THE MODERN ANGLO-BENGALI DICTIONARY

THE MODERN ANGLO BENGALI DICTIONARY

(In 6 Volumes)

(Volume-1)

CHARUCHANDRA GUHA

Publications

KALPAZ PUBLICATIONS

DELHI - 1100052

THE MODERN ANGLO- BENGALI DICTIONARY

ISBN : 81-7835 - 484 - 5 (Set)
ISBN : 81 - 7835 - 485 - 3 (Vol. 1)

Rs. 4500 (Set)

Published in 2007 in India by
Kalpaz Publications
C - 30, Satyawati Nagar,
Delhi - 110052
E-mail : kalpaz@hotmail.com

Laser Typesetting at : Tact Computer, Delhi
Printed at : Mehra Offset Press, Delhi

FOREWORD

by

Dr. Radhakumud Mookerji

M.A.,PH. D., P.R.S., Vidyavaibhava

Author of "A History of Indian Shipping,"
"The Fundamental Unity of India
(From Hindu Sources)," etc.

"The Modern Anglo-Bengali Dictionary" compiled by Mr.Charuchandra Guha of Dacca with the assistance of a competent staff, is a most welcome and opportune addition to the existing literature of lexicons. Justifies its publication not only by the felicity of its design but also by the thoroughness with which the design has been executed. The conception of the design has followed the lines laid down in such standard modern dictionaries as those of Murray, Webster, Whitney, Ogilvie and the like. The execution has uniformly maintained a level of excellence in point of both quality and quantity which is near correspondence to that exhibited in the monumental models mentioned above. All the various shades in the meanings of words have been invariably given ; obscurities are always removed by the light of apposite illustrative quotations ; the freaks of linguistic expression, idioms and the like, receve their due attention ; mythological allusions in current literature have been explained by a brief relation of the stories bearing of them ; technical words in all subjects philosophical scientific or industrial, have been adequately treated and the light of the latest knowledge thrown on them : *as instances we may refer to the treatment of* such philosophical terms,*as category, categorical imperative, absolute, abstract* ; *scientific* terms *like efferent, optical, olfactory nerves, acorus calamus, labeo rohita, magnolia, etc.* ; *and technica*l terms like *mariners compass, plinth, rain-gauge, omnibus, etc.* The selection of suitable Bengali equivalents of these technical words, shows a deep and wide acquaintance with the latest literature on the subjects related thereto. The words coined by modern masters of Bengali literature like Sir Rabindranath Tagore, Principal Ramendrasunder Trivedi, the late Rai Kaliprasanna Gosh Bahadur have been duly appropriated, while that monumental masterpiece of original research just published, Dr. Brajendranath Seas *The Positive Science' of the Ancient* Hindus, a mine of Sanskrit scientific terms, is also laid under contribution. This shows that the compilers have spared themselves no pains in bringing to bear upon their truly arduous task-the equipment of the best modern scholarship which always utilizes the available, up-to-date data and keeps abreast of the latest advances and achievements of research in the various fields of intellectual inquiry. Over and above these the work before us seems to me to be specially commendable for the discovery of bi-lingual equivalents of colloquial and slang words which are eminently deserving of the lexicographer's attention for the not very inconsiderable part they play in the life of a living language.

Thus is intrinsic merits guarantee for utility of this literary venture which both in its plan and execution has faithfully followed the best examples in the literature of lexicons. But apart from this the time of the publication is very opportune and will, with its merits secure for it a good public reception. The Western, and indeed the entire non-Bengali world, have just been awakened to the merits and beauties of the Bengali language as an instrument of human culture by the soul-stirring music of Rabindranath's poetry, and the award to him of the Nobel Prize—the most glorious literary laureal the gift of humanity— has brought a world-wide fame and popularity not only to the poet but also to his mother tongue, to the Bengali language and literature of which the works of the poet are some of the best specimens. There has indeed been a 'discovery of Bengali' by the West just as there was a 'discovery of Sanskrit' by the West in the earlier decades of the nineteenth century with its far reaching effects on the promotion of Hindu learning and culture as embedded in Sanskrit literature, and both the two discoveries may be expected to produce similar results. There has already grown a widespread interest in the Bengali language among the literary circles of the non-Bengali world and translations of Bengali classics into the different languages of the world have become the need of the hour, through as yet but poorly supplied. To this process of popularisation and diffusion of our mother tongue any worker that makes a contribution deserves well to his mother-country and the dictionary compiled by Mr. Charuchandra Guha, which I have been asked to introduce to the public, is as opportune in its appearance as it is useful in its substance and will. I doubt not, easily win for itself its rightful place in the literature of its kind and obtain a worthy circulation among all learners of Bengali whose number is fast developing (from the Governor down wards) for the singular facilities it affords for the acquisition of a bi-linguistic equipment. The work is a great credit to the compiler, Mr Guha, and the able body of his assistance, Mr. Nagendranath Dutt and others whose cordinal co-operation in a common purpose has been fruitful of such happy results. I commed them and their work to the encouragement and support of the public.

BERHAMPORE
(BENGAL) ;
March 12,1916

RADHAKUMUD MOOKERJI

Preface

The word 'Dictionary' is derived from the Latin word *'dictiōnārium'* literally meaning 'a repertory' of *dictiōnēs*, i.e. phrases and words. A dictionary is also called `a lexicon' and hence the science of compiling dictionaries is called `lexicography'.

There are a few types of dictionaries. The most common type of a monolingual dictionary may be defined as: "a book dealing with the individual words (or certain specified classes of them) so as to set forth their orthography, pronunciation, signification and use, their synonyms, derivation and history, or at least some of these factors."

A bilingual dictionary is what enters the forms of one language and defines them, or more often merely gives their equivalents in another language.

The tradition of lexicography is very ancient in India. The earliest work of this class is the *Nighaṇṭu* (of circa 8th cent. B.C.) which is a register of Vedic words classified with their synonyms. Since very old times, many lexicons had been written in Sanskrit, some of which have been lost, but a good number survive. The old Sanskrit lexicons are not dictionaries in the modern sense; they are thesauruses of synonyms, antonyms and homonyms. They are written in metrical forms to facilitate memorising. The compilation of modern dictionaries of Indian languages started with the advent of Europeans, — because of a variety of reasons, — religious, commercial, administrative and later on academic ; In this matter, the case of Bengali is no exception. In the history of Bengali monolingual and bilingual dictionaries (we mean vocabularies and dictionaries in which vacables are arranged in alphabetical order), the oldest known work is the Portuguese-Bengali vocubulary, compiled, in 1743, by the Portuguese missionary Manoel da Assump São, which, however, has now only historical importance. As a result of the establishment of British rule in Bengal, in the middle of the 18th century, and continued activities of the Christian missionaries, bilingual dictionaries, English to Bengali and Bengali to English started being compiled and published. Among the early compilers of bilingual Bengali dictionaries, mention may be made of William Carey (1761-1834) of Srirampur and Ramkamal Sen (1783-1844).

An important landmark in the field of English to Bengali dictionary is *A Modern Anglo-Bengali Dictionary*, of Charuchandra Guha published from Dacca (1915-1919), in three thick volumes (comprising 2537 pages). It is unfortunate that no biographical details about the life and other works of Charuchandra Guha are available. But his dictionary is a laudable achievement,—it is a 'dictionary' and it is 'modern' to the true sense of the terms. It fully conforms to the definition of a dictionary, stated above. Each of the word listed in the Dictionary has been fully treated in fulfilment of the definition.

The scope and comprehensiveness of the Dictionary may be inferred from the subtitle printed on the title pages of the original edition; it reads: "A comprehensive lexicon of bilingual literary, scientific and technical words and terms." The Dictionary displays not less then one thousand illustrations also.

The compiler has taken care to ensure perfect accuracy of the orthography of words, their accentuation, pronunciation and word-divisions. This Dictionary may be called both monolingual and bilingual. If the Bengali parts of the entries are ignored, this may be considered to be a very useful dictionary of the English language.

The primary meaning and various shades of meaning of every word, their idiomatic use and best illustrations in full sentences have been presented. The Bengali parts of the entries are also of no mean importance. The most appropriate Bengali equivalents of the English words have been coined. Though the compiler has selected, in most of the cases, chaste Bengali, i.e. Sanskritized words but, unlike Carey and Sen, he has not cherished any prejudice against foreign loan words used in Bengali since the medieveal age, or the indigenous colqual words and expressions, to facilitate clear understanding of the users of the Dictionary.

In consideration to all the above characteristics, it may safely be stated that Guha's English to Bengali Dictionary stands hardly surpassed even today.

It is, therefore, quite commendable on the part of Kalpaz Publishing House who are engaged in bringing out Indological and other research publications covering a vast area of knowledge, to take up the project of reprinting Guha's Dictionary. I am sure that their venture will be well received and acclaimed by the academicians and wider public alike.

July 10, 2006
New Delhi

SATKARI MUKHOPADHYAYA

Volume - I

THE

MODERN
ANGLO-BENGALI DICTIONARY

A the first letter in the English and some other European alphabets ; ইংরেজী, ল্যাটিন্ প্রভৃতি বর্ণমালার আদ্যক্ষর।

a, (an), *indef. art.* **1.** One ; some one ; any ; each ; এক ; কোন এক, কেহ ; যে কোন ; প্রত্যেক। **2.** *(Used as a prefix)* On ; towards ; in.; into ; to ; as, *aboard* =*on board,* জাহাজে ; *aback*=*towards back,* পশ্চাদ্দিকে ; *once a day*=*once in day,* দিনে একবার ; *apart*=*into parts,* পৃথক্ পৃথক্ ভাগে; *ashore*=*to shore,* তীরাভিমুখে। **3.** *(Mus.)* The sixth tone in the model major scale ; (সঙ্গীত-শাস্ত্র) স্বর-গ্রামের অন্তর্গত মুদারার ষষ্ঠ স্বর "ধা"।

A1. (ā wŭn), *(Naut.)* The symbol indicating a first-class ship in Lloyd's register ; hence, *(colloq.)* first-rate ; excellent ; best ; (নৌ-বিদ্যা) লয়েডের জাহাজের তালিকায় এই সাঙ্কেতিক চিহ্নদ্বারা প্রথমশ্রেণীর জাহাজ বুঝায় ; অতএব, (চলিত ভাষায়) উমদা ; সেরা ; তোফা।

Aardvark.

aard′-vărk (ârd), *n.* The ground-hog or the earth-pig of South Africa ; দক্ষিণ আফ্রিকাদেশীয় জন্তু-বিশেষ, ভূ-শূকর।

aard′-wôlf (ârd-), *n.* The earth-wolf of South Africa ; দক্ষিণ আফ্রিকাবাসী জন্তু বিশেষ, ভূ-বৃক।

Aar′-on (âr-ŭn), *n.* The priestly associate of Moses, mentioned as the first Jewish high priest ; মুসার সহচর জনৈক প্রধান ইয়ুদী পুরোহিত।

Aar′-on's beard, *n.* The name of several plants, having some resemblance to a beard ; esp. the Great St. John's wort ; কয়েক প্রকার ক্ষুদ্র ক্ষুদ্র বৃক্ষের সাধারণ নাম।

Aar′on's rod, *n.* **1.** *(Arch.)* A rod with a serpent twined round it ; (স্থপতি-বিদ্যা) সর্পবেষ্টিত দণ্ডবিশেষ। **2.** The name of several plants, the Golden Rod, etc ; কয়েক প্রকার ক্ষুদ্র ক্ষুদ্র বৃক্ষের সাধারণ নাম।

ȧ-băck′, *adv.* **1.** Backwards ; পশ্চাদ্দিকে। **2.** Against the mast—said of the sails when pressed back by the wind ; (নৌ-বিদ্যা) মাস্তুলের উপর (তাড়িত)। [বায়ুবেগে পশ্চাদ্দিকে তাড়িত বাতবসন (পাইল) সম্বন্ধে কথিত হয়।] **To be taken aback**—To be taken by surprise ; to be greatly astonished ; as, he *was* quite *taken aback* when I told him his plot was found out ; বিস্ময়াভিভূত হওয়া, বিস্ময়বিহ্বল হওয়া ; সহসা অপ্রতিভ হওয়া, থমকিয়া যাওয়া, থতমত খাওয়া, হতভম্ব হওয়া। **To hold aback**—To restrain ; সংযত রাখা। **To stand aback from**—To stand aloof ; to avoid ; দূরে থাকা ; পরিহার করা।

ăb′-ȧ-cŭs, *n.* (Eng. *pl.* ABACUSES, L. *pl.* ABACI) **1.** A frame with balls sliding on wires or strings and used to facilitate arithmetical calculations ; গণনাশিক্ষা দিবার যন্ত্রবিশেষ, গণনা-যন্ত্র (হিঃ কোঃ)।

Abacus.

Doric Capital. a, the abacus.

2. *(Arch.)* The uppermost member or division of the capital of a column, supporting the architrave ; (স্থপতি-বিদ্যা) স্তম্ভের উপরিভাগ বা মাথাল, বোধিকার সর্বোচ্চ ফলক বা বিভাগ, স্তম্ভাগ্রফলক, বোধিকাগ্র (রাঃ রাঃ)।

ȧ-băft′, *adv.* & *prep.* *(Naut.)* Towards the hinder part of a ship ; behind ; (নৌ-বিদ্যা) জাহাজের পশ্চাদ্ভাগে ; পিছে।

ȧ-băn-don (-dŭn), *v. t.* & *n.* **1.** To forsake entirely ; to relinquish all concern in ; as, to *abandon* home, duty ; to give up, as lost ; as, to *abandon* a hopeless enterprise or a sinking ship to resign; as, to *abandon* a post, cares of empire; একান্তভাবে পরিহার করা; সর্ব্বপ্রকার সংস্রব ত্যাগ করা; পরিত্যাগ করা, পরিহার করা; ছাড়িয়া দেওয়া; ত্যাগ করা, বর্জ্জন করা, বিসর্জ্জন করা। **2.** To give up to another's control or mercy; as, he *abandoned* the city to the conqueror; সমর্পণ করা। **3.** To yield one's self completely to a passion or impulse; to give one's self up without attempt at self-control (often in a bad sense); কোন চিত্তরাগ বা প্রবৃত্তির সম্পূর্ণ অধীনতা স্বীকার করা; (পাপ বা দুঃখ স্রোতে) গা ঢালিয়া দেওয়া। ***Noun.*** Careless freedom or ease; as, I was charmed with the *abandon* of her manners; অনায়াস, লীলা, স্বচ্ছন্দাচার, অনাড়ষ্টতা। **—doned,** *adj.* Given up to vice; profligate; extremely wicked; as, an *abandoned* villain; পাপাসক্ত; অভিত্যক্ত, উৎসৃষ্ট, ভ্রষ্টচরিত্র; অতিশয় দুর্বৃত্ত বা দুরাচার। **—ment,** *n.* Total desertion; state of being forsaken; self-surrender; careless freedom of manners; একান্তভাবে পরিত্যাগ, সংত্যাগ; বর্জ্জন; আত্মবিসর্জ্জন; স্বচ্ছন্দচারিতা, মেলামেশায় অনাড়ষ্টভাব। **Abandon one's self to**—Give up one's self to without attempt at restraint; as, he *abandoned* himself to his favourite vice; (পাপস্রোতে বা দুঃখসাগরে) গা ঢালিয়া দেওয়া।

ă-băn-don-ee′ (dŭn-ē), *n.* (*Law*) An underwriter to whom the salvage of wreck is abandoned; (আইন) ভগ্ন জাহাজের মাল যে কর্ম্মচারীর জিম্মায় রাখা হয়।

ă-bāse′, *v. t.* To lower; to humiliate; to degrade; to make base; অবনমিত করা; খর্ব্ব করা, গৌরব-হীন করা; অভিভব করা; হীন করা। **—ment,** *n.* Degradation; humiliation; অধঃপতন, পাতিত্য; গৌরবহানি, পরিভব।

ă-băsh′, *v. t.* To put to shame; to make ashamed or dispirited; to put to confusion; লজ্জিত করা; লজ্জায় জড়সড় করা; লজ্জাকুণ্ঠিত করা। **—ment,** *n.* Confusion from shame; লজ্জাজনিত কুণ্ঠা বা অপ্রতিভতা, সরম-জড়িমা (রবিঃ), সরমসঙ্কোচ, হ্রী-যন্ত্রণা (রঃ)।

ă-băsk′, *adv.* In warm light; basking; উষ্ণালোকে; (রোদ) পোহানের অবস্থায়।

ă-bāte′, *v. t.* & *i.* **1.** To lessen; to diminish; to lower price of; as, to *abate* demand; কমান; প্রশমিত করা; মূল্যহ্রাস করা। **2.** To mitigate (violence); as, to *abate* pain or misery; to weaken energy; উপশম করা; নিস্তেজ করা। **3.** (*Law*) To do away with (nuisance); to frustrate by judicial sentence; to quash (action); as, to *abate* a writ; (আইন) অপসারিত করা; বিচারাদেশ দ্বারা নিষ্ফল করা; বিলোপ করা। ***Verb i.*** To decrease or become less in strength or violence; to fall through; to fail; কমা, হ্রাস হওয়া, উপশমিত হওয়া; ব্যর্থ হওয়া; নিষ্ফল হওয়া।

ăb′-ă-tis, ăb′-ăt-tis, *n.* (*Fort.*) A defence made of felled trees with boughs pointing outwards; (দুর্গ-নির্ম্মাণে) শত্রুহস্ত হইতে আত্মরক্ষার্থ, বহিঃপ্রসারিত শাখাবিশিষ্ট ছিন্নবৃক্ষরচিত উপায় বিশেষ। **—tised,** *adj.*

abattoir′, (*F.*), *n.* A public slaughter-house; কসাইখানা, জবাইখানা, বধস্থলী (অঃ)।

ăbb, *n.* Among weavers, the yarn for the warp; বস্ত্রের অনুপ্রস্থগামী সূত্র, পড়েন।

ăb′-bă, (*Syriac*), *n.* Father; পিতা। *Abba Father = God the Father* (*New Testament*).

ăb′-bă-cy̆, *n.* The dignity, rights, or jurisdiction of an abbot; মঠাধিপতির পদ, অধিকার বা অধিকারভুক্ত স্থান, মঠাধ্যক্ষত্ব।

ăb′-be (-bā), *n.* A Frenchman (originally *abbot*) entitled to wear ecclesiastical dress, esp. without official duties; যাজকীয়পরিচ্ছদ পরিধানে অধিকারী ফরাসীদেশীয় লোক, বিশেষতঃ যাহাকে কোনপ্রকার যাজকীয় কার্য্য করিতে হয় না।

ăb′-bĕss, (*fem. of* ABBOT), *n.* A female superior or governess of a nunnery; (খৃষ্টীয়) মঠাধিকারিণী, বিহারপালিনী, মঠস্বামিনী।

ăb′-bey (-bĭ), *n.* **1.** Buildings occupied by monks or nuns under an abbot or abbess; আশ্রম, মঠ, সঙ্ঘারাম, বিহার, আখড়া। **2.** The church attached to a monastery; মঠ-সংলগ্ন গির্জ্জা বা দেবমন্দির, চৈত্য। **3.** A society of persons of either sex, secluded from the world and devoted to religion and celibacy; the monks or nuns as a body; (খৃষ্টীয়) সন্ন্যাসি-সম্প্রদায় বা সন্ন্যাসিনী-সম্প্রদায়; ভিক্ষু-সঙ্ঘ বা ভিক্ষুণী-সঙ্ঘ।

ăb′-bot (-bŭt), (*fem.* ABBESS), *n.* The head of an abbey or society of monks; মঠাধ্যক্ষ, মঠাধীশ, বিহারপতি, মোহান্ত। **—ba′-tial,** *adj.* Pertaining to an abbey or abbot; মঠ বা মঠাধিকারি-সম্বন্ধীয়। **—ship,** *n.* **Abbot of misrule, Abbot of unreason**—The leader of the Christian revels in the mediæval times; মধ্যযুগে খৃষ্টধর্ম্ম-সংসৃষ্ট আমোদ-প্রমোদের নায়ক।

ăb-brē′-vĭ-āte, *v. t.* **1.** To shorten; to abridge; সংক্ষেপ করা; চুম্বক করা। **2.** (*Math.*) To reduce to the lowest terms, as fractions; (গণিত-শাস্ত্র) নিম্নতম সংখ্যা পরিণত করা (যেমন ভগ্নাংশ), অপবর্ত্তন

করা। —a'-tion, *n.* 1. The act of shortening; সংক্ষেপসাধন, সংক্ষেপণ। 2. A part of a word put for the whole; সংক্ষেপ, শব্দসংক্ষেপ, বাক্য-সংক্ষেপ। 3. (*Math.*) Reduction of fractions to the lowest terms; (গণিত-শাস্ত্র) অপবর্ত্তন (মঃ উঃ)।

A B C, *n.* The elements or rudiments of any subject; উপক্রমণিকা। **A-B-C book** = A primer; প্রাথমিক পাঠ।

ab-di-cate, *v. t.* To formally relinquish, as sovereign power; to renounce formally or by default (a power, office, right, etc.); সিংহাসন ত্যাগ করা; সম্রাস্তপদ বা কার্য্যভার ত্যাগ করা। **—ca-tion,** *n.* The abandonment of an office, power or authority, right or trust; রাজপদত্যাগ, ছত্রচামরত্যাগ, স্বামিত্ববিসর্জন, রাজাসনত্যাগ, রাজপদবিসর্জন, রাজাধিকারত্যাগ।

ăb-dō'-mĕn, *n.* 1. (*Anat.*) The part of the body between the thorax and pelvis; the lower belly; (শারীর-সংস্থান-বিদ্যা) উদর, কুক্ষি, জঠর; তলপেট, বস্তি, নিম্নোদর, পকাধান (সুশ্রুঃ), পক্কাশয় (ঐ)। 2. (*Zool.*) The hinder part of insects, spiders, etc.; (জন্তু-তত্ত্ব) কীট, মাকড়শা প্রভৃতির পশ্চাদ্‌ভাগ।

ab-dŏm'-i-năl, *adj.* & *n.* Pertaining to the lower belly; কুক্ষি বা উদর-সম্পর্কিত, বাস্তেয়। ***Noun.*** A class of fish having the ventral fins under belly; যে মৎস্য-শ্রেণীর পেটের পাখনা পেটের নীচে থাকে। **Abdominal tumour**—গুল্ম।

ab-dŭct, *v. t.* 1. To kidnap; to take away (esp. a woman) by force or fraud; মনুষ্যহরণ করা; বলে বা কৌশলে (বিশেষতঃ স্ত্রীলোক) হরণ করা, ফুসলাইয়া নেওয়া। 2. To draw away, as limb or other part from its natural position হস্তপদাদি বা অঙ্গ অংশ স্বস্থান হইতে প্রত্যাকর্ষণ করা। **—duc'-tion,** *n.* 1. Illegal carrying away of a child, a ward or a wife; অবৈধরূপে মনুষ্যহরণ, (ছলে বলে কৌশলে) শিশু, নাবালক বা পরপত্নী হরণ। 2. The withdrawal of a limb from its natural position; a species of fracture in which the broken parts recede from each other; স্বস্থান হইতে হস্ত পদাদির প্রত্যাকর্ষণ; এক-প্রকার অস্থি-ভঙ্গ, ইহাতে ভগ্ন অংশদ্বয় পরস্পর হইতে দূরে সরিয়া যায়। 3. (*Log.*) A form of argument in which the major premiss is evident, but the minor, and therefore, the conclusion, is only probable; (তর্ক-বিজ্ঞান) একপ্রকার যুক্তি, যাহাতে ব্যাপ্তি-বাক্য স্পষ্ট থাকে; কিন্তু, ব্যাপ্য-পূর্ব্বাবয়ব (উপনয়), অতএব নিগমন, কেবল মাত্র সম্ভাব্য থাকে। **—duc'-tor,** *n.* 1. One who abducts another; মনুষ্যচোর। 2. A muscle that draws away; আকর্ষক মাংস-পেশী, বহির্ণায়ক (হঃ চঃ)।

a-beam' (-bēm), *adv.* On a line at right angles to the ship's length; জাহাজের দৈর্ঘ্যের লম্ব-স্বরূপ রেখার উপরি। **Abeam of us**—Opposite our centre; abreast; আমাদের কেন্দ্রের বিপরীত দিকে; পাশাপাশি।

ā-bē-cē-dā'-ri-ăn, *n.* & *adj.* One who teaches or learns, the alphabet; বর্ণমালা শিক্ষক বা শিক্ষার্থী, বর্ণাধ্যায়ী। ***Adj.*** Pertaining to, or formed by, the letters of the alphabet; hence, rudimentary; বর্ণমালাসংক্রান্ত, বর্ণমালারচিত; প্রাথমিক।

ā-bĕd', *adv.* In or on the bed; শয্যায়, শয্যাস্থ, শয্যোপরি। **Brought abed**—Delivered of a child; প্রসূতবৎসা।

aberglaube, *(G.), n.* Excessive belief; superstition; অন্ধ বিশ্বাস; কুসংস্কার।

ăb-ĕr-rā'-tion, *n.* 1. Deviation from truth or the right path; breaking of rules; moral slip; deviation from a type or standard; সত্যচ্যুতি, বিপথগমন, উন্মার্গগমন; নিয়মভঙ্গ; নৈতিকস্খলন; ব্যভিচার। 2. Partial alienation of reason; intellectual deficiency; বুদ্ধিভ্রম; বুদ্ধি-বৈকল্য। 3. (*Optics*) Non-convergence of the rays of light to one focus; (দৃষ্টি-বিজ্ঞান) অপচার (সাঃ পঃ), বিচলন। 4. *(Astro.)* Displacement of a heavenly body's true position to the observer; (জ্যোতির্বিজ্ঞান) পর্য্যবেক্ষকের দৃষ্টিতে গ্রহনক্ষত্রাদির স্বস্থান হইতে স্থানান্তরে অবস্থিতি-বোধ, ভূচলনসংস্কার (হিঃ কোঃ); অপেরণ (ঐ)। **—er'-rant,** *adj.* 1. Straying from moral standard; ন্যায়পথ-ভ্রষ্ট, সন্মার্গচ্যুত, বিপথগ। 2 Deviating from the natural type; ব্যভিচারী, জাতিরূপাপচারী। **Aberration of light**—আলোকাপচার (সাঃ পঃ)। **Aberration of mind**—তমঃপ্রবেশ (চঃ)।

ā-bĕt', *v. t.* 1. To incite or instigate (a person—often in a bad sense); সাহায্য বা উৎসাহদানে (কুকার্য্যে) উত্তেজিত বা প্ররোচিত করা, প্রোৎসাহিত করা। 2. (*Law*) To counsel or assistin a criminal act; অপরাধজনক কার্য্যে পরামর্শ বা সাহায্যপ্রদান করা **—ment,** *n.* **—ter, -tor,** *ns.* An instigator of an offence or offender; সহায়তাকারী, প্রশ্রয়দাতা, প্রোৎসাহক, প্রবর্ত্তক।

ab extra, (*L.*), *adv.* From outside; বহির্দ্দেশতঃ, বাহির হইতে।

ā-bey'-ănce (-bā-), *n.* Pending state or state of suspension; স্থগিত অবস্থা, মুলতুবী। **To be in or to fall into abeyance**—To be in a state of suspension; as, the property *has fallen into abeyance;* স্থগিত বা মুলতুবী থাকা, যবস্থবে থাকা (রঃ অঃ)।

ăb-hŏr', *v. t.* 1. To shrink from with horror; to hate excessively; to detest; বিভীষিকার সহিত সরিয়া

আসা, ভয়ে সঙ্কুচিত হইয়া সরিয়া আসা ; অতিশয় ঘৃণা করা ; নিরতিশয় অবজ্ঞা করা। **—rĕnce,** *n.* Detestation ; অতিশয় অবজ্ঞা বা ঘৃণা, অতিদ্বেষ। **—rent,** *adj.* **1.** Inspiring disgust ; hateful (of conduct, etc.) ; as, the English are *abhorrent* of cowardice (ভীরুতার প্রতি ঘৃণাশীল) ; বিরক্তিকর ; ঘৃণার্হ, ঘৃণ্য, ঘৃণাশীল, অবজ্ঞেয়। **2.** Inconsistent ; contrary (*to*) ; as, slavery is *abhorrent* to our higher principles ; অসঙ্গত ; বিরোধী, বিরুদ্ধ।

ȧ-bīde', *v.i.* & *t.* **1.** To stay ; to have one's abode ; to dwell—(*at* or *in* a place or *with* a person) ; থাকা ; অবস্থান করা ; বাস করা। **2.** To continue ; to stand firm ; as, let every man *abide in* the same calling ; চলিতে থাকা ; অটল থাকা, স্থির থাকা। ***Verb t.* 1.** To wait for ; to be prepared for ; as, I will *abide* the coming of my lord ; প্রতীক্ষায় থাকা ; প্রস্তুত থাকা। **2.** To be in store for ; as, afflictions *abide* me ; অদৃষ্টে থাকা। **3.** To endure ; to submit to ; as, thou shalt *abide* her judgment ; সহ্য করা ; মানিয়া চলা। **4.** To bear patiently ; to tolerate ; "She could not *abide* Master Shallow." ধৈর্য্যের সহিত সহ্য করা ; বরদাস্ত করা। **—bid'-ing,** *adj.* Permanent ; চিরস্থায়ী। **—bid'-ing-ly,** *adv.* **To abide by**—To act upon ; to remain faithful to ; as, I shall *abide by* your decision ; to stand to ; to adhere to ; as, you should *abide by* what you said at first ; কথানুসারে কায করা, অনুবর্ত্তী বা বশবর্ত্তী হইয়া চলা, পালন করা, মানিয়া চলা, পরিচালিত হওয়া ; অটল থাকা ; অবিচলিত থাকা ; ঠিক থাকা। **To abide one's time**—To wait for an opportune moment ; সুযোগের প্রতীক্ষায় থাকা। **To abide the worst**—To bear patiently the greatest misfortune that might befall ; যতই বিপদ বা দুর্ভাগ্য আসুক না কেন, ধীরভাবে সহ্য করা।

ăb'-i-gail (-gāl), *n.* **1.** (*Lit.*) Father (source) of joy ; (শব্দানুযায়ী) আনন্দজনয়িতা। **2.** A lady's waiting maid ; সহচরী।

ȧ-bil'-i-tў, *n.* **1.** Power (bodily or mental, natural or acquired) ; sufficiency of strength, skill, resources, etc ; capacity ; শক্তি, সামর্থ্য, বিচক্ষণতা, নিপুণতা ; ক্ষমতা। **2.** (*Pl.*) Talents ; mental faculties ; ধীশক্তি ; মনোবৃত্তি সমূহ।

ab initio, *(L.), adv.* From the beginning ; আদ্যবধি, প্রথমাবধি।

ab intra, *(L.), adv.* From within (opp. to ***ab extra***) ; অভ্যন্তর হইতে।

ab invito, (*L.*), *adv.* Unwillingly ; অনিচ্ছাপূর্ব্বক।

ȧ-bi-ō-gĕn'-ĕ-sis, ȧ-bi-ŏg'-ĕn-ў, *n.* A scientific word invented by Prof. Huxley, to indicate the view that living matter can be produced from that which is not in itself living matter ; জড়াৎ জীবোৎপত্তি (সাঃ পঃ), অজীবজনি (হিঃ কোঃ)।

ăb'-jĕct, *adj.* Sunk to a low condition ; degraded ; despicable ; অবনত ; পতিত ; অধম, নীচ, হেয়, অবজ্ঞেয়। **—jec'-tion,** *n.* Meanness of spirit ; abasement ; low state ; নীচতা ; হীনতা ; পতিতাবস্থা, পাতিত্য। **—ly,** *adv.* **—ness,** *n.*

ăb'-jūre, *v. t.* **1.** To renounce on oath (an opinion, cause, etc.) ; to disavow ; as, to *abjure* allegiance to a king ; শপথপূর্ব্বক ত্যাগ করা ; অস্বীকার করা। **2.** To swear perpetual absence from one's country, etc ; জন্মভূমি কিম্বা অন্যস্থল হইতে চিরবিদায় গ্রহণের প্রতিজ্ঞা করা। **—ju-ra'-tion** (-jōō-), *n.* **1.** Renunciation upon oath ; শপথপূর্ব্বক পরিত্যাগ। **2.** A rejection or denial with solemnity ; a total abandonment ; প্রতিজ্ঞাপূর্ব্বক পরিবর্জ্জন বা প্রত্যাখ্যান ; সর্ব্বতোভাবে পরিবর্জ্জন। **—ju'-ra-tŏ-rў,** *adj.* **—jur'-er,** *n.*

ăb-lăc-tā'-tion, *n.* The weaning of a child from the breast ; মাই ছাড়ান।

ăb-lā'-tion, *n.* **1.** A carrying or taking away ; স্থানান্তরীকরণ, অপবাহ। **2.** A removal of any diseased part of the body by surgical operation ; অস্ত্রোপচার দ্বারা রোগদুষ্ট দেহাংশের অপসারণ। **3.** (*Geol.*) The waste of a glacier or rock by melting or water action ; (ভূ-বিদ্যা) দ্রবীভবন বা সলিল-ক্রিয়া দ্বারা হিমানী-নদ বা পাষাণস্তূপ ক্ষয়।

ăb'-lā-tive, *adj.* & *n.* Designating a case of the noun in Sanskrit, Latin and other languages, the fundamental meaning of which is *removal,* or *direction away ;* অপাদানার্থক। ***Noun.*** The sixth case of nouns in Latin and Sanskrit ; অপাদান কারক।

ȧ-blāze', *adv.* & *adj.* **1.** On fire ; glittering brightly ; জ্বলন্ত ; ঝলমল, স্ফুরৎপ্রভাময়। **2.** In a state of ardent desire or glowing excitement ; "The young Cambridge democrats were all *ablaze* to assist Torrijos. বাসনাদীপ্ত, উত্তেজনাদীপ্ত, উদ্দীপ্ত।

ā'-ble, *adj.* **1.** Having sufficient power, strength, force, skill, means, etc. ; capable ; যোগ্য, উপযুক্ত, শক্ত, ক্ষম, সমর্থ, দক্ষ, নিপুণ, কার্য্যদক্ষ ; কার্য্যক্ষম। **2.** Talented ; clever ; ধীমান্, মনীষাসম্পন্ন ; বিচক্ষণ। **3.** Legally qualified ; আইনতঃ যোগ্য। **—bly,** *adv.* With ability ; বিচক্ষণতার সহিত। **Able-bodied**—Having a sound, strong body ; robust ; দৃঢ়িষ্ঠ (উপঃ), বলিষ্ঠ ;

দৃঢ়কায়। **Able-bodied sea-man**—Well-skilled sailor; সুদক্ষ এবং দৃঢ়াঙ্গ নাবিক। **Able-minded**—Possessed of strong intellectual powers; তীক্ষ্ণ মনীষা-সম্পন্ন।

a'-blings, a'-blins, *(Scot.)*, *adv.* Possibly; perhaps; সম্ভবতঃ; হয়ত, বুঝিবা।

ă-bloom', *adv.* In a blooming state; ফুটন্ত, বিকচ অবস্থায়।

ă-blŭsh', *adv.* & *adj.* Blushing; ruddy; সরমরক্তিমগণ্ডে; লজ্জারুণ (রবিঃ)।

ăb-lû'-tion, *n.* **1.** The act of washing or cleansing; (specially) the washing of the body or some parts as a preparation for religious duties; ordinary personal washing; প্রক্ষালন, ধৌতি, জলদ্বারা দেহশুদ্ধি; সন্ধ্যাবন্দনা, নমাজ প্রভৃতি ধর্ম্মকার্য্যে প্রবৃত্ত হইবার প্রাক্কালীন স্নান বা হস্তপদাদি ধৌতকরণ, অভিষেক, অবভৃথ-স্নান, ওজু, জলপাবন, উপমজ্জন; সাধারণ স্নান, আচমন বা হস্তপদাদি ধৌত করণ। **2.** Water used in cleansing; প্রক্ষালনার্থ জল, (সন্ধ্যা, উপাসনাদির পূর্ব্বে) দেহশুদ্ধির জন্য ব্যবহৃত জল, অভিষেকবারি। **—a-ry,** *adj.* **Ablution of the body**—অঙ্গস্নান। **Ablution of the mouth**—আচমন।

ăb'-nĕ-gāte, *v. t.* To renounce (a right or belief); to deny one's self; পরিত্যাগ করা; প্রত্যাখ্যান করা। **—ga'-tion,** *n.* Renunciation or denial; rejection of doctrine; ত্যাগস্বীকার; (কোন) ধর্ম্মমত প্রত্যাখ্যান। **Self-abnegation**—Renunciation of worldly pleasures and giving one's self up for some good cause; আত্মত্যাগ, আত্মোৎসর্গ।

ăb-nŏr'-măl, *adj.* Contrary to rule or usual state; irregular; deviating from the type; নিয়মবিরুদ্ধ, অস্বাভাবিক, বিধিবিরুদ্ধ, সৃষ্টিমার্গবহির্ভূত, বিকট, বিকৃত; অনিয়মিত; সৃষ্টিছাড়া, জাতিরূপাপচারী। **—ly,** *adv.* **—mal'-i-ty,** *n.* **1.** The state or quality of being abnormal; irregularity; নিয়মবিরুদ্ধতা, অনৈসর্গিকতা; অনিয়মিতত্ব। **2.** Something abnormal; অস্বাভাবিক পদার্থ, কিম্ভূতকিমাকার জীব বা বস্তু, বিকট জীব। **—mi-ty,** *n.* Irregularity; deformity; monstrosity; স্বভাববিরুদ্ধতা; বিরূপতা, অঙ্গবিকৃতি; বিকটতা।

ă-board' (-bōrd), *adv.* & *prep.* **1.** Within a ship or boat or in a train; জাহাজে, নৌকায় বা রেলগাড়ীতে। **2.** Alongside; পাশাপাশি। ***Prep.*** On board of; জাহাজোপরি। **He fell aboard of me**—He abused me; সে আমাকে গালাগালি করিয়াছিল। *(Naut.)* **To fall aboard**—To strike against another ship; (নৌ-বিদ্যা) অন্য জাহাজের সহিত ধাক্কা লাগা। **To go aboard**—To embark; জাহাজ, নৌকা প্রভৃতিতে আরোহণ করা। **To keep the land aboard**—তীরের নিকটে নিকটে থাকা। **To lay (a ship) aboard**—যুদ্ধের জন্য নিজ জাহাজ অন্য জাহাজের পাশাপাশি রাখা।

ă-bōde', *n.* **1.** Dwelling-place; residence; বাসস্থান, বসতি; আবাসস্থান (আঃ মঠ), আবাসভবন, অধিষ্ঠান (ইন্দিঃ)। **2.** Stay; as, he fled away without *abode*; অবস্থান।

ă-bŏl'-ish, *v. t.* To do away with; as, to *abolish* laws, customs or institutions; to annul; উঠাইয়া দেওয়া, তুলিয়া দেওয়া, রহিত করা, বাতিল করা; ধ্বংস করা, বিলোপ করা, উচ্ছেদ করা। **—er, —ment,** *ns.*

ăb-ŏ-li'-tion, *n.* **1.** The act of abolishing; as, the *abolition* of slavery; উচ্ছেদসাধন। **2.** An annulling; utter destruction; বিলোপসাধন; বিলোপ। **—ism,** *n.* The principles or measures favouring abolition, esp. of negro slavery; উচ্ছেদের অনুকূল মত বা উপায় সমূহ, বিশেষতঃ দাসত্ব-প্রথার উচ্ছেদসাধনের অনুকূল মত বা উপায় সমূহ। **—ist,** *n.* One who favours abolition, esp. of negro slavery; বিলোপবাদী, বিশেষতঃ দাসত্ব-প্রথার উচ্ছেদ-সাধন-মতাবলম্বী।

ă-bŏm'-i-nă-ble, *adj.* **1.** Detestable; loathsome; odious to the mind; offensive to the senses; গর্হণীয়; জুগুপ্সিত, বীভৎস; নিতান্ত ঘৃণার্হ; জঘন্য। **2.** *(Colloq.)* Annoyingly great; as, his self-conceit is *abominable*; বিকট, উৎকট, অত্যন্ত বিরক্তিকর। **—na'-bly,** *adv.* **—ness,** *n.*

ă-hŏm'-i-nāte, *v. t.* To hate extremely; to loathe; নিরতিশয় ঘৃণা করা; বিজাতীয় ঘৃণা করা। **—na-tion,** *n.* **1.** Detestation; বিজাতীয় ঘৃণা। **2.** Shameful vice; an object of disgust *(to)*; লজ্জাকর ব্যভিচার; ঘৃণার পাত্র।

ăb-ŏ-rĭg'-in-ăl, *adj.* & *n.* Original; primitive; আদিম; আদ্যকালীন। ***Noun.*** An original inhabitant of any land; আদিম অধিবাসী।

ăb-ŏ-rĭg'-in-ēs, *n. pl.* The primitive inhabitants of a country; কোন দেশের আদিম অধিবাসিগণ।

ă-bŏrt', *v. i.* **1.** To miscarry; to bring forth young in an undeveloped state; গর্ভপাত হওয়া; অকালে সন্তান প্রসব করা। **2.** *(Biol.)* To become sterile; to remain undeveloped; to shrink away;—said of individual, or of a race of plants or animals; (জীববিজ্ঞান) বন্ধ্যা হওয়া; অপরিণত থাকা; কোঁকড়াইয়া যাওয়া। **—bor'-tion,** *n.* **1.** Miscarriage; the expulsion of human fetus before the sixth month of pregnancy; গর্ভস্রাব, গর্ভচ্যুতি, গর্ভসংস্রবণ (মঃ সং); ছয় মাসের পূর্ব্বে গর্ভস্রাব (হঃ চঃ), অকাল-প্রসব। **2.** A dwarfed or misshapen creature; খর্ব্ব বা বিকটাকার

জীব। **3.** Failure of a project or action; as, his attempt proved an *abortion*; অসিদ্ধি, নিষ্ফলতা। **—bor′-tive,** *adj.* **1.** Born prematurely; অকাল-প্রসূত। **2.** Fruitless unsuccessful; as, an *abortive* attempt; নিষ্ফল; নিরর্থক। **3.** Imperfectly formed or developed; rudimentary, as organs, etc.; অপরিণত, অপুষ্টাঙ্গ; প্রাথমিক। **—bor′-tive-ly,** *adv.* **—bor′-tive-ness,** *n.* **—ed,** *adj.* **1.** Untimely born; undeveloped; অকালপ্রসূত; অপরিণত, অপুষ্টাঙ্গ। **2.** Rudimentary; as, thorns are *aborted* branches মৌলিক, আদিম। **Criminal abortion**—Abortion by artificial means; (ঘৃণা, লজ্জাদি ভয়ে) অপগর্ভপাত, অপরাধজনক গর্ভপাত, ভ্রূণহত্যা।

ă-bound′ (-bownd), *v.i.* To be in great plenty; to be copiously supplied—*(in, with)*; as, to *abound with* provisions: tigers *abound in* the jungles of Bengal; পর্য্যাপ্ত বা প্রচুর পরিমাণে থাকা; ভুয়িষ্ঠ পরিমাণে বা বহুসংখ্যায় থাকা। **To abound in one's own sense**—To follow one's own judgment independently; স্বাধীনভাবে স্বকীয় বিচারবুদ্ধি অনুসরণ করিয়া চলা।

ă-bout′ (-bowt), *prep.* & *adv.* **1.** Around; as, look *about* you: bind them *about* thy neck; চতুর্দ্দিকে, পরিতঃ, বেড়িয়া। **2.** Near to (in place, size, number, quality, etc.); as, *about* my stature (প্রায়): *about* two thousand (ন্যূনাধিক); সন্নিকটে, প্রায়, কাছাকাছি, কমবেশ। **3.** By or on (one's person); as, I have no money *about* me; সমীপে, কাছে, নিকটে, সঙ্গে। **4.** Here and there; throughout; as, pain lies all *about* the breast; ইতস্ততঃ; সর্ব্বত্র ব্যাপিয়া, জুড়িয়া। **5.** On account of; touching; concerning; as, I know nothing *about* this; জন্য; বিষয়ে; সম্পর্কে, সম্বন্ধে। **6.** Engaged in; as, I must be *about* my father's business; রত, ব্যাপৃত, নিরত। ***Adv.*** **1.** In a circle; circularly; as, the tree was six feet *about*; বেড়িয়া; বেড়ে। **2.** On all sides; around; "And all *about* found desolate;" সর্ব্বত্র; চতুর্দ্দিকে। **3.** On the point of; as, I am *about* to do this; উন্মুখ, উদ্যত। **4.** Here and there; hither and thither; as, wandering *about* from house to house; এখানে সেখানে; ইতস্ততঃ। **5.** Near to in quantity, quality or degree, etc.; as, *about* as high: *about* as large; (সংখ্যা, মাত্রা বা পরিমাণে) কাছাকাছি, নিকটে, ঈষদূন, প্রায়। **6.** Half-round; in the opposite direction; as, to turn one's self *about*; অর্দ্ধ-চন্দ্রাকারে; বিপরীতদিকে। **What are you about?**—What are you engaged in? (Indicates a slight fault-finding) কি করছ হে? [যাহাকে উদ্দেশ করিয়া এই কথাটি বলা হইয়াছে, সে যেন কোন একটা মন্দ কার্য্যে নিযুক্ত আছে, এইরূপ ভাব বুঝায়।] **About-sledge**—The largest hammer used by the smiths; কর্ম্মকারের সর্ব্বাপেক্ষা বৃহৎ হাতুড়ি।

ă-bove′ (-bŭv), *prep., adv., adj.* & *n.* **1.** Higher than; over; as, *above* a ton; উপরি; ঊর্দ্ধে। **2.** Out of the reach of; as, *above* criticism; too great or good for; as, *above* meanness: *above* comprehension (বোধাতীত); অতীত; ঊর্দ্ধে। **3.** Surpassing in number; more than; as, he governed *above* five years; সংখ্যায় অধিকতর; অধিকতর। ***Adv.*** **1.** Overhead or in a higher place; in heaven; মস্তকোপরি, ঊর্দ্ধে; ঊর্দ্ধলোকে। **2.** Earlier in a book or article; as, remarked or said *above*; পূর্ব্বে, অগ্রে। **3.** In a higher rank or place; as, he appealed to the court *above*; ঊর্দ্ধতর স্থান বা পদে। **4.** Besides; in addition; as, over and *above*; ব্যতীত; অধিকন্তু। ***Adj.*** Above-mentioned; above-quoted; as, the *above* few lines; প্রোক্ত, প্রাগুক্ত, পূর্ব্বধৃত। ***Noun.*** The place above: heaven; as, gifts from *above*; ঊর্দ্ধলোক; স্বর্গ। **Above all**—**1.** Chiefly; প্রধানতঃ। **2.** In preference to all other things; সর্ব্বাগ্রে, সর্ব্বোপরি। **Above board**—Above the board or table; hence, openly; without trick or deception; as, an honest man deals *above-board*; প্রকাশ্যে; সর্ব্বজনসমক্ষে; নিষ্কপটে। **Above-cited**—উদ্ধৃত, উপরিধৃত। **Above ground**—Not dead and buried; alive; as, I will have them, if they be *above-ground*; জীবিত; মাটির উপর। **Above-mentioned, above-named, above-quoted** and **above-said**—পূর্ব্বোল্লিখিত, পূর্ব্বোক্ত, প্রাগুক্ত, উপরিকথিত, উপরিধৃত, পূর্ব্ব-কথিত, উল্লিখিত। **Above one's hook**—Beyond one's income; আয়ের অতিরিক্ত। **Above par**—At more than the real or original value; আদি বা প্রকৃত মূল্য অপেক্ষা অধিকতর দরে (কোম্পানীর কাগজ প্রভৃতি সম্পর্কে)। **Above praise**—That can not be praised too highly; প্রশংসার অতীত, নিরতিশয় প্রশংসনীয়। **Above suspicion**—Beyond the reach of calumny; অনিন্দনীয়, নির্ম্মল, নিষ্কলঙ্ক।

ăb-ră-că-dăb′-ră, *n.* A mystical word used in incantations, being written so as to form a triangle, the first line containing the word in full, the one below it

A B R A C A D A B R A
A B R A C A D A B R
A B R A C A D A B
A B R A C A D A
A B R A C A D
A B R A C A
A B R A C
A B R A
A B R
A B
A

omitting the last letter until only one letter remains, and worn as an amulet for the cure of diseases; gibberish; jargon; অক্ষর-রচিত ত্রিভুজাকৃতি তান্ত্রিক "যন্ত্র" বিশেষ—ইহার প্রথম পংক্তিতে সমস্ত শব্দটি লিখিত হয়, তৎপর পর পর ছত্রে শেষ অক্ষরটী ছাড়িয়া দিয়া সর্ব্বশেষে যন্ত্রটীকে একটীমাত্র অক্ষরে পর্য্যবসিত করা হয়—এই যন্ত্রটী রোগনাশক মাদুলি-স্বরূপ ধারণ করা হইয়া থাকে; অর্থহীন বাক্য; পিশাচ-ভাষা, হ য ব র ল।

ab ovo, (*L.*), *adv.* From the very beginning; প্রথমাবধি।

ăb-rāde', *v. t.* To rub or scrape off; to injure (skin, etc.) by violent rubbing; to wear away by friction; ঘষিয়া বা চাঁচিয়া তুলিয়া ফেলা; প্রবল ঘর্ষণ দ্বারা (চর্ম্ম প্রভৃতি) ক্ষয়িত করা; ঘষিয়া ক্ষয় করা। **—ra'-dant,** *n.* A material used for grinding; শাণের জন্য বালি, কাচচুর্ণ প্রভৃতি। **—ra'-sion,** *n.* **1.** The act of wearing or rubbing off; ঘর্ষণদ্বারা ক্ষয়করণ, অবদরণ (হঃ চঃ)। **2.** The substance worn off by attrition; ঘর্ষণহেতু কোন বস্তু হইতে যে পদার্থ পতিত হয়। **3.** *(Surg.)* The scraping off of skin, etc.; the wounded place that results from the scraping off of skin, etc.; (অস্ত্রোপচার-বিদ্যা) চর্ম্মাদি উত্তোলন; ত্বগ্‌ভ্রংস জন্য ক্ষত।

ă-brăn'-chi-ăl, —chi-ate, *adj.* Without gills; (মৎস্যাদি সম্পর্কে) শ্বাস-যন্ত্র-বিহীন।

ă-breast' (-brĕst), *adv.* **1.** Side by side; with the breasts in a line; as, the soldiers rode *abreast*; পাশাপাশি; একের পার্শ্ব অপরের পার্শ্বে এরূপভাবে। **2.** Up to a certain level or degree; keeping up, not behind *(of, with)*; as, to keep *abreast of* the present state of science; নির্দ্দিষ্ট সীমা বা মাত্রা পর্য্যন্ত; সমগতিতে অগ্রসর, তুল্যভাবে অগ্রসর।

ă-bridge', *v. t.* **1.** To shorten; to curtail; to lessen; as, to *abridge* labour; খর্ব্বকরা; কাটা ছাঁটা; কমাইয়া দেওয়া। **2.** To condense; to epitomize, book, etc.; সংক্ষেপ করা; সার-সংগ্রহ করা, চুম্বক করা। **3.** To cut off from; to deprive (persons *of*); as, to *abridge* one of his rights; বিচ্ছিন্ন করা; (কোন কিছু হইতে) বঞ্চিত করা। **—bridg'-ment,** *n.* **1.** Shortening of time, labour, etc.; curtailment (of rights); অল্পকরণ; হ্রাস, কাটা ছাঁটা, সংক্ষেপণ। **2.** Epitome; summary (as of a book); সংক্ষেপ; সংক্ষিপ্ত-সার, সমাহার, সার-সংগ্রহ।

ă-broach' (-brōch), *adv.* Pierced, so as to let the liquor run (of casks); "Hogsheads of ale were set *abroach*;" ফুটা।

ă-broad' (-brâd), *adv.* **1.** Widely; over a wide space; বিস্তৃতভাবে; বিস্তীর্ণ স্থান ব্যাপিয়া। **2.** Out of doors; বাটীর বাহিরে। **3.** In or to foreign countries; বিদেশে, দেশান্তরে। **4.** Before the public at large; here and there; as, there is a rumour *abroad*; সর্ব্বসমক্ষে; যেখানে সেখানে, সর্ব্বত্র। **5.** Wide of the mark; as, you are all *abroad* in your guess; উদ্দিষ্ট বিষয় হইতে তফাৎ। **At home and abroad**—দেশবিদেশে। **The school master is abroad**—Education is diffused among the people; "*The school master is abroad*; and I trust to him, armed with his primer, against the soldier in full military array." জনসমাজে শিক্ষা-বিস্তার হইতেছে। **To get abroad**—To become public; প্রকাশ হইয়া পড়া, ছড়াইয়া পড়া।

ăb'-rō-gāte, *v. t.* To abolish; to repeal; to cancel (laws, customs, etc.); বিলোপ করা, বাতিল করা; রদ করা; রহিত করা। **—ga'-tion,** *n.* The act of repealing; a repeal by the authority; বিলোপসাধন, রহিতকরণ; রদ।

ăb-rŭpt', *adj.* **1.** Steep; precipitous; as, an *abrupt* rock; খাড়া; বিষম, সরলোন্নত, দুরারোহ। **2.** Sudden; hasty; unceremonious; as, an *abrupt* entrance or departure; আকস্মিক; ব্যগ্র, সত্বর, ব্যস্তসমস্ত; রূঢ়, অশিষ্ট। **3.** Unconnected; broken; as, an *abrupt* style; অসম্বদ্ধ, অসংলগ্ন; ভাঙ্গা-ভাঙ্গা।

Abrupt leaf.

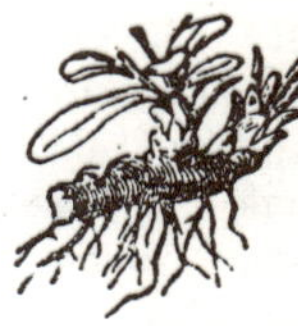
Abrupt root.

4. *(Bot.)* Truncated; as, an *abrupt* leaf or root; (উদ্ভিদ-বিদ্যা) ছিন্নাস্ত। **—ly,** *adv.* In an abrupt manner; খাড়াভাবে, অসম্বদ্ধভাবে, সহসা, অকস্মাৎ, ঝটিতি। **—ness,** *n.*

ăb-rŭp'-tion, *n.* A sudden breaking off; a breaking away of parts from a mass; আকস্মিক ভঙ্গ; কোন বস্তুর কিয়দংশ ভাঙ্গিয়া পড়ন।

Abrus minor—Bead seed tree: শ্বেতকুঁচ (বেলঃ), কাল কুঁচ (ঐ), রতি (ঐ), গুঞ্জা (মঃ উঃ)।

ăb'-scĕss, *n.* A collection of pus formed in a cavity of the body; ব্রণ, ফোড়া স্ফোটক, বিদ্রধি (সুশ্রুঃ)।

ăb-scĭnd', *v. t.* To cut off; কাটিয়া ফেলা।

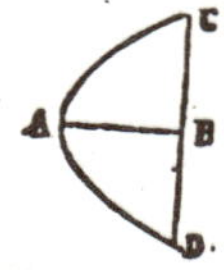

Abscissa. The line A B.

ăb-scĭss', **ăb-scĭs'-să,** (*plu.* ABSCISSES; -SCISSÆ), *n.* The portion of a given line intercepted between a fixed point within it and the ordinate drawn to it from a given point without it ; কোটি (হিঃ কোঃ), ভুজ (ঐ)।

ăb-scĭs'-sion, *n.* **1.** (*Surg.*) A cutting off ; a violent separation ; (অস্ত্রোপচার-বিদ্যা) ছেদন ; প্রবলভাবে বিশ্লেষণ। **2.** (*Rhet.*) An abrupt breaking off in the midst of a sentence ; (অলঙ্কার-শাস্ত্র) কোন বাক্যের মধ্যভাগে আকস্মিক ছন্দোভঙ্গ।

ăb-scŏnd', *v. i.* **1.** To hide or be concealed ; লুক্কায়িত হওয়া বা থাকা। **2.** To depart stealthily, especially, to avoid a legal process ; to decamp ; গোপনে পলায়ন করা, ফেরার হওয়া, গা ঢাকা দেওয়া ; পলায়ন করা। **—er,** *n.* One who absconds ; পলাতক বা ফেরার আসামী।

ăb'-sĕnce, *n.* **1.** The state or time of being away from a place ; the state of being at a distance in place ; অনুপস্থিতি ; বিরহ, বিচ্ছেদ, পরোক্ষ, অসাক্ষাৎ। **2.** Non-existence ; want (*of*) ; as, the *absence* of evidence ; অবিদ্যমানতা, অসদ্ভাব ; অভাব, অপ্রতুল। **3.** Inattention to things present ; abstraction (of mind) ; অমনোযোগ, অনাবিষ্টতা ; চিত্তবিক্ষেপ। **Absence of mind**—Inattentiveness ; অন্যমনস্কতা, চিত্তবিক্ষেপ, আনমন। **In one's absence**—কাহারো অবর্তমানে।

ăb'-sĕnt, *adj.* **1.** Not present ; somewhere else ; অনুপস্থিত, অবর্ত্তমান, গরহাজির ; বিচ্ছিন্ন, অন্যত্র অবস্থিত। **2.** Not-existing ; wanting ; অবিদ্যমান ; হীন, বিরহিত। **3.** Inattentive ; অনাবিষ্ট, অন্যমনস্ক, উন্মনস্ক। **—ee',** *n.* One who absents himself from his country, office or duty, especially, a landlord living away from his estate ; as, an Irish *absentee* ; অনুপস্থিত ব্যক্তি, প্রোষিত (মঃ স্মৃং), প্রবাসী, (বিশেষভাবে) দেশান্তর বা স্থানান্তরবাসী জমিদার। [আয়র্লণ্ডের যে সমস্ত ইংরেজ ভূম্যধিকারী কদাচিৎ তথায় গমনপূর্ব্বক প্রজাপুঞ্জের তত্ত্বাবধান করিয়া থাকেন, তাঁহাদিগকে Irish absentee বলা হয়।] **Absent-minded**—Inattentive ; অন্যমনস্ক, অন্যমনাঃ, আনমনা।

ăb-sĕnt', *v. refl.* To keep one's self away ; দূরে থাকা, প্রবাসে থাকা।

ăb'-sinth, —sinthe, *n.* Spirit combined with extract of wormwood ; আব্‌সিন্‌থ্ (হিন্দি), দোনার কাথের সহিত মিশ্রিত সুরাসার।

ăb'-sō-lūte, *adj.* **1.** Unlimited ; uncontrolled ; unrestricted ; as, *absolute* government (স্বৈরশাসনতন্ত্র) ; অসীমাবদ্ধ ; স্বৈর ; অনিয়ন্ত্রিত, অবাধিত, অবারিত, নির্ব্যূঢ়। **2.** Complete in itself ; perfect ; as, *absolute* beauty ; সর্ব্বাঙ্গসম্পন্ন ; নিখুঁত। **3.** Not relative ; unconditional ; unqualified ; as, *absolute* knowledge ; অনন্যসাপেক্ষ, নিরপেক্ষ, অনাপেক্ষিক ; অবস্থাতীত ; অবিমিশ্র। **4.** Unconditional ; self-existent ; all-pervading and unconditioned ; as, God is *absolute* ; পরম, কেবল, অনাদিসিদ্ধ, দেশকালাতীত, নির্গুণ, শুদ্ধ, নির্বিশেষ, নির্দ্বন্দ্ব, নিরুপাধিক ; স্বয়ম্ভু ; নিরঞ্জন (হেগেল—বিশ্বঃ), তৎস্বরূপ (ঐ)। **5.** (*Gram.*) Standing apart from its usual construction with another word or words ; as, the nominative or ablative *absolute* ; (ব্যাকরণ) (কোন শব্দ) অপর শব্দ বা শব্দসমূহের সহিত সাধারণতঃ যে ভাবে অন্বিত থাকে, তাহা হইতে স্বতন্ত্র ভাবে স্থিত। **6.** (*Chem.*) Pure, unmixed ; as, *absolute* alcohol ; শুদ্ধ, বিশুদ্ধ ; অবিমিশ্র। **—ly,** *adv.* Completely ; arbitrarily ; positively ; unconditionally ; independently ; সম্পূর্ণরূপে ; যথেচ্ছভাবে ; নিশ্চিতরূপে, যথার্থরূপে ; অবস্থাতীতরূপে ; নির্বিশেষ ভাবে। **—ness,** *n.* **Absolute Ego**—পরমাত্মা (হিঃ কোঃ)। **Absolute knowledge**—কেবল জ্ঞান। **Absolute monarchy**—স্বেচ্ছাপরতন্ত্ররাজত্ব (জৈঃ সাঃ)। **Absolute non-existence**—অত্যন্তাভাব (হিঃ কোঃ)। **Absolute right**—নির্ব্যূঢ় স্বত্ব। **Case absolute** or **nominative absolute**—অসমাপিকা ক্রিয়ার সহিত অন্বিত কর্ত্তৃকারক। **The Absolute**—স্বয়ম্ভু, কেবলাত্মা।

ăb-sō-lū'-tion, *n.* A formal setting free from guilt, sentence or obligation ; an ecclesiastical declaration of forgiveness of sins ; নিষ্কৃতি, ক্ষমা, অব্যাহতি, নিস্তার, উদ্ধার ; (খৃষ্টীয় ধর্ম্মযাজকগণ দ্বারা) পাপমোচন, পাপশোধন, পাপক্ষমা, পাপবিমোক্ষণ।

ăb'-sō-lū-tĭsm, *n.* **1.** The principles of absolute government ; স্বৈর বা যথেচ্ছাচারমূলক শাসননীতি, স্বেচ্ছাতন্ত্রতা। **2.** Doctrine of predestination ; মানবের শুভাশুভ পূর্ব্ব হইতেই অপরিবর্ত্তনীয়রূপে নির্দ্দিষ্ট হইয়াছে, এবং আত্মচেষ্টা দ্বারা অদৃষ্টলিপি খণ্ডন করা তাহার সাধ্যাতীত—এইরূপ দার্শনিক বাদ, অদৃষ্টবাদ, দৈববাদ, নিয়তিবাদ। **—tist,** *n.* **1.** An advocate for despotism or absolute government ; স্বেচ্ছাতন্ত্রবাদী। **2.** (*Metaph.*) One who maintains that it is possible to realise a cognition or concept of *the absolute* ; (তত্ত্ববিদ্যা) ব্রহ্মবাদী (হিঃ কোঃ)।

ăb-sŏlve', *v. t.* **1.** To set free or release from some obligation, duty or responsibility ; মুক্ত করা, নিষ্কৃতি দেওয়া, মোচন করা, অব্যাহতি দেওয়া, রেহাই দেওয়া। **2.** (*Rom. law*) To acquit ; to pronounce not guilty ; (রোমীয় আইন) বেকসুর খালাস দেওয়া ; বিচারে নির্দ্দোষ বলিয়া ব্যক্ত করা। **3.** (*Eccles.*) To forgive or grant remission of sins to ; to pronounce forgiveness of sins to ; (খৃষ্টীয় যাজকসমাজের ভাষায়) কোন ব্যক্তির পাপ ক্ষমা করা বা কাহাকে পাপের দায় হইতে অব্যাহতি

দেওয়া ; কোন ব্যক্তির নিকট তাহার পাপক্ষমার বিষয় ঘোষণা করা।

ăb'-sŏ-nănt, *adj.* Discordant ; unreasonable ; অসঙ্গতিপূর্ণ ; যুক্তিবিরুদ্ধ।

ăb-sŏrb', *v. t.* **1.** To drink in ; to imbibe (as a sponge) ; নিপান করা ; শোষণ করা। **2.** To swallow up ; গ্রাস করা, গ্রাস করিয়া ফেলা। **3.** To engross or engage wholly ; as, *absorbed* in study ; মগ্ন করা বা অভিনিবিষ্ট করা। **4.** To take in (heat, light, etc.) by chemical or molecular action ; রাসায়নিক বা আণবিক আকর্ষণ দ্বারা (গ্যাস, আলোক প্রভৃতি) শোষণ করিয়া লওয়া। **—a-bil'-i-ty,** *n.* **—a-ble, —ent,** *adjs.* **—ing,** *adj.* Imbibing, hence, engrossing ; intensely interesting ; শোষণপ্রবণ, চিত্তলয়কর ; অতীব কৌতূহলজনক। **—ing-ly,** *adv.*

ăb-sŏrb'-ĕnt, *n.* **1.** (*Anat.*) One of the vessels in plants and animals that absorb nutriment ; (শারীরসংস্থান বিদ্যা) লসিকা প্রভৃতি যে সকল ক্ষুদ্র ক্ষুদ্র নাড়ী রস শোষণ করে, তাহাদের অন্যতম, শোষক নাড়ী (হঃ চঃ।) **2.** (*Med.*) A substance used for absorbing the acidity of the stomach and the bowels ; (ভৈষজ্য-শাস্ত্র) পক্বাশয় বা অন্ত্রস্থিত অম্লরসশোষক ঔষধ বিশেষ।

ăb-sŏrp'-tion, *n.* **1.** The act or process of causing to disappear ; disappearance through incorporation in something else ; শোষণ, পরিশোষণ, আশোষণ বা আচূষণ ক্রিয়া, চোষণ, চূষা, নিপান (ভাগঃ), শোষণ-ক্রিয়া ; তিরোধান, অন্তর্ধান, লোপ। **2.** Entire occupation of mind ; তদ্গতচিত্ততা, অনন্যমনস্কতা, সমাহিততা, লীনতা। **3.** Sucking in fluid, light, heat, etc., or nutriment ; আলোক, উত্তাপ, দ্রবপদার্থাদি কিম্বা পুষ্টিকর আহারসামগ্রী আশোষণ। **—tive,** *adj.* **—tive-ness, —tiv'-i-ty,** *ns.*

ăb-stain' (-stān), *v.i.* To refrain ; to keep one's self away (*from*) ; বিরত থাকা ; নিবৃত্ত থাকা। **—er,** *n.* One who abstains, especially, from the use of liquor ; a teetotaller ; নিবৃত্তিপন্থী, মদ্যপানত্যাগী, পান-নিবৃত্ত ; মাদকবর্জ্জনকারী। **—stē'-mi-oŭs,** *adj.* **1.** Sparing in diet ; refraining from a free use of food and strong drinks ; temperate ; মিতাহারী ; লঘ্বাহার ; যতাহার। **2.** Very moderate and plain ; spare ; as, an *abstemious* diet (লঘুপথ্য) ; অতি পরিমিত এবং সাদা-সিধা ; লঘু। **3.** Devoted to or spent in abstinence ; as, an *abstemious* life ; সংযমশীল, মিতপানাহারে যাপিত। **—ste'-mi-ous-ly,** *adv.* **—ste'-mi-ous-ness,** *n.* **—stĕn'-tion,** *n.* The act of abstaining or holding aloof ; ক্ষান্তি, বিরতি, সংযম, নিবৃত্তি।

ăb-stêrğ'-ĕnt, *adj.* & *n.* Serving to cleanse ; প্রক্ষালনোপযোগী। ***Noun.*** A substance used in cleansing ; a detergent ; প্রক্ষালনোপযোগী দ্রব্য ; ধাবক, প্রক্ষালক, মলাপকর্ষক।

ăb-stêr'-sion, *n.* Cleansing ; purgation ; প্রক্ষালন ; পরিমার্জ্জন, ক্ষালন।

ăb'-sti-nĕnce (*from*), *n.* **1.** Refraining from indulgence of (appetite, sensual propensities, intoxicating beverages, etc.) ; পানাহার ও ইন্দ্রিয়সেবায় বিরতি, উপরম (হিঃ কোঃ), উপরতি (ঐ), সংযম, নিগ্রহ, জিতেন্দ্রিয়ত্ব। **2.** (*Eccles.*) Refraining from certain kinds of food on certain days ; as, *fish* on fridays ; (খৃষ্টীয় যাজকদের শাস্ত্রমতে) নির্দ্দিষ্ট নির্দ্দিষ্ট দিবসে বিশেষ বিশেষ খাদ্যদ্রব্য বর্জ্জন।

ăb'-sti-nĕnt, *n.* & *adj.* One who abstains ; সংযতাচারী, নিবৃত্তরাগ। ***Adj.*** Refraining from undue indulgence, especially in food and liquor ; পানাহারসংযত।

ăb-străct', *v. t.* **1.** To take away ; to withdraw ; to separate ; as, to *abstract* the attention of any one ; নিবর্ত্তিত করা ; নিষ্কর্ষণ করা ; বিভিন্ন করা, বিশ্লিষ্ট করা, বিযুক্ত করা, পৃথক্ করা। **2.** To draw off interest or attention ; as, my mind was wholly *abstracted* by family matters ; প্রত্যাকর্ষণ করা, প্রত্যাহরণ করা। **3.** To epitomize ; or summarize ; (কোন গ্রন্থের) সার-সঙ্কলন বা সার-সংগ্রহ করা। **4.** To take secretly or dishonestly ; to steal ; as, to *abstract* goods from a parcel ; গোপনে বাহির করিয়া লওয়া, সরাইয়া ফেলা ; অপহরণ করা। **5.** To derive the idea of ; to deduce ; to consider apart from the concrete ; to separate as the qualities or properties of an object in the mind ; উপপাদন করা ; (সাধারণ তত্ত্ব হইতে বিশেষ তত্ত্ব) নির্ণয় করা, নিগমন করা (তর্কঃ) ; বস্তুনিরপেক্ষভাবে চিন্তা করা ; বিষয়বিবিক্তভাবে ভাবা। **—ed,** *adj.* **1.** Separated ; withdrawn in thought ; বাহ্যবিষয় হইতে নিবর্ত্তিত ; প্রত্যাহৃত। **2.** Inattentive to surrounding objects ; absent in mind ; as, an *abstracted* scholar ; তদাকৃষ্টচিত্ত ; তন্ময়। **—ed-ly,** *adv.* **1.** In the abstract ; ideally ; separately ; বস্তুনিরপেক্ষভাবে ; অমূর্ত্তভাবে ; বিষয়-বিবিক্তরূপে। **2.** In an absent-minded manner ; তদাকৃষ্টচিত্তে বা অনন্যমনস্কভাবে। **—ed-ness,** *n.* **—er,** *n.* One who makes an abstract ; সারসংগ্রাহক। **—strac'-tion,** *n.* **1.** The act of separating or withdrawing ; নিষ্কর্ষণ, পৃথক্করণ, নিবর্ত্তন, প্রত্যাকর্ষণ। **2.** The process of stripping an idea of its concrete accompaniments ; বিষয়বিবিক্তকরণ, গুণ ও ভাবকে বস্তু বা বিষয় হইতে পৃথক্রূপে চিন্তন। **3.** An idea or notion of a theoretical character ; something visionary ; as, an *abstraction* monger (কল্পনাব্যব

সায়ী) ; অমূর্ত্ত বিষয়, নিঃসঙ্গ ভাব ; কাল্পনিক বিষয়। **4.** A separation from worldly objects ; a recluse life ; as, a hermit's *abstraction ;* বিষয়ত্যাগ, বিষয়-বৈরাগ্য, প্রত্যাহার ; সংসারাশ্রমবর্জ্জন, সন্ন্যাস। **5.** Absence of mind ; inattention to present objects, occurrences, etc. ; as, a fit of *abstraction ;* তন্ময়তা ; তদ্গতচিত্ততা, অনন্যচিত্ততা। **6.** (*Euphem.*) Purloining ; (মোলায়েম ভাষায়) পরদ্রব্য আত্মসাৎকরণ, সরান।

ăb'-străct, *adj.* & *n.* **1.** Separated from matter ; considered in itself ; abstruse ; ideal ; not practical ; as, an *abstract* idea ; বস্তুনিরপেক্ষ, নির্ব্বিষয়, জড়বস্তু হইতে পৃথক্‌ভূত, বস্তুবিচ্ছিন্ন, অবচ্ছিন্ন (রবিঃ), সূক্ষ্ম, অমূর্ত্ত ; প্রত্যক্, নিরুপাধিক, ত্রিগুণাতীত ; নিগূঢ়, দুরূহ, দুর্জ্ঞেয় ; মনঃকল্পিত ; অব্যবহারিক। **2.** (*Log.* & *gram.*) Expressing a particular quality of an object, viewed apart from the other properties which constitute it ; general, as opposed to particular ; as, *honesty* is an *abstract* word ; [কারণ, *honesty* এই শব্দটী মানবের বহুগুণের মধ্যে একটীমাত্র বিশেষ গুণ প্রকাশ করে ; *reptile* is an *abstract* name, অর্থাৎ *reptile* একটী সাধারণ নাম, ইহা সরীসৃপ্-বর্গের অন্তর্ভুক্ত সর্প, কচ্ছপ, কুম্ভীর, টিক্‌টিকি প্রভৃতি যাবতীয় জাতির সাধারণ নাম।] (ব্যাকরণ ও ন্যায়শাস্ত্র) বিশেষ গুণবাচক, বিশেষ গুণ-প্রকাশক ; সাধারণ, অবিশেষক। **3.** Absent-minded ; প্রত্যাহৃত, অন্যমনস্ক। ***Noun.*** **1.** Essence ; summary ; সংক্ষিপ্তসার ; সার-সংগ্রহ, সংক্ষেপ, সার। **2.** An abstract term or noun ; also an abstract idea ; গুণবাচক পদ বা বিশেষ্য ; ভাববাচকপদ, ভাববাচক শব্দ, বস্তুনিরপেক্ষ ভাব। **Abstract mathematics** or **pure mathematics**—অমূর্ত্তগণিত (হিঃ কোঃ), গণিত-শাস্ত্রের যে শাখায় কোন আকার, আয়তন বা সংখ্যার ধর্ম্ম, স্বতন্ত্র বা ব্যাপকভাবে আলোচিত হয় ; যথা, জ্যামিতি, পাটীগণিত প্রভৃতি ; ইহা *mixed mathematics,* অর্থাৎ জ্যোতি-বিজ্ঞান (astronomy), যন্ত্র-বিজ্ঞান (mechanics) প্রভৃতি হইতে স্বতন্ত্র। **Abstract Noun**—গুণনাম। **Abstract number**—Number used without application to things ; বস্তুনিরপেক্ষ সংখ্যা ; নিরালম্ব বা নির্ব্বিষয় সংখ্যা যথা, ২, ৩, ৪। **Abstract self**—প্রত্যগাত্মা (হিঃ কোঃ)। **An empty abstraction**—A mere ideality ; শূন্যগর্ভ-কল্পনা। **In the abstract**—With reference to theoretical considerations only ; without reference to other associated things ; as, she has no idea of poverty, but *in the abstract* (*Brewer*) ; বস্তুনিরপেক্ষভাবে ; নিঃসঙ্গভাবে, কাল্পনিক ভাবে।

ăb-strūse', *adj.* Hard to understand ; profound ; recondite ; দুর্জ্ঞেয়, দুর্ব্বোধ, দুরধিগম্য, গহন (মঃ ভাঃ) ; জটিল। **—ly,** *adv.* **—ness,** *n.* The state or quality of being difficult to be understood ; দুর্জ্ঞেয়তা, দুরধিগম্যতা।

ăb-sûrd', *adj.* Contrary to reason ; nonsensical ; ridiculous ; incongruous ; অযৌক্তিক, ব্যাহত (সর্ব্বঃ), অসমঞ্জস, যুক্তিবিরুদ্ধ, ন্যায়বিরুদ্ধ ; অর্থশূন্য ; হাস্যাস্পদ ; অসম্বদ্ধ। **—i-tȳ,** *n.* **1.** Folly ; unreasonableness ; মূঢ়তা ; অযৌক্তিকতা, অসঙ্গতি, ব্যাহতি, অসম্ভাব্যতা। **2.** An absurd statement or act ; অযৌক্তিক উক্তি বা কার্য্য। **—ly,** *adv.*

ă-bŭn'-dănce, *n.* **1.** A quantity more than sufficient ; great plenty ; বাহুল্য, অজস্রতা ; প্রাচুর্য্য। **2.** Overflowing emotion ; as, *abundance* of the heart ; উদ্বেল হৃদয়োচ্ছ্বাস। **3.** Affluence ; wealth ; অর্থপ্রাচুর্য্য ; আঢ্যতা, বিভব। **—dant,** *adj.* More than sufficient ; plentiful ; অজস্র, ভূরি, প্রচুর, বহুল ; প্রভূত, ভূয়িষ্ঠ। **—dant-ly,** *adv.*

ab urbe condita, (*L.*) ; (abbr. A. U. C.), *adv.* Counting from the foundation of Rome ; রোমনগরীর প্রতিষ্ঠা-দিবস হইতে গণনায়।

ă-būse', *v. t.* **1.** To misuse ; to make bad use of ; অযথা ব্যবহার করা ; অপব্যবহার করা। **2.** To revile ; to reproach coarsely ; কুৎসা করা, অপবাদ করা, গালাগালি করা ; অপভাষা প্রয়োগ করা, জঘন্য ভাষায় গালি দেওয়া। **3.** To dishonour ; to disgrace ; অসম্মান করা ; অপমান করা। **4.** To violate ; to ravish ; সতীত্বলঙ্ঘন করা ; বলাৎকার করা।

ă-būse', *n.* **1.** Misuse ; improper use or application (*of*) ; as, an *abuse* of our natural powers : *abuse* of words ; অপব্যবহার ; অপলাপ, কু-প্রয়োগ, অশিষ্টপ্রয়োগ। **2.** Ill-treatment of a person (in words) ; তিরস্কার, কুবচন, গঞ্জনা, গালি-গালাজ, কটূক্তি, দুরুক্তি, অপভাষণ। **3.** A corrupt practice or custom ; কদাচার, লোক-বিগর্হিত আচরণ বা ব্যবহার। **4.** Violation ; rape ; as, *abuse* of a female child ; সতীত্বলঙ্ঘন ; বলাৎকার।

ă-bū'-sive, *adj.* **1.** Containing abuse ; reproachful ; as, *abusive* language ; ইতর, গ্লানিপূর্ণ ; নিন্দাত্মক, কুৎসাপূর্ণ। **2.** Practising abuse ; offering harsh words ; as, an *abusive* writer ; দুর্মুখ, নিন্দানিরত, কুৎসাকারী, অপভাষাপ্রয়োগরত ; পরুষকণ্ঠ, কর্কশভাষী। **—ly,** *adv.* **—ness,** *n.*

ă-bŭt', *v. i.* (*on, upon, against.*) To have common boundary with ; to lean on or rest ; as, his lands *abut upon* mine : the building *abuts on* the highway : the bridge *abuts against* the solid rock ; এক সীমাবিশিষ্ট হওয়া, কোন কিছুর উপর অবলম্বিত হওয়া বা ভর দিয়া থাকা। **—ment,** *n.* **1.** The meeting end to end ; junction ; সীমাসংযোগ ; সন্ধিস্থল। **2.** A lateral support ; the solid support for the extremity of a bridge or arch, etc. ; the point of junction between such support and the thing supported ; পিল্পা, পার্শ্বাবলম্ব ; যে কঠিন ইষ্টক বা পাষাণময় অবলম্বের উপর সেতু বা খিলানের প্রান্তভাগদ্বয় ঠেস্ বা ঝোঁক্ দিয়া থাকে ; উক্তরূপ অবলম্ব এবং অবলম্বিত খিলানের সংযোগ বা সন্ধিস্থল। **—ter,** *n.* (*Law*) The owner of the adjoining property ; পার্শ্ববর্ত্তী (লাগাউ) সম্পত্তির মালিক।

ă-bȳss', —bȳsm' (*poet.*), *n.* A bottomless depth or gulf ; any deep immeasurable space ; the lower world ; অতলস্পর্শ খাত ; মহাকাশ ; অধোলোক, রসাতল, নরক। **—bȳs'-măl, —byss'-al,** *adjs.* Bottomless ; infinite ; profound ; অতলস্পর্শ ; অসীম ; অগাধ।

Ab-ȳs-sin'-i-ân, *adj.* & *n.* Of or pertaining to Abyssinia ; এবিসিনিয়া দেশীয়। ***Noun.*** A native of Abyssinia ; হাবসী।

ă-cā'-ci-â (-shi-), *n.* **1.** A genus of elegant trees and shrubs with pinnate leaves ; উপপক্ষ পত্র-বিশিষ্ট বৃক্ষ ও গুল্ম "গণ"। **2.** (*Med.*) Gum Arabic, gum acacia ; (ভৈষজ্য-শাস্ত্র)

Branch of Acacia Arabica.

আরবী-গদ, কিকর (ওয়াট্)। ***Acacia Arabica***—বাব্‌লা, বাবুল, (ওয়াট্)। ***Acacia Catechu***—খদির বৃক্ষ (মঃ উঃ), খয়ের গাছ। ***Acacia Concinna***—কোচাই (বেলঃ)। ***Acacia Farnesiana***—গুইয়া বাবুল (বেলঃ)। ***Acacia Sirissa***—শিরীষ বা শিরীষপুষ্প (মঃ উঃ)।

ăc-ă-dĕm'-ic, *adj.* & *n.* **1.** Belonging to or agreeing with the philosophic school of Plato ; প্লেটো-প্রবর্ত্তিত দার্শনিকমতানুযায়ী। **2.** Belonging to an academy or university ; বিদ্বজ্জনপরিষদ্‌সংক্রান্ত, বিশ্ববিদ্যালয়সংক্রান্ত। **3.** Scholarly ; abstract ; unpractical ; পণ্ডিতোচিত ; অমূর্ত্ত, বিষয়বিবিক্ত ; লোকব্যবহারানভিজ্ঞ, অকার্য্যকর। ***Noun.*** **1.** One who belonged to the school or adhered to the philosophy of Plato ; প্লেটোপ্রবর্ত্তিত মতাবলম্বী প্রাচীন দার্শনিক। **2.** A member or a student of an academy or college ; বিদ্বজ্জনপরিষদের সভ্য,বিদ্বজ্জনসভাধিষ্ঠাতা, কলেজের ছাত্র। **3.** One too much enslaved to the principles of an academy (in painting, etc.) ; (চিত্র, সঙ্গীত প্রভৃতি ললিতকলাচর্চ্চায়) বিদ্বজ্জনপরিষদের অনুমোদিত ধারা ও পদ্ধতির দাসবৎ অনুসরণকারী। **—i-cal,** *adj.* (Same as ACADEMIC). **—ic-al-ly,** *adv.* Theoretically ; unpractically ; অব্যবহারিকরূপে ; অকার্য্যকর ভাবে। **—i-cals,** *n. pl.* University costume ; বিশ্ববিদ্যালয়ের নির্দ্দিষ্ট পরিচ্ছদ। **—ics,** *n. pl.* **1.** Mere theoretical arguments ; ঔপপত্তিক যুক্তিমাত্র। **2.** University robes ; বিশ্ববিদ্যালয়ের পরিচ্ছদ।

ă-căd'-ĕ-mȳ, (*pl.* —MIES), *n.* **1.** The garden near Athens where Plato taught ; hence, Plato's philosophical system ; এথেন্স নগরীর সন্নিকটবর্ত্তী উদ্যানবিশেষ—এই স্থানে গ্রীক দার্শনিক প্লেটো দর্শনশাস্ত্র শিক্ষাদান করিতেন ; প্লেটো প্রবর্ত্তিত দর্শন। **2.** A place of training holding a rank between a college and an elementary school ; a school ; a school for teaching a particular art ; as, Royal Military *Academy* : *Academy* of Music ; উচ্চবিদ্যালয়, প্রবেশিকা-বিদ্যালয় ; বিদ্যালয়, সারস্বত-নিকেতন, চতুষ্পাঠী ; বিশেষ বিশেষ বিদ্যা বা শিল্পশিক্ষার্থ বিদ্যালয়। **3.** A society for cultivating literature, arts, etc., of which membership is an honour ; as, the American *Academy* of Arts and Sciences ; the French *Academy* ; (শিল্প, সাহিত্য, কলাবিদ্যা প্রভৃতির আলোচনার্থ) বিদ্বজ্জনসভা, পণ্ডিতসভা, বিবুধমণ্ডলী, সারস্বতসমাজ বা সারস্বত-পরিষদ্। **—mi'-cian,** *n.* A member of an academy or society for promoting science, arts or literature ; specially, a member of the Royal Academy of Arts ; শিল্প, বিজ্ঞান, সাহিত্য ও ললিতকলানুশীলনপরিষদ্ বা সম্প্রদায়ের সভ্য ; (বিশেষভাবে) রাজকীয় ললিতকলানুশীলনসমিতির সভ্য।

A-cā'-diăn, *adj.* & *n.* Pertaining to Nova Scotia ; নভাস্কশিয়া দেশীয়। ***Noun.*** An inhabitant of Nova Scotia ; নভাস্কশিয়াবাসী।

ăc'-ă-lĕph, -lĕphe, *n.* A name given to a class of marine animals including the medusa, sea-nettle and jelly-fish ; সামুদ্রিক জন্তুশ্রেণী বিশেষ।

Acalypha Indica—মুক্তঝুরী(বেলঃ), মুক্তবর্ষী (বনঃ)।

ă-căn'-thŭs, *n.* **1.** A genus of

(1) (2)

Acanthus of Corinthian capital (2) and its probable origin (1).

prickly plants ; কণ্টকাকীর্ণ বৃক্ষসমূহের "গণ" বিশেষ। **2.** (*Arch.*) An ornament resembling the leaves of *Acanthus spinosus*, used in the capitals of the Corinthian and Composite orders ; গ্রীসদেশীয়

কণ্টকাকীর্ণ বৃক্ষপত্র-সদৃশ স্তম্ভভূষা বিশেষ। *Acanthus ilicifolius*—হরিকুশ

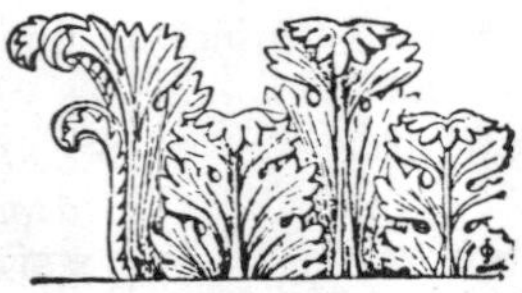

Acanthus of Corinthian capital.

(ওঝাট্), হরকুচকান্ত (ঐ), হরিকাশ (খোরি), সিংহাস্থ (সাঃ পঃ)।

ā-câr'-di-ăc, *adj.* Without a heart; হৃৎপিণ্ডবিহীন।

ā-câr'-pous (-pŭs), *adj.* Not producing fruit; বন্ধ্য, অফল (বৃক্ষ-সম্বন্ধে)।

ā-căt-ă-lĕc'-tic, *adj.* Not defective in the last foot; having the complete number of syllables; as, an *acatalectic* verse; পূর্ণসংখ্যক পদাংশবিশিষ্ট; পূর্ণাঙ্গ শেষ-পংক্তিপাদবিশিষ্ট (কবিতাপংক্তি)।

ă-căt'-ă-lĕp-sȳ, *n. pl.* **1.** Incomprehensibility; অজ্ঞেয়তা (হিঃ কোঃ), অবোধগম্যতা। **2.** The doctrine of the ancient sceptics that human knowledge never amounts to certainty but only to probability; প্রাচীন অজ্ঞেয়বাদী দার্শনিকদিগের প্রবর্ত্তিত মতবিশেষ; এই মতানুসারে বিষয়মাত্রেরই নিশ্চিতজ্ঞান (প্রমা) লাভ মানবের সাধ্যাতীত, সংশয়বাদ (হিঃ কোঃ), অনির্ণয়বাদ (ঐ)। **—lep-tic,** *adj.*

ăc-au-lĕs'-cĕnt (-ä-), *adj.* [also ACAULOUS, ACAULINE.] Having no true stem; নিষ্কাণ্ড (সাঃ পঃ)।

ăc-cēde', *v. t.* (*to*), **1.** To agree or assent *to* (opinion, policy); সম্মত হওয়া, স্বীকার করা, রাজি হওয়া, সম্মতি দেওয়া। **2.** To enter upon an office or dignity; as, **to** *accede* to the throne; কোন সম্ভ্রান্তপদের কার্য্য-ভার গ্রহণ করা। **3.** To join a party; to become added; কোন দলে যোগদেওয়া; যুক্ত হওয়া।

ăc-cĕl'-ĕr-āte, *v. t. & i.* **1.** To increase the speed of; to make quicker; ক্রমশঃ বেগবৃদ্ধি করা, উত্তরোত্তর গতিবৃদ্ধি করা; ত্বরান্বিত করা। **2.** To bring nearer in time; to cause to happen earlier; as, to *accelerate* the ruin of a government; ঘটনার সময় প্রত্যাসন্ন করা; সন্নিকট করা। ***Verb i.*** To add to one's speed; to become swifter; গতি-বৃদ্ধি করা; দ্রুততর হওয়া। **—at-ed,** *adj. (Phys.)* Progressively quicker; as, an *accelerated* motion; (পদার্থবিদ্যা) উত্তরোত্তর দ্রুততর। **—at-ing,** *adj.* Causing progressively quicker motion; as, *accelerating* motion; উত্তরোত্তর দ্রুততর গতিবিধায়ক। **—a'-tion,** *n.* **1.** The act of making quicker or the state of being made quicker; গতি-বর্দ্ধন, গতি-বৃদ্ধি, বেগ-বৃদ্ধি, বর্দ্ধমানতা। **2.** *(Phys.)* The rate of increase of velocity per unit of time; (পদার্থবিদ্যা) নির্দ্দিষ্ট সময়ে যে পরিমাণ গতি বৃদ্ধি হয়। **—a'-tive,** *adj.* Quickening motion; গতিবৃদ্ধিকর। **—a-tor,** *n.* **1.** One who or that which accelerates; গতিবর্দ্ধক ব্যক্তি বা বস্তু। **2.** One of a class of nerves and muscles; শিরা বা পেশীর শ্রেণীবিশেষের একটী। **Acceleration of the moon**—The increase in the moon's mean angular velocity about the earth; চন্দ্রগত্যন্তর (হিঃ কোঃ)। **Acceleration of the planets**—The increased velocity of the planets from aphelion to perihelion; মন্দোচ্চ হইতে নীচোচ্চ পর্য্যন্ত গ্রহগণের ক্রমবর্দ্ধমান গতিবেগ। **Acceleration of the stars.**—The time gained daily by stars over the sun; সূর্য্যের আহ্নিকগতি অপেক্ষা তারার আহ্নিকগতি-বৃদ্ধি।

ăc'-cĕnt, *n. & v. t.* **1.** An inflexion of the voice which gives to each syllable of a word its due pitch with respect to height or lowness; উচ্চারণসময়ে শব্দের অংশবিশেষের উপর প্রযুক্ত জোর, স্বর (মঃ উঃ)। **2.** A mark used in writing, to direct the stress of the voice in pronunciation; ঐ বোধক চিহ্ন, স্বর-চিহ্ন। **3.** Modulation of the voice in speaking; tone; স্বর-বৈচিত্র্য, স্বরলীলা (রবিঃ); ধ্বনি। **4.** *(Pl.)* Language; speech; as, to repeat the *accents* of his sad regret: "My dying *accents* hear;" বাণী, বাক্য; কথা, ভাষা। **5.** *(Mus.)* A stress recurring at intervals (সঙ্গীত-শাস্ত্র) নির্দ্দিষ্ট সময় অন্তে সঙ্গীতে পর্য্যায়ক্রমে যে জোর দেওয়া হয়। ***Verb t.*** **1.** To pronounce or mark with accent; যথাস্থানে জোর দিয়া উচ্চারণ করা, বা স্বর-চিহ্ন চিহ্নিত করা। **—cen'-tu-al,** *adj.* **—cen'-tu-ate,** *v. t.* **1.** To pronounce with an accent; জোর দিয়া উচ্চারণ করা। **2.** *(Fig).* To mark strongly; to emphasize; as, his marriage would strongly *accentuate* the amateur character of his position; (লক্ষণায়) বিশেষভাবে নির্দ্দেশ করা, সুস্পষ্ট করা। **—cen-tu-a'-tion,** *n.* The *acute accent* (´) = উদাত্ত; *the grave accent* (`) = অনুদাত্ত; *the circumflex accent* (⌒ or ʌ) = স্বরিত।

ăc-cĕpt', *v. t.* **1.** To receive, as gift; to receive with favour (an invitation, offer etc.); — with *of*; লওয়া, গ্রহণ করা (যেমন উপঢৌকনাদি); পরিগ্রহ করা। **2.** To accede or assent to; as, to *accept* a treaty, a proposal, an excuse, etc.; সম্মত হওয়া, স্বীকার করা। **3.** To take by the mind; to understand; as, how are these words to be *accepted*; গ্রহণ করা; বুঝা। **4.** To listen favourably to; to grant; "Sweet prince, *accept* their suit." অনুকূলভাবে শ্রবণ করা; প্রার্থনাপূর

করা। **5.** To agree or promise to pay, as a bill of exchange : টাকা দিতে প্রতিশ্রুত হওয়া। **—a-ble,** *adj.* Worth accepting ; pleasing to a receiver ; welcome : as, an *acceptable* present : one *acceptable* to us : পরিগ্রহণীয়, গ্রহণযোগ্য ; আদেয়, মনোজ্ঞ, রুচির, উপাদেয়, সুখদ ; স্বাগত। **—a-ble-ness,** *n.* **—a-bly,** *adv.* **—er, —or,** *ns.* A person who accepts, specifically **(—or),** one who accepts a bill of exchange ; গ্রাহক, পরিগ্রাহক, পরিগ্রহীতা। **Accepted by all**—সর্ব্ববাদিসম্মত।

[ac]-cĕpt'-ănce, *n.* **1.** The act of [ac]cepting ; favourable recep[ti]on ; approval : as, the *accept[an]ce* of a gift, office, doctrine, [e]tc. : পরিগ্রহণ, স্বীকার, অঙ্গীকার, [আ]দান, প্রতিগ্রহ ; সাদরগ্রহণ ; অনু[মো]দন। **2.** Engagement to pay a [b]ill ; টাকা দিবার লিখিত অঙ্গীকার। An accepted bill ; স্বীকৃত হুণ্ডী, [স]াকরাইয়া লওয়া হুণ্ডী (রঃ অঃ)।

[a]c-cĕp-tā'-tion, *n.* A particular sense given to a word or phrase ; its generally recognised meaning : as, my words, in common *acceptation* could never give him provocation : কোন শব্দ বা বাক্যাংশের বিশেষ অর্থ ; (শব্দ বা বাক্যাংশের) চলিতার্থ, শক্তিগ্রহ, অর্থবোধ।

ăc'-cĕss, *n.* **1.** Approach ; admittance ; accessibility ; উপাগম, সমীপাগমন, সন্নিধি-লাভ ; প্রবেশ ; অধিগম্যতা। **2.** Passage ; channel ; doorway ; আগম-পথ, প্রবেশ-মার্গ ; প্রণালী, সঙ্কীর্ণ-পথ ; প্রবেশ-দ্বার, উপসর্পণপথ। **3.** Admission to sexual intercourse ; অভিগম (উপঃ)। **4.** Attack or outburst of illness, anger, emotion, etc. ; as, the first *access* looked like an apoplexy ; পীড়ার আগম, সঞ্চার বা প্রকোপপ্রকাশ। **—ces-si-bil'-i-tŷ,** *n.* Approachableness ; সুগমতা, অভিগম্যতা, সুখসেব্যতা। **—ces'-si-ble,** *adj.* **1.** Approachable ; easy of access ; (স্থানসম্বন্ধে) গম্য, সুগম ; (ব্যক্তি-সম্বন্ধে) অভিগম্য, উপসর্পণীয়, সুখসেব্য (রাঃ তঃ), দর্শন-সুলভ। **2.** Obtainable ; প্রাপ্য, সুলভ। **3.** Open to the influence of ; (with *to*) ; as, minds *accessible to* reason ; কোনও কিছুর প্রভাবাধীন। **—ces'-si-bly,** *adv.*

ăc-cĕs'-să-rŷ, *n.* & *adj.* **1.** A helper in any act ; an accomplice ; সাহায্যকারী, সহায়তাকারী ; সঙ্গী, সহকারী। **2.** Accompaniment ; adjunct ; সহায়, অতিরিক্ত বিষয় ; অনুবন্ধ (মঃ উঃ)। *Adj.* Contributing ; additional ; সহকারী, সাহায্যকারী ; অতিরিক্ত।

ăc-cĕs'-sion (-sĕsh'-ŭn), *n.* **1.** Coming into presence or contact ; the act of becoming joined, (as to a party) ; সমীপাগমন, সম্মিলন ; যোগ, মিলন। **2.** Increase by something added ; that which is added ; বৃদ্ধি, আগম, উপচয় ; উপচিতবস্তু। **3.** The act of coming to or reaching a throne, office or dignity ; সিংহাসনারোহণ, পদ বা মর্য্যাদালাভ, অধিকারপ্রাপ্তি। **4.** (*Law*) Improvement or natural growth of property ; (আইন) সম্পত্তির বৃদ্ধি বা উপচয়। **—al,** *adj.* Additional ; অতিরিক্ত, আনুষঙ্গিক।

ăc-cĕs'-sŏ-rŷ, *adj.* & *n.* **1.** (Of persons) Assisting as a subordinate ; uniting in, and contributing to, a crime, but not as chief actor ; (*usually in a bad sense*) ; as, he was *accessory* in felony ; সহায়ক ; সাহায্যকারী, সহকারী, [অর্থাৎ যদি কোন লোক আপনি অপরাধ না করিয়া অন্য লোককে অপরাধ করিতে পরামর্শ দেয়, বা আজ্ঞা করে, বা অপরাধীকে লুকাইয়া রাখে, তবে তাহাকে *accessory* বলা যায়।] **2.** (Of things) Contributing in a secondary way ; additional ; as, *accessory* sound in music ; আনুষঙ্গিক, অপ্রধান ; অতিরিক্ত, সংযোগী *Noun.* **1.** Something additional and subordinate, as adjunct and accompaniment ; অপ্রধান বা অতিরিক্ত বস্তু, অনুবন্ধ, অনুষঙ্গ। **2.** (*Fine arts.*) A secondary object introduced as illustrative or explanatory of the scene—a mere ornamental part ; (ললিতকলা) একান্তপক্ষে আবশ্যক না হইলেও যে সমস্ত আনুষঙ্গিক ভূষা, অলঙ্কার প্রভৃতি চিত্রাদিতে স্থান লাভ করে [সঞ্চারীভাব (সাঃ দঃ)]। **—ri-ness,** *n.* The state of being or acting in a secondary character ; আনুষঙ্গিকতা, সঞ্চারণা (সাঃ দঃ)। (*Bot.*) **Accessory bud**—(উদ্ভিদ্-বিদ্যা) অতিরিক্ত মুকুল (সাঃ পঃ)।

ăc'-ci-dĕnce, *n.* **1.** The accidence or inflexions of words ; the part of grammar or a book dealing with inflexions ; (ব্যাকরণ) শব্দাদির প্রকৃতি-প্রত্যয় ; ব্যাকরণ বা অন্য যে কোন পুস্তকে শব্দাদির প্রকৃতি প্রত্যয়ের বিষয় আলোচিত হয়। **2.** The elements of any subject ; উপ[ক্রমণিকা], ক্রমণিকা, আদিপ্রকরণ গ্রন্থ।

ăc'-ci-dĕnt, *n.* **1.** Chance or what happens by chance ; an unexpected and unforeseen event ; an unfortunate but unintentional act ; casualty ; mishap ; দৈব-ঘটনা, আকস্মিক ঘটনা ; দৈবদুর্ব্বিপাক ; বিপত্তি, দুর্ঘটনা, বিঘ্ন, ব্যসন, অনিষ্টপাত। **2.** (*Log.*) A property or quality of a thing which is not essential to it, as *whiteness* in paper ; (তর্কবিজ্ঞান) আনুষঙ্গিক বস্তু বা গুণ, অনুষঙ্গ, আকস্মিক উপাধি, আগন্তুক ধর্ম্ম, আকস্মিক গুণ, উপলক্ষণ (হিঃ কোঃ), সমাপত্তি (মঃ উঃ)।

ăc-ci-dĕnt'-ăl, *adj.* **1.** Happening by chance or unexpectedly ; casual ; fortuitous ; as, an *accidental* visit ; দৈবিক ; আপতিক

(সংঃ) ; আকস্মিক ; নৈমিত্তিক। **2.** Not essential ; adventitious ; as, songs are *accidental* to a play ; অপ্রধান, অসমবায়ী (তর্কঃ) ; আগন্তুক। **–ly,** *adv.* Unexpectedly ; by chance ; casually ; not essentially ; unintentionally ; অভাবনীয়রূপে, অপ্রত্যাশিতরূপে ; ঘটনাক্রমে, হঠাৎ, দৈবাৎ, দৈববশে,বিধিবশে, দৈবযোগে ; নৈমিত্তিকরূপে ; অপ্রধানরূপে ; অনিচ্ছাক্রমে। (*Optics*) **Accidental colours**—The colours presented by subjective sensation, not external ; (দৃষ্টি-বিজ্ঞান) ঔপাধিকবর্ণ (হিঃ কোঃ), অর্থাৎ, কোন ব্যক্তি এক খণ্ড সাদা কাগজের উপরিস্থিত একটী রঞ্জিত বিন্দুর প্রতি কিছুক্ষণ দৃষ্টি নিবদ্ধ করত, তৎপর চক্ষু ফিরাইয়া কাগজের অন্য অংশে দৃষ্টিপাত করিলে, প্রাগুক্ত বিন্দুসদৃশ একটী বিভিন্ন বর্ণের বিন্দু প্রতিভাত হইয়া থাকে ; প্রথমোক্ত বিন্দুটী রক্ত কিম্বা কৃষ্ণবর্ণ হইলে, শেষোক্তটী যথাক্রমে সবুজ এবং শ্বেতবর্ণ দৃষ্ট হয় ; এই শ্বেত ও সবুজবর্ণকে 'ঔপাধিক বর্ণ' কহে। (*Painting*) **Accidental lights, Accidentals**—Secondary lights ; effects of light other than ordinary daylight ; (চিত্র-বিদ্যা) ঔপাধিক প্রকাশ (হিঃ কোঃ) ; চিত্রপটে চন্দ্রালোক, বর্ত্তিকালোক, অথবা মেঘান্তরালনিঃসৃত সূর্য্যালোক প্রভৃতির সমাবেশদ্বারা সঞ্জাত ভাব। (*Perspective*) **Accidental points**—(পরিপ্রেক্ষিত) আগন্তুক বিন্দু (হিঃ কোঃ)। **The chapter of accidents**—See CHAPTER.

ac-cip'-i-tral, *adj.* Hawk-like ; keen-sighted ; rapacious ; শ্যেনবৎ ; শ্যেন-চক্ষু (রবিঃ) ; হিংস্রক।

ac-claim' (-clām), *v. t.* & *n.* **1.** To applaud loudly ; প্রশংসাবাদ করা, সাধুবাদ করা। **2.** To declare by acclamation ; to hail ; as, they *acclaimed* him king ; জয়ধ্বনিপূর্ব্বক ঘোষণা করা ; স্বস্তি-বাক্য উচ্চারণ করা, বন্দনা করা, অভিনন্দিত করা। ***Noun.*** Shout of applause ; জয়ধ্বনি, জয়শব্দ।

ăc-clăm-ā'-tion, *n.* Loud and eager assent to a proposal ; shouting in a person's honour ; (*usu. pl.*) as, *long live the king ! vive l' empereur !* কোন প্রস্তাবের অনুমোদনসূচক করতালি, জয়ধ্বনি ইত্যাদি ; জয়ধ্বনি, জয়রব, সাধুবাদ, জয়নাদ, ধন্যবাদ, সাংরাবিণ (মাঃ মাঃ)। **—clam'-ă-tō-rȳ,** *adj.* **Acclamations of joy**—আনন্দ-ধ্বনি। **By acclamation**—করতালি-যোগে।

ăc-clī'-măt-īze, –īse, or **ăc-clī'-māte,** *v. t.* To accustom or habituate to a foreign climate ; to adapt to the peculiarities of a strange climate ; "Young soldiers, not yet *acclimatised,* die rapidly here." (পশু, পক্ষী, উদ্ভিদ্ এবং মনুষ্যকে) দেশান্তরের জলবায়ু বা আবহাওয়া সহনোপযোগী করা; বিদেশীয় শীতাতপসহনশীল করা। **–īz-ā'-tion, –ma-tă'-tion,** *ns.*

ăc-cliv'-i-tȳ, *n.* Upward slope of a hill ; চড়াই, চড়াও (রবিঃ), ক্রমোচ্চ, উৎসঙ্গ (আঃ বঃ)।

ăc-cō-lāde', *n.* A ceremony at the bestowal of knighthood, consisting of an embrace, kiss or stroke on shoulder with the flat of a sword ; নাইট্ উপাধিপ্রদান-কালে, চুম্বন, আলিঙ্গন বা স্কন্ধদেশে অসিফলকাঘাতরূপ ক্রিয়াবিশেষ।

ăc-cŏm'-mō-date, *v. t.* **1.** To adapt ; to conform ; as, to *accommodate* ourselves to circumstances ; উপযোগী করা ; অনুগত করা। **2.** To settle differences between ; to adjust ; as, to *accommodate* differences ; মীমাংসা করা, নিষ্পত্তি করা ; মিট্‌মাট্ করা, আপোষ করা। **3.** To supply or furnish ; to provide with certain conveniences ; to favour ; to find lodging for ; as, to *accommodate* a friend with a loan or with lodging ; যোগান, যোগাড় করা ; প্রয়োজনীয়দ্রব্যপ্রদানে সুবিধা করিয়া দেওয়া ; অনুগ্রহ করা ; বাসস্থানের বন্দোবস্ত করিয়া দেওয়া। **—da-ting,** *adj.* Obliging ; pliable ; lax ; as, an *accommodating* man or disposition ; প্রিয়কারী ; নমনশীল, মৃদুস্বভাব ; স্খলনশীল, স্খলচ্চিত্ত। **—da-ting-ly,** *adv.*

ăc-cŏm-mō-dā'-tion, *n.* **1.** Adaptation ; adjustment (foll. by *to*) ; উপযোগীকরণ ; সুব্যবস্থা। **2.** Obligingness ; প্রিয়কারিতা। **3.** Settlement ; compromise ; মীমাংসা ; নিষ্পত্তি, বিবাদভঞ্জন, আপোষ। **4.** Serviceable thing ; convenience ; কার্য্যোপযোগী বস্তু ; সুবিধা, সুযোগ, আরাম। **5.** A place of residence ; entertainment ; বাসস্থান, আবাসস্থলী ; সৎকার, বিনোদন। **6.** Adaptation of anything to a purpose or meaning different from the original ; (কোন বিষয়) মূল হইতে বিভিন্ন অর্থ বা উদ্দেশ্যের উপযোগীকরণ। **7.** A loan of money ; ঋণ। **Accommodation bill or note**—সিফাশী হুণ্ডী (হিঃ কোঃ)। [অর্থাৎ অপর কোন ব্যক্তির সুবিধার জন্য স্বাক্ষরিত হুণ্ডী বা পত্র।] **Accommodation coach** or **train**—A train stopping at minor or way-stations ; যে গাড়ী আরোহীদিগের সুবিধার জন্য সামান্য সামান্য ষ্টেশনেও থামিয়া থাকে। **Accommodation ladder** (*Naut.*)—A light ladder hung over the side of a ship at the gangway, for use in ascending from, or descending to, small boats ; (নৌ-বিদ্যা) জাহাজের বহির্দ্দেশে সংলগ্ন সিঁড়ি বা মই বিশেষ ; ঐ সিঁড়ির সাহায্যে ক্ষুদ্র ক্ষুদ্র নৌকা হইতে আরোহিগণ জাহাজে আরোহণ কিম্বা জাহাজ হইতে নৌকায় অবরোহণ করিতে পারে ; পোতারোহণী। **Accommodation works**—Works which a railway company is required by law to erect and maintain for the safety of those resident near the line

—they consist of bridges, fences, gates, etc. : রেলপথের সন্নিকটবর্ত্তী অধিবাসিগণের সুবিধার্থে রেলওয়ে কোম্পানী আইনতঃ যে সমস্ত বৃতি (বেড়া), সেতু, দ্বার প্রভৃতি নির্ম্মাণ ও রক্ষা করিতে বাধ্য থাকে।

ăc-cŏm'pá-nȳ(-kûm-), *v. t.* **1.** To go with ;to escort ; to attend,—(*by, with*) ; সঙ্গে যাওয়া, সঙ্গী হওয়া ; প্রহরী বা রক্ষকরূপে সমভিব্যাহারী হওয়া ; সাথী হওয়া। **2.** To co-exist ; to be connected with(said of things); এক সময়ে বর্ত্তমান থাকা, সংযুক্ত থাকা। **3.**(*Mus.*) To perform the accompanying part in a composition : (সঙ্গীত-শাস্ত্র) সঙ্গীতসহায়ক বাদ্যযন্ত্রাদি বাদন করা। **—ni-ment,** *n.* **1.** Appendage ; thing that attends another : অনুবন্ধ, উপকরণ ; আনুষঙ্গিক-পদার্থ। **2.** (*Mus.*) Subsidiary part, vocal or instrumental, usually the latter, as used to support the voice : (সঙ্গীত-শাস্ত্র) গীতি-সহায়ক বাদ্য বা স্বর, উপগান (মালঃ), সঙ্গীতানুগত বাদ্য, উপগা (কাঃ শ্রোঃ), সুরসঙ্গত (জ্যোতিঃ)। **—nist** (or **—nȳst),** *n.* The performer in music who takes the accompanying part : সঙ্গতবাদক। **Accompanied by**—অনুগম্যমান (কৃষ্ণঃ)।

ăc-cŏm'-plĭce, *n.* An associate in a crime (it is followed by *with* before a person, *in* or *of* before the crime) : as, Ram was *accomplice with* Hary *in* the murder *of* Sham : সহাপরাধী, সঙ্গী, সহকারী।

ăc-cŏm'-plish, *v. t.* **1.** To fulfil ; to perform ; to complete ; to finish ; পরিপূর্ণ করা, সম্পন্ন করা ; সম্পাদন করা ; সমাধা করা ; সমাপ্ত করা, সংসাধন করা, সিদ্ধ করা, নিষ্পন্ন করা। **2.** To perfect a person in graceful acquirements; কোন ব্যক্তির অর্জ্জিত জ্ঞান বা শক্তির চরমোৎকর্ষ সাধন করা, গুণসম্পন্ন করা। **—er,** *n.* **—ment,** *n.* **1.** Fulfilment ; completion : সম্পাদন, সাধন, সিদ্ধি ; সমাপ্তি, সমাপন, সমাধা। **2.** Attainment arising from study or practice ; refinement ; grace of manners (*usu. pl.*) : as, *accomplishments* befitting a station ; অভ্যাস বা অধ্যয়ন-লব্ধ গুণরাজি (প্রকৃতি-প্রদত্ত নহে) ; শিষ্টাচার, সভ্যাচার ; (শিষ্টসমাজসম্মত) মাধুর্য্যময় চালচলন। **—plished,** *p. p.* **1.** Completed ; established ; নিষ্পন্ন ; সিদ্ধ। **2.** Complete in acquirements ; having a finished education ; consummate (either in a *good* or *bad* sense) : as, an *accomplished* scholar : an *accomplished* villain ; গুণসম্পন্ন ; কৃতবিদ্য ; উৎকর্ষ-সম্পন্ন, পাকা।

ăc-cord' (-kärd), *n., v. t.* & *i.* **1.** Agreement ; harmony of mind ; consent ; as with full *accord* to our demand ; ঐক্য, একমত ; মনের মিল ; সম্মতি। **2.** Harmony of sounds ; as, the *accord* of tones ; concord ; harmony ; একতান, স্বরসঙ্গতি (রবিঃ) ; সঙ্গতি ; সুসমাবেশ। **3** Voluntary or spontaneous impulse to act ; (used of *persons* and *things*, and preceded by *own*) ; as, of one's own *accord* ; স্বতঃ বা স্বেচ্ছাপ্রণোদিত কর্ম্মপ্রবৃত্তি। **4.** (*Law*) An agreement between parties in controversy, which bars a suit ; মোকদ্দমা আপোষের জন্য সম্মতি। ***Verb t.*** **1.** To grant ; to award ; as, to *accord* due praise ; প্রদান করা ; অর্পণ করা। **2.** To bring to an agreement ; মিলনসংঘটন করা, ঐক্য করা। ***Verb i.*** To agree ; to be in harmony (*with* or *to*) ; as, his disposition *accords with* his look ; মিল হওয়া ; ঐক্য হওয়া। **—ance, —an-cy,** *ns.* Agreement ; conformity ; harmony ; মিল ; অনুবর্ত্তিতা ; সঙ্গতি। **—ant,** *adj.* Agreeing ; conformable ; harmonious (*with* or *to*) ; ঐক্যবিশিষ্ট, অনুযায়ী, অনুবর্ত্তী ; সুসঙ্গত। **—ant ly,** *adv.* **—ing,** *pt. a.* Agreeing ; suitable (*to*) ; অনুবর্ত্তী, অনুযায়ী অনুরূপ ; যথাযোগ্য। **—ing-ly,** *adv.* **1.** Agreeably ; suitably ; অনুসারে, তদনুসারে ; যথানুরূপ। **2.** Consequently ; therefore ; সুতরাং ; অতএব। **According as**—Precisely as ; as, all things are *according as* I gave instruction ; ঠিক যেমন। **According to**—Agreeably to ; on the authority of ; consistent with ; মতানুসারে ; কাহারও কর্ত্তৃত্বে ; অনুযায়ী। **In accordance with**—Agreeably ; অনুসারে। **Of one's own accord**—Voluntarily ; স্বেচ্ছা-ক্রমে, স্বতঃপ্রবৃত্ত হইয়া, স্বেচ্ছামত, গায়ে পড়িয়া। **With one accord**—With unanimity ; একযোগে।

ăc-cŏr'-dĭ-ŏn, *n.* A small musical

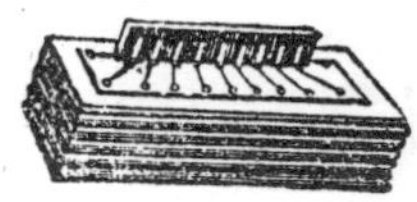

Accordion.

keyed wind instrument with bellows ; বাজা। **—ist,** *n.*

ăc-cŏst', *v. t.* & *n.* To speak first to ; to greet ; প্রথম সম্বোধন করা ; সম্ভাষণ করা, আমন্ত্রণ করা। ***noun.*** Greeting ; opening remark ; সম্ভাষণ ; উদ্বোধন-বাক্য।

ac-couche'-ment, (*F.*), *n.* Lying in ; delivery in child-bed ; প্রসবকাল, প্রসবাবস্থা ; সন্তান-প্রসব।

ac-cou-cheur', (*F.*), য্যা-কু শ্যার্, *n.* A man mid-wife ; ধাত্রীবিদ্যা-ভিজ্ঞচিকিৎসক, কুমারভৃত্যাকুশল ভিষক্, প্রসবতত্ত্ববিৎ পুরুষ (হঃ চঃ)।

ac-cou-cheuse', (*F.*), *n.* A midwife ; ধাত্রী, শল্যহর্ত্রী (চঃ)

ăc-count' (-kōwnt), *n., v. t.* & *i.* **1.** A reckoning ; calculation ; as Julian *account* of time ; হিসাব ; গণনা। **2.** Reckoning of money ;

transactions ; a statement of money received and expended, with balance ; as, he tore the *account* into pieces ; টাকা পয়সার হিসাব ; জমাখরচ, আয়ব্যয় পত্র। 3. Narrative ; statement of facts ; as, an *account* of the French Revolution ; বিবরণ, বিবৃতি, আখ্যান, বৃত্তান্ত ; সত্যবিবরণ। 4. A statement of reason, cause, motive etc. of some events ; reason ; ground ; as, no satisfactory *account* has been given of this phenomenon ; কোন ঘটনার হেতু, কারণ বা উদ্দেশ্য-নির্দ্দেশ, হেতুকথন বা প্রয়োজনবর্ণন ; হেতু ; কারণ, নিমিত্ত। 5. High estimation ; dignity ; as, to stand in one's *account* : men of *account* ; সমাদর, মান্যগণ্যতা ; সম্ভ্রম, কিম্মৎ। 6. Sake ; as, for your *account;* জন্য, খাতির। ***Verb t.*** To regard ; to consider ; as, *account* him as a hero ; গণ্যকরা ; বিবেচনা করা। ***Verb i.*** **1.** To give reckoning (of money held in trust) ; [*to, with* before a person, *for* before a thing] : (গচ্ছিত অর্থের) হিসাব নিকাশ দেওয়া। 2. To give satisfactory reason ; to explain *(for)* ; as, idleness *accounts* for poverty : you must *account* for your impropriety ; সন্তোষজনক হেতুপ্রদর্শন বা কারণ-নির্দ্দেশ করা ; কৈফিয়ৎ দেওয়া। **—ă-bil'-i-ty,** *n.* **—a-ble,** *adj.* 1. Liable to be called on to render an account ; answerable *(for* things, *to* persons) ; দায়ী ; মাল-পত্র বা জিনিষের হিসাবের জন্য দায়ী। 2. Explicable ; হেতু-প্রদর্শন-যোগ্য, কারণ-নির্দ্দেশ-যোগ্য। **—a-bly,** *adv.* **—ant,** *n.* One who keeps, adjusts or is skilled in, accounts ; an officer in a public office, in charge of the accounts ; গণনাকুশল ব্যক্তি, হিসাবনবীশ, হিসাবপরীক্ষক ; হিসাব-পত্ররক্ষক কর্ম্মচারী। **—ant-ship,** *n.* **Accountant General**—The chief accountant in public offices, bank, &c. ; the principal officer of the Accounts Department of a province ; গণনাধ্যক্ষ, প্রধান হিসাব-রক্ষক ; কোনও প্রদেশের হিসাব বিভাগের সর্ব্বপ্রধান কর্ম্মচারী। **Account book**—A book in which accounts are kept ; হিসাববহি, হিসাবের খাতা, গণনাপত্রিকা (রাঃ তঃ)। **Account current**—A running account between parties ; চল্‌তি বা চলিত হিসাব। **In account with**—Having credit relations with ; as, Ram is *in account with* Sham ; দেনা পাওনার সম্বন্ধযুক্ত। **On account of**—For the sake of ; জন্য, নিমিত্ত, হেতু, নিবন্ধন, কারণ, দরুণ, বশতঃ, প্রযুক্ত, বিধায়, বাবত। **On no account**—By no means ; certainly not ; as, *on no account* you should sacrifice your principle ; কোন ক্রমেই নহে ; নিশ্চিতই নয়। **On one's account**—For one's own purpose ; at one's own risk ; as, he began business *on his own account* ; নিজের জন্য ; নিজের ঝুঁকিতে। **On** or **to account**—In the course of a running account ; in part payment ; as, I asked for rupees five *on account ;* চল্‌তি হিসাবে ; কিছু কিছু করিয়া, আংশিকভাবে। **Suspense account**—জাকর। **The great account**—The Day of Judgment ; (খৃষ্টীয় বা মহম্মদীয় ধর্ম্মমতানুসারে) অন্তিম বিচারদিবস। **To be of no account, to be of very little account**—To be of no importance ; as, Corsica was valuable for its timber and mines, but its agriculture *was of no account ;* গণনার যোগ্য না হওয়া, ধর্ত্তব্য না হওয়া। **To bring to account**—To be made to answer for ; "In literature, however, you are seldom *brought to account* for misleading people." দায়ীকরা, কৈফিয়ৎ দিতে বাধ্য করা। **To call to account**—To ask one to say what one has to say in explanation of his conduct ; as, he was *called to account* for his rash conduct ; আত্মপক্ষসমর্থন করিতে অথবা অসঙ্গত আচরণের জন্য কৈফিয়ৎ দিতে বলা। **To find one's account in**—To profit by ; লাভবান্ হওয়া। **To give account**—To find cause ; to explain ; কারণ-নির্দ্দেশ করা ; কৈফিয়ৎ দেওয়া। **To go to one's account**—To be dead; মৃত হওয়া। **To keep an open account**—To keep a running account ; চলিত হিসাব রাখা, লেনাদেনা রাখা। **To lay one's account with**—To expect ; to look forward ; প্রত্যাশা করা; প্রতীক্ষা করা। **To make account of**—To set value upon ; "He *makes* small *account of* beauty." গণ্য করা, মূল্য দেওয়া। **To open an account**—To commence pecuniary transactions with ; হিসাব পত্তন করা। **To send one to one's account**—To kill ; বধ করা, নিকাশ করা। **To take accouut of**—To notice ; লক্ষ্য করা। **To take an account of**—To make a list of ; তালিকা প্রস্তুত করা। **To take into account**—To take into consideration ; ধর্ত্তব্যের মধ্যে আনা। **To turn to account**—To make useful ; as, I must *turn* my time *to account ;* সদ্ব্যবহার করা, কার্য্যকরী করা। **To write off an account**—To cancel ; খারিজ করা, বাতিল করা।

ăc-cou'-tre (-kô-têr), **-têr,** (chiefly used in *p. p.* ACCOUTRED) *v. t.* **1.** To equip ; to attire or array for military service ; সজ্জ করা; বেশভূষায় বা রণসজ্জায় সজ্জিত কর সামরিক কার্য্যের জন্য সেজরচনা ক

—tre-ment, *n.* (Usually in *pl.*) **1.** Equipment ; trappings ; সন্নাহ (ব্রতঃ), সাজসজ্জা ; সজ্জা, ভূষা। **2.** *(Mil.)* A Soldier's outfit, other than arms and garments, as belt, straps & valise ; (সামরিক-শাস্ত্র) অস্ত্র-শস্ত্র ও পরিচ্ছদ ব্যতীত সৈনিকগণের অন্যান্য সজ্জা, যথা—কোমরবন্ধ, চর্ম্মবন্ধ ও চর্ম্ম-পেটক।

ăc-crĕd'-ĭt, *v. t.* **1.** To repose confidence in ; to trust ; to esteem or have high opinion of ; বিশ্বাস ন্যস্ত বা আস্থা স্থাপন করা ; বিশ্বাস করা ; গণ্যকরা, (কাহারও সম্বন্ধে) উচ্চমত বা ধারণা পোষণ করা। **2.** To send out an ambassador with credentials *to* a person, *to* or *at* a court : "Beton was *accredited to* the Court of France ;" বিশ্বাসপত্র বা প্রত্যয়প্রদ নিদর্শনসহ কোন ব্যক্তির নিকট বা বৈদেশিক রাজসভায় দূতপ্রেরণ করা। **3.** To confer authority on ; ক্ষমতার্পণ করা। **—ed,** *adj.* **1.** Officially recognized (persons) ; as, their most *accredited* ministers ; শাসনতন্ত্রদ্বারা স্বীকৃত। **2.** Generally accepted ; orthodox (beliefs, etc.) ; সর্ব্বজনগৃহীত ; গোঁড়া। **—i-tā'-tion,** *n.*

ăc-crĕs'-cĕnt, *adj.* Growing ; ever increasing ; বৃদ্ধিশীল, বর্দ্ধিষ্ণু ; চিরবর্দ্ধমান। **—cĕnce,** *n.* Gradual growth or increase ; ক্রমবৃদ্ধি, ক্রমবর্দ্ধমানতা।

c-crēte', *v. i.* & *adj.* **1.** To grow together, or into one ; একত্র বর্দ্ধিত হওয়া, যুগ্মভাবে বর্দ্ধিত হওয়া। **2.** To adhere ; to be added to ; to form round a nucleus ; সংলগ্ন হওয়া, শ্লিষ্ট হওয়া ; সংযুক্ত হওয়া ; কোন বীজ বা শাঁসের চারিদিকে গড়িয়া উঠা। *adj.* **1.** Characterised by accretion ; as, *accrete* matter ; উপচিত। **2.** *(Bot.)* Grown together into one ; উদ্ভিদ্‌-বিদ্যা) সহজাত। **—crē'-tion,** *n.* The act of increasing by natural growth ; বর্দ্ধন। **2.** An extraneous addition ; as, an *accretion* of earth ; the matter added ; উপচয় ; উপচিত পদার্থ **3.** The growing of separate things (as particles) into one ; পদার্থসমূহের পৃথগ্‌ভূত কণিকাসকলের পিণ্ডাকারে পরিবর্দ্ধন, পিণ্ডীভবন, খণ্ড-সংশ্লেষ। **4.** *(Med.)* A growing together of parts naturally separate, as of the fingers or toes ; (ভৈষজ্য-শাস্ত্র) স্বভাবতঃ পৃথগ্‌ভূত অংশ সমূহের একত্র সংশ্লিষ্ট-ভাবে বর্দ্ধন, যথা, হস্ত পদাঙ্গুলির যৌটক বা সংশ্লেষ (যোড় আঙ্গুল)। **5.** *(Law)* Accession of land to land by the gradual action of natural forces ; the increase of legacy, etc. by share of a failing co-legatee ; (আইন) পয়স্তি হইয়া বা চড়া পড়িয়া ভূ-সম্পত্তির বৃদ্ধি ; সহ-দায় প্রাপ্ত ব্যক্তির অভাবে উত্তরাধিকারীর সম্পত্তি-বৃদ্ধি। **—cre'-tive,** *adj.*

ăc-crue' (-krō), *(to), v. i. (Lit. to grow to)* To arise or spring as a growth or result ; to be added as increase, profit or damage ; as, interest *accrues* to principal ; profit *accrues* to Government from the coinage of copper ; কোন কিছুতে জন্মা, সঞ্জাত হওয়া, উদ্ভূত হওয়া, উৎপন্ন হওয়া, উপজাত হওয়া ; লাভ বা ক্ষতিস্বরূপ বৃদ্ধি পাওয়া, সুদহিসাবে বাড়িয়া উঠা।

ăc-cü-bā'-tion, *n.* A lying or reclining, on a couch ; শায়িত বা অর্দ্ধ-শায়িত অবস্থায় পর্য্যঙ্কোপরি অবস্থিতি।

ăc-cŭm'-bĕnt, *adj.* Leaning or reclining as the ancients at their meals ; ভোজননিরত প্রাচীন গ্রীক্ ও রোমানগণের অনুরূপ পর্য্যঙ্কোপরি অর্দ্ধনিলীন বা অর্দ্ধশয়ান।

ăc-cü'-mü-lāte, *v. t.* & *i.* **1.** To heap up in a mass ; to gain by degrees ; to amass ; as, to *accumulate* wealth ; to collect or bring together ; as, to *accumulate* earth or stones ; রাশীকৃত করা, পুঞ্জীকৃত করা, স্তূপীকৃত করা ; ক্রমশঃ লাভ করা ; জড় করা সঞ্চয় করা ; সংগ্রহ বা একত্রিত করা **2.** *(University)* To take together several degrees at smaller intervals, than is allowed by rules ; (বিশ্ব-বিদ্যালয়) নিয়মিত সময় অপেক্ষা অল্পসময়ের মধ্যে এক সাথে কতিপয় উপাধি গ্রহণ করা। *Verb* To increase greatly (*lit.* & *fig.*) as, public events *accumulate* বহুল পরিমাণে বৃদ্ধি পাওয়া। **—la-tion,** *n.* Collecting ; amassing money-making ; growth of capital by continued interest ; a pile ;

Accumulator.

সঞ্চয়ন, সংগ্রহ ; সঞ্চয়, সমুচ্চয় ; ধনসঞ্চয় ; অবিরাম সুদসংযোগে মূলধনবৃদ্ধি ; রাশি, স্তূপ, পুঞ্জ, উপচয় (মঃ ভাঃ)। **—la-tive,** *adj.* Causing accumulation ; heaping up ; সঞ্চয়কর ; সঞ্চীয়মান। **—la-tive-ly,** *adv.* **—la-tive-ness,** *n.* **—la-tor,** *n.* **1.** One who or that which accumulates ; সঞ্চায়ক, সঞ্চয়কারী। **2.** Money-maker ; ধনসঞ্চয়ী। **3.** Taker of degrees by accumulation ; যে ব্যক্তি একযোগে বিশ্ববিদ্যালয়ের কতিপয় উপাধি গ্রহণ করে। **4.** *(Phys.)* An apparatus for storing electricity ; (পদার্থ-বিদ্যা) তাড়িতসঞ্চায়কযন্ত্র, সঞ্চায়ক (হিঃ কোঃ), বিদ্যুদ্‌-ভাণ্ডার (সাঃ পঃ),

বাহ-ভাণ্ডার (ঐ)। **Accumulation of energy** or **power**—শক্তিসঞ্চয় (হিঃ কোঃ), সামর্থ্যসঞ্চয় (ঐ)।

ăc'-cū-rāte, *adj.* In exact conformity to truth or to a standard; correct; precise; free from error; কোন সত্য, আদর্শ বা নিয়মের সম্পূর্ণ অনুগত; শুদ্ধ; সঠিক, যথার্থ; নির্ভুল। **—ly,** *adv.* Exactly; without mistake; সঠিকভাবে; নির্ভুলরূপে। **—rā-çy̆, —rate-ness,** *ns.* Freedom from mistake; precision; exactness; বিশুদ্ধতা; সঠিকতা; যথার্থতা।

ăc-curse' (-kêrs), *v. t.* To curse; to imprecate; শাপ দেওয়া, অভিশাপ দেওয়া; অভিসম্পাত করা। [অধুনা এই শব্দটী কচিৎ ব্যবহৃত হয়।]

ăc-cŭrsed', —cŭrst', *p. p.* **1.** Doomed to destruction, misery or evil of any kind; as, my life will be *accursed*; lying under a curse; blasted; ruined; হতক, দগ্ধভাল; অভিশপ্ত, শাপগ্রস্ত; বিধ্বস্ত (মৃচ্ছঃ), উৎসন্ন; ধ্বংসপ্রাপ্ত। **2.** Detestable; execrable; as, deed *accursed*; গর্হিত, জুগুপ্সিত, গর্হণীয়; জঘন্য।

ăc-cū'-sā-tive, *adj.* & *n.* (*Gram.*) Corresponding to *objective* case in English; as, an *accusative* case; (ব্যাকরণ) ইংরাজীভাষার কর্ম্মকারকের অনুরূপ। ***Noun.*** A term given to a case of nouns, on which the action of a verb terminates or falls; in English grammar, the *objective* case; সংস্কৃত দ্বিতীয়াবিভক্তি; কর্ম্মকারক। **—ti'-val,** *adj.*

ăc-cūse', *v. t.* **1.** To charge with an offence; to indict; as, to *accuse* one of high crime or misdemeanour; অপরাধী করা; অভিযুক্ত করা। **2.** To charge with a fault; to blame; to censure; (used of persons and things); as, she *accused* her face to face: *accusing* the times is but *accusing* ourselves; দোষী করা; দোষ দেওয়া, অপবাদ দেওয়া; নিন্দা করা, তিরস্কার করা। **—cūs'-ā-ble,** *adj.* Liable to be accused; blamable; (*of*); অভিযোজ্য, অভিযোক্তব্য; দূষ্য, নিন্দনীয়। **—cus'-al,** *n.* **—cus'-ant,** *n.* An accuser; অভিযোগকারী। **—cu-sā'-tion,** *n.* **1.** The act of accusing; অভিশংসন (মিথ্যাভিশংসন, যাজ্ঞঃ, 2389), অভিযোগস্থাপন, দোষারোপণ। **2.** A charge of offence or crime; indictment; as, the *accusation* is murder; অভিযোগের বিষয়; অভিযোগ, পাতকাভিযোগ, অভিযোগ-পত্র। **—cū-sā-tō'-ri-ăl,** *adj.* [(*Law*) *Accusatorial procedure*, etc., in which prosecutor and judge are not the same; যে ব্যবহারবিধিতে অভিযোক্তা এবং বিচারক এক ব্যক্তি নহেন; opposed to *inquisitorial*.] **—cu'-sā-to-ry,** *adj.* Pertaining to, or containing, an accusation; as, *accusatory* language, manner, etc; অভিযোগাত্মক, অপবাদগর্ভ। **—cūsed',** *p.p.* (Used as a *noun*, both singular and plural) One charged with a crime; অভিযুক্ত ব্যক্তি, আসামী, অপরাধী। **—cus'-er,** *n.* One who accuses, esp. one who prosecutes in a court of justice; দোষারোপক, দূষক, অপবাদকারী, ফরিয়াদী, অভিযোক্তা, অভিযোগকারী।

ăc-cŭs'-tŏm, *v. t.* To make familiar by use; to form a habit by practice; (generally with *to*); as, to *accustom* one's self *to* diet; পরিচিত করান, অভ্যাস করান; অভ্যস্ত করা। **—tomed,** *p.p.* Usual; familiar; habituated; প্রায়িক (আপঃ); পরিচিত; অভ্যস্ত।

āce, *n.* **1.** A unit; a single pip on a card or die; as, the *ace* of diamond (রুহিতনের টেক্কা); একক; তাসের টেক্কা বা পাশার পোয়া। **2.** A very small quantity; a particle; an atom; a trifle; as, the creditor will not abate an *ace* of his demand; অতি ক্ষু[দ্র] সংখ্যা; কণা, কণিকা, তিল; পরমাণু কিঞ্চিৎ, যৎসামান্য। **T[o bate an] ace**—To make the lea[st abate]ment; এক তিল বা এক [চু]ল কমান, সূচ্যগ্র পরিমাণও কমান। **Within an ace of**—Within a hair breadth of; (কোন কিছুর) অ[তি] নিকটে।

A-cĕl'-dă-mă (ă-), *n.* **1.** The field in the vicinity of Jerusalem purchased with the bribe which Judas took for betraying his Master, and therefore, called the *field of blood*; খৃষ্ট শিষ্য জুডাস্ বিশ্বাসঘাতকতা পূর্ব্বক গুরুকে শত্রুহস্তে সমর্পণ করিয়া, উৎকোচ স্বরূপ যে অর্থ প্রাপ্ত হয়, তদ্দ্বারা ক্রীত ক্ষেত্র। **2.** (*Fig.*—*common noun*) A field of bloodshed; scene of slaughter; "The system of warfare which had already converted immense tracts into one universal *aceldama*." (লক্ষণায়) হত্যাকলঙ্কিত ভুমি; বধ-স্থলী।

ā-cĕph'-ăl-ous (-ŭs), *adj.* **1** Without the head; বিশিরস্ক (মঃ ভাঃ)। **2.** Recognizing no governing head or chief; নেতৃশূন্য, নায়কবিহীন, শিরঃ-শূন্য (মঃ উঃ)। [3.] (*Bot.*) With the head aborted or cut off; (উদ্ভিদ্-বিদ্যা) অব্যক্তশিরস্ক (সাঃ পঃ)। **4.** (*Prosody*) Wanting the first syllable of foot of the verse; (ছন্দঃশাস্ত্র) প্রথম পদাংশ বা পংক্তিপাদবিহীন।

ăc'-êr-bāte, *v. t.* Same [as] EXACERBATE.

ā-cêrb'-ĭ-ty̆, *n.* **1.** Sourness of taste with bitterness or astringency; harshness; তিক্তকষায় স্বাদ; কটুতা, উগ্রতা, কঠোরপণা। (*Fig.*) Bitterness of speech, manner, or temper; as, there w[as] an *acerbity* in her tone th[at] made me feel extremely uncom[fortable].

fortable ; (লক্ষণায়) বাক্য, ব্যবহার বা প্রকৃতির তিক্ততা।

-**ēr-ous** (-ŭs), **ăc′-ēr-ōse**, *adj.* *Bot.*) Narrow and slender, with a

Acerose leaves—Juniper.

sharp point ; resembling chaff ; (উদ্ভিদ্-বিদ্যা) ক্ষীণ, অনায়ত ও সূক্ষ্মাগ্র ; তুষাকৃতি।

ă-cĕs′-cĕnt, *adj.* (*Lit.* & *fig.*) Turning sour ; hence slightly sour ; as, a disagreeable *acescent* odour resembling that of putrescent milk : their feelings can not but be wounded and *acescent* ; শব্দানুযায়ী এবং লক্ষণায়) অম্লভবনশীল ; ষদম্ল, কটু। **—cence, —cen-cy,** *ns.*

-**ĕ-tăb′-ū-lŭm,** *n.* (*Pl.*—**la**). (*Rom. Antiq.*) A little cup to hold vinegar, sauce, etc., (রোমীয় পুরাতত্ত্ব) সির্কা, ব্যঞ্জন, প্রভৃতির ক্ষুদ্র বাটি। **2.** The socket of the thigh-bone or of joints in insects ; কীটের ঊর্দ্ধাস্থি-কোটর বা অস্থিসন্ধিকোটর।

cēt′-ic, *adj.* Pertaining to or producing vinegar ; চৌক্রিক, চুক্রদ। **ce′-tous,** *adj.* Having a sour taste ; অম্লরস, অম্লস্বাদ। **—i-fi-cā′-tion,** *n.* **—i-fy,** *v. t.* & *i.* To convert into vinegar ; to become sour ; দ্রাবক বা সির্কাতে পরিণত করা হওয়া ; অম্ল হওয়া। **Acetic acid** চুক্রাম্ল, সির্কাম্ল (হিঃ কোঃ), কাঞ্জিক (ঃ সং—প্র), ধান্যাম্ল (রঃ রঃ—প্র), ম্ল (রঃ—প্র)।

ĕt′-ȳ-lēne, *n.* A colourless gas, burning with a bright flame ; উজ্জ্বলশিখাবিস্তারে জ্বলনশীল বর্ণহীন বাষ্পবিশেষ।

a-char′-ne-ment, (*F.*), *n.* Ferocity ; thirst for blood ; ক্রূরতা ; রক্তপিপাসা।

A-chā′-tēs (ă-), *n.* A faithful friend of Aeneas (*Virgil-Aeneid*) ; any faithful friend ; a trusted comrade ; ভার্জ্জিলের ইনিয়াড্ কাব্যের নায়ক ইনিয়াসের আবাল্য-বন্ধু য়্যাকাটেস্ ; অকৃত্রিম বন্ধু বা অকপট সখা ; বিশ্বস্ত সহচর।

āche *n.* & *v. i.* A continuous or abiding pain ; ব্যথা, বেদনা। ***Verb i.*** To suffer continuous or prolonged pain ; ব্যথিত হওয়া, ব্যথা করা, অবিরাম বেদনা বোধ করা। **Ach′-ing,** *adj.* Continuously painful ; যন্ত্রণাদায়ক, অবিরামবেদনাপ্রদ। **Head-ache**—শিরোবেদনা। **Tooth-ache**—দন্তশূল।

ă-chieve′ (-chēv), *v. t.* **1.** To perform ; to accomplish ; সম্পাদন করা ; সুসম্পন্ন করা, সংসাধন করা। **2.** To obtain, or gain, as the result of exertion ; to acquire ; to win ; as, I have *achieved* that reputation ; চেষ্টা বা উদ্যমের ফলে লাভ করা ; অর্জ্জন করা ; লাভ করা। **3.** To reach an end ; as, to *achieve* this end it should lead to war ; উদ্দেশ্য সাধন করা। **—ment,** *n.* **1.** Completion ; accomplishment ; সম্পাদন ; সংসাধন, নিষ্পাদন। **2.** A great or heroic deed ; a feat ; a victory ; অবদান (কুমাঃ, ৭—৫৪), মহৎকৃত্য ; বীরোচিত কর্ম্ম ; রণজয়। **3.** An escutcheon or ensign armorial ; কুলপত্র বা কুলধ্বজ।

ăch-rö-măt′-ic, *adj.* (*Optics*) Free from colour ; transmitting light without decomposing it into its primary colours ; (দৃষ্টি-বিজ্ঞান) বর্ণহীন, নীরঙ্গ, অবর্ণ ; অবিশ্লিষ্টালোক-সঞ্চারী, অর্থাৎ রক্ত, হরিতনীলাদি—মৌলিক বর্ণে বিশ্লিষ্ট না করিয়া আলোক-সঞ্চারণকারী। **—ro′-ma-tism.** *n.* **Achromatic lens**—নীরঙ্গ তাল (হিঃ কোঃ)। **Achromatic telescope** or **microscope**—অবর্ণ দুরবীক্ষণ, তথ্যবর্ণদুরবীক্ষণ যন্ত্র (হিঃ কোঃ), তথ্যবর্ণানুবীক্ষণ যন্ত্র (ঐ)।

ă-chrö′-mă-tīze, *v. t.* To deprive of colour ; বর্ণহীন করা।

ă-cĭc′-ū-lâr, *adj.* Needle-shaped সূচ্যাকার, সূচীনিভ, অনুসূচিক, সূক্ষ্ম সূচ্যগ্র। [Also, ACICULATE, ACICULATED.] **—ly,** *adv.*

ăc′-ĭd, *adj.* & *n.* Sour ; sharp ; biting to the taste ; having the taste of vinegar ; অম্ল ; তীব্র ; টক্ ; চুক্রাস্বাদ, সির্কার মত আস্বাদবিশিষ্ট। ***Noun.*** **1.** A sour substance ; অম্লপদার্থ। **2.** (*Chem.*) A substance, usually sour, which turns vegetable blues to reds and combines with bases to form salts and of which hydrogen is an essential constituent ; (রসায়নশাস্ত্র) দ্রাব, অম্ল (রঃ—প্র), দ্রাবক, তেজাব। **—i-dim′-e-ter,** *n.* An instrument for measuring the strength of acids ; অম্লমানযন্ত্র, অম্লমাপক যন্ত্র (হিঃ কোঃ)। **—i-dim′-e-try,** *n.* The measurement of the strength of acids ; অম্লমিতি (হিঃ কোঃ)। **—ness,** *n.*

ă-cĭd′-ĭ-fȳ, *v. t.* To make acid ; to convert into an acid ; অম্লাক্ত করা ; দ্রাবকে পরিণত করা। **—fi-a-ble,** *adj.* Capable of being converted into acid ; অম্লীভবনক্ষম। **—fi-ca′-tion,** *n.* The act or process of changing into an acid ; অম্লীকরণ।

ă-cĭd′-ĭ-tȳ, *n.* Sourness ; sharpness to the taste ; অম্লতা, অম্লত্ব ; আস্বাদের তীব্রতা। [*Acidity of stomach*—অম্লপিত্ত (সাঃ পঃ)।]

ă-cĭd′-ū-lā-tĕd, *adj.* Made somewhat acid ; অম্লাক্ত, ঈষদম্ল।

ă-cĭd′-ū-lous (-lŭs), *adj.* **1.** Slightly sour ; ঈষদম্ল, কিঞ্চিদম্ল, আম্ল (হিঃ কোঃ)।

2. (*Fig.*) Sour-tempered : as, he is gloomy and *acidulous ;* (লক্ষণায়) কটু-স্বভাব।

ă-cĭn′-i-fōrm, *adj.* Clustered like grapes ; having the form of grapes ; দ্রাক্ষাবদ্-গুচ্ছিত, দ্রাক্ষাবৎ স্তবকিত ; দ্রাক্ষাকার।

ăc-knŏwl′-edge (-ĕj), *v. t.* **1.** To own the knowledge of ; to admit the truth of ; স্বীকার করা ; মানা। **2.** To own the claims or authority of ; to recognize ; as, he was publicly *acknowledged* as the successor to the crown ; কাহারও স্বত্ব অথবা প্রাধান্য স্বীকার করা, মানা ; প্রত্যভিজ্ঞান করা (মঃ ভাঃ)। **3.** To own with gratitude or as an obligation (a gift or service rendered) ; to own, as a benefit ; (ধন্যবাদ বা কৃতজ্ঞতার সহিত) প্রাপ্তি-স্বীকার করা ; উপকার স্বীকার করা। **4.** To own as genuine ; to own or avow in legal form ; প্রকৃত বলিয়া স্বীকার করা ; আইনানুযায়ী স্বীকার করা। **5.** To show recognition by some act, as by a bow, nod, smile, etc. ; to salute ; as, she met him in the street but barely *acknowledged* him ; (প্রণতি, শিরশ্চালন বা মৃদুহাস্য-দ্বারা) পরিচয়জ্ঞাপন করা ; অভিবাদন করা। **—edg(e)-ment,** *n.* **1.** The act of acknowledging ; confession ; avowal ; স্বীকার, অঙ্গীকার ; দোষস্বীকার, অপরাধস্বীকার, একরার ; স্পষ্ট স্বীকার। **2.** The owning of a benefit received ; courteous recognition ; expression of thanks ; উপকার-স্বীকার ; সৌজন্যপূর্ণ স্বীকৃতি ; ধন্যবাদ-জ্ঞাপন। **3.** Something given or done in return for a favour or message ; কোন সংবাদ বা অনুগ্রহের পুরস্কার বা প্রতিদানস্বরূপ প্রদত্ত বস্তু বা অনুষ্ঠিত কার্য্য।

ăc′-mē, *n.* Highest point ; as, the *acme* of joy ; point of perfection ; চূড়ান্ত, পরাকাষ্ঠা ; চরমোৎকর্ষ।

ăc′-nē, *n.* A small hard pimple or tubercle on the face ; মুখব্রণ, মুখদূষিকা (মাঃ নিঃ)।

ă-cŏck′, *adv.* **1.** In cocked fashion (said of the hat) ; টেড়াভাবে। **2.** Defiantly ; অবজ্ঞাপূর্ব্বক।

ăc′-ō-lȳte,—lȳth(e), *n.* **1.** An inferior officer in the Roman Catholic Church who attended the priest and deacons, and

Acolyte.

performed subordinate duties as lighting and bearing candles, etc. ; ক্যাথলিক ধর্ম্ম-মন্দিরে নিযুক্ত পরিচারক বিশেষ। **2.** An attendant ; an assistant ; পরিচারক ; সহকারী।

ăc′-ō-nīte, *n.* **1.** The herb wolf's-bane or monk's-head (*Aconitum Napellus, Aconitum Ferox);* বৎসনাভ (বেলঃ)। **2.** A poisonous extract of the herb ; উক্ত ওষধির বিষাক্ত আরক বা নির্যাস, বিষ, মিঠা-বিষ, কাঠবিষ, মিঠা জহর। **—nit-ic,** *adj.*

ā′-cōrn, *n.* The fruit of the oak ; ওক বৃক্ষের ফল, (আরবী ভাষায়) বালুট (বেলঃ)।

Acorus calamus—Sweet-flag ; শ্বেত বচ (বেলঃ), বচ (ঐ), গোরা বচ (ঐ)।

ā-cŏt-ȳ-lē′-dŏn, *n.* (*Bot.*) A plant which has no seed-lobes or cotyledons ; (উদ্ভিদ্-বিদ্যা) অবীজ-দল (সাঃ পঃ)। **—ous,** *adj.*

ă-cou′-chȳ (-cō-), *n.* A small rodent quadruped allied to the guinea-pig ; গিনীদেশীয় ক্ষুদ্র শূকরবৎ দন্তুর জন্তু বিশেষ।

ă-cous′-tĭc (-cōws-), *adj.* Pertaining to the sense or organs of hearing or the science of sounds ; শ্রবণেন্দ্রিয়সংক্রান্ত, শ্রৌত, ধ্বনি-বিজ্ঞান-বিষয়ক। **—tics,** *n.* (*Usually treated as sing.*) The science of sound and of the phenomena of hearing ; ধ্বনি-বিজ্ঞান, ধ্বনিশাস্ত্র (হিঃ কোঃ), শ্রোত্র-বিদ্যা, নাদ-বিদ্যা।

ăc-quaint′ (-quānt), *v. t.* **1.** To make known ; to make one's self familiar *with* circumstances, etc. ; জ্ঞাত করা, জ্ঞাপিত করা, বিদিত করা ; পরিচিতকরা। **2.** To inform (a person *of* a thing) ; as, to *acquaint* a friend with the particulars *of* an act ; বিজ্ঞাপিত বা অবগত করা। **—ance,** *n.* **1.** The state of having more or less intimate knowledge (used of persons and things) ; পরিচয়, জান শোনা। **2.** A person known to on[e] but not on terms of gre[at] intimacy ; as, he is not a frien[d] only an *acquaintance ;* পরিচি[ত] ব্যক্তি। **3.** The whole body [of] those with whom one is ac[-]quainted (now usually *sing* with *pl.*—**ances**) ; পরিচিত ব্যক্তিবর্গ। **—ance-ship,** *n.* **To make [or] cultivate one's acquaintan[ce]** (*of*)—To endeavour to becom[e] intimate with a person ; কাহা[র] সহিত পরিচিত হইতে চেষ্টা করা, কাহা[র] সহিত পরিচয় প্রসঙ্গ করা।

ăc-quĕst′, *n.* **1.** Acquisitio[n] অর্জ্জন, অর্জ্জিত বস্তু। **2.** (*Law*) Pr[o]perty gained by purchase or g[ift] or otherwise than by inheritanc[e] (আইন) স্বোপার্জ্জিত সম্পত্তি (রঃ অঃ দানসূত্রে প্রাপ্ত সম্পত্তি।

ăc-quĭ-esce′ (-ĕs), *v. i.* **1.** T[o]

agree tacitly ; to accept (the conclusions and arrangements of others) ; মৌনভাবে সম্মত হওয়া ; স্বীকার করা। **2.** To rest satisfied in a state or place ; as, we are not made to *acquiesce* in life and health ; কোন অবস্থায় বা স্থানে সন্তুষ্ট থাকা। **—es'-cence,** *n.* **1.** A silent or passive assent to or compliance with proposals, or measures ; মৌনসম্মতি। **2.** Quiet satisfaction ; as, a life of worldly *acquiescence* will not do ; শান্তিপূর্ণ তৃপ্তি, শান্তভাব। **—es'-cent,** *adj.* Disposed to submit ; assentive ; বশ্য, বশবর্ত্তী, অনুরোধী ; সম্মতিদানশীল। **—es'-cent-ly,** *adv.*

ăc-quïre', *v. t.* To gain by oneself and for oneself ; to get as one's own ; to come into possession of ; as, to *acquire* a title, riches, knowledge, good or bad habits, etc. ; অর্জ্জন করা ; প্রাপ্ত হওয়া ; লাভ করা, অধিকারলাভ করা। **—ment,** *n.* The act of acquiring ; something acquired ; attainment ; (as opposed to natural gift or talent) ; অর্জ্জন ; অর্জ্জিত বস্তু ; প্রাপ্তি। [স্বকীয় চেষ্টা দ্বারা অর্জ্জিত জ্ঞান, বিদ্যা প্রভৃতি, যাহা প্রকৃতি প্রদত্ত নহে।]

ăc-qui-sĭ'-tion, *n.* The act of getting by one's own exertion ; what is acquired ; a gain ; as, learning is an *acquisition,* but memory is a natural gift ; ব্যুৎপত্তিলাভ, অর্জ্জন ; অর্জ্জিত বস্তু (জ্ঞান, বিদ্যা প্রভৃতি) ; প্রাপ্তি। **—quis'-i-tive,** *adj.* **1.** Given to make acquisitions ; অর্জ্জনেচ্ছু। **2.** Acquiring ; (সম্পত্তি) অর্জ্জনে প্রবৃত্তিশীল। **—quis'-i-tive-ness,** *n.* **1.** The state or quality of being acquisitive ; a propensity to acquire a property ; অর্জ্জনশীলতা ; অর্জ্জনপ্রবৃত্তি। **2.** (*Phren.*) The organ, or region of the brain supposed to give rise to this desire ; (মস্তিষ্ক-সামুদ্রিক) মস্তিষ্কের উভয় পার্শ্বান্তর্গত যে অঙ্গ বা বিভাগ বিষয়ার্জ্জনস্পৃহা উৎপাদন করে।

ăc-quit', *v. t.* **1.** To discharge, as a claim or debt ; to clear off ; to pay off ; কোন দাবী বা ঋণ মিটাইয়া দেওয়া ; পরিশোধ করা, শোধ করা ; চুকাইয়া দেওয়া। **2.** To discharge the duties of one's position ; to perform one's part ; as, the soldier *acquitted* himself well in battle ; পদোচিত কর্ত্তব্য পালন করা ; ন্যস্ত কর্ত্তব্য নির্ব্বাহ করা, নির্দ্দিষ্ট কর্ত্তব্য সম্পাদন করা। **3.** To set free from a charge ; to declare (a person) not guilty (of offence) ; মুক্তি দেওয়া, বেকসুর খালাস দেওয়া ; অব্যাহতি দেওয়া। **—tal,** *n.* **1.** The act of acquitting ; a discharge from debt or obligation ; মুক্তি, অব্যাহতি ; ঋণ বা বাধ্যবাধকতা হইতে অব্যাহতি। **2.** A deliverance from the charge of an offence, by verdict, sentence or other legal process ; মুক্তি, অব্যাহতি, খালাস। **3.** Performance of duty ; কর্ত্তব্যসম্পাদন। **—tance,** *n.* **1.** Payment of debt ; ঋণ-পরিশোধ। **2.** A receipt in full ; a writing in evidence of a discharge ; as, *acquittance* roll ; প্রাপ্তি-সূচক রসিদ ; মুক্তি-পত্র, ফারকত।

a'-cre (-cêr), *n.* A measure of land containing 4,840 square yards ; একর (৪,৮৪০ বর্গগজ পরিমিত ভূমি—কিঞ্চিদধিক ৩ বিঘা জমি)। **—age,** *n.* Amount of acres ; acres collectively ; একরের পরিমাণ ; একরসমষ্টি। **—cred,** *p. p.* Possessing landed property ; ভূসম্পত্তিশালী। **—cres,** *n. pl.* Lands or states generally ; ভূ-সম্পত্তি। **Broad acres**—Extensive lands ; বিস্তীর্ণ ভূসম্পত্তি। **God's acre**—A churchyard ; গির্জ্জার প্রাঙ্গণ, সমাধি-স্থান।

ăc'-rid, *adj.* **1.** Sharp or biting to the taste ; bitterly pungent ; irritating ; corrosive ; তীক্ষ্ণ, উগ্র, প্রখর, তীব্রস্বাদ-যুক্ত ; কটু, ঝাল ; উত্তেজক ; ক্ষয়কর। **2.** Of bitter temper or manner ; virulent ; তীব্র ; উগ্র।

ăc'-ri-mō-nȳ, *n.* Bitterness of temper or manner ; স্বভাবের কটুতা, তীব্রতা, উগ্রতা। **—mo'-ni-ous,** *adj.* Bitter-tempered ; virulent (applied to language, temper, manner, etc.) ; তিক্ত-স্বভাব ; তীক্ষ্ণ, দাহক, মর্ম্মান্তিক, অরুন্তুদ (ভাষা, স্বভাব, প্রকৃতি প্রভৃতি সম্পর্কে)। **—mo'-ni-ous-ly,** *adv.* **—mo'-ni-ous-ness,** *n.*

Ac'-ri-tâ (ăc-), *n. pl.* (*Zool.*) Animals without a distinct nervous system ; (জন্তুতত্ত্ব) পরিস্ফুট স্নায়ুজালহীন জন্তুবর্গ।

ăc'-rō-băt, *n.* A rope-dancer ; a tumbler ; রজ্জু-নর্ত্তক, রজ্জুযায়ী, দড়াবাজিকর ; প্লবক (মঃ ভাঃ), কালায়ন (মঃ উঃ)। **—bat'-ic,** *adj.* Pertaining to an acrobat ; কালায়নিক। **—bat'-i-cal-ly,** *adv.* **—ism,** *n.*

ăc'-rō-gĕn, *n.* A cryptogamous plant having perennial stem with growing point at extremity ; (উদ্ভিদ্-বিদ্যা) একজাতীয় অপুষ্পক উদ্ভিদ, যথা শৈবল (moss), পর্ণাঙ্গ (fern), অগ্রবর্দ্ধী (সাঃ পঃ)।

ăc'-rō-lith, *n.* (*Sculpt.*) A statue with the head and extremities of stone, while the trunk is generally made of wood ; (মূর্ত্তি-শিল্প) যে মূর্ত্তির মস্তক ও কর-চরণ প্রভৃতি শরীরের প্রান্তভাগ সকল শিলারচিত এবং শরীরকাণ্ড সচরাচর কাষ্ঠময় হইয়া থাকে।

ă-crŏn'-ȳ-căl, —chăl, *adj.* Rising at sunset and setting at sunrise ; রাত্রিক (তারা) (হিঃ কোঃ)। **—ly,** *adv.*

ă-crŏp'-ō-lis, *n.* A citadel or elevated part of a Greek city, esp. of Athens ; গ্রীসদেশীয় নগরদুর্গ বা সমুন্নত নগরাংশ, (বিশেষতঃ) গ্রীসদেশের রাজধানী এথেন্স্ নগরীর ইতিহাস-বিদিত প্রাচীন দুর্গ।

ă-crŏss', *adv.* & *prep.* **1.** Crosswise ; as, with arms folded *across* ;

আড়াআড়ি ভাবে, ব্যত্যস্ত (মঃ সং, ২—৭২)। 2. From side to side; on the other side; as, was the channel rough when you came *across?* একতীর হইতে অপর তীর; অপরতীরে। ***Prep.*** 1. From one side to another; over; as, a bridge is laid *across* the river; অনুপ্রস্থে, এক প্রান্ত হইতে অপর প্রান্ত পর্য্যন্ত; উপর দিয়া। 2. On the other side of; beyond; as, *across* the sea; অপরতীরে; অপরপার্শ্বে। 3. Transverse to; obliquely against; as, a wind blew *across* me; ছেদকস্বরূপ; আড়ভাবে। 4. Into contact with; as, I came *across* a tiger; সংস্পর্শে।

ă-crŏs'-tic, *n.* & *adj.* 1. A short poem in which the initial or certain other letters of the line, taken in order, spell a word, phrase, or short sentence; (প্রায় অনুরূপ শব্দ) "চিত্র" (সরস্বঃ, ১—৮৩), যে শ্লোক বা কবিতার আদ্য অক্ষর অথবা অন্যান্য নির্দ্দিষ্ট অক্ষরনিচয় ক্রমশঃ সন্নিবিষ্ট করিলে কোন নাম বা সংক্ষিপ্তবাক্য গঠিত হয়; যথা—

কত ফুল হাসে আজ কাননে কাননে;
মধুর মলয় মন্দ বহে ক্ষণে ক্ষণে;
লিখিত সিঁদূর রেখা নভোনীল ভালে;
নীড়ে নীড়ে বিহগেরা সুধাকণ্ঠ ঢালে।

[এই কবিতাটীর প্রতি ছত্রের প্রথম অক্ষর পড়িয়া গেলে "কমলিনী" হয়।]

2. A Hebrew poem in which the lines or stanzas begin with the successive letters of the alphabet; বর্ণমালানুক্রমে লিখিত হিব্রু কবিতা, চৌত্রিশ অক্ষরা স্তুতি, চৌতিশা (প্রাঃ সাঃ)। ***Adj.*** That relates to or contains an acrostic; উক্ত প্রকার কবিতাসম্পৃক্ত বা বিশিষ্ট। **—ti-cal,** *adj.* **—ti-cal-ly,** *adv.*

ăct, *n., v. i.* & *t.* 1. A thing done; a deed; as, an *act* of charity; process of doing; operation; as, in *act* to shoot: in *act* and speech; কৃত কর্ম্ম; কর্ম্ম, কার্য্য, কৃতি; কর্ম্মে নিযুক্ত অবস্থা; প্রক্রিয়া, ক্রিয়া। 2. The main division of a play; as, the 1st *act* of Macbeth; নাটকের অঙ্ক। 3. A law or decree passed by a legislative body, a court of justice, etc.; ব্যবস্থাপক সভাকর্ত্তৃক বিধিবদ্ধ-আইন, বিচারকের আদেশ, প্রভৃতি। 4. (*In Universities*) A thesis maintained by a candidate for a degree, etc.; (বিশ্ববিদ্যালয়ে) উপাধি-প্রার্থিগণকর্ত্তৃক রচিত নিবন্ধ বা অবদান। ***Verb i.*** 1. To exert power; to produce effect; as, the stomach *acts* upon food; ক্রিয়া করা; ফলদায়ী হওয়া। 2. To do the duties of an office temporarily; to serve as; অস্থায়ীভাবে কায করা; কোন কিছুস্বরূপ কায করা। 3. To do things; to perform actions; to behave; as, to *act* generously: to *act* as an interpreter; কায করা; কার্য্য সমাধা করা; চলা, আচরণ করা। 4. To perform on the stage; as, he *acts* very well; অভিনয় করা। ***Verb t.*** 1. To perform as an actor; as, to *act* Macbeth; to personate or assume the office or character of (in a play or in life); as, to *act* the hero: to *act* a fool; কোন নাটকীয় চরিত্রের ভূমিকায় উপস্থিত হওয়া; (অন্য কেহ) সাজা। 2. To feign; to simulate; "With *acted* fear the villain thus pursued;" ভাণ করা; কপটতা করা। **Act of God**—Action of uncontrollable natural forces in causing an accident, as the burning of a ship by lightning; দৈবী আপদ্, আধিদৈবিক আপদ্ (মঃ সং)। **Act of grace**—An act declaring pardon to offenders; মার্জ্জনা-ঘোষণা। [যেমন নব-সম্রাটের অভিষেকোপলক্ষে অপরাধীদিগকে মার্জ্জনা করা হয়।] ***Act' possum***—Same as ***play' possum*** (which see). **Acts of the Apostles**—The fifth book of the New Testament; বাইবেলের New Testamen (নব নিয়ম) এর পঞ্চম পুস্তক। **In act to**—On the very point o doing something; as, *in act to* strike; উন্মুখ, উদ্যত। **To act a part**—To dissemble; ভাণ করা, কপটতা করা। **To act as** or **for**—To do the work of in the absence of another; অন্যের অ পস্থিতিতে তাহার স্থানে কায করা। **act on** or **upon**—To regula one's conduct according (কোন কিছুর) অনুযায়ী বা অনু কায করা। **To act up to** fulfil in practice; ঠিক্ ঠিক করা, প্রতিপালন করা।

ăct'-ing, *adj.* & *n.* Officiating as, an *acting* magistrate; doi alone duties nominally share with others; as, an *acting* manag er; অস্থায়ী; কার্য্যকারী। ***Noun.*** Performance; execution; সাধন সম্পাদন। 2. Dramatic perforn ance; feigning a character r one's own; অভিনয়; ভাণ।

ăc'-tin-ism, *n.* That property the sun's rays by which chem changes are produced, as photography; সূর্য্যরশ্মির যে ধর্ম্মব রাসায়নিক পরিবর্ত্তন সঞ্জাত হয়, (আলোকচিত্রণে) বিকারকতা (হিঃ কে

ăc'-tion, *n.* 1. Operation; exert of energy or influence; as, *action* of heat; ক্রিয়া, ব্যাপার, বৃ কর্ম্মচেষ্টা, কর্ম্মোদ্যোগ। 2. A thi done; a deed; an exploit; feat; (*ethics*) any result of a tivity regarded as proceedin from a moral agent; "T Lord is a God of knowledge, a by Him *actions* are weighe কৃতকর্ম্ম; কার্য্য; অবদান; মহৎক (নীতি-বিজ্ঞান) কর্ম্ম। 3. (*Dram* The event or series of eve represented; the main subj or fable; (নাট্যশাস্ত্র) নাটকীয় ঘ

বা ঘটনাবলী; মুখ্য বিষয় বা মূল উপাখ্যান। 4. Mode of acting; gesture; oratorical management; as, she spoke this speech and marked its sense by *action;* the trained management of the body by domesticated animals; as, the horse has a fine *action;* অভিনয়ভঙ্গী; অঙ্গপ্রত্যঙ্গের গতি, অঙ্গভঙ্গী, বক্তৃতাকালে বিষয়ানুরূপ বা ভাবানুগত-ভাবে বক্তার ভঙ্গী, কণ্ঠস্বর, এবং প্রধানতঃ তদীয় অঙ্গসঞ্চালন; গৃহপালিত জন্তুগণ শিক্ষার ফলে যেরূপ অঙ্গচেষ্টা বা এমন-ভঙ্গী অভ্যাস করে। 5. A legal process or suit; *"Actions* were brought against persons who had defamed the Duke of York." মোকদ্দমা, মামলা। 6. Engagement between troops; as, the guards should be held ready for *action";* যুদ্ধ, বিগ্রহ, সংগ্রাম। 7. Mechanism of a musical instrument; বাদ্য-যন্ত্রের কল-কব্জা। 8. (*Painting & sculpture*) Attitude or position, as expressive of the passion or sentiment depicted; (চিত্র-বিদ্যা ও ভাস্কর্য্য) চিত্রার্পিত মূর্ত্তিতে চিত্তবৃত্তি বা ভাবাবেগদ্যোতক ভঙ্গী বা অঙ্গস্থিতি। [যেমন মানিনী রাধিকা—করলগ্নকপোলারূপে অঙ্কিতা হইয়া থাকেন।] **—a-ble,** *adj.* Liable to a law-suit; as, to call a man a thief is *actionable;* মোকদ্দমা-যোগ্য। **Action and reaction**—ক্রিয়া-প্রতিক্রিয়া, আঘাত-সংঘাত (রবিঃ)। **Action-taking**—Litigious; মামলা-প্রিয়, মামলাবাজ। **Civil action**—A suit or process for some property or money, etc.; দেওয়ানী মোকদ্দমা। **Criminal action**—Prosecution for a crime; ফৌজদারী মোকদ্দমা। **Line of action**—The way or method of performing a deed; কার্য্যপ্রণালী। **To put in action**—To engage in performing a deed; কার্য্যে প্রবৃত্ত বা নিযুক্ত করা।

ăc'-tive, *adj.* 1. Working; effective; কার্য্যকর, ক্রিয়াশীল, সক্রিয়, সচেষ্ট; ফলদায়ক। 2. Energetic; diligent; busy; given to outward action; as, *active* mind: *active* man; উদ্যোগী, উৎসাহী, উৎসাহপূর্ণ; পরিশ্রমী, শ্রমশীল, কর্ম্মঠ, কর্ম্মতৎপর; কর্ম্মরত, কর্ম্ম-ব্যস্ত, অতন্দ্রিত; কার্য্যরত। 3. Agile; nimble; as, an *active* child; চটুল, ক্ষিপ্র, লঘু, চপল; সত্বর, চালাক, চটপটে। 4. Given to action rather than contemplation; practical; কর্ম্মশীল, কর্ম্মময়; ব্যবহারবিদ, ব্যবহারিক (মঃ সং)। 5. Acting upon others; spontaneous; ' Objects which they first believed to be intelligent and *active* are really lifeless and passive;" অপর বস্তুর উপর ক্রিয়াশীল; স্বতঃস্ফূর্ত্ত। 6. (*Gram.*) An epithet of voice in verbs used transitively; (ব্যাকরণ) কর্ত্তৃবাচ্যনিষ্পন্ন। (*Active* verb = সকর্ম্মক ক্রিয়া; *active* voice = কর্ত্তৃবাচ্য।) **—ly,** *adv.* সচেষ্টভাবে, সক্রিয়ভাবে। **—ness,** *n.* **—tiv'-i-ty,** *n.* The state or quality of being active; the exertion of energy; nimbleness; agility; diligence; pursuit of business; the active faculty; as, a man of *activity;* (*pl.*) active forces; spheres of action; কর্ম্মশীলতা, ক্রিয়াশীলতা; কর্ম্মচেষ্টা; ক্ষিপ্রকারিতা, লঘুতা; চটুলতা; কর্ম্মিষ্ঠতা, কর্ম্মঠতা; কর্ম্মানুসরণ; রজোগুণ (হিঃ কোঃ); ক্রিয়াশীল বল; কার্য্যক্ষেত্র। **Active capital** or **wealth**—The wealth or property that may be readily converted into money, and used in commerce; যে ধন অথবা সম্পত্তি অবিলম্বে টাকাতে পরিবর্ত্তন করিয়া কোন ব্যবসায়ে খাটান যায়। **Active commerce**—The commerce which a nation carries on in its own ships, or which is prosecuted by its own citizens (opposed to *passive commerce*); দেশীয় ব্যবসায়িগণ দ্বারা স্বদেশীয় জাহাজে পরিচালিত ব্যবসায় বাণিজ্য (অর্থাৎ বৈদেশিক বণিকগণ দ্বারা নহে।) **Active force, Living force**—ক্রিয়াশক্তি (হিঃ কোঃ)।

ăc'-tŏn, *n.* A jacket of quilted cotton worn under mail; a mail-plated jacket of leather, etc.;

Quilted acton of the 15th century.

তুলাদি-পূরিত কঞ্চুক (কুর্ত্তি) বিশেষ, ইহা লৌহবর্ম্মের নিম্নে পরিহিত হয়; লৌহ-চক্ররাজি-সমন্বিত চর্ম্মাদির কঞ্চুক।

ăc'-tŏr, *n.* One who acts or performs any action; a stage-player; কর্ত্তা, কার্য্যকারক; রঙ্গাজীব, কুশীলব (মৃচ্ছঃ), অভিনেতা, রঙ্গচর (বৃঃ সং), নাটকীয় পাত্র। (*Fem.*) **—tress,** *n.* A female player on the stage; নটী, অভিনেত্রী, নাটকীয় পাত্রী।

ăc'-tu-ăl (-chû-), *adj.* 1. Existing in fact; real; as, the *actual* cost of goods; প্রকৃতপক্ষে বিদ্যমান; বাস্তব, যথার্থ, প্রকৃত। 2. Present; current; as, the *actual* situation of the country; বর্ত্তমান; চলিত। **—al'-i-ty,** *n.* 1. Reality; বাস্তবতা, যথার্থতা। 2. Realism; বস্তুস্বাতন্ত্র্যবাদ (হিঃ কোঃ), জাতিবাস্তবত্ববাদ (ঐ)। 3. (*Pl.*) Existing conditions; বাস্তবাবস্থা। **—ist,** *n.* One who considers actually existing facts and conditions (opp. to IDEALIST); বাস্তববাদী, বাস্তবদর্শী। **—i-za'-tion,** *n.* **—ize,** *v. t.* 1. To make actual; to realise in action; বাস্তব করা; কার্য্যে পরিণত করা। 2. To describe realistically;

স্বভাবসঙ্গতরূপে বর্ণনা করা। **—ly,** *adv.* In fact ; really ; for the time being ; প্রকৃতপক্ষে ; যথার্থতঃ, বাস্তবিকপক্ষে ; সাময়িক ভাবে।

ăc′-tu-â-rȳ (-chû-), *n.* A registrar or clerk, who makes calculations, especially for insurance purposes ; গণনাধ্যক্ষ, বিশেষতঃ, বীমাসংক্রান্তগণনাকুশল ব্যক্তি, বীমা-পরতালক (হিঃ কোঃ)। **—a′-ri-al,** *adj.*

ăc′-tu-āte (-chû-), *v. t.* **1.** To communicate motion to a machine, etc. ; যন্ত্রাদিতে গতি-সঞ্চার করা। **2.** To incite to action ; to inflame ; প্রণোদিত করা, প্ররোচিত করা, প্রবৃত্ত করা ; উদ্দীপিত করা। **—a′-tion,** *n.*

ă-cû′-i-tȳ, *n.* **1.** Sharpness ; as, the *acuity* of a medicine (তীক্ষ্ণবীর্য্যতা) ; তীক্ষ্ণতা। **2.** Acuteness (of disease, wit, acid, etc.) ; তীব্রতা, সূক্ষ্মতা।

ă-cü′-mĕn, *n.* Quickness of perception ; penetration of mind ; sharpness of wit ; ক্ষিপ্রগ্রাহিতা ; সূক্ষ্মদর্শিতা ; তীক্ষ্ণবুদ্ধিতা।

ă-cü′-mi-nāte, *v. t.* & *adj.* To render sharp or keen ; তীক্ষ্ণ বা ধারাল করা। ***Adj.*** Keen ; sharp ; as, *acuminate* leaves ; ছুঁচাল ; সূক্ষ্মাগ্র, সশিখ (সাঃ পঃ)।

ă-cüte′, *adv.* **1.** Sharp ; pointed ; তীক্ষ্ণাগ্র, সূক্ষ্মাগ্র ; সূচীমুখ। **2.** (*Geom.*) Less than a right-angle ; (জ্যামিতি) সমকোণাপেক্ষা ক্ষুদ্রতর, সূক্ষ্ম। **3.** (*Of sensations, senses, intellect*) Quick in catching ; having nice discernment ; sharp-witted ; ক্ষিপ্রগ্রাহী ; কুশাগ্রবুদ্ধি, সূক্ষ্মদর্শী, সূক্ষ্ম বা প্রখর অনুভূতি-সম্পন্ন ; তীক্ষ্ণধী, তীক্ষ্ণবুদ্ধি, প্রখরবুদ্ধি। **4.** (*Of pain*) Keen ; intense ; তীব্র ; উগ্র, প্রবল। **5.** (*Of sounds*) High in pitch ; shrill ; as, an *acute* tone ; (শব্দ-সম্বন্ধে) উদাত্ত ; উচ্চ। **6.** (*Of disease*) Coming sharply to a crisis (opp. to CHRONIC) ; as, an *acute* disease ; (রোগ-সম্পর্কে) আশুসঙ্কটজনক, আশু-সঙ্কট-সঙ্কুল, তীব্র (হঃ চঃ), তরুণ (ঐ)। **—ness,** *n.* **1.** Sharpness of point or edge ; সূক্ষ্মাগ্রতা, ধারালতা। **2.** The faculty of nice discernment ; keenness of penetration ; সূক্ষ্ম-বিচারশক্তি ; কুশাগ্রমতিত্ব, সূক্ষ্মবুদ্ধিতা। **3.** (*Mus.*) Shrillness ; high pitch ; (সঙ্গীত-শাস্ত্র) তীক্ষ্ণতা ; উচ্চতা। **4.** (*Med.*) Violence of a disease ; keenness of pain ; (পীড়ার) তীব্রতা, প্রবলতা ; বেদনার তীব্রতা। **Acute angle** = সূক্ষ্ম কোণ।

ăd′-āğe, *n.* An old saying ; a proverb ; বচন, প্রাচীনোক্তি ; প্রবাদ-বাক্য।

ă-dä′-ği-ō, *adv., adj.* & *n.* (*Mus.*) Leisurely ; slowly ; with grace ; (সঙ্গীত-শাস্ত্র) মৃদুমন্দ ; মন্দমন্দ ; লালিত্য সহকারে। ***Adj.*** Slow ; ধীর, মন্থর। ***Noun.*** A slow movement (in music) ; বিলম্বিতত্ব, বিলম্বিত মূর্চ্ছনা, ঠায়।

Ad′-ăm (ăd-), *n.* **1.** The name of the first man ; the father of the human race, in the Bible ; আদম, আদি মানব ; প্রথমসৃষ্ট পুরুষ। [(প্রাচীন বাইবেল শাস্ত্রানুসারে) ঈশ্বর প্রথমতঃ একটী ধূলিময়ী মূর্ত্তিতে আপনার নিশ্বাস-বায়ু সঞ্চার করত আদিমানব আদমকে সৃষ্টি করেন। তৎপর আদমের দেহাস্থি হইতে ঈভ্ নাম্নী পরমলাবণ্যবতী এক নারী সৃষ্টি করিয়া, উভয়কে নন্দনকল্প ইডেন উদ্যানে স্থাপন করেন। তাহারা শয়তানদ্বারা প্রলুব্ধ হইবার পূর্ব্ব পর্য্যন্ত তথায় নিষ্পাপমনে, নগ্নদেহে বাস করিয়াছিল।] **2.** (*Fig.*) (also *Old Adam*) The unregenerate condition or character ; (লক্ষণায়) মানবের আদি পাপ, মানবের চিত্তগত কুপ্রবৃত্তি। **A-dam′-ic, —i-cal,** *adjs.* **—ite,** *n.* **1.** One descended from Adam ; a human being ; আদমের বংশধর ; মানব। **2.** An imitator of Adam in his nakedness ; an unclothed man ; নগ্নতাবিষয়ে আদমের অনুকরণ-কারী ; দিগম্বর। **3.** A member of any one of the various sects, reputed to have gone naked in their religious assemblies, in imitation of Adam ; ধর্ম্মোন্মত্ত সম্প্রদায়বিশেষভুক্ত ব্যক্তি—এই সম্প্রদায়ভুক্ত উপাসকমণ্ডলী আদি মানব আদমের অনুকরণে নগ্নাবস্থায় তাহাদের ধর্ম্ম-সভায় গমন করিত। **Adam's ale** or **wine**—Humorous name for water ; (কৌতুকচ্ছলে) জল। **Adam's apple**—Projection in the neck under the chin ; কণ্ঠমণি (মঃ উঃ), কাকলক (সুশ্রুঃ), ফল-গ্রন্থি (হঃ চঃ)। [শয়তানের প্ররোচনায় ইডেন-উদ্যানের নিষিদ্ধ ফল ভক্ষণের সময়, ঐ ফলের কতক অংশ আদমের গলায় আটকাইয়া যাওয়াতে তাহার গলদেশে যে স্ফীতি হয়—তাহাই মানবের কণ্ঠমণির উদ্ভবের কারণ, এইরূপ বিশ্বাস হইতে এই শব্দটী উপজাত হইয়াছে।] **Adam's profession** Gardening ; agriculture ; উদ্য রচনা ; কৃষিকর্ম্ম। [আদমের অধঃপত পর ঈশ্বর তাহাকে ইডেন-উদ্যান হ বিতাড়িত করিয়া ভূমিকর্ষণের ক নিয়োজিত করেন।] **A faithfu Adam**—A faithful old servant বিশ্বস্ত পুরাতন ভৃত্য। [মহাকবি সেক্ষপীয়র প্রণীত "As You Like It" নামক নাটকোক্ত ভৃত্য বিশেষ। এই ভৃত্য এক পরিবারে বহুকাল অ বিশ্বস্ততার সহিত কর্ম্ম করিয়া পরে তাহা সুদীর্ঘ জীবনের সমস্ত সঞ্চিত অ প্রভুপরিবারের বিপৎকালে দান করিয় ছিল।] **Not to know a ma from Adam**—To be quite ur acquainted with him ; to unable to recognize him ; কাহা সহিত সম্পূর্ণ অপরিচিত হওয়া ; কাহা চিনিতে অসমর্থ হওয়া। **To beat th offending Adam**—To be fr from sin ; পাপমুক্ত হওয়া।

ăd′-ă-mănt, *n.* **1.** A thing im penetrably hard ; দুর্ভেদ্যপদার্থ বিশেষ। **2.** (Formerly) Loadstone ; অয়স্কান্ত (অপ্রঃ)। **3.** Diamond ; বজ্র, হীরক। **—man′-tine,** *adj.* Made of adamant ; incapable of being broken or penetrated ; impregnable ; বজ্র-নির্ম্মিত, হৈরিক (সাঃ পঃ), বজ্রময় ; কুলিশ-কঠিন ; দুর্ভেদ্য ।

Adansonia Digitata—Baobab, monkey-bread tree or Ethiopian sour gourd ; গোরক্ আম্লি (হিন্দী—বেলঃ) ।

a-dăpt′, *v. t.* **1.** To fit (a person or thing *to* another) ; to make suitable (*to* or *for* a purpose) ; উপযোগী করা ; প্রয়োজনানুরূপ করা, উদ্দেশ্যোপযোগী করা । **2.** To modify so as to fit for a new use ; as, a kind of farm-house, *adapted* out of the old ruin ; নূতন কার্য্যের উপযোগী করিয়া লওয়া । **—ā-bil′-i-tȳ, —a-ble-ness**, *ns.* The state or quality of being adapted ; যোগ্যতা, সংযোজনীয়তা, উপযোগিতা-শক্তি (পাঃ) । **—a-ble**, *a.* Capable of being adapted ; applicable ; যোগ্য, যোক্তব্য ; যোজ্য । **—a′-tion**, *n.* **1.** The act or process of fitting or suiting one thing to another ; উপযোগীকরণ, সংবিধান, যোজনা, যোগ্যতা, উপযোগিতা । **2.** The process of modifying a thing so as to suit a new condition, as the modification of a piece of music to suit a different condition ; the alteration of a dramatic composition to suit a different audience ; নূতন অবস্থার উপযোগীকরণ—যথা, বিভিন্ন অবস্থার উপযোগীকরণার্থ সঙ্গীতের পরিবর্ত্তন ; ভিন্নশ্রেণীর বা ভিন্নদেশীয় শ্রোতৃবৃন্দের উপযোগীকরণার্থ কোন নাটকের ভাব, ভাষা বা ঘটনাসমূহের পরিবর্ত্তন । **—ed-ness**, *n.* **—er**, *n.* One that adapts (in any sense) ; সংযোজক । **—ive**, *adj.* Given to adaptation ; suitable ; সংযোজনশীল ; উপযোগী । **—ive-ness**, *n.*

ad captandum (vulgus), *adv.* & *adj.* Calculated to catch the fancy of the rabble ; ইতর জনতার চিত্তাকর্ষণার্থ । ***Adj.*** Applied also to meretricious attempts to catch popular favour or applause ; as, *ad captandum* (ইতরজনচিত্তাকর্ষক) oratory ; অশিক্ষিত ইতরশ্রেণীর লোকদিগের করতালি ও সাধুবাদলাভার্থ (বক্তার কৃত্রিম প্রয়াস) ।

ădd, *v. t.* & *i.* **1.** To put together ; to join or unite (one thing to another) ; একত্রিত করা ; সংযুক্ত করা, সংযোগ করা, যোগ করা, যোজনা করা, সংযোজিত করা । **2.** To say or write further ; to go on to say or speak ; as, to what I have already said, let me *add* this ; আরও বলা ; বলিতে থাকা । ***Verb i.*** **1.** To be or serve as an addition ; to be added (*to*) ; যোগ হওয়া ; সংযুক্ত হওয়া । **2.** To perform the arithmetical operation of addition ; as, this boy can *add* very rapidly ; সঙ্কলন করা । **Ădd′-a-ble**, *adj.* Capable of being added or added to ; যোজনীয়, যোগার্হ, সঙ্কলনীয় । **To add fuel to the fire, To add fuel to**—To do something that serves to increase excitement or fury ; to give a fresh incitement or provocation to ; "His words *added fuel to* the already excited passion of the mob." জ্বলন্ত অনলে ঘৃতাহুতি বা ইন্ধন প্রদান করা ; ক্রোধের প্রকোপ বা প্রচণ্ডতা বৃদ্ধি করা । **To add in**—To include in a sum ; যোগফলের অন্তর্ভুক্ত করা । **To add to**—To augment ; to increase ; বর্দ্ধিত করা ; বৃদ্ধি করা । **To add up**—To find the sum of ; যোগফল নির্ণয় করা, ঠিক দেওয়া ।

ăd′-dăx, *n.* A species of ox-like antelope ; একজাতীয় কৃষ্ণসার ।

Addax.

ăd-dĕn′-dŭm, (*pl.* ADDENDA), *n.* Thing to be added ; an appendix or addition ; সংযোজনীয় বস্তু ; সংযোজিত বিষয়, পরিশিষ্ট ।

ăd′-dêr, *n.* A small venomous snake ; a viper ; ক্ষুদ্র বিষধর সর্প বিশেষ ; ভুজ্যু (বেঃ সুঃ) । **Adder-bead, Adder-stone**—A stone or bead used by the Druids as an amulet ; এক প্রকার পাষাণ বা কাচনির্ম্মিত অক্ষমালা—এই মালা প্রাচীনকালে ড্রুইড্গণ কর্ত্তৃক সর্প-দংশনের ঔষধস্বরূপ ব্যবহৃত হইত । **Adder-bolt, Adder-fly** or **Flying adder**—Dragon-fly ; ফড়িং (সাঃ পঃ) । **Adder's tongue**—A species of fern ; এক জাতীয় ক্রকচ-পত্র উদ্ভিদ্ ।

ăd-dĭct′, *v. t.* **1.** To devote ; to apply habitually (to a practice) ; to attach closely ; as, to *addict* one's self to intemperance ; নিরত করা, সমর্পণ করা, উৎসর্গ করা ; অনুলগ্ন করা, অভ্যস্ত করা ; আসক্ত করা । **2.** (*Roman law*) To deliver under decree of a court ; hence, (*fig.*) to give over or surrender (*to*) ; (রোমীয় আইন) আদালতের আদেশানুসারে সমর্পণ করা ; অতএব (লক্ষণায়) সমর্পণ করা । **—ed**, *p. p.* Devoted ; closely attached ; নিরত, রত ; আসক্ত, সক্ত, অনুলগ্ন **—ed-ness**, *n.* Devotion ; attachment ; আসক্তি ; অনুরক্তি, রতি ।

ăd-dĭc′-tion, *n.* The state of being given to a habit or pursuit ; devotion ; আসক্তি ; অনুরক্তি ।

ăd-dĭt′-â-mĕnt, *n.* An addition ; thing added ; যোগ ; যুক্ত বস্তু ।

ăd-dĭ′-tion, *n.* **1.** The act or process of adding ; সংযোজন, যোজনা, সঙ্কলন-ক্রিয়া । **2.** The thing added ; সংযোজিত বস্তু । **—al**, *adj.* Added ; supplementary ; সংযোজিত, সংযুক্ত ; ন্যূনতাপূরক, অনুপূরক, অতিরিক্ত । **—al-ly**, *adv.* **In addition to**—Over and above ; অধিকন্তু, অতিরিক্ত ।

ăd′-dle, *adj.*, *n.*, *v. t.* & *i.* **1.** Putrid

(applied to eggs) ; hence, barren ; producing nothing ; পচা (ডিম্ব-সম্বন্ধে) ; অতএব, অনুৎপাদক ; উৎ-পাদিকাশক্তিহীন, বন্ধ্য। **2.** Empty ; vain ; as, that tiresome and *addle* epistle which follows ; শূন্যগর্ভ ; বৃথাড়ম্বরপূর্ণ। **3.** Muddled ; unsound ; as, I wish him one ounce more wit in his *addle* head ; ঘোলা ; বিকৃত। ***Noun.*** **1.** The dry lees of wine ; সুরার শুষ্ক গাদ। **2.** The drainage from dunghill ; mire ; গোময়স্তূপ হইতে নিঃসৃত পঙ্কিল পদার্থের স্রোত ; কর্দ্দম। ***Verb t.*** To muddle ; to confuse (the brain) ; ঘুলাইয়া দেওয়া, আবিল করা ; গোলমাল করিয়া দেওয়া। ***Verb i.*** (*Of eggs*) To grow addle ; (ডিম্ব-সম্বন্ধে) ঘোলা পড়া। **—dled,** *p.p.* Become or made addle as an egg or brain ; ঘোলাপড়া, আবিলীকৃত, আবিলীভূত। **Addle-brained, Addle-headed, Addle-pated,** *adjs.* Dull-witted ; stupid ; মন্দ-বুদ্ধি, হীনবুদ্ধি, মূঢ়মতি ; মূঢ়, নির্ব্বোধ। **The addled parliament**—১৬১৪ খৃঃ অব্দের ৫ই এপ্রিল হইতে ১৬১৫ খৃঃ অব্দের ৭ই জুন পর্য্যন্ত যে পার্লেমেন্টের অধিবেশন হইয়াছিল। এই পার্লেমেন্টে কোন আইন বিধিবদ্ধ হয় নাই বলিয়া, ইহা এই আখ্যা প্রাপ্ত হইয়াছে।

ăd-drĕss', *v. t.* & *n.* **1.** To communicate with (by word or letter) ; to direct speech to ; as, they *addressed* the king ; কাহারও সহিত পত্রাদি ব্যবহার করা বা কথাবার্ত্তা বলা ; কোন ব্যক্তিকে লক্ষ্য করিয়া উক্তি করা। **2.** To court or make suit to, as a lover ; to woo ; as, to prevent the confusion that might arise from our both *addressing* the same lady ; পরিণয়-প্রার্থী হইয়া প্রণয়ালাপ করা ; প্রণয়-লাভার্থ রমণীর আরাধনা করা, বিবাহ-প্রার্থনা করা। **3.** To deliver a speech to a company or meeting ; "Mr. Hunt began to *address* the assembly ;" কোন সভা বা সম্মিলনীতে বক্তৃতা প্রদান করা। **4.** To direct in writing, as a letter ; to superscribe ; শিরোনামা লিখা ; ঠিকানা লিখা। **5.** To prepare one's self ; to apply one's skill or energies (to some work or object); as, they addressed themselves to the task ; (নিজকে) প্রস্তুত করা ; (কোন কার্য্য বা উদ্দেশ্যসাধনে) কোন ব্যক্তির নৈপুণ্য বা শক্তি প্রয়োগ করা। ***Noun.*** **1.** The act of addressing one's self to a person ; "*Sir* is a term of *address.*" সম্বোধন। **2.** Readiness ; skill ; dexterity ; adroitness ; skilful management ; as, the envoy conducted the negotiation with *address* ; সত্বরতা ; নিপুণতা ; কৌশল ; কর্ম্মকুশলতা ; সু-পরিচালনা। **3.** The superscription of a letter ; the name of the person and place to which a letter is directed ; শিরোনামা ; ঠিকানা। **4.** Courtship (generally in *pl.*) ; as, he makes or pays his *addresses* to a lady ; পূর্ব্বরাগ, বিবাহার্থ প্রেমোপাসনা। **5.** Manner of speaking to another ; delivery ; as, a man of pleasing *address* ; বচন-ভঙ্গী ; বক্তৃতা-প্রণালী। **6.** A formal speech of congratulation, respect, thanks, etc. ; a speech ; a formal application to any one or a petition ; অভিনন্দন ; অভিভাষণ, বক্তৃতা ; আবেদন, প্রার্থনা-পত্র। **—ee',** *n.* One to whom a letter is addressed ; (পত্রের) উদ্দিষ্ট ব্যক্তি, পত্রপ্রাপক। **To pay one's addresses to**—To court ; "He was said to be *paying his addresses to* Lady Jane Sheepshanks." বিবাহার্থী হইয়া অনুরাগ প্রার্থনা করা।

ăd-dūce', *v. t.* To cite as a proof or instance ; to bring forward ; as, reasons were *adduced* on both sides ; প্রমাণ বা দৃষ্টান্তস্বরূপ নির্দ্দেশ করা ; উপস্থাপিত করা। **—a-ble, —duc'-i-ble,** *adjs.* Which may be adduced or brought forward ; উপস্থাপনীয়, প্রমাণ-স্বরূপ নির্দ্দেশ্য।

ăd-dŭct', *v. t.* (*Physiol.*) To draw to a common centre (শারীরবিজ্ঞান) এক কেন্দ্রাভিমুখে আকর্ষণ করা। **ăd-dŭc'-tŏr,** *n.* A muscle which draws any part of the body towards the trunk or main axis (opp. to *abductor*) ; যে সকল পেশী শরীরাংশ আকর্ষণপূর্ব্বক সম্মিলিত করে সংযোজক মাংসপেশী। **—tion,** *n.* The act of bringing towards প্রত্যানয়ন। **2.** The act of bringing forward facts ; সত্য উপস্থাপিত করণ।

ăd'-ē-noids (-noyds), *n. pl.* Mass of spongy tissue between the back of nose and throat, often hindering inflation of lungs ; নাসিকার পশ্চাদ্ভাগ এবং কণ্ঠের মধ্যবর্ত্তী শোষণকারী (spongy) বিধানতন্তু সমূহ।

ă-dĕpt', *n.* & *adj.* One fully skilled or well-versed in anything ; a proficient ; as, *adepts* in philosophy ; ওস্তাদ, গুণী, আচার্য্য ; পারদর্শী, নিপুণ, ব্যুৎপন্ন ব্যক্তি। [মধ্যযুগে যে সকল ইয়ুরোপীয় তান্ত্রিক স্পর্শমণি ও সর্ব্বরোগের ঔষধ প্রাপ্তির জন্য লোকসমাজে প্রসিদ্ধি-লাভ করিয়াছিলেন, তাঁহাদিগকে *adepts* বা সিদ্ধ তান্ত্রিক বলা হইত।] ***Adj.*** Completely versed in ; thoroughly proficient ; well-skilled ; সিদ্ধ পারগ, ; পারদর্শী ; সুপটু, নিপুণ।

ăd'-ē-quāte, *adj.* Equal to what is required ; proportionate to the requirements ; as, *adequate* punishment (যথাপরাধ দণ্ড) ; fully sufficient ; যথাযোগ্য, অনুরূপ ; প্রয়োজনানুরূপ, যথানুরূপ, যথোচিত ; পর্য্যাপ্ত ; যথেষ্ট। **—ly,** *adv.* Sufficiently ; suitably ; পর্য্যাপ্তরূপে, যথেষ্টরূপে, যথোচিতরূপে। **—ness, —qua-cy,** *ns.*

A deux, (*F.*), *adv.* For two ; between two ; উভয়ের জন্য ; উভয়ের মধ্যে।

Adhatoda Vasica—বাসক (বেলঃ)।

-here' (-hēâr), *v. i.* **1.** To stick fast or cleave, as a glutinous substance does; as, wax *adheres* to the finger; লাগিয়া থাকা, দৃঢ়রূপে সংযুক্ত হওয়া, আটিয়া যাওয়া, সংযুক্ত হওয়া। **2.** To cleave to a person, party, opinion, practice, etc.; অনুরক্ত থাকা, সঙ্গী, অনুগামী, সমর্থক বা পৃষ্ঠপোষকরূপে অনুরক্ত থাকা, মতানুবর্ত্তী হওয়া, দলভুক্ত হওয়া, কোন অভ্যাসের দাস হওয়া। **—her'-ence,** *n.* The act or state of holding fast (*to* anything or together); attachment (to a person or party); persistence in a practice or tenet; আসঞ্জন (মঃ উঃ), সংযোজন (হঃ চঃ); আসঙ্গ, আসক্তি, প্রসক্তি; সংসক্তি, নিষ্ঠা।

ăd-hēr'-ĕnt (-hēâr-), *adj.* & *n.* **1.** Sticking fast (*to*); লগ্ন, লিপ্ত, নিষ্ঠ। **2.** (*Log.*) Not belonging to the nature of a thing; (তর্কবিজ্ঞান) আনুষঙ্গিক, অসমবায়ী (তর্কঃ)। [যথা "wetness" of a cloth—এই স্থলে "wetness" বা "আর্দ্রতা," বস্ত্রের স্বাভাবিক বা প্রকৃতিগত গুণ নহে, ইহা *adherent* বা অসমবায়ী গুণ।] ***Noun.*** One who adheres to a party, person or system; a follower; a partisan; অনুরক্ত ব্যক্তি; সঙ্গী, অনুগামী; স্বপক্ষভুক্ত ব্যক্তি।

ăd'-hē-sion, *n.* **1.** The act or state of sticking; specially, a sticking together of substances in contact with each other (*adhesion* is generally used in a literal, and *adherence* in a metaphorical sense); আসঞ্জন, অনুলগ্নতা, সংলগ্নতা, সংসক্তি; (বিশেষতঃ) পরস্পর-সংলগ্ন পদার্থ সমূহের সংসক্তি। **2.** Steady attachment of the mind or feeling; fidelity; as, an *adhesion* to vice, error or to a policy; আসক্তি; নিষ্ঠা। **3.** (*Bot.*) The union of parts normally separate; (উদ্ভিদ্-বিদ্যা) অসমসংযোগ (সাঃ পঃ)। **4.** (*Pathol.*) The unnatural union of surfaces consequent upon inflammation; (নিদান-শাস্ত্র) স্ফীতির দরুণ শরীরের অংশ সমূহের অস্বাভাবিক সংযোগ। **—sive,** *adj.* Having the property of adhering; sticky; as, *adhesive* stamps; চট্‌চটে, শ্যান (মঃ উঃ); আঠালো। **—sive-ly,** *adv.* **—sive-ness,** *n.* **1.** The quality or state of being adhesive; viscosity; tenacity; (*lit.* & *fig.*); as, *adhesiveness of* the cement: *adhesiveness to* the principle; (শব্দানুযায়ী এবং লক্ষণায়) সংসক্তি, সংলগ্নতা; আঠালোভাব; দৃঢ়ানুরাগ। **2.** (*Phren.*) The faculty of forming and maintaining attachments to persons; as, *adhesiveness* is strongest and its organ largest in women; (মস্তিষ্ক-সামুদ্রিক) যে বৃত্তিবশতঃ অনুরাগ জাত এবং স্থায়ী হয়, আসঙ্গ-বৃত্তি। **Adhesive plaster**—A plaster of litharge, wax and resin, used for closing wounds; ক্ষতবন্ধের জন্য ব্যবহৃত এক প্রকার চট্‌চটে মলম। **To give in one's adhesion**—To announce one's concurrence; to join as a supporter; (কোন বিষয়ে) সম্মতি জ্ঞাপন করা; সমর্থকরূপে যোগদান করা।

ăd-hĭb'-it, *v. t.* **1.** To take in; as, there were *adhibited* very few; to admit (a person or thing); অন্তর্ভুক্ত করা; প্রবিষ্ট করা। **2.** To put upon; to affix; as, the labels may be *adhibited* to the back of the volumes; লাগান; আঠা দিয়া জুড়িয়া দেওয়া। **3.** To administer remedies; to apply; ঔষধ প্রয়োগ করা; লাগান। **—hi-bi'-tion,** *n.*

ad hoc, (*L.*), *adv.* Arranged for this purpose; special; এতদর্থে বিন্যস্ত; বিশেষ।

ad hominem, (*L.*), *adv.* To the man; মনুষ্যসম্পর্কে। [A phrase applied to an argument founded on the principles or prejudices of a particular person rather than on reasons of truth or logic; এই বাক্যটী সত্য কিম্বা ন্যায়শাস্ত্রমূলক যুক্তি সম্বন্ধে ব্যবহৃত না হইয়া, বরঞ্চ ব্যক্তিবিশেষের মত বা সংস্কারের উপর প্রতিষ্ঠিত যুক্তি সম্বন্ধে প্রযুক্ত হয়।]

ăd-i-ă-băt'-ic, *adj.* (*Phys.*) Impervious to heat or maintaining a constant temperature; (পদার্থবিদ্যা) তাপাবরোধক (হিঃ কোঃ)। **—i-cal-ly,** *adv.*

ăd-i-ăn'-tŭm, *n.* The black Maidenhair; (*Adiantum capillus veneris*) কালিঝাঁপ (যোঃ), হংসরাজ (হিন্দী—বেলঃ)।

ăd-i-ăph'-ŏ-rism, *n.* Latitudinarianism; স্বৈরাচার (হিঃ কোঃ)। **—rist,** *n.* One indifferent about points of theological discussion; উদাসীন, ভেদাভেদরহিত (এপিঃ)।

ā-dieu' (-dü), *int.* & *n.* [*F. a* to and *Dieu* God] Good-bye; বিদায় হই, তবে আসি। ***Noun.*** Farewell; বিদায়। **To bid or say adieu** (*to*)—To take affectionate, regretful or formal leave of; বিদায় গ্রহণ করা। **To make** or **take one's adieu**—To say good bye; বিদায় হওয়া।

ad infinitum, (*L.*), *adv.* Without limit; forever; অনন্ত কাল বা সংখ্যা পর্য্যন্ত, অনাদিপরম্পরা (সাঃ পঃ), অশেষতঃ; অনন্তকালের জন্য।

ad interim, (*L.*), *adv.* & *adj.* For the meantime; for the present; মধ্যবর্ত্তী সময়ের জন্য; আপাততঃ।

ăd'-i-pō-cēre, *n.* A greyish white fatty substance, generated in dead bodies, buried in moist places or submerged in water; জলনিমজ্জিত বা আর্দ্রভূমিতে সমাহিত মৃতদেহজাত ধূসরাভ-শ্বেত বসাময় পদার্থ বিশেষ।

ăd'-i-pōse, *adj.* & *n.* Pertaining to fat; fatty; বসা বা চর্ব্বি-সংক্রান্ত;

বসাময়, মেদস্বী। *N un.* Animal fat ; বসা, মেদ, চর্ব্বি।

ăd′-it, *n.* **1.** An approach, spe. a horizontal entrance to a mine ; আগম, বিশেষতঃ ভূতলের সহিত সমান্তরাল খনিপ্রবেশের সুড়ঙ্গ, খনিপ্রবেশ পথ। **2.** Access ; entrance ; as, some means of *adit* to the Imperial Executive ; আগম ; প্রবেশ।

ăd-jā′-cĕnt, *adj.* Lying near or close *(to)* ; contiguous ; neighbouring ; as, a field *adjacent* to the high-way ; সন্নিহিত, সংনিকৃষ্ট, সমীপবর্ত্তী ; আসন্নবর্ত্তী (কথা সঃ), সংলগ্ন ; নিকটবর্ত্তী। **—cen-cy,** *n.* **Adjacent angles** *(Geom.)*—(জ্যামিতি) সংলগ্ন কোণ (হিঃ কোঃ), সংসক্ত কোণ (ঐ), আসন্ন কোণ।

ăd′-jĕc-tive, *n.* & *adj.* One of the parts of speech, consisting of words joined to nouns to define and limit their signification ; বিশেষণ, গুণবাচক শব্দ। ***Adj.* 1.** Of the nature of an addition or adjunct ; as, the *adjective* word or sentence ; বৈশেষণিক। **2.** Not standing by itself ; dependent ; additional ; as, *adjective* colours or dyes ; অপ্রধান ; অধীন ; অতিরিক্ত। **—ly,** *adv.* **—ti′-val,** *adj.* *(In dyeing)* **Adjective colours**—(রঞ্জনবিদ্যা) যে সকল বর্ণ কষবিধায়ক কোন প্রকার দ্রব্যসংযোগে পাকা করিয়া চিত্রণে ব্যবহার করিতে হয়।

ăd-join′ (-jŏyn), *v.t.* **1.** To join or unite (one thing to another) ; সংলগ্ন করা, সংযুক্ত করা। **2.** To be contiguous to or in contact with ; as, the head of the tomb *adjoins* the west wall ; পাশাপাশি হওয়া, লাগালাগি হওয়া, সংস্পৃষ্ট হওয়া। **—ing,** *pt. adj.* Adjacent ; contiguous ; neighbouring ; "The *adjoining* hospital was sacked." সন্নিহিত ; সংলগ্ন, সংসক্ত, সংনিকৃষ্ট ; সমীপবর্ত্তী, সমীপস্থ।

ăd-journ′ (-jŭrn), *v. t.* & *i.* **1.** To put off ; to postpone ; (properly to another day) ; as, I *adjourn* what I have to say on this topic ; স্থগিত রাখা বা করা ; নির্দ্দিষ্ট দিবস পর্য্যন্ত স্থগিত রাখা বা করা। **2.** To postpone further proceedings to another day ; as, the meeting was *adjourned* for a fortnight ; কার্য্য স্থগিত রাখা, মুলতুবি রাখা। ***Verb i.*** To cease sitting and carrying on business for a time ; to separate in order to meet at another place ; as, the House of Commons *adjourned* at four o'clock ; নির্দ্দিষ্ট বা অনির্দ্দিষ্ট কালের জন্য অধিবেশন বা কার্য্যপরিচালন স্থগিত রাখা ; অন্যস্থানে মিলনের উদ্দেশ্যে পৃথক্ হওয়া। **—ment,** *n.* **1.** The act of adjourning or of putting off till another day or indefinitely ; স্থগিতকরণ, নিরূপিত বা অনিরূপিত কাল পর্য্যন্ত কার্য্যত্যাগ। **2.** The interval during which a public body defers its business ; as, during an *adjournment* of six weeks ; মুলতুবি বা স্থগিত থাকার কাল।

ăd-judge′ (-jŭj), *v. t.* **1.** To adjudicate upon a matter ; to determine ; to settle ; as, the case was *adjudged* in the November term ; কোন বিষয় বিচার করা ; বিচারদ্বারা কোন বিষয় নির্ণয় করা ; নিষ্পত্তি করা। **2.** To award judicially (a thing *to* a person) ; as, the prize was *adjudged* to the victor ; একাধিক প্রতিযোগীর মধ্যে বিচারপূর্ব্বক সর্ব্বাপেক্ষা উপযুক্ত ব্যক্তিকে পুরস্কার প্রদান করা। **3.** To sentence or condemn (any one to a penalty) ; as, the murderer was *adjudged* to penal servitude for life, শাস্তি বা দণ্ডপ্রদান করা। **—judg′-ment,** *n.* The act of judging or deciding by a judicial decision ; judgment ; sentence given ; বিচারদ্বারা নির্ণয় বা নিষ্পত্তি ; সাধ্যসিদ্ধিপাদ (ইঃ উঃ), রায় ; দণ্ড।

ăd-jū′-di-cāte, *v. t.* & *i.* To try and determine judicially ; to adjudge ; বিচারদ্বারা মীমাংসা বা নির্ণয় করা ; বিচারপূর্ব্বক বিভিন্ন প্রতিযোগীর মধ্যে সর্ব্বাপেক্ষা উপযুক্ত ব্যক্তিকে পুরস্কার প্রদান করা। ***Verb i.*** (With *upon*) To sit in judgment and pronounce sentence ; to act as a judge ; as, the court *adjudicated upon* the case ; বিচারাসনে বসিয়া দণ্ডাদেশ প্রদান করা ; বিচারকের কার্য্য করা। **—ca′-tion,** *n.* **1.** The act of determining judicially ; বিচারপূর্ব্বক নির্দ্ধারণ। **2.** Judgment ; judicial sentence ; রায় ; দণ্ড। **—ca-tor,** *n.* One who settles a controverted question or awards the prize in a competition ; বিবদমান প্রশ্নমীমাংসক, যে ব্যক্তি প্রতিযোগীদের মধ্যে বিজয়ী ব্যক্তিকে পুরস্কার প্রদান করেন।

ăd′-jŭnct, *n.* & *adj.* **1.** Something joined to another, and subordinate to it in position, function, etc. ; as, learning is but an *adjunct* to ourselves ; অপ্রধান বিষয়, অঙ্গ। **2.** A person joined to another in some duty or service ; a colleague ; সহায়, সঙ্গী ; সহযোগী। **3.** *(Log.)* An accidental or nonessential quality or property, as *colour* in the body, *thinking* in the mind ; (তর্ক-বিজ্ঞান) অঙ্গ, অপ্রধান গুণ। **4.** *(Gram.)* A word added to qualify or amplify the force of other words ; an amplification of the subject, predicate, etc. ; (ব্যাকরণ) কোন শব্দের গুণপ্রকাশক বা অর্থ-বিস্তারক শব্দ ; বিশেষণ বা ক্রিয়াবিশেষণ, অনুবন্ধ পদ। ***Adj.*** Joined or added to (any thing) ; subordinate ; সংযুক্ত, সম্মিলিত, অনুবন্ধ ; অপ্রধান। **—junc′-tion,** *n.* **—junc′-tive,** *adj.* **—junc′-tive-ly,** *adv.*

ăd-jure′ (-jôr), *v. t.* **1.** To charge any one solemnly or earnestly, under oath, or under the ılty of a curse ; শপথ করান, ়: দেখাইয়া বন্দ বা আদেশ করা। ‍ to request earnestly ; as, his ıds *adjured* him to take ·e care of his life ; সাগ্রহে ন্মা করা। **—ju-ra′-tion,** *n.* ·: act of adjuring ; a solemn ealing to one upon oath ; aı nest appea' ; শপথগ্রহণ করান ; ; ঐকান্তিক অনুরোধ।

ıt′, *v. t.* **1.** To put in order ; ıo *adjust* affairs ; to arrange ; to *adjust* the orthography ; egulate or reduce to system ; ল করা ; যথাস্থানে সন্নিবিষ্ট করা ; ত করা। **2.** To fit ; as, to ıt a garment to the body ; lapt to a standard or pur- ; ঠিক্ লাগানো ; উপযোগী করা।) settle ; to harmonize dis- ncies ; as, to *adjust* ac- s ; মিটানো, নিষ্পত্তি করা ; ঠিক্ **—a-ble, —ive,** *adjs.* **—ment,** harmonising or properly dis- ıg ; settlement ; ব্যবস্থাপন ; ংসা, নিষ্পত্তি, সমাধান, ঠিকঠাক্।

ıt′-âge, *n.* The mouth-piece an artificial fountain ; কৃত্রিম ারার মুখনল।

Adjutant bird.

ăd′-jû-tănt, *n.* & *adj.* **1.** A military officer whose duty it is to assist the superior officers by receiving and communicating orders or the like ; সহকারী সেনানী। **2.** A species of gigantic stork ; হাড়গিলা পাখী। **3.** An assistant or helper ; as, a fine violin must be the best *adjutant* to a fine voice ; সহকারী। ***Adj.*** Helping ; auxiliary ; সহায়ক ; সাহায্যকারী। **—tan-cy,** *n.* **Adjutant-general**—The principal staff-officer in the army ranking next to the commander-in-chief ; জঙ্গীলাটের (মহাসেনাপতির) অব্যবহিত নিম্নপদস্থ সামরিক কর্ম্মচারী বিশেষ।

ăd′-jû-vănt, *adj.* & *n.* Helpful ; auxiliary ; helping ; সাহায্যকারী ; সহায়ক ; সাহায্যপ্রদ। ***Noun.*** A person or thing that helps ; সাহায্যকারী ব্যক্তি বা বস্তু।

ad libitum, ad lib., (*L.*), *adv.* At pleasure ; to the extent of one's wishes ; ইচ্ছামত ; ইচ্ছানুরূপ, যথাভিলাষ, যথাকাম।

ăd-meas′-ure (-mĕzh-ẽr), *v. t.* To ascertain the measure or limits of ; specific., to assign in due shares ; to apportion ; পরিমাপ করা ; বণ্টন করিয়া দেওয়া ; যথোচিত অংশমত বিভাগ করিয়া দেওয়া। **—ment,** *n.* **1.** Applying a measure in order to ascertain or compare dimensions ; মাপন। **2.** Dimensions ; proportions ; পরিমাণ ; অনুপাত।

ăd-mĭn′-ĭ-cle, *n.* **1.** Anything that aids or supports ; an auxiliary ; সাহায্যকারী, সহায়ক ; সহকারী। **2.** (*Law.*) A corroboratory evidence ; (আইন) প্রতিপোষক প্রমাণ।

ăd-mĭn′-ĭs-tẽr, *v. t.* & *i.* **1.** To manage the affairs of (an institution, town, etc.) ; কার্য্য নির্ব্বাহ করা, নির্ব্বাহ করা, পরিচালন করা। **2.** To execute or dispense (justice) ; to furnish or give (a thing *to*) ; as, to *administer* relief ; বিধান করা, বিতরণ করা ; সরবরাহ করা জোগানো। **3.** (*Med.*) To apply medicine to ; to give, as a dose ; as, *administer* this medicine to him ; to direct or cause to be taken as medicine ; (ভৈষজ্য-শাস্ত্র) ঔষধ প্রয়োগ করা ; ঔষধ প্রদান করা (যেমন একমাত্রা ঔষধ) ; ঔষধ সেবন করান বা সেবনের বিধি দেওয়া। **4.** To tender, as an oath *to* ; "Swear...to keep the oath we *administer*." গ্রহণ করান (যেমন শপথ বা হলপ)। **5.** (*Law*) To manage the estate of one who has died intestate ; (আইন) অকৃত-চরম-পত্র মৃত ব্যক্তির (যে ব্যক্তি উইল না করিয়া পরলোক গমন করিয়াছে) সম্পত্তি তত্ত্বাবধান করা। ***Verb i.*** **1.** To contribute (to one's comfort, etc.) ; as, to *administer to* the necessities of the poor ; সাহায্য-দান করা। **2.** To perform the office of an administrator ; as **A** *administers* upon the estate of **B** ; মৃত ব্যক্তির সম্পত্তির তত্ত্বাবধান করা। **—tra′-tion,** *n.* **1.** Management (of any business) ; management of public affairs ; পরিচালন বিধান, নির্ব্বাহ ; সাধারণের কার্য্য নির্ব্বাহ। **2.** Government ; শাসনতন্ত্র। **3.** The executive ; the ministry ; as, a rapid succession of weak *administration* ; শাসকবর্গ ; মন্ত্রিবর্গ। **4.** Application of remedies ; ঔষধ প্রদান, ঔষধপ্রয়োগ। **5.** Dispensation of (justice, sacrament) ; বিচার-বিধান বা সংস্কার-বিধান। **6.** (*Law*) The management of the estate of a deceased person by an executor ; অছিকর্ত্তৃক মৃতব্যক্তির সম্পত্তির রক্ষণাবেক্ষণ। **—tra-tive,** *adj.* Pertaining to the management of affairs ; executive ; শাসন-সংক্রান্ত ; পরিচালনশীল, কার্য্যসম্পাদনকারী, কর্ম্ম-নির্ব্বাহশীল, কার্য্য-নির্ব্বাহক। **—tra-tive-ly,** *adv.* **—tra-tor** (*fem.* -TRIX), *n.* **1.** One who manages or directs the affairs of any institution ; one who performs official duties (of religion, justice, etc.) ; a manager ; অধ্যক্ষ, নির্ব্বাহক, পরিচালক ; সম্পাদক, শাসনকর্ত্তা ; কার্য্যাধ্যক্ষ, কর্ম্মকর্ত্তা । **2.** (*Law*) One officially appointed to manage the estates of a deceased person ; one to whom authority is given to manage an estate ; a trustee ; (আইন) অছি; কোন ব্যক্তির সম্পত্তির তত্ত্বাবধায়ক ; ন্যাসরক্ষক । **–tra-tor-ship,** *n.* **Letters of administration**—A legal document conferring on one the right to act as administrator ; (opposed to *probate*) ; শাসনাধিকারপত্র (হিঃ কোঃ), প্রবন্ধাধিকার-পত্র (ঐ), নির্ব্বাহ-পত্র ।

ăd′-mi-ră-ble, *adj.* Deserving the highest praise ; most excellent ; surprisingly good ; অতিপ্রশংসার্হ, শ্লাঘ্য ; অনুত্তম, অত্যুত্তম ; চমৎকার । **–bly,** *adv.* In an admirable manner ; excellently ; প্রশংসনীয়রূপে, চমৎকারভাবে ; সুষ্ঠু (মঃ উঃ) । **–ness,** *n.*

ăd′-mi-răl, *n.* [From Arabic *amir*=commander, *al*=of the (Faithful, Sea, etc.)] **1.** The commander-in-chief of a country's navy ; a naval officer of the highest rank ; the commander o a fleet ; সর্ব্বপ্রধান নৌসেনাধ্যক্ষ ; সর্ব্বোচ্চপদস্থ নৌসেনানী ; নাবিক-নায়ক, রণপোত-পতি, রণপোতাধ্যক্ষ । [Admiral of the fleet, Admiral, Vice Admiral & Rear Admiral, ইংলণ্ড-দেশে এই চারি-শ্রেণীর Admiral আছেন। ইংলণ্ডের প্রধান Admiral পূর্ব্বে Lord High Admiral নামে অভিহিত হইতেন।] **2.** The ship that carries the admiral ; flagship ; যে রণপোতে সর্ব্বপ্রধান নৌসেনানী অবস্থান করেন ; রণপোতবহরের পতাকাবাহী রণতরী । **–ship,** *n.* **–ty,** *n.* **1.** The board of officials which controls the royal navy (in England, the Lords of Admiralty) ; that branch of the Executive which superintends the navy ; the building in which they meet for business ; রণ-পোত-সচিব-সংসদ, ; সামুদ্রিক-সচিব-সমাজ ; রণ-পোত-মন্ত্রি-সভা-ভবন । **2.** The office of an admiral ; নৌসেনাধ্যক্ষত্ব । **Admiralty Court, Court of Admiralty**—A tribunal having jurisdiction over maritime causes, whether civil or criminal ; সামুদ্রিক বিচারালয় । **The Lord High Admiral**—An officer who superintends all maritime affairs ; সামুদ্রিক ব্যাপারের তত্ত্বাবধায়ক ।

ăd-mi-rā′-tion, *n.* **1.** Agreeable surprise ; wonder mingled with esteem, love or veneration ; শ্লাঘা, প্রশংসা ; সাধুবাদ, শ্রদ্ধা, তারিফ । **2.** (Formerly) Wonder ; (পূর্ব্বে) বিস্ময় । **Note of admiration**—বিস্ময়-বোধক (!) চিহ্ন ।

ăd-mīre′, *v. t.* **1.** To regard with pleased surprise or wonder mingled with approbation, reverence, esteem or veneration ; to take pleasure in the beauty of ; to look on or comtemplate with pleasure ;

"And Enid woke and sat beside the couch, *Admiring* him,........."

প্রশংসা করা, শ্রদ্ধা করা, সমাদর করা, সাধুবাদ করা ; সৌন্দর্য্যদর্শনে পুলকিত হওয়া ; আনন্দিত চিত্তে নিরীক্ষণ বা অনুধ্যান করা । **2.** (Formerly) To view with wonder or surprise ; to wonder at ; (পূর্ব্বে) বিস্মিত বা আশ্চর্য্যান্বিত ভাবে দৃষ্টি করা ; বিস্মিত হওয়া । **–mir′-er,** *n.* One who admires, wonders at, or views with pleasure ; (In common speech) a lover ; প্রশংসাকারী, স্ত্রীজনের ভজনাকারী ; (সাধারণ কথাবার্ত্তায়) প্রেমিক, প্রণয়ী ।

ăd-mis′-sion (-mĭsh-ŭn), *n.* **1.** The act of admitting to a standing or privileges ; sion to enter into a place, etc. ; access ; প্রবেশন, প্রবে ভর্ত্তি । [গৃহাদিতে প্রবেশ সম্বন্ধে *ad* শব্দ প্রয়োগ শুদ্ধ নহে—এরূপ স্থ মাত্র *admittance* শব্দ ব্যবহ **2.** Acceptance into an c position ; institution ; formal *admission* of St. into the number of the a গ্রহণ ; সংস্থাপন । **3.** An ackn ment ; a concession ; a statement admitted ; as, he full *admission* of the স্বীকৃতি ; স্বীকার ; স্বীকৃত বিষয় **bil′-i-ty,** *n.* **–si-ble,** Worthy of being ente (*law*) allowable, as proof ; as, the testimony *missible ;* capable of bei mitted to an office or re গ্রহণ-যোগ্য ; (আইন) গ্রাহ্য ; প্রবেশয়িতব্য । **–si-b.** *n.* **–sive,** *adj.* Tend admit ; স্বীকার-প্রবণ ।

ăd-mit′, *v. t.* **1.** To allo enter (a person or thing or *into* a place ; as; opened the little wind *admit* some air : to *ac* thought *into* the mind ; t entrance to ; as, to *ad.* student *into* college ; to g right of entrance to ; as, th ticket *admits* one ; প্রবেশ করিতে দেওয়া ; ভর্ত্তি করা ; প্রবেশাধিকার দেওয়া । **2.** To allow one to enter on an office or *to* enjoy a privilege ; as, to *admit* an attorney to practise law : to *admit* one to bail ; কোন ব্যক্তিকে বিশেষ অধিকার ভোগ বা পদগ্রহণ করিতে অনুমতি দেওয়া । **3.** To acknowledge or assent to, as an allegation, to confess ; as, he *admitted* his guilt ; to accept as valid or true ;

as if ..ncede ; as, the argument is pen.. *lmitted ;* স্বীকার করা, মানা ; দোষ- ধ.. .কার করা ; ন্যায্য বা যথার্থ বলিয়া 2. .. .র করা ; স্বীকৃত হওয়া। 4. To frie.. ..nit ; to be capable of ; mo.. .ollowed by *of*) ; as, the words প্রা.. o not *admit* of such a construc- Th.. on ; (অন্বয়-সহ নহে) ; অনুমোদন করা ; app.. ., গ্রহণক্ষম হওয়া। **—ta-ble,** *adj.* an e.. **ance,** *n.* 1. The act of admit- শপন .. or letting (one) into a **ăd-jŭ..** ce ; প্রবেশ। 2. (*Law*) The as, .. ving possession to a copy-hold as, .. tate ; (আইন) সম্পত্তিতে অধিকার to r.. দখল-প্রদান। **—ted,** *adj.* 1. Allow- সুশৃঙ্খ.. to enter ; প্রবেশানুমতিপ্রাপ্ত। ব্যবস্থি.. Received as true or valid ; *adjus..* ..owledged ; সত্য বলিয়া ধার্য্য, to ac.. বা স্বীকৃত; সর্ব্ববাদিসম্মত। **—ted-** pose.. *adv.* Confessedly ; স্পষ্টতঃ, 3. T.. ..াদিসম্মতরূপে। **Admitted max-** crepa.. —Granted truths ; সর্ব্ববাদি- cour.. সত্য। **Admitted on all** .কন্দা। ..**ls or sides**—Regarded as *n.* .. by every body ; সর্ব্বজনসম্মত। posi.. **admit of**—To be capable of সীম.. ..aring ; as, this *admits of* no **ăd-j..** ..ay (বিলম্ব-সহ নহে) ; সহ্য (সমাসে)। of.. **..dmit one to bail**—To en- ফোয়.. ..e one on bail ; as, the judge ..*itted* the prisoner *to bail ;* ..ে খালাস দেওয়া।

..**ix',** *v. t.* To add as an ingredient ; to mingle (*with* something) ; উপাদানস্বরূপ যোগ করা ; সংমিশ্রিত করা। **—ture,** *n.* 1. The act of mixing ; সংমিশ্রণ। 2. The compound formed by mixing different substances together ; an alloy ; মিশ্র ; মিশ্রিত-পদার্থ, দ্বন্দ্ব (সাঃ পঃ)।

ăd-mŏn'-ish, *v. t.* 1. To exhort ; to reprove with mildness ; as, *admonish* him as a brother ; উপদেশ দেওয়া ; মৃদু ভর্ৎসনা করা, অনুযোগ দেওয়া। 2. To counsel against wrong practices ; to give warning or advice; (followed by *of, against*) ; "Mosés was sent to reprove and *admonish* the people ;" কদাচার হইতে নিবৃত্ত হইতে পরামর্শ দেওয়া ; সতর্ক করা বা সুপরামর্শ দেওয়া। 3. To instruct or direct ; "Ye choice spirits that *admonish* me ;" উপদেশ দেওয়া বা পরিচালিত করা। 4. To inform ; to remind (*of* a thing) ; to recall to duty ; জ্ঞাত করা, অবগত করা, বিজ্ঞাপিত করা ; স্মরণ করাইয়া দেওয়া ; কর্ত্তব্য কার্য্যে প্রণোদিত করা। **—er,** *n.* **—ment,** *n.*

ăd-mö-ni'-tion, *n.* Warning ; the act of admonishing ; gentle reproof ; expression of authoritative warning, especially in ecclesiastical censure ; সতর্কীকরণ ; অনুবোধন, অনুযোগ ; মৃদুভৎর্সনা ; প্রভুত্ব সহকারে সতর্কীকরণ, বিশেষতঃ, খৃষ্টীয় যাজকগণ কর্ত্তৃক ধর্ম্মচ্যুত ব্যক্তিগণকে প্রভুত্বসহকারে সতর্কীকরণ। **—mon'-i-tor,** *n.* One who admonishes ; a monitor ; উপদেষ্টা ; অনুযোগদাতা। **—mon'-i-to-ry,** *adj.* Conveying admonition ; উপদেশ-গর্ভ, অনুযোগপূর্ণ, সতর্ককর।

ad nauseam, (*L.*), *adv.* To a disgusting extent ; বিতৃষ্ণা না জন্মা পর্য্যন্ত, আঘৃণোদয়।

ăd-noun' (-nōwn), *n.* A word added to a noun, substantive or adjective ; বিশেষ্য বা বিশেষণের সহিত অন্বিত শব্দ।

ă-dô', *n.* Fuss ; troubles ; as, what is here *ado ;* difficulty ; as, with much *ado* he partly kept awake ; গণ্ডগোল, ধুম, ধুমধাম, কোলাহল ; কষ্ট, উদ্বেগ ; গোলমাল, গোলযোগ। **Much ado about nothing**—A great fuss over a petty matter ; বহ্বারম্ভে লঘুক্রিয়া, অনর্থক বহুকোলাহল।

ăd-ö-lĕs'-cĕnce, *n.* Youth or the period of life between puberty and maturity ; তারুণ্য, যৌবনাবস্থা, যৌবনকাল, যৌবনোদ্ভেদ, যুবত্ব (সাঃ পঃ)। (সাধারণতঃ পুরুষের পক্ষে ১৪ হইতে ২৫ বর্ষ বয়স, এবং নারীর পক্ষে ১২ হইতে ২১ পর্য্যন্ত।) **—cent,** *adj.* Growing up from childhood to manhood ; যৌবনোন্মুখ, কিশোর।

A-dō'-nis (ă-), *n.* 1. (*Gr. myth.*) A youth beloved by Venus for his beauty ; গ্রীক পুরাণোক্ত দেবী ভীনাসের প্রণয়পাত্র এডনিস্ নামক পরম-মনোহর যুবক। 2. A pre-eminently beautiful young man ; a beau or dandy ; কার্ত্তিকেয়-কান্ত যুবাপুরুষ, মন্মথ-মনোহর যুবক ; সৌখীন পুরুষ, সুবেশ, ফুলবাবু, নবকার্ত্তিক। 3. (*Entom.*) The butterfly Clifton Blue ; (কীটতত্ত্ব) একজাতীয় নীলবর্ণ প্রজাপতি। 4. (*Bot.*) A genus of plants popularly known as the Pheasant's Eye ; (উদ্ভিদ্-বিদ্যা) "জীবঞ্জীবাক্ষ" নামক ইংলণ্ডীয় পুষ্পতরুবিশেষ। [দেবী Venus যুবক Adonisএর অলৌকিক রূপলাবণ্যে মুগ্ধ হইয়া তাহাকে আত্ম-সমর্পণ করেন। দেবী যুবকের প্রাণে প্রণয়সঞ্চারার্থ অশেষ চেষ্টা করিয়াও সফলকামা হইতে পারেন নাই। অবশেষে এক দিবস মৃগয়াকালে Adonis বন্যবরাহকর্ত্তৃক নিহত হয়। এই Adonisএর রক্তবিন্দু হইতে Pheasant's Eye নামক রক্তপুষ্পপ্রসূতরু উৎপন্ন হইয়াছে—এইরূপ কিম্বদন্তী প্রচলিত আছে।]

ăd'-ö-nīze, *v. refl.* & *i.* 1. To adorn ; to dandify (oneself) ; উৎকৃষ্ট বসন ভূষণে দেহ সজ্জিত করা ; সৌখীন হইয়া পড়া। 2. To play the Adonis ; এডনিসের অনুরূপ রূপ বা পোষাকের বাহার প্রদর্শন করা।

ă-dŏpt', [L. *ad,* to, and *optare* = to choose, desire] *v. t.* 1. To take a stranger into one's family as son, heir, etc. ; পোষ্যপুত্রগ্রহণ করা, দত্তকগ্রহণ করা। 2. To take up (a word, idea, etc.) from some one else, and use it as one's own ; "This view is *adopted* by Dr. Arnold ;" অন্যের মতাদি গ্রহণ করিয়া নিজের মত বলিয়া চালান। 3. To choose for one's practice ; as, his resolutions were *adopted*

-by a small majority ; গ্রহণ করা। **—a-ble,** *adj.* Capable of being adopted ; গ্রহণ-যোগ্য। **—dop′-tion,** *n.* **1.** The act of adopting or the state of being adopted ; specif. voluntary acceptance of a child of other parents to be as one's own child ; as, the *adoption* of a child ; পরিগ্রহ ; দত্তক বা পোষ্য-পুত্র গ্রহণ, পুত্রীকরণ। **2.** Reception ; admission ; as, the *adoption* of a person into a society ; প্রতি-গ্রহণ ; গ্রহণ। **3.** The act of receiving as one's own what is new ; selection ; as, the *adoption* of a new method of agriculture ; গ্রহণ ; নির্ব্বাচন। **—er,** *n.* One who adopts ; an adoptive father ; গ্রহণকারী, গ্রহীতা ; দত্তক-গ্রহণকারী ; **—ive,** *adj.* Due to adoption ; apt to adopt ; as, an *adoptive* son, father, etc. ; গ্রহণ-জনিত ; গ্রহণশীল, পোষ্যপুত্র গ্রহণকারী। **—ive-ly,** *adv.* **Adoptive father** or **mother**—দত্তকগ্রহীতা, পরিগ্রহীতা (কুল্লূঃ) বা দত্তক-গ্রহিত্রী। **Adopted son**—দত্তক-পুত্র। **The country of one's adoption**—Not one's own mother-country but one in which one has settled either for pleasure or business ; "From the public opinion of the *country of his adoption,* Byron had nothing to dread." জন্মভূমি নহে—অথচ চিরদিন বসবাস করিবার ফলে যে দেশকে জন্মভূমির মত গণ্য করা হয়।

ăd-ö-ră′-tion, *n.* **1.** The act of paying honour to a divine being ; worship addressed to a deity ; আরাধন ; অর্চ্চনা, আরাধনা, উপাসনা। **2.** Profound regard and love ; homage paid to one in high esteem ; the highest degree of love, as of a man for a woman ; গভীর শ্রদ্ধা বা প্রেম ; পূজা ; পরম প্রেম, পরমানুরাগ।

ă-dōre′, *v. t.* **1.** To worship, as a deity ; পূজা করা, বন্দনা করা, অর্চ্চনা করা, আরাধনা করা। **2.** To love in the highest degree ; to regard with the utmost respect and affection ; as, the tender soft sex I shall ever *adore* : "The great mass of the population abhorred Popery and *adored* Monmouth." নিরতিশয় প্রেম বা অনুরাগ প্রদর্শন করা, ভজা, ভজনা করা (চন্দ্রঃ) ; দেব-বিগ্রহবৎ সম্মান করা। **—dor′-a-ble,** *adj.* **1.** Worthy of worship or divine honours ; আরাধনীয়, উপাস্য, পূজ্য, সম্মানার্হ। **2.** Worthy of the utmost love or respect ; "That *adorable* Being who governs all." পরম-মাননীয়, পরম শ্রদ্ধেয়, পরম প্রেমাস্পদ। **—dor′-a-bly,** *adv.* **—dor-er,** *n.* **1.** Worshipper ; অর্চ্চক, পূজক, উপাসক, আরাধক। **2.** An ardent admirer ; a lover ; as, I profess myself her *adorer,* not her friend ; একান্ত অনুরক্ত ব্যক্তি ; প্রেমিক, প্রণয়ী।

ă-dŏrn′, *v. t.* To deck or beautify ; to add beauty or lustre to ; to furnish with ornaments ; মণ্ডিত করা, শোভা-সম্পাদন করা, সু-শোভিত করা ; দীপ্তি বা সৌন্দর্য্য-বৃদ্ধি করা ; বিভূষিত করা, অলঙ্কৃত করা। **—ment,** *n.* Decoration ; ornament ; মণ্ডন, শোভা-সম্পাদন ; ভূষা, অলঙ্কার।

ad referendum, (*L.*), *adv.* For further consideration ; পুনর্ব্বিবেচনার জন্য।

ad rem, (*L.*), *adv.* & *adj.* To the point ; to the purpose ; প্রাসঙ্গিক ; উদ্দেশ্যানুরূপ।

ă-drĭft′, *adv.* In a drifting condition ; at the mercy of wind and tide or of circumstances ; "So on the sea, she shall be set *adrift.*" ইতস্ততঃ প্রবমান হইয়া ; ঝটিকা ও স্রোতোবেগ, কিম্বা অবস্থার তাড়নায় লক্ষ্যহীন কিম্বা উদ্দেশ্য-হারা ভাবে চালিত। **To turn one adrift**—To send one away to take his chance ; সংসার-সাগরে ভাসাইয়া দেওয়া।

ă-droit′ (-dr͝oyt), *adj.* Dexterous ; skilful ; active in the use of the hand ; ready in invention or execution ; as, an *adroit* mechanic : an *adroit* reply : দক্ষ ; কুশল, নিপুণ ; লঘুহস্ত ; উদ্ভাবন-শক্তি-সম্পন্ন। **—ly,** *adv.* **—ness,** *n.* Dexterity ; ready skill ; cleverness either bodily or mental ; দক্ষতা ; নৈপুণ্য ; পটুতা, পটিমা (উজ্জ্বলঃ), পাটব (ঐ)।

ă-drȳ′, *adv.* & *adj.* Dry ; thirsty ; শুষ্ক ; তৃষিত, শুষ্ককণ্ঠ।

ăd-scĭ-tĭ′-tious (-shŭs), *adj.* Adopted from without ; additional ; supplemental ; বহির্দ্দেশ হইতে গৃহীত, নৈমিত্তিক (সাঃ পঃ) ; অতিরিক্ত ; ন্যূনতাপূরক। **—ly,** *adv.*

adscriptus glebæ, (*L.*), *adj.* & *n.* Belonging or attached to the soil, as a serf ; ভৌমিক। ***Noun.*** A serf ; ক্ষেত্রকর্ষণকারী ক্রীতদাস।

adsum, (*L.*), *v. i.* I am here ; আমি এখানে।

ăd′-ü-lāte, *v. t.* To flatter basely or slavishly ; চাটুকারিতা করা, চাটূক্তি করা, জঘন্য তোষামোদ করা। **—u-la-tor,** *n.* A servile flatterer ; চাটুকার, স্তাবক। **—u-la-to-ry,** *adj.* Servilely praising ; containing excessive praise or compliment ; as, an *adulatory* address ; চাটুপূর্ণ ; অতি-প্রশংসাগর্ভ, শ্লাঘাসূচক।

ăd-ü-lā′-tion, *n.* Servile flattery ; praise in excess or beyond what is merited ; চাটুকারিতা, চাটূক্তি ; অতিপ্রশংসা, স্তব।

A-dŭll′-ăm-īte, *n.* A member of a party of the more moderate Liberals, who seceded from their own leaders and voted with the Conservatives in 1866 ; পার্লেমেণ্টের যে সমস্ত উদারনীতিক সভ্য ১৮৬৬ খৃঃ অব্দে স্বদলত্যাগ করত রক্ষণশীলদের পক্ষে ভোট দিয়াছিলেন, তাহাদের অন্যতম ব্যক্তি। [মিঃ ব্রাইট্ উক্ত সভ্যগণকে Old

Testamentএ বর্ণিত, Adullamএর গুহাতে নির্ব্বাসিত, Davidএর সহিত সম্মিলিত, দুঃস্থ, পীড়িত এবং ঋণগ্রস্ত ব্যক্তিগণের সহিত তুলনা করিয়াছেন। (I. Sam, xxii. 1, 2.)]

ă-dŭlt′, *n.* & *adj.* A person, animal or plant grown to full size and strength ; পূর্ণ-বয়স্ক ব্যক্তি, জন্তু বা পরিণত বৃক্ষাদি। ***Adj.*** Full-grown ; matured ; প্রবৃদ্ধ, প্রৌঢ়; পরিণত, পরিপক্ক।

ă-dŭl′-têr-ănt, *n.* & *adj.* That which is employed to adulterate anything ; যে বস্তু ভেজালে ব্যবহৃত হয়। ***Adj.*** Employed in adulterating ; ভেজালে ব্যবহৃত।

ă-dŭl′-têr-āte, *v. t.* To falsify or debase by the admixture of baser ingredients ; as, to *adulterate* food, drink, coin, etc. ; to corrupt ; মিশ্রণদ্বারা কৃত্রিম করা, ভেজাল দেওয়া ; দূষিত বা বিকৃত করা। **—a′-tion,** *n.* The act of adulterating or the state of being debased by foreign mixture ; অপদ্রব্য-মিশ্রণ, বিকৃতাবস্থাপ্রাপ্তি। **—a-tor,** *n.* One who debases anything by spurious admixture ; ভেজাল-দাতা, অপদ্রব্যমিশ্রক।

ă-dŭl′-têr-āte, *adj.* **1.** Stained (in conduct or in birth) by adultery ; "The *adulterate* Hastings ;" ব্যভিচার-দুষ্ট, হীনসংসর্গদুষ্ট, অপগর্ভজাত, জারজ। **2.** Spurious ; counterfeit ; কৃত্রিম, ভেজাল ; নকল, মেকি।

ă-dŭl′-têr-īne, *adj.* & *n.* **1.** Born of adultery ; জারজ। **2.** Counterfeit; spurious ; জাল, কৃত্রিম ; মেকি, নকল। **3.** Illegal ; unlicensed ; as, *adulterine* castles, guilds ; অবৈধ ; অননুমত।

ă-dŭl′-têr-ȳ, *n.* Violation of the marriage-bed ; the voluntary sexual intercourse of a married person with one of the opposite sex, either married (*double*) or not (*single*) ; ব্যভিচার ; পারদার্য্য, পরদারাভিগমন, পরস্ত্রীগমন, পতি-লঙ্ঘন, পরপুরুষ-সহবাস, পরপরিগ্রহ (বাৎস্যঃ), পরদারপরায়ণতা (কৃষ্ণঃ), পরদারাভিমর্ষণ (ঐ), অনূঢ়া-লঙ্ঘন। **—er,** *n.* One who commits adultery ; পরস্ত্রীগামী, পারদারিক (কৃষ্ণঃ), পরদার-রত। (*Fem.* ADULTERESS = ব্যভিচারিণী, পরপুরুষ-গামিনী।) **—ous,** *adj.* Pertaining to, or guilty of, adultery ; ব্যভিচার-ঘটিত, ব্যভিচার-দোষে দোষী। **—ous-ly,** *adv.*

ăd-ŭm′-brăl, *adj.* Overshadowing ; shady ; ছায়াবিস্তারী, ছায়াপ্রদ ; সচ্ছায়, ছায়াময়।

ăd-ŭm′-brāte, *v.t.* **1.** To represent in outline ; রেখা-মাত্র দ্বারা প্রদর্শন করা। **2.** To faintly indicate ; "Heaven is *adumbrated* by all positive excellence." ঈষৎ আভাস দেওয়া। **3.** To typify ; to foreshadow ; আদর্শ বা সাদৃশ্য দ্বারা প্রদর্শন করা ; পূর্ব্বাভাস দেওয়া। **—brant,** *adj.* Giving a faint shadow or slight resemblance ; ক্ষীণাভাস-প্রদ। **—bra′-tion,** *n.* A faint sketch ; an outline ; অস্পষ্ট পাণ্ডুলেখ, ক্ষীণ-সাদৃশ্য ; রেখান্যাস (কাব্যঃ)। **—bra-tive,** *adj.*

ad unguem (factus), (*L.*), *adj.* Highly finished ; নিরতিশয় পরিমার্জ্জিত।

ad unum omnes, (*L.*), *adv.* All to a man ; প্রত্যেকেই।

ă-dŭst′, *adj.* **1.** Scorched ; dried up ; parched ; পরিদগ্ধ ; পরিশুষ্ক ; তপ্ত, ভৃষ্ট। **2.** Sunburnt ; as, a tall man, of an *adust* complexion ; রৌদ্রদগ্ধ। **3.** Sallow ; gloomy in features or temperament ; ম্লান ; বিষণ্ণ।

ad valorem, ad val., (*L.*), *adv.* & *adj.* (*Of taxes*) In proportion to the estimated value of goods ; (কর-সম্বন্ধে) সম্পত্তির আনুমানিক মূল্যানুপাতে, মূল্যানুরূপ।

ăd-vănce′, *v. t., i.* & *n.* **1.** To move or put forward ; অগ্রগামী করা বা অগ্রসর করা, এগিয়ে দেওয়া। **2.** To promote or to raise to a higher rank ; as, to *advance* one from the bar to the bench ; উন্নীত করা। **3.** To raise in rate or price ; as, to *advance* the price of goods ; to enhance ; চড়াইয়া দেওয়া ; বৃদ্ধি করা। **4.** To promote the good of ; to improve or make better ; as, to *advance* one's true interest ; উন্নতি-সাধন করা ; উত্তরোত্তর উৎকর্ষ-সাধন করা। **5.** To accelerate (events) ; to hasten ; (ঘটনাদি) সত্বর করা ; ত্বরান্বিত করা। **6.** To put forward (a statement, suggeston, etc.) for acceptance ; as to *advance* an argument ; উপস্থাপিত করা। **7.** To pay money before it is due ; as, to *advance* money ; to supply beforehand ; অগ্রিম দেওয়া ; দাদন দেওয়া, আগাম দেওয়া। ***Verb i.*** **1.** To move or go forward ; as, the troops *advanced ;* অগ্রসর হওয়া, প্রয়াণ করা। **2.** To make progress ; as, to *advance* in wisdom ; উত্তরোত্তর উন্নতি লাভ করা, বৃদ্ধি পাওয়া। **3.** To rise in price ; মূল্য-বৃদ্ধি পাওয়া, মূল্য চড়া। ***Noun.*** **1.** Going forward, or onward ; অগ্রগমন, অগ্রসর, প্রয়াণ। **2.** A gradual progression or improvement (physically, mentally or socially) ; উত্তরোত্তর উৎকর্ষ লাভ। **3.** A rise in amount or price ; as, *advance* in Bank of England rate of discount ; উত্তরোত্তর বৃদ্ধি, মূল্যবৃদ্ধি। **4.** Payment before hand ; loan ; অগ্রিম প্রদান, দাদন, আগাম (বিষঃ) ; কর্জ্জ। **5.** Approach made to gain favour ; "The amours of an empress require the plainest *advances* ;" the first step towards the attainment of a result (usu. in *pl.*) (অনুগ্রহ বা প্রেমলাভার্থ) ঘেসাঘেসি, উপক্রম (বাৎস্যঃ) ; কোন উদ্দেশ্য সিদ্ধির জন্য প্রথম উপক্রম। **—vanced′,** *p. p.* **1.** Moved forward ; in the van or front ;

having reached comparatively a great length of years ; অগ্রগত, অগ্রগামী, পুরোবর্ত্তী ; পরিণত-বয়স্ক প্রৌঢ়। **2.** Far on in progress ; as, the more *advanced* European thinkers ; সমুন্নত। **Advance guard**—A detachment of troops which precedes the march of the main body ; অগ্রবর্ত্তী সেনাদল, নাসীরচর (আঃ বঃ)। **In advance**—Beforehand ; অগ্রিম। **In advance of**—In front of ; ahead of ; পুরোবর্ত্তী ; অগ্রগামী। **In advance of one's age**—Far superior to one's contemporaries ; সামসময়িক মানবমণ্ডলী অপেক্ষা বহুদূর অগ্রসর। **The night is far advanced**—রাত্রি অনেক হইয়াছে। **To make advance in**—To make progress in ; কোন বিষয়ে উন্নতি লাভ করা।

ăd-vănce'-mĕnt, *n.* The act of advancing or the state of being advanced ; as, the *advancement* of knowledge ; improvement ; promotion to a higher place ; উন্নতিসাধন, উন্নতাবস্থা ; উন্নতি, অভ্যুদয়, শ্রীবৃদ্ধি (বিবিধঃ) ; পদোন্নতি, উচ্চপদে উন্নয়ন।

ăd-văn'-tăge, *n.* & *v. t.* **1.** Benefit ; favourable circumstance ; সুবিধা, সুযোগ, কায়দা ; অনুকূল অবস্থা। **2.** Superiority ; mastery (*of, over*) ; "Lest, Satan should get an *advantage* ;" প্রাধান্য ; প্রভুত্ব। **3.** Superiority of state ; benefit ; শ্রেষ্ঠতা ; উপকারিতা, লাভ। ***Verb t.*** **1.** To give an advantage or superiority to ; to favour ; to promote ; সুবিধা দান করা, অপেক্ষাকৃত শ্রেষ্ঠতাপ্রদান করা ; পোষকতা করা ; উন্নীত করা। **2.** To be beneficial to ; to put in a better position ; as, winds do *advantage* trees : to *advantage* a statue by the addition of colour ; হিতকর হওয়া ; উৎকর্ষ সাধন করা। **—ta'-geous,** *adj.* **1.** Causing advantage ; useful ; beneficial ; profitable ; সুবিধাজনক ; কার্য্যকর ; হিতকর ; লাভজনক। **—ta'-geous-ly,** *adv.* **—ta'-geous-ness,** *n.* **To advantage**—Favourably ; in a good light ; উত্তমভাবে ; সুবিধাজনকরূপে। **To have the advantage of**—To be in a more favourable position than some one else ; অপর কোন ব্যক্তি অপেক্ষা অধিকতর সুবিধাজনক অবস্থায় সংস্থিত থাকা। **To show to advantage**—To appear or cause to appear in a conspicuous manner ; প্রকৃষ্টরূপে প্রকাশ করা বা পাওয়া, খোলতাই করা বা হওয়া। **To take advantage of**—To make use of favourable circumstances to the prejudice of another ; অপর ব্যক্তির কোন প্রকার দুর্ব্বলতা বা দুরবস্থার সুযোগ গ্রহণকরত স্বীয়স্বার্থ-সাধন করা। **To take a person at advantage**—To take one by surprise ; অতর্কিতভাবে কাহাকে আক্রমণ করত অপ্রস্তুত করা।

ăd'-vĕnt, *n.* **1.** The coming of Christ ; incarnation ; খৃষ্টাগমন ; নরকলেবরধারণ। **2.** The expected second coming of Christ ; খৃষ্ট-ধর্ম্মাবলম্বিগণকর্ত্তৃক প্রত্যাশিত যীশুখৃষ্টের দ্বিতীয় অবতরণ। **3.** The period including the four Sundays before Christmas ; যীশুখৃষ্টের জন্মোৎসবের (বড় দিনের) পূর্ব্ববর্ত্তী সপ্তাহ-চতুষ্টয়। **4.** Any important arrival ; কোন বিশেষ (জাতি বা ব্যক্তির) আগমনক আবির্ভাব।

ăd-vĕn-tĭ'-tious (-shŭs), *adj.* **1.** Coming from without ; foreign ; accidental ; casual ; as, an *adventitious* idea of terror ; বহিরাগত, ঔপাধিক ; বৈদেশিক, বাহ্য ; আগন্তুক (সাঃ পঃ) ; নৈমিত্তিক, সঞ্চারী (মঃ উঃ)। **2.** (*Law*) Applied to such goods as fall to a man, either by mere fortune or by the liberality of a stranger, not by direct succession ; (আইন) অপুরুষপরম্পরাগত, ভিন্নশাখাগত (সম্পত্তি)। **3.** (*Bot.*) Appearing out of the normal or usual place ; (উদ্ভিদ-বিদ্যা) বটাদি বৃক্ষের শাখা হইতে নিষ্ক্রান্ত শিকড়ের (বটের ঝুরির) মত সাধারণনিয়মবহির্ভূত। **—ly,** *adv.* **—ness,** *n.* **Adventitious root**—(উদ্ভিদ-বিদ্যা) আস্থানিক শিকড় (সাঃ পঃ)।

ăd-vĕn'-ture (-chür), *v. t., i.* & *n.* **1.** To expose to danger ; to imperil oneself ; বিপদাপন্ন করা ; সঙ্কটে ফেলা। **2.** To venture upon ; to take the chance of ; to commit to fortune ; সাহসের উপর নির্ভর করিয়া কোন ঝুঁকিদার বা বিপদ্-সঙ্কুল কার্য্যে প্রবৃত্ত হওয়া ; দৈবের উপর নির্ভর করিয়া কোন কার্য্যে প্রবৃত্ত হওয়া ; অদৃষ্টের হস্তে আত্মসমর্পণ করা। ***Verb i.*** To dare to come or go (*in, into, on, upon,* any place) ; to venture (*on, upon,* an undertaking) ; to take any risk ; যাইতে বা আসিতে সাহসী হওয়া ; কোন ঝুঁকিদার বা বিপৎ-সঙ্কুল কার্য্যে সাহস করিয়া প্রবৃত্ত হওয়া ; সর্ব্বপ্রকার বিপদ্ ও সঙ্কটের মধ্যে অগ্রসর হওয়া, যে কোনরূপ দায় বা ঝুঁকি ঘাড়ে লওয়া। ***Noun.*** **1.** Hazard ; risk ; chance ; বিপদ্, সঙ্কট ; দায়, ঝুঁকি ; দৈব। **2.** A daring or hazardous enterprise ; the encountering of risk ; সাহসিক কর্ম্ম, বিপৎ-সঙ্কুল কার্য্য ; বিপদের সম্মুখীন হওন। **3.** A striking incident or experience ; a remarkable occurrence in one's life ; "To tell all his *adventures* would fill a volume." অদ্ভুত ঘটনা, চরিত (as, দশকুমার চরিত=adventure of ten princes) ; কোন ব্যক্তির জীবনের বিচিত্র ঘটনা বিশেষ। **4.** A novel or unexpected incident ; as, to walk alone in London seemed of itself an *adventure* ; অপ্রত্যাশিত বা অভিনব ঘটনা। **5.** A commercial speculation, especially, speculation in goods sent abroad ; বাণিজ্য-ব্যাপার, বিশেষতঃ বিদেশে মালরপ্তানির ঝুঁকিদার ব্যবসায়। **—ful,** *adj.* **—some,** *adj.*

Given to adventures ; সাহসিক। (SEE VENTURESOME.) **—tur-er,** *n.* **1.** One who seeks adventures, esp., bold, novel, extraordinary enterprise ; অদ্ভুত, বিচিত্র বা বিপৎ-সঙ্কুল কার্য্যান্বেষণকারী। **2.** A soldier of fortune ; ভৃতক সৈন্য, ভাগ্যান্বেষী সৈন্য, যে সৈন্য অর্থ পাইলে, যথা তথা সৈনিকের কর্ম্ম গ্রহণ করে। **3.** One who lives by his wits ; ছলকৌশল বা চালাকি দ্বারা জীবিকার্জ্জনকারী, বিট (বাংস্থঃ)। **4.** A speculator ; ঝুঁকিদার ব্যবসায়ে প্রবৃত্ত ব্যক্তি। **—tur-ess,** *n.* A female adventurer ; a woman on the look-out for a position, esp. by equivocal means ; সাহসিকী বা সাহসিকা ; যে স্ত্রী সন্দিগ্ধ উপায়ে কোন পদলাভের জন্য চেষ্টা করে। **—tur-ous,** *adj.* **1.** Inclined to adventures ; prone to incur risk ; rashly daring ; (applied to persons) ; দুঃসাহসিক-কার্য্যপ্রবণ ; বিপজ্জনক কার্য্যান্বেষী ; অবিমৃষ্যকারী, অসমসাহসী। **2.** Full of hazards ; attended with risk ; (applied to acts) ; সঙ্কট-সঙ্কুল ; বিপজ্জনক। **—tur-ous-ly,** *adv.* **—tur-ous-ness,** *n.*

ăd'-vêrb, *n.* A word that modifies or qualifies an adjective, verb or another adverb, expressing a relation of place, time, circumstance, manner, etc. ; ক্রিয়া-বিশেষণ। **—ver'-bi-al,** *adj.* Pertaining to an adverb ; ক্রিয়া-বিশেষণ-সংক্রান্ত, ক্রিয়া-বিশেষণাত্মক। **—ver'-bi-al-ly,** *adv.*

ad verbum, (L.), *adv.* & *adj.* Word for word ; অক্ষরে অক্ষরে, আক্ষরিক।

ăd'-vêr-să-rŷ, *n.* Opponent ; antagonist ; enemy ; বৈরী, প্রতিদ্বন্দ্বী ; বিপক্ষ ; শত্রু, অরি। **The adversary**—The Devil ; শয়তান।

ăd-vêr-să-'tive, *adj.* (Of words) Expressing opposition or antithesis ; বিরোধবাচক বা বিপরীতার্থক (অব্যয়)। [ব্যাকরণে *but, yet, however* প্রভৃতিকে *adversative conjunctions* কহে, যেহেতু, ইহারা পূর্ব্ব-প্রকাশিত অর্থের সঙ্কোচ-বিধান করে।]

ăd'-vêrse, *adj.* Contrary ; hostile ; (*to*) ; প্রতিকূল ; বিরোধী, বিপক্ষ। **2.** Calamitous ; unfortunate ; injurious ; (*to*) ; as, *adverse* fate or circumstances ; বিপৎ-সঙ্কুল, হানিকর, অনিষ্টকর ; দুর্দ্দৈবপূর্ণ, দৈবোপহত। **3.** Placed opposite ; "And Afric's coast and Calpe's *adverse* height." পরস্পরের বিপরীতদিকে অবস্থিত। **—ly,** *adv.* **—ness,** *n.* (*Law*) **Adverse possession**—(আইন) দখলীয় স্বত্ব।

ăd-vêr'-si-tŷ, *n.* Misfortune ; "Sweet are the uses of *adversity* ;" calamity ; affliction ; trial ; distress ; দুর্দ্দৈব, দুর্ব্বিপাক, দুরদৃষ্ট ; বিপদ্, আপদ্ ; ক্লেশ, যন্ত্রণা ; কষ্ট ; কৃচ্ছ্রতা, দুর্দ্দশা।

ăd-vêrt', *v. t.* To turn the mind or attention ; to refer *to* in speaking or writing ; as, the king's illness was *adverted to* in the House of Commons ; মনোনিবেশ করা, মনোযোগ আকর্ষণ করা ; উল্লেখ করা। **—ĕnce, —ĕn-cŷ,** *ns.* Notice ; attention ; consideration ; লক্ষ্য ; অবধানতা ; বিবেচনা। **—ent,** *adj.* **—ent-ly,** *adv.*

ăd-vêr-tīse', *v. t.* & *i.* To give notice of ; to make generally known ; to announce publicly, especially by a printed notice ; বিজ্ঞাপিত করা, বিজ্ঞাপন দেওয়া ; সাধারণ্যে প্রচার করা ; জাহির করা। ***Verb i.*** To put a public notice in a journal or to announce by placard in a public place ; as, he *advertises* largely in the daily papers ; সংবাদপত্রে বিজ্ঞাপন প্রদান করা, প্রকাশ্যস্থলে বৃহৎ অক্ষরে মুদ্রিত বিজ্ঞাপন আঁটিয়া দেওয়া। **—ment,** *n.* A public announcement, usually by placards or in journals ; বিজ্ঞাপন, সাধারণতঃ সংবাদপত্রসমূহে প্রদত্ত বিজ্ঞাপন। **—tis'-er,** *n.* **1.** One who issues a public notice ; বিজ্ঞাপনদাতা। **2.** A journal or other print in which advertisements are published ; as, *"The Morning Advertiser ;"* যে সকল সংবাদপত্রাদিতে বিজ্ঞাপন প্রকাশিত হয়। **—tis'-ing,** *adj.* Issuing advertisements ; as, an *advertising* agency ; বিজ্ঞাপন-প্রচারী।

ăd-vīce', *n.* **1.** An opinion recommended or offered, as worthy to be followed ; counsel, esp. medical or legal counsel ; উপদেশ ; পরামর্শ, মন্ত্রণা, বিশেষতঃ চিকিৎসক বা ব্যবহারজীবির পরামর্শ। **2.** Information given ; news ; as, we have late *advice* from Paris of the outbreak of a revolution ; প্রদত্ত সংবাদ ; সমাচার। **3.** (*Pl.*) Communications from a distance ; specially in commerce, formal notice of transactions ; দূরবর্ত্তীস্থান হইতে প্রাপ্ত সংবাদ বা বার্ত্তা ; (বাণিজ্য) প্রচলিত প্রথানুযায়ী প্রদত্ত ক্রয়বিক্রয়ের বিজ্ঞাপন বা সংবাদ। **Advice boat**—A small, swift-sailing vessel employed to carry despatches or information ; সরকারী চিঠিপত্র বা সংবাদবাহক দ্রুতগামী ক্ষুদ্র পোত-বিশেষ, বার্ত্তাবাহী পোত।

ăd-vīṡe', *v. t.* & *i.* **1.** To offer counsel to ; উপদেশ দেওয়া, পরামর্শ দেওয়া, মন্ত্রণা দেওয়া। **2.** (*Commer.*) To give information of (an event, transaction) ; to announce ; (followed by *of*); as, the merchants were *advised of* the despatch of goods ; (বাণিজ্য) সংবাদ-প্রদান করা, সমাচার দেওয়া ; বিজ্ঞাপিত করা। **3.** To give notice or information ; to inform ; as, he *advised* the inspector of the murder at once ; সংবাদ-জ্ঞাপন করা। ***Verb i.*** To take counsel ; to join others in deliberating ; (followed by *with*) ; as, I shall *advise with* my friends as to what is to be done ; পরামর্শ লওয়া ; অন্যের সহিত মন্ত্রণা বা পরামর্শে যোগ দেওয়া। **—vĭs-ă-bĭl′-i-ty,** *n.* Advisableness ; expediency ; ঔচিত্য, পরামর্শসিদ্ধতা ; কার্য্যসাধনোপযোগিতা। **—vĭs′-ă-ble,** *adj.* **1.** Proper to be advised or recommended ; prudent ; expedient ; পরামর্শসিদ্ধ ; সমীচীন, যুক্তিযুক্ত, বিজ্ঞোচিত ; কার্য্যসাধক। **2.** Open to advice ; as, pray for an *advisable* and teachable temper ; উপদেশগ্রহণশীল। **—vĭs′-a-ble-ness,** *n.* **—vĭs′-a-bly,** *adv.* **—vĭs′-ed,** *adj.* Deliberate ; considered ; as, an *advised* act or scheme ; সুবিবেচিত ; সুচিন্তিত। **—vĭs′-ed-ly,** *adv.* With deliberation ; heedfully ; purposely ; as, an enterprise *advisedly* undertaken ; বিবেচনাপূর্ব্বক, সুবিচারপূর্ব্বক, সমীক্ষাপূর্ব্বক ; সাবধানতার সহিত ; উদ্দেশ্যপূর্ব্বক। **—vĭs′-ed-ness,** *n.* **—vĭs′-er.** *n.* **1.** One who advises or counsels ; as, the *advisers* of the crown ; উপদেষ্টা, পরামর্শ-দাতা, মন্ত্রণাদাতা। **2.** Also in a bad sense—One who instigates or persuades ; প্রোৎসাহক, প্ররোচক। **—vī′-sŏ-ry,** *adj.* Having power to advise ; giving advice ; as, an *advisory* council ; মন্ত্রণাপ্রদানক্ষম ; মন্ত্রদ বা মন্ত্রণাদায়িনী। **To advise with one's pillow**—To think within one's self ; স্বগত চিন্তা করা।

ad vitam aut culpam, (*L.*), *adv.* During good behaviour ; সদাচার লঙ্ঘন না করা পর্য্যন্ত।

ăd′-vŏ-cāte, *n.* & *v. t.* **1.** One whose profession it is to plead the cause of any one in a court of justice ; a counsel ; উকিল, ব্যবহারজীবী, পরপক্ষবিবাদী ; কৌঁসুলি। **2.** One who speaks in behalf of a cause or proposal, etc. ; a defender ; as, an *advocate* for the oppressed : an *advocate* of free-trade ; পক্ষসমর্থনকারী ; সমর্থক। (*Fem.* ADVOCATESS). ***Verb t.*** To plead in favour of ; to defend by argument before a tribunal ; to recommend publicly ; পক্ষসমর্থন করা ; বিচারালয়ে কাহারো পক্ষে ওকালতি করা ; প্রকাশ্যভাবে কাহারো অনুকূলে বলা বা সুপারিস্ করা। **—ca-cy,** *n.* **1.** The functions of an advocate ; উকিলের কাজ, ওকালতি। **2.** Pleading in support of ; পক্ষসমর্থন, উপরোধ। **—ship,** *n.* **Advocate general**—সর্ব্বপ্রধান সরকারী কৌঁসুলি।

ăd-vow′-sŏn, *n.* The right for presentation to a vacant benefice ; বৃত্তি-ভোগি-যাজক-পদে নিয়োগাধিকার, ধর্ম্মবৃত্তি-দানাধিকার।

ăd-y̆-nā′-mi-ă, *n.* Want of vital force ; physical prostration ; জীবনী-শক্তি-হীনতা ; শারীরিক শক্তিলোপ। **—nam′-ic,** *adj.* Pertaining to debility of the vital powers ; জীবনী-শক্তি-হীনতাসম্বন্ধীয়। **Adynamic fever**—সন্নিপাতজ্বর (সাঃ পঃ)।

ădze, ădz, *n.* & *v. t.* A carpenter's tool like axe with arched blade, used for chipping the surface

Adze.

of timber ; বাইস, বাসী বা বাসি, তক্ষক (মঃ উঃ)। ***Verb t.*** To cut with an adze ; বাইসদ্বারা কাটা।

æ′-dile (ē-), *n.* A magistrate in ancient Rome who superintended public buildings, shows, police, etc. ; প্রাচীন রোমনগরীর উচ্চকর্ম্মচারী বিশেষ,—উক্ত কর্ম্মচারী তামাসা, প্রদর্শনী, পুলিশবিভাগ এবং সরকারী অট্টালিকাসমূহের তত্ত্বাবধায়কতা করিতেন। **—ship,** *n.*

æger, *n.* [*L. sick*] A note certifying that a student is ill ; কোন ছাত্রের অসুস্থতাবিষয়ক ক্ষুদ্রপত্র।

æ′-gis (ē-), (Gr. *aigis,* a goat skin—অজচর্ম্ম) *n.* **1.** The shield of Jupiter or Athene ; জুপিটার বা এথেনী দেবীর চর্ম্ম-ফলক। **2.** (Hence) A protection ; an impregnable defence ; as, under the *ægis* of the British rule ; আশ্রয় ; অলঙ্ঘ্য আশ্রয়-স্থল। [গ্রীক্-পুরাণানুসারে Amalthea নাম্নী এক অজা জিয়াস্‌কে স্তন্য-দানে পালন করে। তিনি কৃতজ্ঞতা প্রদর্শনার্থ উক্ত অজার চর্ম্মদ্বারা স্বীয় উরস্ত্রাণ আচ্ছাদন করিয়াছিলেন।]

Aegle Marmelos—Bengal quince ; শ্রীফল (মঃ উঃ), বিল্ব (ঐ), (বেলঃ)।

ægrotat, (L., *he is sick*), *n.* English university, a medical certificate that a student is too ill to attend at a lecture or examination ; ইংলণ্ডীয় বিশ্ব-বিদ্যালয়স্থ ছাত্রগণের পীড়াবশতঃ অনুপস্থিতির জন্য চিকিৎসকের নিদর্শন-পত্র।

Ae-ō′-li-ăn (ē-), *adj.* Pertaining to Aeolus, the mythic god of the winds ; hence, pertaining to wind ; aerial ; as, an *Aeolian* organ ; (গ্রীক্-পুরাণে বর্ণিত) পবনদেবতা-সম্বন্ধীয় ; অতএব, বায়বীয় ; সমীর-সঞ্জাত। **Aeolian harp** or **lyre**—A stringed instrument producing musical sounds on exposure to wind ; পবন-বীণা, বায়ু-বাদিত বীণা, বায়ব্য-বীণা (অবঃ)।

Ae-ŏl′-ic (ē-), *adj.* & *n.* Pertaining to Aeolis, a district of Asia Minor, colonized by the Greeks ; as, *Aeolic* dialect ; ইয়োলিস্ দেশী ***Noun.*** Aeolic dialect ; ইয়োলিস্ প্রদেশে প্রচলিত উপভাষা।

æ-ŏl′-i-py̆le (ē-), **—pīle,** *n.* instrument for showing the force of steam escaping through a narrow aperture ; বাষ্প-বল-মান য

æ-ō-lŏt′-rō-py̆ (ē-), *n.* Change of physical qualities consequent on change of position ; অবস্থিতি বিপর্য্যয়ের ফলে ভৌতিক ধর্ম্মের বিপর্য্য

চলধর্ম্মতা (হিঃ কোঃ)। **—lo-trop′-ic,** *adj.* Not isotropic ; চলধর্ম্মা।

æ′-ōn (ē-), *n.* **1.** An age of the universe ; immeasurable period ; যুগ ; অপ্রমেয় কাল। **2.** Eternity ; অনন্ত কাল। **3.** (*Platonic Philosophy*) A power existing from eternity ; an emanation or phase of the supreme deity ; অনাদি শক্তি ; পরমেশ্বরের অবস্থাবিশেষ বা বিবর্ত্ত, "বিশ্ববিকাশ"।

-ĕr-āte, *v. t.* **1.** To put air into ; বায়ু-পূরিত করা। **2.** To charge with carbonic acid gas (formerly called *fixed air*) ; কার্ব্বোনিক য়্যাসিড্ বাষ্প-পূরিত করা। **3.** To expose to (the mechanical or chemical) action of the air ; বায়ুদ্বারা ভৌতিক বা রাসায়নিক ক্রিয়া সংঘটিত হইতে পারে—এরূপ স্থানে অনাবৃত রাখা। **—a′-tion,** *n.* **Aerated waters**—কার্ব্বোনিক্ য়্যাসিড্ গ্যাস্ দ্বারা সম্পূরিত বিবিধ প্রকার পানীয়, যথা—সোডা, লেমনেড্, প্রভৃতি।

ā-ē′-rĭ-ăl, *adj.* **1.** Belonging or pertaining to the air or atmosphere ; gaseous ; inhabiting or frequenting the air ; growing, existing or happening in the air ; produced by or in the air ; বায়ব্য, বায়বীয়, বায়ু-মণ্ডলীয় ; বাষ্পীয় ; ব্যোমচর, নভশ্চর, গগন-বিহারী, ব্যোম-বিহারী ; বায়ুজাত, আকাশস্থ, শূন্য-মার্গ-সংঘটিত ; বায়ুজ, বায়ুতে উৎপন্ন। **2.** Consisting of air ; partaking of the nature of air ; as, *aerial* architecture (আকাশকুসুম) প্রভৃত ; অনিলধর্ম্মা। **3.** High ; lofty ; *aerial* spirits ; elevated ; উচ্চ ; আকাশস্পর্শী ; উন্নত। **4.** Light or thin as air ; ethereal ; হাওয়ার মত হাল্কা ; দিব্য, অমূর্ত্ত, অশরীরী, মনঃ-কল্পিত। **—al′-i-ty,** *n.* **—ly,** *adv.* **Aerial roots**—ঝুরি, অবরোহ (রঃ), বায়ব্যমূল (সাঃ পঃ)।

-rie (-ĭ), **ā′-ĕr-ȳ, ey′-rie** (ï-rĭ), **ey′-rȳ**(ĭ-) *n.* **1.** The nest of a bird of prey, esp. eagle that builds high up ; শিকারী পক্ষীর বাসা, উৎক্রোশ পক্ষীর কুলায়। **2.** The brood of a bird of prey ; শিকারী পক্ষীর শাবকসকল। **3.** A human residence perched high on a mountain ; শৈলাবাস।

ā′-ĕr-ĭ-fôrm, *adj.* **1.** Of the form of air ; gaseous ; বায়ুস্বরূপ ; বাষ্পীয়। **2.** Unreal ; অবাস্তব।

ā′-ĕr-ĭ-fȳ, *v. t.* **1.** To change from a solid or liquid state to air or gas ; কঠিন বা তরল অবস্থা হইতে বায়ু বা বাষ্পাকারে পরিণত করা। **2.** To fill or combine with air ; বায়ুদ্বারা পরিপূর্ণ করা বা বায়ুমিলিত করা। **—fi-ca′-tion,** *n.*

ā-ĕr-ō-dȳ-năm′-ics, *n.* The science treating of air in motion ; বায়ু-গতি বিজ্ঞান।

ā′-ĕr-ō-līte, —lĭth, *n.* A meteoric

Aerolite.

stone or meteorite ; উল্কা-প্রস্তর বায়ুপল, ব্যোমাশ্ম (সাঃ প)।

ā′-ĕr-ō-naut (-nät), *n.* One who sails through the air ; a baloonist ; গগন-পর্য্যাটক, ব্যোমবিহারী, বিমানযাত্রী, ব্যোমযায়ী (সাঃ পঃ) ; ব্যোমযান-চালক। **—naut′-ics,** *n.* The science or art of aerial navigation ; গগনপর্য্যটন-কৌশল বা নভোবিহার-বিদ্যা, উড্ডয়ন-বিদ্যা।

ā′-ĕr-ō-plāne, *n.* A light rigid plane used in aerial navigation to oppose sudden upward and downward movement in the air ; hence a *flying machine* using such plane or planes for support,—(the machine is run by a cylinder petrol motor) ; আকাশ-যানবিশেষ, পবন-পক্ষী (হিঃ কোঃ)।

ā′-ĕr-ō-stăt, *n.* **1.** An aviator ; গগন-পর্য্যাটক। **2.** (*Formerly*) A baloonist ; (পূর্ব্বে) ব্যোমযানবিহারী।

ā-ĕr-ō-stăt′-ics, *n.* The science which treats of the weight, pressure, and equilibrium of air and other elastic fluids ; যে বিজ্ঞানে বায়ু এবং অপরাপর স্থিতি-স্থাপক তরল পদার্থের ওজন, চাপ ও সম-সংস্থান বিষয় আলোচিত হইয়া থাকে, স্থিরানিল বিজ্ঞান। **—os-ta′-tion,** *n.* Air-navigation ; গগন-পর্য্যটন, নভো-ভ্রমণ। **—stat′-ic, —stat′-i-cal,** *adjs.*

Æschynomene Aspera—শোলা (বেলঃ), কাঠ শোলা (ঐ), ফুলশোলা (ঐ)।

Æs-cū-lā′-pĭ-ŭs (ĕs-), *n.* The Roman god of medicine ; hence, a physician ; রোমীয় বৈদ্য-দেবতা, রোমীয় ধন্বন্তরি ; ভিষক্, চিকিৎসক। **—an,** *adj.* Relating to the healing art ; medicinal ; চিকিৎসা-শাস্ত্র-বিষয়ক ; ভৈষজ্য।

æs-thĕt′-ics (ĕz-), *n.* The philosophy or theory of taste or of the perception of the beautiful in nature and art ; শোভা-বিজ্ঞান, সৌন্দর্য্য-বিজ্ঞান, রস-সংবেদ-বিদ্যা (হিঃ কোঃ), রস-বিজ্ঞান-রুচি-বিজ্ঞান, রসালঙ্কার (চৌরপঃ) সৌন্দর্য্যতত্ত্বশাস্ত্র (প্রবাসী ১৩২০)। **—ic, —i-cal,** *adjs.* **1.** Pertaining to the appreciation or criticism of the beautiful ; সৌন্দর্য্য-সংবেদ-বিদ্যা-বিষয়ক, রুচি-বিষয়ক, রস-সম্বন্ধী। **2.** Having an appreciation of the beautiful or pleasing ; of refined taste (used of persons, animals) ; সৌন্দর্য্য-বিবেকী (হিঃ কোঃ) ; রসজ্ঞ, রসগ্রাহী। **3.** In accordance with the principles of good taste (used of things) ; সুরুচি-সম্মত। **—i-cal-ly,** *adv.* **—i-cism,** *n.* The aesthetic principles ; pursuit of or devotion to the beautiful in nature and art ; সৌন্দর্য্য-তত্ত্ব, রসতত্ত্ব ; সৌন্দর্য্যানুরাগ। **Æsthetic faculty**—সৌন্দর্য্য-বুদ্ধি, চিত্ত-রঞ্জিনী বৃত্তি (বঙ্কিমঃ)।

æs-thō-phȳs-i-ŏl'-ō-ḡy (ĕs-), *n* The physiology of sensation ; a scientific study of the organs of sensation ; ইন্দ্রিয়জ জ্ঞান (সংবেদন) সম্বন্ধীয় শারীর-বিজ্ঞান ; জ্ঞানেন্দ্রিয় সমূহের বৈজ্ঞানিক আলোচনা।

æs'-ti-văl (ĕs-), **ĕs'-ti-văl,** *adj.* Belonging to or appearing in, summer ; as, *æstival* diseases ; নৈদাঘ, গ্রীষ্মকালীন। **—vate,** *v. t.* To spend the summer ; (*Zool.*) to pass the summer in a state of torpor ; গ্রীষ্মকাল যাপন করা ; (জন্তু-তত্ত্ব) জাড্য বা তন্দ্রিতাবস্থায় গ্রীষ্মকাল যাপন করা। **—va'-tion,** *n.* **1.** The state of torpidity induced by the heat and dryness of summer (opp. to *hibernation*); নিদাঘ-জড়তা। **2.** (*Bot.*) Arrangement of petals in flower-bud before expansion ; (উদ্ভিদ-বিদ্যা) বিকাশের প্রাক্‌কালে কুসুম-কলিকার দল-সংস্থান, কোরক-পত্র-বিন্যাস (সাঃ পঃ)।

æ-ti-ŏl'-ō-ḡy (ē-), *n.* **1.** Assignment of a cause ; কারণ-নির্দ্দেশ। **2.** The science or philosophy of causation ; কারণ-বিজ্ঞান, হেতু-বিজ্ঞান (হিঃ কোঃ)। **3.** The science of the causes and origin of diseases ; নিদান-শাস্ত্র (হিঃ কোঃ)। **—o-log'-i-cal,** *adj.* **—o-log'-i-cal-ly,** *adv.*

ā-fâr', *adv* Far away ; at, to or from a great distance—(often used with *from* preceding, or *off* following) ; তফাতে, বহুদূরে ; অতিদূরে, অতিদূর হইতে।

ăf'-fā-ble, *adj.* **1.** Admitting others to free conversation without reserve ; courteous ; complaisant ; as, an *affable* prince ; অভিগম্য, নিঃসঙ্কোচে আলাপ্য ; শিষ্ট, সৌজন্যপূর্ণ, অমায়িক ; দাক্ষিণ্য-পরবশ, প্রিয়কারী। **2.** Mild ; benign ; as, an *affable* countenance ; সৌম্য, বিনম্র ; সদয়, সকরুণ। **—bil'-i-ty, —ness,** *ns.* Readiness to converse or to be addressed—esp. by inferiors or equals ; benignity ; mildness ; মিষ্টভাষিতা, অমায়িকতা, প্রসন্নতা, দাক্ষিণ্য ; সদয়ভাব ; মৃদুতা, কোমলতা। **—bly,** *adv.*

ăf-fair' (-fâr), *n.* **1.** What has to be done ; business ; কার্য্য, কায, কর্ম্ম। **2.** Matter ; concern ; as, that is my *affair ;* ব্যাপার ; বিষয়। **3.** A partial engagement of troops ; a skirmish ; as, in this little *affair* of the advanced post, Lieut. B was killed ; খণ্ড-যুদ্ধ ; ডিম্ব (মাঃ মাঃ), হাঙ্গামা। **4.** (*Pl.*) Ordinary pursuits of life ; বিষয়-কর্ম্ম, বৈষয়িক বা সাংসারিক ব্যাপার। **Affair of honour**—Duel ; দ্বন্দ্ব-যুদ্ধ। **Affair of love**—An intrigue ; অবৈধ প্রেম, প্রেম-চক্রান্ত, গুপ্তপ্রেম।

ăf-fĕct', *v. t.* **1.** To attack (as disease) ; to act upon contagiously ; আক্রমণ করা ; স্পর্শ-সংক্রামকভাবে ক্রিয়া করা। **2.** To influence ; to act upon (in mind or feelings) ; to touch ; as, the old gentleman seemed to be greatly *affected* therewith ; প্রভাবিত করা, বিচলিত করা, ক্রিয়া করা ; মর্ম্মস্পর্শ করা। **3.** To frequent naturally or habitually ; to haunt (used esp. of animals and plants) ; as, a pavement *affected* by the scorpion for its nest ; বিচরণ করা ; যাতায়াত করা, গতিবিধি করা। **4.** To tend to by affinity or disposition ; as, the drops of every fluid *affect* a round figure ; স্বভাব বা স্বাভাবিক আকর্ষণ হেতু (কোন রূপ আকার ধারণে) প্রবণ বা উন্মুখ হওয়া। **5.** To put on a pretence of ; to assume the character or appearance of ; as, to *affect* ignorance ; ছল করা, ভাণ করা ; কপটতা করা। **6.** To imitate in a constrained and unnatural manner ; "Spencer, in *affecting* the ancients, writ no language ;" অস্বাভাবিকভাবে অনুকরণ করা। **7.** To practise ; to use ; as, to *affect* a costume ; আচরণ করা ; ব্যবহার করা। **—ed,** *adj.* **1.** Assuming or pretending to possess what is not natural or real ; artificial ; as, *affected* manners ; given to false show ; as, an *affected* lady ; কপট, ছদ্ম ; কৃত্রিম ; কৃত্রিম বাহার বা আড়ম্বর প্রদর্শন-প্রিয়। **2.** Attacked ; as by disease ; afflicted ; আক্রান্ত, গ্রস্ত (সমাসে) ; পীড়িত। **3.** Moved or touched in the feelings ; বিচলিত। **4.** Acted upon physically or materially ; as, the water is *affected* even more than the land ; আক্রান্ত। **—ed-ly,** *adv.* **—ed-ness,** *n.* **—fec-ta'-tion,** *n.* Studied display (of) ; false pretence ; artificiality of manners ; (কোন বিষয়ে) কৃত্রিমতাপ্রদর্শন ; মিথ্যা ভাণ, কপটতা, ছল, ভণ্ডামি ; কৃত্রিমাচরণ, কপটাচরণ। **—fec'-tive,** *adj.* Pertaining to the affections ; emotional ; স্নেহানুরাগাদিসম্বন্ধীয় ; আবেগ-পূর্ণ। **—fec'-tive-ly,** *adv.* **—ing,** *adj.* Pathetic ; as, an *affecting* spectacle ; touching ; moving ; as, an *affecting* address ; করুণ ; মর্ম্ম-স্পর্শী, প্রাণস্পর্শী ; চিত্তদ্রবকর, প্রাণ-গলানো। **—ing-ly,** *adv.* **Affected repulse of a lover's caresses**—কুট্টমিত ভাব (সাঃ দঃ)।

ăf-fĕc'-tion, *n.* **1.** The act of influencing or acting upon ; প্রভাবন, বিকরণ (মঃ উঃ)। **2.** An attribute ; a quality or property ; as, figure, weight, etc. are *affections* of bodies ; গুণ ; প্রকৃতি বা ধর্ম্ম। **3.** Bent of mind ; mental state ; any emotion or feeling ; as, the benevolent *affections* (love, esteem, gratitude, etc.) ; inclination ; disposition ; মনোগতি ; মানসিক অবস্থা ; চিত্তবৃত্তি, ভাব ; আসক্তি ; প্রবৃত্তি । **4.** A settled good will ; love ; (*for, toward*) ; as, the *affection* of a parent for his child ; zealous or tender attachment ; প্রীতি ; প্রেম, প্রণয়, স্নেহ, মমতা ; সৌহার্দ্দ্য, অনুরাগ, চিত্তরাগ । **5.** A bodily state ; malady ; disease ; as, a gouty *affection* ; শারীরিক অবস্থা ; ব্যাধি, রোগ, বিক্রিয়া (রঃ) ; পীড়া । **—al,** *adj.* **—ate,** *adj.* **1.** Having great love or affection ; warmly attached ; loving ; fond ; as, an *affectionate* brother ; মমতাপূর্ণ, স্নেহানুগত, স্নেহপ্রবণ, স্নেহগর্ভ ; অনুরাগী ; সপ্রেম ; অনুরক্ত । **2.** Proceeding from affection ; indicating love ; tender ; as, an *affectionate* letter ; প্রণয়-সঞ্জাত ; প্রেমসূচক ; স্নেহময় । **—ate-ly,** *adv.* In an affectionate manner ; সস্নেহভাবে (চন্দ্রঃ), সস্নেহে । **—ate-ness,** *n.* **Affectionate tone** —আর্দ্রস্বর ।

ăf′-fêr-ĕnt, *adj.* Conducting inwards or towards (opp. to *efferent*) ; as, *afferent* nerves (যে শিরাদ্বারা বাহ্যবস্তুর বোধজ্ঞান মস্তিষ্কে নীত হয়) ; মধ্যগ (সাঃ পঃ), অন্তর্ব্বাহী (হিঃ কোঃ), জ্ঞানবাহী (ঐ), প্রতীচীন (ঐ) ।

affettuoso, (It.) *adv.* (*Mus.*) Feelingly ; (সঙ্গীত-শাস্ত্র) ভাবের সহিত ।

ăf-fī′-ănce, *n.* & *v. t.* **1.** Marriage contract or promise ; pledging of faith, esp., plighting of troth in marriage ; বিবাহের চুক্তি বা অঙ্গীকার ; সত্যবাক্যপ্রদান, বিশেষতঃ (বিবাহের) বাগ্দান । **2.** Faith ; trust (*in*) ; শ্রদ্ধা, নিষ্ঠা ; বিশ্বাস, প্রত্যয় । ***Verb t.*** To bind by promise of marriage ; to pledge one's faith to for marriage (usu. *passive*) ; "Tancred was *affianced* to the daughter of Basso ;" বাগ্দান করা ; বিবাহার্থ অঙ্গীকারবদ্ধ হওয়া । **An affianced bride**—বাগ্দত্তা কন্যা ।

ăf-fi-dā′-vit, *n.* (*Law*) A declaration in writing, signed and made upon oath before an authorised magistrate ; (আইন) এফিডেভিট্, শপথ-পত্র (মঃ উঃ), হলফ্‌নামা, সত্যপাঠ-পত্র, স্বীকৃতি-পত্র ।

ăf-fil′-i-āte, *v. t.* **1.** To adopt ; to receive into a family as a son ; hence, to bring into intimate association or close connection ; দত্তক গ্রহণ করা ; পোষ্যপুত্ররূপে গ্রহণ করা ; ঘনিষ্ঠতা বা অন্তরঙ্গতা স্থাপন করা । **2.** (*Law*) To fix the paternity of (an illegitimate child on the putative father) for the purpose of maintenance ; as, a woman is said to *affiliate* a child upon a man ; (আইন) ভরণপোষণের জন্য জারজ সন্তানের পিতৃত্ব নির্দ্দেশ করা । **3.** To receive into a society as a member and initiate into its mysteries, plans, etc. (foll. by *to, with*) ; কোন সম্প্রদায়ের সভ্য-রূপে গ্রহণ করত তৎসম্পর্কীয় রহস্য ও উদ্দেশ্যাদি পরিজ্ঞাত করা । **4.** To adopt societies or institutions as branches ; as, to *affiliate* a school ; সম্প্রদায়, সমিতি, সমাজ বা প্রতিষ্ঠান সমূহকে শাখা-স্বরূপ পরিগ্রহণ করা । **5.** To trace origin to ; মূল অনুসরণ করা, আদি নির্দ্দেশ করা । **fil-i-a′-tion,** *n.* **1.** The act of taking a son ; দত্তকগ্রহণ । **2.** The assignment of a child, as a bastard, to his father ; পিতৃ-নির্দ্দেশ, (যথা, ভরণ-পোষণের জন্য জারজ-সন্তানের জনক-নিরূপণ) **3.** The assignment of anything to its origin ; কোন বিষয়ের মূল নির্দ্দেশ । **4.** The adoption of a smaller society by a larger and more powerful one having the same aim ; বৃহত্তর এবং প্রবলতর শক্তিশালিনী সম্মিলনীকর্ত্তৃক একলক্ষ্যানুসারী ক্ষুদ্রতর সমাজ প্রভৃতিকে অন্তর্ভুক্ত-করণ ।

ăf-fin′-i-tȳ, *n.* **1.** Relationship by marriage [opp. to *consanguinity* or *relation by blood* (সাগোত্রতা) ; foll. by *with, to,* or *between*] ; relations or kindred in general ; বৈবাহিক সম্বন্ধ ; জ্ঞাতি, কুটুম্ব । **2.** Relation ; connection ; close agreement ; as, *affinity* of sounds, of colours ; জ্ঞাতিত্ব-সম্বন্ধ ; সম্পর্ক ; ঐক্য, ঘনিষ্ঠতা । **3.** Structural resemblance (between animals, plants and languages) ; family-likeness ; অঙ্গ-বিন্যাস বা গঠনগত সাদৃশ্য ; পারিবারিক সাদৃশ্য । **4.** (*Fig.*) Similarity of character suggesting family likeness ; (লক্ষণায়) বংশানুগত চরিত্র-সাদৃশ্য । **5.** Liking or attractiveness ; attraction ; প্রীতি, চিত্তহারিত্ব ; আকর্ষণ । **6.** (*Chem.*) Tendency of certain elements to unite with others ; (রসায়ন-শাস্ত্র) অপরাপর মূলপদার্থের সহিত কতিপয় মূলপদার্থের মিলন-প্রবণতা, রসায়ন-প্রীতি (হিঃ কোঃ) ।

ăf-firm′ (-fêrm), *v. t.* & *i.* **1.** To assert positively ; to tell with confidence ; (opp. to *deny*); নিশ্চিত-রূপে বলা ; দৃঢ়বিশ্বাসের সহিত বলা । **2.** (*Law*) To make firm ; to confirm or ratify ; as, the Supreme Court *affirmed* the judgment ; (আইন) দৃঢ় করা ; বলবৎ করা, বাহাল রাখা । **3.** (*Log.* & *gram.*) To make a statement in the affirmative ; (তর্ক-বিজ্ঞান এবং ব্যাকরণ) অস্তিবাচক বাক্য বলা । ***Verb i.*** **1.** To declare strongly or positively ; দৃঢ়রূপে বলা, নিশ্চিতভাবে বলা । **2.** To make a solemn (formal) declaration before a court ; আদালতে শপথ করা, হলফ্ করা । **—a-ble,** *adj.* **—a-bly,** *adv.* **—fir-ma′-tion,** *n.* **1.** The act of affirming (opp. to *negation* or *denial*) ; দৃঢ়তার

সহিত বা নিশ্চিতরূপে কথন। **2.** Confirmation ; ratification ; as, the *affirmation* of a law ; দৃঢ়ীকরণ ; স্থিরীকরণ, সত্যাপন। **3.** An assertion ; a positive statement ; দৃঢ়োক্তি, দৃঢ় বচন ; নিশ্চিতোক্তি, নিশ্চিত-বাক্য। **4.** (*Law*) A solemn declaration by a person who conscientiously declines taking an oath ; (আইন) বিবেক-বিরুদ্ধতা হেতু হলফ্‌গ্রহণে অসম্মত ব্যক্তির সত্য-প্রতিজ্ঞা।

ăf-firm'-ă-tive (-fêrm-), *adj.* & *n.* **1.** Affirming or asserting ; declaratory of what exists ; as, an *affirmative* proposition ; answering 'yes' to a question ; (opp to *negative*) ; as, an *affirmative* answer ; নিশ্চায়ক, নিশ্চিতাত্মক, স্বীকারসূচক, দৃঢ়তাসূচক ; অস্তিত্বজ্ঞাপক, সম্মতিসূচক। **2.** (*Log.*) Expressing agreement of the two terms of a proposition ; (তর্ক-বিজ্ঞান) অন্বয়ী (সাঃ পঃ), সাধর্ম্য। ***Noun.*** **1.** An affirmative proposition ; বিধিবাক্য (হিং কোঃ), অন্বয়ী প্রতিজ্ঞা। **2.** A word or phrase expressing affirmation or assent (*yes, yea, that is so*) ; সম্মতিসূচক বা অস্তিবাচক শব্দ বা পদ। **—ly,** *adv.* **To answer in the affirmative**—To answer 'yes' or 'that is so' ; কোন প্রশ্নের উত্তরে 'হাঁ' বা 'তাইত' বলা।

ăf'-fix, *n.* **1.** Appendage ; addition ; শেষাংশ ; অনুবন্ধ। **2.** (*Gram.*) An addition placed at the beginning or end of a root, stem or word to modify its meaning ; (ব্যাকরণ) প্রত্যয়। **Affix to nouns**—তদ্ধিত। **Affix to verbs**—কৃৎ।

ăf-fix', *v. t.* **1.** To fix ; to fasten (a thing *to, on, upon* another) ; to annex ; to append to ; as, to *affix* a syllable to a word ; লাগান, বদ্ধ করা ; অনুবদ্ধ করা, সংবদ্ধ করা ; সংযুক্ত, সংলগ্ন বা সংযোজিত করা ; পরিশিষ্টরূপে দেওয়া। **2.** To impress (as a seal, stamp) ; as, to *affix* a seal to a deed ; মুদ্রাঙ্কিত করা। **3.** To attach ; to unite or connect with ; as, ideas *affixed* to things ; to *affix* a stigma to a person ; সংযোগ করা ; সংশ্লিষ্ট করা, সংলগ্ন করা। **—ture,** *n.* The act of affixing or fastening to ; সংযোজন।

ăf-flā'-tŭs, *n.* **1.** A breath or blast of wind ; শ্বাস (অঃ), মন্দানিল, ঝঞ্ঝা। **2.** The divine impartation to poets and others of genius, etc. ; প্রেরণা, দৈবজ্ঞান, প্রত্যাদেশ, দৈব-প্রেরণা।

ăf-flict', *v. t.* To distress with bodily or mental suffering ; to trouble ; to harass ; ক্লেশ দেওয়া, মনঃপীড়া দেওয়া, শোক দেওয়া, বিড়ম্বনা করা ; উত্যক্ত করা, বিরক্ত করা ; পীড়ন করা। **—flic'-tion,** *n.* Misery ; distress ; pain ; calamity ; ক্লেশ ; দুর্গতি, উপপ্লব (মঃ ভাঃ), দুর্দ্দশা ; ব্যথা, বেদনা, যন্ত্রণা, সন্তাপ ; বিপদ্‌, আপদ্‌। **—flic'-tive,** *adj.* Painful ; distressing ; যন্ত্রণাদায়ক, পীড়াদায়ক, ক্লেশকর ; দুর্গতিকর। **—flic'-tive-ly,** *adv.*

ăf'-flû-ĕnce, *n.* **1.** A flowing to or towards ; an influx ; প্রবাহ ; আগম, অন্তঃপ্রবাহ। **2.** Abundance ; wealth ; great plenty of worldly goods ; প্রাচুর্য্য, বাহুল্য ; ধনসম্পত্তি, সমৃদ্ধি ; আঢ্যতা।

ăf'-flû-ĕnt, *adj.* & *n.* **1.** Flowing abundantly ; as, *affluent* blood ; প্রচুর পরিমাণে প্রবহমান। **2.** Wealthy ; abounding in goods or riches ; copious ; ধনাঢ্য ; সমৃদ্ধ ; বহুল, ভূয়িষ্ঠ, প্রচুর। ***Noun.*** A tributary stream ; উপনদী (সাঃ পঃ), শাখা (ঐ)।

af'-flŭx, *n.* A flowing towards ; a flow towards a point, esp. of humours ; প্রবাহ ; আগম (বিশেষতঃ রক্ত, শ্লেষ্মাদি সম্পর্কে)।

ăf-fōrd', *v. t.* **1.** To yield or produce as fruit, profit, or results ; as, the earth *affords* grain ; trade *affords* profits ; প্রদান করা, উৎপাদন করা, জন্মান। **2.** To grant or confer ; as, a good life *affords* consolation old age ; দেওয়া, অর্পণ করা, প্রদান করা। **3.** (With *can*) To have the means ; to be rich enough to manage to spare ; as, a m can *afford* a sum yearly charity ; সঙ্গতি থাকা ; উপযুক্ত পরিমাণে ধনসম্পন্ন হওয়া ; ব্যয় সংক্ষেপ করত কার্য্যোপযোগী অর্থের সংস্থান করা। **4.** To be able to stand or bear ; as, his constitution could *afford* such a severe strain ; সহ্য করা।

ăf-fŏr'-ĕst, *v. t.* To convert into a forest or hunting ground অরণ্য বা মৃগয়াভূমিতে পরিণত করা **—a'-tion,** *n.*

ăf-frăn'-chīse, *v. t.* To make free from slavery ; দাসত্বমোচন করা।

ăf-fray' (-frā), *v. t.* & *n.* To disturb or startle from sleep or quiet as a sudden noise does ; (rare ভীত করা, সন্ত্রস্ত করা। ***Nou*** A tumultuous assault or quarr breach of the peace, caused fighting or riot in a pub place ; তুমুল-দ্বন্দ্ব, কলহ বা মারপিট্‌ দাঙ্গাহাঙ্গামা দ্বারা শান্তিভঙ্গ।

ăf-fright' (-frīt), *v. t.* & *n.* T frighten ; to alarm ; as, dream *affright* our souls ; ভয়প্রদর্শ করা, ভীত করা ; ত্রস্ত করা। ***Noun*** Alarm ; terror ; ভয়, শঙ্কা ; ত্রাস।

ăf-frŏnt', *v. t.* & *n.* **1.** To insult openly by language or demeanour ; to offend by insolence ; as, to *affront* one by giving him the lie ; (বাক্যে বা ব্যবহারে) মুখের উপর অসম্মান করা ; ঔদ্ধত্য প্রকাশে ক্ষুণ্ণ করা। **2.** To put to the blush ; to offend the modesty self-respect of ; লজ্জিত করা, লজ্জা ফেলা ; কাহারো লজ্জাশীলতা বা আ সম্মানে আঘাত করা। **3.** To cor front ; to face in defiance ; a to *affront* death ; সম্মুখীন বা মুখ মুখি হওয়া ; সম্মুখে দাঁড়ান। ***Noun*** **1.** An open insult ; as, to off n *affront* ; প্রকাশ্যে অপমান, মুখের উপর অপমান। 2. Offence to one's dignity or modesty ; মর্য্যাদাতিক্রম, লজ্জাশীলতায় আঘাত।

fü'-sion, *n.* 1. Pouring on, sp. of water on the body in one kind of baptism ; আসেক, নিষেক, আসেচন, অভিষেক, বিশেষতঃ, দেহে জলপ্রক্ষেপদ্বারা খৃষ্টীয় ধর্ম্মে দীক্ষাদানের প্রণালী বিশেষ। 2. (*Med.*) The act of pouring water on the body as a curative means, as by a shower-bath, etc. ; (ভৈষজ্যশাস্ত্র) আরোগ্যার্থ পীড়িত ব্যক্তির দেহে সলিল-নিষেক।

a-field' (-fëld), *adv.* 1. To, in, or on the field (of labour or battle) ; মাঠে, ক্ষেত্রে, প্রান্তরে, রণ-ক্ষেত্রে। 2. Away from home ; at a distance ; as, far *afield* ; প্রবাসে ; দূরে। 3. Astray ; বিপথে।

fïre', *adv.* & *adj.* On fire (*lit.* & *fig.*) ; as, the match is left *afire* ; (শব্দানুযায়ী এবং লক্ষণায়) জ্বলন্ত, উদ্দীপ্ত।

flāme', *adv.* & *adj.* In flame ; glowing ; in a glow of light ; (*lit.* & *fig.*) ; (শব্দানুযায়ী এবং লক্ষণায়) জ্বলন্ত অবস্থায় ; জ্বলন্ত ; জাজ্বল্যমান।

-float' (-flōt), *adv.* & *adj.* 1. Borne on the water ; in a floating condition ; on board ship ; in naval service ; প্লবমান ; প্লবমান অবস্থায় ; জাহজোপরি ; নৌ-বিভাগের কার্য্যে। 2. Passing from place to place ; in circulation ; as, a rumour is *afloat* ; সঞ্চারী ; সঞ্চরণশীল। 3. Moving without guide or control ; adrift ; as, our affairs are all *afloat* ; কর্ণধারবিহীন, পরিচালক-শূন্য ; যদৃচ্ছাক্রমে চালিত। 4. Out of debt ; as, your shallowest help will hold me up *afloat* ; ঋণমুক্ত।

-foam' (-föm), *adv.* & *adj.* In a foaming state ; foaming ; ফেনায়িত ভাবে ; ফেনিল।

fond, (*F.*), *adv.* Thoroughly ; fully ; সম্পূর্ণরূপে ; সম্যক্‌রূপে।

ă-fōōt', *adv.* & *adj.* 1. On foot ; পদব্রজে। 2. Astir ; on the move ; চঞ্চল ; চলন্ত বা চলন্ত অবস্থায়। 3. In operation or employment ; as, a design is *afoot* ; প্রারব্ধ, আরব্ধ, প্রবর্ত্তিত।

ă-före', *adv.* & *prep.* (*Naut.*) In front ; in front of ; in the fore part of a vessel ; (নৌ-বিদ্যা) অগ্রে ; কোনকিছুর অগ্রভাগে ; জাহাজের অগ্রভাগে। **Afore-cited, —named, —said**—Cited before ; পূর্ব্বোক্ত, প্রাগুক্ত, পূর্ব্বাভিহিত, পূর্ব্বকথিত, উদ্ধৃত। **Afore-going**—অগ্রগামী, পূর্ব্ববর্ত্তী। **Afore-thought** — পূর্ব্ব-সংকল্পিত। **Afore-time**—পূর্ব্বকালে।

a fortiori, (*L.*), *adv.* With stronger reason ; more conclusively ; বলবত্তর যুক্তি-সহকারে ; নিশ্চিততররূপে, অধিকতর অখণ্ডনীয়রূপে, সুতরাং (হিঃ কোঃ)।

ă-foul' (-fowl), *adv.* & *adj.* In collision ; as, the brig ran *afoul* of the steamer ; entangled ; সংঘর্ষ লাগিয়া ; জড়িত। **To run afoul of**—To come into collision with ; সংঘর্ষ লাগা।

ă-fraid' (-frād), *adj.* In fear ; apprehensive ; fearful ; alarmed ; in fear of the consequence (to oneself) of ; as, to be *afraid* of death ; ভীত ; শঙ্কিত, সশঙ্ক, শঙ্কাশীল ; ভয়াকুল ; ত্রস্ত ; পরিণাম-শঙ্কী। [(*Colloq.*) *I am afraid*—বুঝিবা, আমার আশঙ্কা হইতেছে।] **Afraid of one's shadow**—Greatly alarmed without a cause ; আপনার ছায়া দর্শনে ভয়াকুল, অকারণে মহাভয়যুক্ত।

ă-frĕsh', *adv.* Anew ; newly ; নূতন ; নূতন ভাবে, অভিনবরূপে।

Af-ri-kăn'-dĕr (ăf-), *n.* A native of South Africa born of European (esp. Dutch) settlers ; ইয়ুরোপীয় (বিশেষতঃ ওলন্দাজ) ঔপনিবেশিকের ঔরসে কৃষ্ণাঙ্গী রমণীদিগের গর্ভজাত দক্ষিণ আফ্রিকার অধিবাসী।

ăft, *adj.* & *adv.* (*Naut.*) In, near or towards the stern of a ship ; astern ; (নৌ-বিদ্যা) জাহাজের পশ্চাদ্‌ভাগে ; পাছায়, গলুইয়ের দিকে। **Fore and aft**—From stem to stern ; lengthwise ; জাহাজের এক প্রান্ত হইতে অপর প্রান্ত পর্য্যন্ত ; লম্বালম্বিভাবে।

âft'-êr, *adv.*, *prep.* & *adj.* Later in time ; behind ; afterwards ; as, they came *after* ; উত্তরকালে ; পিছনে, পিছে ; পশ্চাতে, পরে। ***Prep.*** 1. Behind in place ; as, men placed in a line one *after* another ; পশ্চাতে। 2. Later in time (often precedes a clause) ; as, *after* supper (নৈশ-ভোজনান্তে) ; অন্তে, পরে। 3. In pursuit of ; in search of ; with or in desire for ; "As the hart panteth *after* the water-brooks, so panteth my soul *after* thee, O God !" অনুসরণে ; অন্বেষণে ; আকাঙ্ক্ষায়। 4. In imitation of ; after the manner of ; অনুকরণে ; আদর্শানুযায়ী। 5. In allusion to ; as, named *after* Ram ; অনুসারে, ইঙ্গিতে। 6. According to ; as, *after* a fashion ; অনুসারে। 7. Next in importance to ; below in rank or excellence ; as, *after* Shakespear, I class Milton as our greatest poet ; গুরুত্ব-হিসাবে অব্যবহিত নিম্নে ; পদবী বা গুণোৎকর্ষ হিসাবে নিম্নতর স্থানে। 8. Concerning ; as, to enquire *after* a person ; সম্পর্কে, বিষয়ে, সম্বন্ধে। 9. Subsequent to and in consequence of ; পরে এবং ফলে। ***Adj.*** 1. Later in time ; following ; subsequent ; as, *after* period of life : *after* ages ; উত্তরকালীন ; পশ্চাদ্‌বর্ত্তী ; পরবর্ত্তী। 2. (*Naut.*) Hinder ; posterior ; as, *after* cabin ; (নৌ-বিদ্যা) পশ্চাদ্‌বর্ত্তী ; উত্তর। **After age**—A later age or time ; posterity ; (gen. *pl.*) ; উত্তরকাল ; ভবিষ্যদ্‌-বংশধরগণ। **After all**—On the whole ; সব কথা ধরিলে, সব দিক্ দেখিলে, মোটের উপর, নেহাৎ। **After**

birth—সন্তান প্রসবান্তে স্ত্রীলোকের গর্ভাশয় হইতে নির্গত বস্তু, ফুল, জরায়ু, পোত্রী (সাঃ পঃ), গর্ভপরিস্রব (মঃ সং)। **After-brain**—The medulla oblongata ; মেরুদণ্ডের অভ্যন্তরস্থ স্নায়ুরজ্জুর প্রশস্ত অগ্রভাগ, অনুমস্তিষ্ক। **After-crop**—(দ্বিফসলিয়া জমির) দ্বিতীয় বারের ফসল বা শস্য। **After-game**—A subsequent scheme or expedient ; পশ্চাৎ-কৌশল, পশ্চাদুপায়, উত্তরোপায়। **After-glow**—Glow in the West after sunset ; সন্ধ্যারাগ, দিনান্তদীপ্তি। **After-hours**—After the regular hours of work ; দৈনিককার্য্যাবসানে। **After-life**—Future life ; পরকাল। **Aftermost, Aftmost** (*Naut.*)—Nearest the stern ; (নৌ-বিদ্যা) জাহাজের পশ্চাদ্‌ভাগের নিকটতম। **Afternoon**—The time from mid-day to evening ; অপরাহ্ণ, বৈকাল। (*After-noon of life* = জীবনাপরাহ্ণ, শেষবয়স।) **After-pains**—The pains which succeed childbirth ; প্রসবান্তবেদনা, মক্কল (সাঃ পঃ)। **After-piece**—A farce or other similar entertainment ; প্রহসন। **After-shaft**—(জন্তুতত্ব) পরপালক (সাঃ পঃ)। **After-thought**—Reflection after the act ; later expedient উত্তরচিন্তা ; পশ্চাদুপায়। **Afterward (s)**—Later ; subsequently ; পশ্চাৎ, অনন্তর ; তদনন্তর, পরে। **After-wise**—Wise after the event ; কার্য্যান্তে সঞ্জাতবুদ্ধি, অসময়ে জ্ঞানী। **After wit**—Wisdom that comes too late ; উত্তর বুদ্ধি, বিলম্বিত বুদ্ধি। **After one's fancy**—As suits one's fancy ; পসন্দসই, মনোমত। **After the fashion of**—According to the custom and usage of ; কোন রীতি বা পদ্ধতি অনুসারে। **The day, the year after**—The day or year next following ; অব্যবহিত পরবর্ত্তী দিন বা বৎসর। **To be after one's heart**—To be just what an person's desires ; কাহারো মনের মতন হওয়া, পসন্দসই হওয়া। **What are you after ?**—What are you engaged about ? তুমি কি করিতেছ ? (কতকটা দোষ-প্রদর্শনের ভাব বুঝায়।)

ă-gă′, *n.* In Turkey, a commander or chief-officer ; (তুরস্ক-রাজ্যে) সেনানায়ক বা প্রধান রাজকর্ম্মচারী।

ă-gain′ (-găn), *adv.* **1.** Another time ; once more ; আবার, পুনঃ, পুনরায় ; পুনরপি, পুনশ্চ। **2.** On the other hand ; as, the one is my sovereign, the other *again* is my kinsman ; পক্ষান্তরে। **3.** Moreover ; besides ; অধিকন্তু ; এতদ্ব্যতীত। **4.** In return ; back ; in answer ; প্রতিদানে ; ফিরাইয়া ; প্রত্যুত্তরে। **5.** Anywhere else ; as, there is not in the world *again* such a spring as in England ; অন্যত্র। **6.** In response ; as, rocks echoed *again* ; প্রত্যুত্তরে। **Again and again**—Repeatedly ; প্রায়শঃ, পুনঃ পুনঃ, বারম্বার। **As much again**—Twice as much ; দ্বিগুণ পরিমাণ, আরও তত। **Ever and again, Now and again**—Occasionally ; মাঝে মাঝে, কখনও কখনও। **Half as much again**—One-and-a-half time as much ; দেড়গুণ। **To be all one's self again**—To regain one's composure of mind ; পুনর্ব্বার মানসিক স্থৈর্য্যলাভ করা।

ă-gainst′ (-gānst), *prep.* **1.** Opposite to ; facing ; as, *against* the mouth of a river ; (now generally *over against*) ; বিপরীত দিকে ; সম্মুখে। **2.** In opposition to ; as, I am *against* reform ; বিপক্ষে, প্রতিকূলে, প্রতিপক্ষে, বিরুদ্ধে। **3.** In anticipation of ; in provision for ; as, *against* his coming : *against* a rainy day ; আশায়, অপেক্ষায় ; সংস্থানার্থ। **4.** Contrary to ; not in conformity with ; as, it goes *against* my feelings it to censure any woman ; বিরুদ্ধ ; অসঙ্গত। **5.** In contrast to ; as, *against* a dark background ; বৈষম্যে। **6.** Into collision with ; as, to strike *against* a rock ; সংঘর্ষে। **7.** Resting upon ; as, to lean *against* a wall ; ঠেস্ দিয়া। **Against the stream**—Contrary to the flow of the stream ; contrary to the established course ; স্রোতের প্রতিকূলে ; প্রচলিত রীতিনীতির বিরুদ্ধে। **As a set-off against**—(Something) Placed against as equivalent ; পাল্টাদিকে। **To hope against hope**—To hope when there is scarcely any ground for hoping ; আশার কারণের অবর্ত্তমানেও আশা করা।

Agalocha wood—Eagle wood ; অগুরু (বেলঃ)।

Ag′-ă-mi (ăg-) *n.* A South American bird, also called the

Agami.

Trumpeter ; দক্ষিণ আমেরিকাদেশীয় পক্ষি-বিশেষ, তুরিবাদক পক্ষী।

ă-găm′-ic, *adj.* (*Zool.*) Produced without sexual union ; (জন্তু-তত্ব) অমৈথুনজ, অযোনি-সম্ভূত, অনুদ্বাহিত (সাঃ পঃ)।

ăg-ă-mō-gĕn′-ĕ-sis, *n.* (*Biol.*) *n.* A sexual reproduction ; (জীব-বিজ্ঞান) অনুদ্বাহিক সন্তানোৎপাদন। **—ge-net′-ic,** *adj.*

ăg′-ă-mous (-mŭs), *adj.* **1.** (*Biol.*) Having no distinguishable sexual organs ; (জীববিজ্ঞান) অচিহ্ন (সাঃ পঃ), অলিঙ্গ(ঐ)। **2.** (*Bot.*) Cryptogamous ; (উদ্ভিদ্-বিদ্যা) অব্যক্ত-পুষ্পক (ঐ)।

ă-gāpe′, *adv. & adj.* Gaping or open-mouthed, as with wonder or expectation ; হাঁ করিয়া, মুখব্যাদানপূর্ব্বক (বিস্ময় বা প্রত্যাশা হেতু)।

ăg′-ă-ric, *n.* A mushroom ; a name of various fungi (*Agaricus campestris*) ; শিলীন্ধ্র, ছত্রক ; বিভিন্ন-জাতীয় ছত্রকের নাম।

ā-găs′-tric, *adj.* (*Zool.*) Having no distinct alimentary canal ; (জন্তু-তত্ত্ব) অজঠর, অন্নবহনালীবিহীন।

ăg′-āte, *n.* **1.** The name of the several varieties of precious stones ; গন্ধর্ব্বমণি, শবলমণি-বিশেষ, সুলেমানী পাথর (হিঃ কোঃ), গোমেদ (সাঃ পঃ)। **2.** A burnishing instrument used by gold-wire drawers ; স্বর্ণতন্তু নির্ম্মাতৃগণদ্বারা ব্যবহৃত (গন্ধর্ব্বমণিযুক্ত) মার্জ্জন-যন্ত্র বিশেষ।

Agathotes Cherayta—চিরতা (বেলঃ)।

Agati Grandiflora—বক (বেলঃ) অগস্তি (মঃ উঃ), বকপুষ্প (ঐ)।

Agave Americana—American aloe ; বিলাতী আনারস (বেলঃ), জঙ্গলী আনারস (ঐ) গদগাছ (যোঃ), বন আনারস (নৃত্যঃ), বিলাতীকেয়া (ঐ)।

Agave Perfoliata—ঘৃতকুমারী (বেলঃ)।

Agave Vivipera—বাঁশ কেওরা (বেলঃ)।

āge, *n., v. i. & t.* **1.** Length of life or of existence ; the time that any animal or vegetable has lived ; as, the *age* of a man : my *age* is twenty years : *age* of the moon (শুক্লপক্ষীয় তিথি) ; জীবিত কাল, আয়ুঃ ; বয়স, বয়ঃক্রম। **2.** The later part of life, especially as affecting a person's physical powers ; the state of being old ; as, *age* can not wither her : peevishness of *age* ; শেষকাল ; জরা, বার্দ্ধক্য। **3.** One of the stages of life ; as, the life is divided into four *ages* ; শৈশব, যৌবন, প্রৌঢ়, বার্দ্ধক্য প্রভৃতি দশা। **4.** The state of having arrived at maturity ; as, he has come of *age* (সাবালক) ; বয়ঃপ্রাপ্তি, পরিণত বয়স, ব্যবহার-প্রাপ্তি, সাবালকত্ব-লাভ। **5.** A historical epoch ; as, the Golden *age* (সত্যযুগ) : the Iron *age* (কলি যুগ) : the Silver *age* (দ্বাপর যুগ) : the Dark *age* (তামস যুগ, তিমির যুগ) ; যুগ, কল্প। **6.** A generation ; "The way which the *age* follows" ; সাম-সময়িক মানব-সমাজ। **7.** A great length of time ; as, I have not seen you for *ages* ; সুদীর্ঘকাল। **8.** The old people generally ;

> "The hawthorn bush, with seats beneath the shade,
> For talking *age* and whispering lovers made."
> —*Goldsmith.*

বৃদ্ধ-সমাজ, বুড়ার দল। ***Verb i.*** To grow old ; as, he *ages* rapidly ; বাড়িয়া উঠা, বৃদ্ধ হওয়া। ***Verb t.*** To cause to grow old ; বৃদ্ধ করা। **Age′-less,** *adj.* Never growing old ; চিরতরুণ। **Age of discretion** (*Law*) —14 years ; (আইন) ১৪ বৎসর হইতে আরম্ভ। **From age to age** —যুগে যুগে। **Full age** (*Law*)—21 years ; (আইন) পূর্ণ বয়স (২১ বৎসর হইতে আরম্ভ)। **Under age**—Minor; অপ্রাপ্ত-বয়স্ক, নাবালক।

ā′-gĕd, *adj.* **1.** Old ; having lived long ; as, an *aged* oak ; স্থবির বয়োবৃদ্ধ ; প্রাচীন, জীর্ণ। **2.** Of the age of ; as, a man *aged* 20 years ; বয়স্ক।

ā′-gĕn-cy̆, *n.* **1.** Active operation ; action ; instrumentality ; ক্রিয়া ; কার্য্য ; কর্ত্তৃত্ব। **2.** The place of business of an agent ; an establishment for the purpose of doing business for another (usually at a distance) ; as, Reuter's *agency* ; কোন (ব্যবসায়ের) প্রতিনিধির কার্য্যস্থল ; (যৌথ-কারবার প্রভৃতির) প্রতিনিধির কার্য্যালয়। (সাধারণতঃ প্রধান কার্য্যালয় হইতে দূরবর্ত্তী স্থানে থাকে।)

ā-gĕn′-dă, *n.* (*pl.*) **1.** Things to be done ; items of business coming before a meeting ; সম্পাদ্য কার্য্যাবলী ; কোন সভার অধিবেশন-বিশেষের কার্য্য-তালিকা। **2.** (*Pl.* used as *sing.*) A memorandum book ; স্মারক-পুস্তক।

ā′-gĕnt, *n.* **1.** One who or that which acts or exerts power ; কর্ত্তা। **2.** Anything which has the power to produce an effect ; a natural force acting upon matter ; as, a chemical *agent* ; কর্ত্তা, কারক ; সাধিকা-শক্তি। **3.** One who does the actual work ; a substitute, deputy or factor ; কার্য্যকারক ; প্রতিনিধি, চর, গোমস্তা, কুঠিয়াল।

ăg-glŏm′-ēr-āte, *adj., v. t. & i.* Collected into a mass ; পিণ্ডীভূত ***Verb t.*** To cluster or heap together ; পিণ্ডবৎ করা, জড়াইয়া তাল করা, একত্র তাল পাকান। ***Verb i.*** To gather, grow or collect into a ball or mass (*Lit. & fig.*) ; (শব্দানুযায়ী এবং লক্ষণায়) পিণ্ডাকার হওয়া। **—a′-tion,** *n.* **1.** The act of collecting in a mass or of heaping together ; the state of being gathered into a mass ; পিণ্ডীকরণ ; পিণ্ডীভবন। **2.** A collection ; heap ; সঞ্চিতবস্তু ; স্তূপ, রাশি। **—a-tive,** *adj.*

ăg-glū′-ti-nāte, *adj., v. t. & i.* **1.** United as by glue ; cemented together ; (আঠাদ্বারা) সংলগ্নীকৃত ; একত্র সংশ্লিষ্ট। **2.** Consisting of root words combined into compounds but not materially altered as to form or meaning ; অর্থ বা রূপের বিশেষ পরিবর্ত্তন হয় নাই, এইরূপ সমাসবদ্ধ মূলশব্দসমূহসমন্বিত। ***Verb t. & i.*** **1.** To unite or cause to adhere, as with glue ; আঠাদ্বারা আঁটিয়া দেওয় বা জুড়িয়া দেওয়া। **2.** To combine simple words to express compound ideas ; সমাসবদ্ধ পদ রচনা করা। **—na′-tion,** *n.* The act of gluing to gether or the state of cohesion ; সংশ্লেষণ, সংশ্লিষ্টতা। **—na-tive,** *adj.* Adhesive ; চট্‌চটে, সংশ্লেষাত্মক, সংযোজক।

ăg′-grăn-dize, *v. t.* **1.** To increase the power, wealth, rank, or honour (of a person or state) ; কোন ব্যক্তি বা রাজ্যের শক্তি, ধন-সম্পত্তি, পদ বা সম্মান বৃদ্ধি করা। **2.** To embellish ; to exaggerate ; to enlarge or extend ; বিভূষিত করা ; অতিরঞ্জিত করা ; বৃহৎ করিয়া তোলা, বাড়াইয়া তোলা। **—gran′-dize-ment,** *n.* The act of exalting in power, rank, etc. ; exaltation ; enlargement ; গৌরববর্দ্ধন, উন্নয়ন ; অভ্যুদয়, সমুন্নতি ; বিবৃদ্ধি।

ăg′-gră-vāte, *v. t.* **1.** To increase the gravity of (burden, offence, etc.) ; to make worse ; to intensify ; as, to *aggravate* the evils of life ; গুরুতর করা ; আরও মন্দ করা ; গুরুত্ব বৃদ্ধি করা, ভারি করা। **2.** (*Colloq.*) To provoke ; to irritate ; (চলিত ভাষায়) ক্ষেপাইয়া তোলা ; জ্বালান। **—vat-ing,** *adj.* **—va′-tion,** *n.* **1.** The act of making worse or more heinous (used of evils, physical or moral) ; গুরুতরকরণ, ঘোরতরকরণ। **2.** Provocation ; irritation ; উত্তেজনা, প্রকোপন, ক্রোধোদ্দীপন ; অন্তর্দাহ।

ăg′-grē-gāte, *n., adj., v. t.* & *i.* **1.** A mass or assemblage of particulars ; রাশি, পুঞ্জ, সমুচ্চয়, সমবায়, সমূহ, সমষ্টি, সমুদায়, নিচয়। **2.** (*Phys.*) A mass formed by the union of homogeneous particles ; (পদার্থ-বিজ্ঞান) সমজাতীয় কণিকা-সমূহ-রচিত পিণ্ড, রাশি (হিঃ কোঃ)। ***Adj.*** **1.** Formed by the collection of particulars ; সঞ্চিত, পুঞ্জীকৃত, রাশীকৃত, উপচিত, সমবায়ী (মঃ উঃ)। **2.** Total ; collective ; মোট, একুন, সর্ব্বসমেত ; সমষ্টিভূত। ***Verb t.*** **1.** To bring together ; to collect into a sum or mass ; সংগ্রহ করা, জড় করা ; রাশীকৃত করা, পুঞ্জীকৃত করা, সমষ্টিভূত করা। **2.** To unite an individual to an association or company ; দলভুক্ত করা, সমিতিভুক্ত করা। ***Verb i.*** To collect together ; সঞ্চিত হওয়া, মিলিত হওয়া। **—ga′-tion,** *n.* The act or state of being collected into a sum or mass ; collection ; সমাহরণ, রাশীকরণ, সঞ্চয়ন, সঞ্চিতি (মঃ উঃ); সমষ্টি, সংগ্রহ, সমূহ। **In the aggregate**—As a whole ; মোটের উপর, সর্ব্বসাকল্যে।

ăg-grĕss′, *v. i.* & *t.* To make an attack ; to commit the first act of violence ; আক্রমণ করা ; প্রথম আক্রমণে প্রবৃত্ত হওয়া, চড়াও হওয়া। ***Verb t.*** To attack ; আক্রমণ করা।

ăg-grĕs′-sion (-grĕsh-ŭn), *n.* The first attack in a quarrel ; the first act leading to a war or controversy ; প্রথমাক্রমণ ; আক্রমারম্ভ, চড়াও ; প্রথমাপকার। **—sor,** *n.* The person who first attacks ; an assaulter ; প্রথমাক্রমণকারী, প্রথমাপকারকারী, প্রথমদ্রোহী।

ăg-grĕs′-sive, *adj.* Disposed to attack ; making the first attack ; offensive ; as, the minister pursued an *aggressive* foreign policy ; আক্রমণশীল ; প্রথমাক্রমণকারক ; আক্রমণাত্মক। **—ly,** *adv.* **—ness,** *n.* **To assume the aggressive**—To begin the quarrel ; বিবাদ বা বিরোধ বাঁধান।

ăg-grieve′ (-grēv), *v. t.* To give pain or sorrow to ; to grieve ; to oppress (usu. in the passive, as, *to be aggrieved*) ; পীড়া দেওয়া, ব্যথা দেওয়া ; যাতনা দেওয়া, মর্ম্মপীড়া দেওয়া, শোক দেওয়া ; পীড়ন করা।

ă-ghâst′, *adv.* Terrified ; struck with amazement ; ভয়ার্ত্ত, ভয়াকুল, ভয়ব্যাকুল ; বিস্ময়বিহ্বল।

ăg′-ile, *adj.* Quick-moving ; nimble ; active ; as, an *agile* frame : an *agile* tongue ; লঘুগতি ; চট্‌পটে, চটুল, চঞ্চল, চপল ; ক্ষিপ্রকর্ম্মা।

ă-gĭl′-i-ty, *n.* Nimbleness ; quickness of motion ; চটুলতা, চপলতা, চঞ্চলতা ; লঘুগতিত্ব।

ăg′-i-ō, (*It.*), *n.* **1.** The difference in value between one sort of money and another, especially between paper money and metallic coin ; hence, the excess value of one currency over another ; বিভিন্ন প্রকার বা বিভিন্নদেশীয় মুদ্রার মূল্যভেদ, বিশেষতঃ নোট, কোম্পানীর কাগজ প্রভৃতির মূল্যের সহিত ধাতব মুদ্রার মূল্যের তারতম্য ; বাট্টা, ধরাট, অতিরিক্ত মূল্য। **2.** Exchange business ; বিনিময় বা হুণ্ডীর কারবার।

ăg′-i-ō-tāge, *n.* Exchange business ; speculation in stock ; stock-jobbing ; বিনিময় বা হুণ্ডীর কারবার ; কোম্পানীর কাগজের ঝুঁকিদার ব্যবসায় ; কোম্পানীর কাগজের ব্যবসায়।

ă-gist′, *v. t.* To take the cattle of others to graze at a certain sum ; নির্দ্দিষ্ট অর্থ-গ্রহণ করত অন্যের গো-মহিষাদি চারণ করা, রাখালি করা। **—ment,** *n.* **1.** The taking in of cattle or live stock to feed at a rate of so much per head ; প্রত্যেকটীর জন্য নির্দ্দিষ্ট হারে অর্থগ্রহণ করত অন্যের গো মহিষ বা অশ্বাদি জন্তুর চারণ, বা উহাদের আহার্য্য-প্রদান। **2** The price paid for such feeding ; চারণ-শুল্ক। **3.** Any burden, charge or tax ; শুল্ক, কর।

ăg′-i-tāte, *v. t.* **1.** To move to and fro ; to shake or move briskly ; as, the wind *agitates* the sea : to *agitate* water in a vessel ; ইতস্ততঃ সঞ্চালিত করা ; বিক্ষোভিত করা, আলোড়িত করা, হিল্লোলিত করা, সংক্ষোভিত করা (কৃষ্ণঃ), তাড়াতাড়ি নাড়া, কম্পিত করা, তোলা-পাড়া করা। **2.** To disturb or excite into tumult ; to excite the thoughts or feelings ; as, the mind of men is *agitated* by various passions ; বিক্ষুব্ধ করা ; তোলাপাড়া করা, আন্দোলিত করা।

3. To discuss ; to debate (plans, etc.) ; to arouse public attention to, by articles, pamphlets, etc. ; as, each consul forms a party and *agitates* the people in favour of his own views ; আলোচনা করা ; বাদবিতণ্ডা করা ; আন্দোলন করা, বক্তৃতা করিয়া বা খবরের কাগজে লিখিয়া জনসাধারণের মনোযোগ আকর্ষণ করা। **—ta-ted,** *p.p.* Disturbed ; excited ; বিকল, বিক্ষুব্ধ, বিধূনিত, প্রমথিত, আন্দোলিত, হিল্লোলিত, ব্যাকুল, আলোড়িত ; উদ্দীপ্ত। **—ta′-tion,** *n.* **1.** Shaking ; the state of being moved to and fro with violence ; নাড়াচাড়া, বিলোড়ন, বিধূনন ; ক্ষুব্ধতা, বিক্ষোভ, আলোড়িতত্ব। **2.** Mental disturbance (showing itself by physical excitement) ; as, the tidings produced great *agitation ;* ব্যাকুলতা, আকুলতা, উদ্বেগ, চিত্তক্ষোভ, ক্ষোভ, সংক্ষোভ, তোলাপাড়া। **3.** Deliberation ; discussion ; বাদানুবাদ ; বিচার, আলোচনা। **4.** The act of arousing public attention to a political or social question by speeches, etc. ; public excitement ; as, he went on a tour of *agitation ;* রাজনীতিক বা সামাজিক আন্দোলন ; সাধারণের উত্তেজনা, জনক্ষোভ, সংরম্ভ (মঃ ভাঃ)। **—ta-tor,** *n.* **1.** One who keeps up a political agitation ; আন্দোলনকারী, রাজ্য-সংক্ষোভক। **2.** An apparatus for shaking or mixing ; মন্থন-দণ্ড।

ăg′-lĕt, ai′-glĕt (ā-), *n.* **1.** The metal tag of a lace ; ফিতাদির অগ্রভাগে সংযুক্ত ধাতব শল্যক (কণ্টকাকৃতি পদার্থ)। **2.** The spangle or other metallic ornament of dress ; পরিচ্ছদাদিতে সংলগ্ন ধাতুতারা, পরিচ্ছদের চুম্‌কি, ধাতুতারা, শল্যক, প্রভৃতি।

ă-glow′ (-glō), *adv* & *adj.* In a glow of warmth ; flushed ; as, her cheeks were all *aglow* ; দীপ্যমান, উজ্জ্বল, প্রদীপ্ত ; অরুণিত।

ăg′-nail (-nāl), *n.* **1.** Any painful swelling or sore, under, or around the toe or finger-nail ; নখ-রোগ, চিপ্প, চিপ্য (সুশ্রুঃ)। **2.** (Formerly) A corn on the toe or foot ; পদ বা পদাঙ্গুলীর কড়া।

ăg′-nāte, *n.* & *adj.* A kinsman by the father-side ; জ্ঞাতি, সগোত্র, পিতৃকুলের রক্তগত সম্পর্ক। ***Adj.*** Sprung from the same forefather ; akin ; of the same nature ; as, *agnate* words ; স্ববংশজ ; স্বজাতীয় ; সদৃশ। **—nat′-ic,** *adj.* **—na′-tion,** *n.* **1.** Relation by the father's side only (distinct from *cognation*) ; জ্ঞাতিত্ব। **2.** (*Fig.*) Affinity of languages ; ভাষাসমূহের জ্ঞাতিত্ব।

ăg-nō′-mĕn, *n.* **1.** A fourth name sometimes assumed by the Romans ; প্রাচীন রোমবাসিগণ সময় সময় যে চতুর্থ বা অতিরিক্ত নাম গ্রহণ করিতেন। **2.** A nickname ; উপনাম।

ăg-nŏs′-tic, *n.* & *adj.* One who holds that the existence of any thing beyond and behind material phenomena is unknown and (so far as can be judged) unknowable ; অজ্ঞেয়বাদী। ***Adj.*** Pertaining to this theory ; অজ্ঞেয়বাদ-সম্পর্কীয়। **—ti-cism,** *n.* The doctrine of the agnostics ; অজ্ঞেয়তাবাদ (হিঃ কোঃ)।

Ag′-nŭs Căs′-tŭs (ăg-) *n.* The name of a tree once believed to be a preservative of chastity ; সতীত্ব-তরু।

Agnus Dei (obverse side).

Ag′-nŭs Dē′-ī (ăg-), *n.* (Lamb of God) **1.** A title of Jesus ; যীশুখৃষ্টের উপাধি-বিশেষ। **2.** (*Rom Cath. Church*) A figure of a lamb bearing a cross or a flag ; a cake of wax stamped with such a figure, and blessed by the Pope ; ক্রুশ অথবা পতাকাবাহী মেষ-মূর্ত্তি ; পোপ-দ্বারা পবিত্রীকৃত, উক্ত মূর্ত্তি-অঙ্কিত মধুচ্ছিষ্ট (মোম) পিণ্ডবিশেষ।

ă-gō′, *adj.* & *adv.* Past ; gone by ; as, ten years *ago ;* অতীত, গত ; গত হইল, পূর্ব্বে। **Long ago**—Long since ; বহুদিন গত হইল।

ă-gŏg′, *adj.* & *adv.* In eager desire ; astir ; on the move ; (*on, upon, with, for, about*) ; as, they are now *agog* with their republic ; আকুল, আগ্রহান্বিত, উৎকণ্ঠাকুল, সোৎসুক, ব্যাকুল ; অস্থির ; চঞ্চল।

ă-gō′-ing, *adv.* In motion (used only with transitive verbs) ; as, to set a mill *agoing ;* চলন্ত।

ă-gŏn′-ic, *adj.* Making no angle ; অকোণিক (হিঃ কোঃ)। **Agonic line**—অকোণিক রেখা (হিঃ কোঃ)।

ăg-ō-nis′-tic, —ti-căl, *adj.* **1.** Pertaining to athletic contests (especially of Ancient Greece) ; athletic ; hence, combative ; striving to overcome in argument ; (প্রাচীন গ্রীসের) ব্যায়াম, মল্লযুদ্ধ বা মল্লক্রীড়াসংক্রান্ত ; ব্যায়াম বা মল্লক্রীড়া-সংক্রান্ত ; সংগ্রাম-প্রিয় ; তর্ক-যুদ্ধে জয়লাভে যত্নপর। **2.** Strained ; aiming at effect ; as, the modern, *agonistic* paroxysm in literature ; কষ্ট-কল্পিত ; কৃত্রিম, আড়ম্বর, প্রবণ। **—ti-cal-ly,** *adv.*

ăg′-ō-nīze, *v. i.* & *t.* **1.** To suffer violent anguish ; to writhe in anguish ; as, to smart and *agonize* at every pore ; তীব্র যন্ত্রণা বা সন্তাপভোগ করা ; যন্ত্রণায় ছট্‌ফট্ করা। **2.** To contend in the arena ; to wrestle (usually *fig.*) ; মল্লভূমিতে প্রতিদ্বন্দ্বিতা করা ; মল্লযুদ্ধ করা, কুস্তি করা, পাছ্‌ড়া পাছ্‌ড়ি করা, হুড়াহুড়ি করা, ধ্বস্তাধ্বস্তি করা

Verb t. To distress with extreme pain; to torture; as, he *agonized* his mother by his behaviour; তীব্র বেদনা প্রদান করা, মর্ম্মান্তিক যাতনা দেওয়া, নিরতিশয় যন্ত্রণা দেওয়া; পীড়ন করা। **—ni-zing,** *adj.* Causing extreme anguish; suffering agony: তীব্র-সন্তাপ-প্রদ, মর্ম্মান্তিক যন্ত্রণাদায়ক; যন্ত্রণা-ক্লিষ্ট। **—ni-zing-ly,** *adv.*

ăg'-ō-nȳ, *n.* **1.** Extreme bodily suffering or mental pain; মর্ম্মান্তিক যন্ত্রণা, তীব্র বেদনা, তীব্র সন্তাপ। **2.** Paroxysm of pleasure; as, with cries and *agonies* of wild delight; আনন্দোচ্ছ্বাস। **3.** Pangs of death (used in the *pl.*); as, he is in the *agonies* of death; মৃত্যু-যন্ত্রণা, যম-যন্ত্রণা। **Agony column** (in news paper)—The column of advertisements for missing friends, etc.; (পত্রিকায়) নিরুদ্দিষ্ট আত্মীয় প্রভৃতির জন্য বিজ্ঞাপন-স্তম্ভ।

ă-gou'-ti, —tȳ (-gû-), *n.* A hare-like animal common in the West Indies; আমেরিকার দ্বীপপুঞ্জের মূষিকজাতীয় জন্তু বিশেষ।

ă-gră'-ri-ăn, *adj.* & *n.* Pertaining to fields or lands; relating to landed property; ক্ষেত্রসংক্রান্ত, ক্ষেত্রিক, ভূমিবিষয়ক; ভূসম্পত্তিবিষয়ক। ***Noun.*** One in favour of a redistribution of landed property; দেশের সমগ্র ভূসম্পত্তির পুনর্বিভাগের পক্ষপাতী ব্যক্তি। **—ism,** *n.* **—ize,** *v.t.* **Agrarian laws**—(প্রাচীন রোমে) জনসাধারণমধ্যে সাধারণ রাষ্ট্রীয় ভূমির বিতরণ নিয়ামক বিধি। **Agrarian outrage**—প্রজা ভূম্যধিকারীর বিরোধজনিত উপদ্রব।

ă-gree' (-grē), *v. i.* & *t.* **1.** To be of one mind; to come to one mind or opinion; to become friends; as, in the expediency of the law all the parties *agree*; একচিত্ত হওয়া; মিল হওয়া, একমত হওয়া; বন্ধুভাবাপন্ন হওয়া। **2.** To be in harmony in opinions, feelings, conduct, etc.; to live or act together harmoniously; "How dost thou and thy master *agree?*" (কাহারও সহিত) মিলিয়া মিশিয়া থাকা; নির্ব্বিবাদে বাস করা, নির্ব্বিবাদে একযোগে কায করা। **3.** To consent (*to* a proposal, statement, etc.); to concur (*with* a person, *in* an opinion, *as to* a matter); সম্মত হওয়া; রাজি হওয়া, একমত হওয়া। **4.** To be consistent; to be similar; as, this story *agrees* with what has been related by others; ঐক্য হওয়া, সদৃশ হওয়া; অনুরূপ হওয়া। **5.** To suit the constitution of; to do well; as, the same food does not *agree* with every constitution; শারীরিক প্রকৃতির উপযোগী বা অনুকূল হওয়া; শরীরে সহ্য, সহ্য হওয়া। **6.** (*Gram.*) To correspond in number, gender, person or case; as, a verb must *agree* with its nominative; (ব্যাকরণ) (কর্ত্তার) বচন, লিঙ্গ, পুরুষ, ও কারকের সহিত অনুযায়ী হওয়া। ***Verb t.*** To bring (items of accounts) into harmony; (হিসাব) মিল করা। [The transitive use is now obsolete, except in the passive, in the phrase—*It is agreed.*] **—a-ble,** *adj.* **1.** Pleasing to the mind or senses; মনোজ্ঞ, মঞ্জু, মঞ্জুল, মনোরম, প্রীতিপ্রদ, প্রিয়, সৌম্য, শুভ, অভিরাম, অভিমত, হৃদ্য, রম্য, রুচিকর। **2.** (*Colloq.*) Willing or ready to consent; (চলিতভাষায়) সম্মতিদানে ইচ্ছুক বা প্রস্তুত। **3.** Conformable; suitable; (with *to*); as, *agreeable to* all experience; অনুযায়ী; সঙ্গত। **—a-bly,** *adv.* **1.** Suitably; consistently; conformably; (with *to*); উপযোগীরূপে; সঙ্গতরূপে; অনুযায়ীভাবে, অনুসারে। **2.** Pleasingly; প্রীতিপ্রদরূপে, মনোজ্ঞভাবে। **—a-ble-ness,** *n.*

ă-gree'-mĕnt (-grē-), *n.* **1.** A mutual understanding: a convent or treaty; মতের মিলন, মিল; চুক্তি, করার, নিয়ম (কথাসঃ), গিরিমেণ্ট। **2.** Union of opinions, sentiments, &c.; concord; as, good *agreement* subsists among the members of the council; ঐক্য, বনিবনাও; মতৈক্য। **3.** (*Law*) A contract legally binding on the parties making it; an exchange of promises; (আইন) একরার নামা, চুক্তিপত্র; প্রতিজ্ঞাবিনিময়। **4.** (*Gram.*) Concord in gender, number case and person; (ব্যাকরণ) লিঙ্গ, বচন, কারক ও পুরুষের ঐক্য, অন্বয়।

ăg'-ri-cŭl-ture (-chŭr), *n.* The science and art of cultivating the soil; কৃষি, কৃষিকার্য্য, কৃষি-বিদ্যা, বার্ত্তা (মঃ সং)। **—cul'-tur-al,** *adj.* Pertaining to agriculture; connected with tillage of the ground; as, *agricultural* chemistry; কৃষি-বিষয়ক, কৃষি-সংক্রান্ত; ভূমিকর্ষণ সম্বন্ধীয়। **—cul'-tur-ist,** *n.* One skilled in the art of agriculture; a husbandman; কৃষিতত্ত্বজ্ঞ, কৃষিবিদ্; কৃষক, চাষা, ক্ষেত্রিক, কৃষি-জীবী (বিবিধঃ)।

ă-grŏn'-ō-mȳ, *n.* Rural economy; husbandry; কৃষিকর্ম্ম-নির্ব্বাহ; কৃষিকার্য্য। **—mist,** *n.*

ă-ground' (-grownd), *adv.* On the ground; stranded; চড়ার উপর, স্থললগ্ন, তটলগ্ন, সৈকতস্থ; চড়ায় আবদ্ধ। (জলের অল্পতাহেতু চড়ায় আবদ্ধ জাহাজ-সম্বন্ধে ব্যবহৃত হয়।) **To run aground**—To run into a place where the ship lodges on the bottom; চড়ায় লাগা বা আট্‌কিয়া যাওয়া, চড়ায় বাঁধা।

ă-gue' (-gü), *n.* **1.** A malarial fever with cold, hot, and sweating stages; কম্পজ্বর, অনিলজ্বর (সাঃ পঃ), শীতজ্বর (ঐ), পর্য্যায়জ্বর (হঃ চঃ)। **2.** A shivering fit; শীতকম্প। **—gu-ish,** *adj.* **1.** Of the nature of ague; tending to produce ague ; as, the *aguish* listricts of England ; কম্পজ্বরাত্মক ; ম্পজ্বর-কর, কম্পজ্বরজনক। **2.** Quakıg ; shivering ; coming by fits nd starts ; কম্পনশীল ; বেপথুপরিত, পেথুমান ; শীতবেপিত (ভাগঃ); যদৃচ্ছা-ক্রমে আগমনশীল। **–gu-ish-ly,** *adv.* **–gu-ish-ness,** *n.* **Ague-cake**—Enlargement of the spleen of liver caused by ague ; কম্পজ্বর-হেতু প্লীহা বা যকৃদ্‌বৃদ্ধি, বিবর্দ্ধিত প্লীহা।

h, *inter.* An expression of sorrow, regret, surprise, admiraion, contempt and mockery ; া!.হায়! বা বা! মরি মরি! ধিক্!

hâ, *inter.* An interjection exressing surprise, triumph, mockery, etc. ; অহো! আহা হা! আ মরি! হবা! বা! ধিক্! (উচ্চারণভেদে বিভিন্ন ব প্রকাশ করে।)

ead′ (-hĕd), *adv.* **1.** In adance ; in or to the front ; as, y walked *ahead* of us all e way ; অগ্রে ; পূর্ব্বে, আগে আগে। (*Naut.*) Further forward (opp. *astern*) ; as, to lie *ahead* ; নৌ-বিদ্যা) ; জাহাজাদির সম্মুখের দিকে। **go ahead**—To go in adınce ; (*colloq.*) to push forward ; গে আগে যাওয়া ; (চলিত ভাষায়) লয়া অগ্রসর হওয়া। **Ahead of**—advance of ; আগে আগে।

eap′ (-hēp), *adv.* In a heap ; ıddled together (through fear); একত্রীভূত ; (ভয়ে) জড়সড়, পিণ্ডীকৃত।

′-ri-măn (âh-), *n.* The evil enius or demon according to the ualistic doctrine of Zoroaster ; ıe Prince of Darkness and the ternal foe of *Ormuzd,* the King f Light ; জোরায়াস্তরের দ্বিঈশ্বর াদানুসারে কুপ্রবৃত্তির অধিদেবতা ; ইনি অজ্ঞান-তমিস্রার অধীশ্বর, এবং অনাদিকাল ইতে জ্যোতির অধিপতি আউরমজ্‌দেওএর রূপক্রমরূপে বর্ত্তমান আছেন।

huis clos, (*F.*), *adv.* With closed doors ; in private ; রুদ্ধদ্বারে ; গোপনে, নিভৃতে।

ă-hŭll′, *adv.* (*Naut.*) With the sails furled and the helm on the lee side ; (নৌ-বিদ্যা) (ঝড়ের সময়) জাহাজের পাইল গুটাইয়া নির্ব্বাত-পার্শ্বে হাইল বাঁধা অবস্থায়।

aid (ād), *v. t.* & *n.* **1.** To assist ; to help ; সাহায্য করা ; সহায়তা করা। **2.** To promote recovery, etc. ; স্বাস্থ্যাদিলাভে সহায়তা করা। ***Noun.*** **1.** Help ; support ; সাহায্য, সহায়তা ; আনুকূল্য, আশ্রয়। **2.** A helper ; an assistant ; সাহায্যকারী, সহায়তাকারী। **3.** (*Law*) A subsidy or tax granted to the king by Parliament ; an exchequer loan ; (আইন) পার্লেমেণ্ট্ রাজাকে যে অর্থ বা কর মঞ্জুর করিয়া থাকে ; সরকারী তহবিলের ঋণ। **Aid′-ed,** *p. p.* Assisted ; supported ; as, an *aided* school ; সাহায্যপ্রাপ্ত ; সাহায্যকৃত। **Aid′-er,** *n.* A help ; an assistance ; সাহায্যকারী ; সহায়। **Aid′-less,** *adj.* Helpless ; সাহায্যহীন, অসহায়, নিরাশ্রয়।

aide′-de-camp (ād-dē-kong), (also AID′-DE-CAMP ; *pl.* AIDES′-DE-CAMP) *n.* An officer assisting a general by carrying out orders, etc. ; সেনাপতির আজ্ঞাবহ সৈনিক কর্ম্মচারী, সেনাপতিসহায়।

ai′-grĕt (ā-), **ai′-grĕtte′** (ā-), *n.* **1.** A name of the small white heron (usu. *egret*) ; বলাকা-বিশেষ, শ্বেত বক। **2.** A plume or tuft for the head composed of feathers or of gems, etc. ; কিরীটের উপরিস্থিত মণিরচিত চূড়া বা পালকগুচ্ছ।

ai-gûil-lĕtte′ (ā-), *n.* See AGLET.

ail (āl), *v. t.* & *i.* To affect with pain or uneasiness either of body or mind ; to trouble ; to afflict ; as, what *ails* him ? পীড়া দেওয়া, ক্লেশ দেওয়া, মনস্তাপ দেওয়া, সন্তপ্ত করা ; কষ্ট দেওয়া ; ব্যথিত করা। ***Verb i.*** To be ill ; to be indisposed ; as, diarrhœa has prevailed, and the children *ail* ; ব্যথা পাওয়া ; পীড়িত হওয়া, অসুস্থ হওয়া। **Ail′-ment,** *n.* Bodily or mental indisposition ; sickness ; মানসিক বা শারীরিক অসুস্থতা ; ব্যারাম, পীড়া, রোগ।

aim (ām), *v. i., t.* & *n.* **1.** To direct a blow (*at*) ; to discharge a missile (*at*) ; সন্ধান করা ; লক্ষ্যাভিমুখে শরক্ষেপণ করা। **2.** To direct the mind to an object ; to try to gain ; to endeavour ; (followed by *at* or an *infinitive*) ; as, a man *aims at* distinction, or *aims* to be rich ; কোন বিষয়ে মনঃসংযোগ করা ; ধন বা গুণ লাভার্থ লক্ষ্য বা যত্ন করা, কর্ম্ম সমাধার জন্য চেষ্টা করা ; প্রয়াস করা। ***Verb t.*** **1.** To direct a blow or missile, *at* a particular object ; to point a gun, etc. towards (with *at* before the object) ; to level at ; প্রহারার্থ মুষ্টিবদ্ধ হস্তোত্তলন বা শরসন্ধান করা ; লক্ষ্যাভিমুখে বন্দুকাদি আগ্নেয়াস্ত্র নিশানা বা লক্ষ্য করা ; তাক করা। **2.** To direct an act or proceeding against (*at*) ; as, to *aim* a satire or a reflection *at* some person or vice ; লক্ষ্য করা, উদ্দেশ করা। ***Noun.*** **1.** The pointing of a missile ; the direction of anything, as a spear, blow, remarks, discourse, towards a particular point or object ; শরসন্ধান ; নিশানা, উদ্দেশ। **2.** The point intended to be hit ; the object intended to be attained ; as, "Happiness ! our being's end and *aim*." লক্ষ্য, শরব্য ; বাঞ্ছিত বস্তু, ঈপ্সিত বিষয়। **3.** The act of directing the efforts towards an object ; কোন উদ্দেশ্য সাধনে চেষ্টা-প্রয়োগ। **4.** Purpose ; scheme ; as, men are often disappointed of their *aim* ; উদ্দেশ্য, অভিসন্ধি ; মতলব। **Aim′-less,** *adj.* Without aim ; purposeless ; লক্ষ্যহীন,

লক্ষ্য-হারা, লক্ষ্যশূন্য ; উদ্দেশ্যহারা। **Aim′-less-ly,** *adv.* **Aim′-less-ness,** *n.*

aine, (*F.*), *n.* Elder son ; জ্যেষ্ঠ পুত্র।

air (ār), *n.* & *v. t.* **1.** The transparent, invisible, gaseous substance enveloping the earth and breathed by all land animals ; বায়ু, বাতাস, মরুৎ, হাওয়া। **2.** The atmosphere ; the free space above our heads in which birds fly and clouds float ; বায়ুমণ্ডল ; ব্যোম, নভঃ। **3.** A light breeze ; current or draught ; বাত, সমীরণ, অনিল, পবন, গন্ধবহ, মৃদুমারুত, মন্দপবন, মন্দানিল, মৃদুবাত ; বায়ুপ্রবাহ, অনিলপ্রবাহ। **4.** Outward appearance ; look ; as, an *air* of absurdity ; mien ; gesture (expressive of a personal quality or emotion) ; as, with a triumphant *air ;* a graceful *air ;* আকার, ডৌল ; দর্শন ; চেহারা, ঢঙ্গ ; অঙ্গবিক্ষেপ, অঙ্গচেষ্টা। **5.** (*pl.*) Affected manner ; assumed haughtiness ; as, he gave himself *airs ;* চাল ; জাক্, ঠমক্, বড়াই। **6.** Publicity ; "You gave it *air* before me ;" রটনা, লোকপ্রকাশতা। **7.** (*Mus.*) Melody ; tune, especially in harmonized composition; as, a soft *air ;* (সঙ্গীত-শাস্ত্র) সুস্বর ; সুর, তান, রাগ, গৎ, মূর্চ্ছনা। ***Verb t.*** **1.** To expose to the open air ; to ventilate ; as, to *air* clothes : to *air* room ; মুক্ত বাতাসে অনাবৃত রাখা, বায়ু-সঞ্চালনের জন্য উন্মুক্ত রাখা ; বায়ুব্যাপ্ত করা। **2.** To dry or warm at the fire ; as, to *air* liquors ; অগ্নিতাপে শুষ্ক করা, গরম করা। **3.** To go out into the fresh air (usu. *reflex.*) ; বায়ু-সেবনার্থ নির্ম্মল বাতাসে বহির্গত হওয়া। **4.** To show oneself off ; to expose ostentatiously ; as, to *air* one's fine dress ; জাঁক দেখান, জাঁকজমকের সহিত প্রদর্শন করা ; আড়ম্বরপূর্ণভাবে প্রদর্শন করা। **Air′-i-ly,** *adv.* **Air′-i-ness,** *n.* **1.** Openness or exposure to the air ; as, the *airiness* of a country-seat ; প্রবাতত্ব, মুক্ততা। **2.** Gaiety ; sprightliness of motion ; as, the *airiness* of young persons ; প্রফুল্লতা ; লীলাগতি, চটুলতা। **3.** Lightness of style ; as, *airiness* of diction ; রচনাভঙ্গীর লঘুতা। **Air′-less,** *adj.* Void of air ; hence, not open to the air ; stuffy ; বিশুদ্ধ বায়ুহীন ; অতএব, বায়ুচলাচলশূন্য ; ঠাসাঠাসি। **Air′-y,** *adj.* **1.** Composed or consisting of air ; as, *airy* shapes, phantoms ; বায়ুভূত, বায়ুময়, অমূর্ত্ত, অশরীরী। **2.** Relating or belonging to air ; aerial ; as, *airy* region ; বায়ুময়, বায়বীয় ; শূন্য। **3.** Exposed to the open air ; breezy ; as, an *airy* situation ; সুবাত, বায়ুসঞ্চালিত ; বায়ু-বীজিত। **4.** Of thin texture ; light in appearance ; "The *airy* evening dress she wore" সূক্ষ্ম ; হাল্কা, হাওয়ার। **5.** Graceful ; as, *airy* music ; delicate ; ললিত, লীলায়িত ; সুকুমার, সূক্ষ্ম। **6.** Empty ; vain ; imaginary ; as, *airy* threat : *airy* fame : *airy* notions ; শূন্যগর্ভ ; অসার, ফাঁকা ; কাল্পনিক। **7.** Flippant ; superficial ; as, *airy* critics ; speculative ; visionary ; as *airy* metaphysician ; বাকচপল ; পল্লবগ্রাহী ; অনুধ্যানপ্রিয় ; অবাস্তবিক, স্বাপ্নিক। **Air-bed**—A bed for the sick, inflated with air ; পীড়িত ব্যক্তিদের জন্য বায়ু-পুরিত শয্যা, দমের গদি। **Air-bladder**—The swimming bladder of fishes ; মৎস্যের কোষ (পট্কা, বা ফট্কা)। A bladder or sac full of air in an animal or plant ; জন্তু বা উদ্ভিদের দেহের বায়ুপূর্ণ থলি, বায়ুকোষ (প্রঃ বাঃ)। **Air-brake**—A railway brake worked by the pressure of compressed air ; সঙ্কাপিত বায়ুদ্বারা চালিত বাষ্পীয় শকটের চক্রের গতিরো **Air-built**—Erected in the chimerical ; as, *air-built* ho *air-built* castle ; হাওয়ার খাড়া ; ভিত্তিশূন্য, কল্পিত। **Air-** Any small cavity filled wit বায়ু-কোষ। **Air-gun**—A gun projecting balls by the elas force of condensed air ; বায়ু-বন্দু **Air-jacket**—A jacket with ai tight lining, which when inflate supports the wearer in wate সন্তরণার্থ বায়ু-পুরিত অঙ্গরক্ষা (কুর্ত বিশেষ। **Air poise**—An inst ment for weighing air ; বায়ু-মা যন্ত্র। **Air-pump**—A machine

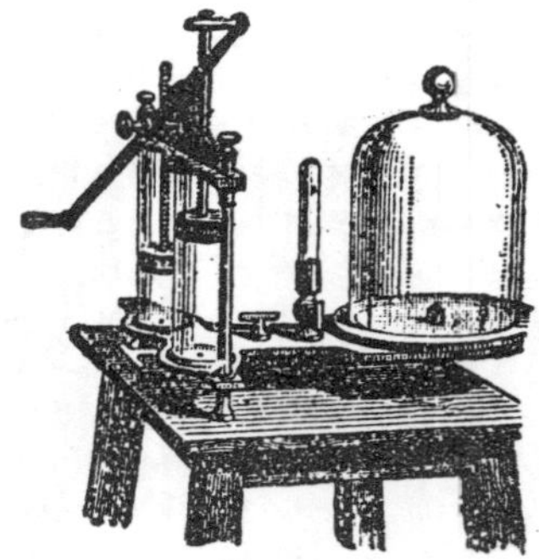

Air-pump.

exhausting the air out of a ve by strokes of a piston ; নিষ্কাশন-যন্ত্র। **Air-shaft**—A p sage for air into a mine, tun etc. ; (খনিমধ্যে) বায়ুপ্রবেশ-পথ। **A ship**—A machine for navigat

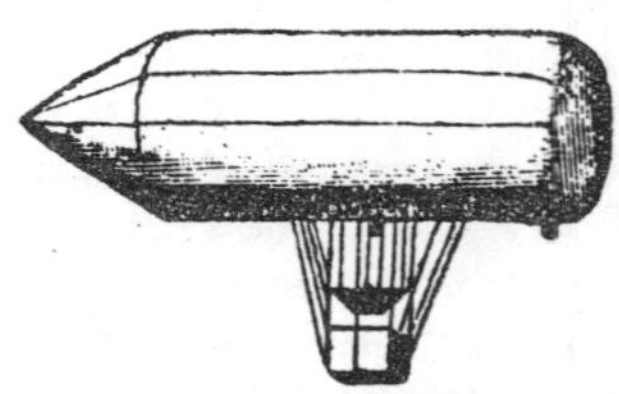

Air-ship.

the air, now, often, a dirigi baloon ; আকাশযান। **Air-ther meter**—A thermometer with instead of mercury ; (পারদের পরিবর্ত্তে) বায়ুপূরিত তাপমান যন্ত্র। **Air-threads**—Threads of gossamer spider seen floating in the air ; ...তন্তু, মাকড়সার জাল। **Air-tight**—So tight as not to admit air ; বায়ুপ্রবেশের পথরুদ্ধ, বায়ববাগম্য (হিঃ কোঃ), দৃঢ়রুদ্ধ। **Air-vessel**—A vessel or tube containing air ; বায়ুকোষ। **In the air**—Prevalent ; as, rumours *in the air* ; সর্ব্বত্র প্রচারিত, সর্ব্বব্যাপ্ত। In an unfixed or uncertain state ; in doubt ; চঞ্চল বা অনিশ্চিত অবস্থায় ; সন্দিগ্ধ অবস্থায়। **To give one's self the airs**—To be conceited or arrogant in behaviour ; (চালচলনে) গর্ব্বিত বা উদ্ধত ভাব প্রকাশ করা, বড়লোকতা ফলান, ঐশ্বর্য্য দেখান, ভড়ং বা ভরক দেখান। **To take air**—To become known ; as, the story has *taken air* ; প্রকাশ হইয়া পড়া। **To take the air**—To go abroad ; to walk or ride out ; বাহির হওয়া ; (বায়ু-সেবনার্থ) অশ্বারোহণে বহির্গত হওয়া, হাওয়া খাইতে বাহির হওয়া।

aisle (īl), *n.* **1.** A lateral division of a church, parallel to and divided by pillars from the nave (central part), choir or transept ; (খৃষ্টীয়) প্রধানধর্ম্মযাজকাধিষ্ঠিত গোল ধর্ম্মমন্দিরের বা সাধারণ ভজনালয়ের অভ্যন্তরস্থ, স্তম্ভশ্রেণীদ্বারা বিভক্ত পক্ষ পার্শ্বভাগ। **2.** A passage between the rows of pews ; (উপাসকগণের) আসন-শ্রেণীর মধ্যবর্ত্তী পথ।

ait (āt), *n.* A small isle, especially in a river ; ক্ষুদ্র দ্বীপ, নদীমধ্যস্থ দ্বীপ।

aitch'-bōne (āch-), *n.* The bone of the rump of an ox ; also the cut-off beef over this bone ; (বৃষের) শ্রোণিফলক ; উক্ত অস্থির উপর হইতে কর্ত্তিত মাংসখণ্ড।

a-jâr', *adv.* **1.** Partly open ; as, the door was standing *ajar* ; ঈষদুন্মুক্ত, অর্দ্ধোদ্ঘাটিত। **2.** In a jarring state ; out of harmony ; as, he is *ajar* with the world ; ঠুকাঠুকিভাবে ; বেমিলে, বেসুরে।

ă-kĭm'-bō, *adv.* (Of the arms) With hands on the hips, and elbows turned outwards ; কটিদেশে হাত রাখিয়া ও কনুই বাঁকাইয়া।

ă-kĭn', *adj.* **1.** Of kin ; related by blood ; (used of persons) ; as, the two families are near *akin* ; স্বজাতীয় ; সগোত্রজ, একবংশোদ্ভূত। **2.** Allied in character ; like each other ; (of things) ; as, envy and jealousy are near *akin* ; সম্বন্ধান্বিত ; সমধর্ম্মা, সদৃশ, স্বরূপ।

a la, (*F.*), *prep.* After the manner or style of ; as, *a la* Russe ; অনুরূপ।

ăl'-ă-băs-têr, *n.* & *adj.* **1.** A marble-like mineral of which artistic and fancy articles are made ; শ্বেতপ্রস্তর বিশেষ, (আরবী ভাষায়) মর্ম্মর আবায়াদ্ (বেলঃ, শ্বেত-স্ফটিক। **2.** A box made of alabaster (for holding unguents) ; প্রলেপ, বিলেপন প্রভৃতি রক্ষার্থ উক্ত প্রস্তরনির্ম্মিত কৌটাবিশেষ। ***Adj.*** Made of alabaster ; white and transparent like alabaster ; as, the *alabaster* effigy : her *alabaster* skin ; শ্বেতস্ফটিক-রচিত ; শ্বেতস্ফটিকবৎ শুভ্র এবং স্বচ্ছ। **—bas'-trine**, *adj.*

a la carte, (*F.*), *adv.* By the bill of fare ; (ভোজনাগারের) ভোজ্যদ্রব্যের তালিকানুসারে।

ă-lăck', **ă-lăck'-ă-dāy**, *inter.* An exclamation expressing sorrow or regret ; খেদসূচক অব্যয়—হায় রে ! হায় ! হায় !! হা হাঃ ! (Written also *alack-the-day.*)

ă-lăc'-rĭ-tȳ, *n.* Cheerfulness ; briskness ; gaiety ; cheerful readiness ; as, the soldiers advanced with *alacrity* to meet the enemy ; হর্ষ, প্রফুল্লতা ; সোদ্যমতা, লঘুতা, ক্ষিপ্রতা ; স্ফূর্ত্তি, উৎসাহ ; উল্লাস, উল্লাসপূর্ণ তৎপরতা।

a la mode, (*F.*), *adv.* & *adj.* According to the fashion ; fashionable ; রীত্যনুসারে, রীত্যনুযায়ী ; লৌকিকাচারানুরূপ। **Alamode silk**—A thin glossy black silk ; চাক্‌চিক্যপূর্ণ কৃষ্ণকৌষেয় বস্ত্রবিশেষ।

ā'-lâr, *adj.* **1.** Pertaining to or having wings ; wing-shaped ; পক্ষসম্পৃক্ত, পক্ষযুক্ত, গরুৎমৎ ; পক্ষাকার। **2.** (*Bot. & Physiol.*) Axillary ; (উদ্ভিদ্ ও শারীরবিজ্ঞান) কক্ষ হইতে উদ্গত, কাক্ষিক (সাঃ পঃ)।

ă-lârm', *n.* & *v. t.* **1.** A call to arms, as on the approach of an enemy ; a warning sound giving notice of approaching danger ; অস্ত্র-গ্রহণার্থ আহ্বান, যুদ্ধার্থ আহ্বান ; বিপৎ-সঙ্কেত, বিপৎ-সূচক ধ্বনি। **2.** A sudden fear excited by an apprehension of danger ; painful suspense ; as, there is nothing in his illness to cause *alarm* ; আশঙ্কা ; আতঙ্ক, ত্রাস, সাধ্বস (মঃ উঃ) **3.** Any mechanical contrivance for awaking persons from sleep or rousing their attention (usually ALARUM) ; প্রবোধ-ঘণ্টা। ***Verb t.*** **1.** To rouse to a sense of danger ; to put on the alert ; to strike with apprehension of danger ; বিপদের সাড়া দেওয়া ; বিপদের সংবাদ দানে সতর্ক করা ; বিপদ্-ভয়ে ভীত করা। **2.** To excite with sudden fear ; as, his ghastly look surprised and *alarmed* them ; ত্রাস উৎপাদন করা, আতঙ্কিত করা **3.** To put in excitement ; to disturb ; as, sellers of fish *alarming* the air with their invitation ; ক্ষুব্ধ করা ; আন্দোলিত করা, বিক্ষোভিত করা। **—ing**, *adj.* Causing apprehension of danger ; আতঙ্কজনক, ভয়াবহ, ভীতিপ্রদ। **—ing-ly**, *adv.* **—ist**, *n.* One who raises alarm, on slight grounds ; a panic-monger ; সামান্য কারণে ভয়োৎপাদনকারী ; আতঙ্ককারক, ত্রাসোৎপাদক। **—larmed'**,

adj. Indicating alarm; as, an *alarmed* look; আতঙ্ক-সূচক।
Alarm-clock—A clock with apparatus that rings loudly at appointed hour; বাদক-ঘড়ী, যে ঘড়ী নির্দ্দিষ্ট সময়ে প্রবল-ধ্বনিতে বাজে।

ă-lăr′-ŭm, *n.* Same as ALARM.

ā′-lă-rȳ, *adj.* Pertaining to wings; পক্ষ-সম্পৃক্ত।

ă-lăs′, *interj.* An exclamation expressive of sorrow, grief, pity, or concern; হায়! হায়!! আহা! অহো! আঃ! ও! আহা!

A-lăs′-tŏr (ă-), Avenging deity; a Nemesis (গ্রীক পুরাণ) প্রতিহিংসা-দেবী; চণ্ডী।

ā′-lāte, *adj.* Having wings; সপক্ষ। (Also ALATED.)

ălb, *n.* A long robe of white linen, reaching to the feet, bound with a girdle, worn by priests; খ্রীষ্টান পুরোহিতগণের আপাদলম্বিত শুক্লবর্ণ পরিচ্ছদবিশেষ।

ăl-bā′-tā, *n.* White metal; German-silver; শ্বেতধাতু; জর্ম্মণ্ সিল্ভার (কৃত্রিম রৌপ্য)।

ăl′-bă-trŏss, *n.* A large, long-winged, web-footed sea-bird of remarkable powers of flight,

Albatross.

found in the Southern Ocean; অতিকায়, দীর্ঘপক্ষ, জালপাদ এবং আশ্চর্য্য-উড্ডয়ন-শক্তি-সম্পন্ন, দক্ষিণমহাসমুদ্রচর পক্ষিবিশেষ।

ăl-bē′-ĭt, *conj.* Be it so; admitting that; even though; notwithstanding; তাহাই হউক, তথাস্তু; স্বীকার করিলেও; যদিও, যদ্যপি; সত্ত্বেও।

ăl′-bèrt, *n.* (Also *Albert Chain.* A kind of watch-chain (from Prince Albert, consort of Queen Victoria); এক প্রকার ঘড়ীর চেইন্। [মহারাণী ভিক্টোরিয়ার পতি প্রিন্স্ আল্বার্টের নামানুসারে।]

ăl-bĕs′-cĕnt, *adj.* Becoming white or whitish; শ্বেতায়মান, পাণ্ডুর।

ăl-bī′-nō, *n.* A person whose skin and hair are abnormally white, and the eyes pink, and unable to bear the ordinary light; an animal having the same peculiarity; অস্বাভাবিক শ্বেতকায়, সাধারণ-আলোকসহনে অক্ষম এবং লোহিত নেত্র-বিশিষ্ট মানব; তদ্রূপ স্বভাববিশিষ্ট জন্তু। **—ness** (*fem.*) **—nism,** *n.*

Al′-bī-ŏn (ăl-), *n.* An ancient name of England; ইংলণ্ডের প্রাচীন নাম, শ্বেতদ্বীপ।

ăl′-bŭm, *n.* **1.** In ancient Rome a white table or board on which public notices were posted; প্রাচীন রোমে ব্যবহৃত শ্বেতবর্ণ ফলক বা কাষ্ঠখণ্ড, ইহার উপরে সরকারী বিজ্ঞাপন লাগান হইত। **2.** A blank book (with ornamental binding) for insertion of autographs, photographs, etc.; হস্তাক্ষর, আলোকচিত্র প্রভৃতি রক্ষণার্থ বিচিত্র-কারুকার্য্যখচিতপ্রচ্ছদপটবিশিষ্ট অলিখিত (সাদা) পুস্তকবিশেষ।

ăl-bū′-mĕn, *n.* **1.** The white of an egg; ডিম্বের শ্বেতাংশ, অণ্ডলাল (সাঃ পঃ), অণ্ডিন (ঐ)। **2.** (*Bot.*) The substance interposed between the skin and embryo of many seeds, of which it usually constitutes the eatable part; (উদ্ভিদ্-বিদ্যা) বহুপ্রকার বীজের ত্বক্ এবং ভ্রূণের মধ্যবর্ত্তী পদার্থ, বীজের এই অংশই সাধারণতঃ আহারোপযোগী হইয়া থাকে, ভ্রূণান্ন (সাঃ পঃ)। **—ize,** *v. t.* (*Phot.*) To coat paper with an albuminous solution (usually in *p. p.*); (আলোকচিত্রণ) অণ্ডলাল-মিশ্রিত জলদ্বারা কাগজ লিপ্ত করা। **—mi-nose, —mi-nous,** *adjs.*

ăl-bū′-mĭ-noid (-noyd), *adj.* & *n.* Like albumen; অণ্ডলালসদৃশ। ***Noun.*** (*Pl.*) A class of organic compounds which form the chief part of the organs and tissues of animals and plants; জীব এবং উদ্ভিদের অঙ্গ এবং বিধান-তন্তু সমূহের প্রধান অংশ-স্বরূপ এক জাতীয় জৈব মিশ্রপদার্থ। (*Proteid* শব্দ দেখ।) **—noi′-dal,** *adj.*

ăl-bû-mĭ-nū′-rĭ-â, *n.* (*Med.*) Presence of albumen in the urine, —generally a symptom of disease of the kidneys; (ভৈষজ্য-শাস্ত্র) একপ্রকার মূত্ররোগ, ইহাতে মূত্রের সহিত অধিক পরিমাণে অণ্ডলাল নির্গত হয়, অণ্ডলাল মূত্র (হঃ চঃ), সাণ্ডলালমূত্র (ঐ)।

ăl-bŭr′-nŭm, ăl′-bŭrn, *n.* (*Bot.*) The whiter and softer part of wood between the inner bark

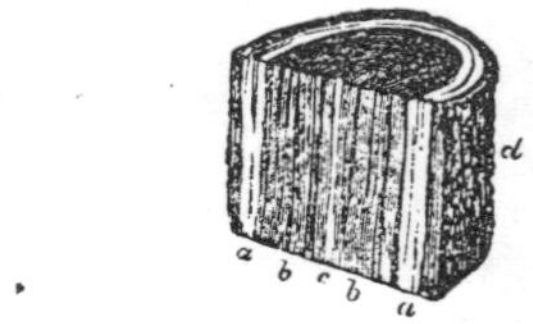

a a, Alburnum or sap-wood. *b b*, Heart-wood. *c*, Pith. *d d*, Bark.

and heart-wood; the sap-wood; (উদ্ভিদ্-বিদ্যা) অন্তর্বল্কল ও কঠিন কাষ্ঠের মধ্যবর্ত্তী কোমল শ্বেতবর্ণ অংশ; কোমল কাষ্ঠ (সাঃ পঃ), সরস কাষ্ঠ (ঐ)।

ăl′-că-hĕst, *n.* Same as ALKAHEST (which see).

ăl-caid′ (-cād), **ăl-cayde′** (-cād), *n.* (In Spain, Portugal, etc.) The commander of a fortress; স্পেন্, পর্টুগাল প্রভৃতি দেশের দুর্গাধিপতি। **2.** The governor or the warden of a prison; কারাধ্যক্ষ, কারারক্ষী।

ăl′-che-mȳ, *n.* The chemistry of the middle ages, esp. the transmutation of the baser metals into gold ; মধ্যযুগের রসায়ন-শাস্ত্র, বিশেষতঃ, নিকৃষ্ট ধাতুকে স্বর্ণে রূপান্তর, সর্ব্বরোগহর ঔষধ আবিষ্কার প্রভৃতি বিষয় যে বিদ্যার প্রধান লক্ষ্য ছিল, কিমিয়া-বিদ্যা, রসসিদ্ধি, রসায়ন (সাঃ পঃ)। **—chem′-ic, —chem′-i-cal,** *adjs.* **—mist,** *n.* One who practises alchemy ; রসসিদ্ধ (রঃ প্রঃ)।

ăl′-cö-hŏl, *n.* **1.** The pure or rectified spirit of wine; সুরাসার, সুরাবীর্য্য। **—hol′-ic,** *adj.* Of, like or containing alcohol ; সুরাসার-সম্পর্কীয়, সুরাসার-ধর্ম্মবিশিষ্ট, সুরাসারযুক্ত। **—ism,** *n.* The action of alcohol on the human system ; a diseased condition, brought about by the continued use of alcoholic liquors ; মানবদেহে সুরার ক্রিয়া; অমিত-পানজনিত ব্যাধি। **—i-za′-tion,** *n.* **—ize,** *v. t.* To convert into alcohol ; to saturate with alcohol ; to rectify ; সুরাসারে পরিণত করা ; সুরাসার সম্পৃক্ত করা ; পরিশোধন করা। **—om′-e-ter,** *n.* An instrument for measuring the alcoholic strength of spirits ; সুরাসারশক্তিমানযন্ত্র।

Al-cö-răn′ (ăl-), *n.* The Koran ; কোরাণ শরিফ্।

ăl′-cöve, *n.* **1.** A recessed portion of a room or a small room opening into a larger one ; (in Spain) a recess for bed ; a vaulted recess in a room-wall ; গর্ভ-কক্ষ, গর্ভ-মণ্ডপ; (স্পেন দেশে) শয়ন-কক্ষ ; দেয়ালের খিলানযুক্ত কুলুঙ্গি। **2.** A small ornamental building with seats, in a garden ; a bower or summer-house ; প্রমোদোদ্যানস্থিত চারুকারুকার্য্যমণ্ডিত আরামমণ্ডপ, কুঞ্জ-কুটীর, উদ্যান-নিকুঞ্জ, নিদাঘভবন।

Al-cy̆′-ö-nē (ăl-), *n.* (Same as HALCYON.)

ăl′-dē-hy̆de, *n.* A colourless volatile fluid of suffocating smell obtained by the oxidation of alcohol ; সুরাসার হইতে প্রস্তুত উদ্বায়ী এবং শ্বাসরোধক গন্ধবিশিষ্ট তরল-পদার্থ বিশেষ।

ăl′-dēr, *n.* A tree usually growing in moist land ; আর্দ্রভূমিজাত বৃক্ষ-বিশেষ।

ăl′-dēr-măn, *n.* A magistrate in English and Irish cities and boroughs, next in dignity to the mayor ; the chief officer of a ward ; ইংলণ্ড ও আয়র্লণ্ডের নগর বা জেলা-সমূহে নগরাধ্যক্ষের নিম্নপদস্থ কর্ম্মচারী ; নগরপাল। **—cy,** *n.* **—man′-ic,** *adj.* **—ry, —ship,** *ns.*

Al′-dīne (ăl-), *adj.* & *n.* Printed by *Aldus Manutius,* a Venetian printer of the 16th century ; খৃষ্টীয় ষোড়শ শতাব্দীতে প্রাদুর্ভূত ভিনিস্-নগর-বাসী য়্যাল্ড্যাস্ মেনুসিয়াস্ নামক মুদ্রাকর দ্বারা মুদ্রিত। ***Noun.*** The name of a certain style of type ; এক প্রকার মুদ্রণের হরফ্।

āle, *n.* **1.** An intoxicating liquor made from an infusion of malt by fermenation, flavoured with hops ; যবসুরা। **2.** A merry-making (in English country places) so called from the liquor drunk ; ইংলণ্ডের পল্লী-সমূহে প্রচলিত "এল্" পানোৎসব। **Ale-house**—A house, where ale is retailed ; hence, a tippling house ; যবসুরা-বিপণি, খুচরা মদের দোকান ; শৌণ্ডিকালয়।

ā-lē-ā-tö-ry̆, *adj.* Depending on the throw of a die or on chance ; as, such an *aleatory* process seemed an unworthy method in arbitrations ; পাশকক্ষেপণাধীন, দৈবায়ত্ত, দৈবাধীন।

ă-lee′ (-ē), *adv.* On the lee or sheltered side of the ship ; away from the wind ; বায়ু-প্রতিমুখ পার্শ্বে ; বায়ুর বিপরীত দিকে।

ăl′-ē-gâr, *n.* Sour ale ; malt vinegar ; অম্লাস্বাদ যবসুরা ; যবসুরাজাত চুক্র (সির্কা)।

ă-lĕm′-bic, *n.* An apparatus formerly used in distilling (now superseded by the *retort* and *worm-still* ;—also used figuratively) ; as, *alembic* of hell ; বক-যন্ত্র (সাঃ পঃ)।

Alembic.

Alembic.

ă-lērt′, *adj.* & *n.* **1.** Watchful ; vigilant ; সাবহিত, সাবধান ; সজাগ, সতর্ক। **2.** Brisk ; nimble ; lively ; as, an *alert* young fellow ; চতুর চট্পটে, তৎপর ; ক্ষিপ্রকর্ম্মা ; সজীব। ***Noun.*** Warning-call ; alarm ; sudden attack ; বিপৎ-সূচক ধ্বনি ; বিপৎসঙ্কেত ; অতর্কিত আক্রমণ। **—ly,** *adv.* **—ness,** *n.* **On the alert**—On the look out ; on the watch ; হুসিয়ার ; (বিপৎ-সম্পর্কে) সতর্ক বা সাবধান।

Aleurites triloba—Candlenut tree ; জঙ্গলী আখরোট (বেলঃ), হিজলী বাদাম (ঐ), বাঙ্গলা আখরোট (খোরী)

Al-ĕx-ăn′-drīne (ăl-), *n.* A kind of verse of six feet or twelve syllables ; (ইংরাজি) পদ্যের ছন্দোবিশেষ।

ă-lĕx-i-phâr′-mic, —tĕr′-ic, *adj.* & *n.* Expelling or counteracting poison ; বিষঘ্ন, বিষঘাতী। ***Noun.*** An antidote against contagion or poison ; স্পর্শসংক্রামক পীড়ানাশক ঔষধ, বিষনাশক ঔষধ।

ăl-frĕs′-cö, *adv.* & *adj.* In the open air ; open-air ; as, an *alfresco* lunch ; মুক্ত-বাতাসে ; মুক্ত বায়ুতে সম্পন্ন।

ăl′-ġē-bră, [Arab. *al-jebr,* the reunion of broken parts, from *jabara,* to reunite] *n.* That branch of mathematics which investigates the relations and properties of numbers by means of general symbols ; বীজগণিত,

অব্যক্তগণিত (হিঃ কোঃ)। **—bra′-ic, —bra′-i-cal,** *adjs.* **—bra′-i-cal-ly,** *adv.* **—bra′-ist,** *n.* One versed in algebra ; বীজগণিতবিদ্, বীজগণিতজ্ঞ। **—ize,** *v. t.* To reduce to algebraic form ; to solve or perform by algebra ; বীজগণিতের ছাঁচে ফেলান ; বীজগণিতের সাহায্যে সম্পাদন বা সমাধা করা।

ăl′-ġid, *adj.* Cold ; chill ; especially, of the cold stage of an ague ; ঠাণ্ডা ; শীতল ; বিশেষতঃ, কম্পজ্বরের শৈত্যাবস্থা সম্বন্ধীয়।

ăl′-gŏ-rĭsm, *n.* The Arabic or decimal system of notation ; আরবদেশীয় প্রথানুসারে (দশমিক) অঙ্ক-লিখন। **Cypher in algorism**—A mere cipher ; a dummy ; সাক্ষি-গোপাল ; মূকসাক্ষি-মাত্র।

ăl-gûâ-zil′, *n.* In Spain, a warrant-officer or sergeant ; স্পেনদেশীয় পেয়াদা বা অধস্তন পোলিশ কর্ম্মচারী।

ăl′-gŭm, *n.* A tree mentioned in the Bible ; (বাইবেলে উল্লিখিত) এক প্রকার অপরিচিত বৃক্ষ বা কাষ্ঠ। [অধ্যাপক মোক্ষমূলর এই শব্দটীকে সংস্কৃত "বল্গুক" শব্দের সহিত অভিন্ন মনে করেন। "বল্গুক" শব্দে চন্দনবৃক্ষ বুঝায়। অধুনাও মালাবার দেশে চন্দনবৃক্ষকে "বল্গুক" কহে।]

Al-hăm′-brâ (ăl-), *n.* The palace of the Moorish kings at Granada, in Spain ; স্পেন্ দেশের অন্তঃপাতী গ্রেণেডা রাজ্যস্থ মুরনৃপতিগণের ইতিহাসবিদিত রাজপ্রাসাদ। **—bresque,** *adj.* After the style of the rich ornamentation of the Alhambra ; য়্যালাম্‌ব্রা প্রাসাদের অতিশোভন সৌধ-মণ্ডনপদ্ধতির অনুবর্ত্তী।

ā′-lĭ-ăs, *adv.* & *n.* Otherwise (called or named) ; as, Smith *alias* Simpson ; ওরফে। ***Noun.*** *(Pl.)* An assumed name ; another name ; ডাকনাম ; অপর নাম, অনন্যাম, নামান্তর।

ăl′-ĭ-bī *n.* & *adv.* (*Law*) The plea that a person charged with a crime was *elsewhere* when it was committed ; as, to prove an *alibi* ; (আইন) স্থানান্তরে স্থিতি, অর্থাৎ ঘটনার সময়ে আসামী অন্যত্র ছিল, এইরূপ হেতুপ্রদর্শন। ***Adv.*** Elsewhere ; as, the prisoner endeavoured to prove himself *alibi* ; অন্যত্র, অন্যস্থানে।

ăl′-ien (-yĕn), *adj.* & *n.* **1.** Foreign ; under foreign allegiance ; বিদেশীয়, বিজাতীয় ; পররাজ্যাধীন। **2.** Wholly different in nature (*from*) ; adverse (*to*) ; repugnant (*to*) ; as, principles *alien* to our religion ; স্বভাব-বিরুদ্ধ ; বিরুদ্ধ, প্রতিকূল ; অসঙ্গতিপূর্ণ। ***Noun.*** **1.** A foreigner ; ভিন্ন দেশবাসী, বিদেশী, বিদেশজাত লোক, বৈদেশিক ব্যক্তি। **2.** One excluded *from* (the citizenship and privileges of a nation) ; জাতীয় বা নাগরিক অধিকার হইতে বঞ্চিত ব্যক্তি।

ăl′-ien (-yĕn), *v. t.* **1.** To transfer the ownership of (often written ALIENE) as, to *alien* lands ; সম্পত্তি বা স্বত্ব হস্তান্তরিত করা। **2.** (*Poet.*) To estrange ; to turn away in feelings or affections ; (কবিতায়) দূরে রাখা, অন্তরিত করা ; স্নেহচ্যুত করা। **—a-bil′-i-ty,** *n.* **—a-ble,** *adj.* Capable of being transferred to another ; হস্তান্তরযোগ্য, পাত্রান্তারযোগ্য।

ăl′-ien-āte (-yĕn-), *v. t.* **1.** To estrange the affections from one who before was loved ; to wean ; as, then my mind was *alienated* from her ; স্নেহচ্যুত করা ; বিচ্ছিন্ন করা, দূরে রাখা, বিশ্লিষ্ট করা। **2.** To transfer, as title, property or right, to another ; সম্পত্তি বা স্বত্ব হস্তান্তর করা, পাত্রান্তর করা। **3.** To turn away ; to divert (*from*) ; as, he was *alienated* from the true religion ; সরাইয়া দেওয়া ; বিষয়ান্তরে প্রেরণ করা, প্রত্যাবৃত্তকরা। **—a′-tion,** *n.* **1.** Act of alienating ; specifically, a transfer of ownership or title ; বিচ্ছিন্নীকরণ, স্বত্ব হস্তান্তরীকরণ। **2.** Estrangement, as of the affections ; বিচ্ছেদ, স্নেহচ্যুতি, বিরাগ, চিত্তবিশ্লেষ। **3.** Derangement of mental faculties ; insanity ; চিত্তবিভ্রম, মস্তিষ্কবিকার ; উন্মাদ।

ăl′-ien-ee (-yĕn-ē), *n.* One to whom transfer of property is made ; যে ব্যক্তির নিকট সম্পত্তি হস্তান্তরীকৃত হয়।

ā′-lĭ-fôrm, *adj.* Wing-shaped ; পক্ষাকৃতি।

ȧ-light′ (-līt), *v. i.* **1.** To dismount (*from* horse) ; to descend (*from* carriage) ; (অশ্ব-পৃষ্ঠ হইতে) অবতরণ করা ; অবরোহণ করা, নামা। **2.** To descend and settle ; to come to earth (from the air) ; as, snow *alights* on a roof : a bird *alights* on a tree ; পতিত হওয়া, পড়া ভূতলে পতিত হওয়া।

ȧ-light′ (-līt), *adj.* (*a*, on & light) Kindled ; on fire ; lighted up ; as, the lamps were *alight* ; প্রদীপ্ত, জ্বলৎ, জ্বলন্ত ; প্রজ্বলিত।

ȧ-lign′ (-līn), **—līne′,** *v. t.* & *i.* To adjust to a line ; as, to *align* the sights (of rifle and the bull's-eye) to bring into line ; to lay or place in a line ; সমসূত্রে যোজনা করা ; রেখাকারে বিন্যাস করা, এক পংক্তিতে বিন্যাস করা ; সমসূত্রে স্থাপন করা। ***Verb i.*** To form in line ; as, the troops *aligned* ; সারি হইয়া দাড়ান, রেখাকারে সজ্জিত হওয়া, পংক্তিবদ্ধ হওয়া। **—ment,** *n.* **1.** Arrangement in a straight or other determined line ; the line of adjustment ; esp., arrangement of soldiers in a line or lines ; সরল নির্দ্দিষ্ট রেখায় বিন্যাস, শ্রেণীবদ্ধভাবে বিন্যাস ; সমাবেশ রেখা, সৈন্য-সমাবেশ রেখা ; বিশেষতঃ, পংক্তিবদ্ধভাবে সৈন্য বিন্যাস। **2.** The ground plan of a railway or other road ; লৌহবর্ত্ম বা অন্য পথের নক্সা বা তল-চিত্র।

ȧ-līke′, *adj.* & *adv.* Similar ; like ; তুল্য, সমান, সদৃশ ; মত, অনুরূপ।

Adv. In like manner ; তুল্যরূপে, সমভাবে ।

ăl′-i-mĕnt, *n.* **1.** Food ; that which nourishes ; hence, the necessaries of life ; means of support ; (also *fig.*) mental sustenance ; খাদ্য, আহার্য্য, ভোজ্য ; পৌষ্টিক ; অতএব, জীবনযাত্রা নির্ব্বাহের জন্য আবশ্যকীয় বস্তু; উপজীবিকা ; (অপিচ লক্ষণায়) যদ্দ্বারা মানসিক পুষ্টি সাধিত হয় । **2.** An allowance for maintenance ; খোরপোষ । **—a′-tion,** *n.* Nourishment ; maintenance ; পোষণ, ণ ; প্রতি-পালন। **—men′-tal** *adj.* **—men′-tal-ly,** *adv.* **—men′-ta-ry,** *adj.* **1.** Nutritious; as, *alimentary* substances ; performing the functions of nutrition ; as, *alimentary canal* ; পৌষ্টিক, পুষ্টিদ ; পোষণ-ক্রিয়া-সাধক বা নির্ব্বাহক । **2.** Providing maintenance ; as, *alimentary endowment* ; জীবনোপায় - প্রদায়ী। **Alimentary canal**—অন্নবহানাড়ী, অন্ননালীমণ্ডল, অন্ননালী (হঃ চঃ) ।

ăl′-i-mō-nȳ, *n.* **1.** Nourishment ; maintenance ; means of living ; পোষণ ; ভরণপোষণ ; জীবনোপায়, উপজীবিকা । **2.** An allowance made to a wife from husband's estate, for her support, upon her divorce or legal separation from him ; বিবাহ-বিচ্ছেদ হেতু বা আইনতঃ পতি-পত্নী পরস্পর বিচ্ছিন্ন হইলে, স্বামীর সম্পত্তি হইতে স্ত্রীর গ্রাসাচ্ছাদনের নিমিত্ত দেয় বৃত্তি, স্ত্রীর খোরপোষ ।

ăl′-i-quănt, *adj.* (*Arith.*) Applied to a number that does not divide another exactly ; (পাটীগণিত) বিষমভাজক ।

ăl′-i-quŏt, *adj.* (*Arith.*) Applied to a part of a number which will divide it exactly, as, 5 is an *aliquot* part of 15 ; যে সংখ্যা বা রাশির অংশবিশেষ দ্বারা ইহা (সেই সংখ্যা) নিঃশেষরূপে বিভাজিত হয়—তৎসম্পর্কে প্রযুক্ত। **Aliquot part**—একাংশ (হিঃ কোঃ) ।

ă-līve′, *adj.* **1.** Having life ; living ; (opposed to *dead*) ; সজীব ; জীবন্ত, জীয়ন্ত । **2.** Fully susceptible to (any sensation or idea) ; as, he is sufficiently *alive* to the beauties of nature, but yet more *alive* to his own interests ; তীক্ষ্ণ অনুভূতি-সম্পন্ন, বোধশক্তি-সম্পন্ন, সচেতন, সজাগ । **3.** In a state of action ; unextinguished ; as, to keep the affections *alive* : to keep the fire *alive* সক্রিয় ; জ্বলন্ত, অনির্ব্বাপিত। **4.** Active ; brisk ; cheerful ; lively ; as, the company were all *alive* ; চপল, চট্‌পটে ; ক্ষিপ্র, ত্বরিত ; হৃষ্ট, উল্লসিত ; উৎফুল্ল । **5.** Swarming (*with*) ; as, a river *alive* with boats ; আকীর্ণ । **6.** Of all living (by way of *emphasis*) ; as, he was the proudest man *alive* ;" সমস্ত লোকের মধ্যে, সমগ্র জগতে । (*Colloq.*) **To look alive**—To make haste ; (চলিত ভাষায়) ফূর্ত্তি করা, জল্‌দি করা ।

ă-liz′-ă-rin, *n.* The red colouring matter of madder ; মঞ্জিষ্ঠার লোহিত-বর্ণ রঞ্জক পদার্থ।

ăl′-kă-hĕst, *n.* The supposed universal solvent of the alchemists ; প্রাচীন রসসিদ্ধ (alchemists) ব্যক্তিগণের সর্ব্বদ্রাবক পদার্থ। [(Also *fig.*) as, an intellectual *alkahest* melting the universe into an idea.]

ăl′-kă-li, *n.* [*Pl.* ALKALIS or ALKALIES] (*Chem.*) One of a class of compounds called bases, including soda, potash, and ammonia, highly soluble in water, producing caustic solutions that neutralize strong acids, and turn yellow litmus to brown, red to blue, etc. ; (রসায়ন-শাস্ত্র) সর্জ্জি, তীক্ষ্ণক্ষার, যবক্ষার প্রভৃতি 'ভাস্ম' পদার্থের সাধারণ নাম ; এই রাসায়নিক পদার্থ জলে দ্রব হয়, তীক্ষ্ণদ্রাবক পদার্থের শক্তি ব্যর্থ করে এবং পীত লিট্‌মাস্ কাগজ বাদামি, এবং লোহিতকাগজ নীল রঙ্গে পরিণত করে, ক্ষার (হিঃ কোঃ) । **—fi-a-ble,** *adj.* **—fy,** *v. t.* & *i.* To convert into or become an alkali ; ক্ষারে পরিণত করা বা হওয়া । **—les′-cence, —les′-cen-cy,** *ns.* **—les′-cent,** *adj.* Slightly alkaline ; ক্ষারাক্ত । **—lim′-e-ter,** *n.* An instrument for measuring the strength of alkalies ; ক্ষারমাপক (হিঃ কোঃ) । **—lim′-e-try,** *n.* **—line,** *adj.* Of alkalis ; having the properties of an alkali ; ক্ষা (হিঃ কোঃ); ক্ষার-স্বভাব । **—loid,** *n.* *adj.* A vegetable principle possessing, in some degree, alkaline properties ; ঈষৎ পরিমাণে ক্ষার-ধর্ম্ম-বিশিষ্ট উদ্ভিজ্জ-বীর্য্য বা সত্ত্ব, উপক্ষার । (*Adj.*) Relatingto or containing alkali ; ক্ষারীয় (হিঃ কোঃ), ক্ষারময় (ঐ), ক্ষারপ্রায় (ঐ) । **—loi′-dal,** *adj.*

Al′-kō-răn (ăl-), *n.* Same as ALCORAN.

all, *adj.*, *n.* & *adv.* **1.** The entire ; as, *all* India : *all* his life ; সর্ব্ব, নিখিল, অখিল, সব, সারা, সমগ্র । **2.** The greatest possible ; as, the train with *all* possible speed ; যতদূর সম্ভব । **3.** (Collectively) The whole number of ; as, *all* men, *all* the men ; সকল, সমস্ত । **4.** Every kind of ; any whatever ; as, to renounce *all* connection ; সর্ব্ব-প্রকার, যাবতীয় ; যে কোন প্রকার। ***Noun.*** **1.** All men ; as, *all* have not the same disposition ; সকল লোক । **2.** The whole ; the total ; (with *of*) ; as, *all* of you ; every one ; everything ; সমস্ত, সমুদায় ; মোট, সমষ্টি ; প্রত্যেক ব্যক্তি ; প্রত্যেক বস্তু । **3.** One's whole property ; "Give *all* thou hast and follow me ;" (কোন ব্যক্তির) সমগ্র সম্পত্তি। ***Adv.*** Wholly ; entirely ; as, it is *all* gone ; altogether ; সমগ্রভাবে, সর্ব্বপ্রকারে ; সম্পূর্ণরূপে, সর্ব্বসমেত ; একবারে, সাকল্যে, সম্যক্‌রূপে, সর্ব্বথা, সর্ব্বতোভাবে । **All-bearing**—সর্ব্ব-প্রসূ । **All-beauteous**—সর্ব্বাঙ্গ-সুন্দর ।

All-beholding — সর্ব্বদর্শী। **All-bestowing**——সর্ব্বপ্রদ, সর্ব্বদ। **All-conquering**—সর্ব্বজিৎ। **All-devouring**—সর্ব্বগ্রাসী, সর্ব্বভক্ষ, সর্ব্বভুক্। **All-enduring**—সর্ব্বংসহ, সর্ব্বসহ। **All Fools' Day**—সব বেকুবের দিন। [কোন কোন ইয়ুরোপীয় জাতির মধ্যে ১লা এপ্রিলকে 'সব বেকুবের দিন' বলা হয়। ঐ দিবস লোককে অপ্রস্তুত করার উদ্দেশ্যে বৃথা নিমন্ত্রণ, চিকিৎসককে বৃথা আহ্বান, প্রভৃতি করিয়া নানা-প্রকার রঙ্গকৌতুক করা হয়।] **All-giver**—সর্ব্বদাতা। **All-glorious**—সর্ব্বতেজোময়। **All-inflaming**—সর্ব্বতাপন। **All-hail**—নমো, বন্দি, স্বাগত। **All-loving**—অনন্ত প্রেমময়। **All-pervading, All-present**—বিভু, সর্ব্বগত, সর্ব্বব্যাপী, সর্ব্বগ, সর্ব্বত্রগ, সর্ব্বযায়ী। **All-preserving**—সর্ব্বপ, সর্ব্বপালক। **All-producing**—সর্ব্বস্রষ্টা। **All-purifying**—সর্ব্বপাবন। **All Saints' Day**—The first of November; a feast dedicated to all the saints in general; নবেম্বর মাসের প্রথম দিবস; "সর্ব্বসিদ্ধ পুরুষ দিবস" নামক খৃষ্টীয় মহোৎসব। **All-seeing**—সর্ব্বদর্শী, সর্ব্বদ্রষ্টা। **All Souls' day**—November 2nd; ২রা নবেম্বর; খৃষ্টধর্ম্মে বিশ্বাসী ব্যক্তিগণের পরলোকগত আত্মার পরিত্রাণের জন্য প্রার্থনার দিবস। **All-wise**—সর্ব্বজ্ঞ, সর্ব্বজ্ঞানময়। **All about**—In all directions; চতুর্দ্দিকে। **All along**—All the way; throughout; সারাপথ; বরাবর, আগাগোড়া। **All and sundry**—All without exception; প্রত্যেক, সকল। **All are not saints that go to the church**—তিলক কাটিলেই বৈষ্ণব হয় না। **All at once**—Suddenly; unexpectedly; হঠাৎ; অপ্রত্যাশিতরূপে। **All but**—Nearly; almost; as, he was *all but* drowned; প্রায়, কাছাকাছি; ঈষদূন। **All covet all lost**—অতি লোভে তাঁতি নষ্ট। **All fours**—A game at cards; এক প্রকার তাসের খেলা। **All in all**—(Used as a *noun* and *adv.*) (*Noun.*) Everything to a person; all that a person desires; as, her good Philip was her *all in all*; সর্ব্বস্ব; বাঞ্ছিতধন, হৃদয়ের ধন, জীবন-সর্ব্বস্ব। Every thing in all respects; সর্ব্বেসর্ব্বা। (*Adv.*) Altogether; সম্পূর্ণরূপে, সর্ব্বৈব। **All is not butter that comes from the cow**—গরুর বাঁট হইতে বাহির হইলেই ক্ষীর ননী হয় না। **All is not gold that glitters**—চক্ চক্ করিলেই সোনা হয় না। **All is up with**—Everything is over with; সব ফুরাইয়া গিয়াছে, দফারফা হইয়া গিয়াছে। **All one**—The same in effect; একই কথা, ফলে এক। **All over**—Spread over every part; wholly; completely; সর্ব্বত্র বিস্তৃত; সর্ব্বতোভাবে; সম্পূর্ণরূপে। **All right**—A phrase expressing assent or approbation; বহুৎ আচ্ছা, বেশ, ঠিক্, তাহাই হউক। **All round**—Not excepting any of the party; with all; কাহাকেও বাদ না দিয়া; সকলের সহিত বা নিকট। In every direction; চতুর্দ্দিকে, সর্ব্বদিক্ ব্যাপিয়া। **All round man**—One who has ability in all departments; সর্ব্বকর্ম্মে দক্ষ ব্যক্তি। **All seems yellow to the jaundiced eye**—ন্যাবা চোখে সব হলদে দেখায়, 'আত্মবৎ মন্যতে জগৎ'। **All's well that ends well**—সব ভাল যার শেষ ভাল। **All the go**—Quite the fashion; quite in vogue; প্রচলিত রীত্যনুযায়ী, রীতি-সম্মত; খুব প্রচলিত। **All the same**—Quite the same thing; একই কথা, কিছুই আসে যায় না। Nevertheless; তথাপি, তৎসত্ত্বেও, তবুও। **All the while**—During the whole time; সবটা সময়। **All the world over**—In every part of the world; পৃথিবীময়, জগৎ-শুদ্ধ, জগৎ-জোড়া। **All told**—All counted; সাকল্যে, সর্ব্বশুদ্ধ। **On all fours**—On four legs or on two legs and two arms or hands; as, to crawl *on all fours*; (পশুর) চারি পায়ের বা (মানুষের) দুই হাত দুই পায়ের উপর। **To be all over with one**—To be done for or dead; দফারফা বা নিকাশ হওয়া। (*Fig.*) **To be, to go, to run on all fours**—To be on the same footing; to be exactly alike; as, this example is *on all fours* with the other; (লক্ষণায়) অনুরূপ বা তুল্যাবস্থ হওয়া, সর্ব্বপ্রকারে মিলা।

Al'-lâh (ăl-ăl), *n.* The name of God among the Mahammedans, আল্লা।

ăl-lāy', *v. t.* **1.** To pacify or appease; as, to *allay* the tumult of the passions; প্রশান্ত করা, শান্ত করা। **2.** To put down or repress (any violence, as heat, wind, etc.); to alleviate (pain, etc.); as, to *allay* the bitterness of affliction; to temper or abate (a pleasure, advantage, etc.); as, benefits are *alloyed* by reproaches; to mitigate; নিবারণ করা; উপশম করা; প্রশমিত করা; লাঘব করা, হ্রাস করা। **—er,** *n.* **—layed',** *adj.* Mixed; mingled; as, gladness *alloyed* with sorrow; tempered; as, judgments are tart unless *allayed* with mercy; মিশ্রিত; বিমিশ্র; কোমলীকৃত।

ăl-lĕge', *v. t.* **1.** To bring forward with positiveness; to assert; as, where much is *alleged,* something must be affirmed; নিশ্চিত রূপে বলা, উক্তি করা; নিঃসন্দিগ্ধভাবে বলা, স্থিরবাক্যে বলা। **2.** To advance, as an argument, plea or excuse; যুক্তি বা ওজর-স্বরূপ উপস্থিত করা, আরোপ করা। **—a-ble,** *adj.* **—le-ga'-tion,** *n.* The act of alleging; specif. act of asserting positively; (*Law*) an assertion (esp. one not proved) ; দৃঢ়োক্তি ; নিশ্চিতোক্তি ; (আইন) (অপ্রমাণিত) উক্তি, অভিযোগ, দোষারোপ। **—leged′**, *p.p.* Produced in court ; asserted but not admitted ; as, an *alleged* murder ; বিচারালয়ে উপস্থাপিত ; আরোপিত। **—leg′-ed-ly,** *adv.*

ăl-lē′-giance (-jăns), *n.* **1.** The duty (of fidelity) of a subject to his sovereign or government ; loyalty ; রাষ্ট্র বা শাসনশক্তির (সরকারের) প্রতি প্রজার কর্ত্তব্য ; রাজভক্তি। **2.** Devotion ; as, *allegiance* to science ; অনুরাগ, নিষ্ঠা, অনুরক্তি, ভক্তি।

ăl′-lē-gō-rȳ, *n.* A description of one thing under the image of another ; রূপকালঙ্কার, ধারাবাহিক রূপক। **—gor′-ic, —gor′-i-cal,** *adjs.* Figurative ; রূপকসংক্রান্ত, রূপকাত্মক, রূপকপূর্ণ, রূপকাকার, লাক্ষণিক। **—gor′-i-cal-ly,** *adv.* **—rist,** *n.* A writer of allegory ; as, John Bunyan is an *allegorist* ; রূপকরচক।

ăl′-lē-gō-rīze, *v. t.* & *i.* To treat as an allegory ; to turn into an allegory ; to make allegories ; as, to *allegorize* the history of a people ; রূপকচ্ছলে বর্ণনা করা ; রূপকাকারে পরিণত করা ; রূপকরচনা করা। ***Verb i.*** To use allegory ; রূপকবাক্য প্রয়োগ করা, লাক্ষণিক বাক্য ব্যবহার করা।

allegretto, (*It.*) *adv.* (*Mus.*) Somewhat briskly ; (সঙ্গীত-শাস্ত্র) কতকটা সতেজে, দ্রুত।

allegro, (*It.*), *adj.*, *adv.* & *n.* (*Mus.*) Lively ; gay ; (সঙ্গীত-শাস্ত্র) দ্রুত, দ্রুতভাবে ; স্ফূর্ত্তিযুক্ত, রঙ্গদার। ***Noun.*** Movement in brisk time ; বাদ্য-যন্ত্রের দ্রুতসঙ্গত, দুন্, জলদ্।

ăl-lē-lū′-iâ-, —iăh, *n.* Song of praise to God ; ঈশ্বরবন্দনা, ঈশ্বরস্তোত্র। (See HALLELUIAH.)

ăl-lē′-vi-āte, *v. t.* To make light ; to relieve ; to mitigate ; লঘু করা ; প্রশমিত করা, উপশম করা ; হ্রাস করা। **—a′-tion,** *n.* The act of removing in part or making easier to be endured ; mitigation ; প্রশমন, লঘূকরণ ; উপশম, লাঘব, শান্তি। **—a-tive, —a-to-ry,** *adjs.* **—a-tor,** *n.* One who or that which alleviates ; শান্তিদাতা, উপশমকারী।

ăl′-ley (-lĭ), (*pl.* ALLEYS), *n.* **1.** A narrow passage, especially a walk or passage in a park or garden, bordered by rows of trees ; সঙ্কীর্ণ পথ, বিশেষতঃ উদ্যান-পথ, উদ্যান-বীথিকা। **2.** A narrow passage or way in a city, as distinct from a public street ; সুঁড়িপথ, অলিগলি।

All-hal′-low(s) (äll-hăl-lōs, -lōz), *n.* All saints ; the saints in heaven collectively ; নিখিল সিদ্ধমণ্ডলী ; দিব্যধামবাসী সিদ্ধপুরুষগণ। **All hallows' day**—All Saints' Day (which see).

ăl-lĭ-ā′-ceous (-shŭs), *adj.* **1.** Of or pertaining to the genus Allium, including garlic, onions, and leeks ; লশুন"গণ" সম্বন্ধীয়। **2.** Having the smell or taste of garlic, etc. লশুনগন্ধ বা লশুনস্বাদ, লশুনবৎ (সাঃ পঃ)।

ăl-lī′-ănce, *n.* **1.** The relation or union between families contracted by marriage ; relationship ; বৈবাহিক সম্বন্ধ ; সম্পর্ক, কুটুম্বিতা। **2.** The union between nations contracted by compact, treaty or league ; দুই বা ততোধিক জাতির মধ্যে সন্ধি বা চুক্তিপত্রদ্বারা সংযোগ, সন্ধিদ্বারা মিলন। **3.** Any sort of union ; সংযোগ, সন্ধি, মিলন। **4.** Community in nature or qualities ; গুণ, ধর্ম্ম বা প্রকৃতিগত ঐক্য, সংশ্রয় (মঃ সং)। **5.** (*Bot.*) A group of allied natural order ; (উদ্ভিদ্-বিদ্যা) সমধর্ম্মবিশিষ্ট নৈসর্গিক বর্গসমূহ।

ăl-lĭ-gā′-tion *n.* (*Arith.*) A rule for finding the price of a compound of ingredients of different values ; (পাটীগণিত). বিমিশ্র প্রক্রিয়া।

ăl′-lĭ-gā-tŏr, *n.* A large carnivorous reptile of the crocodile family, found in America ; আমেরিকা-দেশীয় কুম্ভীরজাতীয় জলজন্তু-বিশেষ।

Alligator.

ăl-lĭt′-êr-āte, *v. t.* To use words that begin with the same letter ; অনুপ্রাসবহুল শব্দ ব্যবহার করা।

ăl-lĭt-êr-ā′-tion *n.* The commencing of two or more words in close connection, with the same letter, or rather the same sound ; as, a *man may make many* friends ; অনুপ্রাস, শব্দচিত্র (সাঃ দঃ) ; যথা, "ললিত লবঙ্গ লতা"। **—lit′-er-a-tive,** *adj.* **—lit′-er-a-tive-ly,** *adv* **—lit′-er-a-tive-ness,** *n.*

Allium ascalonicum—The shallot (which see.)

Allium cepa—The onion ; পিঁয়াজ (বেলঃ), পলাণ্ডু।

Allium porrum—The leek (which see.)

Allium sativum—The garlic ; লশুন (বেলঃ)।

ăl′-lō-cāte, *v. t.* **1.** To distribute or assign ; to allot ; নির্দ্দেশ করা ; বণ্টন করা। **2.** To locate ; নিবেশিত করা, স্থান-নির্দ্দেশ করা। **—ca′-tion,** *n.* **1.** Allotment ; apportionment ; as, the *allocation* of shares in a public company ; বণ্টন ; অংশ-বিভাগ। **2.** The admitting of an item into an account ; an allowance made upon accounts in the exchequer ; হিসাবে নূতন বিষয় (দফা) সংযোগ ; রাজকোষের হিসাবের উপর ধরাট।

ăl-lō-cū′-tion, *n.* A formal address or exhortation by a general to his soldiers ; hence (in *R. C. Church*), a public address by the Pope to his clergy ; অভিভাষণ, সম্ভাষণ, সম্বোধন ; (রোমান ক্যাথলিক্ ধর্ম্মসমাজের) যাজক-সম্প্রদায়সমীপে পোপের অভিভাষণ।

ăl-lō′-dĭ-ŭm, *n.* (*Law.*) Free-hold estate ; estate held in absolute independence, without acknowledgment to a superior ; (opp. to *feudum*) ; (আইন) যে ভূমি ভোগের জন্য কোনপ্রকার খাজানা বা রাজস্ব দিতে কিম্বা বশ্যতা স্বীকার করিতে হয় না ; নিষ্কর সম্পত্তি, অনধীন সম্পত্তি, লাখেরাজ। **—al,** *adj.* Free of rent or service (opp. to *feudal*) as, *allodial* land (নিষ্কর-ভূমি) ; নিষ্কর, লাখেরাজ, অনধীন। **—al-ism,** *n.* **Allodial land belonging to a Brahmin**—ব্রহ্মোত্তর।

ăl-lŏg′-ă-mȳ, *n.* (*Bot.*) Cross-fertilization ; (উদ্ভিদ্-বিদ্যা) পরনিষেক।

ăl-lŏp′-ă-thȳ, *n.* A system of medicine, the object of which is to produce in the bodily frame, another condition of things than that in or from which the disease has originated ; (opposed to *Homœopathy*—like is cured by like) বষম চিকিৎসা-বিধান ; এই বিধান মতে বিসদৃশ ক্রিয়া উৎপাদন দ্বারা কোনও রোগের শক্তি নষ্ট করিতে চেষ্টা করা হয়। **—lo-path′-ic,** *adj.* Of or pertaining to allopathy ; অসদৃশ-চিকিৎসা-সংক্রান্ত বা বিষয়ক। **—lo-path′-i-cal-ly,** *adv.* **—thist,** *n.* One who practises allopathy ; অসদৃশ-ব্যবস্থানুরাগী চিকিৎসক।

ăl-lŏt′, *v. t.* To distribute by lot ; to parcel out in parts or portions ; to set apart as one's share ; to assign *(to)* ; অংশক্রমে বা খণ্ডে খণ্ডে বিভাগ করা, বণ্টন করা, অংশ বিলি করা ; অংশ বিভাগ করা ; অংশ পৃথক্ করা ; প্রদান করা, নির্দ্দেশ করা। **—ment,** *n.* **1.** Apportioning ; assignment ; অংশ-নিরূপণ, অংশ-বিভাগ, অংশ-কল্পনা, প্রকল্পন (মঃ সং) ; ভাগ, অংশ, হিস্যা। **2.** The destiny allotted to one ; lot in life ; fate ; as, no man is born into this world without his particular *allotment ;* নিয়তি ; বিধাতার বিধান ; ভাগ্য, অদৃষ্টলিপি। **3.** A small piece of land let out for cultivation ; চাষের জন্য বিলিকরা ক্ষুদ্র ভূমিখণ্ড।

ăl′-lō-thē-ĭsm, *n.* The worship of strange gods ; পরদেবোপাসনা।

ăl-lŏt′-rō-pȳ, *n.* (*Chem.*) The property of existing in two or more conditions which are distinct in their physical or chemical relations ; (রসায়ন-শাস্ত্র) কোন কোন প্রাকৃতিক পদার্থের দুই বা ততোধিক অবস্থায় অবস্থিতিরূপ ধর্ম্ম, বহুরূপতা (হিঃ কোঃ)। **—lo-trop′-ic, —lo-trop′-i-cal,** *adjs.* **—rop-ism,** *n.*

ăl-lōw′, *v. t.* & *i.* **1.** To own or acknowledge ; as, to *allow* the truth of a proposition ; to accept as true ; স্বীকার করা, মানা ; সত্য বলিয়া গ্রহণ করা। **2.** To grant, give, afford or yield ; to assign ; প্রদান করা, অধিকার দেওয়া, দেওয়া, নির্দ্দেশ করিয়া দেওয়া ; অর্পণ করা। **3.** To permit ; to grant license to ; অনুমতি দেওয়া, অধিকার দেওয়া, অনুজ্ঞা প্রদান করা ; সনন্দ প্রদান করা। **4.** To approve of ; hence, to sanction ; as, to be *'allowed* by a court of justice ; অনুমোদন করা ; মঞ্জুর করা। **5.** To grant something, as an addition or deduction ; as, to *allow* a sum for leakage ; বাদসাদ দেওয়া, ধরাট দেওয়া, হিসাবে না ধরা। ***Verb i.*** To concede ; to make allowance ; (often with *of*) ; ত্যাগ করা, ছাড়িয়া দেওয়া ; মুজারা দেওয়া, বাদসাদ দিয়া লওয়া, হিসাবে না ধরা। **—a-ble,** *adj.* Permissible ; not forbidden ; not unlawful or improper ; অনুজ্ঞেয়, স্বীকারযোগ্য ; অনিষিদ্ধ ; বৈধ, সঙ্গত, সমীচীন। **—a-bly,** *adv.* **—ble-ness,** *n.* **To allow for**—To take into consideration any counteracting cause ; (দোষ) বাদসাদ দিয়া লওয়া। **To allow of**—To permit ; to admit ; অনুমতি দেওয়া ; গ্রহণ করা, আসিতে দেওয়া।

ăl-lōw′-ănce, *n.* & *v. t.* **1.** Permission ; sanction ; tolerance ; as, without the King's will or State's *allowance :* as, *allowance* of slavery ; অনুমতি, অনুজ্ঞা ; অনুমোদন ; সহন, প্রশ্রয়। **2.** Abatement ; as, after making the largest *allowance* for fraud ; deduction ; discount ; বাদসাদ ; ধরাট, দস্তুরী ; ব্যাজ, বাটা। **3.** Acknowledgment ; assent to the truth of an opinion ; স্বীকৃতি, সম্মতি ; সায়, রাজি। **4.** A stated quantity, as of money or of food or drink, allowed for maintenance ; a definite sum or amount granted to meet any requirements ; বৃত্তি, ভাতা, বরাদ্দ ; নির্দ্দিষ্ট বৃত্তি। ***Verb t.*** To put upon a fixed allowance, esp of food and drink ; to supply (anything) in limited quantities ; নির্দ্দিষ্ট হারে ভাতা বা বৃত্তির ব্যবস্থা করা ; পরিমিত পরিমাণে সরবরাহ করা। **To make allowance for**—To allow for (see above).

ăl-lōy′, *n.* & *v. t.* **1.** A mixture of metals ; মিশ্রধাতু, দ্বন্দন (রঃ প্রঃ), উপধাতু। **2.** A baser metal mixed with a finer ; খাইদ, ভাঁজ। **3.** The quality, or comparative purity, as of gold or silver ; স্বর্ণ বা রৌপ্যের উৎকর্ষের মাত্রা বা আপেক্ষিক বিশুদ্ধতা। **4.** (*Fig.*) Evil mixed with good ; as, there is no happiness without *alloy ;* (লক্ষণায়) মঙ্গলের সহিত সংমিশ্রিত অমঙ্গল, ভালমন্দের সমাবেশ। ***Verb t.*** **1.** To mix metals ; to reduce the purity of, by mixing with a less valuable substance ; ধাতুসকল

ংমিশ্রিত করা ; খাইদ্ বা ভাঁজ দেওয়া, উৎকৃষ্ট ধাতুর সহিত নিকৃষ্ট ধাতু মিশ্রিত করা। **2.** To debase or impair by mixture ; to moderate ; as, to *alloy* pleasure with misfortune ; অপকৃষ্ট পদার্থের মিশ্রণদ্বারা উৎকৃষ্ট পদার্থের বিশুদ্ধতা হ্রাস করা ; পরিমিত বা প্রশমিত করা। **Alloy of gold and silver**—চন্দহেম (রঃ প্রঃ)। **Alloy of silver and copper**—চন্দ্রার্ক (রঃ প্রঃ), তারার্ক (ঐ)। **Unalloyed happiness**—অবিমিশ্র সুখ, নির্ম্মল সুখ।

all′-seed (-sēd), *n.* Name of various plants producing much seed ; বহুবীজপ্রসূ বিভিন্ন প্রকার উদ্ভিদের সাধারণ নাম।

all′-spīce, *n.* **1.** An aromatic spice called also Jamaica pepper or Pimenta ;—its odour and flavour are supposed to combine those of cinnamon, nutmegs and cloves, hence the name ; জ্যামেকা দ্বীপজাত, 'পিমেণ্টা' নামক সুগন্ধি মসলা বিশেষ—যাহা জয়িত্রী, লবঙ্গ, দারুচিনির সুবাস-বশিষ্ট বলিয়া বিবেচিত হইয়া থাকে, শীতল-চিনি (কেণ্ডিঃ)। **2.** Other aromatic shrubs ; as, Carolina *all-spice ;* অন্যান্য প্রকার সুরভি গুল্ম।

al-lude′ (-lôd), *v. t.* To refer covertly or indirectly (*to*) ; to hint at, by remote suggestions ; as, the story *alludes to* a recent transaction ; পরোক্ষ-ভাবে উল্লেখ করা, উদ্দেশ করা, কটাক্ষ করা ; আভাস দেওয়া।

al-lure′ (-lôr), *v. t.* **1.** To tempt by a lure or bait ; to draw or try to draw by some proposed pleasure or advantage ; as, rewards *allure* men to brave danger ; to entice ; চার বা টোপদ্বারা প্রলোভিত করা ; ফুস্লান ; প্রলুব্ধ করা, প্রলোভিত করা। **2.** To fascinate ; to charm ; as, some were *allured* by the modern, others reverenced the ancient ; মোহিত করা ; বিমুগ্ধ করা ; **—lur′-er,** *n.* **—lur′-ing,** *adj.* Tempting ; enticing ; attracting ; মনোমুগ্ধকর ; লোভনীয় ; চিত্তাকর্ষক। **—lur′-ing-ly,** *adv.* **—ment,** *n.* Temptation ; enticement ; "Adam, by his wife's *allurement,* fell", প্রলোভন ; প্ররোচন, ফুসলান।

ăl-lū′-sion, *n.* A covert, implied or indirect reference (*to*) ; a reference by a speaker to some striking incident or passage which serves to illustrate the subject at hand ; as, a classical *allusion* ; পরোক্ষভাবে উল্লেখ, লক্ষ্য, উদ্দেশ ; ইঙ্গিত, কটাক্ষ, ধ্বনি (সাঃ দঃ)। **—sive,** *adj.* **1.** Containing an allusion (*to*) ; উদ্দেশক, লক্ষ্যসূচক, ইঙ্গিতদ্যোতক। **2.** Abounding in allusions ; উদ্দেশ-পূর্ণ, লক্ষ্যপূর্ণ। **—sive-ly,** *adv.* **—sive-ness,** *n.*

ăl-lu′-vi-ăl (-lô-), *adj.* Deposited or thrown up by the action of waves ; washed away from one place and deposited in another ; as, *alluvial* soil ; পাললিক ; পলল-ময়, পলি-পড়া।

ăl-lu′-vi-ŏn (-lô-), *n.* **1.** The wash or flow of the sea against the shore, or of a river on its banks ; বেলাভূমি বা তীরোপরি সাগর বা নদীর প্রবাহ। **2.** An inundation ; a flood ; জলপ্লাবন ; বন্যা। **3.** The matter deposited by a flood ; জল-প্রবাহ দ্বারা সমানীত মৃত্তিকাদি। **4.** (*Law*) The formation of new land by the action of flowing water ; (আইন) চরাভূমি, চর, পয়স্তি।

ăl-lu′-vi-ŭm (-lô-), *n.* A deposit of earth, sand, etc., left by flood ; পলল, পলি, পুলিন।

ăl-lȳ′, *v. t.* **1.** To unite by marriage, treaty, league or confederacy ; (followed by *to* or *with* ; generally used in the passive form or reflexively.) বৈবাহিক-সম্বন্ধে বদ্ধ করা, বিবাহ-সূত্রে সম্পর্ক-স্থাপন করা, সন্ধি-সূত্রে সম্বদ্ধ করা, মৈত্রী স্থাপন করা। **2.** To connect, as by resemblance or friendship ; পরস্পর-সাদৃশ্য হেতু দুইটী বস্তুর মধ্যে সম্পর্ক-স্থাপন করা, বন্ধুত্ব-বন্ধনে বদ্ধ করা। **Allied to**—Connected with ; সংযুক্ত, সংবদ্ধ।

ăl-lȳ′, *n.* **1.** A prince or state united by treaty or league ; as, Lewis had spared no effort to gain so valuable an *ally* ; মিত্ররাজা, মিত্র-রাজ্য। **2.** An auxiliary ; as, science, instead of being the enemy of religion, becomes its *ally ;* সহকারী, সাহায্যকারী। **3.** Anything akin to another by structure, etc. ; গঠন প্রভৃতি বিষয়ে অন্য-বস্তুর অনুরূপ দ্রব্য।

ăl-lȳ′, *n.* A choice marble or taw used by boys in playing ; মর্ম্মরপ্রস্তর-নির্ম্মিত উৎকৃষ্ট ক্রীড়া-গুলিকা (গুলি)।

ăl′-mâ-ğĕst, *n.* **1.** A great astronomical treatise of Ptolemy ; মিসরদেশীয় পণ্ডিত টলেমিকৃত জ্যোতিষ-শাস্ত্র বিষয়ক মহাগ্রন্থ। **2.** Other books on astrology and alchemy ; ফলিত জ্যোতিষ অথবা কিমিয়া বিদ্যা-সংক্রান্ত অন্যান্য গ্রন্থ।

ăl′-mâh, —mĕh, —mĕ, (Arab, *al-mah,* learned) *n.* An Egyptian dancing-girl ; মিসর-দেশীয়া নর্ত্তকী।

Alma Mater (*L. Lit.* The bounteous mother), *n.* A name given by students to the universities and schools where they have been trained ; ছাত্রগণ স্ব স্ব বিদ্যালয় বা বিশ্ববিদ্যালয়কে এই নামে অভিহিত করিয়া থাকে। [জননী যেমন স্তন্যদানে শিশুকে পরিপোষণ করেন, বিশ্ব-বিদ্যালয় প্রভৃতিও তদ্রূপ জ্ঞানপীযূষ-প্রদানে শিক্ষার্থীর মানসিক শক্তি-সমূহ পরিপুষ্ট করে।]

ăl′-măn-ăc, —ăck, *n.* An annual calendar of months and days, with astronomical and other data ; পঞ্জিকা, পাঁজী। **Almanac-maker**—পঞ্জিকাকার।

ăl′-mănd-ïne, *n.* A garnet of violet tint ; ধূমল- (বেগুণে) বর্ণ বৈক্রান্ত মণি, নীলগন্ধিক ।

Al-might′-ÿ (äl-mīt-), *adj.* **1.** All-powerful ; সর্ব্বশক্তিমান্, অনন্ত-সামর্থ্যবান্, সর্ব্বশক্তিধর । **2.** (*Slang.*) Exceedingly great ; as, such *almighty* nonsense ; (ইতর ভাষায়) মস্ত, ডাহা । **—i-ness,** *n.* Omnipotence ; সর্ব্বশক্তি-মত্তা । **The Almighty** —The omnipotent God ; সর্ব্বশক্তিমান্ পরমেশ্বর, সর্ব্বশক্তিসমন্বিত ঈশ্বর ।

al′-mond (â-mŭnd), *n.* **1.** The fruit of the almond tree ; বাদাম । **2.** Anything almond-shaped ; specifically, one of the tonsils ; বাদামের মত আকৃতি-বিশিষ্ট যে কোন

Almond.

পদার্থ ; তালুপার্শ্ব-গ্রন্থি, তালুগ্রন্থি (হঃ চঃ) অলি-জিহ্বার উভয়-পার্শ্বস্থ বাদামাকৃতি ক্ষুদ্র মাংস-খণ্ড-যুগল । **Almond oil**—A bland, fixed oil obtained from almonds ; বাদাম তৈল । **Almond tree**—বাদাম বৃক্ষ । **Almond tumbler**—A kind of pigeon ; এক-জাতীয় কপোত ।

ăl′-mŏnd-ïne (-mŭnd-), *n.* (See ALAMNDINE.)

ăl′-mŏn-êr, *n.* A person whose office it is to distribute alms ; ভিক্ষাবিতরণকারী কর্ম্মচারী । **—ry,** *n.* **1.** The place where alms are distributed ; ভিক্ষা-বিতরণস্থলী, সত্র, দানশালা (মঃ ভাঃ) । **2.** The place where an almoner resides ; ভিক্ষা-বিতরণকারীর আবাসভবন ।

ăl′-mōst, *adv.* & *adj.* Very nearly ; well-nigh ; প্রায়, নিকট ; কল্প, ঈষদূন । [It qualifies also a noun ; as, his *almost* impudence.]

alms (âmz), *n.* (Used as *sing.*) Money, food, clothing, etc. given as a gratuity to relieve the poor ; charity ; দরিদ্রকে প্রদত্ত অন্নবস্ত্রঅর্থাদি ; অন্নবস্ত্রাদিদান, ভিক্ষা । **Alms-box, —chest**—A box for the reception of money and provision to be given in alms ; ভিক্ষাধার, দানাধার । **Alms-house**—A house endowed for the support and lodging of the poor ; অনাথাশ্রম, দরিদ্রশালা, পুণ্যগৃহ (রঃ) । **Alms-man**—One supported by charity ; ভিক্ষুক, ভিক্ষোপজীবী ।

ăl′-mŭg, *n.* See ALGUM.

ăl′-oe (-ō), *n.* **1.** A genus of plants with erect spikes of flowers and bitter juice ; ঘৃতকুমারী প্রভৃতি গুল্মাদি । **2.** (*Pl.*) A purgative drug procured from the juice of aloes ; ঘৃতকুমারী প্রভৃতির রস হইতে প্রস্তুত বিরেচক ঔষধ । ***Aloe Americana*** —গদগাছ (যোঃ) । ***Aloe litoralis***—কুমারীলতা (বেলঃ) । ***Aloe Socotrina ;***—মুসাব্বর (ওয়াট্) । ***Aloes wood***—অগুরু কাষ্ঠ (বেলঃ) ।

ăl-ō-ĕt′-ĭc, *n.* & *adj.* A medicine containing aloes ; ঘৃতকুমারী বা মুসাব্বর মিশ্রিত ঔষধ । ***Adj.*** Pertaining to aloes ; ঘৃতকুমারী বা মুসাব্বর-সম্পর্কীয় ।

ă-lŏft′, *adv.* & *prep.* **1.** High up ; overhead ; (*lit.* & *fig.*) ; (শব্দানুযায়ী এবং লক্ষণায়) উর্দ্ধে, স্বর্গে ; মস্তকোপরি, শিরোপরি । **2.** (*Naut.*) In the top ; at the mast-head ; (নৌ-বিদ্যা) উপরে, নৌ-পৃষ্ঠে ; মাস্তলাগ্রে ।

ă-lōne′, *adj.* & *adv.* **1.** Solitary ; single ; একাকী, একেলা, একক, একা ; নির্জ্জন, বিজন । **2.** Of or by itself ; solely ; as, he *alone* remained ; সঙ্গি-শূন্য, একমাত্র ; কেবল । ***Adv.*** Only ; exclusively ; কেবল কেবল-মাত্র ; একান্তে, নিঃসঙ্গভাবে নির্জ্জনে, বিরলে, নিরলে । **To let** or **leave alone**—To suffer to remain, in the present state ; হস্তক্ষেপ না করা, বাধা না দেওয়া, যে ভাবে আছে—সেইভাবে থাকিতে দেওয়া ।

ă-lŏng′, *adv.* & *prep.* **1.** By the length ; lengthwise ; লম্বালম্বি, অনুদৈর্ঘ ; অনুলম্বভাবে । **2.** Onward ; forward ; as, let us walk *along* ; বরাবর, অগ্রে ; সম্মুখভাগে । ***Prep.*** By the length of ; by the side of ; "*Along* the lawn where scattered hamlets rose" ; লম্বালম্বি, অনুমার্গে ; পার্শ্বে । **Along-shore**—By the shore or coast ; তীরপথে । **Along-side**—Close to the side of ship ; জাহাজের পাশাপাশি । **Along-side of**—Side by side with ; পার্শ্বদেশে, পাশাপাশি, সঙ্গে সঙ্গে । **Along with** —In company with ; in conjunction with ; একসঙ্গে ; একযোগে । **To get along**—To advance ; উন্নতি করা, অগ্রসর হওয়া ।

ă-loof′ (-lōf), *adv.* Away ; apart ; (*lit.* & *fig.*) ; (শব্দানুযায়ী এবং লক্ষণায়) দূরে, তফাতে, কিয়দ্দূরে ; পৃথক্ হইয়া, বিরলে, অন্তরে । **—ness,** *n.* **To hold, keep** or **stand aloof**—To abstain ; to keep clear ; to take no part ; বিরত থাকা ; দূরে থাকা, তফাত থাকা, সরিয়া থাকা ; যোগ না দেওয়া ।

ă-lŏp′-ĕ-çÿ, ăl-ō-pē′-ci-ă (-shĭ-), *n.* (*Med.*) Loss of the hair ; baldness ; (ভৈষজ্য-শাস্ত্র) ইন্দ্রলুপ্ত ; খালিত্য, টাকরোগ ।

ă-loud′ (-lowd), *adv.* Loudly ; উচ্চৈঃস্বরে ; উচ্চরবে, চেঁচিয়া ।

ă-lōw′, *adv.* (*Naut.*) In or into the lower part of a vessel ; (নৌ-বিদ্যা) জাহাজের নিম্নতলে বা নিম্নতলাভ্যন্তরে ।

ălp, *n.* **1.** A high mountain ; mountain peak ; উচ্চগিরি ; উচ্চ-শিখর, উচ্চগিরিচূড়া । **2.** (In Switzerland) The green pasture-land on the mountain side ; (সুইজারল্যাণ্ড)

পর্ব্বত-পার্শ্বস্থ হরিৎ গোচারণ-ভূমি। 3. (*Pl. Prop. Noun.*) The great mountain ranges in Switzerland; সুইজার্‌লেণ্ড্‌-দেশস্থিত সুমহান্‌ পর্ব্বতরাজি।

ăl-păc′-ă, *n.* **1.** A kind of llama with long woolly hair; সুদীর্ঘ ঊর্ণা-বিশিষ্ট পেরুদেশীয় মেষ-বিশেষ। **2.** Its

Alpaca.

wool; a kind of cloth made of its wool; উক্ত মেষের পশম; ঐ পশমে প্রস্তুত বস্ত্র, আলপাকা কাপড়।

Al′-phă (ăl-), *n.* **1.** The first letter in the Greek alphabet answering to A, and used to denote the beginning; "I am *Alpha* and Omega" (*i. e.* the beginning and the end; আদি ও অন্ত); গ্রীক বর্ণমালার আদ্য অক্ষর (ইংরাজি A অক্ষরের অনুরূপ)। **2.** (*Astron.*) The chief star of a constellation; তারা-প্রকোষ্ঠের সর্ব্বপ্রধান তারা।

ăl′-phă-bĕt, *n.* **1.** The letters of a language arranged in the customary order; বর্ণমালা, অক্ষরমালা, বর্ণমাতৃকা, বর্ণক্রম। **2.** The first rudiments; as, the very *alphabet* of our law; মূল-সূত্র, উপক্রমণিকা। **—ā′-ri-ăn**, *n.* Learner of the alphabet; বর্ণমালাশিক্ষার্থী। **—bet′-ic, —bet′-i-cal**, *adjs.* Of, in the order of, expressed by, the letters of the alphabet; বর্ণমালা-সংক্রান্ত, বর্ণানুক্রমিক, বর্ণমালানুযায়ী, বর্ণমালা-দ্বারা ব্যক্ত। **—bet′-i-cal-ly**, *adv.*

Al′-pīne (ăl-), *adj.* Of or pertaining to the Alps or any lofty mountain; very high; আল্প্‌স্‌ পর্ব্বতীয়, আল্প্‌স্‌ পর্ব্বত-সংক্রান্ত, অত্যুচ্চ-পর্ব্বত-সম্পৃক্ত; অত্যুচ্চ। **—pin-ist**, *n.* A climber of the Alps; আল্প্‌স্‌-পর্ব্বতারোহী।

Alpinia allughas—তারা (বেঙ্গঃ)।

Alpinia galanga—সুগন্ধ-বচ(বেঙ্গঃ)।

al-read′-ȳ (-rĕd-), *adv.* **1.** Before the present time; beforehand; ইতঃপূর্ব্বে; পূর্ব্বে। **2.** By this time; এতক্ষণে।

ăl′-sīke, *n.* A species of clover; এক জাতীয় ঘাস।

al′-sö, *adv.* In addition; further; besides; অধিকন্তু; আরও, ও; আর, এবং।

Alstonia scholaris—ছাতিম গাছ (বেঙ্গঃ)।

ălt, *n.* (*Mus.*) High notes of the scale; (সঙ্গীত-শাস্ত্র) উচ্চতান। (*Fig.*) **In alt**—In an exalted frame of mind; (লক্ষণায়) মনের উচ্চাবস্থায়।

al′-târ, *n.* **1.** A block, pile, table, stand or other raised structure, with a plane top, on which to place or sacrifice offerings to a deity; বেদী, চৈত্য, স্থণ্ডিল, আয়তন। **2.** The communion table; ধর্ম্মমন্দিরস্থ যে কাষ্ঠাসনের নিকট উপবিষ্ট হইয়া

Altar.

খৃষ্টীয় উপাসকগণ "প্রভুর ভোজনের" প্রসাদ গ্রহণ করেন। **Altar-piece**—A picture or ornamental screen behind the altar in a church; খৃষ্টীয় ধর্ম্মমন্দিরস্থ বেদীর পশ্চাদ্দিক-স্থিত আলেখ্য বা লতাপুষ্পাদিবিচিত্রিত তিরস্করণী (পর্দ্দা)। **To lead to the altar**—To marry; বিবাহ করা।

al′-târ-āge, *n.* The offerings made upon the altar or to a church; বেদীর উপর রক্ষিত নৈবেদ্য, বলি, উপহার, প্রভৃতি।

ălt-ăz′-i-mŭth, *n.* An instrument for determining the altitude and azimuth of heavenly bodies; জ্যোতিষ্ক-সকলের উন্নতাংশ ও দিগংশকোটি পরিমাপের জন্য যন্ত্রবিশেষ, দৃগ্‌-যন্ত্র (হিঃ কোঃ)।

al′-têr, *v. t.* & *i.* To make some change in; to modify; to change entirely or materially; অন্যথা, অন্যরূপ বা প্রকারান্তর করা; রূপান্তর করা; পরিবর্ত্তন করা, বদলান। ***Verb i.*** To become, in some respect, different; to vary; ভিন্ন প্রকার হওয়া; অন্যবিধ হওয়া। **—a-ble**, *adj.* Able to be altered; capable of being altered; পরিবর্ত্তনীয়, রূপান্তর-করণীয়, রূপভেদকরণীয়; পরিবর্ত্তনক্ষম, পরিবর্ত্তনসহ। **—a-bil′-i-ty, —a-ble-ness**, *ns.* **—a-bly**, *adv.* **—a-tive**, *adj.* Tending to alter; পরিবর্ত্তনশীল, বিকারী, পরিবর্ত্তনকর। **To alter one's course**—To make change in one's conduct; স্বভাব পরিবর্ত্তন করা।

al-têr-ā′-tion, *n.* **1.** The act of altering or making some change; পরিবর্ত্তন। **2.** The state of being altered; changed condition; পরিবৃত্তি; পরিবর্ত্তিত অবস্থা।

ăl′-têr-cāte, *v. i.* To dispute vehemently, warmly or angrily; to wrangle (*with*); কলহ করা, বিবাদ করা; গোলমাল করা, তক্‌রার করা। **—ca′-tion**, *n.* Wordy strife; a vehement or angry dispute; a noisy controversy; কলহ, বিবাদ; বাগ্‌যুদ্ধ, বিতণ্ডা; বচসা (বিষঃ), তক্‌রার।

alter ego, [*L. Lit.* other I] One's other self; specif., a confidential or bosom friend; ইতর আত্মা (হিঃ কোঃ); প্রাণসখা, অভিন্নহৃদয়, দ্বিতীয়হৃদয় ("ত্বমসি মে হৃদয়ং দ্বিতীয়ং")।

ăl′-têr-nāte, *v. t.* & *i.* **1.** To perform or arrange by turns or in succession; পর্য্যায়ক্রমে (একটীর

পর অপরটী সম্পাদন করা, পরম্পরাক্রমে সম্পন্ন বা বিন্যাস করা। **2.** To interchange (one thing) alternately *with, by* another; পর্য্যায়ক্রমে পরিবর্ত্তন করা। ***Verb i.*** (Of two or more things) To happen by turns; to succeed each other by turns, in time or space; পর্য্যায়ক্রমে সংঘটিত হওয়া; পর্য্যায়ক্রমে অনুবর্ত্তন করা। **—na′-tion,** *n.* The reciprocal succession or occurrence of things in time or place; as, the *alternation* of day and night; পর্য্যায়ক্রমে আগমন, পরম্পরানুবর্ত্তন, অন্যোন্যানুগমন, পর্য্যায়ক্রম, পর্য্যায়।

ăl-têr′-nāte, *adj.* (Of things of two kinds) Coming each after one of the other kind; one after the other; পর্য্যায়াগত; একান্তরিত। **—ly,** *adv.* In an alternate manner; পর্য্যায়ক্রমে, একান্তরিতভাবে। (*Math.*)

Alternate leaves.

Alternate angles, Alternate series—(গণিত-শাস্ত্র) একান্তর কোণ (হিঃ কোঃ); একান্তর শ্রেণী (ঐ)। (*Bot.*) **Alternate leaves**—বিপর্য্যস্ত-পত্র (সাঃ পঃ), একান্তরিত পত্র (ঐ)।

ăl-têr′-nă-tive, *adj.* & *n.* Offering a choice of two things; as, an *alternative* proposal; দুইটী বিষয়ের মধ্যে যে কোন একটী নির্ব্বাচনীয়, পাক্ষিক, বৈকল্পিক। ***Noun.*** Permission to choose between two things; either of the two possible courses; as, I had no (other) *alternative;* অন্যতর নির্ব্বাচনের অনুমতি; উপায়ান্তর, গত্যন্তর। **Alternative** (in *grammatical sense)*—বিকল্প, বিভাষা। **Alternative conjunctions** — *either — or, neither—nor,* etc.; বৈকল্পিক অব্যয়।

Althæa rosea—Hollyhock; গুলখয়ের (হিন্দী-বেলঃ)।

ăl-though′ (-thō), *conj.* Be it so; suppose that; admit all that; notwithstanding; তা'হউক; যদিও, যদ্যপি; তথাপি, কিন্তু; সত্বেও।

ăl′-ti-tūde, *n.* **1.** The elevation of an object above its foundation, the ground or the sea level; height; as, the *altitude* of a mountain; সাগর-পৃষ্ঠ হইতে উচ্চতা; উচ্চতা, উচ্ছ্রায়, উত্তুঙ্গতা, উৎসেধ। **2.** (*Geom.*) The length of the perpendicular from the vertex to the base; (জ্যামিতি) উন্নতাংশ (হিঃ কোঃ)। **3.** The highest point or degree; চূড়ান্ত সীমা, পূর্ণমাত্রা, পরাকাষ্ঠা। **4.** (*Pl.*) Elevated regions; উচ্চস্থান। **5.** (*Fig.*) High rank, superiority in wealth; exalted position; "Your *altitude* offends the eyes of those who want the power to rise;" (লক্ষণায়) উচ্চপদ, উন্নত অবস্থা; অভ্যুদয়, সমুন্নতি।

ăl′-tō, *n.* (*Mus.*) High tone; (সঙ্গীত-শাস্ত্র) তারাগ্রামের স্বর।

ăl-to-gĕth′-êr (-tōō-), *adv.* Wholly; completely; totally; সর্ব্বথা; সর্ব্বতোভাবে, সম্পূর্ণরূপে; সমগ্রভাবে।

Alto-relievo—Battle of Centaurs and Lapithæ.

alto-relievo, —rilievo, (*It.*) (*Sculp.*) High relief; (ভাস্কর-বিদ্যা) সমতল পৃষ্ঠ হইতে মূর্ত্তির উচ্চ উদ্গম।

ăl′-trû-ĭsm, *n.* The devotion to others or to humanity; পরোপকারবাদ, পরার্থবাদ, পরার্থপরতা (বিবিধঃ), হিতবাদ। **—ist,** *n.* One who practises or advocates altruism; (opp. to *egoist*); হিতবাদী, পরহিতব্রত। **—is′-tic,** *adj.* Benevolent; beneficent; হিতকারী; পরোপকারী, পরার্থপরতামূলক (বিবিধঃ)। **—is′-ti-cal-ly,** *adv.*

ăl′-ŭm, *n.* A double sulphate of aluminium and potassium; ফিটকিরি, স্ফটিকারী (সাঃ পঃ), ফুল্লিকা (ঐ), স্ফুটিকা (ঐ), সৌরাষ্ট্রী (ঐ), ফুল্লতুবরী। **A-lu′-mi-nous,** *adj.*

ă-lu′-mi-nă (-lō-), *n.* The only oxide of aluminium, the most abundant of the earths; এলুমিনিয়াম ধাতুমিশ্রিত রাসায়নিক পদার্থবিশেষ।

ăl-û-mĭn′-i-ŭm, or **ă-lû′-mi-nŭm,** *n.* A white, malleable, very light metal, not oxidized in the air, used for instruments and as an alloy; এলুমিনিয়াম ধাতু।

ă-lŭm′-nŭs, *n.* (*L* = a foster child; *pl.*—NI.) The nursling or pupil of a school or university; ক্রোন বিদ্যালয় কিম্বা বিশ্ববিদ্যালয়রূপিণী জননীর দুগ্ধপোষ্য শিশু, ছাত্র।

ăl′-vē-ă-rȳ, *n.* **1.** A bee-hive or something resembling a bee-hive; মধুচক্র বা মধুচক্রবৎ পদার্থ। **2.** (*Anat.*) The hollow of the external ear; (শারীর-সংস্থান বিদ্যা) কর্ণরন্ধ্র।

ăl′-vē-ō-lāte, —lăt-ĕd, *adj.* Honeycombed; pitted with small cavities; মধুচক্র-বিশিষ্ট; ক্ষুদ্র-রন্ধ্রযুক্ত।

ăl-vē′-ō-lŭs, *n.* A small cavity; hence, the socket of a tooth; an air-cell of the lungs; a cell of a honey-comb, etc.; ক্ষুদ্র গর্ত্তবিশেষ; দন্তকোটর, দন্তমূল (সাঃ পঃ); ফুসফুসের বায়ুকোষ; মধুচক্রাদির কোষ।

ăl′-wāys̆, *adv.* **1.** At all times; on all occasions; perpetually; continually; as, God is *always* the same; সর্ব্বদা, অনুবেল, অনুদিন, অনিবার, অনিশ; সর্ব্বকালে, নিরন্তর; বরাবর, (আঃ মঠ), বেদম্ (*Colloq*), নিরবধি, চিরদিবস; সতত, প্রতিনিয়ত। **2.** Regularly at stated intervals; as often as occasion recurs; invariably; as, he *always* comes home on saturday; নিয়ত, নির্দ্দিষ্ট সময়ান্তে; যখন আবশ্যক হয় তখনই; নিত্য।

ăm, the first person singular present indicative of the verb *to be.*

ă-main′ (-mān), *adv.* **1.** In or with full force; with all one's might; vehemently; "Silent he stood, then laughed *amain;*" সবলে; সজোরে; সতেজে, প্রচণ্ডভাবে। **2.** In all haste; as, there came two men running *amain;* at once; ঝটিতি, সত্বর, দ্রুত; তৎক্ষণাৎ।

ă-măl′-găm, *n.* **1.** Any mixture of a metal with mercury; as, gold or copper *amalgam*; পারদমিশ্র ধাতু, রস ধাতু, পারদমেল (হিঃ কোঃ), আমলগামলা। **2.** (*Fig.*) A mixture or compound of different things; (লক্ষণায়) মিশ্র, মিশ্রিত পদার্থ।

ă-măl′-gă-māte, *v. t., i. & adj.* **1.** To combine mercury with other metal; পারদের সহিত অন্যধাতু মিশ্রিত করা। **2.** To compound two things together; মিশ্রিত করা। ***Verb i.*** To mix together intimately; to become united; অন্তরঙ্গভাবে মিশা; মিলিত হওয়া। ***Adj.*** Combined, especially of languages; যুক্ত, মিলিত (সাধারণতঃ ভাষা-সম্পর্কে)। **—ma′-tion,** *n.* **1.** The act or process of compounding mercury with another metal; পারদমেলন (হিঃ কোঃ), পারদ-মেলন-ক্রিয়া। **2.** The mixing of different elements, races, societies, etc.; complete union; মিশ্রণ, যোগ; সম্পূর্ণ মিলন। **—ma′-tive,** *adj.* **—ma-tor,** *n.*

ă-măn-ū-ĕn′-sis, *n.* One who writes from dictation; শ্রুতলেখক, লিপিকর।

ăm′-ă-rănth, *n.* **1.** An imaginary flower supposed never to fade; (কবি-কল্পিত) অম্লানপুষ্প, পারিজাত। **2.** A genus of ornamental plants, of which the Prince's Feather and Love-lies-bleeding are species; গুল মকমল (ওয়াট), কেদারীচুয়া, জোনাই (প্রবোধ), কর্ণাখ্য প্রভৃতি পুষ্পবৃক্ষ। **3.** A purple colour; আনীললোহিতবর্ণ। **—ran′-thine, —ran′-tine,** *adjs.* **1.** Pertaining to amaranth; অম্লানপুষ্প-সম্বন্ধীয়। **2.** Unfading, as the poetic amaranth; undying; as, the only *amaranthine* flower on earth is virtue; (কবি-বর্ণিত অম্লানপুষ্পবৎ) অম্লান, চিরতরুণ; অমর। **3.** Of a purplish colour; as, *amaranthine* glosses came over them; আনীল-রক্তবর্ণ।

Amarantus atropurpureus—লালনটিয়া (বেলঃ)।

Amarantus campestris—মেঘনাদ (বেলঃ)।

Amarantus fasciatus—টুনটুনি নটিয়া (বেলঃ), বন নটিয়া (ঐ)।

Amarantus Gangeticus—লাল শাক (বেলঃ), রাঙ্গাশাক (ঐ), লাল নটিয়া (বোঃ) নটিয়া খাড়া (ঐ), ডেঙ্গোশাক (ঐ)।

Amarantus lanceolatus—বাঁশপাতা নটিয়া (বেলঃ)।

Amarantus oleraceus—সাদা নটিয়া (বেলঃ)।

Amarantus polygamus—চাঁপানটিয়া (বোঃ)।

Amarantus spinosus—কাঁটা নটিয়া (খোরী)।

Amarantus tenuifolius—ঝিন্টি নটিয়া (বেলঃ)।

ăm-ă-rȳl′-lis, [Gr. *Amaryllis,* name of a country girl] *n.* A genus of autumn-flowering bulbous plants; সুখদর্শনাদি (সাঃ পঃ)।

Amaryllis Grandiflora—সুখদর্শন (বেলঃ)।

Amaryllis.

ă-măss′, *v. t.* To make into a heap; to accumulate (esp. riches); স্তূপাকার করা, রাশীকৃত করা; (ধন) সঞ্চয় করা। **—mas′-sed,** *p.p.* Heaped up; সঞ্চিত, রাশীকৃত। **—ment,** *n.*

ăm-ă-teur′ (-têr), *n. & adj.* **1.** One who cultivates any study or art for the love of it, and not professionally; যে ব্যক্তি সখ করিয়া চিত্র, সঙ্গীত, প্রভৃতি বিদ্যার অনুশীলন করে। **2.** One who has a taste for the arts; কলানুরাগী, শিল্পানুরাগী। ***Adj.*** Done by or in any way pertaining to an amateur; as, *amateur* theatre; অবৈতনিক কলা-চর্চ্চাকারিকৃত, সখের। **—ish,** *adj.*

ăm′-ă-tive, *adj.* Disposed to loving; amorous; প্রেমাসক্ত, প্রেমানুরাগী, প্রণয়াসক্ত; কান্দর্পিক, কামুক, রসিক। **—ness,** *n.* (*Phren.*) The faculty supposed to influence sexual desire; (মস্তিষ্ক-সামুদ্রিক) মস্তিষ্ক-মধ্যস্থ উদ্গাত অংশ বিশেষ। [এই স্থানটী শৃঙ্গারভাবের উদ্দীপন-স্থল বলিয়া মস্তিষ্ক-সামুদ্রিকগণ নির্দ্দেশ করিয়া থাকেন।] **—to′-ri-al,** *adj.* **—to′-ri-al-ly,** *adv.* **—to-ry,** *adj.* Pertaining to a lover, or to sexual love; as, *amatory* potions; প্রেমিক বা নাগর-সম্পর্কীয়, প্রণয়-সম্পৃক্ত, কামোদ্দীপক, শৃঙ্গার-বিষয়ক, কান্দর্পিক, প্রেমব্যঞ্জক।

ăm-au-rō′-sis (-ā-), *n.* A partial or total loss of sight from loss of power in the optic nerve, (without external change in the eye) ; তিমির (হঃ চঃ), দৃষ্টিহীনতা (ঐ), কাচ (সাঃ পঃ) । **—rot′-ic,** *adj.*

ă-maze′, *v. t.* & *n.* To overwhelm with wonder ; to astound or greatly astonish ; বিস্ময়-বিহ্বল করা, বিস্ময়াবিষ্ট করা ; হতবুদ্ধি করা । ***Noun.*** (*Poet.*) Extreme astonishment ; (কবিতায়) পরমবিস্ময়, নিতান্ত বিস্ময় । **—maz′-ing,** *pt. adj.* Astounding ; wonderful ; great beyond expectation ; বিস্ময়কর ; আশ্চর্য্যপূর্ণ ; আশাতীত বৃহৎ । *n.* **—maz′-ing-ly,** *adv.* **—ment,** *n.* Overwhelming wonder, due to mere surprise or admiration ; মহাবিস্ময় ।

Am′-ă-zŏn (ăm-), *n. pl.* **1.** A fabulous race of female warriors in Scythia ; এশিয়া মাইনরের অন্তর্বর্ত্তী সিথিয়াদেশীয় কবি-কল্পিত রণ-রঙ্গিণী রমণীসমাজ । **2.** A female warrior ; রণরঙ্গিণী রমণী । **3.** A strong masculine woman ; a virago ; as, troops of fierce *Amazons,* who .....stop and beat and plunder passengers......... ; পুরুষস্বভাব-স্ত্রী, প্রগল্‌ভা স্ত্রী ; উগ্রচণ্ডা নারী, রণচণ্ডী । **—zo′-ni-an,** *adj.*

ăm-bā′-gēs, *n. pl.* Roundabout ways ; circumlocution ; আঁকাবাঁকা পথ ; বাক্যভঙ্গি, পেঁচানো কথা । **—gious,** *adj.*

ăm-băs′-să-dŏr, *n.* A minister of the highest rank sent to a foreign court to represent his sovereign or country ; an official messenger ; কোন বিদেশীয় রাষ্ট্র হইতে অপর-রাজ্যে দৌত্যকার্য্যে প্রেরিত উচ্চপদস্থ সচিব, রাজদূত ; সরকারী সংবাদ-বাহক । **—do′-ri-al,** *adj.* **—dress,** *n.* A female ambassador ; an ambassador's wife ; রাজ-দূতী ; রাজদূত-পত্নী । **—ship,** *n.*

ăm′-bêr, *n.* A yellow translucent resin found chiefly on the south shore of the Baltic (used for ornaments and burns with an agreeable odour) ; বল্‌টিক্ সমুদ্রের দক্ষিণকূলে প্রাপ্ত শিলীভূত পীতাভ রাল (রজন) বিশেষ, তৈলস্ফটিক, তৃণমণি, চন্দনরস (জ্যোতিঃ) । **Amber-seed**—Musk seed, used to perfume hair-oil, pomatum, etc. ; কেশতৈল, বিলেপন, প্রভৃতি সুগন্ধীকরণার্থ মসকদানা ।

ăm′-bêr-gris, *n.* A wax-like substance (light, opaque and ash-coloured) found floating in tropical seas, and in the intestines of the sperm-whale, odoriferous and used in perfumery ; তিমি-মৎস্যের অন্ত্রে মোমের ন্যায় গাঢ় যে শ্বেত, কৃষ্ণ, ধূসর বা বিচিত্র বর্ণবিশিষ্ট সুগন্ধি-দ্রব্য উৎপন্ন হয়, অম্বরী (যোঃ), অম্বর (ঐ) । **Tobacco perfumed with ambergris**—অম্বরী তামাক (যোঃ) ।

ăm-bi-dĕx′-têr, *adj.* & *n.* Able to use both hands with equal facility ; উভয়হস্তকুশল, উভয়হস্তদক্ষ । ***Noun.*** **1.** A person able to use the left hand as well as the right ; উভয়হস্তকুশল ব্যক্তি, সব্যসাচী । **2.** A double-dealer ; দ্বৈধকারী, দ্বিপক্ষ-পাতী । **—ter′-i′-ty,** *n.* **1.** The power of using both hands alike ; উভয়হস্তকুশলতা, সব্যসাচিত্ব । **2.** (*Fig.*) Superior cleverness ; many-sidedness ; (লক্ষণায়) শ্রেষ্ঠ নৈপুণ্য ; সর্ব্বতোমুখী প্রতিভা । **3.** Double-dealing ; দ্বৈধীভাব, দ্বিপক্ষপাতিত্ব, কপটাচার । **—ous, —trous,** *adjs.* **—trous-ly,** *adv.* **—trous-ness,** *n.*

ăm′-bi-ĕnt, *adj.* Surrounding ; circumfused ; as, the *ambient* air : *ambient* cloud ; ব্যাপক, পরি-বেষ্টক ; পরিব্যাপ্ত ।

ăm-bi-gū′-i-tȳ, *n.* Double meaning ; an expression capable of more than one meaning ; দ্ব্যর্থ, সন্দিগ্ধার্থ, কূটার্থ ; দ্ব্যর্থ বাক্য, একাধিক অর্থ সম্বলিত বাক্য ।

ăm-big′-ū-ous (-ŭs), *adj.* **1.** Obscure ; indistinct ; admitting more than one interpretation ; equivocal ; doubtful ; অস্পষ্ট ; লক্ষিত ; দ্ব্যর্থবোধক ; কূটার্থ (সাঃ পঃ) ; সন্দিগ্ধার্থক । **2.** Of doubtful classification ; as, rocks of *ambiguous* character ; অনিশ্চিতশ্রেণীবিভাগসম্পৃক্ত । **—ly,** *adv.* **—ness,** *n.*

ăm′-bit, *n.* **1.** A circuit or compass ; esp. a space surrounding a house, castle, town, etc. ; precincts ; পরিধি, চক্র ; বিশেষতঃ গৃহ, দুর্গ বা নগরের চতুর্দ্দিগস্থ প্রান্তর ; প্রান্ত-রেখা । **2.** Bounds ; limits ; (*fig.*) extent ; compass of words, thoughts, etc. ; as, the *ambit* of words, which a language possesses ; সীমানা ; সীমা ; (লক্ষণায়) প্রসার ; বাক্য বা অর্থের প্রসার ।

ăm-bi′-tion, *n.* **1.** The desire of power, honour, fame, excellence ; গৌরব-লালসা, যশোলিপ্সা, উচ্চাকাঙ্ক্ষা, উচ্চাভিলাষ, অভ্যুদয়েচ্ছা । **2.** The object of strong desire ; অদম্য অভিলাষের বিষয় । **—less,** *adj.* **—tious,** *adj.* **1.** Aspiring to high position ; strongly desirous ; উচ্চাভিলাষী, অভ্যুদয়েচ্ছু ; প্রবলাকাঙ্ক্ষাপূর্ণ । **2.** Springing from or indicating ambition ; pretentious ; showy ; উচ্চাভিলাষজাত, উচ্চাকাঙ্ক্ষাসূচক ; অনুচিতদাবিকারী ; আড়ম্বরপূর্ণ । **—tious-ly,** *adv.* **—tious-ness,** *n.*

ăm′-ble, *v. i.* & *n.* **1.** To move with a peculiar pace, as a horse, by lifting two feet on one side together ; (অশ্ব-পক্ষে) এক পার্শ্বের চরণদ্বয় একসঙ্গে তুলিয়া মৃদুগতিতে চলা, প্লুতগতিতে চলা । **2.** To ride an ambling horse ; to ride at an easy pace ; (also *fig.* as, how fast your thoughts *amble*) ; প্লুত বা ধোরিত গতিশীল অশ্বে আরোহণ করা ; মৃদুগতিতে অশ্বচালনা করা । ***Noun.*** The pace of an ambling horse ; an easy pace ; as, a fine easy *amble* ; অশ্বের ধোরিত গতি ; লীলা-গতি, মৃদুগতি । **—bler,** *n.* **1.** A horse or mule which ambles ;

ধোরিতগতিবিশিষ্ট অশ্ব বা অশ্বতর, মৃদুগামী অশ্ব, বিশেষতঃ ধোরিতগতি-শিক্ষাপ্রাপ্ত অশ্ব। **2.** One who rides an ambling horse ; উক্ত প্রকার অশ্বের আরোহী। **—bling,** *adj.* **—bling-ly,** *adv.*

am-bly̆-ö′-pi-â, *n.* Impaired vision (the first stage of *amaurosis*) ; দৃষ্টিশক্তিহীনতা। Also, **am′-bly-o-py,** *n.* **—op′-ic,** *adj.*

am′-bö, *n.* (*Pl.* -s, -NES.) A name the pulpit or reading-desk in ly Christian churches ; প্রাচীন য় ধর্ম্মমন্দিরস্থ বেদী বা পাঠ মঞ্চ।

-brö′-si-â, *n.* (Skr. *amritas*) . (*Class. Myth.*) The fabled food f the gods, (as *nectar* was their drink), which conferred immortality on those who partook of it ; (গ্রীক-পুরাণ) অমরত্ব-প্রদায়ী দেব-ভোজ্য, ত্রিদশাহার, দেবান্ন, অমৃত, পীযূষ। **2.** (*Fig.*) Something exquisitely delightful to the taste or smell ; as, the whole company had tasted the *ambrosia* of her lips ; (লক্ষণায়) পরম সুস্বাদু বা সুরভি বস্তু, অমৃতোপম বস্তু। **3.** Bee-bread ; as, bee had collected its *ambrosia* om flowers ; (মধুমক্ষিকা-আহরিত) পুষ্প-পরাগ। **—al,** *adj.* Immortal ; ivine ; divinely fragrant ; divinely eautiful ; as, *ambrosial* curls ; মর ; দিব্য ; অমৃত-সুরভি, স্বর্গীয় সুবাস-য় ; দিব্যলাবণ্যময়। **—al-ly,** *adv.* **an,** *adj.*

-bry̆, *n.* A closed recess in the all of ancient churches, in which red utensils were deposited ; nce, a place for keeping vic-ls ; a pantry or cupboard ; dresser ; প্রাচীন খৃষ্টীয় ধর্ম্ম-মন্দিরে তৈজসপত্রাদি রাখিবার কুলুঙ্গী-খাদ্যাধার ; রুটি এবং অন্যান্য ীর প্রকোষ্ঠ ; থালাবাসন রাখি-র বা আলমারি।

-lănce, *n.* A moving hos- following an army and ded to succour the wounded, as soon as possible ; a covered vehicle for conveying the wounded off the field of battle ; আহত যোদ্ধৃগণের জন্য চলন্ত রুগ্নাবাস ; রণক্ষেত্র হইতে আহত সৈন্যদিগকে স্থানান্তরী-করণার্থ যান, আহত-যান।

Ambulance-waggon (British army).

ăm-bû-lā′-tion, *n.* The act of walking ; পরিভ্রমণ।

ăm′ bû-lā-tō-ry̆, *adj.* & *n.* **1.** Pertaining to or suitable for walking ; moving from place to place ; movable ; as, an *ambulatory* court ; ভ্রমণ-বিষয়ক, ভ্রমণোপযোগী ; চলিষ্ণু, চরিষ্ণু ; পর্য্যটনশীল, পরিক্রমশীল। **2.** (*Law*) Not fixed, but capable of being altered ; revocable ; as, a will is *ambulatory* until the death of the testator ; (আইন) অস্থির, পরিবর্ত্তনসহ ; বদকরণযোগ্য, প্রত্যাহরণীয়, খণ্ডনীয়। ***Noun.*** A place for walking in ; esp. a covered way ; an arcade ; a cloister ; পরিভ্রমণ স্থল, লতাদি আচ্ছাদিত পথ ; অলিন্দ ; মঠমধ্যস্থ ছন্নপথ।

ăm-bŭs-cāde′, *n., v.t.* & *i.* **1.** A lying in wait in order to attack by surprise ; অরাতিগণকে অতর্কিতভাবে আক্রমণের জন্য নিভৃতস্থানে অবস্থিতি, প্রচ্ছন্নাবস্থান। **2** The place where troops lie in wait ; an ambush ; শত্রুর অপেক্ষায় সৈন্যগণের লুক্কায়িত থাকিবার নিভৃতস্থান ; ঝোপ, আড়াল। **3.** A body of troops lying in ambush ; নিভৃতস্থানে লুক্কায়িত সৈন্যদল। ***Verb t.*** To conceal in ambush ; to attack from a covert or lurking place ; শত্রুগণকে অতর্কিতভাবে আক্রমণ করার জন্য নিভৃতস্থানে অবস্থান করা ; গুপ্ত বা প্রচ্ছন্নস্থান হইতে বহির্গত হইয়া আক্রমণ করা। ***Verb i.*** To lie in ambush ; শত্রুর অপেক্ষায় ওৎ করিয়া থাকা বা লুক্কায়িত থাকা।

ăm′-bûsh, *n., v. t.* & *i.* A military disposition consisting of troops concealed in a wood in order to fall unexpectedly upon an enemy ; the concealed station where troops lie in wait ; অতর্কিত-ভাবে আক্রমণার্থ অরণ্য-মধ্যে প্রচ্ছন্নভাবে সৈন্য-সন্নিবেশ ; অতর্কিত আক্রমণের জন্য নিভৃত স্থান। ***Verb t.*** To conceal troops ; to lie in wait for ; to attack from an ambush ; (only in *p. p.*) ; নিভৃতস্থল হইতে আক্রমণার্থ সৈন্য লুক্কায়িত রাখা ; অতর্কিতভাবে আক্রমণার্থ শত্রুর প্রতীক্ষা করা ; নিভৃত-স্থল হইতে আসিয়া আক্রমণ করা। ***Verb i.*** To lie in wait ; to lurk ; শত্রুর আশায় লুক্কায়িত থাকা ; ওৎ করিয়া থাকা। **—ment,** *n.* **To lay an ambush**—To attack from an ambush ; গুপ্তস্থান হইতে হঠাৎ আক্রমণ করা। **To lie in ambush**—To lie concealed in order to attack by surprise ; সহসা আক্রমণার্থ লুক্কায়িত থাকা, উপশয়স্থ হওয়া (শিশুঃ)।

ame damnee, (*F.*), *n.* [*Lit.* a damned or lost soul] A willing and devoted tool or slave of another ; সম্পূর্ণ আয়ত্তাধীন ব্যক্তি, দাসানুদাস।

â-meer′ (-mër), **â-mir′,** *n.* The title of various Mohammedan rulers in Afghanistan ; a Mohammedan nobleman ; a chief ; কাবুলের আমীর ; মোস্লেম্ জাতীয় সম্ভ্রান্ত পুরুষ ; সর্দ্দার।

ȧ-mēl′-iö-rāte, *v. t.* & *i.* To make better ; to improve ; as, in every human being there is a wish to *ameliorate* his own condition ; উৎকর্ষ সাধন করা ; উন্নতি-

করা, শ্রীবৃদ্ধি করা। ***Verb i.*** To grow better ; অপেক্ষাকৃত ভাল হওয়া, উন্নত হওয়া, উৎকর্ষপ্রাপ্ত হওয়া। **—ra′-tion,** *n.* The act or process of making better ; improvement ; উন্নতিসাধন, উৎকর্ষ-সম্পাদন ; উন্নতিলাভ, উন্নতি, শ্রীবৃদ্ধি। **—ra-tive,** *adj.* **—ra-tor,** *n.*

ă-mĕn′, *inter., v.t. & n.* An expression used at the end of prayers, meaning *so be it* ; তথাস্তু, এবমস্তু, তাহাই হউক, স্বস্তি। ***Verb t.*** To say "amen" to ; hence, to ratify solemnly ; "তথাস্তু" বলা ; বিধিপূর্ব্বক দৃঢ়ীভূত করা। ***Noun.*** **1.** A title of Christ—The faithful one ; সত্যব্রত ও বিশ্বাসি-শিরোমণি যীশুখৃষ্ট। **2.** The word 'Amen !' at the end of a prayer, etc ; শান্তিঃ, শান্তিঃ, শান্তিঃ।

ă-mē′-nă-ble, *adj.* **1.** Liable to answer ; responsible (*to* law, etc.) ; কৈফিয়তের জন্য দায়ী ; দায়ী। **2.** Liable *to* (punishment, charge, claim, etc.) ; as, your property being *amenable* to all claims upon the company ; দায়ী, যোগ্য, অর্হ (সমাসে)। **3.** Capable of being tested by (*to*) ; as, *amenable* to the touch ; পরীক্ষণীয়। **4.** Disposed to respond or submit ; tractable ; as, a high-spirited people not *amenable* to discipline ; বশ্য ; সুসাধ্য, সাধ্য। **—bil′-i-ty, —ness,** *ns.*

ă-mĕnd′, (*e* out, *menda,* akin to Skr. *mändä,* fault), *v. t. & i.* **1.** To abandon evil ways ; "*amend* your ways and your doings ;" মন্দ অভ্যাস ত্যাগ করা, কুপথ ত্যাগ করা। **2.** To correct an error in the text of a book or document ; কোন পুস্তক বা দলিলাদির ভ্রমসংশোধন করা, পরিশোধন করা। **3.** (*Law*) To correct or rectify an error in a legal document ; to make professed improvements in a measure before Parliament ; as, to *amend* a bill ; (আইন) দলিল দস্তাবেজ শুদ্ধ বা সংশোধন করা ; পার্লেমেণ্টে উপস্থাপিত আইনের পাণ্ডুলিপি সংশোধন করা। **4.** To make better ; পূর্ব্বাপেক্ষা ভাল করা। ***Verb i.*** To reform oneself ; to become better, by rectifying manners or morals ; আত্মসংশোধন করা ; স্বভাব চরিত্র সংশোধন-দ্বারা পূর্ব্বাপেক্ষা ভাল হওয়া। **—a-ble,** *adj.* Capable of being corrected or bettered ; সংশোধনীয়। **—a-to-ry,** *adj.* **—ment,** *n.* **1.** Correction of faults ; reformation ; improvement ; as, her works are so perfect that there is no place for *amendments* ; সংশোধন ; সংস্কার ; উন্নতিসাধন, উৎকর্ষসাধন। **2.** (*Law*) The correction of error in a writ or process ; (আইন) দলিলাদির সংশোধন। **3.** An alteration proposed to be made in the draft of any bill (before a legislature) or in the terms of any motion under discussion ; a proposed alteration in the terms of a resolution brought forward at a public meeting ; কোন আইনের পাণ্ডুলিপিতে প্রস্তাবিত পরিবর্ত্তন বা সংশোধন ; কোন সভার প্রস্তাবসমূহের প্রস্তাবিত পরিবর্ত্তন।

amende honourable, (*F.*), *n.* Public apology and reparation ; "The Edinburgh Review made *amende honourable* to Burns" প্রকাশ্য ক্ষমাপ্রার্থনা এবং ক্ষতিপূরণ।

ă-mĕnds′, *n.* (*Pl.* now treated as *sing.*) Compensation for a loss or injury ; reparation ; restitution ; as, he was determined to make some little *amends* for the injury he had formerly done ; ক্ষতিপূরণ ; প্রতিকার, প্রতিবিধান ; প্রত্যর্পণ, প্রতিদান। **To make amends**—To give adequate compensation ; উপযুক্ত পরিমাণে ক্ষতিপূরণ করা।

ă-mĕn′-i-tȳ, *n.* **1.** The quality of being pleasant or agreeable (of places, aspect, climate, etc.) ; civility ; gentleness (of perso[ns,] habits, etc.) ; প্রীতিপ্রদভাব, মনোজ্ঞ শীলতা, সৌজন্য ; নম্রতা, ভদ্রত[া]। **2.** (*Pl.*) Pleasant ways or manners ; pleasures ; delights ; as, th[e] *amenities* of authors : *amenitie[s]* of home life ; মনোরমভাব, মাধুর্য্য সুখ ; আনন্দ।

ă-mĕn-ŏr-rhœ′-â (-rē-), *n.* A[n] obstruction of the menses [from] other causes, than pregnanc[y or] old age ; ঋতু-কৃচ্ছ্র, রজঃস্[তম্ভ]। **—al,** *adj.*

ăm′-ĕnt, *n.* See CATKIN. [—] **ta′-ceous,** *adj.* (Also **ă-[men]tŭm,** *n.* **—ti-form,** *adj.*)

ă-mêrce′, *v. t.* **1.** To fine ; as, th[e] court *amerced* the criminal i[n] the sum of £100. (The penalt[y] or fine may be introduced b[y] *in, with,* or *of*) ; জরিমানা কর[া], অর্থদণ্ড করা। **2.** To punish i[n] general ; "Millions of spirit[s] for his fault *amerced* of Heaven ;" শাস্তি প্রদান করা। **—a-ble, —mer[-]ci-a-ble,** *adjs.* **—ment,** *n.* A fi[ne] inflicted on an offender at t[he] discretion of the court ; জরিমা[না,] অর্থদণ্ড।

A-mĕr′-i-căn (ă-), *adj. & n.* [Be]longing to the continent of Ame[r]ica or to the United States ; মার্[কিন] দেশ বা যুক্তরাজ্য-সম্পর্কীয়। ***Noun.*** [A] native of America of Europ[ean] descent ; esp., a citizen of [the] United States ; ইয়ুরোপীয় ব[ংশ]সম্ভূত আমেরিকার অধিবাসী ; [যুক্ত]রাজ্যের নাগরিক অধিকারপ্রাপ্ত ব্যা[ক্তি]।

ăm′-ĕ-thȳst, *n.* A precious s[tone,] a kind of quartz, pur[ple or] violet ; একপ্রকার বহুমূল্য রাজাবর্ত্তমণি (আলোহিত নীলবর্ণ[)]। **—ine,** *adj.* **Oriental amet[hyst,]** A rare violet variety of sa[pphire] রাজাবর্ত্তমণি।

ă′-mi-ă-ble, *adj.* **1.** Exci[ting or] tending to excite love or [...]

ovely ; pleasing ; প্রীতিজনক ; কমনীয় ; মনোরম, মনোজ্ঞ, কান্ত, রুচির, প্রীতিপ্রদ। **2.** Having sweetness of temper ; lovable ; as, an *amiable* girl : *amiable* disposition ; মধুর-স্বভাব, মাধুর্য্যময় ; প্রিয়। **—bil′-i-ty,** *n.* Pleasing quality of heart and behaviour ; loveliness ; সুশীলতা ; মনোজ্ঞতা, কমনীয়তা, মাধুর্য্য। **bly,** *adv.* **—ness,** *n.* **Amiable x** or **fair sex**—স্ত্রী-জাতি।

ıi-ăn′-thŭs, —tŭs, *n.* **1.** A riety of flexible asbestos or untain-flax ; একপ্রকার শঙ্খ-তা। **2.** A green fibrous chrysolite ; হরিতাশ্ম।

ăm′-i-că-ble, *adj.* **1.** Friendly ; peaceable ; মৈত্র, সৌহার্দ্দপূর্ণ ; শান্ত। **2.** Done in a friendly spirit ; বন্ধুভাবে কৃত। **—bil′-i-ty, —ness,** *ns.* The quality of being amicable ; friendliness ; মৈত্রী ; সৌহার্দ্দ, সখ্য, বন্ধুতা। **—bly,** *adv.* **An amicable settlement**—আপোষে মিটমাট।

ăm′-ĭce, *n.* **1.** A hood, or cape with a hood, (made of, or lined with, fur) formerly worn by the clergy ; প্রাচীনকালীন ধর্ম্মযাজক-সম্প্রদায়ের শিরোবস্ত্র বা পৃষ্ঠাচ্ছাদন বসন। **2.** A badge worn by the French canons on the left arm ; ফরাসী দেশের ধর্ম্মাধ্যক্ষ-বিশেষদিগের বামহস্তে পরিহিত চিহ্নবিশেষ। **3.** A square of white linen folded diagonally, worn at first on the head, but now about the neck and shoulders by the priests of the Roman Catholic Church ; রোমান্ ক্যাথলিক্ পুরোহিতগণের গ্রীবা ও স্কন্ধদেশে পরিহিত ক্ষৌম শ্বেতক্ষৌম বস্ত্র। (পূর্ব্বে উক্ত মস্তকে পরিধান করা হইত।)

icus curiæ, (*L.*), *n.* A nd of the court, *i.e.*, a person ourt who informs the judges rrors he has noticed ; a terested adviser ; বিচারালয়ের ারী ব্যক্তি, অর্থাৎ যে ব্যক্তি কোন দোষ বা ত্রুটির কথা বিচারকগণের কর্ণগোচর করে ; নিঃস্বার্থ পরামর্শদাতা।

ă-mid′, ă-midst′, *prep.* In the middle or centre of ; as, he died *amidst* a circle of friends ; among ; in the course of ; as, *amidst* the splendour and festivity of a court ; (*amid* is used chiefly in poetry) ; মধ্যভাগে, মধ্যে, মধ্যস্থানে, মাঝে, অভ্যন্তরে ; ভিতরে ; চলিতেছে এই অবস্থায়। **From amidst**—মাঝখান থেকে।

ăm′-i-dĭn, *n.* The soluble matter of starch ; starch in a state of solution ; শ্বেতসারের দ্রবণীয় পদার্থ ; শ্বেতসার দ্রবণ।

ă-mid′-ships, *adv.* (*Naut.*) In the middle of a ship ; (নৌ-বিদ্যা) জাহাজের মধ্যভাগে।

â-mir′, *n.* See AMEER.

ă-miss′, *adj.* & *adv.* Wrong ; faulty ; improper ; as, it may not be *amiss* to ask advice ; অন্যায় ; দূষণীয় ; অযৌক্তিক, অযুক্ত, অসঙ্গত। ***Adv.*** Faultily ; wrongly ; as, the king may exercise *amiss* his proper powers ; untowardly ; দুষ্যভাবে, সাপরাধে ; অন্যায়-রূপে ; বিসদৃশভাবে। **To come amiss**—To come in an unfavourable moment ; অসময়ে ঘটা বা আসা। **To take amiss**—To take offence at ; to take unkindly ; ত্রুটিগ্রহণ করা, দোষগ্রহণ করা, রুষ্ট হওয়া ; অপ্রিয়-ভাবে গ্রহণ করা।

ăm′-i-tў, *n.* Friendship ; harmony ; friendly relations (between societies, nations, etc.) ; as, Great Britain was in league and *amity* with all the world ; মৈত্রী, মিত্রতা ; ঐক্য ; প্রীতি, সদ্‌ভাব।

ăm′-mē-têr, *n.* An instrument for measuring the force of electric currents ; তড়িদ্বলমাপকযন্ত্র, বিদ্যুৎপ্রবাহের বলমাপনার্থ যন্ত্র-বিশেষ।

ăm-mō′-ni-â, *n.* A colourless gas with pungent smell and strong alkaline reaction (called also *spirit of hartshorn*) ; এক প্রকার বর্ণহীন, তীব্র-গন্ধ এবং উগ্রক্ষারীয়-প্রতিক্রিয়াবিশিষ্ট বাষ্প ; চুলিকা বাষ্প, ক্ষারিণ বায়ু (হিঃ কোঃ)। **—ac,** *adj.* & *n.* Pertaining to, or of the nature of, ammonia ; ক্ষারিণবায়ু-সম্পৃক্ত, ক্ষারিণবায়ুধর্ম্মা। (*Noun*) Gum ammonia ; ঔষধ ও প্রলেপে ব্যবহৃত এক প্রকার গদ। **—at-ed, —ni-al,** *adjs.* **Liquid ammonia**—A solution of ammonia in water ; তরল ক্ষারিণ। **Sal Ammoniac**—A hard white crystalline salt of ammonia ; নিশাদল, চুলিকা (রঃ প্রঃ), চুলিকা লবণ, (রঃ সঃ—প্রঃ) নবসার (ঐ)। [জুপিটার এমোনের মন্দিরসান্নিধ্যে উষ্ট্রের পুরীষ হইতে আরবগণ প্রথমতঃ চুলিকালবণ প্রস্তুত করে বলিয়া প্রসিদ্ধি।]

ăm-mŏ′-ni-â-phōne, *n.* An instrument by means of which ammonia is inhaled in order to improve the voice ; কণ্ঠস্বরের উন্নতির জন্য চুলিকাবাষ্প-শ্বসনার্থ যন্ত্র-বিশেষ।

ăm′-mŏn-īte, *n.* The fossil shell of an extinct genus of molluscs,

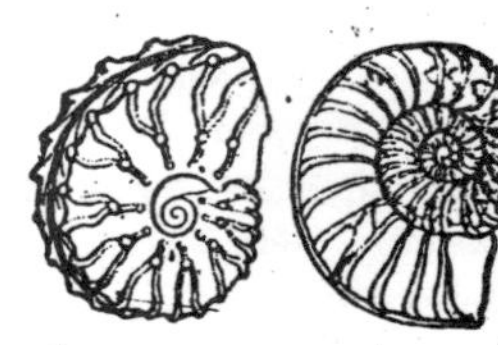

Ammonites.

coiled in a plane spiral ; শিলীভূত শম্বুক, স্বর্ণনাভ (মঃ ভাঃ)।

ăm-mū-ni′-tion, *n.* **1.** (Formerly) Military stores or provisions of all kinds ; (পূর্ব্বে) যাবতীয় যুদ্ধোপকরণ, খাদ্য-সম্ভার প্রভৃতি। **2.** (Now) Powder, shells, shot, bombs, etc. ; (বর্ত্তমানে) বারুদ, গোলাগুলি, বোমা, প্রভৃতি। **Ammunition bread, shoes, etc.**—Such as are contracted for by government and supplied to the soldiers ; রুটি, পাদুকা প্রভৃতি

যে সমস্ত জিনিষ সরকারী ঠিকাদার কর্ত্তৃক সৈনিকদিগকে সরবরাহ করা হয়।

ăm-nē'-si-â, *n.* Loss of memory ; forgetfulness ; স্মৃতিলোপ, স্মৃতিহীনতা ; বিস্মৃতি।

ăm'-nĕs-tў, *n.* & *v.t.* **1.** An act of oblivion ; a general pardon of the offences of subjects against government ; the proclamation of such pardon ; বিস্মরণ ; রাজবিরুদ্ধাচারী প্রজাবর্গের সাধারণ অপরাধ-মার্জ্জনা ; রাজক্ষমা-ঘোষণা । **2.** An intentional over-looking ; স্বেচ্ছাকৃত উপেক্ষা। ***Verb t.*** To grant amnesty to ; to pardon ; (রাজনৈতিক অপরাধীদিগকে) ক্ষমা করা ; মার্জ্জনা করা।

ăm'-ni-ŏn (*pl.* **—ni-a**), *n.* The innermost membrane enclosing the fœtus before birth ; গর্ভস্থ ভ্রূণের অন্তস্তম আবরক-ঝিল্লী।

ă-mœ'-bâ (-mē-), *n.* A class of microscopic animalcule perpetually changing shape ; সতত আকার-পরিবর্ত্তনশীল আণুবীক্ষণিক সূক্ষ্ম প্রাণি-বর্গ। **—bi-form, —boid,** *adjs.*

ăm-œ-bæ'-ăn (-ē-bē-), *adj.* Alternately answering ; as *amœbæan* exchange of witticisms between the Bench and the Bar ; পর্য্যায়-ক্রমে উত্তরদানকারী, উত্তরপ্রত্যুত্তরাত্মক।

ăm-œ-bæ'-ŭm (-ē-bē-), *n.* A poem containing alternating verses, designed to be sung by two persons, one in answer to the other ; তরজা।

Amomum cardamomum—Cardamom ; এলাচি।

Amomum dealbatum—বড় এলাচি (বেলঃ ;—শ্রীহট্টে জন্মে)।

Amomum subulatum—এলাচি (বেলঃ ;—খাসীয়া পর্ব্বতে জন্মে)।

ă-mŏng' (-mŭng), **—mongst'** (-mŭngst), *prep.* **1.** In the midst of ; surrounded by ; as, *among* the thickest trees ; মধ্যে, অভ্যন্তরে ; বেষ্টিত। **2.** In the number or class of ; as, blessed thou art *among* women ; সমাজে, জাতি-মধ্যে। **3.** By the joint action or consent of ; as, settle it *among* yourselves ; মিলিতভাবে, সর্ব্বসম্মতি-ক্রমে। **4.** To each of ; as, he gave five rupees to be divided *among* you ; প্রত্যেককে। **5.** Reciprocally ; as, they quarrelled *among* themselves ; পরস্পরের সহিত।

Amoora rohituka—তিক্তরাজ (বেলঃ)।

ăm'-ō-rous (-rŭs), *adj.* **1.** Having a propensity to love or to sexual enjoyment ; inclined to love ; কান্দর্পিক, আদি-রসাশ্রিত, কামরসিক, কামী, কামুক ; প্রণয়প্রবণ, প্রেমশীল। **2.** In love ; enamoured ; (usu. with *of*) ; "Thy roses *amorous* of the moon ;" প্রেমানুরক্ত, প্রণয়াসক্ত ; প্রেমমুগ্ধ, মোহিত। **3.** Of, relating to, or produced by, love ; প্রণয়-ঘটিত, প্রেমজ, কামজ। **—ly,** *adv.* In the way of love ; fondly ; কামুক-ভাবে, মুগ্ধভাবে ; সানুরাগে। **—ness,** *n.* Fondness of the opposite sex ; lovingness ; কামুকতা, কামজ ভাব, কামভাব ; প্রেমমুগ্ধতা, প্রেমাসক্তি।

Amorphophallus campanulatus—Telinga potato ; ওল (বেলঃ), কন্দ (ঐ)।

ă-mŏr'-phous (-phŭs), *adj.* **1.** Of irregular shape ; shapeless ; unshapen ; অনিয়তাকার ; আকাররহিত ; নিরবয়ব (সাঃ পঃ)। **2.** Anomalous ; unclassifiable ; নিয়ম-বহির্ভূত, বিধি-বিরুদ্ধ ; অশ্রেণীনির্দ্দেশযোগ্য। **3.** (*Min.* & *Chem.*) Uncrystallized ; unorganized ; (খনিজ-বিদ্যা, রসায়ন-শাস্ত্র) অর্কতারহিত (সাঃ পঃ), অনাকিক ; অব্যূহবদ্ধ। **—ly,** *adv.* **—ness, —phism,** *ns.*

ă-mŏr'-tīse, —tīze, *v. t.* **1.** (*Law*) To alienate in mortmain, *i. e.*, to convey (property) to a corporation—(see *mortmain*) ; কোন সনন্দ-প্রাপ্ত সমাজের নিকট ভূ-সম্পত্তি প্রভৃতি হস্তান্তরিত করা, মালিকিস্বত্ব বিক্রয় করা। **2.** To extinguish (debt) usually by means of a sinking fund ; প্রতিবর্ষে নির্দ্দিষ্ট পরিমাণ অর্থসঞ্চয়দ্বারা (ঋণ) পরিশোধ করা। **—ti-za'-tion,** *n.*

ă-mount' (-mownt), *v.i.* & *n.* **1.** To come *to* (so much) ; as, the bill *amounts to* ten rupees ; মোট, একুন বা সমষ্টিতে হওয়া। **2.** To be equivalent (in significance) *to* ; as, his love of mischief *amounted* almost *to* madness ; গুরুত্বে সমান হওয়া, ফলে দাঁড়ান। ***Noun.*** **1.** The sum or total of two or more sums or quantities ; মোট, একুন, সমষ্টি, মোটসংখ্যা। **2.** Quantity ; as, a considerable *amount* ; পরিমাণ। **3.** Full value ; significance or import ; as, the *amount* of the testimony is this ; পূর্ণ মূল্য ; গুরুত্ব, তাৎপর্য্য, ফল।

ă-mour' (-môr), *n.* A love-affair usually an illicit love-affair ; an intrigue ; প্রণয়-ব্যাপার ; অবৈধ-প্রণয় ; গুপ্তপ্রণয়, গুপ্তপ্রেম, প্রণয়চক্র।

ă-mou-rĕtte' (-mô-), *n.* Petty love affair ; নগণ্য প্রণয়-ব্যাপার।

amour-propre, (*F.*), *n.* Self-esteem ; self-conceit ; vanity ; as, to wound one's *amour-propre* (কাহারো আত্ম-সম্মানে আঘাত করা) ; আত্মাদর, আত্ম-সম্মান, আত্মাভিমান ; অহমিকা ; দেমাক।

ăm-pere' (-pāâr), *n.* (*Phys.*) The standard unit of current in electrical measurement ; (পদার্থবিজ্ঞান) তাড়িত-প্রবাহের একক। [ফরাসী তাড়িতবিজ্ঞানবিৎ Ampereএর নামহইতে এই শব্দটী গৃহীত হইয়াছে।]

ăm'-pêr-sănd, *n.* The sign (&) ; এই চিহ্ন (&)। [Also *amperzand, ampussy-and* and *ampassy.*]

Am-phib'-i-ă (ăm-), *n. pl.* Animals capable of living both under water and on land, intermediate between reptiles and fishes, ...

frogs, newts, etc. ; উভচরপ্রাণী, স্থল-জলচর (যথা মৎস্যাদি)। **—an,** *n.* **—ous,** *adj.* **1.** (Of animals, plants) Living both on land and in water ; উভচর, জলস্থলবাসী। **2.** Suited for, or connected with, both land and water ; জলস্থল-বাসযোগ্য ; জলস্থল-সম্পৰ্কীয় বা সম্বন্ধীয়। **3.** Of a mixed nature ; combining two classes, offices, qualities, etc. ; as, *amphibious* dress, code, etc. ; মিশ্র-প্রকৃতিক ; উভয়শ্রেণী-সম্পৰ্কীয়।

am-phib-i-ŏl′-ö-ġy̆, *n.* That branch of zoology treating of Amphibia ; জন্তুতত্ত্বের যে শাখায় উভচর প্রাণীদিগের বিষয় আলোচিত হয়, উভচরতত্ত্ব।

ăm-phi-bŏl′-ö-ġy̆, —phib′-ŏ-ly̆, *n.* Quibble ; a phrase of uncertain meaning ; ambiguous wording ; "The Duke yet lives that Henry shall depose." (*i. e.* who shall depose Henry, or whom Henry shall depose) ; বাক্‌ছল ; দ্ব্যর্থবোধক বাক্য ; অনিশ্চিতার্থক বাক্য। **—phib-o-log′-i-cal,** *adj.* **—phib-o-log′-i-cal-ly,** *adv.*

am-phic′-ty̆-ŏns (ăm-), *n. pl.* An assembly or council of deputies from the different states of Greece ; প্রাচীন গ্রীসদেশের অন্তর্ভুক্ত ভিন্নরাজ্যের প্রতিনিধিবর্গের সভা। **—on′-ic,** *adj.*

Amphidonax karka—নল (বেলঃ)।

am′-phi-găm, *n.* (*Bot.*) A plant with no distinct sexual organs ; (উদ্ভিদ্‌-বিদ্যা) অলিঙ্গ বা অচিহ্নিত তরু। **—phig′-a-mous,** *adj.* Cryptogamous ; (which see).

am′-phi-gö-ry̆, —gou′-ry̆ (-gō-), *n.* A nonsensical composition ; a meaningless rigmarole ; অর্থশূন্য রচনা ; অসার কথা, নিরর্থক বাক্য।

am-phi-ŏx′-ŭs, *n.* The fish called the Lancelet ; এক জাতীয় মৎস্য। [ইহা মস্তিষ্ক, রক্ত ও পৃষ্ঠাস্থিবিহীন।]

am-phip′-ö-dâ (ăm-), *n. pl.* An order of Crustacea, with feet of two kinds ; (চিঙ্গড়ীমাছ, কাকড়া প্রভৃতি) দ্বিজাতীয় পদশ্রেণীযুক্ত, দৃঢ়াবরণবিশিষ্ট প্রাণিবর্গ। **—dan, —dous,** *adjs.*

ăm-phip′-rö-sty̆le, *adj.* & *n.* Having pillars both in front and behind ; with portico at both ends ; সম্মুখ এবং পশ্চাদ্দেশে স্তম্ভরাজি-যুক্ত ; উভয়প্রান্তে মণ্ডপ- (গাড়ী-বারান্দা) শোভিত। ***Noun.*** An amphiprostyle temple or edifice ; উভয়পার্শ্বে মণ্ডপশোভিত মন্দির বা অট্টালিকা।

ăm-phis-bæ′-nâ (-bē-), *n.* **1.** A fabulous serpent with head at each end and moving either way ; (পৌরাণিক) দুমুখো সাপ, শঙ্খিনী সাপ। **2.** (*Zool.*) (proper noun) A genus of worm-like lizards ; (জন্তু-তত্ত্ব) কীটবৎ কৃকলাসশ্রেণী।

ăm-phi-thē′-ă-tre (-tēr), *n.* **1.** An oval or circular building with rows of seats rising behind and above each other, round a central open space or *arena* ; রঙ্গভূমি বা উন্মুক্ত-স্থানের চতুর্দ্দিগ্‌বর্ত্তী ক্রমোচ্চ আসন-শ্রেণী-সমন্বিত বৃত্ত বা বৃত্তাভাসাকার অট্টালিকা।

Amphitheatre.

2. A semi-circular, rising gallery in a theatre ; অর্দ্ধচন্দ্রাকৃতি ক্রমোচ্চ-আসন-শ্রেণীবিশিষ্ট রঙ্গমণ্ডপস্থ মঞ্চ। **3.** (*Fig.*) The scene of a contest ; (লক্ষণায়) বিবাদ-মঞ্চ। **—at′-ri-cal,** *adj.*

Am-phit′-ry̆-ŏn (ăm-), *n.* [From Molière's comedy in which Amphitryon gives a great dinner.] A host or entertainer ; ভোজদাতা, আমন্ত্রয়িতা।

ăm′-phö-râ, *n.* A two-handled vessel, used by the ancients for holding wine, oil, honey, etc.;

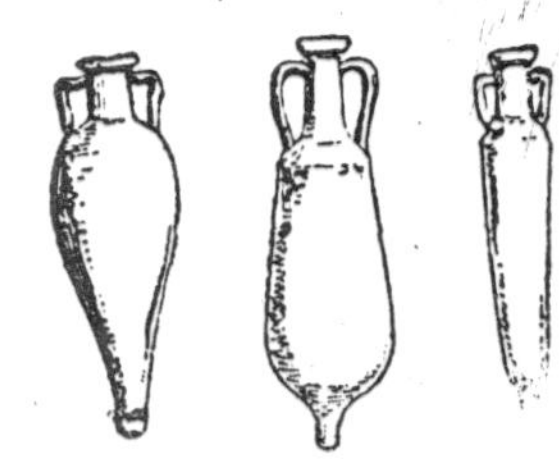

Amphoræ.

গ্রীক ও রোমানদিগের (সুরা, মধু, প্রভৃতি রাখিবার) দ্বিকর্ণ-পাত্র বা ঘট। **—ral,** *adj.*

ăm-phŏr′-ic, *adj.* (*Med.*) Like the sound produced by blowing into a large vessel with a small mouth ; as, *amphoric* resonance ; (ভৈষজ্য-শাস্ত্র) ক্ষুদ্রমুখ কূপীর ভিতর ফুৎকার দিলে যে প্রকার শব্দ হয় তদ্রূপ। [ফুসফুস্ বা হৃৎপিণ্ড পরীক্ষণসময়ে উল্লিখিত শব্দ অনুভূত হয়।]

ăm′-ple, *adj.* **1.** Spacious ; widely extended ; roomy ; as, *ample* room ; প্রকাণ্ড, সুবিস্তীর্ণ ; সুপরিসর ; বিশাল। **2.** Abundant ; plentiful ; quite enough ; as, *ample* fortune, justice ; প্রচুর, প্রভূত ; পর্য্যাপ্ত ; যথেষ্ট। **3.** Copious ; not concise ; as, an *ample* narrative ; বহুল, পুষ্পল ; বিস্তৃত। **—ness,** *n.* Sufficiency ; abundance ; প্রাচুর্য্য, বাহুল্য, অজস্রতা ; পর্য্যাপ্তি। **—ply,** *adv.* Sufficiently ; abundantly ; প্রচুর-রূপে, পর্য্যাপ্তরূপে ; সবিস্তারে।

ăm′-pli-ă-tive, *adj.* (*Log.*) Extending a simple conception ; adding to what is known ; (তর্ক-বিজ্ঞান) সহজ বা অবিমিশ্র বিভাবনার বিস্তারক ; উপবৃংহক (হিঃ কোঃ)। [যথা, "পদার্থ" একটী সহজ বা আত্মপ্রত্যয়লব্ধ বিভাবনা। "সমস্ত পদার্থ আকর্ষণ-শক্তি-বিশিষ্ট" এইরূপভাবে "পদার্থ" শব্দটীকে বিস্তারিত করার নাম উপবৃংহণ।]

ăm′-pli-fy̆, *v.t.* & *i.* **1.** To enlarge (story, statement, etc.) ; to expand ; প্রসঙ্গবিস্তার করা, সবিস্তারে বর্ণনা করা ; পল্লবিত করা। **2.** To extend or increase (anything immaterial) in amount, dignity, etc. ; বর্দ্ধিত করা, বৃদ্ধি করা, বিস্তৃত করা, সম্প্রসারিত করা। ***Verb i.*** **1.** To speak or write diffusely ; (often with *on, upon*) ; as, to *amplify on* or *upon* a subject ; সবিস্তারে বর্ণনা বা রচনা করা। **2.** To magnify ; to exaggerate ; as, the description *amplified* by invention ; বিস্তারিত করা ; অতিরঞ্জিত করা, অতিশয়োক্তি করা। **–fi-ca′-tion,** *n.* **1.** Enlargement ; extension ; বৃদ্ধি, প্রসারণ ; বিস্তৃতি, ব্যাপ্তি। **2.** Diffusive description ; বিস্তৃত বর্ণনা, প্রসঙ্গ-বিস্তার। **3.** Exaggerated representation ; অতিরঞ্জিত বর্ণনা। **–fi-er,** *n.* **–plif′-i-ca-tive, –plif′-i-ca-to-ry,** *adjs.*

ăm′-pli-tude (-chüd), *n.* **1.** Width ; breadth ; largeness ; as, the *amplitude* of heaven and earth ; বিস্তার ; প্রশস্ততা ; প্রকাণ্ডতা, বিশালতা। **2.** (*Fig.*) Largeness of mind ; breadth of thought ; extent of intellectual powers ; as, ***amplitude*** of mind, comprehension, etc. ; (লক্ষণায়) চিত্তের প্রসার, উদারতা, মহত্ব ; চিন্তার প্রসার ; মানসিক শক্তির প্রসার। **3.** Sufficiency ; abundance ; as, *amplitude* of the Divine benignity ; প্রাচুর্য্য, পর্য্যাপ্তি ; অজস্রতা। **4.** Splendour ; dignity ; excellence ; as, religion is the ***amplitude*** of our moral nature ; শ্রী, সমৃদ্ধি ; গৌরব ; চরমোৎকর্ষ। **5.** (*Astron.*) An arc of the horizon intercepted between the true east or west point and the centre of the sun, or star, at its setting and rising ; (জ্যোতির্বিজ্ঞান) উদয়াস্ত-কালীন সূর্য্য বা নক্ষত্রের কেন্দ্রস্থল এবং পূর্ব্ব বা পশ্চিমদিগ্‌বিন্দুর মধ্যস্থিত দিগ্বলয়ের চাপাংশ, অগ্রাংশ (হিঃ কোঃ), অগ্রচাপাংশ (ঐ)।

ăm-pûl′-lâ, *n.* (*Pl.* AMPULLÆ) **1.** A Roman narrow-necked vessel having two handles ; প্রাচীন রোমনগরীর দ্বিকর্ণ এবং অপ্রশস্তগল ভাণ্ডবিশেষ। **2.** A vessel for holding consecrated oil or for other sacred uses ; পূতৈতল রক্ষণার্থ অথবা অন্যান্য পবিত্র কার্য্যের জন্য ব্যবহৃত ভাণ্ডবিশেষ। **3.** (*Biol.*) Any membranous bag shaped like a leathern bottle, as the dilated end of a vessel or duct in animal ; (জীব-বিজ্ঞান) চর্ম্ম-কূপীর মত ঝিল্লী-পুট (থলি)। [যেমন, প্রবাহিকা, নালী বা শিরার প্রসারিত মুখ।]

ăm′-pü-tāte, *v. t.* **1.** To prune or lop off, as branches or tendrils ; (বৃক্ষশাখাদি) ছেদন করা, ছাঁটা, ছাঁটিয়া ফেলা। **2.** To cut off (a limb or a part of an animal body) ; অঙ্গচ্ছেদন করা। **–ta′-tion,** *n.* (*Surg.*) The operation of cutting off a limb ; (অস্ত্রোপচার-বিদ্যা) অঙ্গচ্ছেদন, ছেদ্য-ক্রিয়া। **–ta′-tor,** *n.*

ă-mŭck′, –mŏk′, *adv.* (Used only in the phrase—*To run amuck*—To run about in a frenzied thirst for blood ; to attack all and sundry ; শোণিত-পিপাসায় উন্মত্ত হইয়া ধাবিত হওয়া ; নির্ব্বিচারে সকলকে আক্রমণ করা।) [ভাঙ্গ বা অহিফেনের নেশায় উন্মত্তবৎ মালয়দ্বীপবাসিগণ কখন কখন ছোরা বা তরবারী হস্তে "Amuck, a-muck" শব্দে ধাবমান হইয়া সম্মুখে যাহাকে পায় তাহাকেই বধ করিয়া থাকে।]

ăm′-ü-lĕt, *n.* (*Lit.* & *fig.*) Anything worn as charm against evil ;

Amulet.

(শব্দানুযায়ী এবং লক্ষণায়) মাদুলি, কবচ, রক্ষাকবচ, তাবিজ।

ă-müse′, *v. t.* **1.** To entertain or divert the mind from serious business with trifles ; to occupy the mind with agreeable objects ; to tickle the fancy of ; চিত্তবিনোদন করা, আমোদ প্রদান করা ; চিত্তরঞ্জন করা ; কৌতূহলোদ্দীপ্ত করা। **2.** To delude ; to beguile ; as, he *amused* his followers with idle promises ; বিনোদন করা, ভুলান ; সম্মোহিত করা। **–mus′-a-ble, –mus′-ive,** *adjs.* **–mus′-ing,** *adj.* Pleasing ; diverting ; as, an *amusing* story ; চিত্তবিনোদক, আমোদপ্রদ, কৌতুকপ্রদ, অনুরঞ্জক। **–mus′-ing-ly,** *adv.*

ă-müse′-mĕnt, *n.* **1.** Pleasurable diversion ; entertainment ; pastime ; রঙ্গ ; বিনোদন ; আমোদপ্রমোদ। **2.** Excitement of risible faculty ; a tickling of the fancy ; as, much *amusement* was excited by his recital ; হাসিতামাসা, পরিহাস, কৌতূহল, ক্রীড়াকৌতুক, তামাসা, আমোদ-প্রমোদ ; রঙ্গরস, কেলি, নর্ম্ম।

ăm-ŷg-dăl′-ĭc, *adj.* Obtained from almonds ; as, *amygdalic* acid ; বাদাম হইতে প্রস্তুত বা প্রাপ্ত।

ă-mŷg′-dă-loid (-lōyd), *adj.* & *n.* Almond-shaped ; বাদামাকার। ***Noun.*** An igneous rock, containing mineral nodules of almond-shape ; বাদামাকৃতি ক্ষুদ্র ক্ষুদ্র খনিজ-পিণ্ডসমন্বিত অগ্ন্যুদ্ভূত প্রস্তরখণ্ড।

Amygdalus communis—Almond tree ; বাদামগাছ (বেলঃ))

ăm-ŷ-lā′-ceous (-shŭs), *adj.* Pertaining to starch ; starchy ; শ্বেতসার সংক্রান্ত ; শ্বেতসারোদ্ভব, শ্বেতসারধর্ম্মী।

ăm′-ŷ-loid (-lōyd), *adj* & *n.* Starchy ; শ্বেতসারময়। ***Noun*** Starchy food ; শ্বেতসারপ্রধান খাদ্য।

ăn, *adj.* See A.

ăn′-â, *adv.* (*Med. presc.*) An equal quantity of each (often written āā) ; as, *Pulv. Rhei* et *Zingib.* ℥ij = Powder of rhuburb a ginger of each two drachms.) (ঔষধ ব্যবস্থাপত্রে) সমপরিমাণে।

n'-ă, n. (Pl. ANAS) 1. A collection of a person's memorable sayings ; উক্তি-সংগ্রহ। 2. (Collect. pl.) Anecdotes or literary gossips about a person ; কোন ব্যক্তির সম্পর্কে সাহিত্যিক গল্পগুজব বা উপাখ্যানাবলী।

in-ă-băp'-tist, *n.* 1. One who baptises over again ; যে ব্যক্তি দ্বিতীয়বার জল-সংস্কার গ্রহণ করে। 2. Name of a sect which arose in Germany in 1521 ; ১৫২১ খৃঃ অব্দে জর্ম্মণিদেশে প্রতিষ্ঠিত সম্প্রদায়বিশেষ। **—tism,** *n.* 1. A second baptism ; (খৃষ্টীয়-ধর্ম্মে) পুনর্ব্বার জল-সংস্কার ; পুনর্মজ্জন। 2. The doctrine of the anabaptists ; যৌবনমজ্জনবাদ। **—tis-tic, tis-ti-cal,** *adjs.*

'-ă-băs, *n.* The climbing fish ('nabas scandenes) ; কই মাছ (প্ত)।

ăb'-ă-sis, *n.* A military advance, especially that of the expedition of Cyrus the younger, against his brother Artaxerxes, king of Persia, described by Xenophon, in his famous work "The ANABASIS" ; সামরিক অভিযান, বিশেষতঃ প্রাচীন গ্রীক্ সাহিত্যিক জেনোফোনের সুবিখ্যাত "Anabasis" নামক গ্রন্থে বর্ণিত, পারস্যরাজ Xerxesএর বিরুদ্ধে তদীয় ভ্রাতা সাইরাসের অভিযান।

'n-ăb'-ŏ-lism, *n.* The building-up process in the protoplasm of the living organism, as opposed to *Katabolism,* or the breaking-down process ; জীবদেহস্থিত পদার্থের সংগঠন-ক্রিয়া, অর্থাৎ যে ক্রিয়াদ্বারা অনুলোমভাবে ভুক্তদ্রব্য জৈব-পদার্থে পরিণত হয়, অনুলোম-পরিণাম (সাঃ পঃ)।

Anacardium occidentale—Cashew-nut ; হিজ্‌লী বাদাম (খোরী), কাজু বাদাম (ঐ)।

ăch'-rŏ-nĭsm, *n.* The erroneous reference of an event, custom, etc. to a wrong date ; an error in the computation of time ; a thing out of harmony with the present ; [The term is used when anything is dated too early.] কোন আচার পদ্ধতি বা ঐতিহাসিক ঘটনা ভ্রমপ্রযুক্ত অযথার্থ সময়ে স্থাপন বা উল্লেখ ; আকালিক স্থাপনা, অকালানুযায়িতা, কালাতিক্রম-দোষ ; কাল-বিপর্য্যয়, কালগণনাবিপর্য্যয়, কালসংখ্যাবিপর্য্যয়। [কোন চিত্রকর কুরুক্ষেত্রের চিত্রে মার্টিনি হেনরী বন্দুক সন্নিবেশিত করিলে *Anachronism* বা 'আকালিক স্থাপনা' হইবে।] **—a-chron'-ic, —nis'-tic,** *adjs.*

ăn-ă-clăs'-tic, *adj.* 1. (*Optics*) Pertaining to, or produced by, the refraction of light ; as, *anaclastic* curves ; (দৃষ্টি-বিজ্ঞান) (আলোক) তির্য্যগ্‌গমনসঞ্জাত, তির্য্যগ্‌গমন-সংক্রান্ত। 2. Springing back ; as, *anaclastic* glasses ; তির্য্যগ্‌গমনশীল।

ăn-ă-clăs'-tics, *n.* That part of optics which treats of the refraction of light ; আলোক-বিজ্ঞানের যে শাখায় তির্য্যগ্‌-গামী রশ্মি-সম্বন্ধে আলোচিত হয়, রশ্মি-শাস্ত্র (হিঃ কোঃ)।

ăn-ă-cŏn'-dă, *n.* 1. A large snake found in Ceylon ; সিংহলদ্বীপের বৃহৎ সর্প। 2. A large South American Boa ; দক্ষিণ আমেরিকাদেশীয় অজগর সর্পবিশেষ। 3. Any large snake that crushes its prey ; অজগরজাতীয় বৃহৎ সর্প বিশেষ।

A-năc-rē-ŏn'-tic (ă-), *adj.* & *n.* 1. In the manner or metre of the Greek poet Anacreon's lyrics ; গ্রীস-দেশীয় প্রাচীন কবি Anacreonএর গীতি-কবিতার পদ্ধতি বা ছন্দানুকরণে রচিত। 2. Convivial ; amatory ; উৎসবসম্বন্ধীয়; শৃঙ্গাররসপ্রধান। ***Noun.*** 1. A litttle poem in praise of love and wine ; সুরা ও প্রেম-বিষয়ক ক্ষুদ্র কবিতা। 2. A poem after the manner of Anacreon ; কবি Anacreonএর কবিতার অনুরূপ কবিতা, শৃঙ্গার-রসপূর্ণ কবিতা।

ăn'-ă-dĕm, *n.* A garland, fillet or wreath ; a chaplet or crown of flowers ; মালা, মালিকা, শিরোবন্ধ ; শিরোবেষ্টন-মাল্য, গর্ভক, পুষ্প-কিরীট, কুসুম-মুকুট।

ăn-ăd'-rŏ-mous (-mŭs), *adj.* Ascending rivers (from the sea) to spawn (said of fishes, as the salmon, shad) ; (ইলিষ প্রভৃতি মৎস্য-সম্বন্ধে) ডিম্ব-মোচনার্থ নদীপ্রবাহ-প্রতিকূলগামী।

ă-næ'-mi-ă (-nē-), *n.* (*Med.*) Lack of blood ; unhealthy paleness ; (ভৈষজ্য-শাস্ত্র) রক্তাভাব, রক্তাল্পতা ; মুখপাণ্ডুতা। **—mic,** *adj.* Bloodless ; রক্তশূন্য।

ăn-æs-thĕ'-si-ă(-ēs-),*n.* Insensibility ; স্পর্শহানি। **—æs'-the-tise,** *v. t.* To render insensible to the feeling of pain (*lit.* & *fig.*) ; (শব্দানুযায়ী এবং লক্ষণায়) স্তম্ভক-ঔষধ প্রয়োগে বেদনাবোধ লোপ করা, অনুভব-শক্তি-হীন করা। **—thet'-ic,** *adj.* & *n.* Deadening or destroying sensibility; স্পর্শহর, বেদনারোধক। (*Noun*) A substance producing insensibility to pain, as chloroform ; স্তম্ভনচূর্ণ (বাসঃ প্রঃ), যোগচূর্ণ (দশঃ প্রঃ)। **—thet-i-za'-tion,** *n.*

ăn-ă-gĕn'-ĕ-sis, *n.* (*Physiol.*) A reproduction or regeneration of tissue ; (শারীর-বিজ্ঞান) বিধানতন্তু-সমূহের পুনরুৎপাদন বা পুনরুজ্জীবন।

ăn'-ă-glÿph, *n.* (*Sculp.*) An ornament in low relief and embossed in precious stone or metal ; (ভাস্কর-বিদ্যা) বহুমূল্য ধাতু বা প্রস্তরোপরি অল্প উদ্গাতভাবে ক্ষোদিত ভূষা বা অলঙ্কার। **—glyph'-ic,** *adj.* Pertaining to the art of embossing in relief ; বহুমূল্য প্রস্তরোপরি অল্পোদ্গাত অলঙ্কার-ক্ষোদনবিষয়ক।

ăn-ăg-nŏr'-i-sis, *n.* Denouement in a drama ; নাটকীয় আখ্যানের রহস্যোদ্ঘাটন, নিষ্ঠা, (মঃ উঃ), নির্বহণ (দশরূঃ), কার্য্য (ঐ)।

ăn-ă-gŏ'-gē, *n.* 1. A spiritual or

allegorical interpretation (of words) ; আধ্যাত্মিক ব্যাখ্যা। **2.** An elevation of mind to things celestial ; ভাবসমাধি। **–gŏg′-i-cal,** *adj.* **–gŏg′-i-cal-ly,** *adv.*

ăn′-ă-grăm, *n.* [*Lit.* the letters of a word read backwards] The transposition of the letters of a word or phrase ; কোন শব্দের অক্ষর-সকলের বিভিন্ন প্রকার সমাবেশদ্বারা নূতনশব্দ গঠন, অক্ষর-বিপর্য্যয়। [যেমন, "Mary" হইতে "Army", "Evil" হইতে "Live"] **–gram′-ma-tism, –gram′-ma-tist,** *ns.* **–gram′-ma-tize,** *v. t.* To form into an anagram ; একই শব্দের অক্ষরদ্বারা বিভিন্ন শব্দ গঠন করা। **–mat′-ic, –mat′-i-cal,** *adjs.* **–mat′-i-cal-ly,** *adv.*

ā′-năl, *adj.* Pertaining to, or situated, near the anus ; as, the *anal* fin in fishes ; গুহ্যদ্বার-সম্বন্ধীয়, পায়ু-সন্নিহিত।

ăn′-ă-lĕcts, ăn-ă-lĕc′-tă, *n. pl.* A collection of literary fragments ; literary gleanings ; (usually as a title) ; ভিন্ন ভিন্ন গ্রন্থ হইতে সঙ্কলিত অংশ সমূহ ; সাহিত্য-সংগ্রহ, রচনা-সংগ্রহ।

ăn-ă-lĕp′-tic, *adj.* & *n.* Restorative ; strengthening ; বৃংহণ, তেজোদায়ক ; বলদায়ক। ***Noun.*** A restorative medicine ; বৃংহণ ঔষধ, তেজোবৰ্দ্ধক বা বলদায়ক ঔষধ।

ăn′-ă-logue (-lŏg), *n.* An analogous or parallel word or thing ; সদৃশ বা অনুরূপ শব্দ, সদৃশ বস্তু। [যেমন Sanskrit "নাভি" is an *analogue* to the English word "*Naval*".] (*Rhet.*) *Analogue* = (অলঙ্কার-শাস্ত্র) যমকালঙ্কার।

ă-năl′-ŏ-ġy, *n.* **1.** A resemblance of relations ; an agreement or likeness between things in some circumstances or effects, when the things are otherwise entirely different ; as, *analogy* between things : one thing has an *analogy to* or *with* another ; সম্বন্ধগত সাদৃশ্য, অনুধৰ্ম্মতা ; দুই বা ততোধিক বস্তুর মধ্যে উপমানগত ঐক্য, সাদৃশ্য বা অনুরূপত্ব। [As, learning *enlightens* the mind ; অর্থাৎ চক্ষু যে প্রকার আলোকের সাহায্যে বস্তুনিচয় দর্শন করিতে পারে, মনও তদ্রূপ জ্ঞানের সাহায্যে অজ্ঞাত বিষয় সকল বুঝিতে সক্ষম হয়। এখানে আলোকের সহিত চক্ষুর যে সম্বন্ধ, জ্ঞানের সহিত মনেরও সেই সম্বন্ধ ; অর্থাৎ "আলোক" ও "জ্ঞানের" সম্বন্ধগত সাদৃশ্য বা analogy সূচনা করা হইতেছে।] **2.** (*Log.*) A process of reasoning from parallel cases ; (তর্ক-বিজ্ঞান) উপমান (হিঃ কোঃ), অনুধৰ্ম্মতা (ঐ), সাদৃশ্য (ঐ)। **3.** (*Math.*) Proportion or similarity of ratios ; (গণিত-শাস্ত্র) অনুপাত, সাজাত্য (হিঃ কোঃ)। **4.** (*Biol.*) A resemblance of form or function, between organs or parts, essentially different ; (জীব-বিজ্ঞান) মূলতঃ বিসদৃশ শারীর-যন্ত্র বা দেহাংশ-সমূহের মধ্যে বৃত্তি বা আকারগত সম্বন্ধ বা অনুরূপতা, বৃত্তিসাম্য (সাঃ পঃ)। **5.** (*Gram.*) Conformity (of words) to the spirit, structure or general rules of a language ; (ব্যাকরণ) ভাষার সাধারণ শব্দরূপ-পদ্ধতি বা গঠন-প্রণালীর সহিত (নূতন) শব্দের গঠন বা বিভক্তিসংযোগসাদৃশ্য, ব্যুৎপত্তি বা বিভক্তিগত সাদৃশ্য। **–gist,** *n.* **1.** One occupied with analogies ; শব্দের সম্বন্ধগতসাদৃশ্য বিষয়ে অনুসন্ধানরত ব্যক্তি। **2.** One of a class of philosophers who saw in words images of the thing they expressed ; যে সকল দার্শনিক কোন শব্দের ভিতর উক্ত শব্দের বাচ্য পদার্থের রূপদর্শন করিতেন—তাহাদের অন্যতম, যে দার্শনিক নামের মধ্যে রূপের আভাস দর্শন করিতেন, সাদৃশ্যবাদী। **–gize,** *v. t.* & *i.* **1.** To represent by analogy ; দৃষ্টান্তদ্বারা সাদৃশ্য প্রদর্শন করা। **2.** To show to be analogous ; (দুই বস্তুর) সাদৃশ্য প্রমাণ করা, সাদৃশ্য প্রদর্শন করা। **3.** To employ analogy ; উপমান যুক্তি প্রয়োগ করা। (*Verb i.*) To be in harmony (*with*) ; মিল বা ঐক্য হওয়া, সদৃশ হওয়া। **–gous,** *adj.* Similar ; parallel ; (*to*) ; সদৃশ, অনুরূপ, অনুধৰ্ম্মা (হিঃ কোঃ) ; সমবৃত্ত (সাঃ পঃ), সমফলক। **–gous-ly. –lŏg′-ic,** *adj.* Of, or pertaining to, analogy ; সাদৃশ্যগত। **–lŏg′-i-cal,** *adj.* According to, or expressing, an analogy ; as, we have words which are proper and not *analogical* ; সাদৃশ্যানুযায়ী ; সাদৃশ্য বা সমতাবাচক। **–lŏg′-i-cal-ly,** *adv.*

ăn′-ă-lȳse, –lȳze, *v. t.* **1.** To examine minutely the constitution of ; (বস্তুর) গঠন-প্রণালী সূক্ষ্মরূপে পরীক্ষা করা। **2.** (*Chem.*) To ascertain the elements of a compound ; to resolve a compound into its elements ; (রসায়ন-শাস্ত্র) কোন যৌগিক-পদার্থের উপাদানভূত পদার্থনিচয় নির্ণয় করা ; বিশ্লেষণ করা। **3.** To find, show, the essence of (treatise etc.) ; পুস্তকাদির সার-সংগ্রহ করা, সারমর্ম্ম প্রকটন করা। **4.** (*Gram.*) To resolve a sentence into its grammatical elements ; (ব্যাকরণ) বাক্য-বিশ্লেষণ করা। **–ly-ser, –ly-zer,** *ns.* One who or that which analyses ; বিশ্লেষক। **–lyz′-a-ble,** *adj.* Capable of being analysed ; বিশ্লেষণীয়।

ă-năl′-ȳ-sis, (*pl.* **–sēs**) *n.* **1.** The resolution or separation of a thing (physical, mental or mere conceptional) into its constituent elements or component parts ; বিশ্লেষণ (সাঃ পঃ), বিভাজন, অনুক্রম-চর্চ্চা, ব্যাস-ক্রিয়া (সাঃ পঃ)। [*Opp.* to *synthesis* = সংযোজন, সংশ্লেষণ।] **2.** (*Log.*) The tracing of things to their sources and resolving of knowledge into its original principles ; (তর্ক-বিজ্ঞান) তত্ত্ব-বিভাগ (হিঃ কোঃ), অবয়ব-বিচার (ঐ)। **3.** A brief methodical illustration of the principle of a science ; a brief abstract of a subject ; a table of the principal heads of a continued discourse ; a synopsis ; কোন বিজ্ঞানের মূল-তত্ত্বের রীতি- বা প্রণালীবদ্ধ সার-সংক্ষেপ, সারার্থ-প্রকাশ ; কোন বিষয়ের সার-সংগ্রহ ; কোন ক্রমিক সন্দর্ভের প্রধান প্রধান আলোচ্য বিষয় ; সংক্ষিপ্ত-সার। **4.** (*Gram.*) The resolution of a sentence into its grammatical components ; (ব্যাকরণ) কোন বাক্যের মূল অংশসকল পৃথকীকরণ, বাক্য-বিশ্লেষণ। **5.** (*Chem.*) The process of decomposing a compound with a view to determining either (*a*) what elements it contains (*qualitative analysis*), or (*b*) how much of each element is present (*quantitive analysis*) ; (রসায়ন-শাস্ত্র) উপাদানভূত মৌলিক পদার্থনিচয় নির্ণয়ার্থ যৌগিক পদার্থের বিশ্লেষণ (জাতি- বা গুণ-বিশ্লেষণ), অথবা উপাদানভূত মৌলিক পদার্থের পরিমাণ-নির্ণয়ার্থ বিশ্লেষণ (পরিমাণ-বিশ্লেষণ)।

ăn′-ă-lyst, *n.* One skilled in (usually chemical) analysis ; বিশ্লেষণ-পটু, (সাধারণতঃ) রাসায়নিক বিশ্লেষণ-নিপুণ।

ăn-ă-lŷt′-ĭc, —ĭ-căl, *adjs.* **1.** Pertaining to analysis ; বৈশ্লেষণিক। **2.** Employing analytical method ; বিশ্লেষণ-প্রণালী-[illegible]জক। **3.** (*Gram.*) Using separate words instead of inflexions ; বিভক্তিহীনশব্দপ্রয়োগকারী। **—al-ly,** *adv.* **—ics,** *n. pl.* The science of analysis ; বিশ্লেষণতত্ত্ব। **Analytic Geometry, Analytical Geometry**—বীজ-জ্যামিতি (হিং কোঃ)।

Anamirta cocculus—কাকমারী (বেলঃ)।

ăn-ăm-nē′-sĭs, *n.* Recollection, especially of previous existence ; [illegible]ত, পূর্ব্বজন্মের স্মৃতি, জাতিস্মরতা। **—nes-tic,** *adj.*

ăn-ă-mŏr′-phō-sĭs, —sy, *n.* **1.** (*Perspective*) A distorted drawing (or representation of an image) on a plane or curved surface, which appears regular and in proportion from one point of view, and deformed from another ; a deformation of an image ; (পরিপ্রেক্ষিত) যে সমতল অথবা বক্রীভূত ফলকের উপর অঙ্কিত চিত্র এক দিক হইতে দৃষ্ট হইলে বিকৃত ও বিকটাকার—কিন্তু স্থানান্তর হইতে দৃষ্ট হইলে সৌষ্ঠব-সম্পন্ন ও যথানুপাত বলিয়া প্রতিভাত হয়, বিকৃত ছায়া; প্রতিকৃতির বিকৃতি। **2.** (*Bot.*) An abnormal transformation ; (উদ্ভিদ্-বিদ্যা) বিরূপতা-প্রাপ্তি।

ă-nā′-năs, —nă, *n.* The pine-apple (*Ananas sativus*) ; আনারস।

ăn-ăn′-drous (-drŭs), *adj.* (*Bot.*) Without stamens ; (উদ্ভিদ্-বিদ্যা) পুংকেশরবিহীন, অপুংকেশর।

ăn′-ă-pæst (-pĕst), *n.* (*Prosody*) A foot consisting of two short syllables, followed by one long ; (ছন্দঃশাস্ত্র) যে কবিতার প্রতিপদে প্রথম দুইটী শব্দাংশ লঘু ও তৃতীয়টী গুরু থাকে, সগণ। **—pæs′-tic,** *adj.*

ă-năph′-ō-râ, *n.* (*Rhet.*) The repetition of the same word or phrase in several successive clauses ; "Where is the wise ? where is the scribe ? Where is the disputer of this world." (অলঙ্কার-শাস্ত্র) পুনরাবৃত্তি-অলঙ্কার।

ăn′-ârch, *n.* (*Poet.*) The author of anarchy ; the leader of a revolt ; (কবিতায়) রাজ্যসংক্ষোভক, রাজনীতিক বিপ্লবপন্থী ; বিদ্রোহের নায়ক।

ăn′-ârch-ŷ, *n.* Absence of government ; a state of society when there is no law or supreme power ; hence, disorder ; confusion ; অরাজকতা ; রাজ্যবিপ্লব, প্রজা-বিপ্লব ; বিশৃঙ্খলা ; গোলমাল। **—ism,** *n.* The principles or practice of anarchists ; the theory that all government is an evil ; বিপ্লববাদ ; অরাজকতাবাদ। **—ist,** *n* One who admits of no ruling power ; one who upsets settled order ; a nihilist ; বিপ্লবপন্থী, বিপ্লববাদী ; রাষ্ট্র-বিপ্লবকারী, বিপ্লবকারী ; রাজ্য-বিপ্লবকারী।

ă-năr′-chĭc, —chĭ-căl, *adj.* Pertaining to anarchy ; lawless ; বিপ্লব-ঘটিত ; উচ্ছৃঙ্খল।

ăn-âr′-throus (-thrŭs), *n.* **1.** (*Zool.*) Without joints ; (জন্তুতত্ত্ব) সন্ধিহীন। **2.** (*Gr. Gram.*) Used without the article ; (গ্রীক-ব্যাকরণ) বাক্যার্থ-নির্ণায়ক অব্যয়শব্দবিহীন।

ăn-ă-sâr′-că, *n.* A dropsical affection ; জলোত্তরণ (সাঃ পঃ), সর্ব্বাঙ্গী-শোথ (হঃ চঃ)। **—cous,** *adj.*

ăn-ă-stăt′-ĭc, *adj.* In relief ; উদ্গাত-ভাবে। **Anastatic printing**—A method of printing from reliefs on zinc-plates ; খোদিত অক্ষর-মালা প্রভৃতির প্রতিলিপি দস্তা-ফলকে উঠাইয়া মুদ্রণের প্রণালীবিশেষ।

ă-năs-tō-mō′-sĭs, *n.* (*Anat.* & *Bot.*) The inosculation of vessels, or the opening of one vessel into another ; (শারীর সংস্থান-বিদ্যা এবং জীব-বিজ্ঞান) এক রক্তবহানাড়ীর অন্য নাড়ীতে প্রবেশ। **—năs′-tō-mōse** *v. t.*

ă-năth′-ē-mă, *n.* **1.** Anything accursed or consigned to damnation ; an object of curse ; অভিশাপের পাত্র ; অভিশপ্ত বস্তু। **2.** Curse of God ; ঈশ্বরের অভিশাপ। **3.** A solemn ecclesiastical curse excommunicating a person or denouncing a doctrine or practice ; কোন ব্যক্তিকে ধর্ম্মসমাজ হইতে বহিষ্করণ, কোন মতবাদ বা রীতির অনিষ্টতা জনসাধারণের নিকট ঘোষণা-কালে ধর্ম্মযাজকগণ কর্তৃক অভিশাপ প্রদান। **4.** A curse or imprecation ; denouncement of evil ; শাপ, অভিশাপ, অভিসম্পাত ; আক্রোশন। **—tize,** *v. t.* & *i.* To pronounce an anathema against ; to curse ; অভিশাপ বাক্য উচ্চারণ করা ; অভি-সম্পাত করা।

ă-năt′-ō-cĭsm, n. Compound interest ; চক্র-বৃদ্ধি।

ăn-ă-tŏm′-ic, —i-căl, *adj.* Belonging to or connected with the study or practice of anatomy or dissection ; শারীরসংস্থানবিদ্যাসম্পৃক্ত, ব্যবচ্ছেদ বিষয়ক। **—i-cal-ly,** *adv.*

ă-năt′-ō-mȳ, *n.* **1.** The art of artificially separating the different parts of an organized body to discover their position, structure, etc. ; dissection ; শরীর-ব্যবচ্ছেদ; শবব্যবচ্ছেদ। **2.** The science of bodily structure ; শারীর সংস্থান-বিদ্যা, অঙ্গবিনিশ্চয় বিদ্যা। **3.** A treatise on this science ; শারীরসংস্থানবিদ্যা বিষয়ক গ্রন্থ। **4.** Arrangement of the parts of the body of animals or plants ; as, to investigate the *anatomy* of insects ; উদ্ভিদ্ কিম্বা জীবদেহের বিভিন্নঅংশসমূহের বিন্যাস। **5.** Detailed examination ; analysis ; as, an *anatomy* of a poem, discourse, etc.; সূক্ষ্ম-পরীক্ষা ; বিশ্লেষণ। **6.** A skeleton with the skin left ; a mummy ; অস্থি-পঞ্জর, কঙ্কাল ; (সুগন্ধি ভেষজ প্রভৃতি দ্বারা রক্ষিত) শবদেহ, শুষ্কশব। **7.** A living being reduced to skin and bone ; an emaciated creature ; অস্থিচর্ম্মসারজীব; কঙ্কালসার জীব। **—mist,** *n.* **1.** One who practises, or is skilled, in the art of dissecting bodies (esp. human bodies) ; শারীর-সংস্থান-বিদ্যা-বিশারদ, শরীরব্যবচ্ছেদকারী। **2.** (*Fig.*) An analyser ; as, an *anatomist* of human nature ; (লক্ষণায়) বিশ্লেষক। **—mize,** *v. t.* **1.** To dissect animal or plant ; কোন জন্তু বা উদ্ভিদের অঙ্গব্যবচ্ছেদ করা। **2.** (*Fig.*) To analyse ; as, they have split and *anatomized* the doctrine of free government ; (লক্ষণায়) বিভাজন করা, বিশ্লেষণ করা।

ăn′-bŭr-ȳ, am′-bŭr-ȳ *n.* A soft tumour on horses or oxen ; অশ্ববৃষাদির স্ফোটক।

ăn′-cĕs-tor (-têr), (Fem. ANCESTRESS.) *n.* A progenitor ; a forefather ; পূর্ব্বপুরুষ ; পিতৃপুরুষ। **—ces′-tral,** *adj.* Of, belonging to or inherited from, ancestors ; as, *ancestral* property ; পিতৃ-পৈতামহিক, পৈত্রিক, পূর্ব্বপুরুষগণ হইতে উত্তরাধিকারসূত্রে প্রাপ্ত। **—try,** *n.* Ancestral lineage ; line or body of ancestors or progenitors ; hence, distinguished or ancient descent ; বংশাবলী ; পিতৃ-পিতামহগণ, পুরুষ-পরম্পরা ; আভিজাত্য, কৌলিন্য।

ăn′-c͟hŏr, *n.* **1.** An (iron) implement for holding a ship, etc. at rest in the water ; নঙ্গর, লঙ্গর। **2.** (*Fig.*) That which gives the feeling of stability or security ; a source of confidence ; "Cast all your cares on God, that *anchor* holds ;" (লক্ষণায়) আশ্রয়, আশ্রয়-স্থল, শরণ ; বিশ্বাসের স্থল। **Anchor-ground**—Ground suitable for anchoring ; নঙ্গর ফেলিবার উপযোগী স্থান। **Anchor-hold**—The hold or fastness of an anchor ; security ; নঙ্গর-বন্ধ ; নির্বিঘ্নতা। **Anchor-plate** — A heavy piece of timber or metal serving as a point of support for the cables of suspension-bridge, etc. ; দোদুল্যমান সেতু-প্রভৃতির শৃঙ্খলসমূহের অবলম্বন-স্বরূপ গুরুভার কাষ্ঠ বা ধাতুখণ্ড। **Anchor-watch**

Anchor.

—The watch set while the ship lies at anchor ; নঙ্গর-বন্ধ জাহাজের প্রহরি-বর্গ। **At anchor**—নঙ্গর-বন্ধ। **To be, lie or ride at anchor**—To remain steady in the water without drifting ; নঙ্গর ফেলিয়া থাকা। **To cast anchor**—To drop an anchor into water to keep a sh[ip] at rest ; জাহাজ ভিড়াইবার উদ্দে[শ্যে] জলে নঙ্গর ফেলা। **To take u[p] anchor**—নঙ্গর তোলা। **To weig[h] anchor**—To take up the ancho[r] so as to sail away ; জাহাজ ছাড়িবা[র] উদ্দেশ্যে নঙ্গর তোলা।

ăn′-c͟hŏr, *v. t.* & *i.* **1.** To secure a ship by an anchor ; জাহাজ নঙ্গরবদ্ধ করা, নঙ্গর ফেলিয়া দৃঢ়সংবদ্ধ করা। **2.** (*Fig.*) To fix firmly ; as, let us *anchor* our hopes upon his goodness ; (লক্ষণায়) সংবদ্ধ করা। ***Verb i.*** **1.** To cast anchor ; to come to anchor ; নঙ্গর ফেলা ; নঙ্গরবদ্ধ হওয়া। **2.** (*Fig.*) To fix one's attention, thought, &c. ; "Posthumous *anchors* upon Imogen ;" (লক্ষণায়) মনঃসংযোগ করা। **—a-ble,** *adj.* F[i]t for anchorage ; নঙ্গর ফেলিবার উপযোগী। **—age,** *n.* **1.** The act of anchoring or the state of lying at anchor ; নঙ্গর-ফেলন, জাহাজাদির নঙ্গরবদ্ধাবস্থা। **2.** A place suitable for anchoring, or where ships anchor ; a hold for an anchor ; নঙ্গরের উপযোগী স্থান ; নঙ্গর-বন্ধন-স্থান, নঙ্গর-স্থান। **3.** (*Fig.*) Something to depend upon ; as, he was the *anchorage* of my hopes ; (লক্ষণায়) নির্ভর বা আশ্রয়ের স্থল, আশ্রয়-নিকেতন।

ăn′-c͟hō-rĕss, —crĕss, *n.* A female anchoret ; তপস্বিনী, সন্ন্যাসিনী।

ăn′-c͟hō-rĕt, —rīte, *n.* **1.** A hermit ; a recluse ; তপস্বী, তাপস; যতি, সন্ন্যাসী, উদাসীন (কপালঃ), আরণ্যক। **2.** A person of secluded habits ; নির্জ্জ[নতাপ্রিয়] ... নতাপ্রিয় ব্যক্তি। **—ret′-ic, —ret′-i-cal,** *adjs.*

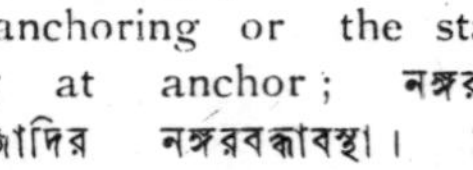

Anchovy.

ăn-chō′-vȳ, *n.* A small fish of [the] herring family ; সুস্বাদু ক্ষুদ্র (সামু[দ্রিক]) মৎস্য বিশেষ। **Anchovy-pear**

st Indian fruit eaten like the go ; পশ্চিমভারতীয় দ্বীপপুঞ্জজাত বিশেষ।

hy-lö'-sis, —ky̆-lö'-sis, *n.* The immovable state of a nt : সন্ধির অনম্যতা বা স্তব্ধতা। The union of two or more eparate bones to form a single bone ; দুই বা ততোধিক পৃথক্ পৃথক্ অস্থির একত্রসংযোগ বা সম্মিলন। **an'-hy-lose, an'-ky-lose,** *v.t.* & *i.*

ncien regima, (*F.*), *n.* The ime before the French revolution ; ফরাসী-বিপ্লবের পূর্ব্ববর্ত্তী কাল।

n'-cient (-shěnt), *adj.* & *n.* . Old ; belonging to times long ast ; especially applied to the mes before the fall of the Roman Empire ; (opposed to *modern*) ; as, *ncient* days ; প্রাচীন ; পুরা, পুরাকালীন, পূর্ব্বকালীন ; বিশেষতঃ রোম-সাম্রাজ্যধ্বংসের পূর্ব্ববর্ত্তী সময়সম্পর্কে প্রযুক্ত। 2. Having existed, lived, ong ; of great age ; as, an *ancient* forest : *ancient* city ; পুরাতন, চিরন্তন ; প্রবৃদ্ধ। ***Noun.*** 1. An aged living being, esp. a venerable man or woman ; an ancestor ; প্রাচীন ব্যক্তি, বিশেষতঃ প্রাচীন পুরুষ বা বর্ষীয়সী স্ত্রী ; পূর্ব্বপুরুষ। 2. (*Pl.*) The civilized peoples of antiquity, esp. the classical nations ; (commonly with *the*) ; (opp. to the *moderns*) ; also the ancient authors of Greece and Rome ; hence, a classic ; প্রাচীনকালের সুসভ্য জাতিসমূহ, বিশেষতঃ প্রাচীন গ্রীক ও রোমান প্রভৃতি জাতি ; গ্রীস ও রোমের প্রাচীন গ্রন্থকারগণ ; উচ্চশ্রেণীর গ্রন্থ বা গ্রন্থকার। **—ly,** *adv.* In ancient times ; of yore ; পুরাকালে ; প্রাচীন সময়ে। **—ness,** *n.* **—ry,** *n.* 1. Antiquity ; old-fashioned style ; প্রাচীনত্ব ; সেকেলে রীতি। 2. Ancient lineage ; dignity of birth ; প্রাচীন বংশাবলী ; বংশমর্য্যাদা, কৌলিন্য। **The Ancient of Days**—The Almighty (from His being existent from eternity) ; পুরাণ পুরুষ, সর্ব্বশক্তিমান্ পরমেশ্বর।

ăn'-cil-lă-ry, *adj.* (*Lit.* Pertaining to a maid servant) Subservient ; subordinate ; (*to*) ; (পরিচারিকার মত) অনুগত ; অধীন।

ăn'-cŏn, *n.* (*Physiol.*) **1.** Elbow ; (শারীর-বিজ্ঞান) কফোণি, খুঁচি। **2.** (*Arch.*) The quoin of a wall or rafter ; (স্থপতি-বিদ্যা) প্রাচীর বা বর্গার বহিষ্কোণ।

and, *conj.* **1.** A simple particle expressing the relation of connection ; এবং, ও, আরও। **2.** Expressing continuous repetition ; as, they walked two *and* two (= by twos) ; পৌনঃপুন্য-সূচক। **3.** Expressing a difference of quality between things of the same class ; as, there are women *and* women (= of different sorts) ; একশ্রেণী-ভুক্ত বস্তুনিচয়ের মধ্যে গুণবৈষম্য-সূচক। **4.** Expressing a consequence or sequel ; as, I said go, *and* he went ; পরিণাম বা পৌর্ব্বাপর্য্যসূচক। **And also**—And in addition ; তথা। **And so forth**—And others ; and the rest ; and similar things ; [the abbreviation *etc.* (*et cetera*) or &c. is usually read *and so forth*] ইত্যাদি ; প্রভৃতি ; প্রমুখ।

and ante, (*It.*) *adv.* & *n.* (*Mus.*) Moderately slow ; (সঙ্গীত-শাস্ত্র) মৃদুভাবে। ***Noun.*** Movement in moderately slow time ; খুব জলদও নয়, খুব ঢিমেও নয়—এরূপভাব।

ănd'-ir-ŏn, *n.* A utensil for supporting fire-wood when burning in a fire-place ; অগ্নি-কুণ্ডে দহ্যমান কাষ্ঠখণ্ড-ধারণার্থ যন্ত্র-বিশেষ।

ăn-drœ'-ci-ŭm (-drē-), *n.* The stamens taken collectively ; পুং-কেশর-শ্রেণী, পুংনিবাস (সাঃ পঃ)।

Andrographis paniculata—কালমেঘ (বেলঃ)।

ăn-drŏg'-y̆-nous (-nŭs), *adj.* **1.** Uniting both sexes in one ; being male and female ; hermaphrodite ; দ্বিলিঙ্গক ; স্ত্রী পুং উভয়-চিহ্নবিশিষ্ট ; অর্দ্ধনারীপুরুষ। **2.** (*Bot.*) With stamens and pistils in the same flower or on the same plant ; (উদ্ভিদ্-বিদ্যা) একই পুষ্প বা বৃক্ষমধ্যে পুংকেশর এবং গর্ভকেশরবিশিষ্ট, স্ত্রীপুংসক (সাঃ পঃ)। **—ny,** *n.*

ăn'-droid (-droyd), **—droi-dēs** (-droy-), *n.* An automaton resembling a human being ; as, he constructed an *androides* capable of playing at chess ; স্বয়ংচল মানবমূর্ত্তি, যন্ত্রাদিদ্বারা চালিত মানব-মূর্ত্তি, যন্ত্রনর।

An-drŏm'-ĕd-â (ăn-), *n.* (*Astron.*) A northern constellation supposed to represent the figure of a woman chained ; (জ্যোতির্বিজ্ঞান) উত্তর-গোলার্দ্ধস্থিত তারাপ্রকোষ্ঠ বিশেষ—এই নক্ষত্রপুঞ্জ শৃঙ্খলিতা নারীমূর্ত্তিরূপে অঙ্কিত হইয়া থাকে। **Andromedæ**—*a*—উত্তরভাদ্রপদ (হিঃ কোঃ)।

ăn-drŏph'-ă-gi, *n.* See ANTHROPOPHAGI.

Andropogon muricatus—বেণা ঘাস (বেলঃ)। [ইহার মূলকে খস্‌খস্ কহে।]

Andropogon schœnanthus—Lemon-grass or sweet-rush ; গন্ধ-বেণা (বেলঃ)।

Andropogon sorghum—জুয়ার।

ăn'-ĕc-dōte, *n.* **1.** A short narrative of a particular or detached incident of an interesting nature ; গল্প, আখ্যান, আখ্যায়িকা, উপাখ্যান। **2.** (*Pl.*) Unpublished narrative or details of history ; অপ্রকাশিত ঐতিহাসিক বিবরণ। **3.** Anecdotes collectively ; আখ্যানাবলী, আখ্যান-মঞ্জরী। **4.** (Humorously) Garrulous old age ; (কৌতুকচ্ছলে) বাচালতা বা বাবদূকতাপূর্ণ বৃদ্ধাবস্থা। **—dot-age,** *n.* **—dot-al, —dot'-i-cal,** *adjs.* **—dot-ist,** *n.* A relater of anecdotes ; আখ্যায়িকা-কথক, গল্প-কথক।

ă-nēle′ (rare), *v. t.* **1.** To anoint ; অনুলিপ্ত করা। **2.** To give extreme unction to ; (খৃষ্টীয় সমাজের প্রথানুসারে) অন্তিমসময়ে তৈল-মর্দ্দন করা।

ă-nĕm′-ō-grăph, *n.* An instrument for recording on paper the direction and force of wind ; যে যন্ত্রের সাহায্যে কাগজের উপর বায়ুর বল এবং দিক্ লিখিত হয়। **—graph′-ic,** *adj.*

ăn-ē-mŏg′-ră-phȳ, *n.* A description of the wind ; বায়ু-বিবরণ।

ăn-ē-mŏm′-ē-têr, *n.* An instrument for measuring the force of the wind ; অনিলবলমান যন্ত্র। **—try,** *n.*

ă-nĕm′-ō-nē, *n.* (*Bot.*) A genus of plants, especially wind-flower ;

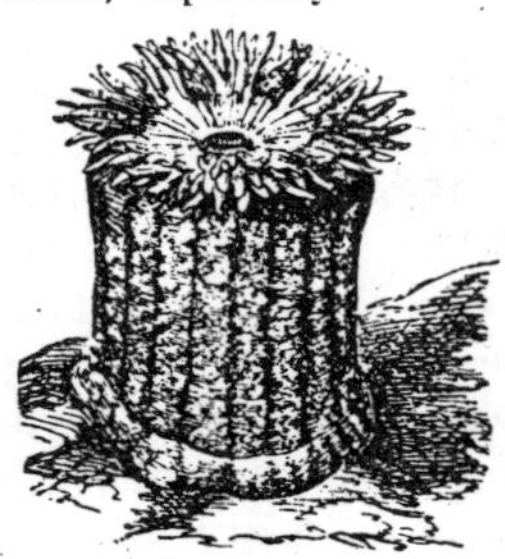

Sea anemone.

(উদ্ভিদ-বিদ্যা।) এক শ্রেণীর উদ্ভিদ, বিশেষতঃ ইংলণ্ডীয় অনিল-পুষ্প।

ăn-ē-mŏph′-ĭ-lous (-lŭs), *adj.* (*Bot.*) Wind-fertilized ; as, *anemophilous* plants ; (উদ্ভিদ-বিদ্যা—পুষ্পসম্পর্কে) বায়ুমেলক (সাঃ পঃ), বায়ুদ্বারা গর্ভাধান-প্রাপ্ত।

ă-nĕnt′, *prep.* About ; concerning ; in respect to ; as, I know nothing *anent* this particular ; বিষয়ে ; সম্বন্ধে ; সম্পর্কে।

ăn′-ĕr-oid (-ōyd), *adj.* & *n.* Containing no liquid,—(said of a kind of barometer) ; তরল পদার্থ-বিহীন। ***Noun.*** A barometer that measures air-pressure by its action on the elastic top of a metallic box exhausted of air, and not by the height of the fluid column ; ধাতুনির্ম্মিত ঘটিকা-যন্ত্রাকৃতি (watch-shaped) বায়ুচাপমান-যন্ত্রবিশেষ, অপারদচাপমান, অপারদ চাপ-মাপক, অনার্দ্র বায়ুভারমাপক (হিঃ কোঃ)।

ăn′-eu-rĭsm (-ū-) **—rȳsm,** *n.* A morbid dilatation of an artery ; ধমনীর দুর্ব্বলতা বশতঃ রক্ত রুদ্ধ ও ধমনী প্রসারিত হইয়া যে কোমল রক্তবর্ণ অর্ব্বুদ উৎপন্ন হয়, ধমন্যর্ব্বুদ (হঃ চঃ), ধমন-শোথ। **—ris′-mal, —rys′-mal,** *adjs.*

ă-new′ (-nū), *adv.* Over again ; in a new form ; afresh ; as, to aim *anew ;* পুনঃ, আবার, পুনরায় ; নূতন আকারে ; নবভাবে।

ăn-frăc-tu-ŏs′-ĭ-tȳ (-chû-), *n.* Sinuosity ; circuitousness ; as, the *anfractuosities* of the brain ; (usually *pl.*) winding passages, or channels ; (also *fig.*) intricacy ; as, the *anfractuosities* of their mind ; কুটিলতা ; আঁকাবাঁকাভাব ; (সাধারণতঃ বহুবচন) আঁকাবাঁকাপথ বা প্রণালী, ঘুরানো পথ ; (লক্ষণায়) জটিলতা। **—frac′-tu-ous,** *adj.*

ăn′-gĕl, *n.* **1.** A divine messenger ; one of an order of spiritual beings, superior to man in power and intelligence ; দেবদূত, স্বর্গীয়-দূত, দেবানুচর ; সিদ্ধ, গন্ধর্ব্ব, যক্ষ,

Angel fish.

বিদ্যাধর, দেবযোনি। **2.** A lovely or innocent being ; a darling (usually a woman) ; "A ministering *angel* thou" : she is an *angel ;* সুরূপ বা সৎস্বভাব পুরুষ ; লাবণ্যবতী রমণী, শুচিস্বভাবা নারী ; প্রেয়সী। **3.** A minister of loving offices ; an attendant spirit ; "Brutus, as you know, was Cæsar's *angel ;*" প্রীতিপূর্ণকার্য্য-সাধক ; রক্ষাকারী দেবদূত। **4.** An old English gold coin varying in value from 6*s.* 8*d.* to 10*s.* bearing a figure of the archangel Michael piercing a dragon ; স্বর্গীয়দূত মাইকেলের প্রতিকৃতিযুক্ত ইংলণ্ডের প্রাচীন স্বর্ণমুদ্রা বিশেষ—ইহার মূল্য ৬ শিলিং ৮ পেন্স হইতে ১০ শিলিং। **—gel′-ic, —gel′-i-cal,** *adjs.* Pertaining to, or resembling angels ; like an angel ; of superhuman qualities ; heavenly ; divine ; দেবদূত-সম্পৃক্ত ; দেবদূত সদৃশ ; অলৌকিক গুণসম্পন্ন ; স্বর্গীয় ; দিব্য। **—gel′-i-cal-ly,** *adv.* **—hood,** *n.* **Angel-bed**—A bed without posts ; খুঁটি বা স্তম্ভবিহীন শয্যা। **Angel-fish**—A kind of shark ; এক জাতীয় হাঙ্গর। **To write like an angel**—To write a very good hand ; অতি সুন্দর হস্তাক্ষরে লিখা। To compose beautifully ; "Who *wrote like an angel,* but talked like poor Poll ;" সুন্দর রচনা করা।

ăn-gĕl′-ĭ-câ, *n.* An aromatic plant used in cooking and medicine (*Angelica archangelica*) ; also, the confection made from this plant ; রন্ধনকার্য্য ও ঔষধাদিতে ব্যবহৃত একপ্রকার সুগন্ধি উদ্ভিদ ; উক্ত উদ্ভিদ্ হইতে প্রস্তুত মিষ্টদ্রব্য বিশেষ।

ăn-gĕl-ŏl′-ă-trȳ, *n.* Angel-worship ; দেবদূতার্চ্চনা।

ăn-gĕl-ŏl′-ō-gȳ, *n.* A discourse on angels ; a doctrine as to angels ; দেবদূত সম্বন্ধীয় আলোচনা ; দেবদূততত্ত্ব।

ăn-gĕl-ŏph′-ă-nȳ, *n.* The actual appearance of an angel to man ; দেবদূতাবির্ভাব।

ăn′-gĕl-ŭs, *n.* A devotional exercise commemorating the incarnation of Jesus Christ ; রোমান ক্যাথলিক সম্প্রদায়ের মধ্যে,

অবতরণস্মৃতি-সূচক প্রাভাতিক, মাধ্যাহ্নিক এবং সায়ংকালীন কীর্ত্তন-বিশেষ।

an′-gêr (ăng-), *n.* & *v. t.* A violent passion excited by a real or supposed injury to oneself or others; rage; ক্রোধ, কোপ, রাগ, মন্যু; রোষ, অমর্ষ। ***Verb t.*** To excite to wrath; to enrage; to provoke; as, you have both pleased and *angered* me; ক্রোধাবিষ্ট করা; রুষ্ট করা; প্রকোপিত করা।

ăn′-gĭ-nâ, *n.* (*Med.*) Severe sore-throat; quinsy; (ভৈষজ্য-শাস্ত্র) গলা-বেদনা (হঃ চঃ); তালুমূল বা গলার প্রদাহ (ঐ)। **Angina pectoris**—Heart-stroke; অতিপরিশ্রম-হেতু শ্বাস-রোধ-সহকৃত বক্ষঃস্থলের আক্ষেপ-রোগ বিশেষ, হৃৎশূল (হঃ চঃ)।

ăn-gĭ-ō-câr′-pous (-pŭs), *adj.* (*Bot.*) Having the fruit in an envelope not constituting part of the calyx; (উদ্ভিদ্-বিদ্যা) কুণ্ড (calyx) হইতে স্বতন্ত্র আবরণের অভ্যন্তরে নিহিত ফলবিশিষ্ট, গুপ্ত-কূটি (সাঃ পঃ), গুপ্ত-লিঙ্গী (ঐ)।

ăn′-gĭ-ō-spêrm, *n.* (*Bot.*) A plant which has its seeds inclosed in a seed-vessel (opp. to *gymnosperm*); (উদ্ভিদ্-বিদ্যা) যে বৃক্ষের বীজ বীজ-কোষের মধ্যে আবদ্ধ থাকে, গুপ্ত-ডিম্বক (সাঃ পঃ)।

an′-gle (ăng-), *n.* **1.** The space included between two meeting lines or planes; দুইটী সম্মিলিত রেখা বা তলের মধ্যস্থিত স্থান। **2.** (*Geom.*) The degree of inclination of two lines to each other; (জ্যামিতি) কোণ। **3.** The projecting corner (of a building, etc.); (অট্টালিকাদির) প্রলম্বিত কোণ। **Acute angle**—ন্যূন কোণ, সূক্ষ্ম কোণ। **Angle-iron**—A piece of iron shaped like an angle used for strengthening a frame-work; ঠাঁট বা কাঠাম দৃঢ়ী-করণার্থ কোণাকৃতি লৌহখণ্ড। **Angle-wise**—*v.* Angularly; কোণাকুণি-ভাবে। **Obtuse angle**—বিষম কোণ, অধিক কোণ। **Right angle**—সমকোণ।

an′-gle (ăng-), *v. t.* To fish with hooks and bait; (*lit* & *fig.*); (foll. by *for*); as, modesty is the only sure bait, when you *angle* for praise; (শব্দানুযায়ী এবং লক্ষণায়) বড়শীদ্বারা মৎস্য বিদ্ধ করা, ছিপে মাছ ধরা, ছিপ ফেলা। **—gler,** *n.* **1.** One who angles or fishes with a rod; যে ব্যক্তি বড়শীদ্বারা মৎস্য বিদ্ধ করে, মৎস্য-ভেদক। **2.** A British fish (called also Sea Devil) that prays upon small fish; এক-জাতীয় মৎস্য। **—gling,** *n.* The art of fishing with rod and line; বড়শীদ্বারা মৎস্য বিদ্ধকরণ।

Angler.

An′-gles (ăng-), *n. pl.* An ancient Low-German tribe, that settled in Britain (where they formed the kingdoms of Northumbria, Mercia & East Anglia); প্রাচীন জর্ম্মণ জাতি বিশেষ—এই জাতি ইংলণ্ডে আবাস-স্থান স্থাপন করে।

An′-glĭ-cân (ăng-), *adj.* & *n.* Pertaining to England or the English nation or to the established Church of England; ইংলণ্ড, ইংরাজজাতি বা ইংলণ্ডের ধর্ম্মসমাজ-সম্পর্কীয়। ***Noun.*** An adherent of the reformed Church of England, esp. of the High Church principles; ইংলণ্ডের সংস্কারপ্রাপ্ত ধর্ম্ম-সমাজের সভ্য। **—ism,** *n.* **1.** Adherence to the doctrine and discipline of the reformed Church of England; ইংলণ্ডের সংস্কারপ্রাপ্ত ধর্ম্মসমাজের মতবাদ এবং শাসনব্যবস্থার প্রতি নিষ্ঠা। **2.** Attachment to England and English institutions; ইংলণ্ডানুরাগ, ইংলণ্ডীয় প্রতিষ্ঠানসমূহের প্রতি অনুরাগ।

Anglice, (*L.*), *adv.* In English; ইংরাজীতে।

An′-glĭ-cĭsm (ăng-), *n.* **1.** An English idiom; a peculiarity of the English language; ইংরাজীভাষার রীতিসিদ্ধ প্রয়োগ; ইংরাজীভাষার বিশেষত্ব। **2.** English political principles or methods of administration; ইংলণ্ডীয় রাজনীতি বা শাসনপদ্ধতি। **—cize,** *v. t.* To make English in form or character; ইংরাজী ভাবাপন্ন করা।

An′-glō (ăng-), *adj.* English; ইংরাজী, ইঙ্গ (অন্য শব্দের সহিত যোগে ব্যবহৃত হয়)। **Anglo-American**—Half-English and half-American; ইঙ্গ-মার্কিণ। **Anglo-Indian**—A native of England born or residing in India; ভারতবর্ষে জাত বা ভারতবাসী ইংরাজ। **Anglo-Saxon**—The old English (people and language) before the Norman conquest; নর্ম্মাণগণকর্ত্তৃক ইংলণ্ডবিজয়ের পূর্ব্বকালীন ইংরাজজাতি বা ইংলণ্ডীয় ভাষা। **2.** A person (wherever found) descended from any of the races of the British Isles; ব্রিটিশদ্বীপপুঞ্জবাসী যে কোন জাতি হইতে উদ্ভূত ব্যক্তি।

An-glō-mā-nĭ-ă (ăng-), *n.* Excessive admiration of the English customs, etc.; ইংলণ্ডীয় রীতিনীতি বা আচারপদ্ধতি প্রভৃতির প্রতি নিরতিশয় অনুরাগ, ইংরাজী-নেশা।

An-glō′-phō-bĭ-ă (ăng-), *n.* An excessive hatred to, or dread of English people, customs, etc.; ইংরাজ-বিদ্বেষ, ইংরাজ-ভীতি, ইংরাজি আচারপদ্ধতির প্রতি বিদ্বেষ।

an-gō′-lă, —ră (ăng-), *n.* A fabric made from the wool of the Angora-goat or an imitation of it; য়্যাঙ্গোরা ছাগের পশম হইতে প্রস্তুত বস্ত্র-বিশেষ, কৃত্রিম এঙ্গোলা বস্ত্র।

an′-grў (ăng′-), *adj.* **1.** Enraged; wrathful; resentful; (followed by *at, with* before a person and *at, about* before a thing); ক্রুদ্ধ, সরোষ, জাতক্রোধ, সক্রোধ, ক্রোধাক্রান্ত, রোষাবিষ্ট; রাগান্বিত, খাপ্পা (*Colloq.*) কুপিত; রুষ্ট, কোপাবিষ্ট। **2.** Moved or excited by anger; wearing the marks of anger; as, *angry* sky, words, countenance, etc.; ক্রোধোদ্দীপ্ত; রোষরক্ত, রোষ-কষায়িত। **3.** Inflamed and painful, as a sore; as, the gouty toe is very *angry*; বেদনা ও প্রদাহযুক্ত। **—gri-ly,** *adv.*

an-guil′-lous (ăng-gwĭl-lŭs), *adj.* Of the nature of an eel; eel-like; বাইনমৎস্যপ্রকৃতিক; বাইনমৎস্যবৎ।

an′-guine (ăng-gwĭn), *adj.* Snake-like; সর্পবৎ, সর্প-সদৃশ।

an′-guish (ăng-gwĭsh), *n.* Extreme pain, either of body or mind; নিদারুণ-যন্ত্রণা, দুঃসহ যাতনা, তীব্র মনোবেদনা, নিদারুণ সন্তাপ।

an′-gü-lâr (ăng-), *adj.* **1.** Having an angle or sharp corner; pointed; কোণ-বিশিষ্ট, কৌণিক; সূক্ষ্মাগ্র, সূচাগ্র। **2.** Forming an angle; placed at, or in an angle; কোণগঠনকারী; কোণস্থিত। **3.** Measured by an angle; as, *angular* distance; কোণদ্বারা পরিমিত। **4.** Ungraceful; awkward; (of action); as, his gestures were *angular*; মাধুর্য্যশূন্য; বিসদৃশ, কদাকার। **5.** Wanting suavity; cantankerous; as, *angular* nature: an *angular* man; লালিত্যহীন; বে-আড়া, বিরূপ। **—lar′-i-ty,** *n.* The quality or state of being angular; crankiness; কোণবিশিষ্টতা; মাধুর্য্য-শূন্যতা। **—ly,** *adv.*

an′-gü-lāte (ăng-), *adj.* & *v. t.* Formed with corners; of an angular form; as, *angulate* stem, leaves, etc.; কোণ-বিশিষ্ট, সকোণ; কোণাকার। ***Verb t.*** To make angular; কোণ-বিশিষ্ট করা। **—la′-tion,** *n.*

ăn-hē-lā′-tion, *n.* Shortness of breath; a panting; শ্বাসকষ্ট, শ্বাসরোধ; ঘনশ্বাস।

ăn-hў′-drous (-drŭs), *adj.* (*Chem.*) destitute of the water of crystallisation; (রসায়ন-শাস্ত্র) নির্জল, নিরুদক, অনার্দ্র (হিঃ কোঃ)।

ȧ-nigh′ (-nī), *prep.* & *adv.* Near (*to*); নিকটে।

ăn′-il, *n.* The indigo-plant or the dye; নীলগাছ বা উদ্ভিজ্জজাত নীল।

ăn′-īle, *adj.* Old-womanish; imbecile; as, not *anile* conjecture, but sound evidence of events; বৃদ্ধাস্ত্রীবৎ, জরতীতুল্য; ক্ষীণ, দুর্ব্বল।

ănil′-i-tў, *n.* Old-womanishness; dotage; বৃদ্ধার ভাব; জরাজীর্ণেন্দ্রিয়তা।

ăn′-i-line, *n.* A colourless oily liquid, the source of many dyes, obtained originally from indigo, but now chiefly from coal-tar; আলকাতরা হইতে প্রস্তুত তৈলবৎ এবং বর্ণহীন তরল পদার্থ বিশেষ।

ăn-i-măd-vêr′-sion, *n.* The utterance of criticsm (usually of a hostile kind); censure; reproof; comment; সমালোচন; নিন্দা, তিরস্কার; দোষারোপণ; সমালোচনা।

ăn-i-măd-vêrt, *v. i.* **1.** To take note; to remark; (commonly foll. by *that*); as, I *animadvert that* you are in the house of a great lady; অবধান করা, লক্ষ্য করা; মতপ্রকাশ করা। **2.** To comment critically; to express censure or blame; (with *on, upon*); সমালোচনা করা, তিরস্কার করা, দোষারোপণ করা।

ăn′-i-măl, *n.* & *adj.* **1.** An organized being endowed with life, sensation and voluntary motion; জীব, প্রাণী, জন্তু। **2.** An inferior or irrational being, as distinguished from man; a quadruped; a beast; নীচ জন্তু, ইতর জন্তু; চতুষ্পদ জন্তু, পশু; জানোয়ার। **3.** (Contemptuously) A man of beastly propensities; পাশব-স্বভাব ব্যক্তি, নরপশু। ***Adj.*** **1.** Belonging or relating to the functions of animal spirits; জান্তব, জৈব। **2.** Pertaining to the merely sentient part of a living being, as distinguished from the intellectual, rational or spiritual part; carnal; as, *animal* passions or appetites; পাশব, পাশবিক; ঐন্দ্রিয়। **3** Of, pertaining to, or consisting of, the flesh of animals; (as opp. to vegetable); as, *animal* oil, cream, butter, etc.: *animal* food; মাংস সম্বন্ধীয়, মাংসগঠিত। **Animal electricity**—The electricity that is developed in certain animals, as the torpedo and a kind of eel; জৈব-তাড়িত। **Animal food**—Food consisting of flesh or other, portions of animals; আমিষাহার, মাংসাহার। **Animal heat**—The constant temperature maintained within the bodies of living animals; জীবিতপ্রাণিদেহের উষ্ণতা, উষ্মা। **Animal kingdom**—One of the three principal divisions into which all natural bodies are divided;—the others being the *vegetable* and *mineral* kingdoms; নিখিল প্রাণিবর্গ, জীবসৃষ্টি। **Animal magnetism**—Mesmerism; জীবদেহের চুম্বকত্ব, মেস্মরতত্ত্ব। **Animal soul**—The soul which is characteristic of an animal; (in human being, it is distinguished from the *rational* soul, which alone has existence apart from the body); জীবাত্মা, মনোময় কোষ, (হিঃ কোঃ), কামরূপ (ঐ)। **Animal spirits**—Natural buoyancy of spirits; cheerfulness; animation; উল্লাস; প্রফুল্লতা; স্ফূর্ত্তি, তেজস্বিতা, ওজস্বিতা, সজীবতা। **Animal world**—

প্রাণিজগৎ, জীবজগৎ। **Animal symbolical** :—Ant (মিতব্যয়িতা, ভবিষ্যদৃষ্টি); ape (অপরিচ্ছন্নতা); Asp (যীশুখৃষ্ট); ass (নির্ব্বুদ্ধিতা); bat (অন্ধতা); bear (বদ-মেজাজ, অসভ্যতা); bee (শ্রমশীলতা); boar (একগুয়েমি, মলিনতা); butterfly (আমোদপ্রমোদময় জীবন); camel (বশ্যতা); catling (ক্রিয়াশীলতা); cock (সাহস); crocodile (কপটতা); crow (দীর্ঘজীবন); cuckoo, stag (অসতী-পতিত্ব); dog (বিশ্বস্ততা, কদর্য্য অভ্যাস); dove (শুচিতা, অহিংসা); duck (প্রতারণা); eagle (রাজপ্রতাপ, প্রত্যাদেশ); elephant (বুদ্ধিমত্তা, অতিগুরুতা); fly (দুর্ব্বলতা, তুচ্ছতা); goat (কামুকতা); goose (আত্মম্ভরিতা); grasshopper (কাঠফড়িং—বার্দ্ধক্য); hare (ভীরুতা); hen (মাতৃস্নেহ); hog (অশুচিতা); horse (দ্রুততা, মাধুর্য্য); lamb (শুভ্রচরিত্রতা); lark (প্রফুল্লতা, হর্ষোৎফুল্লতা); leopard (পাপ); lion (বীরোচিত সাহস); monkey (চাতুরী, চালাকি); mule (একগুয়েমি); nightingale (নিঃসহায় অবস্থা); ostrich (নির্ব্বুদ্ধিতা); owl (জ্ঞান); ox (অহঙ্কার); peacock (গর্ব্ব); pigeon (ভীরুতা); puppy (অসার তর্জ্জন-গর্জ্জন) rat (প্রজননশীলতা); raven (দুরদৃষ্ট); serpent (জ্ঞান); sheep (নির্ব্বুদ্ধিতা, ভীরুতা); swallow (সুদিনের বন্ধু); swan (লীলাগতি, মাধুর্য্য); tortoise (সতীত্ব); turkey-cock (রাজকর্ম্মচারিগণের ঔদ্ধত্য); vulture (লুণ্ঠন); wolf (নিষ্ঠুরতা); ইত্যাদি। **The cries of animals** :—Apes *gibber*; asses *bray*; bears *growl*; bees *hum* (গুণ গুণ); bitterns *boom*; bulls *bellow* (গর্জ্জন); canaries *sing*; calves, sheep *bleat*; cats *mew* (মিউমিউ); cocks *crow*; cows *low* (হাম্বারব); crows *caw* (কা কা); dogs *bark* (ঘেঁউ ঘেঁউ); doves *coo* (কূজন); ducks *quack* (প্যাঁক্ প্যাঁক্); eagles *scream*; frogs *croak* (রটন, মক মক); geese *cackle*; hares *squeak*; kittens *mew*; larks *sing*; owls *hoot* or *scream*; oxen *bellow*; parrots *talk* (বুলি); peacocks *scream* (কেকারব); pigs *grunt* (ঘুঁৎঘুঁৎ); snakes *hiss* (ফোঁস্ ফোঁস্); sparrows *chirp* (কাকলী, বিরাব); swallows *twitter* (কিচিরমিচির); wolves *howl* (ঘোঙ্‌রানি)। **Animals sacred to special deities** :—Apollo (নেকড়ে বাঘ, কাক); Æsculapius (সর্প); Bacchus (দ্বীপী); Diana (হরিণ); Isis (গো-বৎস); Hercules (মৃগ); Juno (ময়ূর, মেষশাবক); Jupiter (উৎক্রোশ পক্ষী); Mars (অশ্ব, গৃধ্র); Mercury (কুক্কুট); Minerva (পেচক); Neptune (বৃষভ); Venus (কপোত, রাজহংস, চটক পক্ষী); Vulcan (সিংহ); ইত্যাদি। So the following beasts are sacred to the different Hindu Gods:—পবন (হরিণ); যম (কাক, মহিষ); গণেশ (মূষিক); কার্ত্তিকেয় (ময়ূর); লক্ষ্মী (পেচক); মনসা (সর্প); শীতলা (মার্জ্জার); চন্দ্র (শশক); গঙ্গা (মকর); দুর্গা (সিংহ); কালী (শৃগাল); ইত্যাদি।

ăn-i-măl'-cūle, *n.* A microscopic animal; কীটাণু, সূক্ষ্মপ্রাণী (যোঃ)।

ăn-i-măl'-cŭl-ĭsm, *n.* The theory which seeks to explain certain physiological phenomena by means of animalcules, as that they are the germs of life, that they are the cause of diseases; কতকগুলি নির্দ্দিষ্ট শারীরিক অবস্থা (যেরূপ পীড়াদি) কীটাণুদ্বারা সঞ্জাত হয়—এইরূপ মতবাদ। **—ist,** *n.* One versed in the knowledge of animalcules; কীটাণুতত্ত্ববিদ্।

ăn'-i-măl-ĭsm, *n.* **1.** Animal activity; physical exercise and enjoyment; শারীরিকক্রিয়া; ব্যায়াম, দৈহিক-সুখ। **2.** Sensuality; পাশবিকতা, ইন্দ্রিয়সুখপরতন্ত্রতা। **3.** The doctrine which views men as mere animals; মানব শুদ্ধ পশুমাত্র—এইরূপ দার্শনিক বাদ। **—i-za'-tion,** *n.* **—ize,** *v. t.* **1.** To convert into animal substance; জান্তবপদার্থে পরিণত করা। **2.** To sensualize; to rouse the sexual passion of; পশুভাবাপন্ন করা; পাশবিক ভাব জাগরিত করা, কামভাব উদ্দীপ্ত করা। **—mal'-i-ty,** *n.* **1.** The animal nature; vital power; পশু-স্বভাব; জীবনীশক্তি। **2.** The merely animal nature as distinguished from moral and spiritual; as, sank in the lowest depth of *animality* and ignorance; শুদ্ধপাশবিকপ্রকৃতি। **3.** The animal world; জীবজগৎ।

Anima mundi, (*L.*), *n.* The soul of the world; বিশ্বাত্মা।

ăn'-i-māte, *adj.* & *v. t.* Living; lively; সজীব, সচেতন; জীবন্ত। ***Verb t.*** **1.** To breathe life into; জীবনসঞ্চার করা, উজ্জীবিত করা। **2.** To impart liveliness or interest to; অনুপ্রাণিত করা। **3.** To inspire, or actuate; to stir up; প্রোৎসাহিত করা; উত্তেজিত করা। **—mat-ed,** *adj.* **1.** Endowed with animal life; living; জীবিত; জীয়ন্ত। **2.** Lively; vigorous; full of spirit; as, an *animated* discussion; সজীব, প্রাণপূর্ণ; তেজোপূর্ণ; উদ্দীপনাপূর্ণ। **—mat-ing,** *adj.* Life-giving; enlivening; জীবনপ্রদ; অনুপ্রাণক। **—mat-ing-ly,** *adv.* **—ma'-tion,** *n.* **1.** Enlivenment; sprightliness; জীবনসঞ্চার, অনুপ্রাণন; স্ফূর্ত্তি। **2.** Liveliness; briskness; as, he recited the story with great *animation*; সজীবতা; তেজস্বিতা, উল্লাস, উৎফুল্লতা। **—ma-tor,** *n.* One who or that which animates, quickens or inspires; জীবনসঞ্চারক, অনুপ্রাণক, উত্তেজক। **Animated nature**—The animal world; প্রাণিবর্গ। **Suspended animation**—The temporary suspension of the vital functions (as in the case of persons all but drowned) ; (জলমগ্নপ্রায় ব্যক্তির) সাময়িকভাবে জীবনীক্রিয়ার নিরোধ।

an′-i-mĕ, *n.* A resin exuding from a tropical American tree, used in making varnish ; আমেরিকাদেশজাত এক প্রকার বৃক্ষের নির্যাস, ইহা বার্ণিশ (কুঙ্কুভ) প্রস্তুত-করণে ব্যবহৃত হয়।

ăn′-i-mism, *n.* (*a*) The hypothesis of Pythagoras and Plato, of a force, immaterial but inseparable from matter, and giving to matter its life and form and movements ; (*b*) the attribution of living soul to inanimate objects and natural phenomena ; (*c*) spiritualism ; spiritualism as opposed, to *materialism* ; (ক) পিথাগোরাস্ ও প্লাতো-প্রবর্ত্তিত দার্শনিক মত—এই মতানুসারে সর্ব্বভূতের সহিত ওতপ্রোতভাবে-সম্মিলিত একটী চৈতন্যশক্তি নিখিল ভূতবর্গের রূপ, প্রাণ ও গতি প্রদান করিতেছে, জীবদেহপার্থক্যবাদ (হিঃ কোঃ) ; (খ) বৃক্ষশিলাদি অচেতন পদার্থ ও ঝঞ্ঝা, বিদ্যুৎ প্রভৃতি নৈসর্গিক ব্যাপার মনুষ্যের মত ব্যক্তিত্ব ও প্রাণবিশিষ্ট বলিয়া নির্দ্দেশ, ক্রমোন্নতিশীল জীবাত্ম-বিশ্বাস (সাঃ পঃ), জড়-চৈতন্যবাদ, সর্ব্বসজীবত্ববাদ (হিঃ কোঃ) ; (গ) প্রেততত্ব ; অধ্যাত্মবাদ। **—mist,** *n.* One who holds the doctrine of animism ; সর্ব্বজীবত্ববাদী, প্রেতবাদী, অধ্যাত্মবাদী। **—mis′-tic,** *adj.*

ăn-i-mŏs′-i-tȳ, *n.* Active enmity ; (*against, between*) ; প্রবল শত্রুতা, বিরোধ, বৈরভাব, বিদ্বেষ।

ăn′-i-mŭs, (*L.* = the mind, mental impulse, disposition.) *n.* Animating spirit or temper, usually of a hostile character ; hence, animosity ; as, the *animus* that actuates the policy of a foreign country ; উদ্দীপক ভাব, উদ্দীপনা ; বিদ্বেষ।

animus furandi, (*L.*) *n.* The intention of stealing ; চুরির অভিপ্রায়।

ăn′-i-ŏn, *n.* A name given by Faraday to an electro-negative element, which (in electro-chemical decompositions) is evolved at the positive pole of a battery ; (opp. to *cation*) ; সুকণা (সাঃ পঃ), বিকণা (ঐ)।

ăn′-ise, *n.* An umbelliferous plant bearing aromatic seeds ; মিঠাজিরা গাছ।

ăn′-i-seed (-sēd), *n.* The seed of the anise ; মৌরি, মিঠাজিরা, মিশ্রেয়া (বনঃ)।

ăn-i-sĕtte′, *n.* A liqueur flavoured with aniseed ; মৌরি-সুবাসিত সুরা।

ăn′-kêr (ang-), *n.* A Dutch liquid-measure, containing about 10 wine gallons ; হলণ্ড দেশীয় তরল পদার্থের পরিমাপ বিশেষ।

ăn′-kle (ang-), **—cle,** *n.* The joint which connects the foot with the leg ; পায়ের গোড়ালি, গুল্ফ, ঘুণ্টক (মঃ উঃ), ঘুণ্টিকা (ঐ), অঙ্ঘ্রি-স্কন্ধ (ঐ)।

ăn′-klĕt (ang-), *n.* An ornament, as a ring of metal for the ankle ; পায়ের মল, নূপুর, মঞ্জীর।

ăn′-nă, *n.* The sixteenth part of a rupee ; এক আনা।

ăn′-năl-ist, *n.* A writer of annals ; ইতিবৃত্ত-লেখক, কাহিনী-লেখক।

ăn′-năls, *n.* **1.** A narrative of events written year by year ; as, the *annals* of revolution ; বর্ষানুক্রমিক কাহিনী বা ঘটনাবিবরণী, প্রতিবার্ষিক বৃত্তান্ত। **2.** Historical records generally ; ইতিহাস, ইতিবৃত্ত, ইতিকথা। **—nal-ist,** *n.* A writer of annals ; বর্ষানুক্রমিক বৃত্তান্ত-লেখক, ইতিবৃত্ত-লেখক।

ăn′-nates, *n. pl.* The first year's revenue of a see or benefice, paid to the pope ; ক্যাথলিক-সম্প্রাদায়ভুক্ত ধর্ম্মাধ্যক্ষের (বিশপ) এলাকার প্রথম বৎসরের উপস্বত্ব, যাহা পোপকে প্রদান করা হয়।

ăn-neal′ (-nēl), *v. t.* **1.** To subject to great heat and then cool slowly, as glass, steel or other metal, with a view to rendering it less brittle ; to temper ; to toughen ; ভঙ্গুরতা-হ্রাসের নিমিত্ত কাচ, ইস্পাত, কিম্বা অন্যবিধ ধাতুকে প্রথমতঃ অত্যুষ্ণ অগ্নিতে স্থাপন করত, তৎপর ক্রমশঃ শীতল করা, তপ্তশীতল করা ; যথোচিত কঠিন করা ; পানি দেওয়া। **2.** To heat, as glass or tiles, in order to fix colours ; রঙ্গ লাগাইবার নিমিত্ত কাচ, টালি প্রভৃতি উত্তপ্ত করা। **—er,** *n.* **—ing,** *n.* The process of applying heat to make metals, glass etc., less brittle ; ভঙ্গপ্রবণতাহ্রাসের জন্য ধাতু, কাচ প্রভৃতি উত্তপ্তকরণ, নিষেক (সাঃ পঃ), অভিষেক (রঃ প্রঃ), স্নপন (ঐ), মজ্জন (ঐ)।

ăn-nĕc′-tĕnt, *adj.* Connecting ; as, *annectent* link ; সংযোজক।

An-nĕl′-i-dă (ăn-), *n.* The class of red-blooded worms ; চক্রিত কৃমি (সাঃ পঃ)। **An′-nĕ-lid,** *n.* & *adj.* **—dan,** *adj.* & *n.*

ăn-nĕx′, *v.t.* **1.** To affix ; to append (*to* book, etc.) ; সংযুক্ত করা ; পরিশিষ্ট রূপে সংযোজিত করা। **2.** To add as a subordinate part ; to unite, as a smaller thing to a greater ; to take possession of (territory etc.) ; as, he *annexed* a province to his kingdom ; অপ্রধান অংশরূপে ভুক্ত বা যোগ করা ; অন্তর্ভুক্ত করা ; স্বাধিকারভুক্ত করা। **3.** To attach or connect as an attribute, consequence, etc. ; as, to *annex* a punishment to a guilt ; কোন কিছুর গুণ বা পরিণামস্বরূপ সংলগ্ন বা সংযোগ করা। **—a′-tion,** *n.* The act of connection ; the act of attaching as a territorial dependency ; appropriation ; সংযোজন ; স্বরাজ্যভুক্তকরণ, স্বাধিকারভুক্তকরণ ; আত্মসাৎকরণ। **—a′-tion-ist,** *n.*

ăn-nĕx′, —nexe′ (-nĕx), *n.* **1.** An addition to a document ; as, to which I add these two *annexes* ; দলিলের পরিশিষ্ট। **2.** A subsidiary building to a main building ; উপভবন, উপপ্রাসাদ।

ăn′-nĭ-cŭt, ăn′-ĭ-cŭt, *n.* [Tamil *anai kattu* ; dam-building.] A dam or mole made in a stream for maintaining and regulating irrigation ; কৃষিক্ষেত্রে জলসেচনসৌকর্য্যার্থ নদীতে যে বাঁধ দেওয়া হয়।

ăn-nī′-hĭl-āte, *v.t.* **1.** To blot out of existence ; to reduce to nothing ; অস্তিত্ববিলোপ করা, সমূলে নির্ম্মূল করা, বিলোপ করা, বিলয় করা ; প্রধ্বংস করা, । **2.** To make null and void ; "*Annihilate* law, and moral order is no more ;" নাকচ করা, বাতিল করা । **3.** (*Theol.*) To destroy the soul as well as the body ; (খৃষ্টীয়-ধর্ম্মশাস্ত্র) সত্তানাশ করা । **—a-tor,** *n.* One who or that which annihilates ; as, fire-*annihilator* ; প্রলয়কারী, উচ্ছেদ-সাধক, নির্ম্মূলক ।

ăn-nī-hĭl-ā′-tion, *n.* **1.** The act of reducing to nothing ; utter destruction, or the state of being reduced to nothing ; শূন্যীকরণ ; বিলোপন, সংহরণ, নির্ম্মূলন ; বিলোপ, সংহার, নিরন্বয়নাশ । **2.** (*Theol.*) The destruction of the soul as well as of the body ; (খৃষ্টীয়-ধর্ম্মশাস্ত্র) সত্তানাশ । **—ism,** *n.* The doctrine that the soul will be annihilated after death ; সত্তানাশবাদ । **—ist,** *n.* One who believes in annihilationism ; সত্তানাশবাদী । **The annihilation of the world**—প্রলয় ।

ăn-nĭ-vêr′-să-rỹ, *adj.* & *n.* Returning with the year at a stated time ; annual ; as, an *anniversary* feast ; বাৎসরিক, সাম্বৎসরিক ; বার্ষিক । ***Noun.*** **1.** The yearly return of a date on which any notable event took place ; সাম্বৎসরিক দিন । **2.** The celebration which takes place at such annually recurring dates ; সাম্বৎসরিক উৎসব, বছরকী (*colloq.*) ।

Anno ætatis suæ, *(L. phr.)* In the——year of his or her age ; কোন স্ত্রী বা পুরুষের——বৎসর বয়সে ।

Anno Domini, [*L. phr.* In the year of the Lord (Jesus Christ.) সংক্ষেপে A. D.] In the year of the Christian era ; খৃষ্টাব্দে ।

Anno Mundi, *n.* [*L. phr.* সংক্ষেপে A. M.] In the year of the world ; (খৃষ্টীয় শাস্ত্রানুসারে) পৃথিবীর সৃষ্ট্যব্দে, জগদব্দে ।

ăn′-nö-tāte, *v. t.* & *i.* To explain or criticize by notes ; as, to *annotate* the works of Bacon ; টীকা টিপ্পনি লিখিয়া কোনও গ্রন্থের অর্থ প্রকটন করা, (কোন গ্রন্থের) টীকা করা, ভাষ্য করা । ***Verb i.*** (With *on, upon*) To make notes or comments ; টীকা টিপ্পনি করা, অন্বয়-মুখে ব্যাখ্যা করা । **—tat-ed,** *adj.* Furnished with notes ; সটীক, সভাষ্য । **—ta′-tion,** *n.* A note added by way of comment or explanation (usually in the plural) ; টীকা, টিপ্পনি, ভাষ্য, ব্যাখ্যা । **—ta-tor,** *n.* A commentator ; টীকাকার, ভাষ্যকার, টিপ্পনিলেখক ।

ăn-nounce′ (-nownce), *v. t.* **1.** To proclaim ; to intimate the approach of ; as, the birth of Christ was *announced* by an angel ; ঘোষণা করা, সাধারণ্যে প্রচার করা ; আগমন জ্ঞাপন করা । **2.** To make known (without words) to the senses or mind ; as, Queen Elizabeth's arrival was *announced* through the country by a peal of cannon ; জ্ঞাপন করা, বিজ্ঞাপিত করা । **—ment,** *n.* Proclamation ; publication ; বিঘোষণ, জ্ঞাপন ; ঘোষণা, প্রচার ।

ăn-noỹ′, *v.t.* **1.** To disturb or irritate ; to tease ; ত্যক্ত করা, উত্যক্ত করা ; উদ্বেজিত করা, ক্ষ্যাপান্ । **2.** To harass ; to molest ; বিরক্ত করা, উপদ্রব করা ; পীড়ন করা । **—ance,** *n.* Molestation ; vexation ; disgust ; পীড়ন, উপদ্রব ; বিরক্তি ; বিতৃষ্ণা ।

ăn′-nü-ăl, *adj.* & *n.* **1.** Returning every year ; বার্ষিক । **2.** Lasting for one year or continuing one yearly season ; as, *annual* plants, tickets, etc. ; বর্ষস্থায়ী, বর্ষজীবী, বর্ষব্যাপী, ঋতুজীবী । **3.** Reckoned by the year ; as, the *annual* motion of the earth ; বর্ষানুসারে গণিত । ***Noun.*** **1.** A plant that lives but one year ; বর্ষজীবিউদ্ভিদ, ওষধি, বর্ষায়ুঃ (যোঃ) । **2.** A book, etc. published yearly ; বার্ষিক পুস্তক, বার্ষিক বিবরণী । **—ly,** *adv.* Yearly ; প্রতিবর্ষে, বর্ষে বর্ষে ।

ăn-nü′-ĭ-tănt, *n.* One who holds an annuity ; বার্ষিকবৃত্তিপ্রাপ্ত ব্যক্তি ।

ăn-nü′-ĭ-tỹ, *n.* **1.** A yearly allowance ; বার্ষিক বৃত্তি । **2.** A periodical payment of money, amounting to a fixed sum in each year, and continuing for a certain period (called a *certain annuity*), or for an uncertain period (called a *contingent annuity*), or a *life annuity*, when the period is determined by the duration of one or more lives ; নির্দ্দিষ্ট সময়ান্তে অর্থপ্রদানের ব্যবস্থা—এইরূপ ব্যবস্থায় নির্দ্দিষ্টকাল পর্য্যন্ত প্রতি বৎসর নির্দ্দিষ্ট সংখ্যক মুদ্রা প্রদান করা যায় (নির্দ্দিষ্ট বার্ষিক বৃত্তি), অথবা অনির্দ্দিষ্ট কালের জন্য নির্দ্দিষ্ট-সংখ্যক মুদ্রা প্রদত্ত হয় (অনির্দ্দিষ্ট বার্ষিক বৃত্তি), কিম্বা এক অথবা ততোধিক ব্যক্তিকে যাবজ্জীবন নির্দ্দিষ্ট বৃত্তি প্রদান করা হয় (আজীবন বার্ষিক বৃত্তি) ।

ăn-nŭl′, *v. t.* To abolish ; to cancel ; (used of laws, decrees, decision of courts, established rules, etc.) ; as, to *annul* laws of inestimable values to our liberties ; রহিত করা ; রদ করা, লোপ করা, বাতিল করা ; নাকচ করা । **—ment,** *n.*

ăn′-nü-lăr, *adj.* Having the form of a ring ; ring-like ; অঙ্গুরীয়াকার, মণ্ডলাকার, গোলাকার, বলয়াকার,

চক্রাকার; অঙ্গুরীয়সদৃশ। **–ly,** *adv.* (*Astron.*) **Annular eclipse**—An eclipse of the sun in which a ring of light is visible round the dark body of the moon; (জ্যোতির্বিজ্ঞান) যে সূর্য্যগ্রহণে চন্দ্রের সমগ্র ছায়া সূর্য্য-মণ্ডলের উপর পতিত হয়, এবং সূর্য্যের অনাবৃত অংশ জ্যোতির্বলয়াকারে চন্দ্র-ছায়ার চতুষ্পার্শ্বে দৃষ্ট হইয়া থাকে, বলয়গ্রাস (সাঃ পঃ), কঙ্কণ-গ্রাস, নিরোধ (বৃঃ সং)। **Annular space**—The space between the inner and outer surfaces of a cylinder; কোন নল বা চুঙ্গির বহিঃপৃষ্ঠ ও অন্তঃপৃষ্ঠের মধ্যবর্ত্তী অবকাশ।

ăn′-nü-lāte, –lāt-ĕd, *adj.* Furnished with rings; marked with rings; formed of rings; চক্রিত, বলয়িত; বলয়াঙ্কিত; বলয়রচিত। **–la′-tion,** *n.*

ăn′-nü-lĕt, *n.* **1.** A small ring; অঙ্গুরীয়ক, চক্রক। **2.** (*Arch.*) A small fillet encircling a column; (স্থপতি-বিদ্যা) বলয়াকৃতি স্তম্ভাগ্রবেষ্টনী, কম্পক (রাঃ রাঃ), আলিঙ্গক (ঐ)।

ăn′-nü-loid (-loyd), *adj.* Ring-like; অঙ্গুরীয়াকৃতি। **–lose,** *adj.* Furnished with rings; composed of rings; চক্রিত; বলয়-রচিত।

ăn′-nü-lŭs, *n.* (*Pl.* ANNULI) A ring or ring-like body; অঙ্গুরীয় বা তদাকার পদার্থ। (*Bot.*) **Annulus of Ferns**—(উদ্ভিদ্-বিদ্যা) নিক্ষেপবলয় (সাঃ পঃ)। **Annulus of moss**—ভেদন-বলয় (ঐ)। **Annulus of equisetum**—পর্ব্ববলয় (ঐ)।

ăn-nŭn′-ci-āte (-shî-), *v. t.* To proclaim; to announce, as coming or ready; ঘোষণা করা, বিজ্ঞাপিত করা; কাহারো আগমনাদি ঘোষণা করা।

ăn-nŭn-ci-ā′-tion (-shî-), *n.* **1.** Announcement; ঘোষণা, বিজ্ঞাপন, জ্ঞাপন। **2.** The announcement of the incarnation, made by the Angel Gabriel to the Virgin Mary; স্বর্গদূত জেব্রায়েল কর্ত্তৃক কুমারী মেরীর নিকট যীশুখৃষ্টের নরকলেবর ধারণের সমাচার প্রচার। **3.** The festival celebrated by the Church of England, of Rome, etc. (on 25th March) in memory of this announcement to Mary; Lady-day; ২৫শে মার্চ্চ—এই দিবস ইংলণ্ডের খৃষ্টীয়-সমাজ এবং রোমান-ক্যাথলিক সমাজে যীশু-খৃষ্টের অবতরণ-বার্ত্তা ঘোষণার স্মৃতি-উৎসব অনুষ্ঠিত হইয়া থাকে; খৃষ্টাবতরণ-উৎসব।

ăn-nŭn′-ci-ā-tŏr (-shî-), *n.* **1.** One who announces; ঘোষণাকারী, বিজ্ঞাপক। **2.** An indicator (as in a hotel) showing in which direction attendance summoned by bell or telephone is needed; এক প্রকার ঘণ্টাযুক্ত তাড়িতবার্ত্তাবহযন্ত্র, ইহা সাধারণতঃ হোটেল প্রভৃতিতে সংযোজিত হয়, ইহা দ্বারা কোন্ কক্ষ হইতে কাহাকে ডাকা হইতেছে, তাহা নির্দ্দেশ করা যায়।

annus mirabilis—**1.** The year of wonders; চমকপ্রদ ঘটনাবলীর বৎসর, অর্থাৎ ১৬৬৬ খৃঃ অব্দ। এই বৎসর লণ্ডননগরীর চিরস্মরণীয় ভীষণ অগ্নিকাণ্ড সংঘটিত হয়, এবং ইংরাজগণ ওলন্দাজদিগকে যুদ্ধে পরাভূত করেন। **2.** The title of a poem written by John Dryden in 1667; কবি জন্ ড্রাইডেন রচিত কবিতা বিশেষ।

ăn′-ōde, *n.* (*Electr.*) Positive pole or that surface by which the galvanic current enters the body undergoing decomposition; (opposed to *cathode*); (তাড়িত-বিজ্ঞান) ধন-ধ্রুব (সাঃ পঃ), আগম (ঐ), সুদ্বার (ঐ)।

ăn′-ō-dȳne, *n.* & *adj.* **1.** Any medicine which allays pain, as an opiate or narcotic; বেদনাপ্রশমক ঔষধ, বেদনানিবারক (হঃ চঃ)। 2. Anything that soothes the mind; মানস-সন্তাপ প্রশমক। ***Adj.*** Serving to assuage pain; "The *anodyne* draught of oblivion"; soothing; বেদনাপ্রশমক; উপশমক, সন্তাপহর, সান্ত্বনাপ্রদ।

ā-noint′ (-noynt), *v. t.* **1.** To pour oil upon; to smear or rub over with oil; তৈল মর্দ্দন করা; তৈল মালিশ করা। **2.** To consecrate, especially a king, priest or prophet by unction, or the use of oil; "*Anoint* Hazel to be king of Syria;" প্রতিষ্ঠাপিত করা, বিশেষত রাজা, পুরোহিত অথবা কোন ঈশ্বর প্রেরিত পুরুষকে অভিমন্ত্রিত তৈল, অভ্যঞ্জন বা বিলেপন মর্দ্দনদ্বারা অভিসংস্কৃত বা প্রতিষ্ঠাপিত করা।

ā-nŏm-ă-lis′-tic, –ti-cal, *adj.* **1.** Irregular; departing from established rules; নিয়মবহির্ভূত, নিয়মবিরুদ্ধ, অনিয়মিত; ব্যভিচারী, অতিচারী। **2.** (*Astron.*) Pertaining to the angular distance of a planet from its perihelion; (জ্যোতির্বিজ্ঞান) কেন্দ্রিক (সাঃ পঃ)। **–ti-ly,** *adv.*

ā-nŏm′-ă-lous (-lŭs), *adj.* **1.** Deviating from a general rule; irregular; নিয়মবহির্ভূত; বিধিবিরুদ্ধ, অনিয়মিত। **2.** Abnormal; সৃষ্টিনিয়ম-বহির্ভূত। **The anomalous equation of a planet**—মন্দফল (কেঃ গিঃ)। **–ly,** *adv.* **–ness,** *n.*

ā-nŏm′-ă-lȳ, *n.* **1.** Deviation from the common rule; irregularity; সাধারণ নিয়মের ব্যতিক্রম, ব্যভিচার, অবিধি, অব্যবস্থা, অনিয়ম, বিশৃঙ্খলা। **2.** Unevenness of motion, condition, etc.; গতি-বৈষম্য, অবস্থা বৈষম্য। **3.** (*Gram.*) Irregularity; (ব্যাকরণ) নিপাতন (মঃ উঃ)। **4.** (*Astron.*). The angular distance of a planet from its perihelion, as seen from the sun; নীচোচ্চের কৌণিক অন্তর, কেন্দ্র (সাঃ পঃ)। **Argument of anomaly**—মন্দকেন্দ্র (কেঃ গিঃ)। **Mean anomaly**—মধ্যকেন্দ্র (সাঃ পঃ)। **True anomaly**—স্ফুট-কেন্দ্র (ঐ)।

ā-nŏn′, *adv.* Soon; presently; ত্বরা, অবিলম্বে; ঝটিতি। **Ever and anon**—Every now and then; সর্ব্বদা, সারাক্ষণ, অনুদিন।

Anona reticulata—Bullock's heart ; নোনা আতা (যোঃ)।

Anona squamosa—Custard-apple ; আতা (যোঃ)।

ăn'-ŏ-nўm, *n.* **1.** A person who remains nameless ; অনামী। **2.** A pseudonym ; কৃত্রিম নাম, কাল্পনিক নাম। **—nym'-i-ty,** *n.* The state of being anonymous ; অনামকতা।

ă-nŏn'-ў-mous (-mŭs), *adj.* **1.** Of unknown name ; বেনামী, নামরহিত, উড়ো। **2.** Of unknown authorship ; (গ্রন্থাদি-সম্বন্ধে) অজ্ঞাতনামা লেখকরচিত, অনামক। **—ly,** *adv.* **—ness,** *n.*

ăn'-ŏ-rĕx-ў, *n.* (*Med.*) Want of appetite ; (ভৈষজ্য-শাস্ত্র) ক্ষুধাহীনতা, অগ্নিমান্দ্য, অরুচি।

ăn-ŏs'-mi-ă, *n.* (*Med.*) A loss of the sense of smell ; (ভৈষজ্য-শাস্ত্র) ঘ্রাণশক্তিহীনতা, নাসাহুণ (সাঃ পঃ)।

ă-oth'-ĕr (ă-nŭth-), *adj.* & *pron.* Not the same ; different ; অপর ; ভিন্ন, আলাহিদা। ***Pron.*** **1.** One more ; an additional one ; as, try *another* : আরও একটা ; অতিরিক্ত একটা। **2.** Any other ; any different person ; "Let *another* praise thee, not your own mouth ;" অন্য কিছু বা অন্য কেহ ; অন্য কোন ব্যক্তি। **One another**—Reciprocal ; as, love *one another ;* অন্যোন্য, পরস্পর। **One with another**—Taken all together ; taken at average ; মোটের উপর ; গড়পড়তায়। **Such another**—Another of the same sort ; এইরূপ আর একটা।

ăn'-sĕr-ĭne, *adj.* **1.** Relating to or resembling a goose ; রাজহংস-সম্পর্কীয়, রাজহংসসদৃশ। **2.** Of the nature of a goose ; silly ; রাজহংস-স্বভাব ; নির্ব্বোধ, বোকা।

ăn'-swer (-sêr), *n.* **1.** Something said or written in return to a question, call or address, etc. ; reply ; প্রত্যুক্তি, প্রত্যুত্তর ; উত্তর। **2.** A reply to a charge ; a defence ; as, at my first *answer* no man stood with me ; জবাব ; সমর্থন। **3.** A responsive action ; "Contraction is an *answer* to stimulus ;" সাড়া। **4.** The thing done in return ; retaliation ; প্রতিদান ; প্রতিফল, প্রতিশোধ। **5.** A solution ; the result of a mathematical operation ; মীমাংসা, সমাধান ; (গণিত-শাস্ত্র) উত্তর, ফল।

ăn'-swer (-sêr), *v. t.* & *i.* **1.** To reply to ; to respond to ; উত্তর দেওয়া ; সাড়া দেওয়া। **2.** To reply an accusation ; কোন অভিযোগের জবাব দেওয়া। **3.** To make a suitable return for anything said or done ; কোন কার্য্য বা উক্তির জন্য যথাযোগ্য প্রতিদান করা। [Thus, to *answer* a prayer or petition, is to grant, if it be deemed right, what it solicits ; সঙ্গত মনে হইলে, কাহারও আবেদন বা প্রার্থনা মঞ্জুর করা। To *answer* the door-bell, is to go and see who has rung it and what his object is in visiting the house ; ঘণ্টাধ্বনি শ্রবণে দ্বারদেশে গমন করত, কে কি উদ্দেশ্যে আসিয়াছে, তাহা নিরূপণ করা। To *answer* a legitimate claim on one's purse, is to pay it ; পরিশোধ করা। To *answer* the evil-doer, is to punish him ; দুষ্কর্ম্মের জন্য কাহাকে শাস্তি-প্রদান করা। To *answer* an enemy's fire in battle, is to fire back at him ; যুদ্ধে গোলার প্রত্যুত্তরে গোলাবর্ষণ করা।] **4.** To be suitable for ; to serve for ; as, the measure *answered* its end : money *answereth* all things ; কায চালান ; কার্য্যোপযোগী হওয়া। **5.** To correspond to ; to agree with ; মিলা ; অনুযায়ী হওয়া। **6.** To solve as a mathematical problem ; (গণিতে) কোন প্রশ্নের সমাধান করা। **7.** To face ; as, fire *answers* fire ; সম্মুখীন হওয়া। **8.** To refute ; as, none can *answer* me ; খণ্ডন করা, প্রতিবাদ করা। ***Verb i.*** (foll. by *to, for.*) **1.** To reply ; to speak or write by way of return ; প্রত্যুত্তর দেওয়া ; প্রত্যুত্তরে বলা বা লিখা। **2.** To be responsible ; দায়ী থাকা, জবাবদিহী হওয়া। **3.** To be fit or suitable ; to suit ; as, gypsum *answers* as a manure on some soils ; উপযোগী হওয়া ; যোগ্য হওয়া। **—a-ble,** *adj.* **1.** Responsible ; accountable ; দায়ী ; জবাবদিহী। **2.** Capable of being answered ; admitting of a (usually satisfactory) reply ; উত্তর-যোগ্য ; উত্তর-সহ। **—a-ble-ness,** *n.* **—a-bly,** *adv.* Suitably ; in due proportion ; যথানুরূপ ; যথানুপাতে। **Evasive answer**—টাল বাহানা, অজুহাৎ। **Lame answer**—Unsatisfactory answer ; অসন্তোষজনক উত্তর। **Plain answer**—সাফ্ জবাব, স্পষ্ট জবাব। **To answer for**—(*a*) To be accountable for ; জবাবদিহী থাকা, দায়ী থাকা। (*b*) To undertake responsibility for ; দায়িত্ব গ্রহণ করা। **To answer the call of nature**—মল-মূত্র ত্যাগ করা। **To answer to**—(*a*) To be known by ; as, I *answer to* that name ; পরিচিত হওয়া। (*b*) To correspond to ; অনুরূপ হওয়া। (*c*) To act in accordance with or in obedience to ; as, do the strings *answer* to thy noble hand ? অনুযায়ী ভাবে বা বশবর্ত্তী হইয়া কায করা। **To answer to a name**—To have the name of ; অমুক নাম থাকা।

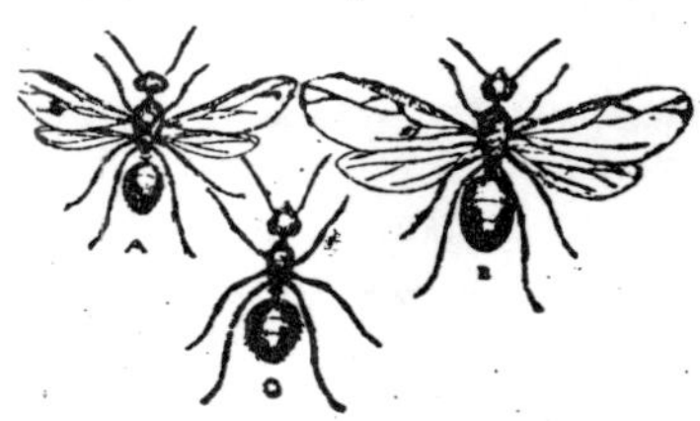

Ants.
(A) Male. (B) Female (C) Worker.

ănt, *n.* A small social insect

celebrated for industry ; পিপীলিকা, পিঁপড়া। **Ant-eater**—A name of

Ant-eater.

several animals which feed upon ants ; বিভিন্নজাতীয় পিপীলিকাভুক্‌ প্রাণীর সাধারণ নাম, বজ্রকীট (*Pangolin*)।

Ant-bear or Great Ant-eater.

Ant-fly—Winged ant used as a bait in angling ; বড়শীতে ব্যবহৃত এক প্রকার সপক্ষ-পিপীলিকা। **Ant-hill**—The mound or heap raised over an ant's nest ; বল্মীক, উইঢিপি। **Ant-catcher, Ant-thrush**—Names of birds of the thrush family living on ants ; পিপীলিকাভুক্‌ সারসশ্রেণী। **White-ant**—A very destructive social insect, also called termite ; উই (যোঃ)।

ănt-ăc′-id, *adj.* & *n.* Counteracting acidity ; অম্লত্ব-প্রতিষেধক, অম্লপিত্তঘ্ন। ***Noun.*** A remedy for acidity in the stomach ; অম্লত্বপ্রতিষেধক ঔষধ।

ăn-tăg′-ō-nĭsm, *n.* **1.** Active opposition (*to, against* a thing ; *between* two things) ; বিপক্ষতা, প্রতিপক্ষতা, প্রতিকূলাচরণ, বিরোধ, প্রতিদ্বন্দ্বিতা। **2.** Opposing principle ; বিরুদ্ধ মত।

ăn-tăg′-ō-nĭst, *n.* An opponent ; an adversary ; বিপক্ষ, বিরোধী ; প্রতিপক্ষ, প্রতিদ্বন্দ্বী। **—nis′-tic, —nis′-ti-cal,** *adjs.*

ăn-tăg′-ō-nīze, *v.t.* **1.** To contend with ; to struggle against ; to oppose actively ; [in England, used only of like forces ; in U. S. a person may *antagonize* (oppose) a measure] ; বিরোধ করা ; প্রতিকূলাচরণ করা ; বাধা দেওয়া। **2.** To counteract or neutralize the action of (any force) ; নিরাকৃত করা। **3.** (*Colloq.*) To make an opponent of ; (চলিত ভাষায়) প্রতিকূলাচারী করা।

ăn-tăl′-gic, *adj.* & *n.* (*Med.*) Alleviating pain ; বেদনাপ্রশমক। ***Noun.*** An anodyne ; বেদনাপ্রশমক ঔষধ।

ănt-ăl′-kă-lī, *n.* (*Chem.*) A substance which neutralizes an alkali ; (রসায়ন-শাস্ত্র) ক্ষারশিথিলকারক পদার্থ।

ănt-ăph-rō-dĭs′-ĭ-ăc, *adj.* & *n.* Preventive of venereal desire ; কামনিবারক। ***Noun.*** A medicine that quells or lessens the venereal desire ; কামনিবারক বা কামপ্রশমক ঔষধ।

ănt-ârc′-tĭc, *adj.* Southern ; of south polar regions ; দক্ষিণ দিক্‌-সংক্রান্ত, অবাচ্য ; কুমেরুসম্বন্ধীয়, যাম্য। **Antarctic Circle**—A small circle of the earth described around the Southern pole at a distance from it of 23° 28′ ; যাম্য বৃত্ত (সাঃ পঃ), কুমেরুবৃত্ত, উদীচ্যেতর বৃত্ত, দক্ষিণবৃত্ত (হিঃ কোঃ)।

ăn-tē-cēd′-ence, *n.* **1.** Precedence (in time or causul relation) ; পূর্ব্ববর্ত্তিতা, প্রাগ্‌ভাব (হিঃ কোঃ)। **2.** (*Astron.*) Retrograde motion ; (জ্যোতির্বিজ্ঞান) বক্রগতি (হিঃ কোঃ)।

ăn-tē-cēd′-ĕnt, *adj.* & *n.* **1.** Previous (*to*) ; prior (*to*) ; as, an event *antecedent* to the deluge ; প্রাক্‌কালীন ; পূর্ব্ববর্ত্তী, পূর্ব্বগামী। **2.** Presumptive ; ***a priori*** ; as, an *antecedent* improbability ; অনুমান-সিদ্ধ ; প্রাগ্‌জ্ঞান-সিদ্ধ। ***Noun.*** **1.** A thing or circumstance which goes before in time or order ; as, a long chain of *antecedents* ; পূর্ব্ববর্ত্তী বিষয় বা অবস্থা। **2.** The earlier events of one's life ; past history of a person ; as, if we would know what a man really is, we must know his *antecedents ;* গত জীবনের ঘটনাবলী পূর্ব্ব বিবরণ, পূর্ব্ব ইতিহাস, পূর্ব্বচরিত **3.** (*Log.*) The part of a conditional proposition on which the other depends (introduced by *if* or some equivalent word, opp. to *consequent*) ; (তর্ক-বিজ্ঞান) পূর্ব্ব (হিঃ কোঃ), কোন আপেক্ষিক বাক্যে যে অংশের উপর অপর অংশ নির্ভর করে। **4.** (*Gram.*) A noun, clause or sentence to which a following (relative) pronoun or adverb refers ; as, *Gautama,* who was called Buddha ;—here *Gautam* is *antecedent* of who ; (ব্যাকরণ) পূর্ব্বপদ। **5.** (*Math.*) The first term of a ratio ; as *a* : *b* ;—here *a* is the *antecedent* ; (গণিত-শাস্ত্র) কোন নিষ্পত্তির প্রথম সংখ্যা। **—ly,**

ăn′tē-chăm-bêr, *n.* A room leading to the chief apartment ; যে ক্ষুদ্র কক্ষ হইতে প্রধান কক্ষে উপস্থিত হওয়া যায়, বাহিরের কামরা, উপসভোপগৃহ।

ăn′tē-chăp-ĕl, *n.* The outer part at the west end of a chapel ; উপাসনা-মন্দিরের পশ্চিমপ্রান্তের

ăn′-tē-dāte, *n.* & *v. t.* ... before the true time ; ... তারিখ। ***Verb t.*** **1.** To ... earlier date than the r... to (document, event, etc.) ; তারিখের পরিবর্ত্তে পূর্ব্বের তারিখ দেওয়া। **2.** To precede in ... পূর্ব্বে সংঘটিত হওয়া। **3.** To ... pate ; "No hostile hand ... *antedate* my doom ;" পূর্ব্বে ... পারা।

·-tē-dī-lū'-vĭ-ăn, *adj.* & *n.* Be-
re the flood or deluge in Noah's
e; belonging, existing or
rring to the time before the
od; hence, very antiquated;
imitive; as, an *antediluvian*
hicle; (বাইবেলে বর্ণিত) মহাপ্লাবনের
র্ব্বকালীন; প্রলয়-প্রাক্কালিক; সেকেলে;
তি প্রাচীন। ***Noun.*** One who
ved before the deluge; an
old-fashioned person; also a
ery old person; মহাপ্লাবনের
র্ববর্ত্তী লোক; মান্ধাতার আমলের
কি, সেকেলে লোক; অতি বৃদ্ধলোক,
ড়ীকাক। **–al,** *adj.*

-tē-lōpe, *n.* A deer-like rumi-
nt genus of animals; কৃষ্ণসার, পৃষৎ,
া, সারঙ্গ (spotted), অজিন-যোনি।

te meridiem, (*L. phr.*) (সংক্ষেপে
m.) Between midnight and
on; পূর্ব্বাহ্ণ (রাত্রি ১টার পর হইতে
দিবস ১২টা পর্য্যন্ত)।

ē-mŭn'-dāne, *adj.* Existing or
urring before the creation of
world; সৃষ্টির পূর্ব্বে বর্ত্তমান, সৃষ্টির
র্ব সংঘটিত।

ē-nā'-tăl, *adj.* Existing before
h; জন্মের পূর্ব্বে বর্ত্তমান।

n'-nă, (*Pl.* ANTENNÆ.), *n.*
ensory organ found in pairs
the heads of insects, etc.,
ularly called *horns* or
s); (কীটপতঙ্গের) শুঁয়া, শৃঙ্গ,
f. দ্বিরেফ)। **–nal, –na-ry,**
r-ous. *adjs.*

ŭp'-tial (-shăl), *adj* Oc-
before marriage; prece-
marriage; as, *antenuptial*
n; বিবাহের পূর্ব্বে সংঘটিত বা
বিবাহের পূর্ব্ববর্ত্তী।

ĕn'-dĭ-ŭm, *n.* The screen
it of the altar; (খৃষ্টীয় ধর্ম্ম-
) বেদীর সম্মুখস্থ পর্দ্দা।

pē'-nŭlt, *n.* The last syllable
word except two; অন্তিম
শব্দের পূর্ব্ববর্ত্তী পদাংশ। **–nul'-
nate, *adj.* Pertaining to the
last syallable but two; অন্তিম
পদাংশদ্বয়ের পূর্ব্ববর্ত্তী পদাংশসম্বন্ধীয়,
উপান্ত-পূর্ব্ববর্ত্তী, পূর্ব্বোপান্ত।

ăn'-tē-păst, *n.* A foretaste; specif.
a first course to whet the ap-
petite; পূর্ব্বস্বাদ; বিশেষতঃ ক্ষুধা-বৃদ্ধির
জন্য প্রথম যে ব্যঞ্জনাদি পরিবেষিত হয়।

ăn-tē-prăn'-dĭ-ăl, *adj.* Before din-
ner; মধ্যাহ্ন-ভোজনের পূর্ব্ববর্ত্তী।

ăn-tē'-rĭ-or (-ĕr), *adj.* **1.** Prior;
going before; (with *to*); পূর্ব্ববর্ত্তী;
অগ্রবর্ত্তী। **2.** Towards the front;
fore; as, the *anterior* part of
the mouth; অগ্রবর্ত্তী; সম্মুখস্থ।
–i-ty, *n.* **–ly,** *adv.*

ăn'-tē-rōōm, *n.* A room leading
to another; উপপ্রকোষ্ঠ, অগ্রকক্ষ।

ănt-hē'-lĭ-ŏn, *n.* A luminous ring
or nimbus projected on a cloud
or fog-bank, opposite to the sun
(when rising or setting); সূর্য্যের
বিপরীত দিগ্‌বর্ত্তী জ্যোতির্ম্মণ্ডল, উপসূর্য্য,
(সাঃ পঃ), প্রতিসূর্য্য (বৃঃ সং)।

ăn-thĕl-mĭn'-tĭc, *adj.* & *n.* Cap-
able of destroying or expelling
intestinal worms; কৃমিঘ্ন। ***Noun.***
A medicine given against intes-
tinal worms; কৃমিনাশক ঔষধ।

ăn'-thĕm, *n.* **1.** A sacred song; a
portion of the Scriptures or of
the Liturgy set to sacred music
and sung; সূক্ত, স্তোত্র, ভজন;
বাইবেলের অংশবিশেষ—যাহা গীত হয়।
2. Song of praise or gladness;
প্রশংসা-গীতি, আনন্দ-গীতি।

ăn-thē'-mĭ-ŏn, *n.* The ornamental
series used in Greek or Roman

Anthemion.

decoration; গ্রীক্ ও রোমান স্থাপত্য-
শিল্পানুযায়ী সৌধ-ভূষা-বিশেষ।

Anthemis nobilis—Chamomile;
বাবুনা ফুল (খোরাসানী)।

Anthemis pyrethrum—Indian
pellitory; আকরকরা (বেলঃ), আকার-
করভ (ঐ)।

ăn'-thĕr, *n.* (*Bot.*) The part of
the stamen containing the pollen

b.b. Anthers.

or fertilizing dust; (উদ্ভিদ-বিদ্যা)
(পুষ্পের) পুংকেশরের অগ্রভাগ, পরাগ-
পূর্ণ শীর্ষভাগ, পরাগকোষ (সাঃ পঃ)।

ăn-thē'-sĭs, *n.* (*Bot.*) The opening
or bursting of the flower; (উদ্ভিদ্-
বিদ্যা) পুষ্পবিকাশকাল (সাঃ পঃ)।

ăn-thŏl'-ō-ġў, *n.* **1.** A collection of
flowers of literature, *i.e.*, beautiful
passages from authors; a collec-
tion of choice poems, esp. epi-
grams (by various authors);
সাহিত্য-পুষ্পসংগ্রহ; প্রাচীনসাহিত্যরথি-
গণের রচনা হইতে কুসুম-সুকুমার বচন-
সমূহ সংগ্রহ। **2.** Literary collection;
সাহিত্য-সংগ্রহ, চয়নিকা। **–gist,** *n.*

An'-tho-nў (ăn-tŏ-), *n.* **1.** St. An-
thony, the patron saint of swine-
herds; শূকরপালকগণের রক্ষয়িতা
সিদ্ধপুরুষ এণ্টোনি। **2.** (Common
noun) The smallest pig of a
litter; একবার প্রসবের সর্ব্বকনিষ্ঠ
শূকর-শিশু। **St. Anthony's fire**—
Erysipelas; বিসর্প রোগ।

ăn'-thŏ-phore (-fŏr), *n.* (*Bot.*) The
stalk which in some flowers
raises the receptacle above
the calyx; (উদ্ভিদ-বিদ্যা) পুষ্পবহ
(সাঃ পঃ)।

ăn'-thră-cīte, *n.* A hard, compact
variety of coal; একজাতীয় কঠিন
এবং নিরেট কয়লা।

ăn'-thrăx, *n.* **1.** A malignant boil
or carbuncle; বিস্ফোটক বা পৃষ্ঠব্রণ।

2. A malignant pustule caused in man by infection from animals; বিষাক্ত ফুস্কুড়ি, সপুয ব্রণ। 3. Splenic fever of sheep and cattle; মেষ ও গো-মহিষাদির প্লীহা-বৃদ্ধিজনিত জ্বর।

ăn-thrö-pŏg′-ë-nȳ, *n.* A study of the origin of man; মনুষ্যোৎপত্তির আলোচনা।

ăn-thrö′-pö-glŏt, *n.* An animal that has a tongue resembling that of man, as a parrot; নর-জিহ্ব জন্তু, যথা শুক পক্ষী।

ăn-thrö-pŏg′-ră-phȳ, *n.* That branch of physical geography which treats of the actual distribution of human race; মানব জাতির বিভিন্ন দেশে অবস্থান বিষয়ক প্রাকৃতিক ভূগোলের শাখা।

ăn′-thrö-poid (-pŏyd), *adj.* & *n.* Resembling man; মানবসদৃশ। ***Noun.*** A being that is human in form only, esp. an anthropoid ape; মানবাকৃতি জীব বা বানর।

ăn-thrŏp′-ö-līte, *n.* A fossil man; শিলীভূত মানব।

ăn-thrö-pŏl′-ö-ğȳ, *n.* The whole science of man; the physiological and psychological science of man; মানববিজ্ঞান; নৃতত্ত্ব, নরতত্ত্ব। **—po lög′ i cal,** *adj.* **—pol′-o-gist,** *n.* One who writes or studies anthropolgy; মানব-তত্ত্বজ্ঞ, নৃতত্ত্ববিদ্।

ăn-thrö-pŏm′-ĕ-trȳ, *n.* The measurment of the human body; মানবমিতি।

ăn-thrö-pö-mŏr′-phize, *v. t.* To attribute a human form or personality to (God, etc.); (ঈশ্বরাদিতে) নরত্ব-আরোপ করা। **—phism,** *n.* The representation of the Deity under a human form or with human attributes and affections; ভগবানে নরপ্রকৃতি বা নররূপারোপ, সগুণবাদ, সাকারেশ্বরবাদ, নরত্ব-আরোপ। **—phist,** *n.* **—phous,** *adj.* Of human form; নররূপী।

ăn-thrö-pŏph′-ă-gous (-gŭs), *adj.* Feeding on human flesh; নর-মাংসভোজী। **—gi,** *n. pl.* Man-eaters; নরমাংসাশিগণ, রাক্ষসগণ। **—gy,** *n.* The eating of human flesh; নর-মাংস ভোজন।

ăn′-tĭ-âr, (Javanese *antjar*), *n.* **1.** The Upas-tree of Java; যবদ্বীপের চাঁদলা বৃক্ষ, যমবৃক্ষ। **2.** A virulent poison obtained from the juice of the Upas tree; চাঁদলা বৃক্ষের বিষাক্ত নির্যাস।

ăn-ti-băc-chī′-ŭs, *n.* (*Prosody*) A foot of three syllables, the two first long and the last short; (ছন্দঃশাস্ত্র) ত গণ (— — ⏑)।

ăn-ti-bil′-i-ous (-ŭs), *adj.* Counteractive of biliousness; পিত্তঘ্ন, পিত্তনাশক।

ăn′-tic, *adj.* & *n.* Grotesque; fantastic; bizarre; উদ্ভট; অদ্ভুত; অপরূপ। ***Noun.*** (Usu. *pl.*) **1.** A Grotesque posture or trick; বিকট অঙ্গ-ভঙ্গি, মস্করামি। **2.** A mountebank; a clown; ধড়ীবাজ; ভাঁড়, বিদূষক।

An′-ti-christ, ăn′-ti-christ (ăn-), *n.* **1.** A great antagonist, person or power, expected to precede Christ's second coming; "As ye have heard that *Antichrist* shall come;" যীশুখৃষ্টের দ্বিতীয় আবির্ভাবের পূর্ব্বে, যে মহাপরাক্রমশালী খৃষ্ট-বিরোধী ব্যক্তি অথবা শক্তি আবির্ভূত হইবে বলিয়া খৃষ্টানগণ প্রত্যাশা করিয়া থাকেন। **2.** A false Christ (common noun); জাল খৃষ্ট। **3.** The Pope (so called by Luther and many Protestants); পোপ। **—christ-i-an,** *adj.* Pertaining to Antichrist; opposed to Christianity; খৃষ্ট-বিরোধি-সম্পর্কীয়; খৃষ্টধর্ম্মবিরোধী। **—christ-i an ism,** *n.*

ăn-tĭc′-i-pāte, *v. t.* **1.** To realise beforehand; to forestall (a person or thing); as, to *anticipate* the pleasures of an entertainment; to expect (a event, *that* it will happen as, I never *anticipated* su disaster; পূর্ব্বাববোধ করা, পূর্ব্বসিদ্ধ করা, পূর্ব্বাস্বাদ করা; পূর্ব্বাভাস পাওয় প্রত্যাশা করা। **2.** To cause t happen earlier; to accelerate as, to *anticipate* one's ruin সত্বর সংঘটিত করা; ত্বরান্বিত করা **3.** To use in advance; to spend (money) before it i properly available; as, do no *anticipate* your income; য সময়ের পূর্ব্বে ব্যবহার করা; (ৎ সঙ্গতরূপে প্রাপ্য হইবার পূর্ব্বে ব্যয় ক **—pant,** *adj.* & *n.* Operating advance; looking forward; pectant; পূর্ব্বাহ্ণে কার্য্যসাধক; প্রত্য আশান্বিত। (*Noun.*) An antici tor; প্রত্যাশী। **—pa-tive,** *adj.* **—** **tive-ly,** *adv.*

ăn-tĭc-i-pā′-tion, *n.* **1.** The ac placing or considering so thing beforehand or before proper time; পূর্ব্বে স্থাপন, অগ্রে চি **2.** Foretaste; realisation bef hand; as, the *anticipation* the joys of heaven; পূর্ব্বা পূর্ব্বাববোধ, পূর্ব্বাবধারণ। **3.** Int foreconception; intuition; cognition; as, many men themselves up to the first cipations of their minds; প্রত্যয়লব্ধ পূর্ব্বজ্ঞান; সহজজ্ঞান বিভাবন। **4.** The act of forward to; expectation; করণ; প্রত্যাশা। **5.** (*Me* occurrence of certain phe before the usual time; (বৈ যথাসময়ের পূর্ব্বে কোন কোন প্রকাশ। **—pa tor,** *n.* **—** **ry,** *adj.*

ăn-ti-clī′-măx, *n.* **1.** (*Rh* sentence in which the first increase in force, and terminate in something important and striking; "

comes Dalhousie, God of War, Lieutenant Colonel to the Earl of Mar ;" (opposed to *climax*—সংস্কৃত সারালঙ্কারের বিপরীত) ; (অলঙ্কার-শাস্ত্র) যে বাক্যের ভাবসকল প্রথমতঃ ক্রমশঃ উৎকর্ষতা লাভ করিয়া, তৎপরে উত্তরোত্তর অপকর্ষতা প্রাপ্ত হয়, গুরুচণ্ডালী-দোষ। **2.** A descent or fall in contrast to a previous rise ; as, the latter years of his life were only an *anticlimax ;* সমৃদ্ধি বা উন্নতির অবস্থা হইতে পতন।

ăn-ti-clī′-năl, *adj.* Inclining in opposite direction ; পরস্পরের

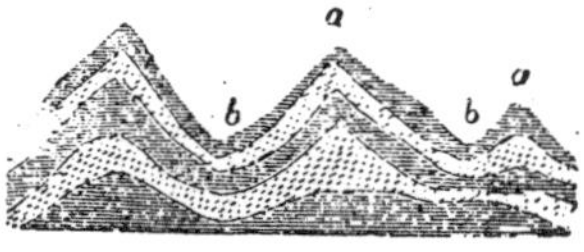

a a a, anticlinal line. *b b,* synclinal line.

বিপরীতদিকে আনত। *(Geol.)* **An anticlinal line** or **axis**—The line from which the strata dip in opposite directions ; (ভূ-বিদ্যা) নিম্নদিকে আনত বিপরীত দিগ্‌গামী তরঙ্গরাজির মত স্তর-বিশিষ্ট শৈলরেখা।

ăn′-ti-cȳ-clōne, *n.* A rotatory outward flow of air from atmospheric area of high pressure ; প্রতীপবাতাবর্ত্ত (সাঃ পঃ), প্রতীপাবর্ত্ত (ঐ), প্রতিচক্রবাত (ঐ), প্রতিচক্রাবর্ত্ত। **—clon-ic,** *adj.* **—clon i-cal-ly,** *adv.*

Antidesma paniculata—খুদীজাম (বেলঃ)।

ăn′-ti-dōte, *n.* **1.** A medicine given to counteract the effects of poison or an attack of disease ; (with *against, for, to*) ; বিষঘ্ন, প্রতিবিষ। **2.** Whatever acts for the counteraction of any evil ; as, an *antidote* against infidelity ; বিঘ্ননাশক। **—dot-al, —dot-i-cal,** *adjs.* Having the quality of, or serving as, antidote ; বিষান্তক, বিষাপহ।

ăn-ti-dȳ-sĕn-tĕr′-ic, *adj.* & *n.* Efficacious against dysentery ; আমাশয়ান্তক। ***Noun.*** A remedy for dysentery ; আমাশয়ঘ্ন ঔষধ।

ăn ti-fē′-brīle, *adj.* & *n.* Tending to cure fever ; জ্বরঘ্ন। ***Noun.*** A febrifuge ; জ্বরসংহারক ঔষধ।

ăn′-ti-gŏd, *n.* One opposed to God, as a rival deity ; ঈশ্বর-বিরোধী, ঈশ্বরের প্রতিদ্বন্দ্বী, শয়তান।

ăn-til′-ō-ġȳ, *n.* Contradiction in terms ; বিরোধোক্তি, উক্তিবিরোধ।

ănti-mă-căs′-sâr, *n.* A covering for chairs, sofas, pillows, etc., to protect them from grease in the hair, আরাম-কেদারা, উপাধান, প্রভৃতির আবরণ।

ăn′-ti-mŏ-nȳ, *n.* A brittle metallic substance of a bluish white colour ; বরনাগ, (সাঃ পঃ), অঞ্জনক (ঐ), অন্তমনীক (মবাঃ)। **Antimony sulphide**—নীলাঞ্জন (সাঃ পঃ), সৌবীরাঞ্জন (ঐ)।

ăn-ti-nō′-mi-ăn, *adj.* & *n.* Opposed to the obligatoriness of moral law ; pertaining to the Antinomians ; নৈতিক-নিয়মের বিরুদ্ধাচারী ; উক্ত মতাবলম্বী নীতিবিরুদ্ধাচারী সম্প্রদায়বিশেষসম্পর্কীয়। ***Noun.*** One who maintains that the moral law is not binding on the Christians ; খৃষ্টধর্ম্মাবলম্বিগণের পক্ষে ঈশ্বরের দশাদেশ পালনের কোনও প্রয়োজনীয়তা নাই, এবং অধিকতম পরিমাণে ঈশ্বরের ক্ষমা ও অনুগ্রহ লাভের জন্য পাপসঞ্চয় কর্ত্তব্য—এবম্বিধ মতাবলম্বী খৃষ্টীয় সম্প্রদায়-বিশেষভুক্ত ব্যক্তি। **—tin′-o-mism,** *n.*

ăn-tin′-ō-mȳ, *n.* **1.** A contradiction in a law or between two laws ; নিয়ম-বিরোধ, পরস্পর-বিরোধ (হিঃ কোঃ), ন্যায়বিরোধ (ঐ)। **2.** A conflict of authority ; বচনবিরোধ (হিঃ কোঃ)। A paradox ; বিরোধাভাস (হিঃ কোঃ), কূট (ঐ)।

ăn-tip′-ă-thȳ, *n.* Constitutional or settled aversion (*against, to, between,* persons) ; সহজ-দ্বেষ, বিদ্বেষ, স্বাভাবিক শত্রুতা, বিতৃষ্ণা, বিরাগ, ঘৃণা, বিরূপভাব। **—ti-pa-thet′-ic,** *adj.* Opposed in nature or disposition ; (*to*) ; having a constitutional aversion to (a thing) ; স্বভাববিরুদ্ধ, প্রকৃতিবিরুদ্ধ ; দৈহিকপ্রকৃতিবিরুদ্ধ। **—ti-path′-ic,** *adj.* **1.** Of contrary character ; (*to*) ; বিরুদ্ধভাবাপন্ন। **2.** (*Med.*) Having or producing contrary symptoms ; (ভৈষজ্য-শাস্ত্র) বিরুদ্ধ-লক্ষণবিশিষ্ট, বিরুদ্ধ-লক্ষণোৎপাদক।

ăn-ti-phlŏ-ġis′-tic, *adj.* & *n.* Reducing inflammation ; প্রদাহ-প্রশমক। ***Noun.*** A medicine allaying inflammation ; প্রদাহ-নিবারক ঔষধ।

ăn′-ti-phŏn, —phōne, *n.* **1.** Alternate singing or chanting ; খৃষ্টীয়-ধর্ম্মমন্দিরের পর্য্যায়-সঙ্গীত বা স্তোত্রপাঠ। **2.** Prose or verse composition sung alternately by two choirs ; খৃষ্টীয় ধর্ম্মমন্দিরস্থ কীর্ত্তন-সম্প্রদায় কর্ত্তৃক পর্য্যায়ক্রমে গীত গদ্য বা পদ্য রচনা। **—tiph′-ō-nal,** *adj* & *n.* **1.** Sung alternately ; পর্য্যায়ক্রমে গীত। **2.** Responsive in sound ; as, a peal of the organ is *antiphonal* to a flourish of trumpets ; প্রতিধ্বনিকারী। (*Noun.*) An antiphonal collection ; পর্য্যায়সঙ্গীত-সংগ্রহ। **—tiph′-o-nal-ly,** *adv.*

ăn-tiph′-ō-nă-rȳ, *n.* A book containing a collection of antiphones ; পর্য্যায়গীতি-সংহিতা।

ăn-tiph′-ō-nȳ, *n.* **1.** A musical response ; সঙ্গীতচ্ছলে প্রত্যুত্তর। **2.** Alternate singing or chanting ; পর্য্যায়ক্রমে গান। **3.** A response or echo ; সাড়া, প্রতিধ্বনি।

ăn-tip′-ō-dēs, (*Sing.* ANTIPODE), *n. Pl.* **1.** Those who live on the side of the globe diametrically opposite ; পৃথিবীর পরস্পর বিপরীত পৃষ্ঠবাসী লোকসকল, কুদলান্তরবাসী (সাঃ পঃ)। **2.** Places diametrically opposite to each other, especially region opposite to our own ; কুদলান্তর দেশ (সাঃ পঃ), প্রতিপাদ স্থান (ঐ)। (*Sing.*) The exact opposite (*of, to*) ; (কোন ব্যক্তি বা বিষয়ের) ঠিক্ বিপরীত। **—dal, —dē'-an,** *adjs.*

ăn'-ti-pōpe, *n.* One who usurps the papal power in opposition to the pope ; পোপের বিরুদ্ধাচারী।

ăn-ti-quā'-ri-ăn, *adj.* & *n.* Connected with the studies of antiquities ; pertaining to antiquaries ; প্রত্নবিদ্যাবিষয়ক ; প্রত্নতাত্ত্বিক। ***Noun.*** **1.** A drawing-paper of large size ; এক প্রকার বৃহদায়তন চিত্রাঙ্কণের কাগজ। **2.** An antiquary ; প্রত্নতত্ত্বজ্ঞ। **—ism,** *n.* **—ize,** *v. i.*

ăn'-ti-quă-rȳ, *n.* One devoted to the study of ancient times through their relics, as remains of ancient habitations, early monuments, statues, coins, inscriptions, etc. ; one who searches for and collects the relics of antiquity ; প্রত্নতত্ত্ববিদ্, প্রত্নতত্ত্বজ্ঞ, প্রত্নবিদ্, পুরাতত্ত্বজ্ঞ ; প্রত্নতত্ত্বানুসন্ধায়ী, পুরাণতত্ত্ববিদ্ (আঃ মঠ)।

ăn'-ti-quāte, *v. t.* To make obsolete, especially to abolish as out of date ; অপ্রচলিত করা, বিশেষতঃ পুরাতন বলিয়া বাতিল বা রহিত করা। **—quat-ed,** *p. p.* Grown old ; obsolete ; out of use ; as, an *antiquated* law ; পুরাকালীন, প্রাচীন ; অপ্রচলিত ; অব্যবহার্য্য।

ăn-tīque' (-tēk), *adj.* & *n.* Of old times ; old-fashioned ; archaic ; প্রাচীনকালীন ; সেকেলে, প্রাচীনধরণের ; অপ্রচলিত, অব্যবহৃত। ***Noun.*** **1.** Relic of ancient art or of times (esp. works of Grecian and Roman antiquity) ; পুরাকালীন শিল্প বিশেষ, বিশেষতঃ প্রাচীন রোম ও গ্রীসের কীর্ত্তিচিহ্ন। **2.** A kind of type like this—**antique** ; একপ্রকার মুদ্রণের হরফ। **—ly,** *adv.* **—ness,** *n.* **The antique**—Antique style ; প্রাচীন লেখকদিগের অনুযায়িনী রচনা-পদ্ধতি।

ăn-tiq'-ui-tȳ (-tĭk-wĭ-), *n.* **1.** Ancientness ; as, a family of great *antiquity;* প্রাচীনত্ব। **2.** Old times; esp. time before the Middle Ages ; former ages ; as, Cicero was the greatest orator of *antiquity ;* বহুপূর্ব্বকাল, পুরাকল্প, পুরাকাল ; বিশেষতঃ মধ্যযুগের পূর্ব্ববর্ত্তী-কাল ; প্রাচীন যুগ। **2.** The ancients ; the people of ancient times ; as, the fact is admitted by all *antiquity ;* প্রাচীন-বর্গ ; পুরাকালের লোক। (*Pl.*—QUITIES.) Ancient institutions, customs or events ; the remains or relics of ancient times ; পুরকালের প্রতিষ্ঠান, রীতি-নীতি, আচার-পদ্ধতি, ঘটনাবলী প্রভৃতি ; প্রাচীন স্মৃতি চিহ্ন বা ধ্বংসাবশেষ-সমূহ।

ăn-ti-săb-bă-tā'-ri-ăn, *adj.* & *n.* Opposed to the observance of Sabbath ; রবিবাসর-বিশ্রাম-বিরোধী। ***Noun.*** One who is opposed to the observance of the Sabbath ; যে ব্যক্তি রবিবার বিশ্রাম দিবস বলিয়া অস্বীকার করে।

ăn-tis'-cians (-tĭsh-ĭ-ăns), *n. pl.* The inhabitants of the earth living on the opposite sides of the equator and whose shadows at noon are cast in contrary directions ; বিষুবরেখার উভয় পার্শ্ববাসী লোক—ইহাদের দেহচ্ছায়া মধ্যাহ্নকালে পরস্পরের বিপরীত দিকে পতিত হয়।

ăn-ti-scŏr-bü'-tic, *n.* A remedy for scurvy ; শীতাদরোগ-প্রতিষেধক (লেবু প্রভৃতি)।

ăn-ti-scrip'-tur-ăl (-chûr-), *adj.* Opposed to the doctrines of Scripture or to its authenticity ; বাইবেল গ্রন্থোক্ত মতবাদের বিরোধী, বাইবেল গ্রন্থের প্রামাণিকতার বিরোধী।

ăn-ti-sĕp'-tic, *adj.* & *n.* **1.** Counteracting putrefaction ; পচননিবারক (হঃ চঃ)। **2.** (*Fig.*) Preventing moral decay ; (লক্ষণায়) নৈতিক অবনতিনিবারক। ***Noun.*** A substance which resists putrefaction ; পচন-নিবারক ঔষধ। **—ti-cal,** *adj.*

ăn-ti sō'-cial (-shăl), *adj.* Averse to society ; opposed to the principles on which society is based ; অসামাজিক ; সমাজব্যবস্থার বিরোধী, সমাজদ্বেষী, সমাজবিরোধী। **—ist,** *n.*

ăn-ti-spăs-mŏd'-ic, *adj.* & *n.* Preventing or allaying spasms or convulsions ; আক্ষেপনিবারক, আক্ষেপ-প্রশমক। ***Noun.*** A medicine so used ; আক্ষেপ-নিবারক ঔষধ।

ăn'-ti-spăst, *n.* (*Prosody*) A foot of four syllables, the first and fourth short and the second and third long (⏑ — — ⏑) ; (ছন্দঃশাস্ত্র) বাক্যাংশচতুষ্টয়বিশিষ্ট কবিতার পাদ-বিশেষ, ইহার প্রথম ও চতুর্থ বাক্যাংশদ্বয় লঘু এবং দ্বিতীয় ও তৃতীয় গুরু হইয়া থাকে।

ănt-i-thē'-ist, *n.* One opposed to belief in the existence of God ; অনীশ্বরবাদী। **—is'-tic,** *adj.* **—the'-ism,** *n.*

ăn-tith'-ĕ-sis, *n.* (*Pl.* ANTITHESES) **1.** Opposition ; contrast ; (*of, between* two things) ; বিরোধ ; বৈপরীত্য, বৈভিন্ন্য। **2.** (*Rhet.*) An opposition or contrast of words or sentiments ; as, the prodigal *robs* his heir, the miser *robs* himself ; বিরোধালঙ্কার, বিরোধাভাস। **3.** A counter-thesis ; a counter-proposition ; প্রতিপক্ষ ; প্রতিপ্রতিজ্ঞা, উত্তর-পক্ষ (বিশঃ)। **4.** The direct opposite (*of, to*) ; as, rhyme is sometimes taken as the *antithesis* of reason ; ঠিক বিপরীত। **—ti-thĕt'-ic, —ti-thet'-i cal,** *adjs.* Of the nature of antithesis ; directly opposite ; consisting of two opposites ; বিরোধালঙ্কারাত্মক ; বিপরীত, বিরুদ্ধ ; পরস্পরবিরোধী ভাব-সম্পন্ন। **—ti-thet'-i-cal-ly,** *adv.*

ăn'-ti-trāde, *n.* A tropical wind blowing steadily in a direction opposite to the trade-wind ; বাণিজ্য-সমীরের বিপরীত দিকে প্রবাহিত পবন, প্রতিবাণিজ্য-বায়ু।

ăn-tĭ-trin-ĭ-tā rĭ ăn, *n* One opposed to the doctrine of the Trinity ; ঈশ্বর পিতা, পুত্র ও পবিত্রাত্মা—এই ত্রিমূর্ত্তিতে বিরাজ করেন, এইরূপ মতবাদের বিরুদ্ধমতাবলম্বী। **—ism,** *n.*

ăn'-tĭ-tȳpe, *n.* That which corresponds to something else, as a stamp does to the die ; প্রতিবিম্ব-মূল, আদর্শ।

ănt'-lêr, *n.* The entire horn or any branch of the horn of a stag or deer ; হরিণশৃঙ্গ, মৃগশৃঙ্গ, শৃঙ্গ-শাখা। **—lered,** *adj.* Furnished with antlers ; শৃঙ্গী।

ăn-tŏ-nŏ-mā'-sĭ-ă, *n.* (*Rhet.*) The substitution of an epithet or the name of an office or dignity, etc. for a person's proper name ; as, *his grace* for an archbishop : *his lordship* for a nobleman ; also, the use of a proper name to express a general idea ; as, in calling an orator a *Cicero* : a wise judge a *Daniel* ; (অলঙ্কার-শাস্ত্র) কোন ব্যক্তির নামের পরিবর্ত্তে তদীয় উপাধি, পদ বা পদগৌরব ব্যবহার ; সাধারণভাবপ্রকাশার্থ নামের ব্যবহার, লক্ষণা (আঃ বঃ)।

A-nŭ'-ră (ă-), *n. pl.* Tailless amphibia, as the frog and toad ; পুচ্ছহীন উভচরবর্গ (যথা মণ্ডূকাদি), অপুচ্ছী, (সাঃ পঃ), অপুচ্ছাঙ্কুর (প্রঃ বাঃ)।

ā'-nŭs, *n.* The circular opening at the lower extremity of the alimentary canal ; গুহ্য, পায়ু, গুহ্যদেশ, গুহ্যদ্বার, মলদ্বার।

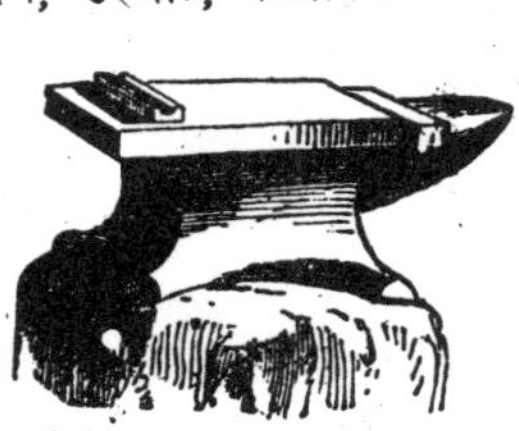

Anvil.

ăn'-vil, *n.* **1.** An iron block upon which the smith hammers and shapes the metal ; (also, *fig.* as, stomach is the *anvil* where our health is forged) ; নেয়ান্, নেয়াই, হ্যাই, কুট, স্থুনা, শূর্ম্মি। **2.** (*Physiol.*) A bone of the ear ; (শারীর-বিজ্ঞান) কর্ণের অস্থি-বিশেষ। **On** or **upon the anvil**—To be in a state of discussion ; as, he has now *on the anvil* another scheme ; (কোন ব্যবস্থা প্রভৃতি) আলোচনাধীন অবস্থায় থাকা।

an-xĭ'-ĕ-tȳ (ăng-zī-), *n.* **1.** Uneasiness ; অস্থিরতা, ব্যগ্রতা, উৎকণ্ঠা। **2.** Solicitous desire ; concern ; ব্যাকুলতা, আকুলতা, উদ্বেগ।

anx'-ious (ăng-shŭs), *adj.* **1.** Troubled ; uneasy (*about*) ; earnestly desirous ; being in a painful suspense ; উদ্বিগ্ন ; উৎকণ্ঠিত, উতালা ; ব্যগ্র, ব্যাকুল ; আকুলিত, উৎসুক। **2.** Causing anxiety ; worrying ; (applied to things) ; as, an *anxious* business ; (*anxious seats, benches*—Those set apart for anxious enquirers.) ; উৎকণ্ঠাপ্রদ ; উদ্বেগজনক। **—ly,** *adv.* In anxious manner ; উতলাভাবে, ঔৎসুক্যসহকারে।

ăn'-ȳ, *adj., pron.* & *adv.,* **1.** One indifferently out of many ; as, I ask *any* one to answer my question ; যে কোন। **2.** Some ; an indefinite number or quantity ; as, are there *any* witnesses present ? কতিপয় ; কোন অনির্দ্দিষ্ট সংখ্যা বা পরিমাণ। **3.** Whatever of all is chosen ; every ; as, *any* chemist will tell you ; যে কোন, যে কেহ ; প্রত্যেক। ***Pron.*** (It is often used, both in singular and plural, as a pronoun, the person or thing being understood.) Anyone ; anybody ; যে কেহ ; যে কোন ব্যক্তি, যে সে। ***Adv.*** To any extent ; in any degree ; before you go *any* further, at all ; যে কোন মাত্রায় ; যে কোন পরিমাণে ; মোটেই। **Any more**—Anything additional ; as, I do not need *any more* ; আর কিছু। Further ; as, I do not think *any more* about it ; আর অধিক। **At any rate, in any case**—Whatever may be the state of affairs ; anyhow ; যাহাই ঘটুক না কেন, যে কোনও অবস্থায় ; যে কোন প্রকারে।

ăn'-ȳ-bŏd-ȳ, *n.* Any one ; any person ; যে কেহ ; যে কোন ব্যক্তি। **Anybodies**—Ordinary people ; as, two or three *anybodies* ; সাধারণ লোক।

ăn'-ȳ-how, *adv.* & *conj.* **1.** In any way whatever ; at any rate ; যে কোন প্রকারে, যেন তেন প্রকারেন ; যাহাই ঘটুক না কেন। **2.** At haphazard ; as, he does his work *anyhow* ; যা তা করিয়া, এলোমেলোভাবে। ***Conj.*** In any case ; at least ; যাহাই হউক ; অন্ততঃ।

ăn'-ȳ-thing, *n.* & *adv.* Whatever thing ; a thing, no matter which ; a thing of any kind ; যে কোন দ্রব্য ; যাহা কিছু একটা ; যে কোন রকমের জিনিষ। ***Adv.*** In any measure ; to any extent ; as, if he be *anything* young ; যতই ; যতদূর। **Anything but**—Not at all or in any respect ; "The battle was a rare one and the victory *anything but* secure ;" মোটেই না, আদবেই না। **Anything like**—In any respect ; at all ; as, I cannot give *anything like* a fair sketch of his trials ; কোন বিষয়ে ; একেবারে, মোটেই।

ăn'-ȳ-time, *adv.* **1.** At any period ; as, the soldiers are liable to be called out *anytime* ; যে কোন সময়, যখন তখন। **2.** Frequently ; repeatedly ; পুনঃ পুনঃ ; বারম্বার, প্রায়শঃ।

ăn'-ȳ-wāy, —wāys, *adv.* At all ; in any case ; একেবারে ; যাহাই হউক।

ăn'-ȳ-where, (-whâr), *adv.* In any place ; কোন স্থানে, কুত্রাপি।

ăn′-ȳ-wīse, *adv.* In any way ; at all ; as, *anywise*, a good relation ; কোন প্রকারে ; আদৌ ।

A-ō′-ni-ăn (ā-), *adj.* Pertaining to Aonia, in Bœtia, or to the Muses who were supposed to dwell there ; বিয়োশিয়াপ্রদেশান্তর্গত এয়োনিয়া নামক স্থানসংক্রান্ত, অথবা তৎস্থানবাসনী বাগ্‌দেবীগণবিষয়ক । **Aonian fount**—The fountain of Aganippe, at the foot of the mount Helicon, sacred to the Muses ; বাগ্‌দেবীগণের অধিষ্ঠান-স্থল হেলিকন-শৈলের পাদদেশবর্ত্তী 'এগানিপি' নামক উৎস ।

ā′-ö-rist, *adj.* & *n.* [*Gr. aoristos*, indefinite—*a* not, and *horizo*, limit.] (*Greek Gram.*) Implying no limitation ; (গ্রীক-ব্যাকরণ) অনির্দ্দিষ্ট । ***Noun.*** A tense of the Greek verb which denotes simply that an action or occurrence took place in an indefinite past time ; অনির্দ্দিষ্ট সময়বোধক ক্রিয়ার কাল, অনিশ্চিত কালবাচক ক্রিয়াপদ, অনদ্যতনভূত । **–ic, –i cal,** *adjs.*

ā-ŏr′-tă, *n.* (*Anat.*) The great artery or trunk of the arterial system, issuing from the left ventricle of the heart ; (শারীর-সংস্থান-বিদ্যা) যে বৃহৎ ধমনী হইতে ফুস্‌ফুসের ধমনী ব্যতীত অন্যান্য ধমনীসমূহ বহির্গত হইয়াছে এবং যদ্দারা হৃৎপিণ্ড হইতে দেহের সর্ব্বত্র শোণিত সঞ্চারিত হয়, মহাধমনী (হঃ চঃ), বৃহদ্ধমনী (ঐ) । **–tic,** *adj.*

a outrance, (*F.*) *adv.* To the death ; মরণপণ ।

ă-pāce′, *adv.* With speed ; swiftly ; quickly ; as, he pushed on *apace* : our friendship ripens *apace* ; দ্রুতপাদসঞ্চারে ; দ্রুতগতি ; শীঘ্রগতি, তূর্ণ ।

ăp′-ăn-āge, *n.* Same as APPANAGE.

ă-pârt′, *adv.* (followed by *from*) **1.** Separately ; independently ; as, consider the two propositions *apart* ; স্বতন্ত্রভাবে, পৃথগ্‌ভাবে ; স্বাধীনভাবে । **2.** Aside ; away ; as, lay *apart* all filthiness ; একধারে ; দূরে । **3.** In two or more parts ; asunder ; to pieces ; as, to take a piece of machinery *apart* ; দুই বা ততোধিক ভাগে ; বিশ্লিষ্টভাবে, বিচ্ছিন্ন ভাবে ; ভাগে ভাগে, খণ্ডে খণ্ডে । **To set apart**—To reserve ; পৃথক্ করিয়া রাখা, স্বতন্ত্র করিয়া রাখা ।

ă-pârt′-mĕnt, *n.* **1.** A room in a building ; কক্ষ, প্রকোষ্ঠ, কুঠরী, ঘর । **2.** (*Pl.*) A set of rooms ; প্রকোষ্ঠশ্রেণী । **The inner apartment**—অন্দরমহল, অন্তঃপুর, শুদ্ধান্ত ।

ăp′-ă-thȳ, *n.* **1.** Insensibility to suffering ; বেদনাবোধহীনতা । **2.** Passionless existence ; ভাববিহীনতা, উত্তেজনাশূন্যতা, বৈরাগ্য, অরতি, জড়িমা, উদাসীনতা, তটস্থতা, নিরামর্ষতা । **–thet′-ic, –thet′-i-cal,** *adjs.* Void of feeling ; passionless ; indifferent ; ভাববিহীন ; অনুরাগশূন্য, বিরাগী ; উদাসী । **–thet′-i-cal-ly,** *adv.*

āpe, *n.* & *v. t.* **1.** A tailless monkey ; লাঙ্গুলশূন্য বানর, খর্ব্বপুচ্ছ কপি । **2.** One who imitates servilely ; a mimic ; দাসবৎ অনুকরণকারী ; যে ব্যক্তি অপরের নকল করে । ***Verb t.*** To imitate servilely ; to mimic ; as, how he *apes* his sire ; নীচভাবে বা দাসবৎ অনুকরণ করা ; অপরের নকল্ করা ।

Ape.

[To lead apes in hell—অবিবাহিতা বৃদ্ধাগণ মরণান্তে প্রেতলোকে বানরগণের পথ প্রদর্শনের কার্য্যে নিযুক্ত হয়—কৌতুকচ্ছলে এরূপ বলা হইয়া থাকে ।] **To play the ape**—To mimic ; ভেঙ্গচান, নকল করা । **To put an ape into one's hood** or **cap**—To make a fool of one ; বেকুব সাজান, বোকা সাজান ।

ă-peak′ (-pēk), *adv.* & *adj.* Vertical, as oars, etc. ; (নৌ-বিদ্যা) খাড়া (যেমন দাঁড় প্রভৃতি রাখা হয়) । [Spelt also *apeek.*]

ā-pĕp′-sȳ –si-ă, *n.* Defective digestion ; lack of digestive power ; মন্দাগ্নি, পরিপাকশক্তিশূন্যতা ; অগ্নিমান্দ্য, বদ্‌হজম ।

apercu, (*F.*), *n.* A brief outline a rough estimate ; সংক্ষিপ্ত রেখাপাত খসড়া নকসা ।

ă-pē′-ri-ĕnt, *adj.* & *n.* Gently purgative ; মৃদুবিরেচক, মৃদুভেদক (সাঃ পঃ), সুখরেচক । ***Noun.*** A laxative medicine ; মৃদুবিরেচক ঔষধ ।

ă-pĕr′-i-tive, *adj.* & *n.* Same as APERIENT.

ăp′-ēr-ture (-chür), *n.* **1.** An opening ; a gap ; a passage perforated or cleft ; ছেদ ; ছিদ্র, রন্ধ্র ; ফাটল । **2.** (*Optics*) The space through which light passes in optical instruments ; (দৃষ্টি-বিজ্ঞান) দৃষ্টি-বিজ্ঞান সম্বন্ধীয় যন্ত্র সকলের আলোক প্রবেশ-পথ ।

āp′-ĕr-ȳ, *n.* A mimicry ; an apish performance ; ভেঙ্গচানি ; মর্কটবৎ অভিনয় ।

ā-pĕt′-ăl-ous (-ŭs), *adj.* (*Bot.*) Without petals ; (উদ্ভিদ-বিদ্যা) অদল (সাঃ পঃ) ।

ā′-pĕx, *n.* (*Pl.* APICES, APEXES.) The tip, top, point or angular summit of anything ; অগ্র, শির, শিখা, শিখর, চূড়াগ্র । **2.** (*Geom.*) The vertex of a triangle or cone ; (জ্যামিতি) শীর্ষ । **3.** (*Bot.*) The end farthest from the point of attachment, or base of an organ ; (উদ্ভিদ্-বিদ্যা) অন্তিম (সাঃ পঃ) । (*Astron.*) **Apex of the earth's motion**—That point of the heavens towards which the earth is moving in its orbit ; ভুগতি-মূর্দ্ধা (হিঃ কোঃ) ।

ă-phā'-ṡi-ă, *n.* Loss of speech, as the result of cerebral affection ; মস্তিষ্ক-বিকৃতি হেতু বাক্‌শক্তি লোপ, বাক্‌রোধ (হঃ চঃ) ।

ă-phēl'-iŏn, *n.* (*Astron.*) That point of a planet's or comet's orbit which is farthest from the sun ; (opposed to *perihelion*) ; গ্রহ বা ধূমকেতুর কক্ষের যে বিন্দু সূর্য্য হইতে সর্ব্বাপেক্ষা দূরবর্ত্তীস্থানে অবস্থিত আছে ; সূর্য্যোচ্চ, (হিঃ কোঃ), অপহেলিক (সাঃ পঃ), মন্দোচ্চ (ভৌমাদির—ঐ) ।

ă-phē-li-ō-trŏp'-ic, *adj.* (*Bot.*) Turning away from the sun ; (said of leaves, etc.) ; (উদ্ভিদ-বিদ্যা) সূর্য্যবিমুখ (সাঃ পঃ) (পত্রাদি-সম্বন্ধে উক্ত হয়) । **—ot'-ro-pism,** *n.* The habit of bending from the sunlight, (said of certain plants) ; বিরুদ্ধমুখ-বৃদ্ধি (সাঃ পঃ) ।

ăph'-ē-sis *n.* (*Gram.*) The gradual loss of an unaccented vowel at the beginning of a word ; (as *squire* for *esquire*) ; (ব্যাকরণ) কোন শব্দের আদিস্বরবর্ণের লোপ । **—tize,** *v.t.*

ă phĕt'-ic, *adj.* Shortened by dropping a letter or syllable from the beginning of a word ; আদিভাগ হইতে কোন অক্ষর বা পদাংশ লোপদ্বারা খর্ব্বীকৃত ।

Male and Female (enlarged). Wheat-Aphides.

ā'-phis, (*Pl.* APHIDES) A plant-louse ; উদ্ভিজ্জ কীটবিশেষ ।

ă-phō'-ni-ă, —ny̆, *n.* Total loss of voice ; speechlessness ; বাক্‌শক্তি-লোপ ; বাক্‌শক্তিহীনতা ।

ăph'-ō-riṡm, *n.* A short pithy maxim ; a definition ; কারিকা, সূত্র, বচন ; সংজ্ঞা । **—ris'-mic, —ris'-tic,** *adjs.* **—ris' tic-al ly,** *adv.*

ăph-rō-diṡ'-i-ăc, *n.* & *adj.* A drug producing venereal desire ; বাজীকরণ, কামোদ্দীপক ঔষধ। ***Adj.*** Increasing the appetite for sexual connection ; কামাগ্নি-সন্দীপক, বাজীকর, কামোৎপাদক, কামোদ্দীপক, কামোত্তেজক ।

Aph-rō-dī'-tē (ăf-), *n.* **1.** The Greek Goddess of love called by the Romans Venus ; (গ্রীক-পুরাণ) রতিদেবী । **2.** (*Astron.*) The star Aphrodite ; (জ্যোতির্বিজ্ঞান) আফ্রজিত (সাঃ পঃ) ।

ă-phy̆l'-lous (-lŭs), *adj.* (*Bot.*) Naturally leafless ; (উদ্ভিদ্-বিদ্যা) স্বভাবতঃ পত্রহীন ।

ā'-pi-ă-ry̆, *n.* A place where bees are kept ; a bee-house ; মধুমক্ষিকা-শালা ; মধুমক্ষিকাপালনস্থল । **—a -ri-an,** *adj.* Relating to bees ; মধু-মক্ষিকাসংক্রান্ত, মাক্ষিক । **—rist,** *n.* A bee-master ; মধুমক্ষিকাপালক, মৌমাছিরক্ষক ।

ăp'-i-căl, *adj.* Belonging to an apex ; placed at the tip ; শিখরীয় ; চূড়াগ্রে স্থাপিত ।

ā'-pi-cŭl-ture (-chūr), *n.* Bee-keeping ; মধুমক্ষিকা-পালন

ă-piece' (-pēs), *adv.* To each ; as the share of each ; as, an orange *apiece* ; each by itself ; severally ; as, these cost a shilling *apiece* ; প্রত্যেকে ; প্রত্যেকের ভাগে, প্রতি অংশে ; পৃথক্ পৃথক্ ; এক একটী ।

Apium graveolens—Celery · ভূতজাত (হিন্দী-বেলঃ) ।

Apium involucratum—রাঁধুনি (বেলঃ) ।

A'-pis (ā-), *n.* A bull to which divine honours were paid by the ancient Egyptians who worshipped him as a symbol of Osiris ; প্রাচীন মিশরবাসিগণকর্ত্তৃক পূজিত ওসিরিস্ দেবতার প্রতীক (চিহ্ন) স্বরূপ বৃষভবিশেষ ।

ăp-ish, *adj.* Of the nature or appearance of an ape ; ape-like in manner ; hence, foolish ; silly ; as, this is but *apish* sophistry ; মর্কটবৎ ; মর্কটস্বভাব, মর্কটবৎ, আচরণ-শীল ; নির্ব্বোধ ; বোকা । **—ly,** *adv.* **—ness.** *n.*

ă-plomb' (-plŏm), *n.* **1.** The state of being perpendicular or true to the plumb-line ; ঋজুভাব, খাড়াভাব । **2.** Self-possession springing from perfect self-confidence ; আত্ম-সংস্থতা, আত্মনিষ্ঠা, ধীরচিত্ততা ।

ăp-nœ-'ă (-nē-), *n.* (*Med.*) Suffocation, as in the case of swoon ; (ভৈষজ্য-শাস্ত্র) শ্বাস-রোধ (হঃ চঃ) ।

ă-pŏc'-ă-ly̆pse, *n.* **1.** The revelation delivered to St. John, in the isle of Patmos, forming the last book of the New Testament ; বাইবেল গ্রন্থের "নব নিয়ম" এর অন্তর্গত শেষ পুস্তক, এই গ্রন্থোক্ত বিষয় St. John পেটমোস্ দ্বীপে প্রত্যাদেশরূপে প্রাপ্ত হন, প্রত্যাদেশ পুস্তক, আসমানি-কিতাব । **2.** Revelation ; disclosure ; as, the new *apocalypse* of nature ; প্রকাশ ; উদ্ঘাটন । **—lyp'-tic, —lyp'-ti-cal,** *adjs.* **—lyp'-ti-cal-ly,** *adv.*

ăp-ō-câr'-pous (-pŭs), *adj.* (*Bot.*) Having the several pistils of the same flower separate ; (উদ্ভিদ্-বিদ্যা) পৃথক্ ফলীয় (সাঃ পঃ), পৃথক্-কিঞ্জলী (ঐ) ।

ă-pŏc'-ō-pē, *n.* (*Gram.*) The cutting off of the last letter or syllable of a word ; as, *th* for the ; (ব্যাকরণ) কোন শব্দের শেষ অক্ষর বা পদাংশের লোপ, অন্ত্যাক্ষরলোপ, পদান্তচ্ছেদ ।

ă-pŏc'-ry̆-phă, *n.* Certain writings which are received by some Christians as an authentic part of the Holy Scriptures, but are rejected by others ; খৃষ্টীয় ধর্ম্মবিষয়ক

যে সমস্ত প্রাচীন রচনার প্রামাণিকতা-বিষয়ে সন্দেহ প্রকাশ করা হয়;—বাইবেলের ইংরাজি অনুবাদে এই সকল সন্দিগ্ধ অংশ পরিবর্জিত হইয়া থাকে। **—phal,** *adj.* Pertaining to the apocrypha ; of doubtful authenticity ; hence, false ; sham ; fictitious ; doubtful ; উক্ত গ্রন্থাবলী-সম্পর্কীয় ; অপ্রামাণিক, অপ্রমাণসিদ্ধ ; অসত্য ; কৃত্রিম ; কাল্পনিক, কল্পিত ; সন্দিগ্ধ।

Ap′-ŏdă, (ăp-), *n. pl.* Birds, reptiles or fish without feet or ventral fins ; অপদী। **—ŏ-dăl,** *adj.* Footless ; পদহীন।

ăp-ŏ-deic′-tic (-dîc-), **—ti căl, —dic′-tic, —dic-ti-câl,** *adj.* (*Log.*) Evident beyond contradiction ; clearly established ; (তর্ক-বিজ্ঞান) স্বতঃসিদ্ধ (হিঃ কোঃ), স্বয়ং-প্রমাণ (ঐ) ; স্পষ্টরূপে প্রতিষ্ঠাপিত।

ăp′-ŏ-gee (-jē), *n.* **1.** (*Astron.*) The point in the orbit of the moon or any planet farthest from the earth ; (জ্যোতির্বিজ্ঞানে) পৃথিবী হইতে চন্দ্র বা অন্য গ্রহকক্ষের দূরতম বিন্দু, মন্দোচ্চ (চন্দ্রসূর্য্যের—সাঃ পঃ), অপপার্থিব (ঐ), ভূম্যুচ্চ (হিঃ কোঃ)। **2.** (*Fig.*) The most distant spot ; the highest point ; (লক্ষণায়) দূরতম স্থান ; সর্ব্বোচ্চ বিন্দু। **—ge-an,** *adj.*

ăp-ŏ-laus′-tic (-läs-), *adj.* Self-indulgent ; অসংযত।

A-pŏl-lō (ă-), *n.* The god of poetry, music, medicine, archery and augury ; গ্রীকপুরাণোক্ত এপোলো-দেব—ইনি প্রাচীন গ্রীক ও রোমানগণ-কর্তৃক কাব্য, সঙ্গীত, আয়ুর্ব্বেদ, ধনুর্ব্বেদ এবং শাকুন-শাস্ত্রের অধিদেবতারূপে পূজিত হইতেন। **The Apollo Belvedere**—A celebrated statue of Apollo, in the Belvedere Gallery of the Vatican, at Rome, esteemed as one of the noblest representations of the human frame ; রোমনগরীস্থ ভ্যাটিক্যান্ প্রাসাদে রক্ষিত এপোলোদেবতার মর্ম্মরময়ী মূর্ত্তি—এই মূর্ত্তিটী মানবীয় সৌন্দর্য্য ও মাধুর্য্যের পরাকাষ্ঠা বলিয়া প্রশংসিত হইয়া থাকে।

A-pŏl′-lȳ-ŏn (ă-), *n.* The devil ; শয়তান।

ă-pŏl-ŏ-ğĕt′-ic, *adj.* & *n.* Regretfully acknowledging or excusing fault or failure ; vindicatory ; ক্ষমাসূচক, ত্রুটী-স্বীকারসূচক, অনুনয়সূচক, ক্ষমা-প্রার্থনাসূচক ; পক্ষ-সমর্থক। ***Noun.*** (*Pl.*) Argumentative defence, esp. of Christianity ; বাদানুবাদদ্বারা পক্ষসমর্থন, বিশেষতঃ যুক্তিতর্ক প্রয়োগদ্বারা খৃষ্টধর্ম্ম-সমর্থন। **—al,** *adj.* **—al-ly,** *adv.*

ă-pŏl′-ŏ-ğist, *n.* One who makes an apology ; one who speaks or writes in defence of another, esp. of Christianity ; ত্রুটি-স্বীকার-কারী ; পক্ষসমর্থক, খৃষ্টধর্ম্ম-সমর্থক।

ă-pŏl′-ŏ-ğize, *v. t.* To acknowledge some fault or offence, with expression of regret for it ; (*for*) ; ক্ষমা প্রার্থনা করা, ত্রুটী স্বীকার করা, মাপ চাওয়া, ঘাট মানা (*colloq.*)

ăp′-ŏ-logue (-lŏg), *n.* Moral fable ; নীতিকথা, নৈতিক উপদেশপূর্ণ উপাখ্যান।

ă-pŏl′-ŏ-ğy, *n.* **1.** A regretful acknowledgment of some offence ; an assurance that no offence was intended ; ত্রুটী বা স্বদোষ-স্বীকার ; ক্ষমা-প্রার্থনা, পরিহার। **2.** Vindication ; explanation ; "Bishop Watson's *Apology* for the Bible ;" সমর্থন ; কৈফিয়ত। **3.** A make-shift ; a substitute ; as, to swallow a hasty *apology* for a dinner ; উপস্থিত কার্য্যোপযোগী কোন বস্তু বা উপায় ; দোষ ফুরানোগোছের জিনিষ।

ăp′-oph-thegm (-ŏ-thĕm), **—ŏ-thegm** (-thĕm), *n.* A terse saying ; a pithy maxim ; অল্পাক্ষর-গ্রথিত নীতিবাক্য, সুভাষিত (হিঃ কোঃ) ; বচন, বাক্য। **—theg-mat′-ic, —theg-mat′-ic-al,** *adjs.*

ăp-ŏ-plĕc′-tic, *adj.* Pertaining to or causing apoplexy ; suffering from, or tending to, apoplexy ; মৃগী বা সন্ন্যাসরোগ-উৎপাদক, সন্ন্যাসরোগ-সংক্রান্ত ; সন্ন্যাস-রোগ-গ্রস্ত, সন্ন্যাসরোগ-প্রবণ।

ăp′-ŏ-plex-ŷ (-plĕk-sî), *n.* A malady arresting the powers of sense and motion, usually caused by the effusion of blood or serum in the brain ; সন্ন্যাসরোগ।

ăp-ŏ-sĭ-ŏ-pē′-sis, *n.* (*Rhet.*) A figure of speech in which the speaker breaks off suddenly ; (অলঙ্কার-শাস্ত্র) ক্রমভঙ্গদোষ।

ă-pŏs′-tă-sȳ, *n.* An abandonment of religious faith, vows, principles or party ; স্বধর্ম্মত্যাগ, স্বমতত্যাগ, স্বপক্ষত্যাগ, স্বধর্ম্মস্খলন, স্বধর্ম্ম-চ্যুতি।

ă-pŏs′-tāte, *n.* & *adj.* **1.** One who forsakes religious faith ; a pervert ; স্বধর্ম্মত্যাগী ; যে ব্যক্তি উৎকৃষ্ট স্বধর্ম্ম ত্যাগকরত অপকৃষ্ট পরধর্ম্ম গ্রহণ করে। **2.** One who deserts his party, principles, etc. ; a renegade ; স্বদলত্যাগী ব্যক্তি, স্বমতত্যাগী ব্যক্তি ; স্বধর্ম্মদ্রোহী ব্যক্তি। ***Adj.*** **1.** Unfaithful to religious principles ; rebellious ; স্বধর্ম্মদ্রোহী ; স্বপক্ষদ্রোহী। **2.** Deserting principles or party ; perverted ; as, *apostate* abilities ; স্বপক্ষত্যাগী ; স্বধর্ম্মত্যাগী। **—ta-tize,** *v. i.* To become an apostate (*from* the original faith, *to* another) ; স্বধর্ম্ম বা স্বমত ত্যাগ-করত অন্যধর্ম্ম বা অন্যমতাবলম্বী হওয়া, স্বপক্ষ ত্যাগ করা।

a posteriori, (*L.*), *adv.* & *adj.* Applied to reasoning from effects to causes ; (opposed to *a priori*) ; inductive or empirical ; অভিজ্ঞতা-মূলক (যুক্তিপ্রণালীসম্বন্ধে প্রযুক্ত), কার্য্য হইতে কারণের অনুমানসম্পর্কে প্রযুক্ত ; (অর্থাৎ ধূমরূপ কার্য্য বা ফলদর্শনে অগ্নির অবস্থিতি অনুমান) ; আনুমানিক, পরীক্ষা-প্রসূত, উপার্জ্জিত (হিঃ কোঃ), অভ্যস্ত (জ্ঞান) (ঐ)।

ă-pŏs′-til, —tille, *n.* A marginal note or annotation ; পার্শ্বলিখিত টিপ্পনি বা মন্তব্য।

ă-pos′-tle (-pŏs'l), *n.* **1.** One sent forth ; a messenger, esp. any of the twelve disciples whom Christ sent forth to preach the Gospel ; প্রেরিত পুরুষ ; বার্ত্তাবহ ; বিশেষতঃ যে দ্বাদশজন পার্ষদকে যীশু খৃষ্টধর্ম্ম প্রচারার্থ প্রেরণ করেন—তাঁহাদের অন্যতম, খৃষ্টপার্ষদ। **2.** The first successful Christian missionary in a country ; one who has extraordinary success as a missionary ; as, Judson

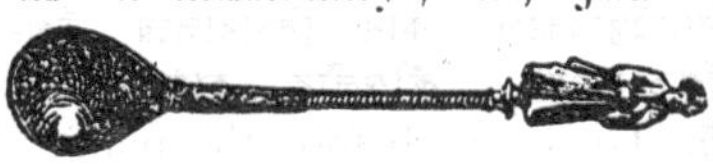

Apostle's spoons.

the *apostle* of Burma ; কোন দেশের সর্ব্বপ্রথম কৃতকার্য্য খৃষ্টধর্ম্ম-প্রচারক ; যে ব্যক্তি প্রচারকের কার্য্যে অসাধারণ কৃতকার্য্যতা লাভ করিয়াছেন। **3.** A leader of a great reform ; as, an *apostle* of temperance ; কোন সংস্কারের নেতা। **Apostle's spoons**—Silver spoons with figures of apostles on handles ; খৃষ্টপার্ষদগণের প্রতিমূর্ত্তিযুক্ত হাতল-বিশিষ্ট রৌপ্য-চামচ বিশেষ।

ă-pŏs′-tŏ-late, *n.* **1.** The office or dignity of an apostle ; খৃষ্টপার্ষদের পদ বা পদগৌরব। **2.** The leadership of a propaganda ; কোন বিশেষ মত-প্রচারের নেতৃত্ব।

ă-pŏs-tŏl′-ic, *adj.* Pertaining to the apostles ; of the character of an apostle ; খৃষ্টপার্ষদগণ-সম্পৃক্ত ; খৃষ্টপার্ষদ-প্রকৃতিসুলভ। **2.** Of the Pope ; as, the *apostolic* see, succession ; পোপ-সম্বন্ধীয়। **—tol′-ic-al,** *adj.*

ă-pŏs′-trŏ-phē, *n.* **1.** *(Rhet.)* A sudden turning away from the ordinary course of a public speech to address some person, (often dead or absent) ; an exclamatory address ; প্রাসঙ্গিক বিষয় পরিত্যাগ করত সহসা কোন (মৃত বা অনুপস্থিত) ব্যক্তির উদ্দেশ্যে অভিভাষণ ; সম্বোধনালঙ্কার, ভাবোচ্ছ্বাসপূর্ণ অভিভাষণ। **2.** *(Gram.)* The mark (') showing the omission of a letter or letters in a word ; the sign of possessive case in English ; (ব্যাকরণ) শব্দ-সঙ্কোচন বা শব্দ-বিলোপের চিহ্ন ; সম্বন্ধ-কারকের চিহ্ন। **—trŏph′-ic,** *adj.*

ă-pŏs′-trŏ-phīze, *v.t.* **1.** *(Rhet.)* To address with or in an apostrophe ; (অলঙ্কার-শাস্ত্র) সহসা প্রসঙ্গ পরিবর্ত্তন-পূর্ব্বক কোন ব্যক্তি বা বস্তুর উদ্দেশ্যে অভিভাষণ করা। **2.** To omit one or more letters of a word ; to mark the omission of letters with the sign (') ; এক বা একাধিক অক্ষর-লোপদ্বারা শব্দ-সঙ্কোচ করা ; শব্দ-লোপ-সূচক চিহ্নে চিহ্নিত করা।

ă-pŏth′-ĕ-căr-ȳ, *n.* One who prepared and sold drugs for medicinal purposes; (now a *druggist* or *pharmaceutical chemist*) ; যে ব্যক্তি ঔষধ প্রস্তুত করত বিক্রয় করিত, ভৈষজ্যকারী। **Apothecary's weight**—ঔষধবিক্রেতার ওজন।

ăp-ŏ-thē′-cē-ŭm, *n.* The spore-case in lichens ; বৃক্ষাদিতে জাত শৈবলের রেণুস্থালী, রেণুস্থালী (সাঃ পঃ)।

ăp′-ŏ-thegm (-thĕm), *n.* Same as APHOTHEGM.

ăp-ŏ-thē′-ŏ-sis, *n.* **1.** Deification ; canonization ; the act of placing a prince or other distinguished person among the heathen deities ; as, the *apotheosis* of Romulus ; দেবত্বারোপণ (হিঃ কোঃ), মোক্ষ-প্রাপ্ত সিদ্ধপুরুষশ্রেণী-ভুক্তকরণ ; কোন নৃপতি কিম্বা প্রসিদ্ধ ব্যক্তিকে দেব-সমাজভুক্ত করণ। [রোমনগরীর সুপ্রসিদ্ধ ব্যক্তিদিগকে প্রায়শঃ এইরূপে সম্মানিত করা হইত।] **2.** The glorification or exaltation of a principle, practice etc. ; as, the *apotheosis* of chivalry ; মত বা আচার প্রভৃতি মহিমান্বিতকরণ, মহিমাবর্দ্ধন। **3.** (Loosely) Release from earthly life ; as, the *apotheosis* of Christ ; (অসাবধানে) সংসার-বন্ধন-বিমুক্তি। **—o-size,** *v. t.* To exalt to the dignity of a deity ; দেবত্ব আরোপ করা।

ăp-pall′, —pal′, *v. t.* To dismay ; to terrify ; শঙ্কিত করা, ভীতি-সঞ্চার করা ; ত্রাস জন্মান। **—pall′-ing,** *adj.* Dismaying ; shocking ; as, an *appalling* sight ; ভয়াবহ, ভয়ঙ্কর, ত্রাসজনক ; ভীষণ। **—ing-ly,** *adv.*

ăp′-păn-āge, ăp′-ă-nāge, *n.* **1.** The provision made for the maintenance of the younger children of kings, princes, etc. ; জ্যেষ্ঠেতর রাজসন্তানগণের জন্য নির্দ্দিষ্ট বৃত্তি বা ভূসম্পত্তি। **2.** A dependency ; as, Ireland is the most valuable *appanage* of our empire ; অধীন রাজ্য। **3.** A natural accompaniment or attribute ; "Wealth should be the *appanage* of wit :" স্বভাবসিদ্ধ অনুষঙ্গ, গুণ বা ধর্ম্ম।

ăp-pă-rā′-tŭs, *n.* (*Sing.* & *pl.* rarely *pl.*-TUSES.) **1.** The mechanical requisites for scientific or other work ; বৈজ্ঞানিক-যন্ত্র, পরীক্ষা-যন্ত্র (হিঃ কোঃ)। **2.** The organs by which natural processes are carried on ; as, the digestive *apparatus* ; শারীরিক-যন্ত্র। **Critical apparatus** or **apparatus criticus**—Materials for the critical study of an author, document, etc. ; কোনও গ্রন্থ বা দলিল প্রভৃতি সূক্ষ্মরূপে আলোচনার জন্য (অভিধান প্রভৃতি) উপকরণ।

ăp-păr′-ĕl, *n.* & *v. t.* **1.** An ornamental embroidery on ecclesiastical vestments ; ধর্ম্মযাজকগণের পোষাকের উপর চিকণ কায। **2.** *(Naut.)* The outfit of ship, as sails, rigging, etc. ; (নৌ-বিদ্যা) জাহাজের পাইল, দড়া, প্রভৃতি। **3.** Garments ; dress ; as, piece-goods, *apparel*, etc. for sale by auction ; পোষাক, পরিচ্ছদ ; বেশ। ***Verb t.*** To dress or clothe ; to attire ; to dress with external ornaments ; (generally used in the *p.p.*) ; as, trees *apparelled* with flowers : "*Apparelled* in celestial light ;" পরিচ্ছদ-শোভিত করা, বসনাবৃত

করা ; বিভূষিত করা, অলঙ্কৃত করা ; সজ্জিত করা, বিমণ্ডিত করা।

ăp-păr′-ĕnt, *adj.* **1.** That may be seen ; visible to the eye ; manifest ; palpable ; চক্ষুঃ-গ্রাহ্য ; দৃশ্য ; প্রত্যক্ষগোচর ; স্ফুট, সুস্পষ্ট, ব্যক্ত। **2.** Seeming (in distinction from *true* or *real*) ; as, *apparent* motion (স্ফুট বা স্পষ্ট গতি) ; *apparent* time (স্ফুট বা স্পষ্ট কাল) ; স্ফুট, আপাত, বাহ্য, প্রতীয়মান। **—ly,** *adv.* Manifestly ; seemingly ; in appearance ; as, they found the Emperor *apparently* frank ; স্পষ্টতঃ ; বাহ্যতঃ ; দৃষ্টতঃ। **Heir-apparent**—(*Law*) One whose right to an estate is indefeasible, if he survive the ancestor ; (আইন) প্রকৃত উত্তরাধিকারী। **Heir apparent to a throne**—যুবরাজ।

ăp-pă-ri′-tion, *n.* **1.** Appearance, esp. of a supernatural being ; a spectre ; a phantom or ghost ; ভূত পিশাচাদির আবির্ভাব ; ছায়া-মূর্ত্তি ; অপচ্ছায়া, উপচ্ছায়া, ভূত, প্রেত, অপদেবতা। **2.** (*Astron.*) The first appearance of a star or other luminary after having been invisible or obscured ; অপ্রকট বা অদর্শনের পর তারকা প্রভৃতি জ্যোতিষ্কের প্রথমোদয়, তারোদয় (হিঃ কোঃ)। **—al,** *adj.*

ăp-păr′-i-tŏr, *n.* **1.** A servant of an officer ; (*Rom. Ant.*) a public servant of a Roman magistrate ; রাজকর্ম্মচারীর অনুচর ; (রোমীয় প্রত্নতত্ত্ব) প্রাচীন রোমের শাসনবিভাগের উচ্চ-কর্ম্মচারিবিশেষের ভৃত্য। **2.** An officer of a civil or an ecclesiastical court ; যাজকীয় বা সাধারণ বিচারালয়ের কর্ম্মচারিবিশেষ। **3.** A beadle in an university ; বিশ্ববিদ্যালয়ের নিম্নপদস্থ কর্ম্মচারিবিশেষ।

ăp-peal′ (-pēl), *v. t.* **1.** To call to a higher tribunal for deliverance from the decision of a lower ; নিম্নআদালতের নিষ্পত্তির বিরুদ্ধে উচ্চতর আদালতে প্রার্থনা করা, পুনর্বিচার-প্রার্থনা করা। **2.** To call upon a recognized authority to vinidicate one's right or decide in one's favour in a dispute ; to make earnest request (*to* a person, *for* a thing) ; বৈধক্ষমতাপ্রাপ্ত কোন ব্যক্তির নিকট বা বিচারালয় প্রভৃতিতে স্বপক্ষ সমর্থন বা অনুকূল নিষ্পত্তিলাভের জন্য আবেদন করা ; সকাতরে প্রার্থনা করা, সনির্ব্বন্ধ অনুরোধ করা। **3.** To prove attractive ; as, these pictures do not *appeal* to me ; চিত্তাকর্ষক হওয়া। **4.** To call to a witness for corroboration ; to call attention *to* (some testimony) ; কোন বিষয় সমর্থনের জন্য সাক্ষী তলব করা ; (কোন বিশেষ সাক্ষ্য বা প্রমাণের প্রতি) দৃষ্টি আকর্ষণ করা। **To appeal to the country**—To dissolve Parliament and ask the electors to send up new representatives ; পার্লেমেণ্ট মহাসভা-ভঙ্গের জন্য রাজাকে পরামর্শ প্রদান করা এবং নির্ব্বাচকগণকে নূতন প্রতিনিধি নির্ব্বাচনের জন্য অনুরোধ করা।

ăp-peal′ (-pēl), *n.* **1.** (*Law.*) The transference of a case from an inferior to a higher court, in the hope of reversing the decision of the former ; also the mode of such proceeding and the right of taking it ; (আইন) পুনর্বিচার প্রার্থনা (যোঃ), পরাবর্ত্ত-ব্যবহার (প্রঃ বাঃ) ; নিম্নআদালতের বিচারের বিরুদ্ধে উচ্চতর আদালতে আবেদনের, অধিকার, পুনর্বিচার-প্রার্থনা-পদ্ধতি। **2.** An earnest request ; an entreaty ; সনির্ব্বন্ধ প্রার্থনা ; অনুনয়। **3.** Recourse ; resort ; as, an *appeal* to arms ; আশ্রয়গ্রহণ ; অবলম্বন। **—a-ble,** *adj.* That can be appealed against ; as, the cause is *appealable* ; উচ্চতর আদালতে বিচারযোগ্য, পুনর্বিচার-গ্রাহ্য।

ăp-pear′ (-pēr), *v. i.* **1.** To come or be in sight ; to be or become visible ; দৃষ্টিপথে আবির্ভূত হওয়া, প্রত্যক্ষগোচর হওয়া ; দৃষ্টিগোচর হওয়া। **2.** To be manifest ; to be plain ; as, more clearly their excellences must *appear* ; প্রকট হওয়া ; স্পষ্ট হওয়া। **3.** To seem ; to look like ; প্রতিভাত হওয়া ; বোধ হওয়া। **4.** To present one's self formally before a tribunal ; to act as counsel ; as, no pleader *appeared* for the accused ; বাদী-প্রতিবাদী বা উকীল-ব্যারিষ্টাররূপে কোন বিচারালয়ে উপস্থিত হওয়া ; কৌঁসুলীর কার্য্য করা। **5.** To come before the public ; to be published ; as, a great writer *appeared* at that time : several works have already *appeared* ; অবতীর্ণ হওয়া ; প্রকাশ হইয়া পড়া ; প্রকাশিত হওয়া।

ăp-pear′-ănce (-pēr-), *n.* **1.** The act of coming into sight ; as, the *appearance* of the sun above the horizon ; a coming into the presence of a person or persons ; as, he made his first *appearance* on the stage ; উদয় ; আবির্ভাব। **2.** Outward look ; mien ; as, a man of noble *appearance* ; চেহারা ; আকৃতি, আকার, রূপ, দর্শন, ডৌল। **3.** Semblance ; as, we are often deceived by *appearances* ; আভাস (বেদান্ত), বিবর্ত্ত (ঐ), প্রতিভাস (ঐ), বিকাশ (বিশ্বঃ)। **4.** An apparition ; a phantom ; as, an *appearance* in the sky ; ছায়া, অপচ্ছায়া ; অপদেবতা। **To all appearance**—So far as can be seen ; "John Bull *to all appearance* is a plain downright matter-of-fact man ;" যতদূর দেখা যায়। **To keep up** or **save appearances**—To preserve a fair outward show ; বাহিরের ঠাট বজায় রাখা, অপরের সমক্ষে সুশোভন আচরণ করা। **To put in an appearance**—To appear in person ; স্বয়ং উপস্থিত হওয়া, স্বয়ং হাজির হওয়া।

ăp-pease′ (-pēz), *v. t.* To pacify ; to quiet (strife, disorder, etc.) ; to satisfy (appetite, thirst, etc.) ; to dispel (anger or displeasure) ; to soothe or allay (mental suffering) ; প্রশান্ত করা, ঠাণ্ডা করা ; নিবৃত্তি করা, তুষ্ট করা ; বিদূরিত করা ; শান্ত করা । **—peas′ a-ble,** *adj.* Capable of being calmed or pacified ; প্রশমনীয় । **—ment,** *n.*

ăp-pĕl′-lănt, *n.* & *adj.* One who appeals to a higher court against the decision of a lower one ; (opposed to *respondent*) ; (উচ্চতর আদালতে) পুনর্ব্বিচারপ্রার্থী, পরাবর্ত্তপ্রার্থক । ***Adj.*** Concerned with appeals ; as, the jurisdiction of this court is *appellant* ; appealing (to a higher tribunal) ; as, *appellant* parties ; পুনর্বিচার-সংক্রান্ত ; পুনর্বিচার-প্রার্থী ।

ăp-pĕl′-lāte, *adj.* Taking cognizance of appeals ; as, *appellate* jurisdiction ; আপিলী মোকদ্দমা শুনিবার ক্ষমতাবিশিষ্ট । **Appellate court**—আপীল আদালত ।

ăp-pĕl-lā′-tion, *n.* A name, title or designation, given ; আখ্যা, অভিধা, উপাধি ।

ăp-pĕl′-lă-tive, *adj.* & *n.* Designating a class ; common (as opposed to *proper*) ; জাতিবাচক, শ্রেণীবাচক ; সাধারণ । ***Noun.*** (*Gram.*) Common noun or name as, man is the *appellative* of the whole human race ; সাধারণ নাম । 2. Title ; appellation ; উপাধি ; নাম । **—ly,** *adv.*

ăp-pĕnd′, *v. t.* **1.** To hang on ; to attach, as a pendant ; "If amulets do work.........upon those parts whereunto they are *appended* ;" ঝুলাইয়া দেওয়া ; লট্‌কান্‌ । **2.** To annex ; to add in writing by way of appendix ; সংযোজিত করা, সংলগ্ন করা ; পরিশিষ্টরূপে সংযোগ করা । **—age,** *n.* The thing attached ; addition ; accompaniment ; সংযোজিত বস্তু ; উপাঙ্গ ; অনুষঙ্গ । **—aged,** *adj.* Furnished with an appendage ; সোপাঙ্গ ।

ăp-pĕnd′-ănt, *adj.* & *n.* **1.** Hanging or attached to ; annexed ; as, the seal *appendant* by a silken cord ; লট্‌কান, সংলগ্ন ; সংযোজিত । **2.** (*Law.*) Attached to a possession or tenure as an additional right ; as, an advowson *appendant* to the possession of a manor ; (আইন) অতিরিক্ত স্বত্বরূপে কোন মূল সম্পত্তি বা জোতের সহিত সংলগ্ন । ***Noun.*** Anything attached to another, as incidental or subordinate to it ; an adjunct ; নৈমিত্তিক বস্তু, উপাঙ্গ ; অনুবন্ধ ।

ăp-pĕn-dī-cī′-tĭs, *n.* (*Med.*) Inflammation of the vermiform appendix ; (ভৈষজ্য শাস্ত্র) অন্ত্রোপাঙ্গপ্রদাহ ।

ăp-pĕn′-dix, (*Pl.* APPENDIXES, APPENDICES), *n.* **1.** Any subsidiary addition to a book or document ; পরিশিষ্ট । **2.** A small process developed from the surface of any

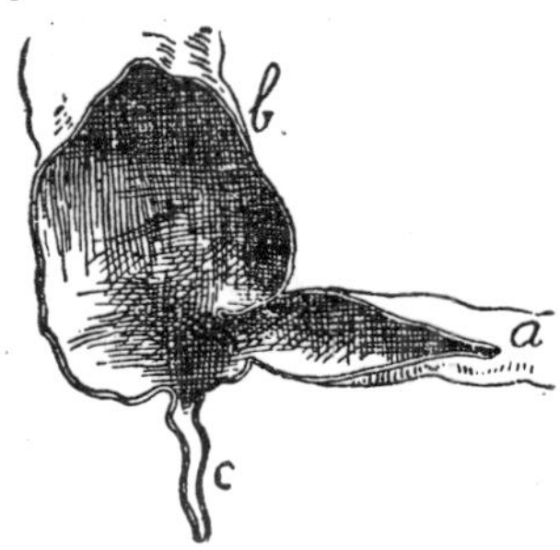

Appendix.
a, Ileum, or end of small intestine ; *b*, Cæcum or beginning of large intestine ; *c*, Appendix

organ (esp. the **vermiform appendix** of the intestines) ; শারীরিক যন্ত্র সমূহ হইতে উদ্ভূত উপাঙ্গ, বিশেষতঃ, অন্ত্র-দেশের কীটাকৃতি উপাঙ্গ ।

ăp-pêr-cĕp′-tion, *n.* **1.** Mind's perception of itself ; self-consciousness ; আত্মবোধ, নিজবোধ (হিঃ কোঃ) ; অন্তর্বোধ (ঐ) । **2.** Mental perception ; recognition ; মানস প্রত্যক্ষ ; প্রত্যভিজ্ঞান ।

ăp-pêr-tain′ (-tān), *v.t.* (foll. by *to*) **1.** To pertain to ; to relate to ; as, things *appertaining* to this life ; (কোন কিছুর) অন্তর্গত হওয়া, (কোন কিছুর সহিত) অন্বিত বা সংস্পৃষ্ট থাকা ; সম্বন্ধ-বিশিষ্ট হওয়া । **2.** To be related to ; সম্বন্ধান্বিত হওয়া । **3.** To belong as a possession or right to ; অধিকারভুক্ত হওয়া । **4.** To be proper or appropriate to ; উপযুক্ত হওয়া, উপযোগী হওয়া ।

ăp′-pē-tĕnce, —tĕn-cȳ, *n.* **1.** A longing for ; a desire ; esp. an ardent desire ; (*of, for, after*) ; লালসা ; স্পৃহা ; আকুল বাসনা । **2.** Affinity for ; (কোন কিছুর জন্য) স্বাভাবিক আকর্ষণ । **3.** Instinctive inclination or propensity ; (as, in aquatic fowls to enter into water) ; স্বাভাবিক আসক্তি বা প্রবৃত্তি ।

ăp′-pē-tĕnt, *adj.* Eagerly desirous ; longing ; (*after, of*) ; বাসনাকুল ; তৃষাকুল ।

ăp′-pē-tīte, *n.* **1.** The desire to fulfil the natural functions of the body ; craving for food ; hunger ; (*for*) ; দৈহিক অভাব বা বাসনাতৃপ্তির জন্য আকাঙ্ক্ষা ; ক্ষুধা, ক্ষুৎপিপাসা ; বুভুক্ষা । **2.** Relish ; as, *appetite* bestowed upon the poor classes, that they may like what they eat ; তার, আস্বাদ । **3.** Strong desire ; eagerness or longing ; "If God had given to eagles an *appetite* to swim ;" স্পৃহা, তৃষ্ণা, তৃষা ; কামনা । **—tīze,** *v. t.* To make hungry ; ক্ষুধার উদ্রেক করা । **—tiz-er,** *n.* **—tiz-ing,** *pt. adj.* Whetting appetite ; ক্ষুধাকারী, ক্ষুধাবৃদ্ধিকর, ক্ষুধাবর্দ্ধক, রুচিকর, রুচিপ্রদ ।

ăp-plaud′ (-plăd), *v.i.* & *t.* To express approval in a loud or lively manner ; সাধুবাদ করা, বাহবা

দেওয়া। *Verb t.* To express approval of in an audible manner; to approve of; to praise; সাধুবাদ করা; অনুমোদন করা; সুখ্যাতি করা। **—er,** *n.*

ăp-plause' (-plăz), *n.* Approbation loudly expressed; acclamation; ধন্যবাদ, সাধুবাদ, জয়ধ্বনি, জয়রব; অনুমোদন বা প্রশংসা-সূচক করতালি প্রভৃতি।

ăp-plau'-sive (-plä-), *adj.* Approbative; expressive of approval; সাধুবাদসূচক; ধন্যবাদজ্ঞাপক।

ap'-ple (ăp'l) *n.* **1.** The round firm fleshy fruit of a rosaceous tree; আপেল ফল, সেও ফল, সেব (যোঃ)। **2.** (*Bot.*) Any inferior fleshy many-celled fruit; as, the *balsam-apple*: the *custard-apple,* etc.; (উদ্ভিদ-বিদ্যা) যাবতীয় মাংসল ও বহু-কোষবিশিষ্ট ফল। **Apple-blossom**—সেওমুকুল। **Apple-brandy, Apple-jack**—A spirit distilled from cider; সেওফল হইতে প্রস্তুত মদিরা বিশেষ। **Apple-john** (also **john-apple**)—A kind of apple said to keep two years and to be best when shrivelled and withered; এক প্রকার সেও ফল—যাহা শুষ্কাবস্থায় অধিকতর সুস্বাদু হইয়া থাকে। **Apple of discord**—A golden apple contended for by Juno, Minerva and Venus; hence, a subject of contention and envy; জুনো, মিনার্ভা এবং ভীনাস্ যে সুবর্ণময় সেওফলের অধিকার লইয়া কলহ করিয়াছিলেন; অতএব, দ্বেষ ও বিরোধের বিষয়। **Apple of love** or **love-apple**—Tomato; বিলাতি বেগুণ। **Apple of Sodon** or **Dead Sea fruit**—A fruit described by old writers as externally of fair appearance, but turning to smoke and ashes when plucked; প্রাচীন গ্রন্থকারগণ-বর্ণিত ফল বিশেষ, এই ফল দেখিতে অতীব সুন্দর; কিন্তু, বৃন্তচ্যুত করিলেই ধূম ও ভস্মে পর্য্যবসিত হয়। **Apple of the eye**—The pupils; hence, any cherished object; as, he was the *apple of his eye;* কনীনিকা; নয়নমণি। **Apple-pie bed**—A bed in which the sheets are so folded that a man cannot get his legs down; যে বিছানার চাদর এরূপ ভাবে ভাঁজ করিয়া রাখা হয় যে, তাহাতে শয়ন করিতে গেলে পা ছড়ান যায় না। **Apple-pie order**—Perfect order; extreme neatness; as, she keeps the house in *apple-pie order;* অতি সুশৃঙ্খলা; নিরতিশয় পারিপাট্য বা পরিচ্ছন্নভাব।

ăp-pli'-ănce, *n.* **1.** The act of applying; প্রয়োগ। **2.** A thing applied as a means to an end; apparatus; device; as, to use various *appliances;* কার্য্য বা উদ্দেশ্যসাধনোপযোগী বস্তু বা বিষয়; উপায়; কৌশল।

ăp'-pli-că-ble, *adj.* Capable of being applied; having reference *to*; appropriate *to;* প্রযোজ্য, প্রয়োগার্হ; প্রাসঙ্গিক; যথোপযোগী।

—bil'-i-ty, *n.*

ăp'-pli-cănt, *n.* One who applies for something; a petitioner; a candidate; প্রার্থী; আবেদনকারী, দরখাস্তকারী; পদপ্রার্থী।

ăp-pli-că'-tion, *n.* **1.** The act of applying; as, *application* of plaster, liniment, etc; the putting of one thing to another; as, *application* of heat to the bulb; (foll. by *to*); প্রয়োগ; সংযোজন। **2.** The employment of means, to gain an end; as, the *application* of the loadstone to navigation; উদ্দেশ্যসিদ্ধির উদ্দেশ্যে উপায়-প্রয়োগ। **3.** The bringing of a general rule etc., to bear upon a particular case; the use of the principles of one science for the purpose of enlarging another; as, the *application* of Algebra to Geometry; কোন একটী বিশেষ বিষয়ে সাধারণ নিয়ম খাটান, উপনয় (হিঃ কোঃ), অতিদেশ (মঃ উঃ), উপযোগ (হিঃ কোঃ); অপর বিজ্ঞানের মূলতত্ত্বসমূহ প্রকটনের জন্য কো বিজ্ঞানের মূলতত্ত্ব-প্রয়োগ। **4.** The capacity of being practicall applied; relevancy; as, this h no *application* to present circu stances; কার্য্যতঃ প্রযুক্ত হইবার শক্তি প্রাসঙ্গিকতা। **5.** The act of appl ing one'self closely to a tas diligence; attention; as, so *application* to other studies; প্রগ অভিনিবেশ; তৎপরতা; মনঃসংযো **6.** A soliciting or petitioning as, he made an *application* for a appointment; a request; th document containing a request: as, his *application* was filed: দরখাস্ত, আবেদন; প্রার্থনা, যাচ্ঞা, নিবেদন; আবেদনপত্র।

ăp-plȳ', *v. t.* & *i.* **1.** To lay on; to put one thing to another; as, to *apply* the hand to the breast; স্থাপন করা; এক বস্তু উপর অপর বস্তু রাখা। **2.** To administer remedy, etc. *to*; প্রয়োগ করা, লাগান। **3.** To use or employ for a particular purpose; to devote *to*; as, to *apply* a sum of money to the payment of a debt; নিযুক্ত করা; ন্যস্ত করা। **4.** T make use of; as, to *apply* th testimony to the case; ব্যবহা করা। **5.** To set oneself closely t to direct the attention *to*; to the mind upon; "*Apply* t' heart to instruction;" কোন গাঢ়ভাবে অভিনিবিষ্ট করা; মনো আকর্ষণ করা; (কোন বিষয়ে) নিবেশ করা। *Verb i.* **1.** suit; to agree; to have re ence (*to*); as, this argum *applies* well *to* the case; উ যোগী হওয়া; মিল হওয়া; সম্পর্ক থাকা **2.** To make request; to solicit; to address oneself *to* for help, etc.; as, to *apply* to a friend for information; অনুরোধ করা; প্রার্থনা করা, যাচ্ঞা করা; আবেদন করা।

point′ (-poynt), *v. t.* **1.** To nominate (a person *to* an office) ; মনোনীত করা। **2.** To fix by mutual agreement ; to fix the time and place of ; as, for a meeting ; উভয়ের সম্মতিদ্বারা নির্দ্ধারিত করা ; ধারণ করা, সময় এবং স্থান স্থির করা। **3.** To ordain authoritatively ; to prescribe (a thing *that* it shall be) ; নির্দ্দিষ্ট করা, নিরূপিত করা ; বিধান করা। **4.** (*Law*) To declare the destination of a property ; (আইন) দান উদ্দেশ্যে সম্পত্তির নিয়োগ হইবে তাহা নির্দ্দেশ করা। **—ee,** *n.* **1.** A person nominated to an office ; কোন পদে মনোনীত ব্যক্তি। **2.** (*Law*) One in whose favour a power of appointment is executed ; যে ব্যক্তির অনুকূলে সম্পত্তি-নিয়োগপত্র সম্পাদিত হয়। **—ment,** *n.* **1.** The act of appointing ; নিয়োজন, নিয়োগ, বিনিয়োগ। **2.** An office held by a person appointed ; as, he holds a high *appointment* in the Civil Service ; চাকুরী, পদ। **3.** Assignment ; engagement ; as, they made an *appointment* to meet at six o'clock ; নির্দ্দেশ, নিরূপণ ; প্রতিশ্রুতি। **4.** Decree ; ordinance ; direction ; order ; as, it is our duty to submit to divine *appointments* ; বিধান ; বিধি ; নির্দ্দেশ ; ব্যবস্থা। (*pl.*) Equipment or outfit, as for a ship, army, etc. ; furniture ; সজ্জা ; আসবাব। **By appointment**—As arranged before ; পূর্ব্ব-বন্দোবস্ত অনুযায়ী, পূর্ব্বকথা মত। **To keep or break an appointment**—To appear, or fail to appear, at a fixed place and time ; নির্দ্দিষ্ট সময়ে বা নিরূপিত স্থানে আসিতে সমর্থ বা অসমর্থ হওয়া। **To make an appointment**—To fix by mutual agreement ; as, they *made an appointment* to meet at six o'clock ; কথাবার্ত্তা বলিয়া স্থির করা।

ăp-pōr′-tion, *v. t.* To assign as due share (*to*) ; to allot ; to portion out ; as, to *apportion* time among many employments ; বণ্টন করিয়া দেওয়া ; বিভাগ করিয়া দেওয়া ; অংশ করিয়া দেওয়া। **—ment,** *n.* The act of allotting in suitable shares ; বণ্টন, ভাগ, নামজারী।

ăp′-pō-site (-zit), *adj.* Appropriate *to* ; very applicable ; well-put ; (foll. by *to*) ; as, this agreement is very *apposite* to the case ; সঙ্গত, উপযোগী, প্রাসঙ্গিক ; সুপ্রযোজ্য ; সুপ্রযুক্ত। **—ly,** *adv.* **—ness,** *n.*

ăp-pō-si′-tion, *n.* **1.** The act of placing one thing to another ; application ; as, the *apposition* of the seals of witnesses ; স্থাপনা, যোজনা। **2.** Placing side by side ; juxtaposition ; পার্শ্বসংস্থাপন ; নিকট-সংস্থিতি। **3.** (*Gram.*) The addition of one substantive to another, as an attribute or complement ; as, Cicero, *the orator* lived in the 1st century ; (here *orator* is in *apposition* with Cicero) ; (ব্যাকরণ) উদ্দেশ্যবিধেয়ভাবে স্থিতি, দুই বিশেষ্য পদকে (উদ্দেশ্যবিধেয়ভাবে) এক-কারকান্তর্গতকরণ, একান্বয়। **—al,** *adj.*

ăp-praise′ (-prāz), *v.t.* To fix price for ; to assign a money value to ; (esp. as an official valuer) ; as, to *appraise* the goods and estate of a deceased person ; মূল্য-স্থির করা ; মূল্য-নিরূপণ করা; মূল্য-নির্দ্দেশ করা। [সরকারি কর্ম্মচারীকর্ত্তৃক মূল্য-নির্দ্ধারণ বুঝায়।] **—prais′-ēr,** *n.* A person appointed and sworn to estimate the value of property ; স্থাবর বা অস্থাবর সম্পত্তির মূল্য-নির্দ্ধারক কর্ম্মচারী। **—ment,** *n.* Valuation by an official ; সরকারী কর্ম্মচারিকর্ত্তৃক মূল্য-নিরূপণ।

ăp-prē′-ci-ā-ble, *adj.* **1.** Capable of being estimated ; মূল্যাবধারণযোগ্য, পরিমেয়। **2.** Perceptible ; sensible ; as, an *appreciable* quantity ; ইন্দ্রিয়-গ্রাহ্য ; অনুভবযোগ্য। **—bly,** *adv.*

ăp-prē′-ci-āte, *v. t.* & *i.* **1.** To value at a proper price ; to estimate justly (worth, quality, amount of) ; as, to *appreciate* the motives of their enemies ; to estimate aright ; as, to *appreciate* the magnitude of the danger ; মূল্যাবধারণ করা ; গুণগ্রহণ করা, মূল্য বুঝা ; পরিমাণ করা, সম্যক্ অবধারণ করা। **2.** To esteem duly or adequately ; to find excellence in ; as, the mental culture necessary to *appreciate* Homer ; to be sensitive to or sensible of ; as, the power of bees to *appreciate* colour ; যথোচিত গুণ-গ্রহণ করা ; যথোচিত মর্য্যাদা করা ; অনুভূতি-সম্পন্ন হওয়া, অনুভব করা। **3.** To raise in value ; as, a sudden peace should *appreciate* the money ; মূল্যবৃদ্ধি করা, দর চড়াইয়া দেওয়া। ***Verb i.*** To rise in value ; (opp. to *depreciate*) ; as, the coin of the country *appreciates* ; দাম চড়া, দর বাড়া। **—a-tive, —a-to-ry,** *adjs.* Manifesting appreciation ; as, *appreciative* audience ; *appreciatory* praise ; গুণগ্রাহী, মর্ম্মজ্ঞ ; গুণগ্রহণ-সূচক। **—a-tive-ly,** *adv.*

ăp-prē-ci-ā′-tion, *n.* **1.** The act of estimating (qualities) ; true estimation ; deliberate judgment ; মূল্যাবধারণ, গুণগ্রহণ ; প্রকৃত মূল্যাবধারণ ; সুচিন্তিত মীমাংসা। **2.** Adequate estimation ; as, his *appreciation* of Henry's character ; যথোচিত গুণগ্রহণ। **3.** A rise in value (opp. to *depreciation*) ; মূল্য-বৃদ্ধি।

ăp-prē-hĕnd′, *v t.* **1.** To arrest ; to seize ; (esp. a criminal to bring him to justice) ; গ্রেপ্তার করা ; ধরা। **2.** To perceive by the senses or intellect ; to recognise ; to understand ; "What bliss human desire can seek or apprehend ;" উপলব্ধি করা, অনুভব করা, অবধারণ করা ; বুঝা, মনে করা ; হৃদয়ঙ্গম করা।

3. To look forward to : to expect (mostly things adverse); to anticipate with fear or dread ; to fear ; as, to *apprehend* the evil which impended ; (কোন কিছুর জন্য) প্রতীক্ষা বা আশা করা ; (প্রধানতঃ প্রতিকূল অবস্থা) সশঙ্কচিত্তে প্রতীক্ষা করা ; আশঙ্কা করা । **—er,** *n.*

ăp-prē-hĕn′-si-ble, *adj.* Capable of being grasped by the senses or intellect ; (*by, to*) ; ইন্দ্রিয়-গ্রাহ্য, অধিগম্য, অনুভাব্য, উপলভ্য । **—bil′-i-ty,** *n.*

ăp-prē-hĕn′-sion, *n.* **1.** The seizure of a person, ship, etc. ; arrest ; বলপূর্ব্বক ধরণ ; গ্রেপ্তার । **2.** Grasping of ideas (with the intellect) ; conception ; intellection ; অবগতি (হিঃ কোঃ), অবধারণ ; সমবধারণ ; বুদ্ধিক্রিয়া । **3.** Understanding ; ability to understand : as, a man of quick *apprehension* ; উপলব্ধি, বোধ ; বোধশক্তি । **4.** Fear as to what may happen ; dread ; শঙ্কা, আশঙ্কা ; অভিশঙ্কা, ভীতি ।

ăp-prē-hĕn′-sive, *adj.* **1.** Pertaining to, or fitted for, sensuous or mental perception ; as, *apprehensive* faculties ; অনুভূতিসম্বন্ধীয়, সমবধারণসম্বন্ধীয়, অবগতিবিষয়ক সমবধারণসমুচিত । **2.** Perceptive ; quick to learn ; intelligent ; sharp ; (foll. by *of*) ; ইন্দ্রিয়-গ্রাহ্য ; ক্ষিপ্রগ্রহণশীল ; বুদ্ধিমান ; তীক্ষ্ণধী, সূক্ষ্মদর্শী । **3.** Anticipative of something adverse ; usually fearful (*of* thing, *for* a person or *for* his safety) ; শঙ্কিত, শঙ্কান্বিত ; সশঙ্ক, সভয় । **—ly,** *adv.* **—ness,** *n.*

ăp-prĕn′-tĭce, *n.* & *v. t.* A learner of a craft ; one bound by legal agreement to serve another person for a certain time, with a view to learn an art, trade or profession ; hence, an unskilled novice ; শিক্ষার্থী ; শিক্ষানবীশ ; নূতনব্রতী ; আনাড়ী লোক। ***Verb t.*** To bind as an apprentice ; কোন প্রকার শিল্প, ব্যবসায় প্রভৃতি শিক্ষাদানার্থ কাহাকে চুক্তিপত্রদ্বারা আবদ্ধ করা । **—ship,** *n.*

ăp-prīse′, *v. t.* **1.** To give notice, verbal or written ; to inform ; (foll. by *of*) ; (*passive*) to be aware of ; লিখিত বা মৌখিক সমাচার দেওয়া, এত্তাহার প্রদান করা, এত্তেলা দেওয়া ; বিজ্ঞাপিত করা, গোচরে আনা ; অবগত থাকা । **2.** To appreciate ; as, he *apprises* peace ; মর্য্যাদাবোধ করা ।

ăp-proach′ (-prōch), *v.i.* & *t.* **1.** To come or go near in place or time ; to advance nearer ; প্রত্যাসন্ন হওয়া, সন্নিকট হওয়া, নিকটবর্ত্তী হওয়া, ঘনিয়ে আসা ; অগ্রসর হওয়া । **2.** To approximate in quality, character, etc. ; (with *to*) ; প্রায় সমতুল্য হওয়া, কাছাকাছি হওয়া । ***Verb t.*** **1.** To come near to ; to draw nearer to ; as, to *approach* the city ; youths *approaching* manhood ; নিকটে আসা, কাছাকাছি আসা ; সান্নিধ্য-প্রাপ্ত হওয়া । **2.** (*Mil.*) To make approaches to ; (সামরিক-শাস্ত্র) অগ্রসর হওয়া, প্রয়াণ করা । **—a-bil′-i-ty, —a-ble-ness,** *ns.* **—a-ble,** *adj.* Accessible ; উপসর্পণীয় ।

ăp-proach′ (-prōch), *n.* **1.** The act of coming or drawing near ; সমীপাগমন, অভিগমন, আগম, উপগম । **2.** A means of approach ; avenue ; as, brocade lined the *approach* ; প্রবেশোপায়, প্রবেশপথ , ছায়াবীথিকা । **3.** An approximation ; as, a nearer *approach* to human type ; সন্নিকর্ষণ । **4.** (*Mil.* in *pl.*) The entrenchments enabling besiegers to draw closer to the besieged ; অবরোধকারিগণের দুর্গসান্নিধ্যে অগ্রসরের জন্য আবরণ, উচ্চ প্রাকার ।

ăp′-prō-bāte, *v. t.* To approve formally ; to sanction ; অনুমোদন করা ; দৃঢ় করা । **—bā′-tion,** *n.* Sanction ; approval ; দৃঢ়ীকরণ, স্থিরীকরণ ; অনুমোদন ।

ăp′-prō-bā-tō-rȳ, *adj.* Containing or expressing approbation ; commendatory ; অনুমোদনজ্ঞাপক, অনুমোদনসূচক, সম্মতিজ্ঞাপক ; প্রশংসাসূচক। **—tive-ness,** *n.* (*Phren.*) Love of praise ; (মস্তিষ্ক-সামুদ্রিক) ; প্রশংসানুরাগ।

ăp-prō′-pri-āte, *adj.* **1.** Peculiar to ; (with *to*) ; as, honour *appropriate to* the sovereign only ; নিজস্ব । **2.** Fitted or suitable ; proper ; (*to, for*) ; as, prayer *appropriate for* the great solemnity ; সমুচিত, যথাযোগ্য, যথোচিত, উপযুক্ত, উপযোগী ; যুক্তিযুক্ত, সঙ্গত । **—ly,** *adv.* In a proper manner ; যথাবিহিতরূপে । **—ness,** *n.*

ăp-prō′-pri-āte, *v. t.* **1.** To take possession of ; to take to oneself ; অধিকার করা, আত্মসাৎ করা ; নিজস্ব করা । **2.** To devote or assign to a special use or purpose ; (*to, for*) ; বিশেষ উদ্দেশ্য-সাধনে নিয়োজিত করা । **—a′-tion,** *n.* Application to a special use or purpose ; বিশেষ কার্য্য বা উদ্দেশ্যে নিয়োগ । **—a-tive,** *adj.* **—a-tor,** *n.*

ăp-prôv′-ăl, *n.* Approbation ; অনুমোদন, সম্মতি, স্বীকৃতি ।

ăp-prôve′, *v. t.* & *i.* **1.** To admit the excellence of ; to think well of ; as, to *approve* the measures of administration ; শ্রেষ্ঠতাস্বীকার বা অনুমোদন করা । **2.** (*Reflex.*) To prove partially ; as, he had approved himself a great warrior ; কতকাংশে প্রমাণিত করা । **3.** To sanction officially ; to confirm ; to ratify ; as, to *approve* the decision of a court-martial ; মঞ্জুর করা ; দৃঢ়ীভূত করা ; বাহাল করা। ***Verb i.*** To pronounce to be good ; to judge favourably ; (often with *of*) ; ভাল বলিয়া বলা ; অনুকূলভাবে বিচার করা । **—proved,** *adj.* Tried ; esteemed ; commended ; as, an *approved* medicine ; পরীক্ষিত ; অনুমত, আদৃত ; প্রশংসিত। **Approved bill**—গৃহীত হুণ্ডী । T

approve of—To pronounce or consider good ; অনুমোদন করা, ভাল বিবেচনা করা।

ăp-prôv′-êr, *n.* **1.** One who commends or pronounces good ; অনুমোদনকারী। **2.** One who turns king's (queen's) or state's evidence ; an informer ; যে ব্যক্তি আত্মদোষ স্বীকারপূর্ব্বক সহাপরাধীদিগের বিরুদ্ধে সাক্ষ্য প্রদান করে, রাজসাক্ষী ; গুপ্ত-সংবাদ-দাতা।

ăp-prŏx′-i-māte, *adj.* **1.** Very near ; closely situated ; nearly resembling ; কাছাকাছি ; আসন্ন, নিকটতম, উপশ্লিষ্ট ; প্রায় অনুরূপ। **2.** Nearly true or accurate ; fairly correct ; as, an *approximate* result ; শুদ্ধকল্প ; শুদ্ধপ্রায়। **—ly,** *adv.*

ăp-prŏx′-i-māte, *v. t.* & *i.* **1.** To bring near ; to cause to approach ; "To *approximate* the inequality of riches to the level of nature ;" কাছাকাছি আনা ; প্রত্যাসন্ন করা। **2.** To come close to ; to approach closely ; as, the telescope *approximates* perfection ; সন্নিহিত হওয়া, নিকটবর্ত্তী হওয়া ; সন্নিকটে আসা। *Verb i.* To come near ; আসন্ন হওয়া, কাছাকাছি হওয়া। **—ma′-tion,** *n.* **1.** A drawing, moving or advancing near ; an approach ; আসন্নতা ; উপগম। **2.** (*Math.*) A continual approach to a correct result ; (গণিত-শাস্ত্র) আসন্নক্রিয়া (ইঃ কোঃ)। **3.** An approach to a correct estimate, calculation or conception or to a given quality, quantity, etc. ; সংনিকর্ষণ। **—ma-tive,** *adj.* **—ma-tive-ly,** *adv.*

ap-pur′-tĕ-nănce (-pêr-), *n.* Something belonging to another thing as principal ; an appendage ; অঙ্গীভূত বস্তু ; উপাঙ্গ। A contributory adjunct ; an accessory ; অনুবন্ধ ; অতিরিক্ত বস্তু।

ap-pur′-tĕ-nănt (-pêr-), *adj.* & *n.* Belonging, as a property or legal right (*to*) ; appropriate (*to*) ; pertinent (*to*) ; সম্পত্তি বা বৈধ অধিকারস্বরূপ সংলগ্ন ; সমুচিত ; প্রাসঙ্গিক। *Noun.* A thing appertaining ; a belonging ; উপকল্প, আনুষঙ্গিক বস্তু বা বিষয়, উপাঙ্গ ; আসবাব।

ā′-pri-cŏt, *n.* An orange-coloured stone fruit of delicious taste, allied to the plum ; খুবানী, জরদ আলু।

A′-pril (ā-), *n.* The fourth month of the English year ; ইংরাজী বর্ষের চতুর্থ মাস। **April-fool**—One who is sportively imposed upon by others on the first day of April ; এপ্রিল মাসের প্রথম দিনে যাহাকে কৌতুকচ্ছলে বোকা সাজান হয়। **April-fool day**—1st of April ; ১লা এপ্রিল। **April gentleman**—নববিবাহিত পুরুষ।

a priori, *adv.* & *adj.* **1.** (*Log.* & *Phil.*) Reasoning from causes to effects ; deductively ; (opposed to *a posteriori*) ; কারণ হইতে কার্য্য অনুমান পূর্ব্বক, প্রাগ্‌জ্ঞান হইতে ; নিগমন ভাবে, আনুমানিক ভাবে। **2.** (*Kant*) (Knowledge) Independent of all experiences ; (জর্ম্মণ দার্শনিক ক্যাণ্টের মতে) স্বতঃসিদ্ধ, সহজাত (জ্ঞান)। [দেশ, কাল, নিমিত্ত প্রভৃতি আত্মপ্রত্যয়-লব্ধ ভাবসমূহ অবলম্বনে যে যুক্তি উপস্থাপিত হয়, ক্যাণ্ট্ তাহা *a priori* বলিয়া নির্দ্দেশ করিয়াছেন।] **3.** (*Loosely*) Presumptively ; in accordance with one's previous knowledge ; (অসাবধানে) আনুমানিকভাবে ; পূর্ব্বজ্ঞানানুযায়ী।

ā′-pron (-prŭn), *n.* **1.** A garment worn in front of the body to protect clothes, etc. ; দেহের সম্মুখভাগ-আবরক বস্ত্র-বিশেষ, পরিচ্ছদ-পরিরক্ষক বসন। **2.** An official dress ; as, a bishop's or freemason's *apron* ; পদবি-সূচক বসন। **3.** A leather covering for the legs in an open carriage ; অনাবৃত শকটে ব্যবহৃত চর্ম্মময় পদাবরণ বিশেষ, জঙ্ঘাত্রাণ, পদত্রাণ। **Apron-husband**—One that meddles with his wife's business ; যে স্বামী স্ত্রীর কার্য্যকর্ম্মে হস্তক্ষেপ করে। **Apron-man**—A mechanic ; শিল্পী, কারিগর। **Apron-string**—The string with which an apron is tied on ; যে রজ্জুদ্বারা পরিচ্ছদাবরক বহির্বসন বদ্ধ করা হয়। **To be tied to the apron-string (of a wife, mother, etc.)**—To be unduly controlled by her ; to be wholly under her influence ; অনুচিতরূপে স্ত্রী বা জননীদ্বারা চালিত হওয়া ; সম্পূর্ণরূপে স্ত্রী বা জননীর প্রভাবাধীন হওয়া। To be continually in a woman's company ; স্ত্রীলোকের আঁচলে আঁচলে ঘুরা, আঁচল-ধরা হওয়া, মা কিম্বা স্ত্রীর হাতের পুতুল হওয়া।

ăp-rō-pos′ (-pō), *adj.* & *adv.* **1.** Opportunely or opportune ; to the purpose ; সময়োচিতভাবে, সময়োচিত ; ঠিক উদ্দেশ্যের উপযোগী। **2.** With regard *to* ; in respect *of* ; by the way "But *apropos* ! Hast thou seen that girl ?" সম্পর্কে ; বিষয়ে ; ভাল কথা।

apse (ăps), *n.* (*Arch.*) A portion of any building semicircular or polygonal in plan, and having a

Apse—Laach, Germany.

dome or vaulted roof ; (স্থপতি-বিদ্যা) খিলান বা গুম্বজযুক্ত ছাদবিশিষ্ট অর্দ্ধচন্দ্র বা পঞ্চভুজাকার হর্ম্ম্যাংশ।

ăp′-si-dăl, *adj.* **1.** (*Arch.*) Of or pertaining to the apse of a church ; (স্থপতি-বিদ্যা) খৃষ্টীয়ধৰ্ম্মমন্দির-সংলগ্ন অৰ্দ্ধচন্দ্র বা পঞ্চভুজাকৃতি উপমন্দির-সম্বন্ধীয়। **2.** (*Astron.*) Of the apsides (of an orbit) ; (জ্যোতির্বিজ্ঞান); উচ্চরেখা-সম্বন্ধীয় (হিঃ কোঃ)।

ăp′-sis, *n.* (*Pl.* APSIDES.) Aphelion and perihelion of a planet or the apogee or perigee of the moon ;

Apsis.

মন্দ (সাঃ পঃ), মন্দোচ্চ (ঐ), উচ্চনীচস্থান (হিঃ কোঃ)। **Line of apsides**—The straight line joining these two points ; মন্দোচ্চ রেখা (সাঃ পঃ)।

ăpt, *adj.* **1.** Suited or adapted for a purpose ; fit ; উদ্দেশ্যোপযোগী ; উপযোগী। **2.** (*Of language*) Suitable to express ideas ; expressive (of thoughts, remarks, etc.) ; appropriate to the occasion ; apposite ; (ভাষা-সম্পর্কে) ভাব-প্রকাশোপযোগী ; দ্যোতক (চিন্তা, মন্তব্য, প্রভৃতি সম্বন্ধে) ; সময়োচিত, কালোপযোগী, কালোচিত ; আপ্ত (মঃ উঃ) ; প্রাসঙ্গিক। **3.** (Of things) Having a habitual tendency ; (বস্তু-সম্পর্কে) (অভ্যস্তভাবে) প্রবণ। **4.** (Of persons) Customarily disposed ; (ব্যক্তি-সম্পর্কে) স্বভাবতঃ উন্মুখ, প্রবণ। **5.** Ready to learn ; quick-witted ; prompt ; as, the *apt* scholar : men are *apt* at devising means of easing their toils ; শিক্ষানুরাগী উপস্থিত-বুদ্ধি ; তৎপর। **Apt′-ly,** *adv.* **Apt′-ness,** *n.* **1.** Suitableness ; appropriateness ; উপযোগিতা ; যথাযোগ্যতা। **2.** (Of persons or things) ; Inclination ; proneness ; as, the *aptness* of iron to rust : *aptness* to be frightened at trifling accidents ; আসক্তি ; প্রবণতা, উন্মুখতা, ঝোঁক। **3.** Quickness of apprehension ; proficiency ; ক্ষিপ্রগ্রাহিতা ; পারদর্শিতা।

ăp′-tĕr-ous (-ŭs), *adj.* **1.** (*Zool.*) Wingless ; (জন্তু-তত্ত্ব) পক্ষ-শূন্য। **2.** (*Bot.*) Destitute of membranous expansions ; (উদ্ভিদ্-বিদ্যা) ঝিল্লিক প্রসারবিহীন।

ăp′-tĕr-ȳx, *n.* A New-Zealand bird, about the size of a goose, with merely rudimentary wings

Apteryx.

and no tail ; (native name *Kiwi*) ; নবজিলণ্ডদ্বীপবাসী পক্ষিবিশেষ।

ăpt′-i-tūde, *n.* **1.** The quality of being fit for a purpose or position ; suitableness ; কার্য্যোপযোগিতা, উদ্দেশ্যোপযোগিতা, পদোপযোগিতা ; উপযোগিতা। **2.** Natural tendency ; disposition ; স্বাভাবিক প্রবৃত্তি ; আসক্তি, উন্মুখতা, প্রবণতা, প্রবৃত্তি। **3.** Talent *for* any pursuit ; ability ; intelligence ; quick-wittedness ; কার্য্যোপযোগী বুদ্ধি ; ক্ষমতা ; বুদ্ধি ; প্রত্যুৎপন্নমতিত্ব।

ā′-quā, *n.* The Latin word for water ; hence, liquid ; solution ; জল ; তরল পদার্থ ; দ্রব। ***Aqua fontana***—Spring-water ; প্রস্রবণ-বারি। ***Aqua fortis***—The nitric acid (of commerce) ; তাম্রদ্রাব (সাঃ পঃ)। ***Aqua regia***—A mixture of nitric and hydrochloric acids, able to dissolve gold and platinum ; স্বর্ণ ও প্লাটিনাম দ্রবকরণে সমর্থ তাম্রদ্রাব ও লৌহদ্রাবমিশ্র, শঙ্খদ্রাব (সাঃ পঃ), শঙ্খদ্রাবরস (ঐ)। ***Aqua vitæ***—[*L.* Water of life.] Brandy or other ardent spirit ; ব্রাণ্ডী, হুইস্কী প্রভৃতি উগ্রবীর্য্য সুরা।

ā-quā-mā-rine′ (-rēn), *n.* & *adj.* A bluish-green beryl ; নীলাভ-হরিদ্বর্ণ মণিবিশেষ, রোচক, পারিভদ্রক। ***Adj.*** Bluishgreen ; sea-coloured ; নীলাভ-হরিত ; আনীল-হরিত।

ā-quā′-ri-ŭm, *n.* (*Pl.* -UMS, -RIA.) **1.** An artificial pond or tank for the keeping of live aquatic plants and animals ; মৎস্য এবং শৈবলাদিরক্ষণার্থ কৃত্রিম পুষ্করিণী ব জলাধার। **2.** A place of publi entertainment containing suc tanks ; উক্তপ্রকার জলাশয়াদিযু পুরোদ্যান প্রভৃতি।

A-quā′-ri-ŭs (ă-′ *n.* The elever sign of the zodiac which t sun enters on the Jan. 2 (the water-bearer) ; কুম্ভরাশি।

ā-quăt′-ic, *adj.* & *n.* **1.** Pertaini to water ; living in or fr quenting water, as, *aquat* plants, animals (জলজন্তু) ; জলী জলজ, জলচর। **2.** Pertaining pastime in or on water ; a *aquatic* sports ; জলক্রীড়া বা জ বিহার-সংক্রান্ত। ***Noun.*** (*Pl.*) Spor conducted in or upon wate জলক্রীড়া, জলকেলি, জলবিহার, বা নৌ দৌড় প্রভৃতি জলপৃষ্ঠে অনুষ্ঠিত ক্রীড়

ā′-quā-tint, —tin′-tā, *n.* A k of engraving on copper the use of a resinous solut and nitric acid ; তাম্রদ্রাব এবং স্থ দ্রব্যের জলদ্বারা তাম্রখণ্ডোপরি চিত্রোৎ করণের প্রণালীবিশেষ।

ăq′-ue-dūct (-wē-), *n.* **1.** artificial channel, esp. an vated structure of mas for the conveyance of from one place to another one for supplying large with water) ; পরীবাহ, জল-বা **2.** (*Physiol.*) A small canal,

he head of mammals ; (শারীর-
ান) ক্ষুদ্র নালী বিশেষতঃ স্তন্যপায়ী
ীবর্গের মস্তকস্থ নালী।

Aqueduct.

-quē-ous (-ŭs), *adj.* **1.** Watery ; লীয়, সজল, জলময়। **2.** Produced y the action of water ; as, *ueous* rocks ; জলবাহিত শিলা-াদিদ্বারারচিত। **Aqueous humour the eye**—চক্ষুঃমল। **Aqueous our**—জলীয়বাষ্প, জলীয়রস।

ıi līne (-wē-). *adj.* **1.** Of an ıe ; শ্যেন বা উৎক্রোশ পক্ষি-সম্বন্ধীয়। Eagle-like ; as, an *aquiline* se (খগ-নাসা, শুক-নাসা) ; উৎক্রোশ-।

ıŏs′-i tŷ, *n.* Wateriness ; লতা, জলীয়তা, জলভাব।

ăb (ăr-), *n.* **1.** A native of abia ; আরবদেশীয় লোক। **2.** An ab horse ; আরবদেশীয় ঘোটক, জ, আর্বা। **City Arab, Street ıb**—A homeless little wander- a child of the street ; পরিত্যক্ত কবালিকা ; গৃহহীন বালকবালিকা।

·besque′ (-bĕsk), *n.* & *adj.* A ration in colour or low relief fanciful intertwining of ıts, leaves and scroll-work

Arabesque.

কাল্পনিক লতা, পাতা, ফল, এবং বিশিষ্ট চিত্রিত বা উৎকীর্ণ ার, আরবালঙ্কার। ***Adj.*** Ara- fantastic ; আরব্য ; অপরূপ।

·bi-ăn (ă-), *adj.* Of Arabia ; **Arabian nights**—A collection of fabulous stories ; আরব্য-রজনী, আরব্যোপন্যাস।

Ar′-ă-bic (ăr-), *n.* & *adj.* The language of the Arabs ; আরবী ভাষা। ***Adj.*** Arabian ; আরবা। **Arabic numerals**—The figures 1, 2, 3, 4, etc. ; আরব্যপ্রণালীর সংখ্যা ১, ২, ৩, ৪, ইত্যাদি।

Ar′-ă-bist (ăr-), *n.* One well-versed in the Arabic language or literature ; আরব্যভাষাবিদ্, আরব্য-সাহিত্যবিদ্।

ăr′-ă-ble, *adj.* & *n.* Fit for tillage ; কৃষি-যোগ্য, কর্ষণোপযোগী। ***Noun.*** Land for tillage ; (opp. to *pasture* or *woodland*) ; কর্ষণোপযোগী ভূমি।

A-răch′-ni-dă (ă-), *n. pl.* (*Zool.*) A class of animals comprising spiders, scorpions and mites ; (জন্তু-তত্ত্ব) ঊর্ণনাভশ্রেণী, ঊর্ণনাভাদি।

ă-răch′-noid (-noyd), *adj.* & *n.* (*Bot.*) Covered with long cobweb-like hairs ; (উদ্ভিদ্-বিদ্যা) লূতাতন্তুবৎ দীর্ঘরোমাবৃত। ***Noun.*** A semi-transparent thin membrane lining the dura matter, and enveloping the brain and spinal cord ; মস্তিষ্ক এবং কশেরুকার মজ্জা-আবরক লূতাতন্তুবৎ অর্দ্ধস্বচ্ছ ঝিল্লী-বিশেষ, মধ্যমাত্রিকা (হঃ চঃ)।

Ar-ă-mā′-ic (ăr-), *n.* The language of Syria ; সিরিয়া দেশের ভাষা।

âr′-bă lĕst, –list, –blăst, *n.* A crossbow ; বক্রচাপ, চক্রধনু। **–er,** *n.* A crossbow-man ; বক্রধনুর্দ্ধর।

âr′ bi-têr, *n.* (*Fem.* ARBITRESS.) **1.** A judge ; a person appointed by two parties to settle dispute ; an umpire ; বিচারকর্ত্তা ; মধ্যস্থ ; সালিশ, স্থেয় (রাঃ তঃ), প্রমাণপুরুষ (মঃ ভাঃ)। **2.** One who has entire control (of) ; as, *arbiter* of the whole world ; চূড়ান্ত বিচারক, সর্ব্ব-নিয়ন্তা, বিধাতা। **–tral,** *adj.*

âr′-bi-trāge, *n.* (*Comm.*) "The process of equalisation of prices in different business centres by buying bills of exchange or stocks in the cheaper market and selling in the dearer ;" যে নগরের বাজারে সস্তা তথায় ক্রয় এবং যে নগরে মহার্ঘ তথায় বিক্রয়-করত হুণ্ডী, কোম্পানীর কাগজ প্রভৃতির মূল্য-সমীকরণ।

âr-bit′-ră-mĕnt, –rē-mĕnt, *n.* The act of deciding of a dispute by an arbiter ; an authoritative or absolute decision ; as, the *arbitrament* of the sword ; (অস্ত্রদ্বারা বিবাদ-মীমাংসা) ; সালিশদ্বারা নিষ্পত্তি, মধ্যস্থতা ; শেষ মীমাংসা।

âr′-bi-tră-rŷ, *adj.* **1.** Derived from mere opinion ; as, *arbitrary* notions of right and justice ; হাত-গড়া, মন-গড়া। **2.** Done according to one's own will or discretion ; capricious ; as, *arbitrary* decision or punishment ; স্বেচ্ছানুরূপ সম্পাদিত ; খামখেয়ালীভাবের। **3.** Having no control ; absolute in power ; despotic ; as, *arbitrary* government ; স্বেচ্ছাচারী ; স্বৈরবৃত্ত ; যথেচ্ছাচারী। **–ri-ly,** *adv.* **–ri-ness,** *n.*

âr′-bi-trāte, *v. t.* & *i.* To settle by, or submit to, arbitration ; মধ্যস্থতাদ্বারা নিষ্পত্তি করা, সালিশ মানা। ***Verb i.*** To act as an arbitrator or umpire ; to mediate ; (*in* a dispute, *between* parties) ; সালিশের কার্য্য করা ; মধ্যস্থতা করা। **–tra′-tion,** *n.* The settlement of a dispute by an arbiter ; সালিশী। **–tra′-tor,** *n.* See ARBITER. **–tra′-tor-ship,** *n.* **Arbitration of exchange**—The operation of converting the currency of one country into that of another (by means of other currencies intervening between the two) ; মধ্যবর্ত্তী কোন প্রকার মুদ্রাদ্বারা এক দেশের মুদ্রা দেশান্তরের মুদ্রাতে বিনিময়।

âr′-bŏr, *n.* **1.** The spindle or axle on which a wheel revolves ; অক্ষ।

2. The main support of a machine ; অক্ষদণ্ড।

âr-bŏ-rā'-ceous (-shŭs), *adj.* Tree-like ; wooded ; তরুতুল্য ; জঙ্গলাকীর্ণ।

âr-bō'-rē-ăl, —ous (-ŭs), *adj.* Connected with trees ; living on or among trees ; frequenting woods ; as, *arboreal* animals ; বৃক্ষসম্পৃক্ত, তরুসম্পর্কীয়, বানস্পত্য ; বৃক্ষবাসী ; বনচর, কাননচারী।

âr-bŏ-rĕs'-cĕnt, *adj.* **1.** Tree-like in growth or general appearance ; বৃক্ষবৎ বর্দ্ধনশীল, তরুনিভ। **2.** (*Arch.*) Branching out ; (স্থপতি-বিদ্যা) শাখায়িত। **—cence,** *n.*

âr'-bŏ-ri-cŭl-türe, *n.* The cultivation of trees and shrubs ; তরু-গুল্মাদির চাষ। **—tur-al,** *adj.***—tur-ist,** *n.*

âr-bŏ-ri-zā'-tion, *n.* A tree-like growth or appearance in minerals, fossils, etc. ; কোন প্রকার খনিজ পদার্থ বা শিলীভূত জন্তু প্রভৃতির দেহে বৃক্ষাকৃতি চিত্রের আবির্ভাব।

âr-bŏr-vī'-tæ (-tē), *n.* A popular name of several evergreens ; কতিপয় চিরহরিত উদ্ভিদের সাধারণ নাম।

âr'-bour (-bêr), *n.* A retreat covered with vines, branches of trees, or other plants, for shade ; a bower ; কুঞ্জ, নিকুঞ্জ ; লতামণ্ডপ, লতাগৃহ, ছায়াকুঞ্জ, নিকুঞ্জগেহ, নিকুঞ্জমন্দির। **—boured,** *adj.*

âr'-bü-tŭs, *n.* A genus of shrubs or trees, including the strawberry-tree ; ষ্ট্রবেরি প্রভৃতি কতিপয় বৃক্ষ বা গুল্মের সাধারণ নাম।

ârc, *n.* Any part of the circumference of a circle or other curve ; চাপ, বৃত্তখণ্ড।

âr-cāde', *n.* **1.** (*Arch.*) A series of arches supported by columns or piers ; (স্থপতি-বিদ্যা) স্তম্ভরাজির উপর অবলম্বিত তোরণশ্রেণী, তোরণাকার ছাদ-বিশিষ্ট পথ। **2.** A passage arched over ; তোরণপথ। **3.** Any covered walk, esp. with shops along one or both sides ; এক বা উভয় পার্শ্বে বিপণিশ্রেণীবিশিষ্ট আচ্ছাদিত পথ। **—cad'-ed,** *adj.*

Ar-cā'-di-ăn (âr-), *n.* & *adj.* A native of Arcadia (a mountainous district of Greece taken as the ideal region of rural contentment); hence, an ideal rustic ; গ্রীস্-দেশের অন্তঃপাতী আর্কেডিয়া প্রদেশের অধিবাসী ; আদর্শ পল্লীবাসী। [আর্কেডিয়া পল্লী-জীবনের সুখশান্তির আদর্শ নিকেতন ছিল বলিয়া প্রসিদ্ধি।] ***Adj.*** Ideally rural ; as, *arcadian* bliss ; আদর্শ পল্লী-সমুচিত। **Arcadian youth**—A block-head ; মূর্খ, নির্ব্বোধ।

âr-cā-nŭm, *n.* (Usually used in the plural, ARCANA.) A profound secret ; a mystery ; as, inquiries into the *arcana* of the Godhead ; গূঢ় রহস্য, নিগূঢ় তত্ত্ব, গুহ্য বিষয় ; রহস্য।

ârch, *n.* **1.** (*Arch.*) A curved structure either capable of bearing weight or merely ornamental ; (স্থপতি-বিদ্যা) খিলান। **2.** An archway ; তোরণনিম্নস্থপথ। **3.** A curvature in the shape of an arch ; as, the delicate *arch* of her feet ; তোরণাকৃতি বক্রতা। **4.** An arched roof ; hence, the heavens ; "How is that immeasurable *arch* upheld ?" খিলান-বিশিষ্ট ছাদ ; নভোমণ্ডল। **Arch-roof**—A vaulted roof ; খিলান-বিশিষ্ট ছাদ। **Archway**—A vaulted passage; খিলানের নিম্নস্থ রাস্তা। **A triumphal arch**—বিজয়তোরণ।

ârch, *v. t.* & *i.* **1.** To cover with an arch ; to furnish with an arch ; তোরণ বা তোরণমালা দ্বারা আচ্ছাদিত করা ; তোরণ-সমন্বিত করা। **2.** To form into an arch or vault ; to curve ; as, the horse *arched* his neck ; তোরণাকৃতি করা ; বক্র করা, বাঁকান। ***Verb_i.*** To form an arch ; খিলানাকৃতি হওয়া, বক্র হওয়া। **Arched,** *adj.*

ârch, *adj.* **1.** Chief ; pre-eminent ; principal ; as, an *arch* rogue ; (but now rarely used wi[th] the hyphen) ; প্রধান, মুখ্য ; [...] **2.** Cunning ; clever ; as, an [...] fellow ; silly ; saucy ; spor[tive] mischievous ; (now u[...] of women and child[ren])

Arch.

as, her *arch* look ; her ways ; চতুর ; চালাক, সে[...] নির্ব্বোধ ; ঠেঁটা ; দুষ্ট, দুরন্ত। **—ly, —ness,** *n.* Slyness without m[...] shrewdness ; waggishness ; [...] রালি ; চাতুর্য্য ; বৈদগ্ধ্য, রঙ্গপ্রিয়তা,

âr-chæ'-ăn (-kē-), *adj.* C[...] earliest geological period ; [...] বিষয়ক আদিযুগসম্বন্ধীয়, আর্কিক (স[...] আদিম (ঐ)।

âr-chæ-ŏl'-ŏ-ġȳ (-kē-), *n.* [...] systematic study of antiqui[ties] esp. the scientific study of remains and monuments of pre-historic period ; প্রত্নবিদ্যা, [...] হাস-চিহ্ন বিদ্যা (হিঃ কোঃ)। **—o-ġi-an, —ol'-o-ġist,** *ns.* **—o-ic, —o-log'-i-cal,** *adjs.*

âr-cha'-ic, —i-căl, *adj.* [...] quated ; as, an *archaic* w[...] primitive ; (of language) no l[onger] in common use, but still ret[ained] for special purposes ; অ[...] প্রাচীন ; অপ্রচলিত, আর্ষ। **—ly,** *adv.*

âr-cha'-ism, *n.* **1.** An archaic [...] or expression ; অপ্রচলিত [...] বাক্য, আর্ষপ্রয়োগ। **2.** The ret[ention] or imitation of what is [...] obsolete in language, art, অধুনা অপ্রচলিত ভাষা, শিল্প প্র[...] রক্ষণ বা অনুকরণ। **—ist,** *n.* **—i[stic,]** *adj.*

in t|ă-ize, *v. t.* To make or ...ar archaic : অপ্রচলিত করা, প্রা ...লিত বোধ হওয়া।

...ăn'-gĕl, *n.* **1.** An angel of the ...est order ; সর্ব্বোচ্চশ্রেণীভুক্ত ...ত ; মুখ্যশ্রেণীর দেবদূত। **2.** A ...of fancy pigeon ; একজাতীয় ...র কপোত। **3.** A kind of dead-...ettle ; একজাতীয় উদ্ভিদ্, পীতপর্ণী।

...gel'-ic, *adj.*

...ch-bish'-op (-ŭp), *n.* The ...ghest dignitary in an epis-...pal church ; (often called *metropolitan* or *primate*) ; প্রধান খৃষ্টীয় ধর্ম্মাচার্য্য। **—ric,** *n.*

...-dea'-con (-dē-kn), *n.* An ...esiastical dignitary next in ...below a bishop ; বিশপের ...হিত নিম্নপদস্থ খৃষ্টীয় আচার্য্য, সহ-ধর্ম্মাচার্য্য। **—ship,** *n.*

...dea'-con-rȳ (-dē-kn-), *n.* ...office, jurisdiction or resi-...ce of an archdeacon ; সহকারী ...চার্য্যের পদ, অধিকার বা আবাস-ভবন।

...-dī'-ō-cēse, *n.* The see or ...sdiction of an archbishop ; ...ণ্ডের সর্ব্বপ্রধান খৃষ্টীয় ধর্ম্মাচার্য্যের ...াট বা অধিকার।

...-dŭch'-ĕss, *n.* The wife of ...archduke ; a daughter of the ...peror of Austria ; অষ্ট্রীয়া-...টের পুত্রবধূ ; অষ্ট্রিয়ার সম্রাট-কন্যা।

...-dūke', *n.* A titular dignity ...the sons of the Emperor ...Austria ; অষ্ট্রিয়া সম্রাটের পুত্র। ...m, **—duch'-y,** *ns.* **—duc'-** *adj.*

...-ĕn'-ē-mȳ, *n.* Chief enemy ; ...an ; প্রধান শত্রু ; শয়তান।

...-ēr, *n.* **1.** One who shoots ...bow and arrows ; ধানুষ্ক, ..., ধানুকী, ধনুভৃৎ। **2.** The ninth ...cal constellation, *sagit-...s* ; ধনুরাশি। **—y,** *n.* **1.** The ...r skill of shooting with a ...and arrow ; ধনুর্বিদ্যা, ধনুর্বেদ। ...*ollect.*) Bows, arrows, etc. ; as, an *archery*-manufacturer ; ধনুঃ, শর প্রভৃতি।

âr'-chē-tȳpe, *n.* The original pattern or model ; a prototype ; "The House of Commons, the *archetype* of all the representative assemblies ;" মূল আদর্শ, আদিম নমুনা ; আদিরূপ। **—typ-al, —typ'-i-cal,** *adjs.*

ârch-fiend' (-fēnd), *n.* Satan ; শয়তান।

âr-chi-dī-ăc'-ō-năl, *adj.* Pertaining to an archdeacon ; সহকারী ধর্ম্মাচার্য্য-সম্বন্ধীয়।

âr-chi-ē-pis'-cō-păl, *adj.* Pertaining to an archbishop ; ইংলণ্ডের সর্ব্বপ্রধান খৃষ্টীয়ধর্ম্মাচার্য্যসংক্রান্ত।

âr'-chil, *n.* A rich violet colour obtained from certain lichens ; কতিপয় শৈলেয় হইতে প্রাপ্ত ধূমল-(বেগুণি) বর্ণ রঞ্জক পদার্থ।

âr-chi-măn'-drīte, *n.* A superior of a monastery or convent in Greek Church ; খৃষ্টীয় ধর্ম্ম-সমাজের গ্রীক্ শাখান্তর্গত মঠ- বা বিহারাধিপতি।

Ar-chi-mē'-dē-ăn (âr-), *adj.* Pertaining to Archimedes, the celebrated mathematician of ancient Greece ; প্রাচীন গ্রীসের সুবিখ্যাত

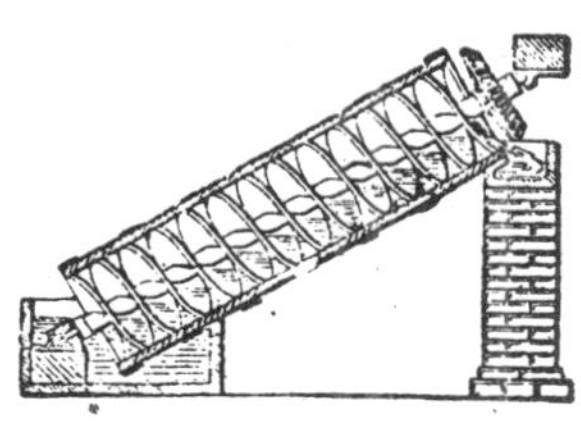

Archimedean screw.

গণিতজ্ঞ আর্কিমিডিস্ সম্বন্ধীয়। **Archimedean Screw**—An instrument for raising water, formed by winding a tube into the form of a screw around a cylinder ; জলোত্তলন যন্ত্রবিশেষ।

âr-chi-pĕl'-ă-gō, *n.* (*Pl.* ARCHIPELAGOS), The Aegean sea (between Greece & Asia Minor) ; a sea with many islands ; a group of islands ; ঈজীয়্যান্ সাগর ; দ্বীপবহুল সমুদ্র, দ্বৈপসাগর ; দ্বীপপুঞ্জ।

âr'-chi-tĕct, *n.* **1.** A person skilled in the art of building ; one who prepares plans of edifices and superintends work ; স্থপতি, সৌধশিল্পী ; প্রাসাদাদির নক্সা প্রস্তুতকারক বা নির্ম্মাণ-কার্য্য পরিদর্শক। **2.** A designer or maker ; a contriver ; as, he is the *architect* of his own fortunes ; গঠনকর্ত্তা, নির্ম্মাতা ; রচক। **3.** A designer of a complex structure ; esp. the Creator ; as, the great *Architect* of nature ; জটিল অট্টালিকাদির পরিকল্পনাকারী ; (বিশেষতঃ) স্রষ্টা, জগৎস্রষ্টা, সৃষ্টিকর্ত্তা। **—tec'-tive,** *adj.*

âr-chi-tĕc-tŏn'-ic, —i-cal, *adj.* **1.** Pertaining to, or skilled in, architecture ; স্থপতি-বিজ্ঞান-সংক্রান্ত, সৌধশিল্পজ্ঞ। **2.** Constructive ; as, *architectonic* functions ; নির্ম্মাণাত্মক। **—ics,** *n.* The science of architecture ; স্থপতি-বিজ্ঞান।

âr'-chi-tĕc-tūre, *n.* **1.** The art or science of building edifices for human use ; গৃহনির্ম্মাণবিদ্যা, স্থপতি-বিজ্ঞান, সৌধশিল্প। **2.** A method or style of building , স্থাপত্যরীতি। **3.** A building ; as, an *architecture* of stone ; অট্টালিকা। **4.** Construction ; workmanship ; as, in ingenious *architecture*, the birds and the bees have been competitors ; গঠন ; কারুকৌশল। **—tur-al,** *adj.*

âr'-chi-trāve, *n.* **1.** (*Arch.*) The lower division of an entablature or that part which rests immediately on the column ; অট্টালিকার মাথাড়ির নিম্নভাগ—যাহা স্তম্ভের অব্যবহিত উপরে থাকে, উত্তর (রাঃ রাঃ), অধঃপ্রস্তার (ঐ)। **2.** A collective name for the various parts (arch, lintels, etc.) which surround a window or doorway ; দ্বার বা বাতায়নের চতুষ্পার্শ্ববর্ত্তী উপস্তম্ভ (বাজু), দ্বারপিণ্ডী, প্রভৃতি।

âr′-chive, *n.* (Usu. *pl.*) A place in which public records are kept ; public records ; the *archives* of a family or country ; দপ্তরখানা, মহাফেজখানা, অক্ষপটল ; সরকারী দলিল পত্রাদি (বঃ উঃ)।

âr′-chiv-ist, *n.* A keeper of archives or records ; সরকারী দলিল পত্রাদি রক্ষক, মহাফেজ।

âr′-chi-vōlt, *n.* The ornamental band of mouldings on the face of an arch ; তোরণের সম্মুখভাগস্থ কারুকার্য্য-মণ্ডিত বেষ্টনী বিশেষ।

âr′-chŏn, *n.* **1.** One of the nine magistrates of Athens ; এথেন্সের নয়জন প্রধান শাসকের অন্যতম। **2.** A ruler or presiding spirit ; শাসনকর্ত্তা, অধ্যক্ষ।

ârc′-tic, *adj.* Of the north pole ; northern ; সুমেরুসংক্রান্ত ; উদীচ্য। **Arctic circle**—A circle parallel to the equator, 23° 28′ from the north pole ; উদীচ্য বৃত্ত (সাঃ পঃ), সুমেরু বৃত্ত (ঐ)। **Arctic ocean**—উত্তর মহাসাগর, সুমেরু সমুদ্র। **Arctic regions**—The lands surrounding the north pole ; সুমেরু প্রদেশ।

Arc-tū′-rŭs (ârc-), *n.* The brightest star in the constellation Boötes ; sometimes the Great Bear itself ; স্বাতীনক্ষত্র ; (কখন কখন) সপ্তর্ষিমণ্ডল।

ârc′-ū-āte, —āt-ĕd, *adj.* Bent or curved in the form of a bow ; arched ; ধনুকাকার, বক্র ; বঙ্কিম, সাচীকৃত।

âr′-dĕnt, *adj.* **1.** Hot ; burning ; as, *ardent* spirit (distilled liquors) (পরিস্রুত সুরা, হুইস্কী, ব্রাণ্ডী প্রভৃতি) ; fiery ; parching ; as the *ardent* sun : *ardent* fever (অভিন্যাস জ্বর) ; উত্তপ্ত, উষ্ণ ; জ্বলন্ত ; অগ্নিময়, জ্বালাকর ; দাহকারী। **2.** Fierce ; "With flashing fire his *ardent* eyes were filled ;" glowing ; প্রচণ্ড, রৌদ্র ; উদ্দীপ্ত, জ্বলন্ত। **3.** Warm ; fervent (applied to passions & affections); eager ; zealous ; as, *ardent* love, temper, passion, desire, etc. ; অনুরাগপূর্ণ ; আকুল, ব্যগ্র ; উদ্দীপনাপূর্ণ ; আগ্রহপূর্ণ। **—den-cy,** *n.* **—ly,** *adv.* **—ness,** *n.*

âr′-dour (-dêr), *n.* **1.** Fierce or burning heat ; as, the *ardour* of the sun's rays ; প্রচণ্ড উত্তাপ। **2.** Warm emotion ; fervour ; zeal ; as, he pursues study with *ardour* : they fought with *ardour* ; প্রবল অনুরাগ ; উৎসাহ, উদ্দীপনা ; আগ্রহ।

âr′-dū-ous (-ŭs), *adj.* **1.** Steep ; hard to climb ; "Those *arduous* paths they trod ;" সরলোন্নত, খাড়া ; দুরারোহ। **2.** Hard to achieve ; laborious ; as, an *arduous* task ; দুষ্কর, দুঃসাধ্য, কঠিন ; শ্রমসাধ্য **—ly,** *adv.* **—ness,** *n.*

are (âr), *v. i.* The present tense plural of the verb *to be*, *art* being the second person, singular ; ভূধাতুর বর্ত্তমানকালবাচক বহুবচন (হই, আছি ; হও, আছ ; হয়, আছে)।

are (âr), *n.* The unit of French square measure ; ফরাসী দেশীয় বর্গীয় পরিমাপের একক, ১০০ বর্গ মিটার বা ১১৯·৬ বর্গগজ পরিমিত বর্গক্ষেত্র।

ā′-rē-ā, *n.* **1.** Any open space, as the floor of a building, etc. ; an open space within any enclosure ; অঙ্গন ; বেষ্টিতভূমি। **2.** The site on which a building stands ; বাস্তু। **3.** The sunken space around the basement of a building ; অট্টালিকার তলপত্তনের চতুষ্পার্শ্ববর্ত্তী (গরাদবেষ্টিত) নিম্নভূমি। **4.** A tract of the earth's surface ; a region ; as, a vast uncultivated *area* ; ভূখণ্ড ; অঞ্চল, প্রদেশ। **5.** The surface included within any given lines ; superficial extent ; কোন সীমাবেষ্টিত স্থানের পরিমাণ ; উপরিভাগের বিস্তার। **6.** (*Geom.*) The superficial contents of any figure ; as, the *area* of a triangle ; (জ্যামিতি) ক্ষেত্রফল, পরিমাণফল। **7.** Extent ; scope ; range : as, a wide *area* of thought : whole *area* of life ; প্রসার ; দৌড়, পাল্লা ; বিস্তার, সীমা।

Ar′-ē-cā (ăr-), *n.* (*Bot.*) A genus of palms, one species of which produces the areca-nut ; (উদ্ভিদবিদ্যা) গুবাকাদি। **Areca-nut**—Betel-nut ; সুপারী, গুবাক, পূগ, ক্রমুক, অকোট।

a-rē′-nā, *n.* [*L. arena*, sand, the sand-strewn place of combat.] **1.** The inclosed space in the central part of the Roman amphitheatre in which combats took place ; প্রাচীন রোমীয় রঙ্গক্ষেত্রের মধ্যভাগস্থ মল্লভূমি। **2.** (*Fig.*) A scene or sphere of contest ; as, an *arena* of controversy, debate, etc. ; (লক্ষণায়) রঙ্গভূমি (কৃষ্ণঃ), সংগ্রামস্থল, বিবাদক্ষেত্র ;

ăr-ē-nā′-ceous (-shŭs), *adj.* Sandy ; sand-like ; বালুকাময়, বেলিয়া ; ধূলিনিভ।

ăr′-ē-nōse, *adj.* Same as ARENACEOUS.

ā-rē′-ō-lā, *n.* (*Pl.* AREOLÆ.) **1.** A very small area, as that between the veins of a leaf or nervures of an insect's wing ; অতি ক্ষুদ্র স্থান। **2.** A coloured circular spot such as that surrounding the human nipple ; রঞ্জিতমণ্ডল, চুচুকের চতুষ্পার্শ্ববর্ত্তী কৃষ্ণাভ মণ্ডল। **3.** (*Physiol.*) The interstice in the tissue ; (শারীর-বিজ্ঞান) ব্যূহতন্তুর মধ্যবর্ত্তী ক্ষুদ্র রন্ধ্র বিশেষ। **—lar,** *adj.* **—late,** *v. t.* **—la′-tion,** *n.*

Ar-ē-ŏp′-ā-gīte, —gist (ăr-), *n.* A member of the court of Areopagus, the highest court of Athens ; এথেন্স নগরীর সর্ব্বোচ্চ ধর্ম্মাধিকরণের অন্যতম বিচারপতি।

Ar-ē-ŏp′-ā-gŭs (ăr-), *n.* [*Gr. Areios pagos*, hill of Mars.] The highest judicial court at Athens, so called because its sessions were held on Mars' hill ; এথেন্স্-নগরীর সর্ব্বোচ্চ বিচারালয় বিশেষ, মার্স্ পর্ব্বতে উক্ত বিচারালয়ের অধিবেশন হইত।

âr'-gă-lă *n.* The adjutant-bird ; হাড়গিলা।

âr'-gă-li, *n.* An Asiatic wild sheep, remarkable for its large horns ; মধ্য-এসিয়ার বন্য-মেষবিশেষ।

ârgănd-lămp, *n.* [Invented by M. Argand, 1789.] A lamp with a cylindrical wick allowing an inside and outside current of air, which greatly increases the brilliancy of the flame ; নলাকার বর্ত্তিকাবিশিষ্ট দীপ। **Argand burner**—A gas-burner on the same principle ; উক্ত প্রণালীতে নির্ম্মিত বাষ্পীয় দীপের মুখ।

Argemone Mexicana—Yellow thistle—বড় শিয়াল কাঁটা (বেলঃ)।

âr'-gĕnt, *n.* & *adj.* **1.** (*Herald.*) Silver colour in armorial bearings ; (কুল-বিদ্যা) কুলচিহ্নস্থ রজত বা শুভ্র বর্ণ। **2.** (*Fig.*) Whiteness like that of silver ; "The polished *argent* of her breast ;" (লক্ষণায়) রজত-শুভ্রতা। ***Adj.*** Made of silver ; bright like silver ; silvery white ; "Yonder *argent* fields above ;" রজতরচিত ; রজতোজ্জ্বল, রজতনিভ ; রজত-শ্বেত।

âr-gĕn-tif'-ĕr-ous (-ŭs), *adj.* Yielding or containing silver ; রৌপ্যদ, রজতোৎপাদক।

âr'-gĕn-tine, *adj.* & *n.* Of, pertaining to, or made of, silver ; silvery ; as, the *argentine* rays of the moon ; রৌপ্যসম্বন্ধীয়, রজতনির্ম্মিত, রজতবৎ। ***Noun.*** **1.** Imitation silver ; কৃত্রিম রৌপ্য। **2.** The silvery scales of fish used in making artificial pearls ; কৃত্রিম মুক্তা-নির্ম্মাণে ব্যবহৃত রৌপ্যবৎ মৎস্য-শল্ক। **3.** (*Zool.*) A genus of small fishes with silvery scales ; (জন্তু-তত্ত্ব) রৌপ্যবৎ শল্কবিশিষ্ট মৎস্য শ্রেণীবিশেষ। **4.** (*Miner.*) Slate-spar ; (খনিজ-বিদ্যা) এক জাতীয় প্রস্তর।

âr'-gĭl, *n.* Clay or potter's earth ; মৃত্তিকা, কুলাল-মৃত্তিকা। **—lā'-ceous,** *adj.* Of the nature of clay ; clayey ; মৃত্তিকাধর্ম্মা ; মৃত্তিকাবিশিষ্ট, মৃণ্ময়।

Ar'-gō (âr-), *n.* **1.** The name of the ship which carried Jason and his companions (54) to Colchis in quest of the golden fleece ; জেসন্ ও তাঁহার সঙ্গিগণ যে জাহাজে আরোহণ করত স্বর্ণ মেষলোমের অনুসন্ধানে কলসিসে গমন করেন। **2.** (*Astron.*) The constellation Argo-Navis ; (জ্যোতির্বিজ্ঞান) তারা প্রকোষ্ঠ বিশেষ, নৌ (সাঃ পঃ)।

âr'-gŏl, *n.* Unrefined tartar ; a hard crust, formed on the sides of vessels in which wine has been kept ; মদ্যকিট্ট ; মদ্যভাণ্ডের গাত্রে সঞ্চিত অশোধিত লাবণিক পদার্থ বিশেষ। [ইহা রঞ্জন-কার্য্যে ব্যবহৃত হয়।]

âr'-gŏn, *n.* A constituent element of our atmosphere discovered in 1894 ; বায়ুমণ্ডলের উপাদানভূত মৌলিক পদার্থবিশেষ। [রেমজে ও রেলে ১৮৯৪ খৃঃ অব্দে উহা আবিষ্কার করেন।]

Argonaut.

Ar'-go-naut (âr-gō-nāt), *n.* One of the legendary heroes who sailed with Jason in the ship Argo, for the golden fleece ; প্রাচীন গ্রীসদেশীয় উপকথায় উক্ত যে বীরবৃন্দ জেসনের সহিত স্বর্ণ মেষ-লোমের অন্বেষণে "আর্গো" নামক জাহাজে কলসিসে গমন করিয়াছিলেন, তাহাদের অন্যতম। **2.** A genus of cephalopod molluscs including the 'paper-nautilus' ; মুণ্ডপদী কম্বোজ-শ্রেণী। **—nau'-tic,** *adj.*

âr'-gō-sȳ, *n.* A merchant vessel of the largest size ; (esp. of Ragusa & Venice) ; "Venetian marchants with deep-laden *argosies* ;" বৃহৎ বাণিজ্যপোত।

âr'-got (-gŏt, or -gō), [*F.*], *n.* The conventional slang of thieves and vagabonds ; cant ; slang ; চোর দস্যুদিগের মধ্যে প্রচলিত সাঙ্কেতিক ভাষা ; অপভাষা ; নীচভাষা, ইতরভাষা।

âr'-gue (-gū), *v. t.* & *i.* **1.** To debate or discuss ; to treat by reasoning ; as, he *argued* the case very ably ; তর্কবিতর্ক করা, বাদানুবাদ করা, বাগ্‌বিতণ্ডা করা, বিচার করা ; যুক্তি-প্রদর্শন করা। **2.** To prove or evince ; to show reasons for ; as, the order visible in the universe *argues* a divine cause ; to indicate ; প্রমাণ করা, স্পষ্টরূপে প্রদর্শন করা ; হেতু প্রদর্শন করা ; নির্দ্দেশ করা। ***Verb i.*** To offer reasons to support or overthrow a proposition, opinion, etc. ; to reason ; (*with, against* a person, *for, against, about,* a thing) ; যুক্তি-প্রদর্শন করা ; তর্কবিতর্ক করা। **—gu-a-ble,** *adj.* Capable of being argued ; admitting argument ; যুক্তিযুক্ত ; যুক্তিসহ। **—gu-er,** *n.* **To argue a person into or out of**—To persuade him into or out of a certain course of action ; কোন ব্যক্তিকে কোন বিষয়ে প্রবৃত্ত বা কোন বিষয় হইতে নিবৃত্ত করা। **To argue a thing away**—To get rid of it by argument ; যুক্তিদ্বারা উড়াইয়া দেওয়া।

âr'-gū-mĕnt, *n.* **1.** Reason

advanced *(for, against,* a proposition, measure, etc.) ; যুক্তি, নয় (হিঃ কোঃ)। **2.** (*Log.*) The middle term of a syllogism ; (তর্ক-বিজ্ঞান) হেতু, লিঙ্গ (হিঃ কোঃ)। **3.** A debate ; a discussion of a question ; as, the *argument* is not about things, but names ; বিতর্ক, বাদ-বিতণ্ডা, বাদানুবাদ, উপপত্তি ; সওয়াল (*Colloq.*)। **4.** The summary of the subject-matter of a book ; as, I will give you the *argument* of the play ; (কোন গ্রন্থের) সংক্ষিপ্ত-সারমর্ম, মুল-আখ্যানের সংক্ষেপ। **—men-ta'-tion,** *n.* A methodical reasoning ; a debate ; শৃঙ্খলাবদ্ধ যুক্তি, বিচারণা ; তর্কবিতর্ক। **—men-ta'-tive,** *adj.* Logical ; capable or fond of arguing ; as, *argumentative* history ; ন্যায়ানুগত ; যুক্তিক্ষম, তর্ক-প্রিয়। **—men-ta'-tive-ness,** *n.*

ár-gū-mĕn'-tŭm, [*L.*], *n.* **1.** An argument ; যুক্তি। **Argumentum ad hominem**—[An argument to the man.] An argument that takes advantage of the character or situation of the opponent ; প্রতিপক্ষের চরিত্র বা অবস্থার সুযোগ-গ্রহণকরত যে যুক্তি প্রদর্শিত হয়, ধর্ম্মহানিবিভীষান্যায় (হিঃ কোঃ)। **Argumentum ad ignorantiam**—An argument founded on the ignorance of an opponent ; প্রতিপক্ষের অজ্ঞানতার উপর প্রতিষ্ঠিত যুক্তি, প্রবচন-ন্যায় (হিঃ কোঃ)। **Argumentum ad judicium**—An appeal to the common sense of mankind ; জনতাবুদ্ধি-ন্যায় (হিঃ কোঃ)। **Argumentum ad verecundiam**—An appeal to a person's modesty ; ত্রপান্যায় (হিঃ কোঃ), প্রীতিন্যায় (ঐ), ভক্তিন্যায় (ঐ)। **Argumentum baculinum**—An appeal to force ; শস্ত্রন্যায় (হিঃ কোঃ)।

Ar'-gŭs (âr-), *n.* A fabulous person with a hundred eyes ; hence, a very vigilant person ; a watchful guardian ; গ্রীকপুরাণোক্ত শতনেত্র-পুরুষ ; তীক্ষ্ণদৃষ্টিসম্পন্ন পুরুষ ; সতর্ক অভিভাবক। **Argus-eyed**—Extremely watchful or sharp-sighted ; অত্যন্ত সতর্ক বা সজাগ, তীক্ষ্ণ-দৃষ্টিসম্পন্ন।

âr-güte', *adj.* **1.** Subtle ; shrewd ; sharp ; (of persons, actions, etc.) ; সূক্ষ্ম ; চতুর, বিদগ্ধ, বিচক্ষণ ; তীক্ষ্ণ-বুদ্ধি। **2.** Shrill ; (of sounds) ; কর্কশ। **—ly,** *adv.* **—ness,** *n.*

âr'-ğyr'-i-â, *n.* Silver-poisoning ; রৌপ্যবিষদুষ্টি।

aria (*Ital.*) *n.* (*Mus.*) Air ; সুর।

A'-ri-ăn (ā-), *n.* & *adj.* One who adheres to the doctrine of Arius of Alexandria, who denied the *consubstantiality* of Christ ; এরিয়্যানপন্থী, একেশ্বরবাদী। [এরিয়্যাস্ খৃষ্টীয় চতুর্দ্দশ শতাব্দীতে এলেকজেন্দ্রিয়া নগরীতে যাজকের কার্য্য করিতেন। [খৃষ্ট ঈশ্বরসৃষ্ট ; কিন্তু ঈশ্বরের সহিত একাত্ম ও অভিন্ন নহেন, তিনি এই মত প্রচার করিয়া গিয়াছেন।] ***Adj.*** Pertaining or adhering to Arius or his doctrines ; এরিয়্যস্ বা তদীয় মত সংক্রান্ত। **—ism,** *n.* **—ize,** *v. t.* & *i.*

ăr'-id, *adj.* **1.** Dry ; parched ; as, *arid* white salt ; *arid* body ; (*fig.*) uninteresting ; as, *arid* studies ; শুষ্ক ; উপতপ্ত, পরিদগ্ধ ; (লক্ষণায়) নীরস। **2.** (Of ground) Barren ; bare ; as, *arid* waste, sands ; অনুর্ব্বর ; অনাবৃত। **A-rid'-i-ty, —ness,** *ns.*

ā'-ri-ĕl, *n.* A species of gazelle in western Asia and Africa ; পশ্চিম এশিয়া এবং আফ্রিকাবাসী হরিণ বিশেষ।

A'-ri-ēs (ā-), *n.* The Ram, the first of the twelve signs of the zodiac ; মেষরাশি।

ȧ-right' (-rīt), *adv.* In a right way or form ; rightly ; সম্যক্‌রূপে, যথোচিত ভাবে ; ঠিক বা নির্ভুলভাবে, নির্দ্দোষরূপে।

ăr'-il, ă-ril'-ŭs, *n.* An extra covering of the seed ; জয়িত্রী প্রভৃতি বীজের উপচ্ছদ, প্রকৃত বীজাবরণোপযোগ (সাঃ পঃ)।

ă-ril'-lōde, *n.* A false aril ; অপ্রকৃত বীজাবরণোপযোগ (সাঃ পঃ)।

ȧ-rīse', *v. t.* **1.** To ascend, as vapours do ; to appear from below the horizon, (as the sun, the moon, the stars) ; to become visible ; to come into notice ; as, a cloud *arose* ; উত্থিত হওয়া, উঠা ; উদিত হওয়া ; দৃষ্টিগোচর হওয়া, দৃষ্টিপথারূঢ় হওয়া ; লক্ষ্যের বিষয়ীভূত হওয়া। **2.** To spring up ; to present itself ; as, errors *arose* ; questions which *arose* in the Privy Council ; উদ্ভূত হওয়া ; উপস্থাপিত হওয়া। **3.** To be born ; as, there *arose* a great master of painting ; to originate ; as, comfort *arose* from reflection ; জাত হওয়া, জন্ম গ্রহণ করা ; উৎপত্তি-লাভ করা। **4.** To get up from sitting or repose ; as, all the audience immediately *arose* ; to get up from sleep or rest ; as, he generally *arises* early in the morning ; উঠিয়া দাঁড়ান ; নিদ্রোত্থিত হওয়া, শয্যাত্যাগ করা। **5.** To rise from the dead ; to return to life from the grave ; (now poetic) ; পুনর্জীবিত হওয়া ; কবর হইতে উত্থিত হওয়া।

ȧ-ris'-tȧ, *n.* (*Bot.*) The awn or beard of grain and grasses ; (উদ্ভিদ্-বিদ্যা) শস্যশূক (ধান্য প্রভৃতির শুঙ্গা)।

ăr-is-tŏc'-rȧ-çy̆, *n.* **1.** (*Lit.*) The government of a state by its best citizens ; as, the *aristocracy* of Venice ; a form of government in which the chief power lies in the hands of those who are most distinguished by birth or fortune ; as, to change the *artistocracy* into an absolute monarchy ; শ্রেষ্ঠ নাগরিকগণকর্ত্তৃক রাষ্ট্র-শাসন ; অভিজাততন্ত্র, সম্ভ্রান্ততন্ত্র। **2.** The ruling body of nobles ; the nobles ; as, between the *aristocracy* and the working people had sprung up a middle class; অভিজাত শাসক-সম্প্রদায়; সম্ভ্রান্ত-সম্প্রদায়। **3.** The best representatives of learning, intellect, etc.; পাণ্ডিত্য, মনীষা প্রভৃতিতে শীর্ষস্থানীয় ব্যক্তিগণ। **Cold shades of aristocraçy**—The unsympathetic patronage of the great; সম্ভ্রান্ত জনগণের অনুরাগশূন্য অনুগ্রহ।

ă-ris′-tŏ-crăt, *n.* One of a ruling oligarchy; a noble; hence a person of haughty and overbearing temper and manners; as, a born *aristocrat*; সম্ভ্রান্ত-বংশীয় শাসকগণের অন্যতম; সম্ভ্রান্ত পুরুষ; মানী, কুলাভিমানী। **—ism,** *n.*

ăr-is-tŏ-crăt′-ic, —i-căl, *adj.* **1.** Pertaining to, or attached to, aristocracy; আভিজাতিক। **2.** Befitting an aristocrat; grand; stylish; as, rooms more *aristocratic* than those in which she lived; সম্ভ্রান্ত জনোচিত; জাঁকোলো; বাহ্যাড়ম্বরপ্রিয়। **—al-ly,** *adv.*

Ar-is-tŏ-lŏ′-chi-ă (ăr-), *n.* A genus of gynandrous plants; অর্কমূলাদি (সাঃ পঃ)। ***Aristolochia Indica***—ঈশের মূল (বেলঃ)।

Ar-is-tŏ-tē′-li-ăn (ăr-), *adj.* Pertaining to Aristotle, or to his system; প্ল্যাটোর শিষ্য সুপ্রসিদ্ধ গ্রীক্ দার্শনিক এরিষ্টোটল্ সম্বন্ধীয়।

ă-rith′-mĕ-tic, *n.* **1.** The science of numbers; the art of computation by figure; পাটীগণিত; অঙ্কবিদ্যা। **2.** A treatise of computation; পাটীগণিত পুস্তক। **Ar-ith-met′-i-cal,** *adj.* **Ar-ith-met′-i-cal-ly,** *adv.* **ti′-cian,** *n.* **Arithmetical progression**—A series of numbers increasing or decreasing by a common difference; [*e. g.* 1, 2, 3, 4, etc. 9, 7, 5, 3, etc.] ব্যক্ত শ্রেণী (হিং কোঃ), সমান্তর শ্রেঢ়ী। **Political arithmetic**—Statistics relating to the condition of a country; কোন দেশের জনসাধারণের সংখ্যা, অবস্থা, আয়ব্যয় প্রভৃতির বিবরণ-সংগ্রহ। **Universal arithmetic**—Algebra; বীজ-গণিত।

ăr-ith-mŏm′-ĕ-têr, *n.* A calculating machine; গণনা-যন্ত্র।

Arius gagora—ঘাঘট মাছ (গুপ্ত)।

ârk, *n.* **1.** A chest; a box; as, a meal *ark*; সিন্দুক, পেটিকা; মঞ্জুষা। **2.** (*Scrip.*) The wooden coffer containing the tables of the Jewish law; (also called *Ark of the Covenant, Ark of Testimony*); ইয়ুদীদিগের ধর্ম্ম-সম্বন্ধীয় বিধি-রক্ষণার্থ কাষ্ঠময় আধার বিশেষ। **3.** The covered floating vessel in which Noah was saved at the Deluge; hence, a place of refuge; as, no safety out of the *ark* of church; বাইবেলোক্ত প্রলয় বা মহাপ্লাবন সময়ে যে আবৃত পোতোপরি আশ্রয়-গ্রহণকরত নোওয়া রক্ষা-লাভ করিয়াছিলেন; আশ্রয়-স্থল। **To touch** or **lay on the ark**—To touch irreverently what is held to be sacred; ভক্তিশূন্যভাবে পবিত্র বস্তু স্পর্শ করা।

ârm, *n.* **1.** The upper limb of the human body from the shoulder to the hand; ভুজ, বাহু। **2.** Anything resembling an arm; the forelimb of an animal; as, *arm* of apes, bears, etc; a main branch or limb of a tree; as, a huge vine with *arms* outspread; a narrower portion projecting from the main body; as, the *arm* of the sea: the *arms* of the mountain; one of the two rails at the sides of a chair, sofa etc.; ভুজাকৃতি বস্তু; জন্তুর সম্মুখের পদদ্বয়; বৃক্ষের প্রধান শাখা; সাগর, পর্ব্বত প্রভৃতির বাহু বা শাখা; কেদারা প্রভৃতির বাজু। **3.** (*Fig.*) Power; authority; as, the *arm* of the law; (লক্ষণায়) ভুজবল, বাহুবল, ক্ষমতা; কর্ত্তৃত্ব। **Arm-chair**—A chair with side-supports; হাত-কেদারা, বাজুদার কুর্শি। **Arm-holes**—The holes in a garment through which the arm is put; পরিচ্ছদে বাহু প্রবেশের ছিদ্র। **Arm in arm**—With one's arm interlocked with that of another; পরস্পরের বাহুতে বাহু জড়াইয়া। **Arm-pit**—The pit or hollow under the arm; কক্ষ, বগল। **Fore-arm**—The part of the human body from the elbow to the hand; প্রকোষ্ঠ। **Infant in arms**—Infant too young to walk; কোলের শিশু, কোলের ছেলে। **Right arm**—The arm on the right side; দক্ষিণ হস্ত, ডান হাত। (*Fig.*) Main support or assistance.

"Sir Lancelot, my *right arm*
The mightiest of my knights;"

(লক্ষণায়) প্রধান অবলম্বন বা সহায়, দক্ষিণহস্ত। **To keep at arm's length**—To avoid familiarity with; দূরে রাখা, অধিক ঘনিষ্ঠতা করিতে না দেওয়া। **To take the arm**—To accept one's invitation; কাহারো নিমন্ত্রণ গ্রহণ করা। **With folded arms**—বাহুতে বাহু জড়াইয়া। **With open arms**—Cordially; আন্তরিকতার সহিত।

ârm, *n.* (*Usu. pl.*) **1.** Instruments of offence used in war; weapons; as, a lesson in cleansing *arms*; armour; mail; as, to shine in brazen *arms*: অস্ত্রশস্ত্র; আয়ুধ, প্রহরণ; বর্ম্ম, কবচ; লৌহময় তনুত্রাণ। **2.** Active hostilities; fighting; as, a cessation of *arms*: suspension of *arms*; যুদ্ধ-কার্য্য; যুদ্ধ। **3.** Military profession; service as a soldier; as, to take up the profession of *arms*; সৈনিকবৃত্তি; সৈনিকের কর্ম্ম। **A passage of (at) arms**—An exchange of blows by armed opponents; যুদ্ধে অস্ত্রবিনিময়। (*Fig.*) A controversial bout; (লক্ষণায়) তর্কযুদ্ধ, মসীযুদ্ধ। **Bred to arms**—Educated to the profession of a soldier; যুদ্ধবিদ্যায় শিক্ষিত। **College of Arms**—The Herald's

College by which armorial bearings are granted ; কুলজ্ঞ-সমাজ। **Fire-arms**—Those requiring gunpowder, such as guns and pistols ; (opp. to sword, spear, etc.) ; আগ্নেয়াস্ত্র। **In arms**—Sword in hand ; prepared to fight ; অসিহস্তে ; যুদ্ধার্থ প্রস্তুত। **In open arms**—Fighting openly ; প্রকাশ্য যুদ্ধে রত। **Small-arms**—Those not requiring carriage ; (opp. to artillery) ; যে সমস্ত ক্ষুদ্র ক্ষুদ্র অস্ত্রশস্ত্র বহনার্থ শকটের আবশ্যক হয় না, যথা তরবারি, ঢাল প্রভৃতি। **Stand of arms**—A complete set of arms for one soldier ; একজন সৈন্যের সমগ্র অস্ত্রশস্ত্র। **To arms**—Be ready for fight ; যুদ্ধার্থ প্রস্তুত হও। **To bear arms**—To serve as a soldier ; সৈনিকের কার্য্য করা। **To carry arms**—To wage war ; যুদ্ধ চালান। **To lay down arms**—To surrender ; to give up the struggle ; অস্ত্র সমর্পণ করা, আত্ম-সমর্পণ করা ; যুদ্ধ হইতে নিবৃত্ত হওয়া। **To stand to one's arms against**—To continue fighting ; যুদ্ধ চালান। **To take up arms**—To rise in hostility ; to draw the sword ; (also fig.) ; অস্ত্রধারণ করা ; যুদ্ধে প্রবৃত্ত হওয়া। **To turn one's arms against**—To attack ; আক্রমণ করা। **Under arms**—Standing or marching arms in hand ; in battle array ; অস্ত্রহস্তে দণ্ডায়মান বা সশস্ত্রভাবে যুদ্ধযাত্রাকারী ; ব্যূহ-বদ্ধ। Enrolled for military service ; as, the state has a million men *under arms* ; সৈনিকের কার্য্যের জন্য তালিকাভুক্ত।

ârm, *v. t.* & *i.* **1.** To cover (a man or horse) with armour or mail ; to provide (a man, garrison, ship, etc.) with weapons ; বর্ম্মাবৃত করা ; অস্ত্রশস্ত্র যোগান। **2.** To furnish with requisites, tools or appliance for a work (of person or animal) ; কোন কার্য্যের জন্য আবশ্যকীয় দ্রব্য বা যন্ত্রাদি যোগান **3.** To furnish with protective covering ; to plate (*with*) for strength ; as, to *arm* the hilt of a sword ; রক্ষাপ্রদ আবরণদ্বারা সজ্জিত করা ; লৌহপ্রভৃতির পট্টদ্বারা দৃঢ়ীভূত করা **4.** (*Fig.*) To fortify (in a moral sense) ; as, I am *armed* so strong in honesty ; to furnish (a man) with qualities, attributes, etc. ; as, she is *armed* with beauty ; (লক্ষণায়) (নৈতিকভাবে) সুদৃঢ় করা শক্তিসমন্বিত করা ; গুণ, ধর্ম্ম প্রভৃতি দ্বারা সমন্বিত করা। **5.** To furnish a magnet with an armature ; চুম্বকত্ব-রক্ষক কৌশল দ্বারা চুম্বক সুদৃঢ় করা। ***Verb i.*** To arm oneself ; to take up arms ; অস্ত্রশস্ত্রে সজ্জিত হওয়া ; অস্ত্রধারণ করা

âr-mä′-dă, *n.* A fleet of ships of war ; esp. the "Invincible Armada" sent by Philip II of Spain against England in 1588 ; রণপোতবহর ; বিশেষভাবে ১৫৮৮ খৃ অব্দে যে স্পেনদেশীয় অজেয় রণপোত-বহর ইংলণ্ড আক্রমণের জন্য প্রেরিত হইয়াছিল।

âr-mă-dil′-lō, *n.* A small American burrowing animal, with

Yellow-footed armadillo.

body encased in a bony armour ; আমেরিকাদেশীয় বর্ম্মধারী ক্ষুদ্র জন্তু বিশেষ, বর্ম্মিল (অভিঃ)।

âr′-mă-mĕnt, *n.* **1.** A military force (usu. naval) equipped for war ; "William's whole *armament* had crossed the channel ;" যুদ্ধার্থ সজ্জিত সেনা (বিশেষতঃ নৌ-সেনা)। **2.** Military equipments ; esp. great guns on board a man-of-war ; as, their *armament* will consist of 12 guns ; যুদ্ধোপকরণ; বিশেষতঃ রণপোতস্থ সুবৃহৎ কামানশ্রেণী। **3.** The process of equipping for war ; যুদ্ধার্থ সজ্জিতকরণ।

âr′-mă-tūre, *n.* **1.** Arms ; armour ; অস্ত্রশস্ত্র ; বর্ম্ম। **2.** Anything serving as a defence, as the prickles and spines of plants, and horns of animals ; আত্মরক্ষণোপযোগী বস্তু, যথা—বৃক্ষের কণ্টক, জন্তুর শৃঙ্গ, দন্ত, প্রভৃতি। **3.** A piece of soft iron placed in contact with the two poles of a magnet ; চুম্বকের উভয় ধ্রুবসংযোগকারী চৌম্বকশক্তি-প্রবর্দ্ধক লৌহ-দণ্ড, চুম্বকত্ব-রক্ষক (হিঃ কোঃ)।

arme blanche, (*F.*), *n.* A cavalry sword or lance ; সাদি-সৈন্যের বর্শা বা তরবারি।

armed (ârmd), *p. p.* **1.** Furnished with arms ; fully equipped for war ; অস্ত্রশস্ত্রে সুসজ্জিত, হাতিয়ার-বন্ধ (*colloq.*) ; রণসজ্জায় সুসজ্জিত। **2.** (Of animal) Furnished with horns, teeth, etc. ; (of plants) furnished with thorns, prickles, etc. ; (of things) plated, or cased with any thing giving strength or efficiency ; as, *armed* finger : *armed* eye (one with magnifying glass) ; (জন্তু-সম্পর্কে) শৃঙ্গ-দন্তাদি অস্ত্র-বিশিষ্ট ; (উদ্ভিদাদির পক্ষে) শূককণ্টকাদিযুক্ত ; (বস্তু-সম্পর্কে) লৌহাদির পত্রমণ্ডিত, দৃঢ়াবরণ-রক্ষিত। **3.** Having arms ; (chiefly in combination) ; as, long-*armed* ; *armed*-chair ; ভুজবিশিষ্ট, সভুজ।

Ar-mē′-ni-ăn (âr-), *n.* & *adj.* **1.** A native of Armenia ; আর্ম্মেণিয়াবাসী। **2.** An adherent of the Armenian Church ; আর্ম্মেণিয়ান্ ধর্ম্ম-সমাজভুক্ত ব্যক্তি। ***Adj.*** Pertaining to Armenia ; আর্ম্মেণিয়াদেশসংক্রান্ত, আর্ম্মাণী। **Armenian bole**—A bright-red clay found in Armenia and used medicinally ; আর্ম্মেণিয়া-দেশীয় লোহিত-মৃত্তিকাবিশেষ, মুলতানী (কেঃভিঃ), মুলতানী মাটী (ঐ)। **Armenian stone**—A soft blue carbonate of copper ; a commercial name for lapis lazuli ; আৰ্ম্মাণী পাথর, নীলসস্যক ; রাজাবর্ত্ত মণি (বাণিজ্য নাম)।

Armeniaca vulgaris—Apricot ; খুবানী, জরদ আলু (বেলঃ)।

âr'-mi-ğêr, *n.* An esquire ; one entitled to bear heraldic arms ; বৰ্ম্ম-বাহক ; কুল-চিহ্ন ধারণে অধীকারী, কুলীন।

âr-mil'-lă, *n.* A bracelet, now esp. in archæology ; বলয়, কঙ্কণ।

âr'-mil-lă-rỹ, *adj.* Pertaining to, or resembling, a bracelet ; বলয়নিভ। **Armillary sphere**—A skeleton celestial globe of metal rings representing equator, tropics, etc. ; নভোমণ্ডলস্থ প্রধান প্রধান বৃত্তসমূহের আপেক্ষিক অবস্থান-প্রদর্শক-যন্ত্রবিশেষ, ভূভগোল, গোলযন্ত্র (সাঃ পঃ)।

Ar-min'-i-ăn (âr-), *n.* & *adj.* An adherent of Arminius, a Dutch theologian, who opposed the view of Calvin, esp. on predestination ; আৰ্ম্মিণিয়াসের মতাবলম্বী। [ধৰ্ম্ম-সংস্কারক আৰ্ম্মিণিয়াস্ মধ্যযুগে হলণ্ডদেশে আবির্ভূত হন ; নিয়তিবাদ প্রভৃতি কতিপয় বিষয়ে তিনি কেলভিনের বিরুদ্ধ মত পোষণ করিতেন।] *Adj.* Pertaining to, or follawoing, the doctrine of Arminius ; আৰ্ম্মিণিয়াসের মত-সম্বন্ধীয়, বা তন্মতাবলম্বী। **—ism,** *n.*

âr'-mi-stice, *n.* A temporary suspension of hostilities by agreement of both parties ; a truce ; উভয় পক্ষের সম্মতিতে অল্প সময়ের জন্য যুদ্ধবিশ্রান্তি, যুদ্ধবিরতি ; অবহার (মঃ ভাঃ)।

ârm'-lĕt, *n.* **1.** A piece of armour for the arm ; বাহুত্রাণ। **2.** An ornament worn on the upper arm ; অঙ্গদ, বাজু, অনন্ত। **3.** A small inlet of the sea or branch of a river ; as, an *armlet* of the sea ; সাগরশাখা, নদীশাখা।

âr-moire' (-mwâr), *n.* A cupboard ; an ambry ; থালা বাসন রাখিবার তাক বা আলমারী ; রুটি এবং অন্যান্য খাদ্যসামগ্রী রাখিবার প্রকোষ্ঠ।

âr-mō'-ri-ăl, *adj.* & *n.* Pertaining to heraldic arms ; কৌলিন্যচিহ্ন-সংক্রান্ত। *Noun.* A book containing coats of arms ; as, the French *armorial* : the Spanish *armorial* ; কৌলিন্য-চিহ্নপূর্ণ পুস্তক।

âr'-mour (-mêr), *n.* **1.** A defensive covering worn in fighting ; mail ; বৰ্ম্ম, কবচ ; বারবাণ। **2.** (*Fig.*) Anything fitted to prove a defence ; "Whose *armour* is his honest thought ;" বর্ম্ম। **3.** Heraldic insignia ; কৌলিন্য-চিহ্ন। **4.** The steel or iron sheathing of a ship of war ; রণপোতের লৌহময় আবরণ। **5.** A diver's water-tight suit ; ডুবারীর জল-প্রবেশ-পথরুদ্ধ পরিচ্ছদ। **6.** A protective covering of plants and animals ; জীব বা উদ্ভিদের দেহরক্ষক আবরণ। **—er,** *n.* **1.** A manufacturer of arms ; অস্ত্রনির্ম্মাতা, অস্ত্রকারক, শস্ত্রকার। **2.** An official in charge of the arms of a ship or regiment ; রণপোত বা সেনা-পল্টনের অস্ত্ররক্ষক কৰ্ম্মচারী। **Armour-bearer**—One who carries the armour of another ; বৰ্ম্মবাহক। **Armour-plate**—One of the iron or steel-plates with which the sides of vessels of war are covered ; গোলাদ্বারা অভেদ্য করণের উদ্দেশ্যে পোতপার্শ্বে বা দুর্গের বহিঃ-প্রাচীরে প্রতিবদ্ধ লৌহপট্ট (লোহার পাত)। **Armour-proof**—Proof against weapons ; অস্ত্রদ্বারা অভেদ্য।

âr'-mour (-mêr), *v. t.* To furnish with a protective covering ; বৰ্ম্মাবৃত করা। **To buckle on one's armour**—To gird up one's loins ; কোমর বাঁধা, যুদ্ধার্থ প্রস্তুত হওয়া।

âr'-mour-ỹ (-mêr-) **âr'-mor-ỹ** (-mêr-), *n.* **1.** The place where arms are kept ; an arsenal ; অস্ত্রাদি রাখিবার স্থান ; অস্ত্রাগার। **2.** (U. S.) A manufactory of arms ; (যুক্তরাজ্যে) অস্ত্রনির্ম্মাণশালা।

âr'-mỹ, *n.* **1.** An organized body of men armed for war ; সৈন্য, বাহিনী, চমূ, ফৌজ, কটক, অনীক। **2.** A body of men organised for a purpose ; as, the Salvation *Army* (মুক্তি-ফৌজ) ; কোন উদ্দেশ্য-সাধনের জন্য সম্মিলিত ব্যক্তিগণ, সেনা। **3.** A great number ; vast multitude ; as, an *army* of locusts : an *army* of words ; বহুসংখ্যা ; অগণিত সংখ্যা। **Army-corps**(-kōr)—A main division of an army in the field ; রণক্ষেত্রে অবতীর্ণ সেনাদলের বৃহৎ বিভাগ বিশেষ। **Army-list**—The official list of the commissioned military officers ; সৈনিককৰ্ম্মচারিগণের সরকারী তালিকা। **Standing army**—A permanent army of professional soldiers ; স্থায়ি-সৈন্য। **The army**—The whole of the regular troops (or land-forces) of a state ; the military service ; কোন দেশের সমগ্র সৈন্য (অথবা স্থল-সৈন্য) ; সামরিক কার্য্য।

âr'-ni-că, *n.* **1.** A genus of plants including mountain-tobacco ; গিরি-তাম্রকূটাদি। **2.** A medicine especially tincture prepared from this ; গিরিতাম্রকূট বৃক্ষ হইতে প্রস্তুত ঔষধ বা আরক বিশেষ।

âr-nŏt'-tō, ân-nŏt'-tō, *n.* **1.** *Bixa Orellana*, a small tree, a native of tropical America ; লটকন্ (কানাই)। **2.** The dye or colouring matter obtained from the seeds of this plant ; উক্ত বৃক্ষের বীজ হইতে প্রাপ্ত রঙ্গ বা রঞ্জক পদার্থ। [ইহা দ্বারা মাথম, রেশম প্রভৃতি কমলা-রঙ্গে রঞ্জিত হয়।]

ă-rō'-mă, *n.* **1.** An agreeable odour ; a sweet smell ; সুগন্ধ, সৌরভ ; সুবাস, ধূপ, আমোদ (উজ্জ্বলঃ), পরিমল। **2.** A subtle pervasive quality or charm ; as, copyright spoils the native *aroma* of the popular tale ; সূক্ষ্ম এবং ব্যাপ্তিশীল গুণ বা সৌকুমার্য্য। **3.** A delicate (intellectual or moral) quality ; সুকুমার (নৈতিক বা মানসিক) গুণ।

ăr-ō-măt′-ic, *adj.* & *n.* Fragrant; sweet-scented; spicy; সুরভি; সুগন্ধ; সুবাসিত। ***Noun.*** **1.** A substance or plant emitting a spicy odour; a fragrant drug; সৌরভ-সঞ্চারক দ্রব্য বা উদ্ভিদ্; সুগন্ধি ভেষজ। **2.** (*Pl.*) Spices; সুগন্ধি মসলা।

ă-rō′-mă-tīze, *v. t.* To impart a spicy flavour to; to season with spice; সুবাসিত করা, সুবাস সঞ্চার করা; সুগন্ধি মসলাদ্বারা স্বাদু করা। **—ma-ti-za′-tion,** *n.*

ă-round′ (-rownd), *adv.* & *prep.* **1.** On every side; in every direction; as, the signs of the time are all *around*; চতুষ্পার্শ্বে; চতুর্দ্দিকে। **2.** Here and there; with no fixed direction; at random; all about; as, to travel *around*; somewhere near; as, to stand *around*; যথা তথা; দিগ্‌বিদিক্ শূন্য-ভাবে; যদৃচ্ছাক্রমে; ইতস্ততঃ; নিকটবর্ত্তী কোন স্থানে। ***Prep.*** **1.** On or along the circuit; as, *around* the wall are heroes, lovers and kings; encircling; as, passing the tape *around* each of the pulleys; মণ্ডলোপরি, মণ্ডলপথে; বেড়িয়া। **2.** Surrounding; enveloping; as, he put his arms *around* my neck; পরিবেষ্টিতভাবে; আবেষ্টিতভাবে। **3.** On all sides of; in all directions from; as, all *around* us: the prospects *around* me; চতুষ্পার্শ্বে; (কোন কিছু হইতে) চতুর্দ্দিকে। **4.** (*U. S.*) Hither and thither over; at random; through; as, to travel *around* the country; (মার্কিণ যুক্ত-রাজ্য) ইতস্ততঃ; যদৃচ্ছাক্রমে; ভিতর দিয়া।

ă-rouse′ (-rowz), *v. t.* To awaken; to stir up into activity; জাগ্রত করা, জাগান; উত্তেজিত করা, উদ্বোধিত করা। **—roused′,** *adj.* উন্নিদ্র, শয্যোত্থিত।

âr′-quē-bŭs, *n.* Same as HARQUEBUS.

ăr′-răck, *n.* A spirituous liquor distilled from the fermented sap of the cocoa-palm or from rice and sugar; আরক, ধান্যেশ্বরী, ধেনোমদ, তাড়ি, গুড়াসব।

ăr-raign′ (-rān), *v. t.* & *i.* **1.** To indict before a tribunal; to accuse; অভিযোগের জবাব দিবার জন্য অভিযুক্ত ব্যক্তিকে আদালতের সম্মুখে দাঁড় করা; অভিযুক্ত করা। **2.** To find fault with; to call in question (action, statement, etc.); as, they will not *arraign* you for want of knowledge; দোষারোপ করা; সন্দেহ প্রকাশ করা, অবিশ্বাস করা। **—ment,** *n.*

ăr-rānge′, *v. t.* & *i.* **1.** To put in proper order; to dispose; as, olives, pomegranates, plums, etc. tastefully *arranged* on silver dishes; to draw up in ranks or line of battle; শৃঙ্খলাবদ্ধ করা, গুছান; বিন্যাস করা, সাজান; ব্যূহরচনা করা। **2.** To adjust; to settle (a dispute, conflicting claims, etc.); as, to *arrange* the terms of a bargain; সংবিধান করা; ঠিক করা, বন্দোবস্ত করা, ব্যবস্থা করা, মীমাংসা করা। **3.** To settle the order, manner, etc. of a thing to be done; to plan beforehand; "The acts done should be *arranged* with the Rajah;" কার্য্যের ক্রম বা প্রণালী স্থির করা; পূর্ব্ব হইতেই পরামর্শ করিয়া স্থির করা। **4.** (*Mus.*) To adapt a composition to voices or instruments for which it was not originally written; as, to *arrange* an opera for the piano (পিয়ানোর সুরের সহিত কোন গীতি-নাট্য সঙ্গত করা); (সঙ্গীত-শাস্ত্র) নূতন ভাবে শব্দসমূহের বিন্যাস এবং পরিবর্ত্তনপূর্ব্বক সঙ্গীতাদিকে অভিনব বাদ্য ও সুরের সহিত সঙ্গত করা। ***Verb i.*** To come to an agreement (*with* a person, *about* a thing); to come to terms; "We can not *arrange* with our enemy at this conjuncture; এক মত হওয়া; চুক্তি বা সর্ত্ত ঠিক করত বিবাদ মীমাংসা করা। **—ment,** *n.* **1.** The act of disposing in order; orderly disposition; order; সংবিধান, বিরচন; রচনা; বিন্যাস। **2.** A settlement by agreement; an adjustment of debatable matters; as, the parties have made *arrangement* of their dispute; আপোষ; মিটমাট, রফা। **3.** Preparations of successful performance; as, *arrangement* for the flight; বন্দোবস্ত, আয়োজন।

ăr′-rănt, *adj.* Notorious; downright; thorough-paced; as, an *arrant* rogue, knave, nonsense; বিখ্যাত (মন্দ অর্থে); পুরা, ডাহা; পাকা। **—ly,** *adv.*

ăr′-răs, *n.* A rich tapestry fabric; a hanging-screen placed round the walls of household apartments; সূচিদ্বারা উত্তোলিত নানা বর্ণের মূর্ত্তিবিশিষ্ট পর্দ্দা বা গৃহসজ্জাবরণ; গৃহের দেয়ালে লট্‌কানো পর্দ্দা। **—rased,** *adj.*

ăr-ray′ (-rā), *v. t.* **1.** To marshal; to draw up for battle; "A force of 12,000 fighting men were *arrayed* in Hyde Park;" রচনা করা, সমাবেশ করা; ব্যূহবদ্ধ করা। **2.** (*Law*) To impanel a jury; as, the jury are *arrayed* by the sheriff; (আইন) জুরিগঠন করা। **3.** To dress up with display; to adorn; to deck; as, the woman was *arrayed* in purple and scarlet colour; (also *fig.*) to clothe (in qualities, etc.); "In fear and love thy heart *array*;" সুসজ্জিত করা, জমকালো পোষাক পরান, মণ্ডিত করা; বিভূষিত করা; (অপিচ লক্ষণায়) গুণাদিদ্বারা অলঙ্কৃত করা।

ăr-ray′ (-rā), *n.* **1.** Order of battle; as, in battle *array*; ব্যূহ। **2.** The arming of the militia; as, a new plan of the commission of *array*; স্বদেশরক্ষিসৈন্যগণকে অস্ত্রশস্ত্র প্রদান। **3.** A military force; the militia of a country or city; as, the whole *array* of the city of London ; সৈন্যবল ; কোন জেলা বা নগর-রক্ষার্থ যে সৈন্যদল তোলা হয়। **4.** An imposing series ; as, an *array* of cliffs : an *array* of figures : বিস্ময়োৎপাদক বস্তুপরম্পরা। **5.** (*Poet.*) Outfit ; dress ; "Dressing by the Moon, in loose *array* ;" (কবিতায়) সাজসজ্জা ; পরিচ্ছদ, পোষাক। (*Law*) The act of impanelling a jury ; the jury thus summoned to attend the court ; (আইন) জুরিদল-গঠন ; নির্ব্বাচিত জুরিগণ। **In evil array**—In a bad condition ; মন্দ অবস্থায়।

ăr-rear′ (-rēr), *n.* **1.** A debt remaining unpaid ; অনাদায়ী ঋণ। **2.** (*Pl.*) Outstanding liabilities, amounts, etc. ; debts ; as, to obtain my *arrears* of pay ; বাকী, বকেয়া ; ঋণ। **In arrear** or **arrears**—Behind hand ; in debt ; as, I am two or three letters *in arrears* ; পশ্চাতে ; ঋণ-জাল বদ্ধ। **In arrears of**—Behind ; as, science was in *arrears of* the art ; পশ্চাতে।

ăr-rear′-āge (-rēr-), *n.* **1.** Backwardness ; পশ্চাদ্‌বর্ত্তিতা। **2.** Unpaid balance ; বাকী টাকা, বকেয়া, বাকী। **3.** (*Pl.*) Debts ; ঋণ।

ăr-rĕct′, *adj.* **1.** (Of the ears) Pricked up ; erect ; (কর্ণসম্বন্ধে) খাড়া ; উৎকর্ণ। **2.** (*Fig.*) On the alert ; (লক্ষণায়) সতর্ক।

ăr-rĕst′, *v. t.* & *n.* **1.** To stop the course of ; as, to *arrest* the current of a river ; রোধ করা, বাধা দেওয়া, গতিরোধ করা, স্তম্ভিত করা। **2.** (*Law.*) To seize a person by legal authority ; as, to *arrest* a thief ; (আইন) ধৃত করা, গ্রেপ্তার করা। **3.** To catch the attention of ; মনোযোগ আকর্ষণ করা। ***Noun.*** Stoppage ; check ; hindrance ; as, an *arrest* of development ; স্তম্ভ, প্রতিবন্ধ, আটক ; গতিরোধ ; বাধা। **4.** (*Law.*) The restraining of one's person to answer a suspected crime ; also, custody ; imprisonment ; as, a month's *arrest* : to suffer *arrest* ; গ্রেপ্তার, আসেধ (মঃ উঃ) ; অবরোধ, আটক ; কয়েদ। **—ment,** *n.* **—res′-tive,** *n.* **Arrest of judgment**—(*Law*) The staying or stopping of judgment after verdict, on ground of legal cause ; কোন আইনঘটিত কারণে রায় স্থগিত করণ, নির্ণয়রোধ। **Process of arrest**—গ্রেপ্তারি পরওয়ানা। **Under (an) arrest**—Under legal restraint ; গ্রেপ্তারবদ্ধ।

arriere-ban, (*F.*), *n.* **1.** A general proclamation by which the old French kings summoned their vassals for the purpose of war ; যে ঘোষণা প্রচারদ্বারা প্রাচীন ফরাসী নৃপতিগণ রাজকীয় ভূসম্পত্তিভোগি-প্রজাগণকে যুদ্ধাদিকার্য্যে সাহায্যার্থ আহ্বান করিতেন। **2.** (*Fig.*) Any general summons issued by an authority ; (লক্ষণায়) কোন ক্ষমতা-প্রাপ্ত ব্যক্তিকর্ত্তৃক সাধারণ আহ্বান।

arriere-pensee, (*F*), *n.* Ulterior motive ; mental reservation ; নিগূঢ় উদ্দেশ্য ; ভাব-গুপ্তি।

ăr′-ris, *n.* A sharp edge formed by angular contact of two planes or curved surfaces ; প্রস্তর, ধাতু প্রভৃতির ফলকদ্বয়ের কৌণিক সংযোগে যে তীক্ষ্ণ প্রান্ত বা কিনারা গঠিত হয়।

ăr-rīv′-ăl, *n.* **1.** A coming to the end of a journey or to a destination ; আগমন, উপস্থিতি। **2.** Appearance upon a scene ; as, the natives, on our *arrival*, civilly gave way for us ; আবির্ভাব। **3.** The person or thing that comes ; as, Ram and Syam were the last *arrivals* ; আগত ব্যক্তি বা বস্তু। **4.** (*Colloq.*) New-born child ; "The new *arrival* is a little daughter; (চলিত ভাষায়) নবজাত শিশু।

ăr-rīve′, *v. i.* **1.** (*Lit. & fig.*) To come to destination or end of journey (foll. by *at.*) : (শব্দানুযায়ী এবং লক্ষণায়) পৌঁছান, উপস্থিত হওয়া। **2.** To reach ; to attain (*at*) ; as, he *arrived* at manhood ; উপনীত হওয়া ; প্রাপ্ত হওয়া, লাভ করা। **3.** To occur ; to happen, as an event : as, such misfortunes had *arrived* : to come ; to be present, as time ; as, at length the hour *arrived* ; সংঘটিত হওয়া ; ঘটা ; সমাগত হওয়া ; উপস্থিত হওয়া।

ăr′-rö-gănt, *adj.* Overbearing ; haughty ; presumptuous ; প্রগল্‌ভ, প্রভুত্বকারী ; উদ্ধত, গর্ব্বিত, দাম্ভিক ; ধৃষ্ট, অবিমৃষ্য। **—gance,** *n.* Proud contempt of others ; conceitedness ; presumption ; ঔদ্ধত্য ; দম্ভ, গর্ব্ব, মদ, দর্প, স্পর্দ্ধা ; প্রগল্‌ভতা। **—ly,** *adv.*

ăr′-rö-gāte, *v. t.* **1.** To assume unduly or presumptuously ; to make undue claims (from vanity) to right or merit ; অসঙ্গতরূপে বা দাম্ভিকতা-সহকারে অতিরিক্তদাবী করা ; অনুচিতদাবী করা। **2.** To attribute to or demand for, without just reason ; সঙ্গত কারণ ব্যতিরেকে আরোপ করা বা কোন কিছুর জন্য দাবী করা। **—ga′-tion,** *n.*

arrondissement, (*F.*), *n.* An administrative sub-division of a French department ; ফরাসী দেশের বিভাগ বিশেষ ; [রাষ্ট্রবিপ্লবের পর ফরাসীদেশ নিম্নলিখিতমত বিভক্ত হয়, যথা :—Departmet ; প্রদেশ ; Arrondissement ; বিভাগ · Canton ; জেলা ; Commune ; উপবিভাগ।]

ăr′-row (-rö), *n.* **1.** A pointed missile, usually feathered and barbed, to be shot from a bow ; শর, বাণ, তীর, সায়ক, ইষু, পত্রী, বিশিখ, কলম্ব। **2.** An arrow-shaped index, pin or ornament ; বাণাকৃতি শঙ্কু বা ভূষা। **—y,** *adj.* Moving like, or resembling, an arrow ; swift ; darting ; as, sharp sleet of *arrowy* showers : *arrowy* tongues of defiance ; সায়ক-গতি, শর-সদৃশ ; দ্রুত-গামী ; দ্রুতবেগে উড্ডয়নশীল। **Arrow-head**—The head or pointed part of an arrow ; বাণাগ্র, ফলক। **Arrow-headed characters**—Cuneiform characters ; কীলকাকৃতি অক্ষর (see CUNEIFORM)। **The broad arrow**—The arrow-head-shaped mark, used by the British Board of Ordnance, and placed upon government stores ; সরকারী মালের উপর বাণাকৃতি চিহ্ন।

ăr′-row-rōōt (-rö-), *n.* A plant from which a nutritious starch is prepared ; আরারুট, তবক্ষীর (দ্রব্যগুণ), তালক্ষীর (ঐ)।

arse (ârs), *n.* The buttocks or rump of an animal ; (পশ্বাদির) শ্রোণি, নিতম্ব। **Heavy arse**—A lazy fellow ; অলস লোক।

âr′-sĕ-năl, *n.* A public establishment for the storage or manufacture of weapons and ammunition ; রাজকীয় (সরকারী) অস্ত্রাগার, আয়ুধাগার, অস্ত্রশালা, শিলখানা।

âr′-sĕ-nic, *n.* A brittle steel-green chemical substance ; ইস্পাতের মত সবুজবর্ণ ভঙ্গপ্রবণ রাসায়নিক পদার্থ বিশেষ, তালসত্ত্ব (রঃ রঃ প্রঃ), সিকতা-সুধা (সাঃ পঃ), তালক (ঐ), আর্জনিক (মনীঃ)। **White arsenic**—দারমোজ, শঙ্খবিষ, শেঁকোবিষ। **Arsenic trisulphide,** As_2S_3—হরিতাল।

âr-sĕn′-ic, *adj.* **1.** Of or pertaining to arsenic ; তালীন (সাঃ পঃ)। **2.** Applied to compounds in which arsenic combines as a pentad ; যে সমস্ত রাসায়নিক পদার্থের সহিত তালক পঞ্চবন্ধনরূপে সংযুক্ত হয়—তৎসম্বন্ধে প্রযুক্ত। **—i-cal,** *adj.* **—sē′-ni-ous,** *adj.*

âr′-sŏn, *n.* The wilful setting on fire of another's house, ship, etc., or one's own, when insured ; স্বেচ্ছাপূর্ব্বক অপর ব্যক্তির গৃহ, ইমারত, পোত প্রভৃতি দাহ, অথবা বীমা-[illegible] করার উদ্দেশ্যে স্বগৃহ প্রভৃতি দাহ, গৃহদাহ, ঘর-জ্বালানি, গৃহদাহাপরাধ।

ârt. The second person singular, indicative mood, present tense, of the verb *to be ;* ভূধাতুর বর্ত্তমান কালের মধ্যম পুরুষের একবচন, হও।

ârt, *n.* **1.** The practical application of the principles of any science ; কারুশিল্প, কলা, শিল্পশাস্ত্র। **2.** An acquired faculty of any kind ; a knack ; as, the *art* of selection : *art* of saying things well ; অর্জ্জিত বৃত্তি ; পটুতা। **3.** Human skill ; human workmanship ; (opp. to *nature*) ; "*Art* pre-exists in nature and nature is reproduced in *art* ;" কর্ম্ম-কৌশল, কলাকৌশল ; মনুষ্য-হস্ত-রচিত কার্য্য, শিল্প। **4.** A system of rules serving to facilitate the carrying out of certain principles : (opp to *science*) ; as, the *art* of war ; যে নিয়ম নিচয়ের সাহায্যে কতিপয় মূল-তত্ত্ব কার্য্যে পরিণত করা সুগম হয়, নীতি। **5.** A craft ; as, the fishermen can not employ their *art* in a troubled sea ; ব্যবসায়। **6.** (*Pl.*) Those branches of learning taught in the academical course of colleges ; as, Master of *Arts ;* যে সমস্ত শাস্ত্রের শাখা কলেজে অধ্যাপিত হয়। **7.** (*Pl.*) An artifice ; a cunning device ; wile ; trick ; as, the *arts* which ladies sometimes condescend to employ for captivation ; ছল ; চালাকি ; ফিকির, কল, ফন্দী ; চাতুরী, কারসাজি। **Art-union**—An association for the advancement of art ; শিল্প-সমিতি। **Black art**—Magic ; ইন্দ্রজাল, যাদুবিদ্যা। **Fine arts**—Those arts in which the mind and imagination are chiefly concerned ; ললিত কলা, সুকুমার কলা (সঙ্গীত, চিত্র-বিদ্যা প্রভৃতি)। **The liberal arts**—The seven branches of learning ; সপ্তাঙ্গ বিদ্যা, যথা :—ব্যাকরণ, ন্যায়, অলঙ্কার, পাটীগণিত, জ্যামিতি, সঙ্গীত, জ্যোতিষ। **To have art and part**—To be connected either in the design or execution ; as, I had no *art and part* in it (অর্থাৎ এই বিষয়টী আমার মাথা হইতে বাহির হয় নাই, অথবা কার্য্যটীও আমার দ্বারা সম্পন্ন হয় নাই) ; কোন কার্য্যের উদ্ভাবনে বা সম্পাদনে সংসৃষ্ট থাকা। **Useful, mechanical or industrial arts**—The arts in which the hands and body are more concerned than the mind, (as in making clothes and utensils) ; কার্য্যকরী শিল্প, যান্ত্রিক শিল্প, শ্রমশিল্প, শ্রমসাধ্য-শিল্প।

Ar′-tĕ-mis (âr-), *n.* The goddess of the moon and of hunting ; (গ্রীক-পুরাণোক্ত) চন্দ্রমণ্ডল ও মৃগয়ার অধিষ্ঠাত্রী দেবী।

Artemisia Indica—দমনক পুষ্প (বৃঃ সং)।

Artemisia vulgaris—নাগদোনা (বেলঃ)।

âr-tē′-ri-ăl-ize, *v. t.* **1.** To convert venous into arterial (blood) by exposure to oxygen in the lungs ; ফুস্‌ফুসস্থ অম্লজান বাষ্পের সংস্পর্শে শৈরিক রক্তকে ধামনিক রক্তে পরিণত করা। **2.** To furnish with an arterial system ; ধমনী-জালসমন্বিত করা।

âr-tē-ri-ŏt′-ō-mȳ, *n.* The opening of artery for blood-letting ; also dissection of arteries ; রক্ত-মোক্ষণার্থ ধমনী-কর্ত্তন ; ধমনীচ্ছেদন, ধমনীব্যবচ্ছেদ।

âr′-tĕr-ȳ, *n.* One of the vessels or tubes by which blood is conveyed from the heart to all parts of the body ; ধমনী, রক্তবাহিনী, বায়ুবাহিনী (সাঃ পঃ), রক্তবহানাড়ী, রোহিণী, জীবিতজ্ঞা। **—te′-ri-al,** *adj.* Pertaining to artery ; ধামনিক। **Arterial drainage**—A system of drains ramifying like an artery ; ধমনীবৎ শাখা-প্রশাখা বিশিষ্ট জল-নিকাশ-ব্যবস্থা।

Ar-tē′-si-ăn (âr-), *adj.* Of or pertaining to Artois in France ;

ফরাসীদেশস্থ আরত্তোয় নামক স্থান-সংক্রান্ত। **Artesian wells**—Wells made by boring into the earth till water is reached, and, which, from internal pressure, flow like a fountain ; অন্তর্জলোৎস কূপ।

âr't'-fûl, *adj.* **1.** Cunning ; crafty ; deceitful ; (said of persons and actions) ; চালাক, চতুর ; ফিকিরী, ফন্দিবাজ ; শঠ, ধূর্ত্ত, প্রতারণাপূর্ণ, ফেরেব্বাজ। **2.** Done by art ; artificial ; as, they may render back *artful* thunder ; শিল্পকৃত ; কৃত্রিম। **—ly,** *adv.* **—ness,** *n.*

âr-thrī'-tis, *n.* The inflammation of the joints ; gout ; সন্ধিপ্রদাহ (হঃ চঃ), সন্ধিবাত (ঐ), গ্রন্থি-প্রদাহ ; গেটে বাত। **—thrit'-ic,** *adj.*

Ar-thrŏp'-ŏ-dă (âr-), *n.* (*Zool.*) Animals with jointed feet, (comprising spiders, insects, etc.) ; (জন্তু-তত্ত্ব) পর্ব্বপদী (সাঃ পঃ), গ্রন্থিপদ (ঐ), গ্রন্থিপদী (ঐ)।

âr'-ti-chōke, *n.* An esculent plant somewhat resembling a thistle ; হতিচোখ (সাঃ পঃ), হাতিচোখ (প্রবোধ)।

âr'-ti-cle, *n.* & *v. t.* **1.** A particular commodity or substance ; as, salt is a necessary *article* ; দ্রব্য, সামগ্রী, জিনিষ। **2.** Each of the distinct heads or points of an agreement, treaty, etc. ; as, *articles* of agreement ; each of the distinct charges of an accusation ; as, certain *articles* presented against him ; সর্ত্ত ; অভিযোগের প্রত্যেক দফা। **3.** A literary composition forming an independent portion of a journal, newspaper, etc. ; as, a leading *article* ; (সংবাদপত্রাদির) প্রবন্ধ **4.** A paragraph or section of any document ; কোন দলিলের অংশ বা অনুচ্ছেদ বিশেষ। **5.** (*Gram.*) One of the three words *a, an, the,* used before nouns to limit or define their application ; (ব্যাকরণ) বিশেষ্য স্বভাব-নিরূপক অব্যয়শব্দ। **6.** The very moment, esp. of death ; "Roman citizens made their wills only in the *article* of death ;" তন্মুহূর্ত্ত, মৃত্যু-মুহূর্ত্ত। ***Verb t.*** **1** To bind by articles of covenant or stipulation ; as, to *article* an apprentice to a mechanic চুক্তি বা করার দ্বারা বদ্ধ করা। **2.** To indict ; to accuse ; "He shall be *articled* against in the High Court of Admiralty ;" যথাবিধানে অভিযুক্ত করা ; অভিযুক্ত করা। **3.** To draw up in distinct particulars ; as, all his errors and follies were *articled* against him ; দফাক্রমে মুসাবিদা করা। **—cled,** *p. p.* Bound by articles ; indentured, as an apprentice ; as, an *articled* clerk ; চুক্তিবদ্ধ, করারবদ্ধ ; চুক্তিপত্রদ্বারা বদ্ধ। **Articles of Association**—Whenever a joint-stock company is formed a printed list of rules for its conduct must be prepared. These are its Articles of Association ; (সমবায়ের) সংসৃষ্টি-পত্র, অনুষ্ঠান-পত্র। **Articles of war**—The code of rules and regulations for the regulation of the army ; সেনাদলসংক্রান্ত-নিয়মাবলী।

âr-tic'-ū-lâr, *adj.* Pertaining to the joint ; সন্ধিস্থল-সম্বন্ধীয়।

Ar-tic-ū-lā'-tă (âr-), *n.* Animals having a jointed structure but no internal skeleton ; গ্রন্থি গঠিতাঙ্গ কঙ্কালহীন জীববর্গ (যথা, পতঙ্গ, বোঁটাদি), গ্রন্থ্যাধার দেহ (প্রঃ বাঃ)।

âr-tic'-ū-lāte, *adj.* & *n.* **1.** Formed of joints ; jointed ; গ্রন্থিল, গ্রন্থিত, জোড়া-যুক্ত ; সন্ধিবদ্ধ, সন্ধিযুত। **2.** Distinctly uttered ; distinguishable ; as, an *articulate* speech ; স্পষ্টরূপে উচ্চারিত ; প্রভেদ্য, পরিচ্ছেদ্য। ***Noun.*** One of the Articulata ; যে জীব-বর্গের দেহ গ্রন্থিসমূহ দ্বারা গঠিত, তাহাদের কোন একটি, গ্রন্থিল (প্রঃ বাঃ)। **—ly,** *adv.* **—ness,** *n.*

âr-tic'-ū-lāte, *v. t.* & *i.* **1.** To joint ; to unite by means of joints ; সন্ধিবদ্ধ করা ; সন্ধি দ্বারা সংযুক্ত করা। **2.** To utter distinct syllables or words ; to pronounce distinctly ; সুস্পষ্ট বাক্যাংশ বা বাক্য উচ্চারণ করা ; সুস্পষ্ট উচ্চারণ করা। ***Verb i.*** To speak distinctly ; স্পষ্টরূপে কথা বলা। **—la'-tion,** *n.* **1.** The act of jointing ; সন্ধি-বন্ধন, গ্রন্থন। **2.** Joint ; পর্ব্ব, গ্রন্থি, সন্ধি। **3.** Articulate utterance or speech ; স্পষ্টোচ্চারণ, শব্দ-ব্যঞ্জন। **4.** A consonant ; ব্যঞ্জনবর্ণ।

âr'-ti-fīce, *n.* **1.** Crafty device ; skilful contrivance ; উপায়, ফিকির ; কৌশল, কল, ফন্দি, কারসাজি, কূট-রচনা (কথা সঃ)। **2.** Skill ; address ; চাতুর্য্য ; নৈপুণ্য, দক্ষতা। **—tif'-i-cer,** *n.* **1.** A skilful or artistic worker ; a handicraftsman ; শিল্পী ; কারিগর। **2.** A deviser or inventor ; "The great *Artificer* of all that moves ;" উদ্ভাবক, পরিকল্পনাকারী। **Artificer of the universe**—The Creator ; বিশ্ব-স্রষ্টা, জগৎ-স্রষ্টা।

âr-ti-fi'-cial (-shăl), *adj.* **1.** Made or contrived by art ; as, an *artificial* peacock (যন্ত্রময়ূর—কাদঃ) ; not natural ; as, *artificial* light ; not real ; as, *artificial* diamond ; মনুষ্যকৃত, কৃত্রিম ; অনৈসর্গিক ; নকল, ঝুঁটা। **2.** Feigned ; not genuine or natural ; as, *artificial* tears ; ছলনা-পূর্ণ, কপটতাপূর্ণ, ছদ্ম ; কৃত্রিম, কৃতক। **3.** Real but produced by art ; as, *artificial* ice, grasses ; নৈসর্গিক অথচ মনুষ্যকৃত। **—ci-al'-i-ty, —ness,** *ns.* **—ize,** *v. t.* **—ly,** *adv.*

âr-til'-lĕr-ȳ, *n.* (No plural.) **1.** (*Formerly*) Weapons of war ; "Jonathon gave his *artillery* unto his lad" (I sam. xx 40) ; (পূর্ব্বে)

যুদ্ধাস্ত্র। 2. (*Now*) Cannon; ordnance; (বর্ত্তমানে) তোপ, কামান; ভারি যুদ্ধাস্ত্র, গোলাগুলি, আগ্নেয়াস্ত্র। 3. The branch of an army which manages the cannon in war; গোলন্দাজ সৈন্য। 4. The science of gunnery; কামান-পরিচালন বিদ্যা। **—ist,** *n.* Gunner; গোলন্দাজ। **Artillery-man**—A man who manages a great gun in firing; গোলন্দাজ সৈনিক। **Artillery-train**—A number of pieces of ordnance mounted on carriages, ready for marching; যুদ্ধক্ষেত্রে প্রেরণার্থ শকটজাত গোলাগুলি প্রভৃতি।

âr'-ti-săn, —zăn, *n.* A handicraftsman; a mechanic; কারিগর, শিল্পী, শিল্পকারক; কারুক, কর্ম্মকার।

ârt'-ist, *n.* One who practises one of the fine arts, esp. painting; যে ব্যক্তি সঙ্গীত, চিত্রাদি যে কোন প্রকার ললিতকলার অনুশীলন করে, কলাকুশল ব্যক্তি, শিল্পী, চিত্রকর, ভাস্কর, স্থপতি, প্রভৃতি; কলাকোবিদ (হিঃ কোঃ)।

âr-tiste' (-tēst), (*F.*), *n.* One who makes a fine art of his employment, as an artistic cook, hairdresser, opera-dancer, etc.; যে ব্যক্তি ললিতকলার মত তদীয় ব্যবসায়ের অনুশীলন করে, কলাবিদগ্ধ (বাৎস্যাঃ), কলাকুশল, ওস্তাদ, নট, সূপকার, কেশপ্রসাধক প্রভৃতি স্বীয় স্বীয় ব্যবসায়ে উৎকর্ষসম্পন্ন ব্যক্তি।

âr-tis'-tic, —ti-căl, *adjs.* Pertaining to art or artists; trained in art; conformable to art; characterised by art; শৈল্পিক, শিল্পিসম্বন্ধীয়; কলাকুশল; কলাশাস্ত্রানুযায়ী; কলাকৌশলপূর্ণ। **—ti-cal-ly,** *adv.*

ârt'-lĕss, *adj.* 1. Unskilful; uncultured; অকৌশলী, অচতুর; অজ্ঞ। 2. Clumsy; as, *artless* pillars; বেডৌল, কদাকার। 3. Guileless; simple; ingenuous; as, *artless* mind: *artless* tale; সরল, অমায়িক, অকপট, সাদা; শুচিস্বভাব, মুগ্ধ-স্বভাব। **—ness,** *n.* Simplicity; মুগ্ধতা।

Artocarpus integrifolius—Jack-fruit tree; কাঁটাল (বেলঃ)।

Artocarpus lacoocha—ডেফল (বেলঃ)।

ā-rŭm, *n.* A genus of endogenous plants; বহিঃসার উদ্ভিদ্‌গণ, কচু, মানকচু প্রভৃতি। **Arum lily**—Cultivated white lily; উদ্যানজাত শ্বেত-কুমুদ।

Arundo karka—নল (বেলঃ)।

Ar'-ȳ-ăn (ār-), *n.* & *adj.* [Skr. *Arya*, noble, eminent] 1. A member of that division of the human race which includes the Hindus and Persians as its eastern branch, and the Celts, the Greeks and Italians as its western; আর্য্যজাতি। 2. The language of the original Aryans (called also Indo-European, Indo-Germanic); আদিম আর্য্যজাতির ভাষা। ***Adj.*** Of or pertaining to the Aryans; as, the *Aryan* languages; আর্য্য, আর্য্যজাতি-সম্বন্ধীয়, আর্য্যভাষা-সম্বন্ধীয়। **—ize,** *v. t.*

ăs, *adv., conj.* & *rel. pron.* 1. Like; similar to; "You shall be *as* gods knowing good or evil;" মতন; সদৃশ, তুল্য। 2. In the same manner; in proportion to; in accordance with; as, I love you *as* I did; তদনুরূপ; তদনুপাতে; তদনুসারে। 3. While; when; at the same time; as, he trembled *as* he spoke; যৎকালে; যখন; তৎসময়ে। ***Conj.*** 1. For example; for instance;—used to introduce illustrative sentences or citations; thus; দৃষ্টান্ত-স্বরূপ, উদাহরণ-স্বরূপ; দৃষ্টান্তস্থলে, যথা। 2. In the idea, character or condition of; as, virtue considered *as* virtue: this actor will appear *as* Hamlet; রূপে। 3. Since; "*As*, the wind was favourable, I had an opportunity of surveying this amazing scene;" যে হেতু। ***Rel. pron.*** That; "Give such things *as* you please;" যাহা, যাহারা, যে গুলি। **As far as**—To the extent; as, *as far as* I can see; যতদূর। **As follows**—Thus and for instance; as, he spoke, *as follows;* এইরূপ, নিম্নোক্ত বা নিম্নলিখিত মত। **As for, As to**—In or with regard or respect to; concerning; *as for* him, I despise him; সম্বন্ধে; সম্পর্কে। **As if, As though**—Like what it would be if; "It seemed *as if* the restoration of Corsica was at hand;" যেন। **As it is**—As matters actually stand; as, it is better, however, *as it is;* যেমন আছে। **As it were**—As if it were so; if one might so put it; as, I heard *as it were* the sound of thunder; যেন; বলিলেও বলা যায়। **As much**—The same; as, give him *as much* as he wants; ঠিক তাই, ঠিক সেই পরিমাণ, যতটা। **As soon as**—Whenever; যেই মাত্র, যে মুহূর্ত্তে। **As well**—Also; in addition; as, you must answer the next question *as well;* আরও; অধিকন্তু। **As well as**—And; also; "Anointed with nectar *as well as* poison;" এবং, ও; অথচ। **As yet**—Up to the present time; up to this time; "They had, *as yet*, had no food;" অদ্যাপি; এখনও, এখন পর্য্যন্তও।

ăs-ă-fĕt'-i-dă, —fœt-i-dă, (-fĕt-), *n.* A concentrated resinous gum with strong smell of garlic, used in medicine and cookery; হিঙ্গ, হিঙ্গু (রঃ প্রঃ), রামঠ (ঐ)। **White asafœtida**—সিত রামঠ (ঐ)।

ăs-bĕs'-tīne, *adj.* Pertaining to asbestos; incombustible; শৈলপলিতা-সংক্রান্ত; অদাহ্য।

ăs-bĕs'-tŏs, *n.* A fibrous mineral that can be woven into an incombustible fabric ; এক প্রকার অংশুময় (আঁশযুক্ত) অদাহ্য খনিজ পদার্থ, শঙ্খপলিতা (ওয়াট্)। **—tic, —tous** *adjs.*

As-căr'-i-dēs (ăs-), *n. pl.* A genus of intestinal worms ; thread-worms ; কয়েক জাতীয় অন্ত্র-মধ্যস্থ কৃমির সাধারণ নাম ; ক্ষুদ্র কৃমি (সাঃ পঃ), মহীলতার ন্যায় কৃমি (হঃ চঃ)।

ăs-cĕnd', *v. t.* & *i.* **1.** To go or move upwards upon ; to climb ; as, to *ascend* a hill or ladder ; to move toward the source ; as, to *ascend* a river ; উঠা ; আরোহণ করা ; (নদী প্রভৃতির) উৎপত্তিস্থানের দিকে অগ্রসর হওয়া। **2.** To mount upon ; as, to *ascend* the throne ; অধিরোহণ করা। ***Verb i.*** **1.** To mount ; (of things) to rise ; আরোহণ করা ; (বস্তু-সম্পর্কে) উত্থিত হওয়া, উর্দ্ধে উঠা। **2.** To rise in thought, degree of quality, social stations, etc. ; "We shall *ascend* beyond laws to a lawgiver ;" (গুণ, সামাজিক পদমর্য্যাদা বা চিন্তারাজ্যে) উত্থিত হওয়া, উর্দ্ধে উঠা। **3.** To go backward in the order of time ; to proceed from modern to ancient times ; as, our enquiries *ascend* to the remotest antiquity ; কালের হিসাবে পশ্চাদ্‌বর্ত্তী হওয়া ; আধুনিক কাল হইতে প্রাচীন সময়ের দিকে অগ্রসর হওয়া। **—ance, —an-cy, —en-cy,** *ns.* Dominant control ; sway (*over*) ; as, custom has an *ascendency* over the understanding ; প্রভুত্ব, কর্ত্তৃত্ব ; প্রাধান্য।

ăs-cĕnd'-ănt, —ĕnt, *adj.* & *n.* **1.** Rising ; উর্দ্ধগ, অধিরোহী, উদীয়মান। **2.** (*Astron.*) Rising towards the zenith ; (জ্যোতির্বিজ্ঞান) 'খমধ্য' অভিমুখে উদীয়মান। **3.** (*Astrol.*) Just above the eastern horizon ; (ফলিত জ্যোতিষ) লগ্নস্থলবর্ত্তী। **4.** Predominant ; ruling ; superior ; প্রধান, প্রবল ; শাসনকারী ; শ্রেষ্ঠ, উচ্চ। ***Noun.*** **1.** Predominance ; supremacy ; as, one man has the *ascendant* over another ; প্রাধান্য, প্রভুত্ব ; শ্রেষ্ঠতা, আধিপত্য। **2.** (*Astrol.*) The horoscope or that sign of the zodiac which rises above the horizon at the time of a child's birth ; জন্মকালে যে রাশি দিক্ চক্রবালে উদিত হয়, জাতকরে জন্মলগ্ন। **3.** Ancestor ; (opposed to *descendant*) ; পূর্ব্বপুরুষ। **Lord of the ascendant**—The planet which rules in the house of the ascendant ; লগ্নাধিপতি গ্রহ। One who has such power or influence ; ভাগ্যনিয়ন্তা। **To be in the ascendant**—To be supreme ; to have commanding power or influence ; প্রবল হওয়া, প্রভাবশালী হওয়া ; প্রভুত্বকারী হওয়া।

ăs-cĕn'-sion, *n.* **1.** The act of ascending ; a rising ; উত্থান, উর্দ্ধগমন ; উদয়। **2.** (*Specif.*) The visible ascent of Jesus Christ on the 40th day after his resurrection ; পুনরুত্থানের ৪০ দিবসান্তে সর্ব্বলোকসমক্ষে খৃষ্টের স্বর্গারোহণ। **—al,** *adj.* **Ascension day**—The day on which the ascension of Christ is commemorated ; the Holy Thursday ; খৃষ্টের স্বর্গারোহণ দিবস ; পবিত্র বৃহস্পতিবার। **Ascensional difference**—চরান্তর (সূঃ দ্বিঃ), লগ্নভুজ (মঃ উঃ)। **Oblique ascension**—ক্রান্ত্যংশ (সূঃ দ্বিঃ), স্বদেশোদয় (সাঃ পঃ)। **Right as censions**—The distance of a heavenly body from the first point of Aries measured upon the equator ; লঙ্কোদয় (সাঃ পঃ), নিরক্ষোদয় (ঐ)। **Right ascension in degrees**—বিষুবাংশ (সিঃ তঃ বিঃ)।

ăs-cĕn'-sive, *adj.* **1.** Rising ; progressive ; উদীয়মান ; বর্দ্ধিষ্ণু, উন্নতিশীল। **2.** (*Gram.*) Increasing the force ; intensive ; (ব্যাকরণ) অভিপ্রায় বা অর্থ-বিস্তারক ; আতিশয্য-বাচক।

ăs-cĕnt', *n.* **1.** The act of rising ; upward movement ; esp. the going up a mountain, stairs, a river, etc. ; উর্দ্ধগমন ; উর্দ্ধগতি ; বিশেষতঃ পর্ব্বত, সোপানাবলী প্রভৃতিতে আরোহণ কিম্বা নদীর উৎপত্তিস্থানের দিকে অগ্রসর। **2.** The way or means by which one may ascend ; a slope ; a flight of steps ; আরোহণ-মার্গ ; প্রবণ-ভূমি ; অধিরোহণী, সোপানশ্রেণী। **3.** (*Fig.*) Rise in thought, rank, etc. ; advancement ; as, his *ascent* to the most eminent dignities of the republic : Italians are in *ascent* ; (লক্ষণায়) জ্ঞানোন্নতি, পদোন্নতি, ইত্যাদি ; উন্নতি, অভ্যুদয়।

ăs-cĕr-tain' (-tān), *v. t.* To find out ; to make sure of ; নির্দ্ধারণ করা, অবধারণ করা ; অবনিশ্চয় করা, নির্ণয় করা, নিরূপণ করা, নিশ্চয় করা, স্থির করা, ঠাহর করা (*colloq.*)। **—able,** *adj.* Capable of being certainly known ; নির্ণেয়, নির্দ্ধার্য্য, নিরূপণীয়। **—ment,** *n.* An acquirement with certainty ; a finding out ; as, the positive *ascertainment* of its limits ; নিরূপণ ; নির্দ্ধারণ, নির্ণয়।

ăs-cĕt'-ic, *adj.* & *n.* Severely abstinent ; austere ; as, an *ascetic* course of the severest abstinence ; কঠোর বৈরাগ্যপূর্ণ ; কঠোর-ব্রত। ***Noun.*** A hermit ; a recluse ; যতি, সন্ন্যাসী, বৈরাগী, তাপস, তপস্বী, উদাসী ; বনবাসী, আরণ্যক। **—i-cal,** *adj.* **—i-cal-ly,** *adv.* **—i-cism,** *n.* The condition, practice, or mode of life of ascetics ; তপশ্চর্য্যা, বৈরাগ্য, কঠোর সাধনা, তপশ্চরণ।

ăs'-ciăns, (from Gr. *a,* not and *skia,* shadow) *n. pl.* The inhabitants of the torrid zone who twice a year have the sun directly overhead at noon ; গ্রীষ্মমণ্ডলের অধিবাসিগণ, অচ্ছায়। [বৎসরে দুইবার সূর্য্য ঠিক মস্তকোপরি অবস্থান করে বলিয়া তাহাদের দেহচ্ছায়া পতিত হয় না।]

As-cĭd′-i-ŭm (ăs-), *n.* **1.** (*Zool.*) A genus of molluscs ; (জন্তু-তত্ত্ব) কম্বোজ-বর্গের অন্তর্ভুক্ত (জন্তু-সমূহের) 'গণ' বিশেষ । **2.** (*Bot.*) A pitcher-shaped appendage found in some plants ; (উদ্ভিদ্-বিদ্যা) আরু (সাঃ পঃ) ।

Ascidium.

ăs-cī′-tēs, *n.* A collection of serous fluid in the cavity of the abdomen ; জলোদর রোগ (বৃঃ সং) ।

ăs-crībe′, *v. t.* **1.** To attribute ; to impute ; to assign (*to*) ; আরোপ করা ; উদ্দেশ করিয়া বলা ; কারণ নির্দ্দেশ করা । **2.** To consider as belonging to (a person or thing) ; "They *ascribe* honour to God." কোন ব্যক্তির গুণ, স্বভাব বা অধিকারস্বরূপ কিম্বা কোন বস্তুর অঙ্গীভূত বলিয়া বিবেচনা করা । **–crib′-a-ble,** *adj.* Attributable ; আরোপণীয়, নির্দ্দেশ্য । **–crip′-tion,** *n.*

ā-sĕp′-tic, *adj.* & *n.* Not liable to putrefaction ; অপচনীয় । ***Noun.*** A non-putrescent substance ; অপচনশীল পদার্থ ।

ā-sĕx′-ū-ăl, *adj.* (*Biol.*) Without sex ; as, *asexual* reproduction ; (জীব-বিজ্ঞান) অযুগ্মাহিক (সাঃ পঃ), অলিঙ্গ (ঐ), অচিহ্নিত (ঐ) । **–ly,** *adv.*

As-gärd′ (ăs-), *n.* The heaven of Scandinavian mythology ; স্কেণ্ডেনেভিয়ার পুরাণে বর্ণিত দেবলোক ।

ăsh, *n* **1.** A forest-tree with silver-grey bark, and close-grained wood ; ইংলণ্ড-দেশীয় রজতধূসরবল্কল-বিশিষ্ট আরণ্য-তরু বিশেষ । **2.** The wood of this ; ঐ বৃক্ষের কাঠ ।

ăsh, *n.* **1.** (Usu. in *pl.*) The powdery residue left after the combustion of any substance, as of wood, coal, etc. ; ভস্ম, ছাই, বিভূতি । **2.** (*Pl.*) The remains of the human body when burnt ; hence, a dead body or corpse ; "The pale *ashes* of the house of Lancaster ;" শ্মশানভস্ম, চিতাভস্ম ; অতএব শব, মৃতদেহ । **Ash-colour**—A colour between brown and grey ; ছাইরঙ, ভস্মবর্ণ । **Ash-fire**—A low fire used in chemical operations ; ক্ষীণাগ্নি, ভস্মাচ্ছাদিত অগ্নি । **Ash-furnace**—A furnace used in glass-making ; কাচ-নির্ম্মাণ-চুল্লী । **Ash-Wednesday**—The first day of Lent ; (from the Roman Catholic custom of sprinkling ashes on the penitents' head) ; রোমান ক্যাথলিক সম্প্রদায়ের লেণ্ট্ পর্ব্বের প্রথম দিবস । উক্ত দিবস অনুতপ্ত ব্যক্তিগণের মস্তকে ভস্ম ছড়ান হইয়া থাকে । **Pale as ashes**—Very pale ; বিবর্ণ, পাণ্ডুবর্ণ, পাংশুবর্ণ । **To lay in ashes**—To reduce to ashes ; to burn to the ground ; as, a great fire broke out and *laid* the town *in ashes* ; ভস্মসাৎ করা ; দাহ করিয়া ভূমিসাৎ করা । **To reduce to ashes**—ভস্মীভূত করা, ভস্মাবশেষ করা ।

ā-shamed′ (-shāmd), *p. p.* Abashed or disconcerted by consciousness of guilt ; (foll. by *of*) ; as, you ought to be *ashamed of* your conduct ; লজ্জিত, লজ্জায় ম্রিয়মাণ বা অধোমুখ ।

ăsh′-ĕn, *adj.* Pertaining to an ash-tree ; made of ash ; "Each his *ashen* bow unbent ;" আশবৃক্ষ-সম্বন্ধীয় ; আশকাষ্ঠ-নির্ম্মিত ।

ăsh′-ĕn, *adj.* Of ashes ; ash-coloured ; pale ; as, the *ashen* hue of age ; ভস্মসম্বন্ধীয়, ভাস্মন ; পাংশুল, পাংশুবর্ণীয় ; বিবর্ণ, মলিন ।

ăsh′-lär, –lêr, *n.* Hewn or squared stone ; also masonry made of stones ; কর্ত্তিত প্রস্তর, চতুর্ভুজাকারে কর্ত্তিত প্রস্তরখণ্ড ; ঐ প্রস্তরের স্থাপত্যকার্য্য ।

ā-shore′ (-shōr), *adv.* To, on, shore ; তীরে, উপকূলে ।

ăsh′-ȳ, *adj.* Of ashes ; covered with ashes ; ash-coloured ; pale ; ভস্মসম্বন্ধীয় ; ভস্মাবৃত, ভস্মাচ্ছাদিত ; পাংশুল ; বিবর্ণ, পাণ্ডুবর্ণ, পাণ্ডুর ।

A-si-ăt′-ic (ā-shĭ-), *adj.* & *n.* Pertaining to Asia ; as, the *Asiatic* Society ; (এশিয়া মহাদেশের সাহিত্য, প্রত্নতত্ত্ব, প্রভৃতি আলোচনার জন্য কলিকাতা মহানগরীতে প্রতিষ্ঠিত পরিষদ্ বিশেষ) এশিয়া-মহাদেশীয় । ***Noun.*** A native of Asia ; এশিয়াবাসী ।

ā-sīde′, *adv.* & *n.* **1.** To, on, one side ; as, to stand *aside* ; off ; away ; as, to put one's cares *aside* ; একপাশে, একদিকে ; দূরে ; তফাতে । **2.** Privately ; so as not to be heard by others ; "Then lords and ladies spake *aside* ;" নির্জ্জনে, নিরলে, বিজনে, নিভৃতে ; একান্তে স্বগত, আত্মগত, জনান্তিকে । ***Noun.*** Words spoken aside, esp. spoken, by an actor and supposed not to be heard by the audience ; স্বগত বাক্য, বিশেষতঃ অভিনেতার জনান্তিকোক্তি । **To set aside**—To quash (a verdict) ; to overthrow ; রহিত করা ; রদ করা ।

ăs′-i-nīne, *adj.* Pertaining to, of the nature of, asses ; as, *asinine* nature ; stupid ; গর্দ্দভোচিত, রাসভীয় ; নির্ব্বোধ, জড়-বুদ্ধি । **–nin′-i-ty,** *n.*

ăsk, *v. t.* & *i.* **1.** To make a request for ; as, *ask* him to do this ; to solicit ; as, *ask* a favour of him ; অনুরোধ করা, বলা, শুধান (*colloq.*) ; প্রার্থনা করা, যাচ্ঞা করা । **2.** To claim ; to require ; as, what price do you *ask* ; দাবী করা ; চাওয়া । **3.** To put a question to ; to call for an answer to ; as, *ask* him a question : *ask* him the time ; জিজ্ঞাসা করা, প্রশ্ন করা ; উত্তর চাওয়া । **4.** To invite ; as, to *ask* (guests) to a wedding or entertainment ; নিমন্ত্রণ করা । ***Verb i.*** **1.** To request or petition (foll. by *for* before an object) ; as, to *ask for* bread ; প্রার্থনা করা, যাচ্ঞা

করা, মাগা, ভিক্ষাকরা। **2.** To make enquiry; (foll. by *after*); as, why do you *ask after* my name; সন্ধান লওয়া, জিজ্ঞাসা করা। **Ask′-ing,** *adj.* & *n.* Requesting; inquiring; silently expressing a desire; as, *asking* eye; অনুনয়-পূর্ণ; প্রশ্নকারী, জিজ্ঞাসু; মৌনভাব-জ্ঞাপক। (*Noun*) **1.** A petition; as, it may be had for the *asking*; আবেদন, প্রার্থনা। **2.** Publication in church of banns of marriage; খৃষ্টীয়-ধর্ম্মমন্দিরে প্রস্তাবিত বিবাহের বিজ্ঞাপন প্রচার। **To ask in church**—To publish the banns in marriage; প্রস্তাবিত বিবাহের বিষয় বিজ্ঞাপিত করা।

ă-skănce′, —skănt′, *adv.* Sideways; obliquely; out of one corner of the eye; আড়নয়নে, বক্রভাবে; কুটিলনেত্রে; আড়চোখে, তেরছনয়নে (প্রাঃ সাঃ)। **To look askance**—To look suspiciously; "Both were *looked askance* by the authority;" সন্দেহের চোখে দেখা।

ă-skew′ (-skü), *adv.* & *adj.* Obliquely; asquint (used of the eye); as, to look *askew*, *i.e.* not straight in the face; তির্য্যগ্‌ভাবে; কুটিলভাবে, কুটিলনেত্রে, আড়চোখে। ***Adj.*** Oblique; awry; (used of other things); বক্র, কুটিল; তির্য্যক্‌।

ă-slănt′, *adv.* & *prep.* Obliquely; slantingly: আড়ভাবে, বক্রভাবে; টের্চাভাবে। ***Prep.*** Athwart; slanting across; "There is a willow grows *aslant* a brook;" আড়ভাবে; প্রবণভাবে।

ă-sleep′ (-slēp), *adv.* **1.** In or into a state of sleep; as, he fell *asleep*; inactive; as, when appetite is *asleep*; into a state of inactivity; as, their apprehensions were laid *asleep*; নিদ্রিত, সুপ্ত, সনিদ্র, নিদ্রাগত, অবসুপ্ত, ঘুমিয়ে, ঘুমে, নিদ্রাবেশে; জড়-অবস্থায়, নিশ্চেষ্ট-ভাবে; নিষ্ক্রিয়ভাবে। **2.** (*Fig.*) Dead; "Concerning those who are *asleep*, sorrow not;" (লক্ষণায়) মৃত, চিরনিদ্রিত, অনন্ত নিদ্রায় নিদ্রিত। **3.** (Of limbs) Benumbed; "Leaning long upon any part maketh it numb, and as we call it, *asleep*;" (অঙ্গ-প্রত্যঙ্গ-সম্পর্কে) অবশ, আড়ষ্ট, জড়ীভূত।

ă-slōpe, *adj.* or *adv.* Sloping; crosswise; ক্রমাবনত, গড়ানিয়া; আড়া-আড়ি, আড়াআড়ি-ভাবে।

ăsp, *n.* **1.** A small hooded poisonous serpent of Egypt and adjacent countries; চক্রক (মঃ উঃ),

The common asp.

চক্রমণ্ডলী (ঐ), কালসর্প (ফঃ হিঃ), বালিষ্টিয়া সাপ (ঐ)। **2.** (*Poet.*) Any venomous serpent; (কবিতায়) যে কোন বিষধর সর্প।

ăs-păr′-ă-gŭs, *n.* A plant in garden the tender shoots of which are eaten (*Asparagus officinalis*); (আরবীয়ভাষায়) হেন্‌ইয়ান্‌ (বেলঃ)। ***Asparagus bean***—বরবটী (প্রবোধঃ)। ***Asparagus racemosus***—শতমূলী।

ăs′-pĕct, *n.* **1.** Gaze; sight; as, his *aspect* was bent on the ground; দর্শন; দৃষ্টি। **2.** Fronting or looking in a given direction: as, the house has a southern *aspect*; মুখ, রোক্‌। **3.** Appearance, especially to the mind; look; view; as to present a thing in its favourable or true *aspect*; রূপ, আকৃতি; আভাস; দৃশ্য। **4.** Countenance; mien; air; "With grave *aspect* he rose;" আকার; চেহারা; ভাব, ভঙ্গী। **5.** (*Astrol.*) The position of one planet with respect to another; ফলিত জ্যোতিষ) গ্রহগণের দৃষ্টি (বৃঃ সং)। **Aspect of planets at birth**—দশা (বৃঃ সং)।

ăsp′-ĕn, *n.* & *adj.* The Asp tree; (হিন্দি) বেদ্‌-ই-মজনুন গাছ। ***Adj.*** **1.** Of or like the aspen tree; উক্ত বৃক্ষসম্বন্ধীয় বা বিষয়ক। **2.** Quivering; "His beard shook horrid with such *aspen* malady;" কম্পিত, কম্পী।

ăs-pĕr-gil′-lŭm, —lŭs, *n.* (In Roman Catholic Churches) The brush for sprinkling holy water on the people; পবিত্র বারি প্রোক্ষণার্থ রোমান ক্যাথলিক ধর্ম্ম-মন্দিরে ব্যবহৃত কূর্চ্চবিশেষ।

ăs-pĕr′-i-tȳ, *n.* **1.** Roughness of surface; unevenness; as, the pores and *asperities* of bodies; কর্কশতা, অমসৃণতা; বন্ধুরতা, উচ্চাবচত্ব। **2.** Severity (of weather); bitter coldness; as, the great *asperity* of climate in winter; (ঋতুর) কঠোরতা; নিদারুণ শৈত্য। **3.** Sharpness or harshness (of temper); bitterness; as, *asperity* of character; (স্বভাবের) কর্কশতা, রূঢ়তা, রুক্ষতা, কঠোরতা; কটুতা, উগ্রতা, তিক্ততা।

ă-spêr′-mous (-mŭs), *adj.* Without seed; বীজবিহীন।

ăs-perse′ (-pêrs), *v. t.* **1.** To sprinkle (*with*); to scatter over; সেচন করা; ছিটান, ছড়ান। **2.** To bespatter (a person or character, *with* damaging reports); লেপন করা। **3.** To slander; to calumniate; "With blackest crimes *aspersed*;" কুৎসা করা; নিন্দা করা, অপবাদ করা, কলঙ্ক রটনা করা। **—per′-sion,** *n.* **1.** A sprinkling, as with water or dust; সেচন। **2.** The spreading of calumnious reports; calumny; কুৎসাপ্রচার; কলঙ্ক, নিন্দা, অপবাদ, গ্লানি, কুৎসা, দুর্নাম। **—per′-sive,** *adj.*

ăs-pêr-sō′-ri-ŭm, *n.* A vessel for holy water; পবিত্রোদক-পাত্র।

ăs′-phălt, —phălt-ŭm, *n.* **1.** A smooth hard bituminous substance ; শিলাজতু। **2.** A mixture of bitumen, pitch and sand for pavements, etc. ; শিলাজতু, আলকাত্‌রা ও বালি মিশ্রণে প্রস্তুত (ইমারতাদির) লেপবিশেষ। **—ic,** *adj.*

ăs′-phō-dĕl, *n.* **1.** A genus of liliaceous plants ; রজনী-গন্ধাদিবর্গভুক্ত পুষ্পবৃক্ষসমূহের 'গণ' বিশেষ। **2.** (*Poet*) Immortal flower in Elysium ; (কবিতায়) অম্লানপুষ্প, পারিজাত।

ăs-phȳx′-i-ă, —phȳx-ȳ, *n.* Suspended animation due to lack of oxygen in blood ; suffocation ; মূর্চ্ছা ; শ্বাস-স্তম্ভ, শ্বাসরোধ। **—i-al,** *adj.* **—i-a-ted,** *p. p.* Suffocated ; শ্বাসরুদ্ধ।

ăs′-pic, *n.* A venomous serpent ; বিষধর-সর্প বিশেষ। [কবিতায় ব্যবহৃত হয়।]

ăs′-pic, *n.* A savoury meat-jelly ; মাংসের সুস্বাদু ঘনরস।

ăs-pīr′-ănt, *n.* One who aspires (*to, for, after*) ; অর্থী, প্রার্থী, আকাঙ্ক্ষী, অভিলাষী, উচ্চপদপ্রয়াসী।

ăs′-pi-rāte, *adj.* & *n.* Pronounced with a breathing or blended with the sound of *h* ; মহাপ্রাণের সহিত উচ্চারিত ; 'হ' ধ্বনির সহিত উচ্চারিত। ***Noun.*** A consonant pronounced with a breathing ; the sound of *h* ; মহাপ্রাণ, মহাপ্রাণ বর্ণ ; 'হ' ধ্বনি।

ăs′-pi-rāte, *v. t.* **1.** To prefix or add to (any sound) the *h* sound or a similar breathing ; (কোন ধ্বনির) আদিতে বা সহিত "হ" ধ্বনি বা মহাপ্রাণ উচ্চারণ সংযোগ করা, যথা— "End"কে "Hend" এইভাবে উচ্চারণ করা। **2.** To draw out gas from a vessel ; (কোন) পাত্র হইতে বাষ্প নিষ্কাশিত করা।

ăs-pi-rā′-tion, *n.* **1.** The act of breathing ; শ্বাসগ্রহণ। **2.** The action of aspirating ; "হ" ধ্বনি বা মহাপ্রাণসহকৃত উচ্চারণ। **3.** Ardent desire (*for, after,* what is elevated or spiritual) ; উচ্চাকাঙ্ক্ষা, উচ্চাভিলাষ, মহতী আশা। **—pir′-a-to-ry,** *adj.*

ăs′-pi-rā-tor (-tėr), *n.* **1.** An apparatus for drawing air, gas etc. through a tube ; বায়ুচোষক (হিঃ কোঃ)। **2.** An instrument for drawing pus from abscesses ; পূযচোষক। **3.** A winnowing-machine ; শূর্প, কুলা।

ăs-pīre′, *v. i.* **1.** To desire earnestly ; (*to, after, at*) ; ব্যগ্রভাবে আকাঙ্ক্ষা করা, স্পৃহা করা, অভিলাষ করা। **2.** To mount up ; to ascend ; to tower ; as, flames *aspire* ; অধিরোহণ করা ; উত্থিত হওয়া ; উচ্চ হইয়া উঠা। **—pir′-ing,** *adj.* Ambitious ; উচ্চাভিলাষী। **—pir′-ing-ly,** *adv.*

ă-squint′, *adv.* & *adj.* Obliquely ; awry ; আড়ভাবে, টেড়াভাবে ; আড়চোখে, টেড়া।

ăss, *n.* **1.** A well-known quadruped of the horse family, with long ears ; গর্দ্দভ, রাসভ, খর, গাধা। **2.** (*Fig.*) A dull, heavy, stupid fellow ; a blockhead ; (লক্ষণায়) নির্ব্বোধ, বেকুব, বোকা ; গাধা। **An ass in a lion's skin**—A fool that apes the wise man ; সিংহ-চর্ম্মাবৃত গর্দ্দভ, অর্থাৎ যে ব্যক্তি মূর্খ হইয়াও হাস্যোদ্দীপকভাবে জ্ঞানী ব্যক্তির অনুকরণ করে। **Asses' bridge**—[Euclid I. 5.] ইউক্লিডের জ্যামিতির প্রথম পুস্তকের পঞ্চম প্রতিজ্ঞা। [প্রথম শিক্ষার্থিগণের নিকট ইহা অত্যন্ত দুরূহ বোধ হয়, তজ্জন্য।] **Do not take an ass to the haystack**—কাঙ্গালকে শাকের আঁটি দেখাইতে নাই। **The ass waggeth his ears**—গাধা কান নাড়ছে, অর্থাৎ কোন মূর্খ ব্যক্তি কথাবার্ত্তায় আপনাকে মহাজ্ঞানী বলিয়া প্রমাণিত করিতে চেষ্টা করিতেছে। **To mount the ass**—To become bankrupt ; দেউলিয়া হওয়া।

ăs′-să-gai (-gā), *n.* A slender spear of hard wood used by tribes in South Africa ; a light javelin ; দক্ষিণ আফ্রিকার আদিম জাতি সমূহের বড়শা বিশেষ ; একপ্রকার লঘু বড়শা।

ăs-sail′ (-sāl), *v. t.* (*Lit.* & *fig.*) **1.** To make hostile attack upon ; (শব্দানুযায়ী এবং লক্ষণায়) আক্রমণ করা। **2.** To overwhelm with questions ; প্রশ্নের পর প্রশ্ন জিজ্ঞাসা করিয়া অভিভূত করা। **—a-ble,** *adj.* Capable of being attacked or invaded ; আক্রমণীয়। **—ant,** *n.* One who attacks a person or thing ; আক্রমণকারী।

ăs-săs′-sin, *n.* **1.** One who undertakes to kill treacherously ; গুপ্ত ঘাতক, গুপ্তহত্যাকারী। **2.** (*Hist.*) A Moslem fanatic in the time of the Crusades, sent by the *Old Man of the Mountains,* to murder Christians ; জেরুজেলেম্ উদ্ধারার্থ খৃষ্টীয় অভিযানের সময়, পর্ব্বতবাসী বৃদ্ধ (সেখ আল্-জাবাল) খৃষ্টানদিগকে গোপনে হত্যা করার জন্য যে সমস্ত ধর্ম্মোন্মত্ত ব্যক্তিকে প্রেরণ করিত, তাহাদের অন্যতম।

ăs-săs′-sin-āte, *v. t.* To murder by treacherous violence ; গুপ্তভাবে হত্যা করা। **—si-na′-tion,** *n.* A killing by treacherous violence ; secret murder ; উপাংশুবধ ; গুপ্তহত্যা। **—si-na-tor,** *n.* An assassin ; গুপ্তহন্তা, গুপ্তহত্যাকারী।

ăs-sault′ (-sălt), *n.* & *v. t.* **1.** A violent onset ; an onslaught ; (*lit.* & *fig.*) ; as, an *assault* upon the constitution of government ; (শব্দানুযায়ী এবং লক্ষণায়) আক্রমণ ; প্রচণ্ড আক্রমণ। **2.** A sudden and vigorous attack on a fortified post ; as, to carry by *assault* ; দুর্গাদির উপর সহসা প্রচণ্ডবেগে আক্রমণ। **3.** (*Law*) An attempt to beat another without touching his person, as by lifting the fist or a cane in a threatening manner, including menacing words ; as, *assault* and battery ; [If the blow aimed takes effect it is a *battery*] ; (আইন) মারিবার উদ্যোগ, চড়াও (লাঠি প্রভৃতি উঠাইয়া ভয় প্রদর্শন করিলেই আইনমত "*assault*" বা 'চড়াও' হয়।) ***Verb t.*** **1.** To make a violent attack upon ; (*lit.* & *fig.*) ; (শব্দানুযায়ী এবং লক্ষণায়) প্রচণ্ডভাবে আক্রমণ করা, চড়াও করা। **2.** To fall on with force ; to assail ; as, the cries of babes newborn *assault* his ears ; সজোরে পতিত হওয়া ; আক্রমণ করা। **3.** To attack a fortress by sudden rush ; সহসা প্রচণ্ডবেগে দুর্গ আক্রমণ করা। **—a-ble,** *adj.*

ăs-say′ (-sā), *n.* **1.** The trial of the weight, value, purity, etc. of metals ; ধাতুর ওজন, মূল্য বিশুদ্ধি প্রভৃতি পরীক্ষা, ধাতুর গুণাগুণ পরীক্ষা, পরখ, যাচাই। **2.** The metal to be so tried ; পরীক্ষণীয় ধাতু। [*Essay* & *Assay* are radically the same word ; but now *assay* is used for the testing of metals while *essay* is used for bodily or mental attempts.] **Assay-master**—An officer who tests gold or silver coin or bullion ; যে কর্ম্মচারী স্বর্ণ বা রৌপ্যের মুদ্রা বা তাল যাচাই করেন।

ăs-say′ (-sā), *v. t.* & *i.* **1.** To try the purity of precious metals ; (স্বর্ণ-রৌপ্যাদি) মূল্যবান ধাতুর গুণাগুণ পরখ করা, যাচাই করা। **2.** To attempt or endeavour ; চেষ্টা করা। **—a-ble,** *adj.* **—ing,** *n.* The act or art of testing metals, ores, in order to ascertain the quantity of gold or silver or any other metal present in them ; পরখকরণ, যাচাই-করণ।

ăs-sĕm′-blāge *n.* **1.** The act of bringing or coming together ; association ; সম্মিলন, সমানয়ন ; সংঘ, সমুচ্চয়, সংহতি, সংঘাত, সমবায়, সন্নিপাত, সঞ্চয়। **2.** A concourse of persons ; a collection of particular things ; as, a political *assemblage* : an *assemblage* of ideas ; জনসংঘ, জনতা ; সমাহার, সমবায়।

ăs-sĕm′-ble, *v. t.* & *i.* To bring or call together ; to congregate ; একত্র করা, একত্র আহ্বান করা, জড় করা ; সমবেত করা, মিলিত করা। ***Verb i.*** To meet or come together ; to collect ; সমবেত হওয়া, সম্মিলিত হওয়া ; একত্র হওয়া।

ăs-sĕm′-blȳ, *n.* **1.** A company or collection of human beings in the same place, usually for the same purpose ; especially a deliberative body ; a legislative council ; সভা, সমাজ, সংসদ্ ; বিশেষতঃ আলোচনা সভা ; ব্যবস্থাপক সভা। **2.** (*Mil.*) A military call by drum or bugle ; ভেরী বা বংশীনাদদ্বারা সামরিক আহ্বান। **Assembly-room**—A room in which persons assemble, especially for dancing ; মিলন-মন্দির, নৃত্যশালা, নাটমন্দির। A room in which the members of the Legislative Council meet for deliberation ; ব্যবস্থাপক সভার সভ্যদিগের সভা-কক্ষ, সভামণ্ডপ, সভাগৃহ, উপস্থান-গৃহ (মঃ ভাঃ)। **General Assembly**—The supreme church judicature of the established Free Church of Scotland ; ধর্ম্ম-সম্বন্ধীয় বিষয় মীমাংসার্থ স্কটলণ্ড-দেশীয় সর্ব্বপ্রধান যাজকীয় ধর্ম্মাধিকরণ। (*Law*) **Unlawful assemsly**—(আইন) বে-আইনি জনতা, অবৈধজনতা।

ăs-sĕnt′, *v. i.* To agree (*to* a proposal) ; to defer (*to* a desire) ; to express agreement (*to* statement, opinion) ; to acquiesce ; স্বীকার করা ; কাহারো ইচ্ছার অনুগত হওয়া ; একমত হওয়া ; সায় দেওয়া, সম্মত হওয়া, রাজি হওয়া। **—er,** *n.*

ăs-sĕnt′, *n.* **1.** An agreement to a proposal ; সম্মতি, সায়। **2.** Mental acceptance or approval ; (distinguished from *consent*) ; as, I must honestly confess my full *assent* to the doctrine ; স্বীকার, অনুমোদন। **Royal assent**—The assent of the sovereign to a bill, passed by the Parliament ; (ইংলণ্ডে) পার্লেমেণ্ট মহাসভাকর্ত্তৃক অনুমোদিত আইনের পাণ্ডুলিপিতে রাজসম্মতি।

ăs-sĕn-tā′-tion, *n.* An obsequious or servile assent (to the opinion of other) ; মনযোগানিয়া ভাবের সায়, হীনানুমোদন, হীনানুগত্যসূচক সম্মতিপ্রদান।

ăs-sĕn′-tient (-shent), *adj.* & *n.* Assenting ; accordant ; অনুমোদনশীল ; সম্মতিশীল। ***Noun.*** One who assents ; সম্মতিদাতা।

ăs-sêrt′, *v. t.* **1.** To insist upon or vindicate a (disputed) claim to (anything) ; as, to *assert* one's rights, independance ; নিজস্বত্ব বা দাবী রক্ষা বা প্রতিপাদন করা, স্বপ্রতিষ্ঠার চেষ্টা করা। **2.** To affirm positively ; to declare ; জোরের সহিত বলা, দৃঢ়রূপে বলা, নিশ্চয়পূর্ব্বক বলা ; খ্যাপন করা। **—a-ble, —ive,** *adjs.* **—ive-ly,** *adv.* **—ser′-tion,** *n.* **1.** An affirmation ; a positive statement ; নিশ্চয় কথন, খ্যাপন (উজ্জ্বলঃ) ; নিশ্চিত বাক্য বা উক্তি। **2.** Insistence upon a right ; স্বাধিকার প্রতিষ্ঠার জন্য নির্ব্বন্ধাতিশয়। **Self-assertion**—Insistence on the recognition of one's claims ; স্বপ্রতিষ্ঠার জন্য নির্ব্বন্ধাতিশয়। **To assert oneself**—To insist upon one's rights or claim ; নিজ স্বত্ব বা দাবী প্রতিষ্ঠার জন্য চেষ্টা করা। To thrust oneself forward unduly ; স্বপ্রতিষ্ঠার চেষ্টা করা।

ăs-sĕr′-tor (-têr), **—sêrt′-êr,** *n.* **1.** One who maintains or defends ; a champion : as, Greeks were famous *asserters* of liberties ; রক্ষাকর্ত্তা, সমর্থক, রক্ষক। **2.** One who makes positive declaration ; নিশ্চিত কথক।

ăs-sĕss′, *v.t.* **1.** To fix the amount of tax, fine, etc. ; করধার্য্য করা, করনির্দ্ধারণ করা, অর্থদণ্ডের পরিমাণ

নির্দ্ধারণ করা। **2.** To estimate the value of a property for taxation; কর বসাইবার জন্য সম্পত্তির মূল্য ধার্য্য করা। **3.** To impose a fine or tax upon (a person, community); (usually *in, at,* before the amount); অর্থদণ্ড করা, কর বসান। **—a-ble,** *adj.* **—a-bly,** *adv.* **—ment,** *n.* **1.** The determination of the amount of taxation, fine, etc.; কর-নির্দ্ধারণ, কর-নিরূপণ, অর্থদণ্ডের পরিমাণ নিরূপণ। **2.** A valuation of property, income, etc., for the purpose of taxation; করধার্য্য করার উদ্দেশ্যে, সম্পত্তি, আয়, প্রভৃতির মূল্য বা পরিমাণ অবধারণ। **3.** The specific sum levied; "*Assessment* received from land-holders directly;" (সদরজমা, মালগুজারি); কর, মালগুজারি (হিঃ কোঃ)। **Account of assessment, receipts and balances**—জমা ওয়াশিল ও বাকীর হিসাব (রঃ অঃ)। **Free of assesment**—নিষ্কর, লাখেরাজ।

ăs-sĕs′-sor (-sêr), *n.* **1.** One who sits as an assistant or adviser to a judge or magistrate; বিচারকের সহকারী বা পরামর্শদাতা, সভাচর, সভাসদ (ব্যঃ মাঃ), সদস্য। **2.** One who assesses taxes or estimates the value of property for taxation; করনির্দ্ধারক, করনির্ণায়ক। **—ship,** *n.* **—so′-ri-al,** *adj.*

ăs′-sĕts, *n. pl.* **1.** (*Law*) The property of a deceased or insolvent person, considered as chargeable for all debts; মৃত বা ঋণ পরিশোধে অসমর্থ ব্যক্তির (দেউলিয়ার) ঋণ-পরিশোধের জন্য ত্যক্ত সম্পত্তি, শেষ ধন (হিঃ কোঃ), জায়দাদ (রঃ অঃ), স্থিত (ঐ)। **2.** The entire property of a person or company which may be made liable for his or their debts; কোন ব্যবসায়ী বা বণিক্ সমিতির সর্ব্ববিধ সম্পত্তির সমষ্টি। **Personal assets**—আসবাব, মালপত্র।

ăs-sĕv′-ĕr-āte, *v. t.* To declare solemnly; প্রতিজ্ঞাপূর্ব্বক বলা, দৃঢ়রূপে বলা। **—a′-tion,** *n.* Positive assertion or affirmation; solemn declaration; নিশ্চিতোক্তি, দৃঢ়োক্তি; সত্য-বাক্য।

ăs-sib′-i-lāte, *v. t.* To give a hissing sound to; হিস্-ধ্বনি সহ উচ্চারণ করা। **—la′-tion,** *n.*

ăs-si-dū′-i-tȳ, *n.* **1.** Constant or close application to any business or enterprise; close attention; diligence; as, the labour and *assiduity* with which he acquired his eloquence; উদ্যোগ, অধ্যবসায়, উদ্যম, প্রযত্ন; গভীর অভিনিবেশ; যত্নপরতা। **2.** (*Pl.*) Constant attentions; as, the *assiduities* of their zealous love; অবিশ্রান্ত অনুরাগ-প্রদর্শন।

ăs-sid′-ū-ous (-ŭs), *adj.* Persevering; unwearingly diligent; অধ্যবসায়ী; অক্লান্ত-কর্ম্মা। **—ly,** *adv.* **—ness,** *n.*

ăs-sign′ (-sīn), *v.t.* & *n.* **1.** To allot as a share to; to apportion; বিলি করা; অংশক্রমে ভাগ করিয়া দেওয়া, বণ্টন করা। **2.** (*Law*) To transfer or make over (esp. personal property) to another; (আইন) হস্তান্তরিত করা, অর্পণ করা। **3.** To allot (a place) to a person; as, he *assigned* to his men their several posts; (স্থান) নির্দ্দিষ্ট করিয়া দেওয়া। **4.** To fix; to determine; as, I cannot *assign* the day; নিরূপণ করা, স্থির করা; নির্দ্দেশ করা। **5.** To point out exactly; to specify; as, the locality which tradition has *assigned* for the place; নিশ্চিত বা নির্ভুলভাবে নির্দ্দেশ করা; বিশেষভাবে নির্দ্দেশ করা। **6.** To ascribe (a reason) *to,* or as accounting *for* anything; as, sundry reasons are *assigned for* his silence; আরোপ করা, নির্দ্দেশ করা। **7.** To bring forward or offer something (as a reason, etc.); উপস্থাপিত করা, প্রদর্শন করা। ***Noun.*** A person to whom property or any right is legally transferred; যে ব্যক্তিকে কোন সম্পত্তি বা বৈধ অধিকার অর্পণ করা হয়। **—a-ble,** *adj* Capable of being allotted, specified or shown; বিভাজ্য, নির্দ্ধার্য্য, নির্দ্দেশ্য। **—or,** *n.* One who makes over a right or property; স্বত্ব বা সম্পত্তি অর্পণকারী।

ăs-sig′-năt (pronounced also ăs-sîn-yâ), *n.* Paper money issued by the revolutionary government of France (1789—96) on security of the state lands; ফরাসী সাধারণতন্ত্র (১৭৮৯—৯৬) কর্ত্তৃক রাষ্ট্রাধিকারভুক্ত ভূমির জামিনে যে ঋণ-স্বীকারপত্র বাহির করা হইয়াছিল।

ăs-sig-nā′-tion, *n.* **1.** The act of allotting; apportionment; অংশ-নিরূপণ, অংশ-চিহ্নীকরণ, নির্দ্দেশন; বণ্টন। **2.** A formal transference of a right or property; স্বত্ব বা সম্পত্তি হস্তান্তর। **3.** An appointment of time or place for meeting (used chiefly of love-interviews, and now commonly in a bad sense); a tryst; as, a lady going to an *assignation* (অভিসারিকা); সঙ্কেতীকরণ; অভিসার, সঙ্কেত (মঃ উঃ), সঙ্কেতস্থান (ঐ), সঙ্কেত-নিকেতন। **4.** An attribution of origin; as, *assignation* of the bronze weapons; উৎপত্তি-নির্দ্দেশ। **5.** Paper money; a bill; নোট; হুণ্ডী।

ăs-sign-ee′ (-sīn-ē), *n.* **1.** One appointed to act for another; an agent or representative; প্রতিনিধি; স্থলাভিষিক্ত ব্যক্তি। **2.** One to whom a right or property is made over; যে ব্যক্তির নিকট সম্পত্তি হস্তান্তরিত হয়। **Official assignee**—A government officer in charge of a bankrupt's property; দেউলিয়া ব্যক্তির সম্পত্তির ভারপ্রাপ্ত সরকারী কর্ম্মচারী।

ăs-sign′-mĕnt (-sīn-), *n.* **1.** Allotment; বিলি, বণ্টন, বিনিয়োগ, বিভাগ,

অংশ। **2.** Legal transference; সম্পত্তি প্রভৃতি হস্তান্তর। **3.** A document effecting the transfer of a right or property; হস্তান্তর পত্র। **4.** Attribution; allegement (of reasons); আরোপণ; (কারণ) নির্দ্দেশ।

ăs-sim′-i-lāte, *v. t.* & *i.* **1.** To make alike; to cause to resemble; (*to, with*); সমান করা, একরূপ করা; সদৃশ করা। **2.** To absorb and incorporate into the system; (*lit.* & *fig.*); (শব্দানুযায়ী এবং লক্ষণায়) দৈহিক উপাদানে পরিণত করা, ভুক্তদ্রব্যাদি রক্ত মাংস অস্থি প্রভৃতিতে পরিণত করা। *Verb i.* To be converted into the substance of the body by digestion; পরিপাকক্রিয়ার ফলে দৈহিক উপাদানে পরিণত হওয়া। **—la-ble,** *adj.* **—la′-tion,** *n.* (Foll. by *to* or *with.*) **1.** The act or process of making or becoming like or identical; resemblance; সদৃশীকরণ, সদৃশীভবন; সাদৃশ্য। **2.** The absorption of nutriment into the system; ভুক্ত অন্নাদির রক্ত মাংসাদিতে পরিণতি, দেহসাৎকরণ, সমীকরণ। **—la-tive, —la-to-ry,** *adjs.*

ăs-sist′, *v. t.* & *i.* To help or aid সাহায্য করা, সহায়তা করা। *Verb i.* **1.** To lend aid; সাহায্য প্রদান করা। **2.** To be present at (a ceremony, entertainment, etc.), as a spectator; "If Tacitus had *assisted* at this assembly;" দর্শকরূপে (ক্রিয়াকাণ্ড বা ভোজ তামাসাদিতে) উপস্থিত থাকা। **—ance,** *n.* Help; aid; succour; সাহায্য; সহায়তা; আনুকূল্য। **—ant,** *n.* & *adj.* A helper; a means of help; aid; as, rhymes merely as *assistants* to memory; সাহায্যকারী, সহকারী, সাহায্যদাতা; সহায়; সাহায্য। (*Adj.*) Aiding or helpful (*to*); সহায়ক।

ăs-sīze′ *n.* **1.** A statute or ordinance regulating weights, measures and price of articles sold in the market; as, the *assize* of measure: *assize* of bread and ale; hence, the statutory price of bread and ale; মাপ, বাটখারা এবং দ্রব্যাদির মূল্য নিয়ামক আইন বিশেষ; অতএব রুটি বা যবসুরার বিধি-নির্দ্ধারিত মূল্য। **2.** The periodical sessions, held in each county of England, for administering civil and criminal justice, by judges acting under special commissions; বিলাতের প্রাদেশিক দায়রা আদালতের বিচারাধিবেশন। **Great assize**—The last judgment; (খৃষ্টীয় ও মহম্মদীয় ধর্ম্মমতে) অন্তিমবিচার-দিবস।

ăs-sīz′-êr, *n.* An officer who has the care or inspection of weights and measures, etc. of articles to be sold; মাপ ও বাটখারা প্রভৃতি পর্য্যবেক্ষক ও তত্ত্বাবধায়ক সরকারী কর্ম্মচারী।

ăs-sö′-cia-ble (-shă-), *adj.* That may be connected in thought *with*; সম্মিলনযোগ্য, সংযোজনীয়। **—bil′-i-ty, —ness,** *ns.*

ăs-sö′-ci-āte (-shî-), *n.* & *adj.* **1.** A companion, (implying intimacy or equality); a mate; সাথী, পার্শ্বচর, সহচর, সহযোগী, পারিপার্শ্বিক; সখা, বয়স্য। **2.** A partner as in business; a confederate in a league; অংশীদার; সন্ধিবদ্ধ মিত্র। **3.** A subordinate member of an association; as, an *associate* of the Royal Academy; সহযোগী সভ্য। **4.** Anything found in conjunction with another; সংযুক্ত বস্তু। *Adj.* **1.** Joined in companionship, function or dignity; as, an *associate* judge or professor; সহযোগী। **2.** Joined in a league; সন্ধিবদ্ধ। **—ship,** *n.*

ăs-sö′-ci-āte (-shî-), *v. t.* & *i.* **1.** To join (persons, things, or one with another); সম্মিলিত করা, সংযুক্ত করা। **2.** To connect in idea; চিন্তাদ্বারা সম্মিলিত করা। **3.** To make oneself a partner in a matter; কোন বিষয়ে সহযোগী হওয়া। *Verb i.* **1.** To have intercourse (*with*); সংসর্গ থাকা, মিলামিশা থাকা। **2.** To combine for a common purpose; এক উদ্দেশ্যে মণ্ডলীবদ্ধ হওয়া। **—a-tive,** *adj.* **—a-tor,** *n.* **—a-to-ry,** *adj.*

ăs-sö-ci-ā′-tion (-shî-), *n.* **1.** The act of combining together for a common purpose; league; সম্মিলন, সংযোগ, সংযোজন, সহযোগিতা; দুই বা ততোধিক রাজ্য বা ব্যক্তির সম্মিলন। **2.** An organized body of persons (for some common purpose); as, the British *Association* for the cultivation of science; সভা, সমাজ, সমিতি; সম্মিলনী, সংসদ্, পরিষৎ, দরবার, মণ্ডলী। **3.** Fellowship; intimacy; সাহচর্য্য। অন্তরঙ্গতা। **Association of ideas**—Mental connection between an object and ideas related to it; ভাবসাহচর্য্য (হিং কোঃ), প্রত্যয়-সহচর (ঐ), উদ্বুদ্ধ-সংস্কার (মঃ ভাঃ)। **A deed or articles of association**—SEE ARTICLE.

ăs-soil′ (-sōyl), *v. t.* **1.** (*Archaic*) To absolve from sin; to pardon; পাপ ক্ষমাকরা; ক্ষমা করা। **2.** To acquit (by sentence of court); to set free; (*of, from*); মুক্তি দেওয়া; খালাস দেওয়া। **3.** To atone for; প্রায়শ্চিত্ত করা। **—mènt,** *n.*

ăs′-sö-năṅce, *n.* **1.** A correspondence in sounds between two words or syllables; স্বরসঙ্গতি, ধ্বনি-সাদৃশ্য। **2.** (*Pros.*) The rhyming of one word with another in the accented vowel and those which follow, but not in the consonants; as, *penitent, reticence*; (ছন্দঃ-শাস্ত্র) এক প্রকার ছন্দঃ—যাহাতে কোন শব্দের স্বরচিহ্নযুক্ত স্বরবর্ণ এবং তৎপরবর্ত্তী স্বরবর্ণসমূহের সহিত অপর শব্দের তৎ তৎ বর্ণের মিল থাকে,

কিন্তু ব্যঞ্জনবর্ণে কোন প্রকার মিল থাকে না। 3. A partial correspondence; আংশিক মিল। **—nant,** *adj.*

ăs-sŏrt′, *v. t.* & *i.* **1.** To classify or arrange in sorts; as, to *assort* goods; শ্রেণীবিভাগ করা, জাতিবিভাগ করা, বাছাই করা, কিসিম করা। **2.** To furnish (a store or shop) with a suitable variety of goods; to make up of articles likely to suit a demand; as, to *assort* a cargo; উপযোগী মালদ্বারা সজ্জিত করা; কাটুতি হইবার সম্ভাবনা আছে এরূপ জিনিষ দ্বারা সাজাইয়া রাখা। ***Verb i.*** **1.** To fall into a class; to suit well or ill with; কোন শ্রেণীতে পড়া; উপযোগী বা অনুপযোগী হওয়া। **2.** To associate with; to consort; সম্মিলিত হওয়া, মিলা; মিলিত হওয়া। **—ment,** *n.* **1.** Classification into kinds or classes; বাছাইকরণ, বিন্যাস, শ্রেণীবিভাগ। **2.** An assorted set of different varieties or various things; as, an *assortment* of silk, goods, etc.; (দোকান প্রভৃতিতে সাজানো) রকমারি জিনিষ বা হরেক রকমের জিনিষ।

ăs-suage′ (-swāj), *v. t.* To mitigate; to soothe, as heat, pain or grief; to pacify, as passion or tumult; to satisfy, as appetite or desire; প্রশমিত করা, হ্রাস করা; উপশম করা; প্রশান্ত করা, সান্ত্বনা করা, নিবৃত্তি করা। **—ment,** *n.*

ăs-sūme′, *v. t.* **1.** To take upon oneself, as aspect, air; as, the cloud *assumed* the figure of an animal; পরিগ্রহ করা। **2.** To take for granted or without proof; to suppose as a fact; ধরিয়া লওয়া; মানিয়া লওয়া। **3.** To simulate; to pretend to possess; as, to *assume* the garb of humility; কৃত্রিমভাব ধারণ করা, ভণ্ডামি করা, কপটতা করা, কপটভাব পরিগ্রহ করা; কোনকিছু আছে বলিয়া ভাণ করা। **4.** To usurp; to appropriate; "Trembling they stand, while Jove *assumes* throne;" বলপূর্ব্বক অধিকার করা; আত্মসাৎ করা। **5.** (*Law*) To undertake or promise; (আইন) ভারগ্রহণ করা বা প্রতিশ্রুত হওয়া। **—sum′-a-ble,** *adj.* **—sumed′,** *p. p.* Supposed; pretended; as, an *assumed* character; কৃত্রিম; ছদ্ম, কৃতক, কপট।

ăs-sūm′-ing, *adj.* Taking much upon oneself; arrogant; ধৃষ্ট, দাম্ভিক, স্পর্দ্ধান্বিত; উদ্ধত।

ăs-sump′-tion, (-sŭm-), *n.* **1.** The act of taking upon one's self; as, the *assumption* of authority; a laying claim to undue importance; arrogance; পরিগ্রহণ; প্রগল্‌ভতা; ঔদ্ধত্য। **2.** The taking of anything for granted; a supposition; (বিনা প্রমাণে) গ্রহণ; অনুমান, অভ্যুপগম (হিঃ কোঃ)। **3.** Ascent or reception into heaven; as, the *assumption* of Elias; esp. the ascent of the Virgin Mary into heaven; hence, the feast in commemoration of this event, held on the 15th of August; স্বর্গারোহণ, স্বর্গধামে পরিগ্রহণ; বিশেষতঃ যীশুজননী কুমারী মেরীর স্বশরীরে স্বর্গারোহণ; অতএব কুমারী মেরীর স্বর্গারোহণ-স্মৃতি ভোজ।

ăs-sump′-tive (-sŭm-), *adj.* **1.** Taken for granted; বিনা প্রমাণে স্বীকৃত। **2.** Arrogant; উদ্ধত।

as-sur′-ănce (ă-shôr-), *n.* **1.** A positive declaration; a pledge of confidence; প্রত্যয়জনন; নিশ্চিত-বাক্য। **2.** Firm persuasion; a full confidence or trust; certainty; প্রতীতি; দৃঢ়প্রত্যয়, পূর্ণবিশ্বাস, ভরসা; নিশ্চয়তা। **3.** Firmness of mind; self-confidence; as, brave men meet danger with *assurance*; মানসিক স্থৈর্য্য; আত্ম-প্রত্যয়। **4.** Audacity; impudence; as, his *assurance* is intolerable; প্রগল্‌ভতা; ধৃষ্টতা। **5.** A contract for the payment of the value of a property in the event of its being lost or for the payment of a specified sum on a person's death; (insurance); as, life *assurance*; (জীবন বীমা): fire or marine *insurance*; বীমা। **To make assurance doubly sure**—To make, as sure as possible; যতদূর সম্ভব নিশ্চিত করা।

ăs-sure′ (a-shôr), *v. t.* **1.** To make safe *from, against* (risks); to insure; ক্ষতি বা অনিষ্টের সম্ভাবনা হইতে নিরাপদ করা; বীমা করা। **2.** To make secure; to establish securely; as, the two chiefs who most *assured* his throne; নিরাপদ করা; সুপ্রতিষ্ঠিত করা। **3.** To make certain (of future events, etc.); to ensure; কৃতনিশ্চয় করা, স্থিরনিশ্চয় করা; সুনিশ্চিত করা। **4.** To give confidence to; to encourage; as, to *assure* the penitent; বিশ্বাস উৎপাদন করা, প্রত্যয়-জন্মান; উৎসাহদান করা, সাহস দেওয়া। **5.** To make (a person) sure *of* (a fact, *that* it is); to tell (a person) confidently *of* (a thing); স্থির-বিশ্বাস জন্মান; সুনিশ্চিতভাবে বলা। **—sured′,** *adj.* **1.** Made sure or certain; কৃতনিশ্চয়। **2.** Confident; bold; as, to proceed with an *assured* easy air; presumptuous; as, an air of *assured* ignorance; সুনিশ্চিত; সাহসিক; প্রগল্‌ভ। **—sur′-ed-ly,** *adv.* **—sur′-ed-ness,** *n.* **—sur′-er,** *n.* One who insures his life; বীমাকারী। **—sur′-ing,** *adj.* **—sur′-ing-ly,** *adv.*

ăs-sûrg′-ĕnt, *adj.* **1.** (*Bot.*) Rising obliquily; as, *assurgent* leaves; (উদ্ভিদ্‌-বিদ্যা) তির্য্যগ্‌ভাবে উত্থায়ী। **2.** Aggressive; as, *assurgent* priesthood; চড়াওকারী।

As-sy̆r-i-ŏl′-ö-ġy̆ (ăs-) *n.* The study of the language, history and antiquities of Assyria ; এসিরিয়া দেশের ভাষা, ইতিহাস এবং প্রত্নতত্ত্ব-চর্চ্চা। **—gist,** *n.* **—o-log′-i-cal,** *adj.*

ă-stăt′-ic, *adj.* Having no tendency to remain in a fixed position ; অস্থিতিক, অস্থিতি-প্রবণ, আসক্ত (হিঃ কোঃ)। **Astatic needle**—One unaffected by the earth's magnetism ; যে সূচীর উপর পার্থিব চুম্বক ক্রিয়া করে না, অস্থিতি-প্রবণ সূচী।

ăs′-têr, *n.* A genus of plants with showy radiated flowers ; সমুজ্জ্বল নক্ষত্রাকৃতি পুষ্পবিশিষ্ট বিভিন্ন-জাতীয় বৃক্ষের সাধারণ নাম।

ăs′-têr-isk, *n.* & *v. t.* A little star ; esp. the figure of a star (thus *), used in printing and writing ; ক্ষুদ্র নক্ষত্র ; তারকাকৃতি চিহ্ন (*)। ***Verb t.*** To mark with an asterisk ; উক্ত চিহ্নে চিহ্নিত করা।

ăs′-têr-ĭsm, *n.* **1.** (*Astron.*) A group or cluster of stars; জ্যোতি-বিজ্ঞান) নক্ষত্রপুঞ্জ, ধিষ্ণ্য (বঃ মিঃ), নক্ষত্র (সূঃ সিঃ) তারাপুঞ্জ (হিঃ কোঃ)। **2.** A group of three asterisks placed thus (⁂) to direct attention to some passage; পুস্তকাদির অংশ বিশেষে মনোযোগ আকর্ষণের জন্য ত্রিতারা চিহ্ন।

ă-stêrn, *adv.* **1.** (*Naut.*) In, at, or toward the hinder part of a ship ; as, to go *astern* ; (নৌ-বিদ্যা) জাহাজের পশ্চাদ্ভাগে, পাছায়। **2.** Away ; behind ; as, a gale of wind *astern* ; backwards ; as, the current drove us far *astern* ; দূরে ; পশ্চাতে ; পশ্চাদ্দিকে।

ăs′-têr-oid (-ōyd), *adj.* & *n.* Star-shaped ; as, the woody *asteroid* form ; নক্ষত্রাকৃতি। ***Noun.*** **1.** The name of the small planets revolving round the sun between the orbits of Mars and Jupiter ; মঙ্গল ও বৃহস্পতির কক্ষের মধ্যবর্ত্তী পথে সূর্য্যের চতুর্দ্দিকে আবর্ত্তনশীল ক্ষুদ্র উপগ্রহ সমূহ, গ্রহক (সাঃ পঃ), অপ-গ্রহক (ঐ), অবান্তর গ্রহ (হিঃ কোঃ)। **2.** A kind of firework ; তারা বাজি। **—al,** *adj.*

ăs-thē-ni′-ă, ăs′-thē-ny̆, *n.* Debility ; want of strength ; দৌর্ব্বল্য ; শক্তিহীনতা।

ăsth′-ma (ăs-mâ or ăz-mâ), *n.* A disease of respiration, characterised by difficult breathing, cough etc. ; শ্বাসকাশ (সাঃ পঃ), শ্বাসরোগ (ঐ), হাঁপানি কাশি। **—mat′-ic,** *adj.* & *n.* Pertaining to, suffering from, or good against, asthma ; শ্বাসকাশরোগ-সম্বন্ধীয়, শ্বাসরোগ-পীড়িত, শ্বাসরোগ-নিবারক। (*Noun*) A person suffering form asthma ; শ্বাসরোগী। **—mat′-i-cal,** *adj.* **—mat-i-cal-ly,** *adv.*

ă-stig′-mă-tĭsm, *n.* A structural defect in the eye, preventing rays of light from being brought to a common focus on the retina ; নকুলান্ধতা (সুশ্রুঃ), অসমদৃষ্টি (হিঃ কোঃ। **—mat′-ic,** *adj.* Affected with or remedying astigmatism ; as, *astigmatic* eye, lenses ; নকুলান্ধ, নকুলান্ধতারোগ-নাশক।

ă-stir′ (-stêr), *adj.* & *adv.* **1.** On the stir ; in motion ; চঞ্চল, অস্থির, ব্যস্ত-সমস্ত ; চলন্ত। **2.** Out of bed ; শয্যোত্থিত। **3.** In excitement ; উত্তেজিতাবস্থায়, উদ্দীপ্ত।

a-stŏm′-ă-tous (-tŭs), **ăs′-tō-mous** (-mŭs), [*a,* without & *stoma,* mouth.] *adj.* Not possessing mouth ; মুখহীন।

ăs-tŏn′-ish, *v. t.* To amaze ; to surprise ; আশ্চর্য্যান্বিত করা ; বিস্ময়াপন্ন করা, তাক লাগান (*colloq.*), অবাক করা। **—ing,** *adj.* Amazing ; wonderful ; অত্যাশ্চর্য্য ; চমৎকার। **—ing-ly,** *adv.* **—ment,** *n.* An intense degree of surprise ; পরম বিস্ময়, মহাবিস্ময়।

ăs-tound′ (-tównd), *v. t.* To shock with alarm or surprise ; to strike dumb with amazement ; স্তব্ধ করা, স্তম্ভিত করা, চমৎকৃত করা বিস্ময়াকুল করা, হতভম্ব করা ; অবাক করা। **—ing,** *adj.* Astonishing ; বিস্ময়কর।

ă-strad′-dle (-stră-), *adv.* In a straddling position ; with one leg on either side ; astride ; as, to sit *astraddle* a horse. ; পদদ্বয় বিস্তার করিয়া ; দুই দিকে দুই পা ছড়াইয়া ; চড়িয়া।

ăs′-tră-găl, *n.* **1.** (*Arch.*) A small moulding round the top or bottom of columns ; (স্থপতি-বিদ্যা) স্তম্ভের ঊর্দ্ধ বা অধোভাগস্থ ক্ষুদ্র বেষ্টন-বলয়, কুমুদ (রাঃ রাঃ)। **2.** (*Gun.*) A ring encircling a cannon near the mouth ; (কামান-নির্ম্মাণে) কামান-রন্ধ্রের সন্নিকটস্থ স্থান পরিবেষ্টক বলয় বিশেষ।

ăs-trăg′-ă-lŭs, *n.* (*Anat.*) The ball of the ankle-joint ; গুল্ফ-সন্ধিগোলক, গুল্ফাস্থি (হঃ চঃ)।

ăs′-tră-khan (-kăn), *n.* The skin of young lambs from Astrakhan in Russia with wool like fur ; রুশিয়ার অন্তঃপাতী আস্ত্রাকান দেশ হইতে সমানীত মেষশাবকের চর্ম্ম।

ăs′-trăl, *adj.* Connected with, consisting of, coming from, the stars ; starry ; নক্ষত্রীয়, নাক্ষত্র, নক্ষত্র-সম্পর্কীয়, নক্ষত্রজাত ; নক্ষত্রময়। **Astral body**—The spiritual appearance of the human form ; a wraith ; a double ; সূক্ষ্ম শরীর ; লিঙ্গ দেহ ; আতিবাহিক দেহ। **Astral lamp**—A lamp that throws no shadow on the table below ; ছায়াবিহীন প্রদীপ। **Astral plane**—ভুবর্লোক (হিঃ কোঃ), পিতৃলোক (ঐ), প্রেতলোক (ঐ)। **Astral spirits** —নক্ষত্র ও গ্রহলোকবাসী দেবযোনি বিশেষ।

ă-stray′ (-strā), *adv.* & *adj.* Out of the right way ; wandering ; বিপথে ; উদ্ভ্রান্ত। **To go**

astray—To go out of the right way ; বিপথগামী হওয়া, উন্মার্গগামী হওয়া। **To lead astray**—To lead in a wrong way ; বিপথে চালিত করা।

ă s-trĭct′, *v. t.* **1.** To bind up ; to compress ; বদ্ধ করা ; সঙ্কুচিত করা। **2.** To make costive ; কোষ্টবদ্ধতা জন্মান। **3.** To bind morally and legally ; নীতি বা আইনের বন্ধনে বদ্ধ করা। **—tric′-tion,** *n.* **1.** (*Med.*) The act of binding close with ligatures ; the stopping of a flow of blood ; constriction ; (ভৈষজ্য-শাস্ত্র) বন্ধনীদ্বারা-বন্ধন ; রক্তস্রাব-নিরোধ ; সঙ্কোচন। **2.** Constipation কোষ্ঠ-কাঠিন্য, কোষ্ঠবদ্ধতা। **—tric′-tive,** *adj.*

ă-strīde′, *adv.* & *prep.* With legs apart, as a man when on horse-back ; (ঘোড়ায় চড়িবার মত) দুই পার্শ্বে পা ঝুলাইয়া, পা ফারক করিয়া। ***Prep.*** With one leg on each side of ; "Kim sat *astride* the gun Zam zammah :" চড়িয়া।

ăs-trĭnġe′, *v. t.* To bind together (*the organic tissue*); to compress ; hence to constipate ; বন্ধন করা ; সঙ্কুচিত করা ; কোষ্ঠবদ্ধ করা।

ăs-trĭn′-ġĕnt, *adj.* & *n.* **1.** Binding ; contracting (opposed to laxative) ; styptic ; as, an *astringent* taste ; ধারক ; কোষ্টবদ্ধকর, সংকোচক; স্তম্ভক, কষায়ান্বিত, কষা। **2.** (*Fig.*) Severe ; austere ; as, *astringent* type of virtue ; (লক্ষণায়) উগ্র, দারুণ ; কঠোর। ***Noun.*** An astringent medicine ; কোষ্টবদ্ধকর ঔষধ, সঙ্কোচক ঔষধ, রক্তরোধক ঔষধ (ডাঃ হিঃ)। **—gen-cy,** *n.* **—ly,** *adv.*

ăs′-trīte, ăs′-trō-īte, *n.* A gem known to the ancients ; star-stone ; প্রাচীনগণের নিকট পরিচিত মণিবিশেষ ; তারকা-মণি।

ăs′-trō-lābe, *n.* An instrument formerly used for taking the altitudes of the sun or stars ; সূর্য্য অথবা নক্ষত্রের উচ্চতামাপক পূর্ব্বকালীন যন্ত্রবিশেষ, নক্ষত্রযন্ত্র (হিঃ কোঃ)।

ăs-trŏl′-ā-trȳ, *n.* The worship of the stars ; নক্ষত্রপূজা, তারার্চ্চনা।

ăs-trŏl′-ō-ġȳ, *n.* **1.** (*Formerly*) Practical astronomy,—also called *Natural Astrology*—the practical application of astronomy to the prediction of events natural *or* moral ; (পূর্ব্বে) ব্যবহারিক জ্যোতিষ, প্রাকৃত জ্যোতিষ—অর্থাৎ ঝঞ্ঝা, বৃষ্টি প্রভৃতি প্রাকৃতিক ঘটনানিচয় এবং মানবের সৎকার্য্য এবং কুকার্য্যের পূর্ব্বাভাস প্রাপ্তির জন্য জ্যোতির্বিজ্ঞানের প্রয়োগ। **2.** The art of judging of the reputed occult and non-physical influences of the stars upon human affairs, also called *judicial Astrology* ; ফলিত জ্যোতিষ, অর্থাৎ গ্রহগণের অবস্থানাদি দ্বারা মানবের শুভাশুভ-নির্ণয় বিদ্যা। **—ger,** *n.* One who practises astrology ; দৈবজ্ঞ, গণক, জ্যোতির্ব্বিদ, গ্রহবিপ্র। **—gize,** *v. t.* & *i.* **—tro-log′-ic, —tro-log′-i-cal,** *adjs.* **—tro-log′-i-cal-ly,** *adv.*

ăs-trŏn′-ō-mȳ, *n.* **1.** The science of the heavenly bodies ; জ্যোতিষ, জ্যোতির্বিদ্যা, জ্যোতির্বিজ্ঞান, সিদ্ধান্ত-জ্যোতিষ (সাঃ পঃ), খগোল-বিদ্যা (আঃ বঃ)। **2.** A treatise on, or text-book of, the science ; জ্যোতির্বিজ্ঞান-বিষয়ক গ্রন্থ। **—mer,** *n.* One skilled in the knowledge of the heavenly bodies ; জ্যোতিষিক (সাঃ পঃ)। **—tro-nom′-ic, tro-nom′-i-cal,** *adjs.* **—tro-nom′-i-cal-ly,** *adv.*

ăs-tūte′, *adj.* Crafty ; cunning ; subtile ; shrewd ; sagacious ; চালাক, বিদগ্ধ ; চতুর ; বিচক্ষণ ; সেয়ানা ; তীক্ষ্ণ-বুদ্ধি। **—ly,** *adv.* **—ness,** *n.*

ă-sŭn′-dẽr, *adv.* Apart ; into parts ; separately ; খণ্ডে খণ্ডে ; খণ্ডশঃ ; পৃথক্ পৃথক্। **As poles asunder**—See POLES. **To tear asunder**—To tear to pieces ; টুক্‌রা টুক্‌রা করিয়া ছিঁড়িয়া ফেলা।

ăs′-wail (-wāl), *n.* The Marhatta name of Indian sloth-bear ; ভল্লুক, ঋক্ষ।

Aswail.

ă-sȳ′-lŭm, *n.* **1.** A sanctuary ; a place of refuge, esp. for debtors and criminals (from which they could not be removed without sacrilege) ; "From every *asylum* ruffians sallied forth to plunder and stab ;" আশ্রয়-স্থল ; ঋণগ্রস্ত বা অপরাধিগণের আশ্রয়-স্থলী। [পূর্ব্বকালে গ্রীস্ প্রভৃতি দেশের দেবালয়ে এবং পরবর্ত্তীকালে ইংলণ্ড প্রভৃতি দেশের ধর্ম্ম-মন্দিরে উক্ত ব্যক্তিগণ আশ্রয়-গ্রহণ করিত।] **2.** A secure place of refuge ; a shelter ; "A port where his ships might find an *asylum*." নির্ব্বিঘ্ন আশ্রয়স্থল, নিবাস ; আশ্রম, সত্র (রাঃ তঃ)। **3.** An institution for the shelter and support of a class of afflicted, destitute, or unfortunate persons, esp. the lunatics ; অনাথাশ্রম, কুষ্ঠাশ্রম, বাতুলাশ্রম, পাগ্‌লা-গারদ, উন্মাদাগার।

ă-sȳm-mĕt′-ri-căl, *adj.* Not symmetrical ; অসমমাত্রিক।

ă-sȳm′-mē-trȳ, *n.* The want of symmetry or proportion between the parts of a thing ; কোন বস্তুর অংশ, সমূহের মধ্যে সামঞ্জস্য বা সমানুপাতের অভাব, অসমমাত্রা, অসৌষ্ঠব।

ăs′-ymp-tōte (-ĭm-), *n.* (*Math.*) A line which approaches nearer and nearer to a given curve but does not meet it within a finite distance ; (গণিত-শাস্ত্র) অসীম-পথ (হিঃ কোঃ), উপগা (ঐ), স্পর্শোন্মুখ (সাঃ পঃ)। **—tŏt′-ic,** *adj.*

ă-sўn'-dĕ-tŏn, *n.* (*Rhet.*) A figure that omits the conjunction; as, I came, I saw, I conquired; (অলঙ্কার-শাস্ত্র) যে অলঙ্কারে সংযোগ-সূচক অব্যয় শব্দের লোপ হয়।

ăt, *prep.* A preposition which expresses the relations of :—**1.** Presence, nearness in place or time, or direction toward ; এই অব্যয় শব্দ দ্বারা নিম্নোক্ত সম্বন্ধ সমূহ প্রকাশিত হয় :—স্থিতি, নৈকট্য অথবা অভিমুখসূচক অব্যয় শব্দ—এ, তে, ইত্যাদি। **2.** Proximity ; নৈকট্য ; as, *at* the door (দ্বারসমীপে) ; *at* school (বিদ্যালয়ে)। **3.** State or condition দশা বা অবস্থা ; as, *at* ease (আরামে) ; **4.** Employment or action ; কাযকর্ম্ম, বৃত্তি ; as, *at* work, *at* play (কার্য্যে ক্রীড়াতে)। **5.** Time, age, or order ; সময়, যুগ, ক্রম ; *at* as, ten o'clock (১০ টায়) : *at* first (প্রথমতঃ, প্রথমে)। **6.** Source, occasion, reason, consequence or effect ; উৎপত্তি, উপলক্ষ, হেতু, পরিণাম, কার্য্য ; as, *qt* the news (সংবাদে) : *at* the command (আদেশে)। **7.** Direction toward an object or end ; অভিমুখ ; as, to aim *at* a mark (লক্ষ্যাভিমুখে)। **At all**—In any degree ; in the least ; "She has no character *at all* ;" বিন্দুমাত্র ; আদৌ, মোটেই। **At arms**—Furnished with arms, used only in the phrase, *a man at arms*) ; অস্ত্রশস্ত্রে সুসজ্জিত। **At grass**—grazing ; ঘাস খাইতেছে অবস্থায়। **At hand**—Near (in time or place) ; সমীপে, নিকটে, কাছে, কাছাকাছি। **At home**—In one's own house ; in one's own country ; as, the government *at home* and abroad ; নিজের বাটীতে, স্বগৃহে ; স্বদেশে। Accessible to callers ; as, he makes it a point to be *at home* on sunday afternoons ; সাক্ষাৎ করার মানসে আগত ব্যক্তিগণকে দর্শনদানে তৎপর। (*Fig.*) Familiar ; conversant ; (*with*) ; as, he was quite *at home with* it ; (লক্ষণায়) সুবিদিত ; সুপরিচিত। **At it**—Hard at work, fighting etc. ; busy ; কঠিন পরিশ্রমে রত, যুদ্ধে রত, ইত্যাদি ; ব্যস্ত। **At large**—At liberty ; unconfined ; as, the prisoner was set *at large* ; মুক্ত ; স্বাধীন ভাবে। Generally ; as the country *at large* must be consulted ; সার্ব্বজনিকভাবে, সাধারণভাবে। **At last**—After long continuance of efforts, hopes, etc. ; অবশেষে, পরিশেষে। **At least**—নিদেন, অন্ততঃ। **At meal**—Eating ; আহারে। **At most**—হদ্দমুদ্দ, বড়জোর। **At once, All at once**—Promptly ; without delay ; এই মুহূর্ত্তে, তাড়াতাড়ি, তৎক্ষণাৎ ; অবিলম্বে। **At pleasure**—With uncontrolled freedom ; অবাধে, স্বচ্ছন্দে, খুসীমত। **At that** (American)—Moreover ; অধিকন্তু, অপিচ। **To come** or **get at**—To reach ; প্রাপ্ত হওয়া, উপনীত হওয়া।

ăt'-ă-băl, *n.* A kind of kettle-drum or tabour used by the Moors ; মূরদিগের দামামা বা নাগারা বিশেষ।

ăt-ă-răx'-i-ă, —răx-ў, *n.* Freedom from disturbance of mind ; উদাসীনতা, ভাববিহীনতা, উদ্বেগশূন্যতা, অক্ষোভ, শান্তভাব।

ăt'-ă-vĭsm, *n.* **1.** Resemblance to remote ancestors rather than to parents ; অতিদূরবর্ত্তী পূর্ব্বপুরুষগণের সহিত সাদৃশ্য, পূর্ব্বপিণ্ডানুকৃতি (হিঃ কোঃ)। **2.** (*Med.*) Recurrence of a disease after intermission of some generations ; (ভৈষজ-শাস্ত্র) কয়েক পুরুষ বিরামের পর কৌলিক পীড়ার পুনরাবির্ভাব, অধিসংক্রান্তি (হিঃ কোঃ), অধিসঞ্চার (ঐ)। **—vis'-tic,** *adj.*

ă-tăx'-ic, *adj.* The natural animal function ; স্বাভাবিক শারীরিক ক্রিয়া।

ăt'-ăx-ў, ă-tăx-i-ă, (*Path.*) Irregularity of animal functions or of the symptoms of disease ; (নিদান-শাস্ত্র) শারীরিক ক্রিয়ার বৈষম্য, রোগলক্ষণনিচয়ের বৈষম্য। **Ataxic fever**—A malignant typhus fever ; এক প্রকার উৎকট সান্নিপাতিক জ্বর। **Locomotor ataxy**—Constitutional unsteadiness in the use of legs, arms, etc. ; হস্তপদাদি সঞ্চালনে স্বাভাবিক অস্থিরতা।

āte, See EAT.

atelier, (*F.*), *n.* A workshop ; a studio ; শিল্পগৃহ, কর্ম্মশালা, কলাভবন ; চিত্রকরদিগের কার্য্য-গৃহ।

ăth-ă-nā'-sў, —si-ă, *n.* Deathlessness ; অমরত্ব।

Ath-ă-nā'-siăn (ăth-), *adj.* Relating to Athanasius, the famous archbishop of Alexandria, in the fourth century ; বিশপ এথেনেসিয়াস্ বা তদীয় মতবাদসম্বন্ধীয়।

ā'-thē-ĭsm, *n.* Disbelief in the existenee of God ; godlessness ; অনীশ্বরবাদ, নিরীশ্বরবাদ ; নাস্তিকতা। **—ist,** *n.* One who disbelieves in the existence of God ; নিরীশ্বরবাদী, অনীশ্বরবাদী, নাস্তিক। **—ist'-ic, —is'-ti-cal,** *adjs.* Pertaining to or containing atheism ; godless ; as, *atheistic* or *atheistical* doctrines ; নিরীশ্বরবাদবিষয়ক, নিরীশ্বর-বাদাত্মক। **—is'-ti-cal-ly,** *adv.*

ăth'-ĕl-ĭng, æth'-ĕl-ĭng (ĕth-), *n.* A member of a noble or royal family ; অভিজাতবংশীয় ব্যক্তি, রাজবংশীয় ব্যক্তি।

ăth-ĕ-næ'-ŭm, (-nē-), **—ăth-ĕ-nē'-ŭm,** *n.* **1.** (*Cap.*) A temple of Athene, at Athens, where scholars and poets read their works and instructed students ; প্রাচীন গ্রীসের শিল্প, কলা এবং সাহিত্যের অধিষ্ঠাত্রী দেবী এথেনীর মন্দির। **2.** A literary or scientific club ; সাহিত্য-পরিষদ্ বা বৈজ্ঞানিক সমিতি। **3.** A reading-room ; a library পাঠকক্ষ, পাঠাগার, গ্রন্থাগার।

A-thē'-nē (ă-),

knowledge, etc., corresponding to the Roman Minerva ; প্রাচীন গ্রীসের বিজ্ঞান, কলাশাস্ত্র প্রভৃতির অধিষ্ঠাত্রী দেবী।

A-thĕ'-ni-ăn (ă-), *adj.* & *n.* Relating to Athens, the capital of Greece ; গ্রীসদেশের রাজধানী এথেন্স্ সম্বন্ধীয়। ***Noun.*** A native of Athens ; এথেন্স্ নগরবাসী। **Atheni-an Bee**—Plato ; গ্রীক্ দার্শনিক প্লেটো। [রচনার মাধুর্য্য ও মনোহারিত্বের জন্য প্লেটো এই আখ্যালাভ করিয়াছেন।]

ăth-ĕr-ō'-mă, *n.* A tumour filled with sebaceous matter ; মেদময় অর্ব্বুদ (জাঃ হিঃ)।

ă-thirst' (-thĕrst), *p.p.* **1.** Thirsty ; তৃষিত, তৃষাতুর, তৃষ্ণার্ত্ত, সতৃষ্ণ। **2.** (*Fig.*) Earnestly desirous or longing (*for*) ; as, *athirst* for fame of war ; (লক্ষণায়) ব্যাকুল, লোলুপ, পিপাসু।

ăth'-lēte, *n.* **1.** A competitor in the physical exercises, (as running, leaping, boxing, wrestling) that formed part of the public games of Greece and Rome); মল্লাদিক্রীড়ায় প্রতিযোগী। **2.** A physically powerful or vigorous man ; ব্যায়ামিক (ভাগঃ), মল্ল, পালোয়ান, কুস্তিগির। **3.** (*Fig.*) An intellectually strong man ; a vigorous contender ; as, a proved *athlete* of debate ; (লক্ষণায়) মহাবুদ্ধিশালী ব্যক্তি ; শক্তিসম্পন্ন তর্ক-যোদ্ধা।

ăth-lĕt'-ic, *adj.* & *n.* **1.** Pertaining to athlets or the exercises practised by them ; মল্ল-সম্বন্ধীয়, ব্যায়াম-সম্বন্ধীয়। **2.** Physically powerful ; বলশালী, বলবান। ***Noun.*** *(Pl.)* The practice of physical exercises ; ব্যায়ামানুশীলন। **—i-cal-ly,** *adv.* **—i-cism,** *n.* **Athletic sports**—মল্লক্রীড়া।

at home, *n.* A reception of guests (within certain hours) at one's home ; (নির্দ্দিষ্ট কালের মধ্যে) নিমন্ত্রিত ব্যক্তিদিগের অভ্যর্থনা, প্রীতি সম্মিলনী।

ă-thwart', *prep.* & *adv.* **1.** Across ; from side to side of ; "*Athwart* the thicket lone ;" (বিজন কুঞ্জের এধারে ওধারে) ; আড়ভাবে, টের্‌চা ; এপাশে ওপাশে। **2.** (*Naut.*) Across the line of a ship's course ; as, a fleet standing *athwart* our course ; (নৌ-বিদ্যা) কোন জাহাজের গমনপথের সহিত আড়ভাবে। ***Adv.*** **1.** Across ; from side to side, usually obliquely ; কোণাকোণিভাবে ; তির্য্যগ্‌ভাবে। **2.** Crosswise ; "All *athwart* there come a post from Wales....." আড়ভাবে। **Athwart hawse**—Across the stem of another ship at anchor ; নঙ্গরবদ্ধ অপর জাহাজের অগ্রভাগের পাশ কাটিয়া।

ă-tilt', *adv.* Set on tilt ; অশ্বারোহণে উদ্যত-শূল হইয়া। **To run** or **ride atilt**—In encounter on horseback with thrust of lance, (now usually figurative of controversial encounters, foll. by *at, with, against*); অশ্বোপরি উদ্যত-শূল হইয়া।

ăt-lăn'-tēs, *n. pl.* (*Arch.*) Figures or half-figures of men used instead of columns to support an entablature ; (স্থপতি-বিদ্যা) অট্টালিকার মাথাড়ীর অবলম্বন-স্তম্ভ স্বরূপ পূর্ণ বা অর্দ্ধোদ্গত মানবমূর্ত্তি।

At-lăn'-tic (ăt-), *adj.* & *n.* Pertaining to Mount Atlas on which the heavens were fabled to rest ; hence applied to the ocean between Europe and Africa on the east and America on the west ; অতলান্তিক। ***Noun.*** The Atlantic Ocean ; অতলান্তিক মহাসাগর।

At-lăn'-tis (ăt-), *n.* According to the ancients, a vast island in the Atlantic Ocean ; প্রাচীন গ্রীক্ লেখকদিগের মতানুসারে অতলান্তিক মহাসাগরগর্ভে নিমগ্ন মহাদ্বীপ বিশেষ। **New Atlantis**—The title of a Lord Bacon's book depicting an ideal commonwealth ; আদর্শ প্রজাতন্ত্রের বর্ণনা-সম্বলিত লর্ড বেকনকৃত গ্রন্থবিশেষ।

At'-lăs (ăt-), *n.* **1.** One of the Titans who attempted to storm heaven, and was condemned to bear the earth on his shoulders ; গ্রীক পুরাণানুসারে যে সমস্ত দৈত্য স্বর্গরাজ্য বিধ্বস্ত করিতে চেষ্টা করে, তাহাদের অন্যতম—দেবরাজ জোভ্ এট্‌লাসের স্কন্ধে পৃথিবী চাপাইয়া দিয়া তাহাকে শাস্তি প্রদান করেন। **2.** A volume of maps ; দেশালেখ্যমালা, ভূচিত্রাবলী, মানচিত্রাবলী। **3.** A large size of drawing-paper (34″ × 26″) ; এক প্রকার বড় আকারের চিত্র আঁকিবার কাগজ। **4.** A silk-satin manufactured in the East ; এক প্রকার রেশমী সাটিন। **5.** (*Physiol.*) The uppermost cervical vertebra, supporting the skull ; (শারীর-বিজ্ঞান) করোটির অবলম্বনস্বরূপ মেরু-দণ্ডের অগ্রভাগ, গ্রীবার প্রথম কশেরুকা।

ăt'-mŏs-phēre, *n.* **1.** The spheroidal gaseous envelope surrounding any heavenly body, esp. the mass of aeriform fluid surrounding the earth ; যে কোন জ্যোতিষ্কের চতুষ্পার্শ্ববর্ত্তী বাষ্প-মণ্ডল, বায়ুমণ্ডল (সাঃ পঃ), অন্তরীক্ষমণ্ডল (ঐ), অন্তরীক্ষ (ঐ)। **2.** Any gaseous medium ; as, an *atmosphere* of cold oxygen ; যে কোন বাষ্পময় মধ্যবর্ত্তী বস্তু। **3.** The air of any particular place ; as, the suffocating *atmosphere* of a small apartment ; কোন বিশেষ স্থানের বায়ু। **4.** (*Fig.*) Mental or moral environment ; as, an *atmposhere* of freedom ; (লক্ষণায়) নৈতিক বা মানসিক পারিপার্শ্বিক অবস্থা বা অবস্থা-বেষ্টনী। **5.** The pressure of 15lbs on a square inch ; as, Hydrogen was liquefied under a pressure 650 *atmospheres* ; প্রতিবর্গ-ইঞ্চ পরিমিত স্থানে ১৫ পাউণ্ড চাপ। **—pher'-ic, —pher'-i-cal,** *adjs.*

Atmospheric stone—Meteor; ব্যোমাশ্ম (সাঃ পঃ)।

ă-tŏll′, *n.* A ring-shaped coral-reef enclosing a lagoon; সমুদ্র-তীরস্থ জলাশয়বেষ্টক প্রবাল-বলয়, অবাল (সাঃ পঃ)।

ăt′-ŏm, *n.* **1.** A body too small to be divided; পরমাণু। **2.** Any thing extremely small; a minute quantity; as, there was not an *atom* of water: not an *atom* of sense; অতি ক্ষুদ্র পরিমাণ, কণা। **—ism**, *n.* Same as, ATOMIC PHILOSOPHY, see under ATOMIC. **—ist**, *n.* A holder of atomic theory or philosophy; পরমাণুবাদী, পরমাণু-সিদ্ধান্ত সমর্থক। **—is-tic**, *adj.* Of atomic philosophy; পরমাণুবাদ-বিষয়ক। **—i-za′-tion**, *n.* **—ize**, *v. t.* To reduce to atoms; পরমাণুতে পরিণত করা। **—i-zer**, *n.* (*Med.*) An instrument for reducing liquids to fine spray; (ভৈষজ্য-শাস্ত্র) যে যন্ত্রদ্বারা তরল পদার্থ (জল, পুষ্পসার, প্রভৃতি) সূক্ষ্ম কণিকাকারে পরিণত হয়।

Atomizer.

Group of atoms—আণবিক ব্যূহ।

ă-tŏm′-ĭc, *adj.* Pertaining to, consisting of, atoms; পরমাণু-বিষয়ক, পরমাণুময়। **—i-cal-ly**, *adv.* **Atomic philosophy**—The doctrine of the formation of all things from individual particles endued with gravity and motion; 'বিশ্বের যাবতীয় পদার্থ পরমাণ সমবায়ে গঠিত—(কণাদের বৈশেষিক দর্শনের অনুকরণে) ডেমক্রিটাস প্রবর্ত্তিত উক্তরূপ দার্শনিক বাদবিশেষ, পরমাণুবাদ (হিঃ কোঃ)। (*Chem.*) **Atomic theory**—The theory that all elements consist of individual atoms of definite relative weight and that atoms of different elements unite with each other in fixed proportions; বিভিন্ন পদার্থের পরমাণু সমূহ নির্দ্দিষ্ট অনুপাতে পরস্পরের সহিত সম্মিলিত হয়—এবম্বিধ রাসায়নিক মতবাদ, পরমাণু-সিদ্ধান্ত (হিঃ কোঃ)। **Atomic weight**—The weight of an atom of an element, as compared with that of an atom of hydrogen, taken as standard; উদজান বাষ্পের এক পরমাণুর সহিত তুলনায় কোন পদার্থের এক পরমাণুর গুরুত্ব, পরমাণুভার (হিঃ কোঃ)।

ăt-ŏ-mĭc′-ĭ-tȳ, *n.* The combining capacity of an element, *i. e.* the number of atoms of hydrogen with which one of its atoms normally combines; equivalence; পরমাণুযোগমান (হিঃ কোঃ), পরমাণুশক্তি (ঐ), পরমাণুতা (ঐ); সংযোগশক্তিসাম্য।

ăt′-ŏm-ȳ, *n.* **1.** An atom; a mote; as, a beam of light crowded with driving *atomies*; পরমাণু; ত্রস রেণু। **2.** A tiny being; a pigmy; "You spiteful little *atomy*"; অতিসূক্ষ্মজীব; অতি ক্ষুদ্রকায় মানব। **3.** An imaciated body; a skeleton; "You starved blood hound! Thou *atomy* thou!" কঙ্কালসার-দেহ; নর-কঙ্কাল।

ă-tōne′, *v. t.* & *i.* **1.** To expiate; to make amends for (a fault or loss); প্রায়শ্চিত্ত করা; ক্ষতিপূরণ করা, প্রতিবিধান করা। **2.** To bring into concord; to reconcile; "In him God and man were perfectly *atoned*"; ঐক্য করা; সামঞ্জস্য বিধান করা। ***Verb i.*** To harmonize; "They well *atone* with this more serious mood;" সঙ্গতি বিশিষ্ট হওয়া। **—ment**, *n.* **1.** (*Originally properly at-one-ment*); agreement; (rare); (খুব প্রচলিত নহে) ঐক্য। **2.** Amends; expiation; ক্ষতিপূরণ; প্রায়শ্চিত্ত। **3.** (*Theol.*) The reconciliation of God and man by means of the incarnation and death of Jesus Christ; reconciliation; (খৃষ্টীয় ধর্ম্ম-শাস্ত্র) যীশুখৃষ্টের নরকলেবর ধারণ ও মৃত্যুর ফলে ঈশ্বরের সহিত মানবের পুনর্ম্মিলন; পুনর্ম্মিলন।

at one, *adv. phr.* **1.** In agreement with each other; as, to make *at-one*; একমতে, মতৈক্যে। **2.** Of the same opinion; as, on these points we are *at one*; একমতাবলম্বী।

ă-tŏn′-ĭc, *adj.* & *n.* **1.** (*Gram.*) Unaccented; as, an *atonic* vowel; (ব্যাকরণ) অস্বরিত। **2.** (*Path.*) Wanting tone or vital energy; as, an *atonic* disease; (নিদান-শাস্ত্র) বলহীন, জীবনীশক্তিহীন। ***Noun.*** An unaccented word, (esp. in *Gr. Gram.*); অস্বরিত শব্দ।

ăt′-ŏ-nȳ, *n.* (*Path.*) Want of tone or vital energy; (নিদান-শাস্ত্র) নির্বীর্য্যতা, দৌর্ব্বল্য, জীবনীশক্তি-হীনতা। **Atony of the bladder**—বস্তিকুণ্ড (সাঃ পঃ)।

ă-tŏp′, *adv.* & *prep.* At the top; above; as, a black mass *atop*; শীর্ষে; ঊর্দ্ধে। ***Prep.*** On the top of; as, rushing *atop* the waves; উপরে।

ăt-ră-bĭl′-ious (-yŭs), *adj.* Affected by black bile; melancholy; acrimonious; পিত্তরোগগ্রস্ত; বিষণ্ণঃ কটুস্বভাব। **—ness**, *n.*

ăt-ră-mĕn′-tăl, *adj.* Inky; as, black as ink; as, *atramental* galls; মসীময়; মসীকৃষ্ণ। **At′-ra-ment**, *n.*

ă-trĭp′, *adv.* (*Naut.*) (Of anchor) Just lifted from the ground in weighing; (নৌ-বিদ্যা) (নঙ্গর-সম্বন্ধে) ভূমি হইতে সবে মাত্র উত্তোলিত।

ā′-trĭ-ŭm, *n.* (*Pl.* ATRIA; ATRIUMS. **1.** The central court of a Roman house; প্রাচীন রোমবাসিগণের ভবনের প্রধান অঙ্গন। **2.** A covered portico; esp. before a church-door; আচ্ছাদিত গাড়ীবারান্দা, বিশেষত

গির্জ্জার সম্মুখস্থিত গাড়ী বারান্দা। **3.** (*Anat.*) The main cavity of the auricle of the heart ; (শারীর সংস্থান-বিদ্যা) হৃৎ-কোষ্ঠের প্রধান গহ্বর।

ă-trō′-cious (-shŭs), *adj.* **1.** Heinously wicked ; execrable ; আসুর, নৃশংস ; নিরতিশয় মন্দ, ঘোরপাপী। **2.** (*Colloq.*) Very bad ; as, *atrocious* handwriting ; (চলিত ভাষায়) ভারি বদ, অতি বিশ্রী। **—ly,** *adv.* **—ness,** *n.*

ă-trŏc′-i-tȳ, *n.* **1.** Heinous wickedness ; নৃশংসতা, বীভৎসতা, ক্রূরতা। **2.** (Often used in the *pl.*) Excessively cruel deeds ; "The *atrocities* which attend a victory ;" ঘোর নৃশংস কার্য্য। **3.** (*Colloq.*) A very bad blunder ; as, *atrocities* committed in spelling ; (চলিত ভাষায়) বিষম ভুল, মারাত্মক ভুল।

ăt′-rō-phȳ, *n., v. t. & i.* A wasting away through imperfect nourishment ; emaciation ; ক্ষীণতা ; অঙ্গ-কৃশতা, একাঙ্গ বা সর্ব্বাঙ্গের শীর্ণতা। ***Verb t. & i.*** To cause to waste away, or become abortive ; ক্ষয়িত করা বা হওয়া ; নিষ্ফল হওয়া।

ăt′-rō-pin, ăt′-rō-pīne, *n.* A poisonous alkaloid found in the deadly night-shade ; বেলেডোনা হইতে প্রাপ্ত বিষাক্ত ক্ষারপদার্থ বিশেষ। [এই ঔষধ প্রয়োগে চক্ষুর তারকা বিস্তারিত হয়।]

ăt-tăch′, *v. t. & i.* **1.** (*Law*) To seize (a person or property) by the authority of a writ of attachment ; (আইন) ঋণের দায়ে কোন ব্যক্তিকে গ্রেপ্তার করা বা তদীয় সম্পত্তি ক্রোক করা। **2.** To tack on ; to fasten (a thing *to* another) ; to fix (anything immaterial) *to* ; সংলগ্ন করা ; বাঁধা, সংবদ্ধ করা, বদ্ধ করা ; সংযোগ করা, আঁটা (*colloq.*)। **3.** To join *oneself to* (a company, expedition, etc.) ; যোগদান করা। **4.** To win or attract the attachment of ; (with *to*) ; "God by various ties *attaches* man to man ;" অনুরাগ আকর্ষণ করা, অনুরাগ লাভ করা, স্নেহ বা প্রীতিলাভ করা। **5.** To add as an attribute ; to attribute ; as, the importance they *attach* to their own service ; গুণ বা ধর্ম্মস্বরূপ সংযোগ করা ; আরোপ করা। ***Verb i.*** (With *to*) To adhere ; to be joined or bound up with ; to fall or come *upon* ; as, the loss should *attach* upon the delinquency ; সংযুক্ত হওয়া, সংবদ্ধ হওয়া, সংলগ্ন হওয়া, সংশ্লিষ্ট হওয়া ; বিজড়িত হওয়া ; পতিত হওয়া, আপতিত হওয়া। **—a-ble,** *adj.* ক্রোকযোগ্য। **To attach importance, weight, etc.**—To hold a thing to be of great importance or value ; গুরুতর মনে করা, মূল্যবান জ্ঞান করা।

ăt-tâ-che′ (-shā), (*F.*), *n.* One attached to the suite of an ambassador ; সহযোগী রাজদূত।

ăt-tăch′-mĕnt, *n.* **1.** The act of fastening or taking on ; connexion ; বন্ধন ; সংযোজন। **2.** Affection ; devotion ; fidelity ; অনুরাগ, আসক্তি, প্রসক্তি, রাগ, অনুরক্তি, সম্প্রীতি, সঙ্গ, আসঙ্গ ; নিষ্ঠা ; সত্যানুরাগ। **3.** Something attached to any object (as a machine, etc.) ; as, a sewing-machine *attachment* ; সংস্পৃষ্ট বা সংসক্ত বস্তু। **4.** A legal seizure ; the writ commanding such a seizure ; ক্রোক ; ক্রোকের পরওয়ানা।

ăt-tăck′, *v. t. & n.* (*Lit. & Fig.*) **1.** To fall upon with force or arms ; to assault ; (শব্দানুযায়ী এবং লক্ষণায়) আপতিত হওয়া ; আক্রমণ করা। **2.** (Of disease) To seize upon ; to begin to affect ; (of physical agents) to begin to destroy ; to waste ; (রোগাদি-সম্পর্কে) আক্রমণ করা ; সঞ্চার হওয়া ; (জড়বস্তু সম্পর্কে) ক্ষয় করিতে আরম্ভ করা ; ক্ষয় করা। ***Noun.* 1.** An offensive operation ; an onset ; (also *fig.*) ; as, an *attack* upon a character ; আক্রমণ, অভিগ্রহ (মঃ উঃ)। **2.** A fit or bout of illness ; as, an *attack* of giddiness ; পীড়ার আক্রমণ।

ăt-tain′ (-tān), *v. t. & i.* To reach by effort ; to gain ; to achieve or accomplish ; উদ্যমদ্বারা লাভ করা ; প্রাপ্ত হওয়া ; সম্পাদন করা, সমাধা করা। ***Verb i.*** (With *to*) To arrive at ; to reach ; পৌঁছা ; প্রাপ্ত হওয়া। **—a-bil′-i-ty,** *n.* **—a-ble,** *adj.* Capable of being attained ; লভ্য, গম্য, সাধ্য, আয়ত্তগম্য, প্রাপ্তব্য। **—a-ble-ness,** *n.* **To attain majority**—To attain full age (21 years) ; সাবালক হওয়া, বয়ঃপ্রাপ্ত হওয়া, প্রাপ্ত-ব্যবহার হওয়া।

ăt-tain′-dêr (-tān-), *n.* The legal consequences of judgment of death or outlawry pronounced in respect of treason or felony : *viz* forfeiture of estates, extinction of civil rights, etc. ; রাজবিদ্রোহাদি গুরুতর অপরাধে শাস্তিপ্রাপ্ত ব্যক্তির সম্পত্তি বাজেয়াপ্তি ও স্বত্বাধিকার বিলোপ প্রভৃতি।

ăt-tain′-mĕnt (-tān-), *n.* **1.** The act of reaching or acquiring by effort ; প্রাপ্তি, সিদ্ধি, লাভ, অবাপ্তি। **2.** Anything acquired by continued effort ; esp. a personal accomplishment ; অনবরত চেষ্টার ফলে যাহা লব্ধ বা প্রাপ্ত হইয়াছে, অর্জ্জন ; বিশেষতঃ অর্জ্জিত গুণ।

ăt-taint′ (-tānt), *v.t.* **1.** To subject to attainder ; রাজবিদ্রোহাদি গুরুতর অপরাধে দোষী করা। **2.** To stain ; to sully (lustre, purity, etc.) ; কলঙ্কিত করা ; কলুষিত করা। **3.** To seize upon or attack, as a disease ; to infect with (corruption, poison, etc.) ; (রোগ-সম্পর্কে) আক্রমণ করা ; বিষজনক বা হানিকর পদার্থদ্বারা দূষিত করা।

ăt′-tăr, *n.* [Pers. *atar,* essence Arab. *utur,* aroma ; cf. otto.]

A fragrant essential oil from rose-petals ; আতর।

ăt-tĕm'-pêr, *v. t.* **1.** To qualify by admixture ; as, to *attemper* spirits with water ; মিশ্রণদ্বারা প্রশমিত করা। **2.** To modify the temperature of ; as, the shadow of the tree *attempered* the sunshine ; তাপ প্রশমিত করা। **3.** To mitigate or assuage (passion, harshness) ; to soothe ; উপশম করা; প্রশমিত করা। **4.** To make fit or suitable (*to*) ; as, discourses *attempered* to hearer's capacities ; to attune *to* ; "High airs *attempered* to vocal strings ;" উপযুক্ত করা, উপযোগী করা ; সুর মিলান, সঙ্গত করা। **—ment,** *n.*

ăt-tempt' (-tĕmt), *v. t.* & *n.* **1.** To use one's endeavour to do (some action) ; to try ; যত্ন করা ; চেষ্টা করা। **2.** To venture upon ; as, to *attempt* the seas ; সাহসে ভর করিয়া সঙ্কটসঙ্কুল কার্য্যে প্রবৃত্ত হওয়া। **3.** To make an attack or assault *upon* ; as, to *attempt* the enemy's camp ; আক্রমণ করা। ***Noun.*** An endeavour ; an effort to gain a point ; an attack ; প্রয়াস, চেষ্টা ; উদ্যোগ, যত্ন, প্রযত্ন ; আক্রমণ। **To attempt the life of**—To try to kill ; কোন ব্যক্তির বধসাধনে চেষ্টা করা।

ăt-tĕnd', *v. t.* & *i.* **1.** To turn one's ear to ; "My tale *attend* ;" to turn the mind to ; to consider ; as, I shall *attend* your request ; কর্ণপাত করা ; অবধান করা ; বিবেচনা করা। **2.** To minister to the sick ; as, hired nurses *attended* infected people ; to pay professional visits to a patient, as a medical man ; রোগীর শুশ্রূষা করা ; চিকিৎসকরূপে রোগী দেখিতে যাওয়া। **3.** To wait upon, as a servant or attendant ; to escort or accompany (for rendering service) ; as, His Highness was *attended* by a train of nobles ; পরিচর্য্যা করা, খিদমৎ করা (*Colloq.*) ; শরীর রক্ষা করা, অনুযাত্রী হওয়া। **4.** (Of things) To follow close upon ; to accompany ; as, a measure *attended* with ill effects ; (বস্তু-সম্পর্কে) অনুগমন করা ; সহকৃত হওয়া। **5.** To be present at (a church, school, lecture, etc.) ; উপস্থিত থাকা। ***Verb i.*** **1.** To turn the energies *to* ; to apply oneself *to* ; as, to *attend* diligently *to* work ; to take care of ; (with *to*) ; as, the clergyman has his own flock to *attend to* ; শক্তি প্রয়োগ করা ; প্রবৃত্ত হওয়া ; তত্ত্বাবধান করা। **2.** To be ready for service ; to be in waiting ; (with *on, upon*) ; as, *attending on* drunk people ; to *attend upon* the committee ; সেবার্থ প্রস্তুত হওয়া ; পরিচর্য্যা করা।

ăt-tĕnd'-ănce, *n.* **1.** The act of attending or waiting on ; the act of being present at ; (attendance *on* or *upon* person, *at* lecture) ; মনোযোগ, অবধান, উপচার (হেঃ চিঃ), পরিচর্য্যা, শুশ্রূষা ; উপস্থিতি। **2.** The number of persons present ; as, a greatly increased *attendance* ; উপস্থিত ব্যক্তিগণের সংখ্যা। **3.** A train ; a retinue ; সহচরবর্গ ; অনুযায়িবর্গ (রঃ), অনুযাত্রিদল। **To dance attendance on**—See DANCE. **In attendance**—Waiting upon ; শুশ্রূষারত, পরিচর্য্যারত। **Attendance-officer**—One whose duty it is to see that children attend school ; বালকবালিকাগণ নিয়মমত বিদ্যালয়ে উপস্থিত হয় কি না—এই বিষয় যিনি দৃষ্টি রাখেন।

ăt-tĕnd'-ănt, *n.* & *adj.* **1.** One who waits upon or accompanies another ; a servant ; as, two ladies with *attendants* aided our escape ; অনুযায়ী, অনুচর, পরিচর, শুশ্রূষাকারী ; খিদমৎগার (*colloq.*), পরিচারক। **2.** An accompaniment ; a concomitant ; as, melancholy is a common *attendant* on poetic genius ; আনুষঙ্গিক বস্তু ; সহচর। ***Adj.*** **1.** Accompanying ; closely consequent ; (*on, upon*) ; as, *attendant* circumstances ; আনুষঙ্গিক ; সহগামী। **2.** Waiting upon ; ministrant ; (*on, upon*) ; as, gentlemen *attendant* on a great Earl ; পরিচর্য্যারত ; সেবারত। **3.** Present ; as, an *attendant* crowd ; সমাগত, উপস্থিত।

ăt-tĕn'-tion, *n.* **1.** The act or state of attending ; earnest regard or consideration ; মনোযোগ প্রদান, মনোযোগ, মনোনিবেশ ; শ্রদ্ধা, সম্মান। **2.** Observant care ; notice ; as, to soften their rude manners by a benignant *attention* to their morals ; দৃষ্টি ; লক্ষ্য, অবধান। **3.** (*Pl.*) Ceremonious politeness ; courtesy ; as, he received all the *attentions* which hospitality could devise : *attentions* paid to a stranger ; আদর, সমাদর, যত্ন ; শিষ্টাচার। **To come to** or **stand at attention**—To assume a prepared military attitude ; যুদ্ধার্থে প্রস্তুতভাবে অবস্থান করা। **To pay attention** or **one's attentions to**—To court ; বিবাহার্থ প্রেমোপাসনা করা।

ăt-tĕn'-tive, *adj.* **1.** Steadily applying one's mind ; heedful ; observant ; মনোযোগী ; অবহিত, অভিনিবিষ্ট, একাগ্রচিত্ত ; পর্য্যবেক্ষণশীল। **2.** Polite ; courteous ; as, very *attentive* to the ladies ; শিষ্ট ; শিষ্টাচারসম্পন্ন। **—ly,** *adv.* In an attentive manner ; মনোযোগপূর্ব্বক, প্রণিধান পূর্ব্বক, সাবহিত, নিবিষ্টমনে, মনোনিবেশপূর্ব্বক, মনোযোগপূর্ব্বক, একাগ্রচিত্তে। **—ness,** *n.*

ăt-tĕn'-ū-ănt, *adj.* & *n.* Making thin, as fluids ; diluting ; বিদ্রাবক, বিলায়ক ; কৃশকারক, তনুকরণশীল। ***Noun.*** A medicine that dilutes the fluids ; বিদ্রাবক ঔষধ।

ăt-tĕn'-ū-ate (-āt), *v.t.* & *i.* **1.** To

make thin or slender ; পাতলা করা, অনিবিড় করা। **2.** To make thin in consistency ; to render less dense ; as, salt may *attenuate* earth ; অঘন করা। **3.** To reduce in force, effect, amount, etc. ; as, to *attenuate* the tediousness : to *attenuate* appetite, emotion ; হ্রাস করা, লাঘব করা। ***Verb i.*** To become thinner or weaker ; কৃশতর বা দুর্ব্বল হওয়া। **—a-ted,** *adj.* **—a′-tion,** *n.* **1.** The act of making thin or slender ; emaciation ; কর্শন ; তনুকরণ (মঃ উঃ)। **2.** Diminution of density ; diminution in force, intensity, etc. ; ঘনত্ব-হ্রাস ; শক্তি-লাঘব।

ăt-tĕn′-ū-āte, *adj.* Slender ; rarefied ; refined ; সূক্ষ্ম, কৃশ ; বিরল; মার্জ্জিত।

ăt-tĕst′, *v. t.* & *i.* **1.** To bear witness to ; to certify ; as, to *attest* the copy of a document ; সাক্ষ্যদ্বারা সমর্থন করা ; সত্য বলিয়া নির্দ্দেশ করা। **2.** To put a person on oath or solemn declaration ; কোন ব্যক্তিকে সত্য প্রতিজ্ঞা করান। **3.** To be proof of ; to vouch for ; "The ruins of Palmyra *attest* its ancient magnificence" ; কোন বিষয়ে সাক্ষ্য বা প্রমাণ প্রদর্শন করা ; নিশ্চয় করিয়া বলা। ***Verb i.*** To bear witness *to* ; সাক্ষ্য দেওয়া। **—er, —or,** *ns.*

ăt-tĕs-tā′-tion, *n.* **1.** The act of testifying ; evidence ; as, the truth appears from the *attestation* of witnesses ; a formal declaration by signature, oath, etc. ; সত্যতা-প্রতিপাদন ; প্রমাণ ; তস্‌দিক (*Colloq.*)। **2.** Administration of an oath ; শপথ-গ্রহণ করান। **Attestation of the court**—আদালতের সহিমোহরযুক্ত করণ।

At′-tic (ăt-), *adj.* & *n.* Of or pertaining to Attica, in Greece, or to its principal city Athens ; গ্রীসদেশস্থ এটিকা বা তদ্দেশের প্রধাননগরী এথেন্স্‌ সম্বন্ধীয়। ***Noun.*** Attic dialect ; Greek spoken by the Athenians ; এটিকার উপভাষা ; এথেন্সে কথিত গ্রীকভাষা। **Attic Bee**—Sophocles ; গ্রীসদেশীয় প্রসিদ্ধ নাট্যকার সফোক্লিস্‌। [রচনার মাধুর্য্য ও মনোহারিত্ব হেতু ইনি এই আখ্যা প্রাপ্ত হইয়াছিলেন।] **Attic faith**—An inviolable faith ; অলঙ্ঘ্য অঙ্গীকার। **Attic Muse**—Xenophon ; গ্রীক্‌ ঐতিহাসিক জেনোফন্‌। **Attic order**—A term applied to the small pillars decorating a low story at the top of a building ; কোন অট্টালিকার উপরিভাগস্থ অনুচ্চ-তলের ভূষা-স্বরূপ ক্ষুদ্রস্তম্ভশ্রেণী। **Attic salt, Attic wit**—Refined wit ; মার্জ্জিত রসিকতা। **Attic style**—A pure, chaste and elegant style ; বিশুদ্ধ, মার্জ্জিত এবং মাধুর্য্য-পূর্ণ রচনাপদ্ধতি।

ăt′-tic, *n.* A low story erected over a principal generally decorated with pilasters and a cornice ; the highest story of a house, or a room in it ; a garret ; চন্দ্রপ্রাসাদ (কথাঃ সং,) চন্দ্রশালা (বৃঃ সং) ; প্রাসাদাদির সর্ব্বোচ্চ তল ; চিলেঘর।

ăt′-ti-cĭsm, *n.* **1.** The style and idiom of Athens ; এথিনীয় ভাষার রচনা-পদ্ধতি বা রীতিসিদ্ধ প্রয়োগ। **2.** Refined amenity of speech ; সভ্যজনোচিত সুমার্জ্জিত ভাষা। **3.** Attachment to Athens ; এথেন্স্‌ নগরীর প্রতি অনুরাগ। **—cize,** *v. t.*

ăt-tīre′, *v. t.* & *n.* To dress ; to array ; to adorn (with elegant or splendid garments) ; সজ্জিত করা ; ভূষিত করা ; (সমুজ্জ্বল পরিচ্ছদে) সুশোভিত করা। ***Noun.*** Dress ; clothes ; apparel, esp. ornamental clothing ; পোষাক ; বসন, বাস ; পরিচ্ছদ, বেশ, সাজ। **—ment, —tir′-ing,** *ns.*

ăt′-ti-tūde, *n.* **1.** A position assumed to serve a purpose ; a posture ; ঢঙ্গ, ভঙ্গি, হাবভাব ; সংস্থিতি, অঙ্গস্থিতি। **2.** Settled behaviour (indicating feeling or opinion) ; as, an *attitude* of devotion ; ভাব। **—tu′-di-nal,** *adj.* **Attitude of mind**—Settled mode of thinking ; মানসিকভাব। **To strike an attitude**—To assume an affected attitude ; to assume it theatrically ; কৃত্রিম হাবভাব বা ভঙ্গী ধারণ করা ; নাটকোচিত ভাবভঙ্গী ধারণ করা।

ăt-ti-tū′-di-nīze, *v. t.* To strike an attitude ; to speak, write or behave affectedly ; "In every line he wrote Cicero was attitudinizing for effect ;" কৃত্রিম হাবভাব বা ভঙ্গি প্রদর্শন করা ; কৃত্রিম ভাবে লিখা বলা বা আচরণ করা।

ăt-tor′-ney (-têr-nî), *n.* **1.** One appointed to act for another in business or legal matters ; আম্‌মোক্তার। **2.** A practitioner in a court of law, preparing the case for the barrister or counsel whose privilege it is to plead and argue ; (also called public attorney or attorney-at-law) ; যে আইনব্যবসায়ী কৌঁসুলিদিগের জন্য মোকদ্দমাসংক্রান্ত কাগজপত্র প্রস্তুত করেন এবং সময়বিশেষে পক্ষসমর্থনও করিয়া থাকেন। **—ship,** *n.* **Attorney-General**—A legal officer empowered to act in all cases in which the state is a party ; ইংলণ্ডের সর্ব্বপ্রধান সরকারী কৌঁসুলি। **Power of attorney**—আম্‌মোক্তারনামা। **Special power of attorney**—খাস আম্‌মোক্তারনামা।

ăt-trăct′, *v. t.* **1.** To draw to or toward ; আকর্ষণ করা, প্রত্যাকর্ষণ করা। **2.** To draw forth and fix upon oneself (mind, eyes, etc.) ; to invite or allure ; as, to *attract* notice : to *attract* admirers ; চিত্তহরণ করা ; চিত্তাকর্ষণ করা, প্রলুব্ধ করা। **—a-bil′-i-ty,** *n.* **—a-ble,** *adj.*

ăt-trăc′-tion, *n.* **1.** The act or faculty of drawing to oneself ; আকর্ষণ, টান (*colloq.*)। **2.** The force which draws, or tends to draw, bodies or their particles to each other ; আকর্ষণী-শক্তি। **3.** That which attracts ; (*lit.* & *fig.*) an attracting quality ; as, she had new *attractions* every time he saw her ; আকর্ষণকারী, আকর্ষক ; (শব্দানুযায়ী এবং লক্ষণায়) মনোমুগ্ধকর গুণ, স্ত্রীলোকের চিত্তাকর্ষক মাধুর্য্য। **—tive,** *adj.* Having the power of attracting ; (esp. *fig.*) alluring ; as, *attractive* graces, eyes ; চিত্তহারী, চিত্তাকর্ষক, মনোহারী ; লোভনীয়। **—tive-ly,** *adv.* **—tive-ness,** *n.* (*Phys.*) **Adhesive attraction**—(পদার্থ-বিজ্ঞান) সংলগ্নাকর্ষণ (হিঃ কোঃ)। **Attraction of gravitation**—গুরুত্বাকর্ষণ (হিঃ কোঃ)। **Capillary attraction**—কৈশিকাকর্ষণ। **Chemical attraction**—রাসায়নিক আকর্ষণ (হিঃ কোঃ)। **Magnetic attraction**—চুম্বকাকর্ষণ (হিঃ কোঃ)। **Molecular attraction**—আণবিক আকর্ষণ।

ăt′-tri-būte, *n.* **1.** A quality or property ; গুণ, ধর্ম্ম। **2.** (*Gram.*) An attributive word ; (ব্যাকরণ) গুণবাচক শব্দ। **3.** A characteristic quality ; স্বভাবসিদ্ধ গুণ। **4.** (*Fine arts*) A symbol of office or dignity attached to any figure ; as, the trident is the *attribute* of Shiva ; (ললিত কলা) দেবদেবী প্রভৃতির চিত্রাদিতে সংযোজিত কার্য্য বা মর্য্যাদার নিদর্শন চিহ্ন।

ăt-trib′-ūte, *v. t.* **1.** To ascribe as belonging or appropriate *to* ; to refer effect *to* its cause ; আরোপ করা ; কারণ নির্দ্দেশ করা। **2.** To assign *to* (time or place) ; (সময় বা স্থান) নির্দ্দেশ করা। **—tri-bu′-tion,** *n.* **1.** The act of attributing ; that which is ascribed ; আরোপণ ; আরোপিত বিষয়। **2.** Authority or function granted to a ruler, court, etc. ; as, within the limits of its *attributions* it makes laws ; শাসনকর্ত্তা, আদালত প্রভৃতির উপর অর্পিত ক্ষমতা বা কর্ত্তব্যকার্য্য। **—ta-ble,** *adj.* Ascribable ; আরোপ্য।

ăt-trib′-ū-tive, *adj.* & *n.* Pertaining to, or expressing, an attribute ; গুণাত্মক, গুণবাচক। ***Noun.*** (*Gram.*) A word expressing an attribute, (usually an adjective or its equivalent) ; (ব্যাকরণ) বিশেষণ প্রভৃতি গুণবাচক শব্দ। **—ly,** *adv.*

ăt-tri′-tion, *n.* **1.** The act of rubbing out ; abrasion ; ঘর্ষণ ; ঘর্ষণজনিত ক্ষয়। **2.** (*Theol.*) Sorrow for sin arising from fear of punishment ; (খৃষ্টীয় ধর্ম্ম-শাস্ত্র) শাস্তির ভয়হেতু পাপের জন্য যে সন্তাপ সঞ্জাত হয়। **—ted,** *adj.* Worn by friction ; ঘর্ষণদ্বারা ক্ষয়প্রাপ্ত।

ăt-tūne′, *v. t.* **1.** To tune or put into tune ; সুর বাঁধা, সমস্বর করা, সুর মিলান, একসুরে বাঁধা। **2.** (*Lit.* & *fig.*) To make accordant to bring into musical accord *to* ; as, to *attune* our aims to the divine will ; (শব্দানুযায়ী এবং লক্ষণায়) ঐক্য করা, মিল করা ; সুরসঙ্গতি করা।

aubade, (*F.*), *n.* A musical announcement of the dawn ; a sunrise song ; উষাগমনগীতি ; সূর্য্যোদয়-গীতি।

au-berge (ä-bêrj), (*F.*), *n.* An inn ; সরাই, পান্থশালা। **—ber′-gist,** *n.* An inn-keeper ; সরাইরক্ষক।

au′-bêr-gine (ä-), *n.* The brinjal ; বেগুন, বার্ত্তাকু।

au′-būrn (ä-), *adj.* Golden brown ; স্বর্ণাভ পিঙ্গল, কপিশ, শ্যাব (আঃ বঃ)।

auc′-tion (ăc-), *n.* & *v. t.* A public sale of articles to the highest bidder ; নিলাম। ***Verb t.*** To sell by auction ; নিলামে বিক্রয় করা। **Dutch auction**—An auction at which the auctioneer starts with a high price and comes down till he meets with a bidder ; যে নিলামে নিলামকারী উচ্চমূল্যে ডাক আরম্ভ করে এবং কেহ না ডাকা পর্য্যন্ত মূল্য কমাইতে থাকে।

auc′-tion-eer′ (ăc-shŏn-ēr), *n.* & *v. i.* One who is licensed to sell by auction ; সরকারী সনন্দপ্রাপ্ত নিলামদার, নিলামদার। ***Verb i.*** To conduct auctions ; নিলামকার্য্য নির্ব্বাহ করা।

au-da′-cious (ä-dā-shŭs), *adj.* **1.** Daring ; bold ; as, an *audacious* speaker ; ধৃষ্ট ; প্রগল্‌ভ। **2.** Impudent ; insolent ; as, an *audacious* traitor ; দুর্বিনীত ; দৃপ্ত, উদ্ধত। **—ci-ty, —ness,** *ns.* **1.** Boldness ; confidence ; সাহসিকতা ; নিঃশঙ্কভাব। **2.** Rashness ; recklessness ; as, the desperate *audacity* of his spirit ; হঠকারিতা ; বেপরওয়া ভাব। **3.** Impudence ; shamelessness ; as, he was shocked at his *audacity* ; ধৃষ্টতা, প্রগল্‌ভতা ; দুর্বিনীতত্ব। **—ly,** *adv.*

au′-di-ble (ä-), *adj.* Able to be heard ; perceptible to the ear ; as, an *audible* voice or whisper ; শ্রোতব্য, শ্রুতিযোগ্য, শ্রুতিগোচর, শ্রুতিগ্রাহ্য ; শ্রাব্য, শ্রোতব্য, শ্রবণগোচর, কর্ণগোচর। **—bil′-i-ty, —ness,** *ns.* **—bly,** *adv.*

au′-di-ĕnce (ä-), *n.* **1.** The act of hearing ; শ্রবণ। **2.** Judicial hearing ; (মোকদ্দমার) শুনানি। **3.** A formal interview (granted by a superior to an inferior) ; as, to demand an *audience* of his sovereign ; দর্শন (রাঃ তঃ—৬ষ্ঠ অঃ—৪৩ শ্লোক)। **4.** An assembly of listeners ; as, he lectured to large *audiences* ; also, readers of a book ; as, the book is published with no thought of *audience* ; শ্রোতৃবর্গ ; পাঠকবর্গ। **Audience-chamber**—দর্শন-গৃহ (মঃ সং, ৭ অঃ, ১৪৫, কুল্লূক), গৃহভদ্রক (গেত্রঃ),

শ্রবণমন্দির (কেন্ডিঃ)। **Audience of leave**—Farewell interview; বিদায়কালীন সাক্ষাৎ। **To give audience**—To give ear; কোন ব্যক্তির বক্তব্য শ্রবণে সম্মত হইয়া তাহাকে দর্শন দান করা।

au-dĭ-ŏm′-ë-têr (ä-), *n.* An instrument by which the power of hearing can be measured; শ্রুতিশক্তি পরিমাপক যন্ত্রবিশেষ।

au′-dĭ-phōne (ä-), *n.* An instrument which, pressed against the upper teeth, assists hearing; শ্রুতিসহায়ক যন্ত্রবিশেষ।

au′-dĭt (ä-), *n.* & *v. t.* **1.** An official examination of accounts; হিসাবপরীক্ষা, সরকারী আয়ব্যয় পরীক্ষা। **2.** (*Fig.*) A searching examination of accounts, esp. the Day of Judgment; "Calling thee to a fearful *audit*;" (লক্ষণায়) পুঙ্খানুপুঙ্খরূপে হিসাব পরীক্ষা, (বিশেষার্থে) অন্তিমবিচার দিবস। **3.** A periodical settlement of accounts between landlord and tenants; প্রজা-জমিদারের মধ্যে নির্দ্দিষ্ট সময়ান্তে হিসাবপত্র বা দেনাপাওনা মীমাংসা। ***Verb t.*** To examine accounts officially; সরকারী কর্ম্মচারীরূপে আয়ব্যয় পরীক্ষা করা। **—di-tor,** *n.* **1.** A hearer or listener; as, the galleries were filled with *auditors*; শ্রোতা। **2.** A person appointed and authorized to examine accounts; আয়ব্যয়-পরীক্ষক। **—di-to′-ri-al,** *adj.* Connected with an audit; আয়ব্যয়-পরীক্ষাসংক্রান্ত। **—di-tor-ship,** *n.* **—di-tress,** *n.* (*Fem.*). **Audit ale**—A kind of ale of special quality brewed at the English Universities; ইংলণ্ডীয় বিশ্ববিদ্যালয়সমূহে প্রস্তুত মদ্যবিশেষ [পূর্ব্বে পুণ্যাহদিবসে ব্যবহৃত হইত]। **Audit day**—A day when rents are paid; পুণ্যাহ। **Audit-house, —room**—An appendage to a cathedral for the transaction of business; বৈষয়িক-ব্যাপার নির্ব্বাহার্থ খৃষ্টীয় মহাধর্ম্মমন্দিরসংলগ্ন উপগৃহবিশেষ। **Audit-office**—The office in which the public accounts are audited; হিসাব পরীক্ষার জন্য সরকারী কার্য্যালয়।

au-dĭ′-tion (ä-), *n.* **1.** The act of hearing; শ্রবণ। **2.** The power or faculty of hearing; শ্রুতিশক্তি।

au′-dĭ-tĭve (ä-), *adj.* Concerned with hearing; শ্রবণ-সম্পৃক্ত।

au-dĭ-tö′-rĭ-ŭm (ä-), *n.* **1.** The part of a public building occupied by the audience; নাট্যশালা, সভাগৃহ প্রভৃতিতে শ্রোতৃবৃন্দের উপবেশনের জন্য নির্দ্দিষ্ট স্থান। **2.** The reception room of a monastery; মঠের অভ্যর্থনা-কক্ষ।

au′-dĭ-tŏ-rŷ (ä-), *adj.* & *n.* Relating to, or connected with, hearing; as, *auditory* nerve; received by the ear; as, *auditory* perception of the report; শ্রাবণ, শ্রৌত; কর্ণদ্বারা গৃহীত। ***Noun.*** **1.** Audience; শ্রোতৃবর্গ। **2.** An auditorium; নাট্যমন্দিরাদিতে শ্রোতৃমণ্ডলীর জন্য নির্দ্দিষ্ট স্থান। **Auditorial passage**—শকুলী, শ্রুতিবিবর, শ্রবণপথ।

au fait (ö-fā), (*F.*), *adj.* Conversant; instructed; পরিচিত, বিদিত, অবগত; উপদিষ্ট। **To be au fait in** or **at**—To be thoroughly conversant with; to be expert or skilful in; সুপরিচিত থাকা, সম্পূর্ণরূপে অবগত থাকা; দক্ষ বা নিপুণ হওয়া। **To put a person au fait of**—To instruct thoroughly in; কাহাকে কোন বিষয়ে সম্পূর্ণরূপে শিক্ষা বা উপদেশ প্রদান করা।

Au-gë′-ăn (ä-), *adj.* Filthy (like the stables of Augeas, which Hercules cleansed by turning the river Alpheus through them); [ইলিশ্ প্রদেশের রাজা অজিয়াসের গোশালায় ৩ হাজার গাভী ও বলীবর্দ্দ অবস্থান করিত। ৩০ বৎসরকাল-যাবৎ উহার আবর্জ্জনা পরিস্কৃত হয় নাই। মহাবীর হার্‌কিউলিস্ এলফীয়াস্ নদীর স্রোতঃ তন্মধ্য দিয়া প্রবাহিত করত উক্ত গোশালার পরিচ্ছন্নতাসাধন করেন] (অজিয়াসের গোষ্ঠেরমত) মলভূয়িষ্ঠ। **To cleanse the Augean Stables**—To remove some long standing nuisances and abuses; বহুদিনসঞ্চিত উৎপাত ও দুর্নীতি দূরীভূত করা।

au′-gêr (ä-), *n.* **1.** A carpenter's tool for boring holes in wood; (সূত্রধরের) আস্ফোটনী, বেধনিকা, তুরপুণ, বর্ম্মা, আগর। **2.** An instrument for boring in the strata of the earth; as, some sand was brought by the *auger*; ভূস্তর-ভেদক যন্ত্র বিশেষ।

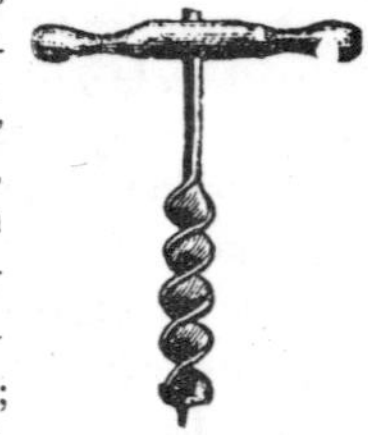

Auger.

aught (ät), *n.* & *adv.* Anything; any part; কোন কিছু; কিঞ্চিৎ, বিন্দু-বিসর্গ। ***Adv.*** To any extent; যত দূর সম্ভব। **For aught I know**—As far as I know; আমি যতদূর জানি।

aug′-mĕnt (äg-), *n.* (*Gram.*) The prefixed vowel to the past tenses of verbs in Sanskrit and Greek; (ব্যাকরণ) সংস্কৃত ও গ্রীক ভাষায় অতীত কালের ক্রিয়াপদের আদিতে যুক্ত স্বরবর্ণ, আগম (মঃ উঃ)।

aug′-mĕnt (äg-), *v. t.* & *i.* To make greater (in size, number, amount); to increase; বৃহত্তর করা; উপচয় করা, বাড়ান, বৃদ্ধিকরা। ***Verb i.*** To increase; বৃদ্ধি পাওয়া, বাড়া। **—a-ble,** *adj.* **—men-ta′-tion,** *n.* Increase; extension; বর্দ্ধন, বৃদ্ধি, উপচয়; প্রসার।

aug-mĕnt′-ă-tĭve (äg-), *adj.* & *n.* **1.** Having the property of increasing; বর্দ্ধনশীল। **2.** (*Gram.*) Having the quality of augmenting; (ব্যাকরণ) বৃদ্ধিশীল। ***Noun.*** A word that expresses greatness; বৃহত্ত্বপ্রকাশক শব্দ। (As, Maharaja, *maha* = great, and *raja* = king.)

au′-gur (ä-gêr), *n.* A religious official among the Romans, whose duty was to foretell future events by observing various actions of birds and also by other signs and omens ; hence, a soothsayer or diviner ; শাকুনিক (বিঃ পুঃ), শকুনজ্ঞ, নিমিত্তজ্ঞ ; দৈবজ্ঞ, গণক। **—gu-ral,** *adj.* **1.** Pertaining to augurs or augury ; শকুনজ্ঞ-সম্বন্ধীয়, শাকুন, শাকুনিক, ভাবী শুভাশুভ-সূচক। **2.** Significant of the future ; as, portents *augural* ; ভবিষ্যসূচক। **—ship,** *n.*

au'-gur (ä-gêr), *v. t.* & *i.* **1.** To predict ; to anticipate ; (said of persons) ; as ; I did *augur* all these to him beforehand ; ভবিষ্যৎ কহা ; পূর্ব্বাববোধ করা। **2.** To betoken ; (said of things) ; as, all these elaborate preparations *augur* mischief ; সূচনা করা। ***Verb i.*** To conjecture from signs or omens ; as, do we *augur* from sparrow ; নিমিত্তাদি দর্শনে ভাবী শুভাশুভ অনুমান করা। **To augur ill, well**—To have bad or good expectations (*of, for*) ; সৌভাগ্য বা দুর্ভাগ্যের আশায় থাকা।

au'-gur-y̆ (ä-gêr-), *n.* **1.** The practice of divining from the flights of birds, etc. ; শকুনজ্ঞান, শকুন-রুত জ্ঞান (বৃঃ সং), নিমিত্তজ্ঞান, শকুন-বিদ্যা, কাকচরিত্র-বিদ্যা। **2.** An augural rite or ceremony ; শাকুনক্রিয়া। **3.** An omen ; prognostication ; as, from their flight strange *auguries* she drew ; দুর্নিমিত্ত ; ভবিষ্যসূচনা। **4.** Presage ; promise ; as, he gave little *augury* of his future greatness ; পূর্ব্বসূচনা ; আশা।

au-gŭst' (ä-), *adj.* Majestic ; venerable ; imposing ; as, to shed that *august* blood ; মহিমান্বিত, প্রবলপ্রতাপান্বিত ; বহুমানাস্পদ ; সুমহান্। **—ly,** *adv.* **—ness,** *n.*

Au'-gŭst (ä-), *n.* The eighth month of the English year, named after Augustus Cæsar ; ইংরেজী বৎসরের অষ্টম মাস (শ্রাবণের শেষার্দ্ধ ও ভাদ্রের প্রথমার্দ্ধ)।

Au-gŭs'-tăn (ä-), *adj.* & *n.* **1.** Connected with the reign of Augustus Cæsar, the palmy period of Latin literature ; রোম সম্রাট্ অগাষ্টাস্ সীজরের রাজত্ব বা তদীয় সাময়িক। **2.** Classical ; উচ্চশ্রেণীর। ***Noun.*** A writer of the Augustan age of any literature ; কোন দেশের জাতীয় সাহিত্যের সমৃদ্ধি-যুগের লেখক। [সম্রাট্ অগাষ্টাসের সময়ে রোম নগরীতে ভার্জ্জিল্, ওভিড্, লুক্রেশিয়াস্ প্রভৃতি জগদ্বিখ্যাত সাহিত্যরথিগণ প্রাদুর্ভূত হইয়াছিলেন ; এই কারণে যে কোন জাতীয় সাহিত্যের সমৃদ্ধিযুগ 'Augustan age, বলিয়া আখ্যাত হয়।]

Auk.

auk (äk), *n.* A web-footed sea-bird with short wings, found in the northern seas ; উত্তরসাগর-চর জালপাদ পক্ষি-বিশেষ।

au'-lic (ä-), *adj.* Pertaining to a royal court ; রাজসভাসংক্রান্ত। **Aulic Council**—The personal council of the emperor of the old German empire, now, the council managing the war department of Austria ; প্রাচীন জর্ম্মণ সম্রাট্সমূহের নিজস্ব মন্ত্রণাসভা, (বর্ত্তমানে) অষ্ট্রিয়া দেশের সামরিক বিভাগ পরিচালক সভা।

au naturel, (*F.*), *adv.* & *adj.* (Cooked) In the simplest way ; অত্যন্ত সাদাসিদাভাবে (রাঁধা)।

aunt (ânt), *n.* The sister of one's father or mother ; a uncle's wife ; পিসী, মাসী, পিতৃস্বসা, মাতৃস্বসা ; খুড়ী, জেঠাই, খুল্লতাত বা পিতৃব্য-পত্নী, জ্যেষ্ঠতাতপত্নী, মামী, মাতুলানী। **Aunt Sally**—A game at fairs, in which players throw sticks at a pipe in the mouth of a wooden woman's head ; মেলাস্থানের ক্রীড়াবিশেষ—এই ক্রীড়াতে ক্রীড়কগণ একটী কাষ্ঠময়ী নারীমূর্ত্তির মুখসংলগ্ন নলের উপর যষ্টি নিক্ষেপ করিয়া থাকে।

au pied de la lettre, (*F.*), *adv.* Literally ; অক্ষরে অক্ষরে, আক্ষরিকভাবে।

au'-ră̆ (ä-), *n.* **1.** Any subtle emanation from any substance, as, flowers, etc. ; কোন বস্তু হইতে নিঃসৃত সূক্ষ্ম পদার্থবিশেষ (যেমন কুসুমের সুবাস), তন্মাত্র (সাংখ্য-দর্শন)। **2.** (*Electr.*) A current of air caused by the discharge of electricity from a sharp point ; (তাড়িত-বিজ্ঞান) কোন বস্তুর সূক্ষ্মাগ্র বিন্দু হইতে নিঃসৃত তাড়িতদ্বারা সঞ্জাত বায়ু-প্রবাহ। **3.** (According to the spiritualists) an essence emanated from living beings affording an atmosphere for the operations of occult phenomena ; (আত্মিকগণের মতে) জীবদেহ-নিঃসৃত চিন্ময় জ্যোতিঃপুঞ্জ, ইহাদ্বারা একটী অদৃশ্য ভা-মণ্ডল সৃষ্ট এবং নানাপ্রকার অলৌকিক ক্রিয়া সম্পাদিত হয়। **4.** (*Path.*) A sensation, as of a current of cold air rising from some part of the body to the head—a premonitory symptom in epilepsy and hysterics ; (নিদান-শাস্ত্র) মূর্চ্ছা, অপস্মার প্রভৃতির আক্রমণের পূর্ব্বে শরীরের কোন ভাগ হইতে মাথার দিকে শীতল বায়ুর প্রবাহ উঠিতেছে—এরূপ (সির্ সির্) বোধ করণ, নিম্নাঙ্গ হইতে উর্দ্ধগামী সির সির অনুভব।

au'-răl (ä-), *adj.* Pertaining to the ear ; received by the ear ; কর্ণসম্বন্ধীয়, শ্রৌত ; শ্রুতিলব্ধ। **—ly,** *adv.*

au-rē'-li-ă̆ (ä-), *n.* **1.** (*Biol.*) The chrysalis or pupa of an insect, esp. of a butterfly ; (জীব-বিজ্ঞান) প্রজাপতি প্রভৃতির কোষস্থ অবস্থা (স্বর্ণবর্ণের জন্য—এই নাম)। **2.** (*Zool.*) A genus of phosphorescent marine animals ; কয়েক জাতীয় জ্যোতিঃস্ফুরক সামুদ্রিক প্রাণীর সাধারণ নাম। **—an,** *adj.* & *n.* Pertaining to an aurelia ; golden ; as, a deep *aurelian* hue ; উক্ত প্রাণীসংক্রান্ত ; হৈম। (*Noun*) A collector or breeder of insects ; পতঙ্গ-সংগ্রাহক, কীটপালক।

au-rē′-ō-lă (ä-), **au′-rē-ōle** (ä-), *n.* **1.** (*R. C. C.*) The celestial crown worn by a martyr, virgin or preacher, as victor over the world, the flesh or the devil ; (রোমান ক্যাথলিক ধর্ম্মসমাজ) ধর্ম্মার্থে জীবন উৎসর্গকারী ব্যক্তি, ব্রহ্মচারিণী কুমারী অথবা শয়তানজয়ী প্রচারক অমরধামে যে স্বর্গীয় কিরীট লাভ করেন। **2.** (*In fine arts*) The circle of light depicted round the head or the whole body of a sacred personage ; hence, a glorifying halo ; "In his countenance was recognized *aureola* of a saint ; (ললিতকলা) ভামণ্ডল, দ্যুতিমণ্ডল (কৃষ্ণঃ কঃ) ; ছটামুকুট। **3.** An actual halo of light esp. that seen in eclipses ; সূর্য্য কিম্বা চন্দ্রের চতুর্দ্দিকস্থ প্রভামণ্ডল, গ্রহণসময়ে দৃষ্ট জ্যোতির্ম্মণ্ডল।

au revoir, (*F.*), *adv.* Good-bye till we meet again ; পুনঃ সাক্ষাৎ পর্য্যন্ত বিদায়।

au′-ric (ä-), *adj.* **1.** Pertaining to gold ; হৈম। **2.** (*Chem.*) In which gold combines as a triad ; as, *auric* chloride or oxide ; (রসায়ন-শাস্ত্র) যে রাসায়নিক মিশ্রণে স্বর্ণ ত্রিবন্ধনরূপে সংমিশ্রিত হয়, তৎসম্বন্ধীয়।

au′-ri-cle (ä-), *n.* **1.** The external ear of animals ; বহিঃকর্ণ, শ্রুতিমণ্ডল (অঃ), শ্রোত্র। **2.** Either of the two upper cavities of the heart into which the blood comes from the veins ; কোষ্ঠ (সাঃ পঃ), রক্তগ্রাহক-হৃদ্‌মী (ঐ), হৃৎপিণ্ডের পেশীময় গহ্বরদ্বয়, হৃৎকর্ণ (হঃ চঃ), হৃৎকোষ। **—cled,** *adj.*

au-ric′-ū-lă (ä-), *n.* A garden flower sometimes called *bear's ear* from the shape of its leaves ; উদ্যানপুষ্পবিশেষ।

au-ric′-ū-lâr (ä-), *adj.* **1.** Pertaining to the ear ; শ্রাবণ, শ্রৌত, শ্রৌত্র। **2.** Told privately in the ear ; as, an *auricular* confession ; গোপনীয়, নিভৃতে কথিত। **3.** Pertaining to the auricle of the heart ; হৃৎকোষসম্বন্ধীয়। **—ly,** *adv.* **Auricular witness**—One who relates what he has heard ; যে সাক্ষী শ্রুত বিষয় বিবৃত করে। **Auricular finger**—The little finger (as the one most easily inserted in the ear) ; কনিষ্ঠাঙ্গুলী (সহজে কর্ণরন্ধ্রে প্রবিষ্ট হয় বলিয়া)।

au-ric′-ū lāte (ä-), *adj.* With ear-shaped projections ; as, an *auriculate* leaf ; কর্ণাকৃতি প্রলম্বিত অংশ সমূহযুক্ত।

au-rif′-er-ous (ä-rĭf-ĕr-ŭs), *adj.* Yielding or producing gold ; containing gold ; স্বর্ণদ, স্বর্ণসূ ; স্বর্ণপূর্ণ, স্বর্ণগর্ভ, কনকময়।

au′-ri-fōrm (ä-), *adj.* Ear-shaped ; having the form of the human ear ; কর্ণাকার ; মনুষ্য-কর্ণাকৃতিবিশিষ্ট।

au′-rist (ä-), *n.* An ear-specialist ; কর্ণরোগবিশেষজ্ঞ, কর্ণ-চিকিৎসক।

au′-rōchs (ä-), *n.* **1.** An extinct wild ox ; অধুনা-লুপ্ত বন্যবৃষ-বিশেষ।

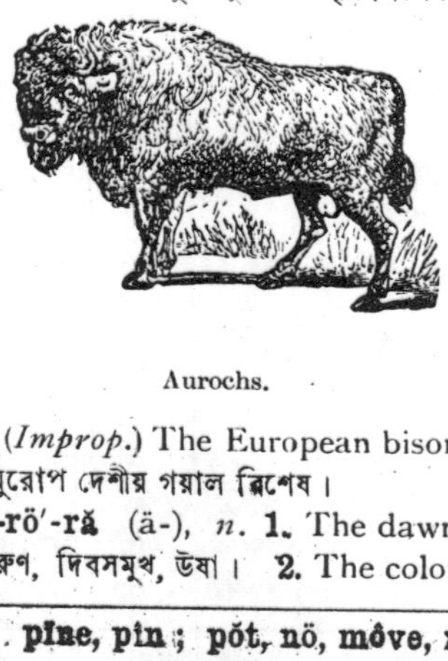

Aurochs.

2. (*Improp.*) The European bison ; ইয়ুরোপ দেশীয় গয়াল বিশেষ।

au-rō′-ră (ä-), *n.* **1.** The dawn ; অরুণ, দিবসমুখ, উষা। **2.** The colour of the sky at sun-rise ; উষারাগ, অরুণিমা। **Aurora Australis**—The southern lights ; কুমেরু-জ্যোতিঃ (হিঃ কোঃ), অবাচী উষা (ঐ)। **Aurora Borealis**—Shooting

Aurora Borealis.

lights of varied colours seen in the northern parts of heavens, generally called the northern lights ; উদীচী উষা (সাঃ পঃ), সুমেরু-জ্যোতিঃ (হিঃ কোঃ)।

Au-rō′-ră (ä-), *n.* The Roman goddess of the morning, represented as rising out of the ocean in a chariot, her rosy fingers dropping gentle dew ; রোমকদিগের উষাদেবী সাগর হইতে উত্থিতা হইতেছেন, এবং তদীয় গোলাপবর্ণ অঙ্গুলী সকল হইতে নীহারবিন্দু স্খলিত হইতেছে—এরূপভাবে অঙ্কিতা হইয়া থাকেন।

au-rō′-răl (ä-), *adj.* **1.** Belonging to or resembling the dawn ; আরুণ, অরুণীয়, অরুণপ্রতিম, উষাসদৃশ। **2.** Roseate ; rosy ; as, "Her cheeks suffused with an *auroral* blush ;" অরুণবর্ণ ; গোলাবি।

au′-rous (ä-rŭs), *adj.* (*Chem.*) With gold univalent in its composition ; (রসায়ন-শাস্ত্র) স্বর্ণ এক-বন্ধনরূপে সংযুক্ত।

au′-rŭm (ä-), *n.* Gold ; স্বর্ণ, কনক, সুবর্ণ, হেম, কাঞ্চন।

aus-cŭl-tā′-tion (äs-), *n.* **1.** The act of listening to ; শ্রবণ। **2.** (*Med.*)

An examination of diseases by listening to the movements of heart, lungs, etc. by means of the ear or stethoscope ; (ভৈষজ্য-শাস্ত্র) কর্ণ অথবা আকর্ণন-যন্ত্র সহযোগে হৃৎপিণ্ড ও ফুস্‌ফুসের শব্দশ্রবণে রোগ-নিরূপণ। **—tor,** *n.* **—to-ry,** *adj.*

aus′-pi-cāte (äs-), *v. t.* & *i.* To initiate with pomp and ceremony ; "To *auspicate* all their proceedings ;" মহাসমারোহসহকারে অনুষ্ঠান বা আরম্ভ করা। ***Verb i.*** To augur ; ভবিষ্যৎ কহা।

aus′-pĭce (äs-), *n.* **1.** A divining or taking of omens by observing birds ; an augury ; পক্ষীর গতি পর্য্যবেক্ষণ দ্বারা ভবিষ্যৎ শুভাশুভ নির্ণয়, শকুন-বিদ্যা। **2.** (*Pl.*) Protection ; patronage ; favourable influence arising from the presence of some person ; আশ্রয় ; পৃষ্ঠপোষকতা ; শুভপ্রভাব।

aus-pi′-cious (äs-pĭ-shŭs), *adj.* **1.** Having omens of success or favourable issue ; predicting, as good ; as, an *auspicious* occasion (মঙ্গলকাল—শকুঃ) ; মঙ্গলময়, শুভ, শুভদ, মঙ্গলপ্রদ, মঙ্গল্য, মাঙ্গলিক, কুশলময় ; কল্যাণসূচক। **2.** Prosperous ; fortunate ; (applied to persons) ; সুভগ, কল্যাণশ্রীযুক্ত ; সৌভাগ্য-শালী। **3.** Favourable; propitious ; (applied to persons or things) ; অনুকূল, শুভঙ্কর ; সুপ্রসন্ন। **—ly,** *adv.* **—ness,** *n.* The quality of being auspicious ; মঙ্গলশ্রী, কল্যাণকারিতা।

aus-tēre′ (äs-), *adj.* **1.** Harsh in flavour ; as, *austere* fruits or wine ; উগ্রস্বাদযুক্ত। **2.** Harsh ; stern ; severe ; as, an *austere* master or look ; কঠোর ; উগ্র ; দারুণ। **3.** Severely and scrupulously truthful ; stringently moral ; strict ; সত্যব্রত, সত্যসন্ধ ; কঠোর-ন্যায়নিষ্ঠ ; কঠোরাচারী। **4.** Severely simple ; একান্ত অনাড়ম্বর, বিলাস-শূন্য। **—ly,** *adv.* **—ness,** *n.* **—ter′-i-ty,** *n.* **1.** Severity of manners or life ; harsh discipline ; strictness ; asceticism ; কঠোরতা ; কঠোর শিক্ষা ; কাঠিন্য, কার্কশ্য ; কঠোর তপশ্চর্য্যা। **2.** Plainness ; severe simplicity ; সাদাসিধাভাব ; কঠোর অনাড়ম্বরতা।

aus′-trăl (äs-), *adj.* Southern ; as, *austral* land, অবাচীন, দক্ষিণদিকস্থ।

Aus-tral-a′-sian (äs-trăl-ā-shĭ-ăn), *adj.* & *n.* Relating to Australasia (Australia & adjoining islands) ; অষ্ট্রেলেশিয় দ্বীপ-পুঞ্জ সম্বন্ধীয়। ***Noun.*** A native of Australasia ; অষ্ট্রেলেশিয় দ্বীপবাসী।

Aus-trā′-li-ăn (äs-), *adj.* & *n.* Pertaining to Australia ; অষ্ট্রেলিয়া দেশীয়। ***Noun.*** A native of, colonist or resident in, Australia ; অষ্ট্রেলিয়ার ঔপনিবেশিক, অষ্ট্রেলিয়া-বাসী।

au-thĕn′-tic (ä-), **—ti-căl,** *adj.* **1.** Genuine ; authoritative ; of undisputed origin ; as, an *authentic* report or register ; প্রকৃত, খাঁটি ; অকৃত্রিম, প্রমাণ-সিদ্ধ ; মৌলিক। **2.** Trustworthy ; as, this man always sent *authentic* information ; প্রত্যয়যোগ্য, বিশ্বাস্য। **—ti-cal-ly,** *adv.* **—tĭc′-i-ty,** *n.* The quality of being authentic or true ; genuineness ; যাথার্থ্য, প্রামাণ্য, প্রামাণিকতা, মৌলিকতা ; সত্যতা, অকৃত্রিমতা।

au′-thŏr (ä-), *n.* **1.** The originator (of a condition of things or events); the first mover ; creator ; as, God is the *author* of the universe ; প্রবর্ত্তক ; চালক ; স্রষ্টা, কর্ত্তা। **2.** The writer of an original book, treatise, etc. ; মৌলিক গ্রন্থকার, গ্রন্থকর্ত্তা, গ্রন্থরচয়িতা, প্রণেতা লেখক, রচক, রচয়িতা। **—ess,** (*n fem.*). A female author ; গ্রন্থকর্ত্রী, গ্রন্থ-রচয়িত্রী, গ্রন্থলেখিকা। **—tho′-ri-al,** *adj.*

au-thŏr′-i-tā-tive (ä-) *adj.* **1.** Commanding ; imperative ; as, an *authoritative* tone : an *authoritative* declaration of pardon ; প্রভুত্বব্যঞ্জক ; আদেশাত্মক, শাসনাত্মক, আজ্ঞাজ্ঞাপক। **2.** Possessing authority ; as, an *authoritative* edition of the Bible ; প্রমাণগর্ভ, প্রামাণিক, কর্ত্তৃত্ব-সম্পন্ন। **—ly,** *adv.* **—ness,** *n.*

au-thŏr′-i-tȳ (ä-), *n.* **1.** Power or right to enforce obedience ; as, the *authority* of a king over his subjects ; বিধিসঙ্গত অধিকার, কর্ত্তৃত্ব। **2.** Delegated power ; "He carried in him an *authority* from God." অর্পিত বা প্রদত্ত ক্ষমতা। **3.** Weight of testimony ; creditability ; as, the *authority* of scriptures ; প্রমাণতা (মঃ ভাঃ), প্রামাণিকতা ; প্রামাণ্য, বিশ্বাস্যতা। **4.** The body exercising power or command ; the executive powers ; (generally *pl.*) ; as, the provincial *authorities* sent copies to the municipal *authorities* ; কর্ত্তৃপক্ষ, শাসক-বর্গ। **5.** A book, quotation, considered to settle a question ; as, I cannot here give references and *authorities* for my statements ; প্রামাণিক পুস্তক, প্রামাণিক বাক্য বা উক্তি। **6.** Influence of character, office, etc. ; mental or moral superiority ; as, the *authority* of a crowd of illustrious names : historian of no *authority* ; পদ, স্বভাব প্রভৃতি জনিত প্রভাব, প্রতিপত্তি ; মানসিক বা নৈতিক শ্রেষ্ঠতা। **7.** A person whose opinion is accepted, esp. an expert on a subject ; a standard author ; প্রামাণিক ব্যক্তি ; প্রামাণিক গ্রন্থকার।

au′-thŏr-ize (ä-), *v. t.* **1.** To give authority to ; to commission (a person to do) ; to give a right to act ; as, to *authorize* commissioners to settle the boundary of the state ; ক্ষমতাপ্রদান করা, ক্ষমতার্পণ করা ; নিয়োগ করা ; ভারার্পণ করা।

2. To warrant ; to sanction ; as, idioms *authorized* by usage ; অনুমোদন করা ; সমর্থন করা। **3.** To give ground for ; to justify a thing ; as, all virtue lies in a power of denying our own desires, where reason does not *authorize* them ; হেতু প্রদর্শন করা ; প্রমাণ বাক্য, চিরাগত ব্যবহার বা লোকমতদ্বারা প্রতিষ্ঠিত বা সিদ্ধ করা। **—i-za-ble,** *adj.* **—i-za'-tion,** *n.* The act of giving authority ; ক্ষমতার্পণ। **Authorized by reason**—যুক্তিসিদ্ধ। **Authorized by the Sastras**—শাস্ত্রসিদ্ধ। **Authorized by usage**—ব্যবহারসিদ্ধ।

au'-thŏr-shĭp (ä-), *n.* **1.** Occupation or career as a writer ; গ্রন্থকর্তৃত্ব, রচকত্ব। **2.** Source ; origin (of a book) ; as, the *authorship* of a book or review : the *authorship* of the riots ; প্রভব, উৎপত্তিস্থল ; মূল, আদিকারণ।

au-tō-bĭ-ŏg'-rā-phȳ (ä-), *n.* Biography or memoirs of a person written by himself ; the act of writing the story of one's own life ; আত্ম-জীবনী, আত্মচরিত, স্বরচিত জীবন বৃত্তান্ত; আত্মজীবনী বিরচণ। **—pher,** *n.* One who writes his history ; আত্মজীবনীকার। **—o-graph'-ic, —o-graph'-i-cal,** *adjs.* Pertaining to autobiography ; আত্ম-জীবনী-সংক্রান্ত।

au'tō-câr (ä-), *n.* A road vehicle driven by mechanical power ; স্বয়ংবহ যান, যন্ত্র-চালিত শকট।

au-to-čeph'-a-lous (ä-tō-sĕph-ā-lŭs), *adj.* **1.** Having a head ; স্বনায়ক-সমন্বিত, নেতৃসমন্বিত। **2.** (Of bishop, churches, etc.) Independent ; (খৃষ্টীয় ধর্ম্মাধ্যক্ষ বা ধর্ম্মসমাজসম্পর্কে) স্বাধীন।

au-tŏch'-thŏn (ä-), (*pl.* -THONS, -THONES), *n.* Aborigines ; আদিম অধিবাসী। **—thon'-ic, —tho-nal, —tho-nous,** *adjs.* **—tho-nism, —tho-ny,** *ns.*

au'-tō-crăt (ä-), *n.* An absolute sovereign ; one who rules with undisputed sway ; as, the *autocrat* for the breakfast table ; স্বৈরনৃপতি ; স্বয়মীশ্বর (মঃ উঃ) ; অবিসম্বাদিত আধিপত্যকারী। **—toc'-ra-cy,** *n.* **1.** An absolute government by one man ; autonomy ; স্বৈরতন্ত্র (সাঃ পঃ), অনিয়ন্ত্রিত স্বাম্য (হিঃ কোঃ), স্বৈর রাজ্য (ঐ) ; স্বৈরিতা (ঐ)। **2.** Controlling influence ; প্রভু-শক্তি। **—crat'-ic, —crat'-i-cal,** *adjs.* Absolute ; holding independent and arbitrary powers of government ; স্বৈর ; অনিয়ন্ত্রিতশাসন-শক্তি-বিশিষ্ট। **—crat'-i-cal-ly,** *adv.* **Autocrat of all the Russias**—A title of the Czar ; রুশিয়ার জারের উপাধিবিশেষ।

au-tŏc'-rā-trīce (ä-), **—trīx,** *n.* A female autocrat ; the title of the empresses of Russia ruling in their own right ; স্বৈরশাসিকা, স্বৈররাজ্ঞী ; রুষসম্রাজ্ঞীগণের উপাধিবিশেষ।

au-to-da-fe, (*pl.* AUTOS-DA-FE) [*Port.* Act of the faith.] *n.* **1.** A sentence of the Inquisition ; অপধর্ম্মসেবী (পোপের বিরুদ্ধবাদী) ব্যক্তিগণের প্রতি স্পেনদেশীয় রোমান ক্যাথলিক ধর্ম্মাধিকরণের দণ্ডাজ্ঞা। **2.** Execution of this sentence, esp. burning of the heretics ; "The Inquisition with its horrible *autos-da-fe;*" উক্ত বিচারালয়ের দণ্ডাজ্ঞা কার্য্যে পরিণত করণ, বিশেষতঃ, উক্ত আদালতের বিচারাদেশক্রমে অপধর্ম্মসেবি-ব্যক্তিকে সর্ব্বজন সমক্ষে জীবন্ত-দাহন।

au-tog'-e-nous (ä-tŏj-ĕ-nŭs), *adj.* Self-generated ; স্বয়ংজাত। **—ly,** *adv.*

au'-tō-grăph (ä-), *adj. n.,* & *v. t.* In one's own handwriting ; as, an *autograph* letter ; স্বহস্তলিখিত। ***Noun.*** **1.** A person's own hand-writing ; especially signature ; স্বহস্তাক্ষর, স্বহস্তলেখ ; স্বাক্ষর। **2.** The author's own manuscript ; গ্রন্থকারের স্বহস্তলিখিত পাণ্ডুলিপি। **3.** A copy produced by autography ; স্বহস্ত-লিখিত প্রতিলিপি, শিলাফলকে অঙ্কিত স্বহস্তাক্ষর হইতে মুদ্রিত অনুলিপি। ***Verb t.*** **1.** To write with one's own hand ; to copy by autography ; স্বহস্তে লিখা ; শিলাফলকে অঙ্কিত স্বহস্তাক্ষরের প্রতিলিপি তোলা। **2.** To sign ; "He *autographs* the admiral's book ;" স্বাক্ষর করা। **—ic, —i-cal,** *adjs.* **—i-cal-ly,** *adv.*

au-tŏg'-rā-phȳ (ä-), *n.* **1.** The act of writing with one's own hand ; a person's own hand-writing ; স্বহস্তে লিখন ; স্বহস্তাক্ষর। **2.** A process in lithography by which a writing or drawing is transferred from paper to stone ; লিথোগ্রাফির যে প্রক্রিয়া বিশেষের সাহায্যে কাগজের লিখিত অংশ শিলাফলকোপরি স্থানান্তরিত করা হয়।

au-tō-măt'-ic (ä-), *adj.* **1.** Self-acting ; working of itself, as a machinery; as, an *automatic* goose (যন্ত্রহংস) ; স্বয়ংবহ (সুঃ সিঃ) ; স্বয়ংচল। **2.** Mechanical ; unconscious ; not voluntarily ; (applied to animal action) ; as, *automatic* movements or functions ; যন্ত্র-চালিতবৎ ; স্বতঃপ্রবৃত্ত (হিঃ কোঃ) ; ইচ্ছা-নিরপেক্ষ, সহজ। **—i-cal,** *adj.* **—i-cal-ly,** *adv.*

au-tŏm'-ā-tĭsm (ä-), *n.* **1.** Involuntary action ; অনিচ্ছাকৃত ক্রিয়া, স্বতঃসঞ্জাত ক্রিয়া। **2.** The doctrine that animals are a kind of automata, acting mechanically and not voluntarily ; জন্তুসকল একজাতীয় স্বয়ংবহ যন্ত্রের মত—এইরূপ দার্শনিক বাদ। **3.** Unthinking routine ; নিত্যকর্ম্মের যন্ত্রবৎ আবর্ত্তন। **4.** The faculty of originating action or motion ; ক্রিয়া বা গতি-উৎপাদিনী বৃত্তি।

au-tŏm'-ā-tŏn (ä-) (*pl.* AUTOMATA, AUTOMATONS.) *n.* **1.** A self-acting machine ; a piece of mechanism with concealed motive power ; স্বয়ংবহ যন্ত্র (সুঃ সিঃ), স্বয়ংচল যন্ত্র, স্ব-শক্তি চালিত-যন্ত্র ; অদৃশ্য যন্ত্র শক্তি-

চালিত যন্ত্র বিশেষ। 2. A living being whose actions are involuntary or without active intelligence; যে জীব কোন প্রকার বিচার-বুদ্ধি প্রয়োগ না করিয়া কলের পুতুলের মত কাজ করিয়া যায়, যন্ত্র-পুত্তলিকা, কলের পুতুল।

au-to-mo′-bile (ä-tŏ-mö-bïle), *n.* A motor-car or vehicle of similar kind; an autocar; যন্ত্র-বিমান; হাওয়া গাড়ী।

au-tŏn′-ŏ-mȳ (ä-), *n.* **1.** The right of self-government; political independence of a city or a state; as, administrative *autonomy;* স্বায়ত্ত শাসনের অধিকার; স্বরাজ। **2.** Personal freedom; ব্যক্তিগত স্বাধীনতা। **3.** (In Kantian philosophy) Freedom of the will; (ক্যাণ্টের দর্শনে) স্বাতন্ত্র্য (নীতি), (হিঃ কোঃ)। **4.** A self-governing community; স্বয়ং-শাসিত সমাজ। **—mous,** *adj.* Of, possessed of, autonomy; স্বতন্ত্র, স্বাধীন, স্বায়ত্ত।

au′-tŏp-sȳ (a-), **—si-ă,** *n.* **1.** Personal observation or inspection; স্বয়ংকৃত পর্য্যবেক্ষণ বা পরিদর্শন। **2.** (*Med.*) Post-mortem examination; (ভৈষজ্য-শাস্ত্র) মৃত্যুর কারণাদি নির্দ্ধারণের জন্য শবদেহ-ব্যবচ্ছেদ, শবদেহ পরীক্ষা। **3.** (*Fig.*) Critical dissection; (লক্ষণায়) সমালোচনা-মূলক ব্যবচ্ছেদ।

au′-tö-tȳpe (ä-), *n.* & *v. t.* **1.** Facsimile; (হস্তাক্ষর প্রভৃতির) যথাযথ প্রতিলিপি। **2.** A permanent photographic printing process for reproducing works of art; আলোক-চিত্রণের প্রক্রিয়া বিশেষ। ***Verb t.*** To reproduce, as a picture by this process; উক্ত উপায়ে কোন আলেখ্যের প্রতিলিপি তোলা।

au′-tumn (ä-tŭm), *n.* **1.** The third season of the year; (August, Sept. and Oct.); শরৎ, শরৎকাল। **2.** (*Fig.*) The period of abatement or decline; "Dr. Preston was now entering into the *autumn* of the Duke's favour"; the decline of human life; (লক্ষণায়) পতন বা অবনতির কাল; মানবজীবনের অবনতি।

au-tŭm′-năl (ä-), *adj.* **1.** Belonging to, or produced in, autumn; শারদ, শারদীয়, শরৎকালীন, শরৎকালে উৎপন্ন। **2.** Maturing or blooming in autumn; শরৎকালে পক্কাবস্থাপ্রাপ্ত বা প্রস্ফুটনশীল। **3.** Past the prime of life; as, an *autumnal* matron; বিগত-যৌবন, প্রৌঢ়-বয়স্ক। **Autumnal Equinox**—See EQUINOX.

aux-il′-iă-rȳ (äg-zĭl-), *n.* & *adj.* **1.** A helper; an assistant; a confederate; সহায়ক; সাহায্যকারী; সহকারী। **2.** (*Gram.*) A verb used to form moods, tenses and voices of other verbs; (*have, be, may, can, do, must, shall* and *will*); (ব্যাকরণ) সহায়ক ক্রিয়াপদ। **3.** (*Pl.*) (Auxiliaries or auxiliary troops.) Foreign troops in the service of a nation at war; যুদ্ধে ব্যাপৃত জাতির অধীনে নিযুক্ত বৈদেশিক সৈন্যদল, মিত্রসৈন্য। ***Adj.*** Helpful to; assisting; subsidiary; সাহায্যপ্রদ; সহায়ক; সাহায্যকারী।

ă-vail′ (-vāl), *v. t.* & *i.* To help; to benefit; "What will skill *avail* us against numbers?" সাহায্য করা; উপকার করা। ***Verb i.*** To afford help; to be of value or profit; to be of use or advantage; as, medicine will not *avail* to check the disease; সাহায্য প্রদান করা; লাভকর বা মূল্যবান্ হওয়া; কার্য্যকারী হওয়া, কাযে লাগা, উপকারে আসা, অভীষ্ট-সিদ্ধ হওয়া, প্রয়োজনানুরূপ হওয়া। **To avail oneself of**—To profit by; to take advantage of; as, I *have availed myself of* the very first opportunity; (কোন কিছুদ্বারা) লাভবান হওয়া; সুযোগগ্রহণ করা।

ă-vail′ (-vāl), *n.* Profit; advantage; used only in the phrase *of avail; without avail; to little avail;* লাভ; সুবিধা, সুযোগ, হিত, গুণ, ফলদায়কতা, উপকারিতা, কার্য্যকারিতা।

ă-vail′-ă-ble (-vāl-), *adj.* **1.** Profitable; advantageous; (*law*) valid; "All laws are *available* by consent;" (archaic except in *law*); লাভজনক; উপকারী, হিতকর, সুবিধা-জনক; (আইন) বৈধ, সিদ্ধ। **2.** Capable of being used; at one's disposal; within one's reach; ব্যবহারযোগ্য; কাহারও কর্ত্তৃত্বাধীনে; কাহারও আয়ত্তাধীনে। **3.** Accessible; প্রাপ্য, প্রাপণীয়, প্রাপ্তব্য, লভ্য, অধিগম্য। **—bil′-i-ty, —ness,** *ns.* **1.** The state or quality of being available; অভীষ্ট-সাধনশক্তি, লাভজনকত্ব, উপযোগিতা, প্রাপ্তব্যতা। **2.** Validity; সিদ্ধতা, প্রমাণ-সিদ্ধতা, ব্যবহার-সামর্থ্য। **—bly,** *adv.*

ăv′-ă-lanche (-lănsh), *n.* **1.** A vast body of snow, earth and ice etc., descending swiftly from a mountain; a snow-slip; পর্ব্বতগাত্র-স্খলিত বিপুল তুষারস্তূপ, হিমপাতিক (সাঃ পঃ), অবলাংশ (হিঃ কোঃ) হিমনিস্যন্দ (আঃ বঃ)। **2.** (*Fig.*) A sudden irresistible descent of anything; "Unable longer to endure such *avalanche* of forgeries;" (লক্ষণায়) প্রচণ্ডবেগে আকস্মিক পতন।

ă-vă′-ni-ă, *n.* An imposition or exaction by the Turkish government; তুর্কী শাসনতন্ত্র কর্ত্তৃক অবিশ্বাসিগণের উপর কর-সংস্থাপন, অথবা তাহাদের নিকট হইতে অর্থ আদায়।

ă-vant′-cou-ri-er (-vâng-kô-rēr), *n.* One who runs or rides before; esp. (in *pl.*) the scouts or advance-guard; নাসীরচর, যুদ্ধে বিপক্ষের সন্ধান লইবার নিমিত্ত চর; অগ্রগামী দূত বা অশ্বারোহী; চর।

ă-vant-guard (-văn-gârd), *n.* The van or advanced body of an army ; নাসীরচর, অগ্রবর্ত্তী সেনাদল ।

ăv'-ă-rĭce, *n.* **1.** Covetousness ; cupidity ; an insatiable desire of gain ; লোভ ; অর্থলালসা, ধনলোভ, ধনতৃষ্ণা, অর্থলিপ্সা ; লাভলিপ্সা, অর্থ-গৃধ্নুতা; ধনপিশাচিকা (মঃ উঃ) । **2.** (*Fig.*) An eager desire to get or keep; as, all are taught an *avarice* of praise ; (লক্ষণায়) তৃষ্ণা, লালসা, লিপ্সা । **—ri'-cious,** *adj.* Greedy of gain ; covetous ; অর্থগৃধ্নু, অর্থলোলুপ, ধনলুব্ধ, লাভলিপ্সু ; লোভী, লোলুপ, লুব্ধ, লিপ্সু । **—ri-cious-ly,** *adv.* **—ri-cious-ness,** *n.*

ă-vâst', *inter.* (*Naut.*) Stop ; cease ; (নৌ-বিদ্যা) থামাও ! গতিবন্ধ কর !

ăv-ă-târ', *n.* **1.** (*Hindu Myth.*) The descent of a deity to the earth in incarnate form ; incarnation ; কলেবরধারণপূর্ব্বক দেবদেবীর মর্ত্তে অবতরণ ; অবতার । **2.** (*Fig.*) Manifestation ; display ; phase ; "Wit and sense are but different *avatars* of the same spirit ;" (লক্ষণায়) প্রকাশ; বিকাশ; বিবর্ত্ত, বিভাব ।

ă-vaunt' (-vänt), *inter.* Be gone ; depart ; (an exclamation of contempt or abhorrence equivalent to "Get thee gone"); দূর হও ! ভাগো !

ā'-vē, *inter.* Welcome ; farewell ; a shout of welcome or farewell ; স্বাগত ! বিদায় ! স্বস্তি ! জয়োহস্তু ! **Ave-bell**—A bell rung when Ave Maria is to be said ; "এভি মেরিয়া" কীর্ত্তন কালে যে ঘণ্টা বাদিত হয় । **Ave Maria**—A salutation and prayer to the Virgin Mary, as mother of God (used in the Roman Catholic Church) ; রোমান ক্যাথলিক ধর্ম্মসমাজে প্রচলিত দেবজননী কুমারী মেরীর স্তুতি বা বন্দনা ।

ă-věnge', *v. t.* To inflict retribution ; to take vengeance for injury done to ; প্রতিকার করা ; প্রতিশোধ লওয়া, দাদ লওয়া (*colloq.*), প্রতিফল দেওয়া, প্রতিহিংসা করা ।

ă-věn'-tū-rine, *n.* **1.** A kind of glass containing gold-coloured spangles ; সোণালি রঙ্গের চুমকিবসানো কাচ বিশেষ । **2.** (*Miner.*) A variety of quartz resembling this glass ; (খনিজ-বিদ্যা) উক্ত কাচসদৃশ শিলা-স্ফটিক বিশেষ ।

ăv'-ĕ-nue (-nū), *n.* **1.** A way of access or approach ; প্রবেশপথ, প্রবেশমার্গ, তোরণ । **2.** An approach to a country-house bordered by trees ; a road-way marked by trees or other objects at regular intervals ; উভয়পার্শ্বে তরুপংক্তি রোপিত পল্লীভবনের প্রবেশমার্গ ; তরুবীথিকা (রবিঃ), ছায়াপথ (প্রবোধ), বনধারা (বিক্রঃ) । **3.** A wide street ; (*U. S.*) ; as, the fifth *avenue* in Newyork ; (মার্কিণ যুক্তরাজ্যে) সুপ্রশস্ত রাজপথ, রথ্যা । **4.** (*Fig.*) Means of access ; "There are no *avenues* to the public service opened for talent ;" (লক্ষণায়) লাভ বা প্রাপ্তির উপায় । **An avenue of mango trees**—চূতবীথি ।

ă-vêr', *v. t.* **1.** To assert ; to affirm ; নিশ্চিতরূপে বলা ; দৃঢ়তার সহিত বলা । **2.** (*Law*) To prove a plea ; to offer the proof of a plea ; (আইন) কোন হেতুবাদ প্রমাণিত করা ; কোন হেতুবাদের প্রমাণ উপস্থাপিত করা । **—ra-ble,** *adj.* **—ment,** *n.* Affirmation ; positive assertion ; as, publishing *averments* ; নিশ্চয় কথন, দৃঢ়োক্তি ; নিশ্চিত বাক্য ।

ăv'-êr-āge, *n.* & *adj.* **1.** A mean proportion ; a medial sum, or quantity, made out of unequal sums or quantities ; মধ্যানুপাত ; গড় । **2.** Apportionment of the loss of a ship, cargo, etc. ; (as in the *general average*) ; ঝঞ্ঝা প্রভৃতি দুর্ঘটনা ঘটিলে জাহাজের মাস্তুলছেদন, মাল প্রভৃতি নিক্ষেপ দ্বারা ইচ্ছাপূর্ব্বক জাহাজের যে ক্ষতি করা হয়—মালিকগণের মধ্যে তাহার অংশানুক্রমিক বিভাগ । **3.** Any loss or damage to ship or cargo from unavoidable causes (as in the phrase *particular average*) ; অপরিহার্য্য কারণবশতঃ জাহাজ বা তদভ্যন্তরস্থ মালের ক্ষতি । **4.** Money paid by those who have received their goods in safety to indemnify the others whose goods had been thrown over-broad in a storm (as in the *petty average*) ; ঝঞ্ঝা হইতে জাহাজ রক্ষার জন্য যে সমস্ত মাল সমুদ্রে নিক্ষিপ্ত হইয়াছে, তাহার মালিকগণের ক্ষতিপূরণের জন্য, যাহাদের মাল নিরাপদে পৌঁছিয়াছে তাহাদের নিকট হইতে গৃহীত অর্থ । ***Adj.*** Containing a mean proportion ; of the usual standard ; as, an *average* amount of rain : an *average* rate of interest ; গড়পড়তা; সাধারণ, মাঝামাঝি । **On** or **upon an average**—In the aggregate ; মোটে, গড়ে, মোটামুটি, গড়পড়তায় ।

ăv'-ĕr-āge, *v. t.* To amount on an average to ; to estimate the average of ; গড়পড়তায় হওয়া ; গড়নির্ণয় করা ।

Averrhoa carambola—Chinese gooseberry ; কামরাঙ্গা (বেলঃ) ।

Averrhoa dulcis—মিঠা কামরাঙ্গা (বেলঃ) ।

ăv-ĕ-r-r u n-c a'-tor (-rŭng-cā-têr), *n.* An instrument for pruning trees, having two blades, fixed on a long rod and worked by a string or wire ; বৃক্ষশাখা ছাঁটিবার যন্ত্র বিশেষ ।

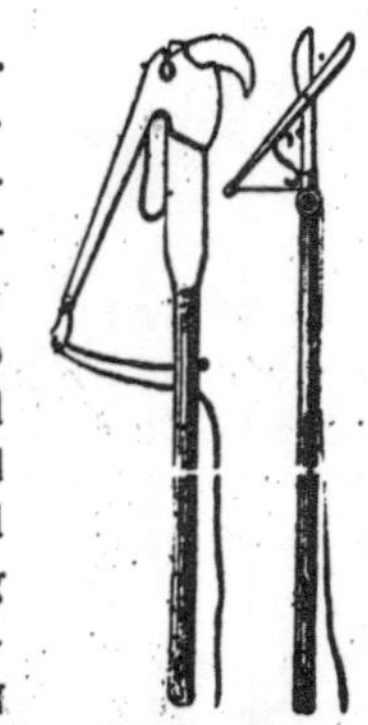

Averruncator.

ă-vêrse′, *adj.* Opposed ; disinclined (*to, from*) ; reluctant ; unwilling to do ; as, *averse* alike to flatter or offend ; বিরোধী, প্রতিকূল; বিমুখ, বিমনা; বীত-শ্রদ্ধ, বিতৃষ্ণ, পরাঙ্মুখ ; অনিচ্ছুক, নারাজ। **—ness,** *n.*

ă-vêr′-sion, *n.* **1.** Opposition or repugnance of mind ; dislike ; antipathy ; (*to, from, for*) ; প্রতিকূলতা, বিতৃষ্ণা, বিরাগ, অনিচ্ছা ; জুগুপ্সা, বিমুখীভাব, বিদ্বেষ, বিমুখতা, পরাঙ্মুখতা, অপ্রবৃত্তি ; দ্বেষ। **2.** Unwillingness to do ; (কোন কার্য্যে) অনিচ্ছা। **3.** The object of dislike or repugnance ; "Pain their *aversion*, pleasure their desire ;" বিরাগের কারণ, বিতৃষ্ণার পাত্র।

ă-vêrt′, *v. t.* **1.** To turn away (eyes, thoughts) from ; as, to *avert* the eyes from an object ; প্রতিনিবৃত্ত করা। **2.** To ward off ; as, how can the danger be *averted* ; বাধা দেওয়া, ফিরান, নিবারণ করা। **—a-ble, —i-ble,** *adjs.* **—er,** *n.*

ā′-vi-ăn, *adj.* Pertaining to birds ; as, the mammalian and *avian* remains ; পক্ষি-সম্বন্ধীয়।

ā′-vi-ă-rȳ, *n.* A place for keeping birds ; a bird-house ; পক্ষিশালা, পক্ষিগৃহ; কুলায়িকা (অঃ), বিটঙ্ক (ঐ)।

ā′-vi-āte, *v. t.* To manage or travel in dirigible balloon, airship, flying-machine, etc. ; ব্যোমযান, ব্যোমপোত প্রভৃতি পরিচালনা করা বা তদুপরি আরোহণ করত আকাশপথে বিচরণ করা। **—a′-tion,** *n.* Managing or travelling in airship, etc. ; ব্যোমপোত প্রভৃতি চালনা, ব্যোমপোতারোহণে গগন-পর্য্যটন। **—a′-tor,** *n.*

ăv′-id, *adj.* Eager ; greedy (*of, for,*) ; as, *avid* of gold ; ব্যগ্র ; লোলুপ। **—ly,** *adv.*

ă-vid′-i-tȳ, *n.* Greediness ; strong appetite ; (applied to the sense); eagerness ; ardent desire (applied to the mind) ; as, *avidity* to know the causes of things ; অতিলোভ, লোলুপতা, গৃধ্নুতা ; প্রবল বুভুক্ষা ; আগ্রহ ; লালসা, তৃষ্ণা।

ā-vi-fau′-nă (-fä-), *n.* The birds of any district or country ; কোন দেশ বা জেলার পক্ষি-সমূহ।

ă-vi′-sō, *n.* Advice-boat ; সংবাদ-বাহিনী তরণী।

avizandum, *n.* (*Scot. law*) Private consideration ; (স্কটলণ্ডদেশীয় আইন) ব্যক্তিগত বা বেসরকারীভাবে বিবেচনা। [To take any case *avizandum* is to take it for the private consideration of the judges outside the court.]

ăv-ō-cā′-tion, *n.* **1.** A distraction ; "He devoted himself, with less *avocation*, to prayer;" চিত্তবিক্ষেপ। **2.** Vocation ; calling ; as, the wandering *avocation* of a shepherd ; ব্যাপার, ব্যবসায়, কর্ম্ম ; বৃত্তি।

ăv′-ō-cĕt, —sĕt, *n.* A wading

Avoset.

bird allied to snipe ; ইয়ুরোপদেশীয় দীর্ঘচঞ্চু পক্ষিবিশেষ।

ă-void′ (-voyd), *v. t.* & *i.* **1.** To shun ; to refrain from (doing a thing) ; to evade ; to escape ; বর্জ্জন করা, পরিহার করা ; প্রতিনিবৃত্ত হওয়া ; কাটিয়ে চলা (*colloq.*), গড়াইয়া যাওয়া (*colloq.*), এড়ান ; রক্ষা পাওয়া, পরিত্রাণ পাওয়া, রেহাই পাওয়া। **2.** (*Law*) To defeat (pleading) ; to quash (sentence) ; (উকীলের তর্ক) ব্যর্থ করা, নিষ্ফল করা ; (দণ্ড) রদ করা, রহিত করা। **—a-ble,** *adj.* That may be avoided ; পরিহার্য্য, বর্জ্জনীয়। **—ance,** *n.* The act of avoiding or shunning ; বর্জ্জন, পরিহার। A vacancy (of an office or benefice) ; "The *avoidance* of the office of such governor-general by death ;" কর্ম্মখালি, বিশেষতঃ ধর্ম্মযাজকগণের কর্ম্মখালি।

ăv-oir-du-pois′ (-êr-dŭ-pŏys), *n.* **1.** A system of weights of which one pound contains sixteen ounces, while in troy weight there are only twelve ounces ; ইংলণ্ডদেশীয় ওজন প্রণালীবিশেষ—এই প্রণালীতে ১৬ আউন্সে এক পাউণ্ড হয়। **2.** (*U. S.*) Weight ; heaviness ; as, a woman of much *avoirdupois* ; (মার্কিণ যুক্তরাজ্য) ওজন; গুরুত্ব।

ă-vouch′ (-vowch), *v. t.* **1.** To assert with positiveness ; to affirm ; as, that is so constantly *avouched* by many ; দৃঢ়তার সহিত বলা ; নিশ্চয়রূপে বলা। **2.** To vindicate ; to guarantee ; as, if it were not *avouched* by the full evidence ; সমর্থন করা ; কোন কিছুর জন্য জামিন বা দায়ী হওয়া। **3.** To acknowledge deliberately ; "Thou hast *avouched* the Lord this day to be thy God ;" ভাবিয়া চিন্তিয়া স্বীকার করা। **—ment,** *n.*

ă-vow′, *v. t.* **1.** To declare openly ; as, a man *avows* his principles ; প্রকাশ্যে ঘোষণা করা, মুক্তকণ্ঠে ঘোষণা করা। **2.** To admit ; to confess ; (*reflex.* & *pass.*) ; স্বীকার করা ; (দোষাদি) স্বীকার করা, কবুল করা (*collq.*)। **3.** To admit oneself to be ; as, he *avows* himself the author ; কোন কিছু বলিয়া স্বীকার করা। **—a-ble,** *adj.* **—al,** *n.* An open or frank declaration ; অকপট স্বীকার। **—vowed-ly,** *adv.* In an avowed manner ; openly ; স্পষ্টতঃ ; প্রকাশ্যতঃ, অকপটভাবে।

ă-vŭl′-sion, *n.* **1.** A tearing asunder ; বিদারণ। **2.** (*Law*) The sudden removal of land by flood etc. to another person's estate; জলের ক্রিয়াদ্বারা সহসা এক ব্যক্তির ভূমি হইতে মৃত্তিকাস্খলিত হইয়া অপর ব্যক্তির ভূমির উপর সঞ্চয়ন।

ă-vun′-cu-lar (-vŭng-cū-lêr), [L. *vunculur*, an uncle] *adj.* Of, or resembling, an uncle; পিতৃব্য বা মাতুল সম্বন্ধীয়, পিতৃব্যোপম, মাতুলোপম।

ă-wait′ (-wāt), *v. t.* **1.** To wait for; to expect; প্রতীক্ষা করা, অপেক্ষা করা; প্রত্যাশা করা। **2.** To be in store for; as, glorious reward *awaits* the good; সঞ্চিত থাকা, ভাগ্যে থাকা।

ă-wake′, (-wāk), *v. t., i.* & *adj.* **1.** To rouse from sleep; জাগরিত করা, নিদ্রাভঙ্গ করা। **2.** (*Fig.*) To rouse; as, that *awoke* the ire of of his master; "*Awake* the soul to loftiest thoughts;" (লক্ষণায়) প্রবুদ্ধ করা, উদ্বুদ্ধ করা। ***Verb i.*** **1.** To cease to sleep; জাগরিত হওয়া, জাগা, নিদ্রোত্থিত হওয়া। **2.** (*Fig.*) To become active; as, to *awake* from sloth; (লক্ষণায়) প্রবোধিত হওয়া, উদ্বুদ্ধ হওয়া। ***Adj.*** Roused from sleep; not asleep; vigilant; নিদ্রোত্থিত; সজাগ; সক্রিয়, জাগরূক, হুসিয়ার। **—wak′-a-ble,** *adj.* Capable of being awakened; প্রবোধ্য। **Awake to**—Aware of; as, he was *awake to* the danger; পরিজ্ঞাত, অবগত। **To be awake to** (anything)—To become conscious of it; পরিজ্ঞাত হওয়া। **Wide awake**—Thoroughly roused from sleep; সম্পূর্ণসজাগ।

ă-wak′-ĕn (-wākn), *v. i.* & *t.* To become awake; to cease to sleep; উন্নিদ্র হওয়া; জাগরিত হওয়া। ***Verb t.*** To rouse from sleep, (*lit.* & *fig.*); জাগরিত করা, উদ্বুদ্ধ করা, প্রবোধিত করা, (শব্দানুযায়ী এবং লক্ষণায়)।

ă-wak′-en-ing (-wākn-), *n.* & *adj.* **1.** The act of *awaking*; প্রবোধন, উদ্বোধন, জাগরণ, নিবোধন। **2.** A revival of religion; ধর্ম্মজগতে নব-জাগরণ। ***Adj.*** Rousing from sleep (*lit.* & *fig.*); জাগ্রৎ (শব্দানুযায়ী এবং লক্ষণায়)। **—ly,** *adv.*

ă-wârd′, *v. t.* **1.** To adjudge; as, the arbitrator *awarded* damages to the complainant; বিচারপূর্ব্বক প্রদান করা। **2.** To grant; to assign; মঞ্জুর করা; নির্দ্দেশ করা, অংশমত বিভাগ করিয়া দেওয়া।

ă-wârd, *n.* **1.** Judicial decision; the decision of arbitrators in a case submitted; as, we cannot expect an equitable *award* where the judge is a party; বিচার-নিষ্পত্তি; সালীশদিগের নিষ্পত্তি। **2.** Payment or penalty assigned by this decision; বিচার নিষ্পত্তির ফলস্বরূপ প্রদত্ত অর্থ বা শাস্তি। **3.** The document conveying such decision; as, all the arbitrators signed the *award*; রায়, সালীশগণের নিষ্পত্তিপত্র। **—er,** *n.*

ă-wâre′, *adj.* Conscious; knowing (*of, that*); as, he was *aware of* the danger; অবগত, বিদিত; জ্ঞাত, পরিজ্ঞাত।

ă-way′ (-wā), *adv.* **1.** To or at a distance from the place, person or thing in question (*lit.* & *fig.*); অনুপস্থিত, দূরে, অন্তরে, তফাতে (*colloq.*) (শব্দানুযায়ী এবং লক্ষণায়)। **2.** Aside; in another direction; as, the axis of the rotation is inclined *away* from the sun; এক পার্শ্বে; অন্যদিকে। **3.** Constantly; continuously; সর্ব্বদা; অবিরাম। **4.** Without delay; অবিলম্বে। **Fire away**—Proceed at once to fire; begin immediately; গুলি চালাও; এখনি আরম্ভ কর। (Away is sometimes used without the verb, as, **away with**—Take away; তফাৎ কর, দূর কর।) **There away**—In that direction; there about; ঐ দিকে; ঐ স্থানের কাছাকাছি। **To do away with**—To make an end of anything; নিকাশ করা, লোপ করা। **To fall away**—To desert; পরিত্যাগ করা। **To make away with**—To destroy; নিকাশ করা, শেষ করা, ধ্বংস করা। **To work away**—To go on working; কায করিতে থাকা। **Wither away**—Wither are you going away; তুমি কোথায় যাইতেছ?

awe (ä), *n.* Reverential fear; solemn wonder; ভক্তিমিশ্রিত ভীতি, সম্ভ্রম (কথা সঃ); গভীর বিস্ময়। **Awe′-less, awe′-some,** *adjs.* **Awe-struck**—Struck with awe; ভয়ার্ত্ত, ভয়বিপ্লুত।

awe (ä), *v. t.* To inspire with veneration or simple dread; ভয়ার্ত্ত করা, ভয়াকুল করা, ভক্তিভাব সঞ্চার করা।

aw-fûl (ä-), **1.** Inspiring awe; as, an *awful* reverence for antiquity; ভীতিপ্রদ, ভীতিকর। **2.** Worthy of profound respect; "His truth, His *awful* holiness;" গভীর সম্মানার্হ। **3.** Sublimely majestic; "Swell *awful* silence on shady hills;" মহিমাময়। **4.** (*Slang.*) Frightful; as, an *awful* bonnet; (ইতর ভাষায়) বিকট, ঘোর, ঘোরদর্শন। **—ly,** *adv.* **—ness,** *n.*

ă-while′, *adv.* For a short time কিয়ৎ কালের নিমিত্ত, অল্প সময়ের জন্য, ক্ষণকালের জন্য।

awk′-ward (äk-wêrd), *adj.* **1.** Not dexterous; bungling; আনাড়ি, অপটু; অনিপুণ। **2.** Clumsy (used of persons and thing); ungraceful; inelegant; as, an *awkward* boy: *awkward* courtesy; কদর্য্য; মাধুর্য্যহীন; অভব্য। **3.** Embarrassing; as, a long and *awkward* process; হতবুদ্ধিকর। **4.** Ill-adapted for use; কদাকার, বিরূপ, অপরূপ। **3.** Troublesome; as, an *awkwrad* customer; বিরক্তিদায়ক, ঝঞ্ঝাটে

(*colloq.*)। **—ly,** *adv.* **—ness,** *n.* Clumsiness ; ungracefulness in manners ; want of dexterity in the use of hands or instruments ; কদর্য্যতা, স্থূলতা ; অভব্যতা ; অপটুতা, অনিপুণতা।

awl (äl), *n.* [Skr. ârä] A pointed instrument for piercing small holes, esp. used by shoemakers, saddlers, etc. ; (চর্ম্মকারের) স্থচি, আর (মঃ উঃ), চর্ম্মপ্রভেদিকা, তুরপুণ, বেধনিকা। (*Bot.*) **Awl-shaped**—(উদ্ভিদ্-বিদ্যা) ত্রপুণাকৃতি (সাঃ পঃ)।

awn (än), *n.* The bristle or beard of barley, oats, grasses, etc., শূক, শস্য-শূক, (ধান্য প্রভৃতির) শুঙ্গা, শুঁয়া। **Awned, awn'-less,** *adjs.*

awn'-ing (än-), *n.* **1.** A covering of canvas or other cloth spread over any place as a protection from the sun's rays ; চাঁদোয়া, শামিয়ানা, চন্দ্রাতপ, বিতান। **2.** A covering of canvas, tarpaulin, etc. spread over a boat, to keep off the sun's rays ; a canvas roof, esp. above the deck of a vessel ; নৌকার ছৈ, বরক (আঃ বঃ) ; ক্যাম্বিস কাপড়ের ছাদ, বিশেষতঃ জাহাজের পাটাতনের উপরিস্থ ক্যাম্বিসের ছাদ। **3.** (*Naut.*) The part of the poop-deck beyond the bulk-head of the cabin ; পোত-কক্ষের কাষ্ঠময় আবরণের বহির্দ্দেশস্থিত, এবং জাহাজের পশ্চাদ্‌ভাগবর্ত্তী উর্দ্ধতলের অংশ-বিশেষ।

a-wry' (-rī), *adv.* & *adj.* **1.** Crookedly ; askew ; asquint ; সাচি, বক্রভাবে, তির্য্যগ্‌ভাবে ; সকটাক্ষ ; কুটিলনেত্রে, তেরছনয়নে, আড়চোখে। **2.** Amiss ; improperly ; "*Draws awry* by her charms ; বিপথগ ; কুটিলস্বভাব, বক্রস্বভাব ; বক্রভাবে, কুটিলভাবে। **To look awry**—To look askance (*lit.* & *fig.*) ; (শব্দানুযায়ী এবং লক্ষণায়) আড়চোখে চাওয়া। **To go, run awry**—To do wrong ; অন্যায় কায করা।

ăx, axe (ăx), *n.* A tool or instrument of iron or steel for hewing timber, felling trees, chopping wood, etc. ; পরশু, কুঠার, টঙ্ক, কুড়ালি। **An axe to grind**—Some private purpose to serve (*U. S.*) ; (মার্কিণ যুক্ত-রাজ্য) ব্যক্তিগত উদ্দেশ্য। **To deserve** or **get an axe**—To deserve to be beheaded as a traitor, with an axe ; as, they were perjured traitors who richly *deserved axes* ; শিরশ্ছেদের উপযুক্ত হওয়া, শিরশ্ছেদ হওয়া। **To hang up one's axe**—To retire from business ; কার্য্য হইতে অবসর গ্রহণ করা। **To lay the axe at the root** (of)—মূলে কুঠারাঘাত করা। **To put the axe in the helve**—To solve a puzzle ; প্রহেলিকা সমাধান করা।

ăx'-i-ăl, *adj.* **1.** Pertaining, or relating to, an axis ; as, *axial* skeleton ; কাক্ষিক। **2.** Of the nature of, resembling, an axis ; around an axis ; কক্ষ-স্বভাব, কক্ষ-সদৃশ ; কক্ষের চতুষ্পার্শ্ববর্ত্তী। **—i-ty,** *n.* **—ly,** *adv.* (*Bot.*) **Axial embryo**—(উদ্ভিদ্-বিদ্যা) মাধ্যভ্রূণ (সাঃ পঃ)। (*Phys.*) **Axial line**—The line in which the magnetic force passes from one pole of a horse-shoe magnet to the other (Farady) ; (পদার্থ-বিজ্ঞান) অক্ষরেখা (হিঃ কোঃ)।

ăx'-il, *n.* The upper angle between a leaf and the stem it springs from, or between a branch and the trunk ; (উদ্ভিদ্-বিদ্যা) পত্র এবং যে কাণ্ড হইতে পত্র উদ্ভূত হইয়াছে, তন্মধ্যবর্ত্তী উর্দ্ধতর কোণ, অথবা শাখা ও কাণ্ডের মধ্যবর্ত্তী কোণ, কক্ষ।

ăx'-ile, *adj.* (*Bot.* & *physiol.*) Belonging to the axis ; (জীব-বিজ্ঞান ও শারীর-বিজ্ঞান) কাক্ষিক।

ăx-il'-iă, *n.* (*Pl.* AXILLAE.) An armpit ; কক্ষ, বগল।

ăx'-il-lâr, *adj.* Same as AXILLARY.

ăx'-il-lă-rў, *adj.* Pertaining to the armpit ; (*Bot.*) in, growing from, the axil ; কাক্ষিক ; (উদ্ভিদ্-বিদ্যা) কক্ষস্থ (সাঃ পঃ)। (*Bot.*) **Axillary bud**—(উদ্ভিদ্-বিদ্যা) কাক্ষিক মুকুল (সাঃ পঃ)। **Axillary stipule**—কাক্ষিক উপতৃণ (সাঃ পঃ)।

ăx'-i-ŏm, *n.* **1.** A self-evident truth ; স্বতঃসিদ্ধ বস্তু, স্বয়ংসিদ্ধ (হিঃ কোঃ)। **2.** An established principle in some art or science ; a principle universally received ; সাধারণ সিদ্ধান্ত (হিঃ কোঃ) ; সর্ব্বজন গৃহীত মূলনীতি। **—o-mat'-ic, —o-mat'-i-cal,** *adjs.* **—o-mat'-i-cal-ly,** *adv.*

ăx'-is, *n.* (*Pl.* AXES) **1.** A straight line, real or imaginary, passing through a body, on which it revolves, or may be supposed to revolve ; অক্ষ, অক্ষরেখা, দণ্ড (সাঃপঃ)। **2.** A straight line from the end to end of a body ; কোন বস্তুর উভয়-প্রান্তসংযোজক সরল রেখা। **3.** (*Physiol.*) The central core of an organ or organism ; (শারীর-বিজ্ঞান) অঙ্গ বা অঙ্গীর কেন্দ্রস্থল। **4.** (*Bot.*) The central line or column about which other parts are arranged ; the stem ; (উদ্ভিদ্-বিদ্যা) মধ্যরেখা বা স্তম্ভ ; কাণ্ড। **5.** (*Geogr.*) **Axis of a continent**—(ভূগোল) কশেরুকা (সাঃ পঃ)। **Axis of a crystal**—ধ্রুবরেখা (ঐ)। **Axis of rotation**—ভ্রমণাক্ষ (হিঃ কোঃ), মেরুদণ্ড (সাঃ পঃ), অক্ষদণ্ড (ঐ), ধ্রুবযষ্টি (ঐ), অক্ষরেখা (ঐ)। **Major axis**—বৃহৎ ব্যাস (হিঃ কোঃ), দীর্ঘ ব্যাস (সাঃ পঃ), দীর্ঘাক্ষ (ঐ)। **Minor axis**—হ্রস্ব ব্যাস (সাঃ পঃ), হ্রস্বাক্ষ।

ăx'-le (ăxl), **ax'-le-tree** (ăxl-trē), *n.* The pin or spindle upon or with which, a wheel revolves ; অক্ষাগ্র, চক্রদণ্ড।

ăx'-ŏ-lŏtl, *n.* A tailed amphibian found in the lakes of Mexico (it is esteemed a great luxury by its inhabitants) ; মেক্সিকোদেশীয় সপুচ্ছ উভচর জন্তু বিশেষ।

ay (ī), **aye** (ī), *inter.* & *n.* Yea ; yes ! indeed ! হাঁ ! বটে ! ঠিক ! যথার্থ ! বাস্তবিক ! ***Noun.*** An affirmative answer ; স্বীকৃতি-সূচক উত্তর । **The ayes have it**—The affirmative voters are in majority; সম্মতি-প্রকাশক ভোটদাতৃগণের সংখ্যা প্রতিপক্ষ হইতে অধিকতর হইয়াছে ।

ā'-yâh, *n.* A waiting woman or lady's maid ; আয়া ।

aye (ā), **ay** (ā), *adv.* Always ; ever ; on all occasions ; (used mostly in poetry) ; সর্ব্বদা ; নিরন্তর, সকল সময় । **For aye**—For ever ; চিরদিনের জন্য ।

Aye-aye.

aye'-aye (ī-ī), *n.* A squirrel-like animal of the size of a cat, found only in Madagascar ; মাদাগাস্কার দ্বীপবাসী জন্তু বিশেষ, ইহা দেখিতে কাঠ বিড়ালের মত এবং আকারে প্রায় বিড়ালের সমান হইয়া থাকে ।

A-zā'-lē-ă (ă-), *n.* A genus of flowering shrubby plants, natives of China and N. America, remarkable for the beauty and fragrance of their flowers ; চীন এবং উত্তর আমেরিকাজাত সুন্দর এবং সুরভি পুষ্পবিশিষ্ট কয়েক জাতীয় গুল্মের সাধারণ নাম ।

ăz'-ă-rōle, *n.* The Neapolitan medlar—a shurb of Southern Europe ; also its fruit ; ইয়ুরোপের দক্ষিণভাগস্থ প্রদেশ সমূহে জাত গুল্ম বিশেষ ; ঐ বৃক্ষের ফল ।

ăz'-i-mŭth, *n.* (*Astron.*) The arc of the heavens extending from the zenith to the horizon, which it cuts at right angles ; (জ্যোতির্বিজ্ঞান) আশাংশ (সাঃ পঃ), দিগংশ কোটি (হিঃ কোঃ), দিঙ্‌মণ্ডল (আর্য্যঃ) । **—al,** *adj.* **—al-ly,** *adv.* **Azimuth circle** or **vertical circle**—দিগংশ যন্ত্র (মাঃ বঃ) ।

ă-zō'-ic, *adj.* **1.** Having no trace of life ; জীবনলেশহীন, নির্জীবক । **2.** (*Geol.*) Containing no organic remains ; (ভূ-বিদ্যা) জৈব পদার্থের লেশ বিহীন ।

ăz'-ōte, *n.* The former name of nitrozen; যবক্ষারজান বাষ্পের পূর্ব্বনাম ।

A-zot'-ic, *adj.* **—o-tize,** *v. t.* To imbue with nitrogen ; to deprive of life ; যবক্ষারজান বাষ্পদ্বারা পরিপূরিত করা ; জীবনহীন করা ।

ăz'-ōth, *n.* The alchemists' name for mercury ; মধ্যযুগের ইয়ুরোপীয় তান্ত্রিকগণ প্রদত্ত পারদের নাম ।

Az'-râ-ēl (ăz-), *n.* In Mahomedan mythology, the angel of death ; মহম্মদীয় পুরাণোক্ত মরণ দূত ।

az'-ure (ā-zhūre), *adj., n.* & *v. t.* **1.** Sky-blue ; আশমানি । **2.** (*Fig.*) Cloudless ; serene ; "Those *azure* moments when the clouds broke from his mind ;" (লক্ষণায়) মেঘমুক্ত, নির্ম্মেঘ ; প্রশান্ত । ***Noun.*** **1.** The fine blue colour of the sky ; as, in robes of *azure* ; আশমানি রঙ্ । **2.** Unclouded vault of heaven ; as, on heaven's *azure* ; নির্ম্মেঘ নীলাকাশ । **3.** Bright blue pigment ; উজ্জ্বল নীলবর্ণ রঞ্জক-পদার্থ বিশেষ । **4.** Lapis lazuli ; লাজবর্দ, সুনীলক, রাজাবর্ত্ত (রঃ প্রঃ) । ***Verb t.*** To colour blue ; নীলবর্ণে রঞ্জিত করা । **—ured,** *adj.*

ăz'-ȳ-gous (-gŭs), *adj.* & *n.* Not yoked or joined with another ; অযুগ্ম । ***Noun.*** (*Physiol.*) An organic part not existing in pairs ; (শারীর-বিজ্ঞান) অযুগ্ম দেহাংশ ।

B

B, **1.** The second letter and the first consonant in the English alphabet ; ইংরাজী বর্ণমালার দ্বিতীয় অক্ষর । **2.** (*Mus.*) The seventh note of the scale of C major ; (সঙ্গীত-শাস্ত্র) স্বরগ্রামের অন্তর্গত মুদারার সপ্তম স্বর "নি" । **Not to know a B from a bull's foot**—To be grossly ignorant or illiterate ; ক অক্ষর গোমাংস হওয়া ।

baa (bâ), *n.* & *v. i.* The cry or bleating of a sheep ; মেষরব, ভ্যাঁ ভ্যাঁ শব্দ । ***Verb i.*** To cry or bleat as a sheep ; as, he treble *baas* for help ; মেষবৎ চীৎকার করা, ভেড়ার মত ভ্যাঁ ভ্যাঁ শব্দ করা ।

Bā'-ăl, *n.* (*Pl.* Baalim) **1.** Chief male deity of the Phœnicians ; ফিনিশীয় জাতীর সর্ব্বপ্রধান দেবতা । **2.** A false god ; অলীক দেবতা (cf. অলীকনলঃ—নৈষঃ) । **—ism,** *n.* ঘোর পৌত্তলিকতা । **—ist, —ite,** *ns.*

băb'-ble, *v. i.* **1.** To talk half articulately, incoherently or excessively ; as, a child *babbles* ; to prattle ; অর্দ্ধস্ফুট রবে কথা বলা, আধ আধ কথা বলা, বক্‌ বক্ করা ;

প্রলাপ করা, বাচালতা করা। **2.** To make a constant murmuring noise as streams, etc. ; কল কল শব্দ করা, তর তর রব করা, কুলু কুলু ধ্বনি করা, মর্ম্মর ধ্বনি করা। **3.** To tell or let out secrets ; as, the queen impatiently *babbled* the plot ; গুপ্ত কথা ব্যক্ত করা, পেটের কথা ফাঁস করিয়া ফেলা। **—blêr,** *n.* **1.** An idle talker ; a chatterer ; বাচাল, বাবদুক ; প্রলাপী, জল্পক। **2.** A teller of secrets ; গুপ্তকথা প্রকাশকারী। **3.** A long-legged Thrush ; শরালী জাতীয় দীর্ঘপদ পক্ষিবিশেষ। **—bling,** *n.* **—ment,** *n.*

băb′-ble, *n.* **1.** Unmeaning prattle ; জল্প, প্রলাপ, বালভাষিত অর্দ্ধস্ফুট বাক্য, আধো আধো কথা। **2.** Murmur of running water ; কুলু কুলু ধ্বনি।

bābe, *n.* *(Poet.)* **1.** An infant ; (কবিতায়) শিশু, দুগ্ধপোষ্য শিশু, কচি ছেলে বা মেয়ে, খোকা বা খুকী। **2.** *(Fig.)* A childish person ; (লক্ষণায়) ছেবলা। **Babes in Christ**—New-made converts to Christianity ; খৃষ্টধর্ম্মে নবদীক্ষিত ব্যক্তিগণ।

bā′-bĕl, *n.* **1.** *(Cap.)* The city and tower in Shinar (where the confusion of languages took place ; *Gen.* XI.) ; hence, a lofty structure ; (often *l. c.*) visionary plan ; বাইবেল গ্রন্থে উল্লিখিত শীনারদেশস্থ বুরুজ বা নগরী—যেখানে ভাষা বিভ্রম ঘটিয়াছিল ; [বেবেলবাসিগণ স্বর্গারোহণের অভিপ্রায়ে একটী বুরুজ নির্ম্মাণ করে। ঈশ্বর ইহাতে ক্রুদ্ধ হইয়া ধৃষ্টতার জন্য শাস্তি দিবার মানসে তাহাদিগের মধ্যে ভাষার পরিবর্তন সংঘটন করেন। বাইবেলোক্ত উপাখ্যানে ইহাই পৃথিবীবাসী জাতি সমূহের ভাষাভেদের কারণ বলিয়া নির্দ্দিষ্ট হইয়াছে। —জেনেসিস্—১১ অধ্যায়।]. অতএব উচ্চপ্রাসাদাদি ; কাল্পনিক উপায়। **2.** A scene of confusion ; as, a perfect *babel* ; গোলমালের স্থান ; কোলাহল পূর্ণ স্থান। **3.** A noisy assembly ; a meaningless noise ; as, grinding *babel* of the street ; তুমুল কোলাহলপূর্ণ সভা ; কলরব, হট্টগোল।

băb-ī-rous′-să (-rôs-), **—rŭs′-să,** [Malaya *babi*, hog & *rusa*, deer.] *n.* The East Asiatic wild hog with upturned horn-like tusks ; বন্য বরাহ।

bä′-boo, —bû, *n.* **1.** A Hindu gentleman ; হিন্দুজাতীয় ভদ্রলোক। **2.** An Indian English writing clerk ; ইংরাজী জানা ভারতবর্ষীয় কেরাণী। **3.** A Hindu title equivalent to Mr. or Sir ; বাবু। **4.** A half-anglicised Hindu ; (অবজ্ঞার্থে) ইংরাজিভাবাপন্ন হিন্দু।

Baboon.

bă-bōōn′, *n.* A large African and South Asiatic monkey ; বৃহৎকায় বানরবিশেষ, হনুমান।

bă-bouche′ (bōōsh), *n.* [Pers. *paposh, pa,* foot & *posh,* covering) A Turkish or oriental slipper ; তুরস্ক বা প্রাচ্যদেশীয় পাদুকা বিশেষ।

bā′-bȳ, *n.* **1.** A very young child of either sex ; an infant in arms ; শিশু, খোকা, খুকী, খুকুমণি ; কোলের ছেলে। **2.** Anything small of its kind ; "Turrets beside which the leaning tower of Pisa is a *baby* ;" কোন জাতীয় ক্ষুদ্র বস্তু। **—ish** *adj.* **—ish-ness, —ism,** *ns.* The characteristic of a *baby* ; a childish mode of speech or action ; শিশু-স্বভাব ; ছেলেমি *(Colloq.)*, ছেবলামি *(Colloq.)*। **—hood,** *n.* The period of infancy ; শৈশব, বাল্যাবস্থা, বাল্য। **To smell of the baby**—To be childish ; ছেলেমানুষ হওয়া।

Băb′-ȳ-lŏn, *n.* The capital of the Chaldean Empire ; hence, any great and luxurious city ; কেলডিয়া সাম্রাজ্যের রাজধানী ; অতএব যে কোন বিলাসব্যসনপূর্ণ মহানগরী। **The modern Babylon**—London, (on account of its wealth, luxury and dissipation) ; লণ্ডন। [প্রাচীন বেবিলোন নগরীর সদৃশ বিলাস, ব্যসন ও সমৃদ্ধির লীলাভূমি বলিয়া মহানগরী লণ্ডনকে সময় সময় এই আখ্যা প্রদান করা হইয়া থাকে।] **—lon′-ic, —lo′-nish,** *adjs.*

Băb-ȳ-lō′-nĭ-ăn, *adj.* & *n.* **1.** Of or pertaining to Babylon ; hence, *(fig.)* huge ; gigantic ; as, the *Babylonian* baggage ; বেবিলোন নগরীয় ; (লক্ষণায়) প্রকাণ্ড ; বিরাট। **2.** Like the confusion of tongues at Babel ; noisily confused ; as, "The confused jargon of the *Babylonian* pulpits" ; বেবেলের ভাষাবিভ্রমবৎ ; কোলাহলপূর্ণ। ***Noun.*** **1.** An inhabitant of Babylon ; বেবিলোনবাসী। **2.** An astrologer ; —(because the Chaldeans were remarkable for the study of astrology) ; জ্যোতির্ব্বিদ্। (প্রাচীন কেলডীয়াবাসিগণ জ্যোতিষশাস্ত্র অনুশীলনে অতীব উন্নতি সাধন করিয়াছিলেন।)

băc-că-lau′-rē-āte (-lä-), *n.* The university degree of a bachelor of arts ; বি, এ, উপাধি। **Baccalaureate sermon**—A farewell discourse delivered in some American colleges to a graduating class ; আমেরিকার কোন কোন বিশ্ববিদ্যালয়ে উপাধি প্রদানের প্রাক্কালে ছাত্রগণের নিকট যে বিদায়কালীন বক্তৃতা প্রদত্ত হয়।

baccara, —rat (-râ), *n.* *(F.)*, A gambling card game ; একপ্রকার তাসের দ্যূত-ক্রীড়া।

băc′-cāte, *adj.* *(Bot.)* Bearing berries ; berry-shaped ; (উদ্ভিদ্-বিদ্যা) জাম বা তদনুরূপ ফল-প্রসূ ; জাম বা তদ্বৎ ফলাকৃতি।

băc′-chă-năl, *n.* & *adj.* **1.** A devotee (priest or votary) of Bacchus ; hence, a drunken reveller ; সুরাদেবতা ব্যাকাসের উপাসক ; অতএব, মদ্যসেবক, মাতাল, সুরামোদী। **2.** A dance or song in honour of Bacchus : সুরাদেবতার সম্মানার্থ নৃত্য বা সঙ্গীত। ***Adj.*** Of or like Bacchus or his rites ; riotous ; roystering ; সুরাদেবতা বা তদীয় ক্রিয়াকাণ্ড-সম্পর্কীয় বা সদৃশ ; মদোল্লাসী; কোলাহলকারী।

Băc-chă-nā-li-ă, *n. pl.* Festival of Bacchus ; drunken revelry ; সুরাদেবতার সম্মানার্থ পানোৎসব ; মদোল্লাস, সুরাপানোৎসব।

Băc-chă-nā-li-ăn, *adj.* & *n.* Of Bacchanals ; riotous ; drunken ; পানোন্মত্তদল সম্বন্ধীয় ; কোলাহলকারী ; পানোন্মত্ত। ***Noun.*** A drunken reveller ; a tippler ; পানোন্মত্ত ব্যক্তি ; সুরামোদী। **—ism,** *n.*

Băc′-chănt, *n.* & *adj.* A priest or votary of Bacchus ; a reveller ; সুরাদেবতা ব্যাকাসের পুরোহিত বা উপাসক; সুরাপানোল্লাসী; মদ্যোল্লাসী। ***Adj.*** Wine-loving ; সুরাপ্রিয়।

Băc-chăn-tē, *Fem.* (Often used in the *pl.* BACCHANTES.) *n.* A priestess of Bacchus ; a female bacchanal ; ব্যাকাস দেবতার পুজিকা, পানোন্মত্তা স্ত্রী। **—chantic,** *adj.*

Bacchus.

Băc′-chŭs, *n.* The Greek god of wine ; গ্রীসদেশীয় সুরা-দেবতা।

băc-cĭf′-ĕr-ous (-ŭs), *adj.* Bearing or producing berries ; জাম বা তদ্বৎ ফল-প্রসূ।

băc′-cĭ-fêrm, *adj.* Berry-shaped ; জাম বা তদ্বৎ ফলাকৃতি।

băc-cĭv′-ō-rous (-rŭs), *adj.* Eating or subsisting on berries ; as, *baccivorous* birds ; জাম বা তদ্রূপ ফলাহারী।

băch′-ă-răch, *n.* An excellent wine named from Bacharach, a town on the Rhine ; রাইন্ নদীর তীরবর্ত্তী ব্যাক্যারেক নগরীতে প্রস্তুত উৎকৃষ্ট মদিরাবিশেষ।

băch′-ĕ-lor (-lêr), (*Fem.* maid, spinster.) *n.* **1.** An unmarried man ; অবিবাহিত পুরুষ, অনূঢ় পুরুষ, কুমার, অকৃতদার। **2.** One who has taken the first degree of a university ; as, a *bachelor* of arts ; বিশ্ববিদ্যালয়ের সর্ব্বপ্রথম উপাধিধারী বা ধারিণী (বি, এ; বি, ই; বি, এস্, সি, প্রভৃতি উপাধিধারী বা ধারিণী)। **3.** (*Hist.*) A knight serving under another's banner ; hence, a simple knight not belonging to a special order ; অপর নাইটের পতাকাতলে যুদ্ধকারী যুবক নাইট্ ; সাধারণ নাইট্। **—hood, —ship, —ism,** *ns.* **Bachelor's buttons**—Various button-shaped flowers, esp. the double buttercup ; বিভিন্ন জাতীয় বোতামাকৃতি পুষ্প, বিশেষতঃ কতিপয় যবক্ষেত্রজাত পুষ্প, সুপুষ্পক (মঃ উঃ), গোলটোপ। **Bachelor's wife**—The ideal wife of which a bachelor dreams ; অবিবাহিত ব্যক্তির স্বপ্নলোকবাসিনী আদর্শ পত্নী। **To wear a bachelor's button**—To remain unmarried ; অবিবাহিত থাকা।

băc′-il-lă-rȳ, *adj.* **1.** Pertaining to, or consisting of, little rods (in tissue, membrane) ; ক্ষুদ্র দণ্ড-সম্পর্কীয়, ক্ষুদ্রদণ্ডবিশিষ্ট। **2.** Connected with bacilli ; রোগবীজাণুসম্পৃক্ত।

bă-cĭl′-li-fôrm, *adj.* Rod-shaped ; দণ্ডাকৃতি।

bă-cĭl′-lŭs, (*pl.* BACILLI), *n.* A genus of microscopic rod-like vegetable organism, some of which are found in the diseased tissues in anthrax, phthisis, etc. ; রোগজনক উদ্ভিজ্জাণু বিশেষ, জীবাণু, বীজাণু।

băck, *n.* & *adj.* **1.** The hinder part of the body in men and the upper part in beasts ; পৃষ্ঠ, পিঠ। **2.** The part behind or farthest from the front ; the rear part of a thing ; as, the *back* of a house, book, etc. ; পশ্চাদ্দেশ ; পশ্চাদ্দিক্। **3.** The body as needing clothes ; as, he has no clothes on his *back* (*back and belly*—clothing and food ; গ্রাসাচ্ছাদন) ; দেহ। **4.** The side of any object away from the spectator ; as, the *back* of an island, hill, village, etc. ; দূরবর্ত্তী পার্শ্ব। **5.** The part of a cutting tool on the opposite side from its edge ; as, the *back* of a knife, saw, etc. ; ছুরি প্রভৃতির ধারাল পার্শ্বের বিপরীত ভাগ, পৃষ্ঠভাগ। **6.** A football player stationed behind ; as, full-*back* : half-*back* ; পশ্চাদ্দিকে সংস্থাপিত পাদগোলক- (ফুটবল) ক্রীড়ক। ***Adj.*** **1.** Situated behind ; remote ; outlying ; as, to take a *back* seat ; পশ্চাদ্দিকে অবস্থিত ; অতি দূরবর্ত্তী ; প্রান্তবর্ত্তী, দূরস্থ। **2.** Being in arrear ; overdue ; as, *back* rent (বাকী খাজানা) ; বাকী-পড়া, বকেয়া ; সাবেক। **3.** Reversed ; counter ; as, *back* current : *back* door ; বিপর্য্যস্ত ; বিপরীত। **Back and belly**—Before and behind ; all over ; as, to beat a man *back and belly* ; অগ্রে পশ্চাতে ; সর্ব্বাঙ্গে। Clothes and food ; as, to give a man *back and belly* ; গ্রাসাচ্ছাদন। **Backbone**—The vertebral column ; the spine ; পৃষ্ঠাস্থি, শিরদাঁড়া (*colloq.*), কশেরুকা ; পৃষ্ঠবংশ, মেরুদণ্ড. The main support or axis ; the chief strength ; as, the lofty mountains are the *backbone* of a country ; প্রধান অবলম্বন ; মুখ্য বল। (*Fig.*) Firmness of character ; moral principle ; as, he has no *backbone* in him ; (লক্ষণার্থ) চরিত্রবল ; ধর্ম্মবুদ্ধি। [**To the backbone**—Thoroughly ; নিতান্ত, ডাহা, হাড়েহাড়ে।] **Backdoor**—*n.* & *adj.*

A door at the back part of a building; a private passage; পশ্চাদ্দ্বার; গুপ্তদ্বার, খিড়কীদ্বার। (*Adj.*) Clandestine: as, *backdoor* intrigues: গুপ্ত, প্রচ্ছন্ন। **Background**—The ground in the rear or behind; পশ্চাদ্‌ভূমি। The part of a picture, scene or description that serves as a setting to chief figures or objects; (চিত্র-বিদ্যা) কোন প্রতিকৃতি। চিত্রিত মূর্ত্তিশ্রেণীর পশ্চাদ্‌ভূমি, পটভূমিকা (রবি), আলেখ্যের ভূমি। (*Fig.*) A place of obscurity or retirement; as, to stand or be left in in the *background*; (লক্ষণায়) অপ্রকাশ্য স্থল, অপ্রকট স্থান, আড়াল। **To keep in the background**—Not to bring prominently into view; পশ্চাদ্দেশে রাখা বা থাকা (যেন জনসাধারণের বিশেষ দৃষ্টিতে না পড়ে—এরূপ স্থানে রাখা বা থাকা)। [**To keep one's self in the background**—To keep one's self out of sight; আড়ালে থাকা। **To place in the backround**—To make of little consequence; পশ্চাতে ফেলা, আড়ালে ফেলা।] **Back-handed**—With the hand turned backward; as, a *backhanded* blow; পশ্চাদাবর্ত্তিত (হস্ত)। Unfair; indirect; sarcastic; as, a *backhanded* compliment; অন্যায়; অসরল; বিদ্রূপপূর্ণ। Sloping back or to the left; as, *back-handed* writing; বামদিকে হেলানো। **Back-handwriting**—Handwriting with the letters sloped backward; পশ্চাদ্দিকে হেলানো হস্তাক্ষর। **Back set**—A setting bak; a reverse; as, they have got many *back-sets* one after another; প্রতিহতি; ভাগ্যবিপর্য্যয়। Counter-current; as, the *backset* caused by the overflow; প্রতিকূল স্রোত, বিপরীত প্রবাহ। **Back-sight**—(Survey) A sight or reading taken backwards; (জরীপ) পশ্চাদ্দিকে বিলোকন। The sight of a rifle nearer the stock; বন্দুকের স্থুলপ্রান্তের নিকটবর্ত্তী নিশানার চিহ্ন। **Backstairs**—Back or private stairs of a house; (বাটীর) পশ্চাতের সিঁড়ি বা গুপ্ত সোপানাবলী। Secret; underhand; unfair; as *backstairs* influence; গুপ্ত, লুক্কায়িত; তলে তলে; অসঙ্গত। **Back-stays**—The ropes slanting abaft from the masthead to the sides of a ship; জাহাজের মাস্তুলাগ্রভাগ হইতে পার্শ্ব পর্য্যন্ত প্রসারিত এবং কিঞ্চিৎ পশ্চাৎদিকে হেলানো রজ্জু-শ্রেণী। **Back-sword**—A sword with one sharp edge; এক পার্শ্বে ধার বিশিষ্ট অসি। A stick with a basket-handle used in rustic amusements; পল্লীর আমোদোৎসবে ব্যবহৃত সাবরণ হাতলবিশিষ্ট দণ্ডবিশেষ। **Backwash**—To clean the oil from wool after combing; আঁচড়াইবার পর পশম হইতে তৈল তোলা। **Back-water**—Water thrown by the paddles of steam-boats, etc.; বাষ্পীয় পোত প্রভৃতির ক্ষেপণি-ফলকদ্বারা পশ্চাদ্দিকে নিক্ষিপ্ত জলরাশি। A currentless water beside a stream and fed by its back-flow; বাঁধদ্বারা আবদ্ধ জলরাশি। A creek communicating with the sea by barred outlets: যে খাড়ী অথবা সাগরশাখার জল তীরদেশের স্থানে স্থানে উপল ও ধূলিস্তর দ্বারা রচিত প্রবেশ-পথে সমুদ্রে গমনাগমন করে। **Back way**—Bypath; (*lit.* & *fig.*) roundabout way; অলিগলি; (শব্দানুযায়ী ও লক্ষণায়) আঁকা বাঁকা পথ। **Back-woods**—Remote uncleared forest-land; অতিদূরবর্ত্তী বনভূমি, প্রত্যন্তবন, প্রত্যন্তপ্রদেশ। **On one's back**—Laid up; শয্যাশায়ী। Prostrate; helpless; ধরাশায়িত, সাষ্টাঙ্গে পতিত; নিরাশ্রয়, নিঃসহায়। **The back of my hand to you**—I will have nothing more to do with you; তোমার সহিত সমস্ত সংস্রব বিচ্ছিন্ন করিলাম। **Thrown on own's back**—Completely worsted; সম্পূর্ণরূপে পরাভূত। **To give the back**—To quit; ত্যাগ করা, বিমুখ হওয়া। **To have on one's back**—To be burdened with; প্রপীড়িত হওয়া। **To pay back**—To wreak vengeance; প্রতিশোধ লওয়া। **To see one's back**—To get rid of a person; (কোন ব্যক্তির হাত হইতে) মুক্ত হওয়া। **To turn one's back upon**—To run away from; to abandon; মুখ ফিরান, বিমুখ হওয়া; পরিহার করা। **To turn the back**—To go away; to flee: পৃষ্ঠপ্রদর্শন করা; রণে ভঙ্গ দেওয়া। **To turn the back on** or **upon one**—To forsake or neglect one; কাহাকে ত্যাগ করা বা কোন ব্যক্তির প্রতি বিমুখ হওয়া। **With one's back to the wall**—Hard-pressed; প্রপীড়িত।

băck, *n.* **1.** A large flat-bottomed ferry-boat; একপ্রকার প্রকাণ্ড খেয়া নৌকা। **2.** A large tube or vessel (used in brewing or distilling, etc.): মদ্য চোলাই প্রভৃতির কার্য্যে ব্যবহৃত বৃহৎ পাত্র বা গামলাবিশেষ।

băck, *v. t.* & *i.* **1.** To furnish with a back or backing; as, to *back* a book; পৃষ্ঠভাগ সংযুক্ত করা, পশ্চাদ্‌ভাগ দৃঢ় করা। **2.** To cause to move backwards; as, to *back* oxen; পশ্চাদ্দিকে চালিত করা, পশ্চাদ্দিকে তাড়িত করা। **3.** To support; to maintain; as, to *back* a friend; সহায়তা করা; পৃষ্ঠপোষকতা করা। **4.** To bet upon; as, to *back* a race-horse; বাজি রাখা। **5.** To write upon the back of; as, to *back* a letter; to endorse; as, to *back* a note or legal document; পৃষ্ঠে লিখা; দলিলাদির পৃষ্ঠে নাম সহি করা। **6.** To ride upon; to mount; as, to *back* a horse; আরোহণ করা; চড়া। **7.** To adjoin behind; as, the chalk cliffs which *back* the beach; পশ্চাদ্দিকে সংলগ্ন

থাকা। *Verb i.* To move or go back; as, the horse refuses to *back;* হটা, পশ্চাদ্দিকে যাওয়া। **Back'-er**—One who backs or supports; পৃষ্ঠপোষক, সমর্থক। (*Naut.*) **To back an anchor**—To lay down a small anchor ahead of a larger one; (নৌ-বিদ্যা) বৃহত্তর নঙ্গরের অগ্রভাগে ক্ষুদ্র নঙ্গর সংযুক্ত করা। **To back down**—To abandon claim; দাবী ত্যাগ করা। **To back out of**—To retreat or withdraw (from an undertaking, etc.); to retreat; (প্রতিশ্রুতি পালন হইতে) পশ্চাৎপদ হওয়া; পিছাইয়া যাওয়া। (*Naut.*) **To back the sails**—To arrange the sails so as to cause the ship to move astern; (নৌ-বিদ্যা) পশ্চাদ্দিকে জাহাজ চালিত করার জন্য পাল সাজান। **To back up**—To lend support or assistance to; সাহায্য করা, সমর্থন করা, পৃষ্ঠপোষণ করা। **To back water**—To reverse a boat's motion with oar; দাঁড়ের সাহায্যে নৌকার গতি ফিরান।

băck, *adv.* **1.** In, to or toward the rear; as, to stand *back;* পশ্চাতে, পশ্চাদ্দিকে। **2.** Into the past; into or in an earlier position or condition; as, to go *back* to barbarism; অতীতকালে; পূর্ব্বাবস্থায়, পূর্ব্ব দশায়, পূর্ব্বস্থলে। **3.** In a state of restraint or hindrance; as, to keep oneself *back;* সংযতাবস্থায়, প্রতিবদ্ধাবস্থায়। **4.** In return; as, what have I to give you *back?* প্রতিদানে। **5.** Ago; since; as, sixty years *back;* আগে, পূর্ব্বে; গত হইল। **6.** Away from a promise; as, to go *back* from or upon one's word; প্রতিশ্রুতি হইতে পিছাইয়া। **7.** In concealment or reserve; as, to keep *back* the truth; গোপনে, হাতে। **8.** At a distance; as, *back* from the road; অল্পদূরে। **9.** Behindhand; as, a week *back* in their rent; পশ্চাদ্‌বর্ত্তী। **Back and edge**—Tooth and nail; যথাসাধ্য, প্রাণপণ, উঠিয়া পড়িয়া। **Back and forth**—To and fro; ইতস্ততঃ। **Backbite**—To speak ill of (in one's absence); to slander; পরোক্ষ বা অসাক্ষাতে কাহারো নিন্দা করা; অপবাদ করা। **Backbiting**—Secret slandering; পরোক্ষে পরদোষকীর্ত্তন; পরীবাদ, পৈশুন্য (মঃ ভাঃ)। **Backslide**—To slide back; to relapse into sin; স্বধর্ম্মভ্রষ্ট হওয়া, স্বধর্ম্মচ্যুত হওয়া; পুনর্ব্বার পাপপঙ্কে নিপতিত হওয়া। **Backslider**—An apostate; a renegade; স্বধর্ম্মচ্যুত ব্যক্তি; স্বধর্ম্মভ্রষ্ট ব্যক্তি। **Backsliding**—A falling back in principle or practice; apostasy; স্বধর্ম্মচ্যুতি; স্বধর্ম্মত্যাগ।

băck-găm'-mŏn, *n.* A game played by two persons on a board with dice and men (pieces); ফলকোপরি দুই ব্যক্তির পাশা এবং গুটির ক্রীড়াবিশেষ, চর্ম্মপট্টিকা ক্রীড়া (মঃ ইঃ)।

băck'-ing, *n.* **1.** The act expressed by the verb *to back* in its various senses; পশ্চাদ্দিকে স্থাপন, পশ্চাদ্দিকে চালনা, পৃষ্ঠপোষকতা, বাজি বা পণ রাখন, দলিলাদির পৃষ্ঠে নামসহিকরণ, আরোহণ। **2.** A body of supporters; পৃষ্ঠপোষকদল। **3.** The material used to form a thing's back or support; কোন বস্তুর পৃষ্ঠভাগ বা অবলম্বন গঠনার্থ উপকরণ। **4.** (*Book-binding*) The preparation of the back of a book, with glue, etc., before putting on the cover; (পুস্তক বাঁধাইর কাযে) মলাট লাগাইবার আগে শিরীস প্রভৃতিদ্বারা পুস্তকের পৃষ্ঠভাগের আবরণ প্রস্তুত করণ।

băck'-stitch (-stĭch), *v. t. & i.* To sew with overlapping stitches; একটী টাঁকের কতক অংশ অপর টাঁকের উপর রাখিয়া সেলাই করা।

băck'-ward (-wẽrd), **—wards** (wẽrds), *adv.* **1.** With the back in advance; as, to ride or move *backward;* পশ্চাদ্দিকে। **2.** Toward or on the back; in past time; ago; as, some reigns *backward;* পূর্ব্বে, আগে; অতীত সময়ে; গত হইল। **3.** From a better to a worse state; as, public affairs go *backward;* ক্রমশঃ মন্দাবস্থায়। **4.** In a reverse manner, way or direction; from the end to the beginning; as, to read *backward;* উল্টাদিকে, বিপরীত ভাবে; শেষ হইতে প্রথম দিকে। **5.** On the back or with the back downward; as, thou wilt fall *backward;* চিৎ হইয়া।

băck'-ward (-wẽrd), *adj.* **1.** Directed to back or rear; as, *backward* glances; পশ্চাদ্দিকে প্রেরিত বা পরিচালিত। **2.** Reversed; repeated from the end to the beginning; as, *backward* prayer; বিপর্য্যস্ত; উল্টাদিক হইতে আবৃত্ত, উল্টা, প্রতীপ, বিপরীত। **3.** Unwilling; sluggish; dilatory; shy; reluctant; as, the nobility were not *backward* with presents of the same nature; অনিচ্ছুক, নারাজ; মন্দগতি; দীর্ঘসূত্র; কুণ্ঠিত, সঙ্কোচপূর্ণ; পরাঙ্মুখ, পশ্চাৎপদ। **4.** Late or behind in time; as a *backward* season; বিলম্বিত, পশ্চাদাগত। **5.** Dull; behind in progress; as, a *backward* learner: a *backward* country; জড়-বুদ্ধি, নির্ব্বোধ; পশ্চাৎপদ, অনুন্নত। **—ness,** *n.*

băck-war-dā'-tion (-wẽr-), (*Stock Exchange*) The percentage paid by a seller of stock for right of delaying delivery (see CONTANGO); কোম্পানীর কাগজের অংশ অর্পণে বিলম্বের জন্য বিক্রেতা ক্রেতাকে শতকরা যে ধরাট প্রদান করিয়া থাকে, হর্জানা (হিঃ কোঃ)।

ba'-con (băcn), *n.* The back and sides of a pig salted and smoked; শূকরের পৃষ্ঠ ও পার্শ্বভাগের শুষ্ক এবং লবণাক্ত মাংস, বল্‌‌র (আপ্তে) **To save one's bacon**—To escape death or injury; আত্মরক্ষা করা,

নিজের গা বাঁচান। **To sell one's bacon**—To sell one's flesh or body ; আত্মদেহ বিক্রয় করা।

Bā-cō'-ni-ăn, *adj.* & *n.* Pertaining to Lord Bacon, or his system of philosophy ; inductive ; experimental ; লর্ড বেকন বা তৎপ্রবর্ত্তিত দর্শন-শাস্ত্র সম্বন্ধীয় ; বিশেষ হইতে সামান্যের সিদ্ধান্তমূলক ; পরীক্ষা-প্রসূত। ***Noun.*** A follower of Bacon ; লর্ড বেকনের মতাবলম্বী। **—ism,** *n.*

ba'-con-ȳ (băc'n-), *adj.* Bacon-like ; fatty ; বল্লূরবৎ ; চর্ব্বিযুক্ত।

băc-tē'-ri-ŭm, *n.* (*Pl.* BACTERIA) A genus of rod-shaped microscopic organism found in decomposing infusions of organic bodies ; নানাপ্রকার পীড়াবীজাণুর সাধারণ নাম, অনুদণ্ডক (সাঃ পঃ)। **—ol'-o-gist,** *n.* **—ol'-o gy,** *n.* The science relating to bacteria ; জীবাণু-তত্ত্ব। **—ter'-i-al,** *adj.*

băc'-ū-line, *adj.* Of or pertaining to the rod or to punishment by caning or flogging ; as, *baculine* argument ; যষ্টি বা বেত্রদণ্ড সম্বন্ধীয়।

băd, *adj.* & *n.* (*com.* worse ; *super.* worst) **1.** Opposite of good ; wicked ; unprincipled ; depraved ; malicious ; (as, man, heart, disposition, etc.) ; বদ, অসৎ ; দুষ্ট ; নীতিজ্ঞান-বর্জ্জিত ; ভ্রষ্ট ; বিদ্বেষ-পূর্ণ। **2.** Immoral ; vicious ; (as life, conduct, etc.) ; দুশ্চরিত্র ; পাপিষ্ঠ, পাপাসক্ত, দুর্জ্জন, দুঃশীল। **3.** Evil ; pernicious ; (as influence, example, habits) ; মন্দ, কু ; অনিষ্টকর। **4.** Ill or infirm ; in pain ; অসুস্থ, দুর্ব্বল ; বেদনাগ্রস্ত। **5.** Unwholesome or noxious ; (as air, climate, food) ; অস্বাস্থ্যকর, অপকারক, অহিতকারক। **6.** Defective ; (as crop) ; অসম্পূর্ণ। **7.** Poor or sterile ; (as soil) ; অনুর্ব্বর, উষর। **8.** Unfortunate ; unhappy ; (as issue, marriage) ; ভাগ্যহীন ; আনন্দশূন্য, সুখশূন্য। **9.** Painful ; unfavourable ; distressing ; (as news) ; যন্ত্রণাপূর্ণ ; অশুভ ; দুঃখজনক। **10.** Incompetent or inefficient ; (as workman) ; অনুপযুক্ত, অযোগ্য। **11.** Debased ; (as coin) ; অপকৃষ্ট, মেকি। ***Noun.*** **1.** Ill fortune ; as, to take the *bad* with the good ; দুরদৃষ্ট। **2.** The wrong side of an account ; হিসাবের ক্ষতির দিক। **3.** Ruin ; as, to go to the *bad* ; ধ্বংস। **Bad'-dish,** *adj.* **Bad'-ness,** *n.* **Bad blood**—Ill feeling ; বৈরভাব, রেষারেষি, দ্বেষ, হিংসা। **Bad book**—Disfavour ; কুদৃষ্টি। **Bad debts**—Debts that cannot be realised ; যে ঋণ কোন দিন আদায় হইবে এইরূপ আশা নাই। **Bad faith**—Treachery ; বিশ্বাসঘাতকতা। **Bad form**—Want of breeding ; শিক্ষাভাব। **(A) bad hand (at)**—আনাড়ী। **Bad shot**—A wrong guess ; ভুল অনুমান। **Bad-tempered**—বদ্-মেজাজী। **To be on bad terms**—To disagree ; মতদ্বৈধ হওয়া। **To go bad**—To decay ; ক্ষয়প্রাপ্ত হওয়া, জীর্ণ হওয়া, নষ্ট হওয়া। **To go to the bad**—To be ruined ; ধ্বংসমুখে যাওয়া, উচ্ছন্ন যাওয়া, গোল্লায় যাওয়া (*colloq.*)। **To the bad**—To a bad condition ; to ruin ; to the wrong side of an account ; in deficit ; মন্দাবস্থায় ; ধ্বংসমুখে ; কোন হিসাবের ক্ষতির দিকে ; কম্‌তিতে। **With bad grace**—Unwillingly ; অনিচ্ছার সহিত।

badge (băj), *n.* **1.** A distinctive emblem or mark (formerly of knight), now worn as a sign of office or membership in some society, etc. ; as, the *badge* of a policeman ; পরিচয়-ব্যঞ্জক চিহ্ন, লিঙ্গ, মুদ্রা (রাঃ তঃ), ব্যঞ্জনা (রঃ)। **2.** Something characteristic ; a token ; "Sweet mercy is nobility's true *badge* ; স্বভাবসিদ্ধ বিষয় ; নিদর্শনচিহ্ন, অভিজ্ঞান, লক্ষণ, চাপরাস। **Badgeman**—Alms-house man ; দরিদ্রাশ্রমবাসী। **Badge of honour**—সম্মান-চিহ্ন। **Badge of infamy**—কলঙ্ক-চিহ্ন। **Badge of slavery**—দাসত্ব-চিহ্ন।

badg'-êr (băj-), *n.* & *v. t.* **1.** A burrowing quadruped related to the bear ; ভল্লুক জাতীয় জন্তুবিশেষ, বিজ্জু (হিঃ কোঃ)। **2.** A painting-brush made of its hair ; উক্ত জন্তুর লোম-নির্ম্মিত চিত্রকরের তুলিকা। ***Verb t.*** **1.** To tease or annoy, as a badger, when baited ; কুকুর-তাড়িত বিজ্জুর মত বিরক্ত বা জ্বালাতন করা। **2.** To tease or irritate persistently ; ত্যক্ত বিরক্ত করা, হাড়ে হাড়ে জ্বালাতন করা।

Badger.

Badger-baiting or **drawing**—Setting dog to draw a badger from its (artificial) hole ; বিজ্জুকে গর্ত্ত হইতে বাহির করার উদ্দেশ্যে কুক্কুর নিযুক্ত করণ। **Badger-legged**—Having legs of unequal length ; অসমপদবিশিষ্ট। [বিজ্জুর পদ সকল অসমান—সাধারণ লোকের এই ভ্রান্ত বিশ্বাস।]

badg'-êr (băj-), *n.* An itinerant licensed dealer in provisions ; hawker ; ঘুরিয়া ঘুরিয়া খাদ্য দ্রব্য বিক্রয়ের অধিকার-প্রাপ্ত ব্যক্তি ; ফেরিওয়ালা।

bă-di-nāge', *n.* Playful or light raillery ; banter ; as, the playful *badinage* of a king's mistress ; লঘূক্তি (মঃ ইঃ), তরল পরিহাস ; নর্ম্মালাপ, রঙ্গরস।

băd'-lȳ, *adv.* **1.** Poorly ; defectively ; as, a *badly* furnished apartment ; হীনভাবে ; অপূর্ণরূপে, অসম্যক্‌রূপে। **2.** Incorrectly ; faultily ; as, he speaks English very *badly* ; অশুদ্ধরূপে ; দোষ-যুক্তভাবে, কদর্য্যভাবে।

3. Immorally ; wickedly ; as, *badly* conducted people ; অন্যায়রূপে ; মন্দভাবে, কুভাবে। 4. Cruelly ; unkindly ; as, he is *badly* beaten ; নিষ্ঠুরভাবে ; নির্দ্দয়ভাবে। 5. (*Colloq.*) Much ; greatly ; as, I want to see you *badly* ; (চলিত ভাষায়) অত্যন্ত ; অতিশয়। **To be badly off**—To be in straitened circumstances ; দুরবস্থায় পতিত হওয়া।

băd'-mĭn-tŏn, *n.* **1.** A game with net, rackets and shuttlecocks ; এক প্রকার ক্রীড়া। **2.** A cooling summer drink ; গ্রীষ্মকালীন পানীয় বিশেষ।

băf'-fle, *v. t.* **1.** To disconcert ; to frustrate or defeat ; নিষ্ফল বা পণ্ড করা ; বিফল করা, পরাস্ত করা, পরাজিত করা, প্রতিহত করা। **2.** To elude ; to foil ; কৌশলে পরিহার করা, এড়ান ; কৌশলে ব্যর্থ করা। **–fler,** *n.* **–fling,** *adj.* **–ment,** *n.* **Baffling winds**—Variable winds ; অস্থির বাতাস, পরিবর্ত্তনশীল পবন। **To baffle description**—To be beyond description ; বর্ণনাতীত হওয়া।

băft, băf'-tâ, *n.* A coarse stuff usually of cotton originally made in India ; বাপ্তা কাপড়।

băg, *n.* **1.** A receptacle of flexible material with an opening at the top ; a small sack ; ব্যাগ, থলি, তোড়া ; ভস্ত্রা, পুট (মঃ ইঃ), পুটলি। **2.** Money-bag ; as, the covetous man likes to count over his *bag* ; টাকার থলি। **3.** An udder ; a dug ; as, cows with good *bags* ; গবাদির স্তন, পালান ; বাঁট। **4.** A sac (in the body of animal), containing honey, poison, etc. ; মধু, বিষ প্রভৃতি পূর্ণ জীবদেহস্থ আধার-কোষ বিশেষ। **5.** *(In the languge of sportsmen)* The animals bagged or obtained ; as, a good *bag* (গৃহে সমানীত প্রচুর পরিমাণ শিকার) ; (শিকারিগণের ভাষায়) শিকারে যে সকল জন্তু পাওয়া যায় বা থলিয়াজাত করা হয়। **6.** (*Comm.*) A fixed or customary quantity of goods in a sack ; as, a *bag* of coffee ; (বাণিজ্য) ছালা, বস্তা। **Bag'-gy,** *adj.* Resembling a bag ; as, *baggy* trousers ; puffy ; as, *baggy* cheeks ; থলিয়াবৎ ; স্ফীত। **Bag and baggage**—With all belongings, esp. of utter expulsion ; as, get away with your *bag and baggage* ; তল্পি তল্পা (সহিত), পুঁটলা পুঁটলি (সহিত)। **Bag-man**—A commercial traveller ; ভ্রমণকারী সওদাগর। **Bag-wig**—An eighteenth century wig, with the back-hair enclosed in a bag ; অষ্টাদশ শতাব্দীর পরচুলা বিশেষ—এই পরচুলার পশ্চাদ্দিকস্থ কেশরাশি একটী থলিয়ার ভিতর আবদ্ধ থাকিত। **A bag of bones**—A very lean person ; কঙ্কালসার বা অস্থিচর্ম্মসার ব্যক্তি। **In the bottom of the bag**—As the last resource ; শেষ উপায় স্বরূপ। **The whole bag of tricks**—Every device ; everything ; all the lot : প্রত্যেক রকম কৌশল ; প্রত্যেক জিনিষ ; সবটা। (*Colloq.*) **To give one the bag or sac**—To dismiss a person from employment ; (চলিত ভাষায়) পদচ্যুত করা, বরতরফ করা। **To let the cat out of the bag**—To reveal a secret, esp. involuntarily ; গুপ্ত কথা ব্যক্ত করা, পেটের কথা ফাঁস করিয়া ফেলা।

băg, *v. t.* & *i.* **1.** To put into a bag or bags ; to store up generally ; as, the day on which they shall *bag* their hops; থলিয়ায় পুরা ; ভাণ্ডারজাত করা। **2.** To kill game ; as, he *bagged* two wolves ; শিকার করা। **3.** (*Colloq.*) To catch ; to steal ; as, *bagging* fowls ; (চলিত ভাষায়) ধরা ; চুরি করা। *Verb i.* To swell out, as a bag ; to bulge ; থলিয়ার মত ফাঁপা ; স্ফীত হওয়া, ফাঁপিয়া উঠা। **Bag'-ging** *n.* **1.** The act of putting into bags ; থলিয়াজাত করণ। **2.** The cloth or other materials for bags ; থলিয়ানির্ম্মাণে ব্যবহৃত বস্ত্র বা অন্যান্য উপকরণ।

băg, *v. t.* To cut (wheat, etc.) with a hook or scythe ; কাস্তে দ্বারা যব প্রভৃতি শস্য কাটা।

bă-gasse' (-găs), *n.* The refuge of the sugarcane after crushing ; আক মাড়ার পর যে ছোবড়া থাকে।

băg-ă-telle' (-tĕl), *n.* **1.** A trifle; a negligible amount ; অকিঞ্চিৎকর বস্তু, নগণ্য পরিমাণ পদার্থ। **2.** A light piece of music ; এক প্রকার সঙ্গীত। **3.** A minor game of billiard kind ; ক্রীড়া বিশেষ।

băg'-gāge, *n.* **1.** The portable equipment of an army ; সৈন্যদিগের পরিচ্ছদ, শিবির, তৈজসপত্র, খাদ্যসম্ভার, প্রভৃতি। **2.** The trunks, valises, etc. which one carries along with him on a journey ; জাহাজ বা রেলযাত্রী প্রভৃতির সঙ্গীয় মালপত্র, মোট, [বর্ত্তমানে এই অর্থে *luggage* শব্দ ব্যবহৃত হয়]। **3.** A good-for-nothing woman ; a strumpet ; নিষ্কর্ম্মা স্ত্রীলোক ; বেশ্যা, জলপাত্র (*slang.*)

bagn'-io (bân-yŏ), *n.* **1.** A bathing house (not now in England) ; স্নানাগার। **2.** An oriental prison ; প্রাচ্যদেশীয় কারাগার। **3.** A brothel ; বেশ্যালয়, বেশ্যাবেশ্ম, গণিকাভবন।

băg'-pīpe, –pīpes, *n.* A musical wind instrument, now used chiefly in Scotland; এক প্রকার বাদ্য-যন্ত্র, বর্ত্তমানে প্রধানতঃ স্কটলণ্ডের অন্তর্গত হাইলেণ্ড প্রদেশে ব্যবহৃত হয়, স্কটলেণ্ড দেশীয় সুষির যন্ত্র বিশেষ। **–pip-er,** *n.*

ghlander's bagpipe.

baignoire, *n.* (*F.*) A box at the theatre on the level of the stalls ; রঙ্গালয়ের আসন বিশেষ।

bah (bâ-), *inter.* An interjection of contempt : অবজ্ঞাসূচক অব্যয় পদ বিশেষ—বা ! বেশ !

bail (bāl), [L. *bajulare,* to bear a burden.] *n.* & *v. t.* **1.** The security for a prisoner's appearance, on giving which he is released pending trial ; জামিন। **2.** The person or persons who become(s) surety for a prisoner's appearance in court ; জামিনদাতা বা জামিনদাতৃগণ। ***Verb t.*** **1.** To admit to bail ; to release (a person) on security given for his appearance ; জামিনে মুক্তি দেওয়া ; উপস্থিত হইবার জন্য জামিন লইয়া অব্যাহতি দেওয়া। **2.** To secure liberation of, by becoming security for ; জামিনে মুক্ত করা (বন্দী কারাগারের ভিতরে থাকিলে)। **3.** To deliver (goods) in trust ; জিনিষ গচ্ছিত রাখা। **Bail′-a-ble,** *adj.* Admitting of bail, (of an offence) ; জামিনযোগ্য। **Bail-bond**—A bond by which bail or security is given ; জামানত নামা, জামিন নামা। **Bail for good conduct**—ফেয়াল জামিন (রঃ অঃ)। **Bail for personal appearance** — হাজির জামিন (রঃ অঃ), দর্শনপ্রতিভূ (যাজ্ঞঃ)। **To admit to bail**—জামিনে মুক্তি দেওয়া। **To bail over to keep the peace**—To require surety from a person for his keeping the peace ; শান্তি রক্ষার্থ জামিন চাওয়া। **To give leg bail**—To run away, (used jocularly) ; দৌড়িয়া পলায়ন করা। **To go bail**—To act as bail or surety ; জামিন হওয়া। To vouch for a thing ; as, I will *go bail* for that ; (কোন বিষয়ে) সাক্ষ্য প্রদান করা। **To stand bail**—To become security for one's appearance in a court ; as, he could get no one to *stand bail* for him ; (আসামীকে) আদালতে উপস্থিত করিবার জন্য জামিন হওয়া। To be a surety ; প্রতিভূ হওয়া।

bail (bāl), [L. *baculam,* a stick.], *n.* **1.** The outer line of a fortification formed of stakes ; the wall of a castle-court ; দুর্গাদির বহির্দ্দেশস্থ কীলক-নির্ম্মিত বৃতি ; পরিখাদি বেষ্টিত দুর্গ-প্রাঙ্গণের প্রাকার। **2.** A pole or bar separating horses in an open stable ; উন্মুক্ত অশ্বশালাস্থ অশ্বগণকে পৃথক্ করণার্থ দণ্ড-বিশেষ। **3.** A little bar laid on the tops of the stumps in cricket ; ক্রিকেট ক্রীড়ায় উইকেটের উপরিদেশে স্থাপিত ক্ষুদ্র কাষ্ঠ-খণ্ড। **Bail′-er,** *n.* A ball bowled so as to hit the bails at cricket ; যে বল এইরূপভাবে করা হয়—যাহাতে উইকেটের উপরিস্থিত কাষ্ঠখণ্ডে আঘাত করে।

bail (bāl), [OE *began,* to bend.], *n.* **1.** The hoop-handle of a kettle or similar vessel ; কেটলি প্রভৃতির হাতল। **2.** (*Australia*) A frame holding cow's head at milking ; (অষ্ট্রেলিয়াতে) দোহনের সময় গাভীর মস্তক-ধারণের জন্য কৌশল বিশেষ।

bail (bāl), *v. t.* To confine (rare) ; আবদ্ধ করা (অপ্রঃ)। **To bail up**—(*Australia*) To hold a cow's head during milking ; (অষ্ট্রেলিয়াতে) গো-দোহন সময়ে গাভীর মস্তক আবদ্ধ করা।

bail, (bāl), *v. t.* To throw water out of a boat with pails, etc. ; as, to *bail* out a boat ; সেচনীদ্বারা নৌকা প্রভৃতি হইতে জল সেচন করা। **Bail′-er,** *n.*

bail-ee′ (bāl-ē), *n.* (*Law*) The person to whom goods are committed in trust ; (আইন) যাহার হস্তে দ্রব্যাদি গচ্ছিত হয়।

bai′-ley (bā-lĭ), *n.* The outer wall of a castle ; পরিখাদি-বেষ্টিত ভবনের বহিঃ-প্রাকার। **Old Bailey**—The central criminal court in London ; প্রাচীন লণ্ডন নগরীর প্রধান ফৌজদারী আদালত।

bail′-ie (bāl-ĭ), *n.* A Scotch municipal magistrate, corresponding to an English alderman ; ইংলণ্ডের নগরপালের অনুরূপ স্কটলণ্ডদেশীয় নাগরিক কর্ম্মচারী বিশেষ।

bail′-iff (bāl-ĭf), *n.* **1.** An officer under sheriff, appointed to make arrests, collect fines, summon juries, etc. ; শেরিফের অধীনস্থ কর্ম্মচারি-বিশেষ, উক্ত কর্ম্মচারী আদালতের আদেশ-ক্রমে গ্রেপ্তার, জরিমানা আদায়, জুরিদিগকে আহ্বান প্রভৃতি কার্য্য করিয়া থাকেন, যষ্টিধর (আঃ বঃ)। **2.** A land-holder's steward ; জমিদারের কার্য্যাধ্যক্ষ। **3.** An agent of the lord of a manor ; ইংলণ্ডদেশীয় সম্ভ্রান্ত-বংশীয় ভূম্যধিকারীর কার্য্যকারক।

bail′-i-wick (bāl-), *n.* The jurisdiction of a bailiff ; শেরিফের অধীনস্থ নাজিরের এলাকা।

bail′-mĕnt (bāl-), *n.* **1.** The delivery of goods in trust ; দ্রব্যাদি গচ্ছিত করণ। **2.** The act of bailing a person accused ; আসামীকে জামিনে খালাস করণ।

bail-ŏr′ (bāl-), *n.* One who delivers goods to another for a stated purpose ; নির্দ্দিষ্ট উদ্দেশ্যে পরহস্তে দ্রব্যাদি সমর্পণকারী।

bails′-măn (bāls-), *n.* One who gives bail for another ; জামিনদাতা।

bain-marie′, (*F.*), *n.* A vessel of hot water in which stewpans are stood to warm ; উষ্ণজলপূর্ণ পাত্রবিশেষ—ইহাতে অন্য পাত্র রাখিয়া মৃদুসন্তাপে তদভ্যন্তরস্থ দ্রব্য সিদ্ধ করা হয়।

Bai-răm, *n.* The name of two Mohammedan festivals, (Lesser and Greater) of which one is held at the close of the fast called *Ramzan* and the other seventy days after ; ঈদ, বকরীদ।

bairn (bārn), *n.* (*Scot.* & *Dial. Eng.*) A child ; "Think on your *bairns* and wives ;" সন্তান, ছেলে-পিলে (*colloq.*)।

bait, [Icel. *baita,* to cause to bite.] *v. t.* & *i.* **1.** To harass and provoke (wild animals) with dogs ;

as, to *bait* a bear, bull, etc. ; কুকুর লেলাইয়া উত্যক্ত করা। **2.** To give food and drink to (horses) on journey ; ভ্রমণকালে (অশ্বগণকে) খাদ্য ও পানীয় প্রদান করা। **3.** To put food on or in (hook, trap, etc.) ; (বড়শী, বাগুড়া প্রভৃতিতে) টোপ, চার প্রভৃতি দেওয়া। ***Verb i.*** To stop (at an inn) on a journey ; বিশ্রাম ও জলযোগের জন্য (পান্থশালায়) থামা।

bait (bāt), *n.* **1.** An attractive morsel of food placed on a hook or in a trap to allure fish or other animals ; মৎস্য অথবা অন্যান্য জন্তুকে বড়শী অথবা বাগুড়ায় বিদ্ধ অথবা আবদ্ধ করণার্থ ব্যবহৃত খাদ্য বা অনুবিধ পদার্থ, চার, টোপ। **2.** (*Fig.*) An allurement ; (লক্ষণায়) প্রলোভন। **3.** A halt in a journey for refreshment or rest ; "They make a stage of thirty miles without a *bait* ;" বিশ্রাম কিম্বা জলযোগের জন্য পথিমধ্যে অবস্থিতি।

baize (bāz), *n.* A coarse woollen stuff, employed chiefly for curtains, cover, etc. ; পর্দ্দা, আবরণ প্রভৃতির জন্য একপ্রকার স্থূল পশমী বস্ত্র, পট্টু।

bāke, *v. t.* & *i.* **1.** To cook by dry heat in closed place or on hot surface (not by direct exposure to fire) ; চুল্লীর ভিতর, কয়লার উপর, অথবা প্রস্তর খণ্ড কিম্বা ধাতু পাত্রোপরি সেঁকিয়া পাক করা, সেঁকা। **2.** To harden by heat ; as, to *bake* bricks : the sun *baked* the mud ; উত্তাপ দ্বারা কঠিন করা। **3.** To harden by cold, (as frost does) ; as, the earth *baked* with frost ; শৈত্যপ্রয়োগ-দ্বারা শক্ত করা। ***Verb i.*** To undergo the process of baking ; to become firm or hard with heat ; as, the ground *bakes* in the hot sun ; (রুটি) পক্ক হওয়া ; উত্তাপে শুষ্ক ও কঠিন হওয়া। **Bakehouse**—A house or room for baking bread or for making loaf-sugar ; রুটি নির্ম্মাণশালা, পূপশালা (মঃ সং), পরিষ্কৃত শর্করাখণ্ড প্রস্তুত করণার্থ গৃহ। **Bakestone**—A flat stone or plate of iron on which cakes are baked in the oven ; যে চ্যাপ্‌টা পাথর কিম্বা লোহার পাতের উপর রাখিয়া চুল্লীর ভিতর রুটি সেঁকা হয়। (*Colloq.*) **Only half-baked**—Deficient in sense ; half-witted ; (চলিতভাষায়) অপরিপক্ক ; অপরিণত-বুদ্ধি।

bāk′-ēr, (*fem.* BAKERESS), *n.* **1.** A professional bread-maker ; পূপকার, রুটিওয়ালা। **2.** A kind of artificial fly used in fishing ; মৎস্য শিকারে ব্যবহৃত কৃত্রিম মক্ষিকাবিশেষ। **—y,** *n.* **Baker-legged, —kneed**—Knock-kneed ; সংহতজানু (মঃ উঃ)। [অর্থাৎ চলিবার সময় যাহার জানুদ্বয় পরস্পরের সহিত ঠোকাঠুকি লাগে।] **Baker's dozen**—[The 13th loaf being huckster's profit] Thirteen ; তের।

bāk′-ing, *n.* **1.** The process of preparing bread ; রুটি-সেঁকন। **2.** The bread baked at a time ; "Susan with her plate of *bakings* ;" একবারে যে পরিমাণ রুটি সেঁকা হয়। **Baking-powder**—A substitute for yeast ; সুরামণ্ডের (গাঁজলা উঠা মদের ফেনার) পরিবর্ত্তে ব্যবহৃত পদার্থ-বিশেষ।

băk′-sheesh (-shĭsh), **—shish,** *n.* Present of money ; tip ; (no article is used before this word) ; অর্থ-পুরস্কার ; বকশিশ।

Bā′-laam (-lăm), *n.* **1.** Name of the prophet whose history is narrated in *numbers xxii-xxiv* ; প্রাচীন বাইবেল গ্রন্থোক্ত ভাববাদী বিশেষ। **2.** (*Slang.*) A matter kept in stock to fill up gaps in newspaper ; (ইতর ভাষায়) সংবাদ-পত্রের শূন্যস্থান-পূরণার্থ যে সমস্ত সংবাদ বা প্রবন্ধাদি হাতে রাখা হয়।

băl′-ănce, *n.* **1.** An apparatus for weighing ; তুলা, তরাজু, তুলাদণ্ড, নিক্তি। **2.** The regulating gear of a clock or watch ; ঘড়ির স্পন্দন-(টক্ টক্ শব্দ) নিয়ামক চক্রশ্রেণী। **3.** (*Astron.*) The zodiacal constellation (*Libra* or the *Scales*) ; (জ্যোতির্বিজ্ঞান) তুলা রাশি। **4.** (*Fig.*) The means by which actions and principles are weighed and estimated ; as, the victory depended long in doubtful *balance* ; (লক্ষণায়) কার্য্য, মূলতত্ত্ব প্রভৃতি তুলনার উপায়। **5.** Power to decide ; authoritative control ; as, England held the *balance* with a strong hand ; মীমাংসার ক্ষমতা ; প্রভুত্ব। **6.** Equilibrium ; steady position ; as, the *balance* of the planets and the sun ; সাম্যাবস্থা, সমতা, সাম্য, তুল্যাবস্থা ; স্থিরতা। **7.** The difference between the Dr. and Cr. sides of an account ; an equality between the sums total of the two sides of an account ; as, the *balance* shows the increase of debts ; অবশিষ্ট, জেরবাকী ; জমা ও খরচের সমষ্টির সমতা। **8.** A weight used as a counterbalance in weighing ; a counterpoise ; (also *fig.*) a thing of equal influence or value ; "If France had ceased to be a *balance* to Spain ;" যে ওজন দ্বারা ভারসাম্য সাধিত হয় ; প্রতিমান ; (অপিচ লক্ষণায়) সমমূল্য বা সমক্ষমতাবিশিষ্ট বস্তু। **9.** (*Art.*) A harmony of design and proportion ; (কলাবিদ্যা) চিত্রের পরিকল্পনা ও বিভিন্ন অংশের সুসমাবেশ বা সঙ্গতি। **Balance in hand**—The sum of money remaining over after realizing all assets and discharging all liabilities ; সমস্তপ্রাপ্য আদায় ও ঋণ পরিশোধের পর হস্তে যে টাকা স্থিত থাকে, রোকড়বাকী (হিঃ কোঃ)। **Balance of power**—International equilibrium ; আন্তর্জাতিক শক্তি-সামঞ্জস্য। [কোন রাজ্যকেই এইরূপ প্রাধান্য লাভ করিতে দেওয়া হয়না যদ্দারা অপর রাজ্যের স্বাধীনতা সঙ্কটাপন্ন হইতে পারে।] **Balance of trade**—An estimation of the difference of value between the exports and imports of a country ; কোন দেশের

আমদানী ও রপ্তানি মালের মূল্যের প্রভেদ অবধারণ। **Balance-sheet**—A sheet of paper showing a summary and balance of accounts ; উদ্বর্ত্ত পত্র, পাকা চিঠা। **Balance-thermometer**—তাপমাপক তুলা (হিঃ কোঃ)। **Balance-wheel**—A wheel in a clock or chronometer which regulates motion ; ঘড়ী বা নাড়ীমান যন্ত্রের স্পন্দন বা গতি নিয়ামক চক্র বিশেষ, কালক্রমচক্র (হিঃ কোঃ), ক্রমসাধক চক্র (ঐ)। **Cash-balance**—মজুত বাকী। **To be thrown off one's balance**—To be irresolute ; সংশয়াকুল হওয়া। **To hold** or **keep the balance even**—To preserve a fair equality ; দুই পক্ষের মধ্যে সমতা রক্ষা করা, নিরপেক্ষভাব অবলম্বন করা। **To lose one's balance**—To fall physically ; to be upset mentally ; টলিয়া পড়া ; মন টলিয়া পড়া, মানসিক স্থৈর্য্য লোপ হওয়া, বিচলিত হওয়া। **To strike a balance**—To calculate the exact difference, if any, between the two sides of an account ; জমাখরচ মিলান। **To tremble** or **hang in the balance**—To be uncertain ; to be in a critical state ; অনিশ্চিত অবস্থায় থাকা, সংশয় দোলায় দোদুল্যমান হওয়া ; সঙ্কটাপন্ন অবস্থায় থাকা।

băl'-ănce, *v. t.* & *i.* **1.** To place or weigh in the scales ; (*fig.*) to estimate the two sides or aspects of anything ; নিক্তিতে ওজন করা ; (লক্ষণায়) কোন বিষয়ের উভয় দিক বিবেচনা বা আলোচনা করা। **2.** To compare in relative force, importance or value, etc. ; to weigh (two things) against each other ; বিভিন্ন বস্তুর আপেক্ষিক শক্তি, গুরুত্ব বা মূল্য তুলনা করা ; দুইটী বস্তু পরস্পরের সহিত তুলনা করা। **3.** To equal in number, weight force, etc. ; to counteract ; as, one species of attraction *balances* another ; সমান হওয়া ; প্রতিরোধ করা। **4.** To settle and adjust, as an account ; to equalize the total debits and credits of accounts ; as, this credit *balances* the account ; হিসাব ঠিক করা বা মিলান ; জমা খরচ মিলান। **5.** To keep steady or erect ; to poise ; "Strong men *balancing* chest of drawers upon their heads ;" স্থির রাখা, খাড়া রাখা ; সমভারাবস্থায় স্থির রাখা। ***Verb i.*** **1.** To be in equipoise ; to be equal with ; দুইদিকে সমভার হওয়া ; সমতুল হওয়া। **2.** To waver ; to hesitate ; সংশয় দোলায় দোলায়িত হওয়া ; ইতস্ততঃ করা। **3.** (*Dancing*) To move toward a person or couple and then back ; (নৃত্য) কোন ব্যক্তি বা নর্ত্তক-নর্ত্তকীযুগলের অভিমুখে নৃত্যচ্ছলে অগ্রসর হইয়া পরে পশ্চাদ্দিকে আসা। **4.** To be equal in debits and credits, as accounts ; জমা খরচ মিলা। **—a-ble**, *adj.* **—ancer**, *n.* A tumbler ; an acrobat ; ডিগ্‌বাজীকর ; রজ্জুনর্ত্তক। **—ment**, *n.* **Accouut balances**—Two sides are equal ; জমাখরচ মিল আছে।

băl'-ăs, *n.* A species of ruby ; একজাতীয় পদ্মরাগ মণি। [পারস্যের অন্তর্গত বাদখাসান জেলায় পাওয়া যায়।]

bă-laus'-tine (-lâs), *n.* The red rose-like flower of the wild pomegranate ; (used as an astringent when dried) ; আরণ্য-দাড়িম্বের মত রক্তবর্ণ গোলাব সদৃশ পুষ্প।

băl'-cō-nȳ, *n.* **1.** A platform projecting from the wall of a house or room, supported by pillars, brackets or consoles and inclosed by a parapet ; বারাণ্ডা, অলিন্দ (মেঘঃ)। **2.** (*Theatr.*) The tire of seats generally between the dress-circle and gallery ; (রঙ্গালয়) প্রাচীরোদগত মঞ্চোপরি উপর্য্যুপরি বিন্যস্ত আসন-শ্রেণী।

bald, *adj.* **1.** With scalp wholly or partly hairless ; কেশহীন, নেড়া, টাকপড়া, খল্বাট (কেঙ্গিঃ)। **2.** (Of animals, mountains, trees, etc.) Hairless ; featherless ; treeless ; leafless ; napless ; (জন্তু, বৃক্ষ, পর্ব্বতাদি সম্বন্ধে) নির্লোম ; পালকশূন্য ; তরুশূন্য ; নিষ্পত্র, পত্রহীন ; তন্তু- (আঁশ) হীন। **3.** (Of horse) Marked with white, esp. on the face ; (অশ্ব-সম্বন্ধে) শ্বেতবর্ণ-চিহ্ন যুক্ত, (বিশেষতঃ মুখে)। **4.** (Of style) Destitute of ornament ; unadorned ; as, to the preface to his *bald* translation ; bare ; jejune ; monotonous ; (রচনাপদ্ধতি-সম্বন্ধে) অলঙ্কারহীন ; অনলঙ্কৃত ; সাদাসিধা ; অন্তঃসারশূন্য, নীরস ; একঘেঁয়ে। **5.** (Of bad qualities) undisguised ; palpable ; as, *bald* baseness, egotism ; অপ্রচ্ছন্ন ; সুস্পষ্ট। **Bald'-ly**, *adv.* **Bald'-ness**, *n.* Absence or loss of hair, esp. from the head ; খালিত্য (সুশ্রুঃ), ইন্দ্রলুপ্ত। **Bald head, Bald-pate**—One who has a bald head ; also, a kind of pigeon ; কেশ-শূন্য মনুষ্য, টাক-পড়া লোক, টেকো ; একপ্রকার পারাবত।

băl'-dă-chin, —chi-nō, —quin (-kin), *n.* **1.** (*Formerly*) Rich brocade ; (পূর্ব্বে) এক প্রকার বহুমূল্য গুলবাহার রেশমী কাপড়। **2.** A structure in the form of a canopy, either supported on columns or suspended from the roof, and placed above an altar, throne or doorway ; স্তম্ভোপরি অবলম্বিত ও ছাদ হইতে বিলম্বিত, বেদী রাজসিংহাসন বা দ্বারোপরিবিস্তৃত বিতান বা চন্দ্রাতপ-বিশেষ।

Baldachin.
From St. Peter's, Rome.

băl'-dêr-dăsh, *n.* **1.** (*Formerly*) A worthless mixture, especially of liquors ; (পূর্ব্বে) অসার মিশ্র পদার্থ (বিশেষতঃ সুরা প্রভৃতির) । **2.** Senseless jargon ; nonsense : অর্থশূন্য প্রলাপ ; বাজে কথা, নিরর্থক কথা, বকবক্ ।

bald′-mon-ey (-mŭn-ĭ), *n.* An umbelliferous plant with yellowish flowers ; এক প্রকার পীতবর্ণপুষ্পবিশিষ্ট ছত্র-পুষ্পী উদ্ভিদ্ ।

bal′-dric, —drick, *n.* A belt for sword, bugle, etc., hung from shoulder to opposite hip ; তরবারি, রণ-বংশী প্রভৃতির জন্য উপবীতাকারে বিলম্বিত চর্ম্মপট্টি বিশেষ । **—wise,** *adv.*

bāle, *n.* Misery ; calamity ; destruction ; evil ; দুর্দ্দশা ; বিপদ্ ; ধ্বংস ; অমঙ্গল । **Bale′-ful,** *adj.* Mischievous ; destructive ; as, *baleful* birds ; pernicious ; malignant ; as, the *baleful* dog-star ; অনিষ্টজনক, অনর্থকারক ; ধ্বংসকারী ; সাংঘাতিক ; অশুভ । **Bale′-ful-ly,** *adv.* **Bale′-ful-ness,** *n.*

bāle, *n.* & *v. t.* A bundle or package of goods for storage or transportation ; বস্তা, গাঁইট । ***Verb t.*** To make up into bales or bundles ; as, cotton has been *baled* and sent down to the seaport ; বস্তাবন্দী করা, গাঁইটবন্দী করা ।

bāle, *v. t.* To throw water out of a boat with buckets ; সেচনীদ্বারা জল সেচা । **To bale up**—To scoop up ; জল সেচা ।

bă-leen′ (-lēn), *n.* Whale-bone ; তিমি মৎস্যের অস্থি ।

bāle′-fīre, *n.* **1.** A great fire in the open air ; মুক্তস্থানে প্রজ্বালিত বৃহৎ অগ্নি । **2.** A beacon-fire ; সঙ্কেতাগ্নি । **3.** Any great fire ; a bonfire ; বৃহৎ অগ্নি ; বহ্ন্যুৎসব ।

balk (bäk), **baulk** (bäk), *n., v. t.* & *i.* **1.** A ridge left unploughed ; জমির আল । **2.** A large beam or rafter ; esp. a tie-beam of a house ; বৃহৎকড়িকাষ্ঠ, বর্গা ; আড়কাঠা । **3.** A hindrance or disappointment ; a check ; "A *balk* to the confidence of bold undertaker ;" বাধা, প্রতিবন্ধ, ব্যাঘাত, মনোভঙ্গ ; প্রতিহতি । ***Verb t.*** **1.** To miss intentionally ; to shun ; as, I will not *baulk* your house ; (also *fig.*) to pass over ; to ignore ; "No topic is *baulked* if it come uppermost ;" ইচ্ছাপূর্ব্বক পরিহার করা ; এড়ান ; (অপিচ লক্ষণায়) উপেক্ষা করা ; অগ্রাহ্য করা । **2.** To refuse (anything offered as food or drink) ; as, he never *baulked* his glass ; (খাদ্য বা পানীয়) প্রত্যাখ্যান করা । **3.** To avoid (a duty, responsibility, etc.) ; কর্ত্তব্য, দায়িত্ব প্রভৃতি এড়ান, উপেক্ষা করা, অবহেলা করা, পরিহার করা । **4.** To hinder or thwart (a person, action, etc.) ; to check (feelings) ; to disappoint (expectations) ; to frustrate ; বাধা দেওয়া, ব্যর্থ করা ; (আবেগ) রোধ করা ; নিরাশ করা ; বিফল করা । ***Verb i.*** To stop short ; to jib ; to shy ; as, the horse *balks* ; চলিতে চলিতে হঠাৎ থামা ; পাশের দিকে ফিরা ; (ভয়াদি হেতু) হঠাৎ চমকিয়া এক পাশে সরিয়া যাওয়া ।

ball, *n.* **1.** Any round body or mass ; as, a *ball* of twine, snow, etc. ; যে কোন প্রকার গোলাকার বস্তু, পিণ্ড, গোলক । **2.** Any celestial body ; the globe ; জ্যোতিষ্ক ; ভূমণ্ডল । **3.** Any part of a thing that is rounded or protuberant ; as, the *ball* of the thumb ; কোন বস্তুর গোলাকার বা ন্যুব্জ অংশ । **4.** Any solid missile (not always spherical) for cannons and other fire-arms ; কামানাদি আগ্নেয়াস্ত্র হইতে নিক্ষেপণীয় সীসক বা লৌহ নির্ম্মিত গোলাকার, নলাকার বা মোচাকার গোলা গুলি প্রভৃতি, গোলাগুলি । **5.** A globular body to play with ; ক্রীড়া-গোলক, কন্দুক । **6.** A general name for games in which a ball is thrown, kicked or knocked ; ব্যাট্‌বল, ফুটবল প্রভৃতি ক্রীড়া, গোলক্রীড়া (হরিঃ) । **7.** A throw or delivery of the ball at cricket ; ক্রিকেট (দণ্ড-কন্দুক ক্রীড়া) খেলায় ক্রীড়া-গোলক নিক্ষেপ । **Ball-and-socket**—A joint in which a ball moves within a socket so as to admit of motion in every direction within certain limits ; একপ্রকার সন্ধি (জোড়া), ইহাতে একটী গোলক কোটরের ভিতর সঞ্চালিত হইয়া নির্দ্দিষ্ট সীমার মধ্যে যে কোন দিকে গতির সাহায্য করে । **Ball-bearing**—A mechanical device for lessening the friction of axle-bearings by means of small loose metal balls ; ক্ষুদ্র ক্ষুদ্র অসংশ্লিষ্ট ধাতব গোলক সকল দ্বারা চক্র-দণ্ড এবং তৎসংলগ্ন অবলম্ব-দণ্ডাংশের ঘর্ষণ-হ্রাসার্থ যান্ত্রিক কৌশল বিশেষ । **Ball-cartridge**—A cartridge containing both powder and ball ; যে টোটার ভিতর গুলি ও বারুদ উভয়ই থাকে । **Ball-cock, Ball-tap**—An automatic cistern-tap with a floating ball ; প্লবমান গোলকবিশিষ্ট জলকুণ্ডের স্বয়ং-বহ নল-বিশেষ । **Ball-flower**—An architectural ornament ; স্থাপত্য ভূষা-বিশেষ । **Ball of the eye**—(Formerly) The pupil ; (now) the entire eye-ball ; (পূর্ব্বে) কনীনিকা, চক্ষুর তারা ; (বর্ত্তমানে) অক্ষিগোল (মঃ উঃ), অক্ষি-গোলক । **Ball of the foot**—The rounded part at the base of the great toe ; পদাঙ্গুষ্ঠের মূলদেশস্থ গোলাকার অংশ । **The ball is with you**—It is your turn ; এখন তোমার পালা । **To have the ball at one's feet**—To have a thing in one's power ; (কোনও বস্তু) স্ববশে বা নিজের আয়ত্তাধীনে থাকা । **To take up the ball**—To take one's turn in conversation ; নিজের পালার সময় কথা বলা । **To keep the ball up or rolling**—To keep conversation or an undertaking from flagging ; কথোপকথনের কৌতূহল সজীব রাখা, কোন কার্য্যের উৎসাহ অক্ষুণ্ণ রাখা ।

ball, *n.* A social assembly for dancing ; নৃত্যসম্মিলনবিশেষ। **Ball-room**—A room for balls ; নৃত্যশালা। **To open the ball**—To lead first dance ; প্রথম নৃত্য পরিচালনা করা। (*Fig.*) To commence operations ; কার্য্যারম্ভ করা।

ball, *v. i.* & *t.* To gather (itself) into a ball ; as, the snow *balls* ; পিণ্ডীভূত হওয়া, বর্ত্তুলাকারে পরিণত হওয়া। ***Verb t.*** To make (snow etc.) into a ball ; to wind (thread) into a ball ; (বরফের) গুলি পাকান ; সূতার গুটি পাকান, পিণ্ডাকারে পরিণত করা বা গুটান।

băl′-lăd, *n.* A light simple song of any kind ; a poem in short stanzas narrating some popular story ; গেয়পদ (সাঃ দঃ) ; লোকপ্রিয়-গাথা, ছড়া, পাঁচালি। **—ry,** *n.* **Ballad-monger**—A seller or maker of ballads ; গাথাবিক্রেতা, গাথারচক।

băl-lade′ (-lâd), *n.* A form of French versification, sometimes imitated in English ; ফরাসীদেশীয় কবিতারচনা-পদ্ধতি। **Ballade royal**—Stanzas of seven or eight lines of ten syllables ; দশ-সংখ্যক পদাংশ-সমন্বিত সপ্ত বা অষ্ট পংক্তিবিশিষ্ট শ্লোকবিশেষ।

băl′-lăst, *n.* **1.** Any heavy substance, as stone, iron, etc., placed in the hold of a ship to secure stability ; জাহাজ স্থির রাখিবার জন্য তলদেশে রক্ষিত প্রস্তর, লৌহখণ্ড, প্রভৃতি গুরুভার পদার্থসমূহ। **2.** Gravel, broken stone, etc., used to form the bed of a rail-road ; রেলপথের মধ্যস্থানে নিক্ষিপ্ত কঙ্কর, প্রস্তর-খণ্ড প্রভৃতি। **3.** The sand carried in bags in the car of a balloon, to steady it ; ব্যোমযান স্থির রাখার নিমিত্ত তৎসংলগ্ন রথোপরি নীত বালুকাপূর্ণ থলিসমূহ। **4.** (*Fig.*) That which gives stability in morals or politics ; as, the *ballast* of sound legislation ; যদ্দ্বারা নৈতিক বা রাজনীতিক বিষয়ে স্থিরতা সাধিত হয়। **A man of no ballast, The man wants a ballast**—An unsteady man ; চঞ্চল-মতি ব্যক্তি, অস্থিরচিত্ত ব্যক্তি।

băl′-lăst, *v. t.* **1.** To steady, as a vessel, by putting heavy substances in the hold ; তলদেশে গুরুভার বস্তু স্থাপনকরত জাহাজাদি স্থির রাখা। **2.** To fill in the bed of a railroad, etc. ; কঙ্কর, প্রস্তরখণ্ড, প্রভৃতি দ্বারা রেলপথের উভয় রেলের মধ্যবর্ত্তী স্থান পূর্ণ করা। **3.** (*Fig.*) To steady morally or mentally ; "Charity must *ballast* the heart" ; নৈতিক বা মানসিকবিষয়ে স্থির বা অটল রাখা। **—ing,** *n.*

ballerina, [*pl.* BALLERINE, BALLERINAS,] (*It.*), *n.* A female dancer ; নর্ত্তকী।

băl′-lĕt (or bă-lā), *n.* A combined performance of professional dancers on the stage ; হাবভাব পূর্ব্বক নৃত্য, লাস্য।

ballet d'action, (*F.*), *n.* A pantomimic dance ; সংদার যাত্রার নৃত্য।

băl-lis′-tă, *n.* An ancient military engine, for hurling stones and other missiles ; পুরাকালে ব্যবহৃত পাষাণাদিক্ষেপক বৃহৎ সামরিক যন্ত্র-বিশেষ। **—tis,** *adj.*

ballon d'essai, (*F.*), *n.* (*Lit.* a trial balloon) A statement circulated to test opinion ; জনসাধারণ বা পররাষ্ট্র সমূহের মতামত পরীক্ষার জন্য প্রচারিত উক্তি, রাজনীতিক ব্যবস্থা প্রভৃতি।

Balloon.

băl-loon′, *n.* & *v. i.* **1.** An air-tight envelope of paper, silk, etc. which, when inflated with light gas, rises in the air ; ব্যোমযান, বেলুন, বিমান। **2.** (*Arch.*) A large ball on the top of a pillar, pier, etc. ; (স্থপতি-বিজ্ঞান) স্তম্ভাদির উপরিস্থিত প্রকাণ্ড গোলক। **3.** (*Chem.*) A large hollow, glass globe used in distillations ; (রসায়ন-শাস্ত্র) পরিস্রবণ কার্য্যে ব্যবহৃত শূন্যগর্ভ গোলক বিশেষ। ***Verb i.*** **1.** To ascend in a balloon ; ব্যোমযানে আকাশ মার্গে আরোহণ করা। **2.** To swell out like a balloon ; as, her gown *ballooning* behind him ; ব্যোমযানের মত ফুলিয়া বা ফাঁপিয়া উঠা। **—er, —ist,** *ns.* An aeronaut ; ব্যোমযাত্রী।

băl′-lŏt, *n.* & *v. i.* **1.** A small ball, ticket or paper used in secret voting ; গুপ্ত মতপ্রদানে ব্যবহৃত গুটিকা, চিরকুট বা কাগজ, গুপ্তানুমতি-সূচক গুলিকা প্রভৃতি। **2.** The system of secret voting by small balls or tickets ; গুটিকা বা চিরকুটদ্বারা গুপ্ত মতপ্রদানপদ্ধতি। ***Verb i.*** To give secret vote ; (*for, against*) ; গোপনে মত প্রদান করা। **Ballot-box**—A box in which voting ballots are deposited ; যে বাক্সে নির্ব্বাচনমতদানের গুটিকা সকল রক্ষিত হয়, গুটিকাধার। **To ballot for**—To select (officials etc.) by secret voting ; গোপনে মত প্রদানদ্বারা (রাজকর্ম্মচারী প্রভৃতি) নির্ব্বাচন করা।

băl′-lŏt, *n.* A small bale of 70 to 120lbs. ; ৭০ হইতে ১২০ পাউণ্ড পর্য্যন্ত ওজনের ক্ষুদ্র বস্তা।

băl′-lŏt-āge, *n.* In France, the second ballot to decide between the two candidates who have come nearest to the legal majority ; (ফরাসীদেশে) দুই জন প্রার্থীর মধ্যে কাহার পক্ষের ভোট বিধি-নির্দ্দিষ্ট ভোট সংখ্যার আধিক্যের সর্ব্বাপেক্ষা নিকটবর্ত্তী—তন্নিরূপণার্থ দ্বিতীয়বার গুটিকা দ্বারা গোপনে ভোট প্রদান।

balm (bâm), *n.* **1.** A fragrant and medicinal exudation from certain trees ; কতিপয় বৃক্ষের সুগন্ধি

ও ভেষজগুণ-সম্পন্ন নির্যাস। 2. A fragrant ointment, (soothing pain or healing wounds, etc.); (বেদনাপ্রশমক বা ক্ষতনাশক) সুরভি মলম। 3. (*Fig.*) A healing or soothing influence; as, the *balm* of sleep; (লক্ষণায়) তাপহারিণী বা শান্তিদায়িনী শক্তি। 4. The name of several aromatic plants; কতিপয় সুগন্ধি উদ্ভিদের সাধারণ নাম, রামতুলসী (খোরী) (Common balm or *Melissa officinalis*)। **Balm'-i-ness,** *n.* **Balm cricket** — The European cicada; ইয়ুরোপদেশীয় ঝিঁঝিঁ পোকা, ঝিল্লী বিশেষ।

băl-mŏr'-ăl, *n.* 1. A kind of woollen petticoat; স্ত্রীলোকের অন্তর্বাস (ঘাঘরার নীচে পরিধেয়) বিশেষ। 2. A Scotch cap; স্কটলণ্ড দেশে ব্যবহৃত একপ্রকার টুপী। 3. A kind of boot lacing in front; একপ্রকার বুটজুতা।

bâlm'-ÿ, *adj.* 1. Deliciously mild; fragrant; (said of air, weather, etc.); মৃদুমধুর; সুগন্ধি, সুবাসময়। 2. Delicately fragrant; as, *balmy* firs; মৃদুসৌরভময়। 3. Of healing virtue; as, *balmy* medicines; রোগনাশক, স্বাস্থ্যজনক। 4. Yielding balm; সুগন্ধি নির্যাসপ্রদ।

bal'-săm, *n.* 1. Any plant of the genus *impatiens*; দোমটী (যোঃ), দোপাটী (ঐ) প্রভৃতি পুষ্পবৃক্ষ। 2. An aromatic resinous product; সুরভি নির্যাস-বিশেষ। 3. (*Fig.*) A healing or soothing agency; "From friendship's source the *balsam* flows;" (লক্ষণায়) প্রশমক বা আরোগ্যজনক বস্তু। **—if'-er-ous,** *adj.* **—sam'-ic,** *adj.* Deliciously fragrant; soothing; মধুরসুরভি; স্নিগ্ধকর, আরামপ্রদ, তাপহর। **—sam'-i-cal-ly,** *adv.*

bal'-ti-mōre, *n.* A common American bird; (from its being of the same colour with Lord Baltimore's coat of arms); আমেরিকাদেশীয় পক্ষি-বিশেষ — মস্তক কৃষ্ণবর্ণ এবং দেহের অবশিষ্ট ভাগ কমলাবর্ণ।

Baltimore-bird and nest.

băl'-ŭs-têr, *n.* A small pillar used as a support to the rail of a staircase; সোপানবৃতির (রেল) অবলম্বনস্বরূপ ক্ষুদ্র স্তম্ভ, সিঁড়ির রেলের পিল্লা বা থাম্বা। **—tered,** *adj.*

băl'-ŭs-trāde, *n.* A row of little pillars, united by a coping, serving as a fence for staircases, etc.; সিঁড়ি প্রভৃতির পিল্লাদার রেল, প্রগ্রীব (রাঃ তঃ)।

băm, *n.* & *v. t.* (*Slang.*) A hoax; (ইতর ভাষায়) ফাঁকি। ***Verb t.*** To deceive; to cozen; ছলনা করা; ফাঁকি দেওয়া।

bambino (*It.*), *n.* The image of infant Jesus in swaddling clothes shown in the Italian churches at Christmas; বড়দিন উপলক্ষে ইতালীদেশীয় খৃষ্টীয় ধর্মমন্দিরে প্রদর্শিত শৈশববস্ত্র-পরিহিত শিশু-যীশুর মূর্ত্তি।

băm-boo' (-bô), *n.* A genus of tropical giant grasses; বংশ, বাঁশ, বেণু। **Bamboo-manna**—বংশলোচন (ওয়াটু), বংশকর্পূর (মঃ ভাঃ)।

băm-boo'-zle, *v. t.* (*Slang.*) To deceive by trickery; to hoax; to mystify or confound; (ইতর ভাষায়) ছলনা করা; ফাঁকি দেওয়া; চোখে ধূলি দেওয়া, ঠকান, বিড়ম্বিত করা। **—ment,** *n.* **To bamboozle out of**—To take away (something) trickishly from a person; ঠকাইয়া লওয়া।

băn, *n., v. t.* & *i.* 1. A public proclamation or edict; ঘোষণা, অনুশাসন। 2. An ecclesiastical anathema; interdict; "Beneath the *ban* of Pope and church;" ধর্ম্মযাজকগণের অভিশাপ; পোপকর্ত্তৃক ধর্ম্মযাজকগণকে উপাসনাদি দেবকার্য্য সম্পন্ন করিতে প্রতিষেধ। 3. Interdiction; prohibition; as, under *ban* to touch; নিষেধ; প্রতিষেধ। 4. A sentence of outlawry; as, *ban* of the Holy Roman Empire; আইনের আশ্রয় হইতে বহিষ্কার-দণ্ড। ***Verb t.*** To interdict or prohibit (a thing or person); নিষেধ করা, প্রতিষেধ করা। ***Verb i.*** To curse; অভিসম্পাত করা।

băn, *n.* A title of the viceroy of Croatia and Slavonia; ক্রয়াশিয়া এবং স্লেবোনিয়ার রাজপ্রতিনিধির উপাধি বিশেষ।

băn'-ăl, *adj.* Commonplace; trite; সামান্য; তুচ্ছ, অকিঞ্চিৎকর।

bă-năl'-i-tÿ, *n.* Triteness; a commonplace; তুচ্ছতা; সামান্য বিষয়।

bă-nâ'-nă, *n.* A tropical fruit tree (allied to plantain); also its finger-shaped fruit growing in clusters; কদলী বৃক্ষ, কলা গাছ; কলা, কদলী, রম্ভা।

Băn'-bur-ÿ-cāke (-bêr-), *n.* A kind of spiced cake made at Banbury; বেনবারি নামক স্থানে প্রস্তুত সুগন্ধি মসল্লাযুক্ত পিষ্টক বিশেষ।

ban'-cō (băng-), *n.* (*Comm.*) The difference between the price of money at a bank and its value outside; ধনাগারে এবং ধনাগারের বাহিরে অর্থের মূল্যের প্রভেদ।

bănc, ban'-cŭs (băng-), *n.* A bench on which judges sit; বিচারাসন। **In banc, In banco**—Applied to sittings of a Superior Court of Common Law as a full court ; লণ্ডন-নগরীস্থ উচ্চতর বিচারালয়ের বিচারক-গণের পূর্ণাধিবেশন সম্বন্ধে প্রযুক্ত।

bănd, *n.* **1.** That which binds ; a fetter ; বন্ধনী ; শৃঙ্খল। **2.** (*Book-binding*) Straps at the back holding the sheets together ; (পুস্তক-বাঁধাই) পুস্তক বাঁধিবার সময় যে ফিতাদ্বারা পশ্চাদ্দিক হইতে পাতাগুলি বাঁধা হয়। **3.** A flat strip of thin material ; পাতলা জিনিষের চ্যাপ্টা সরু এবং লম্বা টুকরা। **4.** A strap forming the part of a garment ; (*pl.*) two strips of linen hanging from the neck as a part of clerical, legal or academic dress ; পরিচ্ছদের অঙ্গীভূত বন্ধনী বিশেষ ; ধর্ম্মযাজক, বিচারক বা বিশ্ববিদ্যালয়ের সভ্যগণের পরিচ্ছদের গলদেশ হইতে বিলম্বিত ক্ষৌমবস্ত্রের দীর্ঘ এবং অনতিপ্রশস্ত খণ্ডদ্বয়। **5.** An organized company ; a troop, (said of armed men, robbers, assassins, etc.) ; দল, সম্প্রদায়, মণ্ডলী ; সৈন্যদল, দস্যুদল প্রভৃতি। **6.** A company of musicians ; esp. that attached to a regiment of the army ; বাদ্যকর সম্প্রদায় ; সেনা-পল্টনের বাদকদল। **Bandbox**—A slight box, of pasteboard or paper, for caps, bonnets, etc. ; টুপি প্রভৃতি রাখার জন্য পুরু কাগজ-নির্ম্মিত বাক্স। [**To look as if one came out of a bandbox**—To look extremely neat ; তক্ তকে ঝক্ ঝকে দেখান।] **Bandmaster**—The conductor of a band of music ; বাদকদলের নেতা। **Band of Hope**—A name of associations of young men pledging themselves to total abstinence from the use of intoxicating liquors ; সুরাপানত্যাগী যুবক-সমিতি, আশাবাহিনী সমিতি। **Bandsman**—A musician who plays in a band ; বাদ্যকর-সম্প্রদায়ভুক্ত বাদক। **Bandstand**—A platfrom for the use of a band of musicians ; বাদ্য-স্থান (প্রবোধ), বাদ্য-মঞ্চ। **German band**—Any itinerant open-air musician ; ভ্রমণকারী সুগায়ক।

bănd, *v. t.* & *i.* To bind or tie with a band ; বন্ধনীদ্বারা সংবদ্ধ করা। ***Verb i.*** To unite ; to confederate for some common purpose ; একত্র হওয়া ; দলবদ্ধ হওয়া।

bănd'-ăge, *n.* & *v. t.* A fillet or strip of woven material, used in dressing and binding up wounds, etc. ; ক্ষতাদির বস্ত্র বন্ধনী, পট্টিকা, পটী (হঃ চঃ)। ***Verb t.*** To tie up (wound etc.) with a bandage বস্ত্রবন্ধনীদ্বারা (ক্ষতাদি) বন্ধন করা। **—ag-ing,** *n.*

băn'-dăn'-nă, —ă, *n.* A richly-coloured yellow or white spotted handkerchief ; হলদে বা সাদা ফুট ফুট দাগযুক্ত জমকালো, রঙ্গের রুমাল।

băn'-deau (-dö), *n.* A fillet for binding woman's hair ; স্ত্রীলোকের চুল বাঁধিবার ফিতা।

bănd'-ĕ-rōle, *n.* **1.** A little flag or streamer carried at the mast-head of a ship ; ক্ষুদ্র পতাকা, কেতু, কেতন। **2.** A flag displayed at the funerals of great men ; বরেণ্য ব্যক্তিগণের অন্ত্যেষ্টি-ক্রিয়া কালে প্রদর্শিত পতাকা বিশেষ।

băn'-di-coot, *n.* A large Indian rat ; ভারতবর্ষ ও সিংহলদ্বীপবাসী বৃহৎকায় মূষিক বিশেষ, ঘুঁস (কেণ্ডিঃ)।

băn'-dit, (*pl.* BANDITTI, BANDITS), *n.* An outlaw ; hence, a lawless desperate marauder ; a brigand ; (esp. in organized gangs) ; আইনের আশ্রয় হইতে বঞ্চিত ব্যক্তি ; অতএব রাহাজান, লুটিয়ারা, দস্যু, ডাকাত।

băn'-dŏg, *n.* **1.** A chained dog ; শৃঙ্খলিত কুক্কুর। **2.** A mastiff ; a bloodhound ; বৃহৎকায় কুক্কুর বিশেষ ; ডালকুত্তা।

băn-dō-leer' (-lēr), **—lier'** (-lēr), *n.* A shoulder-belt with cartridge-loops ; টোটা রাখিবার কোঠরশ্রেণী-সমন্বিত স্কন্ধ-পট্টিকা।

băn'-dō-line (-lēn), *n.* A gummy preparation for fixing the hair or moustache ; কেশ বা গোঁফ কঠিন করিবার জন্য একপ্রকার আটালো জিনিষ।

băn'-dȳ, *v. t.* **1.** To throw or strike (a ball) to and fro, as in the games of tennis, etc. ; (ক্রীড়া-গোলক) আঘাতপূর্ব্বক ইতস্ততঃ সঞ্চালিত করা। **2.** To give and receive reciprocally (blows, words, compliments, etc.) ; কথা কাটাকাটি করা, উত্তর প্রত্যুত্তর করা, বাগ্‌যুদ্ধ করা, বাগ্‌বিতণ্ডা করা, বিনিময় করা, পরস্পর আদান প্রদান করা। **3.** To discuss "Let not known truth be *bandied* in disputation ;" চর্চ্চা করা, আন্দোলন করা।

băn'-dȳ, *n.* **1.** A club bent at the lower part for striking a ball at play ; a hockey-stick ; নিম্নভাগে বক্র ক্রীড়াযষ্টি বিশেষ ; হকি খেলার যষ্টি। **2.** (*Orig.*) A special form of tennis ; hockey ; (প্রথমে) একপ্রকার টেনিস্ খেলা ; হকি খেলা।

băn'-dȳ, *n.* A carriage or buggy, used in India ; ভারতবর্ষের গাড়ী-বিশেষ, বগী।

băn'-dȳ, *adj.* Crooked ; bent ; (of legs) ; কুটিল ; বক্র, বাঁকা। **Bandy-legged**—Having crooked legs ; বক্রপাদ, প্রগতজানুক, বিরলজানুক।

bāne, *n.* **1.** A deadly poison ; প্রাণ-নাশক বিষ। [Now only used in combinations, as *ratsbane, henbane.*] **2.** Any cause of ruin ; harm ; woe ; বিনাশের হেতু, ধ্বংসের কারণ ; অনিষ্ট ; দুঃখ। **Bane'-ful,** *adj.* Having poisonous qualities ; destructive ; noxious ; বিষাক্ত, বিষময় ; প্রাণঘাতী, সাংঘাতিক, মারাত্মক ; অনিষ্টকর। **Bane'-ful-ness,** *n.*

băng, *v. t.* & *i.* **1.** To beat with a resounding blow ; to thump ; (যষ্টি বা দণ্ডদ্বারা) আঘাত করা ; সশব্দে আঘাত করা, দুম্ করিয়া আঘাত করা। **2.** (*Lit.* & *fig.*) To beat as with a club ; to thrash or drub ; (শব্দানুযায়ী এবং লক্ষণায়) প্রহার করা,

উত্তমমধ্যম দেওয়া ; ঠেঙ্গান। **3.** To shut (a door) with a noise ; দুম্ করিয়া বন্ধ করা, ঝনাৎ করিয়া বন্ধ করা। **4.** (*Colloq.*) To excel ; to surpass ; as, he will *bang* all the others ; (চলিত ভাষায়) সদ্গুণে অতিক্রম করা ; ছাড়াইয়া যাওয়া। ***Verb i.*** **1.** To strike noisily ; as, he was *banging* on the piano ; সশব্দে আঘাত করা। **2.** To move with a spring or bound ; লাফাইয়া চলা।

băng, *n.* **1.** A heavy resounding blow ; a thump ; দুম্‌শব্দে আঘাত ; দুম্‌শব্দ, ঝন্ ঝন্, ঝনৎকার। **2.** A sudden explosive noise, as the report of fire-arms ; আকস্মিক স্ফোটন শব্দ।

băng, *adv.* With sudden impact ; abruptly ; completely ; explosively ; আকস্মিক সংঘাতে ; সহসা ; পুরা ; সশব্দে স্ফোটনপূর্ব্বক। **To go bang**—To explode ; সশব্দে ফুটা।

băng, *n.* & *v. t.* A front hair cut square across the forehead ; ললাটদেশের সম্মুখভাগস্থ সোজাভাবে কাটা চুল। ***Verb t.*** To cut the front hair straight across forehead ; উক্ত প্রকারে চুল কাটা। **Bang-tail**—A horse with the tail cut straight across ; যে অশ্বের পুচ্ছ সোজাভাবে কাটা হইয়াছে।

ban′-gle (băng-), *n.* A ring, bracelet, or anklet ; অঙ্গুরী, বালা, বলয়, কঙ্কণ, মল, মঞ্জীর। **–gled,** *adj.* Adorned with bangles ; বলয়-শোভিত।

băn′-i-ăn, –yăn, *n.* **1.** A Hindoo trader ; হিন্দু মহাজন, বেণিয়া। **2.** An Indian flannel jacket ; বেনিয়ান, অঙ্গরক্ষা, ফ্ল্যানেলের জামাবিশেষ। **3.** (In Bengal) A broker to a European house (usually called *sircar*) ; (বঙ্গদেশে) মুৎসুদ্দি, সরকার। **Banyan days**—Among seamen are those days on which no meat is served out to them ; যে সকল দিনে নাবিকগণকে মাংস দেওয়া হয় না। [হিন্দুমহাজনগণের মৎস্যমাংস-বর্জ্জন হইতে এই বাক্যটী গৃহীত হইয়াছে।] **Banyan hospital**—A hospital for animals ; পশুপক্ষী প্রভৃতির জন্য আরোগ্য-শালা। **Banyan-tree**—An Indian tree of the *fig* family ; বটবৃক্ষ।

băn′-ish, *v. t.* **1.** To condemn (a person) by public sentence to leave the country ; to exile ; (*from, out of*) ; নির্ব্বাসনদণ্ড প্রদান করা ; দেশান্তরিত করা, নির্ব্বাসিত করা। **2.** To dismiss from one's presence or mind ; সম্মুখ হইতে তাড়াইয়া দেওয়া বা মন হইতে দূর করা। **–er,** *n.* **–ment,** *n.* Exile ; নির্ব্বাসন।

băn′-is-têr, *n.* (Usually *pl.*) A slender upright post guarding the side of a staircase ; সিঁড়ির রেলের পিল্লা।

băn′-jō, *n.* A stringed musical instrument having a head like a tambourine and a neck like a guitar ; সারঙ্গের মত বাদ্যযন্ত্র বিশেষ। **–ist,** *n.*

bank (băngk), *n.* **1.** A mound, pile or ridge of earth, raised above the surrounding plain ; anything shaped like a mound or ridge of earth ; মৃত্তিকার স্তূপ, মাটির ঢিবি, পোস্তা, বাঁধ, জাঙ্গাল, প্রাকার ; বাঁধের মত যে কোন বস্তু। **2.** A steep acclivity, as the slope of a hill, or the side of a ravine, etc. ; (পর্ব্বতাদির) চড়াই, উৎসঙ্গ (আঃ বঃ), উৎসেধ। **3.** The sloping margin of a river ; the ground near a river ; কূল, তীর, পুলিন, কিনারা ; তট, তীরভূমি। **4.** A shoal, shelf or shallow ; কচ্ছ (সাঃ পঃ), অগভীর স্থান। **5.** (*Mining*) The ground at the top of the shaft ; (খনির কায) খনির সুড়ঙ্গের উপরিভাগস্থ ভূমি।

bănk (băngk), *v. t.* & *i.* **1.** To raise a mound ; to fortify with a bank ; জাঙ্গাল বাঁধা, বাঁধ দেওয়া ; বপ্রদ্বারা সুরক্ষিত করা। **2.** To heap or pile up ; স্তূপীকৃত করা, পুঞ্জীকৃত করা। ***Verb i.*** To rise in banks, as snow, clouds, etc. ; (with *up*) ; বাঁধ বা জাঙ্গালের মত উচ্চ হইয়া উঠা।

bank (băngk), *n.* **1.** A bench for rowers in a galley ; also, a tier of oars ; দাঁড়ীগণের বসিবার আসন ; এক সারি দাঁড়। **2.** (*Law*) The bench or seat of justice ; as, *Bank* Royal = King's Bench ; (আইন) বিচারাসন। **3.** (*Mus.*) A row of keys in an organ ; (সঙ্গীত-শাস্ত্র) অর্গেননামক বাদ্যযন্ত্রের চাবির সারি। **4.** (*Print.*) The table on which sheets are laid before or after printing ; (মুদ্রণ) মুদ্রণের পূর্ব্বে কিম্বা পরে যে মেজের উপর কাগজ রাখা হয়।

bank (băngk), *n.* **1.** (*Orig.*) A money-dealer's table or counter ; an establishment for the custody, loan, exchange or issue of money ; (পূর্ব্বে) মহাজনের টাকা-পয়সা গণিবার মেজ ; ধনাগার। **2.** The funds of a gaming establishment ; দ্যূতক্রীড়ক-সম্প্রদায়ের ধনভাণ্ডার।

bănk (băngk), *v. t.* & *i.* To deposit in a bank ; as, he *banked* £500 ; ধনাগারে সঞ্চিত বা গচ্ছিত রাখা, ব্যাঙ্কে জমা দেওয়া। **Bank′-a-ble,** *adj.* Receivable at a bank ; ধনাগারে গ্রহণীয়। **Bank′-er,** *n.* The keeper or manager of a bank ; মহাজন, সাহু-কার (হিঃ কোঃ)। **Bank′-ing,** *n.* **1.** The business or employment of a banker ; রোকড়ি কাজ, ধন-ব্যবহার। **2.** Fishing on a sea bank (esp. Newfoundland) ; সমুদ্রতীরে মৎস্যশিকার। **Bank-bill**—A bill drawn by one bank on another ; হুণ্ডী, টীপ (রঃ অঃ), বরাত (ঐ)। **Bank-book**—A book containing a customer's account with the bank, (also *pass-book*) ; ব্যাঙ্কের খাতা। **Bank-note**—A promissory note issued by a bank, and payable to bearer on demand ; ব্যাঙ্কের নোট (ঋণ-স্বীকার পত্র) ।

bank′-rŭpt (băngk-), *n., v.t.* & *adj.* A person declared to be unable to pay his debts, or who has failed to pay his debts ; নিঃস্ব, দাউলিয়া, ফতুর। ***Verb t.*** To make insolvent ; দাউলিয়া করা, নিঃস্ব করা। ***Adj.*** Unable to pay debts ; insolvent ; bereft *of* or wanting *in* (some quality, etc) ; ঋণ পরিশোধে অক্ষম ; দাউলিয়া ; বিহীন, বিরহিত। **—cy,** *n.* **1.** The state of being actually or legally bankrupt ; ঋণ-পরিশোধে অক্ষমতা, নিঃস্বতা, দাউলিয়া অবস্থা। **2.** Complete loss of (some good quality, esp. reputation) ; সর্ব্বনাশ।

băn′-nêr, *n.* **1.** A cloth-flag on a pole, used as a standard of an emperor, king, lord, etc., or for war ; পতাকা, নিশান, ধ্বজ, ধ্বজা, ধ্বজপট, বৈজয়ন্ত, রণপতাকা। **2.** The flag of a country ; জাতীয় পতাকা। **3.** An ensign borne in religious and political demonstration ; রাজনীতিক বা ধর্ম্ম-সম্বন্ধীয় শোভাযাত্রাদিতে বাহিত (সাধারণতঃ) দণ্ডদ্বয়ের মধ্যবর্ত্তী পতাকা। **4.** (*Fig.*) Anything used as a symbol of principles ; "Dynamite has become the *banner* of revolutionary party ;" (লক্ষণায়) নিদর্শন। **—nered,** *adj.* **To raise one's banners**—To enter into war ; সমরে প্রবৃত্ত হওয়া।

băn′-nêr-ĕt, *n.* **1.** One knighted on the field for valour ; বীরত্বের পুরস্কারস্বরূপ রণক্ষেত্রে যাহাকে 'নাইট্' উপাধিতে ভূষিত করা হয়। **2.** A knight having vassals under his banners ; যে নাইটের আহ্বানে অধীনস্থ সামন্তগণ যুদ্ধার্থ সমবেত হয়।

băn′-nêr-ŏl, *n.* A banner borne at the funerals of great men and placed over the tomb ; সম্ভ্রান্ত-ব্যক্তিগণের অন্ত্যেষ্টিক্রিয়াকালে বাহিত পতাকাবিশেষ — ইহা সমাধিস্থানোপরি স্থাপিত হয়।

băn′-nŏck, *n.* A flat round cake made of oat or barley-meal ; চাপাটি।

banns, (bănz), *n. pl.* The proclamation in church of an intended marriage, (to give opportunity of objection) ; খৃষ্টীয় ধর্ম্মমন্দিরে প্রস্তাবিত বিবাহের ঘোষণা।

ban′-quĕt (băng-), *n., v. t.* & *i.* A sumptuous feast, usually ceremonial, or state feast, followed by speeches ; ভোজ, ভোজোৎসব, মহাভোজ, যে উৎসবভোজের অন্তে বক্তৃতাদি প্রদত্ত হয়। ***Verb t.*** To entertain at a banquet ; ভোজ প্রদান করা। ***Verb i.*** To regale oneself ; to carouse (with *on*) ; ভোজ খাওয়া, চর্ব্ব্য, চোষ্য, লেহ্য, পেয় আহার করা ; অতিরিক্ত মদ্য পান করা। **—er,** *n.*

băn-quette′ (quĕt), *n.* **1.** A raised way behind rampart, etc., for firing from ; গুলি বর্ষণের জন্য প্রাকারাদির পশ্চাদ্‌বর্ত্তী উচ্চপথ। **2.** The low bench behind the driver in a French omnibus ; ফরাসী দেশীয় বিশ্বম্বহ শকটের চালকের পশ্চাদ্দিক্‌স্থিত অনুচ্চ আসন।

băn′-shee (-shē), **—shie** (-shē), *n.* A supernatural being whose wail portends death in a house ; (Irish and Scotch) ; মৃত্যু-সংবাদ-বাহিকা পরী-বিশেষ। [স্কট্‌লণ্ডের অন্তর্গত হাইলেণ্ড এবং আয়র্লণ্ডের কোন কোন স্থানের কৃষকদিগের মধ্যে এই বিশ্বাস প্রচলিত ছিল যে, কোন ব্যক্তির মৃত্যুর প্রাক্কালে, উক্ত পরী তদীয় গৃহের গবাক্ষতলে উপবিষ্টা হইয়া মৃত্যুসঙ্গীত গান করিত।]

băn′-tăm, *n.* **1.** A small variety of the domestic fowl ; একজাতীয় ক্ষুদ্রকায় গৃহকুক্কুট। **2.** A small but spirited person ; খর্ব্বকায় অথচ তেজস্বী ব্যক্তি।

băn′-têr, *n.* & *v. t.* Humorous ridicule ; good humoured raillery ; pleasantry ; ঠাট্টা, বিদ্রূপ ; পরিহাস ; রঙ্গরস, তামাসা, আমোদ কৌতুক। ***Verb t.*** To make fun of (a person) ; to jest at ; ঠাট্টা, করা পরিহাস করা, কৌতুক করা ; ব্যঙ্গ করা। **—y,** *adj.*

bănt′-îng, *n.* A system of diet for reducing obesity, superfluous fat, etc. ; শরীরের স্থূলতা, অতিরিক্ত মেদ, প্রভৃতি হ্রাসের জন্য আহার-প্রণালী বিশেষ।

bănt′-lîng, *n.* A young child ; a brat ; ছোকরা ; ছোঁড়া, চেঙ্গরা (*colloq.*)।

băn′-tû, *n.* A name applied sometimes to the South African family of languages and races ; দক্ষিণ আফ্রিকার ভাষা এবং জাতি সমূহ সময় সময় এই নামে অভিহিত হইয়া থাকে।

banx′-ring (băngks-), *n.* A Javanese squirrel-like insectivorous animal ; কাঠবিড়ালের মত যবদ্বীপবাসী কীটভুক্ জন্তু বিশেষ।

Banyan-tree.

băn′-yăn, *n.* See BANIAN ; (কেবল "বটবৃক্ষ" অর্থে ব্যবহৃত হয়।)

bā′-ō-băb, *n.* A gigantic African tree, (called also monkey-bread) ; আফ্রিকা-দেশজাত প্রকাণ্ড বৃক্ষ বিশেষ, গোরখ আম্লি (খোরী), বিলাতি আম্লি (ফার্ম্মিঃ)।

băp′-tism, *n.* **1.** The application of water to a person as a sacrament or religious ceremony by which he is initiated to the visible Church of Christ ; জল-প্রক্ষেপ বা জলে নিমজ্জন দ্বারা খৃষ্টধর্ম্মে দীক্ষা-প্রদান, খৃষ্টধর্ম্মে দীক্ষার জন্য জল-সংস্কার। **2.** The ceremony of naming church-bells and ships ;

খৃষ্টীয় ধর্ম্ম-মন্দির এবং জাহাজ প্রভৃতির নামাকরণ উৎসব। **—tis'-mal,** *adj.* **—tis'-mal-ly,** *adv.* **Baptism of blood**—Martyrdom ; ধর্ম্মার্থ আত্ম-বলিদান। **Baptism of fire**—A soldier's first battle ; কোন সৈনিকের প্রথম যুদ্ধ, রণভূমিতে অগ্নি-দীক্ষা।

băp'-tist, *n.* **1.** One who baptizes, esp. applied to John, the fore-runner of Christ ; দীক্ষাদাতা, বিশেষভাবে, যীশুখৃষ্টের আগমন-বার্ত্তা-প্রচারক যোহন। **2.** One of a sect (formerly called ANABAPTISTS by the opponents) which holds that baptism ought to be adminis-tered to believers only and by immersion ; শিশুগণের দীক্ষার বিরোধী, এবং দীক্ষাকালে অবগাহনের পক্ষপাতী সম্প্রদায়ভুক্ত ব্যক্তি, যৌবনমজ্জনবাদী।

băp'-tis-têr-ỹ, —trỹ, *n.* **1.** The part of a church (formerly a separate building), used for baptism ; খৃষ্টীয় ধর্ম্মমন্দিরস্থ দীক্ষাদানস্থলী। **2.** The large tank used for immersion in Baptist churches; ব্যাপ্টিষ্ট্ সম্প্রদায়ের ধর্ম্মমন্দিরস্থ অবগাহন-কুণ্ড।

băp-tīze', *v. t.* **1.** To administer the rite of baptism to : খৃষ্টধর্ম্মে দীক্ষাদান করা। **2.** To denominate ; "Chalk-and-water, which for the purpose of sale, was *baptized* milk." নামাকরণ করা, অভিহিত করা, নাম দেওয়া। **3.** To purify ; to elevate ; "Sorrow had *baptized* her ;" বিশুদ্ধ বা পবিত্র করা ; উন্নত করা। **—tiz'-er,** *n.* One who baptizes ; দীক্ষাদাতা।

bâr, *n.* **1.** A straight piece of wood, metal or other material, long in proportion to its breadth ; as, the *bars* of a fence or gate; a rod ; গরাদ, শলাকা, কীলক ; দণ্ড। **2.** A rod of iron or wood used to fasten a door, gate, etc. ; অর্গল, পরিঘ, হুড়কা, খিল। **3.** An ingot of precious metal ; মূল্যবান ধাতুর পিণ্ড। **4.** A bank of sand, silt, etc., across the mouth of a river or harbour ; চর (সাঃ পঃ)। **5.** A barrier closing a road, gateway, etc. ; as, the *bars* of York ; বেড়া। **6.** (*Law*) (*a*) A plea or objection arresting an action or claim ; as, it is no *bar* to the validity of a claim ; (আইন) যে হেতুবাদদ্বারা কোন মোকদ্দমা বা দাবি স্থগিত থাকে। (*b*) The place in court where prisoners are stationed for arraignment, trial or sentence; hence, the court itself ; as, trial at *bar* ; আসামীর কাঠগড়া ; আদালত। (*c*) The whole body of barristers or lawyers ; as, the members of the *bar* ; the legal profession ; ব্যবহারজীবি-সম্প্রদায় ; আইন-ব্যবসায়। **7.** Any tribunal ; as, the *bar* of public opinion ; যে কোন বিচারালয়। **8.** The rail dividing off the space to which non-members may be admitted on business ; as, the *bar* of the House of Commons ; পার্লেমেণ্ট সভা-মণ্ডপের বৃতি-বিশেষ,—যদ্দারা সভ্যগণ ব্যতীত অন্যলোকের প্রবেশের স্থান বিভক্ত হইয়া থাকে। **9.** The room or counter, in or over, which liquors are served in a public-house, hotel, etc.; সুরাবিপণির যে কক্ষে অথবা যে মেজের উপর দিয়া সুরাপায়ীদিগকে মদ্য প্রদান করা হয়। **10.** (*Mus.*) A vertical line across the staff ; (সঙ্গীত-শাস্ত্র) স্বরলিপির সমান্তরাল রেখা সকলের উপরিস্থ লম্বমান রেখা। **Bar-bell**—An iron bar with a ball at each end, used in gymnastics ; উভয়প্রান্তে গোলকবিশিষ্ট ব্যায়ামের দণ্ডবিশেষ। **Barmaid**—A female waiter at the bar of a tavern ; সুরাগৃহের পরিচারিকা। **Barwood**—A red wood from Gaboon imported for dyeing, etc. ; রঞ্জনাদি কার্য্যের জন্য গেবূন হইতে আনীত লোহিত-বর্ণ কাষ্ঠ বিশেষ। **A case at bar**—A case present before the court ; আদালতে উপস্থাপিত মোকদ্দমা। **At the bar**—In open court ; প্রকাশ্য আদালতে। **To be called to the bar**—To be admitted as a barrister ; কৌন্সুলিরূপে গৃহীত হওয়া। **To be called within the bar**—To be appointed King's (or Queen's) counsel ; রাজার (বা রাণীর) কৌন্সুলি নিযুক্ত হওয়া। **To cross the bar**—To die ; মরা। **To join the bar**—To get enrolled as a pleader ; ব্যবহারজীবি-শ্রেণী ভুক্ত হওয়া। **Trial at bar**—(*English law*) A trial before the full court of judges ; (ইংলণ্ডীয় আইন) বিচারকগণের পূর্ণাধিবেশনে বিচার।

bâr, *v. t.* **1.** To fasten (doors, etc.) with bars ; অর্গলবদ্ধ করা। **2.** To shut up or confine (a person or thing) by bars ; কাঠগড়ায় বদ্ধ করা। **3.** To prohibit (a person) from ; to deprive of ; "I will *bar* no honest man my house ;" বারণ করা, নিষেধ করা ; বঞ্চিত করা। **4.** To take exception to ; to set aside ; "But this I humbly beg to *bar* ;" আপত্তি করা ; রহিত করা। **5.** To block up (a path, etc.) ; রোধ করা, আটক করা। **6.** (*Law*) To arrest or stay (a process, party) by legal objection ; স্থগিত রাখা, মুলতবী রাখা। **7.** To mark with stripes or lines ; ডোরা কাটা। **Barred by limitation**—তামাদি, খারিজ। **Barring out**—The act of excluding a schoolmaster from school by barricading the doors and windows—mode of school-boy-rebellion ; দরজা জানালা বন্ধ করিয়া শিক্ষককে বিদ্যালয়-গৃহে প্রবেশে বাধা প্রদান—বিদ্যালয়ে বালকগণের এক-প্রকার বিদ্রোহ।

bâr, *n.* A large European sea-fish ; ইয়ুরোপদেশীয় অতিকায় সামুদ্রিক মৎস্য বিশেষ।

bâr-ă-lip-tŏn, *n.* See BARBARA.

bârb, *n.* & *v. t.* **1.** A beard or

anything in animals resembling it ; শ্মশ্রু বা জীবদেহস্থিত তৎসদৃশ কোন প্রকার বস্তু। **2.** A chin-piece of a nun's head-dress ; খৃষ্টীয় সন্ন্যাসিনীর অবগুণ্ঠনের চিবুকাচ্ছাদন-বস্ত্র বিশেষ। **3.** The points standing backwards in an arrow or a fish-hook ; বড়শী প্রভৃতির হুল বা কড়া, বড়শীর ফলা। **4.** (*Fig.*) Sting ; as, the burning *barb* of his remorses ; (লক্ষণায়) শেল। **5.** (*Bot.*) A hooked hair ; (উদ্ভিদ্‌-বিদ্যা) পক্ষ্মন্, কড়িয়া (অভিঃ)। ***Verb t.*** To furnish (an arrow, hook, etc.) with barbs ; তীর, বড়শী প্রভৃতিতে হুল লাগান। **Barbed steed**—A horse in armour ; কবচাবৃত অশ্ব, যুদ্ধসজ্জায় সজ্জিত অশ্ব। **Barbed wire**—Wire for fences with prickles at intervals ; কণ্টকযুক্ত তার।

bârb, *n.* Breeds of horse and pigeon imported from Barbary ; **উত্তর আফ্রিকার অন্তর্গত বার্ব্বারী হইতে আনীত অশ্ব এবং কপোত।**

bâr'-bă-ră, *n.* (*Log.*) The first word of the Scholastic mnemonic lines, for the first mood of the first figure in syllogism ; (তর্ক-বিজ্ঞান) কতিপয় স্মরণসহায়ভূত কবিতার প্রথম শব্দ, এই শব্দদ্বারা তিনটী অন্বয়ব্যাপ্তি প্রতিজ্ঞাবিশিষ্ট ন্যায়বাক্য সূচিত হইয়া থাকে। [BARALIPTON শব্দদ্বারা দুইটী অন্বয়ব্যাপ্তি ও একটী ব্যাপ্য প্রতিজ্ঞাবিশিষ্ট ন্যায় বাক্য নির্দ্দিষ্ট হইয়া থাকে।]

bâr-bā'-ri-ăn, *n.* & *adj.* **1.** (*Etymol.*) A foreigner, whose language and customs differ from the speaker's; (ব্যুৎপত্তিগত অর্থ) বিদেশী, পরদেশী। **2.** (*Hist.*) One not a Greek ; one outside the Roman Empire ; a non-christiar ; (ইতিহাস) গ্রীস ভিন্ন অন্যদেশীয় লোক ; রোম সাম্রাজ্যের বহির্দ্দেশবাসী লোক ; অখৃষ্টান লোক। **3.** A rude, wild, uncivilized person ; অসভ্য বা বর্ব্বর ব্যক্তি, নৃশংস, বর্ব্বর বা পাশব প্রকৃতির লোক। **4.** An uncultured person ; one having no literary culture ; অশিক্ষিত ব্যক্তি ; সাহিত্যরসানভিজ্ঞ ব্যক্তি। ***Adj.*** Rude ; uncultured ; uncivilized ; রূঢ় ; অশিক্ষিত, বর্ব্বর ; অসভ্য।

bâr-băr'-ic, *adj.* Rude or rough like the barbarians or their art or taste ; বর্ব্বরোচিত, বর্ব্বরসংক্রান্ত, অসভ্য, জমকালো অথচ সুরুচিসম্মত নহে।

bâr-bâ-rism, *n.* **1.** A mixing of foreign or vulgar expressions in talk or writing ; কথায় বা রচনায় ম্লেচ্ছ বা গ্রাম্য-ভাষার সংমিশ্রণ, ম্লেচ্ছিতা (মঃ ইঃ)। **2.** A non-classical word or idiom ; বর্ব্বরোক্তি, ম্লেচ্ছোক্তি। **3.** Absence of culture ; uncivicilized ignorance and rudeness ; বর্ব্বরতা, অসভ্যতা ; অসভ্যজনোচিত রূঢ়তা।

bâr-băr'-i-tŷ, *n.* **1.** Savage cruelty ; inhumanity ; ক্রূরতা ; অমানুষিকতা, নৃশংসতা, বর্ব্বরতা। **2.** (*With pl.*) A barbarous or cruel act ; as, wholesale *barbarities* ; barbaric style or taste ; নৃশংস বা বর্ব্বরোচিত কার্য্য ; বর্ব্বরোচিত রচনা-পদ্ধতি।

bâr'-bâ-rīze, *v. t.* & *i.* **1.** To make barbarous ; ম্লেচ্ছভাবাপন্ন করা, অসভ্য করা। **2.** To corrupt (language) ; (ভাষা) দূষিত করা। ***Verb i.*** To become barbarous ; to speak or write like a barbarian ; অসভ্য হওয়া, বর্ব্বরতা প্রাপ্ত হওয়া ; বর্ব্বরের মত কথা বলা বা লিখা। **—ri-za'-tion,** *n.*

bâr'-bă-rous (rŭs), *adj.* **1.** (Of language) Not Greek, nor Latin ; hence, not classical or pure ; (ভাষা-সম্পর্কে) গ্রীক কিম্বা লাটিন ভিন্ন; (অতএব) বর্ব্বর, ম্লেচ্ছ, অসংস্কৃত, অপপ্রয়োগ-বহুল। **2.** (Of people) Non-Greek ; outlandish ; living outside the Roman Empire ; (sometimes) not christian ; heathen ; (লোক-সম্পর্কে) অগ্রীক ; বিদেশীয় ; রোম সাম্রাজ্যের বহির্দ্দেশবাসী ; (কখন কখন) অখৃষ্টান ; পৌত্তলিক। **3.** Uncivilized ; uncultured ; rude ; (of men, manners, products, etc.) ; অসভ্য ; অশিক্ষিত ; অশিষ্ট। **4.** Cruel ; inhuman ; as, *barbarous* aspects of war ; নিষ্ঠুর ; অমানুষিক। **—ly,** *adv.* **—ness,** *n.*

bâr'-bāte, *n.* (*Bot.* & *Zool.*) Having hairy tufts ; (উদ্ভিদ্‌ ও জন্তু-তত্ত্ব) কেশবৎ গুচ্ছবিশিষ্ট।

bâr'-bĕ-cue (kü), *n.* & *v. t.* **1.** A hog, ox, or other large animal roasted or broiled whole for a feast ; কোন ভোজোপলক্ষে ভর্জ্জিত বা দগ্ধ আস্ত শূকর, বৃষ বা অন্যবিধ বৃহৎকায় জীব। **2.** A large wooden or iron frame-work for smoking or broiling (meat, fish) ; ধূম বা অগ্নির সাহায্যে মৎস্য বা মাংস পক্করণার্থ লৌহ বা কাষ্ঠময় কাঠাম বিশেষ। **3.** (*U. S.*) A large social entertainment, (in the open air) at which animals are roasted whole ; (মার্কিণ-যুক্তরাজ্যে) অনাবৃত স্থানে সম্পন্ন ভোজোৎসব—যাহাতে আস্ত মেষ, বৃষ, শূকর প্রভৃতি ভর্জ্জিত হইয়া থাকে। **4.** A floor for drying coffee-beans ; যে প্রাঙ্গণে কাফির দানা রৌদ্রে শুষ্ক করা হয়। ***Verb t.*** To roast or broil (an animal) whole ; আস্ত বৃষ, শূকর প্রভৃতি ভর্জ্জিত বা অগ্নি-পক্ক করা।

bâr'-bĕl, *n.* A large European fresh-water fish ; ইয়ুরোপদেশীয় বৃহৎকায় মৎস্য বিশেষ। **—beled,** or **—belled,** *adj.*

bâr'-bêr, *n.* One who shaves and trims a customer's beards, hair, etc., (now, usu. *hair-dresser*) ; নাপিত, ক্ষৌরকার, নরসুন্দর। **Barber-monger**—A fop (*shakes.*) ; ফুলবাবু। **Barber-shop**—নাপিত-গৃহ, নাপিতশালা, ভাণ্ডি-শালা।

bâr'-bĕr-rŷ, ber'-bĕr-rŷ (bŭr-), *n.* A shrub with yellow flowers and oblong red berries ; পীতপুষ্প গুল্মবিশেষ। **Indian barberry**—দারু-হরিদ্রা (খোরীঃ)।

bâr′-bĕt, *n.* A bird with tufts of bristles at the base of its bill ; এক জাতীয় পক্ষী।

Collared Barbet.

bâr-bette′ (-bĕt), *n.* A mound of earth or a platform, within a fort or in a ship on which heavy guns are mounted ; বৃহৎ কামানসকল স্থাপনের জন্য দুর্গ বা রণপোতাভ্যন্তরস্থিত মৃত্তিকাস্তূপ বা মঞ্চবিশেষ।

bâr′-bĭ-căn, *n.* The outer defence to a city or castle, especially a double-tower over a gate or bridge ; শত্রুর প্রবেশ-নিরোধার্থ নগরোপান্তে নির্মিত দুর্গবিশেষ, বিশেষতঃ দুর্গদ্বার বা সেতুর উপর নির্মিত যুগ্মবুরুজ, উপদুর্গ।

bâr′-büle, *n.* A minute barb or beard ; পক্ষ্মক (সাঃ পঃ)।

Barbus puntio—পুঁটি (গুপ্তঃ)।

Barbus ticto—তিত পুঁটি (গুপ্তঃ)।

bâr′-că-röle, —rolle (-röl), *n.* A song sung by Venetian gondoliers ; ভেনিস নগরীর তরণীচালকদিগের গান বিশেষ।

bârd, *n.* **1.** A poet or singer, among the ancient Celts, (who used to compose and sing verses in honour of heroes and their deeds) ; কুশীলব, স্তুতিজীবী, মাগধ, ভাট, চারণ। **2.** A poet generally ; as, the *bard* of Avon ; কবি। **Bard′-ic,** *adj.* **Bard′-ling,** *n.* A poetaster ; ক্ষুদ্র কবি, মন্দ কবি।

bârd, *n.* An armour for the breast and flanks of a war-horse ; যুদ্ধাশ্বের কবচ। **Bard′-ed,** *adj.*

bāre, *adj.* & *v. t.* **1.** (Of the body) Unclothed ; naked ; (শরীর-সম্বন্ধে) বিবস্ত্র, বিবসন, দিগম্বর ; নগ্ন, উলঙ্গ, লেংটা (*colloq.*)। **2.** (Of sky, earth etc.) Without clouds, vegetation, etc. ; (আকাশ, পৃথিবী প্রভৃতি সম্পর্কে)। নির্মেঘ, উদ্ভিজ্জহীন। **3.** Unadorned ; plain ; as, *bare* narration : *bare* truth ; অনলঙ্কৃত ; সাদাসিধা। **4.** Unfurnished ; uncovered ; as, *bare* castles : *bare* boards ; অসজ্জিত ; অনাবৃত। **5.** (Of cloth) Threadbare ; (বস্ত্র-সম্বন্ধে) ছিন্ন, জীর্ণ। **6.** (Of weapons) unsheathed ; (অস্ত্র-সম্বন্ধে) নিষ্কুষিত, উলঙ্গ। **7.** Destitute ; indigent ; needy ; (with of) ; as, *bare* I was born : *bare* of attributes ; নিঃস্ব ; অকিঞ্চন ; অভাবগ্রস্ত। **8.** Mere ; simple ; only ; "The *bare* necessaries of life" ; শুদ্ধ ; মাত্র ; কেবল। ***Verb t.*** To uncover ; to unsheathe (a weapon) ; to reveal or disclose ; "*Bare* my swelling heart ;" to strip (*of, from*) ; অনাবৃত করা ; নিষ্কুষিত করা ; প্রকাশিত করা ; নগ্ন করা। **Bareback**—(Of a horse) Without saddle ; (অশ্ব-পক্ষে) অনাবৃত-পৃষ্ঠ। **Barebone**—A lean skinny person ; কাহিল লোক, কঙ্কালসার ব্যক্তি। **Barefaced**—Without beard, etc. ; without mask or vizard ; অজাতশ্মশ্রু, শ্মশ্রুগুম্ফহীন ; মুখসবিহীন, মুখাবরণবিহীন। (*Fig.*) Shameless ; impudent (of persons, actions, etc.) ; (লক্ষণায়—ব্যক্তি, কার্য্য, প্রভৃতি সম্বন্ধে) নির্লজ্জ ; ধৃষ্ট, প্রগল্‌ভ, বেহায়া। **Bare′-faced-ly,** *adv.* **Bare′-faced-ness,** *n.* **Barefooted**—Without shoes or stockings ; নগ্নপদ। **Barehead, Bareheaded**—With the head uncovered, esp. as a token of respect ; অনাবৃতমস্তক।

barege, (*f.*) *n.* A light silky dress-fabric resembling gauze ; সূক্ষ্ম এবং জালাকার রেশমী বস্ত্র বিশেষ।

bāre′-lŷ, *adv.* **1.** Nakedly ; উলঙ্গভাবে। **2.** Clearly ; plainly ; as, the question is put *barely* ; অপ্রচ্ছন্নভাবে ; স্পষ্টভাবে, পরিষ্কাররূপে। **3.** Only just ; scarcely ; as, so faint as to be *barely* recognizable ; সবেমাত্র ; কষ্টে সৃষ্টে, কদাচিৎ।

bāre′-nĕss, *n.* Nakedness ; baldness ; scantiness ; নগ্নতা ; আভরণহীনতা ; অপ্রাচুর্য্য।

bāre′-sârk, (*lit.* bare-shirt), *n.* & *adv.* A wild Norse warrior ; নরওয়েদেশীয় দুর্দ্দান্ত সৈনিক। ***Adv.*** Without armour ; বর্ম্মবিহীন দেহে।

bâr′-gain (-gĭn), *v. i.* & *t.* **1.** To haggle (*with* a person) over terms of give and take ; দরদস্তুর করা। **2.** To stipulate (*with* a person *for* a thing) ; (কোন বিষয়ের জন্য কাহারো সহিত) চুক্তি বা করার করা। ***Verb t.*** To transfer for a consideration ; to barter ; হস্তান্তরিত করা ; এক দ্রব্যের বিনিময়ে অন্য দ্রব্য দেওয়া। **To bargain away**—To part with, as the result of a bargain ; ছাড়িয়া দেওয়া। **To bargain for**—To count on in advance ; to expect ; পূর্ব্ব হইতেই আশা করা ; প্রতীক্ষা করা।

bâr′-gain (-gĭn), *n.* **1.** An agreement between two parties, settling what each shall give and take ; চুক্তি, সংবাদ (মঃ ভাঃ), সময় (আঃ বঃ), করার, পণ। **2.** An advantageous agreement or purchase ; as, to buy a thing at a *bargain* ; সুবিধাজনক চুক্তি, সুলভে ক্রয়। **Into the bargain**—Over and above what is stipulated ; moreover ; ফাও স্বরূপ, লাভের উপর ; অধিকন্তু। **To make the best of a bad bargain**—To take misfortune cheerfully ; প্রফুল্লচিত্তে দুর্ভাগ্য গ্রহণ করা। **To strike a bargain**—To come to terms over a purchase ; কোন বস্তু ক্রয়সম্বন্ধে দরদস্তুর ঠিক করা।

bârge, *n.* **1.** A pleasure-boat ; প্রমোদতরণী, কেলি-নৌকা, বজরা, ময়ূরপঙ্খী, ক্রীড়া-নৌকা। **2.** A flat-bottomed freight-boat for canals and rivers ; প্রশস্ততল মালের নৌকা। **3.** The second boat of a man-of-war, for the use of the chief officers ; প্রধান প্রধান কর্ম্মচারিগণের ব্যবহারার্থ রণপোতসংলগ্ন দ্বিতীয় তরী। **Barge-couple**—Two gable beams; ঢালুছাদ বিশিষ্ট ঘরের পাশকপালীর প্রান্তবর্ত্তী কাষ্ঠদ্বয়।

bâr-gee′ (-jē), *n.* The man in charge of a barge ; বজরার মাঝী।

băr′-ĭc, *adj.* Of barium ; ভারক বা ভারিয়ম সম্পর্কীয়।

bă-ril′-lă, *n.* **1.** A plant cultivated in Spain, Sicily, etc. for its ashes ; স্পেন, সিসিলি এবং কেনারী দ্বীপপুঞ্জজাত বৃক্ষ বিশেষ, সজ্জী (হিং কোঃ)। **2.** An impure alkali produced by burning the dried plant, which is impure carbonate of soda ; সজ্জিকাক্ষার।

băr′-i-tōne, *n.* See BARYTONE.

bā′-rĭ-ŭm, *n.* A white metallic element, the basis of the alkaline earth baryta ; শ্বেতবর্ণ ধাতব মূল পদার্থবিশেষ, ভারক (সাঃ পঃ), ভারিয়ম (হিং কোঃ)।

bârk, *n.* **1.** The rind or outer sheath of the trunk and branches of trees; বল্কল, বাকল, ত্বক্। **2.** Quinine ; (also Peruvian or Jesuits' *bark*) ; কুইনাইন। **3.** (*Slang.*) The human skin ; (ইতর ভাষায়) মনুষ্য-চর্ম্ম। **Bark-bound**—Hindered in growth by tight bark ; বল্কলদ্বারা দৃঢ়বদ্ধ হওয়াতে বর্দ্ধনে বাধাপ্রাপ্ত।

bârk, *v. t.* **1.** To strip the bark from ; to peel ; বল্কল তুলিয়া ফেলা ; খোসা ছাড়ান। **2.** To rub off the skin (esp. from the shins and joints) ; ঘষিয়া চামড়া তোলা। **3.** To abrade ; ঘষিয়া বা চাঁচিয়া তুলিয়া ফেলা। **4.** To encrust ; as, to *bark* the roof of a hut ; বল্কলাচ্ছাদিত করা, কঠিন আবরণে আচ্ছাদিত করা।

bârk, barque (bârk), *n.* **1.** A three-masted vessel without a mizen topsail (usu. barque) ; ত্রিমাস্তুলবিশিষ্ট

Barque.

পোতবিশেষ। **2.** (*Poet.*) Any sailing vessel or boat, (usu. bark) ; (কবিতায়) পালের জাহাজ বা নৌকা।

bârk, *v. i.* & *n.* **1.** To make the sharp explosive noise (of dogs, foxes, etc.) ; (with *at*) ; ঘেউ ঘেউ করা, কুকুরের মত চীৎকার করা। **2.** To clamour or agitate to no effect ; (কোন কিছুর বিরুদ্ধে) বৃথা চীৎকার করা, হৈ চৈ করা। **3.** (*Colloq.*) To cough ; (চলিতভাষায়) কাঁশা। ***Noun.*** **1.** The usual cry of dogs, foxes, etc. ; কুক্কুর, শৃগাল প্রভৃতির রব, ঘেউ ঘেউ শব্দ, খেউ খেউ শব্দ। **2.** The sound of gun-fire; বন্দুকের আওয়াজ। **3.** (*Colloq.*) A cough ; কাঁশির শব্দ। **Barking dogs seldom bite**—(*Proverb*) যত গর্জ্জে তত বর্ষে না, অসারের তর্জ্জন গর্জ্জন সার। **His bark is worse than his bite**—He scolds and abuses roundly, but does not bear malice or do mischief ; সে স্পষ্টভাবে গালিগালাজ ও তিরস্কার করে, কিন্তু কোন প্রকার অসূয়া, দ্বেষ পোষণ বা অনিষ্ট করে না। **To bark (against) at the moon**—To agitate to no effect ; বৃথা আন্দোলন করা।

bârk′-ẽr, *n.* **1.** An animal that barks ; hence, a noisy assailant ; ঘেউ ঘেউ শব্দকারী জন্তু ; অতএব হৈ চৈ কারী। **2.** A shop or auction tout ; দোকানের বা নীলামের দালাল। **3.** (*Slang.*) A pistol ; a cannon ; (ইতর ভাষায়) পিস্তল ; কামান।

bâr′-ley (-lĭ), *n.* A well-known grain much used for food and for making malts ; বার্লি, যব। **Barley-corn**—A grain of barley ; যবের দানা। The third part of an inch ; এক ইঞ্চির তৃতীয়াংশ। **Barley-sugar**—A confection usually in twisted sticks ; এক প্রকার মিষ্টদ্রব্য। **Barley-water**—Soothing decoction of pearl-barley for invalids ; বার্লির জল। **John Barley Corn**—A personification of malt liquor ; মূর্ত্তিমান যবসুরা। **Pearl-barley**—See PEARL.

bârm, *n.* The froth of beer, etc. ; yeast ; leaven ; বীয়র প্রভৃতি মদ্যের ফেন, গাঁজলা, সুরামণ্ড, সুরাবীজ (ভাবঃ প্রঃ), মণ্ডোদক ; খামি, কিণ্ব ; খমীর। **Barm′-y,** *adj.*

Bâr′-mĕ-cīde, *n.* & *adj.* One who offers imaginary food or illusory benefits ; যে ব্যক্তি মায়িক খাদ্য বা কাল্পনিক সুবিধা প্রদানের প্রস্তাব করে। ***Adj.*** Illusory ; imaginary ; disappointing ; মায়িক ; কাল্পনিক ; নৈরাশ্যজনক। [আরব্যোপন্যাসোক্ত রাজপুত্র বারমিসাইড সাকাবাক নামক এক ভিক্ষুককে নিমন্ত্রণপূর্ব্বক স্বগৃহে আনিয়া, তাহার সম্মুখে পরিহাসচ্ছলে মহার্ঘ অথচ শূন্য ভোজনপাত্র সকল স্থাপন করেন।] **A Barmecide feast**—A feast where there is nothing to eat ; any illusion of plenty ; যে ভোজে কোন প্রকার আহারের আয়োজন থাকে না, বেল্লিকের নিমন্ত্রণ ; মায়া, ছলনা।

bârn, *n.* A store-house for corn, hay, etc. ; hence, an unadorned house; গোলাবাড়ী, শস্যাগার ; সাজসজ্জাহীন গৃহ। **Barn-door**—The large door of a barn ; (humorously) a target too large to be missed ; শস্যাগারের প্রকাণ্ড দ্বার ; সুবৃহৎ লক্ষ্য—অর্থাৎ যাহা বিদ্ধকরণে বিফল হওয়া একরূপ অসম্ভব। **Barn-owl**—The white church-owl ; শ্বেতবর্ণ পেচকবিশেষ

Barn-yard—Farm-yard ; কৃষিক্ষেত্র বাটীকার প্রাঙ্গণ।

bâr′-nă-cle, *n.* **1.** A conical shell-fish found on the bottoms of ships, and on planks or stones under water ; একজাতীয় শম্বুক, গুগ্‌লী। **2.** A sort of goose found in the Arctic seas ; উত্তর সমুদ্রচর হংস বিশেষ। **3.** A follower that cannot be shaken off ; যে সঙ্গীকে কোন প্রকারে ছাড়ানো যায় না। **4.** (*Usu. pl.*) The pincers placed on the nose of horses to coerce them into quiet for shoeing, etc. ; নাল লাগাইবার সময় বা অন্য কোন কারণে ঘোড়াকে শান্ত রাখার উদ্দেশ্যে উহার নাকে যে চিম্‌টা লাগান হয়। **5.** (*Pl.*) (*Colloq.*) Spectacles ; (চলিতভাষায়) চসমা।

bă′-rō-grăph, *n.* A self-recording barometer ; বায়ুভারমাপক (হিঃ কোঃ)। [এই যন্ত্র কাগজের উপর বায়ুমণ্ডলের চাপের পরিমাণ অঙ্কিত করিয়া দেয়।]

bă-rŏl′-ō-ġȳ, *n.* The science of weight ; ভার-বিজ্ঞান।

băr-ŏm′-ē-têr, *n.* An instrument for measuring the weight or pressure of the atmosphere ; বায়ুভারমাপক (হিঃ কোঃ), বায়ুচাপমানযন্ত্র, বায়ুমান। **—o-met′-ric, —o-met′-ri-cal,** *adjs.* **Aneroid barometer**—অনার্দ্র বায়ুভারমাপক (হিঃ কোঃ)। **Cistern barometer**—কুণ্ডবায়ুভারমাপক (হিঃ কোঃ)। **Mountain barometer**—শৈলবায়ুভারমাপক। **Siphon barometer** — বক্র বায়ুভারমাপক (হিঃ কোঃ)।

băr-ō-mĕt′-rō-grăph, *n.* A barograph ; স্বয়ংবায়ুভারসূচক (হিঃ কোঃ)।

băr′-ŏn, *n.* A peer of the realm ; ইংলণ্ডের সম্ভ্রান্ত পুরুষ বিশেষ। **—age,** *n.* The whole body of barons or peers ; the nobility ; অভিজাত সম্প্রদায় বিশেষ ; সম্ভ্রান্ত-সম্প্রদায়। **Baron of beef**—Two sirloins left uncut at the backbone; অবিযুক্ত গোপার্শ্ব মাংস।

băr′-ŏn-ĕss, *n.* A baron's wife ; also, a lady who holds the baronial title in her own right ; ব্যারণ-পত্নী ; ব্যারণেস-উপাধিধারিণী।

băr′-ŏn-ĕt, *n.* A member of the lowest hereditary titled order, next below a baron and above a knight ; ব্যারণের নিম্নতর উপাধিধারী ব্যক্তি। [ব্যারণেট্‌গণ সাধারণ জনশ্রেণীর অন্তর্ভুক্ত।] **—age,** *n.* **1.** The collective body of baronets ; ব্যারণেট্‌-সম্প্রদায়। **2.** A list of the order of the baronets ; ব্যারণেট্‌গণের তালিকা এবং তাঁহাদের সংক্ষিপ্ত বিবরণ সম্বলিত পুস্তকবিশেষ।

băr′-ŏn-ĕt, *v. t.* To raise to the rank of a baronet ; ব্যারণেট্‌ পদবীতে উন্নীত করা।

băr′-ŏn-ĕt-ċy, *n.* The rank or patent of a baronet ; ব্যারণেটের পদবী বা সনন্দপত্র।

bă-rō′-nĭ-ăl, *adj.* Pertaining to a baron ; ব্যারণ-সম্বন্ধীয়।

băr′-ŏ-nȳ, *n.* **1.** A baron's domain, rank and tenure ; ব্যারণের জমিদারী, পদবী এবং জোত। **2.** (*Ireland*) A territorial division ; (আয়র্লণ্ডে) দেশের বিভাগবিশেষ। **3.** (*Scot.*) A large manor ; (স্কট্‌লণ্ডে) বড় জমিদারী।

bâ-roque′ (-rŏk), *adj.* & *n.* Irregularly shaped ; grotesque ; odd ; অপরূপ ; কিম্ভূতকিমাকার ; অদ্ভুত। ***Noun.*** A whimsical style of ornamentation ; এক প্রকার অদ্ভুত ধরণের মণ্ডন পদ্ধতি।

bă-rouche′ (-rôsh), *n.* A four-wheeled carriage with a falling top and seats as in a coach ; একপ্রকার চারি চাকার ফিটন গাড়ী।

bâr′-quen-tīne (-kĕn-), *n.* A three-masted vessel ; ত্রি-মাস্তুল পোত বিশেষ।

băr′-răck, *n.* & *v. t.* A building or set of buildings, for soldiers, esp. when in garrison, (usu. *pl.*) ; সেনানিবাস। ***Verb t.*** To locate in barracks ; সেনানিবাসে স্থানদান করা।

băr′-ră-cōōn, *n.* A set of sheds or enclosure for slaves, convicts, etc. ; ক্রীতদাস বা বন্দিগণের বাসের জন্য চালাঘরশ্রেণী বা বেষ্টিত স্থান, দাসনিবাস।

băr-ră-cū′-dă, —cou′-tă, (-cōō-), **—cōō′-tă,** *n.* An Australian large sea-fish ; অষ্ট্রেলিয়াদেশীয় বৃহৎকায় মৎস্য বিশেষ।

bâr′-rage (-râzh), *n.* The act of barring or damming ; the artificial bar, esp. one in the Nile ; সেতু-বন্ধন ; জল-প্রবাহ-রোধার্থ বাঁধ, সেতুবন্ধ, জাঙ্গাল (বিশেষতঃ মিশর দেশস্থ নীল নদীর)।

băr′-ră-tŏr, *n.* (*Law*) A vexatious litigant ; a malicious raiser of discord ; (আইন) মামলাবাজ ; যে ব্যক্তি দ্বেষপূর্ব্বক বিরোধ বাঁধায়।

băr′-ră-trȳ, *n.* **1.** The practice of exciting and encouraging lawsuits and quarrels ; কলহ কিম্বা মামলা মোকদ্দমায় উৎসাহদান। **2.** (*Marine law*) Fraud or criminal negligence on the part of the master or mariners of a ship to the prejudice of the owner ; পোতাধ্যক্ষ বা নাবিকগণের প্রতারণা বা অপরাধজনক অবহেলা—যদ্দারা পোতস্বামী ক্ষতিগ্রস্ত হয়।

barred, *p. p.* **1.** Marked with bars ; শলাকা-চিহ্নিত। **2.** (Of harbour) Obstructed with sandbar ; (পোতাশ্রয়-সম্বন্ধে) বালির বাঁধদ্বারা অবরুদ্ধ।

băr′-rĕl, *n.* & *v. t.* **1.** A cylindrical wooden vessel bulging in the middle, formed of staves bound with hoops ; পিপা। **2.** The capacity of such a cask, (usually from 30 to 45 gallons) ; পিপার ধারণ-শক্তি। **3.** The metal tube of a gun ; বন্দুকের নল বা নাল। **4.** A cylinder ; as, the *barrel* of a watch ; চোঙ্গ, বেলন, দণ্ড, স্তম্ভবৎপদার্থ। ***Verb t.*** To put or store up, in a barrel ; পিপায় রাখা। **—reled, —relled,** *adj.* **Barrel-bellied**—Having a well-rounded belly ; লম্বোদর, টোওল (*colloq.*)।

băr′-rĕn, *adj.* & *n.* **1.** Bearing no children; as, a *barren* woman (বন্ধ্যা স্ত্রী); বন্ধ্য, বাঁজা। **2.** Producing no vegetation; sterile; as, *barren* land; অনুর্ব্বর, উষর; অনুৎপাদক। **3.** Without fruit or seed; as, *barren* trees or plants; ফলবীজশূন্য। **4.** Fruitless; unprofitable; as, they shed *barren* tears at a tragedy; নিষ্ফল; অলাভজনক, নিরর্থক। **5.** (Of persons) Mentally dull; stupid; (ব্যক্তি-সম্বন্ধে) জড়-বুদ্ধি; মূঢ়। ***Noun.*** A barren tract of land; অনুর্ব্বর ভূখণ্ড। **—ly,** *adv.* **—ness,** *n.*

băr′-rĕt, *n.* A little flat cap, esp. the biretta; একপ্রকার ক্ষুদ্র চ্যাপ্টা টুপি।

băr-ri-cāde′, —cā′-dō, *n.* & *v. t.* **1.** A hastily-formed rampart of casks, earth, trees, logs of wood, etc., designed to impede the advance of a suddenly declared foe; আকস্মিক শত্রুর গতিরোধার্থ পিপা, মৃত্তিকা, বৃক্ষ, কাষ্ঠখণ্ড প্রভৃতি দ্বারা ব্যস্ততা-সহকারে নির্ম্মিত বপ্রবিশেষ। **2.** Any barrier; অবরোধ, প্রতিবন্ধ। ***Verb t.*** To stop up, as a passage; to obstruct; প্রতিরোধ করা; অবরোধ করা।

băr′-ri-ēr, *n.* & *v. t.* **1.** A fence serving to bar the advance (of persons) or to prevent access; প্রতিবন্ধ। **2.** Any obstruction; as, constitutional *barriers*; বাঁধা, বিঘ্ন। **3.** A fence or railing to mark the limits of a place or to keep back a crowd; বেড়া। **4.** A limit or boundary; সীমা, সীমানা। **5.** The gate at which customs are collected; শুল্কগ্রহণ-দ্বার। ***Verb t.*** To close or shut with a barrier; বেড়াদ্বারা বন্ধ করা।

bâr′-rĭng, *prep.* Excepting; leaving out of account; as, nobody else, *barring* the a thor, knew; ব্যতীত, ছাড়া; ব্যতিরে ।

băr′-ris-têr, *n.* A counsel admitted to plead at the bar and undertake the public trial of causes; ব্যবহারজীবী, কৌঁসুলী।

băr′-row (-rō), *n.* **1.** A grave-mound; a tumulus; সমাধি স্তূপ; সমাধির উপরিস্থ মৃত্তিকাস্তূপ।

băr′-row (-rō), *n.* **1.** A rectangular frame for the carrying of load by two or more men; a stretcher; a bier; ভারি দ্রব্য বহনার্থ খট্টা-(খাঙা) বিশেষ; পীড়িত, আহত বা মৃত ব্যক্তিকে বহনার্থ খট্টা বিশেষ; শব বহনার্থ খট্টা বিশেষ, মরার খাট। **2.** A two-wheeled hand-cart; হাত-গাড়ী, ঠেলা-গাড়ী।

băr′-row (-rō), *n.* A castrated hog; শূকর, বিশেষতঃ ছিন্নমুষ্ক শূকর। **2.** A long sleeveless flannel garment for infants; শিশুদিগের আস্তিনবিহীন ফ্লানেলের জামা বিশেষ।

bâr′-têr, *v. i.*, *t.* & *n.* To traffic by exchanging one commodity for another; এক দ্রব্যের বিনিময়ে অপর দ্রব্য দেওয়া। [দ্রব্যের বিনিময়ে টাকা পয়সা দিলে *purchase* বলা হয়।] ***Verb t.*** To exchange (frequenntly for an unworthy consideration,—sometimes followed by *away*); as, to *barter away* goods or honour; বিনিময় করা, অদল বদল করা (সচরাচর অতি তুচ্ছ পদার্থের বিনিময়ে)। ***Noun.*** **1.** Trade by exchange of commodities; truck বিনিময়-ব্যবসায়, অদলবদল, প্রতিপণ; পরিবর্ত্ত, প্রতিভাণ্ড, পরিদান। **2.** An arithmetical rule for computing the value of different commodities; বিনিময়-নিয়ম। **—er,** *n.*

bâr′-ti-zăn, *n.* A small overhanging turret projecting from the angles of a square-tower or the parapet of a building; চতুষ্কোণ বুরুজ হইতে বা কোন অট্টালিকার আবক্ষ-উচ্চ প্রাচীর হইতে প্রলম্বিত ক্ষুদ্র বুরুজ বিশেষ।

bâr′-tŏn, *n.* **1.** A farmyard; কৃষিক্ষেত্র বাটীকার প্রাঙ্গণ। **2.** A demesne farm; খামার।

bā-rȳ′-tā, *n.* (*Chem.*) The monoxide of barium; (রসায়ন-শাস্ত্র) ভারীতা (হিঃ কোঃ), ভারক (সাঃ পঃ)। **—ryt′-ic,** *adj.*

bā-rȳ′-tēs, *n.* (*Miner.*) Barium sulphate, generally called *heavy spar* or *barite*; (খনিজ-বিদ্যা) গন্ধকীয়-ভারক।

băr′-ȳ-tōne, băr′-i-tōne, *n.* **1.** A deep-toned male voice between bass and tenor; ভারী স্বর। **2.** A singer with such a voice; যে গায়ক উক্ত প্রকার স্বরে গান গায়। **3.** (*Gr. Gram.*) A word without the acute accent on the last syllable; (গ্রীক ব্যাকরণ) যে শব্দের শেষ শব্দাংশে উদাত্ত স্বর থাকে না।

bā′-săl, *adj.* **1.** Relating to, or formed by, the base; ভিত্তিসম্বন্ধীয়; ভিত্তিদ্বারা গঠিত। **2.** (*Fig.*) Fundamental; as, *basal* characteristic; (লক্ষণায়) মৌলিক, ভিত্তিস্বরূপ, মূলীভূত।

bă-sâlt′, *n.* A dark-coloured, igneous rock; একপ্রকার কৃষ্ণবর্ণ আগ্নেয় প্রস্তর—সচরাচর স্তম্ভাকারে দৃষ্ট হইয়া থাকে।

băs′-ăn, băz′-ăn, *n.* The skin of a sheep tanned in oak or larch-bark; (ওক্ বিম্বা লার্চ্চবৃক্ষের বক্কল জলে) সংস্কৃত মেষচর্ম্ম।

basbleu, (*F.*), *n.* A blue-stocking; a literary lady; শিক্ষাগর্ব্বিতা নারী; বিদুষী।

băs′-cūle, *n.* An arrangement in bridges by which one portion balances another; সেতুর মধ্যস্থ সংবিধান বিশেষ—যদ্দ্বারা এক অংশ অপরাংশের সহিত তুলিত হয়। **Bascule-bridge**—A counterpoised or balanced drawbridge; এক প্রকার সেতু—তুলা-যন্ত্রের মত এই সেতুর এক দিক নত করিলে অপর দিক উত্থিত হয়, তুলাসেতু।

bāse, *n.* **1.** That on which anything stands or depends ; a support ; a bottom ; foundation ; ভিত্তি, গোড়া ; অবলম্ব, আশ্রয় ; তল ; পত্তন, ভিত্তিভূমি, বুনিয়াদ। **2.** (*Fig.*) Fundamental principle ; a groundwork ; মূলতত্ত্ব ; মূলসূত্র। **3.** (*Arch.*) The part of a column between the shaft and the pedestal or pavement ; (স্থপতি-বিদ্যা) স্তম্ভের পাদদেশ বা নিম্নাংশ, উপস্তম্ভ (মঃ ইঃ), কুম্ভক (রাঃ রাঃ)। **4.** A pedestal ; পাদপীঠ, পীঠ (রাঃ তঃ), বেদিকা (রাঃ রাঃ), অধিষ্ঠান (ঐ)। **5.** (*Chem.*) The positive or the non-acid component of a salt ; (রসায়ন-শাস্ত্র) ভস্ম (হিঃ কোঃ)। **6.** (*Dyeing*) A substance used as a mordant ; (রঞ্জন-বিদ্যা) যে বস্তুর সংযোগে রঙ্গ পাকা করা হয়। **7.** (*Geom.*) The line or surface constituting that part of a figure on which it is supposed to stand ; (জ্যামিতি) ভূমি (হিঃ কোঃ), আধার (ঐ)। **8.** (*Mil.*) A place or tract of country from which the operations of an army proceed and supplies are furnished ; (also *base of operation*); (সামরিক-শাস্ত্র) যে স্থান হইতে সামরিক অভিযান অগ্রসর এবং খাদ্যাদি সরবরাহ করা হয়, মূলস্থান। **9.** (*Math.*) The number from which a mathematical table is constructed ; (গণিত-শাস্ত্র) কোনপ্রকার গণন-প্রণালী বা ঘাতাঙ্কগণন পদ্ধতির প্রারম্ভ-সংখ্যা (যেমন দশমিক গুণনপ্রণালীতে—১০)। **10.** (*Bot. & zool.*) The end at which an organ is attached to trunk ; (উদ্ভিদ্ ও জন্তু-বিদ্যা) ফল, পত্র বা কোন অঙ্গের যে প্রান্ত কাণ্ডের সহিত সংলগ্ন থাকে। **11.** A starting place or goal in various games ; বিভিন্নপ্রকার ক্রীড়ার যাত্রাস্থলী বা গন্তব্য-স্থান। **12.** (*Survey*) A baseline ; (জরিপ) ভূমিরেখা।

bāse, *adj.* **1.** (*Originally*) Of small height ; as, *base* shrubs ; (পূর্ব্বে) খর্ব্ব, অনুচ্চ। **2.** Alloyed with inferior metal ; debased ; as, a *base* coin ; খাইদ-মিশ্রিত, কূটক (যাজ্ঞঃ) ; মেকি। **3.** Morally low ; cowardly ; selfish ; despicably mean ; (of persons, actions, habits, etc.) ; অধম, পতিত ; ভীরু ; স্বার্থপর ; নীচ, হীন, ইতর, ঘৃণ্য, হেয়, অবজ্ঞেয়, পামর, জঘন্য। **4.** Befitting an inferior person ; menial ; as, *base* servitude ; নীচ-জনযোগ্য ; হীনজনোচিত। **5.** Deep or grave in sound ; গম্ভীর। **6.** (*Of language*) Not classical ; as, *base* Latin ; (ভাষা-সম্বন্ধে) অপকৃষ্ট, প্রাকৃত। **Base'-ly,** *adv.* **Base'-ness,** *n.* **Base-born**—Born out of wedlock ; জারজ। Of low or humble birth ; অন্ত্যজ, হীনবংশজাত। **Base-court**—The outer court of a castle ; the court behind a farm-house ; দুর্গাদির বহিঃপ্রাঙ্গণ ; কৃষিক্ষেত্র-বাটীকার পশ্চাদ্দিগের প্রাঙ্গণ। **Base tenant**—A tenant holding land which he will lose if a certain contingent event occurs ; কোন অনিশ্চিত ঘটনা ঘটিলে যে প্রজা ভূমির অধিকার হইতে বঞ্চিত হয়।

bāse, *v.t.* To lay or form a foundation for ; to establish securely ; ভিত্তিস্থাপন করা ; প্রতিষ্ঠিত করা।

bāse-ball, *n.* A game at ball (the U. S. national game) ; কন্দুক-ক্রীড়াবিশেষ (মার্কিণ যুক্তরাজ্যের জাতীয় ক্রীড়া)।

bāse'-lĕss, *adj.* Groundless ; unfounded ; অমূলক ; ভিত্তিহীন। **—ness,** *n.*

Basella alba—White nightshade ; সফেদ পুঁই (বেলঃ)।

Basella cordifolia—রক্তপুঁই (বেলঃ)।

bāse'-mĕnt, *n.* (*Arch.*) The lowest or fundamental part of a structure ; esp. the lowest story sunk below ground level (of a building) ; (স্থপতি-বিদ্যা) তলপত্তন (রাঃ রাঃ), অট্টালিকাদির ভূনিম্নবর্ত্তী সর্ব্বনিম্ন তল, তলঘর (কেঙিঃ), অন্তর্ভৌম প্রাসাদতল।

băsh, *v. t.* To strike with a heavy blow that tends to smash ; প্রচণ্ডভাবে আঘাত করা।

bă-shaw', *n.* The earlier form of the Turkish title, PASHA ; তুরস্কদেশীয় সম্ভ্রান্তব্যক্তিদের উপাধিবিশেষ বর্ত্তমানে "পাশা" লিখিত হয়।

băsh'-ful, *adv.* Shy ; shame-faced sheepish ; লাজুক ; লজ্জাবান, সলজ্জ সব্রীড় ; মুখচোরা, মেনিমুখো (*colloq.*) **—ly,** *adv.* **—ness,** *n.* The quality of being bashful ; লজ্জাশীলতা, শালীনতা

băsh'-i-ba-zouk' (-ē-bă-zōk), *n.* A mercenary soldier belonging to the irregular troops of the Turkish army, notorious for plundering and brutality ; তুরস্ক-দেশীয় অনিয়ত সৈনিক। **—er-y,** *n.*

bā'-sic, *adj.* **1.** Fundamental ; as, *basic* principle ; মৌলিক। **2.** (*Chem.*) Relating to base ; having the amount of base atomically greater than that of the acid ; (রসায়ন-শাস্ত্র) ভাস্মিক (হিঃ কোঃ) ; দ্রাব পদার্থের পরমাণু অপেক্ষা অধিকতর ভস্মপরমাণু-বিশিষ্ট।

bā-sĭc'-i-tŷ, *n.* An acid's relative power of combining with bases ; ভস্মের সহিত অম্লের আপেক্ষিক সম্মিলন-শক্তি, ভাস্মিকতা (হিঃ কোঃ)।

băs'-il, *n.* The name given to some aromatic herbs of the mint family ; পুদিনা জাতীয় কতিপয় ওষধির সাধারণ নাম। **Garden basil, Sweet basil**—বাবুই তুলসী (খোরী)। **Hoary basil, Wild basil**—সাদাতুলসী (খোরী)। **Holy basil**—কৃষ্ণতুলসী (খোরী)।

băs'-il, *n.* Same as BASAN.

bă-sil'-ic, *adj.* (Of the vein) Starting from elbow and discharging into axillary vein ; (শিরা-সম্বন্ধে) যে শিরা কফোণি (কনুই) হইতে কাক্ষিক শিরা পর্য্যন্ত বিস্তৃত হইয়াছে—তৎসম্পর্কীয়।

bă-sil'-i-că, *n.* **1.** (*Originally*) A royal residence ; (পূর্ব্বে) রাজপ্রাসাদ।

2. (*Rom. Antiq.*) A large oblong hall, with double colonnades and a semicircular apse at the end for law courts and public assemblies; (রোমীয় প্রত্নতত্ত্ব) যুগলস্তম্ভশ্রেণী এবং অর্দ্ধবৃত্তাকার দরদালানবিশিষ্ট আয়তক্ষেত্রাকার বিশালায়তন বিচারগৃহ বা সভামণ্ডপ বিশেষ। 3. Such a building used as a Christian Church; খৃষ্টীয় ধর্ম্মমন্দিররূপে ব্যবহৃত উক্তপ্রকার অট্টালিকা। 4. (In Rome) One of the seven churches founded by Constantine; (রোম নগরীতে) সম্রাট্ কনষ্টেনটাইন্ কর্ত্তৃক প্রতিষ্ঠিত সপ্ত ধর্ম্মমন্দিরের অন্যতম।

bă-sĭl′-i-cŏn, —cŭm, *n.* A kind of ointment; মোম, আলকাতরা, রজন, জলপাইয়ের তৈল ও চর্ব্বিদ্বারা প্রস্তুত মলম বিশেষ।

băs′-i lisk, *n.* **1.** A fabulous serpent whose hissing would drive away all other serpents, and whose

Basilisk (hooded).

breath, and even look, was fatal; (also, cockatrice); কবিকল্পিত সর্পবিশেষ—ইহার ফোঁস ফোঁস শব্দে অন্য সর্পসকল ত্রাসে পলায়ন করিত। ইহার নিঃশ্বাস মারাত্মক ছিল বলিয়া কথিত আছে। **2.** A small American lizard with a hollow crest which can be inflated at will; আমেরিকাদেশীয় সচূড় ক্ষুদ্রকায় গোধিকাবিশেষ—এই জন্তু ইচ্ছামত চূড়া স্ফীত করিতে পারে।

ba′-sin (bāsn), *n.* **1.** A small vessel, usually circular, for holding water, designed for washing or other purpose; জলপাত্র, বাটী, খর্পর (বঃ প্রঃ), কোশা। **2.** A tract of country drained by a river and its tributaries; নদীমাতৃক দেশ, অববাহিকা (সাঃ পাঃ)। **3.** A circular or oval valley; গোলাকার বা ডিম্বাকার উপত্যকা। **4.** A hollow receptacle containing water; কুণ্ড, জলাশয়। **5.** A dock with flood-gates; জলপ্রবাহ-প্রবেশের দ্বারবিশিষ্ট পোত-সংস্কার স্থান। **6.** A land-locked harbour; a bay; স্থলরুদ্ধ পোতাশ্রয়স্থান; উপসাগর। **—ful,** *adj.* (*Geog.*) **Basin catchment**—(ভূগোল) সংগ্রহণ-প্রদেশ (হিঃ কোঃ), কোশা (সাঃ পঃ), কোশিকা (ঐ)। **Basin drainage**—পরিবাহ-ক্ষেত্র (হিঃ কোঃ)।

băs′-i-nĕt, băs′-nĕt, *n.* A light steel head-piece; ইস্পাতনির্ম্মিত লঘু উষ্ণীষবিশেষ।

bā′-sis, (*Pl.* BASES.), *n.* **1.** The foundation of any thing; the base; গোড়া, বুনিয়াদ, ভিত্তি; মূল। **2.** The groundwork; the first or fundamental principle; মূলভিত্তি; মূলতত্ত্ব। **3.** Main ingredient; প্রধান উপাদান। **4.** Common ground for negotiation, argument, etc.; সন্ধি, তর্ক প্রভৃতির সাধারণ ভিত্তি।

băsk, *v. i.* **1.** To revel in warmth or light (esp. in the sun, fire-light, etc.); উত্তাপ ও আলোকে (বিশেষতঃ অগ্নির আলোক, সূর্য্যালোক, প্রভৃতিতে) আমোদ প্রমোদ করা, রৌদ্র সেবন করা। **2.** To lie in warmth; রোদ পোহান, আগুন পোহান। **3.** (*Fig.*) To be at ease and thriving under benign influence; as, to *bask* in the sunshine of royal favour; (লক্ষণায়) প্রেম, অনুগ্রহ, সমৃদ্ধি প্রভৃতির সুখজনক প্রভাবের ভিতর আরামে জীবনযাপন করত উত্তরোত্তর উন্নতি লাভ করা। **Bask′-ing,** *adj.*

băs′-kĕt, *n.* & *v. t.* **1.** A vessel of wickerwork made of osiers, canes, rushes, etc.; চুপড়ী, ঝুড়ি, টুকরি, চাঙ্গারী, করণ্ড, মঞ্জুষা। **2.** The quantity which fills a basket; as, a *basket* of cherries; (also *basketful*); এক ঝুড়ি। ***Verb t.*** **1.** To put in a basket; ঝুড়ির মধ্যে রাখা। **2.** To throw into the waste-paper basket; to reject as unsuitable; "Your handwriting will cause our sub-editor to *basket* your communications;" ফাঁস কাগজের ঝুড়িতে নিক্ষেপ করা; অব্যবহার্য্য বলিয়া ফেলিয়া দেওয়া। **Basket-hilt**—A hilt with a covering wrought like basket-work to protect the hand; বংশবেত্রাদিনির্ম্মিত তরবারির মুষ্টি। **Basket-work** — Wickerwork; ঝুড়িতৈয়ারীর কায, বংশবেত্রাদির কায। **The pick of the basket**—The best of the lot; সবার সেরা।

ba′-son (bāsn), *n.* Same as BASIN.

Basque (bâsk), *adj.* & *n.* Pertaining to the people or language of Biscay; বিস্কে উপসাগরের চতুষ্পার্শ্ববর্ত্তী প্রদেশ, তৎস্থানবাসী বা তৎস্থানের ভাষাসম্পর্কীয়। ***Noun.*** **1.** A native of Biscay; বিস্কেবাসী লোক। **2.** The language spoken by the Basque people; ব্যাস্ক্ জাতির ভাষা। **3.** (*Com. noun*) A short continuation of a lady's bodice below the waist; কটির নিম্নদেশে বিলম্বিত স্ত্রীলোকের কঞ্চুলিকার অংশ বিশেষ।

bas-re-lief′ (bâ-rē-lēf), **băss′-rē-lief′** (-lēf), *n.* Low relief; sculpture-work, figures of which project less than half of their true proportions; অল্পমাত্র উদ্গত ভাস্করকার্য্য; যে মূর্ত্তিশিল্পের কার্য্যে মূর্ত্তি প্রভৃতির অর্দ্ধাপেক্ষা অল্পতর অংশ উদ্গত করা হয়।

băss, *n.* The name of various British and American sea-fishes, allied to the *Perch*; ইয়ুরোপ ও আমেরিকা দেশীয় বিভিন্ন প্রকার মৎস্যের সাধারণ নাম।

băss, *n.* The inner bark of the lime or linden used for mats, hassocks, baskets, etc.; জম্বীর বৃক্ষের অন্তর্বল্কল।

băss, *adj.* & *n.* (*Mus.*) Of low pitch ; (সঙ্গীত-শাস্ত্র) গম্ভীর। ***Noun.*** The lowest part in musical composition ; male voice which sings this part ; খাদ ; নিম্নস্বর। **Bass-viol**—A stringed instrument used for playing bass ; a violoncello ; খাদসুর বাজাইবার বাদ্য-যন্ত্র বিশেষ ; বেহালার মত বাদ্যযন্ত্র বিশেষ।

băs'-sĕt, *n.* A short-legged small hound ; একপ্রকার খর্ব্বপাদ এবং ক্ষুদ্র-কায় কুকুর।

băs'-sĕt, *n.* An obsolete card-game ; একপ্রকার অপ্রচলিত তাস-ক্রীড়া।

băs'-sĕt, *n.* & *v. i.* (*Geol.*) The edge of a geological stratum at the surface of the ground ; (ভূ-বিদ্যা) পৃথিবীর পৃষ্ঠে প্ররূঢ় ভূ-স্তর-প্রান্ত। ***Verb i.*** To crop out at the surface ; ভূপৃষ্ঠে প্ররূঢ় হওয়া।

băs'-sĕt-hŏrn, *n.* A tenor clarinet ; একপ্রকার বংশী।

băs'-si-nĕt, *n.* A hooded wicker-cradle or perambulator ; বাঁশ বা বেতের তৈয়ারী ছেলেদের ঢাকনিওয়ালা দোলা বা গাড়ী।

băs-sōōn', *n.* A wind instrument of the double reed kind ; এক প্রকার বংশী।

basso relievo, (*It.*) *n.* Same as BASS-RELIEF.

băst, *n.* **1.** The inner bark of the lime or linden tree ; জম্বীর বৃক্ষের অন্তর্বল্কল। **2.** Other flexible fibrous barks ; এবম্প্রকার অন্যান্য নমনীয় অংশু- (আঁশ) বিশিষ্ট বল্কল, বল্কল্ (সাঃ পঃ), অংশু (ঐ)।

băs'-tard (-tĕrd), *n.* & *adj.* **1.** An illegitimate or natural child ; জারজ সন্তান, বিজাতক, অসতীসুত, কুলটাপুত্র। **2.** Any thing spurious, counterfeit or false ; কৃত্রিম, জাল, মেকি বা নকল জিনিষ। ***Adj.*** **1.** Illegitimate ; জারজ, অপগর্ভজাত, দো-আঁশলা (*Colloq.*)। **2.** Spurious ; not genuine ; adulterated ; কৃত্রিম; মেকি, জাল, নকল ; ভেজাল। **–i-za'-tion,** *n.* **–ize,** *v. t.* To declare illegitimate ; জারজ বলিয়া ঘোষণা করা। **–tar-dȳ,** *n.* Illegitimacy ; জারজত্ব।

Bastard teak—পলাশ (খোরীঃ)।

bāste, *v. t.* To beat soundly ; to cudgel ; বেদম প্রহার করা ; লাঠি দ্বারা আঘাত করা, লগুড়াঘাত করা, লাঠিপেটা করা (*Colloq.*)।

bāste, *v. t.* To moisten (roasting meat) with melted butter, fat, etc. to prevent burning ; (ভাজা করার সময় মাংসে) ঘৃত, চর্ব্বি, প্রভৃতি দেওয়া।

bāste, *v. t.* To sew or tack together with long loose stitches ; সেলাইয়ের আগে টেকিয়া লওয়া।

băs-tile' (-tēl), **–tille'** (-tēl), *n.* **1.** A small fortress ; ক্ষুদ্র দুর্গ বা কেল্লা। **2.** (*Cap.* **–tille.**) The prison-fortress built in Paris in the 14th century and destroyed in 1789 ; প্যারীস নগরীর সুবিখ্যাত দুর্গ বা কারাগার। [ফরাসী বিপ্লবের প্রারম্ভে উন্মত্ত জনসাধারণ বেষ্টিল দুর্গ আক্রমণ করে। তাহারা ১৭৮৯ খৃষ্টাব্দের ১৮ই জুলাই দিবস উক্ত কারাগার অধিকার করত, অচিরে উহা ভূমিসাৎ করিয়াছিল।]

băs-ti-nā'-dō, –nāde', *n.* & *v. t.* A form of punishment by caning on the soles of the culprit's feet ; চীন, তুরস্ক প্রভৃতি দেশে প্রচলিত দণ্ডপ্রদানের প্রণালী বিশেষ। এই প্রথানুসারে অপরাধীর পদতলে বেত্রাঘাত করা হয়। ***Verb t.*** To cane on the soles of feet ; পদ-তলে বেত্রাঘাত করা।

băs'-ti-ŏn, *n.* (*In fort.*) A huge mass of earth faced with sods, brick or stones, standing out from a rampart of which it forms the main portion ; বুরুজ, দুর্গপ্রাকার হইতে বহিরুদ্গত (পঞ্চভুজাকৃতি) মৃত্তিকাস্তূপ—ইহা প্রাকারের একটি প্রধান অঙ্গ বলিয়া পরিগণিত হইয়া থাকে। **–oned,** *adj.*

băs'-ȳl, *n.* (*Chem.*) A body which unites with oxygen to form a *base* ; (রসায়নশাস্ত্র) যে পদার্থ অম্লজান বাষ্পের সহিত সম্মিলিত হইয়া ভস্মে পরিণত হয়।

băt, *n.* A nocturnal mouse-like quadruped with membranous wings ; বাদুড়, জতু, চর্ম্মচটক, জতুকা, ভঙ্গারী (আঃ বঃ)। **Bat-fowling**—The catching of birds by night when at roost ; রাত্রে দাঁড়ে বসিলে পক্ষি-ধরণ।

băt, *n.* & *v. t.* **1.** A wooden implement (with rounded handle and flattened blade) used to strike a ball in cricket ; also, a batsman ; ক্রীকেট খেলার উপকরণ বিশেষ (চ্যাপ্টা ডাণ্ডা) ; ব্যাটধারী। **2.** Part of a brick with one whole end ; a kind of sundried brick ; ইষ্টকখণ্ড (যাহার একপ্রান্ত অভগ্ন থাকে); সূর্য্যতাপে কঠিনীকৃত ইষ্টক বিশেষ। ***Verb i.*** To strike or hit a ball with a bat, esp. in cricket ; ক্রীকেট প্রভৃতি ক্রীড়ায় ক্রীড়াদণ্ড দ্বারা বল তাড়না করা। **Batter, Batsman**—One who wields the bat at cricket ; ক্রীকেট-খেলায় যে ব্যক্তি ব্যাট্-দ্বারা বল তাড়না করে।

bă-tā'-tă, –tās, *n.* The sweet potato (*Batatas edulis*) ; শকরকন্দ আলু, মিঠা আলু। ***Batatas paniculata***—ভুঁইকুমড়া (বেলঃ), ভূমিকুষ্মাণ্ড।

Bă-tā'-vi-ăn, *n.* & *adj.* An inhabitant of ancient Batavia or of modern Holland ; a Dutchman ; প্রাচীন ব্যাটেভিয়াবাসী ; (বর্ত্তমান) ওলন্দাজ। ***Adj.*** Pertaining to Batavia or Holland ; প্রাচীন ব্যাটেভিয়া বা হলন্দ দেশ সংক্রান্ত।

batch (băch), *n.* **1.** The quantity of bread produced at one baking ; একবারে যে পরিমাণ রুটি সেঁকা হয়। **2.** A number of persons or things put or treated together ; a set ; দল, গণ, সঙ্ঘ ; শ্রেণী, তাড়া।

bāte, *v. t.* & *i.* **1.** To strike off a part of ; to deduct ; as, I will not *bate* a jot of ; ছাটিয়া ফেলা ; বাদ দেওয়া, ছাড়িয়া দেওয়া। **2.** To restrain ; to diminish ; as, he *bated* his breath a little ; সংযত করা ; হ্রাস করা। ***Verb i.*** To fall off in force or intensity ; as, his energy did not *bate* a jot ; ক্ষীণ হওয়া, হ্রাসপ্রাপ্ত হওয়া।

bāte, *n.* & *v. t.* An alkaline lye (used by tanners) to make the hides supple ; চর্ম্ম কোমল করণার্থ ক্ষারজল বিশেষ। ***Verb t.*** To steep (hides) in this ; ক্ষারজলে (চর্ম্ম) ডোবান।

bāth, *n.* **1.** The act of washing ; ধৌতকরণ। **2.** Immersion in liquid, air, etc. ; অবগাহন, স্নান। **3.** The water or other liquid used for bathing ; a wash or lotion ; স্নানার্থ জল কিম্বা অন্য তরল-পদার্থ, প্রক্ষালন বারি ; ঔষধ জল। **4.** A vessel or apartment arranged for bathing in ; (usu. *pl.*) a series of such apartments ; as, a fondness for *baths* ; স্নান-পাত্র, স্নানাধার, স্নানাগার, স্নানশালা ; (সাধারণতঃ বহুবচন) স্নানকক্ষশ্রেণী। **Bath of blood**—Carnage ; রক্তগঙ্গা, বহু নরহত্যা। **Bath-room**—A room to bathe in ; স্নানগৃহ (মঃ ভাঃ), যন্ত্রধারাগৃহ, (মেঃ দূত)। **Order of the Bath**—A high order of British knight-hood ; (so called from the bath which preceded installation); as, *C. B.* (Companion of the Bath); ইংলণ্ডের অভিজাতশ্রেণী বিশেষ—এই উপাধিপ্রাপকগণকে উপাধিপ্রাপ্তির পূর্ব্ব দিবস সন্ধ্যাকালে অবগাহন করিতে হইত। **Vapour-bath**—ভাপ্‌রা, বাষ্প-স্বেদ, বাষ্পাভিষেক, বাষ্পস্নান।

Bāth, *n.* A town in Somerset named from its hot springs and resorted to for medical bathing ; সমরসেটের অন্তঃপাতী উষ্ণপ্রস্রবণ-বহুল নগর বিশেষ—উক্ত নগরে আরোগ্য-লাভের উদ্দেশ্যে স্নানার্থ গমন করা হয়। **Bath-brick**—A preparation for cleaning metal ; ধাতু পরিষ্কারের উপকরণ বিশেষ। **Bath-chair**—A large wheeled chair for invalids at Bath ; বাথ নগরে সমাগত রুগ্নব্যক্তি-দিগের জন্য চক্রযুক্ত কেদারা বিশেষ।

bāthe, *v. t.* & *i.* **1.** To wash by immersion ; স্নান করা, অবগাহন করা। **2.** To moisten all over (with tears, perspiration, etc.) ; স্নাত করা, ধৌত করা, সিক্ত করা। **3.** To immerse in (fire, air, light, etc.) ; to envelope ; "The rosy shodows *bathe* me." (অগ্নি, বাতাস, আলোক প্রভৃতিতে) স্নাত বা নিমজ্জিত করা ; পরিবেষ্টিত করা। ***Verb i.*** To plunge or immerse oneself in water or other liquid ; to take a bath ; as, to *bathe* in a sacred river ; জল কিম্বা অন্যবিধ তরল পদার্থে নিমজ্জিত থাকা, জলবৎ পদার্থদ্বারা পরিস্নাত বা পরিবেষ্টিত হওয়া ; স্নান করা।

bāth'-êr, *n.* One who takes a bath, esp in sea or river ; স্নাতক, স্নায়ী, স্নাতা, বিশেষতঃ যে ব্যক্তি নদী কিম্বা সমুদ্রে স্নান করে।

bāth-ing, *n.* The act of taking a bath ; স্নান, অবগাহন, অভিষেক, মজ্জন, নিমজ্জন, প্লাবন

bă-thŏm'-ĕ-têr, *n.* A spring balance for measuring the depth of water ; জলের গভীরতামাপক যন্ত্র।

bā'-thŏs, *n.* (*Rhet.*) A descent from the sublime to the ridiculous ; anticlimax ; (অলঙ্কার-শাস্ত্র) (বাক্যাদির) গুরুগম্ভীরভাবে আরম্ভ এবং অকস্মাৎ হাস্যোদ্দীপকভাবে পতন (যথা—দুগ্ধফেননিভ শয্যা হইতে ধপাৎ করিয়া পড়িয়া গেলাম) ; (বাক্যের) উত্তরোত্তর অপকর্ষতা, গুরুচণ্ডালী দোষ। **—thet'-ic,** *adj.*

bă-thym'-ĕ-trў, *n.* The art or science of measuring depths in the sea ; সাগর-গভীরতা-মান বিদ্যা।

bāt'-ing, *prep.* Excepting ; except ; as, *bating* this, I know nothing ; ছাড়া ; ব্যতীত, ব্যতিরেকে।

bȧ-tiste' (-tēst), *n.* A fine cotton muslin like cambric in texture ; কেম্ব্রিকের মত অতি সূক্ষ্ম ক্ষৌম বস্ত্র বিশেষ।

bă'-tŏn, *n.* & *v. t.* **1.** A staff of office ; as, a marshal's *baton* ; the truncheon of a constable ; দণ্ড ; রুল, সোঁটা। **2.** (*Herald.*) A truncheon in shield ; (কুল-বিদ্যা) চর্ম্মফলকোপরিস্থ দণ্ডবিশেষ। **3.** (*Mus.*) The light stick or wand with which a leader beats time ; (সঙ্গীত-শাস্ত্র) বাদ্যকরের কাঠি। ***Verb t.*** To strike with a truncheon ; as, they would be *batoned* by the police ; দণ্ডাঘাত করা।

Bă-trā'-chi-ă, *n. pl.* (*Zool.*) The order of amphibians which includes the frogs, toads, etc. ; (জন্তু-তত্ত্ব) উভচর জন্তুর বর্গ বিশেষ,—মণ্ডূক (বেঙ্), স্থূল মণ্ডূক (কোলা বেঙ্) প্রভৃতি উক্ত বর্গভুক্ত। **—an,** *adj.*

băt'-tă, *n.* An extra allowance, on special grounds to English officers, soldiers, etc., serving in India ; ভারতবর্ষের ইংরেজ রাজকর্ম্মচারী এবং সৈনিক কর্ম্মচারী প্রভৃতিকে বিশেষ কারণে যে অতিরিক্ত ভাতা প্রদান করা হয়

băt-tăl'-ion (-yŏn), *n.* **1.** A large body of men in battle array ; যুদ্ধার্থ সজ্জিত সৈন্যদল, ব্যূহবদ্ধ সৈন্যদল। **2.** A body of infantry (or engineers) forming the part of a regiment ; কর্ণেলের অধীনস্থ সেনাদলের (পল্টন) অঙ্গীভূত পদাতিক সৈন্য (বা সামরিক পূর্ত্তবিশারদ) দল। **God is for the big battalions**—শক্তির সর্ব্বত্র জয়।

băt'-tĕls, *n. pl.* (In the University of Oxford) The whole college accounts for board, lodgings, rates, etc. ; (অক্সফোর্ড বিশ্ববিদ্যালয়ে) কলেজের ছাত্রগণের আহার, বাসস্থান-প্রভৃতি বাবত খরচের হিসাব।

bat'-ten (bătn), *n.* **1.** A strip of sawed timber (usu. 7 inches broad and $2\frac{1}{2}$ inches thick, 6 ft. or more long) used for flooring ; গৃহ-তলাচ্ছাদনোপযোগী কাষ্ঠ-ফলক

(সাধারণতঃ ৭ ইঞ্চি প্রস্থ, ২½ ইঞ্চি পুরু, ৬ ফিট কিম্বা ততোধিক লম্বা)। **2.** (*Naut.*) A strip of wood used in fastening the edges of a tarpaulin to the deck, also around masts to prevent chafing ; (নৌ-বিদ্যা) জাহাজের পাটাতনের সহিত ত্রিপলের প্রান্ত সংবদ্ধকরণার্থ এবং ঘর্ষণজনিত ক্ষয় নিবারণের হেতু মাস্তুলের চতুষ্পার্শ্বে যে কাষ্ঠখণ্ড সংযুক্ত করা হয়। **3.** A bar of wood used for clamping boards of door, etc. ; দরজা প্রভৃতির তক্তাসকল যোগ করিবার কাঠের বাতা। (*Arch.*) **Batten door**—A door made of narrow boards, held together by cross-pieces nailed to them ; (স্থপতি-বিদ্যা) অপ্রশস্ত কাষ্ঠফলক সকল নির্ম্মিত দ্বার বিশেষ—উক্ত কাষ্ঠফলক সমূহ আড়ভাবে সম্বদ্ধ প্রেকে-আঁটা কাষ্ঠখণ্ড সকল দ্বারা সংযুক্ত থাকে।

bat′-ten (bătn), *v.t.* To strengthen with battens ; উক্ত প্রকার কাষ্ঠখণ্ড-দ্বারা সুদৃঢ় করা। (*Naut.*) **To batten down**—To close the hatches (during a storm, fire, etc.) ; (ঝড়, অগ্নি প্রভৃতির সময়) জাহাজের পাটাতনের ফাঁক বন্ধ করা।

bat′-ten (bătn), *n.* A movable bar in silk-loom striking in or closing the weft ; রেশম ধুনিবার তাঁতের যে দণ্ড পড়েনের উপর আঘাত করে।

bat′-ten (bătn), *v. i. & t.* To grow fat (esp. in ease and luxury) ; হৃষ্টপুষ্ট হওয়া, ভোগ বিলাসের ফলে মোটাসোটা হওয়া। ***Verb t.*** To make fat by plenteous feeding ; to fatten ; প্রচুর আহার প্রদান করত হৃষ্টপুষ্ট করা ; স্থূল করা।

băt′-tĕr, *v. t. & i.* **1.** To beat repeatedly and violently so as to bruise or shatter ; পুনঃ পুনঃ আঘাত করিয়া ছেঁচিয়া ফেলা বা চুরমার করা। **2.** To operate against (walls, etc.) with artillery ; (প্রাচীর প্রভৃতির গাত্রে) কামানের গোলাবর্ষণ করা। **3.** To beat out of shape ; to indent ; পিটিয়া বিকৃত করা ; খাঁজ কাটা। **4.** (*Print.*) To deface (type) by use ; (মুদ্রণ) ব্যবহারদ্বারা (হরফের) উপরিভাগ ক্ষয় করা। ***Verb i.*** To beat repeatedly, esp. with violence ; (with *about, down, in*) ; ঘন ঘন প্রহার করা, কুটা, ঠুকা, পেটা। **Battering charge**—The haviest charge of powder ; দাগিবার পূর্ব্বে কামানে পূর্ণ পরিমাণ বারুদ ভরাট। **Battering-ram**—An ancient military engine used for battering down walls ; প্রাচীর ভঙ্গকরণার্থ প্রাচীনকালে ব্যবহৃত যুদ্ধযন্ত্র বিশেষ। **Battering-train**—A set of siege-guns ; অবরোধার্থ অতিগুরুভার কামানশ্রেণী।

băt′-tĕr, *v. i.* (Of wall, etc.) To incline from the perpendicular ; (প্রাচীরাদি সম্পর্কে) ঢালু হওয়া।

băt′-tĕr, *n.* **1.** A mixture of flour, eggs, milk, etc., beaten together and used in cookery ; (রন্ধনার্থ) ডিম, দুধ এবং আটার লপ্সী, লেই বা কাই। **2.** (*Print.*) A bruise on the face of type ; (মুদ্রণ) অক্ষরের মুখের ক্ষয়।

băt′-tĕr-ȳ, *n.* **1.** (*Law*) The unlawful beating of another or even the slightest touching of his person or clothes in a menacing manner ; (আইন) অবৈধভাবে অন্য ব্যক্তিকে প্রহার, এমন কি শত্রুভাবে তাহার অঙ্গ বা বস্ত্রাদি স্পর্শ, মারপিট, প্রহার। **2.** An apparatus for generating voltaic electricity ; তড়িতোৎপাদক যন্ত্র, তড়িৎ কোষাবলী, তড়িদ্-ঘটমালা (হিঃ কোঃ), প্রবাহ-ভাণ্ডার (সাঃ পঃ)। **3.** (*Mil.*) A number of guns arranged for united action ; a raised work on which cannons are mounted ; এক যোগে গোলাবর্ষী কামানশ্রেণী ; কামান স্থাপনের মঞ্চ বা বপ্রাদি, দমদমা (কেভিঃ)। **4.** Hammered brass or copper vessels ; পিটিয়া গড়া তামা কিম্বা পিতলের বাসন।

băt′-ting *n.* **1.** The act of striking with a bat ; ব্যাট (ক্রীড়াদণ্ড) দ্বারা আঘাত করণ। **2.** Cotton fibre prepared in sheets for quilt, etc. ; লেপ প্রভৃতি প্রস্তুত করিবার জন্য পাটকরা তুলা।

băt′-tle, *n.* **1.** A combat between large organized forces ; রণ, যুদ্ধ, সমর, আহব, আয়োধন, সংগ্রাম, লড়াই (*Colloq.*)। **2.** A struggle ; a contest ; as, the *battle* of life (জীবন-সংগ্রাম) ; সংগ্রাম ; বিগ্রহ। **Battle-array**—The order of troops arranged for battle ; ব্যূহ, বল-বিন্যাস, সৈন্য-সমাবেশ, সৈন্য-রচনা, রণরচনা। **Battle-axe**—A weapon like an axe, formerly used in battle; পট্টিশ, পরশু। **Battle-cry**—War-cry ; সিংহনাদ, রণরব। **Battte-field**—The field or ground on which a battle is fought ; রণভূমি, রণক্ষেত্র, রণাঙ্গন। **Battle-piece**—A picture or literary description of a battle-scene ; রণভূমির চিত্র বা যুদ্ধবর্ণনা। **Battle royal**—A general melee or engagement ; a free fight ; দাঙ্গা ; হাঙ্গামা। **Battle-ship**—A war-ship of the first-class ; প্রথম শ্রেণীর যুদ্ধ জাহাজ, রণপোত, সমরপোত। **Drawn battle**—A battle in which neither party gains the victory; যে যুদ্ধের ফল অনিশ্চিত। **Line of battle**—Troops or ships drawn up to fight ; যুদ্ধার্থ শ্রেণীবদ্ধ সৈন্য-সকল বা রণপোত-শ্রেণী। **Pitched-battle**—A battle planned beforehand and fought on chosen ground ; পূর্ব্ব সংকল্পিত যুদ্ধ, যে যুদ্ধ পূর্ব্বে সংকল্পিত হয় এবং নির্ব্বাচিত স্থানে সম্পাদিত হইয়া থাকে। **To give battle**—To attack ; to engage ; আক্রমণ করা ; যুদ্ধে ব্যাপৃত করা। **To give the battle**—To grant victory ; জয়প্রদান করা। **To join or do battle**—To fight ; যুদ্ধে প্রবৃত্ত হওয়া, যুদ্ধ করা।

băt′-tle, *v. t.* To struggle *with* or *against* (difficulties, the waves, etc.) ; সংগ্রাম করা।

băt′-tle-dōre, *n.* **1.** A child's toy, consisting of a light flat bat for striking a ball or shuttlecock ; বালকদিগের ক্রীড়াদণ্ড বিশেষ। **2.** A wooden instrument like-canoe paddle used in baking, washing, etc. ; চুল্লীর ভিতর পাঁউরুটি স্থাপন-প্রভৃতি কার্য্যের জন্য বৈঠার ন্যায় কাষ্ঠ-দণ্ডবিশেষ ।

băt′-tle-mĕnt, *n.* **1.** A wall pierced with openings, or made notch-like, for military purposes or

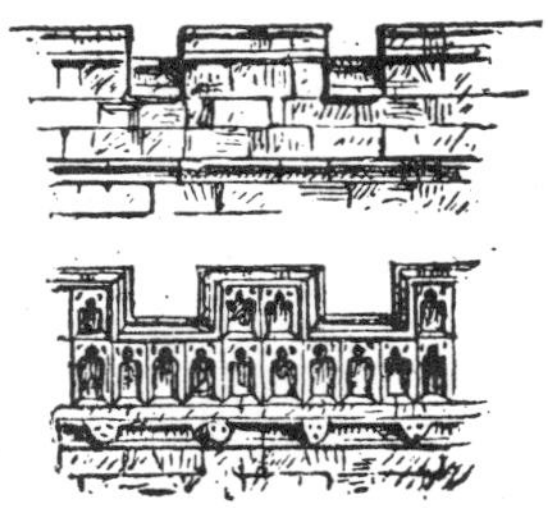

Battlements.

for ornament ; সামরিক উদ্দেশ্য-সাধন বা স্থাপত্যমণ্ডনের জন্য সচ্ছিদ্র বা দন্তুর (ফাঁকযুক্ত বা খাঁজকাটা) প্রাচীর-বিশেষ, দন্তুর-বৃতি। **2.** The towering roof of heaven ; আকাশপটল।

battue (*F.*), *n.* **1.** The act of beating the woods, bushes, etc., for game; শিকার বাহির করার জন্য বন, ঝোঁপ, প্রভৃতি তাড়না। **2.** A shooting party on this plan ; উক্ত উপায়ে শিকারকারীর দল। **3.** A wholesale slaughter (esp. of unresisting crowds); এক-সঙ্গে বহুহত্যা।

bau′-ble (băbl), *n.* **1.** A showy trinket ; সুদৃশ্য অকিঞ্চিৎকর বস্তু, চকচকে জিনিষ। **2.** A court-fool's emblem ; a stick with a head with asses' ears carved at the end of it ; বিদূষকের চিহ্ন বা নিদর্শন; গর্দ্দভকর্ণ নরমস্তকাগ্র দণ্ড-বিশেষ। [পূর্ব্বকালে ইয়ুরোপের রাজা বা জমিদারগণের ভাঁড় বা বিদূষকগণ উক্তপ্রকার দণ্ড ধারণ করিত।] **3.** A trifle; a toy; a thing of no worth ; তুচ্ছ বস্তু; খেলনা; অকিঞ্চিৎকর বস্তু।

Jester's bauble.

Bauhinia purpurea—দেবকাঞ্চন (বেলঃ)।

baulk (băk), *n.* Same as BALK.

baw-bee′ (bă-bē), *n.* A half-penny ; অর্দ্ধপেনি।

bawd (băd), *n.* **1.** A procuress ; কুট্টনী, কুটনী, দূতী। **2.** Obscene talk ; অশ্লীল আলাপ।

bawd′-rŷ (băd-), *n.* **1.** The practice of a bawd ; কুট্টনীর ব্যবসায়। **2.** Obscene or filthy talk ; অশ্লীল আলাপ, কুৎসিত কথাবার্ত্তা।

bawd′-ŷ (băd-), *adj.* Obscene ; filthy (of language) ; (ভাষা-সম্পর্কে) অশ্লীল; কুৎসিত, কদর্য্য। **—i-ness,** *n.* **Bawdy-house**—A brothel ; বেশ্যালয়, গণিকা-ভবন।

bawl (băl), *v. i., t.* & *n.* To cry out loudly ; (with *out, against, for*) ; চীৎকার করা। ***Verb t.*** To shout at the top of one's voice ; উচ্চৈঃস্বরে ঘোষণা করা। ***Noun.*** A loud prolonged cry ; চীৎকার, সোরগোল।

bawn (băn), *n.* **1.** The fortified court of a castle ; গড়বন্দী অট্টালিকার অঙ্গন। **2.** A cattlefold ; গো-মহিষাদির খোঁয়াড়।

bay (bā), *adj.* & *n.* Reddish brown ; as, a *bay* horse ; পাটল, আরক্ত, পিঙ্গল। ***Noun.*** A reddish brown horse ; পাটলবর্ণ অশ্ব।

bay (bā), *n.* **1.** A kind of tree or shrub ; একজাতীয় বৃক্ষ বা গুল্ম। **2.** (*Pl.*) An honorary crown or garland of victory, originally made of laurel branches, with its berries ; hence, heroic or poetic fame ; as, scholars' *bay* ; গ্রীস্ প্রভৃতি দেশে রণজয়ী বীর বা শ্রেষ্ঠ কবিগণের সম্মানস্বরূপ প্রদত্ত উক্ত বৃক্ষপত্রের মুকুট বা মালিকা ; বীরত্বের গৌরব, কবিত্ব-খ্যাতি, কবি-যশঃ। **Bay-rum**—A perfume made from the leaves of bay ; উক্ত বৃক্ষের পত্র হইতে প্রস্তুত সুগন্ধি দ্রব্য বিশেষ। **Crowned with bays**—বিজয়-মুকুট-সুশোভিত।

bay (bā), *n.* **1.** An arm of the sea, bending into the land ; উপসাগর। **2.** A recess in a range of hills etc. ; গিরিমালা প্রভৃতির পরাবর্ত্তন। **Bay-salt**—Salt obtained from sea-water by evaporation ; সমুদ্র-জল হইতে বাষ্পীকরণক্রিয়াদ্বারা প্রস্তুত লবণ। **Bay-state**—State of Massachusetts (U. S.) ; মার্কিণযুক্ত-রাজ্যের অন্তঃপাতী মেসাচুসেট্ প্রদেশ।

bay (bā), *n.* **1.** An opening in a wall esp. the space between two columns ; প্রাচীরের ফাঁক, স্তম্ভদ্বয়ের মধ্যবর্ত্তী অবকাশ। **2.** Any recess; as, horse-*bay*=the stall for a horse) ; বি শ্রা ম স্থ লী। **Bay-window**—A window jutting outwards; বহির্নির্গত বাতায়ন। [ইহা সাধারণতঃ, অর্দ্ধ-ষড়ভুজ বা অর্দ্ধ পঞ্চভুজাকৃতি হইয়া থাকে।] **Sick-bay**—The part of a ship's main deck used as a hospital ; জাহাজের পাটাতনের অংশ বিশেষ—ইহা রুগ্নাবাস স্বরূপ ব্যবহৃত হইয়া থাকে।

Bay-window.

bay (bā), *n.* **1.** The deep prolonged barking of a dog when pursuing ; শিকারের পশ্চাৎধাবিত কুকুরের গভীর চীৎকার। **2.** The combined cry of hounds in conflict with a hunted animal ; শিকারের সহিত সংগ্রামে নিরত কুকুরদলের মিলিত চীৎকার ধ্বনি। **3.** State of one obliged to face antagonist or a difficulty when escape has become impossible ;

"Embolden'd by despair, he stood at *bay.*" কোণঠাসা অবস্থা, বিপদ্দ্বারা সমাচ্ছন্ন বা বিপক্ষ কর্ত্তৃক আক্রান্ত হইয়া নিরুপায় অবস্থায় শত্রুর সম্মুখীন হইতে বাধ্য হইবার ভাব। **To drive or bring to bay**—To drive or pursue so as to compel one to stand at bay; কোণঠাসা করা। **To hold one at bay**—To keep in check; সংযত রাখা। **To keep at bay**—To keep an enemy from closing in; শত্রুকে নিকটে আসিতে না দেওয়া।

bay (bā), *v. i.* & *t.* To bark, as a dog at his game; পশুশিকার-কালে কুক্কুর যেরূপ চীৎকার করে, তদ্রূপ চীৎকার করা। ***Verb t.*** To bark at; to pursue with barking; to keep an enemy from closing in; ঘেউ ঘেউ শব্দ করা; ঘেউ ঘেউ শব্দে কাহারও পিছু পিছু ছুটা; শত্রুকে নিকটে আসিতে না দেওয়া। **To bay the moon**—To bark at the moon; চাঁদের দিকে চাহিয়া ঘেউ ঘেউ করা।

Bāy'-ârd, *n.* **1.** A chivalrous person; শৌর্য্য, দাক্ষিণ্যাদি গুণোপেত ব্যক্তি। [জনৈক সুবিখ্যাত ফরাসীবীরের নাম। উক্ত বীরের চর্ম্ম-ফলকে "*Le chevalier sans peur et sans reproche*;" "নির্ভীক, নিষ্কলঙ্ক বীর" এই বাক্যটী অঙ্কিত ছিল।]

bāy'-ŏ-nĕt, *n.* & *v. t.* **1.** A dagger at the end of a musket or rifle; সঙ্গীন। **2.** (*Pl.*) Soldiers armed with this; as, 2000 *bayonets*; সঙ্গীনধারী সৈন্য। ***Verb t.*** **1.** To stab with a bayonet; সঙ্গীনদ্বারা বিদ্ধ করা। **2.** To coerce by military force; (with *into*); "You send troops to *bayonet* us *into* submission; সামরিক শক্তি-প্রয়োগে বশীভূত করা। **The bayonet** or **bayonets**—Military force; as, under the rule of *the bayonet*; সামরিক শক্তি, অস্ত্রবল। **To fix bayonet**—সঙ্গীন চড়ান।

bă-zaar' (-zâr), **—zâr,** *n.* **1.** An oriental market; বাজার, হট্ট, হাট। **2.** A fancy fair; মোহন মেলা।

bdel'-lĭŭm (dĕl-), *n.* A gummy substance of an agreeable odour brought from the East; গুগ্‌গুল্ (মঃ উঃ), দেবধূপ।

bē, *v. substantive.* **1.** To exist; to occur; to live; বিদ্যমান থাকা; বর্ত্তমান থাকা; বাঁচিয়া থাকা। **2.** To remain; to continue; as, let it *be*; থাকা; চলিতে থাকা। ***Verb copulative.*** To coincide in identity with; as, thou *art* the man; to amount to; as, twice two *is* four; to cost; as, it *is* nothing to me; to signify; as, what *are* those pears; কাহারও সহিত অভিন্ন হওয়া; মোটে হওয়া; ক্ষতি হওয়া; বুঝান। ***Verb auxiliary.*** Used in forming the passive voice of transitive verbs; as, he *is* or *has been* disturbed; সকর্ম্মক ক্রিয়ার কর্ম্ম-বাচ্য নিষ্পন্ন করিতে ব্যবহৃত হয়। **Be about**—Be here and there around; ইতস্ততঃ ঘুরিয়া বেড়ান। **Be at**—To be engaged in; নিযুক্ত থাকা, প্রবৃত্ত থাকা, কোন কার্য্যে রত হওয়া। **Be after** — Be in search of; অনুসন্ধানে থাকা। **Be-all and end-all** — The sole end or purpose; একমাত্র লক্ষ্য বা উদ্দেশ্য। The whole thing; জীবন-সর্ব্বস্ব। **Be it so**—Let it be as you wish; তথাস্তু, তাহাই হউক। **Be off**—To go away off; দূর হওয়া, চলিয়া যাওয়া। To be separated from a thing; খুলিয়া বা খসিয়া যাওয়া। **Be off with you**—(*Colloq.*) Go away; (চলিত ভাষায়) দূর হও। **Be· that as it may**—However that may be; সে যাহাই হউক। **To be up to**—To be competent for; having sufficient knowledge in; "The man *was* not *up to* his business;" কোন কাযের উপযুক্ত হওয়া; কোন বিষয়ে যথাযোগ্য জ্ঞান-সম্পন্ন হওয়া। **To be for**—To be in favour of; to be proper or fit for; স্বপক্ষে বা অনুকূলে থাকা; উপযোগী হওয়া, উপযুক্ত হওয়া। **To be in**—To be present in; উপস্থিত থাকা। **To be in with**—To be near to; to be on terms of friendship or intimacy; নিকটে থাকা; বন্ধুত্বসূত্রে আবদ্ধ থাকা।

beach (bēch) *n.* & *v. t.* **1.** Water-worn pebbles; সলিলক্ষত উপলরাশি। **2.** The shore of the sea, lake, or large river; the strand; সাগর, হ্রদ বা নদীর তট, বিশেষতঃ, উপলবিষম সৈকত, বালুকাসৈকত, উপলময় উপকূল; পুলিন, সৈকত, কিনারা, তট, উপকূল, বেলা। ***Verb t.*** To run a boat or ship ashore; নৌকা প্রভৃতি তটোপরি তাড়িত করা। **Beached,** *p.p.* Run on shore as a boat or ship; জাহাজ নৌকা প্রভৃতি তটোপরিতাড়িত। **Beach'-y,** *adj.* Pebbly; উপলময়। **Beach-comber**—A long rolling wave; সুদীর্ঘ লোলকল্লোল। A settler on the islands of the Pacific; প্রশান্ত মহাসাগরস্থ দ্বীপবাসী। **Beach-master**—An officer superintending disembarkation of troops; যে কর্ম্মচারী জাহাজ হইতে সৈন্যগণের তটাবতরণ সময়ে তত্ত্বাবধায়কতা করেন।

bea'-con (bēcn), *n.* & *v. t.* **1.** A signal fire or light on a height; শৈলোপরি বা উচ্চস্থানে প্রজ্বালিত বিপৎ-সূচক অগ্নি, আকাশদীপ (অঃ বঃ)। **2.** A signal station; as, erection of *beacons* at suitable distances; সঙ্কেত-স্থলী। **3.** A light-house; আলোকমঞ্চ, আলোক-মন্দির। **4.** (*Fig.*) A guide or warning; "Modest doubt is called the *beacon* of the wise;" (লক্ষণায়) পথপ্রদর্শক, বিপদ্-বিজ্ঞাপন। ***Verb t.*** **1.** To give light to; to light up; "That *beacons* the darkness of heaven;" আলোক দান করা; আলোকিত করা, উজ্জ্বলিত করা। **2.** To furnish or supply with beacons; (with *off, out*);

বিপৎ-সূচক চিহ্ন সমন্বিত করা, বা উক্ত চিহ্ন প্রদান করা।

bead (bēd), *n.*, *v. t.* & *i.* **1.** A small ball (esp. of glass) pierced for threading and worn for ornament, or used in a rosary for counting prayers ; কাচ, স্বর্ণ প্রভৃতি নির্ম্মিত হারগুলিকা, গুলী, গুলিকা, গুটিকা, দানা, মালা। **2.** A drop of liquid ; "Cold *beads* of midnight dew ;" a bubble ; বিন্দু, ফোঁটা ; বুদ্বুদ। **3.** The small knob forming the front sight of a gun ; as, to draw a *bead* upon=(to take aim at) ; বন্দুকের নালীর উপরিস্থিত ধাতুগুলিকা,—বন্দুক ছুড়িবার পূর্ব্বে ইহার সাহায্যে লক্ষ্য স্থির করা হইয়া থাকে। **3.** (*Arch.*) A small globular ornament like a string of beads ; a semicircular moulding ; (also *beading*) ; (স্থপতি-বিদ্যা) হারগুলিকার মত স্থাপত্যালঙ্কার বিশেষ, গুল্‌চী (কেণ্ডিঃ); অর্দ্ধচন্দ্রাকৃতি বন্ধ, কুমুদ (রাঃ রাঃ)। ***Verb t.*** To furnish or adorn with beads ; to string together ; হারগুলিকাদ্বারা অলঙ্কৃত করা ; একত্র গ্রথিত করা। ***Verb i.*** To form or grow into beads ; গুলিকাকারে পরিণত হওয়া। **Bead-house**—An almshouse for poor people ; দরিদ্রাশ্রম, দানশালা (স্বভাঃ)। **Bead-roll**—(*Rom. C. Church*) A list of persons to be specially prayed for ; (রোমান ক্যাথলিক ধর্ম্মসমাজে) যে সকল মৃত ব্যক্তির আত্মার সদ্গতির জন্য নির্দ্দিষ্ট সংখ্যক বার প্রার্থনা বা মালাজপ করিতে হইবে—তাহাদের তালিকা। A list of names ; a catalogue ; নামের তালিকা ; ফর্দ্দ। **Beads man**—A man who prays for another, esp one paid or endowed to pray for others ; an almsman ; প্রার্থনার জন্য নিযুক্ত ব্যক্তি, বিশেষতঃ, অপর ব্যক্তির মঙ্গল-প্রার্থনার জন্য নিয়োজিত ব্যক্তি ; ভিক্ষোপজীবী। **Bead-tree**—Azadirachta Indica মহানীম (ওয়াট্)। **String of beads**—জপমালা; অক্ষমালা। **To say, tell** or **count one's beads**—To offer prayers ; মালাজপ করা।

bea'-dle (bē-dl), *n.* **1.** A mace-bearer ; আসাসোঁটা ধারী। **2.** An inferior officer of a court, a parish, a college, etc. ; আদালত, যাজকপল্লী বা কলেজ প্রভৃতির নিম্নকর্ম্মচারিবিশেষ। **—dom,** *n.* Red-tapism ; সরকারী কার্য্যালয়-সমূহের দীর্ঘসূত্রতা বা নিয়ম-ব্যবস্থা।

bead'-ȳ (bĕd-), *adj.* **1.** (*Of eyes*) Small, round and glittering ; (অক্ষি-সম্পর্কে) ক্ষুদ্র, বর্ত্তুল এবং চাক্‌চিক্যময়। **2.** (*Of liquids*) Full of bubbles ; frothy ; (তরল পদার্থ সম্বন্ধে) বুদ্বুদময় ; ফেনিল।

bea'-gle (bē-), *n.* **1.** A small hunting-dog, tracking by scent ; ক্ষুদ্র শিকারী কুক্কুর। **2.** A spy ; a bailiff ; গুপ্তচর, গোয়েন্দা ; নাজীর।

beak (bēk), *n.* **1.** The bill or nib of a bird ; চঞ্চু, তুণ্ড। **2.** Anything pointed like a beak ; a peak ; চঞ্চুর মত সূক্ষ্ম বা উদ্গত যে কোন বস্তু ; গিরিচূড়া। **3.** A hooked nose ; খগ-নাসা। **4.** The projection at the prow of ancient war-ships ; a spout ; চঞ্চ্বাকার পোতমুখ ; পাত্রাদির নল, নল। **Beaked,** *adj.* Having a beak ; pointed ; চঞ্চু-বিশিষ্ট ; চঞ্চুবৎ সূক্ষ্মাগ্র।

beak (bēk), *n.* (*Slang.*) A magistrate ; "If I have to make my bow to the *beak*." ; (ইতর ভাষায়) ম্যাজিষ্ট্রেট, শাসনকর্ত্তা।

beak'-êr (bēk-), *n.* **1.** A large drinking cup with a wide mouth ; বৃহৎ পানপাত্র, চষক (রঘুঃ)। **2.** A vessel of thin glass used by chemists ; রাসায়নিক পরীক্ষায় ব্যবহৃত কাচপাত্র বিশেষ।

beam (bēm), *n.*, *v. t.* & *i.* **1.** A long piece of iron or squared timber in a house or shipbuilding ; কড়িকাঠ, কড়ি, আড়কাঠ, জাহাজ বা গৃহ-নির্ম্মাণে ব্যবহৃত সুদীর্ঘ চতুষ্কোণ কাষ্ঠখণ্ড। **2.** The pole or bar of a balance ; তুলাদণ্ড, দাঁড়ি। **3.** The main trunk of a stag's horn ; মৃগশৃঙ্গের প্রধান কাণ্ড। **4.** The pole of a carriage which passes between the horses ; গাড়ীর বোম, শকট-দণ্ড, কূবর (গোভিঃ), যুগন্ধর (মঃ ভাঃ)। **5.** The shank or straight part of an anchor ; নঙ্গরদণ্ড। **6.** The chief timber of a plough ; লাঙ্গলের দণ্ড, হলদণ্ড, ঈষাদণ্ড। **7.** A cylinder in a loom, on which warp and cloth are wound ; তাঁতের নরাজ। **8.** A lever in steam engine connecting the piston rod and the crank ; বাষ্পীয় যন্ত্রের নল-দণ্ড এবং (কফোণি সদৃশ) বক্রদণ্ড সংযোজক দণ্ড-যন্ত্র। **9.** (*Pl.*) Horizontal cross-timbers of a ship supporting the deck and joining the sides ; জাহাজের পার্শ্বদ্বয়-সংযোজক অথবা পাটাতনের অবলম্বন স্বরূপ কাষ্ঠ স্তম্ভ সমূহ। **10.** A ray or pencil of light ; অংশু, রশ্মি, কিরণ, আলোক-লেখা। **11.** Radiance ; bright look ; smile ; "Her cheek all purple with the *beam* of youth ;" জ্যোতিঃ, দীপ্তি, প্রভা ; উজ্জ্বল-দৃষ্টি ; মন্দ-হাস্য। ***Verb t. & i.*** To send forth light ; to emit in rays ; to shine ; আলোক বিকীর্ণ করা, কিরণচ্ছটায় বিকীর্ণ হওয়া ; আলোকিত হওয়া ; ঝলমল করা। **Beam'-i-ness,** *n.* **Beam'-ing,** *adj.* Emitting beams ; radiant ; কিরণবর্ষী ; উজ্জ্বল, ঝলমল। **Beam'-y,** *adj.* **1.** Shining ; radiant ; as, *beamy* eyes ; উজ্জ্বল ; জ্যোতির্ম্ময়। **2.** (*Of ships*) Broad in the beam. (জাহাজ-সম্পর্কে) বিস্তীর্ণ, প্রকাণ্ড। **On her beam-ends**—On her side almost capsizing ; (পোত-সম্বন্ধে) এক পার্শ্বে এত হেলিয়া গিয়াছে, যেন উল্টাইয়া যায় যায়। (*Fig.*) Utterly at a loss ; hard up ; (লক্ষণায়) নিরুপায়, উপায়ান্তরশূন্য ; টানাটানিতে। **Thrown on my beam-ends**—Driven to my last shift ; শেষ উপায় অবলম্বন করিতে

বাধ্য। **To kick or strike beam**—To prove the lighter; to be defeated; তুলনায় হাল্‌কা হওয়া (ঠিকরে উঠিয়া অর্থাৎ অপর দিকে গুরুভার চাপানহেতু পাল্লার সহিত তুলাদণ্ডের ঠক্কর লাগা); পরাস্ত হওয়া।

bean (bēn), *n.* Name of plants bearing seeds in long pods; a well-known kind of nutritious pulse; কলাই প্রভৃতি শস্য; কুল্মাষ। **Bean-feast**—An annual dinner given by employers to their work-people; (বিলাতে) মনীবগণ শ্রমজীবিদিগকে বৎসর বৎসর যে ভোজ প্রদান করিয়া থাকেন। **Bean-fed**—In high spirits; পূর্ণোৎসাহে।

bear (bār), *v. t.* (In stock exchange) To attempt to lower the price of; as, to *bear* railway stock; (কোম্পানীর কাগজ সম্পর্কে) মূল্য হ্রাস করিতে চেষ্টা করা।

bear (bār), *n.* **1.** A wild animal covered with rough shaggy hairs; ভল্লুক, ভালুক, ঋক্ষ। **2.** A rough unmannerly person; রূঢ়, অসভ্য এবং অসামাজিক ব্যক্তি। **3.** The name of the two constellations (the *Great Bear* and the *Little Bear*); সপ্তর্ষি (হিঃ কোঃ) লঘু সপ্তর্ষি। **4.** One who sells stocks for future delivery hoping to buy

Polar bear.

it cheap meanwhile; যে ব্যক্তি লাভ করিবে আশায় ভবিষ্যতে কোন নির্দ্দিষ্ট তারিখে অর্পণের চুক্তিতে কোম্পানীর কাগজ বিক্রয় করে, এবং ইতিমধ্যে সুলভ মূল্যে ক্রয়ের চেষ্টা করে। **Bear'-ish,** *adj.* রূঢ়স্বভাব। **Bear-baiting**—The sport of setting dogs to attack a bear chained to a stake; কুক্কুর লেলাইয়া ভল্লুকতাড়না। **Bear-garden**—A place where bears are kept for sports; ভল্লুকশালা। A scene of strife and tumult; তুমুল কোলাহলপূর্ণ স্থান। **Bear-leader**—A travelling companion of a man of distinction; সম্ভ্রান্তব্যক্তির দেশভ্রমণের সঙ্গী। **Bear's Breech**—Acanthus; হরিকুশ। **Bear's grease**—Pomade; কেশ-সংস্কারে ব্যবহৃত সুগন্ধি স্নেহ-পদার্থ (মলম) বিশেষ। **Bear-skin**—The skin of a bear used as a wrap; ভল্লুক-চর্ম্ম। A coarse shaggy woollen cloth for overcoats; একপ্রকার স্থূল লোমশ পশমী বস্ত্র। A tall furry cap worn by soldiers; সৈনিকদিগের একপ্রকার লম্বা পশমী টুপি। **To play the bear**—To behave rudely and roughly; রূঢ় বা কর্কশভাবে ব্যবহার করা।

bear (bār), *v. t.* & *i.* **1.** To support or hold up; ধারণ করা। **2.** To carry or convey; বহন করা। **3.** To endure; to tolerate; to suffer; সহ্য করা, সহা; দুঃখভার বহন করা; কষ্টভোগ করা। **4.** To sustain or be responsible for (a cost, responsibility, etc.); (ব্যয়, দায়িত্ব, প্রভৃতির) ভার বহন করা, দায়ী হওয়া। **5.** To possess mentally; to entertain; "The ancient grudge I *bear* him;" মনে রাখা; পোষণ করা। **6.** To possess or carry as a mark of authority or distinction; as, to *bear* a name, sword or badge; কর্ত্তৃত্ব বা গৌরবের নিদর্শন স্বরূপ ধারণ করা। **7.** To allow or admit of; "The style will not *bear* examination;" সহা। **8.** To hold, maintain or have (a property or attribute); "The relation the nobles *bore* to the throne;" ধারণ করা, থাকা। **9.** To give; to bring forward; as, to *bear* testimony; প্রদান করা; উপস্থাপিত করা। **10.** To manage, wield or direct; "Thus must thou thy body *bear*;" to behave; (with the reflexive pronoun); as, he *bore* himself nobly; পরিচালনা করা, চালনা করা, সন্ধান করা; চলা, আচরণ করা। **11.** To push, thrust or drive; "*Bearing* him off over his horse's tail;" ঠেলিয়া দেওয়া, তাড়না করা। **12.** To bring forth or produce; as, to *bear* fruits or children; to yield; as, to *bear* interest; উৎপাদন করা, প্রসব করা; জন্মান। ***Verb i.*** **1.** To produce, as fruits; to be fruitful; as, the tree continues to *bear*; উৎপন্ন করা; ফলবান্ হওয়া, ফলন্ত হওয়া। **2.** To suffer, as with pain; "But man is born to *bear*;" কষ্ট ভোগ করা। **3.** To relate or refer; (with *on* or *upon*); as, how does this *bear on* this question; সম্পর্ক থাকা, সংস্পৃষ্ট থাকা, সংস্রব থাকা। **4.** To press; (with *on*, *upon* or *against*); to maintain one's ground (*against* difficulties); পীড়ন করা, প্রপীড়িত করা; আপনার স্থান বা কোট বজায় রাখা। **5.** To be situated as to the point of compass; as, the land *bears* N. by E.; দিক্ সম্পর্কে অবস্থিত থাকা, সংস্থিত হওয়া। **Bear'-a-ble,** *adj.* **To bear against**—To lean against; কোন কিছুর উপর হেলান দিয়া থাকা। To approach for attack or seizure; আক্রমণ বা ধৃতকরণের জন্য অগ্রসর হওয়া। **To bear a hand**—To lend a hand; to help; সাহায্য প্রদান করা; সহায়তা করা। **To bear arms against**—To fight against; কাহারো বিরুদ্ধে অস্ত্রধারণ করা। **To bear away**—To carry away as winner; জয় করিয়া লইয়া যাওয়া। (*Naut.*) To change the course of a ship, esp. to leeward; (নৌ-বিদ্যা); জাহাজের গতি পরিবর্ত্তন করা। **To bear**

away the palm, prize, etc.—To be victorious ; জয়ী হওয়া। **To bear back** or **backwards**—To retreat ; পলায়ন করা। **To bear date**—To have the mark of time when written or executed ; লিখন বা সম্পাদানের তারিখ যুক্ত হওয়া। **To bear down**—To overcome or crush by force ; পরাস্ত করা, দলন করা। **To bear down on** or **upon**—To press grievously or adversely ; দলন করা, মর্দ্দন করা। (*Naut.*) To proceed with force towards ; (নৌ-বিদ্যা) সবেগে অগ্রসর হওয়া। **To bear fruit**—To produce good results ; সুফলপ্রসূ হওয়া, সফল হওয়া। **To bear hard**—To press or urge ; চাপিয়া ধরা। **To bear in**—To tend toward ; উন্মুখ হওয়া। **To bear in mind**—To keep in memory ; মনে রাখা। (*Naut.*) **To bear in with**—To run or tend toward ; as, a ship *bears in with* the land ; (নৌ-বিদ্যা) ধাবিত বা উন্মুখ হওয়া। **To bear off**—To carry off, as a prize ; পুরস্কারাদি জিতিয়া লওয়া। (*Naut.*) To remove to a distance ; as, to *bear off* a boat ; (নৌ-বিদ্যা) দূরে সরাইয়া নেওয়া। **To bear one company**—To accompany ; সঙ্গী হওয়া। **To bear one's cross, To bear the cross**—To endure the agonizing physical and mental sufferings of which the cross was the symbol ; দুঃসহ অথবা মর্ম্মান্তিক মানসিক বা শারীরিক যন্ত্রণা ভোগ করা। **To bear one's self**—To behave or acquit oneself ; চলা, আচরণ করা। **To bear out**—To defend to the last ; to support ; to corroborate ; as, his friends will *bear out* him ; সমর্থন করা ; দৃঢ় করা ; বলবৎ করা। **To bear through**—To conduct or manage ; পরিচালনা করা, নির্ব্বাহ করা। **To bear up**—To support ; to keep from falling ; ধারণ করা ; পড়িতে না দেওয়া। (*Naut.*) **To bear up for**—To sail for (a place) ; (কোন স্থানের অভিমুখে) জাহাজ চালান। **To bear with**—To endure ; to be indulgent to ; সহ্য করা, বরদাস্ত করা (*Colloq.*) ; প্রশ্রয় দেওয়া, আসকারা দেওয়া (*Colloq.*)। **To bring to bear**—To apply ; খাটান, প্রয়োগ করা।

beard (bērd), *n.* & *v.t.* **1.** The hair that grows on the lips and chin of a man ; শ্মশ্রু, দাঁড়ি। **2.** The awn of a corn or grass ; শস্যের শূক, শূঁয়া, ভুঙ্গ, ধান্যশূক। **3.** The gills of oyster ; শুক্তির শ্বাস-যন্ত্র (কানকো)। **4.** The barb of an arrow ; বাণের কড়া, তীরের ফলা। **5.** The bristles on the beaks of birds ; পক্ষীর চঞ্চুর উপরিস্থ লোমসমূহ, শূক। ***Verb t.*** **1.** To take by the beard ; (esp. in anger or contempt) ; দাঁড়ি ধরিয়া টানা। **2.** To oppose openly ; to set at defiance ; প্রকাশ্যে বিরুদ্ধাচারী হওয়া, মুখের উপর বাধা দেওয়া ; তুচ্ছ করা। **Beard'-ed,** *adj.* Having beard ; prickly ; barbed ; শ্মশ্রুল ; শূকবিশিষ্ট ; সকণ্টক। **Beard'-less,** *adj.* **Beard'-less-ness,** *n.* **To one's beard**—In one's face ; openly ; মুখের উপর ; প্রকাশ্যভাবে। **To beard the lion in his den**—To attack a fierce enemy in his own quarters ;

> "Dar'st thou then,
> *To beard the lion in his den,*
> The Douglas in his Hall ?"

কোন প্রবল শত্রুকে স্বগৃহে আক্রমণ করা। **To take one by the beard**—To attack resolutely ; কৃত-সংকল্প হইয়া আক্রমণ করা।

bear'-ĕr (bār-), *n.* **1.** One who carries ; a porter ; বাহক, বহনকারী ; মোটবাহক। **2.** One who helps to carry a corpse to the grave ; শব-বাহক। **3.** (*India*) Palanquin-carrier ; also, a house servant charged with the care of his master's clothes, furniture, etc. ; (ভারতবর্ষে) শিবিকা-বাহক, পাল্কী-বাহক ; বেহারা। **4.** One who brings a letter, message, rumours, etc. ; পত্র-বাহক, সংবাদ-বাহক, জনরব-প্রচারক, ইত্যাদি।

bear'-ing (bār-), *n.* & *adj.* **1.** The act of carrying ; বহন। **2.** The act of bringing forth (offspring, fruit, etc.) ; উৎপাদন। **3.** Mien ; behaviour ; ভঙ্গি, আকার, চেষ্টা (সং সং) ; আচরণ। **4.** Relation ; as, what is the *bearing* of this on the argument ; aspect ; as, consider this in all its *bearings* ; সংস্রব, সম্বন্ধ ; ভাব, অবস্থা। **5.** Patient endurance ; ধৈর্য্য, সহিষ্ণুতা। **6.** Import ; effect ; force ; as, to change the *bearing* of a word ; অর্থ ; মর্ম্ম ; শক্তি। **7.** (*Pl.*) Those parts of a machine which bear the friction ; যন্ত্রের যে অংশ সকল ঘর্ষণের বেগ সহ্য করে। **8.** (*Herald.*) A single charge or device ; as, armorial *bearings* ; (কুল-বিদ্যা) চর্ম্ম-ফলকোপরি অঙ্কিত কুলচিহ্ন। **9.** (*Pl.*) The relative positions of surrounding objects ; দ্রষ্টার চতুর্দ্দিকস্থ পদার্থ নিচয়ের দিক্-সম্পর্কে অবস্থিতি। ***Adj.*** Without postage ; as, a *bearing* letter ; টিকেট-শূন্য। **To bring one to his bearings**—To bring one to his senses ; কাহারও চৈতন্যোদয় করা। **To lose one's bearings**—To become puzzled ; দিগ্‌ভ্রান্ত হওয়া, বিভ্রান্ত হওয়া, হতবুদ্ধি হওয়া। **To take bearings**—To ascertain on what points of compass objects lie ; দিঙ্‌নির্ণয় করা।

beast' (bēst), *n.* **1.** Any four-footed animal ; চতুষ্পদ জন্তু, পশু, শ্বাপদ (beast of prey)। **2.** Any irrational animal, as opposed to man ; মানবেতর জন্তু। **3.** A brutal, savage man ; a degraded person ; নর-পশু ; পতিত ব্যক্তি। **Beast'-hood,** *n.* **Beast'-li-ness,** *n.* Beastly quality ;

gluttony; drunkenness; obscenity; পাশবিকতা; ঔদরিকতা; মত্ততা; অশ্লীলতা। **Beast'-ly,** *adj.* **1.** Like a beast or its ways; brutal; পশুসংক্রান্ত; পাশব, পশুস্বভাব। **2.** Disgusting; dirty; "A *beastly* walk through the Borough;" abominable; as, *beastly* weather; বিতৃষ্ণাজনক; কুৎসিত, কদর্য্য; জঘন্য। **Beast of burden**—ভারবাহী পশু, বাহন। **Beast of prey**—শ্বাপদ। **The beast**—Antichrist; খৃষ্টীয় শাস্ত্রমতে যীশুখৃষ্টের দ্বিতীয় আগমনের পূর্ব্বে যে খৃষ্টবিরোধী আবির্ভূত হইবে। The animal nature in man; (মানবের) পাশবিক ভাব, পশু-ধর্ম্ম।

beat (bēt), *v. t.* & *i.* **1.** To strike repeatedly; পুনঃ পুনঃ আঘাত করা। **2.** To punish by blows; to thrash; প্রহার করা, মারা; তাড়না করা, ঠেঙ্গান (*Colloq.*)। **3.** To strike or brush, as water, wind; "*Beat* with perpetual storm;" (চলিতভাষায়) আঘাত করা, মৃদুভাবে স্পর্শ করিয়া যাওয়া। **4.** To hammer into any form; "They did *beat* the gold into thin plates;" ধাতুখণ্ড পিটিয়া ইচ্ছানুযায়ী আকার প্রদান করা। **5.** To pound; to pulverize; as, to *beat* pepper, spices, etc.; গুঁড়া করা; চূর্ণ করা। **6.** To tread as a path; as, to *beat* the streets=(to walk up and down); পথ চলা, পাইচারী করা। **7.** To switch (an egg, etc); to make into a batter; as, *beat* together equal quantities of honey and water; ফেটান। **8.** To overcome in a contest, race, game, etc.; to surpass; to leave behind; as, he *beats* them all at swimming; পরাস্ত করা; অতিক্রম করা; পশ্চাতে ফেলা। **9.** To strike (water, bushes, etc.) in order to rouse game; মৎস্য বা পশু-শিকার কালে জলে আঘাত করা বা জঙ্গল ঠেঙ্গান। **10.** To exercise severely; to perplex; as, it *beats* me to make it out; বুঝিবার পক্ষে অত্যন্ত শক্ত হওয়া; হতবুদ্ধি করা। **11.** To flap the wings—said of birds); পাখসাট মারা। *Verb i.* **1.** To strike repeatedly; to knock vigorously or loudly; as, to *beat* at the door; বারম্বার আঘাত করা; সজোরে বা সশব্দে ধাক্কা দেওয়া, ঘা দেওয়া। **2.** To throb; to palpitate; as, my heart *beats* with transport of joy; ধুক্ ধুক্ করা, দুর্ দুর্ করা; স্পন্দিত হওয়া। **3.** To dash or fall with force, as rain, wind, waves, etc.; "The winds *beat* at the crazy casement;" সজোরে পতিত হওয়া, প্রচণ্ডবেগে আঘাত করা। **Beat'-en,** *adj.* **1.** Vanquished; as, *beaten* army; পরাজিত, দলিত, নিষ্পিষ্ট। **2.** Worn by use; trodden; as, a *beaten* track, path etc.; ব্যবহার দ্বারা ক্ষয়প্রাপ্ত; পদদলিত। **3.** Hammered into thin foil; as, *beaten* gold; পিটিয়া পাতলা পাতের মত কৃত। **4.** Exhausted; tired out; as, *beaten* horse; অবসন্ন; ক্লান্ত। **Beat'-ing,** *n.* **1.** Punishment by blows; a flogging; তাড়ন, প্রহার; বেত্রাঘাত। **2.** Exercising the brain; মাথা ঘামানো। **3.** The whipping up of a fluid; তরল পদার্থ ফেটানো। **4.** A pulsating or throbbing; দুরু দুরু শব্দ, স্পন্দন, ধুকধুকি। **To beat about**—To try to find; অন্বেষণ করা, বহুপ্রকারে অনুসন্ধান করা। **To beat about the bush**—To approach a subject circuitously; জঙ্গল ঠেঙ্গাইয়া বেড়ান, সোজা পথে না যাইয়া ঘুরা ফিরা করা, সোজাসুজি কথা না বলিয়া ঘুরাইয়া পাকাইয়া বলা। **To beat an alarm**—To give notice of danger by beat of drum; ঢাক বাজাইয়া বিপদ্-বার্ত্তা জ্ঞাপন করা। **To beat (or sound) a parley**—To beat a drum or sound a trumpet for holding a conference with an enemy; যুদ্ধকালে শত্রুর সহিত পরামর্শ করার জন্য ঢক্কা বা বংশীবাদন করা। **To beat a retreat**—To retreat; পলায়ন করা। (পূর্ব্বে পলায়ন কালে ঢক্কা বাদিত হইত।) **To beat black and blue**—To bruise; মারিয়া কালশিরা পাড়িয়া দেওয়া। **To beat down**—To force or drive downward by hammering—হাতুড় দিয়া পিটিয়া বসান। To break down by heavy blows; to demolish; সজোরে আঘাত করিয়া ভাঙ্গিয়া দেওয়া; ধ্বংস করা। To overthrow (an institution, opinion etc.); উৎপাতিত করা, বিপর্য্যস্ত করা, বিধ্বংস করা। To force down (a price) by haggling; দরদস্তুর করিয়া দাম কমান। **To beat hollow**—To vanquish completely; সম্পূর্ণরূপে পরাজিত করা। **To beat in**—To drive in by force; সবলে প্রবিষ্ট করা। To break in by blows; to batter in; আঘাত করিয়া ভাঙ্গা; পুনঃ পুনঃ আঘাত করিয়া ঢুকান। **To beat into**—To teach or instil into by repetition of instruction; বারম্বার আবৃত্তি করত মনের মধ্যে ঢুকান। **To beat off**—To repel or drive back; প্রতিক্ষেপ করা, পশ্চাতাড়িত করা। **To beat out**—To extend by hammering; hence, to amplify; as, to *beat out* one's thoughts; পিটিয়া বাড়ান; [illegible] করা। **To beat out**—To trace out a path by treading it first; কোন পথ পূর্ব্বে চলিয়া পরে পদচিহ্ন দ্বারা অনুসরণ করা। To drive out; to expel; বিতাড়িত করা; বাহির করিয়া দেওয়া। To thresh (corn); (শস্যাদি) মাড়া। To overpower completely; সম্পূর্ণরূপে পরাভূত করা। **To beat the air**—To struggle in vain; হাওয়ার সঙ্গে লড়াই করা, বৃথা চেষ্টা করা। **To beat the bounds**—To mark boundaries by striking certain points with rods; (বৃক্ষলতাদি

প্রাকৃতিক পদার্থ-নিচয়ে) দণ্ডদ্বারা বিভিন্ন স্থানে আঘাত করত সীমা-চিহ্নিত করা। **To beat the brains, head, etc.**—To think persistently and laboriously ; মাথা ঘামান। **To beat the devil's tattoo**—To strike on a table or other flat surface (usually signifying impatience) ; অঙ্গুলীদ্বারা মেজ, কেদারা প্রভৃতি, অথবা পায়ের অঙ্গুলীদ্বারা মাটি ঠুকা। **To beat the dust**—To take in too little ground with his fore legs, as a horse ; দৌড়িবার সময় সম্মুখের পদদ্বারা অত্যল্প পরিমাণ মৃত্তিকা গ্রহণ করা। To perform his curvets too precipitately or too low ; অত্যন্ত ক্ষিপ্র বা অনুচ্চ ভাবে প্রথমতঃ সম্মুখের পদদ্বয় উত্তোলিত করিয়া এবং তাহা ভূমি স্পর্শ করার পূর্ব্বে পশ্চাতের পদদ্বয় তুলিয়া (অশ্বের) লম্ফ প্রদান করা। **To beat the Dutch**—To be very astonishing ; অত্যন্ত চমকপ্রদ হওয়া। **To beat the general**—To give notice to soldiers to march ; সৈন্যদিগকে অগ্রসর হইবার জন্য আদেশ দেওয়া। **To beat the streets**—To walk up and down ; রাজপথে পাইচারী করা। **To beat the tattoo**—To give the signal for retiring to quarters ; সৈন্যদিগকে সেনানিবাসে আহ্বান করার নিমিত্ত ঢক্কা-বাদন করা। **To beat time**—To note time in music by a movement of the hand or baton ; তাল রাখা, তাল ঠুকা। **To beat to a mummy**—To beat to a senseless mass ; মারিয়া হাড় গুঁড়া করিয়া দেওয়া, বা মৃতপ্রায় করা। **To beat to quarters**—To give the signal on board warships for every man to go to his proper station ; জাহাজের প্রত্যেক ব্যক্তিকে তদীয় নির্দ্দিষ্ট স্থানে গমন করিতে সঙ্কেত করা। **To beat up**—To attack suddenly ; to alarm or disturb ; as, to *beat up* an enemy's quarters ; সহসা আক্রমণ করা ; সন্ত্রস্ত বা সংক্ষুব্ধ করা। **To beat up for recruits**—To go about to get helpers or participators ; কোন দুঃসাহসিক কার্য্যে সাহায্যকারী বা সহযোগী সংগ্রহের উদ্দেশ্যে উদ্যম সহকারে নানাস্থানে গমন করা। **To beat upon**—To strike upon continuously ; কোন কিছুর উপর পুনঃ পুনঃ আঘাত করা। **To beat up one's quarters**—To come upon a visit unexpectedly ; অপ্রত্যাশিতভাবে কাহারও সহিত সাক্ষাৎ করিতে আসা। **To beat up the quarters of**—To arouse ; to disturb ; জাগরিত করা ; বিক্ষুব্ধ করা। **To leave the beaten track**—To depart from the common practice ; সাধারণ নিয়মবহির্ভূত কার্য্য করা। **To tread the beaten track**—To act according to the established rule ; চিরপ্রচলিত প্রথার অনুসরণ করা। **Dead beat**—Completely exhausted ; নিরতিশয় ক্লান্ত।

beat (bēt), *n.* **1.** A stroke or blow ; আঘাত। **2.** A stroke upon a drum ; the signal given thereby ; ঢক্কায় আঘাত ; ঢক্কাধ্বনি দ্বারা সঙ্কেত প্রদান। **3.** A pulsation ; a throb ; স্পন্দন ; দুর্ দুর্ শব্দ, ধুক্ ধুক্ শব্দ, ঘড়ির টিক্ টিক্ শব্দ। **4.** The round or course (esp. of a sentinel or constable on duty) ; চৌকিদারের পাহারার বা পিয়নের চিঠি বিলির সীমানা, (বিশেষতঃ কার্য্যে নিযুক্ত প্রহরী বা কনেষ্টবলের) গমন-চক্র, রোঁদ। ***Adj.*** (*Colloq.*) Wearied ; (চলিত ভাষায়) শ্রান্ত। **By beat of drum**—ঢেঁটরা পিটিয়া।

beat'-êr (bēt-), *n.* **1.** One who or that which strikes ; a punisher ; one who beats a drum ; আঘাতকারী ; শাস্তিদাতা, দণ্ডদাতা ; ঢক্কাবাদক। **2.** A man employed to rouse game ; যে ব্যক্তি জঙ্গল ঠেঙ্গাইয়া শিকারীদিগের জন্য পশু বাহির করে। **3.** A crushing instrument ; পেষণযন্ত্র।

bē-ă-tif'-ic, —i-căl, *adj.* Making blessed ; কল্যাণপ্রদ, নিঃশ্রেয়সকর।

bē-ăt-i-fi-cā'-tion, *n.* **1.** The act of making or being blessed ; কল্যাণদান, কল্যাণপ্রাপ্তি। **2.** (*R.C.Ch.*) The first step to canonisation ; announcement that a dead person is in heavenly bliss ; (রোমান ক্যাথলিক ধর্ম্মসমাজে) সিদ্ধশ্রেণী মধ্যে আরোপণের প্রথম সোপান ; অমুক পরলোকগত ব্যক্তি স্বর্গে পরমানন্দময় অবস্থা প্রাপ্ত হইয়াছেন—ইত্যাকার ঘোষণা, দিব্যজনত্বারোপণ (আঃ বঃ)।

bē-ăt'-i-fȳ, *v. t.* **1.** To make blessed or happy ; কল্যাণবান্ করা, পরমানন্দপূর্ণ করা। **2.** (*R. C. Ch.*) To pronounce (a person) to be in enjoyment of heavenly bliss ; (কোন ব্যক্তি) স্বর্গে পরমানন্দময় অবস্থা লাভ করিয়াছেন—ইহা ঘোষণা করা।

bē-ăt'-i-tūde, *n.* **1.** Supreme blessedness ; আনন্দ-ঘন অবস্থা, পরমানন্দ। **2.** (*Pl.*) The blessings pronounced by Christ in the Sermon on the Mount ; পর্ব্বতোপরি উপদেশ প্রদান কালে যীশুখৃষ্টের শ্রীমুখ হইতে উচ্চারিত আশীর্ব্বচন। **Final beatitude**—অপবর্গ (ভাগঃ), কৈবল্য (মঃ ভাঃ) সিদ্ধি, নিঃশ্রেয়স (মঃ সং), পরমগতি, পরমপদ, অনুত্তমাগতি, কল্যাণ।

beau (bō), *n.* (*Pl.* BEAUX) **1.** A dandy ; a fop ; সুবেশী, ফুলবাবু, সুভগম্মন্য (আঃ বঃ) ; সৌখিন (ভ্রাঃ বিঃ)। **2.** A lady's man ; a lover ; a sweet-heart ; রমণীর সহচর ; প্রেমিক ; প্রণয়ী। **Beau ideal**—The highest conceivable type of excellence or beauty ; সৌন্দর্য্য বা সদ্গুণের চরম আদর্শ।

beau monde, (*F.*), *n.* The fashionable society ; সৌখিন সমাজ।

beaune (bōn), *n.* A red burgandy wine ; বারগেণ্ডী প্রদেশে প্রস্তুত লোহিত-বর্ণ মদিরা বিশেষ।

beau'-te-ous (bū-tē-ŭs), *adj.* Beautiful ; সুন্দর। (প্রধানতঃ কবিতায় ব্যবহৃত হয়।) **—ly,** *adv.* **—ness,** *n.*

beau'-ti-fûl (bü-), *adj.* **1.** Delighting the eye or ear ; সুন্দর, রমণীয়, পেশল, মনোহর, মঞ্জু, মঞ্জুল, ললাম, শোভন, শোভাময়, সুদর্শন, সুরূপ, অভিরাম, কমনীয়, সুশ্রী, চারু, চমৎকার, কান্ত, রুচির, রম্য, মুগ্ধ। **2.** Morally or intellectually impressive ; as, *beautiful* conduct ; charming ; satisfactory ; মনোজ্ঞ, মুগ্ধকর ; মোহন ; সুখদ। **—ly,** *adv.*

beau'-ti-fȳ (bü-), *v. t.* To make beautiful ; to adorn ; সুশোভিত করা ; মণ্ডিত করা, সজ্জিত করা।

beau'-tȳ (bü-), *n.* **1.** That which delights the eye, the ear, or the mind ; রূপ, লাবণ্য, বিভ্রম, সৌন্দর্য্য, মনোহারিত্ব, চারুতা, শোভা, সুষমা। **2.** A particular grace or excellence ; a beautiful trait or feature ; as, that is the *beauty* of it ; বিশেষ শ্রী, উৎকর্ষ বা বরেণ্যতা ; কমনীয় বিশেষত্ব। **3.** A beautiful woman ; as, all the admired *beauties* of Verona ; সুন্দরী। **Art of heightening beauty**—কৌমারযুগ (বাৎস্যঃ)। **Beauty-sleep**—A sleep before midnight ; প্রথম রাত্রির নিদ্রা। **Beauty-spot**—A spot to heighten beauty ; a foil ; মুখমণ্ডলের কান্তিবর্দ্ধক চিহ্ন বা ধাতুখণ্ড ; টিপ্। A beautiful scene ; "Hill-streams and waterfalls rank among the *beauty-spots* of this world" ; সুন্দরদৃশ্য। **Beauty and the Beast**—ফরাসী দেশীয় উপকথা বিশেষের নায়ক এবং নায়িকা। [সুন্দরী (Beauty) পিতার জীবন রক্ষার জন্য পশুর (Beast) সহিত বাস করিতে সম্মত হয়। সুন্দরীর প্রেমে পশুর যাদু ঘুচিয়া যায় এবং সে পরম মনোহর রাজপুত্রের কলেবর প্রাপ্ত হয়। অবশেষে সুন্দরীর সহিত তাহার পরিণয় হয়।]

beaux yeux, (*F.*), *n.* Charms ; attractive look ; fair face ; মনোহারিত্ব, মুগ্ধতা; সুন্দর চেহারা; সুন্দর মুখ।

bea'-vêr (bē-), *n.* **1.** An amphibious rodent, valuable for its fur ; also, its fur ; বীবর ; বীবরের লোম। **2.** A hat made of its fur ; বীবরের লোমনির্ম্মিত টুপি। **3.** The part of a helmet which covers the face ;

Beaver.

মুখের নিম্নভাগ আচ্ছাদক শিরস্ত্রাণের অংশবিশেষ। [মুখের উপরিভাগ আবরকের নাম *Visor*]।

bea'-ver-teen (bē-vêr-tēn), *n.* A cotton twilled cloth with piles of loops ; একজাতীয় স্থূল কার্পাস বস্ত্র।

bē-calm' (-câm), *v. t.* **1.** To make calm (sea, etc.) ; শান্ত করা, নিস্তব্ধ করা, প্রশান্ত করা, ঠাণ্ডা করা। **2.** (*Naut.*) To deprive (a ship) of wind ; (usu. in the passive) ; as, to be *becalmed* = (to lie motionless for want of wind ; বায়ুর অভাবে নিশ্চল অবস্থায় থাকা) ; (নৌবিদ্যা) (জাহাজকে) নির্ব্বাত করা।

bē-cause' (-cäz), *adv.* & *conj.* By reason of ; on account of ; তদ্ধেতু, যেহেতু, কেননা ; কারণ, জন্য, দরুণ।

bĕc-că-fī'-cō, *n.* A small migratory bird, esteemed by Italians as a delicacy ; ইতালীবাসিদিগের আহার্য্য ক্ষুদ্র প্রব্রজনশীল পক্ষিবিশেষ।

bē'-cha-mĕl (-shă-), *n.* A rich, white sauce, thickened with cream ; (from the inventor's name) ; দুগ্ধ, সর প্রভৃতির সংযোগে প্রস্তুত শ্বেতবর্ণ ব্যঞ্জনবিশেষ।

bechedemer, (*F.* lit. a sea-spade) *n.* A sea-slug ; a Chinese dainty ; সমুদ্র-শম্বুক ; চীনদেশীয় রসনাতৃপ্তিকর খাদ্য বিশেষ।

bĕck, *n.* A small brook ; a mountain stream ; নালা ; গিরিনদী।

bĕck, *n., v. t.* & *i.* **1.** A significant nod or motion of the head or hand ; ইঙ্গিতসূচক মস্তকনতি, সঙ্কেত, ইঙ্গিত, ইসারা, শিরশ্চালন প্রভৃতি। **2.** A gesture of salutation or respect ; a bow ; অভিবাদন বা সম্মানসূচক অঙ্গভঙ্গী ; প্রণাম, প্রণতি, নমস্কার। ***Verb t.*** To beckon (a person to approach) ; মস্তক নত করিয়া আহ্বান করা। ***Verb i.*** **1.** To make a mute signal by nodding or shaking ; শিরনতি অথবা হস্ত বা মস্তকদ্বারা ইঙ্গিত করা। **2.** To make slight bow ; to courtesy ; (Scotch) ; ঈষৎ মস্তক নত করিয়া নমস্কার করা, অভিবাদন করা ; নতজানু হইয়া (বিলাতের স্ত্রীলোক বা বালকের মত) নমস্কার করা। **To have at one's beck, To be at the beck and call of**—To be at one's command; কাহারো আদেশের বশবর্ত্তী বা আজ্ঞাবহ থাকা, ডাকের আগে খাড়া থাকা।

bĕck'-ĕt, *n.* (*Naut.*) A simple contrivance for securing loose ropes, tackle or spars ; (নৌ-বিদ্যা) জাহাজের ছিন্ন মাস্তুলাদির কাষ্ঠখণ্ড প্রভৃতি রক্ষণার্থ সংবিধান বিশেষ।

beck'-on (bĕckn), *v. t.* & *i.* To make a significant sign to ; to summon by a motion of the hand ; ইঙ্গিত করা, ইসারা করা ; হাতছানি দিয়া আহ্বান করা। ***Verb i.*** To make a mute signal with the head, hand, finger, etc. ; কোন বিষয় জ্ঞাপন বা আভাস প্রদানের অভিপ্রায়ে হস্ত বা মস্তক সঞ্চালন করিয়া ইসারা বা ইঙ্গিত করা।

bē-cloud' (-clowd), *v.t.* **1.** To cover with clouds ; to make misty ; মেঘাচ্ছন্ন করা ; কুজ্ঝটিকাচ্ছন্ন করা। **2.** To obscure ; to darken ; "These fine words with which we *becloud* unpleasant fact ;" অস্পষ্ট করা ; অন্ধকারাচ্ছন্ন করা।

bē-come' (-cŭm), *v. i.* & *t.* **1.** To come into being ; হওয়া। ***Verb t.*** To suit ; to befit ; to look well on ; উপযোগী হওয়া ; উপযুক্ত হওয়া ; শোভা পাওয়া,

সাজা, মানান। **—com′-ing,** *adj.* Appropriate ; graceful ; as, a low and *becoming* tone ; যথাযোগ্য, সমঞ্জস (মঃ উঃ), সুশোভন, ভব্য, সমীচীন, মানানসই ; মাধুর্য্যময়। **—com′-ing-ness,** *n.* Graceful propriety ; সুশোভনতা। **The becoming**—Decorum ; as, a fine sense of *the becoming* ; শীলতা, ভব্যতা, শোভনতা। **To become of**—To be the fate of ; কপালে ঘটা।

bĕd, *n.* **1.** A thing to sleep on ; a mattress ; as, a feather-*bed* ; a framework with mattress and covering ; বিছানা, সংস্তর (আঃ বঃ) ; গদি, তল্প ; শয্যা, পর্য্যঙ্ক। **2.** A litter ; তৃণাদিরচিত পশুশয্যা। **3.** Conjugal union ; marriage ; "George, the eldest son of his second *bed* ;" দাম্পত্য-মিলন ; পরিণয়। **4.** A smooth or level piece of ground in a garden, (usually somewhat raised) ; "*Beds* of hyacinth and roses ;" ফুলের কেয়ারী। **5.** The bottom of the sea, river, etc. ; as, the *bed* of a river ; সমুদ্রতল, নদীগর্ভ। **6.** (*Geol.*) A layer or a stratum ; (ভূ-বিদ্যা) স্তর, পাষাণস্তর। **7.** That on which anything rests ; a basis ; যাহার উপরে অন্য কিছু অবস্থিত থাকে ; ভিত্তিভূমি। **8.** The foundation of a road or railway ; রাস্তা বা রেলপথের ভিত্তি। **Bed and board**—Entertainment with lodging and food ; আহার এবং বাসস্থান। Connubial relation ; as, she sought divorce from *bed and board* ; দাম্পত্য-সম্বন্ধ। **Bed-chair**—A chair for the sick ; রোগীদিগের জন্য কেদারাবিশেষ। **Bed-chamber**—A room in which to sleep ; শয়নগৃহ (শকুঃ), শয়নকক্ষ, শয্যাকক্ষ। [*Ladies of the bed-chamber* = ইংলণ্ডেশ্বরীর সম্ভ্রান্ত-বংশীয়া অষ্ট সহচরী।] **Bed-clothes**—Sheets pillows, etc., of a bed ; বিছানার চাদর, বালিশ, প্রভৃতি। **Bed-fast**—Bed-ridden ; শয্যাগত। **Bed-fellow**—A person who shares one bed ; শয্যাসঙ্গী। **Bed-gown**—A woman's night-dress ; স্ত্রীলোকের নৈশ-পরিচ্ছদ। **Bed-hangings**—Cushion ; গদি। **Bed-head**—The head-end of a bed ; শিয়র, শিথান। **Bed-key**—A wrench for unfastening bedstead ; খট্টা খুলিবার জন্য পেঁচটানা যন্ত্র বিশেষ। **Bed-maker**—An old man or woman tending college-rooms in the English universities ; অক্সফোর্ড ও কেম্ব্রিজ বিশ্ববিদ্যালয়ে যে বৃদ্ধ পুরুষ বা বৃদ্ধা স্ত্রীলোক কলেজের কক্ষসকল তত্ত্বাবধান করে। **Bed-pan**—An invalid's chamber utensil for use in bed ; শয্যাগত রোগীদিগের (মলমূত্রাদি ত্যাগের জন্য) ব্যবহারার্থ পাত্র বিশেষ। **Bed-post**—The upright support of a bed ; খাটের পায়া। **Bed-ridden**—Confined to bed by age or sickness ; বার্দ্ধক্য বা ব্যাধিপ্রযুক্ত শয্যাশায়ী। **Bed-rock**—The solid rock underneath superficial formations a firm foundation ; বাহ্যস্তর শ্রেণীর নিম্নস্থ কঠিন পাষাণস্তূপ ; দৃঢ়ভিত্তি। Sound reasons or principles ; অভ্রান্ত যুক্তি বা মূলতত্ত্ব। **Bed-room**—A sleeping apartment ; শয়নকক্ষ। **Bed-sore**—A sore produced by long lying in bed ; দীর্ঘকাল রোগ-শয্যায় শায়িত থাকায় রোগীর দেহে যে ক্ষত উৎপন্ন হয়, শয্যাক্ষত। **Bed-spread**—Coverlet ; শয্যাস্তরণ। **Bed-stead**—A frame (wood or metal) of a bed ; খট্টা, পর্য্যঙ্ক, তক্তপোষ, খাটিয়া (*Colloq.*), পালঙ্ক। **Bed-tick**—A large bag or case without the material for stuffing it ; গদির খোল। **Bed-time**—The hour for going to bed ; শয়ন-কাল, শয়ন-সময়। **Bed of down, flowers, roses, etc.**—A comfortable or easy position ; পুষ্পশয্যা, গোলাবের বিছানা, সুখ এবং আরামের অবস্থা। **Bed of honour**—The grave of a soldier who has fallen in battle ; যুদ্ধে নিহত সৈনিকের সমাধি। **Bed of Justice**—The throne of the king in the Parliament of Paris ; also, a sitting at which the king was present ; ১৭৮৯ খৃষ্টাব্দের ফরাসী বিপ্লবের পূর্ব্বে যে সিংহাসনে উপবেশন করত ফরাসী নৃপতি রাজকার্য্য পর্য্যালোচনা করিতেন ; যে ফরাসী পার্লেমেণ্টের অধিবেশনে ফরাসী নৃপতি স্বয়ং উপস্থিত থাকিতেন। **Bed of thorns**—A situation of great anxiety and apprehension ; অত্যন্ত শঙ্কা ও উৎকণ্ঠা-জনক অবস্থা, কণ্টকশয্যা। **Death-bed**—মৃত্যুশয্যা। **Defiler of other's beds**—পরস্ত্রীগামী, পারতল্পিক (আঃ বঃ), পরতল্পগ। **Marriage-bed**—দাম্পত্য-শয্যা। **Narrow-bed**—Grave ; কবর। **Between you and me and the bed-post**—যেন তৃতীয় ব্যক্তি শুনিতে না পারে। **To be brought to bed**—See ABED. **To go to bed**—To retire for the night ; রাত্রিতে শয়ন করিতে যাওয়া। **To keep one's bed**—To be ill ; পীড়িত বা শয্যাশায়ী হওয়া। **To leave one's bed**—To recover from sickness ; আরোগ্য লাভ করা। **To lie in the bed one has made**—To take consequences of one's own acts ; স্বকার্য্যের ফলভোগ করা। **To make a bed**—To arrange it and make it fit for use ; শয্যারচনা করা। **To put to bed with a shovel**—To bury ; সমাহিত করা। **To smoothe the bed**—To make easy the dying moment ; মৃত্যু-যন্ত্রণা লাঘব করা। **To take to one's bed**—To become ill ; পীড়িত হইয়া পড়া।

bĕd, *v. t & i.* **1.** To put to bed ; to lodge for the night ; শয্যায় স্থাপন করা ; রাত্রের জন্য বাসস্থান প্রদান করা। **2.** To furnish (a person) with a bed ; to lay in bed ; (with *up, down,* etc.) ; বিছানা দেওয়া ; শয্যায় শায়িত করা। **3.** To plant deeply ; গভীরভাবে রোপণ করা। **4.** To lay in any hollow place ; to embed ; as, to *bed* a stone ; কোন ফাঁক জায়গাতে বসান ; প্রোথিত করা। **5.** To lay in order ; স্তরে স্তরে সজ্জিত করা। ***Verb i.*** **1.** To stratify ; স্তরবদ্ধ হওয়া। **2.** To go to bed ; to cohabit ; "If he be married and *bed* with his wife" ; শয়ন করা ; অভিগমন করা। **3.** To lie on for support ; as, the rails *bed* on the ballast ; অবলম্বিত হওয়া।

bē-dăb′-ble, *v. t.* To stain or splash, with dirty liquid, blood, etc. ; (রক্ত কিম্বা ময়লা জল দ্বারা) লিপ্ত বা নিষিক্ত করা।

bē-daub′ (-däb), *v. t.* **1.** To smear with paint, etc. ; রঙ্গ প্রভৃতি লেপন করা। **2.** To ornament clumsily ; to bedizen ; অনিপুণভাবে অলঙ্কৃত করা ; জমকালোভাবে সাজান।

bē-dăz′-zle, *v. t.* To dazzle or make dim by a strong light ; ঝলসিয়া দেওয়া, তীব্র আলোকদ্বারা চক্ষু ধাঁধিয়া দেওয়া।

bĕd′-dêr, *n.* **1.** One who puts to bed ; one who litters cattle ; যে ব্যক্তি শয্যায় স্থাপন করে ; যে ব্যক্তি গো-মহিষাদির শয়নার্থ তৃণশয্যা রচনা করে। **2.** Plants suited for flowerbed ; ফুলের কেয়ারীর উপযোগী বৃক্ষ সকল।

bĕd′-dĭng, *n.* **1.** A bed and its furniture (mattress, bed-clothes, etc.) ; বিছানা পত্র। **2.** A litter for cattle ; গো মহিষাদির শয়নার্থ বিস্তৃত তৃণরাশি। **3.** A bottom layer or foundation ; নিম্নদেশবর্ত্তী স্তর বা ভিত্তি। **4.** (*Geol.*) Stratification ; (ভূ-বিদ্যা) স্তরীভবন।

bē-dĕck′ *v. t.* To deck out ; to adorn ; "Heaven was *bedecked* with stars ;" সজ্জিত করা, শোভিত করা ; বিভূষিত করা, মণ্ডিত করা।

bĕd′-ē-guar (-gär), *n.* A moss-like excrescence on rose-bushes ; গোলাবের গুল্মে জাত শৈবলবৎ অস্বাভাবিক উদ্গত অংশ।

bē′-dĕl, —dĕll, *n.* A beadle in English universities ; ইংলণ্ডের বিশ্ব-বিদ্যালয়সমূহের নিম্নপদস্থকর্ম্মচারিবিশেষ।

bē-dĕv′-il, *v. t.* **1.** To treat with diabolical violence or abuse ; to bewitch ; পৈশাচিক ব্যবহার করা, ভূতগ্রস্ত করা ; যাদু করা। **2.** To spoil ; to corrupt ; "A room and furniture *bedeviled* by taste ;" নষ্ট করা ; দূষিত করা। **3.** To drive frantic ; to worry ; as, he did *bedevil* the poor man ; পাগল করিয়া তোলা ; জ্বালাতন করা। **—ment,** *n.* **1.** Possession by an evil spirit ; ভূতাবেশ। **2.** Maddening trouble ; confusion ; উন্মাদকর উপদ্রব ; গোলযোগ।

bē-dew′ (-dü), *v. t.* To moisten by drops ; to cover with dew ; to sprinkle ; আর্দ্র করা ; শিশির-সিক্ত করা ; ছিটান।

bē-dight′ (-dīt), *v.t.* To array ; to adorn ; বসন ভূষণে সজ্জিত করা ; মণ্ডিত করা।

bē-dĭm′, *v. t.* To make dim (the eye, sight, mind, etc.) ; নিষ্প্রভ করা, ঝাপ্‌সা করা (*Colloq.*), অস্পষ্ট করা, ম্লান করা।

bē-dĭz′-en (-dĭz'n), *v. t.* To dress out gaudily ; জমকালো পোষাকে সাজান, সমুজ্জ্বল বেশভূষায় সুশোভিত করা, সুসজ্জিত করা।

bĕd′-lăm, *n.* [Corrupted from BETHLEHEM.] **1.** The Hospital of St. Mary of Bethlehem, used as lunatic asylum ; বাতুলাশ্রমরূপে ব্যবহৃত বেথলেহেমস্থিত সেণ্ট মেরীর রুগ্নাবাস। **2.** Any mad-house ; বাতুলাশ্রম, বাতুলালয়, পাগলা-গারদ, ক্ষিপ্তনিবাস। **3.** (*Fig.*) Any scene of wild uproar ; (লক্ষণায়) তুমুল কোলাহলপূর্ণ স্থান। **—ite,** *n.* A lunatic ; a madman ; ক্ষিপ্ত, উন্মাদ, বাতুল ; পাগল। **Jack or Tom O'Bedlam**—A madman ; পাগল।

bĕd′-ou-in (-ô-), *n.* & *adj.* A wandering Arab ; an Arab of the desert ; a gipsy ; বেদুইন আরব ; যাযাবর আরব, ইহারা মরুভূমির উপর তাঁবু খাটাইয়া বাস করে ; বেদিয়া, হাঘড়িয়া। ***Adj.*** Wandering ; যাযাবর। **—ism,** *n.*

bē-drăb′-ble, *v. t.* To make wet and dirty, with rain and mud ; বৃষ্টি এবং কর্দ্দমদ্বারা সিক্ত বা পঙ্কিল করা।

bē-drăg′-gle, *v. t.* To soil by drawing along on mud (as garments) ; (বস্ত্রাদি) কাদা বা ময়লার উপর দিয়া টানিয়া লইয়া মলিন করা।

bē-drench′ (-drĕnsh), *v. t.* To drench or wet thoroughly ; ভিজাইয়া দেওয়া, স্নাত করা।

bē-drŏp′, *v. t.* To sprinkle as with drops ; ছিটান।

bē-duck′ (-dŭk), *v. t.* To plunge (one) under water ; to immerse ; চুবকানি দেওয়া, ডুবান।

bē-dŭng′, *v. t.* To apply dung to ; to manure ; গোময়লিপ্ত করা ; সার দেওয়া।

bē-dŭst′, *v. t.* To sprinkle with dust ; to soil ; ধূলি প্রক্ষেপ করা ; ধূলি ধূসরিত করা, মলিন করা।

bee (bē), *n.* **1.** A four-winged stinging social insect which

Male or drone. Worker-bee.

produces honey and wax ; মধুমক্ষিকা, অলি, মৌমাছি, ভ্রমর, দ্বিরেফ, মধুকর, ষট্‌পদ, ক্ষুদ্রা, সরঘা, মধুব্রত, মধুপ, ভৃঙ্গ, শিলীমুখ। [প্রত্যেক মধুচক্রে তিন শ্রেণীর মক্ষিকা বাস করে। পুংমক্ষিকা, কর্ম্মি-মক্ষিকা (ক্লীব), রাণী মক্ষিকা। রাণী মক্ষিকার আকার অন্যান্য মক্ষিকা অপেক্ষা বৃহত্তর।]

Female or queen.

পুংমক্ষিকাগণ রাণী মক্ষিকার ডিম্বোৎপাদনে সহায়তা করিয়া মৃত্যুমুখে পতিত হয়। রাণী মক্ষিকা এক কালে প্রতি দিন ২,০০০ এবং বৎসরে গড়ে প্রায় একলক্ষ ডিম্ব প্রসব করে।] **3.** (*Colloq.*) A busy worker ; (চলিত ভাষায়) কার্য্যে ব্যাপৃত বা নিবিষ্ট ব্যক্তি। **4.** An assemblage of persons who engage in united labour for the benefit of individual or family (*American*) ; as, a quilting *bee* : husking *bee* ; (কোন ব্যক্তি বা পরিবারের) হিতসাধিনী সমিতি। **Bee-bread**—The pollen of flowers collected as food for their youngs ; পুষ্পপরাগ, ফুলরেণু, কুসুমরজঃ। **Bee-garden**—An apiary ; মক্ষিকাগৃহ, ভৃঙ্গোদ্যান। **Bee-hive**—A box or case for holding bees ; অলিকুলের বাসের জন্য যে বাক্স, তোরঙ্গ বা ঝুড়ি রক্ষিত হয়, মধুচক্র, মধুক্রম, মৌচাক। **Bee-line**—The shortest (straight) line between two places; সোজাপথ, ঋজুপথ। **Bee-master**—One who keeps bees ; মধুমক্ষিকাপালক। **Bees-wax**—The wax collected by bees ; মোম, মধূচ্ছিষ্ট, শিকথ (অঃ), শিকথক (ঐ), মধূথ। **To have a bee in one's (head) bonnet**—To be somewhat crazy; to be full of fancies; ছিট থাকা, মাথাপাগলা হওয়া ; খেয়ালপূর্ণ হওয়া।

beech (bēch), *n.* A large forest tree ; প্রকাণ্ড আরণ্য বৃক্ষবিশেষ। **Beech'-en**, *adj.* **Beech'-y**, *adj.* **Beech-mast**—The nuts of the tree ; উক্ত বৃক্ষের ফল।

beef (bēf), *n.* The flesh of an ox or cow ; গোমাংস। [*Pl.* BEEVES=oxen.] **Beef'-y**, *adj.* **1.** Like beef ; গোমাংসবৎ। **2.** Solid ; mascular ; stolid ; শক্ত ; পেশল ; বোকা, হাঁদা। **Beef-eater**—An eater of beef ; hence, a fleshy person ; গোমাংসভোজী, গোখাদক ; অতএব মাংসল লোক। A yeoman of the royal guard in England ; ইংলণ্ডেশ্বরের শরীররক্ষক। A warder of the Tower of London ; লণ্ডন নগরীর ইতিহাসবিদিত কারাগারের রক্ষী। **Beef-steak**—A thick slice of beef for grilling or frying ; ভর্জ্জনোপযোগী গোমাংসখণ্ড। **Beef-tea**—Beef-juice or broth for invalids ; রুগ্ন ব্যক্তিদের আহারার্থ গোমাংসের রস, যুস বা সুরুয়া।

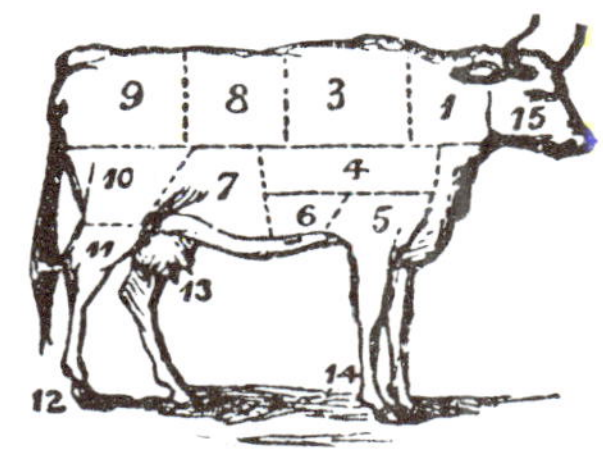

Beef.

1. neck ; 2. shaking-piece ; 3. chine ; 4. ribs ; 5. clod ; 6. brisket ; 7. flank ; 8. loin, sirloin ; 9. rump ; 10. round ; 11. leg ; 12. foot ; 13. udder ; 14. shin ; 15. cheek.

Beef-witted—Dull or heavy in wits ; stupid ; মন্দবুদ্ধি, স্থূলবুদ্ধি, গোমূর্খ; মূঢ়। **Beef-wood**—The red timber of an Australian tree ; গৃহসজ্জা প্রস্তুতকরণোপযোগী অষ্ট্রেলিয়া দেশীয় কাষ্ঠবিশেষ। **Roast-beef**—শূল্য গোমাংস (আঃ বঃ)।

Bē-ĕl'-zē-bŭb, *n.* **1.** The devil, or a devil ; শয়তান, অপদেতা। **2.** (In *P. L.*) The fallen angel next to Satan in power and crime ; (প্যারাডাইস লষ্ট নামক গ্রন্থে) ক্ষমতায় এবং পাপের গুরুত্বে শয়তানের অব্যবহিত নিম্নস্থানীয় স্বর্গভ্রষ্ট দেবদূত বিশেষ।

been (bĕn), *p. p.* of BE.

beer (bēr), *n.* **1.** A liquor made of malt and hops ; যবাদি হইতে প্রস্তুত মদ্যবিশেষ, যবসুরা। **2.** Any fermented liquor or drink ; as, nettle-*beer* : ginger-*beer* ; যে কোন গাঁজলা উঠা তরল পদার্থ বা পানীয় দ্রব্য। **Beer'-y**, *adj.* Of or like beer ; partly drunk with beer ; যবসুরা-সম্বন্ধীয়, যবসুরাবৎ ; বীয়ার পানে অল্পমাতাল। **Beer-house**—A house licensed to sell beer ; যবসুরা-বিক্রয়-গৃহ। **Beer-money**—Money given to British soldiers or ants, etc., in lieu of beer ; সৈনিক কিম্বা ভৃত্যগণকে বীয়ার মদের পরিবর্ত্তে যে অর্থ প্রদান করা হয়। **Beer and skittles**—Pleasure, happiness and satisfaction ; আমোদ প্রমোদ, সুখ এবং আনন্দ। **Small-beer**—Weak beer ; নিস্তেজ যবসুরা। (*Fig.*) Trifling matters ; (লক্ষণায়) অকিঞ্চিৎকর বিষয়। **To think no small beer of**—To have a high opinion of ; উচ্চ মত বা ধারণা পোষণ করা।

beest'-ings (bēst-ingz), **biest'-ings** (bēst-ingz), *n.* The first milk given by a cow after calving ; প্রসবের পর প্রথম প্রথম গাভীর যে দুগ্ধ দোহন করা হয়, গাভীর গাঁজলা দুধ।

bees'-wing (bē-z), *n.* A film of shining scales of tartar formed in port and other wine ; hence, old wine ; পোর্ট কিম্বা অনুরূপ মদিরায় জাত এক প্রকার উজ্জ্বল শল্কবৎ সুরা-কিট্ট ; পুরাতন মদিরা।

beet (bēt), *n.* A plant with succulent root, for making sugar ; পালঙ্ক শাক, বীট-পালং। [শ্বেত-বর্ণ পালঙ্ক হইতে চিনি প্রস্তুত হয় এবং লোহিত-জাতীয় পালঙ্ক-শাক আহার করা হইয়া থাকে।] **Beet-root**—The root of the beet ; বীট-পালং।

bee'-tle (bē), *n.* & *v. t.* **1.** A heavy wooden mallet ; গুরুভার, কাষ্ঠ-মুদ্গর বিশেষ। **2.** A wooden pestle or bat for meshing potatoes, beating linen, etc. ; মুষলাকৃতি (হামান দিস্তার দণ্ড) কাষ্ঠময় যন্ত্র বিশেষ,—ইহার সাহায্যে আলু, কার্পাস বস্ত্র প্রভৃতি কুট্টিত বা বিঘট্টিত করা হইয়া থাকে, মুদ্গর। *Verb t.* To beat with a beetle ; উক্ত যন্ত্রদ্বারা বিঘট্টিত করা। **Beetle-brain, Beetle-head**—A blockhead ; নির্ব্বোধ লোক।

bee'-tle (bē-), *n.* A general name for insects having a horny wing-cover ; কঠিন পক্ষাচ্ছাদনবিশিষ্ট কীট-বর্গের সাধারণ নাম, গোবরে পোকা, কাচ পোকা (যোঃ), প্রভৃতি।

k-beetle—Cockroach ; আর-া (সাঃ পঃ) ।

bee'-tle (bē-), *v. t.* **1.** To hang or jut over, (of brows, cliffs, etc.) ; as, a *beetling* rock ; প্রলম্বিত হওয়া, ঝুঁকিয়া থাকা, উদ্গত হওয়া । **2.** To hang threateningly, (of fate etc.) ; as, the justice of states *beetling* over his head ; আশঙ্কাজনকভাবে বিলম্বমান হওয়া । **Beetle-browed**—Having prominent brows ; sullen ; উন্নতভ্রূ (আঃ বঃ) ; ভ্রূকুটি-কুটিল ।

bē-fall', *v. t. & i.* To happen to (a person, race, etc.) ; as, the disaster which then *befell* the human race ; (কাহারও উপর) পতিত হওয়া, (কাহারও ভাগ্যে) ঘটা । ***Verb i.*** To happen ; to come to pass ; ঘটা, সঙ্ঘটিত হওয়া ; উপস্থিত হওয়া ।

bē-fit', *v. t.* To be suited to or fit for ; to agree with ; to become ; as, duties *befitting* his princely station ; উপযুক্ত হওয়া, যোগ্য হওয়া ; খাটা ; উপযোগী হওয়া, সাজা, মানানসই হওয়া । **—ting**, *adj.* Suitable ; becoming ; উপযুক্ত, যথাযোগ্য ; মানানসই । **—ting-ly**, *adv.*

bē-fog', *v. t.* **1.** To envelop in fog ; কুজ্ঝটিকাচ্ছন্ন করা । **2.** To obscure ; to mystify ; অস্পষ্ট করা ; রহস্যাবৃত করা । **—ged**, *p. p.*

bē-fool', *v. t.* To make a fool of ; to dupe ; আহাম্মক বানান, বোকা বানান ; ভাড়ান, ঠকান, ভুলান ।

bē-fōre', *prep., adv. & conj.* **I.** In front of ; as, *before* our door ; ahead of ; as, *before* him sound the drums ; সম্মুখে ; অগ্রে । **2.** Preceding in time ; as, I will return *before* six o'clock ; পূর্ব্বে । **3.** Open to ; at the disposal of ; as, he had the world *before* him ; (কাহারো) সম্মুখে উন্মুক্ত ; (কাহারো) আয়ত্তাধীন । **4.** Previous to or earlier than (a point of time, date or event) ; as, he would be back *before* dark : three years *before* this time ; (কোন ঘটনা, সময় বা তারিখের) পূর্ব্বে বা অগ্রে । **5.** Superior to ; in precedence of ; as, he is *before* his competitors in power ; in preference to ; as, health is preferred *before* disease ; rather than ; as, he would die *before* yielding ; উৎকৃষ্টতর ; অগ্রে ; তুলনায় অধিকতর আদরণীয় ; বরং । **6.** Under the cognisance of ; in presence of ; as, a case *before* the magistrate : he confessed *before* his countrymen ; বিচারাধীন, এলাকার মধ্যে ; সাক্ষাতে । ***Adv.*** **1.** In front ; ahead ; as, the battle was *before* and behind ; সামনে (*Colloq.*), সম্মুখে ; অগ্রে । **2.** In time past ; previously ; already ; as, he is more reserved than *before* ; অতীতকালে ; পূর্ব্বে ; ইতঃপূর্ব্বে । ***Conj.*** **1.** Previous to the time when ; পূর্ব্বে যখন । **2.** Rather than ; as, he will starve *before* he will steal ; বরং । **Before long**—শীঘ্র, অনতিবিলম্বে । **Before now**—ইতঃপূর্ব্বে । (*Naut.*) **Before the mast**—As a common sailor ; (নৌ-বিদ্যা) সাধারণ নাবিকের মত । [কারণ সাধারণ নাবিকগণ সম্মুখের মাস্তুলের অগ্রবর্ত্তী স্থানে বাস করে ।] **Beforetime**—Formerly ; পূর্ব্বকালে । (*Naut.*) **Before the wind**—Sailing directly with the wind ; অনুকূল বায়ুবেগে পাইল তুলিয়া অগ্রসর (হওয়া) ।

bē-fōre'-hănd, *adv. & adj.* In anticipation ; in advance ; আগায় ; অগ্রিম । **To be beforehand with**—To anticipate or forestall ; (কাহারো ভাবগতিক বুঝিয়া) পূর্ব্ব হইতে ব্যবস্থা করা, আগে থাকিতেই কোন কায করা ।

bē-foul' (-fowl), *v. t.* To make foul ; to cover with filth, (often moral filth) ; as, to *befoul* one's own nest ; কলুষিত করা ; মলিন করা, কলঙ্কিত করা ।

bē-friend' (-frĕnd), *v. t.* To act as a friend to ; to favour ; to help ; বন্ধুবৎ ব্যবহার করা ; অনুগ্রহ করা ; মিত্রভাবে আনুকূল্য করা, বন্ধুভাবে সহায়তা করা ।

bĕg, *v. t. & i.* **1.** To ask (bread, money, etc.) as a charity ; যাচ্ঞা করা, ভিক্ষা করা । **2.** To make petition to ; to entreat ; as, to *beg* a person to grant a favour ; সবিনয়ে প্রার্থনা করা ; মিনতি করা, অনুনয় করা, প্রার্থনা করা । **3.** To take for granted without proof ; as, to *beg* the question ; ধরিয়া লওয়া, বিনা প্রমাণে তর্কস্থলে স্বীকার করিয়া লওয়া । ***Verb i.*** **1.** To ask alms (esp. habitually) ; to live by asking alms ; ভিক্ষা করা ; ভিক্ষাবৃত্তি দ্বারা দিনপাত করা । **Beg'-ging**, *n.* **Begging the question**—(*Log.*) Assuming the truth of the matter in dispute, (the fallacy of *petitio principii*) (তর্ক-বিজ্ঞান) যে বিষয় প্রমাণ করিতে হইবে তাহা প্রমাণিত বলিয়া ধরিয়া লওন, সাধ্যাভ্যুপগম (হিঃ কোঃ), প্রতিজ্ঞাভ্যুপগম (ঐ) । **To beg excuse, leave, pardon, etc.**—A courteous or apologetic mode of asking what is expected ; কাহারো নিকট কোন কিছু চাহিতে হইলে শিষ্টাচার পূর্ব্বক এই বাক্য প্রয়োগ করিতে হয় । [(I) **beg your pardon**—কোন ব্যক্তির সহিত কথাবার্ত্তার সময় তাহার কোন কথা শুনিতে বা বুঝিতে না পারিয়া তাহাকে সেই কথাটী পুনরায় বলার জন্য অনুরোধ করিতে হইলে ইংলণ্ড দেশের শিষ্টাচারের নিয়মানুসারে *I beg your pardon* কথাটী বলিতে হয় ।] **To beg off**—To obtain by entreaty the release of (any one or of oneself) from a penalty ; অনুনয় বিনয় করিয়া কোন প্রকার শাস্তি হইতে (কাহাকে) পরিত্রাণ করা বা (নিজে) পরিত্রাণ পাওয়া । **To go a-begging**—Said of situations, offices,—in need of men to fulfil them, of things,—offered for sale and finding no purchaser ; as, grapes are plentiful there that they go *"a-begging"* ; কাযকর্ম্ম সম্বন্ধে—কর্ম্ম প্রার্থীর আবশ্যক হওয়া ; জিনিষপত্র সম্বন্ধে—(প্রাচুর্য্য বশতঃ) ক্রেতার অভাব হওয়া।

bĕ-găd′, *inter.* By God ; (not in polite use) ; ঈশ্বরের শপথ ; (শিষ্ট-প্রয়োগ নহে)।

bĕ-gĕt′, *v. t.* **1.** To procreate ; to generate ; (said of a father, sometimes of both parents) ; জন্মদান করা ; প্রজনন করা। **2.** To occasion ; to give rise to ; as, one falsehood usually *begets* a necessity for dozen others ; সংঘটন করা ; উৎপাদন করা, জন্মান। **—ter,** *n.* A procreator ; জনয়িতা, জন্মদাতা, উৎপাদক, জনক। **—ting,** *n.*

bĕg′-gar (-gêr), *n.* & *v. t.* **1.** One who begs ; one who lives by begging ; যাচক, ভিক্ষুক ; ভিক্ষোপজীবী। **2.** A poor man or woman ; কাঙ্গাল, কাঙ্গালিনী, ভিখারী, ভিখারিণী। **3.** (Contemptuously) A mean or low fellow ; (অবজ্ঞাচ্ছলে) অপদার্থ লোক, ভিক্ষা-মানব (পাণিঃ), সামান্য ব্যক্তি, ইতর লোক। *Verb t.* **1.** To exhaust the means of ; to impoverish ; নিঃস্ব করা ; কাঙ্গাল করা। **2.** To exhaust ; to reduce to silence ; as, it *beggars* description ; নিঃশেষিত করা ; মূক করা, নির্ব্বাক করা, নিস্তব্ধ করা। **—hood,** *n.* **—li-ness,** *n.* **—ly,** *adj.* **1.** Indigent ; poverty-stricken ; befitting a beggar ; mean ; contemptible ; নিতান্ত নিঃস্ব, অকিঞ্চন ; দারিদ্র্য-গ্রস্ত ; ভিক্ষুকযোগ্য ; অধম, নীচ, সামান্য, ইতর ; হেয়। **2.** Destitute of meaning ; as, *beggarly* arguments, conception, etc. ; অর্থশূন্য, মূল্যহীন। **—y,** *n.* **1** The act of begging ; mendicancy ; extreme poverty ; penury ; ভিক্ষাকরণ, ভিক্ষণ (মঃ ভাঃ) ; ভিক্ষাচর্য্য, যাচকবৃত্তি, ভিক্ষাটন ; নিতান্ত দৈন্য ; দারিদ্র্য। **2.** Beggars collectively ; "Scoffing at the hungry *beggary* ;" a resort of beggars ; "The fetid *beggaries* of Bethnal ;" ভিক্ষুক-দল ; ভিক্ষুকগণের সমাগমস্থল। **Beggar-my-neighbour**—A game at cards ; এক প্রকার তাসের খেলা। **Beggars must not be choosers**—ভিক্ষার চাউল কাঁড়া আর আকাঁড়া।

bĕ-gin′, *v. i.* & *t.* **1.** To do the first act ; to take the first step ; to commence ; কোন কার্য্যের সূত্রপাত করা ; কোন বিষয়ে প্রথম উপায় অবলম্বন করা ; আরম্ভ করা। **2.** To start speaking ; to speak ; "The Arch-Enemy, breaking the horrid silence, thus *began* ;" বলিতে আরম্ভ করা ; বলা। **3.** To come into existence ; to originate ; "Before this world *begun* ;" উদ্ভূত হওয়া ; উপজাত হওয়া। *Verb t.* **1.** To enter on ; to take the first step of ; as, they *began* their reigns at the same time ; প্রবৃত্ত হওয়া ; (কোনও কার্য্যের) সূত্রপাত করা। **2.** To give origin to ; to create ; as, he *began* the dynasty ; প্রবর্ত্তন করা ; সৃষ্টি করা। **To begin at**—To start from a point ; (কোন স্থান বা সীমা হইতে) আরম্ভ করা। **To begin the world**—To start in life ; সংসারে প্রবেশ করা, প্রথম জীবিকার্জ্জনে প্রবৃত্ত হওয়া। **To begin upon**—To set to work at ; কোন কার্য্যে লাগিয়া যাওয়া। (*Colloq.*) **To begin upon a person**—To assail a person ; (চলিত ভাষায়) কোন ব্যক্তিকে আক্রমণ করা। **To begin with**—In the first place ; at the outset ; প্রথমতঃ ; আদৌ, সর্ব্বাগ্রে।

bĕ-gin′-nêr, *n.* **1.** An originator ; a founder ; as, *beginner* of a dynasty, war, etc. ; প্রবর্ত্তক ; প্রতিষ্ঠাতা। **2.** A novice ; a tyro ; প্রথম শিক্ষার্থী ; শিক্ষানবীশ, (কোন কার্য্যে) নূতনব্রতী।

bĕ-gin′-ning, *n.* **1.** The time at which anything begins ; আরম্ভকাল। **2.** The first cause ; origin ; source ; "I am the *beginning* and the end ;" মূল কারণ ; আদি ; উৎপত্তিস্থল, আদ্যক্ষেত্র। **3.** Commencement ; আরম্ভ, প্রারম্ভ, সমারম্ভ। **4.** The earliest proceedings, (often in *pl.*) ; as, great fortunes acquired from small *beginnings* ; সূত্রপাত। **—less,** *adj.* Without beginning ; অনাদি। **The beginning of the end**—The commencement of an approaching disaster ; সর্ব্বনাশের সূত্রপাত।

bĕ-gird′ (-gĕrd), *v. t.* To gird round ; to encircle ; কটিবন্ধ দ্বারা বেষ্টিত করা, মেখলাবদ্ধ করা ; পরিবেষ্টিত করা, পরিবৃত করা, ঘেরা (*Colloq.*), বেষ্টিত করা।

bĕ-gone′ (-gŏn), *inter.* Get you gone ; be off ; get away ; চলিয়া যাও ; দূর হও, তফাৎ হও ; ভাগো।

bĕ-gō′-ni-ă, *n.* A genus of tropical plants, bearing beautiful flowers, cultivated in hot-houses ; উদ্ভিদের "গণ" বিশেষ,—ইহার অন্তর্ভূত কয়েক জাতীয় বৃক্ষ কাচসমাচ্ছাদিত উদ্ভিদগৃহ এবং পুষ্পপাত্রে রোপিত হইয়া থাকে।

bĕ-grīme′, *v. t.* To soil deeply with dirt ; পঙ্কলিপ্ত করা, কর্দ্দমাক্ত করা।

bĕ-grudge′ (-grŭj), *v. t.* To grudge ; to envy (one) the possession of ; গজ্‌গজ্ করা (*Colloq.*) ; দ্বেষপ্রদর্শন করা।

bĕ-guile′ (-gīl), *v. t.* To delude or overreach by guile or craft ; to deceive ; as, these lights that *beguile* travellers ; to deprive of ; to cheat out of ; as, infants are *beguiled* of their right ; ঠকান ; প্রতারণা করা, প্রবঞ্চনা করা, ছলনা করা ; বঞ্চিত করা ; ঠকাইয়া লওয়া। **2.** To charm ; to divert ; to amuse ; "It *beguiled* attenton ;" "By sports are all their cares *beguiled* ;" মোহিত করা ; বিনোদন করা ; আমোদিত করা, প্রমোদিত করা। **3.** To divert attention from ; to while away or pass (time) ; as, he took a book to *beguile* the tedious hours ; বিষয়ান্তরে মন প্রেরণ করা ; (সময়) অতিবাহিত করা, (সময়) কাটাইয়া দেওয়া, (সময়) ক্ষেপ করা ।

beg'-uine (bā-gĕn), *n.* One of an order of females (in Holland and Germany), who, without taking the monastic vows, devote themselves to works of piety and charity,—they live in houses called *beguinages;* হলণ্ড এবং জর্ম্মণী-দেশীয় গৃহবাসিনী সন্ন্যাসিনী-সম্প্রদায় বিশেষ—ইঁহারা দানধ্যানাদি কার্য্য জীবনের ব্রত-স্বরূপ গ্রহণ করিয়া থাকেন।

bē-gŭm, *n.* A Mohammedan princess or lady of high rank ; বেগম, নবাবজাদী, সম্ভ্রান্ত মুসলমান পুরমহিলা।

bē'-half (-hâf), *n.* Support ; defence ; favour ; (used only in prepositional phrases) ; পোষকতা ; সমর্থন ; পক্ষ, তরফ। **On or in behalf of**—In the interest of ; as a friend or defender of ; কাহারো পক্ষে, কাহারো মঙ্গলার্থ ; বন্ধু বা রক্ষকস্বরূপ।

bē-hāve', *v. reflex.* **1.** To conduct one's self ; to act ; as, he *behaved* himself with gallantry ; চলা, আচরণ করা ; কার্য করা। **2.** To show good manners ; to conduct oneself with propriety ; (said of children or young people) ; as, if you cannot *behave* yourself, you had better stay at home ; শিষ্টাচার প্রদর্শন করা ; শিষ্টাচার রক্ষা করিয়া চলা, ভদ্রসমাজে যথাযোগ্য ভাবে চলা ; (যুবক ও বালকদিগের পক্ষে)। **—haved',** *p. p.* (with *well-, ill-*) Having good or bad manners or conduct ; শিষ্টাচার-সম্পন্ন, শিষ্টাচারশূন্য। **—hav'-iour,** *n.* **1.** Deportment ; manners ; (sometimes) good manners ; as, aversion to *behaviour* ; আচার-ব্যবহার, চালচলন ; আদবকায়দা ; (কখন কখন) শিষ্টাচার। **2.** Moral conduct ; treatment shown to or towards others ; সদাচার ; অন্যের প্রতি আচরণ। **3.** The way in which a ship, machine, substance, etc., acts or works ; as, the *behaviour* of a ship in a storm : জাহাজ, যন্ত্র প্রভৃতি যে ভাবে চলে বা কার্য্য করে। **During good behaviour**—As long as one remains blameless in the discharge of one's duties ; সদাচার লঙ্ঘন না করা পর্য্যন্ত, যাবৎ সদ্ব্যবহার অক্ষুণ্ণ থাকিবে। **Upon one's good behaviour**—Liable to be called to account in case of misconduct ; অসদাচরণ করিলে জবাবদিহী হইতে বাধ্য।

bē-head' (-hĕd), *v. t.* To sever the head from ; to kill by cutting off the head : শিরশ্ছেদ করা ; মাথা কাটা।

bē-hē-mŏth, *n.* An animal, probably the hippopotamus, described in Job ; hence, a very large and strong animal ; পুরাতন বাইবেল গ্রন্থের জব নামক পুস্তকে বর্ণিত জন্তু বিশেষ, (সম্ভবতঃ) সিন্ধুঘোটক ; (অতএব) বলবান এবং বৃহৎকায় জন্তু।

bē-hĕst', *n.* A command ; a mandate ; an injunction, (poetical) ; "Hastened to obey his lord's *behest.*" আদেশ, আজ্ঞা ; উপদেশ ; হুকুম, নিদেশ, অনুজ্ঞা।

bē-hīnd', *adv., prep.* & *n.* **1.** Remaining after the others have gone ; as, to stay, leave *behind* ; কোন ঘটনা, কার্য্য বা ক্রিয়ার শেষে অবস্থিত। **2.** Back in time ; in the past ; "My grief lies onward and my joy *behind* ;" সময় হিসাবে পশ্চাতে ; অতীত, গত। **3.** Kept back ; not yet brought forward ; still to come ; as, stronger evidence is *behind* : comical scence is still *behind* ; ভবিষ্যতের ব্যবহারের জন্য রক্ষিত ; এতাবৎ অনুপস্থাপিত ; অনাগত। **4.** Towards the rear ; backward ; as, to look *behind* ; পশ্চাতে, পশ্চাদভিমুখে ; পেছনে (*Colloq.*)। **5.** In arrears ; as, he is *behind* in his rent ; বাকীর দায়ে। **6.** Slow ; (of a watch, clock, etc.) ; (ঘড়ী, টেঁক ঘড়ী প্রভৃতি সম্পর্কে) মন্থর। ***Prep.*** **1.** In a place left by one who has gone on ; as, she stayed *behind* me for a few days ; in existence ; in life ; প্রস্থিত ব্যক্তির স্থানে ; বর্ত্তমান ; জীবিত। **2.** After ; "*Behind* him rode two gallant esquires ;" inferior to (in progress, attainment, etc.) ; as, they are *behind* their neighbours in knowledge : *behind* the age ; পরে ; অপেক্ষাকৃত-হীন, পশ্চাৎপদ। **3.** In or to the rear of ; to the back or farther side of ; as, the sun has sunk *behind* the mountain ; পশ্চাতে, পেছনে (*Colloq.*); অপর পার্শ্বে। **4.** Subsequent to ; later than ; as, *behind* time ; তৎপরে ; অপেক্ষাকৃত বিলম্বে। ***Noun.*** Posterior ; পশ্চাদ্দেশ। **Behind one's back**—Without one's knowledge ; অজ্ঞাতসারে, অগোচরে, অসাক্ষাতে, পরোক্ষে। **Behind the scenes**—In private ; out of sight ; যবনিকার অন্তরালে ; অগোচরে, অদৃশ্যভাবে। **Behind the times**—Antiquated ; পুরাতন, সেকেলে। **Behind time**—Late ; নিরূপিত সময়ের পরে। **To go behind one's words, etc.**—To look for secret motives on his part ; কোন ব্যক্তির কথার ভিতরের রহস্য আবিষ্কারের জন্য চেষ্টা করা। **To fall behind**—Not to keep up ; সমকক্ষ হইতে না পারা, পশ্চাৎপদ হওয়া। **To put behind**—To refuse to consider ; বিবেচনা করিতে অস্বীকার করা।

bē-hīnd'-hănd, *adv.* & *adj.* **1.** In arrears (financially) ; in debt ; বাকীর দায়ে ; দেনাদার। **2.** Backward ; dilatory ; tardy ; as, *behindhand* in studies ; পশ্চাৎপদ ; দীর্ঘসূত্র ; গৌণ, মন্দগতি। **3.** Behind the times ; as, she was ten years *behindhand* in dress ; বর্ত্তমান সময় হইতে পশ্চাৎপদ, সেকেলে। **To be**

behind-hand—To lag : পিছে পড়িয়া থাকা।

bë-höld′, *v. t., i. & inter.* To receive the impression of (anything) by sight ; to see ; নিরীক্ষণ করা, অবলোকন করা ; দর্শন করা। ***Verb i.*** To attend ; to take notice ; অবধান করা ; লক্ষ্য করা। [In this sense, used chiefly in the imperative.] ***Inter.*** Lo ! (used to call attention) ; তাকাও ! দেখ দেখ ! **—er,** *n.* A looker-on ; a spectator ; দর্শনকারী ; সন্দর্শক, দর্শক।

bë-hold′-en (-höld'n), *adj.* Under obligation to ; বাধিত, ঋণী, কৃতজ্ঞতা-পাশে বদ্ধ।

bë-hoof′ (-hôf), *n.* Use ; benefit ; advantage ; (in phrases, *to, for, on behoof* of) ; আবশ্যক ; লাভ, উপকার, ইষ্ট ; সুবিধা।

bë-hôve′, —hoove′ (-hôv), *v. t.* (Used impersonally with *it,* as the subject ; as *it behoves us.*) To be fit or proper *to ;* to be incumbent *upon* ; যথাযোগ্য হওয়া, যথোচিত হওয়া, সাজা ; অবশ্যপালনীয় হওয়া।

beige (bāzh), *n.* A fabric of undyed and unbleached wool ; অধৌত এবং অরঞ্জিত পশম হইতে প্রস্তুত বস্ত্র বিশেষ।

bë′-ïng, (*Verbal noun* of BE), *n.* **1.** Existence ; life ; "In Him we live and move, and have our *being* ;" অস্তিত্ব, সত্তা ; জীবন। **2.** That which has life ; a living existence ; as, a human *being* ; জীব, প্রাণী ; জীবন্ত সত্তা। **3.** Constitution ; nature ; essence ; গঠন ; প্রকৃতি ; সার বস্তু। **4.** Anything that exists ; person ; সত্তাবান জীব বা বস্তু ; ব্যক্তি। **For the time being**—আপাততঃ। **The Supreme Being**—God ; পরমেশ্বর, পরমপুরুষ, পরব্রহ্ম।

bë-jew′-ël (-jü-), *v. t.* To ornament or deck with jewels ; মণি-মণ্ডিত করা, রত্নখচিত করা, রত্ন-ভূষিত করা। **—elled,** *p. p.* Ornamented with jewels ; মণিময় (বাৎস্যঃ)।

bë-lā′-bour (-bêr), *v.t.* **1.** To beat soundly ; to thrash ; গুরুতর প্রহার করা, উত্তম মধ্যম দেওয়া (*Colloq.*) ; তাড়না করা, ঠেঙ্গান (*Colloq.*)। **2.** (*Fig.*) To assail with words ; "He has *belaboured* that great poet character ;" (লক্ষণায়) বাক্য বাণদ্বারা বিদ্ধ করা।

bë-lāte′, *v. t.* To make late ; to delay ; দেরী করা ; বিলম্ব করা। **—lat′-ed,** *p. p.* **1.** Benighted ; "Some *belated* peasant sees ;" পথিমধ্যে রাত্রি আগত, নিশাপ্রাপ্ত। **2.** Coming too late ; নিরূপিত সময়াপেক্ষা বিলম্বে আগত।

bë-laud′ (-läd), *v. t.* To load with praise ; অতি প্রশংসা করা।

bë-lay′ (-lā), *v. t.* (*Naut.*) To fasten a rope by winding it round a pin or cleat ; (নৌ-বিদ্যা) পেনা (কাষ্ঠ বা লোহের সচ্ছিদ্র গুটি বা বাতা) বা জাহাজস্থ লোহ বা কাষ্ঠময় কীলকের চতুর্দ্দিকে জড়াইয়া রজ্জু বদ্ধ করা। **Belay that** or **there** (sailor's slang)—Stop ! that is enough ! থাম ! খুব হয়েছে ! **Belaying pin**—A strong pin round which ropes are belayed on ; রজ্জু জড়াইবার জন্য লৌহ বা কাষ্ঠময় কীলক।

belch (bëlsh), *v. t., i. & n.* **1.** To eject (wind) from the stomach violently ; উদ্গার দেওয়া। **2.** To emit (wind, fumes, etc.) ; (of volcano, cannon, etc.) ; (আগ্নেয়-গিরি বা কামানের ন্যায় ধূম, ভস্ম প্রভৃতি) উদ্গিরণ বা উৎক্ষেপ করা। **3.** To utter noisily or drunkenly abusive or foul talk (often with *out*) ; as, to *belch out* blasphemies ; উচ্চৈঃস্বরে বা মদমত্তভাবে গালাগালি করা বা অশ্লীল কথা উচ্চারণ করা। ***Verb i.*** **1.** To eructate ; উদ্গার দেওয়া, ঢেঁকুর তোলা (*Colloq.*)। **2.** To eject its contents, as a gun ; as, *belching* flames : "Rusty fire locks *belch* after him ;" উদ্গীর্ণ হওয়া, উদ্বমিত হওয়া। ***Noun.*** Eructation ; উদ্গিরণ, উদ্গার।

belch′-êr *n.* (bëlsh-), A particoloured handkerchief ; নানা বর্ণে বিচিত্রিত রুমাল বিশেষ।

bël′-dăm, —dāme, *n.* **1.** An old woman ; a hag ; বৃদ্ধা ; কুরূপা বৃদ্ধা। **2.** A virago ; কোপন-স্বভাবা নারী, উগ্রচণ্ডা, চণ্ডী।

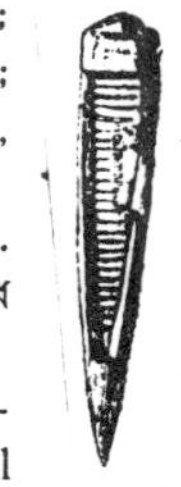
Belemnite.

bë-lea′-guer (-lë-gêr), *v.t.* To besiege ; অবরোধ করা। **—ment,** *n.*

bë-lĕm′-nïte, *n.* A tapering sharp-pointed fossil bone of extinct cuttle fish ; অধুনালুপ্ত সমুদ্রজিভ্ মৎস্যের ক্রম-সূক্ষ্মাগ্র শিলীভূত অস্থি।

belesprit, (*F.*), *n.* (*Pl.* BEAUX-ESPRITS) A man of wit ; সুরসিক পুরুষ।

bël′-frÿ, *n.* A place where bells hang in a church ; খৃষ্টীয় ধর্ম্মমন্দিরের যে স্থানে ঘণ্টা দোদুল্যমান থাকে, খৃষ্টীয় ধর্ম্মমন্দির-সংলগ্ন বা মন্দির হইতে স্বতন্ত্র ঘণ্টাশৃঙ্গ (বুরুজ), ঘণ্টাঘর, ঘণ্টাগার।

Bë′-lï-ăl, *n.* **1.** The spirit of evil ; মূর্ত্তিমান পাপ। **2.** (In *Paradies Lost*) One of the fallen angels ; (মিল্টন কৃত "স্বর্গচ্যুতি" নামক গ্রন্থে) স্বর্গভ্রষ্ট ঈশ্বর-দূতগণের অন্যতম। **A son** or **man of Belial**—A worthless or wicked person ; a reprobate ; নরাধম, দুরাচার ; পাপিষ্ঠ ব্যক্তি।

bë-lie′ (-lï), *v. t.* **1.** To give a false notion of ; to misrepresent ; মিথ্যা ধারণা প্রদান করা ; মিথ্যা বর্ণনা করা। **2.** To fail to act up to (one's promise) ; প্রতিশ্রুতি পালনে অসমর্থ হওয়া। **3.** To slander ; to defame ; (*with, in*) ; কুৎসা প্রচার করা, অপবাদ করা ; মানহানি করা।

bë-lief (-lëf), *n.* **1.** Trust or confidence *in* ; বিশ্বাস, প্রত্যয়, প্রতীতি **2.** (*Theol.*) Faith or a firm persuasion of the truths of religion

(খৃষ্টীয় ধর্ম্মশাস্ত্র) ধর্ম্ম-মতাদিতে বিশ্বাস, শ্রদ্ধা (মঃ উঃ)। **3.** The object of belief; hence, opinion; persuation; as, it is my *belief* that you will be richer; বিশ্বাসের বিষয়, শ্রদ্ধার বিষয়; (অতএব) মত; ধর্ম্মমত। **4.** Acceptance (of a statement or fact) as true; as, his statements are unworthy of *belief*; (উক্তি বা উপপত্তি) সত্য বলিয়া গ্রহণ। **5.** Intuition; সহজজ্ঞান, আত্মপ্রত্যয়লব্ধ জ্ঞান। **The Belief**—Apostle's Creed; খৃষ্টপার্ষদগণের ধর্ম্মমত।

bĕ-lieve′ (-lēv), *v. t.* & *i.* **1.** To give credence to; to accept (a statement) as true; (কোন বিষয়ে) আস্থাস্থাপন্ন করা; (কোন উক্তি) সত্য বলিয়া গ্রহণ করা। **2.** To think; to be of opinion; বিবেচনা করা, অনুমান করা; মতাবলম্বী হওয়া। ***Verb i.*** **1.** (With *in* or *on*) To have faith or confidence; আস্থা বা বিশ্বাস থাকা। **—liev′-a-ble,** *adj*, **—liev′-er,** *n.* **1.** One who believes; বিশ্বাসী। **2.** One who has faith in the doctrines of religion; esp. a Christian; কোন ধর্ম্মে বিশ্বাসী, আস্তিক; (বিশেষতঃ) খৃষ্টধর্ম্মে বিশ্বাসী। **To make believe**—To pretend; ভাণ করা।

bĕ-līke′, *adv.* Perhaps; probably, (often ironical); সম্ভবতঃ; হইলেও হইতে পারে।

bĕ-lit′-tle, *v. t.* **1.** To make small; to dwarf; as, the hills *belittle* the sheet of water; ক্ষুদ্র করা, হ্রাস করা; খর্ব্ব করা, ন্যূন করা। **2.** To depreciate; as, he *belittled* the victory of Port Arthur; অনাদর করা।

bĕll, *n.* **1.** A hollow metallic vessel which emits a clear musical sound when struck by the clapper or tongue; ঘণ্টা, ঘণ্টিকা। **2.** Anything in the form of a bell, as the cup of a flower; "In a cowslip's *bell* I lie;" ঘণ্টাকৃতি বস্তু, ঘণ্টাকৃতি পুষ্প। **3.** A bell rung to tell the time on board ships; জাহাজে কালনির্দ্দেশের জন্য যে ঘণ্টা বাদিত হয়। **Bell-founder**—A maker or caster of bells; যে ব্যক্তি ঘণ্টা ঢালাই করে, ঘণ্টানির্ম্মাতা, ঘণ্টাকর। **Bell-foundry**—A place where bells are cast; ঘণ্টানির্ম্মাণের কারখানা, ঘণ্টাসন্ধানশালা (আঃ বঃ)। **Bell-glass**—A bell-shaped glass cover for plants; ক্ষুদ্র বৃক্ষ আচ্ছাদনার্থ ঘণ্টাকৃতি কাচাবরণ বিশেষ। **Bell-jar**—A bell-shaped glass jar used in chemical laboratory; রাসায়নিক পরীক্ষাগারে ব্যবহৃত ঘণ্টাকৃতি পাত্র। **Bell-man**—One who rings a bell; a town-crier; যে ব্যক্তি রাজপথে ঘণ্টাধ্বনি করে; নগরের ঘোষক। **Bell-metal**—A mixture of copper and tin; কাংস্য। **Bell-pepper**—A species of pepper; কাফ্রী মরিচ (ওয়াট্)। **Bell-punch**—A kind of hand punch provided with a bell; ঘণ্টাযুক্ত টিকিট কাটিবার যন্ত্র। **Bell-ringer**—One who rings a church or town bell at stated times; ধর্ম্মমন্দির বা নগরের ঘণ্টাবাদক, ঘাণ্টিক (মঃ ভাঃ)। **Bell-roof**—A roof shaped like a bell; ঘণ্টাকৃতি ছাদ। **Bell-tower**—A tower containing bells; ঘণ্টাঘর। **Bell-wether**—A leading sheep of a flock with a bell on its neck; hence, a chief or leader; as, you *bell-wether* of the mob; a noisy clamorous fellow; গলদেশে ঘণ্টাযুক্ত পালের অগ্রগামী মেষ; অতএব দলপতি, চাঁই, দলের সর্দ্দার; কোলাহলকারী লোক। **Death-bell, Passing-bell**—A bell sounded at the funeral of a person; মৃত্যু-ঘণ্টা, কোন ব্যক্তির অন্ত্যেষ্টিক্রিয়াকালে যে ঘণ্টা বাদিত হয়। **Small tinkling bells**—কিঙ্কিণী (আঃ বঃ), ঘুঙ্গুর। **To bear** or **carry away the bell**—To carry off the prize; পুরস্কার জিতিয়া লওয়া। **To curse by bell, book and candle**—(An ecclesiastical cursing formula) To excommunicate; (ধর্ম্মযাজকগণ-কর্ত্তৃক) সমাজ-বহিষ্কৃত করা। [এইরূপ সমাজচ্যুতির কালে ঘণ্টা-বাদন, ধর্ম্মগ্রন্থ-বিশেষ হইতে পাঠ, মোমবাতি নির্ব্বাপণ প্রভৃতি কার্য্য করা হইত।] **To lose the bell**—To lose the prize in a contest; প্রতিযোগিতায় পুরস্কার লাভে অসমর্থ হওয়া।

bĕll, *v. t.* To furnish with a bell; ঘণ্টাযুক্ত করা, ঘণ্টা ঝুলাইয়া দেওয়া। **Bell-the-cat**—A nickname given to Archibald Douglas, Earl of Angus; স্কটলণ্ডের অন্তঃপাতী আঙ্গাস নামক স্থানের আর্ল আর্কিবেল্ড ডগলাসের উপনাম। ["স্কটলণ্ডের অধীশ্বর তৃতীয় জেমস ককরেন (Cochrane) নামক জনৈক স্থপতিকে আর্ল উপাধিতে ভূষিত করিলে, তদ্দেশের সম্ভ্রান্ত সমাজ অত্যন্ত ক্ষুব্ধ হইয়া এই বিষয়ে পরামর্শের জন্য সভায় সম্মিলিত হন। কিন্তু তাহাদের মধ্যে কে প্রথম মার্জ্জারের গলায় ঘণ্টা বাঁধিবেন (অর্থাৎ ককরেনের শরীরে প্রথম হাত তুলিবেন), তদ্বিষয়ে সকলে ইতস্ততঃ করিতেছিলেন, তখন ডগলাস সগর্ব্বে বলিয়া উঠিলেন আমি মার্জ্জারের গলায় ঘণ্টা বাঁধিব। তদবধি তিনি Bell-the-cat আখ্যাপ্রাপ্ত হইয়াছেন।]

bĕll, *v. i.* & *n.* To roar; to bellow as a stag or duck at rutting-time; চীৎকার করা, ডাকা; মদাবস্থা-প্রাপ্ত হরিণ কিম্বা হংসীর মত ডাকা। ***Noun.*** The cry of a stag, etc. at rutting; মদাবস্থাপ্রাপ্ত মৃগাদির রব।

bĕll, *n.* A bubble formed in a liquid; "*Bells* of air in a champagne glass;" বুদ্বুদ।

bĕl-lă-dŏn′-nă, *n.* **1.** A poisonous plant which yields a useful medicine; বিষাক্ত ভেষজ বৃক্ষ বিশেষ। **2.** A drug prepared from this plant; উক্ত বৃক্ষ হইতে প্রস্তুত ঔষধ বিশেষ।

belle (bĕl), *n.* (Feminine of BEAU.) A young handsome woman; the reigning beauty of a place; রূপসী, তরুণী; কোন স্থানের প্রধানা সুন্দরী।

belles-letters (bĕl-lĕtr), (*F.*), *n.* (*Pl.*) Pleasing literature including poetry, romance, etc. ; সুকুমার সাহিত্য—কাব্য, উপন্যাস, ইতিহাস, সমালোচনা প্রভৃতি।

bĕl-lĕt′-rist, *n.* A lover of belles-letters ; সুকুমার সাহিত্যানুরাগী। **—le-tris′-tic,** *adj.*

bĕl′-li-cōse, *adj.* Inclined to war or contention ; সমরপ্রিয়, কলহপ্রিয়, যুযুৎসু, সংগ্রামিক, সামরিক, ঝগড়াটে (*Colloq.*), বিবাদশীল। **—cos′-i-ty,** *n.* **—ly,** *adv.*

bĕl-lĭg-ĕr-ĕnt, *adj.* & *n.* Carrying on war ; waging war যুধ্যমান ; সমরে প্রবৃত্ত। ***Noun.*** **1.** A nation, party or state waging regular war ; সমররত জাতি, দল বা রাষ্ট্র। **2.** Any opponent engaged in conflict ; সমরে প্রবৃত্ত প্রতিপক্ষ। **—en-cy,** *n.* **—ly,** *adv.*

Bĕl-lō′-nă, *n.* **1.** The Roman goddess of war ; রোমানদিগের রণদেবী, রণচণ্ডী। **2.** A spirited woman of commanding presence ; উগ্রচণ্ডা, মহাতেজস্বিনী নারী।

bĕl′-low (-lō), *v. i.* & *n.* **1.** To roar as a bull or cow when excited ; উত্তেজিত ষাঁড়ের মত গর্জ্জন করা। **2.** (Of human beings) To vociferate ; to clamour ; (contemptuous) ; as, a bully *bellowing* for more drink ; (মনুষ্যপক্ষে) গর্জ্জন করা ; কোলাহল করা, চেঁচান (*Colloq.*) ; (অবজ্ঞাসূচক)। **3.** To shout or roar from pain ; আর্ত্তনাদ করা। **4.** To roar ; (said of thunder, cannon, wind, sea, etc.) ; গর্জ্জন করা। ***Noun.*** A roar, as of a bull ; a loud deep cry ; বৃষাদির গর্জ্জন ; উচ্চরব, উচ্চনাদ, গর্জ্জন।

bĕl-lows (-lōs), *n.* (*pl.*) **1.** An instrument for producing a current of air (as for blowing a fire, organ, etc.) ; ভস্ত্রা, ভস্ত্রিকা, যাঁতা, চর্ম্মপ্রসেবিকা, বায়ুদ্গারযন্ত্র, ধমন (কক্ষঃ)। **2.** (*Fig.*) That which fans the fire of passions, discord, etc. ; (লক্ষণায়) যাহা হিংসা-ক্রোধাদি উদ্দীপ্ত করে। **3.** The lungs ; ফুস্‌ফুস্।

bĕl′-lȳ, *n., v. t.* & *i.* **1.** That part of the human body, containing the bowels ; the corresponding part in animals ; the abdomen ; উদর, জঠর, পেট, তুণ্ড ; কুক্ষি ; বস্তি, তলপেট। **2.** The stomach, as the receptacle of food ; as, *belly* is not filled with fair words ; hence appetite ; gluttony ; অন্নাশয়, আমাশয় ; (অতএব) ক্ষুধা ; ঔদরিকতা। **3.** The womb ; "Before I formed thee in the *belly* ;" গর্ভ। **4.** The interior cavity of anything ; as, out of the *belly* of hell ; (কোন বস্তুর) গহ্বর, কোষ্ঠ। **5.** The bulging part of anything ; as, the *belly* of a flask ; (কোন বস্তুর) উদ্গাতাংশ বা স্ফীত ভাগ। **6.** The front, inner or lower surface of anything ; (opp. to *back*) ; as, the *belly* of the violin ; কোনও বস্তুর সম্মুখ, মধ্য বা নিম্নভাগ। ***Verb t.*** To cause to swell out (of sails) ; ফুলাইয়া তোলা (পাইল সম্পর্কে)। ***Verb i.*** To bulge out (usually of sails, etc., with *out*) ; স্ফীত হওয়া, ফুলিয়া উঠা, উদ্গাত হইয়া উঠা। **Belly-ache**—Colic; উদরবেদনা, বায়ুশূল (হঃ চঃ), উদরশূল (সুশ্রুঃ)। **Belly-band**—The girth which fastens the saddle of a horse ; ঘোড়ার জিন বাঁধিবার পেটী। **Belly-god**—A glutton ; উদরসর্ব্বস্ব, ঔদরিক। **Bellyful**—A sufficiency of food ; খাদ্যের প্রাচুর্য্য ; উদর-পূর্ণ আহার, আকণ্ঠভোজন, একপেট। A sufficiency ; as, the nation had a *bellyful* of fighting ; প্রাচুর্য্য। **Belly-pinched**—Starving ; অনশনক্লিষ্ট। **Belly-timber**—Food ; provisions ; ক্ষুধানলের ইন্ধন, খাদসামগ্রী ; খাদ্য-সম্ভার। **Belly worship**—Gluttony ; ঔদরিকতা, উদরম্ভরিতা, পেটুকতা। **The belly has no ears**—বুভুক্ষিত ব্যক্তি উপদেশ শুনে না।

bĕ-lŏng′, *v. t.* **1.** To be the property or part of ; as, India *belongs* to Great Britain ; অধিকার-ভুক্ত বা অঙ্গীভূত হওয়া, অন্তর্গত হওয়া, অন্তর্ভূত হওয়া। **2.** To appertain (to) ; to be the business or affairs of ; as, it *belongs* to him to prove his tittle ; (কোন কিছুর সহিত) সংসৃষ্ট হওয়া ; কাহারও কার্য্য বা বিষয় হওয়া। **3.** To be a member of a family, society or nation ; as, he *belongs* to the Maratta race ; কোন পরিবার, জাতি বা সমাজভুক্ত হওয়া। **4.** To be a native or inhabitant of a place ; as, Dr. J. C. Bose *belongs* to Bengal ; কোন দেশের মৌলিক অধিবাসী বা স্থায়ী বাসিন্দা হওয়া। **—ings,** *n. pl.* **1.** A person's property ; possessions ; one's luggage ; (কোন ব্যক্তির) বিষয়-সম্পত্তি ; অধিকৃত বস্তু সমূহ ; তল্পিতল্পা (*Colloq.*), আসবাব পত্র। **2.** (*Colloq.*) Relations ; family ; (চলিত-ভাষায়) জ্ঞাতি, কুটুম্ব ; পরিবার। **3.** Appendage or accessory of another ; as, all these *belongings* of the firm ; অনুবন্ধ, আনুষঙ্গিক বস্তু।

bĕ-lov′-ĕd (-lŭv-), *p. p.* & *n.* Greatly loved ; dear to the heart ; (generally followed by *of*, *by*) ; প্রিয়তম ; দয়িত, সুভগ। ***Noun.*** One who is much beloved ; a darling ; (with *my, his,* etc.) ; বল্লভ,-কান্ত, মনচোরা, প্রাণনাথ, প্রাণেশ্বর ; যাদুমণি।

bĕ-low′ (-lō), *prep.* & *adv.* **1.** Lower (in place) than ; নিম্নে, নীচে, তলে, তলায়। **2.** Down the stream from ; as, *below* that junction of the rivers ; ভাটীর দিকে, নিম্নাভিমুখে, সমুদ্রাভিমুখে। **3.** Too low to be affected by ; as, *below* flattery ; অস্পৃশ্য। **4.** Lower in rank, dignity, etc. than ; as, a man far *below* in station ; lower in excellence ; inferior to ; as, performance is *below* excellence ; সম্ভ্রম, পদমর্য্যাদা, প্রভাব বা উৎকর্ষতায় নিম্নে ; উৎকর্ষে হীন ; হীনতর । **5.** Lower in amount, weight, value, etc. than ; as, *below* the average, normal, etc. ; ওজন, পরিমাণ ইত্যাদিতে অল্পতর । **6.** Unworthy of ; unbefitting ; as, *below* attention, regard, etc. ; অযোগ্য ; অশোভন। ***Adv.*** **1.** In a lower place ; beneath ; নিম্নতর স্থানে ; তলে । **2.** On the earth ; under heaven ; as, *below* in human climes ; ভূতলে, ধরাতলে ; আকাশতলে । **3.** In hell ; as, realms *below* অধোলোকে । **4.** Downstairs ; on a lower room ; সিঁড়ির নীচে ; নীচের কোঠায় । **5.** In a lower rank or grade ; as, the court *below* (নিম্ন আদালত); পদবী, পদ বা ক্ষমতা হিসাবে নিম্নতর স্থানে । **6.** At the foot of a page ; later in a book or writting ; as, the passages alluded to *below* ; পৃষ্ঠার নীচে ; পরবর্ত্তী অংশে বা পৃষ্ঠায়। **Below the mark**—Below the standard ; আদর্শ হইতে নিম্নে।

bĕlt, *n.* & *v. t.* **1.** A girdle ; মেখলা, কোমরবন্ধ, কটিবন্ধ। **2.** A broad strip of anything ; any encircling strip ; ফালি ; পটি, বন্ধনী । **3.** (*Mech.*) A broad flat strap of leather passing around two wheels and communicating motion from one to the other ; (যন্ত্র-বিজ্ঞান) চক্রযুগলের প্রান্তবেষ্টক চর্ম্মময় পটি বিশেষ—যদ্দারা চক্র হইতে চক্রান্তরে গতি সঞ্চারিত হয় । **4.** A strait ; as, Great and Little *Belts* ; প্রণালী । ***Verb t.*** **1.** To encircle ; to encompass ; বেষ্টন করা ; মেখলাবেষ্টিত করা । **2.** To gird on (a weapon, etc.) ; (অস্ত্রাদি) বাঁধা । **3.** To thrash with a belt ; as, he had *belted* your shoulders ; কোমরবন্ধ দ্বারা আঘাত করা । **Belt of calm**—(ভূগোল) নির্ব্বাত বলয় (সাঃ•পঃ) । **Belt of Orion**—ইল্বক (অমরঃ) । **To hit below the belt**—To fight unfairly ; অন্যায় যুদ্ধ করা ।

bĕl-ū'-gă, *n.* A species of fish ; একপ্রকার মৎস্য ।

bĕl vĕ-dere' (-dēr), *n.* **1.** A pavilion or raised turret to view the scenery from ; শীতল সন্ধ্যানিল সেবন বা চতুর্দ্দিকের দৃশ্যাবলী দর্শনোপযোগী মণ্ডপ বা উচ্চ বুরুজবিশেষ । **2.** (In France) A summer-house (in a park or garden) ; (ফরাসীদেশে) (উপবন বা পুরোদ্যানমধ্যস্থিত) নিদাঘনিবাস ।

bē'-mă, *n.* A stage or platform from which speakers addressed the assembly in Athens ; প্রাচীন এথেন্স নগরীর বক্তৃতা-মঞ্চ ।

bē-mīre', *v. t.* To cover or stain with mud ; কর্দ্দমাক্ত করা, কর্দ্দমময় করা, পঙ্কলিপ্ত করা ।

bē-moan' (-mōn), *v. t.* To weep or moan for ; to lament ; ক্রন্দন করা, শোক করা ; খেদ করা, আক্ষেপ করা, বিলাপ করা ।

bē-mock' (-mŏk), *v. t.* To mock at ; to deride ; বিদ্রূপ বা ব্যঙ্গ করা ; ঠাট্টা করা, উপহাস করা ।

bē-mūse', *v. t.* To muddle or stupefy ; "A parson much *bemused* in beer ;" গোলমালে ফেলা, স্তম্ভিত করা ।

bĕn, *adv., prep.* & *n.* Within ; in ; in the parlour or chamber ; ভিতরে ; মধ্যে ; কক্ষে বা বৈঠকখানায় । ***Prep.*** Into the inner part of a house ; গৃহাভ্যন্তরে । ***Noun.*** The inner room ; অন্তর্কক্ষ। **But and ben**—In the outer and inner aparatments ; সদরে অন্দরে। **Over far ben**—Too intimate ; অত্যন্ত অন্তরঙ্গ।

bĕnch, *n.* **1.** A long seat of wood or stone ; দীর্ঘ-আসন, বেঞ্চি। **2.** A long working table ; as, a carpenter's *bench* ; সূত্রধর বা কারিগরের কাজ করিবার মেজ, ছুঁতারের বাঁক, সূত্রধরের পাটা। **3.** A seat in a boat ; তরীর মধ্যস্থিত উপবেশন স্থান, পীঠিকা । **4.** (*Law*) (*a*) A judge's seat in court ; hence, the office or dignity of a judge ; as, to be raised to the *bench* ; (আইন) ধর্ম্মাসন, বিচারাসন ; বিচারকের পদ বা পদমর্য্যাদা । (*b*) The persons who sit as judges collectively ; a court ; as, in the opinion of the full *bench* ; বিচারকগণ ; ধর্ম্মাধিকরণ, আদালত, এজলাস, অধিকরণ-মণ্ডপ (মৃচ্ছঃ) । **5.** A ledge in masonry or earth-work ; পাকা গাঁথুনী বা মাটির কাজের তাক । **Bĕnch'-ĕr,** *n.* **1.** A senior member of the Inn of Court ; বিলাতের ব্যবহার-জীবি-সমাজের বয়োজ্যেষ্ঠ সদস্য । **Bench-mark**—A mark cut by surveyors at places where heights have been taken ; আমিনগণ যে সকল স্থানের উচ্চতা পরিমাপ করে—তৎতৎ স্থলে যে সকল চিহ্ন কাটিয়া রাখে। **Bench-warrant**—A warrant issued by a judge rather than a magistrate ; বিচারকের পরোয়ানা । **Bench and bar**—বিচারক ও ব্যবহারজীবিবর্গ। **A full bench**—হাইকোর্টের সকল বিচারকগণের বৈঠক, কামেল এজলাস (রঃ অঃ) । **To be raised on the bench**—To be made a judge or bishop ; বিচারপতি বা ধর্ম্মাধ্যক্ষের পদে প্রতিষ্ঠিত হওয়া ।

bĕnd, *v. t.* & *i.* **1.** To curve or make crooked ; to crook by straining ; as, to *bend* a bow ; বাঁকান, অনৃজু করা ; বক্রীকৃত করা ; নমিত করা, নোয়ান (*Colloq.*) । **2.** To incline ; to turn ; as, to *bend* the mind ; প্রবণ করা, ঝুঁকান ; হেলান, ফিরান । **3.** To apply closely or with interest ; to direct ; "To mischief mortals *bend* their will." প্রগাঢ়-ভাবে অভিনিবিষ্ট করা ; চালিত করা । **4.** To cause to yield ; to subdue ; as, his spirit was not to be *bent* ; বশীভূত করা ; দমন করা । **5.** (*Naut.*) To tie ; to fasten on ; as, to *bend* a rope ; (নৌ-বিদ্যা) বাঁধা ;

দৃঢ়রূপে বদ্ধ করা। *Verb i.* **1.** To crook or be curving; to bow; বাঁকিয়া যাওয়া, বক্র হওয়া; নমিত হওয়া, আবর্জ্জিত হওয়া (কুমাঃ)। **2.** To incline in any direction; to trend; ঝুঁকিয়া থাকা; উন্মুখ হওয়া, ঝুঁকা। **3.** To stoop; (with *to, before, towards*); দেহ নত করা; অবনত হওয়া, হেট হওয়া। **4.** To apply oneself vigorously; as, to *bend* to the oars; সোৎসাহে কার্য্যে প্রবৃত্ত হওয়া। [*Bent on mischief*—জিঘাংসু। *Bent on religion*—ধর্ম্মপরায়ণ। *Bent on revenge*—প্রতিচিকীর্ষু। *A bent bow*—বক্রীকৃত ধনু, মণ্ডলীকৃত ধনু।] **Bend′-a-ble,** *adj.* **To be bent**—To be determined; স্থিরসংকল্প হওয়া। **To bend the brows**—To frown or scowl; (গভীর চিন্তায় বা ক্রোধে) ভ্রূকুটি করা, ভ্রূভঙ্গি করা, ভ্রূকুঞ্চিত করা, চোখ রাঙ্গান।

bĕnd, *n.* **1.** A curve; as, a *bend* in a road or river (রাস্তার মোড় বা নদীর বাঁক); a turning; বাঁক; মোড়। **2.** (*Naut.*) A knot (of various kinds); (নৌ-বিদ্যা) গ্রন্থি, গাঁট। **3.** (*Herald.*) A band stretching diagonally across a shield; (কুল-বিদ্যা) কুলফলকোপরি কোণাকুণিভাবে বিস্তৃত বন্ধনী বিশেষ। **Bend-leather**—The best quality of sole leather—the thickest leather used for soles; (জুতার গোড়ালীর জন্য) স্থূলচর্ম্ম।

bē-neath′ (-nēth), *prep.* & *adv.* **1.** Under; underneath; lower in place than; at the foot of; নীচে, নিম্নে; তলে; নিম্নতর স্থানে; পাদে, পাদদেশে। **2.** Overburdened with or oppressed by; গুরুভারাক্রান্ত, প্রপীড়িত। **3.** Lower in rank, dignity or excellence than; unworthy of; unbecoming; পদ, সম্মান, গৌরব বা উৎকর্ষে নিম্নতর স্থানে; অযোগ্য; অশোভন। *Adv.* **1.** In a lower place; নিম্নতর স্থানে। **2.** Below; on the earth, as opposed to heaven; নীচে; ভূতলে। **Beneath contempt**—Not worth despising; অবজ্ঞারও অযোগ্য। **Beneath one's dignity**—মর্য্যাদার হানিকর বা অযোগ্য। **Beneath one's notice**—অবধানের অযোগ্য, লক্ষ্য করার অযোগ্য।

bĕn′-ĕ-dick, *n.* A name for a newly married man, especially a confirmed bachelor who marries; (from *Benedick* in Shakespear's *Much ado about nothing*); নববিবাহিত পুরুষ, নবোঢ় ব্যক্তি, বিশেষতঃ যে ব্যক্তি চিরকুমারব্রত অবলম্বন করিয়া পশ্চাৎ দারপরিগ্রহ করে।

bĕn′-ĕ-dict, *n.* Same as BENEDICK.

bĕn-ĕ-dĭc′-tine (-ĭn), *n.* & *adj.* **1.** A member of the order of monks founded by St. Benedict in the sixth century. They wear black clothing and are called black-monks, also black friars; খৃষ্টীয় সিদ্ধপুরুষ বেনিডিক্ট-কর্ত্তৃক ৬ষ্ঠ শতাব্দীতে প্রতিষ্ঠিত সন্ন্যাসি-সম্প্রদায়ভুক্ত ব্যক্তিবিশেষ। এই সম্প্রদায়ভুক্ত সন্ন্যাসিগণ কৃষ্ণবর্ণ পরিচ্ছদ পরিধান করিয়া থাকেন, এবং কৃষ্ণাম্বর সন্ন্যাসী নামে কথিত হন। **2.** A cordial or liqueur formerly distilled at Fecamp and made by benedictine monks; বিনেডিক্টিন সম্প্রদায়ভুক্ত সন্ন্যাসিগণ কর্ত্তৃক প্রস্তুত উত্তেজক পানীয় বা আসব বিশেষ। *Adj.* Pertaining to the monks of St. Benedict or his monastic rule; উক্ত সম্প্রদায়ের সন্ন্যাসী বা মঠের নিয়ম-সম্বন্ধীয়।

bĕn-ĕ-dĭc′-tion, *n.* **1.** The act of invoking a blessing; আশীর্ব্বাদ-প্রার্থনা। **2.** Blessing; a solemn or affectionate invocation of happiness; আশীর্ব্বাদ, কল্যাণবচন, মঙ্গলবাক্য, আশীর্ব্বচন; স্বস্তি, নন্দী (নাটকে), প্রশস্তি (দশরূঃ), আশিস্। **3.** The short prayer, generally at table at the end of church service, or as special Roman catholic service; উপাসনাদির অন্তে শান্তিবাক্য, মঙ্গলবাক্য, মঙ্গলবাদ। **—tive,** *adj.* Tending to bless; আশীর্ব্বাদসূচক। **—to-ry,** *adj.* Expressing benediction; as, a *benedictory* prayer; আশীর্ব্বাদজ্ঞাপক, কুশলসূচক, শুভাকাঙ্ক্ষাজ্ঞাপক।

bĕn-ĕ-făc′-tion, *n.* **1.** A kindly or generous action; a benefit or blessing; উপকারসাধন, হিতসাধন; উপকার, কল্যাণ, কুশল। **2.** A gift for charitable purpose; a grant; লোক-হিতকর কার্য্যে দান; দান, বৃত্তি। **—tor,** *n.* (*fem.* -TRESS.) **1.** A friendly helper; উপকারক, উপকারী, হিতকারী, প্রিয়কারী। **2.** One who bestows a benefit (esp. to a charitable or religious institution); সাহায্যকারী (বিশেষতঃ অনাথ-আশ্রম, ধর্ম্মমন্দির প্রভৃতিতে সাহায্য প্রদানকারী)।

bē-nĕf′-ic, *adj.* (*Astrol.*) **1.** Of favourable influence; as, the moon forms *benefic* aspects; (ফলিত জ্যোতিষ) শুভ। **2.** Beneficent; benign; as, *benefic* truce; উপকারী; অনুগ্রহশীল, অনুগ্রহজনক, মঙ্গলময়।

bĕn′-ĕ-fice (-fĭs), *n.* An ecclesiastical living; যাজকীয় বৃত্তি অথবা খৃষ্টীয় ধর্ম্মমন্দিরের উচ্চতর পদ। **—ficed,** *adj.* Holding a benefice; যাজকবৃত্তিভোগী।

bē-nĕf′-i-cĕnce, *n.* The practice of doing good; active kindness; charity; হিতকারিতা, পরোপকারিতা, লোকোপকার; দয়া বা সাধুতার কার্য্য; দানশীলতা, বদান্যতা। **—cent,** *adj.* Doing good; showing active kindness; পরোপকারী, হিতসাধক, হিতকারী, হিতকর; দানশীল, বদান্য। **—cent-ly,** *adv.*

bĕn-ĕ-fi-cial (-shăl), *adj.* **1.** Advantageous; profitable; উপকারজনক, সুবিধাজনক, হিতকর, শুভজনক, ইষ্টজনক; লাভজনক। **2.** (*Law*) Enjoying the usufruct; as, he is the *beneficial* owner of the property; (আইন) কোন সম্পত্তির উপস্বত্বভোগী বা অধিকারী, জীবনস্বত্বভোগী। **—ly,** *adv.*

bĕn-ĕ-fī'-ci-ă-rȳ (-shî-), *n.* & *adj.* **1.** The holder of an ecclesiastical living ; যাজনবৃত্তিধারী। **2.** The receiver of benefits : উপকারপ্রাপক, দানগ্রাহী। **3.** The holder of a feudal benefice ; a feudatory ; অধীন ভূম্যধিকারী ; সামন্ত। ***Adj.*** Holding by feudal tenure ; as, a *beneficiary* chief ; সামন্ত-তন্ত্রের নিয়মানুসারে সম্পত্তি ভোগদখলকারী।

bĕn'-ĕ-fĭt, *n., v. t.* & *i.* **1.** An advantage ; a profit ; as, for the *benefit* of ; হিত, মঙ্গল, ইষ্ট, সুবিধা ; লাভ, অর্থ। **2.** Act of kindness ; gift ; "Forget not all his *benefits* ;" উপকার ; অনুগ্রহ, প্রসাদ। **3.** A performance (at a theatre or game etc.) the profits of which are given to a particular person or charitable object ; as, *benefit* night : *benefit* match ; যে ক্রীড়া বা নাট্যাভিনয় প্রভৃতির আয় কোন ব্যক্তি বিশেষকে বা জনহিতকর কার্য্যে প্রদত্ত হয়। ***Verb t.*** To do good to ; to be of profit to ; as, exercise *benefits* health ; উপকার করা, কল্যাণ করা ; উপকারে আসা। ***Verb i.*** To get advantage ; to receive benefit ; সুবিধা পাওয়া ; উপকার পাওয়া, উপকৃত হওয়া। **Benefit-club, Benefit-society**—A club or society for mutual insurance against illness or old age ; পীড়িত-বা বৃদ্ধাবস্থায় পরস্পরের সাহায্যের জন্য সভা বা সমিতিবিশেষ। **—er,** *n.* One who confers a benefit ; উপকারক। **Benefit of clergy, Benefit of peerage**—See CLERGY, PEERAGE.

bĕ-nĕv'-ō-lĕnce, *n.* **1.** A disposition to do good ; a charitable feeling ; good will ; পরোপকারশীলতা ; শুভানুধ্যান, শুভচিন্তন, উপচিকীর্ষা, হিতৈষণা ; সদয় ভাব, প্রীতি। **2.** An act of kindness ; a grant of money ; as, the companies gave great *benevolences* ; দয়ার কার্য্য ; অর্থদান। **3.** (*Eng. Hist.*) A forced loan or tax illegally exacted by the kings of England ; ইংলণ্ডের স্বৈর-নৃপতিগণকর্ত্তৃক বলপূর্ব্বক সংগৃহীত ঋণ বা কর বিশেষ।

bĕ-nĕv'-ō-lĕnt, *adj.* Desirous of doing good ; charitable ; generous ; উপকারসাধনেচ্ছু, উপচিকীর্ষু, হিতৈষী ; দানশীল ; উদার। **—ly,** *adv.*

Bĕn-gal, *n.* A province of India ; বঙ্গদেশ। **Bengal light**—A firework used for signals ; সমুদ্রে সঙ্কেতার্থ ব্যবহৃত সমুজ্জল আলোক বিশেষ। **Bengal stripes**—Striped ginghams, originally brought from Bengal ; একপ্রকার ডোরা-কাটা কাপড় (পূর্ব্বে বঙ্গদেশ হইতে বিলাতে প্রেরিত হইত)। **Bengal tiger**—The tiger proper ; শার্দ্দূল, সুন্দরবনের প্রকাণ্ড ব্যাঘ্র।

Bĕn-gal'-ee (-ē), **Bĕn-gal'-i,** *n.* & *adj.* **1.** The language of Bengal ; বঙ্গভাষা। **2.** A native of Bengal ; বঙ্গবাসী। ***Adj.*** Pertaining to Bengal ; বঙ্গীয়।

bĕ-night'-ĕd (-nīt-), (*p.p.* of verb *benight,* which is now obsolete) ; **1.** Overtaken by night ; রাত্রি প্রাপিত, নিশাক্রান্ত, বিশেষতঃ দিবসের কোন কার্য্যসমাপন বা নির্দ্দিষ্ট পথ অতিক্রম করিবার পূর্ব্বে রাত্রি আগত। **2.** Involved in intellectual or moral darkness ; ignorant ; as, a *benighted* country ; অজ্ঞানান্ধকারাচ্ছন্ন, অজ্ঞানতিমিরান্ধ ; অজ্ঞানগ্রস্ত, অজ্ঞাননিমগ্ন, অজ্ঞ।

bĕ-nign' (-nīn), *adj.* **1.** Of a kind disposition ; gracious ; "Creator bounteous and *benign* ;" দয়ালু, সুমনাঃ ; করুণাময়। **2.** Gentle ; mild ; as, a *benign* Quaker ; salubrious ; as, *benign* climate, weather, etc. ; শান্ত ; সৌম্য ; স্বাস্থ্যজনক। **3.** (*Astrol.*) Favourable (as opposed to *malign*) ; (ফলিত জ্যোতিষ) অনুকূল, শুভ। **4.** (*Of diseases*) Of a mild type ; (রোগ-সম্পর্কে) মৃদু-প্রকৃতিক। **—ly,** *adv.* **—nig'-ni-ty,** *n.* Kindness of disposition ; kindliness ; (now attributed to superiors) ; as, such a fatherly *benignity* of look ; দয়ালুতা, মৃদুতা, সুপ্রসন্নতা ; সদয়ভাব।

bĕ-nig'-nănt, *adj.* **1.** Kindly or kind to inferiors ; gracious ; benevolent ; as, a *benignant* sovereign ; দয়ালু, সদয়, অনুগ্রহশীল ; প্রসন্ন ; পরহিতৈষী। **2.** Salutary ; as, *benignant* influence ; শুভ, মঙ্গলজনক। **—ly,** *adj.* **—nan-cy,** *n.*

Benincasa cerifera—Gourd ; কুমড়া (বেলঃ), চালকুমড়া (ঐ)।

bĕn'-i-sŏn, *n.* Benediction ; blessing, especially of God ; আশীর্ব্বাদ, আশিস ; ঈশ্বরাশীর্ব্বাদ।

Bĕn'-jă-mĭn, (From Jacob's youngest son, Gen. XLII. 4.), *n.* The youngest child ; a darling ; সর্ব্বকনিষ্ঠ সন্তান ; যাদুমণি।

bĕn'-jă-mĭn, *n.* (*Slang.*) A kind of men's over-coat ; as, a grave professor in a smooth drab *benjamin* ; (ইতর ভাষায়) ইংলণ্ডের পুরুষগণের পরিধেয় লম্বা কোর্ত্তা বিশেষ।

bĕn'-jă-mĭn, *n.* A gum ; benzoin ; একপ্রকার আঠা ; কপি-তৈল। **Benjamin tree**—A tree yielding benzoin ; উদম্ব বৃক্ষ (ওয়াট্)। A North American shrub with aromatic bark ; উত্তর-আমেরিকা দেশজাত সুগন্ধি-বল্কল-বিশিষ্ট তরু বিশেষ।

bĕn'-nĕt, *n.* The herb bennet or the yellow avens of Europe ; পীতবর্ণ পুষ্পবিশিষ্ট ইয়ুরোপ দেশীয় তরুবিশেষ।

bĕnt, *n.* Twist ; inclination ; leaning or bias ; tendency ; মোচড় ; আসক্তি, প্রবৃত্তি ; ঝোঁক ; প্রবণতা। **To the top of one's bent**—To one's heart's content ; প্রাণ ভরিয়া।

bĕnt, *n.* **1.** Various grass-like reeds, rushes, etc. ; (used collectively in *sing.* or *pl.*) ; নানা প্রকার শর, এড়কা, নল, খাগড়া, প্রভৃতি। **2.** The stiff flower-stalk of grasses ; also, couch-grass ;

বিভিন্ন জাতীয় ঘাসের কঠিন পুষ্প-বৃন্ত-সমূহ ; দূর্ব্বা। **3.** A grassy plain ; তৃণাচ্ছাদিত প্রান্তর। **To go** or **take to the bent**—To avoid danger, creditors, etc. ; বিপদ, পাওনাদার প্রভৃতি এড়ান।

Bĕn′-thăm-ĭsm, *n.* The doctrine that the greatest happiness of the greatest number is the guiding principle of ethics ; (from *Jeremy Bentham*) ; অধিকতম লোকের অধিকতম সুখই নীতি বিজ্ঞানের মূল অনুশাসন—এইরূপ মত, হিতবাদ। **–ite,** *n.*

bentrovato, (*It.*), *adj.* Well-invented ; প্রশংসনীয়রূপে উদ্ভাবিত।

bē-numb′ (-nŭm), *v.t.* **1.** To make (any part of the body) insensible or torpid, (usu. of cold) ; অবশ করা, নিস্পন্দ করা, শিথিল করা, অচেতন করা, অনুভব-শক্তি হ্রাস করা। **2.** To paralyse (mind, feelings or action) ; to stupefy ; আড়ষ্ট করা, জড়ীভূত করা, নিস্তেজ করা ; স্তম্ভিত করা। **–numbed′,** *adj.* **–numbed′-ness, –numb′-ment,** *ns.*

bĕn′-zēne, –zine, *n.* A liquid obtained from coal-tar, used to remove grease spots ; চর্ব্বির দাগ তুলিবার জন্য আলকাতরা হইতে প্রস্তুত তরল পদার্থ বিশেষ।

bĕn-zōin′, *n.* A fragrant aromatic resin, obtained from a tree of Sumatra or Java ; লোবান (খোরী), দেবধূপ (ঐ), কপিতৈল (ভাবঃ প্রঃ), শিলাপুষ্প (মঃ উঃ), অশ্মপুষ্প (অঃ)।

bĕn′-zō-line (-lĭn), *n.* Impure benzoin ; অপরিশোধিত লোবান।

bē-paint′ (-pānt), *v. t.* To smear or cover with paint ; to tinge or colour ; রঞ্জিত করা ; রঙ্ মাখান।

bē-queath′ (-quēth), *v. t.* **1.** To leave (property) by will ; ইচ্ছাপত্র-দ্বারা দান করা, উইলক্রমে দান করা, চরম-পত্র দ্বারা (সন্তান সন্ততির জন্য) সম্পত্তি রাখিয়া যাওয়া। **2.** To transmit to posterity (example, etc.) ; ভবিষ্যদ্বংশধরগণের মধ্যে সংক্রামিত করা। **–a-ble,** *adj.* **–al, –er, –ment,** *ns.*

bē-quĕst′, *n.* **1.** The act of leaving by will ; চরম-পত্রদ্বারা দান। **2.** The thing bequeathed, esp. personal property ; a legacy ; ইচ্ছাপত্র দ্বারা দত্ত বস্তু ; উইলক্রমে দত্ত বস্তু বা ধন।

bē-reave′ (-rēv), *v. t.* To rob ; to deprive (esp. by death) ; to make destitute ; (with *of* before the person or thing taken away); বলপূর্ব্বক বঞ্চিত করা, কাড়িয়া লওয়া ; বিরহিত করা, বিহীন করা ; বিচ্যুত করা, নিরাশ্রয় করা, বিধুর করা। **–ment,** *n.* Deprivation ; esp. the loss of a beloved by death ; বিয়োগ, বৈধুর্য্য, বিধুরতা ; প্রিয়জন-বিয়োগ

bêrg, *n.* (Short for) Iceberg ; হিমশিলা (হিঃ কোঃ), হিমপাতিকা।

bêr′-gā-mŏt, *n.* **1.** A tree of orange or lemon kind ; লেবু বা কমলা জাতীয় বৃক্ষ-বিশেষ। **2.** A perfume extracted from its fruit ; উক্ত বৃক্ষের ফল হইতে প্রস্তুত সুগন্ধি দ্রব্য বিশেষ। **3.** A kind of pear ; একপ্রকার নাসপাতি।

ber-gere′, (*F.*), A style of chair or sofa ; এক ধরণের কেদারা বা উপবেশন-খট্টাবিশেষ।

bĕr′-ĭ-bĕr-ĭ, *n.* A dangerous wasting disease prevalent in India ; শোথরোগবৎ ভারতীয় ব্যাধিবিশেষ। উক্ত রোগাক্রান্ত ব্যক্তিগণের শরীরে বেদনা আড়ষ্টতা, ও অঙ্গপ্রত্যঙ্গের শক্তিহীনতা, প্রভৃতি নানা লক্ষণ প্রকাশ পায়।

bē-rīme′, –rhȳme′, *v. t.* To write verses about ; কোন বিষয়ে কবিতা লিখা।

Bĕrke-le′-ian (bŭrk-lē-ăn), *adj.* Relating to Bishop Berkeley or his philosophy, which denied the objective existence of the material world ; বিশপ বার্কি বা তৎপ্রবর্ত্তিত মায়াবাদ-সম্বন্ধীয়।

Bêr′-lin, *n.* An old-fashioned four-wheeled covered carriage ; (also *berline*) ; এক প্রকার চারি-চাকার গাড়ী। **Berlin black**—A black varnish ; এক প্রকার কাল রঙ্গের বার্ণিশ। **Berlin warehouse**—A shop for berlin wool ; বার্লিন পশমের দোকান। **Berlin wool**—A fine wool for knitting ; বুনিবার উপযোগী এক প্রকার সুন্দর রঙ্গীন পশমী সূতা।

bêrm, berme (bêrm), *n.* A ledge in a fortification between the ditch and the base of the parapet ; দুর্গের পরিখা এবং আবক্ষ উচ্চ প্রাচীরের মধ্যবর্ত্তী আলি (আইল)।

bêr′-rȳ, *n.* & *v. i.* **1.** A small juicy fruit containing seeds ; as, black-*berry* ; বীজবহুল ক্ষুদ্র সরস ফল, নিরস্থিক ফল (বিশ্বঃ), কোলি (সাঃ পঃ), বার্ত্তাকীয় (ঐ)। **2.** (*Popularly*) Any small round juicy fruit without stone ; (লৌকিক ভাষায়) বীজ বা আঁঠি-শূন্য যে কোন প্রকার ক্ষুদ্র সুগোল সরস ফল। **3.** One of the eggs of fish or lobster ; মৎস্য বা চিংড়ি মৎস্যের ডিম্বের এক একটী দানা। ***Verb i.*** **1.** To come into berries ; উক্ত ক্ষুদ্র ফল ধরা। **2.** To gather berries ; উক্ত ফল সংগ্রহ করা। **In berry**—Said of a hen-lobster carrying her eggs ; (চিংড়ীমৎস্য সম্বন্ধে) ডিম্বযুক্ত।

bersaglieri, (*It.*), *n.* Italian sharp-shooters ; ইতালী দেশীয় সিদ্ধ-হস্ত বন্দুকধারী সৈন্যগণ।

bêr′-sêrk, –sêrk-êr, *n.* A wild Norse warrior fighting with mad frenzy ; উন্মত্তভাবে যুদ্ধকারী নরওয়ে দেশের যোদ্ধাবিশেষ। ইহারা রণোন্মত্ত হইয়া যুদ্ধ করে।

bêrth, *n.* & *v. t.*, (*Naut.*) **1.** (*a*) A convenient sea-room for a ship ; (নৌ-বিদ্যা) অন্য জাহাজ প্রভৃতির সহিত সংঘর্ষ না লাগিয়া নিরাপদে চলিতে পারে, সমুদ্রগামী জাহাজের চতুষ্পার্শ্বে তৎপরিমাণ স্থান। (*b*) A place where a ship lies at anchor or at a wharf ; জাহাজের নঙ্গর-স্থান বা জেটিতে

বাঁধিবার স্থান। (*c*) A sleeping place in a ship, railway-car, etc. ; জাহাজ বা রেলগাড়ীর কামরা বা শয়ন-স্থান। **2.** A post or situation, (especially a good comfortable one) ; (ভাল) চাকুরী বা পদ, (বিশেষভাবে) মোটা মাহিয়ানার চাকুরী। ***Verb t.*** **1.** To moor a ship in a suitable place ; সুবিধাজনক স্থানে জাহাজ নঙ্গর করা। **2.** To provide sleeping place for ; (জাহাজ, রেলগাড়ী প্রভৃতিতে) শয়নের স্থান প্রদান করা। **To give a wide berth to**—To keep away from ; to avoid ; দূরে থাকা, দূর হইতে প্রণাম করা ; এড়ান। **To tumble into a nice berth**—To get a nice situation ; ভাল চাকুরী পাওয়া।

bêr′-thă, berthe (bêrth), *n.* A woman's shoulder-cape or deep falling collar ; স্ত্রীলোকের স্কন্ধাচ্ছাদক বস্ত্র বা গলবন্ধ বিশেষ।

Bêr-til-lŏn′-sȳs′-tĕm, *n.* A method of identifying criminals by physical description, measurements, etc. ; (after Bertillon—French anthropologist) ; শারীরিক বর্ণনা, পরিমাপ, প্রভৃতিদ্বারা অপরাধিগণের পরিচয়ের প্রণালী বিশেষ।

bĕr′-ȳl, *n.* A light-blue precious stone ; ফিকে নীল রঙ্গের প্রস্তরবিশেষ, ফিরোজা (ফঃ হিঃ)।

bē-seech′ (-sēch), *v. t.* **1.** To ask earnestly for, (esp. leave, etc.) ; to solicit or beg ; মিনতি করা ; অনুনয় করা। **2.** To supplicate ; to implore (a person, to do a thing) ; সকাতরে প্রার্থনা বা কাকুতি মিনতি করা ; (কোন কার্য্য করিবার জন্য কাহাকে) প্রার্থনা করা, যাচ্ঞা করা। **—er,** *n.* **—ing,** *adj.* Suppliant (of look, tone, etc.) ; অনুগ্রহপ্রার্থী। **—ingly,** *adv.*

bē-seem′ (-sēm), *v. t.* To suit ; to befit ; to be worthy of ; (with *well* or *ill*) ; যোগ্য হওয়া, উপযুক্ত হওয়া, সঙ্গত হওয়া ; যথাযোগ্য হওয়া ; সাজা, শোভা পাওয়া। **—ing,** *adj.* Becoming ; befitting ; comely ; মানানসই ; যথাযোগ্য ; সুশোভন। **—ing-ly,** *adv.* **—ing-ness,** *n.*

bē-sĕt′, *v. t.* **1.** To set or stud (anything) with ornaments ; (only in *p. p.*) : "A robe of azure *beset* with drops of gold :" খচিত করা, বসান। **2.** To surround ; to hem in ; to besiege ; "Let thy troops *beset* our gates :" বেষ্টিত করা ; সমাবৃত করা, পরিবৃত করা ; ঘেরা (*Colloq.*), অবরোধ করা। **3.** To set upon on all sides ; to assail ; to harass ; (of difficulties, temptation, etc.) ; প্রপীড়িত করা ; আক্রমণ করা ; উপদ্রব করা, আকুলিত করা। **4.** To waylay ; পথে লুকাইয়া থাকিয়া অকস্মাৎ আক্রমণ করা। **—ment,** *n.* **1.** The state of being hemmed in (by obstacles) ; বেষ্টিত ভাব। **2.** A besetting sin ; যে পাপ অনুক্ষণ প্রলুব্ধ করে। **—ting,** *adj.* Habitually attending ; সতত সহচর।

bē-shrew′ (-shrô), *v. t.* To wish a curse upon ; অমঙ্গল বা অকল্যাণ ইচ্ছা করা।

bē-sīde′, *prep.* **1.** Close to ; near ; by ; নিকটে ; সন্নিকটে ; পার্শ্বে। **2.** On a level with ; compared with ; as, capable of taking rank *beside* that of Shakespeare ; সমকক্ষ ; তুলনায়। **3.** Wide of (mark, question, etc.) ; লক্ষ্য বা মূল বিষয় হইতে দূরে। **Beside one's self**—Out of one's wit or senses ; আত্মহারা।

bē-sīdes′, *adv.* & *prep.* Over and above ; in addition ; moreover ; otherwise ; অধিকন্তু, আরও ; এতদ্‌তিরিক্ত ; অপিচ ; অন্যথা। ***Prep.*** Over and above ; in addition to ; as well as ; except ; এতদ্ব্যতীত, তার উপর, উপরন্তু ; অধিকন্তু, ইহার উপর ; আরও ; বিনা, ব্যতীত ব্যতিরেকে, ছাড়া, ভিন্ন। **To be besides one's self with joy**—আহ্লাদে আটখানা হওয়া, আনন্দে আত্মহারা হওয়া, আনন্দে মাতিয়া উঠা।

bē-siege′ (-sēj), *v. t.* **1.** To lay siege to ; to surround with armed forces ; অবরোধ করা ; সশস্ত্র সৈন্যদ্বারা বেষ্টিত করা। **2.** To throng round ; to block up ; as, the people have *besieged* the doors of the place ; (কোন কিছুর চতুর্দ্দিকে) জনতা বা ভিড় করা ; পথ, প্রভৃতি অবরোধ করা। **3.** To assail with (importunate) requests ; as, who daily and nightly *besieged* Heaven with supplication ; অনবরত প্রার্থনাদ্বারা প্রপীড়িত করা। **—ment,** *n.* **—sieg′-er,** *n.*

bē-slăv′-êr, *v. t.* **1.** To defile or cover with slaver ; লালাক্লিন্ন করা, লাল মাখান। **2.** To flatter fulsomely ; তোষামোদ করিতে করিতে বিতৃষ্ণা জন্মান।

bē-slŏb′-bêr, *v. t.* **1.** To wet and befoul with saliva ; to beslaver ; লালাস্রাব করা, লালায়িত বা লালাবিলিপ্ত করা ; লালাদ্বারা মলিন করা। **2.** To kiss effusively ; অজস্র চুম্বন বৃষ্টি করা।

bē-slŭb′-bêr, *v. t.* To bedaub or besmear ; লেপন করা, অনুলিপ্ত করা।

bē-smear′ (-smēr), *v. t.* **1.** To smear with greasy or sticky substance ; as, *besmeared* with sandal juice (চন্দন-চর্চ্চিত) ; *besmeared* with blood (রক্তাক্ত) ; তৈলাক্ত, আঠালো বা মলিন পদার্থদ্বারা বিলিপ্ত করা, বিলেপিত করা, চর্চ্চিত করা, লেপন করা, মাখান।

bē-smirch′ (-smêrch), *v. t.* **1.** To soil ; to discolour (with smoke, soot, mud, etc.) ; to dim the lustre of ; মলিন করা, ময়লা করা ; কজ্জলিত করা, ধূমদিগ্ধ করা, বিবর্ণ করা ; নিষ্প্রভ করা।

bē-smŭt′, *v. t.* To blacken with soot ; কজ্জলিত করা (দুর্বঃ)।

bē′-sŏm, *n.* & *v. t.* A brush made of twigs ; a broom ; সম্মার্জ্জনী ; ঝাঁটা (*Colloq.*), খেঙরা (*Colloq.*)।

Verb t. To sweep (with *away, out*) ; ঝাঁটাইয়া ফেলা । **Besom-head**—A block-head ; জড়-বুদ্ধি, আহাম্মক (*Colloq.*) ।

bë-sŏt′, *v. t.* To make sottish (by drink) ; to make dull or stupid ; প্রমত্ত করা ; হতবুদ্ধি করা । **—ted,** *adj.* **—ted-ly,** *adv.* **—ted-ness,** *n.*

bë-span′-gle (-spăng-), *v. t.* To sprinkle or adorn with spangles or glittering objects ; চুম্‌কি বসান, চক্‌চকে বস্তুদ্বারা সাজান ।

bë-spăt′-têr, *v. t.* **1.** To spatter over, with mud, filth, etc. ; কর্দ্দম-লিপ্ত করা, পঙ্কিল বা সমল করা, মল-দূষিত করা । **2.** To asperse ; কলঙ্ক রটনা করা, অপবাদ করা, কলঙ্ক-কালিমা লেপন করা ।

bë-speak′ (-spēk), *v. t.* & *n.* (past. *bespoke* ; *p. p. bespoke, bespoken.*) **1.** To engage beforehand ; as, to *bespeak* a seat in a coach ; to order (goods) ; পূর্ব্ব হইতে বন্দোবস্ত করিয়া রাখা ; কোন জিনিষের ফরমাইস দেওয়া । **2.** To give evidence of ; to indicate ; "Hamlet's soliloquy *bespeaks* the reflective mind ;" to augur ; as, that *bespeaks* war and danger ; প্রমাণিত করা ; সূচনা করা ; ভবিষ্যৎ-সূচনা করা, আভাস দেওয়া । **3.** To speak to ; to address ; (*poetic*) ; উক্তি করা ; কাহাকে সম্বোধন করিয়া বলা । ***Noun.*** Among actors, a benefit (when a particular play is bespoken or chosen) ; অভিনেতার পুরস্কারের জন্য অভিনয় । **—er,** *n.* **Bespoke boot-maker, dress-maker, etc.**—*i. e.* as opposed to ready-made dealer ; অর্থাৎ যাহারা ফরমাইস মত পোষাক পরিচ্ছদ প্রস্তুত করে ।

bë-spec′-kle (-spĕkl), *v. t.* To variegate with specks or spots ; বিচিত্রিত করা, শবলীকৃত করা, ফুট ফুট চিহ্নযুক্ত করা, নানা বর্ণে বিচিত্রিত করা, কর্বূরিত করা ।

bë-sprĕnt′, *p. p.* Sprinkled with ; scattered about ; (poetic) ; প্রোক্ষিত ; আস্তৃত ।

bë-sprin′-kle (-spring-), *v. t.* To sprinkle or strew over ; (*with* liquid, powdery substance, etc.) ; প্রক্ষেপ করা, সিঞ্চন করা, ছড়ান, ছিটান ।

Bĕs′-së-mêr-prŏc′-ĕss, *n.* (From S. H. Bessemer the inventor.) A process of making steel from cast iron, by passing currents of air through it when molten, so as to carry off carbon and other impurities ; (hence, *bessemer iron, bessemer steel*) ; খরলোহের মধ্যে বায়ুপ্রবাহ চালনাদ্বারা অঙ্গার প্রভৃতি অবিশুদ্ধ পদার্থ দূরীভূত করত ইস্পাত প্রস্তুতের প্রণালী বিশেষ ।

bĕst, *adj., n.* & *adv.* (Superlative of *good, well*). **1.** Of the highest excellence ; having good qualities in the highest degree ; অত্যুত্তম, সর্ব্বোন্নত, সেরা, সর্ব্বোত্তম, সর্ব্বোৎকৃষ্ট, অনুত্তম, সর্ব্বপ্রথম শ্রেষ্ঠ-গুণসম্পন্ন, পরমগুণসম্পন্ন । **2.** (Of persons) Most kind or beneficent ; (of things) most appropriate or desirable ; (লোক-সম্পর্কে) পরম-কারুণিক, পরম-উপকারী ; (বস্তু-সম্পর্কে) যোগ্যতম, শ্রেষ্ঠ । **3.** Most ; largest ; অধিকতম ; বৃহত্তম । ***Noun.*** **1** (*Pl.*) The best people ; as, to weep with the *best* ; শ্রেষ্ঠ ব্যক্তিগণ । **2.** (*Sing.*) Best clothing ; as, dressed in their Sunday *best* ; সর্ব্বোৎকৃষ্ট পরিচ্ছদ । **3.** Best state or condition ; "It exhibits man at his *best* ;" সর্ব্বাপেক্ষা ভাল ভাব বা অবস্থা । ***Adv.*** In the highest degree ; most ; as, *best* beloved ; in the most excellent way ; to the fullest extent ; অধিকতম পরিমাণে ; অত্যন্ত ; সর্ব্বোৎকৃষ্টভাবে, শ্রেষ্ঠভাবে ; পূর্ণ পরিমাণে । **Best maid**—The bride's maid at a wedding ; বিবাহকালে কন্যার প্রধানা সহচরী । **Best man**—The principal groomsman at a wedding ; (বিবাহকালে) বরের প্রধান সহচর, নীতবর । **At best**—On the most hopeful view ; যতদূর সম্ভব ভালভাবে দেখিলে বা ধরিয়া লইলে । **Bad is the best**—No good event possible ; কোন শুভঘটনা সম্ভবপর নয় । **For the best**—Intended for the best results ; সর্ব্বোৎকৃষ্ট ফলের জন্য অভিপ্রেত । **I were best**—It would be most advantageous for me ; আমার পক্ষে অত্যন্ত সুবিধার বিষয় হইত । **Of the best**—Of the best quality or sort ; উৎকৃষ্ট শ্রেণীর, উৎকৃষ্ট রকমের । **To do one's best**—To do all one can ; যথাসাধ্য চেষ্টা করা । **To the best**—To the utmost extent (of one's power, knowledge, etc.) ; যথাসাধ্য, যতদূর সম্ভব । **The best is the enemy of the good**—Too high standard bars progress ; উচ্চতম আদর্শ উন্নতির প্রতিবন্ধকস্বরূপ । **To have the best of it**—To have the advantage, in a contest, transaction etc. ; কোন ব্যাপারে বা কোন বিরোধে নিজের পক্ষে সুবিধা থাকা । **To make the best of one's way**—To go as fast as possible ; যতদূর সম্ভব শীঘ্র যাওয়া । **To make the best of both worlds**—To manage so as to get the good things on earth and be sure of a good place in heaven ; এইরূপভাবে চলা যাহাতে পার্থিবজীবনে সুখ-সম্পদ ভোগ করা যায় এবং পরকালেও স্বর্গবাস সুনিশ্চিত থাকে । **To make the best of things**—To be contented ; সন্তুষ্ট থাকা । **To put one's best leg** or **foot foremost**—To do one's best to get on ; স্বীয় উন্নতি সাধনের জন্য প্রাণপণ চেষ্টা করা । **To the best of one's power**—As far as one's power allows ; যথা-শক্তি, যতদূর ক্ষমতায় কুলায় । **With the best**—As well as anyone ; অন্য দশজনের মত ।

bĕst, *v. t.* (*Colloq.*) To get better of ; to outdo ; (কথিত ভাষায়) বলবত্তর হওয়া ; ছাড়াইয়া যাওয়া ।

bē-stead′ (-stĕd), *v. t.* To avail ; to be of use to ; "Vain Philosophy ! little hast thou *bestead*, save to perplex the head ;" কার্য্যকর হওয়া ; কাযে লাগা । [Usu. in *p. p. bestead* or *bested*=placed or circumstanced, (with *ill, hard*, etc.) ; "Many far worse *bestead* than ourselves ;" অবস্থিত ।]

bĕs′-tiăl, *adj.* **1.** Like a beast ; brutish ; পশুবৎ ; পশু-স্বভাব । **2.** Depraved ; lustful ; obscene ; চরিত্র-ভ্রষ্ট ; কামাসক্ত, পশুবৎ কামুক ; অশ্লীল । **—ize,** *v. t.* To brutalize ; পশুবৎ করিয়া তোলা । **—ly,** *adv.* **—tial′-i-ty** *n.* **1.** Irrationality ; stupidity ; অযৌক্তিকতা ; মূঢ়তা । **2.** Disgusting vice ; জঘন্য পাশবাচার, পাশবিকতা । **3.** Unnatural connection with a beast ; পশু-মৈথুন ।

bĕs′-ti-ā-rȳ, *n.* A treatise on beasts ; esp. one of the moralizing treatises written during the Middle Ages ; পশুবিষয়ক গ্রন্থ ; মধ্যযুগে ইয়ুরোপে বাস্তব ও কবিকল্পিত পশুসমূহের কাহিনী-পূর্ণ যে একশ্রেণীর পুস্তক প্রচলিত ছিল, তাহার অন্যতম ।

bē-stick′, *v. t.* To stick over ; to pierce ; (সুতীক্ষ্ণ অস্ত্রে) বিদ্ধ করা ; ভেদ করা ।

bē-still′, *v. t.* To make quiet ; to still ; শান্ত করা ; নিস্তব্ধ করা ।

bē-stir′ (-stêr), *v. refl.* To stir up ; to manifest activity ; to busy oneself ; আলোড়িত করা ; তৎপরতা প্রকাশ করা ; কার্য্যে ব্যস্ত হওয়া ।

bē-stow′(-stō), *v. t.* **1.** To deposit ; to stow ; "He *bestowed* it in a pouch ;" সঞ্চিত করা ; চাপিয়া বা ঠাসিয়া বোঝাই করা । **2.** To lodge ; to quarter ; "See that the women are *bestowed* in safety ;" বাসস্থান দেওয়া ; অস্থায়ী বাসস্থানের বন্দোবস্ত করিয়া দেওয়া । **3.** To employ in an occupation ; to devote for a purpose ; কোন কার্য্যে নিযুক্ত করা ; কোন উদ্দেশ্যে নিয়োগ করা । **4.** To confer as a gift, present, etc. ; (*on* or *upon* a person) ; "The empire is on us *bestowed* ;" দান করা, প্রদান করা । **—al,** *n.* **1.** Disposal ; অর্পণ, সম্প্রদান । **2.** Presentation ; gift ; উপহার-প্রদান ; উপহার । **—er, —ment,** *ns.*

bē strew′ (-strê), *v. t.* To strew (a surface) with ; to scatter (things) about ; আস্তৃত করা, আস্তীর্ণ করা ; ছড়ান ।

bē-strīde′, *v. t.* To stand over (a place) with legs astride ; to sit upon (a horse etc.) with legs astride ; পা ফাঁক করিয়া দাঁড়ান ; চড়িয়া বসা । **2.** (*Fig.*) To stand over to defend ; "When I *bestride* thee in the war ;" (লক্ষণায়) রক্ষা করার জন্য দণ্ডায়মান হওয়া, রক্ষা করা । **3.** To step over ; to stride over or across ; as, to *bestride* a threshold ; ডিঙ্গাইয়া যাওয়া ; লঙ্ঘন করা ।

bĕt, *n., v. t. & i.* **1.** A wager ; পণ বাজি । ***Verb t. & i.*** To lay or stake a bet or wager ; বাজি রাখা, পণ করা, বাজি ফেলা । **Bet′-ting,** *n.* পণ-ক্রিয়া । **A betting-book**—A book for entering bets in ; যে পুস্তকে পণ-সংক্রান্ত বিষয় লিপিবদ্ধ করা হয় । **An even bet**—An equal chance ; উভয়দিকে জয়লাভের সমান সম্ভাবনা । **You bet** (*Colloq.*)—Be assured ; (চলিতভাষায়) নিশ্চিন্ত হও, খাতিরজমা থাকো (*Colloq.*) ।

bē′-tă, *n.* **1.** The second letter of the Greek alphabet ; গ্রীক বর্ণমালার দ্বিতীয় অক্ষর । **2.** (*Astron.*) Used to mark the second star in a constellation ; (জ্যোতির্বিজ্ঞান) এই শব্দটী তারাপুঞ্জের অন্তর্ভূত দ্বিতীয় নক্ষত্রটীকে নির্দ্দেশ করিতে ব্যবহৃত হয় ।

bē-tāke′, *v. refl.* **1.** To commit oneself to some course or means ; কোনপ্রকার বিশেষ পন্থা বা উপায় অবলম্বন বা আশ্রয় করিতে (নিজকে) আবদ্ধ করা । **2.** To convey oneself (*i.e.* go) to a place or person ; as, he *betook* himself to Calcutta ; কোন স্থানে বা কোন ব্যক্তির সন্নিকটে গমন করা ।

bē′-tel (-tle), **bē′-tle,** *n.* The leaf of a plant ; (also, *betel pepper, betelvine*) ; পান, তাম্বূলপত্র, নাগবল্লীপত্র । [**Betel-nut**—A mistaken name for the *areca nut.*] **Betel seller**—তাম্বূলিক, পানওয়ালা ।

bete noire, (*F.*), *n.* [Lit. a black beast] A bugbear ; জুজু ।

bĕth′-ĕl, *n.* **1.** A house of worship ; a hallowed place ; উপাসনাস্থলী, পূজার্চ্চনার স্থান ; পবিত্র স্থান । **2.** A church for dissenters ; খৃষ্টীয় সম্প্রদায় বিশেষের উপাসনা-মন্দির ।

bĕ-thĕs′-dă, *n.* A nonconformist chapel ; খৃষ্টীয় ধর্ম্মসম্প্রদায় বিশেষের উপাসনা-মন্দির ।

bē-think′, *v. refl.* **1.** To call to mind ; to recollect ; (with *of* or *that*) ; to think ; to consider ; মনে আনা ; (ভাবিয়া) স্মরণ করা ; চিন্তা করা ; বিবেচনা করা । **2.** To take into one's head (to) ; মনোমধ্যে সহসা কোন ভাব উদয় হওয়া, কোনরূপ খেয়ালে চাপা ।

bē-tīde′, *v. t. & i.* (Only in 3rd. pers., often imperative) To happen to ; as, woe *betide* the wanderer ; ঘটা, সঙ্ঘটিত হওয়া, আপতিত হওয়া । ***Verb i.*** To happen ; to befall ; as, whatever *betide* ; ঘটা ; (ভাগ্যে) ঘটা ।

bē-tīmeś′, *adv.* **1.** Early in the year ; early in life ; early in the morning ; seasonably ; বৎসরের প্রথমভাগে ; জীবনের প্রথমভাগে ; প্রত্যূষে ; সুসময়ে, সময়মত । **2.** In a short time ; soon ; forthwith ; অল্পদিনের মধ্যে ; শীঘ্র, অচিরে ; অমনি, তৎক্ষণাৎ ।

betise, (*F.*), *n.* A foolish remark or action ; silliness ; নির্ব্বোধের মত মন্তব্য বা কার্য্য ; নির্বুদ্ধিতা ।

bĕ-tō'-kĕn, *v. t.* To give evidence of ; to show ; as, he *betokened* fine sensibility ; প্রমাণিত করা ; প্রদর্শন করা । **2.** To augur ; to give promise of ; as, a dark cloud often *betokens* a storm ; সূচনা করা ; আভাস দেওয়া, পূর্ব্বসূচনা করা ।

bĕ-tŏn', *n.* A kind of concrete, composed of sand, lime and cement ; চূণ, বালি এবং ক্ষুদ্র ক্ষুদ্র প্রস্তরখণ্ডের মিশ্রণে প্রস্তুত ইমারতের মসল্লা বিশেষ ।

bĕt'-ŏ-nȳ, *n.* A purple-flowered plant ; আলোহিত নীলবর্ণ পুষ্পপ্রসূ পাদপবিশেষ ।

bē-tray' (-trā), *v. t.* **1.** To give up treacherously (a person or a thing *to* enemy) ; বিশ্বাসঘাতকতাপূর্ব্বক শত্রু-হস্তে সমর্পণ করা, ধরাইয়া দেওয়া । **2.** To prove false to ; as, to *betray* a person or a cause ; বিশ্বাসঘাতক বলিয়া প্রতিপন্ন হওয়া, প্রভুদ্রোহী বা রাজ-দ্রোহী বলিয়া প্রতিপন্ন হওয়া । **3.** To lead astray ; to mislead ; as, his wit has *betrayed* him to heresy ; বিপথগামী করা ; ভ্রান্তপথে পরিচালিত করা । **4.** To disclose or divulge a secret ; বিশ্বাসঘাতকতাপূর্ব্বক গুপ্ত বিষয় প্রকাশ করা । **5.** To reveal involuntarily ; "She tries to hide the love her eyes *betray* ;" অনিচ্ছা-সত্ত্বে প্রকাশ করিয়া ফেলা । **6.** To show signs of ; to exhibit ; as, a temple like this *betrayed* great antiquity ; চিহ্ন প্রদর্শন করা ; প্রদর্শন করা । **—al,** *n.* The act of betraying ; শত্রুহস্তে সমর্পণ । **—er,** *n.*

bē-trŏth', *v. t.* To bind with a promise to marry ; (usu. in the *p.p.*) ; পরিণয়ার্থ প্রতিজ্ঞাবদ্ধ করা, বাগ্‌দান করা । **—al, —ment,** *ns.* Engagement for marriage ; বিবাহের চুক্তি বা অঙ্গীকার, বিবাহ-সম্বন্ধ, বাগ্দান ।

bē-trŏth'-ĕd, *adj.* & *n.* Affianced ; বাগ্‌দত্ত বা বাগ্‌দত্তা, দত্তা (বাৎস্যঃ) । ***Noun.*** One engaged for marriage ; বাগ্‌দত্তা কন্যা বা বাগ্‌দত্ত বর ।

bĕt'-tĕr, *adj., adv., n., v. t.* & *i.* (Comparative of *good, well.*) **1.** Of greater excellence ; of superior value or use ; শ্রেষ্ঠতর ; অপেক্ষাকৃত অধিকতর মূল্যবান বা কার্য্যকর । **2.** More useful or suitable (of things) ; kinder (of persons) ; অধিকতর উপযোগী বা কার্য্যকর (বস্তু-সম্পর্কে) ; অধিকতর দয়ালু (ব্যক্তি-সম্পর্কে) । **3.** Larger ; more ; বৃহত্তর ; অধিকতর । ***Adv.*** **1.** In a superior manner ; preferably ; অপেক্ষাকৃত ভাল বা শ্রেষ্ঠভাবে ; বরং । **2.** In a higher degree ; as, I know him *better* than any of you ; অধিকতর পরিমাণে । ***Noun.*** **1.** Mastery or superiority (followed by *of*) ; as, to get the *better of* an enemy ; প্রাধান্য, শ্রেষ্ঠতা । **2.** One's superior (in merit, rank or station etc.—usu. in *pl.*) ; as, he will grow as proud as his *betters* ; (গুণ, পদ বা সামাজিক পদমর্য্যাদায় কোন ব্যক্তি অপেক্ষা) শ্রেষ্ঠতর ব্যক্তি, গুরুজন । ***Verb t.*** **1.** To improve (physically, socially, financially, etc.) ; as, girls marry to *better* themselves ; to ameliorate ; as, to *better* their condition ; উন্নতিসাধন করা ; উত্তরোত্তর ভাল করা । **2.** To surpass ; to excel ; "Each day still *betters* other happiness ;" ছাড়াইয়া যাওয়া ; (অন্যকে) সদ্‌গুণে অতিক্রম করা । ***Verb i.*** To improve ; শ্রেষ্ঠতর হওয়া, উন্নত হওয়া । **—ment,** *n.* Improvement ; amelioration ; উৎকর্ষ-সাধন ; উন্নতিসাধন । **Better-feelings**—Higher self ; সৎপ্রবৃত্তি, সাত্ত্বিক ভাব । **Better half**—Wife ; অর্দ্ধাঙ্গ । **Better part**—Most ; অধিকাংশ, প্রায় সমস্ত । **For better or for worse**—Indissolubly ; as, they were united *for better* and *worse* ; অবিচ্ছেদ্যরূপে । **Had better**—Would find it wiser to ; বরং, (করা) ভাল ছিল, (করিলে) ভাল হইত । **So much the better**—ভাল হইত । **The better**—Advantage ; superiority ; সুবিধা ; শ্রেষ্ঠতা । **To be all the better for**—To be so much the more to the benefit of ; ততটা অধিক উপকারে আসা । **To be better off**—To be richer ; to be more comfortable ; পূর্ব্বাপেক্ষা অধিকতর ধনশালী হওয়া ; অধিকতর সুখসুবিধা ভোগ করা । **To be better than one's word**—To do more than one had promised ; কথার চেয়ে কাজে অধিক দেখান । **To get better**—To recover ; আরোগ্যলাভ করা । **To get the better of**—To defeat ; to gain the advantage over ; পরাস্ত করা ; প্রাধান্য লাভ করা । **To think better of**—To reconsider favourably ; to form a better opinion ; কোন বিষয়ে পুনর্বিবেচনা করা ; কোন বিষয়ে পূর্ব্বাপেক্ষা ভালমত পোষণ করা ।

bĕt'-têr, bĕt'-tŏr, *n.* One who bets ; যে ব্যক্তি বাজি বা পণ রাখে ।

bĕt'-tȳ, *n.* **1.** A short bar used by burglars to force open doors ; a jemmy ; সিঁধেল চোরদিগের দরজা ভাঙ্গিবার লৌহনির্ম্মিত নাতিদীর্ঘ দণ্ড-বিশেষ ; সিঁধকাটি । **2.** A man who busies himself with a woman's house-hold duties ; যে ব্যক্তি স্ত্রীলোকের গৃহস্থালীর কার্য্যে হস্তক্ষেপ কর

bē-tween' (-twēn), *prep.* & *a.* **1.** In the middle of two ; দুইএর মধ্যে । **2.** From one to another of ; "If things should go so *between* them ;" পরস্পরের মধ্যে । **3.** Intermediate to ; as, a baronet is *between* a knight and a baron ; মধ্যবর্ত্তী । **4.** In common to ; as, they had one pair of stockings *between* them ; by the united action of ; as, *between* them they killed the man ; উভয়ের মধ্যে সাধারণ ; একযোগে । **5.** Expressing reciprocal relation ; as, the same opposition *between* science and religion ; অন্যোন্যের সহিত সম্বন্ধবাচক । **6.** Confined to as, *between* you and me (তোমাতে আমাতে) ; সীমাবদ্ধ। **7.** To and from ; as, the steamers plying *between* London and Brighton ; এক স্থান হইতে অন্য স্থানে। **8.** Taking one and rejecting the other of ; as, to choose *between* two courses ; একটী গ্রহণ এবং অপরটী অগ্রাহ্য করিয়া। ***Adv.*** **1.** Midway ; in the midst ; মাঝামাঝি ; মধ্যে। **2.** At intervals ; as, visits short and far *between* ; মাঝে মাঝে, সময় সময়। **Between ourselves**—In confidence ; আমাদের মধ্যে (তৃতীয় ব্যক্তি যেন না শুনে), গোপনে। **Between the cup and the lip**—Of dashed hopes ; কোন বিষয় কার্য্যে পরিণত না করা পর্য্যন্ত সবই অনিশ্চিত। **Between the devil and the deep sea**—In a dilemma ; উভয় সঙ্কটে। **Between the lights**—In the twilight ; অতি প্রত্যূষে বা প্রদোষে। **Between two fires**—Between two menacing dangers ; জলে কুমীর ডাঙ্গায় বাঘ এইরূপ অবস্থায়। **Between two lights**—Under cover of darkness ; অন্ধকারে গা ঢাকা দিয়া। **Between whiles**—In the intervals ; at intervals ; ইত্যবসরে ; সময় সময়। **Betwixt and between**—In the middle position ; মাঝামাঝি, আধাআধি। **Few and far between**—At wide intervals ; বহু সময় ব্যবধানে দুই এক বার। **To go** or **stand between**—To act as a mediator ; to be a protector ; মধ্যস্থ হওয়া ; রক্ষক বা তত্ত্বাবধায়ক হওয়া।

bĕ-twixt′ *prep.* Poetic or archaic for BETWEEN.

bĕv′-ĕl, *n., adj., v. t. & i.* **1.** An instrument for taking or setting off angles ; বাটাম্ বা মাটাম্। **2.** An inclination (at an angle) ; ঢালু, প্রবণতা। ***Adj.*** Oblique ; slanting ; মাটামাকৃতি ; ঢালু, প্রবণ। ***Verb t.*** To slope the edge or surface of ; কোন কিছুর কিনারা বা পৃষ্ঠ ঢালু করা। ***Verb i.*** To slant ; হেলিয়া পড়া। **Bevel-gear**—যে সকল যন্ত্রের চক্রসকল

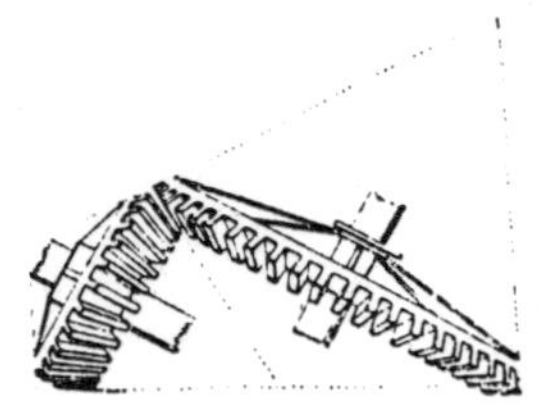

Bevel-gear.

পরস্পরের সহিত কোণাকোণিভাবে সংস্থিত থাকে। **Bevel-wheels**—Clogged wheels with working face oblique to axis ; একপ্রকার দন্তুর চক্র।

bĕv′-ĕr-āge, *n.* A drinking liquor ; পানীয় দ্রব্য।

bĕv′-ȳ, *n.* A flock of birds, (esp. of quails, larks, etc.) ; a company of ladies, of roes, etc. ; বিহঙ্গশ্রেণী, পাখীর ঝাঁক ; রমণীদল, যূথ (উজ্জ্বলঃ), মৃগযূথ, প্রভৃতি।

bĕ-wail′ (-wāl), *v. t. & i.* To wail over ; esp. to utter wailings over the dead ; to lament loudly ; উচ্চৈঃস্বরে খেদ প্রকাশ করা ; (মৃতের জন্য) বিলাপ করা ; রোদন করা। ***Verb i.*** To lament ; to mourn ; শোক প্রকাশ করা ; খেদ করা। **—a-ble,** *adj.* **—er,** *n.* **—ment,** *n.* Lamentation ; বিলাপ।

bĕ-wāre′, *v. i. & t.* To be on one's guard ; to take care ; (followed by *of, lest*) ; সতর্ক থাকা ; সাবধান হওয়া। ***Verb t.*** To take care of ; to take care for ; তত্ত্বাবধান লওয়া, সাবধান হওয়া ; যত্ন লওয়া।

bĕ-weep′ (-wēp), *v. t.* To weep over ; to bedew with tears ; চক্ষুর জল ফেলা, অশ্রুপাত করা ; অশ্রুসিক্ত করা।

bĕ-wil′-dĕr, *v. t.* To perplex greatly ; to confuse ; হতবুদ্ধি করা, ভেবাচেকা লাগান (*Colloq.*), বিহ্বল করা ; ব্যাকুলিত করা, ব্যাকুল করা, বিভ্রান্ত করা, দিশাহারা করা। **—dered,** *adj.* Confused ; বিভ্রান্ত, দিশাহারা। **—ing,** *adj.* **—ing-ly,** *adv.* **—ment,** *n.* Perplexity ; confusion ; চিত্তবৈকল্য (মঃ ভাঃ) ; কিংকর্ত্তব্যবিমূঢ়তা, বৈক্লব্য, সম্মোহ, মোহ, বিস্ময়, মূঢ়তা, ব্যামোহ।

bĕ-witch′ (-wĭch), *v.t.* **1.** To affect by witchcraft or magic ; to put a spell on ; মন্ত্রমুগ্ধ করা ; যাদু করা। **2.** To charm ; to delight exceedingly ; সম্মোহিত করা, বিমোহিত করা, বিমুগ্ধ করা, মন্ত্রমুগ্ধ করা ; পরম-পুলকিত করা। **—er,** *n.* **—er-y,** *n.* Fascination ; সম্মোহন। **—ing,** *adj.* **—ing-ly,** *adv.* **—ment,** *n.* Fascination ; power of charming ; কুহক, যাদু, মোহ, মন্ত্রমুগ্ধতা ; মোহিনীশক্তি।

bĕ-wray′ (-rā), *v. t.* To reveal involuntarily ; অনিচ্ছাক্রমে ব্যক্ত করা।

bey (bā), *n.* A Turkish governor of a province or district ; তুরস্ক-দেশের প্রদেশ বা জেলার শাসন কর্ত্তা।

bey′-lic (bā-), *n.* The dominion or jurisdiction of a bey ; তুরস্ক-দেশীয় শাসনকর্ত্তার অধীনস্থ স্থান।

bĕ-yŏnd′, *prep., adv. & n.* **1.** On the farther side of ; অপর পার্শ্বে, ওপারে। **2.** Farther on than ; আরও সম্মুখে, আরও আগে। **3.** Later than ; past ; as, we arrived an hour and a half *beyond* our time ; অপেক্ষাকৃত পরে ; অতীত। **4.** Out of the grasp or reach of ; as, *beyond* comprehension (বোধাতীত) ; দুরধিগম্য। **5.** Exceeding ; superior to ; more than ; as, *beyond* all size ; অতীত ; শ্রেষ্ঠতর ; অধিকতর। **6.** Over and above ; besides ; as, they do nothing *beyond* their stated services ; অধিকন্তু ; ব্যতীত, ব্যতিরেকে, ভিন্ন। ***Adv.*** Farther away ; at a distance ; দূরে ; তফাতে। ***Noun.*** That which is beyond the present life ; বর্ত্তমান জীবনের অতীত কোন কিছু। **Beyond one's self**—Besides one's self ; আত্মহারা।

Beyond one's senses—অতীন্দ্রিয়। **Beyond seas**—Abroad ; দূরদেশে, সাতসমুদ্র তের নদীর পারে। **From beyond**—দূর হইতে। **The back of beyond**—The remotest corner of ; the world ; a great way off ; পৃথিবীর সুদূরতম প্রান্ত ; বহুদূর। **The beyond**—The future life ; the unknown ; পারলৌকিক জীবন ; অজ্ঞাত লোক। **To look beyond**—To misunderstand ; ভুল বুঝা।

bĕz'-ănt, *n.* A gold coin current in Europe from 9th century ; নবম শতাব্দী হইতে প্রচলিত ইয়ুরোপীয় স্বর্ণ-মুদ্রা বিশেষ। (রৌপ্য-নির্ম্মিত বেজান্ট্‌ও প্রচলিত ছিল।)

bĕz'-ĕl, *n.* **1.** A groove or rim which holds the jewel in a finger-ring or the glass of a watch, etc. ; অঙ্গুরীয়কের যে স্থানে হীরক প্রভৃতি মূল্যবান প্রস্তর, অথবা টেঁক ঘড়ীর যে খাঁজে কাচ বসান হয়, মণিবন্ধন (মঃ উঃ)। **2.** The oblique face of a cut-gem ; পল-কাটা মণির হেলানো পল। **3.** The sloped edge of a chisel, etc. ; বাটালি, রাঁদা প্রভৃতির হেলানো ধারাল ভাগ।

bĕ-zique' (-zēk), *n.* A simple game at cards ; এক প্রকার তাসের খেলা।

bē'-zoar (-zōr), *n.* A concretion found in the intestines of ruminant animals ; রোমন্থনকারী জন্তুগণের অন্ত্রমধ্যে প্রাপ্ত কঠিন পদার্থের পিণ্ড, গোরোচনা (bovine)।

bhăng, băng, *n.* A variety of hemp ; a narcotic drug ; ভাঙ্গ ; ভাঙ্গ হইতে প্রস্তুত নিদ্রাজনক ঔষধ।

bī'-ăs, *n.* & *v.t.* **1.** A weight lodged on one side of a bowl or ball ; বলের একপার্শ্বে সংবদ্ধ ভারী দ্রব্য। **2.** An inclination ; propensity ; prejudice ; as, a natural *bias* to evil ; ঝোঁক, প্রবণতা ; আসক্তি, স্বাভাবিক প্রবৃত্তি ; পক্ষপাত। **3.** Any special influence that sways the mind ; কোন বিশেষ প্রভাব—যদ্দারা মন প্রভাবিত হয়। **4.** A wedge-shaped cloth taken out of the waist of a dress to diminish its circumference ; কোর্ত্তার বেড় কমাইবার জন্য কোমর হইতে যে কাজলার আকার বস্ত্রখণ্ড কর্ত্তিত হয়। *Verb t.* To incline to one side ; to influence (often unduly or unfairly) ; একদিকে ঝোঁকান ; পক্ষপাতযুক্ত করা। **To cut cloth on the bias, To cut cloth bias**—To cut obliquely across the texture ; বুনটের কোণাকোণি বা টের্চাভাবে কাপড় কাটা।

bĭb, *v. i.* To sip to drink frequently ; চুক্ চুক্ করিয়া গেলা, চুমুক দিয়া পান করা ; পুনঃ পুনঃ মদ্য পান করা। **Bĭb'-bĕr,** *n.* A tippler ; (usu. in combination, as wine-bibber) ; মদ্যপায়ী, সুরাপায়ী। **Bĭb'-bing,** *n.*

bĭb *n.* **1.** A piece of cloth worn over the breast by children ; দুগ্ধাদি পানের সময় শিশুর পোষাক রক্ষার্থ বক্ষে যে বস্ত্রখণ্ড বাঁধা হয়। **2.** An article of dress worn by the adults over the breast ; পরিণতবয়স্ক ব্যক্তিগণ বক্ষোপরি যে এক প্রকার বস্ত্রখণ্ড পরিধান করিয়া থাকে। **Best bib and tucker**—The best clothes ; উৎকৃষ্ট পরিচ্ছদ।

bĭb, *n.* A kind of fish, allied to the cod ; কড্ জাতীয় মৎস্য বিশেষ।

bī-bā'-cious (-shŭs), *adj.* Addicted to drinking ; পানাসক্ত।

bī-băc'-i-ty, *n.* Tippling ; অতিরিক্ত পানাভ্যাস।

Bī'-ble, *n.* **1.** The Scriptures of the Old and New Testament ; খৃষ্টানদের ধর্ম্মগ্রন্থ, বাইবেল। **2.** An authoritative text-book ; "The Annual bids fair to become my political *bible* ;" বিজ্ঞান-বিশেষের মূলসূত্রসমন্বিত প্রামাণিক-গ্রন্থ। **Bib'-li-cal,** *adj.* **Bib'-li-cal-ly,** *adv.* **Bib'-li-cist,** *n.* **Bib'-list,** *n.* One well-versed in the Bible ; one who makes Bible the sole rule of faith ; বাইবেলজ্ঞ ; যে ব্যক্তি ধর্ম্ম-সংক্রান্ত বিষয়ে একমাত্র বাইবেলের অনুশাসন মানিয়া চলে। **Bible-Christian**—A member of the sect so called ; খৃষ্টীয় সম্প্রদায়-বিশেষের সভ্য। **Bible-clerk**—A student in some Oxford colleges who reads lessons in chapel ; অক্সফোর্ডের কোন কোন কলেজে যে ছাত্র ধর্ম্ম-মন্দিরে পাঠ করে। **Bible-reader**—One employed to read the Bible from house to house ; ঘরে ঘরে বাইবেল পাঠের জন্য নিযুক্ত ব্যক্তি।

bĭb-li-ŏg'-ră-phȳ, *n.* **1.** The history of books, their authorships, editions, etc. ; গ্রন্থ, গ্রন্থকার, গ্রন্থের সংস্করণ প্রভৃতি সম্বন্ধে বর্ণনা, বিবরণী বা ইতিহাস, গ্রন্থবিবরণী। **2.** A list of books of any author, printer, country or subject ; কোন গ্রন্থকার, মুদ্রাকর দেশ বা বিষয়-সম্পর্কীয় গ্রন্থ-তালিকা। **—o-graph'-i-cal,** *adj.*

bĭb-li-ŏl'-ă-tĕr, —trist, *n.* A worshipper of books, especially the Bible ; গ্রন্থোপাসক, পুস্তক-পূজক, বাইবেল-পূজক। **—try,** *n.* Book-worship, esp. of the Bible ; গ্রন্থপূজা, বিশেষতঃ বাইবেল পূজা।

bĭb-li-ŏl'-ō-ğȳ, *n.* **1.** Bibliography ; গ্রন্থ-বিবরণ, গ্রন্থ-বর্ণনা। **2.** Biblical literature ; বাইবেল-সম্বন্ধীয় সাহিত্য।

bĭb-li-ō-mā'-ni-ă, *n.* A rage for possessing (curious) books ; book-madness ; দুষ্প্রাপ্য এবং অদ্ভুত গ্রন্থসমূহ সংগ্রহের বাতিক ; পুস্তকবাতিক। **—ac,** *n.* An enthusiastic collector of books ; উৎসাহপূর্ণ পুস্তকসংগ্রাহক। **—ni'-a-cal,** *adj.*

bĭb-li-ŏp'-ĕ-ğȳ, *n.* The art of book-binding ; পুস্তক বাঁধাইর কায। **—gist,** *n.* A book-binder ; দপ্তরী, যে পুস্তক বাঁধে।

bĭb'-li-ō-phĭl(e), —ŏph'-i-list, *n.* A lover of books ; গ্রন্থানুরাগী, গ্রন্থ-প্রেমিক।

bĭb'-li-ō-pōle, bĭb-li-ŏp'-ŏ-list, *n.* A book-seller ; পুস্তক-বিক্রেতা।

—o-pol′-ic, —o-po′-lar, *adjs.* **—op′-o-ly,** *n.* Book-selling ; পুস্তক-বিক্রয়।
bĭb-lĭ-ō-thē′-că, *n.* A library ; পুস্তকাগার। **—cal,** *adj.* পুস্তকালয়-সম্বন্ধীয়। **—oth′-e-ca-ry,** *n.*
bĭb′-ū-lous (-lŭs), *adj.* **1.** Absorbent of moisture ; as, *bibulous* paper, sponges, etc. ; রস-শোষণ-শীল। **2.** Addicted to drinking ; পানাসক্ত, নেশাখোর। **—ly,** *adv.*
bī-căm′-êr-ăl, *adj.* Having two (legislative) chambers ; (ব্যবস্থাপক) সভাকক্ষদ্বয়-সমন্বিত।
bī-căp′-sū-lăr, *adj.* Having two capsules ; দ্বিবীজকোষ।
bī-câr′-bŏn-āte, *n.* A substance containing a double portion of carbonic acid ; দ্ব্যঙ্গারাম্ল।
bīce, bīse, *n.* A blue or green pigment prepared from smalt ; কোবাল্টদ্বারা রঞ্জিত কাচ-চূর্ণ হইতে প্রস্তুত নীল বা হরিদ্বর্ণ রঞ্জনপদার্থ বিশেষ।
bī-cĕn′-tē-nă-rȳ, *adj.* & *n.* Of or pertaining to two hundred years ; দ্বিশতাব্দীয়। ***Noun.*** The two-hundredth anniversary of an event ; দ্বিশতাব্দীতম উৎসব।
bī-cĕn-tĕn′-nĭ-ăl, *adj.* & *n.* Lasting or occurring every two hundred years ; দ্বিশতাব্দীকালস্থায়ী, প্রতি দ্বিশাতাব্দী অন্তে সংঘটিত। ***Noun.*** Bicentenary ; দ্বিশতাব্দীতম উৎসব।
bī-cĕph′-ă-lous (-lŭs), *adj.* Having two heads ; দ্বিশীর্ষ, দ্বিশিরস্ক।
bī′-cĕps, *n.* (*Anat.*) A muscle having two heads ; esp. the upper arm flexor ; দ্বিমূলপেশী (হঃ চঃ), দ্বিমুণ্ড (ঐ) ; বিশেষতঃ বাহুর উপরিভাগস্থ পেশীবিশেষ--যাহার ক্রিয়াদ্বারা বাহু নত করা যায়। **—cip′-i-tal,** *adj.*
bĭck′-êr, *v. i.* & *n.* **1.** To quarrel ; to wrangle ; ঝগড়া করা, কলহ করা ; খুঁটুরমুটুর করা, গোলমাল করা (*Colloq.*)। **2.** To brawl ; to patter ; (of *stream, rain, etc.*) ; কলকল ছল ছল রবে প্রবাহিত হওয়া, কুলুকুলুনাদে প্রবাহিত হওয়া ; টিপ্ টিপ্ শব্দ করা। **3.** To flash ; to glitter, (of *light, flame, etc.*) ; দপ্ করিয়া জ্বলিয়া উঠা ; চক্‌চক্ করা, ঝলমল করা। ***Noun.*** Angry contention ; a quarrel ; গোলমাল, কোলাহল, কলহ ; দ্বন্দ্ব, বিবাদ।
bī-cŭs′-pĭd, *n.* & *adj.* A premolar tooth ; পেষণদন্ত (খাঃ)। ***Adj.*** Having two points or cusps ; দ্বিমুখবিশিষ্ট।
bī′-cȳ-cle, *n.* & *v. i.* A two-wheeled velocipede ; দ্বিচক্রযান, বাইসিকেল। [*Colloq.* also called *bike.*] ***Verb i.*** To ride on a bicycle ; দ্বিচক্রযানে আরোহণ বা ভ্রমণ করা। [Also *bike colloq.*] **—clist,** *n.* One who rides a bicycle ; দ্বিচক্রযানচালক।
bĭd, *v. t., i.* & *n.* To offer (a price) for ; as, he *bade* her half the price she asked ; মূল্যপ্রদানের প্রস্তাব করা। **2.** To proclaim ; as, to *bid* the banns ; (বিবাহবার্ত্তা) ঘোষণা করা। **3.** To call in ; to invite (to a feast, wedding, etc.) ; "I made a feast, I *bid* him come ;" আমন্ত্রণ করা ; নিমন্ত্রণ করা। **4.** To salute (a person with welcome, farewell, etc.) ; (বিদায় বা অভ্যর্থনাসূচক) অভিবাদন করা। **5.** To order ; to command ; as, I *bid* him sit down ; আদেশ করা ; অনুজ্ঞা করা। ***Verb i.*** To make an offer (*for* a thing) ; as, to *bid* at an auction ; ডাকা। ***Noun.*** An offer of price, esp. at an auction ; (নিলামের) ডাক। **Bid′-da-ble,** *adj.* Obedient ; বাধ্য, আজ্ঞানুবর্ত্তী। **Bid′-der,** *n.* One who offers a price at an auction ; যে ব্যক্তি নিলামে ডাকে। [*The highest bidder*—নিলামে যে ব্যক্তি সর্ব্বোচ্চ ডাক ডাকে।] **Bid′-ding,** *n.* Invitation ; injunction ; command ; নিমন্ত্রণ ; আদেশ, হুকুম ; অনুজ্ঞা। [*Bidding prayer*—Inviting a congregation to join in prayers ; উপাসকমণ্ডলীকে উপাসনার্থ আহ্বান।] **A bid for freedom**—A bold attempt at escape ; পলায়নের জন্য সাহসপূর্ণ চেষ্টা। **To bid defiance to**—To defy openly ; প্রকাশ্যে তুচ্ছ করা, তুচ্ছ করা। **To bid down**—নিলামে ডাক কমান। **To bid fair**—To seem likely ; সম্ভব বলিয়া বোধ হওয়া। **To bid up**—নিলামে ডাক চড়ান।
bīde, *v. t.* & *i.* (Poet. for *Abide.*) **To bide one's time**—To await best opportunity ; সুযোগের প্রতীক্ষা করা, সুসময়ের প্রতীক্ষা করা।
bī-ĕn′-nĭ-ăl, *adj.* & *n.* Lasting for two years ; happening once in two years ; as, a *biennial* election ; দ্বিবর্ষী, দ্বিবর্ষজীবী (সাঃ পঃ) ; দ্বৈবার্ষিক। ***Noun.*** A plant that lasts but two years ; দ্বিবর্ষজীবী উদ্ভিদ্। **—ly,** *ddv.*
bienseance, (*F.*), *n.* Decorum ; propriety ; as, much attention is paid to *bienseance* ; শীলতা, ভব্যতা ; শোভনতা।
bier (bēr), *n.* A frame used for carrying the dead ; শবযান, শবরথ, শব-শিবিকা, মরার খাটুলী।
biest′-ings (bēst-), *n.* See BEESTINGS.
bĭf′-fĭn, *n.* A variety of cooking apple ; একপ্রকার রন্ধনোপযোগী সেওফল।
bī′-fĭd, bĭf′-ĭ-dāte, *adj.* Cleft or divided into two parts ; দ্বিখণ্ডিত দ্বিধাবিভক্ত, দ্বিকর্ত্তিত (সাঃ পঃ)।
bī-flō′-rāte, bī-flō′-rous (-rŭs), *adj.* Two-flowered ; দ্বিপুষ্পপ্রসূ, দ্বিপুষ্পবিশিষ্ট।
bī′-fōld, *adj.* Two-fold ; দ্বিগুণিত, দোহারা, দ্বিবিধ।
bī-fō′-lĭ-āte, *adj.* Having two leaves ; দ্বিপত্রী (সাঃ পঃ), দ্বিপর্ণী।
bī′-fôrm, *adj.* Having two forms or bodies ; দ্বিমূর্ত্তিযুক্ত, দ্বি-আকৃতিক।
bī-fur′-cāte (-fêr-), **bī-fur′-cā-tĕd** (-fêr-), *adj.* Having two branches ; দ্বিশাখ (সাঃ পঃ), দ্বিবাহুযুক্ত।

bĭ-fur′-cāte (-fêr-), *v. i.* To divide into two branches ; দুই শাখায় বিভক্ত করা। **—ca′-tion,** *n.* A division into two branches ; the branches or one of them ; দ্বিশাখায় বিভাগ ; শাখা-সকল বা তন্মধ্যে একটী।

big, *adj.* **1.** Grown up ; large ; as, a *big* girl ; of great size or bulk ; as, *big* shop ; বয়স্ক, বড়, বৃহৎ, প্রকাণ্ড ; বিপুল, বড় ; বৃহদাকার, মহাকায়, মস্ত (*Colloq.*)। **2.** Pregnant ; as, *big* with child ; (also *fig.*) full of something important ; as, *big* with design, issue, etc. ; গুর্ব্বিণী, গর্ভিণী, সসত্বা ; (অপিচ লক্ষণায়) গুরুতর বিষয়পূর্ণ। **3.** Great ; important ; as, a *big* man ; মহান্ ; গুরুতর। **4.** Boastful ; arrogant ; as, *big* words (লম্বাচৌড়া কথা) : *big* looks : to talk *big* (লম্বাচৌড়া কথা বলা) ; দাম্ভিক ; গর্ব্বপূর্ণ, উদ্ধত। **Big′-ness,** *n.* **Big-horn**—A species of sheep inhabiting the Rocky Mountains ; রকি-পর্ব্বতচারী মেষ বিশেষ। **Big-wig**—A man of high standing or importance ; বড় মানুষ।

big′-ă-mȳ, *n.* The crime of having two wives or husbands at once ; স্বামী বা স্ত্রীর পক্ষে পরস্পরের জীবিতাবস্থায় অন্য দার বা পতি গ্রহণের অপরাধ, দ্বিপত্নীকরণ, দ্বিপতীকরণ। **—mist,** *n.* A man or woman with two wives or husbands ; দ্বিভার্য্য, দ্বিপত্নীক, দ্বিভর্ত্তৃকা, দ্বিপতিকা। **—mous,** *adj.*

bigg, big, *n.* A kind of barley ; এক প্রকার যব।

big′-gin, *n.* A child's cap ; a night cap ; শিশুর টুপী ; নিশাকালে ব্যবহার্য্য টুপি।

bight (bīt), *n.* **1.** A bend of the coast ; a small bay ; (সাগরের) বাঁক ; ক্ষুদ্র উপসাগর। **2.** A loop or coil of a rope ; রজ্জুর ফাঁস বা কুণ্ডলী।

Bĭg-nō′-ni-ă, *n.* **1.** A genus of tropical plants with trumpet-shaped flowers ; সানাই বাঁশীর মত পুষ্পবিশিষ্ট গ্রীষ্ম-মণ্ডল-জাত বিবিধ প্রকার

Bignonia.

তরুর সাধারণ নাম। (ফরাসী নৃপতি চতুর্দ্দশ লুইএর পুস্তকাগারের অধ্যক্ষ *Abbe Bignon*এর নামানুসারে।)

Bignonia Indica—মোরঙ্গ (হিন্দি—বেলঃ)।

Bignonia redicans—দ্বিকোণপুষ্প (অভিঃ)।

Bignonia suaveolnes—পারুল (বেলঃ)।

Bignonia suberosa—নীমি চাম্বেলি (হিন্দি-বেলঃ), আকাশ নীম (ঐ)।

big′-ŏt, *n.* One unreasonably or blindly devoted to a creed or party ; গোঁড়া লোক, ধর্ম্মান্ধ ব্যক্তি। **—ed,** *adj.* Unreasonably and obstinately devoted to some creed or opinion ; ধর্ম্মান্ধ, গোঁড়ামি-পূর্ণ। **—ed-ly,** *adv.* **—ry,** *n.* Blind zeal, esp. in religion ; intolerance ; ধর্ম্মান্ধতা, গোঁড়ামি ; পরমতে অসহিষ্ণুতা।

bi-jou′ (bē-zhô), (*plu.* BIJOUX), (*F.*), *n.* A trinket ; a jewel ; ক্ষুদ্র অলঙ্কার ; রত্ন। **—jou-te-rie′,** *n.* Jewelry, trinkets, etc. ; অলঙ্কার, ক্ষুদ্র অলঙ্কার প্রভৃতি।

bīke, *n.* & *v. t.* An abbreviation for BICYCLE.

bī-lā′-bi-āte, *adj.* Two-lipped ; ওষ্ঠাকার (সাঃ পঃ)।

bī-lăt′-êr-ăl, *adj.* Having two sides ; pertaining to two sides ; দ্বিপার্শ্বযুক্ত ; দ্বিপার্শ্বিক (জাহিঃ)।

bĭl-bĕr-rȳ′, *n.* A shrub and its dark blue berries ; এক প্রকার ক্ষুদ্র গুল্ম এবং তজ্জাত ঘননীলবর্ণ ফল।

bĭl′-bō, *n.* **1.** A rapier ; a sword ; কিরিচ্ ; তরবারি, তলোয়ার। **2.** (*Pl.* BILBOES.) A sort of stocks or shackles for offenders ; বন্দী বা অপরাধিগণকে বদ্ধ করার জন্য এক প্রকার তুড়ুং বা বেড়ী।

bīle, *n.* **1.** A yellow bitter fluid secreted by the liver ; পিত্ত। **2.** Anger ; peevishness ; as, to stir one's *bile* ; রাগ ; খিট্‌খিটে মেজাজ, রুক্ষ প্রকৃতি, চিড়্ চিড়ে স্বভাব। **Bil′-i-a-ry,** *adj.* Of or conveying the bile ; পিত্ত-সম্বন্ধীয়, পৈত্তিক, পিত্ত-প্রবাহী। **Bil′-ious** (î-ûs), *adj.* **1.** Pertaining to, affected by, or arising from, bile ; as, *bilious* fever, patient, etc. ; পৈত্তিক, পিত্তরোগ-গ্রস্ত, পিত্তজ, পিত্ত-বিকারগ্রস্ত। **2.** Ill-tempered ; peevish ; বদ মেজাজী (*Colloq.*) ; রুক্ষস্বভাব, খিট্‌খিটে-স্বভাব-বিশিষ্ট। **Bil′-ious-ness,** *n.* **Bile-duct**—পিত্তপ্রণালী (হঃ চঃ), পিত্তবাহীনাড়ী (ঐ)। **Bile-stone**—পিত্তনালীতে জাত কঠিন পদার্থ।

bilge (bĭlj), *n.*, *v. i.* & *t.* **1.** The protuberant part of a cask at the middle ; পিপার মধ্যভাগের স্ফীতাংশ। **2.** The breadth of a ship's bottom ; জাহাজের তলদেশের প্রস্থ। **3.** The foulness that collects in a ship's bottom ; জাহাজের তলদেশে সঞ্চিত ময়লা। ***Verb i.*** **1.** (*Naut.*) To spring a leak by a fracture from the bilge ; (নৌ-বিদ্যা) জাহাজের তলদেশ ফাটিয়া ছিদ্র বা ফুটা হওয়া। **2.** To swell out ; ফুলিয়া উঠা। ***Verb t.*** To stave in a ship's bottom ; জাহাজের তলদেশে ছিদ্র বা ফুটা করা। **Bilge-water**—The stinking water collected in the bottom of a ship ; জাহাজের তলদেশে সঞ্চিত দূষিত জল।

bĭ-lin′-gual ' (-lĭng-gwăl), *adj.* Containing, or expressed in, two languages ; as, a *bilingual* dictionary ; দ্বিভাষাবিশিষ্ট, দ্বৈভাষিক। **–guist,** *n.* One who speaks two languages ; দ্বৈভাষিক, যে ব্যক্তি দুই ভাষায় কথা বলিতে পারে।

bĭ-lĭt′-êr-ăl, *adj.* Consisting of two letters ; as, a *biliteral* root of a Sanskrit verb ; দ্বিবর্ণাত্মক, দ্ব্যক্ষর।

bilk, *v. t.* **1.** To cheat or defraud ; to evade payment of (a debt, bill, etc.) ; ভাড়ান, ছলনা করা ; পাওনাদারদিগকে ভাড়ান। **2.** To give the slip to ; to evade ; as, to *bilk* an assignation ; ফাঁকি দিয়া পালাইয়া যাওয়া ; এড়ান।

bill, *n.* & *v. i.* **1.** The beak of a bird ; চঞ্চু, চঞ্চুপুট, তুণ্ড, ত্রোটি। **2.** A narrow promontory ; as, Selsea *Bill* ; অপ্রশস্ত অন্তরীপ। **3.** (*Naut.*) The point of the fluke of an anchor ; (নৌ-বিদ্যা) নঙ্গরের নিম্নাংশ বা হুলফলা (যাহা কর্দ্দমে প্রোথিত হয়)। ***Verb i.*** To join bills, as doves ; to caress in fondness ; কপোত কপোতীর মত প্রেমাবেশে চঞ্চুতে চঞ্চু ঘর্ষণ করা ; আদর করা, সোহাগ করা। **To bill and coo**—To interchange caresses ; as doves and lovers ; পরস্পরকে আদর করা, (পক্ষি-পক্ষে) পরস্পরের চঞ্চুতে চঞ্চু ঘর্ষণ করত কুজন করা।

bill, *n.* **1.** A hook-shaped cutting instrument ; (also *bill-hook*) ; কাস্তে, দা, কর্ত্তরিকা, দাত্র (মঃ ভাঃ)।

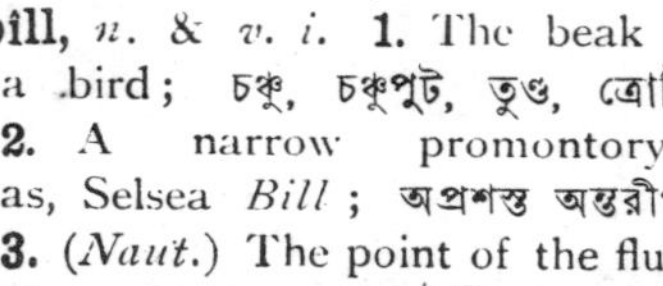

Bill.

2. An ancient military weapon ; a halberd ; পূর্ব্বকালীন যুদ্ধাস্ত্র বিশেষ ; পরশু, পট্টিশ। **Bill-man**—A soldier armed with a bill ; পট্টিশধারী।

bill, *n.* & *v. t.* **1.** The draft of a proposed Act of Parliament ; the draft of a proposed law ; পার্লেমেণ্টের প্রস্তাবিত আইনের পাণ্ডুলিপি ; কোন প্রস্তাবিত আইনের পাণ্ডুলিপি। **2.** A written statement, (esp. of a plaintiff's case) ; নালিশের আরজি, দরখাস্ত, দাবিপত্র (রঃ অঃ), ফরিয়াদ (ঐ), অভিযোগলেখ। **3.** An account of money due or of goods purchased ; দেয় টাকা বা ক্রীত জিনিষের হিসাব। **4.** A placard for advertisement ; programme ; সুবৃহৎ অক্ষরে মুদ্রিত বিজ্ঞাপন-পত্র ; কার্য্য-তালিকা। ***Verb t.*** **1.** To announce by a bill ; বিজ্ঞাপন দ্বারা ঘোষণা করা। **2.** To stick bills on ; বিজ্ঞাপন লাগান। **A true bill**—The words written by a grand jury on a bill of indictment (in accusation against a prisoner) that there is a sufficient evidence to warrant a trial ; বিলাতে অভিযোগ-পত্র প্রথমতঃ বিশেষ জুরির নিকট পেশ করা হয়—এবং মোকদ্দমা চলিতে পারে এইরূপ প্রমাণ পাইলে ঐ জুরি উক্ত পত্রের পৃষ্ঠে "True bill" এই কথাগুলি লিপিবদ্ধ করেন। **Bill at sight** ; দর্শনী হুণ্ডী (হিঃ কোঃ)। **Bill-book**—A book (in commerce) in which all bills received and accepted are entered ; বিলের খাতা। **Bill-broker**—One who negotiates the discounting of bills ; হুণ্ডীর দালাল **Bill of costs**—A statement of the charges of an attorney or solicitor in conducting a client's business ; উকীল, এটর্ণি প্রভৃতি মোক্কেলকে মোকদ্দমার খরচের যে ফর্দ্দ প্রদান করেন। **Bill of exchange**—A note which authorizes the bearer to demand a sum of money at a time and place, in consideration of value received ; হুণ্ডী, বরাত চিঠি। **Bill of fare**—The list of dishes or articles of food ready to be supplied (in a hotel) ; হোটেল বা ভোজনাগারে প্রস্তুত ব্যঞ্জনাদি ভোজ্যদ্রব্যের তালিকা। (*Fig.*) Programme ; (লক্ষণায়) কার্য্য-তালিকা। **Bill of health**—A certificate of state of health on board a ship of passengers and crew given to the captain before sailing ; জাহাজ বন্দর ত্যাগ করার পূর্ব্বে পোতাধ্যক্ষকে যাত্রী ও নাবিকগণের স্বাস্থ্য-সম্বন্ধে যে নিদর্শন পত্র দেওয়া হয়। **Bill of lading**—A ship-master's detailed receipt to consignor ; জাহাজে প্রেরিত মালের রসিদ। **Bill of mortality**—An official account of the births and deaths occurring in a certain district within a certain time ; জন্মমৃত্যুর সরকারী তালিকা। **Bill of rights**—A summary of rights and privileges claimed by a people ; কোন জাতির স্বত্ব বা বিশেষ অধিকারের সারমর্ম্ম। **Bill of sale**—A formal instrument for the conveyance or transfer of goods and chattels ; কবালা, বিক্রয়-পত্র। [*Bill of conditional sale*—কট-কবালা।] **Bill of sight**—An entry at the custom house of imported goods of which the importer does not know the quality or quantity ; মালের পরিমাণ বা রকম সম্বন্ধে জ্ঞাত না থাকিলে যে নিদর্শনপত্রের বলে আমদানীকারক শুল্কাগারের কর্ম্মচারিগণের সাক্ষাতে ঐ মাল খুলিয়া পরীক্ষা করিতে পারে। **Bill of store**—A license from the custom authorities to re-import british goods formerly exported ; রপ্তানীকৃত (বৃটিশ) মাল পুনর্ব্বার আমদানি করার জন্য শুল্কাগারের কর্ত্তৃপক্ষগণের অনুমতি-পত্র। **Bill-sticker**—One who sticks or posts up bills ; যে ব্যক্তি বিজ্ঞাপন লাগায়। **Dishonoured bill**—ফিরতা হুণ্ডী (ফঃ হিঃ)। **Duplicate of a bill**—পৈঠ (হিঃ কোঃ)। **Triplicate of a bill**—পরপৈঠ (ঐ)। **To find a true bill**—To find the charge to be true ; অভিযোগ সত্য বলিয়া নির্ণয় করা।

bil′-lĕt, *n.* & *v. t.* **1.** A small paper or note in writing ; ক্ষুদ্র লিপি, লিপিকা। **2.** An official requisition upon a person for the lodging of a soldier ; সৈনিকদিগের বাসস্থানের বন্দোবস্ত করার জন্য সরকারী পরওয়ানা। **3.** Destination ; গন্তব্যস্থান। **4.** Appointment ; situation ; চাকুরী ; পদ। ***Verb t.*** To quarter, as soldiers ; সৈনিকের বাসস্থান নির্দ্দেশ করা। **Every bullet has its billet**—(see BULLET.)

bil′-lĕt, *n.* **1.** A small log of wood used as fire-wood ; জ্বালানি কাষ্ঠের খণ্ড, ইন্ধন। **2.** A small bar of metal ; ক্ষুদ্র ধাতুর বাট। **3.** (*Arch.*) An ornament in Norman architecture resembling billets of wood either square or round ; (স্থপতি-বিদ্যা) নর্ম্মান স্থাপত্য-রীতির অনুযায়ী ক্ষুদ্র ক্ষুদ্র নলাকার বা সমচতুষ্কোণাকার স্থাপত্য-ভূষা বিশেষ।

billet doux (-dô-), (*F.*), *n.* A love-letter ; প্রেমপত্র, মদনলেখ, প্রণয়লিপি।

bil′-liards (-yêrdz), *n.* **1.** A game played with cues and ivory balls on a cloth-covered table ; দণ্ড এবং হস্তিদন্ত-নির্ম্মিত ক্ষুদ্র ক্ষুদ্র কন্দুকদ্বারা বস্ত্রাচ্ছাদিত ফলকোপরি ক্রীড়াবিশেষ, বিলিয়ার্ড খেলা। **Billiard-marker**—One who attends on players at billiards and records the progress of the same ; যে ব্যক্তি বিলিয়ার্ড ক্রীড়কদিগের সঙ্গে থাকিয়া ক্রীড়ার ফলাফল লিপিবদ্ধ করিয়া থাকে।

bil′-lings-gate, *n.* Foul abusive language ; as, to deal in *billingsgate* ; ইতর ভাষা, অশ্লীল ভাষা, কুৎসিত গালি। [লণ্ডননগরীস্থ Billingsgate নামক মৎস্যের বাজারের মৎস্য-বিক্রেত্রীদিগের অশ্লীল কথাবার্ত্তা হইতে এই শব্দটী উক্ত অর্থে গৃহীত হইয়াছে।]

bil′-lion (-yŏn), *n.* **1.** A million of millions ; নিখর্ব্ব। **2.** (In U. S.) A thousand millions ; (মার্কিণ যুক্তরাজ্যে) বৃন্দ। **—aire′,** *n.* নিখর্ব্ব বা বৃন্দ সংখ্যক ধন- (ডলার বা পাউণ্ড) পতি।

bil′-low (-lö), *n.* & *v. i.* **1.** A great wave or surge of the sea ; উত্তাল তরঙ্গ, কল্লোল, সাগর-লহরী। **2.** (*Poet.*) The sea ; (কবিতায়) কল্লোলমালী, সাগর। **3.** A great wave or flood of anything ; মেঘ, অগ্নি, সৈন্য প্রভৃতির কল্লোল বা প্লাবন। ***Verb i.*** To roll in large waves ; move in billows ; কল্লোলিত হওয়া; কল্লোলে কল্লোলে প্রবাহিত হওয়া। **—lowed,** *adj.* **—y,** *adj.*

bil′-lȳ, *n.* **1.** A policeman's club ; পুলিশ কনেষ্টবলের যষ্টি। **2.** (*Austral.*) A kettle ; (অষ্ট্রেলিয়ায়) কটাহবিশেষ, কেটলী।

bil′-lȳ, *n.* A companion at arms ; সমর-সহচর, সহযোধ।

bil′-lȳ-boy, *n.* An one-masted flat-bottomed trading ship ; এক-মাস্তুলবিশিষ্ট প্রশস্ততল বাণিজ্যপোতবিশেষ।

bil′-lȳ-cŏck, *n.* A kind of round-crowned felt hat ; (পুরুষের ব্যবহার্য্য) এক প্রকার গোলাকৃতি নেমদার টুপী।

bil′-lȳ-goat, (-göt) *n.* A male goat ; পাঁঠা, ছাগ।

bī-lö′-bāte, bī′-lobed (-lōbd), **bī-lŏ-bü-lar** (-lêr), *adj.* Having two lobes ; as, a *bilobate* leaf ; দ্বিখণ্ড-যুক্ত, দ্বিখণ্ডিত (সাঃ পঃ)।

bī-lŏc′-ü-lar (-lêr), *adj.* Divided into two cells or compartments ; দ্বিকোষ্ঠ, দ্বিগর্ভ (সাঃ পঃ)।

bil′-tŏng, *n.* Strips of sundried meat ; রৌদ্রে শুষ্ক মাংসের ফালি।

bĭm′-ă-nă, *n.* An animal having two hands ; দ্বিহস্তপ্রাণী, দ্বিকরী

bĭm′-ă-nous (-nŭs), **bĭm′-ă-năl,** *adj.* Having two hands or two-handed ; দ্বিহস্তবিশিষ্ট।

bim′-bö, *n.* A kind of punch ; জল মদিরাদিদ্বারা প্রস্তুত পানীয় বিশেষ।

bī-mĕt′-ăl-lism, *n.* A system of coinage in which two metals (usually gold and silver) are used at a fixed relative value one to another ; যে মুদ্রা-ব্যবহারের পদ্ধতিতে পরস্পরের আপেক্ষিক মূল্য নির্দ্ধারিত দুইটী ধাতু (সাধারণতঃ স্বর্ণ ও রৌপ্য) ব্যবহৃত হইয়া থাকে। **—lic,** *adj.* **—list,** *n.* An advocate of bimetallism ; দ্বিধাতু পরিমাণবাদী (হিঃ কোঃ)।

bī-mŏnth′-lȳ, *adj.* Once in two months ; (also) twice a month ; as, a *bimonthly* magazine ; দ্বৈমাসিক (দুই মাসে একবার) ; পাক্ষিক।

bĭn, *n.* **1.** A receptacle for corn, coal, dust, bottled wine, etc. ; as, a coal *bin* ; শস্য, কয়লা, বালি, মদ্য-বোতল প্রভৃতির পাত্র বা স্থালী। **2.** The wine from a special bin ; বিশেষ আধারে রক্ষিত মদিরা। **3.** A partition in a cellar for wine-bottles ; মদিরাপূর্ণ বোতল সকল রক্ষণার্থ ভূনিম্নস্থ মদ্য-ভাণ্ডারের প্রকোষ্ঠ বিশেষ।

bī′-nă-rȳ, *adj.* Compounded or composed of two ; twofold ; double ; involving pairs ; দুই বস্তুর মিশ্রণে উৎপন্ন, দুই বস্তু দ্বারা গঠিত ; দ্বিগুণিত ; দ্বিগুণ ; যুগলাত্মক। **Binary compound**—দুইটী মূল পদার্থের মিশ্র, অথবা একটী মূল-পদার্থ এবং তৎসদৃশ ক্রিয়াশীল একটী যৌগিক পদার্থের মিশ্র, কিম্বা মৌলিক পদার্থের মত ক্রিয়াশীল দুইটী যৌগিক পদার্থের মিশ্র, দ্বৈদেহিক সম্মিলন (হিঃ কোঃ)। **Binary stars**—পরস্পরের অথবা উভয়ের সাধারণ গুরুত্ব কেন্দ্রের চতুর্দ্দিকে আবর্ত্তনশীল নক্ষত্র-যুগল। **Binary theory**—যে রাসায়নিকবাদ অনুসারে উদজানবাষ্প যাবতীয় দ্রাবক পদার্থের, এবং ধাতুসমূহ সমগ্র লবণ পদার্থের উপাদান বলিয়া গৃহীত হইয়া থাকে।

bī′-nāte, *adj.* Growing in pairs ; double ; যুগ্ম ; দ্বিগুণিত।

bīnd, *v. t., i.* & *n.* **1.** To tie ; বন্ধন করা, বাঁধা। **2.** To restrain ; to confine ; আটক করা ; রুদ্ধ করা, আবদ্ধ করা। **3.** To encircle round, (*about, with*) ; to wreathe (head etc.) with something (*round, on*) ; জড়ান, বেষ্টন করা ; মাল্য প্রভৃতি দ্বারা বেষ্টিত করা। **4.** To tie up or put a bandage on ; as, to *bind* up a wound ; পট্টি বান্ধা, বস্ত্রবন্ধনী বাঁধা। **5.** To sew together and put a cover ; as, to *bind* a book ; পুস্তক বাঁধা, জিল করা। **6.** To lay under an obligation ; কৃতজ্ঞতাপাশে বদ্ধ করা। **7.** (*Law.*) To place under legal obligation ; to indenture ; as, to *bind* an apprentice: to *bind* one to appear in court ; (আইন) আইন-গঠিত দায়িত্বের অধীন করা ; চুক্তি-পত্র দ্বারা (নির্দ্দিষ্ট সময়ের জন্য কায করিতে) বদ্ধ করা। **8.** To ratify ; as, to *bind* a bargain ; পাকা করা, দৃঢ় করা, বলবৎ করা। **9.** To make costive ; as, certain drugs *bind* the bowels ; কোষ্ঠবদ্ধ করা। **10.** To sew a border on ; as, to *bind* a garment or carpet ; সেলাই করিয়া (পাড়, ফিতা প্রভৃতি) লাগান। ***Verb i.*** **1.** To cohere in a mass ; as, clay *binds* by heat ; একত্র লগ্ন হওয়া, খণ্ড-সংশ্লেষ হওয়া। **2.** To grow hard or stiff ; দৃঢ় বা শক্ত হইয়া উঠা। **3.** To be obligatory ; অবশ্য-পালনীয় হওয়া। **4.** To produce constipation ; কোষ্ঠ-কাঠিন্য জন্মান। **5.** To tie up, especially to tie sheaves up ; "They that reap must sheaf and *bind* ;" বাঁধা, বিশেষতঃ ঘাস প্রভৃতির আটি বাঁধা। ***Noun.*** **1.** Indurated clay between coal strata ; কয়লার স্তরসমূহের মধ্যবর্ত্তী কঠিনীভূত মৃত্তিকা। **2.** (*Bot.*) See BINE. **3.** (*Mus.*) A curved line between two notes to be sounded continuously ; (সঙ্গীত-শাস্ত্র) স্বরলিপিতে ক্রমান্বয়ে বাজাইবার দুইটী সুরের মধ্যবর্ত্তী বক্র-রেখা। **Bind′-er,** *n.* **1.** One who binds ; বন্ধনকারী। **2.** A book-binder ; যে ব্যক্তি পুস্তক বাঁধে, দপ্তরী। **3.** One who binds sheaves of grain ; যে ব্যক্তি শস্যের আটি বাঁধে। **4.** Anything that binds, as cord, rope or band ; a bandage ; দড়ি, রশি, প্রভৃতি যাহা দ্বারা বাঁধা যায় ; পট্টি, বস্ত্র-বন্ধনী। **5.** Tie-beam ; গৃহের যে আড়কাঠায় স্তম্ভ সকল আবদ্ধ থাকে। **6.** A broad bandage applied around the abdomen after delivery ; প্রসবান্তে উদরে বন্ধনার্থ বন্ধনী বিশেষ। **7.** A kind of long fencing-withe or flexible twigs ; বেড়া বাঁধিবার লম্বা কঞ্চির ছোট বেতি বা সরু নরম ডাল। **8.** A wisp of straw for binding sheaves ; the part of a reaping-machine for tying bundles of grain ; শস্যের আটি বাঁধিবার তৃণরজ্জু ; শস্য-কর্ত্তক যন্ত্রের যে অংশে শস্যের আটি বাঁধা হয়। **9.** A loose cover for unbound newspapers, etc. ; সংবাদ-পত্র প্রভৃতির মোড়ক বা আবরণ। **Bind′-er-y,** *n.* A book-binder's establishment ; দপ্তরীর কারখানা, পুস্তকবাঁধাইর দোকান। **Bind′-ing,** *adj.* & *n.* **1.** Restraining ; obligatory ; দমনকারী ; অবশ্য-করণীয়। **2.** Astringent ; কোষ্ঠকাঠিন্যজনক। (*Noun.*) **1.** Bandage ; বস্ত্রবন্ধনী। **2.** Cover of a book ; পুস্তকের মলাট। **Half-bound**—Bound with leather at the back and corners only ; (পুস্তকের) কেবল পৃষ্ঠ এবং কোণসকল চামড়াদ্বারা বাঁধানো। **I will be bound**—I will be responsible for the statement ; আমি এই উক্তির জন্য দায়ী থাকিব। **To bind down**—মুচলেকাদ্বারা বদ্ধ করা। **To bind in**—(*Lit.* & *fig.*) To inclose ; to surround ; "A costly jewel *bound in* with diamonds ;" (শব্দানুযায়ী এবং লক্ষণায়) পরিবেষ্টিত করা ; ঘেরা, বলয়িত করা। **To bind over**—To put under bonds to do something, as to appear in court, to keep the peace, etc. ; আদালতে উপস্থিতি, শান্তিরক্ষা প্রভৃতির জন্য মুচলেকায় আবদ্ধ করা। **To bind to**—To contract ; চুক্তিদ্বারা আবদ্ধ করা। **To bind up in**—To cause to be wholly engrossed with ; to be absorbed in ; "Seeing that his life is *bound up in* the lad's life ;" অভিনিবিষ্ট করা ; নিমগ্ন থাকা।

bīnd′-weed (-wēd), *n.* Kinds of convolvulus and other climbing plants ; হরিণপদী লতা, কলমী শাক, প্রভৃতি।

bīne, *n.* The slender stem of a climbing plant ; (written also *bind*) ; আরোহী বা বৃক্ষাশ্রয়ী উদ্ভিদের কোমল কাণ্ড।

bĭn′-nă-cle, *n.* The compass-box of a ship ; জাহাজের দিগ্‌দর্শনযন্ত্র-রক্ষণার্থ আধার।

bĭn′-ŏ-cle, *n.* See BINOCULAR.

bĭn-ŏc′-ū-lar (-lêr), *adj.* & *n.* Adapted for two eyes ; উভয় নেত্রদ্বারা দর্শনোপযোগী, দ্বিনেত্রিক। ***Noun.*** A field or opera-glass for using with both eyes at once ; দুনলী দুরবীণ (হিঃ কোঃ)। **–ly,** *adv.*

bī-nō′-mi-ăl, *n.* & *adj.* (*In algebra*) An expression or quantity of two terms connected by the sign + or – ; (বীজগণিতে) যোগ বা বিয়োগ চিহ্নদ্বারা সংযুক্ত দ্বিমান বা দ্বিমাত্রা বিশিষ্ট বীজগণিতের রাশি। ***Adj.*** Consisting of two terms ; দ্বৈরাশিক। **Binomial co-efficient**—দ্বিপদগুণক (হিঃ কোঃ)। **Binomial equation**—দ্বিপদ সমীকরণ (ঐ)। **Binomial expression**—দ্বিপদমান (ঐ)। **Binomial theorem**—দ্বিপদ সিদ্ধান্ত (ঐ)।

bī-ō-gĕn′-ĕ-sis, bī-ŏg′-ĕ-nȳ, *n.* The doctrine that living matter arises always from living matter ; কেবলমাত্র জীব হইতেই জীবের উৎপত্তি হইতে পারে—এইরূপ মত, জীবাৎ জীবোৎপত্তি (সাঃ পঃ), জীবজনি (হিঃ কোঃ)।

bī-ō-grăph-ee′ (-ē), *n.* A person whose life is written ; যে ব্যক্তির জীবনী লিখিত হয়।

bī-ŏg′-ră-phȳ, *n.* **1.** The written life of a person ; জীবনচরিত, জীবন-বৃত্তান্ত, চরিতাখ্যান, জীবনবৃত্ত, জীবনী। **2.** The branch of literature dealing with the lives of persons ; জীবনচরিতবিষয়ক সাহিত্যের শাখা। **3.** The life history of any living being ; যে কোন প্রাণীর জীবনের ইতিহাস। **–o-graph′-ic, –o-graph′-i-cal,** *adjs.* **–pher,** *n.* A writer of lives ; জীবনীলেখক, চরিতাখ্যায়ক, জীবনীকার।

bī-ŏl′-ō-ġy̆, *n.* The science of life ; জীব-তত্ত্ব, জীব-বিজ্ঞান, জীব-বিদ্যা, জীবন-বিদ্যা। **–gist,** *n.* **–o-log′-ic, –o-log′-i-cal,** *adjs.* **–o-log′-i-cal-ly,** *adv.*

bī′-ō-plăsm, –plăst *n.* Germinal matter ; জীবন-পদার্থ।

bī′-ō-scōpe, bī′-ō-grăph, *n.* An animated picture machine for screen projection ; যে যন্ত্রের সাহায্যে মনুষ্য, পশু, পক্ষী প্রভৃতির জীবন্ত চিত্র প্রদর্শিত হয়, জীবন্ত-চিত্র প্রদর্শক যন্ত্র।

bĭp′-ă-rous (-rŭs), *adj.* Bringing forth two at a birth ; যমজ-প্রসূ, যুগলপ্রসবকারিণী।

bĭp′-âr-tīte, *adj.* Divided into two parts ; having two corresponding parts ; দ্বিখণ্ডিত ; পরস্পরের অনুরূপ অংশদ্বয়বিশিষ্ট।

bī′-pĕd, *n.* & *adj.* An animal having two feet, as man ; দ্বিপদ জীব। ***Adj.*** Having two feet ; দ্বিপাদ। (Also BIPEDAL).

H. Farman's biplane.

bī′-plāne, *n.* An aeroplane made of two planes, one above the other ; এক প্রকার আকাশযান, ইহাতে উপরি উপরি দুইটি সমতল মঞ্চ আছে।

bī-pō′-lar (-lêr), *adj.* Having two poles ; দ্বিধ্রুবীয় (হিঃ কোঃ)।

bī-quăd-răt′-ic, *n.* & *adj.* A quantity twice squared or raised to the fourth power ; বর্গের বর্গ। ***Adj.*** Of the fourth power ; চতুর্গুণিত। **Biquadratic equation**—দ্বিবর্গাত্মক সমীকরণ।

birch (bêrch), *n.* & *v. t.* **1.** A tree common in England ; ইংলণ্ডদেশীয় বৃক্ষ বিশেষ, ভুর্জ্জ বৃক্ষ। **2.** A twig or bundle of its twigs used for flogging school-boys ; উক্ত বৃক্ষের ক্ষুদ্র শাখা বা শাখা-গুচ্ছ-নির্ম্মিত গুরু-মহাশয়ের বেত্র। ***Verb t.*** To flog with a birch ; to flog ; উক্ত তরু-শাখা নির্ম্মিত বেত্রদ্বারা আঘাত করা ; বেত্রাঘাত করা। **Birch′-en,** *adj.*

bird (bêrd), *n.* & *v. i.* **1.** The name of the feathered race ; পক্ষী, খগ, বিহঙ্গম, অণ্ডজ, দ্বিজ, বিহগ, পাখী খগচর, পতত্র, পতগ, শকুন্ত, গরুত্মৎ **2.** (*Fig.*) A girl ; a maiden

"And by my word ! the bonny *bird*
In danger shall not tarry."

(লক্ষণায়) বালিকা, কুমারী ; তরুণী। ***Verb i.*** To catch or snare birds ; পক্ষী ধরা, ফাঁদ পাতিয়া পাখী ধরা। **Bird-cage**—A cage for birds ; পিঞ্জর, পঞ্জর, কুলায়িকা। **Bird-call**—An instrument for imitating the cry of birds in order to allure or decoy them ; পক্ষীদিগকে প্রলুব্ধ বা জালবদ্ধ করণার্থ পক্ষিরবানুকারী বংশীবিশেষ। **Bird-catcher**—One who catches birds ; পক্ষি-শিকারী, পাশী (অপঃ), শাকুল (বৃঃ সং)। **Bird-cherry**—A species of wild shrub bearing fruits fit only for birds ; এক প্রকার গুল্ম,—ইহার ফল পক্ষিগণ আহার করিয়া থাকে। **Bird-fancier**—One who collects, breeds and deals in birds ; পক্ষী-সংগ্রাহক, পক্ষিব্যবসায়ী, বিহঙ্গপালক। **Birding-piece**—A fowling piece ; পক্ষিশিকারার্থ ক্ষুদ্র বন্দুকবিশেষ। **Bird-lime**—A sticky stuff spread on twigs to catch birds ; এক প্রকার আঠা—ইহা ডালে লাগাইয়া পক্ষী ধৃত করা হয়। **Bird of Jove**—The eagle ; উৎক্রোশ পক্ষী। **Bird of Juno**—The peacock ; ময়ূর। **Bird of Paradise**—A kind of bird of New Guinea and adjacent islands with splendid plumage ; নন্দনপক্ষী। **Bird of prey**—ভাস (অঃ)। **Bird's-eye**—A kind of manufactured tobacco ; এক প্রকার সূক্ষ্মভাবে কর্ত্তিত তৈয়ারী তামাক। **Bird's-eye view**—A general view (of town, district) from above as might appear to a flying bird ; a resume of a subject ; ক্ষিপ্র দর্শন, (উড্ডীয়মান পক্ষীর মত) উপরি উপরি দেখা, মোটা-মুটি দেখা, ভাসা ভাসা দেখা ; (কোন বিষয়ের) সংক্ষিপ্তসার। **Bird's nest**—পাখীর বাসা, নীড়, কুলায়। **Bird-witted**—Flighty ; চঞ্চল। Passing rapidly from one subject to another ; অস্থির-চিত্ত। **A bird of ill omen**—A person who is regarded as unlucky ; ভাগ্যহীন পুরুষ, অভাগা। One who is in the habit of bringing ill news ; কুসংবাদবাহক, দুর্ম্মুখ। **A bird of passage**—A migratory bird ; প্রব্রজনশীল পক্ষী। (*Fig.*) One who shifts from place to place ; (লক্ষণায়) যে ব্যক্তি সর্ব্বদা স্থান পরিবর্ত্তন করে। **Birds of a feather**—People of like character ; সম-প্রকৃতির লোক, সমভাবের লোক। [*Birds of a feather flock together*—চোরে চোরে মাসতুতো ভাই, "ভাবো ভাবং নিগচ্ছতি"।] **A bird in hand is worth two in the bush**—A certainty is better than contingency ; হস্তগত একটী বস্তু সম্ভাবিত দুইটী অপেক্ষা আদরণীয়, বরং অদ্য কপোতঃ শ্বঃ ময়ূরাৎ (বাৎস্যঃ)। **A little bird told me**—I came to learn it in a way I will not reveal ; কি ভাবে কথাটা আমি জানিতে পারিলাম, তাহা আমি প্রকাশ করিব না। **Jail-bird**—See JAIL **To kill two birds with one stone**—To gain two ends at once ; এক ঢিলে দুই পাখী মারা, একসঙ্গে রথ দেখা ও কলা বেচা।

bī′-rēme, *n.* An ancient vessel with two tiers of oars ; দুই সারি দাঁড় বিশিষ্ট প্রাচীন কালীন দীর্ঘ পোত বিশেষ।

bi-rĕt′-tă (bē-), **ber-rĕt′-tă** (bā-), *n.* A square cap worn by some of the clergy ; ধর্ম্মযাজকদিগের সমচতুষ্কোণ টুপী বিশেষ।

birth (bêrth), *n.* **1.** The act of being born, (generally applied to human beings) ; as, the *birth* of a son ; জন্ম, উৎপত্তি, সম্ভব (কুমাঃ)। **2.** The dignity of a family ; noble lineage ; "Elected without reference to *birth*, but solely for qualifications ;" বংশমর্য্যাদা, কুল-গৌরব ; কৌলিন্য। **3.** The act of bringing forth ; as, she had two children at a *birth* ; প্রসব, উৎপাদন, জনন। **4.** That which is born or produced ; জাতক বা জাতবস্তু। **5.** Origin ; beginning ; as, the *birth* of an empire ; মূল, উৎপত্তি, উদ্ভব, যোনি, আদি ; প্রারম্ভ, সূত্রপাত। **Birth-day**—The day of one's birth ; the anniversary of that day ; জন্মদিন, জন্মতিথি ; জন্মোৎসব। **Birth-day book**—A book for entering friends' birth-days ; যে পুস্তকে বন্ধুগণের জন্মদিন লিপিবদ্ধ করা হয়। **Birth-day honours**—Titles given on the king's birth-day ; রাজার জন্মদিন উপলক্ষে প্রদত্ত উপাধি। **Birth-day presents**—Presents given on one's birth-day ; জন্মদিনের উপহার। **Birth-mark**—A mark on one's body at or from birth ; জাতকের জন্ম-চিহ্ন। **Birthplace**—Place where one is born ; জন্মস্থান, জন্মভূমি, জন্মক্ষেত্র (কথা সঃ)। **Birth-rate**—Percentage of birth to population of a country ; দেশের লোকসংখ্যার অনুপাতে জন্ম-সংখ্যা। **Birthright**—The rights to which one is born ; the rights belonging to one as a human being ; as, liberty is the *birthright* of the human species ; জন্মগত অধিকার, জন্মজাতস্বত্ব ; মানব বলিয়া মানবের যে অধিকার তাহা। **Birthwort**—ঈশেরমূল (বনঃ)। **At a birth**—একবার প্রসবে। **By birth**—কুলে, বংশে, জাতিতে। **Blind from birth**—জন্মান্ধ। **New birth**—Re-generation or commencement of a religious life ; নবজীবন, ধর্ম্ম-জীবনারম্ভ। **Of high birth**—কুলীন, মহাকুলজাত। **Pride of birth**—কুলাভিমান। **To give birth to**—To produce ; জন্মদান করা, প্রসব করা।

bĭs′-cuit (-kĕt), *n.* **1.** A kind of hard dry bread in small cakes ; একপ্রকার শুষ্ক কঠিন রুটি, বিস্কুট। **2.** Porcelain or earthenware after baking, but before glazing and painting ; বর্ণক লাগান (কাচের সূক্ষ্ম স্তরদ্বারা আচ্ছাদন) এবং চিত্রণের পূর্ব্বাবস্থায় মাটী বা চীনামাটীর বাসন। **A biscuit-throw**—A short distance ; অল্পদূর। **Meat-biscuit**—মাংসমিশ্রিত বা মাংসপূরিত বিস্কুট।

bise (bēz), *n.* A keen dry North-wind in Switzerland and South France ; সুইজারলণ্ড বা ফরাসীদেশের দক্ষিণভাগে প্রবহমান একপ্রকার শুষ্ক কন্‌কনে উত্তর পবন।

bī-sĕct′, *v. t.* To cut or divide into two equal parts ; সমদ্বিখণ্ডিত করা, সমদ্বিভাগ করা। **—sec′-tion,** *n.* The act of dividing into two equal parts ; সমদ্বিখণ্ডীকরণ, সমদ্বি-ভাগ (হিঃ কোঃ)। **—sec′-tor,** *n.* The bisecting or dividing line ; সমদ্বিখণ্ডকারী রেখা।

bī-sĕx′-ū-ăl, *adj.* Having the organs of both sexes in one individual ; দ্বিলিঙ্গ (সাঃ পঃ), (পুষ্প-সম্বন্ধে) পুংকেশর এবং গর্ভকেশর বিশিষ্ট, (জীব-সম্বন্ধে) ডিম্বাশয় এবং মুষ্কবিশিষ্ট।

bish′-op (-ŭp), *n.* **1.** The spiritual head or governor of a diocese ; খৃষ্টীয়-ধর্ম্মাধ্যক্ষ। **2.** A mitre-shaped piece in the game of chess ; (দাবা-খেলায়) পিল, গজ। **3.** A beverage, being a mixture of wine, oranges or lemons, and sugar ; মদিরা, কমলা বা পাতিলেবু এবং শর্করাসহযোগে প্রস্তুত সরবতবিশেষ। **—ric,** *n.* The office and jurisdiction of a bishop ; বিশপের পদ বা অধিকার। **Bishop's-weed seed** — জোয়ান (বেলঃ)। **The bishop has put his foot in it**—Said of milk or porridge that is burnt, or meat over-roasted ; পোড়া লাগা দুধ ও মণ্ডাদি এবং ভাজায় পোড়া-লাগা মাংস-সম্বন্ধে কথিত হয়। [পূর্ব্বকালীন খৃষ্টীয়-ধর্ম্মাচার্য্যগণের বিধর্ম্মিদহনে জলন্ত উৎসাহ হইতে গৃহীত।]

bis′-mŭth (bĭs- or bĭz-), *n.* A red-dish white metal ; রক্তাভ শ্বেতধাতু বিশেষ, বিস্মিতক (সাঃ পঃ), বিষমদ (মনীঃ)।

bī′-sŏn, *n.* A kind of wild ox of North America ; উত্তর আমেরিকা-দেশীয় বন্য বৃষবিশেষ, গয়াল (লিডেকার), বন-গো (বেলঃ), গৌরী গাই (হিন্দি)।

bisque (bĭsk), *n.* (*In tennis*) The right of scoring one point without winning it at any time in the set ; টেনিসে এক প্রস্থ খেলায় যে অঙ্কসমূহ লব্ধ হয়—তদতিরিক্ত এক অঙ্ক লাভের অধিকার।

bisque (bĭsk), *n.* (A corruption of *biscuit.*) Unglazed white-porcelain ; কাচের সূক্ষ্ম স্তরদ্বারা অনাচ্ছাদিত শ্বেতবর্ণ চীনা মাটি।

bĭs-sĕx′-tĭle, *n.* A leap-year ; ইংরাজী (৩৬৬ দিনের) প্রতি চতুর্থ বৎসর—যখন ফেব্রুয়ারী মাস ২৯ দিনে ধরা হয়, অধিবর্ষ (হিঃ কোঃ), বৃদ্ধি বর্ষ (খঃ)।

bĭs′-têr, —tre, *n.* & *adj.* A dark-brown pigment prepared from soot ; কজ্জল হইতে প্রস্তুত গাঢ় পিঙ্গল-বর্ণ রঞ্জন-পদার্থ।

bis′-tou′-rȳ (-tū-), *n.* A surgeon's scalpel ; অস্ত্র-চিকিৎসকের ছুরিকাবিশেষ।

bĭt, *n.* **1.** A small piece or morsel of food ; এক কামড়, এক গ্রাস (খাদ্য)। **2.** A small piece of anything ; a fragment ; a part ; টুকরা ; খণ্ড ; অংশ। **3.** Any small coin ; as, four penny-*bit* ; সিকি, দোয়ানি প্রভৃতি ক্ষুদ্র মুদ্রা। **4.** A piece of scenery actual or painted ; "There are several *bits* at Volmontone to delight an artist ;" বাস্তব বা চিত্রিত দৃশ্য। **5.** A short passage in a book ; কোন পুস্তকের ক্ষুদ্র অংশ। **6.** Somewhat ; as, he was a *bit* of a poet ; অল্পকিছু, কতকটা। **7.** A little while ; as, wait a *bit* ; অল্পক্ষণ। **A bit of**—Rather ; বরং। **Bit by bit**—Piecemeal ; gradually ; খণ্ডশঃ ; ক্রমশঃ। **A bit of one's mind**—A good scolding ; তীব্র তিরস্কার। *To give a bit of one's mind*—To speak candidly ; অকপটে মনোভাব প্রকাশ করা, প্রাণ খুলিয়া কথা বলা।] **Not a bit of it**—By no means ; কোন ক্রমেই নহে, আদবেই না।

bĭt, *n.* & *v. t.* **1.** The iron of a bridle ; লাগামের লৌহময় অংশ, খলীনঃ (পঞ্চতঃ), আধান (তৈত্তিঃ সং)। **2.** The boring piece of a drill ; তুরপুণ যন্ত্রের যে লৌহময় অংশদ্বারা ছিদ্র করা হয়। **3.** The cutting iron of a plane ; রেঁদার যে লৌহময় অংশদ্বারা কাটা যায়। **4.** The part of a key which enters the lock ; চাবির যে অংশ তালার ভিতরে প্রবিষ্ট করান হয়। **5.** The cutting part of pincers ; সাঁড়াশীর যে অংশদ্বারা কাটা যায়। ***Verb t.*** **1.** To put bit in the mouth (of horses) ; (ঘোড়ার) মুখে খলীন লাগান। **2.** To restrain ; সংযত রাখা, বশে রাখা। **3.** To accustom to the bit ; খলীনে অভ্যস্ত করা। **To draw bit**—To stop ones horse by pulling at the rein ; hence, to stop or slacken speed ; লাগাম টানিয়া ঘোড়া থামান ; অতএব থামান বা গতির বেগ হ্রাস করা। **To take the bit in the teeth**—To go beyond restraint ; দুর্দ্দান্ত হইয়া উঠা।

bitch (bĭch), *n.* **1.** The female of the dog, wolf, fox, etc., (usually, bitch-fox, bitch-wolf) ; কুক্কুরী, শৃগালিকা, নেকড়াবাঘিনী। **2.** A harlot ; "Him you call a dog and her a *bitch* ;" বেশ্যা।

bīte, *v. t., i.* & *n.* **1.** To seize or crush with the teeth ; দংশন করা, দন্তদ্বারা ছেদন করা, দন্তবিদ্ধ করা। **2.** To sting or suck, (of serpent, flea, etc.) ; (সর্পাদি-সম্বন্ধে) ছোবল মারা, (মশকাদির পক্ষে) রক্ত চুষা, কামড়ান। **3.** (*Lit.* & *fig.*) To cause sharp pain to ; as, pepper *bites* the mouth ; (শব্দানুযায়ী এবং লক্ষণায়) তীব্র যন্ত্রণা দেওয়া। **4.** To corrode or blight ; as, *air-bitten* ; *frost-bitten* ; ক্রমশঃ ক্ষয় করা, খাইয়া ফেলা, মুশড়াইয়া দেওয়া। **5.** (*Colloq.*) To cheat ; "The workman saw my ignorance and *bit* me as they pleased ;" (চলিতভাষায়) ঠকান। ***Verb i.*** **1.** To wound with the teeth ; দংশন করা। **2.** To be pungent ; as, it *bites* like pepper ; ঝাল বোধ হওয়া। **3.** To take a bait into the mouth, as a fish does ; to take a tempting offer ; টোপ গেলা ; প্রলোভনে পড়া। **4.** To hold fast ; as, the anchor *bites* ; দৃঢ়রূপে সংবদ্ধ হওয়া। ***Noun.*** **1.** The grasp of anything by the teeth or mouth ; দংশন, কামড়ান। **2.** The wound made by the teeth or other organ of the mouth ; দশনক্ষত, দন্তক্ষত। **3.** A morsel of food ; as, a *bite* of bread ; এক গ্রাস খাদ্য। **4.** A piece bitten out ; কামড়াইয়া কাটা টুকরা। **5.** The taking of bait by fish ; মৎস্যের টোপ গ্রাসকরণ। **6.** (*Lit.* & *fig.*) A grip ; a hold ; (শব্দানুযায়ী এবং লক্ষণায়) শক্তরূপে ধরণ ; ধৃতি। **7.** A trick or cheat ; চাতুরী, ছলনা। **Bit'-er,** *n.* **1.** One who bites ; দংশনকারী। **2.** A cheat ; a swindler ; "The *biter* bit ;" ঠক ; শঠ। **To bite in**—To corrode copper or steel-plates, as nitric acid does in the process of etching ; তামা বা ইস্পাতের পাত খাইয়া দেওয়া (সাধারণতঃ তাম্রদ্রাবদ্বারা রেখা অঙ্কিত করিয়া ঐরূপ করা হইয়া থাকে)। **To bite one's lips**—To control one's anger, etc. ; দন্তদ্বারা ওষ্ঠাধর চাপিয়া ক্রোধ প্রভৃতি দমন করা। **To bite the dust** or **ground**—To fall and die ; to be defeated ; ধরাশায়ী হইয়া মৃত্যুমুখে পতিত হওয়া ; পরাভূত হওয়া। **To bite the thumb at**—To show contempt for ; বৃদ্ধাঙ্গুষ্ঠ প্রদর্শন করা

bīt'-ing, *adj.* **1.** Apt to bite ; দংশনোন্মুখ। **2.** Causing sharp pain ; as, a *biting* jest ; sharp ; severe ; pungent ; sarcastic ; তীব্র যন্ত্রণাপ্রদ, মর্ম্মান্তিক ; তীব্র ; উগ্র ; কটু ; বিদ্রূপাত্মক।

bit'-tēr, *adj.* & *n.* **1.** Tasting like wormwood or quinine ; তিক্ত। **2.** Piercing ; severe ; as, a *bitter* cold day ; কনকনে ; দারুণ, যন্ত্রণাদায়ক। **3.** Harsh ; as, a *bitter* reproach ; relentless ; কর্কশ ; নির্দ্দয়, নিষ্করুণ। **4.** Causing grief ; দুঃখদায়ক। ***Noun.*** **1.** Any substance having a bitter taste ; তিক্তবস্তু। **2.** (*Pl.*) Liquor impregnated with wormwood etc., taken as stomachics ; অগ্নিবৃদ্ধিকর তিক্ত পানীয় ঔষধ। **—ish,** *adj.* Somewhat bitter ; ঈষৎ তিক্ত। **—ly,** *adv.* **—ness,** *n.* **1.** Hatred ; enmity ; বিদ্বেষ ; শত্রুতা। **2.** Sorrow ; deep distress ; সন্তাপ ; মহা বিড়ম্বনা। **Bitter-beer**—Same as BITTER (in the plural). **Bitter-gourd**—উচ্ছে (প্রবোধ)। **Bitter-sweet**—The Woody Nightshade ; একজাতীয় বিষাক্ত গুল্ম। **To the bitter end**—To the last extremity ; শেষ বা চরমসীমা পর্য্যন্ত।

bit′-têrn, *n.* A bird of the heron kind ; ক্রৌঞ্চ।

bi-tü′-mên, *n.* A name applied to various inflammable mineral substances, as naphtha, petroleum, asphaltum ; অশ্ম (রঃ রঃ সঃ প্রঃ), অদ্রিজ (ঐ), শিলাজতু (ঐ), শিলাধাতু (ঐ), গিরিজতু (রঃ প্রঃ), গিরিসানুজ (ঐ), গিরি (ঐ), শৈলজ (ঐ), শৈলেয় (বৃঃ সং), শিলাঞ্জন (সুশ্রুঃ)। **—mi-nate, —mi-nize,** *vs. t.* **—mi-na-ted, —mi-nous, —mi-nif′-er-ous,** *adjs.*

bi′-valve (-vălv), **bi′-valved** (-vălvd), **bi-vălv′-ü-lar** (-lêr), **bi-vălv′-ous** (-ŭs), *n.* & *adj.* **1.** A molluscous animal with hinged double valves or shells ; দ্বিপুটক জন্তু (যেমন ঝিনুক)। **2.** A reed-vessel with two valves ; দ্বিপুটক বীজ-কোষ। ***Adj.*** Having two valves or shells ; দ্বিপুটক, দ্বিখোল (সাঃ পঃ), দ্বিকপাট (ঐ), দ্বিফলক (জাহিঃ)।

biv′-ou-ăc (-ö-), *n.* & *v. i.* The temporary encampment of soldiers or travellers for the night without tents or covering :

"In the world's broad field of battle
In the *bivouac* of life."

নিশাকালে অনাবৃত স্থানে (তাঁবু ব্যতিরেকে) সেনানিবাস বা পথিকদিগের আড্ডা-স্থাপন। ***Verb i.*** To encamp for the night without tents or covering ; to pass the night in the open air ; তাঁবু বা অন্য কোন প্রকার আচ্ছাদন ব্যতিরেকে রাত্রির জন্য অনাবৃত স্থানে আড্ডা লওয়া ; মুক্ত-প্রান্তরে যামিনী যাপন করা।

bi-week′-lȳ (-wēk-), *adj.* & *n.* Occurring or appearing once every two weeks, but usually twice in every week ; পাক্ষিক, সপ্তাহে দুইবার প্রকাশিত বা সংঘটিত। ***Noun.*** **1.** A fortnightly publication ; পাক্ষিক পত্র। **2.** A paper appearing twice every week ; সপ্তাহে দুইবার প্রকাশিত সংবাদপত্র।

Bixa orellana—লটকন (বেলঃ)।

bi-zarre′ (-zâr), *adj.* Eccentric ; grotesque ; odd ; মাথাপাগলা ; কিম্ভুত কিমাকার ; বিকট, অপরূপ, অদ্ভুত, সৃষ্টিছাড়া। **—rie′,** *n.*

blăb, *v. t.* & *i.* To talk much ; to disclose unthinkingly or from love of talking ; "And yonder a vile physician *blabbing* the case of his patient ;" বাচালতা করা, বাজে বকা ; অবিবেচকের মত গুপ্ত কথা প্রকাশ করিয়া ফেলা। ***Verb i.*** To talk indiscreetly ; অবিবেচকের মত কথা বলা। **Blab′-ber,** *n.* One who blabs ; a tattler ; a tell-tale ; বাচাল, বাবদূক ; জল্পক, বহুভাষী ; যে অপর ব্যক্তির গুপ্ত কথা প্রকাশ করে।

blăck, *adj., n.* & *v. t.* **1.** Of the darkest colour ; colourless ; কাল, কৃষ্ণ, অসিত ; অবর্ণ। **2.** Enveloped or shrouded in darkness ; as, a *black* night ; ঘনান্ধকারাচ্ছন্ন, তিমিরাবগুণ্ঠিত। **3.** Dark-skinned ; dark-clothed ; কৃষ্ণকায় ; কৃষ্ণাম্বর। **4.** Unclean ; foul ; অপরিষ্কার ; মলিন। **5.** Dismal ; cruel ; mournful ; calamitous ; ঘোর ; ক্রূর ; বিষাদময় ; বিপৎপূর্ণ। **6.** Atrociously wicked : disgraceful ; নিরতিশয় দুর্বৃত্ত, কৃষ্ণকর্ম্মা (অঃ) ; কলঙ্কজনক। **7.** Threatening ; sullen ; foreboding ; ভীতি-সঞ্চারক ; অন্তঃক্রোধী ; অমঙ্গল-সূচক। **8.** Implying disgrace ; as, a *black* mark ; কলঙ্কসূচক। ***Noun.*** **1.** Black colour ; as, the cloth has a good *black* ; কৃষ্ণ-বর্ণ। **2.** Black paint, dye or varnish ; কৃষ্ণবর্ণ রঞ্জন পদার্থ বা বার্ণিশ। **3.** A negro ; কাফ্রী। **4.** A black garment or dress ; as, she wears *black* ; কৃষ্ণবস্ত্র বা কৃষ্ণপরিচ্ছদ। **5.** A stain ; a spot ; কলঙ্ক ; দাগ। **6.** Particle of soot ; কজ্জল-কণিকা। **7.** The dark smut which attacks wheat ; গোধূম ক্ষয়কারী কৃষ্ণবর্ণ ছত্রাক। ***Verb t.*** **1.** To make black ; কৃষ্ণবর্ণে রঞ্জিত করা, মলিন করা। **2.** To polish with blacking ; (জুতা প্রভৃতিতে) কালি লাগান, কালি বুরুস করা। **Black′-ness,** *n.* **Black-a-moor**—A negro (male or female) ; কাফ্রী (পুরুষ বা স্ত্রী)। **Black and blue**—Discoloured with bruise ; (প্রহার-জনিত) কালদাগযুক্ত, কাল্‌সিটে পড়া। **Black and tan**—A dog so coloured ; কৃষ্ণ-পিঙ্গল কুক্কুর। **Black antimony**—শূর্ম্মা (ওয়াট্)। **Black art**—Necromancy ; magic ; প্রেতবিদ্যা, প্রেত-সিদ্ধি ; যাদুবিদ্যা, ইন্দ্রজাল, ভোজবিদ্যা। **Blackball**—(*Noun*) প্রতিকূলে ভোট দিবার জন্য কৃষ্ণবর্ণ গুটিকা। **Blackball**—(*v. t.*) To vote against by putting a black ball into a ballot box ; ভোট লইবার বাক্সে কৃষ্ণবর্ণগুটিকা প্রদান করত কাহারও প্রতিকূলে মত প্রদান করা। **Black-beer,** *n.* A black syrupy beer ; Dantzig beer ; একপ্রকার কৃষ্ণবর্ণ আসববৎ যবসুরা ; প্রুশিয়ার অন্তর্গত ডেণ্ট্‌জিগ নামক সমুদ্রতীরবর্ত্তী নগরীতে প্রস্তুত যবসুরা। **Black beetle** — A cockroach ; তৈলপায়ী, তেলাপোকা, আরসলা।

Black berry.

Blackberry—The berry of the bramble ; ইংলণ্ডদেশীয় ক্ষুদ্র ফলবিশেষ, আংচ্ছু (ফঃ হিঃ)। **Blackbird**—A species of thrush of a black colour ; ইংলণ্ডদেশীয় পক্ষিবিশেষ। A kidnapped negro slave ; অপহৃত কাফ্রী কৃতদাস। **Black-board**—A board used for writing on with chalk ; বিদ্যালয়-গৃহে ব্যবহৃত কৃষ্ণবর্ণ-কাষ্ঠফলক। **Black book**—An official book (generally bound in black) containing the names of persons suspect or liable to punishment ; সন্দিগ্ধ বা দণ্ডার্হ ব্যক্তিদের সরকারী তালিকা-পুস্তক। **Black-browed**—Having black eye-brow ; gloomy ; dismal ; কৃষ্ণভ্রূ ; বিষণ্ণ ; ঘোর। **Black cap**—A cap put on by judges when passing sentences of death ; প্রাণদণ্ডের আদেশ-প্রদানের অব্যবহিত পূর্ব্বে বিচারকগণ যে কৃষ্ণবর্ণের টুপি পরিধান করিয়া থাকেন। A British bird with a sweet note ; এক-প্রকার ইংলণ্ড দেশীয় পক্ষী। **Black caraway**—কালিজিরা (ওয়াট্)। **Black cattle**—Oxen, cows, etc., reared for slaughter, in distinction from dairy-cattle ; বধার্থ পালিত গবাদি পশু। **Black coat**—A clergyman (familiarly called, as a soldier is called a *red-coat*) ; ধর্ম্মযাজক। **Black death**—The fourteenth century plague which ravaged Europe and Asia,—so called from the black spots which appeared on the skin ; ইয়ুরোপ ও এশিয়া মহাদেশব্যাপী চতুর্দ্দশ শতাব্দীর ভীষণ মহামারী রোগ। **Black draught**—The popular name for a purgative medicine ; একপ্রকার বিরেচক ঔষধ। **Black eye**—An eye discoloured with bruise ; আঘাতের দরুণ কালদাগযুক্ত চক্ষু। A dark eye ; কৃষ্ণতার নয়ন। **Black-faced**—Having a black, dark or gloomy face or aspect ; কালোমুখ, মলিন, বিষণ্ণবদন। **Black flag**—The flag of a pirate ; জলদস্যুগণের কৃষ্ণবর্ণ পতাকা। The black flag hoisted at the execution of a criminal ; প্রাণদণ্ডে দণ্ডিত ব্যক্তির বধকালে যে কৃষ্ণবর্ণ পতাকা উত্থিত করা হয়। **Black friar**—A friar of the Dominican order, so named from the colour of his garment ; ডমিনিক্যান সম্প্রদায়ভুক্ত কৃষ্ণাম্বর সন্ন্যাসী। **Blackguard,** *adj., n.* & *v. t.* Low ; scurrilous ; নীচ, ইতর ; অশ্লীলভাষী। (*Noun.*) A scoundrel ; a foul-mouthed person ; দুর্বৃত্ত ; অশ্লীলভাষী ব্যক্তি। [পূর্ব্বে রাজা বা সম্ভ্রান্ত ব্যক্তির বাটীর বাসন-মাজা ভৃত্য, চোর, ডাকাত, ভবঘুরে প্রভৃতিকে blackguard বলা হইত।] (*Verb t.*) To call blackguard ; to abuse in scurrilous language ; ইতর বলিয়া গালি দেওয়া ; অশ্লীল ও কদর্য্য ভাষায় গালাগালি করা। **Black-hole**—A military lock-up ; সামরিক কারাগার, অন্ধকূপ। **Black Hole Massacre**—অন্ধকূপ হত্যা। **Black-lead**—Graphite ; কৃষ্ণসীস। **Black-leg**—A swindler ; a turf-swindler ; ঠক, জুয়াচোর ; ঘোড়দৌড় খেলার জুয়ারি। A strike-breaker ; ধর্ম্মঘটকারিগণের মধ্যে যে ব্যক্তি ধর্ম্মঘট ভঙ্গ করে। **Black letter**—The old English letter ; প্রাচীন ধরণের ইংরেজী অক্ষর। **Black-list,** *n.* & *v. t.* A list of persons who have become bankrupt ; a list of defaulters ; দেউলিয়া ব্যক্তিগণের তালিকা ; বাকিদারের তালিকা। A list of suspicious persons deserving of censure or punishment ; সন্দিগ্ধব্যক্তিগণের তালিকা, দণ্ডনীয় বা তিরস্কারযোগ্য ব্যক্তিগণের তালিকা। (*Verb t.*) To put in a black-list ; অপরাধী বা সন্দিগ্ধচরিত্র লোকের তালিকায় ভুক্ত করা। **Blackmail,** *n.* & *v. t.* A tribute exacted by freebooters for protection from pillage ; পূর্ব্বকালে ইংলণ্ডের উত্তর এবং স্কটলণ্ডের দক্ষিণাঞ্চলে লুণ্ঠন হইতে অব্যাহতি দানের জন্য লুণ্ঠনকারিগণ যে কর আদায় করিত। A hush-money paid for not disclosing discreditable secret ; an extortion of money by means of intimidation ; আখ্যাতিজনক গুপ্তকথা অপ্রকাশিত রাখার জন্য প্রদত্ত অর্থ ; ভয়-প্রদর্শনদ্বারা গৃহীত অর্থ। (*Verb t.*) To force to make payment by threats ; ভয় প্রদর্শন করিয়া অর্থপ্রদানে বাধ্য করা। **Black Maria**—A prison-van ; বন্দি-শকট, কারাগারের শকট। **Black Monday**—Easter Monday ; ইষ্টার পর্ব্বীয় সোমবার। The monday on which school reopens ; বন্ধের পর বিদ্যালয় খোলার দিনের সোমবার। **Blackplum**—কালজাম (ওয়াট্)। **Black Rod**—The usher of the Chapter of the Garter and of the House of Lords, so called from the black rod which he carries ; নাইটস অব দি গার্টার নামক সম্ভ্রান্ত সমাজের এবং পার্লেমেণ্টের লর্ড সভার কৃষ্ণদণ্ডধর দৌবারিক। **Black salt**—নীলকাচ (রঃ প্রঃ)। **Black sheep**—A disreputable member of a family ; a scoundrel ; কুলকলঙ্ক, কুলকজ্জল ; দুরাচার, দুর্জ্জন। **Blacksmith**—A smith who works in iron ; লৌহকার, লোহার কামার। **Black-snake**—A harmless nonpoisonous reptile ; একপ্রকার বিষহীন সর্প। **Blackthorn**—The sloe-tree ; এক প্রকার বন্য জামগাছ। **Black-y**—Negro ; কাফ্রী। **Black zedoary**—কালাহলদি (ওয়াট্)। **In black**—In mourning ; শোকপরিচ্ছদ-পরিহিত। **In black and white**—In written or printed characters ; কাগজে কলমে, লিখিত বা মুদ্রিত অক্ষরে। **To be in any one's black books**—To have incurred any one's displeasure ; কাহারও বিরাগভাজন হওয়া। **To be deep in one's black books**—To be quite out of his favour ; কাহারো অনুগ্রহ হইতে সম্পূর্ণরূপে বঞ্চিত হওয়া। **To black out**—To obliterate ; মুছিয়া ফেলা, বিলোপ করা। **Washing the black of a Moor white**—Engaged upon a hopeless and useless task ; অসম্ভব বা অনর্থক কার্য্যে রত।

blăck'-ĕn, *v. t.* & *i.* **1.** To make black ; কাল করা। **2.** To darken ; to sully ; অন্ধকারাচ্ছন্ন করা ; কালিমালিপ্ত করা। **3.** To defame ; মানহানি করা। ***Verb i.*** To grow black or dark ; কাল হওয়া, মলিন হওয়া।

blăck'-ing, *n.* A substance used for polishing leather, shoes, etc. ; জুতার কালি।

blăd'-dêr, *n.* **1.** A thin sac or bag in animal bodies which contains the urine, bile, etc. ; মূত্রাধার, মূত্রাশয়, মূত্রকোষ, ক্লোম (সাঃ পঃ), (মৎস্য-সম্পর্কে) পটুকা। **2.** (*Fig.*) Anything inflated or hollow ; a wordy man ; a wind-bag ; (লক্ষণায়) বায়ু বা বারিদ্বারা স্ফীত বস্তু ; বাকসর্ব্বস্ব ব্যক্তি ; শূন্যাধার, শূন্যকুম্ভ। **4.** A blister ; a pustule ; ফোস্কা ; ফুস্কুরী। **—y,** *adj.*

blāde, *n.* **1.** A spire of grass ; পত্র, পত্রাংশ (সাঃ পঃ), ফলক (ঐ), তৃণপত্র। **2.** The cutting part of an instrument ; as, the *blade* of a sword ; a sword ; অস্ত্রের ফলা, ধারা ; তরবারি। **3.** The flat part of an oar, bat, spade, etc. ; দাঁড়, ব্যাট্, কোদালি প্রভৃতির পাত বা প্রশস্ত অংশ। **4.** A flat bone of the shoulder ; অংসফলক (সুশ্রুঃ)। **5.** One of the principal rafters of a house ; গৃহের প্রধান বর্গা সকলের মধ্যে একটী। **6.** A gay dashing young fellow ; "A *blade* whom I took for a decent tailor ;" প্রফুল্লচিত্ত এবং সাহসী যুবক। **Blād'-ed,** *adj.* **Blade-bone**—The flat bone in the shoulder ; স্কন্ধাস্থি, অংসফলকাস্থি।

blague, (*F.*), *n.* Pretentiousness ; অতিগ্রাহিতা।

blain (blān), *n.* A boil ; a pustule ; ব্রণ ; স্ফোটক, ফোস্কা, ফুস্কুরি।

blāme, *v. t.* & *n.* **1.** To find fault with ; to reproach ; দোষারোপ করা ; তিরস্কার করা, ভৎসনা করা। **2.** To fix the responsibility on ; দায়িত্ব চাপান। ***Noun.*** **1.** Censure ; পরীবাদ, নিন্দা। **2.** Fault ; crime ; sin ; দোষ ; অপরাধ ; পাপ। **3.** Responsibility of bad result ; দুষ্কর্ম্মের দায়িত্ব। **Blam'-a-ble,** *adj.* Deserving of blame ; দূষ্য, নিন্দনীয়, নিন্দার্হ, গর্হনীয়। **Blam'-a-ble-ness, Blam'-er,** *ns.* **Blam'-a-bly,** *adv.* **To be to blame**—To deserve censure ; নিন্দা বা তিরস্কারের যোগ্য হওয়া। **To lay the blame**—To accuse ; দোষারোপ করা।

blāme'-fûl, *adj.* Deserving censure ; নিন্দনীয়, নিন্দার্হ। **—ly,** *adv.* **—ness,** *n.*

blāme'-lĕss, *adj.* Innocent ; নির্দ্দোষ, অনিন্দ্য, শুদ্ধ, অজুগুপ্সিত, নিরপরাধ। **—ly,** *adv.* **—ness,** *n.*

blāme'-wor-thȳ (-wêr-), *adj.* Deserving blame ; নিন্দার্হ, দোষার্হ। **—thi-ness,** *n.*

blanch (blănsh), *v. t.* & *i.* **1.** To whiten ; to bleach ; as, to *blanch* linen ; শুক্লবর্ণ করা, শ্বেতবর্ণ করা, ধবলিত করা, সাদা করা, ফরসা করা (*Colloq.*) ; ধোলাই করা (*Colloq.*)। **2.** To blanch (plants) by depriving the light ; (আলোকহীন স্থানে বৃক্ষাদি রাখিয়া) শ্বেতবর্ণ করা। **3.** To whiten by peeling ; as, to *blanch* almonds ; খোসা ছাড়াইয়া সাদা করা। **4.** To whitewash, (with *over*) ; "*Blanch over* the blackest and most absurd things ;" দোষক্ষালন করা। ***Verb i.*** **1.** To grow or become white ; সাদা হইয়া যাওয়া, শুভ্র হওয়া। **2.** To grow pale with fear or cold ; ভয় বা শীতে বিবর্ণ বা পাণ্ডুবর্ণ হওয়া।

blanc-mange' (blä-mänzh), *n.* A kind of white jelly ; শুভ্রবর্ণ মোরব্বা বিশেষ।

blănd, *adj.* **1.** Soft ; gentle ; kind ; as, a *bland* temper ; polite in manners ; affable ; কোমল, মেদুর ; নম্র, শান্ত, ধীর, মৃদু ; দয়ার্দ্র ; শিষ্ট, সৌজন্যপূর্ণ ; মিষ্টভাষী। **2.** Mild ; as, *bland* oil ; not stimulating ; as, a *bland* diet ; স্নিগ্ধ ; অনুত্তেজক। **Bland'-ly,** *adv.* **Bland'-ness,** *n.*

blăn'-dish, *v. t.* To flatter ; to coax ; মিষ্ট কথা দ্বারা মনোরঞ্জন করা ; মিষ্টকথা দ্বারা ভুলান। **—ment,** *n.* (Usu. in *pl.*) Soft words and artful caresses ; winning expressions or actions ; প্রিয়বাক্য, মিষ্টবচন, প্রেমালাপ, তোষামোদ, আদর ; সোহাগ, যত্ন (রমণী-সম্বন্ধে), হাবভাব, বিলাস, বিভ্রম।

blank (blăngk), *adj.* **1.** Pale ; colourless ; "*Blank* moon ;" পাণ্ডুর ; বিবর্ণ। **2.** Not written or printed on ; as, *blank* paper ; সাদা, অলিখিত, অমুদ্রিত। **3.** Having empty spaces for signature or detail ; as, *blank* cheques, documents, etc. ; নাম স্বাক্ষরাদির জন্য শূন্য-স্থান বিশিষ্ট। **4.** Empty ; void ; bare ; as, *blank* space, day, etc. ; শূন্য ; ফাঁক, খালি ; অনাবৃত। **5.** Void of interest, hopes or expression ; as, to live a *blank* existence ; নীরস, ঘটনাশূন্য, আশাশূন্য, নিষ্ফল, ভঙ্গীহীন, ভাবশূন্য। **6.** Absolute ; downright ; as, a *blank* terror, despair, etc. ; অবিমিশ্র ; নিরবচ্ছিন্ন, শুদ্ধ। **7.** Unrhymed ; as, a *blank* verse (অমিত্রাক্ষর ছন্দ) ; অমিত্রাক্ষর। **Blank'-ly,** *adv.* **1.** Without expression ; as, to look *blankly* ; ভঙ্গীশূন্য ভাবে, শূন্যদৃষ্টিতে। **2.** Flatly ; as, he denied *blankly* ; স্পষ্টভাবে। **Blank'-ness,** *n.* **Blank cartridge**—A cartridge containing no ball ; গুলিহীন টোটা। **Blank cheque**—A cheque with amount left for the payee to fill in ; যে হুণ্ডীর টাকার সংখ্যার স্থান প্রাপক বা গ্রাহকদ্বারা পূরণের জন্য খালি রাখা হয়। **Blank shot**—Shot from which no balls are discharged ; ফাঁকা আওয়াজ।

blank (blăngk), *n.* **1.** A void space ; শূন্য স্থান, শূন্য। **2.** An empty space in a written or printed document ; মুদ্রিত বা লিখিত কাগজে পরে পূরণের জন্য যে স্থান ফাঁক রাখা হয়। **3.** A lottery ticket that gains no prize ; চিঠি খেলার যে টিকেটে পুরস্কার পাওয়া যায় না। **4.** Bull's eye of a target ; hence, anything aimed at ; চাঁদমারির শুক্লবর্ণ লক্ষ্য-চিহ্ন ; (অতএব) লক্ষ্য। **5.** A time without incident ; a thing without meaning ; ঘটনাশূন্য সময় ; অর্থশূন্য বিষয়। **In blank**—With an essential portion left to be filled in ; as, to make out a cheque *in blank* ; প্রধান প্রধান বিষয়গুলি অন্য ব্যক্তি দ্বারা পূরণের জন্য খালি রাখিয়া।

blan'-kĕt (blăng-), *n.* & *v. t.* A woollen covering for a bed ; কম্বল। ***Verb t.*** **1.** To cover with a blanket ; কম্বলাবৃত করা। **2.** To toss in a blanket as by way of punishment ; (শাস্তি-স্বরূপ) কম্বলের চারিকোণে ধরিয়া তদুপরিস্থ মনুষ্যকে সহসা উৎক্ষেপণ করা। **3.** To take the wind out of the sails of (another vessel) by passing to windward ; (অন্য জাহাজের) বাতাসের দিকে জাহাজ চালনা করিয়া সেই জাহাজের পালের বাতাস বন্ধ করা। **—ing,** *n.* **1.** Material for blankets ; কম্বলের কাপড়। **2.** The punishment of tossing in a blanket ; কম্বল হইতে উৎক্ষেপণ-দণ্ড। **A wet blanket**—A damper ; a kill-joy ; নিরুৎসাহকারী ; যাহার আগমনে স্ফূর্ত্তি বা প্রফুল্লতা নষ্ট হয়। **Born on the wrong side of the blanket**—Illegitimate ; জারজ।

blâre, *v. i., t.* & *n.* To make sound of trumpet ; ভেঁপুর মত ধ্বনি করা, উচ্চনাদ করা। ***Verb t.*** To utter loudly ; উচ্চৈঃস্বরে ঘোষণা করা, উচ্চনাদে ঘোষণা করা। ***Noun.*** A sound like that of a trumpet ; a roar ; ভেঁপুর মত ধ্বনি ; গর্জ্জন।

blâr'-ney (-nĭ), *n., v. t.* & *i.* Smoothly flattering talk ; খোসামুদে কথা, মনস্তুষ্টিকর বাক্য, মনভুলানো কথা। ***Verb t.* & *i.*** To use cajoling talk ; to beguile with flattery ; খোসামুদে কথা বলা ; তোষামোদ-বাক্যদ্বারা চিত্তহরণ করা, মিষ্ট কথায় ভুলান। **Blarney-stone**—A stone in the castle Blarney, in Ireland, conferring a cajoling tongue on whoever kisses it ; আয়র্লণ্ডের ব্লার্নিদুর্গের প্রাচীর-সংলগ্ন প্রস্তর খণ্ড। [কথিত আছে উহা চুম্বনে চাটুবাক্য বলিবার ক্ষমতা জন্মে।]

blase, (*F.*), *adj.* Exhausted by enjoyment ; cloyed ; tired of pleasure ; অতিতৃপ্ত ; ভোগাসক্তি-রহিত ; বীতস্পৃহ, বীতরাগ, ভোগক্লান্ত।

blăs-phēme', *v. t.* & *i.* **1.** To utter impiety against (God or anything sacred) ; ভগবান বা পবিত্র বস্তু সম্বন্ধে ভক্তিশূন্যভাবে নিন্দাবাদ করা। ***Verb i.*** To utter impious words ; to talk profanely ; ভক্তিশূন্য কথা বলা ; দেবনিন্দাসূচক কথা বলা। **—phem'-er,** *n.* One who blasphemes ; দেবনিন্দক, দেবদ্বেষী, পাষণ্ড। **—phe-mous,** *adj.* Profane ; impious ; দেবনিন্দাত্মক ; অপুণ্য, অমেধ্য, পাপীয়, ভক্তিহীন। **—phe-mous-ly,** *adv.*

blăs'-phĕ-my̆, *n.* Wicked language regarding God or anything held sacred ; দেবনিন্দা, ঈশ্বরনিন্দা, দেবাপবাদ, পবিত্র বস্তু বা ব্যক্তি সম্বন্ধে অপবাদ।

blăst, *n., v. t.* & *i.* **1.** A strong gust of wind ; প্রবল বাত্যা, ঝাপ্‌টা বাতাস, দমকা বাতাস। **2.** The sound made by blowing a wind-instrument ; also, the sound made by the blowing of a steam whistle ; বায়ু বা ফুৎকারদ্বারা বাদিত বাদ্যযন্ত্রের ধ্বনি ; জাহাজ প্রভৃতির পোঁ পোঁ শব্দ। **3.** A blowing up by gunpowder ; an explosion ; also, the charge used for this purpose ; বারুদদ্বারা উড়াইয়া দেওন ; সশব্দ-স্ফেটন ; (পর্ব্বতাদি) বিদারণ করিতে যে পরিমাণ বারুদ ব্যবহৃত হয়। **4.** A sudden pernicious effect upon animals and plants ; a blight ; মড়ক ; ধসারোগ। ***Verb t.*** **1.** To wither or shrivel (plant, animal, etc.) ; ক্ষয় করা, ধ্বংস করা, নাশ করা, বিশুষ্ক করা, কোকড়াইয়া দেওয়া, মুশড়াইয়া দেওয়া। **2.** To visit with the wrath of heaven ; to curse ; (often with *God* understood as *subject*) ; ঈশ্বরের ক্রোধদ্বারা বিদগ্ধ করা ; অভিশাপ করা। **3.** To confound by a loud din ; "Trumpeters, with brazen din, *blast* you the city's ears :" ভীম শব্দদ্বারা স্তব্ধ করা (কাণে তালি লাগান)। **4.** To blow up (rocks etc.) by gunpowder ; (পর্ব্বত প্রভৃতি) বারুদদ্বারা বিদীর্ণ করা বা উড়াইয়া দেওয়া। ***Verb i.*** To be blighted or withered ; শুকাইয়া যাওয়া, মুশড়িয়া যাওয়া, পরিম্লান হওয়া। **Blast'-ed,** *adj.* **Blast'-ing,** *n.* **Blast-furnace**—A smelting furnace into which compressed hot air is blown ; বাত্যাসহায় চুল্লী (প্রবাসী, ১৩১৯ সন), স্বাভাবিক অবস্থায় খনি হইতে উত্তোলিত বিমিশ্র-লৌহ হইতে বিশুদ্ধ লৌহ নিষ্কাশনার্থ চুল্লী বিশেষ। এই চুল্লীতে ঘনীভূত উষ্ণ বায়ু-সঞ্চার করিয়া বিশুদ্ধ লৌহ পৃথক করা হয়। **In full blast**—In full operation ; পুরাদমে, পূর্ণবেগে। **Out of blast**—Not at work ; বন্ধ।

blā'-tănt, *adj.* Bellowing as beast ; noisy ; clamorous (of speaking) ; পশুর মত গর্জ্জনশীল ; কলরবপূর্ণ ; কোলাহলপূর্ণ। **—ly,** *adv.*

blāze, *n., v. i.* & *t.* **1.** A bright glowing flame or fire ; সমুজ্জ্বল অগ্নি-শিখা, অগ্নি। **2.** An outburst ; a violent display ; as, a *blaze* of wrath ; উচ্ছ্বাস ; প্রচণ্ড প্রকাশ **3.** Clear or full light, as of noon ; as, the *blaze* of publicity ; পূর্ণালোক, স্পষ্টালোক। **4.** A glow of bright colour ; বর্ণের দীপ্তি বা উজ্জ্বলতা। **5.** A white spot on the face of a horse or ox ; অশ্ব কিম্বা বৃষের মুখোপরিস্থ শ্বেতচিহ্ন। 6. A spot made on trees by chipping off a piece of the bark ; সীমা কিম্বা পথ নির্দ্দেশার্থ বৃক্ষগাত্রে কর্ত্তিত চিহ্ন। *Verb i.* 1. To burn with bright flame ; উজ্জ্বল শিখা বিস্তারে প্রজ্বলিত হওয়া। 2. To shine brightly ; to be resplendent ; উজ্জ্বল দীপ্তি বিকিরণ করা ; দীপ্তিশালী হওয়া, জাজ্বল্যমান হওয়া। 3. To burn with excitement or passion ; as, his anger too easily *blazed* forth : উত্তেজনায় উদ্দীপ্ত হওয়া। 4. To show bright colours ; দীপ্তবর্ণ প্রদর্শন করা। *Verb t.* 1. To mark (a tree) by chipping off a piece of bark ; also, to indicate (a path) by such a mark ; (বৃক্ষের) বল্কলের অংশবিশেষ তুলিয়া চিহ্ন রাখা ; বিশেষতঃ বৃক্ষাদিতে চিহ্ন কাটিয়া (পথ প্রভৃতি) প্রদর্শন করা। 2. To proclaim as with a trumpet ; as, the secret might soon be *blazed* ; ঢাক ঢোল বাজাইয়া প্রচার করা। **Blaz'-ing,** *adj.* **Blazing indiscretion** — Rash and conspicuous piece of candour ; জ্বলন্ত অবিবেচকতার কার্য্য। **In a blaze**—On flame ; exicted or exasperated ; জ্বলন্ত, উদ্দীপ্ত ; উত্তেজিত। **Go to blazes**—Go to hell ; (used in imprecation) (ইতরভাষায়) নরকে যাও, রসাতলে যাও, চুলোয় যাও। (*Slang*) **Like blaze**—Impetuously ; (ইতর ভাষায়) প্রচণ্ডভাবে। (*Slang*) **To blaze away**—To continue firing rifles etc. ; (ইতর ভাষায়) আগ্নেয়াস্ত্র হইতে ক্রমাগত গুলিগোলা বর্ষণ করা। **To blaze up**—To burst up in anger ; ক্রোধে জ্বলিয়া উঠা।

blāz'-êr, *n.* 1. One who proclaims ; "*Blazer* of crime ;" যে দেশ বিদেশে সংবাদ প্রচার করে। 2. A bright-coloured jacket for boating, golf, etc. ; নৌকাদৌড়, গল্ফ্‌ক্রীড়া প্রভৃতিতে ক্রীড়কগণ যে উজ্জ্বল বর্ণের জামা পরিধান করিয়া থাকে। 3. (*Slang*) An outrageous lie ; (ইতরভাষায়) জ্বলন্ত মিথ্যা কথা।

bla'-zon (blăzn), *n.* & *v. t.* 1. A heraldic shield ; coat of arms, bearings or banner ; কুলচিহ্নাঙ্কিত চর্ম্ম (ঢাল) ; বর্ম্মোপরি ব্যবহৃত কুলমর্য্যাদাসূচক চিহ্ন, কুলচিহ্নাঙ্কিত পতাকা। 2. A correct description of heraldic or armorial bearings ; কুলচিহ্নসমূহের যথাযথ বর্ণনা। 3. A record of virtues or excellencies ; a pompous display ; সদ্‌গুণ বা শ্রেষ্ঠতার বিবরণ ; আড়ম্বরপূর্ণ প্রদর্শন। *Verb t.* 1. To paint, or describe (heraldic bearings) in proper terms ; কুলমর্য্যাদাসূচক চিহ্ন-সমূহ যথাযথরূপে অঙ্কন বা বর্ণন করা। 2. To depict in colours ; to adorn ; উজ্জ্বল বর্ণে-চিত্রিত করা ; ভূষিত করা। 3. To display ; to exhibit conspicuously ; to proclaim ; "*Blazing* our injustice everywhere ;" প্রদর্শন করা ; জাজ্বল্যমানরূপে প্রদর্শন করা ; প্রচার করা। **—er,** *n.* 1. One who blazons coats of arms ; a herald ; কুলমর্য্যাদাসূচক চিহ্নাদি চিত্রক বা বর্ণনাকারী ; কুলাচার্য্য। 2. One who proclaims ; প্রচারক, ঘোষণাকারী। **—ment,** *n.* **—ry,** *n.* 1. The art of describing or painting heraldic devices, armorial bearings, etc. ; কুলচিহ্ন-বর্ণন, ব্যাখ্যান ও অঙ্কন-বিষয়ক বিদ্যা, বংশপরিচয়-বিদ্যা। 2. A brightly coloured display ; সমুজ্জ্বল বর্ণরঞ্জিত দৃশ্যোদ্ঘাটন।

bleach (blēch), *v. t.* & *i.* To make white ; to whiten (linen, etc.) by exposure to sunlight or by chemical process ; ধবল করা ; ধোলাই করা, সূর্য্যকিরণ বা রাসায়নিক প্রক্রিয়াদ্বারা শুভ্র করা। *Verb i.* To become white ; to become pale or pallid ; সাদা হওয়া, শ্বেতবর্ণ ধারণ করা ; বিবর্ণ বা পাণ্ডুবর্ণ ধারণ করা। **Bleached',** *adj.* Whitened ; শুভ্রীকৃত, ধবলিত, ধৌত। **Bleach'-er,** *n.* **Bleach'-er-y,** *n.* A place where bleaching is done ; ধোলাইখানা। **Bleaching powder**—Chloride of lime ; বিরঞ্জন-চূর্ণ (হিঃ কোঃ)।

bleak (blēk), 1. Exposed ; windswept ; as, *bleak* hills, fields, etc. ; শীত ও বায়ুর প্রকোপে উন্মুক্ত ; বায়ুতাড়িত। 2. Cheerless ; dreary ; "*Bleak* edge of poverty ;" বিষাদময় ; নিরানন্দ, উদাস। 3. Cold and chilly ; (usu. of wind or weather) ; হিমশীতল, কন্‌কনে ঠাণ্ডা। **Bleak'-ness,** *n.*

bleak (blēk), *n.* A small white river-fish ; নদীচর ক্ষুদ্র শ্বেতবর্ণ মৎস্য-বিশেষ। Also called BLAY.

blear (blēr), *adj.* & *v. t.* Dim-sighted ; sore or inflamed ; filmy (চক্ষুসম্বন্ধে) ক্ষীণদৃষ্টি ; ক্ষত বা প্রদাহযুক্ত ; পর্দ্দাপড়া, আবরণযুক্ত। *Verb t.* 1. To make sore or watery, as the eyes ; to dim or blur (the sight) ; চক্ষু ঘোলা বা ঝাপ্‌সা করা ; ক্ষীণদৃষ্টি করা। 2. (*Fig.*) To throw dust in the eyes ; to deceive ; (লক্ষণায়) চক্ষে ধূলি দেওয়া ; ঠকান। **Blear-eyed**—Having blear eyes ; প্রদাহযুক্ত চক্ষুবিশিষ্ট, ক্লিন্নাক্ষ (মঃ উঃ)। Dull of perception ; short-sighted ; ক্ষীণবুদ্ধি ; অস্পষ্টদর্শী, অদূরদর্শী।

bleat (blēt), *v. t.* & *n.* To cry as a sheep, goat or calf ; ভেড়ার মত ডাকা, ভেড়া, ছাগল বা বাছুরের মত রব করা। *Noun.* The cry of a sheep, goat or calf ; (contemptuously) human utterances ; মেষরব ; (অবজ্ঞাচ্ছলে) মনুষ্যের ম্যান্ ম্যান্। **Bleat'-ing,** *n.* মেষরব, ভ্যা ভ্যা শব্দ। **To bleat out**—To speak feebly or foolishly ; ম্যান্ ম্যান্ করা।

blĕb, *n.* A blister on the skin ; a bubble in water or glass ; ফোস্কা ; কাচ বা জলের উপর ক্ষুদ্র বুদ্বুদ। **Bleb'-by,** *adj.*

bleed (blēd), *v. i.* & *t.* 1. To emit blood ; (said of a part of the body, a wound, etc.) ; রক্ত ক্ষরিত হওয়া, রক্তস্রাব হওয়া। 2. To suffer wounds or violent death, (often for a cause); "Caesar must *bleed* for it;" আঘাতজনিত যন্ত্রণা ভোগ করা, মৃত্যুযন্ত্রণা ভোগ করা। **3.** (Of plants) To emit sap when wounded; (বৃক্ষ-সম্বন্ধে) আঘাত লাগিলে রস, আঠা বা নির্যাস ক্ষরিত হওয়া। **4.** To lose money freely; to pay lavishly; to suffer extortion; "Hang those City fellows they must *bleed*;" অজস্র অর্থক্ষয় হওয়া; মুক্তহস্তে অর্থ ব্যয় করা; নিষ্পীড়িত হইয়া অর্থ প্রদান করা। ***Verb t.*** **1.** To draw or let blood from (surgically); অস্ত্রদ্বারা রক্ত বাহির করা। **2.** To extort money from; as, they *bled* him freely for this fund; পীড়ন পূর্ব্বক টাকা আদায় করা, অর্থশোষণ করা। **The heart bleeds**—(কাহারো) দুর্দ্দশা দর্শনে বা করুণাবশে হৃদয় বিদীর্ণ হওয়া, মর্ম্মান্তিক যন্ত্রণাভোগ করা, বুক ফাটিয়া যাওয়া।

bleed′-ing (blēd-), *n.* & *adj.* The flowing of blood (from a wound); the operation of letting blood; রক্তপাত, অসৃক্স্রাব; বিস্রাবণ (মঃ উঃ), রক্তমোক্ষণ, অসৃকবিমোক্ষণ। ***Adj.*** **1.** Emitting blood; গলদ্-রক্ত। **2.** Full of deep pity or compasson; as, *bleeding* hearts, thoughts, etc.; গভীর করুণাপূর্ণ।

blĕm′-ish, *v. t.* & *n.* To mark with deformity; to mar or spoil the beauty of; to sully or stain; as, to *blemish* reputation; বিকৃত করা; সৌন্দর্য্য নষ্ট করা; কলঙ্কিত করা, কালিমালিপ্ত করা। ***Noun.*** A stain; flaw; fault; slur; দাগ; ছিদ্র; খুঁৎ; কলঙ্ক।

blench (blĕnsh), *v. i.* & *t.* To start back; to shrink; "*Blench* not at thy chosen lot;" চমকিয়া পিছে হটা; সঙ্কুচিত হওয়া বা জড়সড় হওয়া। ***Verb t.*** To close the eyes to; to blink; as, to *blench* one's merits; চোখ বুঝিয়া থাকা; দেখিয়া না দেখা।

blĕnd, *v. t., i* & *n.* To mix (things) together (esp. sorts of tea, wines, etc. to get a certain quality); মিশ্রিত করা। **2.** To mix components so as to be inseparable and indistinguishable; গুলা। ***Verb i.*** To mingle intimately; to form a harmonious mixture; গাঢ়ভাবে মিশ্রিত হওয়া; গুলা। **2.** To pass imperceptibly into each other (especially, of colours); ক্রমেক্রমে অপ্রত্যক্ষভাবে একটী অপরটীতে বিলীন হওয়া [বিশেষতঃ বর্ণ-সম্বন্ধে—কোন একটী বর্ণ অপরটীতে এইরূপভাবে বিলীন হওয়া যে কোথায় প্রথমটী শেষ অথবা দ্বিতীয়টী আরম্ভ হইয়াছে তদবধারণে অসমর্থ হওয়া।] ***Noun.*** A mixture; a mixture made of various sorts of tea, spirits, tobacco, etc.; মিশ্র; বিভিন্ন প্রকার চা, সুরা প্রভৃতি তরল পদার্থের মিশ্র। **Blend′-ing,** *n.* The act of mingling; সংমিশ্রণ।

blende (blĕnd), *n.* Native sulphide of zinc; আকরোদ্ভূত গন্ধক-খর্পরক।

Blĕn′-heim (-ĕm), *n.* A kind of spaniel (from *Blenheim* house, the seat of the Duke of Marlborough, in England); এক-জাতীয় কুকুর। **Blenheim-orange**—A golden-coloured apple; স্বর্ণবর্ণ সেওফল।

blĕn-nor-rhe′-ă (-nö-rē), **–rhœ′-ă** (-rē-), *n.* An inordinate flow of mucus; শ্লৈষ্মিক ঝিল্লী হইতে অধিক পরিমাণে স্রাব-নিঃসরণ।

blĕn′-nȳ, A small spiny-finned sea-fish; একপ্রকার ক্ষুদ্রকায় সামুদ্রিক মৎস্য।

blĕss, *v. t.* **1.** To consecrate by religious rite, esp. food; "The bishop had *blest* the meat;" ধর্ম্মক্রিয়া দ্বারা পূত করা (বিশেষভাবে খাদ্য-সম্বন্ধে)। **2.** To confer prosperity or happiness upon; to grant divine favour to; "The quality of mercy......is twice *blest*, it *blesseth* him that gives and him that takes," সুখ সমৃদ্ধি-সম্পন্ন করা; ঈশ্বরানুগ্রহ দান করা। **3.** To invoke God's blessing upon; to wish well to; আশীর্ব্বাদ করা, আশিস্ করা; কল্যাণ বা শুভকামনা করা, মঙ্গলকামনা করা। **4.** To praise; to glorify; to extol; "*Bless* the Lord, O my soul;" গুণগান করা; মহিমা ঘোষণা করা; গুণকীর্ত্তন করা। **5.** To esteem or account happy; to congratulate oneself; (*with, in, that*); সুখী বলিয়া গণ্য করা; ধন্য মনে করা। **6.** (Euphemistically or ironically) To curse; "Fuming, *blessing* himself;" (মোলায়েম ভাষায় বা রহস্যচ্ছলে) অভিসম্পাত করা। **God bless me, Bless my soul, etc,**—Exclamations of surprise or indignation; (বিস্ময় বা ক্রোধ-সূচক চীৎকার) আ কপাল! হরি হরি! ত্রাহি মাম্। **Bless you**—ষাট্ ষাট্ [সাধারণতঃ হাঁচির পর বলা হয়।] **To bless with, To be blessed with**—To be in one's possession; কাহারও অধিকৃত বা অধিগত থাকা।

blĕss′-ĕd, blĕst, *adj.* **1.** Hallowed; consecrated; পবিত্র, শুদ্ধ, পূত; পবিত্রীকৃত। **2.** Bringing or imparting happiness; as, *blessed* ignorance; blissful; সুখদ, সুখময়; আনন্দময়। **3.** Revered; adorable; মান্য; পূজ্য, অর্চ্চনীয়। **4.** Fortunate; happy; "*Blessed* thou be, among women;" সুভগ, ভাগ্যবান; সুখী, ধন্য। **5.** Beatified; as, *blessed* spirits; in paradise; অপবর্গপ্রাপ্ত; স্বর্গগত। **–ly,** *adv.* **–ness,** *n.* Happiness; heavenly joy; enjoyment of divine favour; সুখ, শ্রেয়ঃ, কল্যাণ, নিশ্রেয়স; পরমানন্দ, স্বর্গীয় সুখ, অপবর্গ, ঈশ্বরানুগ্রহ; দেবানুগ্রহ-ভোগ। **Single blessedness** — (Jocularly) The unmarried life ; the life of celibacy ; "Grows, lives and dies in *single blessedness* ;" (রহস্যচ্ছলে) অবিবাহিত জীবন ; অনূঢ়াবস্থা, কৌমার্য্য, আজন্ম কৌমার ব্রত। **To your blessed lotus feet**—শ্রীচরণকমলেষু।

blĕss'-ing, *n.* **1.** A declaration or invocation of divine favour ; a benediction ; a bestowal of divine favour ; ঈশ্বরাশীর্ব্বাদ ঘোষণা, ঈশ্বরের আশীর্ব্বাদ প্রার্থনা ; আশিস্, আশীর্ব্বাদ, আশীর্ব্বচন ; ঈশ্বরানুগ্রহদান। **2.** A beneficent gift of God, nature, etc. ; a thing one is glad of ; a boon ; ভগবৎকৃপা, ঈশ্বরপ্রসাদ, কল্যাণ, প্রকৃতির দান ; তুষ্টিজনক বিষয় ; বর। **To ask a blessing**—To say grace before meal ; আহারের পূর্ব্বে ঈশ্বরাশীর্ব্বাদ প্রার্থনা করা।

blĕth'-êr, blăth'-êr, *v. i.* & *n.* To talk loquacious nonsense ; বক্ বক্ করা, বাচলামি করা। ***Noun.*** A garrulous nonsense ; অর্থশূন্য প্রলাপ। **–ing,** *adj.* Foolishly talkative ; বাচাল।

blew'-its (blü-), *n.* A kind of edible mushroom ; একপ্রকার আহারোপযোগী ছত্রাক (ব্যাঙের ছাতা)।

blight' (blīt), *v. t.* & *n.* **1.** To prevent the growth of ; to nip in the bud ; ধ্বংস করা, বৃদ্ধির ব্যাঘাত করা ; অঙ্কুরেই বিনষ্ট করা। **2.** To exert baleful influence on ; to destroy the happiness of ; to mar ; as, to *blight* one's prospects ; অনিষ্টকর প্রভাব বিস্তার করা; (কাহারও) সুখ শান্তি নষ্ট করা, শ্রীভ্রষ্ট করা ; বিনাশ করা, নষ্ট করা। ***Noun.*** **1.** A disease that suddenly nips or destroys plants ; উদ্ভিদের রোগ-বিশেষ, ধসা-রোগ। **2.** A close hazy state of the atmosphere ; বায়ুমণ্ডলের বদ্ধ এবং কুজ্ঝটিকাচ্ছন্ন ভাব। **3.** Any obscure and malignant influence ; anything which withers hopes or prospects ; অশুভ প্রভাব ; আশাভরসা-নাশক বিষয়। **4.** A species of aphis ; এক জাতীয় শস্যনাশক কীট। **Blight'-ing,** *adj.* **Blight'-ing-ly,** *adv.*

blīnd, *adj., v. t.* & *n.* **1.** Without sight or the power of seeing ; অন্ধ, দৃষ্টিশক্তিহীন। **2.** Lacking in discernment or foresight ; as, authors are *blind* to their own defects ; destitute of intellectual or moral light ; দূরদৃষ্টিশূন্য, অদূরদর্শী ; বিবেকশূন্য, জ্ঞানান্ধ, তামসিক, অন্ধধী (মঃ উঃ)। **3.** Not well-marked or easily seen ; hidden ; concealed ; as, a *blind* path : *blind* ditch ; অন্ধকারময় ; নিভৃত ; গুপ্ত। **4.** Intricate ; as, a *blind* maze in a wood ; কুটিল, সঙ্কুল, গহন। **5.** Reckless ; as, *blind* fury, speed, etc. ; mechanical ; not ruled by purpose ; as, *blind* forces ; প্রমাদী, দৃক্‌পাতহীন ; যন্ত্রবৎ ; উদ্দেশ্যবিহীন। **6.** Having no opening for light or passage ; as, a *blind* door, wall, etc. ; আলোকপথ-শূন্য। **7.** Open only at one end ; as, a *blind* lane ; কেবল একদিকে উন্মুক্ত। **8.** Unintelligible ; as, the *blind* passage in a book ; illegible ; a *blind* writing ; দুর্ব্বোধ, দুরধিগম্য, অবোধ্য, অজ্ঞেয় ; দুষ্পাঠ্য। ***Verb t.*** **1.** To make blind ; to deprive the sight of ; অন্ধ করা ; দৃষ্টিহীন করা। **2.** To rob of judgement ; to deceive ; বিচার-মূঢ় করা ; প্রতারণা করা। **3.** To darken ; to obscure ; অন্ধকারাচ্ছন্ন করা ; ঝাপ্‌সা করা, অস্পষ্ট করা। **4.** To put out of sight ; to conceal ; চক্ষুর অন্তরাল করা ; লুকান। ***Noun.*** **1.** Anything which obstructs the light or sight ; a screen for a window, esp. on roller ; দৃষ্টি বা আলোকরোধকারী বস্তু ; জানালার পরদা বা তিরস্করণী, ঝিলিমিলি (Venetian blind)। **2.** Anything to conceal one's real design ; a subterfuge ; a pretext ; "These verses were only a *blind* to conceal the dangerous design ;" চোখের ঠুলি ; ফন্দি, কৌশল ; ছল। **Blind'-ed,** *adj.* [*Blinded by rage*—ক্রোধান্ধ। *Blinded by passion*—কামান্ধ।] **Blind'-er,** *n.* **1.** One that blinds ; যে বা যাহা অন্ধ করে। **2.** A blinker for a horse ; অশ্বের নেত্রবন্ধনী। **Blind'-ly,** *adv.* **1.** In a blind way ; অন্ধবৎ। **2.** Heedlessly ; gropingly ; recklessly ; অসতর্কভাবে ; আঁধারে হাতড়াইয়া ; অবিবেচকের মত। **Blind'-ness,** *n.* **1.** Want of sight ; অন্ধত্ব, দৃষ্টিহীনতা। **2.** Want of intellectual or moral discernment ; folly ; recklessness ; অজ্ঞানতা, বিবেকশূন্যতা ; নির্ব্বুদ্ধিতা ; হঠকারিতা। **Blind bud**—One that bears no bloom ; যে মুকুল হইতে পুষ্পোৎপত্তি হয় না। **Blind-coal**—Coal burning without flame ; যে কয়লা জ্বলিবার সময় শিখা-বিস্তার করে না। **Blind ditch**—A ditch that cannot be easily seen ; যে গর্ত্ত সহজে দৃষ্ট হয় না। **Blind faith**—অন্ধবিশ্বাস, কুসংস্কারজনিত অন্ধ-বিশ্বাস। **Blind lane**—A lane closed at one end ; বদ্ধগলি, একদিকেমাত্র খোলা গলি। **Blind-lantern**—A dark-lantern ; চোরা লণ্ঠন। **Blind letter, man, reader, etc.**—Ill-addressed letter and the officials dealing with such letters ; অশুদ্ধ বা অস্পষ্ট শিরোনামাযুক্ত পত্র, ডাকঘরের যে সকল কর্ম্মচারী উক্ত পত্রের বিলি বন্দোবস্ত করেন। **Blind-man's buff**—A well-known game ; কাণামছি খেলা, চোখবাঁধা খেলা, অঙ্গুলীতাড়িতকা ক্রিয়া (বাৎস্যঃ)। **Blind-man's holiday**—The time before candles are lighted ; গোধূলি বেলা। **Blind side**—A person's weak point ; the unguarded side of a person ; কোন ব্যক্তির স্বভাবের দুর্ব্বলতা ; কোন ব্যক্তির অরক্ষিত পার্শ্ব। **Blind-stitch** — Sewing visible only on one side ; একদিকে দেখা যায় এমন সেলাই। **Blind to**—Unmindful of ; দৃক্‌পাতশূন্য।

Blind-window—One that admits no light ; আলোক প্রবেশের পথশূন্য বাতায়ন. **Blind-worm**—Slow-worm, একপ্রকার সরীসৃপ, কেচুয়া (ফঃ হিঃ)। **Blind at night**—নিশান্ধ। **Blind of (an) one eye**—একচক্ষুহীন, কাণা। **Blind darkness**—অন্ধতম। **Born blind**—জন্মান্ধ। **Colour-blind**—বর্ণান্ধ। **Love is blind, Cupid is painted blind**—প্রণয় অন্ধ, প্রেমের অঞ্জন চক্ষুতে মাখিয়া দেখিলে সবই সুন্দর দেখায়।

blĭnd'-āge, *n.* (*Mil.*) A screen in fortification, sieges, etc. to protect from the enemy's firing ; দুর্গস্থিত সৈন্যগণের রক্ষার্থ তিরস্করণী বিশেষ।

blĭnd'-fōld, *adj.* & *adv.* **1.** Having the eyes bandaged ; আবৃতনেত্র, বদ্ধচক্ষু, রুদ্ধদৃষ্টি। **2.** Without perception or forethought ; reckless ; as, sailing *blindfold* ; জ্ঞানশূন্য ; দৃক্‌পাতশূন্য।

blĭnd'-fōld, *v. t.* **1.** To cover the eyes with bandage ; চক্ষু বাঁধিয়া দেওয়া। **2.** To darken the understanding ; as, prejudice *blindfolded* him ; বুদ্ধি ঘুলাইয়া দেওয়া।

blink', *v. i., t.* & *n.* **1.** To twinkle with the eye ; চোখ মিট্ মিট্ করা। **2.** To see with the eyes half-shut ; অর্দ্ধনিমীলিত নেত্রে নিরীক্ষণ করা। **3.** To wink for an instant ; ক্ষণেকের জন্য চক্ষু বন্ধ করা। **4.** To shine with unsteady light ; to twinkle ; as, the stars began to *blink* ; মিট্ মিট্ করিয়া জ্বলা, ঝিকমিক করা ; টিম টিম করা। ***Verb t.*** **1.** To shut the eyes to ; to ignore ; to evade ; as, to *blink* the question ; কোন কিছু দেখিয়া না দেখা ; অগ্রাহ্য করা ; উপেক্ষা করা। **2.** To blindfold ; "With the sun *blinking* my eyes ;" অন্ধীভূত করা। ***Noun.*** A glimpse or glance ; a momentary gleam ; চাহনি, কটাক্ষ ; ক্ষণিক দীপ্তি। **Blink'-ard**, *n.* **1.** A person who blinks ; যে ব্যক্তি চোখ্ মিট্ মিট্ করে। **2.** One who is stupid or obtuse ; "Calling himself an ass and a *blinkard* ;" মূঢ় ব্যক্তি, স্থূলবুদ্ধি ব্যক্তি। **Blink'-er**, *n.* (Usu. *pl.*) Flaps of leather on a horse's bridle to prevent him from seeing sideways ; অশ্বের উভয় পার্শ্বস্থ দৃশ্যরোধকারী বল্গা-সংলগ্ন নেত্রাবরণ বিশেষ। **Ice-blink**—A shining whiteness about the horizon ; reflection of distant ice-fields ; দিক্‌চক্রবালের চতুষ্পার্শ্ববর্ত্তী উজ্জ্বল ধবলিমা ; দূরবর্ত্তী বরফস্তূপের প্রতিফলিত প্রভা।

bliss, *n.* **1.** Gladness ; joy ; enjoyment ; সুখ ; আনন্দ ; ভোগ। **2.** Perfect joy ; blessedness ; hence, paradise ; "The path to *bliss* abounds with many a snare ;" পূর্ণানন্দ, অখণ্ডানন্দ ; স্বর্গীয় আনন্দ, ধন্যতা, কল্যাণ, শ্রেয়ঃ, অপবর্গ, মঙ্গল, পরমগতি, নিশ্রেয়স ; অতএব স্বর্গ। **Bliss'-ful**, *adj.* **Bliss-ful-ly**, *adv.* **Bliss'-ful-ness**, *n.*

blis'-têr, *n., v. t.* & *i.* **1.** A watery bladder on the skin ; a pustule ; ফোস্কা ; ফুস্‌কুরি, জলপূর্ণ ব্রণ, বিস্ফোট (সুশ্রুঃ), বিস্ফোটক (ঐ), পিটক (চঃ)। **2.** A similar swelling on the surface of plants, metals or a painted surface ; বৃক্ষ, ধাতুফলক বা কোন বস্তুর চিত্রিত পৃষ্ঠোপরি ফুস্কুরীবৎ স্ফীতি। **3.** A plaster applied to raise a blister ; ফোস্কা উৎপাদনের জন্য বস্ত্রলিপ্ত মলম। ***Verb. t.*** **1.** To raise a blister on ; ফোস্কা তোলা। **2.** To give pain to or injure by a blister ; "Whose sole name *blisters* our tongue ;" ফোস্কা তুলিয়া যন্ত্রণা দেওয়া বা ক্ষত করা। ***Verb i.*** To become covered with blisters ; সর্ব্বাঙ্গে ফোস্কা উঠা। **—y**, *adj.* **Blister-beetle, Blister-fly**—An insect used for raising blisters ; ফোস্কা-উৎপাদক কীট বিশেষ, তেলিনী পোকা।

blīthe, *adj.* Gay ; merry ; joyous ; (chiefly in poetry) ; হৃষ্ট, হর্ষোৎফুল্ল ; উল্লসিত; আনন্দময়, পুলকপূর্ণ, প্রফুল্লচিত্ত। **Blithe'-ly**, *adv.* **Blithe'-ness**, *n.* **Blithe'-some**, *adj.* Merry ; cheery ; প্রফুল্ল ; উৎফুল্ল। **Blithe'-some-ly**, *adv.* **Blithe'-some-ness**, *n.*

blĭz'-zard (zêrd), *n.* A furious blinding storm of wind and snow ; প্রবল হিমবাত্যা, তুষারঝঞ্ঝা। **—ly, —ous**, *adjs.*

bloat (blōt), *v. t.* & *i.* **1.** To make turgid ; to cause a swelling on the surface of ; স্ফীত করা ; ফুলাইয়া তোলা, ফাঁপাইয়া তোলা। **2.** To puff up ; to make vain ; "*Bloat* him up with praise ;" গর্ব্বে স্ফীত করা ; দাম্ভিক করা। ***Verb i.*** To become turgid ; to swell ; স্ফীত হইয়া উঠা ; ফুলিয়া উঠা।

bloat (blōt), *v. t.* To dry (herrings) in smoke ; ধূঁয়াতে মাছ শুকান। **Bloat'-er**, *n.* (Also, *bloated herring.*) A smoke-dried herring ; ধূমদ্বারা শুষ্কীকৃত হেরিং মৎস্য।

bloat'-ĕd (blōt-), **bloat** (blōt), *adj.* **1.** Swollen or inflated, esp. with gluttony and self-indulgence ; স্ফীত, বিশেষতঃ অমিতভোজন বা বিলাসের ফলে স্থূলদেহ। **2.** Unduly large ; of excessive size ; as, *bloated* mass, armaments, etc. ; বিরাট ; বিপুলায়তন। **3.** Puffed up with pride ; pampered ; as, the *bloated* aristocracy ; গর্ব্বস্ফীত ; অপরিমিত ভোগবিলাসতৃপ্ত।

blŏb, *n.* **1.** A drop of liquid ; এক বিন্দু তরল পদার্থ। **2.** A small roundish mass ; ক্ষুদ্র গোলাকার পিণ্ড। **3.** A spot of colour ; রঙ্গের দাগ।

blŏb'-bêr, *adj.* Thick or swollen (said of the lips) ; (ওষ্ঠাধর-সম্পর্কে) স্থূল অথবা স্ফীত। **Blobber-lipped**—With thick protruding lips ; স্থূল এবং উদ্গাত ওষ্ঠাধরবিশিষ্ট।

blŏck, *n.* & *v. t.* **1.** A large heavy piece of wood or stone ; a stump ; স্থূলকাষ্ঠ, কুঁদো, গুঁড়িকাঠ ; স্থূণা, স্থাণু। **2.** A bulky piece of anything ; কোন বস্তুর প্রকাণ্ড খণ্ড। **3.** The piece of wood on which the condemned were beheaded ; যে কাষ্ঠ-

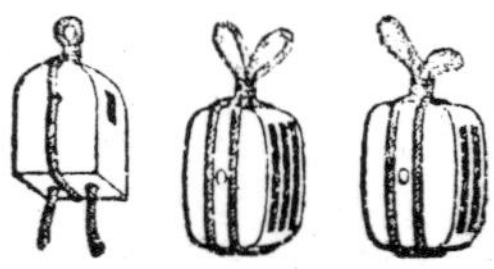

Blocks.

খণ্ডোপরি প্রাণদণ্ডে দণ্ডিত ব্যক্তিগণের শিরচ্ছেদ করা হইত, বধ্যকাষ্ঠ। **4.** The mould on which hats, bonnets, etc. are shaped ; যে ছাঁচের উপর রাখিয়া টুপি প্রভৃতি নির্ম্মিত হয়। **5.** A cluster of buildings bounded usually by four streets ; also, a square or portion of a city inclosed by streets ; ভবনশ্রেণী, সাধারণতঃ রাজপথচতুষ্টয়দ্বারা বেষ্টিত ভবনশ্রেণী ; নগর-চত্বর। **6.** A pulley or system of pulleys mounted in a case ; কোন আধারের উপর আরোপিত কপিকল বা কপিকলশ্রেণী। **7.** A piece of wood engraved for printing ; মুদ্রাঙ্কণের জন্য উৎকীর্ণ কাষ্ঠফলক। **8.** A stone prepared for building ; অট্টালিকাদি নির্ম্মাণের জন্য প্রস্তুত প্রস্তরখণ্ড। **9.** An obstruction ; a stoppage of traffic or progress ; (also, *stumbling block*) ; বাঁধা, বিঘ্ন ; সংরোধ, অবরোধ, প্রতিবন্ধক। **10.** (*Cricket*) The spot where a batsman places his bat to guard his wicket ; (also, centre) ; (ক্রিকেট ক্রীড়ায়) যে স্থানে ব্যাট রাখিয়া ব্যাটধারী উইকেট রক্ষা করে। **11.** A hard-hearted person ; পাষাণ-হৃদয় ব্যক্তি। ***Verb t.*** **1.** To obstruct passage, etc. ; to put obstacles in the way of progress, etc. ; পথাবরোধ করা, আটক করা ; উন্নতির পথে কণ্টক প্রদান করা। **2.** To shape (hats) ; কাঠের ছাঁচের উপর রাখিয়া টুপি তৈয়ার করা। **3.** (*Parliament*) To announce opposition to a bill ; (পার্লেমেণ্টে) কোন প্রস্তাবিত আইনের প্রতিবাদ করা হইবে বলিয়া ঘোষণা করা। **4.** (*Cricket*) To stop (a ball) with the bat ; ক্রীড়াদণ্ড (ব্যাট্) দ্বারা ক্রীড়াগোলকের (বলের) গতিরোধ করা। **5.** (*Bookbinding*) To emboss the covers of books ; পুস্তকের মলাট (প্রচ্ছদ-পট) উদ্গত অক্ষর বা চিত্রে সুশোভিত করা। **Block'-ish,** *adj.* Like a block ; stupid ; dull ; কাষ্ঠখণ্ডের মত ; স্থূল-বুদ্ধি, জড়-বুদ্ধি ; মন্দ-বুদ্ধি। **Block-book**—A book printed from engraved blocks ; খোদিত ফলক হইতে মুদ্রিত পুস্তক। **Block-chain**—A kind of endless chain used in bicycles etc. ; দ্বিচক্রযান প্রভৃতির অন্তহীন শৃঙ্খল। **Blockhead**—Dolt ; নির্ব্বোধ ব্যক্তি। **Block-house**—A building of heavy logs of wood forming a kind of fort ; also, a house of squared logs ; গুরুভার কাষ্ঠখণ্ড-নির্ম্মিত দুর্গ বিশেষ ; সমচতুষ্কোণাকারে কর্ত্তিত কাষ্ঠখণ্ড সমূহদ্বারা নির্ম্মিত গৃহ। **Block-printing**—The process of printing from wooden block ; খোদিত কাষ্ঠখণ্ড হইতে মুদ্রণের প্রণালী। **Block-system (on railway)**—A system of working trains, by which no train may enter a section till it is clear ; যে ব্যবস্থানুসারে রেলপথের কোন অংশে কোনরূপ প্রতিরোধজনক বস্তু থাকা পর্য্যন্ত কোন বাষ্পীয় শকট তথায় প্রবেশ করিতে পারে না। **Barber's block**—A wooden head for wigs ; পরচুলা রাখার জন্য কাষ্ঠময় মস্তক। **A chip of the old block**—A child like its father, especially in character ; বাপের মত বেটা, পিতার অনুরূপ সন্তান। **In block**—As a whole ; wholesale ; সবটা ; পাইকারী। **To block out**—To sketch roughly ; to plan ; মোটামুটি নকসা করা ; নক্সা করা। **To Block up, in**—To confine ; অবরোধ করা। **To cut blocks with a razor**—To waste ingenuity, etc. ; অযথা সূক্ষ্ম বুদ্ধি ব্যয় করা, স্থূল বিষয়ে প্রয়োগ করিয়া ক্ষুরধার বুদ্ধি নষ্ট করা।

blŏck-āde', *n.* & *v. t.* **1.** A blocking up of harbour, town, etc., by hostile forces or ships ; শত্রু পক্ষীয় সৈন্য বা জাহাজাদিদ্বারা পোতাশ্রয়, নগর প্রভৃতি অবরোধ। **2.** An obstruction to passage ; an imprisonment by snow, etc. ; বাঁধা, বিঘ্ন ; বরফ দ্বারা আটক। ***Verb t.*** **1.** To shut up a town or fortress by troops or ships ; জাহাজ বা সৈন্যদ্বারা কোন নগর বা দুর্গ অবরোধ করা। **2.** To obstruct door, view, etc. ; দ্বার, দৃষ্টি প্রভৃতি রোধ করা। **Paper blockade**—A blockade declared but not made effective ; যে অবরোধের বিষয় কেবল কাগজপত্রে ঘোষিত হয়,—কিন্তু কার্য্যে পরিণত হয় না। **To raise a blockade**—To cease blockading ; অবরোধ হইতে বিরত হওয়া। **To run a blockade**—To evade a blockading force ; অবরোধকারী সৈন্যদলকে পরিহার করা।

blŏck-ād'-ēr, *n.* One who blockades ; a blockading vessel ; অবরোধকারী, অবরোদ্ধা ; অবরোধকারী রণপোত।

blōke, *n.* (*Colloq.*) A man ; a fellow ; a chap ; (চলিত ভাষায়) লোক ; বেটা ; মরদ।

blŏnd, blonde (blŏnd), *adj.* & *n.* **1.** (Of complexion) Fair ; গৌরবর্ণ, সুশ্রী। **2.** (*Of hair*) Auburn-coloured ; স্বর্ণাভ-পিঙ্গলবর্ণ। ***Noun.*** A person with fair hair and complexion, (esp. a woman, spelt *blonde*) ; নীলাক্ষ, গৌরবর্ণ পুরুষ, নীলনয়না গৌরাঙ্গী। **Blond lace**—A kind of silk-lace, (usu. *blonde*) ; একপ্রকার রেশমী ফিতা।

blood (blŭd), *n.* & *v. t.* **1.** The red fluid circulating through the veins and arteries of men and animals ; রক্ত, শোণিত, রুধির, অসৃক্, ক্ষতজ। **2.** The sap of plants ; the juice of anything, esp. if red ; "He washed his clothes in the *blood* of grapes ;" গাছের রস ; কোন কিছুর রস, বিশেষতঃ রক্তবর্ণ রস। **3.** Taking of life ; murder ; "*Blood* doth *blood* demand ;" sacrifice ; as, by the *blood* of Christ ; guilt of bloodshed ; "His *blood* be on us, and on our childern ;" জীবননাশ ; হত্যা ; বলিদান ; রক্তপাত-হত্যাপরাধ। **4.** Temperament ; passion ; mettle ; as, his *blood* is up ; প্রকৃতি, স্বভাব, মেজাজ ; রাগ ; তেজঃ, বীর্য্য। **5.** Consanguinity ; kinship ; "They proved the *blood* but were refused the land ;" relations ; "He loved justice more than his *blood* ; সপিণ্ডতা, সগোত্রতা ; জ্ঞাতিত্ব ; কুটুম্ব। **6.** Family ; race ; পরিবার ; কুল, বংশ। **7.** Noble birth ; good family ; as, the pride of *blood* ; কৌলিন্য ; উচ্চ-বংশ। **8.** Good breed or pedigree ; as, a *blood* horse ; উৎকৃষ্ট জাতি। **8.** The sensual or animal nature ; "Nor gives it satisfaction to our *blood* ;" দৈহিক প্রকৃতি, দেহ-ধর্ম্ম। **9.** A dandy ; a man of fashion ; as, the *bloods* of the city ; সৌখিন লোক ; ফুল বাবু *Verb t.* **1.** (*Surg.*) To let blood ; to bleed ; (অস্ত্রোপচার-বিদ্যা) রক্তপাত করা ; রক্তমোক্ষণ করা। **2.** To give (hounds or soldiers) a taste or sight of blood ; শিকারী কুকুরকে প্রথম রক্তের স্বাদ গ্রহণ করিতে দেওয়া, সৈন্যদিগকে প্রথম রক্ত দর্শন করান। **Blood′-less,** *adj.* Without blood ; hence, lifeless ; রক্তশূন্য ; অতএব জীবন-শূন্য। **2.** Unfeeling ; cruel ; নির্ম্মম ; নিষ্ঠুর। **3.** Without blood-shed ; as, a *bloodless* victory ; রক্তপাতশূন্য, রক্ত-লেশহীন। **4.** Pale ; pallid ; as, a *bloodless* image of despair ; বিবর্ণ ; ম্লান, পাণ্ডুর। **Blood′-less-ly,** *adv.* **Blood-baptism**—The martyrdom of those who had not been baptised ; শোণিত-দীক্ষা। [ধর্ম্মার্থ আত্মবলিদানকারী যথারীতি দীক্ষিত না হইলেও খৃষ্টধর্ম্মে দীক্ষার ফললাভ করে।] **Blood-bought**—Gained at the price of life ; রক্তপাত-লব্ধ, রক্তমূল্যে ক্রীত। **Blood-guilty**—Guilty of murder or blood-shed ; হত্যাপরাধী, খুনী। (Whence, **–guilt-i-ness,** *n.*) **Blood-heat**—The ordinary heat of blood in the healthy human body (about 98′-60 *F.*) ; মানব-শোণিতের স্বাভাবিক উষ্ণতা। **Blood-horse**—A thorough bred horse ; উৎকৃষ্ট অশ্ব-বংশোদ্ভব ঘোটক। **Blood-hot**—Excited for blood-shed ; রক্তপাতের জন্য উত্তেজিত, খুনী। As warm as blood (in its natural temperature) ; (স্বাভাবিক অবস্থায় মানব) শোণিতবৎ-উষ্ণ। **Blood-hound**—A large keen-scented fierce kind of dog ; প্রখরঘ্রাণশক্তি-বিশিষ্ট শিকারী কুক্কুর, ডালকুত্তা। A detective ; a spy ; as, the *blood-hounds* of the law ; গোয়েন্দা, টিক্-টিকি ; গুপ্তচর। **Blood-letting**—The surgical removal of a patient's blood ; রক্তমোক্ষণ, রুধিরাভিস্রবণ, অসৃগ্-বিমোক্ষণ। **Blood-money**—A reward for bringing about the death of another ; a reward to witness for securing capital sentence ; money paid to the next of kin (as compensation) for the slaughter of a relative ; কোন ব্যক্তিকে হত্যা করিয়া যে পুরস্কার লাভ করা যায় ; প্রাণদণ্ডের উপযোগী প্রমাণ প্রদান করিতে পারিলে সাক্ষীকে যে পুরস্কার দেওয়া হয় ; হত ব্যক্তির নিকটতম আত্মীয়কে (ক্ষতিপূরণস্বরূপ) যে অর্থ প্রদান করা যায়। **Blood-orange**—An orange with red juice ; লোহিতবর্ণ রসবিশিষ্ট কমলালেবু। **Blood-poisoning**—A bad state of the blood resulting from poisonous matter getting into it, (esp. through wound) ; রক্তদুষ্টি। **Blood-rain** — রক্তবৃষ্টি। **Blood-red** — Red like blood ; রক্তারুণ। **Blood-relation** — One related by blood, not by marriage ; জ্ঞাতি, সগোত্র, একবংশ। **Bloodshed**—The shedding of blood ; slaughter ; রক্তপাত, রক্তারক্তি ; হত্যা, খুন। [*Bloodshedder*—A murderer ; a man-slayer ; খুনী ; হত্যাকারী, নরঘাতক।] **Blood-shot**—(Of the eye) Red and inflamed with blood ; কষায়িত (চক্ষু)। **Blood-stained**—Stained with blood ; guilty of murder ; রক্তকলঙ্কিত, শোণিতদিগ্ধ (মঃ ভাঃ) ; নরহত্যাপরাধী। **Blood-stone**—Kinds of precious stones spotted or streaked with red ; heliotrope ; মূল্যবান প্রস্তর, রক্ত পাষাণ ; এক প্রকার ফুট ফুট লোহিত দাগবিশিষ্ট গাঢ় হরিদ্বর্ণ মণি। **Blood-sucker**—An animal that sucks blood, especially, the leech ; রক্তশোষক, জোঁক, জলৌকা। (*Fig.*) An extortioner ; a sponger ; (লক্ষণায়) পীড়নকারী, অর্থশোষণকারী, রক্তশোষক ; পরভাগ্যোপজীবী, চাটুকার। **Bloodthirsty**—Eager to shed blood ; cruel ; sanguinary ; রক্তপিপাসু, রুধির-পিপাসু, রুধির-লালস ; নির্দ্দয় ; জিঘাংসু। **Blood-vessel**—A vein or artery ; রক্তবহানাড়ী (হঃ চঃ), রক্ত-বাহিনী, অসৃগ্বহা (অঃ), ধমনী। **Blood-wite**—A penalty for murder ; নরহত্যার জন্য শাস্তি। **Blood-worm**—A small red earth worm used by anglers ; বড়শীর টোপ-স্বরূপ ব্যবহৃত লোহিতবর্ণ কীটবিশেষ। **Bad blood**—Ill-feeling ; বৈরভাব, বিদ্বেষ ভাব। **Blood and iron**—Military compulsion ; সামরিক বল-প্রয়োগ। **Blood and iron policy**—War-policy ; রণনীতি। **Blood is thicker than water**—The tie of kindred is real ; রক্তের বন্ধন

(আত্মীয়তার বন্ধন) আর সকল বন্ধন হইতে শ্রেষ্ঠতর। **Blood is up**—Passion is excited; ক্রোধ উদ্দীপ্ত হইয়াছে। **Blood royal** or **the blood**—Royal family; রাজবংশ। **Blue blood**—Aristocratic birth; আভিজাত্য। (See BLUE.) **Flesh and blood**—The animal nature; দৈহিক প্রকৃতি, দেহধর্ম্ম, রক্তমাংসের শরীর। **My own flesh and blood**—Near kindred—children, brothers, sisters, etc.; আমার নিজের পুত্রকন্যা, ভ্রাতা, ভগিনী বা অন্যান্য নিকটতম আত্মীয়গণ। **Fresh blood**—New members admitted to a society; কোন সম্প্রদায়ের নূতন সভ্য। **Half-blood**—Relationship through only one parent; পিতৃ কিম্বা মাতৃ-সম্পর্কে কুটুম্বিতা। [*Of half-blood*—বৈমাত্র, বৈপিত্র, ভিন্নোদর।] **In blood**—In full vigour; full of life; পূর্ণোৎসাহে; তেজঃপূর্ণ। **In cold blood**—Calmly and deliberately; বিনা উত্তেজনায়, ভাবিয়া চিন্তিয়া। **In hot blood**—In temper or excitement; উত্তেজনাবশে। **Out of blood**—Not vigorous; lifeless নিস্তেজ; নির্জীব। **To make blood boil**—To provoke indignation and anger; রক্ত উষ্ণ করিয়া তোলা, রাগে গর গর করা। **To make one's blood creep**—To fill one with owe and terror; ভয় এবং ত্রাসে অভিভূত করা। **To take one's blood**—To kill him; হত্যা করা। **Whole blood**—Relationship by both father and mother; পিতৃমাতৃ উভয়-সম্পর্কে কুটুম্বিতা।

blood'-ȳ (blŭd-), *adj., adv.* & *v. t.* **1.** Relating to, composed of, like, blood; রক্তসম্বন্ধীয়, রক্তগঠিত, শোণিত-তুল্য, শোণিতোপম। **2.** Smeared or stained with blood; as, a *bloody* hand; bleeding; as, *bloody* nose; রক্তাক্ত, শোণিত-রঞ্জিত; গলদ্‌-রক্ত। **3.** Blood-thirsty; cruel; blood-guilty; as, *bloody* villains; রক্তপিপাসু; নিষ্ঠুরস্বভাব, নির্দ্দয়, নৃশংস; রক্তপাতাপরাধী। **4.** Of the colour of blood; blood-red; as, *bloody* flag; রক্তবর্ণ; রক্তারুণ। **5.** (In foul language) Damned, contemptible, etc.; as, a *bloody* rascal; (কদর্য্য ভাষায়) নারকীয়, ঘৃণিত, জঘন্য। **6.** Involving or loving much bloodshed; রক্তপাত-সংসৃষ্ট, প্রচুর রক্তপাতামোদী। **7.** Sanguinary; as, *bloody* battle; রক্তপূর্ণ। ***Adv.*** Very; exceedingly; abominably, (as an intensive); অত্যন্ত, ভারি; নিতান্ত; জঘন্যভাবে। ***Verb t.*** To make blood-red; to stain with bloodshed; রক্তাক্ত করা, রক্তরঞ্জিত করা; রক্তপাত দোষে কলঙ্কিত করা। **–i-ly,** *adv.*—**i-ness,** *n.* **Bloody assizes**—The infamous assizes held by judge Jeffries in 1685; ইতিহাস-প্রসিদ্ধ নির্ম্মম বিচারক জেফ্রিসের বিচারাধিবেশন। **Bloody bones**—A children's bugbear; জুজু। **Bloody-flux**—Dysentery; রক্তাতিসার (হঃ চঃ), রক্তামাশয় (ঐ)। **Bloody-hand**—A red hand, (the armorial device of a baronet); রক্তাক্তহস্ত। [ব্যারোণেট উপাধিধারী ব্যক্তির কুলচিহ্ন।] **Bloody-minded**—Having a cruel disposition; ক্রূরস্বভাব। **Bloody-sweat**—A sweat accompanied by a discharge of blood; রক্ত-মিশ্রিত ঘর্ম্ম। **Bloody urine**—Hæmaturia; সরক্তমূত্র (হঃ চঃ), রক্তমেহ (ঐ)। **Bloody wedding**—St. Bartholomew's slaughter in 1752; ১৭৫২ খৃষ্টাব্দের সেণ্ট বার্থলমিউর হত্যাকাণ্ড—এই হত্যাকাণ্ড নৃপতি ৪র্থ হেনরীর বিবাহ-ভোজের সময় অনুষ্ঠিত হইয়াছিল।

bloom, *n.* & *v. i.* **1.** The blossom or flower of a plant; (used collectively); মুকুল, কোরক, কলিকা, পুষ্প, কুসুম। **2.** The opening of flowers; the flowering state; পুষ্প-প্রস্ফুটন; পুষ্পের বিকাশাবস্থা। **3.** The state or time of beauty, freshness and vigour; prime; perfection; সৌন্দর্য্য, নবীনতা ও সজীবতার কাল; তারুণ্য, নবযৌবন; চরমোৎকর্ষ। **4.** Flush; glow; the roseate hue of the cheek; বর্ণদীপ্তি; দীপ্তি; কপোলরাগ, গণ্ডদেশের গোলাবি বর্ণ। **5.** The delicate powdery coating on grapes, plums, etc.; আঙ্গুর বা বদরীজাতীয় ফলের সূক্ষ্ম বালুকাবৎ আবরণ। **6.** A kind of raisin; একপ্রকার কিস্‌মিস্‌। ***Verb i.*** **1.** To be in flower; to bear flowers; মুকুলিত হওয়া, বৌল ধরা; কুসুমিত হওয়া। **2.** To come into full beauty; to glow; পূর্ণ-লাবণ্যে সুশোভিত হওয়া; দীপ্তিবিস্তার করা। **3.** To culminate; to flourish; চরমসীমায় উপনীত হওয়া; শ্রীসমন্বিত হওয়া। **Bloom'-ing,** *adj.* Bright; shining; in the prime of youth; flourishing; উজ্জ্বল; দীপ্ত; নব-যৌবন-শ্রী সমন্বিত, নবযৌবনাঢ্য; শ্রীসমন্বিত। **2.** Flowering; ফুটন্ত, বিকাশী, বিকচ, কুসুমিত। **3.** (*Slang*) Often euphemistic for *bloody*; (ইতরভাষায়) ঘৃণিত, জঘন্য। **Bloom'-ing-ness,** *n.* **Bloom'-less,** *adj.* **Bloom'-y,** *adj.* **In bloom**—Flowering; ফুটন্ত। **To take the bloom off (a thing)**—To deprive of its freshness; নবীনতা নষ্ট করা।

bloom, *n.* A mass of crude iron hammered into thick bar; স্থূল এবং খর্ব্ব দণ্ডাকারে পেটা অপরিষ্কৃত লৌহ।

bloom'-ēr, *n.* [After Mrs. Bloomer of New York who introduced this costume.] **1.** A female costume of short skirts and trousers, (usualy plural); স্ত্রীলোকের একপ্রকার পোষাক। **2.** A woman who wears this dress; ঐ প্রকার পরিচ্ছদ-পরিহিতা নারী।

blŏs'-sŏm, *n.* & *v. i.* **1.** A flower-bud; the flower that precedes fruit; the flowers of a plant, collectively; কুসুমকলিকা, পুষ্পকোরক, কুট্‌মল, মুকুল; বৌল, ফলজনক মুকুল; বৃক্ষের পুষ্পরাজি। **2.** Early stage of growth; as, the first *blossom* of that literature ; promise ; উন্নতি বা বৃদ্ধির প্রথম অবস্থা, উন্মেষ ; আশা। *Verb i.* 1. To put forth flowers ; to bloom ; to flower ; মুকুলিত হওয়া, কুসুমিত হওয়া ; প্রস্ফুটিত হওয়া ; ফুল্ল হওয়া। 2. To flourish and prosper ; সমৃদ্ধ হওয়া, শ্রীসমন্বিত হওয়া। **Blos'-somed,** *adj.* **Blossom-faced, —nosed**—Bloated ; স্ফীত, গর্ব্বিত।

blŏt, *v. t.* & *i.* 1. To spot or stain with ink ; মসী-লিপ্ত করা। 2. To impair ; to soil ; "It *blots* thy beauty ;" নষ্ট করা, ক্ষতি করা ; মলিন করা। 3. To tarnish ; to sully ; "*Blot* not thy innocence with guiltless blood ;" কলঙ্কিত করা ; কলুষিত করা। 4. (With *out*) To efface or obliterate (writing) ; to annihilate ; to destroy ; "Persian monarchy had been *blotted out* by Alexander ;" মুছিয়া ফেলা ; বিলুপ্ত করা, উচ্ছেদ করা ; নির্ম্মূল করা। 5. To obscure ; to shadow ; as, the moon was *blotted* by the earth's shade ; নিষ্প্রভ করা ; ছায়াবৃত করা। 6. To cover with worthles writing ; "Here are a few of the unpleasantest words that ever *blotted* paper ;" বাজে কথা লিখিয়া পূর্ণ করা। 7. To dry with blotting paper ; শোষ কাগজ দ্বারা শুকাইয়া ফেলা। *Verb i.* To take a blot ; as, the paper *blots* easily ; to make an erasure ; শোষ লওয়া ; ঘষিয়া তুলিয়া ফেলা। **Blot'-ter,** *n.* **Blotting paper**—An absorbent paper for drying wet ink-marks; শোষ কাগজ, ব্লটিং কাগজ। **Blotting-case, —pad, —book**—A case or cover enclosing blotting-paper ; শোষ কাগজের আধার, ক্ষুদ্র গদি বা পুস্তক।

blŏt, *n.* 1. A spot or stain of ink, mud, etc. ; দাগ, চিহ্ন। 2. An obliteration ; an erasure ; মুছন, বিলোপ ; অপহার, অপনয়ন। 3. A spot on reputation ; a disgrace ; a blemish ; কলঙ্ক ; অপমান, অপযশ ; খুঁত। **Blot'-ty,** *adj.* **A blot on the escutcheon**—A disgrace in a family record ; বংশের কলঙ্ক।

blŏt, *n.* 1. A piece liable to be taken at backgammon ; ব্যকগ্যামন ক্রীড়ায় অরক্ষিত গুটিকা। 2. A weak point in one's procedure ; "Here the critic has hit a *blot* ;" কোন ব্যক্তির কার্য্য-প্রণালির কোন বিষয়ে অঙ্গহানি।

blŏtch, *n.* & *v. t.* 1. A pustule or eruption upon the skin ; a boil ; ব্রণ, আঁচিল, দাগ, ফুসকুড়ি, লোমফুট, ফোস্কা, দাগ, ত্বকপুষ্প (অঃ), ত্বগঙ্কুর (ঐ) ; ফোঁড়া। 2. A large irregular spot of ink or colour ; রঙ্গ বা কালির দাগ। 3. (*Slang*) Blotting-paper ; (ইতর-ভাষায়) শোষ কাগজ। *Verb t.* To mark or cover with blotches ; জুবড়ান। **Blotch'-ed,** *adj.* **Blotch'-y,** *adj.*

blŏt-tesque' (-tĕsk), *adj.* Done with heavy blotted touches, (of a piece of painting or description) ; (চিত্রাদি পক্ষে) ধ্যাবরানো।

blouse (blowz), *n.* 1. A light loose upper garment, worn by wormken and children ; আলখিল্লা, পুরুষদের একপ্রকার ঢিলা জামা। 2. A kind of light loose-fitting bodice, belted at waist, for women ; স্ত্রীলোকদিগের ঢিলা আঙ্গিয়া। **Bloused,** *adj.*

blow (blö), *v. i.* & *n.* 1. To flower ; to blossom ; to bloom ; ফুল্ল হওয়া, কুসুমিত হওয়া ; মুকুলিত হওয়া ; ফুটা। *Noun.* A blossoming ; as, in full *blow* ; প্রস্ফুটন। **Blown,** *adj.* In bloom ; ফুটন্ত, পুষ্পিত।

blow (blö), *n.* 1. A forcible stroke with the fist, or any instrument ; আঘাত, ঘা, চোট, ঘাত, প্রহার, কিল, ঘুষি। 2. (*Pl.*) Combat ; fighting ; as, to come to *blows* ; সংগ্রাম, হাতাহাতি ; যুদ্ধ। 3. A sudden calamity ; a disaster ; a shock ; আকস্মিক দুর্ঘটনা ; দুর্বিপাক ; ধাক্কা। **At a (one) blow**—Suddenly ; in one operation ; হঠাৎ ; এক ধাক্কায়, এক চোটে, একবারের চেষ্টায়, এক কোপে। **To come to blows, To exchange blows**—To fight, (said of individuals, nations, etc.) ; হাতাহাতি করা, ঘুষাঘুষি করা, যুদ্ধে প্রবৃত্ত হওয়া। **To strike a blow**—To take vigorous action ; বিশেষরূপে প্রতিবিধান করা। **To strike a blow against**—To oppose ; বিরুদ্ধে দণ্ডায়মান হওয়া, বাঁধা দেওয়া। **To strike a blow for**—To help ; সাহায্য করা। **Without striking a blow**—Without a struggle ; বিনাযুদ্ধে, নির্ব্বিবাদে।

blow (blö), *v. i.* 1. To move rapidly, as air ; as, the wind *blows* ; প্রবাহিত হওয়া, বহা। 2. To send forth a strong current of air, from the mouth or from a pair of bellows ; ফুৎকার দেওয়া, ফুঁ দেওয়া, (ভস্ত্রা হইতে) বায়ুপ্রবাহ নির্গত করা 3. To sound on being blown into, as a trumpet ; ফুঁ দিলে ভেঁপুরমত বাজিয়া উঠা। 4. To pant ; to breathe hard ; হাঁপান ; কষ্টে নিশ্বাস ফেলা। 5. (Of whales, etc.) To eject air and water ; (তিমি মৎস্য-সম্পর্কে) শিরোরন্ধ্র হইতে বায়ু এবং জলধারা উৎক্ষেপণ করা। 6. To be carried or driven by the wind ; as, the dust *blows* in from the street ; বাত্যাতাড়িত হওয়া। 7. (*Colloq.*) To brag ; to storm ; (চলিত-ভাষায়) বড়াই করা ; রাগে গর্ গর্ করা। **To blow hot and cold**—To be vacillating ; to appear both to favour and to oppose ; সংশয়ে দোলায়িত হওয়া, দ্বিধা করা ; যুগপৎ স্বপক্ষ ও বিপক্ষ অবলম্বন করিতেছে এরূপ বোধ হওয়া, এক চোখে কাঁদা এক চোকে হাসা, এক মুখে দুরকম কথা বলা। **To blow over**—To pass away without effect ; to cease ; as, the storm is *blown over* ; (ঝড়-সম্বন্ধে) বহিয়া

যাওয়া, (বিপৎ-সম্বন্ধে) কাটিয়া যাওয়া, দূর হওয়া, বিক্ষিপ্ত হওয়া, উড়িয়া যাওয়া ; ক্ষান্ত হওয়া, থামা। **To blow up**—To burst ; to explode ; বিদীর্ণ হওয়া ; উড়িয়া যাওয়া ;

blow (blō), *v. t.* **1.** To produce a current of air with the mouth or by other means ; বায়ুস্রোত প্রবাহিত করা, ফুৎকার দেওয়া, বাতাস দেওয়া। **2.** To drive by a current of air ; to impel ; as, the tempest *blew* the ship ashore ; বায়ুবিতাড়িত করা ; ঠেলিয়া ফেলা। **3.** To sound (a wind instrument) by the breath ; ফুঁ দিয়া বাজান। **4.** To clear of contents by forcing air through ; as, to *blow* one's nose ; ঝাড়া। **5.** To burst or shatter by (usually with *up, down, open,* etc.) ; as, to *blow up* a building ; আগ্নেয়াস্ত্র বা বিস্ফোরক পদার্থদ্বারা উড়াইয়া দেওয়া, ধ্বংস করা, বিদীর্ণ করা। **6.** (*Slang*) To expose ; as, to *blow* one's private doings ; (ইতর ভাষায়) প্রকাশ করা। **7.** To shape or form by inflation ; as, to *blow* bubbles, glass, etc. ; ফুৎকারদ্বারা ফুলাইয়া নানা আকারে গঠন করা। **8.** To put out of breath ; as, to *blow* a horse ; অতিশয় ক্লান্ত করা। **9.** (*Slang*) To curse ; to confound ; (ইতর-ভাষায়) অভিশাপ দেওয়া ; ভেবাচেকা লাগান। **10.** To inflate with pride ; to puff up ; as, *blown* up with popularity ; অহঙ্কারে স্ফীত করা ; গর্ব্বিত করা। **11.** To deposit eggs on or in ; "To suffer the flesh-fly *blow* my mouth ;" কোন কিছুর উপর বা ভিতরে ডিম পাড়া। **Blow-milk**—মাখনতোলা দুগ্ধ। **To blow a cloud**—To smoke a pipe ; ধূম পান করা। **To blow great guns**—To blow a violent gale ; তুফান ছুটান। **To blow off steam**—To get rid of superfluous energy ; (অনাবশ্যক শক্তি) ছাড়িয়া দেওয়া। **To blow one's brains out**—To shoot him through the head (with fire-arms) ; গুলি করিয়া মস্তক ভেদ করা। **To blow one's own trumpet**—To sound one's own praise ; নিজের ঢাক নিজে বাজান। **To blow out**—To extinguish by a current of air ; বায়ু প্রবাহদ্বারা নির্ব্বাপিত করা, ফুঁ দিয়া নিবান। **To blow the coals or the fire**—To stir up strife ; কলহ বা বিরোধ উস্কাইয়া তোলা। **To blow up**—To inflate ; as, to *blow up* a bubble ; to puff up ; as, *blown up* with conceits ; ফুলাইয়া তোলা ; (গর্ব্ব, আত্মম্ভরিতা, প্রভৃতি দ্বারা) স্ফীত করা। To excite ; as, to *blow up* a contention ; উদ্দীপ্ত করা, উত্তেজিত করা। To scatter by an explosion ; as, to *blow up* a fort ; (বারুদ, বোমা, প্রভৃতি দ্বারা) বিদীর্ণ করা, উড়াইয়া দেওয়া। (*Colloq.*) To scold violently ; as, to *blow up* a person ; (চলিত ভাষায়) তীব্র তিরস্কার করা। **To blow upon**—To bring into discredit ; to render stale ; অপদস্থ করা, অপমানিত করা ; পর্য্যুষিত বা বিস্বাদ করা। To tell tales of ; to expose ; "The credit of these witnesses had been *blown upon* ;" কাহারো অপবাদসূচক গল্প প্রচার করা ; প্রকাশ করা।

blow (blō), *n.* **1.** A violent blowing of wind ; a gale ; বহন ; প্রবল ঝড়, ঝঞ্ঝাবাত, প্রভঞ্জন। **2.** The act of forcing air from the mouth or bellows ; as, have a *blow* at the flute ; ফুৎকার-প্রদান, বাতাস-প্রদান, ধমন (সং ভাঃ)। **3.** The spouting of a whale ; তিমি মৎস্যের শিরোরন্ধ্র হইতে বায়ু ও সলিলোৎক্ষেপ। **4.** A boast ; a vaunting ; গর্ব্ব ; বড়াই। **Blow-fly**—The Meat fly ; যে সকল বিভিন্ন জাতীয় মক্ষিকা ডিম পাড়িয়া মাংস দূষিত করে, তাহাদের সাধারণ নাম। **Blow-hole**—The nostril of a whale ; তিমি মৎস্যের নাসা-রন্ধ্র। The vent for air, smoke, etc., in an underground passage, tunnel, etc. ; সুড়ঙ্গ প্রভৃতি হইতে ধূম, বাতাস, প্রভৃতি নির্গমের পথ। **Blow-out**—An outbreak of anger ; ক্রোধোচ্ছ্বাস। (*Slang*) Abundant meal ; feast ; (ইতরভাষায়) প্রচুর আহার ;

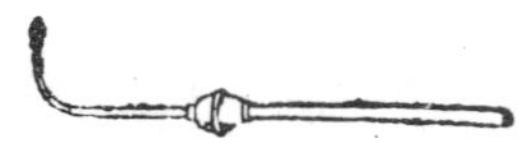

Blowpipe.

ভোজ। **Blowpipe**—A tube used to blow a current of air through a flame ; অগ্নি শিখার ভিতর দিয়া বায়ু-প্রবাহ প্রবাহিত করার জন্য নল বিশেষ, ফুকনী (হিঃ কোঃ), বক্রনাল (রঃ প্রঃ)। A tube used in glass-blowing ; ফুৎকারদ্বারা কাচের জিনিষ তৈয়ার করিবার নল।

blow′-êr, (blō-), *n.* **1.** One who or that which blows ; spe. a whale ; যে ফুৎকার দেয় বা যদ্দ্বারা ফুৎকার করা হয়, ধমক (সং উঃ) ; বিশেষতঃ তিমি-মৎস্য। **2.** An apparatus for increasing a fire's draught ; (চুল্লী বা অগ্নিকুণ্ডে) অগ্নির তেজোবৃদ্ধি-করণার্থ যন্ত্র বিশেষ। **3.** An escape of gas through a fissure in a coal-mine ; কয়লার খনির রন্ধ্র বা ফাটলদ্বারা বাষ্পনির্গম। **4.** (*Colloq.*) A boaster ; (চলিত-ভাষায়), দাম্ভিক, উচ্চভাষী।

blown (blōn), *p. p.* **1.** Driven or tossed by the wind ; বাত্যাতাড়িত, বাতান্দোলিত। **2.** Swollen ; inflated ; (also, blown up) ; স্ফীত ; বায়ুপূরিত। **3.** Stale ; worthless ; পর্য্যুষিত, নষ্ট ; অসার। **4.** Out of breath ; tired ; বে-দম ; ক্লান্ত। **Blown upon**—Having bad reputation ; damaged ; দুর্নামগ্রস্ত ; ক্ষতিগ্রস্ত।

blow′-ȳ (blō-), *adj.* Windy ; wind-swept ; বাত্যাময় ; বাত্যাবিতাড়িত।

blowzed (blowzd), **blowz′-ȳ,** *adjs.* Ruddy-faced ; coarse-looking ;

(of hair, dress) dishevelled ; লোহিত-বদন ; স্থূলকায়, অমার্জ্জিত ; আলুলায়িত।

blŭb, *v. i.* (*Slang*) To shed tears ; (ইতরভাষায়) চোখের জল ফেলা।

blŭb'-bêr, *v. i.* & *t.* To weep and sob noisily ; to cry in a childish manner ; ক্রন্দন করা, রোদন করা, ফোঁপাইয়া ফোঁপাইয়া কাঁদা ; শিশুর মত রোদন করা। ***Verb t.*** To utter broken words or cries (with *out, forth*) ; to wet or disfigure the face with weeping ; কাঁদিতে কাঁদিতে ভাঙ্গা ভাঙ্গা স্বরে কথা বলা, ফোঁপাইতে ফোঁপাইতে কথা বলা ; কাঁদিয়া মুখ ফুলান বা ভিজান। **Blubber-lip**—A swollen, protruding lip ; স্ফীত, উদ্গত ওষ্ঠ।

blŭb'-bêr, *n.* **1.** The fat of whales, etc. ; তিমি কিম্বা তাদৃশ বৃহৎ সামুদ্রিক জন্তুর মেদ কিম্বা বসা। **2.** A jelly-fish or Medusa ; সামুদ্রিক মৎস্য বিশেষ। **3.** The act of weeping ; ক্রন্দন, রোদন।

blû'-chêrs, *n.* A strong leather half-boot or high-shoe ; (after the Prussian General Blücher) ; একপ্রকার দৃঢ় বুট জুতা।

bludg'-eon (blŭj-ŏn), *n.* & *v. t.* A short thick heavy-headed stick ; লগুড়, মুদ্গর, গদা, যষ্টি, সোঁটা, পরিঘ (মঃ ভাঃ), ঠেঙ্গা। ***Verb t.*** To strike repeatedly with this ; পুনঃ পুনঃ লগুড়াঘাত করা, ঠেঙ্গান।

blue (blū), *adj., n.* & *v. t.* **1.** Of the colour of the clear sky or the deep sea ; আসমানি, নীল, শ্যাম, শ্যামল। **2.** Low-spirited ; melancholy ; as, to feel *blue* ; স্ফূর্ত্তিহীন ; বিমর্ষ, নিরানন্দ। **3.** Severe or over-strict in morals ; as, *blue* and sour religionists ; কঠোরব্রত। **4.** (Of women) Pedantic ; learned ; (abbreviation of blue-stockings) ; শিক্ষাভিমানিনী ; পণ্ডিতা। ***Noun.*** **1.** Blue colour ; নীলবর্ণ। **2.** Blue pigment ; নীলবর্ণরঞ্জক পদার্থ। **3.** Blue powder used by laundresses ; রজকিনীগণ কর্ত্তৃক ব্যবহৃত নীল-চূর্ণ। **4.** The sky ; নীলাকাশ। **5.** The sea ; নীলাম্বুরাশি (রঃ)। **6.** (*Pl.*) The Royal Horse Guards ; রাজকীয় অশ্বারোহী রক্ষিসৈন্যদল। **7.** The colour or member of a political party ; রাজনৈতিক দলবিশেষের চিহ্ন বা সভ্য। **8.** An English University athlete ; ইংলণ্ডীয় বিশ্ববিদ্যালয়ের মল্ল-ক্রীড়ক। **9.** A pedantic woman ; a bluestocking ; বিদ্যাভিমানিনী স্ত্রীলোক ; বিদুষী। ***Verb t.*** **1.** To make blue ; নীলবর্ণ করা। **2.** To treat (linen) with blue (in laundering) ; কাপড় ধোলাই করিবার সময় নীলমিশ্রিত জলে চোবান। **Bluebeard**—A merciless tyrant ; নির্দ্দয় অত্যাচারী। [ফরাসী গ্রন্থকার চার্লস্ পেরল্টের কথাগ্রন্থোক্ত ব্লু বেয়ার্ড নামক দানব। এই দানব ক্রমান্বয়ে বহুপত্নীর প্রাণসংহার করত একটী গুপ্ত কক্ষে লুক্কায়িত রাখে। তাহার সর্ব্বশেষ পত্নী প্রবল কৌতূহলাক্রান্ত হইয়া সেই কক্ষদ্বার উন্মুক্ত করিলে, ব্লুবেয়ার্ডের লোমহর্ষকর রহস্য প্রকাশিত হয়। এই শেষোক্তা পত্নীর ভ্রাতৃগণ ব্লুবেয়ার্ডকে শমনসদনে প্রেরণ করে।] **Blue-black**—Black with a tinge of blue ; নীলাভ-কৃষ্ণ। **Blue blood**—High birth ; সম্ভ্রান্ত বংশ, কৌলিন্য, আভিজাত্য। **Blue-book**—One of the official reports of Parliament and the Privy Council ; পার্লেমেণ্ট মহাসভা ও প্রিভি কাউন্সেলের

Bluebottle.

কার্য্যবিবরণী। **Bluebottle**—The blue corn-flower ; নীলবর্ণ পুষ্পবিশেষ A (nickname for) policeman ; পুলিশ। **Blue-butterfly**—নীলমাছি (ষোঃ)। **Blue-cap**—A salmon one year old ; এক বৎসর বয়সের স্যামন মৎস্য। The blue titmouse ; নীলবর্ণ ক্ষুদ্র পক্ষিবিশেষ। The Scotch ; স্কটলণ্ডবাসিগণ। **Blue-coatboy**—A scholar of the charity schools, esp. of the Christ Hospital in London ; দরিদ্র বিদ্যালয়ের, বিশেষতঃ লণ্ডন নগরীস্থ খ্রীষ্ট হাস্পাতালের ছাত্র। **Blue-devils, The blues** (*Colloq.*)—Hypochondria ; low spirits ; as, in a fit of *the blues* ; (চলিত-ভাষায়) বিমর্ষতা, বিষাদ-রোগ ; অবসাদ, স্ফূর্ত্তিহীনতা। **Blue-disease**—Cyanosis ; নীল-পাণ্ডু (হঃ চঃ), নীলরোগ (ঐ)। **Blue expanse**—নীল বিস্তার। **Blue-eyed**—নীলাক্ষ। **Blue-eyed maid**—Minerva ; গ্রীসদেশীয় বাণীদেবী মিনার্ভা। **Blue-fish**—The shark ; হাঙ্গর মৎস্য। **Blue funk**—(*Slang*) Tremulous dread ; (ইতরভাষায়) ভয়ে থরহরি কম্পমান অবস্থা, মহাভয়। **Blue-gown**—Harlot ; গণিকা। **Blue-gowns**—A term given to Scottish paupers ; স্কটলণ্ড দেশের নিঃস্ব ব্যক্তিগণ। **Blue-grass**—A grass found in Europe and America having great value as pasturage ; গোগ্রাসের অতীব উপযোগী আমেরিকা এবং ইয়ুরোপদেশীয় তৃণ বিশেষ। **Blue Hen State**—The state of Delaware ; মার্কিণ যুক্তরাজ্যের অন্তর্গত ডেলাওয়ার রাজ্য। **Blue-jacket**—A seaman in the navy ; নাবিক। **Blue jay**—মণিকণ্ঠ, কিকিদিবি (আঃ)। **Blue-light**—A firework used for signals ; সঙ্কেতসূচক আতস বাজী। **Blue murder**—More terror or alarm than real danger ; as, to shout *blue murder* ; যতটা বিপদ্ নয় তদপেক্ষা অধিকতর ত্রাস কিম্বা ভয়। **Blue-nose**—An inhabitant of Nova Scotia ; নভাস্কশিয়াবাসী। **Blue-Peter**—A signal flag for sailing ; পোতচালনের সঙ্কেতসূচক পতাকা। [*To* *fly the blue Peter*—(জাহাজের পক্ষে) ছাড়িবার জন্য প্রস্তুত হওয়া।] **Blue-pill**—একপ্রকার পারদমিশ্রিত বটিকা। **Blue-ribbon**—The ribbon worn by members of the order of the Garter; ইংলণ্ডের সম্ভ্রান্ত সম্প্রদায়-বিশেষভুক্ত ব্যক্তিগণের পরিহিত নীলবর্ণ ফিতা। The greatest distinction; the first prize; সর্ব্বোচ্চ সম্মান; প্রথম পুরস্কার। The sign of teetotalism; মাদকদ্রব্য পরিহারের চিহ্ন। **Bluerock**—A kind of pigeon; একপ্রকার কপোত পক্ষী। **Bluestocking**—A learned lady; শিক্ষিতা-মহিলা, বিদুষী। [১৪০০ খৃঃ অব্দে ভেনিস নগরীতে ভদ্রলোক ও ভদ্রমহিলাগণের এক সমিতি প্রতিষ্ঠিত হয়। এই সমিতির সভ্য ও সভ্যাগণ নীলবর্ণ মোজা পরিধান করিতেন। ভেনিস নগরীর সমিতি ১৫৯০ খৃষ্টাব্দে লুপ্ত হইলে পর, প্যারী নগরীতে ঐরূপ একটী সভা স্থাপিত হয়। ১৭৮০ খৃঃ অব্দে ফরাসীদেশের অনুকরণে ইংলণ্ডেও একটী সমিতি গঠিত হয়। মিসেস মণ্টেগ্ নাম্নী জনৈক বিদুষী মহিলা তাঁহার সান্ধ্য-সম্মিলনীতে ঐ সমিতির চিহ্ন (নীলবর্ণ মোজা) পরিধান করিতেন।] **Blue-stone, Blue-vitriol** — Sulphate of copper; তুঁতে, তুত্থক। **Blue talk**—Indecent conversation; অশ্লীল কথাবার্ত্তা। **Blue-water**—Open sea; বাহির দরিয়া। **Indigo blue**—নীলীনীল (সাঃ পঃ)। **In the blues**—Dispirited; হতোৎসাহ, স্ফূর্ত্তিহীন। **Light blue**—আনীল। **Man in blue**—A policeman; পুলিশ কনেষ্টবল। **Once in a blue moon**—Very rarely; কদাচিৎ, কৃচিৎ। **Prussian blue**—হরিত-নীল (সাঃ পঃ)। **The blue and yellow**—Edinburgh Review; এডিনবরা রিভিউ নামক সাময়িক পত্রিকা। **To drink till all is blue**—To drink to drunkenness; চতুর্দ্দিকস্থ পদার্থ-সমূহ নীলবর্ণ না দেখা পর্য্যন্ত মদ্যপান করা, পূর্ণ মাতাল না হওয়া পর্য্যন্ত মদ্যপান করা। **To look blue**—To look depressed or low-spirited; ভগ্নোৎসাহ হইয়া পড়া। **True blue**—Staunch and unwavering (in one's faith, principles, etc.); hence, genuine; real; (বিশ্বাস, প্রেম, ধর্ম্মমত প্রভৃতিতে) অচল, অটল, (Cf. নীলীরাগ—উজ্জ্বল-নীলমণি); বিশুদ্ধ; প্রকৃত। **True blue will never stain**—A really noble heart will never disgrace itself; প্রকৃত মহাপ্রাণ ব্যক্তি কখনও অযোগ্য বা কলঙ্কজনক কার্য্য করিবে না।

blŭff, *adj., n., v. t.* & *i.* **1.** (Of a ship) Vertical in the bows; (of a coast) cliffy in outline; (জাহাজ সম্বন্ধে) পোতাগ্রদেশ সরলোন্নত; (উপকূল-সম্বন্ধে) খাড়া, সরলোন্নত। **2.** (Of person, manner, action, etc.) Surly; churlish; gruff; blunt; উগ্রপ্রকৃতি, পরুষ; কর্কশ, রুক্ষ; উগ্র, কড়া, রূঢ়, অভব্য; দুর্বিনীত। ***Noun.*** A high and steep bank or headland; উচ্চ এবং সরলোন্নত উপকূল বা অন্তরীপ। ***Verb t.*** **1.** To try to frighten an opponent, and make him throw up his hand at cards; নিজের হাতে খেলা আছে বলিয়া ভয়-প্রদর্শনে বিপক্ষকে প্রতিনিবৃত্ত করিতে চেষ্টা করা। **2.** To impose on by a show of boldness or strength; কৃত্রিম সাহস ও শক্তি দেখাইয়া অন্যের চক্ষে ধূলি দেওয়া। ***Verb i.*** To practise this policy; উক্ত নীতি অবলম্বন করা। **Bluff'-y,** *adj.*

blŭff, *n.* Boastful swagger; empty pretence or make-believe; "The whole is a *bluff* to influence the election;" হাঁক-ডাক, তর্জ্জন গর্জ্জন; শূন্য ছল বা ভাণ।

blü'-ish, *adj.* Somewhat blue; ঈষৎ নীল, নীলাভ, আনীল। **—ness,** *n.*

blŭn'-dêr, *v. i., t.* & *n.* **1.** To move blindly or stupidly; to stumble (with, *on, along*); অন্ধ বা নির্ব্বোধের মত চলা; হোচট খাওয়া। **2.** To make a gross mistake; বিষম ভুল করা। ***Verb t.*** **1.** To utter stupidly, (with *out*); মূর্খের মত বলা। **2.** To mismanage (a business); to confuse; মন্দভাবে পরিচালনা করা; গোলমাল করিয়া ফেলা। ***Noun.*** A stupid or careless mistake; a gross error; উৎকট ভ্রম; প্রমাদ, বিষম ভ্রম, স্খলিত (শকুঃ)। **—er,** *n.* **Blunderhead**—A stupid fellow; নির্ব্বোধ ব্যক্তি, আহাম্মক লোক। **To blunder away**—To waste by mismanagement; বেবন্দো বস্তের দরুণ নষ্ট করা। To throw away (opportunity, etc.); সুযোগ হারান।

blŭn'-dêr-bŭss, *n.* An ancient short gun with a large bore; বৃহৎ রন্ধ্রবিশিষ্ট একপ্রকার প্রাচীন কালীন বন্দুক।

blunge (blŭnj) *v. t.* To mix (clay, flint-powder, etc.), up with water (in pottery); (কুম্ভকারের বাসনের জন্য) মৃত্তিকা এবং প্রস্তর-চূর্ণ জলের সহিত মিশ্রিত করা। **Blung'-er,** *n.* A wooden blade for mixing clay in potteries; মৃত্তিকা, প্রস্তর-চূর্ণ এবং জল একত্র মিশ্রিত করার জন্য কাঠের বৈঠাবিশেষ। **Blung'-ing,** *n.*

blŭnt, *adj., v. t.* & *n.* **1.** (Of a tool) Without edge or point; not sharp; ভোঁতা; অশাণিত। **2.** Dull; not sensitive; (of intellect, perception); অপ্রখর-বুদ্ধি, স্থূলবুদ্ধি; জড়-বুদ্ধি, জড়-মস্তিষ্ক। **3.** Plain-spoken; abrupt of manner; curt; স্পষ্টবক্তা, ঠোঁটকাটা (*Colloq.*); অভব্য; কাটা, ত্বরিত। ***Verb t.*** **1.** To make less sharp (an edge or point); ভোঁতা করা, ধার নষ্ট করা, তীক্ষ্ণতা বা প্রাখর্য্য নষ্ট করা। **2.** To make dull (the feelings or faculties); বুদ্ধি ভোঁতা করা, চিত্ত-বেগ মন্দীভূত করা। ***Noun.*** **1.** A short thick needle; একপ্রকার ছোট মোটা সূঁচ। **2.** (*Slang*) Ready money; as, I will remit the *blunt* immediately; (চলিত ভাষায়) রোক-টাকা। **Blunt'-ish,** *adj.* **Blunt'-ly,** *adv.* **1.** Obtusely, (shaped, etc.); স্থূলভাবে। **2.** Rudely; curtly; plainly; রূঢ়ভাবে;

অল্পকথায়; স্পষ্টাক্ষরে। **Blunt′-ness,** *n.* 1. Dullness of point or edge; স্থূলতা, অতীক্ষ্ণতা, অপ্রখরতা। 2. Outspokenness; rudeness; স্পষ্টবাদিতা; রূঢ়তা।

blur (blêr), *n.* & *v. t.* 1. A dark spot; a smear of ink, etc.; কাল দাগ; কালি প্রভৃতির লেপ। 2. Dimness; confused effect; অস্পষ্টতা; ঝাপ্সাভাব। 3. A moral stain or blot; কলঙ্ক-চিহ্ন, কলঙ্ক-কালিমা। *Verb t.* 1. To smear (clear writing etc.) with ink, etc.; to disfigure; জোবড়ান; বিকৃত করা। 2. To dim (perception of); to darken; অস্পষ্ট করা, ঝাপ্সা করা; ঘোরালো করা, আঁধার করা। 3. To blot or blemish (the purity, beauty or truth of); মলিন করা, কলুষিত করা, কলঙ্কিত করা। **To blur out**—To efface (writing etc.); মুছিয়া ফেলা।

blurt (blêrt), *v. t.* To utter suddenly or unadvisedly, (with *out*); ধা করিয়া বলিয়া ফেলা, ফস্ করিয়া বলিয়া ফেলা, অবিবেচকের মত বলিয়া ফেলা। **Blurt′-ing,** *adj.* **To blurt out**—To utter indiscreetly; ভাল মন্দ বিচার না করিয়া হঠাৎ বলিয়া ফেলা, কথা ফাঁস করিয়া ফেলা।

blŭsh, *v. i.* 1. To become red in the face from shame or modesty; লজ্জায় মুখমণ্ডল অরুণ বর্ণ ধারণ করা। 2. (*Fig.*) To be ashamed, (*at, for*); as, I *blush for* what has followed; (লজ্জায়) লজ্জিত হওয়া। 3. To become red or roseate; রক্তিমাভ হওয়া, লোহিত বা গোলাবি বর্ণ ধারণ করা। **Blush′-ing,** *adj.* 1. Ruddy; roseate; রক্তিম; গোলাবি। 2. Modest; সলজ্জ, হ্রী-পরিগত।

blŭsh, *n.* 1. The reddening of the face caused by shame, modesty, confusion, etc.; লজ্জা, ব্রীড়াদি ভাব জনিত গণ্ডস্থল ও মুখমণ্ডলের রক্তিমা, কপোলরাগ। 2. A rosy colour or glow; a flush of light; লোহিত-বর্ণ, গোলাবিবিভা; অরুণালোকচ্ছটা। 3. Glance; glimpse; as, at the first *blush*=at the first glance (প্রথম দৃষ্টিতে); দৃষ্টিক্ষেপ, চাহনি; ত্বরিত দৃষ্টি। **Blush′-ful,** *adj.* Bashful; modest; লজ্জারক্তিম, সরমরক্তিম, সলজ্জ; ব্রীড়াবনত, লজ্জাবিনম্র। **Blush′-less,** *adj.* Shameless; impudent; নির্লজ্জ, লজ্জাহীন; ধৃষ্ট। **To put to the blush**—To put to shame; লজ্জিত করা, লজ্জায় ফেলা।

blŭs′-têr, *v.i., t.* & *n.* 1. (Of wind, waves, etc.) To blow boisterously; (বাতাস, ঢেউ, প্রভৃতি সম্পর্কে) প্রচণ্ডবেগে প্রবাহিত হওয়া। 2. To talk noisily and overbearingly; to bully or swagger; তর্জ্জন গর্জ্জন করা, ধুম্ ধাম্ করা; বড়াই করা। *Verb t.* (With *out, forth*) To utter with noisy violence; (*reflex.*) to storm (oneself) into (anger, etc.); সদম্ভে উচ্চারণ করা, তর্জ্জন গর্জ্জন করা; ক্রোধে গর্জ্জন করা। *Noun.* 1. A stormy blast; a boisterous blowing; ভীম প্রভঞ্জন, প্রবল বাত্যা; ভীম গর্জ্জনে ঝঞ্ঝাবহন। 2. Angry self-assertion; noisy boastful language; threats; ধূমধাম, দর্পোক্তি, বড়াই, স্পর্দ্ধাবাক্য; তর্জ্জন গর্জ্জন; ভয়প্রদর্শন। **—er,** *n.* **—ing,** *adj.* 1. Stormy; tempestuous; ঝটিকা-সঙ্কুল; ঝঞ্ঝাগর্জ্জিত। 2. Loud talking; swaggering; তর্জ্জনগর্জ্জনকারী; দম্ভপূর্ণ। **—ing-ly,** *adv.*

bö, boh (bö), *inter.* An exclamation used to startle or frighten; ঐ জুজু! **You can't say bo** or **boo to a goose**—You cannot open your mouth, (said of shy or timid person); তুমি এত ভয়াতুর বা লাজুক যে মুখ ফুটিয়া একটি কথাও বলিতে পারনা।

bō′-a, *n.* 1. A large non-poisonous species of serpents; অজগর, বাহস (তৈত্তিঃ)। 2. A snake-like coil of fur, worn round the neck, by ladies; ইয়ুরোপ এবং আমেরিকার মহিলাগণের ব্যবহৃত লোম, পালক বা

Boa.

তাদৃশ পদার্থে নির্ম্মিত সর্পাকৃতি গলবেষ্টনী বিশেষ। **Boa-constrictor**—অজগর।

Bö-ă-nêr′-gĕs, *n. pl.* The name given by Christ to James and John; hence, (as a *sing.*), a loud vociferous preacher or orator; খৃষ্টপার্ষদ জেমস্ ও যোহনের খৃষ্টদত্ত নাম; (অতএব একবচনে) উচ্চকণ্ঠ বক্তা বা প্রচারক। (*pl.* -GES, -GESSES.)

boar (bör), *n.* 1. The uncastrated male of swine; শূকর, বন্যবরাহ। 2. Its flesh; বরাহমাংস। **Boar′-ish,** *adj.* Swinish; brutal; cruel; শূকরবৎ; পশুবৎ; নির্দ্দয়।

board (börd), *n., v. t.* & *i.* 1. A broad piece of wood; a thin plank; কাষ্ঠফলক, কাষ্ঠপট (ভাবঃ প্রঃ); পাতলা তক্তা। 2. A table spread for meals; (আহার করিবার) মেজ। 3. Food served at the table; daily meals provided at the contract price; as, to pay for *board* and lodging; আহার্য্য; চুক্তি-দ্বারা নির্দ্ধারিত মূল্যে যে দৈনিক আহার্য্য যোগান হয়। 4. A table at which a council is held; hence, body of persons (as a committee); as, a *Board* of Directors: the *Board* of Revenue; মন্ত্রণাসভার মেজ, অতএব সভা, সমিতি, সমাজ। 5. The deck or side of a ship or boat ; জাহাজের পার্শ্ব বা পাটাতন। 6. A table or frame for a game ; as, a chess-*board* ; খেলিবার মেজ বা ছক। 7. A kind of thick stiff paper ; as, paste-*board* : card-*board* ; শক্ত মোটা কাগজ, পিস্‌বোর্ড। 8. One of the two stiff covers on the side of a book ; পুস্তকের মলাট। 9. (*Pl.*) The stage of a theatre ; রঙ্গমঞ্চ। [*To go upon the boards*—To enter upon the theatrical profession ; রঙ্গমঞ্চে প্রবেশ করা, নাটকের দলে যোগ দেওয়া।] ***Verb t.*** 1. To cover with board ; তক্তা বিছাইয়া দেওয়া, তক্তাদ্বারা মোড়াইয়া দেওয়া, কাষ্ঠফলকাচ্ছাদিত করা। 2. To supply with food and lodging at a fixed rate ; নির্দ্দিষ্ট হারে খোরাকি লইয়া আহার্য্য প্রদান করা। 3. To come alongside (a ship, usu. to attach) ; to force one's way on board a ship ; (জাহাজের) সংস্পর্শে আসা ; বলপূর্ব্বক জাহাজে প্রবেশ করা। 4. To embark on ; জাহাজে আরোহণ করা। ***Verb i.*** To live in a house at a certain rate for meals ; to be supplied with food and lodging at a fixed rate ; নির্দ্দিষ্ট হারে খোরাকি দিয়া কোন বাটীতে বাস করা ; নির্দ্দিষ্ট হারে অর্থ প্রদান করিয়া আহার ও বাসস্থান পাওয়া। **Board'-a ble,** *adj.* **Board'-er,** *n.* 1. One who pays to lodge and have his meals in another's family ; যে ব্যক্তি নির্দ্দিষ্ট হারে টাকা দিয়া অন্য ব্যক্তির বাটীতে আহার ও বাস করে। 2. One who boards (an enemy's) ship ; যে ব্যক্তি বলপূর্ব্বক (শত্রুর) জাহাজে আরোহণ করে। 3. A school boy at a boarding school ; ছাত্রাবাস-সমন্বিত বিদ্যালয়ের ছাত্র। **Above board**—See ABOVE. **Board and (by) board** (*Naut.*)—Side by side ; পাশাপাশি। **Boarding house**—A house where persons board ; হোটেল। **Boarding school**—A school, where scholars board and lodge ; ছাত্রাবাস-সমন্বিত বিদ্যালয়। **Board-school**—A school under the management of a School Board ; কার্য্যনির্ব্বাহক সভার তত্ত্বাবধানাধীন বিদ্যালয়। **Board-wages**—Wages allowed to servants in place of food ; ভৃত্যদিগকে খোরাকি বাবত যে টাকা দেওয়া হয়। **By the board**—By the ship's side ; জাহাজের পার্শ্বদিক দিয়া। **To go by the board**—To suffer complete destruction ; সম্পূর্ণ বিধ্বস্ত হওয়া, বিনষ্ট হওয়া। **To enter on the boards**—To inscribe the name of a student on a tablet in a college as a student ; কলেজের কাষ্ঠফলকে ছাত্রের নাম খোদিত করা। **To run on board of, To fall on board of**—To make an attack ; to fall upon (a person or thing) ; আক্রমণকরা ; আপতিত হওয়া।

boast (bōst), *v. i., t.* & *n.* To extol oneself ; to brag (*of, about*) ; to vaunt ; গর্ব্ব করা, দম্ভ করা, দর্প করা ; আত্মশ্লাঘা করা ; বড়াই করা। ***Verb t.*** 1. To speak of with pride or ostentation ; গর্ব্বের সহিত বলা, বড়াই করিয়া বলা। 2. To possess as thing to be proud of ; as, to *boast* a name ; গৌরবজনক বস্তুর অধিকারী হওয়া। ***Noun.*** 1. A vain-glorious statement ; tall talk ; self-exaltation in words ; দম্ভোক্তি ; লম্বাচৌড়া কথা ; আত্মশ্লাঘা। 2. An occasion of pride ; as, the *boast* of fame ; গর্ব্বের হেতু বা উপলক্ষ। **Boast'-er,** *n.* **Boast -ful,** *adj.* Given to boasting ; full of boasting ; self-praising ; গর্ব্বিত, দৃপ্ত ; গর্ব্বপূর্ণ, সগর্ব্ব ; আত্মশ্লাঘী। **Boast'-ful-ly,** *adv.* **Boast -ful-ness,** *n.*

boast'-ing (bōst-), *n.* & *adj.* Vain-glorious speaking ; শ্লাঘন, বিকত্থন, (মঃ ভাঃ), দাম্ভিকতা, বড়াই। ***Adj.*** Vaunting ; bragging ; সগর্ব্ব ; আত্মশ্লাঘাপূর্ণ।

boat (bōt), *n., v. t.* & *i.* 1. A small open vessel (with sails or oars) ; নৌকা, তরী, তরণী, ডিঙ্গি (*Colloq*), কিস্তি (*Colloq.*)। 2. A small steamer ; as, a steam-*boat* : mail-*boat* ; ক্ষুদ্র জাহাজ, ক্ষুদ্র পোত। 3. A boat-shaped dish for sauce, etc. ; চাটনি প্রভৃতি রাখিবার নৌকাকৃতি পাত্র। ***Verb t.*** To place or carry in a boat ; as, to *boat* goods, oars, etc. ; নৌকায় চালান দেওয়া, নৌকায় প্রেরণ করা, নৌকাতে রাখা। ***Verb i.*** To go or sail in a boat ; to row ; নৌকায় বিচরণ করা ; দাঁড় টানিয়া চলা। **Boat'-a-ble,** *adj.* Navigable by boats ; নৌকা চলাচলের উপযোগী, নাব্য (রঃ)। **Boat'-age,** *n.* Carriage by boat ; also, a charge for such carriage ; নৌকাযোগে গমন ; নৌকা-ভাড়া। **Boat'-ing**—Rowing as an amusement ; নৌকাবিহার, নৌকাদৌড়। **Boat-bill**—A South-American heron ; দক্ষিণ আমেরিকার দীর্ঘচঞ্চু পক্ষিবিশেষ। **Boat-fly, -bug**—A species of water-bug ; জলচর কীট বিশেষ। **Boat-hook**—A hook fixed to a long pole and used to push or pull a boat ; নৌকা ঠেলিবার বা টানিবার আঁকড়ষী বা আঁকড়া। **Boat-house**—A shed at water's edge for keeping boats ; জলের কিনারায় নৌকা রাখিবার ঘর। **Boatman**—A man who manages a boat ; দাঁড়ী, মাল্লা, ক্ষেপণিক (বাসবঃ), ভাড়াটিয়া নৌকার মাঝি। **Boat-race**—A race between rowing boats ; নৌকা-দৌড়। **Boatswain**—(Pronounced bōt swān or bōsn) A ship's officer who has charge of the boats, sails, riggings, etc. ; (জাহাজের) টিণ্ডাল (রাধা কুঃ)। **In the same boat**—With like risks, etc. ; তুল্য বিপৎ প্রভৃতির অধীন। **To**

have an oar in another's boat—To meddle with the affairs of others ; অন্য লোকের ব্যাপারে হস্তক্ষেপ করা। **To take boat**—To embark ; জাহাজে চড়া, জাহাজে উঠা।

bŏb, *n., v. t.* & *i.* **1.** Any little round thing that plays loosely at the end of a string, chain, etc. ; a pendant ; দুল, দোলক ; ঝিলমিল। **2.** A bunch of lob-worms used to catch fish ; বড়শীর টোপের উপযোগী কীটের থোবা। **3.** The weight on a pendulum, plumb-line or kite-tail ; দোলক, ওলনদড়ী বা ঘুড়ির লেজে যে ভারি জিনিষ লাগানো হয়। **4.** A short jerking motion ; as, a *bob* of the head ; ঝাঁকনি, নাড়া। **5.** A knot of hair ; a tassel-shaped curl ; কেশগুচ্ছ ; রেশমী ঝাঁপা বা থোবার মত কোকড়ানো চুল। **6.** A horse's docked tail ; অগ্রভাগ-কর্ত্তিত অশ্ব-লাঙ্গুল। **7.** The burden of a song ; গানের ধুয়া, ধ্রুবক। **7.** A light blow ; a tap ; মৃদু আঘাত ; ঠুকনি। **8.** (*Slang*) A shilling ; (ইতর ভাষায়) এক শিলিং। **9.** A bunch of flowers ; a nosegay ; পুষ্পগুচ্ছ ; ফুলের তোড়া। ***Verb t.*** **1.** To strike with a blow ; to rap ; আঘাত করা, ঠুকা ; ঘা দেওয়া। **2.** To gain by fraud ; ঠকাইয়া লাভ করা। **3.** To cut short ; as, to *bob* a horse's tail ; ছোট করা, খর্ব্ব করা, খাট করা। **4.** To move in a short jerking manner ; as, he *bobbed* his head ; (মস্তকাদি) নাড়া, ঝাঁকা। ***Verb i.*** **1.** To play (*to* and *fro, up* and *down*) ; ঝুলা, দুলা। **2.** To angle with a bob ; to angle by giving the hook a jerking motion in the water ; কীটের থোবার টোপ গাঁথিয়া বড়শী ফেলা ; ছিপদ্বারা জল নাড়া চাড়া করিয়া বড়শী ফেলা। **3.** To curtsy ; জানু নত করিয়া নমস্কার করা। **Bob-wig**—A wig with short curls ; খর্ব্ব এবং কুঞ্চিত কুন্তল বিশিষ্ট পরচুলা। **Dry bob**—A boy at Eton who devotes himself to cricket, football, etc. ; ইটন বিদ্যালয়ের যে ছাত্র ক্রীকেট, ফুটবল প্রভৃতি ক্রীড়ায় রত থাকে। **Light bob**—A soldier of the light infantry ; লঘু অস্ত্রধারী পদাতিক সৈনিক। **Wet bob**—A boating Etonian ; ইটন বিদ্যালয়ের নৌকাচালন-পারদর্শী ছাত্র। **To bear a bob**—To join in the chorus ; ধুয়াতে যোগ দেওয়া। **To give the bob**—To make a fool of ; বোকা সাজান।

Bŏb'-ă-dĭl, *n.* A braggart ; গর্ব্বকারী, দম্ভকারী। [বেন জনসন কৃত *Every Man in his Humour* নামক গ্রন্থের চরিত্র বিশেষের নাম।]

bŏb'-bêr-ȳ, *n.* Disturbance ; row ; গোলমাল ; হল্লা (*Colloq.*)। [হিন্দি "বাপ্‌রে" শব্দ হইতে গৃহীত।]

bŏb'-bin, *n.* **1.** The spool upon which sewing thread is wound ; a reel ; টানার নালী (বিশঃ) ; সূতার নাটা বা নাটাই (গ্রী), কাঠিম। **2.** A reel round which wire is coiled ; তার কুণ্ডলিত করিয়া রাখিবার নাটাই। **3** A small bar and string for raising door latch ; কপাটের খিল তোলার জন্য রজ্জুসংলগ্ন ক্ষুদ্র দণ্ডবিশেষ। **Bobbin-lace**—Pillow lace ; বালিশের ঝালর।

bŏb'-bi-nĕt, *n.* A kind of fine netted lace made by machines ; কলে প্রস্তুত সূক্ষ্ম জালাকার ঝালর বিশেষ।

bŏb'-bĭsh, *adj.* Well ; in good spirit ; (as in *pretty bobbish*) ; বেশ ; স্ফূর্ত্তিতে।

bŏb'-bȳ, *n.* A nick-name for a policeman ; পুলিশ। [পুলিশ বিভাগের সংস্কারক স্যর রবার্ট্ পীলের ডাকনাম হইতে গৃহীত।]

bŏb'-ŏ-link, (-lĭngk), *n.* A North American singing-bird ; উত্তর আমেরিকার গায়ক পক্ষিবিশেষ।

bŏb'-slĕd, –sleigh (-slā-), *n.* Two short sleighs coupled together and used in drawing logs, etc. ; ভারি কাষ্ঠ খণ্ড প্রভৃতি টানার জন্য বরফের উপর চলিবার উপযোগী ক্ষুদ্র জোড়া-গাড়ী।

bŏb'-stay (-stā), *n.* A rope to fasten down the bowsprit of a ship to the stem : যে রজ্জুদ্বারা জাহাজের সম্মুখবর্ত্তী পাইল তুলিবার উদ্গাতদণ্ড পোতাগ্রভাগের সহিত সংবদ্ধ করা হয়।

bŏb'-tail (-tāl), *n.* & *adj.* A horse or dog with its tail cut short ; ছিন্ন-পুচ্ছাগ্র কুক্কুর বা অশ্ব। ***Adj.*** Same as BOBTAILED. **–tailed,** *adj.* With tail cut short ; ছিন্ন-পুচ্ছাগ্র। **Tag rag and bob-tail**—The rabble ; ইতর শ্রেণী।

bōde, [illegible] To be the omen of ; to portend ; to foreshow ; ভাবী শুভাশুভ প্রকাশ করা ; নিমিত্তাদিদ্বারা পূর্ব্বসূচনা করা, পূর্ব্বাভাস দেওয়া ; পূর্ব্বলক্ষণ প্রদর্শন করা। ***Verb i.*** To be ominous ; to foretell (evil) ; অমঙ্গল সূচনা করা ; (অশুভের) পূর্ব্বাভাস দেওয়া। **Bode'-ful,** *adj.* Ominous ; portending or threatening evil ; দুর্নিমিত্তজ্ঞাপক, অশুভ ; অমঙ্গলসূচক, কুলক্ষণাক্রান্ত। **Bode'-ment,** *n.* An omen ; a foreboding ; prognostication ; পূর্ব্ব লক্ষণ, শুভাশুভ লক্ষণ, শকুন, নিমিত্ত ; পূর্ব্বসূচনা, ভবিষ্যসূচনা ; ভাবি চিহ্ন, ভাবি লক্ষণ।

bodega, *n.* (*S.P.*) A cellar or shop selling wine only ; যে দোকানে বা মদ্য-ভাণ্ডারে কেবলমাত্র সুরা বিক্রীত হয়।

bŏd'-ice (-ĭs), *n.* A close-fitting upper part of a woman's dress, down to waist ; also, an inner vest worn over stays ; স্ত্রীলোকের পরিচ্ছদের কটি পর্য্যন্ত বিলম্বিত যে অংশ আঁটাভাবে শরীরে লাগিয়া থাকে ; কঞ্চুলিকা, কঞ্চুকী, কাঁচুলি, স্ত্রীলোকের আঙ্গিয়া।

bŏd'-ied (-ĭd), *adj.* Having a body ; embodied, (usu. in composition) ; দেহবিশিষ্ট ; দেহবদ্ধ।

bŏd'-ĭ-lĕss, *adj.* **1.** Having no body ; incorporeal ; as, a *bodiless* spirit ; দেহশূন্য ; অমূর্ত্ত, অশরীরী। **2.** Separated from the body ; as, *bodiless* heads ; দেহ হইতে বিযুক্ত।

bŏd'-ĭ-lȳ, *adj.* & *adv.* Of or belonging to the body or physical nature ; as, *bodily* fear, illness, etc. ; শারীরিক, দৈহিক, আঙ্গিক, কায়িক। ***Adv.*** **1.** In the body ; in person ; as, he is *bodily* present ; দেহে ; স্বশরীরে। **2.** Entirely ; as a whole ; as, cut out *bodily* ; সম্পূর্ণরূপে ; সমগ্রভাবে। **Bodily fear**—Apprehension of physical injuries ; শারীরিক অত্যাচারের ভয়।

bŏd′-kin, *n.* **1.** A small pointed instrument for piercing holes in cloth ; গুণস্‌চ, কাটা। **2.** A long pin for fastening hair ; লম্বা চুলের কাটা, গুজিকাঠি। **To ride, sit** or **travel bodkin**—To sit closely wedged between two persons ; দুইজনের মধ্যে চাপিয়া বসা, দুইজনের মধ্যে ঠেসাঠেসি করিয়া বসা।

Bŏd-lei′-ăn (-lē-), *adj.* & *n.* Of or pertaining to Sir J. Bodley or the celebrated library at Oxford bearing his name ; স্যর জে বড্‌লি বা তদীয় নামীয় অক্‌সফোর্ড বিশ্ববিদ্যালয়ের সুবিখ্যাত পুস্তকাগার-সম্বন্ধীয়। ***Noun.*** The Oxford University Library ; অক্‌স্‌ফোর্ড বিশ্ববিদ্যালয়ের পুস্তকাগার।

bŏd′-ȳ, *n.* **1.** The physical or material frame of man or any animal ; (often contrasted with the *soul*) ; কায়, দেহ, শরীর, অঙ্গ, গাত্র, বপুঃ, তনু, কলেবর, মূর্ত্তি, বিগ্রহ, গা (*Colloq.*)। **2.** The main portion, trunk or stem of anything ; কাণ্ড (শরীর-সম্বন্ধে), স্কন্ধ, কাণ্ড, (বৃক্ষ সম্বন্ধে), প্রধান অঙ্গ (সৈন্য-সম্বন্ধে), প্রধান বিভাগ (দেশ-সম্বন্ধে)। **3.** A person ; a human being ; (generally with *some, any, no*) ; ব্যক্তি, লোক ; মনুষ্য। **4.** A collective whole or totality ; a corporation ; as, a legislative or clerical *body* ; সমুদয়, সঙ্ঘ, সমূহ, দল, বৃন্দ, নিবহ, ঘোষ ; সমবায়। **5.** A general collection ; as, a *body* of facts, laws, etc. ; সাধারণ সংগ্রহ। **6.** A compact quantity or mass ; amount ; bulk ; as, a *body* of land extending thirty miles ; a material thing ; as, a floating *body* : a light *body* ; জড়পদার্থের রাশি বা পিণ্ড (হিঃ কোঃ), পরিমাণ ; আয়তন ; জড়পদার্থ। **7.** A society, league or fraternity ; as, a defensive *body* ; a military force ; সম্প্রদায়, মণ্ডলী ; সৈন্যদল। **8.** The part of upper garment minus the sleeves and collar ; গলবেষ্টনী বা আস্তিন-শূন্য পরিচ্ছদের উপরিভাগ। **9.** (*In Geometry*) Any solid figure ; (জ্যামিতি) ঘনক্ষেত্র, বস্তু (হিঃ কোঃ)। **10.** Consistency or density ; strength ; (of colours, wine, paper, etc.) ; গাঢ়তা, ঘনত্ব ; সার, বল। **Body-cloth**—A rug to cover horses, etc ; অশ্বাদির গাত্র-বস্ত্র বা কম্বল। **Body-colour**—Pigment possessing body or a certain degree of consistnece, substance and tinging power ; কতক পরিমাণ ঘনত্ব, গাঢ়ত্ব বা রঞ্জন-শক্তি-সম্পন্ন রঞ্জক-পদার্থ। [উজ্জ্বলবর্ণ সমাবেশ করার পূর্ব্বে তৈলচিত্রাদিতে ঐরূপ রঙ্গ দেওয়া হয়।] **Body-guard**—A guard for the person, (esp. of a king or dignitary) ; a retinue or escort ; দেহরক্ষক, শরীররক্ষী, শরীর-রক্ষক ; রক্ষিদল, অনুযাত্রিবর্গ। **Body-politic**—The state ; an organized society ; রাষ্ট্র ; ব্যবস্থাবদ্ধ সমাজ বা সম্প্রদায়। **Body-servant**—A valet ; খানসামা, ভৃত্য, পরিচারক। **Body-snatcher**—An exhumer of corpse for dissection ; ব্যবচ্ছেদার্থ সমাধি হইতে শবদেহোত্তোলনকারী। **In a body**—All together ; সকলে মিলিয়া, সমস্তে, একজোটে। **The body of Christ**—The church of which Christ is the head ; খৃষ্টীয় ধর্ম্ম-সমাজ—খৃষ্ট যাহার মস্তক স্বরূপ। **To keep body and soul together**—To remain alive ; কায়ক্লেশে দিনপাত করা, কষ্টেসৃষ্টে জীবন ধারণ করা।

bŏd′-ȳ, *v. t.* **1.** To provide with a body ; to embody ; দেহবিশিষ্ট করা, শরীরী করা ; দেহবদ্ধ করা। **2.** To give mental shape to, (with *forth*) ; "Imagination *bodies forth* the forms of things unknown ;" মানসমূর্ত্তিরচনা করা। **3.** To typify, (with *forth*) ; as, he *bodies forth* the age ;" প্রকৃতিনির্দ্দেশক ধর্ম্ম, গুণ বা বিশেষ লক্ষণ সুস্পষ্টরূপে প্রকাশ করা। **4.** To indicate ; সূচনা করা, প্রদর্শন করা। **To body out**—To give a body to ; দেহবিশিষ্ট করা।

Bœ-o′-tian (Bē-ö-shî-ăn), *adj.* & *n.* Of Bœotia in ancient Greece, proverbial for the dullness of its inhabitants ; stupid ; dull ; গ্রীস-দেশের অন্তর্গত বিয়োশীয়া প্রদেশীয় ; আহাম্মক, বোকা ; স্থূলবুদ্ধি। [বিয়োশীয়া-বাসিগণ অত্যন্ত স্থূলবুদ্ধি ছিল বলিয়া কথিত আছে।] ***Noun.*** A stupid person ; নির্ব্বোধ লোক।

Bo-er (Bö-êr), (formerly Boor), *n.* A Dutch settler or farmer in South Africa ; দক্ষিণ আফ্রিকার ওলন্দাজ ঔপনিবেশিক বা কৃষক, বোয়ার।

bŏg, *n.* & *v. t.* A piece of wet spongy ground ; a marsh ; swamp ; তলতলে ভূমি, অনূপ ; জলা ; বিল। ***Verb t.*** To sink or submerge in bog ; (usu. passive) ; পঙ্কে নিমগ্ন করা, বিলে ডুবাইয়া দেওয়া। **Bŏg′-gȳ,** *adj.* Marshy ; swampy ; জলাময় ; বিলপূর্ণ। **Bog-trotter**—One who lives in a boggy country ; hence, a nickname for Irishmen ; অনূপদেশবাসী ; আয়র্লণ্ডবাসী।

bŏg, *n.* A privy, (vulgar) ; পায়খানা (ইতর ভাষায়)।

bö′-gey (-gî), **bö′-gȳ** *n.* (pl. -GEYS, -GIES) **1.** The devil ; শয়তান। **2.** A hobgoblin ; ভূত। **3.** A bugbear ; জুজু।

bŏg′-gle, *v. i.* **1.** To start with fright ; to shy ; to be startled ; থমকে দাড়ান ; (অশ্বাদির পক্ষে) ভয় পাইয়া চমকিয়া এক পাশে সরিয়া দাঁড়ান ; ভয়ে চমকিয়া উঠা। **2.** To hesitate ; to demur ; (*at, about*) ; দ্বিধা বা

ইতস্ততঃ করা ; থতমত খাওয়া। **3.** To play fast and loose ; to equivocate ; নিতান্ত চঞ্চল প্রকৃতি বা অব্যবস্থিতচিত্তের মত কার্য্য করা ; দ্ব্যর্থ-বাক্য প্রয়োগ করা। **4.** To fumble ; to bungle ; হাতড়াইয়া বেড়ান ; আনাড়ির মত কায করা।

bö′-gie (-gî) ; **bö′-gey** (-gî), *n.* The name given to the framework supporting the front portion of locomotive engine or railway carriage ; বাষ্পীয়যন্ত্র বা বাষ্পীয়-শকটের সম্মুখভাগের অবলম্বন-স্বরূপ কাঠাম বিশেষ। [এই কাঠাম একটী কীলক দ্বারা উক্ত সম্মুখভাগের সহিত সংযুক্ত থাকায় বাষ্পীয়শকট বক্রপথে চলিবার সময় ঝাঁকুনি বা ধাক্কা কম লাগে, এবং শকটের বর্ত্মচ্যুত হওয়ার ও বিশেষ আশঙ্কা থাকে না।] **Bogie-carriage, —engine, etc.**—A carriage, engine, etc., mounted on these ; উক্ত প্রকার কাঠামের উপর আরোপিত শকট বা বাষ্পীয়-যন্ত্র।

bö′-gle, *n.* **1.** A phantom ; a goblin ; অপচ্ছায়া ; ভূত। **2.** A bugbear ; a scarecrow ; জুজু ; কাকাদি দূরীকরণার্থ ছিন্ন বস্ত্রাদি নির্ম্মিত মূর্ত্তি।

bö′-gŭs, *adj.* Sham ; fictitious ; spurious ; কৃত্রিম ; নকল, জাল ; মেকি।

bö′-hea′ (-hē), *n.* A black tea of lowest quality ; এক প্রকার নিকৃষ্ট কৃষ্ণবর্ণ চা।

Bö-hē′-mi-ăn, *n.* & *adj.* **1.** A native of Bohemia ; বোহিমিয়াবাসী। **2.** A gipsy ; বেদিয়া। **3.** A person, (esp an artist, literary man, etc.) who leads a free or irregular life ; যে ব্যক্তি, বিশেষতঃ যে চিত্রকর বা সাহিত্যিক সামাজিক রীতিনীতির ধার ধারে না এবং যথেচ্ছভাবে জীবন কাটায়। ***Adj.*** Of free and easy habits, manners, etc. ; যথেচ্ছাচারী, উচ্ছৃঙ্খল, প্রচলিত সামাজিক রীতিনীতির বিরুদ্ধাচারী বা উপেক্ষা-প্রদর্শনকারী। **—ism,** *n.* **—ize,** *v. i.*

boil (bo̅yl), *v. i.* & *t.* **1.** To bubble with heat ; to be in ebullition ; (উত্তাপে) ফুটিয়া উঠা, স্ফুটিত হওয়া, ফুটা ; টগ্‌বগ্ করা। **2.** To bubble ; as, the billows *boil* ; বুদ্বুদপূর্ণ হওয়া। **3.** To be exicted with passion ; to be hot ; as, his blood *boils* with anger ; রাগে গর্ গর্ করা ; অত্যন্ত রাগিয়া উঠা, রাগে রক্ত টগ্‌বগ্ করিয়া উঠা। ***Verb t.*** **1.** To cause (a liquid) to bubble with heat ; উত্তাপদ্বারা জল প্রভৃতি ফুটাইয়া ফেলা। **2.** To cook or dress in boiling water ; as, to *boil* meat ; to cleanse (cloth etc.) in boiling water ; to prepare by boiling ; as, to *boil* sugar ; গরম জলে সিদ্ধ করিয়া পাক করা ; উষ্ণ জলে বস্ত্র প্রভৃতি পরিষ্কার করা ; সিদ্ধ করিয়া প্রস্তুত করা। **3.** To lessen (the bulk) by boiling ; to condense ; জ্বাল দিয়া কমাইয়া ফেলা ; ঘন করা। **4.** (*Fig.*) To epitomize ; (লক্ষণায়) সংক্ষেপ করা। **To boil away**—To evaporate in boiling ; বাষ্পাকারে পরিণত হওয়া। **To boil over**—To run over the top of a vessel, (of liquid) ; উথলাইয়া পড়া, উপচিয়া পড়া। **To keep the pot boiling**—To get a living ; কোন প্রকারে জীবিকা-নির্ব্বাহ করা।

boil (bo̅yl), *n.* **1.** An act of boiling ; as, give the sauce a minute's *boil* ; সিদ্ধকরণ। **2.** The boiling point ; (esp. *on, at, to* the boil) ; স্ফুটনাঙ্ক।

boil (bo̅yl), *n.* An inflamed suppurating tumour ; বিস্ফোটক, ফোঁড়া। **A blind boil**—One that fails to come to a head ; যে ফোঁড়া মুখ নিয়া উঠে না।

boil′-êr (bo̅yl), *n.* **1.** One who boils ; যে সিদ্ধ করে। **2.** A vessel for boiling water in ; esp. a vessel (of riveted wrought-iron plates) in which steam is generated ; জল গরম করার পাত্র ; বিশেষতঃ বাষ্পীয়-যন্ত্রের বাষ্প প্রস্তুতের জন্য প্রেক-বদ্ধ পিটা লৌহের ফলকদ্বারা নির্ম্মিত বৃহৎ কুণ্ড, বাষ্পজনক (হিঃ কোঃ)। **3.** A tank attached to a kitchen-range ; রন্ধনশালা-সংলগ্ন জলকুণ্ড। **4.** A laundry vessel ; ধোপার কাপড় সিদ্ধ করিবার পাত্র। **5.** A vegetable, fruit, etc. suited for boiling ; সিদ্ধকরণোপযোগী ফল বা তরকারী।

boil′-ing, (bo̅yl), *adj.* & *n.* **1.** Heated to the point of bubbling ; স্ফুটনাঙ্ক পর্য্যন্ত উষ্ণীকৃত। **2.** Bursting with passion, etc. ; inflamed ; ক্রোধোদ্দীপ্ত ; ক্রোধ-প্রজ্বলিত। ***Noun.*** The act of bubbling up ; tumultuous agitation ; inflammation, fever, etc. ; স্ফুটন ; তুমুল আন্দোলন ; প্রদাহ, জ্বর, প্রভৃতি। **—ly,** *adv.* **Boiling point**—The temperature at which a liquid boils, (water at sea-level at 212° Fahr., 100°C) : যে পরিমাণ উত্তাপে তরল পদার্থ বাষ্পাকারে পরিণত হয়, স্ফুটনবিন্দু, স্ফুটনাঙ্ক। **Boiling spring**—A spring which gives out very hot water ; উষ্ণকুণ্ড (হিঃ কোঃ), উষ্ণ প্রস্রবণ। **The whole boiling** (*Slang*)—The whole lot ; (ইতর ভাষায়) সবটা। **To be at the boiling point**—To be very angry ; অত্যন্ত ক্রুদ্ধ হওয়া।

bois′-ter-ous (bo̅ys-têr-ŭs), *adj.* **1.** Violent ; rough ; (of wind, waves, etc.) stormy ; প্রচণ্ড, প্রবল, ভীম ; উত্তাল ; ঝটিকা-বিক্ষুব্ধ। **2.** Too rough or clamorous ; turbulent, (of person speech, behaviour, etc.); কোলাহলকারী, গর্জ্জনকারী ; অতিশয় কর্কশস্বভাব, উদ্দাম। **—ly,** *adv.* **—ness,** *n.*

bōld, *adj.* **1.** Daring ; courageous ; fearless ; (of persons, works, actions, etc.) ; সাহসীক ; অকুতোভয় ; নির্ভীক। **2.** Too forward ; audacious ; presumptuous ; অত্যন্ত সপ্রতিভ ; ধৃষ্ট ; প্রগল্‌ভ, দুর্ব্বিনীত। **3.** Showing vigour of conception or expression ; forcible ; as, *bold* imagination, drawing, description, etc. ; কল্পনা বা দ্যোতনা-সম্পর্কে তেজোব্যঞ্জক ; সজীব। **4.** Striking to the eye ; well-marked ; in high relief ; as, *bold* patterns ;

writing a *bold* hand ; দৃষ্টি-আকর্ষক ; সুপরিস্ফুট ; সুস্পষ্ট, সুপ্রকট। **5.** (*Naut.*) Prominent ; steep ; as, a *bold* shore, rock, etc. ; also, deep, (said of water near a steep shore) ; (নৌ-বিদ্যা) খাড়া ; উদ্গাত ; গভীর। **Bold′-ly,** *adv.* **Bold′-ness,** *n.* **Bold-faced**—Impudent ; lacking modesty ; ধৃষ্ট ; নির্লজ্জ, দুর্বিনীত। **Bold stroke**—A bold effort suddenly or unexpectedly produced ; আকস্মিক বা অপ্রত্যাশিত সাহসিক উদ্যম। **As bold as brass**—Impudent ; ধৃষ্ট। **To make bold**—To take the liberty (to do a thing) ; (কোন কাজ করিতে) সাহস করা। **To make bold will**—To deal with ; আলোচনা করিতে সাহসী হওয়া। **To make so bold as**—To presume ; to venture ; অগ্রেই সাহস করা ; সাহসী হওয়া। **To show a bold front**—To defy ; তুচ্ছ করা।

bōle, *n.* **1.** The stem or trunk of a tree : গাছের গোড়া, কাণ্ড। **2.** A fine clay highly coloured by iron ; একপ্রকার লাল মাটি।

bōle, *n.* (Scotch.) A recess in a wall ; an opening to admit light, air, etc. ; দেয়ালের খোঁদল ; আলো ও বাতাস প্রবেশের ছিদ্র।

bolero, *n.* **1.** (*Sp.*) A lively Spanish dance ; স্পেনদেশীয় নৃত্য বিশেষ। **2.** A ladies' short, sleeveless jacket ; স্ত্রীলোকদিগের আস্তিনবিহীন কঞ্চুকবিশেষ।

bō′-līde, *n.* A large meteor ; a fire-ball ; বৃহৎ উল্কাপিণ্ড ; অগ্নি-পিণ্ড।

bōll, *n.* A rounded seed-vessel, esp. of flax or cotton ; গোলাকার বীজকোষ ; বিশেষতঃ শণ বা কার্পাসের বীজ কোষ। **Bolled,** *adj.*

bŏl′-lârd, *n.* A wooden or iron post on a ship or quay for fastening ropes to ; জাহাজের বা জাহাজ লাগাইবার স্থানের যে লোহ বা কাঠের খোঁটায় দড়ী বাঁধা হয়।

bō-lŏm′-ĕ-têr, *n.* An instrument used to measure small differences in temperature ; তাপের সামান্য বৈভিন্ন্য পরিমাপের জন্য যন্ত্র বিশেষ।

bōl′-stêr, *n.* & *v. t.* A long stuffed pillow to support the sleeper's head in a bed ; also, a cushion for leaning or sitting upon ; লম্বা বালিশ, তাকিয়া ; বসিবার বা হেলান দিবার গদি বিশেষ। **2.** A pad or support in many machines and instruments ; নানাপ্রকার কল ও যন্ত্র-সংলগ্ন নরম গদি বা অবলম্বন। ***Verb t.*** (Usu. with *up*) **1.** To support with a bolster or pillow ; hence, to prop up ; to support ; তাকিয়া বা বালিশদ্বারা ঠেস দিয়া রাখা ; (অতএব) অবলম্বনদ্বারা খাড়া রাখা ; ধারণ করা। **2.** To aid and abet ; সাহায্য করা, দুষ্কর্ম্মে সহায়তা করা। **3.** To pad ; to puff ; (with *out, up*) ; কোন নরম জিনিষ ঠাসিয়া ভরা ; ফুলাইয়া তোলা। **4.** (Among school-boys) To belabour with bolsters ; (বিদ্যালয়ের ছাত্রদিগের মধ্যে) লম্বা বালিশদ্বারা বারম্বার প্রহার করা। **—er,** *n.*

bōlt, *n., v. t.* & *i.* **1.** A short, heavy, blunt-headed arrow shot from a cross-bow ; এড়ো ধনুর ভোঁতা এবং খাট শর। **2.** A thunderbolt ; as, a *bolt* of heaven ; বজ্র, অশনি, কুলিশ। **3.** A stout pin with a screw-head ; বল্টু, পেরেক। **4.** A sliding catch or fastening, for a door or gate ; অগল, খিল, দ্বারকন্টক (অঃ)। **5** The portion of a lock which is shot or withdrawn by the key ; তালার যে অংশ চাবিদ্বারা সরান হয়। ***Verb t.*** **1.** To discharge or drive forth ; ক্ষেপণ করা, চালনা করা। **2.** To gulp down unchewed ; as, to *bolt* food ; গ্রাস করা। **3.** To fasten (door, etc.) with bolt ; to fasten together with bolts ; (দরজা প্রভৃতিতে) অর্গল দেওয়া ; বল্টুদ্বারা আটকান। **4.** (*U. S.*) To break away from a political party ; as, to *bolt* a party nomination ; কোন রাজনীতিক দল ত্যাগ করিয়া চলিয়া যাওয়া। ***Verb i.*** **1.** To start off suddenly ; to come or go suddenly ; as, to *bolt* into or out of the room ; চম্পট দেওয়া ; হঠাৎ আসা, হঠাৎ চলিয়া যাওয়া। **2.** To strike or fall suddenly ; হঠাৎ আঘাত করা বা পতিত হওয়া। **3.** (Of a horse) To break away from the rider's control ; (অশ্বপক্ষে) আরোহীর শাসন না মানিয়া যথেচ্ছভাবে ছুটিয়া চলা। **Bolt-rope**—A rope sewed all round the edge of a sail to prevent tearing ; পাল যাহাতে ছিড়িয়া না যায়, তজ্জন্য ইহার চতুষ্পার্শ্বে যে রজ্জু সেলাই করিয়া দেওয়া হয়। **A bolt from the blue**—Something sudden and unexpected ; বিনামেঘে বজ্রাঘাত। **Cupid's bolt**—কন্দর্পশর, মদন বাণ। **To bolt in**—To shut in by bolting door ; দরজায় খিল দিয়া ভিতরে বন্ধ করিয়া রাখা। **To bolt out**—To exclude by bolting door ; দরজা বন্ধ করিয়া ভিতরে প্রবেশ করিতে না দেওয়া।

bōlt, *adv.* (With *upright*) ; As straight as a bolt ; suddenly ; straight ; শরের মত খাড়াভাবে ; হঠাৎ ; সোজাভাবে, খাড়াভাবে।

bōlt, *n.* **1.** A sudden spring or start ; as, the horse made a *bolt* ; হঠাৎ চম্‌কিয়া লম্ফ প্রদান। **2.** A running away ; as, he contemplated a *bolt* to America ; চম্পট। **3.** Act of swallowing up ; গিলন।

bōlt, boult (bōlt), *v. t.* **1.** To sift ; to pass through a sieve or bolting cloth ; (with *out*) ; চালা, ছাঁকা ; মোটা কাপড় দ্বারা চালা। **2.** To examine by sifting ; to investigate ; (মন্দ হইতে ভাল) বাছিয়া ফেলা ; পরীক্ষা করা, অনুসন্ধান করা। **Bolting-cloth**—Cloth used for sifting flour ; ময়দা চালিবার কাপড়। **To bolt to the bran**—To examine thoroughly ; to discover any thing important ; পুঙ্খানুপুঙ্খরূপে অনুসন্ধান করা ; গুরুতর কোন কিছু আবিষ্কার করা।

bölt'-êr (bölt), *n.* **1.** One who bolts ; esp. a horse given to bolting ; যে ব্যক্তি চম্পট দেয় ; যে ঘোড়া আরোহীর শাসন না মানিয়া যথেচ্ছভাবে চলে। **2.** One who sifts meal, etc., (also *boulter*) ; যে ময়দা প্রভৃতি চালে। **3.** A sieve or strainer ; ময়দাচালনী, ছাকনী, ঝাঁঝরী।

bö'-lŭs, *n.* A round mass of any thing ; esp. a large pill ; কোন জিনিষের পিণ্ড ; ঔষধের গুলি, মোদক (সুশ্রুঃ)।

bomb (bŏm), *n.* A hollow iron ball or globe containing explosives ; a shell ; কামানের গোলা ; বোমা। **Bomb-lance**—A harpoon with an explosive in its head ; শীর্ষদেশে বিস্ফোরক-পদার্থ সমন্বিত তিমি মৎস্যাদি শিকারের বল্লম বিশেষ। **Bomb-proof**—A shelter strong enough to resist shells ; কামানের গোলা দ্বারা দুর্ভেদ্য স্থান বা আশ্রয়। **Bomb-shell**—(Now usu. *shell*) An artillery bomb ; বিস্ফোটক পদার্থপূর্ণ কামানের গোলা।

bŏm'-bârd, *v. t.* **1.** To batter with shot and shell, (especially of war-ship attacking town) ; অনবরত গোলাগুলি বর্ষণ করা। [নগর-ধ্বংসে নিযুক্ত রণপোত শ্রেণী সম্পর্কে বিশেষভাবে ব্যবহৃত হয়।] **2.** (*Fig.*) To assail persistently with abuse, argument, etc. ; (লক্ষণায়) নানা প্রকার যুক্তি তর্ক বা কটূক্তি দ্বারা অনবরত আক্রমণ করা। **—bar-dier,** *n.* A non-commissioned officer in the British artillery ; বিনা সনন্দে নিযুক্ত ইংলণ্ডীয় গোলন্দাজ সৈন্যের কর্ম্মচারী বিশেষ, গোলন্দাজ সৈন্য। **—ment,** *n.* A continuous attack with shot and shell ; অবিরাম গোলাগুলি বর্ষণ দ্বারা আক্রমণ, বিমর্দ্দন (আঃ বঃ)।

bŏm-bâr'-dŏn, —dö-ne (-nā), *n.* A brass instrument, of the trumpet kind ; also, a brass reed-stop on the organ; পিত্তল নির্ম্মিত গভীর-নিনাদী বাদ্যযন্ত্র বিশেষ ; অর্গেণ যন্ত্রের অংশ বিশেষ।

bŏm-bă-sin' (-zēn), **—zine** (-zēn), *n.* A twilled fabric of silk (or cotton) and worsted ; (much used for mourning) ; (শোকপরিচ্ছদ-নির্ম্মাণে ব্যবহৃত) রেশম ও পশম কিম্বা কার্পাস ও পশমের মিশ্রণে প্রস্তুত বস্ত্র বিশেষ।

bŏm'-băst, *n.* Originally, cotton-wool used as stuffing for garment ; hence, inflated high sounding words, or turgid language ; (পূর্ব্বে) পোষাকের ভিতর ঠাসিবার জন্য তুলা ; শব্দাড়ম্বর, দীর্ঘ পদ বিন্যাস, অপ্রতীত শব্দ প্রয়োগ, বাগাড়ম্বরপূর্ণ ভাষা। **—bas'-tic,** *adj.* High sounding ; inflated ; উচ্চধ্বনি প্রকাশক ; অসার বাগাড়ম্বরময়, শব্দাড়ম্বর-বহুল। **—bas'-ti-cal-ly,** *adv.*

Bŏm'-băx, *n.* The silk cotton tree ; শিমুল গাছ, শাল্মলী বৃক্ষ। ***Bombax Malabaricum***—রক্ত শিমুল (বেলঃ)।

Bŏm-bay'-duck (-bā-dŭk), *n.* See BUMMALO.

bon, bonne, (*F.*), *n.* French for, *good* ; (ফরাসীভাষায়) ভাল।

bö'-nă-fī-de, *adv.* & *adj.* In good faith ; sincerely ; genuinely ; সরল বিশ্বাসে ; কোন প্রকার ছলনা বা প্রবঞ্চনা না করিয়া, সরলতার সহিত ; খাঁটিভাবে, অকৃত্রিম ভাবে। ***Adj.*** Real ; sincere ; genuine ; as, *bonafide* poverty ; a *bonafide* inhabitant ; প্রকৃত ; অকৃত্রিম ; আসল, খাঁটি।

bö'-nă-fī-dēs, *n.* (*Law*) Honest intentions ; sincerity ; (আইন) সদভিপ্রায়, সদ্বুদ্ধি ; সরলতা।

bŏ-năn'-ză, *n.* & *adj.* (*U. Colloq.*) A mass of ric ore; "When pocket of rich ore is struck the mine is said to be in *bonanza* ;" a stroke of fortune ; (মার্কিন যুক্তরাজ্যের চলিত ভাষায়) বহুমূল্য খনিজ বিমিশ্র ধাতু ; সৌভাগ্যোদয়। **Bonanza farm**—বহুধনপ্রসূ কৃষিক্ষেত্র ; যে কৃষিক্ষেত্রে আধুনিক বৈজ্ঞানিক যন্ত্রাদি ব্যবহৃত হয়।

bonbon, *n.* (*F.*), A sweet-meat ; a sugar-plum ; এক প্রকার মিঠাই ; চিনির মিঠাইবিশেষ।

bŏnd, *n.* & *v. t.* **1.** Anything that binds ; a band ; a cord ; a chain ; as, a *bond* of love (প্রণয়-পাশ) ; বন্ধনী, বন্ধন, বাঁধন ; পটি ; দড়ি, রজ্জু ; পাশ। **2.** (*Pl.*) Chains ; imprisonment ; শৃঙ্খল, নিগড় ; বন্দিত্ব। **3.** A tie or connection ; a cause of union ; বন্ধন, সম্বন্ধ ; মিলনের কারণ, সংযোগের কারণ। **4.** Moral or political obligation ; নৈতিক বা রাজনীতিক বাধ্যবাধকতা। **5.** A legal deed to carry out certain conditions ; চুক্তিপত্র। **6.** A writing or obligation to pay a sum ; তমসুক, বন্ধকী-পত্র, ঋণপত্র, ঋণলেখ্য, খত। **7.** A government promissory note ; debenture ; গভর্ণমেণ্টের ঋণস্বীকারপত্র ; রেলওয়ে, মিউনিসিপালিটি, পোর্টট্রাষ্ট বা কোন ব্যবসায়ী কোম্পানীকর্ত্তৃক গৃহীত কর্জ্জের ঋণস্বীকার পত্র। **8.** The arrangement of stones or bricks so that they overlap each other and form a solid structure ; গাঁথুনি। **9.** (*Chem.*) A unit of chemical attraction ; as, oxygen has two *bonds* of affinity ; রাসায়নিক আকর্ষণের একক, বন্ধন (হিঃ কোঃ)। ***Verb t.*** **1.** To bind together bricks, stones, etc. ; গাঁথুনি করা। **2.** To put imported goods in the custom warehouses till the duties on them are paid ; শুল্ক পরিশোধ না হওয়া পর্য্যন্ত আমদানী মাল শুল্কাগারে আটক রাখা। **Bondholder**—A person who holds a bond for money lent ; ঋণদাতা, উত্তমর্ণ। **Bondman**—One who is bound or who gives security for another ; প্রতিভূ। **Bond of arbitration**—সালিসনামা (রঃ অঃ)। **In bond**—Stored under charge of Customs till the importer has paid his duty; আমদানীকারী মাশুল আদায় না করা পর্য্যন্ত শুল্কাগারে রক্ষিত। **Security bond**—জামিননামা, জামিনী তমসুক (রঃ অঃ)। **To give bond for**—To secure payment of by giving a bond; to mortgage; তমসুক দেওয়া; বন্ধক দেওয়া।

bŏnd, *adj.* In a state of slavery or servitude: দাসত্ব শৃঙ্খলে আবদ্ধ। **Bondmaid, Bondswoman, Bond-woman**—A female slave; ক্রীতদাসী। **Bondman, Bondsman, Bondslave, Bondservant** — A person in a state of slavery; ক্রীতদাস। **Bond-service** — The slavery: দাসত্ব।

bŏnd, *n.* A league; a confederation; সমবায়; সমিতি, সঙ্ঘ।

bŏnd'-āge, *adj.* **1.** Slavery; দাসত্ব। **2.** Imprisonment; কারাবাস, বন্দি দশা। **3.** Obligation; বাধ্যতা।

bŏnd'-ĕd, *adj.* Secured by a bond, as duties; চুক্তিপত্র দ্বারা শুল্কাদি সুরক্ষিত। **Bonded store** or **warehouse**—A licensed warehouse or store in which goods liable to government duties may be lodged or stored; আবগারী মাশুল বা শুল্কাগারের শুল্ক আদায় না হওয়া পর্য্যন্ত যে গৃহে মাল মজুত রাখা হয়। **Bonded goods**—Goods placed at the bonded warehouse; উক্ত সরকারী গৃহে রক্ষিত মাল। **—er,** *n.*

bōne, *n.* & *v. t.* **1.** A firm, hard substance, forming the skeleton of an animal body; অস্থি, হাড়, (মৎস্য-সম্পর্কে) কাঁটা। **2.** A piece of bone; অস্থিখণ্ড। **3.** Somethi[ng] made of bone; অস্থিনির্ম্মিত দ্রব্য। **4.** (*Pl.*) The bones collectively; the body; as, my old *bones* can still bear this; the mortal remains; as, his *bones* were laid there; অস্থি-সমূহ; দেহ; দেহাবশেষ। **5.** Pieces of bones held between the fingers of the hand and rattled together to keep time to music; তাল ঠুকিবার জন্য অস্থিখণ্ড সমূহ। **6.** Dice made of bone, or ivory; অস্থি বা হস্তিদন্ত নির্ম্মিত পাশা। **7.** Whalebone; a piece of whalebone for a corset; তিমি মৎস্যের অস্থি; স্ত্রীলোকের কাঁচুলীর জন্য তিমি মৎস্যের অস্থিখণ্ড। **8.** A bone with meat adhering to it; as, a knuckle-*bone*; মাংসযুক্ত অস্থি। ***Verb t.*** **1.** To take out the bones from meat, fish (in cookery); as, to *bone* a turkey; (মাংসাদির) হাড় বাহির করা, মৎস্যের কাঁটা বাছিয়া ফেলা। **2.** To put whalebone into; স্ত্রীলোকের কাঁচুলির ভিতর তিমি মৎস্যের হাড় বসান। **3.** To fertilize with bone; অস্থিদ্বারা উর্ব্বরতা সম্পাদন করা। **Bone-ash**—অস্থিভস্ম। **Bone-black**—Animal charcoal; হাড়ের কয়লা। **Bone-dust**—অস্থিচূর্ণ। **Bone-lace**—A kind of lace; একপ্রকার ঝালর। **Bone-mill**—অস্থি চূর্ণ করার কল। **Bone-setter**—One who sets broken or dislocated bones, esp. without being a qualified surgeon; অস্থি-সংযোজক, ভগ্নাস্থি-সংযোজক, বিশেষতঃ যে ব্যক্তি অস্ত্রচিকিৎসাবিদ্যায় শিক্ষিত না হইয়াও ভগ্ন বা সন্ধিচ্যুত অস্থি সংযোজন করে। **Bone-shaker**—রবরনির্ম্মিত চক্রবেষ্টনীবিহীন দ্বিচক্রযান। **A bone of contention**—A subject of dispute; বিবাদের বিষয়, বিতর্কনীয় বস্তু। **A bone to pick with someone**—A controversy or dispute with someone; কোন ব্যক্তির সহিত বিরোধ। **A skin and bone**—A thin person; [কৃশ]কায় ব্যক্তি, কঙ্কাল-সার ব্যক্তি। [B]**red in the bone**—Ineradicable; অনুৎপাটনীয়, মজ্জাগত। **To make no bones of**—To have no scruples in regard to some thing; to publish openly; কোন বিষয়ে সংকোচ বা দ্বিধা না করা; প্রকাশ্যে প্রচার করা। **To the bone**—Penetrating; কন্‌কনে (শীত-সম্বন্ধে), তীব্র।

bŏn'-fīre, *n.* **1.** A triumphal fire; উৎসবাগ্নি, বিজয়াগ্নি, অগ্ন্যুৎসব, বহ্ন্যুৎসব। **2.** A fire for consuming rubbish; আবর্জ্জনা দগ্ধ করার জন্য অগ্নি।

bonhomie, (*F*), *n.* Easy good nature; pleasant and easy manner; সুশীলতা, সহজসারল্য; মনোরম এবং লীলাপূর্ণ ভাব।

bŏn'-ĭ-fāce, *n.* An inn-keeper; সরাইওয়ালা। [Farquhar কৃত "The Beaux' Stratagem" নামক মিলনান্ত নাটকের চরিত্র হইতে গৃহীত।]

bon marche, (*F.*), *n.* A cheap shop; cheap; যেদোকানে সুলভ মূল্যে জিনিষ ক্রয় করা যায়; সস্তা।

bon-mot, (*Pl. bons mots*) *n.*, (*F.*), A witty saying; a witty repartee; সরস পরিহাস বাক্য, সরস প্রত্যুত্তর; নর্ম্মভাষিত (আঃ বঃ), নর্ম্মালাপ।

bonne, *n.* (French-properly a good woman) Nursemaid; governess; দাই, আয়া, পরিচারিকা; শিক্ষয়িত্রী।

bonne bouche, (*pl.* ***bonnes bouches***) *n.* (*F.*) A delicious morsel or mouthful; a titbit, especially to end up with; এক গ্রাস মুখরোচক খাদ্য; খাদ্য দ্রব্যের উৎকৃষ্টাংশ, বিশেষতঃ আহারের শেষভাগে যাহা পরিবেষণ করা হয়।

bŏn'-nĕt, *n.* & *v. t.* **1.** A soft elastic woollen cap worn by men in Scotland; স্কটলণ্ডের পুরুষদিগের পরিধেয় এক প্রকার কোমল পশমী টুপী। **2.** A covering for the head worn by women; স্ত্রীলোকের মস্তকাবরণ বিশেষ। **3.** Anything resembling a bonnet in shape or use; a protective cap in various machines; মস্তকাবরণ সদৃশ কোন বস্তু; বিভিন্ন প্রকার যন্ত্রের আবরণ। **4.** A wire covering over a chimney top; ধূমনির্গম-নলের

Bonnet.

অগ্রভাগোপরি তারের আবরণ। 5. The metal cover or shield over the motor of an automobile ; হাওয়া-গাড়ীর কলের উপরিস্থিত ধাতব আবরণ। 6. An accomplice of a gambler, auctioneer, etc. ; জুয়ারী, নিলামকারী প্রভৃতির দালাল। 7. An additional piece of canvas attached to a sail to catch more wind ; অধিকতর পরিমাণে বাতাস ধরিবার জন্য পাইলের সহিত যে অতিরিক্ত ক্যাম্বিস্ সংযুক্ত করা হয়। 8. The second stomach of ruminants ; রোমন্থনকারী জন্তুগণের দ্বিতীয় পাকস্থলী। ***Verb t.*** 1. To put a bonnet on (a person) ; কাহারও মস্তকে টুপী পরাইয়া দেওয়া। 2. To crush a man's hat over his eyes ; কাহারও চক্ষুর উপর টুপী চাপিয়া ধরা। **—ed,** *adj.* **Bonnet-rouge**—The red cap of liberty of the extremists of the French Revolution ; ফরাসী চরমপন্থী বিপ্লবকারীদের স্বাধীনতার চিহ্ন-স্বরূপ রক্তবর্ণ টুপী। **To fill a person's bonnet**—To equal him in any respect ; যে কোন বিষয়ে কাহারও সমকক্ষ হওয়া। **To have a green bonnet**—To have failed in business ; কারবারে দেউলিয়া হওয়া। **To rive the bonnet of**—To excel ; উৎকর্ষে অতিক্রম করা।

bŏn'-nŷ, *adj.* (Spelled *bonnie* by the Scotch) 1. Handsome ; beautiful ; pleasant-looking ; attractively lively and graceful ; "Till *bonny* Susan sped across the plain ;" রূপবান্ ; সুন্দর ; প্রিয়দর্শন ; কান্ত, অভিরাম। 2. Gay ; merry ; frolicsome ; প্রফুল্ল ; আমুদে ; কেলিপর, ক্রীড়ারঙ্গী। **—ni-ly,** *adv.* **—ni-ness,** *n.* Handsomeness ; সৌন্দর্য্য, রূপ।

bonton, (*F.*), *n.* Good breeding ; the fashionable world ; সভ্যতা, সদাচরণ ; সৌখিন-সমাজ।

bō'-nŭs, *n.* 1. A premium ; something in addition to what is due ; উপরিলাভ ; অতিরিক্ত প্রাপ্য। 2. An extra dividend to shareholders ; অংশীদারগণকে প্রদত্ত অতিরিক্ত লভ্যাংশ। 3. Distribution of profits to insurance policyholders ; জীবন-বীমাকারীদিগের মধ্যে লাভের টাকা বিতরণ। 4. A sum paid to an employee in addition to his wages ; কর্ম্মচারীদিগকে বেতনের অতিরিক্ত যে পারিতোষিক প্রদান করা হয়।

bon vivant, (*F.*), *n.* A jovial companion ; a gourmand ; নর্ম্ম-সখা, আমোদ-পূর্ণ সহচর ; ঔদরিক।

bon voyage, (*F.*) A good journey to you ; আপনার যাত্রা শুভ হউক।

bōn'-ŷ, *adj.* 1. Consisting of bones ; pertaining to bones ; full of bones ; having large strong bones ; অস্থিময় ; অস্থিসম্বন্ধীয় ; অস্থিপূর্ণ ; বৃহৎ এবং দৃঢ় অস্থিবিশিষ্ট। 2. With little flesh ; স্বল্প মাংসযুক্ত।

bŏnze, *n.* A Japanese or Chinese Buddhist priest ; চীনা ব জাপানী বৌদ্ধ যাজক বা পুরোহিত, ফুঙ্গী।

bōō, booh (bōō), *interj.*, *v. t.* & *i.* A sound expressive of disapprobation or contempt ; ধিক্ ধিক্ ! ছি ! ছি !! ***Verb t. & i.*** To hoot a speaker ; কোন বক্তাকে টিট্‌কারী দেওয়া।

bōō'-bŷ, *n.* 1. A stupid fellow ; বোকা। 2. The last boy in a school-class ; a dunce ; বিদ্যালয়ের কোন শ্রেণীর সকলের নীচের ছাত্র ; গণ্ডমূর্খ। 3. Kinds of gannet ; বিভিন্ন জাতীয় সামুদ্রিক হংস। **—ish,** *adj.* **Booby prize**—কোন কোন খেলায় সর্ব্বনিকৃষ্ট অল্প সংখ্যক ক্রীড়ককে যে পুরস্কার দে[illegible] হয়। **Booby trap**—সর্ব্বপ্রথম যে দ্বার উন্মুক্ত করে—যেন তাহার উপর প হইতে পারে, তদুদ্দেশ্যে কক্ষদ্বারোপরি স্থাপিত দ্রব্যাদি। **A booby will never make a hawk**—গাধা পিটিয়া ঘোড়া করা যায় না।

bōō'-dle, *n.* 1. A crowd ; pack ; lot ; জনতা ; দল ; সমূহ। 2. Money paid for political bribery, etc. ; রাজনীতিক উৎকোচের জন্য প্রদত্ত অর্থ। 3. A card game ; একপ্রকার তাসের খেলা।

bŏŏk, *n.* & *v. t.* 1. A collection of sheets of paper, blank, written or printed, fastened together ; বহি, পুস্তক, কেতাব (*Colloq.*)। 2. A literary composition ; a treatise ; সাহিত্যিক রচনা ; গ্রন্থ। 3. A division of a volume ; as, the tenth *book* of "Paradise Lost ;" অধ্যায়, সর্গ, খণ্ড, পর্ব্ব, কাণ্ড। 4. A register or record ; খাতা, হিসাব বহি। 5. The Bible ; বাইবেল। 6. (*Fig.*) Any source of instruction, (real or imaginary) ; as, *book* of fate : *book* of life ; (লক্ষণায়) (প্রকৃত বা কাল্পনিক) শিক্ষালাভের উপায়। 7. (*Pl.*) Merchants' account ; সওদাগরের হিসাব বহি। 8. A libretto ; গীতিনাট্য প্রভৃতির শব্দসমূহ যে পুস্তকে নিবদ্ধ থাকে। 9. One's bets in a race ; ঘোড় দৌড়ে কোন ব্যক্তির বাজির সংখ্যা। ***Verb t.*** 1. To enter, write or register in a book ; খাতাতে লিখা, পাকা খাতায় তোলা, তালিকাভুক্ত করা। 2. To engage seat etc., in theatre, coach etc., by previous payment ; পূর্ব্বে টাকা দিয়া রঙ্গালয় বা গাড়ী প্রভৃতিতে আসনাদির বন্দোবস্ত করা। 3. To issue railway tickets ; রেলযাত্রীকে টিকেট দেওয়া। 4. To take railway ticket ; রেলওয়ের টিকেট লওয়া। 5. To enter and pay for the transmission of (goods, etc.) by any conveyance ; রেলগাড়ী প্রভৃতিতে প্রেরণের জন্য মাল প্রভৃতির নাম ঠিকানাদি খাতায় লিখাইয়া ভাড়া দেওয়া। **Book'-ful,** *adj.* Full of book-learning ; ignorant of men or life ; পুঁথি-পড়া ; সংসার জ্ঞানানভিজ্ঞ, লোকব্যবহারানভিজ্ঞ। **Book'-ish,** *adj.* 1. Fond of study ; গ্রন্থানুরাগী, অধ্যয়নরত। 2. Acquainted with books only ; পুঁথিপড়া। **Book'-less,** *adj.* Without books ; unlearned ; গ্রন্থহীন ; বিদ্যাহীন। **Book-binder**—One who binds books ; দপ্তরী, যে ব্যক্তি পুস্তক বাঁধে।

Book-case—A case with shelves for books ; পুস্তকাধার, পুস্তক-রক্ষণী। **Book-debt**—A debt standing against a person in an account-book ; খাতার বাকী বা দেনা। **Book-hunter**—যে ব্যক্তি সাগ্রহে পুস্তক সংগ্রহ করে, গ্রন্থবাতিকগ্রস্ত ব্যক্তি। **Booking clerk**—টিকিট বাবু। **Booking office**—A place where passengers and parcels are booked ; রেল, ষ্টীমার প্রভৃতির টিকিট বা পার্শেল করিবার ঘর। **Book-keeper**—One who keeps the account of a merchant or public office, etc. ; ব্যবসায়ী বা সরকারী কার্য্যালয় প্রভৃতির হিসাবরক্ষক। **Book-keeping**—হিসাব-রক্ষণ-পদ্ধতি। **Book-learned**—পুঁথি-পড়া পণ্ডিত, পুঁথিগত জ্ঞানে জ্ঞানী। **Book-learning** — গ্রন্থগত বিদ্যা, কেতাবি বিদ্যা। **Book-let**—A little book ; পুস্তিকা। **Book-maker**—One who writes or publishes books ; a compiler ; গ্রন্থ-লেখক, গ্রন্থকার, গ্রন্থপ্রকাশক ; গ্রন্থ-সঙ্কলক। One who wagers on the defeat of horse in a race ; যে ব্যক্তি ঘোড়দৌড়ে ঘোড়ার উপর বাজি রাখে। **Book-making**—The art or practice of compiling books ; পুস্তক-সঙ্কলন। Betting on horse races ; ঘোড়দৌড়ে বাজি রাখন। **Book-man**—A scholar ; a student ; পণ্ডিত ; ছাত্র। **Book-mark**—Something placed in a book to mark a particular page ; পুস্তকের পৃষ্ঠা বিশেষ নির্দ্দেশ করিবার চিহ্ন। **Book-mate**—A schoolfellow ; সমপাঠী, সহপাঠী, সহাধ্যায়ী, সতীর্থ। **Book-muslin**—A fine kind of muslin folded in booklike way when sold ; এক প্রকার সূক্ষ্ম কার্পাসবস্ত্র (মসলিন্)—যাহা পুস্তকের মত ভাঁজ করিয়া বিক্রয় করা হয়। **Book-oath**—An oath made on the Bible ; বাইবেল স্পর্শ করিয়া শপথ। **Book-plate**—নিজের নাম ধামাদি সম্বলিত কাগজ খণ্ড,—যাহা পুস্তকের মলাটের ভিতরের দিকে লাগান হয়। **Book-post**—The arrangement in the post office by which books, printed matters, etc., are conveyed at a special rate ; ডাক-বিভাগের যে বন্দোবস্ত অনুসারে পুস্তক, মুদ্রিত সংবাদ-পত্র ইত্যাদি অল্প মাশুলে প্রেরিত হয়। **Bookseller**—পুস্তক বিক্রেতা। **Bookselling**—পুস্তক বিক্রয়। **Book-shelf**—A shelf on which books are placed ; পুস্তক রাখিবার তাক বা দেরাজ। **Book-shop**—পুস্তকের দোকান। **Book-stall, Book-stand**—A stall or stand where books are offered for sale ; (রেলওয়ে ষ্টেশন প্রভৃতিতে) যে মেজের উপর বিক্রেয় পুস্তক সাজাইয়া রাখা হয়। **Book-trade** — পুস্তকের কারবার। **Book-worm**—A worm that eats holes in books ; পুস্তক ছিদ্রকারী কীট। A student closely attached to study ; অতিরিক্ত অধ্যয়নশীল ব্যক্তি, গ্রন্থকীট (রবিঃ)। **Book of good counsel**—হিতোপদেশ। **Book of life, Book of fate**—A list of those who shall be saved ; (খৃষ্টীয় ধর্ম্মমতে) যাহারা পরিত্রাণ প্রাপ্ত হইবে, তাহাদের তালিকা। **Book of reference**—অভিধান প্রভৃতি। **(A) sealed book**—A book, the contents of which are kept secret ; যে পুস্তকের লিখিত বিষয় অন্যের নিকট গুপ্ত রাখা হয়। **The book of books**—Bible ; বাইবেল। **Without book**—Without authority ; from memory ; অপ্রামাণিক ভাবে ; স্মৃতিশক্তির উপর নির্ভর করিয়া। **Beware of a man of one book**—Never attempt to convert the statement of one who is special in his subject ; বিশেষজ্ঞ ব্যক্তির স্বকীয় বিষয়-সম্বন্ধে কোন উক্তির প্রতিবাদ করিতে চেষ্টা করিও না। **That does not suit my book**—That does not accord with my arrangements ; তাহা আমার বন্দোবস্ত অনুযায়ী নহে। **To be in somebody's bad** or **black book**—To be in disfavour with him ; কাহারও বিরাগভাজন হওয়া। **To be in some body's good book**—To be in favour with him ; সুনজরে থাকা, অনুগ্রহভাজন হওয়া। **To bring (one) to book**—To call to account ; কৈফিয়ৎ চাওয়া। To take to task ; তিরস্কার করা। **To say ones lessons out of book**—To repeat one's lessons from memory ; পাঠ মুখস্থ বলা। **To speak by the book**—To speak with minute exactness, পুঙ্খানুপুঙ্খরূপে বলা। **To take a leaf out of another's book**—To follow his example ; to imitate him ; কাহারো দৃষ্টান্ত অনুসরণ করা ; কাহারো অনুকরণ করা। **To take one's name off the books**—To withdraw from a club ; কোন পরিষৎ বা সভা হইতে নাম তুলিয়া লওয়া। **To talk like a book**—পুস্তকের ভাষায় কথা বলা।

bōom, *n.* & *v. t.* **1.** A long pole or spar by which the bottom of a sail is stretched or extended ; পাইলের নিম্নভাগ প্রসারিত করিবার লম্বা দণ্ড, পাইল ছড়াইবার দণ্ড। **2.** A chain or barrier of timber across a river or mouth of a harbour to prevent ships from passing in ; জাহাজের প্রবেশ নিরোধার্থ পোতাশ্রয়ের মুখে বা নদীতে কাঠফলক বা শৃঙ্খল দ্বারা যে প্রতিবন্ধক স্থাপন করা হয়। ***Verb t.*** To extend or push with a boom or pole, (generally with *out, off*) ; as, to *boom out* a sail : to *boom off* a boat ; দণ্ড দ্বারা প্রসারিত করা বা ধাক্কা দেওয়া।

bōom, *v.i* & *n.* **1.** To hum or buzz ; to make a deep resonant sound ; to make a loud hollow sound ; "Alarm guns *booming* through the night air." গুণ্ গুণ্ করা, ভোঁ ভোঁ শব্দ করা, গুঞ্জন করা ; গম্ভীর নির্ঘোষ বা নিনাদ করা ; গর্জ্জন করা। **2.** To make the bittern's cry ; ক্রৌঞ্চ-পক্ষীর ন্যায় রব

করা। **3.** To move with booming noise, as a ship under full sail; পুরা পাইলভরে জাহাজের ন্যায় বেগে সোঁ সোঁ করিয়া ধাবিত হওয়া। ***Noun.*** **1.** A hollow roar, as of waves, cannon, etc.; গভীর নির্ঘোষ, কল্লোল, কামান প্রভৃতির গর্জ্জন। **2.** The cry of the bittern or the buzz of the beetle; ক্রৌঞ্চ পক্ষীর রব, গোবরে পোকার ভোঁ ভোঁ শব্দ।

Bōom, *v. t., i* & *n.* **1.** To cause to advance rapidly in price; as, to *boom* rail-road or mining shares; হঠাৎ বাজার গরম করিয়া তোলা। **2.** To push anything into sudden prominence; সহসা কোন জিনিষ খুব চল্‌তি করিয়া তোলা, হুহু শব্দে চালান। **3.** To win sudden popularity for an invention, cause, etc., by advertising; to launch with eclat; বিজ্ঞাপন দ্বারা কোন আবিষ্কার বা বিষয় সহসা জনপ্রিয় করিয়া তোলা; মহাসমারোহের সহিত কোন বিষয়ের উদ্বোধন করা। ***Verb i.*** To have rapid growth in market value or popular favour; হঠাৎ কোন জিনিষের বাজার গরম হইয়া উঠা, সহসা জনসাধারণের নিকট আদরণীয় হইয়া উঠা। ***Noun.*** sudden activity or development; as, a *boom* in coffee; হু হু শব্দে চলন বা বাড়িয়া উঠন।

bōom′-ĕr-ăng, *n.* A curved hard wood missile, used by the natives of Australia so balanced, that when thrown to a distance, it returns towards the thrower; অষ্ট্রেলিয়াবাসীদের ব্যবহৃত অর্দ্ধচন্দ্রাকৃতি সুদৃঢ় কাষ্ঠ-নির্ম্মিত প্রহরণ বিশেষ,—ইহা নিক্ষিপ্ত হইলে পুনঃ প্রত্যাবৃত্ত হইয়া নিক্ষেপকারীর হস্তে পতিত হয়।

bōon, *n.* & *adj.* **1.** A request; the thing asked for; প্রার্থনা; প্রার্থিত বস্তু। **2.** A favour granted; a gift; a grant or benefaction; প্রদত্ত অনুগ্রহ; অনুগ্রহ, দান; বর। **3.** A blessing; as, every perfect *boon* is from above; কল্যাণ। ***Adj.*** **1.** Kind; bounteous; benign; (said of nature, air, life, etc.); সদয়; বদান্য; সহৃদয়। **2.** Congenial; gay; jolly; as, a *boon* companion; আনন্দদায়ক; হৃষ্টচিত্ত; উৎফুল্ল, সদানন্দ। **Boon companion**—A convivial companion নর্ম্মসখা, বিট (কথা সঃ)।

Bōon, *n.* The useless vegetable matter from dressed flax; পরিষ্কৃত শণের অসার অংশ।

bōor, *n.* **1.** A peasant; কৃষক, চাষা। **2.** A clumsy, ill-bred or unrefined countryman; an illiterate fellow; অমার্জ্জিত বা অশিষ্ট ব্যক্তি; নিরক্ষর লোক। **3.** A Boer; দক্ষিণ আফ্রিকার ওলন্দাজ ঔপনিবেশিক, বোয়ার। **Boor′-ish,** *adj.* **Boor′-ish-ness.** *n.*

bōose, See BOOZE.

bōot, *n.* & *v. t.* **1.** An outer covering for the foot, usually all or partly of leather, coming above ankle; চর্ম্মপাদুকা বা উপানৎ বিশেষ, বুট জুতা। **2.** An instrument of torture for compressing the legs, formerly used to extort confession; পূর্ব্বকালে অপরাধিগণের স্বীকারোক্তি গ্রহণের জন্য পদ-নিষ্পীড়ক যন্ত্র বিশেষ। **3.** A box or luggage receptacle in a coach under guard's and coachman's seat; (ভাড়াটীয়া গাড়ীর) কোচম্যানের আসনের নীচে মালপত্রাদি রাখিবার আধার বা পেটক বিশেষ। **4.** A cover of leather or rubber cloth for the driving seat of a vehicle to pr[illegible] from rain and mud; গাড়ীচা[illegible] বসিবার স্থান বৃষ্টি এবং কর্দ্দম হইতে রক্ষার নিমিত্ত চামড়া বা রবারের আবরণ। **5.** (*Pl.* but used as a singular) A male servant in a hotel who cleanses boots, runs messages, etc.; হোটেলের যে ভৃত্য, বুটজুতা বুরুস এবং সংবাদ বহন ইত্যাদি কার্য্য করে। ***Verb t.*** To put boots on; বুটজুতা পায়ে দেওয়া। **Boot′-ed,** *adj.* Having boots on; equipped for riding; বুটজুতা-পরা; অশ্বারোহণের জন্য সজ্জিত। **Boot-black**—One who blacks boots; যে বুটজুতায় কালি দেয়। **Boot-closer**—One who sews the upper leathers of boots; যে ব্যক্তি বুটের উপরের চর্ম্মসকল সেলাই করিয়া সংযুক্ত করে। **Boot-jack**—An instrument for taking off boots; বুটজুতা খুলিবার যন্ত্র বিশেষ। **Boot-last, Boot-tree**—The last or wooden mould on which boots are made to keep their shape; বুটজুতা তৈয়ার করিবার কাঠের ফর্ম্মা বিশেষ। **Boot and saddle**—The signal of cavalry to mount; অশ্বারোহী সৈন্যগণকে (অশ্বারোহণ করিতে) সঙ্কেত। **Clumsy boot**—An awkward careless person; আনাড়ি অসাবধান লোক। **Six feet in his boots**—Quite six feet high; ঠিক ছয় ফুট লম্বা (জুতার উপর ছয় ফুট)। **Sly boot**—A cunning artful person; ধূর্ত্ত বা চালাক লোক। **To die in one's boots**—To be cut off in midst of health; পূর্ণ যৌবনে মৃত্যু মুখে পতিত হওয়া। **To get or give the boot**—To be dismissed or dismiss from employment; চাকুরী হইতে বরখাস্ত হওয়া বা করা। **To have one's heart in one's boots**—To be in a state of extreme terror; নিতান্ত ভয়ার্ত্ত হওয়া, প্রাণটী হাতে করিয়া থাকা। **To put the boots on the wrong leg**—To give credit or blame to the wrong party; যে ব্যক্তি প্রকৃতপক্ষে প্রশংসা বা নিন্দার যোগ্য তাহাকে প্রশংসা বা নিন্দা না করিয়া অপর ব্যক্তিকে করা।

bōot, *v. t.* & *n.* To profit; to advantage; to avail; লাভবান্ করা; উপকার করা; কাজে লাগান। [Generally used impersonally, as, *it boots us little*: *what boots* it.] ***Noun.*** Profit ; gain ; advantage ; লাভ ; উপকার ; সুবিধা। **Boot′-less,** *adj.* Unprofitable ; useless ; unavailing ; as, I will follow him no more with *bootless* prayers ; অলাভজনক ; নিরর্থক ; নিস্ফল। **Boot′-less-ly,** *adv.* **To boot**—In addition ; over and above ; to the good ; অধিকন্তু ; অতিরিক্ত, উপরন্তু ; লাভের অঙ্কে। **To make boot of**—To gain ; লাভ করা।

bōōt-ee′ (-ē), *n.* A kind of lady's boot ; infants' wool boot ; মহিলাদিগের এক প্রকার অনুপদীনা, স্ত্রীলোকদিগের উপানৎ বিশেষ ; শিশুদিগের পশমী বুটজুতা।

bō-ō′-tēs, *n.* A northern constellation containing the star Arcturus ; উত্তর দিকস্থ তারাপুঞ্জ—স্বাতী নক্ষত্র এই তারাপুঞ্জের অন্তর্ভুক্ত। [*Bootes* = *a* = স্বাতী (হিঃ কোঃ)।]

booth, *n.* **1.** A house or shed erected with boughs, branches, etc., for temporary occupancy ; বৃক্ষশাখাদি নির্ম্মিত অস্থায়ী কুটীর। **2.** A covered stall in market ; a tent at fair ; হাটের চালা ; মেলার টাট বা তাঁবু। **Polling booth**—A shelter for voting at election ; নির্ব্বাচনকালে ভোটদাতৃগণের অস্থায়ী আশ্রয়।

bōō-tȳ′, *n.* Plunder ; spoil (of war) ; লুণ্ঠিত দ্রব্য ; (যুদ্ধে) লুণ্ঠিত দ্রব্য। **To play booty**—To join with others in order to cheat one player ; to practise collusion ; একজন খেলোয়াড়কে ঠকাইবার মানসে অপর খেলোয়াড়ের সঙ্গে জোট বাঁধা ; প্রতারণার উদ্দেশ্যে যোগ সাজস করা।

booze, *v. i.* & *n.* To drink largely ; অপরিমিত মদ্য পান করা। ***Noun.*** Drink ; drinking bout ; পানীয় ; মদ্যপান-কোলাহল। **Booz′-y,** *adj.*

bō-peep′ (-pēp), *n.* A simple play among children in which one peeps from behind something and cri Bo" ; বালকদিগের একপ্রকার লুকোচুরি খেলা—ইহাতে একটী বালক পশ্চাদ্দিক হইতে উঁকি মারিয়া হঠাৎ "বো" শব্দ করে।

bō-raç′-ic, *adj.* Pertaining to, or produced from, borax ; as, *boracic* acid (সোহাগাম্ল) ; সোহাগা-সংক্রান্ত, সোহাগাজাত।

bŏr′-āge, *n.* A hairy leaved plant having pretty blue flowers used to flavour claret-cup ; নীলপুষ্প তরু বিশেষ—ইহা দ্বারা ক্লেরেট সুরা সুবাসিত করা হয়। **Country borage**—পাথরচুর (বেলঃ)।

bō′-răx, *n.* A native salt in white powder or crystal when pure ; সোহাগা, টঙ্ক (রঃ প্রঃ), টঙ্কন (কাদঃ), রঙ্গক্ষার (অঃ), টঙ্কনক্ষার (রঃ প্রঃ), ক্ষাররাজ (ঐ), মালতীতীরসম্ভব (ঐ)।

bŏr′-bō-rygm (-rîm), **-rȳg-mŭs,** *n.* A rumbling or gurgling noise produced by wind in the bowels ; পেটের ডাক, উদরের গুর গুর শব্দ।

Bŏr-deaux′ (-dö), *n.* Claret wine of Bordeaux, a great city in the southwest of France ; ফ্রান্সের দক্ষিণ পশ্চিমে অবস্থিত বোর্ডো-নগরে উৎপন্ন রক্তবর্ণ সুরা বিশেষ। **Bordeaux mixture**—তুথক্, চূণ এবং জল সহযোগে প্রস্তুত উদ্যান-বৃক্ষ সমূহের ছত্রাকাদিনাশক মিশ্র বিশেষ।

bŏr′-dĕl, *n.* A house for prostitution ; গণিকালয়, বেশ্যালয়।

bŏr′-dêr, *n. v. i,* & *t.* **1.** The outer edge of anything, as of a garment ; verge ; brink ; অঞ্চল, পাড় ; প্রান্ত ; ধার, কিনারা। **2.** A boundary ; a frontier district ; সীমান্ত রেখা ; সীমান্ত প্রদেশ, প্রত্যন্ত দেশ। **3.** A stripe arranged along near the edge of something, as an ornament or finish ; হাঁসিয়া, সঞ্জাব। **4.** A narrow flower-bed ; অপ্রশস্ত কেয়ারি। ***Verb i.*** **1.** To be contiguous or adjacent, (with *on* or *upon*) ; সংলগ্ন থাকা, প্রান্তবর্ত্তী হওয়া, লাগাও হওয়া। **2.** To approach ; to come near to ; সন্নিহিত হওয়া ; কাছাকাছি হওয়া, সদৃশ হওয়া। ***Verb t.*** **1.** To be near or close to ; কোন কিছুর সমীপবর্ত্তী হওয়া। **2.** To be close to the edge or confines of ; to be contiguous to ; as, the region *borders* a forest ; প্রান্তবর্ত্তী হওয়া ; লাগালাগি হওয়া। **3.** To serve as a border for ; পাড়ের কায করা। **4.** To adorn with a border ; পাড় বসান, ঝালর দেওয়া, সঞ্জাব লাগান, হাঁসিয়া লাগান। **—less,** *adj.* **Border-land**—Land on the frontiers of two adjoining countries ; পরস্পর-সংলগ্ন দুই দেশের মধ্যবর্ত্তী স্থান। { প্রায়শঃ লক্ষণায় ব্যবহৃত হয়।] **The border of a city**—নগরোপান্ত। **The border of a garment**—বস্ত্রাঞ্চল। **The border of a wood**—বনান্ত।

bŏr′-dêr-êr, *n.* One who dwells on or near a frontier, (especially a dweller on region between England and Scotland) ; সীমান্ত-প্রদেশবাসী, বিশেষতঃ ইংলণ্ড ও স্কট্লণ্ডের মধ্যবর্ত্তী প্রদেশবাসী লোক।

bōre, *v. t., i.* & *n.* **1.** To pierce so as to make a hole ; (also *Verb i.*) ; তুরপুন প্রভৃতি দ্বারা ছিদ্র করা। **2.** To force a narrow and difficult passage through ; as, to *bore* one's way through a crowd ; অতিকষ্টে ঠেলিয়া পথ করিয়া চলা। **3.** To perforate the strata of the earth in search of coal or other valuable minerals ; কয়লা কিম্বা অন্যান্য মূল্যবান খনিজ পদার্থের জন্য ভূস্তরে ছিদ্র করা। **4.** To push another out of the course ; (ঘোড়দৌড়ে এক ঘোড়ায় অপর ঘোড়াকে ধাক্কাদিয়া দৌড়-চক্রের বাহির করিয়া দেওয়া। **4.** (Of horse) To thrust the head out ; (also *Verb i.*) ; (অশ্ব-সম্পর্কে) মস্তক নিষ্ক্রান্ত করা। ***Noun.*** **1.** A perforation ; ছিদ্র, রন্ধ্র। **2.** The hollow of a gun, cannon, pistol or other firearm ; বন্দুক, কামান প্রভৃতি আগ্নেয়াস্ত্রের কোঠর।

3. The interior diameter of a tube or gun-barrel ; নল অথবা কামানের নলের অভ্যন্তরের ব্যাস। 4. A tool for making a hole by boring ; ছিদ্র করণার্থ যন্ত্র বিশেষ, তুরপুন, বেধনী, বেধনিকা। 5. A small deep hole made in earth to find water, oil, etc. ; জল, তৈল প্রভৃতি আছে কি না, পরীক্ষার জন্য ভূমিতে যে ক্ষুদ্র অথচ সুগভীর গর্ত্ত করা হয়। 6. A person that annoys and wearies ; a twaddler ; যে ব্যক্তি বিরক্ত করে বা অবসাদ জন্মায়, বালাই ; যে ব্যক্তি অনবরত বাজে কথা বকিয়া কান ঝালাপালা করিয়া তোলে। 7. An annoyance ; বিরক্তিজনক বস্তু, উৎপাত। **Bor'-ing,** *n.* **blue bore**—মেঘের ফাঁক—যাহার ভিতর দিয়া নীলাকাশখণ্ড দৃষ্ট হয়।

böre, *v. t.* To weary or annoy ; অবসাদ জন্মান, বিতৃষ্ণা জন্মান, বিরক্ত করা।

böre, *n.* A great rushing up of the tide into a river mouth ; বান, কটালের বান।

böre, *p. p.* of bear—to bring forth.

bö'-rë'-ăl, *adj.* Pertaining to the north or north-wind ; উদীচ্য, উত্তরপবনসম্পর্কীয়।

Bö'-rë-ăs, *n.* The God of the north wind [*Cap.*] ; the north wind [*common noun*] ; উত্তর বায়ুর অধিষ্ঠাতৃ দেবতা ; উত্তর পবন।

böre'-cöle, *n.* A loose open-headed variety of cabbage ; এক প্রকার বাঁধা কপি।

böre'-dom (-dŭm), *n.* State of being bored ; a state of ennui ; বিরক্তি বা বিতৃষ্ণার ভাব ; অবসাদ, ভোগবিতৃষ্ণা।

bör'-êr, *n.* 1. A piercing tool ; one that bores ; esp. a horse that bores ; ভেদনযন্ত্র, তুরপুন; যে ব্যক্তি তুরপুন দ্বারা ছিদ্র করে; বিশেষতঃ ঘোড়দৌড়ে যে ঘোড়া অপর ঘোড়াকে ঠেলিয়া দৌড়-চক্র হইতে বাহির করিয়া দেয়। 2. Kinds of boring insects ; নানাপ্রকার ছিদ্রকারী কীট।

bö'-ric, *adj.* Of boron ; বোরক-সম্বন্ধীয়। (See BORON.)

bŏrn, *p. p.* & *adj.* 1. Brought forth ; possessing stated qualities from birth ; inherited ; as, a *born* liar ; জাত, সম্ভূত, উদ্ভূত, ভূমিষ্ঠ, প্রসূত ; জন্ম হইতে বিশেষ গুণসমূহের অধিকারী ; উত্তরাধিকার সূত্রে প্রাপ্ত। 2. Destined to be ; কোন কিছু হইবার জন্য পূর্ব্ব হইতে নির্দ্দিষ্ট। **A born fool**—আজন্ম মূঢ়। **Born again**—Regenerated ; (আধ্যাত্মিকভাবে) নবজন্মপ্রাপ্ত, দ্বিজ। **Born-blind**—জন্মান্ধ। **Born days**—(*Colloq.*) Lifetime ; (চলিত ভাষায়) জীবিত কাল, জীবন। **Born in the purple**—Of princely birth ; high-born ; রাজবংশজাত ; উচ্চবংশজাত। **Born under a lucky star**—Destined to good luck ; শুভলগ্নজাত। **Born with a silver spoon in one's mouth**—born in wealth and luxury ; প্রচুর বিলাস বিভব সম্পন্ন ব্যক্তির গৃহে জাত। **High born**—কুলীন। **Ill-born**—হীনজাত, অন্ত্যজ।

borne, *p. p.* of *bear.*

bö'-rŏn, *n.* A nonmetallic element ; অধাতক রাসায়নিক মূলপদার্থ বিশেষ, বোরক (সাঃ পঃ), টঙ্ক (হিঃ কোঃ)।

bor'-ough (bŭ-rö) *n.* 1. A corporation town ; স্বায়ত্ত-শাসন এবং রাজদত্ত অন্যান্য বিশেষ অধিকার প্রাপ্ত ইংলণ্ডীয় নগর। 2. A town that sends members to Parliament ; পার্লেমেণ্ট মহাসভায় সভ্যপ্রেরণের ক্ষমতাপ্রাপ্ত নগর। 3. The collective body of citizens or inhabitants of a borough ; as, the *borough* voted to lay a tax ; উক্তপ্রকার নগরের অধিবাসি **A close** or **pocket borough**—এক ব্যক্তির অধিকারভুক্ত নগরী—যথা হইতে পার্লেমেণ্ট মহাসভায় সভ্য-প্রেরণ কেবল তাহার আয়ত্তাধীন ছিল। **Rotten borough**—১৮৩৩ খৃষ্টাব্দের নির্ব্বাচন-সংস্কার সম্বন্ধীয় বিধি-প্রবর্ত্তনের সময় অতি অল্পসংখ্যক নির্ব্বাচক থাকা সত্ত্বেও যে নগরের নির্ব্বাচন-অধিকার বর্ত্তমান ছিল। **To own** or **buy a borough**—To get the power of controlling election of members to Parliament ; পার্লেমেণ্ট মহাসভার সভ্য নির্ব্বাচনের ক্ষমতা আয়ত্ত করা।

borough-English, *n.* A custom in some ancient English boroughs, by which land and tenements descend to the youngest son or to the youngest brother instead of the eldest ; ইংলণ্ডের প্রাচীন কয়েকটী নগরীতে প্রচলিত প্রথা বিশেষ,—এই প্রথানুসারে ভূসম্পত্তি কনিষ্ঠ পুত্র বা কনিষ্ঠ ভ্রাতা প্রাপ্ত হইয়া থাকে।

bŏr'-row (-rö), 1. To get on loan money or property ; ধার করা (*Colloq.*), কর্জ্জ করা, ঋণ করা। 2. To copy or imitate ; to adopt ; as, to *borrow* the style of another ; নকল করা, অনুকরণ করা ; গ্রহণ করা। 3. To derive ; প্রাপ্ত হওয়া। **—er,** *n.* 1. One who borrows ; ঋণগ্রহীতা, অধমর্ণ। 2. An imitator ; a plagiarist ; অনুকরণকারী ; পররচনাপহারক, গ্রন্থ-তস্কর। **—rowed,** *adj.* Taken on loan ; counterfeit ; assumed ; ঋণ-লব্ধ; নকল, কৃত্রিম; কপট। **Borrowed feathers** or **plumes**—Such ornaments as do not belong to the wearer ; দাঁড়কাকের ময়ূরপুচ্ছ, পরকীয় বেশ ভূষা, কৃত্রিম রূপ বা বাহার। **Borrowed hair**—পরচুলা, কৃত্রিম কেশ। **Borrowing days**—এপ্রিল মাসের মাঝামাঝি ৩ দিন। [সাধারণতঃ ঠাণ্ডা ও ঝটিকাপূর্ণ হইয়া থাকে।] **To borrow troubles**—To be needlessly troubled ; অকারণে ব্যতিব্যস্ত হওয়া।

Bŏr-stăl scheme or **system,** *n.* [From Borstal Prison, Kent.] A system under which juvenile offenders are given special treatment to save them from growing into habitual criminals and are helped in finding work after leaving prison ; যে

ব্যবস্থানুসারে যুবক-বন্দিসকল কারাগারের পুরাতন বন্দিগণ হইতে পৃথক্ স্থানে রক্ষিত হইয়া জীবিকার্জ্জন এবং চরিত্র সংশোধনের উপযোগী শিক্ষা প্রাপ্ত হয়, এবং কারাগার ত্যাগের পর যাহাতে তাহারা কোন কর্ম্মে নিযুক্ত হইতে পারে তদ্বিষয়ে চেষ্টা করা হইয়া থাকে।

bŏrt, *n.* Diamond fragments made in cutting ; হীরকের পল কাটিবার কালে যে ক্ষুদ্র ক্ষুদ্র হীরকখণ্ড পতিত হয়।

bŏr'-zoi (–zōy), *n.* The Russian wol-fhound ; রুষ দেশীয় শিকারী কুক্কুর বিশেষ। [নেকড়া বাঘ শিকারে বিশেষ চতুর।]

bŏs'-căge, –kāge, *n.* Masses of trees or shrubs ; a thick foliage ; a grove or thicket ; নিবিড় তরু পুঞ্জ ; ঘনপত্রগুচ্ছ ; কুঞ্জ, উপবন।

bŏsh, *n.* (Used also as *interj.*) Nonsense ; foolish talk ; trash ; humbug ; বাজে কথা ; অর্থশূন্য বাক্য ; আবর্জ্জনা ; ফাঁকি।

bŏsh, *v. t.* (*School slang*) To make a fool of ; to tease ; (বিদ্যালয়ের বালকদিগের ইতরভাষায়) আহাম্মক বানান, বোকা সাজান ; ক্ষেপান। **All bosh**—কুলাভরা ছাই।

bŏsk, bŏs'-kĕt, bŏs'-quet (-kĕt), *n.* A thicket ; a grove ; a shrubbery ; তরু-গহন ; কুঞ্জ ; গুল্মোদ্যান, গুল্মবাটিকা।

bŏsk'-ȳ, *adj.* Woody or bushy ; তরুসমাকীর্ণ, গুল্মবহুল।

bŏs'-om (-ŭm), *n., adj. & v. t.* **1.** The breast of a human being ; বক্ষঃস্থল, উরস, ভুজান্তর। **2.** Embrace ; fold ; as, within the *bosom* of the church ; আলিঙ্গন, ভুজবেষ্টন ; বেষ্টনী। **3.** The part of the dress worn upon the breast ; বক্ষোদেশাবরক পরিচ্ছদাংশ, বক্ষস্ত্রাণ, বক্ষোঃবস্ত্র। **4.** The heart, thoughts, desires, etc. ; "Anger resteth in the *bosom* of the fools ;" secret thought ; "She finds not the *bosom* of my purpose ;" অন্তঃকরণ, মর্ম্মস্থল, চিন্তা, বাসনা প্রভৃতি ; নিভৃত চিন্তা। **5.** The interior ; as, the *bosom* of the earth ; অভ্যন্তরভাগ। **6.** The surface of a lake or ground ; ধরাতল, ধরাপৃষ্ঠ, হ্রদের উপরিভাগ। ***Adj.*** Intimate ; confidential ; beloved ; as, a *bosom* friend ; অন্তরঙ্গ ; বিশ্বস্ত ; প্রিয়। ***Verb t.*** To conceal ; "Of Como *bos'med* deep in chestnut groves ;" লুক্কায়িত রাখা। **Bosom-friend**—A very intimate friend ; অন্তরঙ্গ বন্ধু, প্রাণসখা, পরাণবন্ধু (গীতাঞ্জঃ), সুহৃত্তম (উজ্জ্বলঃ)। **To take to one's bosom**—To marry ; বিবাহ করা।

bŏss, *n. & v. t.* **1.** A protuberance ; স্ফীতাংশ, উদ্গতাংশ। **2.** A knob or stud ; বর্ত্তুল, টোপ, গুল। **3.** (*Arch.*) An ornamental projection often richly carved and placed at the intersection of vault-ribs ; (স্থপতি-বিজ্ঞান) খিলানযুক্ত ছাদের সন্ধিস্থানের উদ্গত অলঙ্কার বিশেষ।

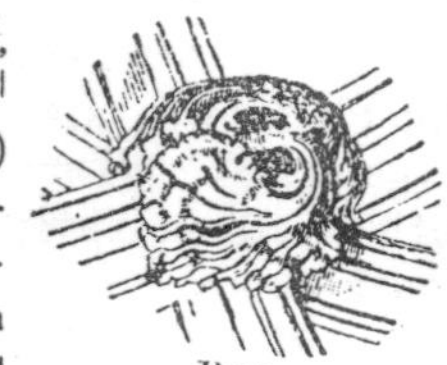

Boss.

4. (*Mech.*) The enlarged part of a shaft, on which a wheel is keyed ; (যন্ত্র-বিজ্ঞান) দণ্ডের যে স্ফীত অংশে চক্র সংযুক্ত করা হয়। ***Verb t.*** To ornament with bosses ; উদ্গাত অলঙ্কারে ভূষিত করা। **Boss'-y,** *adj.* Ornamented with bosses ; উদ্গাতালঙ্কারভূষিত, কারুকার্য্যভূষিত।

bŏss, *n. & v. t.* **1.** (*Slang*) A master ; a person in authority ; (ইতর ভাষায়) কর্ত্তা, প্রভু, মনিব, [illegible]ওয়ালা ; প্রভুশক্তিসম্পন্ন ব্যক্তি। [illegible] (*U.S.*) The manager of a political organization ; (মার্কিণ যুক্তরাজ্যে) কোন রাজনীতিক আন্দোলনের পরিচালক। ***Verb t.*** **1.** To manage ; to be master or manager of ; পরিচালনা করা ; প্রভু বা পরিচালক হওয়া। **2.** To hold mastery over ; কোন কিছুর উপর কর্ত্তৃত্ব করা। **To boss the show**—To be supreme director of an enterprise ; কোন কর্ম্মের সর্ব্বপ্রধান পরিচালক হওয়া।

bŏss'-ing, *n.* A coat of boiled oil spread over earthenware to hold the colour ; রঙ্গ ধরাইবার জন্য মাটির বাসনের উপর যে তপ্ত-তৈলের লেপ দেওয়া হয়।

bŏs'-ton (-tŭn), *n.* A game at cards, somewhat similar to whist ; এক প্রকার তাসের খেলা।

Bŏs-wĕll'-i-ăn, *adj.* Relating to or characterstic of Boswell, the biographer of Dr. Johnson ; ডাক্তার জনসনের জীবনী-লেখক বজ্‌ওয়েলের ন্যায় বা তাঁহার প্রকৃতির অনুরূপ। **Bŏs'-wĕll-ĭsm,** *n.* The style of Boswell ; বজ্‌ওয়েলের রচনা-পদ্ধতি। ***Boswellia thurifera***—গন্ধবিরজা (বেলঃ)।

bŏt'-bŏtt, See BOTS, BOTTS.

bŏt'-ă-nȳ, *n.* **1.** The science of plants ; উদ্ভিদ-বিদ্যা, বৃক্ষায়ুর্ব্বেদ। **2.** A book which treats of the science of botany ; উদ্ভিদ্-বিদ্যাবিষয়ক পুস্তক। **Bo-tan'-ic, Bo-tan'-i-cal,** *adjs.* **Bo-tan'-i-cal-ly,** *adv.* **–nist,** *n.* One versed in botany, (knowledge of plants) ; উদ্ভিদ্ বিদ্যাবিৎ, উদ্ভিদ্‌বেত্তা, বনস্পতিবেত্তা। **–nize,** *v.* To collect plants with the object of examining them scientifically ; to study botany ; বৈজ্ঞানিক পরীক্ষার জন্য বৃক্ষ গুল্মাদি সংগ্রহ করা ; উদ্ভিদ-বিদ্যার অনুশীলন করা। **Botanic physician**—যে বৈদ্য প্রধানতঃ গাছ-গাছড়া ও শিকড় হইতে প্রস্তুত ঔষধ ব্যবহার করে। **Botanical garden**—উদ্ভিদ্ বিদ্যা অনুশীলনের উপযোগী বৃক্ষ গুল্মাদি যে উদ্যানে জন্মান হইয়া থাকে। **Botany Bay**—অষ্ট্রেলিয়ার পূর্ব্বোপকূলে স্থিত বন্দীদিগের সুবিখ্যাত উপনিবেশ।

bō-târ'-gō, –gă, *n.* A relishing food made of mullet or tunny roe ; মৎস্য-ডিম্বদ্বারা প্রস্তুত সুস্বাদু খাদ্য-বিশেষ।

botch (bŏch), *n. & v. t.* A patch added clumsily ; a bungled work ;

বিশ্রীভাবে সেলাই করা তালি ; আনাড়ীর কায। ***Verb t*** To make a clumsy patch ; to repair badly ; বিশ্রীভাবে তালি লাগান ; খারাপভাবে মেরামত করা। **Botch'-er,** *n.*

bŏt'-flȳ, *n.* A family of dipterous insects that deposit their

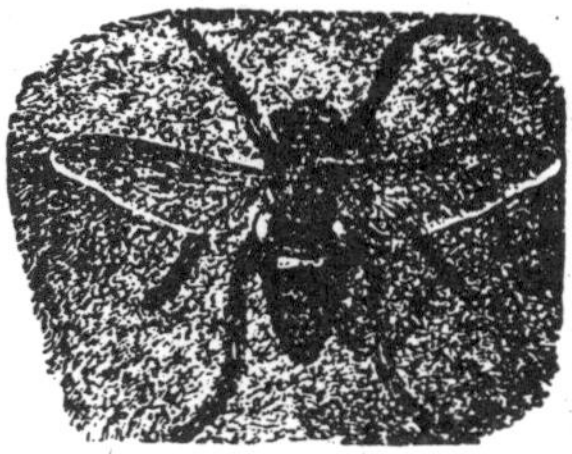

.Bot-fly

eggs on cattle ; এক শ্রেণীর মক্ষিকা, যাহারা গো-মহিষাদির গাত্রে ডিম পাড়িয়া থাকে।

bŏth, *adj., pron., adv. & conj.* The two ; not only one ; as, *both* the brothers were dead ; উভয় ; দুইই। ***Pron.*** The two ; the pair ; as, *both* are dead ; দুইই ; উভয়েই। ***Adv.*** Equally ; as, he is *both* dead and buried ; উভয়তঃ, সমানতঃ। ***Conj.*** As well ; also ; "Malice mars logic and charity *both* ;" on the one side ; ও, আরও ; অপিচ ; এক পক্ষে।

bŏth'-er, *v. t., i. & n.* To annoy ; to trouble ; to perplex ; বিরক্ত করা ; উত্যক্ত করা, ত্যক্ত করা, জ্বালাতন করা ; ঝঞ্ঝাটে ফেলা। ***Verb i.*** To be troublesome ; to worry one's self ; to feel anxiety ; বিরক্তিকর হওয়া ; ত্যক্ত বোধ করা ; উদ্বেগ বোধ করা। ***Noun.*** Worry ; embarrassment ; উৎপাত, ঝঞ্ঝাট ; বালাই। **—a'-tion,** *n.* Petty vexation or annoyance ; (often used as an exclamation) ; বিরক্তি, ঝঞ্ঝাট, জ্বালা, উপদ্রব। **—er,** *n.* **—some,** *adj.* **Bother-head**—Stupid ; স্থূল-বুদ্ধি।

bŏth'-ȳ, bōōth'-ȳ, *n.* A wooden hut or humble cot ; (in Scotland) a rude hut or barrack for unmarried servants ; কাঠের ঘর, দরিদ্রের পর্ণশালা, কুঁড়ে ঘর ; (স্কটলণ্ডে) অবিবাহিত ভৃত্যদের বাসের জন্য কুটীর-শ্রেণী।

bō'-tree (-trē), *n.* The name given to the Pipal tree in Ceylon held sacred by the Buddhists ; সিংহলদ্বীপস্থ বোধিদ্রুম।

bŏts, bŏtts, *n.* (Generally in the plural) A parasitic worm ; এক প্রকার পর-দেহ-পুষ্ট কীট [অশ্বের অন্ত্রে এবং গো-মহিষাদির গাত্রে জন্মে]। **The botts**—ঐ প্রকার আভ্যন্তরীণ কীট দ্বারা জাত অশ্বরোগ।

bŏt-tine' (-tēn), *n.* A small boot ; a lady's boot ; ক্ষুদ্র বুট জুতা ; মহিলাদিগের বুট জুতা।

bŏt'-tle, *n.* **1.** A narrow-necked vessel for liquids ; বোতল, কাচকূপী (সাঃ পঃ)। **2.** The amount of liquid contained in a bottle ; as, to drink a *bottle* of wine ; এক বোতল। **3.** (*Fig.*) Intoxicating liquor ; as, to drown one's reason in the *bottle* ; (লক্ষণায়) মত্ততাজনক তরল পদার্থ, সুরা। **Bottle-brush**—A cylindrical brush for cleansing interior of bottles ; বোতল পরিষ্কার করিবার জন্য লম্বা নলাকার বুরুস। A kind of plant ; এক প্রকার গাছ, বোতল-বুরুষ (প্রবোধ)। **Bottle-friend**—A friend in drinking ; এক গ্লাসের ইয়ার, মদের ইয়ার। **Bottle-glass**—বোতল প্রস্তুতের উপযোগী একপ্রকার গাঢ় সবুজবর্ণ কাচ। **Bottle-gourd**—অলাবু, লাউ (প্রবোধ)। **Bottle-holder**—One who attends upon a boxer or pugilist at a prize-fight ; মুষ্টিযোদ্ধা বা মল্লযোদ্ধার অনুচর। A supporter ; পৃষ্ঠপোষক, সাহায্যকারী। **Bottle-nose**—A swollen nose ; a whale having a beaked snout ; স্ফীত-নাসা ; চঞ্চুবৎ নাসাবিশিষ্ট তিমি মৎস্য। **Bottle-washer**—A chief agent ; a factotum ; প্রধান কার্য্যকারক ; সর্ব্বকর্ম্ম সাধনে নিযুক্ত ব্যক্তি। **Feeding** or **nursing bottle**—শিশুদিগের দুগ্ধপানের নিমিত্ত রবরের চুষনি-যুক্ত বোতল। **Over the bottle**—While drinking ; মদ্যপান কালে। **The bottle**—The practice of drinking ; সুরাপান। Strong drink in general ; সর্ব্বপ্রকার উগ্র পানীয়, মদ্য, মদিরা, সুরা। **To bring up on the bottle**—To rear a child by means of a feeding-bottle ; স্তনের দুধ না দিয়া বোতলের দুধ দ্বারা শিশু-পালন করা। **To pass the bottle of smoke**—To give countenance to conventional lie ; প্রচলিত মিথ্যা কথায় সায় দেওয়া।

bŏt'-tle, *v. t.* **1.** To store in bottles ; বোতলজাত করা, বোতলে পুরিয়া রাখা। **2.** (*Fig.*) To shut up or in ; as, the German fleet is believed to be *bottled up* at home ; (লক্ষণায়) আবদ্ধ করা, ঘিরিয়া ফেলা বা রাখা, রুদ্ধ করা, প্রবেশ করিতে না দেওয়া। **To bottle up**—To conceal ; to restrain for a time (resentment etc.) ; গোপন করা ; কিছু সময়ের জন্য দমন করিয়া রাখা, সংযত করা।

bŏt'-tle, *n.* A bundle of hay or straw ; ঘাস বা খড়ের আঁটি। **To look for a needle in a bottle of hay**—To make a hopeless search ; বৃথা অন্বেষণ করা, খড়ের গাদায় সূচ খুঁজা।

bŏt'-tŏm, *n., v. t., i. & adj.* **1.** The lowest part of anything ; the foot ; তলদেশ, অধোভাগ ; পাদ, পাদদেশ। **2.** The posterior or the sitting part of human body ; পশ্চাদ্দেশ, অধোদেশ, নিতম্ব। **3.** The seat of a chair ; কুর্শি বা কেদারায় বসিবার স্থান। **4.** The bed of a river, lake or sea ; as, a rocky *bottom* ; নদী, সমুদ্র বা হ্রদের তলদেশ। **5.** Lowlying land ; নিম্নভূমি। **6.** (*Naut.*) The keel of a ship ; hence, the vessel itself; "My ventures are not in one *bottom* trusted;" (নৌ-বিদ্যা) জাহাজের যে অংশ সাধারণতঃ জলের নীচে থাকে; জাহাজ। **7.** Foundation; origin; পত্তন, ভিত্তি; উৎপত্তি, মূল। **8.** The essential character; reality; as, to get to the *bottom* of a thing; মৌলিক প্রকৃতি; বাস্তবিকতা। **9.** Native strength; power of endurance; as, the horse has good *bottom*; স্বাভাবিক শক্তি বা বল; সহিষ্ণুতা। **10.** Dregs; গাদ, তলানি। **11.** The last place in a list or class; the lower end of a table; কোন তালিকা বা শ্রেণীর সর্ব্বনিম্ন স্থান; মেজের যে প্রান্তে পদগৌরব হিসাবে নিকৃষ্ট ব্যক্তি উপবেশন করে। ***Verb t.*** **1.** To furnish with a bottom; as, to *bottom* a chair; তলা লাগান। **2.** To base (argument, etc.); (যুক্তি প্রভৃতি) প্রতিষ্ঠিত করা, কোন ভিত্তির উপর দাঁড় করান। **3.** To understand fully; to sound; তলাইয়া বুঝা; অভিপ্রায় অবগত হওয়া। ***Verb i.*** To rest upon as its ultimate support; মূলভিত্তির উপর দণ্ডায়মান হওয়া। ***Adj.*** **1.** Lowest; last; as, one's *bottom* dollar; নিম্নতম; সর্ব্বশেষ। **2.** Fundamental; মৌলিক। **3.** Alluvial; পলিপড়া। **—less,** *adj.* **1.** Without a bottom, (as chair); তলাশূন্য। **2.** Unfathomable; baseless; as, a *bottomless* abyss; অতল-স্পর্শ; অতল (গীতাঞ্জঃ), অগাধ। **—tomed,** *p. p.* **At bottom**—In reality; fundamentally; প্রকৃতপক্ষে; মূলে। **False bottoms**—Crazy or leaky vessels; ফাটা বা ফুটা জাহাজ। **From the bottom of heart**—Without reservation; হৃদয়ের অন্তস্তল হইতে, হৃদয়ের গভীরতম প্রদেশ হইতে। **In the bottom of**—In the inmost part of; গভীরতম প্রদেশে, অন্তস্তলে। **To be at the bottom of**—To be the cause or source of; কোন কিছুর কারণ বা মূল হওয়া, কোন কিছুর গোড়ায় থাকা। **To bet your bottom dollar**—To stake all; সর্ব্বস্ব পণ করা। **To bottom up**—To get upside down; উল্‌টিয়া যাওয়া, বিপর্য্যস্ত হওয়া। **To get to the bottom of a matter**—To ascertain the entire truth; প্রকৃত ব্যাপার নিরূপণ করা। **To go to the bottom**—To sink; ডুবিয়া যাওয়া। **To probe** or **sift out to the bottom**—To scrutinize; তন্ন তন্ন করিয়া দেখা। **To stand in one's bottom**—To be independent; স্বাধীন হওয়া, আত্মনির্ভরশীল হওয়া। **To touch bottom**—To reach the lowest point; গভীরতম প্রদেশ প্রাপ্ত হওয়া।

bŏt'-tŏm, *n.* A ball of thread wound up together; সুতার গুটি।

bŏt'-tŏm-rȳ, *n.* A system of lending money to ship-owner, for purposes of voyage, on security of the ship,—if the ship is lost by perils of the sea, the lender loses the money; জাহাজ বন্ধক রাখিয়া ঋণ-প্রদান (জাহাজ সমুদ্রে মারা গেলে ঋণদাতার টাকা মারা যায়), পোত বন্ধক (আঃ বঃ)।

boudoir, (*F.*), *n.* A lady's small private room; ভদ্রমহিলার নিজস্ব-কক্ষ, স্ত্রীলোকের নিভৃত প্রকোষ্ঠ।

bouffant, (*F.*) *adj.* Puffed out; স্ফীত।

bough (bow̄), *n.* An arm or branch of a tree, especially a large arm or main branch; তরু-শাখা, বিটপ, ডাল।

bought (bŏt), *p. p.* of BUY (which see).

bougie, (*F.*), *n.* **1.** A wax-candle (from Bugia, a town of North Africa, whence these candles were first imported); মোমবাতি (আফ্রিকার বিউজিয়া নগর হইতে প্রথম এই বাতি আমদানি হয়)। **2.** A long, thin, flexible surgical instrument for exploring, dilating, etc., the passages of the body; দেহের বিভিন্ন নাড়ী (অন্ত্র, গলনালী, মূত্রমার্গ প্রভৃতি) পরীক্ষা বা প্রসারিত করিবার জন্য দীর্ঘ, কোমল এবং নমনীয় যন্ত্রবিশেষ, মূত্রসঙ্কোপহারিণী শলাকা, বর্ত্তিকা (ঠাকুর)।

bouillabaisse, (*F.*), *n.* A rich fish-stew; নানা মসল্লাসংযোগে পক্ক মৎস্যের ঝোল, দমপোক্ত।

bouilli, (*F.*), *n.* A stewed or boiled meat; দমপোক্ত বা সিদ্ধ মাংস।

bouillon, (*F.*), *n.* **1.** Broth; soup; মাংসের সুরুয়া, সুপ; মাংসের ক্কাথ (খাঃ)। **2.** (Dress) Puffed fold; পরিচ্ছদ, স্ফীত বস্ত্রভঙ্গ বা বস্ত্রপুট, পোষাকের ফুলানো পাট।

boul'-dêr (bōl-), *n.* **1.** A water-worn rounded stone of considerable size; বর্ত্তুলীকৃত সলিলক্ষত সুবৃহৎ পাষাণ-খণ্ড। **2.** A large erratic block of weather-worn stone; গণ্ডশৈল (সাঃ পঃ)। **Boulder-clay, —drift, —formation**—These are geological terms with reference to ice-age; ভূ-বিদ্যার তুষারযুগ-সম্বন্ধীয় পারিভাষিক শব্দ সমূহ।

boublevard, (*F.*), *n.* A broad street borderd with rows of trees; তরুশ্রেণী সুশোভিত প্রশস্ত বর্ত্ম, রথ্যা।

bouleversement, (*F.*), *n.* Complete overthrow; a turning upside down; সম্পূর্ণরূপে উৎপাতন; বিপর্য্যাস, বিপর্য্যয়।

boul'-têr (bōl-), *n.* A long stout fishing line to which many hooks are attached; বহুবড়শিযুক্ত লম্বা শক্ত সূতা।

bounce (bow̄ns), *v. i., t., n. & adv.* **1.** To leap or spring suddenly and with noise; ঝুপ্ করিয়া লাফ দেওয়া। **2.** To throw oneself about; (কোন বিষয়) চেষ্টা করিয়া দেখা। **3.** To rebound; ঠিকরাইয়া আসা, প্রতিক্ষিপ্ত হওয়া। **4.** To burst noisily or angrily, etc., into or out of room; হুস্ করিয়া প্রবেশ করা বা বাহির হওয়া। ***Verb t.*** **1.** To talk big ; লম্বাচৌড়া কথা বলা, দর্পোক্তি করা, আস্ফালন করা। **2.** To cause to rebound ; ঠিকরান। **3.** To eject violently, as from a room ; বলপূর্ব্বক বাহির করিয়া দেওয়া। **4.** To bully ; to scold ; শাসান, ধমকান; তিরস্কার করা। ***Noun.*** **1.** A sudden leap or bound ; a rebound ; আকস্মিক লম্ফ ; প্রতিঘাত, প্রতিক্ষেপ। **2.** A boast ; a bold lie ; a swagger ; গর্ব্ব, দর্প ; প্রগল্‌ভ মিথ্যা বাক্য ; বড়াই, আস্ফালন। ***Adv.*** Suddenly ; noisily ; as, to come *bounce* into a room ; সহসা, হঠাৎ ; সশব্দে, হঠ্‌ করিয়া, হন হন করিয়া। **To be kept on the bounce**—To be kept in a state of great mental agitation and anxiety ; নিরতিশয় মানসিক উদ্বেগ ও উৎকণ্ঠায় থাকা।

bounc'-êr (bowns-), *n.* **1.** A boaster ; a liar ; a bold lie ; দাম্ভিক, স্পর্দ্ধাকারী ; মিথ্যাবাদী ; প্রগল্‌ভ মিথ্যা বাক্য। **2.** Something big of its kind ; as, the stone must be a *bouncer* ; কোন জাতীয় বস্তু শ্রেণীর মধ্যে সর্ব্বাপেক্ষা বৃহত্তম।

bounc'-ing (bowns-), *adj.* Plump and healthy ; large and heavy ; হৃষ্টপুষ্ট, স্থূলাঙ্গ ; প্রকাণ্ড, স্থূল। **—ly,** *adv.*

bound (bownd), *n.* & *v. t.* **1.** A limit of territory or estate ; a boundary ; প্রান্তসীমা ; সীমা। **2.** (Usually plural) Limitation ; restriction ; সীমাবন্ধন ; বাঁধা। ***Verb t.*** **1.** To set bounds to ; সীমা-নির্দ্দেশ করা। **2.** To limit ; to restrain ; সীমাবদ্ধ করা, পরিমিত করা ; বাধা দেওয়া। **3.** To be the boundary of ; (কোন স্থানের) সীমা-স্বরূপ হওয়া। **Bound'-a-ry,** *n.* A visible limit ; border ; the limit-line ; চতুঃসীমা, সহরদ্দ; প্রান্তদেশ; সীমারেখা। **Bound'-less,** *adj.* Unlimited ; vast ; unconfined ; অনন্ত, অসীম ; বিশাল, প্রশস্ত ; অপার, নিষ্পার, নিঃসীম। **Out of the bounds**—Beyond limits set by school rules ; বিদ্যালয়ের নিয়ম দ্বারা নির্দ্দিষ্ট সীমার বাহিরে। **To break bounds**—To go beyond what is reasonable or allowable ; সীমার বাহিরে যাওয়া, মাত্রা ছাড়াইয়া যাওয়া। **To bring within bounds**—To reduce to a moderate degree ; পরিমিত করা, সীমাবদ্ধ করা। **To go beyond the bounds of**—To exceed the limits of ; সীমা লঙ্ঘন করা। **To know no bounds**—To be limitless ; সীমা না থাকা, অসীম হওয়া।

bound (bownd), *v. i.* & *n.* (Of balls, etc.) **1.** To rebound ; ঠিকরান, প্রতিহত হওয়া। **2.** To jump ; লম্ফঝম্প দেওয়া। **3.** To move with a sudden spring or leap ; to leap ; লাফাইয়া লাফাইয়া চলা ; লম্ফ প্রদান করা। ***Noun.*** **1.** A spring ; a jump ; a springy movement upward or forward ; লম্ফ ; ঝম্প ; হেলিয়া দুলিয়া চলন। **2.** (Of ball, etc.) Recoil ; প্রতিহতি। **By leaps and bounds**—By startingly rapid speed ; বিস্ময়কর বেগে।

bound (bownd), *adj.* Ready to start ; prepared ; destined ; যাত্রার জন্য প্রস্তুত ; প্রস্তুত ; নির্দ্দিষ্ট।

bound'-ên (bownd-), *adj.* **1.** Obliged ; বাধিত। **2.** Binding ; as, *bounden* duty ; অবশ্যপালনীয়।

bound'-êr (bownd-), *n.* **1.** One that limits ; সীমানির্দ্ধারক। **2.** (*Slang*) An inherently vulgar person ; (ইতর ভাষায়) ইতর ব্যক্তি।

boun'-te-ous (bown-tē-ŭs), *adj.* **1.** Liberal ; munificent ; বদান্য, দানশৌণ্ড ; দানশীল, মুক্তহস্ত। **2.** Plentiful ; প্রচুর। **—ly,** *adv.* **—ness,** *n.*

boun'-ti-fûl (bown-), *adj.* **1.** Liberal ; দানশীল। **2.** Plentiful ; প্রচুর, প্রভূত। **—ly,** *adv.* **—ness,** *n.*

boun'-tŷ (bown-), **1.** Liberality ; munificence ; বদান্যতা ; দানশীলতা। **2.** The gift bestowed ; প্রদত্ত বস্তু, দান। **3.** A premium given to encourage men to enlist, or to encourage trade ; as, *bounty-fed* products. ; সরকারী কার্য্যে ভর্ত্তি হইতে উৎসাহিত করিবার জন্য লোকদিগকে যে অর্থ পুরস্কার প্রদান করা হয়, ব্যবসায়-বাণিজ্যে উৎসাহ প্রদানের যে অর্থ প্রদান করা হয়। **—ti-ful,** *adj.* **—ti—hood,** *n.*

bou-quet' (bô-kā), **1.** A nosegay ; a bunch of flowers ; ফুলের তোড়া ; পুষ্পগুচ্ছ, কুসুমস্তবক। **2.** An aroma ; as, the *bouquet* of wine ; সুবাস, আমোদ।

bourg (bôrg), *n.* Same as BURGH, BOROUGH.

bour-geois' (bŭr-jö, -joys), *n.* A size of type between long primer and brevier ; ছাপার ক্ষুদ্র অক্ষর (এই পুস্তকের বাঙ্গালা অক্ষর)।

bour-geois' (bôrzh-wä), *n.* & *adj.* A member of the shop-keeping middle-class ; মধ্যবিত্ত শ্রেণীর ব্যবসায়ী লোক। ***Adj.*** Characteristic of the middle-class ; মধ্যবিত্ত শ্রেণীর স্বভাবসুলভ।

bourgeoisie (bôrzh-wä-zē), (*F.*), *n.* The middle-class ; মধ্যবিত্ত শ্রেণী।

bour'-geon (bôr-jŭn), *n.* & *v. i.* (See BURGEM.)

bourn (bōrn), **bourne** (bōrn), *n.* A boundary ; goal ; "That undiscovered country from whose *bourn*, no traveller returns ;" সীমা ; চরমগম্য স্থান। **Bourn'-less,** *adj.*

bourn (bōrn), *n.* A small brook ; ক্ষুদ্র স্রোতস্বতী।

bourse (bôrs), *n.* A money-market, especially that of Paris ; টাকার বাজার, বিশেষতঃ প্যারী নগরীস্থ কোম্পানীর কাগজ ক্রয়বিক্রয়ের স্থান।

bouse (bôz), *n.* & *v. i.* See BOOSE.

bout (bowt), *n.* **1.** A turn at work or exercise ; as much of an action as can be performed at one time ; পালা, বার, ক্ষেপ, পর্য্যায় ; কোন কাজের যে অংশ একেবারে সম্পাদন করা যায়। **2.** A fit of drinking or illness ; মত্ততা, পীড়ার ক্ষণস্থায়ী আক্রমণ। **3.** A trial of strength ; শক্তি-পরীক্ষা। **A drinking bout**—মদ্যপানোৎসব।

bö'-vīne, *adj.* **1.** Pertaining to oxen or cows ; ox-like ; গোজাতীয়, গব্য ; গোসদৃশ। **2.** Inert ; sluggish ; জড়, নির্জীব ; মন্থর।

bow (bō), *n.* & *v. t.* **1.** A curve ; বক্ররেখা। **2.** The rainbow ; রামধনু, ইন্দ্রচাপ। **3.** A weapon for shooting arrows ; ধনুক, কার্ম্মুক, কোদণ্ড, চাপ, শরাসন। **4.** Fiddlestick ; বেহালাদি বাদ্য যন্ত্রের ছড়। **5.** An instrument used for turning a drill ; প্রস্তরভেদক বজ্রসূচী ঘুরাইবার দণ্ড। **6.** The part of a yoke which embraces the animal's neck etc. ; যোয়ালের যে অংশ দ্বারা পশুর গলদেশ প্রভৃতি বেষ্টিত হয়। **7.** A looped knot of ribbon ; a neck-tie ; ফিতার ফাঁসযুক্ত গ্রন্থি ; গলবন্ধনী। **8.** (*Pl.*) Bow-compass ; see BELOW. ***Verb t.*** To perform or play with the bow ; ছড় দ্বারা বাজান। **Bow-boy**—Cupid ; পুষ্পধন্বা। **Bow-compasses**—A small pair of compasses for describing circles with ink or pencil ; বৃত্তাঙ্কনের যন্ত্র বিশেষ। **Bow-head**—Greenland whale ; গ্রীণলণ্ডের তিমিমৎস্য। **Bow-legged**—Having crooked legs ; বক্রজঙ্ঘ, বক্রপাদ, সংহত-জানু। **Bow-pen**—Bow-compasses, one leg of which carries a drawing pen ; একপ্রকার বৃত্তাঙ্কনের যন্ত্র,—যাহার এক পদে অঙ্কনোপযোগী কলম সংযুক্ত থাকে। **Bow-saw**—A narrow saw stretched like bow-string on wooden frame ; কাঠের কাঠামের উপর ধনুর জ্যার মত সংবদ্ধ অপ্রশস্ত করপত্র (করাত) বিশেষ। **Bow-shot**—The distance to which a bow can send an arrow ; শরগম্য দূরতা, এক তীর, বাণ-পথ। **Bow-string**—The string by which a bow is drawn ; জ্যা, ধনুকের ছিলা, ধনুগুর্ণ, মৌর্ব্বী, শিঞ্জিনী। A string used by the Turks for strangling offenders ; তুরস্কদেশীয় অপরাধীদিগকে ফাঁসি দিবার রজ্জুবিশেষ, পাশদণ্ড। **Bow-window**—(See *Bay window*) [*A carder's bow*—তুলা ধুনিবার ধনুক। *A pellet bow*—গুলাল। *Bow-drill*—বর্ম্মা। *Twang of a bow*—জ্যাঘোষ।] **Draw not your bow till your arrow is fixed**—Have every thing ready before you begin ; কার্য্যারম্ভের পূর্ব্বে সমস্ত প্রস্তুত রাখিও। **To be too much of the bow-hand**—Not to be sufficiently dexterous ; উপযুক্ত পরিমাণ দক্ষতা না থাকা। **To draw a bow at a venture**—To attack with a random remark ; অন্ধকারে ঢিল ছোড়া, আন্দাজের উপর কোন মন্তব্য প্রকাশ করা। **To draw the long bow**—To make extravagant statements ; অসম্ভব উক্তি করা, অত্যুক্তি করা। **To fit the arrow to the bow**—শরাসনে শর সন্ধান করা। **To have a second string to one's bow**—To have more resources than one ; কোন উদ্দেশ্য-সিদ্ধির জন্য একাধিক উপায় থাকা।

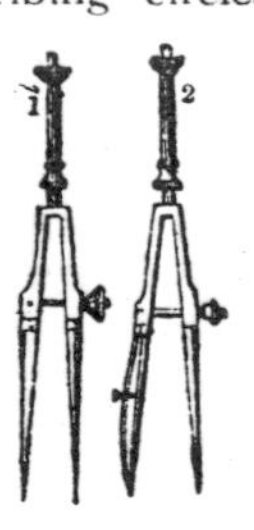

1. Bow-compasses.
2. Bow-pen.

bow, *v. t., i.* & *n.* **1.** To bend ; to inflect ; নত করা ; বক্র করা, বাঁকান। **2.** To turn ; to incline ; ফিরান ; উন্মুখ করা। **3.** To bend the body forward, (esp. as a mark of respect, courtesy or submission) ; প্রণিপাত করা, প্রণতি করা, মস্তক নত করা, নমস্কার করা, অভিবাদন করা। **4.** To express by bowing ; as, to *bow* one's thanks ; to usher (in or out) with bowing ; প্রণিপাত পূর্ব্বক প্রকাশ করা ; সসম্মান-অভিবাদন-পূর্ব্বক অভ্যাগত ব্যক্তিকে কোন গৃহে প্রবিষ্ট করা বা গৃহ হইতে বহির্গত করা। ***Verb i.*** **1.** To stoop ; নত হওয়া, নোয়া। **2.** To bend the head or body in reverence, submission, civility, etc. ; (often with *down*) ; প্রণতি করা, নমস্কার করা, অভিবাদন করা। **3.** To curve ; বাঁকিয়া যাওয়া। ***Noun.*** A bending of the head or body in saluting a person ; প্রণাম, প্রণতি, প্রণিপাত, নমস্কার, অভিবাদন, কুর্ণিশ (*Colloq.*), নতি, নমন। **A bowing acquaintance**—A slight aquaintance ; সামান্য পরিচিত ব্যক্তি। **To make one's bow**—To retire ceremoniously ; to leave the stage ; অন্তর্হিত হওয়া, শিষ্টাচার-প্রদর্শন পূর্ব্বক বিদায় হওয়া ; (রঙ্গ মঞ্চ হইতে) প্রস্থান করা।

bow, *n.* **1.** The rounded fore-end of a boat or ship ; the stem or prow ; জাহাজের মাথা বা আগা-গলুই ; পোতাগ্র। **2.** One who rows in forward part of a boat ; যে ব্যক্তি আগাগলুইর কাছে বসিয়া দাঁড় টানে। **Bowline**—A rope to keep the sail close to the wind ; পালের টানা-দড়ি। **Bow-oar**—The rower nearest the bow or his oar ; যে ব্যক্তি গলুইর খুব নিকটে থাকিয়া দাঁড় টানে ; তাহার দাঁড়।

bowd'-lêr-īze (bōd-), *v. t.* To expurgate ; অশ্লীল বা আপত্তিকর অংশ পরিবর্জ্জন করিয়া কোন পুস্তক প্রকাশ করা। [১৮১৮ খৃঃ অব্দে Thomas Bowdler নামক জনৈক প্রকাশক শেক্ষপীয়রের এক পরিশোধিত সংস্করণ প্রকাশিত করেন—তাঁহার নাম হইতে এই শব্দটী গৃহীত হইয়াছে।] **—i-ser, —ism, —i-za-tion,** *ns.*

bow'-ĕl, *n.* & *v. t.* **1.** One of the intestines ; নাড়ী। (Singular only in medical use). **2.** (*Pl.*) Entrails ; inside of body ; অন্ত্র, নাড়িভুড়ি, আঁতড়ি ; দেহের অভ্যন্তর ভাগ। **3.** The interior part of anything ; as, the *bowels* of the earth ; (কোন

জিনিষের) অভ্যন্তর, গর্ভ, উদর, কুক্ষি। **4.** Compassion ; as, nobody of softer *bowels* ; অনুকম্পা, স্নেহ, মমতা। ***Verb t.*** To eviscerate ; নাড়িভুঁড়ি বাহির করা। **—less,** *adj.* Without pity ; নির্ম্মম, নিষ্করুণ।

bōw'-êr, *n.* One of the two anchors (best and small) carried at the bow of a ship ; পোতাগ্রস্থিত নঙ্গরদ্বয়ের একটী।

bow'-êr, *n.* **1.** A cottage ; কুটীর, পর্ণশালা। **2.** A chamber ; a boudoir ; "Her *bower* may suit thee ill ;" কক্ষ ; মহিলাগণের সুসজ্জিত নিভৃত প্রকোষ্ঠ। **3.** A covered place in a garden formed of boughs and branches ; an arbour ; a summer-house ; তরুমণ্ডপ, লতামণ্ডপ, লতাবিতান, লতাগৃহ, লতাভবন, লতাবলয় (আপ্তে), বৃক্ষবাটিকা ; কুঞ্জগৃহ ; নিদাঘ বাটিকা, নিকুঞ্জ, কুঞ্জগৃহ, নিকুঞ্জ-মন্দির। **—y,** *adj.* Full of bowers ; shady ; leafy ; নিকুঞ্জময় ; ছায়াময় ; পত্রবহুল। **Bower-bird**—অষ্ট্রেলিয়া দেশীয় পক্ষিবিশেষ, ইহারা শুক্তি ও উজ্জ্বল পালক দ্বারা পরিশোভিত করিয়া কুঞ্জবৎ নীড় নির্ম্মাণ করিয়া থাকে। **Bower of bliss**—আনন্দকানন।

bōw'-êr, *n.* One of the two cards (right bower or left) at euchre ; তাস ক্রীড়াবিশেষে রঙ্গের গোলাম (*right bower*), অথবা রঙ্গ যে বর্ণের সেই বর্ণের অপর গোলাম (*left bower*)।

bow'-ie-knife (bō-î-nīfe), *n.* A long broad knife, used as a weapon ; এক প্রকার দীর্ঘ এবং প্রশস্ত ছুরিকা।

bowl (bōl), *n.* **1.** A concave vessel to hold liquids, etc. ; পেয়ালা, বাটি, খর্পর (কথাঃ সঃ), চমূ, সম্পুট। **2.** A drinking vessel ; পান-পাত্র, চষক (রঃ)। **3** The contents of a full bowl ; এক বাটী বা এক পেয়ালা। **4.** The hollow part of a spoon, etc. ; চামচ, নিক্তি প্রভৃতির খোল বা গর্ভ। **The bowl**—convivial drinking ; মদ্য-পানোৎসব।

bowl, (bōl), *n.* **1.** A wooden ball made slightly out of spherical shape to make it run a curved course ; বক্রপথে চালনোপযোগী বর্ত্তুল-প্রায় কাষ্ঠ কন্দুক বিশেষ, ভাঁটা। **2.** The game played with such bowls ; কন্দুক-ক্রীড়া বিশেষ।

bowl (bōl), *v.t.* & *i.* **1.** To play with bowls ; ভাঁটাদ্বারা খেলা করা। **2.** To roll (ball, hoop) along ground ; মাটীতে (কন্দুক, শিশুদিগের ক্রীড়া-চক্র) গড়াইয়া দেওয়া। **3.** To go along by revolving or by means of wheels fast and smoothly ; as, we were *bowled* rapidly along the road ; গড়াইয়া চলা, চাকার উপর দিয়া গড়াইয়া দ্রুতভাবে এবং নিঃশব্দে চলিয়া যাওয়া। **4.** To deliver the ball to be played by the batsman at cricket ; ক্রীকেট খেলায় বল করা। **5.** To pelt or strike with anything rolled ; কোন কিছু গড়াইয়া আঘাত করা। **Bowl'-er,** *n.* **1.** One who plays at bowls ; কন্দুক-ক্রীড়ক। **2.** One who bowls the ball in cricket ; ব্যাটবল খেলায় যে ব্যক্তি বল করে। **To bowl (a player) out in cricket**—To put out a batsman by knocking down a stump in bowling ; (ব্যাট্‌বল খেলায়) বল করিয়া "আউট" করা বা মারা। (*Fig.*) To stop in successful career ; (লক্ষণায়) জীবনের সমৃদ্ধির অবস্থায় হঠাৎ উন্নতির পথ রোধ করিয়া দেওয়া। **To bowl down**—To knock down wicket ; কন্দুক নিক্ষেপ করত (ব্যাট-বল খেলায়) কীলক উল্টাইয়া দেওয়া। **To bowl off**—To knock off bails or stu[mps] ; বলদ্বারা কীলক সকল অথবা ত[দুপরিস্থ] ক্ষুদ্র কাষ্ঠ খণ্ড উল্টাইয়া ফেলা। **To bowl over**—To knock down ; ধাক্কা মারিয়া মাটীতে ফেলিয়া দেওয়া। (*Fig.*) To disconcert ; to render helpless ; (লক্ষণায়) পণ্ড করা ; অসহায় করা।

bowl'-ing (bōl-), *n.* The act or art of playing with bowls ; the style of a bowler at cricket ; ভাঁটা দ্বারা খেলা বা ঐ খেলার কৌশল ; ক্রীকেট ক্রীড়ায় কন্দুক নিক্ষেপকারীর কন্দুক চালনা-পদ্ধতি। **Bowling crease**—যে রেখার পশ্চাত হইতে কন্দুক নিক্ষেপকারী কন্দুক ক্ষেপণ করে। **Bowling-green**—A lawn for playing bowls ; কন্দুক-ক্রীড়ার জন্য সমতল তৃণ-ভূমি।

bow'-măn (bō-), *n.* An archer ; ধনুর্দ্ধর, ধানুকী।

bow'-măn (bō-) *n.* Oarman nearest the bow ; যে দাঁড়ী পোতাগ্র সন্নিহিত স্থানে উপবিষ্ট হইয়া দাঁড় চালনা করে।

bow'-sprit (bō-), *n.* A spar running out from a ship's stem, to which forestays are fastened ; পোতাগ্র হইতে প্রলম্বিত দণ্ড বিশেষ—ইহাতে পাইলের টানা দড়ি বাঁধা হইয়া থাকে।

Bow-street (bō-strēt), *n.* A street near Covent Garden with the chief metropolitan police court ; লণ্ডন নগরীস্থ কভেণ্ট গার্ডেন নামক স্থানের নিকটবর্ত্তী রাজপথবিশেষ,—এই পথে লণ্ডন নগরীর সর্ব্বপ্রধান পুলিশ আদালত প্রতিষ্ঠিত আছে। **Bow Street runner, officer**—Old names for police officer ; পূর্ব্বে পুলিশ কর্ম্মচারিগণ এই নামে অভিহিত হইতেন।

bow'-wow, *n.* & *adj.* **1.** An onomatopoetic name for dog or its bark ; an imitation of dog's bark ; কুকুরের ধ্বন্যাত্মক নাম, কুকুরের ডাক, ঘেঁউ ঘেঁউ শব্দ ; কুকুরের ডাকের অনুকরণ। ***Adj.*** Onomatopoetic ; as, a *bow-wow* word ; ধ্বন্যাত্মক।

bŏx, *n.* **1.** The name of the several species of small evergreen shrubs, especially the one with small dark leathery leaves, much used in garden borders ; কতিপয় জাতীয় চিরহরিৎ গুল্মের সাধারণ নাম, বিশেষতঃ ঘোর সবুজবর্ণ চর্ম্মবৎ পত্র বিশেষ,—যদ্দ্বারা উদ্যান-বৃতি প্রভৃতি রচিত হয়। **2.** A tree remarkable for the hardness and smoothness of its wood and used by turners, engravers, etc.; এক প্রকার বৃক্ষ,—ইহার কঠিন এবং মসৃণ কাষ্ঠ খোদাই কার্য্যের জন্য ব্যবহৃত হইয়া থাকে।

bŏx, *n.* & *v. t.* **1.** A receptacle or case usually lidded of wood, cardboard, or metal and of various shapes; বাক্স, সিন্দুক, পেটারা, মঞ্জুষা, ডিবা। **2.** The quantity that a box contains; একটী বাক্সে যে পরিমাণ জিনিষ ধরে। **3.** A driver's seat on a coach, (from the box under it); গাড়ীর উপরে শকট-চালকের বসিবার স্থান, কোচ-বাক্স। **4.** A money-chest; টাকার সিন্দুক। **5.** (In theatre and other places of amusement) A small enclosure with several seats; (রঙ্গালয় বা অন্যান্য আমোদ প্রমোদের স্থানে) কতিপয় আসন-সমন্বিত বৃতি-বেষ্টিত স্থল। **6.** Something resembling a box; as, a jury *box*: a witness *box*; বাক্সের আকৃতিবিশিষ্ট কোন জিনিষ। **7.** A hut for sentry or signal-man; সান্ত্রী বা সঙ্কেতকারীর ক্ষুদ্র কুটীর। **8.** A small country-house for fishing, shooting, etc.; মৎস্য ও পক্ষি-শিকার প্রভৃতির জন্য ক্ষুদ্র পল্লী-বাটিকা। **9.** A protective case in various machines; বিভিন্ন যন্ত্রাদির আবরণস্বরূপ ক্ষুদ্র পেটক। **10.** A present in a box; a present; as, a Christmas *box*; বাক্সের ভিতরের উপহার; উপহার। ***Verb t.*** **1.** To provide with a box; to put into a box; বাক্সযুক্ত করা; বাক্সবন্দি করা, বাক্সের ভিতর রাখা, বাক্সজাত করা। **2.** To squeeze together; to confine; রাখা; একত্র চাপিয়া আবদ্ধ করা। **3.** To lodge (document) in law-court; আদালতে দলিল দাখিল করা। **4.** To divide off from other compartment; অন্য কামরা হইতে পৃথক্ করা। **Boxing day**—The day after Christmas day, when boxes or presents are given; খ্রীষ্টমাস পর্ব্বের পরদিন, ঐ দিবস উপহার বিতরণ করা হয়। **Box-keeper**—An attendant on the boxes of a theatre or other public amusement; নাট্যালয়ের বৃতিবেষ্টিত স্থান-রক্ষক। **In a box**—In an embarrassing position; in difficulty; হাঙ্গামে; সঙ্কটে। **In the wrong box**—Out of one's place; out of one's element; নিজের অধিকারের বাহিরে; নিজের কোটের বাহিরে (জল হইতে উত্তোলিত মৎস্যের মত)। **To box a fox**—To rob an orchard; বাগান হইতে ফল লুণ্ঠন করা। **To box Harry**—(Among commercial travellers) To shirk the *table'd Hôte*, and take something substantial at tea-time to save expense; (ভ্রমণকারী সওদাগরের-দিগের মধ্যে) খরচ বাঁচাইবার জন্য হোটেলের নিয়মিত খাদ্য গ্রহণ না করিয়া চা-পানের কালেই সারবান বস্তু আহার করা। **To box off**—To divide into small compartments; ক্ষুদ্র ক্ষুদ্র কুঠরীতে বিভাগ করা। **To box the compass**—(*Naut.*) To rehearse the points in correct order; দিগ্‌নির্ণয় যন্ত্রের ৩২টী দিগ্‌বিন্দু যথাক্রমে বলিয়া যাওয়া। (*Fig.*) To make a complete turn; একবার ঘুরিয়া আসা।

bŏx, *n. v. t.* & *i.* A blow with the open hand in the ear; মুষ্টি-প্রহার, মুষ্ট্যাঘাত, চড়, চপেটাঘাত। ***Verb t.*** To strike with the hand open or closed; মুষ্টি প্রহার করা, ঘুষি মারা, মুষ্ট্যাঘাত করা, চপেটাঘাত করা। ***Verb i.*** To fight with the fists, usually in padded gloves or merely for exercise; মুষ্টিযুদ্ধ করা, মোটা দস্তানা পরিয়া মুষ্টিপ্রহার কৌশল শিক্ষা করা। **Box'-er,** *n.* **1.** A pugilist; মুষ্টি-যোদ্ধা। **2.** A member of Chinese anti-foreign secret society; চীনদেশীয় বিদেশি-বিদ্বেষী গুপ্ত-সমিতির সভ্য বিশেষ। **Box'-ing,** *n.* A combat with the fist; মুষ্টিযুদ্ধ, মুষ্টামুষ্টি, ঘুষাঘুষি। **Boxing-match**—A pugilistic encounter; a prize-fight; মুষ্টিযুদ্ধে প্রতিযোগিতা; পণ রাখিয়া মুষ্টিযুদ্ধ। **To box a tree**—To make an incision or hole in a tree for the purpose of procuring the sap; রস-সংগ্রহের উদ্দেশ্যে বৃক্ষগাত্রে গর্ত্ত বা বৃক্ষের ত্বক্‌ছেদ করা।

bŏy, *n.* **1.** A male child; a son; "My only *boy* fell by the side of great Dundee;" বালক, কুমার, কিশোর, ছোকরা; ছেলে, পুত্র। **2.** A familiar term of addressing or speaking of grown up persons; বয়োবৃদ্ধ অন্তরঙ্গ ব্যক্তির প্রতি সম্বোধন-বাক্য। **3.** A servant; a slave; a male native in various countries with subject races; চাকর, ভৃত্য; ক্রীত-দাস; বিভিন্ন পরাধীন জাতির দেশের পুরুষ। **Boy'-hood,** *n.* The state of being a boy; বালকত্ব, কৌমার, শৈশব, বাল্য, কুমারত্ব। **Boy'-ish,** *adj.* Proper to boys; বালকোচিত। Spirited; puerile; তেজস্বী; বাল-সুলভ। **Boy'-ish-ly,** *adv.* **Boy'-ish-ness,** *n.* **Boy's brigade**—বালক-সেনা। [গ্লাস্‌গো নগরবাসী Sir William Smith ১৮৮৩ খৃঃ অব্দে বালকদিগের চরিত্রে গুরুজনে সম্মান, আদেশানুবর্ত্তিতা, আত্ম-সম্মান, প্রভৃতির ভাব বিকশিত করিবার উদ্দেশ্যে উক্ত সমিতি প্রতিষ্ঠিত করেন।] **Boy-scout**—See SCOUT. **Boy's love**—A popular name for southern wood; কাষ্ঠবিশেষ **Boy's play**—Trifling; ছেলেখেলা তুচ্ছ-বিষয়।

bŏy-yâr', bŏy-ârd', *n.* A member of a Russian aristocratic order; রুষদেশীয় সম্ভ্রান্ত-শ্রেণী বিশেষ ভুক্ত ব্যক্তি।

bŏy'-cŏtt, *v.t.* & *n.* **1.** To combine against (a landlord, tradesman, employer or other person) to withhold social or business relations from him and to deter others from holding such a relation; ভূস্বামী, ব্যবসায়ী, মনিব

বা অন্য ব্যক্তির সহিত সর্ব্ববিধ সামাজিক বা ব্যবসায়সম্পর্কীয় সম্বন্ধ বিচ্ছিন্ন করিবার উদ্দেশ্যে দল বাঁধা বা তদ্রূপ সম্পর্করক্ষা করিতে অপর লোককে ভয় প্রদর্শন পূর্ব্বক বাধা প্রদান করা। **2.** To combine in abstaining from buying and selling goods etc. with the object of punishing a person or a class ; কোন ব্যক্তি বা সম্প্রদায়কে শাস্তি দিবার মানসে তৎসহ ক্রয় বিক্রয়ে বিরত হইবার জন্য দলবদ্ধ হওয়া। [আয়র্লণ্ডের ভূস্বামী ক্যাপ্টেন Boycottএর প্রতি তদীয় প্রতিবেশীগণ এইরূপ ব্যবহার করিয়াছিল।] ***Noun.*** Social and business interdiction for the purpose of coercion ; সমাজচ্যুতি, সংস্রব-রাহিত্য, পরিবর্জ্জন, বহিষ্কার, পর-পণ্য বর্জ্জন, ব্যবসায়-সম্পর্কিত-সম্বন্ধচ্ছেদ। **—er,** *n.*

brăb′-ble, *v. i.* & *n.* To engage in paltry noisy quarrel ; অকিঞ্চিৎকর বিষয়ে ঝগড়া করা, তুচ্ছ বিষয়ে কলহ ও কোলাহল করা। ***Noun.*** Wrangle ; quarrel ; বিতণ্ডা ; ঝগড়া, কোন্দল। **—ment,** *n.*

brāce, *n.* & *v. t.* **1.** That which holds anything tight ; a cincture

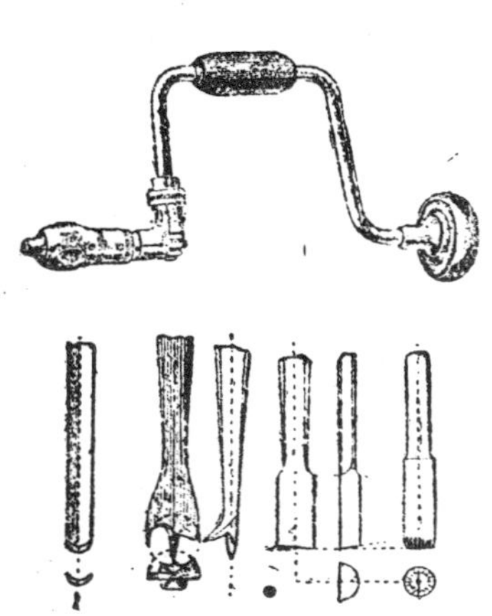

Bit-brace and bits.

or bandage ; বেষ্টনী, বন্ধনী, কটিবন্ধ ; বস্ত্রবন্ধনী। **2.** A pair or couple ; as, a *brace* of ducks ; যুগল, যোড়া, মিথুন, যুগ্ম, দ্বয়। **3.** (*Priting*) A mark connecting two or more words or lines (}) ; (মুদ্রাঙ্কণ) বন্ধনী। **4.** (*Naut.*) A rope attached to a yard for trimming sails ; (নৌ-বিদ্যা) পাইলের টানা-দড়ী। **5.** A handle for holding and turning bits, etc. ; তুরপুন, বর্ম্মা প্রভৃতি যন্ত্র ঘুরাইবার হাতল। **6.** Suspenders or trousers ; পাজামা টানা দিয়া রাখিবার জন্য বস্ত্রের সরু ফালি নির্ম্মিত যে বন্ধনী কাঁধের উপর ঘুরাইয়া বাঁধা হয়, পাজামা-বন্ধনী। **7.** The thong for turning drum ; ঢাক প্রভৃতির চামড়ার দোয়াল। **8.** A thick strap which supports a carriage on wheels ; যে বস্ত্র বা চর্ম্মের স্থূল এবং সরু ফালি-দ্বারা চক্রের উপর শকট ধৃত হইয়া থাকে। **9.** Tightness; আঁটসাঁটভাব,অশিথিলতা। **10.** A strengthening piece of iron or timber ; দৃঢ়তা-বিধায়ক কাষ্ঠ বা লৌহখণ্ড (যথা গৃহের ঠাটে কোণা-কোণি যে কাঠ লাগান হয়)। ***Verb t.*** **1.** To fasten tightly ; to make tight and firm ; to give firmness to ; to strengthen ; as, to *brace* the nerves ; কষিয়া বাঁধা ; শক্ত ও দৃঢ় করা ; দার্ঢ্য প্রদান করা ; বল-সঞ্চার করা। **2.** To support ; to prop ; as, to *brace* a beam in a building ; ধরিয়া রাখা, পড়িতে না দেওয়া ; অবলম্বন দ্বারা খাড়া রাখা, ঠেকো দেওয়া। **3.** To couple together ; যুগ্ম করা, জোড়া করা। **4.** (*Naut.*) To move by braces ; (নৌ-বিদ্যা) টানা-দড়ী দ্বারা (পাইল) চালান। **Brac′-ing,** *adj.* Giving strength or tone ; as, a *bracing* north wind ; স্বাস্থ্য ও বলপ্রদ।

brāce′-lĕt, *n.* **1.** An orn for the wrist or arm ; ।, বলয়, বালা, চূড়ী। **2.** A defensive armour for the arm ; বাহু-রক্ষিণী, বাহুত্রাণ। **3.** (*Slang*) Handcuff ; (ইতর ভাষায়) হাত-কড়া।

brāc′-ēr, *n.* **1.** A band or bandage ; বন্ধনী, পট্টি, বন্ধনের ফিতা। **2.** A wrist-guard in archery and fencing ; শরাভ্যাস এবং অসি-ক্রীড়ায় প্রকোষ্ঠ-রক্ষিণী, গোধা (অমরঃ)। **3.** A medicine as a tonic, which gives tone to any part of the body ; বলবর্দ্ধক বা পুষ্টিকারক ঔষধ।

brach (brăch or brăsh), *n.* A dog for the chase ; a bitch-hound ; শিকারী কুকুর ; শিকারের কুকুরী।

brā′-chi-ăl, *adj.* Of or belonging to the arm ; বাহু-সম্বন্ধীয়, বাহু-সংক্রান্ত, বাহব। **2.** Resembling an arm ; বাহু-সদৃশ।

brăch-ȳ-cē-phăl′-ic, **brăch-ȳ-cĕph′-ă-lous** (-lŭs), *adjs.* Short-headed ; of skulls with breadth at least four-fifths of length ; of persons or races with such skull ; খর্ব্বশির ; যে করোটির প্রস্থ দৈর্ঘ্যের অন্ততঃ $\frac{4}{5}$ অংশ তৎসম্বন্ধীয় ; উক্ত করোটি বিশিষ্ট ব্যক্তি বা জাতি সম্পৃক্ত, প্রশস্ত-করোটী (সাঃ পঃ)।

brā-chȳg′-rā-phȳ, *n.* Stenography ; সংক্ষেপে লিখন-প্রণালী।

bră-chȳl′-ō-gȳ, *n.* Brevity ; incorrectness of speech due to excessive condensation ; স্বল্পাক্ষরতা, বাক্যের সংক্ষিপ্ততা ; অত্যন্ত সংক্ষেপহেতু বাক্যের ভ্রম-দুষ্টতা।

brăck′-ĕn, *n.* A fern abundant on heaths, etc. ; any large fern ; (collectively) mass of ferns ; পর্ণাঙ্গ (সাঃ পঃ) ; অতিকায় পর্ণাঙ্গ ; পর্ণাঙ্গ-সমুচ্চয়।

brăck′-ĕt, *n.* & *v. t.* **1.** A shelf with slanting under-prop for hanging against wall ; প্রাচীর হইতে উদ্গত তাক, নাগদন্ত (কথা সঃ)। **2.** The projecting device for supporting a lamp ; a gas-pipe projecting from the side of a wall ; বাতি রাখিবার

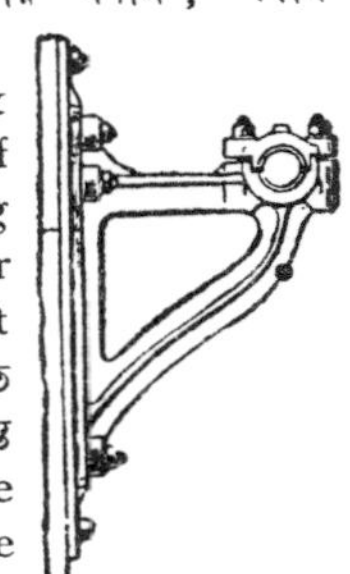

Wall Bracket.

তাক ; প্রাচীর হইতে উদ্গত গ্যাসের বাতির নল। **3.** A side-piece of gun-carriage supporting trunnion; কামানের কর্ণদ্বয় ধারণার্থ কামানবাহী শকটের পার্শ্ব-কাষ্ঠ। **4.** (*Printing*) A mark used in pairs for enclosing words, figures, etc. ; —( ) [ ] { }— (মুদ্রাঙ্কণ) বন্ধনী। ***Verb t.*** **1.** To enclose in brackets ; বন্ধনীবদ্ধ করা, বন্ধনীর মধ্যে স্থাপন করা। **2.** To couple names with a bracket in a list of successful candidates to denote equal merit ; to couple (names, etc.) with a brace, implying connection or equality ; "Only four times beaten for both prizes, as often *bracketed* ;" তুল্য গুণ বা যোগ্যতা বুঝাইবার জন্য পরীক্ষোত্তীর্ণ ব্যক্তিদের তালিকায় দুই বা ততোধিক নাম এক বন্ধনীর মধ্যে সংযোজিত করা ; সমতা বা সম্বন্ধসূচনার্থ (নাম প্রভৃতি) এক বন্ধনীর মধ্যে সংযুক্ত করা। **—ed,** *adj.* Equal ; তুল্য, সমান।

brăck′-ish, *adj.* Saltish,—applied to water mixed with salt ; (জল-সম্বন্ধে) ঈষৎ লবণাক্ত, লোনতা, লোনা, লবণযুক্ত। **—ness,** *n.*

brăct, *n.* A leaf growing upon the flower-stalk ; পুষ্পবৃন্তে জাত অস্বাভাবিক পত্রবিশেষ, মঞ্জরী-পত্র (সাঃ পঃ)। **Brac′-te-al, Brac′-te-ate,** *adjs.* [*L. bracten*, a thin plate of metal.]

brăd, *n.* A slender nail without a head ; একপ্রকার মাথা-শূন্য ক্ষুদ্র পেরেক। **Brad-awl**—An awl for brad ; ক্ষুদ্র পেরেকে বসাইতে ছিদ্র করিবার জন্য তুরপুনবিশেষ।

brăd-ȳ-pĕp′-sȳ, *n.* Slow digestion ; মন্দাগ্নি।

brae (brā), *n.* A hill-side ; a slope ; পর্ব্বত-পার্শ্ব, সানু ; প্রবণভূমি।

brăg, *v. i.* & *n.* To indulge in boastful talk ; to boast or bluster ; আত্মশ্লাঘা করা ; গর্ব্ব করা, বড়াই করা, আস্ফালন করা। ***Noun.*** **1.** Boastful talk ; a boasting ; the thing boasted of ; "Beauty is nature's *brag* ;" দর্পোক্তি ; বড়াই ; গর্ব্বের বিষয়। **2.** A game at cards very like poker ; একপ্রকার তাস খেলা।

brăg-gă-dō′-ci-ō (shi), *n.* **1.** A boaster ; a swaggerer ; আত্মশ্লাঘা-কারী, গর্ব্বকারী ; দাম্ভিক। **2.** Empty boasting ; mere brag ; অহঙ্কার ; দম্ভ, দর্প, গর্ব্ব, বড়াই। [কবি স্পেন্সারের "Faery Queen" নামক কাব্যোক্ত Braggadocchio নামক গর্ব্বিত ব্যক্তির নাম হইতে শব্দটি গৃহীত হইয়াছে।]

brăg′-gârt, *n.* & *adj.* A boaster ; দাম্ভিক ব্যক্তি, গর্ব্বকারী। ***Adj.*** Boastful ; দম্ভপূর্ণ।

braid (brād), *n.* & *v. t.* **1.** Entwined hair ; plait ; বেণী ; কবরী (গীতঃ), ধম্মিল্ল (ঋতুঃ)। **2.** A narrow band, etc. entwined with the hair ; চুল বাঁধিবার ফিতা। **3.** Silk, thread, etc. woven into a band ; রেশমী ফিতা প্রভৃতি। ***Verb t.*** **1.** To plait ; to interweave (hair, flowers, thread, etc.) ; বুনা, বিনানি করা, বুনট করা ; গাঁথা, গুম্ফিত করা, পাকান। **2.** To arrange hair in braids ; বেণী রচনা করা। **3.** To confine hair etc., with ribbon ; ফিতা দ্বারা চুল বাঁধা। **4.** To trim or edge with braid ; পাড় লাগান, ঝালর দেওয়া, কিনারায় ফিতা লাগান। **Braid′-ed,** *adj.* **Braided hair**—কপর্দ্দ (মঃ উঃ), জটাজূট। **To braid St. Catherine's tresses**—To lead a virgin-life ; চিরকুমারী থাকা।

Braid′-ĭsm (brād-), *n.* Hypnotism ; সম্মোহন-বিদ্যা। [সম্মোহন-বিদ্যার শীলনকারী James Braid এর নাম হ গৃহীত।]

br[illegible]l (brāl), *n.* & *v. t.* **1.** A piece of soft leather to bind up a hawk's wings ; বাজ পক্ষীর পক্ষ বন্ধনার্থ কোমল চর্ম্মখণ্ডবিশেষ। **2.** (*Pl. Naut.*) The ropes used to gather up the foot and leeches of the sails preparatory to furling ; গুটাইবার পূর্ব্বে যে রজ্জুসকল দ্বারা পাইলের উভয় পার্শ্ব এবং নিম্নদেশ জড় করা হয়। ***Verb t.*** To haul up by the brails, (used with *up*) ; উক্ত রজ্জুসমূহ দ্বারা পাইলের নিম্নপ্রান্ত ও পার্শ্বদ্বয় একত্র জড় করা।

braille (brāl), *n.* & *v. t.* A system of writing or printing for the blind in which the characters are represented by raised dots ; অন্ধগণের জন্য এক প্রকার মুদ্রণ বা লিখনপ্রণালী। ইহাতে অক্ষর সকল উত্তোলিত বিন্দু সমূহ দ্বারা প্রদর্শিত হইয়া থাকে। [উদ্ভাবক Louis Braille এর নাম হইতে গৃহীত।]

brain (brān), *n.* & *v. t.* **1.** The whitish mass of nervous matter occupying the cavity of the skull in man and other vertebrate animals ; মস্তিষ্ক, মগজ, ঘিলু (*Colloq.*), মস্তলুঙ্গ (সুশ্রুঃ), মস্তক-স্নেহ (অঃ)। (মস্তিষ্ক-পদার্থ সম্পর্কে বহুবচন, এবং সমগ্র মস্তিষ্ক অঙ্গ-স্বরূপে এক-বচন হয়)। **2.** Understanding ; the intellect or the intellectual power ; "The *brain* devise laws ;" বুদ্ধি, মেধা ; ধীশক্তি। ***Verb t.*** To dash out the brains of ; (আঘাত দ্বারা) মস্তিষ্ক বাহির করা, মাথার ঘি বাহির করিয়া ফেলা। **Brain′-ish,** *adj.* Hot-headed ; উষ্ণমস্তিষ্ক। **Brain′-less,** *adj.* Without brains or understanding ; silly ; thoughtless ; মস্তিষ্কহীন, বুদ্ধিহীন ; মন্দবুদ্ধি ; বিবেচনাশূন্য, নির্ব্বোধ। **Brain′-y,** *adj.* Acute ; clever ; সূক্ষ্ম-বুদ্ধি ; চালাক, চতুর, মাথাওয়ালা। **Brain-born**—মস্তিষ্কপ্রসূত, কল্পনা-প্রসূত। **Brain-fag**—Nervous exhaustion ;

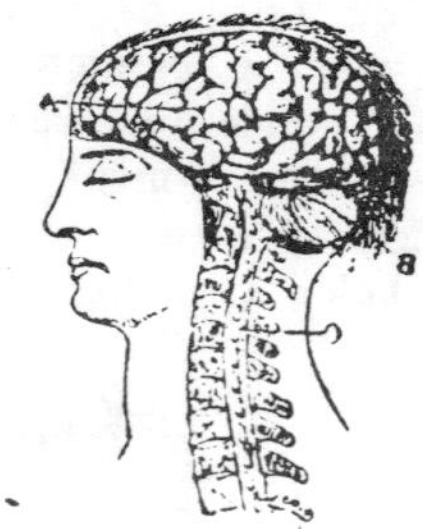

Section of human head showing brain. A. Cerebrum. B. Cerebellum C, Spinal-cord.

স্নায়বিক অবসাদ বা ক্লান্তি। **Brain-fever**—An inflammation of the brain substance itself; মস্তিষ্ক-ঝিল্লীপ্রদাহ (হঃ চঃ), মস্তিষ্কাবরণ-প্রদাহ (ঐ)। **Brain-pan**—The skull; cranium; মাথার খুলী; করোটী। **Brain-sick**—Diseased or disordered in the understanding; mad; বিকৃত-মস্তিষ্ক; উন্মাদ। **Brain work**—Mental work; মানসিক শ্রম। **On the brains**—Constantly in one's thought; সর্ব্বদা মনোমধ্যে জাগরিত। **To blow out one's brains**—To shoot him in the head; মস্তকে গুলি করা। **To cudgel** or **rack one's brains**—To think hard; কোন প্রশ্ন সমাধানের জন্য মাথা ঘামান, মস্তিষ্ক আলোড়ন করা। **To suck** or **pick one's brains**—To appropriate the results of his thoughts; কাহারো চিন্তাপ্রসূতফল আত্মসাৎ করা। **To turn one's brains**—To make giddy; মাথা ঘুরাইয়া দেওয়া। (*Fig.*) To bewilder; (লক্ষণায়) হতবুদ্ধি করা, বিভ্রান্ত করা।

braird (brărd), *n.* & *v. i.* The first shoots of corn or other crop; অঙ্কুর। ***Verb i.*** To come up in fresh shoots; অঙ্কুরিত হওয়া।

braise, braize (brāz) *v. t.* To stew or broil in a covered kettle or pan; ঢাকনি-দেওয়া কেটলী বা কটাহে মৃদু সন্তাপে সিদ্ধ করা বা ঝলসান।

braize (brāz), *n.* A fish of uniform red-colour; লোহিতবর্ণ মৎস্য বিশেষ।

brāke, *n.* Same as BRAKEN.

brāke, *n.* **1.** A species of fern; একপ্রকার পর্ণাঙ্গ। **2.** A thicket of brambles; a place over-grown with brush-wood, brambles, etc.; brush-wood; "He stayed not for *brake* and stopped not for stone; কণ্টকবন, কণ্টকগহন; গুল্মগহন; ঝোঁপ।

brāke, *n.* **1.** A toothed instrument to break the woody part of flax and hemp; পাট, শণ, প্রভৃতি আঁচড়াইবার যন্ত্র। **2.** An instrument for peeling off willow-bark; উইলো বৃক্ষের ত্বক-ছাড়াইবার যন্ত্র বিশেষ। **3.** A baker's kneading machine; রুটি প্রস্তুতকারীর ময়দা দলিবার যন্ত্র। **4.** An instrument to crush and extract the juices from fruits, vegetables, etc.; শাকসবজি, ফল, প্রভৃতির রস-নিষ্কর্ষণার্থযন্ত্র বিশেষ। **5.** A heavy harrow; একপ্রকার ভারি চতুষ্কোণ বিদা বা আঁচড়া-মই। ***Verb t.*** To crush flax, hemp by beating; শণ বা পাট আঁচড়ান।

brāke, *n.* **1.** A contrivance for stopping or retarding the motion of carriage-wheels or railway-cars; শকটচক্র বা রেলগাড়ীর গতিরোধক বা গতিহ্রাসকর কৌশলবিশেষ, গতিরোধক (হিঃ কোঃ)। **2.** A cart or a kind of waggonet; এক প্রকার ক্ষুদ্র শকট। **3.** Same as *brake van*, (see below). **Brakeman, brakesman**—One that manages the brake on railroad; যে ব্যক্তি গতিরোধক-যন্ত্র সংযোজন করত রেলগাড়ী থামায়। **Brake-van**—The van or car in a railway train wherein the brake is worked; the guard's compartment; in a passenger-train usually the luggage-van; রেলগাড়ীর যে কক্ষে গতিরোধক কল চালিত হয়; বাষ্পীয়-শকট রক্ষকের কক্ষ; যাত্রীর সঙ্গীয় মাল রাখিবার জন্য যাত্রী-গাড়ীর সংলগ্ন মাল-গাড়ী। **Brake-wheel**—যে চক্রে উক্ত কল সংযোগ করা হয়, গতিরোধক চক্র (হিঃ কোঃ)।

Brâ'-mah-prĕss, (-mä), *n.* A hydrostatic press of imm[illegible] power, invented by Jo[illegible] Bramah of London; লণ্ডননগ[illegible]সী জোসেফ ব্রামাকর্ত্তৃক উদ্ভাবিত মহাশক্তিশালী জলপীড়ন যন্ত্র।

brăm'-ble, *n.* A wild prickly shrub bearing black-berries; any rough prickly shrub; গৌরীফলপ্রসূ কণ্টক-গুল্ম বিশেষ; কাঁটাবন। **—bly**, *adj.*

brăm'-blĭng, *n.* A bird nearly allied to the chaffinch; কলস্বর পক্ষিবিশেষ।

brăn, *n.* **1.** The husk of ground grain; তুষ, ভুষি, ধান্য-কল্ক। **2.** The coarser part of anything; কোন জিনিষের অসার বা নিকৃষ্ট অংশ। **Bran-new**—SEE BRAND-NEW.

brancard, (*F.*), *n.* A horse-litter; অশ্বের শয়নার্থ বিস্তৃত বিচালী।

branch (brănsh), *n.*, *v. t.* & *i.* **1.** A bough of a tree; শাখা, ডাল, বিটপ। **2.** Anything like a limb of a tree; as, the *branch* of a river; বৃক্ষ-শাখাবৎ কোন বস্তু। **3.** A section or department of a subject; as, *branches* of knowledge; শাখা, কাণ্ড, খণ্ড, বিভাগ। **4.** Any subordinate division of a business; কোন ব্যবসায়ের শাখা। **5.** A line of family descent; কোন বংশের শাখা। ***Verb t.*** **1.** To divide or form into branches; শাখায় বিভক্ত করা, শাখান্বিত করা। **2.** To adorn with needle-work representing branches, flowers or twigs; "A dress all *branched* and flowered with gold;" সূচী-কর্ম্ম দ্বারা উত্তোলিত পুষ্পপল্লব, শাখা প্রভৃতি দ্বারা বিশোভিত করা। ***Verb i.*** **1.** To spread in branches; to spread out branches, as a plant; শাখান্বিত হওয়া; শাখাবিস্তার করা। **2.** To divide into separate parts or subdivisions; বিভিন্ন অংশ বা বিভাগে বিভক্ত হওয়া। **Branch'-y**, *adj.* With many branches; শাখা-বহুল। **Branch-let**—A little branch; ক্ষুদ্র শাখা। **Branch of a river**—শাখানদী। **Branch-office**—শাখা-কার্য্যালয়। **Root and branch**—Thoroughly; radically; সম্পূর্ণরূপে; সমূলে। [Used also as an adjective.]

bran'-chĭ-ăe (brăng-kĭ-ā), *n.* (*pl*). The gills; মাছের কান্‌কো বা ফুল্‌কো। **—al,—ate,** *adjs.*

brănd, *n.* & *v. t.* **1.** A burning piece of wood ; a charred log or stick ; জলন্ত কাষ্ঠখণ্ড ; অর্দ্ধদগ্ধ কাষ্ঠখণ্ড। **2.** A mark made with a hot iron ; পোড়া লোহার দাগ, ছেঁকা। **3.** A trade-mark made by burning or otherwise, as on a cask ; জলন্ত লৌহখণ্ড কিম্বা অন্য উপায়ে পিপা প্রভৃতির উপর যে ব্যবসায়-চিহ্ন দেওয়া হয়। **4.** Quality ; grade ; as, a good *brand* of flour ; প্রকার, রকম ; শ্রেণী। **5.** A stigma ; any mark of infamy or vice ; as, a *brand* of private vice ; চিহ্ন, দাগ ; কলঙ্ক। **6.** An iron stamp for burning a mark in ; যে জলন্ত লৌহমুদ্রাদ্বারা দাগ দেওয়া হয়। **7.** A sword (so called) from its glitter—poetic) ; তরবারি, অসি। **8.** A disease in vegetables or blights of grain crops, (as mildew, rust, smut) ; শস্যরোগ, ধসারোগ। ***Verb t.*** **1.** To burn or mark with a hot iron ; তপ্ত লৌহ দ্বারা দগ্ধ বা চিহ্নিত করা। **2.** To stigmatize ; কলঙ্কিত করা, দাগী করা। **3.** To inpress on the memory ; স্মৃতিপটে অঙ্কিত করা। **Brand'-ed,** *adj.* **Brand'-er,** *n.* **Brand-new**—Quite new ; টাট্‌কা নূতন, তকতকে, ঝক্‌ঝকে নূতন, আনকোরা নূতন [যেন এইমাত্র কামারের হাপর বা অগ্নিকুণ্ড হইতে বহির্গত হইয়াছে]।

brăn'-dish, *v. t.* & *n.* To wave or flourish (a weapon) ; (অস্ত্রাদি) সঞ্চালন করা বা ঘূরান, ভাঁজা (মুদ্গার প্রভৃতি)। ***Noun.*** A wave or flourish ; (অস্ত্রের) ঘূর্ণন।

brănd'-ling, *n.* **1.** The young of a salmon ; স্যামন মৎস্যের শাবক। **2.** A small red worm used as a bait by anglers ; বড়শীর টোপস্বরূপ ব্যবহৃত রক্তবর্ণ ক্ষুদ্র কীট বিশেষ।

brăn'-dy̆, *n.* & *v. t.* A strong distilled liquor ; তীব্র মদিরা বিশেষ, ব্রাণ্ডি। ***Verb t.*** **1.** To mix with brandy ; ব্রাণ্ডির সহিত সংমিশ্রিত করা। **2.** To refresh with brandy ; ব্রাণ্ডি দ্বারা আপ্যায়িত করা। **Brandy-ball**—A kind of sweet ; মিষ্টদ্রব্য বিশেষ। **Brandy-fruit**—Fruit preserved in brandy and sugar ; মদিরা এবং শর্করা-রসে রক্ষিত ফল। **Brandy-pawnee**—(Hindi Pani = water) Brandy with water ; ব্রাণ্ডি-পাণি। **Brandy-snap** — Gingerbread waters ; আর্দ্রককচূর্ণবাসিত মিষ্ট পিষ্টক বিশেষের চাকতি।

bran'-gle (brăng-), *n.* & *v. i.* A wrangle ; a squabble ; কলহ ; হুড়াহুড়ি। ***Verb i.*** To wrangle ; কলহ করা, ঝগড়া করা, কোন্দল করা।

brăsh, *n.* **1.** A rash or eruption ; হামাদি রোগ। **2.** A heap of fragments ; খণ্ড বস্তুর স্তূপ। **Watery brash**—মুখদিয়া জল-উঠা রোগ, বুক-জ্বালা রোগ।

bra'-sier, *n.* Same as BRAZIER.

brăss, *n.* & *adj.* **1.** A yellow metal composed of copper and zinc ; পিত্তল, কাকতুণ্ডী (সাঃ পঃ), রীতি (ঐ), রীতিকা (ঐ)। **2.** (*Pl.*) Utensils, ornaments or other articles of brass ; পিত্তলের বাসন, তৈজনপত্র, অলঙ্কারাদি। **3.** An inscribed sepulchral table of brass ; পিত্তলনির্ম্মিত উৎকীর্ণ সমাধিফলক। **4.** (*Fig.*) Effrontery ; shamelessness ; (লক্ষণায়) ধৃষ্টতা ; লজ্জাহীনতা। **5.** (*Slang.*) Money ; (ইতর-ভাষায়) পয়সা-কড়ি। ***Adj.*** Made of brass ; পিত্তল-নির্ম্মিত। **Brass'-y,** *adj.* & *n.* **1.** Like brass in colour, sound, taste ; পিত্তলবর্ণ, পিত্তলধর্ম্মা। **2.** Impudent ; unfeeling ; pitiless ; লজ্জাহীন ; নির্ম্মম ; নির্দ্দয়, নিষ্করুণ। (*Noun.*) brass-soled golf-club ; পিত্তল মাথা-বাঁধানো গোল্‌ফ্ খেলার দণ্ড। **Brass farthing**—Least possible amount ; অনুমাত্র, বিন্দুমাত্র। **Brass filings**—রীতিচূর্ণ। **Brass founder**—A maker of articles in brass ; a maker of articles in cast brass ; পিত্তলের দ্রব্যনির্ম্মাতা ; পিত্তলের ঢালাইকর। **Brass-plate**—দরজা প্রভৃতির উপরে স্থাপিত (নাম, ব্যবসায় প্রভৃতি অঙ্কিত) পিত্তল-ফলক। **Oxide of brass**—রীতিপুষ্প (আঃ বঃ)। **The brass**—The brass instruments of a musical band ; বাদকদলের পিত্তল-নির্ম্মিত বাদ্যযন্ত্রাদি। **The brass-band**—A set of musicians with brass instruments ; পিত্তলনির্ম্মিত বাদ্যযন্ত্র-বাদনকারী বাদকসম্প্রদায়।

brăs'-săge, *n.* The mint charge for coining money ; (now called *seigniorage*) ; মুদ্রা প্রস্তুত করিবার জন্য টাকশালার মাশুল।

brăt, *n.* A child, so called in contempt ; as, a beggar's *brat* ; (তুচ্ছার্থে) বালক, ছোড়া, ছোকরা, চেঙ্গরা।

brăt'-tice (-tĭs), **brăt'-tish-ing,** *ns.* A wooden partition as in the shaft of a coal-mine ; কয়লার খনির সুড়ঙ্গমধ্যস্থ কাষ্ঠময় বৃতি। **2.** A fence put round dangerous machinery ; বিপজ্জনক যন্ত্রাদির চতুর্দ্দিকবর্ত্তী বৃতি।

bră-vā'-dō, *n.* A show of courage ; a boastful threat ; a bold front ; আস্পর্দ্ধা ; ধমক, দাবানি (*Colloq.*) ; দৃঢ়তার সহিত বাঁকিয়া দাঁড়ানের ভাব।

brāve, *adj., n.* & *v. t.* Courageous ; bold ; dauntless ; (opposed to *cowardly*) ; সাহসী, সাহসিক ; অকুতোভয় ; নির্ভীক। ***Noun.*** **1.** A bold daring person ; "None but the *brave* deserve the fair ;" শূর, বীর। **2.** A Red-Indian warrior ; উত্তর আমেরিকার আদিম অধিবাসী যোদ্ধা। ***Verb t.*** To challenge ; to defy ; to encounter with courage ; "Rise from the shades and *brave* me on the field ;" যুদ্ধার্থ আহ্বান করা ; তুচ্ছ করা ; সাহসের সহিত সম্মুখীন হওয়া। **Brave'-ly,** *adv.* **Brave'-ness,** *n.* **Brav'-er-y,** *n.* **1.** Fearlessness ; intrepedity ; নির্ভীকতা, সাহসিকতা ; শূরতা, শূরত্ব, বীর্য্য, বীরত্ব। **2.** Splendour ; ostentation ;

finery; "There stood our guide decked out with *braveries*;" জাকজমক; আড়ম্বর; বেশভূষা, আভরণ। **To brave it out**—To carry oneself defiantly under suspicion or blame; নিন্দা বা সন্দেহ তুচ্ছ করিয়া স্বকার্য্য সাধনে অগ্রসর হওয়া।

brā′-vō, *n.* (*Pl.* Bravoes) A hired assassin; a murderer; a desperado; অর্থ প্রদানে নিযুক্ত গুপ্ত হত্যাকারী; হত্যাকারী, আততায়ী; গুণ্ডা, গোঁয়ার লোক।

brâ′-vō, *interj.* Well done; সাবাস, বাহবা, সাধু! সাধু!! ধন্য! ধন্য!! [অভিনেতা বা গায়ককে *bravo*, অভিনেত্রী বা গায়িকাকে *brava* এবং গায়ক বা নাট্যসম্প্রদায়কে *bravi* বলা সঙ্গত।]

brâ-vu′-rä (-vô-), *n.* **1.** Brilliant or ambitious execution; অতিশোভন সম্পাদন, জাঁকজমকের সহিত সম্পাদন। **2.** A passage of music requiring exceptional powers; সবিশেষ ক্ষমতার সহিত সম্পাদ্য গীতাংশ।

brawl (bräl), *v. i.* & *n.* **1.** To make a loud noise or disturbance; to squabble; গোলমাল করা, কোলাহল করা; ঝগড়া করা, কলহ করা, কোন্দল করা। **2.** (Of streams) To flow with a murmuring noise; কল্ কল্ ছল্ ছল্ রবে প্রবাহিত হওয়া। ***Noun.*** **1.** A noisy quarrel; a squabble; গোলমাল, কোন্দল; কলহ, ঝগড়া। **2.** Murmuring sound of rushing; স্রোতস্বতীর কল্ কল ছল্ ছল্ ধ্বনি। **Brawl′-ing**, *adj.* **Brawl′-ing-ly**, *adv.*

brawn (brän), *n.* **1.** The flesh of a boar; শূকর-মাংস। **2.** Boar's flesh boiled and pickled; লবণ-জলে রক্ষিত সিদ্ধ শূকর-মাংস। **3.** Muscular part of the body; মাংসপেশী। **4.** The strength of the muscle; পৈশিক শক্তি। **Brawn′-y**, *adj.* **1.** Fleshy; muscular; strong; মাংসল; দৃঢ়-পেশীবিশিষ্ট; দৃঢ়। **2.** Hard; unfeeling; as, a *brawny* conscience; কঠোর; নির্ম্মম।

bray (brā), *v.i.*, *v.t.* & *n.* To make loud harsh noise like an ass; গর্দ্দভের মত চীৎকার করা। ***Verb t.*** To make any harsh discordant noise; "And varying notes the war-pipes *brayed*;" ঘর্ঘর ধ্বনি করা। ***Noun.*** **1.** The harsh cry of an ass; রাসভ-রব। **2.** Any harsh grating sound; ঘর্ঘর রব। **Bray′-er**, *n.* **To bray out**—To utter harshly; কর্কশস্বরে বলা।

bray (brā), *v.t.* To pound; to beat small, especially with pestle and mortar; গুড়া করা, চূর্ণ করা; হামান-দিস্তায় চূর্ণ করা, থেঁতো করা, থেঁতলান।

bray′-êr (brā-), *n.* An instrument to spread ink in printing; (মুদ্রাঙ্কণ) কালি লাগাইবার যন্ত্র বিশেষ।

brāze, *v. t.* **1.** To ornament with brass; to colour like brass; পিত্তলমণ্ডিত করা; পিত্তলের মত রঙ্গ করা। **2.** To solder with an alloy of brass and zinc; পিত্তল এবং দস্তার মিশ্রণ দ্বারা ঝালা দেওয়া। **Braz′-ing**, *n.*

bra′-zen (brāzn), *adj.* & *v. t.* **1.** Made of brass; পিত্তলনির্ম্মিত, পৈত্তল। **2.** Strong and yellow like brass; পিত্তলবৎ কঠিন এবং পীতবর্ণ। **3.** Impudent; immodest; shameless; ধৃষ্ট; দুর্বিনীত; নির্লজ্জ। ***Verb t.*** (With *out*) **1.** To face impudently; উদ্ধতভাবে সম্মুখীন হওয়া। **2.** To harden or make reckless; কঠিন করা, বেপরওয়া করা। **3.** Impudently to maintain; নির্লজ্জের মত (কুকার্য্যের) সমর্থন করা। **–ly**, *adv.* **Brazen age**—দ্বাপর যুগ। **Brazen faced**—Impu[illegible]; shameless; ধৃষ্ট; নির্লজ্জ, বেহায়া

brā′-zier (-zhêr), *n.* Worker in brass; কাঁসারী। **–zi-er-y**, *n.*

brā′-zier (-zhêr), *n.* A pan holding lighted charcoal; জ্বলদঙ্গার রক্ষণার্থ পাত্রবিশেষ, অঙ্গার-ধানিকা (আঃ বঃ)।

brä′-zil wōōd—A very heavy reddish wood, growing in Brazil and used in dyeing red; বকমকাষ্ঠ (খোরী)। **Brazil-nut**—(ব্রাজিল দেশীয়) বাদাম বিশেষ।

breach (brēch), *n.*, *v. t.* & *i.* **1.** A breaking or neglect (of rule, duty, contract, someone's privileged rights or promise, esp. to marry); (নিয়ম, কর্ত্তব্য, চুক্তি, অধিকার, প্রতিশ্রুতি, বিবাহের অঙ্গীকার) লঙ্ঘন, ভঙ্গ, উল্লঙ্ঘন, অতিক্রম। **2.** (*Naut.*) Breaking of waves, as over a vessel; (নৌ-বিদ্যা) কল্লোলভঙ্গ, তরঙ্গভঙ্গ। **3.** Breaking of relations; separation; quarrel; সুহৃদ্‌ভেদ; সম্বন্ধ-ভঙ্গ, মনোভঙ্গ, বিচ্ছেদ, বিয়োগ; কলহ। **4.** A gap in a fortification made by artillery; "Once more unto the *breach*, dear friends, once more;" কামানের গোলার আঘাতে প্রাচীরাদির রন্ধ্র বা ফাটোল। **5.** A whale's leap clear out of water; জল হইতে তিমি মৎস্যের উল্লম্ফন। ***Verb t.*** To make an opening or gap in; to break through; as, to *breach* the walls of a city; তোপদ্বারা ভগ্ন করা; বিদীর্ণ করা। ***Verb i.*** To leap clear out of water, (said of a whale); (তিমি-মৎস্য সম্বন্ধে) জল হইতে শূন্যে লাফাইয়া উঠা। **A clean breach**—Rolling of the waves over the vessel, without breaking; জাহাজের উপর অভঙ্গভাবে তরঙ্গ-সঞ্চালন। Conveying away of masts and everything on deck; মাস্তুল এবং পাটাতনের উপরিস্থিত যাবতীয় পদার্থ তরঙ্গ দ্বারা নীত হওন। **Breach of close**—Trespass; অনধিকার প্রবেশ। **Breach of faith**—A failure to keep an expressed or implied promise; প্রতিজ্ঞাভঙ্গ, অঙ্গীকারভঙ্গ, সত্যচ্যুতি। A betrayal of confidence; বিশ্বাসভঙ্গ, বিশ্বাসঘাতকতা। **Breach of promise**—সত্য-ভঙ্গ, বিবাহের চুক্তি-ভঙ্গ। **Breach of the peace**—শান্তিভঙ্গ।

bread (brĕd), *n.* **1.** A food made of flour; রুটি, পাওরুটী। **2.** Food;

sustenance ; খাদ্য ; আহার-সামগ্রী, আহার্য্য। 3. Livelihood ; as, to earn one's *bread* ; জীবিকা। **Blithe bread**—সন্তানের জন্মোপলক্ষে নিমন্ত্রিত ব্যক্তি এবং কাঙ্গালিগণের মধ্যে যে ভোজ্য দ্রব্য বিতরিত হয়। [ইংলণ্ডের প্রাচীন প্রথা।] **Bread-basket**—A basket for holding bread ; রুটীর টুকরী। (*Slang.*) The stomach ; (ইতর-ভাষায়) পক্কাশয়, পাকস্থলী। **Bread-fruit**—প্রশান্ত মহাসাগরের দ্বীপ সমূহে

Bread-fruit.

উৎপন্ন বৃক্ষবিশেষের ফল, রুটিকা বৃক্ষের ফল, পূতফল। **Bread study**—Any branch of study taken up as a means of gaining a livelihood ; জীবিকার্জ্জনের উপায় বিধানের জন্য যে বিদ্যা শিক্ষা করা হয়, অর্থকরী বিদ্যা। **Breadstuff**—যে বস্তু হইতে রুটি প্রস্তুত হয়। **Bread-winner**—A person that supports a family ; পরিবারের অন্নসংস্থানকারী, পরিবার-প্রতিপালক। **Bread and butter**—Bread-slices spread with butter ; a necessary food ; a livelihood ; মাখন ও রুটী ; প্রয়োজনীয় আহার্য্য ; জীবিকা। **Bread and butter miss**—A school-girl ; বিদ্যালয়ের বালিকা। **Bread and butter science**—অর্থকরী বিদ্যা। **Bread and cheese**—Barest necessaries of life ; যদ্দ্বারা কেবলমাত্র কষ্টে স্বষ্টে জীবন-যাত্রা নির্ব্বাহ হইতে পারে। **Bread and cheese marriage**—Marriage to a man who is too poor to give his wife anything more than the bare necessaries of life ; দরিদ্র ব্যক্তির সহিত বিবাহ। **Bread buttered on both sides**—Easy prosperity ; very fortunate circumstances ; সুখ-সমৃদ্ধি ; অতীব সমৃদ্ধির অবস্থা। **To know which side one's bread is buttered**—To know where one's interest lies ; নিজের স্বার্থ কোথায় রহিয়াছে তাহা জানা। **To make one's bread**—To earn a living ; উদরান্নের সংস্থান করা, জীবিকার্জ্জন করা। **To take bread and salt**—To bind oneself by oath ; প্রতিজ্ঞা-বদ্ধ হওয়া। **To take the bread out of one's mouth**—To deprive of the means of living ; রুটি মারা (*Colloq.*)। To say something which another was on the point of saying ; কাহারও মুখের কথা কাড়িয়া লওয়া।

breadth (brĕdth), *n.* **1.** Broadness ; measure from side to side ; বিস্তার ; প্রস্থ, পরিসর, ওসার, বহর। **2.** A piece of cloth etc. of full breadth ; সম্পূর্ণ ওসারের কাপড় প্রভৃতি। **3.** Extent ; distance ; room ; বিস্তার ; দূরত্ব ; স্থান। **4.** Largeness of mind, view, etc. ; মন বা মতের প্রশস্ততা। **5.** Liberality ; catholicity ; toleration ; মহানুভবতা ; উদারতা, ঔদার্য্য ; পরমত-সহিষ্ণুতা। **6.** (*Painting*) A broad effect ; (চিত্র-বিদ্যা) চিত্রের মুখ্য বিশেষত্ব সমূহ সুস্পষ্ট করণার্থ প্রচুর বর্ণ, সমুজ্জ্বল আলোক, নিবিড়চ্ছায়া প্রভৃতির সমাবেশ। **Breadthways, Breadthwise**—প্রস্থে।

break (brāk), *v. t. & i.* **1.** To part or separate with violence or force ; to divide into two or more parts ; as, to *break* a rope or chain ; বিদীর্ণ করা, ছিঁড়িয়া ফেলা ; ভাঙ্গিয়া ফেলা, ভেদ করা, খণ্ডন করা, ত্রুটিত করা, বিদারণ করা, সম্ভেদ করা। **2.** To lay or burst open anything closed ; as, to *break* a package of goods ; খুলা, ভাঙ্গিয়া খুলা। **3.** To violate or infringe ; ব্যতিক্রম করা, লঙ্ঘন করা, ভঙ্গ করা। **4.** To interrupt ; to destroy the continuity of ; as, to *break* silence ; to *break* one's journey (প্রয়াণভঙ্গ করা) ; বাধা বা ব্যাঘাত জন্মান ; ভঙ্গ করা। **5.** To destroy the completeness of ; to remove a part from ; as, to *break* a set ; সম্পূর্ণতা নষ্ট করা ; অঙ্গহীন করা। **6.** To throw into disorder ; as, the cavalry were not able to *break* the British squares ; ছত্রভঙ্গ করা। **7.** To shatter to pieces ; চূর্ণবিচূর্ণ করা, চুড়মার করা। **8.** To diminish the force of ; to lighten the effects of a fall ; as, he looked about for some shrubs to *break* his dreadful fall ; বেগ হ্রাস করা ; পতনের চোট কমান। **9.** To exchange for other money or smaller currency ; as, to *break* a ten-rupee note ; (নোট্, চেক প্রভৃতি) ভাঙ্গান। **10.** To impart, as news or information ; as, to *break* the news gently to the widow ; to divulge ; সংবাদ প্রদান করা ; কথা প্রকাশ করা, কথা ভাঙ্গা। **11.** To tame ; to subdue ; to make tractable or manageable ; পোষ মানান ; বশ করা ; দমন করা। **12.** To make bankrupt ; to ruin ; দেউলিয়া করা ; সর্ব্বনাশ করা। **13.** To dismiss from office ; as, I see a great officer *broken* ; পদচ্যুত করা, বরখাস্ত করা। ***Verb i.*** **1.** To divide into two or more pieces ; to burst asunder ; টুটিয়া যাওয়া, ভগ্ন হওয়া ; খণ্ড খণ্ড হইয়া ভাঙ্গিয়া যাওয়া। **2.** To open spontaneously, as a bubble, tumour, etc. ; আপনা হইতে ফাটিয়া যাওয়া। **3.** To burst forth violently, as a storm, rain or thunder ; কোন কিছু ফাটিয়া প্রবলবেগে নির্গত হওয়া বা ছুটা। **4.** To be scattered ; as, the clouds are *breaking* ; বিক্ষিপ্ত

হওয়া। **5.** To dawn ; as, when the day *breaks* ; প্রভাত হওয়া, ফর্সা হওয়া। **6.** To decline in health or strength ; ভগ্নস্বাস্থ্য হওয়া, দুর্ব্বল হওয়া। **7.** To be overwhelmed with sorrow or grief ; as, my heart is *breaking* ; (দুঃখে) বুক ফাটিয়া যাওয়া, হৃদয় বিদীর্ণ হওয়া। **8.** To be bankrupt ; দেউলিয়া হওয়া। **9.** To terminate friendship ; সম্বন্ধ রহিত হওয়া, বন্ধুত্ব বিচ্ছেদ হওয়া। **10.** To fail in musical quality ; as, the singer's voice *breaks* ; স্বরভঙ্গ হওয়া। **To break a butterfly on (upon) a wheel**—To employ great exertions for insignificant ends ; মশা মারিতে কামান দাগা। **To break a horse, to break a horse to the rein**—To train a horse ; ঘোড়াকে সোয়ার লওয়ান। **To break a jest**—To utter a jest ; তামাসা করা, পরিহাস বা বিদ্রূপ করা। **To break a journey**—To stop before the journey is accomplished ; গন্তব্য স্থানে পৌছিবার পূর্ব্বেই পথিমধ্যে থামা। **To break a lance with**—To enter into a contest with ; to argue against ; প্রতিপক্ষের সহিত সংগ্রাম করা ; কাহারো পক্ষে বা কোন বিষয়ে যুক্তিতর্ক করা। **To break a law**—To violet or neglect a law ; বিধি লঙ্ঘন করা, আইন ভঙ্গ করা। **To break away**—To free one's self from restraint ; to escape ; to make a sudden exit ; as, the dog *broke away* from the chain ; (শৃঙ্খল হইতে) মুক্ত হওয়া ; পলায়ন করা ; হঠাৎ চলিয়া যাওয়া। **To break bread with**—To be entertained by ; কাহারও দ্বারা ভোজে আপ্যায়িত হওয়া। **To break cover**—To come out of a hiding place as a game when hunted ; ব্যাধ-তাড়িত জন্তুর ন্যায় গুপ্তস্থান হইতে বাহির হইয়া আসা। **To break down**—To crush ; to overwhelm ; চূর্ণবিচূর্ণ করা, ভাঙ্গিয়া ফেলা ; অভিভূত করা। To open a way through, by breaking ; ভাঙ্গিয়া পথ করা। To collapse ; ভাঙ্গিয়া পড়া। To fail in an undertaking ; as he *broke down* in the midst of his speech ; কোন বিষয়ে অকৃতকার্য্য হওয়া। To lose control over one's feelings ; আবেগের বশীভূত হওয়া। **To break fast**—To partake of food after abstinence, especially in the morning ; উপবাসের পর প্রথম আহার করা, প্রাতরাশ করা। **To break forth**—To come out suddenly ; সহসা নির্গত হওয়া। **To break ground**—To open the ground as for planting ; to plough ; বৃক্ষাদি রোপণের জন্য ক্ষেত্র প্রস্তুত করা ; চাষ করা। To begin siege operations ; to begin to execute any plan ; অবরোধ আরম্ভ করা ; কোন কার্য্য বা উদ্দেশ্য সাধনে প্রবৃত্ত হওয়া। (*Naut.*) To release the anchor from the bottom ; (নৌ-বিদ্যা) নঙ্গর তোলা। **To break in**—To force in ; ভাঙ্গিয়া প্রবেশ করা। To discipline ; শিক্ষিত করা, সায়েস্তা করা। **To break in, in upon, into**—To enter violently or unexpectedly ; বলপূর্ব্বক প্রবেশ করা, অপ্রত্যাশিতভাবে প্রবেশ করা। To interpose abruptly in a conversation ; হঠাৎ উপস্থিত হইয়া কথা বার্ত্তায় বাঁধা বা ব্যাঘাত জন্মান। **To break loose**—To extricate or free oneself by force ; বন্ধন ছিন্ন করিয়া বাহির হওয়া। **To break of**—To rid of ; to cause to abandon ; as, I will *break you of* this nasty habit ; মুক্ত করা, ত্যাগ করান, ছাড়ান। **To break off**—(*v. t.*) To separate by breaking ; ভাঙ্গিয়া ফেলা। To abandon ; to put a stop to ; পরিত্যাগ করা ; ক্ষান্ত করা, বিরত করা। (*v. i.*) To become separated by rupture ; (ঝগড়া বা মনোমালিন্য হেতু) বিচ্ছিন্ন হওয়া। To desist or cease suddenly ; বিরত হওয়া, ক্ষান্ত হওয়া। **To break one's mind**—To give expressions to one's thoughts ; মনোভাব প্রকাশ করা, মনের কথা ভাঙ্গা। **To break one's spirit**—To dishearten or discourage one ; ভগ্নোদ্যম করা, নিরুৎসাহ করা। **To break on the wheel, To break upon a wheel**—See WHEEL. **To break open**—To open by breaking ; ভাঙ্গিয়া খুলা। **To break out**—To take out by breaking ; ভাঙ্গিয়া বাহির করা। To burst forth suddenly ; to issue ; as, the sun *broke out* and brightened all the landscape ; (কোন কিছু ভেদ করিয়া) সহসা নির্গত হওয়া ; বহির্গত হওয়া। To escape from restraint ; as, the horse *broke out* of the stable ; (কোন প্রকার আটক ভাঙ্গিয়া) পলায়ন করা। To appear suddenly, as a fire, war or disease ; হঠাৎ আবির্ভূত বা প্রাদুর্ভূত হওয়া। **To break over**—To transgress ; to overleap ; to disregard ; as, the cattle *broke over* the fence into my garden ; অতিক্রম করা ; উল্লঙ্ঘন করা ; অমান্য করা। **To break Priscian's head**—To violate the rules of grammar ; ব্যাকরণের মাথায় লাঠি মারা, ব্যাকরণ-দুষ্ট পদ প্রয়োগ করা। [খৃষ্টীয় পঞ্চম শতাব্দীতে ইয়ুরোপে Priscian নামে একজন শ্রেষ্ঠ বৈয়াকরণ বর্ত্তমান ছিলেন।] **To break the back of**—To dislocate the joints of the back with too heavy a burden ; ভারী বোঝা চাপাইয়া কাহারও পিঠ ভাঙ্গিয়া দেওয়া। To disable thoroughly ; সম্পূর্ণরূপে অক্ষম করা। **To break the camel's back**—To be the last thing that brings about a fearful calamity ; as, the local rate is the last straw to *break the camel's back* ; ভীষণ বিপৎ সংঘটনের জন্য আর যে টুকু অবশিষ্ট থাকে, তাহা পূর্ণ করিবার কারণ স্বরূপ হওয়া। **To break the**

heart—To crush or overwhelm (one) with grief ; দুঃখে হৃদয় বিদীর্ণ করা। **To break the ice**—To get over the initial shyness or reserve ; "As *the ice was now broken*, every member of the company felt more at ease ;" কোনও কথা বলিতে প্রথম প্রথম যে কুণ্ঠা ও সঙ্কোচ বোধ হয়, তাহা অতিক্রম করা। **To break the neck of**—To destroy the main force ; to destroy ; ঘাড় ভাঙ্গিয়া দেওয়া, জোর কমান ; বিনষ্ট করা। **To break through**—To make an opening through by violence ; বলপূর্ব্বক ভেদ করা। To fail to fulfil ; to disregard ; (অঙ্গীকারাদি) ভঙ্গ করা, লঙ্ঘন করা ; অমান্য করা। To pass violently through ; as, to *break through* the enemies' line ; বলপূর্ব্বক অতিক্রম করা, (ব্যূহাদি) ভেদ করা। **To break up**—To open forcibly ; বলপূর্ব্বক উন্মুক্ত করা। To dissolve or put an end to a meeting ; (সভা) ভঙ্গ করা। To dismiss ; to depart ; চলিয়া যাওয়া ; বিদায় হওয়া। To become separated into parts ; as, the ice *breaks up* in the river ; খণ্ড খণ্ড হইয়া ভাঙ্গিয়া পড়া। To be dispersed or dissolved ; বিক্ষিপ্ত হওয়া, বিলীন হওয়া। To be impaired in health ; স্বাস্থ্যভঙ্গ হওয়া। **To break upon**—To dawn upon ; to be revealed to one ; প্রকাশিত হওয়া ; সহসা প্রকটিত হওয়া। **To break wind**—To give vent to or void wind from the anus ; অধোবায়ু মোচন করা। **To break with**—To cease to be friends with ; to quarrel or part with ; বন্ধুত্ব ভঙ্গ হওয়া ; কলহ করিয়া বিচ্ছিন্ন হওয়া।

break (brāk), *n.* **1.** The state of being broken ; ভগ্নাবস্থা। **2.** A rupture ; a breach ; as, a *break* of friendship ; মনোভঙ্গ ; ভঙ্গ। **3.** A broken place ; an interruption of continuity ; an irregularity ; ফাঁক, ভগ্নস্থান ; ছেদ, বিচ্ছেদ, অন্তরায়, ব্যাঘাত, বিরাম, বিরতি, নিরতি ; ব্যতিক্রম। **4.** A line drawn in printing for noting an omission or suspension of the sense ; (মুদ্রাঙ্কণ) কোন স্থানের অর্থের ব্যাঘাত বা শব্দের লোপ বুঝাইবার জন্য যে রেখা অঙ্কিত হয়। **5.** The dawn ; as, the *break* of day ; প্রত্যূষ, ঊষাকাল, অরুণোদয়। **6.** A brake for vehicles ; চক্রগতিরোধক যন্ত্র বিশেষ। **7.** A large four-wheeled vehicle ; চারিচাকার প্রকাণ্ড গাড়ী। **8.** (*Billiards*) The points scored continuously ; ক্রমান্বয়ে অর্জ্জিত অঙ্ক।

break'-āge (brāk-), *n.* **1.** A breaking ; খণ্ডন, ভেদন, ভঙ্গ। **2.** Damage by breaking ; ভাঙ্গার দরুণ ক্ষতি। **3.** An allowance for things broken accidentally or in transportation or use ; দৈবক্রমে, কিম্বা ব্যবহার বা স্থানান্তরিত করিবার সময়ে কোন জিনিষ ভাঙ্গিয়া গেলে তজ্জন্য যে বাদসাদ দেওয়া হয়।

break'-dōwn (brāk-), *n.* **1.** A collapse ; সম্পূর্ণ পতনাবস্থা। **2.** An accident ; দুর্ঘটনা। **3.** A failure of health or power ; স্বাস্থ্য বা শক্তির হ্রাস, জীবনীশক্তির সম্পূর্ণ অবসাদন। **4.** A negro dance ; কাফ্রিদিগের নৃত্য বিশেষ। **Break-down gang**—রেলওয়ে দুর্ঘটনার পর যে সকল লোক ভগ্নাবশেষ স্থানান্তরিত করে। [উচ্চারণ ব্রাক্ ডাউন্]।

break'-ẽr (brāk-), *n.* **1.** One who or that which breaks ; ভঞ্জক, [illegible]কারী, লঙ্ঘনকারী। **2.** A heavy [illegible]an-wave broken on rocks or the shore : "The *breakers* were right beneath her bows ;" শৈল বা তটে প্রতিহত ভগ্নোর্ম্মি, ভঙ্গ (রঃ)। [*Breakers ahead*—A cry of danger ; বিপৎসূচক ধ্বনি।] **3.** (*Naut.*) A small keg or water cask ; (নৌ-বিদ্যা) জল রাখিবার জন্য ক্ষুদ্র পিপা।

break'-făst (brĕk-), *n.*, *v.i.* & *t.* The first meal in the day ; প্রাতর্ভোজন, প্রাতরাশ, ছোট হাজরি (*Colloq.*)। ***Verb i.*** To eat the first meal in the day ; প্রাতর্ভোজন করা, প্রাতরাশ করা। ***Verb t.*** To furnish with breakfast ; প্রাতর্ভোজন প্রদান করা। **—ed, —less,** *adjs.*

break'-nĕck (brāk-), *adj.* Steep and dangerous ; extremely hazardous ; খাড়া এবং বিপজ্জনক ; নিতান্ত সঙ্কটজনক, ঘাড়-ভাঙ্গা।

break'-ŭp (brāk-), *n.* Disruption ; decay ; disintegration ; disbandment ; ভঙ্গ ; ক্ষয় ; বিশ্লেষণ ; দলভঙ্গ।

break'-vōw (brāk-), *n.* One who habitually breaks his vows ; পুনঃ পুনঃ প্রতিজ্ঞা-ভঙ্গকারী।

break'-wa-tẽr, (brāk-), *n.* Any contrivance, as a mole, etc., built to break the force of waves ; তরঙ্গের বেগ নিরোধক বাঁধ বা প্রাচীরাদি, জলবেগ নিবারণের জন্য পোস্তা, প্রভৃতি।

bream (brēm), *n.* A small yellowish fresh-water fish ; নদী প্রভৃতির জলচর পীতবর্ণ ক্ষুদ্র মৎস্যবিশেষ।

bream (brēm), *v. t.* To clear a ship's bottom by means of fire ; অগ্নিদ্বারা জাহাজের তলদেশ পরিষ্কার করা।

breast (brĕst), *n.* & *v. t.* **1.** The soft protuberant milk-secreting organ in woman ; স্তন, কুচ, উরোজ, উরসিজ, বক্ষোজ, পয়োধর, মাই (*Colloq.*)। **2.** The fore part of the body between the neck and the belly in men and animals ; বক্ষঃ, বক্ষঃস্থল, উরঃ। **3.** The heart ; the seat of the affections and passions ; হৃদয় চিত্ত, অন্তঃকরণ ; মর্ম্মস্থল। **4.** Anything resembling a breast ; as, the *breast* of a hill ; বক্ষঃসদৃশ যে কোন বস্তু। ***Verb t.*** To bear the breast against ; to oppose manfully ; to contend with ; as, to *breast* the storm and waves ; বুক পাতিয়া দেওয়া ; বীরের মত সম্মুখীন হওয়া ; সংগ্রাম করা । **Breast-bone**—বুকের চ্যাপটা এবং পাতল হাড় বিশেষ, ইহা দ্বারা পাঁজর সকল সংযুক্ত হয় । **Breast-deep**—বুকের সমান গভীর । **Breast-high** — আবক্ষঃ উচ্চ । **Breast-knot**—(পুষ্প-গুচ্ছবৎ) ফিতার গ্রন্থি,—বক্ষোপরি পরিহিত হয় । **Breast-pin** — বুকে পরিবার জন্য মণিখচিত গুঁজি বিশেষ । **Breast-plate**—A piece of armour covering breast ; উরস্ত্রাণ, বক্ষস্ত্রাণ । The lower shell of turtle, tortoise, etc. ; কূর্ম্ম, (কাছিম), কঠা (কাঠা) প্রভৃতির নীচের দিকের খোল । Inscription plate on coffin ; শবাধারের উপরিস্থ উৎকীর্ণ ফলক । **Breast-wheel**—জলবেগচালিত চক্র বিশেষ ।

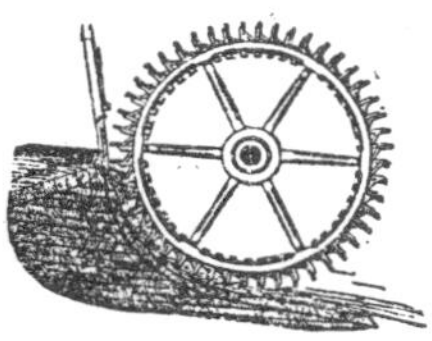

Breast-wheel.

Breast-work—A hastily constructed temporary defence or parapet a few feet high ; শত্রুগণ হইতে আত্মরক্ষার জন্য ক্ষিপ্রহস্তে নির্ম্মিত আবক্ষঃ উচ্চ প্রাচীর, প্রগণ্ডী (মঃ ভাঃ) । **A child at the breast**—দুধের ছেলে, দুগ্ধপোষ্য শিশু, স্তনন্ধয় (কাব্য সাঃ) । **To make a clean breast of**—To make full confession ; সমস্ত কথা অকপটে খুলিয়া বলা, অকপটে দোষ স্বীকার করা । **To take the breast**—To begin to take mother's milk ; মাতৃস্তন্য পান করিতে আরম্ভ করা ।

breath (brĕth), *n.* **1.** The air taken into and expelled from the lungs ; নিঃশ্বাস-প্রশ্বাস । **2.** The power of breathing freely ; as, I am out of *breath* ; দম । **3.** A single respiration or the time of making it ; as, to say inconsistent things in the same *breath* ; একবার শ্বাস-প্রশ্বাস ক্রিয়ায় যে সময় লাগে । **4.** (*Fig.*) That which gives or strengthens life ; life ; (লক্ষণায়) প্রাণবায়ু ; জীবন । **5.** A single word ; the slightest effort ; as, a *breath* can make them as a *breath* has made ; একটী মাত্র কথা ; অনুমাত্র চেষ্টা । **6.** A slight movement of air ; a very slight breeze ; as, *breath* of wind ; শ্বশ্বাস ; মৃদুমন্দ সমীরণ, মন্দানিল । **7.** Odour ; as, the *breath* of flowers ; সৌরভ । **8.** A whisper ; as, not a *breath* was heard ; মৃদুস্বর, শ্বাস-প্রশ্বাসের শব্দ । **Below** or **under one's breath**—In low tones ; in a whisper ; মৃদুস্বরে ; চুপে চুপে । **Breath of life** — The soul ; প্রাণবায়ু । **In a breath**—একশ্বাসে । [*All in a breath*—Without taking breath ; একশ্বাসে ।] **Out of breath**—Not able to breathe quick enough ; exhausted ; তাড়াতাড়ি, উর্দ্ধ শ্বাসে ; পরিশ্রান্ত, অবসন্ন । **The breath of one's nostril**—Something as valuable as life itself ; প্রাণতুল্য মূল্যবান বস্তু । **To draw breath**—To breathe ; to live ; শ্বাসপ্রশ্বাস ক্রিয়া নির্ব্বাহ করা ; বাঁচিয়া থাকা । **To take away one's breath**—To cause surprise and consternation ; বিস্ময়বিহ্বল করা । **To take breath**—To pause ; to rest a while ; দম লওয়া, হাঁপছাড়া ; ক্ষণেকের জন্য বিশ্রাম করা । **To waste breath**—To talk vainly ; বৃথা বাক্যব্যয় করা । **With bated breath**—With breath restrained from reverence or fear ; (ভয় বা সম্মানাধিক্য-হেতু) রুদ্ধশ্বাসে ।

breathe, (brēth) *v. t.* & *i.* **1.** draw in and expel air from lungs ; শ্বাস-প্রশ্বাসের ক্রিয়া নির্ব্বাহ করা । **2.** To send out (new life into) ; to infuse ; অনুপ্রাণিত করা, সঞ্জীবিত করা, অনুজীবিত করা ; অনুপ্রবিষ্ট করা । **3.** To utter softly ; to whisper ; as, he softly *breathed* thy name ; মৃদুস্বরে বলা ; চুপে চুপে বলা । **4.** To exhale ; as, the flowers *breathe* odours ; বাষ্পাকারে নিঃসৃত করা, উদ্গিরণ করা । **5.** To exhibit ; to manifest ; as, to *breathe* simplicity ; প্রদর্শন করা ; প্রকাশ করা । **6.** To suffer to take or recover breath, (as a horse) ; to give rest to ; নিঃশ্বাস ফেলিতে দেওয়া ; হাঁপ ছাড়িতে দেওয়া । ***Verb i.*** **1.** To inhale or exhale air ; শ্বাস গ্রহণ বা মোচন করা । **2.** To live ; বাঁচিয়া থাকা, জীবিত থাকা । **3.** To seem to live ; জীবিত বলিয়া বোধ হওয়া । **4.** To speak softly ; (of wind) to blow softly ; আস্তে আস্তে বা চুপে চুপে কথা বলা ; (বায়ু-সম্পর্কে) মৃদুমন্দ প্রবাহিত হওয়া । **To breathe again**—To be relieved from an anxiety ; উৎকণ্ঠা হইতে মুক্ত হওয়া, হাঁপ ছাড়িয়া বাঁচা । **To breathe freely**—To be at ease ; আরামে থাকা । **To breathe into**—To infuse ; অনুপ্রবিষ্ট করা, সঞ্চার করা । **To breathe one's last**—To die ; to expire ; মৃত হওয়া ; প্রাণবায়ু ত্যাগ করা । **To breathe out**—To eject by breathing ; নিঃসৃত করা । **To breathe short**—To breathe quickly from great anxiety ; অতিশয় উৎকণ্ঠা বা উদ্বেগ বশতঃ ঘন ঘন শ্বাস ত্যাগ করা । **To breathe upon**—To tarnish ; to soil ; মলিন করা ; ময়লা করা, নোঙ্গরা করা ।

breath'-ėr (brēth-), *n.* A short spell of exercise ; অল্পক্ষণস্থায়ী অতিশ্রমসাধ্য ব্যায়াম ।

breath'-ing (brēth-), *n.* & *adj.* **1.** Respiration ; শ্বাস-প্রশ্বাস, শ্বসন । **2.** Inspiration ; as, the *breathings* of the spirit ; অনুপ্রাণন । **3.** Air in gentle motion ; মন্দপবন, ধীরসমীর (গীতঃ) । **4.** Aspiration ; secret prayer ; as, earnest desires and *breathings* after that blessed state ; উচ্চাভিলাস, উচ্চাকাঙ্ক্ষা ; নিভৃত প্রার্থনা । **5.** Utterance ;

as, I am sorry to give *breathing* to my purpose ; বাক্যে প্রকাশ, উচ্চারণ। 6. A stop ; a delay ; বিরাম ; বিলম্ব। 7. Signs (') (') indicating that the initial vowel is or is not aspirated ; মহাপ্রাণচিহ্ন। *Adj.* Life-like, (said of statue, etc.) ; সজীববৎ (মূর্ত্তি প্রভৃতি সম্পর্কে)। **Breathing hole**—গবাক্ষ। **Breathing time**—Time to breathe or pause ; শ্বাস ফেলিবার অবকাশ।

breath'-less, (brĕth-) *adj.* 1. Lifeless ; dead ; জীবন-শূন্য ; মৃত। 2. Out of breath ; বে-দম। 3. Holding the breath, on account of fear, expectation or intense interest ; (ভয়, আশা বা অতিকৌতূহল বশতঃ) রুদ্ধশ্বাস। 4. Unstirred by wind ; অবাতবিক্ষুব্ধ। **—ly,** *adv.* Pantingly ; হাঁপাইতে হাঁপাইতে। 2. In suspense ; উৎকণ্ঠাকুলভাবে। **—ness,** *n.*

brĕd, *p. t.* & *p. p.* of BREED ; জাত, জনিত, উৎপাদিত, পুষ্ট।

breech (brēch), *n.* & *v. t.* 1. The lower part of the body behind ; the buttocks ; শ্রোণি, নিতম্ব, জঘন। 2. The back part of a rifle or gun barrel ; বন্দুকাদির পশ্চাদ্ভাগ। 3. (*Pl.* **—es**) Short trousers fastened below knee and now used only for riding or in court costume, etc. ; (অশ্বারোহণে বা রাজদরবারে ব্যবহৃত) এক প্রকার খর্ব্ব পাজামা—যাহা জানুর নীচে বাঁধা হয়, জঙ্ঘাবরণ, জাঙ্গিয়া। *Verb t.* 1. To put into breeches ; পাজামা পরান। 2. To whip on the breech ; নিতম্বে বেত্রাঘাত করা। **Breech'-less,** *adj.* **Breech-loader, Breech-loading gun**—যে বন্দুক বা কামানের পশ্চাদ্ভাগে গুলি বা টোটা ভরা যায়। **To wear the breeches**—(Said of a wife) To usurp the authority of the husband ; স্বামীর উপর কর্ত্তৃত্ব করা।

breech'-ing (brēch-), *n.* 1. That part of a horse's harness attached to the saddle and hooked on the shafts ; ঘোড়ার সাজের অংশ বিশেষ। 2. A strong rope to prevent a cannon from recoiling too much when fired ; দাগিবার পর কামানের ঠিকরনের বেগ নিবারণের জন্য যে দৃঢ় রজ্জু ব্যবহৃত হয়। 3. The act of whipping on the breech ; নিতম্বদেশে বেত্রাঘাত।

breed (brēd), *v. t., i.* & *n.* 1. To procreate ; to generate ; প্রসব করা ; জন্মদান করা। 2. To propagate ; সন্তান বৃদ্ধি করা, বংশ বৃদ্ধি করা। 2. To nurse or foster ; লালন-পালন করা, পোষণ করা। 4. To train up ; to educate ; শিক্ষা দেওয়া ; শিক্ষিত করা। 5. To produce ; উৎপাদন করা। *Verb i.* 1. To be pregnant ; গর্ভবতী হওয়া। 2. To be produced or multiplied ; উৎপন্ন হওয়া, বৃদ্ধি পাওয়া, সংখ্যা-বৃদ্ধি পাওয়া। 3. To raise a breed or kind ; বাচ্চা তোলা। 4. To have birth ; জন্মলাভ করা। *Noun.* 1. A race or progeny from the same parents or stock ; বংশ, জাতি, সন্তানসন্ততি। 2. A family with hereditary qualities ; পুরুষপরম্পরাগত গুণসমন্বিত কুল বা পরিবার। **Breed'-er,** *n.* **Breed'-ing,** *n.* 1. The act of generating or bringing forth ; জন্মদান, উৎপাদন। 2. The raising of a breed or breeds ; শাবক উৎপাদন বা বাচ্চা তোলন। 3. Education ; behaviour ; good manners ; শিক্ষা ; ব্যবহার, আচরণ ; শিষ্টাচার। **Close breeding, in and in breeding**—একপিতৃকুলজাত স্ত্রী এবং পুরুষের সংসর্গে সন্তান বা শাবকোৎপাদন। **Cross breeding**—Breeding from male and female of different lineages ; বিভিন্ন বংশীয় পুরুষ ও স্ত্রীর সংসর্গে সন্তান বা শাবকোৎপাদন। **Good breeding**—Politeness ; শিষ্টাচার। **Of a good breed**—সুজাত, উত্তমজাতীয়। **To be bred in the bone**—মজ্জাগত হওয়া, হাড়ে হাড়ে থাকা। **To breed in and in**—To marry always among near relations ; সর্ব্বদা ঘনিষ্ঠ সম্পর্কের মধ্যে বিবাহ করা। **To raise a breed**—পশ্বাদির পাল তৈয়ার করা।

breeze (brēz), **breese** (brēz), *n.* The gadfly ; the horsefly ; দংশক, দাঁশ, বনমক্ষিকা ; গোমক্ষিকা।

breeze (brēz), *n.* 1. A gentle wind ; মৃদু বায়ু, মন্দ পবন, মন্দানিল, মৃদুমারুত, হাওয়া (*Colloq.*), ধীরসমীর (গীতঃ)। 2. (*Slang.*) Quarrel ; a display of temper ; "And Femmy, who expected a *breeze*, told his wife to behave quietly ;" (ইতর-ভাষায়) কলহ ; রাগপ্রকাশ। **Land breeze**—Wind blowing from the land generally at night ; স্থলানিল (সাঃ পঃ), স্থলপবন (হিঃ কোঃ)। **Sea breeze**—A breeze or wind blowing generally in the day time, from the sea ; সমুদ্র-পবন (হিঃ কোঃ), সাগরানিল (সাঃ পঃ)।

breeze (brēz), *n.* Small cinders, coke-dust, etc., used by brickmakers ; ইষ্টক-প্রস্তুতকারিগণ কর্ত্তৃক ব্যবহৃত ক্ষুদ্র ক্ষুদ্র কাঠের কয়লা, কোক কয়লার চূর্ণ, প্রভৃতি।

breez'-y (brēz-), *adj.* 1. Pleasantly windy ; wind-swept ; as, a *breezy* day in May ; মনোরম বায়ু-সেবিত, সুপ্রবাত (আঃ বঃ) ; মন্দানিলবীজিত। 2. (*Fig.*) Fresh ; lively ; jovial ; নবীন ; সজীব ; উল্লাসকর। **—i-ly,** *adv.* **—i-ness,** *n.*

brĕnt'-gōōse, brănt'-gōōse, *n.* A small species of wild goose visiting Britain in winter ; (শীতকালে ইংলণ্ডে আগত) এক প্রকার বন্য হংস, বালি হাঁস।

brĕst'-sŭm-mêr, breast'-sŭm-mêr (brĕst-), *n.* A beam supporting the point of a building, etc., after the manner of a lintel ; যে কড়িকাঠ দরজার মাথালের কাঠের মত ইমারতাদির সম্মুখভাগ ধারণ করিয়া থাকে।

bretelle, (*F.*), *n.* An ornamental suspender-like shoulder-strap ; কারুকার্য্যশোভিত স্কন্ধ-পট্ট (পাজামা আটক করিবার ফিতার মত)।

brĕth'-rĕn, *n.* Plural of BROTHER.

Brĕt'-ŏn, *adj.* & *n.* Relating to Brittany or the language of its people ; ব্রিটেনী বা তৎপ্রদেশীয় ভাষা-সম্বন্ধীয়। ***Noun.*** The native language of Brittany in France ; ফরাসী-দেশের অন্তর্গত ব্রিটেনী প্রদেশের ভাষা।

bretwalda, (*F.*), *n.* The chief of the kings of heptarchy, who exercised a certain undefined influence over the others ; প্রাচীন ব্রিটন দ্বীপের সপ্ত এঙ্গ্‌লো-সেক্‌সন নৃপতি-গণের মধ্যে সর্ব্বপ্রধান ব্যক্তি।

brēve, *n.* **1.** Authoritative letter from the sovereign or pope ; সম্রাট বা পোপ (রোমান ক্যাথলিক ধর্ম্ম-সম্রাট) দ্বারা প্রেরিত শাসনাত্মক লিপি। **2.** (*Prosody or grammar*) A short syllable ; (ছন্দঃ-শাস্ত্র বা ব্যাকরণ) লঘূচ্চারণ বিশিষ্ট শব্দাংশ।

brĕ-vĕt', *n.* & *v. t.* **1.** A document conferring a favour from a sovereign or a government ; যে পত্রে কোন রাজা বা শাসনতন্ত্র কোন ব্যক্তিকে কোনরূপ প্রসাদ বা অনুগ্রহ অর্পণ করেন। **2.** A military commission that entitles an officer to rank above his pay ; as, a *brevet* rank ; যে ক্ষমতা-পত্র দ্বারা সামরিক বিভাগের কোন কর্ম্মচারীকে তিনি যে পদবীর বেতন প্রাপ্ত হইতেছেন, তদপেক্ষা উচ্চতর পদবীগ্রহণের অধিকার অর্পণ করা হইয়া থাকে। **3.** An honorary or nominal position ; অবৈতনিক বা সম্মানসূচক পদ বিশেষ। ***Verb t.*** To confer brevet rank on or upon ; কাহাকে উক্তরূপ পদবী প্রদান করা। **—cy**, *n.*

brē'-vĭ-ă-rȳ, *n.* **1.** An epitome ; সংক্ষিপ্তসার। **2.** A book containing the daily service of the Roman Catholic and Greek Churches to be recited by those in orders ; রোমান ক্যাথলিক এবং গ্রীসীয় ধর্ম্ম-সমাজভুক্ত যাজকদিগের নিত্য-পঠনীয় প্রার্থনা-পুস্তক।

brē'-vĭ-āte, *n.* A brief statement or summary ; সংক্ষিপ্তসার, সার-সংগ্রহ।

brē'-vier (-vēr), *n.* (*Printing*) A size of type between bourgeois and minion ; মুদ্রাঙ্কনের ক্ষুদ্র হরফ (অক্ষর) বিশেষ। [এই অভিধানের ইংরেজি হরফ অপেক্ষা অব্যবহিত ক্ষুদ্রতর।

brĕv'-ĭ-tȳ, *n.* Shortness of expression ; conciseness ; "*Brevity* is the soul of wit ;" সংক্ষিপ্ততা ; স্বল্পাক্ষরতা, অনতিকালস্থায়িত্ব।

brew (brô), *v. t.*, *i.* & *n.* **1.** To make beer, ale, etc., by steeping, boiling, and fermentation ; যবসুরা প্রভৃতি প্রস্তুত করা। **2.** To make (tea, punch, etc.,) by infusing or mixing ingredients ; নানাদ্রব্য বা নানাদ্রব্যের ক্বাথ মিশ্রিত করিয়া (চা, সরবৎ প্রভৃতি) প্রস্তুত করা। **3.** To concoct ; to plot ; as, to *brew* mischief ; উদ্ভাবন করা, পাকাইয়া তোলা ; ষড়যন্ত্র করা। ***Verb i.*** To be a brewer ; মদ্যপ্রস্তুতকারীর কায করা। **2.** To be set on foot or preparing ; সূচিত হওয়া, সুরু হওয়া, পাকাইয়া উঠা। ***Noun.*** The mixture formed by brewing ; চুয়ানো মদ। **Brew'-er**, *n.* One who brews ; মদ্য প্রস্তুতকারী, শুঁড়ী। **Brew'-er-y**, *n.* A place for brewing ; মদের ভাঁটিখানা।

brew'-āge (brô-), *n.* Mixed liquor ; drink brewed ; মিশ্রিত মদ্য ; চুয়ানো মদ্য।

brī'-ăr, *n.* See BRIER.

Brī-ā'-rē-ăn, *adj.* Relating to Briareus, a mythological hund[red] handed giant ; hence, hun[dred]-handed or many handed ; গ্রীক্ পুরাণে বর্ণিত শতভুজ দানব ব্রীয়ারাস সম্বন্ধীয় ; শতভুজ, বহুবাহু।

brībe, *n.* & *v. t.* Money etc., offered to procure (often illegal or dishonest) action in favour of the giver ; allurement ; উৎকোচ, ঘুস ; পারিতোষিক। ***Verb t.*** To induce or influence by a bribe ; to give a bribe to ; উৎকোচ দ্বারা প্রলুব্ধ বা প্রভাবিত করা ; উৎকোচ প্রদান করা, ঘুষ দেওয়া। ***Verb i.*** To give a bribe to a person ; (কোন ব্যক্তিকে) ঘুষ দেওয়া। **Brib'-a-ble**, *adj.* **Brib'-ee**, *n.* **Brib'-er**, *n.* **Brib'-er-y**, *n.* The practice of giving or taking bribes ; উৎকোচ প্রদান বা গ্রহণ, উৎকোচ-চর্য্যা।

bric'-ă-brăc, *n.* Old and rare articles, such as, china and curios ; প্রাচীন আসবাব এবং দুষ্প্রাপ্য চিনা বাসন, ব্যজন প্রভৃতি আজব জিনিষ।

brick, *n.*, *v. t.* & *adj.* **1.** A rectangular block of sundried or burnt clay, used in building, etc. ; ইষ্টক, ইট। **2.** Bricks collectively ; ইষ্টক রাশি। **3.** A brick-shaped loaf or a block of tea, etc. ; ইষ্টকাকৃতি রুটি, বা চা পাতার স্তূপ। **4.** A child's wooden toy building-block ; শিশুদিগের খেলার ঘর প্রস্তুতের জন্য ক্ষুদ্র ক্ষুদ্র কাঠের ইট। **5.** (*Slang.*) A generous or kind person ; a merry person ; "He is a dear little *brick* ;" ভাল মানুষ, মাটীর মানুষ; মজার লোক। ***Verb t.*** **1.** To lay, pave or construct with bricks ; ইট বিছান, ইষ্টক দ্বারা বাঁধা বা গাঁথিয়া তোলা। **2.** To imitate or counterfeit a brick wall on ; চূণ বালির আস্তরের উপর রঙ্গ দিয়া, এবং ইটের মত কিনারা তুলিয়া ইষ্টক প্রাচীরের অনুকরণ করা। ***Adj.*** Built of bricks ; as, *brick* wall ; ইষ্টক-নির্ম্মিত। **Brick'-y**, *adj.* ইষ্টক-নির্ম্মিত, ইষ্টক সদৃশ বা ইষ্টকবর্ণ। **Brickbat**—A piece of brick, especially as missile ; ইষ্টকখণ্ড, পাটকেল। **Brick-clay**—চিক্‌নামাটি। **Brickdust**—Dust made by pounding bricks ; সুরকী। A colour like that of brick-dust ; শুরকির বর্ণ। **Brick-field**—ইটখোলা। **Brick-kiln**—ইটের পাঁজা, ইষ্টকচুল্লী। **Brick-layer**—রাজমিস্ত্রী। **Brick-tea**—নিকৃষ্টশ্রেণীর চাপাতা এবং মেষ-রক্তের সংমিশ্রণে প্রস্তুত ইষ্টকাকার খণ্ড-বিশেষ। [রুষদেশের নিম্নশ্রেণীর লোকগণ ব্যবহার করে।] **Brick-work**—A structure formed of bricks ; masonry works ; ইটের গাঁথুনী ; ইমারতি-কর্ম্ম। **Like bricks, Like a thousand of bricks** — Vigorously ; with goodwill ; সোৎসাহে ; প্রীতির সহিত। **To brick up**—ইটদ্বারা বুজাইয়া দেওয়া। **To have a brick in one's hat**—To be drunk ; নিশায় বিভোর হওয়া। **To read like a brick**—To read hard ; অতিশয় অধ্যয়ন করা। **Vitrified brick**—ঝামা ইট।

bri-cōle′ (brē), (*F.*), *n.* **1.** An indirect stroke in tennis and billiards ; টেনিস ও বিলিয়ার্ড ক্রীড়ায় গৌণ আঘাত। **2.** (*Mil.*) Harness worn by men for dragging guns where it is impossible to use horses ; (সামরিক শাস্ত্র) অশ্বের অগম্যস্থানে কামান বহনার্থ সৈনিকগণ যে অশ্বসজ্জা পরিধান করিয়া থাকে।

brīd′-ăl, *n.* & *adj.* A nuptial festival ; a marriage ; বিবাহোৎসব ; বিবাহ, উদ্বাহ। ***Adj.*** Belonging to a bride or wedding ; as, *bridal* ornaments ; বৈবাহিক বা কন্যা-সম্বন্ধীয়, বিবাহ-সম্বন্ধীয়। **—ly,** *adv.* **Bridal garment**—বধূবস্ত্র (মঃ ভাঃ), আনন্দ-পট (অঃ)।

brīde, *n.* A woman about to marry or a newly-married woman ; বিবাহের কন্যা, কনে (*Colloq.*), পাত্রী, নবোঢ়া, নবভার্য্যা, নববধূ, নবপত্নী। **Bridecake**—বিবাহ উপলক্ষে সমাগত নিমন্ত্রিত ব্যক্তিগণকে যে পিষ্টক বাটিয়া দেওয়া হয়, এবং বিবাহান্তে যাহা বন্ধু-বান্ধবগণের নিকট প্রেরিত হয়। **Bride-chamber**—বাসর ঘর, নবদম্পতির শয়ন-মন্দির, কৌতুকাগার (কুমাঃ)। **Bride-groom**—A man at, or soon before or after, his marriage ; বর, পাত্র, নববিবাহিত পুরুষ। **Bridesmaid, bridemaid**—A woman or girl who attends a bride at marriage ceremony ; নবোঢ়া কন্যার সহচরী, জন্যা (রঃ)। **Bridesman, Brideman**—A bride-groom's attendant ; the best-man ; বরের সহচর ; নীতবর, জন্য।

brīde′-wĕll, *n.* A house of correction ; a gaol ; চরিত্র-শোধনাগার ; কারাগার। [প্রাচীন লণ্ডননগরীস্থ St. Bride বা St. Bridget এর কূপের সন্নিকটবর্ত্তী Bridewell নামক প্রাচীন কারাগারের নাম হইতে এই শব্দটি গৃহীত হইয়াছে।]

bridge (brĭj), *n.* & *v. t.* **1.** A passage built over water, railway, etc. ; সেতু, সাঁকো, পুল। **2.** The upper bony part of a nose ; নাসা-বংশ, নাসিকাদণ্ড, নাকের শির-দাঁড়া। **3.** The movable piece over which violin strings are stretched ; বেহালার সোয়ারি, তন্ত্র-ধারক কাষ্ঠখণ্ড। **4.** A platform on a ship where the captain stands to direct the vessel ; জাহাজের উপরিস্থ যে মঞ্চে দণ্ডায়মান হইয়া পোতাধ্যক্ষ পোত পরিচালন তত্ত্বাবধান করেন। ***Verb t.*** **1.** To bridge over ; সেতু নির্ম্মাণ করা, সেতুবন্ধ করা, পুল বাঁধা। **2.** To find a way out of or over, as a difficulty ; (কোন বিপদ্ হইতে) নিষ্ক্রমণের পথ পাওয়া। **Bridge-head**—A work commanding the bridge nearest the enemy ; শত্রুর স[illegible]হিত সেতু-প্রান্তে স্থিত দুর্গবপ্রাদি। [illegible]lge of boats—নৌসেতু। **Bridge of gold, Golden bridge**—Easy retreat provided for beaten enemy ; পরাজিত শত্রুগণের জন্য নিষ্কণ্টকীকৃত পলায়ন-পথ। **To make a bridge of gold for any one**—To enable one to retreat from a false position without loss of dignity ; (কাহারও জন্য) স্বর্ণসেতু নির্ম্মাণ করা, কোনরূপ গোলমাল হইতে মানে মানে রক্ষা পাওয়াইয়া দেওয়া।

bridge (brĭj), *n.* A card game of Russian origin resembling whist ; একপ্রকার তাস খেলা।

brī′-dle, *n.*, *v. t.* & *i.* **1.** The head-reins of horses ; বল্গা, লাগাম, প্রগ্রহ, রশ্মি। **2.** A restraint ; a curb ; সংযম ; নিরোধ। ***Verb t.*** **1.** To put bridle on (horse, etc.) ; অশ্বাদির মুখে লাগাম লাগান। **2.** To curb ; to restrain ; as, to *bridle* the passions ; দমন করা ; সংযত করা, বশে আনা। ***Verb i.*** To assume a dignified or offended air or manner, (usu. foll. by *up*) ; "Whenever you tell her she is handsome she *bridles* ;" ক্ষুন্ন, গর্ব্বিত বা অভিমান-ব্যঞ্জক ভাব ধারণ করা, অভিমানে বা অবজ্ঞাচ্ছলে গ্রীবা বাঁকান। **Bridle-path, Bridle-road**—অশ্ব-চালনের উপযোগী পথ (গাড়ীর জন্য নহে)। **To give horse the bridle, To lay the bridle on horse's neck**—To abandon control ; লাগাম ছাড়িয়া দেওয়া।

bri-dōōn′, *n.* A light snaffle and rein of a military bridle ; সৈনিকদিগের অশ্বের অবান্তর লাগাম।

brief (brēf), *adj.* **1.** Short in duration ; ক্ষণস্থায়ী, ক্ষণিক, অচিরস্থায়ী। **2.** Concise ; succinct ; terse ; সংক্ষিপ্ত ; স্বল্পাক্ষর, অল্পাক্ষরগ্রথিত ; ছাঁটাছোটা, সামাসিক (মঃ সং)। **Brief′-ly,** *adv.* **Brief′-ness,** *n.* **In brief**—In short ; সংক্ষেপে। **To be brief**—To speak shortly ; সংক্ষেপে বলিয়া যাওয়া।

brief (brēf), *n.* & *v. t.* **1.** A short or concise writing ; an epitome ; সংক্ষিপ্ত লিখন, সার-লিপি ; সার-সংগ্রহ, সংক্ষিপ্ত-সার, সংক্ষেপ। **2.** (*Law*) A summary of facts and law-points of a case drawn up for counsel ; (আইন) মোকদ্দমার বৃত্তান্ত এবং আইন-ঘটিত বিষয়ের সারলিপি, যাহা কৌসলির

ব্যবহারের জন্য মুসাবিদা করা হয়, বিবাদ-তত্ত্ব (আঃ বঃ)। **3.** A formal letter on the matter of discipline to a person or community from the Pope ; কোনও সম্প্রদায় বা ব্যক্তি বিশেষের উপর রোমীয় ধর্ম্মসম্রাট পোপের শাসন-সম্পর্কীয় অনুশাসনপত্র বিশেষ। ***Verb t.*** **1.** To reduce facts etc. to a brief ; কৌসলির ব্যবহারের জন্য কোন মোকদ্দমার বৃত্তান্ত এবং আইন-ঘটিত বিষয়ের সারলিপি প্রস্তুত করা। **2.** To instruct barrister by a brief ; উক্ত সারলিপিদ্বারা কোন কৌসলিকে মোকদ্দমা সম্বন্ধে উপদেশ দেওয়া। **Brief'-less,** *adj.* Without much practice ; as, a *briefless* barrister ; মোকদ্দমা-শূন্য ; পসারহীন। **To accept a brief in behalf of**—To espouse the cause of ; কাহারো পক্ষ অবলম্বন করা। **To hold brief for**—To be retained as a counsel for ; to argue in favour of ; কোন পক্ষে কৌসলী নিযুক্ত থাকা ; কাহারও পক্ষে তর্ক (বা ওকালতি) করা

brī'-êr, brī'-ar (-êr), *n.* A prickly plant or shrub ; the wild rose ; কাঁটা গাছ, কণ্টকগুল্ম, কণ্টকবৃক্ষ ; আরণ্য গোলাব। **Sweet brier**—সুগন্ধ পত্র এবং পুষ্প-বিশিষ্ট আরণ্য গোলাব বিশেষ।

brī'-êr, brī'-ar (êr), *n.* The White Heath, of which the root is used for tobacco pipes ; আরণ্য-গুল্ম বিশেষ, ইহার মূল দ্বারা ধূমপানের নল প্রস্তুত হইয়া থাকে, শুকচিনা (খোরী)।

Brig.

brig, *n.* A two-masted square-rigged vessel ; দ্বিমাস্তুল পোতবিশেষ।

bri-gāde', *n.* & *v. t.* **1.** A body of troops, cavalry or infantry, consisting of several regiments, commanded by a general officer ; কতিপয় পল্টন (regiment) দ্বারা গঠিত সেনাপতির অধীনস্থ সুবৃহৎ অশ্বারোহী বা পদাতিক সৈন্যদল, বাহিনী। **2.** An organised body of men wearing a uniform ; as, fire *brigade* ; একরূপ পরিচ্ছদধারী ব্যবস্থাবদ্ধ কর্ম্মিদল। ***Verb t.*** To form into a brigade or brigades ; উক্তপ্রকার এক বা ততোধিক সৈন্যদলে গঠিত হওয়া।

brig-a-dier' (-dēr), *n.* (Fully BRIGADIER GENERAL) The officer who commands a brigade ; বাহিনীপতি। (মেজর জেনেরেল এবং কর্ণেলের মধ্যবর্ত্তী পদবী।)

brig'-ănd, *n.* A highwayman a bandit ; a robber ; রাহাজান ; লুটেরা ; দস্যু, ডাকাত। **—age, —ism,** *ns.*

brig'-ăn-tīne, *n.* A small two-masted vessel ; দ্বিমাস্তুল ক্ষুদ্র পোত বিশেষ। (পূর্ব্বে ইয়ুরোপীয় জলদস্যুগণ ব্যবহার করিত।)

bright (brīt), *adj.* **1.** Shining ; ভাস্বর, দীপ্তিমান্, উজ্জ্বল, জ্যোতির্ম্ময়, দীপ্ত, সপ্রভ। **2.** Transparent ; clear ; স্বচ্ছ ; নির্ম্মল, বিমল। **3.** Attractive; resplendent with charms; চিত্তাকর্ষক, মনোহর, রুচির ; লাবণ্যোজ্জ্বল। **4.** Quick-witted ; "Great in arm and *bright* in art ;" ধীমান্, উজ্জ্বলধী, ক্ষিপ্রবুদ্ধি। **5.** Lit up with joy, hope, etc. ; cheerful ; আনন্দপ্রদীপ্ত, আশাদীপ্ত ; প্রফুল্ল। **6.** Glorious ; "In the *brightest* annals of a female reign ;" মহিমোজ্জ্বল, গৌরব-দীপ্ত। **7.** Clear ; স্পষ্ট, বিশদ। **8.** Of brilliant colour ; as, *bright* red ; দীপ্তবর্ণ। **Bright'-en,** *v. t.* & *i.* **Bright'-ly,** *adv.* **Bright'-ness,** *n.*

Bright's Disease (brīts dĭz-ēz), *n.* A granular degeneration of the kidneys ; মূত্রাশয়ের পীড়াবিশেষ। ইহাতে মূত্রের মধ্যে অণ্ডলালের উদ্ভব হয়। আবিষ্কারক ডাক্তার ব্রাইটের নাম হইতে এইরূপ নাম।

brill, *n.* A kind of flat-fish resembling turbot ; মৎস্যবিশেষ।

bril'-liant (-lyănt), *adj.* **1.** Bright ; sparkling ; দীপ্তিমান্ ; ঝলমল, উজ্জ্বল, চাকচিক্যময়। **2.** (*Fig.*) Splendid ; as, *brilliant* parts ; talented ; "Fontenelle was both *brilliant* and far-sighted ;" (লক্ষণায়) উজ্জ্বল ; প্রতিভাশালী। **—liance, —lian-cy,** *ns.* **—ly,** *adv.*

bril'-liant (-lyănt), *n.* **1.** A diamond of the finest cut, consisting of lozenge-shaped facets alternating with triangles ; অতি-সুন্দর পল-কাটা হীরক। **2.** The smallest size of types used in English printing ; ইংরেজী মুদ্রণের সর্ব্বাপেক্ষা ক্ষুদ্র-হরফ।

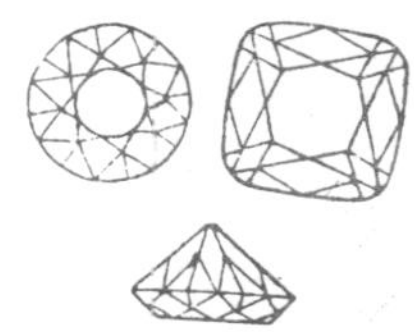

Brilliant.

bril'-lian-tīne (-lyăn-), *n.* **1.** A cosmetic for hair ; কেশমসৃণকর স্নেহপদার্থ বিশেষ। **2.** A glassy dress-fabric like alpaca ; আলপাকার মত একপ্রকার চকচকে কাপড়।

brim, *n.* *v. t.* & *i.* **1.** The edge, margin or brink of anything ; প্রান্ত, কিনারা, ধার, পার্শ্ব। **2.** The edge of a vessel ; কানা। **3.** The rim of a hat ; টুপীর বহির্বিলম্বিত প্রান্ত বা কিনারা। ***Verb t. & i.*** To fill ; to be full to the brim, (*lit.* & *fig.*) ; ছাপিয়ে পড়া ; (শব্দানুযায়ী এবং লক্ষণায়) ছাপাইয়া পড়া, কানায় কানায় পূর্ণ করা বা হওয়া। **Brim'-ful,** *adj.* Full to the brim ; complete ; কানাকানায় পূর্ণ ; আতট পূর্ণ, ছাপাছাপি। **Brim'-less,** *adj.* **Brim'-mer,** *n.* A full cup ; কানায় কানায় পূর্ণ পেয়ালা। **To brim over**—To overflow ; ছাপিয়ে পড়া, উপচিয়া পড়া।

brim'-stōne, *n.* & *adj.* **1.** Sulpher ; গন্ধক, গুল্‌ষারি (মণীঃ), গন্ধপাষাণ (অঃ)

2. A virago ; "A tragedy queen, and a *brimstone* to boot :" আগুণখাকী। **Brimstone-butter-fly**—গন্ধকবৎ পীতবর্ণ প্রজাপতিবিশেষ।

brin'-dĕd, brin'-dled, brin'-dle, *adjs.* Of a brownish or tawny colour with streaks of other colour ; ভিন্নবর্ণের ডোরা বিশিষ্ট পাটল বা পিঙ্গলবর্ণ, শবল। **Brin-dled cow**—শবলী (মঃ উঃ), শবলা (ঐ), চিত্রাঙ্গী গাভী।

brīne, *n.* & *v. t.* **1.** Saltwater ; লোণাজল, লবণোদক। **2.** The sea or ocean ; লবণাম্বুরাশি (রঃ), সমুদ্র, লবণাব্ধি। **3.** Tears (*poet.*) ; অশ্রু-বারি, চোখের জল, নয়নসলিল, অশ্রুজল (কবিতায়)। ***Verb t.*** To steep or saturate in brine ; as, to *brine* hay ; লবণজল দ্বারা সিক্ত করা, লবণ-জলে ডোবান। **Brin'-y,** *adj.* Of, like, pretaining to, brine or the sea ; লবণসম্বন্ধীয়, লবণবৎ, লবণাক্ত, সমুদ্র-সম্বন্ধীয়, সমুদ্রবৎ। **Brine-pan**—বাষ্পী-করণ ক্রিয়াদ্বারা লবণ প্রস্তুতকরণার্থ লৌহ-কটাহ বা অগভীর কুণ্ডবিশেষ। **Brine-pit**—লবণোৎস, লবণকূপ, লবণকুণ্ড।

bring, *v. t.* **1.** To fetch ; to carry ; লইয়া আসা ; আনা, আনয়ন করা। **2.** To procure ; as, to *bring* honours and glory ; প্রাপ্ত হওয়া, লাভ করা, অর্জ্জন করা, পাওয়া। **3.** To persuade or induce ; as, I cannot *bring* myself to believe ; প্ররোচিত বা প্রবর্ত্তিত করা। **4.** To lead ; to conduct ; as, I will *bring* you where you shall have music ; চালিত করা ; লইয়া যাওয়া। **5.** To sell for ; to fetch ; as, what does coal *bring* per ton ; মূল্যে বিক্রীত হওয়া ; দাম হওয়া। **To bring about**—To cause to happen ; to accomplish ; সংঘটন করা, ঘটান ; সাধন করা। **To bring back**—To call to mind ; স্মরণ করা, মনে আনা। To restore ; প্রত্যর্পণ করা, প্রত্যানয়ন করা, ফিরাইয়া দেওয়া। **To bring down**—To cause to come down ; নামান। To kill or wound ; হত বা আহত করা। To humble ; to humiliate ; as, to *bring down* high looks ; অবনত করা, অবনমিত করা ; নামাইয়া দেওয়া, হীন করা, গর্ব্ব খর্ব্ব করা। To lower (price) ; (মূল্য) কমান বা হ্রাস করা। **To bring down the house** (*Colloq.*)—To cause or elicit tumultuous applause ; (চলিতভাষায়) হাততালি এবং বাহবার তুফান ছুটান। **To bring forth**—To give birth to ; to produce ; প্রসব করা ; জন্মান, উৎপাদন করা। **To bring forward**—To exhibit ; to introduce ; প্রদর্শন করা ; উপ-স্থাপিত করা। To carry sum of one page's figures to the next page ; এক পৃষ্ঠার অঙ্কের সমষ্টি অন্য পৃষ্ঠায় টানিয়া আনা, জের টানা, ইজা দেওয়া। To promote ; to forward ; উন্নীত করা ; অগ্রসর করা। **To bring home**—To prove conclusively ; নিঃসংশয়িতরূপে প্রমাণ করা। To cause to appreciate by personal experience ; সম্পূর্ণ হৃদয়ঙ্গম করান। **To bring in**—To introduce, (as bill, custom, etc.) ; উপস্থাপিত করা, প্রবর্ত্তন করা। To import ; আমদানি করা। To pronounce (guilty or not guilty) ; as, to *bring in* a verdict ; (দোষী বা নির্দ্দোষ বলিয়া) ব্যক্ত করা। To take to an appointed place ; কোনও নির্দ্দিষ্ট স্থানে লইয়া যাওয়া। To produce, as income ; to realize, as profit ; (আয় স্বরূপ) উৎপাদন করা ; (মুনাফা বা লাভ স্বরূপ) আদায় করা। **To bring off**—To bear or convey away ; as, to *bring off* man from a wreck ; বহি নিয়া যাওয়া, স্থানান্তরিত করা। To clear from condemnation ; to rescue from wreck, etc. ; (দোষ বা নিন্দা হইতে) মুক্তি বা অব্যাহতি দান করা ; ধ্বংস বা বিনাশ হইতে রক্ষা করা। To conduct enterprise to a success ; (কোন ব্যাপার বা কর্ম্মে) সিদ্ধিলাভ করা। **To bring on**—To cause to advance or begin ; অগ্রসর করান, আরম্ভ করান। To originate ; উদ্ভূত করা, উৎপাদন করা। To induce ; প্রবৃত্তি লওয়ান। **To bring one on one's way**—To accompany or attend one ; সঙ্গী হওয়া, পরিচারক-রূপে সঙ্গে যাওয়া। **To bring out**—To express ; to expose ; ব্যক্ত করা ; প্রকাশ করা। To introduce (a girl) to society ; কোন বালিকাকে সভ্য-সমাজে পরিচিত করাইয়া দেওয়া। To publish ; (পুস্তক) প্রকাশ বা প্রচার করা। **To bring over**—To convey across ; পার করা, অপর তীরে লইয়া যাওয়া। To convert ; to cause to change sides or an opinion ; দীক্ষিত করা ; পক্ষ-পরিবর্ত্তন করান, আত্মপক্ষে আনা, মত পরিবর্ত্তন করান। **To bring round**—To restore to consciousness ; to recover ; চৈতন্য সম্পাদন করা ; আরোগ্য করা, রোগমুক্ত করা, স্বাস্থ্যলাভ করান। **To bring through**—To save ; রক্ষা করা (রোগীকে)। **To bring to**—To check the motion of (a ship by making the sails counteract each other) ; (পাইল সাজাইয়া জাহাজের) গতিরোধ করা। To come to a stop ; থামিয়া যাওয়া। To restore to consciousness ; to resuscitate ; সংজ্ঞা-সম্পাদন করা ; পুনরুজ্জীবিত করা। **To bring to light**—To reveal ; প্রকাশ করা। **To bring to pass**—To cause to happen ; ঘটান, সংঘটন করা। **To bring to play**—To cause to act ; to set in motion ; to give scope to ; কাজ করান ; চালিত করা ; কোন প্রবৃত্তি বা শক্তির বিকাশের জন্য প্রসার দেওয়া। **To bring under**—To subdue ; পরাভূত করা, বশীভূত করা। **To bring up**—To nurse ; to rear ; to educate ; লালন পালন করা ; প্রতি-পালন করা ; শিক্ষা দেওয়া, মানুষ করা। To anchor (ship) ; to come to a stop ; (জাহাজ) নঙ্গর করা ;

থামিয়া যাওয়া। To cause to stop suddenly, (as a horse); as, he *brought up* his horse short; হঠাৎ থামান। To pull up; টানিয়া তোলা। To call attention again to; (কোন বিষয়ে) পুনরায় মনোযোগ আকর্ষণ করা। To raise; as, to *bring up* a subject; উত্থাপন করা। To lay before a meeting; সভায় উপস্থাপিত করা। To continue (accounts, etc.) to a further point; হিসাব টানা, জের টানা। **To bring up the rear**—To come last; সর্ব্বশেষে আসা। **To bring word**—To bring intelligence; সংবাদ আনয়ন করা।

brink, *n.* **1.** The edge or margin of a steep place or abyss; কোন দুরারোহ স্থান বা অতলস্পর্শ খাতের ধার বা কিনারা। **2.** The border of water, especially when steep; as, the *brink* of a river; তীর, কূল, তট, কিনারা, প্রান্ত। **On the brink of**—On the point of; as, *on the brink of* ruin; মুখে, উন্মুখ অবস্থায়।

brio, (*It.*), *n.* (*Mus.*) Vivacity; (সঙ্গীত-শাস্ত্র) সজীবতা।

bri-quette' (-kĕt), **bri'-quet** (-kĕt), *n.* A block of compressed coal-dust (for fuel); সঙ্কাপিত কয়লার চূর্ণের বৃহৎখণ্ড।

brisk, *adj., v. t. & i.* **1.** Lively; active; quick (usually of movement); agile; as, *brisk* pace: *brisk* wind; স্ফূর্ত্তিময়; কর্ম্মঠ, চপল, চটুল, চঞ্চল, চটপটে, চতুর; ত্বরিৎ, ক্ষিপ্র, তৎপর; চঞ্চল, লঘু। **2.** Full of life and spirit; vivacious; প্রাণপূর্ণ, উৎসাহপূর্ণ; তেজস্বী। **3.** Enlivening; keen; as, *brisk* air; স্ফূর্ত্তিপ্রদ; তীব্র, তীক্ষ্ণ। **4.** Effervescing, as liquors; as, *brisk* cider; ফেনায়মান, বুদ্‌বুদায়মান, ফেনিল। ***Verb t. & i.*** (Usually with *up*) To make or become brisk; সজীব বা চটপটে করা বা হওয়া। **Brisk'-ly,** *adv.* In a brisk manner; হন্ হন্ করিয়া। **Brisk'-ness,** *n.*

bris'-kĕt, *n.* That part of the breast of animal which lies next to the ribs; পশুর পঞ্জর-সংলগ্ন বক্ষোমাংস।

bris'-tle (brĭsl), *n., v. t. & i.* **1.** One of the stiff coarse hairs on hog's back and sides; শূকরের পৃষ্ঠ বা পার্শ্বদেশের দৃঢ়লোম, কুঁচি, স্টা (কিরাতঃ)। **2.** A short stiff hair of other animals; the short-cropped beard of man or similar appendage of plants; অপরাপর জন্তুর খর্ব্ব ও সুদৃঢ় লোম; মানুষের ছাঁটা দাড়ি, (উদ্ভিদ-সম্বন্ধে) অনুকণ্টক (সাঃ পঃ)। ***Verb t.*** **1.** To cause to stand upright (hair, etc.); কণ্টকিত করা। **2.** To erect in defiance or anger: অবজ্ঞা বা ক্রোধে কণ্টকিত করা। ***Verb i.*** **1.** To rise up or stand in on end like bristles; কণ্টকিত হইয়া উঠা, রোম কাঁটা দিয়া উঠা, রোম খাড়া হওয়া, রোমাঞ্চিত হওয়া, সংহৃষ্ট হওয়া। **2.** To appear as if covered with bristles; কণ্টকিত বলিয়া বোধ হওয়া। **—tled,** *adj.* **—tli-ness,** *n.* **—tly,** *adj.* **To bristle up**—To show anger or defiance; ক্রোধ বা স্পর্দ্ধায় শরীর কণ্টকিত হইয়া উঠা। **To set up one's bristle**—To show temper; ক্রোধে দেহ কণ্টকিত হওয়া।

Bri'-tain (-tăn), *n.* (also *Great Britain*) England, Wales, and Scotland; শ্বেতদ্বীপ। **Great Britain**—ইংলণ্ড, ওয়েল্‌স্ ও স্কটলণ্ড। **Greater Britain**—ইংলণ্ড, ওয়েল্‌স্, স্কটলণ্ড ও উপনিবেশ সমূহ। **—tan-ic,** *adj.*

Bri-tăn'-ni-ă, *n.* **1.** The personification of Britain; ব্রিটে জননী। **2.** A white metal, alloy of tin, antimony, bismuth, copper, etc., resembling silver, (also called Britannia metal); শুভ্রবর্ণ মিশ্র-ধাতুবিশেষ।

Brit'-ish, *adj.* **1.** Of the ancient Britons; প্রাচীন ব্রিটিশবাসী সম্বন্ধীয়। **2.** Of Great Britain or its inhabitants, (especially in political connexion); গ্রেটব্রিটেন বা তদ্দেশবাসি সম্বন্ধীয় (বিশেষভাবে রাজনীতি সম্পর্কে) **The British**—The British soldiers, people, etc.; ইংরেজ সৈন্য বা ইংলণ্ড, স্কটলণ্ড এবং আয়র্লণ্ডের অধিবাসী। **—er,** *n.* A native of Great Britain, as opposed to American; গ্রেটব্রিটেনের অধিবাসী। **—ism,** *n.* A word, phrase or idiom used in Great Britain and not in the United States, etc.; যে শব্দ, বাক্যাংশ, বা বাগ্‌ধারা কেবলমাত্র গ্রেট্‌ব্রিটেনে ব্যবহৃত হয় (মার্কিণ যুক্তরাজ্যে নহে)।

Bri'-tŏn, *n.* One of the races found by Romans in South England; রোমানগণ দক্ষিণ ইংলণ্ডে যে সমস্ত জাতি প্রাপ্ত হন—তাহাদের অন্যতম। **2.** A native of Great Britain or of the British Empire; গ্রেটব্রিটেন বা ব্রিটীশ-সাম্রাজ্যের অধিবাসী। **North Briton**—Scotsman; স্কট্‌লণ্ডবাসী।

brit'-tle, *adj.* Easily broken; fragile; ভঙ্গুর, ক্ষণ-ভঙ্গুর, ভঙ্গদ, ঠুনকা (*Colloq.*), ঠুনকো (ঐ); ভঙ্গপ্রবণ। **—ness,** *n.*

britzs'-kă (brĭts-), **britz'-kă, brits'-kă,** *n.* A long open carriage that may be closed at pleasure; একপ্রকার সুদীর্ঘ উন্মুক্ত শকট—ইহা যখন ইচ্ছা বন্ধ করিতে পারা যায়।

broach (brōch), *n. & v. t.* **1.** A spit for roasting meat; শিক্‌ কাবাবের শলা। **2.** A spire or steeple; গির্জ্জার চূড়া। **3.** A boring bit; ছিদ্র করিবার যন্ত্র। **4.** A start of a young stag's head; তরুণ হরিণের নবোদ্গত শৃঙ্গ। **5.** A rod or pin sharpened at both ends used by thatchers; ফোড়কাঠি। ***Verb t.*** **1.** To tap a cask; মদ্যাদি বাহির করিবার জন্য পিপায় ছিদ্র করা। **2.** To begin discussion of (a subject) ; "Failing in that we *broached* the third point ; to moot ; to publish first ; (কোন বিষয়ে) আলোচনা আরম্ভ করা, কথা পাড়া ; কোন বিষয়ে আলোচনার জন্য প্রশ্ন উত্থাপন করা ; সর্ব্বপ্রথম প্রকাশ করা। **Broach'-er,** *n.*

broach (brōch), *v. i.* & *t.* To turn a vessel to windward, (used only in the phrase *to broach to*) ; বাতাসের অভিমুখে জাহাজ ঘুরাইয়া রাখা।

broad (bräd), *adj.* **1.** Extended from side to side ; wide ; প্রশস্ত ; বিস্তৃত, চওড়া। **2.** In breadth ; as, this wall is 6ft. *broad* ; প্রস্থে। **3.** Extensive ; as, *broad* lands ; বিস্তীর্ণ। **4.** Full ; clear ; explicit ; as, *broad* day-light (স্পষ্ট দিবালোক) : *broad* facts, hints, etc. ; পরিপূর্ণ ; পরিষ্কার, স্বচ্ছ ; স্পষ্ট, সুপ্রকট। **5.** Coarse ; indelicate ; vulgar ; as, a *broad* story : *broad* joke or humour ; স্থূল ; শীলতা-বর্জ্জিত ; অভব্য অমার্জ্জিত। **6.** Tolerant ; liberal ; as, a *broad* rule ; পরমত-সহিষ্ণু ; উদার। **7.** Bold or vigorous in style or effect ; (রচনা, চিত্রাদির ভাব প্রভৃতি সম্পর্কে) সুস্পষ্ট, সুপরিস্ফুট। **8.** Plain strongly marked; as, *broad* Scotch accent ; স্পষ্ট ; সুস্পষ্ট। **9.** General ; comprehensive ; সাধারণ ; ব্যাপক। **10.** Main ; essential ; as, *broad* outlines ; প্রধান ; মৌলিক। **Broad'-ways, Broad'-wise,** *advs.* **Broad-arrow**—(↑) ব্রিটিশ শাসনতন্ত্রের দ্রব্যজাতের উপরি প্রদত্ত বাণাগ্রাকৃতি চিহ্নবিশেষ। **Broad-bill**—The wild duck ; বন্য হংসবিশেষ। **Broad-blown**—Full blown ; পূর্ণ বিকশিত। **Broad-brim**—A broad-brimmed quaker hat ; quaker ; কোয়েকার সম্প্রদায় ভুক্ত ব্যক্তিগণের পরিধেয় প্রশস্ত-প্রান্ত টুপিবিশেষ ; কোয়েকার সম্প্রদায়ভুক্ত ব্যক্তি। **Broad church**—ইংলণ্ডীয় ধর্ম্ম-সমাজের উদারমতাবলম্বী বিভাগ বিশেষ। **Broad-cloth** — বনাত। **Broad-gauge** — See GAUGE. **Broad-glass**—বাতায়নের কাচ। **Broad-sheet** — একদিকে মুদ্রিত বৃহৎ কাগজ-খণ্ড। **Broad-silk** — রেশমের কাপড় (অর্থাৎ ফিতা নহে)। **Broad-sword**—A sword with a broad-blade ; প্রশস্ত ফলক-বিশিষ্ট তরবারি।

Broadsword.

broad, *n.* & *adv.* **1.** The broad part of anything ; as, the *broad* of an oar ; কোন বস্তুর প্রশস্ত অংশ। **2.** An expansion of a river ; নদীর বিস্তৃত অংশ। ***Adv.*** **1.** Widely ; as, to speak *broad* ; বিস্তৃতভাবে। **2.** Plainly ; স্পষ্টরূপে। **Broad awake** — Wide awake ; সম্পূর্ণ সজাগ।

broad'-căst (bräd-), *n., adj., adv.* & *v. t.* A scattering of seeds with the hand ; হস্তদ্বারা বীজ বিক্ষেপ। ***Adj.*** Scattered wide ; widely diffused ; যথেচ্ছ বিক্ষিপ্ত (যেমন বপনকালীন বীজাদি) ; বহুদূর বিস্তৃত। ***Adv.*** By scattering freely with the hand ; in a widely dispersed manner ; "For sowing *broadcast* seeds of crime ;" হস্তদ্বারা যথেচ্ছভাবে বিক্ষেপ পূর্ব্বক ; বহু বিস্তৃতভাবে। ***Verb t.*** To sow in this manner ; to disseminate widely ; হস্তদ্বারা চতুর্দ্দিকে ছড়াইয়া বীজ বপন করা ; দেশময় ছড়াইয়া দেওয়া।

broad'-en (brädn), *v. i.* & *t.* To grow broad ; to become broader ; প্রশস্ত হইয়া উঠা ; প্রশস্ততর হওয়া। ***Verb t.*** To make broad or broader ; প্রশস্ত বা বিস্তৃততর করা।

broad'-sīde (bräd-), *n.* **1.** The side of a ship above the water ; জলের উপরিস্থিত জাহাজের অংশ, পোতপার্শ্ব। **2.** A discharge of all the guns on one side of a ship at one time ; জাহাজের এক পার্শ্বস্থ কামান শ্রেণী হইতে যুগপৎ গোলা-বর্ষণ। **3.** Same as *broad-sheet* above.

brŏb'-dĭng-năg, (Often incorrectly BROBDIGNAG) *n.* The land of giants ; অতিকায় মানবের দেশ। (Swift কৃত Gulliver's Travels নামক গ্রন্থ-বর্ণিত মহাকায় মানবের দেশ।) **—nag'-i-an,** *adj.* Colossal ; gigantic ; "The houses...have the appearance of *brobdingnagian* bee-hives ;" অতিকায়, প্রকাণ্ড ; সুবিশাল, বিরাট।

brō-cāde', *n.* **1.** A silk or satin stuff woven with raised figures and gold and silver threads ; জরীর গুলবাহার কাপড়, জরীর বুঁটাদার রেশমী কাপড়। **2.** (In India) A cloth of gold and silver ; কিংখাব, কার্ম্মিক বস্ত্র (আঃ বঃ)। **—cad'-ed,** *adj.*

brō-cāde', *v. t.* To work with raised pattern ; রেশমের কাপড়ের উপর জরীর ফুল পাতা প্রভৃতি তোলা।

brŏc'-ârd, *n.* An elementary law or principle ; a short proverbial rule ; a canon ; মূল নীতি-বাক্য ; মূল বিধি-বাক্য ; শাস্ত্রীয় বিধি বা ব্যবস্থা

brŏc'-cō-li, *n.* A cultivated cabbage with edible flower-head ; ফুলকপি বিশেষ, শিগু।

brō-chure' (-shôr), *n.* A stitched booklet ; ক্ষুদ্রপুস্তিকা।

brŏck (brŏk), *n.* **1.** A badger ; বিজ্জু। **2.** A dirty stinking fellow ; নোংরা লোক।

brŏck'-ĕt, *n.* A red male deer two years old with straight horns ; দ্বিবর্ষ বয়স্ক সরল-শৃঙ্গ লোহিত-বর্ণ পুংজাতীয় মৃগশিশু।

brôg, *n.* An awl ; তুরপুন।

brogue (brōg), **1.** Coarse shoe ; এক প্রকার নিকৃষ্ট জুতা। **2.** The pronunciation of English peculiar to the Irish ; আয়র্লণ্ডবাসীদের ইংরেজী উচ্চারণ।

broil (broyl), *n., v. t.* & *i.* A quarrel ; a tumult ; কলহ, ঝগড়া ; গণ্ডগোল, চেঁচামিচি (*Colloq.*)।

broil (brŏyl), *v. t.* & *i.* **1.** To cook meat on fire or gridiron ; অগ্নিতে বা ঝাঁঝরীর উপর মাংস পাক করা। **2.** To make very hot (of person in the sun, etc.) ; রৌদ্রতাপে উত্তপ্ত করা, দগ্ধ করা। ***Verb i.*** **1.** To be subjected to a strong heat, like meat over the fire ; দগ্ধ হওয়া, ভর্জ্জিত হওয়া। **2.** To be greatly heated ; to be greatly excited, as by passion ; as, he *broiled* with impatience ; অত্যন্ত উত্তপ্ত হওয়া ; অতিমাত্রায় উত্তেজিত হওয়া।

broil (brŏyl), *n.* Broiled meat ; ঝলসানো মাংস।

bro'-ken (brökn), *adj.* **1.** Divided into fragments ; as, a *broken* dish ; ভাঙ্গা, ভগ্ন। **2.** Rough ; as, a *broken* ground ; বন্ধুর, অসমান। **3.** Strained apart ; as, *broken* friendship ; বিচ্ছিন্ন। **4.** Made infirm or weak ; as, a *broken* soldier ; অবসন্ন, ভগ্নদেহ, জরাজীর্ণ। **5.** Subjugated ; as, a *broken* horse ; বশীকৃত। **6.** Crushed ; blighted ; as, her *broken* love or life ; নিষ্পেষিত, চূর্ণবিচূর্ণ ; বিশুষ্ক, বিনষ্ট। **7.** Violated ; as, a *broken* promise : a *broken* law ; লঙ্ঘিত। **8.** Ruined financially ; made bankrupt ; as, a *broken* bank ; সর্ব্বস্বান্ত, নিঃস্ব ; দাউলিয়া অবস্থা-প্রাপ্ত। **9.** Imperfectly spoken, as by a foreigner or on account of emotion ; as, *broken* words at parting ; ভাঙ্গা-ভাঙ্গা, (আবেগ বশতঃ) গদ্‌গদ্। **—ly,** *adv.* **Broken-down**—Broken to pieces ; খণ্ড বিখণ্ডীকৃত। Decayed ; জীর্ণ, শীর্ণ। Reduced to poverty ; নিঃস্ব, সর্ব্বস্বান্ত। **Broken English** — Imperfect English ; ত্রুটীযুক্ত ইংরেজী, ভাঙ্গাভাঙ্গা ইংরেজী। **Broken-hearted**—ভগ্নহৃদয়, ভগ্নমানস (মঃ উঃ), ভগ্নাশ। **Broken-meat**—Fragments of meat or other food ; মাংস বা অন্যান্য খাদ্যদ্রব্যের খণ্ড। **Broken money**—Small change ; ভাঙ্গা পয়সা, খুচরা পয়সা। **Broken numbers**—ভগ্নাংশ। **Broken sleep**—ভাঙ্গা ঘুম। **Broken tea**—চালিবার সময় চালুনীর নীচে যে চা পড়ে। **Broken weather**—আকাশের অনিশ্চিতাবস্থা। **Broken wind**—অশ্বের শ্বাসকষ্ট রোগ।

brö'-kêr, *n.* **1.** A dealer in secondhand furniture, etc. ; পুরাতন গৃহসজ্জা বা আসবাব বিক্রেতা। **2.** A middle man or intermediary in bargains ; দালাল। **3.** Agent ; গোমস্তা, কার্য্যকারক। **—age,** *n.* **1.** The business of a broker ; দালালের কাজ। **2.** The commission charged for a transaction by a broker ; দালালি।

brö'-măl, *n.* A chocolate preparation from cocoa ; কোকোয়া হইতে প্রস্তুত পানীয় বিশেষ।

brö'-mă, *n.* A colourless oily liquid obtained by the action of bromine on alcohol ; সুরাবীর্য্যের উপর অরুণকের ক্রিয়ার ফলে যে বর্ণহীন তৈলবৎ তরল পদার্থ প্রাপ্ত হওয়া যায়।

brö-mă-tŏl'-ŏ-ğў, *n.* The science of aliments ; খাদ্য-বিজ্ঞান।

brö'-mic, *adj.* Containing bromine in chemical composition ; রাসায়নিক সংমিশ্রণে অরুণক বিশিষ্ট।

brö-mide', **brö-mide'-print,** *n.* A photograph on paper coated with emulsion of bromide of silver in gelatine ; ব্রমাইড্ অব্ সিলভার এবং শিরিষের মিশ্রদ্বারা বিলেপিত কাগজের উপর যে আলোক চিত্র পরিস্ফুট করা হয়। **Bromide enlargement**—উক্ত প্রকার কাগজের উপর বিবর্দ্ধিত আলোক চিত্র।

brö'-mine (-mîn), *n.* A non-metallic element ; অধাতব মূলপদার্থ বিশেষ, অরুণ (সাঃ পঃ), অরুণক (ঐ) বরমীন (মনীঃ), ব্রম (হিঃ কোঃ)।

brŏn'-chi (brŏng-), **bron'-chi-ă** (brŏng-), *ns. pl.* (Singular BRONCHUS) The ramifications of the windpipe which carry air into the lungs ; কণ্ঠনালীর শাখা প্রশাখা, যাহা ফুসফুসে প্রসারিত হইয়াছে। **—al,** *adj.*

bron'-chī-tis (brŏng-) *n.* An inflammation of the bronchial mucous membrane ; কণ্ঠনালীর শাখা প্রশাখার শ্লৈষ্মিক ঝিল্লীর প্রদাহ, বায়ুনলীভুজপ্রদাহ (হঃ চঃ)।

bron'-chö-çēle (brŏng-), *n.* A swelling of the thyroid gland ; গলগণ্ড (হঃ চঃ)।

bron'chŏph'-ŏ-nў (brŏng-), *n.* (*Med.*) A loud, clear, thrilling sound in the chest detected by auscultation ; (ভৈষজ্য-শাস্ত্র) রোগীর বক্ষঃস্থল কর্ণ বা আকর্ণন যন্ত্রদ্বারা পরীক্ষা করিলে, যেন নলের ভিতর দিয়া কথা বলিতেছে এইরূপ অনুভব।

bron'-chŏt-ŏ-mў (brŏng-), *n.* (*Surg.*) An incision into the windpipe ; (অস্ত্রোপচার বিদ্যা) ছুরিকাদি অস্ত্রদ্বারা শ্বাসনালীর উপরিভাগ মাত্র কর্ত্তন।

brŏnze *n., adj.* & *v. t.* **1.** A brown alloy of copper and tin ; তাম্র ও রঙ্গমিশ্রিত ধাতুবিশেষ, বর্ত্তলোহ। **2.** A statue, bust, etc., cast or wrought in bronze; "Old Roman and French *bronzes*" বর্ত্তলোহ নির্ম্মিত বা বর্ত্তলোহের ঢালাই-করা মূর্ত্তি, প্রভৃতি। **3.** The colour of bronze ; a colour to imitate bronze ; বর্ত্তলোহের বর্ণ ; বর্ত্তলোহের অনুকরণকারী বর্ণ। ***Adj.*** Made of bronze ; coloured like bronze ; বর্ত্তলোহনির্ম্মিত ; বর্ত্তলোহবৎ বর্ণে রঞ্জিত। ***Verb t.*** **1.** To give the appearance of bronze to ; to make brown ; বর্ত্তলোহবৎ করা ; কপিশবর্ণ করা, পিঙ্গলবর্ণ করা। **2.** To make brown by exposure of the skin to the sun ; রৌদ্রতাপে অনাবৃত রাখিয়া কপিশবর্ণ করা। **3.** To make hard or unfeeling ; "The lawyer who *bronzes* his bosom instead of his forehead ;" নির্ম্মম বা কঠিন করা। **Bronz'-y,** *adj.* **Bronze age**—দ্বাপর যুগ। **powder**—A metallic imitating bronze ; বর্ত্তলৌহ অনুকরণের জন্য ধাতু-চূর্ণ।

brooch (brōch), *n.* **1.** An ornamental clasp with a pin for fastening dress ; পরিচ্ছদ আঁটিবার জন্য শঙ্কুযুক্ত এবং শোভাজনক আঁকড়া বিশেষ। **2.** A painting all of one colour ; একরঙ্গের চিত্র।

brōōd, *n., v. i. & t.* **1.** The birds or other egg-produced animals of one hatching ; যে কয়েকটী অণ্ডজ প্রাণী বা পক্ষিশাবক এককালে তা(প) দিয়া ফুটান হয়। **2.** Offspring ; "The lion roars and gluts his tawny *brood* ;" শাবক, ছানা, বাচ্চা, পোত, অর্ভক। **3.** (Usually contempt. colloq.) Children ; as, a woman with a *brood* of children ; (সাধারণতঃ অবজ্ঞার্থে) একপাল ছেলে মেয়ে, কাচ্চা বাচ্চার দল। **4.** A number ; "New *brood* of false witnesses ;" এক দল। **5.** Species ; বিশেষ জীবশ্রেণী। ***Verb i.*** **1.** To sit, as hen on eggs ; মুর্গী প্রভৃতির ন্যায় ডিমের উপর বসা। **2.** To hang close over or on, as night, etc. ; পক্ষের ছায়ায় আবৃত করা, উপরে চাপিয়া বসা। **3.** To meditate sullenly ; as, to *brood* over misfortune ; উদ্বিগ্ন বা বিষণ্ণ মনে চিন্তা করা, মনে গর্ গর্ করা। ***Verb t.*** **1.** To hatch ; to sit over, cover, and cherish ; তা' দেওয়া ; বাচ্চার উপর বসা, পক্ষদ্বারা আচ্ছাদিত করা বা পালন করা। **2.** To think anxiously or moodily upon ; উদ্বিগ্ন মনে চিন্তা করা। **Brood'-i-ness,** *n.* **Brood'-ing-ly,** *adv.* **Brood'-y,** *adj.* Wishing to sit or incubate, (said of hen) ; তা(প) দিতে বা ডিম ফুটাইতে ইচ্ছুক।

brōōk, *n.* A small stream, (smaller than a river but larger than a rivulet) ; ক্ষুদ্র স্রোতস্বতী। **Brook'-let,** *n.* Rivulet ; নালা।

brōōk, *v. t.* To put up with ; to tolerate; সহ্য করা, সহিয়া নেওয়া; সহা (প্রায়শঃ নাস্তিবাচক বাক্যে ব্যবহৃত হয়।)

brōōm, *n. & v. t.* **1.** A yellow-flowered shrub growing on sandy banks or waste grounds ; বালুকাভূমি বা পতিতজমিতে উৎপন্ন পীতপুষ্প গুল্ম বিশেষ, দেবধান্য (যোঃ), দেবধান (ঐ)। **2.** A besom ; শোধনী, ঝাঁটা, খেংরা (*Colloq.*), ঝাড়ু, মার্জ্জনী। ***Verb t.*** To sweep with a broom ; ঝাঁটা দ্বারা ঝাড়ু দেওয়া, ঝাঁটান, ঝাঁট দেওয়া। **Broom'-y,** *adj.* **Broomstick**—সম্মার্জ্জনী দণ্ড, ঝাঁটার দাণ্ডা। **New broom**—A newly appointed official ; নব নিযুক্ত কর্ম্মচারী। **New brooms sweep clean**—Those newly appointed to an office find fault with and want to sweep away old customs ; নবনিযুক্ত কর্ম্মচারিগণ দোষ ধরিয়া থাকেন এবং প্রাচীন রীতিনীতির আমূল পরিবর্ত্তন সাধন করিতে তৎপরতা প্রদর্শন করেন। **To marry over the broomstick**—To be irregularly married ; রীতিবিরুদ্ধরূপে বিবাহিত হওয়া।

brōse *n.* A Scotch dish made by pouring boiling water on oatmeal ; যইএর ছাতুতে অত্যুষ্ণ জল ঢালিয়া যে একপ্রকার খাদ্য প্রস্তুত করা হয়। **Athole brose**—A mixture of whisky and honey ; হুইস্কী এবং মধুমিশ্রিত পানীয় বিশেষ।

brŏth, *n.* A decoction of vegetables and meat in water ; water in which something, especially meat, has been boiled ; a thin soup ; মাংসাদির যূষ ; ক্কাথ, সুরুয়া, মাংসরস ; পাতলা সূপ।

brŏth'-ĕl, *n.* A house of ill-fame ; বেশ্যালয়, গণিকাভবন, বেশ (কথা সঃ), বেশ্যাস (অঃ), বেশগৃহ, চাকলা (ফঃ ইঃ), বারাঙ্গনালয়, বারবধূগৃহ।

broth'-ĕr (brŭth-), **1.** A male person who has the same father and mother with another ; ভ্রাতা, সহোদর, সোদর। [*Half brother*—A male by one of the parents only ; বৈমাত্রেয় (রঃ), বৈপিত্রেয় ভ্রাতা, অন্য পিতৃজভ্রাতা।] **2.** A fellow member of a religious society ; ধর্ম্মভ্রাতা, এক ধর্ম্মসম্প্রদায়ভুক্ত ব্যক্তি। **3.** One of the same society, rank, profession, or denomination ; স্বসম্প্রদায়ভুক্ত ব্যক্তি, স্বশ্রেণীর লোক, সমব্যবসায়ী, এক নাম বা আখ্যাধারী। **4.** Vocative of sovereigns to each other ; রাজন্যবর্গের পরস্পরের প্রতি সম্বোধন পদ। **5.** One that resembles another in manners and disposition ; স্বভাব ও আচরণে সমতুল্য ব্যক্তি। [*Pl.* BROTHERS, BRETHREN. Brethren is used only in the wider meanings of the word.] **–less,** *adj.* **–like,** *adj.* **–ly,** *adj.* Belonging to a brother ; kind ; affectionate ; ভ্রাতৃসম্বন্ধীয়, ভ্রাতৃক, ভ্রাতৃসুলভ ; সদয় ; স্নেহপূর্ণ। **Brother Benedict**—A married man ; বিবাহিত পুরুষ। **Brother Birch**—A fellow school master ; সহযোগী গুরুমহাশয়। **Brother blade**—A fellow soldier ; সহযোদ্ধা। **Brother-in-law**—The brother of one's husbond or wife ; the husband of one's sister ; শ্যালক, দেবর, ভাশুর; ভগিনীপতি। **Brother germain**—সহোদর ভ্রাতা। **Brother Jonathan**—An American ; আমেরিকাবাসী। **Brother-quill**—A fellow author ; সহগ্রন্থকার। **Elder brother**—অগ্রজ। **Uterine brother**—অন্য পিতৃজ ভ্রাতা। **Younger brother**—অনুজ।

broth'-ĕr-hōōd (brŭth-), *n.* **1.** Fraternal tie; friendly alliance ; ভ্রাতৃত্ব, সৌভ্রাত্র ; মৈত্রী। **2.** Companionship ; সহকারিতা, সাহচর্য্য। **3.** An association for any purpose ; as, the *brotherhood* of St. George ; সমিতি, সম্প্রদায়, সঙ্ঘ। **4.** A class of individuals of the same profession or occupation ; as, the legal or medical *brotherhood;* সমব্যবসায়ী লোক বৃন্দ, এক শ্রেণীভুক্ত ব্যক্তিবর্গ।

brough′-am (brô-ăm or brôm), *n.* A one-horse closed carriage ; এক ঘোড়ার (ঢাকা) গাড়ী। [After the first Lord Brougham.]

brow, *n.* 1. The prominent ridge over the eye ; the arch of hair over eye ; ভ্রূ ; ভ্রূলতা, ভ্রূধনু। 2. Forehead ; কপাল, ললাট, ভাল। 3. The edge or projection of a cliff ; as, the *brow* of a precipice ; শৈলপ্রান্ত, দুরারোহ পর্ব্বতের প্রলম্বিত অংশ। 4. The upper portion of a slope (in road) ; প্রবণ ভূমির উর্দ্ধভাগ। 5. (*Fig.*) The general air of the countenance ; "Satan with contemptuous *brow* replied ;" (লক্ষণায়) আকার, ইঙ্গিত। **Brow′-less,** *adj.* Without shame ; নির্লজ্জ। **To knit the brow**—ভ্রূকুঞ্চিত করা, ভ্রূভঙ্গী করা।

brow′-beat (-bēt), *v. i.* To bear down with haughty stern looks and words ; as, to *browbeat* a witness ; চোখ রাঙ্গাইয়া বা ধমক দিয়া দমান বা দাবিয়া রাখা।

brown, *adj., n., v. t. & i.* 1. Of the colour given by mixing orange and black ; বাদামি, পিঙ্গল, কপিশ, কটা। 2. Dark-complexioned ; sun-burnt ; অগৌরবর্ণ ; রৌদ্র-দগ্ধ। *Noun.* 1. A colour of various shades resulting from the mixture of red, black and yellow ; কপিলবর্ণ, কপিশবর্ণ, পিঙ্গলবর্ণ, গোমূত্রবর্ণ (সাঃ পঃ) খদিরবর্ণ (ঐ)। 2. The brown pigment ; কপিশবর্ণ রঞ্জন পদার্থ। 3. (*Slang*) A copper coin ; (ইতর ভাষায়) তাম্রমুদ্রা। *Verb t. & i.* To make or become brown ; পিঙ্গলবর্ণ করা বা হওয়া। **Brown′-ish,** *adj.* Slightly brown ; ঈষৎ পিঙ্গল, আকপিশ। **Brown′-ness,** *n.* **Brown Bess**—প্রাচীনকালে ব্যবহৃত বন্দুকবিশেষ। **Brown bread**—আচালা ময়দার রুটী, লালরুটী। **Brown hemp**—মেস্তাপাট (বেলঃ)। **Brown, Jones, and Robinson**—মধ্যবিত্ত শ্রেণীর ইংরেজ প্রতিনিধি। **Brown paper**—মোটা কাগজ, মুড়িবার কাগজ। **Brown study** — Absent-minded reverie ; now esp. an idle and purposeless reverie ; অন্য মনস্কভাবে চিন্তা ; জাগ্রৎ স্বপ্ন, দিবাস্বপ্ন। **Brown sugar**—অর্দ্ধ পরিষ্কৃত চিনি, লাল চিনি। **To astonish the Browns**—কোন ব্যক্তির পক্ষে বিরক্তিকর হইতে পারে, তদ্বিষয়ে গ্রাহ্য না করিয়া কোন কথা বলা বা কায করা। **To do brown**—To cheat ; ছলনা করা, চোখে ধূলি দেওয়া।

brown′-ie (-ĭ), *n.* 1. A domestic spirit or goblin of benevolent character doing household work secretly ; গৃহস্থের মঙ্গলকারী দেবযোনি বিশেষ, উক্ত দেবযোনি গোপনে গৃহকার্য্য সমাধা করিয়া রাখে।

browse, *n., v. i. & t.* 1. Tender branches and shoots of trees and shrubs fit for cattle to eat ; গবাদি পশুর খাদ্যোপযোগী বৃক্ষ গুল্মাদির কোমল শাখা এবং পল্লব। 2. The act of browsing ; গবাদি পশুর কোমল শাখা পল্লব প্রভৃতি ভক্ষণ। *Verb i.* To pasture ; to feed on the shoots and leaves of plants ; চরা ; তরুণ শাখা পল্লবাদি ভক্ষণ করা। *Verb t.* To feed thus ; গোচারণ করা, চরান, গবাদি পশুকে কোমল শাখা পল্লবাদি ভক্ষণ করান।

bru′-in (brô-), *n.* A bear ; ভল্লুক, ঋক্ষ। "Reynard the fox" নামক উপকথার ভল্লুকের নাম হইতে গৃহীত।

bruise (brōz), *n., v. t. & i.* A hurt with a blunt or heavy instrument ; a contusion ; ভোতা এবং ভারি অস্ত্রের আঘাত ; আঘাত, চোট, ঘৃষ্ট ব্রণ (হঃ চঃ), কালশিরা (ঐ)। *Verb t.* 1. To crush by beating, pounding or squeezing ; to contuse ; as, to *bruise* the bark of a tree with a stone ; ছেঁচা, মাড়া ; থেঁতলান। 2. To batter (wood, metal, etc.) ; পিটান, কুটা। 3. To pound ; to grind small ; গুঁড়া বা চূর্ণ করা ; খণ্ড খণ্ড করা। 4. To ride recklessly, (with *along*) ; দিগ্‌বিদিক শূন্য হইয়া অশ্বচালনা করা। 5. (*Fig.*) To disable ; (লক্ষণায়) অপারগ করা, অক্ষম করা। *Verb i.* To box ; to fight with the fists ; মুষ্টিযুদ্ধ করা ; ঘুষাঘুষি করা। **Bruis′-er,** *n.* 1. One who or that which bruises ; কুট্টক, প্রহারকারী। 2. A boxer ; a prize-fighter ; মুষ্টিযুদ্ধকারী ; মল্ল।

bruit (brôt), *n. & v. t.* (*Archaic*) A report ; rumour ; (অপ্রচলিত) সংবাদ ; জনরব, রটনা। *Verb t.* (*Archaic*) To spread report abroad ; to noise abroad ; (অপ্রচলিত) সংবাদ প্রচার করা ; রটনা করা।

bru-maire, (*F.*), *n.* The second month of the calendar adopted by the French Republic ; ফরাসী সাধারণ তন্ত্রদ্বারা পরিগৃহীত পঞ্জিকার দ্বিতীয় মাস।

brū′-măl, *adj.* Belonging to the winter ; শীতকালীন।

brŭm′-mă-gĕm, *adj.* (*Slang & Colloq.*) Showy but worthless ; sham ; counterfeit ; (ইতরভাষায়, চলিতভাষায়) চটকদার, জমকালো ; কৃত্রিম ; মেকি, ঝুঁটা। [Birmingham নগরে নানা প্রকার চটকদার জিনিষ প্রস্তুত ও বিক্রীত হয় বলিয়া Brummagem (Birmingham শব্দের অপভ্রংশ) শব্দে ঐ প্রকার জিনিষ বুঝায়।]

bru′-mous (brô-mŭs), *adj.* Wintry ; foggy ; শীতকালীন ; কুজ্ঝটিকাচ্ছন্ন।

bru-nette′ (brô-nĕt), *n. & adj.* A girl or woman with a somewhat brown or dark colour ; শ্যামাঙ্গী, শ্যামা। *Adj.* Having a dark tint ; তাদৃশ বর্ণ বিশিষ্ট।

brŭnt, *n.* 1. The heat of an onset or battle ; যুদ্ধ বা আক্রমণের প্রচণ্ড অবস্থা। 2. The force of a blow ; as, the heavy *brunt* of a cannon ball ; a shock of any kind ; আঘাতের চোট ; ধাক্কা। **To bear the brunt of**—To endure the main shock or force of; (কোন কিছুর) প্রচণ্ডতা বা প্রধান বেগ সহ্য করা, বড় ধাক্কা সাম্‌লান।

brŭsh, *n., v. t.* & *i.* **1.** An implement for sweeping or rubbing, generally made of bristles, hair, wire, etc.; as, a cloth *brush*; বুরুস, কুঁচি, মার্জ্জনী, অবলেখন (কৌশঃ)। **2.** A kind of hair-pencil used by painters; তুলিকা, ইষিকা, চিত্রকরের বর্ত্তি। **3.** A painter; চিত্রকর। **4.** The tail of a fox; শৃগাল-পুচ্ছ। **5.** The act of brushing; as, to give one's clothes a *brush*; বুরুস লাগান, বুরুস করণ। **6.** Skirmish; a collision; as, to have a *brush* with the enemy; খণ্ড-যুদ্ধ, ডিম্ব (মঃ উঃ); সংঘর্ষ। **7.** A thicket; ঝোপ, গুল্ম। **8.** (*Electricity*) A brushlike discharge of sparks; বুরুসবৎ তাড়িৎস্ফুলিঙ্গ নির্গম। **9.** A piece of metal ending in wires or strips securing good metallic connexion; প্রান্তদেশে তার বা ধাতুর ফালি সংযুক্ত ধাতু খণ্ড—ইহা দ্বারা উৎকৃষ্ট ধাতব সংযোগ সংসাধিত হয়। **10.** A quick ride; "Let us enjoy a *brush* across the country;" দ্রুত অশ্বচালনা। **11.** A striated bundle of light-rays, usually of feeble intensity; আলোক-রশ্মিচ্ছটা—সাধারণতঃ অপ্রখর হইয়া থাকে। ***Verb t.*** **1.** To sweep or rub with a brush; বুরুস করা, অবলেখন করা। **2.** To graze or touch lightly in passing; স্পর্শ করিয়া বা ছুঁইয়া যাওয়া। **3.** To paint with a brush; তূলিকাদ্বারা চিত্রিত করা। **4.** To ruffle; to excite; ব্যস্তসমস্ত করা; উত্তেজিত করা। ***Verb i.*** To move in haste; to move lightly; as, to *brush* past a person; ঝাঁ করিয়া চলিয়া যাওয়া; নিঃশব্দ পদসঞ্চারে চলিয়া যাওয়া। **Brush-burn**—ঘর্ষণজনিত ক্ষত, ঘৃষ্ট ব্রণ। **To brush along**—To move swiftly; হন্‌হন্‌ করিয়া চলিয়া যাওয়া। **To brush away**—To remove as with a brush; (কুঁচিদ্বারা) ঝাড়িয়া ফেলা। (*Fig.*) To ignore; to pass over; (লক্ষণায়) অগ্রাহ্য করা; উপেক্ষা করা। **To brush on**—To move on; অগ্রসর হওয়া। **To brush over**—To paint lightly; ফিকে রঙ্গদ্বারা চিত্রিত করা। **To brush up**—To furbish; to renew; to improve; মাজিয়া ঘসিয়া লওয়া, চক্‌চকে করা; নূতন করা; উৎকর্ষ সাধন করা, চান্‌কান, রঙ্গ ফেরান, জিলা করা। (*Fig.*) To renew one's memory of; (লক্ষণায়) স্মরণ করাইয়া দেওয়া।

brŭsh'-wood (-wûd), *n.* **1.** Small trees and shrubs growing together; ঝোপ, গুল্ম। **2.** Branches of trees cut off; গাছের ছোট ছোট কাটা ডাল।

brusque (brŭsk), *adj.* Blunt; abrupt in manner; rude; as, a *brusque* man: *brusque* style; রোখা; রুক্ষ, অশিষ্ট, অভব্য; রূঢ়। **Brusque'-ly,** *adv.* **Brusque'-ness, Brusque'-rie,** *ns.*

Brŭs'-sĕls, *n.* A city of Belgium giving its name to a kind of carpet, a kind of lace, etc.; বেলজিয়াম দেশের প্রধান নগর,—উক্ত নগরীতে প্রস্তুত গালিচা বা ফিতা। **Brussels-sprouts** — A kind of cabbage; একপ্রকার বাঁধা কপি, গাছ-কপি (প্রবোধ)।

bru'-tăl (brô-), *adj.* **1.** Of or pertaining to the beasts; পাশবিক। **2.** Sensual; rude; coarse; ferocious; পাশব; রূঢ়; স্থূল; ক্রূর, হিংস্র, নৃশংস। **—i-za'-tion,** *n.* **—ize,** *v. t.* & *i.* **—ly,** *adv.* **—t. '-i-ty,** *n.*

brute (brôt), *adj.* & *n.* **1.** Not gifted with reason; বিবেকবুদ্ধিহীন, বুদ্ধিহীন, প্রজ্ঞাহীন। **2.** Senseless; unconscious; "Not walking statues of clay not the sons of *brute* earth;" অচেতন, জড়; সংজ্ঞাহীন। **3.** Irrational; stupid; sensual; bestial; cruel; as, *brute* violence; মূঢ়; জড়-বুদ্ধি; ইন্দ্রিয়পরবশ, কামাতুর; পাশব; নিষ্ঠুর, ক্রূর, নির্দ্দয়, নৃশংস। **4.** Coarse; uncivilized; "A great *brute* farmer from Liddesdale;" স্থূল, অমার্জ্জিত; অসভ্য। ***Noun.*** **1.** A lower animal; a beast; মানবেতর জন্তু, তির্য্যকপ্রাণী; পশু, জানোয়ার। **2.** A brutal person; a savage; নরপশু; অসভ্য লোক। **3.** The lower nature in man; পাশবপ্রকৃতি, দুষ্প্রবৃত্তি। **Bru-ti-fi-ca'-tion,** *n.* **Bru'-ti-fy,** *v. t.* **Bru'-tish,** *adj.* **Bru'-tish-ly,** *adv.* **Bru'-tish-ness,** *n.*

brutum fulmen, (*L.*), *n.* Empty threat; blank cartridge; মিথ্যা ভয় প্রদর্শন, ফাঁকা আওয়াজ; ফাঁকা টোটা।

bru'-tŭs (brô-) *n.* A style of wig; এক ধরণের পরচুলা। [সাধারণ তন্ত্র-স্থাপনের জন্য আত্মোৎসর্গকারী প্রাচীন রোমান বীর ব্রুটাসের কেশের অনুকরণ।]

brȳ-ŏl'-ŏ-ḡy, *n.* The study of mosses; শৈবলবিদ্যা।

brȳ'-ŏ-nȳ, *n.* A genus of climbing plants; কতিপয় লতিকার সাধারণ নাম।

Bubale.

bŭ'-bā-lē, *n.* A large antelope of Egypt; ইজিপ্ত দেশীয় অতিকায় কৃষ্ণসার।

bub'-ble (bŭb-l), *n., v. i.* & *t.* **1.** A small vesicle of water or other fluid filled with air; বুদ্বুদ,

জলবিম্ব। **2.** An air-filled cavity in solidified liquid, as glass, amber, etc. ; কাচ বা তৈলস্ফটিক প্রভৃতির মধ্যস্থ বুদ্বুদ। **3.** Anything unsubstantial or unreal ; delusion ;

> "Seeking the *bubble* reputation
> Even in the cannon's mouth."

অসারবস্তু, অনিত্য পদার্থ ; মায়া, ভ্রান্তি। **4.** A fraudulent scheme ; as, the South Sea *bubble* ; জুয়াচুরির ফন্দি। **5.** The sound or appearance of boiling ; জল ফুটনের শব্দ, টগবগানি। ***Verb i.*** **1.** To rise in bubbles ; বুদ্বুদাকারে উত্থিত হওয়া। **2.** To run with a gentle gurgling noise ; as, a *bubbling* stream ; কলকলরবে বহিয়া যাওয়া। ***Verb t.*** **1.** To make the sound of bubbles ; টগ্‌বগ্ করা। **2.** (*Now rarely used*) To cheat ; to deceive ; (বর্ত্তমানে ক্বচিৎ ব্যবহৃত হয়) ঠকান; প্রতারণা করা। **—bler,** *n.* **—bling,** *adj.* Emitting or exhibiting bubbles ; উদ্বুদ্বুদ। **—bly,** *adj.* **Bubble and squeak**—Meat and cabbage fried together ; একত্র ভাজা মাংস এবং বাঁধা কপি। **To bubble over with anger, mirth, etc.**—রাগে গর্ গর্ করা, আনন্দে উচ্ছ্বসিত হইয়া উঠা।

bŭb′-bȳ, *n.* A familiar or affectionate term of address to a small boy ; খোকা, যাদুমণি।

bü′-bö, *n.* (*Pl.* BUBOES.) An inflammatory swelling of the glands in the groin or arm-pit ; বংক্ষণ-স্ফীতি, বাঘী রোগ, ব্রধ্ন (হঃ চঃ), বিদারিকা (চঃ)। **—bon′-ic,** *adj.* Pertaining to buboes ; accompanied by buboes ; ব্রধ্ন-সম্বন্ধীয় ; ব্রধ্ন-সংযুক্ত, ব্রধ্ন-সহকৃত। **Bubonic plague**—একপ্রকার মহামারী রোগ,—যাহাতে বংক্ষণদেশ (কুচ্‌কী) স্ফীত হইয়া থাকে।

bü-bŏn′-ö-cēle, *n.* A hernia of the groin ; বংক্ষণ দেশের কোষচ্যুতি।

bŭc′-căl, *adj.* Pertaining to the cheek ; গণ্ড সম্বন্ধীয়, কাপোল।

bŭc-că-neer′ (-nēr), *n.* & *v. i.* A name given to certain English and French piratical adventurers, who in the 17th and 18th centuries, combined to make depredations on the Spaniards in America ; a pirate ; যে সকল ইংরাজ ও ফরাসী জলদস্যু সপ্তদশ ও অষ্টাদশ শতাব্দীতে আমেরিকাবাসী স্পেনিয়ার্ডগণের ধনরত্ন লুণ্ঠন করিত ; জলদস্যু, সাগরদস্যু। ***Verb i*** To be a sea-robber ; জলদস্যুতা করা, বোম্বেটিগিরি করা। **—ing,** *n.* **—ish,** *adj.*

bŭc′-ci-nā-tor (-têr), *n.* A flat thick chin-muscle ; গণ্ডদেশের পেশী বিশেষ—যাহার সাহায্যে বাঁশী প্রভৃতি বাজান যায়।

Bü-cĕn′-taur (-tär), *n.* A fabulous monster,—half man, half ox ; অর্দ্ধ-বৃষ, অর্দ্ধ মানবাকৃতি গ্রীক পৌরাণিক অসুর, বৃষাসুর।

Bü-cĕph′-ă-lŭs, *n.* **1.** The famous war-horse of Alexander the Great ; মহাবীর অলীকসন্দরের সুবিখ্যাত যুদ্ধাশ্ব। **2.** A riding horse ; আরোহণোপযোগী অশ্ব।

Buchanania latifolia—পিয়াল (বেলঃ)।

buck (bŭk), *n.* **1.** A male of a fallow-deer, reindeer, chamois, antelope, hare and rabbit ; পুংজাতীয় হরিণ, বল্গাহরিণ, স্মেয়ছাগ (রুরু), কৃষ্ণসার, শশক, এবং (সচরাচর) ধূসরবর্ণ ক্ষুদ্র শশক। **2.** A gay, dashing young fellow ; a fop ; a dandy ; ইয়ার, নাগর; খোস-পোষাকী বাবু ; ফুলবাবু। **Buck′-ish** *adj.* **Buck′-ish-ly,** *adv.* **Buck-shot**—A large kind of shot used in shooting deer ; হরিণ শিকারে ব্যবহৃত বড় রকমের গুলি। **Buck-shot rule**—সশস্ত্র কনেষ্টবল দ্বারা আয়র্লণ্ড শাসন। **Buckskin**—Leather made of buck's skin ; মৃগচর্ম্ম, অজিন। (*Pl.*) Breeches made of it ; উক্ত চর্ম্ম-নির্ম্মিত জঙ্ঘাবরণ। **Buck-tooth**—A projecting tooth ; উঁচ্চাত দন্ত

bŭck (bŭk), *v. i.* & *t.* (Of a horse or mule) To jump vertically with back arched, head down and the feet drawn together (to throw off its rider) ; (আরোহীকে ফেলিয়া দিবার উদ্দেশ্যে অশ্বাদির) পিঠ বাঁকাইয়া, মাথা নীচু করিয়া, এবং চারি পা একত্র গুটাইয়া লাফ দেওয়া। ***Verb t.*** To throw by bucking ; উক্ত প্রকার লম্ফ প্রদান করত আরোহীকে ফেলিয়া দেওয়া। **Buck-jumper**—উক্ত প্রকারে লম্ফপ্রদানশীল অশ্ব। **To buck off**—To throw rider thus ; ঐ প্রকারে লম্ফ প্রদান দিয়া আরোহীকে ফেলিয়া দেওয়া। **To buck up**—(*Slang*) To busy one's self ; (ইতর ভাষায়) উঠিয়া পড়িয়া লাগা। To make haste ; তাড়াতাড়ি করা।

buck (bŭk), *n.* A basket for trapping eels ; বাইন মাছ ধরিবার ঝুড়ি।

buck (bŭk), *n.* & *v. t.* **1.** A lye in which clothes are soaked in bleaching, or in which they are washed ; রজকের বস্ত্রাদি সোঁদাইবার ক্ষার জল, বোল জল। **2.** Clothes washed in that liquor ; সুন্দি করা বস্ত্রাদি। ***Verb t.*** To soak or wash in lye,—a process in bleaching ; ক্ষার জলে (বস্ত্রাদি) ভিজান, সুন্দি করা। **Buck-basket**—সুন্দি করিবার বস্ত্রাদির পেটক। **Buck-bean**—আরক্ত পুষ্পস্তবকবিশিষ্ট জলজ উদ্ভিদবিশেষ।

buck′-ĕt (bŭk-), *n.* & *v. t.* **1.** A small tub, pail or vessel in which water is drawn or carried ; বাল্‌তি, জলপাত্র, জলদ্রোণি, আহাব (ঋক্)। **2.** The piston of a pump ; দমকলের দণ্ড, নলদণ্ড। **3.** A cavity on the rim of a water wheel ; the scoop of a dredging machine ; জলবেগচালিত চক্রের বেষ্টনীর রন্ধ্রবিশেষ ; (নদী-গর্ভস্থ) কর্দ্দমোত্তলন যন্ত্রের খনিত্র। **4.** The leather socket for a whip, carbine or lance ; (শকট-চালকের)

কষা রক্ষণার্থ চর্ম্মময় কোটর, বন্দুক বা বল্লম রক্ষণার্থ চর্ম্মময় আধার বিশেষ। 5. The socket for the stump in an artificial leg or arm ; কৃত্রিম হস্ত বা পদের কোটর—যাহার ভিতর ছিন্নাবশিষ্ট হস্ত বা পদ প্রবিষ্ট করা হয়। *Verb t.* 1. To ride hard ; hence (*Colloq.*) to drive or push forward rapidly, (also *v. i.*) ; অতিরিক্ত মাত্রায় ঘোড়া দৌড়ান ; (অতএব চলিত ভাষায়) তাড়াতাড়ি সম্মুখের দিকে তাড়িত করা বা ঠেলিয়া দেওয়া। 2. (*Rowing*) To row hurriedly ; বেগে দাঁড় টানা। **—ful,** *adj.* **Bucket-shop**—যে কার্য্যালয়ে কোম্পানীর কাগজ, শস্য, কেরাসিন প্রভৃতির মূল্য সম্পর্কে স্ফূর্ত্তি খেলা হয়। **Fire bucket**—অগ্নি নির্ব্বাপণের জন্য জলবহণার্থ দ্রোণি। **To give the bucket**—To give the sack ; বরখাস্ত করা। (*Slang*) **To kick the bucket**—To die ; (ইতর ভাষায়) পটল তোলা।

buc'-kle (bŭck'l), *n., v. t. & i.* **1.** A metallic link for fastening straps, etc. ; চর্ম্মরজ্জু প্রভৃতি বন্ধনার্থ কড়া বিশেষ, বন্ধনাঙ্গুরী, উপানবন্ধন, কুড়ুপ। **2.** (*Obs.*) A curl of hair ; (অপ্রচলিত) অলকগুচ্ছ। *Verb t.* **1.** To fasten with a buckle, (often *up, on*) ; উক্তপ্রকার কড়াদ্বারা আঁটা। **2.** (With *to*) To prepare for ; to start vigorously ; "Hereupon cartwright *buckled* himself *to* the employment ;" কোন কার্য্যের জন্য প্রস্তুত করা ; কোমর বাঁধিয়া লাগা। *Verb i.* **1.** (*Scotch*) To join in matrimony ; (স্কটলণ্ডে) বিবাহ-বন্ধনে বদ্ধ হওয়া। **2.** To bend or bulge out ; to crumple up (under pressure) ; নমিত হওয়া, বক্র হওয়া ; কোঁকড়াইয়া যাওয়া। **3.** To contend ; to join in close fight ; সংগ্রাম করা ; ঘেষাঘেষি যুদ্ধে প্রবৃত্ত হওয়া। **To buckle on one's armour**—To prepare for a conflict ; সংগ্রামের জন্য প্রস্তুত হওয়া, হাতিয়ার বাঁধা। **To buckle to**—To engage with zeal ; কোমর বাঁধিয়া লাগা।

buck'-ler (bŭk-lêr), *n. & v. t.* **1.** A small round shield usually held by a handle ; ক্ষুদ্র চর্ম্মফলক বা ঢাল। **2.** A protection ; a protector ; রক্ষণ, রক্ষা, আশ্রয় ; রক্ষক। *Verb t.* To depend ; to protect ; রক্ষা করা ; ত্রাণ করা। **To give the bucklers**—To yield ; শত্রুহস্তে আত্মসমর্পণ করা (বড় প্রচলিত নহে)। **To take up the bucklers**—To enter the lists ; রণাঙ্গনে অবতীর্ণ হওয়া।

buck'-ră (bŭk-), *n.* A negro term for a white man ; কাফ্রিদের ভাষায় শ্বেতকায় মনুষ্য। [কাফ্রি-ভাষায় Buckra শব্দের অর্থ দৈত্য বা ক্ষমতাশালী ব্যক্তি।]

buck'-răm (bŭk-), *n. & adj.* **1.** A coarse linen cloth stiffened with gum ; মোমজামার মত বস্ত্রবিশেষ, স্থূল-পট্ট। **2.** Stiffness in manners ; চাল-চলনের আড়ষ্টতা বা অস্বচ্ছন্দতা। *Adj.* Stiff ; precise ; as, *buckram* dames ; আড়ষ্ট, রুক্ষ ; অতি সূক্ষ্ম বিচারী।

buck-wheat (bŭk-whēt), *n.* A kind of edible grain ; একপ্রকার বড় দানাদার গম, ফুলন (পঞ্জাব), রাজাত (লাদক)।

bü-cŏl'-ic, *adj. & n.* Pertaining to the tending of cattle ; pastoral ; rustic ; গোচারণ-সম্বন্ধীয়, গোষ্ঠ-বিষয়ক ; আহীরীয়, গোরাখাল-বিষয়ক, গোপ-বিষয়ক ; পল্লী-বিষয়ক। *Noun.* (*Pl.*) Pastoral poems ; as, the *bucolics* of virgil ; গোষ্ঠ-গীতি, গোপাদি বিষয়ক কাব্য।

bŭd, *n., v. i. & t.* **1.** An unexpanded leaf or flower ; অঙ্কুর, প্ররোহ (মঃ টঃ), কোরক, কলিকা, কলি, কুঁড়ি, কুট্মল, মুকুল (সাঃ পঃ), জালক (আঃ বঃ), চোক। **2.** A germ ; anything still undeveloped ; বীজাণু ; ভ্রূণ, অপরিণত বস্তু। *Verb i.* To put forth buds ; মুকুলিত হওয়া। *Verb t.* To graft by inserting the bud of a plant under the bark of another tree ; অপর বৃক্ষের বল্কলের নিম্নে কোন বৃক্ষের চোক প্রবিষ্ট করিয়া কলম করা, চোক কলম করা। **Bud'-ed,** *adj.* **Bud'-less,** *adj.* **Bud'-y,** *adj.* **Bud-scale**—মুকুলশল্ক (সাঃ পঃ)। **To nip in the bud**—To destroy at the very beginning of growth ; অঙ্কুরে বিনষ্ট করা।

bŭd'-dĭng, *adj. & n.* **1.** Producing buds ; মুকুলপ্রসূ। **2.** Being in the condition of a bud ; মুকুলিত, মুকুলায়মান (কৃষ্ণ কঃ)। **2.** Being in an early stage of growth ; as, a *budding* orator : *budding* poet (অঙ্কুরোদ্গত কবি) ; অঙ্কুরোদ্গত। *Noun.* **1.** The act or process of producing buds ; কুট্মলোদ্গম, পরিস্ফুরণ। **2.** A mode of grafting in which a leaf-bud is inserted as a graft instead of a young shoot ; চোক কলম করণ।

budge (bŭj), *v. i. & t.* To stir ; "I'll not *budge* an inch, boy ;" to move off ; নড়া, সরা ; চলা। *Verb t.* To move ; নাড়া, সরান। **Budg'-er,** *n.*

budge (bŭj), *n. & adj.* The dressed fur of lambs, used to trim scholars' cloaks ; মেষ-শাবকের শোধিত এবং সলোম চর্ম্ম—যদ্দারা পূর্ব্বে ইংলণ্ডীয় পণ্ডিতবর্গের ঢিলা জামা সজ্জিত করা হইত। *Adj.* Scholastic ; pedantic ; stiff ; পণ্ডিত-সমুচিত ; পাণ্ডিত্যাভিমানী ; কঠোর, কড়া।

budg'-ĕt (bŭj-ĕt), *n.* **1.** A little bag, generally of leather ; ক্ষুদ্র থলিয়া। **2.** A store ; a stock ; as, a *budget* of inventions ; ভাণ্ডার ; সংগ্রহ, সঞ্চয়। **3.** The annual estimate of revenue and expenditure of the British nation by the Chancellor of the Exchequer in the House of Commons ; প্রধান রাজস্বসচিব কর্তৃক পার্লেমেণ্টে উপস্থাপিত ব্রিটীশ জাতীর বার্ষিক আয়ব্যয়ের বিবরণী। **4.** A private person's estimate of his annual income and expenditure ; বার্ষিক আয়ব্যয়ের বিবরণ। **—ar-y,** *adj.* **To open the budget**—ব্যবস্থাপক সভায় আগামী বর্ষের আনুমানিক আয়ব্যয়ের হিসাব উপস্থাপিত করা।

buff (bŭf), *n.* & *adj.* **1.** A stout velvety dull-yellow leather of buffalo or ox-hide ; এক প্রকার দৃঢ় এবং নিষ্প্রভ পীতবর্ণ, মকমলবৎ বৃষ বা মহিষচর্ম্ম, বফ্ চর্ম্ম। **2.** The human skin ; "Stripping ourselves to the *buff* we hung up our steaming clothes ;" মনুষ্য-চর্ম্ম। **3.** A dull light yellow colour ; ফিকে পীতবর্ণ, হরিতকী বর্ণ (সাঃ পঃ)। **4.** (*Med.*) The coagulated coating on blood drawn from fever patients ; জ্বররোগীর দেহ হইতে নিঃসৃত রক্তের উপরে যে আপীত কঠিন স্তর দৃষ্ট হয়। ***Adj.*** **1.** Made of buff ; বফ্ চর্ম্মে নির্ম্মিত। **2.** Light yellow ; হরিতকী-বর্ণ। **3.** (*Fig.*) Naked ; (লক্ষণায়) নগ্ন। **Buff'-y,** *adj.* **Buff-coat**—পুরাকালীন সৈনিকদের অসিঘাত-নিবারক কঞ্চুক বিশেষ। **Buff-stick, —wheel**—পালিশের কার্য্যে ব্যবহৃত বফ্ চামড়ায় মোড়া চাকা বা ছড়ি বিশেষ। **To be in buff**—To be naked ; নগ্ন থাকা।

buff (bŭf), *v. t.* To polish (metal) with buff ; বফ চর্ম্ম দ্বারা ধাতু দ্রব্য পালিশ করা।

1. Head of Cape buffalo.
2. Head of Indian buffalo.

bŭf'-fă-lō, *n.* A species of wild ox ; মহিষ, কাসর। **Buffalo-headed**—নির্ব্বোধ, জড়বুদ্ধি।

bŭf'-fĕl-dŭck (-dŭk), *n.* A small duck ; এক জাতীয় ক্ষুদ্রকায় মরাল।

bŭff'-êr, *n.* A contrivance attached to railway carriages, etc., to deaden the force of a

Buffer.

concussion ; সংঘট্টনের বেগ মন্দীভূত করণার্থ বাষ্পীয় শকট প্রভৃতিতে সংলগ্ন কৌশল বিশেষ। **A buffer state**—দুইটী বৃহৎ দেশের মধ্যবর্ত্তী নিরপেক্ষ ক্ষুদ্র রাজ্য—যদ্দ্বারা উভয় রাজ্যের মধ্যে যুদ্ধ-বিগ্রহাদির সম্ভাবনা হ্রাস হয় (যথা, রুষ এবং ভারতের মধ্যবর্ত্তী আফগানিস্তান)।

bŭf'-fêr, *n.* (*Slang*) An old-fashioned incompetent fellow ; a foolish fellow ; (ইতর ভাষায়) সাবেক ধরণের নিষ্কর্ম্মা লোক ; বোকা লোক, অকর্ম্মণ্য লোক।

bŭf'-fĕt, *n., v. t.* & *i.* **1.** A blow with the hand ; a cuff ; মুষ্ট্যাঘাত, চপেটাঘাত ; ঘুষি, কিল, চড়, চাপড়। **2.** Hardships ; trials ; "Fortune's *buffets* and rewards ;" দুর্দ্দশা ; কষ্ট। ***Verb t. & i.*** **1.** To blow with the hand or fist ; to thump ; ঘুষি-মারা, মুষ্ট্যাঘাত করা ; সজোরে আঘাত করা, সংগ্রাম করা। **2.** To contend against ; বিরুদ্ধাচরণ করা, সংগ্রাম করা। **3.** To muffle bells ; ধ্বনি মন্দীভূত করিবার জন্য ঘণ্টা আবৃত করা।

bŭf'-fĕt, *n.* **1.** A kind of cupboard for holding plates, china, etc. ; চীনের বাসন, থালা প্রভৃতি রাখিবার তাক। **2.** A place for refreshments ; জলযোগের সামগ্রী রাখিবার স্থান।

bûf'-fō, (*It.*), *n.* The comic actor of an opera ; a comic singer ; যাত্রাদলের সং ; যে ব্যক্তি হাসির গান গায়।

bŭf'-fōōn, *n.* & *v. i.* A wag or jester ; a clown ; a mimic ; ভাঁড় ; বিদূষক, হাসক (রঃ), বৈহাসিক (বাংস্য) ; হরবোলা, মস্করা। ***Verb i.*** To play the buffoon ; ভাঁড়ামি করা, মস্করামি করা। **—er-y,** *n.* The jests and pranks of a buffoon ; ভাঁড়ামি, মস্করামি। **—ish,** *adj.*

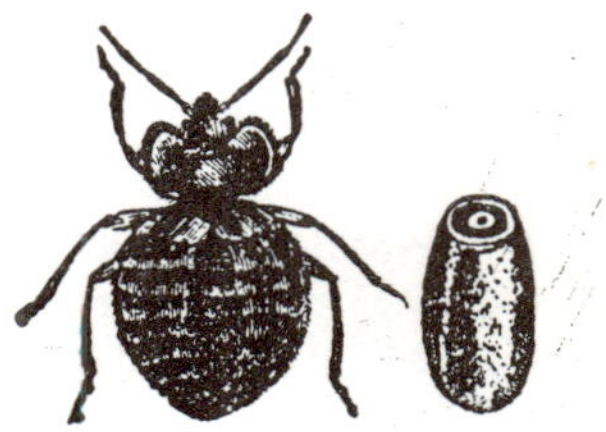

Bedbug, magnified. Egg of bug.

bŭg, *n.* A flat ill-smelling blood-sucking insect infesting beds ; শয্যাকীট, ছারপোকা। **Bug'-gy,** *adj.*

bŭg'-bear (-bār), **bŭg'-ă-bōō,** *n., adj.* & *v. t.* A spectre or hobgoblin ; জুজু। ***Adj.*** Terrifying ; "Such *bugbear* thoughts ;" ভীষণ, ভয়ঙ্কর। ***Verb t.*** To alarm with idle fear ; মিথ্যাভয় প্রদর্শন দ্বারা ভীত করা।

bŭg'-gêr, *n.* (*Law*) **1.** A sodomite ; লৌণ্ডাবাজ (*Slang*), অস্বাভাবিক অভিগমনকারী, পুংমৈথুনকারী, পশুমৈথুনকারী। **2.** A fellow ; a beggar ; a chap ; a beast ; বেটা, লোকটা ; ভিক্ষুক ; ছোকরা ; পশু। **—y,** *n.*

bŭg'-gȳ, *n.* An one-horsed light carriage ; এক ঘোড়ার হাল্‌কাগাড়ী, বগী গাড়ী।

bū'-gle *n.* & *v. i.* **1.** A brass instrument like small trumpet used for military signal ; রণশৃঙ্গ, রণবংশী। **2.** A hunting horn, originally a buffalo horn ; শিকারীর শিঙ্গা, বিষাণ। ***Verb i.*** To sound a bugle ; বংশীধ্বনি করা, শিঙ্গা বাজান। **—gler,** *n.*

bū'-gle, *n.* **1.** Kinds of plants ; বিভিন্ন জাতীয় বৃক্ষের সাধারণ নাম। **2.** An elongated glass-bead, usually black ; পরিচ্ছদাদির শোভা-সম্পাদনার্থ নলাকৃতি (সাধারণতঃ) কৃষ্ণবর্ণ কাচমালা।

bü'-glĕt, *n.* A bicyclist's small bugle ; দ্বিচক্রবানারোহীর ক্ষুদ্র বংশী।

buhl (bül), *n.* **1.** Unburnished gold, brass, tortoise shell, etc., cut in ornamental patterns for inlaying; নানাপ্রকার নমুনায় কর্ত্তিত অপরিকর্ম্মীকৃত স্বর্ণ, পিত্তল, কচ্ছপকম্বু, প্রভৃতি—যদ্দ্বারা গৃহসজ্জাদি পরিগঠিত করা হইয়া থাকে। **2.** Articles of furniture ornamented in this style ; উক্ত প্রকার অলঙ্কারদ্বারা খচিত গৃহসজ্জা বা আসবাব। **Buhl'-work,** *n.* [Boule নামক আসবাব নির্ম্মাতার নাম হইতে গৃহীত।]

build (bĭld), *v. t.* & *n.* **1.** To construct and raise ; গাঁথিয়া খাড়া করা, গড়িয়া তোলা, গড়া। **2.** To increase the power and stability of ; to consolidate ; as, to *build up* one's constitution ; শক্তি বা স্থায়িত্ব বৃদ্ধি করা ; সংহত করা। **3.** To establish ; as, to *build* a reputation ; to make gradually, (often with *up*,—system, empire, reputation) ; দৃঢ়ভিত্তির উপর প্রতিষ্ঠিত করা ; ক্রমশঃ গঠিত করা। **4.** To base (hopes, etc.) upon ; to rely upon ; প্রতিষ্ঠিত করা ; নির্ভর করা। ***Noun.*** The style of construction ; make ; as, the *build* of a ship ; নির্ম্মাণ-প্রণালী, গঠন-পদ্ধতি ; গঠন। **Build'-er,** *n.* **1.** One who builds, as a carpenter, shipwright, or a mason; নির্ম্মাতা (মিস্ত্রী, রাজমিস্ত্রী, পোতনির্ম্মাতা, স্থপতি)। **2.** A contractor for building houses ; যে ঠিকাদার গৃহ নির্ম্মাণের ভার গ্রহণ করে। **Build'-ing** *n.* **1.** An edifice ; a house ; ইমারত, কোঠা, অট্টালিকা ; ভবন। **2.** Act of building ; নির্ম্মাণ। **To build in**—To inclose by building ; গাঁথিয়া ঘিরিয়া ফেলা। **To build up**—To close up by building ; as, to *build up* door ; গাঁথিয়া বুজাইয়া দেওয়া। To erect any edifice ; গাঁথিয়া তোলা।

bŭlb, *n.* & *v. i.* **1.** The nearly spherical underground stem of lily, onion, hyacinth, etc., sending roots downwards and leaves etc., upwards ; (পলাণ্ডু কুমুদ প্রভৃতির) বর্ত্তুলপ্রায় মূল, কন্দ (সাঃ পঃ), শঙ্ককন্দ (ঐ)। **2.** A leaf-bud detaching itself from stem and becoming separate plant ; গেঁউ, কোল-কাণ্ড (সাঃ পঃ), পুট-কাণ্ড (ঐ)। **3.** Any protuberance or enlargement resembling such ; কন্দাকার স্ফীতি। **4.** The dilated part of a glass' tube ; as, the *bulb* of a thermometer ; কাচনলের বিস্ফারিত অংশ। ***Verb i.*** To swell into bulbs; to swell ; গেঁউ বাহির হওয়া ; স্ফীত হওয়া, ফুলিয়া উঠা। **Bul-ba'-ceous, Bulb'-ar, Bulbed,** *adjs.* **Bulb-if'-er-ous,** *adj.* *(Bot.)* Growing from bulbs ; কন্দজ। **Bulb'-ose, Bulb'-ous, Bulb-y,** *adjs.* **Bulb of the eye**—অক্ষিগোলক। **Bulb of the spinal cord**—The medulla oblongata ; গ্রীবাপৃষ্ঠের অভ্যন্তরস্থিত মস্তিষ্কের অংশ।

bŭl'-bĕl, —bil, *n.* A small auxiliary bulb ; ক্ষুদ্র কাক্ষিক কন্দ, অণ্ডিকা (সাঃ পঃ)।

bûl'-bûl *n.* The Persian nightingale ; বুল্‌ বুল্‌ পাখী।

bulge (bŭlj), *n., v. i.* & *t.* **1.** Convex part ; irregular swelling ; as, the *bulge* in a wall ; ন্যুব্জ অংশ; ন্যুব্জতা। **2.** (*Naut.*) The bilge in a vessel ; (see BILGE.) **3.** The bilge or protuberant part of a cask ; পিপার ন্যুব্জ অংশ। ***Verb i.*** To swell out ; to swell outwards irregularly ; as, the ball *bulges* ; স্ফীত হওয়া ; ন্যুব্জ হওয়া। ***Verb t.*** To extend bag, etc., by stuffing it ; কোন কিছু দ্বারা ঠাসিয়া (থলিয়া প্রভৃতি) স্ফীত করা। **Bul'-gi-ness,** *n.* **Bul'-gy,** *adj.*

bŭl'-ğer, *n.* A wooden golf-club with a convex face ; (গোল্‌ফ্ ক্রীড়ার) ন্যুব্জমুখ কাষ্ঠখণ্ড।

bü'-li-mŷ, bü-lĭm'-ĭ-ă, *n.* **1.** An unnatural hunger ; অস্বাভাবিক ক্ষুধা। **2.** (*Fig.*) Voracity (for books etc.) ; (লক্ষণায়) গ্রন্থাদি পাঠের জন্য বুভুক্ষা।

bŭlk, *n., v. i.* & *t.* **1.** Magnitude of material substances ; mass ; size ; as, a ship of great *bulk* ; extent ; জড়বস্তুর আয়তন ; মাত্রা ; আকার ; বিস্তার, পরিসর। **2.** The greater part or number of ; as, the *bulk* of a debt ; প্রধান ভাগ। **3.** The whole cargo in the hold of a ship ; the hold of a ship ; জাহাজের গোলে বোঝাই মাল ; জাহাজের খোল। ***Verb i.*** To grow large ; to seem or appear large or important ; "The fame of Warburton possibly *bulked* larger for the moment ;" বিশাল হওয়া ; বিশাল বা গুরুতর বলিয়া প্রতীয়মান হওয়া। ***Verb t.*** To pile in heaps (fish) ; (মৎস্যাদি) স্তূপীকৃত করা, পুঞ্জীকৃত করা। **Bulk'-i-ness,** *n.* **Bulk'-y,** *adj.* Large ; too large ; unwieldy ; প্রকাণ্ড, বৃহৎ ; বিশাল, বিপুল ; স্থূল, অতিভারী। **In bulk**—Loose ; not in package ; খোলা, আল্‌গাভাবে ; বাঁধা নহে। **To break bulk**—To begin unloading ; মাল খালাস করিতে আরম্ভ করা। **To load in bulk**—To put the cargo (grains etc.) loose ; শস্য প্রভৃতি বোঝাই করা। **To sell in bulk**—To sell in large quantities, as it is in the hold ; থাওকো বিক্রী করা, বিনা ওজনে বিক্রী করা।

bŭlk'-head (-hĕd), *n.* (*Naut.*) Any of the upright partitions separating the various compartments of a vessel ; (নৌ-বিদ্যা) যে সমস্ত কাষ্ঠপ্রাচীর দ্বারা জাহাজের বিভিন্ন কক্ষ (কামরা) বিভক্ত হইয়া থাকে।

bûll, *n., adj., v. i.* & *t.* **1.** An uncastrated male of the ox or any bovine animal ; বৃষ, ষাঁড়, বৃষভ, পুঙ্গব, বলীবর্দ্দ। **2.** The male of whale, elephant, and other large animals ; তিমি, হাতী প্রভৃতি বৃহদাকার জন্তুর পুং জন্তু। **3.** A rough fierce man ; ষণ্ডা, ষণ্ডামার্ক। **4.** (*Astron.*) Taurus, the second of the twelve signs of the zodiac ; (জ্যোতির্বিজ্ঞান) বৃষরাশি। **5.** (*Stock exchange*) One who operates in expectation of a rise of stock ; (কোম্পানীর কাগজের কারবারে) ভবিষ্যতে মূল্য বৃদ্ধি পাইবে এই আশায় যে ব্যক্তি কোম্পানীর কাগজ ক্রয় বা অন্যপ্রকার উপায় অবলম্বন করিয়া লাভের ব্যবস্থা করে। ***Adj.*** Like that of a bull ; male ; large ; loud ; obstinate ; বৃষবৎ ; পুংজাতীয় ; প্রকাণ্ড ; ভীমনাদী ; অদম্য। ***Verb i.*** To take or desire the bull ; (গাভীপক্ষে) ষাঁড় লওয়া, সঙ্গিনী হওয়া। ***Verb t.*** (*Stock exchange*) To try to raise the market price of ; as, to *bull* bonds or stocks ; কোম্পানীর কাগজের মূল্যবৃদ্ধির চেষ্টা করা। **Bull-baiting**—কুক্কুর লেলাইয়া বৃষভ উত্তেজিত করণ। **Bull-beggar**—জুজু। **Bull-calf**—A male calf ; পুং বৎস, এড়ে বাছুর। A simpleton ; নির্ব্বোধ লোক। **Bull-dog**—An English dog of remarkable courage, formerly employed in baiting bulls ; ডালকুত্তা। A tenacious and courageous person; নির্ভীক নাছোড়বান্দা লোক। University proctor's attendant ; ইংলণ্ডদেশীয় কোন বিশ্ববিদ্যালয়ের তত্ত্বাবধায়কের অনুচর। A pistol or revolver of a certain pattern ; একপ্রকার বন্দুক বা পিস্তল। **Bull-fight**—উত্তেজিত বৃষের সহিত সশস্ত্র পুরুষের যুদ্ধ—স্পেনদেশের আমোদ বিশেষ। **Bull-finch**—A small singing bird ; গায়ক পক্ষিবিশেষ। A kind of hedge hard to jump ; দুর্লঙ্ঘ্য বৃতি। **Bull-fly**—দংশ, ডাঁশ। **Bull-frog**—বৃহদাকার মণ্ডূক বিশেষ। **Bull-head**—নদীচর মৎস্য বিশেষ। **Bull-headed**—Obstinate ; impetuous ; blundering ; ঠেঁটা, ষণ্ডা ; চণ্ড ; ভ্রমান্ধ। **Bull-ring**—স্পেনদেশীয় বৃষভ-যুদ্ধের রঙ্গভূমি। **Bull's eye**—A police man's lantern ; চোরা লণ্ঠন। A round piece of glass in a lantern ; লণ্ঠন-সংলগ্ন গোলাকৃতি কাচ-খণ্ড। A circular or oval opening for air and light ; আলো ও বাতাস প্রবেশের জন্য গোল বা ডিম্বাকৃতি রন্ধ্র। (*Naut.*) A thick round glass let into a ship's ports or decks to admit light ; (নৌ-বিদ্যা) আলোক প্রবেশের জন্য জাহাজের পার্শ্ব, পাটাতন প্রভৃতিতে যে গোলাকার স্থূল কাচখণ্ড নিবদ্ধ করা হয়। A boss of glass formed at the centre of a blown glass sheet ; ফুৎকার দ্বারা প্রস্তুত কাচ ফলকের মধ্যদেশে গঠিত স্ফীত বিশেষ। The centre of a target ; a shot that hits it ; শরব্যের কেন্দ্রস্থল ; যে গুলি দ্বারা শরব্যের কেন্দ্রস্থল বিদ্ধ হয়। A kind of sweet meat ; একপ্রকার মিঠাই। **John Bull**—A humorous name for the English collectively ; also an Englishman ; ইংরাজ জাতি ; ইংরাজ [Dr. Arbuthnotএর ব্যঙ্গাত্মক রচনা বিশেষে ইংরাজগণকে এই কৌতুক-পূর্ণ উপনাম দেওয়া হইয়াছে।] **A bull in a china shop**—A reckless or purposeless destroyer ; লণ্ডভণ্ড-কারী। **To take the bull by the horns**—To meet a difficulty regardless of the consequences that will follow ; ফলাফল না ভাবিয়া বিপদের সম্মুখীন হওয়া।

bûll, *n.* A letter or edict of the pope ; (রোমান ক্যাথলিক সম্প্রদায়ের) মহাধর্ম্মাধ্যক্ষের আদেশ পত্র।

bûll, *n.* A ludicrous inconsistency or blunder in speech ; বাক্যের হাস্যকর ভ্রম বা অসংলগ্নতা।

bûl′-lă, *n.* **1.** A round metal ornament worn by ancient Roman children ; প্রাচীন রোমানশিশুদের গোলাকার অলঙ্কার (ধুকধুকি) বিশেষ। **2.** Anything rounded or globular ; গোলাকার বা বর্ত্তুলাকার পদার্থ। **3.** A leaden seal attached to a papal edict ; রোমান ক্যাথলিক সম্প্রদায়ের মহাধর্ম্মাধ্যক্ষের আদেশ পত্রের উপর সীসার মোহর।

bûl′-lāce, *n.* A wild plum-tree or fruit ; বন্য বদরী বৃক্ষ বা ফল।

bûl′-lāte, *adj.* (*Bot.* & *Physiol.*) Blistered-looking; inflated ; puckered ; (উদ্ভিদ-বিদ্যা ও শারীরবিজ্ঞান) ফোস্কা-পড়া ; স্ফীত ; কোঁকড়ানো, কুঞ্চিত।

bûl′-lĕt, *n.* **1.** A shot ; বন্দুকের গুলি। **2.** A plumb or sinker in fishing ; বড়শী-সংলগ্ন সীসকগুলি। **Bullet-headed**—Impetuous ; obstinate ; গোঁয়ার ; ঠেঁটা। **Bullet-proof**—Proof against bullets ; বন্দুকের গুলিদ্বারা অভেদ্য। **Every bullet has its billet**—Fate must have its way ; অদৃষ্টের হাত এড়াইবার জো নাই, কপালে যাহা আছে, তাহা ঘটিবেই।

bûl′-lĕ-tĭn, *n.* & *v. t.* **1.** A short official statement of some (passing) public event ; an official report respecting the health of some great personage ; কোন সাময়িক ঘটনার সংক্ষিপ্ত সরকারী বিবরণ ; কোন গণ্য মান্য বা উচ্চপদস্থ ব্যক্তির পীড়ার অবস্থা সম্বন্ধে সরকারী সমাচার। **2.** A periodical publication ; esp., one containing the proceedings of a society ; সাময়িক পত্রিকা ; বিশেষতঃ যে সাময়িক পত্রে বিদ্বজ্জন মণ্ডলীর কার্য্য-বিবরণী প্রকাশিত হয়। ***Verb t.*** To make known as by a bulletin ; উক্ত রূপ সরকারী বিবরণ প্রচার দ্বারা বিজ্ঞাপিত করা।

bûl′-lion (-lyŏn), *n.* & *adj.* **1.** Gold or silver in the mass before coining or manufacture ; সোণা বা রূপার তাল, ইট, বাট, থাল, চাক্তি, অমুদ্রিত স্বর্ণ বা রৌপ্যপিণ্ড, হিরণ্য। **2.** A heavy twisted fringe, often covered with gold and silver wire ; জরির ঝালর। ***Adj.*** Made of solid or real gold or silver ; নিরেট বা খাঁটি

সোণা বা রূপার তৈয়ারী। **—ist,** *n.* An advocate of an exclusive metallic currency ; কেবল মাত্র ধাতব মুদ্রা প্রচলনের পক্ষপাতী।

bûll'-ock (-ŏk), *n.* A castrated bull ; an ox ; ছিন্নমুষ্ক বৃষ ; বলীবর্দ্দ, বলদ। **Bullock's heart**—নোনা আতা (যোঃ)।

bŭl'-lȳ, *n.* & *v. t.* **1.** A noisy blustering fellow ; an insolvent tyrannical fellow ; (among boys) a coward and tyrant ; তর্জ্জন গর্জ্জনকারী ; গুণ্ডা, ষণ্ডা ; (বালকদিগের মধ্যে) ভীরু অথচ অত্যাচারী। **2.** A ruffian hired to beat or intimidate any one ; ভাড়াটিয়া গুণ্ডা। ***Verb t.* 1.** To overwhelm with bluster or menace ; "He had obtained his place by *bullying* the Lords of Treasury ;" তর্জ্জন গর্জ্জন বা ভয় প্রদর্শনদ্বারা অভিভূত করা। **2.** To frighten into or out of ; ভয় প্রদর্শনে কোন ি য়ে প্রবৃত্ত বা কোন বিষয় হইতে নিবৃত্ত ক

bûl'-lȳ, *adj.* & *interj.* (*E ecially in U. S.*) Capital ; first-rate ; চমৎকার ; সেরা। **Bully for him, you, etc.**—Bravo ; বাহবা ! সাবাস।

bûl'-lȳ, *n.* (*Eton.*) Scrummage in foot-ball ; (ইটন-বিদ্যালয়ে) ফুটবল খেলায় হুড়াহুড়ি বা ধ্বস্তাধ্বস্তি।

bûl'-lȳ, *adj.* Tinned beef, (also *bully beef*) ; টিনে রক্ষিত গোমাংস।

bûl'-rŭsh, *n.* A large strong water rush ; নল, শর, বাজরা (ওয়াট)।

bŭlse, *n.* A bag or purse ; a certain quantity of diamonds and other valuables ; থলিয়া, টাকার থলিয়া ; নির্দ্দিষ্ট পরিমাণ হীরক বা অন্যান্য মূল্যবান জিনিষ।

bŭl'-wark (-wêrk), *n.* & *v. t.* **1.** A rampart ; a fortification ; a mole ; a break-water ; বপ্র, প্রাকার ; কেল্লা, কোট, গড় ; দুর্গাদি, উপদুর্গ ; পাষাণের বাঁধ ; জলপ্রবাহ নিরোধক প্রাচীরাদি। **2.** (*Fig.*) Any means of defence ; "Our naval strength is a *bulwark* to the nation ;" (লক্ষণায়) আশ্রয়-দুর্গ, আশ্রয়স্থল, রক্ষণ-সাধন, সংশ্রয়-স্থান। **3.** (*Naut.*) The side of a ship above the level of the deck ; (নৌ-বিদ্যা) পাটাতনের উপরিস্থিত জাহাজের পার্শ্ব। ***Verb t.*** To fortify with a bulwark or rampart ; to protect ; বপ্র বা প্রাকারদ্বারা সুরক্ষিত করা ; রক্ষা করা।

bŭm, *n* Backside ; buttocks ; পশ্চাদ্দেশ, পাছা ; নিতম্বদেশ। **Bum-bailiff**—নায়েবনাজির। **Bum-boat**—জাহাজে টাটকা খাদ্য দ্রব্য সরবরাহ করিবার জন্য নৌকা বিশেষ।

bŭm, *v. i.* & *n.* To make a murmuring or humming sound ; গুণ্ গুণ্ শব্দ করা, গুঞ্জন করা, ভোঁ ভোঁ করা। ***Noun.*** A humming sound ; গুঞ্জন, গুণ্ গুণ্ শব্দ, ভোঁ ভোঁ শব্দ।

bŭm' ble, *n* A beadle ; যাজক পল্লীর নিম্নপদস্থ কর্ম্মচারী। [ডিকেনস্‌বৃ চ Oliver Twist নামক গ্রন্থোক্ত Bumb e নামক যাজক পল্লীর নিম্নকর্ম্মচারীর নাম হইতে গৃহীত।] **—dom,** *n.* Fussy official pomposity, esp. as displayed by officers of petty corporation, vestries, etc. ; যাজকপল্লী প্রভৃতির ক্ষুদ্র ক্ষুদ্র কর্ম্মচারীর ধূমধাম এবং আড়ম্বর।

bŭm'-ble-bee (-bē), *n.* A large kind of bee ; ভোমরা।

bŭm'-bō, *n.* A cold punch of rum with sugar, nutmeg, etc. ; শর্করা, জাতিফল (জায়ফল), রম মদ্য প্রভৃতির মিশ্রণে প্রস্তুত সরবৎ বিশেষ।

bŭm'-mă-lō, *n.* A small marine Asiatic fish used in India as a relish, (also called Bombay duck) ; এক প্রকার সামুদ্রিক মৎস্য।

bŭm'-mă-ree (-rē), *n.* A middle man in the Billingsgate fish-market ; লণ্ডন নগরীস্থ বিলিঙ্গ্‌সগেট নামক বাজারে যে মধ্যবর্ত্তী ব্যক্তি মৎস্য ব্যবসায়িগণের নিকট হইতে বহু পরিমাণ মৎস্য ক্রয় করত, ক্ষুদ্র ক্ষুদ্র মৎস্য বিক্রেতৃগণের নিকট বিক্রয় করে।

bŭm'-mêr, *n.* An idle worthless fellow ; a loafer ; অলস অকর্ম্মা লোক ; যে টোঁ টোঁ করিয়া বেড়ায়, ভবঘুরে।

bŭmp, *v. t., i.* & *n.* To push ; to throw down (boxes, etc.) against or on (a wall, person, floor, etc.) ; to strike heavily against ; ধাক্কা দেওয়া ; দুম্ করিয়া ফেলা ; সজোরে আঘাত করা, ঠক্কর দেওয়া, ঠুকা, কুটা। ***Verb i.* 1.** To come in violent contact with something ; সজোরে ধাক্কা লাগা, দুম করিয়া পড়া। **2.** To go along with repeated bumps ; ধপ্ ধপ্ করিয়া যাওয়া। **3.** (*Boat-racing*) To overtake ; (নৌকা দৌড়) অতিক্রম করা, লাগাইল ধরা। ***Noun.* 1.** A dull-sounding blow ; knock ; collision ; ধপাৎ শব্দ, দুম্‌দাম্ শব্দ ; ঠক্কর, ঠুকা ; সংঘট্ট। **2.** A swelling caused by it ; আঘাতজনিত স্ফীতি, গুটি। **3.** (*Phrenl.*) A protuberance on the skull which phrenologists associate with affections of the mind, etc. ; (মস্তিষ্ক-সামুদ্রিক) করোটির উপরিস্থ স্ফীতি বিশেষ। মস্তিষ্ক সামুদ্রিকগণের মতে ইহার সহিত চিত্তরাগ প্রভৃতির সংশ্রব রহিয়াছে। **4.** (*Boat-racing*) The touch of a boat by the next,—a win for the latter ; (নৌকা দৌড়) পশ্চাতের নৌকাদ্বারা সম্মুখের নৌকা স্পর্শ—ইহাতে শেষোক্ত নৌকার জয় বুঝায়।

bŭmp, *v. t.* & *n.* To make bittern's cry ; ক্রৌঞ্চ পক্ষীর মত ধ্বনি করা। ***Noun.*** Bittern's cry ; ক্রৌঞ্চ পক্ষীর রব, ক্রৌঞ্চধ্বনি।

bŭmp'-êr, *n.* & *v. t.* **1.** A cup or glass filled to the brim ; কানায় কানায় পূর্ণ পেয়ালা বা পানপত্র। **2.** A brimful glass of wine ; পরিপূর্ণ সুরাপাত্র, পরিপূর্ণ চষক। **3.** A game in which the scoring is all on one side ; যে খেলায় একপক্ষের লোকেরাই সমস্ত জয়াঙ্ক (রন্ প্রভৃতি) লাভ করিয়া থাকে। **4.** A crowded house at a theatre ; নাট্যগৃহ পরিপূর্ণ শ্রোতৃবৃন্দ। ***Verb t.*** To fill to the brim ; কানায় কানায় পূর্ণ করা।

bŭmp'-kĭn, *n.* An awkward, heavy country fellow ; পাড়াগেঁয়ে লোক, চাষারিয়া, অসভ্য লোক।

bŭmp'-tious (-shŭs), *adj.* (*Colloq.*) Self-assertive ; self-conceited ; forward ; (চলিত ভাষায়) আত্মপ্রাধান্য-স্থাপনশীল; আত্মাভিমানী, আত্মশ্লাঘাকারী; প্রগল্ভ। **—ly,** *adv.* **—ness,** *n.*

bŭn, bunn (bŭn), *n.* A kind of sweet cake ; মিষ্ট পিষ্টক বিশেষ।

bŭn, *n.* 1. A rabbit ; খরগোশ, শশক। 2. A squirrel ; কাঠ বিড়াল।

bŭnch, *n., v. t. & i.* A cluster of things growing or fastened together ; গুচ্ছ, স্তবক, তোড়া, (of flowers), কাঁদি (of plaintains), ছড়া, থ'লো, গোছা, থোপ, থোবা। ***Verb t.*** 1. To make into bunches ; স্তবক বা তোড়া প্রস্তুত করা। 2. To gather dress into folds ; পরিচ্ছদাদি ভাঁজে ভাঁজে একত্র করা। ***Verb i.*** To cling together ; to cluster, as into bunches ; একত্র সংলগ্ন হওয়া ; থ'লো বাঁধা, গুচ্ছবদ্ধ হওয়া, স্তবকিত হওয়া। **Bunch-'y,** *adj.* **Bunch of flowers** — কুসুমস্তবক, পুষ্পস্তবক, পুষ্পগুচ্ছ।

bun'-combe (bŭng-kŭm), *n.* See BUNKUM.

bund (bo͞ont), *n.* League ; confederacy ; esp. the confederation of German states ; বন্ধন, যোগ ; সন্ধি ; বিশেষতঃ জর্ম্মণ রাজ্যসমূহের সন্ধিসূত্রে সম্মিলন।

bŭnd, *n.* An embankment against inundation ; বাঁধ।

Bun'-dĕs-răt, (bo͞on), **—răth,** *n.* The federal council of the German Empire ; জর্ম্মণ সাম্রাজ্যের অন্তর্গত সন্ধিসূত্রে সম্মিলিত রাজ্যসমূহের মন্ত্রণাসভা। ইহাতে ২৬টী রাজ্য হইতে ৫৮ জন সভ্য প্রেরিত হন।

bŭn'-dle, *n., v.t. & i.* A number of things fastened or put together ; a roll ; as, a *bundle* of paper ; a set of sticks, iron rods, etc., bound up ; a set of parallel fibres, nerves, etc. ; বাণ্ডিল, পুলিন্দা, বোঁচকা, গাঁঠরী, তল্পি, বস্তা, পুঁটুলি, কলাপ ; তাড়া; আঁটি ; গুচ্ছ। ***Verb t.*** 1. To tie, or make up into, a bundle ; আঁটি বাঁধা, পুলিন্দা করা। 2. To place or send (especially a person) in a hurry or unceremoniously ; "They *bundled* me and my gallant second into our hackney-coach ;" তাড়াতাড়ি বিদায় করিয়া দেওয়া। ***Verb i.*** 1. To throw confusedly into any receptacle ; ব্যস্ততার সহিত কোন কিছুর ভিতর পুরা। 2. To pack up one's things for a journey ; জিনিষ-পত্র বাঁধা, তল্পিতল্পা বাঁধা। 3. To go hurriedly or in confusion, (with *away, off, out*) ; ব্যস্তসমস্ত হইয়া চলিয়া যাওয়া। **To bundle off**—To send a person off in hurry ; তাড়াতাড়ি বিদায় করিয়া দেওয়া। **To bundle out**—To expel summarily ; কোনপ্রকার লৌকিকতা প্রদর্শন না করিয়া তাড়াতাড়ি তাড়াইয়া দেওয়া।

bŭng, *n. & v. t.* 1. The large stopper of the hole in a cask ; পিপার ছিদ্রের বড় কাক্ বা ছিপি, গুঁজি, মুদ্রা (ভাবঃ প্রঃ)। 2. The hole for filling the cask ; পিপার ছিদ্র। ***Verb t.*** 1. To stop up (cask) with a bung ; to close up ; (পিপার) গুঁজিদ্বারা ছিদ্র বন্ধ করা ; বন্ধ করা। 2. (*Slang*) To throw (stones) ; (ইতর ভাষায়) ঢিল ছোড়া। **Eyes bunged up**—আঘাতজনিত স্ফীতিহেতু অথবা অক্ষিরন্ধ্র হইতে নির্গত স্রাবদ্বারা বদ্ধদৃষ্টি।

Bungalow.

bun'-ga-low (bŭng-gă-lō), *n.* A thatched or tiled house usually surrounded by a veranda ; বাঙ্গলা ঘর। **Dak bungalow**—ডাক বাংলা।

bun'-gle (bŭng-), *v. i., t. & n.* To act in a clumsy, awkward manner ; (আনাড়ীর মত) কদর্য্য ভাবে কায করা। ***Verb t.*** 1. To make or mend clumsily ; to manage awkwardly ; কদর্য্যভাবে সারা বা গড়া ; কদর্য্যভাবে সম্পন্ন করা। 2. To blunder over ; to fail to accomplish (task) ; কোন কাজ করিতে ভুল করা ; কোন কাজ সমাধা করিতে বিফল হওয়া। ***Noun.*** 1. A clumsy or awakward performance ; a botch ; নোংরা কাজ, কাঁচা কাজ ; তালি। 2. A gross blunder ; বিষম ভুল, প্রমাদ, স্খলিত। **—gler,** *n.* A clumsy awakward workman ; আনাড়ী, অকৃতী, অদক্ষ, অনিপুণ, বা অপটু ব্যক্তি, কাঁচা লোক। **—gling,** *adj.*

bŭn'-ion (-yŏn), *n.* Same as BUNYON.

bunk (bŭngk), *n.* 1. A wooden case or box, serving for a seat in the day-time and for a bed at night ; দিবাভাগে উপবেশন ও নিশাকালে শয়নোপযোগী কাষ্ঠাধার বিশেষ। 2. One of a series of sleeping berths arranged over each other ; পরস্পরের উপরি সজ্জিত শয্যা-ফলকশ্রেণীর একটী। 3. A recess in a ship's cabin ; জাহাজের কামরার নিভৃত স্থান।

bun'-kêr (bŭng-), *n.* 1. A large bin or similar receptacle ; as, a coal *bunker* ; বৃহৎ আধার। 2. A sandy hollow in a golf-course ; গোল্ফ ক্রীড়া-প্রাঙ্গণস্থ বালুকাময় গর্ত্ত।

bŭn'-kŭm, *n.* An empty claptrap oratory ; a bombastic speech-making for show ; sophistry ; বাহবা বা করতালি লাভার্থ শূন্যগর্ভ বক্তৃতা ; বাগাড়ম্বরপূর্ণ বক্তৃতা ; কুতর্ক, জল্প (হিঃ কোঃ)।

bŭn'-nȳ, *n.* A pet name for a rabbit ; শশকের আদরের নাম।

Bŭn'-sĕn, –sĕn'ȿ, *adj.* Invented by Prof. Bunsen of Heidelberg ; হিডেলবার্গনিবাসী অধ্যাপক ব্যানসেনকর্ত্তৃক উদ্ভাবিত। **Bunsen battery**—এক প্রকার তাড়িত কোষ। **Bunsen burner, Bunsen lamp**—অধ্যাপক ব্যানসেনকর্ত্তৃক উদ্ভাবিত অত্যুষ্ণ উত্তাপ-সঞ্চারক প্রদীপ বিশেষ।

bŭnt, *n.* **1.** A parasitic disease of wheat and other grains ; smut ; গোধুম কিম্বা অন্যান্য শস্যের রোগ বিশেষ ; ছেতো। **2.** A cavity or bagging part of a fishing net, sail, etc. ; পাইল, জাল, প্রভৃতির ঝোলা।

bŭnt, *v. t., i.* & *n.* To strike or push with horns or head ; to butt ; গুঁতা দেওয়া বা আঘাত করা ; ঢু মারা। ***Noun.*** A push ; ধাক্কা, ঢু।

bŭnt'-ĕr, *n.* A woman who picks up rags in the street ; a low woman ; নেক্ড়া-কুড়ুনি ; ইতর স্ত্রীলোক।

bŭn'-ting, *n.* A thin woollen stuff used chiefly for flags ; flags ; পতাকা প্রস্তুতোপযোগী সূক্ষ্ম পশমী বস্ত্র-বিশেষ ; পতাকাশ্রেণী।

bŭn'-ting, *n.* The popular name of a number of birds, closely allied to finches and sparrows ; চটকজাতীয় কতিপয় প্রকার পক্ষীর সাধারণ নাম।

bŭn'-yŏn, *n.* (*Med.*) A lump or inflamed swelling in the ball of the great toe ; (ভৈষজ্য-শাস্ত্র) গুঞ্জন (হঃ চঃ), বৃদ্ধাঙ্গুলীর নিম্নেজাত ক্ষুদ্র মাংসপিণ্ড বা তৎস্থানের প্রদাহজনক স্ফীতি।

buoy (boy̆), *n.* & *v. t.* **1.** An anchored float showing navigable

Buoy.

course or reefs, etc. ; নাব্য বা নাবিকের সঙ্কটস্থল প্রদর্শক প্লবমান কুম্ভবিশেষ, বয়া। **2.** Something that will keep a person afloat in water, (also *fig.*) ; জল নিমগ্ন ব্যক্তির জীবন রক্ষার্থ প্লববিশেষ, বিপদ্‌ভঞ্জক, জীবনরক্ষক (ব্যক্তি বা বস্তু), (অপিচ লক্ষণায়)। ***Verb t.*** (Usu. with *up*). **1.** To keep afloat ; ভাসাইয়া রাখা, ডুবিতে না দেওয়া। **2.** To bring to the surface of ; ভাসাইয়া তোলা। **3.** (*Fig.*) To bear up ; to sustain ; to uplift ; to keep from sinking in despondency ; "Hearts sunk down are not to be *buoyed up* ;" (লক্ষণায়) ভাসাইয়া রাখা ; ধারণ করা ; উত্তোলন করা ; নিরাশা-সাগরে ডুবিতে না দেওয়া, আশ্বাসিত করা। **4.** (With *out*) To fix buoys ; to mark with buoys ; জলোপরি বয়া বা প্লবমান কুম্ভ বসাইয়া যাওয়া ; প্লব বা কুম্ভদ্বারা চিহ্নিত করা। **Buoy'-age,** *n.* **Buoy'-an-cy,** *n.* **1.** The capacity of floating on the surface of water or in the atmosphere ; the floating power of liquids to keep objects afloat ; প্লবনশীলতা ; প্লবনশক্তি (হিঃ কোঃ)। **2.** (*Hydros.*) The loss of weight by immersion in liquid ; (জল-বিজ্ঞান) জলমজ্জনহেতু গুরুত্বহ্রাস। **3.** (*Fig.*) Lightness of spirit ; vivacity ; cheerfulness ; (লক্ষণায়) চিত্তের লঘুতা ; সজীবতা, স্ফূর্ত্তি ; উৎফুল্লতা, উল্লাস। **Buoy'-ant,** *adj.* **1.** Having the quality of floating in fluid ; প্লবনশীল। **2.** Light-hearted ; cheerful ; as, *buoyant* spirits ; লঘুচিত্ত ; হর্ষোৎফুল্ল, উল্লসিত। **Buoy'-ant-ly,** *adv.* **Buoy'-ant-ness,** *n.* **Life-buoy**—See LIFE.

bur (bêr), **burr** (bêr), *n.* **1.** The prickly flower-head or seed-vessel of certain plants which sticks to clothes ; গুকরা (মঃ উঃ)। **2.** A person hard to shake off ; any inconvenient adherent ; কণ্টকস্বরূপ ব্যক্তি ; বালাই।

bŭr'-ble', *v. t.* To simmer with rage, mirth ; রাগে গর্ গর্ করা বা আনন্দে উচ্ছ্বসিত হওয়া।

bur'-bŏt (bêr-), *n.* An eel-like flat-headed, bearded fresh-water fish ; মাগুর জাতীয় মৎস্য বিশেষ।

bur'-den (bêrdn), **bur'-then** (bêr-thn), *n.* & *v. t.* **1.** A load ; a weight ; বোঝা ; ভার। **2.** The carrying capacity of a ship ; weight of the cargo ; জাহাজের বোঝাই বা ভরট ; জাহাজে বোঝাই মালের ওজন। **3.** Bearing of loads ; as, beast of *burden* ; ভারবহন। **4.** That which is grievous, wearisome or oppressive ; গুরুতর, ক্লান্তিকর অথবা দুর্ব্বহ বস্তু বা বিষয়, গলগ্রহ। **5.** The load of taxation, etc. which one has to pay to the government, (usu. in *pl.*) ; "Here the public *burdens* were heavy ;" রাজসরকারে দেয় করভার। ***Verb t.*** To encumber with weight ; to oppress with anything grievous ; ভারাক্রান্ত করা, ভারচাপান, ভারগ্রস্ত করা, ঘাড়ে বোঝা চাপান ; প্রপীড়িত করা ; কর ধার্য্য করা। **–some,** *adj.* Oppressive ; wearing ; পীড়াদায়ক ; দুর্ব্বহ। **–some-ly,** *adv.* **–some-ness,** *n.* **A beast of burden**—See BEAST. **Burden of proof**—প্রমাণের ভার। [কাহারো বিরুদ্ধে কোন অভিযোগ করিলে অভিযোগকারীর পক্ষে উপযুক্ত প্রমাণ প্রদর্শনদ্বারা তাহার সত্যতা প্রমাণিত করণের দায়িত্ব।]

bur'-den (bŭrdn), *n.* The chorus of a song ; gist ; as, the *burden* of a speech ; গানের ধুয়া ; মূল আখ্যান বা বিষয়, সংক্ষিপ্তসার, আখ্যান-বস্তু।

bur'-dock (bêr-dŏk), *n.* A prickly plant ; ভাঁটুই।

bū'-reau (-rō), *n.* (*Pl.* -REAUX.) **1.** A writing table or chest of drawers ; লিখিবার মেজ অথবা দেরাজ। **2.** An office ; a government department ; কার্য্যালয়, দফ্‌তরখানা ; সরকারী বিভাগ। [ইংলণ্ড ব্যতীত ইয়ুরোপের অন্যান্য দেশে bureau বলিতে শাসনতন্ত্রের উচ্চতম বিভাগ বুঝায়,—যথা

bureau of the ministers for foreign affairs.]

bü-reau'-crā-cy̆ (-rö-), *n.* **1.** The system by which the public service of a country is carried on in department, each under the control of a head; officialism; এক এক জন প্রধান কর্ম্মচারীর অধীন বিভিন্ন বিভিন্ন বিভাগদ্বারা দেশের শাসন-কার্য্য নির্ব্বাহের পদ্ধতি বিশেষ, কর্ম্মচারিতন্ত্র; রাজকর্ম্মচারিগণের কায়দা-কানুন। **2.** Officials collectively; কর্ম্মচারিবর্গ। **—crat, —cra-tist,** *ns.* A member of bureaucracy; official confirmed in a narrow and arbitrary routine; কর্ম্মচারি-তন্ত্রভুক্ত কর্ম্মচারী; সংকীর্ণ এবং যথেচ্ছা-চার মূলক নিত্যকার্য্যব্যবস্থার প্রতি দৃঢ়বদ্ধ কর্ম্মচারী। **—crat'-ic, —crat-i-cal,** *adjs.* **—crat'-i-cal-ly,** *adv.*

bü-rette' (-rĕt), *n.* A graduated glass tube for measuring small quantities; অল্প মাত্রায় তরল পদার্থ পরিমাপের জন্য ক্রমচিহ্নিত কাচনল বিশেষ।

burg'-āge (bêrg-), *n.* A tenure by which houses or lands are held in boroughs, cities and towns, at a certain yearly rent; (ইংলণ্ডে) পার্লেমেণ্ট মহাসভায় সভ্য প্রেরণাধিকার-প্রাপ্ত নগর, বৃহৎ নগর বা সামান্য নগরীতে নির্দ্দিষ্ট বার্ষিক রাজস্বপ্রদানে ভূমি বন্দোবস্ত গ্রহণের পদ্ধতি বিশেষ।

bur'-gee (bêr-jē), *n.* A swallow-tailed flag; a small tapered pennant used by yachts, etc.; চাতকপুচ্ছাকৃতি ধ্বজাবিশেষ; প্রমোদ-তরণীতে ব্যবহৃত ক্রম সূক্ষ্মাগ্র ক্ষুদ্র কেতন বিশেষ।

bur'-gee (bêr-jē), A kind of small coal for furnaces; চুল্লীতে ব্যবহারের জন্য ক্ষুদ্র ক্ষুদ্র কয়লার খণ্ড।

bur'-geon (bêr-jŏn), *n.* & *v. t.* A young shoot or sprout; মুকুল, অঙ্কুর। ***Verb t.*** To put forth young shoots; অঙ্কুরিত হওয়া। (Same as BOURGEON.)

bur'-gĕss (bêr-), *n.* **1.** An inhabitant of a borough with full municipal rights; a citizen; পূর্ণ স্বায়ত্বশাসনাধিকার প্রাপ্ত নগরের অধিবাসী; নগরবাসী, নাগরিক, পুরবাসী। **2.** A member of Parliament for a borough, coroporate town or university; পার্লেমেণ্টে সভ্য প্রেরণে ক্ষমতাসম্পন্ন বা স্বায়ত্বশাসনাধিকারপ্রাপ্ত নগরী হইতে কিম্বা বিশ্ববিদ্যালয় হইতে পার্লেমেণ্টে প্রেরিত সভ্য। **3.** A magistrate of a borough; উক্ত প্রকার নগরীর শাসনকর্ত্তা। **—ship,** *n.*

burgh (bŭ-rö) *n.* The Scotch word corresponding to the English borough or corporate town; পার্লেমেণ্ট মহাসভার নির্ব্বাচনাধিকার বা স্বায়ত্বশাসনের ক্ষমতাপ্রাপ্ত নগর। [স্কটলেণ্ডে এই অর্থে ব্যবহৃত হয়।]

Burgh'-er, *n.* An inhabitant of a borough; a citizen or freeman; পার্লেমেণ্ট মহাসভায় সভ্য প্রেরণের ক্ষমতাসম্পন্ন নগরীর অধিবাসী; নগরবাসী, পুরবাসী, নাগরিক অধিকার-প্রাপ্ত ব্যক্তি। **Bur'-ghal,** *adj.*

bur'-glăr (bêr-), *n.* One who breaks into a house by night with intent to commit felony; ভিত্তিচৌর, সন্ধিচৌর, কপাটঘ্ন, সিঁদেল চোর, সন্ধি-তস্কর, সন্ধিহারক (আঃ বঃ), সন্ধিচ্ছেদক (মৃচ্ছঃ)। **—gla-ri-ous,** *adj.* **—gla-ri-ous-ly,** *adv.* **—gla-ry,** *n.* Breaking into a house by night; সিঁদেলচুরি, সন্ধিছেদন (মৃচ্ছঃ)।

bur'-gle (bêr-), *v. i.* & *t.* To commit burglary; সিঁদ কাটিয়া চুরি করা, গৃহভঙ্গ করা। ***Verb t.*** To enter or rob a house burglariously; চুরির অভিপ্রায়ে পরগৃহে প্রবেশ করা, গৃহ ভাঙ্গিয়া জিনিষ পত্র অপহরণ করা।

bur'-gō-măs-têr (bêr-), *n.* **1.** A chief magistrate of a municipal town in Holland or Germany, corresponding to Mayor in England and the United States; জার্ম্মেনী বা হলণ্ডের স্বায়ত্বশাসনাধিকার প্রাপ্ত নগরীর প্রধান শাসনকর্ত্তা। (ইংলণ্ড বা যুক্তরাজ্যের Mayor শব্দের অনুরূপ)। **2.** An aquatic bird common in arctic regions; সুমেরু প্রদেশবাসী জলচর পক্ষিবিশেষ।

bur'-gö-nĕt (bêr-), **—gă-nĕt,** *n.* A visored helmet; a steel cap; মুখাবরণ সমন্বিত শিরস্ত্রাণ বিশেষ; ইস্পাত নির্ম্মিত শিরস্ত্রাণ।

bur'-gōo (bêr-), *n.* A dish made of boiled oatmeal seasoned with salt, butter and sugar, used by seamen; সিদ্ধ যইএর সহিত মাখন, চিনি এবং লবণ সহযোগে প্রস্তুত নাবিকদিগের খাদ্য বিশেষ।

Bur'-gŭn-dy̆ (bêr-), *n.* A richly flavoured wine, mostly red, made in Burgundy; বারগাণ্ডি প্রদেশে প্রস্তুত (সাধারণতঃ) লোহিতবর্ণ সুবাসিত মদিরা বিশেষ। **Burgundian blow**—Decapitation; শিরশ্ছেদ।

bur'-i-ăl (bĕr-), *n.* Depositing a dead body under earth, (usually with attendant ceremonies); funeral; মৃতদেহ ভূগর্ভে প্রোথিত করণ; সমাধি; অন্ত্যেষ্টি ক্রিয়া, সৎকার, প্রেতকর্ম্ম। **Burial ground**—A cemetery; সমাধিভূমি, কবরস্থান, গোরস্থান।

Bŭr'-i-dăn's ăss, *n.* A man of indecision; যে ব্যক্তি কোন কার্য্য করিতে দ্বিধা বা ইতস্ততঃ করে। [গ্রীক দার্শনিক Buridan বলিয়াছেন যদি একটী ক্ষুধিত গর্দ্দভকে সর্ব্বপ্রকারে সমান দুইটি ঘাসের আঁটির মধ্যে স্থাপন করা যায়, তবে ইহা কোন্‌টীতে অগ্রে মুখ দিবে তদ্বিষয় নিশ্চয় করিতে না পারিয়া, অনাহারে মৃত্যুমুখে পতিত হইবে।]

bü'-rin, *n.* The cutting tool of an engraver on metal; ধাতুফলকে

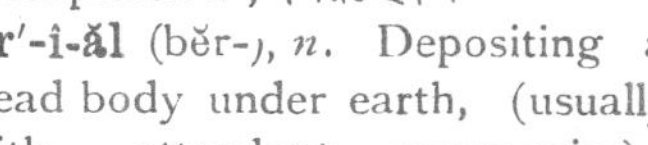

Burin.

খোদাইর কায করিবার উপযোগী যন্ত্র-বিশেষ। **—ist,** *n.*

burke (bêrk), *v. t.* **1.** To murder by suffocation ; to put an end to quietly ; শ্বাসরোধ করিয়া হত্যা করা ; চুপি চুপি নিকাশ করিয়া ফেলা। **2.** To avoid ; to hush up ; as, to *burke* a parliamentary question ; to suppress (rumour, book, etc.) ; ফেলিয়া রাখা ; চাপা দেওয়া, চাপিয়া রাখা, বন্ধ করা। [Burke নামক জনৈক আয়র্লণ্ডবাসী চিকিৎসকগণের নিকট মৃতদেহ বিক্রয়ার্থ কয়েক ব্যক্তিকে গলা চাপিয়া হত্যা করিয়া ১৮২৯ খৃঃ অব্দে প্রাণদণ্ডে দণ্ডিত হয়।]

burl (bêrl), *n.* & *v. t.* A knot in wool, or thread or cloth ; পশম, সূতা বা কাপড়ের ক্ষুদ্র ক্ষুদ্র গ্রন্থি বা গের। ***Verb i.*** To pick knots, loose threads, etc. from, as in finishing cloth ; গ্রন্থি, অবান্তর সূত্র, প্রভৃতি বাছিয়া ফেলিয়া সমাপ্ত বস্ত্র পরিষ্কার করা। **Burl'-y,** *adj.* Knotty ; গ্রন্থিপূর্ণ।

bŭr'-lăp (bêr-), *n.* A coarse canvas for wrappings, etc. ; মুড়িবার জন্য বা অন্যান্য কার্য্যে ব্যবহারের জন্য মোটা ক্যাম্বিস কাপড়। [সচরাচর plural এ ব্যবহৃত হয়।]

bur-lesque' (bĕr-lĕsk), *adj.* & *n.* **1.** Tending to excite laughter ; jocular ; comical ; হাস্যোদ্দীপক ; কৌতুকপূর্ণ ; হাস্যকর। **2.** Bombastic ; mockserious ; বাগাড়ম্বরপূর্ণ ; বিদ্রূপাত্মক অথচ গম্ভীর। ***Noun.*** **1.** A ludicrous representation ; a grotesque satire ; হাস্যোদ্দীপক অভিনয়, কৌতুক নাট্য ; বিকট বিদ্রূপ। **2.** A ludicrous imitation ; a caricature ; a travesty ; (কোন রচনার) হাস্যোদ্দীপক অনুকরণ ; হাস্যোদ্দীপক বিকট চিত্র ; ব্যঙ্গ কাব্য, কৌতুক নাট্য।

bur-lesque' (bêr-lĕsk), *v. t.* To make ridiculous by representation ; to turn into burlesque ; "They *burlesqued* the prophet Jeremiah's words ;" ব্যঙ্গাত্মক অনুকরণ করা, হাস্যজনক অনুকরণ করা ; প্রহসনে পরিণত করা।

bur-lĕt'-tă (bêr-), *n.* A comic opera ; a musical farce ; হাস্যোদ্দীপক নাটক ; সংগীতবহুল প্রহসন বিশেষ।

bur'-lŷ (bêr-), *adj.* **1.** Sturdy ; bulky ; corpulent ; বলবান ; স্থূল ; স্থূলকায়। **2.** Coarse and rough ; boisterous ; as, it was the orator's own *burly* way of nonsense ; রূঢ়, কর্কশ ; তর্জ্জন গর্জ্জনকারী, ধুম্‌ধাম্ কারী।

burn (bêrn), *n.* A small stream or brook ; a spring or fountain ; ক্ষুদ্র স্রোতস্বতী ; উৎস বা নির্ঝর। [স্কট্‌লণ্ড এবং উত্তর ইংলণ্ডে ব্যবহৃত।]

burn (bêrn), *v. t., i.* & *n.* **1.** To consume with fire ; to reduce to ashes by fire ; দগ্ধ করা ; ভস্মীভূত করা। **2.** To put to death by fire ; অগ্নিতে দগ্ধ করিয়া বিনাশ করা। **3.** To scorch or injure by fire ; as, to *burn* meat in roasting it ; to *burn* one's fingers ; to expose to the action of fire ; as, the sun *burns* the plants ; অগ্নিতে দগ্ধ করা, পোড়া লাগান ; অগ্নিপক্ক করা। **4.** To harden by heat ; as, to *burn* bricks ; to make into or produce by heat ; as, to *burn* lime-stone ; অগ্নিতাপে কঠিন করা ; (পোড়াইয়া) প্রস্তুত করা। **5.** To affect with a burning sensation ; to produce an effect like that of fire ; as, ardent spirits *burn* the stomach : fever *burns* a patient ; প্রদাহ জন্মান ; জ্বালান, দহন করা, পোড়াইয়া দেওয়া। **6.** (*Surg.*) To cauterize ; to brand ; (অস্ত্রোপচার বিদ্যা) কষ্টিক বা উত্তপ্ত লৌহদ্বারা পোড়াইয়া দেওয়া, পোড়া লোহার ছেঁকা দেওয়া, দাগ দেওয়া ; দাহ কর্ম্ম করা (সুশ্রুঃ), অগ্নিকর্ম্ম করা। **7.** (*Chem.*) To make acid, etc., eat its way into (some material) ; to combine with oxygen ; (রসায়নশাস্ত্র) তীব্র দ্রাবক পদার্থ দ্বারা খাইয়া দেওয়া ; অঙ্গারজান বাষ্পের সহিত মিশ্রিত করা। **8.** To give a sensation of pain ; যন্ত্রণা বোধ করান। ***Verb i.*** **1.** To be on fire ; to blaze ; to glow ; as, the fuel *burns* ; জ্বলা ; প্রজ্বলিত হওয়া ; দীপ্ত হওয়া। **2.** To give light ; as, the candle *burns* : gas *burns* ; আলোক প্রদান করা। **3.** To suffer from, or to be injured by, fire or great heat ; "Your meat doth *burn* ;" পোড়া লাগা। **4.** To be inflamed with passion or desire ; to be hot or passionate ; as, to *burn* with anger or love (ক্রোধে প্রজ্বলিত হওয়া বা প্রেমানলে দগ্ধ হওয়া) প্রজ্বলিত হওয়া, দগ্ধ হওয়া ; উদ্দীপ্ত হওয়া, উত্তেজিত হওয়া। **5.** To be affected with a sensation of heat or burning pain ; to feel excess of heat ; as, the face *burns* : the patient *burns* with fever ; জ্বালাবোধ করা ; জ্বলা, দগ্ধ হওয়া। ***Noun.*** A sore or mark on the body made by burning ; পোড়ার দাগ, পোড়া ঘা। [*Burn* is produced by heated solid, *scald* by heated liquid.] **Burn'-a-ble,** *adj.* Capable of being burnt ; দহনীয়, দাহ্য, জ্বলনীয়। **Burn'-er,** *n.* **1.** A person who burns or sets fire to anything ; দাহক, অগ্নিদ, প্রজ্বালক। **2.** The part of a lamp or the jet-piece from which the flame issues ; the part that holds the wick ; দীপাদির যে অংশ হইতে শিখা উত্থিত হয় ; বর্ত্তিমুখ। **Burn'-ing,** *adj.* & *n.* **1.** Very hot ; as, the *burning* sun ; অত্যুষ্ণ, জ্বলদগ্নিনিভ। **2.** Powerful ; vehement ; as, *burning* zeal : "Every *burning* word he spoke." শক্তিশালী ; প্রচণ্ড, জ্বলন্ত। **3.** Causing general excitement ; as, a *burning* question ; সাধারণের উত্তেজনাজনক। (*Noun*) Conflagration ; inflammation ; জ্বলন, উজ্জ্বলন, সন্তাপন ; প্রদাহ, দাহন। **Burning crown**—A crown of red-hot iron set on the head of regicides ; রাজহন্তাদিগের শিরোপরি যে

জলন্ত লৌহমুকুট সন্নিবেশ করা হইত। **Burning ghat**—শ্মশান ঘাট। **Burning-glass**—আতসী কাচ, দাহক কাচ। **Burning ground**—শ্মশান। **Burning of a dead body**—শবদাহ। **Burning of mind** — মনস্তাপ। **Burnt offering**—আহুতি, হোম, বৈতানিক। **Burnt out of home and house, etc.** — Driven out of house etc. by the burning of it ; গৃহদাহের জন্য গৃহ হইতে বিতাড়িত। **Heart-burning** — অন্তর্দাহ। **A burnt child dreads the fire**—ঘর পোড়া গরু সিঁদুরে মেঘ দেখে ভয় পায়, চূণ খেয়ে মুখ পুড়িলে দধি দেখে ভয় করে। **Money burns a hole in pocket**—Money clamours to be spent ; টাকা পয়সা পকেট ফুরিয়া বাহির হইয়া যাইতে চায়। **To burn (hung) an effigy**—কোন ব্যক্তিকে অপমানিত করিবার উদ্দেশ্যে তাহার কুশ-পুত্তলিকা বা প্রতিকৃতি দাহন করা বা ঝুলাইয়া দেওয়া। **To burn blue**—To burn with a blue flame ; নীল শিখা বিস্তার করিয়া জ্বলা। **To burn day-light**—To burn candles in the day-time ; দিবসে মোমের বাতি জ্বালা, অপব্যয় করা। **To burn in**—To eat into by burning as fire ; পোড়াইয়া খাইয়া দেওয়া। **To burn one's boats** or **bridges**—To cut off all means of retreat ; প্রত্যাবর্ত্তন বা পলায়নের উপায় না রাখা। **To burn one's fingers**—To suffer for meddling or interfering in other affairs ; পরের ব্যাপারে হস্তক্ষেপ করার দরুণ ক্ষতিগ্রস্ত হওয়া। **To burn out**—To consume the contents of ; পোড়াইয়া নিঃশেষ করা। **To burn the candle at both ends**—To overtax the energies so as to injure the health ; অতিরিক্ত মানসিক পরিশ্রম দ্বারা স্বাস্থ্য নষ্ট করা। **To burn the planks**—To remain long sitting ; বহুক্ষণ বসিয়া থাকা। **To burn the water**—To spear salmon by torchlight ; মশালের আলোকে স্যামন মৎস্য শিকার করা। **To burn together**—গলিত ধাতু দ্বারা দুইটী ধাতু-ফলক একত্র জোড়া দেওয়া। **You cannot burn a candle at two ends**—You cannot do two opposite things at the same time ; এক সময়ে দুইটী বিপরীত কার্য্য করিতে পার না, অর্থাৎ যদি তুমি গভীর নিশীথে নিদ্রা যাও, তবে অতি প্রত্যূষে গাত্রোত্থান করিতে সক্ষম হও না, তুমি এক সময়ে ঈশ্বর ও শয়তানকে সেবা করিতে পার না।

bur'-nĕt (bêr-), *n.* The common name of certain brown-flowered plant ; কপিশবর্ণ পুষ্পপ্রসূ কতিপয় বৃক্ষের সাধারণ নাম।

bur'-nish (bêr-), *v. t., i. & n.* To polish by friction ; to make bright by rubbing ; প্রমার্জ্জিত করা, ঘষিয়া চকচকে করা ; জিল্লা দেওয়া। ***Verb i.*** To take polish ; পালিশের উপযোগী হওয়া। ***Noun.*** Gloss ; polish ; lustre ; চাক্‌চিক্য ; মসৃণতা, জিল্লা ; উজ্জ্বলতা, দীপ্তি। **—er,** *n.*

bur'-nous (bêr-nôs), **bur'-nouse** (bêr-nôs), *n.* **1.** A cloaklike garment worn by the Arabs ; আরবদিগের শিরোবসন সমন্বিত পরিচ্ছদ বিশেষ। **2.** A kind of mantle worn by ladies ; মহিলাদিগের পরিধেয় অঙ্গাবরণ বিশেষ।

burr (bêr), **bur** (bêr), *n.* **1.** A ring of iron on a lance or spear ; বর্শা বা বল্লমের মুষ্টি-দেশস্থ লৌহবলয়। **2.** A knot on a tree ; a knob at the base of a deer's horn, etc. ; গাছের গাঁইট ; মৃগশৃঙ্গাদির মূল-দেশস্থ স্ফীতাংশ। **3.** The sweetbread ; পাকাশয়ের নিম্নস্থিত গ্রন্থির আকার যন্ত্রবিশেষ, ইহা হইতে রস ক্ষরিত হইয়া পরিপাক ক্রিয়ার সাহায্য করে, ক্লোম (হঃ চঃ)। **4.** The lobe of the ear ; কর্ণলতিকা, কর্ণপত্রক, কর্ণলতা, কর্ণের বহির্ভাগ। **5.** A siliceous rock used for mill-stones ; (also burr stone) ; এক প্রকার বেলে পাথর (যাহা হইতে জাঁতা প্রস্তুত হয়)। **6.** Whetstone ; শাণ পাথর। **7.** A kind of lime stone ; a partly vitrified brick ; চূণা পাথর ; ঝামাটে ইট। **8.** A halo round the moon or other heavenly bodies ; চন্দ্রাদি জ্যোতিষ্কের চতুর্দ্দিকস্থ জ্যোতির্মণ্ডল। **9.** A strong rough guttural sounding of the letter *r* ; a whirring sound ; "র" অক্ষরের কর্কশ কণ্ঠ্য উচ্চারণ ; সোঁ সোঁ শব্দ। **10.** A rough ridge left on cut or punched metal or paper ; ছেনিদ্বারা ছিদ্র-করা ধাতু বা কাগজের কাটা বা আব্‌ড়ো-খাব্‌ড়ো কিনারা বা আলি। ***Verb t.*** To pronounce with a burr or guttural sounding of the letter *r* ; to speak without clear articulation ; অর অর্ শব্দে "র" অক্ষর উচ্চারণ করা ; অস্পষ্ট উচ্চারণ করা।

bŭr'-rock (rŏk), *n.* A small weir or dam in a river to direct the stream to fishtrap ; মাছ-ধরা ঘুনিতে নদীস্রোত চালিত করিবার জন্য ক্ষুদ্র বাঁধ।

bŭr'-row (-rō), *n., v. i. & t.* A hole in the ground excavated by foxes, rabbits, etc., for shelter and habitation ; শশকাদির গর্ত্ত, বিবর। ***Verb i.*** **1.** To excavate a hole under ground to lodge in ; (বাসের জন্য) ভূগর্ভে গর্ত্ত করা। **2.** To dwell in a hole or concealed place ; গর্ত্ত বা লুক্কায়িত স্থানে বাস করা, বিবরে বাস করা। **3.** To retire out of sight ; to hide ; চক্ষুর অন্তরালে যাওয়া ; লুকাইয়া যাওয়া। **4.** To work a way under ground ; ভূনিম্নে খনন করিয়া পথ প্রস্তুত করা, সুড়ঙ্গ কাটা। **5.** (*Fig.*) To investigate mysteries, etc. ; (লক্ষণায়) রহস্য উদ্ঘাটন করিতে চেষ্টা করা, নিগূঢ়তত্ত্ব উদ্‌ঘাটনের জন্য অনুসন্ধান করা। ***Verb t.*** To construct by burrowing ; গর্ত্তখননদ্বারা গঠন করা।

bur'-sar (bêr-sêr), *n.* **1.** A treasurer or cash-keeper of a college ;

কলেজের ধনরক্ষক। **2.** A student in the Scottish university or school to whom a stipend or bursary is paid ; স্কটলণ্ড্‌দেশীয় বিশ্ববিদ্যালয়ের বৃত্তিভোগী ছাত্র। **—sa′-ri-al,** *adj.* **—sa-ry,** *n.*

burst (bêrst), *v. i., t.* & *n.* **1.** To break or fly open suddenly and with violence ; বিদীর্ণ হওয়া, সশব্দে ফাটিয়া যাওয়া, ফাটিয়া উড়িয়া যাওয়া। **2.** To break into some sudden expression of feeling, as of the heart in reference to the violence of grief, desire, passion, etc. ; as, to *burst* into song, tears ; বিদীর্ণ হওয়া, ফাটিয়া বাহির হওয়া, সহসা নির্গত, নিঃসৃত বা উৎসারিত হওয়া। **3.** To be opened forcibly ; as, the boil, bud *bursts* : the door *burst* in or open ; উদ্ভিন্ন হওয়া, স্ফুটিত হওয়া। **4.** To be full to overflowing ; as, to *burst* with joy, envy, pride, etc. ; ছাপাইয়া পড়া, উপচিয়া পড়া, উচ্ছ্বসিত হওয়া। **5.** To become suddenly manifest ; to appear suddenly ; as, to *burst* into flame : to *burst* upon the view ; সহসা প্রকাশিত হওয়া ; সহসা আবির্ভূত হওয়া। ***Verb t.*** **1.** To break open suddenly or by violence ; to send powder, shell, case, etc. violently asunder ; as, to *burst* a cannon ; বিদীর্ণ করা ; সশব্দে স্ফুটিত করা। **2.** To make way in or out by force ; সবলে প্রবেশ করা বা নিষ্ক্রান্ত হওয়া। **3.** To open suddenly ; as, to *burst* a door ; সহসা উদ্ঘাটিত করা। ***Noun.*** **1.** An act of bursting ; বিদারণ। **2.** A sudden breaking forth ; হঠাৎ নির্গম। **3.** A sudden opening on the view ; a stretch "Here is a fine *burst* of country ;" সহসা দৃষ্টিপথে উদ্ঘাটন ; বিস্তার। **4.** Result of bursting ; as, a *burst* in a bar of iron ; ভঙ্গ। **5.** An explosion ; eruption ; outbreak ; সশব্দ স্ফোটন ; উদ্গিরণ ; উদ্ভঙ্গ, প্রাদুর্ভাব। **6.** A spurt ; আকস্মিক প্রবল উদ্যম। **7.** A bout of drunkenness ; "A good week's *burst* ;" সুরাপানোৎসব। **8.** A continuous gallop ; অশ্বের ক্রমাগত প্লুতগতি। **A burst up**—A collapse ; a failure ; পতন, বিনাশ ; দেউলিয়া হইয়া পড়ন। **To burst in**—To force one's way violently into ; জোর করিয়া পথ করা, বল পূর্ব্বক প্রবেশ করা। **To burst into blossom**—To begin to blossom ; কুসুমোদ্গম হওয়া। **To burst into laughter**—মুখ ফাটিয়া হাসি বাহির হওয়া। **To burst into tears**—To fail a-crying ; চক্ষু ফাটিয়া অশ্রু নির্গত হওয়া। **To burst open**—ভাঙ্গিয়া খুলিয়া ফেলা। **To burst out**—To force one's way out violently ; সবলে বহির্গত হওয়া। To exclaim ; চীৎকার করিয়া বলা। To appear suddenly ; সহসা আবির্ভূত হওয়া। **To burst up**—To explode ; সশব্দে বিদীর্ণ হওয়া। To become bankrupt ; দেউলিয়া হওয়া।

bur′-ỹ (bĕr-), *v. t.* **1.** To cover out of sight, as a corpse, in a grave, a tomb or the ocean ; (মৃত্তিকার মধ্যে) গোর দেওয়া, কবর দেওয়া, সমাধিস্থ করা, সলিলসমাধি প্রদান করা। **2.** (Of clergy) To perform funeral rites ; (খৃষ্টীয় যাজক সম্পর্কে) অন্ত্যেষ্টি ক্রিয়া সম্পাদন করা। **3.** To put under ground ; as, to *bury* alive ; মাটীতে পুতিয়া ফেলা, সমাহিত করা, ভূপ্রোথিত করা। **4.** To hide in oblivion ; as, to *bury* an injury ; to consign to obscurity ; বিস্মৃতির গর্ভে নিমজ্জিত করা ; অতীতের অন্ধকারে নিমজ্জিত করা। **5.** To put away finally ; to forget ; পরিণামে পরিত্যাগ করা ; ভুলিয়া যাওয়া। **6.** To hide in the earth (treasure etc.) ; to conceal by covering ; (ধনাদি) মাটীর মধ্যে লুকাইয়া রাখা ; চাপা দেওয়া, ঢাক্‌নি দেওয়া, ঢাকা দেওয়া। **7.** (*Fig.*) To lose by death ; as, she *buried* her husband two years ago ; (মৃত্যুহেতু) হারান। **8.** To withdraw from view ; as, to *bury* one's face in one's hands ; লুকান। **Burying-ground, —place**—Graveyard ; cemetery ; সমাধি প্রাঙ্গণ ; কবরস্থান, গোরস্থান। **To bury the hatchet**—To remove quarrel ; to cease strife ; হাতিয়ার রাখিয়া দেওয়া ; বিবাদ হইতে বিরত হওয়া। [শত্রুর সহিত শান্তি সংস্থাপিত হইলে আমেরিকার আদিম অধিবাসিগণ রণকুঠার ভূপ্রোথিত করিয়া থাকে।]

bur′-ỹ (bĕr-), *n.* A delicate kind of pear of several varieties ; কয়েকপ্রকার সুকোমল নাসপাতি ফল।

bŭs, (*pl.* BUSES) *n.* An abbreviation of OMNIBUS (which see.)

bŭs′-bỹ, *n.* A military hat worn in the British army, consisting of a fur hat with a coloured bag overhanging and topped with a pompon ; ইংলণ্ডীয় সৈন্যগণের পরিধেয় লোমনির্ম্মিত টুপি বিশেষ। এই টুপির পশ্চাদ্দিকে একটী রঙ্গীন থলিয়া দোদুল্যমান এবং উপরে একটী চূড়া থাকে।

bûsh, *n.* & *v. t.* **1.** A thick shrub ; a thicket ; ঝোপ, ঝাড় ; নিবিড় গুল্ম। **2.** A shrublike branch of a tree ; ঝোপের মত গাছের ডাল। **3.** A bunch of ivy (as sacred to Bacchus) hung out at vintner's door or as a tavern sign ; শৌণ্ডিক গৃহ বা সুরাবিপণির দ্বারে বিলম্বিত আইভিলতিকাগুচ্ছ। **4.** A luxuriant growth of hair, whisker, etc. ; শ্মশ্রু, কেশ প্রভৃতির প্রাচুর্য্য। **5.** A fox's tail ; শৃগালপুচ্ছ। **6.** A woodland ; a wild uncultivated district, especially in the colonies ; বনভূমি ; অকৃষ্ট অরণ্য প্রদেশ, বিশেষতঃ উপনিবেশসমূহে। ***Verb t.*** **1.** To support with bushes ; as, to *bush* peas ; বৃক্ষ শাখা দ্বারা ধৃত রাখা। **2.** To se (ground) with bushes (to frustrate net-poaching) ; (গোপনে জালদ্বারা পশু শিকার করিতে না পারে তজ্জন্য) ভূমিতে ঝোপ ঝাড় লাগান। 3. To cover seeds by means of the bush-harrow ; বিদার ফাঁকে ফাঁকে ডালপালা ভরিয়া বিদা দিয়া বীজ ঢাকিয়া ফেলা। **Bush-fighting**—ঝোপে জঙ্গলে মারামারি, বৃক্ষগুল্মাদির পশ্চাৎ হইতে যুদ্ধ, অনিয়মিত যুদ্ধ, অব্যবস্থিত সমর। **Bush-harrow**—এক প্রকার বিদা,—যাহার ফাঁকে ডালপালা ভরিয়া দেওয়া হয়। **Bushman**—A woodsman ; বনবাসী, জাঙ্গলিক। A settler in a new country as Australia ; নবাবিষ্কৃত দেশের ঔপনিবেশিক (যথা অষ্ট্রেলিয়ার)। An aboriginal of the Bushman land near the Cape of Good Hope ; উত্তমাশা অন্তরীপের সন্নিকটবর্ত্তী বুশম্যানল্যাণ্ড নামক স্থানের আদিম অধিবাসী। **Bush ranger**—অষ্ট্রেলিয়া মহাদ্বীপে যে দস্যু বা পলাতক বন্দী ঝোপে বাস করিয়া থাকে। **Good wine needs no bush**—চেনা বামুনের পৈতার দরকার নাই। **One beats the bush but another has the hair**—কেহ মরে জল সেঁচে কেহ খায় কৈ। **You are beating the bush for nothing**—বৃথা জঙ্গল ঠেঙ্গাইয়া বা খেদাইয়া বেড়াইতেছ, সোজাসোজি কথা না বলিয়া ঘুরা ফিরা করিতেছ।

bûsh, *n.* & *v. t.* A lining of harder metal inserted into the nave of a wheel or other cricular orifice ; a perforated plug ; ঘর্ষণের ক্ষয় হ্রাসের জন্য চক্রনাভি বা অন্য গোলাকার রন্ধ্রের অভ্যন্তরে যে কঠিনতর ধাতুর পাত সন্নিবিষ্ট করা হয় ; সচ্ছিদ্র গুঁজি। *Verb t.* To furnish with a bush or lining ; উক্তপ্রকার পাতদ্বারা মণ্ডিত করা।

bûsh'-ĕl, *n.* A dry measure of eight gallons ; ফল শস্যাদি মাপিবার পরিমাণ বিশেষ — প্রায় ৯৷৷০ সের। **—ful,** *adj.* **To measure other's corn by one's own bushel**—To judge others by oneself ; আত্মবৎ মন্যতে জগৎ। **Under a bushel**—Secretly ; গোপনে।

busi'-ness (bĭz-nĕs), *n.* **1.** Employment ; occupation ; profession ; as, his *business* was that of a merchant ; কায-কর্ম্ম ; ব্যবসায় ; পেশা। **2.** Buying and selling ; bargaining ; as, doing a great *business* ; ব্যবসায় ; কারবার। **3.** Regular work ; as, hours of *business* ; নিয়মিত কার্য্য। **4.** A commercial house ; a firm ; ব্যবসায়-নিকেতন ; বাণিজ্যশালা। **5.** Proper duty ; what belongs to one to do ; task ; province ; as, analysis is not the *business* of the poet ; কর্ত্তব্য ; নির্দ্দিষ্ট কার্য্য ; কার্য্য ; কার্য্য-ক্ষেত্র। **6.** Object ; intention ; cause of coming ; as, what is your *business* ; উদ্দেশ্য ; অভিপ্রায় ; আগমনের উদ্দেশ্য। **7.** An affair ; matter ; বিষয় ; ব্যাপার। **8.** The right of interposing ; as, what *business* has a man with the disputes of others ; হস্তক্ষেপের অধিকার। **9.** Thing needing attention ; agenda ; as, the *business* of the meeting ; প্রণিধানযোগ্য বিষয় ; কার্য্য-তালিকা। **10.** (*Theatre*) Action, as distinguished from words ; dumb-show ; as, comic *business* ; নাটকে অঙ্গসঞ্চালন, হাবভাব, অঙ্গভঙ্গি ; মূক-অভিনয়। **—like,** *adj.* Systematic ; practical ; prompt ; well-ordered ; প্রণালীবদ্ধ ; ব্যাবহারিক, কার্য্যকর ; সত্বর ; সুশৃঙ্খল, সুবিন্যস্ত। **Business man**—A man engaged in commerce ; ব্যবসায়ী লোক। A man used to dealings with men and matters ; পাকা বিষয়ী লোক। **Good business**—Well done ; বেশ করেছো, সাবাস। **Man of business**—কাজের লোক। An agent ; an attorney ; গোমস্তা ; এটর্ণী। **Mind your own business**—নিজের চরকায় তৈল দেও। **On business**—With definite purpose ; কার্য্যব্যপদেশে, কার্য্যানুরোধে। **To do one's business, to do the busines for a man**—To kill, destroy, or ruin him ; কাহাকে মারিয়া ফেলা, কাহারও দফা রফা করা। **To make a thing one's business**—To devote one's attention to it ; to see that it is done ; কোন বিষয়ে মনোযোগ প্রদান করা, কোন কার্য্যের ভার লওয়া ; কোন কার্য্য যাহাতে সম্পন্ন হয়, তৎপ্রতি দৃষ্টি রাখা। **To go about one's business**—To go off ; চলিয়া যাওয়া। **To mean business**—To be in earnest ; to have serious attention to it ; প্রকৃতপ্রস্তাবে লাগা ; প্রকৃতপক্ষে কোন বিষয়ে মনোনিবেশ করা। **To send one about his own business** — To dismiss promptly ; তাড়াতাড়ি বিদায় করিয়া দেওয়া।

bŭsk, *n.* A piece of steel, whalebone or wood, worn by women in front of their stays ; ইয়ুরোপীয় স্ত্রীলোকদিগের অঙ্গরক্ষার (আঙ্গিয়ার) সম্মুখভাগসংলগ্ন কাঠ কিম্বা তিমি মৎস্যের অস্থিখণ্ড। (ইহার সাহায্যে আঙ্গিয়ার সম্মুখভাগ শক্ত করা হয়।)

bŭs'-kin, *n.* **1.** A kind of boot reaching to the knee, worn to protect the leg against thorns, mud, etc. ; হাঁটুর সমান উচ্চ বুট-জুতা। **2.** A very thick-soled boot worn by the ancient tragic actors of Greece and Rome to lend them height, (opposed to the *sock*, worn by comedians) ; প্রাচীন গ্রীস ও রোমের বিয়োগান্ত নাটকের অভিনেতাদিগের ব্যবহৃত অতি উচ্চ তলাযুক্ত বুটজুতা। **3.** The tragic vein ; a tragedy ; "Great *Fletcher* never breads in *buskin* here ;" বিয়োগান্ত নাটকের ভাব বা ধারা ; বিয়োগান্ত নাটক। **—kined,** *adj.*

Buskin of Bacchus.

buss (bŭs), *n.* & *v. t.* A kiss; a salute with the lips; চুম্বন; চুম্বন বা অধর স্পর্শ দ্বারা অভিবাদন। ***Verb t.*** To kiss; to salute with the lips; চুম্বন করা; অধর স্পর্শদ্বারা অভিবাদন করা।

buss (bŭs), *n.* A small vessel used in herring-fishing; হেরিং-মৎস্য শিকারের জন্য ক্ষুদ্র পোত।

bŭst, *n.* **1.** The sculptured figure of a person, showing only the head, shoulders and breast; মস্তক হইতে বক্ষঃস্থল পর্য্যন্ত অর্দ্ধ শরীরের প্রতিমূর্ত্তি, মানবদেহের উর্দ্ধাংশের প্রতিমা, পূর্ব্বার্দ্ধ-প্রতিমা (আঃ বঃ)। **2.** The upper part of the human body; a woman's bosom; মানবদেহের উর্দ্ধভাগ; স্ত্রীলোকের বক্ষঃস্থল। **Bust'-ed,** *adj.*

bŭs'-tard (-têrd), *n.* A genus of large swift-running birds: the great bustard is the largest European bird; জঙ্গলীকপোত (হিন্দি-বেলঃ), এবং তৎশ্রেণীভুক্ত পক্ষি-সকলের সাধারণ নাম। **Indian bustard**—তোক্দার (হিন্দি-বেলঃ)।

bus'-tle (bŭsl), *v. i., t.* & *n.* **1.** To bestir oneself; to move noisily; as, to *bustle* through the crowd; কর্ম্ম-ব্যস্ত করা; হুটহাট করিয়া চলা। **2.** To make show of activity; to hurry about; কার্য্যতৎপরতা প্রদর্শন করা; ব্যস্তভাবে ছুটাছুটি করা। ***Verb t.*** To make others hurry or work hard; তাড়াতাড়ি কায করান, অতিরিক্ত খাটান। ***Noun.*** An excited activity or fuss; tumult; stir; দৌড়ধাব; গোলমাল, কোলাহল, হুলস্থূল; ব্যস্ততা, ধুমধাম, ছুটাছুটি। **—tler,** *n.* A stuffed pad or cushion worn on the back below the waist, by women, to give fulness to the skirts; ইয়ুরোপীয় স্ত্রীলোকদিগের জঘন-বসন স্ফীত করিবার জন্য ক্ষুদ্র তল্প (গদি) বিশেষ। **—tling,** *adj.*

bus'-ў (bĭz-), *adj.* & *v. t.* **1.** Occupied; engaged in something; ব্যাপৃত; ব্যস্ত। **2.** Actively employed; occupied without cessation; constantly in motion; as, *busy* hammers; কর্ম্মনিরত; কর্ম্মোদ্যুক্ত, নিরন্তর ব্যাপৃত; ব্যস্ত সমস্ত, নিরন্তর ক্রিয়াশীল। **3.** Fussy; meddling with the affairs of others; officious; mischievous; কোলাহলকারী, হৈচৈ-কারী; অন্য ব্যক্তির ব্যাপারে হস্তক্ষেপ-কারী; অনধিকার চর্চ্চা; অনিষ্টকারী। **4.** Crowded with business or activities, (said of places and times); as, a *busy* street: to-morrow is a *busy* day; কর্ম্মকোলাহলময়, কর্ম্মবহুল। ***Verb t.*** To make or keep busy; to occupy oneself (one's hands, eyes, etc.—used chiefly with reflexive pronouns); কর্ম্মব্যস্ত রাখা; (কাহাকে) কার্য্যে ব্যাপৃত করা। **—i-ly,** *adv.* **Busy about nothing**—বৃথা কাযে ব্যস্ত। **Busy-body**—An officious meddlesome person; a mischief-maker; যে ব্যক্তি গায়ে পড়িয়া অন্যের ব্যাপারে হস্তক্ষেপ করে; অনিষ্টকারী। **Busy-minded** — Having an active mind: ব্যস্তমনাঃ।

bŭt, *adv., prep., negative relative pronoun* & *conj.* Only; merely; as, she is *but* a child; কেবল, শুধু; সবেমাত্র, মাত্র। ***Prep., neg. rel. pron. & conj.*** **1.** Except; if not; short of; if it were not that; as, no one *but* me: what can he do *but* die; ভিন্ন, ব্যতীত, ছাড়া, ব্যতিরেকে,; যদি না; কোনকিছু অপেক্ষা কম; তাহা না হইলে। **2.** Otherwise than; as, I cannot *but* do it; (ইহা) ছাড়া অন্যরূপ। **3.** Who or that not; as, no one *but* knows that; কে না। **4.** (After negative) That; as, ten to one *but* was you; (নাস্তিবাচক শব্দের পর) তাহা। **5.** On the contrary; nevertheless; however; yet; বরং, অপীচ, পরন্তু, তৎসত্ত্বে; যাহাহউক, পক্ষান্তরে; অধিকন্তু, কিন্তু, তথাপি। **But and ben,** See BEN. **But for**—Had it not been for না হইলে। **Last but one**—সর্ব্ব শেষটীর অব্যবহিত পূর্ব্ববর্ত্তীটী।

bŭt, *n.* & *v. t.* An objection আপত্তি। ***Verb t.*** To utter or use buts; as, *but* me no buts; পুনঃ পুনঃ 'কিন্তু' শব্দ উচ্চারণ বা ব্যবহার করা।

butch'-êr (bûch-), **1.** One who slaughters animals for food; কসাই, শৌনিক। **2.** A dealer in meat; মাংস-বিক্রেতা, মাংস বিক্রয়জীবী। **3.** (*Fig.*) A judge, general, etc., who has men killed needlessly or brutally; (লক্ষণায়) যে বিচারক বা সৈন্যাধ্যক্ষ অনর্থক বহুলোকের প্রাণদণ্ড বিধান করেন। **4.** A salmon-fly; মক্ষিকাবিশেষ। ***Verb t.*** **1.** To slaughter animals, for food or market; (মাংস বিক্রয়ার্থ বা ভক্ষণার্থ) পশু হত্যা করা। **2.** To slaughter (people) wantonly or cruelly; কসাইয়ের মত নির্দ্দয় ভাবে নরহত্যা করা। **3.** To ruin by bad reading or editing; to damage by harsh criticism; (পুস্তকাদি) কদর্য্যভাবে পাঠ বা সম্পাদন দ্বারা নষ্ট করা; কঠোর সমালোচনা দ্বারা ক্ষতি করা। **—ly,** *adj.* **—y,** *n.* **1.** Shambles (in barracks, camp, ship, etc.); সৈন্যাগার বা জাহাজাদির কসাইখানা। **2.** Needless or cruel slaughter of people; carnage; massacre; নির্দ্দয়ভাবে বহুলোক নিধন; নৃশংস হত্যা; বহুনরহত্যা।

Butea frondosa—পলাশ (বেলঃ)।

bŭt'-lêr, *n.* A male servant who has the care and management of wines, plates, etc., in a great house; the head servant; বড়লোকের বাড়ীর চাকর বা খানসামা, ভাণ্ডারী, রেকাবদার; প্রধান ভৃত্য। **—ship,** *n.*

butt (bŭt), *n.* **1.** A large wine or ale cask (108 to 140 gallons); মদের বড় পিপা। **2.** The thicker end, especially of tool or weapon ; কোন অস্ত্রের বা যন্ত্রের স্থূল প্রান্ত, কুঁদা। **3.** The larger end of a piece of timber, or of a fallen tree ; পতিত বৃক্ষের বা তক্তার বৃহত্তর প্রান্ত। **4.** A piece of land left unploughed at the end of a field ; ক্ষেত্রপ্রান্তস্থ অকর্ষিত ভূমি। **5.** A sort of hinge used in hanging doors ; এক প্রকার কবাটের কব্জা। **6.** The thickest and stoutest part of tanned ox-hides, used for soles of shoes, harness, etc. ; শোধিত বৃষ চর্ম্মের স্থূল ও দৃঢ়তম অংশ—যদ্দ্বারা পাদুকাতল, অশ্বসজ্জা প্রভৃতি প্রস্তুত হয়। **7.** A joint where the ends of two objects come squarely together ; দুইটী বস্তুর প্রান্তের সন্ধিস্থল।

bŭtt (bŭt), *n.* **1.** A mound behind a target ; শরব্যের পশ্চাদ্‌বর্ত্তী মৃত্তিকা-স্তূপ। **2.** (*Pl.*) A shooting range ; বন্দুকাদির পাল্লা। **3.** A target ; a mark to be shot ; লক্ষ্য ; শরব্য। **4.** End ; aim ; object ; উদ্দেশ্য ; লক্ষ্য ; অভিপ্রায়। **5.** A person at whom ridicule, jest or contempt is directed ; as, the *butt* of the company ; ঠাট্টা, বিদ্রূপ বা উপহাসের পাত্র। **6.** A push or thurst given by the head of an animal ; as, the *butt* of a ram ; শৃঙ্গাঘাত, গুঁতা, ঢু।

butt (bŭt), *v. t.* & *i.* **1.** To strike with the head, as a ram ; (also *v. i.*) ; ঢু মারা। **2.** To make (a joint) by joining end to end without overlapping ; প্রান্তে প্রান্তে মিলাইয়া জোড়া দেওয়া। ***Verb i.*** **1.** To jut ; উদ্গাত হওয়া। **2.** To abut on ; লাগাও হওয়া।

bŭt′-têr, *n.* & *v. t.* **1.** An oily substance obtained from cream নবনীত সদৃশ কোন বস্তু। **3.** (*Fig.*) Fulsome flattery ; "You have been daubed over by the dirty *butter* of his applause ;" (লক্ষণায়) ন্যক্কারজনক তোষামোদ। [c.f. তৈল in our তৈলমর্দ্দন।] ***Verb t.*** To smear with butter ; to cook or sauce with butter ; মাখন মাখাইয়া দেওয়া ; মাখনদ্বারা পাক করা, মাখনদ্বারা সুস্বাদু করা। **–y,** *adj.* & *n.* Having the quality or appearance of butter ; নবনীতবৎ, মাখনসদৃশ। (*Noun.*) **1.** An apartment in which wines, liquors, and provisions are kept ; যে কক্ষে মদ্য প্রভৃতি পানীয় এবং খাদ্যদ্রব্য রক্ষিত হয়। **2.** In some colleges a room where refreshments are kept ; (কোন কোন কলেজে) যে কক্ষে ফল, তামাক, পানীয় এবং জলযোগের দ্রব্য বিক্রয়ার্থ রক্ষিত হয়। **Butter-boat**—ভোজনকালে যে নৌকাকৃতি পাত্রে ঘৃত, মাখন, প্রভৃতি রাখা হয়, মাখনদান। **Buttercup**—উজ্জ্বল পীতবর্ণ পান-পাত্রবৎ পুষ্পপ্রসূ তরুবিশেষ। **Butter-fingers**—(*Slang*) One who lets drop anything he ought to hold ; (ইতর ভাষায়) ননীর আঙ্গুল, অর্থাৎ যে ব্যক্তি অসাবধানতাবশতঃ হাত হইতে জিনিষ ফেলিয়া দেয়। **Butter-fish**—কাণিপাব্‌দা। **Butter-fly**—প্রজাপতি। A showily dressed, vain and gaudy person ; ফুলবাবু। A fickle person ; a trifler ; চপলমতি ব্যক্তি, তরলমতিব্যক্তি ; তুচ্ছকারী। [*Butter-fly-kiss*—A kiss with one's eye-lashes ; অক্ষি পক্ষ্মদ্বারা চুম্বন অর্থাৎ মৃদু স্পর্শ করণ।] **Butter-knife**—মাখন কাটিবার জন্য (রৌপ্যাদি নির্ম্মিত) ভোঁতা ছুরি, নবনীতকর্ত্তরিকা। **Butterman**—A man who makes or sells butter ; নবনীত প্রস্তুতকারী fore-tooth ; উপরের পাটির বৃহৎ দন্ত। **Butter-tree**—আফ্রিকাদেশীয় বৃক্ষ বিশেষ—ইহার বীজ হইতে নবনীতবৎ পদার্থ প্রাপ্ত হওয়া যায়, নবনীত বৃক্ষ। **Butter-woman**—নবনীত বিক্রেত্রী, মাখনওয়ালী, গোয়ালিনী, গোপী। **Buttery-hatch**—ভোজ্যবিতরণের জন্য ক্ষুদ্র দ্বার বিশেষ। **Clarified butter**—ঘৃত, সর্পি। **Butter to butter is no relish**—কেবল চাট্‌নি খাইয়া পেট ভরে না। **Fine words butter no parsnips**—Mere professions are valueless ; মিষ্ট কথায় পেট ভরে না। **He knows on which side is bread buttered**—He knows his self-interest ; সে তাহার নিজের বুঝ ষোল আনা বা কড়ায় গণ্ডায় বুঝে। **He looks as if butter would not melt in his mouth**—He looks like a dolt ; তাহাকে নিতান্ত গোবেচারার মত দেখায়। **To butter one's bread on both sides**—To live a most comfortable and luxurious life ; অতিসুখসচ্ছন্দে জীবন-যাত্রা নির্ব্বাহ করা। **To have one's bread buttered for life**—To be well provided for ; সারাজীবন সুখে স্বচ্ছন্দে চলিতে পারে এরূপ ব্যবস্থা হওয়া।

bŭt′-têr-ine (-în), *n.* An artificial butter prepared from animal fat with some other ingredients intermixed ; চর্ব্বি ও অন্যান্য কতিপয় দ্রব্যের সহযোগে প্রস্তুত কৃত্রিম নবনীত বিশেষ, কৃত্রিম মাখন।

bŭt′-têr-is, *n.* A farrier's tool for paring hoofs of horses ; অশ্বের খুর কাটিবার যন্ত্র বিশেষ।

bŭt′-tock (-tŏk), *n.* & *v. t.* **1** The rump or the protuberant part behind ; নিতম্ব, জঘন, শ্রোণি, প্রোথ। **2.** The convexity of a ship behind, under the stern ; জাহাজে-রদেশের স্থূলতা। **3.** in wrestling ; মল্ল... ***Verb t.*** ...

but'-ton (bŭtn), *n., v. t.* & *i.* **1.** A knob or ball or disk sewn to garment to fasten it or for ornament ; বোতাম । **2.** A bud ; a germ of a plant ; মুকুল ; অঙ্কুর । **3.** An unopened mushroom ; অস্ফুট ছত্রাক । **4.** A knob, handle or catch, as in electric bell ; বৈদ্যুতিক ঘণ্টা প্রভৃতির হাতল, ঘুণ্টি বা আঁকড়া । **5.** A small bar revolving on pivot as door-fastening ; অর্গল, ফিরকি । **6.** A small rounded body ; ক্ষুদ্র গোলাকার বস্তু । **7.** (*Pl. used* as a singular.) A liveried page ; নির্দিষ্ট পরিচ্ছদ পরিহিত বালভৃত্য । [*Also a boy in buttons.*] ***Verb t.*** **1.** To attach a button or buttons ; বোতাম লাগান । **2.** To fasten with a button or buttons ; to inclose or make secure with buttons, (often with *up*) ; বোতাম দ্বারা আটকান ; বোতামদ্বারা বন্ধ করা । ***Verb i.*** To be fastened by a button or buttons ; to be capable of being buttoned ; এক বা ততোধিক বোতামদ্বারা বন্ধ হওয়া ; বোতাম লাগাইবার যোগ্য হওয়া । **–less, –toned, –y,** *adjs.* **Button-hole,** & *v. t.* **1.** A hole or loop to admit a button ; বোতামের ঘর, পুঁটে-ঘরা । **2.** (*Fig.*) Flowers worn in button-hole ; (লক্ষণায়) বোতামের ছিদ্রে পরিহিত পুষ্পগুচ্ছ । **3.** A small mouth ; ক্ষুদ্র মুখ । (*Verb t.*) To seize a man by the button or button-hole and detain him in conversation against his will ; to bore ; বোতাম বা বোতামের ছিদ্রে ধরিয়া কথাবার্ত্তা বলিয়া কোন ব্যক্তিকে ইচ্ছার বিরুদ্ধে আটক করিয়া রাখা ; বিরক্ত করা বা বিতৃষ্ণা জন্মান । **Not to care a button**—Not to feel the slightest concern or regard ; [illegible]

the exterior of a wall, etc. ; দেয়াল প্রভৃতির পোস্তা । **2.** Any prop or support ; উপস্তম্ভ, আশ্রয়, আলম্ব (আঃ বঃ), ঠেস, ঠেকা । ***Verb t.*** **1.** To support by buttress ; to prop ; পোস্তা বাঁধিয়া সুরক্ষিত করা ; অবলম্বন দেওয়া । **2.** To support by argument ; "Some of the facts concerning America *buttressed* their arguments ;" যুক্তিতর্ক দ্বারা সমর্থন করা ।

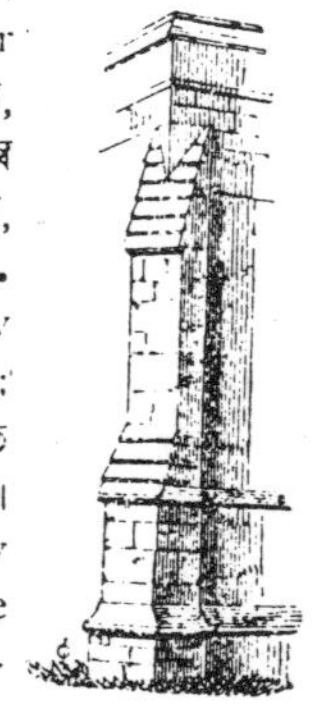

Buttress.

bux'-om (bŭk-sŭm), *adj.* Plump ; jolly ; comely ; গোলগাল, হৃষ্টপুষ্ট, টুকটুকে, মোটাসোটা, নাদুসনুদুস্ (*Colloq.*) ; উৎফুল্ল, উল্লাসপূর্ণ ; সুশ্রী । **–ness,** *n.*

buy (bī), *v. t.* **1.** To obtain by paying a price (usually money) ; to purchase ; (opposed to *sell*) ; অর্থ বিনিময়ে প্রাপ্ত হওয়া ; ক্রয় করা, খরিদ করা । **2.** To serve to procure ; to acquire or procure for any kind of equivalent ; as, to *buy* favour by flattery : প্রাপ্তির সাহায্য করা ; বিনিময়ে লাভ করা । **3.** To get by some sacrifice ; as, dearly *bought* love ; (কোন প্রকার ত্যাগ বা ক্ষতি স্বীকার করিয়া) প্রাপ্ত হওয়া । **4.** To gain over (a person) by bribery ; (কাহাকে) উৎকোচদ্বারা বশীভূত করা । **Buy'-a-ble,** *adj.* That can be bought ; ক্রেতব্য, ক্রেয় । **Buy'-er,** *n.* One who buys ; ক্রেতা । **To buy in**—To purchase a stock ; কোম্পানীর কাগজ খরিদ করা । To buy for the owner at a public sale, especially when an insufficient (claim, claimant, blackmailer, etc.) ; দাবির টাকা শোধ করিয়া মুক্তিলাভ করা, দাবিদার বা দস্যুকে টাকা দিয়া মুক্ত হওয়া । To release from military service by payment ; টাকা দিয়া সৈনিকের কায হইতে মুক্ত করা । **To buy off a person**—To cause a person to desist from opposition by pecuniary or other consideration ; কোন ব্যক্তিকে অর্থ প্রদান বা অন্য কোনপ্রকারে বশীভূত করিয়া প্রতিকূলতাচরণে বিরত করা । **To buy on credit**—To purchase, on a promise, to make payment at a future day ; ধারে কেনা । **To buy out**—To pay a person to give up post, property, etc. ; সম্পত্তি, চাকুরী প্রভৃতি ছাড়িয়া দিবার জন্য কাহাকেও টাকা দেওয়া । **To buy over**—To bribe ; উৎকোচ দেওয়া, ঘুষ দেওয়া । **To buy the refusal of anything**—বায়না করিয়া রাখা [অর্থাৎ বায়নাদাতা ক্রয় করিবার অধিকার স্বেচ্ছায় ত্যাগ না করিলে বায়না-গ্রহীতা অন্যের নিকট বিক্রয় করিতে পারিবে না ।] **To buy up**—To purchase the hole commodity of a substance for speculative purposes ; ভবিষ্যতে অধিক মূল্যে বিক্রয়ের উদ্দেশ্যে কোন জিনিষ সমস্ত ক্রয় করিয়া রাখা, রাখী করা ।

buzz (bŭz), *v. i., t.* & *n.* **1.** To make a low humming sound, as bees ; গুন্ গুন্ শব্দ করা, গুঞ্জন করা, ভন্ ভন্ করা, ভ্যান্ ভ্যান্ করা, ভোঁ ভোঁ শব্দ করা । **2.** To speak with a low hissing voice ; ফিস্ ফিস্ করিয়া কথা বলা । ***Verb t.*** **1.** To move or hover about annoyingly like blue-bottle ; গুন্ গুন্ করিয়া ঘুরিয়া বেড়ান, ভন্ ভন্ করিয়া ঘুরা । **2.** To whisper ; to circulate ; ফিস্‌ফিস্ করিয়া কথা বলা ; কাণাঘুষা করা । **3.** To utter by speak-

সজোরে নিক্ষেপ করা। *Noun.* **1.** A continuous humming noise, as of bees ; as, the constant *buzz* of a fly ; গুণ্‌গুণ্ শব্দ, গুঞ্জন, ঝঙ্কার, ভন্‌ভন্ শব্দ, ভ্যান্‌ভ্যানি (*Colloq.*)। **2.** A low whispering hum passing through a crowd ; জনতার কলকল ধ্বনি, কলরব, কিলকিলা শব্দ। **3.** A whisper ; a report spread secretly and cautiously ; "There is a certain *buzz* of a stolen marriage ;" কাণাকাণি ; কাণাঘুষা। **4.** A downy beetle ; a fishing-fly like it ; এক প্রকার গোবরে পোকা ; মৎস্য ধরিবার ফড়িং বিশেষ। **Buzz'-er,** *n.* A steam-whistle ; জাহাজ, রেলগাড়ী প্রভৃতির শিটি।

bŭz'-zard (*-zêrd*), *n.* **1.** A bird of prey of the falcon family ; এক প্রকার বাজজাতীয় পক্ষী। **2.** A block-head ; a dunce ; নির্ব্বোধ ; মূর্খ।

bȳ, *prep.* & *adv.* **1.** Near ; close to ; as, sit *by* me ; কাছে ; সমীপে, নিকটে। **2.** Along ; in passing along ; through ; via ; avoiding ; passing ; as, *by* the nearest way : to pass him *by* : to go *by* a church ; বরাবর ; বরাবর যাইতে যাইতে ; মধ্যদিয়া ; হইয়া ; ছাড়িয়া ; অতিক্রম করিয়া। **3.** Denoting the author, producer, agent, means, instrument, or cause of ; as, Sakuntala *by* Kalidas : the city was destroyed *by* fire : to travel *by* rail : to live *by* bread : profit is made by commerce : to take *by* force ; দ্বারা, দিয়া, কর্ত্তৃক, পূর্ব্বক। **4.** According to ; as, this appears *by* his own account ; অনুসারে। **5.** At the rate of ; in the quantity of ; as, to sell cloth *by* the yard, milk *by* the quart, egg *by* the dozen ; হিসাবে ; পরিমাণে। **6.** During the course of ; as, *by* day : *by* night ; ভাগে, যোগে, কালে। **7.** As soon as ; not later than ; as, *by* this time, the sun had risen : *by* now : *by* the time ; যেই মাত্র, যেই মুহূর্ত্তে ; (নির্দ্দিষ্ট) সময়ের পরে নয়। **8.** With reference to ; in respect of ; as, he did well *by* her ; সম্বন্ধে ; সম্পর্কে। **9.** Against ; বিরুদ্ধে। *Adv.* **1.** Near ; at hand ; as, to stand *by* : unto the neighbouring castle *by* ; নিকটে ; সমীপে, সন্নিধানে। **2.** Aside ; in reserve ; as, let them lay their helmets *by* : to put or lay *by* ; এক পার্শ্বে ; ভবিষ্যতের জন্য রক্ষিত। **3.** With verbs of motion *by* conveys the notion of *passing* and with reference to time, *by* is equivalent to *past* ; as, they marched *by* : all that is gone *by* ; চলিয়া ; গত। **Better by far**—Much better ; শত গুণ ভাল, ভাল। **By Birth**—জাতিতে। **By chance**—দৈবাৎ, দৈবক্রমে। **By day**—দিবাভাগে। **By degrees**—ক্রমে ক্রমে। **By dint of**—By the force or operation of ; (কোন কিছুর) শক্তিতে, সাহায্যে বা বলে। **By hundreds**—শত শত। **By land**—স্থলপথে। **By night**—নিশাযোগে, রজনীযোগে। **By no means**—কোন মতেই না। **By note**—মুখস্থ করিয়া, কণ্ঠস্থ করিয়া। **By one's self**—Without any one else near ; solitary ; alone ; একাকী ; নির্জ্জনে ; একান্তে, বিরলে। **By sea**—জলপথে, সমুদ্রপথে। **By ten o'clock**—ঠিক দশটার সময় বা তাহার কিছু পূর্ব্বে। **By the bye**—In passing ; প্রসঙ্গক্রমে, কথাচ্ছলে, ভাল কথা, ও হো হো। **By the dozen**—ডজন্ ডজন। **By then**—ততক্ষণে। **By the way**—As one goes ; প্রসঙ্গক্রমে, ও ওহো। **By this**—When that event happened ; ঐ ঘটনার কালে। **By this time**—এত ক্ষণে। **By turns**—Alternately ; পর্য্যায়ক্রমে। **By way of joke**—ঠাট্টাচ্ছলে। **By what means**—কি করিয়া। **Day by day**—দিনের পর দিন, দিন দিন, প্রতিদিন। **One by one**—একে একে। **It is sold by the maund**—মণ হিসাবে বিক্রয় হয়। **To be by way of knowing every-body**—To profess, or be supposed, to know every body ; সবলোকের সহিত জানাশোনা আছে এরূপ ভাবগতিক দেখান। **To come by**—To get possession of ; to obtain ; অধিকার লাভ করা ; প্রাপ্ত হওয়া। **To stand by**—To support ; সমর্থন করা।

bȳ, bȳe, *adj.* & *n.* Subordinate ; incidental ; secondary ; out-of-the-way ; secret ; as, *by*-effects : a *by*-consideration ; অপ্রধান ; আনুষঙ্গিক ; গৌণ ; সাধারণ পথ বা প্রণালীর বহির্ভূত ; গোপনীয়। *Noun.* **1.** A thing not directly aimed at ; something not the direct object of regard ; as, the duty by the *bye* ; গৌণকর্ম্ম ; গৌণ-উদ্দেশ্য। **2.** (*Cricket*) Run scored for ball that passes batsman and wicket-keeper ; কোন কন্দুক (বল) ব্যাটধারী এবং উইকেট রক্ষককে অতিক্রম করিলে তজ্জন্য যে 'দৌড়' লাভ হয় **By-corner**—A private corner ; গুপ্ত কোণ। **By-election** — উপনির্ব্বাচন। [অর্থাৎ সাধারণ নির্ব্বাচনে নির্ব্বাচিত ব্যক্তি পদ পরিত্যাগ করিলে বা মৃত্যুমুখে পতিত হইলে তাহার স্থল পূরণের জন্য যে উপনির্ব্বাচন হয়।]

bȳ ănd bȳ, *adv.* & *n.* Before long ; অবিলম্বে, অচিরাৎ। *Noun.* The future ; ভবিষ্যৎ কাল।

bȳ'-blow (*-blō*), *n.* **1.** A side blow at some one else than the main opponent ; প্রধান প্রতিদ্বন্দ্বীর স্থলে অন্য ব্যক্তিকে যে আঘাত করা হয়। **2.** A bastard child ; জারজ সন্তান।

bȳ'-ĕnd, *n.* Private end ; secret purpose or advantage ; গুপ্ত অভিসন্ধি ; গূঢ় অভিপ্রায়, গুপ্ত উদ্দেশ্য, গুপ্ত সুবিধা।

bȳ'-gone (*-gŏn*), *adj.* & *n. pl.* **1.** Past ; gone by ; departed ; অতীত ; গত ; অন্তর্হিত। **2.** Antiquated ; সেকেলে, প্রাচীন ধরণের,

অপ্রচলিত। *Noun. Pl.* The past; the past offences; as, let *by-gones* be *by-gones* (গতস্য শোচনা নাস্তি); অতীত কাল, গত বিষয়; পূর্ব্বকৃত অপরাধ।

bȳ'-law (-lä), **bȳe-**, *ns.* A regulation made by a local incorporated body for the regulation of its own affairs or the affairs entrusted to its care; মিউনিসিপালিটি প্রভৃতি কর্ত্তৃক বিধিবদ্ধ আইন, উপবিধি, উপধর্ম্ম (যঃ সং)। [By-law শব্দের *by* শব্দটী ডেনমার্ক-দেশীয়, উক্ত ভাষায় উহার অর্থ "সহর"।]

bȳ'-nāme, *n.* **1.** A nickname; ডাকনাম, উপনাম। **2.** Secondary name; গৌণ নাম।

bȳ'-păst, *adj.* Gone by; past; elapsed; গত; অতীত; অতিক্রান্ত।

bȳ'-päth, —way (-wā), *ns.* **1.** A private path; গুপ্তপথ, অপ্রকাশ্য রাস্তা বা শুঁড়ি পথ। **2.** Indirect course or means; as, *by-paths* of history; গৌণ উপায় বা গতি।

bȳ'-play (-plā), *n.* **1.** Action apart from the main course of events; নাটকের উপাঙ্গ, (অঙ্গভঙ্গি প্রভৃতি)। **2.** A dumb show of minor characters on the stage; অপ্রধান নাটকীয় চরিত্র সমূহের মৌন-প্রদর্শন।

bȳ'-prŏd-ŭct *n.* Something produced incidentally in manufacturing something else; কোন বস্তু প্রস্তুত করণের সময় আনুষঙ্গিক ভাবে যে অন্য বস্তু প্রাপ্ত হওয়া যায়, উপসর্গ (হিঃ কোঃ), উপোৎপাদন। [যথা, গ্লিসিরিণ সাবানের এবং খৈল তেলের উপোৎপাদন।]

byre, (-bīr), *n.* A cow-house; গোগৃহ, গোশালা।

bȳs'-sŭs, *n.* **1.** A cloth of exceedingly fine texture and fabric of flax, used by the ancients; প্রাচীনকালে ব্যবহৃত অতি সূক্ষ্ম বস্ত্র। **2.** A tuft of silky filaments by which some molluscs adhere to rock; সূক্ষ্ম পট্টসূত্রবৎ অংশু বা তন্তু-গুচ্ছ,—যদ্দারা শম্বুকাদি প্রস্তরে সংলগ্ন থাকে।

bȳ'-stănd-êr, *n.* One who stands near; a spectator; নিকটে দণ্ডায়মান ব্যক্তি; দ্রষ্টা, দর্শক।

bȳ' street (-strēt), *n.* A side street; উপপথ।

bȳ'-way (-wā), *n.* **1.** A secluded road or track; গুপ্ত পথ, নিভৃত পথ। **2.** A short cut; সোজা পথ। **3.** A less known department of any subject; কোন বিষয়ের অপ্রসিদ্ধ বা অল্পমাত্র জ্ঞাত বিভাগ।

bȳ-word (-wêrd), *n.* **1.** A proverb; a common saying; জনপ্রবাদ, প্রবাদ বাক্য; প্রবচন। **2.** An object of common derision; সাধারণের উপহাস পাত্র।

bȳz'-ănt, *n.* Same as BEZANT.

Bȳ-zăn'-tine (-tīn), *n.* & *adj.* **1.** Inhabitants of Byzantium or Constantinople; (প্রাচ্য রোমরাজ্যের রাজধানী) কনষ্টাণ্টিনোপল নিবাসী। *Adj.* Of the style of architecture, etc., developed in the Eastern Empire; প্রাচ্য রোম-সাম্রাজ্যে বিকাশ-প্রাপ্ত স্থাপত্য-রীতি প্রভৃতি সম্বন্ধীয়।

C

C, **1.** The third letter of the English alphabhet; ইংরাজী বর্ণমালার তৃতীয় অক্ষর। **2.** (*Mus.*) The first note of the natural major scale; (সঙ্গীত-শাস্ত্র) স্বরগ্রামের অন্তর্গত মুদারার প্রথম স্বর "সা"। **3.** (*In argument*) The third hypothetical person or thing; (তর্ক) কল্পিত তৃতীয় ব্যক্তি বা বস্তু। **4.** (*Algeb.*) The third known quantity; (বীজগণিত) পরিজ্ঞাত তৃতীয় রাশি। **5.** As a numeral *C* stands for Latin *centum* or 100; *C* ল্যাটিন ভাষার *centum* (একশত) শব্দের সংক্ষেপ-স্বরূপ ব্যবহৃত হয় (যথা—*CC*=200)।

Câ-'ā-bâ, *n.* (*Arabic*) The Mahommedan temple at Mecca, specially a small cubical oratory within, adored by Mahommedans as containing the black stone, said to have been given by an angel to Abraham; মক্কা নগরীস্থিত কাবা নামক সুপ্রসিদ্ধ ধর্ম্মমন্দির, বিশেষভাবে উক্ত মন্দিরাভ্যন্তরস্থ ক্ষুদ্র প্রার্থনা-মণ্ডপ, ইহাতে মুসলমানগণদ্বারা অর্চ্চিত সুপবিত্র কৃষ্ণপ্রস্তর অবস্থিত আছে। এই প্রস্তর এব্রাহেম জনৈক দেবদূতের নিকট হইতে প্রাপ্ত হন বলিয়া উল্লিখিত আছে।

căb, *n.* & *v. t.* (Abbreviated from CABRIOLET.) An one-horsed covered hackney carriage with two or four wheels; a hansom; দুই বা চারি চাকা বিশিষ্ট এক ঘোড়ার আবৃত গাড়ি; একপ্রকার দুই চাকার গাড়ী—এই প্রকার গাড়ীর চালক পশ্চাৎ-দিকের উচ্চ আসনে উপবিষ্ট থাকে। *Verb t.* To go in a cab; as, I'll *cab* it to White Hall; উক্তপ্রকার গাড়িতে যাওয়া। **Cab-man**—উক্ত-প্রকার গাড়ির চালক। **Cab-rank**—উক্তপ্রকার গাড়ির সারি। **Cab-tout**—যে ব্যক্তি উক্তপ্রকার গাড়ী ডাকিয়া অথবা গাড়ী হইতে আরোহীর মালপত্র নামাইয়া পয়সা রোজগার করে।

că-băl', *n.* & *v. i.* **1.** A small party united for some secret designs;

কুচক্রিদল। 2. Secret plot; intrigue; গুপ্ত মন্ত্রণা, কুমন্ত্রণা, গূঢ় মন্ত্রণা, কূটযুক্তি; চক্রান্ত, চক্র। 3. The committee for foreign affairs under Charles II; ইংলণ্ডের রাজা দ্বিতীয় চার্লসের পররাষ্ট্রসভা। [১৬৭১ খৃঃ অব্দে দ্বিতীয় চার্লসের রাজত্বকালে বিচিত্র ঘটনা-সম্মিলনে যে পাঁচজন মন্ত্রী দ্বারা (Clifford, Arlington, Buckingham, Ashley and Lauderdale) মন্ত্রিসভা সংগঠিত হয়, তাহাদের নামের আদ্য অক্ষর যোগে *cabal* শব্দ রচিত হওয়ায় তদবধি ঐ বলিতে কুচক্রিদল বুঝায়।] ***Verb i.*** To form a party for a secret purpose; to plot; গুপ্ত অভিসন্ধি সাধনার্থ দলবদ্ধ হওয়া; চক্রান্ত করা, কূট-মন্ত্রণা করা।

căb'-ă-lă, -bă-, *n.* **1.** The designation of a mystic system of philosophy, theosophy and magic, current among the Jews; ইয়ুদিদিগের মধ্যে এক সময়ে প্রচলিত ভাবযোগ, ব্রহ্মবিদ্যা এবং তান্ত্রিক ক্রিয়াকাণ্ডের নাম। [ইহারা "সর্ব্বং খল্বিদং ব্রহ্ম" বাদের প্রচারক ছিল এবং বাইবেল গ্রন্থের অদ্ভুত আধ্যাত্মিক ব্যাখ্যা প্রদান করিত।] **2.** Mystic interpretation; esoteric doctrine; occult lores; "Eager he read whatever tells of magic, *cabala*, and spells;" নিগূঢ় ব্যাখ্যা; নিগূঢ় মতবাদ; গুপ্তবিদ্যা, গুহ্যতত্ত্ব। **—lism,** *n.* **—list,** *n.* One who professes acquaintance with, and faith in, the Jewish mystic doctrine of the cabala; ইয়ুদী তন্ত্রবিৎ, ইয়ুদী তান্ত্রিক। **—lis'-tic,** *adj.* **1.** Pertaining to the cabala; ইয়ুদীদিগের গুপ্তবিদ্যা সম্বন্ধীয়। **2.** Mystic; occult; গুপ্ত, নিগূঢ়; গূঢ়ার্থ, গুহ্য, পরমগহন।

căb'-ă-rĕt, *n.* A tavern; a liquor shop; মদিরাগৃহ, মদ্য বিক্রয় স্থান; শুঁড়িখানা।

căb'-as (-â), *n.* (Fr. often written as CABA) A lady's flat work-basket or reticule; মহিলার হস্ত-পেটিকা বা জালনির্ম্মিত থলিয়া।

căb'-bāge, *n.* & *v. i.* A culinary vegetable of several varieties; কপিশাক। ***Verb i.*** To form a head like that of a cabbage in growing; বাঁধাকপির মত মাথা বাঁধিয়া উঠা। **Cabbage-butterfly**—শ্বেতবর্ণ প্রকাণ্ড প্রজাপতি বিশেষ, ইহার অণ্ডোৎপন্ন কিরা কপিজাতীয় শাক ধ্বংস করে। **Cabbage-net**—কপি সিদ্ধ করিবার ক্ষুদ্র জাল বিশেষ। **Cabbage palm**—তালজাতীয় বৃক্ষ বিশেষ, ইহার অগ্রপল্লব কপিশাকের মত খাদ্যরূপে ব্যবহৃত হয়। **Cabbage-rose**—একজাতীয় গোলাব ফুল। **Cabbage-worm**—কতিপয় কীট ও প্রজাপতির কপিধ্বংসকারী কিরা বিশেষ।

căb'-bāge, *v. t.* & *n.* To purloin; to retain cloth left after cutting a garment; "Your tailor, instead of shreds, *cabbages* whole yards of cloth;" আত্মসাৎ করা; জামা প্রভৃতি কাটিবার পর যে কাপড় উদ্বৃত্ত থাকে তাহা আত্মসাৎ করা। ***Noun.*** The cloth so appropriated; উক্তপ্রকারে আত্মসাৎ-করা কাপড়।

căb'-in, *n.*, & *v. t.* **1.** A cottage or small house; a hut; কুটীর, ছোট ঘর; অস্থায়ী ক্ষুদ্র গৃহ। **2.** A room in a ship for officers and passengers; (উচ্চশ্রেণীর) যাত্রী এবং জাহাজের কর্ম্মচারিগণের কামরা, পোতকক্ষ, মন্দির (রাধা কুঃ)। ***Verb t.*** To confine in a small place; "I am cribbed, *cabined*, and confined;" সংকীর্ণ স্থানে রুদ্ধ করা। **Cabin-boy**—জাহাজের যাত্রী এবং কর্ম্মচারিগণের পরিচারক।

căb'i-nĕt, *n.* **1.** A closet; a small room; ক্ষুদ্র নির্জ্জন কক্ষ, নিভৃতাগার; ক্ষুদ্র প্রকোষ্ঠ। **2.** A private room for consultations; মন্ত্রণাকক্ষ, মন্ত্রণাগৃহ। **3.** A case with drawers etc., for keeping valuables or displaying curiosities; মূল্যবান বা চমকপ্রদ দ্রব্যাদি রাখিবার দেরাজ বিশেষ। **4.** The collective body of ministers of a state; মন্ত্রিসভা, সচিববর্গ, মন্ত্রিবর্গ। **5.** A council room of twelve or twenty chief ministers of a state; কোন রাষ্ট্রের ১২ কি ২০ জন প্রধান মন্ত্রির জন্য মন্ত্রণাগৃহ। **6.** Those ministers collectively; মন্ত্রিসভা। **Cabinet-council**—মন্ত্রিসভার অধিবেশন। **Cabinet edition**—পুস্তকের ক্ষুদ্র পরিপাটী সংস্করণ বিশেষ। **Cabinet-makers**—বিচিত্র দ্রব্যাদি নির্ম্মাতা, আসবাব নির্ম্মাতা। **Cabinet-photograph**—কার্ড অপেক্ষা বড় আকারের আলোকচিত্র।

cā'-ble, *n.*, *v. t.* & *i.* **1.** The rope or chain to which a ship's anchor is attached; জাহাজের কাছি বা শৃঙ্খল। **2.** The wire rope used for the support of some suspension bridge; ঝুলানো সেতু ধারণের জন্য ধাতবরজ্জু বিশেষ। **3.** The wire rope used for submarine telegraphs; as, a telegraphic *cable*; সাগরতল-বার্ত্তাবহের ধাতব রজ্জু। **4.** A submarine or under-ground line containing insulated wires; অপরিচালক পদার্থ-বেষ্টিত ধাতবরজ্জু সমন্বিত সাগরতল বা ভূগর্ভস্থ তাড়িত বার্ত্তাবহ। **5.** A cable message; সাগরতলস্থ তারযোগে প্রেরিত বার্ত্তা। **6.** (*Arch. and goldsmiths' work*) A rope-shaped ornament; (স্থপতি-বিদ্যা এবং স্বর্ণকারের কার্য্য) রজ্জুর আকৃতি সৌধ ভূষা, দড়াহার প্রভৃতি। ***Verb t.*** **1.** To fasten with a cable; কাছিদ্বারা বাঁধা। **2.** To telegraph by submarine cable; as, to *cable* a message across the Atlantic; সাগরতলস্থ তারযোগে বার্ত্তা প্রেরণ। **3.** To fill the flutes of a column with cable-moulding; রজ্জুবৎ অলঙ্কারদ্বারা স্তম্ভগাত্রস্থ নালী সকল পূর্ণ করা। ***Verb i.*** To send a message by the submarine telegraph cable; as, he *cables* today; সাগরনিম্নস্থ তারযোগে তাড়িত বার্ত্তা প্রেরণ করা। **Cable-laid rope**—তিনগুণবিশিষ্ট তিনটী রজ্জু একত্র পাকাইয়া

যে রজ্জু রচিত হয়। **Cable-moulding**—স্তম্ভগাত্রস্থ নালী সকলের রজ্জুবৎ ভূষা, রজ্জুবৎ সৌধালঙ্কার। **To bend the cable**—To make it fast to the anchor ; নঙ্গরে কাছি লাগান। **To pay out the cable, To slip the cable**—To let it run out ; কাছি ছাড়িয়া দেওয়া।

cā′-ble-grăm, *n.* A message by submarine cable ; সাগরতলস্থ তার-যোগে প্রেরিত সমাচার।

că′-blĕt, *n.* A little cable ; a cable-laid rope less than 10 inches in circumference ; ক্ষুদ্র রজ্জু ; তিনগুণবিশিষ্ট তিনটী রজ্জু একত্র পাকাইয়া ১০ ইঞ্চি অপেক্ষা অল্প পরিধিবিশিষ্ট যে রজ্জু রচিত হয়।

că-bŏb′, *n.* (Arab kabab) Meat cooked in small pieces with ginger, garlic, etc. ; কাবাব।

că-bōō′-dle, *n.* (*Slang, U. S.*) The lot, (usually in the phrase "*the whole caboodle*") ; যুক্তরাজ্যের ইতর ভাষায়। তাবৎ, বেবাক।

că-bōōse′, *n.* A cooking room on a ship's deck, usually called the galley ; জাহাজের পাকশালা, জাহাজের রান্নাঘর।

căb-ri-o-let (-rē-ō-lā), see CAB.

că-cā′-ō, *n.* The chocolate tree ; দক্ষিণ আমেরিকা ও আমেরিকার দ্বীপ-পুঞ্জজাত বৃক্ষবিশেষ, ইহার বীজ হইতে চকোলেট নামক পানীয় প্রস্তুত হয়।

cach′-ă-lŏt (căsh-), *n.* The sperm whale ; একজাতীয় তিমি মৎস্য, ইহার মাথার খুলিতে শ্বেতবর্ণ বসাময় পদার্থ থাকে।

cache (căsh), *n.* & *v. t.* A hiding place for treasure, provisions, ammunitions, etc. ; ধনরত্ন, খাদ্যসম্ভার কিম্বা গোলাগুলি লুকাইবার স্থান। 2. The stores so hidden ; উক্ত স্থানে লুক্কায়িত ধনরত্ন, খাদ্যসম্ভার প্রভৃতি। ***Verb t.*** To place in cache ; উক্তপ্রকার নিভৃত স্থানে লুকায়িত রাখা।

cache-peigne, (*F.*), *n.* Flowers, ribbons, etc. placed behind a woman's hat, but under the brim ; স্ত্রীলোকের টুপির পশ্চাদ্‌ভাগে কিনারার নীচে যে কৃত্রিম পুষ্প, ফিতা প্রভৃতি সংলগ্ন করা হয়।

ca-chet′ (kâ-shā), *n.* A stamp ; the seal of a letter ; মোহর ; চিঠির উপরের গালামোহর। **Lettre de cachet**—ফরাসী নৃপতির গুপ্ত গালা-মোহরযুক্ত পরওয়ানা বিশেষ,—ইহার বলে বিনা বিচারে লোককে কারারুদ্ধ করা হইত।

că-chĕx′-ȳ *n.* An ill-conditioned state of body or mind ; রক্ত-দুষ্টিবশতঃ সর্ব্বাঙ্গীণ বিকৃত অবস্থা, শারীর-বিকার, ধাতু-বিকৃতি, মানসিক অসুস্থতা।

căch′-in-nāte, *v. t.* To laugh loudly ; উচ্চহাস্য করা, অট্টহাস্য করা। **—na-tion,** *n.* **—na-to-ry,** *adj.*

că-chou′ (-shōō), *n.* A pill used by smokers to sweeten breath ; নিশ্বাস সুরভি করার জন্য তাম্রকূটসেবিগণকর্ত্তৃক ব্যবহৃত বটিকা বিশেষ।

că-chü′-chă, *n.* A Spanish dance ; স্পেনদেশীয় নৃত্য-বিশেষ।

că-cique′ (-sēk), *n.* American-Indian native chief ; আমেরিকার প্রাচীন অধিবাসীদিগের সর্দ্দার।

cack′-le (kăkl), *n.* & *v. i.* The sound of a goose or hen ; হংসী বা কুক্কুটীর রব, কঁ্যাক কঁ্যাক শব্দ, প্যাঁক প্যাঁক শব্দ। ***Verb i.*** 1. To make such a sound ; প্যাঁক প্যাঁক শব্দ করা। 2. To giggle ; খিল খিল করিয়া হাসা। 3. To chatter or prate ; বক্ বক্ করা।

căck′-lêr, *n.* A fowl that cackles ; প্যাঁক প্যাঁক রবকারী পক্ষী।

căc-ō-dē′-mŏn, *n.* 1. An evil spirit ; ভূত, প্রেতাত্মা। 2. A poisonous compound ; একপ্রকার বিষাক্ত মিশ্র পদার্থ।

căc′-ō-ē-pȳ, *n.* Bad pronunciation ; কদর্য্য উচ্চারণ।

căc-ō-ē′-thēs, *n.* Ill habit ; an itch for doing something unadvisable ; কদভ্যাস ; অসঙ্গত কার্য্য করিবার জন্য কণ্ডূয়ন। ***Cacoethes scribendi***—রচনাকণ্ডূয়ন।

că-cŏg′-ră-phȳ, *n.* Bad writing or spelling ; কদর্য্য হস্তাক্ষর বা বর্ণ-বিন্যাস।

că-cŏl′-ō-ġȳ, *n.* 1. Bad choice of words or pronunciation ; নিকৃষ্ট শব্দ নির্ব্বাচন বা কদর্য্য উচ্চারণ।

că-cōōn′, *n.* A large seed of a tropical American plant ; আমেরিকার উষ্ণ-মণ্ডলজাত বৃক্ষ বিশেষের বীজ। [এই বীজ হইতে নস্যাধার, সুগন্ধি দ্রব্যের কৌটা প্রভৃতি নির্ম্মিত হয়।]

că-cŏph′-ō-nȳ, *n.* 1. Ill sound ; কর্কশ ধ্বনি, কোঁ কোঁ শব্দ। 2. (*Mus.*) A combination of discordant sounds ; (সঙ্গীত-শাস্ত্র) বিস্বর সমূহের সম্মিলন। **—nous,** *adj.* Harsh-sounding ; কর্কশারাবী, শ্রুতিকটু, দুঃস্বন (মঃ ভাঃ)।

căc′-tŭs, *n.* Any plant of the order cactaceæ; নাগফণাদি (সাঃ পঃ) বর্গভুক্ত বৃক্ষ সমূহের একটী। [এই সমস্ত বৃক্ষ নিষ্পত্র ও কণ্টকবহুল হইয়া থাকে।] ***Cactus Indicus***—নাগফণা। [Prickly pear বা ফণিমনসার বৃক্ষ ও নাগফণাদি (cactus) বর্গের অন্তর্ভূত।]

Sharp-angled cactus.

căd, *n.* 1. (*Slang*) An omnibus conductor ; (ইতর ভাষায়) অম্‌নিবাস্ গাড়ীর চালক। 2. A low vulgar fellow ; ইতর লোক, দুর্বৃত্ত।

că-dăs′-trăl, *adj.* Pertaining to landed property ; ভূসম্পত্তি সম্বন্ধীয়। **—tre, —ter,** *ns.* A public register of the lands of a country for fiscal purposes ; রাজকীয় জরিপের চিঠা। **Cadastral survey** or **plan**—A survey on a large and complete scale ; দেশব্যাপী বিরাট জরিপ, ক্ষেত্রবদ্ধ জরিপ (য়োঃ), প্রত্যেকের অধিকারে যত জমি থাকে তাহার মাপ, থাকবস্তা (যোঃ)।

că-dăv′-êr-ous (-ŭs), *adj.* Corpse-like ; deadly pale ; শবসদৃশ ; মরণমলিন। **—ness,** *n.*

căd′-die (-dî), *n.* A golf-player's attendant ; an errand boy ; গোলফ্ ক্রীড়কের সহচর ; সংবাদবাহক বালক।

căd′-dis, -dice (dîs), (*Pl.* -dies), *n.* The larva of the may-fly, used as bait ; বড়শীর টোপরূপে ব্যবহৃত মক্ষিকা-বিশেষের কিরা।

căd′-dў, *n.* A small box for keeping tea ; চা রাখিবার ক্ষুদ্র পেটক।

cāde, *n.* A cask or barrel ; পিপা।

cā′-dence (-dĕns), *n.* **1.** A fall of the voice in reading or speaking ; (পাঠ বা বক্তৃতাকালে) কণ্ঠ-স্বরের বিরাম বা পতন। **2.** A rhythmical modulation of voice or any sound ; as, music of bells in *cadence* sweet ; স্বরসংক্রম (মূর্চ্ছঃ), স্বর-পরিবর্ত্তন, স্বর-বিবর্ত্তন, স্বর-বৈচিত্র। **3.** Rhythm ; শ্রুতিমধুর শব্দপ্রবাহ, স্বর-প্রবাহ। **4.** (*Mus.*) The close of a musical phrase ; (সঙ্গীত-বিদ্যা) গানের সম।

cā′-dĕn-cў, *n.* **1.** The descent of younger branch ; জ্যেষ্ঠেতর পুত্র-গণের বংশানুক্রম। **2.** (*Herald.*) The relative status of younger sons ; (কুলবিদ্যা—ইংলণ্ডে) জ্যেষ্ঠেতর পুত্রগণের মধ্যে আপেক্ষিক মর্য্যাদা।

cā′-dĕnt, *n.* Falling ; declining ; স্রংসী ; পতনশীল।

că-dĕn′-ză, (*It.*), *n.* A flourish of music at the close of a movement ; গানের কর্ত্তব।

că-dĕt′, *n.* **1.** A younger brother or son ; the youngest son ; "The *cadet* of an ancient and noble family ;" কনিষ্ঠ ভ্রাতা বা পুত্র ; সর্ব্বকনিষ্ঠ পুত্র। **2.** One who serves as a private soldier to become an officer ; a student in a naval or military college ; সামরিক কর্ম্মচারিরূপে নিযুক্ত হইবার উদ্দেশ্যে যে ব্যক্তি সৈন্যদলে সাধারণ সৈনিকের কার্য্য করে ; নৌ বা সামরিক বিদ্যালয়ের ছাত্র।

cadge (căj), *v. t.* To go about begging or peddling ; ভিক্ষা বা ফেরি করিয়া বেড়ান।

cadg′-êr (căj-), *n.* **1.** One who brings butter, eggs, poultry and the like to the market from the country ; যে ব্যক্তি গ্রাম হইতে মাখন, ডিম, কুক্কুট প্রভৃতি বাজারে বিক্রয়ার্থ আনয়ন করে। **2.** A street-hawker ; ফেরিওয়ালা। **3.** A beggar ; a loafer ; ভিক্ষুক ; ভবঘুরে, যে ব্যক্তি টোঁ টোঁ করিয়া ঘুরে। **4.** One who gets his living in a questionable manner ; "The gentleman *cadger* ;" যে ব্যক্তি সন্দিগ্ধ উপায়ে জীবিকা অর্জ্জন করে।

cā′-dî, *n.* A judge in Mohammedan countries ; কাজী।

Căd-mē′-ăn, —mī′-, *adj.* Relating to Cadmus, who introduced the original Greek alphabet ; আদিম গ্রীক্ বর্ণমালার প্রবর্ত্তক ক্যাড্‌ম্যস্ সম্বন্ধীয়। **Cadmean victory** — জেতাবিজেতা উভয় পক্ষে বহু সৈন্যক্ষয় সংঘটিত হওয়ার পর যুদ্ধ জয়। [ফিনিসীয় বীর Cadmus কর্ত্তৃক উপ্ত নাগদন্ত হইতে যে সমস্ত সশস্ত্র পুরুষ উত্থিত হইয়াছিল, তাহারা পরস্পরের সহিত যুদ্ধ করিয়া পাঁচজন ব্যতিরেকে অপর সকলেই মৃত্যুমুখে পতিত হয়।]

căd′-mi-ŭm, *n.* A white metal occurring in zinc ores ; অশোধিত দস্তাতে বর্ত্তমান শ্বেতবর্ণ ধাতু বিশেষ, কদম্বক (সাঃ পঃ)।

că′-dre, *n.* **1.** Framework ; scheme ; কাঠাম ; ব্যবস্থা। **2.** Permanent establishment of a regiment forming nucleus for expansion at need ; কোন পল্টনের স্থায়ী সৈন্য এবং কর্ম্মচারিবৃন্দ—(যুদ্ধাদির কালে) আবশ্যক মত যাহার প্রসার করা যাইতে পারে।

Caduceus.

că-dū′-cē-ŭs, *n.* The winged staff of Mercury ; রোমীয় দেবদূত মার্কারীর সপক্ষ দণ্ড।

că-dū′-cous (-cŭs), *adj.* Falling early as leaves or flowers ; আশু-পতনশীল। **—ci-ty,** *n.* **1.** Caducous quality ; transitoriness ; আশু-পতন (সাঃ পঃ) ; ক্ষণস্থায়িত্ব।

cæ′-cŭm (sē-), *n.* A bag containing only one opening, connected with intestine ; বৃহৎ অন্ত্রের সহিত সংযুক্ত এক দিকে খোলা থলিয়া বিশেষ, অন্ধান্ত্র (হঃ চঃ)।

Cæsalpinia sappan—Sappan wood—বকম কাঠ।

Cæ′-săr (sē-), *n.* **1.** The cagnomen of the Roman dictator Caius Julius Cæsar ; প্রাচীন রোমের সুপ্রসিদ্ধ নেতা কেয়াস জুলিয়াস সীজারের উপাধি। **2.** Any Roman emperor ; যে কোন রোম সম্রাট। **3.** Any autocrat or absolute monarch ; স্বেচ্ছাচারী রাজা। **—sa′-re-an, —sa′-ri-an,** *adjs.* **Cæsarean operation**—উদরের পার্শ্ব কাটিয়া জরায়ু হইতে সন্তান বাহির করণ। [জুলিয়াস সীজারকে এইরূপে মাতৃগর্ভ হইতে মোচন করা হইয়াছিল বলিয়া প্রবাদ আছে।] **Cæsar's wife must be above suspicion**—জুলিয়াস সীজরের পত্নী পম্পিয়ার নাম কেয়াস ক্লডিয়াসের বিরুদ্ধে কোন অভিযোগে জড়িত হইলে,—তিনি পম্পিয়াকে অপরাধিনী বলিয়া বিশ্বাস না করিলেও—সীজরের স্ত্রী সর্ব্বপ্রকার সন্দেহের অতীত হইবে—এই হেতুতে তাহাকে পরিত্যাগ করিলেন।

cæ-sū′-ră (sē-), *n.* A pause in a verse ; যতি, পাঠচ্ছেদ (অঃ)।

Caeteris paribus—Other things being equal ; অন্যান্য বিষয় তুল্য হইলে।

că-fe′ (-fā), *n.* A coffee-house ; a restaurant ; কাফি পান করিবার স্থান, পানাগার ; সাধারণ ভোজনাগার। **Cafe and lait**—দুগ্ধ-শূন্য কাফি। **Cafe′-chantant**—যে উদ্যান বা সঙ্গীত-শালায় চা, মিঠাই প্রভৃতি জলযোগের দ্রব্য পরিবেষণ করা হয়। **Cafe-noire**—Strong-coffee (without milk) ; a brown colour ; (দুগ্ধ-শূন্য) উগ্র বা তেজাল কাফি ; কপিশ বর্ণ।

căf-fē'-ic, *adj.* Pertaining to, or obtained from, coffee ; as, *caffeic* acid ; কাফি সম্বন্ধীয়, কাফি হইতে প্রাপ্ত।

căf-fē'-ine (-ĭn), *n.* A vegetable alkaloid found in coffee and tea plants ; কাফি এবং চাগাছে প্রাপ্ত ক্ষারময় পদার্থ বিশেষ, কাফি বা কাওয়ার বীর্য্য (হঃ চঃ)।

Căf'-fre (-fêr), *n.* See KAFIR.

căf'-tăn, *n.* A Persian or Turkish vest ; তুরস্ক অথবা পারস্যদেশীয় হাতকাটা জামা বা ফতুয়া বিশেষ।

cāge, *n.* & *v. t.* **1.** A box or case made of wood and wire for confining birds or beasts ; খাঁচা, পিঞ্জর, পঞ্জর। **2.** A prison ; a place of confinement for malefactors ; "His father had never a house but a *cage* ;" কারাগার ; বন্দিশালা, কয়েদখানা। **3.** (*Mining*) A cage-like structure in which miners stand while being raised from, or lowered into, a mine ; (খনির-কার্য্যে) খনি হইতে উপরে উঠিবার সময় বা খনিতে নামিবার কালে খননকারিগণ যে পিঞ্জরাকৃতি মঞ্চের উপর দণ্ডায়মান থাকে। **4.** Open framework of various kinds ; নানাপ্রকারের খোলা ঠাট বা কাঠাম। ***Verb t.*** To confine or keep in a cage ; খাঁচায় রাখা, পিঞ্জরাবদ্ধ করা। **Cageling**—A bird confined in a cage, especially a young bird ; খাঁচার পাখী, পিঞ্জরাবদ্ধ পক্ষী বা পক্ষিশাবক।

Cain (cān), *n.* A murderer ; a fratricide ; নরহন্তা ; ভ্রাতৃহন্তা। [আদমের পুত্র Cain তদীয় ভ্রাতা এবেলকে হত্যা করিয়াছিলেন।] **Cain-coloured**—Reddish ; তাম্রবর্ণ, রক্তাভ। [ভ্রাতৃহন্তা কেইন এবং যীশুখৃষ্টের বিশ্বাসঘাতক শিষ্য জুদাসের কেশ আরক্ত ছিল বলিয়া কিম্বদন্তী প্রচলিত আছে।]

Cain'-īte (cān-), *n.* **1.** A descendant of Cain ; কেইনের বংশধর। **2.** (*Pl.*) A small gnostic sect of the second century ; দ্বিতীয় শতাব্দীর ইয়ুদীতান্ত্রিক সম্প্রদায় বিশেষ। [ইহারা ইয়ুদীদিগের ঈশ্বরকে প্রকৃত ঈশ্বরের বিরোধী বলিয়া জ্ঞান করিত এবং কেইন প্রমুখ (ইয়ুদী-) ঈশ্বরদ্রোহিগণের অর্চনা করিত।]

cai-nō-zō'-ic (cā-), *adj.* Of the third geological period ; ভূতত্ত্বের তৃতীয় যুগ-সম্বন্ধীয়, নব্যজীবক (সাঃ পঃ)।

că-ique' (-ēk), *n.* A light kind of boat used upon the Bosphorus ; বস্‌ফোরাস্ প্রণালীতে চালিত লঘু তরণী বিশেষ।

cairn (cārn), *n.* Pyramid of rough stones, as memorial, sepulchre, land-marks, etc. ; স্মৃতি-স্তম্ভ, সমাধি-স্তম্ভ বা সীমাচিহ্নরূপে ব্যবহৃত মোচাকার অমসৃণ পাষাণখণ্ডের স্তূপ।

cairn'-gōrm (cārn-), *n.* A yellow or wine-coloured precious stone ; পীত বা মদিরাবর্ণ মূল্যবান প্রস্তর বিশেষ।

cais'-sŏn (căs-), *n.* **1.** An ammunition chest or wagon ; বারুদ, গোলাগুলি প্রভৃতি রাখিবার সিন্দুক বিশেষ। **2.** A wooden chest with bombs, to bury beneath the path, etc., of an enemy, and explode under him ; শত্রুকে উড়াইয়া দিবার উদ্দেশ্যে তদীয় গমনপথে প্রোথিত বোমাপূর্ণ কাঠের বাক্স। **3.** A wooden case or frame sunk in the beds of rivers, etc., to keep out the water during the laying of the foundation of a bridge, etc. ; সেতু প্রভৃতির ভিত্তিস্থাপনকালে জলপ্রবেশের পথ রুদ্ধ করার উদ্দেশ্যে যে কাষ্ঠময় আধার বা কাঠাম নদীগর্ভে বসানো হয়। **4.** A boat-shaped vessel used as a dock-gate ; পোত-সংস্কারস্থানে জলপ্রবেশ রোধার্থ নৌকাকৃতি পোত।

cai'-tiff (cā-), *n.* & *adj.* A mean despicable fellow ; হীনপ্রকৃতির লোক, ইতর লোক, ঘৃণার্হ লোক। ***Adj.*** Mean ; base ; cowardly ; নীচাশয় ; অধম, ইতর ; কাপুরুষবৎ।

Cajanurs Indicus—অড়হর (বেল ৭)

căj'-ē-pŭt, -ū-, *n.* A medicinal volatile oil (*Malay*) ; একপ্রকার উদ্বায়ী ভেষজ তৈল, কাজুপাতী (যোঃ)।

că-jōle', *v. t.* To persuade or soothe by flattery, deceit, etc. ; ছল-চাতুরীদ্বারা প্ররোচিত করা, ছল-চাতুরীদ্বারা প্রতীতি জন্মান, ফুসলান, ভুলান, মিষ্ট কথায় প্রতারিত করা। [Cajole a person *into* doing something, cajole a person *out of* something, or cajole something *out of* a person.] **—jol'-er-y,** *n.* Coaxing ; wheedling ; deceitful persuasion ; মনভুলানো কথা-দ্বারা প্ররোচিত করণ ; খোসামোদ ; ছলনা-পূর্ণ প্ররোচনা। **—jol'-ing, —ment,** *ns.*

cāke, *n.* & *v. i.* **1.** A small mass of dough baked ; অগ্নিতে সেকা ক্ষুদ্র ময়দার তাল। **2.** A small flattish loaf of bread ; একপ্রকার চ্যাপ্টা পাঁউরুটি এবং ক্ষুদ্র চাপাটি। **3.** A thin hard baked kind of eaten bread ; একপ্রকার কড়াভাজা রুটী **4.** A kind of bread compounded with fruit, etc. ; পিষ্টক, পিঠা, পূপ। **5.** Anything resembling a cake in form ; as, a *cake* of soap ; যে কোন পিষ্টকাকৃতি বস্তু, পিণ্ড, ডেলা, পাটালি, টিক্‌লি, চাক্‌তি, পিষ্ট (ধাঃ—প্রঃ), পিষ্টী (রঃ চুঃ—প্রঃ) পিষ্টিক (রঃ—প্রঃ)। ***Verb i.*** To become coagulated or formed into a cake ; ডেলা পাকান, তাল পাকান, পিণ্ডীভূত হওয়া, ঘনীভূত হওয়া, জমাট বাঁধা, জমিয়া ডেলা বাঁধা। **Ague-cake** — See AGUE. **Oil-cake**—See OIL. **An obsequial** or **funeral cake**—পিণ্ড। **My cake is dough**—My plan has failed ; আমার মতলব ব্যর্থ হইয়াছে। **The land of cakes**—স্কট্‌লণ্ড। **To take the cakes**—To carry off the honours ; পুরস্কার জিতিয়া লওয়া। **You cannot both have** or **keep your cake and eat it**—You cannot do the impossible ; তুমি অসম্ভব সম্ভব করিতে পার না।

căl'-ă-bar (-bêr), **—bêr,** *n.* The fur of the grey squirrel ; ধূসরবর্ণ মার্জ্জারের রোম।

căl'-ă-băsh, *n.* **1.** The common gourd (plant or fruit) ; অলাবু, তুম্বা, কদু। **2.** The fruit of the American calabash tree ; আমেরিকা

Calabashes.

দেশীয় অলাবু বৃক্ষের ফল। **3.** A cup or utensil made of the shell enclosing the fruit of the above tree ; অলাবুপাত্র, অলাবুর খোল হইতে প্রস্তুত কমণ্ডলু, ভিক্ষাপাত্র প্রভৃতি।

că-lā'-dĭ-ŭm, *n.* A genus of plants of the arum family ; নানাপ্রকার কচু।

căl-ă-man'-co (-mang-kō), *n.* A glossy Flemish woollen stuff much used in the eighteenth century ; হলণ্ড্‌দেশে প্রস্তুত চকচকে পশমী বস্ত্র বিশেষ, অষ্টাদশ শতাব্দীতে ইহার বহুল প্রচলন ছিল।

căl'-ă-măn'-dêr, *n.* A very valuable cabinet wood native of South East India and Ceylon ; দক্ষিণ পূর্ব্ব ভারতবর্ষ এবং সিংহলদ্বীপে জাত একপ্রকার বহুমূল্য কাষ্ঠ, ইহা দ্বারা মূল্যবান আসবাব তৈয়ারী হয়। [Also called *Coromondal wood.* সিংহলদ্বীপে প্রচলিত নাম কেলুমেদিরীয়।]

căl'-ă-măr-ȳ, *n.* A popular name applied to numerous forms of cuttle fish and cephalopoda ; বিভিন্ন প্রকার সমুদ্রজিভ্‌ (সাঃ পঃ) বা মুণ্ডপদীর নাম।

căl'-ăm-băc, *n.* Agollocha ; অগরু কাষ্ঠ।

căl'-ă-mine (-mĭn), *n.* An important British ore of zinc ; এক প্রকার অবিশুদ্ধ দস্তা, খর্পর (রঃ—প্রঃ), রসক (ঐ), কারবেল্লক (রঃ রঃ সঃ—প্রঃ), দদ্দুর (ঐ), ক্ষিতিকিট্ট (রঃ—প্রঃ), তাম্ররঞ্জক (ঐ), রসোদ্ভব (ঐ), রীতিকৃত (ঐ)।

căl'-ă-mint, *n.* Kinds of aromatic herbs ; বিবিধ জাতীয় সুগন্ধি ওষধি।

căl'-ă-mīte, *n.* A fossil plant ; শিলীভূত উদ্ভিদ্‌ বিশেষ।

că-lăm'-ĭ-tous (-tŭs), *adj.* **1.** Producing, or attended with, distress or misery ; বিপজ্জনক, দুর্দ্দৈবপূর্ণ, ব্যসনোপেত। **2.** Wretched ; দুঃখজনক, ক্লেশপূর্ণ।

că-lăm'-ĭ-tȳ, *n.* **1.** Any great misfortune or cause of misery ; বিপদ্‌, বিপাক, ব্যসন, দারুণ দুর্ব্বিপাক। **2.** Deep misery ; দারুণ ক্লেশ, দুঃখ, বিপত্তি।

căl'-ă-mŭs, *n.* **1.** The Indian cane ; বেতস, বেত, বানীর, বেত্র, বঞ্জুল। **2.** The reed pen used by the ancients in writing ; প্রাচীনগণের ব্যবহৃত শরনির্ম্মিত লেখনিবিশেষ, খাগড়ার কলম। **3.** (*Music*) A reed-flute ; (সঙ্গীত) বংশী, বেণু। **4.** (*Scripture*) A sort of reed or sweet-scented wood mentioned in the Scriptures as brought from India ; বাইবেল গ্রন্থে উক্ত ভারতবর্ষ হইতে সমানীত বেত্র বা সুগন্ধি কাষ্ঠ বিশেষ।

că-lăsh', *n.* **1.** A light pleasure or travelling carriage ; এক প্রকার হাল্কা গাড়ী। **2.** A hood for a lady's head ; স্ত্রীলোকের মস্তকাবরণ বিশেষ।

căl'-căr, *n.* (*Bot.*) A hollow tube or spur at the base of a petal or corolla ; (উদ্ভিদ্‌-বিদ্যা) পুষ্পের দল বা মুকুটবৎ অন্তরাবরণের নিম্নভাগস্থ শূন্যগর্ভ নল বা কণ্টক বিশেষ, কোষ-কণ্টক (সাঃ পঃ)।

căl-cā'-rē-ous (-ŭs), *adj.* Consisting of or containing calcium carbonate or carbonate of lime ; চূণে (*Colloq.*), চূর্ণকময়, চূর্ণময়।

căl-că-rif'-êr-ous (-ŭs), *adj.* Lime-yielding ; calciferous ; চূর্ণদ, চূর্ণোৎপাদক ; চূর্ণসারদ।

căl-cē-ō-lā'-rĭ-ă, *n.* Kinds of plant with flowers like ancient slippers ; প্রাচীন কালীন উপানদাকৃতি পুষ্পপ্রসূ বিবিধ প্রকার বৃক্ষ।

căl'-cē-ō-lāte, *adj.* (*Bot.*) Slipper-shapped ; উপানদাকৃতি (সাঃ পঃ)।

căl'-cĭc, *adj.* Pertaining to, derived from, or containing, calcium or lime ; চূণে, চূর্ণজ, চূর্ণময়।

căl-cĭf'-êr-ous (-ŭs), *adj.* Yielding carbonate of lime ; চূর্ণসারোৎপাদক।

căl'-cĭ-fȳ, *v. t.* & *i.* To convert into lime ; চূণে পরিণত করা। ***Verb i.*** To be converted into lime ; চূর্ণে পরিণত হওয়া। **—cif'-ic,** *adj.* **—fi-ca'-tion,** *n.*

căl-cīne', căl'-cīne, *v. t.* & *i.* **1.** To reduce to calx or chalky powder by the action of heat ; ভস্ম করা, উত্তাপপ্রয়োগে খড়িময় চূর্ণে পরিণত করা। **2.** To oxidize, as a metal by the action of heat ; জারণ করা। ***Verb i.*** To become a calx or powder by heat ; উত্তাপ প্রয়োগের ফলে ধাতুভস্মে বা চূর্ণে পরিণত হওয়া। **—ci-na'-tion,** *n.* **1.** The operation of expelling from a substance by heat, either water or volatile matter combined with it ; ভস্মীকরণ (প্রঃ)। **2.** The operation of reducing a metal to an oxide ; জারণ (রঃ—প্রঃ)।

căl'-cīte, *n.* Native carbonate of lime ; চূণাপাথর, খড়িমাটী প্রভৃতির প্রধান উপাদান, সফেদ-সুর্ম্মা (হিঃ কোঃ), চূর্ণসার।

căl'-cĭ-ŭm, *n.* (*Chem.*) An element ; a yellow metal, the basis of lime ; (রসায়ন-শাস্ত্র) মূল পদার্থ বিশেষ, খটিক (সাঃ পঃ) ; চূর্ণের মূল উপাদানস্বরূপ পীতবর্ণ ধাতুবিশেষ।

călc-spâr, *n.* Same as CALCITE.

căl'-cū-lă-ble, *adj.* That may be calculated or ascertained by calculation ; গণনীয়, গণিতব্য, সংখ্যেয় (মঃ ভাঃ), গণেয় (নৈষঃ), গণ্য, পরিগণনীয়।

căl'-cū-lāte, *v. t.* & *i.* **1.** To compute ; to reckon up in number

গণনা করা, খতান (*Colloq.*) ; সংখ্যা করা, হিসাব করা। **2.** To divine or prognosticate by the situation of the planets at a certain time ; "A cunning man did *calculate* my birth ;" কোন নির্দ্দিষ্ট সময়ে গ্রহাদির অবস্থানদৃষ্টে ভাবী শুভাশুভ নিরূপণ করা। **3.** To adjust for a purpose ; as, to *calculate* a system of laws for the government ; কোন উদ্দেশ্য সাধনের উপযোগী করা। **4.** To ascertain beforehand by exact reckoning ; পূর্ব্বেই সঠিকভাবে গণিয়া নির্ণয় করিয়া রাখা। **5.** To plan deliberately ; ভাবিয়া চিন্তিয়া ঠিক করা, পূর্ব্বাপর বা অগ্র পশ্চাৎ বিবেচনা করিয়া ঠিক করা। **6.** (*U. S.*) To suppose ; to believe ; (মার্কিণ-যুক্তরাজ্যে) অনুমান করা, গণ্য করা ; বিশ্বাস করা। ***Verb i.*** To reckon ; to prognosticate ; to estimate ; গণনা করা ; ভাবী শুভাশুভ সূচনা করা ; আনুমাণিক ব্যয় নির্দ্ধারণ করা। **—lat-ed,** *p. p.* **1.** Worked out by reckoning ; গণিত, সংখ্যাত। **2.** Fitted ; adapted ; suited ; উপযুক্ত ; উপযোগী ; যোগ্য। **—lating,** *adj.* **1.** Of or pertaining to arithmetical calculation ; গণন-সম্বন্ধীয়। **2.** Having the power of arithmetical calculation ; গণন-ক্ষম। **3.** Given to forethought ; deliberately selfish and scheming ; as, cool *calculating* disposition ; পরিণামদর্শী, অগ্রপশ্চাৎ বিবেচনাশীল ; মতলবী, হিসাবী। **—la'-tion,** *n.* **1.** Computation ; গণনা, সংখ্যান, হিসাব। **2.** The result got by reckoning ; গণনা-ফল। **3.** Forecast ; অগ্রনিরূপণ, পূর্ব্বাঙ্কপাত। **—la-tor,** *n.* **1.** One who computes or reckons ; গণক, গণনাকারী। **2.** A set of tables for using in calculations ; গণনসহায়ক নামতা বিশেষ। **3.** A calculating machine ; গণন-যন্ত্র। **Calculating machine** — যে যন্ত্রের সাহায্যে বিশুদ্ধরূপে যোগ, বিয়োগ প্রভৃতি অঙ্ক করা যায়।

căl'-cū-lous (-lŭs), *adj.* Of or suffering from stone or calculus ; অশ্মরীরোগ সংক্রান্ত, অশ্মরীরোগগ্রস্ত, আশ্মরিক (সুশ্রুঃ), শার্করিক।

căl'-cū-lŭs, *n.* **1.** (*Med.*) The medical term for what is popularly known as stone ; (ভৈষজ্য-শাস্ত্র) শিলা (হঃ চঃ), অশ্মরী (ঐ), পাথর, মূত্রাশয়, বৃক্ক প্রভৃতিতে যে পাথর বা শিলা উপজাত হয়। **2.** A particular method of calculation ; গণনপ্রণালী বিশেষ, কলন (হিঃ কোঃ)। **Calculus of finite difference**—পরিচ্ছিন্নান্তর কলন (ঐ)। **Calculus of variation**—বৈশেষিক কলন (ঐ)। **Differential calculus**—ব্যাস-গণিত (সাঃ পঃ), চলগণিত (বাপুঃ), সূক্ষ্ম-গণিত (আঃ বঃ), চল বা অত্যল্প সংখ্যা-সমূহের অনুপাতের পরিমাণদ্বারা গণিত-বিষয়ক প্রশ্নানুসন্ধানের পদ্ধতি বিশেষ। **Infinitesimal calculus**—অত্যল্প কলন (হিঃ কোঃ)। **Integral calculus**—সমাসগণিত (সাঃ পঃ), সমাহার গণিত (ঐ), চলরাশি-কলন (হিঃ কোঃ), দুই বা ততোধিক অনির্ণীত পরিমাণ (magnitude) এর অত্যল্প পরিবর্ত্তনের অনুপাত হইতে বিচারদ্বারা উক্ত পরিমাণ-সমূহ নির্ণয়ের প্রণালী বিশেষ।

caldarium, (*L.*), *n.* The Roman hot bath-room ; প্রাচীন রোমের উষ্ণ-স্নানাগার।

căl'-drŏn, *n.* See CAULDRON.

Căl-ē-dō'-nĭ-ă, *n.* The ancient Latin name of Scotland ; স্কট্‌লণ্ড্ দেশের প্রাচীন ল্যাটিন নাম। (বর্ত্তমানেও কবিতায় ব্যবহার আছে)। **—an,** *adj.* & *n.* Of or pertaining to ancient Scotland ; প্রাচীন স্কট্‌লণ্ড্ দেশ-সম্বন্ধীয়। (*Noun*) A native of ancient Scotland ; a Scotchman ; প্রাচীন স্কট্‌লণ্ডের অধিবাসী ; স্কট্‌লণ্ড্-বাসী।

căl-ē-fā'-cient (-shĕnt), *adj.* & *n.* Producing warmth ; উষ্ণতা-জনক। ***Noun.*** A medical agent producing warmth ; উষ্ণতাজনক ঔষধ বিশেষ। **—fac'-tion,** *n.* **—fac'-tive,** *adj.*

căl-ē-făc'-tō-rȳ, *adj.* & *n.* Producing warmth ; উষ্ণতাজনক। ***Noun.*** A heated seating room in a monastery ; (খৃষ্টীয়) মঠমধ্যস্থ উষ্ণীকৃত উপবেশন কক্ষ।

calembour (*F.*), *n.* Pun ; দ্ব্যর্থক শব্দ, শব্দশ্লেষ (শিশুঃ)।

căl'-ĕn-dar (-dêr), *n.* & *v. t.* **1.** An almanac ; পঞ্জিকা। **2.** A register of persons and things ; a list of criminal cases which stand for trial ; a register of the names of prisoners ; ব্যক্তি বা বস্তুর আনুক্রমিক তালিক, পঞ্জী, তালিকা, ফিরিস্তি, তপশিল ; বিচার্য্য ফৌজদারী মোকদ্দমার তালিকা ; অপরাধিগণের নামের খাতা। ***Verb t.*** **1.** To register ; to enter in a list ; খাতায় তোলা ; তালিকাভুক্ত করা। **2.** To arrange ; to analyse ; to index ; as, to *calendar* documents ; শৃঙ্খলাবদ্ধ করা ; বিশ্লেষণ করা ; নির্ঘণ্ট প্রস্তুত করা। **Calendar clock**—যে ঘড়ি কেবলমাত্র ঘণ্টা মিনিট প্রভৃতি প্রদর্শন করে না, পরন্তু বার, মাস, এমন কি সময় সময় তিথি এবং বৎসর পর্য্যন্ত নির্দ্দেশ করিয়া থাকে। **Calendar month**—সৌর মাস।

căl'-ĕn-dêr, *n.* & *v. t.* **1.** A machine consisting of two rollers for pressing cloth and paper smooth and glossy ; কাপড় বা কাগজ মসৃণ বা চকচকে করিবার জন্য যন্ত্র বিশেষ, চক্রযন্ত্র (মঃ ইঃ), নরাজ। **2.** One who pursues the business of calendering ; যে ব্যক্তি উক্ত যন্ত্রের সাহায্যে কাপড় বা কাগজ মসৃণ বা চকচকে করে। ***Verb t.*** To press cloth, paper, etc. in a calender or roller machine to smoothe it ; নরাজদ্বারা বস্ত্র, কাগজ প্রভৃতি মসৃণ বা চকচকে করা।

căl'-ĕn-dêr, *n.* A mendicant Dervish of Persia and Turkey ;

পারস্য এবং তুরস্ক দেশীয় ভিক্ষোপজীবী দরবেশ বিশেষ।

căl'-ĕnds, *n.* The first day of each month in ancient Roman calendar ; প্রাচীন রোমীয় পঞ্জিকার প্রতি মাসের প্রথম দিবস। (Written also KALENDS). **The Greek Calends** — Never ; কখনও না। [গ্রীক্‌দিগের ভিতর calends শব্দের ব্যবহার ছিল না।] **To fix any thing for the Greek Calends**—To postpone it indefinitely ; অনির্দ্দিষ্টকালের জন্য স্থগিত রাখা।

Că-lĕn'-dŭ-lă, *n.* A genus of composite plants ; গাঁদা জাতীয় ফুল। ***Calendula officinalis***—Marigold ; গাঁদা ফুল, বিলাতি গাঁদা (যোঃ)।

căl'-ĕn-tūre, *n.* A kind of fever or delirium occurring on board ship in hot climates, in which sailors imagine the sea to be green fields and will throw themselves into it ; জ্বরজ বা জ্বরবিকারজনিত উন্মাদ রোগ বিশেষ। উষ্ণমণ্ডলে জাহাজের নাবিকগণ এই রোগে আক্রান্ত হইয়া, হরিৎ ক্ষেত্রভ্রমে সমুদ্রবক্ষে ঝম্পপ্রদান করিয়া থাকে।

calf (câf), *n.* (*Pl.* CALVES.) **1.** The young of the cow or of the bovine family of animals ; গোবৎস, বৎস, বাছুর। **2.** A leather made of the skin of the calf ; a fine light-coloured leather used in book-binding ; as, to bind books in *calf* ; পরিশোধিত গোবৎস চর্ম্ম ; পুস্তক বাঁধাইর কাযে ব্যবহৃত ফিকে রঙের মিহি চামড়া বিশেষ। **3.** The young of elephant, deer, whale, etc. ; করভ, মৃগ-শিশু, তিমি মৎস্যের শাবক প্রভৃতি। **4.** (*Colloq.*) Any silly person ; a dolt ; (চলিত ভাষায়) গোমূর্খ ; মূঢ়, জড়-বুদ্ধি। **5.** A small island near a larger one ; বৃহত্তর দ্বীপের সন্নিহিত ক্ষুদ্র দ্বীপ। **6.** (*Naut.*) A floating piece of ice ; (নৌ-বিদ্যা) প্রবমান তুষার খণ্ড। **Box-calf**—বুট নির্ম্মাণে ব্যবহৃত এক প্রকার উৎকৃষ্ট গোবৎস-চর্ম্ম। **Calf kneed**—Knock-kneed ; সংহতজানু (অঃ)। **Calf-love**—Childish love affairs ; অল্প-বয়স্ক বালকবালিকার মধ্যে ক্ষণস্থায়ী উচ্ছ্বাসপূর্ণ প্রেম। **Calf's teeth**—Milk teeth ; দুধে দাঁত। **Calves-foot jelly**—গো বৎসের পা জলে সিদ্ধ করত যে ক্বাথ প্রস্তুত করা হয়। **Golden calf**—Wealth as an object of worship ; ধন (অর্চ্চনাস্পদভাবে।) [Moses সিনাই পর্ব্বত হইতে চলিয়া গেলে পর Aaron ইয়ুদিদিগের অর্চ্চনার জন্য এক স্বর্ণময় গোবৎসবিগ্রহের প্রতিষ্ঠা করেন। এই ঘটনা হইতে—Golden calf শব্দের উক্ত অর্থটী গৃহীত হইয়াছে।] **Moon-calf**—See MOON. **Sea-calf**—Seal ; শীল মৎস্য। **A cow in or with calf**—Pregnant cow ; গর্ভবতী গাভী। **To eat the calf in the cow's belly**—কালনেমির মত লঙ্কা ভাগ করা। **To slip her calf**—To suffer abortion ; (গাভী পক্ষে) গর্ভপাত হওয়া।

calf (câf), *n.* (*Pl.* CALVES.) The fleshy hinder part of leg-shank ; জঙ্ঘাদেশের পশ্চাদ্ভাগস্থ মাংসের অংশ, পিণ্ডিকা (সাঃ পঃ), পিণ্ডলী। ঐ), পিণ্ডক (যাজ্ঞঃ), পায়ের ডিম, জঙ্ঘাপিণ্ড (সেলঃ)।

Căl'-i-băn, *n.* A savage ; a boor ; অসভ্য ; নরপশু, বর্ব্বর। [সেক্ষপীয়রকৃত 'Tempest' নাটকের ক্যালিভান নামক চরিত্রের নাম হইতে এই শব্দটী গৃহীত হইয়াছে।]

căl'-i-brāte, *v. t.* **1.** To ascertain the internal diameter of a gun or any tube ; বন্দুক, কামান, নল বা চুঙ্গী প্রভৃতির আভ্যন্তর-ব্যাস নিরূপণ করা। **2.** To determine or rectify the graduation of, as of the various graduated instruments ; বিভিন্ন প্রকার ক্রমাঙ্কিত যন্ত্রের ক্রমাঙ্ক-নির্ণয় বা সংশোধন করা। **—bra'-tion**, *n.*

căl'-i-bre (-bêr), **—bêr**, *n.* **1** The diameter of a body ; as, the *calibre* of a column ; ব্যাস। **2.** The diameter of the bore of a fire-arm ; বন্দুকাদি আগ্নেয়াস্ত্রের অভ্যন্তরের ব্যাস। **3.** Compass or extent of mind ; mental capacity ; "Coming from the man of their *calibre* they were highly mischievous ;" মনের প্রসার ; মানসিক ক্ষমতা, বোধশক্তি। **Calibre-compass**—See CALIPERS.

căl'-i-cle, *n.* (*Biol.*) A small cup-like body ; (জীব-বিজ্ঞান) ক্ষুদ্র পানপাত্রের অনুরূপ অঙ্গবিশেষ।

căl'-i-cō, *n.* (*Pl.* -COES.) **1.** A plain white cloth made from cotton ; শ্বেতবর্ণ কার্পাস-বস্ত্র। [পূর্ব্বে এইরূপ বস্ত্র মালাবার উপকূল হইতে ইয়ুরোপে রপ্তানি হইত।] **2.** Printed cotton cloth coarser than muslin ; মসলিন অপেক্ষা মোটা ছিটের কাপড়। (যুক্ত-রাজ্যে শেষোক্ত অর্থে ব্যবহৃত হয়।) **Calico-printing**—উক্ত প্রকার শ্বেত কার্পাসবস্ত্রের উপর নানাপ্রকার নমুনা মুদ্রিত করিয়া ছিট প্রস্তুত করণ।

căl'-i-păsh, *n.* The part of a turtle next to the upper shell, containing a gelatinous substance of a dull greenish tinge ; কূর্ম্মের উপরের খোলার ভিতরের দিকে যে মলিন সবুজবর্ণ তৈলাক্ত পদার্থ সংলগ্ন থাকে।

căl'-i-pee, (-pē) *n.* The part of a turtle which belongs to the lower shell containing a gelatinous substance of a light yellowish colour ; কূর্ম্মের বুকের খোলার ভিতরের দিকে যে মৃদু পীতবর্ণের তৈলাক্ত পদার্থ থাকে।

căl'-i-pêrs, *n.* (*Pl.*) Compasses with bowed legs, used for measuring the internal or external diameter of any round body ; গোলাকার বস্তুর বাহ্য বা আভ্যন্তর ব্যাস পরিমাপক যন্ত্রবিশেষ, বেড়ীকম্পাস, পরিমাণ-পরকার (হিঃ কোঃ)।

cā'-liph, —lĭf, *n.* A title of the successors of Mahommed both as temporal and spiritual rulers ; মহম্মদের বংশধরগণের উপাধিবিশেষ, খলিফা। [বর্ত্তমানে তুরস্কের সুলতানগণ এই উপাধি গ্রহণ করিয়াছেন।] **—li-phate**, *n.*

ca'-lix, *n.* See CALYX.

calk (cäk), *v. t.* See CAULK.

calk (cäk), *v. t.* To cover the back of a drawing, etc., with chalk for the purpose of transferring a copy of it ; প্রতিলিপি তুলিবার উদ্দেশ্যে চিত্রাদির পৃষ্ঠ খড়িদ্বারা আবৃত করা।

calk (cäk), *v. t.* & *n.* To provide with sharp iron to prevent horse-shoe or boot from slipping ; পিচ্ছিল পথে পদস্খলন নিবারণের উদ্দেশ্যে ঘোড়ার নাল বা বুট জুতায় তীক্ষ্ণ লৌহখণ্ড সংযোগ করা। ***Noun.*** A pointed piece of iron on a horse-shoe, etc. to prevent slipping ; পিচ্ছিলপথে পদস্খলন নিবারণের উদ্দেশ্যে ঘোড়ার নাল প্রভৃতিতে যে তীক্ষ্ণাগ্র লৌহখণ্ড সংযোজিত করা হয়।

cal'-kin (cä-kĭn or căl-), *n.* Same as CALK.

call, *v. t.* & *i.* **1.** To command or request to come or be present ; ডাকা, আহ্বান করা। **2.** To urge ; to invite ; as, to *call* a minister to be the pastor of a church ; to nominate ; নির্ব্বন্ধাতিশয় সহকারে বলা ; আহ্বান করা ; মনোনীত করা। **3.** To demand presence of ; as, to *call* a witness ; তলব করা। **4.** To rouse from sleep ; as, *call* me in the morning ; জাগ্রত করা। **5.** To convoke an assembly ; সভা আহ্বান করা। **6.** To denominate ; to designate ; "If you would but *call* me Rosalind ;" অভিহিত করা, নামে ডাকা ; আখ্যাত করা, নাম রাখা। **7.** To consider ; to regard, as, you *call* it mean ; বিবেচনা করা ; গণ্য করা। **8.** To invoke ; to appeal to ; "I *call* God for a witness ;" আহ্বান করা ; দোহাই দেওয়া। **9.** To read over ; "No Parish clerk who *calls* the psalms so clear ;" আবৃত্তি করা। ***Verb i.*** (With *at, to, after, out, up, down.*) **1.** To speak in a loud voice ; to address by name ; উচ্চৈঃস্বরে কথা বলা ; নাম ধরিয়া ডাকা। **2.** To make a short visit, (with *at, for, upon*) ; দেখা করিতে যাওয়া, সাক্ষাৎ করা। **3.** To make a demand or request ; চাওয়া, দাবী করা, প্রার্থনা করা। **Called to one's account**—Removed by death ; ইহলোক হইতে অন্তর্হিত। **To call again**—To call a second time ; পুনরায় ডাকা। **To call a person names**—To abuse him ; কোন ব্যক্তিকে গালি দেওয়া। **To call a spade a spade**—See SPADE. **To call at**—To make a short stop on way, (said of ships) ; (জাহাজসম্বন্ধে) পথিমধ্যে অল্প সময়ের জন্য থামা। To pay a short visit to ; অল্পকালের জন্য কোন স্থানে গমন করা, সাক্ষাৎ করিতে যাওয়া। **To call attention to**—To direct attention to ; মনোযোগ আকর্ষণ করা। **To call away**—To turn aside ; to divert ; নিবর্ত্তিত করা ; বিষয়ান্তরে প্রেরণ করা। **To call back**—To revoke ; to withdraw ; ফিরাইয়া লওয়া, প্রত্যানয়ন করা, প্রতিনিবৃত্ত করা, প্রতিসংহার করা ; প্রত্যাহার করা। **To call down**—To pray for ; প্রার্থনা করা। To imprecate ; to rebuke ; to censure ; অভিশাপ দেওয়া ; তিরস্কার করা ; নিন্দা করা। **To call for**—To require or desire the attendance (of persons) ; (কোন ব্যক্তিকে) ডাকা বা উপস্থিত হইতে আহ্বান করা। To give an order for a thing to be supplied ; কোন জিনিষের ফরমাইস দেওয়া। (*Fig.*) To desire anxiously ; (লক্ষণায়) আকুলভাবে আকাঙ্ক্ষা করা। To demand ; to need ; চাওয়া ; আবশ্যক করা। (*Colloq.*) To call or make visit in any place in order to fetch away a person or an article ; as, I will *call for* her or a parcel ; (চলিত ভাষায়) কোন বস্তু বা লোককে আনিবার জন্য কোন স্থানে যাওয়া। **To call for a trump**—তাস খেলায় নিজের সঙ্গীকে রঙ্গ খেলিবার জন্য ইঙ্গিত করা। **To call forth**—To elicit ; as, to *call forth* all the faculties of the mind ; উদ্দীপন করা, অন্তর্নিহিত শক্তি উদ্বোধিত করা। **To call in**—To collect ; as, to *call in* debts or money ; সংগ্রহ করা। To withdraw from circulation ; প্রচলন বন্ধ করার উদ্দেশ্যে (মুদ্রাদি) উঠাইয়া লওয়া, গুটাইয়া লওয়া। To summon to one's house ; to invite to come together ; as, to *call in* neighbours ; কাহারও বাটীতে আহ্বান করা ; একযোগে আসিবার জন্য আমন্ত্রণ করা। To pay a short visit, (with *to, at, of,* places, *on, of,* persons); অল্প সময়ের জন্য কোন স্থানে যাওয়া, কাহারও সহিত সাক্ষাৎ করিতে যাওয়া। **To call in doubt** or **question**—To dispute the authority or authenticity of a statement ; কোন উক্তির প্রামাণিকতা বা সত্যতা সম্বন্ধে তর্ক বা প্রশ্ন উত্থাপন করা। **To call into being** or **existence**—সৃষ্টি করা, অস্তিত্ব প্রদান করা। **To call into play**—To give scope for ; ক্রিয়ার জন্য প্রসার দেওয়া। **To call off**—To summon away ; to divert ; ডাকিয়া লইয়া যাওয়া ; বিষয়ান্তরে প্রেরণ করা। To make a short visit to ; অল্প সময়ের জন্য অবস্থান করা। [যে সকল জাহাজ পথিমধ্যে কোন বন্দরে অল্প কালের জন্য অবস্থান করে, তাহাদের সম্বন্ধে প্রযুক্ত হয়। Call at এবং call off এর মধ্যে প্রভেদ এই যে call off বলিলে জাহাজ ঠিক বন্দরে না লাগিয়া অনতিদূরে নঙ্গর করিয়া রহিয়াছে এইরূপ বুঝায়।] **To call on, upon**—To make a short visit to ; দেখা করিতে যাওয়া। To appeal to ; to invite ; to request earnestly ; as, to *call upon* a person to make a speech ; আবেদন করা ; আহ্বান করা ; সনির্বন্ধ অনুরোধ করা। To solicit payment or make a demand of a debt ; পাওনা চাওয়া ; ঋণের টাকার দাবী করা। To invoke or pray to ; to worship ; as, to *call on* or *upon* God ; আহ্বান করা, প্রার্থনা করা ; অর্চনা করা। **To call out**—To call loudly ; to ejaculate ; চীৎকার করিয়া ডাকা, উচ্চৈঃস্বরে বলা ; আবেগোচ্ছ্বসিত কণ্ঠে সহসা বলিয়া ফেলা। To elicit ; প্রকট করা, ব্যক্ত করা। To challenge to a duel ; দ্বন্দ্বযুদ্ধে আহ্বান করা। To summon to service ; কার্য্যের জন্য আহ্বান করা। **To call over**—To recite a roll of names or a list of items ; নাম ডাকা, নাম বা বিষয়ের তালিকা যথাক্রমে উচ্চৈঃস্বরে পড়িয়া যাওয়া। (*Colloq.*) **To call over the coals**—To reprove ; to find fault with ; (চলিত ভাষায়) তিরস্কার করা ; দোষ প্রদর্শন করা। **To call (something) one's own**—To claim or consider as one's own ; নিজস্ব বলিয়া দাবী বা গণ্য করা। **To call the jury**—বাক্স হইতে যে অনুক্রমে তোলা হইয়াছে তদনুসারে জুরীদিগের নাম ডাকা। **To call the plaintiff**—প্রকাশ্য আদালতে (পেয়াদা কর্ত্তৃক) উচ্চৈঃস্বরে বাদীর নাম ডাকা। **To call to account**—To demand an account from ; কৈফিয়ত তলব করা, জবাবদিহী করা। **To call to another's mind**—To bring to recollection of another ; to remind another of a thing ; অন্যের স্মৃতিপথে আনয়ন করা ; অন্য ব্যক্তিকে কোন বিষয় স্মরণ করাইয়া দেওয়া, মনে পাড়িয়ে দেওয়া। **To call to mind**—To bring to one's recollection ; to remember ; স্মৃতিপথে আনয়ন করা ; স্মরণ করা। To revive in memory ; স্মৃতি পথে আরূঢ় হওয়া। **To call to order**—To open a meeting ; সভার উদ্বোধন করা। To intimate to any person or persons at a meeting that he is or they are transgressing the rules of debate ; বাদানুবাদের নিয়মভঙ্গ দ্বারা সভার কার্য্যে ব্যাঘাত জন্মাইয়াছে এই কথা সভাস্থ এক বা ততোধিক ব্যক্তিকে জ্ঞাপন করা। **To call to the bar**—To grant license to practise as a barrister in any of the courts of law ; কৌঁসুলীর কার্য্য করিতে অধিকার প্রদান করা। **To call up**—To bring into view or recollection ; as, to *call up* the image of a desired friend ; দৃষ্টিপথে আনয়ন করা, স্মৃতি পথে আরূঢ় করা। To bring into action or discussion ; to demand the consideration of ; as, to *call up* a bill before a legislative body ; কার্য্যে পরিণত করা, আলোচনার বিষয়ীভূত করা ; কোন বিষয়ের বিবেচনার জন্য দাবী করা। To require the payment of instalments of a loan subscribed to ; ঋণদানের জন্য অঙ্গীকৃত অর্থের কিস্তির টাকা চাওয়া। To summon to arise ; জাগরিত হইবার জন্য আহ্বান করা। **To call upon a prisoner**—অভিযুক্ত ব্যক্তি দোষী সাব্যস্থ হইলে কেন সে দণ্ডপ্রাপ্ত হইবে না, এই কথা তাহাকে জিজ্ঞাসা করা।

call, *n.* **1.** A vocal address or summons or invitation ; ডাক, আহ্বান, আমন্ত্রণ। **2.** A cry ; a shout ; চীৎকার ; নিনাদ। **3.** A signal of bugle, etc. ; a signalling whistle ; রণ শিঙ্গাদ্বারা সঙ্কেত ; রণবংশী। **4.** An invocation or prayer for help or relief ; দুঃখমোচনের জন্য প্রার্থনা, দোহাই। **5.** A divine summons to any office or duty ; (কোন পদ গ্রহণ বা কর্ত্তব্য পালনে) ঈশ্বরের আহ্বান, দেবতার ডাক। **6.** A summons or invitation ; তলব, আহ্বান, আমন্ত্রণ। **7.** Duty ; need ; occasion ; as, you have no *call* to blush ; কর্ত্তব্য ; আবশ্যক, প্রয়োজন ; উপলক্ষ। **8.** Demand for money, esp. for unpaid capital from a company's share-holders ; টাকার দাবি, বিশেষতঃ সমবায়ের অংশীদারগণের নিকট মূলধনের অপরিশোধিত অর্থ প্রদানের জন্য আহ্বান। **9.** A demand ; a claim ; "Dependence is a perpetual *call* upon humanity ;" দাবি ; দাওয়া। **10.** A short visit ; অল্প সময়ের জন্য সাক্ষাৎ বা দর্শন। **11.** The cry of a bird to its mate or young ; কূজন, বিহঙ্গ-কাকলী। **12.** (*Fowlery*) A noise or cry in imitation of a bird ; a pipe to call birds by imitating their cry ; (পক্ষি-শিকার) পক্ষিরবানুকারী শব্দ ; পক্ষিরবানুকারী বংশী বিশেষ। **13.** (*Hunting*) A note blown on the horn to encourage the hounds ; (মৃগয়া) কুক্কুরদিগকে উৎসাহিত করিবার জন্য শিঙ্গাদ্বারা বিশেষ সুরবাদন। **14.** (*Naut.*) A whistle or pipe used by the boatswain or his mate to summon sailors together ; (নৌ-বিদ্যা) যে শিটী মারিয়া বা ভেঁপু বাজাইয়া জাহাজের টিণ্ডাল বা তদীয় সহকারিগণ অন্যান্য নাবিকদিগকে একত্র করে। **15.** (Stock-exchange) Option of claiming stock at a given date ; (কোম্পানীর কাগজের কারবার) নির্দ্দিষ্ট তারিখে কোম্পানির কাগজ দাবি করিবার ইচ্ছাধীনতা। **At call**—ধনাগারে (ব্যাঙ্ক) গচ্ছিত যে অর্থ যখন অভিরুচি তোলা যাইতে পারে তৎসম্বন্ধে at call প্রযুক্ত হয়। **Call-bird**—A decoy-bird ; বন্য পক্ষিগণকে ভুলাইয়া জালপাশ-সমাকীর্ণ পুষ্করিণীতে আনয়নের জন্য গৃহপালিত পক্ষিবিশেষ। **Call-boy**—যে বালক নাটকের অভিনেতৃগণকে ডাকিয়া আনে। **Call-day, call-night**—যে দিবস বা রাত্রিতে ব্যবহার-শাস্ত্র শিক্ষার্থী ছাত্রদিগকে কৌঁসুলীর শ্রেণীতে ভুক্ত করা হয়। **Call-loan, call-money**—যে অর্থ যখন অভিরুচি ফিরিয়া চাওয়া যাইতে পারে। **Call-notes**—পক্ষিগণ যে কাকলীদ্বারা পরস্পরের সহিত মনোভাবের আদান প্রদান করে। **Call of duty**—কর্ত্তব্যানুরোধ, কর্ত্তব্য কার্য্যের প্রেরণা। **Call of nature**—বাহ্য প্রস্রাবের বেগ। **Call of the house**—পার্লেমেণ্ট মহাসভা কিম্বা অন্য কোন ব্যবস্থাপক সভার প্রত্যেক সভ্যগণকে উপস্থিতির জন্য

অলজ্ঘনীয় আহ্বান। [পার্লেমেণ্ট বা ব্যবস্থাপক সভায় সমগ্র সভ্যের মত জ্ঞাত হওয়া আবশ্যক হইলে এইরূপ করা হইয়া থাকে।] **Within call**—ডাক শোনা যায় এমন দূরে।

căll'-ẽr, *n.* **1.** One who calls; আহ্বানকারী, আমন্ত্রণকারী। **2.** A person who pays call or visit; যে ব্যক্তি দেখা বা সাক্ষাৎ করে।

căl'-lêr, *n.* **1.** (*Scotch.*) Cool; refreshing; as, *caller* day: *caller* air; শীতল; শ্রান্তি-নিবারক। **2.** Fresh; as, *caller* herrings; টাট্‌কা।

Callichrous pabda—পাব্‌দা (গুপ্তঃ)।

căl-lig'-ră-phŷ, *n.* Beautiful handwriting; handwriting; সুন্দর হস্তাক্ষর; হস্তাক্ষর। **—li-graph'-ic,** *adj.* **—pher, —phist,** *ns.*

căll'-ing, *n.* **1.** The act of one who calls; আহ্বান। **2.** Divine summons to salvation or self-devotion; মুক্তি বা আত্মোৎসর্গের জন্য ভগবদাহ্বান। **3.** Occupation; profession; trade; বৃত্তি; পেশা; ব্যবসায়। **4.** A body of persons following any calling; "Not to impose celibacy on whole *callings*;" কোন ব্যবসায়ে নিযুক্ত জনগণ, সমব্যবসায়ী ব্যক্তিবর্গ।

Căl lĭ' ō-pē, *n.* The Muse that presides over eloquence and heroic poetry; (গ্রীকপুরাণোক্ত) বাগ্মিতা ও বীরগাথার অধিষ্ঠাত্রী বাগ্‌দেবী।

căl'-li-pêrs, *n.* See CALIPERS.

căl-lis-thĕn'-ic, *adj.* Relating to callisthenics or exercise for health or bodily symmetry; স্বাস্থ্যলাভ বা অঙ্গসৌষ্ঠব সম্পাদনার্থ ব্যায়াম বিষয়ক।

căl-lis-thĕn'-ics, *n.* The art or science of healthful exercise for the body and limbs to promote gracefulness and strength; স্বাস্থ্যলাভের জন্য বা অঙ্গসৌষ্ঠব সম্পাদনার্থ ব্যায়াম-কৌশল।

căl-lŏs'-i-tŷ, *n.* **1.** State or quality of being callous; (*fig.*) lack of sensibility or feeling; স্পর্শানভিজ্ঞতা; (লক্ষণায়) অনুভব শক্তিহীনতা, অনুরাগ-শূন্যতা। **2.** Abnormal hardness or thickness of the skin; চর্ম্মের অস্বাভাবিক দার্ঢ্য বা স্থূলতা। **3.** A hard or thickened spot or protuberance; কড়া, কিণ (মঃ ভাঃ)।

căl'-lous (-lŭs), *adj.* **1.** Hardened; indurated; as, a *callous* ulcer: a *callous* hand; কঠিনীভূত; দৃঢ়ীভূত। **2.** Unfeeling; insensible; hardened in feeling; "It is an immense blessing to be perfectly *callous* to ridicule;" নির্ম্মম; বেদনাবোধশূন্য; কঠোরচিত্ত, নির্দ্দয়, কঠিন। **—ness,** *n.*

căl'-low (-lō), *adj.* **1.** Destitute of feather; unfledged; পালকবিহীন; অজাতপক্ষ। **2.** Youthfnl; immature; তরুণ; অপরিপক্ব, অনভিজ্ঞ, কাঁচা।

căl'-lŭs, *n.* **1.** (*Med.*) Callosity; (ভৈষজ্য-শাস্ত্র) কড়া। **2.** (*Anat.*) A bony material formed while bone-fracture heals; (শারীর-সংস্থান-বিদ্যা) ভগ্নাস্থিসংযুক্ত হইবার কালে যে অস্থিময় পদার্থ উপজাত হয়।

calm (câm), *n.* **1.** Stillness; quiet; "The wind ceased and there was a great *calm*;" নিস্তব্ধতা; নীরবতা। **2.** Serenity; মনঃপ্রসাদ, নিরুদ্বেগ। (*Geog.*) **The belt of calms**—(ভূগোল) নির্ব্বাতমণ্ডল (সাঃ পঃ)।

calm (câm), *adj.* **1.** Still or quiet; নীরব, নিস্তব্ধ, শান্ত, প্রশান্ত, স্থির, নিঝুম (*Poet.*), অচঞ্চল, নিথর (*Poet.*), স্তিমিত, নিষ্কম্প, নিশ্চল, অনুত্তরঙ্গ, নিবাত। **2.** Undisturbed by passion; not agitated or excited; quiet; tranquil; স্থির; বিশ্রব্ধ; শান্ত, প্রশান্ত, অব্যাকুল, নির্ব্বিকার; স্থিতধী, স্থিতপ্রজ্ঞ, অক্ষুব্ধ। **Calm'-ly,** *adv.* **Calm'-ness,** *n.* **1.** Quietness; stillness; tranquility; নিস্তব্ধতা; নীরবতা; প্রশান্তি, শান্তভাব। **2.** Uuruffied state; quietness; স্থৈর্য্য, শম, শান্তভাব; নির্ব্বিকারত্ব, অক্ষোভ।

calm (câm), *v. t.* & *i.* To make calm; to pacify; as, to *calm* contending kings; নিস্তব্ধ করা; প্রশান্ত করা, স্থির করা। ***Verb i.*** (Always with *down*) To become calm; as, the tempest now began to *calm down*; শান্ত হওয়া, স্থির হওয়া।

calm'-a-tive (căl-mă-tĭv), *adj.* & *n.* Calming; sedative; প্রশান্তকর; অবসাদক। ***Noun.*** A calming agent; অবসাদক ঔষধ।

căl'-ō-mĕl, *n.* Chloride of mercury much used in medicine; রসকর্পূর (রঃ চিঃ—প্রঃ), ভস্মসূত (রসঃ চিঃ—প্রঃ), শ্বেতভস্ম (ঐ), কর্পূররস (রঃ প্রঃ সুঃ—প্রঃ)।

Calophyllum inophyllum—সুলতানা চম্পা (হিন্দি—বেলঃ)।

căl-ō-rĕs'-cĕnce, *n.* (*Phys.*) The change of heat rays to light rays; (পদার্থ-বিদ্যা) তাপরশ্মির আলোকরশ্মিতে পরিবর্ত্তন, তাপরশ্মিপ্রকাশ (হিঃ কোঃ)।

că-lŏr'-ic, *n.* & *adj.* Heat; তাপ। ***Adj.*** Pertaining to caloric; উষ্ণতা-সম্বন্ধীয়। **Caloric engine**—উষ্ণবায়ুচালিত যন্ত্র।

că-lŏr'-i-dŭct, *n.* A tube or duct for conducting heat; তাপবাহিনী নলিকা (হিঃ কোঃ), তাপবাহিকা।

căl'-ō-rie (-rē), *n.* The unit of heat according to French standard; ফরাসীদেশীয় পরিমাণানুযায়ী তাপাঙ্ক। [অর্থাৎ এক কিলোগ্রাম (২½ পাউণ্ড) জলের উষ্ণতা শতাঙ্কিত তাপমান যন্ত্রের ১ অঙ্ক বৃদ্ধি করিতে হইলে যে পরিমাণ উত্তাপের প্রয়োজন হয়।]

că-lŏr-i-fā'-cient (-shĭ-ent), *adj.* See CALORIFICIENT.

că-lŏr'-i-fere (-fāre), *n.* An apparatus for conveying and distributing heat; তাপবাহী যন্ত্র (হিঃ কোঃ)।

căl-ō-rif'-ic, *adj.* Causing heat; heating; তাপজনক (হিঃ কোঃ); তাপক। **Calorific rays**—তাপজনক কিরণ।

că-lŏr-i-fi-cā'-tion, *n.* Production of heat, esp. animal heat; তাপোৎপাদন, বিশেষতঃ জৈব তাপোৎপাদন।

că-lŏr-i-fi′-cient (-shŭnt), **că-lŏr-i-fi′-ĕnt,** *adjs.* **1.** Heat-producing ; তাপজনক। **2.** (*Physiol.*) Applied to foods which being rich in carbon are supposed to give rise to heat in the animal body by oxidation ; (শারীর-বিজ্ঞান) মেদ প্রভৃতি যে সমস্ত অঙ্গার-প্রধান খাদ্যদ্রব্য দ্বারা মানবদেহে তাপ উপজাত হয়—তৎসম্বন্ধে প্রযুক্ত।

căl-ŏ-rim′-ĕ-têr, *n.* An instrument for measuring the specific heat of a body ; উষ্ণতামাপক (হিঃ কোঃ), তাপমান (সাঃ পঃ)।

căl-ŏ-rim′-ĕ-trȳ, *n.* Measurement of the quantity of heat in bodies ; উষ্ণতামিতি (হিঃ কোঃ)।

că-lŏr-i-mō′-tor (-têr), *n.* A galvanic instrument for evolving caloric ; তাপোৎপাদনের জন্য বৈদ্যুতিক যন্ত্রবিশেষ, বিদ্যুত্তাপকারক (হিঃ কোঃ)।

Că-lŏt′-rŏ-pis, *n.* A genus of plants, natural order Asclepiadaceæ ; আকন্দাদি। ***Calotropis gigantea***—White Calotropis ; শ্বেত আকন্দ (যোঃ), শ্বেতার্ক (ঐ)।

că-lotte′ (-lŏt), *n.* The plain round skull-cap worn by the clergy of the Roman Catholic Church, etc. ; রোমান ক্যাথলিক পুরোহিত প্রভৃতির প্রান্তহীন টুপীবিশেষ। (মুসলমানদিগের টুপির মত)।

căl′-ŏ-tȳpe, *n.* A photographic process ; আলোকচিত্রণের প্রণালী বিশেষ।

căl′-trăp, cal′-trŏp, *ns.* **1.** An instrument armed with four spikes, so arranged that one always stands upright, used to obstruct the progress of an enemy's cavalry or of the besiegers of a fortification ; লৌহকীলক (প্রেক) চতুষ্টয়বিশিষ্ট যুদ্ধযন্ত্রবিশেষ, চতুঃশূল (আঃ বঃ)। [এই যন্ত্রটী এইরূপ ভাবে নির্ম্মিত যে একটী কীলক সর্ব্বদাই খাড়াভাবে থাকে। ইহাদ্বারা অশ্বারোহী সৈন্য এবং দুর্গাবরোধকারিগণের গতিরোধ করা হয়।] **2.** (*Bot.*) The common name of Tribulus ; (উদ্ভিদ্-বিদ্যা) গোক্ষুর (সুশ্রুঃ), গোখুর (ঐ)। **Water caltrop**—পানিফল (খোরী)।

căl′-ū-mĕt, *n.* **1.** A kind of pipe used by the North American Indians for smoking tobacco ; উত্তর আমেরিকার আদিম অধিবাসীদিগের তাম্রকূট পানের নলবিশেষ (হুকা)। **2.** A symbol of peace ; শান্তি-নিদর্শন বিশেষ। **To smoke the calumet together**—To make peace ; শান্তিস্থাপন করা।

că-lŭm′-ni-āte, *v. t.* To slander ; কুৎসা রটনা করা, অপবাদ করা অখ্যাতি করা, দুর্নাম করা। **—a′-tion —a-tor,** *ns.* **—a-to-ry,** *adj.*

că-lŭm′-ni-ous (-us), *adj.* Given to or marked by calumny ; অপবাদ-রত, অপবাদগর্ভ, গ্লানিকর, কুৎসাশীল, গ্লানিসূচক, কলঙ্ককর। **—ly,** *adv.*

căl′-ŭm-nȳ, *n.* False accusation ; slander ; মিথ্যা অভিযোগ ; অপবাদ, অখ্যাতি, কলঙ্ক, পরীবাদ, নিন্দাবাদ, পৈশুন্য, বদনাম (*Colloq.*)।

căl′-vă-rȳ, *n.* **1.** The place where Christ was crucified on a small hill near Jerusalem ; জেরুজেলেম নগরীর সন্নিকটবর্ত্তী যে ক্ষুদ্র শৈলে যীশুখৃষ্ট ক্রুশবিদ্ধ হইয়াছিলেন। **2.** A representation of the crucifixion of Christ in the open air ; উন্মুক্তস্থানে ক্রুশবিদ্ধ যীশুর প্রতিমূর্ত্তি প্রদর্শন। [রোমান ক্যাথলিক দেশসমূহে নগরোপকণ্ঠস্থিত ক্ষুদ্র শৈলোপরি ক্রুশবিদ্ধ যীশুর প্রতিমূর্ত্তি প্রতিষ্ঠিত হইয়া থাকে।] **3.** (*Herald.*) A cross set upon the steps ; (কুল-বিদ্যা) সোপানোপরি স্থাপিত ক্রুশবিশেষ।

calve (câv), *v. i.* & *t.* **1.** To give birth to a calf ; বৎস প্রসব করা। **2.** (*Fig.*) To bring forth ; "The grassy clods now *calved* ;" to bear ; (লক্ষণায়) উৎপাদন করা ; প্রসব করা। **3.** (*Iceberg*) To break off from a glacier, (also *v. t.*) ; (হিমশৈলসম্বন্ধে) তুষারনদী হইতে বিচ্যুত হওয়া। ***Verb t.*** To bear ; to bring forth ; বাচ্চা দেওয়া ; বিয়ান, বিয়ন।

Căl′-vĭn-ĭsm, *n.* **1.** The doctrines of the great Genevan religious reformer, John Calvin (1509-1564); সুইজারলেণ্ড দেশের অন্তঃপাতী জেনাভা নগরীর সুপ্রসিদ্ধ ধর্ম্ম-সংস্কারক ক্যালভিনের ধর্ম্মমত। [ক্যালভিনের মতে ভগবান পূর্ব্ব হইতেই নির্দ্দিষ্ট সংখ্যক ব্যক্তিকে মুক্তির জন্য নির্ব্বাচিত করিয়াছেন, এতদ্ভিন্ন অপর সকলের অদৃষ্টে চিরনিরয় বাসের ব্যবস্থা করা হইয়াছে।] **2.** Adherence to Calvin's doctrines ; ক্যালভিনের মতানুবর্ত্তিতা। **—ist,** *n.* **—is′-tic, —is′-ti-cal,** *adjs.* **—is′-ti-cal-ly,** *adv.* **—ize,** *v. t.*

calx (călks), *n.* (*Pl.* CALXES or CALCES.) **1.** (*Chem.*) The substance left after a metal or mineral has been subjected to violent heat or calcination ; ভস্ম (রঃ রঃ সঃ—প্রঃ), ধাতুভস্ম (হিঃ কোঃ), দগ্ধধাতুচূর্ণ, খাক, জারা, খড়ী বা চূণ। **2.** (*Glass-making*) Broken glass which is restored to the pots ; (কাচনির্ম্মাণে) যে সকল ভাঙ্গা কাচের টুকরা পুনরায় পাত্রে রক্ষিত হয়। **Calx of brass**—রীতিকুসুম (প্রঃ), কুসুমাঞ্জন (মঃ উঃ)। **Calx of gems**—বজ্রভস্ম (রঃ রঃ সঃ—প্রঃ)। **Calx of iron**—তীক্ষ্ণভস্ম (রঃ রঃ সঃ—প্রঃ)। **Calx of mercury**—সূতভস্ম (ঐ)। **Calx of silver**—রৌপ্যমল। **Calx of tin**—বঙ্গভস্ম (রঃ নঃ মাঃ—প্রঃ)।

că-lȳc-i-flō′-răl, —rous (-rŭs) also **—rāte,** *adjs.* (*Bot.*) Having stamens and petals inserted in calyx ; বহির্বাসনিবদ্ধ পুংকেশর পুষ্পফলধারী, কুণ্ডাধারপুষ্পী (সাঃ পঃ)। **—i-form,** *adj.* (*Bot.*) Having the form or appearance of a calyx ; কুণ্ডবৎ (সাঃ পঃ)।

căl′-ȳ-cle, *n.* (*Bot.*) An accessory calyx outside the true one ; পুষ্পের উপবহির্বাস। **—coid, —coi′-de-ous, —cled,** *adjs.*

cā'-lȳx, *n.* **1.** The outer covering or leaf-like envelope of a flower ; পুষ্পের বহিরাবরণ বা পত্রবৎ আচ্ছাদন, কুণ্ড (সাঃ পঃ), বহির্বাস

Various forms of calyx.

(ঐ), বহিরাবরণ (ঐ), দলকোষ (আঃ বঃ), হরিদ্‌বর্ণ পুষ্পদলাবরণ (ঐ), পুষ্পচ্ছদ, পুষ্পকুণ্ড, পুষ্পকোষ, পুষ্পাবেষ্টন। **2.** (*Physiol.*) A cup-like cavity or organ ; (শারীরবিজ্ঞান) কুণ্ড বা বাটীর মত দেহযন্ত্র বিশেষ।

căm, *n.* **1.** (*Mach.*) A projecting part of a wheel so shaped as to convert circular into reciprocal or variable motion ; (যন্ত্র) প্রলম্বিত চক্রাংশ বিশেষ ; ইহার সাহায্যে চক্রবৎগতি অগ্রপশ্চাৎ বা বিষম গতিতে পরিবর্ত্তিত হয়। **2.** A ridge or mound of earth (*Prov. Eng.*) ; (প্রাদেশিক ইংরাজী) মাটির ঢিপি, মৃত্তিকা-স্তূপ।

căm-ă-ră-de-rie' (-d'rē), (*F.*), *n.* Loyalty to one's associates ; good fellowship ; সঙ্গীর প্রতি অনুরাগ ; সদ্বন্ধু-সাহচর্য্য।

că-mă-ril'-lă, *n.* **1.** The private audience chamber of a king, courtiers, priests ; as, encircled with a dangerous *camarilla* ; রাজা, যাজক বা অমাত্যগণের গুপ্ত মন্ত্রণাকক্ষ। **2.** A cabal ; a clique ; a junto ; কুচক্রি-সভা ; কুচক্রিদল ; রাজকার্য্যে দোষ আবিষ্কারের জন্য গুপ্তসভা।

căm'-bêr, *n., v. i.* & *t.* **1.** (*Shipbuilding*) An upward convexity of a deck or other surface ; as, she has a high *camber* ; (পোত-নির্ম্মাণ) জাহাজের পাটাতন বা অন্য কোন কিছুর পৃষ্ঠোপরিস্থ ন্যুব্জতা। **2.** (*Arch.*) A slightly arched beam ; (স্থপতিবিদ্যা) ঈষদ্ বক্র কড়িকাঠ। ***Verb i.*** To curve upward ; উর্দ্ধদিকে বক্রীভূত হওয়া। ***Verb t.*** To curve shipplanks ; to arch slightly ; জাহাজের তক্তা বক্র করা ; ঈষদ্ বক্র করা, অল্প-বাঁকান। **Camber-beam** — (*Arch.*) A slightly arched beam ; ঈষদ্ বক্র কড়িকাঠ।

Căm'-bêr-wĕll-Beau-tȳ, (-bū-), *n.* A butterfly ; প্রজাপতি।

căm'-bĭst, *n.* One skilled in the science of exchange ; a dealer in bills of exchange ; (অর্থাদির) বিনিময়বিজ্ঞানবিৎ ; হুণ্ডি ব্যবসায়ী। **—ry,** *n.* The science of exchange, weight, etc. ; বিনিময়বিজ্ঞান, ভারবিজ্ঞান, প্রভৃতি।

căm'-bĭ-ŭm, *n.* A larger tissue formed between the wood and the bark of the exogenous plants ; বহির্জনি উদ্ভিদের কাষ্ঠ এবং বল্কলের মধ্যস্থলে গঠিত সূত্রবৎ পদার্থ বিশেষ, পরবর্ত্তী স্তর (সাঃ পঃ), পরিণামী (ঐ)।

căm-bōōse', *n.* Same as CABOOSE.

căm'-brĕl, *n.* A butcher's bent wood or iron to hang carcases on ; নিহত পশুর দেহ টাঙ্গাইবার জন্য মাংসবিক্রেতৃগণের বক্র লৌহ বা কাষ্ঠখণ্ড বিশেষ।

Căm'-brĭ-ă, *n.* The ancient Latin name of Wales ; ওয়েলেস্ দেশের প্রাচীন ল্যাটিন নাম। **—an,** *adj.* & *n.* **1.** Pertaining to Wales ; ওয়েলেস্‌দেশ সম্বন্ধীয়। **2.** (*Geol.*) Belonging to the lowest sub-division of the rocks lying below the Silurian in Wales and Cumberland ; (ভূ-বিদ্যা) ওয়েলেস্ এবং ক্যাম্বারলেণ্ডের সিলুরিয়্যানের স্তরের নিম্নবর্ত্তী প্রস্তরের সর্ব্বনিম্ন উপরিভাগ সম্বন্ধীয়। (*Noun*) **1.** A Welshman ; ওয়েলেস্‌দেশীয় লোক। **2.** (*Geol.*) The Cambrian formation ; সিলুরিয়্যান স্তরের নিম্নবর্ত্তী প্রস্তরের সর্ব্বনিম্ন উপরিভাগ। **Cambrian age**— শম্বুকযুগ (অভিঃ)।

căm'-brĭc, *n.* & *adj.* A kind of fine white linen ; সূক্ষ্ম এবং শ্বেতবর্ণ-ক্ষৌমবস্ত্র বিশেষ, শ্বেতাংশু বিশেষ, সূক্ষ্ম-পট্ট-বস্ত্র বিশেষ, শ্বেত কার্পাস বস্ত্র। ***Adj.*** Pertaining to fine white linen ; উক্ত প্রকার ক্ষৌম-বস্ত্র সম্বন্ধীয়। [Flandersএর অন্তঃপাতী Cambray নামক স্থানে প্রথম প্রস্তুত হয়।]

cāme, *n.* A grooved slip of lead as used in lattice windows ; জাফরীর জানালায় ব্যবহৃত খাজ-কাটা সীসার টুকরা।

cāme, *v. i.* Did come, *p.t.* of *come* ; আসিয়াছিল।

căm'-ĕl, *n.* **1.** A large ruminant quadruped of Asia and Africa with one or two humps, used as a beast of burden and for riding ; উষ্ট্র, উট (*Colloq.*), ক্রমেলক, মহাঙ্গ, ময়, বণিগ্বহ (অঃ) দ্বিককুদ (Bactrian), দীর্ঘগ্রীব, ধূম্র (তৈত্তিঃ)। [আরব দেশীয় উষ্ট্রের একটী, বহ্লিক দেশীয় উষ্ট্রের দুইটি ককুদ (hump) থাকে।] **2.** A water-tight machine placed beneath a vessel for floating it over shoals ; অগভীর জলময় স্থানে জাহাজ ভাসাইবার জন্য তন্নিম্নে স্থাপিত জল-প্রবেশ-রুদ্ধ্-শূন্য যন্ত্র বিশেষ। **3.** A thing hard to believe or accept ; "Ye blind guides, which strain at a gnat and swallow a *camel* ;" অসম্ভব গল্প, নলিনী-পত্রে দণ্ডায়মানা ষোড়শী কামিনী হস্তিগ্রাস করিতেছে এরূপ বিষয়। **—eer,** *n.* **1.** One who drives or rides a camel ; উষ্ট্র চালক, উষ্ট্রারোহী। **Camel-backed**— Hump-backed ; কুব্জ-পৃষ্ঠ। **Camel-bird**—A name given to the ostrich ; উটপক্ষী। **Camel corps**— উষ্ট্রারোহী সৈন্য। **Camel's hair,** *adj.* & *n.* Made of camel's hair or of squirrel's tail-hairs ; উষ্ট্র-লোম-নির্ম্মিত, কাষ্ঠমার্জ্জারের পুচ্ছ-লোম-বিনির্ম্মিত। (*Noun.*) A paint brush made of squirrel's tail hairs ; কাঠবিড়ালের পুচ্ছ লোম-নির্ম্মিত তুলিকা বিশেষ। **Camel swallower** — A credulous person ; বিশ্বাস-প্রবণ ব্যক্তি, যে ব্যক্তি অসম্ভব গল্পে বিশ্বাস করে। **A she camel**—উষ্ট্রী, উষ্ট্রিকা। **The young of camel**—উষ্ট্রশাবক, করভ। **To break the camel's back**—To be the last thing which causes a catastrophe ; শোচনীয় পরিণামের শেষ কারণ হওয়া।

că-měl'-li-ă, *n.* A species of evergreen shrubs from China and Japan ; চীন ও জাপানদেশীয় চিরহরিৎ গুল্ম বিশেষ।

că-měl'-ō-pârd, *n.* The giraffe ; জিরাফ।

căm'-ěl-rȳ, *n.* Troops mounted on camels ; উষ্ট্রারোহী সৈন্য।

căm'-ē-ō, *n.* A precious stone carved in relief ; উদ্গতকারু-কার্য্য-খোদিত মণি বিশেষ। [উক্ত প্রকার মণির দুইটী বা ততোধিক বিভিন্ন বর্ণের স্তর থাকা আবশ্যক। রত্নোপরি উৎকীর্ণ চিত্রাদির যথাযোগ্য স্থানে ঐ সমস্ত স্তরের বর্ণরাজি প্রকটন দ্বারাই মণিকারের শিল্প-কৌশল প্রদর্শিত হইয়া থাকে।]

căm'-ê-ră, *n.* **1.** (*Arch.*) An arched roof or covering ; a vault ; (স্থপতি-বিদ্যা) খিলান বিশিষ্ট ছাদ বা আবরণ ; খিলান। **2.** A judge's chamber ; বিচারকের খাস কামরা। **3.** The variety of camera-obscura used by photographers ; আলোক চিত্রকারিগণের যন্ত্র বিশেষ (নিম্নে দেখ)। **Camera lucida**—দূরবর্ত্তী পদার্থ নিচয়ের প্রতি-বিম্বিত চিত্র কাগজের উপরে উৎপাদন করত, তদঙ্কন সৌকর্য্যার্থ যন্ত্র বিশেষ। ছায়াচিত্র ক্যামেরা (হিঃ কোঃ)। **Camera obscura**—অন্ধকার কক্ষ বা পেটকাভ্যন্তরস্থিত শ্বেতবর্ণ পদার্থের উপরি-ভাগে বহিঃস্থিত পদার্থের প্রতিকৃতি প্রক্ষেপার্থ যন্ত্র বিশেষ, প্রতিবিম্ব ক্যামেরা (হিঃ কোঃ)। (*Law*) **To hear in camera**—To hear a cause privately in the judge's own room instead of in open court ; (আইন) প্রকাশ্য আদালতে বিচার না করিয়া বিচারকের নিজস্ব কক্ষে (খাস কামরায়) কোন (অশ্লীল) মোকদ্দমার বিচার করা।

Căm-êr-ō'-ni-ăn, *n.* **1.** A follower of Richard Cameron or his doctrines ; স্কটলণ্ড দেশীয় ধর্ম্মসংস্কারক রিচার্ড কেমেরণ্ সম্বন্ধীয়। **Cameronian regiment**—The 26th regiment of the British army ; ব্রিটিশ সৈন্যদলের ২৬ সংখ্যক পল্টন।

căm-i-sāde', căm-i-sa'-dō, *n.* **1.** A shirt worn by soldiers over their armours during night attack ; নিশাকালীন আক্রমণে সৈনিকগণ বর্ম্মোপরি যে কঞ্চুক পরিধান করিয়া থাকে। **2.** A night attack ; সৌপ্তিক (মঃভাঃ), নৈশাক্রমণ।

căm'-i-sōle, *n.* A woman's loose morning gown or jacket ; (ইংলণ্ডীয়) স্ত্রীলোকের প্রভাতকালে পরিধেয় ঘাগরা বা অঙ্গ-রক্ষা বিশেষ।

căm'-lět, *n.* A cloth originally made of camel's hair but now chiefly of wool and goat's hair ; এক প্রকার বস্ত্র। [পূর্ব্বে উষ্ট্র লোম হইতে প্রস্তুত হইত, বর্ত্তমানে ছাগলোম ও পশম হইতে প্রস্তুত হয়।]

căm'-mŏck, *n.* (*Bot.*) Kinds of yellow-flowered plant ; পীতবর্ণ পুষ্প-প্রসূ বিভিন্ন জাতীয় বৃক্ষ।

căm'-ō-mīle, cham'-ō-mīle, *n.* A bitter plant used in medicine ; তিক্ত ভেষজ বৃক্ষ বিশেষ, বাবুনা ফুল (খোরী)।

Că-mŏr'-ră, (*It.*), *n.* A secret society of Naples organised early in the ninteenth century ; উনবিংশ শতাব্দীর প্রথম ভাগে নেপল্‌স্ নগরীতে প্রতিষ্ঠিত গুপ্ত সমিতি বিশেষ। **—rism,** *n.* **—rist,** *n.*

cămp, *n. v. i. & t.* **1.** A place where troops are lodged in tents, etc. ; সেনা-সন্নিবেশ-স্থল। **2.** A collection of tents, huts, etc. for shelter ; as, forming a *camp* in the neighbourhood of Boston ; an encampment ; আশ্রয়ের জন্য পর্ণগৃহ বা পট-মণ্ডপ শ্রেণী ; সেনানিবাস, সেনাবাস, ছাউনি, সেনানিবেশ, শিবির, স্কন্ধাবার (আঃ বঃ)। **3.** Military service or life ; as, courts and *camps* ; সামরিক কর্ম্ম, সামরিক জীবন। **4.** Temporary quarters of nomads, gypsy, travellers, etc. ; হাঘড়িয়া, যাযাবর এবং ভ্রমণকারিগণের অস্থায়ী আবাস। **5.** A great number ; অগণিত সংখ্যা। **6.** The body of persons encamped ; শিবিরে সন্নিবেশিত সৈন্যদল। **7.** Adherents of a doctrine ; "No one has reached a way out of the great *camp* of old ideas ;" কোন বিশেষ মতাবলম্বী ব্যক্তি সমূহ। **8.** (*Agric.*) A mound of earth under which potatoes and other vegetables are stored, as a protection against frost ; (কৃষি-বিজ্ঞান) যে মৃত্তিকা স্তূপের নিম্নে আলু প্রভৃতি তরকারী তুষার হইতে রক্ষার জন্য রক্ষিত হয়। ***Verb i.*** To encamp ; to lodge in a camp (often with *out*) ; ছাউনি ফেলা, শিবির সন্নিবেশ করা ; ছাউনিতে বাস করা। ***Verb t.*** To lodge an army in tents ; শিবির সমূহে সৈন্যদলের বাসের সংস্থান করা। **A division in the camp**—গৃহবিচ্ছেদ, আত্মবিরোধ। **Camp-bed, —chair**—একপ্রকার হালকা খাট বা কেদারা, যাহা ইচ্ছামত গুটাইয়া রাখা যায়। **Camp-boy**—শিবিরানুচর বালক। **Camp-fever**—মোহজনক সান্নিপাতিক জ্বর। **Camp-follower**—সৈন্যদলের অনুযাত্রী ভৃত্য, খাদ্যদ্রব্য বিক্রেতা (বিক্রেত্রী) প্রভৃতি, লশ্বন (হর্ষঃ), সেনানুচর। **Camp-meeting**—খোলা ময়দানে ধর্ম্ম-সংক্রান্ত সভার অধিবেশন। **Flying camp**—দ্রুতবেগে একস্থান হইতে অপর স্থানে গমনের জন্য সৈন্যদল। **To camp out**—To lodge in a camp in the open ; খোলা ময়দানে তাঁবুতে বাস করা। **To pitch a camp**—To set up the tents or huts of a camp ; শিবির সন্নিবেশ করা, ছাউনি করা, তাঁবু ফেলা। **To strike camp**—To take down the tents or huts of a camp ; সেনা-বাসের তাঁবু উঠাইয়া লওয়া, শিবির-ভঙ্গ করা।

câm-pa'-gna (-pân-yâ), *n.* **1.** An open level tract of country

মুক্ত এবং সমতল প্রদেশ। **2.** The level district in Italy near Rome ; রোম-নগরের সন্নিকটবর্ত্তী সমতল ভূভাগ-বিশেষ।

căm-paign′ (-pān), *n.* & *v. i.* **1.** A large open field ; সুবিস্তীর্ণ মুক্ত প্রান্তর, খোলা ময়দান। **2.** (*Mil.*) A continuous series of military operations ; the time during which an army keeps the field ; as, the *campaign* lasted six months ; (সামরিক-শাস্ত্র) অবিচ্ছিন্ন সামরিক কার্য্য-কলাপ ; যে সময় ব্যাপিয়া সৈন্যদল যুদ্ধে নিরত থাকে, যুদ্ধ-কাল। **3.** (*Pol.*) An organised series of operations ; esp. an attempt to rouse public opinion for or against a policy ; (রাজনীতি) প্রণালীবদ্ধ কার্য্য-পরম্পরা ; বিশেষতঃ কোন শাসননীতির স্বপক্ষে বা বিপক্ষে জনমত উদ্দীপনের চেষ্টা। ***Verb i.*** To serve in a campaign ; দীর্ঘ সময় ব্যাপী যুদ্ধে সৈনিকের কার্য্য করা। **—er,** *n.* One who has served in several campaigns ; a veteran ; যে ব্যক্তি দীর্ঘসময়ব্যাপী বহু যুদ্ধে সৈনিকের কার্য্য করিয়াছে ; রণপ্রবীণ, প্রাচীন সৈনিক, বৃদ্ধ সৈনিক। **Political campaign**—নির্ব্বাচিত হইবার উদ্দেশ্যে নির্ব্বাচনপ্রার্থী যে সমস্ত সভার অধিবেশন ও বিজ্ঞাপনাদি প্রচার করে।

căm-pā′-nă, *n.* **1.** A church-bell ; গির্জ্জার ঘণ্টা। **2.** The pasque-flower ; পুষ্পবিশেষ। **3.** (*Arch.*) One of the guttæ of the Doric architecture ; (স্থপতি-বিজ্ঞান) স্থাপত্য ভূষাবিশেষ। **—paned′, —pan′-i-form,** *adjs.* (*Bot.*) Bell-shaped ; (উদ্ভিদ্-বিদ্যা) ঘণ্টাকৃতি।

căm-pă-nē′-rō, *n.* (*Zool.*) The bell-bird of South America ; দক্ষিণ আমেরিকাদেশীয় পক্ষিবিশেষ।

căm-pă′-ni-ă, *n.* Same as CAMPAIGN.

căm-pă-ni′-le (-nē-lā), *n.* (*Arch.*) A bell-tower, usually one detached from a church ; ঘণ্টামণ্ডপ, বিশেষতঃ খৃষ্টীয় ধর্ম্ম-মন্দির হইতে বিচ্ছিন্ন ঘণ্টামণ্ডপ।

căm-pă-nŏl′-ō-ġy, *n.* The subject or science of bells or bell-ringing ; ঘণ্টা-বিদ্যা, ঘণ্টা-বিজ্ঞান। **—gi-cal,** *adj.* **—gist,** *n.*

căm-păn′-ū-lă, *n.* A genus of plants with bell-shaped flowers, usually blue or white ; ঘণ্টাকৃতি পুষ্পবিশিষ্ট কতিপয় জাতীয় পুষ্পতরুর সাধারণ নাম। **—ceous,** *adj.* **—late,** *adj.* (*Bot.* & *Zool.*) Bell-shaped ; (উদ্ভিদ্-বিদ্যা এবং জন্তু-বিজ্ঞান) ঘণ্টাকৃতি (সাঃ পঃ), ঘণ্টাকার (ঐ)। **Campanulate corolla**—উপঘণ্টস্তর (সাঃ পঃ)।

căm-pea′-chy-wood (-pē-chi-wûd), *n.* Logwood ; মেক্সিকদেশীয় রক্তবর্ণ কাষ্ঠবিশেষ, কুচন্দন (মঃ উঃ)।

căm-pĕs′-trăl, —tri-ăn, *adjs.* Growing in, or pertaining to, fields ; ক্ষেত্রজ, ক্ষেত্রিক।

căm′-phine (-phēn), *n.* Rectified oil of turpentine ; পরিস্রুত তার্পিণ তৈল।

căm′-phor (-phêr), A white translucent crystalline volatile substance with aromatic smell and bitter taste ; কর্পূর, স্ফটিকাভ্র (মঃ উঃ), সিতাভ্র, ঘনসার, হিমবালুকা। **—phor′-ic,** *adj.* **—pho-ra′-ceous,** *adj.* **Borneo camphor**—ভীমসেনী কর্পূর। **Camphor-oil**—কর্পূর-তৈল। **Camphor-tree**—কর্পূরবৃক্ষ। **Camphor wood**—গন্ধি কাষ্ঠ (ওয়াট্)

căm′-phor-āte (-phêr-), *v. t.* & *n.* To impregnate or treat with camphor ; কর্পূরবাসিত করা, কর্পূর-পূরিত করা। ***Noun.*** A salt of camphoric acid ; কর্পূরদ্রাবকের লবণ বিশেষ। **—at-ed,** *adj.* Combined or impregnated with camphor ; কর্পূর বাসিত, কর্পূরসম্পূরিত।

căm′-pi-ŏn, *n.* A plant,—the popular name of the *Lychnis* ; এক জাতীয় পুষ্পবৃক্ষ।

cămp′-shĕd, *v. t.* To face with campshot ; স্তম্ভ বা কাষ্ঠফলক সকল দ্বারা নদীতট আচ্ছাদিত করা।

căm′-wood (-wûd), *n.* A hard red West-African wood yielding dye ; পশ্চিম আফ্রিকা দেশজ লোহিতবর্ণ-রঞ্জকপদার্থ-প্রদ বৃক্ষ বিশেষ।

căn, *n.* & *v. t.* A vessel for holding liquids, usually of metal, esp. tin ; as, an oil *can* : a milk *can* ; ধাতবপাত্র, টিনের পাত্র। ***Verb t.*** To preserve by putting in sealed cans ; as, to *can* meat, fish or fruit ; সীল-আঁটা টিনের পাত্রে পুরিয়া মৎস্য, মাংস বা ফল তাজা রাখা।

Can′-ner-y, *n.* A place where meat, fish, fruit, etc. are canned ; যে স্থানে মৎস্য, মাংস, ফল প্রভৃতি তাজা রাখার জন্য পাত্রে বদ্ধ করা হয়। **Can′ning,** *n.* The act or process of preserving, meat, fish, fruit, etc., by sealing up in cans or tins ; বায়ু-প্রবেশ-পথ-শূন্য টীনের কৌটার ভিতর মাংস, মৎস্য, ফলাদি সংরক্ষণ বা সংরক্ষণ-প্রণালী। **Can-buoy,** *n.* A small buoy employed to mark out shoals and rocks ; ক্ষুদ্র বয়া বিশেষ। **Can-dock**—The water lily ; কুমুদ।

căn, *Aux. v.* **1.** To be able to ; to be permitted to ; as, I *can* go, but do not wish to ; সমর্থ হওয়া, পারা, পারক হওয়া। **2.** To feel inclined to ; as, I *could* laugh for joy ; প্রবৃত্তি বোধ করা।

Cā′-naan (-năn), *n.* The part of Palestine west of the Jordan ; Palestine ; Paradise ; জর্ডন নদীর পশ্চিম তীরস্থিত প্যালেষ্টাইন দেশের অংশ বিশেষ ; প্যালেষ্টাইন দেশ ; স্বর্গ। **—ite,** *n.* **—it-ish,** *adj.*

Căn′-ă-dă, *n.* & *adj.* A British province in North America ; উত্তর আমেরিকার অন্তঃপাতী ইংরেজাধিকৃত প্রদেশ বিশেষ। ***Adj.*** Pertaining to or from Canada ; ক্যানাডা দেশীয়, ক্যানেডাদেশাগত। **Canada balsam**—গন্ধবিরজা (খোরী)।

Că-nā′-di-ăn, *adj.* & *n.* Pertaining to Canada ; ক্যানেডাদেশীয়। ***Noun.*** A native or inhabitant of Canada ; ক্যানেডা দেশবাসী।

că-naille′ (-näl- or -nâ-yă), *n.* The mob ; the vulgar rabble ; জনতা, প্রাকৃত লোক ; ইতর জন।

că-năl′, *n.* & *v. t.* **1.** An artificial water-course for navigation or for irrigating land ; খাল, পয়ঃপ্রণালী, কুল্যা, খাত। **2.** (*Anat.*) A duct in the body for the passage of liquids or solids ; as, the alimentary *canal* ; (শারীরসংস্থান-বিদ্যা) দ্রব বা কঠিন পদার্থবাহী শরীরস্থ নালী, অন্ন-বহা নালী। **3.** (*Zool.*) A groove in a shell for protrusion of breathing-tube ; (জীব-বিজ্ঞান) শম্বুক প্রভৃতির খোলে শ্বাসনালী নির্গমনার্থ নালী বিশেষ। ***Verb t.*** To make canal through ; to provide with canals ; কোন স্থানের উপর দিয়া খাল কাটিয়া নেওয়া ; খাল কাটিয়া দেওয়া। **Canal-boat**—খালে চলিবার নৌকা। **Canals of Mars**—মঙ্গল-গ্রহের খাত সমূহ। [যাহা মঙ্গলগ্রহবাসী বুদ্ধিমান জীবদ্বারা খনিত বলিয়া অনুমিত হইয়া থাকে।]

căn-ă-lic-ū′-lāte, —lāt-ĕd, *adj.* Striated ; অনুখাতিত (সাঃ পঃ)। **—lus,** *n.*

că-năl-ī-zā′-tion, *n.* The construction of canals ; খাল-খনন।

căn′-ă-līze, *v. t.* To make a canal through ; to convert into a canal ; কোন স্থানের উপর দিয়া খাল কাটিয়া নেওয়া ; খালে পরিণত করা।

că-nard′ (-nâr or -nârd), [*F.* canard = duck] *n.* An absurd story set afloat as news ; a false report ; আজগবী খবর ; মিথ্যা সংবাদ। [Cornelissen নামক জনৈক সুরসিক ফরাসী জনসাধারণের বিশ্বাস-প্রবণতা পরীক্ষার্থ সংবাদপত্রে প্রকাশ করেন যে, তাহার ২০টি হংসের মধ্যে একটী কাটিয়া ফেলিলে, অবশিষ্ট ১৯টী হংস মিলিয়া তাহাকে উদরসাৎ করে। তৎপর অন্য একটী হংস কাটিয়া দেওয়া হইলে অবশিষ্ট ১৮টী মিলিয়া তাহাকে ভক্ষণ করে। এইরূপে তিনি এক একটী হংস কাটিতে থাকেন, আর অবশিষ্ট জীবিত হংস সকল তাহাকে ভক্ষণ করে। এইরূপে ১৯শ তম হংসটী কাটিয়া দিলে, পর সর্ব্বশেষ জীবিত হংসটি তাহাকে গলাধঃকরণ করে। ইহা হইতে প্রমাণিত হইল যে শেষোক্ত হংসটী ১৯টী কই প্রকৃতপক্ষে ভক্ষণ করিয়াছে। উপর্যুক্ত ঘটনা হইতে canard শব্দের প্রচলিত অর্থ উদ্ভূত হইয়াছে।]

Căn′-ă-rese (-rēs), *adj.* & *n.* Pertaining to Canara in Western India ; পশ্চিম ভারতের অন্তঃপাতী ক্যানারা নামক স্থান সম্বন্ধীয়। ***Noun.*** A native of Canara ; the language of the Dravidian group ; ক্যানারাবাসী ; দ্রাবিড় ভাষা।

Canarium strictum—গুগ্গুল্ ধূপ (বেলঃ)।

că-nā′-rȳ, *adj.* & *n.* **1.** Pertaining to the Canary islands ; ক্যানেরী দ্বীপ সম্বন্ধীয়। **2.** Of a pale yellowish colour : as, *canary* stone ; অনুজ্জ্বল পীতবর্ণবিশিষ্ট। ***Noun.*** **1.** A light sweet wine from the Canary islands ; ক্যানারী দ্বীপ হইতে সমানীত লঘু এবং সুস্বাদু সুরা বিশেষ। **2.** A yellow feathered song-bird ; পীতবর্ণ পালক-বিশিষ্ট গায়ক পক্ষিবিশেষ। **3.** A yellow fishing-fly ; মৎস্য শিকারের জন্য পীতবর্ণ কীটবিশেষ। **Canary-bird**—A canary ; পীতবর্ণ পক্ষিবিশেষ, ক্যানারী পাখী। (*Slang*) A jail-bird ; (ইতর ভাষায়) পুরাতন কয়েদী। (*Slang*) A mistress ; (ইতর ভাষায়) উপপত্নী। (*Slang*) Guinea ; (ইতর ভাষায়) এক গিনি (গিনির রঙ্ ক্যানারী পাখীর পালকের মত হলদে বলিয়া)। **Canary-creeper**—মৃদু পীতবর্ণপুষ্পপ্রসূ লতা-বিশেষ। **Canary-grass**—একপ্রকার ঘাস,—ইহার বীজ ক্যানারী পক্ষীর খাদ্যরূপে ব্যবহৃত হয়। **Canary-wood**—দক্ষিণ আমেরিকা হইতে সমানীত ফিকে কমলা বর্ণের কাষ্ঠবিশেষ।

că-năs′-têr, *n.* (*Orig.*) **1.** A rush-basket in which tobacco used to be packed ; (পূর্ব্বে) যে শর-নির্ম্মিত পেটকে তামাকু বস্তাবন্দী করা হইত। **2.** A species of cut tobacco ; একপ্রকার কাটা তামাক।

căn′-căn, *n.* A kind of indescent French dance ; ফরাসীদেশীয় অশ্লীল নৃত্য বিশেষ।

căn′-cĕl, *v. t.* & *n.* **1.** To blot out by drawing lines across ; to blot out ; কাটা ; মুছিয়া ফেলা, অপহ্নব করা। **2.** To annul or destroy ; রদ করা, বাতিল করা, ধ্বংস করা। **3.** To neutralize ; to make up for ; "The latter kindness may *cancel* a greater previous wrong ;" শমিত করা ; ক্ষতিপূরণ করা। **4.** (*Print.*) To suppress ; as, the book-sellers agreed to have the leaf *cancelled* ; (মুদ্রাঙ্কণ) চাপিয়া রাখা। **5.** (*Math.*) To strike out common factors from the numerator and denominator ; (গণিত-শাস্ত্র) কাটা ; অপবর্ত্তন করা (লীলাঃ)। ***Noun.*** The deletion and reprinting of a part of a book ; the part suppresed and reprinted ; "It was his pride to read these *cancels* to his friend ;" কোনও পুস্তকের অংশ বিশেষের পরিবর্জ্জন এবং পুনর্মুদ্রণ ; পরিবর্জ্জিত এবং পুনর্মুদ্রিত অংশ। **—la′-tion,** *n.* **A pair of cancels**—টিকিট কাটিবার সাঁড়াশী।

căn′-cĕl-lāte, *adj.* (*Bot.* & *Zool.*) Marked with cross lines ; reticulated ; (উদ্ভিদ্ ও প্রাণি-বিদ্যা) জালবৎ রেখাঙ্কিত ; জালাঙ্কিত (সাঃ পঃ)।

căn-cĕl′-lī, *n.* (*Anat.*) A reticulated structure existing in bones ; (শারীরসংস্থান-বিদ্যা) অস্থি-মধ্যস্থ জালাঙ্কিত অঙ্গ। **—lous,** *adj.* (*Anat.*) Made up of cancelli ; (শারীরসংস্থান-বিদ্যা) উক্তপ্রকার জালাঙ্কিত অঙ্গবিশিষ্ট।

căn′ cêr, *n.* **1.** (*Cap.*) A genus of crustaceans or crabs ; কর্কটাদি। **2.** (*Cap.*) (*Astron.*) (*a*) One of the signs of the zodiac ; কর্কট রাশি। (*b*) A constellation between Gemini and Leo ; মিথুন ও সিংহ

রাশির মধ্যবর্ত্তী তারা প্রকোষ্ঠ। **3.** (*Med.*) A malignant spreading tumour eating the part it is in, and recurring when removed ; (*fig.*) any evil acting similarly ; "The incurable *cancer* of the soul ;" একপ্রকার দূষিত অর্ব্বুদ, কর্কটরোগ (ডাঃ), ঘুরঘুরে ঘা ; (লক্ষণায়) দুষ্টক্ষতবৎ যে কোনও প্রকার কদাচার (আলস্য, উৎকোচগ্রহণ প্রভৃতি)। **—ate,** *v. t.* **—a'-tion,** *n.* **—ous,** *adj.* **Calms of cancer**—কর্কমণ্ডল (হিঃ কোঃ)। **Tropic of cancer**—See TROPIC.

căn'-croid (-croid), *adj.* & *n.* **1.** Crab-like ; কর্কটবৎ। **2.** Like a cancer ; as, a *cancroid* tumour ; দুষ্টক্ষতবৎ। ***Noun.*** **1.** A crustacean of the crab family ; কর্কট জাতীয় জন্তু। **2.** A disease like cancer ; কর্কটরোগের অনুরূপ রোগ বিশেষ।

căn-dĕ-la'-brŭm, (*Pl.* CANDELABRA ; also *sing.* CANDELABRA, *pl.* CANDELABRAS.) *n.* (*Antiq.*) A tall ornamental candlestick or lampstand ; a large branched candlestick ; a chandelier ; (প্রত্নতত্ত্ব) কারুকার্য্যখচিত সুদীর্ঘ দীপপাদপ বিশেষ ; শাখায়িত সুবৃহৎ দীপ-গাছা, শাখাবিশিষ্ট আলোকদান ; ঝাড়, ফরাসী ঝাড়(ফঃ হিঃ), দীপাধার, কৌমুদীবৃক্ষ(অঃ), দীপবৃক্ষ (রঃ)।

căn-dĕnt, *adj.* Heated to whiteness ; glowing with heat ; as, a *candent* vessel ; অত্যুত্তপ্ত, অত্যুষ্ণ ; তাপপ্রদীপ্ত (হিঃ কোঃ)।

căn-dĕs'-cĕnce, *n.* Incandescence ; a white heat ; তাপপ্রদীপ্তভাব ; অত্যুত্তাপ। **—cent,** *adj.* Glowing with white heat ; অত্যুত্তাপ বশতঃ শ্বেতদীপ্তিময়।

căn'-dĭd, *adj.* **1.** Unbiased ; as, a *candid* opinion ; পক্ষপাতশূন্য, নিরপেক্ষ। **2.** Open ; frank ; খোলা ; স্পষ্টভাষী, সরল, সাদা, উদার, নিষ্কপট, শুদ্ধশীল, শুদ্ধমতি, বিমলাত্মা। [*Candide* — *Candidus* = white.] **—ly,** *adv.* **—ness,** *n.* **A candid friend** — যে ব্যক্তি বন্ধুত্বের দাবীতে সরলতার ভাণ করিয়া অপ্রীতিকর কথা বলে।

căn'-dĭ-dāte, *n.* One who puts himself or is put forward for appointment to an office or honour ; অর্থী, প্রার্থী, পদপ্রার্থী, উমেদার, কর্ম্মপ্রার্থী, পরীক্ষার্থী। [*From L. candidus* = white ; প্রাচীন রোমে পদপ্রার্থিগণ শ্বেত পরিচ্ছদ পরিধান করিতেন।] **—da-cy, —da-ture, —ship,** *ns.*

căn'-died (-dĕd), *p. p.* See CANDY.

căn'-dle, *n.* **1.** A cylindrical body of tallow, wax, etc., enclosing a wick for giving light ; বাতী, বর্ত্তিকা, মোমবাতি। **2.** (*Fig.*) Anything which affords light ; a luminary ; as, by these blessed *candles* of the night ; (লক্ষণায়) আলোকপ্রদ বস্তু ; জ্যোতিষ্ক। **3.** A unit of light-measurement ; আলোক-পরিমাণের একক। **Candle-berry tree**—উত্তর আমেরিকাদেশীয় বৃক্ষবিশেষ। **Candle-bomb**—জলপূর্ণ কাচের বোমাবিশেষ—বাতীর শিখায় ধরিলে ইহা বিদীর্ণ হয়। **Candle-coal**—Same as CANNEL COAL (which see). **Candle-ends**—The ends of a burned down candle ; fragments ; মোমবাতি পুড়িয়া শেষ হইলে যে সকল টুকরা অবশিষ্ট থাকে ; টুকটাক জিনিষ। **Candle-fish** — সামুদ্রিক মৎস্যবিশেষ, ইহা মোমবাতির মত প্রজ্বালিত করা হইয়া থাকে, উলাচোন (খোরী)। **Candle-holder**—One who or that which holds a candle ; one that assists ; যে ব্যক্তি বা যাহা বাতি ধারণ করে, মশালধারী ; সাহায্যকারী, সহায়। **Candle-light**—The light of a candle ; the time when candles are lighted ; dusk ; বাতির আলো, দীপালোক ; সাঁঝের প্রদীপ জ্বালিবার সময়, প্রদোষ, গোধূলি, সাঁঝ। **Candle-nut**—বাঙ্গলা আখ্রোট (খোরী)। **Candle-power**—The illuminating power of a candle [the usual standard is a spermaceti candle burning 120 grains per hour, used for the measuring of other artificial light] ; মোমবাতির দীপ্তিপ্রদানশক্তি, প্রকাশশক্তি (হিঃ কোঃ)। **Candlestick** — শামাদান, দীপ-বৃক্ষ (রঃ), দীপাধার, দীপ-পাদপ (অঃ), দীপগাছা। **Candle-waster**—যে ব্যক্তি গভীর রাত্রি পর্য্যন্ত অধ্যয়ন করে। **Candle-wood**—উত্তর আমেরিকাদেশীয় বৃক্ষ বিশেষের কাষ্ঠ। **Electric-candle**—তড়িতদীপক (হিঃ কোঃ)। **Roman candle**—একপ্রকার আতসবাজী, এক প্রকার নলবাজী,—যাহা হইতে রঙ্গীন গোলকসকল নিক্ষিপ্ত হয়। **Tallow-candle**—চর্ব্বির বাতি। **Wax-candle**—মোমবাতি। **Is not fit to hold a candle to**—Is not fit to be compared with ; তুলিত হইবার যোগ্য নহে। **Sale by inch of candle**—নীলামের প্রণালী বিশেষ—ইহাতে এক ইঞ্চি বাতি জ্বলিবার সময় পর্য্যন্ত ডাকিবার সময় থাকে। **The game is not worth the candle**—The result is not worth the trouble or cost of it ; পরিশ্রমের বা অর্থব্যয়ের অনুরূপ ফল পাওয়া যায় নাই। **To burn the candle at both ends**—See BURN. **To hold a candle to the devil**—To aid or countenance that which is wrong ; to do knowingly what is wrong ; অন্যায় বিষয়ে সাহায্য বা উৎসাহদান করা ; জ্ঞানতঃ অন্যায় কার্য্য করা। **To hold the candle**—To assist in a subordinate position ; অধস্তন কর্ম্মচারীরূপে সাহায্য করা। **To smell of the lamp or candle**—To manifest great pains and long study by night ; অত্যন্ত কষ্ট এবং সুদীর্ঘকালব্যাপী নৈশ অধ্যয়নের ভাব প্রকাশ করা। **To sell by inch of candle**—নিলামে বিক্রয় করা। **To vow a candle to the devil**—To propitiate the devil by a bribe ; সয়তানকে উৎকোচ প্রদানে প্রসন্ন করা।

căn′-dle-măs, *n.* A festival on the second day of February in honour of the purification of the Virgin Mary, so called from the number of candles used ; ২রা ফেব্রুয়ারী তারিখে অনুষ্ঠিত খৃষ্টীয় পর্ব্ব বিশেষ।

căn′-dock (-dŏk), *n.* The yellow water-lily ; পীতবর্ণ কুমুদপুষ্প।

căn′-dour (-dêr), *n.* Openness of heart ; impartiality ; সরলতা, সারল্য অকপটতা, আর্জ্জব, চিত্তের ঔদার্য্য, দাক্ষিণ্য, শুচিতা ; পক্ষপাতশূন্যতা।

căn′-dŷ, *n., v. t.* & *i.* Crystallized sugar ; a conserve or confection of sugar ; খণ্ডমিছরি ; চিনির লাড্ডু বা মণ্ডা, খণ্ডমোদক (আঃ বঃ)। ***Verb t.*** **1.** To conserve or boil in sugar ; as, to *candy* fruit ; চিনির শিরায় ডুবাইয়া তাজা রাখা বা সিদ্ধ করা। **2.** To form into crystals ; as, to *candy* sugar ; দানা বাঁধান। **3.** To cover or incrust with crystals, as of ice ; as, the cold brook *candied* with ice ; দানাদ্বারা আবৃত করা। ***Verb i.*** **1.** To become coated with sugar ; শর্করাবৃত হওয়া। **2.** To become crystallized or congealed ; দানা বাঁধা, জমাট হওয়া। **Candy-sugar**—মিছ্‌রি। **Candy-tuft**—একপ্রকার বৃক্ষ।

căn′-dŷ, *n.* A weight, at Madras 500 pounds, at Bombay 560 pounds ; মান্দ্রাজ, বোম্বাই প্রভৃতি প্রদেশের ওজন বিশেষ, খংড়ি (কেন্ডিঃ)।

cāne, *n.* & *v. t.* **1.** A term applied to the stems of some palms, grasses and other plants ; বেত্র, বানীর, বেতস, অভ্রপুষ্প, বিদুল, বঞ্জুল। **2.** Sugarcane ; as, *cane* sugar ; ইক্ষু। **3.** A walking-stick ; a staff ; ছড়ি ; যষ্টি, বেত্রযষ্টি। **4.** A measure of length used in some parts of Europe ; ইয়ুরোপের কোন কোন দেশের দৈর্ঘ্যের মাপ বিশেষ। **5.** A stick of sealing-wax, sulphur, glass ; গালা, গন্ধক বা কাচের দণ্ড। ***Verb t.*** **1.** To beat with a cane ; as, he was *caned* by a brutal tutor ; বেত্রাঘাত করা, বেত মারা, বেত্র প্রহার করা। **2.** To insert cane into chair-frame ; বেত দিয়া ছাওয়া, বেত দিয়া মোড়া। **Can′-ing,** *n.* A thrashing with a cane ; বেত্রাঘাত। **Can′-y,** *adj.* Pertaining to canes ; abounding with canes ; বেত্র-সম্বন্ধীয় ; বেতস-বহুল। **Cane-brake**—বেতসবন, বানীর নিকুঞ্জ (গীতঃ), বঞ্জুল-কুঞ্জ (ঐ)। **Cane-chair**—যে কেদারায় বসিবার স্থান বেত্র-নির্ম্মিত। **Cane-mill**—ইক্ষু-পীড়ন-যন্ত্র। **Cane-press** — আক-মাড়া কল। **Cane-sugar**—ইক্ষু-জাত শর্করা। **Cane-trash**—আকের গোয়া

Că-nĕl′-lă *n.* A genus of aromatic trees ; কয়েকজাতীয় সুগন্ধি বৃক্ষের সাধারণ নাম।

că-nĕph′-ŏ-rŭs, *n.* A sculptured Greek youth or maid, bearing a basket on head at the feast of Demeter ; ডিমিটারের ভোজপর্ব্বে প্রদর্শিত প্রস্তর-রচিত মস্তকে পেটকবাহী তরুণ বা তরুণী গ্রীকমূর্ত্তি।

că-nĕs′-cĕnt *adj.* Growing white ; hoary ; শ্বেতায়মান ; শ্বেত।

cangue (căng), **căng,** *n.* A heavy wooden board worn round the neck by Chinese criminals ; চীন দেশীয় বন্দিগণের গলদেশে পরিহিত স্থূল-কাষ্ঠফলক বিশেষ।

căn′-hŏŏk, *n.* A contrivance for slinging a cask ; পিপা তুলিবার ও নামাইবার জন্য কৌশল বিশেষ।

că-nic′-ū-lă, *n.* (*Astron.*) The Dog-star ; (জ্যোতির্বিজ্ঞান) সীরীয়াস নামক অত্যুজ্জ্বল নক্ষত্র, শ্বতারা (হিঃ কোঃ)। **—lar,** *adj.* **Canicular days**—৩রা জুলাই এবং ১১ই সেপ্টেম্বরের মধ্যবর্ত্তী উষ্ণ দিবস সকল। **Canicular year**—মিসর দেশীয় বৎসর।

cā-nīne′, *adj.* & *n.* **1.** Pertaining to the dog ; dog-like ; কুক্কুর সম্বন্ধীয়, শৌবন, শৌন ; কুক্কুর তুল্য। **2.** (*Med.*) Unnatural ; unsatiable ; (ভৈষজ্য-শাস্ত্র) অস্বাভাবিক ; অতৃপ্ত। ***Noun.*** (*Anat.*) A canine tooth ; (শারীরসংস্থান-বিদ্যা) শ্বদন্ত, শৌবন দন্ত (সাঃ পঃ)। **Canine appetite**—অতৃপ্ত বুভুক্ষা। **Canine laugh**—A sardonic laugh ; কাষ্ঠ-হাস্য। **Canine letter**—'*R*' অক্ষর। **Canine tooth** — কৃন্তন-দন্ত এবং পেষণ-দন্ত সকলের মধ্যবর্ত্তী সূক্ষ্মাগ্র দন্ত সমূহের একটী, শ্বদন্ত, শৌবন দন্ত।

Cā′-nis *n.* A genus of carnivorous mammals ; মাংসাশী এবং স্তন্যপায়ী জন্তু শ্রেণী বিশেষ। **Canis major**—The Great Dog, a constellation of 32 stars in the southern hemisphere ; দিব্য-শ্বান্‌ (সাঃ পঃ), লুব্ধক (হিঃ কোঃ), মৃগব্যাধ (সাঃ পঃ)। **Canis minor**—The Little Dog, a constellation of 14 stars in the northern hemisphere ; তারা প্রকোষ্ঠ বিশেষ। ***Canis aureus***—The jackal ; শৃগাল (বেলঃ)।

căn′-is-têr, *n.* **1.** A small basket of rushes, reeds or the like ; খর, নল, খাগড়া, বা তদ্বৎ বস্তু নির্ম্মিত ঝুড়ি বা চুপড়ী। **2.** A small box, usually of metal for tea, shot, etc. ; কানেস্ত্রা, ডিবা। **3.** (*R. C. Church*) A vessel holding waters before consecration ; (রোমান ক্যাথলিক ধর্ম্ম সমাজ) উৎসর্গীকরণের পূর্ব্বে যে পাত্রে রুটিকা রক্ষিত হয়। **4.** Same as, CANISTER SHOT below. **Canister shot**—কামান হইতে ছুড়িবার উপযোগী গুলিপূর্ণ আধার বিশেষ। ইহার পাল্লা অল্প এবং ছুড়িবার সময় আধারটী ফাটিয়া গুলিসকল ছড়াইয়া পড়ে।

can′-kêr (căng-), *n.* & *v. t.* **1.** An ulcer or a collection of ulcers in the mouth ; মুখ মধ্যস্থ দুষ্টব্রণ বা ক্ষত সমূহ, মুখক্ষত, নালী ঘা, আঁতের ঘা। **2.** A worm that eats into plants ; ফলপুষ্পাদিনাশক কীট, শূক কীট। **3.** (*fig.*) Anything that corrodes or destroys ; a corrupting influence ; "The *canker* of enemy and faction ;" (লক্ষণায়) ক্ষয়কর বস্তু, ধ্বংসজনক বস্তু ; দূষিত প্রভাব। **4.** A disease of fruit-trees causing the bark to rot and fall off ; ফলবৃক্ষের ধসা রোগ। **5.** A disease of horse's foot ; অশ্বের পদ-রোগ বিশেষ। **6.** A kind of wild, worthless rose ; নিকৃষ্ট আরণ্য গোলাব বিশেষ। ***Verb t.*** To consume with canker ; to infect ; to corrupt ; পোকা ধরা, ক্ষয় করা ; রোগ-দূষিত করা ; দূষিত করা, কলুষিত করা, বিষাক্ত করা। **–kered,** *adj.* **–kered-ly,** *adv.* **–ous, –y,** *adjs.* **Canker-fly** — একপ্রকার ফলনাশক কীট। **Canker-rash** — একপ্রকার স্পর্শ-সংক্রামক জ্বর। [ইহাতে কণ্ঠে ঘা জন্মে।] **Canker-worm** — বৃক্ষাদি নাশক কীট, শূক কীট (আঃ বঃ)।

căn'-nă, *n.* **1.** A plant with bright yellow, red, or orange flowers and ornametal leaves ; বৈজয়ন্তী (প্রবোধ), জয়ন্তী বৃক্ষ (ঐ), সর্ব্বজয়া (বেলঃ)। **2.** An Italian measure of length equal to 6 or 7 feet ; ইতালি দেশে প্রচলিত দৈর্ঘ্যের পরিমাপ বিশেষ।

căn'-nă-bĭn, *n.* (*Chem.*) A poisonous resin obtained from *cannabis Indica* ; (রসায়ন-শাস্ত্র) গাঁজা হইতে প্রস্তুত বিষাক্ত রজন বিশেষ।

căn'-nă-bĭs, *n.* A genus of urticaceous plants, yielding the hemp ; গাঁজা, ভাঙ্গ প্রভৃতির গাছ। ***Cannabis Indica, Cannabis sativa***—The Indian hemp ; সিদ্ধি, গাঁজা, ভাঙ্গ।

căp'-nĕl, *n.* A bituminous coal burning with a bright flame and used in making coal oils and gas ; (also cannel coal) ; এক প্রকার কয়লা, ইহা উজ্জ্বল শিখা-বিস্তারে প্রজ্বলিত হয়—ইহা হইতে কয়লা, তৈল এবং গ্যাস প্রস্তুত হয়, গ্যাসকয়লা, কানি কয়লা (ফঃ হিঃ)।

căn'-nĭ-băl, *n.* & *adj.* A human being that eats human flesh ; any animal feeding on its own species ; নরমাংসভুক মানব, পুরুষাদ (মঃ ভাঃ), নৃভুজ্ (ভট্টিঃ), আদমখোর (*colloq.*) ; যে জন্তু স্বজাতীয় জন্তুর মাংস ভক্ষণ করে। ***Adj.*** Relating to cannibalism ; as, *cannibal* ferocity ; রাক্ষসোচিত, নৃশংস। **–ism,** *n.* (*Fig.*) Barbarity ; atrocities ; (লক্ষণায়) বর্ব্বরতা, নৃশংসতা ; জিঘাংসুতা। **–is'-tic,** *adj.*

căn'-nĭ-kĭn, *n.* A small drinking vessel ; ক্ষুদ্র পান পাত্র।

căn'-non (-nŭn), *n.* **1.** A large gun or a piece of ordnance ;

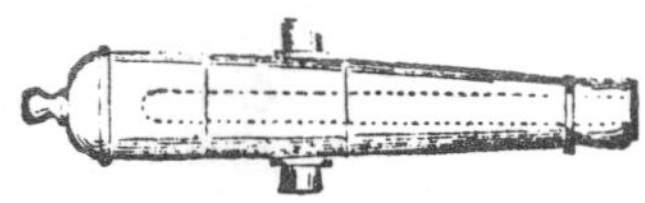

Cannon.

কামান, তোপ। **2.** (*Mech.*) A hollow cylinder moving independently on a shaft ; (যন্ত্র-বিজ্ঞান) দণ্ডোপরি স্বাধীনভাবে ঘূর্ণ্যমান শূন্যগর্ভ চোঙ্গ বিশেষ। **3.** (*Billiards*) A stroke in which the player hits both the red and his opponent's ball ; (মেজ-খেলা) যে আঘাতে ক্রীড়ক লোহিত কন্দুক এবং প্রতিপক্ষ ব্যক্তির কন্দুক উভয়টিকেই আঘাত করে। **4.** A smooth round bit for a horse ; অশ্বের সুগোল এবং মসৃণ খলীন (লাগামের লৌহময় অংশ) বিশেষ। **5.** A sausage-shaped, properly a horizontal, curl ; চোঙ্গাকার কেশগুচ্ছ, (সঙ্গতভাবে) মস্তকের অগ্রভাগের সহিত সমান্তরাল কেশগুচ্ছ। **–ry,** *n.* Artillery ; কামান সমূহ, গোলন্দাজ সৈন্য। **Cannon-ball** — কামানের গোলা। **Cannon-bit**—সুগোল এবং মসৃণ খলীন বিশেষ। **Cannon-bone**—নলাকার অশ্বজঙ্ঘাস্থি বিশেষ। **Cannon-metal** — তাম্র ও রঙ্গের মিশ্রণে প্রস্তুত ধাতু বিশেষ। **Cannon-proof**—কামানের গোলাদ্বারা অভেদ্য। **Cannon-shot** — কামানের গোলা, কামানের পাল্লা।

căn'-non (-nŭn), *v. t.* & *i.* **1.** To discharge cannon ; তোপ দাগা। **2.** To make a cannon at billiards (only *verb i.*) ; বিলিয়ার্ড খেলায় একসঙ্গে লোহিত কন্দুক ও প্রতিপক্ষ ব্যক্তির কন্দুক আঘাত করা। **3.** To come into collision ; to strike and rebound ; সংঘৃষ্ট হওয়া ; ধাক্কা লাগিয়া ঠিকরিয়া উঠা বা আসা, ধাক্কা দিয়া ঠিকরাইয়া দেওয়া।

căn-non-āde' (-nŭn-), *n.*, *v. t.* & *i.* **1.** A continuous gun-fire ; অবিশ্রান্ত গোলাবর্ষণ। **2.** A loud noise like a cannonade ; গুড়ুম্ গুড়ুম্ শব্দ, কামান গর্জ্জন। ***Verb t.*** To attack or batter with artillery ; তোপদ্বারা আক্রমণ করা, অবিশ্রান্ত কামানের গোলাবর্ষণ করা। ***Verb i.*** To discharge cannon ; তোপ দাগা। **–eer', –ier',** *ns.* A man who manages, or fires, cannon ; গোলন্দাজ।

căn'-nŏt, *v. i.* To be unable ; না পারা, অসমর্থ হওয়া, অপারক হওয়া। **I cannot away with this**—I detest it ; আমি ইহা ঘৃণা করি।

căn-nū-lă, *n.* A surgical tube used for various purposes (esp. for injecting or withdrawing fluids) ; ক্ষত হইতে পূজ রসাদি দূরীকরণার্থ নল, দেহাভ্যন্তরে ঔষধাদি প্রবেশ করাইবার নল। **–lar,** *adj.* Having the form of a tube ; চোঙ্গের আকার, নলাকার।

căn'-nȳ, căn'-nie (-nĭ), *adj.* **1.** Shrewd ; artful ; worldly-wise ; বিচক্ষণ ; কৌশলী, চালাক, সেয়ানা ; সংসার-জ্ঞানাভিজ্ঞ, বিষয়-বুদ্ধিসম্পন্ন। **2.** Cautious ; prudent ; সতর্ক, হুসিয়ার ; বিবেচক। **3.** Skillful ; expert ; সুচতুর, নিপুণ ; দক্ষ। **4.** Natural ; moderate ; not extortionate ; স্বাভাবিক ; মধ্যপন্থী ; অপীড়ক। **5.** Gentle ; circumspect ; শান্ত ; চৌকস, সর্ব্বদর্শন। **6.** Easy ; comfortable ; as, edge me into some *canny* post ; সহজ ; সুখদায়ক, আরামপ্রদ। **7.** Possessed of supernatural power ; "*Canny* Elshie ;" অলৌকিক শক্তিসম্পন্ন, অতিমানুষ শক্তি-সম্পন্ন। **–ni-ly,** *adv.* **–ni-ness,** *n.* **No canny**—Not safe ; not fortunate (*Scot.*) ;

বিঘ্নসঙ্কুল ; ভাগ্যহীন। **To ca'canny**—To go or act cautiously ; সাবধানে অগ্রসর হওয়া বা কায করা।

că-noe' (-nö), *n.* & *v. i.* **1.** Originally a boat of bark or skins

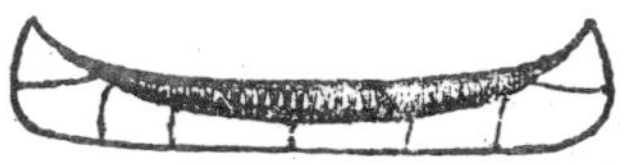

Canoe.

used by savages ; অসভ্য লোকদিগের চর্ম্ম বা বল্কল নির্ম্মিত নৌকা, ডোঙ্গা, ডিঙ্গী, শাল্‌তি। **2.** A light boat propelled by a paddle ; হালকা নৌকা বিশেষ। *Verb i.* To paddle a canoe ; বৈঠাদ্বারা নৌকা চালনা করা। **To paddle one's own canoe**—To mind one's own affair ; নিজের চরকায় তেল দেওয়া।

căn'-ŏn, *n.* **1.** A law or rule in general ; বিধি, নিয়ম, ব্যবস্থা, কানুন (*Colloq.*)। **2.** The general law governing the treatments of a subject ; as, six *canons* of Hindu Arts ; চিত্র, সঙ্গীত, সমালোচনা, প্রভৃতি বিষয় বিজ্ঞান-সম্মতভাবে আলোচনা করিতে হইলে যে সকল সাধারণ নিয়মের অনুবর্ত্তী হইয়া চলিতে হয়। **3.** (*Eccl.*) A rule in ecclesiastical matters ; a decision of matters in religion ; ধর্ম্মসংক্রান্ত নিয়ম ; ধর্ম্ম-ব্যবস্থা, ধর্ম্ম-বিধি। **4.** The list of Bible books accepted by Christian Churches ; খৃষ্টীয় ধর্ম্মসমাজ সমূহ দ্বারা স্বীকৃত বাইবেলের অন্তর্গত পুস্তক সমূহের তালিকা। **5.** The rules of a religious order ; the book containing such rules ; ধর্ম্ম-সম্প্রদায়ের নিয়মাবলী ; উক্ত নিয়মাবলীর পুস্তিকা, ধর্ম্ম-সংহিতা। **6.** A list of Saints canonised ; খৃষ্টীয় সিদ্ধপুরুষ-গণের তালিকা। **7.** A member of a Cathedral chapter ; খৃষ্টীয় মহাধর্ম্ম-মন্দিরের যাজক বিশেষ। **8.** The part of the Mass containing words of consecration ; রোমান ক্যাথলিক খৃষ্টীয় ধর্ম্মসম্প্রদায়ের (শেষ ভোজন নামক) উপাসনার "উৎসর্গ" অঙ্গ। **9.** (*Mus.*) A species of musical composition ; (সঙ্গীত-শাস্ত্র) এক প্রকার সঙ্গীত। **10.** (*Print.*) The largest size of type with a specific name ; (মুদ্রণ) সর্ব্বাপেক্ষা বৃহৎ মুদ্রণের হরফ। **11.** The part of a bell by which it is suspended ; ঘণ্টার অংশ বিশেষ—যদ্দ্বারা ইহা টাঙ্গান হইয়া থাকে। **12.** An instrument used in binding up wounds ; ক্ষতস্থান বাঁধিবার সময় ব্যবহৃত যন্ত্রবিশেষ। **13.** A rule for compounding medicines ; ঔষধ মিশ্রণের নিয়ম বা বিধি। **—ess,** *n.* A woman who enjoys prebend without having to make religious vows ; যে স্ত্রীলোক ধর্ম্মব্রত গ্রহণ ব্যতিরেকেও ধর্ম্মবৃত্তি ভোগ করে। **Ca-non'-ic,** *adj.* Same as CANONICAL (*archaic*). **Ca-non'-i-cal,** *adj.* **1.** According to a canon or canons ; included in the canon of Scriptures ; as, *canonical* hours : *canonical* books ; ধর্ম্মনিয়মানুগত ; বাইবেলের গৃহীত পুস্তকসমূহের অন্তর্ভূত। **2.** (*Mus.*) In the canon form ; সঙ্গীত রচনাবিশেষ বিষয়ক। **3.** Of a Cathedral chapter or a member of it ; মহাধর্ম্মমন্দিরের যাজক-সভা বা উক্ত সভার সভ্য-সংক্রান্ত। **4.** Accepted ; authoritative ; গৃহীত ; প্রামাণিক। **Ca-non'-i-cal-ly,** *adv.* **Ca-non'-i-cal-ness,** *n.* **Ca-non'-i-cals,** *n. pl.* See CANONICAL DRESS below. **—ic'-i-ty,** *n.* **—ist,** *n.* **—is'-tic,** *adj.* **—i-za'-tion,** *n.* The act of canonizing a person ; the state of being canonized ; সিদ্ধপুরুষ শ্রেণীভুক্তকরণ ; সিদ্ধাবস্থা। **—ize,** *v. t.* **1.** (*Eccl.*) To enrol in the list of saints ; as, Thomas Becket was *canonized* ; খৃষ্টীয় সিদ্ধপুরুষশ্রেণীভুক্ত করা। **2.** To regard as a saint ; সিদ্ধপুরুষরূপে গণ্য করা। **3.** To recognise (book) as cononical ; বাইবেলের অন্তর্ভূত পুস্তক স্বরূপ স্বীকার করা। **4.** To sanction or ratify by Church authority ; খৃষ্টীয় ধর্ম্ম-সমাজের কর্ত্তৃপক্ষগণকর্ত্তৃক অনুমোদন বা বলবৎ করা। **—ry,** *n.* **Canonical books** or **scriptures**—মহাধর্ম্মমন্দিরস্থ যাজক-সভাদ্বারা গৃহীত বাইবেলের পুস্তক সমূহ। **Canonical dress** — যাজক সভাসম্মত যাজকীয় পরিচ্ছদ, যাজকবেশ (আঃ বঃ) [সময় সময়, যে কোন ব্যবসায়াবলম্বী ব্যক্তিগণের পরিচয়জ্ঞাপক পরিচ্ছদ।] **Canonical Epistles**—The seven Catholic epistles ; খৃষ্টধর্ম্ম সম্বন্ধে সাতটী পত্র (অর্থাৎ জেমস্‌এর একটী, পিটারের দুইটী, যোহনের তিনটী ও জুদের একটী)। **Canonical hours**—খৃষ্টীয় ধর্ম্মবিধি অনুসারে দিবসের যে যে নির্দিষ্ট বেলা পূজোপসনার জন্য নিরূপিত হইয়াছে। **Canonical obedience**—উচ্চতর শ্রেণীর যাজকগণের প্রতি নিম্ন শ্রেণীস্থ যাজকগণের বশ্যতা। **Canonical punishments** — ধর্ম্ম-সমাজ যে সমস্ত শাস্তি প্রদান করিতে পারে (যথা, সমাজচ্যুতি), ধর্ম্ম-দণ্ড। **Canon-law**—রোমান ক্যাথলিক খৃষ্টীয় ধর্ম্ম-সমাজের শাসন-ব্যবস্থা নিয়মিত করিবার জন্য বিধি, খৃষ্টীয় ধর্ম্ম-বিধি। **Canon of the Mass**—(*R. C. Church*) ; রোমান ক্যাথলিক খৃষ্টানদিগের (শেষ ভোজন) উপাসনার অঙ্গবিশেষ। **Canon residentiary**—যাজকসভার যে সভ্য সমস্ত বৎসরে বা বৎসরের মধ্যে কিছুকাল মহাধর্ম্মমন্দিরে বাস করেন। **Honorary canon** — মহাধর্ম্মমন্দিরস্থ-যাজকসভার-সম্মানিত সভ্য বিশেষ (অর্থাৎ যাহাকে কোনও কায করিতে হয় না অথবা বৃত্তি প্রভৃতি প্রদত্ত হয় না।) **Minor canon** (*Ch. of Eng.*)—মহাধর্ম্মমন্দিরস্থ উপযাজক বিশেষ।

ca'-non, *n.* See CANYON.

că-nŏph'-i-list, *n.* **1.** A lover of dogs ; কুক্কুরানুরাগী।

că-nō'-pŭs, *n.* (*Astron.*) A bright star in the southern constellation *Argo* ; অগস্ত্য (সাঃ পঃ)।

căn'-ŏ-pȳ, *n.* & *v. t.* **1.** A covering over a throne, bed, person, etc. ; চন্দ্রাতপ, চাঁদোয়া, সামিয়ানা, বিতান, তিরস্করণী। **2.** (*Fig.*) Any over-hanging shelter ; sky, etc. ;

as, the cloud *canopy* above us may be thick enough to shut out the light of the stars ; (লক্ষণায়) যে কোনরূপ শিরোপরি বিস্তৃত আবরণ ; আকাশ, প্রভৃতি। **3.** (*Arch.*) A roof-like projection over a niche, tomb, statue ; (স্থপতি-বিদ্যা) কুলুঙ্গি, সমাধিভবন, বা প্রস্তর-মূর্ত্তির বহির্বিলম্বিত ছাদের মত আচ্ছাদন। ***Verb t.*** To cover with a canopy ; চন্দ্রাতপাবৃত করা।

că-nō′-rous (-rŭs), *adj.* Melodious ; musical ; as, birds that are most *canorous* ; সুস্বর, সুকণ্ঠ ; মধুর, শ্রুতি-মধুর, সুললিত, শ্রুতিসুখকর। **—ness,** *n.*

cănt, *n., v.t. & i.* **1.** An inclination ; slope ; as, the helm had been lashed with a small *cant* to leeward ; হেলন ; প্রবণতা, ঢালুভাব। **2.** A toss, thrust or push with a sudden jerk ; as, to give a ball a *cant* ; সহসা উৎক্ষেপণ, সবলে তাড়ন বা ধাক্কা প্রদান, ঠুকা, ধাক্কা। **3.** (*Arch.*) An external angle or quoin of a building ; a bevel ; (স্থপতি-বিদ্যা) বাহ্যকোণ, অট্টালিকার বহিঃস্থ কোণ ; ঢালুভূমি। **4.** (*Coopering*) One of the segments forming a side-piece in the head of a cask ; (পিপানির্ম্মাণ) পিপার অগ্রভাগের চাপাকৃতি কাষ্ঠখণ্ডদ্বয়ের একটী। **5.** A segment of the rim of a wooden cog-wheel ; কাষ্ঠময় দন্তুর চক্রবেষ্টনীর খণ্ডবিশেষ। ***Verb t.*** **1.** To bevel off ; to tilt over ; as, to *cant* a cask ; ঢালু করা ; কাৎ করা, হেলান। **2.** To toss ; to push sideways ; as, to *cant* a ball ; উৎক্ষেপণ করা ; এক পার্শ্বে ঠেলিয়া দেওয়া। **3.** To cut off an angle, as of a square piece of timber; কোণ কাটিয়া লওয়া। ***Verb i.*** **1.** To take inclined position ; হেলিয়া পড়া, কাৎ হওয়া। **2.** (*Naut.*) To swing round ; (নৌ-বিদ্যা) ঘুরা, পাক খাওয়া আবর্ত্তিত হওয়া। **Cant board**—ঢালু কাষ্ঠফলক।

cănt, *n., adj. & v. i.* **1.** An affected mode of speaking ; কৃত্রিম-ভাবে কথা কহিবার ভঙ্গী বা ধরণ, কথার ছাঁদ। **2.** The language peculiar to a sect ; কোন সম্প্রদায়ের নিজস্ব ভাষা। **3.** Hypocritical sanctimoniousness ; hypocrisy ; as, they shall hear no *cant* from me ; কপট সাধুতা, বিড়াল-তপস্বীর ভাব, মর্কট-বৈরাগ্য (চৈঃ চঃ) ; ভণ্ডামি। **4.** Barbarous jargon peculiar to thieves, rogues, and beggars ; a kind of slang ; চোর গুণ্ডা ও ভিক্ষুকদিগের মধ্যে প্রচলিত অপভাষা বিশেষ ; একপ্রকার ইতর ভাষা। ***Adj.*** Pertaining to, containing, or of the nature of, cant ; as, *cant* words ; অপভাষা-সম্বন্ধীয়, অপভাষাত্মক, অপভাষাবহুল। ***Verb i.*** **1.** To speak whiningly ; প্যান্‌প্যান্ করা, ঘ্যান্‌ঘ্যান্ করা, নাকি-স্বরে কথা বলা। **2.** To use the language of thieves, etc. ; to use any slang jargon ; চোরদস্যুদের ভাষায় কথা কহা ; ইতর-ভাষায় কথা বলা। **3.** To make hypocritical pretentions to goodness ; as, the rankest rogue that ever *canted* ; ভণ্ডামি করা, কপট সাধুতা দেখান, মর্কট বৈরাগ্য প্রদর্শন করা। **Cant′-er,** *n.*

cănt, *n. & v. t.* A call for bidders at a public sale ; an auction ; ক্রেতৃগণকে নিলামে আহ্বান ; নিলাম। ***Verb t.*** **1.** (*Archaic*) To sell by auction ; (অপ্রচলিত) নিলামে বিক্রয় করা। **2.** To determine by bidding at an auction ; as, "Two monks were outvying each other in *canting* the price of an abbey ;" নিলামে ডাকিয়া স্থির করা।

cân't, A colloquial contraction for *cannot* ; চলিত-ভাষায় cannot (পারি না) শব্দের সংক্ষেপ।

Căn′-tăb, *n.* An abbreviation of CANTABRIGIAN (which see).

Căn-tā′-bri-ăn, *adj.* Pertaining to Cantabria on the bay of Briscay in Spain ; স্পেনদেশের অন্তঃ-পাতী কেন্‌টেব্রিয়ানামক স্থান সম্বন্ধীয়।

Căn-tā-brig′-i-ăn, *n. & adj.* A native or resident of Cambridge ; a member of the Cambridge University ; কেম্ব্রিজ নগরীর স্থায়ী বা অস্থায়ী অধিবাসী ; কেম্ব্রিজ বিশ্ববিদ্যালয়ের উপাধিধারী। ***Adj.*** Of or relating to Cambridge or its university ; কেম্ব্রিজ বা তন্নগরস্থিত বিশ্ববিদ্যালয়-সম্পর্কীয়।

căn′-tă-li-vêr, —lē-vėr, *n.* Same as CANTILEVER (which see).

căn-tă′-loup (-lôp), *n.* A kind of melon ; একপ্রকার ফুঁটি।

căn-tan′-ker-ous (-tăng-kêr-ŭs), *adj.* Perverse ; quarrelsome ; cross-grained ; malicious ; as, the *cantankerous* old ; বিকৃতস্বভাব ; ঝগড়াটে ; বে-আড়া ; পিশুন, দ্রোহবুদ্ধি। **—ly,** *adv.* **—ness,** *n.*

căn-tâ′-tâ, *n.* (*Mus.*) A poem set to music ; a kind of short oratoris, or lyric drama set to music but not acted ; (সঙ্গীত-শাস্ত্র) সঙ্গীতের সুর দেওয়া কবিতা, গীতিকাব্য ; সুর দেওয়া বক্তৃতা বা গীতিনাট্য—যাহা অভিনীত হয় না।

can-ta-tri′-ce (căn-tă-trē-chā or cân-tâ-trēs), *n.* (*Mus.*) A professional woman singer ; (সঙ্গীত-বিদ্যা) পেশাদারিণী গায়িকা।

căn-teen′ (-tēn), *n.* **1.** (*Mil.*) A soldier's vessel for carrying drink ; (সামরিকশাস্ত্র) সৈন্যের পানপাত্র। **2.** A box of cooking utensils for use in camp ; শিবিরে ব্যবহারার্থ রন্ধন কার্য্যে ব্যবহারোপযোগী তৈজসপূর্ণ পেটিকা। **3.** Provision and liquor shop in a camp or barracks ; শিবির অথবা সেনা-বারিকের খাদ্যদ্রব্যের দোকান, সেনা-বারিকের সুরাবিপণি।

căn′-têr, *n., v. i. & t.* **1.** An easy gallop ; অশ্বের প্লুতগতিবিশেষ, অর্দ্ধ-পুলায়িত (মঃ .উঃ)। **2.** A rapid passing over ; as, a rapid *canter* in the times over all the topics ;

দ্রুতবেগে অতিক্রম। *Verb i.* To move in a canter; অর্দ্ধপুলায়িত গতিতে অগ্রসর হওয়া। *Verb t.* To make a horse go thus; অর্দ্ধপুলায়িত গতিতে অশ্বচালনা করা। **To win in a canter**—(*In horse-racing*) To be so far ahead of the field as to be under no necessity of urging the horse at the post; hence, (*fig.*) to overcome an opponent easily; (ঘোড়দৌড়ে) প্রতিযোগীর অশ্বদিগকে বহু পশ্চাতে ফেলিয়া আসাতে, নিজ বিজয় বিষয়ে কৃতনিশ্চিত হওয়ায়, অতি দ্রুতবেগে অশ্ব চালনার আবশ্যক না হওয়া; (লক্ষণায়) সহজে বাজি জিতা, অনায়াসে শত্রুকে পরাভূত করা।

Căn′-têr-bur-ŷ (-bĕr-), *n.* **1.** A city in England and the seat of the Archbishop of Canterbury; ইংলণ্ডের নগরবিশেষ—ক্যাণ্টারবারীর মহা-ধর্ম্মাধ্যক্ষের শ্রীপাট। **2.** (*l. c.*) A stand with partitions for holding books, portfolios, etc.; পুস্তক, আল্‌গা কাগজ প্রভৃতি রাখার জন্য বিভিন্ন কোঠায় বিভক্ত ক্ষুদ্র মেজবিশেষ। **Canterbury bell**—একজাতীয় ঘণ্টাফুল। **Canterbury gallop**—অশ্বের প্লুতগতি-বিশেষ। **Canterbury tale**—A tale told to relieve the weariness of a journey; পথশ্রান্তি নিবারক গল্প। [প্রাচীন ইংরেজ কবি চসারের কেন্‌টারবারী গল্পগুচ্ছোক্ত তীর্থযাত্রিগণদ্বারা কথিত গল্প হইতে শব্দটী গৃহীত হইয়াছে।] A cock-and-bull story; আষাঢ়ে গল্প।

căn-thăr′-i-dēs, *n. pl.* Spanish flies, used for blistering; স্পেন-দেশীয় ফোস্কা উৎপাদক কীটবিশেষ, তেলেনী মক্ষিকা (হঃ চঃ)। **—dal,** *adj.* **—din, —dine,** *n.* The active principle of blistering flies; উক্ত কীটের সত্ত্ব।

căn′-thă-ris, *n.* A beetle; গোবরে পোকা।

căn′-thŭs, *n.* The angle formed by the meeting of the eye-lids; অপাঙ্গ, নেত্রোপান্ত, নয়নকোণ।

căn′-ti-cle, *n.* **1.** One of the Prayer-Book hymns; প্রার্থনা পুস্তকের স্তোত্রবিশেষ। **2.** (*Pl.*) The song of songs or song of Solomon; সোলোমোনের গীতি। **3.** A little song or hymn; ক্ষুদ্র গীতি বা স্তোত্র।

căn′-ti-lĕ-vêr, —tă-li-vêr, —tă-lĕ-vêr, *n.* A bracket projecting from the wall for supporting a balcony, a cornice, or the like; বারাণ্ডা, আলিসা প্রভৃতির অবলম্বন স্বরূপ প্রাচীর সংলগ্ন আড়া বিশেষ **Cantaliver bridge**—উক্তপ্রকার আড়ার উপর নির্ম্মিত সেতু।

căn′-til-lāte, *v. t.* To chant; to recite with musical tones; গান করা, কীর্ত্তন করা; স্বর সংযোগে আবৃত্তি করা। **—la′-tion,** *n.*

căn′-tle, *n.* **1.** A piece; a part; খণ্ড; অংশ। **2.** The hind-bow of a saddle; ঘোড়ার জিনের বক্র পশ্চাদ্‌ভাগ।

căn′-tō, *n.* **1.** The divisions of a song or poem; উল্লাস, উচ্ছ্বাস, তরঙ্গ, পর্ব্ব, স্কন্ধ, খণ্ড, কাণ্ড। **2.** (*Mus.*) The highest vocal part in concerted music; soprano; (সঙ্গীত-শাস্ত্র) ঐকতানবাদ্যে সর্ব্বোচ্চস্বর বিশিষ্ট অংশ; বামাকণ্ঠোত্থিত সর্ব্বোচ্চ স্বর, জিলস্বর।

căn′-tŏn, *n.* **1.** A small portion or district of territory, constituting a distinct state or government, as in Switzerland; কোন দেশের ক্ষুদ্র অংশ বা বিভাগ বিশেষ,—যাহা স্বতন্ত্র রাজ্য বা শাসন-তন্ত্ররূপে পরিগণিত হইয়া থাকে। [যেমন সুইজরলণ্ড্ দেশে।] **2.** The inhabitants of a canton; উক্ত প্রদেশ-বাসিগণ। **3.** A small portion; a division; ক্ষুদ্র অংশ; বিভাগ। **4.** A distinct part or division; as, the *cantons* of a flag; স্বতন্ত্র অংশ বা বিভাগ। **5.** (*Herald.*) A square division less than a quarter in the upper corner of a shield; (কুল-বিদ্যা) ঢালের উপরের কোণে (ঢালের) চতুর্থাংশ অপেক্ষা ক্ষুদ্রতর সমচতুষ্কোণ ক্ষেত্রবৎ বিভাগ বিশেষ। **—al,** *adj.*

căn′-tŏn, *v. t.* **1.** To divide into small parts or districts; ক্ষুদ্র ক্ষুদ্র বিভাগ বা জেলায় বিভক্ত করা। **2.** (*Mil.*) To allot quarters to troops; (সামরিকশাস্ত্র) সৈন্যদিগের বাসস্থান বিলি বন্দোবস্ত করিয়া দেওয়া। **—toned,** *adj.* (*Arch.*) **1.** Ornamented at the corners with projecting pilasters; (স্থপতি-বিদ্যা) প্রাচীরোদ্গত স্তম্ভদ্বারা কোণদেশ অলঙ্কৃত। **2.** (*Herald.*) Having a charge in each of the four corners; (কুল-বিদ্যা) (চতুষ্কোণের) প্রতিকোণে কুল-চিহ্নাঙ্কিত।

căn′-tŏn-mĕnt, *n.* A part of a town or village assigned to troops; in India also a permanent military station; গ্রাম বা নগরের যে অংশে সৈন্যগণ বাস করে; (ভারতবর্ষে) সেনানিবাস, ছাউনী।

căn-tōōn′, *n.* A kind of strong cotton stuff or fustian; স্থূল কার্পাস বস্ত্র বিশেষ।

căn′-tŏr, *n.* A singer; esp. the leader of a church-choir; গায়ক; (বিশেষভাবে) খৃষ্টীয় ধর্ম্মমন্দিরের গায়ক-দলের নেতা।

căn-tō′-ri-ăl, *adj.* Pertaining to a precentor or to the north side of the choir; খৃষ্টীয় ধর্ম্মমন্দিরের প্রধান গায়ক সম্বন্ধীয়, খৃষ্টীয় ধর্ম্মমন্দিরস্থ কীর্ত্তনস্থলীর উত্তরপার্শ্ব সম্বন্ধীয়।

căn-tō′-ris, *adj.* Pertaining to a cantor; খৃষ্টীয় ধর্ম্মমন্দিরস্থ প্রধান গায়ক সম্বন্ধীয়।

Căn′-tü-ăr, *n.* Signature of the Archbishop of Canterbury; কেন্টারবেরী নগরীস্থ প্রধান ধর্ম্মাধ্যক্ষের স্বাক্ষর।

căn′-trăp, —trip, *n.* (*Scot.*) A charm; a trick; (স্কটলণ্ড্) যাদু; কৌশল, চাতুরী।

căn′-tŷ, *adj.* (*Scot.*) Lively and cheerful; as, the *canty* dame;

(স্কট্‌লণ্ড) সজীব, প্রফুল্ল, উৎফুল্ল, স্ফূর্ত্তি-পূর্ণ। **—ti-ness,** *n.*

căn′-văs, *n.* & *adj.* **1.** A strong unbleached cloth of hemp or flax used for sails, tents, etc.; ক্যাম্বিস কাপড়, শণের চট। **2.** A clear, unbleached cloth, woven regularly in little squares, used for tapestry works; বুটিদার পর্দ্দার কাযের জন্য ব্যবহৃত বস্ত্রবিশেষ। **3.** (*Naut.*) The sails of a ship; as, to spread as much *canvas* as the ship will bear; (নৌ-বিদ্যা) জাহাজের পাইল, বাতবসন (মঃ ইঃ)। **4.** A tent; as, I should enjoy the prospect of being on horse-back and under *canvas* again; তাঁবু, শিবির, পটবাস। **5.** A picture; "Touched the glowing *canvas* into life;" পট, চিত্রপট। ***Adj.*** Made of canvas; ক্যাম্বিস বস্ত্র-নির্ম্মিত। **Canvas-back**—উত্তর আমেরিকার সামুদ্রিক হংস বিশেষ। **Canvas-bag**—শাণপুট (আঃ বঃ)। **Canvas-city**—A military encampment; শিবির-নগরী, বস্ত্র-নগরী (আঃ মঠ) সেনানিবাস। **Canvas-stretcher**—যে কাঠের কাঠামে চিত্রাঙ্কণের জন্য পট প্রসারিত করা হয়। **To get** or **receive the canvas**—An obsolete phrase signifying 'to be dismissed'; পদচ্যুত হওয়া (অপ্রচলিত)।

căn′-vass (-văs), *v. t., i.* & *n.* **1.** To examine thoroughly; to scrutinize; as, to *canvass* the votes cast at an election; পুঙ্খানুপুঙ্খরূপে পরীক্ষা করা; তন্নতন্ন করিয়া অনুসন্ধান করা। **2.** To examine by discussion; to debate; as, an opinion that we are likely soon to *canvass*; আলোচনা দ্বারা ভালমন্দ নির্ণয় করা; তর্কবিতর্ক করা, বাদবিতণ্ডা করা। **3.** To go through in the way of solicitations; to solicit votes from; as, to *canvass* a district for votes, for subscription, etc.; কোন কিছু প্রার্থনা বা যাচ্ঞা করিতে করিতে স্থানে স্থানে যাওয়া; অনুকূলমত (vote) প্রার্থনা করা। ***Verb i.*** To seek or go about to solicit votes or interest, or to obtain mercantile orders, etc.; as, to *canvass* for a firm; অনুকূলমত বা অন্য কোন প্রকার স্বার্থ-সিদ্ধির অভিপ্রায়ে স্থানে স্থানে পর্য্যটন করা, কিম্বা কোন জিনিষের ক্রেতা সংগ্রহের জন্য চেষ্টা করা। ***Noun.*** **1.** Close inspection; as, a *canvass* of votes; পুঙ্খানুপুঙ্খরূপে পর্য্যবেক্ষণ। **2.** Discussion; আলোচনা। **3.** Solicitation; as, no previous *canvass* was made for me; প্রার্থনা, যাচ্ঞা। **—er,** *n.* One who canvasses; যে ব্যক্তি অনুকূলমত কিম্বা ক্রেতাদি সংগ্রহের জন্য চেষ্টা বা পর্য্যটন করে। **—ing,** *n.*

căn′-yon (-yŭn), *n.* A deep gorge with stream; সংকীর্ণ এবং সুগভীর পার্ব্বত্য খাত।

căn-zo′-ne (-tsö-nā), *n.* (*Mus.*) A song or air in two or more parts, with passages of fugue and imitation; (সঙ্গীত-শাস্ত্র) এক প্রকার সঙ্গীত।

căn-zö-nĕt′, *n.* (*Mus.*) A short light song; ক্ষুদ্রগীতি, ঠুংরি (ফঃ হিঃ) টপ্পা (ঐ)।

caout′-chouc (kô-chôk), *n.* India-

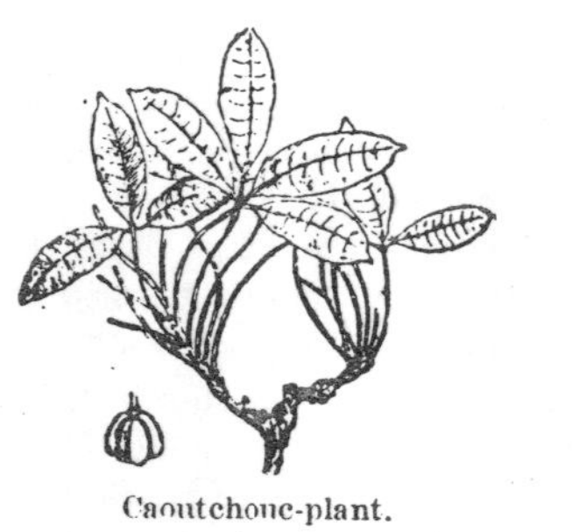

Caoutchouc-plant.

rubber; রবর। **Vulcanised caoutchouc**—গন্ধকী রবর (হিঃ কোঃ)।

căp, *n.* **1.** A covering for the head; (a woman's head-dress of muslin, a boy's head-dress); টুপি, টোপর, তাজ, শিরস্ক (স্ত্রীলোকের শিরোপা বা মস্তকাবরণ, বালকের টুপি)। **2.** The badge or ensign of some dignity, especially of the cardinalate; "He'll make his *cap* coequal with the crown"; কোন সম্ভ্রান্তপদসূচক চিহ্ন বা পতাকা। **3.** A respectful uncovering of the head; as, he that will give a *cap* and make a leg in thanks; সম্মানার্থ মস্তকাবরণ উন্মোচন। **4.** The highest (of things and persons); as, the *cap* of fools (মূর্খচূড়ামণি); চূড়ামণি। **5.** A cap-like covering, natural or added for various purposes; টোপরের মত আবরণ (স্বভাবজাত বা বিভিন্ন উদ্দেশ্য সাধনে সংযুক্ত)। **6.** (*Arch.*) The uppermost of any assemblage of parts; as, the *cap* of a column, door, etc.; (স্থপতি-বিদ্যা) শীর্ষভাগ। **7.** (*Herald.*) The cap of state carried before the sovereign at his coronation; (কুল-বিদ্যা) ইংলণ্ডেশ্বরের অভিষেককালে তদগ্রে বাহিত রাজমুকুট। **8.** (*Naut.*) A square piece of wood placed over the head or upper end of a mast; (নৌ-বিদ্যা) মাস্তুলের শীর্ষ বা উর্দ্ধপ্রান্তে স্থাপিত সমচতুষ্কোণ কাষ্ঠখণ্ড। **9.** A percussion cap (see BELOW.) **10.** A conical paper bag; মোচাকার কাগজের থলি। **11.** A large size of writing paper; as, fools *cap*; বড় আকারের লিখিবার কাগজ। **Cap′-ful,** *adj.* Enough to fill a cap; টুপিপূর্ণ। **Capcase**—ভ্রমণকারীর ক্ষুদ্র পেটক। **Cap-paper**—একপ্রকার মোটা কাগজ। **Cap-square**—কামানের উভয় কর্ণদ্বয় আচ্ছাদক স্থূল লৌহ-পট্ট। **Cap-stone**—শীর্ষপ্রস্তর। **A capful of wind**—a light puff of wind; দমকা বাতাস। **A feather in one's cap** (see FEATHER.) **Cap and bells** — (ইয়ুরোপে) ভাঁড় বা বিদূষকের সাজ। **Cap and feather**

day—Childhood ; শৈশব। **Cap in head**—Humbly ; বিনীত ভাবে, তটস্থ হইয়া। **Cap of liberty**—রোমের ক্রীতদাসদিগকে দাসত্ব-মুক্তির নিদর্শনস্বরূপ যে মোচাকার টোপর প্রদান করা হইত। [বর্ত্তমানে—সাধারণ তন্ত্রের পক্ষপাতিগণের চিহ্ন।] **Cap of maintenance**—ইংলণ্ডেশ্বরগণের অভিষেককালে তাহাদের অগ্রে যে রাজমুকুট বাহিত হয়। **Football cap**—মকমলের টুপি ; ক্রীড়ক দলে প্রবেশের চিহ্নবিশেষ। **Percussion cap**—টোটা প্রভৃতি বিস্ফোরক পদার্থ প্রজ্বালিত করিবার জন্য তাম্রনির্ম্মিত ক্ষুদ্র চোঙ্গ বিশেষ। **Scotch cap**—হাইলেণ্ডবাসিগণের পরিচ্ছদের অংশ বিশেষ। **I must put on my considering cap**—আমি বিশেষ বিবেচনার পর এই বিষয়ে শেষ উত্তর প্রদান করিব। **If the cap fits, wear it**—If the remark applies to you, apply it to yourself ; মন্তব্যটী তোমার সম্পর্কে প্রযোজ্য হইলে প্রয়োগ করিও। **To gain the cap**—To obtain a bow from another out of respect ; অপর ব্যক্তির নিকট হইতে সসম্মান অভিবাদন লাভ করা। **To pull caps**—To quarrel like two women, who pull each other's caps ; টুপি টানাটানি করিয়া স্ত্রীলোকেরা যেরূপ ঝগড়া করে তদ্রূপ কোন্দল করা। **To set one's cap at**—(Of a woman) To try to captivate ; to try to obtain as a husband ; (স্ত্রীলোক-সম্পর্কে) মুগ্ধ করিতে চেষ্টা করা ; পতিরূপে লাভ করিতে চেষ্টা করা। **Your cap is all on one side**—You are in an ill humour : তোমার মেজাজ খারাপ আছে।

căp, *v. t. & i.* **1.** To put a cap upon ; to provide with a cap or cover ; as, to *cap* a post : টুপি পরান, টোপর পরান ; টুপি বা অন্য কোনও প্রকার আবরণ দ্বারা আচ্ছাদিত করা। **2.** To confer a university degree on (*Scot.*) ; (স্কটলণ্ড) বিশ্ববিদ্যালয়ের উপাধি প্রদান করা। **3.** To salute by removing the cap ; as "Tom......*capped* the proctor with the profoundest of bows ;" টুপি তুলিয়া অভিবাদন করা। **4.** To render complete ; to crown ; as, he *capped* this exploit by another still more audacious ; সমাপ্ত করা, সমাধা করা ; সম্পূর্ণতা প্রদান করা। **5.** To match ; to outdo or surpass ; সমকক্ষ হওয়া ; অতিক্রম করা, ছাপাইয়া উঠা। **6.** To put a percussion cap on the nipple of a gun ; বন্দুকের মুখে (বোঁটায়) ক্ষুদ্র তামার চোঙ্গ লাগান। ***Verb i.*** To take off the cap in salutation ; অভিবাদন কালে টুপি তোলা। **I cap to that**—I assent to it ; আমি এই বিষয়ে সম্মত আছি। **To cap texts or proverbs**—To quote texts or proverbs alternately in emulation or contest ; পরস্পরের সহিত প্রতিযোগিতার জন্য শাস্ত্রবচন বা প্রবাদবাক্য দ্বারা উত্তর প্রত্যুত্তর করা। **To cap the climax**—To say or do something extraordinary ; অসম্ভব কথা বলা বা অসম্ভব কার্য্য করা। **To cap the glove**—To surpass everything ; সবকে অতিক্রম করা। **To cap verses**—To quote verses in turn ; কবির লড়াই করা, কবিতার পংক্তি উদ্ধার করত উত্তর প্রত্যুত্তর করা, তরজার লড়াই করা।

cā'-pă-ble, *adj.* **1.** Having ability, power, or skill to do ; susceptible ; (usually followed by *of*) ; as, *capable of* pain ; শক্ত, ক্ষম, শক্য, সমর্থ, সম্পাদনে পটু ; গ্রাহক, সংবেদনীয়, গ্রহণক্ষম, বেদনক্ষম। **2.** Gifted ; competent ; qualified ; as, a *capable* judge ; স্বাভাবিক বুদ্ধিবিশিষ্ট ; কর্ম্মক্ষম, উপযুক্ত ; যোগ্য, লায়েক (*Colloq.*)। **3.** Legally qualified or competent ; as, a bastard is not *capable* of inheriting an estate ; আইনতঃ যোগ্য বা ক্ষমতাবান। **4.** Wicked enough for (with *of*) ; "They are *capable of* being incendiaries ;" কোন দুষ্কর্ম্ম সাধনে সমর্থ। **—bil'-i-ty,** *n.* Capacity ; কার্য্য-শক্তি, ক্ষমতা, সামর্থ্য, যোগ্যতা। **—ness,** *n.*

că-pā'-cious (-shŭs), *adj.* **1.** Roomy ; spacious ; as, a *capacious* vessel ; বিশাল ; বিপুল, প্রশস্ত। **2.** (*Fig.*) Comprehensive ; liberal ; as, a *capacious* mind ; (লক্ষণায়) ব্যাপক ; উদার। **—ly,** *adv.* **—ness,** *n.*

că-păc'-i-tāte, *v. t.* **1.** To render capable ; সমর্থ করা। **2.** To furnish with legal powers ; as, to *capacitate* one for an office ; আইনসঙ্গত ক্ষমতা প্রদান করা।

că-păc'-i-tȳ, *n.* **1.** The power of receiving or containing ; as, the *capacity* of the exhausted cylinder ; ধারণ-শক্তি, প্রস্থি (প্রঃ)। **2.** (*Fig.*) Comprehensiveness of mind ; the receptive faculty ; (লক্ষণায়) চিত্তের প্রসার ; যে শক্তিদ্বারা ইন্দ্রিয়াদিপ্রদত্ত জ্ঞান গৃহীত হয়, গ্রহণ-শক্তি। **3.** Capability ; opportunity to do or of doing ; as, the *capacity* of blessing the people ; শক্যতা, কার্য্যশক্তি, সামর্থ্য, শক্যত্ব, শক্তি ; কার্য্য করিবার সুযোগ। **4.** Position ; character ; as, to work in the *capacity* of a carpenter (সূত্রধররূপে) ; in the *capacity* of a friend (বন্ধুভাবে) ; পদ ; রূপ, স্বরূপ, ভাব। **5.** Measure of capacity ; মাপ, পরিমাণ। **6.** (*Law*) Legal competency ; "He had been restored to his *capacity* of governing ;" (আইন) বৈধ ক্ষমতা। **Capacity for heat**—উত্তাপ শোষণ শক্তি। **To the extent of one's capacity**—যথাশক্তি।

căp-á-pie' (-pē), *adv.* From head to foot ; as, he was armed *cap-a-pie* ; পা হইতে মাথা পর্য্যন্ত, আপাদমস্তক, নখশিখান্ত, আনখশিখ।

că-păr'-i-sŏn, *n.* & *v. t.* **1.** An ornamental covering for a horse ;

horse's trappings ; as, their horses clothed with rich *capar-isons* ; কারুকার্য্য-খচিত অশ্বাবরণ ; অশ্ব-সজ্জা, জিন-পোষ (ফঃ হিঃ), অশ্বালঙ্কার, কুথ (আঃ বঃ)। 2. (*Fig.*) Equipment ; outfit ; as, my heart groans beneath the gay *capar-isons* ; (লক্ষণায়) সজ্জা ; সাজ-গোজ, সাজসজ্জা। *Verb t.* 1. To cover with a cloth, as a horse : অশ্বাদির পৃষ্ঠ কারুকার্য্য-খচিত বস্ত্রে আচ্ছাদিত করা। 2. To dress richly ; as, I am *caparisoned* like a man ; জাঁকাল পোষাক পরান, বহুমূল্য পরিচ্ছদে সজ্জিত করা, মহার্ঘ বস্ত্রে সুসজ্জিত করা।

cāpe, *n.* 1. A piece of land running into the sea ; অন্তরীপ। 2. A kind of wine from the Cape of Good Hope ; উত্তমাশা অন্তরীপ হইতে সমানীত মদিরা বিশেষ। **Cape wine**—দক্ষিণ আফ্রিকায় প্রস্তুত মদিরা বিশেষ। **The Cape**—Cape of Good Hope ; উত্তমাশা অন্তরীপ।

cāpe, *n.* A kind of small cloak covering the shoulders ; a sleeveless cloak ; স্কন্ধদেশাবরক প্রাবরণ, স্কন্ধচ্ছদ (আঃ বঃ) ; আস্তীন-শূন্য শ্লথ পরিচ্ছদ বিশেষ।

cāpe, *v. i.* (*Naut.*) To head or point ; to keep a course ; as, the ship *capes* south-west by south ; (নৌ-বিদ্যা) কোন দিকে যাওয়া, অভিমুখীন হওয়া ; কোন নির্দ্দিষ্ট পথে চলা।

că'-pĕ-line (-lĭn), *n.* 1. A hood worn by ladies going out to an evening party ; মহিলাগণ সান্ধ্য-সম্মিলনে যাইবার কালে যে শিরোবস্ত্র পরিধান করিয়া থাকেন। 2. A surgical bandage for the head ; মস্তকের ক্ষত বন্ধনী বিশেষ।

că-pĕl'-lă, *n.* A brilliant star in the constellation Auriga ; ব্রহ্মহৃদয় (সাঃ পঃ)।

căp'-ĕl-lĕt, *n.* A tumour-like swelling on a horse's elbow or on the back part of his hock ; কফোণি বা পশ্চাৎপদের নিম্নভাগস্থ গ্রন্থিতে অর্ব্বুদবৎ স্ফীতি বিশেষ।

că-pĕll'-mies-têr (mĭs-), **kă-,** *n.* A choirmaster ; খৃষ্টীয় ধর্ম্মমন্দিরস্থ কীর্ত্তন সম্প্রদায়ের নেতা।

că'-pêr, *n.* 1. A bramble-like South European shrub ; দক্ষিণ ইয়ুরোপে জাত কণ্টক গুল্ম বিশেষ। [*Capparis spinosa*—ক্রকচ (অমরঃ), টাউর-কাঁটা গাছ, করীর (দ্রব্য গুণ), কেবির (বেলঃ)]। 2. (*Pl.*) The flower-bud of the caper-bush used for pickling ; আচার প্রস্তুতে ব্যবহৃত উক্ত গুল্মের পুষ্পকলিকা।

că'-pêr, *n.* & *v. i.* A frolicsome leap ; fantastic proceeding ; as, we that are true lovers, run into strange *capers* ; ক্রীড়াচ্ছলে উল্লম্ফন, কুর্দ্দন (মঃ উঃ) ; আজগুবীকাণ্ড, অদ্ভুত ব্যাপার। *Verb i.* To leap in a sprightly manner ; "He *capers*, he dances, he has eyes of youth ;" লাফালাফি ছুটাছুটি করা, নেচে কুঁদে বেড়ান। **—er,** *n.* **To cut a caper**—To dance or act fantastically ; লক্ষঝম্প করা, নর্ত্তন কুর্দ্দন করা, নেচে কুদে বেড়ান, আজগুবী কাণ্ড করা।

că-pêr-cail'-zie (-căl-zĭ), *n.* A species of grouse (also CAPERCAILLIE) ; এক জাতীয় বন্য কুক্কুট।

că'-pĭ-ăs, *n.* A writ of arrest ; (also *writ of capias*) ; গ্রেপ্তারি পরওয়ানা।

căp-ĭl-lā'-ceous (-shŭs), *adj.* Thread-like ; সূত্রবৎ।

căp-ĭl-laire' (-lāre), *n.* 1. A kind of syrup prepared with maidenhair ; কালিঝাঁপ সহযোগে প্রস্তুত আসব বিশেষ। 2. Any syrup flavoured with orange flowers ; কমলাপুষ্প-বাসিত আসব (সিরাপ) বিশেষ।

că-pĭl'-lă-mĕnt, *n.* A filament ; আঁশ, তন্তু।

căp'-ĭl-lă-rŷ, *adj.* & *n.* Hair-like ; very slender ; কেশনিভ (সাঃ পঃ), কৈশিক (ঐ), কৈশী (ঐ) ; অতি সরু। *Noun.* 1. A fine vessel or canal ; সূক্ষ্ম নাড়ী বা নালী বিশেষ, কৈশিক নালী (সাঃ পঃ)। 2. One of the smallest vessels connecting the arteries and veins ; ধমনী এবং শিরাসংযোজক অতি ক্ষুদ্রতম নাড়ী বিশেষ, শরীরের অভ্যন্তরস্থ কেশের ন্যায় সূক্ষ্ম সূক্ষ্ম নাড়ী, কৈশিকা (হঃ চঃ)। **—lar'-i-ty,** *n.* **Capillary attraction, Capillary repulsion**—কৈশিক নালীতে তরল পদার্থের উথান পতন, কৈশিকাকর্ষণ (সাঃ পঃ), কেশাকর্ষণ (হিঃ কোঃ), কেশনিরাকরণ (হিঃ কোঃ), কৈশিক বিপ্রকর্ষণ।

căp'-ĭ-tăl, *n.* (*Arch.*) The head or upper portion of a column ; স্তম্ভের শীর্ষ বা উর্দ্ধ ভাগ, বোধিকা (রাঃ রাঃ)।

căp'-ĭ-tăl, *adj.* & *n.* 1. Relating to the head ; মস্তক-সম্বন্ধীয়। 2. Involving loss of life ; punishable by death ; as, *capital* sentence ; প্রাণহানিঘটিত ; বধদণ্ডার্হ, বধদণ্ডযোগ্য, প্রাণদণ্ডার্হ। 3. Vitally injurious ; fatal ; as, *capital* error ; সাংঘাতিক ; মারাত্মক। 3. First in importance ; chief ; as, a *capital* article in religion ; metropolitan ; as, a *capital* town or city ; মুখ্য ; প্রধান ; রাজধানীস্বরূপ। 5. (*Colloq.*) Excellent ; first class ; as, *capital* singer or player ; (কথিতভাষায়) চমৎকার ; সবার সেরা। 6. Original ; principal ; as, *capital* stock or fund ; মূলস্বরূপ, পুঁজিস্বরূপ ; আসল। *Noun.* 1. The seat of governmet ; the head city of any country ; রাজধানী ; কোন দেশের সর্ব্বশ্রেষ্ঠ নগর। 2. Money or wealth employed in trade, manufactures, etc. ; মূলধন, পুঁজি, ধনমূল (অঃ), ধন (যাজ্ঞঃ), আসল, পরিপণ, নীবী (অমরঃ)। 3. (*Fig.*) Means of influence or of increasing one's power ; as, to make a *capital* out of something ; প্রভাব বা ক্ষমতা বৃদ্ধির উপায়। 4. Capital letters (see below). **—ly,** *adv.* **Capital letter**—ইংরাজী বড় হাতের অক্ষর। **Capital offence**—প্রাণদণ্ডার্হ অপরাধ। **Capital punishment** — প্রাণদণ্ড, বধদণ্ড, মৃত্যুদণ্ড, চরমদণ্ড। **Circulating** or **floating capital**—শ্রম-শিল্প ইত্যাদির কার্য্যে যে কাঁচা মাল ব্যবহৃত হয় এবং শ্রমজীবী প্রভৃতিকে যে বেতন বা টাকা দেওয়া হয়, ভ্রমণশীল বা প্লবমান মূলধন, মূল উপাদান, চলপুঁজি (হিঃ কোঃ), অস্থায়ী পুঁজি (ঐ)। **Fixed capital**—(যন্ত্র ইমারত প্রভৃতি) স্থায়ী মূলধন, স্থায়ী পুঁজি (হিঃ কোঃ), অচল পুঁজি (ঐ)। **To live on one's capital**—পুঁজি ভাঙ্গিয়া খাওয়া। **To make capital out of**—To turn to advantage; সুবিধা করিয়া লওয়া, ইষ্টসিদ্ধির উপায় করিয়া লওয়া। **To speak in capitals**—To speak with emphasis; জোরের সহিত বলা।

căp′-i-tăl-ism, *n.* The possession of capital; the system under which capitalists flourish; ধনস্বামিত্ব, মূলধনাধিকারিত্ব; যে ব্যবস্থাধীনে ধনস্বামিগণ উত্তোরোত্তর শ্রীবৃদ্ধি প্রাপ্ত হন।

căp′-i-tăl-ist, *n.* One who has money for investment, usually a man of large property which is employed in business; পুঁজিওয়ালা (হিঃ কোঃ), মহাজন, ধনস্বামী (কাশিঃ), ধনী।

căp′-i-tăl-ize *v. t.* **1.** To convert into or use as capital; মূলধনে পরিণত করা, মূলধনস্বরূপ ব্যবহার করা। **2.** To estimate or assess the present value of an income or annual payment; as, to *capitalize* pension, rents, etc.; আয় বা বার্ষিক দেয় অর্থের বর্ত্তমান মূল্য হিসাব বা আদায় করা। **—i-za′-tion,** *n.*

căp′-i-tāte, —tāt-ĕd, *adj.* (*Bot.*) **1.** Having a distinct or round head; (উদ্ভিদ্-বিদ্যা) বর্ত্তুল-শিরা। **2.** (*Bot.*) With clustered flowers, etc.; (উদ্ভিদ্-বিদ্যা) গুচ্ছিত পুষ্পবিশিষ্ট।

căp-i-tā′-tion *n.* **1.** Numeration by the head; মস্তক হিসাবে গণনা। **2.** A tax or imposition upon each head or person; laying of a tax of so much per head; প্রত্যেক ব্যক্তির উপর নির্দ্ধারিত মাথট বা কর; জনপ্রতি নির্দ্দিষ্ট কর স্থাপন। **Capitation grant**—কতিপয় বিশেষ সর্ত্ত-পালনে সম্মত প্রত্যেক ব্যক্তিকে সরকার কর্ত্তৃক নির্দ্দিষ্ট সংখ্যক মুদ্রা-প্রদান।

Căp′-i-tŏl, *n.* **1.** The temple of Jupiter, at Rome, built on the Capitoline hill, where the Senate met; রোমনগরীস্থ ক্যাপিটলাইন পর্ব্বতোপরি নির্ম্মিত জুপিটার দেবতার মন্দির। উক্ত মন্দিরে সেনেট্‌সভার অধিবেশন হইত। **2.** The building in which the Congress of the United States meets; also the building in which the legislature of a state holds its session; মার্কিণ যুক্তরাজ্যের মহাসমিতির অধিবেশন-গৃহ; মার্কিণ যুক্তরাজ্যের অন্তর্ভুক্ত কোন কোন রাজ্যের ব্যবস্থাপক সভার অধিবেশন-গৃহ। **—to-line,** *adj.* **Capitoline games**—জুপিটার দেবতার সম্মানার্থ রোমনগরীতে প্রতিবর্ষে মহাসমারোহে সম্পাদিত মল্ল-ক্রীড়া প্রভৃতি।

că-pit′-ū-lar (-lêr), *adj.* **1.** Of an ecclesiastical chapter; যাজকসভা-সংক্রান্ত। **2.** (*Bot.*) Growing in small heads, as the dandelion; (উদ্ভিদ্-বিদ্যা) শিরোনিভ (সাঃ পঃ)। **3.** (*Physiol.*) Of a terminal protuberance of bone; (শারীর-বিজ্ঞান) অস্থির মস্তকাকার প্রবর্দ্ধন সম্বন্ধীয়। **—la-ry,** *n.* A collection of civil and ecclesiastical laws, esp. of the Frankish Kings; রাজকীয় বা যাজকীয় বিধি-সংগ্রহ (বিশেষতঃ ফ্রাঙ্ক নৃপতিগণের)।

că-pit′-ū-lāte, *v. i.* To surrender on certain conditions, drawn up under various heads; as, the Irish after holding out a week, *capitulated*; কতিপয় বিশেষ সর্ত্তে সমর্পণ করা, সন্ধিসর্ত্তে সমর্পণ করা। **—la′-tion,** *n.* **1.** The act of surrendering to an enemy upon stipulated terms or condition; an agreement; condition; বিশেষ সর্ত্তাধীনে শত্রুহস্তে সমর্পণ; চুক্তি; করার, সর্ত্ত। **2.** The treaty or instrument containing the conditions of surrender; সমর্পণের সর্ত্ত সম্বলিত সন্ধি বা সন্ধি-পত্র।

cā′-pŏn, *n.* & *v. t.* A castrated cock; ছিন্ন-মুষ্ক কুক্কুট, মুর্গীর খাসী, খাসীমোরগ। **—ize,** *v. t.* To castrate as a fowl; মুর্গী প্রভৃতি ছিন্নমুষ্ক করা।

căp-ō-nier′ (-nēr), *n.* A covered passage across the ditch of a fort; দুর্গপরিখামধ্যস্থ প্রচ্ছন্ন পথ।

că-pŏt′, *n.* & *v. t.* A winning of all the tricks of cards at the game of piquet, and scoring forty; তাসক্রীড়া বিশেষে প্রতিপক্ষের সমস্ত তাস জিতিয়া লওন। ***Verb t.*** To win all the tricks from, at piquet; উক্ত ক্রীড়ায় সমস্ত তাস জিতিয়া লওয়া।

că-pote′ (-pōt), *n.* A soldier's or traveller's, etc. long cloak with hood; সৈনিক, ভ্রমণকারী, প্রভৃতির মস্তকাবরণসমন্বিত সুদীর্ঘ প্রাবরণ বিশেষ।

căp′-ric-ă-cid, [*L. caper,* goat] *n.* A fatty acid obtained from butter, cocoanut oil, etc. having a slightly goat-like smell; নবনীত, নারিকেল তৈল প্রভৃতি হইতে প্রাপ্ত বসাময়, ঈষৎ ছাগ-গন্ধী অম্ল বিশেষ।

că-price′ (-prēs), **1.** An unaccountable sudden change of mind or conduct; a fancy; a whim; a freak; চিত্তচাঞ্চল্য, চপলতা; সখ; খেয়াল; মর্জ্জি। **2.** Capricious habit or disposition; as, the folly and *caprice* of the present age; চপলস্বভাব, অস্থিরচিত্ততা, অব্যবস্থিতচিত্ততা।

că-pri′-cious (-shŭs), *adj.* Guided by whim; fickle; inconstant; irregular: "The lower animals are *capricious* in their affections, aversions and sense of beauty;" খেয়ালের বশ; অস্থির-চিত্ত, চঞ্চল-স্বভাব,

চঞ্চলচিত্ত, অব্যবস্থিতচিত্ত ; অস্থির, চপল ; অনিয়মিত। **—ly,** *adv.* **—ness,** *n.*

Căp′-ri-cŏrn, *n.* **1.** (*Astron.*) The tenth sign of the zodiac ; (জ্যোতির্বিজ্ঞান) মকর রাশি, আকোকের (সাঃ পঃ)। **2.** A southern constellation represented by a figure with its forepart like a goat and hindpart like a fish ; দক্ষিণনভোমণ্ডলস্থ তারা-প্রকোষ্ঠ বিশেষ। **Tropic of Capricorn**—See TROPIC.

căp-ri-fi-cā′-tion, *n.* A process intended to accelerate the ripening of the fig and to improve the fruit by subjecting them to puncture by wild fig gall-insects ; বন্য আঞ্জীর বৃক্ষস্থ লাক্ষা কীটদ্বারা ক্ষুদ্রক্ষুদ্র ছিদ্র করাইয়া আঞ্জীরফল শীঘ্র পাকাইবার এবং ঐ ফলের উৎকর্ষ বিধানের প্রণালী বিশেষ।

căp′-rīn, căp′-rine (-rīn), *adj.* [L. *caper*, goat] Pertaining to a goat ; like a goat ; অজসম্বন্ধীয় ; অজসদৃশ, ছাগ-সদৃশ।

căp′-rine (-rîn), *n.* A substance found in butter which with butyrine and caprone, gives it its peculiar taste and odour ; নবনীতের উপাদানভূত পদার্থ বিশেষ।

căp′-rī-ōle, *n.* & *v. i.* A caper ; a leap or kick without advancing ; ছাগবৎ লম্ফ ; (অশ্বপক্ষে) লম্ফ বা পদাঘাত। ***Verb i.*** To perform a capriole ; to leap ; to caper ; উক্তপ্রকার লম্ফ প্রদান করা ; লম্ফদেওয়া ; ছাগবৎ লম্ফ প্রদান করা।

căp′-rōne, *n.* A flavouring oil from butter ; নবনীত হইতে প্রাপ্ত তৈল বিশেষ--ইহাদ্বারা নবনীত স্বাদবিশিষ্ট হয়।

Căp′-si-cŭm, *n.* **1.** A genus of plants producing hot capsules and seeds ; the Guinea-Pepper ; the chillies ; বিভিন্ন প্রকার মরিচ-জাতীয় বৃক্ষের সাধারণ নাম ; গিনিদেশের মরিচ ; লঙ্কামরিচ, লঙ্কা। **2.** (*l. c.*) The prepared fruit ; মরিচের আচার প্রভৃতি। ***Capsicum frutescens***—লঙ্কা-মরিচ (বেলঃ)। ***Capsicum grossum***—কাফ্রীমরিচ (বেলঃ)।

căp-sīze′, *v. t., i.* & *n.* To upset or overturn, as a ship, boat, etc. ; উল্টাইয়া দেওয়া, বিপর্য্যস্ত করা। ***Verb i.*** To be upset or capsized ; as, take care the boat does not *capsize* ; উল্টাইয়া যাওয়া। ***Noun.*** An upset ; an overturn ; বিপর্য্যাস ; উল্টানি।

căp′-stăn, *n.* A movable upright block of timber round which a rope or coil is made to coil when raising an anchor or a heavy weight ; পোতাগ্রস্থিত ঘূর্ণনশীল কাষ্ঠনির্ম্মিত যন্ত্রবিশেষ। দণ্ডদ্বারা এই যন্ত্রে

Capstan.

রজ্জু-কুণ্ডলিত করিয়া নোঙ্গর প্রভৃতি ভারি জিনিষ উত্তোলিত করা হয়। **To man the capstan**—নোঙ্গর প্রভৃতি তুলিবার জন্য উক্ত যন্ত্রের কাছে নাবিকদিগকে প্রস্তুত রাখা। **To rig the capstan**—উক্তযন্ত্রের কোঠরসকলে দণ্ড সংযোজনপূর্ব্বক উহাকে পরিচালনার্থ প্রস্তুত করা।

căp′-sūle, *n.* **1.** (*Bot.*) A dry many-seeded seed-vessel which opens by valves ; এক প্রকার শুষ্ক বহুবীজপূর্ণ বীজাধার (পক্কাবস্থায় যাহার খোলকের ভিন্ন ভিন্ন খণ্ডসকল ফাটিয়া ছড়াইয়া পড়ে), বীজকোষ, বীজাধার, উপপেটক (সাঃ পঃ), নীরস ফল (বিশ্বঃ)। **2.** (*Anat.*) A membranous envelope or sac ; (শারীরসংস্থান-বিদ্যা) থলির ন্যায় ঝিল্লী (হঃ চঃ), কোষ-বন্ধনী (জাহিঃ)। **3.** (*Chem.*) A small, shallow saucer of clay or porcelain, for evaporating, etc. ; (রসায়ন-শাস্ত্র) বাষ্পীকরণ প্রভৃতি কার্য্যোপযোগী ক্ষুদ্র চীন বা মৃণ্ময় পাত্র। **4.** (*Med.*) A small gummy envelope for nauseous medicines ; (ভৈষজ্য-শাস্ত্র) ঘৃণাকারজনক বটীকাদির আঠালো পদার্থে নির্ম্মিত আবরণ বিশেষ। **5.** (*Mil.*) The shell of a metallic cartridge ; (সামরিক শাস্ত্র) ধাতুনির্ম্মিত টোটার বহিরাবরণ। **6.** A metallic cap or cover for the mouth of a bottle ; বোতলের ধাতুনির্ম্মিত টোপর বা ঢাক্‌নিবিশেষ। **—su-lar,** *adj.*

Capsule.

căp′-tain (-tăn), *n.* **1.** One who has authority over others ; a chief ; a leader ; অধ্যক্ষ ; কর্ত্তা, সর্দ্দার, দলপতি, চাঁই (*Colloq.*) ; নেতা, নায়ক। **2.** One skilled in war ; an experienced commander ; a great soldier ; as, foremost *captain* of his time ; সমর-কুশল ব্যক্তি, যুদ্ধবিদ্যাবিশারদ ব্যক্তি ; অভিজ্ঞ সেনানায়ক ; লব্ধপ্রতিষ্ঠ সৈনিক পুরুষ। **3.** (*Army*) The military officer who commands a company of infantry, cavalry or artillery ; (স্থল-সৈন্য) সৈন্যাধ্যক্ষ (মেজর ও ল্যাফ-ট্যানেণ্টএর মধ্যবর্ত্তী উপাধিধারী)। **4.** (*Navy*) An officer in the navy commanding a ship of war ; the commander of a vessel ; (নৌ-সৈন্য) রণপোতাধ্যক্ষ ; পোতপরিচালক। **5.** A master or commander of a merchant vessel ; বাণিজ্যপোতাধ্যক্ষ, নাখোদা (রাধাকুঃ), দরিয়াসারং (ঐ)। **6.** The foreman of a body of workmen ; শ্রমজীবিগণের অগ্রণী বা নেতা। **7.** The head-boy of the highest class ; সর্ব্বোচ্চ শ্রেণীর সর্ব্বপ্রথম ছাত্র। **8.** The head of any number of persons engaged in any game or sport ; ক্রীড়কদিগের অগ্রণী। **—cy,** *n.* The rank, post, or commission of a captain ; সৈন্যাধ্যক্ষত্ব, রণপোতাধ্যক্ষত্ব। **—ship,** *n.* **1.** The rank or condition of a captain ; সৈন্যাধ্যক্ষত্ব। **2.** Skill in military affairs ; সামরিক বিষয়ে পারদর্শিতা, সমরকৌশল। **—less,** *adj.* **Captain-General** — The commander-in-chief of an army ; প্রধান সেনাপতি। **To come captain Stiff over a person**—To behave arrogantly towards any one ; কাহারো প্রতি উদ্ধত ব্যবহার করা।

căp'-tain (-tān), *v. t.* To be the captain of ; to lead ; as, who will again *captain* the team ; অধ্যক্ষ হওয়া ; পরিচালনা করা।

căp'-tion, *n.* **1.** The act of seizing ; specially, a legal arrest ; ধরণ ; গ্রেপ্তার। **2.** (*Law*) A certificate attached to, or written on, a document, stating when, where, and by what authority, it was taken, found or executed ; (আইন) দলীলে সংলগ্ন বা দলীলের উপর লিখিত নিদর্শন পত্র। ইহাতে কখন, কোন্ স্থানে এবং কাহার আদেশবলে দলীলটী গৃহীত, প্রাপ্ত এবং সম্পন্ন হইয়াছে— তৎসমস্ত বর্ণিত থাকে। **3.** (*U. S.*) The heading of a chapter, articles, etc. ; (মার্কিণ যুক্তরাজ্যে) পরিচ্ছেদ বা প্রবন্ধাদির শিরোনাম।

căp'-tious (-shus), *adj.* **1.** Fallacious; sophistical ; as, a *captious* and tempting question ; ensnaring; ভ্রমসঙ্কুল, ভ্রান্তিপূর্ণ ; কুতর্কপূর্ণ, বাক্‌ছলপূর্ণ ; ফাঁদে ফেলানোগোছের, ঠকানিয়া। **2.** Ready to take offence or catch at faults ; fond of taking exception ; as, a *captious* and suspicious age ; পরদোষ-গ্রহণ-তৎপর, ত্রুটীগ্রহণপটু; ছিদ্রান্বেষী, দোষদর্শী, ছিদ্রানুসন্ধায়ী, ছলগ্রাহী। **—ly,** *adv.* **—ness,** *n.*

căp'-ti-vate, *v. t.* To charm ; to engage the affections of ; to fascinate ; মোহিত করা, মুগ্ধ কর ; চিত্তরঞ্জন করা, চিত্তহরণ করা, মনোহরণ করা ; বিমুগ্ধ করা। **—vat-ing,** *adj.* Fascinating ; winning ; মোহময়, মনোমুগ্ধকর, মুগ্ধকারী ; হৃদয়হারী, চিত্তহারী (বাংস্থঃ), মনোহারী, চিত্তবিমোহন

căp'-tive, *n.* & *adj.* **1.** A person or animal taken prisoner, especially in war ; one kept in confinement or under restraint ; one who is unable to escape ; যুদ্ধে বন্দীকৃত মনুষ্য বা অশ্বাদি পশু ; বন্দী ; পলায়নে অসমর্থ ব্যক্তি। **2.** (*Fig.*) One who is captivated ; "Venus' *captive* and my slave ;" (লক্ষণায়) বিমুগ্ধ ব্যক্তি। ***Adj.*** **1.** Made prisoner in war ; kept in bondage or confinement ; যুদ্ধে বন্দীকৃত ; বন্দীভূত। **2.** (*Fig.*) Subdued by love ; charmed ; (লক্ষণায়) প্রেমপাশ-বদ্ধ ; বিমুগ্ধ। **3.** Of or like a prisoner ; as, *captive* state ; serving to confine ; as, *captive* chains ; বন্দিবিষয়ক, বন্দিতুল্য ; বন্দিকারী। **—tiv'-i-ty,** *n.* Imprisonment ; bondage ; বন্দিদশা ; বন্ধনাবস্থা, দাসত্ব। **Captive balloon**—রজ্জুদ্বারা ভূমির সহিত সংবদ্ধ ব্যোমযান বিশেষ।

căp'-tor (-têr), *n.* [*L.* a catcher (of animals)] One who takes by force, as a prisoner or prize ; especially one who takes a prize at sea ; (যুদ্ধে) বন্দিগ্রাহী, লুণ্ঠিত দ্রব্য গ্রহণকারী ; বিশেষতঃ সমুদ্র মধ্যে শত্রু পক্ষীয় রণপোত-গ্রহণকারী।

căp'-türe, *n.* & *v. t.* **1.** The act of seizing or taking possession of (by force or stratagem) ; arrest ; as, the *capture* of an enemy, vessel or a criminal ; বন্দীকরণ ; গ্রেপ্তার। **2.** The thing or person seized ; a prize ; বন্দীকৃত বস্তু বা ব্যক্তি ; ধৃত রণপোত। ***Verb t.*** To make captive ; to seize as a capture ; বন্দী করা, পাকড়ান (*Colloq*) ; (যুদ্ধে) লুণ্ঠিত দ্রব্যস্বরূপ গ্রহণ করা, শত্রুর রণপোত ধরা।

Căp'-ü-chin (-shēn), *n.* **1.** A Franciscan monk so called from the hood he wears ; খৃষ্টীয় সন্ন্যাসী সম্প্রদায়ভুক্ত ব্যক্তি বিশেষ। **2.** (*l. c.*) A woman's cloak and hood ; স্ত্রীলোকের গাত্র বা মস্তকাবরণ। **Capuchin monkey, Capuchin pigeon**—এক জাতীয় বানর বা কপোত। ইহাদের শিরোদেশের রোম বা পালক মস্তকাবরণের মত শোভা পাইয়া থাকে।

caput mortuum—[*L.* dead head] *n.* **1.** A term for residuum of any substance after distillation or sublimation ; তলানি, ছাঁকনা, গাদ। **2.** (*Fig.*) Worthless residue ; (লক্ষণায়) অসার অবশিষ্টভাগ।

căp-ȳ-bä'-ră, *n.* A large South American rodent allied to the Guinea-pig ; ব্রাজিল দেশীয় ইন্দুরবৎ দক্ষিণ আমেরিকাবাসী বৃহৎকায় দন্তর জন্তু বিশেষ।

câr, *n.* **1.** A small two-wheeled carriage drawn by one horse ; a cart ; একাশ্ববাহিত ক্ষুদ্র শকটবিশেষ, দুই চাকার গাড়ী ; শকট। **2.** (*Poetic*) A chariot ; as, the *car* of Juggarnath ; (কবিতায়) বিমান, রথ, স্যন্দন। **3.** A carriage for running on rails ; a tram-car (England) ; রেলের উপর চলিবার উপযোগী গাড়ী ; ট্রামগাড়ী (ইংলণ্ডে)। [ইংলণ্ডে শুধু ট্রামগাড়ী বুঝায়। আমেরিকায় ট্রামগাড়ী ও রেলগাড়ী উভয়ই বুঝায়।] **4.** The part of a balloon in which æronauts sit ; ব্যোমযানের যে অংশে গগনপর্য্যটকগণ উপবেশন করিয়া থাকেন। **Car-man**—Carter ; শকটচালক। **The car festival**—রথযাত্রা।

Că-răb'-i-doe (-dē), *n. pl.* A large family of beekes ; গোবরে পোকার "বর্গ" বিশেষ।

căr'-ă-bīne, *n.* See CARBINE.

căr-ă-bi-neer', —nier' (-nēr), *n.* A soldier armed with a carbine ; ক্ষুদ্র বন্দুকধারী সৈনিক [৬ সংখ্যক Dragoon Guards সৈন্যদলকে *Carabineers* বলা হয়।]

căr′-ă-căl, *n.* A kind of lynx, a native of Africa and Asia ; আরণ্য মার্জ্জারবিশেষ।

Caracal.

că̆r′-ă-cōle, –cōl, *n.* & *v. i.* **1.** A half turn which a horseman makes either to the right or left ; (অশ্বারোহিকর্ত্তৃক) বাম বা দক্ষিণদিকে (অর্দ্ধ) পার্শ্বাবর্ত্তন। **2.** A winding stair ; ঘুরানো সিঁড়ি, পাক-সিঁড়ি। ***Verb i.*** To execute half turns to the right or left ; to wheel ; বাম বা দক্ষিণদিকে (অর্দ্ধ) পার্শ্বাবর্ত্তন করা ; ঘুরা।

că-rafe′ (-răf), *n.* A glass water-bottle for the table ; ভোজনকালে মেজের উপর রক্ষিত জলপূর্ণ কাচের বোতল।

căr′-ă-mĕl, *n.* **1.** Burnt sugar used for colouring spirits, wines, etc. ; সুরা, সুরাসার, প্রভৃতি রঞ্জনার্থ দগ্ধ শর্করা। **2.** A kind of confectionary ; একপ্রকার মিষ্টদ্রব্য।

că-răm-bō′-lă, *n.* The acrid pulpy fruit of a small East Indian tree ; কামরাঙ্গা।

căr′-ă-pāce, *n.* The thick shell which protects the body of the tortoise or turtle, crab, etc. ; কূর্ম্ম, কুলীরক (কাঁকড়া) প্রভৃতির খোল, কূর্ম্ম-পৃষ্ঠ, ঢাল (সাঃ পঃ)।

căr′-ăt, *n.* **1.** A measure of weight for precious stones, about $3\frac{1}{5}$ grains ; বহুমূল্য প্রস্তরাদি পরিমাপের মাত্রা বিশেষ (প্রায় ৩$\frac{১}{৫}$ গ্রেণ), রক্তিকা (প্রকৃতপক্ষে ক্যারেটের অর্দ্ধভাগ)। **2.** A measure of the purity of gold, pure gold being 24 carats ; বিশুদ্ধ স্বর্ণকে ২৪ ক্যারেট ধরিয়া তত্তুলনায় স্বর্ণের বিশুদ্ধতার মাত্রা বিশেষ। (As this is 18 carat gold—অর্থাৎ এই স্বর্ণে ২৪ ভাগের ১৮ ভাগ খাঁটি সোণা এবং ৬ ভাগ খাঁইদ আছে ; অর্থাৎ ৩ ভাগ বিশুদ্ধ সোণা ও এক ভাগ খাঁইদ আছে।) [আফ্রিকা দেশজাত carob বৃক্ষের বীজকে carat বলে। এই বীজ প্রথমতঃ স্বর্ণ ও পরে হীরকের ওজনে ব্যবহৃত হইত। স্বর্ণের ওজনে নির্দ্দিষ্ট পরিমাণ (যথা এক পাউণ্ড অথবা এক আউন্স ট্রয়) স্বর্ণের $\frac{১}{২৪}$ ভাগকে carat কহে। খাইদের পরিমাণ-নির্ণয়ের জন্য নির্দ্দিষ্ট পরিমাণ স্বর্ণ ২৪ ভাগে বিভক্ত করা হয়,—যথা ২২ ক্যারেট স্বর্ণে $\frac{২}{২৪}$ ভাগ খাইদ আছে।]

căr′-ă-văn, *n.* **1.** A company of merchants, pilgrims, etc., travelling together for mutual security in crossing desert parts of Asia and Africa ; আফ্রিকা এবং এশিয়া মহাদেশের মরুপ্রদেশ অতিক্রমকালে নির্বিঘ্নতার জন্য সম্মিলিত বণিক্ বা ভ্রমণকারীর দল, বণিক্-কটক (দশঃ), বণিক-সার্থ (ভাগঃ), সার্থ (মঃ ভাঃ), শকট-সার্থ (পাতঃ পাণিঃ)। **2.** A large covered cart or waggon for the conveyance of wild beasts for exhibition ; a large close carriage or any kind of house on wheels ; "I have never seen such a fat boy in or out of a *caravan* ;" প্রদর্শনীর জন্য বন্যজন্তুসমূহ বহনোপযোগী আচ্ছাদিত বৃহৎ শকটবিশেষ ; প্রকাণ্ড আচ্ছাদিত শকট বা চক্রোপরিস্থাপিত গৃহবিশেষ। **–eer′,** *n.* The leader of a caravan ; বণিক্-কটক-নায়ক, সার্থবাহন (কথা সঃ), সার্থপাল (মার্কঃ পুঃ) সার্থপতি (হেমঃ পরিঃ)। **–van′-sa-ry, –van′-se-ra, –van′-se-rai,** *ns.* A kind of inn in eastern countries where caravans put up for the night ; (পারস্য প্রভৃতি দেশে) বণিক্-কটকের রাত্রি যাপনের জন্য সরাইবিশেষ, পান্থনিবাস, পথিকাশ্রম (আঃ বঃ)।

căr′-ă-vĕl, căr′-vĕl, *n.* (*Hist.*) **1.** A kind of light sailing-vessel, chiefly Spanish and Portuguese, of 15th and 17th centuries একপ্রকার হাল্কা জাহাজ। **2.** A small fishing vessel ; মৎস্যশিকারার্থ ক্ষুদ্র পোতবিশেষ।

căr′-ă-wāy, *n.* **1.** A biennial aromatic plant and its seeds : কাওরা (যোঃ), কারোয়া, বিলাতি জিরা (ঐ) শা-জিরা (Indian), উদ্গার-শোধন (ভাব প্রঃ)। **2.** A cake or sweet-meat, containing caraway seeds ; বিলাতি জীরার বীজমিশ্রিত পিষ্টকবিশেষ। **Black caraway**—কালিজিরা (ওয়াট্)।

câr′-bīde, *n.* A compound of carbon with a metal ; ধাতুমিশ্রিত অঙ্গার।

câr′-bīne, căr′-ă-bīne, *n.* (*Mil.*) **1.** A short fire-arm for cavalry use ; (সামরিকশাস্ত্র) অশ্বারোহী

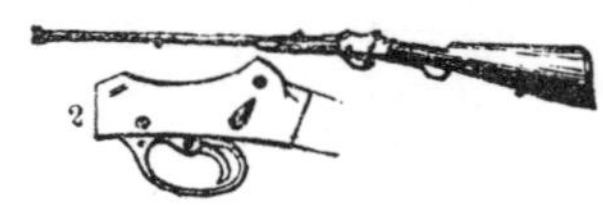

Carbine, Carbine lock.

যোদ্ধৃগণের ক্ষুদ্র বন্দুকবিশেষ, লঘুবন্দুক। **2.** (*Mil.*) A soldier armed with a carbine ; (সামরিকশাস্ত্র) লঘু বন্দুকধারী সৈনিক। **–bi-neer′,** *n.*

câr-bŏl′-ĭc, *adj.* Pertaining to, or derived from, carbon ; অঙ্গার-সম্বন্ধীয়, অঙ্গারজাত। **Car′-bo-lize,** *v. t.* **Carbolic acid**—আলকাতরা হইতে প্রস্তুত সংক্রামকরোগের বীজ-নাশক অম্লবিশেষ।

câr′-bŏn, *n.* **1.** A non-metallic element present in all organic compounds ; অঙ্গার (সাঃ পঃ), কারবন (মণীঃ)। **2.** (*Electr.*) A charcoal pencil used on one form of electric lighting ; (তাড়িতবিজ্ঞান) একপ্রকার বিদ্যুদ্-দীপে ব্যবহৃত অঙ্গারময় সূচী বিশেষ। **–bo-na′-ceous, –bon′-ic,** *adjs.* Pertaining to or composed of carbon ; অঙ্গার সম্বন্ধীয়, অঙ্গার-রচিত। **–if′-er-ous,** *adj.* Producing or containing carbon or coal ; অঙ্গারগর্ভ। **–i-za′-tion,** *n.* The act or process of carbonizing; অঙ্গারোৎপাদন। **—ize,** *v. t.* **1.** To make or convert into carbon; অঙ্গারোৎপাদন করা, অঙ্গারে পরিণত করা। **2.** To reduce to charcoal or coke; অঙ্গার বা কোক কয়লায় পরিণত করা। **3.** To cover papers with carbon for taking copies; প্রতিলিপি গ্রহণের জন্য কাগজ অঙ্গারলিপ্ত করা। **Carbon-paper**—পত্রের প্রতিলিপি গ্রহণার্থ অঙ্গারলিপ্ত কাগজ, কারবন কাগজ। (*Photo.*) **Carbon-printing**—(আলোকচিত্রণে) স্থায়ী আলোকচিত্র মুদ্রণের পদ্ধতি বিশেষ, কারবনচিত্রণ। **Carbonic acid**—অঙ্গারাম্ল (সাঃ পঃ), অঙ্গারক দ্রাবক (ঐ)। **Carboniferous age, era** or **period**—অঙ্গারযুগ (অর্থাৎ যে যুগ বা অব্দে বর্ত্তমানে অঙ্গারাবস্থাপ্রাপ্ত উদ্ভিদ্ সকল বিদ্যমান ছিল)। **Carboniferous system** or **formation**—যে প্রস্তরপরম্পরা দ্বারা অঙ্গারযুগের স্তর সকল রচিত হইয়াছে (কয়লা, চূণাপাথর, বালুকাপ্রস্তর প্রভৃতি)।

câr-bō-nâ′-rō, *n.* (*Pl.* -RI.) A member of a secret political society established in Italy in the beginning of the last century with the object of setting up a republic; উনবিংশ শতাব্দীর প্রথম ভাগে ইতালীদেশে প্রজাতন্ত্র প্রতিষ্ঠার উদ্দেশ্যে যে রাজনীতিক গুপ্ত সমিতি সংগঠিত হইয়াছিল তাহার সভ্য। [Carbonaro শব্দের ব্যুৎপত্তিগত অর্থ অঙ্গারদাহক (charcoal burners)]

câr′-bŏn-āte, *n.* & *v. t.* A chemical compound formed by the union of carbonic acid with a base; অঙ্গারাম্ল ও কোন প্রকার ভস্মের সংযোগে উৎপন্ন রাসায়নিক মিশ্র পদার্থ বিশেষ। ***Verb t.*** To form into carbonate; উক্তপ্রকার মিশ্রপদার্থে পরিণত করা। **—at-ed,** *adj.* **Carbonate of Lime**—খড়ি। **Carbonate of Potash**—যবক্ষার (রঃ প্রঃ)। **Carbonate of Soda**—সজ্জিকাক্ষার (রঃ প্রঃ) সাজি (ওয়াট্), সাজিমাটী (ঐ)।

câr′-boy, *n.* A large coloured glass-bottle protected with a basket-work; বেত্র বংশাদিনির্ম্মিত আবরণে রক্ষিত বৃহৎ রঙ্গীন কাচের বোতল, ইহাতে গন্ধকদ্রাবক প্রভৃতি দ্রব্য রক্ষিত হয়। [From Pers. *qurabh*, Bengali form কার্ব্বা।]

câr′-bun-cle (-bŭng-), **1.** A red precious stone (formerly of many kinds, *e. g.* ruby); লোহিতবর্ণ মণি, লাল (ফঃ হিঃ), সর্পমণি (মঃ উঃ)। (পূর্ব্বে বিভিন্নপ্রকার রক্তবর্ণ প্রস্তর বুঝাইত;—যথা পদ্মরাগ।) **2.** (*Now*) The name given to almandine, a variety of garnet,—cut with concave surfaces (it has a dark colour); (বর্ত্তমানে) বৈক্রান্ত মণিবিশেষ। **3.** (*Med.*) A malignant tumour or ulcer differing from a boil in having no central core; a pimple on the nose or face; (ভৈষজ্য-শাস্ত্র) পৃষ্ঠাঘাত প্রভৃতি প্রদাহ ও দূষিত ব্রণ (হঃ চঃ), দাহিকা (ঐ); বৃথব্রণ। **—cled, —cu-lar,** *adjs.* (*Carbuncular eruption*—জাবিনী (সাঃ পঃ)। **Carbuncle of the scalp**—ইরিবিল্লী (সাঃ পঃ)।

câr′-bū-rĕt, *v. t.* To combine (any element) chemically with carbon; to impregnate with carbon; অঙ্গারের সহিত (যে কোন মৌলিক পদার্থের) রাসায়নিক সংমিশ্রণ করা; অঙ্গার দ্বারা সম্পূরিত করা। **—tor, —ter,** *ns.*

câr′-că-nĕt, *n.* A collar of jewels; মণিময় কণ্ঠবেষ্টিকা, মণিমালা।

câr′-cass, —case, (-kăs), *n.* **1** A dead body; a corpse; (now used of human body only in contempt); as, to pamper his own *carcass*; (অবজ্ঞাচ্ছলে) শব; মৃতদেহ। **2.** The body of a slaughtered animal without head, limbs, or offal; নিহত জন্তুর মস্তক, পদ এবং অন্যান্য অব্যবহার্য্য অংশ ব্যতিরিক্ত দেহাংশ। **3.** (*Fig.*) The skeleton or framework; as, the *carcass* of a house or ship; (লক্ষণায়—পোত, গৃহ প্রভৃতির) পঞ্জর, কঙ্কাল, ঠাট, কাঠাম। **5.** (*Mil.*) A kind of fire-ball from gun for igniting buildings; as, a discharge of *carcasses* and bombshells; (সামরিকশাস্ত্র) প্রাসাদাদি প্রজ্বালিত করিবার জন্য দাহ্যপদার্থপূর্ণ কামানের গোলাবিশেষ।

câr-ci-nŏl′-ō-ġy, *n.* The department of zoology dealing with crustaceans; প্রাণি-বিজ্ঞানের যে বিভাগে কর্কট প্রভৃতি বর্ম্মধারী জীবগণের বিষয় আলোচিত হইয়া থাকে।

câr-ci-nō′-mă, *n.* A cancer; শর্করার্ব্বুদ (সাঃ পঃ)।

cârd, *n.* & *v. t.* A toothed instrument for combing wool or flax and for raising nap on cloth; শণ বা পাট আঁচড়াইবার চিরুণী বিশেষ, ঊর্ণামার্জ্জনী। ***Verb t.*** To comb with a card; to cleanse; as, to *card* wool: to *card* a horse; আঁচড়ান, পরিষ্কার করা; ধুনা।

cârd, *n.* **1.** A piece of pasteboard with painted figures and points in it for playing with (also called PLAYING CARD.); তাস **2.** A visiting card; কাহারো সহিত সাক্ষাৎ করিবার জন্য নাম ধামাদি লিখিত বা মুদ্রিত যে স্থূল কাগজখণ্ড ব্যবহৃত হইয়া থাকে, নামপত্র (আঃ বঃ)। **3.** The programme of any sports, especially races; ক্রীড়াদির কার্য্যতালিকা, বিশেষতঃ ঘোড়দৌড়ের কার্য্যতালিকা। **4.** A flat piece of thick paper or pasteboard for various purposes; as, post-*card*; বিভিন্ন কার্য্যোপযোগী স্থূল কাগজখণ্ড। **5.** A printed or written notice, rules, etc., for hanging in window or on wall; প্রাচীর বা গবাক্ষে টাঙ্গাইবার জন্য লিখিত বা মুদ্রিত বিজ্ঞাপন, নিয়মাবলী প্রভৃতি। **6.** (*Naut.*) A circular sheet of paper on which the points of the compass are marked; (নৌ-বিদ্যা) যে বৃত্তাকার

কাগজখণ্ডে দিক্‌সকল চিহ্নিত হইয়া থাকে, দিগ্‌ভাগ-পত্র। **Card-basket**—A basket for keeping visiting cards; নামপত্র রক্ষণার্থ পেটক বিশেষ। A basket made of card-board; স্থূলকাগজ নির্ম্মিত পেটক বিশেষ। **Card-board** — স্থূলকাগজ বিশেষ। **Card-case**—নামপত্র রাখিবার আধার বিশেষ। **Card-sharper**—যে ব্যক্তি তাসখেলায় প্রতারণা করে। **Card-table**—তাস খেলিবার মেজ। **A great card**—A big wig; a man much talked about and admired; হোমড়াচোমড়া লোক; বড় লোক। **A knowing card**—A sharp fellow; চালাক লোক, সেয়ানা। **A loose card**—A worthless fellow; অকর্ম্মণ্য লোক। **A queer card**—An eccentric person; মাথা-পাগলা লোক, অদ্ভুত লোক। **A sure card**—An undertaking which will be sure to succeed; যে কার্য্যে সিদ্ধিলাভ সুনিশ্চিত। A person sure to command success; যে ব্যক্তির সফলতালাভ সুনিশ্চিত। **House of cards**—তাসের ঘর (অসার এবং বিঘ্নসঙ্কুল ব্যবস্থা, ব্যবসায় প্রভৃতি সম্পর্কে ব্যবহৃত হয়)। **That was my best trump card** — My best chance; তাহা আমার ইষ্টসিদ্ধির প্রধান সুযোগ ছিল। **The card**—The correct thing; what is expected; as, 10s. is about *the card*; সঠিক বিষয়; প্রত্যাশিত বস্তু বা বিষয়। **The card of one's house**—The man of mark; প্রতিষ্ঠাবান ব্যক্তি, গণ্যমান্য ব্যক্তি। **To count on one's cards**—To anticipate success under the circumstances; অবস্থা বিবেচনায় সিদ্ধিলাভের আশা করা। **To cut cards**—তাস কাটা। **To deal cards**—তাস দেওয়া বা বাঁটা। **To go in with good cards**—To have excellent grounds for expecting success; কৃতকার্য্যলাভের আশা করার প্রকৃষ্ট কারণ বর্ত্তমান থাকা। **To have the cards in one's hands**—To have everything under one's control; সব বিষয় নিজের আয়ত্তাধীন থাকা। **To make a mislead at cards**—বাঁটে গণ্ডগোল করা। **To play one's best card**—To do that which one hopes most likely to command success; যাহাতে ইষ্টসিদ্ধির সমধিক সম্ভাবনা সেইরূপ কার্য্য করা। **To play one's cards badly** — To manage or project unskillfully; আনাড়ীর মত কায করা। **To play one's cards well**—To make no error; to act shrewdly; নির্ভুলভাবে কায করা; বিচক্ষণের মত কায করা। **To show one's card**—To let out one's plans; হাতের তাস বিপক্ষকে দেখাইয়া ফেলা, কাহারও মতলব বা অভিসন্ধি ফাঁস করিয়া ফেলা। **To speak by the card**—To speak with elegance and to the point; সুষ্ঠুরূপে ও প্রাসঙ্গিকভাবে কথা বলা। **To shuffle the cards**—তাস ভাঁজা, তাসা। **To throw up the cards**—To cease the struggle; to confess defeat; সংগ্রামে বিরত হওয়া; হার মানা।

câr'-dă-mom (-mŭm), *n.* **1.** The capsules of certain tropical plants which form an aromatic spice; এলাচি। **2.** A plant which produces cardamoms; এলাচিগাছ, এলালতা (রঃ)।

câr'-dĭ-ăc, *adj.* & *n.* **1.** (*Anat.*) Of the heart; of the upper orifice of the stomach; as, the *cardiac* arteries; (শারীর-সংস্থান-বিদ্যা) হৃদয় সম্বন্ধীয়; হৃদ্দ্বার (হৃৎপিণ্ডের নিকটবর্ত্তী আমাশয়ের উপরের মুখ) সম্বন্ধীয়। **2.** (*Med.*) Exciting action in the heart, through the medium of the stomach; stimulant; (ভৈষজ্য-শাস্ত্র) হৃৎপিণ্ডের ক্রিয়োত্তেজক (হৃঃ চঃ); বলপ্রদ, দীপন। ***Noun.*** (*Med.*) A heart stimulant; a cordial; (ভৈষজ্য-শাস্ত্র) হৃৎপিণ্ডের বল-বিধায়ক ঔষধ; হৃদ্‌বলদ (সাঃ পঃ)।

câr'-dĭ-găn, *adj.* & *n.* A knitted woollen jacket named after the Earl of Cardigan; একপ্রকার পশমের বুনা জামা।

Cardinal.

câr'-dĭ-năl, *adj.* & *n.* Fundamental; chief; principal; as, the *cardinal* doctrine in one's faith; মৌলিক মুখ্য; প্রধান। ***Noun.*** **1.** One of the ecclesiastical princes who constitutes the pope's council; রোমান ক্যাথলিক ধর্ম্ম-সম্রাট পোপের সভাসদ্‌। **2.** A woman's short cloak with a hood; স্ত্রীলোকের শিরচ্ছদবিশিষ্ট শ্লথ পরিচ্ছদ বিশেষ।

Cardinal's hat.

—ate, —ship, *ns.* **—ly,** *adv.* Fundamentally; মূলতঃ, প্রধানতঃ। **Cardinal bird**—আমেরিকার ঘোর রক্তবর্ণ গায়ক পক্ষি-বিশেষ। **Cardinal flowers**—See LOBELIA. **Cardinal numbers**—মুখ্যাঙ্ক (হিঃ কোঃ), ১, ২, ৩ ইত্যাদি একাদি সংখ্যা। **Cardinal points**—চারিদিক (উত্তর, দক্ষিণ, পূর্ব্ব, পশ্চিম), কাষ্ঠা (মঃ ভাঃ)। **Cardinal virtues**—Justice, prudence, temperance and fortitude; মুখ্যধর্ম্ম চতুষ্টয়,—ন্যায়নিষ্ঠা, বিজ্ঞতা, মিতাচার, সহিষ্ণুতা।

cârd'-ĭng, *n.* The process of preparing staple for spinning; (তূলা) ধুনন।

câr'-dĭ-ō-grăph, *n.* An apparatus for recording the motions of the heart; হৃৎস্পন্দনজ্ঞাপক যন্ত্র। **—graph'-ic**, *adj.*

câr′-di-oid (-ŏyd), *n.* A heart-shaped algebraic curve ; বীজগণিতের হৃদয়াকার বক্রবিশেষ, হৃদয়াকার (সাঃ পঃ)।
câr-di-ŏm′-ĕ-trȳ, *n.* Measurement of the heart as, by percussion or auscultation ; অঙ্গুলীবিঘাতন, আকর্ণনযন্ত্র সহযোগে কিম্বা কর্ণসংযোগে হৃৎপিণ্ডের অবস্থা নির্ণয়।
câr-dī′-tis, *n.* Inflammation of the tissues of the heart ; হৃৎপ্রদাহ (হঃ চঃ), হৃৎপিণ্ডের প্রদাহ (ঐ)।
câr′-dŏl, *n.* A yellow oily liquid extracted from the shell of the cashew-nut; কাজু বাদামের খোসা হইতে প্রস্তুত পীতবর্ণ তৈলাক্ত তরল পদার্থ বিশেষ।
câr-doon′, *n.* The prickly artichoke used in cookery and as a salad ; রন্ধনে ব্যবহৃত সকণ্টক হাতিচোখ বিশেষ।
câr-dŏph′-ă-ġi, *n.* (*Pl.*) Thistle eaters ; donkeys ; কণ্টকগুল্মভোজী ; গর্দ্দভ সকল।
câr-dü′-ŭs, *n.* Thistle ; কণ্টকগুল্ম।
câre, *n.* & *v. i.* **1.** A burdensome sense of responsibility ; anxiety ; concern ; গুরুতর দায়িত্ব ; উদ্বেগ ; উৎকণ্ঠা, ভাবনা, যত্ন, চিন্তা। **2.** Charge ; management ; "The *care* of all the churches ;" ভার ; পরিচালন, তত্ত্বাবধারণ, নির্ব্বাহ, তত্ত্বাবধায়কতা, রক্ষণাবেক্ষণ। **3.** Caution ; heed ; pains ; "Thank thee for thy *care* and honest pains ;" সতর্কতা, সাবধানতা ; অবধানতা, মনোযোগ, দৃষ্টি, খবরদারি ; শ্রম, কষ্ট। **4.** The object of watchful attention ; "Is she thy *care* ?" সবিশেষ মনোযোগের সহিত তত্ত্বাবধানের বিষয়। ***Verb i.*** **1.** To be anxious or solicitous ; to be concerned or interested ; to have regard ; উদ্বেগপূর্ণ হওয়া, চিন্তিত হওয়া, ভাবা, চেষ্টিত হওয়া, যত্নবান হওয়া ; দৃক্পাত করা, ভ্রূক্ষেপ করা, গণ্য করা ; গ্রাহ্য করা। **2.** To be inclined or disposed ; to like ; as, not *caring* to observe the wind ; উন্মুখ হওয়া, প্রবণ হওয়া ; পছন্দ করা। **Care-cloth**—রোমান ক্যাথলিক গির্জ্জাতে নব-বিবাহিত ব্যক্তির গাত্র যে সূক্ষ্ম ক্ষৌমবস্ত্রে আবৃত করা হয়। **Care-crazed**—চিন্তাজর্জ্জরিত। **Care-laden**—চিন্তাভারাক্রান্ত। **Care-taker**—যে ব্যক্তি কোন বিষয়ের ভার গ্রহণের জন্য নিযুক্ত হয়,—বিশেষতঃ যে ব্যক্তি কাহারও অনুপস্থিতিকালে তাহার বাটীর রক্ষণাবেক্ষণকার্য্যে নিযুক্ত হয়। **Care-worn**—চিন্তাক্লিষ্ট। **Care killed the cat**—বিড়ালের ৯টী প্রাণ আছে বলিয়া কথিত, কিন্তু গুরুতর চিন্তা ও উদ্বেগে তাহাও নষ্ট হয়। **Care of**—(Abbrev. c. o.) হাতে, মারফত। **Not to care a bit, fig, pin, straw**—To care little or nothing ; ভ্রূক্ষেপ না করা, অনুমাত্রও গ্রাহ্য না করা। **To care for**—To have regard for ; মান্য, গ্রাহ্য করা, গণ্য করা। **To take care**—To be careful or cautious ; সাবধান হওয়া, সতর্ক হওয়া। **To take care of**—To look after with care ; তত্ত্বাবধান করা, রক্ষণাবেক্ষণ করা, খবর লওয়া।
câre′-fûl, *adj.* **1.** Full of care ; anxious ; ভাবনাকুল ; চিন্তামগ্ন, উদ্বেগপূর্ণ, উদ্বিগ্ন। **2.** Filling with care or solicitude ; painful ; ভাবনাপীড়িত, সচিন্ত, চিন্তাকুল ; যন্ত্রণাপ্রদ। **3.** Painstaking ; cautious ; যত্নপর ; সাবহিত, অবহিত, সতর্ক, সাবধান, হুসিয়ার (*Colloq.*)। **4.** Attentive to support or protect ; রক্ষণাবেক্ষণে মনোযোগী। **5.** Showing or done with care or attention ; as, *careful* consideration ; মনোযোগসূচক, সযত্নে বা সাবধানে সম্পাদিত। **—ly,** *adv.* **—ness,** *n.*
câre′-less (-lĕs), *adj.* **1.** Free from care or anxiety ; hence cheerful ; উদ্বেগশূন্য, নিশ্চিন্ত, ভাবনাহীন, বীতচিন্ত, বে-পরওয়া (*Colloq.*) ; উৎফুল্ল। **2.** Undisturbed ; অনুদ্বেজিত, অবিক্ষুব্ধ। **3.** Having no care ; negligent ; যত্নশূন্য ; অমনোযোগী, সহেল। **4.** Without thought or purpose ; as, a *careless* expression ; চিন্তাশূন্য, উদ্দেশ্যবিহীন, উদাস। **—ly,** *adv.* **—ness,** *n.*
că-reen′ (-rēn), *v. t.* & *i.* To turn on one side, as a ship, for the purpose of repairing, cleaning etc. ; জীর্ণ-সংস্কার বা পরিষ্কার করিবার উদ্দেশ্যে (জাহাজ) কাৎ করিয়া রাখা। ***Verb i.*** To incline to one side, as a ship under a press of sail ; (পাইল ভরে জাহাজের মত) কাৎ হওয়া। **—age,** *n.* **1.** The act of careening a ship ; জীর্ণ-সংস্কারাদির জন্য জাহাজ কাৎ করিয়া রাখন। **2.** (*Naut.*) Expense of careening ships ; (নৌ-বিদ্যা) (জীর্ণসংস্কারাদির জন্য) জাহাজ কাৎ করার খরচ। **3.** A place for careening ; জীর্ণসংস্কারের জন্য জাহাজ কাৎ করিবার জায়গা।
că-reer′ (-rēr), *n.* & *v. i.* **1.** A rapid running ; speed in motion ; "Full merrily hath...this *career* been run ;" দ্রুতধাবন ; বেগ। **2.** General course of action or movement ; course or progress through life ; "Brief, brave and glorious was his young *career* ;" কার্য্যকলাপের সাধারণ গতি ; জীবন-গতি, জীবন-ব্যাপার। **3.** The flight of a hawk about 120 yards; বাজপক্ষীর ন্যূনাধিক ১২০ গজ পরিমিত উড্ডয়ন। ***Verb i.*** To run or move rapidly ; as, *careering* gayly over the curling waves ; দ্রুতবেগে ধাবিত হওয়া, দ্রুতবেগে চলা।
că-ress′ (-rĕs), *n.* & *v. t.* An act of endearment ; an embracing or touching with tenderness ; as, "Wooed her with soft *caresses* ;" সোহাগ, আদর ; সুকোমল স্পর্শ বা আলিঙ্গন, আশ্লেষ, পরিরম্ভ, লালন (মঃ উঃ)। ***Verb t.*** To treat with tokens of fondness or affection ; to touch or speak to in a loving manner ; আদর করা ; প্রেম বা

সোহাগভরে কথা বলা বা স্পর্শ করা। **–ing,** *adj.* **–ing-ly,** *adv.*

că'-rĕt, *n.* A mark thus (∧) to show in written compositions that something has been omitted in a line ; লিখিত রচনার কোন পংক্তিতে কোন কথা ছাড় পড়িয়াছে—ইহা প্রদর্শন করিবার জন্য ইত্যাকার (∧) চিহ্ন বিশেষ, পুরক (আঃ বঃ)।

că'-rĕx, *n.* A genus of plants including the sedges ; নদী বা সাগরতীরে জাত নানাপ্রকার তৃণের সাধারণ নাম।

câr'-gō, *n.* The lading or freight of a ship or other vessel ; জাহাজ প্রভৃতির বোঝাই মাল।

căr'-gōōse, *n.* The crested grebe ; একপ্রকার পক্ষী।

că-ri-ā'-mă, *n.* A long-legged South American bird which preys upon snakes ; দক্ষিণ আমেরিকাবাসী দীর্ঘপদ অহিভুক্ পক্ষিবিশেষ।

Căr'-ib, *n.* One of the aboriginal inhabitants of the Southern West Indian islands ; পশ্চিমভারতীয় দ্বীপ-পুঞ্জের প্রাচীন অধিবাসী। **–be'-an,** *adj.* **–bee,** *n.*

căr'-i-bou (-bô), *n.* The American reindeer ; আমেরিকার বন্যহরিণ।

carica papaya—পেপে (বেলঃ)।

căr'-i-că-türe, *n.* & *v. t.* A grotesque representation of a person or thing by over-emphasis on characteristic traits ; (pictorial, literary or mimetic) ; হাস্যোদ্দীপক সাদৃশ্য প্রদর্শন, বীভৎস চিত্র, বিকৃত চিত্র, বিকৃতি, উপহাস্য চিত্র (আঃ বঃ), ব্যঙ্গ-চিত্র, নকসা, ব্যঙ্গ-কাব্য। ***Verb t.*** To represent with ridiculous exaggeration ; to burlesque ; হাস্যোদ্দীপক চিত্রাদিদ্বারা সাদৃশ্য প্রদর্শন করা, ব্যক্তি বা বস্তুর হাস্যোদ্দীপক অনুরূপ প্রদর্শন করা ; হাস্যোদ্দীপক বা বিদ্রূপাত্মক অভিনয় করা, ব্যঙ্গ-চিত্র অঙ্কিত করা। **–tu-rist,** *n.*

căr'-i-cous (-cŭs), *adj.* Resembling a fig ; as, *caricous* tumour ; আঙ্গীর ফলবৎ।

că'-ri-ēs, *n.* (*Med.* & *Bot.*) Decay of the bones or teeth, or of vegetable tissue ; (ভৈষজ্য-শাস্ত্র এবং উদ্ভিদ্-বিদ্যা) অস্থিক্ষয়, দন্তক্ষয়, অস্থির ক্ষতরোগ (জাহিঃ), কৃমি-দন্ত (সাঃ পঃ), উদ্ভিদের তন্তুক্ষয়।

că'-ri-ous (ŭs), *n.* Decayed (esp. of bones, teeth) ; ক্ষয়িত, ক্ষয়প্রাপ্ত, গলিত, জীর্ণ, (বিশেষভাবে দন্ত ও অস্থি-সম্পর্কে)।

căr'-il-lón, *n.* **1.** A set of bells rung either by hand or mechanically ; হস্ত বা যন্ত্রদ্বারা বাদিত ঘন্টা-শ্রেণী। **2.** An air played on bells ; ঘন্টাশ্রেণীতে বাদিত গানের গৎ। **3.** A small musical instrument producing bell-like effects ; ঘন্টাবৎ নিনাদী ক্ষুদ্র বাদ্য-যন্ত্রবিশেষ।

că-rī'-nă, *n.* (*Bot.*) A keel-like structure in a plant or animal ; উদ্ভিদ্ অথবা জন্তুর নৌমেরুদণ্ডবৎ দেহাংশ বিশেষ, নৌমেরুদণ্ড (সাঃ পঃ)। **–nal,** *adj.* **Car'-i-nate, Car'-i-nat-ed,** *adjs.*

căr'-i-ōle, *n.* A small open carriage ; ক্ষুদ্র অনাবৃত শকটবিশেষ।

carissa carandas—করমচা (বেলঃ)।

cârk'-ing *adj.* Distressing ; perplexing ; as, *carking* cares ; বিড়ম্বনাজনক, সন্তাপজনক ; হতবুদ্ধিতাজনক।

cärl, carle (cărl), *n.* **1.** A rude man ; a fellow ; রূঢ় ব্যক্তি ; ইতর ব্যক্তি। **2.** A kind of hemp ; একপ্রকার শণ। **3.** A quantity of food (*Pl.*) ; কিছু পরিমাণ খাদ্য।

câr'-lin, câr'-line (-lîn), *n.* An old woman ; বৃদ্ধা স্ত্রীলোক।

câr'-line (-lîn), *n.* A kind of thistle ; একপ্রকার কন্টক গুল্ম।

Câr'-list, *n.* A supporter of the claims of Don Carlos and his heirs to the Spanish throne ; যে ব্যক্তি ডন-কার্লোস এবং তদীয় উত্তরাধিকারিগণের স্পেনদেশীয় রাজ-সিংহাসনে দাবী সমর্থন করে।

câr'-lock (-lŏk), *n.* A Russian isinglass obtained from the bladder of the sturgeon ; মৎস্য বিশেষের পটকা হইতে প্রস্তুত রুশিয়া দেশের শিরিস বিশেষ।

Câr'-lō-vin'-gi-ăn, *adj.* & *n.* Relating to the second French dynasty founded by Charlemagne ; সার্লেমেন কর্তৃক প্রতিষ্ঠিত দ্বিতীয় ফরাসী রাজবংশ সম্পর্কীয়। ***Noun.*** One of the second French dynasty founded by Charlemagne ; সার্লেমেন কর্তৃক প্রতিষ্ঠিত দ্বিতীয় ফরাসীরাজবংশের অন্যতম নৃপতি। **Carlovingian dynasty**—সম্রাট সার্লেমেন কর্তৃক প্রতিষ্ঠিত রাজবংশ।

Câr-lȳl'-ĭsm, *n.* Principles, literary manner, and mannerism of Carlyle ; কার্লাইলের মত, সাহিত্যিক রীতি এবং উৎকট রীতিপ্রিয়তা। **–e-an, –i-an,** *adjs.*

căr'-mâ-gnole (-nîöl), *n.* **1.** A song and dance popular during the first French Revolution ; প্রথম ফরাসী বিপ্লবকালে প্রচলিত জনপ্রিয় নৃত্যগীত বিশেষ। **2.** The dress worn by the Jacobins during the Revolution ; ফরাসীবিপ্লব-সময়ে বিপ্লব-পন্থিগণ যে পরিচ্ছদ পরিধান করিত। **3.** The wearer of such a dress ; a violent revolutionist : উক্ত পরিচ্ছদধারী ; প্রচণ্ড বিপ্লববাদী। **4.** The bombastic reports of the French successes in battle ; ফরাসীগণের যুদ্ধে জয় সম্বন্ধে বাগাড়ম্বরপূর্ণ সংবাদ।

câr'-măn, *n.* See CAR.

Câr'-mĕl-īte, *n.* **1.** (*Eccl. Hist.*) A member of a mendicant order of friars (established in Mount Carmel in the 12th century) ; শ্বেতাম্বর খৃষ্টীয় সন্ন্যাসি-সম্প্রদায় বিশেষ। **2.** A fine woollen stuff usually grey ; (সাধারণতঃ) ধূসরবর্ণের পশমী বস্ত্র।

Câr'-mĕl-īte, Câr'-mĕl-in, *adjs.* Pertaining to the order of Carmelites ; উক্ত সন্ন্যাসি-সম্প্রদায় সম্পর্কীয়।

câr-min'-ă-tive, *adj.* & *n.* Curing flatulence ; warming ; as, *carminative* hot seeds ; বায়ুনাশক (সাঃ পঃ), (উদরের) বায়ুনিঃসারক, বাতঘ্ন, বায়ুঘ্ন ; তাপজনক, উষ্ণতাসঞ্চারক। ***Noun.*** A medicine to remedy colic and flatulence ; বায়ুদোষনাশক ঔষধ, উদরবায়ুনিঃসারক ঔষধ।

câr′-mīne, *n.* & *adj.* **1.** A rich red colour with a shade of purple ; অলক্তবর্ণ, আলতার মত লাল রঙ্। **2.** A crimson pigment from cochineal ; লাক্ষা হইতে প্রস্তুত রক্তবর্ণ রঞ্জন পদার্থ বিশেষ, অলক্ত, আলতা, যাবক। ***Adj.*** Of that colour ; অলক্তবর্ণ। **—min′-ic,** *adj.*

câr′-mŏt, *n.* (*Alchem*) The matter of which the philosopher's stone was believed to be composed ; (মধ্যযুগের রসায়ন-শাস্ত্র) স্পর্শমণির মূল উপাদান।

câr′-nāge, *n.* **1.** The flesh of slain animals ; dead bodies ; নিহত জন্তুর মাংস ; শবরাশি। **2.** A great slaughter or massacre ; as, made great *carnage* of them ; বহু নরহত্যা, জনহত্যা।

câr′-năl, *adj.* **1.** Sensual ; fleshy ; sexual ; as, not sunk in *carnal* pleasure ; ইন্দ্রিয়জ ; দৈহিক ; কামজ, পাশবিক। **2.** Not spiritual ; worldly ; অনাত্ম, পার্থিব ; সাংসারিক, ঐহিক। **—ism, —nal′-i-ty,** *ns.* **—ize,** *v.t.* **—ly,** *adv.* **Carnal desire**—কাম। **Carnal knowledge**—সংসর্গ (আঃ বঃ)।

câr′-năl-līte, *n.* A pink-colourd mineral obtained from the Strassforth salt mines ; ষ্ট্রেসফর্থনগরীস্থ লবণখনি হইতে প্রাপ্ত লোহিতবর্ণ খনিজ পদার্থ বিশেষ।

câr-năs′-si-ăl, *adj.* & *n.* (*Anat.*) Adapted to eating flesh ; (শারীরসংস্থান-বিদ্যা) মাংসাহারোপযোগী। ***Noun.*** A carnossial tooth ; মাংসকৃৎদন্ত (সাঃ পঃ)।

câr-nā′-tion, *n.* & *adj.* **1.** A rosy pink colour ; গোলাবি রং। **2.** (*Pl.* PAINTING) The flesh-tints ; মাংসবর্ণ। ***Adj.*** Of rosy pink colour ; গোলাবিবর্ণ। **—tionel,** *adj.*

câr-nā′-tion, *n.* (*Bot.*) Cultivated kinds of Clove pink ; (উদ্ভিদ্-বিদ্যা) মাংসবর্ণ পুষ্প বিশেষ, গুলনার (ফঃ হিঃ)।

Carnation.

câr-nau′-bă (-nă-ŏ-), *n.* (*Bot.*) The Brazilian waxpalm ; (উদ্ভিদ্-বিদ্যা) ব্রাজিলদেশীয় তালজাতীয় বৃক্ষবিশেষ।

câr′-nĕl, *adj.* Chaotic ; shapeless ; বিশৃঙ্খলাপূর্ণ ; অবয়বশূন্য।

căr-nĕl′-iăn, *n.* (*Min.*) A variety of chalcedony, of a deep red, flesh-red, or reddish-white colour ; (খনিজ-বিদ্যা) গাঢ়লোহিতবর্ণ, মাংসবর্ণ, কিম্বা রক্তাভ শ্বেত, সীসমণি বিশেষ, রুধিরাক্ষ।

câr′-nē-ous (-ŭs), *adj.* Fleshy ; as, *carneous* fibres ; মাংসময়।

câr′-ney (-nî), *n.* A disease of horses ; অশ্বরোগবিশেষ।

câr-ney′ (-nî), *n.* & *v. t.* (*Slang*) Flattery ; (ইতর-ভাষায়) তোষামোদ। ***Verb t.*** To flatter ; তোষামোদ করা।

câr-ni-fĕx, (*Antiq.*) A public executioner at Rome ; (প্রত্নতত্ত্ব) প্রাচীন রোমনগরীর জল্লাদ বা ঘাতক।

câr′-ni-fȳ, *v. t.* & *i.* To form into flesh ; মাংসে পরিণত করা, মাংসল করা। ***Verb i.*** To form flesh ; মাংসে পরিণত হওয়া। **—fi-ca′-tion,** *n.* The act or process of carnifying ; মাংসে পরিণত করণ।

câr′-ni-văl, *n.* **1.** A season of festivity and revelry observed in Roman Catholic countries just before Lent ; রোমানক্যাথলিকদিগের মহা আড়ম্বরপূর্ণ ধর্ম্মোৎসব। **2.** (*Fig.*) A riotous revelry ; gala ; "Love in the sacred halls held *carnival* ;" (লক্ষণায়) তুমুল কোলাহল, মদ্যপানোৎসব ; আড়ম্বরপূর্ণ উৎসব।

Câr-nĭv′-ō-ră, *n.* (*Pl.*) An order of flesh-eating animals ; মাংসাশী জন্তুর বর্গ, ক্রব্যাদ (সাঃ পঃ), মাংসাশী, মাংসাদ।

câr-ni-vōre, *n.* Carnivorous animal or plant ; মাংসাশী জন্তু বা উদ্ভিদ্।

câr′-nĭv-ō-rous (-rŭs), *adj.* Feeding on flesh ; মাংসাশী।

câr′-nȳ, *n.* & *v. t.* See CARNEY.

căr′-ŏb, *n.* A leguminous tree or its fruits ; একজাতীয় বৃক্ষ অথবা তজ্জাত ফল।

căr′-ŏl, *n. v. t.* & *i.* **1.** A joyous song ; warble ; as, it was the *carol* of a bird ; আনন্দ-গীতি ; কাকলী, কূজন। **2.** A song of praise or devotion ; as, a Christmas or Easter *carol* ; স্তুতি-গীতি, বন্দনাগীতি, ভজনগান। ***Verb t.*** To praise or celebrate in song ; মহিমাকীর্ত্তন করা, স্তুতি গান করা। ***Verb i.*** To sing, esp. to sing joyfully ; গান করা, আনন্দোৎফুল্ল কণ্ঠে গান করা।

Căr′-ō-line (-lîn), *n.* **1.** Of Charlemagne ; সার্লেমেন্ সম্বন্ধীয়। **2.** Pertaining to Charles I & II of England ; ইংলণ্ডের নৃপতি প্রথম ও দ্বিতীয় চার্লস সম্বন্ধীয়।

Carolingian, *n.* See CARLOVINGIAN.

căr-ō-lĭt′-ic, —lȳt′-, *adj.* (*Arch.*) Adorned with sculptured leaves or branches ; (স্থপতি-বিদ্যা) উৎকীর্ণ পত্র বা শাখাবিমণ্ডিত।

că-rŏt′-id, *n.* & *adj.* One of the two great arteries conveying blood to the head ; মস্তকে শোণিত বহনকারী গ্রীবার বৃহৎ ধমনীদ্বয়ের অন্যতর। ***Adj.*** (also, **-al**) Pertaining to or near the carotid ; উক্ত ধমনী-সংক্রান্ত বা সন্নিহিত।

căr'-ö-tĭn, *n.* (*Chem.*) A red tasteless substance, extracted from the carrot ; (রসায়ন-শাস্ত্র) গাজর হইতে নিষ্কষিত রক্তবর্ণ এবং আস্বাদ-বিহীন পদার্থ বিশেষ।

că-rous'-ăl (-rowz-), *n.* A feast or festival ; a noisy drinking bout ; ভোজ, মহোৎসব ; মহাকোলাহলপূর্ণ মদ্যপানোৎসব।

că-rouse' (-rowz), *n.* & *v. i.* A drinking match ; a carousal ; মদ্যপানে প্রতিযোগিতা ; কোলাহলপূর্ণ মদ্যপানোৎসব। ***Verb i.*** To drink freely and heartily ; to revel ; অতিরিক্ত মদ্য পান করা ; মদ্য পানোৎসব করা।

cârp, *n.* A fresh water herbivorous fish ; রোহিতাদি মৎস্য।

cârp, *v. t.* To censure ; to find fault petulantly, (usually followd by *at*) ; "And *at* my actions *carp* or catch ;" নিন্দা করা ; দোষ ধরা, খুঁত ধরা, ছিদ্রান্বেষণ করা।

câr'-păl, *adj.* Pertaining to the carpus ; মণিবন্ধ সম্বন্ধীয়।

cârp'-êr, *n.* One who carps : a caviller ; দোষদর্শী ; ছলগ্রাহী।

cârp'-ing, *adj.* & *n.* Cavilling ; captious ; as, *carping* critic ; দোষদর্শী ; ছিদ্রান্বেষী। ***Noun.*** The act of cavilling ; a cavil ; দোষ-দর্শন ; দোষদৃষ্টি।

car'-pe-di-em, *n.* (*L.*) Enjoy the present day ; improve the time ; দিন গেলে আর ফিরিয়া আসিবে না, ইহা ভাবিয়া যতটা পার ভোগ করিয়া লও ; বর্ত্তমান সময়ে যাহা পার সুবিধা করিয়া লও।

câr'-pĕl, *n.* A simple pistil or one of the parts of a compound pistil ; ফুলাণু (সাঃ পঃ), কিঞ্জল্ক (ঐ)। **—la-ry,** *adj.*

câr'-pĕn-têr, *n.* & *v. i.* A worker in timber ; a framer or builder of houses and ships ; সূত্রধর, সূত্রকার (রঃ), তক্ষক, বর্দ্ধকি (মঃ উঃ), ছুতার (*Colloq.*) ; গৃহনির্ম্মাতা, পোতনির্ম্মাতা। ***Verb i.*** To do a carpenter's work ; ছুতারের কাজ করা। **—ing,** *n.* **—try,** *n.* The art of cutting, framing, or joining, timber ; কাষ্ঠ-শিল্প, তক্ষ-কর্ম্ম (আশ্বঃ শ্রৌঃ)। **Carpenter-ant**—একজাতীয় পিপীলিকা বা মধুমক্ষিকা,—যাহারা বৃক্ষগাত্রে ছিদ্র করিয়া বাস করে।

căr'-pĕt, *n.*& *v. t.* **1.** A thick fabric, usually woollen, used for covering floors, stairs, etc. ; গালিচা, দুলিচা (বিশ্বঃ), চিত্রাস্তরণ (আঃ বঃ), শতরঞ্চ (কার্পাসনির্ম্মিত)। **2.** A soft smooth covering resembling or suggesting carpet ; "The grassy *carpet* of this plain ;" গালিচার মত মসৃণ এবং কোমল আস্তরণ বিশেষ। ***Verb t.*** **1.** To cover with a carpet ; গালিচামণ্ডিত করা। **2.** (*Colloq.*) To call a (servant) into the parlour, etc. to be reprimanded ; to reprimand ; "They had done nothing ! Why are they *carpeted* ?" (কথিত ভাষায়) (চাকরকে) তিরস্কার করিবার উদ্দেশ্যে কোঠায় ডাকিয়া আনা ; ধমক দেওয়া, তম্বি করা। **Carpet-bag**—ভ্রমণকারিগণের ব্যাগ (পূর্ব্বে গালিচার বস্ত্রে প্রস্তুত হইত)। **Carpet-bagger**—যে নির্ব্বাচন-প্রার্থী বা রাজনীতিক আন্দোলনকারী দেশময় বক্তৃতা করিয়া পর্য্যটন করে। **Carpet-bed**—নানা নমুনায় রোপিত খর্ব্ব বৃক্ষাদি-রচিত বাগানের কেয়ারীবিশেষ। **Carpet-dance** — অনিয়মিত নাচের মজলিস্। **Carpet-friend**—কপট বন্ধু। **Carpet-knight**—যে বীরের বীরত্ব রণক্ষেত্রের পরিবর্ত্তে বৈঠকখানাতেই প্রদর্শিত হয়, রমণীরঞ্জক পুরুষ। **Carpet-monger**—সুখপ্রিয় ব্যক্তি, আরামপ্রিয় ব্যক্তি। **Carpet-walk**—তৃণাচ্ছাদিত ভ্রমণ-পথ। **Carpet-way**—কর্ষিতক্ষেত্রের চতুষ্পার্শ্বস্থিত সবুজ তৃণাবৃত ভূখণ্ড। **To be on the carpet**—To be under consideration ; to be the subject of deliberation ; বিবেচনাধীন থাকা ; বিবেচনার বিষয়ীভূত হওয়া। **To come or be brought on the carpet**—To be introduced ; প্রবর্ত্তিত হওয়া।

căr-phŏl'-ŏ-ğŷ, *n.* Delirious fumbling with bed-clothes ; বিকৃত মস্তিষ্ক ব্যক্তির মত শয্যাবস্ত্র হাতড়ান।

câr-pö-ğĕn'-ic, *adj.* Productive of fruit or causing fruit to be developed ; ফল-প্রসূ, ফল-বর্দ্ধন-কর।

câr'-pŏ-līte, *n.* A fossil fruit ; শিলীভূত ফল।

câr-pŏl'-ŏ-ğŷ, *n.* That branch of botany which deals with seeds of fruits ; বীজ বিজ্ঞান, ফল-বিজ্ঞান। **—gist,** *n.* **—po-log'-i-cal,** *adj.*

câr-pŏph'-ă-gous (-gŭs), *adj.* Living on fruits ; ফলাহারী, ফলভোজী।

câr'-pŭs (*L.*). *n.* The wrist ; মণিবন্ধাস্থি, হাতের কব্জা (সাঃ পঃ)।

car'-rack, *n.* See CARACK.

căr'-ri-age (-rĭj), *n.* **1.** The act of carrying, transporting, or conveying ; বহন। **2.** The expense of carrying ; as, how much does the *carriage* amount to ; বহনের খরচ। **3.** The manner of carrying one's self ; behaviour ; as, a reverend *carriage* ; আকার-প্রকার ; চাল-চলন। **4.** A wheeled vehicle ; যান, শকট, গাড়ী। **5.** Management ; execution ; পরিচালন ; সম্পাদন, পালন। **6.** Passing of Parliamentary motion, etc. ; (পার্লেমেন্টের প্রস্তাব প্রভৃতি) বিধিবদ্ধ হওন। **7.** (*Mil.*) The frame on which a gun is mounted and carried, (gun-carriage) ; (সামরিকশাস্ত্র) কামান স্থাপন এবং বহনোপযোগী কাঠাম বিশেষ। **8.** (*Print.*) The frame which carries the inking-rollers ; (মুদ্রণ) কালির রুলের ঠাট। **9.** (*Mach.*) A portion of a machine which moves and carries an object ; as, the log-*carriage* of a sawing machine ; (যন্ত্র) যন্ত্রের যে অংশ কোন বস্তু বহন বা সঞ্চালন করে। **—a ble,** *adj.* Passable by carriages ; শকটদ্বারা গম্য। **A carriage-and-four**—চারিঘোড়ার গাড়ী। **A carriage-and-pair**—দুই ঘোড়ার

গাড়ী। **Carriage-company, Carriage folk**—গাড়ী ঘোড়া রাখিতে সমর্থ ব্যক্তিবর্গ। **Carriage-stand**—গাড়ীর আড্ডা।

căr′-rĭ-êr, *n.* **1.** One who carries ; a messenger ; বাহক ; দূত, সংবাদ-বাহক। **2.** One who is employed to carry goods ; মুটে। **Carrier-pigeon**—পত্রবাহক কপোত।

car′-ri-ole, *n.* See CARIOLE.

căr′-rĭ-ŏn, *n.* & *adj.* The dead or putrefying body or flesh of an animal ; flesh so corrupted as to be unfit for food ; শব, পশ্বাদির মৃত দেহ ; গলিত মাংস, পূতি মাংস। ***Adj.*** Of or pertaining to dead or putrefying carcasses ; feeding on carrion ; শব, মৃতদেহ বা গলিত-মাংস সম্বন্ধীয় ; গলিত মাংসভোজী, পূতি-মাংসভুক্‌। **Carrion-beetle** — শব ভোজী কীট। **Carrion-crow**—ইয়ুরোপের কাক—ইহারা গলিত শব, কীট, ফল, বীজ প্রভৃতি ভক্ষণ করিয়া থাকে।

căr-rŏn-āde′, *n.* A short long-calibred ship's gun ; বৃহৎ রন্ধ্রবিশিষ্ট খর্ব্বাকৃতি কামান।

căr′-rŏt, *n.* An orange-coloured esculent root ; গাজর (ওয়াট্‌)। **—y,** *n.* & *adj.* Red-hair ; a red-haired person ; রক্তবর্ণ কেশ ; লোহিত-বর্ণ কেশবিশিষ্ট ব্যক্তি। *Adj.* **1.** Like carrot in colour or taste ; বর্ণ বা আস্বাদে গাজরবৎ। **2.** (*Fig.*) Having reddish yellow hair ; রক্তাভ পীত কেশবিশিষ্ট।

căr′-rȳ, *v. t.* & *i.* **1.** To convey or transport, (often with *away* or *off*) ; বহন করা, স্থানান্তরে প্রেরণ করা। **2.** To take or bear with one ; as, to *carry* an unborn child ; সঙ্গে নেওয়া বা ধারণ করা। **3.** To transfer ; as, to *carry* the war from Greece into Asia ; to bring forward, as from one page, column, or book, to another ; স্থানান্তরিত করা ; পৃষ্ঠা, স্তম্ভ বা পুস্তকান্তরে স্থানান্তরিত করা, জের টানা, ইজা দেওয়া। **4.** To convey by force ; to impel ; to conduct ; as, passion and revenge will *carry* them too far ; বল-পূর্ব্বক চালিত করা ; অগ্রে ঠেলা ; চালিত করা, বাহিত করা। **5.** To cause to pass ; to transmit ; as, sound is *carried* in the air ; চালিত করা ; প্রেরণ করা। **6.** To prolong ; to continue ; as, to *carry* a road ten miles farther : to *carry* modesty to excess ; প্রবর্দ্ধিত করা, বাড়ান ; পূর্ব্ববৎ চালাইয়া যাওয়া। **7.** To achieve ; to bring to a successful issue ; to win victory for ; as, to *carry* a point, measure, or resolution : to *carry* an election ; সুসম্পন্ন করা ; কৃতকার্য্যতা সিদ্ধি করা ; জয় লাভ ক[illegible] **8.** To gain ; to win ; as, t[illegible]rry a prize ; পাওয়া ; লাভ করা। **9.** To capture ; as, he will *carry* the island ; বলপূর্ব্বক অধিকার করা, হস্তগত করা। **10.** To contain or involve ; to import ; to show or exhibit ; as, he thought it *carried* something of argument ; ধারণ করা, অন্তর্ভূত করা ; মর্ম্ম প্রকাশ করা ; প্রদর্শন করা। **11.** To manage ; to conduct ; as, to *carry* matters with a high hand ; পরিচালনা করা ; নির্ব্বাহ করা। **12.** To behave strangely (with the reflexive pronouns) ; as, to *carry* oneself insolently ; অদ্ভুত ব্যবহার করা। **13.** To endure weight of ; as, ships *carry* sail ; ভার বহন করা। **14.** To persuade ; to influence by words ; as, he *carried* his audience with him ; প্ররোচিত করা ; কথাদ্বারা বশ করা। ***Verb i.*** **1.** To act as a bearer ; to convey anything ; as, to fetch and *carry* ; বাহকের কায করা ; বহা। **2.** To have the power of projecting a ball to a certain distance ; কোন নির্দ্দিষ্ট দূরত্ব পর্য্যন্ত কন্দুক নিক্ষেপে সমর্থ হওয়া। **3.** (*Hunting*) To run on ground that sticks to the feet ; (মৃগয়া) পায়ে আঠার মত লাগিয়া থাকে এরূপ মাটীতে দৌড়া। **4.** To bear the head in a particular manner, as a horse ; বিশেষভাবে শিরোভঙ্গি করা। **5.** (*Naut.*) To loose (mast, etc.) by breakage ; (নৌ-বিদ্যা) (মাস্তুল প্রভৃতি) ভাঙ্গিয়া আল্গা হওয়া। **—ing,** *n.* **—rier,** *n.* See CARRIER above. **Carry-all**—একাশ্ববাহিত লঘু শকট বিশেষ। **To be carried away by one's feelings**—To be overcome by emotion ; আবেগদ্বারা অভিভূত হওয়া। **To carry all before one**—To overcome all obstacles ; to be completely successful or popular ; সর্ব্বপ্রকার বাধা অতিক্রম করা ; সম্পূর্ণ কৃতকার্য্যতা লাভ করা, জন-প্রিয় হওয়া। **To carry anything too far**—To exceed the proper bounds in anything ; কোন বিষয়ে সঙ্গত সীমা অতিক্রম করা, কোন বিষয়ে মাত্রার বাহিরে যাওয়া। **To carry arms**—(*Mil.*) To serve in the army ; (সামরিকশাস্ত্র) সৈনিকবিভাগে কায করা। To hold a weapon in the position for saluting ; অভিবাদনের জন্য নির্দ্দিষ্টভাবে বন্দুকাদি ধারণ করা। **To carry away**—To carry off ; to abduct ; লইয়া যাওয়া ; (বলে, ছলে, কৌশলে) মনুষ্য হরণ করা। To deprive of self-control ; to charm ; to overpower ; as, to be *carried away* by music ; আত্মহারা করা ; বিমুগ্ধ করা ; অভিভূত করা। (*Naut.*) To break off ; to loose ; (নৌ-বিদ্যা) ভাঙ্গিয়া যাওয়া ; বিচ্যুত হওয়া, খসিয়া যাওয়া। **To carry coals**—To bear injuries ; ক্ষতি সহ্য করা। **To carry coals to New castle**—To take things to a place where they already abound ; তেলা মাথায় তেল দেওয়া, কুবেরকে ধন দান করা। **To carry conviction**—To induce a strong belief as to the truth or otherwise of a thing; কোন বিষয়ের সত্যতা বা অলীকতা সম্বন্ধে দৃঢ় প্রত্যয় জন্মান। **To carry fire in one hand and water in the other**—To say one thing and mean another; to flatter; মনে এক কথা মুখে আর কথা বলা; তোষামোদ করা। **To carry forward**—To convey or conduct forward; সম্মুখের দিকে বাহিত বা চালিত করা। To promote; to advance; উন্নতিসাধন করা; অগ্রসর করা। (*Book-keeping*) To transfer from one page, column, or book, to its successor; (হিসাব) পৃষ্ঠা, স্তম্ভ, বা পুস্তকান্তরে স্থানান্তরিত করা, জের টানা। **To carry it off**—To face through; (অসুবিধাজনক অবস্থা) তাচ্ছিল্য করিয়া সম্মুখীন হওয়া, গ্রাহ্য না করিয়া সম্মুখীন হওয়া। **To carry off**—To remove to a distance; স্থানান্তরিত করা। (*Fig.*) To kill (said of a disease); (লক্ষণায়) বিনাশ করা, ধ্বংসমুখে পাতিত করা। To win, as a prize; পুরস্কারাদি লাভ করা। To help to pass; অতিক্রমে সাহায্য করা। **To carry on**—To manage or conduct; as, to *carry on* trade; চালান, পরিচালনা করা। To help forward; to continue to pursue; as, to *carry on* a design; অগ্রসর করা; অনুসরণ করা, চলা। (*Colloq.*) To behave in a certain fashion; (চলিতভাষায়) কোন প্রকার বিশেষভাবে চলা। **To carry one's point**—To gain what one contends for in a controversy; তর্কস্থলে প্রতিপক্ষকে পরাজিত করিয়া স্বমত প্রবল রাখা। To succeed in one's aim; স্বকীয় লক্ষ্য সাধনে কৃতকার্য্য হওয়া। **To carry out**—To put in practice; to continue to the end; to complete; কার্য্যে পরিণত করা; শেষ পর্য্যন্ত চালান; সম্পাদন করা, সমাপ্ত করা। **To carry out one's bat**—(*Cricket*) To leave the crickets without having been put out; (ক্রীকেট খেলায়) শেষ পর্য্যন্ত না মরা (out না হওয়া)। **To carry over**—To induce to join the other party; অপর পক্ষে যোগদানে প্রবৃত্ত করা। (*Stock-exchange*) To put off a settlement of an account to the next account day; পরবর্ত্তী হিসাবের দিন পর্য্যন্ত হিসাব চুকান স্থগিত রাখা। **To carry sail**—To have the sails spread; পাইল বিস্তার করা। **To carry sword**—To carry it in saluting position; অভিবাদনসূচকভাবে তরবারী ধারণ করা। **To carry the colours**—To serve as an ensign; সেনাবিভাগে পতাকাধারীর কার্য্য করা। **To carry the day**—To win the day or contest; সংগ্রাম বা প্রতিদ্বন্দ্বিতায় জয়লাভ করা। **To carry through**—To bring safely out of difficulties; দায় হইতে উদ্ধার করা, বিপদ্ হইতে পার বা উত্তীর্ণ করা। To complete; সম্পাদন করা, সমাধা করা। **To carry up**—To build or raise higher; পূর্ব্বাপেক্ষা উঁচু করিয়া গাঁথিয়া তোলা। **To carry weight**—To be handicapped in horse racing; ঘোড়দৌড়ে সকল প্রতিযোগিগণের সহিত সমসুবিধা বিশিষ্ট হইবার জন্য শ্রেষ্ঠ প্রতিযোগিগণের কতিপয় বিষয়ে অসুবিধা ভোগ করা। To be of importance; গুরুত্ববিশিষ্ট হওয়া। **To carry with one**—To remember; মনে রাখা।

carse (cârs), *n.* In Scotland, a stretch of alluvial land along the banks of some rivers; স্কট্‌লণ্ড্ দেশে নদীতীরবর্ত্তী পলি-পড়া ভূখণ্ড।

cârt, *n., v.t.&i.* **1.** A two-wheeled vehicle for the conveyance of heavy goods; শকট, গোশকট। **2.** A light business wagon used by bakers, etc.; রুটিওয়ালা প্রভৃতির হালকা গাড়ী। ***Verb t.*** To carry in a cart; উক্ত প্রকার শকটে বহন করা। ***Verb i.*** To carry burdens in a cart; to work with a cart; শকটে মাল বহন করা; শকটদ্বারা কায করা। **—er,** *n.* One who drives a cart; গাড়োয়ান, শকটচালক। **Cart-horse**—শকট বহনোপযোগী অশ্ব। **Cart-house**—গাড়ীর ঘর, যানশালা (রং)। **Cart-ladder**—অধিক পরিমাণ মাল বহনের জন্য যে শকটের অগ্র ও পশ্চাদ্দেশে তাক জুড়িয়া দেওয়া হয়। **Cart-load, Cart-ful**—গাড়ী বোঝাই, বহু পরিমাণ দ্রব্য। **Cart-road**—গো-শকট চলার উপযোগী রাস্তা। **Cart-wheel**—গাড়ীর চাকা। **Cart-wright**—শকট-নির্ম্মাতা। **To put the cart before the horse**—To reverse the right order or allocation of things; পর্য্যায় ব্যতিক্রম করা, আগের কায পরে করা।

cârt, [*F.* a card] *n.* (*Lit.*) A card; a bill of fare at a tavern; স্থূল-কাগজখণ্ড; সাধারণ ভোজনাগারের ব্যঞ্জনাদি ভোজ্যদ্রব্যের তালিকা।

cârt'-äge, *n.* The act or cost of carting; গাড়ী বোঝাই করণ, গাড়ী বোঝাইর খরচ।

carte, quarte, (cârt), [*F.* quarte] A fencing position; অসিক্রীড়ায় অবস্থান বিশেষ।

carte blanche, (*F.*), *n.* **1.** A blank paper signed at the bottom with a person's name, given to another person with permission to superscribe what conditions he pleases; hence, unconditional terms; কোন ব্যক্তির নাম সহি-করা সাদা কাগজ,—এইরূপ কাগজ যে ব্যক্তিকে দেওয়া হয়, সে তাহাতে তাহার ইচ্ছানুরূপ সর্ত্ত লিখিয়া লইতে পারে; অতএব অনিয়মিত সর্ত্ত। [কোন ধনাগারের টাকা প্রদানের আদেশ পত্রে (cheque) দাতা টাকার সংখ্যা উল্লেখ না করিয়া কেবল স্বাক্ষর সংযুক্ত করেন এবং গ্রহীতা সেই আদেশ পত্রে স্বেচ্ছানুরূপ টাকার সংখ্যা লিখিয়া লইতে পারেন,—এরূপ স্থলেও ঐ আদেশপত্র carte blanche বলিয়া অভিহিত হয়।] **2.** Full discretionary power; স্বেচ্ছানুরূপ কার্য্য করিবার পূর্ণ ক্ষমতা।

carte-de-visite, (*F.*), *Lit.* **1.** A visting card; সাক্ষাৎ করিবার

(আত্মপরিচয়জ্ঞাপক) স্থূল কাগজ খণ্ড। **2.** A photographic portrait on a small card ($3\frac{1}{2}'' \times 2\frac{1}{4}''$) ; ক্ষুদ্র আকারের আলোকচিত্র।

câr′-tĕl, *n.* **1.** A written challenge to duel ; দ্বন্দ্বযুদ্ধার্থ আহ্বান-পত্র। **2.** An agreement between states at war, for the exchange of prisoners ; exchange of prisoners ; যুদ্ধে রত জাতিদ্বয়ের মধ্যে বন্দি-বিনিময়-পত্র ; বন্দি-বিনিময়। **3.** The manufacturers' union to keep up prices ; জিনিষের দড় চড়া রাখিবার জন্য নির্ম্মাতৃগণের সম্মিলনী।

Câr-tē′-sian (-zĭ-ăn or -zhĭ-ăn), *adj.* & *n.* Of or pertaining to Rene Descartes, or his philosophy, or mathematical methods ; ফরাসী দার্শনিক দেকার্ত্তে, বা তৎপ্রবর্ত্তিত দর্শন-শাস্ত্র কিম্বা গণিতশাস্ত্র বিষয়ক প্রণালী সম্বন্ধীয়। ***Noun.*** An adherent of this philosophy ; উক্ত দার্শনিক মতাবলম্বী। **—ism,** *n.*

Câr-thū′-sian (-zĭ-ăn or -zhĭ-ăn), *n.* **1.** A member of an exceedingly austere religious order founded in France by St. Bruno in 1086 ; ১০৮৬ খৃষ্টাব্দে সেণ্ট্ ব্রিউনো কর্ত্তৃক প্রতিষ্ঠিত ধর্ম্ম-সম্প্রদায়ভুক্ত ব্যক্তি। **2.** A member of the Charterhouse school founded on the site of Carthusian monastery in 1371 ; ১৩৭১ খৃঃ অব্দে কার্থুজিয়ান মঠের বাস্তুতে প্রতিষ্ঠিত "চার্টারহাউজ স্কুল" নামক প্রতিষ্ঠানের সভ্যবিশেষ।

câr′-tĭ-lāge, *n.* A smooth, solid, elastic substance softer than bones; gristle ; তরুণাস্থি ; উপাস্থি। **—lag′-i-nous,** *adj.* **Cartilaginous fish—** তরুণাস্থিময় কঙ্কালবিশিষ্ট মৎস্যশ্রেণী।

câr-tŏg′-ră-phy̆, *n.* The art of map-drawing ; মানচিত্রাঙ্কণ বিদ্যা। **—pher,** *n.* **—to-graph′-ic, —to-graph′-i-cal,** *adjs.*

câr′-tō-măn-cy̆, *n.* Fortune-telling by playing cards ; তাসক্রীড়া দ্বারা ভাগ্যগণনা।

câr′-tŏn, *n.* **1.** A thin kind of paste-board ; a paste-board box ; একপ্রকার মোটা কাগজ মলাট কাগজ ; স্থূলকাগজের বাক্স। **2.** A white disc fixed on the bull's eye of a target ; চাঁদমারির মধ্যস্থলে নিবদ্ধ শ্বেতবর্ণ চক্রবিশেষ।

câr-tōōn′, *n.* & *v. t.* **1.** A design drawn on strong paper for fresco, tapestry, painting, mosaic, etc. ; প্রাচীর গাত্রাঙ্কিত চিত্র, মূর্ত্তিবিশিষ্ট পর্দ্দা প্রভৃতির কায, চিত্রাঙ্কণ, এবং নানাবর্ণের কাচ, মর্ম্মরপ্রস্তর প্রভৃতি দ্বারা শোভিত কারুকার্য্য প্রভৃতির জন্য স্থূল কাগজে অঙ্কিত পরিকল্পনা, নক্সা। **2.** A full-page (or large) illustration on current political events in comic paper ; ব্যঙ্গ-পত্রিকায় প্রকাশিত সামযিক রাজনীতিক ঘটনাবলী ... (বা বৃহৎ) চিত্র, ***Verb t.*** **1.** To ... উক্তপ্রকার পরিকল্পনা অঙ্কন করা। **2.** To represent (persons, events, etc.) in a cartoon ; ব্যঙ্গচিত্র অঙ্কন করা।

câr-touch′, —touche′ (-tôsh), *n.* **1.** (*Arch.*) A scroll ornament on

Cartouch of Ptolemy.

the cornice of a column ; (স্থপতি-বিদ্যা) স্তম্ভের প্রস্তরাগ্রের (আলিসার) উপরিভাগস্থ আবর্ত্তিত (গুটানো) কাগজবৎ স্থাপত্য-অলঙ্কার বিশেষ। **2.** Any inscriptive tablet sculptured so as to represent a half-unrolled sheet of parchment ; অর্দ্ধভাগ আবর্ত্তিত অপরার্দ্ধ অনাবর্ত্তিত একপ্রকার ছাগচর্ম্ম-নির্ম্মিত কাগজখণ্ডের অনুকরণে তক্ষিত শিলালিপি ফলক। **3.** (*Egyptian Antiq.*) An oval figure (on ancient monuments) containing hieroglyphic names and titles of Egyptian kings, etc. ; (মিশরীয় প্রত্নতত্ত্ব) প্রাচীন মিশরদেশীয় নৃপতিগণের চিত্রাক্ষরে লিখিত নাম, উপাধি প্রভৃতি সম্বলিত (প্রাচীন সমাধিস্তম্ভগাত্রস্থ) ডিম্বাকৃতি ক্ষেত্র বিশেষ।

câr′-tridge (-trij), *n.* A charge of explosive for firearms or blasting made up in cases of paper, flannel, metal, etc., (it is called a ball-cartridge, when it contains a projectile, and blank, when no ball or shot is used) ; কার্ত্তুজ, টোটা। **Cartridge-belt—** টোটা রাখিবার জন্য কোটর বিশিষ্ট চর্ম্ম-বন্ধনী। **Cartridge-box—**তোজ্‌দান। **Cartridge-paper—**টোটার আবরণের জন্য মোটা কাগজ, চিত্রাঙ্কণের জন্য মোটা কাগজ, শক্ত খামের জন্য মোটা কাগজ।

câr′-tū-lă-ry̆, *n.* **1.** A collection of records ; a register, as of a monastery ; দলীল-দস্তাবেজ ; খাতা-পত্র, যথা মঠাদির খাতা-পত্র। **2.** An ecclesiastical officer in charge of public records ; সাধারণ কাগজ-পত্রের ভারপ্রাপ্ত যাজক-কর্ম্মচারী।

carum carni—শা-জিরা (যোঃ)।

căr′-un-cle (-ŭng-), (*Eng.*), **că-run′-cū-lă** (-rŭng-), (*Lat.*), *n.* **1.** A small fleshy excrescence, either natural or morbid ; specifically a fleshy excrescence on the head of a fowl, as the wattles of a turkey, etc. ; মাংসময় ক্ষুদ্র সহজ বা রোগজ উদ্ভেদ (হঃ চঃ) ; মোরগের কণ্ঠনিম্নস্থ মাংসময় উদ্ভেদ। **2.** (*Bot.*) A protuberance surrounding the hilum of a seed ; (উদ্ভিদ্-বিদ্যা) বীজের চোক বা মুখের চতুষ্পার্শ্বস্থ উদ্ভেদবিশেষ।

carve (cârv), *v. t.* & *i.* **1.** To cut (some solid material) in order to produce the representation of an object or some decorative design ; to engrave ; to sculpture ; (কাষ্ঠ, প্রস্তর, প্রভৃতি কাটিয়া) মূর্ত্তি প্রভৃতি বাহির করা ; খোদিত করা ; মূর্ত্তি প্রস্তুত করা। **2.** (*Fig.*) To achieve by one's own exertion; as, to *carve* one's way; (লক্ষণায়) স্বকীয় চেষ্টা দ্বারা কোন বিষয়ে সিদ্ধ লাভ করা। **3.** To cut up meat; ভোজনোপবিষ্ট ব্যক্তিগণের জন্য বা রন্ধনের জন্য মাংসাদি কাটা। **4.** To subdivide, (usually with *up*); to apportion; ক্ষুদ্র ক্ষুদ্র অংশে বিভক্ত করা; বণ্টন করিয়া দেওয়া। ***Verb i.*** **1.** To exercise the trade of a sculptor; to engrave or cut figures; ভাস্করের কার্য্য করা; মূর্ত্তি প্রভৃতি খোদিত করা বা কাটিয়া বাহির করা। **2.** To act as a carver (divider of meat) at table; ভোজনোপবিষ্ট ব্যক্তিগণকে পক্ক মাংস কাটিয়া দেওয়া। **Carv′-ing,** *n.* **1.** The act or art of cutting wood, stone, etc.; কাষ্ঠ, প্রস্তর প্রভৃতিতে খোদাই করণ, তক্ষণ-শিল্প (প্রবাসী ১৩১৯)। **2.** Device or figure carved; ক্ষোদিত মূর্ত্তি বা পরিকল্পনা। **To carve one's way**—To make one's way; নিজের পথ করিয়া লওয়া। **To carve out**—To take from a larger whole; to acquire, especially by the sword; বৃহত্তর বস্তু হইতে অংশ কাটিয়া লওয়া; অর্জ্জন করা, বিশেষতঃ তরবারির সাহায্যে লাভ করা। **To cut and carve**—To refine; পরিমার্জ্জিত করা।

câr′-vĕl, *n.* Same as CARAVEL. **Carvel-built**—With the planks all flush, not overlapping; পরস্পরের সহিত সমতলভাবে সংযুক্ত কাষ্ঠফলক সকল সমন্বিত (অর্থাৎ একটী তক্তার প্রান্তের সহিত অপরটীর প্রান্ত মিলিত—এরূপ ভাবে সংযুক্ত)।

câr′v-êr, *n.* **1.** One who carves or works in wood, marble, ivory, etc.; a sculptor or engraver; তক্ষক; ভাস্কর, খোদাইকারক। **2.** One who cuts up meat at table; যে ব্যক্তি ভোজনোপবিষ্ট ব্যক্তিগণকে পক্ক মাংস কাটিয়া দেয়। **3.** A large table knife for carving; ভোজন সময়ে মাংস কাটিবার জন্য বৃহৎ ছুরিকা বিশেষ।

căr-ŷ-ăt′-id, *n.* (*Arch.*) The figure of a female (used instead of a column) supporting an entablature; [corresponding male figures were called Atlantes, Filamones or Persians]; (স্থপতি-বিদ্যা) স্তম্ভশিরশাখাধারিণী স্ত্রীমূর্ত্তি, অট্টালিকার স্তম্ভের পরিবর্ত্তে যে স্ত্রীমূর্ত্তি সর্দ্দাল কার্ণিশাদি সমেত অট্টালিকার মাথাড়ী ধারণ করিয়া থাকে, স্ত্রী-স্তম্ভ।

caryophyllus aromaticus—লবঙ্গ (বেলঃ)।

caryota urens—বনখাজুর (বেলঃ)।

căs-cāde′, *n.* **1.** A water fall; জলপ্রপাত, নির্ঝর, নির্ঝরিকা (সাঃ পঃ)। **2.** A wavy fall of lace, etc.; ঢেউ খেলানো জরি প্রভৃতি।

câs′-că-râ, *n.* A kind of buckthorn; একপ্রকার গুল্ম। ***Cascara sagrada***—কালি বিশেষ বা ইহার বিরেচক ঔষধ স্বরূ

cāse, *n.* **1.** An in ng's occurring; an actual state of affairs; কোন ঘটনার দৃষ্টান্তস্থল, উদাহরণ; প্রকৃত বিষয়। **2.** A position, circumstances, in which one is placed; অবস্থা, দশা, হাল (*Colloq.*)। **3.** (*Med.*) A person's diseased conditions; instance of any disease; a person under medical treatment; (ভৈষজ্য-শাস্ত্র) পীড়িতাবস্থা; কোন পীড়ার দৃষ্টান্ত; চিকিৎসাধীন রোগী। **4.** (*Law*) A suit for trial; a sum of arguments on one side; statement of parties; মোকদ্দমা, মামলা; বিচার্য্য-বিষয়; একপক্ষের যুক্তিতর্কের সমষ্টি। **5.** (*Gram.*) A change in the termination of a noun, etc. to express relation; (ব্যাকরণ) কারক। **Case-law**—নজীরদ্বারা নির্ণীত আইন, নজীরি আইন। **A case in point**—আলোচ্য বিষয়ের সহিত সংস্পৃষ্ট দৃষ্টান্ত, বিবরণ বা বিষয়। **A case of conscience**—যে বিষয়ে, পরস্পর বিরোধী মত সমূহের মধ্যে কোনটী গ্রহণ করিতে হইবে, তাহা বিবেকদ্বারা নিরূপণীয়। **In any case**—যে কোন অবস্থায়, যাহাই হউক না কেন। **In case if**—যদ্যপি, যে স্থলে; পাছে। **In case to**—কোন কার্য্যের জন্য উপযুক্ত অবস্থায়। **In that case**—তাহা হইলে, সেই অবস্থায়, যদি ঐরূপ ঘটে। **In the case of**—Regarding; সম্বন্ধে, সম্পর্কে। **The case**—The fact; the reality; প্রকৃত ঘটনা; বাস্তবিক অবস্থা। **To make a case against**—To substantiate a charge against; কাহারও বিরুদ্ধে কোন অভিযোগ সত্য বলিয়া সপ্রমাণ করা। **To make out a case**—To establish a charge by evidence or argument; প্রমাণ বা যুক্তিপ্রয়োগ দ্বারা কোনও অভিযোগ সাব্যস্থ করা, মোকদ্দমা দাঁড় করা। **To make out one's case**—To prove it; কোন বিষয় সপ্রমাণ করা। **To put the** —To take for examples; ঃ স্বরূপ গ্রহণ করিতে হইলে।

cāse, *n.* & *v. t.* **1.** An enclosure of something, as a box, bag, sheath, etc.; an outer protective covering of watch, seed-vessel, book, etc.; আবরণ; (ঘড়ীর) ঢাক্‌নী, (বীজের) খোসা, পুট, (পুস্তকের) আধার, (তরবারির) কোষ, খাপ, (বালিশের) খোল, ইত্যাদি। **2.** A glass box for showing specimens, curiosities, etc.; কোন জিনিষের নমুনা, আশ্চর্য্য বস্তু, প্রভৃতি প্রদর্শনার্থ কাচের বাক্স। **3.** A box with proper contents; as, a dressing *case*; যথাযোগ্য দ্রব্যজাত পূর্ণ বাক্স। **4.** A frame for plant-growing; বৃক্ষাদির মাচা। **5.** (*Print.*) A receptacle with compartments for holding types (*upper case,* capitals, *lower case,* small letters); হরফ রাখিবার ক্ষুদ্র ক্ষুদ্র প্রকোষ্ঠ বিশিষ্ট কাঠাধার বিশেষ। ***Verb t.*** To put or enclose in a case; to surround *with,* (also with *up, over*); আধারে রাখা; খোল, খাপ প্রভৃতির ভিতর পূরা। **Case-ending**—বিভক্তি। **Case-knife**—যে

ছুরিকা কোষে বা আধারে পুরিয়া নীত হয়। **Case-man**—মুদ্রা-যন্ত্রালয়ে মুদ্রাক্ষর বিন্যাসকারী, বিন্যাসক (আঃ বঃ)। **Case of address**—সম্বোধন কারক। **Case-shot**—টীনের বাক্সে ভরা যে সকল গুলিকা দাহ্য পদার্থ পূর্ণ পলিতা বা নলের সাহায্য ব্যতিরেকে কামান হইতে নিক্ষিপ্ত হয়। **Case-worm**—একপ্রকার কীট। **In good case**—ভাল অবস্থায়। **Printing case**—হরফ রাখিবার নিমিত্ত কোটর বিশিষ্ট কাষ্ঠাধার।

cāse'-hard-en (-hârdn), *v. t.* To harden the surface of, especially to give steel surface to (iron) by chemical process; উপরিভাগ কঠিন করা, বিশেষতঃ রাসায়নিক প্রক্রিয়া দ্বারা (লৌহের) উপরিভাগ ইস্পাতময় করা। **2.** (*Fig.*) To render callous; (লক্ষণায়) কঠিন করা, নির্ম্মম করা। **Case-hardened**—নির্লজ্জ, আত্মসম্মানবিহীন।

cā'-sē-in, *n.* **1.** A proteid or albuminoid,—the basis of cheese; যবক্ষারজান বিশিষ্ট দুগ্ধের সার, ছানা (খাঃ)। **2.** A similar substance found also in certain vegetables; কতিপয় গুল্মাদিতে প্রাপ্ত উক্ত প্রকার পদার্থ। **—ous,** *adj.*

cāse'-māte, *n.* (*Fort.*) A vaulted chamber in the thickness of the rampart of a fortress, with embrasures, through which artillery may be fired; a shell-proof vault to protect the troops, ammunitions, etc.; (দুর্গ) দুর্গপ্রাকার-গাত্রস্থ খিলান বিশিষ্ট এবং কামান দাগিবার রন্ধ্র সমন্বিত কক্ষ বিশেষ; গোলাগুলি এবং সৈন্যগণের রক্ষার জন্য গোলা দ্বারা অভেদ্য কক্ষ বিশেষ। **—ma-ted,** *adj.*

cāse'-mĕnt, *n.* **1.** Properly a small portion of an old fashioned window, made to open on hinges fastened to one of its vertical sides, the rest of the window being fixed; প্রাচীন ধরণের 'জানালার ক্ষুদ্র অংশ বিশেষ—জানালার কোন একটী খাড়া পার্শ্বের সহিত উক্ত অংশ কব্জায় আটা থাকে। **2.** (*Poet.*) A window; "He watched them from the *casement* when they walked"; (কবিতায়) গবাক্ষ, বাতায়ন।

câ'-sërn —serne (-zërn), *n.* (Usually *Pl.*) Small buildings for troops between ramparts and houses of fortress; barracks; দুর্গপ্রাকার ও দুর্গাট্টালিকার মধ্যবর্ত্তী ক্ষুদ্র ক্ষুদ্র গৃহ সমূহ; সৈন্য-নিবাস।

căsh, *n.* & *v. t.* (no *pl*) Ready money; species or bank-notes; রোক টাকা, নগদ টাকা, রোকড়; মুদ্রা, নোট। ***Verb t.*** To turn into money or to exchange for money (note, cheque etc.); to pay money for; নোট, চেক প্রভৃতি ভাঙ্গান; কিছুর পরিবর্ত্তে টাকা প্রদান করা। **Cash'-ier,** *n.* A person in charge of a bank or merchant's cash or money transactions; ধন-রক্ষক, তহবিলদার, খাজাঞ্চি। **Cash-account**—রোকড় হিসাব (হিঃ কোঃ)। **Cash-book**—রোকড় বহি (হিঃ কোঃ)। **Cash-credit**—ব্যক্তিগত জামিনে বা গচ্ছিত টাকার জামিনে ব্যাঙ্ক হইতে টাক তুলিবার অধিকার; রোকড় হিসাব (হিঃ কোঃ)। **Cash transaction**—নগদ লেনাদেনা। **Cash payment**—নগদ মূল্য প্রদান। **Cash price**—নগদ মূল্য। **Hard-cash**—নগদ টাকা। **In cash**—Having or with money; নগদ টাকা হস্তে স্থিত। **Out of cash**—Without money; নগদ টাকা শূন্য।

Căsh, *n.* (*Pl.* CASH) A small Chinese coin perforated and strung on a thread; সূত্রে গ্রথিত চীনদেশীয় সচ্ছিদ্র মুদ্রা বিশেষ

că-shew' (-shô), *n.* A tropical American tree with kidney-shaped, ash-coloured fruit; হিজলী বাদাম (খোরী), কাজু বাদাম (ঐ), কাজু (ঐ)।

căsh-ier' (-ēr), *v. t.* **1.** To dismiss from service or from society; as, they have already *cashiered* several of their followers; চাকুরী হইতে অবসৃত করা, জবাব দেওয়া, সমাজচ্যুত করা, পদচ্যুত করা। **2.** To discard (things); as, they absolutely *cashier* the literal express sense of the words; অগ্রাহ্য করা।

căsh'-mere (-mēr), *n.* **1.** (Also *Cashmere shawl.*) A rich and costly kind of shawl of fine soft wool of *Cashmere goat*; কাশ্মিরী শাল। **2.** The material of it; a fine woollen stuff; তিব্বতদেশীয় ছাগলোম,—যাহা হইতে কাশ্মিরী শাল প্রস্তুত হয়; একপ্রকার সূক্ষ্ম পশমী বস্ত্র। **3.** Any similar shawl; an imitation of the original; কাশ্মিরী শালের অনুরূপ শাল; নকল কাশ্মিরী শাল।

căsh-mĕ-rette' (-rĕt), *n.* A kind of fabric for ladies' dresses made with a soft and glossy surface in imitation of cashmere; ইয়ুরোপীয় স্ত্রীলোকের পরিচ্ছদের জন্য সুকোমল পশমী বস্ত্রবিশেষ।

că-si'-nö (-sē-), *n.* [*It.* a small house] A club-house or public room used for gaming, dancing, music, etc.; নৃত্যগীত ক্রীড়াদির জন্য প্রমোদাগার বিশেষ, প্রমোদাগার, আমোদাগার।

căsk, *n.* & *v. t.* **1.** A wooden vessel of a cylindrical form, usually bulging in the middle formed of carved staves bound together by hoops (a barrel); পিপা। **2.** The vessel and its contents; পিপা এবং তদভ্যন্তরস্থ পদার্থ। **3.** The quantity contained in a cask; a varying measure of capacity; এক পিপায় যে পরিমাণ জিনিষ ধরে; পরিমাপ বিশেষ। ***Verb t.*** To put in a cask; পিপাজাত করা।

căs'-kĕt, *n.* A small box, often of precious meterial and workmanship, for jewels, letters, etc.; রত্নপেটক, সম্পুটক, মণ্ডন-পেটিকা (উজ্জ্বলঃ), অভিনন্দনপত্রাদির জন্য কারু-কার্য্যশোভিত বহুমূল্য আধার।

casque (căsk), [Sp. *casco*, a skull, a helmet.] *n.* A helmet ; শিরস্ত্রাণ।

Căs-săn'-dră, *n.* Prophet of ill ; an unregarded prophet ; অশুভ-বাদী ; যে ভবিষ্যদ্‌বক্তার কথা কেহ গ্রাহ্য করে না। [(গ্রীক-পুরাণ) Cassandra ট্রয়ের অধিপতি প্রায়ামের দুহিতা ছিলেন। দেবতা এপলো তাহার প্রণয়াকাঙ্ক্ষী হইয়া প্রস্তাব করেন ক্যাসাণ্ড্রা তাহার প্রার্থনা পূরণে স্বীকৃতা হইলে তিনি তাহাকে ভবিষ্যৎ কথনের ক্ষমতা প্রদান করিবেন। ক্যাসাণ্ড্রা দেবপ্রসাদে ভবিষ্যৎ কথনের ক্ষমতা প্রাপ্ত হইলেন, কিন্তু এপলোদেবের প্রার্থনা পূরণ করিলেন না। ইহাতে এপলোদেব ক্রুদ্ধ হইয়া তাহাকে অভিশাপ প্রদান করিলেন যে ক্যাসাণ্ড্রা যে সমস্ত ভবিষ্যদ্‌বাণী প্রকাশ করিবেন, তাহা সত্য হইলেও লোকে তাহাতে আস্থা-স্থাপন করিবে না।]

căs-sā'-tion, *n.* (*Law.*) The act of annulling or reversing a judicial sentence ; annulment ; (আইন) দণ্ড রহিতকরণ ; রদ, বাতিল। **Court of cassation**—ফরাসী দেশের সর্ব্বোচ্চ পুনর্ব্বিচারের আদালত।

căs-sä'-vă, *n.* (*It.*) **1.** A plant (of the warmer parts of America) with tuberous roots ; সিমুল আলু (নৃত্যঃ)। **2.** The nutritious starch or flour obtained from the soft roots of the plant ; the bread made from these ; সিমুল আলুর মূল হইতে প্রস্তুত পুষ্টিকর শ্বেতসার বিশেষ ; উক্ত শ্বেতসার হইতে প্রস্তুত রুটি।

cas'-se-rōle (căs-), [*Fr.* a sauce pan] *n.* A heat-proof earthenware vessel in which meat is cooked and served ; মাংস রন্ধনের ও পরিবেষণের জন্য মৃন্ময় পাত্রবিশেষ।

cas'-sia (căsh-ĭ-ă), *n.* **1.** An inferior kind of cinnamon ; Chinese cinnamon ; নিকৃষ্ট জাতীয় দারুচিনি ; চীনদেশীয় দারুচিনি। **2.** (*Cap.*) A genus of leguminous plants yielding senna-leaves ; কয়েক জাতীয় বৃক্ষের সাধারণ নাম—এই বৃক্ষ হইতে সোণামুখী পত্র পাওয়া যায়। ***Cassia acutifolia*** — Bombay senna ; সোণামুখী (বেলঃ)। ***Cassia alata***—দাঁদ মৰ্দ্দ (হিন্দি—বেলঃ)। **Cassia buds**—কয়েক জাতীয় দারুচিনির শুষ্ক মুকুল। **Cassia cinnamon**—তেজ-পাতার গাছ (মঃ উঃ)। ***Cassia elongate***—সোণামুখী (বেলঃ)।

căs'-sock (-sŏk), A long close-fitting garment worn under the gown by some Anglican clergymen or as ordinary attire ; এংলিকান যাজকগণের একপ্রকার আঁট-সাঁট পোষাক—ইহা সাধারণ পোষাকের মত অথবা আলখাল্লার নীচে পরা হয়, জুব্বা (ফঃ হিঃ)। **—socked,** *adj.*

cassolette, [*F.*] *n.* **1.** A vessel for burning perfumes ; সুগন্ধিদ্রব্য জ্বালাইবার পাত্রবিশেষ। **2.** A perfume-box with perforated top ; উপরিভাগে ছিদ্রবিশিষ্ট সুগন্ধি দ্রব্যের আধার বিশেষ।

căs'-sö-wă-rȳ, *n.* [Malay *casuari*] A large cursorial bird, (inhabiting the islands of the Indian Archipelago) resembling,

Crested Cassowary.

and nearly as large as, the ostrich ; ভারতদ্বীপপুঞ্জবাসী বৃহৎকায় ধাবনশীল পক্ষিবিশেষ।

căs-sû-mü'-nâr, [Hindi] *n.* An aromatic, ginger-like root, used as a tonic and stimulant ; সুগন্ধি মূলবিশেষ, দেখিতে আদার মত, বলকারক এবং উত্তেজক, আমহলদী (বেলঃ)।

căst, *v. t.* & *i.* **1.** To throw or fling ; to send or drive off by force ; to hurl ; as, to *cast* dice or lots ; to *cast* net, hook, fly ; নিক্ষেপ করা, ছোড়া ; সবলে তাড়িত করা, ফেলা, ফিকা (*Colloq.*) ; বেগে নিক্ষেপ করা। **2.** To turn ; to direct, as the sight ; as, to *cast* a look or glance ; ফিরান ; পাত করা, ক্ষেপ করা। **3.** To let fall ; to throw off ; as, the trees *cast* their fruit ; a serpent *cast* his skin ; to drop ; to throw away ; as, a horse *casts* shoe ; পাতিত করা ; ত্যাগ করা, মোচন করা ; ক্ষরিত করা, চ্যুত করা ; ছুড়িয়া ফেলা, অনাবশ্যক বলিয়া ছুড়িয়া ফেলা। **4.** To scatter, as seed ; ছড়ান। **5.** To throw on the ground, as in wrestling ; ভূপাতিত করা। **6.** To shed ; to impart ; to reflect ; as, to *cast* light upon a subject ; বিকীর্ণ করা ; প্রদান করা ; প্রতিবিম্বিত করা। **7.** To compute ; to reckon ; to calculate ; as, to *cast* accounts ; গণনাদ্বারা স্থির করা ; গণনা করা ; হিসাব করা। **8.** To form into a particular shape by pouring liquid metal into a mould ; to found ; as, to *cast* cannon, bullet, etc. ; দ্রবধাতু ছাঁচে ফেলিয়া গড়া ; ঢালাই করা। **9.** To overthrow in a law-suit ; to condemn as a criminal ; মোকদ্দমায় পরাজিত করা ; দোষী সাব্যস্ত করা, অপরাধী বলিয়া স্থির করা। **10.** To fix or distribute (the parts of play) among actors ; as, to *cast* parts to actors ; to assign (an actor) for a part ; অভিনেতৃগণের মধ্যে ভূমিকা বিতরণ করা ; অভিনেতৃগণের কে কোন ভূমিকা গ্রহণ করিবে তাহা নির্দ্দেশ করা। **11.** (*Print.*) To stereotype or electrotype ; (মুদ্রণ) বিন্যস্ত অক্ষর হইতে (ঢালাইদ্বারা) মুদ্রণ ফলক তৈয়ার করা। ***Verb i.*** **1.** To throw the line in angling, esp. with a fly-hook ; বড়শী ফেলা।

2. To turn or revolve in the mind ; to consider ; as, this way and that I *cast* to save my friends ; মনে মনে আলোচনা বা চিন্তা করা ; তোলাপাড়া করা। **3.** To receive a form or shape (by melting) ; (দ্রবীভূত হইয়া) আকৃতি বা গঠন প্রাপ্ত হওয়া। **4.** (*Naut.*) To fall off or incline so as to bring a ship to the wind ; (নৌবিদ্যা) জাহাজের পার্শ্ব বাতাসের দিকে আনিবার জন্য জাহাজ সরান বা কাৎ করা। **5.** To warp ; to twist from regular shape ; as, a stuff is said to *cast* or warp when it alters its straightness ; দোমড়াইয়া যাওয়া ; তেওড়াইয়া যাওয়া। **Cast away**—Abandoned ; পরিত্যক্ত। **The die is cast**—See DIE. **To cast about**—To go this way and that, in search for ; to be on the look out for ; ইতস্ততঃ খুঁজিয়া বেড়ান ; হাতড়াইয়া বেড়ান। To devise means (*for, to do, how*) ; উপায় নির্দ্ধারণ করা। **To cast adrift**—To throw in a helpless position ; অকূলে ভাসাইয়া দেওয়া। **To cast a horoscope**—To calculate and prepare a horoscope ; ঠিকুজি প্রস্তুত করা। **To cast anchor**—To drop anchor ; নোঙ্গর ফেলা। **To cast a sheep's eye at one**—To look askance at one ; to look wantonly at one ; কাহারও দিকে আড় নয়নে চাওয়া ; কাহারও প্রতি লম্পটের মত দৃষ্টিক্ষেপ করা। **To cast aside**—To throw aside as useless ; অব্যবহার্য্য বোধে ফেলিয়া দেওয়া। **To cast a slur on** or **upon**—To impute a blame or to reproach ; দোষ বা কলঙ্কারোপ করা, ভর্ৎসনা করা। **To cast a vote**—To give or deposit it ; কাহারও অনুকূলে মত প্রদান বা ন্যস্ত করা। **To cast away**—To throw away ; to turn to no use ; to reject ; ফেলিয়া রাখা ; অব্যবহার করা ; অগ্রাহ্য করা। (*Passive,—of ship*) To be wrecked ; (জাহাজাদিপক্ষে) ধ্বংস হওয়া। **To cast back**—To revert ; প্রত্যাবৃত্ত করা। **To cast beyond the moon**—To form wild conjecture ; অসম্ভব কল্পনা করা। **To cast by**—To throw by ; to reject ; অকর্ম্ম্য বলিয়া ফেলিয়া রাখা ; অগ্রাহ্য করা। **To cast calf**—To miscarry ; to suffer abortion ; অকালে বাচ্চা দেওয়া বা বিয়ন ; গর্ভস্রাব হওয়া। **To cast damp on**—(*Colloq.*) To depress ; দমাইয়া দেওয়া (*Colloq.*), নিরুৎসাহ করা। **To cast down**—To ruin ; to destroy ; to throw down ; ধ্বংস কর ; নাশ করা ; ভূমিসাৎ করা। (*Fig.*) To deject or depress the mind ; (লক্ষণায়) বিরস করা, ভগ্নোদ্যম বা বিষণ্ণ করা। **To cast forth**—To throw out or from an inclosed space ; to emit or send out ; বদ্ধস্থান হইতে বহির্দিকে প্রক্ষেপ করা ; নির্গত বা বাহির করা। **To cast in one's lot with**—To share the fortunes of ; সমসুখদুঃখভাগী হইবার জন্য কাহারো সহিত মিলিত হওয়া। **To cast in one's teeth** or **nose**—To upbraid or reproach him ; to twit ; তিরস্কার করা ; ভর্ৎসনা করা। **To cast into the shade**—To outshine ; নিষ্প্রভ করা, মলিন করা, অতিক্রম করা। **To cast lots**—To determine an event by some arrangement of chances ; গুলি-বাঁট করা, গুটিদ্বারা নির্দ্ধারণ করা। **To cast off**—To discard or reject ; to drive away (persons, things) ; to throw off ; to free one's self from ; ঠেলিয়া ফেলা, ত্যাগ করা ; বিতাড়িত করা ; পরিত্যাগ করা ; নির্ম্মুক্ত করা। (*Hunting*) To leave behind, as dogs ; to let loose or free ; (মৃগয়া) পশ্চাতে ফেলা (কুকুরাদি) ; ছাড়িয়া দেওয়া মুক্ত করা। (*Knitting*) To close loops and make selvedge ; (বুনন-কর্ম্ম) ফাঁস বন্ধ করিয়া কাপড়ের পাড় তৈয়ার করা। (*Naut.*) To loosen from or let go ; as, to *cast off* a vessel in tow ; (নৌ-বিদ্যা) আল্গা করা, ছাড়িয়া দেওয়া। **To cast off copy**—(*Print.*) To estimate the amount of printed matter a certain quantity of manuscript will make ; (মুদ্রণ) হস্তলিখিত কাগজ ছাপায় কতটুকু হইবে তাহা আন্দাজ করা। **To cast one's self on** or **upon**—To surrender ; আত্মসমর্পণ করা। **To cast out**—To reject or turn out of doors ; প্রত্যাখ্যান করা, গৃহ হইতে বহিষ্কৃত করা। To quarrel over ; কোন কিছু নিয়া কলহ করা। **To cast pearls before the swine**—To place things of great value before those who are ignorant of their worth ; ব্যাঙে বনে মুক্তা ছড়ান, বানরের গলায় মুক্তাহার দেওয়া। **To cast spell on**—To bewitch ; to enchant ; মন্ত্রমুগ্ধ করা ; যাদু করা। **To cast to the winds**—To disperse in all directions ; চারিদিকে বিক্ষিপ্ত করা বা ছড়াইয়া দেওয়া। To tear into shreds ; ছিন্নভিন্ন করা। **To cast up**—To calculate ; to reckon ; গণনা করা ; হিসাব করা। To vomit ; to eject ; (*lit.* & *fig.*) ; (শব্দানুযায়ী এবং লক্ষণায়) বমন করা ; উদ্গিরণ করা। To twit or upbraid with ; to throw in one's teeth ; দোষ প্রদর্শন করিয়া তিরস্কার করা, ভর্ৎসনা করা ; কাহাকে মুখের উপর দশ কথা শুনাইয়া দেওয়া। To appear unexpectedly ; হঠাৎ উপস্থিত হওয়া। **To cast young**—To miscarry ; to suffer abortion ; অকালে সন্তান প্রসব হওয়া ; গর্ভস্রাব হওয়া।

cast, *p. p.* **1.** Condemned ; as, a *cast* criminal ; দোষি-সাব্যস্ত। **2.** Condemned by the public ; unsuccessful ; as, so may a *cast* poet write ; জনসাধারণ দ্বারা নিন্দিত ; অকৃতকার্য্য, বিফলকাম। **3.** Made by founding or casting ; as, *cast* iron, steel ; ঢালাই-করা।

câst, *n.* **1.** The act of throwing ; a throw ; especially in angling, the act of throwing the line on the water ; the thing thrown ; as, a *cast* of dreadful dust ; ক্ষেপণ; নিক্ষেপ, পাত ; বড়শী ফেলন ; নিক্ষিপ্ত বস্তু। **2.** The distance passed by a thing thrown ; as, about a stone's *cast* ; ক্ষেপণ-দূরত্ব, পাল্লা। **3.** A throw of dice ; the number thrown at dice ; hence, a state of chance or hazard ; as, it is an even *cast* whether the army should march this way or that ; অক্ষ-ক্ষেপ ; পাশা খেলায় ক্ষেপের অঙ্ক ; অতএব দৈবাধীন অবস্থা। **4.** A motion or turn of the eye ; look ; a squinting ; as, a *cast* of the eye ; দৃষ্টিক্ষেপ ; দৃষ্টি ; কুটিল চাহনি। **5.** The form or shape into which anything or work is thrown or moulded ; a model made by running molten metal or pressing some soft material (wax.etc.) into a mould; (*fig.*) shape ; impression generally ; as, cunning *casts* in clay ; কোন জিনিষ ঢালাই করার সময় যে আকার বা ডৌল দেওয়া হয় ; ছাঁচে দ্রবীভূত ধাতু ঢালিয়া বা মোম প্রভৃতি কোমল জিনিষ ছাঁচের উপর চাপিয়া যে আদর্শ প্রস্তুত করা হয় ; (লক্ষণায়) আকৃতি, ডৌল ; ছাপ **6.** The undigested food thrown up by hawk, owl, etc. ; বাজপাখী, পেচক প্রভৃতি কর্ত্তৃক পরিত্যক্ত অজীর্ণ খাদ্য। **7.** Adding of columns in an account ; calculation ; সঙ্কলন-ক্রিয়া ; গণনা। **8.** An assignment of the parts of a play to the several actors ; a set of actors taking the part in a play ; as, the play was produced with a very strong *cast* ; বিভিন্ন অভিনেতৃগণের অভিনেয় অংশের নির্দ্দেশ ; নাটকের অভিনেতৃবর্গ। **9.** A tinge ; a slight colouring ; as, a *cast* of green ; বর্ণ, রঙ্ ; বর্ণের আমেজ বা আভাস, ঈষৎ রঞ্জন। **10.** Manner ; outward appearance ; as, a peculiar *cast* of countenance ; quality ; as, a *cast* of mind ; ধরণ ; ডৌল, আকার ; ভাব, প্রকৃতি।

Căs-tā'-li-ăn, *adj.* Pertaining to *Castalia,* a spring on mount Parnasus, sacred to the Muses ; hence, poetic ; গ্রীক বাণীদেবীগণের প্রিয় পার্ণেসাস গিরিস্থিত ক্যাসটেলিয়া নামক নির্ঝর-সম্বন্ধীয় ; অতএব কবিত্বপূর্ণ, কাব্যরসপূর্ণ।

căs'-tă-nĕt, *n.* (Usu. *Pl.*) Two small concave shells of ivory or hard wood, shaped like spoon fastened to the thumb, to rattle in time of dancing ; কাষ্ঠ বা হস্তিদন্তে নির্ম্মিত চামচের আকার মন্দিরা বিশেষ, করতারা।

căst'-ă-wāy, *n.* & *adj.* **1.** A reprobate ; পতিত ব্যক্তি, ধর্ম্মভ্রষ্ট ব্যক্তি, জাতিভ্রষ্ট ব্যক্তি, অপাংক্তেয় ব্যক্তি, সমাজ বর্জ্জিত ব্যক্তি। **2.** A ship-wrecked person ; ভগ্ননৌক ব্যক্তি, সাগরতট বা সাগর তলস্থ শৈল সংঘর্ষে ভগ্ন পোতের বিপন্ন যাত্রী। ***Adj.*** **1.** Thrown away ; পরিত্যক্ত। **2.** Worthless ; rejected ; of no value ; অসার, অকর্ম্মণ্য ; অব্যবহার্য্য ; মূল্যহীন।

caste (căst), *n.* **1.** Among the Hindus, rank in society of an exclusive nature, due to birth ; জাতি, বর্ণ (সাঃ পঃ)। **2.** A hereditary (more or less exclusive) class in other countries ; a class or order of society (used of the upper grades) ; সমাজান্তর্গত বিভিন্ন শ্রেণী বা জাতি ; (ভারত ব্যতিরিক্ত অন্যান্য দেশে) (উচ্চ শ্রেণী পক্ষে) বংশানুক্রমিক জাতি। **3.** This system of the division of society ; the position it confers ; জাতি-ভেদ-প্রথা ; জাতি অনুসারে পদমর্য্যাদা। **A low caste man**—অন্ত্যজ। **Distinction of caste**—জাতি ভেদ, বর্ণ ভেদ। **Mixed cast**—বর্ণ সঙ্কর। **Low caste**—নিকৃষ্ট জাতি। **Of the same caste**—স্ববর্ণ। **To lose, renounce, caste**—জাতিচ্যুত হওয়া, জাতি ত্যাগ করা।

căs'-tĕl-lăn, *n.* A governor of a castle ; দুর্গাধিপতি, দুর্গেশ, দুর্গস্বামী দুর্গপতি, দুর্গপাল। **—la-ny,** *n.* The jurisdiction of a castellan ; দুর্গস্বামীর অধিকারভুক্ত স্থান।

căs'-tĕl-lāt-ĕd, *adj.* **1.** Castle-like ; দুর্গবৎ। **2.** Battlemented ; having castles (said of districts etc.) ; তোপ দাগিবার ছিদ্র বা খাঁজ যুক্ত প্রাচীর বিশিষ্ট ; অট্টালঙ্কৃত (আঃ বঃ), শিখরমণ্ডিত (ঐ)।

câst'-êr, *n.* One that casts in any sense, as stones, account, dice, type, cannon, etc. ; ক্ষেপক, গণনাকারী, অক্ষ-ক্ষেপক, হরফ ঢালাইকর, কামান ঢালাইকর, গণক প্রভৃতি। **2.** See CASTOR.

căs'-ti-gāte, *v. t.* **1.** To chastise ; to punish by stripes ; শাস্তি দেওয়া, সাজা দেওয়া ; বেত্রাঘাত করা, কষাঘাত করা। **2.** To punish with blows and words ; প্রহার করিয়া শাস্তি দেওয়া, ভর্ৎসনা করা, বাক্য দণ্ড করা। **3.** To correct and emend book, etc. ; পুস্তকাদি সংশোধন করা। **—ga'-tion,** *n.* (*Lit.* & *fig.*) **1.** Punishment by whipping ; chastisement ; (শব্দানুযায়ী এবং লক্ষণায়) বেত্রদণ্ড ; শাসন, নিগ্রহ, শাস্তি-প্রদান। **2.** Critical scrutiny and emendation ; সূক্ষ্মসমালোচনা এবং সংশোধন। **—ga-tor,** *n.* **—ga-to-ry,** *adj.*

câst'-ing, *n.* **1.** The act of throwing anything ; ক্ষেপণ। **2.** The act of founding ; ঢালাই করণ। **3.** Anything formed in a mould ; ছাঁচে তৈয়ারী জিনিষ। **4.** The taking of impressions, figures, medals, etc. ; মূর্ত্তি, পদক প্রভৃতির ছাপ তোলন। **Casting-net**—খেয়াজাল (গুপ্ত), ফেঁকা জাল (ঐ), ঝাঁথাবুরানি (ঐ), ক্ষেপণী জাল। **Casting voice, vote**—কোন প্রস্তাবের অনুকূলে এবং প্রতিকূলে মত-সংখ্যা সমান হইলে সভাপতি স্বীয় মতের অতিরিক্ত যে আরও একটী মত প্রদান

দ্বারা এক পক্ষের মত সংখ্যা বর্দ্ধিত করত উপস্থিত বিষয়ের মীমাংসা করিয়া থাকেন। **Casting-weight**—দাঁড়ি পাল্লার উভয় দিকে ভার সমান হইলে যে বাটখারা দ্বারা এক দিকের ভার বৃদ্ধি করা হয়।

câst'-i-ron (-ï-êrn), *adj.* & *n.* **1.** Made of iron melted and run into moulds ; খরলৌহ নির্ম্মিত। **2.** Hard ; untiring ; rigid ; কঠিন ; অক্লান্ত ; দৃঢ়। ***Noun.*** Iron shaped by being run into moulds ; খর লৌহ, ঢালা লোহা।

cas'-tle (casl), *n.* **1.** A large fortified building or set of buildings ; a stronghold ; প্রাকার পরিখাদি দ্বারা সুরক্ষিত বৃহৎ অট্টালিকা বা অট্টালিকা-শ্রেণী ; দুর্গ, কোট, কেল্লা সুরক্ষিত স্থান, কোট্ট (কথা সঃ)। **2.** A mansion that was once a stronghold ; the mansion of a noble man or prince ; এক সময়ে প্রাকার, পরিখাদি দ্বারা সুরক্ষিত ছিল এইরূপ প্রাসাদ ; সৌধ, হর্ম্ম্য, প্রাসাদ। **3.** A piece made with battlemented top, used in the game of chess ; (শতরঞ্জ খেলায়) রথ বা নৌকা। **4.** (*Poet. or Rhet.*) A large ship, esp. of war ; (কাব্য বা অলঙ্কারশাস্ত্রে) বিশাল অর্ণবযান, বিশেষতঃ রণপোত। **Castle-builder**—আকাশকুসুম রচক। **Castle-building**—আকাশকুসুম-রচনা, গগননগর নির্ম্মাণ, দিবাস্বপ্ন দর্শন। **Castle-influence**—(আয়র্লণ্ডে) রাজ-পুরুষগণের রাজনীতিক প্রভাব। **A castle in the air**—A scheme that has no solid foundation ; day-dream ; (also called *a castle in Spain*) ; আকাশকুসুম, গগননগর, খপুষ্প, অভ্রপুষ্প (নৈযঃ), খেয়ালি-পোলাও (*Colloq.*) ; দিবাস্বপ্ন, লাখ টাকার স্বপ্ন, মনে মনে লঙ্কাভাগ। **An Englishman's house is his castle**—ইংলণ্ডবাসীর গৃহ তাহার দুর্গস্বরূপ, অর্থাৎ তথায় কাহারও বলপূর্ব্বক প্রবেশের অধিকার নাই। **The castle**—Government system ; শাসনপদ্ধতি। (*Ireland*) **The castle, The Dublin castle**—(আয়র্লণ্ডে) যে দুর্গে আয়র্লণ্ডের রাজপ্রতিনিধির দরবার সম্মিলিত হয় এবং শাসনকার্য্য নির্ব্বাহিত হয়। The officials who administer the government of Ireland ; যে সকল রাজকর্ম্মচারী আয়র্লণ্ড শাসন করেন।

cas'-tle (căsl), *v. t.* & *i.* (*Chess*) To move the king two squares to the right or left and bring up the castle or rook to the square the king has passed over ; (শতরঞ্জ খেলায়) রাজাকে দক্ষিণে বা বামে দুই ঘর সরাইয়া, রাজা যে ঘর অতিক্রম করিয়া গিয়াছে, তাহাতে নৌকা স্থাপন করা, রাজা বাঁধা।

căs'-tled (căsld), *adj.* Having a castle or castles ; built like a castle ; fortified ; দুর্গ-সমন্বিত, দুর্গ-শ্রেণীসমন্বিত ; দুর্গাকারে নির্ম্মিত ; প্রাকার পরিখাদিদ্বারা সুরক্ষিত।

căs'-tor (-têr), [Gr. *Kastor* a beaver] *n.* **1.** Same as CASTOREUM below. **2.** (*Slang.*) A hat, especially made of beaver fur ; (ইতর ভাষায়) টুপি, বিশেষতঃ বীবর লোমনির্ম্মিত টুপি। **3.** A heavy quality of broad-cloth for overcoats ; একপ্রকার মোটা বনাত।

căs'-tor (-têr), **-têr,** *n.* **1.** (*Orig.*) A small vessel with a perforated top for sprinkling pepper or other powdery substance ; a phial or cruet to contain condiments for the table ; (পূর্ব্বে) উপরিভাগে ছিদ্র বিশিষ্ট ক্ষুদ্র ভাণ্ড বিশেষ, ইহা দ্বারা গোল-মরিচ চূর্ণ বা অন্য কোনও চূর্ণ বস্তু ছিটাইয়া দেওয়া হইত ; আচার, মসলা প্রভৃতি পূর্ণ ক্ষুদ্র কাচের বোতল—যাহা ভোজনকালে মেজে রাখা হয়। **2.** A stand to hold a set of cruets (usually *pl.*) ; সিরকাদান, আচারদান প্রভৃতি রাখিবার বৈঠক বিশেষ। **3.** A small wheel on a swivel, attached to the legs of chairs or other articles of furniture ; ঘুরিতে পারে এরূপ আকড়ায় আটা, কেদারা বা অন্যান্য আসবাব সামগ্রীর পায়ায় লাগানো ক্ষুদ্র চাকা।

Castor.

căs'-tor (-têr), *n.* A horny external knob inside a horse's leg, (also called *chestnut*) ; ঘোড়ার পায়ের কড়।

Căs'-tŏr and Pŏl'-lŭx, *n.* (*Astron.*) The constellation Gemini ; জিতুম (সাঃ পঃ), মিথুন (ঐ) **2.** Same as CORPOSANT, which see. **Castor**—পুনর্বসু দ্বিতীয় (হিঃ কোঃ)। **Pollux**—পুনর্বসু (ঐ)।

căs-tö'-rē-ŭm, *n.* An orange-brown substance with strong penetrating odour, found in the inguinal sacs of the beaver ; বীবরের বঙ্ক্ষণ দেশস্থ থলিদ্বয়ে প্রাপ্ত কমলা-লেবুরমত বর্ণবিশিষ্ট উগ্রগন্ধ পদার্থ বিশেষ।

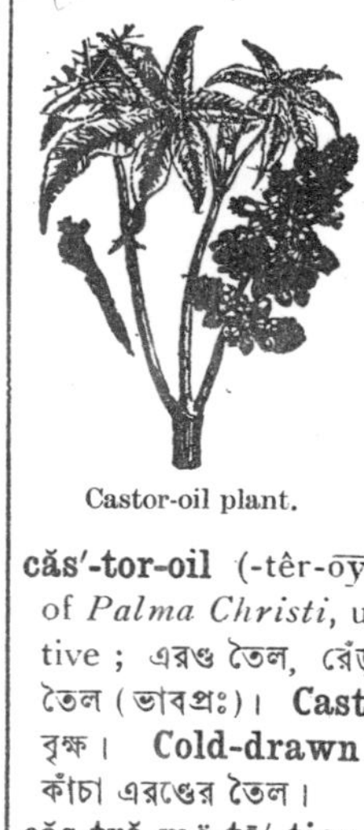

Castor-oil plant.

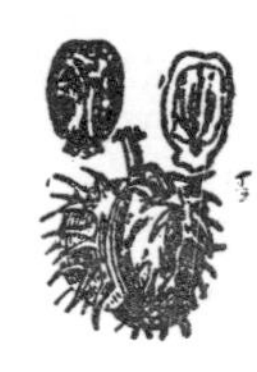

Nut of castor-oil plant.

căs'-tor-oil (-têr-ōyl), *n.* The oil of *Palma Christi*, used as purgative ; এরণ্ড তৈল, রেঁড়ীর তৈল, গন্ধর্ব্ব তৈল (ভাবপ্রঃ)। **Castor-tree**—এরণ্ড-বৃক্ষ। **Cold-drawn castor-oil**—কাঁচা এরণ্ডের তৈল।

căs-tră-mē-tā'-tion, *n.* The art or act of encamping or laying out camps ; শিবির-সন্নিবেশ-বিদ্যা, শিবির-স্থাপন।

căs'-trāte, *v. t.* To remove testicles of ; to emasculate ; বৃষণোৎপাটন করা ; মুষ্কচ্ছেদন করা, খাসী করা (*Colloq*), দামড়া করা (*Colloq.*), খোজা করা (*Colloq.*)। **2.** To expunge obscene passages from a writing ; to expurgate a book ; "The following letter which I have *castrated* in some places ;" কোন রচনার অশ্লীল অংশ তুলিয়া দেওয়া, ছাঁটিয়া দেওয়া ; কোন পুস্তকের দূষিতা অংশ পরিবর্জ্জন করা। 3. (*Fig.*) To deprive of vigour ; to take the spirit from ; (লক্ষণায়) শক্তিহীন করা ; নিস্তেজ করা। **–tra′-tion,** *n.* **1.** Gelding ; মুষ্কচ্ছেদন, বৃষণোৎপাটন, অণ্ডাকর্ষণ, অণ্ডকোষচ্ছেদন (জাহিঃ), বৃষণোৎকর্ত্তন। **2.** Expurgation of a book or writing ; কোন পুস্তক বা রচনার অশ্লীল অংশ পরিবর্জ্জন।

cas′-ü-ăl (căzh-), *adj.* & *n.* **1.** Happening or coming to pass without design ; accidental ; fortuitous ; coming by chance ; as, *casual* breaks in the general system ; নৈমিত্তিক, আগন্তুক, আপতিক ; দৈবিক ; দৈবঘটিত ; দৈবাগত। **2.** Coming at certain times without regularity ; irregular ; as, *casual* expenses ; আকস্মিক ; অনিয়মিত। **3.** Undesigned ; উদ্দেশ্যবিহীন। **4.** Unmethodical ; careless ; superficial ; বিশৃঙ্খল ; অসাবধান ; পল্লবগ্রাহী, ভাসাভাসা, উপরি উপরি। ***Noun.*** A chance or occasional visitor, labourer, pauper, etc. ; দৈবাৎ উপস্থিত, অসময়ে আগত সাক্ষাৎকারী, শ্রমজীবী, দরিদ্র প্রভৃতি। **–ly,** *adv.* **–ness,** *n.* **Casual labourer**—যে ব্যক্তি সময় সময় কায করে। **Casual leave** — হঠাৎ কোন কারণবশতঃ সরকারী আফিস প্রভৃতির কর্ম্মচারিগণকে যে দুই চারি দিন বেতন সহিত বিদায় দেওয়া হয়। **Casual poor**—যে ব্যক্তির সময় সময় দরিদ্রভাণ্ডার হইতে সাহায্য গ্রহণ করিতে হয়। **Casual ward**—দৈবাগত দরিদ্র বা রোগীর জন্য রক্ষিত আরোগ্যশালা বা শ্রমজীবিনিকেতনের অংশ বা বিভাগ বিশেষ।

cas′-ü-ăl-tŷ (căzh-), *n.* **1.** That which comes without design or without being foreseen ; accident ; an unfortunate occurrence ; a disaster ; দৈব ; দুর্ঘটনা ; দুর্দ্দৈব ; দৈবদুর্ব্বিপাক। **2.** (*Pl.*) A list or number of killed, wounded and invalided in a battle, march, etc. ; যুদ্ধ বা যুদ্ধযাত্রা প্রভৃতিতে হতাহত বা অকর্ম্মণ্য ব্যক্তিগণের সংখ্যা বা তালিকা।

căs′-ü-ĭst, *n.* **1.** One who studies and resolves cases of conscience ; ধর্ম্মাধর্ম্মবিচারক। **2.** A sophist ; a quibbler ; তার্কিক, তর্কপ্রবণ ব্যক্তি ; কূটতার্কিক। **–is′-tic, –is′-ti-cal,** *adjs.* **–ist-ry,** *n.* **1.** The science or doctrine of dealing with cases of conscience or of resolving questions of right and wrong in conduct ; ন্যায়ান্যায়বিবেক বিদ্যা, ধর্ম্মাধর্ম্মবিবেক বিদ্যা, ধর্ম্মাধর্ম্মবিচারণ বিদ্যা, ধর্ম্মাধর্ম্মবিচার (হিঃ কোঃ), ধর্ম্মবিচারণা (আঃ বঃ)। **2.** Sophistical or false reasoning or teaching in regard to duties and morals ; কর্ত্তব্য এবং সদাচার সম্বন্ধে কূট নৈয়ায়িক তর্ক বা কুশিক্ষা, কূটতর্ক (হিঃ কোঃ)।

casus belli, *n.* Whatever causes or justifies a war ; যে সমস্ত কারণে যুদ্ধ সংঘটিত হয় বা যুদ্ধে প্রবৃত্ত হওয়া ন্যায় সঙ্গত বলিয়া প্রতিপন্ন হয়।

căt, *n.* **1.** A small domesticated carnivorous animal ; বিড়াল, মার্জ্জার, বিলাই (*Colloq.*), দীপ্তাক্ষ, ব্যাঘ্রাস্য। **2.** (*Zool.*) Any member of the genus *Felis,* as lion, tiger, panther, leopard, the cheetah, etc. ; as, the great *cats* ; (প্রাণি-বিদ্যা) মার্জ্জার'গণ'ভুক্ত জন্তুসকলের যে কোন একটী, যথা ব্যাঘ্র, সিংহ, প্রভৃতি। **2.** A spiteful woman ; a scratching child ; বিদ্বেষপরায়ণা স্ত্রীলোক ; যে শিশু বিড়ালের মত লোককে আঁচড় মারে। **3.** (*Naut.*) A ship usually employed in the coal and timber trade ; a strong tackle or combination of pulleys, to hook and draw up an anchor ; (নৌ-বিদ্যা) সচরাচর কয়লা এবং কাঠের কারবারে নিযুক্ত জাহাজ বিশেষ ; জাহাজের নঙ্গর আঁকড়িয়া ধরিবার বা তুলিবার নিমিত্ত শক্ত কাছি বা সজ্জিত কপিকল সকল। **4.** A six-legged tripod ; ছে-পায়া বিশেষ। **5.** A rope whip with nine knotted tails or lashes, formerly used for flogging sailors and soldiers ; (also *cat-o'-nine-tails*) ; নব্য-সংখ্যক বেত্র বিশিষ্ট রজ্জুবিশেষ,—পূর্ব্বে ইহা দ্বারা নাবিক ও সৈনিকদিগকে বেত্রাঘাত করা হইত, নববলিকা (আঃ বঃ), নব পুচ্ছিকা, কোড়া (রঃ অঃ)। **6.** The game *tip-cat* ; the tapered short stick used in the game ; একপ্রকার ক্রীড়া ; উক্ত ক্রীড়ায় ব্যবহৃত ক্ষুদ্র ক্রমসূক্ষ্ম যষ্টি বিশেষ। **Cat and dog,** *adj.* ঝগড়াটে ; বে-মিল, **Cat and dog life**—বিড়াল কুকুরের মত অহরহ ঝগড়াপূর্ণ জীবন (বিশেষতঃ পতি-পত্নীর মধ্যে)। **Cat-bird**—আমেরিকাদেশীয় মার্জ্জাররাবী পক্ষিবিশেষ, মার্জ্জারপক্ষী। **Cat-call**—রঙ্গালয়ে অপ্রীতি প্রকাশার্থ যে কর্কশ রবে শীস বা শিটি দেওয়া হয়। **Cat-eyed**—কটা-চোখো ; অন্ধকারে দেখিতে সমর্থ। **Cat fall**—যে রজ্জুর সাহায্যে পোতাগ্রদেশ-সন্নিহিত প্রলম্বিত লৌহ বা কাষ্ঠখণ্ডের উপর নোঙ্গর তোলা হয়। **Cat-fish**—আমেরিকা দেশীয় নদীচর বৃহৎ মৎস্য-বিশেষ,—জল হইতে উত্তোলিত হইবার কালে এই মৎস্য বিড়ালের ন্যায় মিউ মিউ শব্দ করিয়া থাকে। **Cat-footed**—নিঃশব্দ ; অলক্ষিত। **Cat-head**—পোতাগ্রদেশ-সন্নিহিত প্রলম্বিত লৌহ বা কাষ্ঠখণ্ড-বিশেষ,—ইহার উপর নোঙ্গর উত্তোলিত ও দৃঢ়সংবদ্ধ করা হয়। **Cat-ladder**—একপ্রকার মই,—যাহা খাড়াভাবে প্রাচীরে লাগান হয়। **Cat-lap**—Any poor drink ; নিস্তেজ পানীয় দ্রব্য—যথা চা ; অমাদক পানীয় দ্রব্য। **Cat-mint**—নীলপুষ্পপ্রসূ সুগন্ধি গুল্ম বিশেষ। **Cat-nap, –sleep**—কেদারায় উপবিষ্ট অবস্থায় ক্ষণস্থায়ী নিদ্রা। **Cat-o'-nine-tails**—See CAT 5. **Cats'-cradle**—শিশুদিগের ক্রীড়াবিশেষ। **Cat's-eye**—বৈদূর্য্য মণি (রঃ রঃ সঃ—প্রঃ)। **Cat's-foot**—আইভিলতা। **Cat's meat**—বিড়ালের জন্য ফেরিওয়ালাগণকর্ত্তৃক বিক্রীত অশ্ব বা তদ্বৎ জীবের মাংস। **Cat's-paw**—A person used a tool by another ; যে জন অপর ব্যক্তি কর্ত্তৃক যন্ত্র-স্বরূপ ব্যবহৃত হয়, ক্রীড়নক, ক্রীড়া পুত্তলিকা। A slight breeze rippling water in places ; জলাশয়ের স্থানে স্থানে বীচিমালা উৎপাদক-মন্দানিল। *To make a cat's paw of*—পরের ভাতে বেগুণ পোড়া, পরের মাথায় কাঠাল ভাঙ্গা। **A cat has nine lives**—বিড়ালের বড় কঠিন প্রাণ, বিড়ালকে সহজে বধ করিতে পারা যায় না। **A cat in the pan**—A falsehood given out as coming from one who did not originate it ; অন্য ব্যক্তির প্রমুখাৎ শ্রুত হইয়াছি এইরূপ ভূমিকা করিয়া কাহারো নিকট যে অলীক কথা বলা হয়। **A cat may look at a king**—A humorous phrase asserting the right of a person in the presence of one much above his position ; বিড়ালও রাজার দিকে তাকাইতে পারে ; অর্থাৎ আমি যেমন তুমিও তেমন, তুমি কি এতই বড়লোক যে তোমার দিকে তাকাইলে বা তোমার সহিত কথা কহিলে তোমার সম্ভ্রমের হানি হইবে। **Care killed the cat**—See CARE. **No room to swing a cat**—Very confined space ; অত্যন্ত সংকীর্ণ স্থান। **The cat is out of the bag**—আসল কথা বেরিয়ে পড়েছে। **To fight like Kilkenny cats**—To fight till each (one) destroys the other ; একজন মৃত্যুমুখে পতিত না হওয়া পর্য্যন্ত যুদ্ধ করা। **To grin like a Cheshire cat**—To show teeth and gums while laughing ; হাসিবার সময় দাঁত এবং দাঁতের মাড়ি দেখান। **To let the cat out of the bag**—To disclose a trick ; to let out secret ; চাতুরী প্রকাশ করিয়া ফেলা ; গুপ্তকথা বাহির করিয়া ফেলা। **To rain cats and dogs**—To pour down incessantly and violently ; মুষলধারে বৃষ্টি পড়া, ঝম্ ঝম্ করিয়া বৃষ্টি পড়া। **To shoot the cat**—To vomit ; বমি করা। **To turn a cat-in-pan**—To make a sudden change of party in politics or religion from interested motives ; স্বার্থসাধনের অভিপ্রায়ে রাজনীতি বা ধর্ম্মসম্পর্কীয় বিষয়ে সহসা একদল ত্যাগ করিয়া অন্য দলে যাওয়া। **To wait for the cat to jump, To see which way the cat jumps**—To watch how things are going to turn before committing oneself ; কোন বিষয়ে আপনাকে আবদ্ধ করিবার পূর্ব্বে ঘটনা কিরূপ দাঁড়ায়, তাহা দেখিবার জন্য অপেক্ষা করা। **Who will bell the cat**—Who will risk his own safety to save his neighbour ? ম্যাও ধরে কে ? [ঈশপের গল্প বিশেষ হইতে গৃহীত। এক সময়ে মার্জ্জার দ্বারা উৎপীড়িত মূষিকবর্গের মধ্যে একটা বুদ্ধিমান মূষিক প্রস্তাব করিল যে মার্জ্জারের গলদেশে একটা ঘণ্টা বাঁধিয়া দেওয়া হউক—তাহা হইলে মূষিকগণ পূর্ব্ব হইতে বিড়ালের আগমনের সংবাদ পাইবে। এখন একটী ক্ষুদ্রজ্ঞানী মূষিক বলিয়া উঠিল "এ কার্য্যের ভার নেয় কে ?"]

căt, *v. t. & i.* **1.** To bring up to the cat-head ; as, to *cat* an anchor ; পোতাগ্রদেশ-সন্নিহিত প্রলম্বিত কাষ্ঠ বা লৌহখণ্ডের নিকট আনয়ন করা। **2.** To flog with a cat-o-nine-tails ; নবসংখ্যক বেত্র সমন্বিত দণ্ডদ্বারা বেত্রাঘাত করা। ***Verb i.*** To vomit (*Colloq.*) ; (কথিত ভাষায়) বমি করা।

căt-ă-chrē'-sis, *n.* Misuse of words or abuse of terms ; a figure in rhetoric when one word is wrongly put for another ; শব্দের অপব্যবহার, পদের অপব্যবহার ; (অলঙ্কারশাস্ত্র) শব্দালঙ্কার বিশেষ,—যাহাতে ভ্রমবশতঃ এক শব্দের স্থলে অপর শব্দ ব্যবহৃত হয়। **—chres'-tic, —chres-ti'-cal,** *adjs.* **—chres'-ti-cal-ly,** *adv.*

căt'-ă-clăsm, *n.* A violent break ; disruption ; বিভেদ ; বিদারণ।

căt'-ă-clÿsm, *n.* **1.** A deluge or extensive overflowing of water ; (little used) ; জল-প্লাবন ; পৃথিবী-প্লাব, মহাবন্যা, আপ্লাব। **2.** (*Geol.*) Any violent physical change involving sudden and extensive alterations of the earth's surface ; (ভূ-বিদ্যা) যে ভীষণ প্রাকৃতিক ঘটনা-বিপর্য্যয়ে পৃথিবীপৃষ্ঠে অকস্মাৎ মহাপরিবর্ত্তন সংঘটিত হয়, ভূত-সংপ্লব, খণ্ডপ্রলয়। **3.** (*Fig.*) A political or social upheaval ; a debacle ; (লক্ষণায়) রাজনৈতিক বা সামাজিক বিক্ষোভ ; বিপ্লব। **—clys'-mal, —clys'-mic,** *adjs.* **—clys'-mist,** *n.*

căt'-ă-comb (-cōm), *n.* **1.** A subterranean cemetery or burying place ; ভূগর্ভস্থ সমাধিক্ষেত্র, অন্তর্ভৌম শবাধার (আঃ বঃ), [এই সমস্ত ভূগর্ভস্থ সমাধিসমূহ আদিম খৃষ্টানগণের সমাধিক্ষেত্র ও আশ্রয়স্থল ছিল। পূর্ব্বে রোমনগরীর সন্নিকটবর্ত্তী সেণ্ট সেবেষ্টিয়ান গির্জ্জার নিম্নস্থ পিতার এবং পলের সমাধি-স্থান সম্বন্ধে প্রযুক্ত হইত।] **2.** (*Usu. pl.*) The subterranean cemeteries in or near Rome ; রোম বা রোমনগরীর সমীপস্থিত ভূগর্ভস্থ সমাধিসমূহ। **3.** Any subterranean receptacle for the bones of the dead ; মৃতব্যক্তির দেহাবশেষ-রক্ষার্থ ভূগর্ভস্থ আধারবিশেষ। **4.** A wine-cellar ; ভূনিম্নস্থ মদ্য-ভাণ্ডার।

căt-ă-dī-ŏp'-tric, —tri-căl, *adjs.* Pertaining to, produced by, or involving, both the reflection and refraction of light ; আলোকের প্রতিফলন এবং পরাবর্ত্তন সংসৃষ্ট, সঞ্জাত বা সম্পর্কীয়। **Catadioptric telescope**—The same as REFLECTING TELESCOPE (which see).

căt-ă-cous'-tics (-cows-), *n.* That part of acoustics which treats of reflected sounds or echoes ; প্রতিধ্বনি-বিদ্যা, প্রতিধ্বনি-শাস্ত্র (হিঃ কোঃ)।

că-tăd'-rō-mous* (-mŭs), *adj.* Living in fresh water and going to the sea to spawn, as the eel ; স্বাদুজলবাসী এবং ডিম্বপ্রসবার্থ সমুদ্রযায়ী।

căt'-ă-falque (-fălc), *n.* **1.** A decorated stage for coffin or effigy of distinguished persons during funeral service ; অন্ত্যেষ্টি-ক্রিয়ার সময় যে কারুকার্য্যখচিত মঞ্চোপরি সুপ্রসিদ্ধ ব্যক্তিগণের শবাধার বা প্রতিকৃতি রক্ষিত হয়। **2.** An open hearse ; a tomb of state ; উন্মুক্ত শবশকট ; আড়ম্বরপূর্ণ সমাধি-স্তম্ভ।

Căt′-ă-lăn, *adj.* & *n.* Pertaining to Catalonia, a province of Spain ; স্পেনদেশের অন্তঃপাতী ক্যাট্যালোনিয়া নামক প্রদেশ সম্বন্ধীয়। ***Noun.*** A native of, and the language spoken in, Catalonia ; ক্যাট্যালোনিয়ার অধিবাসী, ক্যাট্যালোনিয়ার ভাষা।

căt-ă-lĕc′-tic, *adj.* Wanting a syllable in the last foot (of a verse) ; as, a *catalectic* verse ; (পদ্যের) শেষ চরণে একটী পদাংশ হীন, ন্যূনাক্ষর (আঃ বঃ), ন্যূনৈকাক্ষর (মঃ ইঃ), ন্যূনপাদক।

căt′-ă-lĕp-sy̆, *n.* **1.** A sudden suspension of voluntary sensation ; নিস্পন্দ বায়ুরোগ,—ইহাতে কিয়ৎক্ষণ শারীরিক ও মানসিক ক্রিয়া স্তব্ধীভূত থাকে। **2.** (*Philos.*) An apprehension or grasping by the mind ; (দর্শন-শাস্ত্র) ধারণা।

căt-ă-lĕp′-tic, *adj.* & *n.* Pertaining to, affected with, or resembling, catalepsy ; উক্ত রোগসম্পৃক্ত, উক্ত রোগাক্রান্ত, উক্ত রোগসদৃশ। ***Noun.*** A person affected with catalepsy ; উক্ত রোগপীড়িত ব্যক্তি। **2.** (*Philos.*) A mental apprehension ; (দর্শন-শাস্ত্র) ধারণা।

căt′-ă-logue (-lŏg), *n.* & *v. t.* **1.** A complete list or enumeration, (usually alphabetical or under headings, etc.) of men and things, often with particulars added to items ; তালিকা, নির্ঘণ্ট, ফর্দ্দ, ফিরিস্তি প্রভৃতি। ***Verb t.*** To make a list of ; to enter or insert in a catalogue ; তালিকা করা ; তালিকা পুস্তকে ভুক্ত করা। **—logu-er, —log-er,** *ns.*

Că-tăl′-pă, *n.* A genus of trees with heart-shaped leaves and trumpet-shaped flowers ; কয়েক জাতীয় উষ্ণমণ্ডলজাত বৃক্ষের সাধারণ নাম। ইহাদের পাতা পানের ন্যায়, এবং ফুলগুলি দেখিতে সানাই বাঁশীর মত।

că-tăl′-y̆-sis, *n.* (*Chem.*) The effect produced by a substance, that, without undergoing change itself, aids a chemical change in other bodies ; (রসায়ন-শাস্ত্র) স্বয়ং অপরিবর্ত্তিত থাকিয়া, অপর পদার্থ সমূহে রাসায়নিক ক্রিয়া সংঘটিত করে, এবম্বিধ পদার্থের ক্রিয়া, যোগবাহী ক্রিয়া (হিঃ কোঃ)।

căt-ă-ly̆t′-ic, *adj.* Pertaining to, characterized by, or causing, catalysis ; যোগবাহীক্রিয়া-সম্বন্ধীয়, যোগবাহীক্রিয়াত্মক, যোগবাহীক্রিয়া জনক। (*Chem.*) **Catalytic agent**—(রসায়ন-শাস্ত্র) সহায়ক (বরবর মুণি-তত্ত্বত্রয়-ভাষ্য, অচিৎপ্রকরণ—Quoted by Dr. P. C. Roy.)

Catamaran of Madras,

căt-ă-mă-răn′, [Tamil *Kattumaran*, tied logs of wood] *n.* **1.** A raft usually of three logs ; মান্দ্রাজ-দেশে সমুদ্রে ব্যবহৃত ত্রিকাষ্ঠরচিত ভেলা বিশেষ, ভেলা, উড়ুপ, প্লব, শাল্‌তি, ত্রিকাণ্ড ভেলা। **2.** A raft of two boats fastened side by side ; পরস্পরের পার্শ্বসম্বদ্ধ নৌকাদ্বয় রচিত ভেলা বিশেষ। **3.** A quarrelsome woman ; কলহপ্রিয়া স্ত্রীলোক।

căt-ă-mē′-ni-ă, *n.pl.* The monthly courses of women ; menstrual discharges ; menses ; স্ত্রীরজঃ ; আর্ত্তব, রজঃস্রাব, স্ত্রীপুষ্প ; ঋতুস্রাব।

căt′-ă-mīte, *n.* A boy kept for unnatural purposes ; a sodomite's minion ; অস্বাভাবিক অভিগমনের জন্য রক্ষিত বালক ; গাণ্ডু (কেণ্ডিঃ), বাঁটু (শ্রীহট্ট অঞ্চলে), লৌণ্ডা, কুন্তীক (মঃ উঃ)।

căt′-ă-mount (-mownt), **căt-ă-moun′-tain** (-mown-tān), *n.* **1.** The European wild cat ; the leopard ; ইয়ুরোপদেশীয় বন্য মার্জ্জার ; চিতা। **2.** A wild quarrelsome person ; দুর্দ্দান্ত কলহপ্রিয় ব্যক্তি, ঝগড়াটিয়া লোক।

căt′-ă-plăsm, *n.* A plaster or poultice ; লেপ, প্রলেপ, পুল্টিস্, লোপ্‌ত্রী (সাঃ পঃ)।

căt′-ă-pŭlt, *n.*, & *v.t.* & *i.* **1.** A military engine, used by the ancient Greeks and Romans for throwing darts, stones etc. ; সামরিক যন্ত্রবিশেষ,—প্রাচীন গ্রীক ও রোমানগণ এইরূপ যন্ত্রের সাহায্যে বল্লম, পাষাণ প্রভৃতি নিক্ষেপ করিতেন, প্রস্তরাদি অবক্ষেপণের জন্য পূর্ব্বকালীন যুদ্ধযন্ত্রবিশেষ, অবক্ষেপণী (আঃ বঃ)। **2.** A small forked stick having an elastic band fixed to the two prongs for throwing small stones etc. (used by boys) ; লোষ্ট্রক্ষেপণার্থ ফিঙ্গা যন্ত্রবিশেষ, বালকদের ঢিল ছুড়িবার ছিট্‌কিনি কল। ***Verb t. & i.*** To shoot (bird etc.) with this ; উক্ত যন্ত্রদ্বারা পাখী গুলি করা।

căt′-ă-răct, *n.* **1.** A great fall of water over a precipice, as that of Niagara ; জলপ্রপাত, প্রস্রবণ। **2.** A downpour of rain ; a rush of water ; বর্ষণ, অববর্ষণ (কাঃ শ্রৌঃ) ; জলবেগ। **3.** (*Pathol.*) A disease of the eye consisting in an opacity of the crystalline lens or its capsule, producing partial blindness ; (নিদান) চক্ষুর ছানি রোগ, মতিয়াবিন্দু (জাহিঃ), তিমির (সাঃ পঃ), নীলিকা (ঐ), মোতিবিন্দু (কেণ্ডিঃ), মোতিবিম্ব (ঐ), পটল (সুশ্রুঃ)। **4.** (*Mech.*) A steam-engine governor acting by the flow of water ; বাষ্পীয়-যন্ত্রের জলপ্রবাহ চালিত নিয়ামক বিশেষ—ইহার সাহায্যে যন্ত্রমধ্যে বাষ্প, জল প্রভৃতি নীত হয় এবং তদ্দ্বারা গতির সমতা সাধিত হয়।

că-tarrh' (-târ), *n.* A cold affecting the chest, accompanied with an increased secretion of mucus, esp. from the nose ; পীনস (সুশ্রুঃ), প্রতিশ্যায় (সাঃ পঃ), (চলিত ভাষায়) শ্লেষ্মা, কফ-কাসাদি, সর্দ্দি। **—al,** *adj.* **Catarrhal fever**—কফজ্বর (সাঃ পঃ)।

căt'-ăr-rhine (-rïne), **căt'-ă-rhine** (-rïne), *n.* A genus of monkeys ; একজাতীয় বানর। [ইহাদের নাসিকা নিম্নদিকে আনত থাকে।]

că tăs'-tă-sis, *n.* **1.** The part of the Greek drama where the action has reached its height ; গ্রীক নাটকে কাব্যের চরম পরিণতি। **2.** (*Rhet.*) The exordium of a speech ; (অলঙ্কার-শাস্ত্র) বক্তৃতার ভূমিকা। **3.** (*Med.*) Constitution ; condition ; habit of body ; (ভৈষজ্য-শাস্ত্র) শরীরের স্বাভাবিক অবস্থা ; অবস্থা ; দেহের ধাতু (ধাত), দেহ-প্রকৃতি।

că-tăs'-trö-phĕ, *n.* **1.** Denouement or the final event in a romance, drama, etc. ; নাটক বা উপন্যাস প্রভৃতির চরম ঘটনা, (যথা বিয়োগান্ত কাব্য বা নাটকে মৃত্যু, মিলনান্ত কাব্য বা নাটকে পরিণয়), সংহৃতি (সাঃ দঃ), নিষ্ঠা (আঃ বঃ), নির্বহণ (দশরূঃ)। **2.** An unfortunate calamity or disaster ; a disastrous end ; sudden, widespread, or signal, disaster ; দুর্ঘটনা, বিপত্তি ; নিদারুণ পরিণাম, দুঃখ পরিণাম (কেভিঃ) ; উপপ্লব, উৎপাত, ব্যসন। **3.** (*Geol.*) A supposed change in the crust of the earth from sudden physical violence ; (ভূ-বিদ্যা) আকস্মিক প্রাকৃতিক উপপ্লবজনিত ভূ-পঞ্জরের কল্পিত পরিবর্ত্তন। **Cat-a-stroph'-ic, Cat-a-stroph'-i-cal,** *adjs.* **—phism,** *n.* **—phist,** *n.*

că-taw'-bă (-tä-), *n.* **1.** A light-red variety of American grape ; আমেরিকাদেশীয় আলোহিত বর্ণ আঙ্গুর ফল। **2.** A rich-flavoured wine made from this grape ; উক্ত প্রকার আঙ্গুর হইতে প্রস্তুত সুস্বাদু মদিরা।

catch (căch), *v. t.* & *i.* **1.** To capture or seize ; to seize, as in a snare or trap or on a hook ; গ্রেপ্তার করা, পাকড়ান, আটক করা ; ফাঁদে ফেলা, বড়শীতে ধরা। **3.** To reach or get to, in time ; সময় মত কোন স্থানে পৌঁছা। **3.** To be infected with (a cold, a fever, an accident etc.) ; আক্রান্ত হওয়া (সর্দ্দি, জ্বর, দুর্ঘটনা প্রভৃতি দ্বারা)। **4.** To lay hold on forcibly ; to grasp, as with the hand ; to hit or strike (usually with parts specified) ; as, I *caught* him on the nose ; জোর করিয়া ধরা ; মুঠা করিয়া ধরা ; আঘাত করা বা মারা। **5.** To communicate to ; to ignite, (said of fire, combustible) ; as, fire *caught* the next house ; সংক্রামিত হওয়া ; প্রজ্বলিত করা। **6.** To intercept the motion of ; to stop or retard ; to get entangled with or come into contact with ; as, the nail *catches* dress ; to grasp and hold something moving through the air ; as, to *catch* a ball ; গতি রোধ করা ; থামান, বিলম্বিত করা ; জড়িত হওয়া, সংস্পর্শে আসা ; লুফা। **7.** To grasp with the senses or the mind (a meaning, sound, or tune) ; as, to *catch* a melody ; ইন্দ্রিয় বা মনদ্বারা গ্রহণ করা। **8.** To captivate ; as, a vision *caught* my eye ; মোহিত করা, মুগ্ধ করা। ***Verb i.*** **1.** To make captures ; বন্দী করা। **2.** To be ignited, as fire ; to spread ; to be communicated ; as, does the sedition *catch* from man to man ; ধরিয়া উঠা (যেমন আগুন) ; ছড়ান ; সংক্রামিত হওয়া। **3.** To be entangled ; to be fastened ; to take and retain hold ; as, a kite *catches* in a tree ; জড়িত হওয়া ; বদ্ধ হওয়া ; ধরা, ধরিয়া থাকা। **Catch'-a-ble,** *adj.* **Catch'-er,** *n.* **Catch-club**—পর্য্যায় সঙ্গীত গায়ক সম্প্রদায়। **Catch-drain** — পর্ব্বত পার্শ্বস্থ উন্মুক্ত পরিখা বা নর্দ্দমা বিশেষ, অতিরিক্ত জল ধারণার্থ খালের পার্শ্ববর্ত্তী পয়ঃ-প্রণালী বিশেষ। **Catch-fly**—একপ্রকার বৃক্ষ,—ইহার কাণ্ড আঠালো থাকে। **Catchment, catchment-area, catchment basin**—জলকুণ্ড, নদী প্রভৃতির জলাগম ক্ষেত্র। **Catchment basin**—নির্দ্দিষ্ট অববাহিকা (সাঃ পঃ)। **Catch-penny**—অকিঞ্চিৎকর জিনিষ ; গুরু-গম্ভীর নাম বিশিষ্ট অসার ক্ষুদ্র পুস্তিকা ; পয়সা কুড়াইবার ফন্দী। **Catch-pole, Catch-poll** — নাজিরের প্যাদা। **Catchup, catsup** (See *Ketchup*) ছত্রাক, বিলাতি বেগুণ ও আখরোটএর সহিত সির্কা অথবা মদ্য এবং সুগন্ধি মসলা সংযোগে প্রস্তুত ব্যঞ্জন বিশেষ। **Catch-weed**—যে সমস্ত বৃক্ষাদি কোন বস্তুর সংস্পর্শে আসিলে, তাহাতে লগ্ন হইয়া থাকে। **Catch-word**—The first word of a page given at the bottom of the preceding page ; পরপৃষ্ঠার প্রথম শব্দ যাহা পূর্ব্ববর্ত্তী পৃষ্ঠার নিম্নদেশে লিখিত হয়। (Among actors) The last word of the preceding speaker—the cue ; (অভিনেতৃদিগের মধ্যে) পূর্ব্ববর্ত্তী অভিনেতা কর্ত্তৃক উচ্চারিত সর্ব্বশেষ শব্দ। An influential temporary phrase in politics, religion, etc. ; ধর্ম্ম, রাজনীতি প্রভৃতি ব্যাপারে বিশেষ বাণী। যথা 'সাম্য' 'মৈত্রী' 'স্বাধীনতা' ফরাসী বিপ্লববাদিগণের বিশেষ বাণী। **Catch-work** — পর্ব্বতস্কন্ধে জল প্রক্ষেপার্থ কৃত্রিম জলাশয় বিশেষ। **To be caught red-handed**—See RED. **To catch a glimpse of**—To see for a moment ; ক্ষণেকের তরে দেখা। **To catch another's eye**—To attract his attentions ; কাহারও দৃষ্টি আকর্ষণ করা। **To catch at**—To make a sudden and eager attempt to seize (*lit.* & *fig.*) ; (শব্দানুযায়ী এবং লক্ষণায়) কোন কিছু ধরিবার জন্য ব্যগ্রভাবে চেষ্টা করা, ঝাঁপটা মারিয়া ধরিতে যাওয়া। **To catch a Tartar, crab**—See TARTAR, CRAB. **To catch**

away—To snatch away; to take away suddenly; ছিনাইয়া লওয়া; হঠাৎ কাড়িয়া লওয়া। **To catch a weasel asleep**—See WEASEL. **To catch cold (or a cold)**—(Formerly) To be chilled by cold; (now) to contract a cold; to take cold; (পূর্ব্বে) শীত লাগা, শীতার্ত্ত হওয়া; (বর্ত্তমানে) ঠাণ্ডা লাগা; সর্দ্দি লাগা। **To catch fire**—To become inflamed or ignited; to take fire; আগুণ ধরা, আগুণ লাগা, প্রজ্বলিত হওয়া, প্রদীপ্ত হওয়া; জ্বলিয়া উঠা। **To catch hold of**—To take hold of; ধরা। **To catch it**—(*Colloq.*) To get a scolding or beating; to suffer punishment; (চলিত ভাষায়) মার খাওয়া, গাল খাওয়া; শাস্তিভোগ করা। **To catch napping**—See NAPPING. **To catch on**—To fasten on; to seize hold; (কোন কিছুতে) সংযোগ বা সংলগ্ন করা; আকড়াইয়া ধরা। **To catch one a blow**—(*Colloq.*) To inflict a blow on him; (চলিতভাষায়) ঘা দেওয়া। **To catch one in the fact**—To catch one in the very act of committing a crime; হাতে হাতে ধরা। **To catch one on the hip**—To get the advantage on one; to get one under one's power; কাহাকেও সুবিধায় পাওয়া; কাহাকেও বাগে পাওয়া। **To catch one's eye**—To attract one's notice; কাহারও দৃষ্টি আকর্ষণ করা, নজরে পড়া। **To catch one tripping**—To catch one taking a false step; কোনও ব্যক্তি বিপথে পদার্পণ করিতেছে দেখিতে পাওয়া বা ধরিয়া দেওয়া। (*Cricket*) **To catch out**—বল লুফিয়া 'আউট' করা। **To catch the (or one's) breath or air**—To stop one's breathing suddenly and momentarily; হঠাৎ শ্বাসরোধ করা। **To catch the spirit of**—To comprehend the meaning of; কোন কিছুর মর্ম্ম বা তাৎপর্য্য অবধারণ করা। To be inspired with the same feeling; একই ভাবে অনুপ্রাণিত হওয়া। **To catch up**—To snatch up suddenly (*lit.* & *fig.*); (শব্দানুযায়ী এবং লক্ষণায়) খপ্ করিয়া ধরা, ক্ষিপ্রভাবে ধারণ করা। **To catch up with**—To come up with; নাগাইল ধরা।

catch (căch), *n.* **1.** The act of seizing; seizure; specifically the act of catching fish; the number (of fish) or the quantity taken at one time; as, a good *catch* of fish; ধরণ, গ্রেপ্তার; ধৃতি; (বিশেষতঃ) মৎস্য ধরণ; একবারে যে পরিমাণ বা যতগুলি মৎস্য ধৃত হয়। **2.** (*Cricket*) The act of seizing the ball before it touches the ground; also a player who catches; as, he is a sure *catch*; (ক্রীকেট খেলায়) বল লুফন; যে ক্রীড়ক বল লুফে। **3.** A contrivance for checking motion of door, etc.; দরজা, চাকা প্রভৃতি আটক করিবার কৌশল বিশেষ, আঁকড়া। **4.** Something designed to arrest the attention or fancy, etc.; a deception; a surprise; চতুর প্রশ্ন; ফাঁকি; অতর্কিত ঘটনা। **5.** A thing or person caught or worth catching (considered as an object of desire); ধৃত বা ধৃতির উপযুক্ত বস্তু বা ব্যক্তি (অভিলাষের সামগ্রী—এই অর্থে)। **6.** (*Mus.*) Originally, a sound, where each singer, in turn, catches up, as it were, the words from his predecessor, the second singer beginning to sing the first line as soon as the first has finished it, and so on; later, a composition for several voices with arrangement for ludicrous verbal combination; পর্য্যায়ক্রমে গীত সঙ্গীত বিশেষ, এইরূপ সঙ্গীতে প্রত্যেক গায়ক তদীয় পূর্ব্ববর্ত্তী গায়কের দ্বারা গীত অংশ পুনর্ব্বার গাহিতে থাকে; (পরবর্ত্তী কালে) উক্ত প্রকার সঙ্গীতের প্রকার বিশেষ, ইহাতে পরবর্ত্তী ব্যক্তি পূর্ব্ববর্ত্তী ব্যক্তির গীত অংশের হাস্যোদ্দীপক অনুকরণ করে।

catch'-ing (căch-), *n.* & *adj.* The action of the verb 'to catch'; a nervous or spasmodic twisting; ধৃতি, ধরণ, গ্রহণ; খেঁচুনি। ***Adj.*** **1.** Infectious; contagious; as, a disease is *catching*; সংক্রামক; স্পর্শ-সংক্রামক, ছোঁয়াচে, স্পর্শসঞ্চারক (রাঃ তঃ)। **2.** Captivating; charming; attracting; as, a *catching* melody or manner; হৃদয়গ্রাহী; মুগ্ধকর; চিত্তাকর্ষক।

catch'-ȳ (căch-), *adj.* **1.** Tending to catch the fancy or attention; as, *catchy* music; চিত্তাকর্ষক, মনোহর। **2.** Entangling,—usually used figuratively; as, a *catchy* question; জটিল (সাধারণতঃ লক্ষণায় ব্যবহৃত হয়)। **3.** Changeable; fitful; as, a *catchy* wind; অব্যবস্থিত অস্থির; চপল, চঞ্চল।

cāte, *n.* (*Usually pl.*) Luxurious food; dainties; delicacies; সুখাদ্য, দেবভোগ্য খাদ্য; রসনা-তৃপ্তিকর খাদ্য; উপাদেয় খাদ্য সামগ্রী।

căt-ē-c̲h̲ē'-sis, *n.* Primary, oral instruction, as that given to catechumens; প্রাথমিক মৌখিক শিক্ষা।

căt-ē-c̲h̲ĕt'-ic, —i-căl, *adjs.* **1.** Pertaining to oral teaching; মৌখিক শিক্ষাসংক্রান্ত। **2.** Of, pertaining to, or associated with, instruction in the rudimentary Christian doctrines; খ্রীষ্টীয় ধর্ম্মের মৌলিক মতানুযায়ী শিক্ষা সম্বন্ধীয়, উক্ত শিক্ষা সংসৃষ্ট। **3.** Of, pertaining or conforming to, a Church Catechism; খৃষ্টধর্ম্ম সম্বন্ধীয় প্রশ্নোত্তর পুস্তক বিষয়ক, উক্ত পুস্তক সম্পর্কীয়, উক্ত পুস্তকানুযায়ী। **4.** Consisting of, proceeding by, questions and answers; প্রশ্নোত্তরগর্ভ, প্রশ্নোত্তরাত্মক। **—i-cal-ly,** *adv.*

căt-ē-c̲h̲ĕt'-ics, *n.* The art or practice of teaching by question and answer; প্রশ্নোত্তরচ্ছলে শিক্ষাদান-প্রণালী, প্রশ্নোত্তরচ্ছলে শিক্ষাদান-কৌশল।

căt′-ē-chīze, —chīse, *v. t.* **1.** To instruct by question and answer or by the Church Catechism ; প্রশ্নোত্তরচ্ছলে উপদেশ প্রদান করা ; খৃষ্টীয় ধর্ম্মবিষয়ক প্রশ্নোত্তর পুস্তক হইতে উপদেশ প্রদান করা। **2.** To put question to ; কাহাকে প্রশ্ন করা। **—chist, —chiz-er,** *ns.*

căt′-ē-chism, *n.* **1.** A form of instructions by questions and answers ; প্রশ্নোত্তরচ্ছলে শিক্ষাপ্রদানের প্রণালীবিশেষ। **2.** A book containing summary of principles, especially, of religious doctrines in the form of questions and answers ; যে পুস্তকে কোন তত্ত্বের,—বিশেষতঃ ধর্ম্মমতের সারমর্ম্ম প্রশ্নোত্তরচ্ছলে প্রদত্ত হইয়াছে, প্রশ্নোত্তরাবলী, প্রশ্নোত্তর মালা, প্রশ্নোত্তর পুস্তক। **3.** (*Fig.*) A series of questions and answers ; a series of questions put to any one ; (লক্ষণায়) প্রশ্নোত্তরমালা ; জিজ্ঞাসিত প্রশ্নসমূহ। **—chis′-mal,** *adj.*

căt′-ē-chu (-shū), [Malaya, kăchū] *n.* A brown astringent substance, chiefly obtained from Acacia catechu ; খয়ের, খদির-সার, কৎ।

căt-ē-chū′-mĕn, *n.* **1.** One who is under Christian instruction preparatory to admission into the Church ; যে ব্যক্তি খৃষ্টীয় ধর্ম্ম-সমাজে ভুক্ত হইবার জন্য শিক্ষা প্রাপ্ত হইতেছে। **2.** A beginner ; প্রথম শিক্ষার্থী।

căt-ē-gŏr-ē-măt′-ic, *adj.* Capable of being used by itself as a term ; স্বতন্ত্রার্থবাচক। **Categorematic word** — স্বতন্ত্রার্থবাচক শব্দ, স্বতন্ত্রার্থ পদ (হিঃ কোঃ), বাচক পদ (ঐ)।

căt-ē-gŏr′-i-căl, *adj.* **1.** (*Logic*) Admitting no conditions or exceptions ; unconditional ; absolute ; as, a *categorical* proposition (নিরপেক্ষ প্রতিজ্ঞা—সাঃ পঃ) ; (তর্ক-শাস্ত্র) নিরপেক্ষ (সাঃ পঃ) ; অবস্থাতীত ; অনন্যসম্বন্ধ, সম্বন্ধাতীত। **2.** Explicit ; direct ; স্পষ্ট ; প্রত্যক্ষ। **The categorical imperative**—(ক্যাণ্ট প্রবর্ত্তিত নীতি-বিজ্ঞান) নিয়তবিধি (হিঃ কোঃ), পরম বিধি (ঐ), নিরপেক্ষ বিধি (ঐ)। [ক্যাণ্টের মতে নৈতিক বিধির আদেশ বা অনুশাসন সর্ব্বপ্রকার অবস্থা, উদ্দেশ্য বা লক্ষ্যের অতীত। এই পরমবিধিসমূহের প্রামাণিকতা সার্ব্বভৌমিক। ইহারা অচলপ্রতিষ্ঠ নৈসর্গিক বিধি সমূহের অন্তর্ভুক্ত। "এইরূপ ভাবে কর্ম্ম করিয়া যাও যেন তোমার ইচ্ছাপ্রসূত নীতি তোমাদ্বারা গৃহীত হইয়া সার্ব্বভৌমিক নৈসর্গিক নিয়ম সমূহের অঙ্গীভূত হইতে পারে।"]

căt′-ē-gō-rȳ, *n.* (*Logic* & *Philos.*) A term in logic and philosophy applied to certain general classes under which objects of knowledge may be arranged ; (তর্ক-বিজ্ঞান ও দর্শন-শাস্ত্র) জ্ঞানের বিষয় সমূহ যে ব্যাপক বিভাগ সকলে শ্রেণীবদ্ধ করা যাইতে পারে। [আরিস্তোতলের মতে *Category* পদার্থ দশটী :—যথা বস্তু (substance), গুণ (quality), সংখ্যা (quantity), সম্বন্ধ (relation), ক্রিয়া (action), কাল (time), দেশ (space), রাগ (passion), অধিকার (possession), অবস্থা (situation)] **2.** (*Kant*) The conceptions which the mind forms to raise the matter of knowledge received from the senses into an intelligible notion ; ইন্দ্রিয়-সমানীত বিষয় সমূহকে বোধগম্য ধারণায় পরিণত করণার্থ মন যে ভাব সমূহ গঠন করিয়া থাকে, পদার্থ (হিঃ কোঃ)। [ক্যাণ্টের মতে এইরূপ দ্বাদশটী ভাব বা category :—যথা (১) সংখ্যা (quantity)—তদন্তর্ভুক্ত, একত্ব (unity), বহুত্ব (plurality), সমগ্রতা (totality) ; (২) গুণ (quality)—তদন্তর্ভুক্ত বাস্তবিকতা (reality), অনস্তিত্ব (negation), সসীমতা (limitation) ; (৩) সম্বন্ধ (relation), তদন্তর্ভুক্ত—বস্তু (substance), কার্য্যকারণসম্বন্ধ (causality), অন্যোন্য সম্বন্ধ (reciprocity) ; (৪) প্রকারতা (modality) ;—তদন্তর্ভুক্ত সম্ভাব্যতা (possibility), অস্তিত্ব (exsistence), অবশ্যম্ভাবিতা (necessity)] **3.** Class ; order ; division ; শ্রেণী ; পর্য্যায়, বর্গ ; বিভাগ। **—gor′-i-cal,** *adj.* **—rist,** *n.* **—rize,** *v. t.* **Categorical proposition**—নিরপেক্ষ প্রতিজ্ঞা (সাঃ পঃ), নিরপেক্ষ বাক্য (তর্কঃ-বিঃ)।

căt-ē-lĕc′-trōde, *n.* (*Phys.*) A negative electrode or cathode ; (পদার্থবিদ্যা) ঋণাত্মক তড়িদ্দ্বার, কুদ্বার (সাঃ পঃ)।

că-tē′-nă, *n.* [*L.* a chain) A chain or connected series ; শৃঙ্খল, পর্য্যায়, শ্রেণীবদ্ধ বস্তু বা বিষয়পরম্পরা। **Catena patrum**—A series of extracts from commentaries by the Fathers, on particular portion of Scriptures ; প্রাচীন খৃষ্টীয় ধর্ম্মাচার্য্যগণ কর্ত্তৃক প্রণীত বাইবেলের বিশেষ বিশেষ ভাগের ভাষ্য সমূহ হইতে উদ্ধৃত অংশ সমূহ।

căt′-ē-nă-rȳ, căt-ē-na′-ri-ăn, *adjs.* & *ns.* Like or pertaining to a chain, esp. a uniform chain freely suspended between two points ; as, a *catenarian* arch : a *catenary* curve ; শৃঙ্খলবৎ, শৃঙ্খলাকার, শৃঙ্খল সম্বন্ধীয়, বিশেষতঃ দুইটী অবলম্বন বিন্দুর মধ্যে বক্রাকারে দোদুল্যমান শৃঙ্খল সম্বন্ধীয়। ***Nouns.*** A curve formed by a uniform chain hanging freely from two fixed points, not in one vertical plane ; অবলম্বন বিন্দুদ্বয়ের মধ্যে দোদুল্যমান শৃঙ্খলদ্বারা রচিত বক্ররেখা।

căt′-ē-nāte, *v. t.* To connect like links ; শিকলের কড়ার মত সংযোগ করা। **—nat-ed,** *adj.* Chain-like ; শৃঙ্খলসদৃশ। **—na′-tion,** *n.* Connection of links or union of parts, as in a chain ; a regular or connected series ; শৃঙ্খলবৎ গ্রন্থন ; সংযোজন, শৃঙ্খলা, শ্রেণী, পরম্পরা।

cā-têr, *n.* The four of cards or dice ; পাশার চার পো, তাসের চৌকা।

cā-têr, *v. i.* **1.** To purvey food ; to buy provisions, (with *for*) ; ভক্ষ্য-দ্রব্য সরবরাহ করা, খাদ্যদ্রব্য যোগান ;

খাদ্যদ্রব্য ক্রয় করা। **2.** To provide amusement, entertainment, etc. for ; নাচ তামাসা ভোজ প্রভৃতি দেওয়া। **—er,** *n.* **—ess,** *n.*

căt'-ĕr-ăn, *n.* An irregular soldier, marauder or robber of the Scottish Highlands ; hence a brigand ; a cattle-lifter ; স্কট্‌লণ্ডের উত্তর প্রদেশের অনিয়মিত সৈন্য, দস্যু বা লুণ্ঠনকারী ; দস্যু ; গোচোর।

că'-tẽr-cous-in (-cŭzn), *n.* An intimate or good friend ; অন্তরঙ্গ বন্ধু, অকৃত্রিম বন্ধু। **—ship,** *n.* **To be catercousins**—To be on good or familiar terms ; বন্ধুভাবে বাস করা, অন্তরঙ্গভাবে বাস করা।

căt'-ẽr-pĭl-lar (-lẽr), *n* **1.** The elongated worm-like larva of a butterfly or moth ; প্রজাপতি বা তসরে পোকার লম্বা কীরা, তৃণজলৌকা,

Caterpillar.

কীট (সাঃ পঃ), শূককীট (আঃ বঃ), শোঁয়া পোকা। **2.** A rapacious person or one who preys upon the community ; লুণ্ঠক, সমাজের রক্ত-শোষক।

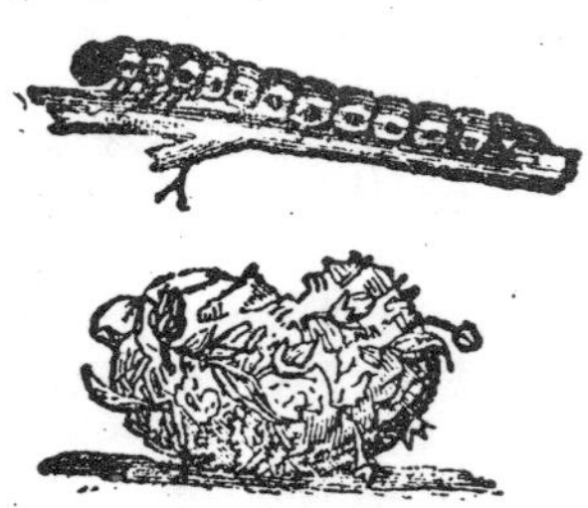

Caterpillar & cocoon.

căt'-ẽr-waul (-wâl), *v. i.* & *n.* **1.** To cry as cats in heat or rutting time ; কামপীড়িত বিড়াল-বিড়ালীর মত চীৎকার করা। **2.** To quarrel like cats ; বিড়ালের মত ঝগড়া করা। ***Noun.*** The shriek or cry of cats at rutting time ; cat's screaming ; কামমোহিত বিড়াল-বিড়ালীর ধ্বনি ; মার্জ্জার রব, ম্যাও ম্যাঁও শব্দ।

cātes, *n. pl.* See CATE.

căt'-gŭt, *n.* A cord of musical instruments etc. made of the intestines of sheep, horse or ass ; মেষ, অশ্ব বা গর্দ্দভের অন্ত্র হইতে প্রস্তুত বাদ্যযন্ত্র প্রভৃতির তন্ত্র, চর্ম্মসূত্র, নাড়ীসূত্র, বীণা বা বেহালাদির তাঁইত, তন্ত্রী, তন্ত্র। **2.** The stringed instruments collectively ; তন্ত্রীবিশিষ্ট বাদ্যযন্ত্র সমূহ। **3.** A coarse corded cloth ; এক প্রকার মোটা কাপড়।

căth'-ă-rist, *n.* A puritan ; শুদ্ধাচারী ব্যক্তি। **—rism,** *n.* **—ris'-tic,** *adj.*

căth'-ă-rīze, *v. t.* To make clean ; esp. to make chemically clean ; পরিশোধিত করা ; বিশেষতঃ রাসায়নিকভাবে বিশোধিত করা।

că-thär'-sis, *n.* (*Med.*) **1.** A natural or artificial purgation of any passage, as of the mouth, bowels, etc ; (ভৈষজ্য-শাস্ত্র) অন্ত্র, অন্নবহনাড়ী প্রভৃতির নৈসর্গিক বা মনুষ্যকৃত শোধন। **2.** An outlet to emotion afforded by drama, etc. ; নাট্যাদি পাঠ বা দর্শন দ্বারা আবেগ স্ফুরণ, রসোদ্রেক (হিঃ কোঃ)।

că-thär'-tic, *adj.* & *n.* (*Med.*) Cleansing the bowels ; purgative ; অন্ত্রশোধক ; বিরেচক, রেচক (সাঃ পঃ), সারক (ভাবঃ প্রঃ), ভেদক (সাঃ পঃ), মলনিঃসারক, কোষ্ঠ পরিষ্কারক, অনুলোমন (ঠাকুর)। ***Noun.*** A purgative medicine ; often a mild purgative ; কোষ্ঠপরিষ্কারক ঔষধ, জোলাপ ; (প্রায়শঃ) মৃদু বিরেচক ঔষধ। **Cathartic acid**—সোণামুখীর তিক্তাস্বাদ এবং বিরেচক নির্যাস।

că-thē'-dră, *n.* **1.** The official seat or throne of a bishop ; hence, the episcopal see or dignity ; খৃষ্টীয় ধর্ম্মাধ্যক্ষের আসন ; অতএব খৃষ্টীয় ধর্ম্মাচার্য্যের অধিকার বা পদগৌরব। **2.** The professional chair of one (a professor or teacher) entitled to teach with authority ; প্রামাণ্য শিক্ষা বা উপদেশ দানের অধিকারী ব্যক্তির (অধ্যাপক বা উপদেষ্টার) আসন। ***Ex cathedra***—ধর্ম্মাসন হইতে, প্রামাণ্য ভাবে।

că-thē'-drăl, *n.* & *adj.* The principal church of a diocese, in which is the seat or throne of a bishop ; বিশপের অধিকারভুক্ত স্থানের মধ্যে সর্ব্বপ্রধান ধর্ম্মমন্দির, মহা ধর্ম্মমন্দির, মহাভজনভবন, মহামণ্ডপ, মহামন্দির। ***Adj.*** Belonging to a cathedral ; খৃষ্টীয়-মহাধর্ম্ম মন্দির সম্বন্ধীয়।

Căth'-ẽr-ĭne-wheel (-whēl), *n.* **1.** (*Arch.*) A window or compartment of a window, of a circular form with radiating spikes ; (স্থপতি-বিদ্যা) ছটার মত বিকীর্য্যমান আর (পাখী) বিশিষ্ট গোলাকার বাতায়ন বা বাতায়নের বিভাগ, সূর্য্যমুখী খিড়কী। **2.** A firework which as it goes off, rotates like a wheel ; চরকী বাজি। **3.** Lateral summersaults ; পার্শ্বের দিকে ডিগবাজী। **To turn Catherine-wheels**—To make a series of summersaults sideways ; পাশের দিকে ক্রমাগত কয়েকবার ডিগবাজী খাওয়া।

căth'-ĕ-tẽr, *n.* A tubular instrument usually of silver, to draw off the urine from the bladder ; মূত্রনিঃসারণার্থ সচ্ছিদ্র শলাকা, মূত্রনিষ্কষক যন্ত্র বিশেষ, মূত্রাকর্ষিণী, আঃ বঃ)।

căth'-ōde, *n.* (*Electr.*) The negative pole of a current, (opposed to *anode*) ; the surface in contact with the negative pole ; (তাড়িত-বিজ্ঞান) বিদ্যুৎপ্রবাহের ঋণধ্রুব ; ঋণধ্রুবের সহিত সংস্পৃষ্ট (কোন কিছুর) উপরিভাগ, বিগম (সাঃ পঃ), নিমল (ঐ), কুম্ভার (ঐ), ঋণধ্রুব (হিঃ কোঃ)। **Că-thŏd'-ic, —o-dal,** *adjs.* **Cathode rays**—কুরশ্মি (সাঃ পঃ), বিয়োগরশ্মি (ঐ)।

căth'-ō-lic, *adj.* & *n.* **1.** Universal or general ; as, so great and *catholic* a war ; বিশ্বজনীন, সার্ব্বলৌকিক, সার্ব্বভৌম। **2.** All embracing ; broad-minded ; tolerant ; liberal ; সর্ব্বানুসারী (হিঃ কোঃ); প্রশস্তমনাঃ, উদারমনাঃ ; পরমতসহিষ্ণু ; উদার। **3.** Orthodox, as opposed to *heterodox* and *sectarian*—applied esp. to the Christian Church before separation into Greek or Eastern and Latin or Western ; গোঁড়া,—গ্রীক অথবা প্রাচ্য এবং ল্যাটিন বা প্রতীচ্য এই দুই সম্প্রদায়ে বিভক্ত হইবার পূর্ব্বকালীন খৃষ্টীয় ধর্ম্মসমাজ সম্বন্ধে বিশেষভাবে প্রযুক্ত। **4.** Belonging to the part of the Latin Church that remained under the Roman obedience after the Reformation ; খৃষ্টধর্ম্মসংস্কারের পর ল্যাটিন খৃষ্টীয়সমাজের যে অংশ পোপের অধীন রহিয়াছিল—তৎসম্বন্ধীয়। **5.** Relating to the Roman Catholics ; রোমানক্যাথলিক সম্প্রদায় সম্বন্ধীয়। ***Noun.*** **1.** A member of the universal Christian Church (founded by Christ and his apostles) ; (খৃষ্ট এবং তদীয় দ্বাদশজন শিষ্যদ্বারা প্রতিষ্ঠিত) সার্ব্বভৌম খৃষ্টীয় ধর্ম্মসমাজের সভ্য। **2.** A member of the Church of Rome ; রোমানক্যাথলিক খৃষ্টীয়ান, রোমক-ধর্ম্মাবলম্বী। **Ca-thol'-i-cal-ly, –ly,** *advs.* **Că-thŏl'-i-cism,** *n.* **Ca-thol'-i-cize,** *v. t.* **Catholic Church**—সার্ব্বভৌম খৃষ্টীয় ধর্মসমাজ ; খৃষ্ট-বিশ্বাসী জনসমাজ। **Catholic Emancipation**—ইংলণ্ড, স্কট্‌লণ্ড এবং আয়র্লণ্ডের রোমানক্যাথলিকগণকে নানাপ্রকার নাগরিক অক্ষমতা ও পক্ষপাতমূলক রাজবিধির কবল হইতে মুক্তিপ্রদান। **Catholic Epistles**—বাইবেলের 'নবনিয়ম' গ্রন্থান্তর্গত লিপিসমূহ। এই সকল লিপি যীশুখৃষ্টের সপ্ত শিষ্য বিভিন্ন ধর্ম্মসমাজের নিকট প্রেরণ করেন। **Catholic King** or **His Catholic Majesty**—স্পেন নৃপতির উপাধিবিশেষ।

căth-ŏ-lĭc'-i-tȳ, *n.* **1.** Liberality of sentiments ; breadth of view ; উদারতা, চিত্তৌদার্য্য ; মতের প্রসার। **2.** Wide prevalence ; বিস্তৃত প্রভাব। **3.** The doctrines or faith of the whole Christian Church ; the doctrine of the Church of Rome ; the religion of the Roman Catholics ; নিখিল খৃষ্টীয় সমাজের ধর্ম্মমত বা ধর্ম্মবিশ্বাস ; রোমীয় সমাজের ধর্ম্মমত ; রোমান ক্যাথলিক ধর্ম্ম।

că-thŏl'-i-cŏn, *n.* (*Med.*) A remedy for all diseases ; a panacea ; (ভৈষজ্য-শাস্ত্র) সর্ব্বরোগহর ঔষধ ; সর্ব্বৌষধি।

Căt'-il-ine (-în), *n.* A profligate conspirator ; দুর্বৃত্ত ষড়যন্ত্রকারী। **–i-li-na'-ri-an,** *adj.* [খৃষ্টপূর্ব্ব ৬৩ অব্দে ক্যাটালিনা নামক এক দুর্বৃত্ত রোমনগরী ধ্বংসের জন্য ষড়যন্ত্র করিয়াছিল।]

căt'-kin, *n.* (*Bot.*) A downy hanging inflorescence of the willow, birch, etc. ; (উদ্ভিদ্-বিদ্যা) তরুশাখা হইতে লম্বমান বিড়াল পুচ্ছাকৃতি হরিৎ পুষ্পস্তবক, শিখা (সাঃ পঃ)।

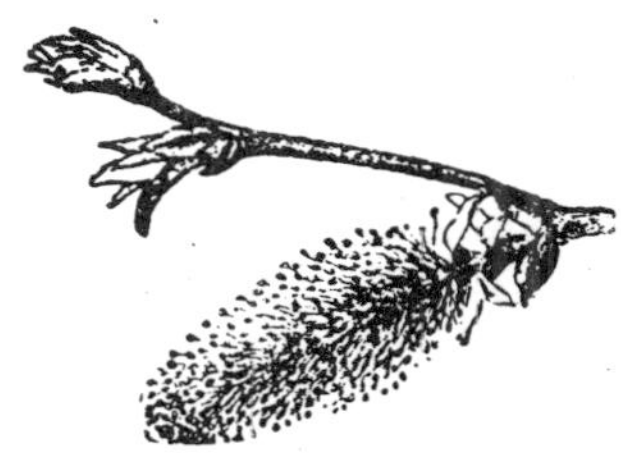

Catkin.

căt'-ling, *n.* **1.** A kitten ; বিড়ালছানা। **2.** Fine cat-gut ; the string of a lute, violin, etc. ; সূক্ষ্মচর্ম্মরজ্জু ; বীণা, বেহালা প্রভৃতির তন্ত, তন্ত্রী। **3.** An amputating knife (spelt also *cat'-lin*) ; অস্ত্রচিকিৎসকগণ দ্বারা অঙ্গচ্ছেদনে ব্যবহৃত কর্ত্তরিকা (ছুরিকা) বিশেষ।

Că-tō'-ni-ăn, *adj.* Resembling Cato ; severe ; প্রাচীন রোমনগরবাসী কঠোরস্বভাব কেটো সম্বন্ধীয় ; কঠোর।

că-tŏp'-tric, –tri-căl, *adjs.* Of or pertaining to a mirror or reflector ; produced by, or depending on, reflection ; দর্পণ বা আলোক পরাবর্ত্তক বিষয়ক ; আলোক পরাবর্ত্তনজাত, পরাবর্ত্তনাধীন। **Catoptric light**—পরাবর্ত্তক প্রভাব (হিঃ কোঃ)। **Catoptric light telescope**—পরাবর্ত্তক-প্রভাদূরবীণ।

că-tŏp'-trics, *n.* The part of optics which treats of reflected light ; দৃষ্টিবিজ্ঞানের প্রতিবিম্ববিষয়ক অঙ্গ, প্রভাপরাবর্ত্তন শাস্ত্র (হিঃ কোঃ)।

cat's'-eye, *n.* See CAT.

căt'-tle, *n. pl.* **1.** Beasts of pasture, especially oxen, bulls, and cows ; sometimes also horses, sheep, etc. ; (*slang*) horses ; গবাদি পশু ; (কখন কখন) অশ্ব, মেষ প্রভৃতি ; (ইতরভাষায়) অশ্ব সমূহ। [গ্রেটব্রিটেনে ষণ্ড, গাভী এবং গোবৎস দিগকে "Black cattle" কহে, পরন্ত ছাগ এবং মেষকে small cattle কহে] **2.** Contemptible persons ; গরুরদল (অবজ্ঞার্থে মনুষ্যকে বলা হয়)। **Cattle-feeder**—গবাদি পশুর খাদ্য-নিয়ামক যন্ত্রবিশেষ। **Cattle-leader**—দুষ্টগরুর নাকে বাঁধিবার আংটা-বিশেষ। **Cattle-lifter**—গো-চোর। **Cattleman**—গোপাল, গোপ, পশুপাল। **Cattle-plague**—গবাদির স্পর্শ-সংক্রামক পীড়া-বিশেষ, গোমড়ক, গোবসন্ত। **Cattle show**—পশুপ্রদর্শনী। **Cattle-trespass**—পরের ক্ষেত্রে গবাদির প্রবেশ। **Herd of cattle**—গোকুল।

Cau-că'-sian (că-), *adj.* & *n.* Belonging to Mount Caucasus or to the neighbouring countries ; ককেসস্ পর্ব্বত বা তৎসন্নিহিত প্রদেশ সম্বন্ধীয়। ***Noun.*** A member of the white race ; Indo-European ; শ্বেতাঙ্গ ; আর্য্যবংশোদ্ভব শ্বেতকায় পুরুষ।

cau'-cŭs (că-), *n.* & *v. t.* (*American*) A private meeting of citizens to agree upon candidates to be proposed for election to officers, or to concert measures for supporting a party ; (আমেরিকায়) রাষ্ট্রীয় পদপ্রার্থিগণের কোন্ কোন্ ব্যক্তিকে নির্ব্বাচিত করিতে হইবে, তদ্বিষয়ে মতৈক্যের জন্য অথবা

দল বিশেষের সমর্থনের উপায় নির্দ্ধারণার্থ নগরবাসিগণের সভাবিশেষ, সভ্যনির্ব্বাচনী সভা। *Verb t.* To organise, to dictate to, by means of this system ; উক্ত সভাদ্বারা ব্যবস্থাবদ্ধ করা বা প্রভুত্ব সহকারে কর্ত্তব্য নির্দ্ধারণ করা।

cau'-dăl (cä-), *adj.* Of or like a tail ; পৌচ্ছ, পুচ্ছবৎ। **—ly,** *adv.*

cau'-dāte (cä-), *adj.* Having a tail ; পুচ্ছবিশিষ্ট, লাঙ্গুলবিশিষ্ট।

cau'-dex (cä-dĕx), *n.* (*Bot.*) The stem of a tree, especially of a palm or tree fern ; (উদ্ভিদ্-বিদ্যা) বৃক্ষের কাণ্ড, বিশেষতঃ তাল বা পর্ণাঙ্গ জাতীয় বৃক্ষের কাণ্ড।

cau'-dle (cä-), *n.* A kind of warm drink, a mixture of wine or ale with eggs, gruel, sugar and spices, for sick persons, especially women in child-bed ; রুগ্ন ব্যক্তি বা অচিরপ্রসূতা স্ত্রীলোকগণের জন্য ডিম্ব, চিনি, মদ্য এবং সুগন্ধি মসলা মিশ্রিত উষ্ণতা-সঞ্চারক পানীয় বিশেষ, অণ্ডাদি মিশ্রিত মদ্যময় পানীয় বিশেষ।

caught (kät), *past tense* & *p. p.* of CATCH.

caul (cäl), *n.* **1.** A kind of net or covering for the hairs ; the hinder part of caps ; কেশাবরক জাল বা আচ্ছাদন ; টুপীর পশ্চাদ্‌ভাগ। **2.** A membrane enveloping the fetus which sometimes covers the head of the child at its birth ; গর্ভস্থ ভ্রূণের দেহাবরক জালবৎ ত্বক্‌বিশেষ, গর্ভবেষ্টন, উল্ব (সাঃ পঃ)। [এই ত্বক্ সময় সময় সদ্যজাত শিশুর মস্তকে জড়াইয়া থাকে। এইরূপ উল্ব সহিত জন্মলাভ করিলে জাতক ভাগ্যবান হয় বলিয়া ইংলণ্ডের লোকগণ বিশ্বাস করিয়া থাকেন। এই উল্বধারক ব্যক্তি কদাচ জলমগ্ন হয় না, এই বিশ্বাস হেতুও ইহা সমাদৃত হইয়া থাকে।]

caul'-drŏn (cäl-), *n.* A large kettle or boiler ; কটাহ।

cau-lĕs'-cĕnt (cä-), *adj.* (*Bot.*) With visible stem ; (উদ্ভিদ্-বিদ্যা) চক্ষুগ্রাহ্য কাণ্ডবিশিষ্ট।

cau'-li-flōw-ēr, *n.* A variety of the cabbage, with large compact fleshy flowerhead ; ফুলকপি।

cau'-līne (cä-), *adj.* (*Bot.*) Growing on, or belonging to, a stem ; (উদ্ভিদ্-বিদ্যা) কাণ্ডজাত, কাণ্ডসম্বন্ধীয়, দণ্ডস্থিত (সাঃ পঃ)।

cau'-lis (cä-), *n.* (*Bot.*) The stem of a plant ; (উদ্ভিদ্-বিদ্যা) ওষধিকাণ্ড (সাঃ পঃ)।

caulk (*kawk*), *v. t.* To stop up seams of a ship with oakum and melted pitch to prevent leaking ; আলকাতরা ও পুরাতন কাছির শণের সাহায্যে জাহাজের ছিদ্র রোধ করা।

cau'-mă (cä-), [Gr. *kauma*, burning heat] *n.* (*Med.*) Great heat, as in fever ; (ভৈষজ্য শাস্ত্র) অত্যুত্তাপ।

caus'-ăl (cäz-), *n.* Pertaining to a cause or expressing a cause ; কারণ সম্পর্কীয়, কারণ বাচক।

cau-sā'-tion (cä-), *n.* **1.** The act of causing ; সংঘটন। **2.** Relation between cause and effect ; কার্য্যকরণ সম্বন্ধ। **3.** The doctrine that all things cause ; কারণবাদ। **—ist,** *n.*

caus'-a-tive (cäz-ă-tĭv), *adj.* **1.** Causing ; সংঘটনকারী। **2.** (*Gram.*) Expressing cause ; (ব্যাকরণ) কারণবাচক, ণিজন্ত।

cause (cäz), **1.** That which produces an effect or contributes to it ; কারণ, হেতু। **2.** A person or thing that occassions something ; কারক, কর্ত্তা। **3.** The ground, reason, or motive for action ; হেতু, উদ্দেশ্য। **4.** (*Law*) The matter about which a person goes to law ; the case of one party in a suit ; (আইন) মোকদ্দমার বিষয় ; মোকদ্দমা। **Cause'-less,** *adj.* **1.** Without a cause ; groundless ; as, a *causeless* and most unjust civil war ; অকারণ ; হেতুশূন্য, অহৈতুক, অহেতুক। **2.** Having no antecedent cause ; fortuitous ; অনাদি, পূর্ব্ববর্ত্তী কারণ বিহীন ; আকস্মিক। **Cause'-less-ly,** *adv.* Without cause ; অকারণে, অহৈতুক, খামকা, (*Colloq.*) অনর্থক, বৃথা, নিরর্থক। **Cause body, Causal body**—কারণ শরীর (হিঃ কোঃ), বিজ্ঞানময়কোষ (ঐ), জ্ঞানদেহ (ঐ)। ***Cause celebre***—বিখ্যাত মোকদ্দমা, (সাধারণতঃ) অতীব কৌতুহলোদ্দীপক ফৌজদারী মোকদ্দমা। **Cause of action**—মোকদ্দমার হেতু, অজুহাত। ***Cause sui***—স্বয়ম্ভু (হিঃ কোঃ), স্বকারণ (ঐ)। **Efficient cause**—নিমিত্ত কারণ। **First cause**—পরম কারণ, সৃষ্টিকর্ত্তা। **Formal cause**—স্থূল কারণ (হিঃ কোঃ)। **Material cause**—উপাদান কারণ, সমবায়িকারণ (আঃ বঃ)। **Primary cause**—নিদান, আদি কারণ, বীজভূত কারণ, আদ্যবীজ। **Relation of cause and effect**—কার্য্যকারণভাব, জন্যজনকভাব, সাধ্যসাধকভাব। **To make common cause (with)**—To join in behalf of a common object ; এক উদ্দেশ্য সাধনে যোগদান করা।

cause (cäz), *v. t.* **1.** To affect as an agent ; to bring about ; to produce ; কোন কিছুর উপর ক্রিয়া করা ; ঘটান ; উৎপাদন করা, জন্মান। **2.** To induce or make (a person or thing *to do*) ; লওয়ান, করান।

causerie, (*F.*), *n.* A newspaper article of an informal or conversational kind, esp. on literary subjects ; সংবাদপত্রের চুটকী-প্রবন্ধ।

causeuse, (*F.*), *n.* A small sofa on which two persons can sit ; দুই জন লোকের বসিবার উপযোগী ক্ষুদ্র পর্য্যঙ্ক।

cause'-way, cau'-sey (cäz-wā, cä-zī), *ns.* & *vs. t.* **1.** A raised way across a low or wet place or marshy ground ; জাঙ্গাল, আলিপথ। **2.** A raised foot-way by a road ; পথিপার্শ্বস্থিত উচ্চ পাদচারণ পথ। *Verb t.* **1.** To pave with cobbles or pebbles ; প্রস্তরখণ্ড দ্বারা মণ্ডিত করা। **2.** To provide with a causeway ; জাঙ্গাল নির্ম্মাণ করিয়া দেওয়া।

caus'-tic (căs-), *adj.* & *n.* **1.** Burning ; corrosive ; destructive of organic tissue ; প্রদাহজনক, দাহক, বিদাহী ; ক্ষয়কর ; জৈব বিধানতন্তুর ধ্বংসকারক। **2.** (*Fig.*) Cutting ; biting ; sarcastic ; (said of language, wit and persons) ; (লক্ষণায়) মর্ম্মচ্ছেদী, মর্ম্মভেদী, মর্ম্মান্তিক, অরুন্তুদ, অন্তর্দাহজনক ; তীব্র ; বিদ্রূপাত্মক। ***Noun.*** A substance which burns and destroys living tissue when brought in contact with it ; দাহক, কাষ্টিক পদার্থ। **—ti-cal-ly,** *adv.* **—tic'-i-ty,** *n.* (দৃষ্টি-বিজ্ঞান) যে বক্ররেখার উপর অপর বক্ররেখা হইতে পরাবর্ত্তিত বা প্রতিবিম্বিত আলোক রশ্মি-সমূহ স্পর্শরেখা (tangent) স্বরূপ পতিত হয়, বক্রাংশুস্পর্শ (হিঃ কোঃ)।

cau'-têr-ize (că-), *v. t.* **1.** To burn or sear with a caustic or hot iron ; দাহক পদার্থ বা তপ্ত লৌহ দ্বারা কোন স্থান দগ্ধ করা। **2.** (*Fig.*) To make callous ; (লক্ষণায়) অনুভূতিশূন্য করা। **—i-za'-tion,** *n.*

cau'-têr-ÿ (că-), **1.** A heated metallic instrument used for searing organic tissue ; জীবদেহস্থ তন্তুসমূহ দগ্ধকরণার্থ উত্তপ্ত ধাতব যন্ত্র বিশেষ। **2.** (*Med.*) A burning or searing of morbid flesh, with a hot iron or caustic ; (ভৈষজ্য-শাস্ত্র) উত্তপ্ত লৌহ বা দাহক ঔষধ দ্বারা রোগদুষ্ট মাংস দগ্ধ করণ, অগ্নি-কর্ম্মণ্য (সাঃ পঃ), দাহকর্ম্ম (ঐ)।

cau'-tion (că-), *n.* & *v.t.* **1.** A word of warning ; a hint or advice to any one to take heed ; সাবধানতা-সূচক বাক্য ; সতর্কতা অবলম্বনের ইঙ্গিত বা পরামর্শ। **2.** The taking of heed ; prudence in regard to danger ; সাবধানতা অবলম্বন ; সাবধানতা, সতর্কতা। **3.** (*Mil.*) A preliminary word of command ; (সামরিক-শাস্ত্র) প্রাথমিক আদেশবাণী। **4.** (*Scotch Law*) Security ; pledge ; bail ; (স্কট্‌লণ্ড্ দেশীয় আইন) প্রতিভূ ; বন্ধক ; জামিন। ***Verb t.*** To warn ; সাবধান করা, সতর্ক করা। **—a-ry,** *adj.* **—tious,** *adj.* Heedful ; careful ; circumspect ; সতর্ক ; সাবধান, হুঁশিয়ার (*Colloq.*) ; চৌকস। **—tious-ly,** *adv.* **—tious-ness,** *n.* **Caution money**—Money deposited as a security for good conduct ; a sum deposited before entering college, by way of security ; সদ্ব্যবহারের জন্য জামিন স্বরূপ গচ্ছিত অর্থ ; কলেজে প্রবেশকালে ছাত্রগণকে যে অর্থ জামিনস্বরূপ গচ্ছিত রাখিতে হয়।

căv-ăl-cāde', *n.* A procession of persons on horseback ; অশ্বারোহিগণের সংযান বা যাত্রা।

căv-ă-lier' (-lër) *n.*, *adj.* & *v. t.* **1.** A horseman, esp. a horse-soldier ; অশ্বারোহী, সাদী, অশ্বারোহী সৈন্য। **2.** A courtly gentleman ; a gallant, esp. one attending upon or escorting a lady ; শিষ্ট ভদ্রলোক ; নারীমোহন (উজ্জ্বলঃ), নাগর, স্ত্রীগণের পরিচর্য্যায় রত পুরুষ। **3** A partisan of Charles I, (as contrasted with a Roundhand) ; ইংলণ্ডেশ্বর প্রথম চার্লসের পক্ষীয় ব্যক্তি। ***Adj.*** Oft-hand ; free and easy ; as, this *cavalier* declaration of the youngman ; haughty ; supercilious ; disdainful ; as, this *cavalier* tone from an unknown person ; হঠাৎ, অচিন্তিত ; অবাধ এবং সহজ ; উদ্ধত ; গর্ব্বিত ; অবজ্ঞাপূর্ণ। ***Verb t.*** To act as escort to (a lady) ; কোন মহিলার শরীররক্ষকের কায করা। **—ly,** *adv.* & *adj.*

căv'-ăl-rÿ, *n.* The collective name for horse-soldiers, (opposed to infantry) ; অশ্বারোহী সেনা, অশ্বানীক, তুরগবল, বাজিসৈন্য, সাদীসৈন্য।

cāve, *n.*, *v. t.* & *i.* **1.** A hollow place in the earth ; গুহা, কন্দর, গহ্বর, দেবখাত, দরী, গুম্ফা, বিবর। **2.** (*Politics*) A secession, or a group of seceders, from a political party, (as from the liberal party in England in 1866) ; (রাজনীতি) রাজনীতিক দলত্যাগ ; কোন রাজনীতিক দলত্যাগী ব্যক্তিবর্গ। ***Verb t.*** To hollow or make into a cave ; to place or inclose as in a cave ; খনন করত গহ্বরে পরিণত করা, গহ্বরে পরিণত করা ; গহ্বরে স্থাপন করা, গুহা-বদ্ধ করা। ***Verb i.*** **1.** To fall as an overturned thing ; উল্টাইয়া পড়া। **2.** To form a political cave or cabal ; রাজনীতিক কুচক্রিদল গঠন করা, কোন রাজনীতিক দল ত্যাগ করিয়া নূতন দল গঠন করা। **Cave-bear**—এক প্রকার লুপ্ত ভল্লুক,—যাহাদের দেহাবশেষ গহ্বরে প্রাপ্ত হওয়া যায়, গুহাঋক্ষ (অভিঃ)। **Cave-dweller**—অনৈতিহাসিক যুগের যে সমস্ত লোক গহ্বরে বাস করিত। **To cave in**—To fall in over a hollow ; to break down ; to collapse ; গর্ত্ত বা গহ্বরের ভিতরের মাটি ধসিয়া পড়া ; ভাঙ্গিয়া পড়া ; ছত্রভঙ্গ হওয়া।

cā'-vē-ăt, *n.* **1.** A warning ; সতর্ক হইবার খবর। **2.** (*Law*) A notice to stop procedure ; (আইন) আদালতের মীমাংসাধীন কোন বিষয় স্থগিত রাখিবার জন্য মোকদ্দমার কোন পক্ষীয় ব্যক্তিকর্ত্তৃক) আদালতে বিজ্ঞাপন।

căv'-ĕn-dish, *n.* Leaf tobacco pressed into cakes ; চাপদ্বারা পিণ্ডাকারে পরিণত তাম্রকূট পত্র।

căv'-êrn, *n.*, *v. t.* & *i.* A subterranean hollow ; ভূগর্ভস্থ গহ্বর, গুহা, কন্দর (সাঃ পঃ), দেবখাত। ***Verb t.*** **1.** To enclose in, as if in a cavern ; as, a hermit *caverned* in a wood ; কন্দরস্থ করা, গুহাবদ্ধ করা। **2.** To hollow out so as to form a cavern ; গহ্বর খনন করা। ***Verb i.*** To lurk or live in a cavern ; গহ্বরে লুক্কায়িত থাকা, গহ্বরে বাস করা। **—ous,** *adj.*

căv'-ess-ŏn (-ĕs-), *n.* A kind of nose-band of iron or other stiff material used in breaking and training horses ; ঘোটকের নাসাবন্ধ।

căv-i-âr', căv-i-āre' (-ē-), *n.* The prepared and salted roe of the sturgeon and other large fish as a relish, (esp. in Russia) ; মৎস্য বিশেষের লবণ মিশ্রিত অণ্ড, লাবণমৎস্যাণ্ড।

căv′-ĭl, *v. i.* & *n.* To raise captious and trifling objections ; to find fault unfairly or without good reason (*at, about*) ; তুচ্ছ বিষয়ে আপত্তি তোলা ; মিথ্যা দোষ আরোপণ করা, অমূলক আপত্তি উত্থাপন করা, খুঁত ধরা। ***Noun.*** A captious or frivolous objection ; a quibble ; তুচ্ছ আপত্তি, খুঁত ; কুতর্ক। **—ling,** *adj.* **—ler,** *n.*

căv′-i-tȳ, *n.* A hollow place ; an empty space within a solid body ; গর্ত ; সংহত পদার্থমধ্যস্থ শূন্যগর্ভ স্থান, কোটর, কুহর, ছিদ্র, রন্ধ্র।

cā′-vȳ, *n.* An American rodent ; আমেরিকাদেশীয় দন্তুর জন্তুবিশেষ।

caw (cä), *n.* & *v. i.* The cry or call of a rook, crow, raven, etc. ; কা কা শব্দ, কাকরুত। ***Verb i.*** (Of rooks, crows, ravens, etc.) To utter their natural cry ; (কাক, দাঁড়কাক প্রভৃতির পক্ষে) কা কা শব্দ করা। **To caw out**—To utter in a cawing tone ; কা কা করিয়া কথা বলা।

Căx′-tŏn, *n.* **1.** A book printed by (William Caxton in 1474) the first English Printer ; ইংলণ্ডের সর্ব্বপ্রথম মুদ্রাকর উইলিয়েম ক্যাক্সটন্ দ্বারা মুদ্রিত পুস্তকবিশেষ। **2.** A kind of type like that used by Caxton ; ক্যাক্সটনকর্তৃক ব্যবহৃত হরফের অনুরূপ হরফ।

cay-enne′ (cā-ĕn), *n.* A very pungent powder obtained from the dried and ground pods and seeds of capsicum ; একপ্রকার অতি-ঝাল লঙ্কামরিচের চূর্ণ। **Cayenne-pepper**—Red pepper ; লঙ্কামরিচ।

Cay′-măn (cā-), **Cai′-măn** (cā-), *n.* A species of south American alligator (with round short muzzle) ; দক্ষিণ আমেরিকার কুম্ভীরবিশেষ।

că-zique′ (-zēk), **că-zic′** (-zēc), *n.* Same as CACIQUE.

cease (sēs), *v. i.* & *t.* **1.** To stop ; to give over ; to desist (*from*) ; থামা, স্থগিত হওয়া ; পরিত্যাগ করা ; নিরস্ত হওয়া, নিবৃত্ত থাকা, বিরত হওয়া, ক্ষান্ত হওয়া। **2.** (Of actions, feelings, phenomena, etc.) To come to an end ; to be at an end ; সমাপ্ত হওয়া ; অবসান হওয়া। ***Verb t.*** To leave off ; to discontinue (one's own action) ; ছাড়িয়া দেওয়া ; বন্ধ করা। **Cease′-less,** *adj.* Without pause or stop ; অবিরল, অবিরাম, অবিশ্রান্ত, বিরামবিহীন (গীতাঞ্জঃ), বিরামহীন (ঐ), নিরবচ্ছিন্ন, নিত্য, সতত, অবিরত, নিরন্তর। **Cease′-less-ly,** *adv.* **Cease′-less-ness,** *n.* **To cease fire**—(*Mil.*) To discontinue firing ; (সামরিকশাস্ত্র) গুলিবর্ষণে নিরস্ত হওয়া। **Without cease**—Incessantly ; অবিরত, অনুক্ষণ, নিরন্তর।

cē′-ci-tȳ, *n.* Blindness (*usu. fig.*) ; অন্ধতা (সাধারণতঃ লক্ষণায়)।

cē-dar (-dĕr), *n.* **1.** A large evergreen tree remarkable for the durability and fragrance of its wood ; একজাতীয় দেবদারু। **2.** The wood of this tree ; উক্ত বৃক্ষের কাঠ। **—darn,** (*poet.*) *adj.* **Indian cedar**—দেবদারু (ওয়াট্)।

cede (sēd), *v.t.* To give up ; esp. to give up a portion of territory ; সমর্পণ করা ; বিশেষতঃ কোন রাজ্যের অংশবিশেষ ছাড়িয়া দেওয়া।

cē-dil′-lă, *n.* A mark written under C to show that it is to be sounded like s ; C এই অক্ষরের "স্" এর অনুরূপ উচ্চারণ সূচনার জন্য তন্নিম্নে যে চিহ্ন (,) লিখিত হয়।

Cedrus Deodara—দেবদারু (বেলঃ)।

cee (sē), *n.* The letter "C" ; এই বর্ণ। **Cee-spring, C-spring**—শকটের প্রধান অংশের অবলম্বনস্বরূপ ইংরেজী "C" অক্ষরের অনুরূপ স্থিতিস্থাপক অংশ বিশেষ।

ceil (sēl), *v. i.* To cover or overlay the inner side of the roof of ; to plaster the roof of (a building or apartment) ; ছাদের ভিতরের দিক মণ্ডিত বা আচ্ছাদিত করা ; দালান বা কোঠার ছাদে আস্তর দেওয়া।

ceil′-ing (sēl-), *n.* **1.** The act of one who ceils a room ; ছাদের ভিতরের পৃষ্ঠ আচ্ছাদন। **2.** The inner roof of a room ; ভিতরের দিকের ছাদ।

cĕl′-ă-dŏn, *n.* **1.** A pale sea-green colour ; সমুদ্রজলবৎ নিষ্প্রভ হরিদ্বর্ণ।

cĕl′-ăn-dīne, *n.* The name of two distinct plants, bearing yellow flowers ; পীতবর্ণ পুষ্পপ্রসূ দুইপ্রকার বৃক্ষ।

cĕl′-ĕ-brănt, *n.* One who performs a solemn rite ; esp. the priest who officiates at the Eucharist ; ধর্ম্ম-সংক্রান্ত ক্রিয়া সম্পাদক ; খৃষ্টের শেষ ভোজন ক্রিয়া সম্পাদক যাজক।

cĕl′-ĕ-brāte, *v. t.* & *i.* **1.** To perform publicly and in due form (any religious ceremony, a marriage, funeral, etc.) ; to solemnize ; উৎসবাদি সম্পন্ন করা, অনুষ্ঠান করা ; বিধি পূর্ব্বক সম্পাদন করা। **2.** To observe with solemn rites (a day, festival, etc.) ; as, to *celebrate* a birth day ; ধর্ম্ম সংক্রান্ত ক্রিয়া কলাপের অনুষ্ঠান করা, বিধি পূর্ব্বক পালন করা। **3.** To publish abroad ; to proclaim ; to extol ; to publish the fame of ; as, to *celebrate* His Throne with hymns ; দেশ বিদেশে প্রচার করা ; ঘোষণা করা, কীর্ত্তন করা ; প্রশংসাদ্বারা বাড়াইয়া তোলা ; খ্যাতি প্রচার করা, যশোগান করা। ***Verb i.*** To officiate at the Eucharist ; খৃষ্টের শেষ ভোজন পর্ব্বে পৌরোহিত্য করা। **—brat ed,** *p. adj.* Distinguished ; renowned ; famous ; বিশ্রুত, খ্যাত, প্রথিত, প্রসিদ্ধ, কীর্ত্তিত ; সুবিখ্যাত ; সুপ্রসিদ্ধ, লোকবিশ্রুত, বিশ্রুতনামা, পুণ্যকীর্ত্তি, দেশবিশ্রুত। **—bra′ tion,** *n.* **Ce-leb′-ri-ty,** *n.* **1.** Fame ; renown ; as, the *celebrity* of Milton ; যশঃ, খ্যাতি ; নাম, রূঢ়ি, প্রতিষ্ঠা। **2.** A celebrated person ; খ্যাতনামা ব্যক্তি, প্রসিদ্ধ ব্যক্তি।

cĕ-lĕr′-ĭ-tŷ, *n.* Swiftness ; speed ; (chiefly used with reference to the actions or movements of living beings) ; দ্রুতত্ব, ত্বরা, ক্ষিপ্রতা ; গতি, বেগ।

cĕl′-ĕr-ŷ, *n.* A plant cultivated for the use of its blanched stalks as a salad and vegetable ; রাঁধুনি (ওয়াট্), ভূতজাত (হিন্দি)।

cĕ-leste′ (-lĕst), *n.* Sky blue colour ; azure ; আসমানী ; নীল।

cĕ-lĕs′-tĭăl, *adj.* & *n.* **1** Of or pertaining to the sky or visible heavens ; as, *celestial* globe or map ; আন্তরীক্ষ, আকাশিক, নভোমণ্ডল-সম্বন্ধীয়, খগোলীয়। **2.** Of or pertaining to the spiritual heaven ; divine ; divinely excellent or beautiful ; স্বর্গীয় ; দিব্য ; দেবোপম সুন্দর বা অত্যুৎকৃষ্ট। ***Noun.*** **1.** An inhabitant of heaven ; দ্যুলোকবাসী, অমৃতলোকবাসী, স্বর্গবাসী। **2.** *(Pl.)* Heavenly objects, bodies, attributes ; স্বর্গীয় বস্তু নিচয়, জ্যোতিষ্ক সমূহ, স্বর্গীয় গুণরাজি। **Celestial**—(কৌতুকচ্ছলে) চীনদেশীয় লোক। **Celestial body**—খমূর্তি, খশরীর। **Celestial Empire**—চীন সাম্রাজ্য। **Celestial sphere**—খগোল (সাঃ পঃ)।

cĕl′-ĭ-bāte, *adj.* & *n.* Not married ; unmarried ; single ; bound to not marry ; অবিবাহিত ; অকৃতদার ; অনূঢ় ; কৌমার ব্রতাবলম্বী। ***Noun.*** One who leads a single life ; a confirmed bachelor or spinster ; one bound by vows not to marry ; অবিবাহিত ব্যক্তি ; চিরকুমার, চিরকুমারী ; আজন্ম কৌমার ব্রতাবলম্বী, কৌমার ব্রতাবলম্বিনী। **–ba-cy,** *n.* Single life, esp. that of a bachelor or one bound by vows not to marry ; অবিবাহিত জীবন, অনুদ্বাহ, অবিবাহিতাবস্থা, অনূঢ়াবস্থা, আজন্ম কৌমার ব্রত।

cĕll, *n.* **1.** *(Hist.)* A small monastery or nunnery dependent on some larger house ; (ইতিহাস) বৃহত্তর মঠ বা ভিক্ষুণী সংঘের অধীনস্থ ক্ষুদ্রতর মঠ বা সন্ন্যাসিনী নিকেতন। **2.** An anchoret's one-roomed dwelling ; সন্ন্যাসীর বাসকক্ষ। **3.** *(Poet.)* A small and humble dwelling ; a cottage ; a lonely nook ; the den of a wild beast ; (কবিতায়) ক্ষুদ্র এবং হীনভবন ; কুটীর ; নিরিবিলি স্থান ; বন্যজন্তুর গুহা। **4** *(Poet.)* Grave ; "Each in his narrow *cell* for ever laid" ; (কবিতায়) কবর। **5.** One of a number of small apartments in a building for a single person (as in a monastery, prison) ; কুঠরী, গুপ্তি (মৃচ্ছ ঃ—কারাগার সম্পর্কে), ক্ষুদ্র কক্ষ, (যথা কারাকক্ষ, মঠকক্ষ)। **6.** One of the compartments in the comb of bees ; মধুচক্রের কোষ। **7.** *(Electr.)* A simple voltaic apparatus with only one pair of metallic elements ; (তাড়িত-বিজ্ঞান) বিদ্যুদ্‌ঘট (হিঃ কোঃ), প্রবাহ কোষ (সাঃ পঃ)। **8.** An enclosed cavity or sac in organized bodies and minerals ; ব্যূহবদ্ধ বস্তু বা খনিজ পদার্থের মধ্যস্থ বেষ্টিত গর্ত্ত বা কোষ। **9.** *(Biol.)* The ultimate element in organic structures ; (জীব-বিজ্ঞান) কোষাণু, কললবিন্দু (হিঃ কোঃ), কললকণ (ঐ), কণ (ঐ), বিন্দু (ঐ), অনুকোষ (হঃ চঃ) প্রাণী ও উদ্ভিদের মূল উপাদান। **10.** *(Bot.)* The loculi of the ovary in plants, etc. ; (উদ্ভিদ্‌বিদ্যা) কোষ (সাঃ পঃ), গর্ভ (ঐ), পরাগোপকোষ।

cĕl′-lar (-lêr), *n.* & *v. t,* **1.** An underground room or vault used esp. for the keeping of provisions and other stores ; ভূনিম্নস্থ ক্ষুদ্র কক্ষ, বিশেষতঃ ভূনিম্নস্থ ভাণ্ডারগৃহ, ভূমিগৃহ (কথা সঃ)। **2.** *(Abbr.* for) Wine cellar ; hence, a person's stock of wine ; ভূনিম্নস্থ মদ্যভাণ্ডার ; অতএব কোন গৃহস্থের বাটীস্থ সঞ্চিত মদ্য। ***Verb t.*** To put into or store up, as in a cellar, (also with *in)* ; ভূনিম্নস্থ ভাণ্ডারে রাখা। **–age,** *n.* Provisions of cellars ; cellars collectively ; ভূনিম্নস্থ ভাণ্ডারের সঞ্চিত ভোজ্য দ্রব্যরাশি ; ভূনিম্নস্থ ভাণ্ডারের শ্রেণী। **Cellar-book** — ভূনিম্নস্থ ভাণ্ডারগৃহে সঞ্চিত মদ্যাদির হিসাব বহি।

cĕl′-lar-êr (-lêr-), *n.* A steward or butler of a monastery or chapter ; one who has charge of the cellar, and provisions ; মঠ বা যাজক পরিষদের ভাণ্ডারী ; ভাণ্ডারী, ভাণ্ডাররক্ষক।

cĕl-lar-ĕt′ (-lêr-), *n.* A case or side-board for keeping wine bottles in dining room ; ভোজনাগারে মদ্য-বোতল সকল রাখিবার টানা দেরাজ বা আধারবিশেষ।

cĕl-lĭf′-êr-ous (-ŭs), **cĕl′-lū-lāt-ĕd, cĕl-lū-lĭf′-êr-ous** (-ŭs), **cĕl-lū-lous** (-lŭs), *adjs.* Same as CELLULAR (which see).

cel′ lö (chĕl-), *n.* (Short for) VIOLIN CELLO (which see).

cĕl -lū-lar (-lêr), *adj.* **1.** Pertaining to, or consisting of, small single rooms or cavities ; ক্ষুদ্র কক্ষ সম্বন্ধীয়, ক্ষুদ্র কক্ষবিশিষ্ট, কোষ সম্বন্ধীয়, কোষ বিশিষ্ট। **2.** *(Physiol.)* Consisting of cells (used of vegetable tissues, opposed to *vascular*) ; (শারীরবিজ্ঞান) কোষাণু বিশিষ্ট, অনুকোষময় (হঃ চঃ)। **Cellular tissue**—কৌষিক ঝিল্লী (হঃ চঃ)।

cĕl′-lūle, *n.* A minute cell or cavity ; ক্ষুদ্র কোষ বা গহ্বর।

cel′-lū-loid (-loyd), *adj.* & *n.* Like cells ; কোষবৎ। ***Noun.*** A compound of cellulose, manufactured in substitution of ivory, bone, coral, etc., for umbrella handles, combs, etc. ; এক প্রকার কৃত্রিম হস্তি দন্ত, অস্থি বা প্রবাল, যদ্দারা, চিরুণী, ছাতার বাট প্রভৃতি প্রস্তুত হয়।

cĕl-lū-lose (-lös), *adj.* & *n.* Full of minute cavities ; অনুকোষপূর্ণ। ***Noun.*** A substance forming the essential part of the solid framework of plants ; বৃক্ষের কঠিন অংশের সারভাগ উৎপাদক পদার্থ বিশেষ,

বৃক্ষাদির দুশ্ছেদ্য স্থিতিস্থাপক মূল উপাদান (হঃ চঃ)।

cĕl'-si-sŭs, *n.* A centigrade scale or thermometer ; শতাংশ চিহ্নিত ক্রমাঙ্কিত মান-যন্ত্র, শতাংশক তাপমান যন্ত্র।

cĕlt, *n.* A chisel or axe-shaped stone or metal implement, employed by prehistoric and primitive peoples ; অনৈতিহাসিক বা প্রাচীন যুগের ব্যক্তিগণের ব্যবহৃত পাষাণময় কুঠার বা বাটালি।

Celt (sĕlt), **Kĕlt,** *n.* A member of one of the peoples akin to the ancient Galli (Bretons, Cornish, Welsh Irish and Gaels) ; প্রাচীন ব্রিটন, ওয়েল্‌স্, প্রভৃতি জাতির লোক।

Celt'-ic (sĕlt), **Kĕlt'-ic,** *adjs.* & *ns.* Of or pertaining to the Celts or their language ; as, *celtic* people, tribes, language ; সেল্ট্ জাতি সম্বন্ধীয়, উক্ত জাতির ভাষা সম্বন্ধীয়। ***Noun.*** A group of languages now spoken chiefly in Brittany, Wales, Ireland and the Scotch Highlands ; ভাষাশ্রেণী বিশেষ, বর্ত্তমানকালে ওয়েল্‌স্, আয়র্লণ্ড্ ও—স্কট্‌লণ্ডের পার্ব্বত্য প্রদেশে প্রচলিত আছে। **—i-cism,** *n.* **—i-cize,** *v. t.* & *i.*

cĕ-mĕnt', *n.* **1.** An adhesive substance for making stones cohere ; মাটী ও চুণ মিশান এক প্রকার গাঁথুনী মসলা, চূর্ণমাটী, বজ্রলেপ, সংঘাত (সাঃ পঃ)। **2.** Any substance used by men or animals for making bodies adhere to each other, as glue, sealing wax, starch, paste, etc. ; সংযোজক বস্তু—আঠা, গালা প্রভৃতি। **3.** (*Fig.*) Bond of union ; principle of union ; as, friendship is the *cement* of two minds ; (লক্ষণায়) মিলন-বন্ধন ; সংযোগ-সূত্র। ***Verb t.*** **1.** To cause to adhere by means of cement ; to unite firmly or closely ; বজ্রলেপ দ্বারা সংযুক্ত করা ; দৃঢ়রূপে সংবদ্ধ করা, আশ্লিষ্ট করা। **2.** To apply cement to (a surface) ; to coat or line with cement, so as to make water-tight ; বজ্রলেপ দ্বারা লিপ্ত করা ; চূণবালিমিশ্রিত মসল্লা দ্বারা আস্তর করা। **3.** (*Fig.*) To unite firmly or closely ; as, to *cement* all parts of the community ; (লক্ষণায়) দৃঢ়রূপে সংযোগ বা সংসৃষ্ট করা। **Portland cement**—বিলাতী মাটি।

cĕm'-ĕ-tĕr-ȳ, *n.* A burial-ground generally ; now, esp. a large public park or ground laid out expressly for the interment of the dead, and not being a churchyard ; শ্মশান, সমাধিক্ষেত্র, প্রেতবন, কবরস্তান, গোরস্তান, পিতৃকানন ; (বর্ত্তমানে) শবদেহ প্রোথিত করিবার জন্য নগরোদ্যান বা পরিবেষ্টিত উপবন।

cĕn'-ō-bīte, *n.* One of a religious order, dwelling in a convent community ; মঠবাসী সন্ন্যাসী, বিহারবাসী।

cĕn'-ō-tăph, *n.* An empty tomb or a monument erected in honour of a person who is buried elsewhere ; অন্যত্র সমাহিত ব্যক্তির সম্মানার্থ শূন্যগর্ভ সমাধি মন্দির বা স্মরণস্তম্ভ।

cense' (sĕns), *v. t.* To perfume with burning incense ; to offer incense to ; প্রজ্বলিত ধূপগন্ধে আমোদিত করা ; (পূজার্চ্চনা বা সম্মানার্থ) ধূপ প্রজ্বলিত করা।

cĕn'-sêr, *n.* A vessel in which incense is burnt,—a thurible ; ধূপপাত্র, ধূপাধার, ধূপভাজন, ধূপদান, ধুনচি, ধূপচি।

cĕn'-sŏr, *n.* **1.** An ancient Roman magistrate drawing up the register or census of the citizens etc. and supervising public morals ; প্রাচীন রোমের উচ্চপদস্থ কর্ম্মচারিবিশেষ—ইনি লোক গণনা এবং নাগরিক জন বৃন্দের নৈতিক চরিত্রাদির পরিদর্শক ছিলেন। **2.** A person expressing opinions on other's morals and conduct ; যে ব্যক্তি অন্যের নৈতিক চরিত্র বা আচরণ সম্বন্ধে মত প্রকাশ করে। **3.** An official empowered to examine all manuscripts, books, journals, before they are published, and to see that they contain nothing heretical, immoral and seditious ; কোন পুস্তক, পাণ্ডুলিপি বা সংবাদপত্রে নীতিবিরুদ্ধ, ধর্ম্মবিরুদ্ধ অথবা রাজদ্রোহকর কোন বিষয় প্রকাশিত হইতে না পারে তজ্জন্য উক্ত পুস্তক, পত্রিকাদি পরীক্ষার্থ ক্ষমতাপ্রাপ্ত রাজকর্ম্মচারী। **4.** The title of various officials in Universities and Colleges ; বিশ্ববিদ্যালয় বা কলেজ সমূহের বিভিন্ন কর্ম্মচারীর উপাধি। **5.** An adverse critic ; প্রতিকূল সমালোচক। **—so'-ri-al,** *adj.* **—so'-ri-ous,** *adj.* **1.** Over-critical ; severe in making remarks on others ; fault-finding (*of*) ; উৎকট সমালোচনা প্রিয়, কঠোর ; মন্তব্য প্রকাশক ; দোষদর্শী। **2.** Implying or expressing censure ; নিন্দাত্মক, গ্লানিকর। **—so'-ri'-ous-ly,** *adv.* **—so'-ri-ous-ness,** *n.* **—ship,** *n.* **Censorship of the press**—যে ব্যবস্থানুসারে ক্ষমতাপ্রাপ্ত সরকারী কর্ম্মচারী প্রকাশিত হইবার পূর্ব্বে সর্ব্বপ্রকার পুস্তক, পুস্তিকা, সংবাদপত্রাদি পরীক্ষা করত আপত্তি জনক পুস্তকাদির প্রচার বন্ধ করিয়া দিতে পারেন।

cĕn'-sure (-shôr), *n.* & *v. t.* The act of finding fault with or condemning as wrong ; hostile criticism ; expression of disapproval or condemnation ; reprimand ; দোষদর্শন, তিরস্কার, গঞ্জনা, ভর্ৎসনা, উপালম্ভ ; বিরুদ্ধ সমালোচনা, পরীবাদ, গর্হণ ; অননুমোদন ; তম্বি (*Colloq.*), বাগ্‌দণ্ড, ধিগ্‌দণ্ড। ***Verb t.*** To express disapproval of ; to criticize unfavourably ; to find fault with ; to condemn ; অননুমোদন করা ; প্রতিকূল সমালোচনা করা ; দোষ ধরা ; তিরস্কার করা, দোষ দেওয়া, নিন্দা করা। **—sur-a-ble,** *adj.* **—sur-a-ble-ness,** *n.*

cĕn'-sŭs, *n.* **1.** The registration of citizens and their property in ancient Rome for purposes of taxation ; কর-সংস্থাপনের জন্য প্রাচীন রোমনগরবাসিগণের নাম এবং তাহাদের সম্পত্তি তালিকাভুক্ত করণ। **2.** An official enumeration of the population of a country ; (in India taken every 10 years) ; **মনুষ্যগণনা, লোকগণনা, আদমসুমারী, প্রজাগণনা।**

cĕnt, *n.* **1.** A hundred ; শত। **2.** (*U. S. Canada, Mexico,* etc.) The one-hundredth of a dollar, (nearly equal to a half-penny) ; (যুক্ত-রাজ্য, মেক্সিকো প্রভৃতি দেশে) ১ ডলারের শতাংশ মূল্যের মুদ্রা বিশেষ (প্রায় অর্দ্ধ পেনির সমান মূল্য।) **Per-cent**—শতকরা। **Cent per cent**—শতকরা শত ; সুদে আসলে সমান।

cĕn'-tăl, *n.* A weight of one hundred pounds avoirdupois, used for corn ; শস্যাদি পরিমাপের জন্য ১০০ পাউণ্ড পরিমিত ওজনবিশেষ।

cĕn'-täur (-tär), *n.* **1.** A fabulous creature, with the head, trunk, and arms of a man, joined to the body and legs of a horse ; গ্রীক পুরাণোক্ত অর্দ্ধ অশ্বাকার দেবযোনি বিশেষ, নরাশ্ব (আঃ বঃ), অশ্বাসুর (ঐ)। **2.** (*Fig.*) An unnatural hybrid creation ; (লক্ষণায়) অস্বাভাবিক সঙ্কর সৃষ্টি। **3.** One of the southern constellations ; দক্ষিণ আকাশস্থ তারা প্রকোষ্ঠ বিশেষ।

cĕn'-tau-rȳ (-tä-), *n.* A name of various plants ; বিভিন্ন প্রকার বৃক্ষের নাম।

cĕn-tē-nā'-ri-ăn, *adj.* & *n.* Of the age of a hundred years ; শতবর্ষ বয়স্ক। ***Noun.*** A person a hundred years old ; শতায়ুঃ, শতবর্ষজীবী।

cĕn'-tē-nă-rȳ, *adj.* & *n.* Of or pertaining to a period of hundred years ; occurring once in every hundred years ; শতাব্দ সম্বন্ধীয় ; শতবর্ষ মধ্যে সংঘটিত। ***Noun.*** **1.** A period, space or age of one hundred years ; a century ; শতবর্ষ ; শতাব্দী। **2.** A centennial anniversary ; a celebration of the completion of a century ; শতবার্ষিক উৎসব ; শতাব্দ উৎসব।

cĕn-tĕn'-ni-ăl, *adj.* & *n.* Of or relating to a space of one hundred years or to its completion ; of a hundred years, standing ; a hundred years old ; শত বার্ষিক, শতবর্ষান্তিক ; শতবর্ষ স্থায়ী ; শতবর্ষ বয়স্ক। ***Noun.*** One hundreth anniversary or its celebration ; শাতবার্ষিক, শাতবার্ষিক উৎসবানুষ্ঠান।

cĕn-tĕn'-ni-ŭm, *n.* A space of one hundred years ; a century ; শতবর্ষ ; শতাব্দ, শতাব্দী।

cĕn-tĕs'-i-măl, *adj.* **1.** Relating to division into hundredths ; as, *centesimal* thermometer ; (শতাঙ্কিত তাপমান যন্ত্র) ; শতাংশিতত্ব সম্বন্ধীয়। **2.** Hundredth ; শততম।

cĕn'-ti-grāde, *adj.* Having a hundred degrees ; graduated into a hundred divisions or equal parts ; শতাংশবিশিষ্ট ; শতাংশ-চিহ্নিত। **Centigrade thermometer**—যে তাপমান যন্ত্রের যম বিন্দু এবং স্ফুটনাঙ্কের মধ্যবর্ত্তীস্থান শতাংশে বিভক্ত হয়, এবং যাহার o অংশে যমবিন্দু এবং শততমাংশে স্ফুটনাঙ্ক অঙ্কিত থাকে, শতাংশী তাপমান যন্ত্র (হিঃ কোঃ)।

cĕn'-ti-grăm, —gramme (-grăm), A weight equal to one-hundredth of a gram ; এক গ্র্যামের শত ভাগের এক ভাগ ওজন।

cĕn'-ti-li-tre, —tĕr, *n.* A measure of volume equal to one hundredth of a litre ; এক লিটরের ($\frac{3}{5}$ ঘন ইঞ্চির কিছু অধিক) শতাংশ।

cĕn-til'-liŏn, *n.* The hundredth power of a million ; এক নিযুতের শততম ঘাত বা সামর্থ্য (১এর ডাহিনে ৬০০ শত শূন্য বসাইলে যে সংখ্যা হয়।)

cĕn'-time (-tēm), *n.* A French coin of the value of one hundredth of a franc ; ফরাসী দেশের মুদ্রাবিশেষ (এক ফ্রাঙ্কের শতাংশ মূল্যের)।

cĕn'-ti-mē-tre (-tĕr), **—ter,** *n.* A measure of length equal to one hundredth of a meter or about two-fifths of an inch ; প্রায় $\frac{2}{5}$ ইঞ্চি পরিমিত ফরাসী দেশীয় দৈর্ঘ্যের মাপ বিশেষ।

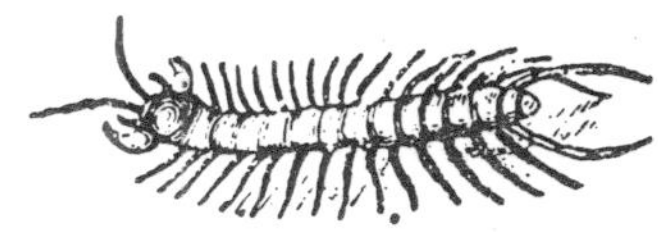

Centipede.

cĕn'-ti-pede (-pēd), *n.* A many-legged insect ; শতপাদ, শতপদী (সাঃ পঃ), শতপাদিকা, বিছা প্রভৃতি।

cĕnt'-nĕr, *n.* A measure of weight used in Germany ; জর্ম্মণী দেশের ওজন বিশেষ (প্রায় ১ হন্দর)।

cĕn'-tō, *n.* A composition formed by joining scraps from other authors ; নানা গ্রন্থ সংগৃহীত কাব্য নানা গ্রন্থকারের রচনার সঙ্কলন বিশেষ।

cĕn'-trăl, *adj.* **1.** Of or pertaining to the centre or middle ; situated, in or proceeding from, the centre ; কেন্দ্রীয়, কৈন্দ্রিক, মধ্যভাগ সম্বন্ধীয় ; মধ্যস্থ, মাধ্য, কেন্দ্রস্থিত, মধ্যগত, কেন্দ্রজাত, কেন্দ্রবর্ত্তী (জিঃ)। **2.** (*Fig.*) Principal ; dominant ; as, the *central* figure ; (লক্ষণায়) প্রধান ; মুখ্য। **—tral'-i-ty,** *n.* **—ly,** *adv.* **—ness,** *n.*

cĕn'-trăl-ĭsm, *n.* Centralization or the centralizing system, esp. in government ; কেন্দ্রীকরণ, বিশেষতঃ শাসন-ব্যবস্থার কেন্দ্রীকরণ। **—ist,** *n.*

cĕn'-trăl-ize, *v. t.* & *i.* **1.** To draw or bring to a central point ; to concentrate (administrative powers) in a single head or centre ; কেন্দ্রাভিমুখীন করা ; কেন্দ্রীকৃত করা, (শাসনশক্তি) একজন নেতা বা প্রধান পুরুষের হস্তে কেন্দ্রীভূত করা। ***Verb i.*** To come together at a centre ; কেন্দ্রীভূত হওয়া। **—i-za'-tion,** *n.* **1.** The act of centralizing or bringing to a centre ; কেন্দ্রীকরণ। **2.** A term indicative of the system of concentrating administrative functions in the hands of the principal departments of the state ; কোন রাষ্ট্রের প্রধান প্রধান বিভাগের হস্তে শাসনকার্য্য কেন্দ্রীকরণের ব্যবস্থা, অধিকারনিমজ্জন (হিঃ কোঃ), কেন্দ্রীকরণ।

cĕn'-tre, —têr, *n., v. t. & i.* **1.** The middle part of a circle or sphere, equally distant from all points on the circumference ; কেন্দ্র। **2.** The middle point or portion of anything ; also a person or thing placed at such a point ; মধ্যবিন্দু, মধ্যস্থল ; মধ্যস্থলবর্ত্তী পুরুষ বা বস্তু। **3.** The point, pivot, axes, or line, round which a body turns or revolves ; যে বিন্দু, শঙ্কু, অক্ষ, বা রেখার চতুর্দ্দিকে কোন বস্তু ঘূর্ণিত বা আবর্ত্তিত হয়, নাভি। **4.** The point of concentration or dispersion ; nucleus ; source ; as, the *centre* of a world's desire ; মধ্যবিন্দু ; গর্ভ, বীজ ; উৎপত্তিস্থল। **5.** The position of equilibrium of a body ; as, the *centre* of gravity ; কোন বস্তুর ভার-সাম্যাবস্থা। **6.** (*Arch.*) The wooden support or mould upon which an arch or dome is supported while building ; (স্থপতি-বিদ্যা) যে কাষ্ঠময় অবলম্বন বা ছাঁচের উপর কোন খিলান বা গুম্বজ নির্ম্মিত হইবার কালে অবলম্বিত থাকে। **7.** (*Mil.*) The main body of troops occupying the space between the two wings ; (সামরিক শাস্ত্র) সৈন্যদলের বাম ও দক্ষিণ পার্শ্বের মধ্যস্থলবর্ত্তী প্রধান অংশ। **8.** Among the Fenians the name given to the head of the organization ; যুক্তরাজ্যের ফেনিয়ানাখ্য ষড়যন্ত্রকারিদলের নেতা। ***Verb t.*** **1.** To place or fix in the centre ; to concenrate (*in, on*) ; কেন্দ্রদেশে স্থাপিত করা, কেন্দ্রদেশে সংবদ্ধ করা ; কেন্দ্রীভূত করা। **2.** To find the centre of ; কেন্দ্র নির্ণয় করা। ***Verb i.*** To be concentrated, as at a centre ; কেন্দ্রীভূত হওয়া। **—less,** *adj.* **—tric, —tri-cal,** *adjs.* **—tri-cal'-i-ty, —tric'-i-ty,** *ns.* **Centre-bit**—ছিদ্র করিবার যন্ত্রবিশেষ, বিলাতি বর্ম্মা। **Centre-piece** — কোন বস্তুর মধ্যস্থলবর্ত্তী অংশ ; বিশেষতঃ মেজ প্রভৃতির মধ্যস্থলে রাখিবার জন্য কারুকার্য্যখচিত রেকাব বা কাচনির্ম্মিত পানপাত্র। **Centre-rail**—দন্তুর চক্রের জন্য পার্ব্বত্যলৌহবর্ত্মে পরিস্থ তৃতীয় লৌহবর্ত্ম। **Centre of gravity** — ভারমধ্য, গুরুত্বকেন্দ্র (হিঃ কোঃ)।

cĕn-trif'-ü-găl, *adj.* Flying or tending to fly off from the centre ; কেন্দ্রাতিগ, কেন্দ্রপরাঙ্মুখ (হিঃ কোঃ), কেন্দ্রাপগামী (ঐ), কেন্দ্রবিসর্পী, মধ্যত্যাগী (সাঃ পঃ)। **Centrifugal force**—কেন্দ্রাতিগাশক্তি, কেন্দ্রবিমুখবল, কেন্দ্র পরাঙ্মুখবল (হিঃ কোঃ), কেন্দ্রাপসারিণীশক্তি (আঃ বঃ), কেন্দ্রের প্রতিমুখীশক্তি (রবিঃ)।

cĕn-trip'-ĕ-tăl, *adj.* Tending toward the centre ; (opposite of *centrifugal*) ; কেন্দ্রাভিমুখ (হিঃ কোঃ), কেন্দ্রোপসর্পী, মধ্যগামী (সাঃ পঃ), কেন্দ্রোন্মুখ (হিঃ কোঃ)। **Centripetal force**—কেন্দ্রাভিমুখিনী শক্তি, কেন্দ্রের অভিমুখীশক্তি (রবিঃ), কেন্দ্রাভিমুখীন বল, কেন্দ্রাভিসারিণীশক্তি (আঃ বঃ) কৈন্দ্রিকাকর্ষণ।

cĕn'-tü-ple, *adj. & v. t.* A hundred-fold ; শতগুণ, শতাবৃত। ***Verb t.*** To increase or multiply a hundredfold ; শতগুণ বৃদ্ধি করা, শতগুণিত করা।

cĕn-tü'-pli-cāte, *adj. & v. t.* Hundred-fold ; শতগুণ। ***Verb t.*** To make a hundred-fold ; শতগুণ করা। **—ca'-tion,** *n.* **In centuplicate**—যে বস্তুর একশত প্রতিলিপি প্রস্তুত হয় তৎসম্বন্ধে প্রযুক্ত।

cĕn-tü'-ri-ŏn, *n.* The commander of century in the Roman army ; any officer in command of 100 men ; রোমীয় সৈন্যদলে শতসংখ্যক সৈন্যের নায়ক ; শতসংখ্যক সৈন্যের নায়ক, শতযোধপতি (আঃ বঃ)।

cĕn'-tü-rȳ, *n.* **1.** (*Rom. Hist.*) A division of the Roman army, originally consisting of 100 men ; রোমীয় সৈন্যদলের বিভাগ বিশেষ, পূর্ব্বে ঐরূপ এক বিভাগ একশত সৈন্য দ্বারা গঠিত হইত। **2.** One of the political divisions of the Roman people for voting ; (there were 193 *centuries*) ; নির্ব্বাচন মত প্রদানার্থ রোম নগরবাসিগণের রাজনীতিক বিভাগ বিশেষ। **3.** Any body of 100 men or soldiers ; শতসংখ্যক সৈন্য। **4.** A group of hundred things ; as, the *centuries* of Bhartrihari ; a hundred "points" in the score of a game, (esp. 100 runs in cricket) ; শতসংখ্যক বস্তুর সমবায়, শতক ; ক্রীড়ার শতবিন্দু (অর্থাৎ রন প্রভৃতি)। **5.** A period of hundred years ; specifically one of the hundred year divisions of the Christian era ; as, the twentieth *century* ; শতবর্ষ ; খৃষ্টীয় শতাব্দী। **Century plant**—বিলাতি আনারস (বেলঃ)।

cĕŏrl, *n.* An old English freeman of the lowest class ; (opposed to a *thane*) ; a churl ; প্রাচীন ইংলণ্ডের নিম্নতম শ্রেণীর স্বাধীন ব্যক্তি ; চাষা।

cĕph'-ā-lăl-ḡȳ, —lăl'-ḡiă, *n.* (*Med.*) Headache ; (ভৈষজ্য-শাস্ত্র) শিরোবেদনা, শিরোঘূর্ণন (সাঃ পঃ)।

cĕ-phăl'-ic, *adj. & n.* **1.** Of or pertaining to the head ; situated in the head ; মস্তক সম্বন্ধীয় ; মস্তকস্থ। ***Noun.*** A medicine for headache or other disorder of the head ; শিরোবেদনা বা অন্যবিধ শিরোরোগের ঔষধ, শিরোবলদ (সাঃ পঃ)।

cĕph'-ā-lō-pŏd, *n.* A mollusc having the arms or tentacles attached to the head, (as the cuttle fishes, nautilus etc.) ; মুণ্ডপদী (সাঃ পঃ), শিরোপদী (ঐ), মুণ্ডগ (ঐ)।

cĕph-ă-lō-thō'-răx, *n.* (*Zool.*) The anterior division of the body in arthropods ; (জন্তুতত্ত্ব) পর্ব্বপদী জন্তুর (মাকড়সা, বৃশ্চিক, কর্কট প্রভৃতির) অঙ্গের অগ্রভাগ ; শিরোবুক্ষ (সাঃ পঃ)।

cĕ-răm'-ĭc, [also KERAMIC] *adj.* Pertaining to pottery ; as, *ceramic* products ; মৃৎশিল্প সম্বন্ধীয়। **—ics, —ist,** *ns.*

cĕr-ăs'-tēs, *n.* The horned viper of Egypt, Palestine, etc. ; মিশর, প্যালেস্তাইন প্রভৃতি দেশীয় সশৃঙ্গ সর্পবিশেষ।

cêr'-bêr-ŭs, *n.* (*Gr. Myth.*) A three-headed dog, fabled to guard the gates of hell ; hence a vigilant custodian, esp. if surly ; গ্রীকপুরাণ বর্ণিত যমপুরীর দ্বার রক্ষক ত্রিশিরাঃ সারমেয় বিশেষ ; সতর্ক প্রহরী (বিশেষতঃ রুক্ষ প্রকৃতির)। **—be're-an,** *adj.* **A sop to Cerberus**—Something given for silencing ; কোন ব্যক্তির মুখবন্ধ করিবার উদ্দেশ্যে প্রদত্ত কোন কিছু।

cēre, *n.* & *v. t.* The naked waxlike membrane that covers the bills of some birds ; কোন কোন পক্ষীর চঞ্চুনিম্নস্থ মোমবৎ ঝিল্লীবিশেষ। ***Verb t.*** To wrap in a cere-cloth ; to wrap a dead body ; মোমজামাদ্বারা আবৃত করা ; মৃতদেহ আবৃত করা। **Cere-cloth**—মোমজামা, সৈকথবসন।

cē'-rē-ăl, *adj.* & *n.* Pertaining to corn or other edible grain ; শস্যাদি সম্বন্ধীয়। ***Noun.*** (*Pl.*) Kinds of corn or grain used for human food ; ধান্য যবাদি শস্য।

cêr-ē-bĕl'-lŭm, *n.* The little or hinder brain ; মস্তিষ্কের পশ্চাদ্ভাগস্থ অধস্তন অংশ, অনুমস্তিষ্ক (সাঃ পঃ), উপমস্তিষ্ক (হঃ চঃ), অবর মস্তিষ্ক (আঃ বঃ)। **—lar,** *adj.*

cêr'-ē-brăl, *n.* (*Anat.*) Of or pertaining to the brain or hemispheres of the brain ; মস্তিষ্ক সম্বন্ধীয়, মস্তিষ্ক বিষয়ক। **Cerebral appoplexy**—মস্তিষ্কের রক্তস্রাব (হঃ চঃ)। **Cerebral letters**—মূর্দ্ধণ্য বর্ণ।

cêr-ē-brā'-tion, *n.* Action of the brain whether conscious or unconscious ; জ্ঞাতসারে বা অজ্ঞাতসারে নিষ্পন্ন মস্তিষ্কের ক্রিয়া। **Unconscious cerebration**—যে মস্তিষ্ক ক্রিয়া অজ্ঞাতসারে নিষ্পন্ন হইলেও, বিচারবুদ্ধিপ্রসূত হইলে যেরূপ হইত তদনুরূপ ফল উৎপাদন করিয়া থাকে [যথা, একটা নাম মনে করিবার জন্য বহু চেষ্টা করিয়াও সফলকাম হইতে পারি নাই, অন্য সময়ে অন্য বিষয় চিন্তা করিতেছি হঠাৎ নামটী মনে পড়িল ; ইহাকেই অজ্ঞাতসারে নিষ্পন্ন মস্তিষ্কের ক্রিয়া কহে।]

cêr'-ē-brŭm, *n.* The brain proper in front of and above the cerebellum ; বৃহদ্ মস্তিষ্ক (গৃহস্থ), অগ্রমস্তিষ্ক (আঃ বঃ)।

cēre'-mĕnt, *n.* (*Usu. pl.*) Waxed wrappings for the dead ; মৃতদেহাচ্ছাদনের জন্য মোমজামা কাপড়।

cĕr-ē-mō'-nĭ-ăl, *adj.* & *n.* Relating to a ceremony ; formal ; ritual ; আনুষ্ঠানিক, অনুষ্ঠানাত্মক ; লৌকিক, বৈধিক, বৈধী ; নৈয়মিক। ***Noun.*** 1. A prescribed system of rites ; formalities observed on any occasion ; অনুষ্ঠান পদ্ধতি ; লৌকিক আচারানুষ্ঠান। 2. The observance of conventional forms in social intercourse ; সামাজিক ব্যবহারে প্রথামূলক আচার পদ্ধতির অনুসরণ। **—ism, —ist,** *ns.* **—ly,** *adv.*

cêr'-ē-mō'-nĭ-ous (-ŭs), *adj.* 1. Pertaining to or consisting of outward forms or rites ; formal ; বাহ্যানুষ্ঠান সম্পৃক্ত, বাহ্য ক্রিয়া কলাপসম্পন্ন ; লৌকিক। 2. Full of ceremony ; accompained with rites, religious or showy ; অনুষ্ঠানপূর্ণ ; (ধর্ম্ম-সম্বন্ধীয় বা সমারোহপূর্ণ) ক্রিয়ানুষ্ঠান সহকৃত। 3. According to prescribed or customary rules or forms ; formally respectful ; punctilious ; as, *ceremonious* bow, politeness, thanks, etc. ; নির্দ্দিষ্ট বা প্রচলিত নিয়ম বা পদ্ধতি অনুযায়ী, যথাবিধি ; লৌকিকভাবে শ্রদ্ধাবান ; আচারানুষ্ঠানাদি পালনে সূক্ষ্মভাবে নিয়মের অনুবর্ত্তী। **—ly,** *adv.* **—ness,** *n.*

cêr'-ē-mŏ-nȳ, *n.* 1. An outward rule or external form in religions ; performance of some solemn act according to prescribed form ; ধর্ম্ম সম্পর্কীয় বাহ্য ক্রিয়া কাণ্ড, ক্রিয়া কলাপ ; যথাবিধানে ধর্ম্মাদি ক্রিয়ার অনুষ্ঠান। 2. Forms of civility ; social behaviour required by strict etiquette ; formality ; শিষ্টাচার বিধি, সৌজন্য রীতি ; সামাজিক ব্যবহার, আচার ; লৌকিকতা। 3. (*Disparagingly*) A formal rite or observance ; an empty form ; as, there is no obligation to use the seal, it is only a *ceremony* ; (অবজ্ঞাচ্ছলে) বাহ্যানুষ্ঠান ; অন্তঃসারশূন্য ক্রিয়া কলাপ। **Master of ceremonies**—যে কর্ম্মচারী রাজকীয় উৎসব প্রভৃতিতে সমাগত ব্যক্তিগণের আচরণীয় বিধি, নিয়ম, শিষ্টাচারাদি সম্বন্ধে তত্ত্বাবধায়কতা করিয়া থাকেন। **To stand upon ceremony**—To insist upon the punctilious observances of formalities or refuse to go on without them ; সামাজিক শিষ্টাচার বা লৌকিকতা পালনের জন্য জেদ করা। **Without ceremony**—Offhand ; unceremoniously ; ফস্ করিয়া ; লৌকিকতার ধার না ধারিয়া।

Ce'-rēs (sē-), *n.* The Roman equivalent of Demeter (*q. v.*), who was worshipped as Goddess of fertility and harvest ; রোমীয় পুরাণোক্ত লক্ষ্মীদেবী।

cêr'-ĭph, *n.* Same as SEREPH.

cē-rise' (-rēz), *adj.* & *n.* Of the colour of the bright red cherry ; রক্তোজ্জ্বলচেরিফলবৎবর্ণবিশিষ্ট। ***Noun.*** A light and clear red colour ; একপ্রকার স্বচ্ছ এবং মৃদু রক্ত বর্ণ।

cē′-rīte, *n.* A very rare metal, the hydrated silicate of cerium ; এক প্রকার দুষ্প্রাপ্য ধাতু।

cē′-ri-ŭm, *n.* A rare metallic element ; একপ্রকার ধাতব মূল পদার্থ, গ্রীক (সাঃ পঃ)।

cē-rō-plăs′-tic, *adj.* Relating to the art of modelling in wax ; modelled in wax ; as, *ceroplastic* figures ; মধূথময় নমুনা প্রস্তুত বা আদর্শ গঠন সম্পর্কীয় ; মধূথরচিত। **—tics,** *n.* **1.** (*Sing.*) The art of modelling in wax ; মধূথ হইতে নানাপ্রকার আদর্শ বা নমুনা প্রস্তুতের বিদ্যা। **2.** (*Pl.*) Wax-works ; মধূথ নির্ম্মিত দ্রব্যজাত।

cē′-rō-sin, *n.* (*Chem.*) A waxy substance obtained from the bark of the sugar-cane ; (রসায়নশাস্ত্র) ইক্ষুর ত্বক্ হইতে প্রাপ্ত মোমবৎ পদার্থ বিশেষ।

cêr′-tain (-tăn), *adj.* **1.** Fixed ; settled ; as, *certain* rate, price, etc. ; স্থির, নিশ্চল ; নির্দ্ধারিত। **2.** Not liable to fail ; unerring ; inevitable ; অব্যর্থ ; ধ্রুব, অবশ্যম্ভাবী ; নিশ্চিত। **3.** Indubitable ; সন্দেহাতীত, অসংশয়িত, নিঃসন্দিগ্ধ। **4.** (*Of persons*) Assured in mind (of a thing that it is so) ; as, to make her *certain* of the sad event ; স্থিরনিশ্চিত, কৃতনিশ্চয়, দৃঢ়নিশ্চয়, নিশ্চিতমনস্ক, নিভ্রান্তচিত্ত, বদ্ধনিশ্চয়। **5.** Sure, (followed by an infinitive) ; নিশ্চিত। **6.** Not specifically named ; some ; one ; অনির্দ্দিষ্ট ; কেহ ; অমুক। **—ly,** *adv.* Infallibly ; fixedly ; undoubtedly ; confidently ; admittedly ; নিশ্চিতরূপে ; দৃঢ়রূপে ; নিঃশংসয়িতরূপে ; নিশ্চয় ; স্পষ্টতঃ। **—ty,** *n.* **1.** A fact or truth unquestionably established ; indubitable prospect ; স্থিরপ্রতিষ্ঠিত সত্য ; নিশ্চিতাশা। **2.** Quality or state of being certain ; absolute conviction ; নিশ্চয়তা, অসন্দিগ্ধতা ; দৃঢ়প্রতীতি, স্থিরবিশ্বাস, দৃঢ়প্রত্যয়। **3.** A thing in actual possession ; হস্তগত দ্রব্য। **For certain** — Assuredly ; নিশ্চিতই। **For, of, to certainty** — Assuredly ; beyond doubt ; নিশ্চিতরূপে ; সন্দেহাতীতরূপে। **To make certain**—পাকা করা।

cêr′-tĭs, *adv.* Certainly ; assuredly ; (poetry or archaic prose) ; নিশ্চিতভাবে ; নিশ্চয়পূর্ব্বক।

cêr-tif′-i-cāte, *n.* & *v. t.* **1.** A written testimony to the truth of a certain fact or facts ; a testimonial of character or definite statement of qualifications ; অভিজ্ঞানপত্র, সত্যাপনপত্র ; উপাধিপত্র, প্রশংসাপত্র (হিঃ কোঃ)। **2.** A legally authenticated voucher or testimony of certain facts ; (sometimes) a kind of license ; as, an attorney's annual *certificate* (সনদ্) ; (আইন) কোন বিষয়ের সত্যতা সম্বন্ধে বিধিসিদ্ধ নিদর্শনপত্র, সত্যতা প্রতিপাদনপত্র, প্রমাণপত্র ; (কখন কখন) সনন্দ, সনদ (প্রভৃতি)। **3.** (*Law*) A writing made in any court to give notice to another court of anything done therein ; (আইন) কোন বিচারালয়ের কার্য্যাবলী অপর বিচারালয়ে বিজ্ঞাপ্তি করিবার জন্য লিখনবিশেষ, প্রমাণ (আঃ বঃ)। ***Verb t.*** **1.** To furnish (*a person*) *with* a certificate ; to authorize or license by, a certificate ; অভিজ্ঞানপত্র প্রদান করা ; অভিজ্ঞানপত্রদ্বারা ক্ষমতা বা অনুমতি প্রদান করা, সনদ দেওয়া। **2.** To verify or attest by certificates ; অভিজ্ঞানপত্রদ্বারা সত্যতা প্রতিপাদন করা। **--ca′-tion,** *n.*

cêr′-ti-fȳ, *v. t.* **1.** To make certain, as a fact ; to give certain information (*of*), (applied to things) ; সুনিশ্চিত করা ; (কোন বিষয়ে) নিশ্চিত সংবাদ জ্ঞাপন করা। **2.** To assure or inform certainly ; নিশ্চিত করিয়া বলা, নিশ্চিত সংবাদ জ্ঞাপন করা। **3.** To testify to in writing ; to declare or attest by a legal certificate ; কোন বিষয়ের সত্যতার প্রতিপোষক কথা লিখিয়া দেওয়া, সত্য বলিয়া লিখা, বিধিসিদ্ধ নিদর্শনপত্রদ্বারা ব্যক্ত করা, কোন বিষয়ের সত্যতা প্রতিপাদন করা। **Certified copy**—সহিমোহরের নকল।

cêr-ti-ō-rā′-ri (-shî-), *n.* (*Law*) A writ issued from a superior court to call up the records of an inferior court ; (আইন) উর্দ্ধতন আদালত হইতে নিম্নতর আদালতের মোকদ্দমার কাগজপত্র তলব করিবার পরওয়ানা।

cêr′-ti-tūde, *n.* (*Law*) Freedom from doubt ; certainty ; নিশ্চয়তা, নিঃসন্দিগ্ধতা ; দৃঢ়প্রতীতি।

cē-rû′-lē-ăn, *adj.* & *n.* Sky-coloured ; deep blue ; আসমানি রঙের, আকাশবর্ণ ; ঘননীলবর্ণ, শ্যামল। ***Noun.*** **1.** Cerulean colour or hue ; আসমানি রঙ্। **2.** (*Humorous*) A blue-stocking ; a blue ; (কৌতুকচ্ছলে) বিদ্যাভিমানিনী স্ত্রীলোক।

cē-rû′-mĕn, *n.* Earwax ; কর্ণমল, কর্ণগূথ, কাণের খইল। **—mi-nif′-er-ous, —mi-nous,** *adjs.*

cē′-ruse (-rûs), *n.* **1.** White lead, used as a pigment ; খনিজ সফেদা। **2.** A cosmetic containing white lead ; খনিজ সফেদাযুক্ত অঙ্গরাগ।

cêr′-vi-căl, *adj.* Of or pertaining to the neck ; গলদেশীয়, গ্রৈব (সাঃ পঃ)।

cêr-vīne, *adj.* Of or pertaining to the deer ; মৃগসম্বন্ধীয়।

cē-săr′-ē-vitch (-vîch), **—witch** (-wîch), *n.* The Tsar's eldest son ; রুশিয়ার জারের জ্যেষ্ঠ পুত্র।

cĕss, *n.* & *v. t.* A tax (now displaced by *rate* in England) ; land tax (in Scotland) ; a tax for a special object (in India) ; as, *roadcess* (পথকর) ; কর ; ভূমিকর (স্কটলণ্ড) ; কোন বিশেষ উদ্দেশ্যে গৃহীত কর (ভারতবর্ষে)। ***Verb t.*** To assess ; to tax ; কর নির্দ্ধারণ করা ; কর বসান।

cĕs-sā′-tion, *n.* Discontinuance; stoppage; নিবৃত্তি, অবসান, বিরতি; বিচ্ছেদ, বিরাম, উপরম, নিবারণ। **Cessation of arms**—যুদ্ধ-নিবৃত্তি।

ces′-sion (sĕ-), *n.* The act of ceding; a yielding or surrender to another rights, property or anything to which one has a title or claim, esp. of a territory by a state; the portion thus surrendered; সমর্পণ; প্রদান, ত্যাগ, উৎসর্গ; অন্য ব্যক্তির নিকট, স্বত্ব, অধিকার সম্পত্তি প্রভৃতি সমর্পণ, রাজ্যখণ্ড সমর্পণ; সমর্পিত ভূখণ্ড। **—ar-y,** *n.*

cĕss′-pit, *n.* A pit for receiving garbage, night-soil, etc.; ময়লার গর্ত্ত, বিষ্ঠাকুণ্ড।

cĕss′-pōōl, *n.* **1.** A small well or excavation made in the bottom of drain to receive the sediments or filth; specif. a well sunk to receive the soil from a water-closet, kitchen, etc., usually so constructed that the solid matter is retained, while the liquid escapes; ময়লা প্রভৃতি দূষিত পদার্থের জন্য নর্দ্দমার নিম্নস্থ ক্ষুদ্র কূপ বা গহ্বর বিশেষ; বিশেষতঃ রন্ধন গৃহ ও পায়খানার ময়লা যে কূপে গৃহীত হয়, মলকুণ্ড, ময়লার গর্ত্ত, সার-ডোবা, পরাডোবা। **2.** (*Fig.*) Any receptacle of filth; as, Seneca speaks of Rome as a *cesspool* of iniquity; (লক্ষণায়) দূষিত বস্তুর আধার, বিষ্ঠাকুণ্ড।

cĕs′-toid(-toyd), *adj.* & *n.* Ribbon-like; ফিতার মত। ***Noun.*** A worm of this kind; ফিতাক্রিমি (সাঃ পঃ)।

cĕs′-tŭs, *n.* **1.** A belt or girdle, as of a bride; কটিবন্ধনী, মেখলা, [(বিশেষ ভাবে) গ্রীক রোমীয় পুরাণোক্ত ভীনাস বা এফ্রোডাইট দেবীর মেখলা; এই মেখলা পরিধানকারীর হৃদয়ে প্রেমভাব উদ্দীপ্ত হইত, রতি-মেখলা, রতিরসনা।] **2.** A covering for the hands of boxers, made of leather bands, loaded with lead or iron; মুষ্টি যোদ্ধাদের চর্ম্মময় অঙ্গুলিত্র।

Ce-ta′-ce-ă (sē-tā-shî-), *n. pl.* (*Zool.*) An order of marine mammals, consisting of the whales, dolphins, etc.; তিম্যাদি (সাঃ পঃ)।

cē-tā′-cean (-shăn), *adj.* & *n.* Of or pertaining to the Cetacea or whales; তিম্যাদি সম্বন্ধীয়। ***Noun.*** A member of the mammalian order containing whales; a whale; তিম্যাদি জন্তু; তিমি।

cē-tē-ō-sau′-rŭs (-sä-), *n.* A gigantic fossil saurian; অতিকায় এবং শিলীভূত শল্কবিশিষ্ট জন্তু বিশেষ।

ceteris paribus, *adv.* Other things being equal; অন্যান্য বিষয় সমান হইলে।

Cey-lon-ese′ (sē-lŏn-ēz), *adj.* & *n.* Of or belonging to Ceylon; সিংহলদ্বীপ সম্বন্ধীয়। ***Noun.*** A native of Ceylon; সিংহলের অধিবাসী।

Cha-blis′ (shă-blē), (*From Chablis in France*) ***n.*** A celebrated white French wine; ফরাসী দেশীয় সুবিখ্যাত শ্বেতবর্ণ মদিরা।

cha′-bouk (chă-bûk), **—bûk** *n.* A long whip (used in the East) in flogging; চাবুক।

chack (chăk), *n.* A light hasty meal; তাড়াতাড়ি নাকে মুখে গুঁজিয়া চারটী ভোজন।

chăc′-mă, *n.* A south African baboon; দক্ষিণ আফ্রিকার বানর বিশেষ।

chad (shăd) *n.* Same as SHAD, (which see).

chāfe, *v. t., i.* & *n.* **1.** To excite heat in by friction; to stimulate to warmth; as, to *chafe* the limbs; রগড়াইয়া গরম করা, রগড়ান, মলা; উষ্ণ করিয়া তোলা। **2.** To rub so as to wear away; to fret; to gall; as, to *chafe* a cable, one's finger; ঘসিয়া ক্ষয় করা; খাইয়া দেওয়া; রগড়াইয়া নুনছাল তোলা। **3.** To fret; to irritate; প্রকোপিত করা, বিরক্ত করা; জ্বালাতন করা। ***Verb i.*** **1.** To be excited or heated; to rage; to fret; as, to *chafe* as at a personal wrong; উত্তেজিত হওয়া, গরম হওয়া; ক্রুদ্ধ হওয়া, চটা; খিট্ খিট্ করা। **2.** To be in violent agitation; to dash as in anger; to rage or boil; বিক্ষুব্ধ হওয়া; ক্রোধে ধাবিত হওয়া; খাপ্পা হওয়া, রাগে টগবগ্ করা। **3.** To be fretted and worn by rubbing; as, cable *chafes*; খাইয়া যাওয়া। ***Noun.*** Rubbing; friction; injury or wear caused by rubbing or friction; রগড়ান; ঘর্ষণ; মর্দ্দন বা ঘর্ষণজনিত ক্ষয় বা আঘাত। **Chafing dish**—তপ্তক (ভাবঃ প্রঃ), কটাহ; অঙ্গার ধানিকা।

chāf′-ēr, *n.* **1.** A vessel for heating water; a saucepan; জল গরম করিবার পাত্র; পাক পাত্র। **2.** A name given to certain beetle, usually the *cockchafer*; একপ্রকার গোবরে পোকা। **—y, *n.***

chaff (chăf), ***n.*** & *v. t.* **1.** The glumes or husks of grains and grasses separated from the seed by threshing and winnowing etc.; তুষ, ভূষি, মুর্ম্মুর, ধান্যকঙ্ক। **2.** (*Fig.*) Refuse; worthless matter; (লক্ষণায়) আবর্জ্জনা; অসার-বস্তু। **3.** Cut hay and straw used for feeding cattle; গো-মহিষাদির খাদ্যের জন্য ক্ষুদ্রাংশে কর্ত্তিত শুষ্ক তৃণাদি। **4.** (*Bot.*) The thin dry leaves or bracts of the flower or grasses; (উদ্ভিদ-বিদ্যা) তৃণপুষ্পের শুষ্ক লঘুদল বা মঞ্জরীপত্র। **5.** (*Colloq.*) Light jesting talk; banter; raillery; as, amidst the *chaff* of a good natured crowd; (চলিতভাষায়) খোসগল্প, চুটকী গল্প; হাসিঠাট্টা; ব্যঙ্গ-কৌতুক। ***Verb t.*** **1.** To mix with chaff; ভূষির সহিত মিশ্রিত করা। **2.** To cut (hay and straw etc.) for fodder; গবাদির খাদ্যের জন্য ঘাস, খড় প্রভৃতি কাটা।

3. (*Colloq.*) To banter : to rail ; (চলিতকথায়) ঠাট্টা করা ; বিদ্রূপ করা। **Chaff'-y,** *adj.* (*Fig.*) Light, empty and worthless as chaff ; as, a *chaffy* load : *chaffy* thoughts, pamphlet, etc. : (লক্ষণায়) ভুষির মত পাতল, শূন্যগর্ভ এবং অসার। **Chaff-bed**—যে গদিতে পালকের পরিবর্ত্তে তুষ ঠাসা হয়। **Chaff-cutter**—যে যন্ত্রের সাহায্যে খড় বা শুষ্ক ঘাস সূক্ষ্মাংশে কর্ত্তিত হয়। **An old bird is not caught with chaff**—বুড়ো শালিককে ভুষি দ্বারা ধরা যায় না, অর্থাৎ পাকা লোককে ফাঁকা কথায় ভুলান যায় না।

chăf'-fẽr, *n., v. i.* & *t.* 1. One who indulges in banter ; বিদ্রূপকারী। 2. Bargaining ; haggling about price ; দরাদরি করণ ; দর কষাকষি করণ। ***Verb i.*** 1. To haggle about terms or price ; দর কষাকষি করা। 2. To talk much and idly ; বেজায় বাজে কথা বকা। ***Verb t.*** To buy and sell ; to exchange as words ; কেনাবেচা করা ; বিনিময় করা, অদলবদল করা। **—er,** *n.*

chăf'-finch (-finsh), *n.* A little British song-bird of the finch family ; কলকণ্ঠ পক্ষিবিশেষ।

cha-grin' (shă-), *n.* & *v. t.* Acute vexation ; ill-humour ; তীব্র বিরক্তি ; অসন্তোষ। ***Verb t.*** To fret ; to vex ; উত্যক্ত করা ; বিরক্ত করা।

chain (chān), *n.* & *v. t.* 1. A series of links or rings (of metal or other material) connected or fitted into one another ; শৃঙ্খল, শিকল, জিঞ্জীর, নিগড়। 2. (*Pl.*) Fetters ; confinement ; নিগড়, বেড়ী ; অবরোধ। 3. Necklace ; watch-guard, etc. ; হার, মাল্য ; টেঁক ঘড়ীর চেইন প্রভৃতি। 4. A connected train or series ; a sequence ; a set (*of* proofs, events, posts, mountains) ; শ্রেণী, পরম্পরা ; অনুক্রম, শৃঙ্খলা, পর্য্যায়, পারম্পর্য্য, মালা, সমূহ, প্রস্থ। 5. (*Survey*) A measuring line of jointed metal-rod, (its length = 66 ft.) : (জরীপ) জরীপের শিকল (৬৬ ফিট লম্বা)। 6. (*Weaving*) The warp ; (বয়নবিদ্যা) পড়েন। 7. (*Naut.*) Same as CHAINPLATE (which see). ***Verb. t.*** 1. To fasten with a chain ; hence to fetter ; to restrain ; to enslave ; as, mind *chained* to passion ; শৃঙ্খলিত করা, শৃঙ্খলবদ্ধ করা ; নিগড়িত করা ; প্রতিরোধ করা ; ক্রীতদাস করা। 2. To obstruct or protect by a chain, as a harbour ; শৃঙ্খলদ্বারা রোধ বা রক্ষা করা। 3. (*Surv.*) To measure with a chain ; (জরীপ) শিকলদ্বারা মাপ করা। **Chain'-less,** *adj.* **Chain-argument** — (*Log.*) A sorites ; ন্যায়শৃঙ্খল (সাঃ পঃ)। **Chain-belt**—বল সঞ্চারার্থ কটিবন্ধাকার শৃঙ্খলবিশেষ। **Chain-bolt**—(*Naut.*) যে সমস্ত বৃহৎ কীলকদ্বারা জাহাজের লৌহপট্ট নিবদ্ধ করা হয়—তন্মধ্যে একটী। **Chain-bridge**—দোদুল্যমান সেতু, ঝুলান সেতু। **Chain-gang** — একত্র শৃঙ্খলিত বন্দিদল। **Chain-guard** — টেঁক ঘড়ীর ঘূর্ণন-নিয়ামক যন্ত্রবিশেষ। **Chain lightning** — শৃঙ্খলাকার বিদ্যুত শিখা। **Chain-man**—জরীপের শিকল বাহক। **Chain-mail**—একত্র গ্রথিত লৌহার কড়া সকল দ্বারা নির্ম্মিত সাঁজোয়া বিশেষ। **Chain-plates** — (*Naut.*) মাস্তুলের অবলম্বনরজ্জুপরম্পরা বাঁধিবার জন্য জাহাজের পার্শ্বদেশে নিবদ্ধ সুদৃঢ় লৌহপট্ট সমূহ। **Chain-pump**—একপ্রকার দমকল, ইহাতে একটী চক্রাকার শৃঙ্খল সংযুক্ত আছে। ইহা জলে নিমজ্জিত থাকে, একটী চক্রোপরি ঘুরাইয়া জল হইতে ঐ শৃঙ্খল উত্তোলিত করা হয়, শৃঙ্খল সঞ্চালিত জলোত্তলনযন্ত্র, ঘটীযন্ত্র (মার্কঃ পুঃ)। **Chain-rule**—পাটীগণিতের শৃঙ্খল নিয়ম। **Chain-shot**—(সামরিকশাস্ত্র) ক্ষুদ্র শৃঙ্খল দ্বারা সংযুক্ত গুলিদ্বয় বা অর্দ্ধগুলিদ্বয়। এইরূপ গুলি পূর্ব্বে রণপোতের রজ্জু কাটিবার জন্য নৌ-যুদ্ধে ব্যবহৃত হইত। **Chain-stitch**—শিকলের কড়ার মত সেলাই। **Chain-wheel**—যে চক্র তৎপ্রান্তনিবদ্ধ শৃঙ্খল সহকারে বল সংক্রামিত করে।

chair (chār), *n.* & *v. t.* 1. A movable single seat of various forms, with a back ; কেদারা, কুর্সি, চৌকী, মাচিয়া। 2. A seat of justice or of authority ; বিচারকের আসন, ক্ষমতাপ্রাপ্ত ব্যক্তির আসন। 3. The seat of a professor, hence his office ; অধ্যাপকের পীঠ বা আসন, (অতএব) অধ্যাপকের পদ বা কার্য্য। 4. The seat of a person presiding at a meeting or assembly ; chairman ; as, to address the *chair* ; সভা বা সমিতির সভাপতির আসন বা কার্য্য ; সভাপতি। 5. (*Railway*) The iron blocks which support the rails of a railroad ; যে সকল ভারী লৌহখণ্ডের উপর লৌহবর্ত্মের লৌহদণ্ড (রেল) সকল অবলম্বিত থাকে। 6. A sedan chair ; জম্পান। ***Verb t.*** 1. To carry publicly in triumph on a chair or seat ; as, they were declared duly elected and were *chaired* through the streets ; মহাসমারোহে জয়োল্লাস সহকারে কেদারায় বা আসনে স্থাপন করত রাজপথে বহন করিয়া নেওয়া। 2. To provide with a chair or chairs ; as, the offices were newly *chaired* ; এক বা ততোধিক কেদারা যোগান। **Chair-bed**—একপ্রকার কেদারা,—আবশ্যকমত ইহাকে শয্যায় পরিবর্ত্তিত করিতে পারা যায়। **Chair-day**—জীবন সন্ধ্যা, বার্দ্ধক্য। **Curule-chair**—See CURULE. **Easy-chair**—See EASY. **Wheel-chair**—See WHEEL. **In the chair**—Acting as chairman ; সভাপতিরূপে। **To leave the chair**—To cease acting as chairman ; to close a meeting ; সভাপতির আসন ত্যাগ করা ; সভা ভঙ্গ করা। **To put in the chair**—To elect as chairman ; সভাপতি পদে বৃত করা, সভাপতিরূপে নির্ব্বাচন করা। **To take a chair**—To take a seat ; to be seated ; আসন গ্রহণ করা ; উপবিষ্ট হওয়া। **To take or leave the chair**—To begin c end the proceedings ; (সভার) কার্য্য আরম্ভ বা শেষ করা। **To take the chair**—To assume the position of chairman ; সভাপতির আসন পরিগ্রহ করা।

chair'-măn (châr-), *n.* (*pl.* -MEN, *fem.* -WOMAN, সভাপত্নী)। **1.** A person chosen to preside over a meeting ; the permanent president of a committee, board, etc. ; সভাপতি, সভানায়ক ; সমিতি, মন্ত্রণা-সভা প্রভৃতির স্থায়ী সভাপতি। **2.** The porter of a sedan-chair ; জম্পান বাহক।

chaise (shāz), *n.* A light open carriage for one or two persons ; এক বা দুইজন লোকের জন্য একপ্রকার হাল্‌কা খোলা গাড়ী।

chăl-cĕd'-ō-nŷ, *n.* A quartz stone of several varieties and of various colours ; সীসমণি। [এসিয়া মাইনরের অন্তঃপাতী *Chalcedon* নামক স্থানের নাম হইতে এই শব্দটী গৃহীত হইয়াছে।]

chăl-cŏg'-ră-phŷ, *n.* The act or art of engraving on copper or brass, esp. for printing ; তাম্র বা পিত্তলের উপর ক্ষোদন, তাম্র বা পিত্তল ফলকোপরি ক্ষোদনশিল্প।

Chal-dē'-ăn (kăl-), *adj.* & *n.* Of or pertaining to Chaldea, or its people ; hence, of or pertaining to astrology, magic, or occult learning ; কেল্‌ডিয়া দেশীয়, কেল্‌ডিয়াবাসি-সম্বন্ধীয় ; অতএব, ফলিতজ্যোতিষ সম্বন্ধীয়, ঐন্দ্রজালিক, গুপ্তবিদ্যা সম্বন্ধীয়। ***Noun.*** A native of Chaldea or Babylon ; hence, an astrologer ; কেল্‌ডিয়াবাসী, বেবিলোন বাসী ; অতএব, জ্যোতির্ব্বিৎ।

chăl'-drŏn, *n.* A coal measure (36 bushels) ; কয়লার মাপ বিশেষ।

cha-let' (shâ-lā). *n.* **1.** A Swiss hut or cottage ; hence, a villa built in the style of a Swiss cottage ; সুইজর্‌লেণ্ড্ দেশীয় কুটীর ; অতএব সুইজর্‌লেণ্ড্ দেশীয় কুটীরের অনুকরণে নির্ম্মিত নগরোপকণ্ঠস্থ উদ্যান-বাটিকা। **2.** A street lavatory, urinal etc ; রাজপথিস্থিত প্রক্ষালনগৃহ, মূত্রত্যাগস্থান, প্রভৃতি।

chăl'-ice (-ĭs), *n.* **1.** A drinking cup or goblet ; esp, the cup used in the celebration of the Eucharist ; পেয়ালা, বাটী, চষক ; বিশেষতঃ খৃষ্টের শেষ ভোজন পর্ব্বানুষ্ঠান উপলক্ষে ব্যবহৃত পান-পাত্র। **2.** (*Poet.*) A flower-cup ; (কবিতায়) পুষ্পকুণ্ড।

chalk (chăk), *n.* & *v. t.* A white soft earthy limestone used for writing and drawing ; খড়ি, কঠিনী, খটিকা, ধাতুপল (আঃ বঃ)। ***Verb t.*** To rub, or mark with chalk ; to manure with chalk ; to whiten with chalk ; hence, to make pale ; খড়িদ্বারা ঘর্ষণ করা, খড়িদ্বারা চিহ্নিত করা ; খড়ীদ্বারা সার দেওয়া ; খড়ি

Chalk forming.

দ্বারা শ্বেতবর্ণ করা ; পাণ্ডুর করা। **Chalk'-y,** *adj.* **Chalk-stone**—খড়ি পাথর **Red-chalk**—গৈরিয়া (মঃ উঃ)। **By long chalk, by long chalks**—অনেকদূর, বহুদূর ; বহু-পরিমাণে। **Chalk for cheese**—Something inferior for a good article ; মধুর পরিবর্ত্তে গুড়, নারিকেল বদলে নরুণ। **To chalk out**—To delineate, esp. by the main features ; আঁকিয়া বা দাগিয়া লওয়া (বিশেষতঃ) মুখ্য মুখ্য বিষয় প্রকটন করা। (*Fig.*) To mark out, as a course to be followed ; (লক্ষণায়) কর্ত্তব্য পথ নির্দ্দেশ করা।

chăl'-lenge (-lĕnj), *v. t.* & *n.* **1.** (*Mil.*) To question or demand countersign from any person approaching or attempting to pass a sentry ; (সামরিকশাস্ত্র) সান্ত্রীর দিকে অগ্রসর হইতেছে বা সান্ত্রীকে অতিক্রম করিয়া যাইতেছে এরূপ ব্যক্তিকে (সান্ত্রী কর্ত্তৃক) পরিচয় জিজ্ঞাসা করা বা সামরিক সঙ্কেত প্রদর্শন করিতে বা সঙ্কেতবাক্য বলিতে আহ্বান করা। **2.** To take exception to evidence, jurors, votes, etc. ; জুরীসম্বন্ধে, ভোট বা প্রমাণাদি সম্বন্ধে আপত্তি উত্থাপন করা। **3.** To call in question ; to dispute ; as, to *challenge* the accuracy of a statement ; আপত্তি উত্থাপন করা ; তর্ক উত্থাপন করা। **4.** To invite to duel, contest or game ; স্পর্দ্ধাপূর্ব্বক দ্বন্দ্বযুদ্ধে আহ্বান করা, কোনরূপ তর্ক যুদ্ধে বা মল্লযুদ্ধে প্রবৃত্ত হইবার জন্য স্পর্দ্ধাপূর্ব্বক আহ্বান করা। **5.** To claim (attention, admiration) ; (প্রশংসা, মনোযোগ প্রভৃতি) দাবী করা। ***Noun.*** **1.** The act of calling to account ; esp. the act of a sentry in demanding the countersign ; আহ্বান ; বিশেষতঃ সামরিক সঙ্কেত বা বাক্যাদির জন্য সান্ত্রী কর্ত্তৃক আহ্বান। **2.** Exception taken to a juror or to a vote ; কোন মোকদ্দমায় জুরীর নির্ব্বাচন সম্বন্ধে বা কোন ভোট সম্বন্ধে আপত্তি উত্থাপন। **3.** An invitation or call to a contest or controversy of any kind, esp. to single combat or duel ; defiance ; কোন বিবাদ বা তর্কবিতর্কে প্রবৃত্ত হইবার জন্য আহ্বান বা আমন্ত্রণ, (বিশেষতঃ) দ্বন্দ্বযুদ্ধে আহ্বান, যুদ্ধার্থ আহ্বান, 'যুদ্ধং দেহি' রবে আহ্বান ; যুদ্ধাহ্বান, সমরাহ্বান (মঃ ভাঃ) **—a-ble,** *adj.* **—leng-er,** *n.*

chal'-lis (shăl-lĭ), *n.* An elegant silk and woollen fabric for ladies' dresses ; স্ত্রীলোকের পরিচ্ছদে ব্যবহৃত একপ্রকার সুন্দর পশমী ও রেশমী কাপড়।

cha-lu-meau' (shă-lû-mō), *n.* A pastoral instrument of music ; a reed ; রাখালের বেণু, বংশী, বাঁশরী ; মুরলী।

Chăl-ŷ-bē'-ăn, *adj.* Pertaining to the Chalybes, an ancient nation of Asia Minor, famous for their skill in working iron ; লৌহকার্য্যে চাতুর্য্যের জন্য সুবিখ্যাত এসিয়া মাইনর-বাসী প্রাচীন জাতি বিশেষ সম্বন্ধীয়।

chă-lўb'-ē-āte, *adj.* Impregnated with iron, esp. as a mineral water or spring ; লৌহময়, লৌহগর্ভ।

chăm, *n.* The sovereign prince of Tartary, (now usually written *Khan.*) ; তাতার দেশের রাজা। **The great cham**—স্বৈর শাসক ; শক্তিশালী লেখক বা সমালোচক।

cha-māde' (shă-), *n.* (*Mil.*) A signal for retreat by beat of drum or sound of trumpet ; (সামরিকশাস্ত্র) রণদুন্দুভি বা সমরতুরিনিনাদ দ্বারা পলায়নের সঙ্কেত প্রদান।

chām'-bēr, *n.* **1.** An apartment ; কক্ষ। **2.** The reception room of a palace ; রাজপ্রাসাদের অভ্যর্থনা-কক্ষ, দর্শন গৃহ (মঃ সঃ)। **3.** (*Pl.*) Set of rooms (for single persons) in larger building ; esp. rooms in the Inns of Court occupied by lawyers ; set of rooms in a block of buildings for offices etc. ; a judge's private room where he sits to hear such cases, and to transact such business, as may be done out of court ; (ভিন্ন ভিন্ন ব্যক্তির জন্য) সুবৃহৎ অট্টালিকাস্থিত কক্ষশ্রেণী ; বিশেষতঃ (ইংলণ্ডে) ব্যবহারজীবিগণের সম্মিলন-ভবনস্থিত কক্ষশ্রেণী ; কার্য্যালয় প্রভৃতির জন্য কক্ষশ্রেণী ; বিচারকের খাস কামরা। **4.** A hall of justice or legislation ; a legislative body ; ব্যবস্থাপক সভার গৃহ, ভবন, বিচারকক্ষ ; ব্যবস্থাপক সভা। **5.** A hollow or cavity ; গর্ত্ত বা রন্ধ্র। **6.** That part of the bore of a gun in which the charge is placed ; (in revolvers) each of the barrels or compartments, which contains charge ; বন্দুকের রন্ধ্রের যে অংশে গুলি বারুদ ভরা হয়, ঘরা, রঞ্জন ঘর ; (পিস্তল পক্ষে) নল। **—bered,** *adj.* **—ing,** *n.* (*Obs.*) Sexual indulgence ; effeminacy ; মৈথুন ; স্ত্রীস্বভাব, নির্ব্বীর্য্যতা। **Chamber-counsel**—যে ব্যবহারজীবী বিচারালয়ে উপস্থিত না হইয়া নিজ বাটীতে মোকেলদিগকে পরামর্শ দিয়া থাকেন। **Chamber-maid** — শয্যাগৃহের পরিচারিকা, কোষ্ঠ দাসী (আঃ বঃ)। **Chamber-man**—শয়নকক্ষের পরিচারক। **Chamber-master**—যে ব্যক্তি বাটীতে বসিয়া পাদুকা ব্যবসায়িগণের জন্য চর্ম্মপাদুকা প্রস্তুত করে। **Chamber-mate**—এক কক্ষবাসী। **Chamber-music**—এক বা ততোধিক ব্যক্তি দ্বারা ক্ষুদ্র কক্ষে সম্পাদ্য সংগীত। **Chamber-pot**—শয্যাগৃহস্থ মূত্রাধার। **Chamber of commerce, agriculture**—বণিক্‌সমিতি, কৃষিসমিতি। **Chamber of deputies**—ফরাসী দেশীয় জনপ্রতিনিধিসভা।

chām'-bēr-lain (-lān or -lĭn), *n.* **1.** An officer having charge of the management of the private chambers of a sovereign or nobleman ; রাজা বা সম্ভ্রান্ত ব্যক্তির নিজস্ব কক্ষ সমূহের তত্ত্বাবধায়ক কর্ম্মচারী, কঞ্চুকী। **2.** A hereditary holder of ceremonial office ; ইংলণ্ডীয় রাজপ্রাসাদের কর্ম্মচারিবিশেষ। **3.** The high steward of a nobleman ; কোন সম্ভ্রান্ত পুরুষের প্রধান কর্ম্মাধ্যক্ষ। **Lord Chamberlain of the household** — ইংলণ্ডেশ্বরের গার্হস্থ্য বিভাগের কর্ম্মচারিবিশেষ—ইনি রাজপ্রাসাদের বহুবিভাগের কর্ম্মাধ্যক্ষতা করিয়া থাকেন—ইনি রাজকীয় রঙ্গমঞ্চস্থ অভিনেতৃবর্গকে অভিনয় সম্বন্ধে অনুমতি প্রদান করিয়া থাকেন।

chă-mē'-lē-ŏn, *n.* **1.** A lizard remarkable for changing its colour and fabled to live on air ; কৃকলাস, বহুরূপী (প্রবাসী ১৩২০

Chameleon.

অগ্রহায়ণ), সরট, কৃলাহক, প্রতিসূর্য্যক (আঃ বঃ)। **2.** (*Fig.*) An inconstant or variable person ; as, he is an intellectual *chameleon* ; (লক্ষণায়) অব্যবস্থিতচিত্ত বা অস্থিরমতি ব্যক্তি, বহুরূপী। **—like, —on'-ic,** *adjs.*

chăm'-fĕr, *n.* & *v. t.* **1.** A small gutter or furrow cut in wood or stone ; পাথরের উপর কাটা জুলি বা খাঁজ। **2.** The surface produced by bevelling off a square edge or corner equally on both sides ; কোন বস্তুর চতুষ্কোণ প্রান্ত বা কিনারা টের্ছাভাবে কাটিলে যেরূপ আকার গঠিত হয়। ***Verb t.*** **1.** To channel ; to furrow ; জুলি কাটা ; খাঁজ কাটা। **2.** To bevel symmetrically a right-angled edge or corner ; কোন বস্তুর সমকোণ প্রান্ত বা কিনারা সমপ্রমাণে টের্চ্ছা করিয়া কাটা।

cham'-ois (shăm-ōy or shăm-wä), **1.** A European wild antelope of goat size ; মেষয় ছাগ, বাতমৃগ বিশেষ। **2.** A soft pliable leather from sheep, goats, deer, etc. ; মেষ, ছাগ, হরিণ প্রভৃতির চর্ম্ম হইতে প্রস্তুত কোমল ও নমনীয় চর্ম্ম বিশেষ।

chămp, *v. t.* & *n.* **1.** To crunch ; চর্ব্বণ করা। **2.** To mash ; to trample under foot ; চূর্ণবিচূর্ণ করা ; পদদলিত করা। ***Noun.*** Chewing action or noise ; চর্ব্বণের কড়মড় শব্দ, চর্ব্বণ।

cham-pagne' (shăm-pāne), *n.* A kind of light, brisk, sparkling wine from Champagne in France ; ফরাসীদেশ হইতে সমানীত সুপ্রসিদ্ধ শ্যাম্পেন মদ্য।

cham paign' (shăm-pāne), *n.* An expanse of flat open country ; মুক্ত সমতল ভূভাগ, সমভূমি, সমস্থল (হিঃ কোঃ)।

chăm'-pêr-tў, *n.* (*Law*) Maintenance of a party in law-suit upon condition of sharing with him the thing of issue if recovered ; (আইন) যদ্দারা কোন মোকদ্দমায় অসংসৃষ্ট ব্যক্তি এই সর্ত্তে বাদী বা প্রতিবাদীপক্ষকে সাহায্য করে—যাহাতে সাহায্যপ্রাপ্ত পক্ষ মোকদ্দমায় জয়লাভ করিলে উক্ত সাহায্যকারী বিরোধীয় বিষয়ের একাংশ প্রাপ্ত হয়।

cham-pi′-gnon (shăm-pîn-yŏn), *n.* A mushroom ; শিলীন্ধ্রী, ছত্রাক।

chăm′-pi-ŏn, *n.* & *v. t.* **1.** A person who fights, argues, etc., for another or for a cause ; যে ব্যক্তি কোন ব্যক্তির জন্য বা কোন কর্ত্তব্য পালনের জন্য সংগ্রামে বা তর্কযুদ্ধে প্রবৃত্ত হয়, বীর, যোদ্ধা, যোধ, ভট (মঃ ইঃ)। **2.** The first in some athletic art or trial of skill ; মল্লক্রীড়াদিতে প্রথমস্থানপ্রাপ্ত ব্যক্তি। **3.** The animal, plant, vegetable, etc., which obtains the first prize in a general competition ; as, five tons of Scotch *champions* ; প্রদর্শনীতে প্রথম পুরস্কার প্রাপ্ত জন্তু, উদ্ভিদ্‌, শাকসব্জী প্রভৃতি। ***Verb t.*** To protect or defend as champion ; (*fig.*) to maintain the cause of ; to stand up for ; বীরের মত রক্ষা বা সমর্থন করা ; (লক্ষণায়) কাহারো পক্ষ সমর্থন করা ; সাহায্যার্থ দণ্ডায়মান হওয়া। **—ess,** (*fem.*) *n.* **—less,** *adj.* **—ship,** *n.*

chance (chăns), *n.*, *adj.*, *v. t.* & *i.* **1.** The happening of an event ; ঘটনাসংঘটন। **2.** An accident ; a casual occurrence ; আকস্মিক ঘটনা ; নৈমিত্তিক ঘটনা, দৈব, দৈবঘটনা। **3.** Probability ; (esp. in *pl.*) fortune ; "If it be thy *chance* to kill me" ; সম্ভাবনা ; ভাগ্য, অদৃষ্ট, কপাল। **4.** An opportunity offered ; সুযোগ, সুবিধা। ***Adj.*** Fortuitous ; incidental ; casual ; as, *chance* companion, meeting ; নৈমিত্তিক ; প্রাসঙ্গিক ; আকস্মিক। ***Verb t.*** To risk ; to venture upon ; (usually with *it* as object) ; "Come what will, I will *chance* it ;" ঝুঁকি লওয়া ; দৈবের উপর নির্ভর করিয়া কোন কার্য্যে প্রবৃত্ত হওয়া। ***Verb i.*** To happen, come or arrive, without design or expectation ; অপ্রত্যাশিত বা অচিন্তিত ভাবে আসা, উপস্থিত হওয়া বা ঘটা, দৈবাৎ ঘটা। **Chanc′-y,** *adj.* **Chance comer**—দৈবাগত ব্যক্তি, অতিথি। **An eye to the main chance**—যাহাতে দুপয়সা প্রাপ্তি হয় সেই দিকে নজর। **By chance**—হঠাৎ, দৈবাৎ ; দৈবক্রমে, দৈব যোগে, দৈববশে, ঘটনাবশে, ঘটনাক্রমে, দৈব সংযোগে। **On the chance**—দৈবের উপর। **The last chance**—শেষ ভরসা। **The main chance**—প্রধান সুযোগ। **To stand a good or fair chance**—To have prospect ; ফললাভের সম্ভাবনা থাকা। **To take one's chance**—To submit to whatever may happen ; অদৃষ্টের হস্তে আত্ম সমর্পণ করা **To try a chance**—To test one's lot ; অদৃষ্ট পরীক্ষা করা।

chăn′-cĕl, *n.* The eastern part of a church reserved for the clergy, choir, etc. and usually railed off ; যাজকবৃন্দ, কীর্ত্তন সম্প্রদায় প্রভৃতির উপবেশনের জন্য নির্দ্দিষ্ট (খৃষ্টীয়) ধর্ম্ম মন্দিরের পূর্ব্বদিকস্থ ভাগ,—মন্দিরের এই অংশ সাধারণতঃ গরাদ-বেষ্টিত থাকে।

chăn′-cĕl-lor (-lêr), *n.* **1.** A state or law official of various kinds ; বিচার বা আইন বিভাগের বিভিন্ন কর্ম্মচারী। **2.** The titular head of a university, (the Vice Chancellor performing all duties) ; বিশ্ববিদ্যালয়াধীশ। **3.** (Scotland) The foreman of a jury ; (স্কটলণ্ডে) জুরিদিগের অগ্রণী। **4.** (*U. S.*) Judge in a statutory court of chancery or equity in various states ; (যুক্তরাজ্য) আমেরিকার বিভিন্ন রাজ্যস্থ যে সকল বিচারালয়ের বিচারক লিখিত ব্যবস্থা দ্বারা মোকদ্দমা নিষ্পত্তি না করিয়া শুদ্ধ ন্যায়ান্যায় দৃষ্টে নিষ্পত্তি করেন। **—ship,** *n.* **Chancellor of an Ecclesiasticel Court**—খৃষ্টীয় ধর্ম্মাধ্যক্ষের আইন সম্বন্ধীয় পরামর্শ দাতা। **Chancellor of the Exchequer**—ইংলণ্ড দেশের রাজস্ব সচিব। **Chancellor of the order of Garter**—ইংলণ্ডীয় অভিজাত সম্প্রদায় বিশেষের কর্ম্মচারী বিশেষ। **Lord Chancellor, Lord High Chancellor**—ইংলণ্ড দেশের সর্ব্বোচ্চ রাজকর্ম্মচারী এবং মন্ত্রিসভার বিশিষ্ট সভ্য।

chance′-med-ley (chăns-mĕd-lĭ), *n.* [*Lit.* mingled chance] (*Law*) The casual killing of a man, not altogether without the killer's fault, though without an evil intent ; ঘটনাক্রমে হত্যাকরণ, অর্থাৎ যেরূপ নরহত্যায় হত্যাকারীর অসদভিপ্রায় না থাকিলেও সে সম্পূর্ণরূপে দোষ নির্ম্মুক্ত নহে। [পথিপার্শ্বস্থ বৃক্ষশাখা ছেদনের সময় যদি ছেদনকারী পথিকদিগকে সাবধান না করে, এবং সেই শাখা পড়িয়া কোন লোক মৃত্যুমুখে পতিত হয়, তবে এইরূপ স্থলে ছেদনকারী ব্যক্তি অপরাধী বলিয়া গণ্য হইবে।]

chăn′-cĕr-ȳ, *n.* **1.** The court presided over by the Lord Chancellor in England ; formerly the highest court of Justice next to Parliament ; now a division of the High Court of Justice ; সর্ব্বপ্রধান বিচারপতি কর্ত্তৃক অধিষ্ঠিত সাধারণ বিচারালয় ; (পূর্ব্বকালে) ইংলণ্ডের মহাসভার নিম্নে সর্ব্বোচ্চ বিচারালয় ; (অধুনা) প্রধান বিচারালয়ের অন্যতম বিভাগ। **2.** An office of public records ; সরকারী দলীলপত্র যে কার্য্যালয়ে রক্ষিত হয়। **In chancery**—উক্ত আদালতের বিচারাধীন। **To get into chancery**—(*Slang*) (ইতর ভাষায়) মুষ্টিযুদ্ধে সম্পূর্ণরূপে প্রতিদ্বন্দীর বাগে পড়া।

chan′-cre (shăng-kĕr), [F. cancer] *n.* A venereal ulcer ; উপদংশ বিষজনিতক্ষত, শিশ্নবিস্ফোট (সাঃ পঃ)। **—crous,** *adj.*

chan′-de-lier (shăn-dĕ-lēr), *n.* An ornamental branched hanging support for several lights ; ঝাড়, দীপবৃক্ষ, দীপপাদপ।

chăn′-dlêr, *n.* **1.** A seller or maker of candles ; মোমবাতি বিক্রেতা, মোমবাতি প্রস্তুতকারী, বাতিকার। **2.** A retail dealer in provisions, groceries, etc. ; মুদী। **—y,** *n.*

chānge, *v. t.*, *i.*, & *n.* **1.** To alter or make different ; to cause to pass from one state to another ; পরিবর্তন করা, রূপান্তরিত করা, প্রকারান্তর করা ; অবস্থান্তরিত করা। 2. To substitute something else for ; to quit one and take another ; as, to *change* the clothes : to *change* carriages on a railway ; এক বস্তুর পরিবর্তে অন্য বস্তু দেওয়া ; এক বস্তু ত্যাগ করিয়া অন্য বস্তু গ্রহণ করা। 3. To give and take reciprocally ; to exchange, (followed by *with*) ; পরস্পর আদান প্রদান করা ; বিনিময় করা, অদল বদল করা। 4. To give or get a smaller or foreign coin for ; টাকা প্রভৃতি ভাঙ্গান। 5. (Of milk, wine) To render sour or tainted ; (দুগ্ধ, মদ্য প্রভৃতি সম্পর্কে) টকিয়ে দেওয়া বা দূষিত করা। *Verb i.* 1. To be altered ; to become different ; পরিবর্ত্তিত হওয়া ; রূপান্তরিত বা অবস্থান্তরিত হওয়া। 2. To pass from one phase to another ; esp. to pass through the phase of new moon ; as, the moon *changes* to-morrow night ; অবস্থান্তর প্রাপ্ত হওয়া, চন্দ্রকলার হ্রাস বৃদ্ধি হওয়া ; বিশেষতঃ অমাবস্যা অতিক্রম করা। *Noun.* 1. Alteration ; variation ; পরিবর্তন ; রূপান্তর। 2. Variety ; বৈচিত্র্য। 3. Exchange ; বনিগ্‌গণের সমাগমস্থল। 4. Small coin ; সিকি, দুয়ানি প্রভৃতি ক্ষুদ্র মুদ্রা, ভাঙ্গানি। 5. The balance of money paid beyond the price of article ; কোন জিনিষের মূল্য স্বরূপ প্রদত্ত অতিরিক্ত অর্থ—যাহা ক্রেতাকে ফেরত দেওয়া হয়। 6. The arrival of the moon at a fresh phase ; the coming of the new moon ; চন্দ্রকলার রূপান্তর ; অমাবস্যা সমাগম, পর্ব্বসন্ধি (রঃ)। 7. (Bell-ringing) (usu. *pl.*) Different orders in which a peal can be rung ; ঘণ্টাশ্রেণী বাজাইবার বিভিন্ন ক্রম ; প্রস্তার (মিউজিক্)। **Change-a-bil′-i-ty, Change′-a-ble-ness,** *ns.* **Change′-a-ble,** *adj.* 1. Irregular ; inconstant ; alterable ; mutable ; fickle ; অনিয়মিত ; অস্থির, অনিত্য ; অব্যবস্থিত ; পরিবর্তনসহ, পরিবর্তনশীল, বিবর্তনশীল ; চপলপ্রকৃতি, তরলমতি, চঞ্চলচিত্ত। 2. Showing different colours under different aspects ; as, cock's wing is *changeable* ; বিভিন্ন অবস্থায় ভিন্ন ভিন্ন বর্ণ প্রদর্শনশীল। **Change′-a-bly,** *adv.* **Change′-ful,** *adj.* (*Poet.*) **Change′-ful-ly,** *adv.* **Change′-ful-ness,** *n.* **Change′-less,** *adj.* Immutable ; নির্ব্বিকার (হিঃ কোঃ)। **Change of air**—বায়ুপরিবর্তন। **Change of life**—বর্ষীয়সী (পঞ্চাশৎ বর্ষীয়া) স্ত্রীলোকদিগের রজো নিবৃত্তির অব্যবহিত পূর্ব্বাবস্থা। **Change of season**—ঋতু পরিবর্তন। **To change colour** or **hue**—To become altered in colour ; (of persons) to turn pale ; to blush ; বিবর্ণ হওয়া ; পাণ্ডুবর্ণ ধারণ করা ; লজ্জায় গণ্ডস্থল আরক্তিম হওয়া। **To change face**—To change countenance ; চেহারা বদলান। **To change for the better** or **worse**—To get a change into a better or worse condition ; পূর্ব্বাপেক্ষা ভাল কি মন্দ অবস্থায় পরিবর্ত্তিত হওয়া। **To change hand**—To pass from one hand to another ; হস্তান্তরিত হওয়া, একের অধিকার হইতে অন্যের অধিকারে যাওয়া। **To change into**—To transform into ; পরিবর্ত্তিত করা, রূপান্তরিত করা। **To change oneself**—To change one's clothes ; কাপড় ছাড়া বা পরিবর্তন করা। **To change one's condition**—To get married ; বিবাহ করা। **To change one's feet**—To change one's shoes ; (*now only Scotch*) ; জুতা পরিবর্তন করা। **To change one's minds**—To alter one's opinion or purpose ; মত বা উদ্দেশ্য পরিবর্তন করা। **To change one's tune**—To alter one's manner of speaking ; স্বর বদলান। **To change places**—To be in the position or rank of another ; অন্যের পদ বা মর্য্যাদা প্রাপ্ত হওয়া। **To change side**—To go over from one side to another ; পক্ষ পরিবর্তন করা। **To change step**—To alter the cadence of the steps in marching ; যুদ্ধ-যাত্রা বা কুচ্‌কাওয়াজ এর সময়ে পদপতনের ধারা পরিবর্তন করা। **To put the changes upon a person**—To deceive ; প্রতারণা করা। **To ring the changes**—To go through all the changes in ringing a peal of bell ; (*fig.*) to go through all the possible variations of any process ; সজ্জিত ঘণ্টাশ্রেণী নানাভাবে বাজান ; (লক্ষণায়) সর্ব্বপ্রকার পরিবর্তনের ভিতর দিয়া অগ্রসর হওয়া। **To take one's change out of**—To take one's revenge on (a person) or for (a thing) ; কোন ব্যক্তির উপর বা কোন বিষয়ের জন্য শোধ তোলা, প্রতিহিংসা লওয়া।

change-ling (chănj-), *n.* 1. A child left or taken in the place of another ; একটী শিশুর পরিবর্তে রক্ষিত বা গৃহীত অপর শিশু। [পরীরা সুন্দর শিশু লইয়া গিয়া তাহার পরিবর্তে একটী নির্ব্বোধ ও কদাকার শিশু রাখিয়া যাইত—এইরূপ বিশ্বাস হইতে শব্দটী উপজাত হইয়াছে।]

chăn′-nĕl, *n.* & *v. t.* 1. A natural or artificial bed of running water ; (প্রাকৃতিক বা কৃত্রিম) প্রণালী (সাঃ পঃ), খাল, খাত (ঐ)। 2. The deeper part of a strait, bay or harbour, etc., where the main current flows ; the bed of a river ; প্রণালী, নদী বা পোতাশ্রয় প্রভৃতির প্রধান এবং গভীরতর অংশ—যথায় স্রোতঃ প্রবাহিত হয় ; নদীগর্ভ। 3. (*Geog.*) A strait or narrow sea between two pieces of land ; as, the English *channel* ; (ভূগোল) দুই স্থলভাগের মধ্যবর্ত্তী সঙ্কীর্ণ জলভাগ, প্রণালী। 4. A tube or duct ; as, the poison *channel* in snake's fangs ; প্রবাহিকা, নালী। 5. Medium ;

agency ; as, the news was conveyed to us by different *channels* ; line of action, thought, etc. ; as, the conversation into this *channel* ; উপায় ; সাধন, কর্তৃত্ব; কার্য্যপ্রণালী, চিন্তাপ্রণালী। ৫. (*Arch.*) A groove or fur as in a column ; স্তম্ভাদির খাঁজ বা নালী। ***Verb t.*** To form a channel in ; to groove ; প্রণালী প্রস্তুত করা ; খাঁজ কাটা।

chăn′-nĕl, *n.* A broad thick plank projecting horizontally from a ship's side abreast of the mast to spread the shrouds and keep them clear of the bulwark ; পোত পার্শ্ব হইতে শায়িত ভাবে প্রলম্বিত স্থূল এবং প্রশস্ত কাষ্ঠ-ফলক—ইহাতে মাস্তুলের অবলম্বন রজ্জু-সমূহ বন্ধন করা হয় বলিয়া ইহারা পাটাতনের উপরিস্থিত জাহাজের পার্শ্ব হইতে আলগা থাকে।

chănt, *v. t., i.* & *n.* **1.** To sing ; গান করা। **2.** To celebrate in song ; (গুণ প্রভৃতি) কীর্ত্তন করা। **3.** To intone ; গানের সুরে কথা কহা। ***Verb i.*** To sing ; গান করা। ***Noun.*** **1.** A song ; melody ; গীত, গান, সঙ্গীত ; সুতান, সুমিষ্ট তান, সুস্বর, কলস্বর। **2.** A short melody with long reciting note for psalms and canticles ; একপ্রকার ভজন, ভজন সঙ্গীত। **3.** A singsong intonation in talk ; সাধারণ কথাবার্ত্তায় সঙ্গীতের স্বর প্রয়োগ। **Chan-tant′,** *adj.* **Chant′-er, (–or),** *ns.* **1.** A singer or songster ; গায়ক। **2.** A precentor ; ভজনালয়ের প্রধান গায়ক। **3.** In bag-pipes, the tube with finger-holes ; স্কটলণ্ড্ দেশীয় সুপ্রসিদ্ধ ব্যাগ-পাইপ বাদ্য যন্ত্রের নল। **4.** A swindling horse-dealer ; জুয়াচোর অশ্ব-ব্যবসায়ী। **To chant a horse**—To sell it fraudulently ; প্রবঞ্চনা করিয়া অশ্ব বিক্রয় করা।

chantage, (*F.*), *n.* Blackmailing ; ভয় প্রদর্শন দ্বারা অবৈধরূপে অর্থ গ্রহণ।

chan-te-relle, (*F.*) *n.* A yellow edible fungus ; একপ্রকার পীতবর্ণ ভোজনোপযোগী ছত্রাক।

chăn′-ti-cleer (-clēr), *n.* A cock ; মোরগ, কুক্কুট।

chân′-trȳ, *n.* **1.** An endowment for priests to sing daily mass for the souls of the donors or others ; দাতা বা অন্য ব্যক্তির পরলোকগত আত্মার সদ্গতির নিমিত্ত প্রতিদিন ভজন সঙ্গীত গাহিবার জন্য যাজকগণকে যে বৃত্তি প্রদত্ত হয়। **2.** A chapel, so endowed ; as, *chantries* were added to churches ; ঐরূপ বৃত্তি প্রাপ্ত ক্ষুদ্র উপাসনা-মন্দির বা ভজনালয়, গীতি-মন্দির (আঃ বঃ)।

chânt′-ȳ, *n.* A sailor's song while heaving ; ভাটিয়াল গান, মাল্লার গান।

cha′-ŏs, *n.* **1.** The confused, inorganised state of primordial matter before the creation of distinct and orderly forms ; সৃষ্টির প্রাক্‌কালীন বিশৃঙ্খল অবস্থা, অপঞ্চীকৃত ভূতস্থিতি, (হিঃ কোঃ), সংপ্লব (ঐ)। **2.** Utter confusion and disorder ; মহাবিশৃঙ্খলা। **–ot′-ic,** *adj.* **–ot′-i-cal-ly,** *adv.*

chăp, *v. t., v. i.,* & *n.* To cause to crack in fissures ; "......no winter's blast *chap* her fair face" ; ফাটান। ***Verb i.*** **1.** To crack or open in silts ; as, the earth *chaps* ; ফাটা (হাত, মুখ প্রভৃতি), বিদীর্ণ হওয়া। **2.** To knock, rap, at a door ; as, to *chap* out (দরজায় ঘা দিয়া কাহাকে ডাকা) ; আঘাত করা, দরজায় ঘা মারা বা ধাক্কা দেওয়া। **3.** To strike, (of a clock, etc.) ; (ঘড়ী প্রভৃতির পক্ষে) বাজা। ***Noun.*** **1.** Cleft, crack or chink, as in the surface of the earth or in the skin ; মাটি বা ঠোঁট, হাত, পা, প্রভৃতির ফাটা, ফাটল। **2.** Stroke, knock, rap ; ঘা, ধাক্কা, ঠক্ ঠক্ শব্দ।

chăp, *n.* **1.** (*Pl.*) (Of animals) The jaws ; চোয়াল, হনু, চিবুক। **2.** (*Sing.*) The lower half of the cheek, esp. of the pigs, as an article of food ; চোয়ালের নিম্নার্দ্ধ ভাগ, বিশেষতঃ শূকর শাবকের—যাহা খাদ্যস্বরূপ ব্যবহৃত হয়। **Chap′-fall-en,** *adj.* নিরতিশয় ক্লান্তি বা দুর্ব্বলতা হেতু লোল-চিবুক ; অতএব স্ফূর্তিহীন, ম্লান, বিষণ্ণ।

chăp, *n.* (*Colloq.*) A youngman ; fellow ; lad ; (চলিতভাষায়) বটু, যুবা ; বেটা ; ছোকরা, ছোঁড়া।

chăp-ăr-răl′, *n.* **1.** A thicket of low evergreen oaks ; অনুচ্চ এবং চিরহরিত ওক বৃক্ষের কুঞ্জ। **2.** A thicket formed by thorny shrubs, brambles, etc. ; কণ্টকবন।

chăp′-bōōk, *n.* See CHAP-MAN.

chāpe, *n.* **1.** The metal plate or mounting of a scabbard ; তরবারির কোষের অগ্রভাগস্থ ধাতুনির্ম্মিত পট্ট। **2.** The tip of a fox's tail ; শৃগাল পুচ্ছের অগ্রভাগ। **3.** The part of a buckle by which it is fastened to a strap or belt ; ধাতুনির্ম্মিত বন্ধনাঙ্গুরীর অংশ বিশেষ,—যদ্দ্বারা ইহা কটিবন্ধন প্রভৃতির সহিত সংবদ্ধ হয়, বন্ধনকীলক (মঃ ইঃ)।

cha-peau′ (shă-pō), *n.* A hat or covering for the head ; শিরস্ত্রাণ, মস্তকাবরণ।

cha-peau-bras (shă-pō-brâ), *n.* A three-cornered flat silk hat of 18th century, which could be carried under the arm ; অষ্টাদশ শতাব্দীতে প্রচলিত একপ্রকার ত্রিকোণ রেশমী টুপি।

chăp′-ĕl, *n.* **1.** A subordinate place of worship, esp. of Christian worship ; ক্ষুদ্র ভজনালয়, (খৃষ্টীয়) মহাধর্ম্মমন্দিরের অধীন ক্ষুদ্র পূজাশালা। **2.** A place of worship in a palace or a private residence ; রাজপ্রাসাদ বা কোন ব্যক্তির ভবনস্থ উপাসনা গৃহ। **3.** (English) Dissenters' place of worship ; প্রচলিত খৃষ্ট ধর্ম্মমত উপাসনা-প্রণালী-বিরোধিসম্প্রদায় বিশেষের উপাসনা মন্দির, সম্মিলন-গৃহ। **4.** A printing office ; an association of workmen in a printing office ; মুদ্রণকার্য্যালয় ; মুদ্রণ-কার্য্যালয়ের কর্ম্মচারিসমিতি। **Chapel of ease**—বৃহৎ যাজক পল্লীর অতিরিক্ত ভজনালয়।

chăp'-ē-lĕt, *n.* A pair of stirrup leather with stirrups ; চর্ম্মরজ্জু সংলগ্ন জিনের রেকাবদ্বয়।

chăp'-ŏl-rȳ, *n.* The district attached to a chapel ; ধর্ম্মমন্দিরের অধিকারভুক্ত স্থান।

chap'-êr-ŏn, (shăp-), *n.* & *v. t.* **1.** A hood or cap formerly worn by nobles and ladies ; (পূর্ব্বকালে) ইংলণ্ডীয় সম্ভ্রান্ত পুরুষ এবং ভদ্রমহিলাগণের মস্তকাবরণ বা শিরস্ত্রাণ বিশেষ। **2.** A married or elderly woman who, for the sake of propriety, accompanies a young unmarried lady to public place as a guide or protector ; প্রকাশ্যস্থলে গমনকালে কোন অবিবাহিতা যুবতীর সহিত শোভনতার জন্য যে বিবাহিতা বা বর্ষীয়সী মহিলা গমন করেন। ***Verb t.*** To act as chaperon to a young lady ; যুবতীর রক্ষক স্বরূপ প্রকাশ্যস্থানে গমনাগমন করা।

chăp'-i-têr, *n.* (*Arch.*) The capital of a column ; স্তম্ভশীর্ষ, বোধিকা (রাঃ রাঃ)।

chăp'-lain (-lān), **1.** An ecclesiastic who conducts divine service in a ship, regiment, public establishment or a family ; জাহাজ, সেনা পল্টন, প্রতিষ্ঠান বা পরিবারের পুরোহিত, ঋত্বিক্। **—cy, —ship,** *ns.*

chăp'-lĕt, *n.* **1.** A garland or wreath of leaves, flowers, gold or gems, etc., to be worn on the head ; শিরোমালা, গর্ভক (মঃ উঃ), শেখর (হরিঃ), উত্তংশ (সাঃ দঃ), কুসুমাবতংসক (মঃ উঃ), মৌলিমাল্য (উজ্জ্বলঃ), মৌলিমালিকা, মৌলিমালা। **2.** A rosary ; জপমালা, অক্ষমালা। **3.** A tuft of feathers on a peacock's head ; ময়ূরশিখা। **4.** A string of eggs in toad, etc. ; কোলাব্যাঙ্গ প্রভৃতির ডিমের ছড়া। **5.** (*Arch.*) A small moulding carved into beads, pearls, etc. ; (স্থপতিবিদ্যা) মালা, মুক্তাফল প্রভৃতির আকারে রচিত ক্ষুদ্র 'বন্ধ' বিশেষ।

chăp'-măn, *n.* One who buys or sells ; a hawker ; ক্রেতা বা বিক্রেতা ; ফেরিওয়ালা। **Chap-book** — পূর্ব্বে ফেরিওয়ালাগণ যে সমস্ত জনপ্রিয় পুস্তক ফেরি করিয়া বেড়াইত, অতএব জনপ্রিয় পুস্তক।

chăp'-têr, *n.* & *v.t.* **1.** An important division of a book or treatise ; hence, limited subject ; part of a narrative, etc. ; as, it is a curious *chapter* in modern history ; অধ্যায়, সর্গ, পরিচ্ছেদ, উচ্ছ্বাস, উল্লাস ; অতএব নির্দ্দিষ্ট বিষয় ; কোন বৃত্তান্ত প্রভৃতির অংশ। **2.** A corporation of clergy ; যাজকসমিতি, যাজক সমাজ। **3.** A head or division of the Acts of Parliament of a single session ; পার্লেমেণ্ট মহাসভার এক অধিবেশন কালে যে সমস্ত আইন বিধিবদ্ধ হয় তাহার শিরোনাম বা বিভাগ। **4.** A meeting of the members of a religious order ; যাজকগণের সভা। ***Verb t.*** To divide into chapters, as a book ; অধ্যায় কিম্বা পরিচ্ছেদে বিভক্ত করা। **Chapter-house**—খৃষ্টীয় মহাধর্ম্মমন্দিরের যে কক্ষে যাজকদিগের সভার অধিবেশন হয়। **The chapter of accidents**—দৈবঘটনা সমূহ। **To give chapter and verse**—To give exact reference to a passage or exact authority for a statement ; কোন উক্তি বা গ্রন্থোদ্ধৃত বাক্যের পোষকতার জন্য যথার্থ প্রামাণ্য, অর্থাৎ গ্রন্থকার বা পুস্তকের নাম, পুস্তক প্রকাশের তারিখ, গ্রন্থের কোন অধ্যায়ে উল্লিখিত উক্তি রহিয়াছে, প্রভৃতি বিবরণ প্রদান করা। **To the end of the chapter**—To the end ; শেষ পর্য্যন্ত।

châr, *n.* A small fish of the trout kind, found in the mountain lakes in Wales ; ওয়েল্‌স্ দেশের পার্ব্বত্য হ্রদবাসী মৎস্য বিশেষ।

châr, *v. t.* & *i.* To burn to charcoal, (also *v. i.*) ; to scorch ; to blacken with fire ; as, to *char* wood ; পোড়াইয়া অঙ্গার করা, অগ্নিদগ্ধ হইয়া অঙ্গারে পরিণত হওয়া ; দগ্ধ করা ; আগুনে পোড়াইয়া কাল করা।

chār, *v. t.* & *i.* Same as CHARE which see.

char-a-bancs' (shâr-ă-bâng), A long, light pleasure van with transverse seats ; লঘু এবং দীর্ঘাকৃতি লীলাযানবিশেষ—ইহার আসনশ্রেণী কোণাকুণিভাবে সজ্জিত থাকে।

chăr'-ăc-têr, *n.* & *v. t.* **1.** A distinctive mark ; a mark engraved or inscribed ; a seal ; a stamp or impression ; পার্থক্যসূচক চিহ্ন ; খোদিত বা উৎকীর্ণ চিহ্ন ; শীলমোহর ; ছাপ বা মোহর। **2.** A letter of the alphabet ; বর্ণ, অক্ষর ; **3.** A person's handwriting ; as, written in a rough unsteady *character* ; হস্তাক্ষর। **4.** (*Nat. Hist.*) Characteristic ; (প্রাণি-বিদ্যা) প্রকৃতি-নির্দ্দেশক ধর্ম্ম বা গুণ। **5.** The peculiar qualities impressed by nature or habit on a person ; স্বভাব, চরিত্র, শীল (আঃ বঃ)। **6.** Good moral qualities ; good reputation ; সদ্গুণ সমূহ ; সুখ্যাতি, সুনাম। **7.** Certificate of qualities ; as, she came to me for her *character* ; প্রশংসা পত্র। **8.** A personage ; বিশিষ্টব্যক্তি। **9.** Imaginary person created by novelist or dramatist ; নাটক বা উপন্যাসের চরিত্র বা পাত্র পাত্রী। **10.** (*Colloq.*) An odd or eccentric person ; মাথা-পাগলা লোক। ***Verb t.*** **1.** To engrave ; to inscribe ; as, the history of nature is *charactered* in his brain ; খোদিত বা উৎকীর্ণ করা। **2.** To delineate ; to describe ; as, you have well *charactered* him ; চিত্রিত করা ; বর্ণনা করা। **—is'-tic,** *adj.* & *n.* **1.** Displaying character ; distinctive ; typical ; (*of*) ; স্বভাবসিদ্ধ,

স্বাভাবিক; বিশেষক, বিশেষত্বদ্যোতক, বৈশেষিক; লাক্ষণিক, প্রকৃতি-নির্দ্দেশক, স্বভাবদর্শক, স্বভাবসূচক, স্বধর্ম্মসূচক, লক্ষণসূচক, বিশেষ গুণবোধক। (*Noun.*) **1.** A distinctive mark, trait or feature; essential peculiarty or quality; বিশেষত্ব দ্যোতক চিহ্ন, গুণ বা সুস্পষ্ট লক্ষণ; মৌলিক বিশেষত্ব বা ধর্ম্ম, স্বভাব (হিঃ কোঃ), অনুভাব (ঐ), বিশেষ গুণ (ঐ)। **2.** (*Math.*) The whole number in a logarithm; ঘাতাঙ্কগণনে সমস্ত সংখ্যা, পূর্ণভাগ, পূর্ণক (হিঃ কোঃ)। **—is'-ti-cal-ly,** *adv.* **—i-za'-tion,** *n.* **—ize,** *v. t.* **1.** To delineate the character or peculiar qualities of (a person or thing); to describe *as*; (কোন ব্যক্তি বা বস্তুর) স্বভাব বা বিশেষ গুণ বর্ণনা করা; লক্ষণ বর্ণনা করা। **2.** To be characteristic of; to impart character to; স্বভাবসিদ্ধ হওয়া; বিশেষ গুণ বা ধর্ম্ম বিশিষ্ট করা। **—less,** *adj.* Without a character; ordinary; without individuality; without any testimonials; চরিত্রহীন; সাধারণ; ব্যক্তিত্বশূন্য; প্রশংসাপত্র বিহীন। **A bad character**—বদমায়েস, কুচরিত্রের লোক। **Character actor, actress**—যে অভিনেতা বা অভিনেত্রী ভাড়, বিদূষক, পাগল বা পাগলিনীর ভূমিকা গ্রহণ করে। **In character**—Appropriate; proper; যথাযোগ্য; সঙ্গত। **Out of caracter**—বেমানানসই; অসঙ্গত।

cha-rade' (shă-rād or -râd), *n.* An enigma the solution of which is a word of two or more syllables each separately significant, the word and its meaning being intended to be discovered from description or dramatic representation; একপ্রকার প্রহেলিকা; প্রত্যেকটী শব্দাংশের স্বতন্ত্র অর্থ আছে, এইরূপ দুই বা ততোধিক শব্দাংশবিশিষ্ট একটী শব্দ এইরূপ প্রহেলিকার উত্তর হইয়া থাকে। শব্দটী এবং ইহার অর্থ উক্তরূপ শব্দাংশ এবং সমগ্র শব্দের বর্ণনা বা অভিনয় হইতে বাহির করিয়া লইতে হয়।

châr'-coal (-cōl), *n.* Coal made by charring or burning wood; the carbonaceous residue of vegetables, animal or combustible mineral substances when they undergo smothered combustion; কাঠ কয়লা; অঙ্গার, অঙ্গারক (সাঃ পঃ), কোকিল (রঃ প্রঃ)। **2.** A charcoal pencil or crayon for drawing; চিত্রাদি কার্য্যের জন্য অঙ্গার-লেখনী।

chāre, chār, *n.* & *v. i.* To work by the day; to do small jobs; ঠিকা কায করা, ঘড় ঝাট দেওয়া, বাসন মাজা প্রভৃতি ক্ষুদ্র ক্ষুদ্র কায করা। ***Noun.*** Work done by the day or in odd jobs; ঠিকা কায; ঘর ঝাট দেওয়া, বাসন মাজা প্রভৃতি কায।

charge (chârj), *v. t., i.* & *n.* **1.** To put a load on or in; to fill with; as, to *charge* a vessel with liquor, etc.; ভার চাপান, বোঝাই করা; কোন কিছুদ্বারা পূর্ণ করা। **2.** To load; as, to *charge* a gun: to *charge* a Leyden jar: to *charge* water with carbon dioxide; ভরা, গুলি বারুদ ভরা, পূরণ করা, সম্পূরিত করা, অনুপ্রবিষ্ট করা। **3.** (*Fig.*) To fill; as, to *charge* memory with facts; (লক্ষণায়) পূর্ণ করা। **4.** To lay on or impose; ভারার্পণ করা, কার্য্যের ভার দেওয়া। **5.** To ask a price for; to set a price on; মূল্য চাওয়া, মূল্যাদি দাবি করা; মূল্য স্থির বা ধার্য্য করা। **6.** To enjoin or command; অনুজ্ঞা করা, আদেশ বা নিষেধাজ্ঞা প্রচার করা। **7.** To put to the account of, as a debt; to enter upon the debit side of an account; কাহারও হিসাবে খরচ লিখা; হিসাবের খরচের জায়গায় লিখা। **8.** To impute as a fault; দোষাদি আরোপ করা। **9.** To accuse; অভিযুক্ত করা। **10.** To subject to a pecuniary obligation or iability; "Money to be *charged* on the revenues of India;" টাকা পয়সার দায়িত্ব চাপান। **11.** To entrust; বিশ্বাস পূর্ব্বক ন্যস্ত করা। **12.** To give direction to; কোন কার্য্য সম্বন্ধে কাহাকে উপদেশ দেওয়া। **13.** To spur one's horse against at full gallop; to attack or assail with impetuosity; নক্ষত্রবেগে অশ্ব ছুটাইয়া শত্রুকে আক্রমণ করা; প্রচণ্ডবেগে ধাবিত হইয়া আক্রমণ করা, প্রচণ্ডবেগে আক্রমণ করা। **14.** To place (a weapon) in position for action; to direct the aim of; as, to *charge* bayonets: when she *charged* her trident, the enemy fled; অস্ত্র উদ্যত করা; অস্ত্র সন্ধান করা। ***Verb i.*** **1.** To make an onset; to rush to an attack; as, to *charge* with fixed bayonets; আক্রমণ করা; আক্রমণার্থ ধাবিত হওয়া। **2.** To demand a price for; To make a debit; মূল্য চাওয়া; কাহারও নামে খরচ লেখা। ***Noun.*** **1.** A material load; বোঝা, ভার। **2.** That which loads a rifle, cannon, etc.; বন্দুক, কামান প্রভৃতিতে যে পরিমাণ গুলি বারুদ ভরা হয়। **3.** (*Electr.*) A quantity of electric fluid communicated to Leyden jar etc.; লিডেন জার প্রভৃতিতে সঞ্চারিত বিদ্যুত রাশি। **4.** (*Her.*) Any device borne upon an escutcheon; (কুল-বিদ্যা) চর্ম্মোপরিস্থ মর্য্যাদা চিহ্ন। **5.** (*Fig.*) A load of trouble, expense, responsibility, etc.; (লক্ষণায়) কষ্টভার, ব্যয়ভার, দায়িত্ব, প্রভৃতি। **6.** Price or cost; ব্যয়, মূল্য। **7.** An impetuous rush or onset; as, the *charge* of the light brigade; প্রচণ্ডবেগে আক্রমণ বা আপতন। **8.** A task or duty laid upon one; responsibility; as, your tutor is every way equal to such a *charge*; ন্যস্ত কর্ত্তব্য; ভার। **9.** Care; custody; management; তত্ত্বাবধান; জিম্মা, হেপাজৎ (*colloq.*), হাওলা (*colloq.*); পরিচালন। **10.** A person or thing committed to one's care or management; ভারার্পিত বস্তু বা ব্যক্তি। **11.** An official instruction given by a judge to a jury; an exhortation given by a bishop to his clergy; বিচারক জুরিদিগকে মোকদ্দমা সম্বন্ধে যে উপদেশ প্রদান করিয়া থাকেন; ধর্ম্মাধ্যক্ষ (বিশপ) তদধীনস্থ যাজকগণকে যে উপদেশ প্রদান করিয়া থাকেন। **12.** Injunction, instruction or command given; অনুজ্ঞা, উপদেশ, আদেশ। **Charge´-a-ble,** *adj.* **1.** That may be charged or imputed; ভারার্পণীয়, আরোপণীয়। **2.** Expensive; costly; (now *obsolete*); ব্যয়সাধ্য; মূল্যবান। **3.** Accusable; অভিযোগার্হ, অভিযোক্তব্য। **4.** Subject to a charge, tax or payment; অর্থদাবী যোগ্য। **5.** Liable to be made an expense; ব্যয়যোগ্য। **Charge´-a-ble-ness,** *n.* **Charge-house**—যে গৃহে বারুদ গুলি ভরিয়া কার্ত্তুজ তৈয়ারী হয়। **Charge-sheet**—যে কাগজে থানায় বন্দীরূপে আনীত আসামীদিগের নাম, তাহাদের বিরুদ্ধে যে অপরাধ আরোপিত হইয়াছে তাহা, এবং অভিযোক্তার নাম লিখিত হইয়া থাকে। **In charge of**—তত্ত্বাবধানে। **It is no charge**—It is of no importance; এটা বড় কিছু গুরুতর নহে; ইহাতে আসে যায় না। **To charge anything on**—To ascribe; আরোপ করা। **To charge in** or **upon**—To throw a burden upon; ভার চাপান, দায়িত্ব চাপান। **To charge one with, To charge oneself with**—To take upon oneself the responsibility of; to undertake; দায়িত্ব গ্রহণ করা; কোন কর্ম্মের ভার গ্রহণ করা। **To give (an object) in charge to a person**—To commit it to his care; কোন বস্তুর ভারার্পণ করা। **To give (a person) in charge**—To hand over to the custody of the police; পুলিশের জিম্মা বা হাওলা করিয়া দেওয়া। **To have, take** or **give the charge of**—To take or give the duty or responsibility of taking care of a person or thing; কোন কার্য্যের ভার বা দায়িত্ব গ্রহণ বা প্রদান করা, জিম্মায় থাকা, রক্ষণাবেক্ষণের ভার গ্রহণ করা। **To lay to one's charge**—To impute to one as a fault; দোষাদি আরোপ করা, কোন অপরাধে অভিযুক্ত করা। **To make a charge at**—To make an onset; প্রচণ্ডবেগে আক্রমণ করা। **To make, give** or **have no charge**—To make of no account; গণ্য না করা; দৃক্‌পাত না করা। **To return a charge**—To put forward an accusation; কোন ব্যক্তির বিরুদ্ধে অভিযোগ উপস্থাপিত করা। **To return to the charge**—To broach the same subject; একই বিষয় পুনরুত্থাপন করা। **To take in charge**—To take upon oneself the responsibility of something; কোন বিষয়ের দায়িত্ব গ্রহণ করা।

charge d' affaires, *n.* A deputy ambassador; an ambassador at a minor court; প্রতিনিধি, রাজদূত; ক্ষুদ্র রাজদরবারে প্রেরিত দূত, নিস্‌ষ্টার্থ (মাঃ মাঃ)।

chârg´-ér, *n.* A military officer's horse; সৈনিক কর্ম্মচারীর অশ্ব।

chăr´-i-lȳ, *adv.* Carefully; frugally; সাবধানে, সতর্কভাবে; মিতব্যয়িতার সহিত।

chăr´-i-ŏt, *n., v. t. & i.* **1.** A car or vehicle used in ancient warfare, racing or public triumphs; রথ, স্যন্দন, বিমান। **2.** A four-wheeled carriage of pleasure or state; লীলা শকট, রাজকীয় শকট। ***Verb t.*** To convey or carry in a chariot; রথোপরি বহন করা, লীলাশকটে বা রাজশকটে বহন করা। ***Verb i.*** To drive or ride in a chariot; রথারোহণে পরিভ্রমণ করা, রথে আরোহণ করা, লীলাশকটে বা রাজশকটে আরোহণ করা।

chăr-i-ŏt-eer´ (-ēr), *n., v. t. & i.* The driver of a chariot or car; সারথি, সূত, যন্তা, রথবাহক, শকটচালক। ***Verb t.*** To drive a chariot or vehcile; রথ বা রাজশকট চালনা করা, কোন ব্যক্তিকে লইয়া রথ চালনা করা। ***Verb i.*** To act as charioteer; to drive; সারথ্য করা; রথ চালনা করা, রাজশকট বা লীলা শকট চালনা করা।

chăr´-i-tă-ble, *adj.* **1.** Liberal in giving to the poor; giving freely; generous; দানশীল, দানশৌণ্ড; মুক্তহস্ত; বদান্য। **2.** Pertaining to, of the nature of, charity; eleemosynary; দান সম্বন্ধীয়, দানাত্মক; দাতব্য। **3.** Favourable; lenient; as, a *charitable* judgment of one's conduct; দাক্ষিণ্যশীল, উদার, অনুকূল; সদয়। **—bly,** *adv.* **Charitable dispensary**—দাতব্য চিকিৎসালয়।

chăr´-i-tȳ, *n.* **1.** Universal love; goodwill; বিশ্বপ্রেম, ভূতানুকম্পা (রঃ); প্রীতি, সদিচ্ছা। **2.** Disposition to think well or judge favourably of others; large heartedness; দাক্ষিণ্য; চিত্তের প্রশস্ততা, উদারতা। **3.** Liberality to the poor; alms giving; generosity; বদান্যতা, দানশীলতা; ভিক্ষাদান; সদাশয়তা, মহানুভবতা, ঔদার্য্য। **4.** Whatever is bestowed gratuitously on the poor for their relief; alms; দান, খয়রাৎ; ভিক্ষা। **5.** Love; kindness; natural affection; প্রেম; দয়ালুতা, করুণা; অনুরাগ। **6.** (*Pl.*) Affections; as, the *charities* of domestic life; স্নেহ, অনুরাগ প্রভৃতি। **Brother** or **sister of charity**—কোন ধর্ম্মসম্প্রদায়ভুক্ত যে পুরুষ বা স্ত্রী দরিদ্রের দুঃখ ভার লাঘব কিম্বা রোগীর শুশ্রূষারূপ মহৎকার্য্যে জীবন উৎসর্গ করিয়াছেন। **Charity-boy,—girl**—দানশালা বা অনাথাশ্রমে পালিত বালক বালিকা। **Cold as charity**—দানশীলতার মত শীতল (অনুরাগবিহীন)। [সাধারণতঃ অনুরাগশূন্যভাবে যে দান কার্য্য নির্ব্বাহিত হয় তৎস্মরণে।] **Charity**

begins at home—স্বজনপ্রীতি হইতে বিশ্বজনীন প্রীতির উদ্ভব হয়।

cha-ri-va′-ri (shâ-rē-vâ-rē), *n*. **1.** (*Music*) A mock serenade of discordant noises made with kettles, pans, tea-trays, etc. used to be performed before the houses of old people who remarried and unpopular persons generally; hence a medley of discordant sounds; a babel of noise; a hubbub; কোন ব্যক্তি বৃদ্ধবয়সে পুনর্ব্বিবাহ করিয়া অথবা অন্য কোন কার্য্য দ্বারা সাধারণের বিরাগভাজন হইলে তাহার গৃহে রাত্রিকালে বহুলোক সমবেত হইয়া কেটলী, কড়াই, চার বারকোষ প্রভৃতি বাজাইয়া যে হট্টগোলের সৃষ্টি করিত; সোরগোল; হট্টগোল; কোলা হল কলরব। **2.** A journal like *Punch* devoted to caricaturing; ব্যঙ্গ-পত্রিকা।

char′-lă-tăn (shâr-), *n*. **1.** A quack; a mountebank; নাড়ীটেপা হাতুড়ে বৈদ্য, কুবৈদ্য; ওঝা। **2.** A pretentious impostor; ভণ্ড, প্রতারক, প্রবঞ্চক। **—ish, —tan′-ic, —tan′-i-cal,** *adjs.*

Charles's Wain (chârlz-iz-wān), *n*. (*Astron.*) A name given to the seven bright stars in Ursa Major; (জ্যোতির্বিজ্ঞান) চিত্র শিখণ্ডী (রাঃ রাঃ), সপ্তর্ষি (হিঃ কোঃ)।

châr′-lȳ, *n*. (*Slang*) A night watch man; (ইতরভাষায়) নৈশ প্রহরী।

châr-lock (-lŏk), *n*. The wild or field mustard; হুড়হুড়িয়া, আদিত্যভক্তা।

char′-lotte, [*F.*] *n*. A pudding of cooked apple covered with bread-crumbs; সেওফলের পিষ্টক বিশেষ। ***Charlotte Russe***—পিষ্টক-বিশেষ।

chârm, *n., v. t.* & *i.* **1.** Words, philters, characters, acting as a spell; যাদুমন্ত্র, যাদু, কুহক, টোনা, মায়া, তুক (*Colloq.*), গুণ (*Colloq.*), আসুরী মায়া। **2.** An amulet; কবজ, তাবিজ, রক্ষাকবজ, মাদুলী। **3.** Fascination; সম্মোহিনী শক্তি, মোহজনক ভাব, মোহিনীশক্তি, সৌন্দ, মাধুর্য্য। **4.** A trinket worn on a watch-chain or girdle; টেঁকঘড়ির শিকল বা কটিবন্ধে সংলগ্ন ক্ষুদ্র অলঙ্কার বিশেষ। ***Verb t.*** **1.** To bewitch; যাদুমন্ত্রদ্বারা বশীভূত করা, যাদু করা, মন্ত্রমুগ্ধ করা। **2.** To captivate; মুগ্ধ করা, বিমোহিত করা। **3.** To yield exquisite pleasure to; পরমানন্দ প্রদান করা। **4.** To allay; to soothe; উপশম করা; সান্ত্বনা করা। ***Verb i.*** **1.** To use spells; যাদুমন্ত্র প্রয়োগ করা। **2.** To act as a charm; যাদুমন্ত্রবৎ ক্রিয়া করা, মন্ত্রশক্তিবৎ কার্য্য করা।

Charmed, *adj.* **Charm′-er,** *n*. **1.** An enchanter; a magician; যাদুকর, মায়াবী; ঐন্দ্রজালিক। **2.** One who fascinates; esp. a beautiful woman; সম্মোহক; মোহিনী, সুন্দরী।

Charm′-ful *adj.* **Charm′-ing,** *adj.* Fascinating; highly pleasing or delightful; as, a *charming* princess; মুগ্ধকর; রমণীয়, রুচির, ললিত, মোহন, চিত্তহারী, মনোমুগ্ধকর, পরমানন্দদায়ক। **Snake-charmer**—অহিতুণ্ডিক, সাপুড়িয়া, তুবড়িওয়ালা। **To bear a charmed life**—To bear a life fortified or protected by a spell or charm; যাদুমন্ত্রদ্বারা অভিরক্ষিত জীবনযাপন করা। [যে ব্যক্তি বারম্বার দৈববলে মৃত্যুহস্ত হইতে আশ্চর্য্যরূপে রক্ষা পায়, তৎসম্বন্ধে প্রযুক্ত হয়।]

châr-nêl, *adj.* Sepulchral; ghastly; শ্মশানতুল্য, সমাধিক্ষেত্রবৎ, সমাধিসম্বন্ধীয়; পৈশাচিক। **Charnel-house**—শবাস্থিসংরক্ষণ স্থান, অস্থিসঞ্চয়স্থল, শবাস্থিশালা।

Chā-rŏn, *n*. (*Gr. Myth.*) A ferryman whose office was to ferry the souls of the deceased over the Styx; (গ্রীকদেশীয় প্রত্নতত্ত্ব) গ্রীক পুরাণোক্ত বৈতরণী নদীর পাটনী। **Charon's boat, ferry, etc.**—মৃত্যুসময়।

châr-poy, *n*. [Hindi] The common light Indian bedstead; চারপায়া।

chârt, *n.* & *v. t.* **1.** An outline map or a tabular statement giving information of any kind; as, a genealogical *chart*; নক্সা বা চিত্র (সাঃ পঃ)। **2.** A marine map or a delineation of coasts, islands, shoals, etc.; সামুদ্রিক মানচিত্র, সমুদ্রচিত্র (আঃ বঃ)। **3.** A record by curves, etc. of fluctuations in temperature, prices, etc.; মূল্য, বায়ুমণ্ডলের উষ্ণতা, প্রভৃতির হ্রাসবৃদ্ধিপ্রদর্শক নক্সা বিশেষ। ***Verb t.*** To make a chart of; নক্সা প্রস্তুত করা। **Chart′-less,** *adj.* **Chart of stars**—তারা চিত্র (হিঃ কোঃ), নক্ষত্র চিত্র (ঐ)।

châr′-têr, *n.* & *v. t.* **1.** A written document delivered by the sovereign or legislature granting rights, privileges, etc., to the people, creating a borough, company, or other corporation; অধিকারপত্র (হিঃ কোঃ), সনদ, সনন্দ, শাসন (যাজ্ঞঃ)। **2.** A special privilege; বিশেষ স্বত্ব বা অধিকার। **3.** (*Com.*) The letting or hiring a vessel by special contract; the contract or instrument whereby a vessel is hired or let; (বাণিজ্য) বিশেষ চুক্তিতে জাহাজ ভাড়া প্রদান বা ভাড়া গ্রহণ; জাহাজ ভাড়ার চুক্তিপত্র। **4.** Documents or deeds conveying landed property; ভূমিদানপত্র, শাসনপত্র। ***Verb t.*** **1.** To grant a charter to; to establish by charter; সনন্দ প্রদান করা; সনন্দ বা শাসনপত্র দ্বারা প্রতিষ্ঠিত করা। **2.** To hire (a ship) by charter-party; (*colloq.*) to hire (a vehicle, etc.); চুক্তিপত্রদ্বারা জাহাজ ভাড়া করা; (চলিত ভাষায়) (গাড়ী প্রভৃতি) ভাড়া করা। **—er,** *n.* **—tered,** *adj.* **Chartered accountant**—রাজকীয় সনন্দপ্রাপ্ত গণনবিদ্যা বিশারদগণের পরিষদ্ হইতে প্রশংসাপত্র-প্রাপ্ত গণন শাস্ত্রবিদ্ ব্যক্তি। **Chartered company** — ইংরেজ অধিকৃত স্থানে ব্যবসায় বাণিজ্য এবং স্থলবিশেষে শাসনকার্য্য পরিচালনের জন্য সনন্দপ্রাপ্ত

বণিক্ সমিতি। **Charter-house**—১৬১১ খৃষ্টাব্দে ইংলণ্ডদেশে প্রতিষ্ঠিত দাতব্য অনুষ্ঠান বিশেষ, বর্ত্তমানে ইংলণ্ড-দেশীয় সুবৃহৎ সরকারী বিদ্যালয় বিশেষ। **Chârter-party**—পোতস্বামীর সহিত বণিগ্‌দিগের জাহাজ ভাড়া করা সম্বন্ধে অথবা জাহাজাদির বোঝাই মাল প্রাপককে নিরাপদে বুঝাইয়া দেওয়া বিষয়ে চুক্তিপত্র; জাহাজ ভাড়ার চুক্তিপত্র।

chârt′-ism, *n.* The principle or practice of the body of political reformers in England, that sprung up about the year 1838, and advocated universal suffrage, annual parliaments, etc.; ইংলণ্ড দেশীয় শ্রমজীবি সম্প্রদায়ের উন্নতি বিধায়িনী সমিতি বিশেষের মত বা অনুষ্ঠান। **–ist,** *n.*

châr-tŏg′-ră-phy̆, *n.* Same as CARTOGRAPHY.

char-treuse′ (shâr-trôz), *n.* [F.] **1.** A liqueur made by the Carthusian monks with aromatic herbs and brandy; কার্থুজিয়ান সন্ন্যাসিগণ কর্ত্তৃক ব্রাণ্ডি এবং সুগন্ধি ওষধিসমূহ সহযোগে প্রস্তুত পানীয় বিশেষ। **2.** A pale apple-green colour; সেওফলেরমত নিষ্প্রভ সবুজ বর্ণ বিশেষ।

châr′-wo-măn (-wû-), *n.* A woman who does odd jobs by the day; ঠিকা ঝি, ঠিকা দাসী।

châr′-y̆, *adj.* **1.** Careful; সতর্ক, সাবধান। **2.** Frugal; stingy; মিত-ব্যয়ী; ব্যয়কুণ্ঠ, কৃপণ। **3.** Shy; মুখচোরা। **–i-ly,** *adv.* **–i-ness,** *n.*

Chă-ry̆b′-dis, *n.* A dangerous whirlpool on the coast of Sicily (now Calofaro) opposite the Italian rock Scylla; ইতালী দেশীয় সিলা নামক পাষাণ পর্ব্বতের বিপরীত দিকস্থিত সিসিলীদ্বীপের উপকূল প্রদেশের বিপৎসঙ্কুল আবর্ত্ত বা ঘূর্ণিজল। **Scylla and Charybdis**—জলে কুমীর ডাঙ্গায় বাঘ।

chāse, *n.* **1.** Pursuit; hunting; the pursuit of a ship; অনুসরণ, অনুধাবন, পশ্চাদ্ধাবন; মৃগয়া; জাহাজের পশ্চাদ্ধাবন। **2.** The ground where game is preserved or hunted; মৃগয়াভূমি, যে ভূমিতে মৃগয়ার্থ পশু রক্ষিত হয়। **3.** The hunted animal or pursued ship; "The *chase* opened fire on the African coast;" শিকার, মৃগ্য (আঃ বঃ), অনুসৃত পোত। **Chase-gun**—রণ-পোতের কামান বিশেষ—তাড়িত শত্রুপক্ষীয় পোতের উপর, বা পশ্চাদ্ধাবিত শত্রুপক্ষীয় পোত হইতে আত্মরক্ষার জন্য, ইহা হইতে গোলা বর্ষিত হয়। **The chase**—মৃগয়া। **To give chase to, To be in chase of, To have** or **hold in chase**—To pursue; অনুসরণ করা; পশ্চাদ্ধাবন করা।

chāse *n.* (*Print.*) A rectangular iron frame used by printers to confine types when set in pages or columns; যে আয়তক্ষেত্রাকার লৌহ নির্ম্মিত কাঠামের (ফ্রেম) মধ্যে মুদ্রাকর-গণ অক্ষর-বিন্যস্ত পৃষ্ঠা বা স্তম্ভসমূহ আবদ্ধ করে।

chāse, *n.* **1.** The part of a gun between the trunnion and the muzzle; কামানের মুখ এবং কর্ণের মধ্যবর্ত্তী স্থান। **2.** A groove cut in the face of a wall, to receive a pipe, etc; দেয়ালের উপর কাটা খাঁজবিশেষ, ইহাতে চুঙ্গী প্রভৃতি বসান হয়।

chāse, *v. t.* **1.** To pursue; to hunt; অনুসরণ করা; মৃগয়া করা। **2.** To drive away; বিতাড়িত করা, অপসারিত করা, বিদূরিত করা। **3.** To cut into the form of a screw; ইস্ক্রুপের আকারে কাটা।

chāse, *v.t.* To emboss or engrave, etc.; বুটা তোলা, খোদিত করা।

chās′-ing, *n.* The art of embossing metals; ধাতুর উপর উদ্গাত কারুকার্য্য।

chās′-êr, *n.* Same as CHASE-GUN above.

chăsm, *n.* **1.** A gap or wide opening in the ground; a cleft or fissure; গভীর গর্ত্ত, গহ্বর, বিবর; ফাটল। **2.** A void space; blank; শূন্যস্থান; ফাঁক। **3.** A break in a chain of facts, narratives, etc.; an interval; ভঙ্গ, বিরাম, ছেদ; অবকাশ। **4.** A breach of relations, feelings, interests, etc between persons or parties; সুহৃদ্‌ভঙ্গ, সম্বন্ধভঙ্গ, মনোভঙ্গ, অনুরাগ-ভঙ্গ, মনান্তর।

chasse (shâs), *n.* A small portion of spirituous liquor taken to remove the taste of coffee, tobacco, etc.; কাফি, তামাক প্রভৃতির স্বাদ দূরীকরণার্থ যে অল্প পরিমাণ মদিরা পান করা হয়।

chasse, [*F.*], *n.* & *v. i.* A kind of gliding step in dancing; নৃত্য বিশেষ। ***Verb i.*** To execute such step or movement; উক্ত প্রকার নৃত্য করা।

Chasselas, (*F.*), *n.* A European white grape, esteemed for the table; একপ্রকার শ্বেতবর্ণ আঙ্গুর ফল।

chasse-pot′ (shâs-pö), *n.* A breech-loading rifle once used in the French army; ফরাসী সৈন্য-দলে ব্যবহৃত প্রাচীন বন্দুক বিশেষ।

chas-seur′ (shâs-êr), *n.* **1.** A hunter; শিকারী। **2.** A light armed foot or cavalry soldier; লঘু অস্ত্রধারী পদাতিক বা অশ্বারোহী সৈনিক।

chas′-sis (shâs-ē), *n.* **1.** The base-frame of gun-carriage, motor-car, etc.; কামানের গাড়ী, হাওয়া-গাড়ী প্রভৃতির নীচের কাঠাম। **2.** A company's stock of motor-cars, motor-buses etc.; কোন কোম্পানীর ভাণ্ডারস্থ সমুদায় হাওয়া গাড়ী, বা যাত্রি-বহনার্থ বৃহৎ হাওয়া গাড়ী প্রভৃতি।

chāste, *adj.* **1.** Pure from unlawful sexual intercourse; virtuous; virgin; pure; (বিবাহিতা স্ত্রী-সম্পর্কে) পতিব্রতা, সতী, সাধ্বী, একচারিণী (বাৎস্যঃ), (পুরুষ-পক্ষে) জিতেন্দ্রিয়, কুমার, সংযতেন্দ্রিয়, ব্রহ্মচারী, স্ত্রীপরাঙ্মুখ, একপত্নীব্রতী, (অবিবাহিতা পক্ষে) কৌমারব্রতচারিণী, ব্রহ্মচারিণী, অনন্য-পূর্ব্বা; ধর্ম্মশীলা; অক্ষতযোনি, কুমারী;

বিশুদ্ধ, নির্ম্মল, শুচি, শুদ্ধ, পবিত্র, নির্দ্দোষ। **2.** Unadorned; simple; refined; pure in taste or style; as, *chaste* style or composition; free from obscenity; অনলঙ্কৃত, অলঙ্কারবিহীন; সাদাসিদা; মার্জ্জিত; সুরুচি (রুচি বা রচনা সম্বন্ধে), বিশুদ্ধ, সাধু, শিষ্ট, সংস্কৃত, প্রাঞ্জল; অশ্লীলতাবর্জ্জিত। **3.** Decent in speech; শিষ্টবাক্, বিনয়ী। **Chaste'-ly,** *adv.* **Chaste'-ness,** *n.* **Chaste-tree**—নিসিন্দা গাছ (খোরী)।

chăs'-ti-tȳ, *n.* **1.** Freedom from unlawful sexual intercourse; virginity: (বিবাহিতা স্ত্রীপক্ষে) সতীত্ব, পাতিব্রত্য ধর্ম্ম (কৃষ্ণঃ), (পুরুষ পক্ষে) ব্রহ্মচর্য্য, জিতেন্দ্রিয়তা, অব্যভিচার, সংযম। **2.** Moral purity; নৈতিক পবিত্রতা। **3.** Simplicity of style or taste; সরল রচনা ভঙ্গী, রুচির সরলতা।

chăs'-tĕn (chāsn), *v. t.* **1.** To correct by punishment; to discipline; শাস্তিপ্রদানে সংশোধন করা, সাজা দেওয়া, তাড়না করা; শাসন করা। **2.** To make chaste in style; to refine; প্রাঞ্জল রচনা করা; পরিমার্জ্জিত করা। **3.** To restrain or moderate; সংযত করা; পরিমিত করা। **—tened,** *adj.* **—ten-er,** *n.*

chăs'-tīse, *v. t.* **1.** To inflict punishment upon for the purpose of correction; to beat; সংশোধনার্থ শাস্তি দেওয়া, শাসন করা; প্রহার করা। **2.** To reduce to order or obedience; to free from faults or excesses; as, the gay, social sense, by decency *chastised*; শৃঙ্খলায় আনা, বশীভূত করা, দমন করা; নির্দ্দোষ করা, অমিতাচার নিবারণ করা। **—ment,** *n.* Corrective punishment; correction; সংশোধনার্থ শাস্তি, সাজা; সংশোধন। **—tis-a-ble,** *adj.* **—tis-er,** *n.*

chăs'-ū-ble, *n.* A sleeveless vestment worn by the priest while celebrating Mass; রোমান ক্যাথলিক পুরোহিতগণ "যীশুর শেষ ভোজন" ক্রিয়ার-অনুষ্ঠান কালে যে আস্তিনহীন আলখেল্লা পরিধান করিয়া থাকেন।

chăt, *v. i.* & *n.* To talk idly or familiarly; গল্পগুজব করা, গাল গল্প করা, গল্প সল্প করা। *Noun.* **1.** Light, familiar talk; conversation; idle talk; বিশ্রম্ভালাপ কথাবার্ত্তা; গল্পগুজব; গালগল্প, গল্পসল্প খোস গল্প। **2.** A name of several small, lively birds of the Warbler family; as, the stone-*chats* কয়েকপ্রকার কলস্বন পক্ষীর সাধারণ নাম। **Chat'-ti-ness,** *n.* **Chat'-ty** *adj.* Given to light familiar talk; talkative; বাচাল; গল্পগুজব প্রিয়।

cha-teau' (shâ-tö-), *n.* **1.** A castle or a fortress in France; ফরাসী-দেশীয় প্রাকারপরিখাদিরক্ষিত প্রাসাদ বা দুর্গ। **2.** A country mansion or a country seat; as, the *chateau* of the Luxemberg; ফরাসী রাজ্যে (রাজা বা সম্ভ্রান্ত ব্যক্তির) পল্লী প্রাসাদ, পল্লী নিকেতন, পল্লীনিবাস বা পল্লীভবন। **Chateau-en-Espagne**—A castle in the air, আকাশ-কুসুম, গগন-নগর।

chat'-e-laine (shăt-ē-lān), *n.* A set of short chains attached to a woman's belt for carrying keys, watch, pencil, etc.; স্ত্রীলোকের কটি-বন্ধ সংলগ্ন শৃঙ্খল পংক্তি, যাহা হইতে চাবি প্রভৃতি ঝুলানো হয়।

cha-toy'-ănt (shā-), *adj.* Changing lustre or colour like that of a cats' eye in the dark; অন্ধকারাচ্ছন্ন স্থানে মার্জ্জারনেত্রপ্রভাবৎ চঞ্চল দীপ্তিময়।

chăt'-tĕl, *n.* (*Law*) Any item of movable or immovable property except the freehold, or the things which are parcel of it; (আইন) নিষ্কর লাখেরাজ সম্পত্তি ব্যতীত অন্যপ্রকার স্থাবর বা অস্থাবর সম্পত্তি, জাইগাদ্।

chăt'-têr, *v. i.* & *n.* **1.** To utter sounds rapidly and indistinctly, as a magpie or a monkey; কিচিরমিচির করা। **2.** To talk rapidly or idly; to jabber; to prate; বকিয়া যাওয়া; কিচ্‌মিচ্ করা, কিলকিলাশব্দ করা; বক্‌বক্ করা, হড়বড় করা। **3.** To sound as the teeth when one shivers; to rattle together; as, with *chattering* teeth and bristling hair upright; দন্তসংঘর্ষণ করা, দাঁত কড়মড় করা; ঘরঘর করা। *Noun.* **1.** Sounds like those of a magpie or monkey; idle talk; কিচিরমিচির শব্দ; বাজে কথা। **2.** Noise made by the collision of the teeth, as in shivering; দন্তসংঘর্ষশব্দ। **—er,** *n* **—ing,** *n.* **Chatter-box**—যে ব্যক্তি সর্ব্বদা কিচ্‌মিচ্ করিয়া বাজে কথা বলে, বাচাল, বাচাট, বাবদূক।

chaud'-mel-lee, (shöd-mĕl-ā), (*Scot. law*) A sudden broil arising from the heat of passion; hence, the wounding or killing of a man in such an affray without premeditation; (স্কট্‌লণ্ডের আইন) হঠাৎ উত্তেজনাহেতু কলহ; অতএব এরূপ কলহে পূর্ব্বসংকল্প ব্যতিরেকে আঘাত করণ বা মনুষ্য হনন।

chauf'-fêr (shäf), *n.* A metal box for holding fire; a portable furnace with air-holes; অগ্নিরক্ষার্থ ধাতব আধার; বায়ু প্রবেশের ছিদ্রবিশিষ্ট বহনোপযোগী চুল্লীবিশেষ, দমচুলা।

chauf-feur' (shä-fêr), (*F.*), *n.* A motorcar driver; হাওয়া গাড়ীর চালক।

chau'-mŏn-tĕl (shö-), *n.* A large kind of pear; একজাতীয় বৃহৎ নাসপাতি ফল। [ফরাসী দেশের Chaumontel গ্রামের নাম হইতে গৃহীত।]

chaus-sure' (shö-sür), (*F.*), *n.* Boot and shoes (esp. for ladies); বুট, জুতা, উপানৎ (বিশেষতঃ ভদ্রমহিলা-গণের জন্য)।

chau'-vin-ĭsm (shö-), *n.* Absurdly exaggerated patriotism or military enthusiasm; [নেপোলিয়ানের পরমোৎসাহী সহচর Chauvin এর নাম হইতে গৃহীত।] উৎকটদেশপ্রেম, উৎকট রণোৎসাহ। **—ist,** *n.*

Chavica Betle—পান (বেলঃ)। ***Chavica Roxburghi*** — পিপুল (বেলঃ)।

chaw (chä), *v. t.* & *n.* To chew ; চিবান। ***Noun.*** A quid of tobacco ; চর্ব্বণের জন্য তামাকের কলি। **Chaw-bacon**—পাঁড়াগেয়েভূত; গোঁয়ার-গোবিন্দ।

cheap (chēp), *adj.* **1.** Low in price ; সস্তা, সুলভ, অল্পমূল্য। **2.** Worthless ; of little account ; mean ; as, you grow *cheap* in every subject's eye ; অসার, তুচ্ছ, অপদার্থ ; নগণ্য ; হীন। **3.** Easily obtained ; অনায়াসলব্ধ। **Cheap'-en,** *v. t.* & *i.* To make or become cheap ; দর কমান, সস্তা করা, সস্তা হওয়া। **Cheap'-er,** *n.* **Cheap'-ly,** *adv.* **Cheap'-ness,** *n.* **Cheap-Jack, Cheap-John** — পুরাতন জিনিষের ফেরিওয়ালা। **Cheap-trip**—অল্প ভাড়ায় রেলপথে ভ্রমণ। **Dog cheap**—অতিসুলভ। **Dirt cheap**—সস্তার চূড়ান্ত, মাটির দরে বিক্রীত। **To be cheap of anything**—To get less than one's deserts ; যতটা (শাস্তি প্রভৃতি) পাওয়া উচিত ছিল তার চেয়ে অল্পেতেই সারিয়া যাওয়া। **To feel cheap**—To be ashamed or insulted ; লজ্জিত হওয়া, অপমানিত হওয়া। **To hold cheap**—To hold of small account ; নগণ্য মনে করা।

cheat (chēt), *v. i., t.* & *n.* **1.** To deceive ; to trick ; to swindle ; প্রতারণা করা, প্রবঞ্চনা করা, তঞ্চকতা করা (*Colloq.*), ছলনা করা, বঞ্চনা করা ; ঠকান, ঠগামি করা ; জুয়াচুরি করা। **2.** To beguile ; as, to *cheat* winter of its dreariness ; ভুলাইয়া লওয়া। ***Verb i.*** To practise fraud or trickery ; ঠকামি করা, ভাড়ান, ধোকা দেওয়া (*Colloq,*), চালাকি করা। ***Noun.*** **1.** A fraud ; a trick ; as, when I consider life, it is all a *cheat* ; ঠকামি, প্রতারণা, বঞ্চনা ; জুয়াচুরি, । **2.** One who cheats or deceives ; ঠক, প্রতারক, শট, জুয়াচোর, ধড়িবাজ। **3.** A card game in which undetected cheating is licensed ; একপ্রকার তাস খেলা—ইহাতে ধরা না যায় এরূপ ঠকামি অনুমোদিত হইয়া থাকে। **Cheat'-able,** *adj.* **Cheat'-ableness, cheat'-er,** *ns.* **To cheat of**—To deceive of ; (কোন কিছু) ঠকাইয়া লওয়া, ভাড়াইয়া লওয়া। **To cheat the devil**—To do evil for gain, and then give it to the church or for other similar purposes ; ধনলাভের উদ্দেশ্যে কুকার্য্য করিয়া অন্যায়লব্ধ অর্থ বা সম্পত্তির কিয়দংশ ধর্ম্মকার্য্যে ব্যয় করা। **To cheat the gallows**—To escape death by being hanged ; কোন প্রকারে ফাঁসীর দায় হইতে রক্ষা পাওয়া। [যাহার ফাঁসী হওয়া উচিত ছিল এরূপ ব্যক্তির পক্ষে প্রযোজ্য।] **To put a cheat upon**—To deceive ; প্রতারণা করা, ঠকান।

check (chĕk), *v. t., v. i., n.* & *adj.* **1.** (*Chess*) To threaten opponent's king at chess ; (শতরঞ্জ ক্রীড়া) কিস্তি দেওয়া। **2.** To restrain or hinder ; to curb ; বাধা দেওয়া, আটক করা ; দমন করা, সামলান। **3.** To verify or examine by comparison with certified data, vouchers, etc. ; to mark as having been examined ; as, to *check* an account : to *check* baggage ; মোকাবিলা করা, পরতাল করা, মিলান ; হিসাবের প্রত্যেক দফা পরীক্ষা করিয়া পার্শ্বে চিহ্ন দেওয়া। **4.** (*Naut.*) To slack or ease off a brace which is too stiffly extended ; (নৌ-বিদ্যা) অত্যন্ত কষাভাবে টানা রজ্জু শিথিল করা। ***Verb i.*** **1.** To make a stop ; to pause ; (with *at*) ; স্থগিত করা ; থামা। **2.** (Of hounds) To stop in losing the scent, or to make sure of it ; (শিকারী কুকুরের পক্ষে) পলায়মান জন্তুর সন্ধান হারাইয়া বা তদ্বিষয়ে সুনিশ্চিত হইবার জন্য থামা। ***Noun.*** **1.** A term in chess when one party obliges the other either to move or guard his king ; (শতরঞ্জ ক্রীড়া) কিস্তি। **2.** A sudden arrest given to motion ; a repulse or rebuff ; হঠাৎ গতিরোধ, আটক, রোধ, নিরোধ ; বাধা, ধাক্কা। **3.** Person or thing that restrains ; নিরোধকারী ব্যক্তি বা বস্তু। **4.** A mark put against an item in a list ; তালিকার প্রত্যেক দফার পার্শ্বে যে চিহ্ন দেওয়া হয়। **5.** (*Banking*) An order for money, (usually written CHEQUE) ; টাকা দিবার আদেশপত্র, চেক্, টাকার বরাত-চিঠি। **6.** (*Falconry*) The forsaking of the proper game by a hawk to follow other birds that cross its flight ; (শ্যেন-বিদ্যা) প্রকৃত শিকার ত্যাগকরত অন্য পক্ষীর অভিমুখে বাজপক্ষীর উড্ডয়ন। **7.** (*Hunt.*) Loss of the scent ; (মৃগয়া) পলায়মান জন্তুর সন্ধান হারান। **8.** A counter used in games at cards (*U.S.*) ; তাসখেলায় ব্যবহৃত মেজবিশেষ (যুক্তরাজ্যে ব্যবহৃত)। **9.** (*War.*) A reverse ; a slight defeat ; (যুদ্ধ) বিপর্য্যায় ; সামান্য পরাজয়। **10.** A small clink or crack ; ছেঁদা, ফুটা। **11.** A token given to railroad passengers, serving to identify them in claiming their luggage etc.; also in theatres etc. a similar token given to those who go out expecting to return ; সঙ্গীয় মাল দাবী করিবার কালে যাত্রিগণকে রেলওয়ে কোম্পানী হইতে প্রাপ্ত যে পরিচয় জ্ঞাপক নিদর্শন প্রদর্শন করিতে হয় ; কিয়ৎক্ষণের জন্য রঙ্গমঞ্চ পরিত্যাগ করিতে হইলে দর্শকদিগকে যে নিদর্শন দেওয়া হয়। **Check'-less,** *adj.* **Check'-y,** *adj.* **Check-book**—ব্যাঙ্কের চেক বহি, ধনাগার হইতে টাকা তুলিবার জন্য আদেশ পত্রের বহি। **Check-clerk**—হিসাব পত্রাদির বিশুদ্ধি পরীক্ষক কেরাণী। **Check-rein**—যে লাগামের সাহায্যে ঘোড়ার মাথা নোয়াইতে বাধা দেওয়া হয়। **Check-roll**—কোন বাড়ীর পরিচারকবর্গের তালিকা, ভৃত্য-তালিকা। **Check-string**—যে রজ্জু টানিয়া গাড়ীর আরোহী চালকের মনোযোগ আকর্ষণ

করিতে পারে। **Check-taker**—নাটক বা রেল গাড়ীর প্রবেশ-অনুমতি-পত্র-সংগ্রাহক কর্ম্মচারী।

check (chĕk), *n.* A pattern (woven or otherwise) made with crossed liners; চৌখুপী ছক প্রভৃতি, চৌখুপী ডোরাবিশিষ্ট কাপড়।

check'-êr (chĕk-), *v. t.* & *n.* **1.** To cheque; চৌখুপী ডোরাবিশিষ্ট করা, ছক কাটা। **2.** To variegate or diversify; as, our minds are, as it were, *checkered* with truth and falsehood; বিবিধ বর্ণে রঞ্জিত বা বিচিত্রিত করা, চিত্রবিচিত্র করা, বৈচিত্র্যপূর্ণ করা। ***Noun.*** **1.** One who checks; a rebuker; নিরোধক; ভর্ৎসনাকারী। **2.** One of the squares of a pattern in squares; চৌখুপী ছিট প্রভৃতির একটী খুপ। **3.** (*Pl.*) Draughts; শতরঞ্জের অনুরূপ ক্রীড়া বিশেষ।

check'-māte (chĕk-), *v. t.* & *n.* **1.** (*Chess*) To put in check, as an opponent's king, so that he cannot be released; (শতরঞ্জ ক্রীড়া) কিস্তি দিয়া মাত করা। **2.** (*Fig.*) To defeat; to frustrate; (লক্ষণায়) পরাভূত করা; বিফল করা, মাত করা (*Colloq.*)। ***Noun.*** **1.** The position in the game of chess when the king is in check and cannot be released; কিস্তি মাত। **2.** (*Fig.*) Final defeat at chess or in any enterprise; দাবাখেলায় বা অন্য কোনরূপ কার্য্যে চরম পরাজয়।

chĕd'-dar (-dêr), *n.* An excellent kind of cheese first made in Somersetshire; সর্ব্বপ্রথম সমারসেট-সায়ারে প্রস্তুত উৎকৃষ্ট পনীর বিশেষ।

cheek (chēk), *n.* & *v.i.* **1.** The side of the face below the eye; গণ্ড, কপোল, গাল, গণ্ডমণ্ডল (কৃষ্ণকঃ)। **2.** (*Pl.*) Those pieces of a machine which form corresponding sides or which are double or alike; as, the *cheeks* of a gun-carriage; jaws of vise; যন্ত্রের দুই পার্শ্বে যে দুইটী অনুরূপ খণ্ড থাকে, অথবা যে যন্ত্রখণ্ড সকল দেখিতে ঠিক একরূপ বা দুই দুইটী করিয়া আছে; পাক সাঁড়াসীর মুখ। **3.** The side post of a door or window; দরজা বা জানালার পার্শ্বের থাম। **4.** Audacity; impudence; effrontery; "He can't have the *cheek* to ask for more;" প্রগল্‌ভতা; ধৃষ্টতা; ঠেঁটামি। ***Verb t.*** (*Slang*) To address saucily; (ইতর ভাষায়) উদ্ধতভাবে কথা বলা। **Cheek'-y,** *adj.* Impudent; audacious; ধৃষ্ট; দুর্বিনীত, প্রগল্‌ভ, ঠেঁটা। **Cheek-bone**—কপোল-ফলক। **Cheek pouch** — বানরের গণ্ডদেশস্থ থলিয়া। **Cheek-tooth** — চর্ব্বণ দন্ত। **Cheek by jowl**—Side by side; very intimate; পাশাপাশি, কাছাকাছি; হরিহর আত্মা। **To one's own cheek**—নিজের ভাগে।

cheep (chēp), *v. t.,* & *n.* To chirp, as a small bird; ক্ষুদ্র পক্ষীর মত চিঁচিঁ শব্দ করা, পিঁ পিঁ শব্দ করা। ***Noun.*** A squeak, as of a mouse; a chirp; মুষিকাদির কিচ্ কিচ্ শব্দ; চিঁ চিঁ শব্দ।

cheer (chēr), *v. t., i.* & *n.* **1.** To gladden; to rejoice; আনন্দিত করা; প্রফুল্ল করা, উৎফুল্ল করা, হৃষ্ট করা, হর্ষোৎফুল্ল করা। **2.** To incite; to encourage; to solace or comfort; as, the proud, he tamed, the penitent he *cheered*; উদ্দীপ্ত করা; প্রোৎসাহিত করা; আশ্বাসিত করা, আশ্বস্ত করা, প্রবোধ দেওয়া। **3.** To applaud with cheer; to urge on, esp. by shouts; as, to *cheer* a public speaker; আনন্দধ্বনি পূর্ব্বক সাধুবাদ করা; আনন্দধ্বনি পূর্ব্বক কোন কার্য্যে উৎসাহিত করা। ***Verb i.*** **1.** To grow cheerful; হর্ষোৎফুল্ল হওয়া, প্রফুল্ল হওয়া। **2.** To utter a cheer or shout of acclamation or joy; আনন্দধ্বনি করা, জয়ধ্বনি করা, সাধুবাদ করা। ***Noun.*** **1.** (*Obs.*) The face; countenance; (অপ্রচলিত) বদনমণ্ডল; চেহারা। **2.** Frame of mind; state of feeling or spirits; as, be of good *cheer*; মানসিক অবস্থা; মেজাজ। **3.** Gaiety; animation; আমোদ; উৎফুল্লতা। **4.** Food; "The table was loaded with good *cheer*;" fare; feast; খাদ্যদ্রব্য, খাদ্যসামগ্রী; খাদ্য; ভোজ। **Cheer'-er,** *n.* **Cheer'-ful,** *adj.* **1.** Contented; in good spirits; lively; animated; সন্তুষ্ট; হৃষ্ট, প্রসন্ন; স্ফূর্তিযুক্ত; উৎফুল্ল, প্রফুল্ল, উল্লসিত। **2.** Animating; pleasant; as the *cheerful* sun; উৎসাহসঞ্চারক, স্ফূর্তিসঞ্চারক; মনোরম। **3.** Willing; ইচ্ছুক। **Cheer'-ful-ly,** *adv.* **Cheer'-ful-ness,** *n.* **Cheer'-i-ly,** *adv.* **Cheer'-i-ness,** *n.* **Cheer'-ing-ly,** *adv.* **Cheer'-less,** *adj.* Without comfort; gloomy; সুখশূন্য; ম্লান, নিরানন্দ, অপ্রসন্ন, বিমর্ষ, অপ্রফুল্ল। **Cheer'-less-ly,** *adv.* **Cheer'-less-ness,** *n.* **Cheer'-y,** *adj.* Cheerful; lively in spirit; প্রফুল্ল; উৎফুল্ল। **The fewer the better cheer**—লোক যত কম হয় ততই প্রত্যেকের ভাগে খাদ্যদ্রব্য অধিক পড়ে। **Three cheers**—সমস্বরে ক্রমাগত জয়ধ্বনি। **To be of good cheer**—To be hopeful; আশায় উৎফুল্ল হওয়া, আশায় বুক বাঁধা। **To make good cheer**—To feast; ভোজ দেওয়া। **To make of good cheer** — To console; সান্ত্বনা দেওয়া।

cheese (chēz), *n.* **1.** Food made of pressed curds; পনীর। **2.** The fruit of mallow; বিলাতি বেড়েলা গাছের ফল। **3.** (*Slang*) Anything good or first-rate in quality; anything genuine; (ইতরভাষায়) সেরা জিনিষ; খাটি জিনিষ। **Chees'-i-ness,** *n.* Stinginess; ব্যয়কুণ্ঠতা। **Cheese-cake**—দধি, চিনি এবং মাখন হইতে প্রস্তুত বা উক্ত দ্রব্য সমূহ পুরিত পিষ্টক বিশেষ। **Cheese-fly**—পনীর কীট। **Cheese-monger** — পনীর ব্যবসায়ী। **Cheese-paring,** *n.* & *adj.* **1.** A paring of cheese rind ; পনীরের ছিলকা বা খোসা। 2. Stinginess ; ব্যয়কুণ্ঠতা। (*Adj.*) Meanly economical ; parsimonious ; as, *cheese-paring* economy ; বখিল ; কঞ্জুষ (ফঃ হিঃ)। **Cheese-vat**—যে স্থানে বা আধারে দধি চাপ দিয়া পনীর প্রস্তুত করা হয়। **Green-cheese**—কাঁচা পনীর। **To get the cheese**—To be disappointed ; নিরাশ হওয়া। **To make cheeses**—(বিদ্যালয়ের বালিকাদিগের পক্ষে) পায়ের উপর ঘুরিয়া, ঘাগরা ফুলাইয়া ভূতলে পতিত হওয়া। **To make the cheese**—To make deap curtsey ; (স্ত্রীলোকের পক্ষে) প্রণতজানু হইয়া অভিবাদন করা।

chees'-ŷ (chēz-), 1. Resembling cheese ; tasting of cheese ; পনীরবৎ ; পনীরস্বাদ। 2. (*Slang*) Stylish ; (ইতরভাষায়) চটকদার।

chee'-tah (chē-tă), *n.* A kind of leopard, tamed in India and trained to hunt deer ; চিতা বাঘ।

chef (shĕf), *n.* 1. The chief or head person ; প্রধান ব্যক্তি, সর্দ্দার। 2. Head cook ; পাচকদলের সর্দ্দার, প্রধান সূপকার।

chef-d'-œuvre', *n.* A masterpiece ; শ্রেষ্ঠ গ্রন্থ, শিল্পকার্য্য, সাহিত্য, রচনা প্রভৃতি।

che'-lă, *n.* (*Zool.*) The pincer-like claw of Crustacea and Arachnida ; (পশুতত্ত্ব) খোলকী এবং উর্ণনাভাদির সাঁড়াশির মত নখর।

chĕm'-i-căl, *adj.* & *n.* Of or relating to the science of chemistry ; রসায়নশাস্ত্রবিষয়ক, রাসায়নিক। ***Noun.*** A substance obtained or used in chemical operations ; রাসায়নিক প্রক্রিয়ায় ব্যবহৃত বা উক্ত প্রক্রিয়া দ্বারা উৎপন্ন পদার্থ বিশেষ, রাসায়নিক পদার্থ। **–ly**, *adv.* **Chemical affinity**—রসায়নপ্রীতি (হিঃ কোঃ), রাসায়নিক সংসর্গ (ঐ)। **Chemical analysis** — রাসায়নিক বিশ্লেষণ। **Chemical attraction**—রাসায়নিক আকর্ষণ। **Chemical combination** — রাসায়নিক সংযোগ, সন্তুয় ক্রিয়া (রঃ প্রঃ), সংহতক্রিয়া (ঐ), সমুত্থান (ঐ)। **Chemical composition**—রাসায়নিক সংঘটন (হিঃ কোঃ)। **Chemical compound**—মিলিত দ্রব্য (রঃ প্রঃ) সংহতভূতার্থ (ঐ)। **Chemical contact** — আরম্ভক সংযোগ (রঃ প্রঃ)। **Chemical examination** — রাসায়নিক পরীক্ষা (হিঃ কোঃ)। **Chemical examiner**—রাসায়নিক পরীক্ষক। **Chemical operation**—রসকর্ম্ম (প্রঃ)। **Chemical principles**—রাসায়নিক সিদ্ধান্ত (হিঃ কোঃ)। **Chemical process**—রাসায়নিক রীতি।

che-mise' (shĕ-mēz), *n.* 1. An undergarment worn by females ; স্ত্রীলোকদিগের সেমিজ, কামিজ। 2. A breast-wall ; আবক্ষঃ উচ্চ প্রাচীর।

chem'-i-sette' (shĕm-î-zĕt), *n.* An undergarment worn over the chemise ; lace, muslin, etc. filling up the opening of dress below throat ; সেমিজের উপরিভাগে পরিহিত অন্তঃপরিচ্ছেদ বিশেষ ; কোন পোষাকের কণ্ঠনিম্নস্থ অনাবৃত অংশাবরক লেস্ বা মসলিন খণ্ড।

chĕm'-ist, *n.* 1. A person skilled in chemistry ; a professor of chemistry ; রসায়নতত্ত্ববিৎ ; রসায়নশাস্ত্রাধ্যাপক, রসবাদী (রঃ প্রঃ), রসায়নবিৎ (ঐ)। 2. A dealer in medical drugs ; ঔষধবিক্রেতা।

chem'-is-trŷ, *n.* 1. The science which treats of the properties of substances both elementary and compound, and of the laws of their combination and action one upon another ; রসায়নশাস্ত্র, রসায়নীবিদ্যা (ধাঃ প্রঃ)। 2. A treatise in chemistry ; রসায়নশাস্ত্র বিষয়ক গ্রন্থ। **Analytical chemistry**—বৈশ্লেষিক রসায়ন (হিঃ কোঃ)। **Applied** or **practical chemistry** — ফলিত রসায়ন, ব্যবহারিক রসায়ন (হিঃ কোঃ)। **Inorganic chemistry**—জড় রসায়ন (হিঃ কোঃ)। **Organic chemistry**—জৈব রসায়ন (হিঃ কোঃ)।

chem'-i-tŷpe, *n.* (*Engraving*) A process by which an impression from an engraved plate is obtained in relief ; (খোদন কার্য্য) ক্ষোদিতফলক হইতে উদ্গত প্রতিলিপি (ছাপ) তুলিবার প্রণালী বিশেষ।

che-nille' (shĕ-nēl), *n.* A tufted cord of silk or worsted, somewhat resembling a caterpillar, used for making hair-nets etc. ; স্ত্রীলোকদিগের কেশাবরণের জাল প্রভৃতি প্রস্তুতের জন্য রেশম বা পশম সূত্রনির্ম্মিত বৃশ্চিকসদৃশ রজ্জু বিশেষ।

Chē-nō-pō'-di-ŭm, *n.* A genus of annual and perennial herbs ; বেতো প্রভৃতি শাক। ***Chenopodium viride***—বেতোশাক (প্রবোধ), বেতুয়া (ঐ)।

cheque (chĕk), *n.* See CHECK.

cheq'-uer, (chĕk-êr), *n.* & *v.* Same as CHECKER.

cheq'-uy (chĕk-î), *n.* Same as CHECKY.

chĕr'-ish, *v. t.* 1. To treat with tenderness and affection ; to foster ; to nurture ; স্নেহ যত্ন করা ; লালন পালন করা ; পোষণ করা, পোষা। 2. To entertain in the mind ; to promote ; হৃদয়ে ধারণ করা, হৃদয়ে পোষণ করা ; বর্দ্ধন করা, শ্রীবৃদ্ধি করা। **–er**, *n.* **Cherished treasure**—আদরের ধন।

che-rōōt' (shē-), *n.* [Tamil *Shurutta*] A kind of cigar with both ends open ; চুরুট।

chĕr'-rŷ, *n.* & *adj.* 1. A well-known stone fruit ; চেরী ফল। 2. A tree producing this fruit ; চেরী বৃক্ষ। 3. The timber of this tree, (esp. black cherry), used in cabinet making ; চেরী কাঠ। ***Adj.*** Like a red cherry in colour ; ruddy ; blooming ; as, a *cherry* lip : *cherry* cheeks ; লোহিত চেরীফলের মত বর্ণ বিশিষ্ট ; লোহিত, আরক্ত ; প্রস্ফুট, যৌবনের সৌন্দর্য্য ও স্ফূর্ত্তি বিকাশী। **Cherry-bob**—এক বৃন্তে জাত

দুইটী চেরী ফল। **Cherry-brandy**—চেরিফলদ্বারা রঞ্জিত গাঢ় লোহিতবর্ণ মদিরা বিশেষ। **Cherry-cheeked**—আরক্তগণ্ড। **Cherry-fair**—চেরীফল বিক্রয়ের জন্য মেলা। **Cherry-laurel**—ইউরোপদেশীয় চিরহরিত গুল্মবিশেষ। **Cherry-pit**—বালকদিগের ক্রীড়াবিশেষ। ইহাতে গর্ত্তমধ্যে চেরীফল সকল নিক্ষিপ্ত হয়। **Cherry-stone**—চেরীফলের আঁটি; চেরীফলের আঁটিদ্বারা ক্রীড়াবিশেষ। **Cherry-ripe** — চেরীফল বিক্রেতার ডাক। **To make two bites of a cherry** — To divide something too small to be worth dividing; অতি ক্ষুদ্র বস্তু ভাগ করা। **To make two bites at a cherry** — To boggle; থতমত খাওয়া।

chĕr′-sö-nese, (-nēz), *n.* A peninsula; (*mostly poet. or rhet.*); (সাধারণতঃ কবিতা ও অলঙ্কার) প্রায়দ্বীপ।

chêrt, *n.* A variety of quartz resembling flint; অগ্নিপ্রস্তরবৎ স্ফটিকবিশেষ। **Chert′-y**, *adj.*

chĕr′-ŭb, *n.* [*Pl.* CHERUBS, CHERUBIM.] **1.** An angelic being next in order to a seraph, and represented as young; দেবদূত বিশেষ। **2.** A beautiful and innocent child; "The youngest a rosy cheeked *cherub* with golden curls."; সুন্দর এবং শুভ্রস্বভাব শিশু। [বর্ত্তমান চিত্রকলায় cherub সুন্দর শিশুর মস্তকরূপে অঙ্কিত হইয়া থাকে।] **Che-ru′-bic, Che-ru′-bi-cal**, *adjs.*

chêr′-vil, *n.* A garden herb used in soup, salad, etc.; উদ্যানজাত ওষধি বিশেষ—ইহা ব্যঞ্জনাদিতে ব্যবহৃত হয়, আতরীলাল (খোরী)।

chess (chĕs), *n.* An ingenious game played on a checkered board; দাবা খেলা, চতুরঙ্গ। **Chess-board**—দাবা খেলার ঘর, শতরঞ্চ খেলার ছক, অষ্টাপদ, পঙ্কলী (মঃ উঃ), পঙ্কমী (অঃ), শারিপট্ট (মঃ উঃ), শারিফলক (ঐ), শারিফল (ঐ)। **Chess-man**—দাবা খেলার গুটি, শারি, সারি (মঃ উঃ), জতুপুত্রক (অঃ), সার, সারিকা, খেলিনী (মঃ ইঃ), খেলনী (ঐ), শার (মঃ উঃ), বল। [*The king of chess*—রাজা; *queen* — দাবা, মন্ত্রী; *bishop*—গজ, পিল; *knight*—অশ্ব; *rook* or *castle* — নৌকা, রথ; *pawn*—পদাতি, বʼড়ে।]

chĕs′-sĕl, *n.* A mould or vat in which cheese is formed; পনীরের ছাঁচ।

chĕst, *n.* & *v. t.* **1.** A large strong box; সিন্দুক। **2.** (*Com.*) A case in which tea, opium, etc., are transported; hence, the quantity which such a case contains; (বাণিজ্য) যে তোরঙ্গে চা, আফিং প্রভৃতি বাণিজ্য দ্রব্য চালান দেওয়া হয়; অতএব, ঐরূপ এক তোরঙ্গে যে পরিমাণ জিনিষ ধরে। **3.** A box for the safe keeping of any requisites; as, a carpenter's *chest*: medicine *chest*: surgeon's *chest*; তোরঙ্গ, সিন্দুক, মঞ্জুষা। **4.** Treasury; coffer; also the fund of money itself; as, a military *chest* was formed; ধনাগার, অর্থাধার; টাকার সিন্দুক; ধনকোষ। **5.** The body enclosed by the ribs and breastbone—the thorax; পঞ্জর, বক্ষঃ, উরস, ভুজান্তর, উরস্থল, ছাতি (*Colloq.*)। ***Verb t.*** To put into a coffin; শবাধারে রাখা। **2.** To deposit in a chest or box; সিন্দুকজাত করা। **Chest of drawers**—দেরাজ। **Chest-wall**—বক্ষঃ, প্রাচীর।

chĕs′-têr-field (-fēld), *n.* A kind of overcoat; একপ্রকার লম্বা কুর্ত্তা।

chest nŭt (chĕs-), *n.* & *adj.* **1.** The seed or nut of the chestnut tree; একপ্রকার ফল। **2.** The tree itself or its timber; উক্তফলবৃক্ষ বা উহার কাষ্ঠ। **3.** A bright reddish brown colour; উজ্জ্বল পিঙ্গলবর্ণ, কপিশবর্ণ। **4.** (*Slang*) A stale anecdote; (ইতরভাষায়) নীরসগল্প। **5.** A horse of chestnut colour; as, her landau with a pair of powerful *chestnuts*; কপিশবর্ণ অশ্ব। ***Adj.*** Of a deep reddish brown colour; as, her rich *chestnut* locks; কপিশবর্ণ। **Water-chestnut**—পানিফল (খোরী)।

cheval (shĕ-văl), *n.* [*Fr. pl.* CHEVAUX.] A horse; hence a support or frame; অশ্ব; অতএব, অবলম্বন, কাঠাম। **Cheval glass**—সমগ্র দেহের প্রতিবিম্ব গ্রহণক্ষম ফ্রেমে আঁটা সুদীর্ঘ দর্পণবিশেষ।

Cheval-de-frise, *n.* (*pl.* CHEVAUX-DE-FRISE) A piece of timber with spikes or spears to stop cavalry etc., in war; সূক্ষ্মাগ্র লোহকীলকপূর্ণ কাষ্ঠফলকবিশেষ — ইহাদ্বারা যুদ্ধকালে অশ্বারোহী সৈন্য প্রভৃতির গতিরোধ করা হয়।

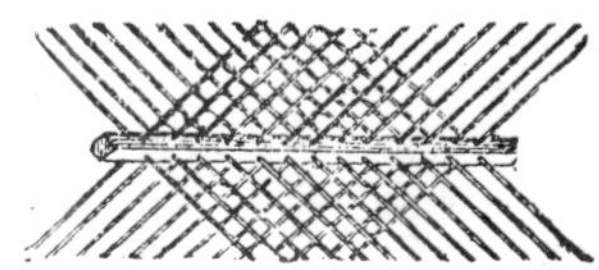

Cheval-de-frise.

chev-a-lier′ (shĕv-ă-lēr), *n.* **1.** A horseman; esp. a knight; সাদী, অশ্বারোহী; বীর পুরুষ। **2.** A member of the certain orders of knighthood; (বিলাতের) কোন কোন সম্ভ্রান্ত সম্প্রদায়ভুক্ত ব্যক্তি। **Chevalier of industry**—যে ব্যক্তি অসদুপায়ে জীবিকার্জ্জন করে, জুয়াচোর। **The Chevalier** or **Chevalier de St. George**—ইংলণ্ডেশ্বর দ্বিতীয় জেম্‌সের পুত্র জেম্‌স্ ষ্টুয়ার্টের নাম। **The young chevalier**—চার্লস এড্‌ওয়ার্ড ষ্টুয়ার্ট।

che-ve-lure, [*F.*] *n.* Hair; arrangment of the hair; কেশ, কুন্তল, চিকুর; কেশবিন্যাস।

chĕv′-i-ŏt, *n.* **1.** A hardy breed of short wooled sheep reared on the Cheviot Hills; ইংলণ্ড এবং স্কট্‌লণ্ড্ দেশের মধ্যবর্ত্তী চিভিয়ট্ নামক পর্ব্বতোপরি পালিত একজাতীয় কঠোর শ্রমসহিষ্ণু মেষ। **2.** A cloth made from their wool; উক্তমেষলোম নির্ম্মিত বস্ত্র।

chev-rette′ (shĕv-rĕt), *n.* A thin goatskin used for gloves; এক প্রকার অম্বুল ছাগচর্ম্ম—ইহাদ্বারা দস্তানা নির্ম্মিত হয়।

chev′-ron (shĕv-rŭn), *n.* **1.** (*Her.*) A bent bar of inverted V shape, in escutcheons; (কুল-বিদ্যা) ইংরেজী V অক্ষর উল্টাইলে যদ্রূপ (∧) হয়—কুল চিহ্নাঙ্কিত চর্ম্মোপরি তদ্রূপ চিহ্নবিশেষ। **2.** (*Mil.*) The distinguishing mark or badge on the sleeves of non-commissioned officers, policemen, etc.; (সামরিকশাস্ত্র) সাধারণ সামরিক কর্ম্মচারী, পুলিশ প্রহরী প্রভৃতির আস্তিনে পরিহিত উক্ত প্রকার (∧) চিহ্ন। **3.** (*Arch.*) The same shape used in decorative art, etc.; (স্থপতিবিদ্যা) উক্ত আকৃতির সৌধভূষা প্রভৃতি।

chev′-ro-tain (shĕv-rö-tān), **–tĕn,** *n.* A small muskdeer; ক্ষুদ্রকায় কস্তুরী মৃগ।

chĕv′-ŷ, chiv′-ŷ, *n., v. t.* & *i.* **1.** A cry used in hunting; মৃগয়াধ্বনি। **2.** A hunt; a chase; মৃগয়া; শিকার। **3.** The game of prisoner's base; একপ্রকার ক্রীড়া। ***Verb t.*** To chase; to pursue; শিকারের অনুসরণ করা; পশ্চাদ্ধাবন করা। ***Verb i.*** To race; to scamper; দ্রুতবেগে ধাবিত হওয়া; ছুটাছুটি করা।

chew (chô), *v. t., i.* & *n.* **1.** To bruise or grind with the teeth; to masticate; চর্ব্বণ করা, চিবান; খাদ্যদ্রব্য চর্ব্বণ করা। **2.** (*Fig.*) To meditate on or upon; as, he *chews* revenge; (লক্ষণায়) মনে মনে ভাবা বা চিন্তা করা। ***Verb i.*** **1.** To perform the action of biting and grinding with the teeth; চর্ব্বণ করা। **2.** To ruminate; to meditate (*on* or *upon*); as, old politicians *chew* on wisdom past; গিলিতচর্ব্বণ করা; কোন বিষয়ে বা বিষয়াবলম্বনে চিন্তা করা। ***Noun.*** That which is chewed; a quid of tobacco; যাহা চর্ব্বণ করা হয়; চিবাইবার জন্য বা মুখে রাখিবার এক কলি দোক্তা, সুখা। **Chew′-er,** *n.* **To chew the cud**—To ruminate; গিলিত চর্ব্বণ করা, রোমন্থন করা, জাওর কাটা (*Colloq.*)। (*Fig.*) To meditate; (লক্ষণায়) চিন্তা করা। **To chew the rag**—See RAG.

chi-an′-ti, (*It.*) *n.* A red wine of Tuscany; (ইতালীর অন্তঃপাতী) টাস্কানী প্রদেশে প্রস্তুত লোহিতবর্ণ মদিরাবিশেষ।

chi-â-rö-scû′-rö, *n.* **1.** (*Fine arts*) That department of painting which relates to light and shade; (লক্ষণায়) চিত্র-বিদ্যার ছায়ালোক বিভাগ। **2.** (*Fig.*) Use of contrast (in literature, criticism, etc.); variation; (লক্ষণায়) (সাহিত্য, সমালোচনা প্রভৃতিতে) বিরুদ্ধ ভাবের সমাবেশ; বৈচিত্র্য। **3.** Light and shade effects in nature; প্রকৃতিতে ছায়ালোক-সন্নিবেশ-সঞ্জাত ভাব।

chī-ăs′-mŭs, *n.* A grammatical figure in which the order of words in the first clause is inverted in the second; as, don't live to eat but eat to live; ব্যাকরণের অলঙ্কার বিশেষ,—ইহাতে প্রথম বাক্যাংশের শব্দের ক্রম পরবর্ত্তী বাক্যাংশে বিপর্য্যস্ত করা হয়।

chi-bouk′ (shî-bûk), **chi-bouque′** (shî-bûk), *n.* A long Turkish tobacco pipe; তুরস্ক দেশীয় দীর্ঘাকৃতি ধূমপানের নল বিশেষ।

chic (shēk), [*F.*], *n.* & *adj.* Artistic skill or dexterity; that which gives an air of superior excellence to a person or thing; কলা-কৌশল, কলা-নৈপুণ্য; (মনুষ্য-পক্ষে) বৈদগ্ধ, বিদগ্ধতা, (বস্তু পক্ষে) কলা-কৌশল-সম্পন্নতা। ***Adj.*** Stylish; বাহ্য-আড়ম্বর প্রিয়।

chī′-că, *n.* A red colour obtained from (*Bignonia chica*) and used by some American Indians to stain their skin; বৃক্ষ বিশেষের পত্র জাত রক্তবর্ণ রঞ্জক পদার্থ বিশেষ,—ইহা দ্বারা আমেরিকার কোন কোন প্রাচীন অধিবাসী দেহ রঞ্জিত করিয়া থাকে।

chi-cane′ (shî-cān), *v. t., i.* & *n.* To quibble over; to cavil at (a thing); to cheat (a person) *into, out of* a thing; কথার মার পেঁচ করা; বাক্ চাতুরী করা; ছলনা করা। ***Verb i.*** To use shifts, cavils and artifices; ফন্দি, বাক্চাতুরী বা কৌশল প্রয়োগ করা। ***Noun.*** Same as CHICANERY below. **–can′-er-y,** *n.* Legal trickery; sophistry; উকিল ব্যারিষ্টারদিগের ফন্দি, চাতুরী বা বাক্ছল; কুতর্ক।

Chickweed.

chick (chîk), *n.* **1.** A young bird before or after hatching; অচিরজাত পক্ষিশাবক। **2.** A child; a term of endearment; শিশু; যাদু, সোণা।

chick-weed (chîk-wēd), *n.* A low creeping weed which birds are fond of; এক প্রকার লতা।

chick′-ĕn (chîk-), *n.* (*pl.* -ENS, -EN.) **1.** The young of various birds; especially of the domestic fowl; its flesh; বিভিন্নপ্রকার পক্ষীর শাবক; বিশেষতঃ কুক্কুট শাবক, মুরগী ছানা; কুক্কুটশাবকের মাংস। **2.** One young and inexperienced; as, I am no *chicken*; অল্পবয়স্ক এবং অনভিজ্ঞ ব্যক্তি। **Chicken-breast** — বক্ষের অস্থির বিকৃতভাবে উদ্গম। **Chicken-broth**—রোগীদের পথ্য-স্বরূপ ব্যবহৃত কুক্কুট শাবক-মাংসের কাথ। **Chicken-hazard**—এক প্রকার পাশা খেলা। **Chicken-heart**—দুর্ব্বলচিত্ত; ভীরু, কাপুরুষ ব্যক্তি। **Chicken-hearted**—ভীরু। **Chicken-pox**—জলবসন্ত, পানিবসন্ত, রসগত মসূরিকা (সাঃ পঃ)। **To count one's chickens before they are hatched**—কালনেমির লঙ্কাভাগ, গাছে না উঠতেই এক কাঁদি।

chick′-ling (chîk-), *n.* A small chicken; ক্ষুদ্র মুর্গী ছানা।

chick′-lĭng (chĭk-), or **chick′-ling-vetch** (chĭk-lĭng-vĕch), *ns.* The common vetch or pea of Europe, extensively cultivated for its seeds ; ইয়ুরোপদেশীয় মটর বিশেষ।
chick′-pea (chĭk-pē), *n.* A dwarf pea largely used for food ; চণক, চানা, বুট, ছোলা।
chic′-ŏ-rȳ, *n.* A blue flowering plant cultivated for its root, (which is ground for use with or instead of coffee); একপ্রকার নীলপুষ্পগ্রস্থ বৃক্ষ।
chīde, *v. t.* & *i.* **1.** To rebuke ; to reprove by words ; to find fault with ; তিরস্কার করা ; ভৎর্সনা করা, গঞ্জনা করা ; দোষ প্রদর্শন করা, মুখ করা (*Colloq.*)। **2.** (*Fig.*) To be noisy about ; "The sea that *chides* the banks of England ; আশে পাশে কোলাহল করা। ***Verb i.*** **1.** To scold ; to contend in angry words ; তিরস্কার করা, ভৎর্সনা করা ; ক্রোধপূর্ণ বাক্যে বাদ প্রতিবাদ করা। **2.** To clamour ; কলরব করা। **Chid′-er**, **Chid′-ing**, *ns.*
chief (chēf), *n.* & *adj.* **1.** The foremost authority ; leader ; ruler ; অগ্রণী, প্রধান ব্যক্তি, মুখ্যপাত্র ; নায়ক, নেতা ; সর্দ্দার, শাসক, পতি, ঈশ। **2.** The headman of a clan, tribe, etc. ; গোষ্ঠিপতি, জাতি বা বংশ বিশেষের প্রধান পুরুষ। **3.** A superior officer ; the head of any department ; উর্দ্ধতন কর্ম্মচারী ; কোন বিভাগের সর্ব্বপ্রধান কর্ম্মচারী বা কর্ত্তা। **4.** (*Her.*) The principal part of the escutcheon occupying the upper third of a shield ; (কুলবিদ্যা)। কুলচিহ্নাঙ্কিত চর্ম্মের প্রধান অংশ। ***Adj.*** **1.** Highest in office or rank ; standing at the head ; principal ; প্রধান, শ্রেষ্ঠ, ধুরন্ধর ; শীর্ষস্থানীয় ; মুখ্য। **2.** Leading ; foremost ; greatest ; as, his *chief* intimate ; নেতৃস্থানীয়, শীর্ষস্থানীয় ; অগ্রগণ্য ; মুখ্যতম। **Chief′-less**, *adj.* **Chief′-ly**, *adv.* Above all ; সর্ব্বোপরি, প্রধানতঃ। **Chief′-dom**, **Chief′-ship**, *ns.* **Chief-justice** — প্রধান বিচারপতি। **In chief**—In the highest place or position ; supreme ; as, commander-*in-chief* ; উচ্চতম স্থান বা পদে ; সর্ব্বপ্রধান, সর্ব্বশ্রেষ্ঠ। **To hold land in chief**—To hold land directly from the sovereign ; সাক্ষাৎ সম্বন্ধে রাজার নিকট হইতে প্রাপ্ত ভূমি ভোগ করা। **Chief tenant** or **tenant-in-chief**—যে ব্যক্তি সাক্ষাৎ সম্বন্ধে রাজার নিকট হইতে প্রাপ্ত ভূমি ভোগ করে।
chief′-tain (chēf-tān), *n.* **1.** A military leader ; a captain (poet) ; সেনানায়ক ; সৈন্যাধ্যক্ষ (কবিতায়)। **2.** The captain or leader of a band of robbers ; দস্যুদলপতি। **3.** The chief of a Highland clan or uncivilized tribe ; স্কট্‌লণ্ডের উত্তরভাগস্থ পার্ব্বত্য ভূখণ্ডনিবাসী গোষ্ঠির সর্দ্দার, অসভ্য জাতির সর্দ্দার। **—cy**, **—ess**, **—ry**, **—ship**, *ns.*
chiff′-chăff, *n.* A bird of warbler family ; একপ্রকার পক্ষী।
chif′-fŏn (shĭf-), [*F.*], *n.* **1.** (Usu. *pl.*) Adornments of female dress, as a bunch of ribbon, lace, etc. ; স্ত্রীলোকের পোষাকের ফিতা, লেইস্ প্রভৃতি। **2.** (*Sing.*) A thin soft silky gauze ; এক প্রকার কোমল সূক্ষ্ম রেশমবৎ গজ কাপড়।
chif-fon-nier′ (shĭf-ŏ-nēr), *n.* **1.** A kind of cabinet with drawers ; এক প্রকার দেরাজযুক্ত আলমিরা। **2.** A rag picker ; a collector of scraps ; নেকড়া কুড়ুনী ; চিরকুট সংগ্রহকারী।
chi-gnon′ (shē-nĭŏng), *n.* A mass of hair natural or artificial, worn by a woman at the back of the head ; বেণী, কবরী, খোপা, ধম্মিল্ল (ঋতুঃ)।
chig′-oe (-ō), *n.* A small species of flea of the West Indies,—it burrows beneath the skin of the human feet and hands ; পশ্চিম ভারতীয় (আমেরিকার) দ্বীপপুঞ্জের কীট বিশেষ—ইহা মনুষ্যের হস্তপদতলে ছিদ্র করিয়া চর্ম্মের ভিতরে বাস করে।
chĭl′-blain (-blān), *n.* An itching sore on hand or foot from exposure to cold ; বিপাদিকা, শীতস্ফোট (হঃ চঃ), নীহার-স্ফোট (ঐ), অতি শীত জনিত অঙ্গুলী প্রভৃতির একপ্রকার প্রদাহ।
chīld, *n.* (*Pl.* CHILDREN.) **1.** A son or a daughter ; পুত্র বা কন্যা, অপত্য, সন্তান। **2.** The unborn or newly born human being ; infant ; গর্ভস্থ শিশু, নবজাত শিশু ; শিশু। **3.** A boy or girl ; ছেলে বা মেয়ে, বালক বা বালিকা। **4.** A follower or adherent of ; as, a *child* of the devil ; অনুবর্ত্তী, অনুগামী, সঙ্গী, দলভুক্ত ব্যক্তি। **5.** A person of immature experience or judgment ; অনভিজ্ঞ বা অপরিপক্কবুদ্ধি ব্যক্তি। **6.** (*Pl.*) The descendants of a man, however remote ; as, the *children* of Israel ; বংশধর। **Child′-hood**, *n.* The time from birth to puberty ; শৈশব, শিশুকাল, বাল্য, বালত্ব। **Child′-ish**, *adj.* **1.** Of, proper to, a child ; as, *childish* innocence ; শিশু বিষয়ক, শিশুজনোচিত। **2.** Silly ; নির্ব্বোধ। **Child′-ish-ly**, *adv.* **Child′-ish-ness**, *n.* **Child′-less**, *adj.* Without children ; নিঃসন্তান, আঁটকুড়া (*Slang*)। **Child-bearing**—সন্তান প্রসব, সন্তানোৎপাদন। **Child-bed**—প্রসবাবস্থা ; সন্তান প্রসব, গর্ভমোচন। **Child-birth**—সন্তান প্রসব, গর্ভবিমোচন ; প্রসব বেদনা। **Child-like**, *adj.* শিশুসুলভ, বালসুলভ। **Child's-play**—ছেলে খেলা, অতি সহজ বিষয় ; তুচ্ছ বিষয়। **Child-widow**—বাল-বিধবা। **Child-wife**—অল্পবয়স্কা স্ত্রী। **Child is the father of the man**—"উঠন্ত মূল পত্তনেই চেন' যায়" অর্থাৎ পরিণত বয়সের গুণাদির অঙ্কুর শৈশবেই দৃষ্ট হয়। **From a child** or **children** — From childhood ; আশৈশব। **Second childhood**—Dotage ; জরা। **To be with child**—To be pregnant ; অন্তঃসত্ত্বা হওয়া। **To get** or **go with child**—To be pregnant ; গর্ভবতী হওয়া।

Chil'-dêr-măs, *n.* The festival of the Holy Innocents,—28th Dec. ; হিরোডের আদেশে নিহত শিশুগণের স্মরণার্থ খৃষ্টীয় পর্ব্ব বিশেষ—২৮শে ডিসেম্বর অনুষ্ঠিত হয়।

chil'-i-ăd, *n.* A thousand ; a period of thousand years ; সহস্র ; সহস্র বর্ষ।

chil'-i-ă-gŏn, *n.* A plane polygon of a thousand angles ; সহস্রাস্র ক্ষেত্র, সহস্রভুজ ক্ষেত্র।

chil'-i-ăsm, *n.* The opinion that Christ will reign bodily upon the earth for 1000 years ; যীশুখৃষ্ট সশরীরে অবতীর্ণ হইয়া এই পৃথিবীতে সহস্রবর্ষকাল রাজত্ব করিবেন—এইরূপ মতবাদ। **—ast,** *n.* **—as'-tic,** *adj.*

chill (chil), *v. t., i., adj.* & *n.* **1.** To make cold ; শীতার্ত্ত করা, শীতপীড়িত করা, শীতল করা। **2.** To depress ; to dispirit ; as, *chilling* his caresses by the coldness of his manners ; ভগ্নোৎসাহ করা, নিরুদ্যম করা ; নিরুৎসাহ করা, ঠাণ্ডা করা। **3.** To harden (molten iron) by contact of cold iron ; শীতল লৌহের সংস্পর্শে (দ্রবলৌহ) কঠিন করা। ***Verb i.*** To grow cold ; to become surface-hardened by sudden cooling while solidifying ; ঠাণ্ডা হওয়া ; জমাট বাঁধিবার সময় হঠাৎ শীতল হইয়া উপরিভাগ কঠিন হওয়া। ***Adj.*** **1.** Unpleasantly cold to feel ; tending to cause shivering ; শীতল ; বেপথুজননপ্রবণ কম্পজননপ্রবণ। **2.** Affected by cold ; shivering with cold ; শীতার্ত্ত ; শীতবেপিত। **3.** Not warm or affectionate ; formal ; as, a *chill* reception ; অনুরাগশূন্য, আবেগশূন্য, প্রাণশূন্য, আন্তরিকতাশূন্য ; লৌকিক। **4.** (*Fig.*) Depressing ; discouraging ; dispiriting ; "*Chill* penury repressed their noble rage ;" (লক্ষণায়) অবসাদকর ; নিরুৎসাহকর, উৎসাহ-ভঙ্গকর ; ভগ্নোদ্যমজনক। ***Noun.*** **1.** A cold sensation ; a shivering with cold ; শৈত্যানুভব ; শৈত্য হেতু কম্প। **2.** Coldness in the air, water, etc. ; জল, বাতাস প্রভৃতির শৈত্য। **3.** A benumbing and depressing influence ; as, a *chill* comes over the assembly ; অবসাদজনক ভাব, অপ্রফুল্লকর ভাব। **Chilled,** *adj.* **Chill'-i-ness,** *n.* **Chill'-ing,** *adj.* **Chill'-y,** *adj.* & *adv.* **1.** Rather cold to feel ; disagreeably cold ; sensitive to cold ; শৈত্যভাবাপন্ন ; ঠাণ্ডা ; শীতানুভবপ্রবণ। **2.** Not genial ; আন্তরিকতা শূন্য, প্রীতিশূন্য, প্রাণশূন্য। (*Adv.*) In a chill or cold manner ; অনুরাগশূন্যভাবে। **To take the chill off**—To give a slight heat ; ঈষদুষ্ণ করা। **To feel chilly**—To be oppressed with coldness ; ঠাণ্ডা বোধ করা, শীত লাগা।

chil'-i, chil'-lŷ, *n.* The pod or fruit of Cayenne pepper ; লঙ্কা-মরিচ।

Chil'-têrn Hŭn'-drĕds, *n.* A hilly district in Buckinghamshire which has belonged to the crown from time immemorial ; বাকিংহামশায়ারের অন্তঃপাতী পার্ব্বত্য উপবিভাগ বিশেষ। [এই স্থানটী স্মরণাতীত কাল হইতে ইংলণ্ডের নৃপতিগণের অধিকৃত হইয়া আসিতেছে। পার্লেমেণ্টের সভ্যগণ প্রত্যক্ষভাবে পদত্যাগ করিতে পারেন না। তাঁহাদের কাহারও পদত্যাগের প্রয়োজন হইলে তাঁহারা, ঐ স্থানের কর্ম্মাধ্যক্ষের নামতঃ বর্ত্তমান পদ গ্রহণ করিয়া, তৎক্ষণাৎ আবার সেই পদ ত্যাগ করেন।] **To apply for the Chiltern Hundreds**—পার্লেমেণ্টের সভ্যপদ পরিত্যাগ করা।

chi-mæ'-ră (-mē-), **chi-mē'-ră,** *n.* **1.** (*Class. Myth.*) A fire-breathing monster with a lion's head, a serpent's tail, and a goat's body ; গ্রীক ও রোমীয় পুরাণোক্ত বিকটাকার অসুর বিশেষ ; ইহার মস্তক সিংহের মত, লাঙ্গুল সর্পবৎ, দেহ ছাগ সদৃশ, এবং ইহার নিশ্বাসে অগ্নি নির্গত হয়। **2.** A fanciful conception ; a mere wild fancy ; as, the *chimera* of an author ; আজগুবি ভাব ; অসম্ভব কল্পনা, শশবিষাণ। **—mer'-ic, —mer'-i-cal,** *adjs.* **—mer'-i-cal-ly,** *adv.*

chīme, *v. t., i.* & *n.* **1.** To cause to sound in harmony ; ঐক্যতান সহকারে বাদন করা। **2.** To strike or cause to sound, as a set of bells ; ঘণ্টাশ্রেণী বাজান। **3.** To make to rhyme ; কবিতার পংক্তির অন্তে উচ্চারণ মিল করা। ***Verb i.*** **1.** To sound in harmony or accord, as bells ; as, to hear bells *chime* ; একতানে বা স্বরসঙ্গতি সহকারে বাজিয়া উঠা। **2.** To be in harmony ; (often with *in with*) ; as, everything *chimed in with* such a humour ; সঙ্গতি বিশিষ্ট হওয়া, মিলা, উপযোগী হওয়া। **3.** To rhyme ; as, his numbers rarely *chime* ; কবিতার পংক্তি অন্তের উচ্চারণ মিল হওয়া। ***Noun.*** **1.** The harmonious sound of bells or other musical instruments ; অনেকগুলি ঘণ্টা বা বাদ্য যন্ত্রের ঐক্যতান। **2.** An apparatus for striking a bell or set of bells ; ঘণ্টা বা ঘণ্টা-পংক্তি বাদনার্থ যন্ত্রবিশেষ। **3.** Harmony ; melody ; rhythm ; স্বর-সঙ্গতি ; সুস্বর ; ছন্দঃ। **4.** Correspondence ; সঙ্গতি, ঐক্য। **To chime in**—To join in harmoniously or in unison (in music) ; ঐক্যতান হওয়া। **To chime in with**—To be in complete accord with ; সম্পূর্ণ মিল হওয়া, এক সুরে বাজা, সুরে সুর মিলা। **To fall into chime with, To keep chime with** — To be in harmonious correspondence ; সঙ্গতি পূর্ণ হওয়া, খাপ খাওয়া (*Colloq.*)।

chime, chimb (chīme), *n.* The projecting rim at the ends of a cask ; পিপার প্রান্তদেশস্থ উদ্গত বেষ্টনী।

chim'-ney (-nĭ), *n.* **1.** A flue or passage for the escape of smoke for fire ; ধূমনির্গমনল ; ধূমনির্গম-নালী, ধূমনালী (আঃ বঃ)। **2.** The pipe or funnel that carries off the smoke or steam of a locomotive engine, steam boat, etc. ; বাষ্পীয়-পোত, বাষ্পীয়শকট, প্রভৃতির ধূম নির্গমনল। **3.** A glass tube protecting the lamp flame ; দীপশিখাবরক কাচনল, চিমনী, দীপের ধূমনির্গমনল। **4.** (*Mountaineering*) A narrow cleft by which cliff may be climbed.; (পর্ব্বতারোহণে) যে সংকীর্ণ ফাটলের সাহায্যে পর্ব্বতে আরোহণ করা যায়। **Chimney-can, Chimney-pot**—ধূমনিবারণের জন্য ধূমনির্গমনলের অগ্রভাগে নিবদ্ধ মৃত্তিকা বা ধাতুপট্টনির্ম্মিত নল বিশেষ। **Chimney-corner**—(শীত-প্রধান দেশে) পূর্ব্বকালীন বৃহদাকার বহ্নিসেবন-স্থলিমধ্যবর্ত্তী (বৃদ্ধ ব্যক্তি প্রভৃতির) উপবেশনস্থান, চুল্লি-কোণ (আঃ বঃ)। **Chimney-piece** — অগ্নি-সেবন-স্থলীর উর্দ্ধ ও চতুষ্পার্শ্বস্থিত কারুকার্য্য-খচিত স্থাপত্য-ব্যবস্থা বিশেষ, চুল্লি-বেষ্টনী (আঃ বঃ)। (*Colloq.*) **Chimney-pot, —hat**—(চলিত কথায়) চোঙ্গাকার কাল রেশমী টুপি—আজকাল বিলাতের পুরুষেরা ব্যবহার করে। **Chimney-shaft** — কোন গৃহের উপরিস্থিত ধূম-নির্গমনালীর অংশ; শিল্পশালা প্রভৃতির সুদীর্ঘ ধূমনির্গমনালী। **Chimney-sweep, Chimney-sweeper** — ধূম-নালী-মার্জ্জক (আঃ বঃ)। **Chimney top**—ধূমনির্গম-নালীর যে অংশ ছাদের উপর উত্থিত থাকে।

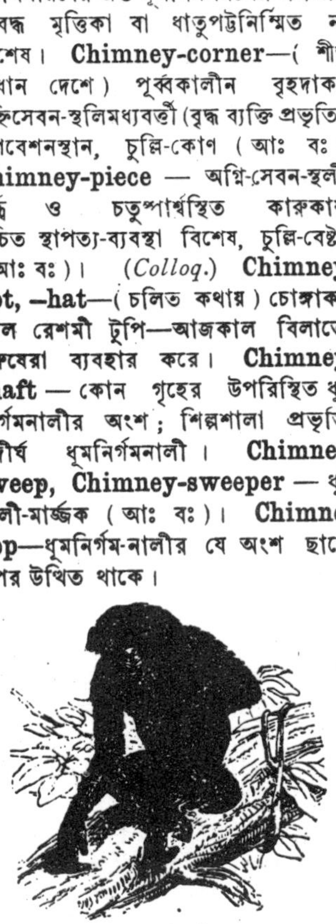

Chimpanzee.

chim-păn′-zee (-zē), *n.* An African ape resembling man ; বনমানুষের মত আফ্রিকা দেশীয় বানরবিশেষ।

chin, *n.* The lower extremity of the face below the mouth ; চিবুক, থুতনী। **Up to the chin, chin-deep**—Deeply immersed in ; গভীরভাবে নিমজ্জিত।

chī′-nă, *n.* **1.** Porcelain ; চিনামাটি। **2.** Things made of this ; crockery in general ; চীনামাটির ভাণ্ডাদি ; দগ্ধমৃণ্ময় ভাণ্ড সমূহ। **China box**—কামিনী ফুল বা ঐ গাছ (যোঃ)। **China-clay**—See KAOLIN. **China-closet**—চীনাবাসন রাখিবার বা প্রদর্শন করিবার কুঠরী। **China grass**—Ramie ; কালখুরা, কঙ্কুরা। **China-mania**—দুষ্প্রাপ্য এবং প্রাচীন চীনা বাসন সংগ্রহের জন্য উৎকট বাতিক বা খেয়াল। **China-root**—চোব চিনির শিকড়। **China-rose**—জবা, ওড্রপুষ্প, রুদ্রপুষ্প। **China-shop**—কাচ, চীনামাটি এবং দগ্ধমৃণ্ময় বাসনের দোকান। **China-ware**—চীনা মাটির বাসন।

chinch, *n.* The bed-bug in America ; আমেরিকার ছারপোকা।

chin-chil′-lă, *n.* **1.** A small South American rodent ; দক্ষিণ আমেরিকার দন্তর জন্তুবিশেষ। **2.** Its soft grey fur ; উক্ত জন্তর ধূসরবর্ণ কোমল রোম।

chin′-cough (-kŏf), *n.* Hooping cough ; ঘুংড়ি কাশি।

chine *n.* **1.** The backbone or spine of an animal ; পশুর শিরদাঁড়া বা পৃষ্ঠবংশ। **2.** A piece of the backbone of an animal, with the adjoining parts, cut for cooking ; রাঁধিবার জন্য কাটা জন্তর শিরদাঁড়া বা ঐ জায়গার নিকটের মাংস। **3.** A ridge ; আল। **4.** The edge or brim of casks, etc. ; পিপা প্রভৃতির ধার বা কানা। **5.** A deep, narrow ravine ; দরী, কন্দর। **Chined,** *adj.*

Chi-nese′ (-nēz), *adj.* Of or pertaining to China ; চীনদেশীয়। **Chinese fire**—আতসবাজীর উপকরণ বিশেষ। **Chinese lantern**—রঙ্গীন কাগজের লণ্ঠন, চীনা লণ্ঠন। **Chinese white**—একপ্রকার সাদা রঙ্গ।

chink, *v. t., i.* & *n.* **1.** To cause to open in cracks or slits ; ফাটান। **2.** To fill up chinks or cracks ; as, to *chink* a wall ; ফাটল বুজান। ***Verb i.*** To open ; to crack ; খুলিয়া যাওয়া ; ফাটা। ***Noun.*** A cleft or rent ; a long narrow opening ; গর্ত্ত, ছিদ্র, রন্ধ্র, ফাঁক, চিড় ; ফাটল। **Chink′-y,** *adj.*

chink, *v. t., i.* & *n.* To cause to jingle as money ; ঝন্‌ঝন্ শব্দ করান। ***Verb i.*** To emit a jingling sound ; ঝন্‌ঝন্ করিয়া উঠা। ***Noun.*** **1.** A sharp sound as of glasses or coins striking together ; ঝন্‌ঝন্ শব্দ, শিঞ্জিত, ক্বণিত, নিক্বণ। **2.** (*Slang*) Ready money ; as, to leave his *chink* to better hands ; (ইতর ভাষায়) রোক্ টাকা, নগদ টাকা।

chintz (chĭnts), **chints,** *n.* Cotton cloth, printed with flowers and other devices, in a number of different colours ; ছিঁট।

chip, *v. t., i.* & *n.* **1.** To cut small pieces *off, from* ; to hew ; খণ্ড খণ্ড করা ; চেলা করা, ফালি করা, ছেদন করা। **2.** To crack or break away (the egg-shells) in hatching, (said of chickens, etc.) ; তা দিয়া ডিম ফুটান। ***Verb i.*** To break, crack or fly off in small pieces, as crockery at the edges ; ভাঙ্গিয়া যাওয়া, ফাটিয়া যাওয়া, ক্ষুদ্র ক্ষুদ্র খণ্ডে উড়িয়া যাওয়া। ***Noun.*** **1.** A thin piece cut from wood, or broken from stone, etc. ; কাঠের চেলা, পাথরের টুকরা, ফালি, খণ্ড। **2.** A thin slice of potato, fruit, etc. ; ফল, বিলাতী আলু, প্রভৃতির চাকলা। **Chip′-py,** *adj.* **1.** Irritable ; খিট্‌খিটে। **2.** Dry ; uninteresting ; শুষ্ক ; নীরস। **To chip at**—To aim a blow at ; to pick a quarrel with ; সন্ধান করা ; গায়ে পড়িয়া ঝগড়া করা। **To chip in**—To interrupt ; বাধা দেওয়া।

A chip of the old block—পিতৃগুণানুরূপ পুত্র, যে ব্যক্তিতে বংশগত বা পারিবারিক বিশেষত্ব বিশিষ্টরূপে প্রকাশ পাইয়াছে।

chĭp, *n.* & *v. t.* A trick in wrestling ; মল্লযুদ্ধের কৌশলবিশেষ। ***Verb t.*** To trip up, (esp. in wrestling) ; হুচট খাওয়ান, (বিশেষতঃ মল্লযুদ্ধে) পা ফস্কাইয়া দেওয়া।

chĭp'-munk (-mŭngk), *n.* A North American squirrel; উত্তর আমেরিকার কাঠবিড়ালী বিশেষ।

chĭp'-pĕn-dāle, *adj.* Applied to a light and elegant style of drawing-room furniture ; লঘু এবং পরিপাটী বৈঠকখানার আসবাব নির্ম্মাণের পদ্ধতি-বিশেষ সম্পর্কে প্রযোজ্য। [অষ্টাদশ শতাব্দীর সুবিখ্যাত আসবাব সামগ্রী নির্ম্মাতা Chippendale এর নাম হইতে গৃহীত।]

chī'-rō-grăph, *n.* A document of various kinds formally written or signed ; প্রচলিত নিয়মানুসারে লিখিত এবং স্বাক্ষরিত বিভিন্ন প্রকার দলিল।

chī'-rō-măn-çȳ, *n.* Divination by the hand ; palmistry ; কর-সামুদ্রিক (হিঃ কোঃ) ; সামুদ্রিক শাস্ত্র।

chī-rŏp'-ō-dȳ, *n.* The art of treating corn, wart, defective nails, etc. on hand and feet ; কড়া, আচিল প্রভৃতির চিকিৎসাতত্ত্ব। **—dist,** *n.*

chirp (chêrp), *v. i., t.* & *n.* **1.** To make a short sharp shrill sound, as is done by small birds or certain insects ; কিচির মিচির শব্দ করা, ঝিঁ ঝিঁ করা। **2.** To talk merrily ; to speak feebly ; উৎফুল্ল-ভাবে কথা বলা ; ক্ষীণস্বরে কথা বলা। ***Verb t.*** To cheer ; কিচির মিচির করিয়া আনন্দ প্রকাশ করা। ***Noun.*** A short, shrill note, as of certain birds or insects ; কিচির মিচির শব্দ, ঝিঁ ঝিঁ শব্দ। **Chirp'-ing,** *adj.* **Chirp'-y,** *adj.* হর্ষোৎফুল্ল। **To chirp up**—To cheer up . প্রফুল্ল করা।

chirr (chêr), *v. i.* & *n.* To chirp, as is done by the cricket or grasshopper ; ঝিঁ ঝিঁ শব্দ করা। ***Noun.*** A prolonged trilling sound ; ঝিঁ ঝিঁ শব্দ।

chĭr'-rŭp, *v. t., i.* & *n.* **1.** To chirp ; কিচির মিচির করা, ঝিঁ ঝিঁ শব্দ করা। **2.** To act as a paid applauder at a theatre, etc. ; পয়সা পাইয়া রঙ্গালয় প্রভৃতিতে বাহবা দেওয়া। ***Noun.*** A series of chirps ; কিচির মিচির শব্দ, ঝিঁ ঝিঁ শব্দ।

chĭs'-ĕl, *n.* & *v. t.* A carpenter's tool to pare or cut ; বাটালি, টঙ্কক। ***Verb t.*** **1.** To cut, engrave, etc. with a chisel ; (often with *out*) ; বাটালি দ্বারা কাটা, খোদা ইত্যাদি কার্য্য করা। **2.** (*Slang*) To cheat ; to defraud ; (ইতর ভাষায়) প্রতারণা করা ; ঠকাইয়া লওয়া। **—elled,** *adj.* Cut with a chisel ; clear-cut, (having clear and sharp outlines) ; as, *chiselled* lip, features etc. ; বাটালিদ্বারা কাটা ; স্পষ্টরূপে কর্ত্তিত, সুস্পষ্ট বহিঃরেখাবিশিষ্ট। **Full chisel**—At full speed, (*Colloq. U. S.*) ; পূরাবেগে।

chĭt, *n.* **1.** A shoot or sprout ; as, the *chits* of corn or potatoes ; প্ররোহ, অঙ্কুর। **2.** A young child ; as, when I was a naughty little *chit* ; ছোঁড়া, ছুঁড়ী। **3.** A young slender woman (*depreciatingly*) ; as, to be in love with a *chit* of fourteen ; (অবজ্ঞাচ্ছলে) কাহিল স্ত্রীলোক।

chit, chit'-tȳ, *n.* A short letter or note ; a certificate given to a servant ; চিঠি, চিরকুট, রুক্কা ; চাকরের প্রশংসাপত্র।

chĭt'-chăt, *n.* A light familiar conversation ; গল্পগুজব, খোসগল্প।

chī'-tin, *n.* A substance forming the horny cover of beetles and crustaceans ; গোবরে পোকা এবং খোলাবিশিষ্ট জীবগণের শৃঙ্গময় দেহাবরণ যে পদার্থ দ্বারা গঠিত হয়, কঞ্চুকিন (সাঃ পঃ)। **—ous,** *adj.*

chil'-têr-lings, *n.* The smaller intestines of swine, etc., fried for food ; (gen. *pl.*) ; শূকরাদির ক্ষুদ্রতর অন্ত্র—যাহা ভাজিয়া খাওয়া হয়।

chiv'-ăl-rȳ (shĭv-), *n.* **1.** (*Obs.*) Cavalry ; সাদী সৈন্য (অপ্রচলিত)। **2.** A body of illustrious mounted soldiers ; gallant gentlemen ; একদল সুবিখ্যাত অশ্বারোহী সৈন্য ; ভদ্রবংশজাত রমণী-রঞ্জক পুরুষগণ, নাগর। **3.** Knighthood ; "The age of *chivalry* is gone ;" মধ্যযুগের নাইটদিগের রীতি বা ধারা। **4.** The characteristics of an ideal knight, such as bravery, honour and courtesy ; আদর্শ নাইটের বিশিষ্ট গুণাবলী—শৌর্য্য, সম্মান এবং শিষ্টাচার। **5.** Devotion to the service of women ; inclination to defend the weaker party ; নারী-সেবানুরাগ ; দুর্ব্বলরক্ষণ-প্রবৃত্তি। **—ric, —rous,** *adjs.* **1.** Of or relating to the age of chivalry regarded as a period in history ; as, *chivalrous* spirit ; শৌর্য্য, দাক্ষিণ্যাদি গুণোপেত নাইটগণের যুগসম্বন্ধীয়। **2.** Belonging to, or characteristic of, the ideal knight ; nobly daring ; gallant ; honourable ; courteous ; আদর্শ নাইট সম্বন্ধীয় ; শূর ; রমণীরঞ্জক ; মর্য্যাদাসম্পন্ন ; শিষ্ট, ভদ্র। **—rous-ly,** *adv.* **—rous-ness,** *n.*

chīve *n.* A small herb allied to onion, (usu. in *pl.*) ; পেঁয়াজের অনুরূপ সবজী বিশেষ।

chlō'-răl, *n.* (*Chem.*) An oily liquid produced from chlorine and alcohol ; কুলহরিণ এবং সুরাসার হইতে প্রস্তুত তৈলবৎ তরল পদার্থ বিশেষ।

chlō-rīde, *n.* (*Chem.*) A compound of chlorine ; কুলহরিণের মিশ্র।

chlō-rine (-rĭn), *n.* (*Chem.*) A greenish-yellow gas obtained from common salt ; হরিণ (সাঃ পঃ), হরিণক (ঐ), কুল হরিণ (মণীঃ)।

chlô'-rō-dȳne *n.* (*Med.*) A patent medicine, narcotic and anodyne ; কলেরা রোগের ঔষধ বিশেষ।

chlō'-rō fôrm, *n.* & *v. t.* A volatile limpid fluid much used in surgery to induce insensibility; সংজ্ঞালোপকর ঔষধ বিশেষ, ক্লোরোফর্ম্। ***Verb t.*** To treat a person with chloroform; to render insensible by chloroform; ক্লোরোফর্ম্ দ্বারা চিকিৎসা করা; ক্লোরোফর্ম্ দ্বারা অজ্ঞান করা।

chlö'-rō-phyll, *n.* The colouring matter of the leaves and other green parts of plants; বৃক্ষের পত্র এবং অন্যান্য সবুজবর্ণ অংশের হরিদ্বর্ণ বর্ণক পদার্থ, পত্রহরিৎ (সাঃ পঃ)।

chlō-rō'-sis, *n.* The green sickness; হরিৎ পীড়া (হঃ চঃ) মৃৎপাণ্ডু (ঐ)। **—rot'-ic,** *n.*

chŏck *n., v. t.* & *adv.* A wedge or block of wood used to stop a cask, wheel, etc. from moving; চাকা, পিপা প্রভৃতি যাহাতে গড়াইয়া না যায়, তজ্জন্য যে কাজলা বা কাঠের টুকরা লাগান হয়। ***Verb t.*** **1.** To wedge a wheel or cask etc., (usu. *up*); চাকা, পিপা প্রভৃতিতে কাজলা বা কুঁদো লাগান। **2.** (*Naut.*) To put a wedge or block into or under; (নৌ-বিদ্যা) কোন কিছুর ভিতরে বা নীচে কুঁদো বা কাজলা প্রভৃতি লাগান। ***Adv.*** Entirely; tightly; পরিপূর্ণভাবে; ঠাসাঠাসি ভাবে। **Chock-full**—(See CHOKE.)

chŏc'-ō-lāte *n.* & *adj.* **1.** A cake of cacao-seed paste; আমেরিকা দেশীয় ফলবিশেষের চূর্ণ হইতে প্রস্তুত পিণ্ড। **2.** A beverage made by dissolving this paste in hot milk or water; উষ্ণ দুগ্ধ বা জলে উক্ত পিণ্ড মিশ্রিত করিয়া প্রস্তুত পানীয়বিশেষ। ***Adj.*** Dark brown; কপিশবর্ণ, গাঢ় বাদামিবর্ণ।

choice (choys), *n.* & *adj.* **1.** The act of choosing; selection; বরণ, মনোনয়ন; নির্ব্বাচন, বাছনি। **2.** The power, right or faculty of choosing; নির্ব্বাচনী শক্তি, নির্ব্বাচনাধিকার, নির্ব্বাচনী বৃত্তি। **3.** The best part; the pick; উৎকৃষ্ট অংশ; বাছা জিনিষ। **4.** Abundance and variety to choose from; as, an unusual *choice* of silk; নানাপ্রকার নমুনা বা প্রাচুর্য্য। **5.** The thing or person chosen or selected; নির্ব্বাচিত বা মনোনীত ব্যক্তি অথবা বস্তু। **6.** Alternative; as, he has no *choice* but to be scientific; গত্যন্তর। ***Adj.*** **1.** Excellent; বরণীয়, উৎকৃষ্ট, সর্ব্বোত্তম, বিশিষ্ট, বরেণ্য, উমদা (*Colloq.*), তোফা (*Colloq.*), সেরা (*Colloq.*), বাছা, সরস, খাসা, চমৎকার। **2.** Appropriate; as, *choice* word and measured phrase; সমুচিত, যথাযোগ্য। **Choice'-ly,** *adv.* **Choice'-ness,** *n.* **At choice**—At pleasure; খুসীমত, ইচ্ছামত, মর্জ্জিমত। **Hobson's choice**—যে জিনিষটী দেওয়া হইতেছে সেইটী নেও—অথবা কোনটী নিও না এরূপ ভাব। **Of choice**—Of worth or value; as, men *of choice*; গণ্য-মান্য। **To have one's choice**—To have the right or privilege of choosing; নির্ব্বাচনের ক্ষমতা বা অধিকার থাকা। **To hold in most rich choice**—To hold in very high estimation; অত্যন্ত শ্রদ্ধা বা সমাদর করা। **To make a choice of**—To choose; to select; মনোনয়ন করা; নির্ব্বাচন করা। **To take one's choice**—To take what one will take or have; নিজের পসন্দমত জিনিষ গ্রহণ করা। **Without choice**—Without distinction; ভালমন্দ নির্ব্বিশেষে, নির্বিচারে, ইতর বিশেষ না করিয়া।

choir (cwīr), *n.* **1.** The band of singers, who perform or lead the musical part of the service in a church; খৃষ্টীয়-ধর্ম্ম-মন্দিরসংসৃষ্ট গায়কসম্প্রদায়। **2.** That part of the church appropriated to the singers; খৃষ্টীয়-ধর্ম্মমন্দিরে গায়কসম্প্রদায়ের উপবেশনস্থল। **3.** The chancel of a cathedral or collegiate church; খৃষ্টীয় মহাধর্ম্মমন্দির বা বৃহৎ মন্দিরের যে স্থানে বেদী থাকে। **Choir-organ** (also chair-organ)—বাদ্যযন্ত্র বিশেষ।

chōke *v. t., i.* & *n.* **1.** To suffocate; to strangle; শ্বাসরোধ করা, গলা টিপি শ্বাস বন্ধ করা; শ্বাসরোধ করিয়া মারা। **2.** To block up; অবরুদ্ধ করা। **3.** To hinder or check the growth or progress; বৃদ্ধি বা উন্নতি রোধ করা। **4.** To suppress or smother any feeling; মানসিক আবেগ নিরোধ করা। **5.** To irritate or offend greatly; as, I was *choked* at this word; জ্বালাতন করা, উত্ত্যক্ত করা, বিরক্ত করা। **6.** To fit tightly; আঁট হইয়া লাগা। ***Verb i.*** **1.** To have the windpipe stopped; শ্বাসনালী বন্ধ হওয়া, শ্বাসরোধ হওয়া। **2.** To be hindered or checked; বাধাপ্রাপ্ত হওয়া। **3.** To stick; as, the words *choked* into his mouth; আটকিয়া থাকা। **Chok'-er,** *n.* One who interrupts or stops; অবরোধকারী, বাধাপ্রদানকারী। **Chok'-y, Chok'-ey,** *adjs.* **Choke-bore**—একপ্রকার কামান—ইহার বন্দুমুখের দিক ক্রমশঃ সূক্ষ্ম হইয়া আসিয়াছে। **Choke-damp**—কূপ, কয়লাখনি, প্রভৃতির বিষাক্ত শ্বাসরোধকর বাষ্প। **Choke-full**—কানায় কানায় পরিপূর্ণ, আকণ্ঠপূর্ণ। **Choke-pear**—(লক্ষণায়) যে বস্তু সহজে গলাধঃকরণ করা যায় না; তীব্র তিরস্কার। **Choking coil**—স্থূল তারের কুণ্ডলী বিশেষ—যদ্দ্বারা দীপশ্রেণীর আলোক মন্দীভূত করা হয়। **White choker**—যাজকগণের শ্বেতবর্ণ গলবন্ধ বিশেষ। **To choke back down**—To repress; to smother down; দমন করা, দমাইয়া দেওয়া; চাপিয়া ফেলা। **To choke off**—To put a stop to; to get rid of; বন্ধ করা; নিষ্কৃতি লাভ করা, উদ্ধার পাওয়া। **To choke up**—To block up a channel; জলনালী রোধ করা।

chōke, *n.* The capillary part of an artichoke; হাতীচোখ গাছের কেশাকৃতি অংশ।

chŏ-læ'-mi-ă (-lē-), **chŏ-lē'-mi-ă** *n.* A disease characterised by the presence of bile in the blood ; রক্তে পিত্তাধিক্য (হঃ চঃ)।

chŏl′-ă-gogue (-gŏg), *n.* A medicine that carries off bile ; পিত্ত-নিঃসারক ঔষধ (হঃ চঃ), পিত্তভেদক (সাঃ পঃ), পিত্তকর (ঠাকুর)।

chŏl′-ẽr, *n.* **1.** Bile ; পিত্ত। **2.** Anger ; heat of temper ; irascibility ; রাগ; কোপ ; রোষপরবশতা। **—ic,** *adj.*

chŏl′-ẽr-ă, *n.* **1.** A disorder with bilious diarrhœa, vomiting, stomach-ache and cramps ; (also called ENGLISH, BILIOUS or SUMMER CHOLERA) ; পিত্তসংযুক্ত উদরাময় রোগ বিশেষ,—বমি, পক্বাশয়ে বেদনা এবং খিঁচুনী এই পীড়ার লক্ষণ। **2.** A non-bilious often fatal disease endemic in India and epidemic in other parts of the world ; ওলাউঠা, বিসূচিকা, মহামারী। (Also ASIATIC, EPIDEMIC, MALIGNANT CHOLERA.) **—a′-ic,** *adj.*

chŏl′-ẽr-ine, *n.* The first stage of *epidemic* cholera ; ওলাউঠার প্রথমাবস্থা।

choose (chōōz), *v. t.* & *i.* **1.** To select out of a greater number ; নির্ব্বাচন করা, মনোনয়ন করা, বরণ করা। **2.** To think proper, (with infinitive object) ; as, he did not *choose* to speak to her in public ; সমীচীন বিবেচনা করা, পছন্দ করা। **3.** (*Colloq.*) To want ; as, do you *choose* any refreshment ; (চলিত ভাষায়) চাওয়া। ***Verb i.*** To make a selection between different things ; নির্ব্বাচন করা। **Choos′-a-ble** or **Choose′-a-ble,** *adj.* **Choos′-er,** *n.* **Choos′-ing-ly,** *adv.* **Cannot choose**—Cannot help ; অন্যথা করিতে পারি না, না করিয়া পারি না। **Not much to choose between**—বড় ইতর বিশেষ নাই। **To choose out**—To pick out ; বাছিয়া নেওয়া, পছন্দ করিয়া লওয়া। **To pick and choose**—To select with careful scrutiny ; পুঙ্খানুপুঙ্খরূপে বিচারপূর্ব্বক নির্ব্বাচন করা।

chŏp, *v. t., i.* & *n.* **1.** To cut with a quick and heavy blow ; to cut (by an axe, cleaver, etc.) into pieces ; to mince (usu. with *off*) ; কোপ মারিয়া কাটা ; কুঠার প্রভৃতি দ্বারা কাটা ; খণ্ড বিখণ্ড করা, চেলা করা, খণ্ড খণ্ড করা। **2.** To utter abruptly ; ফট্ করিয়া বলা। ***Verb i.*** **1.** To make a quick stroke or repeated strokes (with axe, etc.) ; (কুঠার প্রভৃতি দ্বারা) পুনঃ পুনঃ কোপান। **2.** To thrust oneself in ; to enter forcibly ; to break in with a remark ; to intervene (with *in, into*) ; ঠেলিয়া প্রবেশ করা ; জোর করিয়া প্রবেশ করা ; হঠাৎ কোন মন্তব্য প্রকাশ করা ; মাঝে পড়া। ***Noun.*** A piece chopped off ; a slice of mutton or pork, including a rib to be cooked and served by itself ; কোপ দিয়া কাটা টুকরা ; শূকর বা ভেড়ার পাঁজর সহিত মাংসখণ্ড—যাহা রাঁধা হইয়া স্বতন্ত্রভাবে পরিবেষিত হয়, মাংসের চপ, মাংসফালিকা (নৈষঃ)। **Chop′-per,** *n.* **1.** One who chops or cuts into pieces ; a large-bladed short-handled axe ; যে ব্যক্তি কোপাইয়া কাটে ; মাংস ছেদনার্থ ছুরিকা, কর্ত্তরিকা বিশেষ। **Chop-house**—যে ভোজনালয়ে চপ প্রভৃতি বিক্রয় হয় ; যে ভোজনালয়ে সস্তায় আহার করা যায়। **At one chop**—এক কোপে। **To chop at**—To aim a blow at ; অস্ত্রাদি সন্ধান করা। **To chop in**—To intervene in talk ; কথার উপর কথা বলা। To interpolate ; প্রক্ষিপ্ত করা। **To chop in with**—To interrupt with ; বাধা প্রদান করা। **To chop out with**—To give vent to ; প্রকাশ করা। **To chop up**—To cut into small pieces ; কুটিকুটি করিয়া কাটা। **To chop yarns**—To tell stories ; গল্প ফাঁদা।

chop, *v. t., i.* & *n.* **1.** To buy and sell ; to exchange ; কেনাবেচা করা ; বিনিময় করা, অদলবদল করা। **2.** To change ; পরিবর্ত্তন করা, অন্য প্রকার করা, বদলান। ***Verb i.*** **1.** To practise bartering ; বিনিময় করা। **2.** (*Of the wind*) To change or shift its direction suddenly, (with *round, about*) ; (বায়ুপক্ষে) সহসা গতি পরিবর্ত্তন করা। ***Noun.*** An exchange ; a barter ; পরিবর্ত্তন; বিনিময়। **Chop-logic**—Logical argumentation ; তর্কবিতর্ক, ন্যায়ের বিচার, ন্যায়ের কচকচি। **To chop and change**—To buy and sell ; to exchange ; কেনা বেচা করা ; অদলবদল করা। **To chop logic**—To exchange logical arguments and terms ; বাদানুবাদ করা, তর্কবিতর্ক করা।

chŏp, *n.* The jaw; the cavity of the mouth ; চোয়াল ; মুখবিবর। **Chop-fallen**—See CHAPFALLEN. **Chops of the channel**—অতলান্তিক সাগর হইতে ব্রিটিশ প্রণালীতে প্রবেশের পথ।

chŏp, *n.* (India and China) **1.** An official stamp ; a seal ; (ভারতবর্ষে এবং চীনদেশে) সরকারী মোহর ; সীলমোহর। **2.** A license, passport, etc. ; a permit ; as, to receive the *chop* for trade ; সনন্দ, ছাড়পত্র প্রভৃতি ; অনুমতি পত্র। **3.** (*China*) A trade-mark ; a brand of goods ; (চীনদেশে) ব্যবসায়চিহ্ন ; যে ছাপ বা চিহ্ন দ্বারা কোন জিনিষের রকম বুঝা যায়। **Chop of tea**—কতিপয় চাএর বাক্স—যাহাতে একই ভাবে তৈয়ারী ও একই রকমের চা থাকে (একইরূপ ব্যবসায়চিহ্ন থাকে)। **Grand chop**—বন্দরে জাহাজের মাল খালাস।

chŏp′-in, *n.* A liquid measure ; তরল পদার্থের পরিমাপ বিশেষ।

chŏ-pine (-pēn), *n.* A kind of shoe raised above the ground by means of a cork sole or the like ; একপ্রকার জুতা।

chŏp-ping, *adj.* Same as CHOPPY.

chŏp-ping, *adj.* Plump ; গোলগাল।

chŏp-py̆, *adj.* **1.** Running in irregular waves ; উচ্ছৃঙ্খল তরঙ্গ

সঙ্কুল। 2. Full of clefts or cracks; চিড় বা ফাটল পূর্ণ।

chŏp'-stick (-stĭk), *n.* One of two small sticks of ivory or wood, used by the Chinese for conveying food to the mouth; চীনদেশীয়গণ কাঠ বা হাতীর দাঁতের যে দুইটী কাঠিদ্বারা মুখে খাদ্য তুলিয়া দেয় তাহার একটী।

chō'-răl, *adj.* 1. Of or belonging to a choir; sung by a choir; খৃষ্টীয় ধর্ম্মমন্দিরস্থ গায়কসম্প্রদায় সম্পৃক্ত; উক্ত গায়কসম্প্রদায়দ্বারা গীত। 2. Belonging to, or of the nature of, a chorus; sung in chorus; একতানগান সম্বন্ধীয়, একতান-গানাত্মক; সমস্বরে গীত। **—ist**, *n.* একতান গায়ক; ছন্দোবদ্ধ স্তোত্রগায়ক বা রচক।

chō'-răl(e), *n.* A psalm or hymn; ধর্ম্মসঙ্গীত বা স্তোত্র।

chŏrd, *n.* 1. (*Mus.*) Harmonious combination of musical tones; (সঙ্গীতশাস্ত্র) স্বরসঙ্গতি, একতান। 2. A harmonious combination of colours; বিবিধ বর্ণের সুসমাবেশ। 3. A string of a musical instrument, (as of a harp); গুণ, তন্ত্রী, তার। 4. (*Physiol.*) A structure resembling a string; as, spinal *chord*; (শারীর-বিজ্ঞান) তন্ত্রী। 5. (*Geom.*) A straight line joining the extremities of an arc; (জ্যামিতি) জ্যা, পূর্ণ-জ্যা (হিঃ কোঃ), চাপকর্ণ (ঐ)। **Chor'-dal**, *adj.* **To break** or **spread a chord**—To play the notes in succession instead of simultaneously; পর্য্যায়ক্রমে এক একটী স্বর বাজান। **To touch the right chord**—To appeal skilfully to emotion; হৃদয়ের গভীর তন্ত্রী স্পর্শ করা।

chŏr-dee', (-dē), *n.* A painful erection of the penis, under which it is considerably curved; প্রমেহাদি রোগে যন্ত্রণাপ্রদ বক্র লিঙ্গোচ্ছ্বাস।

chō-rē'-ă, *n.* (*Med.*) St. Vitus's dance; তাণ্ডব রোগ (হঃ চঃ)।

chō-ree' (-rē), *n.* A trochee (which see).

chŏr'-ē-ō-grăph, *n.* A designer or arranger of a ballet; নৃত্য-বিশেষের পরিকল্পনাকারী বা বন্দোবস্ত-কারী। **—graph'-ic,** *adj.* **—og'-ra-pher**, *n.* **—og'-ra-phy**, *n.*

chō'-ri-ămb, chō'-ri-ăm-bŭs, *ns.* A metrical foot of four syllables, the first and last long, the two others short (— ⌣ ⌣ —); বাক্যাংশ চতুষ্টয়বিশিষ্ট কবিতার পদ, ইহার প্রথম ও শেষ বাক্যাংশ দুইটী গুরু, এবং অবশিষ্ট দুইটী লঘু হইয়া থাকে। **—am'-bic**, *adj.*

chō'-ric, *adj.* Of or pertaining to a chorus in Greek tragedy; গ্রীক দেশীয় বিয়োগান্ত নাটকের বৃন্দগায়ক সম্বন্ধীয়।

chō'-ri-ŏn, *n.* 1. (*Anat.*) The outermost membrane enveloping the foetus before birth; (শারীর সংস্থান-বিদ্যা) গর্ভস্থ ভ্রূণের বাহ্যাবরণ-ঝিল্লী। 2. (*Bot.*) The external membrane of the seeds of plants; বীজাবরণ (হঃ চঃ)।

chō'-rist, *n*, One who sings in a chorus; বৃন্দগায়ক। **Chor'-is-ter**, *n.* A member of a choir of singers; a choir-boy; খৃষ্টীয় ধর্ম্ম-মন্দিরস্থ গায়কদলভুক্ত ব্যক্তি; খৃষ্টীয় ধর্ম্ম মন্দিরস্থ বালক গায়ক।

chō-rŏg'-ră-phȳ, *n.* Art of describing or mapping a particular region or district; কোন বিশেষ ভূখণ্ড বা বিভাগের বর্ণন বা মানচিত্রাঙ্কণ-কৌশল, প্রদেশবর্ণন (আঃ বঃ)। **—pher**, *n.* **—ro-graph'-ic, —ro-graph'-i-cal**, *adjs.* **—ro-graph'-i-cal-ly**, *adv.*

chō'-roid (-royd), *n.* One of the membranes of the eye; অক্ষি-গোলকাবরক শিরাত্মক ঝিল্লীবিশেষ, কৃষ্ণ-পটল (সাঃ পঃ)।

chō-rŏl'-ō-ğȳ, *n.* The science of geographical distribution of plants and animals; যে শাস্ত্রে জন্তু এবং উদ্ভিদের ভৌগোলিক সংস্থান বিষয় আলোচিত হয়। **—gist**, *n.*

chŏr'-tle, *v. i.* টিপি হাসা।

chō'-rŭs, *n.*, *v. t.* & *i.* 1. *Antiq.*) A band of dancers and singers in religious ceremonies and dramatic performances; also the song sung by them; (গ্রীসদেশীয় প্রত্নতত্ত্ব) প্রাচীন গ্রীসদেশের রঙ্গমণ্ডপ বা ধর্ম্মানুষ্ঠানের গায়ক এবং নর্ত্তক সম্প্রদায়, বৃন্দ (সংগীতঃ); উক্ত সম্প্রদায়দ্বারা গীত সঙ্গীত। 2. A personage who speaks the prologue and comments upon the course of events in Elizabethan drama; রাজ্ঞী এলিজাবেথের সাময়িক নাটকের যে ব্যক্তি প্রস্তাবনাবর্ণন এবং ঘটনা সমূহের সমালোচনা করিত, পার্শ্বস্থ (মঃ উঃ), পারিপার্শ্বিক (ঐ)। 3. A number of persons singing in concert; a choir; ঐক্যতান সঙ্গীত-সম্প্রদায়, বৃন্দগায়ক (সংগীতঃ); খৃষ্টীয় ধর্ম্ম মন্দিরস্থ গায়ক সম্প্রদায়। 4. The burden of a song in which the audience joins; (সঙ্গীত-শাস্ত্র) ধ্রুপদ, ধূয়া, ধ্রুবক, ধ্রুব। *Verb t.* 1. To sing or utter in chorus; সমস্বরে গান করা, মিলিতস্বরে গান করা। 2. To sing the chorus of; (*fig.*) to add an expression of assent, etc. (to another's utterances); কোন সঙ্গীতের ধূয়া গান করা; (লক্ষণায়) ধূয়া করা। *Verb i.* To sing in chorus; to exclaim simultaneously; সমস্বরে গান করা; একযোগে চীৎকার করা।

chose (shōz), *n.* (*Law*) A thing; a piece of personal property (আইন) বস্তু; ব্যক্তিগত সম্পত্তি বিশেষ। **Chose in possession**—প্রকৃতপক্ষে কোন ব্যক্তির অধিকারগত বস্তু।

chou (shōō), *n.* (*Pl.* CHOUX, shōō) A bunch or ornamental knot of ribbon, chiffon, etc. used in woman's dress; স্ত্রীলোকের পরিচ্ছদে ব্যবহৃত কারুকার্য্য সমন্বিত ফিতা প্রভৃতির গ্রন্থি।

chough (chŭf), *n.* A red-legged crow; রক্তপাদ কাক বিশেষ।

chouse (chows), *v. t.* & *n.* To trick ; to swindle, (*of, out of*) ; চাতুরী করা ; ঠকাইয়া লওয়া। ***Noun.*** **1.** A swindler ; a cheat ; a dupe ; জুয়াচোর ; ঠক, প্রতারক, বঞ্চক ; যে ব্যক্তি সহজে প্রতারিত হয়, হবুচন্দ্র। **2.** A trick ; swindle ; sham ; চাতুরী, ছল, কূট ; জুয়াচুরি ; ফাঁকি, ব্যাজ।

chow, *adj.* & *n.* Chinese ; (also *n.*) চীন দেশীয় (লোক)। ***Noun.*** A dog of Chinese bread ; চীনা কুকুর।

chow′-chow, *n.* A Chinese term for any mixture, but in trade circles confined generally to mixed pickles ; মিশ্র ; বিভিন্ন ফলের মিশ্রিত আচার।

chow′-dêr, *n.* A dish made of fresh fish or clams stewed with slices of pork, onions, etc. ; মৎস্য, পলাণ্ডু, শূকর-মাংস-খণ্ড প্রভৃতি সহযোগে প্রস্তুত ব্যঞ্জন বিশেষ।

chow′-ry, *n.* [Hindi, *chaumri*, Skr. *chamar*] A whisk or fly-flapper, made of hair or feather ; চামর, বাল-ব্যজন।

chrē-mă-tis′-tic, *adj.* Of, pertaining to, or occupied in, money-making ; economic ; অর্থসংগ্রহ-সম্পৃক্ত, অর্থসংগ্রহে রত ; অর্থব্যবহার-ঘটিত। **Chrem-a-tis′-tics,** *n.* Political economy ; ধনবিজ্ঞান, অর্থশাস্ত্র।

chrĕs-tō′-măth′-ic, *adj.* Teaching what is useful ; আবশ্যকবিষয়-শিক্ষাপ্রদায়ী।

chrĕs-tŏm′-ă-thy, *n.* A collection of choice passages, esp. with notes, to be used in acquiring a language ; উৎকৃষ্ট রচনাবলী সংগ্রহ।

chrism, *n.* **1.** Consecrated oil, or unguent, used in sacred rites ; ধর্ম্ম কার্য্যে ব্যবহৃত পবিত্র তৈল, বিলেপন প্রভৃতি, অভ্যঞ্জন (মঃ ইঃ)। **2.** A sacramental anointing ; unction ; দীক্ষাসময়ে ব্যবহৃত পবিত্র তৈলাদি ; পূত তৈলাদিদ্বারা অভ্যঞ্জন। **Chris′-mal,** *adj.* **Chris′-ma-to-ry,** *n.* A vessel containing the chrism ; পূত তৈল পাত্র।

chris′-om (-ŭm), *n.* A white robe, put on a child at baptism as a token of innocence ; also used as a shroud if the child died within a month from baptism ; শুভ্র-চিত্তের চিহ্ন স্বরূপ দীক্ষাকালে শিশুকে যে শ্বেতপরিচ্ছদ পরিধান করান হয় ; দীক্ষাপ্রাপ্তির মাসকাল মধ্যে মৃত শিশুর শবাচ্ছাদন বস্ত্র। **Chrisom-babe**—এক মাসের অনধিক বয়স্ক শিশু ; নির্ম্মল চিত্ত শিশু।

Christ, (krīst), *n.* **1.** The Messiah or Lord anointed ; মেসায়া, অভিষিক্ত প্রভু (যাঁহার আগমনের কথা ইয়ুদীদিগের ভাববাণীতে উল্লিখিত আছে—এবং ইয়ুদীগণ যাঁহার অবতরণের প্রতীক্ষা করিতেছে)। **2.** A title (now treated as a name) given to Jesus as fulfilling this prophecy and expectation ; যীশু খৃষ্ট। **3.** A divine ruler ; a saviour ; "Each man must be his own *Christ* or he is no Christian ;" দৈবপ্রেরিত শাসনকর্ত্তা ; ত্রাণকর্ত্তা। **Christ′-hood,** *n.* **Christ′-less,** *adj.* Without Christ or his spirit ; unchristian ; খৃষ্টবিরহিত, খৃষ্টস্বভাব শূন্য ; অখৃষ্টান। **Christ′-like,** *adj.* Like Christ ; exhibiting the spirit of Christ ; খৃষ্টতুল্য ; খৃষ্টস্বভাব। **Christ′-ly,** *adj.* **Christ-cross, Criss-cross** — ক্রুশচিহ্ন, ঢেঁড়াসহি। **Christ-cross-row**—বর্ণমালা।

chris′-ten (krĭsn), *v. t.* & *i.* **1.** To initiate into the Christian church by baptism ; to baptize ; খৃষ্টধর্ম্মে দীক্ষিত করা ; দীক্ষিত করা। **2.** To receive a name at baptism ; দীক্ষাকালে নাম প্রাপ্ত হওয়া। **3.** To give a name to ; to call by the name of ; as, they have *christened* a river after Mr. Whymper ; নামকরণ করা ; কোন বিশেষ নামে ডাকা, অভিহিত করা। **4.** To name and dedicate (bells, ships, etc.) by a ceremony likened to baptism ; দীক্ষার অনুরূপ ক্রিয়াদ্বারা ঘণ্টা, জাহাজ প্রভৃতি নামকরণ করা বা উৎসর্গীকৃত করা। ***Verb i.*** To administer baptism ; to perform the rite of baptism ; জল সংস্কার দ্বারা খৃষ্ট ধর্ম্মে দীক্ষাদান করা ; জল সংস্কার দ্বারা দীক্ষা কার্য্য সম্পাদন করা।

Chris′-ten-dom (krĭsn-dŭm), *n* **1.** The countries professing Christianity taken collectively ; খৃষ্টধর্ম্মাবলম্বী জাতিসমূহের অধ্যুষিত দেশ সমূহ, খৃষ্টীয় দেশ সমূহ, খৃষ্ট রাজ্য। **2.** The whole body of Christians ; the church ; নিখিল খৃষ্ট ধর্ম্মাবলম্বিগণ ; খৃষ্টীয় ধর্ম্মাবলম্বিসমাজ।

Chris′-tiăn (krĭs-), *n.* & *adj.* **1.** One who believes or professes the religion of Christ ; an adherent of Christianity ; খৃষ্টধর্ম্মাবলম্বী ; খৃষ্টান। **2.** (*Colloq.*) A human being as distinguished from a brute ; a respectable person ; (চলিত ভাষায়) মানব ; সম্ভ্রান্ত ব্যক্তি। ***Adj.*** **1.** Pertaining to Christ or his religion ; খৃষ্ট বা তদীয় ধর্ম্মসম্বন্ধীয়। **2.** Following the examples and precepts of Christ ; Christ-like ; kindly ; as, *Christian* piety ; খৃষ্টের দৃষ্টান্ত বা উপদেশ অনুসরণকারী ; খৃষ্ট তুল্য ; করুণাপরবশ। **3.** (*Colloq.*) Civilized ; respectable ; decent ; as, *Christian* food, weapons ; (চলিতভাষায়) সুসভ্য ; সম্ভ্রান্ত ; ভদ্রোচিত। **–ism,** *n.* A Christianity of a sort or form ; খৃষ্টানি। **–i-za′-tion,** *n.* **–ize,** *v. t.* **–ly,** *adj.* & *adv.* **–ti-an′-i-ty,** *n.* **1.** The Christian religion ; খৃষ্টধর্ম্ম, খৃষ্টীয় মত। **2.** Christian condition or quality ; Christian spirit or character ; খৃষ্টধর্ম্মাবলম্বীর অবস্থা বা গুণ ; খৃষ্টধর্ম্মাবলম্বীর ভাব বা প্রকৃতি। **Christian name**—দীক্ষানাম ; ব্যক্তিগত নাম (উপনাম বা পারিবারিক নাম হইতে পৃথক)। **Christian era**—খৃষ্টাব্দ। **Christian science**—চিকিৎসা বিনা কেবল খৃষ্টান-সমুচিত বিশ্বাসবলে রোগপ্রতীকারের প্রণালী বিশেষ। [বোষ্টন নগরবাসিনী Mrs. Eddy কর্ত্তৃক প্রতিষ্ঠিত।

See "*Mesmerism and Christian Science*" by F. Podmore.]

christ′-măs, *n.* & *adj.* (CHRISTMAS DAY) The festival of the Nativity of Christ observed by the Christian church yearly on the 25th December ; খৃষ্টমাস পর্ব্ব, বড়দিন। ***Adj.*** Appropriate to Christmas ; as, *Christmas* book or card ; খৃষ্টমাস পর্ব্বোপলক্ষে ব্যবহারোপযোগী। **Christmas box**—বড়দিন পর্ব্বোপলক্ষে সরকারী কর্ম্মচারীকে (পোলিশ কর্ম্মচারী, ডাকপিয়ন প্রভৃতিকে) যে উপহার বা পারিতোষিক প্রদান করা হয় ; বড়দিনের উপহারপূর্ণ পেটক। **Christmas card**—বড়দিন উপলক্ষে বন্ধু বন্ধুকে যে সমুজ্জলচিত্রশোভিত কার্ড প্রেরণ করে। **Christmas eve**—বড়দিনের পূর্ব্ব-সন্ধ্যা। **Christmas flower, rose**—গুলদাউদি (খোরী), সেবন্তিকা (ঐ), কটুরোহিনী (ঐ)। **Christmas gift**—বড়দিনের উপহার। **Christmas tide**—বড়দিনের সময়। **Christmas tree**—খৃষ্টমাস পর্ব্বোপলক্ষে গৃহ মধ্যে স্থাপিত চিরহবিত তরুবিশেষ—ইহা দীপালোকিত, নানাভূষাবিমণ্ডিত ও বিবিধ উপহারদ্রব্যে সুশোভিত করা হইয়া থাকে।

chris-tŏl′-ă-trȳ, *n.* Worship of Christ as divine ; খৃষ্টপূজা।

chris-tŏl′-ŏ-ġy, *n.* **1.** The branch of Christian theology which treats of the person of Christ ; খৃষ্টীয় ধর্ম্মশাস্ত্রের খৃষ্টতত্ত্ব সম্বন্ধীয় শাখা।

chrŏ′-mă-scōpe, *n.* An instrument for showing the optical effects of colour ; রঙ্গদর্শক (হিঃ কোঃ)।

chrō-măt′-ic, *adj.* **1.** Relating to colour ; রঙ্গসম্বন্ধীয় (হিঃ কোঃ), বর্ণ-বিষয়ক (ঐ)। **2.** Highly coloured ; সুরঞ্জিত। **3.** (*Mus.*) Including notes not belonging to the diatonic scale ; (সঙ্গীত-শাস্ত্র) ত্রয়োদশ স্বরবিশিষ্ট, গ্রামিক। **—i-cal-ly,** *adv.* **Chromatic printing**—রঙ্গীন ছাপাই (হিঃ কোঃ), নানাবর্ণের কালিতে চিত্র প্রভৃতি মুদ্রণ। **Chromatic scale**—ত্রয়োদশ স্বরশ্রেণী (হিঃ কোঃ), বিকৃত স্বরশ্রেণী (মিউজিক)।

chrō-măt′-ics, *n.* The science of colours ; রশ্মিরঙ্গ শাস্ত্র (হিঃ কোঃ)।

chrō-mă-tŏg′-ră-phȳ, *n.* A treatise on colours ; বর্ণবিদ্যা বিষয়ক পুস্তক।

chrō-mă-tŏl′-ŏ-ġy, *n.* The science of, or a treatise on, colours ; রঙ্গ-বিদ্যা, রঙ্গ-বিদ্যা বিষয়ক পুস্তক।

chrō-mă-tŏp′-sȳ, *n.* Any abnormally coloured vision ; অস্বাভাবিক-রূপে রঞ্জিত দৃশ্য।

chrō′-mă-trōpe, *n.* An arrangement in a magic-lantern, consisting of a slide of two circular disks, brilliantly coloured, one of which is made to rotate in front of the other, producing kaleidoscopic movement of colours ; ম্যাজিক-লণ্ঠনের ব্যবস্থা বিশেষ, ইহাতে সমুজ্জলবর্ণে রঞ্জিত দুইটী গোলাকার কাচ-খণ্ড থাকে, ইহারা পরস্পরের সম্মুখে ঘূর্ণিত হইয়া বহুরূপপ্রদর্শক যন্ত্রের মত বর্ণলীলা প্রদর্শন করে ; বর্ণভ্রামক যন্ত্র (হিঃ কোঃ), বিবিধরঙ্গী চক্র (ঐ)।

chro′-mă-tȳpe, *n.* (*Photog.*) A process for procuring coloured photographs ; রঙ্গীন ছায়াচিত্র তুলিবার প্রণালী।

chrōme (krōm), *n.* **1.** The metal chromium ; ক্রোমিয়াম ধাতু, ক্রোম (হিঃ কোঃ)। **2.** A yellow pigment and colour ; পীতবর্ণ, পীতবর্ণরঞ্জক পদার্থ।

chrō′-mic, *adj.* Pertaining to chromium ; ক্রমিয়াম্ ধাতু সম্বন্ধীয়।

chrō′-mīte, *n.* (*Min.*) A black submetallic mineral consisting of oxide of chromium and iron ; (খনিজ বিদ্যা) একপ্রকার খনিজ পদার্থ।

chrō′-mi-ŭm, *n.* A greyish white metallic element ; ক্রোমিয়াম ধাতু, ক্রোম (হিঃ কোঃ)।

chrō′-mō-grăph, *n.* & *v. t.* An apparatus for multiplying copies of written matter ; হস্তলিখিত বিষয়ের বহু প্রতিলিপি তুলিবার যন্ত্রবিশেষ। ***Verb t.*** To copy by this ; উক্তযন্ত্রের সাহায্যে প্রতিলিপি তোলা।

chrō-mō-lith′-ŏ-grăph, *n.* A picture printed in colours from stone ; পাষাণ-ফলক হইতে মুদ্রিত নানাবর্ণে রঞ্জিত আলেখ্য বিশেষ। **—graph′-ic,** *adj.* **—li-thog′-ra-pher,** *n.* **—li-thog′-ra-phy,** *n.* The art of printing in colours from stone ; পাষাণ-ফলক হইতে নানাবর্ণের চিত্রমুদ্রণবিদ্যা।

chrom-ŏ-phō′-tō-grăph, *n.* A photograph in natural colours ; স্বাভাবিকবর্ণের আলোকচিত্র। **—tog′-ra-phy,** *n.* Colour photography ; স্বাভাবিকবর্ণে আলোকচিত্র তুলিবার বিদ্যা।

chrō′-mō-sphēre, *n.* (*Astron.*) The red gaseous envelope round the sun ; (জ্যোতির্বিজ্ঞান) সূর্য্যের চতুর্দ্দিকস্থ লোহিতবর্ণ বাষ্পীয়মণ্ডল, বর্ণ-মণ্ডল (হিঃ কোঃ)।

chrŏn′-ic, *adj.* & *n.* **1.** Lasting a long time ; as, *chronic* disease ; inveterate ; as, *chronic* sufferer, grumbler, etc. ; (রোগাদি সম্পর্কে) দীর্ঘস্থায়ী, চিরকালিক, পুরাতন (হঃ চঃ), প্রাচীন (হঃ চঃ), দৈর্ঘ্যরাত্রিক (চঃ), চির-কালিক (হিঃ কোঃ) ; স্থিরপ্রতিষ্ঠ, বদ্ধমূল **2.** Constant ; as, *chronic* horror of anything ; ক্রমাগত, অবিরত, নিয়ত। **3.** (*Vulg.*) Bad ; dreadful ; severe ; (ইতরভাষায়) বদ্, ভয়ঙ্কর, গুরুতর। ***Noun.*** A chronic invalid or sufferer ; পুরাতন রোগী। **—i-cal-ly,** *adv.* **Chronic disease**—পুরাতন রোগ, চিররোগ (হিঃ কোঃ)।

chrŏn′-i-cle, *n.* & *v. t.* **1.** A continuous register of events in order of time ; a historical record ; সময়ানুক্রমিক লিখিত বিবরণ, কালানুক্রমিক বৃত্তান্ত ; ঐতিহাসিক দলিল **2.** A narrative ; account ; বৃত্তান্ত বিবরণ। **3.** A title of newspapers ; as, the daily *chronicle* ; সংবাদ-পত্রের উপাধি বিশেষ। ***Verb t.*** To enter or record in a chronicle ; ধারাবাহিকভাবে লিপিবদ্ধ করা। **—cler,** *n*

A writer or compiler of a chronicle; a recorder of events; ধারাবাহিক বিবরণ লেখক; বৃত্তান্ত লেখক, ইতিবৃত্ত লেখক। **To chronicle small beer**—To register or notify insignificant events; সামান্য সামান্য ঘটনা লিপিবদ্ধ বা বিজ্ঞাপিত করা।

chronique scandaleuse*—*n. A body of scandalous gossips current at any time and place; কুৎসা রাশি।

c̲h̲rŏn′-ō-grăm, *n.* A phrase, sentence or inscription in which certain letters (usually made conspicuous) express by their numerical values a date or epoch; as, LorD haVe MerCIe Vpon Vs = 50 + 500 + 5 + 1000 + 100 + 1 + 5 + 5 (the date 1666); কোন বাক্য, পদ বা শিলালিপি,—যাহাতে কতিপয় (সাধারণতঃ) সুস্পষ্ট অক্ষরনিচয়ের সংখ্যাঘটিত মানদ্বারা কোন তারিখ বা অব্দ নির্দ্দেশিত হয়। **—mat′-ic, —mat′-i-cal,** *adjs.*

c̲h̲rŏn′-ō-grăph, *n.* An instrument recording time with extreme accuracy; a stop-watch; সময়নির্ণায়কযন্ত্র; একপ্রকার টেঁক্‌ঘড়ী। **—graph′-ic, —graph′-i-cal,** *adjs.*

c̲h̲rō-nŏg′-ră-phȳ, *n.* A description or record of past time; history; প্রাচীনকালের বিবরণ বা প্রামাণ্য লিপি; ইতিহাস। **—pher,** *n.*

c̲h̲rō-nŏl′-ō-ġȳ, *n.* **1.** The science of computing dates; arrangement of events with dates; computation of time; কালগণনবিদ্যা, কালনিরূপণ শাস্ত্র, কালক্রমনির্ণয়ন বিদ্যা, কালানুপূর্ব্বদর্শন বিদ্যা; ধারাবাহিকতা; কালগণনা। **2.** A table or treatise displaying this; কালনিরূপণ তালিকা, কালনিরূপণ পুস্তক। **Chron-o-log′-i-cal,** *adj.* **—ger, —gist,** *ns.* One who investigates the date and order in time of events; কালনিরূপক, ঘটনা সমূহের তারিখ এবং পৌর্ব্বাপর্য্য নির্দ্দেশক।

c̲h̲rō-nŏm′-ĕ-tĕr, *n.* An accurate time-keeper; সূক্ষ্মকালদর্শক যন্ত্র (হিঃ কোঃ), নাড়ীমান (সাঃ পঃ)। **Chron-o-met′-ric, Chron-o-met′-ri-cal,** *adjs.* **—try,** *n.*

c̲h̲rŏn′-ō-scōpe, *n.* An instrument for measuring very short intervals of time, and used in determining the velocity of projectiles; সূক্ষ্ম কালমাপক যন্ত্র-বিশেষ (বন্দুক, কামান প্রভৃতির গুলির গতিবেগ নির্দ্ধারণে ব্যবহৃত হয়), কালান্তর জ্ঞাপক (হিঃ কোঃ)।

c̲h̲rȳs′-ă-lis, —lid, *n.* (*Pls.* -LISES, -LIDS, -LIDES) **1.** (*Nat. Hist.*) The stage into which the larva of most insects passes before becoming an imago or perfect insect; (প্রাণি-বিদ্যা) প্রজাপতি প্রভৃতির পক্ষোদ্গমের পূর্ব্বাবস্থা, কোষস্থ (সাঃ পঃ), কোষবাসী। **2.** (*Fig.*) The shell or case whence the perfect insect bursts; (লক্ষণায়) যে খোল বা আধার হইতে পূর্ণাঙ্গ পতঙ্গ বহির্গত হয়। **3.** (*Fig.*) A transition state; (লক্ষণায়) পরিবর্ত্তনাবস্থা। **—lid, —loid,** *adjs.*

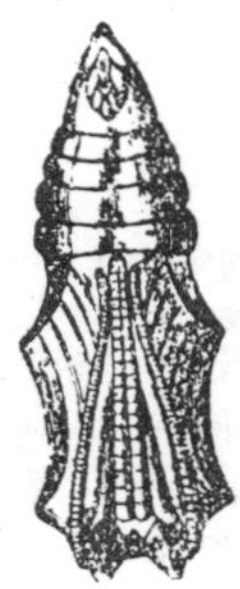

Chrysalis.

Chrysanthemum (Ox-eye-Daisy)
1. Floret of the ray.
2. Floret of the disk.

c̲h̲rȳs-ăn′-thē-mŭm, *n.* A genus of composite plants to which belong the Corn Marigold and Ox-eye Daisy; চন্দ্রমল্লিকাদি, গুল-দাউদী প্রভৃতি পুষ্পবৃক্ষ।

c̲h̲rȳs-ĕl-ĕ-phăn′-tīne, *adj.* Overlaid with gold and ivory, as by ancient Greek sculptors; স্বর্ণ এবং দ্বিরদ-রদ-মণ্ডিত।

c̲h̲rȳs′-ō-bĕr-ȳl, *n.* A yellowish-green gem; পীতাভ হরিদ্বর্ণ মণি-বিশেষ, নারঙ্গা (যোঃ)।

c̲h̲rȳ-sŏg′-ră-phȳ, *n.* **1.** The art of writing in letters of gold; স্বর্ণাক্ষর লিখন-বিদ্যা। **2.** A letter or other writing, executed in letters of gold; স্বর্ণাক্ষর-লিখিত লিপি বা অন্য প্রকার লিখন।

c̲h̲rȳs′-ō-līte, *n.* **1.** (*Formerly*) A name of several different gems of a green colour; (পূর্ব্বে) হরিদ্-বর্ণের বিভিন্ন প্রকার মণি। **2.** (*Now*) The precious olivine; (বর্ত্তমানে) জলপাইএর মত বর্ণবিশিষ্ট বহুমূল্য প্রস্তর বিশেষ।

c̲h̲rȳs′-ō-prāse, *n.* **1.** A apple-green variety of chalcedony; সেওফলের মত সবুজবর্ণ সীসমণি বিশেষ। **2.** (*Formerly*) A golden-green precious stone; (পূর্ব্বে) হেমাভ হরিদ্ বর্ণ বহুমূল্য প্রস্তর বিশেষ, স্বর্ণাঙ্গী।

chŭb, *n.* A common European fresh water fish (little valued as food); ইয়ুরোপ মহাদেশীয় মৎস্যবিশেষ।

chubb (chŭb), *n.* [Also **chubb's lock, chubb lock**] A kind of patent lock; একপ্রকার তালা। [আবিষ্কারক Chubb এর নাম হইতে গৃহীত।]

chŭb′-bȳ, *adj.* Round faced; plump; as, *chubby* cheeks; সুগোল মুখমণ্ডলবিশিষ্ট; গোলগাল, হৃষ্টপুষ্ট, নাদুস্‌নুদুস্। **—bi-ness,** *n.*

chuck (chŭk), *n.* & *v. i.* The call of a hen; মুরগীর ডাক, কুক্কুটধ্বনি। ***Verb i.*** To make a chuckling noise like hen; মুর্গীর মত ডাকা।

chuck (chŭk), *n.* A term of endearment ; as, sweet *chuck* ; আদরের ডাক, যাদুধন।

chuck (chŭk), *v. t.* & *n.* **1.** To strike or give a gentle blow under the chin ; আদর করিয়া চিবুকের নীচে চাপড়ান। **2.** To fling or throw with carelessness and ease ; উদাসীনভাবে বা অনায়াসে ফেলিয়া দেওয়া। ***Noun.*** **1.** A slight sudden tap or blow under the chin ; চিবুকের নীচে মৃদুমৃদু চাপড়। **2.** A toss ; a jerk ; উৎক্ষেপণ ; ঝাঁকুনি। **Chuck-farthing**—Pitch and toss ; মুদ্রাক্ষেপ ক্রীড়া-বিশেষ। (*Slang*) **Chuck it** — Cease ; থাম। **To chuck away**—To waste, lose (chance, etc.) ; অপব্যয় করা, হারান। **To chuck out**—To expel a troublesome person from a meeting, music-hall, etc. ; উপদ্রবকারী ব্যক্তিকে সভা, গীতশালা প্রভৃতি হইতে বাহির করিয়া দেওয়া। **To chuck over**—To discard ; to disinherit ; প্রত্যাখ্যান করা ; উত্তরাধিকারিস্বত্ব হইতে বঞ্চিত করা। **To chuck up**—To abandon in disgust ; বিরক্তির সহিত পরিত্যাগ করা। **To chuck up the sponge**—To give up a contest or attempt ; চেষ্টা বা প্রতিদ্বন্দ্বিতা হইতে নিবৃত্ত হওয়া।

chuck (chŭk), *n.* & *v. t.* A contrivance in lathe and the like for holding work to be operated upon ; কুন্দাদি যন্ত্রমধ্যস্থ ব্যবস্থা বিশেষ—ইহাতে কুন্দিবার সময় বস্তু আরোপিত হয়। ***Verb t.*** To fix (wood etc.) on the lathe ; কুন্দযন্ত্রে কাষ্ঠফলক প্রভৃতি আরোপিত করা।

chuck'-le (chŭkl), *v. i., n.* & *adj.* **1.** To laugh in a suppressed manner ; টিপি টিপি হাসা, মনে মনে হাসা। **2.** To feel inward triumph or exultation ; কোন কার্য্যে সফলতা লাভ করিবার জন্য মনের ভিতর আনন্দ বা উল্লাস ভোগ করা। ***Noun.*** A suppressed laughter ; a laugh of triumph and exultation ; টিপি টিপি হাসি ; বিজয় বা উল্লাসসূচক হাস্য।

chuck'-le, *n.* & *v. t.* Hen's call ; মুরগীর ডাক। ***Verb t.*** To make hen's call ; মুরগীর মত ডাকা।

chuck'-le-head (chŭkl-hĕd) *n.* A blockhead ; a stupid lout ; জড়বুদ্ধিব্যক্তি, গোবর গণেশ।

chuff (chŭf), *n.* A rustic boor ; a surly fellow ; পাড়াগেঁয়ে ; উগ্রপ্রকৃতি লোক। **Chuff'-y,** *adj.*

chŭm, *v. t.* & *n.* To occupy rooms together ; এক কক্ষে বাস করা। ***Noun.*** **1.** A room-mate ; এককক্ষ বাসী। **2.** An intimate friend ; (বন্দী, প্রভৃতি সম্পর্কে) সঙ্গী, অন্তরঙ্গ বন্ধু। **Chum'-mage,** *n.* **1.** The quartering of two or more persons in one room ; এক কক্ষে দুই বা ততোধিক ব্যক্তির বাসনির্দ্দেশ। **2.** The fee demanded from a new chum ; নূতন সঙ্গীর নিকট হইতে যে মাশুল দাবী করা হয়। **Chum'-mer-y,** *n.* The quarters occupied by chums ; কয়েকজন মিলিয়া যে বাটীতে বাস করে, সঙ্গি-নিবাস। **Chum'-my,** *adj.* Intimate ; অন্তরঙ্গ। **New chum** — (অষ্ট্রেলিয়াতে) নূতন ঔপনিবেশক ; নূতন কাঁচা লোক। **To chum one person upon another**—To put as an occupant of the same room ; এক কক্ষবাসী করা। **To chum up with**—To try to make friends with ; বন্ধুত্ব স্থাপনের চেষ্টা করা।

chŭm'-mŷ, *n.* A chimney sweeper's boy ; ধূমনালী-পরিমার্জ্জকের সঙ্গীয় বালক।

chŭmp, *n.* **1.** A short thick piece of wood ; কাঠের কুঁদা। **2.** (*Colloq.*) A block-head ; (চলিতভাষায়) স্থূলবুদ্ধি ব্যক্তি। **3.** Head ; as, off his *chump* ; মস্তক।

chunk (chŭngk) *n.* A thick piece of anything, as wood, meat, etc. ; কোন বস্তুর স্থূল খণ্ড।

church (chêrch), *n., v. t.* & *adj.* **1.** A building set apart for public Christian worship ; (খৃষ্টীয় ধর্ম্মমন্দির, ভজনালয়, গির্জ্জা। **2.** The collective body of Christians ; নিখিল খৃষ্টধর্ম্মাবলম্বিগণ। **3.** The clergy ; যাজক সম্প্রদায়। **4.** A formally organised body of Christian believers worshipping together ; একত্র উপাসনাকারী ব্যবস্থাবদ্ধ খৃষ্টবিশ্বাসী জনসম্প্রদায়। ***Verb t.*** **1.** To bring a woman to a church to have thanks offered for her safe delivery of a child ; কোন স্ত্রীলোকের সুপ্রসবের জন্য ঈশ্বরকে ধন্যবাদ প্রদানার্থ তাহাকে ধর্ম্মমন্দিরে আনয়ন করা। ***Adj.*** Ecclesiastical ; যাজকীয়। **Church'-i-fy,** *v. t.* **Church'-i-ness,** *n.* **Church'-ing,** *n.* **Church'-ly,** *adj.* **Church army**—নিঃস্ব এবং দুশ্চরিত্র ব্যক্তিগণের উদ্ধারসাধনের জন্য ইংলণ্ডীয় ধর্ম্মসমাজের (Church of England) অধীন সম্প্রদায় বিশেষ। **Church-going**—নিত্য ধর্ম্মমন্দিরগামী। **Churchman**—রাজবিধিদ্বারা প্রতিষ্ঠিত খৃষ্টীয় ধর্ম্মসমাজের যাজক ; ধর্ম্মযাজক। **Church militant**—শয়তানের বিরুদ্ধে যুদ্ধে নিরত পৃথিবীবাসী খৃষ্টধর্ম্মাবলম্বী সমাজ। **Church-rate**—ধর্ম্ম মন্দিরের ব্যয় নির্ব্বাহার্থ কর বিশেষ। **Church-service**—খৃষ্টীয় ধর্ম্মমন্দিরের উপাসনা পদ্ধতি ; খৃষ্টীয় ধর্ম্মমন্দিরে ব্যবহৃত প্রার্থনাপুস্তক। **Church-text**—প্রাচীণ ধরণের ইংরাজি অক্ষর। **Church triumphant**—স্বর্গীয় মহিমা-মণ্ডিত নিখিল খৃষ্টীয়সিদ্ধপুরুষগণ। **Church-warden**—খৃষ্টীয় ধর্ম্মমন্দির রক্ষক। (*Colloq.*) A long clay-pipe ; (চলিতভাষায়) একপ্রকার সুদীর্ঘ মৃণ্ময়নল। **Church-woman**—ধর্ম্মসমাজভুক্তা নারী, বিশেষতঃ ইংলণ্ডীয় ধর্ম্মসমাজভুক্তা নারী। A woman who habitually attends church ; যে নারী নিয়মমত খৃষ্টীয় ধর্ম্মমন্দিরের উপাসনাদিতে যোগদান করিয়া থাকেন। **Churchyard**—খৃষ্টীয় ধর্ম্মমন্দিরের প্রাঙ্গণ—ইহার অংশবিশেষ সমাধিক্ষেত্রস্বরূপ ব্যবহৃত হয়। **Established Church** — রাজবিধিদ্বারা প্রতিষ্ঠিত খৃষ্টীয় ধর্ম্মসমাজ। **Fat**

churchyard—বহুজনক্ষয়। **Mother Church**—কোন যাজকপল্লীর আদিম বা প্রধান ধর্ম্মমন্দির; রোমান ক্যাথলিক ধর্ম্মসমাজ এবং ইহার স্বীকৃত শাখা সমূহ। **As poor as a church mouse**—অতীব দরিদ্র। **To go to church**—To attend church service; to get married; ধর্ম্মমন্দিরের উপাসনায় যোগদান করা; বিবাহিত হওয়া।

churl (chêrl), *n.* **1.** A person of low birth; হীনবংশজাত ব্যক্তি। **2.** A peasant; a boor; কৃষক; পাড়াগাঁয়ে লোক। **3.** A selfish miser; as, some rich *churl* hoarding up his wealth; কৃপণ, কঞ্জুস (*colloq.*)। **Churl'-ish,** *adj.* **Churl'-ish-ly,** *adv.* **Churl'-ish-ness,** *n.*

churn (chêrn), *n., v. t.* & *i.* A vessel or machine for making butter; মন্থনভাণ্ড, মন্থনঘটী, মন্থনদণ্ড, মন্থান। ***Verb t.*** **1.** To agitate in churn for the production of butter; নবনীত প্রস্তুত করণার্থ ভাণ্ডস্থ দধি বা সর মন্থন করা। **2.** To agitate with violence or continued motion; মন্থন করা, মথিত করা। ***Verb i.*** To work a churn; মন্থনদণ্ড চালনা করা। **Churn'-ing,** *n.* The act of making butter; মন্থন, মথন, নবনীত প্রস্তুত করণ। **2.** The amount of butter made at once; একবারে যতটা মাখন প্রস্তুত হয়। **Churning-rope**—মন্থনরজ্জু, নেত্র (মঃ ভাঃ)। **Churn-milk**—মাঠা, ঘোল, তক্র। **Churn-staff**—মন্থ, মন্থন, মন্থনদণ্ড।

churr (chêr), *n.* & *v. i.* A low trilled sound; কোন কোন পক্ষীর কম্পনাত্মক মৃদু কূজন। ***Verb i.*** To make such sound; উক্তপ্রকার শব্দ করা।

chŭnt, *interj.* An expression of impatience; তুৎ।

chute (shōōt), *n.* **1.** A fall of water; জলপ্রপাত। **2.** A slope for shooting rubbish down; আবর্জ্জনা নিম্নে নিক্ষেপের জন্য ঢালু।

chut'-ney (nĭ), **—nee** (nē), *n.* An East Indian condiment; চাটনী।

chyle (kīl), *n.* A white milky fluid formed by the action of the pancreatic juice and the bile on the chyme; পিত্ত এবং পাচকরসের ক্রিয়ার ফলে অসম্যক্ পরিপক্ব ভুক্তদ্রব্য যে দুগ্ধবৎ শুভ্র পদার্থে পরিণত হয়, অন্নরস, ধাতুপ (সাঃ.পঃ), পক্করস (হঃ চঃ)। **Chy-li-fac'-tion, —fi-ca'-tion,** *ns.* **Chy'-li-fy,** *v. t.*

chȳ-lü'-ri-â, *n.* A discharge of milky wine; বসামেহ। (এই রোগে 'কাইল' বা অন্নরস মূত্ররূপে নির্গত হয়।)

chyme (kīm), *n.* The pulpy mass of partially digested food in the small intestines after its passage from the stomach; আমাশয়ের ক্রিয়ায় পরিপাচিত মণ্ডবৎ অর্দ্ধজীর্ণ ভুক্ত দ্রব্য, আমরস (হিঃ কোঃ)।

chȳm'-ic, —ist, *n.* See CHEMIST.

cī-bō'-ri-ŭm, *n.* **1.** (*Arch.*) A insulated arched vault on four columns; (স্থপতি-বিদ্যা) স্তম্ভ-চতুষ্টয়োপরিধৃত খিলানবিশিষ্ট ছাদ। **2.** (*R. C. Ch.*) The coffer or case in which the Host is kept; (রোমান-ক্যাথলিক ধর্ম্মসমাজ) যে পেটক বা আধারে খৃষ্টের রক্ত ও মাংসে পরিণত সুরা ও রুটিকা রক্ষিত হয়।

Pupa of the cicada.

Larva of the cicada.

cĭ-cā'-dă, —cā'-lă, *n.* An insect remarkable for its chirping sound; উইচিমড়ে (সাঃ পঃ)।

cĭc'-ă-trice (-trĭs), **—trix,** *n.* **1.** The scar of a healed wound; আরোগ্যান্তে ক্ষতের যে দাগ থাকে, ক্ষত-চিহ্ন (হঃ চঃ), শুষ্কব্রণ (আঃ বঃ)। **2.** A scar on the bark of a tree; বৃক্ষবল্কলোপরিস্থ ক্ষতচিহ্ন। **—tri'-cial, —cose,** *adjs.* **—tri-za'-tion,** *n.* The process of healing over; ত্বগুৎপাদন প্রক্রিয়া। **—trize,** *v. t.* & *i.* **1.** To heal a wound, sore, etc., by inducing a scar; শুষ্ক করিয়া ক্ষতাদি আরোগ্য করা। **2.** To mark with scars; ক্ষতচিহ্নে চিহ্নিত করা। (*Verb i.*) To become healed or covered with skin; ক্ষতাদি আরোগ্য হওয়া, ক্ষতাদি নবোদ্গত চর্ম্মদ্বারা আচ্ছাদিত হওয়া।

cĭc'-ă-tri-cle, —cūle, *ns.* A round white spot on the surface of the yolk-bag of a birds' egg; পক্ষিডিম্বের পীতাংশের আবরণোপরি শ্বেতবর্ণ গোলাকার চিহ্ন বিশেষ।

cĭc'-ē-lȳ, *n.* (*Pl.* -LIES) A genus of umbelliferous plants, allied to *chervil*; আতরী-লালের অনুরূপ ছত্রপুষ্পক উদ্ভিদের 'গণ' বিশেষ।

Cicer ărietinum — Chickpea; বুট, চনক।

cĭ-cē-rō'-nē, *n.* & *v. t.* A guide who shows and explains the antiquities or curiosities of a place to strangers; বিদেশীয়দিগকে কোন স্থানের প্রত্নদ্রব্য বা কৌতুকসামগ্রী প্রদর্শক বা ব্যাখ্যাকারক। ***Verb t.*** To act as a guide to; to show the sights to; প্রদর্শকের কার্য্য করা; দ্রষ্টব্য বস্তু সমূহ প্রদর্শন করান।

cĭc-ē-rō'-ni-ăn, *adj.* & *n.* Pertaining to or after the manner of Cicero; eloquent; প্রাচীন রোমনগরীর সুপ্রসিদ্ধ বক্তা সিসিরোসম্বন্ধীয় বা তদনুবর্ত্তী; বাগ্মিতাপূর্ণ। ***Noun.*** An admirer or imitator of Cicero's style; সিসিরোর রচনাপদ্ধতির অনুকরণকারী বা প্রশংসাকারী।

cicis be o, (*It.*), *n.* (*Pl.* CICISBEI) The recognized gallant of a married woman; a dangler about woman; জার, উপপতি; নাগর। **—ism,** *n.*

Cid (sîd), *n.* (*Sp.* chief, commander; *Ar.* Seyid, lord) **1.** A title given in Spanish literature to Ruy Diaz, count of Bivar, a champion of Christianity against the Moors in the 11th century; স্পেনদেশীয় Ruy Diaz নামক মহাবীরের উপাধি। ইনি একাদশ শতাব্দীতে মুরদিগের অত্যাচার হইতে খৃষ্টধর্ম্মাবলম্বীগণকে রক্ষা করিয়াছেন। [See Southey's *Chronicles of Cid*] **2.** An epic celebrating his exploits; উক্ত বীরের বীরত্ব-কাহিনীপূর্ণ মহাকাব্য। [See translation of *Cid* by T. Ormsby.]

cī'-dêr, *n.* A beverage made from the juice of apples expressed and fermented; সেওফলের রস হইতে প্রস্তুত মদিরা বিশেষ। **Cider-press**—সেওফল হইতে রস নিষ্কর্ষণের জন্য যন্ত্রবিশেষ।

cī-dĕ-vant' (-vŏng), (*F.*), Former; late; পূর্ব্ববর্ত্তী, পূর্ব্বতন; ভূতপূর্ব্ব।

cĭ-gâr', *n.* A compact roll of tobacco leaves for smoking; সিগার, চুরুট। **Cigar-holder**—চুরুটের নল।

cĭg-ă-rette' (-rĕt), *n.* A little roll of finely cut tobacco rolled up usually in thin papers, used for smoking; সরু চুরুট, সিগারেট।

cĭl'-i-ȧ, *n.* **1.** (*Anat.*) The eye lashes; (শারীরসংস্থান-বিদ্যা) পক্ষ্ম, চক্ষুর পাতার লোম। **2.** (*Bot.*) Long hairs on the margin of a plant, leaf, etc.; (উদ্ভিদ্-বিদ্যা) বৃক্ষপত্রাদির কিনারার লম্বা শূঙ্গা। **3.** (*Phys.*) Minute hairlike organs or appendages found on the tissues of some animals; (শারীর-বিজ্ঞান) অধিকাংশ জন্তুর বিধানতন্তুর সূক্ষ্ম কেশবৎ অঙ্গ বা উপাঙ্গ। **—ate, —at-ed,** *adjs.* **—a'-tion,** *n.* **—ry,** *adj.*

cil'-ice (sĭ-lĭs), *n.* A kind of haircloth; লোমনির্ম্মিত বস্ত্র বিশেষ।

Cim-mē'-ri-ăn (sĭm-), *adj.* Of or belonging to the Cimmerians; gloomy; extremely dark; সীমিরী-নামক জাতি সম্বন্ধীয় (প্রাচীন গ্রীকদিগের মতে ঐ জাতি চিরান্ধকারে বাস করিত); অন্ধতমসাচ্ছন্ন; ঘনান্ধকারাবৃত।

cĭn-chō'-nă, *n.* **1.** A genous of trees some of which yield bark

Cinchona.

from which quinine is obtained; একজাতীয় বৃক্ষশ্রেণী—ইহাদের কোন কোন বৃক্ষের বন্ধল হইতে কুইনাইন প্রস্তুত হয়। **2.** The bark itself; উক্ত বৃক্ষসমূহের বন্ধল। **—nism,** *n.* **—nize,** *v. t.*

Cin-cĭn-nā'-tŭs (sĭn-), *n.* A great man in retirement who can be called on in a crisis; অবসরপ্রাপ্ত পুরুষ শ্রেষ্ঠ—যাহাকে মহাশঙ্কটকালে আহ্বান করা যাইতে পারে। [রোমীয় বীর Cincinnatus জাতীয়শঙ্কটকালে হলচালন কার্য্য পরিত্যাগ করিয়া স্বদেশের আহ্বানে দেশনায়কের পদ গ্রহণ করেন।]

cinc'-tūre (sĭngk-), *v. t.* & *n.* **1.** To surround, as with a girdle; to encircle; মেখলাবৎ বেষ্টিত করা; বেষ্টিত করা। ***Noun.*** A belt; a girdle for the waist (*poet.*); কটিবন্ধ; মেখলা, রসনা, চন্দ্রহার, কাঞ্চী। **2.** An inclosure; বেষ্টিতস্থলী। **3.** (*Arch.*) A ring or list at the top and bottom of the shaft of a column; (স্থপতি-বিদ্যা) স্তম্ভের উর্দ্ধ বা নিম্নদেশস্থ বন্ধ বা বেষ্টিকা। **—tured,** *adj.*

cĭn'-dêr, *n.* **1.** The refuse or dross thrown off from iron or other metals in the furnace; গলিত লৌহাদি ধাতু হইতে যে অসার মলভাগ চুল্লীতে পতিত হয়, ধাতুমল। **2.** The residue of coal, wood, etc., after it has ceased to flame or burn; অঙ্গার। **3.** (*Pl.*) Ashes; ভস্ম। **4.** (*Slang*) Brandy, whiskey, etc. taken in tea, soda-water, etc.; (ইতর-ভাষায়) চা, সোডা, প্রভৃতির সহিত যে ব্রাণ্ডি, হুইস্কি, ইত্যাদি পান করা হয়। **—y,** *adj.* **Cinder-path**—ধাতুমলদ্বারা সমাচ্ছাদিত পাদচারণ পথ। **Cinder-sifter**—ভস্ম হইতে অঙ্গার পৃথক করিবার চালুনি বিশেষ।

Cĭn-dêr-ĕl'-lă (sĭn-), *n.* **1.** A person of unrecognized merit or beauty; যে ব্যক্তির গুণ বা সৌন্দর্য্য জনসমাজে আদৃত হয় নাই। **2.** The heroine of a fairy tale; a scullery maid; উপকথা বিশেষের নায়িকা; যে পরিচারিকা বাসন মাজা, রান্নাঘর ঝাঁট দেওয়া প্রভৃতি নীচকার্য্য সম্পন্ন করে। [বালিকা Cinderella মলিনবেশে গৃহস্থালীর নীচকার্য্যে নিযুক্ত থাকিত—এদিকে তাহার বৈমাত্রেয় অগ্রজাগণ সুন্দর সুন্দর পোষাক পরিয়া বলনাচে নৃত্য করিতে যাইত। অবশেষে একজন পরী তাহাকে মোহনবেশে সজ্জিত করত, রাজপ্রাসাদের বলনাচে লইয়া যান, তথায় রাজপুত্র তাহার প্রেমে পতিত হন।] **Cinderella dance**—যে নাচের মজলিস্ মধ্যরাত্রে বন্ধ হয়।

cĭn-ē-măt'-ō-grăph, *n.* See KINEMATOGRAPH.

cĭn-ē-rā'-ri-ă, *n.* A bright flowered composite plant, grown chiefly as green-house or window plants; একপ্রকার উজ্জ্বল বর্ণ বিশিষ্ট পুষ্পপ্রসূ বৃক্ষ—ইহা প্রধানতঃ হরিদ্গৃহ এবং বাতায়ন নিম্নে জন্মান হয়।

cĭn'-ĕr-ă-rȳ, *adj.* Pertaining to ashes; ভস্ম সম্বন্ধীয়, ভাস্ম। **Ce-ner-a'-tion,** *n.* The reducing of anything to ashes by combustion; ভস্মীকরণ। **—e-ra'-ri-um,** *n.* A place for depositing the ashes of the dead after cremation; শবদাহের পর যে স্থানে ভস্ম সঞ্চিত হয়।

Cinerary urn, vase — ভস্ম-রক্ষণ পাত্র।

cĭ-nĕ'-rĕ-ous (-ŭs), *adj.* Ash-coloured ; ashen-grey ; (*said of bird or plumage*) ; ভস্মবর্ণ ; ভস্ম-ধূসর।

Cin-ga-lese' (sĭng-gă-lēz), *n.* & *adj.* A native or language of Ceylon ; সিংহল দ্বীপবাসী ; সিংহল দ্বীপের ভাষা। ***Adj.*** Belonging to Ceylon ; সিংহল সম্বন্ধীয়।

cingulum, (*F.*), *n.* (*Zool.* & *Anat.*) A girdle ; (জন্তুতত্ত্ব এবং শারীর-সংস্থান-বিদ্যা) বেষ্টনী।

cĭn'-nă-bâr, *n.* & *adj.* Red mercuric sulphide or vermilion ; রস-সিন্দূর (হিঃ কোঃ), হিঙ্গুল (রঃ প্রঃ), মণিরাগজ (ঐ), শুকতুণ্ডক (ঐ), চীনেসিন্দূর। **—ba-rine,** *adj.*

cĭn'-nă-mŏn, *n.* & *adj.* A well-known aromatic bark from a tree which abounds in Ceylon ;

Cinnamon.

দারুচিনি, বিজ্জুল (আপ্তে), গন্ধবল্কল (আঃ বঃ), দারুসিতা (ঐ)। ***Adj.*** Cinnamon-coloured ; দারুচিনিবর্ণ। **—mon'-ic, —mom'-ic,** *adjs.* **Cinnamon stone**—পীত বা কপিশবর্ণ বৈক্রান্তমনি, শিখরি। ***Cinnamomum***—দারুচিনি (বেলঃ)। ***Cinnamomum albiflorum***—ডালচিনি। ***Cinnamomum nitidum*** — তেজপাতা।

cinque (sĭngk), *n.* The number five in dice or cards ; তাস বা পাশার পাঞ্জা। **Cinque'-foil,** *n.* (*Bot.*) **1.** A genus of plants with compound leaf of five leaflets ; (উদ্ভিদ-বিদ্যা) পঞ্চপত্রী, পঞ্চপর্ণী। **2.** (*Arch.*) An ornamental foliation having five points or cusps, used in windows, panels, etc. ; (স্থপতি-বিদ্যা) বাতায়ন প্রভৃতির কারুকার্য্যখচিত পঞ্চদল-পুষ্পাকৃতি ভূষা বিশেষ। **Cinque Ports**—ইংলণ্ডের দক্ষিণ পূর্ব্বকোণে অবস্থিত পঞ্চবন্দর। [Sandwich, Dover, Hythe, Romney and Hastings.]

cinquecente, *n.* The Italian style of art, architecture, (of the 16th century) characterised by a reversion to chemical form ; (ষোড়শ শতাব্দীতে) ইটালী দেশীয় কলা বা স্থাপত্যরীতি।

cĭ'-phêr, cÿ'-phêr, *n., v. i.* & *t.* **1.** The arithmetical character **0** ; শূন্য অঙ্ক। **2.** A nonentity ; নগণ্য ব্যক্তি, সাক্ষীগোপাল। **3.** Any Arabic numeral ; a figure ; ১, ২, ৩ প্রভৃতি যে কোন সংখ্যা ; অঙ্ক। **4.** Interlaced initials of person, company, etc. ; কোন সম্প্রদায় বা ব্যক্তির নামের জড়িত আদ্যক্ষর সমূহ। **5.** A secret writing ; গূঢ়লিপি, গূঢ়াক্ষর, গুপ্তলিপি। ***Verb i.*** **1.** To do sums in arithmetic ; পাটীগণিতের অঙ্ক কষা। **2.** To calculate ; গণনা করা। ***Verb t.*** To put into secret writing ; গুপ্ত অক্ষরে লিপিবদ্ধ করা।

Cir-cas'-sian (sêr-căsh-ăn), *adj.* Pertaining to Circasia in Asia ; সারকাসিয়া দেশীয়। ***Noun.*** **1.** A native of Circasia ; সারকাসিয়া দেশবাসী। **2.** (*l.c.*) A woollen cloth ; একপ্রকার পশমী বস্ত্র।

Cir'-cē (sêr-), *n.* A sorceress ; enchantress ; যাদুকরী ; মায়াবিনী। [সার্সী ইটিয়া দ্বীপে বাস করিত। Ulysess উক্ত দ্বীপে অবতরণ করিলে সার্সী মায়াবলে তাহার সঙ্গীদিগকে শূকররূপে পরিণত করে। Ulysess মার্কারিসের প্রদত্ত ঔষধি বিশেষের বলে সার্সীর কুহকপাশ ছেদন করেন।] **—an,** *adj.*

cir-'cĭ-nate (sêr-), *adj.* With leaves rolled up from apex to base ; (উদ্ভিদ-বিদ্যা) শিখা হইতে মূল পর্য্যন্ত জড়িতপত্র বিশিষ্ট, মধ্যাগ্র-জড়িত (সাঃ পঃ)।

cir'-cle (sêr-), *n., v. t.* & *i.* **1.** A plane figure contained by a curved line, every point of which is equally distant from a point within the figure ; the line that bounds a circle ; (জ্যামিতি) বৃত্ত ; মণ্ডল, বলয়, পরিধি, পরিবেষ। **2.** A ring or circlet ; চক্র, বেষ্টনী। **3.** The orbit of a planet ; the orb of a heavenly body ; গ্রহের কক্ষ ; জোতিষ্কের মণ্ডল। **4.** A set ; a coterie ; শ্রেণী ; মহল, সমাজ, মণ্ডলী। **5.** The area of influence, action, etc. ; কার্য্যক্ষেত্র, প্রভাবক্ষেত্র, প্রভৃতি। **6.** A luminous ring in the sky ; a halo ; নভোমণ্ডলস্থ জ্যোতির্বলয় ; ছটামুকুট। **7.** One of the galleries or tiers of seats in a theatre ; রঙ্গমণ্ডপের ক্রমোচ্চ আসন শ্রেণীর একটী। **8.** A territorial division ; রাজ্যের বিভাগ বিশেষ। **9.** A company surrounding a principal person ; কোন প্রধান ব্যক্তির চতুর্দ্দিকস্থ পারিষদবর্গ। **10.** (*Log.*) A fallacy of proving a proposition from another that rests on it for proof ; (তর্ক-বিজ্ঞান) কোন বাক্যের উপর প্রমাণের জন্য নির্ভর করিতেছে—এইরূপ বাক্য হইতে প্রথমোক্ত বাক্য প্রমাণীকরণরূপ তর্কাভাস, চক্রক (সর্ব্বঃ), চক্রাশয় (ঐ)। ***Verb t.*** **1.** To surround ; বলয়িত করা, পরিবৃত করা, পরিবেষ্টিত করা। **2.** To move round ; ভ্রাম্যমাণ করা, বিবর্ত্তিত করা। **3.** To make circular ; গোলাকার করা। ***Verb i.*** To move in a circle (***around, about*** etc.) ; বলয়াকারে আবর্ত্তিত হওয়া। **—cled,** *adj.* **—clet,** *n*

1. A small circle ; ক্ষুদ্র বৃত্ত। **2.** A ring or band (of precious metal or jewels) worn as an ornament, esp. on the head ; স্বর্ণ-রৌপ্যাদি ধাতু বা মণিনির্ম্মিত শিরোবেষ্টনী প্রভৃতি, মৌলিমাল্য। **–cling,** *n.* **Dress circle**—রঙ্গমঞ্চে দর্শকদিগের উপবেশনের জন্য সর্ব্বনিম্নে অবস্থিত এবং সর্ব্বাধিক মূল্যের আসন-শ্রেণী। **Upper** or **family circle**—রঙ্গ-মণ্ডপের অল্প মূল্যের উপরের আসন শ্রেণী। **White circle**—ছায়াপথের প্রাচীন নাম। **To reason** or **argue in a circle**—চক্রক তর্ক করা, অর্থাৎ যাহা প্রমাণ করিতে হইবে তাহাই প্রমাণিত বলিয়া ধরিয়া তর্ক করা। **To square the circle**—To attempt impossibilities ; অসাধ্য সাধন করিতে চেষ্টা করা।

cir′-cuit (sêr-kĭt or sér-kŭt), *n.*, *v. t.* & *i.* **1.** The circumference ; পরিধিরেখা, পরিধি, পরিবেষ। **2.** Area inclosed ; বেষ্টিত স্থান, সীমাবচ্ছিন্ন স্থান। **3.** A roundabout journey ; a circular journey ; a round ; পরিভ্রমণ ; পরিক্রমণ, পরিক্রমা ; রোঁদ। **4.** The journey of a judge or other persons in a particular district for holding courts or performing other stated duties ; বিচারাদি কার্য্যের জন্য নির্দ্দিষ্ট প্রদেশে বিচারপতিদিগের নিয়মিত চক্রভ্রমণ। **5.** Those making the circuit ; the judges and barristers making the circuit, esp. the latter ; যাহারা পরিক্রম করে; (বিলাতের) পরিক্রমকারীবিচারকমণ্ডলী এবং বিশেষতঃ ব্যবহারজীবিগণ। **6.** The district or division of country through which the judge makes his circuit ; দেশের যে জেলা বা বিভাগের মধ্য দিয়া বিচারক পরিক্রম করেন। **7.** (*Electr.*) The path of a voltaic current ; (তাড়িত-বিদ্যা) ভল্টেইক্ তাড়িতপ্রবাহের সঞ্চারপথ, কুণ্ডলী (সাঃ পঃ)। ***Verb t. & i.*** To move in a circle ; to go round ; পরিক্রম করা ; প্রদক্ষিণ করা। **–cu′-i-tous,** *adj.* Roundabout ; indirect ; ঘুরানো, বক্র, আঁকাবাঁকা ; পরোক্ষ। **–cu′-i-tous-ly,** *adv.* **–cu′-i-tous-ness,** *n.* **–cu′-i-ty,** *n.* **To make** or **go the circuit of**—To go round ; to go the round of ; ঘুরিয়া আসা ; চক্র দিয়া আসা। (*Electr.*) **Short circuit** — (তাড়িত-বিজ্ঞান) চালক পদার্থের বিকলতা হেতু অভিপ্রেত পথের পরিবর্ত্তে ক্ষুদ্রতর পথে তাড়িত প্রবাহের সঞ্চার।

cir′-cu-lar (sêr-cŭ-lêr), *adj.* & *n.* **1.** Of the form of a circle ; বৃত্তাকার, গোলাকার, মণ্ডলাকার, চক্রাকার, বলয়াকার। **2.** Moving in or passing over a circle ; মণ্ডলাকারে বা মণ্ডলোপরি আবর্ত্তনশীল। **3.** (*Log.*) Of the nature of arguing or reasoning in a circle ; (তর্ক-বিজ্ঞান) চক্রকাত্মক। **4.** Circuitous ; roundabout ; indirect ; আঁকাবাঁকা, ঘুরানো ; কুটিল; পরোক্ষ। **5.** Addressed to a circle of persons having a common interest ; as, a *circular* letter ; সমস্বার্থ বিশিষ্ট ব্যক্তিমণ্ডলীর নিকট লিখিত। **6.** (*Math.*) Of or like the geometrical circle ; (গণিতশাস্ত্র) বৃত্ত বিষয়ক বা বৃত্ততুল্য। ***Noun.*** Circular letter. (see below.) **–ize,** *v. t.* **–lar′-i-ty,** *n.* **–ly,** *adv.* **Circular letter**—সমস্বার্থ বিশিষ্ট ব্যক্তিগণের নিকট লিখিত সাধারণ লিপি, প্রসিদ্ধিপত্র (কেভিঃ)। **Circular note**—ধনাগারের কর্ত্তা কোন ভ্রমণকারীর অনুকূলে বিভিন্ন বিভিন্ন বৈদেশিক ধনাগারে যে হুণ্ডী প্রদান করেন। **Circular saw**—গোলাকৃতি করাত। **Circular tour**—যে নির্দ্দিষ্ট ভ্রমণ কোন স্থান হইতে আরব্ধ হইয়া তথায় পরিসমাপ্ত হয়।

cir′-cŭ-lāte (sêr-), *v. i.* & *t.* **1.** To go round ; as, blood *circulates* in the body ; সঞ্চালিত হওয়া। ***Verb t.*** **1.** To give currency to ; to diffuse ; প্রচলিত করা ; প্রচারিত করা। **2.** (*Math.*) To recur (said of decimal fraction) ; (গণিত শাস্ত্রে) পুনঃ পুনঃ আগত হওয়া। **Circulating decimal** — পৌনঃপুনিক দশমিক। **Circulating library**—যে গ্রন্থাগার হইতে পাঠকগণ পর্য্যায়ক্রমে পুস্তক গ্রহণ করে, ভ্রাম্যৎ পুস্তকালয় (আঃ বঃ)। **Circulating medium** — যদ্দ্বারা বিনিময় করা যায়, বিনিময় দ্বার।

cir-cŭ-lā′-tion (sêr-), *n.* **1.** Movement of the blood from and to the heart ; also, the circuit of any nutritive fluid through the vessels of animals or plants ; রক্ত-সঞ্চালন (হঃ চঃ), রুধিরাভিসরণ (সাঃ পঃ) ; জন্তু বা উদ্ভিদের দেহে কোন প্রকার পুষ্টিকর তরল পদার্থ সঞ্চালন। **2.** Transmission ; distribution ; পরিচালন, সঞ্চারণ ; প্রচার। **3.** Number of copies sold, esp. of a newspaper ; বিক্রীত পুস্তকাদির সংখ্যা ; সংবাদপত্রের প্রচার। **4.** Currency ; circulating coin, notes, etc. ; as, a boundless paper *circulation* ; প্রচলন ; প্রচলিত মুদ্রা। **–tive,** *adj.* Inclined to or promoting circulation ; প্রচলনোন্মুখ ; প্রচলন-বিধায়ক। **–tor,** *n.* **–to-ry,** *adj.*

cir′-cŭ-lŭs (sêr-), *n.* **1.** A circle or ring ; বৃত্ত, অঙ্গুরীয়ক। **2.** A technical name of various instruments in surgery ; অস্ত্রোপচার-কার্য্যে ব্যবহৃত বিভিন্ন প্রকার অস্ত্রের নাম।

circulus in probando, (*L.*) (A circle in proof.) A form of Petitio Principii ; প্রমাণচক্রক (হিঃ কোঃ)।

cir-cŭm-ăm′-bi-ĕnt (sêr-), *adj.* Going round ; surrounding ; পরিক্রমশীল ; পরিবেষ্টনকারী। **–ence,** **–en-cy,** *ns.*

cir-cŭm-ăm′-bü-lāte (sêr-), *v. t.* & *i.* To walk round (a place, etc.) ; পরিক্রম করা, প্রদক্ষিণ করা, পরিভ্রমণ করা। ***Verb i.*** **1.** To walk about ; to go about ; ইতস্ততঃ পরিভ্রমণ করা ; চতুর্দ্দিকে ভ্রমণ করা। **2.** (*Fig.*) To beat about the bush ; (লক্ষণায়) সোজা সোজি না বলিয়া ঘুরাঘুরি করা। **–la′** *n.* **–la-tor,** *n.* **–la-to-ry**

cir-cŭm-bĕnd′-i-bŭs, (s circumlocution ; পেঁচাও

cir′-cŭm-cīse (sêr-), *v. t.* **1.** To cut off foreskin of, as a Jewish and Mahomedan rite ; লিঙ্গের ত্বক্‌ছেদ করা, সুন্নৎ করা, খত্‌না করা, চণ্ডিক (মালঃ) করা। **2.** To purify ; as, to *circumcise* the heart ; পবিত্র করা। **–cised,** *adj.* **–ci′-sion,** *n.* **The circumcised people**—The Jews ; ইয়ুদী জাতি।

cir-cŭm′-fêr-ĕnce (sêr-) *n.* (*Geom.*) The curved line which forms the boundary of a circle or other closed curve ; a circuit ; পরিধি ; পরিবেষ, মণ্ডল ; পরিবেষ্টন (সাঃ পঃ)। **–en-tial,** *adj.*

cir-cum′-fer-en-tor (sêr-cŭm-fêr-ĕn-têr), *n.* An instrument used by surveyors for taking or measuring angle ; আমীনদিগের কোণগ্রাহক বা কোণমাপক যন্ত্র বিশেষ।

cir′-cŭm-flĕx (sêr-), *n., adj.* & *v. t.* An accent mark (∧) placed only on long vowels to indicate contraction, length, etc. ; (ব্যাকরণ) স্বরিত। ***Adj.*** (*Anat.*) Curved ; (শারীরসংস্থান-বিদ্যা) বক্রীভূত। ***Verb t.*** **1.** To mark or pronounce with a circumflex ; স্বরিত চিহ্নে চিহ্নিত করা, স্বরিত স্বরে উচ্চারণ করা। **2.** To bend or wind round ; বাঁকিয়া দেওয়া, পাক দেওয়া। **–flex′-ion,** *n.*

cir-cŭm′-flū-ĕnt (sêr-), *adj.* Flowing round ; ambient : চতুর্দ্দিকে cavity of the internal ear ; কর্ণকম্বু (সাঃ পঃ)। **2.** (*Bot.*) A spiral-shaped body or organ ; (উদ্ভিদ্‌বিদ্যা) কম্বু (সাঃ পঃ)। **–ate, –at-ed,** *adjs.*

cock (kŏk), *n.* **1.** The male of the domestic fowl ; কুক্কুট, মোরগ, তাম্রচূড়, ঊষাকল। **2.** The male of other birds ; as, *cock*-sparrow ; অন্যান্য পুংপক্ষী। **3.** A weather-cock ; বায়ুর দিঙ্‌-নির্ণায়ক যন্ত্রবিশেষ। **4.** A chief man ; a leader ; "Sir Andrew—the *cock* of the club ;" আবর্ত্তিত করা। **–ra′-tion,** *n.* **–ra-to-ry,** *adj.*

cir-cŭm-jā′-cĕnt (sêr-), *adj.* Lying or situated round ; bordering on every side ; চতুর্দ্দিকে স্থিত ; পরিবেষ্টক। **–cence,** *n.*

cir-cŭm-lō-cū′-tion (sêr-), *n.* The use of many words where few would do ; a round-about expression ; বাগাড়ম্বর, বাগ্‌বিস্তার, বাগ্‌বাহুল্য ; পেঁচাও কথা, বাক্যভঙ্গী। **–al, –a-ry, –loc′-u-to-ry,** *adjs.* **–ist,** *n.* **Circumlocution office**—সরকারী আফিস—যাহাতে কোন বিষয় মীমাংসায় বিলম্ব হইয়া থাকে।

cir-cŭm-năv′-i-gă-ble (sêr-), *adj.* Capable of being sailed round ; জলপথে প্রদক্ষিণযোগ্য। **–gate,** *v. t.* To sail round (esp. the globe or world) ; জলপথে প্রদক্ষিণ করা, ভূপ্রদক্ষিণ করা। **–ga-tor,** *n.* **–ga-to-ry,** *adj.*

cir-cŭm-nū-tā′-tion (sêr-), *n.* (*Bot.*) Successive nodding towards all points of the compass, as in the tendrils of plants ; (উদ্ভিদ্‌বিদ্যা) লতাতন্তু প্রভৃতির ক্রমান্বয়ে সর্ব্বদিকে অভিনমন, ঘূর্ণিগতি (সাঃ পঃ)। **–nu′-tate,** *v. t.*

cir-cŭm-ō′-răl (sêr-), *adj.* Situated around the mouth ; মুখের চতুর্দ্দিকে অবস্থিত।

cir-cum-po′-lar (sêr-cŭm-pō-lêr), *adj.* Round, about, or near, one of the poles ; (ভূবিদ্যা) মেরুর চতুর্দ্দিকস্থ বা সন্নিকটস্থ।

cir-cŭm-scrībe′ (sêr-), *v. t.* **1.** To draw a line round ; চতুর্দ্দিকে সীমারেখাঙ্কিত করা। **2.** (*Fig.*) To restrain ; as, to *circumscribe* royal power ; (লক্ষণায়) সীমাবদ্ধ করা। **3.** (*Geom.*) To describe (a figure) about another figure touching it at certain points, without cutting it ; (জ্যামিতি) একটী ক্ষেত্রের চতুর্দ্দিকে অপর একটী ক্ষেত্র এরূপ ভাবে অঙ্কিত করা, যাহাতে প্রথমোক্ত ক্ষেত্রটী শেষোক্ত ক্ষেত্রকে কর্ত্তিত না করিয়া কতিপয় বিন্দুতে স্পর্শ করে, পরিগত করা। **4.** To define logically ; ন্যায়শাস্ত্রানুগত সংজ্ঞা প্রদান করা। **–scribed′,** *adj.* **–scrib′-er,** *n.* **–scrip′-tion,** *n.* **1.** The act of marking out or imposing limits ; limitation ; restriction ; সীমানির্দ্ধারণ ; সীমাবদ্ধকরণ, সীমাবন্ধন ; নিবন্ধন, নিয়মন। **2.** Boundary ; outline ; সীমা ; বহিঃরেখা। **3.** A district or region of defined limits ; নির্দ্দিষ্ট সীমাবচ্ছিন্ন বিভাগ বা ভূখণ্ড। **4.** An inscription round a coin, seal, etc. ; মুদ্রা, সীলমোহর প্রভৃতির চতুর্দ্দিকস্থ উৎকীর্ণ লিপি।

cir-cum-so′-lar (sêr-cŭm-sō-lêr), *adj.* (*Astron.*) Revolving round, or being near the sun ; (জ্যোতির্বিজ্ঞান) সূর্য্যের চতুর্দ্দিকে আবর্ত্তনশীল, সূর্য্যসমীপবর্ত্তী।

cir′-cŭm-spĕct (sêr-), *adj.* Watchful on every side ; cautious ; prudent ; চৌকস ; সতর্ক ; অবহিত। **–spec′-tion,** *n.* **–spec′-tive,** *adj.* **–spec′-tive-ness,** *n.*

cir′-cŭm-stance (sêr-cŭm-stăns), *n.* & *v. t.* **1.** (*Sing.*) An event or incident ; ঘটনা, ব্যাপার। **2.** The ceremony ; fuss ; as, all the pomp and *circumstance* of a tournament ; অনুষ্ঠান, ক্রিয়াকলাপ ; ঘটা। **3.** (*Pl.*) The surroundings of an action ; অবস্থা। **4.** (*Pl.*) Material welfare ; as, straitened *circumstances* ; সাংসারিক বা আর্থিক অবস্থা। ***Verb t.*** To place in particular relations to other things ; অবস্থায় ফেলা। **Circumstance alters cases**—প্রতি ঘটনার বিশেষ বিশেষ অবস্থার প্রতি লক্ষ্য রাখিয়া কার্য্যপ্রণালীর পরিবর্ত্তন করিতে হয়।

cir-cum-stan′-tial (sêr-cŭm-stăn-shăl), *adj.* & *n.* **1.** Relating to or dependent on circumstances ; not incidental ; অবস্থাঘটিত, অবস্থাধীন ; অপ্রধান, আগন্তুক। **2.** Minute ;

particular ; পুঙ্খানুপুঙ্খ ; সবিশেষ। **3.** Full of pomp or splendour ; আড়ম্বরপূর্ণ, সমারোহপূর্ণ। ***Noun.*** (*Pl.*) Particulars ; esp. adventitious features ; nonessentials ; বিশেষ বিবরণ, বৃত্তান্ত; আগন্তুক ভাব সমূহ ; গৌণ বিষয় সমূহ। **—ly,** *adv.* **—tial′-i-ty,** *n.* **Circumstantial evidence**—কোন ব্যাপারের পূর্ব্বাপর ঘটনাসমূহ দ্বারা যে প্রমাণ হয়, মোকদ্দমার হালাৎ দৃষ্টে যে প্রমাণ হয়, অবস্থা-ঘটিত প্রমাণ, বৃত্তান্ত-ঘটিত-প্রমাণ, অনুমানসিদ্ধ প্রমাণ।

cir-cum-stan′-ti-ate (sêr-cŭm-stăn-shî-āt), *v. t.* To support or confirm by circumstances ; to describe in full detail ; অবস্থা দ্বারা সমর্থিত বা দৃঢ়ীভূত করা ; সবিস্তারে বর্ণনা করা। **—a′-tion,** *n.*

cir-cŭm-văl′-lāte (sêr-), *v. t.* To surround with a rampart or entrenchment ; বপ্রবেষ্টিত করা, পরিখাবেষ্টিত করা। **—la′-tion,** *n.* **1.** The act of surrounding a place, esp. a besieged city, with rampart, etc. ; বপ্র বা প্রাচীর দ্বারা অবরুদ্ধ নগরী প্রভৃতি পরিবেষ্টন। **2.** A rampart or entrenchment constructed round any place by way of defence ; বপ্র, পরিখা।

cir-cŭm-vĕnt′ (sêr-), *v. t.* **1.** To entrap ; ফাঁদে ফেলান। **2.** To over-reach ; ঠকান, প্রতারিত করা। **—ven′-tion,** *n.*

cir-cŭm′-vŏ-lūte (sêr-), *v. t.* To roll or curl round ; ঘূর্ণিত করা, ঘূরান, আবর্ত্তিত করা। **—lu′-tion,** *n.* **1.** A rolling or wrapping round ; আবর্ত্তন, মোড়ন। **2.** A convolution ; a coil ; পাক, গ্রন্থি ; কুণ্ডল। **3.** A sinuous movement ; **কুটিলগতি।**

cir-cum-volve′ (sêr-cŭm-vŏlv), *v.t.* & *i.* To roll or move round ; আবর্ত্তিত করা বা হওয়া, ঘূর্ণিত করা বা হওয়া।

cir′-cŭs (sêr-), *n.* **1.** A circular or oval arena lined with tiers of seats for the exhibition of equestrian or acrobatic performances, etc. ; অশ্বারোহণ, রজ্জু-নৃত্য, এবং নানাপ্রকার ব্যায়ামকৌশল-প্রদর্শনের জন্য ক্রমোচ্চ আসনশ্রেণী বিশিষ্ট অণ্ডাকার বা মণ্ডলাকার রঙ্গভূমি, মণ্ডলরঙ্গ, মণ্ডলাকার রঙ্গভূমি। **2.** A rounded hollow or plain encircled by hills ; শৈলবেষ্টিত বৃত্তাকার সমতলভূমি বা কুণ্ড। **3.** A circular range of houses ; as, Regent *circus* ; মণ্ডলাকারে সজ্জিত ভবন শ্রেণী।

Circus æruginosus—মাঠ চিল (বেলঃ)।

Cirrhina mrigal—মৃগেল (গুপ্তঃ)।

Cirrhina latia—কালবাটা (গুপ্তঃ)।

cir-rho′-sis (sîr-rö-sîs), *n.* A disease of the liver, occurring in spirit drinkers ; মদ্যপায়ীদিগের যকৃত রোগ বিশেষ। **—rhot′-ic,** *adj.*

cĭr′-ri-pĕd(e), *n.* A marine animal, with legs like curl of hair, attached to other bodies ; সামুদ্রিক জন্তু বিশেষ, গুণ্ডপদ।

cĭr′-rŭs, *n.* **1.** (*Bot.*) A tendril ; লতা-তন্তু। **2.** (*Zool.*) A slender appendage, as the fleshy barbel or beard of some fishes ; (জন্তু-তত্ত্ব) সূক্ষ্ম উপাঙ্গ, যথা কোন কোন মৎস্যের দাড়ির মত উপাঙ্গ। **3.** (*Meteor.*) A form of cloud with diverging filaments like lock of hair or wool ; (আবহ বিদ্যা) অলকমেঘ (সাঃ পঃ), উর্ণামেঘ (ঐ), কুণ্ডলমেঘ (হিঃ কোঃ), বিক্ষিপ্ত কার্পাসবৎ মেঘ। **—rose, —rous,** *adjs.*

cĭs-ăl′-pine (-pîn or -pïn), *adj.* On this side of the Alps,—with respect to Rome, *i. e.* south of the Alps ; আল্পস্ পর্ব্বতের যে পার্শ্বে রোমনগরী অবস্থিত—তদ্দিকস্থ, অর্থাৎ দক্ষিণদিকস্থ।

cĭs-mă-rïne′, *adj.* On this side of the sea ; সমুদ্রের এদিকস্থ।

cĭs-ō-ce-ăn′-ic (-shē-), *adj.* On this side of the ocean ; মহাসাগরের এদিকস্থ।

cĭs-pŏn′-tine (-tîn or -tïn), *adj.* On this side of the bridges, viz. in London, north of the Thames ; সেতুর এদিকস্থ।

cĭst, *n.* **1.** (*Archæol.*) A sepulchral chest excavated in rock or hollowed tree-trunks ; (ইতিহাস-চিহ্ন-বিদ্যা) পাষাণ-মধ্যে বা তরুকোটরে খনিত সমাধি সিন্দুক। **2.** (*Gr. Antiq.*) A box or chest for sacred utensils ; (গ্রীসদেশীয় প্রত্নতত্ত্ব) পবিত্র তৈজস দ্রব্য রক্ষণার্থ সিন্দুক বিশেষ।

Cis-ter′-cian (sîs-têr-shân), *adj.* & *n.* (*Eccles.*) Of or belonging to the monastic order, founded at Citeaux, in France, by Robert, abbot of Molesme ; মোলস্মির মঠাধ্যক্ষ রবার্টদ্বারা ফরাসীদেশের অন্তঃপাতী 'সীটো' নামক স্থানে প্রতিষ্ঠিত সন্ন্যাসি-সম্প্রদায় সম্বন্ধীয়। ***Noun.*** A monk of this order ; উক্ত সম্প্রদায়-ভুক্ত সন্ন্যাসী বিশেষ।

cĭs′-têrn, *n.* **1.** An artificial reservoir for holding or storing water or other liquids ; চৌবাচ্চা। **2.** A pond or a natural reservoir ; পুষ্করিণী, জলাশয়, জলকুণ্ড।

cĭs′-tŭs, *n.* A genus of handsome shrubs with large white or red short-lived flowers ; বৃহৎ এবং অল্পকালস্থায়ী শ্বেত ও রক্তবর্ণ পুষ্পপ্রসূ গুল্মশ্রেণী।

cĭt, *n.* A shortened form of citizen, and used as a term of contempt ; সহরিয়া, সহুরে।

cĭt′-ă-dĕl, *n.* **1.** A fortress in or near a city ; নগর-দুর্গ, পুরদুর্গ, অন্তদুর্গ, পুরকোষ্ঠ (মঃ উঃ), নগরোপকণ্ঠস্থ দুর্গ। **2.** (*Fig.*) The last retreat of a hard-pressed party, belief, etc. ; as, the *citadel* of smuggling ; (লক্ষণায়) আশ্রয়দুর্গ, কোট।

cīte, *v. t.* **1.** To summon officially to appear in a court of law ; বিচারালয়ে উপস্থিত হইবার জন্য তলব বা শমন দেওয়া। **2.** To quote (a passage, book or author) in support of a position ; গ্রন্থাদি হইতে উদ্ধৃত করিয়া প্রমাণস্বরূপ প্রয়োগ করা। **3.** To bring forward ; উপস্থাপিত করা, উল্লেখ করা। **Cit′-a-ble,** *adj.* **Ci-ta′-tion,** *n.* **Ci′-ta-to-ry,** *adj.*

cĭth′-ă-ră, *n.* An ancient instrument of the lyre class ; ছতার (সৌরীন্দ্রঃ)।

cĭth′-êr, –êrn, *n.* An instrument of the guitar kind, and played with a quill ; সেতারবৎ যন্ত্রবিশেষ, ছতারা (সৌরীন্দ্রঃ)।

cĭt′-i-zĕn, *n.* **1.** A burgess or freeman of a city ; রাজনীতিক অধিকারপ্রাপ্ত নাগরিক। **2.** A townsman ; পুরবাসী, পৌরজন, নাগরিক, নগরবাসী। **3.** An enfranchised inhabitant of a country (opp. to an *alien*) ; কোন রাষ্ট্রের প্রজা, পৌরজনাধিকারপ্রাপ্ত দেশবাসী, নৈগমিক (সাঃ পঃ)। **4.** Inhabitant (of) ; as, some small forest *citizens* ; অধিবাসী। **–hood,** *n.* **–ship,** *n.* The right of a citizen ; পৌরজনাধিকার, নৈগমিকতা (সাঃ পঃ)। **–ize,** *v. t.* **–ry,** *n.* **Citizen king**—ফরাসীরাজ লুই ফিলিপ (তিনি প্রজাগণকর্ত্তৃক নির্ব্বাচিত হইয়াছিলেন)। **A citizen of the world** — A cosmopolitan ; যিনি সকল দেশকেই স্বদেশ বলিয়া গণ্য করেন, বিশ্বনাগরিক।

cĭt′-rāte, *n.* (*Chem.*) A salt of citric acid ; বীজপূরাম্লজাত লবণ বিশেষ।

cĭt′-ric, *adj.* (*Chem.*) Derived from the citron ; বীজপূরজাত। **Citric acid**—জম্বীর দ্রাব (রঃ প্রঃ), বীজপূরাম্ল (ঐ), মাতুলুঙ্গাম্ল (ঐ), লুঙ্গাম্ল (ঐ)।

cĭt′-rine, *adj.* Lemon-coloured ; টাবালেবুর বর্ণ।

cĭt′-rŏn, *n.* **1.** A fruit resembling a lemon ; a citron tree ; টাবালেবু (ষোঃ), বীজপুর (ঐ) ; ঐ বৃক্ষ। **2.** The pale yellow green or lemon colour ; আপীতবর্ণ বা হরিদাভ পীতবর্ণ।

citrulus colocynthus—মাকাল (বেলঃ)।

citrulus cucurbita—তরমুজ।

citrus aurantium — The orange ; কমলা (বেলঃ)।

citrus bergamia—লেবু।

citrus decumana—বাতাবি লেবু।

cĭt′-ȳ, *n.* **1.** A town or other inhabited place ; নগর, পুরী, পুর, সহর। **2.** The collective body of citizens ; পৌরবর্গ, নাগরিক সমাজ। **–less,** *adj.* **–ward(s),** *adv.* **Celestial City, Heavenly city** or **City of God**—স্বর্গ। **City of a Hundred Towers**—ইটালী দেশ। **City of marts**—লণ্ডন। **City of Palaces**—কলিকাতা। **City of the dead**—শবনগরী, শ্মশান। **City of the Prophet**—মেদিনা। **City of the Seven Hills** or **Eternal city**—রোমনগরী। **City of the Violet Crown**—এথেন্স। **City of Victory**—Cairo (in Egypt) ; কেইরো (মিসর দেশে)। **City Police**—সহর কোতোয়ালী। **Holy city**—জেরুসেলেম, স্বর্গ। **The City** — লণ্ডন মহানগরীর যে অংশে ব্যবসায় বাণিজ্যাদি কার্য্য নির্ব্বাহিত হয়।

cĭv′-ĕt, *n.* & *v. t.* **1.** A small carnivorous animal of Africa and India ; গন্ধমার্জ্জার, গন্ধগোকুলাদি (সাঃ পঃ), বাঘডাসা (বেলঃ), খট্টাস (মঃ উঃ)। **2.** A strong musky

Civet.

perfume obtained from the civet cat ; গন্ধগোকুলার দেহ হইতে প্রাপ্ত মৃগমদগন্ধী গন্ধদ্রব্য বিশেষ, মৃগধর্ম্মজ (গেলঃ)। ***Verb t.*** To perfume with civet ; উক্ত গন্ধদ্রব্য দ্বারা সুরভিত করা।

cĭv′-ic, *adj.* **1.** Pertaining to a city or citizen ; নগর বা নগরবাসী সম্পর্কীয়, নাগরিক। **–i-cal-ly,** *adv.* **Civic crown, garland**—(প্রাচীন রোমে) যুদ্ধে স্বনগরবাসীর জীবনরক্ষাকারীকে গৌরব-প্রদর্শনার্থ দেবদারুপত্র বিরচিত যে মুকুট বা মালিকা উপহার দেওয়া হইত।

cĭv′-il, *adj.* **1.** Of or belonging to or made up of, citizens ; as, *civil* life ; পৌরবর্গসম্বন্ধীয়, পৌরবর্গঘটিত। **2.** Decently polite ; not rude ; ভদ্র ; বিনীত। **3.** Pertaining to ordinary life and affairs, in distinction from military, ecclesiastical, etc. ; সাধারণ জীবন বা বিষয়-সংক্রান্ত, অসামরিক, অযাজকীয় প্রভৃতি। **4.** (*Law*) Pertaining to the private rights of individuals in a community and legal proceedings employed in settling them ; not criminal ; সমাজবদ্ধ ব্যক্তিগণের স্বত্ব বা অধিকারসম্বন্ধীয় এবং স্বত্ব বা অধিকার মীমাংসার্থ মোকদ্দমাদি সম্বন্ধীয় ; দেওয়ানী। **5.** Legally recognized for the purposes of ordinary life, (*said of division of time*) ; as, *civil year* : *civil* day ; সচরাচর জীবন ব্যাপারের জন্য বিধিকর্ত্তৃক স্বীকৃত। **Civil court** — দেওয়ানী আদালত। **Civil day** — সাবন দিন। **Civil death**—(আইন) আইনসঙ্গত স্বত্ব বা অধিকারসম্পর্কে মৃত্যু, সামাজিক মৃত্যু। **Civil Engineering**—See *Engineering.* **Civil imprisonment**—(*Law*) দেওয়ানী ফাটক। **Civil law**—দেওয়ানী আইন। **Civil list**—অসামরিক বিভাগ সমূহে নিযুক্ত কর্ম্মচারিগণের তালিকা ; পার্লেমেণ্ট কর্ত্তৃক ইংলণ্ডেশ্বরের সাংসারিক ব্যয় এবং বৃত্তিবিধানের জন্য প্রতিবৎসর যে অর্থ মঞ্জুর করা যায়। **Civil Servant**—সিভিল সার্ব্বিসের কর্ম্মচারী। **Civil Service**—শাসনতন্ত্রের অসামরিক বিভাগ সমূহ ; অসামরিক বিভাগ সমূহে নিযুক্ত কর্ম্মচারিবর্গ।

Civil struggles, strife, war—অন্তর্দ্রোহ, অন্তর্বিগ্রহ। **Civil suit**—দেওয়ানী মোকদ্দমা। **Indian Civil Service**—ভারতবর্ষীয় শাসনবিচার প্রভৃতি বিভাগের জন্য ইংলণ্ড হইতে নির্ব্বাচিত উচ্চ কর্ম্মচারি-সম্প্রদায়। **The civil war**—ইংলণ্ডদেশে সপ্তদশ শতাব্দীতে পার্লেমেণ্টের সহিত প্রথম চার্লসের যে সংগ্রাম হয়।

cĭ-vĭl'-ĭ-ăn, *n.* **1.** A practitioner, professor or student of Civil Law; a writer or authority on the civil law; (rare); দেওয়ানী আদালতের উকীল, দেওয়ানী আইনের অধ্যাপক বা ছাত্র; দেওয়ানী আইন বিষয়ক প্রামাণ্য গ্রন্থ বা গ্রন্থলেখক। **2.** A member of the Indian Civil Service of the Crown, (also *Indian Civilian.*); ভারতীয় সিভিল সার্ভিসের কর্ম্মচারী। **3.** A person not belonging to the Army or the Navy; অসামরিক বা অনৌ-বিভাগীয় কর্ম্মচারী।

cĭ-vĭl'-ĭ-tỹ *n.* **1.** Ordinary courtesy or politeness; সৌজন্য, শিষ্টাচার, ভদ্রতা, শিষ্টতা, শীলতা। **2.** A polite act or expression; ভদ্র ব্যবহার, শিষ্টবাক্য।

cĭv'-ĭ-līze, *v. t.* **1.** To bring out of barbarism; to enlighten; to refine; সভ্যকরা, জ্ঞানালোকে আলোকিত করা; পরিমার্জ্জিত করা। **2.** To domesticate or tame (wild animals); জন্তু পোষ মানান। **—li-za-ble,** *adj.* **—li za'-tion,** *n.* **1.** The act of making or becoming civilized; সভ্যকরণ; সভ্যতাপ্রাপ্তি। **2.** An advanced state of human society; a particular stage or type of this; as, Egyptian *civilization*; সভ্যতা; কোন বিশেষ সময়ের বা প্রকৃতির সভ্যতা। **—lized,** সভ্যতা প্রাপ্ত। **To civilize away**—To get rid of barbarous habits; সভ্যতা প্রাপ্ত হওয়া।

clack (clăk), *v. i.* & *n.* **1.** To chatter; to cluck or cackle as a hen; to talk loquaciously; কিচির মিচির শব্দ করা; মুরগীর মত ডাকা; বক্‌বক্ করা। **2.** To crack; to rattle; খট্‌খট্ শব্দ করা; ঘ্যানর ঘ্যানর শব্দ করা। ***Noun.*** **1.** A sharp dry, sudden sound; খট্‌খট্ শব্দ। **2.** Senseless chatter; বক্‌বক। **3.** (*Colloq.*) The tongue; (চলিত ভাষায়) জিহ্বা।

clăd, *adj.* Clothed; arrayed; বসনাবৃত; সজ্জিত।

claim (clām), *n.* & *v. t.* **1.** A demand for something as due; দাবী, দাওয়া। **2.** A right or title, (*to* thing, *on* or *upon* person); স্বত্ব, অধিকার। **3.** The piece of land allotted for mining; খনির কার্য্যের জন্য নির্দ্দিষ্ট বা গৃহীত ভূখণ্ড। **4.** (*Life Ins.*) The amount payable upon a life policy at death or a matured endowment policy; (জীবনবীমা) দাবীর টাকা। ***Verb t.*** **1.** To demand as one's due; দাবী করা, দাওয়া করা। **2.** To deserve or have right to; পাওয়ার উপযুক্ত হওয়া, দাবী থাকা। **Claim'-able,** *adj.* **Claim'-ant, Claim'-er,** *ns.* **To lay claim to**—To assert one's right to; কোন ব্যক্তির স্বত্ব বা অধিকার বলিয়া দাবী করা।

clair-au'-di-ence, (clār-ŏ-dî-ĕns), *n.* The faculty of mentally perceiving sounds beyond the range of hearing, (induced under certain mesmeric conditions); অতীন্দ্রিয় শব্দশ্রবণের শক্তি, দিব্যশ্রুতি।

clair-voy'-ance (clār-vоў-ăns), *n.* **1.** The faculty of seeing mentally what is happening or exists out of sight; অপ্রত্যক্ষ বিষয় দর্শন, অতীন্দ্রিয় বিষয় দর্শনের শক্তি, দিব্যদর্শন। **2.** Exceptional insight; as, *clairvoyance* in dramatic affairs; অনন্যসাধারণ অন্তর্দৃষ্টি। **—ant,** *n.*

clăm, *n.* & *v. i.* **1.** A species of bivalve shell-fish; শুক্তি বিশেষ। **2.** A kind of forceps; a clamp; (*usu. pl.*); সাঁড়াশী; একপ্রকার চিমটা। ***Verb i.*** To clog with viscous matter; আঠালো বস্তু দ্বারা লাগান।

clăm'-ănt, *adj.* **1.** Clamorous; noisy; কলরবকারী; কোলাহলপূর্ণ। **2.** (*Fig.*) Crying; urgent; (লক্ষণায়) আশুপ্রতিবিধেয়; জরুরি। **—ly,** *adv.*

clăm'-bêr, *v. i.* & *n.* To climb with difficulty and effort; to creep or crawl up; অতিকষ্টে আরোহণ করা; হাঁচর পাঁচর করিয়া উঠা। ***Noun.*** The act of clambering; অতিকষ্টে আরোহণ। **—er,** *n.*

clăm'-mỹ, *adj.* Soft, moist and sticky; viscous; নরম, আর্দ্র এবং আঠালো; চট্‌চটে। **—mi-ly,** *adv.* **—mi-ness,** *n.*

clăm'-our (-êr), **clăm'-or** (-êr), *n., v. i.* & *t.* **1.** Loud shouting or outcry; vociferation; esp. excited outcry of appeal, complaint, opposition; কলরব; কোলাহল, সোরগোল; উচ্চনাদ। **2.** (*Pl.*) An outburst of noisy utterance; a cry; জনকোলাহল, কোলাহল, কলরব; চীৎকার। ***Verb i.*** **1.** To raise an outcry; (*for, against*); কোন কিছুর জন্য বা বিরুদ্ধে চীৎকার করা। **2.** To demand or call importunately for; কোন কিছুর জন্য কোলাহল সহকারে আন্দোলন করা। ***Verb t.*** To utter; to assert clamorously; কোলাহল করা, গলাবাজি করা। **—er,** *n.* **—ous,** *adj.* **—ous-ly,** *adv.* **—ous-ness,** *n.* **To clamour down**—To silence; চুপ করান।

clămp, *n.* & *v. t.* A heavy foot-step; গুরুপদক্ষেপ বা পদধ্বনি। ***Verb t.*** To tread heavily; গুরু-পাদবিক্ষেপ সহকারে চলা।

clămp, *n.* & *v. t.* A piece of timber or iron used to strengthen anything or fasten work together; আঁকড়া, পতর, বাতা, খিল, গেলাপ, গোঁজ, খোঁটা, পট্টি। ***Verb t.*** To fasten together or strengthen with a clamp or clamps ; বাতা বা আকড়া দ্বারা শক্ত করা বা জোড়া দেওয়া।

clămp, *n.* & *v. t.* A pile of bricks laid up for burning ; a heap of coal for cooking, etc. ; a heap of garden rubbish for burning, etc. ; পোড়াইবার জন্য কাঁচা ইটের পাঁজা ; রন্ধনাদির জন্য কয়লার গাদা ; পোড়াইবার জন্য বা অন্য উদ্দেশ্যে স্তূপীকৃত বাগানের জঞ্জাল।

clăn, *n.* **1.** A number of persons claiming descent from a common ancestor and associated together ; a tribe ; a family ; বংশ, কুল ; গোত্র, গোষ্ঠী ; পরিবার। **2.** A party ; coterie ; set ; সম্প্রদায় ; মণ্ডলী ; শ্রেণী। **3.** A collection of animals, plants, etc. ; a class ; একজাতিভুক্ত জীব, জন্তু বা উদ্ভিদের সমষ্টি, জন্তু বা উদ্ভিদের বর্গ বা পর্য্যায় ; শ্রেণী। **Clan'-nish,** *adj.* **Clan'-nish-ly̆,** *adv.* **Clan'-nish-ness,** *n.* **Clan'-ship,** *n.* **Clans-man**—এক গোষ্ঠীর লোক।

clăn-dĕs'-tine (-tĭn), *adj.* Secret ; private ; underhand ; surreptitious ; গুপ্ত, গূঢ়, গোপন ; প্রচ্ছন্ন ; ভিতর ভিতর, তলে তলে সাধিত ; গোপনে কৃত বা সম্পন্ন। **—ly,** *adv.* **—ness, —tin'-i-ty,** *ns.*

clăng, *n., v. t.* & *i.* A loud resonant ringing metallic sound ; ঝঞ্ঝনা, ঝন্‌ঝন্ শব্দ, টং টং শব্দ, ঝনৎকার, ঝন্‌ঝনা শব্দ, ঠন্ ঠন্ শব্দ। ***Verb t.*** To cause (thing) to make ringing sound ; ঝন্‌ঝন্ করিয়া বাজান, টং টং করা, ঠন্ ঠন্ করা। ***Verb i.*** To emit a loud resonant ringing sound, (esp. of pieces of metals struck together) ; ঝন্ ঝন্ করিয়া উঠা, ঠন্ ঠন্ করিয়া উঠা।

clan'-gor, —gour (klăng-gêr), *n.* A loud resonant ringing sound ; ঝন্ ঝন্ শব্দ, ঝঞ্ঝনা, ঢং ঢং শব্দ। **—gor-ous,** *adj.* **—gor-ous-ly,** *adv.*

clank (klăngk), *n., v. t.* & *i.* A sharp sound, as of heavy pieces of metal ; রুণু ঝুনু শব্দ, ঝনৎকার, টঙ্কার। ***Verb t.*** To cause to sound with a clank ; ঝম্ ঝম্ করিয়া বাজান। ***Verb i.*** **1.** To give out a clank ; রুণু ঝুনু করিয়া বাজা, ঝম্ ঝম্ করিয়া বাজা। **2.** To move with a clanking sound ; ঝন্ ঝন্ করিয়া চলা, ঝম্ ঝম্ করিয়া চলা।

clăp, *n., v. t.* & *i.* **1.** The loud explosive noise of thunder ; a peal, as of thunder ; নির্ঘোষ ; গর্জ্জন, গুড়ুম্ গুড়ুম্ শব্দ। **2.** The noise made by striking the palms ; an applause ; করতালির শব্দ ; হাততালি। **3.** A slap ; a pat ; চপেটাঘাত, চড়, চাপড় ; মৃদু করাঘাত। ***Verb t.*** **1.** To strike the palms of the hands together in applause ; হাততালি দেওয়া, করতালি দেওয়া। **2.** To slap with the palm of the hand, in token of approval or encouragement ; পিঠ চাপড়ান। **3.** To shut (a door, window) with explosive noise ; to slam ; ঝনাৎ করিয়া বন্ধ করা ; ঝপাৎ করিয়া বন্ধ করা। **4.** To flap (wings) ; পাখসাট মারা। ***Verb i.*** **1.** To make a hard explosive noise ; to make a clack or clatter ; গর্জ্জন করা ; পটাৎ পটাৎ করা, ঘ্যানর্ ঘ্যানর শব্দ করা। **2.** To strike with the hands together in applause ; করতালি দেওয়া। **At one clap, At a clap**—At one stroke ; at once ; এক কোপে ; এক বারে। **To clap eyes on**—To get a sight of ; দৃষ্টিগোচর করা। To apply oneself to a task ; কোন কার্য্যে লাগিয়া যাওয়া। **To clap hold of**—To lay hold of promptly ; পট্ করিয়া ধরা। **To clap up**—To make, or settle hastily ; ঝট্ করিয়া তৈয়ার করা, চট্ করিয়া ঠিক করা। To imprison hastily ; ঝট্ করিয়া কয়েদ করা।

clăp, *n.* A venereal disease ; gonorrhœa ; উপদংশঘটিত রোগ বিশেষ ; প্রমেহ।

clăp'-nĕt, *n.* A folding net for taking birds and insects ; পক্ষী ও কীট ধরিবার একপ্রকার জাল।

clăp'-pêr, *n.* **1.** The tongue of a bell ; ঘণ্টালোলা, ঘণ্টার নুড়নুড়ি। **2.** A contrivance for scaring away birds ; পক্ষী তাড়াইবার কল বিশেষ। **3.** One who applauds ; যে ব্যক্তি বাহবা দেয়।

clăp'-pêr-claw (-clă), *v. t.* **1.** To scratch with the hand and nails ; to hit ; আঁচড় মারা ; আঘাত করা। **2.** (*Fig.*) To revile ; to criticize spitefully ; (লক্ষণায়) গালিগালাজ করা ; বিদ্বেষপূর্ণ সমালোচনা করা।

clăp'-trăp, *n.* & *adj.* Language or expression designed to catch applause ; cheap showy sentiment ; বাহবা পাওয়ার জন্য চাতুরীপূর্ণ ভাষা বা বাক্য ; অসার অথচ আড়ম্বরপূর্ণ ভাব। ***Adj.*** Contrived for making a show or gaining applause ; showy but insincere ; as, a *clap-trap* orator ; আড়ম্বর-প্রদর্শন বা বাহবা লাভের জন্য কল্পিত ; কপট ও আড়ম্বরপূর্ণ।

claque (clăk), (*F.*), *n.* **1.** A body of hired applauders in a theatre ; রঙ্গালয়ের ভাড়াটিয়া বাহবা দাতার দল। **2.** A body of subservient followers always ready to applaud their leader ; ধামাধরার দল।

claquer, claquerer, (*F.*), *ns.* A hired applauder ; ভাড়াটিয়া বাহবা দাতা।

clăr'-ence (-ĕns), *n.* A close four-wheeled carriage, with seats for four inside, and two on box ; একপ্রকার চারিচাকার গাড়ী।

clă-rĕn'-dŏn, *n.* (*Print.*) A thick-faced condensed type of various sizes ; একপ্রকার মুদ্রণের হরফ।

clare obscure—(*Paint.*) Light and shade ; (চিত্রবিদ্যা) আলো ও ছায়া।

clăr'-ĕt, *n.* & *adj.* **1.** The name given to the red wine of

Bordeaux ; any light red wine ; (*Slang*) blood ; ফরাসী দেশজাত লোহিতবর্ণ মদিরা বিশেষ ; লাল সরাব ; (ইতরভাষায়) রক্ত। **2.** (*Angling*) An artificial salmon-fly ; (ছিপে মাছ ধরিতে) স্যামন মৎস্য ধরিবার জন্য কৃত্রিমমক্ষিকা বিশেষ। ***Adj.*** Reddish violet ; of the colour of claret ; রক্তাভ ধূমল ; ক্লারেটবর্ণ। **To tap one's claret**—মুষ্ট্যাঘাত করিয়া নাকে রক্ত ছুটান।

clăr'-i-fȳ, *v. t.* **1.** To make clear (obscure subject, etc.) ; প্রাঞ্জল করা। **2.** To free from impurity, (a liquid, butter, air, etc.) ; স্বচ্ছ করা, নির্ম্মল করা, বিশুদ্ধ করা। **—fi-ca'-tion,** *n.* **—fi-er,** *n.* **1.** That which clarifies ; a substance used to clarify liquids, etc. ; বিশোধক পদার্থ ; পরিষ্কারক দ্রব্য। **2.** A vessel in which liquor or juice is clarified ; মদ্যাদি বিশোধিত করিবার পাত্র। **Clarified butter**—ঘৃত।

clăr'-i-nĕt, clar'-i-ŏ-nĕt, *ns.* A wooden single reed instrument played by holes and key ; একপ্রকার বংশী, সানাই, রণবংশী, তুরী।

clăr'-i-ŏn, *n.* & *adj.* **1.** A shrill narrow-tubed trumpet formerly used in war ; পূর্ব্বকালীন রণবংশী বিশেষ। **2.** Any rousing sound ; as, the cock's shrill *clarion* ; যে কোন উদ্বোধনকারী ধ্বনি। ***Adj.*** Loud and clear ; উচ্চনিনাদী।

Clarius magur—মাগুর (গুগুঃ)।

clăr'-i-tȳ, *n.* Clearness ; নির্ম্মলতা, অনাবিলতা, স্বচ্ছতা, প্রাঞ্জলতা।

clā'-rȳ, *n.* A labiate plant cultivated as pot-herb ; একপ্রকার শাক।

clăsh, *v. i., t.* & *n.* **1.** To produce a noise by striking against something ; সংঘট্ট করা, ঠুকাঠুকি করা, ঝঞ্ঝন করা। **2.** To come into violent collision, (with or without noise) ; প্রচণ্ডভাবে সংঘৃষ্ট হওয়া। **3.** To come into or engage in, conflict (*with, against*) ; to interfere, (*with*) ; সংঘর্ষ হওয়া ; হস্তক্ষেপ করা। **4.** To attack with violence, (*at, against, with*) ; প্রচণ্ডবেগে আক্রমণ করা। **5.** To disagree ; মতদ্বৈধ হওয়া, মতের অনৈক্য হওয়া। **6.** To be at variance with ; বিরোধী হওয়া। ***Verb t.*** To strike noisily together ; সংঘট্ট করা। ***Noun.*** **1.** A loud noise, such as is caused by the striking together of weapons ; ঝনৎকার, ঝন্‌ঝনা, চটাচট শব্দ। **2.** Hostile encounter ; সংঘর্ষ। **3.** Disagreement ; মত-বিরোধ, মতদ্বৈধ।

clăsp, *n.* & *v. t.* **1.** A metal fastening of two interlocking parts ; a buckle ; a brooch ; আঁকড়া ; বন্ধনাঙ্গুরী ; স্ত্রীলোকের বক্ষঃস্থলের বসন নিবদ্ধ করণার্থ কারুকার্য্যমণ্ডিত সূচী বিশেষ, বক্ষঃসূচী। **2.** A fastening of the covers of a book ; পুস্তকের প্রচ্ছদপট বন্ধনী। **3.** Taking in the arms ; embrace ; (*fig.*) reach ; as, within the *clasp* of this covenant ; ভুজপাশে বন্ধন ; আলিঙ্গন, আশ্লেষ ; (লক্ষণায়) বেড়। ***Verb t.*** **1.** To secure with a clasp, (usu. *up*) ; to shut or fasten ; আঁকড়া দ্বারা বন্ধ করা ; বন্ধ করা। **2.** To embrace (*lit.* & *fig.*) ; আকড়াইয়া ধরা, আলিঙ্গন করা, পরিরম্ভন করা, (শব্দানুযায়ী এবং লক্ষণায়)। **Clasp'-er,** *n.* **Clasp-knife** — চাকুছুরি, যে ছুরির ফলা মুড়িয়া বাটের ভিতর রাখা যায়। **To clasp one's hands**—To join one's hands by interlocking the fingers ; অঙ্গুলীতে অঙ্গুলী গ্রথিত করত হাত যোড় করা।

class (clăs), *n., v. t.* & *i.* **1.** A division, order or grade of society (according to status) ; শ্রেণী (সামাজিক মর্য্যাদা অনুসারে)। **2.** The caste-system ; caste ; social rank, esp. high rank ; as, the spirit and power of *class* ; জাতিভেদ-প্রথা ; জাতি ; সামাজিক পদ, উচ্চপদবী। **3.** A set of students taught together ; বিদ্যালয়ের শ্রেণী। **4.** A division of candidates according to merit, as a result of examination ; as, to take a *class* (=to take honours) ; গুণানুসারে পরীক্ষোত্তীর্ণ ছাত্রদিগের বিভাগ। **5.** A division of things according to grade or quality ; as, a higher, low, first, etc. *class* ; উৎকর্ষ, অপকর্ষ অনুসারে বস্তুর বিভাগ। **6.** (*Nat. Hist.*) One of the highest groups into which animal, vegetable or mineral kingdom is divided, as, family, genera, species, etc. ; (প্রাকৃতিক ইতিহাস) বর্গ, গণ, পর্য্যায়, শ্রেণী। ***Verb t.*** **1.** To place in a class ; to assign to its proper group ; শ্রেণীবদ্ধ করা ; কোন বস্তুর উপযুক্ত শ্রেণী নির্দ্দেশ করা। **2.** To place (students) in a class for instruction ; to place in a particular class, as the result of examination ; বিদ্যালয়ের শ্রেণীতে ভুক্ত করা ; পরীক্ষোত্তীর্ণ ছাত্রগণের গুণানুসারে শ্রেণীবিভাগ করা। ***Verb i.*** To fall into a particular class or division ; কোন বিশেষ শ্রেণী বা বিভাগে ভুক্ত হওয়া। **Class'-a-ble,** *adj.* **Class-book**—বিদ্যালয়ের শ্রেণীবিশেষের পাঠ্য পুস্তক। **Class-fellow**—সহাধ্যায়ী, সতীর্থ। **Class-man** — (অক্সফোর্ড্ বিশ্ববিদ্যালয়ে) যে ছাত্র সম্মানের সহিত পরীক্ষায় উত্তীর্ণ হইয়াছে। **Class-mate**—সহাধ্যায়ী। **The classes** — ধনী বা শিক্ষিত সম্প্রদায়।

clăs'-sic, *n.* **1.** A Greek and Roman work or author of the highest class ; any ancient Greek and Latin writer ; (now) a writer or literary work of the first rank and admitted excellence ; as, English *classics* ; উৎকৃষ্ট শ্রেণীর গ্রীক বা রোমীয় গ্রন্থ বা গ্রন্থকার ; প্রাচীন গ্রীক ও রোমীয় গ্রন্থকার ; (বর্ত্তমানে) প্রথম শ্রেণীর গ্রন্থকার বা গ্রন্থ। **2.** (*pl.*) The general body of Greek and

Latin literature ; গ্রীক ও লাটিন সাহিত্য। 3. A Greek and Latin scholar ; "A fine *classic*, a youth of promise ;" গ্রীক ও লাটিন সাহিত্যে সুপণ্ডিত ব্যক্তি।

clăs′-sic, –si-căl, *adj.* & *n.* **1.** Of the first class ; প্রথম শ্রেণীর, উচ্চ শ্রেণীর। **2.** Belonging to ancient Greek and Latin authors of the first rank ; as, *classic* poetry ; of the arts and culture of that age ; as, *classic* civilization ; প্রাচীন গ্রীস ও রোমের উচ্চশ্রেণীর গ্রন্থকার সম্বন্ধীয় ; উক্ত যুগের কলাবিদ্যা বা সভ্যতা সম্বন্ধীয়। **3.** Of literary note ; historically famous ; as, *classic* Edinburgh ; সাহিত্যিক হিসাবে বিখ্যাত ; ঐতিহাসিকভাবে বিখ্যাত। **4.** Pure ; chaste ; refined ; as, *classic* style, taste : (opp. to *romantic*) ; বিশুদ্ধ ; সাধু ; পরিমার্জ্জিত। **–cal-i-ty,** *n.* **–cal-ly,** *adv.* **–cal-ness,** *n.* **–si-cism,** *n.* A Latin or Greek form of idiom ; লাটীন বা গ্রীক ভাষার রীতিসিদ্ধ প্রয়োগ। **–si-cist,** *n.* A follower of classical style ; a classical scholar ; an advocate of classical education ; প্রাচীন গ্রীক বা রোমান সাহিত্যিকদিগের রচনাপদ্ধতির অনুসরণকারী ; প্রাচীন গ্রীক ও রোমান সাহিত্যে সুপণ্ডিত ব্যক্তি ; প্রাচীন গ্রীক ও রোমান সাহিত্যবিষয়ক শিক্ষার সমর্থনকারী ব্যক্তি। **–si-cize,** *v.* **Classic races** — ইংলণ্ডের পাঁচটী সুপ্রসিদ্ধ ঘোড়দৌড়ের নাম। (যথা ; Two thousand, One thousand, Derby, Oaks and St. Leger.)

clăs′-si-fȳ, *v. t.* To distribute into classes ; to arrange according to a system ; শ্রেণীবিভাগ করা ; শ্রেণীবদ্ধ করা, প্রণালীবদ্ধ করা। **–fi-a-ble, –fi-ca-to-ry,** *adjs.* **–fi-ca′-tion,** *n.* The act of classifying ; arrangement ; শ্রেণীনির্দ্দেশ, বর্গনির্দ্দেশ ; বিভাগ, শ্রেণীবিভাগ। **–fi′-er,** *n.*

clăss′-ȳ, *adj.* (*Colloq.*) Of superior merit ; (চলিতভাষায়) অধিকতর গুণসম্পন্ন।

clăt′-têr, *n., v. i.* & *t.* **1.** A repetition of abrupt sounds ; ঠক্‌ঠক্, খট্‌খট্, পট্‌পট্। **2.** Noisy talk ; confused din of voices ; সোরগোল, কোলাহল, বাজে কথা ; বক্‌বক্। ***Verb i.*** To strike so as to make a thing rattle ; খট্‌খট্ শব্দ করা, ঠক্‌ঠক্ শব্দ করা, ঘরঘর শব্দ করা। **2.** To talk idly ; বাজে কথা বকা। ***Verb t.*** To make a rattling noise with ; কোন কিছু দ্বারা ঘর্ঘর ধ্বনি করা। **–er,** *n.* **–ing-ly,** *adv.*

clause (cläz), *n.* **1.** A single sentence ; বাক্য ; **2.** *Gram.*) A subordinate portion of a sentence containing a subject and its predicate ; (ব্যাকরণ) উদ্দেশ্য ও বিধেয়ান্বিত বাক্যাংশ। **3.** A separate article, stipulation, or proviso in a legal or formal document ; লেখ্য পত্রাদির দফা, সর্ত্ত বা প্রকরণ। **Clau′-su-lar,** *adj.*

claus′-trăl (cläs-), *adj.* Pertaining to a cloister or religious house ; মঠ বা আশ্রমসম্বন্ধীয়।

clā′-vāte, *adj.* (*Bot.*) Club-shaped ; (উদ্ভিদ-বিদ্যা) গদাকার (সাঃ পঃ)।

clăv′-i-chŏrd, *n.* A musical instrument with strings and keys ; একপ্রকার বাদ্যযন্ত্র।

clăv′-i-cle, *n.* The collar-bone ; অংসফলক, জত্রু (সাঃ পঃ) কণ্ঠাস্থি, অক্ষক (সাঃ পঃ,—সুশ্রু)।

claw (clä), *n.* & *v. i.* **1.** The pointed horny nail of beast's or bird's foot ; (পশুপক্ষীর) নখর। **2.** A foot armed with sharp nails ; থাবা। **3.** The pincers or holders of shell-fish ; শঙ্খ শম্বুকাদি জলজন্তুর সাঁড়াশী বা দীর্ঘ নখর। **4.** Anything resembling the claw ; a contrivance for grappling, holding, etc. ; নখরের অনুরূপ বস্তু ; চিম্‌টা। **5.** (*In contempt*) A hand ; (অবজ্ঞাচ্ছলে) হাত। ***Verb t.*** **1.** To scratch or tear with the nails or pointed instruments ; সূক্ষ্মাগ্র যন্ত্রদ্বারা আঁচড়ান বা বিদারণ করা, আঁচড়ান। **2.** To scratch softly ; সুরসুরি দেওয়া (বড় প্রচলিত নহে)। **Claw hammer**—হাতুড়ী বিশেষ,—ইহার এক প্রান্ত পেরেক খুলিবার জন্য চেড়া থাকে। **Claw-hammer-coat** — একপ্রকার কোর্ত্তা,—ইহার পেছনের দিকের নীচের অংশ চেড়া থাকে। **Claw me and I will claw thee**—আমাকে খুসি কর, আমিও তোমাকে খুসি করিব। **In one's claws**—In one's possessions ; কাহারো থাবার মধ্যে, কাহারো মুঠার মধ্যে। **To claw away**—To scold ; তিরস্কার করা। **To claw off**—To get rid of ; রেহাই পাওয়া। To eat rapidly or voraciously ; তাড়াতাড়ি খাওয়া, পেটুকের মত খাওয়া। **To claw the back of, To claw by the back**—To fawn upon ; তোষামোদ করা, হীনভাবে তোষামোদ করা। **To pare, cut the claws of**—To disarm ; নিরস্ত্র করা।

clay (clā), *n.* & *v. t.* **1.** A stiff tenacious earth,—materials of bricks, pottery, earthenware, etc. ; চিক্কণ মৃত্তিকা (ভাবঃ প্রঃ), কুলালমৃত্তিকা, কৃষ্ণমৃত্তিকা, এঁটেল মাটি। **2.** Mire ; mud ; কর্দ্দম ; কাদা, মাটি। **3.** Earth as the material of the human body ; hence, the human body ; as, your lifeless *clay* ; ক্ষিতি (মানব দেহের উপাদানস্বরূপ) ; মাটির দেহ। ***Verb t.*** To cover or plaster with clay ; to mix clay with ; আঠালো মাটির দ্বারা আবৃত বা লেপন করা ; কোন কিছুর সহিত আঠালো মাটি মিশান। **–ey, –ish,** *adjs.* **Clay-cold**—প্রাণহীন। **Clay-pipe**—মৃণ্ময় ধূমপান নল। **(To be) clay in the hands of the potter**—কুম্ভকারের হাতে কাদার তালের ন্যায়, যাহা ইচ্ছা তাহাই করান যাইতে পারে এরূপ অবস্থায় আসা। **To moisten** or **wet one's clay**—(*Humorous*) To drink ; (কৌতুকচ্ছলে) মদ্য পান করা।

clay′-more (klā-mōr), *n.* The two-edged broadsword of the ancient Scottish Highlanders ; উভয়দিকে

ধার বিশিষ্ট পূর্ব্বকালীন হাইলেণ্ডারগণের খড়্গাবিশেষ।

clean (clĕn), *adj.* & *adv.* **1.** Free from dirt or filth; unsoiled; unadulterated; pure; as, *clean* wheat; untarnished; as, *clean* gold; নির্ম্মল, বিমল; পরিষ্কার, পরিচ্ছন্ন; খাঁটি; শুচি, মেধ্য; বিশুদ্ধ। **2.** Free from weeds or stones, etc.; as, a *clean* field; আগাছা শূন্য, কঙ্করশূন্য। **3.** (*Of paper*) Blank; (of *printer's proof*) having few or no corrections or alterations; অলিখিত, সাদা; (মুদ্রাকরের মুদ্রণী-পত্র সম্পর্কে) সামান্য সংশোধনবিশিষ্ট বা সংশোধনশূন্য। **4.** (*Of precious stones*) Having no interior flaws; (মণি-সম্পর্কে) নিখুঁত। **5.** Pure; chaste; innocent; "Create in me a *clean* heart, O God;" পবিত্র; নির্ম্মল, বিমলাত্মা, শুদ্ধমতি; নির্দ্দোষ, নিষ্পাপ, নিষ্কলঙ্ক। **6.** Free from knots; as, *clean* timber; গাঁইট-শূন্য, অগ্রন্থিল। **7.** Not defiling; fit to be used for food; as, a *clean* animal; শুচি; খাদ্যোপযোগী। **8.** Neatly made; comely; as, *clean* limbs; সুগঠিত; সুন্দর, সুদর্শন। **9.** Sharp (of wit); clever; as, a *clean* trick; তীক্ষ্ণ (বুদ্ধি-সম্পর্কে); চালাক, সাফ্ (*Colloq.*)। **10.** Entire; complete; as, a *clean* sweep; অখণ্ড; সম্পূর্ণ। ***Adv.*** **1.** In a manner free from dirt; পরিষ্কৃতভাবে। **2.** Neatly; dexterously; পরিচ্ছন্নরূপে; নিপুণতার সহিত। **3.** Wholly; সাফ্, বিলকুল (*Colloq.*) **Clean Bill of health**—See BILL. **Clean-bred**—সুশিক্ষিত। **Clean-cut**—সুকর্ত্তিত; সুস্পষ্টভাবে গঠিত। **Clean-fingered**—নিপুণহস্ত; সাধু। **Clean-fish**—সবে মাত্র ডিম্ব ছাড়িয়াছে এরূপ মৎস্য; অজাত-ডিম্ব মৎস্য। **Clean-handed**—শুভ্রচরিত্র। **Clean-limbed** — সুঠাম, সুগঠিত; অঙ্গসৌষ্ঠব সম্পন্ন। **Clean-sweep**—সম্পূর্ণরূপে অব্যাহতি, নিষ্কৃতি। **Clean-timbered** — সুগঠিত। **To have clean hands, To keep the hands clean**—To be innocent of wrong-doing; দোষশূন্য হওয়া। **To keep a clean tongue**—To abstain from offensive or foul talk; কুকথা বলিয়া জিহ্বা কলুষিত না করা। **To make a clean breast**—To make full confession; অকপটে সমস্ত দোষ স্বীকার করা। **To show a clean pair of heels**—To escape by superior speed; বেগে পলায়ন করা।

clean (clēn), *v. t.* To free from dirt, filth or impurity; to cleanse; পরিষ্কার করা, পরিচ্ছন্ন করা, নির্ম্মল করা; শোধন করা। **Clean'-a-ble,** *adj.* **Clean'-er,** *n.* **Clean'-ly,** *adj.* & *adv.* Clean; as, a *cleanly* room; পরিষ্কার। (*Adv.*) In a clean manner; neatly; exactly; পরিষ্কারভাবে; পরিচ্ছন্নভাবে; ঠিকভাবে। **Clean'-li-ness,** *n.* **To clean away, off**—To remove dirt or the like; ময়লা, কর্দ্দম, জঞ্জালাদি পরিষ্কার করা। **To clean down**—To clean by sweeping down; ঝাঁট্ দিয়া পরিষ্কার করা। **To clean out**—To empty or exhaust; খালি করা, নিঃশেষ করা। To make bankrupt; দাউলিয়া করা, নিঃস্ব করা।

cleanse (clĕnz), *v. t.* **1.** To make clean; to free from dirt or filth; পরিষ্কার করা, নির্ম্মল করা; পরিচ্ছন্ন করা, সাফ্ করা (*Colloq.*)। **2.** To free from sin or guilt; to purify; (*of, from*); নিষ্পাপ করা, নির্দ্দোষ করা; পবিত্র করা। **3.** To purge; as, to *cleanse* the bowels: কোষ্ঠ পরিষ্কার করা। **4.** (*Bible*) To cure (leper, etc.): (বাইবেল) আরোগ্য করা (কুষ্ঠ রোগী প্রভৃতি)। **Cleans'-er,** *n.*

clear (clēr), *adj.* & *adv.* **1.** Brilliant; as, the *clear* sun, stars; উজ্জ্বল। **2.** Transparent; blooming; as, *clear* complexion, skin, etc.; free from admixture; bright; as, *clear* colour; স্বচ্ছ; ফুটন্ত, যৌবনের সৌন্দর্য্যবিকাশী; নির্ম্মল, বিমল, অমল; দীপ্ত, সমুজ্জ্বল। **3.** Distinct; plain; easy to understand; পরিস্ফুট, সুস্পষ্ট, বিশদ; স্পষ্টার্থ, স্ফুট; সুখবোধ্য, সরল। **4.** Seeing distinctly; having keen perception; as, *clear* eyes and judgment; স্পষ্টদর্শী, বিমলধী, বিশদবুদ্ধি; সূক্ষ্মদর্শী। **5.** Free from doubt; certain; as, I am not *clear* that the object is a good one; নিঃসন্দিগ্ধ; কৃতনিশ্চয়। **6.** Easily or distinctly heard; as, a *clear* voice; সুস্পষ্ট। **7.** Innocent; unsullied; as, men of *clear* honour; নির্দ্দোষ; নিষ্কলঙ্ক। **8.** Net; as, a *clear* profit; খরচাবাদ, নিট (*Colloq.*), ঝাড়া (*Colloq.*)। **9.** Free from obstacles; open; as, a *clear* view, space, etc.; খোলা, নির্ব্বিঘ্ন, বাধাশূন্য; মুক্ত, অবারিত, উদার। **10.** Free from encumbrance; out of debt; as, five pounds would set me *clear*; ঝঞ্ঝাট মুক্ত; ঋণমুক্ত। ***Adv.*** In a clear manner; brightly; distinctly; audibly; wholly; quite; পরিষ্কাররূপে; উজ্জ্বলভাবে; স্পষ্টভাবে, সুস্পষ্টভাবে; শ্রুতিযোগ্যরূপে; সমগ্রভাবে; সম্পূর্ণরূপে। **Clear-cut**—সুস্পষ্টভাবে কর্ত্তিত; সুস্পষ্টরূপে সীমানির্দ্দিষ্ট। **Clear day or days**—পূরা দিন। **Clear-headed**—বিমলধী। **Clear-fire**—নির্ধূম বা শিখাবিহীন অগ্নি। **Clear side of a ship**—জলপৃষ্ঠ হইতে জাহাজের পাটাতনের কাষ্ঠফলকের উচ্চতা। **Clear-sighted** — সূক্ষ্মদর্শী, দূরদর্শী। **Clear stuff, boards, planks, etc.**—যে কাষ্ঠাদিতে গ্রন্থি নাই। **In the clear**—আভ্যন্তরীণ পরিমাণে; একপ্রান্ত হইতে অপর প্রান্ত পর্য্যন্ত। **The coast is clear**—The causes of danger are over; বিপদের কারণ দূর হইয়াছে, সকল বাধা বিপত্তি অপগত হইয়াছে।

clear (klēr), *v. t.* & *i.* **1.** To render bright or transparent; উজ্জ্বল বা স্বচ্ছ করা। **2.** To free from impurities; to clarify (a liquid)

বিশুদ্ধ করা ; শোধন করা। 3. To elucidate ; as, I have quite *cleared* my meaning ; বোধগম্য করা, সহজ-বোধ্য করা, সুখবোধ্য করা। 4. To free from impediments, obstructions, etc. ; বাধাশূন্য করা, প্রতিবন্ধকশূন্য করা। 5. To settle or discharge a debt, bill, etc. ; as, money sufficient to *clear* all his debts ; ঋণ প্রভৃতি পরিষ্কার করা। ***Verb i.*** **1.** To become clear or bright ; to become free from clouds, mist, etc. ; পরিষ্কার বা উজ্জ্বল হওয়া ; মেঘ-মুক্ত হওয়া, কুঝটিকা মুক্ত হওয়া। **2.** To become transparent ; স্বচ্ছ হওয়া। **3.** To depart, so as to leave the place clear ; চলিয়া যাওয়া। **4.** To dispose of supplies by purchase and sale ; ক্রয়বিক্রয়দ্বারা মাল খালাস করা। **To clear air**—To free from clouds, mists, etc. ; (আকাশ) মেঘ বা কুজ্ঝটিকা মুক্ত করা। **To clear an examination paper** — To dispose of all the questions ; সমস্ত প্রশ্নের উত্তর প্রদান করা। **To clear a ship**—To discharge it of its cargo ; জাহাজের মাল খালাস করা। **To clear away**—To remove ; to leave the place ; স্থানান্তরিত হওয়া ; স্থান ত্যাগ করা। To remove meal from the table ; ভোজনের মেজ হইতে আহার্য্য দ্রব্য স্থানান্তরিত করা। (Of clouds, fogs, etc.) To pass away ; to disappear ; তিরোহিত হওয়া ; অন্তর্হিত হওয়া। **To clear goods**—To pay the custom house dues, duties, etc. ; শুল্কাগারের প্রাপ্য শুল্ক প্রভৃতি প্রদান করা। **To clear off**—To remove an encumbrance ; to get rid of (a debt or claim) ; ঝঞ্ঝাট দূর করা ; (ঋণ বা দায় হইতে) মুক্ত হওয়া। (Of clouds, fogs, etc.) To melt away ; to go off ; (মেঘ, কুজ্ঝটিকা প্রভৃতির পক্ষে) মিলাইয়া যাওয়া, দ্রবীভূত হওয়া ; তিরোহিত হওয়া। **To clear out**—To take or throw out ; to empty ; বাহির করিয়া লওয়া, দূর করিয়া ফেলা ; শূন্য করা। To depart out of a place ; to be off ; প্রস্থান করা ; চলিয়া যওয়া। **To clear ship for action** or **to clear for action**—(*Naut.*) To remove encumbrances from the decks and prepare for an engagement ; যুদ্ধ সজ্জার পূর্ব্বে জাহাজের তল হইতে গতিরোধক। দ্রব্যাদি দূর করা বা সরাইয়া ফেলা। **To clear up**—To brighten up ; উজ্জ্বল করা। To become clear, esp. the weather after rain or storm ; পরিষ্কার হওয়া, বিশেষতঃ ঝড় বা বৃষ্টির পর আকাশ নির্ম্মল হওয়া।

clear'-ance (klēr-ăns), *n.* **1.** The act of making clear ; specif. the clearing of land by the removal of wood, old houses, etc. ; নির্ম্মলী-করণ, পরিষ্করণ ; বন, পুরাতন বাটী প্রভৃতি অপসারিত করিয়া ভূমি পরিষ্করণ। **2.** The clearing of a ship at the Custom House ; also a certificate that this has been done ; permission to sail ; শুল্কা-গারের প্রাপ্য শুল্কাদি প্রদানপূর্ব্বক জাহাজাদি ছাড়িবার অনুমতিলাভ ; উক্ত শুল্ক প্রভৃতি প্রদানের নিদর্শন পত্র, ছাড়চিঠি ; জাহাজ ছাড়িবার অনুমতি। **Clearance sale**—সাবাড়ি বিক্রয়।

clear'-cole (klēr-kōl), *n.* & *v. t.* A preparation of size mixed with white-lead, used in house-painting, etc. ; পাতলা শিরীষ এবং সফেদা মিশ্রিত গৃহাদি-রঞ্জক পদার্থ বিশেষ। ***Verb t.*** To paint with this ; উক্ত রঙ্গ দ্বারা বিলেপিত করা।

clear'-ing (klēr-), *n.* **1.** The act or process of making clear ; brightening ; clarifying ; elucidation ; পরিষ্করণ, সম্মার্জ্জন ; প্রকাশন ; বিশোধন ; স্পষ্টীকরণ। **2.** A piece of land in a primeval forest, cleared for cultivation ; আবাদি ভূমি। **Clearing house**—ইংলণ্ডের মহাজন-গণের প্রতিষ্ঠান বিশেষ—ইহাতে চেক, হুণ্ডি প্রভৃতির বিনিময় হয়। **Railway clearing house**—রেলওয়ে কার্য্যালয়-বিশেষ — ইহাতে বিভিন্ন রেলওয়ে কোম্পানীর মধ্যে পাওনা-দেনার হিসাব পরিষ্কার হয়।

clear'-lŷ (klēr-), *adv.* In a clear manner ; distinctly ; evidently ; পরিষ্কাররূপে ; স্পষ্টরূপে ; ফুটভাবে।

clear'-nĕss (klēr-), *n.* **1.** Transparency or purity of colour of a thing ; স্বচ্ছতা, নির্ম্মলতা, অনাবিলতা। **2.** Distinctness of vision, expression, understanding, etc. ; স্পষ্টতা, বিশদতা, প্রাঞ্জলতা। **3.** Freedom from obstructions ; বাধাশূন্যতা।

cleat (klēt), *n.* **1.** A wedge ; কাজলা, ছেনি, মেক, কীল, কীলক। **2.** (*Naut.*) A piece of wood or iron for fastening ropes upon ; (নৌ-বিদ্যা) রজ্জু বাঁধিবার জন্য জাহাজের ভিন্ন ভিন্ন স্থানে সংবদ্ধ কাষ্ঠ বা লৌহখণ্ড।

cleav'-age (klēv-āj), *n.* **1.** The act of splitting asunder ; the state of being cleft ; as, the *cleavage* between the classes ; বিদারণ, বিভেদন ; সম্ভেদ, বিভঙ্গ, ভেদ। **2.** (*Miner.* & *Geol.*) The manner in which substances tend to split ; (খনিজ-বিদ্যা ও ভূ-বিদ্যা) সম্ভেদ-পদ্ধতি।

cleave (klēv), *v. i.* (*p. t.* CLEAVED, CLOVE, *p.p.* CLEAVED) To stick fast or adhere to ; সংসক্ত হওয়া, সংশ্লিষ্ট হওয়া।

cleave (klēv), *v.t.* & *i.* (*p. t.* CLOVE or CLEFT. *p.p.* CLOVEN or CLEFT) To part or divide by a cutting blow ; to split ; (often with *asunder, in two*, etc.) ; to pierce and penetrate (air, water, etc.) ; ছেদন করা ; বিদারণ করা ; ভেদ করিয়া প্রবেশ করা। ***Verb i.*** **1.** To part ; to crack ; as, the ground *cleaves* by frost ; খণ্ডিত হওয়া ; ফাটিয়া যাওয়া। **2.** To make one's way ; (with *through*) ; ঠেলিয়া অগ্রসর হওয়া। **Cleav'-a-ble,** *adj.* **In a cleft stick**—In a tight place allowing neither retreat nor advance ;

যে স্থল হইতে অগ্রসর কিম্বা পশ্চাৎপদ হওয়া সম্ভবপর নহে—এরূপ স্থানে।

cleav'-êr (klēv-), *n.* **1.** One who splits (wood, etc.); ছেদনকারী। **2.** A butcher's instrument for dividing into joints or pieces; কসাইর দা, কাতান।

cleav'-êrs, cliv'-êrs (klēv-), *n.* (*Used as sing.* or *pl.*) A creeper sticking to clothes; (also called *goosegrass, catchweed,* etc.); একপ্রকার লতাগাছ—যাহা কাপড়ে লাগিয়া থাকে।

cleck (klĕk), *v. t.* To hatch, (*lit.* & *fig.*); তা দেওয়া (শব্দানুযায়ী এবং লক্ষণায়)।

cleek (klēk), *n* An iron headed golf club; লৌহমণ্ডিতাগ্রভাগবিশিষ্ট গল্‌ফ্ ক্রীড়ার দণ্ড।

clĕf, *n.* (*Mus.*) One of the symbols indicating pitch of stave in music; (সঙ্গীত-বিদ্যা) স্বরসংক্রম চিহ্ন।

clĕft, *v. t., i.* & *n.* (*p. t.* & *p. p.* of CLEAVE, which see). ***Noun.*** An opening made by splitting a crack; a fissure; ফাটল; ফাঁক, ফাটা, ফাইট।

clĕg, *n.* The gadfly; দংশক, ডাঁস।

cleis-tō-găm'-ic (klēs-), *adj.* (*Bot.*) Applied to certain small permanently closed flowers, adapted for self-fertilization; (উদ্ভিদ্‌বিদ্যা) কতিপয় আত্মনিষেকোপযোগী চিররুদ্ধ ক্ষুদ্র পুষ্প সম্বন্ধে প্রযুক্ত।

clĕm, *v. t.* & *i.* To waste with hunger; অনাহারে কৃশ করা বা হওয়া।

clĕm'-ă-tis, *n.* The generic name of woody climbing plants; এক শ্রেণীর লতার সাধারণ নাম।

clĕm'-ĕnt, *adj.* **1.** Merciful; kindly; কারুণিক; সদয়, দয়ালু। **2.** (*Of weather or climate*) Mild; gentle; (জল বায়ু, আবহাওয়া প্রভৃতি সম্পর্কে) প্রশান্ত; মৃদু। **—en-cy,** *n.* Mildness or gentleness of temper; mercy; leniency; প্রশান্তভাব, দয়ার্দ্র ভাব; করুণা; দয়ালুতা। **2.** Mildness of weather or climate: (opp. to *inclemency, severity*); জলবায়ু, আবহাওয়া প্রভৃতির শান্ত বা মৃদুভাব।

clĕnch (klĕnsh), **clinch** (klĭnsh), *v. t.* & *i.* **1.** To secure or fasten by a nail; to rivet; প্রেক প্রভৃতি দ্বারা আটা; নাচি দ্বারা আটা। **2.** To close tightly (the fingers, fist, teeth); দৃঢ়বদ্ধ করা, (মুষ্টি) বদ্ধ করা। **3.** To grasp firmly; to clutch; to grip; শক্ত করিয়া ধরা; আঁকড়াইয়া ধরা; মুটাইয়া ধরা। **4.** (*Fig.*) To confirm or settle conclusively (an argument, a bargain, etc.); (লক্ষণায়) স্থির-সিদ্ধান্ত করা, পাকা করা। ***Verb i.*** To interlock closely; to close up tightly, as the hands, teeth; দৃঢ়ভাবে সংগ্রথিত হওয়া; দৃঢ়সংবদ্ধ হওয়া। **Clench'-er,** *n.* A nail, etc. used for clenching; প্রেক প্রভৃতি।

clench (klĕnsh), *n.* **1.** A grip; a clutch; a tight closure of the teeth, fist, etc.; secure fastening of a nail, etc.; মুষ্টিবন্ধ; গ্রাহ; দৃঢ়রূপে ধারণ, মুটাইয়া বা আকড়াইয়া ধরণ; দৃঢ়বন্ধন। **2.** (*Fig.*) Conclusive confirmation of an argument; (লক্ষণায়) কোনও যুক্তির চূড়ান্ত সিদ্ধান্ত।

clĕp'-sȳ-dră, *n.* An ancient clock worked by a flow of water; জলপ্রবাহ দ্বারা চালিত প্রাচীন কালের ঘটিকাযন্ত্র বিশেষ।

Clerodendron infortunatum—ভাঁট (বেলঃ)।

clere'-stō-rȳ (klēr-), *n.* The part of a cathedral-wall which rises clear of the roofs, with series of windows for lighting the interior; ছাদ্ হইতে পৃথগ্‌ভাবে উত্থিত খৃষ্টীয় মহাধর্ম্মমন্দিরের প্রাচীরাংশ বিশেষ। মন্দিরের অভ্যন্তরভাগে আলোক প্রবেশের জন্য এই প্রাচীরাংশ গবাক্ষশ্রেণী-সমন্বিত থাকে।

clêr'-ġȳ, *n.* (THE CLERGY, usu. *pl.*; A CLERGY, *sing.*) The body of men ordained for religious service, in the Christain Church; (opp. to *laity*); যাজকমণ্ডলী, যাজকসম্প্রদায়। **Benefit of clergy**—পূর্ব্বকালে যাজক বা অক্ষরজ্ঞানসম্পন্ন ব্যক্তিগণের সাধারণ বিচারালয়ে বিচারিত না হওয়ার, এবং পরবর্ত্তী সময়ে, প্রথম অপরাধের জন্য ক্ষমালাভের বিশেষ অধিকার। **Clergy-man,** *n.* যাজক। **Clergy-woman,** *n.* ধর্ম্মযাজক-পত্নী, ধর্ম্মযাজকের আত্মীয়া।

clĕr'-ic, *adj.* & *n.* Of or belonging to the clergy; যাজকীয়। ***Noun.*** A clergyman; যাজক।

clĕr'-i-căl, *adj.* & *n.* **1.** Of or pertaining to the clergy; যাজকীয়, ধর্ম্মযাজক সম্বন্ধীয়। **2.** Of or relating to a clerk or penman; as, a *clerical* error; লিপিকর সম্বন্ধীয়, কেরাণী সম্পর্কীয়। **—cal'-i-ty,** *n.* **—ism,** *n.* **—ize,** *v. t.* **—ly,** *adv.*

clerk (klârk), *n.* **1.** A clergyman, a lay officer of parish Church with various duties; যাজক, পাদরী, ধর্ম্মোপদেশক। **2.** One who reads the responses in the English Church service; ইংলণ্ডীয় ধর্ম্মসমাজ সংসৃষ্ট ধর্ম্ম-মন্দিরে উপাসনাকালে যে ব্যক্তি উপাসকমণ্ডলীর মুখপাত্রস্বরূপ উত্তর প্রদান করে। **3.** An officer in charge of the records, correspondence, etc. of court, corporation, etc.; মসীজীবী, কেরাণী। **4.** One able to read or write; a scholar; লিখনপঠনপটু ব্যক্তি; পণ্ডিত ব্যক্তি। **—dom, —er-y, —ship,** *ns.* **—ling,** *n.* A young or petty clerk; ছোকরা কেরাণী, সামান্য কেরাণী। **—ly,** *adj.* & *adv.* **Clerk of the crown**—যে রাজকর্ম্মচারী অপরাধীদিগের বিরুদ্ধে অভিযোগ প্রস্তুত এবং অভিযোগ পাঠ করেন।

clĕv'-êr, *adj.* **1.** Possessing quickness of intellect; talented; মেধাবী; প্রতিভাসম্পন্ন। **2.** Adroit; dexterous; সুনিপুণ; সুদক্ষ, কুশল, নিপুণ, সেয়ানা (*Colloq.*)। **3.** Ingenious; done with skill, (said of doer or thing done); কৌশলী; সুকৌশলে

সম্পাদিত। **4.** (*U. S.*) Good-natured ; amiable ; সৎস্বভাব ; নম্র। **–ish,** *adj.* **–ly,** *adv.* In a clever manner ; চতুরতার সহিত, নিপুণতার সহিত। **–ness,** *n.* The quality of being clever ; নিপুণতা, চাতুর্য্য, দক্ষতা, বাহাদুরী (*Colloq*)।

clew, clue (klü), *n.* & *v. t.* **1.** A ball of thread or yarn, or the thread in it ; also the cocoon of a silk-worm ; গুটির সূতা ; সূতার গুটি ; রেশম কীটের গুটি। **2.** (*Myth.* and *legend*) A ball of thread that guides one's way out of a labyrinth or maze ; hence, that which guides through a chic, perplexity or difficulty ; (গ্রীক ও রোমীয় পুরাণ এবং উপকথায়) যে সূত্রপিণ্ডের সাহায্যে কোন গোলকধাঁধা হইতে বহির্গত হওয়া যায়, (ক্রীটদ্বীপের গোলকধাঁধা হইতে বহির্গত হইবার জন্য ক্রীটরাজ মাইনসের কন্যা Ariadne Theseus কে যে সূত্র প্রদান করেন—তৎস্মরণে) ; যৎসাহায্যে কোন গোলকধাঁধা হইতে বহির্গত হওয়া যায় ; সূত্র। **3.** (*Naut.*) The lower corner of a square sail and the aftmost corner of a fore and aft sail ; সমচতুষ্কোণ পাইলের নিম্নতর কোণ বা জাহাজের সম্মুখ এবং পশ্চাদ্ভাগস্থ পাইলের সর্ব্ব পশ্চাদ্দিকস্থ কোণ। ***Verb t.*** (With *up*) To draw the lower ends of sails to upper yard or mast ready for furling ; গুটাইবার পূর্ব্বে পাইলের নিম্নদিগের প্রান্তদ্বয় মাস্তলের উপর টানিয়া আনা।

cli-che' (klë-shā), *n.* **1.** An electrotype or stereotype plate ; বৈদ্যুতিক ক্রিয়াদ্বারা প্রস্তুত সীসা বা তাম্র নির্ম্মিত অক্ষর ফলক। **2.** (*Fig.*) A hackneyed literary phrase ; সাহিত্যে ব্যবহৃত পুরাতন বাক্য।

click (klĭk), *v. i.* & *n.* To tick ; ঘড়ীর ন্যায় টিক্ টিক্ শব্দ করা। ***Noun.*** **1.** A short sharp sound ; টিক্ টিক্ শব্দ। **2.** A small piece of iron falling into a notched wheel ; হাস্কল।

Click'-er, *n.* **1.** One who or that which clicks ; টিক্ টিক্ শব্দকারী। **2.** A foreman shoemaker who cuts out the leather for boots and shoes ; যে চর্ম্মকার জুতা তৈয়ারীর জন্য চামড়া কাটিয়া দেয়। **3.** (*Printing*) The compositor who distributes the copy among others, makes up the pages, sets up head-lines, etc. ; মুদ্রাকর। **Click-clack, Click-click**—টিক্ টিক্ শব্দ ; বক্‌বক্।

clī'-ĕnt, *n.* **1.** One under the protection or patronage of another ; a dependent ; শরণাগত ব্যক্তি, আশ্রিত ব্যক্তি ; প্রতিপাল্য ব্যক্তি, অনুজীবী। **2.** (*Law*) An employer of a lawyer ; (আইন) মোক্কেল। **3.** An employer of any professional man ; a customer ; চিকিৎসক প্রভৃতির নিযোক্তা ; গ্রাহক, ক্রেতা। **–age,** *n.* **–al,** *adj.* **–ship,** *n.*

clī'-ĕn-tele (-tël), *n.* **1.** A body of clients or dependents ; a following ; আশ্রিতবর্গ ; সহচরবর্গ। **2.** Customers, supporters (of a lawyer, physician, shop, theatre, etc.) ; মোক্কেলবর্গ, ক্রেতৃগণ, পৃষ্ঠপোষকবর্গ।

cliff, *n.* A high, steep rock ; উচ্চ খাড়াপাহাড়। **Cliff'-y,** *adj.* **Cliff'-man**—শৈলারোহণ কুশল ব্যক্তি।

clī măc'-têr-ic, *n.* & *adj.* **1.** A critical stage in human life (according to some, multiples of 7 ; according to others multiples of 9) ; মানবজীবনের সন্ধিসময়। ***Adj.*** Pertaining to such a period ; critical ; উক্ত সময়-সম্বন্ধীয় ; সঙ্কট-সঙ্কুল। **–i-cal,** *adj.* **The grand climacteric**—63rd year of life ; ৬৩ বৎসর বয়স (জীবনের সঙ্কটপূর্ণ সময় বলিয়া বিবেচিত হয়)।

clī'-māte, *n.* **1.** The condition of a country in relation to atmospheric phenomena, as temperature, humidity, etc., as these affect animal or vegetable life ; জলবায়ু, আবহাওয়া। **2.** A region considered with reference to its weather ; as, *climate* unfavourable to British constitution ; (জলবায়ু, আবহাওয়া সম্পর্কে বিবেচিত) ভূখণ্ড। **–mat'-ic, –mat'-i-cal,** *adjs.* **–mat'-i-cal-ly,** *adv.*

clī-mă-tŏg'-ră-phȳ, *n.* A study or description of climates ; জলবায়ুতত্ত্ব অনুশীলন, জলবায়ুর বিবরণ।

clī-mă-tŏl'-ö-ğȳ, *n.* The science which deals with climates and investigates climatic conditions ; জলবায়ুবিজ্ঞান। **–gist,** *n.* **–to-log'-i-cal,** *adj.*

clī'-măx, *n., v. t.* & *i.* **1.** (*Rhet.*) A figure of speech in which the language rises step by step in dignity, importance and force ; (অলঙ্কার-শাস্ত্র) বাক্যালঙ্কারবিশেষ,—ইহাতে কোন বাক্যের শব্দ সমূহ উত্তরোত্তর উৎকর্ষতা লাভ করে, সারালঙ্কার (মঃ উঃ)। **2.** The last or highest term in a rhetorical climax ; hence, the highest point of anything ; the culmination ; acme ; as, the very *climax* of prosperity ; সারালঙ্কার-বাক্যের সর্ব্বশেষ বা সর্ব্বোন্নত শব্দ ; শীর্ষবিন্দু, সর্ব্বোচ্চবিন্দু ; পরাকাষ্ঠা ; চূড়ান্ত সীমা। ***Verb t.*** **1.** To arrange in an ascending gradation ; ক্রমোচ্চভাবে সজ্জিত করা। **2.** To bring to a culmination ; চূড়ান্ত সীমায় আনা। ***Verb i.*** **1.** To rise by successive steps ; ক্রমশঃ উৎকর্ষ প্রাপ্ত হওয়া। **2.** To culminate ; চরমসীমায় উপনীত হওয়া। **To cap the climax**—To surpass everything, as in excellence or in absurdity ; সকলকে অতিক্রম করা।

climb' (klīm), *v. i.* & *t.* **1.** To raise oneself by grasping or by the aid of hands and feet ; to ascend a steep place ; হস্তপদাদির সাহায্যে অতি কষ্টে আরোহণ করা ; আরোহণ করা। **2.** (*Fig.*) To rise in dignity, rank or state, (often with *up*) ; (লক্ষণায়) পদোন্নতি লাভ করা, অবস্থার উন্নতি লাভ করা। 3. (*Of plants*) To creep up by the aid of tendrils or by twining ; লতাগুল্মাদির সাহায্যে আরোহণ করা। 4. (Also *Verb t.*) To mount slowly upwards ; (said of the sun, moon, etc,) ; ধীরে ধীরে উপরে উঠা (সূর্য্য, চন্দ্র প্রভৃতি সম্পর্কে)। ***Verb t.*** 1. To be situated on an ascent ; as, the wood and vineyards *climb* half way up ; উচ্চস্থানে অবস্থিত হওয়া। 2. To ascend (anything steep) by hands and feet ; to get the top of ; to mount ; হস্তপদের সাহায্যে আরোহণ করা ; উপরিভাগে উপনীত হওয়া ; আরোহণ করা। **Climb'-a-ble,** *adj.* **Climb'-er,** *n.* 1. One who or that which climbs ; আরোহণকারী। 2. (*Bot.*) A plant which creeps upwards ; (উদ্ভিদ-বিদ্যা) ব্রততী, লতা। 3. (*Zool.*) One of an order of birds that climbs ; (প্রাণি-বিজ্ঞান) আরোহণক্ষম পক্ষিবর্গের একটী। **Climbing iron**—বৃক্ষারোহণকালে বা তুষার মণ্ডিত প্রবণ-ভূমি আরোহণের সময় বুটজুতায় যে বৃহৎ প্রেকসমূহ নিবদ্ধ করা হয়। **Climbing-perch**—Anabas ; কইমাছ। **To climb down**—To descend by the aid of hands and feet ; হস্তপদাদির সাহায্যে নামা, অবরোহণ করা। (*Fig.*) To retreat from a position taken up ; to give in ; (লক্ষণায়) পশ্চাৎপদ হওয়া ; পরাভব স্বীকার করা। **To climb Parnasus** — To write poetry ; কবিতা রচনা করা।

clinch, *n.* See CLENCH.

cling, *v. i.* (*pt.* & *p. p.* CLUNG) 1. To adhere ; to stick fast ; (with *to* or *together*), সংলগ্ন হওয়া ; সংসক্ত হওয়া। 2. To cleave *to* ; to remain faithful *to* ; as, they still *clung* to the doctrine of non-resistance ; লগ্ন হওয়া ; অনুরক্ত হওয়া, নিষ্ঠ থাকা। **Cling-'ing,** *p. a.* **Cling'-ing-ly,** *adv.* **Cling'-ing-ness,** *n.* **Cling-stone**—এক প্রকার নাসপাতি। **To cling together**—সংলগ্ন থাকা, সংযুক্ত থাকা।

clĭn'-ic, clin'-ique (-ĭc), *n.* (*Med*) The teaching of medicine or surgery at the bedside of a sick person ; রুগ্নব্যক্তির শয্যা-পার্শ্বে ভৈষজ্য-শাস্ত্র বা অস্ত্রোপচারবিদ্যা শিক্ষাপ্রদান

clĭn'-ĭ-căl, *adj.* Pertaining to a sick-bed ; রুগ্নশয্যাসম্বন্ধীয়। **Clinical baptism**—রুগ্নশয্যাশায়ী ব্যক্তিকে দীক্ষা-প্রদান। **Clinical lecture**—রুগ্ন ব্যক্তির শয্যাপার্শ্বে প্রদত্ত ভৈষজ্যশাস্ত্র বা অস্ত্রোপচার বিদ্যাসম্বন্ধে উপদেশ। **Clinical thermometer** — তাপমান যন্ত্র-বিশেষ।

clink (klĭngk), *v. t.*, *i.* & *n.* To make a ringing sound ; (as of (glasses, etc.) ; ঠন্‌ঠন্ করিয়া বাজান বা বাজা। ***Noun.*** 1. A sharp abrupt ringing sound, (as of glasses struck together) ; ঠন্‌ঠন্ শব্দ, টুন্‌টুন্ শব্দ, ঝন্‌ঝন্ শব্দ। 2. (*Colloq.*) Money ; cash coin ; (চলিতভাষায়) টাকাপয়সা ; নগদ টাকা। **Clink'-er,** *n.* One who or that which clinks ; specif. (*pl.*) fetters ; ঝন্‌ঝন্ শব্দকারী ; (বহুবচন) পায়ের শিকল।

clink (klĭng), *n.* A prison-cell ; কারাকক্ষ।

clink'-êr (klĭngk-), *n.* 1. A very hard kind of brick made in Holland ; হলণ্ডদেশে প্রস্তুত এক প্রকার কঠিন ইষ্টক। 2. A brick with surface vitrified by exposure to intense heat in the kiln ; ঝামা। 3. A mass of slag or volcanic lava ; আগ্নেয়গিরি হইতে নিঃসৃত গৈরিক পদার্থ। **Clinker-built** — একটির পার্শ্ব অপরটীর উপরে তামার প্রেকদ্বারা সম্বদ্ধ এইরূপ কাষ্ঠফলকশ্রেণী নির্ম্মিত।

clī-nŏm'-ē-têr, *n.* An instrument for measuring slopes ; প্রবণতা-পরিমাপক যন্ত্র। **—no-met'-ric,** *adj.* **—try,** *n.*

clin'-quant (klĭngk-ănt), *adj.* & *n.* Glittering ; tinselled ; dressed in spangles ; ঝলমল ; চটকদার ; চুমকি-বসানো। ***Noun.*** Tinsel ; false glitter ; চটকদার জিনিষ ; চটক।

Clīō, *n.* (*Class. Myth.*) The Muse of history ; (গ্রীক পুরাণে) ইতিহাসের অধিষ্ঠাত্রী দেবী।

clip, *v. t.* & *n.* 1. To surrouud closely ; নিবিড়ভাবে আলিঙ্গন করা। 2. To grip tightly ; to hold in a tight grasp ; শক্ত করিয়া ধরা ; দৃঢ়-মুষ্টিতে ধরা। ***Noun.*** A clasp for letters, papers, etc. ; চিঠি ও কাগজ পত্রাদি চাপিয়া ধরিয়া রাখিবার আঁকড়া।

clip, *v.t.* & *n.* 1. To cut with shears or scissors, (with *off*, *away*) ; কাঁচিদ্বারা কাটিয়া বা ছাঁটিয়া ফেলা। 2. To cut the hair off ; to cut off (a sheep's wool or fleece) ; চুলছাঁটা ; (মেষের পশম বা লোম) ছাঁটা। 3. To pare off the edge of coin ; মুদ্রার কিনারা কাটিয়া ফেলা। 4. To cut short ; to curtail ; to pronounce inperfectly ; as, *clipping* her words in vehemence ; সংক্ষেপ করা ; কাটা ছাঁটা ; অস্ফুট বা অসম্পূর্ণভাবে উচ্চারণ করা। ***Noun.*** 1. The act of shearing or hair-cutting ; মেষের লোম কর্ত্তন, ছাঁটন। 2. The quantity of wool shorn in one place or in one season ; একস্থানে বা এক মরসুমে যে পরিমাণ পশম ছাঁটা হয়। 3. (*Colloq.*) A blow or stroke with the hand ; as, he hit him a *clip* ; (চলিত কথায়) মুষ্ট্যাঘাত, কিল, চাপড়। **Clip'-per,** *n.* 1. One who clips coin ; যে ব্যক্তি মুদ্রার কিনারা কাটিয়া থাকে। 2. A clipping or cutting instrument ; (*pl.*) scissors ; কাটারী, ছাঁটিবার যন্ত্র ; (বহুবচন) কাঁচি। 3. One who moves swiftly ; a swift horse ; যে ব্যক্তি ছুটিয়া চলে ; দ্রুতগামী অশ্ব। 4. A fast-sailing vessel ; দ্রুতগামী পোত। 5. (*Slang*) A thing excellent of its kind ; as, a real *clipper* of a dog; (ইতরভাষায়), (এক জাতীয় বস্তুর মধ্যে) সবার সেরা। **6.** A small piece clipped off; a shred of cloth; a portion pared from a coin, etc.; ছাঁটা টুকরা; ছাঁটা কাপড়ের টুকরা; মুদ্রা হইতে কর্ত্তিত খণ্ড। **Clip-collector**—যে ব্যক্তি ক্রেতাদের জন্য সংবাদ-পত্র সমূহ হইতে কাটিয়া কোন বিষয়ক ক্ষুদ্র ক্ষুদ্র অংশ সংগ্রহ করে। **To clip any one's wings**—To restrain one's ambition; to lessen one's power of action; কাহারও উচ্চাকাঙ্ক্ষায় বাধা প্রদান করা; কাহারও কার্য্যকারিতা শক্তি খর্ব্ব করা।

clique (klēk), *n.* A small or exclusive party or set; a narrow coterie or circle; (generally used in a bad sense); (মন্দ অভিসন্ধিতে গঠিত) দল; ক্ষুদ্র দল বা মণ্ডলী। **Cli'-quish,** *adj.* **Cli'-quish-ness, Cli'-quism,** *ns.*

Clitoria ternatea—নীল অপরাজিতা, শ্বেত অপরাজিতা (বেলঃ)।

clĭ'-tō-ris, *n.* (*Anat.*) A small organ at the upper part of the vulva, homologous to the penis in the male; (শারীরসংস্থান-বিদ্যা) ভগাঙ্কুর, যোনিলিঙ্গ, ভগলিঙ্গ।

clō-ā'-că, *n.* [*Pl.* -cæ (-sē)] **1.** A sewer; a privy or water closet; নর্দ্দমা, পয়ঃপ্রণালী; পায়খানা। **2.** (*Physiol.*) The excrementary cavity in birds, reptiles and most fishes; (শারীর-বিজ্ঞান) পক্ষী, সরীসৃপ এবং অধিকাংশ মৎস্যের মলাধার। **3.** (*Fig.*) A gathering place of moral evils; দুর্নীতির সমাবেশ-স্থল **—cal,** *adj.*

cloak (klōk), *n.* & *v. t.* **1.** A loose outer garment worn by both sexes over other clothes; একপ্রকার ঢিলা জামা, প্রাবরণ। **2.** A covering; as, under a *cloak* of snow; আবরণ, পর্দ্দা। **3.** (*Fig.*) A pretence; an outward show; as, religion is made a *cloak* to many villains; (লক্ষণায়) ছল, অছিলা (*Colloq.*); অজুহাত; লোক দেখানো ভাব। ***Verb t.*** To cover with or wrap in a cloak; hence, to hide or conceal; to disguise; ঢিলা জামাদ্বারা ঢাকিয়া বা জড়াইয়া রাখা; লুক্কায়িত করা, গোপন করা; প্রচ্ছন্ন করা। **Cloak-room**—যে কোঠায় টুপি, প্রাবরণ প্রভৃতি রাখা হয়; রেলওয়ে ষ্টেশন, রঙ্গালয় প্রভৃতির কক্ষ বিশেষ—যেখানে কিছু সময়ের জন্য জিনিষ পত্র রাখা যাইতে পারে।

clock (klŏk), *n.* An instrument for measuring time, kept in motion by springs, wheels, etc. and recording hours, minutes, etc. by hands on a dial; ঘড়ী, ঘটিকা যন্ত্র। **Clock'-tower**—ঘন্টা ঘর। **Clock-wise**—ঘড়ীর কাঁটা যেই দিকে ঘুরে সেই দিকে। **Clock-work,** *n.* & *adj.* The mechanism of a clock; ঘড়ীর কল। (*Adj.*) Regular; mechanical; নিয়মিত; যন্ত্রবৎ। **Like a clock**—With steady regularity; ঘড়ীর কাঁটার মত। **To go like the clock-work**—To go along smoothly and without a hitch; ঘড়ীর কাঁটার মত চলা। **To know, find, what o' clock it is**—To discover (know) the real state of things; প্রকৃত অবস্থা নির্ণয় করা বা অবগত হওয়া। **To tell the clock**—To count the hour; to record the time; সময় গণনা করা; সময় লিখিয়া রাখা। **When one's clock strikes** — When one's hour comes; যখন কাহারো সময় আসে।

clock (klŏk), *n.* An ornamental pattern worked in silk on the side of a stocking; মোজার পার্শ্বদেশে রেশমের চিকণ কাজ।

clock (klŏk), *v. i.* To cluck; to sit on eggs; to hatch; শাবক-আহ্বানার্থ কুক্কুটীর মত কক্ কক্ শব্দ করা; ডিমের উপর বসা; ডিমে তা দেওয়া। **Clocking-hen**—ডিমে তা দেওয়ায় নিযুক্ত মুর্গী।

clŏd, *n.* & *v. t.* **1.** A lump of any solid matter; specif. a lump of earth or clay; as, *clods* upon a coffin; লোষ্ট্র, ডেলা; মাটির ডেলা। **2.** (*Depreciatively*) The human body, as a mass of clay; as, a breathless *clod*; (অবজ্ঞাচ্ছলে) মানবদেহ। **3.** (*Fig.*) A dull, gross, stupid fellow; a block-head; (লক্ষণায়) জড়-বুদ্ধি ব্যক্তি; স্থূল-বুদ্ধি ব্যক্তি। ***Verb t.*** To pelt with clods; লোষ্ট্র বর্ষণ করা। **Clod'-dish,** *adj.* **Clod'-dish-ness,** *n.* **Clod-hopper**—গোবর গণেশ।

clŏg, *n.* & *v. t.* **1.** A thick piece of wood; a clump; স্থূল কাষ্ঠখণ্ড; কুঁদা। **2.** (*Fig.*) An impediment; a hindrance; (লক্ষণায়) বাধা, প্রতিবন্ধক; আটক। **3.** A wooden solid overshoe or sandal; একপ্রকার খড়ম। ***Verb t.*** **1.** To fasten a heavy block of wood to; to fetter; কোন কিছুতে স্থূল কাষ্ঠখণ্ড সংবদ্ধ করা; শৃঙ্খলিত করা। **2.** To burden; to encumber; to hinder; to impede (actions); ভারাক্রান্ত করা; বোঝা চাপান; বাধা দেওয়া, প্রতিবন্ধক দেওয়া; কার্য্য প্রতিরোধ করা। **3.** To choke up so as to hinder free passage; to obstruct; as, the road was *clogged* with carriages; গতিপথ রোধ করা; আবদ্ধ করা, অবরুদ্ধ করা। **Clog'-gy,** *adj.*

clois'-têr (kloys-), *n.* & *v. t.* **1.** A place of religious seclusion; a monastery or nunnery; নির্জ্জন সাধনাশ্রম; (খৃষ্টীয়) ভিক্ষুসংঘ, খৃষ্টীয় তপস্বিনিগণের মঠ। **2.** A covered walk or arcade often round a quadrangle (with wall on the outer and windows on the inner side), esp. in a convent, or large church; খৃষ্টীয় মঠ, বা বৃহৎ ধর্ম্ম-মন্দিরের গৃহবেষ্টিত চত্বরের চতুর্দ্দিকস্থ আচ্ছাদিত পথ। ***Verb t.*** **1.** To shut up or enclose in a monastic house; মঠে আবদ্ধ করা। **2.** To shut up in retirement; নির্জ্জন বা নিভৃতস্থানে বদ্ধ করা। **3.** To convert into a cloister or convent; মঠাদির মধ্যস্থ

ছদ্মপথ বা ভিক্ষুণী-সংঘে পরিণত করা। **—tered, —tral,** *adjs.* **The cloister**—The monastic life ; আশ্রম-জীবন, খৃষ্টীয় মঠবাসীর জীবন।

cloke (klōk), *n.* & *v. t.* See CLOAK.

clō'-nŭs, *n.* A spasm with violent successive muscular contractions and relaxations ; একপ্রকার আক্ষেপ রোগ। **Clon'-ic,** *adj.* (opp. to *tonic.*)

cloop, *n.* & *v. i.* The sound made by drawing a cork from a bottle ; বোতলের মুখ হইতে কাক বা ছিপি (কর্ক) টানিয়া লইলে যে শব্দ হয়। ***Verb i.*** To make this sound ; উক্তপ্রকার শব্দ করা।

clōse, *adj.* & *adv.* **1.** Shut fast ; as, a *close* carriage ; রুদ্ধ। **2.** Enclosed ; confined ; narrow ; as, *close* alleys, prison : *close* confinement ; প্রাচীরবেষ্টিত; আবদ্ধ ; সংকীর্ণ। **3.** Hidden ; concealed ; as, *close* sins, plots ; secret ; secluded ; as, *close* caverns ; গুপ্ত ; লুক্কায়িত ; গোপন ; নির্জ্জন। **4.** Confined ; stifling (said of air, weather, etc.) ; আবদ্ধ ; শ্বাসরোধকর। **5.** Reserved ; reticent ; as, he was, too *close* to name his circumstances ; অনালাপী ; মৌনী, বাগ্যত। **6.** Stingy ; niggardly ; ব্যয়কুণ্ঠ ; কৃপণ। **7.** Dense or compact ; without interstices or vacuities ; as, *close* writing ; ঘন, নিবিড় ; নীরন্ধ্র, সঙ্কাপিত। **8.** Intimate ; confidential ; as, *close* friend ; অন্তরঙ্গ ; বিশ্বস্ত। **9.** Fitting tightly or exactly ; as, *close* cap, bonnet, etc. ; আঁটসাট। **10.** Exact ; to the point ; as, *close* translation ; accurate ; careful ; as, *close* observer, reasoning ; strict ; minute ; as, *close* examination, attention, etc. ; ঠিক ; যথার্থ ; প্রামাণিক ; সযত্ন ; সঠিক ; পুঙ্খানুপুঙ্খ। **11.** Very near ; immediately adjoining ; (followed by *to*) ; অতি নিকটবর্ত্তী ; আসন্ন। **12.** Leaving no gaps or weak points ; as, *close* reasoning ; অভেদ্য, অকাট্য। ***Adv.*** **1.** In immediate contact ; very near ; (usu. with *stand, sit, lie, hold,* etc.) ; আসন্নভাবে ; অতি সন্নিকটে। **2.** Tightly ; fast ; as, it shuts *close* ; আঁটভাবে ; দৃঢ়ভাবে। **Close'-ly,** *adv.* **Close'-ness,** *n.* **Close to, Close by, Close upon**—Very near, immediate ; অতি নিকটবর্ত্তী ; অব্যবহিত।

clōse, *n.* **1.** An inclosed place ; an enclosure ; বেষ্টিত স্থান ; বৃতি-বেষ্টিতস্থল। **3.** The precinct of a cathedral ; খৃষ্টীয় মহাধর্ম্মমন্দিরের সীমানা। **3.** An entry or passage ; esp. one leading from the street to dwelling houses, out-houses, etc. ; প্রবেশমার্গ, প্রবেশ বা নির্গম পথ ; রাজপথ হইতে বাজবাটী বা বহির্ব্বাটী পর্য্যন্ত পথ। **4.** (*Law*) **To break one's close**—To trespass on his land ; কাহারও ভূমিতে অনধিকার প্রবেশ করা।

clōse, *v. t., i.* & *n.* **1.** To stop up (an opening or channel) ; to shut ; as, to *close* the door, eyes ; রোধ করা ; বন্ধ করা, রুদ্ধ করা। **2.** To bring to an end ; to finish ; as, to *close* an account ; সমাপ্ত করা, শেষ করা ; সম্পন্ন করা। **3.** To unite ; to consolidate ; (usu. with *up*) ; যোগ করা, একত্র করা ; সংহত করা, একত্র সন্নিবিষ্ট করা। **4.** To fill up (a gap or open place) ; to confine ; গর্ত্ত বা ফাঁক বন্ধ করা ; আবদ্ধ করা। ***Verb i.*** **1.** To become shut, (with *upon, over*) ; রুদ্ধ হওয়া, বন্ধ হওয়া। **2.** To terminate ; as, the summer *closes* ; শেষ হওয়া, অবসান হওয়া। **3.** To join ; যুক্ত হওয়া, একত্র হওয়া, সংযুক্ত হওয়া। **4.** To draw near, (*about, on, round, upon*) ; as, they *closed* round him ; hence, to engage in hand to hand fight ; to grapple *with,* as, he *closed* with him and proved too strong ; সন্নিকটে আসা ; বাহুযুদ্ধে প্রবৃত্ত হওয়া ; আঁকড়াইয়া ধরা। **5.** To come to terms or agreement, (*with, upon*) ; চুক্তি বা সর্ত্তে আবদ্ধ হওয়া। ***Noun.*** **1.** Conclusion ; end ; as, to bring the matter to a *close* ; উপসংহার ; অবসান, সমাপ্তি। **2.** A grappling of combatants ; encounter ; বাহুযুদ্ধ ; সম্মুখ যুদ্ধ। **3.** The playground of a school ; বিদ্যালয়ের ক্রীড়াপ্রাঙ্গণ। **Close-banded**—একতাবদ্ধ। **Close-barred** — দৃঢ়-সংবদ্ধ। **Closed-fisted**—কৃপণ, হাতকষা, হাতভারী, ব্যয়কুণ্ঠ, কঞ্জুস (*Colloq.*), বদ্ধমুষ্টি (*Colloq.*)। **Close-grained**—ঘনসংবদ্ধ ; নিরবকাশ। **Close-hauled**—যথাসম্ভব বায়ুর প্রতিকূলে পাইলভরে গমনশীল। **Close-stool**—বাক্সের ভিতরে আঁটা বাহ্যপ্রস্রাবের পাত্র। **Close-tongued**—সংযতবাক্। **A close contest**—যে দ্বন্দ্বে উভয়পক্ষ প্রায় সমবল। **At close quarters**—হাতাহাতি। **At the close of**—শেষে, অন্তে। **Close vote**—উভয় পক্ষে নির্ব্বাচন মত-সংখ্যা প্রায় তুল্য। **Draw to a close**—Be about to end ; শেষ হইয়া আসা। **Follow close upon**—Come immediately after ; অব্যবহিত পরেই বা সঙ্গে সঙ্গে আসা। **To close a bargain**—To make an agreement ; চুক্তি করা। **To close about**—To close in on all sides ; to encompass ; চারিদিকে ঘিরিয়া ফেলা ; পরিবৃত করা। To draw near to ; to come in contact *with* ; সন্নিকটে আসা, সন্নিহিত হওয়া ; সংস্পর্শে আসা। **To close in upon**—To fall upon ; আপতিত হওয়া। **To close one's days**—To die ; মরিয়া যাওয়া, জীবনলীলার অবসান হওয়া। **To close ranks or files**—To bring (soldiers) in close order so as to leave no gaps ; (সৈন্যগণকে) ঘন সন্নিবিষ্ট করা। **To close up** — To confine completely ; সম্পূর্ণরূপে অবরুদ্ধ করা। To complete ; to sum up ; as, we must now *close up* ; সমাপ্ত করা ; স্বল্প কথায় ব্যক্ত করা। To block up ; to fill up ; রুদ্ধ করা, আটক করা ; পূর্ণ করা। **To close with**—To accede to ; to accept ; স্বীকার করা ; গ্রহণ করা। **To close with the land**—(*Naut.*) To approach the land ; (নৌ-বিদ্যা) স্থলের অভিমুখে অগ্রসর হওয়া। **To keep** or **lie close**—To be in hiding ; লুক্কায়িত থাকা। **With closed doors**—In private ; গোপনে, নিভৃতে, রহসি।

clŏs'-ĕt, *n.* & *v. t.* **1.** A small room, esp. for private interviews ; an inner chamber ; নির্জ্জন কক্ষ ; ভিতরের কামরা। **2.** The private council chamber of a monarch ; যে গৃহে রাজা গোপনে বিশেষ বিশেষ ব্যক্তিগণকে দর্শন দান করেন, দর্শনগৃহ (মঃ সং)। **3.** A small side-room for storing utensils, provisions, etc. ; তৈজসপত্র, খাদ্যদ্রব্যাদি রক্ষণার্থ পার্শ্বপ্রকোষ্ঠ। **4.** A water-closet ; একপ্রকার পাইখানা। ***Verb t.*** **1.** To shut up in a closet for private conference or secret treaty ; (esp. in *pass. to be closeted with or together*) ; গুপ্ত পরামর্শ বা সন্ধির জন্য নিভৃত কক্ষে বন্ধ করা। **–ing,** *n.* A private conference ; esp. between two persons ; নিভৃত-মন্ত্রণা, বিশেষতঃ দুই ব্যক্তির মধ্যে গুপ্ত-পরামর্শ। **Bed-closet**—A small bed-room ; ক্ষুদ্র শয়ন কক্ষ। **Closet-play**—যে নাটক পঠিত হয়,—অভিনীত হয় না।

clō'-sure (-zhŭr), *n.* & *v. t.* **1.** The act of shutting ; closed condition ; বন্ধ করণ, রুদ্ধ করণ ; রুদ্ধাবস্থা। **2.** The closing of a debate in the House of Commons by a vote of the House ; পার্লেমেন্টের সাধারণ সভার মতানুসারে কোন বিষয়ে তর্কবিতর্কের অবসান। ***Verb t.*** To apply the closure to (a debate or speaker) ; উক্ত প্রকারে তর্কবিতর্ক বন্ধ করা।

clŏt, *n., v. t.* & *i.* **1.** A semi-solid lump of coagulated liquid, esp. of blood ; সংযত বা জমাট রক্তাদি। ***Verb t.*** To stick together in clots ; চাপ বাঁধা, চাপ বা ডেলা হইয়া লাগিয়া থাকা। ***Verb i.*** To coagulate or curdle, (said of blood, cream, etc.) ; চাপ, ডেলা, জমাট বা সংযত হওয়া (রক্ত সর প্রভৃতি সম্পর্কে), জমাট বাঁধা, জমিয়া যাওয়া। **Clotted hair**—জটা। **Clotted nonsense**—আষাঢ়ে গল্প।

clŏth, *n.* (*Pl.* CLOTHS, CLOTHES) **1.** Any material formed by weaving ; বস্ত্র, কাপড়। **2.** The distinctive dress of any profession, esp. of the clergy ; hence, the clerical profession ; কোন বৃত্তি বা ব্যবসায় অবলম্বনকারিগণের পদোচিত পরিচ্ছদ, বিশেষতঃ যাজকগণের পরিচয়-জ্ঞাপক পরিচ্ছদ ; যাজকের ব্যবসায়। **3.** A table cloth ; (see below). **American cloth**—চামড়ার মত এক প্রকার এনামেল-করা কাপড়। **Cloth-binding**—কাপড়, রেশম প্রভৃতি দ্বারা পুস্তক বাঁধাই। **Table-cloth**—মেজের উপরে দিবার কাপড়, আহার্য্য দ্রব্য সাজাইবার আগে মেজের উপর যে কাপড় বিছানো হয়। **Cloth of estate, state**—সিংহাসন প্রভৃতির উপরিস্থ বিতান বিশেষ। **Cloth of gold, silver**—জরির কাপড়। **The cloth**—যাজকসমাজ ; যাজকের পদ। **To cut the coat according to the cloth**—To keep within the limits of one's means ; আয় বুঝিয়া ব্যয় করা। **To lay the cloth**—ভোজনের জন্য মেজ প্রস্তুত করা।

clōthe, *v. t.* (*p. p.* **clothed, clad**) **1.** To cover with a garment ; to provide with clothing ; to dress ; পরিচ্ছদাবৃত করা ; পোষাক পরিচ্ছদ প্রদান করা ; পরিচ্ছদ দ্বারা সজ্জিত করা। **2.** To invest as with a garment ; as, leaves *clothe* trees ; বস্ত্রের মত আচ্ছাদিত করা। **3.** To put (thoughts or ideas) into words ; to express ; (*in, with*) ; (চিন্তা বা ভাব) বাক্যে প্রকাশ করা ; প্রকাশ করা। **Cloth'-ing,** *n.* Clothes collectively ; apparel ; dress ; বস্ত্রসমূহ ; বেশ, পরিচ্ছদ ; পোষাক।

clothes (klōthz or klōz), *n. pl.* Wearing apparel ; dress ; পরিধান বসন ; পোষাক। **Bed-clothes**—বিছানার চাদর, কম্বল, সুজনী প্রভৃতি। **Clothes-bag, –basket**—পরিচ্ছদাদি রাখিবার আধারবিশেষ (বিশেষতঃ মলিন বস্ত্রাদি ধৌত করিবার পূর্ব্বে যে আধারে রাখা হয়)। **Clothes horse**—কাপড় শুকাইবার একপ্রকার আলনা—ইহার উপর কাপড় রাখিয়া অগ্নিতাপে শুষ্ক করা হয়। **Clothes-line, –rope**—ধৌত বস্ত্রাদি শুষ্ক করণার্থ যে তার বা রজ্জুতে ঝুলাইয়া দেওয়া হয়। **Clothes-man**—পুরাতন পোষাক বিক্রেতা। **In long clothes**—Still in infancy ; এখন পর্য্যন্ত শৈশবাবস্থায়।

clōth'-i-êr, *n.* A maker of cloth ; a seller of cloth or clothes ; বস্ত্রবয়নকারী ; বস্ত্র বা পোষাক বিক্রেতা।

Clotho.

Clō'-thō, *n.* (*Class. Myth.*) The youngest of the three Fates ; গ্রীক-পুরাণোক্ত সর্ব্বকনিষ্ঠা ভাগ্যদেবী।

cloud (klowd), *n., v. t.* & *i.* **1.** A visible mass of condensed watery vapour floating in the atmosphere at some altitude ; মেঘ, জলদ, নীরদ, বারিদ, ঘন, অভ্র, মুদির, পয়োধর, পর্জ্জন্য, বলাহক। [CLOUDS are commonly classified in four kinds,—(*a*) *Cirrus,* (*b*) *Cumulus,* (*c*) *Stratus,* (*d*) *Nimbus.*] **2.** A mass of smoke or dust floating in

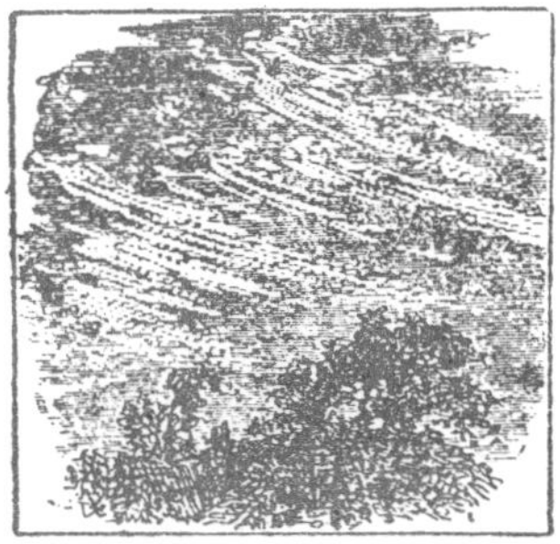

Cloud—Cirrus.

the air ; as, a *cloud* of incense : a *cloud* of smoke ; বাষ্পরাশি, ধূলিপটল। **3.** (*Fig.*) Anything fleeting or unsubstantial ; as, weighing of *clouds* and portioning out of shadows ; (লক্ষণায়) ক্ষণস্থায়ী, অবাস্তবিক বা কাল্পনিক বস্তু। **4.** A dark vein or spot on a transparent material, as in marble, stones, etc. ; hence, a blemish or defect ; as, a *cloud* on one's reputation ; স্বচ্ছপদার্থে কৃষ্ণবর্ণ রেখা বা বিন্দু ; অতএব কলঙ্ক, খুঁত। **5.** A great number (of insects, birds, horsemen, etc., moving together) ; a multitude ; a crowd ; as, *cloud*

Cloud—Cirro-stratus.

of witnesses ; দলবদ্ধভাবে চলন্ত অসংখ্য পক্ষী, কীট, অশ্বারোহী প্রভৃতি ; জনতা ; লোকারণ্য। **6.** A light woollen scarf, (worn by ladies) ; স্ত্রীলোকদিগের একপ্রকার পাতলা পশমী ওড়না, হাওয়ার চাদর। **7.** Any state of obscurity or darkness ; অস্পষ্ট বা ঝাপ্সা ভাব। **8.** Anything that darkens with gloom, trouble, affliction, etc. ; a state of gloom, etc. ; as, a *cloud* of sorrow, suspicion, etc. ; বিষাদমেঘ ; বিষণ্ণাবস্থা, অপ্রসন্নতা। ***Verb t.*** **1.** To darken with clouds ; hence, to overshadow ; to dim ; to obscure ; as, his merits *clouds* every

Cloud—Cumulus.

other : the tears *clouded* her eyes ; মেঘাচ্ছন্ন করা ; ছায়াবৃত করা ; নিষ্প্রভ করা ; অস্পষ্ট করা। **2.** To cast a shadow over ; to darken with trouble ; as, to *cloud* one's

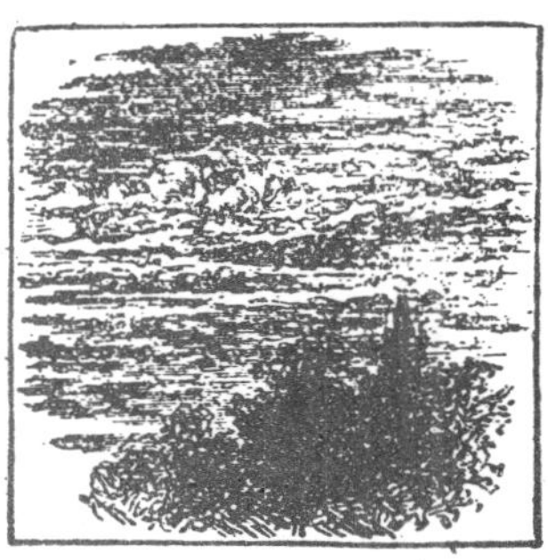

Cloud—Cirro-cumulus.

happiness ; ছায়াবৃত করা ; বিপদ, কষ্ট, ঝঞ্ঝাট দ্বারা আচ্ছন্ন করা। **3.** To cast a slur upon ; to defame ; to sully ; (used of reputation, character, etc.) ; কলঙ্ক আরোপ করা ; মানহানি করা ; কলঙ্কিত করা। **4.** To variegate with colours ; as, to *cloud* yarns ; নানাবর্ণে বিচিত্রিত করা। ***Verb i.*** To become dim or gloomy ; to darken ; (usually with *up, over*) ; অস্পষ্ট হওয়া, ম্লান হওয়া ; অন্ধকারাচ্ছন্ন করা। **Cloud'-less,** *adj.* **Cloud'-less-ly,** *adv.* **Cloud'-less-ness,** *n.* **Cloud'-y,** *adj.* **1.** Pertaining to the clouds ; মেঘ-সম্বন্ধীয়, মেঘাত্মক, মেঘময়, বারিদপূর্ণ। **2.** Dim ; obscure ; indistinct ; (said of ideas, language, etc.) ; অনুজ্জ্বল ; নিষ্প্রভ ; অস্পষ্ট। **3.** Gloomy ; ম্লান, বিষণ্ণ। **Cloud'-i-ly,** *adv.* **Cloud'-i-ness,** *n.* **Cloud'-let,** *n.* A little cloud ; ক্ষুদ্র মেঘখণ্ড। **Cloud-burst**—Violent rainstorm ; বৃষ্টি-সহকৃত প্রবল ঝঞ্ঝা। **Cloud-capt (capped)**—(পর্ব্বত সম্পর্কে) মেঘ-মাল, মেঘ-মালী। **Cloud-kissing**—মেঘচুম্বী, মেঘস্পর্শী। **In the cloud**—In the dreamland ; স্বপ্নরাজ্যে, কল্পনারাজ্যে। **To be under a cloud** — To be in disgrace ; কলঙ্কগ্রস্ত হওয়া। **To blow a cloud**—To smoke a cigar or pipe ; চুরুট খাওয়া, ধূমপান করা।

clough (klŭf or klōw), *n.* A ravine ; a steep valley usually with torrent bed ; দরী ; সরলোন্নত উপত্যকা।

clout (klowt), *n.* & *v. t.* **1.** A piece of cloth, leather, etc. used for mending ; তালির জন্য কাপড় বা চামড়ার টুকরা, মেরামতের জন্য ব্যবহৃত বস্ত্র বা চর্ম্মখণ্ড। **2.** A canvas on a frame as a mark at archery ; a shot that hits the mark ; ক্যাম্বিস্ কাপড়ের তৈয়ারী লক্ষ্য বা শরব্য; যে গুলি লক্ষ্যস্থানে আঘাত করে। **3.** An iron-plate on an axle to keep it from wearing ; ঘর্ষণ জনিত ক্ষয় নিবারণ জন্য অক্ষদণ্ডে সংবদ্ধ লৌহফলক। ***Verb t.*** **1.** To patch (with cloth, leather etc. ; তালি লাগান। **2.** To guard with an iron-plate, as an axle-tree ; also to stud with (broad-headed) nails the soles of shoes ; লৌহফলকদ্বারা অক্ষদণ্ড প্রভৃতি রক্ষা করা ; জুতার তলায় পেরেক লাগান।

clōve, *n.* A bulb of garlic, shallot, etc. ; রসুন প্রভৃতির কন্দ।

clōve, *n.* **1.** The dried flower-bud of a tropical tree, used as a pungent aromatic spice ; (*usu. in pl.*) ; also, the tree itself ; লবঙ্গ ; লবঙ্গ-তরু । **Clove-gilly flower** — একপ্রকার লবঙ্গ-গন্ধ পুষ্প। **Oil of cloves**—লবঙ্গের আতর।

clōve, *n.* A rocky cleft or fissure ; a gap ; a ravine ; (used in place-names) ; ফাটল ; ফাঁক ; গভীর এবং সঙ্কীর্ণ গিরিপথ, দরী।

clō′-ven (-v'n), **clōve,** (*p. t.* & *p. p.* of **cleave,**) *p. adj.* Divided ; split ; খণ্ডিত ; বিদীর্ণ। **Cloven-footed**—খণ্ডিত ক্ষুরবিশিষ্ট। Satanic ; শয়তানী। [প্রথমতঃ গ্রীক পুরাণোক্ত বনদেবতা Pan সম্বন্ধে বলা হইত, (যাহার পা, পায়ের খুর এবং জানু ছাগলের মত ছিল), তৎপর শয়তান সম্পর্কে ব্যবহৃত হইয়া আসিতেছে।]

clō′-vêr, *n.* A genus of plants (called *trefoil,* three-leafed) cultivated for fodder ; পশুর খাদ্যোপযোগী তৃণবিশেষ। **To live** (or **be) in clover**—To live in ease and luxury, (clover being extremely delicious and fattening to cattle) ; ভোগবিলাসের ক্রোড়ে লালিত হওয়া।

clown, *n.* **1.** A countryman ; a rustic or peasant ; পাড়াগেঁয়ে লোক ; চাষা। **2.** A man without culture or refinement ; a boor ; অশিক্ষিত বা অসভ্য ব্যক্তি ; বর্ব্বর। **3.** The fool or buffoon in a play, circus, etc. (*Shaks*) ; a retainer of a court or great house ; নাটক বা সার্কাসের বিদূষক ; ভাঁড়, বৈহাসিক (বাংস্বঃ)। **Clown′-ish,** *adj.* **Clown′-ish-ly,** *adv.* **Clown′-ish-ness,** *n.*

clown′-êr-ȳ, *n.* The performance of a comic clown ; ভাঁড়ামি, মস্করামি।

cloy̆, *v. t.* **1.** To surfeit or satiate (with over-feeding or with richness, sweetness, or sameness of food) ; অতিশয় ভোগের দ্বারা অতৃপ্তি বা অরুচি জন্মান, প্রচুরপরিমাণ মিষ্ট দ্রব্য বা সর্ব্বদা একপ্রকার খাদ্যদ্বারা বিতৃষ্ণা জন্মান। **2.** (*Fig.*) To gratify beyond desire ; to disgust or weary (with excess of anything) ; as, too often preaching *cloys* the people ; (লক্ষণায়) আশাতীতরূপে চরিতার্থ করা, সন্তৃপ্ত করা ; ভোগবিতৃষ্ণ করা, ভোগক্লান্ত করা।

clŭb, *n., v. t.* & *i.* **1.** A thick heavy stick ; a bludgeon ; a stick with one end thicker and heavier than the other ; লগুড় ; গদা, মুগুর। **2.** The crooked-headed stick used in golf ; গোল্‌ফ্ ক্রীড়ায় ব্যবহৃত বক্রাগ্র দণ্ডবিশেষ ; **3.** A playing card of the suit bearing a black trefoil leaf ; (*pl.*) the suit of cards having such figure ; চিরতন ; চিরতনের তাস। **4.** A number of persons associated for the promotion of some common purpose, as of social intercourse, literature, science, politics, etc. ; সভা, পরিষৎ, সমাজ, গোষ্ঠী (বাংস্বঃ)। ***Verb t.*** **1.** To beat with a club ; গদাঘাত করা। **2.** To collect or gather together into one mass or body ; একত্র জড় করা। **3.** To unite for a common end ; to contribute (as one's share) towards a common stock ; এক উদ্দেশ্যে যুক্ত হওয়া ; সাধারণ ভাণ্ডারে নিজের অংশের দেয় চাঁদা প্রভৃতি দেওয়া। **4.** To defray by a proportionate charge ; as, to *club* the expense ; অংশানুসারে অর্থ প্রদান করত ব্যয় নির্ব্বাহ করা ; ***Verb i.*** **1.** To combine together in joint action ; একযোগে কার্য্য করিবার জন্য মিলিত হওয়া। **2.** To pay a proportional share of a common charge ; অংশমতে ব্যয়ভার বহন করা।

Club′-ba-ble, Club′-a-ble, *adjs.* Fit for membership of a club ; sociable ; সমাজের সভ্য হইবার উপযুক্ত ; সামাজিক। **Club′-dom,** *n.* **Club′-less,** *adj.* **Club-foot**—বিকৃত পদ। **Club-headed** — স্থূলবুদ্ধি। **Club-house**—পরিষদ্‌গৃহ, মিলনগৃহ। **Club-law** — পাশববলে শাসন। **Indian club**—মুগুর। **To be on the club** — To receive relief from its funds ; কোনরূপ সভা বা সম্প্রদায়ের ধনভাণ্ডার হইতে সাহায্য পাওয়া। **To club a musket**—To use the butt-end of it as a club ; বন্দুকের কুঁদা লাঠির মত ব্যবহার করা।

cluck (klŭk), *n.* & *v. i.* The guttural cry of a hen (to her chickens) ; শাবক আহ্বানার্থ কুক্কুটীর ধ্বনি। ***Verb i.*** To make the noise of a brooding hen ; শাবক আহ্বানকালে কুক্কুটীর মত ধ্বনি করা।

clue (klü), *n.* See CLEW.

clŭm′-bêr, *n.* A kind of spaniel ; একপ্রকার শিকারী কুকুর।

clŭmp, *n., v. t.* & *i.* **1.** An unshaped piece, as of wood ; a lump ; কুঁদা ; ডেলা, তাল, খণ্ড। **2.** A tuft of trees or shrubs ; গাছ পালার ঝোপ বা ঝাড় ; গুল্ম (বোঃ)। **3.** A thick extra sole on a shoe ; জুতার তলার অতিরিক্ত চামড়া। ***Verb t.*** **1.** To heap or plant together ; পুঞ্জীভূত করা, ঝাড় লাগান। **2.** To provide (boot) with extra thick sole ; জুতার তলায় অতিরিক্ত চামড়া লাগান। ***Verb i.*** To walk or tread heavily ; ধপ্ ধপ্ করিয়া চলা।

clŭm′-sȳ, *adj.* Awkward ; inelegant ; ungainly ; badly constructed ; without skill ; কদাকার ; অমার্জ্জিত, স্থূল, গোব্‌দা (*colloq.*) ; বিসদৃশ ; কুগঠিত ; অনিপুণ, আনাড়ী। **—si-ly,** *adv.* **—si-ness,** *n.*

clunch (klŭnch), *n.* **1.** A lump ; ডেলা। **2.** A soft white limestone used esp. for internal carved work ; একপ্রকার সাদা কোমল চূণা পাথর।

clŭng, *p. p.* of CLING.

Clupea ilisha—ইলিশ মাছ (গুপ্তঃ)। ***Clupea chapra***—চাপিলা মাছ (গুপ্তঃ)।

clŭs′-têr, *n., v. t.* & *i.* **1.** A group of things of the same kind, growing or joined together; a bunch; থলো, কাঁদি ছড়া, স্তবক; গুচ্ছ। **2.** A number of persons, animals or things collected in one place; a crowd; a group; as, a *cluster* of islands, stars, etc.: একস্থানে সম্মিলিত মানব, জন্তু বা বস্তু সমূহ; জনতা; শ্রেণী, দল। ***Verb t.*** To gather or group in a cluster (usu. in *p. p.*); গুচ্ছিত করা। ***Verb i.*** To assemble or collect closely; to form a cluster; একত্র জড় হওয়া; স্তবকিত হওয়া। **Clustered pillar, column**—একত্র গুচ্ছিত কতিপয় অঙ্গুল স্তম্ভ, গুচ্ছিত স্তম্ভ, স্তম্ভ-স্তবক।

clutch (klŭch), *n., v. t.* & *i.* **1.** Tight grip or grasp; দৃঢ়-মুষ্টি। **2.** (*Pl.*) Paw or talons; cruel grasp; থাবা, নখর; নির্দ্দয় হস্ত। **3.** (*Mech.*) A piece of machinery for connecting shafts with each other or with wheels so that they may be disengaged at pleasure; (যন্ত্র-বিজ্ঞান) যন্ত্রের অংশবিশেষ—যদ্দারা চক্রাদি সংযোজক দণ্ড সকল পরস্পরের সহিত বা চক্রের সহিত সংযুক্ত হয়। ***Verb t.*** **1.** To double in the fingers and compress them together; হস্ত মুষ্টি-বদ্ধ করা। **2.** To seize with claws; to seize eagerly; (with *away, off, up*); থাবা দিয়া ধরা; ব্যগ্রতাসহকারে ধরা। **3.** To hold with a tight grasp; as, to *clutch* power; দৃঢ় মুষ্টিতে ধরা। ***Verb i.*** To make an eager effort to seize, (with *up*); ধরিবার জন্ম সাগ্রহ চেষ্টা করা। **In the clutches**—কবলে।

clutch (klŭch), *n.* A laying of or sitting on eggs; ডিম্ব প্রসব করণ, ডিমে তা দেওন।

clŭt′-têr, *n.* & *v. i.* Confused noise; সোরগোল, হট্টগোল। ***Verb i.*** To move with noise or confusion; to make a confused noise; হুড়াহুড়ি করিয়া চলা; সোরগোল করা।

clўp′-ē-ŭs, *n.* The broad shield-like part of some insects' head; কোন কোন কীটের মস্তকের ঢালের মত অংশ। **—e-al, —e-ate,** *adjs.*

clўs′-têr, *n.* A medicine injected into the rectum, to cleanse the bowels; an enema; পিচকারীদ্বারা মলদ্বারের অভ্যন্তরে প্রবিষ্ট ঔষধ; মলদ্বারের পিচকারী।

Cō, *n.* An abbreviation of company; কোম্পানী শব্দের সংক্ষেপ।

coach (cōch), *n., v. t.* & *i.* **1.** A large close carriage with four wheels and with seats inside and outside; চারিচাকার গাড়ী বিশেষ। **2.** A railway carriage; (*U. S.*) a sleeping car; রেলের গাড়ী; (যুক্তরাজ্যে) বাষ্পীয়-শকটের শয্যাসমন্বিত কক্ষ। **3.** A private tutor to prepare for an examination; যে গৃহ-শিক্ষক কোন ছাত্রকে পরীক্ষার জন্ম প্রস্তুত করেন। **4.** An instructor in athletics, esp. boat-race; মল্লক্রীড়া-শিক্ষক, বিশেষতঃ যে ব্যক্তি নৌকা দৌড়ের জন্ম নৌচালকদিগকে শিক্ষাদান করেন। **5.** An apartment in a ship of war under the poop; রণপোতের পশ্চাদ্ভাগের নিম্নস্থ কক্ষ। ***Verb t.*** **1.** To convey in or seat in a coach; চারিচাকার গাড়ীতে বসান বা বহন করা। **2.** To tutor (a pupil) for an examination; to train the crews for a boat-race; কোন ছাত্রকে পরীক্ষার জন্ম প্রস্তুত করা; নৌকা দৌড়ের জন্ম চালকদিগকে শিক্ষাদান করা। ***Verb i.*** To read or study with a coach; পরীক্ষার পূর্ব্বে গৃহশিক্ষকের নিকট অধ্যয়ন করা। **Coach-box**—গাড়ী চালকের বসিবার আসন। **Coach-house**—গাড়ীর ঘর। **Coach-man**—শকটচালক, কোচোয়ান, গাড়োয়ান। **Coach-office**—যে কার্য্যালয়ে যাত্রী-গাড়ীর টিকিট বিক্রয় হয়। **Coach-stand**—ভাড়াটিয়া গাড়ীর আড্ডা। **Coach and four, and six**—চারি-ঘোড়ার গাড়ী, ছয় ঘোড়ার গাড়ী। **To drive a coach and six through an act of Parliament**—To stultify it: পার্লেমেণ্টের আইন ব্যর্থ করা।

cō-ăd-ja′-cĕnt, *adj.* Contiguous, esp. in thought; সন্নিহিত (বিশেষতঃ চিন্তা-সম্পর্কে)। **—cen-cy,** *n.*

cō-ăd′-jū-tănt, *n.* & *adj.* (*Law*) Assistant; সাহায্যকারী ব্যক্তি। ***Adj.*** Mutually assisting; পরস্পরের সাহায্যকারী।

cō-ăd-jū′-tor (-têr), *n.* An assistant; a helper; সহকারী ব্যক্তি; সাহায্যকারী ব্যক্তি।

cō-ăd′-ū-nāte, *v. t.* & *adj.* To combine; সংযোগ করা। ***Adj.*** (*Bot.*) Joined together; (উদ্ভিদ্-বিদ্যা) সংযুক্ত।

cō-ā′-gĕnt, *n.* An assistant; an associate; সহকারী; সহযোগী।

cō-ăg′-ū-lāte, *v. t.* & *i.* To change (blood, milk, etc.) into a soft, solid mass; to curdle or congeal; জমাট বাঁধান; জমান, ঘনীভূত করা। ***Verb i.*** To curdle; to clot; to congeal; জমিয়া যাওয়া; জমাট বাঁধা, চাপ বাধা; ঘনীভূত হওয়া। **—la-bil′-i-ty,** *n.* **—la-ble,** *adj.* Capable of being coagulated; ঘনভবনশীল। **—lant,** *n.* That which produces coagulation; সংযমনকর (সাঃ পঃ)। **—la′-tion,** *n.* The act of coagulating; সংযমন (সাঃ পঃ), ঘনীকরণ। **—la-tive,** *adj.* **—la-tor,** *n.* **—lum,** *n.* A mass of coagulated matter; a clot of blood; ঘনীভূত বস্তু; রক্তের চাপ, দম্বল, সংযত রক্ত (ডাক্তারি)।

coal (kōl), *n., v. t.* & *i.* **1.** A piece of glowing carbon (without flame); a cinder; জ্বলন্ত অঙ্গার; অঙ্গার। **2.** A solid, hard, black, combustible substance dug out of the earth and largely used as fuel ; মৃদঙ্গার, পাথুরিয়া কয়লা, বিলাতী কয়লা (বেলঃ)। *Verb t.* **1.** To supply (a steam-ship, fire, etc.) with coal for fuel ; as, to *coal* a steamer ; কয়লা সরবরাহ করা। **2.** To burn to coal ; পুড়িয়া কয়লা করা। **3.** To mark or delineate with charcoal ; কয়লাদ্বারা চিহ্নিত বা অঙ্কিত করা। *Verb i.* To take in coal ; as, the steamer *coaled* at Southampton ; কয়লা লওয়া। **Coal'-y, Coal'-less,** *adjs.* **Coal-box, —scuttle** — কয়লার আধার। **Coal-field**—কয়লার ক্ষেত্র, মৃদঙ্গারবহুল ক্ষেত্র। **Coal-fish**—A black cod : কৃষ্ণবর্ণ কড্ মৎস্য। **Coal-gas**—কয়লার বাপ। **Coal-heaver**—কয়লার মুটে। **Coal-house**—কয়লার ঘর। **Coaling-station**—যে বন্দরে বাষ্পীয় পোত কয়লা বোঝাই করে। **Coal-master**—কয়লার ক্ষেত্রের ইজারাদার বা স্বত্বাধিকারী। **Coal-mine, —pit**—কয়লার খনি বা আকর। **Coal-tar**—কয়লার আল্কাত্রা। **A cold coal to blow at**—A hopeless task to perform ; নিরুৎসাহজনক কার্য্য। **To blow the coals**—To fan the flames of passion, etc. ; ক্রোধাগ্নি প্রজ্বলিত করা, বিবাদানল প্রজ্বলিত করা। **To carry (or bear) coals**—To do degrading work ; to submit to insult ; অপমানজনক কায করা ; নীরবে অপমান সহ্য করা। **To carry coals to Newcastle**—To do what is absurdly superfluous ; তেলা মাথায় তেল দেওয়া। **To cart (heap or gather) coals of fire on the head**—To return good for evil, and thus to fill an enemy's mind with remorse ; কুব্যবহারের পরিবর্ত্তে সদ্ব্যবহার করিয়া শত্রুকে লজ্জিত করা। **To haul (call or bring) over the coals**—To call to task ; তিরস্কার করা। **To stir coals**—To excite ill-feeling ; কুভাব বা বিদ্বেষ উত্তেজিত করা।

cō-ă-lesce' (-lĕs'), *v. t.* **1.** To grow together ; জোড়া বাঁধিয়া জন্মা, যুগ্মভাবে জাত হওয়া। **2.** To unite into one body or association ; সংযুক্ত হওয়া, সম্মিলিত হওয়া, একদলভুক্ত হওয়া। **—les'-cence,** *n.* Union into one mass ; uniting (of persons or parties) into a single body ; সংশ্লেষ ; সম্মিলন, সংযোগ, একীভাব : **—les'-cent,** *adj.*

cō-ă-li'-tion, *n.* **1.** Union into a body or mass ; সমবায়, সংযোগ, সম্মিলন, একীভাব, সমাগম, সংহতি। **2.** A combination of different individuals, parties or states into one ; বিভিন্ন ব্যক্তি, দল বা রাজ্যের সম্মিলন। **—ist,** *n.*

coal'-mouse, cole-mouse (kōl-mows), *n.* A small dark-coloured bird ; ধূসরবর্ণ ক্ষুদ্র পক্ষি-বিশেষ।

coam'-ing (kōm-), *n.* (*pl.*) The raised border or edges of the hatches of a ship ; জাহাজের চাপ-দরজার আবরণের উন্নত কিনারা।

coarse (kōrs), *adj.* **1.** Composed of large particles ; not fine (opp. to *fine*) ; as, *coarse* thread, cloth, etc. ; common ; inferior ; as, *coarse* fish : *coarse* fare ; মোটা দানাদার ; খর (সাঃ পঃ), স্থূল, ঘন, মোটা ; সাধারণ ; নীরস, অপকৃষ্ট। **2.** (*Of persons*) Unrefined ; as, *coarse* society ; indelicate ; vulgar ; as, *coarse* language ; rude ; rough ; uncivil ; as, *coarse* manners ; অসংস্কৃত, অমার্জ্জিত, অশিষ্ট, রুক্ষ ; অকোমল ; গ্রাম্য, ইতর ; কর্কশ ; রূঢ় ; অভদ্র। **Coarse'-ly,** *adv.* **Coarse'-ness,** *n.* **Coarse-fibred, Coarse-grained**—Having coarse fibres or textures ; মোটা আঁশ বা দানা বিশিষ্ট। (*Fig.*) Wanting in refinement ; (লক্ষণায়) অমার্জ্জিত, অভব্য।

coars'-en (kōrsn), *v. t.* & *i.* To make or become coarse ; মোটা করা বা হওয়া।

coast (kōst), *n.* & *v. i.* **1.** The margin of the land next the sea ; sea-shore ; বেলা (সাঃ পঃ), উপকূল (ঐ) ; সাগরতীর। **2.** A run downhill on a bicycle, with the feet off the pedals ; পাদান হইতে পা তুলিয়া দ্বিচক্রযানযোগে বেগে পাহাড় হইতে অবতরণ। *Verb i.* **1.** To sail (*by, along*) the coast, esp. in sight of land ; to sail from port to port ; সমুদ্রের কূলে কূলে জাহাজে যাওয়া ; বন্দর হইতে বন্দরে জাহাজে যাওয়া। **2.** To bicycle down-hill without pedalling ; পাদান হইতে পা তুলিয়া দ্বিচক্রযানযোগে পাহাড় হইতে নামা। **Coast'-ing,** *n.* **1.** Sailing along the coast ; trading between the ports of a country ; উপকূলে উপকূলে পোত চালন ; কোন দেশের বন্দরে বন্দরে অর্ণবযানযোগে বাণিজ্য করণ। **2.** Delineation of a coast line ; বেলা-রেখাঙ্কন। **Coast'-wards, Coast'-wise,** *advs.* **Coast-guard**—ইংলণ্ডের নৌবিভাগের অধীন উপকূলরক্ষী সৈন্যদল। **Coast-line**—বেলারেখা, তটরেখা, বেলায়তি (সাঃ পঃ), বেলাভূমি (ঐ)।

coat (kōt), *n.* & *v. t.* **1.** An outer garment worn by men, usually of cloth with sleeves ; অঙ্গরাখা, জামা, কুর্ত্তা। **2.** A woman's stout-buttoned overcoat ; স্ত্রীলোকের লম্বা কুর্ত্তা বিশেষ। **3.** An animal's covering of hair, fur, wool, etc. ; পশ্বাদির শরীরাবরক লোম। **4.** Anything that covers or conceals ; as, a *coat* of snow ; a coating ; as, a *coat* of varnish ; আচ্ছাদন, আবেষ্টন, আবরণ, ত্বক্, খোসা ; পোঁচ, লেপ। *Verb t.* **1.** To provide with a coat ; কুর্ত্তা পরান। **2.** To cover with a layer or coating of any substance ; লেপ দেওয়া, লিপ্ত করা। **Coat'-ing,** *n.* **1.** A coat or covering ; a layer of any substance ; ত্বক্, আচ্ছাদন ; আবরণ, লেপ **2.** Cloth for coats ; কুর্ত্তার কাপড়। **Coat-armour, Coat of arms**—Armorial devices ; কুলচিহ্ন, বর্ম্মোপরি

ব্যবহৃত প্রাবরণোপরিস্থ কুলচিহ্ন। **Coat of mail** — উরশ্ছদ, বর্ম্ম, বারবাণ,

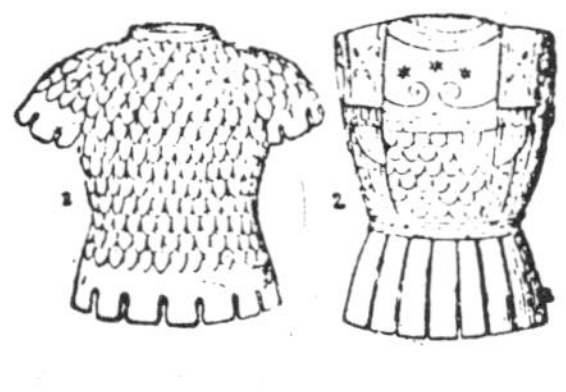

1. Roman. 2. Greek.
Coats of mail.

সাঁজোয়া। **To cut the coat according to the cloth**—(See CLOTH). **To dust one's coat**—To beat him ; প্রহার করা। **To turn one's coat**—To desert one's party ; to apostatize ; স্বদল ত্যাগ করা ; স্বধর্ম্ম বা স্বমত ত্যাগ করা। **To wear the king's coat**—To serve as a soldier ; সৈনিকের কার্য্য করা।

coat-ee′ (kŏt-ē), *n.* A close-fitting military coat with short tails ; সৈনিকগণের ব্যবহৃত কুর্ত্তাবিশেষ।

cō-ă-ti′, *n.* An American carnivorous mammal allied to the raccoon, with long flexible snout ; আমেরিকাদেশীয় স্তন্যপায়ী জন্তুবিশেষ।

coax (kōks), *v. t.* To persuade by flattery or blandishment ; to wheedle ; তোষামোদ করা ; মিষ্ট কথায় ভুলান। **Coax′-er, Coax′-ing,** *ns.* **To coax away, down**—To entice ; ভুলাইয়া লইয়া যাওয়া।

cō-ăx′-ăl, —i-ăl, *adj.* (*Math.*) Having common axis ; (গণিতশাস্ত্র) একাক্ষিক (হিঃ কোঃ)।

cŏb, *n.* **1.** Head ; মস্তক। **2.** A great man ; a leader ; as, he was the *cob* of all this country ; বড়লোক ; নায়ক। **3.** A male swan (also COB-SWAN) ; একজাতীয় বৃহৎ রাজহংস। **4.** A strong stout pony ; হৃষ্টপুষ্ট অশ্ব। **5.** A lump or large piece of coal ; কয়লার বৃহৎ খণ্ড। **6.** A spike on which the kernels of maize grow ; ভুট্টার শীষ।

cŏb, *n.* A composition of clay mixed with straw used for building walls ; প্রাচীর নির্ম্মাণে ব্যবহৃত খড় মিশ্রিত মৃত্তিকা। **Cob′-by,** *adj.*

cō′-bŏlt, *n.* **1.** A reddish-grey metal similar in many respects to nickel ; ধাতুবিশেষ, শ্বেত, সাইতা, গুহ্যক (সাঃ পঃ)। **2.** A deep-blue pigment made from it ; উক্ত ধাতু হইতে প্রস্তুত নীল রঙ্গ বিশেষ। **—bal′-tic, —if′-er-ous,** *adjs.* **—ine** or **—ite,** *n.* A crystallized sulpharsenide of cobalt, of a silver or yellowish colour ; তারামাক্ষিক (রসঃ—প্রঃ)।

cob′-ble (kŏbl), *n.* & *v. t.* **1.** A pebble ; উপল। **2.** (*Pl.*) A roundish lump of coal ; গোলাকৃতি কয়লার খণ্ড। ***Verb t.*** To pave with cobbles; ক্ষুদ্র ক্ষুদ্র প্রস্তর খণ্ডদ্বারা রাস্তা বাঁধা।

cob′-ble (kŏbl), *v. t.* To mend or repair roughly ; to patch up ; specif. to mend shoes ; জোড়া তাড়া দেওয়া, তালি দেওয়া ; জুতা সারা।

cob′-ble, co′-ble (kŏbl), *n.* A small flat-bottomed fishing boat ; জেলে ডিঙ্গি।

cŏb′-blêr, *n.* **1.** A mender of shoes ; জুতা মেরামতকারী। **2.** A clumsy workman ; আনাড়ি বা অনিপুণ কারিকর, অদক্ষ শিল্পী। **3.** (*Colloq.*) A cooling beverage ; একপ্রকার ঠাণ্ডা সরবত। **Let not the cobbler overstep his last**—Let no one presume to interfere in matters of which one is ignorant ; কোন ব্যক্তিকে অনধিকার চর্চ্চা করিতে দিও না।

cō-bĕl-lĭg′-êr-ĕnt, *n.* & *adj.* A nation or state co-operating in warfare ; যে জাতি বা রাষ্ট্র যুদ্ধে সহকারিতা করে। ***Adj.*** Carrying on war in conjunction with another power; অপর শক্তির সহিত সহযোগিতায় যুদ্ধকারী।

cō′-bră (or cŏb′-ră) [cō′-ră-dē-că-pĕl-lō], *n.* A very venomous serpent of the viper family ; গোখুরা সাপ। **Cobra's saffron**—নাগেশ্বর (খোরী), পুন্নাগ।

Cobra-de-capello.

cŏb′-wĕb, *n.* **1.** A spider's network ; also the thread of this ; মাকড়সার জাল ; কৃমি-তন্তু, লূতাতন্তু, মাকড়সার সূতা। **2.** (*Fig.*) Something flimsy ; অসার বা অকিঞ্চিৎকর বস্তু। **3.** An entangling mesh ; as, *cobwebs* of the law ; ফাঁদ, পাশ। **—by, —web-bed,** *adjs.* **—ber-y,** *n.* **To have a cobweb in the throat**—To feel thirsty ; তৃষ্ণা বোধ করা।

cō′-că, *n.* The dried leaf of a South American plant, which being chewed, is said to give great power of fatigue-enduring ; also the plant itself ; দক্ষিণ আমেরিকা মহাদেশীয় বৃক্ষ বিশেষের শুষ্ক পত্র (উহা চর্ব্বণ করিলে ক্লান্তি নিবারিত হয়) ; ঐ বৃক্ষ।

cō′-că-ine, *n.* A drug made from coca leaves producing local insensibility ; কোকা বৃক্ষের পত্র হইতে প্রস্তুত স্থানিক অবসন্নতাজনক ক্ষারবিশেষ। **—in-i-za′-tion,** *n.* **—in-ize,** *v. t.* To render insensible by means of cocaine ; কোকেইন ব্যবহারে অচেতন বা স্পর্শানভিজ্ঞ করা। **—in-ism,** *n.* (*Med.*) A morbid condition produced by excessive use of cocaine ; (ভৈষজ্য-শাস্ত্র) অতিরিক্ত কোকেইন সেবনজনিত রুগ্নাবস্থা।

cŏc-că-ğee′ (-gē), *n.* A cider apple ; একপ্রকার সেওফল।

Coccinea Indica—বিম্বফল (বেলঃ), তেলাকুচা (ঐ)।

Cocculus acuminatus — তিলকোরা (বেলঃ)।

Cocculus cordifolius — গুলঞ্চ (বেলঃ), কন্দগুরুচি।

Cocculus Indicus — কাকমারী (বেলঃ)।

cŏc'-cŭs, *n.* (*Bot.*) One of the carpels or seed vessels of a dry fruit ; (উদ্ভিদ্-বিদ্যা) শুষ্কফলের কিঞ্জলক বা বীজাধারের কোন একটী, গুটিকাফল (সাঃ পঃ)।

Coccystes, *n.* A genus of birds, family Cucelidæ, sub-family Cuculidæ ; চাতকাদি। ***Coccystes melanoleucos***—চাতক (যোঃ)।

cŏc'-cȳx, *n.* (*Anat.*) The lower bone of the vertebral column ; পৃষ্ঠবংশের অধঃপ্রান্তস্থ ত্রিকোণাস্থি, কোকিলচঞ্চু অস্থি, চঞ্চ্বস্থি। **—cyg'-e-al,** *adj.*

cō'-chin, *n.* A breed of large domestic fowls (from Cochin-China) ; একপ্রকার গৃহপালিত কুক্কুট।

cōch'-i-neal (-nēl), *n.* The dried bodies of insects found on Cactus in Mexico and used for making scarlet dye and carmine ; মেক্সিকোদেশীয় শুষ্ক কীট এবং তাহা হইতে প্রস্তুত লোহিতবর্ণ রঞ্জক পদার্থ বিশেষ,—লাক্ষা, ক্রিমিদানা (যোঃ), ক্রিমিদ্রব, অলক্ত। **Cochineal insect** — ইন্দ্রগোপ, শক্রগোপ।

Cochineal insect.

cŏch'-lē-ă, *n.* **1.** (*Anat.*) The spiral cavity of the internal ear ; কর্ণকম্বু (সাঃ পঃ)। **2.** (*Bot.*) A spiral-shaped body or organ ; (উদ্ভিদ্-বিদ্যা) কম্বু (সাঃ পঃ)। **—ate, —at-ed,** *adjs.*

cock (kŏk), *n.* **1.** The male of the domestic fowl ; কুক্কুট, মোরগ, তাম্রচূড়, ঊষাকল। **2.** The male of other birds ; as, *cock*-sparrow ; অন্যান্য পুংপক্ষী। **3.** A weather-cock ; বায়ুর দিঙ্-নির্ণায়ক যন্ত্রবিশেষ। **4.** A chief man ; a leader ; "Sir Andrew—the *cock* of the club ;" প্রধান ব্যক্তি, চাঁই ; সর্দ্দার। **5.** A tap ; নল, নালী। **6.** The indicator of a balance ; নিক্তির কাঁটা। **7.** The hammer in the lock of a fire-arm ; বন্দুকের ঘোড়া। **Cock-boat**—জাহাজের ডিঙ্গী, ক্ষুদ্র নৌকা। **Cock-brained**—লঘুমস্তিষ্ক। **Cock-crowing**—ঊষাকাল। **Cock-eyed**—টেরা। **Cock-fighting, Cock-fight**—কুক্কুটযুদ্ধ (বাংস্তঃ)। **Cock's-comb**—কুক্কুটশিখা, শ্বেতমুর্গা (খোরী), মোরগজটা (প্রবোধ)। **Cock-a-hoop** or **Cock on the hoop**—Triumphant ; exulting ; বিজয়োল্লাসপূর্ণ ; হর্ষোৎফুল্ল, দৃপ্ত। **At** or **on full cock**—(ছুড়িবার পূর্ব্বে) বন্দুকের ঘোড়া উঠান। **Cock and bull story**—আষাঢ়ে গল্প, গাঁজাখুরি গল্প। **Cock of the school** — The leader in games, fighting, etc. ; যে বালক ক্রীড়া বা কলহে নায়কতা করে। **Cock of the walk**—The chief person of a circle, coterie, etc. ; দলের সর্দ্দার, পাড়ার মোড়ল। **Full cock**—(কল প্রভৃতির নল বা মুখ) পুরা খোলা। **That cock won't fight**—That dodge won't answer; ঐ চাতুরী খাটিবে না। **To beat cock-fighting**—(*Colloq.*) To surpass everything else ; (চলিত-ভাষায়) সকলের উপর টেক্কা দেওয়া। **To cry cock**—To claim victory ; জয়ের দাবী করা। **To live like fighting cocks**—To live in luxury ; ভোগবিলাসের মধ্যে বাস করা। **To turn the cock**—To open it ; (কল প্রভৃতির) মুখ বা নল খোলা।

cock (kŏk), *n.* **1.** A turning up (of the nose, etc.) ; (নাসিকা প্রভৃতির) উপরের দিকে উল্‌টানো ভাব, নাকসিটকানি। **2.** A significant turn of the eye ; টেরা চাহনি। **3.** An upward turn given to the brim of a hat ; টুপির কিনারা উপরের দিকে উল্টানি। **Cocked hat**—একপ্রকার টুপি,—ইহার কিনারা উপরের দিকে উল্টানো থাকে। **To knock into a cock or cocked hat**—To be out of shape or recognition ; পরিচয় করিতে পারা যায় না এরূপ হওয়া।

cock (kŏk), *v. t.* & *i.* **1.** To set erect or upright ; খাড়া করিয়া রাখা। **2.** To place, as the hat, on one side of the head ; টুপি প্রভৃতি মাথার একপার্শ্বে টের্চ্চা করিয়া স্থাপন করা। **3.** To turn or set up with an air of pertness ; টুপি প্রভৃতি মস্তকের একপার্শ্বে টের্চ্চা-করিয়া উদ্ধতব্যঞ্জকভাবে পরা। **4.** To draw the hammer of (a fire-arm) fully back and set it for firing ; বন্দুক প্রভৃতির ঘোড়া পশ্চাদ্দিকে টানিয়া ছুড়িবার জন্য প্রস্তুত করা। ***Verb i.*** To strut ; to swagger ; গর্ব্বিতভাবে চলা ; গর্ব্বভরে হেলিয়া দুলিয়া চলা। **To cock the ears**—To prick up the ears in attention, interest, etc. ; কৌতূহলাদি বশতঃ উৎকর্ণ হওয়া। **To cock the eyes**—To give a wink ; কটাক্ষক্ষেপ করা। **To cock the nose** — To turn it up in contempt or indifference ; নাক সিটকান, নাসিকা কুঞ্চিত করা।

cŏck-ă-bŏn'-dȳ, *n.* An artificial fly used by anglers ; বড়শীতে ব্যবহৃত কৃত্রিম টোপ বিশেষ।

cŏck āde', *n.* A knot or ribbon stuck on the hat ; a badge worn on the hat, esp. by the servants of the naval or military officers ; টুপির উপর সংবদ্ধ ফিতা বা ফিতার গ্রন্থি ; টুপির উপর পরিহিত চিহ্ন বিশেষ (বিশেষভাবে নাবিক এবং সামরিক কর্ম্মচারিগণের ভৃত্যগণ পরিধান করিয়া থাকে)। **—ad'-ed,** *adj.*

cŏck'-ă-dōō-dle-dōō', *n.* The cry of the cock ; (*humorous*) a cock ; কুক্কুটধ্বনি ; (কৌতুকচ্ছলে) কুক্কুট।

cŏck-ă-hōōp', *adj.* & *adv.* See under COCK.

Cŏck-aigne', —ayne', (-ān), *n.* **1.** An imaginary country of idleness and luxury ; কল্পিত

ভোগবিলাসের রাজ্য। **2.** London and its suburbs; লণ্ডন নগরী এবং লণ্ডনের সহরতলী।

cŏck-ă-leek'-ie (-lēk-ē), See COCKY-LEEKY.

cŏck-ă-tōō', *n.* Any of the various beautiful birds of the parrot kind, with movable crest; কাকাতুয়া।

cock'-a-trice (kŏk-ă-trīs), *n.* See BASILISK.

Cockchafer.

cŏck'-chāf-êr, *n.* The may-bug or beetle; গোবরে পোকা।

cŏck'-êr, *v. t.* To fondle; to indulge; আদর করা, সোহাগ করা; প্রশ্রয় দেওয়া, আসকারা দেওয়া (*Colloq.*)।

cŏck'-êr, *n.* **1.** A cock-fighter; যে ব্যক্তি মোড়গ দ্বারা লরাই করায়। **2.** A spaniel; নতকর্ণ কুকুর বিশেষ। **According to Cocker**—According to what is correct; শুদ্ধ বিষয়ের অনুযায়ী। [Edward Cocker নামক এক ব্যক্তি একখানি পাটীগণিত প্রকাশ করেন। ঐ গ্রন্থের ৬০ সংস্করণ হইয়াছিল।] According to established rules; প্রচলিত নিয়মানুসারে।

cŏck'-êr-ĕl, *n.* **1.** A young domestic cock; গৃহপালিত ক্ষুদ্র কুক্কুট বিশেষ। **2.** (*Fig.*) A pugnacious young man; "Thou art no such *cockerel* thyself; কলহপ্রিয় যুবক।

cŏck'-hŏrse, *n.* & *adv.* A child's rocking horse or hobby horse; ছেলেদের খেলার ঘোড়া। ***Adv.*** Mounted (on a horse); অশ্বারূঢ় অবস্থায়।

cock'-le (kŏkl), *n.* A reddish-purple flowered plant growing in corn fields, esp. among wheat, (also CORN-COCKLE); লোহিতাভ ধূমল (বেগুণে) বর্ণ পুষ্পপ্রসূ গুল্ম বিশেষ—শস্যক্ষেত্রে জন্মে।

cock'-le (kŏkl), *n.* **1.** Any bivalve mollusc, common on sandy coasts and used for food; also its shell; শুক্তি বিশেষ; ঐ প্রকার শুক্তির কঠিন পৃষ্ঠাবরণ। **2.** A small shallow boat; (also COCKLE SHELL, COCKLE BOAT); একপ্রকার ক্ষুদ্র নৌকা। **Hot cockles**—কাণা মাছি খেলা। **To warm the cockles of one's heart**—To rouse one's inmost feelings; অন্তরের অন্তরতম ভাব জাগরিত করা।

cock'-le (kŏkl), *n.*, *v. i.* & *t.* **1.** A wrinkle or bulge in paper, glass, etc.; বস্ত্র, কাগজ, কাচ প্রভৃতির কুঞ্চন, চুনট বা স্ফীতি। **2.** That part of a hop-kiln or oast where fire is made; (also COCKLE OAST) হপলতা শুষ্ক করিবার বৃহৎ চুল্লির যে অংশে অগ্নি প্রজ্বলিত করা হয়। **3.** A kind of stove for heating apartments, (also COCKLE STOVE); কক্ষশ্রেণী উষ্ণ করণার্থ চুল্লীবিশেষ। ***Verb i.*** (Of *cloth, paper, etc.*) To pucker; to wrinkle; to bulge; কুঞ্চিত হওয়া; কোঁকড়াইয়া যাওয়া; স্ফীত হওয়া। ***Verb t.*** To cause to wrinkle; কুঞ্চিত করা।

cŏck'-lŏft, *n.* A small upper loft next the roof; উপরের ক্ষুদ্র কুঠরী, চন্দ্রশালা (আঃ বঃ), শিরোগৃহ (ঐ)।

cŏck'-ney (-nē), *n.* & *adj.* A native of London (by way of contempt); লণ্ডন সহরবাসী (অবজ্ঞাচ্ছলে)। ***Adj.*** Pertaining to cockney; লণ্ডননগরবাসী সম্পর্কীয়। **—dom**, *n.* **—fy**, *v. t.* **—ish**, *adj.* **—ism**, *n.* **ize**, *v. t.* & *i.*

cŏck'-pit, *n.* **1.** A pit or arena where game-cocks fight; যে বেষ্টিত স্থানে কুক্কুটদিগকে লড়াইয়ের জন্য ছাড়িয়া দেওয়া হয়, কুক্কুট-যুদ্ধস্থলী। **2.** A place in the lower deck of a man-of-war for the wounded in an action; রণপোতের নিম্নতর পাটাতনের স্থান বিশেষ—এই স্থানে নৌযুদ্ধে আহত সৈন্যগণকে রাখা হয়। **The cockpit of Europe**—বেলজিয়ম দেশ। [এই দেশে ইউরোপের অনেক মহাযুদ্ধ সংঘটিত হইয়াছিল।]

cŏck'-roach (-rōch), *n.* Any orthopterous insect, the so-called black beetle, very troublesome in houses; তৈলচোরিকা, আরসলা (সাঃ পঃ), তৈলপায়ী, তেলাপোকা।

cŏck'-sure (-shûr), *adj.* & *adv.* **1.** Absolutely certain; সুনিশ্চিত, নিঃসন্দেহ। **2.** Presumptuous; প্রগল্ভ।

cŏck'-sȳ, cŏx'-ȳ, *adjs.* Saucy; impudent; (school boy's word); বে-আদব, ঠেঁটা; ধৃষ্ট।

cŏck'-tail (-tāl), *n.* & *adj.* **1.** A horse with docked tail; a half-bred horse; কর্ত্তিতপুচ্ছ অশ্ব; দো-আঁশলা ঘোড়া। **2.** A kind of beetle; একপ্রকার গোবরে পোকা। **3.** A person placed above his birth or breeding; বংশ বা শিক্ষা দ্বারা সমাজে যে স্থান পাইবার উপযুক্ত-তদপেক্ষা উচ্চতর স্থানে অবস্থিত ব্যক্তি। **4.** Brandy or gin sweetened with sugar and slightly weakened with water; চিনি এবং জল মিশ্রিত ব্রাণ্ডি বা সরাপ।

cŏck'-ŭp, *n.* **1.** (*Print.*) An initial letter much taller than the rest; (মুদ্রণ) কোন শব্দের অন্যান্য অক্ষরের তুলনায় অনেক দীর্ঘ আদ্যাক্ষর। **2.** A kind of fish; ভেট্‌কী মাছ।

cŏck'-ȳ, *adj.* Same as COCK-SY. **—i-ly**, *adv.* **—i-ness**, *n.*

cŏck-y-leek'-y (kŏk-ī-lēk-ī), *n.* A Scotch soup made of cock boiled with leek; রশুনের মত আনাজের সহিত সিদ্ধ-করা মোরগের ঝোল।

cō'-co, —coa (-kō), *n.* **1.** A palm native of both Indies;

নারিকেল বৃক্ষ। **2.** The fruit of this palm, (also COCOANUT) ; নারিকেল ফল। **3.** (*Humorously*) The human head ; (কৌতুকচ্ছলে) মনুষ্যের মস্তক। **Coco-nut, Cocoa-nut**—নারিকেল। **Coco-nut matting**—নারিকেলের খোসার আঁশ হইতে প্রস্তুত মাদুর বিশেষ। **Coconut oil**—নারিকেল তৈল।

cō′-coa (-kō), *n.* The meat of the cacao roasted and ground ;

Cocoa plant.

also a drink made from this powder ; কেকো ফলের চূর্ণ ; ঐ চূর্ণ হইতে প্রস্তুত পানীয় বিশেষ। **Cocoa powder**—একপ্রকার বারুদ।

cō-coon′, *n., v. t.* & *i.* The round silky case in which the silk-worm and many other larvæ envelope themselves ; কৃমিকোষ, গুটি (সাঃ পঃ), কোষ (ঐ)। ***Verb t.*** To form a cocoon ; গুটি তৈয়ার করা। ***Verb i.*** To wrap in a cocoon ; গুটিতে আবদ্ধ হওয়া। **—er-y,** *n.* A place for rearing silk-worms ; গুটিপোকা পালনের স্থান।

cŏd, *n.* A well-known large sea-fish ; সামুদ্রিক মৎস্য বিশেষ। **Cod-bank**—সমুদ্রগর্ভস্থ চড়া বিশেষ—যেস্থানে কড মৎস্য জড় হয়। **Cod-liver oil**—কড্ মৎস্যের যকৃৎ হইতে প্রাপ্ত তৈল বিশেষ—বলকারক ঔষধরূপে ব্যবহৃত হয়।

cŏd, *n.* **1.** A husk or pod ; খোসা, সুঁটি। **2.** The scrotum ; অণ্ডকোষ। **3.** A pillow ; বালিস।

cod′-dle (kŏdl), *v. t.* & *n.* **1.** To parboil ; মৃদু সিদ্ধ করা। **2.** To treat as an invalid ; to make delicate by over-nursing ; to pamper ; রুগ্ন ব্যক্তির মত সেবা করা ; অত্যধিক শুশ্রূষা করিয়া আদুরে গোপাল করিয়া তোলা ; আদর করা, সোহাগ করা। ***Noun.*** A pampered being ; আদুরে গোপাল।

cōde, *n.* & *v. t.* **1.** Laws collected and arranged, particularly if done by an authority ; সংহিতা, কোন দেশের বিধিবদ্ধ আইন সমূহ, বিন্যস্ত-সংগ্রহ (হিঃ কোঃ)। **2.** A collection of rules and regulations on any subject ; কোন বিষয়-সংক্রান্ত বিধি-সমূহ বা নিয়মাবলী, ব্যবহারবিধি। **3.** A system of words, (*arbitrarily*) used for other words or phrases, to secure brevity and secrecy ; শব্দের সংক্ষেপের জন্য বা কোন কথা গোপন রাখিবার জন্য যে সাঙ্কেতিক শব্দ সমূহ ব্যবহৃত হয়, সাঙ্কেতিক শব্দ। ***Verb t.*** To put in the form of a code ; as, to *code* a telegraphic message ; উক্তরূপ সাঙ্কেতিক শব্দে পরিণত করা। **Code′-less,** *adj.*

cō-dĕc-lĭ-na′-tion, *n.* (*Astron.*) The complement of the declination, (usually called the *North Polar distance*) ; (জ্যোতির্বিজ্ঞান) ক্রান্তির পূরক।

cō-dē′-ine (-în), *n.* An alkaloid obtained from opium ; অহিফেন হইতে প্রাপ্ত ক্ষারময় পদার্থ বিশেষ।

cō′-dĕx, *n.* (*pl.* CODICES.) **1.** A manuscript volume, esp. of the ancient scriptures or of the classics ; পুঁথি বিশেষ, হস্তলিখিত প্রাচীন বাইবেল বা প্রাচীন গ্রীক ও রোমান গ্রন্থকারদিগের পুস্তক। **2.** A body of prescriptions ; ঔষধের ব্যবস্থাপত্র সমূহ।

codg′-ĕr (kŏj-), *n.* **1.** (*Colloq.*) A fellow ; a chap ; (চলিত ভাষায়) বেটা ; ছোঁড়া। **2.** An eccentric old man ; a miserly man ; পাগলাটে বুড়ো ; কঞ্জুষ (*Colloq.*)।

cŏd′-i-cĭl, *n.* A supplement to a will ; উইলের ক্রোড়পত্র, ইচ্ছাপত্রের পরিশিষ্ট। **—cil′-la-ry,** *adj.*

cŏd′-i-fȳ, *v. t.* To reduce (laws) to a code ; to systematize ; সংহিতাবদ্ধ করা ; শৃঙ্খলাবদ্ধ করা। **—fi-ca′-tion,** *n.* **—fi-er,** *n.*

cŏd′-ling, *n.* A young or small cod ; ক্ষুদ্র কড্ মৎস্য।

cŏd-ling, —lin, *n.* A variety of cooking apple ; এক জাতীয় সেওফল।

cō-ĕd-ū-cā′-tion, *n.* Education of boys and girls together in school or college ; স্কুল বা কলেজে এক সঙ্গে বালকবালিকাদিগের শিক্ষাদান, সহাধ্যাপনা। **—al,** *adj.*

cō-ĕf-fĭ′-cient (-shĕnt), *n.* **1.** A joint agent or factor ; সহযোগী বস্তু। **2.** (*Math.*) A number or quantity placed (usually) before and multiplying another quantity known or unknown ; (গণিত-শাস্ত্র) যে সংখ্যা জ্ঞাত বা অজ্ঞাত রাশির (সচরাচর) পূর্ব্বে গুণক স্বরূপ স্থাপিত হইয়া থাকে, গুণ (সাঃ পঃ), প্রকৃতি (ঐ), বর্ণ (ঐ), আরক (ঐ), গুণক (হিঃ কোঃ)।

cœ′-li-ăc (sē-), *adj.* Of or belonging to the belly ; as, *cœliac* artery ; উদর সম্বন্ধীয়।

cō-emp′-tion (-ĕm-), *n.* The act of purchasing the whole quantity of any commodity ; কোন জিনিষ সমস্ত ক্রয় করণ, রাখি করণ, পূর্ব্ব ক্রয়।

cœ-næs-thē′-sis (sē-nēs-), *n.* (*Psychol.*) The vital sense ; (মনস্তত্ত্ব) সামান্য-সংবেদন (হিঃ কোঃ)।

cœ′-nō-bīte (sē-), *n.* See CENOBITE. **—bit′-ic,** *adj.* **—bit′-ism,** *n.*

cō-ē′-quăl, *adj.* & *n.* Equal with one another ; of the same rank, power, importance, etc. ; পরস্পরের তুল্য ; সমক্ষমতাপন্ন, সমগুরুত্ববিশিষ্ট। ***Noun.*** One who is equal with another ; অন্য ব্যক্তির সমকক্ষ ব্যক্তি। **–ly,** *adv.* **–qual'-i-ty,** *n.*

cō-erce' (-êrs), *v. t.* **1.** To restrain by force ; বলপূর্ব্বক সংযত করা, নিরোধ করা, প্রতিরোধ করা, শাসন করা, নিগৃহীত করা। **2.** To compel or enforce ; বাধ্য করা, বলপ্রয়োগদ্বারা বাধ্য করা। **–er-ci-bil'-i-ty,** *n.* **–er'-ci-ble,** *adj.*

cō-êr'-cion (-shŭn), *n.* **1.** Controlling of voluntary agent or action by force ; compulsion ; বলপূর্ব্বক বাধ্যকরণ ; বলপ্রয়োগ, নিগ্রহ, জবরদস্তি (*Colloq.*)। **2.** Employment of force to suppress political disaffection and disorder ; government by force ; রাজনীতিক বিক্ষোভ-দমনের জন্য বলপ্রয়োগ ; বাহুবলে রাজ্যশাসন। **–a-ry,** *adv.* **–ist,** *n.*

cō-êr'-cive (-sĭv), *adj.* That has power or authority ; compulsory ; constraining ; সংযমনকর, নিয়ামক, নিরোধকারী ; বলপ্রয়োগাত্মক ; নিগ্রহাত্মক। **–ly,** *adv.* **–ness,** *n.*

cō-ĕs-sĕn'-tial (-shăl), *adj.* Having the same essence ; এক মূলক।

cō-ē-tā'-nē-ous (-ŭs), *adj.* Of the same age or duration ; contemporary ; সমবয়স্ক, সমকালস্থায়ী ; সামসময়িক।

cō-ē-têr'-năl, *adj.* Equally eternal ; সমনিত্য, সমচিরস্থায়ী, সমসনাতন। **–ly,** *adv.* **–ni-ty,** *n.*

cō-ē'-văl, *adj.* & *n.* Of the same age ; সমকালীন, সমবয়স্ক। ***Noun.*** A contemporary ; সামসময়িক ব্যক্তি।

co-ex-ec'-u-tor (kō-ĕgz-ĕk-ū-têr), (fem. **–trix**) *n.* A joint executor ; সহযোগী কর্ম্মনির্ব্বাহক।

cō-ex-ist' (-ĕgz-), *v. i.* To exist at the same time or in the same place, etc., (*with*) ; যুগপৎ অবস্থান করা, এক স্থানে অবস্থান করা। **–ence,** *n.* Existence ; conjunction ; এককালিকত্ব, সমকালবিদ্যমানতা ; সহভাব (হিঃ কোঃ), সহাস্তিত্ব (ঐ)। **–ent,** *adj.* এককালিক ; সহবর্তী।

cō-ĕx-tĕnd', *v. t.* & *i.* To extend equally with ; সমায়ত হওয়া। ***Verb i.*** To be co-extensive ; সমস্থান ব্যাপিয়া বিস্তৃত থাকা। **–ten'-sion,** *n.* **–ten'-sive,** *adj.* Equally extensive ; সহব্যাপী (জিঃ), সমব্যাপক। **–ten'-sive-ness,** *n.*

cŏf'-fee (-fē), *n.* **1.** A drink made from the seeds of a shrub roasted and ground ; কাফি। **2.** The seeds or berries (either raw or roasted) ; also the shrub yielding this ;

Coffee Tree.

কাফির বীজ ; কাফি গুল্ম। **Coffee-cup**—কাফি পাত্র বা পেয়ালা। **Coffee-house**—কাফি এবং অন্যান্য জলযোগের সামগ্রী বিক্রয়ের দোকান। **Coffee-mill** — কাফি পেষণ যন্ত্র। **Coffee-pot**—কাফি পাত্র। **Coffee-room**—সাধারণ ভোজনাগারের কাফি পানের কক্ষ। **Coffee-tavern**—যে জলযোগের দোকানে কাফি প্রভৃতি অমাদক দ্রব্য বিক্রীত হয়।

cŏf'-fêr, *n.* **1.** A box, esp. for money or valuables ; বাক্স, তোরঙ্গ, বিশেষতঃ অর্থ বা মূল্যবান বস্তুর পেটক, রত্নাধার, মুদ্রাধার। **2.** (*Pl.*) Treasury ; funds ; "*Coffers* of the government had long been empty ;" ধনাগার ; ধনভাণ্ডার। **3.** (*Arch.*) A sunk panel in vaults and domes, etc. ; (স্থপতি-বিদ্যা) গম্বুজ, খিলানবিশিষ্ট ছাদ প্রভৃতির খোপ। **4.** (*Poet.*) A hollow trench across a dry moat ; দুর্গবেষ্টক পরিখার মধ্যস্থ খাদবিশেষ। **5.** A floating dock ; প্রবমান পোতসংস্কার-মঞ্চ। **Coffer-dam**—সেতু প্রভৃতির ভিত্তিস্থাপনকালে জলপ্রবেশের পথ রুদ্ধ করিবার উদ্দেশ্যে যে কাঠময় আধার বা কাঠাম নদীগর্ভে বসান হয়।

cŏf'-fin, *n.* & *v. t.* **1.** A chest in which a corpse is buried ; শবাধার, কাঠমল্ল (প্রঃ বাঃ)। **2.** The whole hoof of a horse below the coronet ; অশ্বের পশ্চাদ্‌ভাগস্থ সমগ্র খুর। **3.** Same as COFFINSHIP. ***Verb t.*** **1.** To inclose in a coffin ; to inclose ; শবাধারে বদ্ধ করা ; বদ্ধ করা। **2.** (*Fig.*) To store away (books, etc.) inaccessibly ; দুষ্প্রাপ্য স্থানে (পুস্তক প্রভৃতি) গুদামজাত করিয়া রাখা। **Coffin-bone** — অশ্বখুর মধ্যস্থ অস্থিবিশেষ। **Coffin-plate**—শবাধারের আবরণোপরি সম্বদ্ধ ধাতুফলকবিশেষ—ইহাতে মৃতব্যক্তির নাম ধামাদি লিখিত থাকে। **Coffin-ship**—সমুদ্রগমনের অনুপযোগী জাহাজ। **To drive** or **put a nail into one's coffin**—To hasten one's death by intemperance, etc. ; অমিতাচার, প্রভৃতি দ্বারা মৃত্যু সন্নিকট করা।

cŏf-fle, *n.* A train of men or beasts ; esp. a gang of slaves chained together ; পশুশ্রেণী, একদল মানুষ ; বিশেষতঃ শৃঙ্খলাবদ্ধ ক্রীত-দাস সমূহ।

cŏg, *n.* & *v. t.* The tooth of a wheel by which it drives another wheel or body ; চক্রদন্ত, চাকার দাঁত, প্রধি-দন্ত। ***Verb t.*** To furnish (a wheel, etc.) with cogs ; চাকা প্রভৃতিতে দাঁত লাগান। **Cogged,** *adj.* **Cog-wheel**—দন্তুর চক্র।

cŏg, *v. t.* To practise certain tricks in throwing dice ; পাশা ক্ষেপণে চাতুরী করা। **Cog'-ging,** *adj.* **To cog a die** or **the dice**—Fraudulently to control their fall ; কপট পাশা খেলা।

cō'-gĕnt, *adj.* Forcible ; convincing ; as, *cogent* reasons, argument, etc. ; প্রবল, অকাট্য, দৃঢ়,

অপ্রতিষেধ্য ; প্রতীতিজনক। **—gen-cy,** *n.* **—ly,** *adv.*

cŏg′-i-tă-ble, *adj.* Thinkable ; conceivable ; ধ্যেয়, চিন্তনীয় ; বিভাব্য।

cŏg′-i-tāte, *v. i.* & *t.* **1.** To think ; to meditate ; চিন্তা করা, অনুধ্যান করা। ***Verb t.*** To think over ; to plan ; ভাবা ; মনে মনে আঁটা। **—ta-tive,** *adj.* **—ta-tive-ly,** *adv.* **—ta-tive-ness,** *n.*

cŏg-i-tā′-tion, *n.* Attentive consideration ; a thought or reflection ; "Fixed in *cogitation* deep" ; ধ্যান, অনুধাবন, সংচিন্তন ; চিন্তা বা বিচারণা, নিদিধ্যাসন।

cō′-gnac (-nīăk), *n.* An excellent quality of French brandy produced at Cognac ; ফরাশী দেশের কনিয়েক নগরীতে প্রস্তুত উৎকৃষ্ট মদিরা বিশেষ।

cŏg′-nāte, *adj.* & *n.* **1.** Allied by blood ; specif. related on the mother's side ; সগোত্র ; (বিশেষভাবে) মাতৃসম্পর্কে সম্পর্কীয়। **2.** (*Of languages*) Of the same family ; (ভাষাসম্বন্ধে) এক পরিবার ভুক্ত। **3.** (*Of words*) Coming from the same root ; (শব্দ সম্পর্কে) অভিন্ন ধাতু হইতে উৎপন্ন। **4.** Of the same kind or nature ; as, Geometry and the *cognate* sciences ; সমপ্রকৃতিক, সমধর্ম্মা, স্বজাতীয়, সম্বন্ধবিশিষ্ট। ***Noun.*** A kinsman ; specif. one related by the mother's side ; (opp. to *agnate*) ; জ্ঞাতি ; (বিশেষভাবে) মাতৃসম্পর্কে সম্পর্কীয় ব্যক্তি। **Cognate object**—ক্রিয়ার সমার্থক কর্ম্মপদ, সাধারণতঃ অকর্ম্মক ক্রিয়ার সহিত অন্বিত কর্ম্মপদ।

cŏg-nā′-tion, *n.* Cognate relationship, esp. in philology ; স্বজাতিত্ব, সগোত্রতা, জ্ঞাতিত্ব (বিশেষতঃ ভাষাবিজ্ঞানে)।

cŏg-ni′-tion, *n.* (*Phil.*) Knowlege from experience or inspection ; পদার্থের জ্ঞান, অবগতি, প্রজ্ঞান। **—al,** *adj.* **—tive,** *adj.* Pertaining to cognition ; জ্ঞানীয় (হিঃ কোঃ), জ্ঞানসম্বন্ধীয় (ঐ), জ্ঞানাত্মক (ঐ), জ্ঞানাংশক। **Cognitive faculties**—জ্ঞানার্জ্জনী বৃত্তিসমূহ।

cŏg′-niz-ā-ble, *adj.* Capable of being known ; জ্ঞেয়, জ্ঞাতব্য। **2.** Coming within the cognizance of the law ; আইনের আমলে আসিবার যোগ্য। **3.** Capable of being judicially tried ; as, *cognizable* case ; আদালতের বিচার্য্য, আদালতের মোতালক। **4.** (I. Cr. P. C.) Liable to be arrested by a Police officer without a warrant ; (ভারতবর্ষীয় ফৌজদারী কার্য্যবিধি আইন) পুলিসের ধর্ত্তব্য (গ্রেপ্তারী পরওয়ানা বিনা পুলিশ কর্ত্তৃক গ্রেপ্তার যোগ্য।)

cŏg′-ni-zance, —sance (-zăns), *n.* **1.** The state of being aware of anything ; অবগতি। **2.** (*Law*) The hearing or trying of a cause ; as, within or under the *cognizance* of ; (আইন) মোকদ্দমার শুনানি, বা বিচারকরণ। **3.** The right of dealing with, or trying a matter legally or judicially ; বিচারের অধিকার, কোন বিষয় সম্বন্ধে আইনসঙ্গত কার্য্য করিবার অধিকার। **4.** A distinctive mark ; a badge ; "To assume as his *cognizance* the Sprig of Broom ;" পরিচয়জ্ঞাপক চিহ্ন ; পদসূচক চিহ্ন।

cŏg′-ni-zănt, *adj.* Being aware of ; অবগত।

cŏg′-nīze, *v. t.* (*Philos.*) To know or perceive ; (দর্শনশাস্ত্র) জানা, প্রত্যক্ষ করা।

cŏg-nŏ′-mĕn, *n.* (*Pls. E.* -MENS ; *L.*—MINA.) (*Rom. Ant.*) The third name or family name of a Roman citizen ; as, Caius Julius *Cæsar* ; (রোমীয় প্রত্নতত্ব) প্রাচীন রোম নগরবাসীর তৃতীয় নাম বা পারিবারিক নাম। **2.** A surname ; উপনাম। **3.** Name ; নাম।

cŏg-nŏs′-ĉi-ble, *adj.* Capable of being known, (esp. in philosophy). ; বিজ্ঞেয়, জ্ঞাতব্য, বোধ্য।

cog-no-vit, (*L.*) *n.* (*Law*) An acknowledgment by a defendant to save expense that the plaintiff's claim is just ; (মোকদ্দমার খরচের দায় হইতে উদ্ধার লাভের উদ্দেশ্যে) প্রতিবাদিকর্ত্তৃক বাদিপক্ষের দাবীর ন্যায্যত স্বীকার।

cō-hăb′-it. *v. i.* To live together, esp. as husband and wife ; বিবাহ ব্যতিরেকে একত্র বাস করা, স্বামীস্ত্রীরূপে একত্র বাস করা, সহবাস করা। **—i-tad′-tion,** *n.*

cō-heir′ (-ār), *n.* A joint heir ; সহোত্তরাধিকারী, দায়াদ।

Cō-here′ (-hēr), *v. i.* **1.** To stick together ; to be united ; সংসক্ত হওয়া, সংশ্লিষ্ট হওয়া ; যুক্ত হওয়া। **2.** To be logically connected or consistent ; ন্যায়শাস্ত্রানুগতভাবে সঙ্গত বা সম্বন্ধবিশিষ্ট হওয়া। **—her′-ence, —her′-en-cy,** *ns.* **1.** Sticking together ; cohesion ; সংসক্তি ; দৃঢ়লগ্নতা। **2.** Logical connexion ; consistency ; ন্যায়শাস্ত্রানুগত সঙ্গতি ; অনুসারিত্ব, অবিরোধ। **—her′-ent,** *adj.* **1.** Sticking together ; cohering ; সংহত ; যুতসিদ্ধ (সাঃ পঃ)। **2.** Connected ; consistent ; সুসম্বদ্ধ ; সঙ্গতিবিশিষ্ট। **—her′-ent-ly,** *adv.*

cō-hĕr′-i-tor (-têr), *n.* A co-heir ; সহোত্তরাধিকারী, দায়াদ। **—it-age,** *n.*

cō-hē′-sion (-zhŏn), *n.* **1.** The act of cohering or sticking together ; সংলগ্নতা, দৃঢ়সংসক্তি। **2.** (*Phys.*) A form of attraction by which particles of bodies stick together ; একপ্রকার আকর্ষণ—যদ্দারা পরমাণু সমূহ পরস্পর সংশ্লিষ্ট হয়, যোগাকর্ষণ (প্রঃ বাঃ), আশ্লেষণ, খণ্ড-সংযোগ (সাঃ পঃ)। **—he′-sive,** *adj.* **—he′-sive-ly,** *adv.* **—he′-sive-ness** *n.*

cō′-hŏrt, *n.* **1.** (*Rom. Antiq.*) A body of soldiers from 300 to 600 in number forming a tenth part of a legion ; (রোমীয় প্রত্নতত্ব) রোমীয় সৈন্যদলের বিভাগবিশেষ, ইহাতে

৩০০ হইতে ৬০০ সৈন্য থাকিত। **2.** A band of warriors ; a band ; যোদ্ধৃদল ; দল। **3.** A group ; কুল (সাঃ পঃ), দল।

coif (koyf), *n.* & *v. t.* **1.** A close-fitting cap covering the top, back and sides of the head ; মস্তকাবরণ বিশেষ, যদ্দারা মস্তকের উপর, পশ্চাদ্‌ভাগ এবং পার্শ্বদ্বয় আবৃত হয়, মুকুট, শিরস্ক। **2.** A white cap formerly worn by a sergeant-at-law ; পূর্ব্বে ইংলণ্ডের এক শ্রেণীর ব্যবহারজীবিগণ যে শ্বেতবর্ণ টুপি পরিতেন। ***Verb t.*** To cover with a coif ; উক্ত টুপী দ্বারা আবৃত করা।

coiffeur, *n.*, (*F.*), A hair-dresser ; কেশপ্রসাধক।

coiffure, *n.* A style or fashion of dressing the hair ; কেশরচনার প্রকার বিশেষ।

coign, coigne (koyn), *n.* **1.** A projecting corner ; বহির্বিলম্বিত কোণ, অস্র। **2.** A wedge ; কাজলা। **Coign of vantage** — সুবিধাজনক স্থান।

coil (koyl), *v. t., i.,* & *n.* To lay up (a cable, rope, etc.) in concentric rings ; to roll up a rope ; পাকান ; কুণ্ডলী করা। ***Verb i.*** **1.** To twist into spiral shape ;

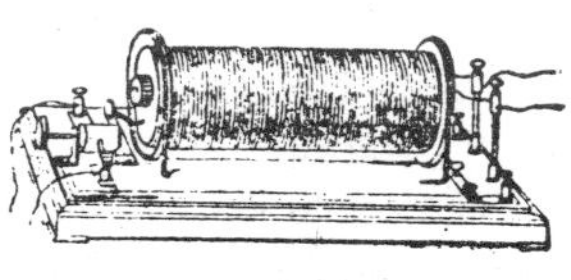

Industrial coil.

কুণ্ডলিত হওয়া। **2.** To move sinuously ; as, he could *coil* unperceived through unsuspected paths ; আঁকিয়া বাঁকিয়া চলা। ***Noun.*** **1.** A length of cable, rope, etc. wounded up (in rings) ; রজ্জুর কুণ্ডলী, বিঁড়া। **2.** A single complete turn of any coiled body, as a snake, the tendril of a plant ; কুণ্ডলী। **3.** (*Elect.*) A spiral wire for the passage of a current ; (তাড়িতবিজ্ঞান) তাড়িতপ্রবাহ সঞ্চারণের জন্য কুণ্ডলিত তার, কুণ্ডলী। **Coil of snake**—ভোগ। **Coil of wire**—তারের গুটি। **Induction coil**—বর্ত্তন গুটিকা (সাঃ পঃ), বর্ত্তন বেষ্টিকা (ঐ), বর্ত্তন বেষ্টন (ঐ)। **Primary coil**—প্রধান গুটি (সাঃ পঃ), প্রধান বেষ্টন (ঐ)। **Secondary coil**—অধীন গুটি (সাঃ পঃ) অধীন কুণ্ডলী (ঐ)।

coil (koyl), *n.* (*Poet.*) Turmoil ; ঝঞ্ঝাট। **Mortal coil**—মানব জীবনের কষ্ট বা ঝঞ্ঝাট।

coin (koyn), *n.* **1.** A piece of metal stamped and current as money ; মুদ্রা, টঙ্ক। **2.** Money ; as, to pay their workmen in *coins* ; টাকা পয়সা, নগদ টাকা। **Coin of the fool**—গোখুর (সাঃ পঃ)। **False coin**—কৃত্রিম মুদ্রা। **To pay one in his own coin**—উপযুক্ত প্রতিশোধ লওয়া।

coin (koyn), *v. t.* **1.** To make money by stamping metal ; মুদ্রা প্রস্তুত করা। **2.** (*Fig.*) To invent ; to fabricate ; (esp. a new word or phrase) ; উদ্ভাবন করা ; গঠন করা, (বিশেষতঃ নূতন শব্দ বা বাক্য)।

Coin'-age, *n.* **1.** The act or process of coining money ; মুদ্রা-প্রস্তুতকরণ। **2.** Coins in use ; প্রচলিত মুদ্রা। **3.** Fabrication ; invention ; গঠন ; উদ্ভাবন। **To coin money**—To earn a large sum of money in a short time ; অল্প সময়ে বহু অর্থ উপার্জ্জন করা।

cö-in-cīde', *v. t.* **1.** To occupy the same portion of space ; সমান স্থান অধিকার করিয়া থাকা। **2.** To occur at the same time ; সমকালে ঘটা। **3.** To agree exactly ; to concur ; একমত হওয়া, সম্পূর্ণ ঐক্য হওয়া ; মতৈক্য হওয়া। **—in'-ci-dence,** *n.* The occupation of the same place ; সমস্থান অধিকার, সন্নিপাত, সমনুপাত (হিঃ কোঃ), সামানাধিকরণ্য। **2.** Exact agreement in substance, character, etc. ; সম্পূর্ণ ঐক্য। **—in'-ci-dent, —den-tal,** *adjs.* **—ci-den-tal-ly,** *adv.*

cö-in-here' (-hēr), *v. i.* **1.** To inhere together ; একত্র লগ্ন থাকা, সংশ্লিষ্ট হওয়া। **2.** To inhere or exist together, as in one substance ; একসময়ে বিদ্যমান থাকা।

coir (koyr), *n.* Coconut fibre, used for ropes, matting, etc. ; নারিকেলের ছোবড়া।

cö-i'-tion, *n.* Sexual intercourse ; মৈথুন, সম্ভোগ, সুরত, সঙ্গম, নিধুবন (গীতঃ), সম্প্রয়োগ (বাৎস্যঃ)।

cöke, *n.* & *v. t.* Coal charred and deprived of volatile matter ; দগ্ধ কয়লা, পোড়া কয়লা। ***Verb t.*** To convert into coke ; পোড়া কয়লায় পরিণত করা।

cŏl'-ăn-dêr, *n.* A perforated vessel used as a strainer in cookery ; চালুনী, ঝাঁঝরী, ছাঁকনী।

cŏl'-chi-cŭm, *n.* Meadow saffron,—a medical plant ; একপ্রকার ভেষজ গুল্ম। [গ্রীক্‌পুরাণোক্ত মিডিয়া নাম্নী মায়াবিনীর বাসস্থানের নাম হইতে গৃহীত।]

cŏl'-cŏ-thâr, *n.* The brown red peroxide of iron used in polishing glass ; কাচ পালিসে ব্যবহৃত রাসায়নিক পদার্থ বিশেষ।

cöld, *adj.* & *n.* **1.** Not warm or hot ; অনুষ্ণ, শীতল, ঠাণ্ডা, অতপ্ত, সহিম, শিশির। **2.** Causing chilliness ; শৈত্যজনক। **3.** Suffering from cold ; শীতার্ত্ত। **4.** Spiritless ; wanting passion, ardour or zeal ; "A *cold* request is entitled to a *cold* answer ;" আবেগহীন ; নিরুদ্যম, নিরুৎসাহ। **5.** Not affectionate, cordial or friendly ; reserved ; "The husband becoming *cold* and averse to her ;" নিঃস্নেহ, স্নেহশূন্য, অনুরাগ-শূন্য, উদাসীন, আন্তরিকতাশূন্য, বন্ধুতা-শূন্য ; অনালাপী। **6.** Chilling ; depressing ; uninteresting ; নিরুৎসাহকর ; অবসাদজনক ; নীরস। **7.** Not affecting the scent strongly ;

মৃদু-গন্ধ। *Noun.* **1.** Chilliness; শৈত্য। **2.** An ailment occasioned by cold; সর্দ্দি। **Cold′-ly,** *adv.* **Cold′-ness,** *n.* **Cold-blast**—চুল্লীর মধ্যে সঞ্চিত শীতল বায়ুপ্রবাহ। **Cold-blooded**—(মৎস্যাদি সম্পর্কে) শীতল রক্তবিশিষ্ট; (লক্ষণায়) জড়, অলস, অনুরাগশূন্য। **Cold-chisel**—ঠাণ্ডা ধাতু কাটিবার জন্য বাটালিবিশেষ। **Cold-colour**—নীল, ধূসর প্রভৃতি বর্ণ। **Cold-cream**—স্নিগ্ধতা এবং মসৃণতা বিধায়ক মসৃণ অভ্যঞ্জন বিশেষ। **Cold-drawn**—অনুত্তপ্ত বীজ হইতে নিষ্পীড়িত (তৈল)। **Cold-feet**—উপযুক্ত জল নিকাশের ব্যবস্থা বিনা অত্যধিক জল সেচন হেতু তরুগুল্মাদির যে অবস্থা হয়। **Cold-hammer**—ঠাণ্ডা ধাতু পেটার উপযোগী হাতুড়ী বিশেষ। **Cold-hearted**—অনুরাগশূন্য। **Cold-pig**—নিদ্রিত ব্যক্তিকে জাগরিত করিবার জন্য তদীয় দেহে শীতল জল প্রক্ষেপ। **Cold-short**—Brittle in its cold state; শীতলাবস্থায় ভঙ্গপ্রবণ, শীত-ভঙ্গুর। **Cold-sore**—জ্বরঠুঁটো। **Cold-steel**—তরবারী, সঙ্গীন প্রভৃতি। **Cold-storage**—অবিকৃত রাখিবার জন্য খাদ্যাদি শীতল স্থানে ভাণ্ডারজাত করণ। **Cold-without**—চিনিশূন্য এবং ঠাণ্ডাজল মিশ্রিত ব্রাণ্ডী বা সুরাসার। **In cold blood**—With deliberate intent; not under the influence of passion; ভাবিয়া চিন্তিয়া; উত্তেজনার বশবর্ত্তী না হইয়া। **Murder in cold blood** or **cold-blooded murder**—উপাংশু হত্যা, ভাবিয়া চিন্তিয়া নরহত্যা। **To catch cold, To take cold**—ঠাণ্ডা লাগা, সর্দ্দি লাগা। **To give the cold shoulder**—To show indifference; ঔদাসীন্য প্রকাশ করা। **To leave out in the cold**—To neglect; তাচ্ছিল্য করা। **To throw cold water on**—To discourage; নিরুৎসাহ করা।

cōle (kōl), *n.* A general name for all sorts of cabbage; কপি জাতীয় শাকের সাধারণ নাম।

cŏl-ē-ŏp′-têr-ă, *n. pl.* A class of insect having an outside horny covering as among the beetles; কোষপক্ষক কীট, যথা, গোবরে পোকা প্রভৃতি। **–al, –ous,** *adjs.* **–ist,** *n.* *coleus amboinicus*—পাথরচুর (বেলঃ)।

cole′-wort (kōl-wêrt), *n.* A variety of cabbage in which the leaves never form a compact head; একপ্রকার কপি—যাহার পাতাগুলি বাঁধে না।

cŏl′-ic, *n.* A severe griping pain in the belly; উদরাক্ষেপ, শূলবেদনা, উদরশূল, বায়ুশূল, শূলরোগ (সাঃ পঃ)। **Col′-ick-y,** *adj.*

cŏl-lăb′-ō-ră-tor (-têr), *n.* An associate in labour, esp. in literary or scientific labour; সহযোগী, সহকর্ম্মী, সহপরিশ্রমী, বিশেষতঃ সাহিত্য বিজ্ঞানানুশীলনে সহযোগী। **–ra′-tion,** *n.*

cŏl-lapse′ (-lăps), *n.* & *v. i.* **1.** A sudden and complete failure; সম্পূর্ণপতন। **2.** A breakdown; ভঙ্গ, পতনাবস্থা। **3.** (*Med.*) Extreme depression or sudden failing of all the vital powers, as the result of disease; জীবনীশক্তির সম্পূর্ণ অবসাদন, হিমাঙ্গ (হঃ চঃ)। *Verb i.* **1.** To fall together suddenly; সহসা সার্ব্বাঙ্গীণ পতন হওয়া, অবসন্ন হওয়া। **2.** To fail suddenly and completely; ভাঙ্গিয়া পড়া, জীবনীশক্তি লোপ হওয়া। **–laps′-i-ble, –laps′-a-ble,** *adjs.* So made as to collapse when required for packing, etc.; আবশ্যকমত গুটাইয়া ক্ষুদ্রস্থানে বদ্ধ করা যাইতে পারে—এইরূপভাবে গঠিত।

cŏl′-lar (-lêr), *n.* & *v. t.* **1.** Something worn round the neck; a neck-band; কণ্ঠবেষ্টিকা; গ্রীবা বেষ্টনী, গলবন্ধ, গলাসি, হাঁসুলি। **2.** The part of a garment round the neck; কোর্ত্তা প্রভৃতির গলদেশ-বেষ্টক অংশ, গ্রীবা-বেষ্টন বস্ত্র। **3.** A badge worn round the neck by knights; নাইট উপাধিধারিগণের কণ্ঠবেষ্টিকা। **4.** Part of a horse's harness that goes round the neck; ঘোড়ার গলাসি। **5.** A leather or metal band round a dog's or prisoner's neck; কুকুরের গলাসি, কারাগারের কয়েদীর গলার হাঁসুলি। **6.** A band of linen, etc. worn round the neck; বস্ত্রাদি নির্ম্মিত গলবেষ্টনী। **7.** The coloured ring or circle round the necks of birds; পক্ষীর কণ্ঠের চতুর্দ্দিকের রঙ্গীন বেষ্টনী। **8.** (*Naut.*) The upper part of a stay; also a rope in the shape of a ring to which a stay is confined; (নৌ-বিদ্যা) মাস্তুলের অবলম্বন রজ্জুর উর্দ্ধভাগ; যে অঙ্গুরীয়াকার রজ্জুতে উক্ত অবলম্বন-রজ্জু সম্বদ্ধ করা হয়। *Verb t.* **1.** To seize by the collar; গলদেশ ধরা, টুঁটি ধরা। **2.** To get control of; আয়ত্ত করা। **3.** To press (meat, etc.) into roll; (মাংস প্রভৃতি) চাপ দিয়া একত্র জড়ান। **–ette′,** *n.* A small collar; ক্ষুদ্র কণ্ঠবেষ্টিকা। **Collar-bone**—See CLAVICLE. **Collar-work**—কঠোর পরিশ্রম। **A collar of brawn**—এক মোড়কে যে পরিমাণ শূকর মাংস রাখা হয়। **Against the collar**—বিঘ্ন স্বত্বেও। **In collar**—In employment; নিযুক্ত। **Out of collar**—Out of employment; বেকার। **To slip the collar**—মুক্ত হওয়া; হাঙ্গামা বা ঝঞ্ঝাট হইতে উদ্ধার পাওয়া।

cŏl-lāte′, *v. t.* **1.** To compare critically, noting the points of agreement or difference; সূক্ষ্ম ভাবে মিলান, মোকাবেলা করা। **2.** To gather and place in order, as the sheets of a book for binding; পুস্তকাদি বাঁধানের নিমিত্ত পত্রসমূহ যথাক্রমে সাজাইয়া রাখা। **3.** To place in or confer a benefice; যাজন কার্য্যে নিযুক্ত করা বা যাজকবৃত্তি প্রদান করা, ধর্ম্মশালায় নিয়োগ করা, সেবায়েৎ নিযুক্ত করা। **–la′-tion,** *n.* **1.** A bringing together for examination and comparison ; ঐক্যকরণ, পরস্পরের সহিত তুলনা কিংবা পরীক্ষার নিমিত্ত একত্রীকরণ। 2. Presentation to a benefice ; যাজকপদে নিয়োগ। 3. The gathering and examination of sheets preparatory to binding ; পুস্তক বাঁধাইবার পূর্ব্বে মুদ্রিত কাগজগুলি একত্রীকরণ এবং পরীক্ষণ। 4. A light repast or luncheon ; জলযোগ, লঘু আহার। **—la′-tive,** *adj.* **—la′-tor,** *n.*

cŏl-lăt′-êr-ăl, *adj.* 1. Placed side by side ; পার্শ্ববর্ত্তী। 2. Acting indirectly ; গৌণভাবে কার্য্যকারী, প্রাসঙ্গিক। 3. Not chief or principal ; as, *collateral* issues ; অপ্রধান, আনুষঙ্গিক। 4. Descending from the same stock or ancestor, opposed to *lineal* ; স্বগোত্রোদ্ভূত, সগোত্র। ***Noun.*** A collateral relation ; সগোত্র সম্বন্ধ, সপিণ্ড, দায়াদ জ্ঞাতি। **—ly,** *adv.*

cŏl′-league (-lēg), *n.* A partner or associate in office ; সহযোগী ; সহকারী, সঙ্গী, সহকর্ম্মকর্তা।

cŏl-league′ (lēg), *v. i.* To join or unite in a law-suit ; to conspire ; কোন মোকদ্দমায় একপক্ষ হওয়া, দল বাঁধা ; ষড়যন্ত্র করা।

cŏl-lĕct′, *v. t.* & *i.* 1. To gather into one body ; to assemble or bring together ; রাশীকৃত করা, সমাহরণ করা, জড় করা ; একত্র করা, গাদা করা। 2. To infer ; উপপাদন করা। 3. To recover one's self-possession ; "I did in time *collect* myself ; স্থৈর্য্যলাভ করা, প্রকৃতিস্থ হওয়া। ***Verb i.*** To assemble together ; to accumulate ; একত্রিত হওয়া, মিলিত হওয়া, জমা হওয়া, জড় হওয়া ; সংগৃহীত হওয়া, সঞ্চিত হওয়া। **—lect′-i-ble,** *adj.* **—lec′-tion,** *n.* 1. The act of collecting ; সঞ্চয়। 2. That which is collected ; সংগ্রহ, সংঘ, সমাহার, সমুচ্চয়, রাশি, সমবায়। 3. A sum collected for a religious or charitable purpose : ধর্ম্ম বা দান কার্য্যের জন্য সংগৃহীত অর্থ। 4. (*Oxford University*) A college examination at the end of each term ; (অক্সফোর্ড বিশ্ববিদ্যালয়) কলেজের বার্ষিক পরীক্ষা। **—lec′-tive,** *adj.* 1. Gathered into a mass ; রাশীকৃত, সংহত, সমবেত, উপচিত, সমাগত। 2. (*Gram.*) Expressing a collection or aggregate of individuals, by a singular form ; সামুদয়িক, সংঘবাচক, সমূহবাচক, সমষ্টিবোধক, বহুত্ববাচক। **—lec′-tive-ly,** *adv.* **—lec′-tive-ness,** *n.* **—lec′-tiv-ism,** *n.* The economic theory of socialism, that industry should be carried on with a collective capital ; যৌথমূলধনদ্বারা শ্রমশিল্পাদির কার্য্য নির্ব্বাহ হওয়া উচিত— সাম্যবাদীদিগের এইরূপ মতবাদ। **—lec′-tiv-ist,** *n.* **—lec′-tor,** *n.* 1. One who collects, as tickets, money, etc. ; সংগ্রাহক, তহশীলদার। 2. A tax-gatherer ; করসংগ্রাহক, করগ্রাহক, করসমাহর্ত্তা (আঃ বঃ)। 3. (*India*) The chief official of a district collecting revenue and holding magisterial power ; জেলার প্রধান রাজপুরুষ, কালেক্টর, করনায়ক (আঃ বঃ)। **—lec′-to-rate,** or **—lec′-tor-ship,** *ns.* The office of a collector ; উক্ত কর্ম্মচারীর আফিস, অধিকার বা পদ, কালেক্টরী। **Collective Noun**—সমূহবাচক বিশেষ্য। **Collective term**—সমষ্টি নাম। **To collect one's self**—To regain self-control ; প্রকৃতিস্থ হওয়া।

cŏl′-lĕct, *n.* A short, comprehensive prayer adapted to a particular day and forming part of a liturgy ; সংক্ষিপ্ত প্রার্থনা বিশেষ।

cŏl-lĕc-tā′-nē-ă, *n. pl.* Collected passages ; (নানা গ্রন্থ হইতে) সংগৃহীত বাক্য সমষ্টি।

cŏl′-lege (-lĕj), *n.* 1. A body of colleagues with common functions and privileges ; একক্রিয় ব্যক্তিগণের সঙ্ঘ বা সম্প্রদায়। 2. A society of scholars or friends of learning, incorporated for study or instruction, esp. in the higher branches of knowledge ; as, the *colleges* of Oxford and Cambridge Universities : বিদ্যোৎসাহী সমাজ, পণ্ডিত সমাজ। 3. An institution for higher education affiliated to the University ; বিশ্ববিদ্যালয়ের অন্তর্ভুক্ত উচ্চ শিক্ষার জন্য বিদ্যালয়, কলেজ। 4. A building or number of buildings, used by a college ; উচ্চবিদ্যালয় গৃহ, উচ্চবিদ্যালয়ের অট্টালিকাশ্রেণী। 5. A place of professional study ; কোন ব্যবসায় অবলম্বনের উপযোগী শিক্ষালাভার্থ বিদ্যালয়। **—le′-gi-an,** *n.* 1. A member of a college, particularly of a literary institution ; সাহিত্য পরিষদের সভ্য, বিদ্যোৎসাহী সমাজের সভ্য। 2. A student in a college ; উচ্চবিদ্যালয়ের ছাত্র, কলেজের ছাত্র, বিদ্যার্থী। **—le′-gi-ate,** *adj.* **College of Heralds**—কুলাচার্য্যমণ্ডলী।

cŏl′-lĕt, *n.* 1. A small collar or neck-band ; কণ্ঠ-বেষ্টিকা। 2. The part of a ring in which a stone is set ; অঙ্গুরীয়কের মণি-বন্ধন স্থান।

cŏl-līde′, *v. i.* 1. To strike or dash against each other ; সংঘৃষ্ট হওয়া, ধাক্কা লাগা, ঠোকাঠুকি লাগা, সংঘট্ট লাগা, নিষ্পিষ্ট হওয়া। 2. To be in conflict ; বিরোধ হওয়া, সংঘর্ষ হওয়া।

Collie.

cŏl′-lie (-lī), *n.* The Scotch shepherd dog ; স্কটল্যাণ্ডদেশীয় মেষ-রক্ষক কুকুর।

cŏl′-lier (-yêr), *n.* **1.** A coal-miner ; কয়লা খননকারী, অঙ্গার-খনক। **2.** A proprietor of coal-mines ; কয়লা খনির স্বত্বাধিকারী। **3.** A vessel employed in the coal trade ; কয়লাবাহী পোত। **4.** A sailor on such ship ; কয়লাবাহি-পোতের নাবিক। **—y,** *n.* A coal-mine ; কয়লার খনি।

cŏl′-li-gāte, *v. t.* To tie or bind together ; "He has discovered and *colligated* a multitude of the most wonderful phenomenon;" একত্র বাঁধা, সংবদ্ধ করা, সংযোজিত করা। **—ga′-tion,** *n.* A binding together ; বন্ধন, সংশ্লেষণ, সংযোজন, সমাবেশ।

cŏl′-li-māte, *v. t.* To bring into the same line, as the axes of telescopes ; to render parallel, as rays of light ; (দূরবীক্ষণ-যন্ত্র) একাক্ষ করা ; (আলোক রশ্মি) সমান্তরাল করা। **—ma′-tion,** *n.* The adjustment of the line of sight of a telescope or astronomical instrument ; দূরবীক্ষণ প্রভৃতি জ্যোতিষিক যন্ত্রের দৃষ্টি রেখা নিয়মীকরণ, একাক্ষী ভবন, লক্ষ্যবীক্ষণ (হিঃ কোঃ)। **—ma-tor,** *n.* **1.** A small attached telescope used to determine errors of collimation ; দূরদর্শন যন্ত্রের দৃষ্টিরেখা নির্ণয়ের ভ্রম সংশোধনার্থ তৎসম্বদ্ধ ক্ষুদ্র দূরদর্শন যন্ত্র বিশেষ। **2.** A tube in spectroscope throwing parallel rays on prism ; ত্রিপার্শ্ব কাচের উপর সমান্তরাল রশ্মিসমূহ প্রক্ষেপকারী বর্ণ-বিশ্লেষণযন্ত্র মধ্যস্থ নলবিশেষ।

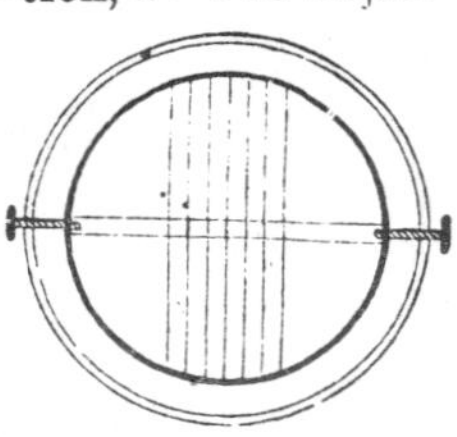

Line collimation.

cŏl-lin′-ē-ar (-êr), *adj.* In the same straight line ; সহরৈখিক, সরৈখিক, একরৈখিক।

cŏl′-lish, *n.* A tool to polish the edge of a sole ; জুতার তলার কিনারা পরিষ্কৃত করিবার যন্ত্র।

cŏl-li′-sion (-zhŏn), *n.* A striking together, as of two hard bodies ; পরস্পর-সংঘর্ষণ, সংঘাত, সম্পাত, সংঘট্ট, টক্কর, প্রতিঘাত, ঠোকাঠুকি। **2.** Antagonism ; বৈপরীত্য, বিরোধ, বিপক্ষতা, প্রতিকূলতা, সংঘর্ষ।

cŏl′-lō-cāte, *v. t.* To set or place ; to arrange ; অবস্থাপিত করা, প্রতিষ্ঠিত করা, সংস্থাপন করা ; বিন্যস্ত করা। **—ca′-tion,** *n.* **Collocation of words**—শব্দ বা পদবিন্যাস।

cŏl-lō-cū′-tion, *n.* Mutual discourse ; পরস্পর কথোপকথন, সম্ভাষণ। **—tor,** *n.* A partaker in talk ; যাহার সহিত কথোপকথন করা হয়।

cŏl-lō′-di-ŏn, *n.* A gummy solution of pyroxylin or gun-cotton in ether, employed in surgery and photography ; অস্ত্রোপচার কার্য্যে এবং আলোকচিত্রণে ব্যবহৃত রাসায়নিক পদার্থ বিশেষ।

cŏl-logue′ (-lōg), *v. t.* To scheme or plot together ; একত্র ফন্দি পাকান, ষড়যন্ত্র পাকান।

cŏl′-loid (-loyd), *n.* & *adj.* A viscid inorganic substance like gelatine ; একপ্রকার অজৈব আটালো পদার্থ, লস্‌লসা (ফঃ হিঃ)। *Adj.* Gluey ; লেই বা শিরীষবৎ।

cŏl′-lŏp, *n.* **1.** A slice of meat ; মাংসের ফালি, চিল্‌তা, মাংসফালিকা (আঃ বঃ)। **2.** A piece ; খণ্ড। **3.** A darling ; আদুরে গোপাল।

cŏl′-lō-quŷ, *n.* **1.** Mutual discourse of two or more persons ; কথোপকথন, কথাবার্ত্তা, সংবাদ, সংলাপ, আলাপ, সম্ভাষণ। **2.** A judicial and legislative court in the Presbyterian Church ; প্রিসবিটেরিয়ান-ধর্ম্ম সম্প্রদায়ের বিচারালয়। **—qui-al,** *adj.* Pertaining to or used in common conversation ; বাচনিক, সাধারণ কথোপকথনে ব্যবহৃত, চলিত, কথিত, কথ্য। **—qui-al-ise,** *v. t.* **—qui-al-ism,** *n.* A colloquial expression, not employed in formal discourse or writing ; কথ্য ভাষায় বাক্যাদি কথনের রীতি বা ধারা। **—quist,** *n.* **Eternal colloquy between the father and the son**—নিত্যলীলা (প্রায় অনুরূপ শব্দ)।

cŏl-lūde′, *v. i.* To conspire in a fraud ; প্রতারণার উদ্দেশ্যে কাহারও সহিত একত্র মিলিয়া ষড়যন্ত্র করা।

cŏl-lū′-sion (-zhŏn), *n.* A secret agreement and co-operation for a fraudulent or deceitful purpose, esp. between ostensible opponents as in law-suit ; প্রতারণার্থ গুপ্ত-সন্ধি, কপট মন্ত্রণা, (বিশেষতঃ মোকদ্দমায় উভয়পক্ষীয় লোকদিগের মধ্যে) যোগ-সাজস্‌, পাকচক্র, ফেরেববাজি (*Colloq.*)। **—sive,** *adj.* **1.** Deceitful ; প্রতারণা-পূর্ণ। **2.** Acting in collusion ; as, *collusive* parties ; ষড়যন্ত্রকারী। **—sive-ly,** *adv.* **—sive-ness,** *n.* **—so-ry,** *adj.*

cŏl′-lŷ, *n.* A kind of dog ; এক প্রকার কুকুর।

cŏl-lŷr′-i-ŭm, *n.* An application to the eye, usu. an eye-water ; কজ্জল, শূর্ম্মা, রসাঞ্জন, অঞ্জন, নেত্ররঞ্জন।

Colocasia antiquorum — গুঁড়ি কচু (বেলঃ), আশুকচু (ঐ), কালকচু (ঐ), বনকচু (ঐ)।

Colocasia Indica—মানকচু (বেলঃ)।

Colocasia nymphæfolia—সরকচু (বেলঃ)।

cŏl′-ō-cŷnth, *n.* **1.** Bitter cucumber ; the tree bearing the fruit ; মাকাল, ইন্দ্রায়ণ ; মাকাল গাছ। **2.** A purgative drug prepared from colocynth ; মাকাল ফল হইতে প্রস্তুত বিরেচক ঔষধ বিশেষ।

cō-logne′ (-lōn), *n.* A perfumed liquid ; সুগন্ধি তরল পদার্থ বিশেষ। **Eau-de-Cologne** — A perfumed spirit first made in Cologne in 1709 by Jean Farina ; অডিকোলন।

Cō-logne′-earth (-lōn-êrth), *n.* একপ্রকার বেগুনে আভাযুক্ত বাদামি রঙ্গের মাটি।

cō′-lŏn, *n.* **1.** A punctuation mark (:) ranking between a period and a semicolon ; বাক্যের ছেদ চিহ্ন বিশেষ। 2. (*Anat.*) That part of the large intestines which extend from the caecum to the rectum ; অন্ধান্ত্র হইতে সরলান্ত্র পর্য্যন্ত বৃহদন্ত্রের অংশ, স্থুলান্ত্র (হঃ চঃ)।

colo′-nĕl (kêr-), *n.* The chief officer of a regiment ; সেনাপ্টনের সর্ব্বপ্রধান কর্ম্মচারী, সেনাবিভাগপতি। **—cy, —ship,** *ns.* His office or rank ; সেনানায়কের পদ বা পদবী।

cŏl-ŏn-nāde′, *n.* A range of columns placed at regular intervals ; স্তম্ভশ্রেণী।

cŏl′-ŏ-nȳ, *n.* **1.** A settlement in a new country ; a body of people who leave home and go and settle in a new country subject to the parent one ; উপনিবেশ, আবাদ (*Colloq.*) ; ঔপনিবেশিকগণ। **2.** A number or body of living creatures or plants growing together ; as, "New *colonies* of birds to people air ;" একত্রবাসী জীবগণ বা একত্র বর্দ্ধিত তরু বা গুল্মরাজি। **3.** People of one nationality or occupation living in a city ; as, the Jewish *colony* in Calcutta ; কোন নগরবাসী সমব্যবসায়ী ব্যক্তিবর্গ, কোন নগরবাসী বিশেষ জাতিভুক্ত জনসম্প্রদায়। **4.** An aggregate of individuals ; জীবসমষ্টি,—যেরূপ প্রবাল প্রভৃতিতে দৃষ্ট হয়। **—ni-sa′-tion, —ni-za′-tion,** *n.* The act of colonizing ; the state of being colonized ; উপনিবেশ স্থাপন ; ঔপনিবেশিকতা। **—nise, —nize,** *v. t.* & *i.* **1.** To plant or establish a colony in ; কোন স্থানে উপনিবেশ সংস্থাপন করা। **2.** To establish in a colony ; কোন উপনিবেশে বাসস্থান সংস্থাপন করা। (*Verb i.*) To settle in ; উপনিবিষ্ট হওয়া। **—nist,** *n.* An inhabitant of a colony ; উপনিবেশবাসী, ঔপনিবেশিক।

cŏ-lō′-nĭ-ăl, *adj.* & *n.* Of or pertaining to colony ; as, *colonial* rights ; উপনিবেশ সম্বন্ধীয়, ঔপনিবেশিক। ***Noun.*** An inhabitant of a colony ; উপনিবেশবাসী। **—ism,** *n.* **Colonial self-government** — ব্রিটিশ উপনিবেশের অনুরূপ শাসন-প্রণালী, ঔপনিবেশিক স্বায়ত্তশাসন। **Colonial office**—শাসনতন্ত্রের যে বিভাগে উপনিবেশ সমূহের ভার অর্পিত হইয়াছে, ঔপনিবেশিক কার্য্যালয়।

cŏl′-ŏ-phŏn, *n.* In early printing the inscription at the end of a book with name, date, etc. ; প্রাচীন পুস্তকের শেষভাগে মুদ্রিত গ্রন্থের নাম, প্রকাশের তারিখ, প্রভৃতি বিবরণ-সম্বলিত লিপিবিশেষ।

cŏl′-ŏ-phŏ-nȳ, *n.* A dark resin distilled from the oil of turpentine ; তার্পিণ তৈল হইতে প্রাপ্ত কৃষ্ণবর্ণ ধূনাবিশেষ। [এসিয়ামাইনরের অন্তঃপাতী Colophon নামক স্থানে প্রথম প্রস্তুত হয়।]

cŏl-ŏs-sē′-ŭm, *n.* Vespasian's amphitheatre at Rome which was the largest in the world ; রোমীয় সম্রাট ভেস্‌পিসিয়ানের অতি বৃহৎ রঙ্গ-ভূমি।

Colosseum.

cŏ-lŏs′-sŭs, *n.* **1.** The gigantic statue of Apollo, which stood astride at the harbour of Rhodes, esteemed as one of the seven wonders of the world ; প্রাচীন কালে রোডস্‌দ্বীপে স্থিত এপলোদেবের অতিকায় মূর্ত্তি,—পৃথিবীর সপ্ত আশ্চর্য্যের অন্তর্গত বলিয়া পরিগণিত। **2.** Any thing best or gigantic ; "The *colossus* of the North (Russia) put its legions in movement ;" উৎকৃষ্ট বা অতিকায় বস্তু। **—sal,** *adj.* **1.** Like a colossus ; gigantic ;

Colossus.

কলোসাসের তুল্য ; অতিকায়, প্রকাণ্ড, বিরাট, বিশাল। **2.** Remarkable ; বিখ্যাত।

col′-our, —or (cŭl-êr), *n., v. t.* & *i.* **1.** A property of light which causes bodies to have different appearances to the eye ; আলোকের গুণবিশেষ—যদ্দারা চক্ষুর নিকট বস্তুসমূহ বিভিন্ন বর্ণবিশিষ্ট বলিয়া প্রতিভাত হয়। **2.** Any hue distinguished from white or black ; রং, বর্ণ। **3.** The hue or colour characteristic of good health ; "And his ear trickled and his *colour* flew ;" সুস্থ ব্যক্তির মুখের গোলাবি আভা। **4.** A paint or pigment ; as, oil *colours* ; রঞ্জন-সাধন দ্রব্য, বর্ণক-পদার্থ। **5.** Pretext ; semblance ; "Which afforded a *colour* for detaining the troops" ; ছল, অছিলা ; আবরণ। **6.** False show ; ভাণ। **7.** The hue of the darker variety of mankind ; অশ্বেতকায় মনুষ্যের বর্ণ। **8.** A colour used as the badge of any party or side ; কোন দল বা পক্ষের চিহ্ন। **9.** (*Phren.*) The faculty of perceiving colour ; (মস্তিষ্ক-সামুদ্রিক) বর্ণবোধিনী বৃত্তি। **10.** (*Law*) An appearance of right ; (আইন) স্বত্ব বা অধিকারের আভাস। **11.** (*Liter.*) Picturesqueness ; (সাহিত্য) অলঙ্কারের বাহুল্য। **12.** (*Pl.*) A flag or standard ; পতাকা, ধ্বজা, নিশান। **13.** Kind ; species ; প্রকার, রকম; জাতি, বর্ণ। ***Verb t.*** **1.** To tinge ; to paint ; রঞ্জিত করা ; চিত্রিত করা। **2.** To disguise ; to misrepresent ; to make plausible ; গোপন করা ; মিথ্যা বর্ণনা করা ; আপাত-রম্য করা। **3.** To exaggerate ; as, to *colour* a fact ; অতিরঞ্জিত করা, রং চড়ান। ***Verb i.*** To turn red in the face ; to blush ; মুখ লাল হইয়া উঠা ; লজ্জায় গণ্ডদেশ আরক্তিম হইয়া উঠা। **—a-ble,** *adj.* Plausible ; having an appearance of right or justice ; counterfeit ; as, a *colourable* imitation ; আপাত-রম্য, আপাত-মনোহর ; আপাত-গ্রাহ্য ; জাল, নকল। **—a-ble-ness,** *n.* **—a-bly,** *adv.* **—a-tion,** *n.* **—ing,** *n.* **1.** Any substance used to give colours ; রঞ্জক পদার্থ। **2.** Manner of applying colours ; রঞ্জনপ্রণালী। **—ist,** *n.* **—less,** *adj.* **1.** Without colour ; বর্ণহীন। **2.** Transparent ; স্বচ্ছ। **3.** Pale ; বিবর্ণ। **4.** Wanting in vividness ; নিস্তেজ। **5.** Impartial ; as, a judicial decision should be *colourless* ; পক্ষপাতশূন্য। **—oured,** *adj.* Tinged ; painted ; রঞ্জিত ; চিত্রিত। **Colour-blind** — বর্ণভেদ-করণে অক্ষম, বর্ণান্ধ। **Colour-box**— রঙের বাক্স। **Colour-man**—A vendor of paints ; রংব্যবসায়ী। **Colour-sergeant** — পতাকারক্ষক সামরিক কর্ম্মচারী বিশেষ। **A fast colour** — পাকা রং। **Coloured people** — অশ্বেতকায় লোক, কাফ্রি বা নিগ্রোজাতি। **Complementary colour** — কোন বর্ণকে শ্বেতবর্ণে পরিণত করিতে হইলে অপর যে সকল বর্ণের আবশ্যক হয়। **Primary colours** or **simple colours** — মূলবর্ণ, — (পূর্ব্বে) রক্ত, কমলা, পীত, সবুজ, নীল, ঘননীল, বেগুনে এই সপ্ত বর্ণ, (বর্ত্তমানে) লাল, সবুজ, বেগুনে, (চিত্রকরদিগের পক্ষে) রক্ত, পীত, নীল। **Secondary colour** — দুইটি মূলবর্ণের মিশ্রণে যে বর্ণ উৎপন্ন হয়। **Water colours** — যে সকল বর্ণ জলের সহিত মিশ্রিত হইয়া চিত্রণে ব্যবহৃত হয়। **To change colour, To lose colour**—To turn pale ; ম্লান হওয়া, বিবর্ণ হওয়া। To blush ; লজ্জায় মুখ আরক্তিম হওয়া। **To colour a stranger's goods**— কোন নগরের শুল্কাগারের মাল, উক্ত নগরবাসী কোন ব্যক্তির নামে লিখাইতে বৈদেশিক বণিক্‌কে অনুমতি দেওয়া। [এইরূপ ব্যবস্থাদ্বারা বৈদেশিক বণিক্ উচ্চতর শুল্ক দিবার দায় হইতে অব্যাহতি পায়।] **To come off with flying colours**—To come off triumphant ; বিজয়ী হওয়া, জয়ডঙ্কা দিয়া আসা, জয়পতাকা উড়াইয়া আসা। **To come out in one's true colours**—To appear in one's real character ; স্বরূপ প্রকাশ করা, স্বমূর্ত্তি ধারণ করা। **To desert one's colours**—To abandon one's post or duty ; কার্য্য ত্যাগ করা বা কর্ত্তব্যকার্য্য পরিত্যাগ করা। To become turncoat ; স্বমত বা স্বপক্ষ পরিত্যাগ করা। **To fight under false colours**—To put forward a false pretence as a cover for one's action ; কৃত্রিম সদ্ভাব দেখাইয়া ভিতরে ভিতরে কাজ সারিয়া লওয়া। **To give colour to** — To give a plausibility to ; আপাত মনোরমভাবে দাঁড় করান। **To hang out false colours**—To put up another's flag ; শত্রুর পতাকা উড্ডীন করা। To pretend to belong to a party other than one really does ; অপর পক্ষের লোক বলিয়া ভাণ করা। **To nail one's colours to the mast**—To commit oneself to some party or plan of action ; কোন পক্ষ বা কার্য্যপ্রণালী অবলম্বন করিবার জন্য নিজেকে আবদ্ধ করা। **To paint in bright** or **lively colours** — উজ্জ্বলবর্ণে চিত্রিত করা। **To put a false colour on a matter**—To put a false construction of it ; কোন বিষয়ের কদর্থ করা। **To see things in their true colours**—To see them as they are ; বস্তুর প্রকৃতপক্ষে যেরূপ, সেরূপভাবে দেখা। **To show one's colours**—To show one's party or character ; কোন্ দলের লোক তাহা প্রদর্শন করা, নিজের স্বভাব প্রদর্শন করা। **To stick to one's colours**—To adhere to one's party or opinion ; স্বকীয় পক্ষে বা স্বমতে অটল থাকা। **To strike one's colours**—To lower one's flag as a sign of submission ; বশ্যতার চিহ্ন স্বরূপ নিজের পতাকা নত করা, অধীনতা স্বীকার করা। **Under colour of**—Under the pretext of ; অছিলায়। **Without colour**— Without disguise ; অকপটে। Without individuality ; ব্যক্তিত্বশূন্যভাবে।

cŏl′-pŏr-teur (-têr), *n.* A hawker, especially one selling tracts and religious books ; ফেরিওয়ালা, বিশেষতঃ যে ব্যক্তি ধর্ম্মগ্রন্থাদি ফেরি করিয়া বেড়ায়। **—tage,** *n.*

cŏl′-stäff, *n.* A staff by means of which a burden is borne by two persons on their shoulders ; যে দণ্ডের সাহায্যে দুই ব্যক্তি কোনরূপ বোঝা বহন করে, ভার-যষ্টি।

cōlt, *n., v. t. & i.* **1.** A young horse properly of the male kind ; অশ্বশাবক। **2.** A young foolish, inexperienced person ; নির্ব্বোধ এবং অনভিজ্ঞ যুবক। **3.** (*Naut.*) A rope used for chastisement in the navy ; নাবিকদিগকে শাস্তি-প্রদানে ব্যবহৃত রজ্জুবিশেষ। **4.** A young player at cricket ; তরুণ-বয়স্ক ক্রিকেট খেলোয়াড়। ***Verb t.*** To beat with a colt ; উক্তপ্রকার রজ্জু দ্বারা আঘাত করিয়া শাস্তি দেওয়া। ***Verb i.*** To frisk like a colt ; অশ্ব-শাবকের মত লাফালাফি বা ছুটাছুটি

করা। Colt'-ish, *adj.* Colt's foot—একপ্রকার পীতবর্ণ পুষ্পপ্রসূ গুল্ম—ইহার পত্র শ্বাসকাসের ঔষধ স্বরূপ ব্যবহৃত হয়। Colt's tooth—An imperfect and superfluous tooth in young horses; অশ্ব শাবকের অতিরিক্ত এবং অপরিণত দন্ত বিশেষ। A love of youthful pleasure; যৌবনসুলভ আমোদ প্রমোদে অনুরাগ। To cast one's colt's tooth—To give up bad habits of infancy; শৈশবের কদভ্যাস ত্যাগ করা। To have a colt's tooth—To be fond of youthful pleasures; যৌবন সুলভ আমোদ প্রমোদে অনুরাগী হওয়া।

cŏl'-tĕr, coul'-têr (kōl), *n.* The cutting iron of a plough; লাঙ্গলের ফাল।

Cŏl'-ū-bêr, *n.* A genus of harmless serpents; একজাতীয় সর্প,—ইহারা লোকের অনিষ্ট করে না। **–brine,** *adj.* Snake-like; esp. like the Coluber genus of harmless snakes; সর্প-সদৃশ; অহিংস্র-সর্প জাতিবিশেষ সদৃশ।

cŏ-lŭm'-bă, *n.* A bird of the order of pigeons; কপোত জাতীয় পক্ষী। **–bal,** *adj.* কাপোতক।

Columba intermedia — কবুতর (বেলঃ), কপোত।

cŏl'-ŭm-bīne, *adj.* & *n.* **1.** Of or like a dove; ঘুঘু-সম্বন্ধীয়, ঘুঘু সদৃশ। **2.** Dove coloured; ঘুঘুবর্ণ। *Noun.* A garden plant of the butter-cup family; উদ্যানজাত বৃক্ষবিশেষ।

Cŏl'-ŭm-bīne, *n.* The heroine in pantomime; সংদার যাত্রার নায়িকা।

cŏl'-umn (-ŭm), *n.* **1.** A pillar; স্তম্ভ, থাম, লাট। **2.** Any thing resembling a column; as. a *column* of smoke; স্তম্ভাকৃতি বস্তু। **3.** A body of troops drawn up in deep files and narrow front; সম্মুখভাগ সংকীর্ণ, এবং পশ্চাদনুক্রমে বহুসংখ্যক পংক্তিতে সজ্জিত সৈন্যশ্রেণী, সূচি-ব্যূহ (আঃ বঃ)। **4.** A body of ships, esp. following one another; পশ্চাদনুক্রমে সজ্জিত রণপোত শ্রেণী। **5.** A perpendicular row of lines in a page or newspaper; গ্রন্থের পৃষ্ঠায় স্তম্ভাকারে সজ্জিত অক্ষর পংক্তি, সংবাদ পত্রের স্তম্ভ। **6.** A perpendicular line of figures; স্তম্ভাকারে সজ্জিত সংখ্যা-পংক্তি। **7.** (*Bot.*) The stamen of a plant when the filaments are united into a tube; (উদ্ভিদ বিদ্যা) নলাকারে সংযুক্ত পুংকেশর সমূহ, পুষ্প-স্তম্ভ (সাঃ পঃ)। **–lum'-nal,** *adj.* Shaped like a column; স্তম্ভাকৃতি (জাহিঃ)। **–lum'-nar,** *adj.* Like a column; স্তম্ভনিভ (সাঃ পঃ)।

Column. (Corinthian.)

Column (Corinthian order).

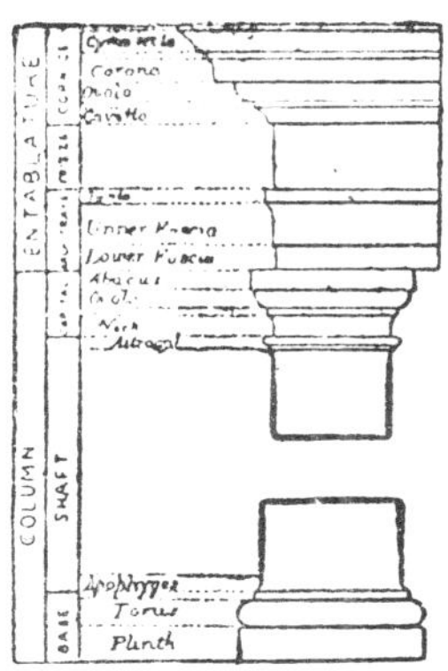

Column (Tuscan).

cŏ-lūre', *n.* (*Astron.*) One of the two great circles intersecting at right angles in the poles of the equator; (জ্যোতির্বিজ্ঞান) উন্মণ্ডল (হিঃ কোঃ), অয়নান্ত বৃত্ত (ঐ), অয়ন প্রোত বৃহৎ বৃত্ত (সাঃ পঃ), অয়নান্তের অহোরাত্র বৃত্ত (ঐ), ধ্রুবপ্রোত বৃত্ত (ঐ)। **Equinoctial colure**—ক্রান্তিপাতবৃত্ত (সাঃ পঃ), বিষুব প্রোতবৃত্ত (ঐ)। **Solstitial colure**—অয়নান্তবৃত্ত (সাঃ পঃ), অয়নান্ত প্রোত বৃত্ত (ঐ)।

cŏl'-ză, *n.* A kind of cabbage from the seeds of which is obtained oil for lamps; একপ্রকার কপি, ইহার বীজ হইতে প্রদীপের তৈল প্রাপ্ত হওয়া যায়।

cō'-mă, *n.* A state of deep lethargy; গভীর সুষুপ্তি, তন্দ্রাদোষ (হঃ চঃ), অতিশয় নিদ্রালক্ষিত রোগ বিশেষ, অচেতনাবস্থা (জাহিঃ), সান্নিপাতিক মূর্চ্ছা (সাঃ পঃ)। **–tose, –tous,** *adj.* **1.** Affected with deep coma; গভীর নিদ্রাচ্ছন্ন, অতি নিদ্রালু, সান্নিপাতিক মূর্চ্ছাযুক্ত। **2.** Drowsy; সংজ্ঞাহীন।

cō'-mă, *n.* **1.** A tuft or bunch of hair like appendages as on some seeds; বীজাদির উপরিস্থ রোমাকার উপাঙ্গ, কেশগুচ্ছ (সাঃ পঃ)। **2.** The nebulous envelope surrounding the nucleus of a comet; ধূমকেতুর চতুর্দ্দিকস্থ নীহারিকাবৎ অস্পষ্ট আবরণ, কেতুনাভি আবরণ (হিঃ কোঃ)

cō'-māte, *n.* A companion; সহচর সহবর্ত্তী, সঙ্গী, সাথী।

cōmb (kōm), *n., v. t.* & *i.* **1.** A toothed instrument for separating and cleaning hair, wool, etc.; also for fastening the hair; কঙ্কতিকা, চিরুণী, অবলেখন, কঙ্কত, প্রসাধনী, কাঁকুই (*Colloq.*); খোপার চিরুণী। **2.** A cock's crest; কুক্কুটের শিখা বা ঝুঁটী, কুক্কুটচূড়া, কুক্কুটশিখা।

3. The crest of a hill or wave ; পৰ্ব্বত বা তরঙ্গের শীর্ষ। 4. Same as honey-comb (which see.) 5. A dry measure ; পরিমাণ বিশেষ। *Verb t.* To separate, arrange or clean by means of comb ; চিরুণী দ্বারা আঁচড়ান, পরিষ্কার বা বিন্যাস করা। *Verb i.* To break with a white foam, as the top of a wave ; শুভ্র ফেন-খণ্ডে ভাঙ্গিয়া পড়া (যেমন তরঙ্গ)। **Combed,** *adj* **Comb′-er,** *n.* **To comb a man's head**—To humiliate a person ; to give him a thrashing ; কোন ব্যক্তির মস্তক নত করা ; কাহাকে উত্তম মধ্যম দেওয়া। **To cut a man's comb**—To take down a man's conceit ; কোন ব্যক্তির গৰ্ব্ব খৰ্ব্ব করা। **To set up one's comb**—To be vain-glorious ; গৰ্ব্বিতভাব ধারণ করা।

cŏm′-băt, *v. t., i.* & *n.* **1.** To contend ; to fight with ; দ্বন্দ্ব করা ; সংগ্রাম করা, যুদ্ধ করা। **2.** To resist ; বাধা দেওয়া, প্রতিরোধ করা। *Verb i.* To contend ; to fight ; সংগ্রাম করা ; যুদ্ধ করা, লড়াই করা। *Noun.* A fight ; a contest ; a struggle for supremacy ; যুদ্ধ ; সংগ্রাম ; বিরোধ। **—a-ble,** *adj.* **—ant,** *adj.* & *n.* Contending ; যুদ্ধকারী, বিরোধী। (*Noun.*) One who engages in combat ; যোদ্ধা, যোধ, বীর, ভট। **—tive,** *adj.* Disposed to engage in combat ; যুযুৎসু, যুদ্ধপ্রিয়। **—tive-ness,** *n.*

combe (kōm), *n.* A hollow among hills ; পৰ্ব্বতসমূহের মধ্যবর্ত্তী গহ্বর।

comb-êr (kōm-), *n.* **1.** One who or that which combs ; যে আঁচড়ায়। **2.** A machine for combing or carding wool ; পশম আঁচড়াইবার বা ধুনিবার যন্ত্র বিশেষ।

cŏm-bĭ-nā′-tion, *n.* **1.** The act of combining ; সম্মিলন, সংশ্রয়, সংহৃষ্টি, সংযোগ, সংহতি। **2.** A union of persons or states to effect some purpose ; ব্যক্তি বা রাজ্য-সমূহের মধ্যে সংযোগ, সম্মিলন, সমবায় বা সন্ধি। **3.** (*Chem.*) A union of substances in compounds with properties differing from theirs ; (রসায়ন-শাস্ত্র) রাসায়নিক সংযোগ। **4.** (*Pl.*) A women's and children's garment consisting of chemise and drawers combined ; স্ত্রীলোকদের বা বালকদিগের এক প্রকার আঁটা পোষাক।

cŏm-bīne′, *v. t.* & *i.* **1.** To join two together ; সংযুক্ত করা, একত্র করা। **2.** To bring into harmonious union ; সম্মিলিত করা। *Verb i.* **1.** To form a union ; সংযুক্ত হওয়া, সম্মিলিত হওয়া। **2.** To agree ; একমত হওয়া, ঐক্য হওয়া। **3.** To coalesce ; মিলিত হওয়া। **4.** (*Chem.*) To unite by affinity ; (রসায়ন-শাস্ত্র) রাসায়নিক আকর্ষণে সম্মিলিত হওয়া। **—bined,** *adj.* **—bined-ly,** *adv.* **—bin′-er,** *n.*

cŏm-bŭs′-ti-ble *adj.* & *n.* **1.** Capable of taking fire and burning ; দাহ্য, জ্বলনশীল। **2.** Easily kindled or excited ; সহজ-কোপন, আশুক্রোধী। *Noun.* Anything that will take fire and burn ; দাহ্য পদার্থ। **—ness,** *n.* **—ti-bil′-i-ty,** *n.* **—tion,** *n.* A burning ; প্রজ্বলন, দহন।

come (kŭm), *v. t.* **1.** To move to a place ; to draw near or approach ; আসা ; সন্নিকটে আসা, অগ্রসর হওয়া। **2.** To arrive ; পৌছা। **3.** To appear ; as, the colour *comes* into the cheeks ; আবির্ভূত হওয়া। **4.** To arrive at some state or condition ; কোনরূপ অবস্থায় উপনীত হওয়া। **5.** To happen ; সমাগত হওয়া, সংঘটিত হওয়া। **6.** To issue ; to proceed ; "The present motion *came* from a gentleman of that country ;" বহির্গত হওয়া, নিঃসৃত হওয়া ; উদ্ভূত হওয়া। **Com′-er,** *n.* One who comes ; আগন্তুক। **A come down**—A fall or abasement ; পতন, অপমান। **Come, come**—Stop (expressing rebuke) ; থাম, থাম (তিরস্কার বাচক)। **Come what may**—Whatever may happen ; যাহাই ঘটুক না কেন। **To come about**—To happen ; ঘটা। **To come across**—To meet accidentally ; ঘটনাক্রমে সাক্ষাৎ হওয়া। **To come across the mind**—To enter into one's mind or thought ; মনে আসা, মনে জাগা। **To come after**—To follow ; অনুসরণ করা। To come in search of ; অনুসন্ধানের জন্য আসা। **To come again**—To return ; প্রত্যাগমন করা, প্রত্যাবর্ত্তন করা। **To come and go**—To have freedom of action ; স্বাধীনভাবে কার্য্য করিবার ক্ষমতা থাকা। **To come at**—To reach ; পঁহুছা। **To come away**—To part or depart ; বিচ্ছিন্ন হওয়া, প্রস্থান করা। **To come between**—To intervene ; মধ্যে আসিয়া পড়া। To estrange ; বিচ্ছিন্ন করা। **To come by**—To obtain ; to gain ; to acquire ; প্রাপ্ত হওয়া ; লাভ করা ; অধিগত করা। **To come close to**—To come near ; নিকটবর্ত্তী হওয়া। To touch one's feelings, interest or reason ; মৰ্ম্মস্পর্শ করা। **To come down**—To descend ; অবতরণ করা, নামা। To be humbled ; অবনত হওয়া। To pay (usually *with*) ; টাকা দেওয়া। **To come down in the world**—To be reduced in circumstances ; দুরবস্থায় পতিত হওয়া। **To come down to**—To descend to ; নামিয়া আসা। To proceed from one generation to another by transmission ; পিতৃপিতামহক্রমে আসা। **To come down upon**—To call to account ; কৈফিয়ত তলব করা। To rebuke ; to punish severely ; তিরস্কার করা ; গুরুতর শাস্তি প্রদান করা। To fall upon ; আক্রমণ করা। To press hard ; চাপিয়া ধরা। **To come forth**—To advance ; অগ্রসর হওয়া। To be published ; প্রকাশিত হওয়া।

To come forward—To move to the front ; সম্মুখবর্ত্তী হওয়া, অগ্রসর হওয়া, পুরোবর্ত্তী হওয়া। **To come from**—To be desended from ; কোন বংশে জাত হওয়া। To be derived from ; উদ্ভূত হওয়া। To be spoken or written ; কোন ব্যক্তি দ্বারা কথিত বা লিখিত হওয়া। **To come home** — To return home ; বাটীতে প্রত্যাবর্ত্তন করা। **To come in**—To enter ; প্রবেশ করা। To arrive ; পঁহুছা। To become fashionable or seasonable ; সময়োপযোগী হওয়া, প্রচলিত হওয়া। To comply ; সম্মত হওয়া। To yield or surrender ; আত্মসমর্পণ করা। To be added or inserted ; যুক্ত হওয়া। To accrue as income or revenue ; লাভ বা রাজস্ব স্বরূপ আগত হওয়া। To have sexual intercourse ; স্ত্রী পুরুষের সংসর্গ হওয়া। To bring forth ; প্রসব করা। **To come in for**—To get share of ; to obtain ; অংশ প্রাপ্ত হওয়া ; প্রাপ্ত হওয়া। **To come in one's way**—To be an obstacle to ; প্রতিবন্ধক স্বরূপ হওয়া। To occur to one's mind ; কাহারও মনে উদয় হওয়া। **To come in sight**—To become visible ; নয়নগোচর হওয়া। **To come into fashion**—To become the prevailing mode ; সাময়িক রীতি হওয়া। **To come into one's head**—To occur to one's mind ; কোন ব্যক্তির মনে উদয় হওয়া। **To come into play** or **operation**—To be brought into use or employment ; ব্যবহারে আসা, ক্রিয়াশীল হওয়া। **To come near**—To be nearly equal to ; প্রায় সমতুল্য হওয়া। **To come of**—To descend or spring from ; (কোন বংশ হইতে) উদ্ভূত হওয়া। To result or follow from ; ফলস্বরূপ আগত হওয়া। **To come off**—To escape ; to get free ; অব্যাহতি পাওয়া ; মুক্তি লাভ করা। To take place ; ঘটা। To part from ; to fall away from ; বিচ্ছিন্ন হওয়া ; স্খলিত হওয়া। **To come off by**—To suffer ; (কষ্ট) ভোগ করা। **To come off from**—To leave off ; পরিত্যাগ করা। **To come on**—To advance ; অগ্রসর হওয়া। To thrive ; উন্নতি করা। To take place ; ঘটা। **To come out**—To move from within to outside ; বাহির হইয়া আসা। To become public ; প্রচলিত হওয়া, প্রকাশিত হওয়া। To end ; শেষ হওয়া। To be introduced into society ; as, she *came out* two seasons ago ; সমাজে পরিচিত হওয়া। To bud ; মুকুলিত হওয়া। To take a position or rank in an examination ; কোন পরীক্ষায় বিশেষ স্থান অধিকার করা। **To come out of**—To proceed ; উদ্ভূত হওয়া। **To come out with**—To give vent to ; প্রকাশ করা। **To come over** — To pass from one place or position to another ; কোন স্থান হইতে স্থানান্তরে গমন করা ; কোন অবস্থা হইতে অবস্থান্তর প্রাপ্ত হওয়া। **To come over to** — To join ; যোগদান করা। **To come round**—To move round a place or sport ; কোন স্থানের চতুর্দ্দিকে আবর্ত্তিত হওয়া। To recover ; আরোগ্য লাভ করা। **To come short**—To be deficient ; ন্যূন হওয়া। To fail to reach a standard ; কোন আদর্শের পক্ষে খাটো হওয়া, বিফল হওয়া। **To come to**—To arrive at a place ; কোন স্থানে পৌঁছা। To reach to a certain state or condition ; কোন বিশেষ অবস্থাপ্রাপ্ত হওয়া। To amount to ; সমষ্টিতে হওয়া। To consent or yield ; স্বীকৃত হওয়া। To recover, as from a swoon ; (মূর্চ্ছা হইতে) চৈতন্য লাভ করা। **To come to a bad end**—To die unnaturally ; অপমৃত্যু ঘটা। **To come to a head**—To suppurate, as a boil ; পুঁজপূর্ণ হওয়া, পাকা। To mature ; পরিপক্ক হওয়া। **To come to an untimely end**—অকালে মৃত্যুগ্রাসে পতিত হওয়া। **To come to a stand still**—To stop ; থামা। **To come to blows**—To fall out ; কলহ করা, হাতাহাতি করা, মারামারি করা। **To come together** — To assemble ; সমবেত হওয়া। **To come to grief**—To meet with disaster or misfortune ; দুরবস্থায় পতিত হওয়া। **To come to hand** — To be received ; হস্তগত হওয়া। **To come to light**—To be disclosed or made public ; প্রকাশিত বা প্রচারিত হওয়া। **To come to one's self**—To recover one's senses ; চৈতন্য লাভ করা, সংজ্ঞা লাভ করা। **To come to pass** — To happen ; ঘটা। **To come to terms** — To make an agreement ; চুক্তি করা, কোন বিষয়ে চুক্তির সর্ত্ত ঠিকঠাক করা। **To come to the front**—To come forward ; সম্মুখে আসা। **To come to the hammer** — To be sold by auction ; নীলামে বিক্রয় হওয়া। **To come to the point**—To address oneself to the matter in hand, without circumlocution ; সোজাভাবে আসল কথা পাড়া। **To come true** — To be found to have been true ; সত্য বলিয়া প্রতিপন্ন হওয়া। **To come under**—To be included under ; অন্তর্ভুক্ত হওয়া। **To come upon** — To attack ; আক্রমণ করা। To meet ; সাক্ষাৎ করা। To hold answerable ; দায়ী করা। **To come up to**—To approach ; নিকটে আসা। To amount to ; সমষ্টিতে দাঁড়ান। **To come up with**—To overtake ; নাগাইল ধরা। **To come with** — To join or be assisted ; যোগদান করা, সাহায্য পাওয়া। To agree to ; সম্মত হওয়া।

come (cŭm), *n.* **1.** Passing to and fro ; ইতস্ততঃ বিচরণ। **2.** Coming down ; অধঃপতন।

cŏ-mē'-dĭ-ăn, *n.* **1.** An actor or player in a comedy ; মিলনান্ত নাটকের অভিনেতা। **2.** A comic actor ; বৈহাসিক। **3.** A writer of comedy ; মিলনান্ত নাটকের রচয়িতা।

cŏ-me-di-enne' (-mā-dĭĕn), *n.* A comedy actress ; মিলনান্ত নাটকের অভিনেত্রী।

cŏ-mē-dĭ-ĕt'-tă, *n.* A slight comedy ; ক্ষুদ্র মিলনান্ত নাটিকা।

cŏm'-ĕ-dȳ, *n.* A stage play of mirthful character chiefly representing the every day life and with a happy ending ; মিলনান্ত নাটক, প্রহসন, হর্ষপ্রধান নাটক।

come'-lȳ (kŭm-), *adj.* Pleasing or agreeable to the sight ; handsome ; **সুদর্শন ; সুন্দর, সুশ্রী**। **2.** Becoming ; "Is it *comely* that a woman pray unto God uncovered ;" সুশোভন। **—li-ness,** *n.* The quality of being comely ; সৌন্দর্য্য, লাবণ্য, শোভনতা।

com'-ĕr (kŭm-), *n.* One who comes ; আগন্তুক। **First comer**—প্রথমাগত ব্যক্তি। **All comers**—সর্ব্বসাধারণ।

cŏ-mĕs'-ti-bles, *n. pl.* Eatables ; আহার্য্য, খাদ্য-সামগ্রী।

cŏm'-ĕt, *n.* A heavenly body belonging to the solar system, having a nucleus surrounded by a luminous envelope, and often luminous tail or train ; ধূমকেতু, কেতুতারা। **—a-ry, Co-met'-ic,** *adjs.* **—og'-ra-phy, —ol'-o-gy,** *ns.* **Comet-finder,** *n* ধূমকেতু-প্রদর্শক দূরবীক্ষণ যন্ত্র।

Comet.

com'-fit (kŭm-fĭt), *n.* **1.** A dry sweet-meat ; শুষ্ক মিষ্ট দ্রব্য, মোদক, উপস্কর। **2.** Any kind of fruit or root preserved with sugar and dried ; শর্করামিশ্রিত শুষ্ক ফলাদি, মোরব্বা।

com'-fort (kŭm-fêrt), *v. t.* & *n.* To console or soothe ; সান্ত্বনা করা, আশ্বস্ত করা, প্রবোধ দেওয়া *Noun.* **1.** Solace ; সান্ত্বনা, আশ্বাস, প্রবোধ। **2.** That which gives ease, enjoyment, etc. ; সুখ বা আরামদায়ক বস্তু, সান্ত্বনাদায়ক বস্তু। **—a-ble,** *adj.* **1.** Consolatory ; আশ্বাসক, সান্ত্বনাদায়ক। **2.** Free from pain or trouble ; উদ্বেগশূন্য। **3.** Tranquil ; "A motherly *comfortable* woman ;" প্রশান্ত। **—a-ble-ness,** *n.* **—a-bly,** *adv.* **—er,** *n.* **1.** One who administers comfort or consolation ; সান্ত্বনাদায়ক ব্যক্তি। **2.** The Holy Spirit as the indwelling, abiding presence of Christ ; (খৃষ্টীয় শাস্ত্রানুসারে) পবিত্রাত্মা **3.** A woollen scarf ; পশমের সূতার তৈয়ারী গলবন্ধ বিশেষ, উলসূতার কম্ফোর্টার। **—less,** *adj.*. **Job's comforter**—যে ব্যক্তি সান্ত্বনার ছলে অধিকতর দুঃখ প্রদান করে।

com'-frey, com'-fry (kŏm- or kŭm-frĭ), *n.* A wild plant formerly much prized as a vulnerary ; ভেষজ গুল্মবিশেষ—পূর্ব্বে ক্ষতাদির ঔষধস্বরূপ ব্যবহৃত হইত।

cŏm'-ic, *adj.* **1.** Relating to comedy, as distinct from tragedy ; মিলনান্ত নাটক সম্বন্ধীয়। **2.** Causing mirth ; হাস্যকর, হাস্যোদ্দীপক। **—i-cal,** *adj.* **—i-cal-ly,** *adv.* **—ness,** *n.*

cŏ-mique' (-mēk), *n.* A comic actor or singer ; হাস্যোদ্দীপক নাটকের অভিনেতা, হাস্যোদ্দীপক সঙ্গীত গায়ক, বৈহাসিক।

cŏ-mĭ'-ti-ă (-shĭ-), *n.* A public assembly of the Roman people for electing officers or passing laws ; প্রাচীন রোমনগরের ব্যবস্থাপক সভাবিশেষ। **—tial,** *adj.*

cŏm'-i-tȳ, *n.* Courtesy ; civility ; শিষ্টাচার, সৌজন্য ; ভদ্রব্যবহার। **Comity of nations** — আন্তর্জাতিক শিষ্টাচার (যদ্দ্বারা একদেশের ব্যবস্থা দেশান্তরে গৃহীত হয়।)

cŏm'-mă, *n.* **1.** The point denoting the shortest pause in reading ; বাক্যের প্রথমচ্ছেদ, কমা চিহ্ন [,]। **2.** (*Mus.*) A small interval ; (সঙ্গীতশাস্ত্র) স্বল্পবিরাম। **Comma bacillus**—একপ্রকার কমাকৃতি রোগবীজাণু—বিসূচিকাগ্রস্ত রোগীর অন্ত্রমধ্যে দৃষ্ট হয়। **Inverted commas**—উদ্ধৃত চিহ্ন (" ")।

cŏm-mănd', *v. t., i.* & *n.* **1.** To order with authority ; হুকুম করা, আজ্ঞা করা, অনুজ্ঞা করা। **2.** To exercise direct authority over ; প্রভুত্ব করা, কর্তৃত্ব করা। **3.** To have control of ; শাসনাধীন রাখা, শাসন করা। **4.** To lead or direct as a general does his army ; নেতৃত্ব করা, অধিনায়কতা করা। **5.** To claim ; "His literary criticism *command* our admiration ;" দাবী করা। **6.** To have at one's disposal ; "If any of us can be of use, you surely ought to *command* us ; আয়ত্তাধীন থাকা, কর্তৃত্বাধীনে থাকা। **7.** To overlook "Strong castles which *commanded* the principal defiles ; এরূপভাবে অবস্থিত থাকা যাহাতে নিম্নবর্ত্তী স্থান সমূহের উপর অধিপত্য বিস্তার করা যায়। **8.** To restrain ; দমন করা। *Verb i.* To have or exercise chief authority ; প্রধান কর্তৃত্ব থাকা, প্রধান কর্তৃত্ব পরিচালনা করা। *Noun.* **1.** The right, power or act of commanding ; কর্তৃত্বের ক্ষমতা বা অধিকার, আদেশ করণ, প্রভুত্ব করণ, আদেশদানের ক্ষমতা বা অধিকার। **2.** A mandate ; an injunction ; বিধি, বিধান, আদেশ ; নিদেশ, নিয়োগ, আজ্ঞা, হুকুম, অনুশাসন (সাঃ পঃ)। **3.** Leadership ; নেতৃত্ব। **4.** A body of troops under the command of a particular officer ; কোন সেনানীর নেতৃত্বাধীন সেনাদল। **5.** The power of overlooking ; সুবিধাজনক উচ্চস্থানে

অবস্থিতি হেতু নিম্নের সমস্ত স্থানের উপর কর্তৃত্ব করণের ক্ষমতা। 6. Supreme power or authority; প্রধান কর্তৃত্ব, একাধিপত্য। 7. Restraint; সংযম। **–a-ble,** *adj.* **–er,** *n.* **1.** One who commands; আদেষ্টা, আজ্ঞাপক। **2.** One who has supreme authority; অধিপতি, প্রধান কর্তা। **3.** A leader; সেনানী, সেনাপতি। **4.** (*Naut.*) An officer who ranks next below a captain; (নৌ-বিদ্যা) পোতাধ্যক্ষের অব্যবহিত নিম্নতর পদবর্তী নাবিক কর্ম্মচারী, পোতনায়ক (সাঃ পঃ)। **5.** A wooden mallet; বৃহৎ কাঠের হাতুড়ী। **–er-in-cheef,** *n.* প্রধান সেনাপতি, জঙ্গীলাট, মহাসেনাপতি। **–er-ship,** *n.* **–ing,** *adj.* **1.** Exercising authority; প্রভুত্বকারী। **2.** Exalted; উচ্চ, উন্নত। **3.** Dominating by superior height or strategic position; as, *commanding* position; অপেক্ষাকৃত উন্নত স্থানে বা সামরিক হিসাবে সুবিধাজনক স্থলে অবস্থানহেতু আধিপত্যকারী। **4.** With wide view of; যে স্থান হইতে চতুর্দ্দিকের দূরবর্ত্তী দৃশ্যসমূহ দৃষ্ট হয়,—তদ্রূপ স্থানে অবস্থিত। **–ing-ly,** *adv.* **–man-dant′,** *n.* A commander, esp. the governor of a fortress; অধ্যক্ষ, সৈন্যাধ্যক্ষ, সেনানায়ক, বিশেষতঃ দুর্গাধ্যক্ষ। **–ment,** *n.* **1.** A command; injunction; আদেশ, হুকুম, আজ্ঞা; অনুজ্ঞা। **2.** Exercise of authority; ক্ষমতা-পরিচালন। **3.** (*Script.*) One of the ten laws or precepts given by God to the Israelites at Mount Sinai; (খৃষ্টীয় শাস্ত্রানুসারে) ঈশ্বরের দশ আদেশের একটী, ঈশ্বরাজ্ঞা। **Command night**—(রাজাদেশে) রঙ্গালয় প্রভৃতির বিশেষ অভিনয় রজনী। **Commander of the faithful**-খলিফাদিগের উপাধি বিশেষ। **At command**—আয়ত্তাধীন, কর্তৃত্বাধীন।

cŏm-măn-deer′ (-dēr), *v. t.* To compel to military service; বলপূর্ব্বক সামরিক কার্য্যে নিযুক্ত করা।

cŏm-măn′-dō, *n.* A party called out for military service, esp. any such raised among the Dutch or Boer colonists for military purpose; সামরিক কার্য্যের জন্য আহুত ব্যক্তিবর্গ, বিশেষতঃ ওলন্দাজ বা বেয়ার ঔপনিবেশিকগণের ভিতর সামরিক উদ্দেশ্যে দলবদ্ধ ব্যক্তিবর্গ।

cŏm-meas′-üre (-mĕzh-), *v. t.* To equal in measure; to coincide with; সমপরিমাণ হওয়া; মিল হওয়া। **–ur-a-ble,** *adj.*

comme-il-faut, *adj.* Well-bred; শিষ্টাচার-সম্পন্ন।

Commelyna communis—কৃসপ্রিয় (বেলঃ)।

cŏm-mĕm′-ŏ-rāte, *v. t.* To preserve the memory of by a special act or observance; to celebrate with honour and solemnity; কোন বিশেষ অনুষ্ঠানদ্বারা স্মৃতি জাগরূক রাখা; স্মৃতি উপলক্ষে উৎসবাদির অনুষ্ঠান করা। **–ra-ble,** *adj.* **–ra′-tion,** *n.* **1.** The act of commemorating; স্মৃতিরক্ষাকরণ। **2.** A celebration designed to honour the memory of some person; স্মৃতি-উৎসব। **3.** The great festival of the Oxford academic year in memory of its founders; অক্সফোর্ড বিশ্ববিদ্যালয়ের প্রতিষ্ঠাতৃবর্গের বাৎসরিক স্মৃতি-উৎসব। **–ra-tive, –ra-to-ry,** *adjs.* **–ra-tor,** *n.*

cŏm-mĕnce′, *v.i.* & *t.* **1.** To begin; আরব্ধ হওয়া, সুরু হওয়া। **2.** To take full degree of; "To *commence* M. A.;" বিশ্ববিদ্যালয়ের ডি, এল্, এম্, এ প্রভৃতি উপাধি গ্রহণ করা। ***Verb t.*** To begin; আরম্ভ করা। **2.** To enter upon; কোন কার্য্যে প্রবৃত্ত হওয়া। **–ment,** *n.* **1.** The beginning; আরম্ভ, প্রারম্ভ, সূচনা, উপক্রম, প্রবর্ত্তন, পত্তন (*Colloq.*)। **2.** The day when the degrees of Masters and Doctors are conferred at Cambridge and United States Universities; কেম্ব্রিজ, অক্সফোর্ড এবং মার্কিন যুক্তরাজ্যের বিশ্ববিদ্যালয়ের ডি, এল্, এম্, এ প্রভৃতি উপাধি প্রদানের দিবস।

cŏm-mĕnd′, *v. t.* **1.** To commit to the care or charge of; কোন্ ব্যক্তির জিম্মায় বা তত্ত্বাবধানে রাখা। **2.** To recommend as worthy of confidence; বিশ্বাসযোগ্য বলিয়া উপস্থাপন করা। **3.** To approve; to praise; অনুমোদন করা; প্রশংসা করা। **4.** To call for notice or attention; প্রণিধান করিতে বলা, মনোযোগ আকর্ষণ করা। **–a-ble,** *adj.* Praiseworthy; প্রশংসনীয়, প্রশস্ত, শ্লাঘনীয়। **–a-bly,** *adv.* **–a-to-ry,** *adj.* **Com′-men-da-tor,** *n.* **–men-da′-tion,** *n.* **1.** Praise; প্রশংসা, সুখ্যাতি, স্তুতি, শ্লাঘা। **2.** Recommendation; সুপারিশ। **3.** That which is the ground of approbation or praise; প্রশংসার বিষয়। **Commend me to**—Remember me kindly to; কাহারও কাছে প্রীতিপূর্ব্বক স্মরণ করিয়া দেওয়া (*Colloq*)। **Commend me to**—Give me by preference; আমাকে বিশেষভাবে দেও।

cŏm-mĕn′-săl, *adj.* & *n.* Eating at the same table; এক মেজে ভোজনকারী, সহভোজী। ***Noun.*** An animal or plant living as another's tenant sharing its food; যে জন্তু বা উদ্ভিদ্ অন্য জন্তু বা উদ্ভিদের দেহে বাস করিয়া তাহাদের খাদ্যের ভাগ গ্রহণ করে। **–sal′-i-ty, –ism,** *ns.* The being commensal; সহভোজিত্ব।

cŏm-mĕn′-sü-ră-ble, *adj.* **1.** Having a common measure; সমপরিমাণ, সমগুণিতক, সাপবর্ত্ত। **2.** Divisible without remainder by the same; একই সংখ্যাদ্বারা অবশিষ্টশূন্য রূপে ভাজ্য। **3.** Proportional; আনুপাতিক। **–bil′-i-ty, –bly,** *advs.* **–ness,** *ns.* **–rate,** *v., t.* & *adj.* To reduce to a common measure; সমগুণিতকে পরিণত করা। (*Adj.*) Equal in measure or extent;

সমপরিমাণ, সমব্যাপী। **—rate-ly,** *adv.* **—rate-ness, —ra'-tion,** *ns.*

cŏm'-mĕnt (Also **—ment'**, in the case of ***Verb i.***), *v. i.* & *n.* **1.** To make critical or explanatory notes; to annotate; টীকা করা; টিপ্পনি লেখা। **2.** To make remarks; মন্তব্য প্রকাশ করা, টিপ্পনী কাটা। ***Noun.*** **1.** A note; টীকা, ব্যাখ্যা। **2.** A remark, observation or criticism; মন্তব্য, সমালোচনা, টিপ্পনী। **—men-ta-tor, —er,** *ns.* An expositor or annotator; টীকাকার, ব্যাখ্যাতা, ভাষ্যকার। **—men-ta'-tion,** *n.*

cŏm'-mĕn-tă-rȳ, *n.* **1.** A comment; মন্তব্য। **2.** A series of explanatory notes on the whole of a work or a detached portion of it; বৃত্তি, টীকা, ভাষ্য, প্রকরণ।

cŏm'-merce (-mêrs), *n.* **1.** Interchange of merchandise on a large scale between nations or individuals; বাণিজ্য, ব্যবসায়। **2.** Social intercourse; "His *commerce* with the world had been small;" লোকসংসর্গ, মেলামেশা। **3.** Sexual intercourse; স্ত্রী-সঙ্গম। **4.** A card game; একপ্রকার তাসের খেলা। **—mer'-cial,** *adj.* Mercantile; বাণিজ্য সংক্রান্ত, বাণিজ্যবিষয়ক। **—mer'-cial-ly,** *adv.* **Commercial college**—ব্যবসায় শিক্ষার জন্য বিদ্যালয়, বাণিজ্য-বিদ্যালয়। **Commercial traveller**—ভ্রমণকারী সওদাগর, যে ব্যক্তি নানা স্থানে পর্য্যটন করত জিনিষের নমুনা দেখাইয়া জিনিষ জোগাইবার আদেশ গ্রহণ এবং প্রতিনিধি নিযুক্ত করে। **Chamber of commerce**—বণিক্ সমিতি।

cŏm-mi-nā'-tion, *n.* **1.** Threatening; তর্জ্জন, ভীতিপ্রদর্শন। **2.** An office in the liturgy of the Church of England, being a recital of God's judgment against sinner; ইংলণ্ডীয় ধর্ম্ম সমাজের ক্রিয়া বিশেষ,—যাহাতে পাপীদিগের প্রতি ঈশ্বরের বিচার সম্বন্ধীয় উক্তির আবৃত্তি করা হয়। **—min'-a-to-ry,** *adj.*

cŏm-min'-gle (-mĭng-), *v. t.* To mingle or mix with; সংমিশ্রিত করা।

cŏm'-mi-nūte, *v. t.* To reduce to minute particles or to a fine powder; পেষণ করা, চূর্ণ করা। **—nut-ed,** *adj.* Fractured; বিচূর্ণিত, ভগ্নাবস্থাপ্রাপ্ত। **—nu'-tion,** *n.* The act of reducing to a fine powder; সংচূর্ণন, মর্দ্দন। **Comminuted fracture**—বিচূর্ণিত ভগ্ন (সাঃ পঃ)। [অস্থি ভগ্ন হইয়া অনেক খণ্ড হইলে তাহাকে 'comminuted fracture' বলে।]

cŏm-mis'-êr-āte, *v. t.* To feel for the miseries of another; পরদুঃখে কাতর হওয়া, পরদুঃখে দুঃখিত হওয়া। **—a-ble,** *adj.* **—a'-tion,** *n.* Concern for the sufferings of others; pity; পরদুঃখে কাতরতা; করুণা, কারুণ্য, অনুকম্পা। **—a-tive,** *adj.* **—a-tor,** *n.*

cŏm-mis-sā'-ri-ăt, *n.* **1.** The department which has the charge of provisioning the army; যে বিভাগের উপর সৈন্যদলের রসদ-সংগ্রহের ভার ন্যস্ত আছে, রসদবিভাগ। **2.** The body of officers charged with such service; সৈন্যদিগের রসদ যোগাইবার ব্যবস্থাকারী কর্ম্মচারিসমূহ। **—ship,** *n.*

cŏm'-mis-să-rȳ, *n.* **1.** One to whom any charge is deputed; যাহার উপর কোন কর্ম্মের ভার অর্পিত হয়। **2.** A deputy; প্রতিনিধি। **3.** An officer representing a bishop and performing his duties in distant parts of the diocese; খৃষ্টীয় ধর্ম্মাধ্যক্ষের প্রতিনিধি বিশেষ। **4.** An officer whose business is to provide food for a body of troops; সৈন্য দলের রসদ সংগ্রাহক কর্ম্মচারী। **5.** In the French Police a superior officer under the may or or profect of Police; ফরাসীদেশের উর্দ্ধতন পুলিশ কর্ম্মচারিবিশেষ। **—sa'-ri-al,** *adj.* **Commissary court**—এডিনবুরার সর্ব্বোচ্চ ধর্ম্মাধিকরণ।

cŏm-mĭs'-sion (-mĭ-), *n.* & *v. t.* **1.** The act of committing, doing or performing; সমর্পণ, সম্পাদন। **2.** The act of intrusting; ভারার্পণ, বিনিয়োগ, সন্নিয়োগ। **3.** That which is committed; ভারার্পিত বস্তু, ন্যস্ত বস্তু। **4.** Power and authority given; আজ্ঞাপত্র, ক্ষমতাপত্র, প্রত্যয়পত্র, অর্পিত ক্ষমতা। **5.** A writing from proper authority given to a person as his warrant for exercising certain powers; ক্ষমতাপত্র। **6.** A certificate conferring military or naval rank and authority; সামরিক বা নাবিক কর্ম্মচারীর নিয়োগ পত্র বা সনন্দ। **7.** A body of persons appointed to perform some duties; as the public service *commision*; কোন বিশেষ কার্য্য সম্পাদনে নিযুক্ত ব্যক্তি-বর্গ, বৈঠক। **8.** The brokerage or allowance made to a factor or agent for transacting business for another; দস্তুরী, দালালি, পারিশ্রমিক, বর্ত্তন। **9.** The committing of (crime, offence, etc.); পাপ-কার্য্য করণ। ***Verb t.*** **1.** To give a commission to; ভারার্পণ করা, বিনিয়োগ করা। **2.** To authorise; ক্ষমতা প্রদান করা। **3.** To order; ফরমাইস দেওয়া। **4.** To give (an officer) command of a ship by means of commission; to order a ship for active service; "The new ships which we *commission* and the new regiment which we raise;" সনন্দদ্বারা কোন নাবিক কর্ম্মচারীকে রণপোতাধ্যক্ষের কার্য্যভার অর্পণ করা; কোন রণপোতের যুদ্ধ-গমন সম্বন্ধে আদেশ প্রদান করা। **—al, —a-ry, —sioned,** *adjs.* **—er,** *n.* **1.** A person who has a commission or warrant to perform some office; কোন কার্য্য নির্ব্বাহার্থ সনন্দ-প্রাপ্ত ব্যক্তি। **2.** A member of a commission, government boards, etc.; কোন বৈঠকের সভ্য, সরকারী কর্ম্মচারিগণের স্থায়ী বৈঠকের সভ্য। **3.** (*India*) The chief officer of a division ; (ভারতবর্ষ) কোন বিভাগের সর্ব্বপ্রধান রাজকর্ম্মচারী, কমিশনর। **—er-ship,** *n.* **Commission agent** or **merchant**—যে ব্যক্তি দস্তুরী লইয়া অন্যের জন্য ক্রয় বিক্রয় করে কিংবা অপরের কারবারের কার্য্যভার গ্রহণ করে। **Commissioned officer**—সনন্দ-প্রাপ্ত সামরিক কর্ম্মচারী, লেফ্‌টেনেন্ট এবং তদূর্দ্ধতর উপাধিধারিগণ। (*Naut.*) **To put a vessel** or **ship into** or **in commission**—To equip and man a government vessel, and send it out on service after it has been laid up ; (নৌ-বিদ্যা) কোন সরকারী জাহাজ সজ্জিত ও নাবিক সমন্বিত করিয়া কোন কার্য্য সাধনে প্রেরণ করা।

cŏm-mis-sion-aire′ (-mĕs-yŏn-âr), *n.* A light errand porter or messenger ; দূত, সংবাদবাহক।

cŏm′-mis-süre, *n.* **1.** A joining ; juncture ; seam ; যোগবন্ধন ; সন্ধি ; সেলাইয়ের জোড় মুখ। **2.** A joint between two bones ; অস্থি-সন্ধি। **3.** The corner of the lips, eyelids, etc. ; ওষ্ঠাধর, অক্ষিপল্লব প্রভৃতির সংযোগ-কোণ। **4.** A suture of the cranium of the skull ; করোটীর বিভিন্ন অংশের সন্ধিস্থল। **5.** Various bands or bundles of white or gray nerve substance, which connect the two hemispheres of the brain ; মস্তকের উভয় গোলার্দ্ধ-সংযোজক শ্বেত বা ধূসরবর্ণ স্নায়ু পদার্থের গুচ্ছ বা বেষ্টনী।

cŏm-mit′, *v. t.* **1.** To give in trust or charge ; as, to *commit* to the sessions ; to consign ; as, to *commit* to flames ; ন্যস্ত করা, সোপর্দ্দ করা, ভারার্পণ করা, সমর্পণ করা ; অর্পণ করা। **2.** To put in charge of a jailor ; as, to *commit* for contempt ; কারাধ্যক্ষের হস্তে সমর্পণ করা। **3.** To perpetrate, as a crime ; (কুকর্ম্ম) করা। **4.** To pledge or bind ; প্রতিজ্ঞাবদ্ধ করা। **5.** To compromise ; to involve ; "The preachers have now *committed* themselves too far to recede ;" সঙ্কটে ফেলা ; বিজড়িত করা। **—ment,** *n.* **1.** The act of committing ; consignment ; ভারার্পণ, সোপর্দ্দ করণ। **2.** A warrant or order for the imprisonment of a person ; কোন ব্যক্তিকে কারারুদ্ধ করিবার আদেশপত্র। **3.** A doing or perpetration ; (কুকর্ম্ম) করণ। **—ta-ble,** *adj.* **—tal,** *n.* **To commit one's self**—To compromise one's self ; আপনাকে দায়গ্রস্ত করা, সঙ্কটে ফেলা বা বিজড়িত করা। **To commit to memory**—To learn by heart ; কণ্ঠস্থ করা, মুখস্থ করা।

cŏm-mit′-tee (-tē), *n.* **1.** A body of persons appointed for a special function ; বিশেষ কার্য্য-নির্ব্বাহের জন্য নিযুক্ত সমিতি। **2.** (*Law*) A person entrusted with a charge of an idiot or lunatic or his estate ; ক্ষিপ্ত বা জড়-বুদ্ধি ব্যক্তি বা তদীয় সম্পত্তির তত্ত্বাবধায়ক

cŏm-mix′, *v. t.* & *i.* To mix or mingle together ; মিশ্রিত করা বা হওয়া। **—ion,** *n.* **—ture,** *n.*

cŏm-möde′, *n.* **1.** A kind of lady's head-dress in use in the time of William and Mary ; ইংলণ্ডের রাজা উইলিয়ম এবং রাজ্ঞী মেরীর সময়ে ব্যবহৃত স্ত্রীলোকদিগের টুপি বিশেষ। **2.** A close-stool ; মলত্যাগের পাত্র। **3.** A chest of drawers ; দেরাজ। **4.** An ornamental cup-board ; কারুকার্য্যখচিত তাক।

cŏm-mö′-di-ous(-ŭs), *adj.* **1.** Suitable or convenient ; উপযোগী, সুবিধাজনক। **2.** Spacious ; as, a *commodious* room ; বিস্তীর্ণ, সুপ্রশস্ত। **—ly,** *adv.* **—ness,** *n.*

cŏm-mŏd′-i-tȳ, *n.* **1.** A useful thing ; আবশ্যক সামগ্রী। **2.** An article of trade ; পণ্য দ্রব্য।

cŏm′-mö-döre, *n.* **1.** A naval officer commanding a few ships of war when these are detached for any purpose from the rest of the fleet ; যে পোতাধ্যক্ষ রণপোত-বহর হইতে কার্য্য-ব্যপদেশে বিশ্লিষ্ট রণপোত সমূহের অধিনায়কতা করেন। **2.** By courtesy, the senior captain when two or more ships of war are cruising in company ; the president in a yachting club ; একত্র বিচরণকারী দুই বা ততোধিক যুদ্ধ জাহাজের অধ্যক্ষের মধ্যে সর্ব্বপ্রধান অধ্যক্ষের শিষ্টাচারসূচক উপাধি ; প্রমোদপোত সমিতির সভাপতি। **3.** The leading vessel of a fleet of merchantmen ; বাণিজ্য পোতশ্রেণীর মধ্যে সর্ব্বাগ্রগামী পোত।

cŏm′-mŏn, *adj.* & *n.* **1.** Belonging equally to ; coming from, or done by more than one ; সাধারণ ; দুই বা ততোধিক লোক হইতে আগত বা দুই বা ততোধিক লোক দ্বারা সম্পাদিত। **2.** General ; সর্ব্বজনীন। **3.** Often met with ; সচরাচর দৃষ্ট। **4.** Ordinary ; সামান্য, প্রাকৃত। **5.** Without rank or position ; as, *common* soldier ; পদবীহীন, সাধারণ। **6.** Of inferior quality ; নিকৃষ্টশ্রেণীর, অধম। **7.** Vulgar or mean ; নীচ, ইতর। **8.** (*Gram.*) Applicable to a whole class ; জাতিবাচক। **9.** (*Math.*) Belonging to two or more quantities ; (গণিত) দুই বা ততোধিক রাশির মধ্যে সাধারণ। ***Noun.*** **1.** An inclosed or uninclosed tract of ground for pleasure, and pasturage, etc., the use of which belongs to the public ; সর্ব্বসাধারণের ব্যবহার্য্য উন্মুক্ত প্রান্তর, গোষ্ঠ, গোচারণ-ভূমি, সাধারণ-ভূমি। **2.** The common people ; সাধারণ লোক। **3.** All below the rank of nobility ; সাধারণ লোকশ্রেণী, প্রাকৃত জন। **—a-ble,** *adj.* **1.** (*Of animals*) That may be pastured in common land ; (জন্তু-সম্পর্কে) সাধারণ ভূমিতে চারণযোগ্য। **2.** (*Of land*) Held in common ;

(ভূমি-সম্পর্কে) অন্যের সহিত সহযোগীতায় অধিকৃত, সাধারণ। **—age,** *n.* **1.** The right of pasturing on a common ; সাধারণ ভূমিতে গোচারণাধিকার। **2.** The right of using anything in common; সাধারণের ব্যবহারাধিকার। **Common Bench, Court of common Pleas**—ইংলণ্ডের উচ্চ আদালতের বিভাগবিশেষ। **Common-book**—স্মারক পুস্তক। **Common crier**—সংবাদ-ঘোষণাকারী। **Common gender**—উভয় লিঙ্গ। **Common hall**—সাধারণ গৃহ। **Common law**—ইংলণ্ডের অলিখিত প্রথামূলক আইন, দেশাচার। **Common Noun**—(ব্যাকরণে) জাতিবাচক বিশেষ্য। **Common prayer**—The liturgy of the Church of England ; ইংলণ্ডীয় ধর্ম্মসমাজের উপাসনারীতি, গীতস্তোত্রাবলী। **Common room**—স্কুল, কালেজ ও তদ্রূপ কোন প্রতিষ্ঠানের যে কক্ষে সমস্ত শিক্ষকগণ মিলিত হন, বিশেষতঃ (অক্সফোর্ড বিশ্ববিদ্যালয়ে) মধ্যাহ্ন ভোজনান্তে যে গৃহে সদস্যগণ মিলিত হন। **Common school**—সাধারণ বিদ্যালয়। **Common seal**—সমবায় প্রভৃতির সীলমোহর। **Common sense**—Normal understanding ; sound practical judgment ; সাধারণ বুদ্ধি ; সহজ বুদ্ধি, স্থূল বুদ্ধি, কাণ্ডজ্ঞান। **Common weal**—জনহিত। **Common woman**—গণিকা, সাধারণ স্ত্রী (সাঃ দঃ)। **In common**—Together ; একযোগে। Equally with others ; অন্যের সহিত সমানভাবে। **Out of common**—অসাধারণ, সৃষ্টি-ছাড়া। **Philosophy of common sense**—যে দার্শনিক মতানুসারে মানবজাতির সর্ব্বজন-স্বীকৃত ধারণাসমূহ পুঙ্খানুপুঙ্খরূপে বিচার বিনা সত্য বলিয়া গৃহীত হইয়া থাকে। **The common good**—The interest of the community at large ; সর্ব্বজনীন স্বার্থ। **The common people**—The people in general ; জনসাধারণ। **To make common cause with**—To have the same interests and aims with ; সমান স্বার্থ ও উদ্দেশ্য থাকা। To join ; যোগদান করা।

cŏm′-mŏn-ăl-tȳ, cŏm-mŏn-ăl′-i-tȳ, *n.* The general body of the people without any distinction of rank or authority ; জনসাধারণ।

cŏm′-mŏn-êr, *n.* **1.** One of the common people ; সাধারণ লোক। **2.** A member of the House of Commons ; ইংলণ্ডের প্রাকৃত সভার সভ্য। **3.** One who has joint right in common ground ; সাধারণ ভূমিরতুল্য স্বত্বাধিকারী। **4.** A student in Oxford University who pays his way independently ; অক্স্‌ফোর্ড বিশ্ববিদ্যালয়ের যে ছাত্র আহারের ব্যয় নিজে নির্ব্বাহ করে।

cŏm′-mŏn-place (-plās), *n., adj., v. t.* & *i.* **1.** An ordinary or common topic ; a trite remark ; সাধারণ প্রসঙ্গ ; নূতনত্বহীন মন্তব্য, নীরস মন্তব্য। **2.** A memorandum ; স্মারক-পুস্তক, সামান্য সন্নিবেশ। ***Adj.*** Common ; trite ; not new ; সাধারণ, সামান্য ; নীরস ; নূতনত্বহীন। ***Verb t.*** To enter in a commonplace book ; স্মারক পুস্তকে লিপিবদ্ধ করা। ***Verb i.*** To extract or publish common places from ; সাধারণ মন্তব্য উদ্ধৃত বা প্রকাশ করা।

cŏm′-mŏns, *n.* **1.** The common people; সাধারণ লোক। **2.** House of Commons ; ইংলণ্ডের প্রাকৃত সভা বা প্রজা সভা। **3.** Food provided at a common table, as in colleges, etc ; কলেজ প্রভৃতিতে একত্রে আহারের জন্য যে খাদ্য যোগান হয়। **4.** Daily fare ; খোরাক, দৈনিক আহার্য্য। **5.** Definite portion of a food supplied at a fixed price ; নিরূপিত মূল্যে যে নির্দ্দিষ্ট পরিমাণ খাদ্যদ্রব্য সরবরাহ করা হয়। **Short commons**—Scant fare ; অপ্রচুর খাদ্য, অপর্য্যাপ্ত খাদ্য সামগ্রী।

cŏm′-mŏn-weal, (-wēl), **cŏm′-mŏn-wealth** (-wĕlth), *n.* **1.** A body politic ; রাষ্ট্র। **2.** A republic ; প্রজাতন্ত্র, সাধারণ তন্ত্র। **3.** A form of government in which the power rests with the people, esp. that in England after the overthrow of Charles I ; প্রজাতন্ত্র শাসনপ্রণালী — এইপ্রকার শাসন-প্রণালী রাজা প্রথম চার্ল্‌সের রাজ্যচ্যুতির পর অল্প সময়ের জন্য ইংলণ্ডে প্রতিষ্ঠিত হইয়াছিল।

cŏm-mō′-tion, *n.* **1.** Physical disturbance ; ভৌতিক বিক্ষোভ। **2.** A disturbance ; tumult ; all public agitation ; rebellion ; গণ্ডগোল, হুলস্থুল ; জনবিক্ষোভ ; বিদ্রোহ।

cŏm-môve′, *v. t.* **1.** To put in motion ; সঞ্চালিত করা, আলোড়িত করা। **2.** To excite ; উদ্দীপ্ত করা।

cŏm′-müne, *n.* **1.** A small territorial district in France under a mayor in the country sometimes embracing a number of villages, while some of the large cities are divided into a number of communes ; ফরাসী দেশে মেয়রের অধীন ক্ষুদ্র বিভাগ। **2.** Similar division elsewhere ; ফরাসী ব্যতিরিক্ত অন্যান্যদেশের উক্তপ্রকার বিভাগ। **3.** The inhabitants of a commune ; উক্ত বিভাগের অধিবাসিবর্গ। **4.** A revolt in Paris in 1871, in favour of communalistic government ; সমাজতন্ত্র প্রতিষ্ঠাকল্পে প্যারী নগরীতে ১৮৭১ খৃঃ অব্দে যে বিদ্রোহ হইয়াছিল। **—mu′-nal,** *adj.* **1.** Of the commune ; ফরাসীদেশের শাসন-সম্পর্কীয় ক্ষুদ্র বিভাগ-সংক্রান্ত। **2.** Of the Paris commune ; প্যারী নগরীর ১৮৭১ খৃষ্টাব্দের বিদ্রোহ সংক্রান্ত। **3.** Of the commonalty ; জনসাধারণ সংক্রান্ত। **—mu-nis′-tic,** *adj.*

cŏm′-müne, *n.* Familiar conversation ; বিশ্রম্ভালাপ, সম্ভাষণ।

cŏm-müne′, *v. i.* **1.** To hold intimate converse with ; অন্তরঙ্গ আলাপ করা। **2.** To partake of the Lord's supper ; খৃষ্টের শেষ ভোজনের স্মৃতিস্বরূপ রুটি ও সুরা গ্রহণ করা। **—mu-nism,** *n.*

cŏm-mū'-ni-cāte, *v. t.* & *i.* **1.** To impart ; to bestow ; to acquaint with ; বিতরণ করা, সঞ্চার করা ; প্রদান করা ; প্রকাশ করা, জ্ঞাত করা। **2.** To admister Holy Communion ; খৃষ্টের শেষ ভোজনের স্মৃতিস্বরূপ রুটি ও মদিরা প্রদান করা। ***Verb i.*** **1.** To have intercourse ; to interchange thoughts ; সংসর্গ করা, যোগাযোগ থাকা, আলাপ পরিচয় থাকা ; মনোভাবের আদান প্রদান করা। **2.** To correspond ; চিঠিপত্র লিখা। **3.** To partake of the Communion ; খৃষ্টের শেষ ভোজনের স্মৃতি স্বরূপ রুটি ও সুরা গ্রহণ করা। **4.** To afford access to ; as, a dining room *communicating* with his bed-room ; প্রবেশ করিতে দেওয়া। **—ca-ble,** *adj.* **1.** That may be communicated or imparted ; জ্ঞাত করণযোগ্য, সঞ্চারযোগ্য। **2.** Communicative ; আলাপ-প্রিয়। **—cant,** *n.* **1.** One who partakes of or receives, Holy Communion ; খৃষ্টের শেষ ভোজন পর্ব্বের স্মৃতিচিহ্নস্বরূপ রুটি ও মদিরা গ্রহণকারী **2.** One who imparts information ; সংবাদদাতা। **—ca-tive,** *adj.* **1.** Inclined to communicate or impart to other ; বিজ্ঞাপক, সঞ্চারকারী, প্রদানশীল। **2.** Talkative ; আলাপপ্রিয়, আলাপী। **—ca-tive-ly,** *adv.* **—ca-tive-ness,** *n.* **—ca-tor,** *n.* **1.** A person or thing that communicates ; সঞ্চারকারী বস্তু বা ব্যক্তি, প্রদাতা, প্রদানকারী, জ্ঞাপনকারী। **2.** A contrivance enabling passengers in a railway carriage to communicate with the guard in cases of danger or accident ; বাষ্পীয় শকটের কক্ষ সমূহে স্থাপিত যন্ত্রবিশেষ,—যৎসাহায্যে যাত্রিগণ বিপদ বা দুর্ঘটনার সময়ে রক্ষককে সংবাদ প্রদান করে, সঙ্কট-সংজ্ঞাপক। **3.** The part of a telegraph-instrument used in sending messages ; তাড়িত-বার্ত্তাবহ যন্ত্রের অংশ বিশেষ,—যৎসাহায্যে বার্ত্তা প্রেরিত হয়, প্রেরক (হিঃ কোঃ), সঞ্চারক (ঐ)।

cŏm-mū-ni-cā'-tion, *n.* **1.** The act of imparting news ; সংবাদ-জ্ঞাপন। **2.** Interchange of thoughts or opinion ; intercourse ; মত বা মনোভাবের আদান প্রদান; পরিচয় প্রসঙ্গ, সংসর্গ। **3.** Correspondence ; চিঠিপত্র। **4.** News ; সন্দেশ, সংবাদ। **5.** Connecting passage or opening ; যাতায়াতের পথ বা দ্বার।

cŏm-mūn'-ion (-yŏn), *n.* **1.** Participation ; সহকারিতা, সহভাগিতা। **2.** Fellowship ; সহযোগিতা। **3.** Intercourse ; interchange of thoughts or opinion ; যোগাযোগ, সংসর্গ ; মত বা মনোভাবের আদান প্রদান। **4.** The celebration of the Lord's supper ; খৃষ্টের শেষ ভোজন নামক ক্রিয়ার অনুষ্ঠান। **5.** A body of Christians who have one common faith and discipline ; কোন বিশেষ সম্প্রদায়ভুক্ত খৃষ্ট-ধর্ম্মাবলম্বিবর্গ, খৃষ্টীয় সমাজ। **—ist,** *n.* One who is of the communion ; এক সম্প্রদায়ভুক্ত খৃষ্ট ধর্ম্মাবলম্বিগণ। **Communion elements**—খৃষ্টের শেষ ভোজন নামক ক্রিয়া অনুষ্ঠানকালে ব্যবহৃত রুটি ও মদিরা। **Communion service**—খৃষ্টের শেষ ভোজন নামক ক্রিয়ানুষ্ঠানকালীন উপাসনা বিশেষ। **Communion table**—খৃষ্টের শেষ ভোজন ক্রিয়ার অনুষ্ঠানকালে যে মেজের নিকটে জানু পাতিয়া উপবেশন করত খৃষ্টীয় উপাসকগণ রুটি ও মদিরা গ্রহণ করেন।

cŏm'-mū-nĭsm, *n.* A theory or condition of things according to which private property should be abolished and all things held in common ; সম্যবাদিগণের মতবাদ বিশেষ—এই মত অনুসারে সম্পত্তিতে ব্যক্তিগত অধিকার লোপ এবং দেশের সমস্ত সম্পত্তিতে সর্ব্বসাধারণের সমান অধিকার প্রতিষ্ঠিত করিতে হইবে। [See NORDOHOFF'S *The Communistic societies of the United States.*] সাধারণস্বত্ববাদ (হিঃ কোঃ), সামাজিত্ববাদ (ঐ), গণতন্ত্র (সাঃ পঃ), সাজ্যিকতা (ঐ)। **—nist,** *n.* One who holds such a principle ; সাধারণস্বত্ববাদী। **—nis'-tic,** *adj.*

cŏm-mū'-ni-tȳ, *n.* **1.** Common possession or enjoyment ; সাধারণাধিকার বা ভোগ। **2.** A body of people having common rights, privileges, or interests or living in the same locality ; গোষ্ঠী, মণ্ডলী, প্রজা, সঙ্ঘ (সাঃ পঃ)। **3.** Society at large ; জন-সাধারণ, জনসমাজ। **4.** Social intercourse ; "There can be no *community* between you and me ;" মেলামিশা, সমাগম। **5.** Likeness ; as, the points of *community* in their nature ; সাদৃশ্য, সমানতা সাধারণতা (রাঃ তঃ)।

cŏm-mūte', *v. t.* & *i.* **1.** To exchange ; বিনিময় করা, পরিবর্ত্তন করা। **2.** To exchange a punishment for one less severe ; "The capital sentence was *commuted* to imprisonment for life." গুরুতর দণ্ডের পরিবর্ত্তে অপেক্ষাকৃত লঘু দণ্ড বিধান করা। ***Verb i.*** To pay or arrange to pay, in gross instead of part by part ; একসঙ্গে দেওয়া বা দেওয়ার বন্দোবস্ত করা। **—mut-a-bil'-i-ty,** *n.* **—mut'-a-ble,** *adj.* Capable of being interchanged ; বিনিময়যোগ্য, পরিবর্ত্তনসহ, পরিবর্ত্তনীয়। **—mut'-a-ble-ness,** *n.* **—mu-ta'-tion,** *n.* **1.** The act of commuting ; change ; বিনিময় ; পরিবর্ত্তন। **2.** The substitution of lesser punishment for a greater ; গুরুতর দণ্ডের স্থলে লঘুতর দণ্ড বিধান। [illegible]le of commutation—স্থানীয়[illegible]র (হিঃ কোঃ), শীঘ্রকেন্দ্র (সাঃ [illegible]

cŏ'-mōse, *a*[illegible]*Bot.*) Ending in hair ; h[illegible], পুচ্ছী (সাঃ পঃ) ; কেশময়, লোমশ।

cŏm′-păct, *adj., v.t.* & *n.* **1.** Closely packed together ; দৃঢ়-সংবদ্ধ। **2.** Solid ; condensed ; সংহত ; ঘনীভূত, নিবিড়, গাঢ়, সান্দ্র। **3.** (*Fig.*) Brief ; (লক্ষণায়) সংক্ষিপ্ত। *Verb t.* **1.** To press closely together ; ঘনীভূত করা, সংহত করা। **2.** To unite or connect firmly ; দৃঢ়-সংলগ্ন করা, দৃঢ়-সংবদ্ধ করা। *Noun.* An agreement between parties ; চুক্তি, করার, নিয়ম, দৃঢ়-সন্ধি। **—ly,** *adv.* **—ness,** *n.* The state of being compact ; সংঘাত, সংহত্ব, সংহতি, সংক্ষেপ।

cŏm-păn′-ion (-yŏn), *n.* A skylight on an upper deck with frames and sashes of various shapes ; জাহাজের কামরা এবং তন্নিম্নবর্ত্তী পাটাতনে আলোক প্রবেশার্থ ব্যবস্থা বিশেষ। **The companion ladder**—জাহাজের পাটাতন হইতে কামরায় গমনাগমনের জন্য সিঁড়ি, জাহাজের পশ্চাদ্‌ভাগস্থ উচ্চ পাটাতন হইতে কর্ম্মচারীদিগের কামরায় উঠিবার সিঁড়ি।

cŏm-păn′-ion (-yŏn), *n.* **1.** One who keeps company or frequently associates with another ; সহচর, সঙ্গী, সাথী, বয়স্য, সহায়ক, সখা, সমভিব্যাহারী। **2.** A knight of lowest rank in certain orders ; as, a *companion* of the Bath ; ইংলণ্ডের কোন কোন সম্ভ্রান্ত-শ্রেণীর সর্ব্বনিম্নপদবীর লোক। **—a-ble,** *adj.* **1.** Fitted to be a companion ; সহচরোপযোগী। **2.** Agreeable ; sociable ; "Each *companionable* guest ;" প্রিয় ; সামাজিক। **—a-bly,** *adv.* **—less,** *adj.* Without a companion ; সহচর বিহীন। **—ship,** *n.* Fellowship ; সাহচর্য্য, সখিত্ব, সখিতা, সহভাব, বয়স্যত্ব।

com′-pă-ny̆ (cŭm-), *n.* & *v. i.* **1.** Fellowship ; society ; friendly intercourse ; সাহচর্য্য ; সঙ্গ, সংসর্গ ; বন্ধুভাবে মিলামিশা। **2.** A companion ; সহচর। **3.** A number of persons assembled ; একত্র সমবেত ব্যক্তিবর্গ, সভা, সমাজ, পরিষৎ, মণ্ডলী, বৈঠক, দল। **4.** Guests or visitors ; as, to invite the *company* to dine ; অতিথি বা অভ্যাগত ব্যক্তি। **5.** An association of persons for the purpose of carrying on some enterprise or business ; ব্যবসায় বাণিজ্যর অভিপ্রায়ে সম্মিলিত ব্যক্তিবর্গ, ব্যবসায়ি-সঙ্ঘ। **5.** (*Colloq.*) Partners in a firm ; (চলিত ভাষায়) বাণিজ্যাগারের অংশীদার। **7.** A subdivision of a regiment of troops under the command of a captain ; কাপ্তানের অধীন সেনাপল্টনের বিভাগ বিশেষ। **8.** The crew of a ship, including the officers ; জাহাজের সমগ্র নাবিকদল ও কর্ম্মচারিবৃন্দ। **9.** The body of actors employed in a theatre ; নাটকের অভিনেতৃবর্গ, নাটকীয় পাত্র ও পাত্রীগণ। *Verb i.* To associate ; সঙ্গ করা। **To be good** or **bad company**—To have or to lack companionable qualities ; দশজনের সঙ্গে মেলামিশা করিবার উপযোগী গুণ থাকা বা না থাকা। **To keep company**—সঙ্গ করা, সংসর্গ করা। **To know a man by his company** — To determine his character by the quality of his friends ; কোন ব্যক্তির সংসর্গ দ্বারা তাহার স্বভাবের পরিচয় পাওয়া।

cŏm-pāre′, *v. t.* & *i.* **1.** To liken or represent as similar ; তুলনা করা, সাদৃশ্য করা। **2.** (*Gram.*) To form comparative and superlative degrees of (adjective and adverb) ; (ব্যাকরণ) বিশেষণের উত্তর তর বা তম যোগ করা। *Verb i.* To bear comparison ; as, this book does not *compare* with that ; তুলনা হওয়া। **Com′-pa-ra-ble,** *adj.* Capable of being compared ; worthy of comparison ; তুল্য, তুলনীয় ; উপমেয়, তুলনার যোগ্য। **Com′-pa-ra-ble-ness,** *n.* **Com′-pa-ra-bly,** *adv.* **—par′-a-tive,** *adj.* & *n.* **1.** Suitable for, or pertaining to, comparison ; তুলনা-সম্বন্ধীয়, তুলনার উপযোগী। **2.** Not positive or absolute ; estimated by comparison ; as, *comparative* claims of pleasures and wisdom ; আপেক্ষিক ; তুলনামূলক। **3.** (*Gram.*) Involving or pertaining to the second of the three degrees of comparison ; উৎকর্ষবাচক (ব্যাকরণ) তর প্রত্যয়ান্তক। (*Noun.*) An adjective inflected, expressing more or less ; (ব্যাকরণে) তর-প্রত্যয়ান্ত বিশেষণ পদ। **—par′-a-tive-ly,** *adv.* **—par′-i-son,** *n.* **1.** The act of comparing ; তুলনাকরণ, মুকাবেলা। **2.** The state of being compared ; সাম্য, সাদৃশ্য, ঔপম্য, উপমা, উপমিত, তুলনা। **3.** (*Gram.*) The inflection of an adjective in its several degrees ; উৎকর্ষাপকর্ষ দ্যোতনার্থ বিশেষণ পদের রূপান্তর সাধন। **4.** (*Rhet.*) A figure by which two things are compard together with regard to some quality or property common to both ; as, *the lake sparkled like a jewel* ; (অলঙ্কার-শাস্ত্র) উপমালঙ্কার, দৃষ্টান্তালঙ্কার, উপমান। **Beyond comparison** — অনুপম, অতুলনীয়। **By way of comparison**—By way of illustration ; উপমাচ্ছলে, উদাহরণচ্ছলে। In comparison with ; তুলনায়। **To compare notes**—To exchange opinions or views ; to compare results of investigation or enquiry ; মতামতের আদান প্রদান করা, মনোভাবের বিনিময় করা ; অনুসন্ধানের ফলাফল তুলনা করা।

cŏm-pârt′, *v. t.* To subdivide ; ক্ষুদ্রতর অংশে বিভাগ করা, অবান্তর বিভাগ করা।

cŏm-pârt′-mĕnt, *n.* **1.** A separate part of a general design ; ছেদ, ভাগ, বিভাগ। **2.** A division of a railway carriage, room, etc. ; রেলগাড়ীর কামরা, কক্ষ, প্রকোষ্ঠ। **3.** A water-tight division of a ship ; জল-প্রবেশ-পথ-শূন্য পোত-প্রকোষ্ঠ।

com′-pass (kŭm-păs), *n.* & *v. t.* **1.** A circuit ; চক্র, মণ্ডল। **2.** Space ;

limit ; area ; স্থান ; সীমা ; সীমাবচ্ছিন্ন স্থান। 3. Circumference ; পরিধি, বেষ্টন। 4. Range or extent ; as, the *compass* of his eye ; গমন-দূরত্ব, বিষয়, প্রসর। 5. Range of a voice ; শব্দের গমন দূরত্ব। 6. An instrument consisting of a magnetised needle, used to steer ships by, etc. ; দিগ্‌দর্শন যন্ত্র, দিঙ্‌নির্ণয় যন্ত্র, মৎস্য-যন্ত্র (রাধাকুঃ)। 7. (*Pl.*) An instrument with two legs for describing circles, etc. ; বৃত্তাদি অঙ্কনের জন্য যন্ত্র বিশেষ, কম্পাস যন্ত্র, কর্কট-যন্ত্র (সাঃ পঃ)। ***Verb t.*** 1. To go round or about ; প্রদক্ষিণ করা। 2. To surround ; to encircle ; পরিবেষ্টিত করা ; পরিবৃত করা। 3. To grasp with the mind ; to comprehend fully ; "Strange forebodings of ill that cannot be *compassed* ;" অবধারণ করা ; উপলব্ধি করা। 4. To accomplish ; সাধন বা সম্পাদন করা। 5. To plot ; as, to *compass* the death of any person ; ষড়যন্ত্র করা। **–a-ble,** *adj.* **Compass-box** — যে কাচাচ্ছাদিত বাক্সের ভিতর দিগ্‌দর্শন যন্ত্রের সূচী ও গোলাকৃতি স্থূল কাগজখণ্ড থাকে। **Compass-card** — দিগ্‌দর্শন যন্ত্রের চক্রাকার স্থূল কাগজ খণ্ড। **Compass-dial**—টেকে রাখার উপযোগী একপ্রকার সূর্য্য ঘড়ী। **Compass-needle** — দিগ্‌দর্শন যন্ত্রের দিঙ্‌নির্ণয়ার্থ সূচী। **Compass-plane**—ন্যুব্জ পৃষ্ঠ বস্তুর উপরিভাগ রাঁদা করার জন্য যন্ত্রবিশেষ। **Compass-saw** — মণ্ডলাকার করপত্র, গোলাকার করাত। **Compass signal** — দিগ্‌ দর্শন যন্ত্রের দিগ্‌বিন্দু সূচক। **Mariner's compass** — A declination compass used in guiding the course of a ship ; পোতের গতিপথ-নির্দ্দেশক দিঙ্‌নির্ণয়-যন্ত্র বিশেষ, মৎস্যযন্ত্র (রাধা কুঃ)। **To fetch a compass**—To go round in circuits ; চক্রাকারে ভ্রমণ করা। **Within compass**—Within fixed limit ; নির্দ্দিষ্ট সীমার মধ্যে।

cŏm-pas'-sion (-pă-), *n.* Sympathy with sufferings and sorrows of others ; পরদুঃখকাতরতা, দয়া, সহানুভূতি, করুণা, কম্পা। **–a-ble,** *adj.* **–ate,** *adj.* Having a tender heart ; merciful ; pitiful ; সকরুণ, পরদুঃখকাতর ; করুণার্দ্র দয়াশীল, সদয়, কারুণিক ; সকৃপ, কৃপালু। **–ate-ly,** *adv.* **–ate-ness,** *n.*

cŏm-păt'-i-ble, *adj.* Consistent ; in harmony with ; অবিরুদ্ধ ; সঙ্গতি-বিশিষ্ট, অনুসারী, সুসঙ্গত। **–bil'-i-ty,** *n.* The quality of being compatible ; সুসঙ্গতি, যোগ্যতা, অনুসারিত্ব। **–bly,** *adv.* **–ness,** *n.*

cŏm-pa'-tri-ŏt, *n.* A fellow country man ; স্বদেশবাসী, স্বদেশীয়, সাংস্থানিক। **–ism,** *n.*

cŏm-peer' (-pēr), *n.* 1. An equal ; সমান ব্যক্তি, সমতুল্যব্যক্তি। 2. A companion ; বয়স্য, সঙ্গী, সহচর।

cŏm-pĕl', *v. t.* 1. (*Poet.*) To drive or urge with force ; বলপূর্ব্বক চালিত করা, প্রবর্ত্তিত করা। 2. To oblige to do any act ; কোন কার্য্য করিতে বাধ্য করা। 3. To exact by rightful claim ; as, he *compelled* a certain admiration from all men ; জোর করিয়া আদায় করা।

cŏm'-pĕnd, *n.* Same as COMPENDIUM.

cŏm-pĕn'-di-ŭm, *n.* An abridgment ; a summary ; সংক্ষেপ ; সংক্ষিপ্তসার, সারসংগ্রহ, সংহিতা ; সারমর্ম্ম। **–ous,** *adj.* Brief but comprehensive (of works and authors) ; সংক্ষিপ্ত, অবিস্তার। **–ous-ly,** *adv.* **–ous-ness,** *n.*

cŏm'-pĕn-sāte, *v. t.* & *i.* To make amends ; to recompense ; ক্ষতিপূরণ করা ; প্রতিকার করা। 2. (*Fig.*) To furnish an equivalent for ; (লক্ষণায়) তুল্যরূপ প্রতিদান করা। 3. (*Mech.*) To make up for the variation to which a pendulum is liable ; (যন্ত্র-বিজ্ঞান) ঘড়ী প্রভৃতির দোলকের দোলনাহেতু সময়ের যে ব্যতিক্রম হয়, তাহা পূরণ বা সংশোধন করা। ***Verb i.*** To make amends ; ক্ষতিপূরণ করা। **–pen'-sa-tive,** *adj.* & *n.* **–pen'-sa-to-ry,** *adj.* **–sa-tor,** *n.*

cŏm-pĕn-sā'-tion, *n.* 1. The act of compensating ; ক্ষতিপূরণ। 2. What is given to supply a loss or make good a deficiency ; হানি-মূল্য, ক্ষতিপূরণ স্বরূপ প্রদত্ত বস্তু, ক্ষতি-পূরণ। **Compensation balance** or **pendulum** — জলবায়ু বা শীতাতপের বৈষম্যহেতু যাহাদের কোন প্রকার ব্যতিক্রম হয় না, তদ্রূপ তুলাযন্ত্র বা দোলক।

cŏm-pete' (-pēt), *v. t.* 1. To strive with others for something ; to rival ; একই বস্তু পাইবার জন্য অপরের সহিত প্রতিযোগিতা করা ; প্রতিদ্বন্দ্বী হওয়া। **–pe-ti'-tion,** *n.* Strife for superiority ; rivalry ; প্রাধান্য লাভের চেষ্টা ; প্রতিদ্বন্দ্বিতা, প্রতিযোগিতা। **–pet'-i-tive,** *adj.* Pertaining to or based on competition ; প্রতি-যোগিতা-সংক্রান্ত, প্রতিযোগিতা-মূলক **–pet'-i-tor,** *adj.* Rival ; প্রতিদ্বন্দ্বী, প্রতিযোগী। **Competition-wallah**— A member of I. C. S, chosen by competition ; প্রতিযোগিতা-মূলক পরীক্ষাদ্বারা নির্ব্বাচিত ভারতীয় সিভিল সার্ব্বিসের কর্ম্মচারী।

cŏm'-pē-tĕnt, *adj.* 1. Fit ; capable ; suitable ; qualified ; কর্ম্ম-ক্ষম, সমর্থ ; কর্ম্মকুশল, লায়েক (*Colloq.*) ; উপযুক্ত, যোগ্য, উপযোগী ; যথোচিত গুণ-সম্পন্ন। 2. (*Law*) Having right or power ; (আইন) ক্ষমতাবান্‌, অধিকারী। 3. Properly belonging ; as, it was *competent* to him to refuse ; সমুচিত, পরিমিত। **–tence, –ten-cy,** *ns.* 1. Fitness ; উপযুক্ততা, শক্তি, সামর্থ্য। 2. Sufficiency of means to live comfortably ; সুখে স্বচ্ছন্দে জীবনযাত্রা নির্ব্বাহের পক্ষে উপযুক্ত সম্পত্তি। 3. Legal power or capacity ; বৈধক্ষমতা বা অধিকার। **–ly,** *adv.*

cŏm-pīle', *v. t.* To select or put together for publication ; সমাহরণ

করা, সঙ্কলন করা, সংগ্রহ করা। **—pi-la′-tion,** *n.* **1.** The act of compiling ; পুস্তক সংগ্রহ। **—pil′-er,** *n.* One who compiles ; সংগ্রহকার, সঙ্কলয়িতা।

cŏm-plā′-cĕnt, *adj.* Satisfied ; আত্মতৃপ্ত, প্রসন্ন, সন্তুষ্ট। **—cence, —cen-cy,** *ns.* Calm contentment ; satisfaction, esp. self-satisfaction ; শান্তি, প্রসাদ, প্রসন্নতা, তুষ্টি, সন্তোষ তৃপ্তি ; পরিতোষ। **—ly,** *adv.*

cŏm-plain′ (-plān), *v. t.* **1.** To express grief or pain ; to murmur ; খেদ করা, বিলাপ করা ; অসন্তোষ প্রকাশ করা। **2.** To make a charge against ; অভিযোগ করা, নালিশ করা। **3.** To announce that one is suffering from (a headache etc.) ; (শিরঃপীড়া প্রভৃতি হইতে) যন্ত্রণা পাইতেছে বলিয়া বলা। **—ant′,** *n.* Plaintiff ; পূর্ব্বপক্ষ, ফরিয়াদী, বাদী, অভিযোক্তা। **—er,** *n.* **—plaint′,** *n.* **1.** An expression of grief, regret or resentment ; দুঃখ-প্রকাশ, বিলাপ। **2.** A formal accusation ; অভিযোগ, নালিশ। **3.** Cause or ground of complaint ; অভিযোগের হেতু বা কারণ। **4.** A bodily ailment ; ব্যাধি, আর্ত্তি, পীড়া, রোগ, আময়। **To lodge a complaint**—To bring an accusation against somebody ; কাহারও বিরুদ্ধে নালিস রুজু করা, মোকদ্দমা দায়ের করা।

cŏm′-plai-sănt (-plā-), *adj.* Desirous of pleasing ; courteous ; প্রসন্নকরণেচ্ছু ; শিষ্ট। **—sance,** *n.* **1.** Politeness ; courtesy ; শিষ্টতা ; ভদ্রতা। **2.** Deference ; as, she is never treated afterwards with any degree of *complaisance* ; শ্রদ্ধা, সম্মান। **—ly,** *adv.* **—ness,** *n.*

cŏm′-plĕ-mĕnt, *n.* **1.** That which completes ; পূরক, অনুপূরক। **2.** (*Gram.*) One or more words joined to another to complete the sense ;' (ব্যাকরণ) অনুপূরক শব্দ। **3.** (*Naut.*) Full number required (to man ship) ; "The *complement* of the fleet was fixed at twelve hundred souls ;" (নৌ-বিদ্যা) জাহাজের নাবিকগণের পূর্ণসংখ্যা। **4.** (*Math.*) What is wanted in an arc or angle to make it up to 90° degrees ; (গণিত-শাস্ত্র) পূরক (হিঃ:কোঃ), কোটি (ঐ)। **—men′-tal,** *adj.* **—men′-ta-ry,** *adj.* & *n.* **1.** Serving to complete ; পূরণকারী, পূরণাত্মক। (*Noun.*) **1.** (*Math.*) The difference between the arc or angle and 90° ; কোণ বা বৃত্তাংশের সহিত ৯০ অংশের প্রভেদ, পূরক (হিঃ কোঃ)।

cŏm′-plĕ-mĕnt, *v. t.* To supply a lack ; to supplement ; অভাব পূরণ করা ; অনুপূরণ করা।

cŏm-plēte′, *adj.* **1.** Perfect ; entire ; সর্ব্বাঙ্গসম্পন্ন, পূর্ণ ; অখণ্ড। **2.** Finished ; as, the edifice is *complete* ; সমাপ্ত, নিষ্পন্ন, সিদ্ধ, সম্পন্ন। **3.** Unqualified ; as, *complete* surprise ; অবিমিশ্র। **—ly,** *adv.* **—ness,** *n.*

cŏm-plēte′, *v. t.* **1.** To perfect ; to furnish or equip fully ; সর্ব্বাঙ্গ নিষ্পন্ন করা ; সুসজ্জিত করা। **2.** To finish ; সমাপন করা, সমাপ্ত করা, পূর্ণ করা, শেষ করা, সাধন করা, সুসম্পন্ন করা। **—ple′-tion,** *n.* The getting through the end ; সমাপ্তি, সমাপন, সাধন, পরিসমাপ্তি, সম্পাদন, পরিপূর্ণতা, নিষ্পত্তি, সমাধা, সম্পন্নতা।

cŏm′-plĕx, *adj.* **1.** Composed of two or more parts or things ; composite ; বিভিন্নাংশাত্মক ; মিশ্র। **2.** Not simple ; intricate ; অসরল ; বিষম, জটিল, দুরূহ। **—ly,** *adv.* **—plex′-i-ty,** *n.* The state of being complex in structure ; intricacy ; বৈষম্য ; নানার্থকত্ব, জটিলতা, মিশ্রতা। **Complex sentence**—গর্ভিত বাক্য।

cŏm-plĕx′-ion (-plĕk-shŏn), *n.* **1.** The colour or hue of the skin, particularly of the face ; শরীরের রং, বিশেষতঃ মুখের রং, মুখরাগ। **2.** (*Fig.*) External aspect ; "Skill in putting off the evil day and in giving a fair *complexion* to the present one ;" (লক্ষণায়) আকার, ভাব, প্রকৃতি, ছায়া। **—less,** *adj.* **Fair complexion**—গৌরবর্ণ।

cŏm-plī′-ănce, *n.* **1.** A disposition to assent to just wishes of others ; submission ; সম্মতি ; বশ্যতা, বশবর্ত্তিতা, বশম্বদত্ব। **2.** Complaisance ; শীল, শিষ্টাচার। **In compliance with**—According to ; কাহারও ইচ্ছা, প্রস্তাব বা প্রার্থনানুসারে, অনুরোধে, বশবর্ত্তী হইয়া।

cŏm-plī′-ănt, *adj.* Submissive ; yielding ; বাধ্য, অনুবর্ত্তী, নম্র, বিনয়ী, বিনীত ; বচনগ্রাহী। **—ly,** *adv.*

cŏm′-pli-cāte, *adj.* Intricate ; difficult to analyse ; জড়িত, জটিল ; দুরূহ।

cŏm′-pli-cāte, *v. t.* To twist or knit together ; to make complex ; জড়িত করা ; জটিল করা, সঙ্কুল করা। **—ca-cy,** *n.* Complexity ; জটিলতা। **—cat-ed,** *adj.* Intricate ; দুরূহ।

cŏm-pli-cā′-tion, *n.* **1.** Involved or intricate perplexity ; entanglement ; জটিলতা ; জড়িতভাব। **2.** Something complicated ; জটিল ব্যাপার। **Complication of a disease**—রোগের উপসর্গ, এক রোগে অপর রোগের বিদ্যমানতা।

cŏm-plĭc′-i-tў, *n.* Partnership in crime ; অপরাধে সংসৃষ্টতা, দুষ্কর্ম্মে সহযোগিতা, সহকারিতা, যোগসাজস।

cŏm′-pli-mĕnt, *n.* & *v. t.* **1.** An expression of regard or praise ; an act implying praise ; প্রশংসাবাদ, স্তুতিবাদ ; সমাদর প্রকাশ। **2.** A ceremonious greeting, (usu. in *pl.*) ; as, to send one's *compliments* to a friend ; নমস্কার, অভিনন্দন। **3.** (*Archaic*) A gift ; gratuity ; (অপ্রচলিত) উপহার, উপায়ন ; পারিতোষিক। ***Verb t.*** **1.** To address with expressions of approbation or respect ; সমাদর প্রকাশ করা,

শ্রদ্ধা প্রকাশ করা, প্রশংসাবাদ করা **2.** To manifest kindness or regard for by a present; as, I was *complimented* with perfumes; উপহার প্রদান পূর্ব্বক (কাহারও প্রতি) শ্রদ্ধা বা সহানুভূতি প্রদর্শন করা। **–men′-ta-ry,** *adj.* Using or passing compliments; expressive of regard or praise; সমাদরসূচক, সম্মান সূচক; প্রশংসাত্মক, অভিনন্দক। **Left-handed compliment** — স্তুতিচ্ছলে উচ্চারিত নিন্দাবাক্য, ব্যাজস্তুতি। **To make one a compliment**—To show one respect; কাহারও প্রতি সম্মান প্রদর্শন করা। **To make one's compliments to**—To offer formal courtesies to; সাদর সম্ভাষণ করা। **To pay** or **present one's compliments**—To give one's respects or greetings; নমস্কার জ্ঞাপন করা। **To return the compliment**—To say or do something pleasant in return for a previous favour; কোনরূপ অনুগ্রহের প্রতিদানে প্রীতিবাক্য বলা বা প্রীতিকর কার্য্য করা।

cŏm′-plĭn, –pline (-plĭn), *n.* (*R. C. Church*) The last service at night recited after sunset; (রোমান ক্যাথলিক ধর্ম্মসমাজ) নৈশ উপাসনাবিশেষ।

cŏm-plȳ′, *v. i.* To consent or conform; স্বীকার করা, অনুমোদন করা, সম্মত হওয়া, অনুবর্ত্তী হওয়া। **To comply with a request**—কাহারও অনুরোধ রক্ষা করা।

cŏm-pō′-nĕnt, *adj.* & *n.* Forming one of the elements of a compound; উপাদানীভূত। ***Noun.*** A constituent; উপাদান, অঙ্গ, ভাগ।

cŏm-pōrt′, *v. t.* & *i.* To behave or bear oneself; আচরণ করা, চলা ***Verb i.*** To agree or accord; as, such wholesale slaughter does not *comport* with our opinion; মিল হওয়া। **–ment,** *n.* Behaviour; ব্যবহার, আচরণ, চালচলন। **To comport with**—To suit; to befit; সাজা; মানানসই হওয়া।

cŏm-pōse′, *v. t.* **1.** To put together; to make up; (now rarely in the active construction); সমাধান করা; গঠন করা। **2.** To write as an author; প্রণয়ন করা, রচনা করা। **3.** To dispose in proper form; "To *compose* is to arrange unequal things;" যথারীতি সজ্জিত করা। **4.** To calm; to quiet; as, *compose* thy mind; স্থির করা; শান্ত করা। **5.** (*Print.*) To place or arrange in proper order as the types in the composing stick; to set up in type (a manuscript); (মুদ্রণকার্য্যে) অক্ষর পংক্তি সজ্জিত বা বিন্যস্ত করা; হস্ত লিখিত বিষয় মুদ্রাক্ষরে নিবদ্ধ করা। **6.** To originate or write as author; মৌলিক রচনা করা। **7.** To adjust (a dispute, etc.); মীমাংসা করা। **8.** (*Mus.*) To set words to music; স্বরসংযোগ করা, সুরযোজনা করা। **–posed′,** *adj.* **1.** Quiet; শান্ত, ধীর। **2.** Settled; সমাহিত, সুস্থির। **–pos′-ed-ly,** *adv.* **–pos′-ed-ness,** *n.* **–pos′-er,** *n.* One who composes (usu. music); গ্রন্থকর্ত্তা, রচক, রচয়িতা।

cŏm-pōs′-ing, *n.* A placing together; বিন্যাস। **Composing frame**—অক্ষরপূর্ণ কাষ্ঠাধার সমূহ দুই দিকে হেলানভাবে রাখিবার জন্য কাষ্ঠনির্ম্মিত কাঠাম বিশেষ। **Composing machine**—অক্ষর বিন্যাসের যন্ত্র। **Composing room** — অক্ষর বিন্যাস-কক্ষ, যে কক্ষে উপবেশন করত মুদ্রাযন্ত্রের অক্ষর-বিন্যাসকগণ অক্ষর-বিন্যাস করে। **Composing stick**—পিত্তলাদি নির্ম্মিত যন্ত্র বিশেষ—যাহাতে একসঙ্গে কয়েক পংক্তি অক্ষর বিন্যাস করা হয়।

cŏm-pōs′-i-tæ (-tē), *n.* (*Bot.*) The largest order of plants with compound flowers; (উদ্ভিদ্-বিদ্যা) ভৃঙ্গরাজাদি (সাঃ পঃ)।

cŏm-pōs′-ite (-ĭt), *adj.* & *n.* **1.** Made of distinct parts; বিভিন্নাংশাত্মক, বিমিশ্র। **2.** (*Archit.*) Composed upon the Ionic grafted upon the Corinthian; (স্থপতি-বিদ্যা) আইয়োনিক এবং কোরিন্থিয় এই উভয় স্থাপত্যরীতি মিশ্রিত। **3.** (*Bot.*) Of the natural order compositæ; (উদ্ভিদ-বিদ্যা) ভৃঙ্গরাজাদি সংক্রান্ত। **4.** (*Ship building*) Constructed partly of wood and partly of iron; (পোতনির্ম্মাণে) কতকাংশ লৌহ এবং কতকাংশ কাষ্ঠ দ্বারা নির্ম্মিত। ***Noun.*** **1.** Anything made up of different parts or elements; a compound; বিভিন্ন অংশাত্মক বস্তু; বিমিশ্রবস্তু। **2.** (*Arch.*) Fifth classical order—Ionic and Corinthian mixed; (স্থপতি-বিজ্ঞান) আইওনিক এবং করিন্থিয়ান স্থাপত্যরীতি মিশ্রণাত্মক সৌধ-নির্ম্মাণ পদ্ধতি বিশেষ **Composite candle**—নারিকেল এবং কতিপয় রাসায়নিক পদার্থের সংমিশ্রণে প্রস্তুত বাতি বিশেষ। **Composite carriage** — (রেলওয়ে) যে গাড়ীতে বিভিন্ন শ্রেণী থাকে।

cŏm-pō-sĭ′-tion, *n.* **1.** The action of putting together or combining; মিশ্রণ, সংযোগ, বিরচন, গ্রন্থন, সংযোজন, সংযোগ, বিন্যাস, সংস্থান। **2.** A thing formed by the combination of two or more substances; a mixture; মিশ্রদ্রব্য; মিশ্রপদার্থ। **3.** Construction; making up; গঠন; নির্ম্মাণ। **4.** Act of writing for practice in any language; art of literary production; প্রণয়ন; সাহিত্য-রচনা। **5.** Formation of words into a compound word; যৌগিক শব্দ গঠন। **6.** Settlement of a debt by an accepted reduction; as, he made a *composition* with his creditor; পাওনাদারের সহিত রফা। **7.** (*Mus.*) The act of composing music guided by scientific rules; (সঙ্গীতশাস্ত্র) বৈজ্ঞানিক নিয়মসম্মত সঙ্গীত বিরচন। **8.** Mental constitution; as, persons who have a touch of madness in their *composition*; মানসিক প্রকৃতি। **–pos′-i-tive,** *adj.* **Composition of forces**—কোন নির্দ্দিষ্ট দিকে ক্রিয়াশীল

দুই বা ততোধিক বলের সমান কার্য্য-কারী একমাত্র বল সংযোজন, বল-সংযোগ (হিঃ কোঃ)।

cŏm-pŏs′-i-tor (-têr), *n.* **1.** One who composes or sets in order ; রচনাকারী, বিরচক, বিন্যাসকারী। **2.** One who sets up type ; মুদ্রা-যন্ত্রের অক্ষর বিন্যাসক ব্যক্তি, মুদ্রাক্ষর-বিন্যাসক (আঃ বঃ)।

compos mentis, (*L.*) *adj.* In one's right mind ; অবিক্ষিপ্ত, প্রকৃতিস্থভাবে, সদজ্ঞানে। ***Non compos mentis***—Not in one's right mind ; অপ্রকৃতিস্থ ভাবে বা অবস্থায়।

cŏm′-pŏst, *n.* & *v. t.* A mixture of various manures ; মিশ্রসার। ***Verb t.*** To manure with compost ; মিশ্রসার দ্বারা (কোন জমিতে) সার দেওয়া।

cŏm-pō′-sure (-zhür), *n.* Settled state of the mind ; calmness ; শান্তি, স্থৈর্য্য, প্রসাদ, গাম্ভীর্য্য, সুস্থিরতা, অসম্মোহ ; স্থির-বুদ্ধিতা।

cŏm-pō-tā′-tion, *n.* The act of drinking together ; a symposium ; সম্পীতি, সহপান, একত্রে পান ; পানসভা, পানগোষ্ঠী। **Com′-po-ta-tor,** *n.*

cŏm′-pōte, *n.* Fruit preserved in syrup ; মোরব্বা।

cŏm′-pound (-pownd), *adj.* & *n.* **1.** Made up of several ingredients ; consisting of several parts ; সংযুক্ত, সঙ্কর, মিশ্রিত ; বিভিন্ন অংশাত্মক। **2.** (*Gram.*) Formed by the aggregation of independent elements ; (ব্যাকরণ) যৌগিক। **3.** (*Bot.* & *Zool.*) Consisting of a combination of individual organism ; বিমিশ্র। ***Noun.*** **1.** A substance made up of two or more elements, ingredients or parts combined ; মিশ্রদ্রব্য, মিশ্রপদার্থ, যৌগিক পদার্থ (সাঃ পঃ)। **2.** (In India) An inclosure containing a house ; (ভারতবর্ষে) বাটীর চতুঃসীমা। **Compound addition, subtraction, etc.** — মিশ্র সঙ্কলন, মিশ্র বিয়োগ, ইত্যাদি। **Compound interest**—চক্রবৃদ্ধি সুদ। **Compound-fracture**—মিশ্রিত অস্থি-ভগ্ন (অর্থাৎ দুই এর অধিক ভাগে ভগ্ন)। **Compound word**—যৌগিক শব্দ, সমাস, সংযুক্তশব্দ।

cŏm-pound′ (-pownd), *v. t.* & *i.* **1.** To unite two or more ingredients in one mass ; বিভিন্ন উপাদান একত্র মিশ্রিত করা। **2.** (*Gram.*) To form into one word by combination of two or more ; (ব্যাকরণ) সমাস-বদ্ধ করা। **3.** To mix or mingle together so as to form one ; to unite or combine ; মিলান, একত্র করা, যোগ করা, মিশ্রিত করা ; সংযোগ করা। **4.** To settle amicably,—as debt by partial payment, subscription by a lump sum, etc. ; মীমাংসা করা, মিটাইয়া ফেলা, রফা করা। **5.** To condone (liability, offence) for money, etc. ; আপোষে রফা করা। ***Verb i.*** **1.** To come to terms of agreement or payment, (followed by *for*) ; as, Cornwall *compounded* to furnish ten oxen for thirty pounds ; চুক্তি বা সর্ত্তের ঠিক্ ঠাক্ করা, কোন বিষয় আপোষে মিট্মাট্ করিবার জন্য কথা-বার্ত্তা ঠিক্ ঠাক্ করা। **2.** To mix up drugs according to the prescription of a physician ; চিকিৎসকের ব্যবস্থা-পত্রানুসারে ঔষধ সকল বিভিন্ন প্রকারে মিশ্রিত করিয়া প্রস্তুত করা। **—er,** *n.* **1.** One who compounds drugs according to a prescription ; ঔষধ পরিবেষক, ঔষধ মিশ্রণ-কারী। **2.** One who attempts to bring persons or parties to terms of agreement ; আপোষে নিষ্পত্তিকারী ব্যক্তি। **3.** One who compounds a debt or obligation ; রফাকারী। **To compound a felony**—To receive back stolen goods upon an agreement not to prosecute the thief ; চোরকে অভিযুক্ত করা হইবে না, এইরূপ সর্ত্তে তাহার নিকট হইতে অপহৃত দ্রব্য পুনরায় গ্রহণ করা।

cŏm-prē-hĕnd′, *v. t.* **1.** To contain ; to include ; সমাবেশ করা, ধারণ করা ; অন্তর্ভুক্ত করা। **2.** To take into the mind ; to conceive ; অনুভব করা, বুঝিতে পারা ; ধারণা করা, অবধারণ করা।

cŏm-prē-hĕn′-si-ble, *adj.* **1.** Capable of being understood ; intelligible ; বুঝিবার যোগ্য, অবধারণীয়, বিভাব্য, বোধগম্য, ধারণাগম্য ; ধারণার বিষয়ীভূত। **2.** That may be included ; গ্রাহ্য, অন্তর্ভুক্ত হইবার যোগ্য। **—bil′-i-ty,** *n.* **—bly,** *adv.*

cŏm-prē-hĕn′-sion, *n.* **1.** Mental capacity to understand ; understanding ; ধীশক্তি ; অনুভব, অবধারণ, উপলব্ধি, বোধ, জ্ঞান, বুদ্ধি, ধারণা, সমাগতি (হিঃ কোঃ)। **2.** Inclusive power ; comprehensiveness ; "Word of the widest *comprehension* ;" অন্তর্ভুক্তকরণের শক্তি ; ব্যাপকতা। **3.** (*Log.*) The intension of a term or the sum of the qualities implied in the term ; (তর্ক-বিজ্ঞান) অর্থব্যাপ্তি (হিঃ কোঃ), অভিব্যাপ্তি। **Comprehension scheme** — পিউরিটান ও এংলিক্যান এই উভয় ধর্ম্মসমাজ ইংলণ্ডীয় ধর্ম্মসমাজের অন্তর্ভুক্তকরণের সঙ্কল্প।

cŏm-prē-hĕn′-sive, *adj.* Quick or sharp of intellect ; embracing or comprising much ; wide ; as, large *comprehensive* ideas ; বুদ্ধিমান, সূক্ষ্মবুদ্ধি, তীক্ষ্ণবুদ্ধি ; ব্যাপক, অভিব্যাপক, অভিব্যাপী ; প্রশস্ত, বিস্তীর্ণ, সামাসিক, উদার। **—ly,** *adv.* **—ness,** *n.* The quality of being comprehensive ; ব্যাপকতা, বিস্তীর্ণতা।

cŏm-prĕss′, *v. t.* **1.** To force into a smaller bulk ; to press together ; সঙ্কুচিত করা ; সঙ্কাপিত করা, চাপ দেওয়া, সম্পীড়িত করা। **2.** To condense ; to concise ; as, to *compress* a book ; ঘনীভূত করা, নিবিড়তাপাদন করা, ঘন-সন্নিবিষ্ট করা ; সংক্ষেপ করা। **—ive,** *adj.*

—pressed′, *adj.* Pressed together ; সঙ্কুলিত, ঘন-সন্নিবিষ্ট।

cŏm′-prĕss, *n.* (*Surg.*) A soft pad for applying pressure ; a piece of wet cloth covered with waterproof bandage, for relief of inflammation ; (অস্ত্রোপচার-বিদ্যা) পটী (হিঃ কোঃ), ক্ষতাদি বন্ধনার্থ জড়ান গদি।

cŏm-prĕss′-i-ble, *adj.* Capable of being compressed ; সঙ্কোচনীয়, সঙ্কোচ্য, সঙ্কোচনশীল, সঙ্কোচ-ক্ষম। **—bil′-i-ty**, *n.* The state or quality of being compressible ; সঙ্কোচ্যতা।

cŏm-pres′-sion (-prĕ-), *n.* Condensation (*lit* & *fig.*) ; হ্রাস, সঙ্কোচন, সম্পীড়ন, আকুঞ্চন, আপীড়ন, সঙ্কাপন, নিবিড়তাপাদন (সাঃ পঃ), সঙ্কোচ।

cŏm-prĕs′-sor (-sêr), *n.* **1.** (*Anat.*) A muscle that compresses some parts ; (শারীর-সংস্থানবিদ্যা) সঙ্কোচক-পেশী। **2.** (*Surg.*) An instrument for compressing a part of the body ; (অস্ত্রোপচার-বিদ্যা) দেহের অংশ-বিশেষ সঙ্কোচনার্থ যন্ত্র-বিশেষ।

cŏm-prīse′, —prīze′, *v. t.* **1.** To contain or include ; ধারণ করা, অন্তর্ভুক্ত করা, অন্তর্গত করা, সামিল করা (*Colloq.*)। **2.** To condense (within limits etc.) ; "The word politics *comprises* itself a difficult study of no inconsiderable magnitude ;" সংক্ষিপ্ত করা। **—pris′-a-ble**, *adj.*

cŏm′-prō-mīse, *v. t.* & *i.* **1.** To settle by mutual concessions ; আপোষে নিষ্পত্তি বা মীমাংসা করা, মিট্‌মাট্ করা, রফা করা। **2.** To involve ; বিজড়িত করা। **3.** To put in hazard ; as, to *compromise* the honours of a nation ; সঙ্কটাপন্ন করা, দায়গ্রস্ত করা। ***Verb i.*** To come to agreement by concessions ; কোন বিষয় মিটমাট করিবার জন্য ঠিকঠাক করা। **—mis-a-ble**, *adj.*

cŏm′-prō-mīse, *n.* **1.** A settlement of a difference by mutual concessions ; আপোষ, মিটমাট, রফা। **2.** Adjustment of conflicting opinions, courses, etc. by modification of each ; পরস্পর বিরোধী মতের সমন্বয়।

cŏmp-trōl′-lêr, *n.* Mis-spelling of controller in some titles ; as, *comptroller* of accounts ; see CONTROLLER.

cŏm-pŭl′-sion, *n.* Force ; forcible constraint ; জবরদস্তি, জুলুম, বলপ্রয়োগ; বাধ্যবাধকতা। **—sive**, *adj.* Having power to compel ; বাধ্যকারী। **—sive-ly**, *adv.*

cŏm-pŭl′-sō-rȳ, *adj.* Enjoined by authority ; enforced ; as, the bondage of *compulsory* worship ; having the power of exercising force ; as, the exercise of any *compulsory* power over them ; অবশ্যপালনীয় ; বাধ্যতামূলক, নিয়ত (প্রবাসী) ; বাধ্যকারী। **—ri-ly**, *adv.*

cŏm-pŭnc′-tion, *n.* The sting or reproach of conscience ; regret ; as, without *compunction* ; আত্মগ্লানি ; অনুশোচনা, অনুতাপ। **—tious**, *adj.* **—tious-ly**, *adv.*

cŏm-pur-ga′-tion (-pêr-), *n.* The custom, in Anglo-Saxon Law, of permitting the accused to call in witnesses to prove his innocency, by joining their oaths to his ; প্রাচীন এংলোস্যাক্সনদিগের বিচার পদ্ধতি বিশেষ—যাহাতে অভিযুক্ত ব্যক্তি তদীয় নির্দ্দোষিতা-সম্বন্ধীয় শপথ-বাক্যের প্রতিপোষকতার জন্য কতিপয় সাক্ষীকে আহ্বান করিতে পারিত।

Com′-pur-ga-tor, *n.* **—to′-ri-al**, *adj.*

cŏm-pūte′, *v. t.* To count ; to calculate ; গণনা করা ; সংখ্যা করা। **—put′-a-ble**, *adj.* Capable of being computed ; সংখ্যেয়, গণনীয়, গণিতব্য। **—put′-er, —put′-ist**, *ns.*

cŏm-pū-tā′-tion, *n.* **1.** Calculation ; গণনা, সংখ্যান। **2.** The amount computed ; গণিত সংখ্যা।

cŏm′-rāde, *n.* An intimate associate ; সহায়, অন্তরঙ্গ, সঙ্গী, সাথী। **—ship**, *n.* **Comrade of a lover**—পীঠমর্দ্দ (মঃ উঃ)।

Cŏm′-tism, *n.* The philosophy of M. Auguste Comte ; ফরাসী দার্শনিক কোমৎ কর্ত্তৃক প্রবর্ত্তিত দর্শন, প্রত্যক্ষবাদ। [কোমৎএর মতে মানবজাতি তিনটী বিভিন্ন অবস্থা অতিক্রম করে. (১) ধর্ম্মসম্বন্ধীয়, (২) দার্শনিক, (৩) প্রত্যক্ষ বা বৈজ্ঞানিক। See J. S. Mill's *Comte and Positivism.*]

Cō′-mŭs, *n.* A god of mirth and revelry ; আনন্দ ও পানোল্লাসের দেবতা বিশেষ।

cŏn, *v. t.* **1.** To study ; পাঠ করা, অধ্যয়ন করা। **2.** To commit to memory ; কণ্ঠস্থ করা।

cŏn, *v. t.* (*Naut.*) To direct how to steer ; জাহাজ কিরূপভাবে চালাইতে হইবে তাহা নির্দ্দেশ করা। **Conning Tower**—গোলাদ্বারা অভেদ্য বেষ্টিত মঞ্চ বিশেষ—এই মঞ্চোপরি লৌহপট্টাচ্ছাদিত পোতের কর্ণধার উপবেশন করিয়া থাকে।

cŏn, *adv.* & *n.* Against ; প্রতিকূলে। ***Noun.*** Opposing argument, voter, etc. ; বিরুদ্ধ যুক্তি, বিরুদ্ধপক্ষীয় ভোটদাতা, প্রভৃতি। **Pros and cons**—Arguments for and against ; স্বপক্ষ ও বিপক্ষ বা অনুকূল ও প্রতিকূল যুক্তি পরম্পরা।

cŏn-ā′-cre (-kêr), *n.* (In Ireland) A system of underletting a portion of a farm for a single crop ; (আয়র্লণ্ডে) একবার শস্য উৎপাদনের জন্য কোন কৃষিক্ষেত্রের অংশবিশেষ বন্দোবস্ত গ্রহণের রীতি।

con amore, *adv.* Zealously ; উদ্যমসহকারে।

cō-nā′-ri-ŭm, *n.* The pineal gland of the brain ; সহস্রার (হীরেন্দ্র)।

cō-nā′-tion, *n.* (*Phil.*) The power or act which directs or impels the effort of any kind, whether muscular or psychical ; প্রবৃত্তি, ইচ্ছাশক্তি, চিকীর্ষা (হিঃ কোঃ), ব্যবসায় (ঐ), কামনা (ঐ)

cō-nā'-tŭs, *n.* Effort of nature; ক্রিয়োন্মুখতা, রজঃ (হিঃ কোঃ)।

cŏn-căt'-ē-nāte, *v. t.* To chain or link together; to unite in a series; পরস্পর-সংযুক্ত করা, শৃঙ্খলাবদ্ধ করা; শৃঙ্খলাকারে গ্রথিত করা, অনুবদ্ধ করা। **—na'-tion,** *n.* **1.** Union in a linked series; শৃঙ্খলাকারে সংযোজন। **2.** A series of things depending on each other; পরস্পর সম্বদ্ধ বস্তু পরম্পরা, শ্রেণী, পংক্তি, শৃঙ্খলা, অনুবন্ধ। **Concatenation of causes**—কারণমালা।

cŏn'-cāve, *adj.* & *n.* Hollow as the inner surface of a bowl

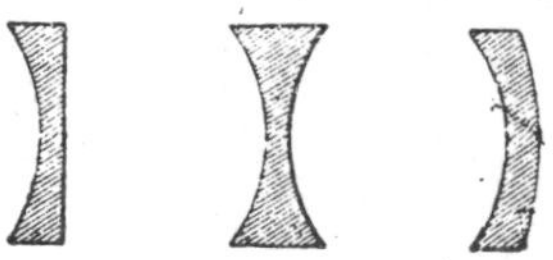

Concave or Plano-concave Lens. Concavo-concave Lens. Concavo-convex Lens.

or sphere; উত্তান (সাঃ পঃ), সংবৃত-মধ্য, পুটাকার, মধ্যনিম্ন, ন্যুব্জ, অন্তর্বর্তুল, নতোদর। ***Noun.*** A curved hollow; an arc or vault; বক্রোদর গর্ত, খিলান। **—cav'-i-ty,** *n.* **—ly,** *adv.*

cŏn-ceal' (-ēl), *v. t.* To keep secret; to keep out of sight; গোপন রাখা, গোপন করা; প্রচ্ছাদন করা, লুকান, ঢাকা, আচ্ছাদন করা। **—cealed',** *adj.* Hidden; লুক্কায়িত, গূঢ়, উপগূঢ়, সাবরণ, প্রচ্ছন্ন, নিভৃত, সংবৃত। **—ment,** *n.* **1.** The act of concealing; সংগোপন, প্রচ্ছাদন, অপহ্নুতি, সংগুপ্তি। **2.** A hiding place; পলায়ন-স্থান।

cŏn-cēde', *v. t.* To admit; to allow to pass undisputed; to grant a right or privilege; "Free trade was *conceded* to the West-Indian Islands;" স্বীকার করা, মানিয়া লওয়া, মঞ্জুর করা, অবাধে চলিতে দেওয়া; স্বত্ব বা অধিকার প্রদান করা।

cŏn-ceit' (-sēt), *n.* & *v. t.* **1.** An overestimation of self; গর্ব্ব, অহঙ্কার, অভিমান, আত্মাভিমান, অহমিকা। **2.** A fancy; "The *conceit* seems to be too preposterous to be thought of as a serious opinion; খেয়াল, অমূলক কল্পনা। ***Verb t.*** **1.** (*Archaic*) To suppose; to judge or imagine; (অপ্রচলিত) অনুমান করা; বিচার করা, কল্পনা করা। **2.** To persuade oneself (that); as, we *conceit* ourselves that we contemplate absolute existency; প্রবৃত্ত করা, লওয়ান। **—ed,** *adj.* Vain; গর্ব্বিত, অহঙ্কারী, উদ্ধত, দৃপ্ত, আত্মাভিমানী, আত্মশ্লাঘাকারী, আত্মম্মন্য। **—ed-ly,** *adv.* **In conceit with**—In accord with; অনুসারে। **Out of conceit with**—Not pleased with; অসন্তুষ্ট।

cŏn-ceiv'-ă-ble (-sēv-), *adj.* That may be understood or believed; বোধগম্য, বুদ্ধি-গ্রাহ্য, চিন্ত্য, ভাব্য, বিভাবনীয়। **—bil'-i-ty,** *n.* **—bly,** *adv.* **—ness,** *n.*

cŏn-ceive' (-sēv-), *v. t.* & *i.* **1.** To receive into the womb; গর্ভধারণ করা, গর্ভগ্রহণ করা। **2.** To understand or comprehend; মনোমধ্যে পোষণ বা ধারণ করা, উপলব্ধি করা, হৃদয়ঙ্গম করা। **3.** To form an idea or conception in the mind; to devise or formulate; as, he first *conceives* then perfects his design; ধারণা করা; উদ্ভাবন করা। ***Verb i.*** **1.** To become pregnant; গর্ভবতী হওয়া, অন্তঃসত্ত্বা হওয়া। **2.** To think (usu. followed by *of*); as, *conceive* of things clearly and distinctly; চিন্তা করা, ভাবা।

cŏn-cĕl'-ē-brāte, *v. t.* (*R. C. Church, of newly ordained priest*) To celebrate mass with ordaining bishop; (রোমান ক্যাথলিক ধর্ম্মসমাজে নবদীক্ষিত পুরোহিতের পক্ষে) দীক্ষা-দানকারী ধর্ম্মাধ্যক্ষের সহিত (শেষ ভোজন নামক) উপাসনাবিশেষে যোগদান করা।

cŏn-cĕl'-tō, *n.* (*Pl.* CONCELTI) An affected phrase; গুরুগম্ভীর বাক্য। **—tism,** *n.*

cŏn'-cĕn-trāte, *v. t.* & *i.* **1.** To bring to a common centre; এককেন্দ্রীভূত করা, সমাহৃত করা। **2.** (*Chem.*) To reduce to a state of great strength or purity; as, spirit of vinegar *concertrated* and reduced to its greatest strength; (রসায়ন-শাস্ত্র) ঘনীভূত করা। **—trat-ed,** *adj.* **—tra'-tion,** *n.* **1.** The act of concentrating or state of being concentrated; কেন্দ্রীকরণ, সংকেন্দ্রণ (হিঃ কোঃ)। **2.** (*Chem.*) The act of increasing the strength of fluids by volatilizing part of their water; (রসায়ন-শাস্ত্র) ঘনীভূত করণ, নিবেশন (হিঃ কোঃ)। **3.** The keeping of the mind fixed on something; ধারণা, অনন্যমনস্কতা, একাগ্রতা (হিঃ কোঃ)। **—tra-tive,** *adj.* Tending to condense or hold together; ঘনীভবনশীল, নিবেশনশীল। **—tra-tive-ness,** *n.*

cŏn-cĕn'-tre (-têr), **—têr,** *v. i.* & *t.* To come to one point as centre; এক কেন্দ্রে মিলিত হওয়া, সমকেন্দ্রিক হওয়া, এককেন্দ্রীভূত হওয়া। ***Verb t.*** To draw or direct to a common centre; সমকেন্দ্রিক করা। **—tric, —tri'-cal,** *adjs.* Having a common centre; সমকেন্দ্রিক (সাঃ পঃ)। **—tri'-cal-ly,** *adv.* **—tric'-i-ty,** *n.* **Concentric fire**—(*Mil.*) Firing concentrated on a point; (সামরিক শাস্ত্র) কোন নির্দ্দিষ্টস্থলে গোলাবর্ষণ।

cŏn'-cĕpt, *n.* (*Log.*) A general notion or idea of a class of objects; (তর্কবিজ্ঞান) সামান্যগ্রহ (হিঃ কোঃ), সামান্য প্রত্যয় (ঐ), প্রত্যয় (ঐ)।

cŏn-cĕp'-tă-cle, *n.* (*Bot.*) A pericarp of one valve; (উদ্ভিদ-বিদ্যা) এক পুটবিশিষ্ট বীজকোষ, গোলককুণ্ড (সাঃ পঃ)।

cŏn-cĕp′-tion, *n.* **1.** The act of conceiving in the womb ; গর্ভাধান, গর্ভধারণ, গর্ভগ্রহণ। **2.** (*Fig.*) First origin of anything ; (লক্ষণায়) অঙ্কুর, উদ্গম। **3.** The formation in the mind of a notion or idea ; a notion ; সমবধারণ, ভাবনা, উপলব্ধি, অনুভব, বিভাবন ; ধারণা। **—al,** *adj.*

cŏn-cĕp′-tive, *adj.* Pertaining to conception ; ধারণা-সম্বন্ধীয়।

cŏn-cĕp′-tū-ăl-ism, *n.* The doctrine in Philosophy that universals have an existence in the mind apart from any concrete embodiment ; মধ্যযুগের দার্শনিক মতবাদ বিশেষ—এই মতানুসারে কোনরূপ মূর্ত্ত প্রতিরূপ ব্যতিরেকেও শ্রেণী, পর্য্যায় প্রভৃতি সাধারণ ভাবসমূহের সত্তা মনোমধ্যে বর্ত্তমান রহিয়াছে বলিয়া গৃহীত হয়, প্রত্যয়-সত্ত্ববাদ (হিঃ কোঃ), সামান্য (ঐ)। **—ist,** *n.* **—ist-ic,** *adj.*

cŏn-cĕrn′, *v. t.* & *n.* **1.** To relate to ; to involve ; সম্বন্ধ থাকা, সম্পৃক্ত হওয়া ; সংসৃষ্ট হওয়া। **2.** To interest one's self ; কোন বিষয়ে অনুরাগী হওয়া, ব্যাপৃত হওয়া। ***Noun.*** **1.** Affair ; বিষয়, প্রয়োজন, ব্যাপার। **2.** Interest ; সম্বন্ধ, স্বার্থ, অনুরাগ। **3.** Solicitous regard ; anxiety ; উদ্বেগসহকৃত যত্ন ; ঔৎসুক্য, ব্যগ্রতা, উদ্বেগ। **4.** Business organization ; as, a banking *concern* ; ব্যবসায়। **5.** (*Colloq.*) A material thing ; "A steel pen which is a very unpliable *concern* ;" (চলিত ভাষায়) জড়বস্তু। **—ed-ly,** *adv.* **—ing,** *prep.* As regards ; সম্বন্ধে, বিষয়ে, ঘটিত, সংক্রান্ত, বাবতে। **—ment,** *n.* **1.** A thing in which one is concerned ; affair ; বিষয় ; ব্যাপার। **2.** Importance ; গুরুত্ব। **3.** Anxiety ; উদ্বেগ। **The whole concern**—All concerned with a particular affair or business ; কোন ব্যাপারে লিপ্ত জনসমূহ। **To feel** or **have a concern in** or **for**—To be or feel interested in ; কোন বিষয়ে অনুরাগ বোধ করা, কোন বিষয়ে সংসৃষ্ট থাকা।

cŏn-cêrt′, *v. t.* & *n.* To arrange by mutual agreement ; to plan ; পরামর্শদ্বারা ঠিক করা ; পরামর্শ করা, মন্ত্রণা করা, উদ্ভাবন করা। ***Noun*** **(con′-).** **1.** Unionor agreement in a scheme or plan ; কোন পরামর্শে মতৈক্য। **2.** Concord ; ঐক্য, মিল। **3.** A musical entertainment in which several voices or instruments take part ; ঐক্যতান সঙ্গীত, ঐক্যতান বাদ্য, নহবৎ। **Concert room**—সঙ্গীতশালা, গন্ধর্ব্বশালা (কথাঃ সঃ)।

cŏn-cêr-ti′-nȧ, *n.* A portable musical wind instrument, with a set of keys at each end ; একপ্রকার বাদ্যযন্ত্র, বাজাবিশেষ।

cŏn-ces′-sion (-sĕ-), *n.* **1.** The act of conceding ; প্রার্থনাপূরণ, অনুমতি, অনুমোদন, অর্পণ, ত্যাগ। **2.** The thing conceded ; grant ; অর্পিতবস্তু ; দান। **—aire′,** *n.* One who has obtained a concession ; the person to whom a concession or privilege has been made ; অধিকারপ্রাপ্ত ব্যক্তি ; কোনরূপ বস্তু বা অধিকার যে ব্যক্তিকে অর্পণ করা হইয়াছে। **—sive,** *adj.* Implying concession ; অনুমোদনসূচক। **—sive-ly,** *adv.*

cŏnch, *n.* **1.** A marine shell ; শঙ্খ, কম্বু। **2.** A shell used by Tritons as a trumpet ; গ্রীকপুরাণোক্ত ট্রিটন্ নামক জলদেবতার শঙ্খ। **Con′-chi-form,** *adj.* Shell-shaped ; শঙ্খাকৃতি। **Con-choid′-al,** *adj.* Shell-like ; শঙ্খকল্প। **Con-chol′-o-gist,** *n.* One who studies, or is versed in, conchology ; শঙ্খবিজ্ঞানবিৎ। **Con-chol′-o-gy,** *n.* That branch of natural history which deals with the shells or molluscs ; শঙ্খ-বিজ্ঞান, শঙ্খ-শাস্ত্র।

con-chif′-ê-rȧ (cŏng-), *n. pl.* A class of mollusc having two shelly valves ; দ্বিখোলবিশিষ্ট কম্বু প্রভৃতি। **—er-ous,** *adj.* Shell-bearing ; শঙ্খোৎপাদী।

cŏn-cierge′ (-syärzh), *n.* A doorkeeper ; a porter ; দ্বার-রক্ষক ; দ্বারবান, দৌবারিক।

cŏn-cĭl′-i-ar* (-êr), **—ă-rȳ,** *adj.* Of or pertaining to an ecclesiastical council ; যাজক-সভাসংক্রান্ত।

cŏn-cĭl′-i-āte, *v. t.* **1.** To reconcile or bring to a state of friendship ; মিলন-সংঘটন করা, বন্ধুত্বে পুনঃ প্রতিষ্ঠিত করা, পুনর্মিলন করান, অনুকূল করা, সুপ্রসন্ন করা, অনুরঞ্জন করা। **2.** To pacify ; সান্ত্বনা করা। **—a-ble,** *adj.* Capable of being reconciled ; প্রসাদ্য। **—a′-tion,** *n.* **1.** Act of conciliating ; তুষ্টিসাধন, অনুরঞ্জন, প্রসাদন। **2.** Reconcilement ; মিলন-সংঘটন, পুনর্মিলন। **—a-tive,** *adj.* **—a-tor,** *n.* A peace-maker ; শান্তি-সংস্থাপক। **—a-to-ry,** *adj.* Tending or calculated to conciliate ; প্রীতি-সাধক, মৈত্রীসূচক, অনুকূল, হৃদয়গ্রাহী, মিলনসাধক, অনুরঞ্জক।

cŏn-cīse′, *adj.* Brief in expression ; স্বল্পাক্ষর, সংক্ষিপ্ত, চুম্বক, অবিস্তীর্ণ অল্পশব্দক, লঘু, সামাসিক (মঃ সঃ), অল্পাক্ষর-গ্রথিত। **—ly,** *adv.* **—ness,** *n.* The quality of being concise ; স্বল্পাক্ষরতা।

cŏn-cĭ′-sion (-zhŏn) *n.* **1.** A cutting off ; ছেদন, কর্ত্তন। **2.** Conciseness ; সংক্ষিপ্ততা, স্বল্পাক্ষরতা।

cŏn′-clāve, *n.* **1.** The room in which Cardinals meet to elect a Pope ; যে কক্ষে উপবেশনকরত কার্ডিন্যালগণ পোপ নির্ব্বাচন করেন। **2.** A private assembly of Cardinals for election of a Pope ; পোপ নির্ব্বাচনার্থ ধর্ম্মাধ্যক্ষদিগের গুপ্তসভা **3.** A private assembly ; গুপ্তসভা, গূঢ়সমাজ। **—clav-ist,** *n.* **To be in conclave**—To be engaged in a secret meeting ; গুপ্ত সমিতিতে নিযুক্ত থাকা বা যোগদান করা।

cŏn-clūde′, *v. t.* & *i.* **1.** To bring to an end ; to close ; সমাপ্ত করা ; অবসান করা ; উপসংহার করা

2. To determine; to settle; "Is it *concluded* he shall be protector;" স্থির করা; নিশ্চয় করা, নির্দ্দিষ্ট করা, অবধারণ করা, বন্দোবস্ত করা, নির্দ্ধারণ করা। 3. To infer, as from premises; "*Concluding* that his life was in danger;" অনুমান করা। 4. To bring about as a result; "If we *conclude* a peace;" সমাধা করা, সম্পন্ন করা। ***Verb i.*** To come to an end; to terminate; সমাপ্ত হওয়া; অবসান হওয়া।

cŏn-clü'-sion (-zhŏn), **1.** Termination; উপসংহার, শেষ, অন্ত, অবসান, সমাপ্তি। **2.** Final decision; result; চূড়ান্ত নিষ্পত্তি, নির্ণয়; পরিণাম, ফল। **3.** (*Log.*) The inferential proposition of a syllogism; (তর্কবিজ্ঞান) সিদ্ধান্ত, অনুমান, নির্ণয়, উপপত্তি, নিগমন (সাঃ পঃ), উপসংহার (ঐ)। **4.** Settling; arrangement; as, *conclusion* of peace; স্থিরীকরণ, সিদ্ধান্ত; ব্যবস্থা। **–sive,** *adj.* Decisive; convincing; চূড়ান্ত, চরম, অকাট্য, অখণ্ড্য, প্রামাণ্য, প্রত্যয়জনক। **–sive-ly,** *adv.* **–sive-ness,** *n.* **In conclusion**—Lastly; সর্ব্বশেষে, পরিশেষে। **To jump to a conclusion** — To come to a conclusion hastily; ঝটিতি কোন সিদ্ধান্তে উপনীত হওয়া। **To try conclusions**—To make experiment or essay of anything; কোন বিষয়ে পরীক্ষা বা চেষ্টা করা।

cŏn-cŏct', *v. t.* To make up of mixed ingredients (soup, drink); to compose; to devise; as, to *concoct* a plot; নানাদ্রব্যের মিশ্রণে প্রস্তুত করা; গঠন করা; পাকান, কল্পনা করা, উদ্ভাবন করা। **–coc'-tion,** *n.* **–ive,** *adj.* **–or,** *n.*

cŏn'-col-or-ous (-kŭl-êr-ŭs), *adj.* (*Zool.*) Of uniform colour; (প্রাণীবিজ্ঞান) এক বর্ণবিশিষ্ট, একরঙ্গা।

cŏn-cŏm'-i-tănce, –tăn-cy̆, *n.* **1.** Co-existence; সহবর্ত্তন, সাহচর্য্য, অন্বয়, সমন্বয়, সঙ্গ, সমবায়, সহবিদ্যমানতা, নিত্যযোগ, সহভাব (হিঃ কোঃ)। **2.** (*R. C. Church*) The co-existence of the body and blood of Christ in either element of the eucharist; (রোমান্ ক্যাথলিক ধর্ম্মসমাজ) খৃষ্টের শেষ-ভোজন স্মৃতি-অনুষ্ঠানে ব্যবহৃত রুটি ও সুরা উভয়ের প্রত্যেকটীতে খৃষ্টের রক্ত ও মাংসের সহবিদ্যমানতা।

cŏn-cŏm'-i-tănt, *adj.* & *n.* Accompanying; conjoined with; আনুষঙ্গিক, সহভাবী (হিঃ কোঃ), সহবর্ত্তী; সমবায়ী, সমবায়িক, সহচারী। ***Noun.*** A connecting or accompanying circumstance; আনুষঙ্গিক অবস্থা।

cŏn'-cŏrd, *n.* **1.** Union in feelings, sentiments, opinions, etc.; agreement; একচিত্ততা, সংযোগ, ঐক্য; মিলন। **2.** (*Gram.*) An agreement between words in gender, number, person or case; (ব্যাকরণ) লিঙ্গ, বচন, পুরুষাদির ঐক্য, অন্বয়। **3.** Treaty; "Abiding by the *concord* of Salamanca;" সন্ধি। **4.** (*Mus.*) An agreeable combination of tones simultaneously heard; (সঙ্গীতশাস্ত্র) ঐক্যতান, সমস্বরতা। **–a-ble,** *adj.*

cŏn-cŏrd'-ănce, *n.* **1.** Agreement; ঐক্য, মিল, অন্বয়। **2.** A book in which the principal words used in any work, as the Scriptures, the Vedas, Shakespeare, etc., are arranged alphabetically, and the book, chapter, verse, act, scene, line or other subdivision in which each word occurs are noted; as, the "Vedic *Concordance*;" যে পুস্তকে কোন গ্রন্থের (যথা বেদ, বাইবেল, সেক্সপীয়রের নাটক প্রভৃতির) প্রধান প্রধান শব্দসমূহ বর্ণমালানুক্রমে প্রদত্ত হইয়া থাকে, এবং তৎ তৎ শব্দগুলি পুস্তকের কোন খণ্ড, অধ্যায়, অঙ্ক, দৃশ্য, বা পংক্তিতে সন্নিবিষ্ট আছে, তাহাও উল্লিখিত থাকে, নির্ঘণ্ট-গ্রন্থ। **–ant,** *adj.* **1.** Agreeing; corresponding; অনুরূপ, সদৃশ, অন্বিত; ঐক্যবিশিষ্ট। **2.** In musical concord; ঐক্যতানবিশিষ্ট। **–ant-ly,** *adv.*

cŏn-cŏr'-dăt, *n.* A treaty or compact between a sovereign and the Pope; কোন দেশের নৃপতি এবং পোপের মধ্যে সন্ধি বা চুক্তি-পত্র।

cŏn'-course (-kōrs), *n.* A crowd; an assembly; ভিড়, জনতা, জন-সংঘ; সমিতি, সমবায়।

cŏn-crĕs'-cĕnce, *n.* (*Biol.*) Growing together; একত্রীভবন (সাঃ পঃ)।

cŏn'-crēte, *adj.* & *n.* **1.** Real; মূর্ত্ত, সাকার, বাস্তব, স্থূল, পরাক্ (হিঃ কোঃ)। **2.** (*Gram.*—of *noun*) Denoting a thing as opposed to a quality, state or action; (ব্যাকরণ—বিশেষ্যের পক্ষে) বস্তু-বাচক। ***Noun.*** **1.** A concrete thing; মূর্ত্তবস্তু, সংহত বস্তু। **2.** A mass of stones, chippings, pebbles, etc., cemented by mortar; খোয়াদ। **–ly,** *adv.* **In the concrete**—In the sphere of reality; মূর্ত্তভাবে, স্থূল জগতে।

cŏn-crēte', *v. t.* & *i.* **1.** To congeal or solidify; জমাট বাঁধান, ঘন করা। **2.** To cover with concrete খোয়াদ দ্বারা আবৃত করা।

cŏn-crē'-tion, *n.* **1.** The act of concreting; coalescence; ঘনীকরণ, পিণ্ডীকরণ; পিণ্ডাকারে পরিণতি, সংহতি, সংঘাত। **2.** A mass concreted; পিণ্ড, তাল। **3.** (*Path.*) A morbid formation in the body; stone; (নিদান-শাস্ত্র) মূত্রযন্ত্র, যকৃদ্ প্রভৃতিতে কোন প্রকার নিরেট পদার্থের সঞ্চয়; পাথরী, অশ্মরী, পিণ্ড (হঃ চঃ)। **4.** (*Geol.*) A mass formed of solid particles; (ভূবিদ্যা) পিণ্ড। **–al, –a-ry.** *adjs.*

cŏn-cü'-bi-nāge, *n.* Cohabiting as man and wife without being married; the state of being a concubine; অবিবাহিতাবস্থায় স্ত্রীপুরুষভাবে সংসর্গ বা সহবাস, সম্ভোগ-সম্বন্ধ মানিত পতিপত্নীভাব; উপপত্নী-সেবা, উপপত্নীত্ব।

cŏn-cü'-bi-nă-ry̆, *adj.* & *n.* Of or sprung from concubinage living in concubinage ; সম্ভোগ সম্বন্ধজাত ; স্ত্রীপুরুষরূপে বাসকারী। ***Noun.*** One living in concubinage ; বিবাহ বিনা সহবাসকারী পুরুষ বা সহবাসকারিণী স্ত্রী।

cŏn'-cū-bīne, *n.* **1.** A woman who cohabits with a man without being married ; a kept mistress ; উপপত্নী, ভোগ্যা-স্ত্রী, স্বৈরিণী ; রক্ষিতা স্ত্রীলোক। **2.** (Among polygamous people) Lawful wife, but of inferior rank or condition ; (বহু বিবাহকারী লোকদিগের মধ্যে) হীনবংশজাতা স্ত্রী। **—bi-nal,** *adj.*

cŏn-cū'-pis-cĕnce, *n.* **1.** Sexual lust ; lechery ; সংসর্গস্পৃহা, ইন্দ্রিয়লালসা; কামুকতা। **2.** (*Bible N. T.*) Desire for worldly things ; বিষয়াভিলাষ, বিষয়বাসনা। **—cent,** *adj.* Libidinous ; eagerly desirous ; আসঙ্গ-লিপ্সু ; কামুক, কামী।

cŏn-cur' (-kêr), *v. i.* **1.** To meet or come together at one point ; to coincide ; এক বিন্দুতে মিলিত হওয়া ; ঠিক একই স্থান অধিকার করা। **2.** To co-operate ; to act jointly ; as, the whole church *concur* in that action ; সহকারিতা করা ; একযোগে কার্য্য করা। **3.** To agree (with) ; একমত হওয়া, মিল হওয়া, সম্মত হওয়া। **—rence,** *n.* Agreement or union in action or opinion ; ঐকমত্য, সহযোগিতা।

cŏn-cŭr'-rĕnt, *adj.* & *n.* **1.** Existing or happening at the same time ; সহগামী। **2.** Conjoined ; সম্মিলিত। **3.** Acting in conjunction ; as, he gives the *concurrent* assistance of his own power ; একযোগে কার্য্যকারী, সহকারী। **4.** (*Geom.*) Meeting in one point ; (জ্যামিতি) একবিন্দু-বিসর্পী। ***Noun.*** That which concurs ; সহগামী বা সহকারী বস্তু। **—rent-ly,** *adv.* **Concurrent lease**—পূর্ব্বের পাট্টার ম্যাদ শেষ হইবার পূর্ব্বে সম্পাদিত নূতন পাট্টা।

cŏn-cŭss', *v. t.* **1.** To shake or agitate violently (*usu. fig.*) "*Concussed* with uncertainty ; সংঘট্টিত করা, বিঘট্টিত করা। **2.** To coerce by threats ; as, he was *concussed* by the crown ; ভয়প্রদর্শনে বাধ্য করা।

cŏn-cŭs'-sion, *n.* **1.** A shaking or agitation ; a shock caused by collision of bodies ; সংঘট্ট ; সংঘট্টজনিত ধাক্কা বা আঘাত, টক্কর। **2.** (*Surg.*) Effect on the brain etc. of a shock ; (অস্ত্রোপচার বিদ্যা) মস্তিষ্ক প্রভৃতিতে সংঘট্টজনিত সংঘাত। **Concussion-bellows**—(সঙ্গীতশাস্ত্র) বাদ্যযন্ত্রের ভস্ত্রা। **Concussion-fuse**—গোলায় সংলগ্ন যে দাহ্যদ্রব্যপূর্ণ নল বা পলিতা কোন কিছুর সহিত সংস্পৃষ্ট হইলে প্রজ্বলিত হইয়া উঠে।

cŏn-demn' (-dĕm), *v. t.* **1.** To censure ; to blame ; তিরস্কার করা, ধিক্কার দেওয়া ; অপসন্দ করা, দোষারোপ করা, নিন্দা করা। **2.** To doom to punishment ; দণ্ডাজ্ঞা দেওয়া। **3.** To convict of guilt ; অপরাধী সাব্যস্ত করা, দোষী সাব্যস্ত করা। **4.** To pronounce to be unfit for use or service ; as, the ship and her cargo were *condemned* ; অব্যবহার্য্য বা অকর্ম্মণ্য বলিয়া স্থির করা, বাতিল করা। **5.** To pronounce to be forfeited ; বাজেয়াপ্ত হইয়াছে বলিয়া প্রচার করা। **6.** To bear witness or evidence against ; to convict ; as, his looks *condemn* him ; বিপক্ষে সাক্ষ্য বা প্রমাণ প্রদান করা ; দোষী সাব্যস্ত করা। **—demned',** **—dem'-na-ble,** *adjs.*

cŏn-dĕm-nā'-tion. *n.* **1.** Censure ; reprobation ; তিরস্কার ; ধিক্কার। **2.** Sentence of punishment ; দণ্ড, শাস্তি। **3.** The ground or reason of condemning ; as, his own conduct is his *condemnation* ; দণ্ডহেতু। **—dem'-na-to-ry,** *adj.* Expressing condemnation ; তিরস্কারবাচক।

cŏn-dĕn-sā'-tion, *n.* **1.** Act of condensing ; state of being condensed ; সংহতি, ঘনীকরণ ; ঘনীভবন (সাঃ পঃ)। **2.** A condensed mass ; ঘনীভূত পিণ্ড।

cŏn-dĕnse', *v. t.* & *i.* **1.** To compress or reduce into a smaller compass ; as, the Bowen process of *condensing* milk ; নিবিড়তাপাদন করা, স্বল্পায়ত করা, ঘনীভূত করা, গাঢ় করা। **2.** To abridge ; সংক্ষেপ করা। **3.** (*Optics*) To concentrate (rays of light) ; (দৃষ্টি-বিজ্ঞান) কেন্দ্রীভূত করা (আলোকরশ্মিসমূহ)। **4.** (*Electr.*) To increase the amount or intensity of (a charge of electricity) ; (তাড়িত-বিদ্যা) (বিদ্যুতপ্রবাহের) পরিমাণ বা তীব্রতা বৃদ্ধি করা। **5.** (*Chem.* & *Phys.*) To reduce into another and denser form,—as to reduce a gas into a liquid and a liquid into a solid ; (রসায়ন-শাস্ত্র ও পদার্থ-বিজ্ঞান) গাঢ়তর রূপান্তর প্রদান করা। ***Verb i.*** To grow or become thick ; ঘনীভূত হওয়া, গাঢ় হওয়া। **—den-sa-bil'-i-ty,** *n.* **—den'-sa-ble,** *adj.*

cŏn-dĕns'-êr, *n.* **1.** One who or that which condenses ; ঘনীভূতকারী ব্যক্তি বা বস্তু, সংক্ষেপকার। **2.** A pneumatic engine or syringe by which air may be compressed ; যে বায়ব্য যন্ত্র বা পিচকারির দ্বারা বায়ু সঙ্কাপিত করা যাইতে পারে, সংহতি-যন্ত্র (আঃ বঃ)। **3.** (*Electr.*) An instrument for concentrating electricity by the effect of induction ; (তাড়িত-বিদ্যা) বিদ্যুদ্‌গাঢ়ীকরণার্থ যন্ত্র বিশেষ, বিদ্যুদ্‌-ভাণ্ড (সাঃ পঃ)। **4.** (*Optics*) A lens or system of lenses by which light is concentrated on one point or object ; (দৃষ্টি-বিজ্ঞান) পরকলা বা পরকলা শ্রেণী,—যৎসাহায্যে কোন এক নির্দ্দিষ্ট বিন্দু বা বস্তুর উপর আলোক কেন্দ্রীভূত করা হয়।

cŏn-dē-scend' (-sĕnd), *v. i.* **1.** To stoop voluntarily from a superior to an inferior position ; to accommodate oneself to an inferior; অনুগ্রহ প্রকাশার্থ উচ্চপদ হইতে অবনত হওয়া; হীনব্যক্তির সহিত তুল্যভাবে মেলামেশা করা, হীনতা স্বীকার করা, অভিমান ত্যাগ করা। 2. To yield; বশীভূত হওয়া, সম্মত হওয়া, প্রসন্ন হওয়া। **To condescend upon**—To specify or mention; উল্লেখ করা, নির্দ্দেশ করা।

cŏn-dē-scen′-sion (-sĕn-), *n.* **1.** Stooping to equality with or courtesy to inferiors; অনুজীবী বা হীনব্যক্তির প্রতি অনুগ্রহশীলতা, হীন ব্যক্তি বা অনুজীবীর প্রতি সাম্যভাব-প্রদর্শন, অভিমান-বিসর্জন। **2.** Courtesy; সৌজন্য, শিষ্টাচার। **3.** Patronizing manner; অনুগ্রহ-ব্যঞ্জক ব্যবহার।

cŏn-dign′ (-dīn), *adj.* Deserved; adequate; as, *condign* punishment; যথার্থ, ওয়াজিব (*Colloq.*), যথাযোগ্য, উপযুক্ত, যথোপযুক্ত, সমুচিত।

cŏn′-dī-mĕnt, *n.* Seasoning for food; sauce; আচার, চাট্‌নি, মসলা; উপস্কর (সাঃ পঃ)। **—men-tal,** *adj.*

cŏn-dī′-tion, *n.* **1.** Quality, state or external characteristic of anything; ভাব, গতি, অবস্থা, দশা, হাল (*Colloq.*)। **2.** A proviso; a stipulation; "In no case could France obtain more favourable *conditions*;" নিয়ম, পণ, সর্ত্ত; করার। **3.** (*Gram.*) A clause expressing a condition; আপেক্ষিক বাক্য। **4.** (*Pl.*) External circumstances; as, the new *conditions* of life; বাহ্যিক অবস্থা। **In** or **out of condition**—In a good or bad state of health, strength and training; ভাল বা মন্দ অবস্থায় (স্বাস্থ্য, শক্তি এবং শিক্ষা-সম্পর্কে)। **To change one's condition**—To marry; বিবাহ করা।

cŏn-dī′-tion, *v. t.* **1.** To make terms; to stipulate; চুক্তি করা, নিয়ম করা, করার করা; স্বীকার করা, সম্মত হওয়া। **2.** To determine; নির্দ্ধারণ করা। **3.** To burden or qualify by a condition; to limit or restrict; "He *conditioned* in his marriage settlement to give her half his goods;" সর্ত্ত করা; সীমাবদ্ধ করা। **4.** (*Commerce*) To test; (বাণিজ্য) পরীক্ষা করা।

cŏn-dī′-tion-ăl, *adj.* **1.** Not absolute; made with limitations; আপেক্ষিক, সাপেক্ষ, সপ্রতিবন্ধক, নৈয়মিক (হিঃ কোঃ), কারণজ (ঐ); সীমাবদ্ধ। **2.** (*Gram.* & *Log.*) Expressing a condition or supposition; (ব্যাকরণ ও ন্যায়শাস্ত্র) সংশয়বাচক, বিকল্পসূচক (আঃ বঃ)। **—al′-i-ty,** *n.* **—ly,** *adv.*

cŏn-dī′-tioned(-shŏnd),*adj.* **1.** Having a certain condition, state or qualities; as, a well *conditioned* ground; কোন বিশেষ অবস্থা-বিশিষ্ট। **2.** Having a specified disposition; বিশেষ স্বভাববিশিষ্ট। **3.** Situated; "In countries well-governed and happily *conditioned*;" অবস্থিত। **4.** Subjected to conditions or limitations; প্রতিবদ্ধ (তিঃ কোঃ), নিয়ত (ঐ), পরিচ্ছিন্ন (ঐ), অবচ্ছিন্ন।

cŏn-dō′-lă-tō-rȳ, *adj.* Expressing condolence; পরিবেদনাসূচক, সমবেদনাসূচক।

cŏn-dōle′, *v. i.* To grieve with; to sympathize; কাহারও দুঃখে দুঃখ প্রকাশ করা; সমবেদনা প্রকাশ করা। **—do′-lence,** *n.* Expression of sympathy; সমবেদনা প্রকাশ।

condominium, *n.* (*Diplom.*) Joint control of a state's affairs vested in two or more states; (কূট রাজনীতি) কোন রাজ্যসংক্রান্ত ব্যাপার সমূহ দুই বা ততোধিক ভারপ্রাপ্ত রাজ্যের সহযোগিতায় নির্ব্বাহ।

cŏn-dōne′, *v. t.* **1.** To pardon; to overlook the offence of (esp. matrimonial infidelity); পাপকর্ম্ম মার্জ্জনা করা, ক্ষমাকরা; কাহারও দোষ উপেক্ষা করা (বিশেষতঃ অবিশ্বাসিনী স্ত্রীর বা পরস্ত্রীতে আসক্ত স্বামীর)। **2.** (*Loosely*) To atone or compensate for; প্রায়শ্চিত্ত করা, ক্ষতিপূরণ করা। **—do-na′-tion,** *n.* **1.** Forgivenes of an offence; ক্ষমা, অপরাধ-মার্জ্জনা। **2.** (*Law*) The forgiving by a husband of his wife or by a wife of her husband for any breach of marital duty, with an implied understanding or condition that it shall not be repeated; (আইন) স্বামী স্ত্রীর নিকট কিম্বা স্ত্রী স্বামীর নিকট কোনরূপ বিশ্বাস-ঘাতকতার অপরাধ করিলে, ঐ অপরাধ দ্বিতীয়বার করা হইবে না এই সর্ত্তে স্বামীকর্ত্তৃক স্ত্রীর কিম্বা স্ত্রীকর্ত্তৃক স্বামীর অপরাধ-মার্জ্জনা।

cŏn′-dor (-dêr), *n.* **1.** A large bird of prey,—vulture of South America; দক্ষিণ আমেরিকাদেশীয় গৃধ্রবিশেষ।

condottiere, *n.* [*It.*] An Italian free-booter; ইতালিদেশীয় লুণ্ঠনকারী।

cŏn-dūce′, *v. t.* To contribute to, or promote, a result; to further; (followed by *to*, or *toward*); কোনরূপ ফল উৎপাদনে আনুকূল্য বা সাহায্য করা, ফলোপধায়ক হওয়া; অগ্রসর করা। **—du′-cive,** *adj.* Tendinig to promote; সহায়তাকর, সাধক, ফলোপধায়ক, জনক, আবহ, প্রয়োজক। **—du′-cive-ness,** *n.*

cŏn′-dŭct, *n.* **1.** Guidance; পথ-প্রদর্শন, পরিচালন। **2.** Manner of carrying business; কার্য্যপ্রণালী। **3.** Deportment usually with more or less reference to its moral quality; as, good or bad *conduct*; আচার, আচরণ, চরিত্র, ব্যবহার, চর্য্যা, বৃত্তি, চালচলন। **4.** Manner of arrangement of parts as in a painting; চিত্রাদিতে বিভিন্ন অংশের সংস্থান-প্রণালী। **5.** (*Mil.*) Generalship; (সামরিকশাস্ত্র) অধিনায়কতা।

cŏn-dŭct′, *v. t.* & *i.* **1.** To bring along or guide; to direct; পথ-প্রদর্শন করা; চালিত করা। **2.** To behave,—with the reflexive; as he *conducted himself* well; চলা,

আচরণ করা। **3.** To command (an army); সৈন্যদলের অধিনায়কতা করা। **4.** To manage; as, to *conduct* a business; পরিচালনা করা, নির্ব্বাহ করা। **5.** (*Mus.*) To lead or direct, as a choir or orchestra, (also *Verb i.*); (সঙ্গীত-শাস্ত্র) ভজনগায়ক দল কিম্বা নাট্যালয় প্রভৃতির বাদকদলকে পরিচালন করা। ***Verb i.*** (*Phys.*) To transmit (also *Verb t.*); তাপ, তাড়িত, প্রভৃতি চালিত করা, সঞ্চালন করা। **—duc′-tion,** *n.* **1.** Passage of heat through any body or of electricity over its entire surface; কোন বস্তুর মধ্যে উত্তাপ সঞ্চালন বা কোন বস্তুর উপরে তাড়িত সঞ্চালন, প্রবাহ, সঞ্চালন (সাঃ পঃ)। **2.** Conducting (of liquid through pipe, etc. esp. of natural processes); নল প্রভৃতির ভিতর দিয়া তরল পদার্থ সঞ্চালন। **—i-bil′-i-ty,** *n.* **—i-ble,** *adj.* Capable of conducting (heat etc.); পরিচালনীয়, পরিচালনক্ষম। **—ive,** *adj.* Capable of conducting; possessing conductivity; পরিচালনক্ষম; পরিচালক। **—iv′-i-ty,** *n.* The power of conducting heat, electricity, etc.; সঞ্চালন-ক্ষমতা (সাঃ পঃ), সঞ্চালনশীলতা (ঐ), পরিচালকতা (প্রঃ বাঃ), চালকতা (হিঃ কোঃ)।

cŏn-dŭc′-tor (-têr), *n.* **1.** A leader; a guide; নায়ক, চালক, নেতা, অধ্যক্ষ; পথপ্রদর্শক। **2.** One who attends the passengers in a tramway-car, etc.; ট্রামগাড়ী প্রভৃতিতে যে কর্ম্মচারী যাত্রীদিগের তত্ত্বাবধান করে। **3.** A manager or director, esp. of a choir; কার্য্য-নির্ব্বাহক, তত্ত্বাবধায়ক, বিশেষতঃ ভজন-সঙ্গীত গায়ক দলের নেতা। **4.** A substance capable of transmitting electricity, heat, etc.; উত্তাপ, তাড়িত, প্রভৃতি সঞ্চালক পদার্থ, প্রবাহক (আঃ বঃ), পরিচালক (সাঃ পঃ), চালক (হিঃ কোঃ)। **5.** A rod at the top of a building conducting electricity away into the earth; অট্টালিকাগ্রস্থিত ধাতব দণ্ডবিশেষ—যদ্দ্বারা ভূতলে তাড়িত চালিত হয়, বিজলীদণ্ড।

cŏn′-duit (-dĭt), *n.* A channel or pipe to lead or convey water, (also *fig.*); পয়ঃপ্রণালী (লক্ষণায়ও ব্যবহৃত হয়), জলের নল।

cŏn-dū′-plĭ-cāte, *adj.* Folded length-wise along the middle; (উদ্ভিদ্-বিদ্যা) মধ্যদিকে লম্বালম্বিভাবে মুদ্রিত, মুদ্রিত (সাঃ পঃ)।

cŏn′-dȳle, *n.* (*Anat.*) A rounded projection at the end of a bone; (শারীর-সংস্থানবিদ্যা) অস্থির প্রান্তে বর্ত্তুলাকৃতি প্রলম্বিত অংশ। **—dy-loid,** *adj.*

cŏn-dȳ-lō′-mă, *n.* A wart-like growth or tumour near the genital organs or the arms; ভগ বা গুহ্যদ্বারে আঁচিলবৎ উপমাংস, শ্লেষ্মাগুটি (হঃ চঃ), কোর (সুশ্রুঃ) অণ্ডকোর (সাঃ পঃ), শ্লৈষ্মিকবটী (জাহিঃ)।

cōne, *n.*, *v. t.* & *i.* **1.** A solid body or figure tapering to a point from a circular base like a sugar-loaf; মোচাকার বস্তু, সূচী (সাঃ পঃ), মোচা (সাঃ পঃ), বৃত্তসূচী (ঐ), সূচ্যাকার শঙ্কু (হিঃ কোঃ), সূচি-ঘনক্ষেত্র (আঃ বঃ)। **2.** The fruit of several evergreen trees as of the pine, fir, etc.; সরল, দেবদারু প্রভৃতি কতিপয় চিরহরিত বৃক্ষের ফল। **3.** (*Zool.*) The English name of any shell of the large tropical molluscous genus Conus; (জন্তু-বিদ্যা) একপ্রকার শম্বুক। **4.** A cone-shaped vessel hoisted as a foul-weather signal; দুর্দ্দিনের সঙ্কেত-স্বরূপ ব্যবহৃত মোচাকৃতি পাত্র বিশেষ। ***Verb t.*** To shape like a cone; মোচাকৃতি করা। ***Verb i.*** To bear cones; উক্তপ্রকার ফলপ্রসূ হওয়া। **Con′-ic, Con′-i-cal,** *adjs.*

Cone.

cōnes, *n.* Name given by bakers to a fine white flour used by them to dust their loaves and troughs; একপ্রকার মিহি ময়দা।

conessi bark—কুটজের ছাল।
conessi seed—ইন্দ্র-যব।

cō′-ney (-nē), *n.* Same as CONY.

cŏn′-făb, *v. t.* & *n.* Colloq. & abbr. of CONFABULATE or CONFABULATION.

cŏn-făb′-ū-lāte, *v. t.* To talk in an easy unrestrained manner; গল্পগুজব করা। **—la′-tion,** *n.* **—la-to-ry,** *adj.*

cŏn-fĕc′-tion, *n.* **1.** Making or preparation by mixture of ingredients; বিভিন্ন উপাদানের সংমিশ্রণে প্রস্তুত করণ। **2.** Thing compounded; esp. a sweetmeat or preparation of fruit preserved in sugar; উক্তপ্রকার মিশ্রিত দ্রব্য; মিষ্টদ্রব্য, মিঠাই, মোরব্বা, উপস্কর, খণ্ডপাক (সাঃ পঃ)। **3.** A piece of fashionable apparel for women, as a mantle, cloak, etc.; "A dainty *confection* of pale blue silk;" স্ত্রীলোকের সৌখিন পোষাক বিশেষ। **—a-ry,** *adj.* & *n.* Of or pertaining to confections or their making; মিষ্টদ্রব্য সম্বন্ধীয়, মিষ্টদ্রব্য-প্রস্তুত বিষয়ক। (*Noun*) A store or place for sweetmeats, etc.; মিষ্টদ্রব্যের ভাণ্ডার।

cŏn-fĕc′-tion-êr, *n.* One whose occupation is to make or to sell sweetmeats, candies, etc.; ময়রা, মোদক, মিঠাইওয়ালা, মিষ্টদ্রব্য-প্রস্তুতকারী, হালুইকর, মিষ্টকার (আঃ বঃ)। **—y,** *n.* **1.** The art of preparing sweetmeats; মিষ্টদ্রব্য প্রস্তুত প্রণালী। **2.** A place where sweet-meats are made or sold; ময়রার দোকান, মিষ্টদ্রব্য প্রস্তুতের স্থান। **3.** Sweetmeats in general; মিষ্টদ্রব্য।

cŏn-fĕd′-êr-ă-cȳ, *n.* **1.** A league, covenant or treaty; an alliance; সন্ধি; সন্ধিসূত্রে মিলন। **2.** Persons, states, or nations united by a league; মিত্রতা-সূত্রে বা সন্ধি-সূত্রে আবদ্ধ ব্যক্তি কিংবা রাজ্যাদি। **3.** (*Law*) A league for an unlawful or evil purpose; a conspiracy;

"*Confederacy* to carry on the work of darkness;" (আইন) অবৈধ অভিপ্রায়ে বা অসদুদ্দেশ্যে সম্মিলন; চক্রান্ত, যোগসাজস।

cŏn-fĕd′-êr-āte, *adj.* & *n.* Allied or united in a league (*lit.* & *fig.*); সন্ধিসূত্রে আবদ্ধ বা সম্মিলিত। ***Noun.*** **1.** An ally (esp. in a bad sense); an accomplice; মিত্র; সহাপরাধী, দুষ্কর্ম্মে সহকারী। **2.** One united in a league; সন্ধিবদ্ধ ব্যক্তি।

cŏn-fĕd′-êr-āte, *v. t.* & *i.* To unite in a league; সন্ধিসূত্রে আবদ্ধ করা বা হওয়া। **—a′-tion,** *n.*

cŏn-fêr′, *v. t.* & *i.* To give or bestow; to grant; সমর্পণ করা; সপে দেওয়া (*Colloq.*); প্রদান করা। ***Verb i.*** To consult together; একত্র পরামর্শ করা। **—en′-tial** *adj.* **—ment,** *n.* **—ra-ble,** *adj.* **To confer on**—To grant some degree or title; উপাধি প্রদান করা। **To confer with**—To hold a consultation with some one; কাহারও সহিত মন্ত্রণা বা পরামর্শ করা।

confer, [*L.*] *v.* (*imper*) Compare; তুলনা কর। (Abbr.—*cf.*)

cŏn′-fêr-ĕnce, *n.* **1.** Consultation; মন্ত্রণা, পরামর্শ। **2.** A meeting for consultation, discussion or adjustment of differences, etc.; মন্ত্রণা-সভা, পরামর্শ-সভা।

cŏn-fêr′-vă, *n.* An aquatic plant; শৈবাল।

cŏn-fĕss′, *v. t.* & *i.* **1.** To admit or own; to acknowledge; as, I *confess* my fault; স্বীকার করা; কবুল করা। **2.** To disclose sins, esp. to a priest with a view to absolution; (also *Verb i.*); পাপ স্বীকার করা, বিশেষতঃ পাপের ক্ষমা পাইবার উদ্দেশ্যে ধর্ম্মযাজকগণের নিকট আত্মদোষ প্রকাশ করা। ***Verb i.*** (*Of the priest*) To hear or receive the confession of a penitent; (ধর্ম্মযাজকের পক্ষে) অনুতপ্ত পাপীর পাপের কাহিনী শ্রবণ করা। **—ed-ly,** *adv.*

cŏn-fes′-sion (-fĕ-), *n.* **1.** Acknowledgment of guilt, failure, etc.; as, the *confession* of Rousseau; স্বীকারোক্তি, একরার, আত্মকথা, দোষস্বীকার। **2.** (*Eccl.*) Act of disclosing sins or faults to a priest; ধর্ম্মযাজকের নিকট স্বীয় পাপ কার্য্যের কথা প্রকাশ করণ, পাপস্বীকার। **Auricular confession**—ধর্ম্মযাজকের নিকট পাপ স্বীকার। **Confession of Augsberg**—মার্টিন লুথারের ধর্ম্মমত—যাহা ১৫৩০ খৃঃ ২৫শে জুন তারিখ মেলাংকথন্ অগস্‌বার্গ নামক স্থানে প্রকটিত করিয়াছিলেন। **Confession of faith**—সূত্রবিশেষ—যাহাতে কোন ধর্ম্মসমাজের মতসমূহ নিবদ্ধ থাকে।

cŏn-fes′-sion-ăl (-fĕ-), *adj.* & *n.* Of or pertaining to confession; স্বীকার-সম্বন্ধীয়, স্বীকারোক্তি-সম্বন্ধীয়। ***Noun.*** A place where a priest sits to hear confessions; যে আসনে উপবেশন করত ধর্ম্মযাজক কোন ব্যক্তির পাপের কাহিনী শ্রবণ করেন।

cŏn-fes′-sion-ist (-fĕ-), *n.* One adhering to a certain confession of faith; কোন বিশেষ ধর্ম্মসমাজের মতাবলম্বী ব্যক্তি।

cŏn-fĕs′-sor (-sêr), *n.* **1.** One who confesses any fault or crime; পাপ বা আত্মদোষ স্বীকারকারী। **2.** One who confesses his religion in face of danger, but does not suffer martyrdom; স্বীয় ধর্ম্মমত ব্যক্ত করিয়া যাহাকে বিপদাপন্ন হইতে হয় কিন্তু জীবনোৎসর্গ করিতে হয় না। **3.** A priest who hears confessions and grants absolution; যে ধর্ম্মযাজক পাপকাহিনী শ্রবণ করেন এবং পাপ হইতে ক্ষমাপ্রদান করেন।

cŏn-fĕt′-tö, *n.* (usu. in *pl.* -TI) Bonbons; sweetmeats; also plaster or paper imitations of bonbons often used by carnival revelers, at wedding, etc.; বন্‌বন্; মিঠাই; কাগজের তৈয়ারী বন্‌বন্,—যাহা বিবাহাদিতে আমোদপ্রিয় ব্যক্তিগণ ব্যবহার করে।

cŏn-fī-dănt′, (*Fem.* CONFIDANTE = সখী, নর্ম্মসখী, সজনী) *n.* A bosom friend, chiefly in love affairs and lighter matter of love; অন্তরঙ্গ বন্ধু, সখা, বয়স্য, নর্ম্মসখা, বিশেষতঃ যাহার নিকট ভালবাসা বা গুপ্ত প্রণয়-কাহিনী বলা হয়।

cŏn-fīde′, *v. t.* & *i.* **1.** To entrust or commit to the charge of; "The execution of the plan was *confided* to Aranda;" বিশ্বাসপূর্ব্বক ন্যস্ত করা। **2.** To impart as a secret; "An opportunity of *confiding* all her perplexities to her friend;" কাহারও নিকট গুপ্তকথা বলা। ***Verb i.*** To believe in with assurance; দৃঢ়বিশ্বাস করা। **To confide to**—To entrust one with—বিশ্বাসপূর্ব্বক ন্যস্ত করা।

cŏn′-fī-dĕnce, *n.* **1.** A firm trust or reliance; বিশ্বাস, প্রত্যয়, নির্ভর, বিশ্রম্ভন (বাংস্যঃ)। **2.** Assured expectation; as, great *confidence* of success; ভরসা, নিশ্চিতাশা। **3.** Overboldness; as, their *confidence* rises from too much credit given to their wits; দুঃসাহস, প্রগল্‌ভতা। **4.** Condition of close intimacy or trust; "A citizen who afterwards was in great *confidence* with Cæsar;" বিশ্বস্ততা, অন্তরঙ্গতা। **Confidence trick (or game)**—জুয়াচুরীর ফন্দিবিশেষ,—যাহাতে বিড়ম্বিত ব্যক্তি অর্থ, অলঙ্কার, প্রভৃতি বিশ্বাসপূর্ব্বক জুয়াচোরের হস্তে ন্যস্ত করিতে প্রলুব্ধ হয়। **To be in one's confidence**—To be trusted by one; কাহারও বিশ্বাস-ভাজন হওয়া। **To have confidence**—To have faith in; কাহারও উপর বিশ্বাস থাকা। **Told in confidence**—Told as a secret; গোপনীয়-ভাবে কথিত, বিশ্বাসপূর্ব্বক কথিত। **To take into confidence**—To admit a person into one's secrets; কাহাকেও বিশ্বাস করিয়া গুপ্ত কথা বলা। **To worm oneself into one's confidence**—To enter gradually by arts and insinuation into the confidence of a person ; নানারূপ ছল কপটতা করিয়া ক্রমে ক্রমে কোন ব্যক্তির বিশ্বাস ভাজন হওয়া ।

cŏn'-fĭ-dĕnt, *adj.* & *n.* **1.** Having full belief ; অসন্দিগ্ধ, নিঃসন্দেহ, পূর্ণবিশ্বাস-পরায়ণ, বিশ্রব্ধ, ছিন্নসংশয়, কৃতনিশ্চয়, দৃঢ়নিশ্চয় । **2.** Relying one one's self ; undaunted ; আত্মনির্ভরশীল, স্বাবলম্বী ; নির্ভয়, নিঃশঙ্ক, সাহসী । **3.** Presumptuous ; conceited ; as, a *confident* slut ; প্রগল্‌ভ ; দৃপ্ত । ***Noun.*** A confidant ; সখা । **—ly,** *adv.* **—ness,** *n*

cŏn-fĭ-dĕn'-tial, *adj.* **1.** Communicated in confidence ; characterised by the communication of secrets ; বিশ্বাসপূর্ব্বক কথিত, অপ্রকাশ্য ; গোপনীয় । **2.** Charged with secret service ; as, a *confidential* clerk ; গোপনীয় কার্য্যের ভারপ্রাপ্ত, বিশ্বস্ত । **—ti-al'-i-ty,** *n.*

cŏn-fĭg-ū-rā'-tion, *n.* **1.** External form or figure due to adjustment of parts ; বহিরাকার, বাহ্যাকৃতি, বাহ্যগঠন, গঠন (সাঃ পঃ), গঠন-প্রণালী (ঐ) । **2.** (*Astrol.*) The relative position of the planets ; the face of the horoscope according to the relative aspects of the planets at any time ; (ফলিত-জ্যোতিষ) গ্রহাদির আপেক্ষিক স্থিতি, সাপেক্ষিক স্থিতি (হিঃ কোঃ), গ্রহকুণ্ডলিকা (মঃ উঃ) ।

cŏn-fĭg'-ūre, *v. t.* To arrange into any form or shape (*usu. fig.*) ; as, *configuring* themselves into human shape ; কোন বিশেষ আকারে বিন্যাস করা, অবয়ববিশিষ্ট করা ।

cŏn'-fīne, *n.* (*usu. pl.*) Boundaries ; frontiers ; প্রান্ত, চতুঃসীমা ; সীমান্ত ।

cŏn-fīne', *v. t.* & *i.* **1.** To shut up ; to imprison ; আবদ্ধ করা, সীমাবদ্ধ করা ; কারারুদ্ধ করা । **2.** (*In. pass.*) To be in child-bed ; সূতিকাগৃহে আবদ্ধ থাকা । ***Verb i.*** To border ; to be contiguous ; সীমায় থাকা ; লাগালাগি থাকা । **Be confined to one's bed** or **room**—Be unable through illness to leave one's bed or room ; (রোগে) শয্যাগত হওয়া, শয্যাশায়ী হওয়া ।

con-fīne'-mĕnt, *n.* **1.** Imprisonment ; কারারোধ, কারাবাস, কয়েদ, বন্ধন । **2.** Restriction from going abroad, esp. by childbirth ; আটক, সূতিকাগৃহে বন্ধাবস্থা, প্রসবাবস্থা । **3.** Restriction ; limitation ; বাধা, নিরোধ ; সীমাবদ্ধতা ।

cŏn-firm' (-fêrm), *v. t.* **1.** To make stronger or firmer ; to strengthen ; প্রবল করা ; দৃঢ় করা, বলবৎ করা । **2.** To assure or ratify ; as, the senate *confirms* the treaty ; সুনিশ্চিত করা, অনুমোদন করা, মঞ্জুর করা, দৃঢ়ীভূত করা । **3.** To corroborate (a statement or evidence) ; সমর্থন করা, পোষকতা করা । **4.** To establish more firmly ; দৃঢ়তররূপে প্রতিষ্ঠিত করা, পাকা করা, বাহাল করা (*Colloq.*) । **5.** (*Eccl.*) To admit into full church privilege ; খৃষ্টীয় ধর্ম্মযাজকের পূর্ণ অধিকার প্রদান করা । **—a-tive,** *adj* **—a-tive-ly,** *adv.* **—a-to-ry,** *adj.* **—firmed',** *adj.* **A confirmed villain**—পাকা বদমায়েস ।

con-fir-mā'-tion (-fêr), *n.* **1.** The act of confirming or strengthening ; স্থিরীকরণ, দৃঢ়ীকরণ । **2.** Corroboration ; convincing testimony ; সমর্থন ; প্রত্যয়জনক প্রমাণ । **3.** The ceremony of admission into full church privilege by a bishop ; খৃষ্টীয় ধর্ম্মসমাজের পূর্ণ অধিকার প্রদান উপলক্ষে ধর্ম্মাধ্যক্ষ কর্ত্তৃক অনুষ্ঠিত ক্রিয়া বিশেষ, প্রতিপাদন (আঃ বঃ) ।

cŏn'-fĭs-cate, *v. t.* **1.** To appropriate to the public treasury ; রাজকোষভুক্ত করা, জব্দ করা, সরকারে খাস করিয়া লওয়া । **2.** To seize as by authority ; as, the police *confiscated* the liquor found in the premises ; বাজেয়াপ্ত করা । **—ca-to-ry,** *adj.*

cŏn-fĭs-cā'-tion, *n.* **1.** Act of confiscating ; বাজেয়াপ্ত করণ, জব্দ করণ, সর্ব্বস্বাপহার । **2.** (*Colloq.*) Legal robbery by or with the sanction of the ruling power ; (চলিতভাষায়) রাজশক্তি কর্ত্তৃক বা রাজশক্তির অনুমোদনে বিধিসিদ্ধ লুণ্ঠন ।

cŏn-flā-grā'-tion, *n.* (*Lit.* & *fig.*) A great destructive fire ; দাহ, মহাজ্বলন, ভীষণ অগ্নিদাহ বা অগ্নিকাণ্ড, দাবানল, মহা অগ্নিদাহ, ব্যাপকাগ্নি ।

cŏn-flā'-tion, *n.* **1.** The action of fusing together ; একত্রে গলিত করণ । **2.** (*Fig.*) The combination of two variant readings of a text into a composite reading ; (লক্ষণায়) দুইটী বিভিন্ন পাঠের সংযোগ ।

con'-flict, *n.* **1.** (*Lit* & *fig.*) Fight or struggle ; যুদ্ধ, বিরোধ, সংঘর্ষ । **2.** Violent collision ; তুমুল সংঘর্ষ । **3.** Variance of principles, etc. ; as *conflict* comprehends all kinds of intellectual hesitation ; মতদ্বৈধ, মতবিরোধ, প্রতিপক্ষতা । **Conflict of laws**—ব্যবস্থা-বিজ্ঞানের শাখাবিশেষ — যাহাতে দুইটী বিভিন্ন রাজ্যে প্রচলিত বিধি সকলের বৈষম্য সংক্রান্ত বিষয় সমূহ আলোচিত হইয়া থকে ।

cŏn-flict', *v. t.* **1.** To strive and struggle ; to contend ; সংগ্রাম, করা ; বিরোধ করা, যুদ্ধ করা । **2.** To clash ; to be incompatible ; সংঘট্টিত হওয়া ; মতদ্বৈধ হওয়া, বিসদৃশ হওয়া, বিরোধী হওয়া । **—flict-ing,** *adj.* Contradictory ; বিরুদ্ধ, বিপরীত, বিরোধী, বিবদমান ।

cŏn'-flū-ĕnce, *n.* **1.** A flowing together ; একত্রে প্রবহন । **2.** Junction of two or more streams of water ; দুই বা ততোধিক স্রোতস্বিনীর সঙ্গমস্থল, সঙ্গম । **3.** A multitude ; "He was with much honour, in sight of a great *confluence* of people ;" জনতা ।

cŏn'-flū-ĕnt, *adj.* & *n.* **1.** Flowing together ; meeting in the course, as two streams, etc.

একত্র প্রবহমান ; সংযোজনশীল। 2. (*Fig.*) Uniting or blending into one ; as, this vast *confluent* tumult ; (লক্ষণায়) সম্মিলিত, সংমিশ্রিত। ***Noun.*** A small stream flowing into a large one ; বৃহৎ স্রোতস্বতী অভিমুখে প্রবহমান ক্ষুদ্র স্রোতস্বতী, উপনদী। **Confluent small-pox**—যে বসন্তে গুটি সকল পরস্পরের সহিত সংশ্লিষ্ট হইয়া যায়, লেপাবসন্ত, সংশ্লিষ্ট বসন্ত।

cŏn′-flŭx, *n.* 1. Flowing together ; a confluence ; একসঙ্গে প্রবহন ; স্রোতঃসঙ্গমস্থল। 2. A large assemblage ; বৃহজ্জনতা, বহুজনসমাগম।

cŏn-fŏrm′, *v. t.* & *i.* To make like in shape or character ; to accomodate ; to adapt ; as, the life of a nation should be *conformed* to certain principles of belief and conduct ; অনুরূপ করা ; সদৃশ করা ; উপযোগী করা। ***Verb i.*** 1. To comply with ; অনুযায়ী হওয়া, অনুবর্ত্তী হওয়া, সদৃশ হওয়া, অনুরূপ হওয়া। 2. To obey ; অনুগত হওয়া। **—ance,** *n.*

cŏn-fŏrm′-ȧ-ble, *adj.* 1. Having the same form ; অনুরূপ, সদৃশ। 2. Agreeable ; consistent ; as, a conclusion *conformable* to our present doctrine ; অনুগত ; অনুযায়ী, যোগ্য, অবিরুদ্ধ, সঙ্গতিবিশিষ্ট। 3. Submissive ; আজ্ঞাবহ, বশ্য, বশংবদ। **—bil′-i-ty,** *n.* **—bly,** *adv.*

cŏn-fŏr-mā′-tion, *n.* 1. Act of conforming ; the particular make or construction of a body ; structure ; আনুরূপ্য, অনুরূপতা ; গঠন ; আকৃতি, আকার, দেহের গঠন। 2. Adaptation ; উপযোগিতা, উপযোগিতা-শক্তি।

cŏn-fŏrm′-ist, *n.* One who conforms with the worship of the Church of England ; ইংলণ্ডীয় ধর্ম্মসমাজের অনুমোদিত উপাসনা প্রণালীর অনুসরণকারী।

cŏn-fŏrm′-i-tȳ, *n.* 1. Resemblance ; আনুরূপ্য, সাদৃশ্য, অনুরূপতা। 2. Compliance ; অনুবৃত্তি, অনুকূলতা, বশ্যতা। **In conformity with**—In accordance with ; কোনও কিছুর অনুসারে।

cŏn-found′ (-fownd), *v. t.* 1. To mix or mingle ; মিশ্রিত করা। 2. To throw into perplexity ; to confuse ; "This difficulty, for a long time, quite *confounded* me ;" কিংকর্ত্তব্যবিমূঢ় করা, হতবুদ্ধি করা, আকুলিত করা, বিহ্বল করা ; বিভ্রান্ত করা। 3. To mistake one for another ; এক ব্যক্তিকে অন্য ব্যক্তি বলিয়া ভ্রম করা। 4. To dismay ; ভীত করা। 5. To defeat (a plan, hope) ; (উপায়, আশা) ব্যর্থ করা। 6. (*Bible*) To put to shame ; (বাইবেল) লজ্জিত করা। **—ed,** *adj.* Confused ; কিংকর্ত্তব্যবিমূঢ়, হতবুদ্ধি। **—ed-ly,** *adv.* **Confound you**—চুলায় যাও।

cŏn-frȧ-têr′-ni-tȳ, *n.* 1. A brotherhood ; সৌভ্রাত্র, ভ্রাতৃত্ব। 2. A society or body of men, generally a religious or charitable one ; সম্প্রদায়, ধর্ম্মসম্প্রদায়, ভ্রাতৃমণ্ডলী, দাতৃ-সম্প্রদায়।

confrere (cŏn-frār), [*F.*], *n.* Fellow member of a profession, scientific body, etc. ; সমব্যবসায়ী, বৈজ্ঞানিক সভাদির সহযোগী সদস্য।

cŏn-front′ (-frŭnt), *v. t.* 1. To stand face to face with, esp. to face hostility ; "It was impossible to *confront* the might of France ;" সম্মুখীন হওয়া। 2. To oppose ; বাধা দেওয়া, প্রতিরোধ করা। 3. To compare ; to contrast ; তুলনা করা ; বৈসাদৃশ্য প্রদর্শন করা। 4. To bring (a person) face to face (with his accusers, etc.) ; "To send a man to the gallows as a traitor without *confronting* him with his accusers ;" মুখামুখি করান, কোন ব্যক্তিকে (তাহার অভিযোক্তা প্রভৃতির) সম্মুখে দাঁড় করান।

Cŏn-fū′-ci-ăn (-shi), *adj.* Of or belonging to Confucius, the Chinese philosopher ; চীনদেশীয় দার্শনিক কন্‌ফিউসিয়াস্ সম্বন্ধীয়। **—ism, —ist,** *ns.*

cŏn-fūse′, *v. t.* 1. To put into disorder ; to disorganize ; গোলমাল করিয়া ফেলা ; বিশৃঙ্খল করা। 2. To obscure ; to render doubtful of meaning or explanation ; "Our ideas of their intimate essences and causes are *confused* ;" অস্পষ্ট করা ; অর্থ অস্পষ্ট করা। 3. To disconcert ; to perplex ; to abash ; আকুলিত করা, হতবুদ্ধি করা ; বিভ্রান্ত করা, ব্যস্ত করা, বিহ্বল করা ; অপ্রতিভ করা, লজ্জিত করা। **—fused′,** *adj.* 1. Perplexed ; বিহ্বল, বিভ্রান্ত, আকুলিত, অপ্রতিভ। 2. Disordered ; বিশৃঙ্খল। **—fus′-ed-ly,** *adv.*

cŏn-fū′-sion (-zhŏn), *n.* 1. Act of confusing ; state of being confused ; disorder ; tumult ; বিশৃঙ্খলকরণ ; গোলযোগ, ব্যস্ততা, হুলস্থূল, বিপ্লব ; বিশৃঙ্খলা ; সোরগোল। 2. Loss of self-possession ; perplexity ; বুদ্ধি-বিকৃতি, চিত্তভ্রান্তি ; বিভ্রম, বিক্লবতা, হতবুদ্ধিতা, অপ্রতিভাবস্থা।

cŏn-fūte′, *v. t.* To co[illegible]o be- of error by argument or p[illegible] মিশ্রিত to prove to be false o[illegible] erroneous ; তর্ক বা প্রমাণদ্বারা ভ্রমপ্রদ[illegible] ; করা ; খণ্ডন করা, নিরাকরণ করা, প্রতি[illegible]ত করা। **—fu-ta′-tion,** *n.* Refuta[illegible]tion ; নিরাকরণ, খণ্ডন (হিঃ কোঃ)।

cŏn′-ḡë, cŏn′-gee (-gë), *n., v. t.* & *i.* 1. (*Archaic*) A bow or courtesy before taking leave or at other times ; বিদায়কালীন নমস্কার ইত্যাদি, প্রণাম। 2. A dismissal without ceremony ; বিনা লৌকিকতায় বরখাস্ত বা কর্ম্মচ্যুতি। ***Verb t. & i.*** 1. To bow or courtesy ; অভিবাদন করা, প্রণিপাত করা। 2. To take leave ceremoniously ; শিষ্টাচারপূর্ব্বক বিদায় লওয়া।

cŏn-geal′ (-jēl), *v. t.* & *i.* 1. To freeze, (also *v. i.*) ; ঘনীভূত করা ব হওয়া। 2. To coagulate ; (also *v. i.*)

to check the flow of ; "As if with horror to *congeal* his blood ;" জমাট বাঁধান বা জমাট বাঁধা, গাঢ় হওয়া, জমিয়া যাওয়া ; প্রবাহরোধ করা। **—a-ble,** *adj.* **—ment,** *n.*

cŏn-gē-lā′-tion, *n.* **1.** Act of congealing ; ঘনীভবন, (শীতে) জমাট বাঁধন। **2.** State of being congealed ; ঘনীভূতাবস্থা। **3.** A congealed mass ; ঘনীভূত পিণ্ড।

cŏn′-ge-ner (jē-nêr or -jĕn-êr), *n.* & *adj.* A thing of the same genus or nature ; একজাতীয় বস্তু, সমধর্ম্মা বস্তু। ***Adj.*** Akin or allied to ; স্বজাতীয়, সম্বন্ধবিশিষ্ট।

cŏn-gē-nĕr′-ic, *adj.* **1.** Of the same genus, kind or race ; এক-জাতিভুক্ত, একবিধ, একজাতীয়, একবংশীয়। **2.** Allied in nature ; সমপ্রকৃতিক।

cŏn-gĕn′-êr-ous (-ŭs), *adj.* Akin in nature or character; সমপ্রকৃতিক।

cŏn-gē′-ni-ăl, *adj.* **1.** Of the same genus or family (*loosely*) ; একজাতীয়, একবংশীয়। **2.** Kindred ; একপ্রকৃতিক। **3.** Sympathetic ; সহানু-…পন্ন। **4.** Naturally adapt-…ited ; "The sea was an …ent never *congenial* to the …rit of Spartan warfare ; প্রকৃতির …গী ; উপযোগী, অনুকূল,অনুযায়ী, …প। **—al′-i-ty,** *n.* **—ly,** *adv.*

…n-gĕn′-i-tăl, *adj.* **1.** Existing from birth ; as, a *congenital* deformity ; সহজ, সহজাত, আজন্মিক। **2.** Natural ; as, a *congenital* disease ; মৌলিক, স্বাভাবিক। **—ly,** *adv.*

…on′-gêr (cŏng-), *n.* The common seaeel, much used for food ; (also CONGER-EEL) ; সামুদ্রিক মৎস্যবিশেষ, সমুদ্রের বাইন মৎস্য, সমুদ্রকুক্ষিকা (আঃ বঃ)।

…ŏn-gē′-ri-ēs, *n.* A collection or heap of particles or bodies ; পুঞ্জ, পিণ্ড, রাশি, স্তূপ।

…ŏn-gĕst′, *v. i.* & *t.* To accumulate to excess ; অত্যধিক পরিমাণে সঞ্চিত হওয়া, জমাট হওয়া। ***Verb t.*** To affect with congestion or overflowing ; as, the traffic was *congested* ; অতিরিক্ত মাত্রায় জড় করিয়া সমাকুল করা, ঘন-সন্নিবিষ্ট করা, পরিমাণাধিক্যদ্বারা প্রপীড়িত করা। **—ges′-tive,** *adj.*

cŏn-gĕs′-tion, *n.* **1.** An unnatural accumulation of blood in an organ deranging its action ; কোন শারীরিক যন্ত্রে অস্বাভাবিক রক্তাধিক্য, রক্তসংগ্রহ। **2.** (*Fig.*) Crowded condition ; as, a *congestion* of traffic on a railway ; (লক্ষণায়) জনাকীর্ণ ভাব, লোকাকীর্ণতা, সঙ্কুলতা।

cŏn-glōbe′, cŏn-glō′-bate, *v.t.* & *i.* To form into a ball or hard round substance ; গোলাকার করা, বর্ত্তুলাকার করা, পিণ্ডীকৃত করা বা পিণ্ডীভূত হওয়া, কন্দুকাকারে গঠন করা। **—glo-ba′-tion,** *n.*

cŏn-glō′-bate, *adj.* Formed into a ball ; পিণ্ডীভূত, বর্ত্তুলীকৃত, কন্দুকা-কারে পরিণত।

cŏn-glŏm′-êr-āte, *adj.* & *n.* **1.** Gathered into a ball or mass ; পিণ্ডীভূত, সংহত, স্তূপীকৃত, কন্দুকাকারে পরিণত। **2.** (*Geol.*) Composed of the fragments of pre-existing rocks cemented together ; (ভূ-বিদ্যা) একত্র সংশ্লিষ্ট প্রস্তরখণ্ড সমূহ দ্বারা রচিত। ***Noun.*** Sort of course rough rock composed of various substances, as pebbles of quartz, flints, etc. ; উপলখণ্ড, অগ্নিপ্রস্তরখণ্ড, প্রভৃতির সংশ্লেষদ্বারা রচিত পাষাণবিশেষ।

cŏn-glŏm′-êr-āte, *v. t.* & *i.* To collect into a coherent mass, (*lit.* & *fig.*) ; (শব্দানুযায়ী ও লক্ষণায়) সংহত করা, পিণ্ডীভূত করা, পুঞ্জীকৃত করা, তাল পাকান, রাশিকৃত হওয়া।

cŏn-glŏm-êr-ā′-tion, *n.* A mixed coherent mass ; রাশি, স্তূপ।

cŏn-glū′-ti-nāte, *v. t.* & *i.* To glue together ; to cause to adhere together ; আঠা দিয়া সংশ্লিষ্ট করা ; জোড়া। ***Verb i.*** To coalesce ; সংযুক্ত হওয়া, সংশ্লিষ্ট হওয়া, জোড়া লাগা। **—na′-tion,** *n.* **—na-tive,** *adj.*

cŏn′-gou (-gō), **—gō,** *n.* A kind of black Chinese tea ; চীনদেশীয় এক-প্রকার কাল রংয়ের চা।

cŏn-grăt′-ū-lāte, *v. t.* To address (a person) with expressions of sympathetic joy on any fortunate event ; to wish joy to ; "You *congratulate* me on the prosperous situation of my affairs ;" অভি-নন্দন করা ; আনন্দ প্রকাশ করা। **—lant,** *adj.* **—la′-tion,** *n.* **1.** Act of congratulating ; হর্ষপ্রকাশ, অভি-নন্দন। **2.** (*Pl.*) Congratulatory expressions ; অভিনন্দনসূচক বাক্য। **—la-tor,** *n.* **—la-to-ry,** *adj.* Expressive of sympathetic joy ; অভিনন্দনসূচক।

cŏn′-grē-gāte, *v. t.* & *i.* To gather or collect together ; সম্মিলিত করা, জড় করা, সমবেত করা। ***Verb i.*** To assemble ; মিলিত হওয়া, জড় হওয়া, একত্র হওয়া।

cŏn-grē-gā′-tion, *n.* **1.** Act of bringing together ; assembly ; সমাহরণ, একত্রীকরণ ; মণ্ডলী, সমাহার সংসদ্, সমবায়, সমাজ। **2.** A body of persons assembled for religious worship ; পূজা, উপাসনাদির উদ্দেশ্যে মিলিত জনমণ্ডলী। **3.** The Jews gathered together in the wilderness during the journey to Canaan ; কানানদেশে যাত্রাকালে অরণ্য-মধ্যে সমবেত ইহুদীগণ। **4.** At the university of Oxford the assembly of masters and doctors ; অক্স্ফোর্ড বিশ্ববিদ্যালয়ের এম্ এ ও ডাক্তার উপাধিধারিগণের সংসদ্। **5.** A permanent committee of the Roman Catholic College of Cardinals ; রোমান ক্যাথলিক ধর্ম্মসমাজের কার্ডিনেলদিগের স্থায়ী পরিষৎ। **—al,** *adj.* **1.** Of or pertaining to a congregation ; পূজা, উপাসনাদির উদ্দেশ্যে সমবেত জনসম্প্রদায় সম্বন্ধীয়। **2.** [*Cap.*] Of or adhering to congregationalism ;

খৃষ্টীয় ধর্ম্মসমাজের (নিম্নবর্ণিত) শাসন-ব্যবস্থা-পদ্ধতিবিশেষ সংক্রান্ত।

con-grē-gā′-tion-ăl-ĭsm (cŏng-), *n.* That system of Church Government which vests all ecclesiastical power, in the assembled brotherhood of each local church ; খৃষ্টীয় ধর্ম্মসমাজের শাসন-ব্যবস্থাপদ্ধতিবিশেষ—যদ্দারা স্থানীয় প্রত্যেক ধর্ম্মসমাজের উপাসকমণ্ডলীর হস্তে সমস্ত যাজকীয় ক্ষমতা অর্পিত হইয়া থাকে। **–ist,** *n.* **–ize,** *v. t.*

con′-grĕss (cŏng-), *n.* **1.** A gathering or assembly ; সভা, পরিষৎ, মহাসভা। **2.** A formal assembly of delegates for the discussion or settlement of some question, esp. (in politics) of envoys or deputies representing sovereign states or sovereigns themselves for the settlement of international affairs ; কোন প্রশ্ন আলোচনা বা মীমাংসার উদ্দেশ্যে প্রতিনিধিগণের সম্মিলন, (বিশেষ ভাবে) (রাজনীতি ক্ষেত্রে) কোন আন্তর্জাতিক প্রশ্নের মীমাংসার জন্য বিভিন্ন রাজা বা রাজ্যের প্রতিনিধিগণের সম্মিলন। **3.** The federal legislature of the United States or its session ; মার্কিণ যুক্তরাজ্যের জাতীয় মহাসমিতি বা ইহার অধিবেশন। **–gres′-sion-al,** *adj.* **–man,** *n.* **Church congress**—ইংলণ্ডীয় ধর্ম্মসমাজের বার্ষিক অধিবেশন। **Indian National congress**—ভারতবর্ষের জাতীয় মহাসমিতি।

con′-grēve (cŏng-), *n. & adj.* **1.** A kind of friction-match (also, CONGREVE MATCH) ; একপ্রকার দেশলাই,—যাহা ঘর্ষণ করিয়া জ্বালান হয়। **2.** An iron rocket for use in war, (also CONGREVE ROCKET) ; একপ্রকার লৌহার হাউই বাজী,—ইহা যুদ্ধে ব্যবহৃত হয়। ***Adj.*** Pertaining to or invented by Sir William Congreve ; স্যর উইলিয়ম কনগ্রীভ্ সম্পর্কীয় বা তদ্দারা আবিষ্কৃত।

con′-grû-ĕnce (cŏng-), **–ĕn-cȳ,** *n.* Agreement ; consistency ; সুসঙ্গতি, মিল, ঐক্য ; সামঞ্জস্য। **–ent,** *adj.* Suitable ; সুসঙ্গত, অনুরূপ, যোগ্য, উপযোগী, সহচর।

con′-gru-ous (cŏn-grû-ŭs), *adj.* Accordant ; harmonious ; সঙ্গত, সঙ্গতিবিশিষ্ট ; অনুসারী। **–gru′-ity,** *n.* Consistency ; correspondence ; সামঞ্জস্য ; অনুরূপতা, সঙ্গতি।

cŏn′-ic, *adj. & n.* **1.** Shaped like a cone ; মোচাকার। **2.** Pertaining to a cone ; বৃত্তসূচী-সংক্রান্ত, কোণিক (অভিঃ)। ***Noun.*** (*Pl.*) That branch of Geometry which treats of the cone and the figures formed by plane section of it ; শঙ্কুছিন্ন-গণিত, সূচিচ্ছেদ গণিত। **–i-cal,** *adj.* **–i-cal-ly,** *adv.* **Conic section**—A curve line formed by the intersection of a cone and plane ; শঙ্কু এবং সমতলের পরস্পরের ছেদন হইতে যে বক্ররেখা উৎপন্ন হয়, শঙ্কু স্পর্শরেখীয় খণ্ড (হিঃ কোঃ), শঙ্কুখণ্ড (আঃ বঃ)।

cō′-ni-fêr, *n.* A cone-bearing tree ; দেবদারু বা তৎপর্য্যায়ভুক্ত বৃক্ষ। **–nif′-er-ous,** *adj.* Bearing cones or seed-vessels of a conical figure, as pine, fir, etc. ; মোচাকৃতি ক্ষুদ্র ক্ষুদ্র ফলপ্রসূ ; দারুক ফলপ্রসূ।

cō′-ni-fôrm, *adj.* Cone-shaped ; মোচাকার।

cō′-nīne, cō-nī′-ine (-în), *ns.* The poisonous alkaloid of the plant hemlock ; হেমলক বৃক্ষের বিষাক্ত নির্যাস।

cŏn-jĕc′-tūre, *n.* **1.** An opinion formed on a very slight evidence ; a guess ; অনুমান ; বিতর্ক, আন্দাজ, আঁচ (*Colloq.*)। **2.** (In textual criticism) Proposal of a reading not actually found in the traditional text ; প্রচলিত গ্রন্থের বহির্ভূত পাঠ প্রচলনের প্রস্তাব। **–tur-al,** *adj.* Depending on conjecture ; said or done by guess ; অনুমানসিদ্ধ ; আনুমানিক।

cŏn-jĕc′-tūre, *v.t. & i.* To guess ; to propose ; as, to *conjecture* a reading ; অনুমান করা ; আন্দাজ করা। ***Verb i.*** To surmise ; অনুমান করা, আঁচা (*Colloq*)। **–tu-ra-ble,** *adj.* **–tu-ra-bly,** *adv.*

cŏn-join′, *v. t. & i.* To join together ; to unite ; একত্র করা ; সংযুক্ত করা। ***Verb i.*** To become joined together ; সংযুক্ত হওয়া।

cŏn-joint′ (-joynt), *adj.* **1.** Connected ; associated ; সংযুক্ত, সংহত ; সংশ্লিষ্ট। **2.** Made up of two or more in combination ; as, a *conjoint* delta ; একত্র সম্বদ্ধ দুই বা ততোধিক বস্তু দ্বারা গঠিত। **–ly,** *adv.*

cŏn-jū′-gal, *adj.* Of or pertaining to marriage ; as, *conjugal* right ; relating to married persons ; as, *conjugal* affection ; বৈবাহিক, বিবাহ-সম্বন্ধীয় ; দাম্পত্য। **–gal′-i-ty,** *n.* **–gal-ly,** *adv.*

cŏn-jū′-gāte, *v. t. & i.* (*Gram.*) To inflect in different forms of voice, mood, tense, person and number ; as, to *conjugate* a verb ; ধাতুর রূপ করা। ***Verb i.*** **1.** To have sexual intercourse ; স্ত্রীপুরুষের সংসর্গ হওয়া। **2.** To become fused ; (জীব-বিজ্ঞান) সংযুক্ত হওয়া।

cŏn′-jū-gāte, *adj. & n.* **1.** United, coupled ; সংযুক্ত ; পরস্পরের সহিত সম্মিলিত। **2.** (*Gram.*) Derived from the same root ; সমব্যুৎপত্তিক, এক ধাতুজ। **3.** (*Math.*) Joined in a reciprocal relation ; (গণিত-শাস্ত্র) বদ্ধ (হিঃ কোঃ), সম্বদ্ধ (ঐ), প্রতিবদ্ধ (ঐ)। **4.** (*Bot.*) Paired ; as, a *conjugate* leaf ; (উদ্ভিদ্-বিদ্যা) যুগ্ম। **5.** (*Biol.*) United in conjugation ; (জীব-বিজ্ঞান) সংযুক্ত। ***Noun.*** **1.** A word kindred in meaning and origin with another word ; ধাতুগত সম্বন্ধবিশিষ্ট নামব্যুৎপত্তিক শব্দ। **2.** (*Math.*) Short for conjugate axis, point, etc. ; (গণিত-শাস্ত্র) সম্বদ্ধাক্ষ (হিঃ কোঃ)।

cŏn-jū-gā′-tion, *n.* **1.** Act of conjugating ; union ; combination ;

সংবন্ধন ; সংযোগ ; সন্ধি। 2. (*Gram.*) A scheme of all the inflexional forms of a verb ; (ব্যাকরণ) ধাতুরূপকরণ, বিভক্তিসংযোগ (হিঃ কোঃ) ধাতুরূপ। 3. (*Bot.*) The union of two distinct cells for reproduction ; (জীব বিজ্ঞান) পুনরুৎপাদনের জন্য দুইটী স্বতন্ত্র কোষের সংযোগ। **—al,** *adj.* **—al-ly,** *adv.*

cŏn-jŭnct′, *adj.* & *n.* **1.** Confined ; joint with another ; as, *conjunct* rights (*Scot. law*) ; সীমাবদ্ধ ; সহভাগী, সংযুক্ত। **2.** Made up of or effected by united elements or persons ; united ; as, a *conjunct* analysis ; একত্রীভূত মূল পদার্থ বা ব্যক্তি দ্বারা গঠিত বা সম্পাদিত। ***Noun.*** A person or thing associated with another ; সংশ্লিষ্ট ব্যক্তি বা বস্তু। **—ly,** *adv.*

cŏn-jŭnc′-tion, *n.* **1.** Connection ; association ; union ; সম্পর্ক, মিলন ; সংশ্রয়, সংসর্গ ; সংযোগ। 2. (*Astron.*) The meeting of two or more planets in the same degree of the zodiac ; রাশি চক্রের এক ভাগে দুই বা ততোধিক গ্রহের সম্মিলন, যোগ বা সঙ্গম, যোগ। **3.** (*Gram.*) A word used to join sentences, clauses or words ; সংযোগ বা সমুচ্চয়ার্থক অব্যয়। **4.** A combination of events or circumstances ; as, a *conjunction* of calamities ; ঘটনা-সম্মিলন। **5.** A combined group of persons or things ; association ; union ; একত্র সংশ্লিষ্ট বস্তু সমূহ, সম্মিলিত ব্যক্তিগণ ; সমিতি ; মিলন। **In conjunction with**—Together with ; একযোগে।

cŏn-jŭnc-ti′-vă, *n.* The mucous membrane covering the eyeball and the inner surface of the lids ; যোজক-ত্বক (হঃ চঃ), চক্ষুর শুক্লমণ্ডল বা শুভ্র আবরণ।

cŏn-jŭnc′-tive, *adj.* & *n.* **1.** Serving to unite ; connective ; সংযোজনকর ; সংযোজক। 2. Done in conjunction ; as, *conjugative* records ; একযোগে সম্পাদিত। **3.** (*Gram.*) Serving to conjunct words or clauses as a conjunction ; uniting the sense as well as the construction ; subjunctive ; as, a *conjunctive* mood ; (ব্যাকরণ) অব্যয়াত্মক ; শব্দের ভাব ও বিন্যাস সংযোজক ; সংশয়াত্মক, সম্ভাবনাত্মক। ***Noun.*** **1.** A conjunctive word ; a subjunctive mood ; অব্যয় শব্দ ; ক্রিয়ার সম্ভাবনা, সন্দেহ বা কল্পনাবাচক অবস্থা। 2. (*Logic*) A conjunctive or conditional syllogism ; (তর্ক-বিজ্ঞান) সংযোজক বা সাপেক্ষ ন্যায়। **—ly,** *adv.* **Conjunctive mood**—ক্রিয়ার সন্দেহ, সম্ভাবনা, বা কল্পনাসূচক অবস্থা। **Conjunctive proposition**—সাবয়ব প্রতিজ্ঞা। **Conjunctive syllogism**—যে ন্যায়ের ব্যাপ্তিবাক্য সাবয়ব প্রতিজ্ঞা হইয়া থাকে।

cŏn-jŭnc-ti-vī′-tis, *n.* (*Med.*) Inflammation of the conjunctiva ; শুক্লমণ্ডল-প্রদাহ (হিঃ কোঃ), অভিষ্যন্দ (সাঃ পঃ)।

cŏn jŭnc′-tūre, *n.* **1.** A combination of important events or circumstances ; a crisis ; গুরুতর ঘটনার সম্মিলন ; সঙ্কট-কাল। 2. (*Astron*) Conjunction ; (জ্যোতির্বিজ্ঞান) শীঘ্র (মঃ উঃ)।

cŏn-jü-rā′-tion, *n.* **1.** Practice of magic ; incantation ; ইন্দ্রজাল বিদ্যার অনুশীলন ; যাদুমন্ত্র। **2.** A charm ; a magic spell ; কুহক ; যাদু, টোনা। **3.** A solemn appeal ; সনির্ব্বন্ধ প্রার্থনা।

cŏn-jūre′, *v. t.* & *i.* **1.** To inplore with solemnity ; "She *conjured* his help ;" সনির্ব্বন্ধ প্রার্থনা করা। **2.** (*Pron.* kŭn-jêr), To constrain as a devil to appear by some spell ; ভূত-নামান। **3.** (*Pron.* kŭn-jêr) To affect by conjuration ; to produce or bring out by the arts of a conjurer ; যাদুমন্ত্রদ্বারা অভিভূত বা মোহিত করা ; ইন্দ্রজাল বা যাদুবলে উৎপন্ন করা। ***Verb i.*** To practise the arts of magic ; to juggle ; যাদুবিদ্যার অনুশীলন করা ; ভেল্কি দেখান, যাদুবিদ্যা প্রদর্শন করা, বাজি দেখান। **To conjure up**—To bring into existence by magic or other tricks ; to cause to appear to the imagination ; as, to *conjure up* a phantom or alarms ; যাদুবলে সৃষ্টি করা ; কল্পনায় প্রতিভাসিত করা। **To put on one's conjuring cap**—To reflect on a question put to him ; জিজ্ঞাসিত প্রশ্ন সম্বন্ধে মনোমধ্যে আলোচনা করা।

con′-jur-er, —or (kŭn-jêr-êr), *n.* **1.** A magician ; one who practises sleight of hand ; যাদুকর, মায়াবী, অভিচারবিৎ, কুহকী, ঐন্দ্রজালিক, বাজীকর ; হস্তকৌশলপ্রদর্শক। **2.** (*Ironical*) An unusually clever person ; as, he is no *conjurer* (far from clever) ; (কৌতুকচ্ছলে) অসাধারণ চালাক লোক।

cŏnk, *n.* (*Slang.*) The nose ; (ইতর ভাষায়) নাক।

cŏn -nāte, *adj.* **1.** Inborn ; innate ; as, *connate* ideas ; স্বভাবসিদ্ধ ; প্রকৃতিগত, নৈসর্গিক, স্বাভাবিক। **2.** Co-eval in origin ; born together ; (said of two or more qualities) ; সহজ, সমকালজ, সহোৎপন্ন (হিঃ কোঃ) ; সহজাত। **3.** (*Bot.* & *Biol.*) United in origin ; as, *connate* leaves (united at the base) ; (উদ্ভিদ্‌বিদ্যা ও জীববিজ্ঞান) একত্রীভূত (সাঃ পঃ), যমজ।

cŏn-năt′-ü-răl, *adj.* **1.** Innate ; natural ; প্রকৃতিগত ; স্বভাবসিদ্ধ, স্বাভাবিক। **2.** Of the same nature ; as, *connatural* things ; সজাতীয়, সমজাতীয়, সমধর্ম্মা, সমপ্রকৃতিক, একভাবাপন্ন। **—ly,** *adv.*

cŏn-nĕct′, *v. t.* & *i.* **1.** To join or link together ; সংযোগ করা, মিলিত করা, লাগান, সংগ্রথিত করা, সংশ্লিষ্ট করা। **2.** To make coherent as, to *connect* arguments ; সুসম্বদ্ধ করা। **3.** To unite as a person by relationship with another ; as, to *connect* one with a party ; সম্বন্ধ-বিশিষ্ট করা। **4.** To associate in idea ; চিন্তায় সম্মিলিত করা। **5.** To have to do with (*pass*) ; সম্পর্ক থাকা, সংশ্লিষ্ট থাকা, সংশ্রব থাকা। ***Verb i.*** **1.** To join ; to have a close relation ; as, this part *connects* with what goes before ; সংযুক্ত হওয়া ; সম্বন্ধবিশিষ্ট হওয়া। **2.** To run in connection ; as, trains and steamers *connect* at a certain place (*U. S.*) ; পরস্পরের সহিত সংযোগে চলা, অবিচ্ছিন্ন ভাবে চলা। **—er, —or,** *ns.* **—i-ble,** *adj.*

cŏn-nĕct′-ĕd, *adj.* **1.** Joined in sequence or order ; as, *connected* ideas ; সংলগ্ন, সংযুক্ত, সুসঙ্গত, সুসম্বদ্ধ। **2.** United by relationship or intimacy ; as, he is well-*connected* ; সম্বন্ধবিশিষ্ট, সংসৃষ্ট, সম্পৃক্ত, সংশ্লিষ্ট, সংক্রান্ত, ঘটিত। **—ly,** *adv.* **—ness,** *n.* **Well-connected**—Related with persons of good position ; "They are fairly descended and *well-connected* ; সম্ভ্রান্তলোকের সম্পর্কীয়, উচ্চপদস্থ ব্যক্তিগণের সহিত সম্বন্ধ-বিশিষ্ট।

cŏn-nĕc′-tion, —nex′-ion(-nĕc-tion), *n.* **1.** Act of connecting ; state of being connected ; সংযোজন ; সংসৃষ্টতা, সমাসক্তি, যোগ, সংযোগ। **2.** A connecting part ; a bond ; as, hot water *connections* ; সংযোজক-অংশ ; সংযোগ-বন্ধন। **3.** Relation of thought or speech ; as, in the same *connection* ; coherence of words or ideas ; চিন্তা ও বাক্যের সম্বন্ধ বা অন্বয় ; বাক্য বা ভাবের সুসম্বদ্ধতা বা সমন্বয়। **4.** A person related by marriage or distant consanguinity ; সম্পর্কীয় ব্যক্তি, জ্ঞাতি, কুটুম্ব। **5.** A relationship by blood or marriage ; as, a man of high *connections* ; relation in a practical way ; as he deplored his *connection* with that man ; sexual relation ; as, criminal *connection* (abbre. *crim. con.*) ; রক্তগত-সম্পর্ক বা বিবাহসূত্রে-সম্পর্ক, সম্বন্ধ ; কুটুম্বিতা ; সংশ্রব, যৌন-সম্বন্ধ, সঙ্গম, সঙ্গ। **6.** A body of persons connected together in some common interest ; as, a business *connection* ; a body of customers ; এক উদ্দেশ্যে সংযুক্ত ব্যক্তিবর্গ; ক্রেতৃবর্গ। **7.** A religious body or sect ; as the Methodist *connection* ; ধর্ম্মসম্প্রদায়, সম্প্রদায়। **8.** The meeting of one means of communication with another, as a railway train or steamboat in order to take on the passengers ; রেলওয়ে, জাহাজ প্রভৃতির সংযোগ। **—al,** *adj.* **In connection (—xion) with**—With reference to ; সম্পর্কে, বিষয়ে। Connected with, as trains, boats, etc., taking on passengers from other ; (রেলওয়ে, জাহাজ প্রভৃতির মত) পরস্পরের সহিত সংযুক্ত।

cŏn-nĕc′-tive, *adj.* & *n.* Connecting ; tending to connect ; সংযোজক, সংযোগী ; সংযোজনশীল। ***Noun.*** (*Physiol.*) Same as CONNECTIVE TISSUE below. **Connective tissue**—যোজক (হঃ চঃ), যে মাংসল অংশদ্বারা পরাগকোষের অংশদ্বয় সংযুক্ত থাকে।

cŏn-nĕx′-ion, *n.* See CONNECTION.

cŏn-nĭv′-ançe (-ăns), *n.* **1.** Act of intentional oversight (with *at, in*) ; tacit or implied consent ; as, done with my *connivance* ; স্বেচ্ছাকৃত উপেক্ষা ; সায়, মৌন-সম্মতি, গোপনে গোপনে সম্মতি, ভিতরে ভিতরে সায়। **2.** (*Law*) Implied or express consent to wrongdoing ; (আইন) অন্যায় কার্য্যে প্রকাশ্য বা অপ্রকাশ্য সম্মতি।

cŏn-nīve′, *v. t.* **1.** To pretend ignorance ; to forbear to notice (folwed by *at*) ; as, he *connived* at the vices of his son ; জানে না বলিয়া ভাণ করা, জ্ঞানপূর্ব্বক উপেক্ষা করা ; উপেক্ষা করা, দেখিয়া না দেখা। **2.** To wink (*at*) ; to look with secret favour or sympathy at ; as, they *connived* at his escape ; অক্ষি-সংকোচ করা, দেখিয়া না দেখা, উপেক্ষা করা ; গোপনে গোপনে অনুগ্রহ করা বা সহানুভূতির চক্ষে দেখা। **—niv′-ent,** *adj.* (*Nat. Hist.*) Convergent ; as, the *connivent* leaves of a flower (having an inward inclination) ; (জীববিদ্যা) এককেন্দ্রাভিমুখীন।

cŏn-nois-seur′(-ĭs-sür),*n.* A critical judge of any art or matter of taste ; কলানাট্যজ্ঞ, রসভাবজ্ঞ, সামাজিক সমজদার, গুণগ্রাহী ব্যক্তি, গুণজ্ঞ, অভিজ্ঞ, বোদ্ধা, তদ্বিদ্য (ন্যায়ঃ দঃ), রসজ্ঞ, মর্ম্মজ্ঞ।

cŏn-nōte′, *v. t.* **1.** To signify along with the primary meaning ; to imply (as a consequence) ; as, punishment *connotes* guilt ; অভিপ্রায় ব্যক্ত করা ; অর্থ প্রকাশ করা, দ্যোতন করা। **2.** (*Log.*) To indicate the attributes implied in a term while denoting the subject ; (তর্ক-বিজ্ঞান) বিষয়-নির্দ্দেশ সহকারে গুণরাজির আভাস দেওয়া। **—no-ta′-tion,** *n.* **1.** Act of connoting ; অর্থ-প্রকটন। **2.** (*Log.*) Sum of attributes forming the meaning of a term ; intension ; (তর্কবিজ্ঞান) জাত্যর্থ (হিঃ কোঃ), জাতিবোধন (ঐ), সামান্যাভিধান, অর্থ-ব্যাপ্তি (হিঃ কোঃ)। **—no-ta-tive,** *adj.* **1.** Implying something in addition ; অতিরিক্ত বস্তুবাচক। **2.** (*Log.*) Expressing connotation ; (তর্ক-বিজ্ঞান) গুণবোধক (হিঃ কোঃ), জাতিবিশিষ্ট ব্যক্তিবোধক (ঐ)। **—ly,** *adv.* (*Log.*) **A connotative term**—(তর্ক-বিজ্ঞান) দ্যোতক (সাঃ পঃ), শক্যতাবচ্ছেদক (ঐ), দ্যোত্য (হিঃ কোঃ)। (*Log.*) **Non-connotative term**—অদ্যোতক নাম।

cŏn-nū'-bi-al, *adj.* **1.** Matrimonial; বৈবাহিক, ঔদ্বাহিক। **2.** Conjugal; দাম্পত্য। **—al'-i-ty,** *n.* **—ly,** *adv.*

cō'-noid (-noÿd), *adj.* & *n.* **1.** Resembling a cone; মোচাকার। ***Noun.*** **1.** (*Geom.*) A solid formed by the revolution of a conic-section about its axis; (জ্যামিতি) মোচাকার ঘন। **2.** Anything shaped like a cone; মোচাকার বস্তু।

con'-quer (kŏng-kêr), *v. t.* **1.** To acquire by fighting; as, to *conquer* a country; যুদ্ধজয় করিয়া লাভ করা, অস্ত্রবলে জয় করা, পরাজিত করিয়া অধীনস্থ করা। **2.** To overcome by force; পরাভূত করা, পরাস্ত করা, পরাজিত করা। **3.** To overcome; as, to *conquer* temptation; জয় করা। **—a-ble,** *adj.*

con'-quer-or(kŏng-kêr-êr), *n.* One who conquers; a victor; জেতা, বিজেতা; বিজয়ীব্যক্তি। **The conqueror**—William I who conqured England; ইংলণ্ডের নৃপতি প্রথম উইলিয়ম। (*Colloq.*) **To play the conqueror** — To play a game decisively; (চলিত ভাষায়) জয় কিম্বা পরাজয় সুনিশ্চিত না হওয়া পর্য্যন্ত ক্রীড়া করা।

con'-quest (kŏng-kwĕst), *n.* **1.** Act of conquering; as, the *conquest* of India; জয়, বিজয়, অভিভব, পরাভব। **2.** That which is conqured; as, the island was their new *conquest*; বিজিত স্থান, পরাভূত দেশ। **3.** A person whose favour or affections have been won; as, he found her an easy *conquest*; যে ব্যক্তির অনুগ্রহ বা অনুরাগ লব্ধ হইয়াছে, যাহার হৃদয় বিজিত বা বশীকৃত হইয়াছে। **To make a conquest** or **a conquest of**—To conquer; জয় করা। To win the favour or affections of (a person); অনুগ্রহ বা অনুরাগ লাভ করা। **The conquest** or **Norman conquest**—নরমাণ্ডীর ডিউক উইলিয়ম কর্ত্তৃক ১০৬৬ খৃষ্টাব্দে ইংলণ্ড বিজয়। **Universal conquest**—দিগ্বিজয়।

cŏn-san'-guine (-săng-gwĭn), *adj.* Same as CONSANGUINEOUS.

cŏn-san-guin'-e-ous (-săng-gwĭn-ē-ŭs), *adj.* Of the same blood; related by birth; সগোত্র, সপিণ্ড; জ্ঞাতি-সম্পর্কীয়, অন্তরঙ্গ, একবংশজাত।

cŏ-san-guin'-i-tȳ (-săng-gwĭn), *n.* **1.** Relationship by blood; জ্ঞাতিত্ব; জ্ঞাতি-সম্বন্ধ, সগোত্রতা। **2.** (*Fig.*) Affinity; (লক্ষণায়) সম্পর্ক।

cŏn'-science (-shĕns), *n.* The moral sense of right and wrong; সদসদ্ বিবেক, ধর্ম্মাধর্ম্ম বিবেক, শুভবুদ্ধি (রবিঃ), কল্যাণ-বুদ্ধি, ধর্ম্ম-বুদ্ধি হিতবুদ্ধি, সংজ্ঞান (আঃ বঃ), চেতনা অনুভব, ইমান (*Colloq.*)। **—less,** *adj.* **Conscience clause** — আইনের প্রকরণ বিশেষ — যদ্দারা আইনের কোন রূপ বিধান কোন ব্যক্তির ধর্ম্ম-বিরুদ্ধ হইলে, সেই ব্যক্তিকে তাহা পালনের দায় হইতে অব্যাহতি দেওয়া হয়। **Conscience money**—কোন ব্যক্তি আয়কর প্রভৃতির দায় হইতে এড়াইবার চেষ্টা করিয়া পরে ধর্ম্মবুদ্ধির তাড়না হেতু অনুতপ্ত হইলে, যে অপ্রদত্ত কর রাজকীয় ধন-ভাণ্ডারে প্রদান করে। **Conscience-proof**—ধর্ম্মবুদ্ধি-শূন্য। **Court of conscience**—লণ্ডন নগরী এবং অন্যান্য ব্যবসায়ের স্থানের আদালত বিশেষ,—এই আদালতে ক্ষুদ্র ক্ষুদ্র ঋণের টাকা আদায়ের জন্য নালিশ করা হয়। **Good** or **clear conscience** — অবিকৃত ধর্ম্মবুদ্ধি; অপঙ্কিল ধর্ম্মবুদ্ধি, নির্ম্মল ধর্ম্মবুদ্ধি। **Guilty** or **bad conscience** — মলিন ধর্ম্মবুদ্ধি, বিকৃত ধর্ম্মবুদ্ধি। **In conscience**—ধর্ম্মভয় করিলে। **In all conscience**—Reasonably; যুক্তিযুক্তরূপে, যুক্তিসিদ্ধরূপে। **My conscience**—A form of oath; ধর্ম্ম। **Qualms of conscience** — Stings of conscience; বিবেক-দংশন, ধর্ম্মবুদ্ধিরতাড়না। **Stricken conscience**—Penitence; অনুশোচনা। **Tender conscience**—Scrupulousness; সংশয়পূর্ণতা। **To have the conscience to** — To have the impudence to; কোন কিছু করার উপযোগী ধৃষ্টতা থাকা। **To make a conscience of**—To act according to the dictates of conscience; ধর্ম্মবুদ্ধির প্রেরণা অনুসারে চলা। **With a clear conscience**—With the consciousness of being guiltless; নিষ্পাপ-চিত্তে।

cŏn-sci-en'-tious (-shĭ-ĕn-shŭs) *adj.* **1.** Actuated by a strict regard to the dictates of conscience; scrupulous; as, a *conscientious* judge; ধর্ম্ম-ভীরু, ন্যায়নিষ্ঠ, ন্যায়পরায়ণ; সদসদ্ বিবেকী, ধর্ম্মাত্মা, শুদ্ধমতি, সংজ্ঞানী। **2.** Governed by conscience; as, a *conscientious* act; ধর্ম্মসঙ্গত, ন্যায়-সঙ্গত। **—ly,** *adv.* **—ness,** *n.*

cŏn-scious (-shŭs), *adj.* **1.** Aware; as, he became *conscious* of his position; জ্ঞাত, অবগত, বিদিত। **2.** having one's mental faculties awake; as, to become *conscious*; সচেতন, সজ্ঞান, জ্ঞানী। **3.** (*Philos.*) Possessed of consciousness; (দর্শন-শাস্ত্র) চেতনা-সম্পন্ন, সংজ্ঞা-সম্পন্ন। **4.** Felt; as, *conscious* guilt; অনুভূত। **5.** Self-conscious (which see). **—ly,** *adv.*

cŏn-scious-nĕss (-shŭs), *n.* **1.** The state of being conscious; চেতনাবস্থা, চৈতন্য, বাহ্যজ্ঞান, হুস, সংজ্ঞা, চেতনা। **2.** Perception; উপলব্ধি, প্রত্যক্ষ-জ্ঞান। **3.** (*Philos.*) The faculty of being conscious as a condition of all thought, feeling and volition; (দর্শন-শাস্ত্র) প্রবোধ, চিৎ (হিঃ কোঃ), সংবিৎ (ঐ), প্রজ্ঞা, বিজ্ঞান, আত্মজ্ঞান। **4.** The totality of thoughts and feelings making up a man's conscious being; যে চিন্তা ও ভাব সমষ্টি দ্বারা কোন ব্যক্তির আত্মবোধসম্পন্ন সত্তা সঞ্জাত হয়। **Moral consciousness** — নৈতিকজ্ঞান।

cŏn-scrībe', *v. t.* To enlist compulsorily; বলপূর্ব্বক তালিকাভুক্ত করা

cŏn'-script, *adj.* & *n.* Enrolled by compulsion ; বলপূর্ব্বক সৈন্য-তালিকাভুক্ত। ***Noun.*** One conscribed to serve as a soldier or sailor ; বলপূর্ব্বক সৈন্য বা নাবিকের তালিকায় ভুক্ত ব্যক্তি। **Conscript father**—রোমনগরীর প্রধান ব্যবস্থাপক সভার সভ্য।

cŏn-scrip'-tion, *n.* A compulsory enlistment of individuals for military or naval service ; বলপূর্ব্বক সৈন্য বা নাবিক তালিকায় ভুক্তকরণ, বল-সমুত্থান।

cŏn'-sĕ-crāte, *adj.* Sacred ; consecrated ; পূত, পবিত্র ; উৎসর্গীকৃত, সংস্কৃত, সুপ্রতিষ্ঠিত।

cŏn'-sĕ-crāte, *v. t.* **1.** Sanctify ; as, reputation *consecrates* opinions ; পূত করা, পবিত্র করা, সংস্কৃত করা। **2.** To appropriate to sacred uses ; to dedicate to the service of God ; as, to *consecrate* a church ; অভিষেক করা, প্রতিষ্ঠা করা ; দেবকার্য্যে উৎসর্গ করা। **3.** To appropriate as to some purpose ; as, a room *consecrated* to old coins ; কোন বিশেষ উদ্দেশ্যের জন্য রাখা। **4.** To set apart to a holy office by sacred rites ; as, to *consecrate* a bishop ; দীক্ষিত করা। **—cra-tor,** *n.* **—cra-to-ry,** *adj.* Serving to consecrate ; পূতকারী, প্রতিষ্ঠাপক।

cŏn-sĕ-crā'-tion, *n.* **1.** Act of consecrating ; dedication with religious rites ; দেবকার্য্যে উৎসর্গীকরণ ; প্রতিষ্ঠাপন, প্রতিষ্ঠা। **2.** Ordination, as of a bishop to a sacred office ; দীক্ষাদান, অভিষেক। **3.** Devotion to some purpose ; কোন বিশেষ উদ্দেশ্যে উৎসর্গীকরণ। **4.** Act of rendering sacred ; পবিত্রীকরণ, সংস্কার।

cŏn-sĕc'-ta-rў, *n.* Deduction ; conclusion ; অনুমান ; নিগমন।

cŏn-sĕ-cū'-tion, *n.* **1.** Inference ; logical sequence ; অনুমান ; পারম্পর্য্য, অনুপূর্ব্ব, পৌর্ব্বাপর্য্য। **2.** Succession, as of events ; অনুক্রম ; ধারাবাহিকতা, পরম্পরা। **3.** (*Gram.*) Sequence of words, tenses, etc. ; (ব্যাকরণ) শব্দ, কাল প্রভৃতির অনুক্রম বা পৌর্ব্বাপর্য্য।

cŏn-sĕc'-ū-tive, *adj.* **1.** Succeeding in a regular order ; following without interval ; ক্রমাগত, ক্রমিক ; ধারাবাহিক। **2.** (*Gram.*) Expressing consequence ; (ব্যাকরণ) অবশ্যম্ভাবী, ফলবাচক। **3.** Following logically ; as, *consecutive* reasoning ; অনুক্রমিক। **—ly** *adv.* In a consecutive manner ; ক্রমশঃ, ধারাবাহিকরূপে, পরপর, ক্রমান্বয়ে। **—ness,** *n.* **Consecutive clause**—(ব্যাকরণ) অবশ্যম্ভাবী ফলবাচক বাক্যাংশ।

cŏn-sē-nĕs'-cĕnce, *n.* A general decay from old age ; জরাজীর্ণতা।

cŏn-sĕn-sū'-ăl, *adj.* **1.** (*Physiol.*) Caused by sensation or sympathy and not by conscious volition ; as, *consensual* actions ; (শারীরবিজ্ঞান) সংবেদানুবিধায়িনী। **2.** (*Law*) Existing by consent ; (আইন) সর্ব্বসাধারণের স্বীকৃতি দ্বারা স্থিত।

cŏn-sĕn'-sŭs, *n.* **1.** Agreement ; concord ; সম্মতি, সর্ব্বসম্মতি, ঐক্য ; ঐকমত্য। **2.** (*Physiol.*) General agreement of different organs of the body in effecting a purpose ; (শারীর-বিজ্ঞান) কোন ক্রিয়া সম্পাদনের জন্য বিভিন্ন বিভিন্ন শারীরিক যন্ত্রের সাধারণ ঐক্য।

cŏn-sĕnt', *v. t.* To agree ; to acquiece in what another proposes or desires ; to yield ; as, my poverty but not my will, *consents,*—Shakes ; সম্মত হওয়া, রাজি হওয়া (*Colloq.*), স্বীকার করা ; সায় দেওয়া, অনুমোদন করা ; বশ্যতা স্বীকার করা।

cŏn-sĕnt', *n.* Accordance with what is done or proposed by another ; compliance ; permission ; as, to gain the *consent* of the king ; সম্মতি, স্বীকৃতি ; সায় ; অনুমতি। **Age of consent**—যে বয়সে কোন্ নির্দ্দিষ্ট কার্য্যে কোন ব্যক্তির সম্মতি বৈধ বলিয়া গণ্য হয়। **Silence gives consent**—মৌনং সম্মতি-লক্ষণং। **With one** or **by common consent**—Unanimously ; সর্ব্বসম্মতিক্রমে।

cŏn-sĕn-tā'-nē-ous (-ŭs), *adj.* **1.** Agreeing ; suited ; consistent ; (generally with *to* or *with*) ; অনুসারী ; অনুরূপ ; সঙ্গতি-বিশিষ্ট। **2.** Unanimous ; একমত। **—ly,** *adv.* **—ne'-i-ty,** *n.* **—ness,** *n.*

cŏn-sĕn'-ti-ĕnt (-shî-), *adj.* **1.** Accordant ; unanimous ; একমত ; একবাক্য। **2.** Giving consent ; (followed by *to*) ; সম্মতি-প্রদানশীল।

cŏn'-sĕ-quence (-kwĕns), *n.* **1.** That which follows as a result ; ফল, পরিণাম। **2.** Logical inference ; অনুমান, নিগমন (আঃ বঃ)। **3.** Connection of causes and effects ; as, by necessary *consequence* ; কার্য্যকারণ-সম্বন্ধ। **4.** Importance ; as, it is of no *consequence* ; গুরুত্ব। **5.** Social rank ; as, men of *consequence* ; সামাজিক পদমর্য্যাদা। **In consequence**—As a result ; পরিণামে, ফলে। **In consequence of**—As the effect of ; ফলস্বরূপ। **Of consequence** — Important ; গুরুত্ব-বিশিষ্ট। Of social distinction ; সামাজিক পদমর্য্যাদাসম্পন্ন, গণ্যমান্য।

cŏn'-sĕ-quĕnt, *n.* & *adj.* **1.** An event which follows another (without implication of causal connexion) ; পরবর্ত্তী ঘটনা। **2.** (*Logic*) The second part of a conditional proposition ; (তর্কবিজ্ঞান) আপেক্ষিক প্রতিজ্ঞার দ্বিতীয় অংশ, অনুবর্ত্তী (হিঃ কোঃ)। **3.** (*Math.*) The second term of a ratio, the first being the antecedent ; (গণিতশাস্ত্র) অনুপাতের দ্বিতীয় রাশি, দ্বিতীয় নিষ্পত্তি (হিঃ কোঃ)। ***Adj.*** **1.** Following as the effect ; (with *on* or *to*) ; ফলস্বরূপ-অনুবর্ত্তী, ফলস্বরূপ-আগত,

ফলীভূত। **2.** (*Logic*) Following as an inference; logically consistent; (তর্ক-বিজ্ঞান) অনুবর্ত্তী; ন্যায়-শাস্ত্রানুযায়ীরূপে সঙ্গতি-বিশিষ্ট।

cŏn-sē-quĕn′-tial (-shăl), *adj.* **1.** Following as an effect or inference; ফল বা অনুমানস্বরূপ অনুবর্ত্তী, আনুষঙ্গিক। **2.** Of the nature of secondary consequence or result; as, *consequential* advantages; ফলীভূত, পরিণামভূত। **3.** Conceited; "Pampered and *consequential* freed man;" দৃপ্ত, গর্ব্বিত। **—ly,** *adv.* **—ti-al′-i-ty,** *n.*

cŏn′-sē-quĕnt′-lȳ, *adv.* & *conj.* As a result; কাজে কাজেই। ***Conj.*** Therefore; তাই, তাহাতে, সুতরাং।

cŏn-sêrv′-ăn-cȳ, *n.* **1.** A court having jurisdiction over a port or river; as, the Thames *conservancy*; বিচারালয় বিশেষ—নদী, বন্দর, প্রভৃতি এই বিচারালয়ের এলাকা-ভুক্ত। **2.** The official preservation of forests, trees, &c.; বন, বৃক্ষ, প্রভৃতি সংরক্ষণ।

cŏn-sêr-vā′-tion, *n.* **1.** The act of conserving; preservation; সংরক্ষণ; রক্ষণ, ক্ষয়-নিবারণ, রক্ষা। **2.** The preserving of fruits or other similar things; ফল প্রভৃতি রক্ষণ। **Conservation of energy or force**—কোন বস্তু বা বস্তু পরম্পরায় সংক্রামিত বল-শক্তির অপচয় হয় না—এইরূপ বৈজ্ঞানিক মত, শক্তি-স্থিতি (হিঃ কোঃ), বল-স্থিতি (ঐ)।

cŏn-sêrv′-ă-tive, *adj.* & *n.* **1.** Tending to preserve; রক্ষণোন্মুখ। **2.** Adhering to the existing institutions or views; as, the *conservative* party of the English Parliament; প্রচলিত রীতিনীতি ও অনুষ্ঠানের প্রতি দৃঢ়ানুরাগী, রক্ষণশীল, নববিদ্বেষী (আঃ বঃ), স্থিতি-পাল (আঃ বঃ)। **3.** Moderate; cautious; as, a *conservative* estimate; পরিমিত; সতর্ক। ***Noun.*** **1.** One who conserves; a preservative; সংরক্ষক; ক্ষয় বা পচন নিবারক বস্তু। **2.** A member of the conservative party; রক্ষণশীল দলের সভ্য। **—tism,** *n.* **1.** The principles of the conservatives; রক্ষণশীল সম্প্রদায়ের মত। **2.** The practice of preserving what is established; রক্ষণশীলতা। **Conservative ministry**—রক্ষণশীল সম্প্রদায়ের সভ্যগণদ্বারা গঠিত মন্ত্রি-সভা।

cŏn-sêr-vă-toire′ (-twâr), *n.* (*F.*) A public school of music; সঙ্গীত-বিদ্যালয়।

cŏn′-sêr-vā-tor (-têr), *n.* **1.** One who preserves; a keeper; সংরক্ষক; রক্ষাকর্ত্তা, পালক। **2.** The official custodian of a building, museum, forests, (India) etc.; সৌধ, চিত্রশালা, বন (ভারতে) প্রভৃতির সংরক্ষক রাজকর্ম্মচারী। **Conservators of the peace**—রাজা, লর্ড চেন্সেলার প্রভৃতি। **Conservator of a river**—নদী, মৎস্য ধরিবার স্থান, প্রভৃতির তত্ত্বাবধায়ক রাজকর্ম্মচারিবিশেষ। **Conservator of forest**—বনবিভাগের উচ্চপদস্থ কর্ম্মচারি-বিশেষ, বনপাল।

cŏn-sêrv′-ă-tŏ-rȳ, *n.* **1.** A greenhouse for the preservation of tender plants; হরিৎগৃহ, উদ্ভিদশালা (প্রবোধ), পুষ্পগৃহ (রঃ)। **2.** A conservatoire; সঙ্গীতবিদ্যালয়।

cŏn′-serve (-sêrv), *n.* **1.** A medicinal preparation to preserve roots or fruits in a fresh state; ঔষধ-বিশেষ,—যদ্দ্বারা ফল মূল তাজা রাখা যায়। **2.** A sweetmeat; মিঠাই।

cŏn-serve′ (-sêrv), *v. t.* To keep safe from loss or decay; ক্ষতি বা ধ্বংস হইতে রক্ষা করা।

cŏn-sĭd′-êr, *v. t.* & *i.* **1.** To think on with care; to meditate on; to contemplate mentally; বিবেচনা করা; পর্য্যালোচনা করা, প্রণিধান করা; ভাবা। **2.** To have regard for; to make allowance for; 'God will *consider* our degenerated integrities;" কোন বিষয় বিবেচনা করা; দোষ বাদসাদ দিয়া লওয়া। **3.** To regard; as, to *consider* wealth of little importance; গণ্য করা। ***Verb i.*** To think seriously or deliberately; গভীরভাবে চিন্তা করা। **All things considered** — On the whole; মোটের উপর। **To consider of**—(*Archaic*) To think over; কোন বিষয় ভাবা।

cŏn-sĭd′-êr-ă-ble, *adj.* **1.** Worth considering; বিবেচ্য। **2.** Worthy of regard; notable; as, a *considerable* man; মাননীয়, গণ্য, পূজ্য, মান্য; বিখ্যাত। **3.** Moderately large; much; as, *considerable* trouble; একরকম বড়; প্রচুর, যথেষ্ট, বিস্তর। **—bly,** *adv.*

cŏn-sĭd′-êr-āte, *adj.* **1.** Mindful of others; thoughtful for others; অন্যের প্রতি মনোযোগী; অন্যের জন্য চিন্তাপর। **2.** (*Archaic*) Careful; prudent; (অপ্রচলিত) সতর্ক; বিজ্ঞ, বিচার-সম্পন্ন। **—ly,** *adv.* **—ness,** *n.*

cŏn-sĭd-êr-ā′-tion, *n.* **1.** Act of considering; attentive thought; reflection; বিবেচনা; পর্য্যালোচনা; ভাবনা। **2.** The ground or reason for conclusion; as, that is a *consideration*; সিদ্ধান্তের হেতু বা বিষয়। **3.** Thoughtful regard for others; as, *consideration* for the poor; যত্ন, মনোযোগ। **4.** (*Law*) Anything given or done as equivalent for what one does or undertakes for another; (আইন) মূল্য, কোন কার্য্যের প্রতিদানে কৃত কার্য্য বা প্রদত্ত বস্তু। **5.** Remuneration; as, for a *consideration*; পুরস্কার। **6.** Importance; গুরুত্ব। **In consideration of**—In view of; on account of; in return for; দৃষ্টে; জন্য; প্রতিদানে। **On no consideration**—On no account; কোন মতেই নহে। **To take into consideration**—To consider; বিবেচনা

করা। **Under consideration**—Under discussion ; বিবেচনাধীন, আলোচনাধীন।

cón-sĭd′-êr-ĭng, *prep.* & *adv.* In view of ; as, *considering* the frailties of human nature ; দৃষ্টে। ***Adv.*** Taking everything into account ; সবদিক ভাবিয়া।

cŏn-sign′ (-sīn), *v. t.* **1.** To make over ; to deliver formally ; to commit, (with *to*) ; as, to *consign* a body to a watery grave ; সমর্পণ করা ; রীত্যনুযায়ী প্রদান করা ; অর্পণ করা। **2.** To send by rail, etc. to an agent ; as, to *consign* goods ; রেলওয়ে প্রভৃতি যোগে প্রেরণ করা, চালান দেওয়া। **3.** To deposit ; as, to *consign* money to a bank ; গচ্ছিত রাখা, জমা রাখা। **—a-ble,** *adj.* **—ee,** *n.* A person to whom goods, etc. are sent for sale or superintendence ; কোন মালের প্রাপক। **—or,** *n.* One who consigns goods to another for sale, etc. ; (মাল) প্রেরক। **To consign to**—To transfer to a place permanently ; স্থায়িভাবে স্থানান্তরিত করা। To cast into ; as, to *consign* a thing *to* the water ; নিক্ষেপ করা, বিসর্জ্জন করা (প্রতিমাদি)। **To consign to oblivion**—To forget ; বিস্মৃতি-সলিলে নিমজ্জিত করা। **To consign to the flames**—To throw into fire ; অগ্নিতে সমর্পণ করা, অগ্নিসাৎ করা। **To consign to the tomb**—To bury ; সমাহিত করা।

cŏn-sĭg-nā′-tion, *n.* **1.** The act of formally giving money to a person legally appointed to receive it ; আইনানুসারে নিযুক্ত ব্যক্তিকে অর্থ-সমর্পণ। **2.** Transmission of goods for sale or custody ; মাল প্রেরণ, মাল চালান করণ। **To the consignation of**—Addressed to as a consignee ; প্রাপকের ঠিকানায় প্রেরিত।

cŏn-sign′-mĕnt (-sīn-), *n.* **1.** Act of consigning ; মাল প্রেরণ। **2.** Goods sent for sale or custody ; চালান, চালানি মাল। **3.** The writing by which anything is delivered ; যে লিখন দ্বারা কোন বস্তু অর্পিত হয়। **4.** Things consigned ; (বাণিজ্যে) প্রেরিত দ্রব্যাদি।

cŏn-sĭl′-ĭ-ĕnt, *adj.* Concurrent ; as, *consilient* inductions ; সহগামী। **—ence,** *n.* **Consilience of induction**—সিদ্ধান্তৈক্য (হিঃ কোঃ), আগমৈক্য (ঐ)।

cón-sĭst′, *v. i.* **1.** To be made up or composed ; (with *of*) ; as, light *consists* of luminous particles ; একযোগে বা মিলনে গঠিত হওয়া। **2.** To lie, (with *in*) ; as, virtue *consists in* being uncomfortable ; থাকা। **3.** To be consistent or harmonious, (followed by *with*) ; "Health *consists with* temperence alone"—Pope ; ঐক্য হওয়া, মিল হওয়া, সঙ্গতি-বিশিষ্ট হওয়া। **—ence, —en-cy,** *n.* **1.** Firmness ; solidity ; দৃঢ়তা ; ঘনতা, সংহতত্ব। **2.** The degree of density ; as, the *consistence* of a syrup ; ঘনতার পরিমাণ। **3.** Harmony in all parts ; congruity ; as, *consistency* of behaviour ; adherence to the same principles of action ; as, the virtue of *consistency* ; সুসঙ্গতি ; সামঞ্জস্য ; ঐক্য, মিল, অবিরোধ, অনুসারিত্ব। **—ent,** *adj.* **1.** Harmonious ; not contradictory ; (generally followed by *with*) ; as law is *consistent with* justice ; সঙ্গতি-বিশিষ্ট, সমান, অবিরুদ্ধ ; অবিপরীত। **2.** Acting up to the same principles ; as, let us lie *consistent* ; একই মূলতত্ত্বের অনুসারী, সঙ্গতি-বিশিষ্ট, সামঞ্জস্যপূর্ণ। **—ly,** *adv.* In a consistent manner ; সঙ্গতভাবে, সামঞ্জস্যের সহিত। **To consist in**—To be comprised in ; থাকা। **To consist of**—To be composed of ; একাধিক বস্তুর সংযোগে বা মিলনে গঠিত হওয়া। **To consist with**—To be consistent with ; সঙ্গতিবিশিষ্ট হওয়া, সামঞ্জস্য থাকা।

cŏn′-sĭs-tŏ-rȳ, *n.* **1.** The council of presbyters or elders ; যাজকবৃন্দগণের সভা। **2.** The ecclesiastical senate consisting of the pope and cardinals ; পোপ এবং কার্ডিন্যালগণ দ্বারা গঠিত যাজক সংসদ্। **3.** The court of a diocesan bishop in the English Church ; ইংলণ্ডীয় ধর্ম্মসমাজের ধর্ম্মাধ্যক্ষের সভা। **4.** (*Lutheran Church*) A body of clerical officers ; (লুথারীয় ধর্ম্মসমাজ), যাজকীয় কর্ম্মচারি-সম্প্রদায়। **—ri-al,** *adj.*

cŏn-sŏ′-cĭ-āte (-shî-), *n.* & *adj.* A partner ; an associate ; অংশী ; সহযোগী, সঙ্গী। ***Adj.*** United in fellowship ; সহযোগিতায় মিলিত।

cŏn-sŏ′-cĭ-āte (-shî-), *v. t.* & *i.* To unite together ; to associate ; একত্র হওয়া ; সঙ্গ করা। ***Verb i.*** To join in fellowship ; সংসর্গ করা, সঙ্গে মিশা। **—a′-tion,** *n.*

cŏn-sŏ-lā′-tion, *n.* **1.** Act of consoling or soothing ; solace ; শোকাপনোদন, শোকাপহরণ, সান্ত্বনা-প্রদান ; সান্ত্বনা, প্রবোধ, শান্তি। **2.** A person or thing giving consolation ; সান্ত্বনা-প্রদায়ক বস্তু বা ব্যক্তি, সান্ত্বনার কারণ। **3.** Consolation prize, race, etc. ; অকৃতকার্য্য ব্যক্তিদিগের সান্ত্বনার জন্য যে পুরস্কার, দৌড়ের সুবিধা, প্রভৃতি প্রদত্ত হয়।

cŏn-sŏl′-ă-tŏ-rȳ, *adj.* Tending to give solace and comfort ; সান্ত্বনা-সূচক, প্রবোধজনক, দুঃখহারক, শোকহারক। **—ri-ly,** *adv.*

cŏn-sōle′, *v. t.* To soothe in mental distress ; to comfort ; সান্ত্বনা দেওয়া ; প্রবোধ দেওয়া। **—sol′-a-ble,** *adj.* That may be comforted ; শমনীয়।

cŏn′-sōle, *n.* **1.** (*Arch.*) An ornamental bracket ; (স্থাপত্য-রীতি) কারুকার্য্যখচিত দেয়ালগিরি, নাগদন্তক, (আঃ বঃ)। **2.** (*Music*) A case enclosing manuals, etc. of an organ; (সঙ্গীতশাস্ত্র) অর্গেন নামক বাদ্যযন্ত্রের চাবির সারি ঢাকিবার জন্য আধার বিশেষ। **Console table, mirr** — তাকের . হায্যে যে মেজ বা আয়না দেয়ালের উপর ঠেস দিয়া রাখা হয়।

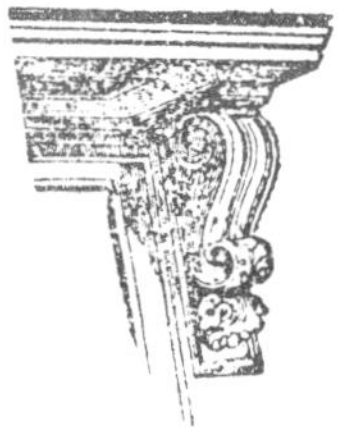
Console supporting cornice.

cŏn-sŏl′-ĭ-dāte, *v. t. & i.* **1.** To make solid; as, to *consolidate* the ground; (*fig.*) to strengthen; as, to *consolidate* power; কঠিন করা, সংহত করা, দৃঢ় করা, জমান, ঘনীভূত করা, সঙ্কাপিত করা; (লক্ষণায়) শক্তিশালী করা। **2.** To unite into one; একত্রীভূত করা, একত্র মিলিত করা, সংযুক্ত করা। **3.** (*Law*) To unite into one comprehensive statute; (আইন) একটা ব্যাপক আইনে সম্মিলিত করা। ***Verb i.*** To become solid; to combine solidly; ঘনীভূত হওয়া, জমাট বাঁধা; দৃঢ়রূপে সংযুক্ত হওয়া, দৃঢ় বদ্ধ হওয়া। **—da′-tion,** *n.* **1.** The act or process of consolidating; দৃঢ়ীকরণ, জমান, সঙ্কাপন। **2.** Combination; একত্রীভবন, মিলন, সংযোজন। **—da-tor,** *n.* **—da-to-ry,** *adj.* **Consolidated annuities**—(consols); বিলাতের কোম্পানীর কাগজ—জাতীয় ঋণের অধিকাংশ ইহার অন্তর্ভুক্ত। ১৭৫১ খৃঃ অব্দে শতকরা বার্ষিক তিনটাকা সুদের কোম্পানীর কাগজে একীভূত করা হয়। **Consolidated fund** — নানাপ্রকার করের সমষ্টি। **Consolidation Acts**—একটী সাধারণ বিধিতে একত্রীবদ্ধ পার্লেমেন্টের কতিপয় বিশেষ বিধি; পার্লেমেন্টের কতকগুলি বিশেষ আইন, ইহা হইতে জাতীয় ঋণের সুদ, রাজার গার্হস্থ্য ব্যয় প্রভৃতির অর্থ প্রদত্ত হয়।

cŏn-sŏls′, *n. pl.* A contraction of CONSOLIDATED ANNUITIES, which see.

consomme, *n.* (*F.*), (*Cookery*) A soup made by boiling meat and vegetables; (রন্ধন-বিদ্যা) মাংস ও তরকারীর যুষ।

cŏn′-sö-nănce, *n.* **1.** Recurrence of similar sounds, (as in a verse); এক রূপ ধ্বনির পুনরাবৃত্তি, (যেমন কবিতায়)। **2.** (*Music*) Agreement in sounds; pleasant accord of sounds produced simultaneously; (সঙ্গীত-শাস্ত্র) সুরের ঐক্য, মিল বা সামঞ্জস্য, সমস্বরতা, অনুসারিতা, স্বরসাম্য, সমবায়িত্ব (মিউজিক)। **3.** Agreement or congruity; harmony; মিল, ঐক্য, অবিরোধ, আনুরূপ্য; ঐক্যতান, স্বর-সঙ্গতি।

cŏn′-sö-nănt, *n.* A letter other than a vowel; a sound requiring a vowel in forming a syllable; ব্যঞ্জনবর্ণ, হলবর্ণ; ব্যঞ্জনধ্বনি। **—nan-tal,** *adj.* **Conjunct consonant**—সংযোগ।

cŏn′-sö-nănt, *adj.* **1.** Accordant; consistent, (with *to* or *with*); as, it is *consonant with* our aim; সঙ্গতি-বিশিষ্ট, অনুসারী, অবিরুদ্ধ, যোগ্য। **2.** Having like sounds; as, *consonant* words; ঐক্যতানিক, সমোচ্চারণ-বিশিষ্ট সমনাদ, একনাদ, সমস্বর। **3.** (*Music*) Harmonising together; as, *consonant* chords; ঐক্যতানিক। **—ly,** *adv.*

cŏn′-sŏrt, *n.* **1.** A husband or wife; স্বামী বা স্ত্রী, পতি বা পত্নী, কলত্র। **2.** (*Naut.*) A ship keeping company with another; (নৌ-বিদ্যা) সহগামী অর্ণবপোত। **—ship,** *n.* Fellowship; সংসর্গ।

cŏn-sŏrt′, *v. t. & i.* To unite; to associate; "He is *consorted* involuntarily with the people"—Hamilton; মিলিত করা, সংসর্গ করা। ***Verb i.*** **1.** To accord; to harmonise; (followed by *with*); as, it does not *consort with* the idea; মিলা, ঐক্য হওয়া; সঙ্গতি-বিশিষ্ট হওয়া। **2.** To associate or keep company; সংসর্গ করা, সঙ্গ করা, মিলিত হওয়া, সহবাস করা। **In consort**—In company; in harmony; মিলিত হইয়া; একসূত্রে। **King or Prince consort** — The husband of a queen (as the title of the late Prince Albert); কোন দেশের রাণীর পতি।

cŏn-spĕ-çĭf′-ic, *adj.* Of the same species; এক জাতীয়।

cŏn-spĕc′-tŭs, *n.* **1.** A general mental view or survey; পরিদর্শন। **2.** A synopsis; a sketch; সংক্ষিপ্ত-সার, চুম্বক, সারসংগ্রহ; স্থূল-কথা।

cŏn-spic′-ū-ous (-ŭs), *adj.* **1.** Open to the view; clearly visible; দৃষ্টি-পথারূঢ়, দৃষ্টিবিষয়ীভূত, পরিদৃশ্যমান; সুস্পষ্ট, প্রত্যক্ষ, প্রতীয়মান, সুপ্রকাশ, প্রকট। **2.** Attracting notice; eminent; noteworthy; as, to play a *conspicuous* part; নেত্রাকর্ষক, প্রকৃষ্ট, সুদৃশ্য, সুদর্শন; সমুন্নত, প্রখ্যাত, বিখ্যাত, প্রসিদ্ধ। **—cu′-i-ty, —ness,** *n.* **—ly,** *adv.* In a conspicuous manner; স্পষ্টরূপে, স্পষ্টতঃ। **Conspicuous for**—Distinguished for; কোন কিছুর জন্য বিখ্যাত। **In a conspicuous place**—প্রকাশ্য স্থানে। **To be conspicuous by one's absence**—অনুপস্থিতি হেতু বিশেষ লক্ষ্যের বিষয়ীভূত হওয়া।

cŏn-spĭr′-ă-çȳ, *n.* **1.** Act of conspiring; ষড়যন্ত্র করণ, কুমন্ত্রণা। **2.** A secret combination of men for an evil or unlawful purpose; plot; ষড়যন্ত্র; পাকচক্র, চক্রান্ত, কুচক্র, ঐকমত্য।

cŏn-spĭr′-ă-tor (-têr), *n.* One who engages in a conspiracy; a plotter; ষড়যন্ত্রকারী; কুচক্রী, চক্রান্তকারী। **—tress,** *n. fem.*

cŏn-spīre′, *v. i. & t.* **1.** To combine secretely for an illegal or evil purpose, *e.g.* treason, murder, etc.; to plot; কুমন্ত্রণা করা, চক্রান্ত করা, গুটি করা (*Colloq.*), জোট বাঁধা; ষড়যন্ত্র করা। **2.** To concur to one end; কোন উদ্দেশ্য সাধনে এক মত হওয়া। ***Verb t.*** To plot; as, to *conspire* one's ruin; উদ্ভাবন করা।

cŏn-spue′ (-spü), *v. t.* To express detestation for the abandonment or abolition of, (as a person or policy) ; (ব্যক্তি) পরিত্যাগ বা (শাসন-নীতি) রহিত করণের জন্য অশ্রদ্ধা প্রকাশ করা।

cŏn′-stă-ble, *n.* A peace officer ; a policeman ; শান্তিরক্ষক ; চৌকিদার, সিপাই পোলিশ, রক্ষী, নাগরিক, কোতোয়াল (কোটাল)। **Special constable** — বিশেষ সময়ে নিযুক্ত শান্তিরক্ষক কর্ম্মচারী, কোন লোক দ্বারা শান্তিভঙ্গের আশঙ্কা থাকিলে শান্তিরক্ষার্থ তাহাকে যে অবৈতনিক কনেষ্টবল নিয়োগ করা হয়। **Constable of France**—প্রাচীন ফরাসী নৃপতিগণের গার্হস্থ্য বিভাগের প্রধান কর্ম্মচারী। **Lord High Constable** or **Constable of Englond**—A similar officer of the English Royal household ; ইংরেজ নৃপতিগণের তদ্রূপ কর্ম্মচারী। বর্ত্তমানে বিশেষ ঘটনা উপলক্ষে অস্থায়িভাবে নিযুক্ত হইয়া থাকেন। **To outrun the constable**—To overstep all bounds of moderation ; to run into debt ; বাড়াবাড়ি করা ; ঋণ করা। **To overrun the constable**—To run into debt ; ঋণ করা, ঋণজালে জড়িত হওয়া।

cŏn-stăb′-ü-lă-rȳ, *adj.* & *n.* Of or relating to constables ; কনষ্টেবল-সম্বন্ধীয়, কোটাল-সম্পর্কীয়। ***Noun.*** The organized body of constables ; কনষ্টেবল সম্প্রদায়, কোটালসম্প্রদায়।

cŏn′-stăn-cȳ, *n.* **1.** Firmness of mind ; fortitude ; স্থৈর্য্য, ধৈর্য্য, দৃঢ়তা ; অধ্যবসায়। **2.** Faithfulness ; as, *constancy* and adherence to Christ ; নিষ্ঠা, স্থিরানুরাগ, দৃঢ় ভক্তি। **3.** Immutability ; fixedness ; অপরিবর্ত্তনীয়তা ; শাশ্বতত্ব, স্থায়িতা, স্থায়িত্ব, সাতত্য।

cŏn′-stănt, *adj.* & *n.* **1.** Unchangeable ; as, the *constant* image of a thing ; অপরিবর্ত্তনীয়। **2.** Steadfast ; resolute ; স্থির, অচল, অটল, স্থায়ী, শাশ্বত, সনাতন, নিত্য, অবিনাশী ; স্থিরমতি। **3.** Faithful ; true ; (with *to*) ; একনিষ্ঠ ; দৃঢ়ানুরক্ত। **4.** Incessant ; perpetual ; as, *constant* chatter ; নিত্য, অবিরত ; সতত, নিয়ত। **5.** Not fickle ; অচঞ্চল। ***Noun.*** (*Physics*) That which remains invariable ; (পদার্থ-বিজ্ঞান) অপরিবর্ত্তনীয় বস্তু। **2.** (*Math.*) A quantity which remains the same throughout a problem ; স্থির রাশি। **—ly,** *adv.* Incessantly ; always ; very often ; সর্ব্বদা ; সতত, অনুক্ষণ ; প্রায়শঃ। **Absolute constant**—(*Math.*) যে রাশির মান সর্ব্বাবস্থায় অপরিবর্ত্তনীয় থাকে। **Arbitrary constant** — ইচ্ছানুসারে যে রাশিতে যে কোন মান আরোপণ করা যাইতে পারে।

cŏn-stăn′-tia (shĭ-ă), *n.* Wine produced on the Constantia farm near Cape town ; কেপ্ টাউনের নিকটবর্ত্তী কনষ্টেন্সিয়া কৃষিক্ষেত্রে প্রস্তুত মদিরাবিশেষ।

cŏn-stĕl-lā′-tion, *n.* **1.** A number of fixed stars grouped within an imaginary outline ; তারা-প্রকোষ্ঠ, তারামণ্ডল, রাশি। **2.** (*Fig.*) An assemblage of splendours or excellencies ; as, a *constellation* of fair ladies ; রূপগুণাদি দ্বারা সমুজ্জ্বল ও শ্রেষ্ঠ মানব বা বস্তুনিচয়ের সমাবেশ। **Constellation of the lion**—সিংহরাশি।

cŏn′-stêr-nāte, *v. t.* **1.** To fill with consternation or dismay ; সন্ত্রস্ত করা, ভয়বিহ্বল করা। **—na′-tion,** *n.* Astonishment ; terror ; বিস্ময়, সন্ত্রাস ; ভয়বিহ্বলতা।

cŏn′-sti-pāte, *v. t.* **1.** To stop by filling up capillary or other passages ; কৈশিকনালী বা অন্যপথ পূর্ণ করিয়া বন্ধ করা। **2.** To render costive ; কোষ্ঠ-বদ্ধ করা, কোষ্ঠকাঠিন্য জন্মান। **—pa′-tion,** *n.* A state of the bowels in which the evacuations are stopped ; costiveness ; কোষ্ঠ কাঠিন্য ; কোষ্ঠবদ্ধতা।

cŏn-stit′-ü-ĕn-cȳ, *n.* **1.** The whole body of voters or electors in a town or country ; কোন নগর বা দেশের নির্ব্বাচক সম্প্রদায়। **2.** A place or a body of residents in a place represented by elected members ; কোন ব্যক্তি যে স্থান হইতে নির্ব্বাচিত হয়, তৎস্থানের অধিবাসিবর্গ। **3.** A body of customers, etc. ; ক্রেতৃবর্গ, প্রভৃতি।

cŏn-stit′-ü-ĕnt, *adj.* & *n.* **1.** Component ; as, the *constituent* parts of water ; উপাদানভূত। **2.** Having the power of electing or appointing ; নির্ব্বাচনক্ষম, নিয়োগক্ষম। **3.** Having the power of framing or revising a constitution ; as, a *constituent* assembly ; কোন নিয়ম গঠন বা সংশোধনের জন্য ক্ষমত প্রাপ্ত। ***Noun.*** **1.** A component part ; উপাদান, অবয়ব (হিঃ কোঃ)। **2.** One who appoints another as his agent or representative প্রতিনিধির নিয়োগকর্ত্তা। **3.** One of those who elect a person to an office as their representative অন্যতম নির্ব্বাচনকর্ত্তা। **Constituent assembly**—১৭৮৮ খৃঃ অব্দে ফরাসী বিপ্লবের সময়ে প্রতিষ্ঠিত জাতীয় সমিতি।

cŏn′-sti-tüte, *v. t.* **1.** To establish ; সংস্থাপন করা, প্রতিষ্ঠিত করা, প্রতিষ্ঠাপিত করা। **2.** To give a legal form to ; as, to *constitute* an assembly ; আইনানুযায়ী আকার প্রদান করা। **3.** To make up ; "Truth and reason *constitute* that intellectual gold that defies destruction ;" গঠন করা, একযোগে গঠিত করা। **4.** To appoint or elect to an office ; as, to *constitute* a man president ; নিয়োগ বা নির্ব্বাচন করা। **4.** To make ; to frame,—(passive) ; "Faculties *constituted* like our own ;" গঠন করা ; রচনা করা। **—tu′-tion,** *n.* **1.** Establishment ; সংস্থাপন, গঠন, সংস্থান। **2.** Nature or character of the body wit regard to strength, health and vitality ; as, a robust *constitution* ; দৈহিক প্রকৃতি, ধাতু, দেহস্বভাব, শারীরিক প্রকৃতি। **3.** The natural condition of the mind ; মনের স্বাভাবিক অবস্থা, মনোভাব, মানসিক প্রকৃতি, প্রকৃতি, মেজাজ। **4.** The mode in which a state is organised ; শাসন-ব্যবস্থার ধারা বা প্রকৃতি। **5.** A system of fundamental principle for the government of a state ; the established form ; রাজ্যশাসনের মূল সূত্র বা নীতিসমূহ ; নিয়মতন্ত্র। **6.** (*Hist.*) A regulation or ordinance ; as, the *constitutions* of Clarendon ; (ইতিহাস) নিয়ম, ব্যবস্থা, বিধান। **–tu′-tion-al,** *adj.* & *n.* **1.** Inherent in, or belonging to, the constitution of body or mind ; as, a *constitutional* malady ; দেহগত, প্রকৃতিগত, স্বভাবসিদ্ধ, সর্ব্বাঙ্গীণ, ধাতুগত, কৌলিক। **2.** Beneficial to one's constitution or health ; as, *constitutional* walks ; স্বাস্থ্যজনক। **3.** In accordance with the constitution of a state or society ; as, *constitutional* reforms ; কোন রাষ্ট্র বা সম্প্রদায়ের অচলপ্রতিষ্ঠ নিয়মসমূহের অনুসারী। **4.** Regulated by or dependent on a constitution ; as, a *constitutional* government ; নিয়মতন্ত্রসম্মত, নিয়মতন্ত্রাধীন। **5.** Pertaining to a political constitution ; as, the *constitutional* history of England ; নিয়মতন্ত্রসম্বন্ধীয়। **6.** Adhering or loyal to the political constitution ; নিয়মতন্ত্রনিষ্ঠ। **7.** Essential ; as, a *constitutional* element of evidence ; মৌলিক, প্রধান। (*Noun*) A walk for the sake of one's health ; স্বাস্থ্যরক্ষার্থ ভ্রমণ বা বায়ুসেবন। **–tu′-tion-al-ism,** *n.* **1.** Adherence to the principles of the constitution ; নিয়মতন্ত্রনিষ্ঠা। **2.** A constitutional form of government ; নিয়মতন্ত্র। **–tu′-tion-al-ist,** *n.* One who advocates a constitutional form of government ; a writer on the political constitution ; নিয়মতন্ত্রের পক্ষপাতী ; নিয়মতন্ত্রসম্বন্ধীয় গ্রন্থ-লেখক। **–tu-tion-al′-i-ty,** *n.* The state of being constitutional, (spec. political) ; নিয়মতন্ত্রতা। **–tu′-tion-al-ly,** *adv.* **1.** Naturally ; as, he was *constitutionally* timid ; প্রকৃতিগত, স্বভাবতঃ, স্বভাবগত। **2.** In accordance with the political constitution ; legally ; নিয়মতন্ত্রানুসারে ; আইনতঃ। **–tu-tion-al-ize,** *v. t.* & *i.* To make constitutional ; নিয়মতন্ত্র সম্মত করা। (*Verb i.*) To take a constitutional walk for health ; স্বাস্থ্যরক্ষার উদ্দেশ্যে ভ্রমণ করা। **Constitutional government** — যে শাসনতন্ত্রে রাজা কতকগুলি অচলপ্রতিষ্ঠ নিয়মের অধীন থাকেন, নিয়মতন্ত্ররাজ্য (জিঃ)। **Constitution of Clarendon** — খৃষ্টীয় ধর্ম্মসমাজের অধিকার নির্দ্দেশক বিধি সমূহ,—১১৬৪ খৃঃ অব্দে ক্লেরেণ্ডন নামক স্থানে নিবদ্ধ করা হয়। **To give a nation a constitution** — To give it fixed laws even to the limitations of the sovereign's rights ; রাজার অধিকার সীমাবদ্ধ করিয়াও কোন জাতিকে অচল প্রতিষ্ঠিত শাসননিয়ম প্রদান করা। **Written costitution**—কোন শাসনতন্ত্রের মূল সূত্র সমূহ সম্বলিত দলিলবিশেষ।

cŏn′-sti-tū-tive, *adj.* **1.** Forming an essential part ; মূল উপাদানীভূত। **2.** Essential ; as, the *constitutive* element of a thing সারভূত, মৌলিক। **3.** Having the power of establishing or creating ; constructive ; গঠনক্ষম ; সংস্থাপক, বিরচনশীল। **4.** Component or constituent ; as, the *constitutive* parts of the drama are six ; উপাদানীভূত। **5.** (*Phys.* & *chem.*) Pertaining to the constitution ; as, the *constitutive* property ; (পদার্থ-বিজ্ঞান ও রসায়নশাস্ত্র) উপাদান বা অবয়ব সম্বন্ধীয়।

cŏn′-sti-tū-tor (-têr), *n.* One who frames a constitution ; ব্যবস্থাপক।

cŏn-strain′ (-strān), *v. t.* **1.** To bind or confine ; to imprison ; বন্ধ করা, আটক করা ; কারারুদ্ধ করা। **2.** To compel ; to force ; বাধ্য করা ; বলপ্রয়োগে বাধ্য করা। **3.** To restrain ; to repress ; দমন করা ; সংযত করা। **4.** To compress ; সঙ্কুচিত করা। **5.** To bring about by compulsion ; as, there is not sufficient testimony to *constrain* his assent ; বল প্রয়োগদ্বারা সাধন করা। **–strained′,** *p. p. adj.* Forced ; cramped ; as, a *constrained* voice ; বাধ্য, প্রতিরুদ্ধ, কষ্ট-কল্পিত ; সঙ্কোচ-জড়িত।

cŏn-straint′ (-strānt), *n.* **1.** Compulsion ; confinement ; necessity ; বাধ্যবাধকতা ; আটক, অবরোধ ; আবশ্যকতা। **2.** Unnaturalness or embarrassment of manne ; as, she welcomed me with a *constraint* ; চালচলনে অস্বাভাবিকতা, অস্বচ্ছন্দতা, বাঁধ বাঁধ ভাব, আটক, কুণ্ঠা, সঙ্কোচ।

cŏn-strict′, *v. t.* To contract or compress ; সঙ্কুচিত করা, সঙ্কাপিত করা। **–stric′-tion,** *n.*, Contraction ; সঙ্কোচন, সঙ্কোচ। **–stric′-tive,** *adj.* **–stric′-tor,** *n.* (*Anat.*) **1.** A muscle which contracts ; (শারীর-সংস্থান-বিদ্যা) সঙ্কোচকপেশী। **2.** A large snake ; অজগর।

cŏn-stringe′ (-strînj), *v. t.* To contract ; to cause to shrink (as an organ, tissue) ; সঙ্কুচিত করা ; (শারীরিক) বিধান-তন্তু সমূহ সঙ্কুচিত করা। **–strin′-gen-cy,** *n.* **–strin′-gent,** *adj.* Causing contraction ; সঙ্কোচক (ঠাকুর)।

cŏn-strŭct′, *v. t.* **1.** To form ; to build ; to make ; as, to *construct* an edifice ; গঠন করা ; নির্ম্মাণ করা ; প্রস্তুত করা। **2.** (*Gram.*) To put together (as words) syntactically ; (ব্যাকরণ) যথাক্রমে শব্দ-বিন্যাস করা। **3.** (*Geom.*) To draw ;

as, to *construct* a circle ; (জ্যামিতি) অঙ্কিত করা। **4.** To devise ; as, to *canstruct* a theory ; উদ্ভাবন করা। **—struc′-tion,** *n.* **1.** The act or process of constructing ; erection ; fabrication ; গঠন, নির্ম্মাণ ; গাঁথিয়া তোলন ; রচনা। **2.** A thing constructed ; নির্ম্মিত বা গঠিত বস্তু **3.** (*Gram.*) The syntactical arrangement of words in a sentence ; (ব্যাকরণ) বাক্যে যথাক্রমে শব্দযোজনা, অন্বয়। **4.** Act of explaining or construing ; as your *construction* of the tenor of the letter ; অর্থ-প্রকটন, মর্ম্মোদ্ঘাটন। **5.** Interpretation ; as, to put a good or bad *construction* upon his refusal ; অর্থ। **6.** (*Geom.*) The act or mode of drawing a figure for solving a problem or proving a proposition ; (জ্যামিতি) অঙ্কন। **—struc′-tion-al,** *adj.* Pertaining to an interpretation ; structural ; অন্বয় বা অর্থসম্বন্ধীয় ; গঠন-গত। **—struc′-tive,** *adj.* **1.** Having the quality to construct or form ; tending to construct ; (opposed to destructive) ; as, *constructive* criticism ; নির্ম্মাণক্ষম, গঠনক্ষম ; নির্ম্মাণাত্মক (হিঃ কোঃ)। **2.** Not directly expressed but inferred ; virtual ; as, a *constructive* intention or permission ; পরোক্ষভাবে ব্যক্ত, অনুমানলব্ধ ; ফলতঃ বটে কিন্তু বাহ্যতঃ নয়। **3.** Of or pertaining to construction ; belonging to the structure of a building ; গঠন-সম্বন্ধীয় ; অট্টালিকার নির্ম্মাণ বা গঠন-গত। **—struc′-tive-ly,** *adv.* **Construction train** — লৌহ-বর্ত্মের নির্ম্মাণ বা জীর্ণ-সংস্কার-কার্য্যের নিমিত্ত লোক ও সরঞ্জাম প্রেরণার্থ বাষ্পীয়-শকট। **To bear a construction**—To allow of a particular interpretation ; বিশেষ অর্থ গ্রহণক্ষম হওয়া, বিশেষ অর্থ-সহ হওয়া। **To put a false construction upon** — To interpret wrongly ; অপ্রকৃত অর্থ করা, ভ্রমপূর্ণ অর্থ করা।

cŏn-strŭc′-tor (-têr), *n.* One who constructs ; (esp.) a supervisor of the construction and repairs of ships, etc. ; নির্ম্মাতা ; পোত প্রভৃতির নির্ম্মাণ- এবং জীর্ণ-সংস্কার-পরিদর্শক কর্ম্মচারী। **—ship,** *n.*

cŏn′-strue (-strô), *v. t.* & *i.* **1.** To arrange words so as to discover the sense of a sentence ; বাক্যের অর্থনির্ণয়ার্থ যথাযথরূপে শব্দ বিন্যাস করা, অন্বয় করা। **2.** To explain the construction of ; as, to *construe* a sentence ; অন্বয়মুখে ব্যাখ্যা করা। **3.** To combine grammatically ; to translate ; ব্যাকরণের নিয়মানুযায়ী সংযোগ করা ; অনুবাদ করা। **4.** To explain the sense of ; to interpret ; as, pleaders can *construe* their pleading ; ব্যাখ্যা করা ; অর্থ করা। ***Verb i.*** **1.** To admit of grammatical analysis ; as, this passage does not *construe* ; অন্বয়-সহ হওয়া। **To construe into**—To interpret into as ; কোন বিশেষ-রূপে অর্থ বা ব্যাখ্যা করা।

cŏn-sŭb-stăn′-tial (-shî-al), *adj.* Of the same substance, essence or nature, (esp. of three Persons in the Godhead) ; সমপ্রকৃতিক সমস্বভাব, এক-তত্ত্ব। **—ti-al′-i-ty,** *n.*

cŏn-sŭb-stăn′-ti-āte (-shî-), *v. t.* & *i.* To unite into one common substance ; এক পদার্থে পরিণত করা। ***Verb i.*** To become combine in one substance ; এক পদার্থে পরিণত হওয়া।

cŏn-sŭb-stăn-ti-ā′-tion (-shî-), *n.* (*Theol.*) The doctrine of the presence of the body and blood of Christ in the sacramental elements ; (খৃষ্টীয় ধর্ম্ম-শাস্ত্র) খৃষ্টের শেষ নৈশ-ভোজনের স্মৃতি-অনুষ্ঠানের সুরা ও রুটিতে তাঁহার রক্ত ও মাংস সহবিদ্যমান রহিয়াছে—এইরূপ মতবাদ।

cŏn′-sue-tūde (-swē-), *n.* **1.** Custom, usage etc. having legal force ; আইনতঃ পালনীয় রীতিনীতি, প্রচলিত বা চিরাগত আচারব্যবহার। **2.** Social intercourse ; সামাজিক মেলামিশা।

cŏn-sue-tū′-di-nă-rў (-swē-), *adj.* & *n.* Customary ; প্রথামূলক। ***Noun.*** A book containing ritual usuages of a monastic house ; কোন আশ্রমের চিরাগত পূজা ও উপাসনা-পদ্ধতির বিবরণ সম্বলিত পুস্তক।

cŏn′-sŭl, *n.* **1.** (*Rom. Antiq.*) One of the two annually elected chief magistrates of the Republic ; (রোমীয় প্রত্নতত্ত্ব) প্রাচীন রোমনগরীর সাধারণ-তন্ত্রের প্রতি বৎসর নির্বাচিত দুই জন প্রধান-শাসন কর্ত্তার অন্যতর। **2.** The title of the three chief magistrates of the French Republic (from 1799 to 1804) ; ফরাসী সাধারণ তন্ত্রের (১৭৯৯ হইতে ১৮০৪ খৃঃ অব্দ পর্য্যন্ত) তিনজন প্রধান শাসনকর্ত্তার উপাধি। **3.** A state agent residing in a foreign town to represent the sovereign and to look after the interests of his states in that country ; বৈদেশিক বাণিজ্যদূত, বৈদেশিক প্রতিনিধি। **4.** The local representative officer of the cyclists' touring club ; দ্বিচক্রযানারোহিগণের ভ্রমণ-সমিতির স্থানীয় প্রতিনিধি। **Consul-general** — কোন দেশ হইতে প্রেরিত প্রধান রাজদূত,—ইনি বিভিন্ন স্থানে প্রতিষ্ঠিত তদ্দেশের বাণিজ্য-দূতগণের উপর কর্তৃত্ব করিয়া থাকেন।

cŏn′-sū-lar (-lêr), *adj.* & *n.* Of the nature of, or pertaining to, a consul ; রোমের প্রধান শাসকসম্বন্ধীয়, বৈদেশিক বাণিজ্য-দূত-সম্বন্ধীয়। ***Noun.*** A Roman of consular rank ; প্রাচীন রোমের অন্যতর প্রধান শাসকের পদবিধারী ব্যক্তি।

cŏn′-sū-lāte, *n.* The office or residence of a (modern) consul ; the office of a (Roman) consul ; বৈদেশিক বাণিজ্যদূতের কার্য্যালয় ; প্রাচীন রোমনগরীর অন্যতর শাসনকর্ত্তার কার্য্যালয়।

cŏn-sŭlt′, *v. t.* & *i.* **1.** To ask the advice of; to seek the opinion of; as, to *consult* a physician; to refer to; as, to *consult* a dictionary; পরামর্শ জিজ্ঞাসা করা, পরামর্শ করা; মত চাওয়া; দেখা (অভিধান প্রভৃতি)। **2.** To have regard to; to consider; as, to *consult* public interest; গণ্য করা; বিবেচনা করা। ***Verb i.*** To take counsel; as, to *consult* with a man or a book; মত বা পরামর্শ গ্রহণ করা, দেখা। **2.** To deliberate together; to confer; একত্র পরামর্শ করা; মন্ত্রণা করা। **—a-tive,** *adj.* **—sul-tee′**, *n.* **To consult one's pillow**—To take a night for reflection; একরাত্রি ব্যাপিয়া ভাবা।

cŏn-sŭlt′-ănt, *n.* **1.** One who consults; পরামর্শগ্রহণকারী। **2.** A consulting physician; (see below). **Consulting physician** or **engineer**—যে চিকিৎসক কিম্বা পূর্ত্তবিদ্যা-বিশারদ জনসাধারণ বা সমব্যবসায়িগণকে পরামর্শ প্রদান করেন।

cŏn-sŭl-tā′-tion, *n.* **1.** The act of consulting; পরামর্শগ্রহণ। **2.** Deliberation of two or more persons with a view to a decision; পরামর্শ, মন্ত্রণা। **3.** A meeting for deliberation or discussion; পরামর্শসভা, আলোচনাসভা। **Consultation fee**—পরামর্শের জন্য দর্শনী।

cŏn-sūme′, *v.t.*& *i.* **1.** To destroy; নষ্ট করা, ধ্বংস করা, ক্ষয় করা। **2.** To use up; to eat up; to exhaust; as, to *consume* provision; to waste; as, to *consume* wealth; ব্যবহার করিয়া নিঃশেষিত করা, ফুরাইয়া দেওয়া; খাইয়া শেষ করা, খাইয়া ফেলা; নিঃশেষিত করা; অপব্যয় করা। ***Verb i.*** To waste away slowly; ক্রমশঃ ক্ষয়প্রাপ্ত হওয়া, অল্পে অল্পে লোপ পাওয়া। **—sumed′**, *p.p. adj.* Used up; eaten up; ব্যবহার দ্বারা নিঃশেষিত; উপভক্ষিত। **—sum′-ed-ly**, *adv.* Excessively; as, laughing *consumedly*; অতিমাত্রায়। **—sum′-er**, *n.* **1.** One who or that which consumes; ধ্বংসকারী, ক্ষয়কর। **2.** (*Polit. Econ.*) The user of the goods or articles produced (opposed to *producer*); (অর্থ-নীতি) উৎপন্ন জিনিষের ব্যবহারকারী, খাদক।

cŏn′-sŭm-māte, *v. t.* **1.** To bring to completion; to accomplish; to finish; as, to *consummate* a business; সমাপ্ত করা; শেষ করা, সমাধা করা; সম্পূর্ণ করা, সম্পন্ন করা, নিষ্পন্ন করা, সিদ্ধ করা। **2.** To complete by sexual intercourse; as, to *consummate* a marriage; বিবাহিত স্ত্রীপুরুষের সহবাস দ্বারা নিষ্পন্ন করা। **—ma-tive**, *adj.* **—ma-tor**, *n.*

cŏn-sŭm′-māte, *adj.* Complete; perfect; as, a *consummate* minister or hypocrite; সম্পন্ন; সর্ব্বাবয়বসম্পন্ন, সর্ব্বাঙ্গসুন্দর, পাকা। **—ly**, *adv.*

cŏn-sŭm-mā′-tion, *n.* **1.** Completion; সমাপ্তি, অবসান, নিষ্পত্তি, সম্পাদন, সিদ্ধি, পরিসমাপ্তি, পরিপূর্ণতা। **2.** The state of full development; perfection; as, the *cosummation* of heathen virtue; সর্ব্বাঙ্গসম্পন্নতা; চরমোৎকর্ষ। **3.** Goal; as, Radicalism has come to its *consummation*; চরমগন্তব্যস্থল। **4.** A consummated or perfected thing; সর্ব্বাঙ্গসম্পন্ন বা চরমোৎকর্ষপ্রাপ্ত বস্তু।

cŏn-sump′-tion (-sŭm-), *n.* **1.** The act of consuming; decay; destruction; waste; ক্ষয়করণ; ক্ষয়; ধ্বংস; অপব্যয়, অপচয়। **2.** Wasting disease; ক্ষয়রোগ, ক্ষয়কাস (সাঃ পঃ), রাজযক্ষ্মা। **3.** (*Polit. Econ.*) The expenditure of the products of industry; the amount of goods consumed; শ্রমশিল্পদ্বারা উৎপন্ন জিনিষের ব্যয়; যে পরিমাণ জিনিষ ব্যয়িত হয়। **Pulmonory consumption**—রাজযক্ষ্মা, ক্ষয়-কাস।

cŏn-sump′-tive (-sŭm-tĭv), *adj.* & *n.* **1.** Tending to consume; destructive; ক্ষয়কারী; বিনাশসাধক। **2.** (*Med.*) Affected with or disposed to consumption; (ভৈষজ্য-শাস্ত্র) ক্ষয়রোগাক্রান্ত, ক্ষয়রোগগ্রস্ত, ক্ষয়রোগোন্মুখ। ***Noun.*** One affected with consumption; as, the spring is bad for *consumptives*; ক্ষয়রোগগ্রস্ত ব্যক্তি। **—ly**, *adv.*

cŏn-tă-bĕs′-cence (-ĕns), *n.* (*Bot.*) Suppression of pollen formation in the anthers of flowers; (উদ্ভিদ্-বিদ্যা) পুষ্পের পরাগকোষে রেণু-গঠন-নিরোধ। **—cent**, *adj.*

cŏn′-tăct, *n.* **1.** A close union or junction of bodies; touch; সংসর্গ, সংযোগ; সংস্পর্শ। **2.** (*Geom.*) The meeting of curves, surfaces, or of a straight line and curve; as, a point of *contact*; (জ্যামিতি) স্পর্শ। **To come in** or **into contact**—To come across; to be brought into connections with; সাক্ষাৎ হওয়া; সংস্পর্শে আসা। **To make** or **break contact**—To complete or interrupt an electric circuit; (hence *contact-maker*, *contact-breaker*); বৈদ্যুতিক প্রবাহের সঞ্চার পথ সম্পূর্ণ বা ভঙ্গ করা।

cŏn-tâ-dī′-nŏ, *n.* (*It*) An Italian peasant; ইতালীদেশীয় কৃষক।

cŏn-tā′-gion (-jŏn), *n.* **1.** The communication of disease by contact direct or indirect; a contagious disease; a matter spreading contagious disease; প্রত্যক্ষ বা পরোক্ষ স্পর্শহেতু রোগ-সংক্রমণ; স্পর্শ-সংক্রান্ত রোগ; স্পর্শ-সংক্রামক রোগ বিস্তারকারী বস্তু। **2.** Moral corruption; "A few eminent men......were exempt from the general *contagion*;" অসাধুতা। **3.** Contagious or catching influence; as, the *contagion* of adventure; সংক্রামক প্রভাব। **—ist**, *n.* One believing in the contagiousness of certain diseases, *i. e.* cholera, plague, etc.; বিসূচিকা, মহামারী, প্রভৃতি রোগের স্পর্শ-সংক্রামকতা বিষয়ে বিশ্বাসী ব্যক্তি।

cŏn-tā'-gious (-jŭs), *adj.* **1.** Communicated by contact ; as, a *contagious* disease ; স্পর্শসংক্রামক, সংক্রামক, ছোঁয়াচে, স্পর্শ-প্রভব (সাঃ পঃ) । **2.** Conveying or generating disease ; as, *contagious* air ; pestilential ; রোগসংক্রমণকারী, রোগোৎপাদী ; মারী বা অনিষ্ট উৎপাদক । **3.** (*Fig.*) Catching ; (লক্ষণায়) সংক্রামক । **—ly,** *adv.* **—ness,** *n.*

cŏn-tain' (-tān), *v. t.* **1.** To hold as contents ; to comprise ; to include ; ধারণ করা ; অন্তর্ভুক্ত করা, অন্তর্ভূত করা ; অন্তর্গত করা। **2.** To be able to hold ; to be equal to ; as, a bushel *contains* four pecks ; ধারণ করিতে সমর্থ হওয়া ; সমান হওয়া । **3.** (*Passive*) To comprehend or include (*within* space or *between* limits) ; as, the space *contained between* the orbits of Mars and Jupiter ; অন্তর্ভুক্ত করা। **4.** (*Geom.*) To enclose ; to include ; as, *contained* angles ; (জ্যামিতি) পরিবেষ্টন করা ; অন্তর্ভুক্ত করা । **5.** (*Arith.* & *Algeb.*) To be divisible by without a remainder ; (পাটীগণিত ও বীজগণিত) কোন রাশিদ্বারা অবশিষ্ট শূন্যরূপে বিভাজ্য হওয়া । **6.** To put restraint upon ; as, he could not *contain* himself for joy ; আত্মসংবরণ করা । **—a-ble,** *adj.*

cŏn-tăm'-i-nāte, *v. t.* To pollute ; as, to *contaminate* the mind ; দূষিত করা, অশুচি করা, কলুষিত করা । **—na'-tion,** *n.* Pollution ; that which contaminates ; অপবিত্রতা, মলিনতা, মালিন্য, কলুষতা ; কলুষ, অপবিত্রতাজনক বস্তু ।

cŏn-tan'-gō (-tăng-), *n.* A sum of money paid to seller of stock for accommodating buyer by putting off the time of payment ; কোম্পানীর কাগজের বিক্রেতা বিক্রীত-কাগজের মূল্য প্রদানের নির্দ্দিষ্ট সময় বাড়াইয়া দিলে, ক্রেতা তাহাকে যে অর্থ প্রদান করিয়া থাকে। **Contango** or **continuation day**—কোম্পানীর কাগজের বাজারে পাক্ষিক হিসাব নিষ্পত্তির পূর্ব্ববর্ত্তী দ্বিতীয় দিবস।

cŏn-temn' (tĕm), *v. t.* To despise ; to disregard ; উপেক্ষা করা, অবজ্ঞা করা, হেয় জ্ঞান করা ; অশ্রদ্ধা করা। **—tem'-ner,** *n.* Scorner ; ঘৃণাকারী, অশ্রদ্ধাকারী ।

cŏn'-tĕm-plāte, *v. t.* & *i.* **1.** To consider with continued attention ; to meditate on ; প্রগাঢ় অভিনিবেশ সহকারে ভাবা ; ধ্যান করা । **2.** To look on attentively ; as, *contemplating* her from head to foot ; অভিনিবেশ সহকারে দর্শন করা । **3.** To expect ; as, to *contemplate* an event that may take place ; to intend ; to plan ; as, to *contemplate* coming at noon ; আশা করা ; অভিপ্রায় করা ; কল্পনা করা। **4.** To regard ; গণ্য করা। ***Verb i.*** To think studiously ; to reflect ; অনুধ্যান করা ; ভাবা। **—pla'-tion,** *n.* **1.** The act of contemplating ; meditation ; musing ; পরিচিন্তন ; ধ্যান ; নিদিধ্যাসন, চিন্তা। **2.** Purpose ; expectation ; as, in *contemplation* ; উদ্দেশ্য ; প্রত্যাশা। **3.** Attentive observation ; as, an object of vision and *contemplation* ; অভিনিবেশ সহকারে পর্য্যবেক্ষণ। **—pla-tor,** *n.* **To have in contemplation**—To purpose or have under consideration ; মনে মনে সঙ্কল্প থাকা, বিবেচনা স্থলে থাকা।

cŏn-tĕm'-plā-tive (-tĭv), *adj.* Reflective ; as, a *contemplative* character ; given to contemplation ; as, a *contemplative* life ; চিন্তাশীল ; ভাবুক, ধ্যানশীল, অনুধ্যানপরায়ণ। **—ly,** *adv.* **—ness,** *n.*

cŏn-tĕm-pō-rā'-nē-ous (-ŭs), *adj.* Existing or happening at the same time ; (followed by *with*) ; সমকালবর্ত্তী, সমকালীন, সমানকালীন, সামসময়িক। **—ly,** *adv.* **—ne-i-ty,** *n.*

cŏn-tĕm'-pō-rā-rȳ, *adj.* & *n.* **1.** Living or occurring together in the same time ; সামসময়িক, সমকালীন। **2.** Equal in age ; "Loves his *contemporary* trees ;" সমবয়স্ক। ***Noun.*** One who lives at the same time with another ; a person of the same age with another ; a newspaper published during the same period ; "We quote from our *contemporary* the Vatican ;" সমকালীন ব্যক্তি, সামসময়িক লোক ; সমবয়স্ক ব্যক্তি ; এক সময়ে প্রকাশিত সংবাদপত্র, সহযোগী **Contemporary with**—Living or existing at the same time with (another) ; সামসময়িক, সমকালবর্ত্তী

cŏn-tĕm'-pō-rīze, *v. t.* To make contemporary ; সমকালবর্ত্তী করা।

cŏn-tĕmpt' (-tĕmt), *n.* **1.** Disdain ; অবজ্ঞা, ঘৃণা, তাচ্ছিল্য, হেলা। **2.** Disgrace ; as, to hold in *contempt* অপমান, অবমাননা। **3.** An act or expression denoting contempt ; "Insult and *contempts* ;" অবজ্ঞাসূচক কার্য্য বা উক্তি। **4.** (*Law*) Disobedience to a sovereign's lawful commands or to the authority of a legislative body ; (আইন) রাজার বৈধ আদেশের অবমাননা, বিধি-প্রতিষ্ঠিত প্রতিষ্ঠানের প্রতি অসম্মানপ্রদর্শন। **Contempt of court**—আদালতের অবমাননা। **To bring** or **fall into contempt** — অপমানিত করা ; অবজ্ঞের হওয়া।

cŏn-tempt'i-ble (-tĕnt), *adj.* Worthy of disdain ; vile ; despicable ; অবজ্ঞেয় ; হেয় ; ঘৃণার্হ, নিন্দার্হ। **—bil'-i-ty,** *n.* **—bly,** *adv.* **—ness,** *n.*

cŏn-temp'-tu-ous (-tĕm-tū-ŭs), *adj.* Showing or expressing disdain ; insolent ; "She was hard... ...cold, *contemptuous* ;" ঘৃণাসূচক, অবজ্ঞাসূচক, অবজ্ঞাপ্রদর্শক ; প্রগল্ভ। **—ly,** *adv.* **—ness,** *n.*

cŏn-tĕnd', *v. i.* & *t.* **1.** To strive ; to compete ; to fight ; to struggle ;

as, *contending* passions ; চেষ্টা করা ; প্রতিযোগিতা করা, প্রতিদ্বন্দ্বিতা করা ; বিবাদ করা ; সংগ্রাম করা। **2.** To strive in debate ; to argue ; "The question, the author would *contend* for ;" তর্কবিতর্ক করা, বাদানুবাদ করা ; বাগ্‌বিতণ্ডা করা। **To contend with one for** or **against a thing**—কোন বিষয়ের অনুকূলে বা প্রতিকূলে কাহারও সহিত বাদানুবাদ করা।

cŏn'-tĕnt, *n.* (Uusually in *plural*) **1.** That which is contained, (with *of*) ; as, the *contents* of a book ; (পুস্তকাদির) অন্তর্লিখিত বিষয় সমূহ, (ভাণ্ডাদির) অভ্যন্তরস্থ বস্তু। **2.** Capacity ; size ; "Ships of great *content*" — Bacon ; ধারণশক্তি ; আয়তন, পরিসর। **3.** (*Gram.*) Area or quantity of space contained within certain limits ; আয়তন। **4.** Real meaning ; প্রকৃত অর্থ, অন্তরার্থ, অন্তর্গতার্থ। **A table of contents**—সূচীপত্র, নির্ঘণ্টপত্র।

cŏn-tĕnt', *n.* Satisfaction ; contentment ; as, to one's heart's *content* (to one's full inward satisfaction ; মনের সাধ মিটাইয়া) ; তুষ্টি ; সন্তোষ।

cŏn-tĕnt', *adj.* & *n.* **1.** Satisfied ; gratified ; তুষ্ট, সন্তুষ্ট, পরিতুষ্ট; পরিতৃপ্ত ; **2.** Willing ; ready ; as, he was *content* to void the house for us ; ইচ্ছুক ; প্রস্তুত। ***Noun.*** (*Pl.*) Those who vote affirmatively ; (generally expressed with word "content") ; যাহারা কোন প্রস্তাবের অনুকূলে মত প্রদান করে। **Content, not content**—ইংলণ্ডের প্রাকৃত সভার সম্মতি বা অসম্মতিবাচক মত। **Non-contents**—ইংলণ্ডের প্রাকৃত সভায় কোন প্রস্তাবের প্রতিকূলে মত প্রদানকারী।

cŏn-tĕnt', *v. t.* To satisfy ; to gratify ; to please ; as, to *content* oneself with a thing ; সন্তুষ্ট করা, পরিতুষ্ট করা ; তৃপ্ত করা, সন্তৃপ্ত করা ; পরিতৃপ্ত করা। **—ed,** *p.p. adj.* Satisfied ; পরিতৃপ্ত, সন্তুষ্ট। **—ed-ly,** *adv.* **—ed-ness, —ment,** *ns.* State of being contented ; সন্তোষ, পরিতৃপ্তি, পরিতুষ্টি।

cŏn-tĕn'-tion, *n.* **1.** Strife ; contest ; controversy ; সংগ্রাম, বিগ্রহ, বিরোধ ; কলহ, বিবাদ, দ্বন্দ্ব ; তর্কবিতর্ক, বাগ্‌বিতণ্ডা, বাদানুবাদ। **2.** Competition ; প্রতিযোগিতা। **3.** A point argued or contended for ; "This then is your *contention* ;" তর্কের বিষয়, বিরোধের বিষয়।

cŏn-tĕn'-tious(-shŭs), *adj.* **1.** Given to contention or strife ; quarrelsome ; কলহরত, বিবাদরত ; ঝগড়াটে (*Colloq.*), কলহপ্রিয়। **2.** Characterized by or involving contention ; বিরোধাত্মক। **—ly,** *adv.* **—ness,** *n.*

cŏn-têr'-mi-nal, *adj.* With a common boundary ; একসীমাবচ্ছিন্ন।

cŏn-têr'-mi-nous (nŭs), *adj.* **1.** Having the same boundary ; একসীমাবচ্ছিন্ন। **2.** Co-extensive ; (in space, time, and meaning) ; সহস্থিত, সহবিদ্যমান, সহবর্ত্তী। **3.** Meeting or touching at their ends (said of two things) ; প্রান্তে প্রান্তে মিলিত বা সংস্পৃষ্ট। **—ly,** *adv.*

cŏn-tĕst', *v. t.* & *i.* **1.** To argue as a point ; to call in question ; "They *contested* the right of the Pope ;" বাদানুবাদ করা ; সন্দেহ বা অবিশ্বাস করা। **2.** To strive earnestly for ; to dispute with arms ; as, to *contest* the crown, field, or victory ; কোন কিছুর জন্য প্রাণপণে চেষ্টা করা ; যুদ্ধ করা। ***Verb i.*** To strive ; to contend ; to emulate ; সংগ্রাম করা ; বিরোধ করা ; প্রতিযোগিতা করা, প্রতিদ্বন্দ্বিতা করা। **—a-ble,** *adj.*

cŏn'-tĕst, *n.* Debate ; dispute ; emulation ; তর্কবিতর্ক ; বাদানুবাদ ; প্রতিযোগিতা।

cŏn-tĕst'-ănt, *n.* One who contests ; বিরোধকারী, প্রতিদ্বন্দ্বী।

cŏn-tĕs-tā'-tion, *n.* **1.** Contention ; dispute ; conflict ; বিবাদ ; তর্কবিতর্ক, বাদানুবাদ ; সংঘর্ষ, বিরোধ **2.** An assertion contended for ; "The appellant's *contestation*... is untenable ; নিশ্চয়-বাক্য। **In contestation**—In dispute ; বিরোধীয়।

cŏn'-tĕxt, *n.* The parts which precede or follow a passage quoted and fix its true meaning ; কোন (পুস্তকাদির) উদ্ধৃত অংশের পূর্ব্ববর্ত্তী বা পরবর্ত্তী অংশ, যাহা উক্ত উদ্ধৃত অংশের অর্থ নির্ণীত করে, বাক্য-সম্বন্ধ, কথাসন্দর্ভ, গ্রন্থসন্দর্ভ, অর্থান্বয়, বাক্যান্বয়, পূর্ব্বাপরসম্বন্ধ, প্রকরণ। **In this context**—In this connection ; এই প্রসঙ্গে।

cŏn-tĕx'-tūre, *n.* **1.** The interweaving of several parts into one body ; texture ; "In the silk ribbons you might plainly see the *contexture* ;" সংগ্রন্থন, বুনন ; জমিন। **2.** A structure ; a fabric ; গঠন ; রচনা। **3.** A connective literary composition ; সুগ্রথিত রচনা। **—tur-al,** *adj.* **—tur-al-ly,** *adv.*

cŏn-ti-gū'-i-tў, *n.* **1.** Contact ; nearness ; সংস্পর্শ ; নৈকট্য, অব্যবধান (হিঃ কোঃ), সান্নিধ্য, সন্নিধি, সমীপতা, সামীপ্য। **2.** (*Psychol.*) Proximity as of ideas either in place or in time ; (মনস্তত্ত্ব) ভাবসমূহের দেশ বা কালগত সান্নিধ্য। **3.** A continuous mass or series ; "Among the *contiguity* of trees ;" পরম্পরা।

cŏn-tig'-ū-ous (-ŭs), *adj.* Touching one another ; next in order ; adjacent ; সংস্পর্শী ; অব্যবহিত পরবর্ত্তী, সন্নিকটবর্ত্তী। **—ly,** *adv.* (*Geom.*) **Contiguous angles** — (জ্যামিতি) সংসক্ত কোণ।

cŏn'-ti-nĕnt, *adj.* **1.** Temperate ; মিতাচারী। **2.** Chaste ; জিতেন্দ্রিয়, ব্রহ্মচর্য্যশীল। **—ly,** *adv.* **—nence,** *n.* **1.** Self-restraint ; temperance ; ইন্দ্রিয়-সংযম, আত্মদমন ; মিতাচার। **2.** Chastity ; ব্রহ্মচর্য্য, জিতেন্দ্রিয়ত্ব।

cŏn′-ti-nĕnt, *n.* One of the grand divisions of land on the globe ; প্রধান ভূভাগ, মহাদেশ, মহাদ্বীপ। **The continent**—The mainland of Europe; ইয়ুরোপের প্রধান ভূভাগ।

cŏn-ti-nĕn′-tăl, *adj.* & *n.* **1.** Of or relating to a continent ; মহাদেশ সম্বন্ধীয়। **2.** Of or pertaining to the mainland of Europe in distinction from the British Isles ; as, a *continental* tour ; ব্রিটিশদ্বীপ ব্যতীত ইউরোপের ভূভাগ সম্বন্ধীয়। **3.** (*American Hist.*) Belonging or relating to America ; as, *continental* congress ; (আমেরিকার ইতিহাস) আমেরিকা-সম্বন্ধীয়। ***Noun.*** An inhabitant of the continent of Europe ; ব্রিটিশদ্বীপ ব্যতিরিক্ত ইয়ুরোপের ভূভাগ-বাসী। **–ism,** *n.* **–ist,** *n.* **–ize,** *v. t.* To impart a continental character to ; (ব্রিটিশদ্বীপ ব্যতীত) ইয়ুরোপীয় ভাব প্রদান করা। **–ly,** *adv.* **Continental system** — ইয়ুরোপের প্রধান ভূভাগের সহিত ইংলণ্ডের বাণিজ্যসম্বন্ধ বিচ্ছিন্ন করিবার জন্য নেপোলিয়নের কল্পনা।

cŏn-tin′-gĕnt, *adj.* & *n.* **1.** Of uncertain occurring ; casual ; as, *contingent* advantages ; অনিশ্চিত; অনিয়ত, নৈমিত্তিক। **2.** Happening by chance ; accidental ; as, *contingent* events ; দৈবিক, দৈবাধীন, দৈবায়ত্ত, দৈবযৌগিক ; আকস্মিক, যদৃচ্ছাজাত। **3.** Conditional ; as, it is *contingent* on the continuance of war ; সাপেক্ষ। **4.** Unessential ; as, *contingent* attributes ; অপ্রধান, আনুষঙ্গিক। **5.** True only under existing conditions; as, *contingent* truths ; কেবল বর্ত্তমান অবস্থায় সত্য। **6.** (*Law*) Dependent on what may or may not occur ; as, *contingent* property ; সম্ভাবিত। ***Noun.*** **1.** An event which may or may not occur ; অনিশ্চিত ঘটনা। **2.** A force contributed to form a part of an army or navy ; স্থলসৈন্য বা নৌসৈন্যদলের অংশ বিশেষ। **–gen-cy,** *n.* **1.** The quality of being contingent or casual ; the possibility of coming to pass ; নৈমিত্তিকতা, অনিশ্চয়তা ; সম্ভাবনা ; **2.** A fortuitous event ; as, the *contingencies* of life ; দৈব, দৈবঘটনা, দৈবযোগ, আকস্মিক ঘটনা, যদৃচ্ছা। **3.** An incidental expense ; "Ever varying *contingencies* of marriage, etc. ;" বাজে খরচ। **4.** A thing which depends on an uncertain event ; অনিশ্চিত বিষয়। **–ly,** *adv.*

cŏn-tin′-ū-ăl, *adj.* **1.** Incessant ; uninterrupted ; অবিরত, অবিরাম, বিরামবিহীন; অবিশ্রান্ত, নিরন্তর, অনবরত, অশ্রান্ত, নিরবচ্ছিন্ন। **2.** Very frequent ; নিয়ত, নিত্য। **–ly,** *adv.* Constantly ; very often ; সতত, সদা, সর্ব্বদা ; নিরন্তর, নিত্য, অষ্টপ্রহর, অহর্নিশ, পদে পদে।

con-tin′-ū-ance (-ăns), *n.* **1.** Act or fact of continuing ; duration ; স্থিতি, স্থায়িত্ব ; স্থিতিকাল। **2.** Stay ; as, during his *continuance* in office ; অবস্থিতি। **3.** Uninterrupted succession ; অনুবৃত্তি। **4.** (*Law*) The deferring of a suit till a future date ; নির্দ্দিষ্ট তারিখ পর্য্যন্ত মোকদ্দমা মুলতুবীরাখন। **Of long continuance**—দীর্ঘস্থায়ী, বহুকালস্থায়ী, বহুদিনস্থায়ী।

cŏn-tin′-ū-ănt, *adj.* & *n.* Capable of a continuous sound ; as, a *continuant* consonant ; (R, F V, S, &c.) ; অবিরাম ধ্বন্যাত্মক। ***Noun.*** A consonant of which sound can be prolonged ; যে ব্যঞ্জনবর্ণের ধ্বনি দীর্ঘ করা যাইতে পারে।

cŏn-tin-ū-ā′-tion, *n.* **1.** Act of continuing ; prolongation ; uninterruption ; successsion ; ক্রমাগত চলন, অবারিত গতি ; প্রবর্দ্ধন ; নিরবচ্ছিন্নতা, অনবচ্ছিন্নতা ; ধারাবাহিকতা, পারম্পর্য্য। **2.** Resumption after an interruption or break ; as, the *continuation* of an action, story or book ; পূর্ব্বানুবৃত্তি। **3.** (*Stock-exchange*) Carrying over an account till the next settling-day ; (কোম্পানীর কাগজ) পাক্ষিক হিসাব-নিষ্পত্তির দিন পর্য্যন্ত হিসাবের জের টানন। **4.** Additional parts ; as, it is the *continuation* of a previous discussion ; অতিরিক্ত অংশ। **5.** (*Pl.*) Trousers, (*slang*) ; (ইতর ভাষায়) পাদচ্ছদ, পাজামা। **Continuation day**—(কোম্পানীর কাগজ) পাক্ষিক হিসাব নিষ্পত্তি দিন।

cŏn′-tin′-ū-ā-tive (-tĭv), *adj.* Tending to continue ; ক্রমাগত চলনশীল।

cŏn-tin′-ū-ā-tor (-tẽr), *n.* One who continues anything (especially a literary work) begun by another ; যে ব্যক্তি অপর ব্যক্তিদ্বারা প্রারব্ধ বিষয় (বিশেষতঃ সাহিত্য গ্রন্থ) পূর্ব্ববৎ চালাইয়া যায়।

cŏn-tin′-ue (-ū), *v. t.* & *i.* **1.** To prolong ; to maintain ; to resume after interruption or break ; পূর্ব্ববৎ চালাইয়া যাওয়া ; রক্ষা করা, ধরিয়া রাখা ; পূর্ব্বানুবৃত্তি করা। **2.** To retain, as in office, etc. ; চাকুরী প্রভৃতিতে রাখা। **3.** (*Law*) To adjourn or put off ; (আইন) স্থগিত রাখা, মুলতুবী রাখা, তারিখ ফেলা। ***Verb i.*** **1.** To remain in a state or place ; to stay ; থাকা ; অবস্থান করা। **2.** To endure ; to last ; "Let what now exists *continue*;" টিকিয়া থাকা ; স্থায়ী হওয়া। **3.** Not to leave off ; as, to *continue* to circulate a news ; to be continued ; চালাইতে থাকা ; ক্রমশঃ প্রকাশ্য হওয়া। **–u-a-ble,** *adj.*

cŏn ti-nū′-i-ty, *n.* **1.** The condition of being continuous ; unceasingness ; uninterruptedness ;

অনুবৃত্তি; ধারাবাহিকতা; বিরামবিহীনতা, অবিচ্ছেদ (আঃ বঃ), নিরবচ্ছিন্নতা; **2.** Perpetuity ; সাততা (আঃ বঃ)। (*Phys.*) **Law of continuity**—(পদার্থ-বিজ্ঞান) পদার্থবিজ্ঞানের তত্ত্ব বিশেষ,—এই তত্ত্বানুসারে কোন বস্তুই মধ্যবর্ত্তী অবস্থা সমূহ অতিক্রম না করিয়া এক অবস্থা হইতে অবস্থান্তর প্রাপ্ত হয় না।

cŏn-tĭn'-ū-ous (-ŭs), *adj.* Joined continuously ; continued ; uninterrupted ; unbroken ; as, *continuous* line ; *continuous* energy ; ব্যবধানরহিতভাবে সংযুক্ত; ধারাবাহিক ; নিরবচ্ছিন্ন, ব্যবধানরহিত ; অবিচ্ছিন্ন। **—ly,** *adv.* **—ness,** *n.* **Continuous brake**—(রেলওয়ে) কোন এক নির্দ্দিষ্ট বিন্দু হইতে চালিত চক্রগতিরোধক পরম্পরা বিশেষ। **Continuous style**—(*Arch.*) (স্থপতি-বিজ্ঞান) স্থাপত্যরীতি বিশেষ,—যাহাতে বাতায়নের প্রকোষ্ঠ-গঠক দণ্ড সমূহ গবাক্ষ-নিম্নস্থ কারুকার্য্যের উপর প্রবর্দ্ধিত হইয়া থাকে।

cŏnt'-līne, *n.* **1.** The space between the strands on the outside of a rope ; রজ্জুর বহির্ভাগের গুণ সমূহের মধ্যবর্ত্তী স্থান। **2.** (*Naut.*) The empty space between the casks stowed side by side ; (নৌ-বিদ্যা) পাশাপাশিভাবে সজ্জিত পিপাশ্রেণীর মধ্যবর্ত্তী স্থান।

cŏn-tŏr'-ni-āte, *adj.* & *n.* With a furrow curved round the edge ; প্রান্তের চতুর্দ্দিকে বক্রীভূত কুঞ্চিতরেখাবিশিষ্ট। ***Noun.*** A medal having a deep furrow on the edge ; প্রান্তদেশের চতুর্দ্দিকে গভীর কুঞ্চিত রেখা-সমন্বিত পদক।

cŏn-tŏrt', *v. t.* To twist ; to writhe ; to distort ; "The feathers are violently *contorted* ;" মোচড়ান ; পাকান, আকুঞ্চিত করা ; বিকৃত করা, বিরূপ করা।

cŏn-tŏr'-tion, *n.* Writhing ; contorted form or state as of the face or body ; distortion ; আকুঞ্চন, মোচড়ান ; মুখ বা দেহের আকুঞ্চিত অবস্থা ; অঙ্গ বিকৃতি। **—ist,** *n.* An acrobat practising contortion of the body ; an artist whose work exhibits contortions ; যে বাজীকর শরীর আকুঞ্চিত করে ; যে শিল্পীর শিল্প-কার্য্যে বিভিন্ন প্রকার আকুঞ্চিত অবস্থা প্রদর্শিত হয়।

cŏn'-tour (-tôr), *n.* & *v. t.* **1.** The outline of a figure ; বাহ্যরেখা, প্রান্ত-রেখা, আকাররেখা(হিঃ কোঃ)। **2.** The artistic quality of outline ; as, he has a sense of *contour* and form ; রেখা-ন্যাসের শিল্প-কৌশল। **3.** The outline of a coast, mountain, mass, etc. ; পর্ব্বতমেখলা, তটের বাহ্যরেখা, প্রভৃতি। ***Verb t.*** To mark with exterior lines ; to make as a road round the contour of a hill ; বাহ্যরেখাদ্বারা চিহ্নিত করা ; কোন পর্ব্বতের বাহ্যরেখার চতুর্দ্দিকে পথ-নির্ম্মাণ করা। **Contour line**—মানচিত্রে সাগরপৃষ্ঠ হইতে সমোচ্চ বিন্দুসমূহের উপর দিয়া যে সকল রেখা অঙ্কিত হয় তাহার একটী, সমোন্নতিরেখা (সাঃ পঃ), আকাররেখা (হিঃ কোঃ)। **Contour map**—যে মানচিত্রে সমোন্নতি-রেখাদ্বারা স্থানের উচ্চাবচতা প্রদর্শিত করা হয়।

cŏn'-trȧ, *prep.* & *n.* Against ; as, pro and *contra* (for and against) ; বিরুদ্ধে। ***Noun.*** **1.** (abbr. con.) An argument against ; as, pros and *cons* (arguments for and against) ; প্রতিকূলযুক্তি। **2.** (*Bookkeeping*) The opposite, esp. the credit side of an account ; (হিসাব) বিপরীতদিক্, বিশেষতঃ জমার দিক্।

cŏn'-trȧ-bănd, *n.* & *adj.* **1.** Illegal traffic ; smuggling ; বেয়াইনি কারবার, আইন না মানিয়া আমদানী বা রপ্তানী করণ ; ঘাট মারণ, মাশুল চুরি-করণ, বিজোড়া মাল আমদানী বা রপ্তানী করণ। **2.** Goods prohibited to be imported or exported ; smuggled goods ; নিষিদ্ধ পণ্যদ্রব্য; বিজোড়া মাল। ***Adj.*** Prohibited to be exported or imported ; as, *contraband* goods ; dealing in contraband ; as, *contraband* trader ; নিষিদ্ধ ; নিষিদ্ধ মাল আমদানী বা রপ্তানিকারী। **Contraband of war**—যুদ্ধকালে যুদ্ধকারী বা নিরপেক্ষ জাতিসমূহ দ্বারা সরবরাহ করণে নিষিদ্ধ দ্রব্য।

cŏn'-trȧ-bănd-ist, *n.* One who deals in contraband goods ; যে ব্যক্তি নিষিদ্ধমাল আমদানী বা রপ্তানী করে।

cŏn'-trȧ-bass (-băs), *n.* The largest instrument of the violin class, also called the double-bass ; বেহালা জাতীয় বৃহত্তম বাদ্য যন্ত্র।

cŏn'-trăct, *n.* **1.** (*Law*) An agreement which binds the parties to a performance ; a bargain ; a convention between states ; (আইন) চুক্তি ; করার, একরার, ক্রয় বিক্রয়ের চুক্তি, ফুরণ (*Collog*), সংবিদ্, সময় (আঃ বঃ) ; বিভিন্ন রাজ্যের মধ্যে চুক্তি। **2.** Act of betrothment ; "The *contract* between the bride and the bridegroom was renewed ;" বাগ্দান। **3.** A writing containing the stipulations ; চুক্তি-পত্র, একরার নামা, অঙ্গীকার-পত্র, নিয়ম-পত্র। **4.** The department of law relating to legal contracts ; আইনের চুক্তি-সংক্রান্ত বিভাগ। **5.** An agreement effecting a transfer of property ; কবালা-পত্র, সম্পত্তি হস্তান্তরপত্র।

cŏn-trăct', *v. t.* & *i.* **1.** To agree upon ; to undertake mutually ; অঙ্গীকার করা ; চুক্তি করা, করার করা। **2.** To betroth ; to enter into ; বাগ্দান করা ; স্থির করা, ধার্য্য করা। **3.** To narrow ; to lessen ; "Selfishness *contracted* their understandings ;" সংকীর্ণ করা ; হ্রাস করা। **4.** To acquire ; to form ; as, to *contract* a habit ; to incur ; as, to *contract* debt ; অর্জ্জন করা ; গঠন করা ; প্রস্তু হওয়া। **5.** To limit ; "Time so *contracts* us that we cannot dwell on all." সীমাবদ্ধ করা। **6.** (*Gram.*) To shorten as a word &c., by omitting or combining some of its elements ; (ব্যাকরণ) কতিপয় অংশের লোপ বা মিলন সাধন করত শব্দ প্রভৃতি সংক্ষিপ্ত করা। 7. To cause to shrink ; সঙ্কুচিত করা। 8. To knit ; as, to *contract* the brow ; কুঞ্চিত করা। ***Verb i.*** 1. To shrink ; to become less ; সঙ্কুচিত হওয়া ; ক্ষুদ্রতর হওয়া। 2. To make a mutual agreement ; to bargain ; চুক্তি করা ; দর দস্তুর ঠিক করা, ফুরণ করা। **–ed,** *p. p. adj.* Compressed, as a muscle ; shrunken, as a brow ; mean ; narrow, as a mind, ideas, &c. ; সঙ্কুচিত ; কুঞ্চিত ; সঙ্কীর্ণ ; অপ্রশস্ত, অনুদার (মন, ভাব, প্রভৃতি)। **–i-bil′-i-ty,** *n.* Capability of being contracted ; সঙ্কুচনীয়তা, সঙ্কুচিষ্ণুতা (সাঃ পঃ), সঙ্কোচশীলতা (হিঃ কোঃ)। **–i-ble,** *adj.* **To contract oneself out of**—To be released of (some obligation) by a special contract ; বিশেষ চুক্তিদ্বারা কোন প্রকার বাধ্যবাধকতা হইতে নিষ্কৃতি পাওয়া।

cŏn-trăc′-tĭle, *adj.* Tending to contract ; as, a *contractile* force of muscle ; সঙ্কুচিষ্ণু (সাঃ পঃ)। **–til′-i-ty,** *n.*

cŏn-trăc′-tion, *n.* 1. Act of contracting ; shrinking ; state of being contracted ; সংকোচন ; আকুঞ্চন, কুঞ্চন ; কুঞ্চিতাবস্থা, 2. (*Gram.*) The shortening of a word by the combination or omission of some of its letters (as in *can't, n'er* &c.) ; (ব্যাকরণ) বর্ণের লোপ বা সংযোজন দ্বারা শব্দের সংক্ষেপ সাধন। 3. A contracted word ; (as, *dep't* for department) ; সংক্ষিপ্ত শব্দ। 4. (*Fig.*) Restriction ; as, *contraction* of one's expense ; (লক্ষণায়) সংকোচ। 5. Act of incurring ; গ্রস্ত হওন।

cŏn-trăc′-tive (-tĭv), *adj.* Tending or serving to contract ; সঙ্কুচিষ্ণু।

cŏn-trăc′-tor (-têr), *n.* 1. One who contracts (esp.) to perform any work or service at a certain price or rate ; চুক্তিকারক, (বিশেষতঃ) ঠিকাদার। 2. That which shortens or narrows ; সংকোচক।

cŏn-trăc′-tū-ăl, *adj.* Relating to, or of the nature of, a contract ; চুক্তিসম্বন্ধীয়, চুক্তিঘটিত।

cŏn′-tră-dance (-dáns), *n.* (Country dance) A dance in which partners are arranged face to face or in opposite lines ; (পল্লি-নৃত্য) একপ্রকার নৃত্য,—যাহাতে সহযোগিগণ পরস্পরের সম্মুখীনভাবে বা পরস্পরের বিপরীত পংক্তিতে সজ্জিত হইয়া থাকে।

cŏn-tră-dict′, *v. t.* 1. To affirm the contrary of ; as, to *contradict* a statement ; to deny ; প্রতিবাদ করা ; অস্বীকার করা। 2. To be directly contrary to ; বিরোধী হওয়া। **–a-ble,** *adj.* **–dic′-tor,** *n.*

cŏn-tră-dic′-tion, *n.* 1. A contrary assertion or statement ; denial ; প্রতিবাদ, বিরুদ্ধবাদ, প্রতীপবচন (মঃ ইঃ), বচনবিরোধ (ঐ), ব্যাঘাত, বিরোধোক্তি, বিরোধী (হিঃ কোঃ) ; অস্বীকার, প্রত্যাখ্যান (মঃ ইঃ)। 2. Incongruity ; inconsistency ; "So brings the argument to a *contradiction* ;" অসামঞ্জস্য ; অসঙ্গতি। 3. Act of opposing or gainsaying ; প্রতিবাদকরণ, অস্বীকারকরণ, নিরাকরণ, বিপ্রতিষেধ। 4. Anything contradictory, (as an act, fact, etc.) ; as, to make *contradictions* consistent ; পরস্পর-বিরোধী বিষয়। **Contradiction in terms**—পরস্পর-বিরোধী উক্তি।

cŏn-tră-dic-tious (-shŭs), *adj.* Given or inclined to contradiction ; তর্কপ্রিয়। **–ly,** *adv.* **–ness,** *n.*

cŏn-tră-dic′-tō-rȳ, *adj.* & *n.* Implying contradiction ; inconsistent ; contrary ; contradictious ; বিরোধাত্মক ; অসঙ্গতি-পূর্ণ ; বিরুদ্ধ (আঃ বঃ), পরস্পর বিরোধী ; তর্কপ্রিয়। ***Noun.*** 1. A contradictory proposition or assertion ; পরস্পর-বিরোধী প্রতিজ্ঞা বা উক্তি। 2. (*Logic*) A proposition which denies or opposes another in all its terms ; (তর্ক-বিজ্ঞান) পরস্পর-বিরোধী প্রতিজ্ঞা। **–ri-ly,** *adv.* **–ri-ness,** *n.*

cŏn-tră-dis-tinc′-tion (-tĭngk-), *n.* Distinction by opposite qualities ; গুণবৈষম্য দ্বারা প্রভেদকরণ।

cŏn-tră-dis-tin′-guish (-tĭng-gwĭsh), *v. t.* To distinguish by a contrast or opposite qualities ; বৈধর্ম্ম বা গুণবৈষম্যদ্বারা প্রভেদ প্রদর্শন করা।

cŏn-trăl′-tō, *n.* & *adj.* (*Mus.*) The highest voice of a male adult or the lowest voice of a female or boy ; (সঙ্গীত-শাস্ত্র) বালক বা স্ত্রীলোকের মিহি স্বর অথবা পুরুষের মোটা স্বর। ***Adj.*** Relating to or possessing the quality of contralto ; উক্ত স্বর সম্পর্কীয়, উক্ত স্বরাত্মক।

cŏn-tră-pō-si′-tion, *n.* 1. A placing over against ; opposition ; contrast ; বিপরীতাবস্থান ; বিরোধ ; বৈষম্য। 2. (*Logic*) A species of conversion, (every Q is R ; therefore No not- R is Q) ; (তর্ক-বিজ্ঞান) একপ্রকার উদ্দেশ্যবিধেয় পরিবর্ত্তন, নিষেধব্যবস্থাপন (হিঃ কোঃ), বিপরীতাবর্ত্তন (সাঃ পঃ)।

cŏn-tră-pŭn′-tăl, *adj.* (*Mus.*) Relating to or according to the rules of counterpoint ; স্বরসঙ্গত সম্বন্ধীয়, স্বরসঙ্গতের নিয়মানুযায়ী। **–tist,** *n.*

cŏn-tră′-ri-ănt, *adj.* Contrary ; opposed, (with *to*) ; বিপরীত ; বিরুদ্ধ।

cŏn-tră-ri′-ē-tȳ, *n.* 1. The quality or state of being contrary ; repugnance ; বৈলক্ষণ্য (আঃ বঃ), বৈপরীত্য (ঐ), বিপর্য্যাস (মঃ ইঃ), বিপরীততা, বিরুদ্ধধর্ম্মতা, বিরোধত্ব ; বিরোধ, ব্যত্যয়। 2. An inconsistency ; discrepancy ; "When there in such *contrariety* of opinion ;" অসঙ্গতি ; বৈসাদৃশ্য, অনৈক্য। 3. (*Logic*)

Contrary proposition ; (তর্ক-বিজ্ঞান) বিপরীত প্রতিজ্ঞা।

cŏn'-tră-ri-wīse, *adv.* **1.** On the other hand ; পক্ষান্তরে। **2.** Conversely ; বিপরীত পক্ষে, ক্রমবিপর্য্যয়ে। **3.** Reversely ; "The wicked... go *contrariwise* ;" বিপথে, উন্মার্গ-গামী হইয়া।

cŏn'-tră-rȳ, *adj., n.* & *adv.* **1.** Opposed ; repugnant ; inconsistent ; বিরুদ্ধ, বাম, বিপরীত ; বিরোধী ; অসঙ্গতি-পূর্ণ। **2.** Opposite in direction ; বিপরীতদিগ্‌বর্ত্তী। **3.** Wayward ; perverse ; as, a *contrary* boy ; একগুঁয়ে ; উচ্ছৃঙ্খল, বেআড়া। **4.** Unfavourable ; as, *contrary* wind or weather ; প্রতিকূল। **5.** The other or opposite (of two things) ; "This is an invention of the *contrary* part ; অন্যতর (বস্তু) বা বিপরীত (বস্তু)। **6.** (*Logic*) Affirming the opposite ; (তর্ক-বিজ্ঞান) বিপরীত ভাব প্রতিপাদক। ***Noun.*** **1.** A thing of opposite qualities ; বিরুদ্ধধর্ম্মাশ্রিত বস্তু। **2.** A fact or quality that is incompatible with another ; বিসদৃশ তথ্য বা গুণ। **3.** (*Logic*) A proposition contrary to another ; বিপরীত প্রতিজ্ঞা। ***Adv.*** In an opposite manner ; in opposition ; "Those act *contrary* to nature ;" বিপরীতভাবে ; বিরুদ্ধে। **–ri-ly,** *adv.* **–ri-ness,** *n.* **Contrary propositions** — পরস্পর-বিরোধী প্রতিজ্ঞাসমূহ। [As, all A is B : no A is B—এই দুইটী পরস্পর-বিরোধী প্রতিজ্ঞা। ইহাদের মধ্যে উভয়টী সত্য হইতে পারে না ; কিন্তু, উভয়টী মিথ্যা হইতে পারে।] **Contrary to**—(*adj.*) Opposite to ; বিরুদ্ধ, বিরোধী। (*Adv.*) In opposition to ; বিরুদ্ধে, প্রতিকূলে। **On the contrary** — On the other hand ; পক্ষান্তরে। **To interpret by contraries**—To understand *yes* for *no* etc. ; হাঁ বলিতে না বুঝা, কিম্বা না বলিতে হাঁ বুঝা। **To the contrary**—To the opposite purpose ; বিপরীত উদ্দেশ্যে।

cŏn-trăst', *v. i.* & *t.* To show marked difference on comparison, (followed by *with*) ; তুলনা দ্বারা বৈসাদৃশ্য প্রদর্শন করা, বৈষম্য বা বৈসাদৃশ্য প্রদর্শন করা। ***Verb t.*** To set in opposition, in order to show the difference between ; বৈসাদৃশ্য বা পার্থক্য প্রদর্শনার্থ তুলনা করা।

cŏn'-trăst, *n.* **1.** Opposition or comparison of things to show their difference ; as, *contrast* enhances the splendour of beauty ; বৈভিন্ন্য বা বৈপরীত্য প্রদর্শনার্থ তুলনা, ব্যতিরেক, বৈষম্য, বৈলক্ষণ্য, বৈসাদৃশ্য। **2.** A thing or person strikingly different from another ; "Pain is the necessary *contrast* to pleasure ;" বিরুদ্ধধর্ম্মাশ্রিত ব্যক্তি বা বিষয়, বিপরীত বস্তু বা বিষয়, প্রতিপক্ষ (মঃ ইঃ)।

cŏn'-trāte, *adj.* Having the teeth set at right angles to the plane (of the wheel) ; (চক্রের) সমতল-পৃষ্ঠের লম্বস্বরূপ দন্তবিশিষ্ট।

cŏn-tră-văl-lā'-tion, *n.* (*Fort.*) A chain of redoubts raised by besiegers to prevent sorties of the garrison ; (দুর্গ) দুর্গস্থিত সৈন্যগণের আকস্মিক আক্রমণ প্রতিরোধের জন্য অবরোধকারিগণ কর্ত্তৃক নির্ম্মিত উপদুর্গশ্রেণী।

cŏn-tră-vene' (-vēn), *v. t.* **1.** To transgress ; ভঙ্গ করা, লঙ্ঘন করা। **2.** To contradict, as a statement ; to be in conflict with ; "Acts which might *contravene* this duty ;" প্রতিবাদ করা ; বিরোধী হওয়া।

cŏn-tră-vĕn'-tion, *n.* Infringement ; ভঙ্গ, লঙ্ঘন।

cŏn-tre-temps' (-tr-tân), *n.* An untoward accident ; an unexpected hitch ; দুর্ঘটনা ; অপ্রত্যাশিত বিঘ্ন বা প্রতিবন্ধক।

cŏn-trib'-ūte, *v. t.* & *i.* To give jointly with others ; to furnish as an article to a newspaper ; to give for a purpose ; to give as a share ; আংশিকভাবে প্রদান করা ; সংবাদপত্রাদিতে প্রবন্ধ প্রদান করা ; কোন উদ্দেশ্যে প্রদান করা ; অংশস্বরূপ দেওয়া। ***Verb i.*** To give a part or share ; to impart aid or influence to a common purpose ; to have a share in any act or effect ; অংশ বা ভাগ দেওয়া ; সাধারণ উদ্দেশ্যে সাহায্য প্রদান করা বা ক্ষমতা প্রয়োগ করা ; কোন কার্য্যে অংশ বা ভাগ থাকা।

cŏn-tri-bū'-tion, *n.* **1.** The act of contributing ; আংশিক দান বা সাহায্য করণ, দান (আঃ বঃ)। **2.** A tax imposed for the support of an army in the field ; রণক্ষেত্র-স্থিত সৈন্যগণের ব্যয়নির্ব্বাহার্থ সংস্থাপিত কর। **3.** Subscription ; চাঁদা, মাথট (*Colloq.*)। **4.** An article or writing sent to a magazine or periodical ; সংবাদ পত্রাদিতে প্রেরিত প্রবন্ধ বা পত্র। **To lay under contribution**—To exact contributions from ; চাঁদা আদায় করা। To derive knowledge from ; নানা গ্রন্থ হইতে অল্প অল্প করিয়া জ্ঞান সংগ্রহ করা।

cŏn-trib'-ū-tor (-têr), *n.* One who contributes ; a writer of articles for magazines, &c. ; আংশিক সাহায্যকারী ; সংবাদপত্রাদির প্রবন্ধ-লেখক। **–to-ry,** *adj.*

cŏn'-trīte, *adj.* Broken-hearted for sin ; penitent ; পাপের জন্য ভগ্ন-হৃদয়, পাপস্মৃতি-পীড়িত ; অনুতপ্ত, শোকাগ্নিসন্তপ্ত (মঃ ইঃ), পশ্চাত্তাপী। **–ly,** *adv.*

cŏn-tri-tion, *n.* Penitence ; অনুতাপ, পশ্চাত্তাপ।

cŏn-trīv'-ance (-ăns), *n.* **1.** The act of contriving or planning ; deceitful practice ; design ; invention ; বিরচন ; ফন্দি ; উপায় (আঃ বঃ) মতলব, ফিকির, যুক্তি ; উদ্ভাবন। **2.** A thing contrived ; a plan ; as, military *contrivances* ; a device (mechanical) ; উদ্ভাবিত বস্তু ; উদ্ভাবনা, কল্পনা ; কৌশল, সংবিধান (মঃ ভাঃ)

3. Inventive capacity ; উদ্ভাবনীশক্তি, হেকমতি (*Colloq.*), হুনর (*Colloq.*)।

cŏn-trive′, *v. t.* & *i.* **1.** To devise ; to plot ; as, to *contrive* murder ; উদ্ভাবন করা ; ষড়যন্ত্র করা। **2.** To bring about ; to effect ; ঘটান ; সাধন করা। ***Verb i.*** To design ; esp. to manage household affairs ; as, to *contrive* well ; কল্পনা করা ; বিশেষতঃ গার্হস্থ্য ব্যাপার নির্ব্বাহ করা। **—triv′-a-ble,** *adj.* **—triv′-er,** *n.* One who contrives ; সংবিধানকারী, উদ্ভাবয়িতা (আঃ বঃ), পরিকল্পক (মঃ ইঃ)।

cŏn-trōl′, *n.* **1.** Restraining power or authority ; sway ; শাসন ; কর্ত্তৃত্ব। **2.** Restraint ; a check ; দমন ; নিরোধ, নিয়ন্ত্রণা (আঃ বঃ)। **3.** A means of verification ; যাথার্থ্য প্রতিপাদনের উপায় বিশেষ। **4.** (Spiritualism) A person, ghost, or spirit believed to actuate the performances of the medium ; (প্রেত-তত্ত্ব) ব্যক্তি, ভূত বা প্রেতাত্মা,—যাহার অনুপ্রেরণায় মাধ্যমিকের কার্য্য সমুহ সম্পাদিত হয় বলিয়া অনুমিত হইয়া থাকে। **Control expreriment**—বৈজ্ঞানিক পরীক্ষা বিশেষ — যদ্দারা পরীক্ষাকারী অন্যান্য পরীক্ষার ফল পরখ ও আয়ত্ত করিতে সমর্থ হয়। ঐ সমস্ত পরীক্ষার কোন একটী বিশেষ অবস্থা বর্জ্জন করত ইহাদের অন্য সমস্ত অবস্থার অনুকরণ দ্বারা, বর্জ্জিত অবস্থাটী অন্য বিষয়সমূহে লক্ষিত ফল-সম্পর্কে কি পরিমাণে দায়ী, তাহা অনুমান করা যাইতে পারে।

cŏn-trōl′, *v. t.*, **1.** To exercise authority over ; to dominate ; to hold in check ; to curb ; as, to *control* oneself or one's passions, etc. ; কর্ত্তৃত্ব করা ; প্রভুত্ব করা ; নিরোধ করা, দমন করা ; সংযত করা। **2.** To check or verify ; as, to *control* receipts, expenditure, accounts, etc. ; হিসাব মিলান, মোকাবেলা করা, যাথার্থ্য প্রতিপাদন করা। **—la-ble,** *adj.* **—ment,** *n.*

cŏn-trōl′-ler, *n.* **1.** One who controls ; শাসনকারী, দমনকারী, নিরোধকারী, নিয়ামক (আঃ বঃ), নিয়ন্তা। **2.** A steward, (esp. of the Royal household) ; গাহর্স্থ্য কর্ম্মাধ্যক্ষ (বিশেষতঃ রাজবাটীর)। **3.** An officer to check the accounts of collectors of the public money, (also spelt *comptroller*) ; হিসাব পরীক্ষক রাজকর্ম্মচারী। **4.** (*British Navy*) A member of the admiralty having the title of Additional Naval Lord and Controller ; (ব্রিটিস নৌ-বল) নৌ-বিভাগের উচ্চ কর্ম্মচারি-বিশেষ। **5.** (*Mach.* etc.) A piece of mechanism that regulates motions, etc. ; (যন্ত্র প্রভৃতি) গতি প্রভৃতি নিয়ামক যন্ত্রাংশ-বিশেষ। **—ship,** *n.* **Controller general**—উচ্চ কর্ম্মচারি বিশেষ।

cŏn-trö-vêr′-sial (-shî-ăl), *adj.* Relating, or open, to controversy ; disputatious ; বিবাদ ঘটিত, বিবাদসহ, বিবাদী, বিবাদ-বিষয়ক ; তর্কবিতর্ক ঘটিত, বিতণ্ডাত্মক। **—ism,** *n.* **ist,** *n.* One given to controversy ; a disputant ; বাদানুবাদ-প্রিয় ; তর্কবিতর্ক-কারী। **—ly,** *adv.*

cŏn′-trö-vêr-sy̆, *n.* **1.** Disputation; debate esp. in writing ; contest ; বাদানুবাদ, তর্কবিতর্ক ; বাগ্‌যুদ্ধ (মঃ ইঃ) বাগ্‌বিরোধ, প্রশ্ন-বিবাদ, বিতর্ক ; বিরোধ, জল্প (হিঃ কোঃ)। **2.** (*Law*) Litigation ; (আইন) মোকদ্দমা। **Without** or **beyound controversy**—নির্বিবাদে, নির্বিরোধে।

cŏn′-trö-vêrt, *v. t.* To dispute by reasoning ; to discuss ; to contradict ; যুক্তি-প্রদর্শন দ্বারা প্রতিবাদ করা ; আলোচনা করা ; প্রতিবাদ করা।

cŏn-tü-mā′-cious (-shŭs), *adj.* **1.** Obstinate ; stubborn ; একগুঁয়ে, ঠেঁটা, বে-আদব ; জেদী। **2.** (*Law*) wilfully disobeying the order of a court ; ইচ্ছা পূর্ব্বক আদালতের হুকুম অমান্যকারী। **—ma′-cious-ly,** *adv.* **—ma′-cious-ness,** *n.*

cŏn′-tü-mă-cy̆, *n.* **1.** Obstinate disobedience or resistance ; অবাধ্যতা, জেদ, একগুঁয়েমি, বে-আদবি। **2.** Wilful disregard of any lawful authority, as of a court ; আদালত প্রভৃতির আদেশ অমান্যতা।

cŏn-tü-mē′-lious (-ŭs), *adj.* Insolent ; proudly rude ; উদ্ধত ; দৃপ্ত। **—me′-li-ous-ly,** *adv.*

cŏn′-tü-mĕ-ly̆, *n.* **1.** Insolent, reproachful, language or treatment ; বাকপারুষ্য, পরিভাষণ (মঃ ইঃ) উদ্ধত ব্যবহার। **2.** Disgrace ; ignominy ; অপমান, অবমাননা ; কলঙ্ক। **3.** Reproach ; তিরস্কার।

cŏn-tüse′, *v. t.* To bruise ; ছেঁচা। **—tu′-sion,** *n.* Severe bruise ; ঘৃষ্টব্রণ, নীলিকা (মঃ ইঃ)।

cō-nŭn′-drŭm, *n.* **1.** A riddle ; প্রহেলিকা, প্রশ্নদূতী (মঃ ইঃ), হেঁয়ালী-সমস্যা। **2.** A hard question ; কঠিন প্রশ্ন।

cŏn′-vă-lesce (-lĕs), *v. i.* To recover health ; রোগ কিম্বা দুর্ব্বলতা হইতে ক্রমশঃ আরোগ্যলাভ করা, সারিয়া উঠা।

cŏn-vă-lĕs′-cĕnt, *adj.* & *n.* Recovering from sickness or debility ; রোগ বা দুর্ব্বলতা হইতে ক্রমশঃ আরোগ্যের দিকে অগ্রসর, রোগাবসানে পুনঃস্বাস্থ্যলাভোন্মুখ। ***Noun.*** One recovering his health after sickness ; রোগান্তে পুনঃ স্বাস্থ্য লাভকারী ব্যক্তি। **—cense,** *n.* Gradual recovery of health and strength ; রোগান্তে ক্রমশঃ স্বাস্থ্যলাভ, আরাম। **Convalescent hospital**—রোগান্তে ক্রমশঃ স্বাস্থ লাভকারী ব্যক্তিগণের জন্য রুগ্নাবাস।

cŏn-vĭc′-tion, *n.* Mode of transmitting heat or electricity by the motion of particles in the heated or electrified body ; উত্তপ্ত বা তাড়িত-সঞ্চারিত বস্তুর কণা-সমূহের চালনা দ্বারা তাপ বা তাড়িত সঞ্চালন-প্রণালী, পরিবাহন (সাঃ পঃ), সংবাহন (ঐ), বহন (হিঃ কোঃ)।

convenance, (*F.*) *n.* (*usu. pl.*) Conventional propriety ; প্রথা-সঙ্গত সমীচীনতা ।

cŏn-vene' (-vēn), *v. t.* & *i.* **1.** To assemble, esp. for a common purpose ; (also *Verb i.*) ; সমাগত করা, সম্মিলিত করা, সমাহ্বান করা ; সমাগত হওয়া, মিলিত হওয়া, সমবেত হওয়া, একত্র হওয়া । **2.** To call together ; to convoke ; সমবেত করা ; সমাহ্বান করা । **3.** To summon to appear before a tribunal ; আদালতে উপস্থিত হইবার জন্য আদেশ করা ।

cŏn-vēn'-ïent, *adj.* **1.** Suitable ; appropriate ; সুবিধাজনক ; উপযোগী । **2.** Not troublesome ; as, if it is *convenient* to you ; অবিরক্তিকর, আরামজনক ।

cŏn-vēn'-ience (ī-ĕns), *n.* **1.** Suitableness ; fitness ; উপযোগিতা ; যোগ্যতা । **2.** An opportunity or advantage ; as, to do something at one's *convenience* ; সুবিধা, সুযোগ, অবসর, ফুরসৎ (*Colloq.*) । **3.** Water-closet ; মলমূত্রাদি ত্যাগের প্রকোষ্ঠ । **4.** (*Pl.*) Material arrangements conducive to personal comforts ; as, necessary *conveniences* for the homestead ; (গৃহাদিতে) শারীরিক সুখস্বচ্ছন্দতা-বিধায়ক ব্যবস্থা ।

cŏn'-vĕnt, 1. A religious community (usu. of women) living together ; মঠ, আশ্রম, ভিক্ষুণী-সংঘ, সন্ন্যাসিনী-নিকেতন । **2.** A building or buildings occupied by them ; ভিক্ষুণী বা সন্ন্যাসিনীগণের আবাসগৃহ বা গৃহশ্রেণী ।

cŏn-vĕn'-ti-cle, *n.* **1.** A secret religious meeting of questionable propriety or decency ; গুপ্ত ধর্ম্মসভা । **2.** Religious meeting of Nonconformists or Dissenters or the place where they meet ; প্রচলিত খৃষ্টধর্ম্মবিরুদ্ধ সম্প্রদায় বিশেষের গুপ্ত ধর্ম্মসভা বা উক্ত সভার অধিবেশন স্থল ।

cŏn-vĕn'-tion, *n.* **1.** Act of summoning an assembly ; সভাহ্বান । **2.** General agreement or tacit consent ; ঐকমত্য, সর্ব্বসম্মতি ; মৌন-সম্মতি । **3.** A rule or usage based on general agreement ; প্রচলিত প্রথা, নিয়ম বা আচার ব্যবহার । **4.** Agreement between parties ; বিভিন্ন দলের মধ্যে মতৈক্য । **5.** A formal assembly, (esp. *Eng. Hist.*) ; নিয়মানুগত সভা, মজলিস । **6.** An extra-ordinary assembly of the House of Parliament without the summons of the sovereign ; রাজাজ্ঞা ব্যতিরেকে পার্লেমেণ্ট মহাসভার বিশেষ অধিবেশন, (যেমন ১৬৬০ খঃ অব্দের পার্লেমেণ্টের অধিবেশন—যাহাতে দ্বিতীয় চার্লসকে সিংহাসনে পুনঃ প্রতিষ্ঠিত করা হয়) । **7.** A compact between commanders of armies in respect to military operations, as the suspension of hostilities, etc. ; সাময়িক যুদ্ধ বিশ্রান্তি প্রভৃতির জন্য উভয় পক্ষের সৈন্যাধ্যক্ষের মধ্যে চুক্তি বা করার ।

cŏn-vĕn'-tion-ăl, *adj.* Settled by tacit consent ; not natural, original or spontaneous ; প্রচলিত প্রথাসম্মত, প্রথামূলক ; লৌকিক (আঃ বঃ), লোকব্যবহারানুগত । **2.** (*Art*) Following tradition ; (শিল্প-শাস্ত্র) প্রচলিত-প্রথানুসারী, গতানুগতিক । **–al'-i-ty,** *n.* **1.** Character of being conventional ; প্রথানুযায়িতা । **2.** A conventional practice; লোক-ব্যবহার, প্রচলিত প্রথা । **–ism,** *n.* Regard for or adherence to that which is received or established by arbitrary agreement ; লোক-ব্যবহারনিষ্ঠা, লোকব্যবহারানুগত্য, গতানুগতিকতা । **–ist,** *n.* **–ize,** *v. t.* **–ly,** *adv.*

cŏn-vĕn'-tū-ăl, *adj.* & *n.* **1.** Of or pertaining to a convent ; আশ্রম-সম্বন্ধীয়, ভিক্ষুণীসংঘসম্বন্ধীয় । **2.** [Cap.] Pertaining to the Conventual Franciscans ; ফ্রান্সিস্কেন সম্প্রদায়ের মঠবাসী সন্ন্যাসিগণ সম্বন্ধীয় । ***Noun.*** **1.** A member or inmate of a convent ; মঠবাসী সন্ন্যাসী, মঠবাসিনী সন্ন্যাসিনী । **2.** [Cap.] R. C. Church—A member of that church of the order of Franciscan friars who live in large convents and follow a mitigated rule, the other branch being the Observants ; ফ্রান্সিস্কেন সম্প্রদায়ের শাখাবিশেষ—এই শাখাভুক্ত সন্ন্যাসিগণ প্রকাণ্ড মঠে বাস করেন এবং অপেক্ষাকৃত অকঠোর নিয়ম পালন করিয়া থাকেন ।

cŏn-verge' (-vêrj), *v. t.* & *i.* **1.** To tend to one point, (*lit.* & *fig.*) কেন্দ্রাভিমুখীন করা । **2.** To cause to tend to one point ; এক কেন্দ্রাভিসারী করা । **–ver'-gence, –ver'-gen-cy,** *ns.* Tendency to one point ; এককেন্দ্রাভিমুখতা (মঃ ইঃ)। **–ver'-gent, –ver'-ging,** *adjs.*

cŏn-vêrs'-ă-ble, *adj.* **1.** Easy and pleasant in conversation ; সদালাপী প্রিয়ম্বদ । **2.** Pertaining to, or suitable for, social intercourse ; মেলা-মেশা সম্পর্কীয়, মেলামেশার উপযোগী । **–bly,** *adv.* **–ness,** *n.*

cŏn-vĕrse', (-vêrs), *v. t.* To talk familiarly ; to discourse ; কথোপকথন করা, কথাবার্ত্তা বলা ; আলাপ করা ।

cŏn'-verse (-vêrs), *n.* **1.** (*Archaic*) **1.** Familiar discourse ; (অপ্রচলিত) কথাবার্ত্তা, কথোপকথন, আলাপ । **2.** Frequent intercourse ; intimate association ; মেলামেশা ; অন্তরঙ্গতা ।

cŏn'-verse (-vêrs), *adj.* & *n.* Opposite ; acting in reverse manner ; বিপরীত, উল্টা ; বিপরীতভাবে ক্রিয়াশীল । ***Noun.*** **1.** Proposition produced by conversion ; *e. g.* the converse of "no virtue is vice" is "no vice is virtue" ; (ন্যায়শাস্ত্র) পরিবর্ত্তিত প্রতিজ্ঞা । **2.** A form of words produced by transposition of some terms of another ; *e.g.* "A quiet day and a noisy night ;" "A noisy day and quiet night ;" কোন বাক্যের শব্দ সমূহের পর্য্যায় ব্যতিক্রম দ্বারা উৎপন্ন বাক্য।

cŏn'-vêr-sance (-săns), **—săn-çy,** *ns.* Familiarity ; বিশেষ জানা শোনা, পরিজ্ঞান (মঃ ইঃ)।

cŏn'-vêr-sănt, *adj.* **1.** Well-acquainted ; সুপরিচিত। **2.** Acquainted by familiar use or study ; versed ; as, duly *conversant* in the Platonic philosophy ; সুপরিজ্ঞাত ; অভিজ্ঞ (আঃ বঃ), ব্যুৎপন্ন, বিশারদ (মঃ ইঃ)। **2.** Concerned ; as, angels *conversant* with man's affairs ; লিপ্ত। **—ly,** *adv.* In a familiar manner ; সুপরিচিত ভাবে, অন্তরঙ্গ ভাবে।

cŏn-vêr-să'-tion, *n.* **1.** Familiar discourse ; talk ; কথাবার্ত্তা, কথোপকথন, গল্পগাছা ; আলাপ, সম্ভাষণ, সংলাপ। **2.** Sexual intercourse ; as, criminal *conversation* ; স্ত্রী-সঙ্গম, স্ত্রী-সম্ভোগ। **—al,** *adj.* **1.** (*Of persons*) Ready to converse; আলাপপ্রিয়। **2.** Pertaining to conversation ; as, a *conversational* style; কথোপকথনসম্পর্কীয়। **—al-ist, —ist,** *ns.* One who excels in conversation ; সংলাপপটু ব্যক্তি, আলাপ-নিপুণ ব্যক্তি। **—al-ly,** *adv.* **In course of conversation** — কথাচ্ছলে, কথায় কথায়। (*Painting*) **Conversation piece**—(চিত্রবিদ্যা) মূর্ত্তিসমুচ্চয়যুক্ত পল্লি-চিত্রপট।

cŏn-vêr-sa-zi-o'-ne (-săt-sî-ō-nā), *n.* A meeting for conversation, generally on literary or scientific topics ; বৈঠক, (বিশেষতঃ) সাহিত্যিক বা বৈজ্ঞানিক বিষয় আলোচনার জন্য বৈঠক।

cŏn-vĕr'-sion, *n.* **1.** Transmutation ; a change from one party or religion to another ; পরিবর্ত্তন, রূপান্তরকরণ, অবস্থান্তরকরণ ; ধর্ম্মান্তর-পরিগ্রহ, স্বধর্ম্ম বা স্বদল ত্যাগ করণ। **2.** (*Theol.*) A radical change of heart or moral character ; (খৃষ্টীয় ধর্ম্ম-শাস্ত্র) মন কিংবা চরিত্রের আমূল পরিবর্ত্তন। **3.** (*Log.*) The inference of one proposition from another by transposing the terms ; উদ্দেশ্য-বিধেয় পরিবর্ত্তন। **4.** (*Law*) (Illegal) Appropriation of something to private use ; the change of bonds, debentures, etc., into others of different character ; (আইন) কোন বস্তু অবৈধভাবে স্বাধিকারভুক্ত করণ ; ঋণ-স্বীকার-পত্র প্রভৃতি ভিন্ন প্রকার পত্রে পরিবর্ত্তন।

cŏn-vêrt', *v. t.* **1.** To change from one state to another ; to transform ; অবস্থান্তরিত করা ; রূপান্তরিত করা। **2.** To turn from one faith, party, etc., to another ; ধর্ম্মান্তর গ্রহণ করা, স্বদল ত্যাগ করত অন্যদল-ভুক্ত হওয়া। **3.** To turn from a bad life to a good holy life ; পাপ-পথ পরিত্যাগ করত পবিত্র জীবন আরম্ভ করা। **4.** To apply to a different purpose ; (esp. *law*) to appropriate illegally ; ভিন্ন উদ্দেশ্যে প্রয়োগ করা ; (বিশেষতঃ আইনে) অবৈধ-রূপে আত্মসাৎ করা। **5.** (*Log.*) To change one proposition into another by transposing the terms ; (তর্ক-বিজ্ঞান) উদ্দেশ্য-বিধেয় পরিবর্ত্তন করা। **6.** To give in exchange for some equivalent ; সমমূল্যের অন্য কিছুর সহিত বিনিময় করা। **To convert into**—To change into ; রূপান্তরিত করা। **To convert to**—To cause to take up (another religion or party etc.) ; (অন্য দল বা ধর্ম্ম) গ্রহণ করান।

cŏn'-vêrt, *n.* A person who turns from one opinion, party or faith to another ; a man turned from sin to holiness ; ধর্ম্মান্তর-গ্রহণকারী, স্বধর্ম্মত্যাগী, ধর্ম্মান্তরগামী, স্বদলত্যাগী ; সাধু বা পবিত্র জীবন আরম্ভকারী।

cŏn-vêrt'-i-ble, *adj.* **1.** Transformable ; capable of being interchanged ; synonymous ; as, *convertible* terms ; পরিবর্ত্তনীয় ; রূপান্তরগ্রহণীয় ; সমার্থক, তুল্যার্থবাচক। **2.** Capable of being converted to a party or religion ; ধর্ম্মান্তর-গ্রহণযোগ্য, অন্য-পক্ষ গ্রহণ-যোগ্য। **3.** Capable of being exchanged for value of different kind ; as, *convertible* paper money (exchangeable for species) ; তুল্য-মূল্য বস্তুতে পরিবর্ত্তনীয়। **—i-bil'-i-ty,** *n.* **—i-bly,** *adv.* Reciprocally ; অঙ্গাঙ্গীভাবে, অন্যোন্যসম্বন্ধভাবে। **Convertible husbandry**—পর্য্যায়ক্রমে শস্য উৎপাদন।

cŏn'-vĕx, *adj.* & *n.* Rising on the interior surface into a round form ; (as opp. to *concave*) ; ন্যুব্জ, বহির্বর্ত্তুল, উন্নতোদর, মধ্যোচ্চ (আঃ বঃ)। ***Noun.*** **1.** A convex part of anything ; কোন বস্তুর বহির্বর্ত্তুল অংশ। **2.** A convex glass or lens ; বহির্বর্ত্তুল কাচ বা তাল। **3.** (*Slang*) A kind of playing-card for cheating ; (ইতর ভাষায়) প্রতারণা করার জন্য তাস বিশেষ। **—vex'-i-ty,** *n.* State or quality of being convex ; the exterior surfaces of a convex body ; মধ্যোচ্চতা (আঃ বঃ), বহির্বর্ত্তুলতা ; বহির্বর্ত্তুল বস্তুর উপরি ভাগ। **—ly,** *adv.*

Convex or plane convex. Convexo-concave. Convexo-convex.

cŏn-vĕx'-ō-cŏn'-câve, *adj.* (*Optics*) Convex on one side and concave on the other ; এক দিকে উন্নত ও অপর দিকে নত, নতোন্নতদর (হিঃ কোঃ), অর্দ্ধচন্দ্রাকৃতি (মঃ ইঃ)। **—plane,** *adj.* Convex on one side and plane on the other; একদিকে সমতল অপরদিকে, উন্নত, সমোন্নতদর (হিঃ কোঃ)। **—vex,** *adj.* Convex on both sides ; যুগলোন্নতদর (হিঃ কোঃ)।

cŏn-vey′ (-vā), *v. t.* **1.** To transport ; to carry ; স্থানান্তরে লইয়া যাওয়া ; বহন করা। **2.** (*Law*) To make over, as property ; to transfer by sealed writing ; প্রদান করা ; কবালাদিদ্বারা হস্তান্তর করা। **3.** To transmit (sound, smell, etc.) ; as, air *conveys* sound ; to cause to pass from one place or person to another ; সঞ্চার করা ; হস্তান্তরিত করা, স্থানান্তরিত করা। **4.** To impart or communicate ; as, words *convey* ideas ; সংক্রমিত করা, সঞ্চার করা। **—a-ble,** *adj.* Capable of being conveyed or transferred ; বহনযোগ্য, হস্তান্তরকরণীয়। **—ance,** *n.* **1.** Transporting ; transmission ; স্থানান্তরীকরণ ; প্রেরণ, বহন। **2.** A vehicle ; যান, বাহন, প্রবহন (মঃ উঃ)। **3.** (*Law*) Transfer of ownership ; স্বত্ব-স্বামিত্ব হস্তান্তরীকরণ। **4.** Communication ; as, *conveyance* of ideas ; সঞ্চার, সংক্রমণ। **5.** A deed by which anything as a property is transferred ; কবালা, হেবা, দানপত্র। **Letter** or **deed of conveyance**—দানপত্র, হস্তান্তরপত্র।

cŏn-vey′-ănc-ĕr (-vā-), *n.* **1.** One who prepares deeds for the transference of property ; যে ব্যক্তি সম্পত্তির হস্তান্তর-পত্র মুসাবিদা করিয়া দেয়। **2.** What effects conveyance of something ; বহনকারী, বাহক।

cŏn-vey′-ănc-ing (-vā-), *n.* The business of drawing deeds for transferring property ; হস্তান্তরপত্র মুসাবিদার কার্য্য।

cŏn-vict′, *v. t.* To prove guilty ; to pronounce guilty, (followed by *of*) ; বিচার করিয়া দোষী সাব্যস্ত করা ; বিচার করিয়া অপরাধী বলা। **2.** To impress (one) with the sense of error or sinfulness ; as, to *convict* men of self-conceit ; ভ্রান্তি বা অপরাধের বিষয়ে প্রতীতি জন্মান।

cŏn′-vict, *n* One found guilty of a crime ; a person undergoing penal servitude ; যে ব্যক্তি বিচারে অপরাধী বলিয়া সাব্যস্ত হইয়াছে, নির্ণীতাপরাধ (আঃ বঃ) ; বন্দী, কয়েদী, আসামী। **—ism,** *n.*

cŏn-vic′-tion, *n.* **1.** The act of convicting or proving guilty of an offence ; দোষী সাব্যস্ত করণ। **2.** (*Law*) The act of convicting a person of an offence ; the state of being convicted ; কোন ব্যক্তিকে অপরাধী সাব্যস্ত করণ ; অপরাধিসাব্যস্ততা। **3.** The act of convincing ; প্রত্যয়-উৎপাদন। **4.** A firm belief ; প্রতীতি, নিশ্চয় (হিঃ কোঃ), দৃঢ়-প্রত্যয়, স্থিরসিদ্ধান্ত। **Summary conviction**—জুরি ব্যতিরেকে জজ বা ম্যাজিষ্ট্রেট কর্ত্তৃক কোন ব্যক্তিকে অপরাধী সাব্যস্তকরণ। **Under conviction**—In the state of awakened consciousness of sin ; স্বকৃত পাপের বোধ উদ্বোধিত অবস্থায়।

cŏn-vic′-tive (-tĭv), *adj.* Tending to produce conviction ; নিশ্চায়ক।

cŏn-vince′ (-vĭns) *v. t.* To persuade by argument ; to satisfy by proof ; to produce moral conviction (of sin) into (with *of*) ; যুক্তি তর্কদ্বারা বিশ্বাস জন্মান ; প্রমাণদ্বারা বুঝান ; (পাপ প্রভৃতি সম্পর্কে) বোধ জন্মান। **—ment,** *n.* **—vinc′-ing,** *adj.* **—vinc′-ing-ly,** *adv.* In a convincing manner ; নিশ্চায়কভাবে। **—vinc′-ing-ness,** *n.*

cŏn-vin′-ci-ble, *adj.* Capable of conviction ; প্রতীতি-জননক্ষম।

cŏn-viv′-i-ăl, *adj.* **1.** Relating to, or befitting, a feast ; social ; ভোজোৎসব-সম্বন্ধীয়, আহারবিহার-সম্বন্ধীয়, ভোজোৎসব-সমুচিত ; সামাজিক। **2.** Jovial ; merry ; আমোদজনক ; প্রফুল্ল। **—al′-i-ty,** *n.* Festivity ; আমোদ, উৎসব। **—ist,** *n.* A person of convivial habits ; আমোদপ্রিয় ব্যক্তি, উৎসবপ্রিয় ব্যক্তি। **—ly,** *adv.*

cŏn-vō-cā′-tion, *n.* **1.** The act of calling or assembling by summons ; আহ্বান। **2.** An assembly ; a meeting ; সভা, সম্মিলনী, মজলিস ; সংসদ, পরিষৎ। **3.** (*Church of England*) Synod of clergy of the province of Canterbury or York ; কেণ্টারবারী বা ইয়র্ক প্রদেশের যাজকদিগের সংসদ। **4.** (University of Oxford & Durham) An academical assembly, in which the business of university is transacted ; বিশ্ববিদ্যালয়ের সভা। **5.** (*India*) An annual meeting of the Senate for conferring degrees ; (ভারতবর্ষে) বিশ্ববিদ্যালয়ের বার্ষিক উপাধি বিতরণী সভা। **—al,** *adj.*

cŏn′-vōke′, *v. t.* To call together ; to convene ; আহ্বানপূর্ব্বক একত্র করা ; সম্মিলিত করা, সমাহ্বান করা।

cŏn′-vō-lūte, *adj.* & *n.* (*Bot.* & *Conch.*) Rolled or wounded together ; coiled ; (উদ্ভিদ্-বিদ্যা এবং শঙ্খতত্ত্ব) জড়ানো, গুটানো ; কুণ্ডলিত। ***Noun.*** A convolution ; a coil ; বলি ; কুণ্ডলী।

cŏn′-vō-lūt-ĕd, *adj.* Folded in tortuous windings ; twisted ; আঁকাবাঁকা ভাঁজযুক্ত ; পেঁচাল।

cŏn-vō lū′-tion, *n.* Act of rolling ; the state of being rolled together ; কুণ্ডলীকরণ ; কুণ্ডলিতাবস্থা (অন্ত্রাদির) পেঁচ, কুণ্ডলী।

cŏn-vŏlve′, *v. t.* & *i.* To roll or wind together ; জড়ান, পাকান, পেঁচান

Convolvulus.

cŏn-vŏl′-vū-lŭs, *n.* A genus of plants including bindweed ; লতাবিশেষ, ক্ষীরবিদারী (আঃ বঃ), মহাশ্বেতা (মঃ ইঃ), ইক্ষুগন্ধা (ঐ), ভুমিকুষ্মাণ্ডক।

Convolvulus pluricaulis—গোরক পান (হিন্দি)। *Convolvulus reptans*—কলমী শাক।

cŏn-voy′, *v. t.* To accompany on the way for protection either by sea or by land; as, a cruiser *convoyed* the ships: "A fresh guard was to *convoy* me to Dijon:" রক্ষি-স্বরূপ সঙ্গে যাওয়া, রক্ষণার্থ সঙ্গে যাওয়া।

cŏn′-voy, *n.* **1.** Act of convoying; escorting for protection; an honourable escort; রক্ষিরূপে অনুগমন; শরীররক্ষাকরণ; সম্মানার্থ অনুগমনকারী শরীররক্ষিবর্গ। **2.** Number of merchants' ships under escort or able to defend themselves; as, a *convoy* was expected from Tunis; রণতরী প্রভৃতি দ্বারা সুরক্ষিত অথবা আত্মরক্ষণে সমর্থ বাণিজ্যপোত শ্রেণী। **3.** A protecting force accompanying ship or property either by sea or land; person or persons, goods, etc. under escort; যে সৈন্যদল জল বা স্থলপথে কোন সম্পত্তি বা অর্ণবপোতের অনুগমন করে; রক্ষিদল দ্বারা রক্ষিত ব্যক্তি, ব্যক্তি সমূহ বা সম্পত্তি।

cŏn vulse′ (-vŭls), *v. t.* **1.** To agitate greatly, (*lit* & *fig.*); আন্দোলিত করা, আলোড়িত করা, বিক্ষুব্ধ করা। **2.** To contract, as the muscular parts of an animal body; দৈহিক পেশীর আক্ষেপ জন্মান, খেঁচা।

cŏn-vŭl′-sion, *n.* **1.** (*Pl.*) A violent involuntary contraction of the muscles; খেঁচুনি, তড়কা (যোঃ), আক্ষেপ (সুশ্রুঃ), অপতন্ত্রক (আঃ বঃ)। **2.** A violent agitation (social or political); commotion; বিক্ষোভ, সংক্ষোভ, তুমুল আন্দোলন; গোলযোগ, বিভ্রাট। **3.** (*Pl.*) A violent fit of laughter; অট্টহাস্য। **–a-ry**, *adj.*

cŏn-vŭl′-sive (-sĭv), *adj.* Attending with or producing convulsions; convulsionary; (*lit* & *fig.*); (শব্দানুযায়ী এবং লক্ষণায়) আক্ষেপ-সহকৃত, আক্ষেপজনক; বিক্ষোভজনক। **–ly**, *adv.*

cō′-nȳ, –ney (-nĭ), *n.* **1.** A rabbit; (*Bible*) a rabbit-like animal of Palestine; শশক; (বাইবেল) পেলেস্টাইন দেশের শশকবৎ জন্তু বিশেষ। **2.** A kind of fish; একপ্রকার মৎস্য। **Coney-catcher** — (*Arch.*) (অপ্রচলিত) জুয়াচোর।

coo, *v. i., t.* & *n.* **1.** To make a low sound as a dove or pigeon; কু কু করা, কূজন করা। **2.** To converse in a loving manner; "Billing and *cooing*;" আদর বা সোহাগভরে কথাবার্ত্তা বলা। ***Verb t.*** To express cooingly; সোহাগজড়িত কণ্ঠে প্রকাশ করা। ***Noun.*** The cry of a dove or pigeon; any similar sound; ঘুঘু বা কপোত পক্ষীর রব; কূজন।

coo′-ey, (-ĭ), **–ee** (-ē), *n.* The cry used as a signal by the Australian aborigines and adopted by the colonists; অষ্ট্রেলিয়ার আদিম নিবাসিগণের সঙ্কেতধ্বনি — যাহা বর্ত্তমানে ঐ দেশের ঔপনিবেশিকগণ গ্রহণ করিয়াছে।

cook (cûk), *n.* One whose occupation is to cook or prepare food; পাচক, সুপকার, রাঁধুনী, বল্লব, রসুইকার (*Colloq.*), বাবুর্চি (*Colloq.*)। **Cook-house**—উষ্ণপ্রধান দেশের অনাবৃত স্থানস্থিত রন্ধনশালা; জাহাজের পাকশালা। **Cook-room**—রন্ধনকক্ষ, রান্নাঘর, রন্ধনগৃহ, পাকগৃহ; জাহাজের পাকশালা। **Cook-shop** — ভোজনালয়। **Too many cooks spoil the broth**—অধিক সন্ন্যাসীতে গাঁজন নষ্ট।

cook (cûk), *v. t.* & *i.* **1.** To prepare as food by heat or fire; পাক করা, রন্ধন করা। **2.** (*Colloq.*) To tamper with or manipulate; as, to *cook* accounts, etc.; (*fig.*) to concoct; as, to *cook up* a story; হাতের কৌশলে বদলান; (লক্ষণায়) মনে মনে পাকান। **3.** (Esp. in *chess*) To ruin (*slang*); (বিশেষতঃ দাবা খেলায়) নষ্ট করা। ***Verb i.*** To undergo cooking; পক্ক হওয়া। **2.** To cook food, etc, by fire; অগ্নিতে খাদ্য প্রভৃতি পাক হওয়া।

Cook′-er, *n.* **1.** A cooking-stove। পাক করিবার চুল্লী। **2.** A vessel for cooking food etc.; পাক-পাত্র; **3.** One who falsifies (accounts, etc.) or concocts; যে ব্যক্তি হিসাব প্রভৃতি জাল করে, যে ব্যক্তি কোন কিছু মনে মনে পাকায়। **4.** An article of food etc. that cooks well: ফল প্রভৃতি খাদ্য দ্রব্য—যাহা সুচারুরূপে পক্ক হয়। **To cook one's goose**—To kill one; to spoil one's chances of success; বধ করা; কাহারও সফলতার আশা নষ্ট করা।

cook′-êr-ȳ (cûk-), *n.* The art or practice of preparing food for the table; রন্ধন-বিদ্যা, পাকপ্রণালী, পাককলা। **Cookery book**—রন্ধনবিদ্যা সম্বন্ধীয় পুস্তক, পাকপ্রণালী বিষয়ক পুস্তক।

cook′-ie (cûk-ē), *n.* **1.** A plain sweet bread (*Scotch.*); একপ্রকার মিঠা পাউরুটি। **2.** (*U. S.*) A small flat cake; (মার্কিন যুক্তরাজ্য) একপ্রকার ক্ষুদ্র চাপাটি।

cook′-ȳ (cûk-), *n.* (*Colloq.*) A (female) cook; রাঁধুনী।

cōol, *adj.* & *n.* **1.** Moderately cold; as, *cool* weather; ঠাণ্ডা, নাতিশীতল, স্নিগ্ধ। **2.** Producing a sensation of cold; as, a *cool* gust; শৈত্যজনক, দেহস্নিগ্ধকর, স্নিগ্ধকর। **3.** Wanting in zeal; self-possessed; unexcited; indifferent; as, a *cool* friend, debater or lover; উদ্যমশূন্য; সংযত-চিত্ত; অনুত্তেজিত; ধীরচেতা, উদাসীন, প্রশান্ত। **4.** Impudent; audacious; as, a *cool* behaviour; ধৃষ্ট; প্রগল্ভ। **5.** (*Colloq.*) Implying a large sum; as, a *cool* thousand; (চলিত কথায় বহু টাকাপয়সা বুঝাইতে) পুরা। **6.** Showing coolness or dislike; as, a *cool* reception; অনুরাগশূন্য, প্রীতিশূন্য, প্রাণশূন্য, আবেগহীন, উদাসীন, অনুৎসুক, অনুৎকণ্ঠিত,

অনাসক্ত। 7. (*Hunting*) Faint; as, a *cool* scent; মৃদু, ক্ষীণ। ***Noun.*** 1. Coolness; শীতলত্ব, শৈত্য। 2. A cool place; cool air or time; as, he rode in the *cool* of the evening; শীতল স্থান; ঠাণ্ডা বাতাস বা সময়। **Cool'-ish,** *adj.* **Cool'-ly,** *adv.* **Cool'-ness,** *n.* **A cool hand**—ধৃষ্ট ব্যক্তি। **A cool thousand or hundred**—একশত বা সহস্র পাউণ্ড রূপ বৃহৎ অর্থ রাশি। **Cool and calculating** — শীতলপ্রকৃতি হিসাবী (লোক)। **Cool as a cucumber**—Perfectly self-possessed; সম্পূর্ণরূপে আত্মসংস্থ। **Cool-headed**—স্থির-বুদ্ধি। **Cool tankard**—সুরা, জল, লেবুর রস প্রভৃতি দ্বারা প্রস্তুত পানীয় বিশেষ।

cōol, *v. t.* & *i.* 1. To make cool; as, ice *cools* water; শীতল করা, ঠাণ্ডা করা। 2. To moderate or allay, as heat, excitement, passion; প্রশমিত করা, ঠাণ্ডা করা, হ্রাস করা। ***Verb i.*** 1. To grow cool; ঠাণ্ডা হওয়া, শীতল হওয়া, জুড়ন। 2. To lose ardour, zeal or affection; নিরুৎসাহ, উদ্যমহীন বা অনুরাগশূন্য হওয়া। **To cool one's copper**—To cool one's throat and mouth parched by drinking; মদ্য পান হেতু শুষ্কতা-প্রাপ্ত মুখ এবং কণ্ঠ ঠাণ্ডা করা। **To cool the heel** — (*Colloq.*) To be kept waiting, as for admission to a patron's house; বড় লোকের সহিত সাক্ষাৎকারের অপেক্ষায় দাঁড়াইয়া থাকা।

cōol'-êr, *n.* A vessel in which something is cooled; as, a butter-*cooler*; দ্রব্যাদি জুড়াইবার বা ঠাণ্ডা করিবার পাত্র।

cōo'-lie (-lĭ), **–lȳ,** *n.* A labourer in India or China; কুলী, মুটে, মজুর। **–ism,** *n.*

cōom, *n.* 1. Soot; ঝুল। 2. Coal-dust; কয়লার গুড়া।

coomb, combe (cōom), *n.* 1. A measure of capacity = 4 bushels; শস্যাদির পরিমাপ বিশেষ। 2. A steep valley running up from the sea-coast; সমুদ্রোপকূল হইতে উত্থিত সরলোন্নত উপত্যকা বিশেষ। 3. A hollow or valley on a hill-side; পর্ব্বত পার্শ্বস্থ গহ্বর বা উপত্যকা বিশেষ।

cōon, *n.* 1. (*U. S.*) A raccoon; উত্তর আমেরিকার মার্জ্জারবৎ সর্ব্বভুক্ জন্তুবিশেষ। 2. A sly fellow; ধূর্ত্ত ব্যক্তি। **A gone coon**—A person whose case is hopeless; যাহার সম্বন্ধে কোন আশা নাই।

cōop, *n.* 1. A basket confining fowls or the small animals; মুর্গী অথবা অন্য ক্ষুদ্র জন্তু রাখিবার পিঞ্জর বা খাঁচা, বীতংস (মঃ ইঃ)। 2. A basket used in catching fish; মাছ ধরিবার ঝুড়ি, ঘুনি।

cōop, *v. t.* 1. To confine in a coop; পিঞ্জরাবদ্ধ করা। 2. To shut up or confine, as persons; আবদ্ধ করা, রুদ্ধ করা। **To coop up in**—To confine in; কোন কিছুর ভিতর রুদ্ধ করা। * * * * *

cōo'-pêr, *n.* & *v. t.* 1. One who makes or repairs tubes, casks, etc.; পিপা, চোঙ্গা প্রভৃতি প্রস্তুত বা মেরামতকারী। 2. A wine cooper; see below. 3. A drink composed half of stout and half of poster; এক প্রকার পানীয়। ***Verb t.*** 1. To make or repair casks, etc.; পিপা, চোঙ্গা, প্রভৃতি প্রস্তুত বা মেরামত করা। 2. To put in casks; পিপাজাত করা। 3. (*Colloq.*) To finish up; "When I was fairly *coopered* up; (চলিত ভাষায়) শেষ করা, সারা করা। **A dry cooper**—যে ব্যক্তি শুষ্কদ্রব্য রাখিবার উপযোগী পিপা প্রভৃতি নির্ম্মাণ করে। **A wet cooper**—যে ব্যক্তি তরল পদার্থ রাখিবার উপযোগী পিপা প্রভৃতি নির্ম্মাণ করে। **A white cooper**—যে ব্যক্তি পরিবার বা দুগ্ধ মন্থনালয়ের ব্যবহারের উপযোগী দোহন-ভাণ্ড, চোঙ্গা প্রভৃতি নির্ম্মাণ করে। **Wine cooper**—মদ্যবিক্রেতা, যে ব্যক্তি মদ্যের গুণাগুণ পরীক্ষা করে, যে ব্যক্তি মদ্য বোতলজাত করে।

cōo'-pêr-āge, *n.* The work or workshop of a cooper; পিপা নির্ম্মাণকার্য্য, পিপা-নির্ম্মাণশালা।

cō-ŏp'-êr-āte, *v. i.* 1. To work conjointly for the same end; এক উদ্দেশ্য সাধনে একযোগে কাজ করা। 2. To concur in producing a result; একই উদ্দেশ্য সাধনে একমত হওয়া, সহকারিতা করা, সহযোগিতা করা, সাহচর্য্য করা। 3. To join in economic cooperation; সমবায়ে যোগদান করা। **–ant,** *adj.* & *n.* Operating together; labouring to the same end; একযোগে কার্য্যকারী; একই উদ্দেশ্য সাধনের জন্য পরিশ্রমকারী। ***Noun.*** Something co-operant; সহকারী বা একক্রিয় ব্যক্তি বা বস্তু। **–a-tor,** *n.*

cō-ŏp-êr-ā'-tion, *n.* 1. Joint assistance to the same end; সাহচর্য্য, সমুত্থান (মঃ সঃ), সমবায়, সংব্যাপার (হিঃ কোঃ), সহব্যাপার (ঐ)। 2. (*Pol. Econ.*) The union of small capitalists for the purposes of purchase, production, etc.; (অর্থ-নীতি) সমবায়।

cō-ŏp'-êr-ā-tive (-tîv), *adj.* Of, tending to, co-operation; সাহচর্য্য-সংক্রান্ত, সমবায়সংক্রান্ত। **Co-operative society**—সমবায়-সংঘ, সমবায়-সম্প্রদায়। [সমবায়ের সভ্যগণ এরূপ সমবায় ভাণ্ডার হইতে আবশ্যক দ্রব্য ক্রয় করেন, এবং ভাণ্ডারের লাভ ও ক্ষতির ভাগী থাকেন।] **Co-operative credit society**—সমবায়ঋণদান সমিতি।

cō-ŏpt', *v. t.* To elect into any body by the votes of its existing members; কোন সম্প্রদায়ের সভ্যগণের 'মত' দ্বারা উক্ত সম্প্রদায়ের সভ্যরূপে নির্ব্বাচিত করা। **–op-ta'-tion,** *n.*

cō-ŏr'-di-nāte, *adj.* & *n.* 1. Equal in rank, degree or importance; সমপদস্থ, সমশ্রেণীভুক্ত, সমগুরুত্ববিশিষ্ট, সমপরিমাণ, সমকক্ষ। 2. (*Gram.*

Opposed to subordinate; (ব্যাকরণ) স্বপ্রধান। **3.** (*Biol.*) Not subordinate, the one to the other, but standing on the same level; (জীববিদ্যা) অঙ্গাঙ্গী। ***Noun.*** (*Math.*) (*Pl.*) Two lines generally at right angles to each other, employed to fix the place of any point; (গণিতশাস্ত্র) দুইটা রেখা—যাহারা পরস্পরের সংযোগে সমকোণ উৎপন্ন করে, এবং যাহাদের সাহায্যে কোন বিন্দুর স্থান নিদ্ধারণ করা যায়, ভুজকোটী (সাঃ পঃ) ভুজযুগ্ম (হিঃ কোঃ)। **—ly,** *adv.* (*Math.*) **Anticomplimentary co-ordinates**—অপূরক ভুজযুগ্ম (হিঃ কোঃ)। **Areal co-ordinates**—ক্ষেত্রফলীয় ভুজযুগ্ম (হিঃ কোঃ)। **Biangular co-ordinates** দ্বিকোণক ভুজযুগ্ম (হিঃ কোঃ)। **Bipolar co-ordinates**—দ্বিধ্রুবীয় ভুজযুগ্ম (হিঃ কোঃ)। **Biradial co-ordinates** — ত্রিজ্যা ভুজযুগ্ম (হিঃ কোঃ)। **Cartisian Co-ordinates** — কার্তীয় ভুজযুগ্ম (হিঃ কোঃ)। **Complementary Co-ordinates**—পূরক ভুজযুগ্ম (হিঃ কোঃ)। **Ecliptic co-ordinates** — দৈর্ঘ্য ভুজযুগ্ম (হিঃ কোঃ)। **Generalized co-ordinates** — সাধারণ ভুজযুগ্ম (হিঃ কোঃ)। **Normal co-ordinates**—ত্রিফলক ভুজযুগ্ম (হিঃ কোঃ)। **Polar co-ordinates**—অক্ষীয় ভুজযুগ্ম (হিঃ কোঃ)।

cö-ŏr'-dĭ-nāte, *v. t.* **1.** To make co-ordinate; সমশ্রেণীভুক্ত করা, সমপদস্থ করা। **2.** To arrange in proper order or classes; to harmonise; যথানুক্রমে বা যথাযোগ্য শ্রেণীতে সন্নিবিষ্ট করা, অঙ্গাঙ্গীভাবে রাখা; সঙ্গতিবিশিষ্ট করা, সমন্বয় করা।

cö-ŏr-dĭ-nā'-tion, *n.* **1.** The act of co-ordinating; সমপদস্থ করণ। **2.** The act of arranging in due rank or order; যথাক্রমে বা যথাস্থানে সন্নিবেশ, অঙ্গাঙ্গীকরণ (সাহিত্য)।

coot, *n.* **1.** A small black water-fowl frequenting lakes and still rivers; কৃষ্ণবর্ণ জলচর পক্ষিবিশেষ। **2.** (*Prov.*) A simpleton; (প্রাদেশিক) নির্ব্বোধ ব্যক্তি। **Bald coot**—জালপাদ জলচর পক্ষিবিশেষ।

cŏp, *n.* A conical ball of thread on a spindle; টাকুতে জড়ানো মোচাকার সূতার গুটি।

cŏp, *n.* (*Slang*) Policeman; পোলিশ কর্ম্মচারী।

cŏp, *n.* (*Slang*) To catch; to capture; ধরা; পাকড়াও করা।

cō-pai'-bă, —vă, *n.* A liquid resinous substance used in medicine; ঔষধরূপে ব্যবহৃত আটালো তরল পদার্থ বিশেষ।

cō'-păl, *n.* Resin used for varnishes; ডামর (যোঃ), কহরোবা (রঃ সঃ)।

cō-pâr'-cĕ-nă-rȳ, —nêr-ȳ, *n.* Joint heirship; সমাংশভাগিত্ব, সমভাগিত্ব, সমভাগিভাব, (দায়ভাগে) সমত্তোরাধিকারত্ব, পৈত্রিক সমানাধিকার। **—ner,** *n.* A joint heir or heiress; পৈত্রিক সম্পত্তিতে সমাংশভাক্ ব্যক্তি, সহদায়াদ, হিস্যাদার, সরিক।

cō-pârt'-nêr, *n.* A sharer; a partaker; অংশীদার, সরিক; সহযোগী, সমবায়ী, বিভাগী, হিস্যাদার। **—ship,** *n.*

cō-pârt'-nêr-ȳ, *n.* Co-partnership; সম্ভূয়সমুথান।

cōpe, *n.* **1.** An ecclesiastical vestment resembling a long cloak worn in sacred ministrations;

Priest wearing cope.

যাজকীয় পরিচ্ছদ বিশেষ। **2.** (*Fig.*) Canopy; as, the *cope* of heaven; (লক্ষণায়) চন্দ্রাতপ। **3.** (Founding) The outer portion of a mould; (ঢালাইর কাজ) ছাঁচের বহির্ভাগ।

cōpe, *v. t.* & *i.* To dress, cover, or furnish with a cope; উক্ত প্রকার যাজকীয় পরিচ্ছদ দ্বারা সজ্জিত, আবৃত বা সমন্বিত করা। ***Verb i*** To hang over like a coping; প্রাচীরের মাথালির পাথরের ম ঝুকিয়া থাকা। **Cope-stone, coping-stone**—A head or top stone; শীর্ষভাগস্থ প্রস্তর, মাথালির পাথর। (*Fig.*) Finishing touch; (লক্ষণায়) সম্পূর্ণতা-প্রদায়ক তুলির রেখা।

cōpe, *v. i.* To strive or struggle with; to match; প্রতিদ্বন্দ্বিতা করা; সমকক্ষ হওয়া, আঁটিয়া উঠা। **To cope with**—To contend with equal strength against; আঁটিয়া উঠা।

cō'-pĕck, *n.* A Russian copper coin worth from $\frac{1}{4}$ to $\frac{1}{3}$ of a penny in English; রুষদেশীয় তাম্র মুদ্রা। (প্রায় ১ পয়সা মূল্যের)

cŏp'-êr, (also HORSE-COPER) A horse dealer; অশ্ব-ব্যবসায়ী।

cŏp'-êr, coop'-êr, *ns.* Floating grog-shop for North-sea fishers; উত্তর সাগরের মৎস্য-শিকারীদিগের জন্য প্রবমান সুরাবিপণি।

Cō-pêr'-nĭ-căn, *adj.* Pertaining to Copernicus or to his astronomical system; কোপারনিকাস বা তৎপ্রতিষ্ঠিত জ্যোতিষিক সংস্থিতি-সম্বন্ধীয়। **Copernican theory** or **system**—কোপার্নিকাস্ কর্ত্তৃক প্রতিষ্ঠিত জ্যোতিষিক বাদ বা সংস্থিতি। তাঁহার মতে গ্রহগণ সূর্য্যের চতুর্দ্দিকে পরিভ্রমণ করিতেছে।

cŏp'-ĭng, *n.* The course of masonry topping a wall; an over-hanging shelf for protecting wall-fruit; প্রাচীর প্রভৃতির মাথাল, কপিশীর্ষ (আঃ বঃ) প্রাকারশৃঙ্গ (মঃ ইঃ); প্রাচীরগাত্রে উৎপন্ন ফল রক্ষা করিবার জন্য দোলায়মান তাক বিশেষ।

cō'-pĭ-ous (-ŭs), *adj.* **1.** Plentiful; প্রচুর, পর্য্যাপ্ত, বহুল, বিস্তর, প্রভূত, অজস্র, পুষ্কল। **2.** Abounding in information; as, a *copious* subject; having a large vocabulary as a language; জ্ঞাতব্যবিষয় পূর্ণ;

বাগ্‌বিস্তারপূর্ণ, শব্দবহুল। **—ly,** *adv.* **—ness,** *n.*

cŏp′-pêr, *n., adj.* & *v. t.* **1.** A metal of a brownish red colour; তাম্র, তামা, তাঁবা, অর্ক (সাঃ পঃ), কমল (ঐ), শুল্ব (ঐ), শুল্বক (ঐ), তুথকসত্ত্ব (ঐ), তাম্রক (ঐ), ভাস্কর (ঐ), রবি (ঐ), নাগমর্দ্দন (ঐ), নীলবিভ্রম (ঐ), হেমগর্ভ (ঐ), নীল (ঐ)। **2.** A copper or bronze coin; a penny, half penny or farthing; তাম্রমুদ্রা, বর্ত্তলৌহ-ধ' নির্ম্মিত মুদ্রা; একপেনি, অর্দ্ধ পেনি ব ফার্দ্দিং। **3.** A vessel or large b ler made of iron or copper; 'for every quarter of malt mashed the *copper* should contain 140 gallons;" লৌহ বা তাম্র-নির্ম্মিত পাক-পাত্র। ***Adj.*** **1.** Mixed with, or made of copper; তাম্র-মিশ্রিত, তাম্রগর্ভ। **2.** Consisting of, or resembling, copper; red-brown; তাম্রপূর্ণ, তাম্রসদৃশ; তাম্র-বর্ণ। ***Verb t.*** To cover with copper; as, to *copper* a ship; তামার পাত দ্বারা মোড়ান, তাম্রমণ্ডিত করা, তাম্রপট্টাচ্ছাদিত করা। **Copper-bit**—একপ্রকার ঝালা দিবার যন্ত্র—ইহার সূক্ষ্ম অগ্রভাগ তাম্র-নির্ম্মিত। **Copper bottomed**—তাম্র-পট্টাচ্ছাদিত-তলদেশ। **Copper-captain** — জাল কাপ্তান। **Copper-head**—আমেরিকা-দেশীয় বিষধর সর্প বিশেষ। **Copper-Indian**—উত্তর আমেরিকার লোহিতবর্ণ আদিম অধিবাসী। **Copper-leaf**—তাম্রপত্র, তম্বুরবিপত্র (সাঃ পঃ)। **Copper-nose**—মদ্য পান হেতু লোহিত-বর্ণ-প্রাপ্ত নাসিকা। **Copper-plate**—তাম্রফলক, তাম্রপট্ট, তাম্রপত্র, শুল্বপত্র (সাঃপঃ), তাম্রশাসন। An impression from a copper-plate; তাম্রশাসনের ছাপ, তাম্রফলকের ছাপ। **Copper-powder**—তাম্রচূর্ণ, শুল্বচূর্ণ (সাঃ পঃ)। **Copper-pyrites**—তাপ্য (সাঃ পঃ), বিমল (ঐ), মাক্ষিক (ঐ)। **Copper-smith** — A worker in copper; যে ব্যক্তি তামার কাজ করে, তাম্রকার, তাম্রিক। **Copper sulphate**—তুথ্যক (সাঃ পঃ), তুথ (ঐ), সস্যক বা শস্যক (ঐ), সস্য (ঐ), ময়ূরগ্রীবতুথ (ঐ), ময়ূরতুথ (ঐ), শিখিগ্রীবতুথ (ঐ), শুদ্ধসত্ত্ব (ঐ)। **Copper-sulphide** — পর্পটী তাম্র (সাঃ পঃ), তাম্রযোগ (ঐ)। **Hot-coppers**—অতিরিক্ত মদ্যপান হেতু শুষ্কীভূত মুখ এবং কণ্ঠ। **To cool one's copper**—See cool.

cŏp′-pêr, *n.* (*Slang*) A police-man; (ইতরভাষায়) পুলিশের লোক।

cŏp′-pêr-ăs, *n.* Sulphate of iron; কাসীস, হীরাকাসীস, হীরাকস।

cŏp′-pice (-pĭs), *n.* A wood of small growth for periodical cutting; বনখণ্ড, উপবন, ঝোপ। A **coppice-wood**—ঝোপ, ঝোড়।

cŏp′-ră, *n.* The dried kernel of coconut; নারিকেলের শুষ্ক শাঁস।

cŏp′-rŏ-līte, *n.* The petrified dung of certain extinct animals; কতিপয় লুপ্ত জন্তুর শিলীভূত মল। **—lit′-ic,** *adj.*

Cŏpt, *n.* A Christian descendant of the ancient Egyptians; প্রাচীন মিশরবাসীদিগের খৃষ্টধর্ম্মাবলম্বী বংশধর।

Cŏp′-tic, *adj.* & *n.* Relating to the Copts; প্রাচীন মিশরবাসীদিগের খৃষ্টধর্ম্মাবলম্বী বংশধরগণ সম্পর্কীয়। ***Noun.*** Language of the Copts; উক্ত বংশধরগণের ভাষা।

cŏp′-ū-lă, *n.* **1.** (*Log.* & *Gram.*) The word which joins the subject and predicate of a proposition; (ব্যাকরণ এবং তর্কবিজ্ঞান) উদ্দেশ্য এবং বিধেয় সংযোজক শব্দ। **2.** (*Anat.*) A connecting part, as a bone, cartilage, etc.; (শারীর-সংস্থান-বিদ্যা) সংযোজক অস্থি, তরুণাস্থি প্রভৃতি। **—lar,** *adj.*

cŏp′-ū-lāte, *v. i.* To unite in sexual intercourse; সঙ্গম করা, স্ত্রীসঙ্গ করা, রমণ করা, মৈথুন করা, শৃঙ্গার করা। **—la-to-ry,** *adj.*

cŏp-ū-lā′-tion, *n.* **1.** Logical or grammatical connection; সংযোগ, সমাহার, সংযোজন। **2.** Sexual union; coition; শৃঙ্গার; রতিক্রিয়া, সুরত, নিধুবন, ব্যবায়, গ্রাম্যধর্ম্ম।

cŏp′-ū-lā-tive (-tĭv), *adj.* & *n.* **1.** Serving to couple or connect; as, (in gram.) a *copulative* conjunction like "and"; সংযোজনাত্মক। **2.** (*Log.* & *Gram.*) Of the nature of a copula; উদ্দেশ্য বিধেয় সংযোজকধর্ম্মা। **3.** (*Zool.* & *Anat.*) Relating to sexual union; (জন্তুবিজ্ঞান এবং শারীরসংস্থান-বিদ্যা) সঙ্গ মসম্বন্ধীয়। ***Noun.*** A copulative conjunction or particle; সংযোজক অব্যয় শব্দ।

cŏp′-ȳ, *n.* **1.** An imitation, transcript, or reproduction of an original; অনুকরণ, নকল, প্রতিলিপি, অনুলিপি। **2.** An individual book or a single set of books containing the works of an author; as, a *copy* of the Bible; এক খণ্ড পুস্তক, এককেতা, একখানি। **3.** A model to be copied; নমুনা, আদর্শ। **4.** Manuscript given to be printed or to be set up in types; মুদ্রাঙ্কণের মুললিপি, মুদ্রিতব্য লিপি। **5.** (*Eng. Law*) A legal instrument or form of tenure by which property is held; (ইংলণ্ডীয় আইন) ইংলণ্ডের ভূম্যধিকারের প্রণালী বিশেষ। **—ist,** *n.* A transcriber; an imitator; প্রতিলিপিকার, লিপিকর, নকলনবীস; অনুকরণকারী। **Copy-book**—আদর্শ-লিপি পুস্তক, প্রতিলিপি পত্রিকা (আঃ বঃ)। **Copy book maxims** or **morality** — সাধারণ নীতিবাক্য। **Copy-hold** — ইংলণ্ডের ভূম্যধিকার-বিশেষ, আয়ত্তাধিকার (আঃ বঃ), পাট্টা-দারী। **Fair** or **clean copy**—পরিষ্কার প্রতিলিপি। **Rough** or **foul copy**—মূল পাণ্ডুলিপি। **To make copy of**—To turn into manuscript for the printer; মুদ্রাঙ্কণের জন্য হস্তলিপি প্রস্তুত করা। **To set a copy**—To write in an exercise book a copy for a learner to imitate; হস্তলিপির পুস্তকে শিক্ষার্থীদিগের

অনুকরণের জন্য আদশলিপি লিখিয়া দেওয়া।

cŏp'-y̆, *v. t.* & *i.* To transcribe or write from the original ; অনুকরণ করা, নকল করা, অনুলিপি প্রস্তুত করা, প্রতিলিপি প্রস্তুত করা। ***Verb i.*** অনুকরণ করা। **Copying-press**—হস্তলিখিত পত্রাদির অনুলিপি তুলিবার জন্য যন্ত্রবিশেষ।

cŏp'-y̆-right (-rït), *n., adj.* & *v. t.* The exclusive right to print or produce, given by law for a limited number of years ; গ্রন্থস্বত্ব, মুদ্রণাধিকার, মুদ্রণস্বত্ব (আঃ বঃ)। ***Adj.*** Related to, or protected by the law of, copyright ; গ্রন্থস্বত্ব সংক্রান্ত, গ্রন্থস্বত্ব আইন দ্বারা রক্ষিত। ***Verb t.*** To secure copyright (for books, etc) ; গ্রন্থস্বত্ব রক্ষা করা।

cō-quet' (-kĕt), *adj.* Coquettish ; সলীল, সবিভ্রম।

cō-quet' (-kĕt), *v. i.* **1.** To love in order to gratify vanity ; হাবভাব প্রদর্শন করা, লীলা বিভ্রম প্রদর্শন করা। **2.** To play or dally (with); as, we have *coquetted* with political crimes ; ক্রীড়া কৌতুক করা, রসরঙ্গ করা। **—ry,** *n.* **1.** Attempt to attract admiration, notice or love ; বিলাস, বিভ্রম, ঠাট্, ঠমক, হাব (আঃ বঃ), লীলা-বিভ্রম। **2.** Attractive prettiness as result of art ; "The house front......one *coquetry* of coloured brick and carved stone ; শিল্পিহস্তসৃষ্ট চিত্তাকর্ষক সৌন্দর্য্য।

cō-quette' (-kĕt), **1.** A woman who trifles with men's affection ; বিলাসিনী, বিলাসবতী, বিভ্রমবতী, রসিকা, রসবতী, রসরঙ্গিনী। **2.** A genus of crested humming birds; এক জাতীয় চূড়াবিশিষ্ট সুশ্রী পক্ষী। **—quet'-tish,** *adj.* **—quet'-tish-ly,** *adv.*

cō-qui'-tō (-kē-), *n.* A beautiful Chillian palm ; চিলিদেশীয় তাল-জাতীয় রম্য বৃক্ষবিশেষ।

cŏr-ă-cle, *n.* An ancient form of boat made by covering a wicker-frame with leather or oil cloth still used in Wales and Ireland ; চর্ম্মাদি দ্বারা আচ্ছাদিত বংশ বেত্রাদি নির্ম্মিত একপ্রকার ক্ষুদ্র নৌকা।

Fisherman with coracle.

cŏr'-ă-coid (-koyd), *adj.* (*Anat.*) Shaped like a crow's beak ; (শারীরসংস্থানবিদ্যা) কাকচঞ্চ্বাকৃতি। **Coracoid process**—স্কন্ধাস্থির কাকচঞ্চুবৎ প্রবর্দ্ধন।

cŏr'-ăl, *n.* & *adj.* **1.** A hard calcareous substance found in the ocean secreted by marine polyps for their common support and habitation and of different colours ; প্রবাল, প্রবালক (সাঃ পঃ) বেলাবল্লী জাত (ঐ), বিদ্রুম, রত্নকন্দ, হেমকন্দল, মুঙ্গা। **2.** Toy of polished coral for children cutting teeth ; শিশুদিগের প্রবালনির্ম্মিত ক্রীড়নক। **3.** Unimpregnated roe of lobster ; অগর্ভাধানপ্রাপ্ত চিংড়ী মৎস্যের ডিম্ব। ***Adj.*** Having a red colour like coral : প্রবালরক্ত। **Coral-island**—প্রবাল-দ্বীপ। **Coral-reef**—প্রবাল-স্তূপ। **Coral-sea** — অষ্ট্রেলিয়া এবং নব হেব্রাইডেস এর মধ্যবর্ত্তী প্রশান্তমহাসাগরাংশ। **Coral-rag** — শিলীভূত প্রবালময়চূর্ণ-প্রস্তর। **Coraltree**—মন্দার বৃক্ষ, মাদারগাছ।

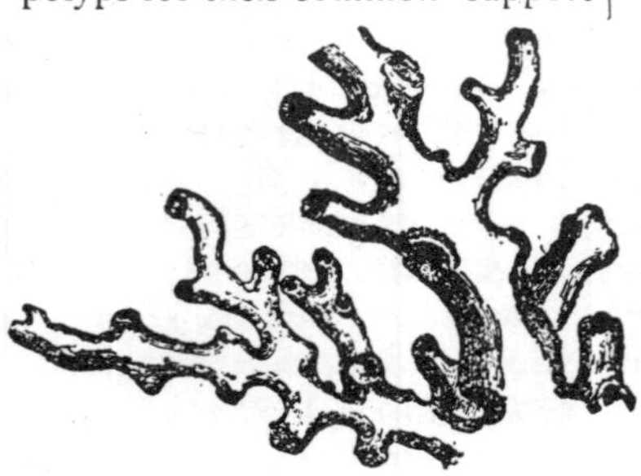

White coral.

cŏr'-ăl-līne, *adj.* **1.** Like, or composed of, coral ; প্রবালনিভ, প্রবাল-মিশ্রিত। **2.** Having the colour of red coral ; প্রবালরক্ত। **Coralline-marble**—প্রবালগর্ভ প্রস্তর। **Coralline-ware** — (সপ্তদশ ও অষ্টাদশ শতাব্দীর) ইতালীদেশীয় লোহিত মৃত্তিকার পাত্রাদি।

cŏr'-ăl-līte, *n.* **1.** A fossil coral ; শিলীভূত প্রবাল। **2.** Skeleton of a single zoophyte ; প্রবালজাতীয় জীব বিশেষের কঙ্কাল।

cŏr'-ăl-loid (-loyd), *adj.* & *n.* Like or akin to coral ; প্রবালনিভ, প্রবাল-কল্প। ***Noun.*** An animal resembling a coral ; প্রবালসদৃশ জন্তু।

coram', *adj.* [*L.*] Before ; in the presence of ; as, *coram* populo (before the people) ; সম্মুখে, সমক্ষে ; সাক্ষাতে।

cŏr'-bie (-bē), *n.* (*Scot.*) A raven or carrion crow ; দাঁড়কাক, গলিত মাংসভোজী কাক।

cŏr'bĕl, *n., v. t.* & *i.* (*Arch.*) A projection from the face of a wall supporting a superincumbent weight ; (স্থপতি-বিজ্ঞান) প্রাচীর হইতে উদ্গত প্রস্তরাদির তোড়া বিশেষ। ***Verb t.*** To support on corbels ; তোড়ার উপর অবলম্বিত রাখা। ***Verb i.*** To project on, or as on a corbel ; তোড়ার উপর প্রলম্বিত হওয়া, তোড়ার উপর যেরূপ থাকে তদ্রূপ প্রলম্বিত হওয়া। **—belled,** *adj.* (*Arch*) **Corbel-table**—তোড়াসমূহের উপর অবলম্বিত গ্রথিত ইষ্টকাদির প্রলম্বিত পংক্তি।

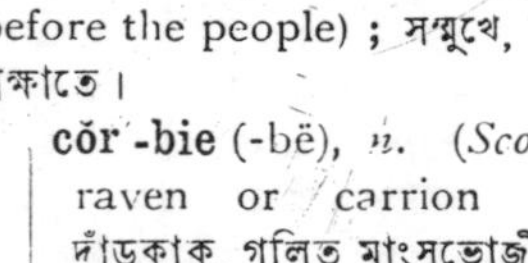

Corbel-table.

cŏrd, *n.* & *v. i.* **1.** A string or small rope ; রজ্জু, রশি, দড়ি। **2.** (*Anat.*) Anything resembling a cord ; as, spinal *cord* ; (শারীর-সংস্থান-বিদ্যা) রজ্জু-সদৃশ বস্তু। **3.** A raised cord-like ribbon ; a ribbed fabric ; রজ্জুর মত ফিতা ; এক প্রকার শির-তোলা কাপড়। **4.** A moral tie, restraint or attraction ; নৈতিকবন্ধন সংযম বা আকর্ষণ। *Verb i.* To bind with cords ; রজ্জুদ্বারা বন্ধন করা। **Cords**—এক-প্রকার শির-তোলা কাপড়ের তৈয়ারী পাজামা।

cŏrd'-āge, *n.* Ropes or cords collectively, esp. the ropes in the rigging of a ship ; রজ্জুসমূহ, জাহাজের দড়া-দড়ি।

cŏr'-dāte, *adj.* Heart-shaped ; হৃৎপিণ্ডাকৃতি, তাম্বুলাকার (সাঃ পঃ)।

cŏrd'-ĕd, *adj.* **1.** Fastened with cords ; রজ্জু-সংবদ্ধ। **2.** Furnished with cords ; রজ্জু-সমন্বিত। **3.** Striped or ribbed with cords ; as, cloth with a *corded* surface ; রজ্জুদ্বারা শির-তোলা।

cŏr-dĕ-lier' (-lĕr), *n.* A franscisсan friar, so named from the knotted cord worn as a girdle ; ফ্র্যান্সিস্কান সম্প্রদায় ভুক্ত সন্ন্যাসী। [এই সম্প্রদায়ভুক্ত সন্ন্যাসিগণ একটী গ্রন্থিযুক্ত রজ্জু কটিদেশে বদ্ধ করিতেন—এই হেতু এই নাম।]

cór'-dĭal, *adj.* & *n.* **1.** Hearty ; sincere ; affectionate ; আন্তরিক, হৃদ্য ; অকপট, অকৃত্রিম ; প্রিয়। **2.** Invigorating ; giving strength or spirit ; as, *cordial* medicine ; উত্তেজক, উৎসাহজনক ; বলকর স্ফূর্ত্তিজনক, তেজোবর্দ্ধক। ***Noun.*** **1.** Any invigorating preparation, as a medicine, food, or drink ; উত্তেজক বা বলকারক ঔষধ, খাদ্য বা পানীয়। **2.** (*Com.*) Aromatized sweetened spirit ; সুবাসিত এবং সুমিষ্ট সুরা। **–di-al'-i-ty,** *n.* Sincere affections and kindness ; heartiness ; অকপট প্রীতি ; আন্তরিকতা, হৃদ্যতা। **–ly,** *adv.*

cordillera, *n.* (*Sp.*) Mountain-ridge, esp. of the Andes ; সুদীর্ঘ গিরিপৃষ্ঠ (বিশেষতঃ আন্দিজ পর্ব্বতের)।

cŏrd'-īte, *n.* A smokeless explosive ; নির্ধূম বিস্ফোরক দ্রব্য বিশেষ।

cŏr'-dŏn, *n.* **1.** (*Fort.*) A row of projecting stones along the line of a rampart ; (দুর্গ) দুর্গ প্রাকারের পার্শ্বস্থ প্রলম্বিত প্রস্তরশ্রেণী। **2.** A line or series of sentries or military posts ; সৈনিক-প্রহরী শ্রেণী, সৈনিকদিগের আড্ডার সারি। **3.** Continuous circle of persons ; as, a crowd kept back by a *cordon* of police ; বৃত্তাকারে সজ্জিত লোক-শ্রেণী, অবিচ্ছিন্ন লোক-চক্র। **4.** (*Sanit.*) Same as SANITARY CORDON below. **5.** Ornamental cord or braid ; শোভাজনক রজ্জু বা ফিতা। **6.** A cord or ribbon worn as a badge of honour or as a decoration of an owner of knighthood ; নাইটগণ কর্ত্তৃক সম্মানসূচক চিহ্ন স্বরূপ পরিহিত ফিতা বা রজ্জু। **7.** Fruit-tree pruned to grow as single stem ; শাখা ছেদন দ্বারা একমাত্র কাণ্ডে পরিবর্দ্ধিত ফলবৃক্ষ। **Sanitary cordon**—সংক্রামক রোগদুষ্ট এবং উক্ত রোগশূন্য বিভাগদ্বয়ের মধ্যে যোগাযোগ নিবারণের জন্য প্রহরি-রক্ষিত রেখা।

Cŏr'-dō-văn, *n.* & *adj.* Leather of Cordova in Spain ; স্পেনদেশস্থ কর্ডোবা নামক স্থানের বিশোধিত চর্ম্ম। ***Adj.*** Of or relating to Cordova in Spain ; স্পেনদেশের অন্তর্গত কর্ডোবা নগরীসম্বন্ধীয়।

cŏr'-dū-roy, *n.* & *adj.* **1.** A thick cotton-stuff corded or ribbed ; শির-তোলা স্থূল কার্পাস বস্ত্র। **2.** (*Pl.*) Breeches or trousers of corduroy ; উক্তপ্রকার বস্ত্র নির্ম্মিত পাজামা। **3.** (*U.S.*) A corduroy road (one made of tree-trunks laid across a swamp) ; (মার্কিণ যুক্তরাজ্য) জলাভূমির উপর বৃক্ষকাণ্ডদ্বারা রচিত বর্ত্মবিশেষ। ***Adj.*** **1.** Made of corduroy ; শির-তোলা কার্পাস কাপড়ের তৈয়ারী। **2.** Ribbed and furrowed like corduroy ; উক্তপ্রকার বস্ত্রের মত শির-তোলা। **3.** Formed of tree-trunks laid across a miry place ; কর্দ্দমস্থানোপরি বৃক্ষকাণ্ড দ্বারা রচিত।

cŏrd'-wain (-wān), *n.* (*Archaic*) Spanish leather ; (অপ্রচলিত) স্পেন-দেশীয় শোধিত চর্ম্ম।

cŏrd'-wain-ĕr (-wān-), *n.* A shoemaker, (now only as guild name &c.) ; জুতা প্রস্তুতকারী, পাদুকাকার।

cōre, *n.* & *v. t.* **1.** The interior part of rock cut out in boring ; পাষাণের সারভাগ। **2.** The inner part containing seeds of fruits, as apple, pear, etc. ; ফলের শাঁস। **3.** The inner part of a thing, as of a column, wall, etc. ; আভ্যন্তরিক অংশ। **4.** (*Fig*) The inmost part ; as, rotten at the *core* ; অন্তরতম অংশ, মর্ম্মস্থল, মজ্জা। **5.** The heart or most vital part ; as, the *core* of a subject ; সারভাগ। **6.** A disease in sheep ; মেষরোগ। **7.** (*Founding*) The internal mould forming a hollow in the casting of metals ; (ঢালাইর কাজ) ধাতু ঢালাই করিবার ছাঁচের ভিতরের অংশ — যৎ সাহায্যে চোঙ প্রভৃতির ছিদ্র করা হয়। **8.** The central strand of a rope ; রজ্জুর মধ্যবর্ত্তী গুণ। **9.** (*Electro magnatism*) A solid bar of iron around which a spiral is wound ; (বিদ্যুচ্চুম্বকত্ব) নীরন্ধ্র লৌহদণ্ড বিশেষ—ইহার চতুর্দ্দিকে তার কুণ্ডলিত করা হয়। ***Verb t.*** **1.** To take out the core or inward part of ; as, to *core* a fruit ; মজ্জা বা শাঁস বাহির করিয়া লওয়া। **2.** (*Founding*) To form by means of a core, as a hole in casting ; (ঢালাইর কাজ) ছাঁচের অভ্যন্তরস্থ ছিদ্র করণোপযোগী ব্যবস্থার সাহায্যে ছিদ্রাদি করা। **3.** To inclose in the core ; অন্তরতম প্রদেশে রুদ্ধ

করা। Cor′-er, *n.* Core′-less, *adj.* **To lie at the very core**—To be situated in the innermost part; অন্তরতম প্রদেশে থাকা। **To the core**—To the innermost part; extending to the heart of anything; অন্তরতম প্রদেশ পর্য্যন্ত; মর্ম্মস্থল পর্য্যন্ত। To the innermost recesses of one's heart; অন্তরের অন্তরতম প্রদেশে, মর্ম্মস্থলে, মর্ম্মে মর্ম্মে।

cō-rē-lā′-tion, *n.* Same as CORRELATION.

cō-rē-li′-gion-ist (-jŭn-), *n.* An adherent of the same religion; একধর্ম্মাবলম্বী।

cō-rē-spónd′-ĕnt, *n.* (*Law*) A man charged with adultery in a divorce case, (the petitioner's wife being the *respondent*): বিবাহবিচ্ছেদের মোকদ্দমায় যে পুরুষ প্রতিবাদিনী স্ত্রীর জার বলিয়া অভিযুক্ত হয়।

corf, *n.* **1.** A basket used in mines; খনির কাজে ব্যবহৃত ঝুড়ি বিশেষ। **2.** A floating cage in which fish etc. are kept alive; এক প্রকার প্লবমান পিঞ্জর—যাহাতে মৎস্য প্রভৃতি জীবিত রাখা হয়।

coria soboxna — স্বর্ণ-খরিজা (গুপ্ত)।

cō-ri-ā′-ceous (-shŭs), *adj.* Consisting of, or resembling, leather; tough; শোধিত-চর্ম্মরচিত, শোধিত চর্ম্মসদৃশ; চর্ম্মবৎ (সাঃ পঃ)।

cō-ri-ăn′-dêr, *n.* (*Bot.*) A plant which produces aromatic seeds; ধনে, ধন্যাক, ধানেয় (আঃ বঃ)।

Cŏ-rin′-thi-ăn, *adj.* & *n.* **1.** Of or relating to Corinth in Greece; গ্রীসদেশের অন্তঃপাতী করিন্থ নগর-সম্পর্কীয়। **2.** (*Arch.*) Relating to the most delicate ornate of the three Greek ORDERS of architecture; (স্থপতি-বিজ্ঞান) গ্রীসদেশীয় স্থাপত্য-রীতি বিশেষ সম্পর্কীয়। ***Noun.*** **1.** A native of Corinth; করিন্থনগরবাসী। **2.** A man of fashion about town; a man of means, who rides his own horse or sails his own yacht, etc.; "The brothers were what, in modern times, we should call Dandies or *Corinthians*;" সহুরে বাবু; সঙ্গতিশালী লোক—যাহার নিজের গাড়ী ঘোড়া, বজরা প্রভৃতি আছে। **3.** (*Pl.*) Either of the two epistles written by St. Paul to the Corinthians; সেণ্ট্ পল করিন্থবাসিগণকে যে দুইটী পত্র লিখেন—তাহার কোন একটী। **—esque,** *adj.* Approximating the Corinthian style; করিন্থীয় স্থাপত্যরীতির প্রায় অনুরূপ। **Corinthian order**—করিন্থীয়স্থাপত্যরীতি—একন্থাস পত্ররাজি শোভিত ঘণ্টাকৃতি স্তম্ভশীর্ষ ইহার বিশেষত্ব।

cŏrk, *n., adj.* & *v. t.* **1.** The bark of a species of oak; একজাতীয় বৃক্ষের বল্কল। **2.** A stopper for a bottle, cut out of a cork; বোতলের ছিপি, কাক। **3.** The cork tree; কাক গাছ। **4.** A piece of cork used as a float by anglers; বড়শীর ফাতনাস্বরূপ ব্যবহৃত কাকের টুকরা। **5.** (*Bot.*) The inner division of the bark in higher plants; (উদ্ভিদ্-বিদ্যা) উচ্চশ্রেণীর বৃক্ষাদির অন্তর্বল্কল। ***Adj.*** Made of cork: as, a *cork* jacket; কাকের তৈয়ারী। ***Verb t.*** **1.** To provide or fit with a cork or float; কাক বা ফাতনা লাগান। **2.** To stop with, or as with, a cork; কাকদিয়া বন্ধ করা, ছিপি দ্বারা বন্ধ করা, কাক আঁটা। **3.** To blacken with a burnt cork; পোড়া কাক দ্বারা কাল করা। **Cork-jacket**—সাঁতার দিবার উপযোগী কাকের তৈয়ারী কুর্ত্তিবিশেষ। **Cork-screw**—বোতলের কাক খুলিবার পেঁচ। **Cork-screw-curl**—কাক খুলিবার পেঁচের মত ফুলের গোছা। **Cork-tree**—কাক-গাছ (যাঃ)। **Cork-wood**—নানাপ্রকার লঘু এবং ছিদ্রবহুল কাষ্ঠ।

cŏrk′-āge, *n.* **1.** Corking or uncorking of bottle; বোতলের কাক লাগান বা খুলন। **2.** A charge for drawing the cork and taking care of bottles of wine bought elsewhere by a guest; কাক খোলার জন্য এবং অন্যস্থানে ক্রীত মদ্যাদি সরাইয়ে পান করার দরুণ, সরাইওয়ালাকে যে অর্থ দিতে হয়।

cŏrk′-ed (-kŏrkt), *adj.* **1.** Stopped with cork; (*of wine*) having the taste of a cork; কাক-আঁটা; (মদ্য-সম্বন্ধে) কাকের আস্বাদ বিশিষ্ট। **2.** Blackend with a burnt cork; পোড়া কাক দ্বারা কাল রঙ্ প্রাপ্ত।

cŏrk′-êr, *n.* **1.** (*Slang*) A conclusive statement or fact; (ইতর ভাষায়) পাকা কথা, শেষ কথা। **2.** A notable lie; মস্ত মিথ্যা কথা।

cŏrk′-ȳ, *adj.* **1.** Like cork; কাকের মত। **2.** (*Fig.*) Light; lively; skittish; as, *corky* humour; (লক্ষণায়) লঘু; সতেজ; চটুপটে।

cŏrm, *n.* (*Bot.*) A bulb-like subterraneous stem; a solid bulb; (উদ্ভিদ্-বিদ্যা) নিরেট কন্দ (সাঃ পঃ); দৃঢ়কন্দ (ঐ), বজ্রকন্দ (ঐ), গেণ্ডু (ঐ)।

cŏr-mō′-rănt, *n.* **1.** A large voracious sea-bird; বৃহৎকায় এবং অতি-ভোজী সামুদ্রিক পক্ষি বিশেষ, সমুদ্র-কাক (আঃ বঃ)। **2.** A greedy or voracious person; উদরসর্ব্বস্ব বা অতিলোভী ব্যক্তি, মহাশন।

cŏrn, *n.* **1.** A small seed as of pepper etc., esp. a seed of cereal plants, as wheat, rye, etc.; শস্য। **2.** (*Collectively*) The seeds of cereal plants; (*U. S.*) maize; ধান্য যবাদি শস্য; (মার্কিণ যুক্তরাজ্যে) ভুট্টা। **3.** (*Collectively*) Cereal plants growing or while still containing the grain; ক্ষেত্রস্থিত শস্য। **4.** A small particle as of sand or salt, etc.; as, a *corn* of sugar-candy; ধূলি, লবণ প্রভৃতির কণা। **Corn-chandler**—খুচরা শস্য বিক্রেতা। **Corn-cob**—জনারের বীজ-যষ্টি। **Corn-cob-pipe**—জনারের বীজযষ্টি দ্বারা নির্ম্মিত ধূমপানের নল। **Corn-crake**—এক প্রকার পক্ষী। **Corn-exchange**—শস্য ব্যবসায়ের স্থান। **Corn-factor**—

পাইকারী শস্যবিক্রেতা। **Corn-field**—শস্য-ক্ষেত্র। **Corn-flag** — বৃক্ষবিশেষ। **Corn-flour**—ময়দা, তণ্ডুল চূর্ণ, ভুট্টা-চূর্ণ প্রভৃতি। **Corn-flower** — শস্যক্ষেত্রে জাত নানাপ্রকার গাছের নাম। **Corn-fly, -moth** — শস্য নাশকারী কীট-বিশেষ। **Corn-in-Egypt**—প্রচুর খাদ্যদ্রব্য সম্ভার (Gen. xiii)। **Corn-land**—শস্যোৎপাদনের উপযোগীভূমি। **Corn-laws**—শস্যব্যবসায়নিয়ামকবিধিসমূহ। [বিশেষতঃ ১৮৪৬ খৃঃ অব্দ পর্য্যন্ত ইংলণ্ডে যে শস্য ব্যবসায় নিয়ামক বিধিসমূহ প্রচলিত ছিল।] **Corn-mill**—শস্য চূর্ণ করিবার কল, জাঁতা। **Corn-rent** — মুদ্রার পরিবর্ত্তে শস্যদ্বারা প্রদত্ত হ্রাস-বৃদ্ধিশীল কর। **Corn-stalks** — অষ্ট্রেলিয়া ও মার্কিণ যুক্তরাজ্যের ঔপনিবেশিকগণের সন্তান।

Indian corn.

cŏrn, *v. t.* To preserve with salt; to sprinkle with salt; লবণ দ্বারা তাজা রাখা; কোন কিছুর উপর লবণ ছিটাইয়া দেওয়া।

cŏrn, *n.* A hard horny excrescence on a toe or foot; পায়ের কড়া, কড়া, কিণ। **To tread on one's corns** — To wound his susceptibilities; কাহারও মনে আঘাত দেওয়া।

cŏrn'-brăsh, *n.* (*Geol.*) A coarse calcareous sand-stone; (ভূ-তত্ত্ব) এক প্রকার চূর্ণকময় বেলে পাথর।

cŏr'-nē-ă, *n.* A horny transparent membrane forming the first part of eye-ball through which light passes; চক্ষুর সম্মুখভাগস্থ স্বচ্ছাবরণ, শ্বেতভাগ (আঃ বঃ), শার্ঙ্গত্বক (হঃ চঃ), স্বচ্ছপটল (সাঃ পঃ), শুক্ল-মণ্ডল (মঃ ইঃ)।

cŏr'-nĕl, *n.* English name for the botanical genus, Cornus; একজাতীয় বৃক্ষ।

cŏr-nĕl'-ĭăn, *n.* Dull red or reddish white chalcedony; মৃদু রক্তিম বা রক্তাভধবল সীসমণি।

cŏr'-nē-ous (-ŭs), *adj.* Horny; hornlike; শৃঙ্গময়, শার্ঙ্গ; শৃঙ্গবৎ।

cŏr'-nĕr, *n., v. t.* & *i.* **1.** The point or place where two converging sides or edges meet; কোণ, অস্র। **2.** A salient or projecting angle, esp., where two streets meet; বহির্বিলম্বিত কোণ, বিশেষতঃ দুইটী রাজপথের সংযোগস্থান। **3.** An outer or inner angle of a building etc.; প্রাসাদাদির বহির্বিলম্বিত বা আভ্যন্তর কোণ। **4.** A secret or retired place; as, done in a *corner*; নির্জ্জন স্থান, নিভৃত প্রদেশ, নিরিবিলি জায়গা, আড়াল, আবডাল। **5.** A region; a quarter; অঞ্চল, প্রদেশ; দিক্‌। **6.** (*Comm.*) The state of things produced by persons who buy up the whole of any stock which compels those who need such stock to buy of them at their own price; "The cotton *corner* in Liverpool has collapsed;" (বাণিজ্য) কেহ কোন জিনিষ সমস্ত পরিমাণ ক্রয় করত ক্রেতৃগণকে তাহার ইচ্ছামত দরে ঐ জিনিষ ক্রয় করিতে বাধ্য করিলে যে অবস্থা হয়। ***Verb t.*** **1.** To provide with corners; to put or set in a corner; কোণবিশিষ্ট করা; কোণে রাখা বা স্থাপন করা। **2.** To drive into a corner, (esp. *fig.*); কোণ ঠাসা করা। **3.** To get command of a stock, so as to be able to put one's own price on it; as, to *corner* petroleum; কোন জিনিষ সম্পূর্ণরূপে নিজের আয়ত্তাধীন করিয়া স্বেচ্ছানুরূপ দরে বিক্রয় করিতে সমর্থ হওয়া। ***Verb i.*** To form a corner in a stock; স্বেচ্ছানুরূপ দরে বিক্রয় করার উদ্দেশ্যে কোন জিনিষ সমস্ত ক্রয় করিয়া ফেলা। **Corner-chisel** — কোণদেশ কর্ত্তনের উপযোগী বাটালি বিশেষ। **Corner-punch** — কোণ চাঁচিবার ছেনি। **Corner-stone**—A stone forming a part of a corner or angle in a wall, esp. such a stone lying at the foundation of a principal angle; প্রাচীর-কোণের অংশস্বরূপ প্রস্তরখণ্ড, বিশেষতঃ প্রধান কোণের ভিত্তিদেশে স্থিত উক্তরূপ প্রস্তর-খণ্ড, আর-প্রস্তর (মঃ ইঃ)। (*Fig.*) Indispensable part; basis; (লক্ষণায়) অপরিহার্য্য অংশ; ভিত্তি। **To cut off a corner**—To make a short cut to avoid a corner; মোড় ফিরিয়া না ঘুরিতে হয়, তজ্জন্য সোজা পথে যাওয়া। **To drive in a corner**—To place in a position of great difficulty and embarrassment; to drive from all subterfuges and excuses; মহা মুস্কিলে ফেলা; কোণঠাসা করা। **To put in the corner**—To put a child in the corner as a punishment; শাস্তিস্বরূপ বালককে গৃহকোণে আবদ্ধ রাখা। **To turn the corner**—To pass round a corner into another road, street, etc.; মোড় ফিরা। (*Fig.*) To pass a critical point (in illness, etc.); (লক্ষণায়) (পীড়া প্রভৃতির) সঙ্কটাপন্ন অবস্থা অতিক্রম করা।

cŏr'-nĕt, *n.* (Also CORNET-A-PISTONS) **1.** A brass or silver wind-instrument capable of producing the notes of the chromatic scale; বাদ্যযন্ত্র বিশেষ, কর্ণেট

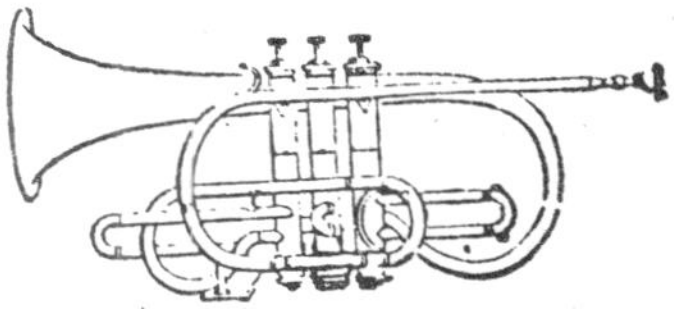

Cornet-a-pistons.

কোহল (আঃ বঃ)। **2.** Conically rolled piece of paper for groceries, etc.; মুদি, পসারী, প্রভৃতির দোকানের মোচাকার ঠোঙ্গা। **-ist,** *n.* A cornet player; উক্ত বাদ্যযন্ত্র বাদক।

cŏr'-nĕt, *n.* **1.** White head-dress of a sister of charity; দরিদ্রের ভগিনীগণের শ্বেতবর্ণ মস্তকাবরণ।

2. (*Formerly*) The officer who carried the colours in a troop of horse, (corresponding to the *ensign* in infantry) ; (পূর্ব্বে) অশ্বারোহিসৈন্যদলের পতাকাবাহী, বৈজয়ন্তিক (আঃ বঃ)। **—cy,** *n.* Commission or rank of a cornet ; উক্ত সৈনিক কর্ম্মচারীর পদ বা পদবী।

cŏr′-nice (-nĭs), *n.* 1. (*Arch.*) The moulding which projects from the top of a wall, column, or entablature ; আলিসা, প্রাকারশেখর (মঃ ইঃ), প্রস্তারাগ্র (রাঃ রাঃ), কার্ণিস। 2. Ornamental moulding round the wall of a room just below the ceiling ; ছাদের আভ্যন্তর পৃষ্ঠের অব্যবহিত নিম্নবর্ত্তী কক্ষ-প্রাচীরের চতুর্দ্দিকস্থ শোভাজনক স্থাপত্য-ভূষা। 3. Over-hanging mass of hardened snow at the edge of a precipice ; খাড়া পাহাড়ের কিনারা হইতে ঝুলানো কঠিন বরফরাশি।

cŏr-nif′-êr-ous (-ŭs), *adj.* (*Geol.*) Producing or containing hornstone ; অগ্নিপ্রস্তরকল্প প্রস্তরোৎপাদী, উক্ত প্রকার প্রস্তরপূর্ণ।

cŏr′-nish, *adj.* Of Cornwall ; কর্ণোয়াল নামক স্থান-সম্বন্ধীয়।

cŏr-nö′-pē-ăn, *n.* Same as CORNET.

cŏrn′-stōne, *n.* A motled kind of limestone found in the old red sandstone formation ; নানা-বর্ণের ফুট্‌কুট্ দাগ বিশিষ্ট চুণাপাথর।

cŏr-nū-cō′-pĭ-ă, *n.* 1. The representation of a horn filled with fruit, flowers, and grain ; an overflowing supply ; ফল, পুষ্প এবং শস্য পরিপূর্ণ শৃঙ্গের প্রতিরূপ বিশেষ, শ্রীপদ্ম (মঃ ইঃ) ; অতিপ্রভূততম দ্রব্য সম্ভার। 2. An ornamental vessel shaped like this ; কারুকার্য্য-শোভিত শৃঙ্গাকার পাত্র বিশেষ। **—an,** *adj.*

cŏr-nūt′-ĕd, *adj.* Having horns ; horn-shaped ; সশৃঙ্গ, শৃঙ্গবিশিষ্ট ; শৃঙ্গাকার।

cŏrn′-ȳ, *adj.* 1. Of or relating to corn ; শস্য সম্বন্ধীয়। 2. Abounding in corn ; শস্যবহুল, শস্যপূর্ণ।

cŏrn′-ȳ, *adj.* Relating to, or having, corns on the feet ; পায়ের কড়া সম্বন্ধীয়, কড়াযুক্ত।

cŏr-ŏl′-lă, *n.* (*Bot.*) The whorl of leaves forming the inner covering of a flower ; (উদ্ভিদ্-বিদ্যা) পুষ্পের অন্তরস্থ আবরণ-গঠনকারী পত্রাবর্ত্ত, অন্তর্বাস (সাঃ পঃ), স্রক (ঐ), অন্তরাবরণ (ঐ), মুকুট (ঐ), গর্ভদল (আঃ বঃ)। **—ceous,** *adj.* **—lene,** *adj.* Resembling a corolla ; মুকুটবৎ (সাঃ পঃ)। **Corollene whorl**—স্রগাবর্ত্ত (সাঃ পঃ)।

cŏr′-ŏl-lă-rȳ, *n.* 1. A deduction or inference from a proposition already demonstrated ; প্রমাণিত প্রতিজ্ঞা হইতে যে অনুমান করা হয়, অনুমান (প্রঃ বাঃ), ফলিত (হিঃ কোঃ), উপসিদ্ধান্ত (ঐ), অপবাহ (মঃ ইঃ)। 2. A natural consequence ; a result ; স্বাভাবিক পরিণাম ; ফল।

cŏ-rō′-nă, *n.* 1. A halo or luminous circle round the sun, moon, etc. ; an anthelion ; চন্দ্র বা সূর্য্যের চারিদিকের বিচিত্রবর্ণবলয় (যোঃ), ছটা-মুকুট ; সূর্য্যের বিপরীত দিগ্‌বর্ত্তী জ্যোতির্মণ্ডল, প্রতিসূর্য্য। 2. A luminous appearance observed during total eclipses of the sun ; সূর্য্যের পূর্ণ গ্রহণের কালে দৃষ্ট জ্যোতির্ম্ময় দৃশ্য। 3. A circular chandelier suspended from the roof of a church ; গির্জ্জার ছাদ হইতে ঝুলানো গোলাকার ঝাড়। 4. (*Anat.*) A crown-shaped part of the body ; (শারীরসংস্থানবিদ্যা) মুকুটাকার দেহাংশ ; (দন্ত, নরকপাল প্রভৃতির শিখরদেশ)। 5. (*Arch.*) The principal member of a cornice with a broad projecting face ; (স্থপতি-বিজ্ঞান) কপোতবন্ধ (রাঃ রাঃ), আলিসা। 6. (*Bot.*) An appendage on the top of a seed or on the inner side of a corolla ; (উদ্ভিদ্ বিদ্যা) পুষ্পের অন্তর্বাসের অভ্যন্তর ভাগের অথবা বীজের উপরের উপাঙ্গ বিশেষ, কিরীট (সাঃ পঃ), নির্য্যূহ (ঐ)।

cŏr′-ŏ-năch, *n.* A dirge, a funeral lamentation among the Highlanders and the Irish ; শ্মশান-গীতি, হাইলেণ্ড্‌ ও আয়র্লণ্ডের অধিবাসিগণের শ্মশানসঙ্গীত।

cŏr′-ŏ-năl, *n.* 1. A crown or coronet ; রাজমুকুট, কিরীট, সম্ভ্রান্ত পুরুষদিগের মুকুট। 2. A garland ; মাল্য, হার, মালিকা।

cŏr′-ŏ-năl, *adj.* 1. Of or relating to the crown of the head ; of, or pertaining to, a corona ; ছটা-মুকুট সম্পর্কীয়, দন্ত, নরকপাল প্রভৃতির শিখর দেশ-সম্বন্ধীয় ; কপোতবন্ধ-সম্বন্ধীয়, পুষ্পের কিরীট-সম্বন্ধীয়। 2. (*Anat.*) Lying in the direction of coronal suture ; (শারীর-সংস্থানবিদ্যা) নরকপালের সেবনী-সন্ধির দিকে অবস্থিত। **Coronal bone**—ললাটাস্থি। **Coronal suture**—সেলাইয়ের জোড়ামুখের মত নরকপালের সন্ধি বিশেষ, নরকপালের সেবনী-সন্ধি (হঃ চঃ)।

cŏr′-ŏ-nāte, —nāt-ĕd, *adj.* (*Bot* & *Zool.*) Having a corona or a crown-shaped part ; (উদ্ভিদ্-বিদ্যা ও প্রাণি-তত্ত্ব) মুকুটাকার অংশবিশিষ্ট।

cŏr-ŏ-nā′-tion, *n.* The act or ceremony of crowning a sovereign or his consort ; অভিষেক, রাজ্যাভিষেক। **Coronation oath**—অভিষেক কালে রাজার শপথ।

cŏr′-ŏ-nêr, *n.* An officer who holds a court of enquiry in a case of sudden death ; (originally) an officer charged with maintaining the rights of the private property of the crown ; কোন ব্যক্তির অপমৃত্যু ঘটিলে যে কর্ম্মচারী মৃত্যুর কারণাদি সম্বন্ধে অনুসন্ধান করেন, শবপরীক্ষক কর্ম্মচারী ; (পূর্ব্বে) যে কর্ম্মচারী রাজার নিজস্ব সম্পত্তি তত্ত্বাবধান করিতেন। **—ship,** *n.* **Coroner's inquest**—করোনারের আদালতে অপমৃত্যুর কারণ সম্বন্ধে অনুসন্ধান।

cŏr′-ŏ-nĕt, *n.* **1.** An inferior crown worn by princes and noblemen; রাজপুত্র বা সম্ভ্রান্ত পুরুষদিগের মুকুট। **2.** A decorative part of a woman's head-dress; স্ত্রীলোকের শোভাসাধক মস্তকাবরণ বিশেষ। **3.** A garland; মাল্য, হার, মালিকা। **4.** The lowest part of a horse's pastern immediately above the coffin; অশ্বখুরের পশ্চাদ্‌ভাগের অব্যবহিত উপরের অংশ। **—ed,** *adj.* Wearing a coronet; belonging to the peerage; সম্ভ্রান্ত লোকের মুকুট পরিহিত; সম্ভ্রান্ত সম্প্রদায়ভুক্ত।

1. Coronet of Prince of Wales. 2. Do. of Princes and Princesses and younger children of the Queen. 3. Do. of a Duke. 4. Do. of a Marquis. 5. Do. of an Earl. 6. Do. of a Viscount. 7. Do. of a Baron.

cŏr′-ŏ-noid (-noyd), *adj.* Hooked or curved like the beak of a crow; as, the *coronoid* process of the lower jaw; কাকচঞ্চুবৎ।

cŏ-rö′-zŏ, *n.* A tree of South America, allied to the Palms; দক্ষিণ আমেরিকার তাল্ জাতীয় বৃক্ষ বিশেষ। **Corozo nut**—উক্ত বৃক্ষের বীজ, — উহা হইতে উদ্ভিজ্জ গজদন্ত নির্ম্মিত হয়।

cŏr′-pŏ-ră, *n. Pl.* of CORPUS which see. **Corpora geniculata**—(*Sing. Corpus geniculatum*) উভয় দর্শন-স্নায়ুপথের প্রান্তের পশ্চাদ্‌বর্ত্তী অর্দ্ধবুদাকার মস্তিষ্কাংশ। **Corpora quadrigemina** — মস্তিষ্কের উপরিভাগস্থিত অর্ব্বুদাকার চারিটি উন্নতাংশ। **Corpora striata**—(Sing. *Corpus striatum* which see).

cŏr′-pŏ-răl, *adj.* **1.** Of, or relating to, the body; দৈহিক, শারীর, কায়িক, শারীরিক। **2.** Personal; "With his *corporal* liberty;" ব্যক্তিগত। **—ly,** *adv.* **Corporal oath**—(তাবা, তুলসী, ক্রুশ প্রভৃতি) পবিত্র বস্তু স্পর্শ করিয়া যে প্রতিজ্ঞা করা হয়। **Corporal punishment**—শারীরিক দণ্ড (যথা, বেত্রাঘাত)।

cŏr′-pŏ-răl, *n.* **1.** The lowest officer of a company of infantry; পদাতিক সৈন্যদলের সর্ব্বনিম্নকর্ম্মচারী, নায়ক। **2.** (*Navy*) A petty officer who attends to police matters under the master-at-arms; (নৌ-বল) নৌবিভাগের নিম্নতর শান্তিরক্ষক কর্ম্মচারী।

cŏr′-pŏ-răl, —răs, *n.* (*Eccles.*) A communion cloth; (যাজকীয় শাস্ত্র) খৃষ্টের শেষ ভোজন নামক স্মৃতি-উৎসবকালে ব্যবহৃত বস্ত্র বিশেষ।

cŏr-pŏ răl′-i-tў, *n.* **1.** Material or corporal existence; materiality; ভৌতিক সত্তা, দৈহিক সত্তা; ভৌতিকতা। **2.** Body; দেহ। **3.** Bodily matters, want etc.; দৈহিক বিষয়, দৈহিক অভাব, প্রভৃতি।

cŏr′-pŏ-rāte, *adj.* **1.** United in a body community or corporation; as, a *corporate* town (=town having municipal rights); সংঘ-বদ্ধ, মিলিত, একত্রীভূত। **2.** Collectively one; সমবেতভাবে এক। **3.** Of or relating to, a body politic; রাষ্ট্র-সংক্রান্ত, রাষ্ট্র-সম্বন্ধীয়। **—ly,** *adv.*

cŏr-pŏ-rā′-tion, *n.* **1.** A body of persons, esp. a body corporate formed and authorized by law to act as a single person; আইন-দ্বারা গঠিত, এবং ব্যক্তি স্বরূপ কার্য্য করিবার অধিকার প্রাপ্ত সভা বা সমাজ, সমবায় (আঃ বঃ)। **2.** (*Colloq.*) Abdomen, esp. when protuberant; (চলিত ভাষায়) তলপেট, বিশেষতঃ যখন স্ফীত বা উদ্গত। **Corporation aggregate**—বহু লোকদ্বারা গঠিত সংঘ। **Corporation sole**—এক ব্যক্তিদ্বারা গঠিত সংঘ, (যথা রাজা, খৃষ্টীয় ধর্ম্মাধ্যক্ষ)। **Municipal corporation** — পার্লেমেণ্টে সভ্য প্রেরণে ক্ষমতাপ্রাপ্ত নগর, ও তদ্‌ব্যতিরিক্ত অন্য নগর বা মহানগরীর নাগরিক কর্ত্তৃপক্ষ।

cŏr′-pŏ-rā-tive (-tîv), *adv.* Pertaining to, or consisting of, a corporation; সংঘবিষয়ক, সংঘাত্মক।

cŏr′-pŏ-rā-tor (-tēr), *n.* Member of a corporatian; সংঘের সভ্য।

cŏr-pŏ′-rē-ăl, *adj.* **1.** Bodily; material; (opposed to *spiritual* or *immaterial*); শারীরিক, দৈহিক, কায়িক, আঙ্গিক, শারীর; ভৌতিক, মূর্ত্ত, স্থূল, মূর্ত্তিধারী। **2.** (*Law*) Tangible; জড়পদার্থাত্মক। **—al′-i-tў,** *n.* State or quality of being corporeal; দেহিভাব, দেহিত্ব। **—ly,** *adv.*

cŏr-pŏ-rē′-i-tў, *n.* **1.** The quality or state of having or being a material body; দেহিত্ব, আঙ্গিতা, শরীরতা, সদেহতা, দেহিভাব। **2.** Physical personality; জড়দেহ।

cŏr′-pŏ-sănt, *n.* A ball of electric light often observed in dark tempestuous night about a ship's rigging,—also called St. Elmo's fire; ঝটিকাময় অন্ধকার রাত্রিতে মাস্তুলাগ্রে (সচরাচর) দৃষ্ট বৈদ্যুতিক আলোকপিণ্ড।

corps (cŏr), *n.* (*pl.* same, pron. körz) One of the largest divisions of an army in the field; a body of troops assigned to a special purpose; রণক্ষেত্রস্থিত সৈন্যদলের বৃহত্তম বিভাগ বিশেষ, সৈন্যগুল্ম (মঃ ইঃ), বাহিনী; কোন বিশেষ উদ্দেশ্যে নিযুক্ত সৈন্যদল। **Corps d'armee**—বৃহৎ সৈন্যদল। **Corps de ballet** — হাবভাবপূর্ব্বক নৃত্যকারী নর্ত্তকদল।

corpse (cŏrps), *n.* The dead body of a human being; শব, কুণপ, মৃতদেহ, মড়া (*colloq.*), লাস (*colloq.*)। **Corpse-bearer**—শববাহক। **Corpse-candle**—গির্জ্জার প্রাঙ্গণের কবরের উপর যে চঞ্চল আলোকশিখা দৃষ্ট হয়—এইরূপ আলোক মৃত্যুসূচনাকারী বলিয়া গণ্য হয়, সমাধি-দীপ।

cŏr'-pū-lĕnt, *adj.* Large or bulky of body; fat; স্থূলকায়; স্থূল, পীন, মেদস্বী। **—lence, —len-cy,** *ns.*

cŏr'-pŭs, *n.* **1.** A body of general collection of writings; রচনা-সংগ্রহ। **2.** (*Physiol.*) Structure of special character in the animal body; (শারীর-বিজ্ঞান) জন্তুদেহের বিশেষভাবের অঙ্গবিন্যাস। **Corpus-callosum**—বৃহদ্ মস্তিকের মূলস্থিত শুভ্রবর্ণ সুদৃঢ় পদার্থ—এতদ্বারা মস্তিস্কের অর্দ্ধবৃত্তদ্বয় সংযুক্ত রহিয়াছে। **Corpus christi**—(রোমান ক্যাথলিক ধর্ম্মসমাজ) ত্রিনিতির রবিবারের বিচারের পরবর্ত্তী বৃহস্পতিবারে অনুষ্ঠিত পর্ব্ববিশেষ। **Corpus delicti**—আইনভঙ্গের কারণ সমূহ **Corpus juris**—[*L*] A body of law; বিধি-সমূহ। **Corpus-luteum**—ডিম্ব অর্থাৎ স্ত্রীবীর্য্য নির্গত হইলে ডিম্বাশয়ে যে চিহ্ন থাকে। **Corpus-striatum**—পেয়ারা ফলের আকার মস্তিষ্কাংশ বিশেষ।

cŏr'-pus-cle (-pŭs-l), **cŏr'-pŭs-cūle,** *ns.* **1.** Minute solid microscopic bodies found in the blood; রক্তাণু, অণুকোষ (হঃ চঃ), কণিকা (সাঃ পঃ), অণুদেহ (হিঃ কোঃ)। **2.** Atom, (esp. of electricity); পরমাণু, বিশেষতঃ তাড়িত পরমাণু।

cŏr-pŭs'-cū-lar (-lêr), *adj.* Pertaining to corpuscles or particles; রক্তাণু-সম্পর্কীয়, কণিকা-সম্বন্ধীয়। **Corpuscular theory of light**—যে মতবাদানুসারে আলোক জ্যোতির্ম্ময় পদার্থ সকল হইতে নিঃসৃত সূক্ষ্ম-কণিকা সমূহের সমষ্টি বলিয়া অনুমিত হয়।

cŏr-râl', *n.* & *v. t.* **1.** A pen or inclosure for animals (in U. S. & Span. Amer.); খোঁয়াড়। **2.** An inclosure formed of wagons by emigrants; ঔপনিবেশিকগণ-রচিত শকটবেষ্টিত স্থান। **3.** A strong inclosure for capturing wild elephant, etc.; বন্যহস্তী ধৃত করণার্থ সুদৃঢ় বেষ্টিত স্থল, খেদা। ***Verb t.*** To form a corral by means of, as wagons; to confine in a corral; শকট প্রভৃতি দ্বারা বেষ্টিত করা; খোঁয়াড়ে বদ্ধ করা, খেদায় আটক করা।

cŏr-rĕct', *v. t.* **1.** To make or set right; to mark the errors of, as a proof-sheet, etc., for amendment; শুদ্ধ করা, নির্দ্দোষ করা, নির্ভুল করা; সংশোধন করা। **2.** To chastise; to cure as a person of an error or fault; শাস্তি দেওয়া; শোধরান, দোষ সংশোধন করা। **3.** To counteract or neutralize, as the hurtful qualities of a thing; "The heat *corrects* the folly of the head;" নিরাকরণ করা; প্রতিক্রিয়া দ্বারা ব্যর্থ করা। **4.** (*Phys.*) To adjust so as to bring to some standard condition; as, to *correct* a reading of the barometer; (পদার্থ-বিজ্ঞান) কোন প্রকার নিয়মবদ্ধ অবস্থায় আনয়নের জন্য ঠিক করা।

cŏr-rĕct', *adj.* **1.** In accordance with a just or conventional standard; as, a *correct* style; proper; right; as, *correct* manners; বিশুদ্ধ, সাধু; সঙ্গত, যথাযথ; সমীচীন। **2.** True; accurate; exact; সত্য, ভ্রমশূন্য; নির্ভুল, ঠিক; যথার্থ। **—ly,** *adv.* **—ness,** *n.* The state of being correct; শুদ্ধি, শুদ্ধতা, যাথার্থ্য। **Corrected knowledge**—প্রমা (হিঃ কোঃ)।

cŏr-rĕc'-tion, *n.* **1.** Act of correcting; amendment; শুদ্ধি, শোধন, শুদ্ধকরণ; সংশোধন। **2.** Punishment; as, a house of *correction*; শাস্তি, সাজা। **3.** An emendation; as, the *correction* on a proof; সংশোধন, কাটাকুটি (*Colloq.*)। **4.** Counteraction of what is hurtful or inconvenient; নিরাকরণ, প্রতিসমাধান (মঃ ইঃ)। **5.** (*Phys.*) A quantity applied by way of correcting; (পদার্থ-বিজ্ঞান) সংশোধনের জন্য প্রযুক্ত সংখ্যা। **—al,** *adj.* **A house of correction**—সংশোধনাগার। **Under correction**—Subject to correction; as, I spoke *under correction* (*i. e.* I may be wrong); ভ্রম হইতে পারে স্বীকার করিয়া।

cŏr-rĕc'-tive (-tĭv), *adj.* & *n.* Having the power to correct or counteract what is wrong or harmful; tending to rectify; সংশোধনক্ষম, শোধক; ভ্রমনিবারক। ***Noun.*** That which corrects or tends to correct; সংশোধক।

cŏr-rĕc'-tor (-têr), *n.* **1** One who or that which corrects; a critic; সংশোধক; সমালোচক। **2.** One who inflicts correction or punishment; শাস্তিদাতা, শাস্তা। **A corrector of the press** — আদর্শ মুদ্রাঙ্কন-পত্র-সংশোধক।

cŏr'-rē-lāte, *n.* One of the two persons or things standing in a reciprocal relation, (as father and son); পরস্পরের সহিত সম্বন্ধযুক্ত ব্যক্তিদ্বয়ের অন্যতর।

cŏr-rē-lāte', *v. t.* & *i.* To place in mutual or reciprocal relation; as, to *correlate* natural phenomena; পরস্পরের সহিত সম্বন্ধবিশিষ্ট করা। ***Verb i.*** To have a reciprocal relation; (followed by ***with*** or *to*); পরস্পরের সহিত সম্বন্ধ-থাকা।

cŏr-rĕl′-ā-tive (-tĭv), *adj.* & *n.* **1.** Having a reciprocal relation; (followed by *with, to*); পরস্পরের সহিত সম্বন্ধবিশিষ্ট, অন্যোন্যসম্বন্ধ (মঃ ইঃ) অন্যোন্যাপেক্ষ, পরস্পরাপেক্ষ, অনুবন্ধী। **2.** Analogous; সদৃশ। **3.** (*Gram.*) Corresponding and regularly used together; as, *either or* are *correlative* words; পরস্পরের অনুসারী এবং নিত্য একত্র ব্যবহৃত। ***Noun.*** **1.** A correlate; পরস্পরের সহিত সম্বন্ধ বিশিষ্ট ব্যক্তিদ্বয়ের অন্যতর। **2.** (*Gram*) Each of two correlative words; (ব্যাকরণ) অন্যোন্যানুগামী শব্দদ্বয়ের অন্যতর। **—re-la′-tion,** *n.* **1.** A mutual relation of two or more things; দুই বা ততোধিক বস্তুর অন্যোন্য-সম্বন্ধ, অনুবন্ধ (হিঃ কোঃ), প্রতিযোগ (ঐ), পরস্পর-সম্বন্ধ (আঃ বঃ)। **2.** State of being so related to each other that one cannot be altered without the other also undergoing change; সহ-পরিবর্তন-সম্বন্ধ। **Correlation of forces**—(পদার্থ-বিজ্ঞান) তাপ, আলোক, তাড়িত প্রভৃতি প্রাকৃতিক শক্তি বা বলনিচয়ের অন্যোন্য নির্দিষ্ট পরিমাণ সম্বন্ধ,—যাহার বলে একটীর তত্তুল্য পরিমাণ অপরটীতে পরিবর্তিত করিতে পারা যায়।

cŏr-rē-spŏnd′, *v. i.* **1.** To be analogous or in harmony; (followed by *with* or *to*); "Their habits *correspond* to their education;" to be similar, (with *to*) "An assembly that *corresponds* to our Parliament, etc.;" সঙ্গতিবিশিষ্ট হওয়া, সামঞ্জস্য থাকা, মিল থাকা; সদৃশ হওয়া, অনুরূপ হওয়া। **2.** To communicate by sending or receiving letters, (followed by *with*); পত্র-ব্যবহার করা। **—ingly,** *adv.*

cŏr-rē-spŏnd′-ence (-ĕns), *n.* **1.** Agreement; congruity; (followed by *with, to* or *between*); ঐক্য, সামঞ্জস্য; সমভাবিতা। **2.** Communication by means of letters; পত্রব্যবহার, পত্র-সংবাদ (আঃ বঃ), পত্রবিনিময় (মঃ ইঃ)। **3.** The letters interchanged between correspondents or contributed to a periodical; চিঠিপত্র, সংবাদপত্রাদিতে প্রেরিত পত্র বা প্রবন্ধ। **Doctrine of correspondences**—সুইডেনবর্গ প্রবর্তিত মত বিশেষ—যাহাতে প্রত্যেক ভৌতিক বস্তু কোন আধ্যাত্মিক সত্য বা ভাবের প্রতীক বা চিহ্ন বলিয়া গণ্য করা হয়।

cŏr-rē spŏnd′-ĕnt, *n.* & *adj.* **1.** One who holds intercourse by letters; পত্র-ব্যবহারকারী। **2.** One who is engaged to transmit regularly news to a newspaper; as, a war *correspondent*; পত্রপ্রেরক। **3.** (*Com.*) A person or firm having regular business relations with another of a remote place; (বাণিজ্য) যে ব্যক্তি বা বাণিজ্যশালার সহিত দূরস্থানবর্তী কোন ব্যক্তি বা বাণিজ্যশালার নিয়মিত ব্যবসায়গত সম্পর্ক রহিয়াছে। ***Adj.*** **1.** Congruous; suitable; সঙ্গতি বিশিষ্ট; উপযোগী। **2.** Corresponding, (followed by *with* or *to*); অনুসারী।

cŏr-rē-spŏnd′-ing, *adj.* **1.** Answering; অনুযায়ী। **2.** Carrying on correspondence; পত্র-ব্যবহারকারী।

cŏr′-ri-dŏr, *n.* (*Arch.*) A main passage in a large building, on which many rooms open; (স্থপতিবিজ্ঞান) দরদালান। **A corridor train** — একপ্রকার বাষ্পীয়-শকট,—যাহাতে আরোহিগণ অবতরণ না করিয়া এক গাড়ী হইতে অপর গাড়ীতে যাইতে পারে।

cŏr′-rie (-rĭ), *n.* A circular hollow on the side of a hill; পর্বত-গাত্রস্থ গোলাকৃতি গহ্বর।

cŏr-ri-gĕn′-dŭm, *n.* A fault or error to be corrected as in a book, etc.; শুদ্ধি-পত্র।

cŏr′-ri gi-ble, *adj.* **1.** Capable of being corrected; সংশোধনীয়, সংশোধিতব্য। **2.** Submissive to correction; docile; as, a *corrigible* boy; শাসনযোগ্য; বশ্য, বাধ্য, অনুগত।

cŏr-rī′-văl, *n.* A fellow rival; প্রতিদ্বন্দ্বী, প্রতিস্পর্দ্ধী (মঃ ইঃ)।

cŏr-rŏb′-ō-rănt, *adj.* & *n.* Giving strength, as a medicine; corroborating, as a fact; বলপ্রদ; সমর্থনকারী।

cŏr-rŏb′-ō-rāte, *v. t.* To confirm as a law, etc.; to make more certain, as a statement, etc., by evidence; দৃঢ় করা, প্রতিষ্ঠাপিত করা; সমর্থন করা, বলবৎ করা, পাকা করা, সুনিশ্চিত করা। **—ra-tive, —ra-to-ry,** *adjs.* **—ra-tor,** *n.*

cŏr-rŏb-ō-rā′-tion, *n.* Act of confirming by further evidence; that which corroborates; প্রতিষ্ঠাপন, সমর্থন, স্থিরীকরণ; যদ্দারা সমর্থন করা হয়।

cŏrŏb′-ō-ree (-rē), *n.* The native dance of the Australian aborigines; অষ্ট্রেলিয়ার আদিম অধিবাসিগণের নৃত্যবিশেষ।

cŏr-rōde, *v. t.* & *i.* To wear away or destroy by degrees, (said of rust, diseases or chemical agents); ক্ষয় করা, খাইয়া ফেলা। ***Verb i.*** To become corroded; ক্ষয় হওয়া, খাইয়া যাওয়া **—ro′-sion,** *n.*

cŏr-rō′-sive (-sĭv), *adj.* & *n.* Having the quality of eating away or destroying (*lit.* & *fig.*); (শব্দানুযায়ী এবং লক্ষণায়) ক্ষয়কর, মর্মান্তিক, অরুন্তুদ, দাহক। ***Noun.*** That which has the quality of corroding; ক্ষয়কারক বস্তু। **—ly,** *adv.* **—ness,** *n.* **Corrossive sublimate**—রসকর্পূর (ঠাকুর)।

cŏr′-rŭ-gāte, *v. t.* & *i.* **1.** To wrinkle; to contract into folds or furrows; (also *v. i.*); সমকুঞ্চিত করা; কুঞ্চিত করা। **2.** To mark with or bend into ridges; as, to *corrugate* plates of iron; ঢেউ

তোলা, তরঙ্গায়িত করা। **—ga′-tion,** *n.* **Corrugated iron**—ঢেউতোলা লোহার চাদর, সমকুঞ্চিত লৌহপট্ট।

cŏr′-rū-ga-tor (-tẹr), *n.* The small muscle situated on each side of the forehead which knits the brow ; ললাটের উভয় পার্শ্বস্থিত ক্ষুদ্র পেশী—ইহা দ্বারা ভ্রু কুঞ্চিত হয়।

cŏr-rŭpt′, *adj.* **1.** Putrid ; decomposed; পচা; গলিত, পূতিগন্ধ (মঃ ইঃ)। **2.** Depraved; wicked ; ভ্রষ্ট; পাপিষ্ঠ। **3.** Open to bribery ; venal ; "The chief judges were *corrupt* and cruel ;" উৎকোচগ্রাহী ; অর্থবশ। **4.** (Of language, text, etc.) Infected with errors or mistakes ; ভ্রমদুষ্ট, ভ্রান্তিবহুল। **—ly,** *adv.* **—ness,** *n.*

cŏr-rŭpt′, *v. t.* & *i.* **1.** To putrefy ; পচান্। **2.** (*Fig.*) To debase or pervert ; "Evil communications *corrupt* good manners ; (লক্ষণায়) বিকৃত করা, দূষিত করা, বিগড়াইয়া দেওয়া। **3.** To bribe ; ঘুষ দেওয়া। **4.** To introduce errors into (language) ; ভ্রমদুষ্ট করা। ***Verb i.*** **1.** To become put d ; পচা। **2.** To become vitiated ; দূষিত হওয়া। **—rup′-tive,** *adj.*

cŏr-rŭpt′-i-ble, *adj.* **1.** Susceptible of corruption ; perishable ; "They held that the World is *corruptible* ;" পচনশীল ; নশ্বর, ধ্বংসশীল। **2.** Capable of moral corruption ; সৎপথ হইতে ভ্রংশনীয়। **—bil′-i-ty,** *n.* **—bly,** *adv.*

cŏr-rŭp′-tion, *n.* **1.** Putrefaction ; পচন, পূতি (মঃ ইঃ)। **2.** Moral deterioration ; depravity ; নৈতিক অবনতি ; অন্তদুষ্টতা (মঃ ইঃ), ভ্রষ্টতা। **3.** Debasement of language ; অপভ্রংশ, অপশব্দ (মঃ ইঃ)। **4.** Bribery ; উৎকোচ, ঘুষ। (*Law*) **Corruption of blood**—(আইন) (পূর্ব্বে) রাজদ্রোহাদি গুরুতর অপরাধে উপযুক্ত ব্যক্তির পক্ষে সম্পত্তি ভোগ, হস্তান্তর বা উত্তরাধিকার সূত্রে প্রাপ্তির অসমর্থতা, অধিকার-লোপ (আঃ বঃ)।

cŏr′-săc, —săk, *n.* Tartar fox ; একপ্রকার খেঁকশিয়াল।

cŏr′-sāge, *n.* The waist or bodice of a woman's dress ; স্ত্রীলোকের পোষাকের কটি, স্ত্রীলোকের জামা।

cŏr′-sair (-sâr), *n.* **1.** A pirate ; জলদস্যু, সাগরডাকু। **2.** A privateering vessel such as those of Barbery coast ; বে-সরকারী যুদ্ধ জাহাজ।

corse (cŏrs), *n.* (*Archaic or poet.*) Corpse ; (অপ্রচলিত বা কবিতায়) মৃতদেহ।

cŏr′-sĕt, *n.* A tight-fitting article of dress, worn principally by woman, to give shape to and support the body ; স্ত্রীলোকের আঁটা জামা, চেলিকা (মঃ ইঃ), চোলী (ঐ), কঞ্চুলিকা (ঐ)। **—ed,** *adj.*

cŏrs′-lĕt, corse′- (cŏrs-), *n.* **1.** A cuirass or armour to cover the body ; উরস্ত্রাণ, উরশ্ছদ, বর্ম্ম, কবচ, সাঁজোয়া। **2.** A garment (usu. tight-fitting) covering the

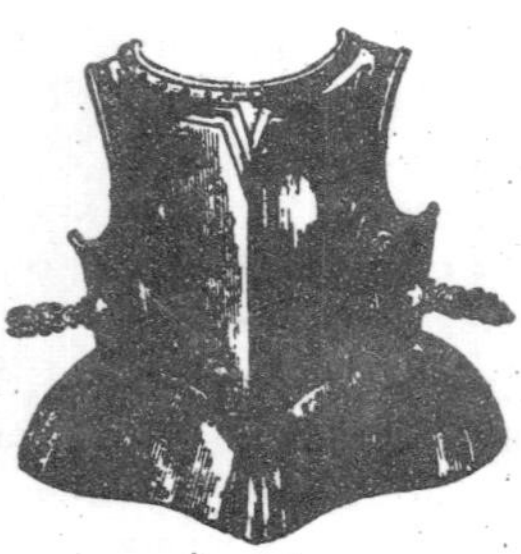

Corslet.

body as distinct from the limbs ; একপ্রকার (সাধারণতঃ আঁটা) হাতকাটা জামা। **3.** (*Zool.*) The thorax ; (প্রাণি-তত্ত্ব) গ্রীবা ও উদরের মধ্যবর্ত্তী শরীরের গহ্বর।

cortege, *n.* [*F.*] A train of attendants ; a procession ; অনুযাত্রিদল, অনুযায়িবর্গ ; শোভাযাত্রা।

cortes, *n. pl.* [*Sp.* & *Port.*] The two chambers constituting the legislative assembly of Spain and Portugal ; স্পেন এবং পর্টুগাল দেশের ব্যবস্থাপক সভা।

cŏr′-tĕx, *n.* (*pl.* -TIUS) **1.** Bark ; বল্কল। **2.** The outer part of an organ, as the kidney ; esp. the outer layer of gray matter of the cerebrum and the cerebellum ; কোন শারীরিক যন্ত্রের বাহ্যাবরণ, বিশেষতঃ বৃহদ্মস্তিষ্ক ও অনুমস্তিষ্কের ধূসরবর্ণ পদার্থের বাহ্যস্তর।

cŏr′-ti-căl, *adj.* (*Bot., Zool.*, etc.) Belonging to the outer part of a plant or animal ; (উদ্ভিদ্-বিদ্যা, প্রাণি-তত্ত্ব প্রভৃতি) বল্কল বা বাহ্যাবরণ সম্বন্ধীয়, বাল্কল।

cŏr′-ti-cāte, —cāt-ĕd, *adj.* Having or resembling bark ; বল্কলবিশিষ্ট, বল্কলসদৃশ।

cŏ-rŭn′-dŭm, *n.* The hardest known mineral except the diamond, generally of a greyish or greenish-brown tint, used for polishing steel and cutting gem ; হীরক ভিন্ন সর্ব্বাপেক্ষা কঠিনতম খনিজ পদার্থ—সাধারণতঃ ধূসর বা হরিদাভ কপিশবর্ণ, কুরুবিন্দ, কুরুন্দ।

cŏr′-ŭs-cāte, *v. i.* To glitter ; to sparkle ; (*lit.* & *fig.*); চক্‌মক্ করা ; ঝিক্‌মিক্ করা, ঝলমল করা, জ্যোতিঃস্ফুরণ করা। **—cant,** *adj.* **—ca′-tion,** *n.* **1.** Act of coruscating ; আলোকস্ফুরণ, ঝলক, চমক। **2.** A brilliant display of ; "He might have illuminated his times with the incessant *coruscation* of his genius ;" প্রতিভাচ্ছটা।

cŏr-vee (-vā), *n.* (Feudal law) Forced unpaid labour exacted by a feudal lord ; (সামন্ততন্ত্র সম্পর্কীয় বিধি) জমিভোগের জন্য প্রজাকে বিনা বেতনে জমিদারের যে কাজ করিয়া দিতে হয়।

côr-vette′ (-vĕt), *n.* (*Naut.*) A flush-decked full-rigged ship of under twenty guns ; (নৌ-বিদ্যা) একপ্রকার যুদ্ধ জাহাজ।

cŏr′-vīne, *adj.* Pertaining to the crow or raven ; কাক-সম্বন্ধীয়, বায়স-সম্পর্কীয়, দাঁড়কাক-সম্বন্ধীয়।

cŏr′ vŭs, *n.* A small constellation adjoining Virgo ; হস্তা (সাঃ পঃ) ।

cŏr′-ȳ-bănt, *n.* A priest of Cybele who celebrated the mysteries with wild dances ; সিবিলি দেবীর পুরোহিত—যিনি উদ্দাম নৃত্য সহকারে দেবীর নিগূঢ় পূজানুষ্ঠান করিতেন। **—ban′-tic, —ban′-tine,** *adjs.* **—ban′-tian,** *adj.*

cŏr′-ȳ-dŏn, *n.* A generic proper name for a rustic in pastoral poetry ; পল্লীগাথায় পল্লীবাসীর সাধারণ নাম।

cŏr′-ȳmb, *n.* (*Bot.*) Species of inflorescence ; a raceme or panicle in which the stalks of the lower flower are longer than those of the other ; (উদ্ভিদ্‌বিদ্যা) একপ্রকার পুষ্পোদ্গম ; উপকিরীট (সাঃ পঃ)। **Co rym′-bose,** *adj.*

Corypha elata—বাটুল (বেলঃ)।

cŏr-ȳ-phae′-ŭs (-phē-), *n.* 1. The leader of a chorus ; বৃন্দগায়ক দলের নেতা। 2. (*Fig.*) A headman ; (লক্ষণায়) নেতা, সর্দ্দার।

Corypha taliera—শ্রীতাল (বেলঃ)।

Corypha umbraculifera—তালী (বেলঃ)।

cō-rȳ′-ză, *n.* Nasal catarrh ; শিরঃ-শ্লেষ্মা।

cŏs, *n.* Lettuce introduced from the island of Cos (now Stanchio) ; কস্ দ্বীপ হইতে সমানীত কাজু বা সালাদ।

cŏs, *n.* Abbreviation of COSINE.

cosaque, *n.* [F.] A bon-bon forming a cracker ; একপ্রকার বন্ বন্ মিঠাই—যাহা পট্‌কার মত ফুটিয়া থাকে, পট্‌কা বন্-বন্।

cōse, *v. i.* To make oneself cosy ; সুখকর বা আরামদায়ক করা।

cō-seis′-măl (-sĭs-), *adj.* & *n.* Of or relating to a simultaneous shock of earth-quake waves ; ভূমিকম্প-তরঙ্গের প্রবাহের সমকালীন কম্পন সম্পর্কীয়। ***Noun.*** A line connecting the points of simultaneous shock from an earth-quake wave ; ভূমিকম্প তরঙ্গের সমকালীনকম্পন-বিন্দু-সংযোজক রেখা।

cŏsh′êr, *v. t.* To pamper ; to coddle up ; অতিশয় প্রশ্রয় দেওয়া ; অতিশয় আদর করিয়া নষ্ট করা।

cō-sig′-nă-tô-rȳ, *adj.* & *n.* Signing jointly ; সহ-স্বাক্ষরকারী ***Noun.*** One who signs, as a treaty, etc. jointly with others ; যে জন অন্য ব্যক্তির সহিত একযোগে সন্ধিপত্র প্রভৃতি স্বাক্ষর করে।

cō′-sīne, *n.* (*Trigon.*) The side of the complement of an arc or angle ; (abbr. *cos.*) ; (ত্রিকোণমিতি) কোটি-জ্যা (সাঃ পঃ)।

cŏs-mĕt′-ic, *Adj.* & *n.* Improving beauty, esp. of the skin ; সৌন্দর্য্যবর্দ্ধক, লাবণ্যার্দ্ধক, অঙ্গকান্তিবর্দ্ধক, দেহবর্ণোজ্জ্বলকারী, কান্তিদ (আঃ ব)। ***Noun.*** A preparation to improve the beauty of skin, hair or complexion ; অঙ্গলেপ, সোন্ধা, অঙ্গরাগ, অভ্যঞ্জন (সাঃ পঃ) বর্ণা (ঠাকুর)।

cŏs′-mic, *adj.* 1. Relating to the whole frame of the universe ; নিখিল-বিশ্ব-ব্যবস্থাসম্বন্ধীয়। 2. Of or pertaining to cosmos ; ব্রহ্মাণ্ড-সম্বন্ধীয়। 3. Orderly ; সুব্যবস্থিত। **—mi-cal,** *adj.* 1. Cosmic ; ব্রহ্মাণ্ডতত্ত্ব-সম্বন্ধীয়। 2. Rising or setting with the sun ; সূর্য্যোদয়ে উদীয়মান ও সূর্য্যাস্তে অস্তগামী। **Cosmic philosophy**—ব্রহ্মাণ্ড-সম্বন্ধীয় দর্শন।

cŏs′-mĭsm, *n.* The system of philosophy based on the doctrine of evolution ; জগত্তত্ত্বনির্ণায়ক শাস্ত্র। **—mist,** *n.*

cŏs-mŏg′-ō-nȳ, *n.* 1. The origin of the universe ; সৃষ্টিপ্রক্রিয়া, জগদুৎপত্তি (মঃ ইঃ)। 2. The doctrine of the origin of the universe ; জগদুদ্ভবতত্ত্ব (আঃ বঃ), জগদুৎপত্তিবাদ (হিঃ কোঃ), সৃষ্টিক্রম (ঐ)। **—mo-gon′-ic, —mo-gon′-i-cal,** *adjs.* **—nist,** *n.* An expounder of the origin of the universe ; জগদুৎপত্তি-ব্যাখ্যাতা, জগদুৎপত্তিবাদী।

cŏs-mŏg′-ră-phȳ, *n.* The description of the earth or of the universe ; the science of the constitution of the universe ; সংসারবৃত্তান্ত, বিশ্ববিবরণ, জগদ্বর্ণন, সৃষ্টিবর্ণন (হিঃ কোঃ) ; বিশ্বব্যবস্থা-বিজ্ঞান, সৃষ্টিবিচার। **—mo-graph′-ic, —mo-graph′-i-cal,** *adjs.* **—pher,** *n.*

cŏs-mŏl′-ō-ġȳ, *n.* The science of the universe ; ব্রহ্মাণ্ডতত্ত্ব (বিশ্বঃ)। **—mo-log′-i-cal,** *adj.* **—gist,** *n.*

cŏs-mō-plăs′-tic, *adj.* Forming the universe ; বিশ্বগঠনকারী।

cŏs-mō-pŏl′-i-tăn, *adj.* & *n.* 1. Belonging to all parts of the world ; সার্ব্বভৌমিক। 2. Free from national prejudices ; জাতিগত সংস্কার-বর্জ্জিত। 3. (*Natur. hist.*) Found in all or most parts, of the world ; (জন্তু-বিদ্যা) পৃথিবীর সর্ব্বাংশে বা অধিকাংশ স্থানে প্রাপ্ত। 4. Characteristic of a citizen of world ; বিশ্বনাগরিক-সুলভ। ***Noun.*** A cosmopolite ; বিশ্বনাগরিক, যে ব্যক্তি সকল দেশকেই স্বদেশ বলিয়া গণ্য করে, সর্ব্ব-মিত্র, (হিঃ কোঃ), জগন্মিত্র (ঐ) বিশ্বপুরবাসী। **—ism,** *n.* **—ize.** *v. t.* & *i.*

cŏs-mŏp′-ō-līte, *n.* & *adj.* 1. A citizen of the world ; বিশ্বনাগরিক। 2. A plant or animal found in all or most parts of the world ; যে জন্তু বা উদ্ভিদ্ পৃথিবীর সর্ব্ব স্থানে বা অধিকাংশ স্থলে দৃষ্ট হয়। ***Adj.*** Free from national prejudices ; জাতীয়সংস্কারবর্জ্জিত। **—litism,** *n.*

cŏs-mō-rā′-mă, *n.* An exhibition of views of all parts of the world ; পৃথিবীর সর্ব্বস্থানের চিত্রপ্রদর্শনী [এই চিত্রসমূহ প্রচ্ছন্ন প্রদীপদ্বারা উজ্জ্বলিত করা হইয়া থাকে।] **—ram′-ic,** *adj.*

cŏs′-mŏs, *n.* 1. The universe as an orderly system ; বিশ্ব, জগৎ, ব্রহ্মাণ্ড। 2. A harmonious system, as of ideas, etc. (*e.g.* that which constitutes the sum total of experience) ; ভাবরাজ্য, মানসজগৎ

3. Order ; harmony ; শৃঙ্খলা, সুব্যবস্থা ; সুসঙ্গতি।

cŏs-mō-thĕt'-ic, *adj.* Believing in the existence of matter, but at the same time denying that the external world has any existence except in consciousness ; জড় পদার্থের অস্তিত্বে বিশ্বাসী ; কিন্তু জাগ্রৎ চৈতন্য ভিন্ন যে অন্যত্র বহির্জগতের কোন সত্তা আছে—এই কথা অস্বীকারকারী।

Cŏs'-săck, *n.* One of a military tribes inhabiting steppes in the south of Russia ; রুশিয়ার কসাক।

cŏs'-sĕt, *n.* & *v. t.* A pet lamb ; a pet ; পালিত মেষ শাবক ; আদুরে গোপাল, যাদুমণি। ***Verb t.*** To fondle ; আদর করা, সোহাগ করা।

cŏst, *n.* **1.** The price paid or charged for a thing ; মূল্য, অর্থ (মঃ ইঃ), দাম, খরচ, খর্চ্চ। **2.** The expenditure of time, labour, etc. ; সময়-ব্যয়, শ্রম-ব্যয়। **3.** (*Law*) (*pl.*) Expenses of a lawsuit ; মোকদ্দমার (আইন) খরচা। **4.** Loss ; "He knows it to his *cost*, good man !" ক্ষতি, হানি। **Cost-less,** *adj.* **Cost-book**—খনির জমাখরচের বহি। **Prime-cost, Cost-price**—ক্রয়মূল্য, আসল দাম, কেনা দাম, পড়তা। **At any cost, At all cost** — At any sacrifice ; যেমন করিয়াই হউক, যতই খরচ হউক না কেন। **At cost price** — At prime-cost ; ক্রয়মূল্যে, কেনা দামে। **At one's cost**—At one's expense ; কাহারও ব্যয়ে, কাহারও ক্লেশ বা অনিষ্ট জন্মাইয়া। **At the cost of**—At the expense of ; ব্যয়ে। **To one's cost**—To one's loss or detriment ; কাহারও ব্যয়ে, কাহার ক্ষতি বা নাশ ঘটাইয়া।

cŏst, *v. i.* **1.** To be of the price of ; as, the book *cost* Rs. 3 ; to cause the expenditure of ; as, it *cost* me much money and labour ; মূল্য হওয়া ; ব্যয় করান। [*Note.* It has no passive, the person is an indirect object ; the price is an adverbial object "*in*" being understood before it.] **2.** To require the expenditure, loss, or suffering of ; as, it *cost* him time ; ব্যয়, ক্ষতি বা ক্লেশ সহ্য করিতে হওয়া। **3.** (*Comm.*) To fix prices ; (বাণিজ্য) মূল্য নির্দ্দিষ্ট করিয়া দেওয়া। **Cost what it may**—At any cost or price ; যতই লাগুক না কেন। **To cost one dear or dearly**—To entail heavy expenditure or loss upon ; to involve a heavy penalty ; গুরুতর ব্যয়-সাধ্য হওয়া, গুরুতর ক্ষতির বিষয় হওয়া ; গুরুতর শাস্তির কারণ হওয়া।

cŏs'-târd, *n.* **1.** A kind of large apple ; একপ্রকার বড় সেওফল। **2.** (*Archaic*) The head ; (অপ্রচলিত) মাথা।

cŏs'-tāte, *adj.* Having ribs ; পঞ্জর-বিশিষ্ট।

cŏs-tēăn, -een (-ēn), *v. i.* (*Min.*) To dig small pits to seek for metallic lodes ; (খনিজ-বিদ্যা) ধাতুরেখা অন্বেষণ জন্য ক্ষুদ্র ক্ষুদ্র গর্ত্ত খনন করা।

cŏs'-têr, *n.* (Abbr. of *coster-monger*) An apple seller ; a hawker who sells fruits ; সেওফল বিক্রেতা ; যে ব্যক্তি ফল প্রভৃতি ফেরি করিয়া বেড়ায়। **Coster-monger**—*n.* & *adj.* **1.** Same as COSTER. (*Adj.*) (*Archaic*) Mean ; mercenary ; (অপ্রচলিত) নীচ ; অর্থলোভী।

cŏs'-tive (-tĭv), *adj.* **1.** Having the bowels bound ; constipated ; আনদ্ধ (মঃ ইঃ), বদ্ধকোষ্ঠ ; কোষ্ঠকাঠিন্য বিশিষ্ট। **2.** (*Fig.*) Niggardly ; (লক্ষণায়) কৃপণ। **–ness,** *n.*

cŏst'-lȳ, *adj.* **1.** Of a high price ; expensive ; দামী, বহুমূল্য, মহার্ঘ, মহার্ঘ ; ব্যয়সাধ্য। **2.** (*Poet.*) Sumptuous ; জাঁকাল। **–li-ness,** *n.*

cŏst'-mă-rȳ, *n.* A perennial aromatic plant ; এক প্রকার বহুবর্ষজীবী সুগন্ধি তৃণ।

cŏs'-tūme, *n.* & *v. t.* **1.** A customary style of dress (including the way of wearing the hair) of a people, class or period ; কোন বিশেষ যুগ বা জাতির পরিচ্ছদের ধরণ। **2.** A complete set of outer garments ; একপ্রস্থ পোষাক, বেশ (মঃ ইঃ) নেপথ্য (ঐ)। **3.** The dress of an actor or an actress in a play ; নাটকের অভিনেতা বা অভিনেত্রীর পোষাক। ***Verb t.*** To provide with a costume or dress ; পোষাক প্রদান করা। **Costume piece**—একপ্রকার নাটকাভিনয় — যাহাতে অভিনেতৃগণ ঐতিহাসিক পরিচ্ছদ পরিধান করিয়া থাকেন।

cŏs-tūm'-ĕr, –i-êr, *n.* One who makes, or deals in, costumes, as for theatres, etc. ; নাটকাদির পরিচ্ছদ প্রস্তুতকারী, নর্ত্তকাদির পরিচ্ছদ ব্যবসায়ী।

Costus speciosus—কিমুক (বেলঃ)।

cō'-sȳ, –zȳ, *adj.* & *n.* Warm and comfortable ; snug ; as, a *cosy* person or place ; সুখদায়ক ; আরামদায়ক, আরামজনক। ***Noun.*** A canopied seat for two. occupying a corner of a room ; দুই ব্যক্তির উপবেশনের উপযোগী কক্ষকোণ-স্থিত চন্দ্রাতপাবৃত আসন বিশেষ। **–si-ly,** *adv.* **–si-ness,** *n.*

cŏt, *n.* & *v. t.* **1.** A den, coop or like shelter for small domestic animals ; গৃহপালিত ক্ষুদ্র জন্তুর খোঁয়াড় বা খোপ। **2.** (*Poet.*) A cottage ; (কবিতায়) কুটীর। ***Verb t.*** To put in a cot ; খোঁয়াড়ে রাখা, খোপে রাখা।

cŏt, *n.* **1.** (*Anglo-Ind.*) A light bed-stead ; (ভারতবর্ষবাসী ইংরেজ সমাজে) চারপায়া, খাট। **2.** (*Naut.*) A hammock ; (নৌ-বিদ্যা) নাবিকদিগের দোলায়মান শয্যা, ঝুলিখাট। **3.** A bed or crib for a child to sleep in ; a bed in children's hospital ; শিশু-শয্যা ; শিশুদিগের রুগ্নাবাসের শয্যা।

cŏt, *n.* Abbreviation of COTANGENT.

cō-tăn'-gĕnt, *n.* (*Trigon.*) The tangent of the complement of an arc or angle ; (ত্রিকোণমিতি) কোটিস্পর্শরেখা (হিঃ কোঃ)।

cōte, *n.* A shed or shelter, esp. for animals ; টং, খোপ, খোঁয়াড়।

cō-tĕm′-pŏ-ră-rȳ, *etc.* See CONTEMPORARY.

cō-tĕn′-ănt, *n.* A tenant in common ; সহযোগী প্রজা।

cō′-tĕ-rie (-rē), *n.* **1.** A circle of familiar friends who meet for social or literary intercourse ; সামাজিক ও সাহিত্যিক বিষয়ে আলাপনার্থ মিলিত অন্তরঙ্গ বন্ধুমণ্ডলী। **2.** A select circle in society ; গুণিজনমণ্ডলী, বিদ্বজ্জনমণ্ডলী।

cō-thur′-nŭs (-thêr), *n.* A boot or buskin worn by the actors in tragedies ; বিয়োগান্ত নাটকের অভিনেতৃগণকর্তৃক পরিহিত জানু-সন্ধি পর্য্যন্ত লম্বিত পাদুকা বিশেষ।

cō-tīd′-ăl, *adj.* Indicating an equal tide-level in different places at the same time ; বিভিন্ন স্থানে সমসময়ে জোয়ারের জলের উচ্ছ্বাস-সূচক, সমসাময়িক উচ্ছ্বাসসূচক। **Co-tidal line**—যে সকল স্থানে জোয়ারের জলের সমসাময়িক উচ্ছ্বাস হয়—তদ্রূপ স্থানসমূহ সংযোজক মানচিত্রের রেখা, সমবৈলিক রেখা।

cō-til′-liŏn, *n.* **1.** Name of several dances ; বিভিন্নপ্রকার নৃত্যের নাম। **2.** Music for this ; উক্তপ্রকার নৃত্যসমূহের উপযোগী বাদ্য।

cŏt′-tāge, *n.* **1.** A labourer's or villager's small dwelling ; কুটীর, কুটী, ছাপরা, উটজ (মঃ ইঃ), পর্ণশালা তৃণকুটীর (আঃ বঃ)। **2.** A small country or suburban house ; ক্ষুদ্র পল্লীগৃহ, নগরোপকণ্ঠস্থ ক্ষুদ্রভবন। **Cottage hospital** — ক্ষুদ্র রুগ্নাবাস। **Cottage loaf**—দুইটী ময়দার তাল দ্বারা তৈয়ারী একপ্রকার রুটি—ইহার ছোটটী বড়টীর উপরে লাগানো থাকে। **Cottage-piano**—A small upright piano ; একপ্রকার ক্ষুদ্র এবং খাড়া পিয়ানো।

cŏt′-tāğ-êr, *n.* **1.** A person who lives in a cottage ; কুটীরবাসী। **2.** A Scottish peasant occupying a house attached to a farm ; কৃষিক্ষেত্র-সংলগ্ন কুটীরবাসী স্কট্‌লণ্ডদেশীয় কৃষক।

cŏt′-têr, *n.* A key, pin or bolt for fastening the parts of a machine, etc. ; যন্ত্রের অংশসমূহ সংবদ্ধ করার জন্য চাবি, গুঁজি, খিল বা কীলক।

cŏt′-ti-êr, *n.* **1.** A cottager ; কুটীরবাসী। **2.** An Irish tenant holding a small farm under cottier tenure ; আয়র্লণ্ডদেশীয় জোতদার প্রজা। **Cottier tenure** — আয়র্লণ্ডদেশের প্রজা।

cot′-ton (cŏt-t′n), *n.* **1.** A soft downy substance growing in the pods of several plants ; কার্পাস, তুলা, রুই। **2.** The cotton plant ; কার্পাস গাছ। **3.** Cloth made of cotton ; কার্পাস বস্ত্র। **4.** Thread spun from cotton ; sewing cotton ; কার্পাসের সূতা ; সেলাইয়ের সূতা **5.** Any cotton-like downy substance growing on other plants কার্পাস ভিন্ন অন্যপ্রকার বৃক্ষে জাত কার্পাসবৎ পদার্থ। **—y,** *adj.* **Cotton-cake**—কার্পাস বীজের ময়দার পিষ্টক। **Cotton-grass**—একপ্রকার ঘাস। **Cotton lord**—প্রকাণ্ড তুলা ব্যবসায়ী। **Cotton paper** — তুলার কাগজ। **Cotton plant**—কার্পাস গাছ। **Cotton-spinner**—যে ব্যক্তি সূতা কাটে ; কাপড়ের কলের স্বত্বাধিকারী। **Cotton-waste**—যন্ত্রাদি পরিষ্কার করার জন্য কার্পাসের আবর্জ্জনা। **Cotton wood**—একজাতীয় প্রকাণ্ড বৃক্ষ। **Cotton wool**—Raw cotton ; কাঁচা কার্পাস। **Cotton yarn**—তুলার সূতা। **Stuffed with cotton**—রুই-ভরা।

Cotton plant.

cot′-ton (cŏt-t′n), *v. i.* **1.** To agree ; to become friendly ; (followed by *together, with*) ; ঐক্য হওয়া ; বন্ধুভাবাপন্ন হওয়া। **2.** To become attached, (with *to*) ; অনুরক্ত হওয়া। **To cotton up**—To make friendly advances ; "You stop here and *cotton up* to the gipsies ;" বন্ধুত্ব করিতে যাওয়া, প্রীতিস্থাপনের চেষ্টা করা।

cot′-ton-ŏc′ră-çȳ (cŏt-t′n-), *n.* The class who have risen to wealth through the cotton-trade ; কার্পাসের ব্যবসায় করিয়া ধনী হইয়াছে—এইরূপ ব্যক্তিগণের শ্রেণী বা সমাজ।

cŏt-ȳ-lē′-dŏn, *n.* **1.** The first leaf or one of the first two leaves developed in a plant ; a seed-leaf ; বৃক্ষের প্রথমোদ্গত পত্র, ভ্রূণপত্র (সাঃ পঃ) ; বীজদল (ঐ)। **2.** A genus of plants including navel wort or kidney wort ; এক জাতীয় বৃক্ষ। **—ous,** *adj.*

cŏt′-ȳ-loid (-lȳd), *adj.* (*Anat.*) Shaped like a cup ; (শারীর-সংস্থান বিদ্যা) বাটীর আকার।

cou′-căl (cōō-), *n.* A genus of common marsh-birds in Africa and India ; কুর্কা এবং তজ্জাতীয় পক্ষী। ***Taccocua sirkee***—A bird belonging to this genus — Bengal sirkee ; কুর্কা (যোঃ), কুরো (ঐ)।

couch (cowch), *n.* **1.** A bed for sleep or repose ; a lounge ; খট্টা, চারপায়া, কৌচ, খাট, পালঙ্ক পর্য্যঙ্ক তল্প (মঃ ইঃ) ; একপ্রকার আরাম কেদারা, শেজ। **2.** The malting floor ; যে মেজের উপরে অঙ্কুরিত করার উদ্দেশ্যে জলে পচানো যব রাখা হয়। **3.** (*Paint.*) A coat of colour, varnish, etc. ; রং, বার্ণিশ প্রভৃতির লেপ। **Couch-grass**—দুর্ব্বা (ওয়াট্)।

couch (cowch), *v. t.* & *i.* **1.** To lay down, (now used only in *p. p.*) ; শায়িত করা। **2.** To heap grain on a floor to promote germination ; অঙ্কুরোদ্গমের জন্য যবাদি

শস্ত্র মেজের উপর কাঁড়ি করিয়া রাখা। 3. To lower as a spear in the position of attack; to level as a gun; বল্লম প্রভৃতি নত করিয়া আক্রমণ করার উপযোগী অবস্থায় ধারণ করা; বন্দুকাদি তাক করা। 4. To express as thought, etc., (with *in*); "All the answers were *couched* in the negative;" ভাষায় ব্যক্ত করা। 5. To remove as cataract by displacing the opaque lens of the eye with a needle; সূচের দ্বারা চক্ষুর উপরের পর্দ্দা তুলিয়া ছানি দূর করা। 6. To conceal as an idea or meaning, etc., (with *in*, *under*); "That lies naturally *couched under* this allegory;" ভাব বা অর্থ প্রভৃতি প্রচ্ছন্ন করা। ***Verb i.*** 1. (*Of animals*) To lie in the lair; (জন্তু-সম্পর্কে) গর্ত্তে শায়িত থাকা। 2. To lie down on a bed or place of repose; বিছানায় বা আরামজনক স্থানে শায়িত থাকা। 3. To crouch or cower, as a beast; (*fig.*) to bow or bend in submission; (পশুর মত) গুটিসুটি মারা; (লক্ষণায়) বশ্যতার চিহ্নস্বরূপ প্রণত হওয়া। 4. To lie in ambush; ওৎ পাতিয়া থাকা। **To couch aperson or a person's eye**—কোন ব্যক্তির চক্ষুর ছানি তুলিয়া ফেলা। **To couch a spear or lance**—See COUCH (3. *v. t.*)

couch (cowch), *n.* (More usually *couch-grass*) A troublesome grass; দুর্ব্বাঘাস (ওয়াটু)।

couch'-ănt (cowch-), *adj.* 1. Lying down or squatting; "His nephew... Lay *anchant* with his eyes upon the thrown Ready to spring;" শায়িত, ভূশয়ানভাবে অবস্থিত। 2. (*Her.*) Lying down with the head raised up, as an animal; (কুল-বিদ্যা) ঈষদুত্তোলিত মস্তকে শয়ান।

cou'-găr (cô-), *n.* A large carnivorous quadruped of the cat kind; মার্জ্জার জাতীয় বৃহৎকায় মাংসাশী জন্তু বিশেষ।

Cougar.

cough (cŏf), *n.* 1. A convulsive effort to expel phlegm, etc. from the air passages; কাশি। 2. A tendency to cough; an ailment causing repeated coughing; কাশের ভাব; কাশরোগ।

cough (cŏf), *v.t.* & *i.* 1. To expel air from the lungs or air-passages by coughing, (with *up*, *out*); কাশা। 2. To say with a cough, (with *out*, *up*); কাশিতে কাশিতে বলা। ***Verb i.*** To expel air or irritating matter from the lungs or air-passages in a noisy and violent manner; কাশা। **To cough down**—To silence as a speaker by coughing; কাশিদ্বারা কোন ব্যক্তিকে চুপ করিয়া দেওয়া।

could (cûd), past tense of CAN.

cou-lisse' (cŏ-lēs), *n.* 1. A side-scene in a theatre; the space between two side-scenes; রঙ্গালয়ের পার্শ্ববর্ত্তী দৃশ্যপট; দুইটী পার্শ্ববর্ত্তী দৃশ্যপটের মধ্যবর্ত্তী স্থান। 2. A groove in which a sluice-gate etc. slides up and down; যে খাঁজের মধ্যে কবাট প্রভৃতি পিছলাইয়া উঠিয়া ও নামিয়া থাকে।

cou-loir' (cô-lwär), *n.* A steep gorge on a mountain-side; পর্ব্বত পার্শ্বস্থ সংকীর্ণ এবং সরলোন্নত গিরিপথ।

cou-lomb' (cô-lŏm), *n.* The unit of electrical quantity; তাড়িতের একক।

coul'-têr (cōl-), **cŏl'-**, *n.* The sharp iron of the plough that cuts the earth; লাঙ্গলের ফাল।

cou'-mă-rin (cō-), *n.* An aromatic substance obtained from the Tonka bean; উদ্ভিজ্জ বিশেষ হইতে প্রাপ্ত সুগন্ধি দ্রব্য বিশেষ।

coun'-cil (cown-), *n.* 1. An assembly for consultation, deliberation or advice; পরামর্শ-সভা, মন্ত্রণা-সভা, সংসদ্, বৈঠক, পঞ্চায়েৎ-জমায়েৎ, মজলিস। 2. An ecclesiastical meeting; যাজকীয়-সভা। 3. A body of men to advise a sovereign or chief magistrate; as, Privy *council*; মন্ত্রিসভা, শাসনবিভাগের উর্দ্ধতন কর্ম্মচারীর মন্ত্রণা-সভা। 4. (*New Test.*) Jewish Sanhedrin; (বাইবেলের নব নিয়ম গ্রন্থে) ইহুদিদিগের সর্ব্বোচ্চ ধর্ম্মাধিকরণ। 5. An administrative body at the head of a corporate town, city, or county; নাগরিক ব্যাপার সমূহ পরিচালনের জন্য সভা। 6. A body assisting the governor of British crown colony or dependency; ব্যবস্থাপক-সভা। 7. A body assisting in carrying on the affairs of an institution; কার্য্যনির্ব্বাহক সভা। **Council-board**—ব্যবস্থাপক সভায় যে মেজের চতুর্দ্দিকে সভ্যগণ উপবেশন করেন। **Council-chamber, —house** — ব্যবস্থাপক সভার গৃহ বা কক্ষ, দেওয়ান-খাস, ইন্দ্রক (আঃ বঃ)। **Council of war** — বিশেষ গুরুতর ঘটনার সময় আহূত সৈনিক কর্ম্মচারিগণের সভা।

coun'-cil-lor (cown-sĭl-lêr), *n.* Member of a council; সভাসদ্, ব্যবস্থাপক সভার সভ্য। **—ship,** *n.*

coun'-sĕl (cown-), *n.* 1. Consultation; deliberation; পরামর্শ, মন্ত্রণা, বিতর্ক; চর্চ্চা। 2. Advice; direction; উপদেশ, পরামর্শ; তত্ত্বাবধান। 3. A barrister; also collectively, the legal advocates united in the management of a case; কৌঁসুলি; কোন মোকদ্দমা পরিচালনের জন্য সম্মিলিত ব্যবহারজীবিবর্গ। **Counsel of perfection** — যে নিষেধ সকলের পক্ষে পালনীয়। **To keep one's own** or

another's counsel—To keep one's own or another's secret; মনের কথা প্রকাশ না করা, মন্ত্রগুপ্তি রাখা।

coun'-sĕl (cŏwn-) *v. t.* To advise; পরামর্শ দেওয়া।

coun'-sel-lor (cŏwn-sĕl-lêr), *n.* 1. An adviser; উপদেষ্টা, পরামর্শদাতা, বুদ্ধিসহায় (মঃ ইঃ), মন্ত্রী, অমাত্য, সচিব। 2. (Ireland) An advising barrister (also counsellor-at-law); (আয়র্লণ্ডে) পরামর্শদাতা কৌঁসুলি।

count (cŏwnt), *n.* 1. Reckoning; computation; গণনা, গন্তি, সংখ্যান; হিসাব। 2. The sum total; সর্ব্বসাকল্য, মোট সমষ্টি। 3. (*Law*) A particular charge in an indictment; (আইন) অভিযোগের কোন বিশেষ দফা, দাওয়া; পূর্ব্ব পক্ষপাদ (মঃ ইঃ)। 4. (*House of Commons*) Adjournment in consequence of a quorum of forty members not being present, (also *count-out*); (প্রাকৃতসভা) পার্লেমেণ্ট সভার অধিবেশনের জন্য ন্যূনকল্পে যে ৪০ জন সভ্যের উপস্থিতি আবশ্যক, উপস্থিত সভ্যসংখ্যা তদপেক্ষা অল্পতর হওয়ার দরুণ সভার কার্য্য স্থগিত রাখন।

count (cŏwnt), *v. t. & i.* 1. To enumerate; to compute; গণা, গন্তি করা, হিসাব করা, গণনা করা; সংখ্যা করা। 2. To include in reckoning; গণনার মধ্যে ধরা। 3. To esteem; to consider; "Must we *count* life a curse, and not a blessing?" গণ্য করা; বিবেচনা করা। ***Verb i.*** 1. To name numerals in order; ১, ২, প্রভৃতি সংখ্যা গণা। 2. To be accounted; as, every vote *counts*; গণনার মধ্যে ধরা। **To count up**—To find the sum of; যোগফল নির্ণয় করা, সমষ্টি নির্ণয় করা। **To count for**—To be worth; মূল্যে হওয়া। **To count kin with one**—(*Scotch*) নিজের বংশাবলীর সহিত অপর ব্যক্তির বংশাবলী তুলনা করা। **To count on** or **upon**—To rely; নির্ভর করা। **To count one's beads**—মালা জপ করা। **To count out the House (of Commons)**—(ইংলণ্ডের প্রাকৃত সভার) সভ্য গণনা করা এবং উক্ত সভ্যগণের সংখ্যা ৪০ হইতে কম হইলে, সভার কার্য্য স্থগিত করা।

count (cŏwnt), *n.* A foreign title of nobility answering to English peer; রুশিয়া প্রভৃতি দেশের অভিজাত ব্যক্তিদিগের উপাধি বিশেষ। **Count'-ship**, *n.*

coun'-te-nance (cŏwn-tĕ-năns), *n.* 1. Features of the human face; চেহারা, আকৃতি (আঃ বঃ) 2. The face; মুখ, বদন, আস্য, আনন, বয়ান। 3. Composure; "The Persian stood and received them with a good *countenance*;" স্থৈর্য্য। 4. Favour; encouragement; কৃপা, অনুগ্রহ, প্রসাদ, আনুকূল্য, মেহেরবানি; উৎসাহ। **His countenance fell**—He looked disappointed; তাহার মুখে নৈরাশ্যের ছায়া পড়িল। **To keep one's countenance**—To maintain composure; to refrain from laughing; গাম্ভীর্য্য রক্ষা করা; হাসি চাপিয়া রাখা। **To keep one countenance** or **in countenance**—To support the confidence of another by one's presence or assistance; স্বয়ং উপস্থিত থাকিয়া বা সাহায্য করিয়া কাহাকে আশ্বস্ত করা। **To put out of countenance**—To make ashamed; to disconcert; লজ্জিত করা; অপ্রতিভ করা, নতানন করা।

coun'-te-nance (cŏwn-tĕ-năns), *v.t.* 1. To sanction; মঞ্জুর করা। 2. To encourage; to abet; প্রোৎসাহিত করা; দুষ্কর্ম্মে সাহায্য করা।

coun'-têr (cŏwn-), *n.* 1. A piece of metal or ivory etc., used for reckoning in games; ক্রীড়াতে গণনার জন্য ধাতু বা গজদন্ত-খণ্ড, গুটিকা (আঃ বঃ)। 2. An imitation coin of base metal; জাল মুদ্রা। 3. A banker's table; a table in a shop on which money is counted and over which business is transacted ব্যাঙ্কওয়ালার মেজ; বণিক্‌ফলক (মঃ ইঃ), গণনাফলক (ঐ), দোকানের যে মেজে টাকা পয়সা গণা এবং কেনাবেচা হয়। **Counter jumper**—দোকানের গোমস্তা বা কর্ম্মচারী, সচিব। **Over the counter**—দোকানে অর্থাৎ বণিক্‌দিগের মিলন-স্থলীতে নহে।

coun'-têr (cŏwn-), *n.* 1. The curved part of the stern of a ship; জাহাজের পশ্চাদ্ভাগের বক্রীভূত অংশ। 2. That part of a horse which lies between the shoulders, and under the neck; অশ্বের স্কন্ধদ্বয়ের মধ্যবর্ত্তী এবং গলদেশের নিম্নবর্ত্তী স্থান।

coun'-têr (cŏwn-) *n.* The back part of a shoe or boot round the heel, (abbr. of *counter-fort*); জুতার গোড়ালির চতুর্দ্দিকস্থ পশ্চাদ্ভাগ।

coun'-têr (cŏwn-), *adj.* 1. Opposite; contrary; as, a *counter* direction or current; বিপরীত; প্রতিকূল। 2. Duplicate; as, a *counter* list; দ্বিতীয়।

coun'-têr (cŏwn-), *v. t. & i.* 1. To encounter; to oppose; to contradict; সম্মুখীন হওয়া; প্রতিরোধ করা; প্রতিবাদ করা। 2. (*Chess*) To meet with a counter-move; (শতরঞ্চ ক্রীড়া) বিপক্ষে চাল দেওয়া। 3. (*Boxing*) To strike with a counter-blow; (মুষ্টিযুদ্ধ) প্রতিঘাত করা। ***Verb i.*** 1. To meet in opposition; শত্রুভাবে সম্মুখীন হওয়া। 2. (*Boxing*) To return a blow while guarding one; (মুষ্টিযুদ্ধ) কোন আঘাত আটকাইয়া তৎসময়ে প্রতিপ্রহার করা।

coun'-têr (cŏwn-), *adv.* 1. In an opposite direction; as, to run, hunt, or go *counter* (*i. e.* in a direction opposite to that taken by the games); বিপরীত

দিকে। 2. In opposition; contrary; as, to act or go *counter* to a rule; বিরুদ্ধে; প্রতিকূলভাবে।
coun'-têr-ăct (cown-), *v. t.* To hinder or frustrate by contrary action; to defeat; প্রতিক্রিয়াদ্বারা ব্যর্থ করা, রোধ করা; পরাহত করা, নিষ্ফল করা, বিফল করা, প্রতিহত করা (মঃ ইঃ)। **—ac'-tion,** *n.* **—ac'-tive,** *adj.*
coun'-têr-ă-gĕnt (cown), *n.* That which counteracts; প্রতিক্রিয়াজনক বস্তু বা শক্তি।
coun'-ter-ap-proach (cown-têr-ăp-prōch), *n.* (*Mil.*) A series of defences thrown up in front of a besieged place; (সামরিকশাস্ত্র) অবরুদ্ধ স্থানের সম্মুখদেশে নির্ম্মিত উপদুর্গ, প্রাচীর, পরিখা প্রভৃতি।
coun'-têr-ăt-trăc'-tion (cown-), *n.* Opposite attraction; rival attraction; প্রত্যাকর্ষণ; বিপরীত আকর্ষণ।
coun'-ter-bal-ance (cown-têr-băl-ăns) *n.* & *v. t.* 1. A weight used to balance another; a counterpoise; বরাবর ওজন, প্রতিতুলা; ভার-সামঞ্জস্য, ভারসাম্য, বিপরীতদিগের তুল্য ভার, ভারসমতা। 2. (*Fig.*) An equivalent or counterbalancing power or influence; (লক্ষণায়) তুল্য-শক্তি বা প্রভাব। *Verb t.* 1. To weigh against with an equal weight; to counterpoise; তুলা-যন্ত্রের অপর পাল্লায় সমান ভার চাপাইয়া ওজন করা; ভার সামঞ্জস্য করা, তুল্যভার করা (মঃ ইঃ)। 2. (*Fig.*) To counteract the power or effect of; (লক্ষণায়) কোন কিছুর শক্তি বা কার্য্য ব্যর্থ করা।
coun'-têr-blăst (cown-). *n.* An energetic declaration against something; তীব্র প্রতিবাদ।
coun-têr-chānge (cown-), *v. t.* & *i.* 1. To exchange; to transpose; পরিবর্ত্তন করা; স্থান বা ক্রম পরিবর্ত্তন করা। 2. To chequer; "Her ivory neck rubies and sapphires *counterchanged* in check;" বিচিত্রিত করা। *Verb i.* To change places; স্থানপরিবর্ত্তন করা।
coun'-ter-charge (cown-têr-chârj), *n.* An opposite charge as against an accuser, etc.; বিপরীত অভিযোগ, পাল্টা অভিযোগ, পাল্টা মোকদ্দমা, প্রত্যভিযোগ (অর্থঃ)।
coun-têr-chârm (cown-) *n.* & *v. t.* A counteracting charm; উল্টা মন্ত্র, পাল্টা যাদু, প্রতিপ্রয়োগ, প্রতিমায়া (মঃ ভাঃ), প্রতিকারমন্ত্র। *Verb t.* To destroy the effect of a charm; যাদু-মন্ত্রের কার্য্য ব্যর্থ করা, মন্ত্রচ্ছেদ করা (মঃ ইঃ)।
coun'-têr-chĕck (cown-), *n.* & *v. t.* 1. A check; বাধা। 2. A check that controls another check, প্রতিরোধ, প্রতিষেধ (মঃ ইঃ)। *Verb t.* To oppose or check by some obstacles; প্রতিরোধ করা, বাধা দেওয়া।
coun'-ter-claim (cown-têr-clām): *n.* A claim one makes to upset another; a claim set up by a defendent in a suit; পাল্টা দাবী; কোন মোকদ্দমার প্রতিবাদিকর্ত্তৃক যে দাবী উপস্থাপিত করা হয়।
coun'-têr-clŏck-wīse (cown-), *adj.* Contra clockwise; ঘড়ীর কাঁটা যে দিকে চলে তাহার বিপরীত-দিকে।
coun'-ter-feit (cown-têr-fĭt), *adj.* & *n.* 1. Not genuine; as, a *counterfeit* coin or writing; জাল, মেকি, নকল, ঝুটা, কুট। 2. Spurious; deceitful; as, a *counterfeit* virtue.; কৃত্রিম; কপট। *Noun.* 1. A thing made in imitation to be passed off as an original; a forgery; মেকি জিনিষ, নকল জিনিষ; জাল, কপট-লেখ্য (মঃ ইঃ)। 2. An imposter; a cheat; (*obs.*); ভণ্ড, ছদ্মবেশী; প্রতারক। 3. A likeness; a counterpart; প্রতিকৃতি; প্রতিরূপ।
coun'-ter-feit (cown-têr-fit), *v. t.* 1. To imitate; অনুকরণ করা। 2. To imitate with a view to deceive; to forge; নকল করা জাল করা; কপটানুকরণ করা, ছল করা। 3. To make (something false or spurious) to pass off as genuine; নকল জিনিষ আসল বলিয়া চালান। 4. To feign; to pretend; ভাণ করা; ছল করা। 5. To resemble; "Sleep *counterfeited* death so well;" সদৃশ হওয়া।
coun'-ter-foil (cown-têr-foyl), *n.* The corresponding part of a bank-check, etc.; টাকার বরাত চিঠির অনুরূপ অংশ প্রভৃতি, চেকের মুড়ি প্রভৃতি।
coun'-têr-fōrt (cown-), *n.* A buttress to support a wall or terrace; দেয়াল বা চাতালের পোস্তা।
coun-têr-ir'-ri-tănt (cown-), *n.* (*Med.*) An irritant substance employed to relieve another irritation or inflammation, (*lit.* & *fig.*); (ভৈষজ্যশাস্ত্র) প্রত্যুত্তেজনা বা প্রত্যুপদাহজনক বস্তু (শব্দানুযায়ী এবং লক্ষণায়) [এই ঔষধ দ্বারা শরীরের একস্থানে উপদাহ জন্মাইয়া অপর স্থানের উপদাহ দূর করা হয়।]
coun'-têr-mănd, (cown-), *v.t.* & *n.* 1. To revoke or annul (a former command); to cancel an order for (goods etc.); to recal; as a person or force by a counter-order; (পূর্ব্বাদেশ) রহিত করা, প্রত্যাদেশ করা; (জিনিষাদির) ফরমায়েস কাটিয়া দেওয়া; বিপরীত আদেশ দ্বারা কোন সৈন্যদল বা ব্যক্তিকে ফিরাইয়া আনা। 2. To oppose; প্রতিরোধ করা। *Noun.* A contrary order; revocation of a command; বিপরীত আদেশ; প্রত্যাদেশ (মঃ ইঃ), আদেশ খণ্ডন।
coun'-têr-mârch (cown-), *n.* 1. A marching back; উল্টাকুচ, প্রত্যভিযান, প্রতিযাত্রা, প্রত্যাবর্ত্তন। 2. A change of measures, etc.; কার্য্য প্রণালীর পরিবর্ত্তন।
coun-têr-mârch' (cown-), *v. i.* To march back; প্রতিযাত্রা করা, প্রত্যভিযান করা।
coun'-têr-mârk (cown-) *n.* 1. An additional mark made for greater

ecurity or surer identification ; অধিকতর নিরাপদ করার জন্য, এবং নিশ্চিততর রূপে পরিচয় করা যাইতে পারে, এই উদ্দেশ্যে যে অতিরিক্ত চিহ্ন দেওয়া হয়। 2. An additional mark on a package of goods belonging to several merchants ; এক বস্তায় একাধিক ব্যবসায়ীর মাল থাকিলে বিভিন্ন মহাজনের মাল পরিচয়ের জন্য যে অতিরিক্ত চিহ্ন দেওয়া হয়। 3. A hall mark added to that of the artificer of old and silver work ; অলঙ্কারাদির পর শিল্পীর চিহ্নের অতিরিক্ত দ্বিতীয় চিহ্ন। 4. A mark added to a medal long after it had been struck, by which the change in its value may be known ; নির্ম্মিত হইবার বহুদিন পরে পদকে যে চিহ্ন সংযুক্ত করা হয় এবং যদ্দ্বারা ইহারা মূল্যের পরিবর্ত্তন জ্ঞাত হওয়া যায়।

coun-têr-mârk' (cōwn-), *v. t.* To furnish with a countermark ; মাল, অলঙ্কার বা পদকাদির উপর উক্তরূপ চিহ্ন সংযুক্ত করা।

coun'-têr-mīne (cōwn-), *n.* 1. (*Mil.*) A mine made to intercept that of the besiegers ; (সামরিকশাস্ত্র) দুর্গ অবরোধকারিগণের বারুদপূর্ণ সুড়ঙ্গে বাধা দিবার জন্য নির্ম্মিত দ্বিতীয় সুড়ঙ্গ। (*Mil.*) A floating or submerged mine used to explode mines previously laid by the enemy ; শত্রু-কর্ত্তৃক জলমধ্যে বা জলোপরি স্থাপিত বিস্ফোরক পদার্থপূর্ণ ভাণ্ড উড়াইয়া দিবার জন্য প্রবমান বা জল-নিমজ্জিত উক্তরূপ দ্বিতীয় ভাণ্ড। 3. A counter-plot ; চাল, ফেরেব, দাগা, ধোকা, প্রতিচক্রান্ত, প্রতিকৌশল।

coun-têr-mīne' (cōwn-), *v. t.* & *i.* To oppose by means of countermine ; বিস্ফোরকদ্রব্যপূর্ণ দ্বিতীয় সুড়ঙ্গ নির্ম্মাণ অথবা জলোপরি বা জলমধ্যে বিস্ফোরক দ্রব্যপূর্ণ ভাণ্ড স্থাপন করিয়া শত্রুর তদ্রূপ উপায় ব্যর্থ করা। To frustrate by secret and opposite measures ; প্রচ্ছন্ন এবং প্রতিকূল উপায় অবলম্বন দ্বারা ব্যর্থ করা। *Verb i.* To make a countermine ; জলমধ্যে বা জলোপরি বারুদপূর্ণ দ্বিতীয় ভাণ্ড স্থাপন করা, বিস্ফোরক দ্রব্যপূর্ণ দ্বিতীয় সুড়ঙ্গ নির্ম্মাণ করা।

coun'-têr-mōve (cōwn-), **—mōve-mĕnt,** *n.* A movement in opposition to another ; বিপরীত চাল।

coun'-têr-mūre (cōwn-), *n.* (*Fort.*) A wall built up behind another wall to take its place if carried ; (দুর্গ) প্রাচীরের পশ্চাদ্দেশে নির্ম্মিত দ্বিতীয় প্রাচীর, প্রথমটী শত্রুর দ্বারা অধিকৃত হইলে, এই প্রাচীর তাহার স্থান অধিকার করে।

coun'-têr pāne (cōwn-), *n.* A bed-cover ; পালঙ্গপোশ, সুজনী, শয্যাপ্রচ্ছদ (মঃ ইঃ), কুথ (আঃ বঃ)।

coun'-têr-pârt (cōwn-), *n.* 1. A corresponding part ; a copy ; অনুরূপ অংশ ; প্রতিমান (মঃ ইঃ), দলিল প্রভৃতির অনুলিপি, প্রতিরূপ, প্রতিকল্প (মৃচ্ছঃ), নকল। 2. (*Law*) Duplicate ; (আইন) চেক প্রভৃতির মুড়ি। 3. A person who closely resembles another ; যে ব্যক্তি দেখিতে অন্য ব্যক্তির প্রায় অনুরূপ। 4. A person or thing complementary to another ; অনুপূরক বস্তু বা ব্যক্তি, প্রতিপূরক (কথাঃ সঃ)।

coun'-têr-plŏt (cōwn-), *n.* A plot to frustrate another ; প্রতিচক্রান্ত, প্রতিকৌশল, প্রতীপমন্ত্রণা (আঃ বঃ)।

coun-têr-plŏt' (cōwn-), *v. t.* To devise a counter-plot ; to defeat, by an opposite plot ; প্রতিচক্রান্ত করা ; প্রতিচক্রান্ত দ্বারা পরাভূত করা।

coun'-ter-point (cōwn-têr-pōynt), *n.* 1. (*Mus.*) Melody added as accompaniment to a given melody ; (সঙ্গীত-শাস্ত্র) কোন নির্দ্দিষ্ট সুরের সহিত সংযুক্ত আনুষঙ্গিক সুর। 2. (*Mus.*) The art or mode of composite melody ; (সঙ্গীত-শাস্ত্র) মিশ্রসুরের কৌশল বা ধারা।

coun'-ter-poise (cōwn-têr-pōyz). *n.* 1. A weight which balances another ; প্রতিমান। 2. An equivalent power or force acting in opposition ; তুল্য পরিমাণ বিরুদ্ধ শক্তি বা বল। 3. Equilibrium ; ভার-সামঞ্জস্য, প্রতিসাম্য (হিঃ কোঃ)।

coun'-ter-poise (cōwn-têr-pōyz), *v. t.* 1. To counterbalance ; সমভার করা, সমতোল করা। 2. To act against with equal power or effect ; to keep in equilibrium ; সমান শক্তির সহিত বিরুদ্ধে কাজ করা ; ভার-সামঞ্জস্য করা। 3. To compensate ; ক্ষতি পূরণ করা।

coun'-ter-poi-son (coōwn-têr-pōy-z'n), *n.* An antidote against a poison ; প্রতিবিষ (অঃ), বিষঘাতী, গরলঘ্ন (মঃ ইঃ)।

coun'-têr-rĕf-ŏr-mā'-tion (cōwn-), *n.* A counteracting reformation ; প্রতিক্রিয়াজনক সংস্কার।

coun'-têr-scârp (cōwn-), *n.* (*Fort.*) The outer slope or wall of a ditch ; (দুর্গ) পরিখার বহির্দিকের ঢালু ভূমি বা প্রাচীর, পরিখা-পর্য্যন্ত (আঃ বঃ)।

coun'-ter-sign (cōwn-têr-sīn), *v. t*, 1. To sign as a writing, etc. in addition to another to attest its authenticity ; কোন দলিলের সত্যতা-নির্দ্দেশের জন্য ইহাতে অন্য ব্যক্তির স্বাক্ষরের সহিত স্বীয় স্বাক্ষর সংযুক্ত করা। 2. To ratify or confirm ; বলবৎ করা, দৃঢ়ীভূত করা, পাকা করা।

coun'-ter-sign (cōwn-têr-sīn), *n.* 1. (*Mil.*) A watch-word given to soldiers, on guard ; (সামরিকশাস্ত্র) প্রহরীর সঙ্কেত-বাক্য, সম্ভাষা (মঃ ইঃ), সংবিদ্ (মঃ ইঃ)। 2. A special sign or mark for authentication ; সত্যতাপ্রমাণীকরণের জন্য বিশেষ চিহ্ন বা অভিজ্ঞান।

coun'-ter-sink' (cōwn-têr-singk), *v. t.* 1. To drill a conical depression in wood or metal to receive the head of a screw, etc. ; পাকওয়ালা পেরেকের মাথা বসাইবার জন্য কাঠ বা ধাতুর উপর গর্ত্ত করা। 2. To cause to sink a screw-head in such a hole; উক্তপ্রকার গর্ত্তে পাকওয়ালা পেরেকের মাথা বসান।

coun-ter-vail' (cown-têr-vāl), *v. t. & i.* **1.** To act against with equal power or effect; to compensate; তুল্য বলে বা ফলে প্রতিক্রিয়া করা; ক্ষতিপূরণ করা। **2.** To avail or prevail against; কোন কিছুর বিরুদ্ধে কার্য্যকর হওয়া বা প্রবল হওয়া। *Verb i.* To be of equal force or weight; তুল্য শক্তি বা গুরুত্ববিশিষ্ট হওয়া।

coun'-ter-weight (cown-têr-wāt), *n.* A weight in an opposition scale; অপরদিকের পাল্লার ওজনের প্রতিমান।

coun'-ter-work (cown-têr-wêrk), **1.** (*Mil.*) A work raised in opposition to those of the enemy: শত্রুর দুর্গ প্রাচীরাদির বিরুদ্ধে নির্ম্মিত দুর্গ প্রাচীরাদি। **2.** A work in opposition to another; প্রতি-কার্য্য।

coun'-ter-work (cown-têr-wêrk), *v. t. & i.* To work in opposition to; to frustrate; বিরুদ্ধে কার্য্য করা; ব্যর্থ করা, বিফল করা। *Verb i.* To work in opposition; বিরুদ্ধে কার্য্য করা।

count'-ess (cownt-), *n.* The wife of an earl or count; আর্ল বা কাউন্টের পত্নী।

count'-ing-house (cownt-ing-hows), *n.* A house or room to keep accounts, etc.; an office; হিসাবখানা, গণনালয়; কার্য্যালয়।

count'-less (cownt-), *adj.* Innumerable; অগণিত, অগণ্য, অসংখ্য।

coun'tri-fied (cown-trî-fīd), **-trȳ-**, *adj.* Rustic in manners, etc.; পাড়াগেঁয়ে, গ্রাম্য।

coun'-trȳ (cŭn-), *n.* **1.** A large tract of land; a region; দেশ; অঞ্চল। **2.** One's native land; জন্মভূমি। **3.** A state; রাষ্ট্র। **4.** Rural district as opposed to a city or town; as, to leave town for the *country*; পল্লীগ্রাম, জনপদ (সাঃ পঃ)। **5.** The people of a state or region; কোন রাজ্য বা দেশের লোক-বৃন্দ। **6.** (*Law*) A jury; as, a trial by the *country*; (আইন) জুরী, সভাসদ (ব্যঃ মাঃ)। **7.** (*Cricket*) Places far from the wickets; (ক্রীকেট ক্রীড়ায়) কীলকত্রয় হইতে বহু দূরবর্ত্তী স্থান। **Country cousin**—পল্লীগ্রামবাসী কুটুম্ব। **Country dance** — নৃত্য বিশেষ — এইরূপ নৃত্যে সহযোগিগণ পংক্তিবদ্ধভাবে পরস্পরের সম্মুখীন হইয়া নৃত্য করে। **Country gentleman** — পল্লীবাসী ভদ্রলোক। **Country house**—পল্লীনিবাস, পল্লী-ভবন। **Country note**—স্থানীয় ব্যাঙ্ক হইতে প্রচারিত ঋণ-পত্র। **Country party**—নগর অথবা হস্ত- বা যন্ত্র-শিল্পের বিরুদ্ধে জনপদ বা কৃষির স্বার্থ-রক্ষার্থ পল্লী-সমিতি বিশেষ। **Country side**—নির্দ্দিষ্ট পল্লীপ্রদেশ বা তৎস্থানের অধিবাসী। **In the country**—(Cricket) Far from the wickets; (ক্রীকেট ক্রীড়ার) কীলকত্রয় হইতে দূর। **An appeal to the country**—An appeal to the body of electors; নিখিল নির্ব্বাচক-বর্গের নিকট আবেদন।

coun'-trȳ-măn (cŭn-), *n.* **1.** One born in the same country with another; স্বদেশবাসী। **2.** A rustic; পাড়াগেঁয়ে লোক, চাষা, জানপদ (মঃ ইঃ), পল্লীবাসী।

coun'-tȳ (cown-), *n.* **1.** (*Gr. Br. & Ir.*) A district separated from the rest of the country for certain administrative purposes; (গ্রেট ব্রিটেন এবং আয়র্লণ্ড) প্রদেশ (সাঃ পঃ), মণ্ডল (মঃ ইঃ)। **2.** Administrative division in most British colonies; অধিকাংশ ইংরেজ উপনিবেশে শাসন-সম্পর্কীয় বিভাগ বিশেষ, প্রদেশ, সুবা। **3.** (*U. S.*) The largest division for local government in all states except Louisiana; (মার্কিণযুক্ত-রাজ্য) লুইসিয়ানা ব্যতীত অন্যান্য রাজ্যে স্বায়ত্ত শাসনের জন্য বিভাগ বিশেষ। **4.** The people of a county; উক্তরূপ বিভাগবাসী জনবৃন্দ। **County borough** — পঞ্চাশ হাজারের অধি[illegible] অধিবাসিবিশিষ্ট এবং পার্লেমেণ্ট মহাসভা[illegible] সভ্যপ্রেরণের ক্ষমতাপ্রাপ্ত, নগর বিশেষ। এইরূপ নগর ১৮৮৮ খৃঃ অব্দ হই[illegible] প্রদেশের সহিত সমশ্রেণীভুক্ত ব[illegible] গণ্য হইয়া আসিতেছে। **County corporate**—গ্রেটব্রিটেন বা আয়লণ্[illegible] যে নগর বা সহরে জেলার মত শেরি[illegible] এবং অন্যান্য শাসনবিভাগীয় কর্ম্মচা[illegible] প্রতিষ্ঠিত আছেন। **County council**-প্রাদেশিক সভা। **County court**-প্রাদেশিক বিচারালয়, বিশেষতঃ ক্ষু[illegible] ঋণের টাকা আদায়ের জন্য বিচারালয়। **County family** — পল্লীপ্রদেশে [illegible] পরিবারের সম্পত্তি ও পৈত্রিক আবাস ভবন আছে। **County Palatine**–See PALATINE. **County town**–প্রদেশের প্রধান নগর।

coup (cô), *n.* **1.** A successful strok[e] or move; সফল আঘাত বা চাল **2.** (*Bil.*) Direct holing of th[e] ball; (বিলিয়ার্ড ক্রীড়ায়) অন্য কন্দুকে সহিত টক্কর লাগাইয়া গর্ত্তে কন্দুকক্ষেপ **Coup-d'etat**—A decisive strok[e] to alter the constitution of [a] country by force, and against, [or] without, the consent of the peopl[e] জনসাধারণের মতের বিরুদ্ধে, বা মত[illegible] না করিয়া বলপূর্ব্বক কোন দেশের শা[সন] ব্যবস্থা পরিবর্ত্তনের জন্য চূড়ান্ত আঘ[াত] আকস্মিকনীতি কৌশল (আঃ বঃ)। **Coup de grace**—A decisive [fi]nishing stroke; চূড়ান্ত আঘাত, খ[illegible] ঘা, ঘাল। **Coup de main**—(*Mi[l.]*) An instantaneous and vigoro[us] attack to capture a positio[n] (সামরিকশাস্ত্র). কোন স্থান অধি[কার] করার জন্য আকস্মিক প্রচণ্ড আক্র[মণ] **Coup d'œil** — Comprehensi[ve] glance; ব্যাপক দৃষ্টি।

coupe (cô-pā), *n.* **1.** A four-whee[led] carriage carrying two in[side] with a seat for the driver o[utside]; একপ্রকার চারিচাকার গা[ড়ি]। **2.** An end compartment o[f a] carriage on British Railway[s]

ব্রিটীশ রেলওয়ে সমূহে বাষ্পীয়-শকটের পশ্চাদ্‌ভাগের কক্ষ।

cou'-ple (cŭpl) *n.* **1.** A band or leash to unite two hounds together; দুইটী কুকুরকে এক সঙ্গে বাঁধিবার জন্য রজ্জু। **2.** A brace; যুগল, মিথুন, যুগ্ম, দ্বন্দ্ব, জোড়া, জুট, দ্বয়। **3.** A man and his wife; দম্পতী, ভার্য্যাপতী (মঃ ইঃ)। **4.** A pair of partners in a dance; নর্ত্তকযুগল। **5.** (*Dynam.*) Two equal and parallel forces acting in opposite direction (ডাইনমো) পরস্পরের বিপরীতদিকে ক্রিয়াশীল সমান এবং সমান্তরাল বলদ্বয়, যুগল (হিঃ কোঃ)।

cou'-ple (cŭpl), *v. t.* & *i.* **1.** To fasten together, (esp. dogs in pairs); এক সঙ্গে বাঁধা (বিশেষতঃ দুইটী কুকুর)। **2.** To chain together; একত্র শৃঙ্খলাবদ্ধ করা। **3.** To unite; সংযুক্ত করা। **4.** To marry, (also *verb i.*) বিবাহ করা বা বিবাহ দেওয়া। **5.** To connect or associate in thoughts or speech; চিন্তায় বা বাক্যে সংযোগ করা। *Verb i.* To pair; to copulate; জোট বাঁধা; সঙ্গম করা।

cou'-plêr (cŭ-), *n.* One or that which couples, as a link, ring, or shackle; সংযোগকারী ব্যক্তি, সংযোজক বস্তু।

cou'-plĕt (cŭ-), *n.* Two lines which rhyme; কবিতার মিলযুক্ত চরণদ্বয়, যুগ্মক (আঃ বঃ)।

cou'-pling (cŭ-), *n.* **1.** Act of bringing or coming together; (*specif.*) sexual union; সংযোজন, যুগলীকরণ; সঙ্গম। **2.** A link connecting two railway carriages; বাষ্পীয় শকটের কক্ষদ্বয় সংযোজক শৃঙ্খল বিশেষ। **3.** (*Mach.*) A device for uniting adjacent parts; (যন্ত্র) সন্নিহিত অংশদ্বয়-সংযোজক কৌশল বিশেষ।

cou'-pŏn (cô-), *n.* A part to be detached or cut out from a ticket, paper, or the like; টিকিট, কাগজ কিম্বা তদ্রূপ বস্তু হইতে পৃথক্‌করণীয় অংশ বিশেষ।

cour'-âge (cŭr-), *n.* Bravery; fearlessness; বীর্য্য, বীরত্ব, সাহস, শৌর্য্য, নির্ভীকতা, হিম্মত (*Colloq.*)। **Dutch courage** — মাতালের সাহস। **Moral courage** — সৎসাহস। **The courage of one's conviction**—নিজের স্থিরধারণা বা বিশ্বাসানুযায়ী কার্য্য করিবার সাহস। **The courage of one's opinions**—কোন বিষয়ে নির্ভীকভাবে স্বমত প্রকাশের সাহস।

cou-ra'-geous (cŭ-râ-jŭs), *adj.* Fearless; intrepid; নির্ভীক, সাহসী; নিঃশঙ্ক, অভীরু, শূর। **—ly,** *adv.* **—ness,** *n.*

cou'-ri-êr (cô-rē-), *n.* **1.** A servant employed to make travelling arragements on the continent; (ইংলণ্ড ব্যতীত) ইয়ুরোপের প্রধান ভূভাগে ভ্রমণের বন্দোবস্ত করিবার জন্য নিযুক্ত ভৃত্য বিশেষ। **2.** A title sometimes given to a newspaper; as, Liverpool *courier*; কোন কোন সংবাদ পত্রের উপাধি। **3.** A messenger sent express with dispatches; দ্রুতগামী সংবাদবাহক, বার্ত্তাহর (মঃ ইঃ), বার্ত্তাবহ (আঃ বঃ), অশ্বারোহী দূত, হরকরা।

course (cōrs), *n.* **1.** The act of moving onward; progress; অগ্রগমন, পুরোগমন; অগ্রগতি, ক্রমোন্নতি। **2.** A path or way traversed; অতিক্রান্ত পথ, পন্থা (জিঃ)। **3.** Pursuit of a game, esp. hares with dogs; শিকারের অনুসরণ। **4.** Direction; a line of procedure; as, to change one's *course*, দিক্; কার্য্য-প্রণালী। **5.** (*Pl.*) Conduct; behaviour; আচরণ, চালচলন, চাল; ব্যবহার। **6.** The ground on which a race is run; as, a race *course*; দৌড়ের মাঠ। **7.** Line of stream; নদীর খাত। **8.** Career; a methodical series; as, a *course* of lectures; জীবন-গতি; পরম্পরা, পর্য্যায়, ধারা, প্রবাহ। **9.** Part of a meal served at a table at one time; আহারের সময়ে একবারে পরিবেশিত ব্যঞ্জন, ব্যঞ্জনের পদ। **10.** Menstrual flux; স্ত্রীলোকের ঋতু, রজঃ। **11.** (*Masonry*) One row or tier of bricks in a wall; (গাথুঁনির কাজ) প্রাচীরের এক পাটি বা প্রস্ত ইট। **12.** (*Naut.*) One of the sails that hangs from a ship's lowest yards; (নৌবিদ্যা) জাহাজের সর্ব্বনিম্ন পাটাতন হইতে লম্বিত পাইল শ্রেণীর একটী। **In due course**—At the proper time; যথাকালে। **In couse of time** — কালক্রমে। **Matter of course**—A natural thing; স্বাভাবিক বিষয়। **Of course** — Naturally; কাজেকাজেই, সুতরাং, নিঃসন্দেহ।

course (cōrs), *v. t.* & *i.* **1.** To hunt; to pursue; শিকার করা; অনুসরণ করা, পিছে পিছে যাওয়া। **2.** To cause to run; as, she would *course* horses and ride them to water; দৌড়ান। **3.** To use (grey-hounds) in coursing; শিকারে (শিকারী কুকুর) ব্যবহার করা। *Verb i.* To run about; as, blood *courses* through veins; to move with speed; ইতস্ততঃ ছুটাছুটি করা; ধাবিত হওয়া।

cours'-êr (cōrs-), *n.* **1.** (*Poet.*) A swift horse; দ্রুতগামী অশ্ব, জবনবাজী (আঃ বঃ)। **2.** One who hunts; শিকারী, শিকারবাজ।

court (cōrt), *n.* **1.** An open area inclosed by buildings or walls; প্রাচীর বা প্রাসাদ-বেষ্টিত অঙ্গন, চত্বর, চক। **2.** A place forming a kind of recess from a public street; রাজপথের সন্নিকটস্থ গৃহবেষ্টিত প্রাঙ্গণ। **3.** (*Camb. Univ.*) A college quadrangle; (কেম্ব্রিজ বিশ্ববিদ্যালয়) কলেজের চত্বর। **4.** A court-like section of a museum etc.; যাদুঘর প্রভৃতির অঙ্গনবৎ অংশ। **5.** An enclosed quadrangular area for games; as, a tennis *court*; a plot of ground marked out for lawn-tennis; ক্রীড়া-প্রাঙ্গণ; আঙা খেলার জন্য চিহ্নিত অঙ্গন। **6.** The residence of a sovereign; রাজবাটী,

রাজভবন, রাজমহল, প্রাসাদ, রাজমন্দির (মঃ ইঃ), রাজকুল (আঃ বঃ)। **7.** The persons who compose a king's retinue or council ; the sovereign and his ministers ; রাজসভাসদ্‌বর্গ, অমাত্য বা পারিষদবর্গ ; নৃপতি এবং তদীয় মন্ত্রিবর্গ। **8.** An assembly held by a sovereign, esp. for state reception, etc. ; অভ্যর্থনাদির জন্য আহুত রাজসভা, দরবার। **9.** The place where justice is administered ; বিচারালয়, ধর্ম্মাধিকরণ, ব্যবহারমণ্ডপ (আঃ বঃ), কাছারী। **10.** The judges or other persons assembled for the hearing and deciding of cases ; বিচারাসনাধিষ্ঠিত বিচারক বা বিচারকবর্গ, আদালত। **11.** The sitting of a judicial assembly ; বিচারাধিবেশন। **12.** Attention directed to gain favour ; courtship ; অনুগ্রহলাভার্থ উপসেবন ; অনুগ্রহযাচ্ঞা, প্রেমযাচ্ঞা, পূর্ব্বরাগ, বিবাহার্থ প্রেমোপাসনা। **13.** The qualified members of a company or corporation ; a meeting of these members ; কোন সংঘ বা সমবায়ের যথোচিত যোগ্যতাসম্পন্ন সভ্যগণ ; উক্ত সভ্যগণের অধিবেশন। **14.** A lodge (in some friendly societies) ; (কোন কোন বান্ধব-সমিতির) মিলনমণ্ডপ। **Court-card**—(*Origin. coat-card*) তাসের প্রত্যেক প্রস্থের রাজা, রাণী ও গোলাম। **Court-guide**—সম্ভ্রান্ত পুরুষগণের নামধামাদি সম্বলিত পুস্তক, নামপঞ্জী। **Court-hand**—লেখায় উকিলী ছাঁদ। **Court-martial** — (*Pl. courts-martial*). নৌ বা সামরিক বিভাগের অপরাধিগণের বিচারের জন্য বিচারালয়, সামরিক বিচারালয়। (*Verb t.*) To try by a court-martial ; সামরিক বিচারালয়ে বিচার করা। [*A drumhead court-martial* — যুদ্ধকালে বিপর্য্যস্ত দুন্দুভির চতুর্দ্দিকে সামরিক বিচারালয়ের অধিবেশন।] **Court-plaster**—কাল রেশমী কাপড় হইতে প্রস্তুত পলস্তারা বিশেষ। **Court-yard**—গৃহাদির চত্বর, প্রাঙ্গণ (আঃ বঃ), অঙ্গন, আঙ্গিনা, উঠান। **Civil court**—দেওয়ানী আদালত। **Criminal court** — ফৌজদারী আদালত। **Court of justice** — ধর্ম্মাধিকরণ, বিচারালয়। **Court of St. James's**—ইংরেজ নৃপতিগণের সভা। **Out of court**—Not entitled to be heard, as a plaintiff (*lit.*), or argument (*fig.*); শ্রোতব্য নয় (বাদীর কথা—শব্দানুযায়ী ; যুক্তি—লক্ষণায়)। **To bring into court**—To seek to adjust by means of litigation ; মোকদ্দমা দ্বারা মীমাংসার চেষ্টা করা। To produce before a court as evidence or authority ; প্রমাণ বা প্রামাণ্য স্বরূপ বিচারকের নিকট উপস্থাপিত করা। **To pay court to**—To try to gain the favour of by flattery etc. ; তোষামোদ প্রভৃতি দ্বারা অনুগ্রহ লাভের চেষ্টা করা, প্রেমযাচ্ঞা করা, বিবাহার্থ প্রেমোপাসনা করা।

court (cört), *v. t.* & *i.* **1.** To try to win the favour of, by flattery, etc. ; তোষামোদ প্রভৃতি দ্বারা অনুগ্রহ লাভের চেষ্টা করা, খোসামোদ করা, আরাধনা করা (আঃ বঃ)। **2.** To woo; প্রেম-যাচ্ঞা করা, ভজা, বিবাহার্থ প্রেমোপাসনা করা। **3.** To try to gain ; as, to *court* popularity ; to seek ; লাভ করিতে চেষ্টা করা ; খুঁজা, চেষ্টা পাওয়া। **4.** To invite as an enquiry etc. ; to allure ; "Flowers.........*court* an angel's feet to tread them down"; আহ্বান করা ; প্রলুব্ধ করা। *Verb i.* To pay courtship ; as, to go *courting* ; প্রেম যাচ্ঞা করা। **To court death** — To summon death ; মৃত্যু আহ্বান করা। **To court insult**—To seek to gain insult ; অপমান ডাকিয়া আনা।

cour'-te-ous (cör-tē-ŭs), *adj.* Civil ; polite ; complaisant ; obliging ; of elegant manners ; ভদ্র, সানুনয় ; শিষ্ট, সভ্য ; দক্ষিণ (আঃ বঃ), প্রিয়কারী ; বিনীত, সবিনয় (মঃ ইঃ) ; সৌজন্যপূর্ণ, সুজন (আঃ বঃ), শীল। **—ly**, *adv.* **—ness**, *n.*

cour'-tē-săn (cör-), **—zăn**, *n.* A prostitute ; বেশ্যা, গণিকা, বারাঙ্গনা সাধারণী, বারবিলাসিনী, রূপাজীবা (মঃ ইঃ) পণ্যস্ত্রী (ঐ)।

cour'-tĕ-sy̆ (cör-), *n.* **1.** Politeness of manners ; complaisance urbanity ; শিষ্টাচার ; সৌজন্য, বিনয়শীলতা ; সভ্যতা, ভব্যতা, দাক্ষিণ্য (আঃ বঃ)। **2.** An act of kindness or civility ; শিষ্টাচারের কার্য্য **3.** Favour ; as. a title given by *courtesy* ; অনুগ্রহ, প্রসাদ। **4.** A curtsy or salutation by a woman ; প্রণতজানু হইয়া স্ত্রীলোকের অভিবাদন। **Courtesy title** — অনধিকারী ব্যক্তিকে শিষ্টাচার পূর্ব্বক যে উপাধি প্রদত্ত হয়, ভদ্রতার অনুরোধে প্রদত্ত উপাধি। **By courtesy**— By favour ; অনুগ্রহে। **Courtesy of England and Scotland**— (*Law.*) পত্নীর মৃত্যুর পর তৎকর্ত্তৃক উত্তরাধিকার সূত্রে প্রাপ্ত বা কোন কোন প্রকার সম্পত্তিতে স্বামীর জীবন-স্বত্ব। **Too much courtesy too much craft**—অতি ভক্তি চোরের লক্ষণ।

court'-ier (cört-yĕr), *n.* **1.** One who attends or frequents the courts of princes ; সভাসদ, অমাত্য, (মুসলমান বাদসাহের পক্ষে) আমীর ওমরাহ। **2.** One who solicits favours ; a refined flatterer ; অনুগ্রহপ্রার্থী, খোসামোদী ; স্তাবক।

court'-ly̆ (cört-), *adj.* **1.** Polite ; elegant ; শিষ্ট ; সুচারু। **2.** Obsequious ; flattering ; বশংবদ ; তোষামোদকারী। **—li-ness**, *n.*

court'-ship (cört-), *n.* The act of wooing or courting for marriage ; বিবাহার্থ ভজনা, বিবাহার্থ প্রেমার্চ্চনা, পূর্ব্বরাগ।

cous'-cous **(sou)** [côz-côz (zô)], *n.* A kind of food used by the natives of Northern Africa ; উত্তর আফ্রিকার অধিবাসিগণের খাদ্য বিশেষ।

cous'-in (cŭzn), **1.** The son or daughter of an uncle or aunt ; সহোদর, সহোদরা, এবং বৈমাত্রেয় ও

বৈপিত্রেয় ভ্রাতা ভগিনী ছাড়া অন্যান্য ভ্রাতাভগিনী। 2. A person or thing akin to another ; পরস্পরের সহিত ঘনিষ্টসম্বন্ধবিশিষ্ট ব্যক্তি বা বস্তু। 3. A title of address used by a sovereign to his nobles or to another sovereign ; রাজা তদীয় অমাত্য ও অপর রাজাকে পত্র লিখিবার সময় যে সম্বোধনপদ ব্যবহার করেন। **—hood, —ship,** *ns.* **—ly,** *adj.* **Cousin-German, First cousin**—সাক্ষাৎ খুড়তুত, পিসতুত, মামাত ভাই বা ভগিনী। **One's second cousin**—পিতার সাক্ষাৎ মামাত, খুড়তুত, পিসতুত, ভাই বা ভগিনীর পুত্র বা কন্যা। **Cousin Betsy**—A dull-headed person ; a half-wit; নির্ব্বোধ ব্যক্তি; ক্ষীণবুদ্ধি ব্যক্তি। **Cousin Michael** or **Michael**—জর্ম্মনীর লোকের কৌতুকজনক নাম। **To call cousins**—To claim kinship (with) ; ঘনিষ্ঠ সম্বন্ধের দাবী করা।

cōve, *n.* **1.** A creek or small bay ; খাড়ি, খল্ল (মঃ ইঃ)। **2.** (*U. S.*) A recess in the side of a mountain ; (মার্কিণযুক্তরাজ্য) পর্ব্বত-পার্শ্বস্থ নিভৃত স্থান। **3.** (*Arch.*) A kind of concave moulding or vault ; (স্থপতি-বিজ্ঞান) একপ্রকার ন্যুব্জাকার বন্ধ বা খিলান।

cōve, *n.* (*Slang.*) A man ; a fellow ; (ইতর ভাষায়) লোকটা ; বেটা।

cōve, *v. t.* (*Arch.*) To arch over ; to slope inwards as a fireplace-side ; বক্রীভূত করা ; অগ্নিসেবনস্থলীর ভিতরের দিকে ঢালু হওয়া।

cov'-ĕ-nănt (cŭv-), *n., v. t. & i.* **1.** An agreement or contract ; a clause in a contract ; চুক্তি, নিয়ম, সময়, সংবিদ, পণ (মঃ ইঃ) ; চুক্তিপত্রের কোন এক দফা। **2.** (*Law*) A contract under seal ; (আইন) চুক্তিপত্র। **3.** (*Bible*) The promise made by God to man on certain conditions ; (বাইবেল) মানবের সহিত ঈশ্বরের চুক্তি। ***Verb t. & i.*** To enter into a formal agreement ; to stipulate ; চুক্তিতে আবদ্ধ হওয়া ; চুক্তি করা। **Solemn League and Covenant** — ১৬৪৩ খৃঃ অব্দের ধর্ম্ম-সংস্কারের বন্দোবস্ত বা অঙ্গীকার,—যদ্দ্বারা ইংলণ্ড ও স্কট্‌লণ্ডে যাজকবৃদ্ধসমাজ প্রতিষ্ঠিত হয়।

cov'-ĕ-nănt-ĕd (cŭv-), *adj.* Bound by a covenant, esp. of Indian Civil Servants ; নিয়মিত (মঃ ইঃ), চুক্তিবদ্ধ, চিহ্নিত (বিশেষতঃ ভারতীয় সিভিল সার্ভিসের কর্ম্মচারিগণের পক্ষে)। **Covenanted service** — যে সমস্ত কর্ম্মচারী পূর্ব্বে পূর্ব্বভারতীয় বাণিজ্য সম্প্রদায়ের (East India Company) সহিত চুক্তিতে আবদ্ধ হইয়া কার্য্যনিযুক্ত হইত এবং যাহারা বর্ত্তমানে ভারত সচিবের সহিত চুক্তিবদ্ধ হইয়া কার্য্যে নিযুক্ত হয়।

cov'-ĕ-nănt-ĕr (cŭv-), *n.* **1.** One who makes a covenant ; চুক্তিবদ্ধ ব্যক্তি, নৈয়মিক (মঃ ইঃ)। **2.** (*Scot. Hist.*) A subscriber to the Scottish National Covenant in 1638 ; (স্কট্‌লণ্ডের ইতিহাস) জাতীয় যাজকবৃদ্ধ সমাজের সমর্থনার্থ যাহারা ১৬৩৮ খৃঃ অব্দে প্রতিজ্ঞাপত্রে স্বাক্ষর করেন।

Cŏv'-ĕn-trȳ, *n.* The name of a town in Warwickshire ; ওয়ারউইক্‌সায়ারের অন্তর্গত সহর বিশেষ। **To send a person to Coventry**—To refuse to associate with him ; কাহারও সহিত সামাজিক সংস্রব ত্যাগ করা, সমাজচ্যুত করা।

cov'-ĕr (cŭv-), *v. t.* **1.** To overspread ; to overlay ; as, to *cover* a book with silk ; আবৃত করা, ঝাঁপা (*Colloq*) ; আচ্ছাদিত করা, মণ্ডিত করা। **2.** To strew ; as, the field was *covered* with dead men ; আস্তৃত করা, আকীর্ণ করা পরিব্যাপ্ত করা। **3.** To clothe ; to envelope ; বস্ত্রাদি পরা ; আবৃত করা। **4.** To extend over ; as, the Roman legions *covered* the country ; বিস্তৃত হওয়া। **5.** To shelter ; "The shady trees *cover* him ;" আশ্রয় প্রদান করা। **6.** To include ; to be co-extensive with ; to suffice to meet as expenses ; অন্তর্ভূত করা ; সমায়তান হওয়া ; ব্যয়াদি সঙ্কুলনের জন্য প্রচুর হওয়া। **7.** To conceal ; "Frank laughed to *cover* his anxiety ;" ঢাকা, লুকান, গোপন করা। **8.** To take exact aim at ; as, to *cover* one with a rifle ; ঠিক লক্ষ্য করা, ঠিক নিশানা করা। **9.** To copulate with ; as, a horse *covers* a mare ; সঙ্গম করা। **10.** (*Mil.*) To stand or march behind ; পশ্চাতে দণ্ডায়মান হওয়া বা যাত্রা করা। **11.** To incubate ; ডিমে তা দেওয়া। **12.** To have command over ; as, one fortress *covers* this territory ; উচ্চস্থানাদিতে অবস্থান হেতু নিম্নবর্ত্তী স্থান সমূহের উপর আধিপত্য করিতে সমর্থ হওয়া। **13.** To pass over ; as, to *cover* a distance ; অতিক্রম করা। **14.** To forget ; to forgive ; "Blessed is he whose sin is *covered.*" XXXIII. ; ভুলিয়া যাওয়া ; ক্ষমা করা। **15.** To put on a headdress ; "*Cover* thy head........"—*Shakes.* ; টুপী, উষ্ণীষ প্রভৃতি পরা। **16.** (*Cricket*) To stand behind another player to stop balls missed by the latter ; অন্য ক্রীড়কের পশ্চাতে দাঁড়াইয়া তাহার নিকট হইতে ভ্রষ্ট কন্দুক থামান। **—ing,** *n.* A cover ; আচ্ছাদন, ঢাকনী, গিলাপ। **Cover-point**—(ক্রীকেট ক্রীড়ায়) যে ক্রীড়ক পয়েণ্টের পশ্চাতে দণ্ডায়মান থাকে ; ঐ ক্রীড়কের স্থান। **To cover in**—To complete the covering of ; আচ্ছাদন পূর্ণ করা। To fill in as a grave, etc., with earth ; কবর প্রভৃতি মাটি দ্বারা পূর্ণ করা। **To cover the buckle** — To make a difficult step in dancing ; নৃত্যে কষ্ট-সাধ্য পদক্ষেপ করা। **To cover the feet**—(*Bible*) মলত্যাগ করা। **To cover up** — To wrap up so as to conceal ; লুকাইবার জন্য ঢাকিয়া ফেলা। **To cover with a gun**—To aim at with a gun ; বন্দুকদ্বারা নিশানা করা।

cov′-ĕr (cŭv-), *n.* **1.** Anything spread over something else ; an envelope ; as, the *cover* of a book or letter ; a lid ; আচ্ছাদনী ; ঢাকনী, আবরণ ; পিধান (আঃ বঃ), মোড়ক, (বালিসের) খোল। **2.** A screen ; a veil ; a disguise ; পর্দ্দা, পট (মঃ ইঃ); অবগুণ্ঠন ; ছদ্মবেশ। **3.** (*Hunting*) A thicket or underwood which shelters or conceals games ; (মৃগয়া) যে গুল্ম বা ঝোপে শিকার লুক্কায়িত থাকে। **4.** Protection ; a shelter ; "His army was under a *cover* ;" আশ্রয় ; রক্ষণ। **5.** (*Com.*) A sum of money sufficient to meet a liability, etc. ; (ব্যবসায়) কোন রূপ দায় প্রভৃতি শোধের পক্ষে প্রচুর অর্থ। **6.** Plate, napkin, etc., laid for each person at table ; as, *covers* were laid for four ; ভোজনে উপবিষ্ট ব্যক্তিগণের জন্য থালা, কাঁটা, চামচ, রুমাল প্রভৃতি। **Cover for**—A pretence for ; কোন কিছুর জন্য ছল। **Cover is laid**—Dinner is prepared ; মধ্যাহ্ন ভোজন প্রস্তুত হইয়াছে। **From cover to cover**—From one board or side of the binding of a book to the other ; পুস্তকের আগাগোড়া। **Under cover or cover of**—Under the pretence of ; ছলে। Under the concealment or protection of ; কোন কিছুর আড়ালে বা আশ্রয়ে। **To address a person under cover to another** — To write to one under an envelope addressed to another ; কোন ব্যক্তির নিকট লিখিত পত্রের খামের ভিতর অন্য ব্যক্তিকে পত্র লিখা।

cov′-ĕr-lĕt (cŭv-), **—lid,** *n.* **1.** The outer cover of a bed ; বিছানার চাদর, শয্যাচ্ছাদন (মঃ ইঃ), উত্তরচ্ছদ (আঃ বঃ)। **2.** A covering ; আচ্ছাদন।

cov′-ĕrt, (cŭv-), *adj.* Secret ; concealed ; as, *covert* attack ; গোপন, নিগূঢ়, ছেদো (*Colloq.*) ; প্রচ্ছন্ন, লুক্কায়িত, চোরা, গুপ্ত, ব্যাজ, ছদ্ম। **—ly,** *adv.*

cov′-ĕrt (cŭv-), *n.* **1.** A sheltering place ; আশ্রয়ের স্থান, সংশ্রয় (মঃ ইঃ)। **2.** A wood affording shelter for games ; যে বনে শিকার আশ্রয় লয়। **3.** (*Pl. Zool.*) Feathers covering the base of the wings and tail of a bird ; পক্ষীর ডানা ও পুচ্ছের বড় বড় পালকের নীচের পরপালক। **Covert-coat**—A short overcoat ; একপ্রকার লম্বা কুর্ত্তা।

cov′-ĕr-türe (cŭv-), *n.* **1.** Covering ; shelter ; defence ; আচ্ছাদন ; আশ্রয় ; রক্ষণ। **2.** (*Law*) The state of a married woman under the protection of her husband ; (আইন) বিবাহিতা স্ত্রীর স্বামীর রক্ষণাধীনাবস্থা, ভর্তৃবশতা।

cov′-ĕt (cŭv-), *v. t.* & *i.* **1.** To desire earnestly ; লোভ করা, লালচ করা। **2.** To long for illegally ; to hanker after ; লালায়িত হওয়া ; লিপ্সু হওয়া। ***Verb i.*** To have an inordinate desire ; অতৃপ্ত বাসনা থাকা। **—a-ble,** *adj.*

cov′-et-ous (cŭv-et-ŭs), *adj.* Inordinately desirous, (usu. with *of*) ; avaricious ; লোভী, লোলুপ, লোভান্বিত (মঃ ইঃ), লুব্ধ (আঃ বঃ) ; লাভলিপ্সু। **—ly,** *adv.* **—ness,** *n.* The quality of being covetous ; লাভলিপ্সা, লালসা, জিঘৃক্ষা (মঃ ইঃ)।

cov′-ey, (cŭv-ē), *n.* **1.** A brood of birds, esp. of partridges ; a small flock of birds ; পক্ষীর শাবক দল, বিশেষতঃ চড়ুই পাখীর শাবক দল ; পাখীর ক্ষুদ্র ঝাঁক। **2.** A company ; a set ; as, a *covey* of ladies ; দল, যূথ ; শ্রেণী।

cov′-in (cŭv-), *n.* A collusive compact ; প্রতারণাপূর্ণ চুক্তি, কপট সংবিদ্ (মঃ ইঃ)।

cöv′-ing, *n.* **1.** The arched piece of a building ; খিলান-বিশিষ্ট অট্টালিকাংশ। **2.** The vertical sides of a fireplace ; অগ্নিসেবনস্থলীর খাড়া দণ্ডায়মান অংশ।

cow, *n.* **1.** The female of the bull or of bovine animals generally ; গাভী, গাই, ধেনু। **2.** The female of an elephant etc ; হস্তিনী, গণ্ডারী প্রভৃতি, স্ত্রীজাতীয় তিমি মৎস্য প্রভৃতি। **Cow′-ish,** *adj.* Like a cow ; ধেনুবৎ। **Cow-bane** — Water hemlock ; এক প্রকার জলজ উদ্ভিদ। **Cow-boy**—A boy having charge of cows ; রাখাল, গোপাল। (*U.S.*) A man in charge of cattle in a ranch ; (মার্কিণ-যুক্তরাজ্য) বাথানের অধ্যক্ষ। **Cow-catcher** — A strong frame in front of a locomotive to remove cows etc. ; গাভী প্রভৃতি দূর

Cow-catcher.

করিবার জন্য বাষ্পীয়-শকটের সম্মুখভাগস্থ সুদৃঢ় কাঠাম বিশেষ। **Cow dung**—গোবর, গোময়, গোপুরীষ। **Cow-field**—গোষ্ঠ। **Cow-fish**—A sea-cow, a kind of American and Indian fish ; একপ্রকার মৎস্য। **Cow grain**—বরবটী (নৃত্যঃ)। **Cow-hage**—কিওয়াচ (বেলঃ), আলকুশী (যোঃ), আত্মগুপ্ত। **Cow-heel**—গাভীর বা বলদের খুরের জেলি। **Cowherd**—গোপালক, গোপ, বল্লব, আভীর, গাভীর রাখাল। **Cow-hide**—The hide of a cow ; গোচর্ম্ম। Leather made of cow-hide ; শোধিত গোচর্ম্ম। A whip of cow's hide ; গোচর্ম্মনির্ম্মিত চাবুক। **Cow-itch, cow (h) age**—আলকেশী, আলকুশী। **Cow-pasture**—বাথান, গোচারণ ভূমি। **Cow-path**—গোবাট। **Cow-shed**—ব্রজ। **Cow-stall**—গোশালা। **Cow-tree**—গোপাদপ।

cow̄, *v. t.* To depress with fear ; ভয়ার্ত্ত করা।

cow̄'-ard (-êrd), *n.* & *adj.* A man destitute of courage ; a timid person ; কাপুরুষ ; ভীরু লোক। ***Adj.*** **1.** Lacking courage ; ভীরু। **2.** Proceeding from fear or timidity ; as, *coward* cries ; ভয় বা ভীরুতা হইতে জাত। **—li-ness,** *n.* **—ly,** *adj.* & *adv.*

cow̄'-ard-ice (-êrd-ĭs), *n.* Timidity ; কাপুরুষতা, ভীরুতা। **Moral cowardice**—নৈতিক সাহসহীনতা (লোকনিন্দার ভয়)।

cow̄'-êr, *v. i.* **1.** To sink by bending the knees ; জানু নত করিয়া মাটীতে পড়িয়া যাওয়া, নতজানু হইয়া ভূতলে পতিত হওয়া। **2.** To shrink through fear ; ভয়ে জড়সড় হওয়া, ভয়ে গুটি সুটি মারা।

cow̄l, *n.* **1.** A monk's hooded gown ; hood of this ; খৃষ্টীয় সন্ন্যাসিগণের মস্তকাবরণ-সমন্বিত পরিচ্ছদ বিশেষ ; উক্ত পরিচ্ছদের মস্তকাবরণ। **2.** A movable chimney-top ; ধূমনির্গম নালীর টোপর—যাহা ইচ্ছামত খোলা যাইতে পারে। **Cowled,** *adj.*

cow̄l, coul (cow̄l), *n.* A vessel for carrying water borne on a pole between two persons ; জলদ্রোণি বিশেষ—যাহা দুই ব্যক্তি দণ্ডের মধ্যে করিয়া বহিয়া নেয়।

cow̄'-pŏx, *n.* Disease on teats of cows communicated to human beings by vaccination ; গো-বসন্ত।

cow̄'-rie (-rĭ), **-rȳ,** *n.* A small shell used as money in Africa and India ; কড়ি, কপর্দ্দক, বরাটক, বরাট।

cow̄'-slip, *n.* Primrose of several varieties ; এক জাতীয় পুষ্পতরু।

The cowslip (Primula veris)

cŏx'-ă, *n.* [*L.*] Hip ; বঙ্ক্ষণ, কুচকী, উরু-সন্ধি। **—al,** *adj.*

cŏx'-comb (-cōm), *n.* **1.** A vain empty-headed fellow ; a fop ; হীন মস্তিষ্ক আত্মস্পর্দ্ধী ব্যক্তি, বক্কেশ্বর ; ফুলবাবু, খোসপোষাকী, নব-কার্ত্তিক। **2.** (*Bot.*) Same as COCKSCOMB. **—comb'-i-cal,** *adj.*

cŏx'-comb-rȳ (-cōm-), *n.* Foppishness ; বাবুগিরি।

cŏx'-swain (-swān), *n.* **1.** The helmsman of a boat ; কাণ্ডারী, কর্ণধার। **2.** A sailor who has charge of a ship's boat and its crew and who usually steers ; সারেঙ্গ। **—less,** *adj.* **—ship,** *n.*

cŏx'-ȳ, *n.* See COCKSY.

coy, *adj.* **1.** Bashful ; modest ; লাজুক, সলজ্জ, মুখচোরা, অপ্রগল্‌ভ (মাঃ বঃ) ; লজ্জাশীল, সরমিলা, (সাধারণতঃ বালক ও যুবতীসম্পর্কে ব্যবহৃত হয়)। **2.** Soft ; hesitating ; মৃদু, কোমল ; দ্বিধাযুক্ত। **3.** (*Of place*) Secluded ; as, the Nile's *coy* source ; নিভৃত, নির্জ্জন। **—ly,** *adv.* **—ness,** *n.*

cōze, *n.* & *v. i.* A snug chat ; সরস গল্পগুজব। ***Verb i.*** To have a chat ; গল্পগুজব করা।

coz'-en (cŭzn), *v. t.* **1.** To cheat ; to deceive ; প্রতারণা করা ; ঠকান, ধোকা দেওয়া, বঞ্চনা করা। **2.** To beguile (in doing) ; ভুলাইয়া কোন কাজ করান।

cō'-zȳ, See COSY.

crăb, *n.* **1.** A well-known crustacean or shell-fish ; কাঁকড়া, কর্কট, কুলীর, জলবিল্ব (মঃ ইঃ), অপত্যশত্রু (ঐ), পঙ্কবাস (ঐ)। **2.** (*Astron.*) Cancer,—a sign in the zodiac ; (জ্যোতির্বিজ্ঞান) কর্কটরাশি। **3.** A machine for hoisting heavy weights ; গুরুভার বস্তু উত্তোলনার্থ যন্ত্রবিশেষ।

Crab.

4. (*Pl.*) At hazard the lowest throw or two aces ; পাশাদির সর্ব্বনিম্নক্ষেপ, অর্থাৎ ২ পো। **Crab-louse**—এক প্রকার উৎকুণ। **Crab-eyes**—মৎস্য-বিশেষের পাকস্থলীতে প্রাপ্ত কঠিন পদার্থ বিশেষ। The scarlet seeds of an East Indian bead-tree ; রতিবীজ, সুনকাইচ (ওয়াট্)। **To catch a crab**—To miss a stroke and fall backwards or to fail to raise the oar clear of the water on the rocovery ; দাঁড় জলে না লাগাতে পশ্চাৎদিকে পড়া, দাঁড় জলে আটকাইয়া যাওয়া। **To turn out crab**—To end in failure ; ব্যর্থপ্রযত্ন হওয়া।

crăb, *v. t.* & *i.* **1.** (Of hawks) To scratch ; to fight with each other ; (বাজপক্ষি-সম্বন্ধে) নখদ্বারা আঁচড়ান, নখাঘাত করা ; পরস্পরের সহিত লড়াই করা (Also *Verb i.*)। **2.** To run down ; to depreciate (*colloq.*) ; (চলিতভাষায়) নিন্দা করা ; তাচ্ছিল্য করা।

crăb, *n.* **1.** A small, wild, very sour apple ; tree bearing this ; (also crab-apple) ; একপ্রকার অম্লাস্বাদ সেওফল, জঙ্গলী সেও ; উক্ত ফলবৃক্ষ। **2.** A peevish morose person ; খিটখিটে অমিশুক লোক।

crăb'-bĕd, *adj.* **1.** Peevish ; sour-tempered ; cynical ; খিটখিটে ;

কড়া, কটুস্বভাব ; মনুষ্যদ্বেষী। 2. (Of writings and authors) Ruggedly intricate ; difficult to make out ; অপ্রাঞ্জল, অপষ্টার্থ ; দুরূহার্থ। 3. Cramped ; irregular ; as, a *crabbed* hand-writing ; জড়িত ; বিশৃঙ্খল, টেরাবাঁকা। **—ly,** *adv.* **—ness,** *n.*

crăck, *n.* & *adj.* 1. A sudd n sharp noise (of a whip, rifle or thunder) ; (বেত্র-সম্পর্কে) সপাং, (বজ্র-সম্পর্কে) কড়মড়, (বন্দুক-সম্পর্কে) পট্‌পট্‌, ঠাঁসঠাঁস, পটাপট্‌ শব্দ। 2. A smart quick blow ; as, a *crack* on the head ; পটাপট্‌ করিয়া আঘাত, সপাং করিয়া আঘাত। 3. (*Scot.* & *Dial.*) Familiar conversation ; (*pl.*) news ; (স্কট্‌লণ্ড্‌ এবং প্রাদেশিক ভাষায়) অন্তরঙ্গ আলাপ ; (বহুবচন) সংবাদ। 4. A partial fracture ; a clink or fissure ; ছিদ্র বা ফাটল ; ভেদ, চিড়, ফুট, ফাটফুট। 5. A good player, horse, etc. ; ভাল খেলোয়াড়, ঘোড়া প্রভৃতি। 6. (*Thieves' slang*) Burglar ; also burglary ; (চোরদিগের ইতর ভাষায়) সিঁধেল চোর ; সিঁধেল চুরি। ***Adj.*** (*Colloq.*) First-rate ; (চলিতকথায়) উমদা, বেড়ে, বাড়িয়া, সেরা। **Crack-brained** — Crazy ; মাথাপাগলা। **Crack of doom**— অন্তিম বিচার দিবসে বজ্রের কড়মড় শব্দ। **In a crack**—In a moment ; ফস্‌ করিয়া, পট্‌ করিয়া, ফট্‌ করিয়া।

crăck, *v. t.* & *i.* 1. To break with sharp abrupt sound ; as, to *crack* a skull or nut ; to fracture partially ; as, to *crack* glass ; মট্‌ করিয়া ভাঙ্গা ; ফাটান, ঠন্‌ঠন্‌ করিয়া ভাঙ্গা। 2. To craze ; to impair the intellect ; পাগল করা ; বুদ্ধি ভ্রংশ করা। 3. To utter smartly ; as, to *crack* a joke ; সরসভাবে উচ্চারণ করা। 4. To drink the contents of ; as, to *crack* a bottle ; ভিতরের জিনিষ পান করা। 5. To snap ; as, to *crack* a whip ; সপাং করিয়া আঘাত করা, পটাপট্‌ করিয়া মারা। 6. To damage ; to ruin ; as, to *crack* reputation or credit ; হানি করা ; নাশ করা। 7. To eulogise ; (with *up*) ; প্রশংসা করা, বাখান করা। 8. To make dissonant, as a voice ; বিকৃতস্বর করা। 9. (*Slang*) To break into ; as, to *crack* a crib (to break into a house, store, etc.) ; (ইতরভাষায়) ভাঙ্গিয়া ভিতরে প্রবেশ করা। ***Verb i.*** 1. To produce a sharp sound ; as, a whip *carcks* ; to break with a sharp noise ; সপাং করিয়া উঠা, পট্‌ করিয়া উঠা ; মট করিয়া ভাঙ্গা। 2. To burst or open into clinks ; ফাটিয়া উঠা, চটা। 3. To become dissonant, as a voice, at the age of puberty ; যৌবনসমাগমে বিকৃতস্বর হওয়া, গলা ভাঙ্গা। **Crack'-a-ble,** *adj.* **To crack a bottle**— To open and drink the contents of a bottle ; বোতল খুলিয়া মদ্য পান করা। **To crack a crust**—To go on fairly well in the world ; to make an income which is sufficient though small ; একরূপ সংসারযাত্রা নির্ব্বাহ করা ; অল্প হইলেও জীবনযাত্রার পক্ষে যথেষ্ট এইরূপ আয় করা। **To crack a joke**—To utter a joke ; ঠাট্টা করা। **To crack a tidy crust** — To make a fair income enabling one to live comfortably ; to succeed in life ; স্বচ্ছন্দে জীবনযাত্রা নির্ব্বাহের উপযোগী আয় করা ; জীবনে উন্নতিলাভ করা। **To crack credit**—বাজার সম্ভ্রম নষ্ট করা। **To crack of**—(*Arch.*) To boast of ; (অপ্রচলিত) কোন বিষয়ে বড়াই করা। **To crack up**—To speak highly of ; উচ্চ প্রশংসা করা।

crack'-ed (crăct), *p. p. adj.* 1. (*Colloq.*) Crazy ; insane ; মাথা পাগলা ; ক্ষ্যাপা, পাগলা। 2. Split ; broken ; ফাটা ; ভাঙ্গা, টুটা, ফুটা।

crăck'-ėr, *n.* 1. One who or that which cracks ; বিদারক। 2. A small firework ; পট্‌কাবাজী। 3. An explosive bonbon ; পট্‌কা বন্‌বন্‌। 4. A hard biscuit ; এক প্রকার শক্ত বিস্কুট। 5. An instrument for cracking ; as, nut *crackers* ; যাঁতা প্রভৃতি। 6. (*Slang*) Smash ; (ইতরভাষায়) চুরমার। 7. A boaster ; a liar ; a lie ; দাম্ভিক ; মিথ্যুক ; মিথ্যা কথা।

crack'-le (crăcl), *v. i.* & *n.* To make slight frequent cracking sounds ; খট্‌ খট্‌ করা, ঠন্‌ ঠন্‌ করা, চিড়্‌ চিড়্‌ করা, চড়্‌ চড়্‌ শব্দ করা। ***Noun.*** 1. A frequent cracking noise ; খট্‌ খট্‌ শব্দ, চট্‌ চট্‌ শব্দ, ঠন্‌ ঠন্‌ শব্দ, চিড়্‌ চিড়্‌ শব্দ, চড়্‌ চড়্‌ শব্দ। 2. Porcelain or glassware having a cracked surface ; উপরিভাগে ফাটা কাচের বাসন বা চিনা বাসন। **Crackle-china, — glass** — See CRACKLE *Noun.*

crăck'-ling, *n.* 1. The giving out of sharp and rapid cracks ; খট্‌ খট্‌ শব্দ করণ। 2. The brown skin of a roasted pork ; ভাজা-করা শূকরের বাদামি রঙ্গের চামড়া।

crăck'-nĕl, *n.* A light crisp biscuit ; একপ্রকার হাল্‌কা কচ্‌মচে বিস্কুট, মুড়মুড়ী (আঃ বঃ)।

crăcks'-măn, *n.* A burglar ; সিঁধেল চোর।

crăck'-ȳ, *adj.* 1. Having cracks ; apt to crack ; ফাটা, দাগযুক্ত ; ভঙ্গপ্রবণ। 2. (*Colloq.*) Crazy ; talkative ; মাথাপাগল ; বহুভাষী, পাগলটে ; বাচাল।

crā'-dle, *n.* & *v. t.* 1. A baby's bed or cot oscillating on rockers ; the place of birth or early nurture ; as, the *cradle* of an art ; শিশুখট্টা (মঃ ইঃ), দোলা ; ঝোল্‌না, হিন্দোলা ; জন্মদোলা। 2. Infancy ; as, from the *cradle* ; শৈশব। 3. A cradle-like framework ; দোলার মত কাঠাম। 4. (*Naut.*) That on which a ship rests during construction or repairs ;

(নৌ-বিদ্যা) জাহাজ মেরামত ও তৈয়ারী করার সময় যে কাঠামে রাখা হয়। 5. (*Agri.*) A frame attached to a scythe to lay corn evenly; (কৃষি-বিজ্ঞান) কর্ত্তিত শস্য সমভাবে রাখিবার জন্য শস্যকর্ত্তনযন্ত্রসংলগ্ন কাঠাম বিশেষ। 6. (*Surg.*) A frame to protect a wound; (অস্ত্রোপচার-বিদ্যা) ক্ষতস্থান-রক্ষার্থ কাঠাম বিশেষ। 7. (*Engraving*) A kind of serrated chisel; (ক্ষোদন বিদ্যা) করাতের মত খাঁজ-কাটা বাটালি। 8. (*Mining*) A gold-washing machine; (খনির কাজ) স্বর্ণ ধৌত করণার্থ যন্ত্র বিশেষ। 9. Cat's cradle; see CAT'S CRADLE below. ***Verb t.*** 1. To place or rock in a cradle; দোলায় রাখা, দোলায় রাখিয়া দোল দেওয়া। 2. To nurture or bring up in infancy; শৈশবকালে লালন পালন করা। 3. To cut and lay (corn etc.) with a cradle-scythe; কাঠামবিশিষ্ট শস্য-কর্ত্তরিকাদ্বারা শস্য কাটা ও সমভাবে রাখা। 4. To place or support in or on a cradle; to raise or transport as a ship by means of a cradle; জাহাজ তৈয়ারী বা মেরামতের সময় কাঠামের উপর বা ভিতরে রাখা; উক্ত রূপ কাঠামের সাহায্যে উত্তোলিত বা চালিত করা। 5. (*Mining*) To wash in a cradle; (খনির কার্য্য) ধৌত করা। **Cat's cradle**—একগাছি রজ্জু দুই হাতের অঙ্গুলির মধ্যে দোলার আকারে জড়াইয়া যে একপ্রকার ক্রীড়া হয়। **From the cradle**—From infancy; আশৈশব। **In one's cradle**—In one's early stage of life; শৈশবে।

cra'-dling, *n.* 1. The act of using a cradle; দোলাব্যবহার করণ। 2. (*Arch.*) A framework of wood or iron; (স্থপতি-বিজ্ঞান) লোহ বা কাঠের কাঠাম।

crăft, *n.* 1. Art; skill; trade or profession; as, a handi-*craft*: a goldsmith's *craft*; শিল্পকলা; চাতুর্য্য, হুনর, নৈপুণ্য; ব্যবসায়, পেশা। 2. Artifice; cunning; fraud; কৌশল, চালাকি; ফাঁকি, ধাঁধাঁ, শঠতা; কৌটিল্য, বৈদগ্ধ (মঃ ইঃ); প্রতারণা, ছল। 3. The members of a trade; সমব্যবসায়ী ব্যক্তিবর্গ। 4. A vessel or a boat; vessels (collectively); জাহাজ, নৌকা; জাহাজশ্রেণী। 5. The implements used in angling; বড়শী ও তৎসংসৃষ্ট যন্ত্রাদি। **Crafts'-man-ship,** *n.* **Craft-brother**—সমব্যবসায়ী লোক। **Craft-guild**—সম ব্যবসায়ী ব্যক্তি বর্গের সংঘ বা সম্প্রদায়। **Craftsman**—কোন ব্যবসায়ে নিযুক্ত ব্যক্তি; শিল্পী, কারিকর। **The craft**—The brotherhood of freemasons; ফ্রিমেশন নামক গুপ্ত সম্প্রদায়। **The gentle craft**—বড়শী দ্বারা মৎস্য শিকার।

crăft'-ŷ, *adj.* Cunning; wily; চালাক; ধূর্ত্ত, শঠ, বিদগ্ধ (আঃ বঃ)। **—i-ly,** *adv.* **—i-ness,** *n.*

crăg, *n.* A steep or rugged rock; a rocky point; খাড়া অথবা বন্ধুর পর্ব্বত; কূট, শৃঙ্গ, শৈলশিখর। **Crag'-ged, Crag'-gy,** *adjs.* **Crag'-ged-ness, Crag'-gi-ness,** *ns.* **Cragsman**—An expert climber of crags; বন্ধুর পর্ব্বতারোহণকুশল ব্যক্তি।

crăg, *n.* (*Geol.*) Gravel or sand mixed with shells; (ভূ-বিদ্যা) শম্বুকাদির সহিত মিশ্রিত বালি বা কঙ্কর।

crake, *n.* & *v. i.* 1. Kinds of birds including corn-crake; এক জাতীয় পাখীর নাম। 2. The cry of the corncrake; উক্ত জাতীয় পাখীর ডাক। ***Verb i.*** To cry out as a crake; উক্ত প্রকার পাখীর মত ডাকা। **Spotted crake**—*Porzana Maruetta*; গুড়্গুড়া (যোঃ), গুড়গুড়ি (ঐ) খয়েরী (হিউম্)।

crăm, *v. t., i.,* & *n.* 1. To stuff; to fill to excess; to thrust in by force; ঠাসা; অপরিমিত মাত্রায় বোঝাই করা; ভর্ত্তি করা, ঠাসা, গাদা। 2. To fill, as with food, beyond satiety; "I was *crammed* with gooseberries;" পেট বোঝাই করিয়া খাওয়ান। 3. To prepare (a person) for an examination by storing his memory with facts; to learn or study as a subject hastily; মুখস্থ করাইয়া পরীক্ষার জন্য প্রস্তুত করা; তাড়াতাড়ি কোন বিষয় শিক্ষা বা পাঠ করা। ***Verb i.*** 1. To eat greedily; পেটুকের মত খাওয়া। 2. To prepare for an examination by cramming; মুখস্থ করিয়া কোন পরীক্ষার জন্য প্রস্তুত হওয়া। ***Noun.*** 1. A crowd; "A prodigious *cram*"—Dickens; ভিড়, জনতা। 2. (*Slang*) A lie; (ইতর ভাষায়) মিথ্যা কথা। 3. The act of cramming, as for an examination; the information acquired py cramming; পরীক্ষার জন্য মুখস্থ করণ; মুখস্থ দ্বারা জ্ঞাত বিষয়। 4. One who crams; যে ব্যক্তি মুখস্থ করে।

crăm'-bō, *n.* 1. A game in which one person gives a word to which another finds a rhyme; একপ্রকার ক্রীড়া—যাহাতে এক ব্যক্তি কোন এক শব্দ বলিলে, অপর ব্যক্তি সেই শব্দের সহিত মিলবিশিষ্ট শব্দ বাহির করে। 2. Rime (in contempt); (অবজ্ঞা-চ্ছলে) কবিতার শব্দের মিল। **Dumb crambo**—এক প্রকার ক্রীড়া—যাহাতে এক পক্ষের লোককে অপর পক্ষের লোকের মনোগত কোন শব্দ আন্দাজ করিয়া বলিতে হয়; দ্বিতীয় পক্ষের লোকেরা কেবল তাহাদের কল্পিত শব্দের সহিত মিলবিশিষ্ট একটী শব্দ প্রথম পক্ষের লোকদিগকে জানিতে দেয়।

crăm'-mêr, *n.* 1. One who crams or stuffs; যে ব্যক্তি ঠাসিয়া ভরে বা গাদা করে। 2. A person who fattens, or an apparatus, used in fattening poultry, etc.; যে ব্যক্তি কুক্কুট প্রভৃতিকে পুষ্ট করে, কুক্কুটাদি পুষ্ট করণে ব্যবহৃত যন্ত্র বিশেষ। 3. One who crams in study; যে ব্যক্তি মুখস্থ করিয়া পরীক্ষার জন্য প্রস্তুত হয়। 4. (*Slang*) A falsehood; (ইতর ভাষায়) মিথ্যা কথা।

crămp, *n.* Contraction of the muscles from sudden chill, strain, etc. ; দৈহিক পেশির আক্ষেপ, খিল, অঙ্গগ্রহ (মঃ ইঃ)। **Cramp-fish,** *n.* The torpedo fish ; একপ্রকার বৈদ্যুতিক শক্তিসম্পন্ন মৎস্য, — এই মৎস্যের স্পর্শে শরীরে বিদ্যুত-স্পর্শের মত অবসন্নতা জন্মে।

crămp, *n.* **1.** A piece of iron bent at the ends to hold together pieces of timber, stone, etc. ; (also cramp-iron) ; লোহার আঁকড়া, পট্টি, বক্রলৌহ (আঃ বঃ)। **2.** A portable kind of iron screw-press for compressing the joints of timber framework ; এক প্রকার পেঁচ বসাইবার যন্ত্র। **3.** Restraint ; hindrance ; "A narrow fortune is a *cramp* to a great mind ;" আটক ; বাধা, প্রতিবন্ধ।

crămp, *adj.* **1.** Difficult to decipher ; as, a *cramp* handwriting ; অপাঠ্য। **2.** Contracted ; confined ; as, a *cramp* corner ; সঙ্কুচিত ; সংকীর্ণ।

crămp, *v. t.* **1.** To affect with spasm ; খিল ধরা। **2.** To confine narrowly, (often with *up*) ; as, a company of puppy-dogs *cramped up* in a box ; সংকীর্ণ স্থানে বদ্ধ করা। **3.** (*Fig.*) To hamper : (লক্ষণায়) বাধা দেওয়া।

crăm′-pŏn, *n.* **1.** A grappling iron ; আঁকড়া। **2.** An iron-plate with spikes for walking on ice etc. ; এক প্রকার প্রেকযুক্ত লোহার পাত—যাহা পায়ে লাগাইয়া অনায়াসে বরফের উপর দিয়া চলা যায়।

crăn, *n.* (*Scot.*) A measure containing $37\frac{1}{2}$ gallons ; (স্কট্‌লণ্ড্) ৩৭২ তোলার পরিমাপ বিশেষ।

crăn′-āge, *n.* Use of a crane ; also the price paid for such use ; ভারোত্তলন-যন্ত্র ব্যবহার ; ভারোত্তলন যন্ত্র ব্যবহারের জন্য যে অর্থ দিতে হয়।

crăn′-bĕr-rȳ, *n.* A wild sour berry ; এক প্রকার অম্ল ফল।

crāne, *n.* **1.** A large wading bird with long legs, neck, and bill :

Crowned Crane.

সারস, বক, বলাকা, দীর্ঘজঙ্ঘ (মঃ ইঃ), ক্রৌঞ্চ। **2.** A machine for raising and removing heavy goods ; ভারোত্তলনযন্ত্র। **3.** A siphon ; বক্রনলিকা। **4.** An overhanging tube for supplying a tender with water, (also *water-crane*) ; বাষ্পীয় শকটের সহিত সংলগ্ন জলবাহিশকটে জল যোগাইবার জন্য বক্রনল বিশেষ। **Crane fly** — Daddy-longlegs ; একপ্রকার মক্ষিকা। **Crane's bill** — একজাতীয় নানাপ্রকার গুল্মের সাধারণ নাম।

crāne, *v. t.* & *i.* **1.** To lift by or as by a crane ; ভারোত্তলন যন্ত্রদ্বারা উত্তোলন করা, ভারোত্তলন যন্ত্রবৎ উত্তোলন করা। **2.** To stretch (the neck) like a crane, (also *Verb i.*) ; বকের মত গলা বাড়াইয়া দেওয়া। **To crane at**—To shrink from a danger or difficulty ; বিপদ্ বা সঙ্কটদর্শনে ভয়ে সঙ্কুচিত হইয়া সরিয়া আসা।

crā-nĭ-ŏl′-ŏ-ġȳ, *n.* The science of the human skull, esp. its conformation in connexion with the separate faculties and properties of the mind ; করোটি-বিজ্ঞান, কপালবিদ্যা (হিঃ কোঃ), কপাল-সামুদ্রিক, কপাল-শাস্ত্র।

crā′-nĭ-ŭm, *n.* **1.** Bones enclosing the brain ; মস্তিষ্ক-পরিবেষ্টক অস্থি-সমূহ, শিরঃকপাল (সাঃ পঃ)। **2.** The skull ; করোটী, কর্পর (মঃ ইঃ)। **—al,** *adj.*

crănk (crăngk), *n.* & *v. t.* **1.** (*Machinery*) An iron axis bent and jointed like an arm, used for changing a rotatory motion into horizontal or perpendicular one or the contrary ; কফোণির (কনুই) আকৃতিবিশিষ্ট যন্ত্রাংশ বিশেষ—ইহাদ্বারা চক্রগতি ভূতলের সহিত সমান্তরাল বা লম্বমান গতিতে পরিণত হয়, অথবা শেষোক্ত গতিদ্বয় চক্রগতিতে পরিণত হয়। **2.** An elbow-shaped connexion in bell-hanging ; ঘণ্টা

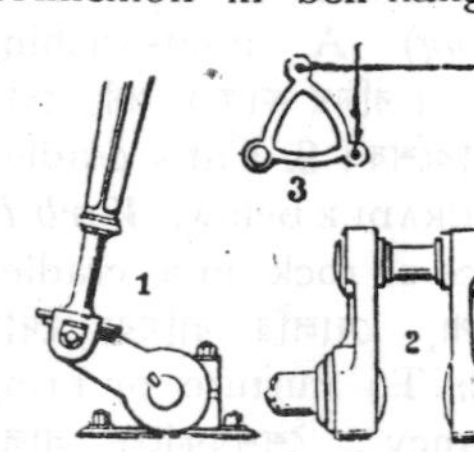

Single crank, Double crank-

ঝুলাইতে যে কফোণির আকার যন্ত্রাংশ সংযোগ করা হয়। **3.** A revolving disc turned by criminals as punishment ; বন্দিগণ শাস্তিস্বরূপ যে চাকা ঘুরায়। ***Verb t.*** To bend into the shape of a crank ; to furnish or fasten with a crank ; কফোণির আকারে বক্র করা ; কফোণির আকার যন্ত্রাংশ সংলগ্ন বা সমন্বিত করা।

crank (crăngk), *n.* **1.** A twisting in speech ; কথার মারপেঁচ, বক্রোক্তি। **2.** A caprice ; খেয়াল, মর্জ্জি। **3.** An eccentric person ; ছিটগ্রস্ত লোক, মাথাপাগলা লোক।

crank (crăngk), *adj.*. Sick ; infirm ; কাতর ; দুর্ব্বল।

crank (crăngk), *adj.* (*Naut.*) Liable to be upset ; (নৌ-বিদ্যা) উল্টাইয়া যাইবার যোগ্য, টলমলিয়া।

cran′-kle (crăng-), *v. i.* & *n.* To bend or twist ; বাঁকিয়া যাওয়া, পাক লাগা। ***Noun.*** A twist ; a crinkle ; পাক, মোচড়, কোঁচকা।

crank′-ȳ (crăngk-), *adj.* **1.** Sickly ; রোগা। **2.** In bad condition ; shaky ; as, do not seat on this chair, it is *cranky* ; জীর্ণাবস্থা প্রাপ্ত ; শীর্ণশীর্ণ। 3. Irritable ; whimsical ; কোপন, খিটখিটে ; খাম-খেয়ালি। Abounding in twists ; tortuous ; as, a *cranky* road ; পেঁচাল ; কাবাঁকা। 5. (*Naut.*) Crank ; নৌ-বিদ্যা) টলমলিয়া। **—i-ly,** *adv.* **i-ness,** *n.*

in'-nŏg, *n.* Ancient lake-dwelling in Scotland and Irĕland ; টলণ্ড এবং আয়র্লণ্ডের প্রাচীন বভবন।

ăn'-nȳ, *n.* A chink ; a cleft ; ছিদ্র, রন্ধ্র ; ফাটোল। **—nied,** *adj.* Full of chinks ; বহু-রন্ধ্র, বহু-ছিদ্র।

āpe, *n.* & *v. t.* **1.** A thin transparent silken fabric, usually dyed black and worn in mourning ; একপ্রকার রেশমী কাপড়, ক্রেপ। **2.** A band of crape worn round a hat etc., as a token of mourning ; শোকচিহ্ন-স্বরূপ টুপী প্রভৃতিতে যে ক্রেপ কাপড়ের টুকরা জড়ান হয়। ***Verb t.*** To drape, clothe, or cover with crape ; ক্রেপ্ বস্ত্রদ্বারা সজ্জিত বা আবৃত করা।

craped (crāpd), *adj.* **1.** Covered, robed, or draped with crape ; ক্রেপ বস্ত্রদ্বারা সজ্জিত বা আবৃত, ক্রেপ কাপড়ের পোষাক পরিহিত। **2.** Crimped ; তরঙ্গায়িত।

crăp'-ū-lĕnt, *adj.* Noted for, or surfeited with, intemperence ; অমিতাচারের জন্য বিখ্যাত, অপরিমিত মদ্যপানতৃপ্ত, মদবিহ্বল (আঃ বঃ)। **—lence,** *n.* **—lous,** *adv.*

crăsh, *v. i., t.,* & *n.* To make a crash or loud clattering noise ; to make or go with a crash ; কড়মড় শব্দ করা ; হুড়মুড় করিয়া চলা, ঘটর মটর করিয়া যাওয়া। ***Verb t.*** **1.** To dash in pieces violently ; to smash ; "......Stone *crashed* the solid bone ;" মড় মড় শব্দে ভাঙ্গিয়া ফেলা ; চূরমার করা। **2.** To force or drive with a crashing noise ; "Knights *crashed* their horses through the brushwood ;" হুড় মুড় শব্দে চালান বা ছুটান। ***Noun.*** **1.** A loud noise as of things falling and breaking at once ; a violent breaking by collision ; কড়মড় শব্দ, মড়মড় শব্দ ; মড়মড় শব্দে ভাঙ্গিয়া পড়ন। **2.** The collapse of a commercial undertaking ; failure ; বাণিজ্যিক ব্যাপারে নিষ্ফলতা ; নিষ্ফলতা। **To go or fall crash**—To go or fall with a crashing noise ; মড় মড় করিয়া ভাঙ্গিয়া পড়া।

crăsh, *n.* A coarse linen cloth for towels etc. ; গামছা প্রভৃতির জন্য এক প্রকার মোটা কাপড়।

crā'-sis, *n.* (*Gr. Gram.*) The contraction of two vowels into a long one or a diphthong ; স্বরবর্ণদ্বয়ের সংকোচনদ্বারা যে একটী দীর্ঘ স্বরবর্ণ উৎপাদিত হয়, যুগ্মস্বর।

crăss, *adj.* **1.** Gross ; coarse ; dense ; (*lit.* & *fig.*); as, *crass* stupidity ; স্থূল ; মোটা ; নিবিড়, গাঢ়। **2.** Stupid, as a person or idea ; মূঢ়। **Crass'-ly,** *adv.* **Crass'-ness,** *n.*

crăs'-si-tūde, *n.* Grossness ; stupidity ; স্থূলতা ; মূঢ়তা।

Cratæva Roxburghii—তিক্ত-শাক।

cratch (crăch), *n.* A grated crib or rack in which hay is put for cattle ; যে খোঁয়াড় বা মাচায় গবাদির জন্য ঘাস রাখা হয়, গড়া।

crāte, *n.* **1.** A box or case usually of wooden slats with interspaces used as a container for goods in transportation ; ফাঁক ফাঁক কাঠের ফালিদ্বারা তৈয়ারী তোরঙ্গ বা আধার, যাহার ভিতর ভরিয়া মাল চালান দেওয়া হয়। **2.** A basket of wickerwork for transporting china-crockery, etc. ; চিনের বাসন, মাটির বাসন, প্রভৃতি চালান দিবার জন্য চাঙ্গারি। **3.** A glazier's frame for carrying glass ; কাচ বহনের জন্য কাচ-শিল্পীর ঠাট। **Crate'-ful,** *adj.*

crā'-têr, *n.* **1.** (*Gr. Antiq.*) A large bowl ; (গ্রীস্‌দেশীয় প্রত্ন-তত্ত্ব) বৃহৎ পানপাত্র। **2.** The mouth of a volcano ; a circular cavity ; জ্বালামুখীর গহ্বর, অগ্নিগহ্বর (সাঃ পঃ), গহ্বর (সাঃ পঃ) ; গোলাকার গহ্বর। **3.** (*Astron.*) A southern constellation called the *cup* ; (জ্যোতির্বিজ্ঞান) দক্ষিণ নভোমণ্ডলস্থ তারা-প্রকোষ্ঠ বিশেষ। **4.** (*Mil.*) The pit left by the explosion of a mine or a shell ; (সামরিকশাস্ত্র) গোলা বা বারুদপূর্ণ সুড়ঙ্গে সশব্দ স্ফোটন দ্বারা উৎপন্ন গর্ত্ত। **—ter'-i-form,** *adj.* Bowl-shaped ; বাটির আকৃতি বিশিষ্ট, চষকাকৃতি।

Crater.

craunch (cränsh), *v. t.* To crunch ; কড়মড় করিয়া চিবান।

crā-văt', *n.* **1.** A neck-cloth ; গলবেষ্টন বস্ত্র, গলবন্ধ, গ্রীবাভরণ (মঃ ইঃ)।

crāve, *v. t.* & *i.* **1.** To implore ; to entreat ; সকাতরে প্রার্থনা করা ; অনুনয় করা। **2.** To ask or beg for ; মাগা, যাচ্ঞা করা, ভিক্ষা করা। **3.** To long for ; to need ; "What the eye views not, the heart *craves* not ;" আশা করা, কামনা করা, আকাঙ্ক্ষা করা ; আবশ্যক হওয়া। ***Verb i.*** To long or hanker eagerly ; to beg (with *for*) ; প্রবল আকাঙ্ক্ষা করা ; যাচ্ঞা করা।

cra'-ven (crāvn), *adj.* & *n.* Cowardly ; faint-hearted ; despicable ; ভীরু, কাপুরুষ ; দুর্ব্বলহৃদয় ; হেয়। ***Noun.*** **1.** A coward ; a spiritless fellow ; ভীরু বা কাপুরুষ লোক ;

নিস্তেজ লোক। 2. A cock that is not game ; যে মুর্গী লড়াইয়ের উপযুক্ত নয়। **—ly,** *adv.* **To cry craven**—To surrender ; আত্মসমর্পণ করা।

craw (crä), 1. The crop of birds or insects ; পক্ষী বা পতঙ্গের প্রথম পাকস্থলী। 2. The stomach of an animal ; জন্তুর পাকস্থলী।

craw'-fish (crä-), *n.* 1. A crustacean of the genus lobster but smaller ; চিঙ্গড়ীর ন্যায় মৎস্য বিশেষ। 2. (*U. S.*) One who retreats from his position ; (মার্কিণ যুক্তরাজ্য) মতত্যাগী ব্যক্তি।

crawl (cräl), *n.* 1. A pen or enclosure in shallow water to contain fish, etc. ; অগভীর জলে মৎস্যাদি আটক করার জন্য খোঁয়াড়। 2. A South African village called *krawl* ; দক্ষিণ আফ্রিকার গ্রাম।

crawl (cräl), *v. i.* & *n.* 1. To move slowly along the ground as a worm ; to move slowly on hands and knees ; গুড়িগুড়ি করিয়া চলা ; হামাগুড়ি দিয়া চলা। 2. To move or walk slowly or timorously ; আস্তে আস্তে বা ভয়ে ভয়ে চলা, চোরের মত চলা। 3. To move or advance abjectly ; হীনভাবে চলা বা অগ্রসর হওয়া। 4. To feel as if insects were creeping over the body ; সড়সড় করা, সুর সুর করা। 5. To spread by extending stems or branches, as a creeper ; লতায়িত হওয়া। 6. To be alive or swarming with crawling things ; as, a corpse *crawls* with worms ; কীরা, পোকা, প্রভৃতি দ্বারা আকীর্ণ হওয়া। ***Noun.*** Act of crawling ; হামাগুড়ি। **Crawl'-y,** *adj.*

crawl'-ēr (cräl-), *n.* 1. One that crawls ; যে হামাগুড়ি দেয়, উরোগামী (মঃ ইঃ)। 2. A crawling cab ; যে গাড়ী ভাড়ার জন্য ঘটর ঘটর করিয়া আস্তে আস্তে চলে।

cray'-fish (crā-), *n.* Same as CRAWFISH.

cray'-ŏn (crā-), *n.* & *v. t.* 1. A pencil of coloured clay, chalk, etc., used in drawing ; চিত্রাঙ্কণে ব্যবহৃত নানা বর্ণের খড়ি বা মৃত্তিকা লেখনী বিশেষ, চিত্রবর্ত্তিকা (মঃ ইঃ)। 2. A crayon-drawing ; উক্তপ্রকার লেখনী দ্বারা অঙ্কন। 3. A carbon point in an electric arc-lamp ; বৈদ্যুতিক প্রদীপবিশেষের অঙ্গারক-সূচী। ***Verb t.*** 1. To draw in crayons ; রঙ্গীন খড়ি বা মৃত্তিকা দ্বারা অঙ্কিত করা। 2. (*Fig.*) To sketch or plan ; (লক্ষণায়) রেখাঙ্কন করা, নক্সা করা, আঁদরা করা।

craze, *v. t., i.,* & *n.* 1. (*Pottery*) To produce small cracks on the surface of ; (মৃৎশিল্প) মৃণ্ময় পাত্রাদির উপরিভাগে ক্ষুদ্র ক্ষুদ্র ফাটার দাগ উৎপাদন করা। 2. To impair the intellect of ; to render insane ; বুদ্ধি-ভ্রংশ করা, বিকৃত-মস্তিষ্ক করা ; পাগল করা, উন্মাদ করা। ***Verb i.*** 1. (*Pottery*) To be minutely cracked as the glazing ; (মৃৎশিল্প) মৃন্ময় ভাণ্ডাদির উপরিভাগে সূক্ষ্ম সূক্ষ্ম ফাটার চিহ্ন দেখা দেওয়া। 2. To become insane ; উন্মত্ত হওয়া, বিকৃত-মস্তিষ্ক হওয়া। ***Noun.*** 1. Mania ; বাতিক। 2. Insanity ; উন্মাদ-রোগ, পাগলামি। **Crazed,** *p. p. adj.* **craz'-ing,** *n.* **Crazing mill**—আকরোত্থিত খনিজমিশ্র বঙ্গ চূর্ণ করণার্থ যন্ত্র।

cra'-zy̆, *adj.* 1. Shaky ; as, a *crazy* ship or building ; জীর্ণ, জর্জ্জরিত। 2. Deranged ; mad ; বিকৃত-মতি ; উন্মত্ত, বাতুল, বিক্ষিপ্ত। 3. Infirm ; sickly ; দুর্ব্বল, জরা-জর্জ্জরিত ; রোগা। **—zi-ly,** *adv.* **—zi-ness,** *n.*

creak (crēk), *n., v. i.* & *t.* A sharp, harsh grating sound ; কচকচি, ঠাস্ ঠাস্ শব্দ, কচাৎ কচাৎ শব্দ, ঘটর ঘটর শব্দ, কড়মড় শব্দ। ***Verb i.*** To make a continued sharp grating noise ; কচকচ্ শব্দ করা, কড়মড় শব্দ করা, কচাৎ কচাৎ শব্দ করা, ঘটর ঘটর শব্দ করা। ***Verb t.*** To cause to creak ; কচাৎ কচাৎ শব্দ করান, ঘটর ঘটর শব্দ করান। **Creak'-y,** *adj.*

cream (crēm), *n.* 1. The oily part of milk which collects on the surface ; সর, মলাই, সন্তানিকা। 2. The part of a liquid that gathers on the surface ; তরল পদার্থের যে অংশ উপরে পর্দার মত পড়ে। 3. A sweatmeat prepared from cream ; সর হইতে প্রস্তুত মিঠাই বিশেষ। 4. The best part of a thing ; আসল ভাগ, সারাংশ, সত্ব 5. A cream like cosmetic or medicinal preparation ; as, a cold *cream* ; সরের মত অঙ্গরাগ বা ঔষধ। 6. The colour of cream ; সরের বর্ণ। 7. A cream-coloured horse, etc. ; সরের বর্ণ ঘোড়া। **Cream'-i-ness,** *n.* **Cream'-y,** *adj.* **Cream-chease** — সর না-তোলা দুগ্ধ হইতে তৈয়ারী পনীর, মালাইর পনীর। **Cream-fruit** — সায়েরালিয়ান নামক স্থানের ফল বিশেষ। **Cream-coloured**—পীতাভ-শ্বেত। **Cream-laid** or **wove paper**—সরের বর্ণ পালিশ ব বুনা কাগজ। **Cream-separator**—দুগ্ধ হইতে সর পৃথক করার জন্য যন্ত্র বিশেষ। **Clotted** or **Devonshire cream**—দুগ্ধ উষ্ণ করিয়া প্রস্তুত সর। **Cream of lime**—বিশুদ্ধ গুঁড়া চূণ। **Cream of tartar** — তিন্তিরাম্ল এবং কাষ্ঠ-ভস্মের ক্ষার।

cream (crēm), *v. i.* & *t.* To form cream or scum as milk or other liquid ; সর পড়া। ***Verb t.*** 1. To cause as milk to form cream ; দুধে সর ফেলা। 2. To take cream from (milk, etc.) by skimming ; সর তোলা, সর উঠান। 3. To take off the choicest part of (anything) ; সারাংশ তুলিয়া লওয়া। 4. To add cream to, as tea, etc. ; চা প্রভৃতিতে সর মিশান। **Cream-faced**—(ভয়ে) পাংশুবর্ণ, পাঙ্গাশবর্ণ।

cream'-ēr (crēm-), *n.* A flat dish for skimming cream from milk ; a machine for separating cream ; দুগ্ধ হইতে সর তুলিবার জন্য থালা বিশেষ ; সর তুলিবার যন্ত্র বিশেষ।

cream'-ẽr-ȳ (crēm-), *n.* **1.** An establishment where cheese, butter, etc. are made and sold ; যে কারখানায় পনীর ও মাখন প্রভৃতি প্রস্তুত ও বিক্রীত হয়। **2.** A place where milk is set for creaming ; যে স্থানে সর তোলার জন্য দুগ্ধ রাখা হয়।

crē'-ance (-ăns), *n.* The cord which secures a hawk while it is being trained ; শিক্ষাদানকালে যে রজ্জুতে বাঁধিয়া বাজপক্ষীকে আটক রাখা হয়।

crease (crēs), *n., v. t.* & *i.* **1.** A line or mark made by folding ; a wrinkle ; ভাজের দাগ ; চুনট, ঊর্মি (মঃ ইঃ), ঊর্ম্মিকা (ঐ)। **2.** (*Cricket*) A line defining the position of the bowler or batsman ; as, a bowling *crease* ; (ক্রীকেট ক্রীড়ায়) বলনিক্ষেপকারী বা ব্যাটধারীর অবস্থান নির্ণায়ক রেখা। ***Verb t.*** **1.** To make a crease or creases in ; as, to *crease* a piece of paper ; to wrinkle ; চুনট করা, তহ করা ; কুঞ্চিত করা। **2.** To crimp ; তরঙ্গায়িত করা। **3.** (*U. S.*) To stun as a horse etc., by shooting ; (মার্কিণ যুক্তরাজ্যে) গুলি করিয়া ঘোড়া প্রভৃতিকে স্তম্ভিত করা। ***Verb i.*** To become creased ; তরঙ্গায়িত হওয়া, কুঞ্চিত হওয়া। **Creas'-y,** *adj.* **Bowling crease**—যে রেখার পশ্চাতে থাকিয়া বলনিক্ষেপকারী বলনিক্ষেপ করে।

crease (crēs), *n.* A Malay dagger ; মালয় দেশবাসীদিগের ছুরিকা বিশেষ, কিরিচ।

crē-āte', *v. t.* **1.** To bring into being or existence ; সৃষ্টি করা, বিরচন করা, রচনা করা। **2.** To cause to produce ; to give rise to ; "Position and climate *create* habits ; ঘটান, উৎপাদন করা ; উদ্ভূত করা। **3.** To originate as a work of thought or imagination as, an actor *creates* a part ; মানস-সৃষ্টি করা। **4.** To invest with a new character, office or rank ; as, to *create* (a man) a peer ; নূতন ভাব, কার্য্য বা পদবী প্রদান করা। **—a'-tive,** *adj.* **—a'-tive-ly,** *adv.* **—a'-tive-ness,** *n.*

crē-ā-tine (-tĭn), *n.* An organic base found in meat-juices ; মাংসের রসে যে জৈব সার পাওয়া যায়।

crē-ā'-tion, *n.* **1.** Act of creating the world ; সৃষ্টি, সর্জ্জন। **2.** The act of making or producing ; বিরচন, উৎপাদন, জনন, নির্ম্মাণ, নির্ম্মিতি (আঃ বঃ)। **3.** Investment with a new character or position ; নূতনভাব বা পদবী প্রদান। **4.** The things created ; the production of the human intellect or imagination ; creatures collectively ; সৃষ্ট বস্তু, চরাচর, সৃষ্টি, দুনিয়া প্রভৃতি ; মানসসৃষ্টি, কল্পনা-প্রসূত বিষয় ; সৃষ্ট জীবগণ। **—ism** *n.* **1.** (*Theol.*) The doctrine of the creation of a soul by God for every human being at birth ; (খৃষ্টীয় ধর্ম্মশাস্ত্র) জন্মকালে ঈশ্বর প্রত্যেক মানবের জন্য এক একটী পৃথক্ আত্মা সৃষ্টি করিয়া দেন—এইরূপ মত, সৃষ্টীশ্বরভেদবাদ (হিঃ কোঃ), প্রতি-জীব সৃষ্টিবাদ (ঐ)। **2.** (*Philos.*) The theory that the earth is created out of nothing ; (দর্শনশাস্ত্র) শূন্য বা অবস্তু হইতে জগত সৃষ্ট হইয়াছে—এইরূপ দার্শনিক বাদ। **—ist,** *n.*

crē-ā'-tor (-tẽr), *n.* **1.** One who creates ; the supreme being ; স্রষ্টা ; সৃষ্টিকর্ত্তা, ঈশ্বর, ধাতা, বিধাতা। **2.** The creator God ; সৃষ্টিকর্ত্তা পরমেশ্বর। **—tress,** *n.* (*Fem.*)

crea'-tūre (crē-), *n.* **1.** A created thing ; সৃষ্টবস্তু, ভূত (মঃ ইঃ)। **2.** A living being ; an animal ; a human being (in contempt, pity or affection) ; প্রাণী ; জন্তু ; জানোয়ার, জীব (মনুষ্য সম্পর্কে—করুণা, স্নেহ বা অবজ্ঞা প্রকাশার্থে)। **3.** One who owns his fortune to another ; a dependent ; a tool ; যে ব্যক্তি অন্য ব্যক্তির নিকট হইতে ধনসম্পত্তি লাভ করে ; আশ্রিত-জন, প্রতিপাল্য ব্যক্তি, উপজীবী ; যন্ত্র। **4.** Something as food, drink, promoting human comfort ; "Good *creature*" ; শারীরিক সুখ স্বচ্ছন্দতাবিধায়ক বস্তু। **5.** (*Humorous*) Whisky, etc. (with *the* before it) ; as, *the creature* ; হুইস্কি প্রভৃতি। **The creature**—হুইস্কি অথবা মাদকদ্রব্য। **Creature comforts**—অন্যান্য শারীরিক সুখ স্বচ্ছন্দতা, আচ্ছা খানাপিনা। **A creature of circumstances**—অবস্থার উপর সম্পূর্ণ নির্ভর-শীল ব্যক্তি।

crea'-tūre-lȳ (crē-), *adj.* Of, or having the qualities of, the creature ; প্রাণিসম্বন্ধীয়, প্রাণি-স্বভাব-বিশিষ্ট।

creche (crāsh), *n.* A public nursery for children ; সাধারণ শিশু-পালনাগার।

crē'-dence (-dĕns), *n.* **1.** Belief ; as, to give *credence* to a story ; বিশ্বাস, প্রত্যয়, শ্রদ্ধা (মঃ ইঃ)। **2.** (*Eccles.*) A communion table on which bread and wine are placed before consecration ; (যাজকীয় শাস্ত্র) উৎসর্গের পূর্ব্বে যে মেজে খৃষ্টের শেষ ভোজনের স্মৃতি উৎসবের রুটি ও সুরা রক্ষিত হয়। **To find credence in**—To be believed in ; বিশ্বাসভাজন হওয়া। **To give credence to**—To believe ; বিশ্বাস করা, আস্থা স্থাপন করা। **A letter of credence**—অনুরোধপত্র, সুপারিশ পত্র, পরিচয় পত্র।

cre-den'-tial (-shĭ-ăl), *n.* **1.** That which gives a title to credit ; বিশ্বাস-জনকপত্র, বিশ্বাসজনকনিদর্শন ; বিশ্বাস্ত পত্র, সনদ। **2.** (*Usu. Pl.*) Letters of recommendation or introduction ; (*lit.* & *fig*) ; (সাধারণতঃ বহুবচন) সুপারিশ পত্র, পরিচয়পত্র,

অভিজ্ঞান পত্র (মঃ ইঃ) (শব্দানুযায়ী এবং লক্ষণায়)।

crĕd'-i-ble, *adj.* Worthy of credit or belief; প্রত্যয়যোগ্য, বিশ্বাস্য, বিশ্বাসার্হ, বিশ্বসনীয়, শ্রদ্ধেয়। **—bil'-i-ty,** *n.* **—bly,** *adv.*

crĕd'-it, *n.* **1.** Belief; faith; trust; প্রত্যয়; শ্রদ্ধা; বিশ্বাস, বিশ্রম্ভ (মঃ ইঃ)। **2.** Reputation; good name; honour; "A citizen of *credit* and renown;" মান, পশার; সুনাম; কীর্ত্তি, খ্যাতি, প্রতিষ্ঠা, ইজ্জত, ভরম, সম্ভ্রম। **3.** Power derived from reputation etc.; প্রতিপত্তি। **4.** Honour; acknowledgment of merit; as, to get *credit* for a meritorious act; a source of honour; as, to be a *credit* to one's family; সম্মান; গুণের সম্মান; সম্মানের হেতু। **5.** (*Comm.*) Sale on trust; mercantile reputation entitlir one to be trusted; the time given for payment of goods sold on trust; as, a long *credit*; (বাণিজ্য) ধার; বাজার সম্ভ্রম; ধারে বিক্রীত জিনিষের মূল্য প্রদানের জন্য নির্দ্দিষ্ট সময়, ম্যাদ, মুদ্দত। **6.** (*Book-keeping*) The acknowledgment of payment by entry in an account; হিসাবে জমা করিয়া টাকার প্রাপ্তি-স্বীকার। **7.** (*Book-keeping*) The side of an account in which payment is entered, (opposed to *debit*); the sum on the credit side of an account; হিসাবের জমার দিক; জমার দিকের টাকার অঙ্ক। **8.** A sum that a person can get from a bank; কোন লোক ধনাগার হইতে যত টাকা পাইতে পারে, তাহার সংখ্যা। **9.** A sum which the administration is empowered by vote of Parliament to borrow and expend in anticipation of the amount voted in the Annual Estimates; বার্ষিক আয়ব্যয় নির্দ্ধারণের সময় মঞ্জুর হইবে আশায় যে টাকা কর্জ্জ করিয়া খরচ করার জন্য পার্লেমেন্টমহাসভা শাসন কর্ত্তৃপক্ষগণকে ক্ষমতা প্রদান করিয়া থাকেন। **A letter of credit**—কোন কার্য্যকারকের নিকট হইতে টাকা পাইবার আদেশ-পত্র। **On or upon credit**—ধারে। **On the credit of**—Upon the security of; কাহারও জামিনে। **To carry to the credit of, (credit to)**—To enter on the credit side of an account; হিসাবের জমার দিকে লিখা। **To give credit to**—To trust; বিশ্বাস করা। **To give one credit for**—To enter as a sum on one's credit; কাহারও হিসাবের জমার দিকেকোন টাকা লিখা। (*Fig.*) To give one honour or praise for; (লক্ষণায়) কোন ব্যক্তিকে প্রশংসা বা সম্মান প্রদান করা। **To take credit to one's self**—To claim honour (for doing something); (কোন কার্য্য সম্পাদনের জন্য) সম্মানের দাবী করা।

crĕd'-it, *v. t.* **1.** To put faith in; বিশ্বাস-স্থাপন করা, আস্থা-স্থাপন করা। **2.** To do honour to; গৌরবান্বিত করা। **3.** (*Book-keeping*) To enter on the credit side of an account; to give credit for; as, to *credit* a sum to a person or to *credit* a person with a sum; হিসাবের জমার দিকে লিখিয়া লওয়া। **4.** (*Fig.*) To give credit for; as, to *credit* a person with a quality; (লক্ষণায়) গুণানুবাদ করা, সুখ্যাতি করা, সুনাম করা। **To credit one with**—To ascribe to one; আরোপ করা। To give one credit for; কোন বিষয়ের জন্য গৌরব প্রদান করা।

crĕd'-it-ă-ble, *adj.* Estimable; honourable; আদরণীয়; সম্মানজনক, মান্য, শ্রদ্ধেয়, শ্লাঘ্য, কীর্ত্তিকর। **—bly,** *adv.*

crĕd'-i-tor (-têr), *n.* **1.** A person to whom a sum of money or debt is due, (opp. to *debtor*); উত্তমর্ণ, মহাজন। **2.** (*Book-keeping*) The credit or right-hand side of an account, (abbr. *Cr.*); হিসাবের ডাহিন বা জমার দিক। **3.** (*Rom. law*) The promise in a contract; (রোমীয় আইন) কোন যুক্তির প্রতিশ্রুতি।

crē'-dō, *n.* A creed or formula of belief; ধর্ম্মমত, ধর্ম্মসূত্র।

crĕd'-ū-lous (-lŭs), *adj.* **1.** Over-ready to believe; unsuspecting; বিশ্বাসপ্রবণ, অতিবিশ্বাসী, আশুবিশ্বাসী, কানপাতলা; সংশয় বা সন্দেহশূন্য। **2.** Based upon or produced from credulity; as, *credulous* exaggerations; অতিবিশ্বাসমূলক, অতিবিশ্বাসজনিত। **—ness,** *n.* **—ly,** *adv.*

crĕ-dū'-li-tў, *n.* Excessive easiness of belief; বিশ্বাসপ্রবণতা, অতি বিশ্বাস, শ্রদ্ধাজাড্য (হিঃ কোঃ)।

creed, (crēd), *n.* **1.** A brief and authoritative summary of the articles of Christian faith, (also *the creed*); খৃষ্টধর্ম্মের মত বা বিশ্বাসের সংক্ষিপ্ত এবং প্রামাণিক সারমর্ম্ম। **2.** A system of religious belief; ধর্ম্মবিশ্বাসের প্রণালীবদ্ধ ব্যবস্থাসমূহ। **3.** Any solemn profession of principles or opinions; অচলপ্রতিষ্ঠ মত বা বিশ্বাস গম্ভীরভাবে বিঘোষণ।

creek (crēk), *n.* **1.** A small inlet, bay or cove; খাড়ি। **2.** A small port or harbour; ক্ষুদ্র বন্দর বা পোতাশ্রয়-স্থলী। **3.** Short arm of a river; নদীর ক্ষুদ্র শাখা। **3.** (*U. S.*) A rivulet; a stream; (মার্কিণ-যুক্তরাজ্য) ক্ষুদ্রনদী; স্রোতস্বতী। **4.** A narrow plain between mountains; পর্ব্বতসমূহের মধ্যবর্ত্তী সঙ্কীর্ণ উপত্যকা।

creel (crēl), *n.* An osier basket, esp. a fisher's; angler's fishing basket; ঝুড়ি, চাঙ্গারি, বিশেষতঃ ধীবরদিগের মৎস্যের ঝুড়ি; মৎস্যবেধকগণের ঝুড়ি।

creep (crēp), *v. i.* & *n.* **1.** To move on the belly as a worm; সরীসৃপের মত বুকে হাঁটিয়া চলা। **2.** To advance slowly, timorously or stealthingly; গুঁড়ি গুঁড়ি

চলা। **3.** (*Fig*) To come up unobserved ; as, despondency began to *creep* over fairer hearts ; (লক্ষণায়) অলক্ষিতে আসা, চোরের মত আসা। **4.** To fawn ; to cringe ; as, a *creeping* sycophant ; তোষামোদ করা ; কাকুতি মিনতি করা, গড়াইয়া পড়া। **5.** (*Of plants*) To grow along the ground, wall or other support ; (উদ্ভিদ সম্বন্ধে) লতায়িত হওয়া। ***Noun*** **1.** Creeping ; বুকে হাঁটিয়া চলন, উরোগমন। **2.** Feeling of horror ; ছম্ ছম্ বোধ। **3.** A low arch under a railway embankment; লৌহবর্ত্মের বাঁধের নীচে অনুচ্চ তোরণ। **4.** A close opening for animals to pass through ; জন্তুদিগের প্রবেশের জন্য সংকীর্ণ ফাঁক। **Flesh creeps**—Feels as if things were creeping over it ; shivers (as a result of fear, horror or repugnance) ; গা সড়নড়ি করা ; গা ছম্ ছম্ করা। **To give one the creeps**—To cause one to shudder ; ভয়ে থর থর করিয়া কাঁপান।

creep′-er, (crēp-) *n.* **1.** One who or that which creeps ; esp. a creeping plant ; যে বা যাহা বুকে হাঁটিয়া চলে, উরোগামী (মঃ ইঃ) ; লতা, বল্লরী, বল্লী, ব্রততী। **2.** A grapnel for dragging the bottom of water ; একপ্রকার নঙ্গর, যাহা জলের তলদেশ ঘসড়াইয়া যায়।

creese (crēs), **crease** (crēs), **kris** *ns.* A Malay dagger having a serpentine blade ; মালয়দ্বীপ বাসিগণের ছুরিকা।

crē-māte′, *v. t.* To dispose of (a human body) by burning ; দাহকর্ম্ম করা, শবদাহ করা, অগ্নি-সৎকার করা। **—ma′-tion,** *n.* Act of cremating ; দহন, দাহ, অগ্নিসৎকার, দাহকর্ম্ম। **—ma′-tion-ist,** *n.*

crē-mā′-tor (-tēr), *n.* A person or furnace cremating dead bodies or rubbish ; দহনকারী, শবদাহক, জঞ্জালদাহক, শ্মশানের চুল্লী, চিতা।

crĕm-ă-tō′-ri-ŭm, crĕm′-ă-tŏ-rŷ, *ns.* A place or establishment for cremation ; শবদাহনস্থলী, শ্মশান।

creme, *n.* (*F.*) Cream ; সর, সার। ***Creme de la creme***—The very pick ; সারাৎসার। ***Creme de menthe***—পুদিনার সার।

crē-mŏ′-nă, *n.* A superior kind of violin formerly made at Cremona in Italy ; একপ্রকার উৎকৃষ্ট শ্রেণীর বেহালা।

crē′-nāte, —nāt-ĕd, *adj.* (*Bot.* and *zool.*) Notched ; indented ; দন্তিল, অতীক্ষ্ণ দন্তিত (সাঃ পঃ) ; খাঁজ-কাটা। **—na′-tion,** *n.*

crĕn′-ă-tūre, *n.* A notch on the edge of a leaf, etc. ; পাতা প্রভৃতির কিনারার খাঁজ।

crĕn′-ĕl, —elle (-ĕl), *n.* A loophole in a parapet through which to dischange musketry ; দুর্গের আবক্ষঃস্থল উচ্চ প্রাচীরের বন্দুক ছুড়িবার রন্ধ্র।

crĕn′-ĕl-āte, —lāte, *v. t.* To furnish with battlements or loopholes ; তোপ বন্দুকাদি দাগিবার রন্ধ্র করা বা উক্তরূপ রন্ধ্রযুক্ত প্রাচীর সমন্বিত করা।

crē′-ōle, *n.* & *adj.* **1.** A native of the West Indies or Spanish America but not of indeginous blood ; পশ্চিম ভারতীয় দ্বীপপুঞ্জ ও স্পেনিশ আমেরিকার উপনিবেশিকগণের বংশধর। **2.** A Negro born in America (now generally called *creole negro*) ; আমেরিকাদেশে জাত কাফ্রী। ***Adj.*** Of or relating to creole descent ; স্পেনিশ আমেরিকা বা পশ্চিমভারতীয় দ্বীপপুঞ্জের কাফ্রীগণের বংশধরগণ সম্পর্কীয়। **Creole whites**—পশ্চিম ভারতীয় দ্বীপপুঞ্জের ইয়ুরোপীয় অধিবাসিগণের বংশধরগণ। **Creole Negro**—আমেরিকা দেশেজাত কাফ্রী বা তদ্দেশের আধিবাসিরূপে পরিগণিত কাফ্রী।

crē′-ō-sōte, *n.* **1.** An antiseptic oily fluid with the smell of smoke ; পচন-নিবারক তৈলাক্ত তরল পদার্থ বিশেষ। **2.** Carbolic acid ; কার্বলিক অম্ল।

crepe, *n.* (*F.*) Crape ; ক্রেপ কাপড়। **Crepe de chine**—কাঁচা রেশম হইতে তৈয়ারী ক্রেপ কাপড়।

crĕp′-i-tāte, *v. i.* **1.** To crackle ; পটপট করা, কড়কড় করা, চিড় চিড় করা। **2.** (*Zool.*) To discharge fluid with sharp report ; চিড় চিড় শব্দে তরল পদার্থ নির্গত করা। **—tant,** *adj.* **—ta′-tion,** *n.*

crē′-pŏn, *n.* A stuff like crape but firmer in texture ; ক্রেপের মত এক প্রকার কাপড়।

crĕpt, See creep.

crē-pŭs′-cū-lar (-lêr), *adj.* **1.** Of or relating to twilight ; dim ; গোধূলি-বেলা সম্বন্ধীয়, সান্ধ্য, প্রাদোষিক ; নিষ্প্রভ। **2.** (*Zool.*) Flying or appearing in the twilight ; (প্রাণি-বিদ্যা) গোধূলিচর। **3.** Imperfectly enlightened ; as, *crepuscular* civilization ; অস্ফুটালোক-প্রাপ্ত।

crē-scen′-dō (-shĕn-), *adv.*, *n.*, & *adj.* (*Mus.*) With a gradually increasing volume of sound, (abbr. *cres.* or *crese.*) ; (সঙ্গীত-শাস্ত্র) ক্রমবর্দ্ধিষ্ণু ধ্বনিসহকারে। ***Noun.*** A gradual increase in the volume of sound ; a passage of music to be played with an increasing volume of tune ; ধ্বনির পরিমাণের ক্রমশঃ বৃদ্ধি ; ক্রমবর্দ্ধিষ্ণু ধ্বনিতে গেয় সঙ্গীতাংশ। ***Adj.*** **1.** (*Mus.*) Gradually increasing in volume ; (সঙ্গীত-শাস্ত্র) ক্রমবর্দ্ধমান ধ্বনি-বিশিষ্ট। **2.** (*Phon.*) Pronounced with increasing force or stress ; (ধ্বনি-বিজ্ঞান) স্বরের উপর ক্রমবর্দ্ধিষ্ণু জোর সহকারে উচ্চারিত।

crĕs′-cĕnt, *n.* & *adj.* **1.** The moon in her increasing state ; চন্দ্রকলা, চন্দ্ররেখা, শিশুশশী, অপূর্ণচন্দ্র, বালেন্দু, বালচন্দ্রমা। **2.** A figure of the new moon as the badge of the Turkish Sultans ; the Turkish power ; Mahommadanism ; as, the crescent and the cross ; তুরস্ক দেশের সুলতানদিগের চিহ্নস্বরূপ চন্দ্রলেখা ; তুরস্কশক্তি ; মুসলমান ধর্ম্ম। **3.** Anything shaped like the crescent moon ; বালেন্দুসন্নিভ বস্তু। **4.** A row of houses in the form of an arc of a circle ; বৃত্তখণ্ডাকারে স্থিত গৃহশ্রেণী। **5.** A disease in a horse's foot ; অশ্বের পদরোগ বিশেষ। **6.** A Turkish musical instrument ; তুরস্কদেশীয় বাদ্যযন্ত্র বিশেষ। **7.** (*Her.*) A bearing in the form of a half-moon ; (কুলবিদ্যা) অর্দ্ধচন্দ্রাকৃতি কুলচিহ্ন। ***Adj.*** **1.** Increasing ; ক্রমবর্দ্ধিষ্ণু। **2.** Of the shape of the crescent ; চন্দ্রলেখাকার।

crĕss, *n.* **1.** A species of plant with pungent edible leaves ; as, garden or water *cress* ; তোরা তেজক, চানসুর, হালিম শাক (ফার্ম্মিঃ)। **2.** Any plant resembling cress ; হালিম শাকের মতন গাছ গাছড়া। **Garden cress**—*Lepidium sativium* চুনসার (বেলঃ), হালিম (বীজ সম্পর্কে), লুট পুটিয়া (পাতাসম্পর্কে)। **Cress-seed**—হারিফ (হিন্দি), রোহিত সর্ষপ (বেলঃ)।

crĕs'-sĕt, *n.* **1.** A fire-pan fixed on the top of a hole ; (*modern*) a fire-basket for giving light on a wharf, etc. ; দণ্ডাগ্রে সংবদ্ধ অগ্নিপাত্র, আকাশদীপ (আঃ বঃ) ; (আধুনিক) জেটি প্রভৃতিতে আলোক প্রদানের জন্য অগ্নিপাত্র। **2.** (*Coopering*) A fire-case used to char the inside of a cask ; (পিপানির্ম্মাণ) পিপার ভিতরের দিক পোড়াইয়া কাল করার জন্য অগ্নিপাত্র বিশেষ। **3.** A chafer ; কটাহ।

crĕst, *n., v. t.* & *i.* **1.** A tuft on the head of a bird or animal ; চূড়া, শিখর, মৌলি, শিখা, কিরীট, শেখর, অবতংস। **2.** A tuft or plume of feathers worn on a helmet ; the apex of a helmet ; a helmet ; শিরস্ত্রাণের উপর পরিহিত পালকগুচ্ছ ; শিরস্ত্রাণের চূড়া ; শিরস্ত্রাণ। **3.** (*Her.*) A device placed over a coat of arms ; বর্ম্মের উপরিস্থ কুলমর্য্যাদাসূচক চিহ্নের চূড়া। **4.** High spirits ; courage ; pride ; as, *crest*-fallen (dejected, abashed, etc.) ; সাহস ; বীর্য্য ; গর্ব্ব। **5.** The rising part of a horse's neck ; the mane ; অশ্বের গলদেশের উত্থিত অংশ ; অশ্বাদির ঘাড়ের লোম। **6.** The top or summit, as of a mountain, etc. ; (পর্ব্বতাদির) চূড়া। **7.** The top of a wave ; তরঙ্গ শীর্ষ। **8.** (*Anat.*) A ridge along the surface of a bone ; (শারীরসংস্থান বিদ্যা) শরীরের অস্থির উন্নত অংশ, অস্থি-শির। **9.** (*Arch.*) The ornamental ridging of a roof, etc. ; (স্থপতি-বিজ্ঞান) ছাদ প্রভৃতির কারুকার্য্য খচিত আলি। ***Verb t.*** **1.** To furnish with a crest ; to serve as a crest to ; চূড়ার কাজ করা ; চূড়াসমন্বিত করা। **2.** To mark with long streaks ; লম্বা লম্বা ডোরাবিশিষ্ট করা। **3.** To reach the top of, as a hill or wave ; পর্ব্বত বা তরঙ্গের চূড়ায় উপনীত হওয়া। ***Verb i.*** To form or rise to, a crest, as a wave ; চূড়া গঠন করা, চূড়ার আকারে উত্থিত হওয়া। **Crest-fallen** — হেঁটমুখ, হতোদ্যম, হৃত-গর্ব্ব।

crē-ta'-ceous(-shŭs), *adj.* Chalky ; of the nature of, or abounding in, chalk ; খটিক-সম্বন্ধীয়, খটিক-ধর্ম্মী, খটিক-বহুল।

crē'-tic, *n.* A metrical foot ; পদ্যের চরণ বিশেষ, শব্দাংশত্রয় বি. ৪ পদ্যের চরণ বিশেষ—ইহার মধ্য শব্দাংশ লঘু এবং প্রথম ও শেষ শব্দাংশদ্বয় গুরু হইয়া থাকে।

crē'-tin, *n.* One of a class of deformed idiots found in the Alpine valleys ; আল্‌স্‌ পর্ব্বতের উপত্যকাবাসী কদাকার এবং আজন্ম-নির্ব্বোধ লোক। **–ism,** *n.* **–ize,** *v. t.* **–ous,** *adj.*

cré-tonne (-tŏn), *n.* [*L.*] A patterned cotton-cloth for upholstery purposes ; পর্দ্দা, লেপ, তোষক প্রভৃতির জন্য ব্যবহৃত একপ্রকার লতা-পাতাযুক্ত সূতার কাপড়।

crē-vasse' (-vȧs), *n.* **1.** A fissure or rent in the mass of a glacier, etc. ; তুষারনদী প্রভৃতির ফাটল বা

Crevasse.

ভঙ্গ, হিমানীদরী। **2.** (*U. S.*) A breach in the embankment of a river ; (মার্কিণযুক্তরাজ্যে) নদীর বাঁধের ভঙ্গ।

crĕv'-ice (-ĭs), *n.* A fissure ; a cleft ; ছিদ্র, রন্ধ্র, ফাইট, অন্ধিসন্ধি; চিড়।

crew, (crô), *n.* **1.** A company of seamen manning a ship or boat ; জাহাজ বা নৌকার নাবিকমণ্ডলী, পোতবাহকগণ, মাঝি সকল, মাল্লা সকল। **2.** A band of armed men ; অস্ত্রধারী ব্যক্তির দল। **3.** A company of people associated together ; লোকমণ্ডলী, জনমণ্ডলী। **4.** A set ; a gang ; শ্রেণী ; দল। **5.** A body of workmen employed in a particular piece of work ; কোন বিশেষ কার্য্যে নিযুক্ত শিল্পিবর্গ।

crew (crö), See CROW.

crew'-ĕl (crö-), *n.* **1.** A kind of fine worsted yarn for tapestry and embroidery ; একপ্রকার মিহি পশমী সূতা—যদ্দারা পর্দ্দার কাপড়ে ফুল, পাতা, প্রভৃতি তোলা হয়। **2.** Crewel-work ; পর্দ্দার উপর মিহি পশমী সূতা দ্বারা ফুলপ্রভৃতিতোলার কাজ, পর্দ্দার উপর চিকণের কাজ।

crib, *n.* **1.** A manger or rack for fodder ; যে গামলা প্রভৃতিতে পশুদিগের খাদ্য দেওয়া হয়, গবাদনী (মঃ ইঃ), দ্রোণী (আঃ বঃ), অশ্বগবাদির ভোজনপাত্রের উপরিস্থ ঘাস রাখিবার তাক। **2.** A child's bed with barred sides ; এক প্রকার শিশু-খট্টা—ইহার চতুর্দ্দিক গরাদদ্বারা বেষ্টিত থাকে। **3.** A stall for oxen ; গোশাল। **4.** A bin for storing grain, salt, etc. ; শস্য, লবণ প্রভৃতি রাখিবার ক্ষুদ্র গোলা। **5.** A framework for supporting a roof or for lining a shaft ; ছাদ, চাল বা স্তম্ভের কাঠাম। **6.** (*Colloq.*) A plagiarism ; a translation or key for the illegitimate use of students ; (চলিত ভাষায়) অন্যের লেখা চুরি ; ছাত্রগণ কর্ত্তৃক অবৈধভাবে ব্যবহারের জন্য অনুবাদ বা অর্থপুস্তক। **7.** (*Card-game*) A set of cards composed of two thrown from the hand of each player (in cribbage) ; তাস খেলার পিট। **8.** A house or shop ; as, to crack a *crib* (= to break into a shop or house as burglar — thieves' cant) ; বাটী বা দোকান। **Crib'-biting**—A horse's habit of seizing the manger with the teeth and at the same time noisily drawing in the breath ; অশ্ব-কর্ত্তৃক খাদ্যপাত্র দাঁত দ্বারা কামড়াইয়া ধরণ এবং তৎসময়ে সশব্দে শ্বাস টানিয়া লওন।

crib, *v. t.* **1.** To shut up in a small space ; সংকীর্ণ স্থানে বদ্ধ করা, রুদ্ধ করা, আটক করা। **2.** To plagiarize ; অপর ব্যক্তির রচনা হইতে চুরি করা। **3.** To supply as a cowshed etc. with cribs or mangers ; গোশালায় গবাদির খাদ্যপাত্র বা ঘাস রাখিবার তাক জোগান।

crib'-bāge, *n.* A game at cards ; এক প্রকার তাস খেলা।

crib'-ble, *n.* A sieve ; চালুনি।

crib'-ri-fôrm, *adj.* Perforated like a sieve (*Anat.* & *Bot.*) ; চালুনীর মত রন্ধ্র-বহুল।

crick, *n.* & *v. t.* A spasmodic affection in the neck, back, etc. ; ঘাড়, পৃষ্ঠ প্রভৃতির আক্ষেপজনক রোগ বিশেষ। ***Verb t.*** To produce a painful stiffness in (the neck etc.) ; গলা প্রভৃতিতে বেদনাযুক্ত আড়ষ্টতা উৎপাদন করা।

crick'-ĕt, *n.* An insect which makes a chirping or creaking sound ; ঝিঁঝিঁ পোকা, ঝিল্লী, ভৃঙ্গারী।

crick'-ĕt, *n.* & *v. i.* A favourite outdoor game played with bats and ball between two parties ; ক্রীকেট ক্রীড়া, দণ্ড-কন্দুক ক্রীড়া। ***Verb i.*** To play cricket ; উক্ত প্রকার ক্রীড়া করা। **—er,** *n.*

crī'-coid (-coyd), *adj.* & *n.* Shaped like a ring ; অঙ্গুরীয়াকার। ***Noun.*** The ring-shaped cartilage of the larynx ; কণ্ঠনালির উর্দ্ধভাগস্থ অঙ্গুরীয়াকার তরুণাস্থি বিশেষ।

crī'-êr, *n.* **1.** One who cries ; an officer who proclaims orders etc. in courts or makes public announcements ; চীৎকারকারী ; নকীব, বিঘোষক, ঘোষণাকারী। **2.** A hawker ; ফেরিওয়ালা।

crī'-key (-kī), *interj.* denoting astonishment ; বিস্ময়বোধক অব্যয়।

crīme, *n.* **1.** The commission of an act forbidden by law ; অবৈধ কার্য্য করণ। **2.** A grave offence ; গুরুতর অপরাধ। **3.** Any great wickedness ; sin ; sinful conduct ; দুষ্কৃত ; অধর্ম্ম, পাপ, কল্মষ, কলুষ ; পাপাচরণ।

crim'-i-năl, *adj.* & *n.* **1.** Of the nature of a crime ; as, a *criminal* connection ; অপরাধাত্মক। **2.** Guilty of a crime ; কোনরূপ অপরাধে দোষী, কৃতাপরাধ, সাপরাধ, গুনাগার। **3.** Relating to crimes ; as, *criminal* law ; (opposed to *civil*) ; অপরাধ বিষয়ক, ফৌজদারী। ***Noun.*** A person guilty of a crime ; a malefactor ; অপরাধী ; দুষ্কর্ম্মকারী। **—ly,** *adv.* **—nal'-i-ty,** *n.* **Criminal conversation** or **connection**—(আইন) বিবাহিতা নারীর সহিত অবৈধ আলাপ বা সংস্রব।

crim'-i-nāte, *v. t.* **1.** To accuse of a crime ; to prove guilty of a crime ; কোন অপরাধে অভিযুক্ত করা ; কোন অপরাধে অপরাধী প্রমাণিত করা। **2.** To blame or censure severely ; to condemn ; তীব্র তিরস্কার করা ; অপরাধী স্থির করা, দোষী করা। **—na'-tion,** *n.* **—na-tive, —na-to-ry,** *adjs.*

crim'-i-ne (-nī), **—ny̆,** *interj.* denoting astonishment ; বিস্ময়বোধক অব্যয়।

crim-i-nŏl'-ŏ-ġy̆, *n.* The science of crime ; অপরাধ-বিদ্যা, অপরাধ-তত্ত্ব।

crim'-i-nous (-nŭs), *adj.* Guilty of a crime ; as, a *criminous* clerk (clergyman) ; কৃতাপরাধ।

crimp, *n.* & *v. t.* One who decoys another into the naval or military service ; (*lit.* & *fig.*) ; (শব্দানুযায়ী এবং লক্ষণায়) ; যে ব্যক্তি নানারূপ প্রলোভনে ভুলাইয়া বা ফাঁকি দিয়া অন্য ব্যক্তিকে নৌ বা সামরিক বিভাগের কার্য্যে নিযুক্ত করে। ***Verb t.*** To decoy for the army or the navy ; to entrap ; নানা প্রকার প্রলোভনদ্বারা ভুলাইয়া নৌ বা সেনা-বিভাগে ভর্ত্তি করান ; ফাঁদে ফেলান।

crimp, *v. t.* **1.** To pinch into plaits or folds ; to frill ; কোঁচান ; চুনট করা। **2.** To corrugate ; তরঙ্গায়িত করা, ঢেউ তোলা। **3.** To gash the flesh of a live-fish with a knife ; ছুরি দ্বারা জীবিত মৎস্যের শরীর গভীর ভাবে কাটা। **4.** To form leather into the required shape ; ইচ্ছানুরূপ আকারে চর্ম্ম গঠন করা।

crim'-son (-z'n), *adj.*, *n.*, *v. t.* & *i.* Deep-red ; ঘনারুণ, শোণ, সুরক্ত, ঘোররক্ত, অলক্তবর্ণ। ***Noun.*** A deep-red colour ; ঘোররক্ত বর্ণ। *Verb t. & i.* To turn deep-red ; ঘোর রক্তবর্ণে রঞ্জিত করা, ঘোর রক্তবর্ণ ধারণ করা।

cringe (crînj), *v. t. & n.* **1.** To shrink ; to cower ; কুঞ্চিত হওয়া ; ভয়ে জড়সড় হওয়া। **2.** To crouch ; to fawn ; as, you should bow to most people but *cringe* to none ; হীনভাবে সঙ্কুচিত হওয়া ; হীনভাবে তোষামোদ করা, কাকুতি মিনতি করা। **3.** To behave obsequiously (to) ; সামান্য লোকবৎ মনযোগানিয়াভাবে চলা। *Noun.* Servile civility ; হীন তোষামোদ, মনযোগানিয়া ভাব।

crin'-gle (crîng-), *n.* (*Naut.*) A ring or eye in a rope of a sail ; (নৌ-বিদ্যা) পাইলের রজ্জুর আংটী বা ছিদ্র।

cri'-nite, *adj.* Hairy ; লোমশ।

Crinium Asiatiticum—সুখদর্শন (বেলঃ), নাগদোনা (ঐ), বিষমণ্ডল (ঐ), লক্ষ্মীনারায়ণ (ঐ)।

cri-noi'-dē-ă (-nŏy-), *n.* An order of extinct lily-shaped zoophites related to some of the star-fish ; তারাপক্ষাদি (সাঃ পঃ), পদ্মপক্ষাদি (ঐ)।

crin'-kle (cring-), *v. t. & i. & n.* To turn or wind ; to twist ; পাকান, জড়ান, পেঁচান ; আঁকাবাঁকা করা বা হওয়া। *Noun.* A wrinkle ; কোচ্কা, চুনট। **—kly,** *adv.*

crin'-kum-cran'-kum (crîng-kŭm-crăng-kŭm), *n. & adj.* A thing full of twists and turns ; (*lit. & fig.*) ; (শব্দানুযায়ী এবং লক্ষণায়) পেঁচান জিনিষ। *Adj.* Full of twists ; পেঁচাল।

cri-nō-lette' (-lŏt), *n.* A contrivance for disbending the back of a woman's skirt ; স্ত্রীলোকের ঘাগরার পশ্চাদ্ভাগ বিস্তারক কৌশল বিশেষ।

cri'-nō-līne, (-lîn) *n.* **1.** A fabric of horse-hair or linen thread ; অশ্বলোম বা ক্ষৌমসূত্র দ্বারা প্রস্তুত বস্ত্র বিশেষ। **2.** A petticoat stiffened with hair, wire, etc. ; লোম, তার প্রভৃতি দ্বারা কঠিনীকৃত ঘাগরা বিশেষ, বেড়াঘাগরা। **3.** A netting round a warship as defence against torpedoes ; জলতলচারী মোচাকার বৃহদ্ গোলা হইতে রণপোত রক্ষার্থ জালের আবরণ বিশেষ।

crī-ō-sphinx (-sfîngks), *n.* (*Egypt. Myth.*) A ram-headed sphinx ; (মিশরদেশীয় পুরাতত্ত্ব) মেষ-মুণ্ড স্ফিঙ্ক্‌স্।

crip'-ple, *n. & v. t.* **1.** A lame person ; পঙ্গু, খঞ্জ, লুলা, লেংড়া, খোঁড়া, পাদবিকল (মঃ ইঃ)। **2.** A temporary staging for cleaning or painting windows ; জানালায় রঙ্ লাগাইবার জন্য বা জানালা পরিষ্কার করিবার জন্য অস্থায়ী মঞ্চ। *Verb t.* **1.** To lame ; পঙ্গু করা, বিকল করা। **2.** (*Fig.*) To disable ; as, to be financially *crippled* ; (লক্ষণায়) বিকল করা, অসমর্থ করা।

crī'-sis, *n.* (*Pl. crises*) **1.** Turning point, esp. of a disease ; সন্ধিসময়, বিশেষতঃ পীড়ার সঙ্কটকাল (অর্থাৎ আরোগ্য বা মৃত্যুসূচক পরিবর্ত্তন)। **2.** A time of difficulty, danger and suspense in commerce, politics, etc. ; সঙ্কট, নিদান।

crisp, *adj., v. t. & i.* **1.** So dry as to be easily broken ; brittle ; কড়কড়া, মরমরা, খড়খড়ে, মচ্মচে, মচমচিয়া ; ভঙ্গ-প্রবণ। **2.** Bracing ; as, *crisp* air ; স্বাস্থ্যজনক। **3.** (*Fig.*) Brisk ; decided in manner ; as, such a *crisp* touch on the piano ; (লক্ষণায়) সজীব ; সুস্পষ্ট। **4.** (*Of hair*) Curly ; কুঞ্চিত। *Verb t. & i.* **1.** To form into curls ; কুঞ্চিত করা বা হওয়া। **Crisp'-ly,** *adv.* **Crisp'-ness,** *n.*

cris-pate, *adj.* (*Bot. & Zool.*) Crisped ; irregular ; (উদ্ভিদ এবং জন্তু-তত্ত্ব) কুঞ্চিত ; বিশৃঙ্খল।

cris-pā'-tion, *n.* **1.** The act of curling ; the condition of being curled ; undulation ; কুঞ্চন ; কুঞ্চিত ভাব ; তরঙ্গায়িত ভাব। **2.** A wrinkling or contraction ; কুঞ্চন।

crisp'-ȳ, *adj.* Curled ; undulated as, a *crispy* lock ; কুঞ্চিত ; তরঙ্গায়িত। **2.** Brittle ; মচমচিয়া, মড় মড়ে। **3.** Brisk ; সতেজ।

criss'-crŏss, *n.* CHRIST-CROSS.

cris'-tāte, *adj.* (*Nat. hist.*) Crested ; সচূড়।

crī-tē'-ri ŏn, *n.* (*Pl. criteria*) A principle or standard by which anything is judged or estimated ; a test ; a rule ; গুণাগুণ নির্ণয়ের আদর্শ, মানদণ্ড, নিকষ (হিঃ কোঃ) ; পরীক্ষা ; বিধি, দাড়া।

cri'-tic, *n.* One who pronounces judgment on anything or person ; a judge of literary or artistic works ; a severe judge or censurer ; one skilled in Biblical criticism ; সমালোচক ; সাহিত্য-সমালোচক ; দোষগুণের কঠোর বিচারক, গুণদোষকোবিদ (আঃ বঃ) ; বাইবেল গ্রন্থের সমালোচনায় নিপুণ ব্যক্তি। **—ti cas'-ter,** *n.* An inferior critic হীন সমালোচক।

crit'-i-căl, *adj.* **1.** Inclined to criticize unfavourably ; censorious ; সমালোচনাপ্রিয় ; দোষদর্শী, ছিদ্রান্বেষী। **2.** Skilful in criticism ; nicely judicious ; সমালোচনানিপুণ ; গুণদোষ-বিচারকুশল (আঃ বঃ), সূক্ষ্মদর্শী। **3.** Relating to or indicating a crisis ; crucial ; dangerous ; as a *critical* condition ; সঙ্কটকাল-সম্বন্ধীয় ; পরীক্ষাত্মক ; সঙ্কট-সঙ্কুল। **4.** Of or relating to critics or criticism ; as, a *critical* examination or essay ; সমালোচনা বা সমালোচক সম্বন্ধীয়, সমালোচনা বিষয়ক। **5.** (*Math. & Phys.*) Marking transition from one state, etc. to another ; (গণিত ও পদার্থবিদ্যা) অবস্থান্তর জ্ঞাপক। **—ly,** *adv.* **Critical philosophy**—জর্ম্মণ

দার্শনিক ইমানুয়্যাল ক্যাণ্ট কর্তৃক প্রবর্ত্তিত সমালোচনামূলক দর্শন।

crit′-i-cism, **1.** The function or work of a critic; সমালোচনা, গুণাগুণজ্ঞান (মঃ ইঃ), গুণাগুণবাদ (আঃ বঃ)। **2.** A critical judgment or examination; সমালোচনামূলক বিচার বা পরীক্ষা, দোষগুণ বিচারণ। **Higher** or **historical criticism**—কোন গ্রন্থের বিরচন, সম্পাদন প্রভৃতি সম্বন্ধীয় প্রশ্নসমূহের ঐতিহাসিক সমালোচনা। **Textual criticism**—বাইবেলের উৎপত্তি, মূলগ্রন্থ, প্রকৃতি প্রভৃতি সম্বন্ধে বৈজ্ঞানিক অনুসন্ধান।

crit′-i-cize, *v. t.* **1.** To examine critically; সমালোচনা করা। **2.** To find fault with; দোষ-প্রদর্শন করা।

cri-tique′ (-tēk), *n.* **1.** Critical essay or notice; গুণাগুণবিচার প্রবন্ধ (আঃ বঃ), সমালোচনা। **2.** Act or art of criticism; সমালোচন, সমালোচন-বিদ্যা।

croak (crōk), *n., v. i.* & *t.* The low harsh sound of a frog or raven; মক্‌মক্ শব্দ, ভেক বা দাঁড়কাকের অনুচ্চ কর্কশ শব্দ, ভেকনাদ (মঃ ইঃ), কা কা রব (ঐ)। ***Verb i.*** **1.** To make a hoarse low sound in the throat as a frog or raven; ভেক বা দাঁড়কাকের মত অনুচ্চ কর্কশ রবে ডাকা, ভেকনাদ করা (মঃ ইঃ)। **2.** To forbode evil; অশুভ সূচনা করা। **3.** (*Slang*) To die; (ইতরভাষায়) মরা। ***Verb t.*** To utter dismally; নিরানন্দজনক স্বরে উচ্চারণ করা। **Croak′-y,** *adj.*

croak′-êr (crōk-) *n.* An animal that croaks; esp. a prophet of evil; যে জন্তু অনুচ্চ কর্কশরবে ডাকে; অশুভ-সূচনাকারী।

crō′-ce-āte (-sĭ-, or -shĭ-); *adj.* Pertaining to saffron; saffron-coloured; কুঙ্কুম-সম্বন্ধীয়, কৌঙ্কুম; কুঙ্কুমবর্ণ, কাশ্মীরজবর্ণ।

crō-chet′ (-shā), *n.* & *v. t.* Fancy knitting-work by means of a small hook; কুশিকাটা দ্বারা বুনা কাজ। ***Verb t.*** To knit in this style; কুশি কাটা দ্বারা বুনা।

crō-cĭd′-ō-līte, *n.* A fibrous opaque mineral in aspect like asbestos; শঙ্খপলিতার মত খনিজ পদার্থ বিশেষ।

crŏck, *n.* **1.** An earthen vessel or pitcher; মৃণ্ময় পাত্র বা কলস, মৃদ্ভাণ্ড **2.** (*Dial.*) A metal pot; (উপভাষা) ধাতব পাত্র। **3.** A broken piece of earthen-ware, as used to cover the hole in a flower pot; মাটীর বাসনের ভাঙ্গা টুকরা।

crŏck, *n.* & *v. i.* **1.** (*Slang*) An inefficient person; (ইতরভাষায়) অকর্ম্মণ্য লোক, অযোগ্য লোক। **2.** A worthless animal, esp. a horse; অকর্ম্মণ্য প্রাণী, বিশেষতঃ অশ্ব। **3.** (*Scot.*) An old ewe; (স্কটলণ্ড) বুড়া ভেড়ী। ***Verb i.*** (*Slang*) To break down; (ইতর ভাষায়) ভাঙ্গিয়া পড়া।

crŏck, *n.* **1.** Soot; ঝুল, ভুষা, কালি। **2.** A low stool; অনুচ্চ কাঠাসন।

crŏck′-ĕr-ȳ, *n.* Earthen-ware vessels; মৃণ্ময় পাত্র সমূহ।

crŏck′-ĕt, *n.* (*Arch.*) Ornaments of leaves, flowers, etc., employed to decorate angles of spires, pinnacles, etc.; (স্থপতি-বিজ্ঞান) চূড়া, শিখর প্রভৃতির কোণ সকলের ভূষণস্বরূপ পত্রপুষ্পাদি।

crŏc′-ō-dīle, *n.* **1.** A large amphibious reptile; নক্র, ঘড়িয়াল, কুম্ভীর, মহামুখ (মঃ ইঃ), অসিদন্ত (ঐ), জলশূকর (ঐ)। **2.** (*Humorous colloq.*) A girl's school-walking two and two in a long file; (চলিত ভাষায় কৌতুকচ্ছলে) এক এক সারিতে দুই জন করিয়া একের পশ্চাতে এক, এইরূপ বহু সারিতে বালিকাদিগের বিদ্যালয়ে গমন। **Crocodile tears**—মায়াকান্না, কপট রোদন, (cf. সাপের চোখে সাঁতার পানি, সতীনের কান্না, মাছের শোকে বিড়ালের কান্না)।

crō′-cŭs, *n.* A bulbous plant with brilliant yellow or purple flowers, তৃণ-কুঙ্কুম, জাফ্রান, কেসর, কাশ্মীরজ, কুঙ্কুমলতা (আঃ বঃ)। **2.** The name of a red or deep yellow-polishing-powder made with oxide of iron; লোহার মরিচা

Corn of crocus.

হইতে প্রস্তুত লাল বা হল্‌দে রঙ্গের পালিশের গুড়া। ***Crocus sativus***—কুঙ্কুম গাছ, কাশ্মীরজ বৃক্ষ, কাশ্মীরজ (বেলঃ)।

Crœ′sŭs (crē-), *n.* A king of Lydia in the 6th cent. B. C. renowned for his vast wealth; hence, a very rich man; লিডিয়ার অধিপতি মহাধনশালী ক্রীসাস্; অতএব ধনকুবের।

crŏft, *n.* **1.** A small piece of arable land adjoining a dwelling house; ভদ্রাসন বাটীর সংলগ্ন কৃষিযোগ্য ক্ষুদ্র ভূমিখণ্ড। **2.** A small holding of a crofter; ক্ষুদ্র কৃষি-ক্ষেত্র।

crŏft′-ĕr, *n.* **1.** One who rents a small holding, esp. in Scotland; যে ব্যক্তি ক্ষুদ্র কৃষিক্ষেত্র দ্বারা জোত গ্রহণ করে। **2.** One of the joint tenants of a holding; কোন কৃষিক্ষেত্রের সহ-প্রজা।

crŏm′-lĕch, *n.* An ancient structure of large stones set on end supporting a stone laid horizontally ; প্রাচীনকালীন স্মৃতিস্তম্ভ

Cromlech.

বিশেষ,—দুইখানি খাড়া পাথরের উপর একখানি পাথর পাতিয়া ইহা নির্ম্মাণ করা হইত।

crōne, *n.* **1.** An old woman ; বৃদ্ধা স্ত্রীলোক, জরতী (আঃ বঃ), বুড়ী। **2.** An old ewe ; বুড়া ভেড়ী।

crō´-nȳ, *n.* An intimate friend ; a chum ; প্রাণের বন্ধু ; ইয়ার।

crōōk, *n., adj., v. t.* & *i.* **1.** A shepherd's or bishop's staff curving at the end ; রাগাল বা ধর্ম্মাধ্যক্ষের বক্রাগ্র যষ্টি। **2.** Anything bent ; বক্রাকৃতি বস্তু। **3.** A hook ; আঁকড়া। **4.** A curve ; a meander ; বাঁক; পাকচক্র, চক্কর, ঘুরপেঁচ। ***Adj.*** Crooked ; বক্র, জিহ্ম, বাঁকা। ***Verb t. & i.*** To bend ; to curve ; বাঁকান, বাঁকিয়া যাওয়া ; বক্র করা, বক্র হওয়া। **Crook-back(ed)**—Hunch-back(ed) ; কুব্জ। **By hook or crook** — By some means or other ; by fair means or foul ; যে কোন উপায়ে ; ভাল উপায়েই হউক বা মন্দ উপায়েই হউক। **On the crook**—(*Slang*) Dishonestly ; (ইতর ভাষায়) কুটিলভাবে, অসাধু ভাবে।

crōōk-ĕd, *adj.* **1.** Curved ; bent ; deformed ; বক্র, জিহ্ম ; বাঁকা, টেরা ; বেডৌল, বিকৃতাঙ্গ। **2.** Perverse ; not straight-forward ; বে-আড়া ; কুটিল, অসরল। **3.** Dishonest ; as, *crooked* dealings ; অসাধু। **—ly,** *adv.* **—ness,** *n.*

crōōn, *v. t.* & *i.* & *n.* To sing in a low voice ; to hum ; গুণ্ গুণ্ স্বরে গান করা ; গুণ্ গুণ্ করা। ***Verb i.*** **1.** To bellow as a bull (*Scot. dial.*); (স্কটলণ্ডের উপভাষায়) ষাঁড়ের মত গর্জ্জন করা। **2.** (*Scot. dial.*) To utter a low plaintive sound ; (স্কট্‌লণ্ড্‌ দেশীয় উপভাষায়) শোকসূচক মৃদু ধ্বনি উচ্চারণ করা। ***Noun.*** A low murmuring or humming sound ; গুণ্ গুণ্ শব্দ।

crŏp, *n.* **1.** The first stomach or craw of a bird ; পক্ষীর প্রথম পাকস্থলী, পক্ষীর গলার থলি, পক্ষি-জঠর (মঃ ইঃ)। **2.** An organ similar to the craw in other animals ; পক্ষীর প্রথম পাকস্থলীর অনুরূপ অন্যান্য জন্তুর শারীরিক-যন্ত্র। **3.** (*Arch.*) A finial ; (স্থপতি-বিজ্ঞান) চূড়া, শিখরাদির উপরিস্থ পত্রপুঞ্জ প্রভৃতি। **4.** The handle or stock of a whip ; as, a hunting *crop* ; চাবুকের ডাঁট। **5.** The top of anything ; "She proceeded to search for them in the *crop* of the wall ;" শীর্ষ, চূড়া, উপরিভাগ। **6.** Produce, esp. of a field or garden ; as, to reap the *crop ;* cultivation ; "Acres in *crop* and grass ;" শস্য, ফসল ; চাষ। **7.** The yield of something during one season ; "The annual rice-*crop* of the states is twenty million tons ; এক মরসুমে উৎপন্ন শস্যাদির পরিমাণ। **8.** The act of cutting hair ; the style of wearing the hair cut close and short ; কেশ-কর্ত্তন ; খর্ব্ব করিয়া চুল ছাটিবার ছাঁদ। **9.** An entire tanned hide ; অখণ্ড শোধিত চর্ম্ম। **10.** A mark made by cropping the ears of animals ; জন্তুগণের কর্ণচ্ছেদন করিয়া যে চিহ্ন রাখা হয়। **11.** A certain cut of meat ; কর্ত্তিত মাংসখণ্ড। **12.** A piece cut off from the end ; as, the rails give a short *crop* from either end ; উভয় প্রান্ত হইতে কর্ত্তিত খণ্ড। **13.** (*Mining*) Tin ore prepared for smelting ; (খনির কাজ) গলাইয়া বিশুদ্ধ ধাতু বাহির করার জন্য প্রস্তুত আকরোত্থিত রঙ্গ্‌। **14.** (*Mining*) The outcrop of a layer, vein etc. ; (খনির কাজ) বহির্দেশে প্রকটিত আভ্যন্তর স্তর প্রভৃতি। **15.** That which is like crop ; as, a *crop* of lies ; শস্যবৎ বস্তু। **Crop´-ful,** *adj.* Having a full crop, or stomach ; (পক্ষিসম্পর্কে) পূর্ণোদর। **Crop-eared**—(জন্তু-সম্পর্কে) ছিন্নকর্ণ ; (মনুষ্য সম্পর্কে) কর্ত্তিত-কেশ। **In, under** or **out of crop**—In, under or out of cultivation ; চাষের অধীন, চাষের বাহিরে।

crŏp, *v. t.* & *i.* **1.** To cut off the end of ; to bite off the tops of (plants, etc.) ; as, the horses *crop* grass ; to reap ; to gather (*lit.* & *fig.*) ; death *crops* the growing boys ; প্রান্তদেশ কাটিয়া ফেলা ; (গাছ প্রভৃতির) আগা কামড়াইয়া কাটিয়া ফেলা ; শস্য কাটা ; সংগ্রহ করা (শব্দানুযায়ী এবং লক্ষণায়)। **2.** To raise a crop from ; to sow plant, etc. ; as, to *crop* a field (*with* barley, etc.) ; ফসল উৎপাদন করা ; বপন করা, ক্ষেত করা। **3.** To clip or cut short as ears, hair or the edges of books, etc. ; চুল ছাঁটা, কাণ কাটা, পুস্তকের কিনারা কাটা। **4.** (*Coal-mining*) To dock ; (কয়লার খনির কাজ) কাটা। ***Verb i.*** **1.** To bite off the tops of plants etc. as an animal ; (জন্তু-সম্পর্কে) গাছ প্রভৃতির আগা কামড়াইয়া কাটা। **2.** To appear unexpectedly (with *out, forth, up*) ; "Cases *crop up* in villas ;" অপ্রত্যাশিত ভাবে ঘটা। **3.** (*Mining* and *Geol.*) To come up to the surface, as a vein etc., (with *up* and *out*) ; (খনির কার্য্য এবং ভূবিদ্যা) উপরিভাগে প্রকাশিত হওয়া।

To crop forth, out, or **up**— To appear or come to light incidentally or unexpectedly ; ঘটনাচক্রে বা অপ্রত্যাশিতভাবে প্রকাশিত হইয়া পড়া।

crŏp′-pêr, *n.* **1.** One who or that which crops ; ছেদনকারী, ছেদক। **2.** A machine for cropping iron rods, etc. ; লৌহদণ্ড প্রভৃতি কাটিবার যন্ত্র বিশেষ। **3.** A person cutting off the nap of cloth etc. ; যে ব্যক্তি বস্ত্রাদির আঁশ বা পশম প্রভৃতি কাটে। **4.** A pigeon with a large crop ; এক প্রকার পারাবত—ইহার গলার থলি অতি বড় হইয়া থাকে। **5.** A person who raises a crop or crops ; শস্যোৎপাদক। **6.** A plant yielding a crop, (with a qualifying word) ; as, a good or bad *cropper* ; ফল- বা শস্যপ্রসূ বৃক্ষ। **7.** (*Slang*) A fall as from a horse-back, etc. ; a failure ; (ইতর ভাষায়) (অশ্ব-পৃষ্ঠ হইতে) পতন ; বিফলতা। **To come, fall** or **get a cropper** — (*Slang*) To fall headlong ; (ইতর ভাষায়) উদ্দামবেগে পতিত হওয়া।

crŏp′-pȳ, *n.* **1.** A person with the hair cut short ; চুল-ছাঁটা লোক। **2.** An Irish rebel of the time of 1798 ; ১৭৯৮ খৃঃ অব্দের আয়র্লণ্ড দেশবাসী বিদ্রোহী।

crō′-quet (-kā), *n.* An open-air game played with mallets balls, hoops and pegs ; মুদ্গর, কন্দুক, চাক্তি এবং খোঁটার দ্বারা মাঠের ক্রীড়া বিশেষ।

rō-quet′ (-kā), *v. t.* & *i.* To send of (another's ball) by striking one's own in contact with it (in croquet) ; নিজের কন্দুকে আঘাত করিয়া তৎসংস্পৃষ্ট অপর কন্দুক দূরে সরাইয়া দেওয়া। **—ed,** *adj* (Pron. krokid.) **—ing,** *n.* (Pron. kroking)

crō-quette (-kĕt), *n.* A fried ball of rice, meat and other ingredients; তণ্ডুল-চূর্ণ মাংস এবং অন্যান্য উপাদানে প্রস্তুত ভর্জ্জিত পিণ্ড।

crōre, *n.* (*Skr.* koti) Ten millions ; as, *crores* of rupees ; কোটি।

crō′-sier, —zier (-zhĭ-êr), *n.* **1.** The pastoral staff of a bishop or abbot ; an archbishop's staff with a cross on the top ; খৃষ্টীয় ধর্ম্মাধ্যক্ষ বা মঠাধ্যক্ষের দণ্ড ; প্রধান ধর্ম্মাধ্যক্ষের অগ্রভাগেক্রুশযুক্ত দণ্ড। **2.** (*Bot.*) The curved top of a young fern ; (উদ্ভিদ-বিদ্যা) তরুণ পর্ণাঙ্গের বক্র অগ্রভাগ। **3.** The constellation called the Southern Cross ; (*obs.*) ; (জ্যোতির্বিজ্ঞান) দক্ষিণীয় চতুষ্পথ (হিঃ কোঃ)।

crŏss, *n.* **1.** An instrument for crucifixion, composed of two pieces of timber placed transversely ; the similar structure on

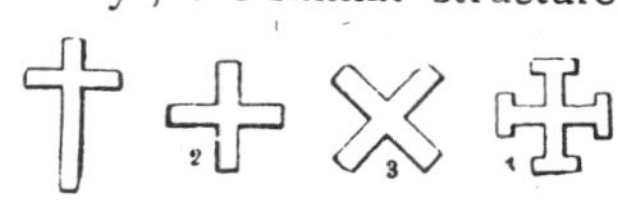

Cross.

which Christ was crucified ; প্রাচীন কালে রোমান প্রভৃতি জাতিদিগের মধ্যে মৃত্যুদণ্ডে দণ্ডিত ব্যক্তিগণের বধের নিমিত্ত পরস্পরের অনুপ্রস্থগামী কাষ্ঠদণ্ডদ্বয়-রচিত যন্ত্র বিশেষ, ক্রুশ ; যে ক্রুশে যীশুখৃষ্ট

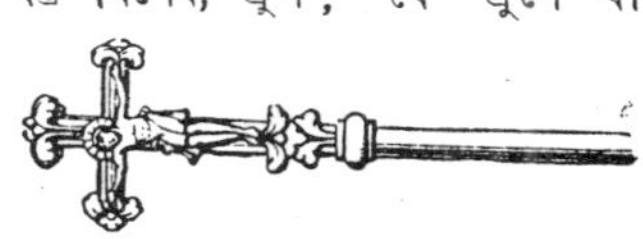

Ornamental cross.

বিদ্ধ হন। **2.** The symbol of the Christian religion ; the Christain religion ; " 'Tis where the *cross* is preached" ; খৃষ্ট ধর্ম্মের চিহ্ন ; খৃষ্ট ধর্ম্ম। **3.** A monument shaped like a cross or surmounted with a cross ; a cross set up in the centre or market place of a town ; a market, (now only local) : ক্রুশাকৃতি স্মৃতিস্তম্ভ, ক্রুশশোভিতাগ্র স্মৃতিস্তম্ভ ; নগরের মধ্যস্থানে বা বাজারে স্থাপিত ক্রুশ ; বাজার। **4.** The crusaders' symbol ; খৃষ্টীয় একাদশ, দ্বাদশ, ত্রয়োদশ শতাব্দীতে মুসলমানদিগের হস্ত হইতে জেরুজালেম নগরী উদ্ধার করণার্থ নিযুক্ত খৃষ্টধর্ম্মাবলম্বী সৈনিক পুরুষদিগের চিহ্ন। **5.** Anything shaped like a cross ; ক্রুশাকৃতি বস্তু। **6.** A staff surmounted by a cross borne before archbishops or in religious processions ; খৃষ্টীয় প্রধান ধর্ম্মাধ্যক্ষ বা ধর্ম্মসম্বন্ধীয় শোভাযাত্রার সম্মুখে বাহিত ক্রুশাগ্রদণ্ডবিশেষ। **7.** (*Herald.*) A bearing representing the Christian symbol or some modification of it ; (কুল-বিদ্যা) ক্রুশাকৃতি কুলচিহ্ন। **8.** A cross-shaped figure or mark used as a badge of an order of knighthood ; as, the grand *cross* ; a wearer of such cross ; সম্ভ্রান্ত সম্প্রদায়ের চিহ্নস্বরূপ ক্রুশচিহ্ন ; উক্ত চিহ্নধারী। **9.** Trial ; affliction ; trouble ; দুঃখদুর্দ্দশা ; পীড়া, যন্ত্রণা ; কষ্ট, ঝঞ্ঝাট। **10.** Any figure, mark or decoration in the shape of a cross ; ক্রুশাকৃতি চিত্র, চিহ্ন বা ভূষা। **11.** The intersection of two lines or ways ; চতুষ্পথ, চৌমাথা। **12.** A thwarting ; an altercation ; ব্যাঘাত, প্রতিবন্ধক, প্রতিরোধ ; বিবাদ। **13.** (*Electr.*) An accidental contact between two conductors ; (তাড়িত-বিদ্যা) পরিচালক পদার্থদ্বয়ের মধ্যে আকস্মিক সংস্পর্শ। **14.** (*Astron.*) The Southern Cross ; (জ্যোতির্বিজ্ঞান) দক্ষিণীয় চতুষ্পথ (হিঃ কোঃ)। **15.** (*Surveying*) A cross-staff ; (ভূমান-বিদ্যা) ক্রুশাকৃতি দণ্ড। **16.** A mixing of breeds in producing animal ; a product of the intermixture of breeds ; (পশুর) সঙ্কর-সন্তানোৎপাদন ; সঙ্কর। **17.** A cross made for a signature of a person unable to write ; অশিক্ষিত ব্যক্তির ঢেড়া সহি। **18.** (*Slang*) Fraud ; (ইতরভাষায়) জুয়াচুরি। **Cross′-let,** *n.* A small cross ; ক্ষুদ্র ক্রুশ। **Cross′-wise,** *adv.* In the form of a cross; across; transversely; perversely; ক্রুশাকারে; অনুপ্রস্থভাবে; আড়াআড়ি; কোণাকোণি। **Cross-bearer**—One who carries the cross before an archbishop or in a procession; যে ব্যক্তি প্রধান ধর্ম্মাধ্যক্ষ বা ধর্ম্মসম্পর্কীয় শোভাযাত্রার অগ্রে ক্রুশ বহন করে, ক্রুশবাহক। One who patiently endures afflictions for the sake of Christ; যে ব্যক্তি যীশু-খৃষ্টের জন্য ধীরভাবে দুঃখ যন্ত্রণা সহ্য করে। **Fiery cross**—স্কট্‌লণ্ডবাসি-গণের সঙ্কেত চিহ্ন বিশেষ। **Grand cross**—সম্ভ্রান্ত সম্প্রদায় সমূহের সর্ব্বোচ্চ শ্রেণীর ভূষা; উক্তরূপ ভূষাভূষিত ব্যক্তি। **Greek cross**—একপ্রকার ক্রুশ—যাহার নীচের দিকের অংশ অপর তিনটী অংশের প্রত্যেকটীর সমান দীর্ঘ। **Latin cross**—একরকম খাড়া ক্রুশ—যাহার নীচের দিকের অংশ অপর ৩টী অংশের প্রত্যেকটী অপেক্ষা দীর্ঘতর **Maltese cross**—একপ্রকার ক্রুশ—ইহার প্রত্যেকটী অংশ সমান লম্বা। [এই সকল অংশ সংযোগস্থলে সংকীর্ণ এবং বহিঃপ্রান্তে প্রশস্ত এবং প্রান্ত সমূহ দন্তাকারে কর্ত্তিত থাকে।] **St. Andrew's cross**—ইংরেজী X অক্ষরের অনুরূপ ক্রুশচিহ্ন **Tau cross**—ইংরাজী T অক্ষরের অনুরূপ St. Anthonyর ক্রুশ। **Victoria cross**—রণক্ষেত্রে অনন্য-সাধারণ বিক্রম প্রদর্শনের জন্য প্রদত্ত গৌর-বসূচক ভূষা। **On the cross**—(Opposed to *on the square*) surreptitiously or unfairly; as, to get anything *on the cross*; গোপনীয়ভাবে, অন্যায়রূপে। Diagonally; কোণাকুণি। **To bear one's own cross**—To endure his own troubles; নিজের দুঃখদুর্দ্দশা ভোগ করা। **To get on the cross**—To become dishonest; অসাধু হওয়া।

crŏss, *v. t. & i.* **1.** To place across or crosswise; as, to *cross* swords (in fighting); to intersect; as, the roads *cross* each other: আড়ভাবে বা কোণাকুণি ভাবে রাখা; পরস্পর ছেদন করা। **2.** To make the sign of the cross upon; as, the pale monk *crossed* his brow; কোন কিছুর উপর ক্রুশ চিহ্ন করা। **3.** To cancel, (usu. with *out* or *off*); কাটা। **4.** To pass over from side to side; এক তীর হইতে অপর তীরে যাওয়া, পার হওয়া, উত্তরণ করা। **5.** To sit across; to bestride (a horse, etc.); চড়িয়া বসা; চড়া। **6.** To carry or take across; as, the general *crossed* his army at this ford; পার করা। **7.** To meet and pass; (also *verb i.*) সাক্ষাৎ হওয়া এবং অতিক্রম করা। **8.** To obstruct; to oppose; বাঁধা দেওয়া; প্রতিরোধ করা। **9.** To cause to interbreed; একজাতীয় বিভিন্নপ্রকার জন্তর সঙ্গমে শাবক উৎপাদন করা। *Verb i.* **1.** To pass across; to intersect; as, at the spot where two roads *cross*; পরস্পরকে আড়ভাবে কর্ত্তন করা; কাটাকাটি করা। **2.** To move from one side to the other; (usu. with *over*); as, he now *crossed over* to the other side; পার হওয়া, উত্তরণ করা। **3.** To be athwart; আড় হওয়া। **4.** To interbreed; একজাতীয় বিভিন্নপ্রকার জন্তর সংসর্গে সন্তান উৎপাদিত হওয়া। **To cross a cheque**—টাকা দিবার আদেশপত্রের উপর ধনাগারের নাম অথবা কেবল "এণ্ড কো" কথাগুলি সংযোজিত করা (এইরূপ স্থলে কেবল এই ধনাগারের মারফত টাকা পাওয়া যায়)। **To cross a fortune teller's hand with silver**—To describe crossing lines on her hand with a silver coin given by the consulter; hence, to give money to; জিজ্ঞাসু ব্যক্তিকর্ত্তৃক অপদেবতা তাড়াইবার উদ্দেশ্যে যাযাবর জাতীয়া গণকিনীর হস্তে রৌপ্যদ্বারা ক্রুশচিহ্ন অঙ্কিত করা; অতএব অর্থপ্রদান করা। **To cross swords**—To engage in conflict; পরস্পরের সহিত যুদ্ধে প্রবৃত্ত হওয়া। **To cross the mind of any one**—To occur in one's mind; মনে উদয় হওয়া। **To cross the path of any one**—To defeat one's purpose; কাহারও মতলব বা উদ্দেশ্য ব্যর্থ করা। **To cross the Rubicon**—To take decisive, unrevocable step; প্রত্যাবৃত্ত বা পশ্চাৎপদ হওয়ার পথ না রাখা। (See Rubicon.)

crŏss, *adj.* **1.** Transverse; intersecting; ব্যত্যস্ত (আঃ বঃ), অনুপ্রস্থগামী, টের্চ্ছা; পরস্পর-ছেদনকারী। **2.** Contrary; opposed; প্রতীপ (আঃ বঃ), প্রতিকূল; বিরুদ্ধ। **3.** (*Colloq.*) Peevish; (চলিতভাষায়) খিটখিটে। **4.** (*Slang*) Dishonest; (ইতরভাষায়) অসাধু। **Cross'-ly,** *adv.* **Cross'-ness,** *n.* **Cross-beam**—এড়োকাঠ, পরিমিত (বেঃ সূঃ)। **Cross-bench**—পার্লেমেণ্ট মহাসভার আসন বিশেষ—যাহাতে স্বাধীন বা নিরপেক্ষ সভ্যগণ উপবেশন করেন। **Cross-bred**—Hybrid; দো-আঁসলা, সঙ্কর। **Cross-case**—পাল্টা মোকদ্দমা। **Cross-entry**—হিসাবের বিপরীত দিকের ভুক্ত বিষয়। **Cross-multiplication,** *n.* তির্য্যগ্ গুণন, বজ্রবধ (সাঃ পাঃ), বজ্রাভ্যাস (ঐ)। **Cross-patch**—দুঃশীল এবং কোপনস্বভাব ব্যক্তি। **Cross-reference**—অধিকতর বিবরণ অবগতির জন্য পুস্তকের এক অংশে অন্য অংশে অনুসন্ধানের জন্য উল্লেখ।

crŏss'-bĕnch, *adj.* Impartial; পক্ষপাতশূন্য, নিরপেক্ষ।

Common crossbill.

crŏss'-bill, *n.* A bird the mandibles of whose bill cross each other at the points; একপ্রকার

পক্ষী, — ইহার চঞ্চুর চিবুকাস্থিদ্বয়ের অগ্রভাগ আড়ভাবে থাকে।

crŏss′-bones (-bōnz), *n.* (*Pl.*) Two thigh or arm bones placed or depicted crosswise, symbolizing death (generally in conjunction with a skull) ; মৃত্যুর চিহ্নস্বরূপ কোণাকুণিভাবে স্থাপিত বা চিত্রিত উরু বা বাহুর অস্থিদ্বয়।

crŏss′-bow (-bō), *n.* A weapon for shooting stone formed by fixing a bow crosswise on a stock ; প্রস্তর নিক্ষেপক যন্ত্র বিশেষ,—ইহা একটী দণ্ডের উপর অনুপ্রস্থ ভাবে একটী ধনু সংবদ্ধ করিয়া নির্ম্মিত হয়, বক্রচাপ (আঃ বঃ). গোলাসন (মঃ ইঃ)।

Crossbow.

crŏss′-breed (-brēd), *n., v. t. & i.* **1.** A breed produced from the parents of different breeds or kinds ; সঙ্কর জাতি, খচ্চর (আঃ বঃ)। **2.** A hybrid ; দোঁ-আসলা। ***Verb t. & i.*** To hybridize ; দোঁ-আসলা করা।

crŏss′-bŭt-tŏck, *n.* A throw in which the wrestler turns his left side to his opponent, places his left-leg across both legs of his opponent and pulls him forward over his hip ; একপ্রকার কুস্তির পেঁচ—যাহাতে কুস্তিগীর তাহার বামদিক প্রতিপক্ষের দিকে ফিরাইয়া থাকে, এবং তাহার বামপদ প্রতিপক্ষের উভয় পদের পশ্চাদ্ভাগে আড়ভাবে স্থাপন করিয়া তাহাকে চিৎ করিয়া ফেলিয়া দেয়।

crŏss′-cŭt, *n.* A cut or path from side to side ; a short cut ; একপার্শ্ব হইতে অপর পার্শ্ব পর্য্যন্ত কাটা পথ ; সোজা পথ, আড় পথ।

crosse (crŏs), *n.* A kind of large battle-dore used in the game of *lacrosse* ; ক্রীড়াবিশেষে ব্যবহৃত দণ্ডবিশেষ, কন্দুকতাড়নী।

crŏss′-ĕx-ăm′-ine (-ĭn), *v. t.* To examine minutely as a witness of the opposite party in a law-suit ; জেরা করা, কূট প্রশ্ন করা। **—i-na′-tion,** *n.* The act of cross-examining ; জেরা, কূট প্রশ্ন।

crŏss fêr-ti-li-zā′-tion, *n.* (*Bot.*) The fertilization of one plant by pollen from another ; উদ্ভিদ্‌ বিদ্যা) এক বৃক্ষের পুষ্পপরাগ অপর বৃক্ষের পুষ্পে নিষেক, পর-নিষেক (সাঃ পঃ)।

crŏss′-fīre, *n.* A firing from two or more parts of a military fire so that the lines of fire cross each other ; আনুপ্রস্থিক অগ্নিবর্ষণ,—ইহাতে রণক্ষেত্রের বিভিন্ন স্থান হইতে গোলাগুলি বর্ষণ করা হয়, এবং গোলাবর্ষণের রেখাসমূহ পরস্পরকে ছেদন করে।

crŏss′-grain (-grān), *n.* A grain running transversely to the regular grain ; পরস্পরের বিপরীতদিগ্‌গামী রগ বা আঁশ।

crŏss′-grained (-grānd), *adj.* **1.** With grain or fibres running irregularly or transversely ; as, *cross-grained* wood ; পরস্পরের বিপরীতদিগ্‌গামী রগ বা আঁশবিশিষ্ট, আড়শিরা, তির্য্যক্‌। **2.** (*Fig.*) Perverse ; untractable ; (লক্ষণায়) বে-আড়া ; অদম্য।

crŏss′-hatch (-hăch), *v. t.* To engrave with parallel lines in two series crossing one another ; to shade (an engraving) by this method ; তির্য্যগ্‌ভাবে পরস্পরচ্ছেদী দুই প্রস্থ সমান্তরাল রেখা দ্বারা উৎকীর্ণ করা ; উক্ত উপায়ে উৎকীর্ণ ফলক ছায়ান্বিত করা।

crŏss′-ing, *n.* **1.** The act of crossing ; উত্তরণ, উল্লঙ্ঘন, অতিক্রমণ। **2.** A point or place where two roads, railways, etc. intersect ; যে স্থান বা বিন্দুতে দুইটী পথ, লৌহবর্ত্ম প্রভৃতি পরস্পরকে ছেদন করে, চতুষ্পথ (আঃ বঃ), চৌমাথা। **3.** A place where a street etc. is crossed by passengers etc. ; যে স্থানে পথিকগণ রাজপথ প্রভৃতি পার হয়, তরণ-পথ। **4.** Opposition ; thwarting ; বাধা, প্রতিবাদ ; বিফলীকরণ। **Crossing-sweeper**—যে ব্যক্তি চৌমাথা ঝাড় দেয়। **A level crossing**—পথ বা লৌহবর্ত্মের অথবা এক সমতলবিশিষ্ট লৌহবর্ত্মদ্বয়ের তরণ-স্থল।

crŏss′-leg-ged (-lĕgd), *adj.* Having the legs across as a person squatting ; with one leg laid across the other as a person sitting on a chair ; ব্যত্যস্ত-পাদ (আঃ বঃ) ; পায়ের উপর পা রাখিয়া উপবিষ্ট, বীরাসনস্থ (আঃ বঃ)।

crŏss′-lĕt, *n.* See in CROSS.

crŏss′-light, (-līt), **1.** A light which crosses the path of another ; যে আলোকের রশ্মিচ্ছটা অপর আলোকের রশ্মিচ্ছটাকে ছেদন করিয়া যায় (অর্থাৎ তদ্দ্বারা দ্বিতীয় আলোক কর্ত্তৃক অনালোকিত স্থান সমূহ আলোকিত হইয়া থাকে।) **2.** The illustration of a subject from another point of view ; "The *cross-lights* of modern philosophy ;" অন্যদিক হইতে কোন বিষয় বিশদীকরণ।

crŏss′-pŭr-pose (-pŭs), *n.* **1.** A contrary or opposing purpose ; that which is inconsistent or contradictory ; বিপরীত উদ্দেশ্য, উল্টা মতলব, বিরুদ্ধ অভিপ্রায় ; অসঙ্গতিবিশিষ্ট বিষয়, পরস্পরবিসম্বাদী বা পরস্পরবিরোধী বিষয়। **2.** (*Pl.*) A popular game carried on by questions and answers ; প্রশ্নোত্তরাত্মক ক্রীড়াবিশেষ। **To be at cross-purposes**—To misunderstand each other ; to act unintentionally counter to each other ; পরস্পরকে ভুল বুঝা ; অনভিপ্রায়ে পরস্পরের বিরুদ্ধে কাজ করা।

crŏss′-quĕs′-tion (-tyŏn), *n. & v. t.* A question put in cross examination ; প্রতিপ্রশ্ন, জেরা, কূটপ্রশ্ন। ***Verb t.*** To cross-examine ; প্রতিপ্রশ্ন করা, জেরা করা। **Cross-questions and crooked**

answers — এক প্রকার প্রশ্নোত্তরাত্মক ক্রীড়া।

crŏss'-road (-rŏd), *n.* **1.** A road running across another ; a road joining to main roads ; a by-road ; যে রাস্তা অন্য রাস্তাকে কাটিয়া যায় ; যে ক্ষুদ্র রাস্তা দুইটী প্রধান রাস্তাকে সংযোগ করে ; উপপথ (মঃ ইঃ), বাজে রাস্তা। **2.** A place of intersection of two or more roads ; দ্বিপথ, চৌমাথা, চতুষ্পথ।

crŏss'-stăff, *n.* **1.** An instrument for taking altitudes of celestial bodies ; জ্যোতিষ্ক-সমূহের উচ্চতা পরিমাপক যন্ত্র বিশেষ। **2.** An instrument to measure offsets in surveying ; পরস্পরচ্ছেদী রেখা যুগল দ্বারা চতুরংশে বিভক্ত পিত্তল-বৃত্তসমন্বিতাগ্র ক্ষেত্রমাপন দণ্ড-বিশেষ।

crŏss'-stitch (-stĭch), *n.* A kind of needle-work in which the stitches are diagonal and in pairs ; a stitch made of two crossing each other ; একপ্রকার সূচের কাজ,—ইহাতে ফোঁড় সকল জোড়ায় জোড়ায় কোণাকুণি ভাবে থাকে ; একপ্রকার ফোঁড়,—যাহাতে একটী ফোঁড় অপরটির উপর কোণাকুণি ভাবে থাকে।

crŏss'-trees (-trēz), *n. pl.* (*Naut.*) Two horizontal cross-timbers at the head of the lower and top-masts ; নিম্নতর মাস্তুল এবং দ্বিতীয় মাস্তুলের উপর শয়ানভাবে স্থিত কাষ্ঠফলকদ্বয়।

Crotalaria juncea—মেস্তা পাট (বেলঃ)।

crotch'-ĕt (crŏch-), *n.* **1.** A hook or hook-like instrument ; আঁকড়া, বা আঁকড়ার মত যন্ত্র, আকর্ষণী (মঃ ইঃ), অঙ্কুশ (ঐ) **2.** A hook for reaping ; শস্য কাটার কালে ব্যবহৃত আঁকড়া বিশেষ। **3.** A hook-like organ of an animal ; জন্তুর আঁকড়ার মত শারীরিক যন্ত্র। **4.** (*Surg.*) A kind of instrument used in extracting the fetus after craniotomy ; (অস্ত্রোপচার-বিদ্যা) মস্তক-সংচূর্ণনের পর যে যন্ত্রের সাহায্যে গর্ভস্থ ভ্রূণকে নিষ্কাশিত করা হয়। **5.** (*Mus.*) A note in music equal to half a minim; (সঙ্গীত-শাস্ত্র) সঙ্গীত-স্বর সূচক চিহ্ন বিশেষ, শৃণি (আঃ বঃ)। **6.** (*Print.*) Bracket (as [ ) ; (মুদ্রণ) বন্ধনী। **7.** A whimsical fancy or conceit ; খেয়াল, মৌজ, উৎকট কল্পনা। **—er,** *n.* One given to some whim, hobby, project or crotchet ; উৎকট কল্পনাপ্রিয় লোক। **—i-ness,** *n* **—y,** *adj.* Whimsical ; of the nature of a crotchet ; খামখেয়ালী, আজবী ; উৎকট কল্পনাপ্রিয়।

crŏ'-tŏn, *n.* A kind of plant yielding croton oil ; জয়পাল (খোরী)। **Croton-oil**—জয়পালের তৈল। ***Croton oblongifolium***— ভুতম কুসুম (বেলঃ)। ***Croton polyandrum***—দুন্তী (বেলঃ)। ***Croton tiglium***—জয়পাল, রেচক (বেলঃ)।

crouch (crowch), *v. i., t.,* & *n.* **1.** To bend or stoop low ; গুড়ি-মারা। **2.** To stoop servilely or meanly; to cringe ; হীনভাবে বা দাসের মত গড়াইয়া পড়া ; ভয়ে বা শ্রদ্ধায় সঙ্কুচিত হওয়া, গুটিসুটি মারা, জড়সড় হওয়া। ***Verb t.*** To bend low in humility or fear ; ভয় বা বশ্যতায় প্রণত হওয়া। ***Noun.*** Act of crouching or stooping ; গুটিসুটি।

croup(e) (crôp), *n.* **1.** The rump of a horse, etc. ; the part behind the saddle ; অশ্বাদির পশ্চাদ্ভাগ, অশ্বনিতম্ব (মঃ ইঃ) ; জিনের পশ্চাদ্দিকের অংশ। **2.** (*Humorously*) The buttocks of a man ; (কৌতুকচ্ছলে) মনুষ্যের নিতম্ব।

croup (crôp), *n.* A disease of the wind-pipe in children accompanied with a hoarse cough and difficult respiration ; শিশুদিগের কণ্ঠনালীর রোগ বিশেষ — এই রোগে স্বরভঙ্গ এবং শ্বাসকষ্ট সঞ্জাত হয়, স্বরঘ্ন (হঃ চঃ)।

crou'-pi-êr (crô-), *n.* **1.** One who watches the cards and collects the money at a gaming table ; যে ব্যক্তি জুয়াখেলার মেজে বসিয়া তাসের দিকে দৃষ্টি রাখে, এবং বাজির টাকা সংগ্রহ করে। **2.** The assistant chairman in a public dinner party ; সাধারণ ভোজের সহকারী সভাপতি।

crow (crō), *n.* **1.** The black bird of the genus corvus ; কাক, বায়স, বলিভুক্ (মঃ ইঃ), চিরঞ্জীবী, (ঐ), প্রাতর্ভোক্তা (ঐ), কাওয়া। **2.** A bar of iron used as a lever, also called crow-bar ; ভারি জিনিষ চারা দিয়া তুলিবার জন্য লৌহদণ্ড। **3.** (*Astron.*) The Southern constellation called corvus ; (জ্যোতির্বিজ্ঞান) হস্তা নক্ষত্র। **Crow-bar**—See CROW **(2.) Crow-berry** — A heath-like shrub ; a fruit got from this ; এক প্রকার গুল্ম ; উক্ত গুল্মজাত ফল। **Crow bill**—Forceps for extracting bullets, etc. ; বন্দুকের গুলি প্রভৃতি টানিয়া বাহির করার জন্য সাঁড়াশী। **Crow-foot** — A name for the species of butter-cups (plants) ; একপ্রকার গাছ, কাকপদ (সুশ্রুঃ)। (*Naut.*) Arrangement of small ropes for suspending awning ; জাহাজের পাটাতন প্রভৃতির উপরে ক্যাম্বিস কাপড় বিস্তারিত করার জন্য ক্ষুদ্র রজ্জুর ব্যবস্থা। (*Mil.*) A caltrop, also called a crow's foot ; (সামরিক শাস্ত্র) পানিফলের আকার যন্ত্র বিশেষ— যাহা পূর্ব্বে শত্রুর গমন-পথে স্থাপিত হইত। A crow's foot ; কাক-পদ। **Crow quill** — A quill of the crow; a steel pen for fine writing ; কাকপক্ষ ; চিকন লিখার জন্য ইস্পাতের তৈয়ারী কলম। **Crow's foot**—Anything of the shape of a crow's foot ; কাকপদাকার বস্তু। (*Pl.*) The wrinkles that appear at the outer corner of the eye ; বার্দ্ধক্য জনিত নেত্র প্রান্তের বলি বা কুঞ্চন, বৃদ্ধাবস্থায়

নেত্রের বহিঃপ্রান্তের মাংসের কুঞ্চন। **Crow's nest**—(*Naut.*) A tub or box at the top-gallant mast-head for the look-out man who watches for whales ; (নৌ-বিদ্যা) জাহাজের মাস্তুল বিশেষের অগ্রস্থ আধার বিশেষ—যেখানে থাকিয়া পর্য্যবেক্ষক তিমি-মৎস্যের জন্য পর্য্যবেক্ষণ করে। **As the crow flies**—In a straight and direct course ; ঠিক সোজা পথ ধরিয়া। **To eat crow**—To be forced to do something extremely disagreeable or humiliatory ; নিতান্ত অপ্রীতিকর বা অপমানজনক কোন কার্য্য করিতে বাধ্য হওয়া। **To have a crow to pluck or pull with anyone**—To have some fault to find with one ; to have a disagreeable matter to settle with him ; কোন লোকের দোষ বাহির করা ; কাহারও সহিত কোন অপ্রীতিকর বিষয় মিটানের আবশ্যক হওয়া।

crow (crō), *n.* **1.** The cry of a cock ; কুক্কুটধ্বনি, মুরগের ডাক। **2.** Joyful cry of an infant ; শিশুর আনন্দ কোলাহল।

crow (crō), *v. t.* (*P.t. crew, crowed, p. p. crowed*) **1.** To cry as a cock ; কুক্কুটের মত ডাকা। **2.** (*Of a child*) To utter joyful cry ; (শিশুর পক্ষে) আনন্দধ্বনি করা। **3.** To boast in triumph ; as, we must not *crow* till we are out of the wood ; বিজয়োল্লাসে গর্ব্ব করা। **To crow over**—To triumph over ; শত্রুর পরাজয়ে বিজয়োল্লাস প্রকাশ করা।

crowd, *n.* **1.** A throng ; a great multitude ; জনতা ; ভিড়, সঙ্কুল লোকারণ্য, জনসংমর্দ (আঃ বঃ), লোকসংঘ (মঃ ইঃ)। **2.** (*Colloq.*) A company ; set ; clique ; (চলিত ভাষায়) দল ; প্রস্থ ; (অসাধু উদ্দেশ্যে বদ্ধ) দল। **3.** A large number of things adjacent to each other ; as, a *crowd* of islands ; পুঞ্জ। **The crowd**—The masses ; জনগণ, জনসাধারণ। **Crowd of sail**—(*Naut.*) A large number of sails hoisted ; যুগপৎ উত্তোলিত বহুসংখ্যক পাইল।

crowd, *v. i.* & *t.* **1.** To collect into a mass, (also *verb t.*) : জড় হওয়া বা করা, সঙ্কুলিত করা। **2.** To force one's way ; as, a man *crowds* into a thronged place ; ঠেলিয়া পথ করা। **3.** (*Naut.*) To hasten ; (নৌ-বিদ্যা) ত্বরান্বিত করা। ***Verb t.*** **1.** To thrust ; to cram ; ঠাসা ; গাদা করা, সঙ্কুলিত করা। **2.** To compress ; as, we stood *crowded* before the picture ; সঙ্কাপিত করা। **3.** To fill to excess ; ছাপাছাপি করিয়া পূর্ণ করা, উপছিয়া পড়ে এরূপ ভাবে ভরা, ঠাসিয়া ভরা। **To crowd out**—To press out ; ঠেলিয়া বাহির করা। [বিশেষতঃ গুরুতর বিষয় সন্নিবেশ করার জন্য সামান্য প্রবন্ধাদি পত্রিকাস্থ না করা।] **To crowd sail**—To hoist an unusual number of sails ; যুগপৎ বহুসংখ্যক পাইল খুলিয়া দেওয়া।

crown, *n.* **1.** A garland for the head given as a reward of victory ; বিজয়ের পুরস্কারস্বরূপ প্রদত্ত শিরোমাল্য। **2.** The state cap of a soverign ; রাজমুকুট, রাজমৌলি (মঃ ইঃ), কিরীট, তাজ। **3.** (*Fig.*) King or queen ; regal power ; (লক্ষণায়) রাজা বা রাণী ; রাজশক্তি। **4.** Any crown-shaped ornament ; মুকুটাকার অলঙ্কার। **5.** A five shilling piece anciently stamped with a crown ; ৫ শিলিং মূল্যের মুদ্রা—পূর্ব্বে এরূপ মুদ্রায় রাজমুকুট মুদ্রিত থাকিত। **6.** The top or the head of a mountain, of a hat, etc. ; মস্তকাগ্র (মঃ ইঃ), মাথার চাঁদি, শেখর, মৌলি, পর্ব্বতের চূড়া বা শেখর, টুপি-মাথা। **7.** Whole head ; মস্তক **8.** The portion of a tooth which appears above the gum দাঁতের যে অংশ মাড়ির উপর দেখা যায়। **9.** (*Arch.*) The vertex of an arch ; (স্থপতি-বিজ্ঞান) তোরণের শিখর দেশ। **10.** A size of paper (15 × 20 inches) ; নির্দ্দিষ্ট আয়তনের কাগজ (১৫ × ২০ ইঞ্চি)। **Crown-colony** — রাজাদ্বারা সাক্ষাৎভাবে শাসিত উপনিবেশ। **Crown-glass**—সর্ব্বোৎকৃষ্ট বাতায়নের কাচ। **Crown-land**—রাজার নিজস্ব ভূসম্পত্তি ও অন্যান্য স্থাবর সম্পত্তি, খাস মহাল। **Crown-law** — ইংলণ্ডের ফৌজদারী আইন। **Crown-lawyer** — সরকারী উকিল। **Crown-office** — ইংলণ্ডের ফৌজদারী আদালত। **Crown-prince** — In Germany, the heir-apparent to the throne ; জর্ম্মাণীর যুবরাজ, যুবরাজ, ভাবি-চক্রবর্ত্তী।

crown, *v. t.* **1.** To invest with a crown or regal authority ; রাজমুকুট প্রদান করা, পট্টাভিষেক করা, রাজক্ষমতা প্রদান করা। **2.** (*Fig.*) To reward or honour ; "Thou hast *crowned* him with glory ;" (লক্ষণায়) গৌরব-মুকুট প্রদান করা, শিরোপা দেওয়া। **3.** To cover, or stand, at the top of ; "Her statue *crowns* a public fountain ;" অগ্রভাগ মণ্ডিত করা, শীর্ষদেশে অবস্থিতি করা। **4.** To complete ; to perfect ; to form chief ornament to ; "Let manhood *crown* what infamy inspired ;" সমাপ্ত করা, সিদ্ধ করা ; চরমোৎকর্ষ সাধন করা ; মুকুট-স্বরূপ হওয়া, চূড়া-স্বরূপ হওয়া। **5.** To bring to a successful issue ; as, to *crown* efforts, wishes, etc. ; সফলতা সম্পাদন করা। **6.** To fill to overflowing ; "The bowls are *crowned* ;" কাণায় কাণায় পূর্ণ করা, উপছিয়া পড়ে এরূপ ভাবে পূর্ণ করা। **7.** (*Draughts*) To make as a piece a king ; ড্রাফ্‌ট্‌স্ ক্রীড়ার কোন গুটিকে রাজা করা। **To crown all**—To give a finishing touch surpassing and confirming everything previous ; সর্ব্বোপরি।

crowned (crownd), *adj.* **1.** Having a crown ; invested or adorned with a crown ; মুকুটিত ; রাজমুকুটপ্রাপ্ত, কিরীট-ভূষিত, কিরীটী, মুকুটধারী, জাত-মুকুটসংস্কার। **2.** Brimful ; "One *crowned* cup to all......" ; কাণায় কাণায় পূর্ণ। **To be crowned with success**—সাফল্য, সার্থকতা বা সিদ্ধিলাভ করা।

crown'-êr, *n.* (*Obs.* or *dial.*) A coroner ; (অপ্রচলিত বা উপভাষায়) শব-পরীক্ষক কর্ম্মচারী।

crown'-ing, *adj.* Highest ; as, *crowning* folly ; চূড়ান্ত, চরম।

croy'-dŏn, *n.* A two-wheeled carriage like a gig ; একপ্রকার দুই চাকার গাড়ী।

cru'-cial (crô-shî-al), *adj.* **1.** Of the shape of a cross ; ক্রুশাকৃতি, ঢেরাকার। **2.** Decisive ; critical ; severe ; as, a *crucial* test or point ; চূড়ান্ত ; চরম ; গুরুতর।

cru'-cian, –sian, (crô-shî-ăn), *n.* A deep yellow-coloured fish allied to the carp, (also called the *crucian carp*) ; এক প্রকার ঘনপীতবর্ণ রোহিত জাতীয় মৎস্য।

cru'-ci-āte (crô-shî-), *adj.* (*Bot.* & *Zool.*) Cruciform as leaves, petals or wings of insects, etc.; (উদ্ভিদ্-বিদ্যা ও জন্তুতত্ত্ব) ক্রুশাকৃতি।

cru'-cĭ-ble (crô-), *n.* **1.** A melting pot used by chemists and others ; ধাতু গলাইবার মুষা বা মুচি, আবর্ত্তনী (আঃ বঃ)। **2.** A basin at the bottom of a furnace to collect the molten metal ; গলিত ধাতুসংগ্রহের জন্য চুল্লীর তলদেশস্থ পাত্র-বিশেষ। **3.** (*Fig.*) A severe trial or test ; "In the *crucible* of pain we are purified ;" (লক্ষণায়) গুরুতর পরীক্ষা, অগ্নি-পরীক্ষা।

cru-cif'-er-ous (crô-sîf-êr-ŭs), *adj.* **1.** Bearing or adorned with the cross ; ক্রুশধারী, ক্রুশ-শোভিত। **2.** (*Bot.*) With four petals in the form of cross ; (উদ্ভিদ্‌বিদ্যা) ক্রুশাকারে বিন্যস্ত দলচতুষ্টয়-বিশিষ্ট।

cru'-cĭ-fix (crô-), *n.* A figure or image of Christ on the cross the cross itself (improperly used) ; ক্রুশবিদ্ধ যীশু খৃষ্ট ; ক্রুশ (অপব্যবহার)।

cru'-ci fixion (crô-sî-fîc-tion), *n* **1.** The act of crucifying ; the death of Christ on the cross ; ক্রুশ-বিদ্ধ-করণ ; খৃষ্টের ক্রুশে মৃত্যু। **2.** Death upon a cross ; ক্রুশে বিদ্ধ হইয়া মৃত্যু। **3.** A picture or representation of the crucifixion of Christ ; ক্রুশবিদ্ধ খ্রীষ্টের প্রতিমূর্ত্তি বা প্রতিকৃতি।

cru'-cĭ-fôrm (crô-), *adj.* Cross-shaped ; as, a *cruciform* flower ; ক্রুশাকার।

cru'-cĭ-fȳ (crô-), *v. t.* **1.** To put to death by nailing hands and feet to a cross ; ক্রুশে বিদ্ধ করা। **2.** (*Fig.*) To mortify ; to subdue ; as, to *crucify* the flesh, sins or passions, etc. ; (লক্ষণায়) অভিভূত করা ; বশীভূত করা, দমন করা।

crude (crôd), *adj.* **1.** Raw ; unrefined ; in a natural state ; as, *crude* sugar or salt ; কাঁচা, অপক্ব (মঃ ইঃ) ; অশোধিত, অসংস্কৃত ; স্বাভাবিক অবস্থায় স্থিত। **2.** Not digested ; অপাচিত, অজীর্ণ। **3.** Unripe as a fruit etc. ; অপক্ব। **4** Immature,—lacking finish ; as, a *crude* design or reasoning ; rough ; rude ; unpolished ; as, a *crude* action, statement, or manners ; অপরিণত ; স্থূল, মোটা ; কর্ক্কশ ; রুক্ষ ; অমার্জ্জিত। **5.** Bare ; as, *crude* facts ; নগ্ন। **6.** (*Gram.*) Uninflected as the form of a word ; (ব্যাকরণ) অরূপান্তরিত। **Crude'-ly,** *adv.* **Crude'-ness,** *n.*

cru'-di-tȳ (crô-), *n.* **1.** The state or quality of being crude ; অপরিণতাবস্থা, রুক্ষতা, অমার্জ্জিত ভাব। **2.** Anything crude or undigested ; অপাচিত বস্তু, অপরিপক্ব বস্তু।

cru'-ĕl (crô-), *adj.* **1.** Hard-hearted ; inhuman ; unmerciful ; পাষাণ-হৃদয়, ক্রূর, নিষ্ঠুর ; অমানুষিক ; নিষ্করুণ, নির্দ্দয়, নৃশংস। **2.** Causing pain or misery ; as, *cruel* weather ; দুঃখযন্ত্রণাজনক। **3.** Painful ; as, *cruel* death ; যন্ত্রণাপূর্ণ। **–ly,** *adv.* **–ty,** *n.* **1.** Inhumanity ; অমানুষিকতা। **2.** A cruel deed or treatment ; নিষ্ঠুর কার্য্য, নির্দ্দয় ব্যবহার।

cru'-ĕt (crô-), **1.** A small glass bottle for holding vinegar, sauce, etc. for the table ; ভোজনকালে শির্কা, আচার প্রভৃতি পূর্ণ যে শিশি মেজের উপর রাখা যায়, শির্কাদান, আচারদান, কূপক (আঃ বঃ)। **2.** (*Eccles.*) Eucharistic flagon ; (যাজকীয়-শাস্ত্র) খৃষ্টের শেষ ভোজনের স্মৃতি-উৎসবের রুটি ও মদিরা রক্ষার্থ পাত্র। **Cruet-stand**—শির্কা, আচার প্রভৃতির শিশি রাখার বৈঠক, কূপকাধার (আঃ বঃ)।

cruise (crôz), *v. i.* & *n.* **1.** To sail to and fro in quest of enemy's ships or for pleasure ; (*lit.* & *fig.*) ; (শব্দানুযায়ী এবং লক্ষণায়) শত্রুর জাহাজের অন্বেষণে পরিক্রম করা, আমোদের জন্য জাহাজে সমুদ্রবক্ষে পরিক্রম করা। **2.** (*Colloq.*) To wander hither and thither on land ; (চলিত ভাষায়) স্থলে ইতস্ততঃ পর্য্যটন বা পরিক্রম করা। ***Noun.*** A sailing up and down in search of enemy's ships or for pleasure ; আমোদের জন্য বা শত্রুর জাহাজের অনুসন্ধানে সমুদ্রবক্ষে পরিক্রম, সমুদ্র-পরিক্রম, সমুদ্র-পর্য্যটন।

cruis'-êr (crôz-), *n.* A person or a ship that cruises ; (*specif.*) a warship adapted for cruising ; সমুদ্রবক্ষে পরিক্রমকারী ব্যক্তি বা জাহাজ ; (বিশেষতঃ) পরিক্রমোপযোগী সমরপোত, সমুদ্র-পর্য্যটক রণপোত, পরিভ্রমণপোত (আঃ বঃ)। **Armoured cruiser**—রণপোত হইতে অপেক্ষাকৃত লঘুতর লৌহপট্টাবৃত আচ্ছাদিত সমুদ্রপর্য্যটক সমরপোত, সাগর-চর। **Protected** or **unprotected cruiser**—সংরক্ষক-পাটাতন সমন্বিত বা বিরহিত পর্য্যটনকারী সমুদ্রপোত।

cruive (crūv), *n.* A wicker trap for catching salmon ; শ্যামন মৎস্য ধরিবার ঘুণি।

crumb (crŭm), *n.* & *v. t.* **1.** A fragment ; a small piece of bread etc. ; টুকরা, খণ্ড ; রুটি প্রভৃতির ক্ষুদ্র টুকরা। **2.** (*Fig.*) A bit ; a particle ; as, a *crumb* of comfort ; (লক্ষণায়) অল্পমাত্র ; কণা। **3.** The soft inner part of a bread, (opposed to *crust*) ; পাউরুটীর ভিতরের শাঁস। ***Verb t.*** **1.** To break into crumbs or fragments ; as, to *crumb* bread ; টুকরা টুকরা করা, খণ্ড খণ্ড করা। **2.** (*Cookery*) To cover or thicken with crumbs ; "A dish of milk well *crumbed* ;" (রন্ধন-বিদ্যা) পাউরুটির গুড়া দ্বারা আবৃত বা ঘনীভূত করা। **Crumb'-y,** *adj.* **Crumb-cloth** — রুটির কণা পড়িয়া গালিচা নষ্ট না হইতে পারে, তজ্জন্য মেজের নিম্নে যে কাপড় রাখা হয়। **To a crumb** — Completely ; exactly ; সম্পূর্ণরূপে ; সঠিকরূপে। **To gather up one's crumb** — (*Dial.*) To regain strength ; (উপভাষায়) পুনরায় শক্তিলাভ করা।

crŭm'-ble, *v. t.* & *i.* To break into small fragments ; গুড়া করা, খণ্ড বিখণ্ড করা, চূর্ণ বিচূর্ণ করা। ***Verb i.*** To fall into small pieces ; to fall to ruin ; to perish ; গুড়া হইয়া পড়া ; ধ্বংসপ্রাপ্ত হওয়া ; বিধ্বস্ত হওয়া।

crŭm'-bly̆, *adj.* Apt to crumble ; friable ; as, *crumbly* soil ; ক্ষয়শীল ; সহজে চূর্ণনীয়, মড়মড়ে।

crŭm'-my̆, *adj.* **1.** (*Slang*) Plump ; comely ; (ইতর ভাষায়) মোটাসোটা, গোলগাল ; সুশ্রী। **2.** Full of crumbs ; soft, as the crumbs bread ; রুটির গুড়া দ্বারা পূর্ণ ; পাউরুটির ভিতরের শাঁসের মত নরম।

crŭm'-pĕt, *n.* A kind of muffin ; একপ্রকার পিষ্টক।

crŭm'-ple, *v. t.* & *i.* To draw or press into wrinkles ; to rumple ; to ruffle ; as, to *crumple* a piece ; of paper ; কুঞ্চিত করা ; চুনট করা ; কোঁকড়ান। ***Verb i.*** To contract ; to shrink after being crushed together ; as, a leaf *crumples* ; সঙ্কুচিত হওয়া ; কোঁকড়াইয়া যাওয়া।

crunch (crŭnsh), *v. t.*, *i.*, & *n.* **1.** To chew with violence or noise, (also *verb i.*) ; কড়মড় করিয়া চিবান। **2.** To grind under foot, (also *verb i.*) ; পদতলে চূর্ণ করা। ***Verb i.*** To force a way with violence and noise through some brittle substance ; মড় মড় শব্দে উপল, বরফ খণ্ড প্রভৃতির ভিতর দিয়া যাওয়া। ***Noun.*** Act of crunching ; কড় মড় শব্দে চর্ব্বণ।

crŭp'-pêr, *n.* **1.** A strap of leather to prevent a saddle from shifting forward ; ঘোড়ার জিন সম্মুখের দিকে সরিয়া আসিতে না পারে তজ্জন্য যে চর্ম্মরজ্জু দ্বারা উহা আবদ্ধ থাকে. পুচ্ছবন্ধ (মঃ উঃ), বালবন্ধ (মঃ ভাঃ), লেন্দি, ডুমচী। **2.** Hind quarters of a horse ; ঘোটকের পশ্চাদ্ভাগ।

cru'-răl (crô-), *adj.* (*Anat.*) Belonging to the leg ; (শারীরসংস্থান-বিদ্যা) উরু বা জঙ্ঘা সম্বন্ধীয়।

crû-sāde', *n.* & *v. i.* **1.** A Christian military expedition of the middle ages for the recovery of the Holy land from the Saracens ; মুসলমানগণের হস্ত হইতে জেরুজালেম নগরী উদ্ধারার্থ মধ্যযুগের খৃষ্টীয় সমরাভিযান। **2.** Any war instigated by the Church for alleged religious ends ; খৃষ্টীয় ধর্ম্ম-যুদ্ধ। **3.** (*Fig.*) Any enterprise undertaken with zeal and enthusiasm ; as, a *crusade* against intemperance ; (লক্ষণায়) অভিযান, সমরাভিযান। ***Verb i.*** To engage in a crusade ; ধর্ম্মাভিযানে প্রবৃত্ত হওয়া। **—sad'-er,** *n.* One who engages in a crusade ; খৃষ্টীয় ধর্ম্মযোদ্ধা, জেরুজালেম নগরীর উদ্ধার-ব্রতী মধ্যযুগের খৃষ্টীয় সৈনিক।

cruse, (crôs), *n.* A pot or jar of earthenware ; মৃন্ময় পাত্র বা ভাণ্ড।

crŭsh, *v. t.* &. *i.* **1.** To break or bruise with pressure ; পেষণ করা, থেঁতো করা, ছেঁচা, বিমর্দ্দিত করা। **2.** To crumple (dress, etc.) by rough handling ; কুঞ্চিত করা, (পোষাক প্রভৃতি) অমসৃণ করা, আবড়ো খাবড়ো করা। **3.** (*Fig.*) To subdue utterly ; (লক্ষণায়) সম্পূর্ণরূপে বশীভূত করা। ***Verb i.*** To make one's way by crushing or pressure ; ভিড় ঠেলিয়া পথ করিয়া লওয়া। **To crush out**—To extinguish ; to stamp out ; নির্ব্বাপিত করা ; উন্মূলিত করা, সমূলে বিনাশ করা। **To crush a cup of wine**—To drink it ; পেয়ালার সমস্তটুক মদ্য পান করা। **To crush a fly on the wheel**—মশা মারিতে কামান দাগা।

crŭsh, *n.* **1.** Act of crushing ; নিষ্পেষণ, বিমর্দ্দন, অবমর্দ্দন। **2.** Violent crowding, (esp. of persons) ; ঠাসাঠাসি, ঘেঁসাঘেঁসি, ঠেলাঠেলি, চাপাচাপি, গাদাগাদি। **3.** (*Colloq.*) A crowded social gathering ; (চলিত-ভাষায়) লোকসঙ্কুল সামাজিকসম্মিলনী। **Crush-room**—রঙ্গালয় প্রভৃতির কক্ষ বিশেষ,—যথায় দর্শকগণ অবকাশ কালে পরিক্রমণ করিয়া থাকেন। **Crush-cap** or **hat**—স্থিতিস্থাপক গুণোপেত টুপি—অর্থাৎ যে টুপি সঙ্কাপিত হওয়ার পর আবার পূর্ব্বাকার ধারণ করে।

crŭst, *n.*, *v. t.* & *i.* **1.** The hard outer part of a bread ; পাউরুটির উপরের ছিলকা। **2.** A hard external coat of anything ; কোন বস্তুর কঠিন বহিরাবরণ, পটল (মঃ ইঃ)। **3.** A hard dry scrap of bread ; রুটির ছিলকা। **4.** The covering of a pie ; পিষ্টকের বহিরাবরণ। **5.** A dry rough incrustation formed over sore in healing ; মামড়ি, চমটি, চিপিটিকা (হঃ চঃ)। **6.** (*Geol.*) The exterior portion of the earth, so far as accessible to our inspection and observation ; (ভূ-বিদ্যা)

পৃথিবীর বহিরাবরণ, ভূত্বক্ (সাঃ পঃ)। **7.** The hard external covering of an animal or plant ; খোলা, খোলক, ছাল, বল্কল। **8.** (*Fig.*) Anything superficial; "Break through the *crust* of his selfishness ;" (লক্ষণায়) বাহ্য বস্তু। ***Verb t.*** To cover with or form into a hard case or crust ; কঠিন বহিরাবরণ দ্বারা আবৃত করা, খোলা দ্বারা আবৃত করা, খোলা গঠিত হওয়া, মামড়িদ্বারা আবৃত করা। ***Verb i.*** To become covered with a crust ; খোলা বা মামড়িদ্বারা আবৃত হওয়া। **Crust of wine**—বোতলের গাত্রে সঞ্চিত সুরাকিট্ট।

Crŭs-tā′-ce-ă, (-shē-), *n. pl.* A division of animals, comprising crabs, shrimps, lobsters, etc., having an external shell ; কর্কট, চিংড়ীমৎস্য প্রভৃতি খোলধারী জীববর্গ, খোলকী (সাঃ পঃ), বর্ম্মধর (আঃ বঃ)। **—cean,** *adj.* & *n.* **—ce-ol′-o-gy,** *n.*

crŭs-tā′-ceous (-shŭs), *adj.* **1.** Crust-like ; খোলার তুল্য। **2.** (*Of animals*) Having a hard covering ; (জন্তু-সম্পর্কে) খোলাবিশিষ্ট, কাম্বক (মঃ ইঃ)। **3.** (*Zool.*) Belonging to the Crustacea ; (জন্তু-বিদ্যা) খোলকীপর্যায়ভুক্ত।

crŭst′-ĕd, *adj.* **1.** Covered with a crust ; খোলা বা মামড়ি দ্বারা আবৃত। **2.** (*Of wine*) Having deposited a crust ; (মদ্য-সম্পর্কে) ন্যস্তসুরাকিট্ট। **3.** (*Fig.*) Antiquated ; venerable ; as, a *crusted* theory ; (লক্ষণায়) প্রাচীন ; শ্রদ্ধার্হ।

crŭst′-ȳ, *adj.* **1.** Like crust ; hard ; খোলার মত ; কঠিন। **2.** Peevish ; surly ; "........Don't be *crusty* ;" খিট্‌খিটে ; কর্ক্কশ, কোপন। **—i-ly,** *adv.* **—i-ness,** *n.*

crutch (crŭch), *n.* **1.** A staff with a cross-piece used by cripples ; পঙ্গু বা খোঁড়ার আশ্রয়-নড়ি। **2.** Support ; prop ; (*lit.* & *fig.*) ; নির্ভর-যষ্টি ; অবলম্বন-দণ্ড, (শব্দানুযায়ীএবং লক্ষণায়)। **3.** (*Naut.*) A contrivance of forked shape ; (নৌ-বিদ্যা) দো-ফেঁকড়া ডালবিশিষ্ট কৌশল বিশেষ। **4.** Cross-piece; এড়োকাঠ। **Crutch′-ed,** *adj.*

Crutched Fri′-ars (crŭcht frī-êrs), *n. pl.* **1.** Minor order of Friar wearing a cross ; ক্রুশধারী সন্ন্যাসি-সম্প্রদায় বিশেষ। **2.** The quarters of this order ; উক্ত সম্প্রদায়ের মঠ।

crŭx, *n.* A puzzle ; কূট বিষয়, হেঁয়ালি, গোলক ধাঁধা।

crȳ, *n.* **1.** A loud noise expressive of pain or suffering ; ক্রন্দন, রোদন, বিলাপ। **2.** A loud calling out of words ; চীৎকার, উৎক্রোশ (আঃ বঃ), আরাব। **3.** Appeal ; entreaty ; "The *cry* of the whole people was for a free Parliament ;" আবেদন, নিবেদন ; প্রার্থনা। **4.** Public notice, as by a hawker of his wares ; (ফেরিওয়ালা প্রভৃতির) ডাক। **5.** A rumour ; "The *cry* goes that you shall marry her ;" জনরব। **6.** Voice of the public ; জনমত। **7.** A political catch-word ; রাজনীতিক বাণী। **8.** A fit of weeping ; as, a good *cry* (an energetic fit of weeping that relieves the feelings); এক চোট ক্রন্দন। **9.** Yelping of hounds in chase ; শিকারের পশ্চাদ্ধাবমান কুকুরের চীৎকার। **Cry-baby**—যে ব্যক্তি শিশুর মত প্যাঁন প্যাঁন ম্যান ম্যান করে। **A far cry**—A long way ; বহু দূর। **Hue and cry**—সোরগোল, চীৎকার। **Cry of tin**—টিন দুমড়াইলে যে শব্দ হয়। **Within cry**—Within calling distance ; ডাকদিলে শোনা যায় এরূপ দূরে, এক ডাকের মধ্যে।

crȳ, *v. t.* & *i.* **1.** To shout or utter loudly ; to exclaim ; উচ্চৈঃস্বরে বলা ; চীৎকার করা, চেঁচান। **2.** To bring to a certain state by weeping ; as, to *cry* oneself to sleep ; কাঁদিয়া কাঁদিয়া কোন বিশেষ অবস্থায় আনা। **3.** To advertise or sell by outcry ; as, *to cry* muffins ; ডাকিয়া ডাকিয়া ফেরি করা, হাঁকা। **4.** To extol ; to praise ; (with *up.*) ; গুণকীর্ত্তন করা ; প্রশংসা করা, তারিফ করা, প্রতিষ্ঠা করা। **5.** To proclaim the banns of (for marriage) ; বিবাহ ঘোষণা করা। ***Verb i.*** **1.** To call out loudly ; to shout ; উচ্চৈঃস্বরে ডাকা ; চীৎকার করা। **2.** To shed tears with or without sound ; to weep or wail; রোদন করা, ক্রন্দন করা, কাঁদা, ফুকরান, অশ্রুমোচন করা ; বিলাপ করা। **3.** To ask (for) ; as, to *cry for* a thing ; (*lit.* & *fig.*) ; (শব্দানুযায়ী এবং লক্ষণায়) কোন কিছুর জন্য প্রার্থনা করা। **4.** (*Of animals*) To give forth the characteristic sound or call ; as, the raven *cries* ; to yelp as a hound ; (জন্তু-সম্পর্কে) স্বাভাবিক স্বরে ডাকা ; শিকারী কুকুরের মত ডাকা। **To cry at the top of the voice**—গলা ফাটাইয়া চীৎকার করা। **To cry cupboard**—To become hungry ; ক্ষুধিত হওয়া। **To cry down**—To decry ; নিন্দা করা, দোষী করা, অপ্রতিষ্ঠা করা। **To cry goods for sale**—ডাকিয়া ডাকিয়া জিনিষ ফেরি করা, জিনিষ হাঁকা। **To cry halves**—To claim an equal share with another ; (with *in*) ; অন্যের সমান অংশ দাবী করা। **To cry in the wilderness**—অরণ্যে রোদন করা। **To cry off**—To withdraw from a bargain ; কোন রূপ চুক্তি হইতে অপসৃত হওয়া। **To cry out**—To exclaim ; চীৎকার করা। **To cry out against**—To complain loudly against ; to censure ; কোন কিছুর বিরুদ্ধে উচ্চৈঃস্বরে অনুযোগ করা ; তিরস্কার করা। **To cry over spilt milk**—To waste time in regretting uselessly ; বৃথা অনুশোচনায় সময় নষ্টকরা। **To cry quits**—To declare one's self clear or even with another, either for past favours or injuries, or as in a contest, and willing to let matters rest as they stand ; কাহারও সহিত দেনা-পাওনা শোধ (কৃতজ্ঞতা বা প্রতিহিংসার শোধ) হইয়াছে বলিয়া ঘোষণা করা। **To cry shame upon**—To protest against, as a person or act ; কোন ব্যক্তির কার্য্যের বিরুদ্ধে প্রতিবাদ করা। **To cry stinking fish**—To condemn one's own wares ; নিজের জিনিষের নিন্দা করা। **To cry to**—To beseech or implore ; সকাতরে প্রার্থনা করা। **To cry up**—To extol ; to speak highly of ; গুণ কীর্ত্তন করা ; উচ্চ প্রশংসা করা। **To cry wolf**—To give alarm without occasion ; বিপদ ঘটিয়াছে বলিয়া মিছামিছি চীৎকার করা। **I cry your mercy**—I beg pardon ; ক্ষমা চাই। **Much cry little wool**—অতিমেঘে অনাবৃষ্টি, যত গর্জ্জে তত বর্ষে না।

crȳ'-ing, *adj.* **1.** Calling out loudly ; lamenting or weeping etc. ; চীৎকারকারী ; রোরুদ্যমান। **2.** Calling for notice ; urgent ; flagrant, as an evil ; মনোযোগ প্রদানের জন্য আর্ত্তনাদকারী ; একান্ত প্রয়োজনীয়, জরুরি ; জাজ্বল্যমান, জ্বলন্ত।

crȳ'-ō-gĕn, *n.* (*Chem.*) Freezing mixture ; a thing mixed with ice to produce cryogen ; শীতজনক মিশ্র (হিঃ কোঃ) ; বরফের সহিত যে জিনিষ মিশাইয়া শীতজনক মিশ্র প্রস্তুত করা হয়।

crȳ'-ō-līte, *n.* A brittle mineral from Greenland etc. ; গ্রীণলণ্ড প্রভৃতি স্থান হইতে সমানীত সমুজ্জল খনিজ পদার্থ বিশেষ।

crȳpt, *n.* A subterranean cell or cave especially beneath a church for burying purposes ; an underground chapel ; গুহা, গুম্ফা, বিশেষতঃ খৃষ্টীয় ধর্ম্মমন্দিরের নিম্নস্থ সমাধি-কোষ্ঠ ; ভূগর্ভস্থ ভজনালয়, আন্তর্ভৌমিক উপাসনা-মন্দির।

crȳp'-tic, *adj.* Secret ; mystical ; নিগূঢ়, গুপ্ত ; গুহ্য।

crȳp'-tō, crȳp-tō-căl'-vin-ist, *n.* One who secretly sympathises with Calvinisim ; যে ব্যক্তি গোপনে গোপনে ক্যালভিন প্রবর্ত্তিত সম্প্রদায়ের প্রতি সহানুভূতি প্রদর্শন করে।

crȳp'-tō-găm, *n.* (*Bot.*) A kind of plant bearing no true flowers, such as lichens, mosses, ferns, etc. ; (উদ্ভিদ-বিদ্যা) অপুষ্পক উদ্ভিদ, অপুষ্পক (সাঃ পঃ)। **–gam'-ic, –tog'-a-mous,** *adjs.* **–tog'-a-mist,** *n.* **–tog'-a-my,** *n.*

crȳp'-tō-grăm, –grăph, *ns.* A thing written in cipher or secret characters; cipher ; সাঙ্কেতিক অক্ষরে লিখিত বিষয় ; সঙ্কেতলিপি, সঙ্কেতলিখন। **–gram'-, graph'-ic,** *adj.* **–tog'-ra-pher,** *n.* **–tog'-ra-phy,** *n.* The act or art of writing in cipher ; সঙ্কেতলিখন, সঙ্কেতলিখনবিদ্যা।

crȳp-tŏl'-ō-gȳ, *n.* Secret or enigmatical language ; গুপ্তভাষা, প্রহেলিকাময় ভাষা।

crȳs'-tăl, *n.* & *adj.* **1.** Pure transparent quartz ; a piece of this material ; স্ফটিক, অর্ক, শুচিমণি, সিতমণি, কাচমণি, কর্পূরাশ্ম, সিতাশ্ম ; স্ফটিকখণ্ড। **2.** (*Poet.*) Anything clear or transparent like crystal, as water, etc. ; (কবিতায়) স্ফটিকস্বচ্ছ বস্তু, যথা জল (cf. স্ফটিক জল)। **3.** A glass of superior composition and manufacture, also called *crystal glass* ; articles made of this kind of glass ; একপ্রকার উৎকৃষ্ট শ্রেণীর কাচ, স্ফটিক-কাচ ; স্ফটিক-কাচ নির্ম্মিত ভাণ্ডাদি। **4.** The glass of a watch-case ; টেঁক ঘড়ির ঢাকনির উপরের কাচ। **5.** (*Chem.* & *Min.*) A regular solid mineral with smooth planes or faces ; (রসায়ন-শাস্ত্র এবং খনিজবিদ্যা) সমতল-পৃষ্ঠ বা পলসমূহ বিশিষ্ট নিয়ত-সংহত এবং নিয়তাকার খনিজ পদার্থ। **6.** (*Her.*) Argent or pearl ; (কুল-চিহ্ন) রৌপ্য বা মুক্তা। ***Adj.*** Made of, or resembling, crystal ; transparent ; clear ; স্ফটিক-নির্ম্মিত, স্ফটিকাভ ; স্বচ্ছ ; নির্ম্মল, অনাবিল। **Crystal glass**—See CRYSTAL 3. **Crystal vision** — স্ফটিকদর্শন, কাচ-সামুদ্রিক। **Rock crystal** — একপ্রকার বিশুদ্ধ স্ফটিক, বিমলমণি।

crȳs'-tăl-line (-līn), *adj.* **1.** Made or composed of crystal ; স্ফটিক-নির্ম্মিত, স্ফটিক-রচিত, স্ফাটিক। **2.** Like crystal ; clear ; transparent ; স্ফটিকনিভ ; বিমল ; স্বচ্ছ। **3.** Of, relating to, or of the nature of, crystal ; স্ফটিক-সম্বন্ধীয়, স্ফটিকাকার। **Crystalline lens** — (শারীর-সংস্থান-বিদ্যা) অক্ষিমধ্যস্থ অর্দ্ধমসূরদল পরিমাণ অতি স্বচ্ছ ঝিল্লী—যৎসাহায্যে আলোকরশ্মি সমূহ কেন্দ্রীভূত হইয়া দৃষ্টি শক্তি জন্মে, অক্ষি-মুকুর (হঃ চঃ), দৃষ্টি (হঃ চঃ), দীপ্তোপল (ঐ)।

crȳs'-tăl-līze, *v. t.* & *i.* **1.** To cause to form crystals ; to form into crystals ; স্ফটিকোৎপাদন করা ; স্ফটিকীভূত করা, দানা বাঁধান। **2.** (*Fig.*) To cause to assume a definite or permanent shape ; "The forms of action......*crystallized* in the law or in the edict ;" (লক্ষণায়) স্থায়ী বা নিয়ত আকার ধারণ করা, দানা বাঁধা। ***Verb i.*** **1.** To be converted into crystals ; to assume a crystalline form ; স্ফটিকীভূত হওয়া ; স্ফটিকাকার প্রাপ্ত হওয়া। **2.** (*Fig.*) To assume a definite and settled form ; as, public opinion *crystallizes* slowly ; (লক্ষণায়) নিয়ত এবং স্থায়ী ভাব ধারণ করা। **–liz-a-ble,** *adj.* **–li-za'-tion,** *n.* The act of forming into crystals ; স্ফটিকীভবন, অর্কতাপত্তি (সাঃ পঃ), ভাস্বতা-পাদন, স্ফটিকীকরণ।

crȳs-tăl-lŏg'-ē-nȳ, *n.* The formation of crystals ; স্ফটিকীভবন। **–lo-gen'-ic,** *adj.*

crȳs-tăl-lŏg'-ră-phȳ, *n.* **1.** The science of crystallization ; স্ফটিক-বিদ্যা, অর্ক-বিদ্যা। **2.** A treatise on the formation of crystals ; স্ফটিক-বিদ্যা সম্বন্ধীয় গ্রন্থ। **–lo-graph'-ic,** *adj.* **–pher,** *n.* One who studies crystallography ; স্ফটিক-বিদ্যা চর্চ্চাকারী।

crȳs′-tăl-loid (-lo̅y̆d), *adj.* & *n.* Like crystal ; crystalline ; স্ফটিক-নিভ; স্ফটিকাকার। ***Noun.*** **1.** (*Chem.*) A substance or body of crystalline structure ; (রসায়নশাস্ত্র) দানাদার বস্তু। **2.** (*Bot.*) A crystal-like particle found in certain cells; (উদ্ভিদ্-বিদ্যা) উদ্ভিদের কোন কোন কোষে প্রাপ্ত স্ফটিক-কণাকার বস্তু।

cte′-noid (tĕ-no̅y̆d), *adj.* & *n.* Comb-shaped, as scales or teeth of certain fishes ; কঙ্কতিকাকার (যেমন কোন কোন মৎস্যের শল্ক এবং দন্ত)। ***Noun.*** A fish with such scales or teeth ; কঙ্কতিকাকার শল্ক বা দন্ত-বিশিষ্ট মৎস্য।

cten-ŏph′-ō-ră (tĕn-), *n. pl.* A sub-class of cœlenterates ; কঙ্কতী (সাঃ পঃ), কঙ্কতদেহী (প্রঃ বাঃ), [যাহাদের দেহ শ্লেষ্মপিণ্ডাকার এবং চিরুণীর ন্যায় দন্তে আবৃত।]

cŭb, *n., v. t.* & *i.* **1.** The young of the fox, bear, wolf, lion, tiger, etc. ; সিংহশিশু, সিংহশাবক, শৃগালশাবক, ব্যাঘ্রশাবক, ভল্লুকশাবক। **2.** An unpolished ill-behaved youth ; অসভ্য এবং বর্ব্বরপ্রকৃতি যুবক, জানোয়ার। ***Verb t. & i.*** To bring forth cubs; (শাবক) প্রসব করা, বাচ্চা দেওয়া। **Cub′-bish,** *adj.* **Cub′-hood,** *n.* **Cub-hunting**—শৃগালশাবক-শিকার।

cŭb′-āge, *n.* **1.** The cubic content of a solid ; the act of finding the content of a solid ; ঘনফল ; ঘনফল-নির্ণয়। **2.** Cubic measure ; ঘনমূলীয় মান।

cŭb′-ă-tūre, *n.* **1.** Finding or determination of cubic contents ; ঘনফল নির্ণয়। **2.** Cubic content ; ঘনফল।

cŭb′-bing, *n.* Hunting of cubs or young foxes ; শৃগাল-শাবক-শিকার।

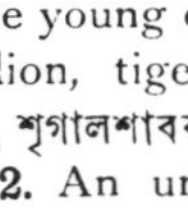

Cube.

cūbe, *n.* & *v. t.* **1.** (*Geom.*) An angular solid body, with six equal square sides ; ছয়টী সমান এবং সমচতুষ্কোণ পার্শ্ববিশিষ্ট ঘনপদার্থ, ষড়স্রক্ষেত্র, ঘন (হিঃ কোঃ)। **2.** A block of anything shaped like a cube ; ঘনাকৃতি বস্তু। **3.** (*Arith.* & *Algeb.*) The third power of a number ; the product of a number multiplied by its square ; as, the *cube* of 3 is 27 ; (পাটীগণিত এবং বীজগণিত) কোন সংখ্যার তৃতীয় ঘাত বা সামর্থ্য ; কোন সংখ্যাকে ইহার বর্গ দ্বারা পূরণ করিলে যাহা হয়। ***Verb t.*** **1.** To raise to the third power or cube ; to find the cube of ; to determine the cubic content of, as a solid ; কোন সংখ্যাকে সেই সংখ্যাদ্বারা ক্রমে দুইবার পূরণ করা, ঘাত করা ; ঘনফল নির্ণয় করা ; সংহত পদার্থের ঘনফল নির্ণয় করা। **2.** To pave with cubes or blocks ; ঘনাকৃতি প্রস্তর খণ্ডাদি দ্বারা আচ্ছাদিত করা। **Cube powder** — ঘনক্ষেত্রাকার দানাবিশিষ্ট বারুদ। **Cube-root**—ঘনফল।

cū′-bĕb, *n.* The small spicy berry of a plant akin to pepper ; কাবাবচিনি।

cū′-bic, *adj.* **1.** Having the shape or property of a cube ; ঘনাকৃতি, ঘনধর্ম্মী। **2.** Of three dimensions ; as, a *cubic* foot ; (abbr. c. or cu.) ; ত্রিপরিমাণ বিশিষ্ট (দৈর্ঘ্য, প্রস্থ ও উচ্চতা), ঘন। **3.** (*Math.*) Of third degree or power ; involving the cubes of numbers ; as, *cubic* equation ; (গণিত-শাস্ত্র) ত্রিঘাত সম্বন্ধীয় ; ঘনমূলীয়, ঘনমূল-ঘটিত। **—bi-cal,** *adj.* **—bi-cal-ly,** *adv.* **Cubic content of a solid**—ঘনফল। **Cubic foot or inches**—ঘনফুট, ঘনইঞ্চি। **Cubic measure**—ঘনমূলীয় মান।

cū′-bi-cle, *n.* A sleeping place ; a small separate compartment for sleep in schools etc. ; শয়নস্থলী ; বিদ্যালয় প্রভৃতির শয়ন-প্রকোষ্ঠ।

cū′-bi-fôrm, *adj.* Of the form of a cube ; ঘনক্ষেত্রাকার।

cū′-bit, *n,* A measure of length, (usually the length of an arm from the elbow to the tip of the middle finger) from 18 to 22 inches ; এক হস্ত।

cū′-bit-ăl, *adj.* **1.** (*Anat.* & *Zool.*) Of or pertaining to the forearm, or the corresponding part in animals ; (শারীর-সংস্থানবিদ্যা ও জন্তু-বিদ্যা) ককোণি হইতে মণিবন্ধ পর্য্যন্ত হস্তাংশ সম্বন্ধীয়, অথবা জন্তুর অনুরূপ অংশ সম্বন্ধীয়। **2.** Of the length of a cubit ; একহস্ত পরিমিত।

cū′-boid (-bo̅y̆d), *adj.* & *n.* Resembling a cube in form ; as, a *cuboid* bone ; ঘনক্ষেত্রাকৃতি, ষট্‌চতুর্ভুজাকার। ***Noun.*** **1.** The cuboid bone ; পাদদেশের ষড়স্র অস্থিবিশেষ। **2.** (*Math.*) A rectangular parallelepiped ; (গণিত শাস্ত্র) সমচতুরস্র সমানান্তর খাত (হিঃ কোঃ)। **—boi′-dal,** *adj.*

cŭck′-ing-stōōl, *n.* A chair on which females for certain offences, as for brawling and scolding, were fastened and ducked ; কোন্দল, ভর্ৎসনা প্রভৃতির শাস্তি দিবার উদ্দেশ্যে যে কেদারায় বাঁধিয়া কোন স্ত্রীলোককে জলে ডুবান হইত।

cŭck′-ŏld, *n.* & *v. t.* **1.** The husband of an adulteress or unfaithful wife ; কুলটা-পতি, অসতী-পতি। **2.** The cow-bird ; একপ্রকার পক্ষী। **3.** The cow-fish ; একপ্রকার মৎস্য। ***Verb i.*** To make a cuckold of ; কোন ব্যক্তির স্ত্রীকে ভ্রষ্টা করা।

cŭck′-ōō, *n.* **1.** A migratory bird so named from its note ; কোকিল, পিক, পরভৃত, বসন্তদূত (মঃ ইঃ)

Cuckoo.

2. The note of a cuckoo or a similar sound ; কূজন। 3. A fool.; a simpleton ; বোকা ; নির্ব্বোধ। **Cuckoo clock**—একপ্রকার ঘড়ী,—ইহা বাজিবার সময় কোকিল-কূজনবৎ ধ্বনি করিয়া থাকে। **Cuckoo-pint** — একপ্রকার কচু জাতীয় গাছ। **Cuckoo-spit** — গ্রীষ্মকালে বৃক্ষগাত্রে দৃষ্ট কীটদেহ নিঃসৃত ফেনবৎ পদার্থ বিশেষ। **Cuckoo shrikes**—কাবাসিয়া (যোঃ)। **Pied crested cuckoo**—চাতক।

cū'-cŭl-lāte, –lāt-ĕd, *adj.* **1.** Hooded ; অবগুণ্ঠিত। 2. (*Bot.*) Shaped like a hood as a leaf, etc. ; (উদ্ভিদ-বিদ্যা) (পত্রাদির পক্ষে) অবগুণ্ঠনাকৃতি। 3. (*Zool.*) Covered with a hood ; (জন্তু-বিদ্যা) অবগুণ্ঠিত।

cū'-cŭm-bêr, *n.* **1.** A kind of long fleshy fruit ; শসা, ক্ষীরা, রাজফল (মঃ ইঃ)। 2. A creeping plant which bears this fruit ; শসা গাছ, ক্ষীরা গাছ। 3. A plant allied to a common cucumber ; শসাজাতীয় গাছ। **Cool as a cucumber**—See COOL.

Cucumis momordica — ফুঁটি (বেলঃ)।

Cucumis sativus—Cucumber ; ক্ষীরা (বেলঃ), শসা (ঐ)।

Cucumis utilissimus — কাঁকুড়, কার্কতি (বেলঃ)।

cū-cŭr'-bit, *n.* A chemical vessel used in distillation etc. ; তির্য্যক পাতন ক্রিয়ায় ব্যবহৃত রাসায়নিক পাত্র বিশেষ। 2. A gourd—plant or fruit ; কুষ্মাণ্ড—লতা বা ফল। **–bi-ta'-ceous,** *adj.*

Cucurbita maxima—সফরী কুমড়া (বেলঃ), মিঠা কদু (ঐ)।

Cucurbita ovifera—চালকুমড়া।

cŭd, *n.* **1.** Food which ruminating animals bring back to the mouth and chew at leisure ; রোমন্থনকারী জন্তুগণ পুনশ্চর্ব্বণের জন্য যে খাদ্য পাকস্থলী হইতে উদ্গীর্ণ করে। 2. A quid of tobacco ; এক কলি দোক্তা, সুখা। **To chew the cud**—To ruminate as animals ; রোমন্থন করা, পুনশ্চর্ব্বণ করা, গিলিতচর্ব্বণ করা। (*Fig.*) To reflect ; to ponder ; (লক্ষণায়) নিবিষ্টচিত্তে ভাবা ; অনুধ্যান করা, তোলাপাড়া করা।

cŭd'-bear (-bār), *n.* **1.** A purple or violet coloured powder used in dyeing ; রঞ্জন কার্য্যে ব্যবহৃত আরক্ত-নীল বা ধূমলবর্ণ চূর্ণ বিশেষ। 2. The lichen from which this substance is got ; একপ্রকার শেওলা গাছ—যাহা হইতে এই রঞ্জন বস্তু পাওয়া যায়।

cŭd'-dle, *v. t., i.,* & *n.* To hug ; to embrace closely ; to fondle ; গাঢ় আলিঙ্গন করা ; বুকে চাপিয়া ধরা ; সোহাগ করা। ***Verb i.*** To lie close or snug together ; to curt oneself up as for sleep ; ঘেঁসাঘেঁসি করিয়া বা বুকে বুকে চাপিয়া থাকা, জড়াজড়ি করিয়া থাকা বা শয়ন করা ; গুটিশুটি মারিয়া ঘুমান। ***Noun.*** A close embrace ; a hug ; প্রগাঢ় আলিঙ্গন ; জড়াজড়ি।

cŭd'-dy, *n.* **1.** A ship's cabin towards the stern ; জাহাজের পশ্চাদ্-ভাগস্থ কক্ষ। 2. Closet or cupboard ; থালা, বাসন রাখিবার তাক বা ক্ষুদ্র প্রকোষ্ঠ।

cŭd'-dy, *n.* **1.** (*Scot.*) An ass or donkey ; (স্কটলণ্ড) রাসভ, গর্দ্দভ। 2. A fool ; বোকা, গাধা। 3. (*Mech.*) A lever mounted on a tripod for lifting stones, etc. ; (যন্ত্র-বিজ্ঞান) ত্রিপদের উপর আরূঢ় দণ্ড-যন্ত্র বিশেষ—যদ্দ্বারা প্রস্তর প্রভৃতি উত্তোলিত করা হয়। 4. The young of the coal-fish ; মৎস্য বিশেষের শাবক।

cudg'-ĕl (kŭj-), *n.* & *v. t.* **1.** A short thick stick of wood ; যষ্টি, লগুড়, দণ্ড, লাঠি। 2. (*Pl.*) Cudgel play ; লাঠি খেলা। ***Verb t.*** To beat with a thick stick ; লগুড়াঘাত করা, যষ্টি দ্বারা আঘাত করা। **Cudgel-play**—লাঠি খেলা। **To cross the cudgel** — To desist from the contest ; লাঠি খেলা হইতে বিরত হওয়া। **To cudgel one's brains (for etc.)** — To exercise one's wits (for) ; to try to think (of) ; মাথা ঘামান, মস্তিষ্ক আলোড়িত করা ; কোন কথা স্মরণ করিতে পুনঃ পুনঃ চেষ্টা করা। **To take up the cudgel for** — To engage in a contest in behalf of ; কাহারও পক্ষ হইয়া বিবাদে প্রবৃত্ত হওয়া।

cŭd'-weed (-wēd), *n.* A plant the flowers of which long retain their beauty ; একপ্রকার গাছ—ইহার পুষ্পের সৌন্দর্য্য দীর্ঘকাল অক্ষুণ্ণ থাকে।

cue (cū), *n.* **1.** The last words of an actor's speech serving as a signal to another to act or speak ; পূর্ব্ব অভিনেতার শেষ কথা (যাহা হইতে ইঙ্গিত পাইয়া পরবর্ত্তী অভিনেতা স্বীয় অংশের অভিনয় করে), ইঙ্গিত-বাক্য। 2. A hint or intimation ; ইসারা, সংজ্ঞা (আঃ বঃ), সঙ্কেত, আভাস, ইঙ্গিত, সন্ধান। 3. The part one is to perform in his turn ; "My *cue* is villainous melancholy" — Shakes. ; the proper course to take ; "His *cue* would be.........to magnify difficulties ;" কোন অভিনেতার পর্য্যায়গত অভিনের অংশ ; কর্ত্তব্যপথ। 4. Humour or disposition of mind ; "Nobody was in the *cue* to dance ;" মানসিক ভাব, মেজাজ। **To give the cue** — To give a hint ; আভাস দেওয়া, ইঙ্গিত দেওয়া। **To take one's cue from**—To take hint as to one's course of action from ; to follow another's lead ; অন্যের ইঙ্গিত ধরিয়া চলা ; অন্যের ধুয়া ধরা।

cue (cū), **1.** A pigtail or long plait of hair ; দীর্ঘ বেণী বা শিখা। 2. A straight rod used in playing billiards ; বিলিয়ার্ড ক্রীড়ায় ব্যবহৃত দণ্ড। 3. (*Humorous*) The tail of an animal ; (কৌতুকচ্ছলে) লাঙ্গুল, লেজ। **Cue'-ist,** *n.* A billiard player ; বিলিয়ার্ড ক্রীড়ক।

cŭff, *n.* **1.** The ornamental part of a sleeve near the hand ; জামার আস্তিনের শোভাসাধক অংশ, আস্তিনের কফ্। **2.** A band of linen worn round the wrist ; ক্ষৌম বস্ত্র খণ্ড—যাহা হাতের কব্জিতে বেষ্টন করা হয়। **3.** A hand cuff ; হাতকড়ি। **cuff'-ed,** *adj.*

cŭff, *v. t., i.,* & *n.* To strike with the fist or the palm ; to beat ; কিল দেওয়া, মুষ্ট্যাঘাত করা, ঘুষি দেওয়া, চড় দেওয়া, চপেটাঘাত করা ; প্রহার করা। ***Verb i.*** To fight ; to scuffle ; মুষ্টামুষ্টি করা ; ধ্বস্তাধ্বস্তি করা, পাছড়াপাছড়ি করা। ***Noun.*** A blow with the fist ; a slap ; কিল, ঘুষি ; চড়, চপেটাঘাত।

cuibono,(*L.*), **1.** For whose benefit ; কাহার উপকারের জন্য। **2.** (*Pop.*) To what purpose ; কি উদ্দেশ্যে।

cui-răss' (kwĭ-), *n.* **1.** A breast-plate and back-plate fastened together ; উরস্ত্রাণ, বক্ষস্ত্রাণ। **2.** Woman's close-fitting sleeveless bodice ; স্ত্রীলোকদিগের একপ্রকার আঁটা হাত-কাটা জামা।

cui-ras-sier' (kwĭ-răs-sĭr), *n.* A horse-soldier armed with a cuirass ; উরস্ত্রাণ-পরিহিত অশ্বারোহী যোদ্ধা, চোলকী।

cui-sine' (kwē-zēn), *n.* **1.** The cooking department ; রন্ধন-বিভাগ। **2.** Manner or style of cooking ; রন্ধনপ্রণালী, রন্ধনরীতি।

cuisse (kwĭsh), **cuish** (kwĭsh), *ns.* (*Hist.*) Thigh-armour ; (*usu. pl.*) ; উরুদেশ আবরক বর্ম্ম বিশেষ, উরুত্রাণ।

cul-de sac, (*F.*), *n.* **1.** A blind alley ; বন্ধ গলি। **2.** (*Anat.*) A natural cavity, tubular vessel etc., open at only one end ; (শারীর-সংস্থানবিদ্যা) একদিকে মুক্ত শরীরস্থ কোষ্ঠ, বা রক্তরসাদি বহা নলাকার নাড়ী প্রভৃতি।

cŭ'-li-nă-rў, *adj.* **1.** Relating to kitchen or cooking ; রন্ধনশালা-সম্বন্ধীয় মহানসিক, রন্ধনসম্বন্ধীয়। **2.** Fit for cooking ; as, *culinary* plants ; রন্ধনোপযোগী।

cŭll, *v. t.* & *n.* **1.** To pick out (flowers, etc.) ; আহরণ করা, চয়ন করা, অবচিত করা। **2.** To select from ; নির্ব্বাচিত করা। ***Noun.*** Something selected ; নির্ব্বাচিত বস্তু বা জন্তু।

cŭl'-lĕn-dêr, *n.* Same as CO-LANDER.

cŭl'-lĕt, *n.* Broken glass for remelting ; পুনরায় গলানের জন্য ভাঙ্গা কাচের টুকরা।

cŭl'-lў, *n.* A silly dupe ; a simpleton ; হবুচন্দ্র ; বোকা।

cŭlm, *n.* Stem or corn or grasses ; নাল (সাঃ পঃ), স্তম্ব (আঃ বঃ)।

Cul-mif'-er-ous, *adj.*

cŭl'-mi-nănt, *adj.* **1.** At or forming the top ; অগ্রভাগস্থ, চূড়াদেশস্থ, চূড়াস্বরূপ। **2.** (Of heavenly body) Being on the meridian ; (জ্যোতিষ্ক-সম্বন্ধে) মধ্যোচ্চগামী (সাঃ পঃ)।

cŭl'-mi-nāte, *v. i.* **1.** To reach the highest point, (*lit.* & *fig.*) ; পরাকাষ্ঠা হওয়া, চূড়ান্ত সীমায় উপনীত হওয়া, শেষ সীমায় পৌঁছা। **2.** (*Astron.*) To come to the meridian ; (জ্যোতির্বিজ্ঞান) যাম্যোত্তর বৃত্তে উপনীত হওয়া। **—na'-tion,** *n.* **1.** Act of culminating ; চূড়ান্ত সীমায় আগমন। **2.** Top ; চূড়া, পরাকাষ্ঠা। **3.** (*Astron.*) The transit of heavenly body over the meridian ; its highest altitude ; (জ্যোতির্বিজ্ঞান) মধ্যাগমন (সাঃ পঃ) ; যাম্যোত্তরবৃত্তস্থান (হিঃ কোঃ)। **Lower culmination**—মধ্যনীচাগমন (সাঃ পঃ)। **Upper culmination**—মধ্যোচ্চাগমন (সাঃ পঃ)। **Culminating point**—মধ্যলগ্ন (সাঃ পঃ), মধ্যভ (ঐ), মধ্যম (ঐ)।

cŭl -pā-ble, *adj.* Blameworthy ; criminal ; as, *culpable* homicide ; নিন্দার্হ, দোষী ; অপরাধযুক্ত, সাপরাধ। **—bil'-i-ty,** *n.* **—bly,** *adv.* **—ness,** *n.*

cŭl'-prit, *n.* **1.** An offender ; দোষী, অপরাধী। **2.** A person arraigned in court for crime ; অভিযুক্ত ব্যক্তি, আসামী।

cŭlt, *n.* **1.** A system of religious belief ; ধর্ম্মপ্রণালী। **2.** Homage ; worship ; as, the *cult* of Apollo ; পূজা, আরাধনা ; অর্চ্চনা।

cŭl'-ti-vāte, *v. t.* **1.** To till ; to prepare for crops ; চাষ করা ; কর্ষণ করা। **2.** (*Fig.*) To refine ; to culture (mind, manners, etc.) ; (লক্ষণায়) পরিমার্জ্জিত করা ; মানসিক উন্নতি সাধন করা। **3.** To practise ; to cherish ; as, to *cultivate* an art, sentiment or swim ; অভ্যাস করা, অনুশীলন করা, চর্চ্চা করা ; পরিপোষণ করা। **—va-ta-ble,** *adj.*

cŭl-ti-vā'-tion, *n.* Cultivating ; cultivated state (*lit.* & *fig.*) ; কর্ষণ, চাষ, অনুশীলন ; সভ্যতা।

cŭl'-ti-vā-tor (-têr), *n.* **1.** One who cultivates ; কৃষাণ, কৃষক, চাষা, ক্ষেত্রিক (আঃ বঃ)। **2.** A kind of harrow for loosening the earth about growing crops ; শস্য গাছের চারিদিকের মাটি ঢিলা করার জন্য বিদা বিশেষ।

cŭl'-trāte, *adj.* Shaped like a pruning knife ; ডাল-ছাঁটা ছুরীর আকার। **—tri-form,** *adj.*

cŭl'-tūre, *n.* & *v. t.* **1.** Tillage ; cultivation ; কর্ষণ ; চাষ। **2.** Rearing of certain animals, as oysters, fish, microbes, etc. ; also the product of such cultivation ; শুক্তি, মৎস্য প্রভৃতির চাষ ; উক্ত চাষের ফলে উৎপন্ন মৎস্য প্রভৃতি। **3.** Improvement or refinement by education and training ; "She neglected the *culture* of understanding ;" অনুশীলন। **4.** Refinement in manners and taste ; সভ্যতা। ***Verb t.*** (*Lit.* & *fig.*) To cultivate ; (chiefly used in *p. p.*) ; চাষ করা, কর্ষণ করা, অনুশীলন করা। **—tur-al,** *adj.* **—tur'-ist,** *n.*

cŭl'-tŭs, *n.* Same as CULT (which see).

cŭl′-vêr, *n.* (*Dial.*) A wood-pigeon ; (উপভাষায়) বন্য-কপোত। **Culver keys**—The cowslip ; এক প্রকার গাছ, কুকসিমা।

cŭl′-vêr-in, *n.* A long cannon of the sixteenth century ; a small fire arm ; ষোড়শ শতাব্দীর দীর্ঘ কামান বিশেষ ; এক প্রকার ক্ষুদ্র আগ্নেয়াস্ত্র।

cŭl′-vêrt, *n.* 1. A transverse drain for the passage of water under a road, canal, etc. ; a conduit ; রাস্তা, খাল প্রভৃতির নীচের জল-প্রণালী ; জল-নালী। 2. A channel for electric cable ; তাড়িত-রজ্জু স্থাপনের জন্য প্রণালী।

cŭm, *prep.* (*L.*) With ; as, *cum grano* (with caution and reserve ; *lit.* with a grain of salt) ; সহিত। **Cum-dividend**—(Abbr. *cum-div.*) অচিরে বিতরণীয় লভ্যাংশ অন্তর্ভুক্ত করিয়া।

cŭm′-bêr, *v. t.* & *n.* To hinder ; to burden ; বাধা দেওয়া ; প্রপীড়িত করা। ***Noun.*** Hindrance ; encumbrance ; বাধা ; ভার, বোঝা, দায়।

cŭm′-bêr-some (-sŭm), *adj.* Unwieldy ; clumsy ; as, *cumbersome* waggons ; troublesome ; ভারি, গুরু-ভার ; গোব্দা ; দুর্ভর (আঃ বঃ), ক্লেশকর, পীড়াদায়ক। **—ly,** *adv.* **—ness,** *n.*

cŭm′-brous (-brŭs), *adj.* Same as CUMBERSOME above. **—ly,** *adv.* **—ness,** *n.*

cŭm′-in, —min, *n.* A plant having aromatic seeds ; জীরা গাছ। **Cumin seed**—জীরা, জীরক।

cŭm′-mêr, kim′-mêr, *ns.* (*Scot.*) A godmother of one's child or god-child ; a female companion ; (স্কটলণ্ড) কোন ব্যক্তির পুত্র বা ধর্ম্ম-পুত্রের ধর্ম্মমাতা ; সখী, সঙ্গিনী।

cŭm′-mêr-bŭnd, *n.* (*Anglo. Ind.*) A girdle or waistband ; কোমরবন্ধ।

cū′-mū-lāte, *v. t.* & *i.* 1. To gather into a heap ; to accumulate ; পুঞ্জীভূত করা ; সঞ্চিত করা। 2. To combine in addition ; as, to *cumulate* one office with another ; (*law*) to combine into one as several actions or defences ; অতিরিক্ত বিষয়স্বরূপ সংযুক্ত করা ; (আইন) বিভিন্ন অভিযোগ বা আত্মপক্ষ-সমর্থনের বিষয় সমূহ একত্র সংযোগ করা। ***Verb i.*** To accumulate ; সঞ্চিত হওয়া। **—la′-tion,** *n.*

cū′-mū-lā-tive (-tĭv), *adj.* 1. Increasing by successive additions; as, *cumulative* force or evidence ; ক্রমশঃ বর্দ্ধনশীল। 2. Tending to gather together or accumulate ; সঞ্চয়নশীল, উপচয়ী (আঃ বঃ)। **—ly,** *adv.* **—ness,** *n.* **Cumulative evidence**—একই মর্ম্মের বহু প্রমাণ। **Cumulative punishment**—দণ্ডের উপর দণ্ড। **Cumulative preference shares**—যেরূপ অংশের অংশীদারগণ চলিত বৎসরের অন্যান্য সুদ বিতরিত হইবার পূর্ব্বেই সুদের অবশিষ্ট টাকা পাইবার অধিকারী হন। **Cumulative voting**—নির্ব্বাচন মত প্রদানের রীতি-বিশেষ — ইহাতে প্রত্যেক মতদাতা, যত সংখ্যক নির্ব্বাচনপ্রার্থী আছেন, তত সংখ্যক মত দিতে পারেন, এবং তিনি ইচ্ছা করিলে কোন বিশেষ ব্যক্তির অনুকূলে তাহার সমস্ত মত প্রদান করিতে পারেন, সামুদয়িক মত।

cū′-mū-lŭs, *n.* (*Pl.—li.*) 1. A heap ; রাশি। 2. A cloud in convex masses piled one upon another ; স্থূলমেঘ, পুঞ্জমেঘ। **—lous,** *adj.* Like cumulus clouds ; স্থূলমেঘবৎ।

cū′-nē-āte, *adj.* & *n.* Wedge-shaped; (applied to arrow-headed characters of the ancient inscriptions of Persia, Assyria, etc.) ; কীলকাকার (পারস্য, এসিরিয়া প্রভৃতি দেশের প্রাচীন উৎকীর্ণ লিপির বাণাগ্রাকৃতি অক্ষর সমূহ সম্বন্ধে বিশেষভাবে প্রযুক্ত)। ***Noun.*** Cuneiform characters or writing ; প্রাচীন পারস্য, এসিরিয়া প্রভৃতি দেশের কীলকাকৃতি বর্ণমালা বা লিখন।

cū-nē′-i-fôrm, *adj.* & *n.* Wedge-shaped ; as, *cuneiform* inscription ; কীলকাকার, কীলকাকৃতি। ***Noun.*** Cuneiform writings in ancient inscriptions of Persia, Assyria, etc. ; প্রাচীন পারস্য, এসিরিয়া প্রভৃতি দেশের কীলকাকৃতি উৎকীর্ণ লিপি।

cŭn′-ning, *adj.* 1. Skilful ; expert ; দক্ষ ; নিপুণ। 2. Ingenious ; as, a *cunning* workmanship ; চাতুর্য্যপূর্ণ, কৌশলপূর্ণ (আঃ বঃ)। 3. Crafty ; artful ; deceitful ; কৌশলী ; সেয়ানা ; ধূর্ত্ত, শঠ। 4. Possessing wit or intelligence; clever ; চতুর, চালাক ; বিচক্ষণ। **—ly,** *adv.*

cŭn′-ning, *n.* 1. Dexterity ; ability ; নৈপুণ্য ; কার্য্যদক্ষতা। 2. Craft ; deceit ; চালাকী, কৌশল, ফন্দী, চাতুরি ; ধূর্ত্তামি, শঠতা।

Cuon Rutilans—বনকুত্তা (বেলঃ)।

cŭp, *n.* 1. A drinking vessel ; as, a tea-*cup* ; বাটি, পেয়ালা, চষক (আঃ বঃ)। 2. (*Med.*) A cupping glass ; (ভৈষজ্যশাস্ত্র) রক্তমোক্ষণার্থ পাত্র বিশেষ। 3. A small cavity in the surface of the ground ; ভূপৃষ্ঠস্থ ক্ষুদ্র গহ্বর। 4. (*Sporting*) An ornamental vessel given as a prize ; (ক্রীড়ায়) পুরস্কারস্বরূপ প্রদত্ত কারুকার্য্যখচিত পাত্র। 5. A cavity like a cup, esp. the calyx of a flower or socket of a bone ; পেয়ালার আকার গর্ত্ত, বিশেষতঃ পুষ্পভাণ্ড, পুষ্পকুণ্ড, পুষ্পকোষ (আঃ বঃ), অস্থি-কোটর। 6. A cupful ; as, a *cup* of tea : half a *cup* ; এক পেয়ালা। 7. Fate ; a portion ; experience ; as, a bitter *cup* : his *cup* (of misery or happiness) was full ; অদৃষ্ট ; ভাগ্য ; অভিজ্ঞতা। 8. The wine of the communion ; the chalice used at the communion ; খৃষ্টের শেষ ভোজনের স্মৃতি-উৎসবে ব্যবহৃত মদিরা ; উক্ত উৎসবে ব্যবহৃত পান-পাত্র। 9. Wine, cider, etc. with different flavourings ; as, a claret *cup* ; বিভিন্নপ্রকার আস্বাদবিশিষ্ট মদ্য, সেওফলের মদিরা প্রভৃতি। **Cup′-ful,** *adj.*

Cup-bearer — মদিরা পরিবেষণকারী ; রাজা বা সম্ভ্রান্ত ব্যক্তির বাটীর কর্ম্মচারি বিশেষ। **Cup-moss**—পেয়ালার আকার উপাঙ্গ বিশিষ্ট তরুশৈবল। **Challenge cup**—রৌপ্য বা স্বর্ণনির্ম্মিত পাত্র,—যাহা ঘোড়দৌড় প্রভৃতিতে বিজেতাকে প্রদত্ত হয়, বিশেষতঃ যে পাত্র বিজয়ী ব্যক্তি পরবর্ত্তী ঘোড়দৌড় প্রভৃতি পর্য্যন্ত নিজ অধিকারে রাখিতে পারে। **Cup and ball**—একপ্রকার ক্রীড়নক,—ইহার অগ্রভাগে একটী পেয়ালা নিবদ্ধ আছে, ঐ পেয়ালায় রজ্জুদ্বারা একটী কন্দুক বাঁধা থাকে, এই কন্দুক উপরে উঠাইয়া আবার পেয়ালায় ধরিয়া একপ্রকার ক্রীড়া করা হয়; উক্তপ্রকার ক্রীড়া। **A cup too low**—In low spirit; স্ফূর্ত্তিহীন মনে। **Cup was full**—Happiness or misery was complete; সুখ বা দুঃখ পূর্ণমাত্রায় হইয়াছিল। **In one's cups**—In a state of intoxication; মাতাল অবস্থায়। **His cup runs over**—He has more than enough; তাহার টাকা পয়সার ছড়াছড়ি, তাহার ধন সম্পত্তি উপচিয়া পড়ে। **There is many a slip between the cup and the lip**—শ্রেয়াংসি বহু বিঘ্নানি, না আঁচালে বিশ্বাস নাই। **We must drink the cup**—We must bear the burden awarded to us; আমাদের অদৃষ্টে যাহা নির্দ্দিষ্ট রহিয়াছে, তাহা আমাদিগকে বহন করিতেই হইবে।

cup, *v. t.* **1.** To draw blood by puncturing the skin and applying cupping glass; ধারাল অস্ত্র দ্বারা চর্ম্মের উপর নানাস্থান কাটিয়া বাটি বসাইয়া রক্ত আকর্ষণ করা, শৃঙ্গীক্রিয়া দ্বারা রক্তমোক্ষণ করা। **2.** (*Golf*) To make a depression in the ground with the club when sending the ball; (গোল্‌ফ্ ক্রীড়া) কন্দুক তাড়নকালে ক্রীড়াদণ্ড দ্বারা ভুমি কতকটা বসাইয়া দেওয়া। **Cup'-ping,** *n.* The operation of drawing blood with a cupping glass to or from the surface of the body to relieve inflammation of internal parts; (ভৈষজ্য-শাস্ত্র) চর্ম্মের উপর একাধিক স্থানে কর্ত্তন করত, কাচের পেয়ালার সাহায্যে রক্তমোক্ষণ, শৃঙ্গীক্রিয়া (সাঃ পঃ), তুম্বীক্রিয়া (ঐ)। **Cupping glass**—পেয়ালার আকার কাচপাত্র বিশেষ,—ধারাল অস্ত্রদ্বারা চর্ম্মের উপর এক সময়ে একাধিক স্থানে কর্ত্তন করত এইরূপ পেয়ালার সাহায্যে রক্তমোক্ষণ করা হয়, শৃঙ্গী (সাঃ পঃ), তুম্বী (ঐ)।

cup'-board (cŭb-bĕrd), *n.* A shelved closet or cabinet for crockery, provisions, etc.; বাসনাদি রাখিবার তাক, অন্নকোষ্ঠ (আঃ বঃ)। **Cup-board love**—Simulated love for the sake of what one can get by it; স্বার্থপূর্ণ কৃত্রিম ভালবাসা। **Skeleton of the cup-board**—See SKELETON.

cū'-pĕl, *n.* & *v. t.* A small vessel for assaying precious metals; স্বর্ণরৌপ্যাদি ধাতুর বিশুদ্ধি পরীক্ষার জন্য ক্ষুদ্র পাত্র বিশেষ, ভাণ্ডিকা (সাঃ পঃ), হুণ্ডিকা (ঐ)। ***Verb t.*** To assay in a cupel; ভাণ্ডিকায় রাখিয়া স্বর্ণ রৌপ্যাদি ধাতুর বিশুদ্ধতা পরীক্ষা করা। **—la'-tion,** *n.*

Cupid.

cū'-pĭd, *n.* **1.** The god of love; রোমীয় পুরাণবর্ণিত কামদেব—নগ্ন শিশু, নগ্ন, হস্তে ধনুর্ব্বাণ, দেবী ভিনাস ইহার মাতা, কন্দর্প, কাম, স্মর, পঞ্চশর, মার, কুসুমেষু, মকরধ্বজ, আত্মভূ, অনন্যজ, মদন, অনঙ্গ মনসিজ, পুষ্পধ্বজ, রতিপতি, মন্মথ, মীনকেতন, প্রদ্যুম্ন, শম্বরারি। **2.** A beautiful boy; মনোহরশিশু, শিশুকন্দর্প।

cū-pĭd'-ĭ-tȳ, *n.* Avarice; covetousness; ধনতৃষ্ণা, ধনলোভ; অর্থগৃধ্নুতা, অর্থলোলুপতা।

cū'-pō-lă, *n.* **1.** A roof having a rounded form; গোলাকৃতি ছাদ, শিখর (রাঃ রাঃ)। **2.** The ceiling of a dome; গম্বুজের ছাদের ভিতরের পিঠ, তোরণ-শীর্ষ (আঃ বঃ), হর্ম্যশিখর (মঃ ইঃ)। **3.** A furnace for melting metals for casting (also *cupola furnace*); ঢালাইর ধাতু গালাইবার চুল্লী। **4.** (*Anat.* & *Zool.*) A dome-like organ or process; শারীরসংস্থানবিদ্যা ও জন্তুবিদ্যা) গম্বুজের আকার শারীরিক যন্ত্র অথবা অস্থির উন্নত বা বিবর্দ্ধিত অংশ।

Cupola

cū'-prē-ous (-ŭs), *adj.* Of or like copper; তাম্রবৎ, তাম্রাকার।

Cupressus Torulosa — দেওদার (বেলঃ)।

cū'-prĭc, *adj.* Containing copper; তাম্রপূর্ণ, তাম্রগর্ভ। **—prif'-er-ous,** *adj.* **—prous,** *adj.*

cū'-pūle, *n.* (*Bot.* & *Zool.*) A cup-shaped organ: পেয়ালার আকার অঙ্গ, ক্ষুদ্র কুণ্ড (সাঃ পঃ)।

cur, (kŭr), *n.* **1.** A degenerate snarling dog; খেঁকি কুকুর, শুনক (আঃ বঃ)। **2.** A contemptible man; হেয় ব্যক্তি, হীন ব্যক্তি।

cu-ra-cao', —coa, (cô-ră-sō), *n.* A liqueur flavoured with orange-peel etc.; কমলার ত্বক প্রভৃতি দ্বারা সুবাসিত সুরা।

cū'-ră-cȳ, *n.* **1.** The office or post of a curate; সহকারী পল্লীযাজকের পদ। **2.** Benefice of a perpetual curate; স্থায়ী সহকারী যাজকের বৃত্তি।

cū-rä'-rē, —ri, *n.* A resinous substance used by the Indians of South America to poison their arrows; একপ্রকার ধূনার মত জিনিষ—যদ্দ্বারা দক্ষিণ আমেরিকার আদিম অধিবাসিগণ তাহাদের অস্ত্রের ফলক বিষাক্ত করিত। **Cu'-ra-rize,** *v. t.*

cŭ'-răs-sow (-sō), *n.* A large South American Turkey-like bird ; দক্ষিণ আমেরিকার কুক্কুটবৎ বৃহৎ পক্ষি-বিশেষ।

cū'-rate, *n.* An assistant to a parish priest ; সহকারী পল্লীযাজক, উপপুরোহিত (মঃ ইঃ)।

cūr'-ā-tive (-tĭv), *adj.* & *n.* Tending to cure (esp. a disease) ; আরোগ্যকর, আরোগ্যসাধক, রোগনাশক, রোগঘ্ন। ***Noun.*** Such a thing ; আরোগ্যজনক বস্তু।

cū-rā'-tor (-têr), *n.* **1.** A person in charge ; a manager ; ভারপ্রাপ্ত ব্যক্তি ; কর্ম্মকর্ত্তা, কর্ম্মাধ্যক্ষ, কার্য্যাধ্যক্ষ। **2.** A custodian of a museum ; যাদুঘরের ভারপ্রাপ্ত কর্ম্মচারী, চিত্রশালাধ্যক্ষ। **3.** (In some European universities) A member of a general or special board of managers ; (কোন কোন ইয়ুরোপীয় বিশ্ববিদ্যালয়ে) সাধারণ বা বিশেষ কার্য্যনির্ব্বাহক সভার সভ্য। **—to'-ri-al,** *adj.* **—ship,** *n.*

curb (kêrb), *n.* & *v. t.* **1.** A chain or strap which serves to guide, restrain or manage a horse ; অশ্বসংযমন রজ্জু বা শৃঙ্খল। **2.** (*Fig.*) A check ; a restraint ; আটক, প্রতিবন্ধক ; প্রতিরোধ। **3.** A support on the edge ; as, a *curb* stone ; প্রান্তদেশের অবলম্বন প্রস্তর। **4.** A structure round the top of a well ; কূপ প্রভৃতির উপরিভাগের চতুর্দ্দিকস্থ প্রাচীর। **5.** A swelling on a horse's leg ; অশ্বপদের স্ফীতি। **6.** An ornamental fender for a fire place ; গৃহমধ্যস্থ অগ্নিসেবনস্থলীর কারুকার্য্যখচিত বৃতিবিশেষ। ***Verb t.*** **1.** To check or restrain as with a curb, (*lit.* & *fig.*) ; প্রতিরোধ করা, সংযত করা, বাধা দেওয়া, দমন করা। **2.** To furnish with a curb or curb-stone ; প্রান্তদেশে পাথর বসান : **Curb'-y,** *adj.* **Curb-roof** — একপ্রকার ছাদ,—ইহার অগ্রভাগ গোলাকৃতি এবং দুই পার্শ্ব হেলানো। **Curb-stone**—নিরোধপ্রস্তর। ***Curculigo Orchioides*** — তালমূলী (বেলঃ)।

cur'-cū-mā (kêr-) *n.* **1.** (*Bot.*) A genus of plants yielding turmeric ; (উদ্ভিদ-বিদ্যা) হরিদ্রাদি। **2.** A plant of this genus ; হরিদ্রাদিগণের যে কোন গুল্ম। **3.** Substance used in curry powder and as a test for alkalis ; হলুদ, হরিদ্রা। ***Curcuma Amad***—আমদ (বেলঃ)। ***Curcuma Angurtifolia***—টিকোর (বেলঃ)। ***Curcuma Aromatica***—বনহলদি (বেলঃ)। ***Curcuma Longa***—হরিদ্রা। **Curcuma paper** — ক্ষার-পদার্থ বর্ত্তমান আছে কিনা ইহা পরীক্ষার জন্য হরিদ্রায় রঞ্জিত কাগজ। ***Curcuma Zedoaria***—শুটি, বনহলদি (বেলঃ)।

curd (kêrd), *n.* **1.** The thickened part of milk ; দধি, দই। **2.** A substance like the curd of milk ; দধিবৎ দ্রব্য। **3.** The edible flowerhead of some plants as cauliflowers, etc. ; ফুলকপি প্রভৃতির ফুল, যাহা আহার করা হয়। **4.** A fatty subtance found between flakes of boiled salmon ; সিদ্ধ স্যামন মৎস্যের সরু আঁশসকলের মধ্যে প্রাপ্ত মেদবৎ পদার্থ। **Curd'-y,** *adj.* **Curd-soap**—সোডা ও চর্ব্বি দ্বারা তৈয়ারী সাবান।

cur'-dle (kêr-), *v. t.* & *i.* **1.** To change into curd ; দধি করা। **2.** To congeal ; জমান। ***Verb i.*** **1.** To be coagulated as milk etc. ; জমিয়া যাওয়া। **2.** To thicken ; গাঢ় হওয়া, ঘনীভূত হওয়া। **To curdle the blood**—To congeal the blood (as with horror) ; রক্ত জমাট করিয়া দেওয়া (ভয়াদি প্রদর্শন দ্বারা)।

cūr'-ā-ble, That may be cured ; সাধ্য, চিকিৎস্য। **Cu-ra-bil'-i-ty,** *n.*

cūre, *n.* **1.** A mode of medical treatment ; as, to resort to the water *cure* ; চিকিৎসা, প্রতীকার (আঃ বঃ)। **2.** The act of healing or the state of being healed ; restoration to health ; as, the *cure* of a disease ; আরোগ্যকরণ, আরোগ্যাবস্থা ; আরোগ্য। **3.** A remedy ; restorative ; as, a *cure* for the headache ; আরোগ্যজনক ঔষধ, ভৈষজ্য ; পুনঃস্বাস্থ্যকর বা বলকর ঔষধ। **4.** (*Eccles.*) Spiritual charge ; as, the *cure* of souls ; the office of a curate ; (যাজকীয় শাস্ত্র) আধ্যাত্মিক ভার ; পল্লীযাজকের পদ, পুরোহিত বৃত্তি (মঃ ইঃ)। **Cure'-less,** *adj.*

cūre, *v. t.* & *i.* **1.** To heal or restore to health, as a patient ; আরোগ্য করা, রোগমুক্ত করা, আরাম করা। **2.** To remedy, as a disease or evil etc. ; প্রতিকার করা। **3.** To prepare for preservation by salting or drying ; as, to *cure* meat, fruit, etc. ; শুষ্ক বা লবণাক্ত করিয়া রক্ষা করা। ***Verb i.*** **1.** To restore health ; পুনঃস্বাস্থ্য লাভ করা। **2.** To become cured or healed ; আরোগ্য লাভ করা, আরাম হওয়া, সারিয়া উঠা। **Cure-all**—A remedy for all diseases ; panacea ; সর্ব্বরোগ-প্রতিকারক ঔষধ ; সর্ব্বরোগহর ঔষধ। A name for various plants ; বিভিন্নপ্রকার গাছ গাছড়ার নাম।

cūre, *n.* (*Slang*) An odd or eccentric person ; সৃষ্টিছাড়া লোক, বাতিকগ্রস্ত লোক।

cure (cū-rā), *n.* (*F.*) A parish priest in France ; ফরাসীদেশের পল্লীযাজক।

cur'-few (kêr-fū), *n.* In former times, a regulation for extinction of fires at a particular time in the evening ; the ringing of a bell for that purpose ; the time fixed for it ; the evening bell (also called the *curfew-bell*) ; [(obs.) a cover for fire ; (অপ্রচলিত) আগুনের ঢাকনি] সায়াহ্নে নির্দ্দিষ্ট সময়ে

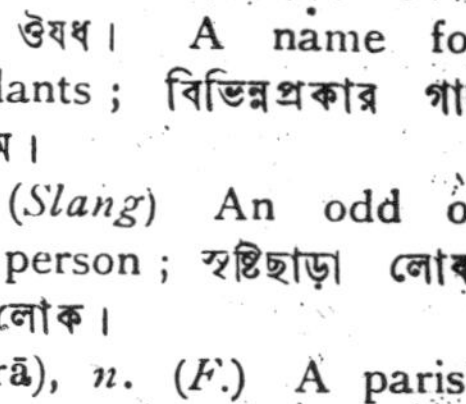

Curfew for fire.

আলোক নির্ব্বাপণের বিধি বিশেষ; উক্ত অভিপ্রায়ে ঘণ্টা-বাদন; উক্তরূপ অগ্নি-নির্ব্বাণের জন্য নিরূপিত কাল; সান্ধ্য-ঘণ্টা, প্রদোষ-ঘণ্টা (আঃ বঃ)।

cū'-ri-ă, *n.* (*L.*) **1.** One of the ten divisions into which any of the three ancient Roman tribes were divided; রোমনগরীর তিনটী প্রাচীন বংশের প্রত্যেকটী যে দশটি বিভাগে বিভক্ত ছিল, তাহার অন্যতম। **2.** The place where the curia met for worship; উক্ত প্রাচীন বংশত্রয়ের বিভাগের পূজাস্থলী। **3.** The Roman Senate House; রোমনগরীর 'সিনেট সভা। **4.** The Senate of ancient Italian towns; ইতালী দেশীয় প্রাচীন নগরী সমূহের সিনেট সভা। **5.** A court of justice (under feudal organization); (সামন্ততন্ত্রের অধীন) বিচারালয় বা ধর্ম্মাধিকরণ। **6.** The papal court; পোপের সভা। **—al,** *adj.* **—ism,** *n.*

cū'-ĭ-ō, *n.* An interesting article or object of art; কৌতুকজনক শিল্প-দ্রব্য, কৌতুক-সামগ্রী।

cū-ri-ŏs'-ĭ-tȳ, *n.* **1.** A strong desire; inquisitiveness; কুতূহল, কৌতূহল; ঔৎসুক্য। **2.** An object of curiosity; a rarity; something strange or curious; as, it is a *curiosity*; কৌতূহলের বিষয়; দুষ্প্রাপ্য বা দুর্লভ বস্তু; কৌতুক সামগ্রী। **Curiosities of literature**—সাহিত্যের চমকপ্রদ বিষয়।

cū'-ri-ous (-ŭs), *adj.* **1.** Very anxious to learn; inquisitive; কৌতূহলী, উৎসুক, কৌতুকাবিষ্ট; অনুসন্ধিৎসু, জিজ্ঞাসু। **2.** Strange; rare; surprising; বিচিত্র, আশ্চর্য্য, আজব, চমৎকার; দুর্লভ, দুষ্প্রাপ্য; চমকপ্রদ, বিস্ময়জনক। **3.** Careful; wrought with skill or elegance; as, a *curious* construction; সতর্ক; শিল্পচাতুর্য্যপূর্ণ। **—ly,** *adv.* **—ness,** *n.*

curl (kêrl), *n.* **1.** A ringlet of hair; অলকগুচ্ছ, চূর্ণ-কুন্তল, কুঞ্চিত কেশগুচ্ছ। **2.** Anything spiral; a spiral form as of smoke etc.; an undulation as in a wood; কুণ্ডলীবৎ বস্তু; কুণ্ডলিত ধূম প্রভৃতি; তরঙ্গায়িত ভাব। **3.** The act of curling; as, a *curl* of the lip (in contempt); the state of being curled; as, to keep the hair in *curl*; কুঞ্চন; কুঞ্চিতাবস্থা। **4.** A disease in potatoes in which the leaves seem curled and shrunk up; আলুগাছের রোগবিশেষ — যাহাতে পাতাগুলি কোঁকড়াইয়া যায়। **Curled hair**—কুটিল কেশ (সাঃ পঃ)।

curl (kêrl), *v. t.* & *i.* **1.** To twist to ringlets; কুঞ্চিত করা, কোঁকড়ান। **2.** To twist or coil into a spiral shape; কুণ্ডলী পাকান। ***Verb i.*** **1.** To bend into spiral form, as hair; to grow in curls as a vine; কোঁকড়ান, কুঞ্চিত হওয়া; কুণ্ডলী পাকাইয়া বাড়িতে থাকা। **2.** To move in a spiral form as smoke, etc.; to bend in a curved form; "Round her slender waist he *curled*;" কুণ্ডলী পাকাইয়া চলা; কুণ্ডলিত হওয়া। **3.** To play at the game of curling; বরফের উপর পাথর চালাইয়া খেলা করা। **Curled,** *adj.* **Curled darlings**—Pampered and petted youths; আদুরে গোপালেরা, আলালের ঘরের দুলালেরা। **To curl up**—To roll up into a curl; কুঞ্চিত হওয়া, কোঁকড়ান। (*Slang*) To collapse; (ইতর ভাষায়) ভাঙ্গিয়া পড়া।

Curlew.

cur'-lew (kêr-lū), *n.* **1.** A wading bird of the snipe tribe; বক জাতীয় পক্ষিবিশেষ, ক্রৌঞ্চ।

curl'-ing (kêrl-), *n.* **1.** Act of curling; কুঞ্চন। **2.** A Scotch game in which large smooth stones are propelled on the ice; স্কটলণ্ড দেশীয় ক্রীড়া বিশেষ—ইহাতে বরফের উপর বড় বড় পাথর চালিত করা হয়। **Curling-irons, —tongs** — চুল কোঁকড়াইবার যন্ত্র, কুন্তল-কুঞ্চক।

curl'-ȳ (kêrl-), *adj.* Having curls; tending to curl; arranged in curls; অলকশোভিত, চূর্ণকুন্তল-শোভিত; কুঞ্চনশীল; কুঞ্চিতভাবে বিন্যস্ত। **—i-ness,** *n.* **Curly pate**—কুঞ্চিত-কেশ ব্যক্তি।

cur-mudg'-eon (kêr-mŭj ŏn), *n.* A miser; কৃপণ। **—ly,** *adj.*

cŭr'-răch, *n.* A coracle; চর্ম্মাচ্ছাদিত ক্ষুদ্র তরণী।

cŭr'-rănt, *n.* **1.** A small kind of dried grapes imported from the Levant; ভূমধ্য সাগরের পূর্ব্বোপকূলস্থ দেশ সমূহ হইতে সমানীত এক প্রকার শুষ্ক আঙ্গুর, মনাক্কা (যোঃ)। **2.** The name of several shrubs and their fruits; করণ্ট (আঃ বঃ), করণ্টফল (ঐ)। **Bengal currant**—করমচা।

cŭr-rĕn-cȳ, *n.* **1.** The time during which a thing is current; প্রচলন-কাল। **2.** (Of money) Circulation; (of ideas, reports, etc.); prevalence; প্রচার, প্রচলন, রেওয়াজ; ব্যাপকতা। **3.** The circulating medium of a country, as coin or notes commonly called money; কোন দেশের প্রচলিত মুদ্রা। **4.** General esteem; সমাদর।

cŭr'-rĕnt, *adj.* **1.** Passing at the present time; as, the *current* year or month; belonging to the present time; as, the *current* issue of a journal; চলিত; উপস্থিত, বর্ত্তমান। **2.** In general circulation amongst the public; as, *current* money, opinion, rumours, etc.; প্রচলিত। **3.** Commonly accepted as true or genuine; as, the *current* meaning of a word ; ব্যবহারিক, চলিত, গতানুগতিক। **—ly,** *adv.* **Current account**—চল্‌তি হিসাব। **Current hand-writing**—দ্রুত হস্তলিপি। **To pass, go or run current**—To be generally accepted as true or genuine ; চলিত হওয়া, লোকসমাজে চলিয়া যাওয়া।

cŭr'-rĕnt, *n.* **1.** A flowing ; a running stream ; a body of air or water moving in a certain direction ; প্রবহন ; প্রবাহ, স্রোতঃ, প্রসরণ (মঃ ইঃ), ধারা। **2.** A course ; as, the *current* of events, opinions or time ; গতি। **3.** (*Elect.*) The passage of an electric fluid from one pole of an apparatus to the other ; (তাড়িত-বিদ্যা) তাড়িত-প্রবাহ।

cŭr'-ri-cle, *n.* A carriage with two wheels and drawn by two horses abreast ; এক প্রকার দুই চাকার গাড়ী, কেলিরথ (মঃ ইঃ)।

cŭr-ric'-ū-lŭm, *n.* **1.** A course of study at a university, school, etc. ; বিশ্ববিদ্যালয় প্রভৃতি দ্বারা নির্দ্ধারিত পাঠ্য বিষয়, পাঠ্য-তালিকা, পঠিতব্য বিষয়।

cŭr'-ri-êr, *n.* A man who dresses and colours leather after it is tanned ; যে ব্যক্তি বিশোধিত চর্ম্ম রঞ্জিত ও চাকচিক্যময় করে, কুরট (মঃ ইঃ)।

cur'-rish (kêr-), *adj.* Like a cur ; spiteful or snappish ; mean-spirited ; নিকৃষ্ট কুকুরবৎ, শ্বশীল (মঃ ইঃ) ; হিংসুক, রাগী, খিট্‌খিটে ; নীচাশয়, হীনচেতা। **—ly,** *adv.* **—ness,** *n.*

cŭr'-rȳ, *n.* & *v. t.* **1.** A highly spiced condiment or sauce much used in India ; মসল্লার বাটনা। **2.** A stew of fowl, fish, etc. cooked with curry ; মৎস্য বা মাংসের ঝোল, ব্যঞ্জন। ***Verb t.*** To flavour or cook with curry powder ; মসল্লার গুঁড়া মিশাইয়া রন্ধন করা বা সুস্বাদু করা। **Curry-paste, —powder**—মসলার বাটনা, মসল্লার গুঁড়া।

cŭr'-rȳ, *v. t.* **1.** To rub or clean as a horse with a curry-comb ; খড়রা দ্বারা অশ্বাদিকে আঁচড়ান বা পরিষ্কার করা। **2.** To dress ; as, to *curry* tanned leather ; চকচকে করা। **3.** To beat ; to thrash ; "I have seen him *curry* a fellow's carcase ;" প্রহার করা ; উত্তম মধ্যম দেওয়া। **To curry favour**—To seek favour or patronage by mean flattery ; হীন তোষামোদ দ্বারা অনুগ্রহ বা আনুকূল্যলাভের চেষ্টা করা।

curse (kêrs), **1.** An imprecation of evil ; malediction ; a profane oath ; a sentence of excommunication ; অভিসম্পাত ; অভিশাপ, শাপ ; অপবিত্র শপথ ; ধর্ম্মসমাজ-বহিষ্কার-দণ্ড। **2.** An accursed object ; "... A *curse* to all the nations ;" অভিশপ্ত বস্তু, ঘৃণার্হ বস্তু। **3.** Anything that brings evil or affliction ; a bane ; as, intemperance is the greatest *curse* of a country ; অশুভজনক বিষয়, কষ্টজনক বিষয় ; অনিষ্ট। **The curse of Cain**—কেইন তাহার ভ্রাতা এবেলকে বধ করার দরুণ, ঈশ্বরের অভিশাপে সমস্ত জগৎময় ভবঘুরের মত ঘুরিয়াছিল। **The curse of Scotland** — (In cards) The nine of diamonds ; রুহিতনের নয়লা। [রুহিতনের নয়লা একপ্রকার তাসের জুয়াখেলার বিজয়ী তাস ; এইরূপ ক্রীড়ায় স্কটলণ্ড দেশের বহু সম্ভ্রান্ত পরিবার সর্ব্বস্বান্ত হন।]

curse (kêrs) *v. t.* & *i.* **1.** To utter a wish of evil against ; to excommunicate ; অভিসম্পাত করা, অভিশাপ দেওয়া ; ধর্ম্মসমাজ হইতে বর্জ্জন করা। **2.** To blaspheme ; দেবনিন্দা করা। **3.** To afflict or harass ; to torment ; (usually in the passive) ; as, to be *cursed* with a bad temper ; উত্যক্ত করা ; নিগৃহীত করা। ***Verb i.*** To utter curses ; to swear ; শপথবাক্য উচ্চারণ করা ; শপথ করা।

curs'-ĕd (kêrs-), **curst** (kêrst), *adj.* & *adv.* **1.** Execrated ; অভিশপ্ত, ঘৃণিত। **2.** Detestable ; damnable ; ঘৃণ্য, জঘন্য ; নারকীয়। **3.** (*Archaic*) Cantankerous, (usually *curst*) ; (অপ্রচলিত) বেআড়া। **—ly,** *adv.* **—ness,** *n.*

cur'-sive (kêr-sĭv), *adj.* & *n.* Running ; as, a *cursive* handwriting (in manuscript), (opposed to *uncial*) ; দ্রুত। ***Noun.*** A writing or manuscript in cursive hand ; দ্রুতহস্তে লিখিত পাণ্ডুলিপি। **Cursive hand**—A running hand ; দ্রুত-হস্ত।

cur'-sö-rȳ (kêr-) *adj.* Hasty ; superficial ; দ্রুত, ক্ষিপ্র, ত্বরিত ; উপর উপর, ভাসা ভাসা, বাহ্য। **—ri-ly,** *adv.* **—ri-ness,** *n.* **Cursory view**—দ্রুত-দৃষ্টি, উপর উপর দেখা।

curt (kêrt), *adj.* **1.** Short ; সংক্ষিপ্ত। **2.** Rudely brief ; as, *curt* answer ; কাটা, রুখা। **Curt'-ly,** *adv.* **Curt'-ness,** *n.*

cur-tail' (kêr-tāl), *v. t.* To cut short ; to abridge ; to lessen ; (*lit.* & *fig.*) to deprive (a person or thing) of something ; কাটা-ছাটা ; সংক্ষেপ করা ; হ্রাস করা, সঙ্কোচ করা ; (শব্দানুযায়ী এবং লক্ষণায়) (কোন ব্যক্তি কিম্বা বস্তুকে) কোন কিছু হইতে বঞ্চিত করা। **—ment,** *n.* The act of curtailing ; সংক্ষেপ, সঙ্কোচ, হ্রাস-করণ। **Curtail-step**—সোপান-শ্রেণীর নিম্নতম ধাপ।

cur'-tain (kêr-tān), *n.* & *v. t.* **1.** A hanging-cloth used as a screen for a window, bed, etc. ; a movable screen for concealing the stage in a theatre ; তিরস্করণী, পর্দ্দা, চি যবনিকা। **2.** (*Fort.*) A plain wall of a fortified place connecting two towers etc. ; (দুর্গ) দুর্গাদি দ্বারা সুরক্ষিত স্থানের বুরুজদ্বয় প্রভৃতি সংযোজক প্রাচীর। **2.** (*Arch.*) The part of a wall of a building between two pavilions, towers, etc.; (স্থপতি-বিদ্যা) মণ্ডপ বুরুজ প্রভৃতির মধ্যবর্ত্তী হর্ম্ম্য-প্রাচীরাংশ। ***Verb t.*** To cover or inclose with curtains, (usually with *off*); to furnish with curtains; তিরস্করণী দ্বারা আবৃত বা বেষ্টিত করা; পর্দ্দা দ্বারা ঘেরা। **Curtain-lecture**—শয্যায় শয়ন করিলে পর পত্নী পতিকে যে তিরস্কার-বাক্য প্রয়োগ করেন, পত্নীর অনুযোগ, শয্যানুশাসন (আঃ বঃ), শয্যা-গঞ্জনা। (*Theatre*) **Curtain-raiser**—(রঙ্গালয়) নাট্যারম্ভের পূর্ব্বে যে সংক্ষিপ্ত বিষয় অভিনীত হয়। **Fire-proof curtain** — রঙ্গমঞ্চ ও রঙ্গমঞ্চ হইতে অগ্নির বিস্তার নিবারণ জন্য ধাতুনির্ম্মিত তিরস্করণী। **Mosquito curtain**—মশারি, মশহরী (আঃ বঃ)। **Behind curtain** — Behind the screen; away from the public view; পর্দ্দার আড়ালে; লোকচক্ষুর অন্তরালে। **The curtain falls, drops** or **is dropped**—যবনিকা পতন। **The curtain rises, is raised**—যবনিকোত্তোলন; নাট্যারম্ভ। **To draw the curtain**—To draw it back or aside to reveal objects; পর্দ্দা সরান। To draw it forward to conceal objects; পর্দ্দা টানিয়া দেওয়া।

cŭr-tâ'-nă, *n.* A pointless sword borne before kings of England at their coronation as emblem of mercy; ইংলণ্ডেশ্বরদিগের অভিষেক-কালে তাহাদিগের অগ্রে বাহিত করুণার নিদর্শনস্বরূপ অসূক্ষ্মাগ্র অসি।

cur'-ti-lāge (kêr-), *n.* Area attached to a dwelling house; বসত-বাটীর সংলগ্ন বা সামিল ভূমি, উদ্বাস্তু।

curt'-sy̆ (kêrt-); **—sey** (-sî), *n.* & *v. i.* A woman's salutation by slightly bending the knees; প্রণতজানু হইয়া স্ত্রীলোকের মত নমস্কার, অঙ্গপ্রণাম (মঃ ইঃ)। ***Verb i.*** To make a curtsey; উক্ত প্রকারে প্রণিপাত করা।

cū'-rule (-rôl), *adj.* Pertaining to any high civic dignity; উচ্চ নাগরিক মর্য্যাদা সংক্রান্ত। **Curule chair**—(*Rom. Antiq.*) An ivory chair somewhat like a camp-stool; (রোমীয় প্রত্নতত্ত্ব) গজদন্ত নির্ম্মিত কেদারা বিশেষ। [কেবল মাত্র Dictators, proctors, consuls, censors প্রভৃতি উচ্চ কর্ম্মচারিগণের ব্যবহারের অধিকার ছিল।]

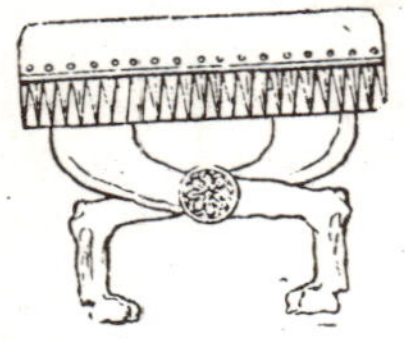

Curule chair.

cur'-vă-türe (kêr-), *n.* **1.** A curving; বক্রতা, জিহ্মতা, বক্রিমা (আঃ বঃ)। **2.** A curve; a bend; বক্র; বক্রতা, আনতি (মঃ ইঃ)। **3.** (*Geom.*) Deviation of a curve from a straight line; (জ্যামিতি) বক্র (হিঃ কোঃ)।

curve (kêrv), *v. t.* & *i.* To bend; to crook; বক্র করা; বক্র হওয়া, বাঁকিয়া যাওয়া।

curve (kêrv), *n.* **1.** An arched line; বক্র-রেখা, ধনুর্মার্গ (মঃ ইঃ)। **2.** A curved thing; বক্রাকার বস্তু।

cur'-vĕt (kêr-), *n.* A horse's leap in which he raises his fore legs together; অশ্বের লম্ফবিশেষ, যাহাতে সে এক সঙ্গে সম্মুখের পদদ্বয় তুলিয়া থাকে, বল্গিত (আঃ বঃ), প্লুত (মঃ ইঃ)।

cur'-vĕt (kêr-), *v. i.* To make a curvet; উক্ত প্রকারে লম্ফ প্রদান করা।

cur'-vi-fōrm (kêr-), *adj.* Having a curved form; বক্রাকৃতি।

cur-vi'-lin-e-ar (kêr-vî-lîn-ē-êr), *adj.* Contained by, or consisting of, curved line or lines; বক্ররেখা দ্বারা পরিবেষ্টিত, বক্ররেখা সমন্বিত, বক্রীয় (হিঃ কোঃ) **—ar'-i-ty**, *n.* **—ly**, *adv.*

cŭs'-cŭs, *n.* Aromatic root of an Indian grass; খসখস, বীরতারা (বেলঃ)।

Cuscuta Reflexa—হল্‌দি আলগুশি লতা (বেলঃ), নীল তার (ঐ), আকাশ-বেল (ঐ)।

cŭsh'-ăt, *n.* The sing-dove; কাঁটিদার ঘুঘু, বন্যকপোত।

cûsh'-ion (-ǒn), *n.* **1.** A pad for sitting, kneeling or resting on, stuffed with wool, hair or other soft material; গদি, তাকিয়া, আস্তরণ, উপাধান (আঃ বঃ)। **2.** A pincushion; আলপিন রাখিবার ছোট গদি। **3.** A pad for woman's hair; মহিলাদিগের চুলে বাঁধিবার নরম গদি। **4.** A pad beneath skirts of a woman's dress; মহিলাদিগের ঘাগরার নীচে পরিহিত নরম গদি। **5.** (*Billiards*) The side of a billiard-table which causes the balls to rebound; (বিলিয়ার্ড ক্রীড়া) বিলিয়ার্ডের মেজের যে পার্শ্বে প্রতিহত হইয়া কন্দুক ঠিকরাইয়া আসে। **6.** (*Mech.*) A body of steam at the end of a cylinder to receive the impact of the piston; (যন্ত্র-বিজ্ঞান) নলদণ্ডের সংঘাত ধারণ করিবার জন্য নলের নিম্নদেশস্থ বাষ্পপুঞ্জ। **7.** Fleshy part of the buttock (of a pig etc.); (শূকর প্রভৃতির) নিতম্বদেশের মাংসল অংশ। **8.** The frog of horse's foot; অশ্বপদতলস্থ স্থিতিস্থাপক-গুণোপেত শৃঙ্গবৎ পদার্থ বিশেষ। **—y**, *adj.* **Cushion-tire**—(Of a bicycle) Robber tubing stuffed with robber shreds; (দ্বিচক্রযানের) রবারের টুকরা দ্বারা ঠাসা রবারের নল।

cŭsh'-ion (-ǒn), *v. t.* **1.** To furnish with cushions; গদি দ্বারা মোড়া। **2.** To cover or conceal, as with a cushion; গদির মত মোড়া বা ঢাকা। **3.** (*Fig.*) To suppress; as, I am prepared to *cushion* the matter; (লক্ষণায়) চাপা দেওয়া, চাপিয়া রাখা, গোপন করা।

cŭsp, *n.* **1.** Apex; peak; অগ্রভাগ; শৃঙ্গ, শিখা, চূড়া। **2.** (*Geom.*) A point at which two branches of a curve meet and stop; দুইটী বক্র রেখার সম্মিলনে উৎপন্ন বিন্দু, সম্মিলন বিন্দু, স্কন্ধ (হিঃ কোঃ)। **3.** (*Arch.*) A projecting point between small arcs in Gothic tracery ; গথিক পদ্ধতির অনুযায়ী দ্বার ও বাতায়নের উপরিস্থ শোভাজনক কারুকার্য্যে ক্ষুদ্র ক্ষুদ্র বৃত্তখণ্ডের মধ্যবর্ত্তী উদ্গত বিন্দু। **4.** (*Bot.*) Pointed end, esp. of a leaf ; (উদ্ভিদ্‌বিদ্যা) সূক্ষ্মান্ত ভাগ (বিশেষতঃ পত্রের)। **5.** (*Astron.*) The point or horn of the crescent moon ; (জ্যোতির্বিজ্ঞান) চন্দ্রকলার সূক্ষ্মাগ্রভাগ বা শৃঙ্গ, অর্দ্ধেন্দু শিখা (মঃ ইঃ), শৃঙ্গ (হিঃ কোঃ)। **Cusp′-ed,** *adj.*

cŭs′-pi-dal, *adj.* Of the nature of a cusp ; সূক্ষ্মাগ্রভাগ (সাঃ পঃ)। **—date, —dat-ed,** *adjs.*

cŭs′-pi-dŏr, —dŏre *n.* (*U. S.*) A spittoon ; (মার্কিণ যুক্ত রাজ্য) পিকদান।

cŭss, *n.* **1.** (*U. S.*) A curse ; (মার্কিণ যুক্ত রাজ্য) অভিশাপ। **2.** A fellow ; a beast (disparagingly) ; ইতরলোক ; পশু।

cŭss′-ĕd-nĕss, *n.* (*U. S.*) Perversity ; (মার্কিণ যুক্ত রাজ্য) নষ্টামি।

cŭs′-tard (-tẽrd), *n.* A mixture of milk and egg sweetened and baked or boiled ; দুগ্ধ, ডিম্ব ও চিনির মিশ্রণে প্রস্তুত সুমিষ্ট পিষ্টক বা ক্ষীর, দুগ্ধাণ্ডমিষ্ট (আঃ বঃ)। **Custard apple**—A West Indian fruit with pulp like custard ; নোনা আতা, আতা (যোঃ) আতৃপ্য (আঃ বঃ)।

cŭs-tō′-di-ăl, *adj.* Relating to custody ; সংরক্ষণ-সংক্রান্ত।

cŭs-tō′-di-ăn, *n.* A keeper ; a guardian ; রক্ষক ; অভিভাবক।

cŭs′-tō-dȳ, *n.* **1.** Charge ; guardianship ; জিম্মা, হেপাজৎ ; সংরক্ষণ, তত্ত্বাবধান। **2.** Imprisonment ; অবরোধ, কারাবাস। **To take into custody**—To arrest ; গ্রেপ্তার করা।

cŭs′-tom (-tŭm), *n.* **1.** Habitual practice ; a regular habit ; রীতি, দস্তর, প্রথা, ধারা ; আচার, ব্যবহার, অভ্যাস, অনুসার (মঃ ইঃ) । **2.** Aggregate of usages or practices regulating social life ; সামাজিক আচার, লোকাচার। **3.** (*Law*) The established usages having the force of law ; (আইন) দেশাচার। **4.** (*Pl.*) The duty imposed by law upon merchandise imported or exported ; শুল্ক, মাশুল, হাসিল। **5.** The practice of frequenting shops. etc for purchasing or giving orders ; business-support or patronage ; জিনিষ ক্রয়ের জন্য বা জিনিষের ফরমাইস দিবার জন্য দোকানে গতিবিধি ; কারবারে পৃষ্ঠপোষকতা। **Custom-house**—An office, esp. in a seaport where customs and duties are collected ; শুল্কশালা, শুল্কস্থান, শুল্কাগার, মাশুলঘর।

cŭs′-tom-ă-rȳ (-tŭm-), *adj.* & *n.* **1.** Habitual ; usual ; conventional ; প্রথামূলক, রীতিসিদ্ধ ; গতানুগতিক ; মামুলি, চলিত। **2.** (*Law*) Subject to or held by payment of customs or dues ; (আইন) কর-সাপেক্ষ, করযোগ্য, শুল্ক-যোগ্য। *Noun.* (Also *custumary*) A book descriptive of the customs or legal usages of a city or country ; কোন নগর বা দেশের রীতিনীতি, আচার, প্রভৃতি যে পুস্তকে বিবৃত হইয়াছে, আচার-গ্রন্থ। **—ri-ly,** *adv.* **—ri-ness,** *n.*

cŭs′-tom-ẽr (-tŭm-), *n.* **1.** A purchaser ; ক্রেতা, গ্রাহক, খরিদদার। **2.** (*Colloq.*) A chap or fellow whom one has to deal with ; (often with some adjectives) ; as, a queer or awkward *customer* ; (চলিতকথায়) যাহার পাল্লায় পড়া যায়—এরূপ লোক।

cŭs′-tŏs, *n.* [*L.*] A guardian ; a keeper ; রক্ষক ; পালক। **Custos rotulorum** — (শব্দানুযায়ী) নাম তালিকাপুস্তক-রক্ষক ; (ইংলণ্ডীয় আইন) কোন দেশের সর্ব্বপ্রধান শান্তিরক্ষক বিচারপতি।

cŭt, *n.* **1.** An opening, cleft, gash, or wound made by an edged instrument ; a surface left by cutting ; as, a smooth *cut* ; (*fig.*) a wound ; shock ; "A cruel *cut* to a troubled conscience ;" অস্ত্রক্ষত ; কাট, ছেদ ; (লক্ষণায়) আঘাত ; ধাক্কা। **2.** Style ; fashion ; as, the *cut* of clothes or face ; ছাঁদ ; গঠন, গড়ন। **3.** An artificial channel or canal ; কৃত্রিম খাল। **4.** A part cut off from the main body ; কর্ত্তিত অংশ। **5.** A straight course or passage ; as, a short *cut* ; সোজা পথ বা রাস্তা। **6.** A block on which a picture is engraved for printing ; যে ফলকে মুদ্রাঙ্কণের জন্য কোন চিত্র উৎকীর্ণ হইয়া থাকে, চিত্র-খোদিত-ফলক। **7.** The act of cutting ; a stroke or blow with a knife, whip, sword, etc. ; কর্ত্তন ; ছুরিকাঘাত, কষাঘাত, তলোয়ারের চোট, খড়্গাঘাত। **8.** The excision or omission of a part, as of a drama ; the part so cut off ; নাটক প্রভৃতির অংশ বর্জ্জন ; উক্তরূপ বর্জ্জিত অংশ, ছাঁইট। **9.** An act or speech that wounds the feeling ; মর্ম্মচ্ছেদী কার্য্য বা বাক্য, মর্ম্মভেদী বাক্য। **10.** A lot ; সমূহ। **11.** A railway cutting ; লৌহবর্ত্মের উভয় পার্শ্বের কাটা জায়গা। **12.** A narrow opening in the floor of the stage of a theatre by which scenes are moved up and down ; রঙ্গমঞ্চের যে কাটা স্থানের ভিতর দিয়া দৃশ্যপট-সমূহ উঠান ও নামান হয়। **A cut above**—একধাপ উচু। **A short cut** — A crossing that shortens the distance, (*lit.* & *fig.*); (শব্দানুযায়ী এবং লক্ষণায়) ঋজুমার্গ (মঃ ইঃ), সোজাপথ, সোজারাস্তা। **Cut and dry,—dried**—তৈয়ারী। **Cut and thrust**—A hand-to-hand fight or struggle ; হাতাহাতি যুদ্ধ। **The cut of one's jib**—One's outward appearance ; বাহ্য আকৃতি। **To draw cuts**—To draw lots with sticks of unequal length ; বিভিন্ন দৈর্ঘ্যের যষ্টিদ্বারা সুরতি খেলা।

cŭt, *v. t.* & *i.* **1.** To wound or penetrate by an edged instrument ; to cleave ; to make an incision into ; as, to *cut* one's finger ; কাটা ; ছেদন করা ; ক্ষত করা । **2.** To separate by cutting ; as, to *cut* a slice of meat ; কাটিয়া খণ্ড খণ্ড করা, কাটিয়া টুকরা টুকরা করা । **3.** To carve ; মাংসাদি খণ্ড খণ্ড করা কুটা । **4.** To trim or pare as hair or nail ; নখ, চুল প্রভৃতি কাটা । **5.** To fell as wood ; to hew as timber ; কাঠ প্রভৃতি কাটা ; কুঠার দ্বারা তক্তা প্রভৃতি ছেদন করা । **6.** To intersect ; as, lines *cut* one another ; ছেদন করা, কাটা । **7.** To fashion or shape by cutting ; as, to *cut* a coat or diamond ; to engrave as a plate, etc. ; to excavate, as a ditch etc. ; কাটিয়া গঠন করা ; ফলক প্রভৃতি খোদিত করা ; (খাল প্রভৃতি) কাটা । **8.** To wound the feelings of ; as, he was *cut* to the quick ; মর্ম্মাহত করা, মনে আঘাত দেওয়া । **9.** To perform ; as, to *cut* a caper, dash, or joke, etc. ; করা । **10.** To absent oneself from ; to avoid ; as, to *cut* a lecture ; অনুপস্থিত থাকা ; পরিহার করা । **11.** To abridge, as a drama ; নাটক প্রভৃতি সংক্ষেপ করা, কাটা ছাঁটা । **12.** To reduce in amount, as rates, prices, etc. ; মূল্য, প্রভৃতি হ্রাস করা । **13.** To divide in two or more parts as a pack of cards ; তাস কাটা । **14.** To mow or reap, as hay, corn, etc. ; ঘাস, শস্য প্রভৃতি কাটা । **15.** To strike, as with a whip, etc. ; চাবুক প্রভৃতি দ্বারা আঘাত করা । **16.** To decline to recognise ; না চিনা । **17.** To renounce, as, to *cut* a connexion ; ছিন্ন করা । ***Verb i.*** **1.** To do the work of an edge tool ; to make an incision ; ধারাল অস্ত্রের কাজ করা ; অস্ত্র বসাইয়া কাটা । **2.** To be divided as by a knife ; as, cheese *cuts* well ; ছুরি প্রভৃতি দ্বারা খণ্ডিত হওয়া । কাটা যাওয়া । **3.** To use a cutting instrument ; ধারাল অস্ত্র ব্যবহার করা । **4.** To pass (with *across, through,* etc..) ; অতিক্রম করা, চলিয়া যাওয়া । **5.** (*Slang*) To run away ; (ইতর ভাষায়) দৌড়িয়া যাওয়া । **6.** To strike with a whip etc. ; চাবুক প্রভৃতি দ্বারা আঘাত করা । **7.** To divide a pack of cards in two parts ; তাস কাটা । **Cut'-ting-ly,** *adv.* **Cut-glass**—Glass with a surface shaped or ornamented by grinding etc. ; বেলোয়ারি কাচ । **Cut-purse** — গাঁইট-কাটা । **Cut-throat** — হত্যাকারী ; গলা-কাটা । **Cut and come again**—Plenty or abundance, (a hospitable phrase) ; প্রাচুর্য্য, খাদ্য-পানীয়ের প্রাচুর্য্য । **To cut across**—To go or pass straight ; সোজা চলিয়া যাওয়া । **To cut a dash or figure**—To make a show ; to be conspicuous ; ভড়ক দেখান, জাঁক দেখান ; (নিজকে) জাহির করা, সুপ্রকট হওয়া । **To cut a joke** — To perform a joke ; ঠাট্টা করা । **To cut a tooth** — To have it appear through the gum as a child ; শিশুর দাঁত উঠান । **To cut capers**—To dance ; to frisk above ; নাচা কুঁদা ; লম্ফ ঝম্প দেওয়া । **To cut down**—To fell as a tree etc. ; গাছ প্রভৃতি কাটিয়া ফেলা । To curtail ; as, to *cut down* expenses ; সঙ্কোচ করা । **To cut in**—To enter abruptly ; হঠাৎ প্রবেশ করা । **To cut lots**—To determine lots by cutting cards ; তাস কাটিয়া ভাগ্য পরীক্ষা করা । **To cut off**—To sever ; to put an end to ; to intercept (communication etc.) ; ছেদন করা ; শেষ করা ; বাধা দেওয়া । **To cut off (a child) with a shilling**—To disinherit by bequeathing a shilling ; চরমপত্র দ্বারা এক শিলিং প্রদান করিয়া কাহাকেও উত্তরাধিকার হইতে বঞ্চিত করা, ত্যাজ্য সন্তান করা । **To cut one dead**—To decline to recognise an acquainted person in public ; কোন পরিচিত ব্যক্তিকে লোকসমাজে চিনিয়াও না চিনা । **To cut one lucky or one's stick**—To go ; যাওয়া । **To cut one's eye, teeth**—To become knowing or sharp ; চালাক বা জ্ঞাতসার হওয়া । **To cut one's way** — To force a passage through opposing forces ; ঠেলিয়া পথ করিয়া লওয়া । **To cut out** — To remove by cutting ; কাটিয়া ফেলা । To supplant ; কৌশলে স্থানচ্যুত করা । To shape (*lit.* & *fig.*) ; (শব্দানুযায়ী এবং লক্ষণায়) গড়া, গঠন করা । (*Naut.*) To seize and carry off (a vessel) from a harbour or from under the fires of an enemy ; (নৌ-বিদ্যা) পোতাশ্রয় হইতে অথবা শত্রুর গোলাবৃষ্টির মধ্যে হইতে (জাহাজ) ধরিয়া লইয়া যাওয়া । **To cut short**—To abridge ; সংক্ষেপ করা । **To cut the coat according to the cloth**—See under CLOTH. **To cut the (Gordian) knot**—To effect anything by shor and strong measures ; কোন গোলমেলে বিষয় সোজাসুজি মীমাংসা করা । [ফ্রিজিয়া দেশের জনৈক কৃষক একটি গ্রন্থি বাঁধিয়া রাখে। এই গ্রন্থির বিষয় এই প্রবাদ প্রচলিত হয় যে ব্যক্তি উহা খুলিতে পারিবে সে সমগ্র এসিয়ার সাম্রাজ্য-লাভ করিবে। মহাবীর অলীকসুন্দর দিগ্বিজয় ব্যপদেশে ফ্রিজিয়ায় আসিলে পর তাহাকে এই গন্থি প্রদর্শিত হয়। অলীকসুন্দর উহা তৎক্ষণাৎ তরবারি দ্বারা দ্বিখণ্ডিত করিয়া বলিলেন, "এই ভাবেই আমরা আমাদের গ্রন্থি ছেদন করিয়া থাকি।"] **To cut the ground from under one**—To leave an adversary no ground to stand on by disproving all his arguments ; প্রতিপক্ষের সমস্ত যুক্তি খণ্ডন করিয়া তাহাকে নিরুপায় করা । **To cut to the heart, To cut to the quick**—To wound the feelings of ; মর্ম্মে আঘাত করা, আঁতে ঘা দেওয়া । **To cut up, to cut in pieces**—To destroy utterly ; to criticize severely ; বিধ্বংস করা ; কঠোর সমালোচনা করা। **To cut up rough**—To be disagreeable or quarrelsome about anything ; কোন বিষয় লইয়া অপ্রীতির সঞ্চার হওয়া, কোন বিষয় লইয়া কলহ করা। **To cut up**—To leave large fortune ; প্রচুর সম্পত্তি রাখিয়া যাওয়া।

cū-tā'-nē-ous (-ŭs), *adj.* Of the skin ; চর্ম্ম সম্বন্ধীয়, চার্ম্মিক।

cutch—কথ (বেলঃ)।

cūte, *adj.* (*Colloq.*) Clever ; (চলিত ভাষায়) চালাক। **Cute'-ly,** *adv.* **Cute'-ness,** *n.*

cū'-ti-cle, *n.* **1.** The epidermis or the scarf-skin ; বাহ্যত্বক, উপত্বক অবভাসিনী (মঃ ইঃ)। **2.** (*Bot.*) Superficial film of plants ; (উদ্ভিদ-বিদ্যা) বৃক্ষাদির বাহিরের পর্দ্দা, কৃত্তিক (সাঃ পঃ)। **—tic'-u-lar,** *adj.*

cū'-tis, *n.* The true skin under the cuticle ; বাহ্যত্বকের নিম্নবর্ত্তী প্রকৃত ত্বক, প্রকৃত-ত্বক (হঃ চঃ)।

cŭt'-lăss, *n.* A broad curving sword used by sailors ; নাবিকদিগের দা বা কাটারি, কর্ত্তরিকা।

cŭt'-lêr, *n.* One who makes or deals in knives or other similar instruments ; ছুরি, কাঁচি প্রভৃতি নির্ম্মাতা বা বিক্রেতা।

cŭt'-lêr-ȳ, *n.* **1.** The business or trade of a cutler ; ছুরি, কাঁচির ব্যবসায়। **2.** Articles made or sold by a cutler ; ছুরি, কাঁচি প্রভৃতি।

cŭt'-lĕt, *n.* A small slice of meat (esp. mutton or veal) for cooking ; রাঁধিবার জন্য মাংসের ফালি (সাধারণতঃ পাঁজর এবং তৎসংলগ্ন মাংস), ভৃষ্ট-ফালিকা (আঃ বঃ)।

cŭt'-têr, *n.* **1.** A person or thing that cuts ; কর্ত্তক, কর্ত্তনকারী। **2.** A soft brick that can be cut to any shape ; এক প্রকার নরম ইট, যাহা যে কোন আকারে কাটা যাইতে পারে। **3.** A small boat used by ships of war ; রণপোত সমূহদ্বারা ব্যবহৃত ক্ষুদ্র নৌকা। **4.** A vessel with one mast and a straight running

Cutter.

bow-sprit, closely resembling a sloop ; একপ্রকার এক মাস্তুলের জাহাজ।

cŭt'-ting, *n.* Act of separating with a sharp-edged instrument ; কর্ত্তন, ছেদন। **Press cutting**—A paragraph etc. cut from a newspaper ; সংবাদপত্র হইতে কর্ত্তিত প্রবন্ধাংশ প্রভৃতি।

cŭt'-tle, *n.* A mollusc which ejects a black fluid to conceal itself (also *cuttle-fish*) ; এক প্রকার কম্বুজ—ইহার শরীর হইতে একরূপ কৃষ্ণবর্ণ তরল পদার্থ নির্গত হইয়া ইহাকে লুক্কায়িত করে, সমুদ্রজিহ্বা (সাঃ পঃ), দশভুজা (আঃ বঃ)। **Cuttle-bone** — Its internal shell, used for polishing ; সমুদ্রফেন, সিন্ধুকফ, হিঙীর।

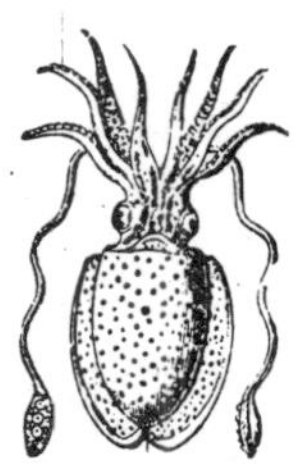

Cuttle-fish.

cŭt'-tȳ, *adj.* & *n.* Abnormally short ; অতি খাটো। ***Noun.*** A short tobacco-pipe ; ধূমপানের ক্ষুদ্র নল। **Cutty-stool** — স্কট্লণ্ড দেশীয় ধর্ম্মমন্দিরের আসন বিশেষ — যাহাতে বসিয়া অসতী নারীগণ প্রকাশ্য তিরস্কার ভোগ করিত।

cŭt'-wa-têr, *n.* **1.** The forepart of a ship's prow that cuts the water ; পোতাগ্রদেশের সম্মুখ ভাগ,—যাহা জল কাটিয়া চলে, তরঙ্গভেদী (আঃ বঃ)। **2.** A structure attached to the pier of a bridge with an edge to resist the action of water ; জলের ক্রিয়া রোধের জন্য সেতুস্তম্ভসংলগ্ন ব্যবস্থা বিশেষ। **3.** A water-fowl ; জলচর পক্ষিবিশেষ।

cŭt'-worm (-wŭrm) *n.* A caterpillar that cuts off young plants level with the ground ; এক প্রকার শুঁয়াপোকা—ইহারা কচি কচি গাছগুলি মাটির সমান করিয়া কাটিয়া ফেলে।

cȳ-ăn'-ic, *adj.* **1.** (*Chem.*) Relating to, or containing, cyanogen ; হরিৎ-নীলবর্ণের প্রধান উপাদান সংক্রান্ত বা যুক্ত। **2.** Blue ; নীল।

cȳ'-ă-nīde, *n.* (*Chem.*) A compound of cyanogen with a metallic base ; (রসায়ন-শাস্ত্র) হরিৎ-নীলের প্রধান উপাদান এবং ধাতু-বিশেষের মিশ্র।

cȳ-ăn'-ō-gĕn, *n.* **1.** (*Chem.*) A compound radically composed of one atom of nitrogen and one atom of carbon ; (রসায়ন-শাস্ত্র) এক পরমাণু নেত্রজন ও এক পরমাণু অঙ্গারকের রাসায়নিক সম্মিলনে উৎপন্ন যৌগিক পদার্থ। **2.** A colourless highly poisonous gas ; এক প্রকার অবর্ণ অতি বিষাক্ত বাষ্প।

cȳ-ă-nŏm'-ĕ-têr, *n.* An instrument for measuring the intensity of the blueness of the sky ; আকাশের নীলিমার গাঢ়তা পরিমাপক যন্ত্র বিশেষ, নীলিমামান।

cȳ-ā-nō'-sis, *n.* Blue jaundice (a disease rendering the skin blue due to defective circulation of the blood) ; নীলরোগ (এই রোগে অসম্পূর্ণ রক্ত সঞ্চালন হেতু চর্ম্ম নীল হইয়া যায়)।

cȳ'-căd, *n.* (*Bot.*) A kind of palmlike plants ; (উদ্ভিদ্-বিদ্যা) তালবৎ একপ্রকার গলজাতীয় বৃক্ষ।

cyc'-la-men, *n.* (*Bot.*) A genus of bulbous plants with beautiful flowers ; (উদ্ভিদ্-বিদ্যা) একজাতীয় সুন্দর পুষ্পপ্রসূ কন্দ।

cȳ'-cle, *n.* & *v. i.* **1.** An orbit in the heavens ; আকাশমণ্ডলের কল্পিত কক্ষ বিশেষ। **2.** The recurrent

Chainless cycle.

period of years, events or phenomena, etc. ; as, the *cycle* of the seasons ; কালচক্র, বর্ষচক্র, ঘটনাচক্র, ঋতু-পর্য্যায়, আবর্ত্ত। **3.** A complete set or series ; a circle ; "He figures among a *cycle* of champions ;" চক্র ; মণ্ডলী। **4.** A long period of years ; an age ; যুগ ; কল্প। **5.** A body of legends connected with some mythical or heroic event or character ; as, the Arthurian *cycle* ; আখ্যায়িকাবলী। **6.** A bicycle, tricycle or similar other vehicles ; দ্বিচক্রযান, ত্রিচক্রযান প্রভৃতি। ***Verb i.*** **1.** To pass through a cycle ; to revolve in cycles ; কোন যুগ অতিক্রম করা ; চক্রে চক্রে আবর্ত্তিত হওয়া। **2.** To ride a bicycle etc. ; দ্বিচক্রযান প্রভৃতি আরোহণ করা। **Metonic** or **Lunar cycle**—১৯ বৎসর কাল—যে সময়ের অন্তে অমাবস্যা ও পূর্ণিমা আবার পূর্ব্ববৎ মাসের সেই সেই তারিখে হইয়া থাকে, চন্দ্রচক্র (হিঃ কোঃ)। **Solar cycle** — ২৮ বৎসর কাল—যে সময়ের অন্তে বার সকল আবার পূর্ব্ববৎ মাসের সেই সেই তারিখে পড়িয়া থাকে, সৌরচক্র।

cȳc'-lic, —li-căl, *adj.* **1.** Of or pertaining to a cycle ; moving in cycles ; যুগসম্বন্ধীয় ; আবর্ত্তমান। **2. (-lic)** Of or relating to a cycle of mythic or heroic events ; as, a *cyclic* poet ; পৌরাণিক আখ্যায়িকাবলী-সম্বন্ধীয়, প্রাচীনকালীন নরদেবগণের কাহিনী-সম্বন্ধীয়। **3.** (*Bot.*) Having the floral leaves arranged in whorls as a flower ; (উদ্ভিদ-বিদ্যা) চক্রাকারে বিন্যস্ত দলসমন্বিত, স্তবকী (সাঃ পঃ)। **Cyclic chorus**—(*Greek Antiq.*) (গ্রীসদেশীয় পুরাতত্ত্ব) নৃত্যগীত সহকারে বেদী প্রদক্ষিণকারী একতান গায়কদল।

cȳ'-cling, *n.* Act of riding a cycle ; দ্বিচক্রযানাদি আরোহণ।

cȳ'-clist, *n.* One who rides a cycle ; দ্বিচক্রযানাদির আরোহী।

cȳ'-clô-grăph, *n.* An instrument for tracing circular area etc. ; বৃত্তাঙ্কন যন্ত্র।

cȳ'-cloid (-cloÿd), *n.* (*Geom.*) A curve described by a point on the radius of a circle within, on or without its circumference as it (the circle) rolls along a straight line ; (জ্যামিতি) চক্রাবর্ত্ত, চক্রাভাস (হিঃকোঃ)। **—cloi'-dal,** *adj.*

cȳ-clŏm'-ĕ-têr, *n.* **1.** An instrument for measuring areas of circles ; বৃত্তের ক্ষেত্রফল পরিমাপক যন্ত্রবিশেষ, বৃত্তমানযন্ত্র। **2.** An instrument for measuring the distance traversed, as by a bicycle ; যে যন্ত্রের সাহায্যে দ্বিচক্রযান প্রভৃতি কতটা স্থান অতিক্রম করিয়াছে তাহা জানা যায়, অতিক্রান্তপথমানযন্ত্র।

cȳ'-clône, *n.* **1.** A rotatory system of winds revolving round a calm centre and advancing ; চক্রবাত্যা (আঃ বঃ), চক্রবাত (হিঃ কোঃ)। **2.** A circular hurricane ; a tornado ; ঝঞ্ঝাবর্ত্ত ; বাতাবর্ত্ত। **3.** (*Astron.*) A rotatory storm in the solar photosphere ; সৌরপ্রকাশ মণ্ডলমধ্যে প্রবাহিত চক্রবাত। **—clon'-ic,** *adj.*

cȳ-clŏ-pæ'-di-ă(-pē-),**—pē'-di-ă,** *n.* Same as ENCYCLOPEDIA.**—dic,** *adj.*

Cy-clŏ-pē'-ăn (sī-), **—clŏ'-pi-ăn,** *adj.* Of or pertaining to Cyclops ; resembling Cyclops ; huge ; একাক্ষ দৈত্যসম্বন্ধীয় ; একাক্ষদৈত্যবৎ ; প্রকাণ্ড।

Cy'-clŏp(s) (sī-), *n.* (*pl.* *-ops, -opses, -opes*) **1.** (*Gr. Myth.*) ; A one-eyed giant ; গ্রীকপুরাণোক্ত একচক্ষু দৈত্যবিশেষ। **2.** A one-eyed person ; একচক্ষু ব্যক্তি।

cȳ-clŏ-râ'-mă, *n.* A circular panorama ; বৃত্তাকারে প্রসারী চিত্রদৃশ্য, বৃত্তাকারে বিস্তৃত চিত্রাবলী।

cȳ-clŏs'-tŏ-mous (-mŭs), *adj.* (*Zool.*) Having a circular mouth ; চক্রতুণ্ডী (সাঃ পঃ)।

cȳ'-clŏ-stȳle, *n.* An apparatus for printing copies of writing ; লিখিত পাণ্ডুলিপির প্রতিলিপি মুদ্রণার্থ যন্ত্রবিশেষ।

Cydonia vulgaris—বিহি, বিহিদানা (বেলঃ)।

cȳg'-nĕt, *n.* A young swan ; তরুণ রাজহংস, বালহংস (আঃ বঃ)।

cȳl'-in-dêr, *n.* **1.** (*Geom.*) A solid figure described by the revolution of a right-angled parallelogram about one of its side which remains fixed ; (জ্যামিতি) বেলন (হিঃ কোঃ), যষ্টিঘনক্ষেত্র (আঃ বঃ)। **2.** A roller-like body, hollow or solid ; নল, চোঙ্গ, বেলন। **3.** (*Mach.*) The chamber of a steam-engine in which the force of steam is exerted on the piston ; (যন্ত্র) বাষ্পীয় যন্ত্রের যে প্রকোষ্ঠে নলদণ্ডের উপর বাষ্পের শক্তি প্রযুক্ত হয়। **4.** (*Print.*) An inking roller of a printing machine ; (মুদ্রণ) ছাপার কলের ডলনা—যাহা ঘুরিয়া অক্ষরে কালি লাগায়। **5.** (*Archæology*) A cylindrical clay-tablet with cuneiform inscriptions buried under Babylonian or Assyrian temples ; a cylindrical stone, used as a seat by the Assyrians ; (ইতিহাস-চিহ্নবিদ্যা) বেবিলোন ও এশিরিয়ার দেবমন্দির সমূহের নিম্নদেশে প্রোথিত কীলকাকার অক্ষরদ্বারা উৎকীর্ণ বেলনাকার মৃন্ময়ফলক ; এশিরীয়াবাসীদিগের বেলনাকার আসন।

cȳ-lin'-dri-căl, *adj.* & *n.* Cylinder-shaped ; নলাকার, বেলনাকার, স্তম্ভবৎ, সমবর্ত্তুল।

cy̆l'-in-droid (-droy̆d), *adj.* & *n.* More or less like a cylinder ; বেলনকল্প। ***Noun.*** A solid body or figure like a cylinder ; বেলনের মত ঘন বা সংহত বস্তু।

cy̆'-mă, *n.* (*Pl.* -MAS) **1.** (*Arch.*) A moulding of the cornice, the profile of which is waving ; কার্ণিসাদির তরঙ্গাকার স্থাপত্যভূষা, পদ্ম (রাঃ রাঃ)। **2.** (*Bot.*) Cyme ; পার্শ্ব-বর্দ্ধ (সাঃ পঃ)।

cy̆-mâr', *n.* **1.** A woman's loose garment ; স্ত্রীলোকের ঢিলা পোষাক। **2.** A bishop's chimere ; খৃষ্টীয় ধর্ম্মাধ্যক্ষের শ্লথ বহিঃপরিচ্ছদ।

cy̆m'-băl, *n.* A basin-shaped musical instrument of brass used in pairs ; কাংস্যতাল, করতাল, মন্দিরা। **—ist,** *n.* A performer on cymbals ; করতালবাদক।

cy̆m'-bă-lō, *n.* (*Mus.*) A stringed instrument of music ; (সঙ্গীত-শাস্ত্র) তন্ত্রিযুক্ত বাদ্যযন্ত্র।

cy̆m'-bi-fôrm, *adj.* (*Bot.* & *Anat.*) Shaped like a boat ; (উদ্ভিদ-বিদ্যা ও শারীরসংস্থান-বিদ্যা) নৌকাকৃতি, নাবাকার (সাঃ পঃ)।

cy̆m-bō-cē-phăl'-ic, *adj.* Having a boat-shaped *i. e.* long and narrow skull ; নৌকাকৃতি করোটী-বিশিষ্ট।

cy̆me, *n.* (*Bot.*) A kind of inflorescence like that of the elder ; (উদ্ভিদ-বিদ্যা) পার্শ্ব-বর্দ্ধ (সাঃ পঃ)।

câr'-năl-līte, *n.* A pink-coloured mineral obtained from the Strassforth salt mines ; ষ্ট্রেসফরথনগরীস্থ লবণখনি হইতে প্রাপ্ত লোহিতবর্ণ খনিজ পদার্থ বিশেষ।

câr-năs'-si-ăl, *adj.* & *n.* (*Anat.*) Adapted to eating flesh ; (শারীরসংস্থান-বিদ্যা) মাংসাহারোপযোগী। ***Noun.*** A carnossial tooth ; মাংসকৃন্তদন্ত (সাঃ পঃ)।

câr-nā'-tion, *n.* & *adj.* **1.** A rosy pink colour ; গোলাবি রং। **2.** (*Pl.* PAINTING) The flesh-tints ; ব্যক্তি — এই সম্প্রদায়ের দার্শনিকগণ, শিল্প, বিজ্ঞান, আমোদ প্রভৃতির বিদ্বেষী ছিলেন। **2.** A sarcastic or surly person ; ব্যঙ্গকারী ব্যক্তি, নিত্য-কোপন ব্যক্তি। **—ism,** *n.*

cy̆n'i-căl, *adj.* Dog-like ; surly ; churlish ; sneering ; misanthropic ; শ্ব-স্বভাব ; নিত্য-কোপন ; কর্কশ, রূক্ষ ; অবজ্ঞাকারী ; মানব-বিদ্বেষী। **—ly,** *adv.*

cy̆n-ō-cĕph'-ă-lŭs, *n.* **1.** A fabulous dog-headed man ; গ্রীক পুরাণ-বর্ণিত কুক্কুরশিরা ব্যক্তি। **2.** (*Zool.*) A dog-faced baboon ; (জন্তু-বিদ্যা) কুক্কুরবদন কপি, শ্বমুখ কপি।

cynoctonum pauciflorum — ছাগলপাটি (বেলঃ)।

cynodon dactylon—দুর্ব্বা (বেল)।

cy̆'-nō-sure (-zhôr) *n.* **1.** The constellation of the Little-Bear ; pole-star ; লঘু সপ্তর্ষি (হিঃ কোঃ) ; ধ্রুবতারা। **2.** (*Fig.*) Guiding star ; "For the guidance of our liberty ; the *cynosure* is our charity" ; (লক্ষণায়) ধ্রুবতারা। **3.** Centre of attraction ; "Rome will be the *cynosure* of the world ;" মুকুটমণি।

cyperus hexastachyus — মুথু (বেলঃ), মুথা (ঐ), ভদ্রমুস্তা (ঐ)

cyperus inundatus — পাটি (বেলঃ)।

cy̆'-phêr, *n.* See CIPHER.

cy pres (sē-prā), *adv.*, *adj.* & *n.* (*Law*) As near as practicable ; as, the court will carry out the testator's intentions *cy pres* ; যথা-সম্ভব কাছাকাছি। ***Adj.*** Approximate ; কাছাকাছি, আসন্ন। ***Noun.*** Approximatian ; আসন্ন হওন।

cy̆'-prĕss, *n.* **1.** A coniferous tree with hard wood and dark foliage ; দারু (হিন্দি-প্রবোধ), দেবদারু (ঐ)। **2.** A branch of this as emblem of mourning ; শোকচিহ্ন স্বরূপ দেবদারু শাখা।

Cyp'-ri-ăn (sĭp-), *adj.* & *n.* **1.** Of or pertaining to Cyprus ; সাইপ্রাস দ্বীপ-সম্বন্ধীয়। **2.** Licentious ; কামাসক্ত লম্পট। ***Noun.*** **1.** A native or inhabitant of Cyprus ; সাইপ্রাস দ্বীপের অধিবাসী। **2.** A licentious person, esp. a prostitute ; "A *cyprian* of the lowest grade" ; কামাসক্ত ব্যক্তি, বিশেষতঃ গণিকা।

Cy-rē'-nā-ic (sĭ-), *adj.* & *n.* Belonging to the school of the Socratic philosopher Aristippus of Cyrene whose doctrine was one of practical hedonism ; সক্রেতিসের মতানুবর্ত্তী সাইরিণবাসী এরিষ্টিপাসের দর্শন সম্বন্ধীয়—ইনি সুখবাদী দার্শনিক ছিলেন। ***Noun.*** A Cyrenaic philosopher ; সাইরিণীয় দার্শনিক।

cy̆st, *n.* **1.** (*Path.*) A bag in animal bodies which includes morbid matter ; (নিদান-শাস্ত্র) পুযকোষ (হঃ চঃ), থলি। **2.** (*Biol.* & *Bot.*) A cell containing embryos etc. ; (জীব বিজ্ঞান ও উদ্ভিদবিদ্যা) ভ্রূণাদির কোষ, থলি (সাঃ পঃ)।

cy̆s'-tic, *adj.* Of the urinary or gall-bladders ; কোষিক, মূত্রনালী বা পিত্তাধার নলী-সম্পর্কীয়, পিত্তকোষ-সম্বন্ধীয়।

cy̆s-tī'-tis, *n.* Inflammation of the bladder ; মূত্রনালী-প্রদাহ।

cy̆s-tŏt'-ō my̆, *n.* (*Surg.*) The operation of cutting into the bladder ; (অস্ত্রোপচার-বিদ্যা) মূত্রাশয়-ছেদন।

czar, tzar (zâr), *n.* The title of the emperor of Russia ; রুশিয়ার অধিরাজ, রুশ-সম্রাট্।

czar'-e-vitch, —witch, tsar'—, (zâr-ĕ-vĭch), *n.* The son of a czar ; রুশিয়ার অধিরাজের পুত্র।

cza-rĕv'-nă (zâ-), **tza—,** (zâ-), *n.* Daughter of a czar ; রুশিয়ার অধিরাজের কন্যা।

cza-ri'-na, tza—, (zâ-rē-nă), *n.* Wife of a czar ; Russian empress ; রুশিয়ার অধিরাণী ; রুশ-সম্রাজ্ঞী।

czech, czekh, (chĕck), *n.* A Bohemian ; বোহেমিয়াবাসী।

THE MODERN ANGLO- BENGALI DICTIONARY

THE MODERN ANGLO BENGALI DICTIONARY

(In 6 Volumes)

(Volume-5)

CHARUCHANDRA GUHA

Publications

KALPAZ PUBLICATIONS

DELHI - 1100052

THE MODERN ANGLO- BENGALI DICTIONARY

ISBN : 81-7835 - 484 - 5 (Set)
ISBN : 81 - 7835 - 489 - 6 (Vol. 5)

Rs. 4500 (Set)

CHARUCHANDRA GUHA

Published in 2007 in India by
Kalpaz Publications
C - 30, Satyawati Nagar,
Delhi - 110052
E-mail : kalpaz@hotmail.com

Laser Typesetting at : Tact Computer, Delhi
Printed at : Mehra Offset Press, Delhi

THE

MODERN
ANGLO-BENGALI DICTIONARY

R, The eighteenth letter of the English alphabet ; ইংরাজী বর্ণমালার অষ্টাদশতম ক্ষর। **The r months**—যে সকল াসের নামের মধ্যে "*r*" অক্ষর আছে September হইতে April পর্য্যন্ত) ই ৮ মাস ঝিনুকের মরসুম। **The hree Rs**—Read·.g, (w)riting nd (a)rithmetic as the basis f elementary education; সামান্য লখন, পঠন এবং অঙ্কশিক্ষা।

a, *n.* The Sun God of ancient Egypt ; প্রাচীন মিসরদেশের সূর্য্যদেব। নি অনন্ত সমুদ্র হইতে জাত হইয়া র্গরাজ্যের উপর আধিপত্য বিস্তার রেন। মিসরদেশের ফেরোয়া (Pharoah) াতিগণ Ra দেবের অন্বয়ে প্রসূত য়া দাবী করিতেন।

b'-bĕt, *n.* **1.** A groove cut longi- linally in a piece of timber to eive the edge of a plank ; a ping cut made on the edge one board so that it may join lapping with another similarly t ; কোন তক্তায় লম্বালম্বিভাবে কাটা জ ; টের্চ্ছাভাবে কাটা তক্তার কিনারা— অনুরূপভাবে কাটা তক্তার সহিত া দেওয়া হয়। **Rabbet-joint**— খাঁজে জোড়া। **Rabbet-plane**— কাটার জন্য একপ্রকার রেঁদা।

-bi (*or* -bī), *n.* A Jewish cher or expounder of the law ; দী পণ্ডিত, ইহুদীদেশীয় স্মার্ত্তপণ্ডিত।

'-bin, *n.* Same as RABBI. **te, —ism, —ist,** *ns.* **—bin'-i-l,** *adj.* **—bin'-i-cal-ly,** *adv.*

răb'-bĭt, *n.* A wooden implement for mixing mortar ; খাম্বিরা মিশাইবার জন্য একপ্রকার কাষ্ঠনির্ম্মিত যন্ত্র।

răb'-bĭt, *n., v. i. & t.* A burrowing rodent allied to the hare ; খ র গো স, শশ, শশক [Syn. লোমকর্ণ, লম্বকর্ণ, মৃদুলোমক।] ***Verb i. & t.*** To hunt, catch or kill (rabbits) ; শশক ধরা, শিকার করা বা বধ করা। **—y,** *adj.* **1.** Realating to, or resembling, a rabbit ; শশকসম্বন্ধীয়, শশকবৎ। **2.** Overrun with rabbits, as a region ; শশকপূর্ণ, শশকোপদ্রুত।

Rabbit.

răb-bĭt, *v. t.* (*Vulg.*) To confound, (*used imperatively as an imprecation*) ; (ইতর ভাষায়) ধ্বংস করা [সাধারণতঃ অভিশাপে ব্যবহৃত হয় (ধ্বংস হও, চুলোয় যাও।)]

răb'-ble (-l), *n.* **1.** A mob ; a confused disorderly crowd ; প্রাকৃত জনসম্মর্দ ; ইতর লোকের ভিড়, ইতর লোকের জনতা। **2.** *The* lower class of people ; ইতরশ্রেণী, প্রাকৃত জন।

răb'-ble (-l), *n.* An iron bar bent at one end for stirring molten metal ; গলিত ধাতু নাড়িবার জন্য বক্রাগ্র লৌহদণ্ড।

răb'-ble-mĕnt (-l-), *n.* (*Now rare*) A rabble ; a confused noise like that of a rabble ; ইতর লোকের জনতা ; সোরগোল হট্টগোল।

Răb-ē-lai'-sĭ-ăn (-lā-), **—læ-** (-lā-), *adj. & n.* Of, relating to, or like, Rabelais, a French humorist, or his writings characterized by exuberant imagination and language and coarse humour and satire ; ফরাসীদেশের সুপ্রসিদ্ধ পরিহাসরসিক গ্রন্থকার রেবেলেস সম্বন্ধীয় বা তদ্বৎ, রেবেলেসের রচনা সম্বন্ধীয়। ***Noun.*** One who admires, or studies, Rabelais ; রেবেলেসের গ্রন্থ অধ্যয়নকারী বা প্রশংসাকারী।

răb'-ĭd, *adj.* **1.** Furious ; extremely violent ; as, *rabid* hate ; প্রচণ্ড ; অত্যুগ্র, বিজাতীয়। **2.** Extreme or unreasonable in opinion ; headstrong ; as, a *rabid* socialist ; উৎকট ; দুর্দম। **3.** Mad as a dog ; ক্ষিপ্ত। **4.** (*Med.*) Of, or relating to, rabies ; (ভৈষজ্যশাস্ত্র) জলাতঙ্ক সম্বন্ধীয়। **—ly,** *adv.* **—ness,** *n.* **Ra-bid'-i-ty,** *n.* **Rabid dog**—ক্ষিপ্ত কুকুর, অলর্ক (সুশ্রুঃ)। **Rabid poison**— আলর্ক বিষ।

rā'-bĭ-ēs, *n.* Hydrophobia ; canine madness ; জলাতঙ্ক ; ক্ষিপ্ত কুকুরাদির দংশনজনিত উন্মাদ।

race (rās), *n.* **1.** (*Rare*) A running ; (কচিদ্ ব্যবহৃত) দৌড়, ধাবন। **2.** A course of the sun or moon ; a career or course of life; as, before he could run his *race* ; চন্দ্র বা সূর্য্যের গতি ; জীবন। **3.** A contest of speed between runners, ships, horses or persons doing anything ; (*pl.*) a meeting for contests in the running of horses ; as, he attended the *races* ; দৌড়, ঘোড়দৌড় ; ঘোড়দৌড় সভা । 4. A strong current or the channel for it ; খরস্রোতঃ, বেগবতী প্রবাহিনী, উহার খাত । 5. The water-course leading to a mill-wheel ; as, a mill-*race* ; জলপ্রবাহচালিত কল যে জলস্রোতঃ দ্বারা চালিত হয় । 6. A channel or slide for a shuttle etc. ; যে নালীর ভিতর দিয়া মাকু আসা যাওয়া করে । **Race ball**—ঘোড়দৌড়ের সংশ্রবে বল নাচ কিম্বা অন্য প্রকার নাচ । **Race-card**—ঘোড়দৌড়ের বিজ্ঞাপন । **Racecourse**—The ground for horse-race ; মাঠ, বীথি (সিদ্ধং মুখে নবসু বীথিষু কশ্চিদশ্বং—শিশুঃ ৫-৬০), কাষ্ঠা, চর্য্যাভূমি । **Racehorse**—দৌড়ের ঘোড়া, জবাশ্ব । **Race-meeting**—যে নির্দ্দিষ্ট দিবস বা দিবস সমূহে কোন নির্দ্দিষ্ট স্থানে ঘোড়দৌড় হইবে বলিয়া স্থিরীকৃত হয় । **Tidal race**—ওঘপ্রবাহ (হিঃ কোঃ) ।

race (rās), *v. i.* & *t.* **1.** To go swiftly; esp., to compete in speed ; দৌড় দেওয়া; বিশেষতঃ দৌড়ে প্রতিযোগিতা করা । **2.** (Of a propeller, paddle-wheel, etc.) To work vigorously from diminished resistance while out of water ; (জাহাজের প্রচালক, চালকচক্র প্রভৃতি সম্পর্কে) জল হইতে উপরে থাকায় প্রতিরোধের ন্যূনতা হেতু সতেজে চলা । ***Verb t.*** **1.** To compete with in speed ; to cause to race or move at full speed ; as, he *raced* his horse against the bicycle : to *race* a yacht ; দৌড়ে প্রতিযোগিতা করা ; পূর্ণবেগে চালান । **2.** To fling *away* as fortune etc. on horse-racing ; ঘোড়দৌড়ে অনেক টাকা উড়ান ।

race (rās), *n.* **1.** A body of individuals sprung from a common stock ; a family or tribe ; বংশ, কুল, অন্বয় ; গোষ্ঠী, পরিবার, গোত্র । **2.** A permanent variety of mankind ; as, the Mongolian *race* ; a genus or variety of animals or plants ; জাতি ; জন্তু বা উদ্ভিদের জাতি, গণ । **3.** Descent ; as, of a noble *race* ; বংশ । **4.** A class of people with some common characteristics ; as the *race* of poets ; সাধারণ গুণ বা লক্ষণবিশিষ্ট লোক শ্রেণী, কুল (cf. কবি কুল) ।

race (rās), *n.* A root as of ginger ; আদা প্রভৃতির মূল ।

ră-ceme′ (-sēm), *n.* (*Bot.*) A species of inflorescence in which a number of flowers with short pedicles stand on a common stem ; (উদ্ভিদ্ বিদ্যা) পুষ্পস্তবক, ফুলের ছড়ি, শীর্ষ (সাঃ পঃ) ।

Raceme.

răc′-ē-mōse, *adj.* (*Bot.* & *anat.*) Resembling a raceme ; as, the *racemose* gland ; (উদ্ভিদ্ এবং শারীরসংস্থান বিদ্যা) ফুলের ছড়ির ন্যায়, শীর্ষবৎ ।

răc′-ĕr, *n.* One that races or contends in a race ; a racehorse ; a bicycle, yacht, etc. used in racing ; যে দৌড়ে প্রতিযোগিতা করে ; ঘোড়দৌড়ের ঘোড়া ; দৌড়ে ব্যবহৃত দ্বিচক্রযান, প্রমোদ পোত, প্রভৃতি ।

ra′-chis, rha′— (rā-), *ns.* **1.** (*Anat.*) The spine or the vertebral column ; (শারীরসংস্থান বিদ্যা) মেরুদণ্ড, পৃষ্ঠবংশ । **2.** (*Bot.*) The petiole of a compound leaf ; (উদ্ভিদ্ বিদ্যা) মিশ্র পত্রের বৃন্ত । **3.** (*Bot.*) A peduncle ; (উদ্ভিদ্ বিদ্যা) পুষ্পদণ্ড । **4.** The shaft of a feather esp. the part bearing the barbs ; পালকের বৃন্ত, পক্ষবৃন্ত, বিশেষতঃ যে অংশে সূক্ষ্ম পার্শ্বিক পালকতন্তু থাকে ।

ră-chi′-tis, *n.* (*Med.*) Rickets ; (ভৈষজ্য শাস্ত্র) বালাস্থিবিকৃতি রোগ ।

rā′-ci-al, *adj.* Of, or relating to, a race or family of men ; জাতীয়, কুলগত, বংশগত, জাতিগত । **—ly,** *adv.*

răck, *n.* & *v. i.* **1.** Thin flying clouds ; বায়ুচালিত লঘু মেঘ রাশি । **2.** Destruction ; as, to go to *rack* and ruin ; ধ্বংস, সর্ব্বনাশ । ***Verb i.*** (Of clouds) To fly or drive before the wind ; (মেঘসম্বন্ধে) উড্ডীন হওয়া, বায়ুচালিত হওয়া । **To go to rack and ruin**—To be ruined ; to fall into utter despair ; ধ্বংসপ্রাপ্ত হওয়া, ভাঙ্গিয়া পড়া, ছারেখারে যাওয়া , নৈরাশ্যে ভাঙ্গিয়া পড়া ।

răck, *n., v. i.* & *t.* **1.** A framework for holding fodder for cattle, horse, etc. ; অশ্ব গবাদির খাদ্য রাখার জন্য তাক । **2.** A framework on or in which articles are laid or arranged ; তাক, আলনা । **3.** A bar with teeth on one side adapted to work into the teeth of a wheel ; এক পাশে দাঁত-কাটা দণ্ডবিশেষ—যাহা কোন চাকার দাঁতের সহিত ক্রিয়া করে । ***Verb i.*** To fill a rack with fodder for cattle, horse, etc. (usu. with *up*) ; অশ্ব গবাদির খাদ্যদ্বারা তাক পূর্ণ করা । ***Verb t.*** **1.** To supply a rack with fodder for (a horse) ; to fasten as an animal to a rack, (with *up*) ; (ঘোড়ার জন্য) ঘাস প্রভৃতি তাকে রাখা ; অশ্ব গবাদি তাকে বাঁধা । **2.** To place as an article in or on a rack ; তাকে বা আলনা কোন জিনিষ রাখা । **Rack-railway**—যে লৌহবর্ত্মের পাতা রেল দুইটি

Rack and pinion.

মাঝখানে একটী দাঁত-কাটা রেইল থাকে। **Rack-saw**—বড় দাঁতওয়ালা করাত। **Rack-wheel**—দন্তুর চক্র।

răck, *v. t.* & *n.* **1.** To stretch or strain unduly ; as, to *rack* one's brains for something to say ; অতিমাত্রায় প্রসারিত করা, ঘামান। **2.** To torture by an instrument which strains the limbs and pulls the joints ; সম্পীড়নযন্ত্র দ্বারা পীড়ন করা। **3.** (Of a disease, mental or bodily agony, etc.) ; To torment ; to cause extreme pain to ; তীব্র যন্ত্রণা দেওয়া ; মর্ম্মান্তিক যাতনা প্রদান করা। **4.** To exact as rent, excessively or oppressively ; to harass with excessive rent ; অতিরিক্ত বা পীড়নপূর্ব্বক খাজানা আদায় করা ; অতিরিক্ত খাজানা দ্বারা প্রপীড়িত করা। **5.** To exhaust as land by excessive use ; অতিরিক্ত ব্যবহার দ্বারা ভূমির উৎপাদিকতা শক্তি নিঃশেষিত করা। ***Noun*.** **1.** An instrument of torture on which the victim's limbs were strained by cords and levers ; পীড়নযন্ত্র বিশেষ—ইহা দ্বারা অপরাধীর দেহ অতিমাত্রায় প্রসারিত করিয়া হস্তপদাদি সন্ধিচ্যুত করা হইত। **2.** A cause of anguish ; pain ; as, the *rack* of gout ; যন্ত্রণার কারণ ; যন্ত্রণা, ব্যথা, যাতনা। **Rack-rent**—(*n.* & *v. t.*) An excessive rent equal, or nearly equal, to the value of the land ; অতিরিক্ত খাজানা। (*Verb t.*) To exact this from (a tenant) or for (a land) ; অতিরিক্ত খাজানা আদায় করা। **Rack-renter**—যে প্রজা অতিরিক্ত খাজানা প্রদান করে ; যে জমিদার অতিরিক্ত খাজানা আদায় করেন। **To be or live at rack and manger**—To be prodigal ; to live extravagantly ; অতিব্যয়ী হওয়া ; অমিত ব্যয় করা। **To be on the rack**—To suffer torture, physical or mental ; যাতনা ভোগ করা। To be in a state of restless activity ; অস্থির থাকা। **To work by rack of eye**—To work with the assistance of the eye alone without line or rule ; কেবল চক্ষুর সাহায্যে কাজ করা।

răck, *n.* Same as ARRACK. (Also, *rack-punch*).

răck, *v. t.* To draw off, as wine etc. from the lees ; গাদ হইতে মদ্য বাহির করা।

răck, *n.* & *v. i.* A quick amble ; অশ্বের গতিবিশেষ, দ্রুত ধোরিত গতি। ***Verb i.*** To amble quickly ; অতি দ্রুত ধোরিত গতিতে চলা।

răck'-ĕt, răc'-quet (-ĕt), *ns.* **1.** A bat used in tennis etc. ; আণ্টাল খেলার ব্যাট। **2.** (*Pl.*) A game played with ball and rackets in a four-walled court ; আণ্টাল খেলা। **3.** A snow-shoe resembling a racket ; বরফের উপর ব্যবহারের জন্য আণ্টাল খেলার ব্যাটের আকার একপ্রকার জুতা। **Racket-ball**—আণ্টাল খেলার বল। **Racket-press**—আণ্টাল খেলার ব্যাটের আকার ঠিক রাখার জন্য একপ্রকার চাপ-কল। **Racket-tail**—আণ্টাল খেলার ব্যাটের ন্যায় পুচ্ছবিশিষ্ট একপ্রকার পক্ষী।

răck'-ĕt, *n.* & *v. i.* **1.** A noise ; clamour ; din ; গোলমাল ; কোলাহল, সোরগোল ; হল্লা। **2.** A scene of bustle or tumult ; social excitement ; dissipation ; as, to go on a *racket* or carouse ; হট্টগোলের স্থান ; সামাজিক বিক্ষোভ ; লাম্পট্য, ভ্রষ্টাচার। **3.** A dodge or trick ; a line of business ; চালাকি, ফাঁকি, ফন্দী ; কার্য্যপ্রণালী। **4.** A trying experience ; ordeal ; as, to stand the *racket* ; কঠোর অভিজ্ঞতা ; অগ্নিপরীক্ষা। ***Verb i.*** **1.** To frolic ; to carouse or dissipate, (often with *about*) ; আমোদ-প্রমোদ করা ; মদের বৈঠকে কোলাহল করা, জঘন্য আমোদ প্রমোদে মত্ত হওয়া। **2.** To move about noisily ; সোর গোল করিয়া ছুটাছুটি করা। **—y**, *adj.* Addicted to making, or marked by, a noise ; কোলাহলরত, কোলাহলকারী, কোলাহলপূর্ণ। **To be on the racket**—To go on the loose ; to be dissipated ; উচ্ছৃঙ্খল ভাবে চলা ; জঘন্য আমোদপ্রমোদে মত্ত হওয়া। **To stand the racket**—To take the consequences ; to be responsible ; দায়িত্ব গ্রহণ করা ; দায়ী হওয়া।

raconteur, (*F.*), *n.* (*Fem.* RACONTEUSE.) A storyteller ; গল্পকথক।

Racoon.

răc-(c)ōōn', *n.* A small American quadruped, valuable for its fur ; আমেরিকা দেশীয় ক্ষুদ্র চতুষ্পদ জন্তু বিশেষ।

ra'-cy̆, *adj.* **1.** Of distinct characteristic, taste or nature ; as, *racy* flavour ; সরস, রসাল, তেজাল। **2.** Distinctively vigorous or spirited ; peculiarly animated ; as, a *racy* person, style of writing, or speaking ; তেজঃপূর্ণ ; সতেজ। **3.** Stimulating ; piquant ; ঝাঁঝাল ; মিঠাকড়া। **—ci-ness**, *n.* **Racy of the soil** — Piquant ; lively ; spirited ; ঝাঁঝাল ; সতেজ ; তেজঃপূর্ণ।

răd, *n.* See RADICAL.

răd'-dle (-l), *n.* & *v. t.* Red ochre ; গৈরিক, গিরিমাটী। ***Verb t.*** To paint with raddle ; to colour coarsely with rouge ; গৈরিক দ্বারা রঞ্জিত করা ; রাগচূর্ণ দ্বারা রঞ্জিত করা।

ra'-di-ăl, *adj.* & *n.* **1.** Of, or relating to, a ray or radius ; কিরণসম্বন্ধীয় ব্যাসার্দ্ধসম্বন্ধীয়। **2.** Grouped, or appearing, like rays or radii ; shooting out as from a centre;

অংশুগত (সাঃ পঃ), অংশুল (ঐ); কেন্দ্রাপসর্পী, কেন্দ্রবিসর্পী। **3.** Of, or relating to, the radius of the forearm; as, *radial* artery, nerve, etc.; প্রকোষ্ঠের কনিষ্ঠাস্থি সম্বন্ধীয়। **4.** Having spokes or radiating lines; আরবিশিষ্ট, বীকীর্য্যমান রেখাসমন্বিত। **5.** Of, or relating to, radium; র‍্যাডিয়াম সম্বন্ধীয়। ***Noun.*** A radial nerve or artery; প্রকোষ্ঠের কনিষ্ঠাস্থির সন্নিহিত শিরা বা ধমনী। **—i-za'-tion,** *n.* **—ize,** *v. t.* To arrange radiately; বিকীর্ণভাবে বিন্যস্ত করা। **—ized,** *p. adj.* **—ly,** *adv.*

rā'-di-ăn, *n.* (*Math.*) An arc of a circle equal to the radius or the angle at the centre measured by it; (গণিতশাস্ত্র) সমত্রিজ্যা-কোণ (হিঃ কোঃ)।

rā'-di-ănt, *adj.* & *n.* **1.** Emitting rays of light; isssuing in beams or rays as light; অংশুল, অংশুমান; প্রকাশবিসর্জক (হিঃ কোঃ), কিরণচ্ছটা-বিসারী। **2.** (Of eyes, looks, etc.) Beaming with joy, love, hope; bright, dazzling or splendid as beauty etc.; হর্ষোৎফুল্ল, আশাপ্রদীপ্ত, আশালোকোজ্জ্বল, প্রেমোজ্জ্বল, আনন্দোজ্জ্বল; চোখঝলসানো, তীব্রোজ্জ্বল, সমুজ্জ্বল, দীপ্ত, ভাস্বর, সপ্রভ, প্রভাময়। **3.** Emitted or transmitted by radiation as heat etc.; বিকিরণশীল। **4.** (*Bot.*) Radiating (উদ্ভিদ্‌বিদ্যা) বিকীর্য্যমান, পরিধিগত (সাঃ পঃ)। ***Noun.*** **1.** The point or object from which light or heat emanates; তাপবিকিরণবিন্দু, কিরণ-বিকিকরণবিন্দু, তাপবিকিরণস্থলী, কিরণবিকিরণস্থলী, কিরণমূল (হিঃ কোঃ), প্রকাশমূল (ঐ)। **2.** (*Astron.*) The apparent focal point of a meteoric shower; (জ্যোতির্বিজ্ঞান) উল্কা সম্পাতমূল (হিঃ কোঃ)। **—ance, —an-cy,** *ns.* State of being radiant; brilliance; vivid brightness; দীপ্তি; প্রভা, ঔজ্জ্বল্য: তীব্রোজ্জ্বলতা। **—ly,** *adv.* **Radiant energy**—প্রকাশবিসর্জক শক্তি। **Radiant heat**—প্রকাশবিসর্জক তাপ (হিঃ কোঃ)। **Radiant point**—A point from which rays or radii proceed; কিরণবিকিরণবিন্দু, ব্যাসার্দ্ধমিলনবিন্দু, কিরণমূল (হিঃ কোঃ), প্রকাশমূল (ঐ)। (*Astron.*) Same as RADIANT, *n.* 2.

rā'-di-āte, *adj.* **1.** Having rays or radial parts; অংশুল, অংশুগত, ব্যাসার্দ্ধসমন্বিত। **2.** (*Bot.*) Diverging from a common centre; (উদ্ভিদ্‌বিদ্যা) বিকীর্ণ। **3.** Radially arranged; বিকীর্ণকিরণপ্রতিমবিন্যস্ত। **—ly,** *adv.*

rā'-di-āte, *v. i.* & *t.* **1.** To emit rays of light or heat; to be radiant; to shine; আলোকরশ্মি বা তাপরশ্মি বিকিরণ করা; উজ্জ্বল হওয়া; দীপ্তি পাওয়া। **2.** (Of light, heat, etc.) To issue or proceed in rays; কিরণস্ফুরণ হওয়া, কিরণ-বিকীর্ণ হওয়া। **3.** To proceed or spread from a central point; প্রসৃত হওয়া, বিকীর্ণ হওয়া, প্রতিস্ফুরিত হওয়া। ***Verb t.*** **1.** To emit in rays as heat or light; বিকীর্ণ হওয়া। **2.** To disseminate as life, joy, love, etc.; বিকীর্ণ করা, ছড়ান, পরিব্যাপ্ত করা। **—a'-tion,** *n.* Act of radiating; state of being radiated; diffusion of rays of light; the emission of rays of light or heat from a body; বিকিরণ (ব্রজঃ হিন্দুঃ); বিকীর্ণতা (ঐ); কিরণবিকিরণ, কিরণস্ফুরণ, রশ্মিবিকিরণ; অংশুপ্রসরণ, প্রসরণ (হিঃ কোঃ), বিসর্জন (ঐ)। **—a-tive,** *adj.*

rā'-di-ā-tor (-têr), *n.* That which radiates; an apparatus for diffusing heat as in a room etc.; বিকিরণকারী; কক্ষ প্রভৃতিতে তাপ-বিকিরণার্থ যন্ত্র বিশেষ, তাপবিকিরণযন্ত্র।

răd'-i-căl, *adj.* & *n.* **1.** Of, relating to, or proceeding from, the root; মৌলিক, মূলজ। **2.** Fundamental; essential; primary as, the *radical* principles of a system; thorough-going; extreme; as, *radical* reform; a *radical* party; মৌলিক; মূলীভূত; আমূল, প্রাথমিক; চরম। **3.** (*Politics*) Of, or relating to, the radicals; (রাজনীতি) আমূল পরিবর্ত্তন-পক্ষপাতিগণ সম্বন্ধীয়। **4.** (*Math*) Of, or relating to, a radix or root; as, a *radical* sign; (গণিতশাস্ত্র) করণ্যাত্মক (হিঃ কোঃ)। **5.** (*Bot.*) Of, relating to, or springing direct from, the root; as, a *radical* leaf; (উদ্ভিদ্‌ বিদ্যা) মূলজ (সাঃ পঃ), কাণ্ডপাদজ (হিঃ কোঃ)। **6.** (*Philol.*) Of, or relating to, the roots of words; ধাতুসম্বন্ধীয়। **7.** (*Mus.*) Belonging to the root of a chord; (সঙ্গীতশাস্ত্র) তন্ত্রীমূল-সম্বন্ধীয়। ***Noun.*** **1.** A root or radical part; a fundamental or basic principle; মূল, মৌলিক অংশ, মূলতত্ত্ব। **2.** (*Philol.*) A root: মূলশব্দ, ধাতু। **3.** (*Chem.*) A fundamental constituent of a compound; (রসায়নশাস্ত্র) মিশ্র পদার্থে মৌলিক উপাদান, মূলক (হিঃ কোঃ) **4.** (*Politics*; also *colloq.* rad.) One who advocates radical reform or extreme changes of a democratic character in the state; (রাজনীতি) আমূল পরিবর্ত্তনের পক্ষপাতী ব্যক্তি। **—ly,** *adv.* **1.** As regards root or origin; naturally; as, *radically* bright; গোড়ায়, মূলে, মূলতঃ; স্বভাবতঃ। **2.** In a radical manner; fundamentally; আমূল; মৌলিকভাবে **Compound radical**—বিবিধ মূলক (হিঃ কোঃ)। **Simple radical**—একাকী মূলক (হিঃ কোঃ)। **Radical axis** — করণ্যাত্মক অক্ষ (হিঃ কোঃ)। **Radical humour, heat, etc.**—(মধ্যযুগীয় দর্শনে এবং বর্ত্তমানে রহস্যচ্ছলে) জীবনরক্ষার পক্ষে একান্ত অপরিহার্য্য উত্তাপ, আর্দ্রতা প্রভৃতি।

răd'-i-căl-ĭsm, *n.* State or quality of being radical ; the principles of radicals in politics ; মৌলিকতা ; চরমসংস্কারপন্থিতা। **–i-za'-tion,** *n.* **–ize,** *v. t.* & *i.* To make, or become, radical esp. in politics ; চরমসংস্কারপন্থী হওয়া, আমূল পরিবর্ত্তনের পক্ষপাতী হওয়া।

răd'-i-cle (-kl), *n.* **1.** (*Bot.*) The minute root of an embryo plant ; a rootlet ; (উদ্ভিদ্ বিদ্যা) বীজমূল, মূলাণু (সাঃ পঃ) ; ক্ষুদ্র মূল, মূলাঙ্কুর। **2.** (*Anat.*) A root-like subdivision of a nerve or vein ; (শারীরসংস্থান বিদ্যা) শিরা বা স্নায়ুর বৃক্ষমূলবৎ অবান্তর বিভাগ। **Ra-dic'-u-lar,** *adj.*

rā-di-ō-ăc'-tive (-tĭv), *adj.* That can affect electrometer etc. by radiation ; (of radium, uranium, polonium, etc.) having power to emit invisible rays that penetrate opaque matter and produce electrical effects ; অংশুবিকিরণদ্বারা বিদ্যুৎমাপক প্রভৃতির উপর ক্রিয়াকরণক্ষম ; (রেডিয়াম, ইউরেনিয়াম, পলনিয়াম, প্রভৃতি সম্পর্কে) অপারদর্শকপদার্থ ভেদকারক ও বৈদ্যুতিক প্রয়োজনক এবং অদৃশ্য কিরণবিকিরণক্ষম। **–tiv'-i-ty,** *n.* The phenomenon associated with substances which spontaneously emit rays of unique penetrating power ; রেডিয়াম, ইউরেনিয়াম, প্রভৃতি অপারদর্শক পদার্থ ভেদকারী স্বতঃকিরণ-বিসারী পদার্থসমূহ সংসৃষ্ট ব্যাপারসমূহ। ১৮৯৬ খৃঃ অব্দে Henri Becquerel নামক জনৈক বৈজ্ঞানিক পরীক্ষা করিয়া দেখিতে পান যে Potassium uranyl sulphateএর রশ্মিসমূহ কৃষ্ণবর্ণে রঞ্জিত কাগজ, ধাতুর পাত, প্রভৃতি ভেদপূর্ব্বক আলোকচিত্রফলকের উপর ক্রিয়া করে। অতঃপর ১৮৯৮ খৃঃ অব্দে Madame Curie উক্ত ধর্ম্মাক্রান্ত Radium এবং Polonium নামক মূলপদার্থদ্বয় আবিষ্কার করেন। এই সকল পদার্থ হইতে ত্রিবিধ আলোক নির্গত হয়। α-rays সমূহ ধনতাড়িত সম্পৃরিত, β-rays সমূহ ঋণ-তাড়িত সম্পূরিত এবং γ-rays সমূহ রঞ্জন আলোকের সদৃশ।]

rā-di-ō-câr'-păl, *adj.* (*Anat.*) Of, or relating to, the radius and the wrist ; (শারীরসংস্থানবিদ্যা) অনু-প্রকোষ্ঠাস্থি এবং মণিবন্ধসম্বন্ধীয়।

ra'-di-ō-grăph, *n.* & *v. t.* **1.** An instrument for measuring and recording the intensity and duration of sunshine ; রৌদ্রের স্থিতি ও প্রখরতা পরিমাপার্থ যন্ত্রবিশেষ, রৌদ্রমান। **2.** An image or picture on a sensitive plate produced by Röntgen rays ; রঞ্জন আলোর সাহায্যে রাসায়নিকদ্রব্যালিপ্ত ফলকে উৎপাদিত চিত্র, রঞ্জনচিত্র। ***Verb t.*** To make such a figure or picture of ; রঞ্জনচিত্র উৎপাদন করা। **–graph'-ic,** *adj.* **–graph'-i-cal-ly,** *adv.* **–og'-ra-phy,** *n.* Art or process, of making radiographs ; রঞ্জন-চিত্রশিল্প, রঞ্জনচিত্রোৎপাদনপ্রক্রিয়া।

rā-di-ŏm'-ē-têr, *n.* An instrument for illustrating the conversion of radiant energy into mechanical force ; একপ্রকার যন্ত্র—যদ্দ্বারা বিকিরণশীল তেজের যান্ত্রিক শক্তিতে পরিবর্ত্তন প্রদর্শিত হয়, বিকীর্ণ-তেজোমাপক। [এই যন্ত্র Sir William Crooks কর্তৃক ১৮৭৩—৭৬ খৃঃ অব্দে আবিষ্কৃত হয়।]

rā-di-ŏph'-ō-ny̆, *n.* Production of sound by radiant light or heat ; বিকিরণশীল তাপ বা আলোকের সাহায্যে ধ্বনি উৎপাদন।

rā-di-ŏs'-cō-py̆, *n.* Direct observation of objects opaque to light by means of Röntgen rays ; রঞ্জন আলোর সাহায্যে সাধারণ আলোকে অদৃশ্য বস্তুসমূহের প্রত্যক্ষদর্শন, রঞ্জনবীক্ষণ।

rā-di-ō-tĕl'-ĕg-răm, *n.* A message sent by wireless telegraphy ; অতারতাড়িত বার্ত্তা।

răd'-ish, *n.* A cruciferous plant with a fleshy root ; this root ; মূলাগাছ ; মূলা, মূলক [Syn. কন্দমূল হরিৎপর্ণ, হরিপর্ণ, পাটীর, পটীর, সেকিম।] [Chin. *Hung-lo-p'eh* ; Germ. *Radieschen* ; Fr. *Radis, rave* ; It. *Ravanello.*]

rā'-di-ŭm, *n.* A new element recently discovered possessing unusual power of radiation, found in pitch-blende and certain kinds of ore ; নবাবিষ্কৃত মূলপদার্থ বিশেষ, এই পদার্থ হইতে স্বতই অবিচ্ছিন্ন ভাবে অদৃশ্যকিরণরাজি নির্গত হয়, কিন্তু তাহাতে উহার কোনরূপ ক্ষয় বা পরিবর্ত্তন পরিলক্ষিত হয় না। [এই মূল পদার্থ Pitch-blende নামক দ্রব্য হইতে Madame Curie তদীয় পতির সহযোগে ১৮৯৮ খৃঃ অব্দে আবিষ্কার করেন। ১০ টন উত্তম পিচব্লেণ্ড হইতে কেবলমাত্র ১ গ্র্যাম বিশুদ্ধ রেডিয়াম পাওয়া যায়। এক গ্র্যাম রেডিয়ামের লবণের মূল্য প্রায় ৩ লক্ষ টাকা। বৈজ্ঞানিক পণ্ডিত Joly অনুমান করেন যে সমগ্র সাগর জলে অন্যূন ১০,০০০ টন রেডিয়াম আছে। এক টন কয়লা দগ্ধ করিয়া যে পরিমাণ শক্তি পাওয়া যায় কেবল মাত্র এক গ্র্যাম রেডিয়াম্ হইতে তৎপরিমাণ শক্তি উৎপন্ন হয়। রেডিয়ামের লবণ সমূহ শ্বেতবর্ণ ও স্বতোদীপ্ত। উহারা অল্পকালের মধ্যেই পীত ও কপিশবর্ণ ধারণ করে, কিন্তু বিশুদ্ধ লবণ সমূহের শুক্লবর্ণ দীর্ঘকাল স্থায়ী থাকে। রেডিয়ামের বাষ্পে দুষ্টক্ষত রোগ আরোগ্য হয়। রেডিয়ামের α and β কিরণ দ্বারা হীরক, কাচ প্রভৃতির বর্ণ পরিবর্ত্তন হয় এবং ইহাদ্বারা অম্লজানবাষ্প অম্লজানসারে (ozone) রূপান্তরিত হইয়া থাকে। রেডিয়ামের লবণ মিশ্রিত জল মৌলিক উপাদান সমূহে বিশ্লিষ্ট হইয়া যায়। রেডিয়াম দ্বারা জড় ও চৈতন্যের প্রকৃত সম্বন্ধ নির্ণীত হইবে এইরূপ আশা করার যথেষ্ট কারণ আছে। See Rutherford, *Radio-activity* 1905 (second ed.) ; Sir Oliver Lodge, *Electrons,* 1906 ; A. T. Cameron, *Radio-Chemistry,* 1910, *and Radium and Radio-activity* ; Joly, *Radio-activity and Geology,*

1909; E.E. Fournier d' Abbe, *The Electron Theory*, 1906; Sir J. J. Thomson, *The Corpuscular Theory of Matter*, 1907; Soddy, *Radio-activity*, 1904; also *Matter and Energy*, 1912 (Home University Library].

ră'-dĭ-ŭs, *n.* (*Pl.*, -DII) **1.** The semi-diameter of a circle or sphere; a radial line from the focus to any point of a curve; ব্যাসার্দ্ধ (ব্যাসার্দ্ধার্দ্ধং নয়েৎ কেন্দ্রাৎ—আর্য্যঃ), বিষ্কম্ভার্দ্ধ (আর্য্যঃ); ত্রিজ্যা (সূঃ সিঃ), ত্রিজীবা (ঐ)। **2.** The shorter or smaller of the two bones of the forearm; a corresponding bone in a beast's foreleg or a bird's wing; কফোণি হইতে মণিবন্ধ পর্য্যন্ত যে দুই খানি অস্থি প্রসারিত আছে, তন্মধ্যে ক্ষুদ্রতর অস্থি, অনুপ্রকোষ্ঠাস্থি (সাঃ পঃ); জন্তুর অগ্রপাদ ও পক্ষীর পাখার অনুরূপ অস্থি। **3.** A circular area as measured by its radius; as, I know everyone within a *radius* of 15 miles; ব্যাসার্দ্ধ দ্বারা পরিমিত বৃত্তাকৃতি স্থান। **4.** Any of the lines diverging from a point like the radii of a circle; something like this, *e. g.* a spoke; কোন বিন্দু হইতে বৃত্তের ব্যাসার্দ্ধবৎ কেন্দ্রাপসর্পীরেখাসমূহের অন্যতম; বৃত্তের ব্যাসার্দ্ধবৎ কোন কিছু, যথা আর, অর। **5.** (*Bot.*) The ray of a flower *e. g.* daisy; also, the radiating branch of an umbel; (উদ্ভিদ্‌বিদ্যা) পুষ্পের অংশ; উপচ্ছত্রের বিকিরণশীল অংশ। **Radius vector**—(জ্যোতি-বিজ্ঞান) কোন আকর্ষক গ্রহ (যথা সূর্য্য) এবং উহার চতুর্দ্দিকে ভ্রাম্যমাণ গ্রহ যে কল্পিত রেখা দ্বারা সংযুক্ত হয়, কর্ণ (হিঃ কোঃ), শ্রুতি (ঐ), চলকর্ণ বা শ্রবণ (সাঃ পঃ); (জ্যামিতি) কোন নির্দ্দিষ্ট বিন্দু হইতে কোন চক্র পর্য্যন্ত অঙ্কিত চলরেখা, নাভিশ্রুতিত্রিজ্যা (হিঃ কোঃ)।

ră'-dĭx, *n.* (*Pl.*, -DICES) **1.** A fundamental number or base in mathematics; as, ten is the *radix* of decimal numeration; মৌলিক সংখ্যা। **2.** (*Philol.*) A root; (ভাষাবিজ্ঞান) ধাতু। **3.** (*Bot.*) The root of a plant; (উদ্ভিদ্ বিদ্যা) মূল, শিকড়। **4.** Original source or cause (of); মূল, মূল কারণ।

răff, Same as RIFF-RAFF.

Răf-fă-ĕl-esque' (-esk), *adj.* Same as RAPHAELESQUE.

răf'-fĭ-ă (-ĭ-), *n.* **1.** A kind of palm; একপ্রকার তালজাতীয় বৃক্ষ। **2.** The fibre got from the leaves of this tree used in tying up plants; উক্ত বৃক্ষের আঁশ—যদ্দ্বারা গাছগাছড়া বাঁধা হয়।

răf'-fish (-ĭsh), *adj.* Worthless; villainous; dissipated; অসার; পামর, লম্পট; ভ্রষ্টচরিত্র। **—ly,** *adv.* **—ness,** *n.*

răf'-fle (-l), *n., v. i. & t.* A kind of lottery sale in which each person deposits a part of the value of things in consideration of the chance of gaining it; একপ্রকার ভাগ্য পরীক্ষার খেলা যাহাতে প্রতি ব্যক্তি কোন জিনিষ লাভ করার আশায় উহার মূল্যের কতক অংশ জমা দেয়, সুর্ত্তি। ***Verb i.*** To enter one's name in a raffle as for an article; সুর্ত্তি খেলায় নাম দেওয়া। ***Verb t.*** To sell by a raffle; সুর্ত্তি দ্বারা বিক্রীত করা।

răf'-fle (-l), *n.* Refuse; rubbish; আবর্জ্জনা; জঞ্জাল, ভগ্ন অট্টালিকা, ইষ্টকাদির স্তূপ, রাবিশ।

răft, *n., v. t. & i.* **1.** An assemblage of logs, casks, etc. fastened together and floated down a stream, as for transport, etc.; চালি। **2.** A floating structure for conveying persons or things esp. in emergencies; ভেলা, ভুরা (East Bengal), মান্দাস, (প্রাঃ সাঃ) [Syn. উড়ুপ, প্লব, কোল, তর্ণি, বহিত্র, বারিপথ, ভেলক, হোড়, ত্রুম, দণ্ডার, তড়ও, প্লবাকা।] **3.** Floating accumulation of trees, ice, etc.; প্লবমান বৃক্ষশ্রেণী, হিমশিলা প্রভৃতি। ***Verb t.*** **1.** To transport on or as a raft; to make into a raft; ভেলায় করিয়া নেওয়া; ভেলা প্রস্তুত করা। **2.** To go along or cross as a river etc. on a raft; ভেলায় নদী প্রভৃতির উপর চলা, বা নদী প্রভৃতি পার হওয়া। ***Verb i.*** To use or work a raft; ভেলা ব্যবহার করা, ভেলা চালান। **Raftsman**—ভেলাচালক।

răft'-ĕr, *n.* One who rafts timber যে ব্যক্তি চালি ভাসাইয়া আনে।

răft'-ĕr, *n. & v. t.* The inclin[ed] roof timber of a house; ক্[রুয়া,] বর্গা, তুলা (শিশুঃ)। ***Verb t.*** **1.** (Usu. in *p. p.*) To furnish with rafters; রুয়া বা বর্গা লাগান। **2.** (*Agri.*) To plough as land so as to turn over the grass side of the ploughed furrow on th[e] land that is left unploughed যাহাতে কর্ষিত মৃত্তিকার তৃণাবৃত অং[শ] অকর্ষিত ক্ষেত্রখণ্ডে উল্টাইয়া পড়ে এরূ[প] ভাবে কর্ষণ করা। **Rafter-bird**—একপ্রকার পক্ষী।

răg, *n.* **1.** A tattered cloth shred; জীর্ণবস্ত্র, ছেঁড়া কাপড়, চী[র,] চীবর, ন্যাকড়া। **2.** (Usu. *Pl.*) Mean or tattered attire; as, to be in *rags*; (*sometimes with a negative*) the smallest scrap of cloth or sail; as, *not* a *rag* to put on; (সাধারণতঃ বহুবচন) জীর্ণবস্ত্র; পাইল বা কাপড়ের অতি ছোট টুকরা। **3.** An irregular piece; remnant; a scrap; as, flying *rags* of cloud; খণ্ড; অবশিষ্ট; টুকরা। **4.** (*Contempt.* or *jocul.*) A handkerchief, curtain, flag, newspaper, etc.; (অবজ্ঞা বা রহস্যচ্ছলে) রুমাল, পর্দ্দা, নিশান, খবরের কাগজ, প্রভৃতি **5.** (*Collective*) A material con[-]sisting of rags used in ma[king] paper; কাগজ তৈরির জন্য ন্য[াকড়া] প্রভৃতি। **6.** (*Rare*) A rough p[ro]jection; (কচিদ্‌ব্যবহৃত) বন্ধুর উদ্গ[ত]

2. To send as goods by rail ; রেলে মাল পাঠান। 3. To place rails on (as a railway route); লৌহবর্ত্মে লৌহদণ্ড (রেল) পাতা বা বসান। **Rail'-ing,** *n.* **1.** A barrier as a fence etc. consisting of a rail or rails and supports ; গরাদ, লৌহবৃতি। **2.** Rails in general ; material for rails ; লৌহবর্ত্মের উপর বিন্যস্ত লৌহদণ্ড ; লৌহদণ্ডের উপকরণ। **Rail'-less,** *adj.* **Rail chair**—লৌহবর্ত্মের শয়ান কাষ্ঠের উপর সম্বদ্ধ লৌহময় ধারণী—যাহার উপর পাতা লৌহদণ্ড সকল অবলম্বিত থাকে। **Railroad**—Railway ; লৌহবর্ত্ম, লোহপথ। **Railway**—*n., v. t. & i.* A road or way constructed with two parallel iron bars along which carriages are carried by steam or horse-power ; রেলপথ, লৌহবর্ত্ম, লৌহপথ। (*Verb t.*) To build railways in (a country etc.) ; (কোন দেশে) লৌহবর্ত্ম প্রস্তুত করা। (*Verb i.*) To travel by rail ; রেলযোগে ভ্রমণ করা। *Railway-less, adj.* **Railway accident**—রেলওয়ে দুর্ঘটনা। **Railway act**—রেলওয়েসংক্রান্ত আইন। **Railway bill**—নূতন লৌহবর্ত্ম নির্ম্মাণের জন্য পার্লেমেন্টে যে প্রস্তাব উপস্থাপিত করা হয়। **Rail-way sub-office** — (Abbr. *R. S. O.*) ; লৌহবর্ত্মের নিকটস্থ স্থান—যথায় কোন বড় ডাকঘরের অধীন ডাকঘর আছে। **At railway speed**—Very swiftly ; speedily ; রেলগাড়ীর মত বেগে ; তূর্ণ। **By rail**—By railway ; রেলযোগে। **Off the rails** — Derailed ; (*fig.*) disorganized ; out of order ; বর্ত্মচ্যুত ; শৃঙ্খলাচ্যুত ; বিশৃঙ্খল।

rail (rāl), *n.* A genus of wading birds ; একজাতীয় পক্ষী।

rail (rāl), *v. i.* To utter insolent or abusive language ; to scoff ; গালি দেওয়া ; বিদ্রূপ করা। **Rail'-er,** *n.*

rail'-ing, *n. & adj.* Insolent and reproachful language ; raillery ; গালি ; বিদ্রূপ। ***Adj.*** Insulting ; abusive ; scoffing ; অপমানজনক ; নিন্দাত্মক ; বিদ্রূপাত্মক। **–ly,** *adv.*

rail'-ler-ў (rāl-êr-), *n.* **1.** Slight satire ; banter ; good-humoured ridicule ; বিদ্রূপ ; ব্যঙ্গ ; পরিহাস ; উপহাস, ঠাট্টা। **2.** A jest ; রহস্য।

rai'-mĕnt (rā-), *n.* Clothing ; dress ; বস্ত্র ; পোষাক, কাপড়চোপড়।

rain (rān), *n.* **1.** Water falling in drops from the atmosphere ; also, the fall of such drops ; বৃষ্টি, জল (*colloq.*) [Syn. খজল, মেঘোদক, আকাশ-সলিল, ঘনাম্বু, বর্ষ, আবৃষ্টি, গোমূত, অভ্রপ্রুষ (ঋক্), পরামৃত, খবারি, পর্জ্জন্য (অন্নাদ্ভবন্তি ভূতানি পর্জ্জন্যাদন্নসম্ভবঃ—গীতা) ; বৃষ্টিপাত। 2. (Usu. *pl.*) A shower of rain ; এক পসলা বৃষ্টি, বর্ষণ, ধারাসম্পাত (heavy shower), ধারাবর্ষণ (*ib.*), ধারাসার (*ib.*)। **3.** (*Pl.* with *the*) The rainy season ; বর্ষাঋতু, বর্ষাকাল, প্রাবৃট্ কাল, প্রাবৃট্। **4.** (*Pl., cap.,* with *the*) The rainy region of the Atlantic 4—10° North latitude ; অতলান্তিক মহাসাগরের যে অংশে প্রচুর বৃষ্টিপাত হয়। **5.** Falling like rain, of liquid, solid particles or bodies ; (*lit.* & *fig.*) ; as, a *rain* of pearls, fire or of kisses or congratulations ; বর্ষণ, বর্ষ, বৃষ্টি [cf. পুষ্পবর্ষণ, চুম্বন-বৃষ্টি, অগ্নিবৃষ্টি]। **Rain'-less,** *adj.* **Rain-bird**—বিভিন্ন প্রকার পক্ষীর সাধারণ নাম ; বিশেষভাবে গ্রীসদেশীয় কাঠঠোকরা পাখী। **Rain-box**—নাট্যমন্দিরে ব্যবহৃত বৃষ্টিরবানুকারী যন্ত্রবিশেষ। **Rain-cloud**—বর্ষপ্রদ মেঘ, পর্জ্জন্য, বর্ষুকাব্দ, বর্ষুকাম্বুদ। **Rain-doctor**—যে ব্যক্তি মন্ত্রাদিদ্বারা বৃষ্টি উৎপাদন করে, হীড়াল (used in parts of East Bengal)। **Raindrop**—বৃষ্টিবিন্দু, বৃষ্টির ফোঁটা। **Rainfall**—A shower or quantities of rain falling within a given area in a given time (usu. reckoned by inches of depth per annum) ; কোন নির্দ্দিষ্ট স্থানে নির্দ্দিষ্ট কালের মধ্যে যে পরিমাণ বৃষ্টিপাত হয়, বৃষ্টিপাত। **Rain-gauge** — বৃষ্টিমানযন্ত্র, বর্ষমা (অর্থঃ)। **Rain-glass** — বায়ুচাপ-মানযন্ত্র। **Rain-maker** — Same as RAIN-DOCTOR. **Rain-pour** — মুষলধারে বর্ষণ, ধারাবর্ষণ। **Rain-proof,** *adj.* বৃষ্টিরোধক। **Rain-tight**—Same as RAIN-PROOF (which see). **Rain tree**—বিলাতী শিরীষ। **Rain-water**—বৃষ্টিজল, বৃষ্টিবারি, মেঘোদক (মৃচ্ছঃ বর্ষাম্বু, বর্ষজল। **Rain-worm**—কেঁচে **Rain or shine**—Whether it rain or not ; বৃষ্টি হউক আর নাই হউক।

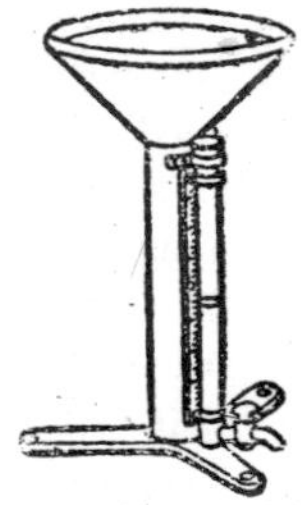

Rain-gauge.

rain (rān). *v. i.* & *t.* **1.** To in drops from coluds, (with *it* nominative) ; বৃষ্টি হওয়া। **2.** send down rain ; as, the sky God *rains* ; বৃষ্টি প্রেরণ করা। **3.** fall or drop like rain ; as, flow *rained* from their hands ; হওয়া, বর্ষিত হওয়া। ***Verb t.*** shower or send down like ra as, to *rain* benefits upon one ; বর্ষণ করা, বৃষ্টি করা। **never rains but pours**—Eve usually happen several togeth জলে জল বাঁধে, ধনে ধন দেখে, পু পুত দেখে। **It rains cats an dogs or pitch-forks**—See CAT.

rain'-bow (rān-bō), *n.* & *adj.* An arc of a circle consisting of all the prismatic colours, appearing in the sky opposite the sun ; রামধনু রামধনুক, ইন্দ্রধনু, ইন্দ্রচাপ, [Syn. সুরে চাপ, শক্রধনু, ইন্দ্রায়ুধ, দেবায়ুধ, হরিহেত (কথমবলোকয়েয়মধুনা হরিহেতিমতীঃ—মাঃ মাঃ), মণিধনু, ত্রিদশায়ুধ, সুরধনু (বৃঃ জাঃ), মেঘধনু, শক্রশরাস কৌশিকায়ুধ, বায়ুফল, রোহিত (straight or imperfect rainb লোহিত (*ib.*), শক্রচাপ (মঃ ভাঃ), কার্ম্মুক (বিক্রঃ), সুরচাপ (বৃঃ

2. To send as goods by rail ; রেলে মাল পাঠান। 3. To place rails on (as a railway route); লৌহবর্ত্মে লৌহদণ্ড (রেল) পাতা বা বসান। **Rail'-ing,** *n.* 1. A barrier as a fence etc. consisting of a rail or rails and supports ; গরাদ, লৌহবৃতি। 2. Rails in general ; material for rails ; লৌহবর্ত্মের উপর বিন্যস্ত লৌহদণ্ড ; লৌহদণ্ডের উপকরণ। **Rail'-less,** *adj.* **Rail chair**—লৌহবর্ত্মের শয়ান কাঠের উপর সম্বদ্ধ লৌহময় ধারণী—যাহার উপর পাতা লৌহদণ্ড সকল অবলম্বিত থাকে। **Railroad**—Railway ; লৌহবর্ত্ম, লোহপথ। **Railway**—*n., v. t. & i.* A road or way constructed with two parallel iron bars along which carriages are carried by steam or horse-power ; রেলপথ, লৌহবর্ত্ম, লৌহপথ। (*Verb t.*) To build railways in (a country etc.) ; (কোন দেশে) লৌহবর্ত্ম প্রস্তুত করা। (*Verb i.*) To travel by rail ; রেলযোগে ভ্রমণ করা। *Railway-less, adj.* **Railway accident**—রেলওয়ে দুর্ঘটনা। **Railway act**—রেলওয়েসংক্রান্ত আইন। **Railway bill**—নূতন লৌহবর্ত্ম নির্ম্মাণের জন্য পার্লেমেণ্টে যে প্রস্তাব উপস্থাপিত করা হয়। **Rail-way sub-office** — (Abbr. *R. S. O.*) ; লৌহবর্ত্মের নিকটস্থ স্থান—যথায় কোন বড় ডাকঘরের অধীন ডাকঘর আছে। **At railway speed**—Very swiftly ; speedily ; রেলগাড়ীর মত বেগে ; তূর্ণ। **By rail**—By railway ; রেলযোগে। **Off the rails** — De-railed ; (*fig.*) disorganized ; out of order ; বর্ত্মচ্যুত ; শৃঙ্খলাচ্যুত ; বিশৃঙ্খল।

rail (rāl), *n.* A genus of wading birds ; একজাতীয় পক্ষী।

rail (rāl), *v. i.* To utter insolent or abusive language ; to scoff ; গালি দেওয়া; বিদ্রূপ করা। **Rail'-er,** *n.* **rail'-ing,** *n. & adj.* Insolent and reproachful language ; raillery ; গালি ; বিদ্রূপ। *Adj.* Insulting ; abusive ; scoffing ; অপমানজনক ; নিন্দাত্মক ; বিদ্রূপাত্মক। **—ly,** *adv.*

rail'-ler-ȳ (rāl-êr-), *n.* 1. Slight satire ; banter ; good-humoured ridicule ; বিদ্রূপ ; ব্যঙ্গ ; পরিহাস ; উপহাস, ঠাট্টা। 2. A jest ; রহস্য।

rai'-mĕnt (rā-), *n.* Clothing ; dress ; বস্ত্র ; পোষাক, কাপড়চোপড়।

rain (rān), *n.* 1. Water falling in drops from the atmosphere ; also, the fall of such drops ; বৃষ্টি, জল (*colloq.*) [Syn. খজল, মেঘোদক, আকাশ-সলিল, ঘনাম্বু, বর্ষ, আবৃষ্টি, গোমূত, অভ্রপ্রুষ (ঋক্), পরামৃত, খবারি, পর্জ্জন্য (অন্নাদ্ভবন্তি ভুতানি পর্জ্জন্যাদন্নসম্ভবঃ—গীতা) ; বৃষ্টিপাত। 2. (Usu. *pl.*) A shower of rain ; এক পসলা বৃষ্টি, বর্ষণ, ধারাসম্পাত (heavy shower), ধারাবর্ষণ (*ib.*), ধারাসার (*ib.*) । 3. (*Pl.* with *the*) The rainy season ; বর্ষাঋতু, বর্ষাকাল, প্রাবৃট্ কাল, প্রাবৃট্। 4. (*Pl., cap.,* with *the*) The rainy region of the Atlantic 4—10° North latitude ; অতলান্তিক মহাসাগরের যে অংশে প্রচুর বৃষ্টিপাত হয়। 5. Falling like rain, of liquid, solid particles or bodies ; (*lit. & fig.*) ; as, a *rain* of pearls, fire or of kisses or congratulations ; বর্ষণ, বর্ষ, বৃষ্টি [cf. পুষ্পবর্ষণ, চুম্বন-বৃষ্টি, অগ্নিবৃষ্টি]। **Rain'-less,** *adj.* **Rain-bird**—বিভিন্ন প্রকার পক্ষীর সাধারণ নাম ; বিশেষভাবে গ্রীসদেশীয় কাঠঠোকরা পাখী। **Rain-box**—নাট্যমন্দিরে ব্যবহৃত বৃষ্টিরবানুকারী যন্ত্রবিশেষ। **Rain-cloud**—বর্ষপ্রদ মেঘ, পর্জ্জন্য, বর্ষুকাব্দ, বর্ষুকাম্বুদ। **Rain-doctor**—যে ব্যক্তি মন্ত্রাদিদ্বারা বৃষ্টি উৎপাদন করে, হীড়াল (used in parts of East Bengal)। **Raindrop**—বৃষ্টিবিন্দু, বৃষ্টির ফোঁটা। **Rainfall**—A shower or quantities of rain falling within a given area in a given time (usu. reckoned by inches of depth per annum) ; কোন নির্দ্দিষ্ট স্থানে নির্দ্দিষ্ট কালের মধ্যে যে পরিমাণ বৃষ্টিপাত হয়, বৃষ্টিপাত। **Rain-gauge** — বৃষ্টিমানযন্ত্র, বর্ষমা (অর্থঃ)। **Rain-glass** — বায়ুচাপ-মানযন্ত্র। **Rain-maker** — Same as RAIN-DOCTOR. **Rain-pour** — মুষলধারে বর্ষণ, ধারাবর্ষণ। **Rain-proof,** *adj.* বৃষ্টিরোধক। **Rain-tight**—Same as RAIN-PROOF (which see). **Rain tree**—বিলাতী শিরীষ। **Rain-water** বৃষ্টিজল, বৃষ্টিবারি, মেঘোদক (মৃচ্ছঃ বর্ষাম্বু, বর্ষজল। **Rain-worm**—কেঁচো **Rain or shine**—Whether it rain or not ; বৃষ্টি হউক আর নাই হউক।

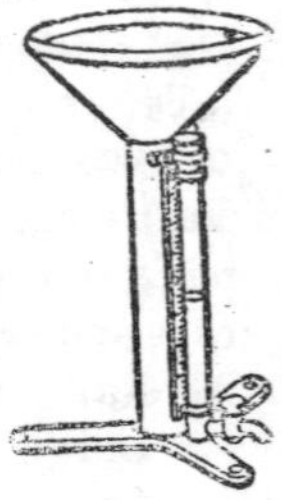

Rain-gauge.

rain (rān). *v. i. & t.* 1. To [fall] in drops from coluds, (with *it* nominative) ; বৃষ্টি হওয়া। 2. [To] send down rain ; as, the sky [or] God *rains* ; বৃষ্টি প্রেরণ করা। 3. [To] fall or drop like rain ; as, flow[ers] *rained* from their hands ; [বর্ষণ] হওয়া, বর্ষিত হওয়া। *Verb t.* [To] shower or send down like ra[in] ; as, to *rain* benefits upon [some]one ; বর্ষণ করা, বৃষ্টি করা। [It] **never rains but pours**—Ev[ents] usually happen several togeth[er] ; জলে জল বাঁধে, ধনে ধন দেখে, পু[ত্রে] পুত দেখে। **It rains cats an[d] dogs or pitch-forks**—See CAT.

rain'-bow (rān-bō), *n. & adj.* A[n] arc of a circle consisting of all the prismatic colours, appearing in the sky opposite the sun ; রামধনু, রামধনুক, ইন্দ্রধনু, ইন্দ্রচাপ, [Syn. সুরে[ন্দ্র]চাপ, শক্রধনু, ইন্দ্রায়ুধ, দেবায়ুধ, হরিহে[তি] (কথমবলোকয়েয়মধুনা হরিহেতিমতীঃ—মাঃ মাঃ), মণিধনু, ত্রিদশায়ুধ, সুরধনু (বৃঃ জাঃ), মেঘধনু, শক্রশরাস[ন] কৌশিকায়ুধ, বায়ুফল, রোহিত (straight or imperfect rainb[ow]) লোহিত (*ib.*), শক্রচাপ (মঃ ভাঃ), কার্ম্মুক (বিক্রঃ), সুরচাপ (বৃঃ

সুরগ্রামণীচাপ, সুরপতিচাপ, সুরপতি-ধনু (মেঘদূঃ), সুরশরাসন (বাসবঃ), সুরগোপচাপ (সারঙ্গঃ পঃ), সুরেশ্বরধনু (কাব্যঃ সাঃ), শক্রকার্ম্মুক (বৃঃ সং), শক্রায়ুধ (ঐ), হরিচাপ (ঐ), ইন্দ্রকার্ম্মুক (ঐ), কার্ম্মুক (বরাহঃ যোগঃ), বাসবচাপ (বিক্রমঃ), আখণ্ডলচাপ (কাদঃ), আখণ্ডলধনু (ঐ), পুরন্দরচাপ (ঐ), শতমন্যুচাপ (ঐ), শতযজ্ঞচাপ (ঐ), ময়ুরপিচ্ছচিত্রচাপ (ঐ), সহস্রাক্ষধনু (রঃ), পুরন্দরধনু (গীতঃ), হরিধনু (গোপালঃ), শুনাশীর-শরাসন (হর্ষঃ)। [আমাদের প্রাচীনগণ ইন্দ্রধনুর উৎপত্তির কারণ পরিজ্ঞাত ছিলেন, তাহার প্রমাণ ঃ—"সূর্য্যস্য বিবিধবর্ণাঃ পবনেন বিঘট্টিতাঃ করাঃ সাভ্রে। বিয়তি ধনুঃ সংস্থানা যে দৃশ্যন্তে তদিন্দ্রধনুঃ" ॥— বরাহমিহির। "সলিল-শীকরাসাররচিতদুর্দ্দিনেষু পর্য্যন্তদিবসকর-কিরণস্তবকরচিতসুরচাপচারুষু"—(কাদঃ)।] *Adj.* Many-coloured; নানাবর্ণ, অনেকবর্ণ, ইন্দ্রায়ুধবর্ণ। **Lunar rainbow**—চন্দ্রকিরণজনিত ইন্দ্রধনু, চন্দ্রীয় চন্দ্রধনু। **Rainbow darter**—এক প্রকার মৎস্য। **Rainbow-trout**—একপ্রকার রুচিরবর্ণ মৎস্য। **Sea-rainbow**—সাগরশীকরে জাত ইন্দ্রধনু। **Secondary rainbow**—গৌণ রামধনু। এইরূপ রামধনুর বর্ণরাজি বিপর্য্যস্ত-ক্রমে বিন্যস্ত থাকে]।

rain'-y (rān-), *adj.* **1.** On, or in which, rain falls; showery; wet; as, *rainy* weather: *rainy* month; বাদলা; বর্ষা; আর্দ্র। **2.** Heavy with, or bringing, rain; as, *rainy* cloud, wind, etc.; বর্ষুক, বর্ষপ্রদ, বৃষ্টিবহুল। **Rainy day**—A day on which rain falls; (*fig.*) a time, esp. of pecuniary difficulty; বাদলা দিন (from Sans. বার্দ্দল); (লক্ষণায়) দুর্দ্দিন। **Rainy-season**—বর্ষাকাল, প্রাবৃটকাল, বর্ষাঋতু [Syn. ঘনাকর, জলার্ণব, জলাগম, ময়ুরোল্লাসক, বার্ষিক্য, চাতকানন্দন, বৃষ্টিকাল, জলদাগম, মেঘাগম, তপান্ত, নভস, ঘনসময়, জলদকাল, তপাত্যয়।]

raise (rāz), *v. t.* **1.** To cause to rise; to lift, as a weight; to set upright; as, to *raise* a post; to awaken; as, to *raise* one from sleep; উত্তোলন করা; তোলা; খাড়া করা; জাগরিত করা, নিদ্রা হইতে উঠান। **2.** To stir up; to rouse; to incite to struggle, war or tumult; as danger *raised* his spirits; উত্তেজিত করা; উদ্বুদ্ধ করা, প্রবুদ্ধ করা; যুদ্ধাদিতে প্রণোদিত বা প্রোৎসাহিত করা। **3.** To call up as a spirit; to bring into life; as, to *raise* one from the dead; ভূত নাবান; পুনর্জীবিত করা। **4.** To build up; গাঁথিয়া তোলা। **5.** To create; to produce; to grow; to breed; সৃষ্টি করা; উৎপাদন করা; জন্মান; বাচ্চা তোলা। **6.** To give rise to, as a smile, blush, etc.; to start; to occasion; as, to *raise* a controversy; to bring forward or suggest for discussion; as, to *raise* a question etc.; to set up; as, to *raise* a claim, demand, etc.; উৎপাদন করা; আরম্ভ করা; জন্মান; উত্থাপন করা; উপস্থাপিত করা। **7.** To utter; to make audible; as, to *raise* a shout, hymn, etc.; উচ্চারণ করা; শ্রবণ-যোগ্য করা। **8.** To collect; to levy; to procure; as, to *raise* a tax, loan, money, troops, etc.; জড় করা; আদায় করা; সংগ্রহ করা। **9.** To elavate in rank, position, etc.; to promote; to make higher or nobler; উন্নীত করা; পদোন্নতি বিধান করা; উচ্চতর বা উন্নততর করা। **10.** To enhance or increase as the price of a thing etc.; মূল্য বৃদ্ধি করা, দাম চড়ান। **11.** To make louder as one's voice; গলা চড়ান, স্বর চড়ান। **12.** (*Naut.*) To come in sight of, as land, ship, etc.; (নৌ-বিদ্যা) দৃষ্টিপথবর্ত্তী হওয়া। **13.** To relinquish; to cause an enemy to relinquish; as, to *raise* a siege, blockade; উঠাইয়া নেওয়া; উঠাইয়া নিতে বাধ্য করা। **Rais'-ing**, *n.* The act of one who raises; সমুদ্ধরণ, সংস্থাপন, উন্নমন, উন্নয়ন। **No one raised his voice**—Nobody spoke; কেহ কথাটী কহিল না। **To raise a cheque**—জুয়াচুরী করিয়া হুণ্ডী প্রভৃতির টাকার অঙ্ক বাড়াইয়া লওয়া। **To raise a cloth**—To make nap on it; কাপড়ের ফুঁপি তোলা। **To raise a dust**—To cause dust to rise; (*fig.*) to cause turmoil; to obscure the truth; ধূলা উঠান; (লক্ষণায়) গোলযোগের সৃষ্টি করা; সত্য আচ্ছন্ন করা। **To raise a laugh** — To make others laugh; অপর সকলকে হাসান। **To raise bread**—To cause to rise with yeast; খমীর দ্বারা রুটি ফুলান। **To raise Cain, hell, the devil, the mischief, etc.**—To make, or cause, disturbance; গোলমাল করা, গোলযোগের সৃষ্টি করা, তুমুল কাণ্ড বাঁধান। **To raise colour**—(In dyeing) To brighten it; রঙ্গ চড়ান। **To raise objection**—আপত্তি উত্থাপন করা। **To raise one from the dead**—To restore him to life; পুনর্জন্ম প্রদান করা। **To raise one's back** — To become obstinate; to rebel; একগুঁয়েমি করা; বিদ্রোহাচরণ করা, অবাধ্য হওয়া। **To raise one's eyes**—To look upwards; উর্দ্ধে দৃষ্টিপাত করা, চোখ তুলিয়া চাওয়া। **To raise one's glass to**—To drink the health of; কাহারো স্বাস্থ্য কামনায় মদ্যপান করা। **To raise one's hat** — To bow; টুপি তুলিয়া অভিবাদন করা। **To raise one's reputation**—To increase it; কাহারো খ্যাতি বৃদ্ধি করা। **To raise the country, city, etc.** — See RAISE, *v. t.*, 2. **To raise the wind**—(*Fig.*) To procure money for some purpose; (লক্ষণায়) কোন উদ্দেশ্যে অর্থ সংগ্রহ করা।

rai'-sin (rā-), *n.* A dried grape; শুষ্ক দ্রাক্ষা, কিসমিস, মনাক্কা (bigger ones) [Arab. *Zabib* ; Fr. *Raisins secs* ; Germ. *Rosinen* ; Russ. *Issur* ; Chin *Kan-pu-tau* ; Ital. *Uve passe.*]

raison d'etat, (*F.*), *n.* Reason of state ; রাষ্ট্রীয় হেতু।

raison d'etre, (*F.*), *n.* Reason or excuse for being ; কোন কিছু অবস্থিতির হেতু বা উপলক্ষ, অস্তিত্বকারণ (হিঃ কোঃ)।

rait (rāt), See RET.

rāke, *n.* **1.** An instrument for collecting hay or straw and smoothing soil etc. ; বিদা। **2.** Any of various instruments resembling a rake for other purposes ; বিদার মত আকৃতি বিশিষ্ট বিভিন্ন প্রকার যন্ত্র।

rāke, *v. t.* & *i.* **1.** To gather, stir, pull *out*, clear *off*, etc. with or as with a rake ; as, to *rake* hay : to *rake out* fire : to *rake off* leaves ; বিদা বা বিদার আকার যন্ত্রদ্বারা জড় করা, উস্কান বা টানিয়া আনা। **2.** To gather together ; as, to *rake together* money ; একত্র করা, জড় করা। **3.** To clean or smooth with a rake ; বিদাদ্বারা পরিষ্কার বা মসৃণ করা। **4.** To search through ; to ransack ; as, to *rake* all history for the information ; অনুসন্ধান করা; তন্ন তন্ন করিয়া খোঁজা। **5.** To scrape or scratch with or as with a rake ; to pass lightly over ; "Like clouds that *rake* mountain summits" ; বিদাদ্বারা আঁচড়ান ; মৃদুমন্দ গতিতে চলা। **6.** (*Mil.*) To enfilade ; to fire in the direction of the length of (a ship) ; (সামরিক-শাস্ত্র) লম্বালম্বিভাবে গোলা বর্ষণ করা ; (শত্রুপোতের) লম্বালম্বিভাবে গোলাবর্ষণ করা। **7.** To sweep with the eyes ; (of a window etc.) to have a commanding view of ; এক পার্শ্ব হইতে অপর পার্শ্ব পর্য্যন্ত চাহিয়া যাওয়া ; (বাতায়ন প্রভৃতি সম্পর্কে) সুবিস্তীর্ণ স্থান দর্শনযোগ্য করা। ***Verb i.*** To use a rake ; to search minutely ; as, to *rake* among, in or into old records ; বিদা দেওয়া ; তন্ন তন্ন করিয়া তল্লাস করা, পুঙ্খানুপুঙ্খরূপে অনুসন্ধান করা। **To rake up**—To revive ; পুনরুজ্জীবিত করা, খুঁচিয়ে তোলা। **To rake up the fire**—To prepare a fire so as to last all night by covering it with a large piece of coal and putting cinders on the top ; পাথুরিয়া কয়লার বড় টুকরা দ্বারা ঢাকিয়া তদুপরি অঙ্গার রাখিয়া অগ্নি রক্ষা করা।

rāke, *n.* A dissipated or dissolute man ; a debauchee ; লম্পট, বদমায়েস ; ভ্রষ্টচরিত্র ব্যক্তি।

rāke, *v. i., t.* & *n.* **1.** (*Naut.*) To incline or slope backward as a mast ; (নৌ-বিদ্যা) পশ্চাদ্দিকে হেলিয়া পড়া। **2.** (Of a ship, its bow or stern) To project at the upper part of the bow or stern beyond the keel ; (জাহাজ, জাহাজের আগা বা পাছা গলুই সম্বন্ধে) পানিতরাসের বাহিরে জাহাজের অগ্র বা পশ্চাদ্ভাগে উদ্গাত হওয়া। ***Verb t.*** To incline backward ; পশ্চাদ্দিকে হেলান। ***Noun.*** Amount of inclination of a thing ; a raking position ; প্রবণতার পরিমাণ ; পশ্চাদ্দিকে প্রবণতা বা পানিতরাসের বাহিরে পোতের অগ্র বা পশ্চাদ্ভাগে উদ্গতি।

rāke'-hĕll, *n.* (*Archaic*) A debauchee or rake ; (অপ্রঃ) লম্পট। **—y,** *adj.* (*Archaic.*)

rāk'-ish, *adj.* Of, or like, a rake ; dissolute ; লম্পটসম্বন্ধীয়, লম্পটবৎ ; ভ্রষ্ট, দুশ্চরিত্র। **—ly,** *adv.* **—ness,** *n.*

rāk'-ish, *adj.* (Of a ship) Seeming to be built for speed and hence open to suspicion of piracy ; smart-looking ; (জাহাজসম্পর্কে) দ্রুতগমনের জন্য নির্ম্মিত বলিয়া প্রতিভাত অতএব জলদস্যুতার জন্য অভিপ্রেত এইরূপ অনুমিত ; চটকদার।

râle, *n.* (*Path.*) An abnormal sound in the lungs ; (নিদান শাস্ত্র) ফুসফুসের একপ্রকার অস্বাভাবিক ধ্বনি।

rallentando, *adv.* Gradually slower (*a musical direction*) ; ক্রমশঃ আস্তে।

răl-li-câr(t), *n.* A kind of two-wheeled vehicle for four persons ; চারি ব্যক্তির জন্য একপ্রকার দুই চাকার গাড়ী।

răl'-lȳ, *v. i., t.* & *n.* **1.** To re-assemble after rout or dispersion ; to renew conflict or fight ; ছত্রভঙ্গ বা পলায়নের পর (সৈন্য) পুনরায় জড় হওয়া ; যুদ্ধ বা বিরোধ পুনরায় আরম্ভ করা। **2.** To come together or assemble as support or for united effort ; as, my party *rallied* round me ; সাহায্যার্থ বা সমবেত চেষ্টার জন্য একত্র হওয়া। **3.** To recover strength, vigour or energy ; to regain health or spirits ; শক্তি, তেজঃ, বল, প্রভৃতি পুনঃপ্রাপ্ত হওয়া ; স্বাস্থ্য অথবা উৎসাহ পুনরায় লাভ করা। ***Verb t.*** **1.** To assemble or bring together as troops after dispersion or rout ; to cause to fight again ; ছত্রভঙ্গ বা পলায়মান সৈন্যদল পুনরায় একত্র করা ; পুনরায় যুদ্ধে প্রবৃত্ত করা। **2.** To bring together for support or common action ; as, he *rallied* his party round him ; সাহায্যার্থ বা সমবেত কার্য্যের জন্য একত্র করা। **3.** To revive ; to rouse ; as, to *rally* one's powers or faculty ; পুনরুজ্জীবিত করা ; উদ্দীপ্ত করা, উদ্বুদ্ধ করা, প্রবুদ্ধ করা, জাগরিত করা। ***Noun.*** **1.** The act of rallying or forming into a reorganized body ; reunion for fresh effort ; ছত্রভঙ্গ সৈন্যদল প্রভৃতি পুনরায় একত্রীকরণ ; নবোদ্যমের জন্য পুনঃ সমাগম। **2.** Recovery of health, strength or vigour ; স্বাস্থ্য, শক্তি, তেজঃ, প্রভৃতি পুনঃপ্রাপ্তি। **3.** A set-to in boxing, racket, etc. ; (মুষ্টিযুদ্ধ, আণ্টাল প্রভৃতি খেলায়) আঘাতের দ্রুত বিনিময়।

răl'-lȳ, *v. t.* To attack with raillery ; to banter ; বিদ্রূপবাণ বর্ষণ করা,

বাঙ্গ করা, উপহাস করা, ঠাট্টা করা। **—ing,** *adj.* **—ing-ly,** *adv.*

ăm, *n.* **1.** A male sheep ; ভেড়া, মেষ, মেড়া [Syn. মেঢ্র, উরভ্র, উরণ, উরণক, সংসফাল, সংফাল, মেঠ, হুড়, হুড়ু, এড়ক, মেণ্ড, মেণ্ঢ, মেণ্ঢক, অবি, ঊর্ণায়ু, বৃষ্ণি, রোমশ, লোমশ]। **2.** (*Astron., cap.*) The zodiacal sign Aries ; (জ্যোতিবিজ্ঞান) মেষরাশি। **3.** A warship with a steel-beak at the bow for charging the side of other ships ; also, such a beak ; শত্রুপোতের পার্শ্বভাগে আক্রমণের জন্য অগ্রভাগে ইস্পাতনির্ম্মিত চঞ্চ্বাকৃতি প্রলম্বিত অংশবিশিষ্ট রণপোত ; উক্তরূপ প্রলম্বিত অংশ। **4.** Same as BATTERING RAM. **5.** A hydraulic engine ; জলীয় শক্তি দ্বারা চালিত যন্ত্র। **6.** The falling weight of a pile-driving machine ; খোঁটা বসাইবার যন্ত্রের পতনশীল ভারি অংশ। **7.** The plunger of a hydrostatic press, force-pump, etc. ; জলচাপযন্ত্র, দমকল, প্রভৃতির চাপপ্রদায়ক নিরেট চোঙ্গ। **8.** A rammer ; মুদ্গর, দুরমুষ। **Ram's head**—একপ্রকার অর্কিড ; বুট, ছোলা। **Ram's horn**—মেষশৃঙ্গ ; মৎস্য ধুইবার জন্য পার্শ্বদেশে ছিদ্রবিশিষ্ট বাক্স ; একপ্রকার জাল ; একপ্রকার গুল্ম ; ভারোত্তোলন যন্ত্রে সংলগ্ন একত্রসংশ্লিষ্ট আঁকড়া।

Ram.

m, *v. t. & i.* **1.** To strike against violently ; as, to *ram* one's head against a wall ; (*naut.*) to drive a ram against or through (a ship) ; জোরে আঘাত করা ; (নৌ-বিদ্যা) রণপোতের লৌহময় চঞ্চ্বাকৃতি অগ্রভাগ চালাইয়া দেওয়া। **2.** To beat down as soil etc. into solidity with wooden block etc. ; to make firm as a post etc. by ramming soil round it ; কাঠের মুদ্গর দ্বারা আঘাত করিয়া মাটী প্রভৃতি শক্ত করা ; চারিদিকের মাটী দুরমুষ প্রভৃতি দ্বারা পিটিয়া খোঁটা প্রভৃতি শক্ত করিয়া বসান। **3.** To drive as a pile etc. *down, into,* etc. by heavy blows ; সজোরে আঘাত করিয়া খোঁটা প্রভৃতি বসান। **4.** To force into a place by pressure ; as, to *ram* clothes into a bag ; ঠাসিয়া ঢুকান। **5.** To force in as a charge in a gun ; বন্দুকে বারুদ প্রভৃতি গাদা। **6.** To cram or stuff as with stuffing etc. ; ঠাসা, ভরা। ***Verb i.*** To use a rammer ; দুরমুষ বা মুদ্গর ব্যবহার করা। **Ram′-mer,** *n.* **1.** One that rams or drives ; an instrument for driving anything with force or beating earth into solidity ; তাড়নকারী ; মুদ্গর, দুরমুষ। **2.** A rod for forcing in the charge of a gun ; বন্দুকে বারুদ প্রভৃতি ঠাসিবার শিক, গাদনকাঠি। **Ram-rod**—Same as RAMMER, *n.* 2. **To ram an argument home**—To put sufficient stress on it ; কোন যুক্তির উপর বিশেষ জোর দেওয়া।

Răm-â-dăn′, *n.* The ninth month of a Mohammedan year in which a fasting during daytime on each day is strictly observed ; মোসলমানদিগের রমজান মাস।

rā′-măl, *adj.* (*Bot.*) Of, relating to, or proceeding from a branch ; (উদ্ভিদ্ বিদ্যা) শাখাসম্বন্ধীয়, শাখাস্থ, শাখাপ্রসূত।

răm′-ble (-bl), *v. i.* & *n.* **1.** To walk, ride or sail from place to place without any definite object in view ; to rove ; উদ্দেশ্যবিহীনভাবে ইতস্ততঃ বিচরণ করা ; ইতস্ততঃ পর্য্যটন করা, পরিক্রম করা। **2.** To talk, write or discourse disconnectedly ; অসম্বদ্ধভাবে কথা বলা, অসংলগ্ন প্রলাপ করা, অসংলগ্নভাবে লিখা। ***Noun.*** A going or moving from place to place, without any determinate business ; উদ্দেশ্যবিহীনভাবে ইতস্ততঃ ভ্রমণ, পর্য্যটন, পরিক্রম।

răm′-blêr, *n.* **1.** One ...bles ; পথিক, পর্য্যটক, ভ্র... **2.** One of a climbing grou... roses, esp. the crimson rambl... একপ্রকার রক্তবর্ণ লতানিয়া গোলাপ।

răm′-bling, *adj.* **1.** Roving ; wandering ; বিচরণশীল ; পর্য্যটনশীল। **2.** Desultory ; incoherent, as a talk, etc. ; অসংলগ্ন ; অসম্বদ্ধ ; খাপছাড়া। **3.** Climbing as plants ; লতানিয়া। **4.** Irregularly planned as a street, house, etc. ; বিশৃঙ্খলভাবে পরিকল্পিত। **—ly,** *adv.*

răm′-ĕ-kin, —quin, *ns.* A small slice of bread covered with a mixture of cheese and eggs ; পনীর ও ডিমের মিশ্রদ্বারা আবৃত রুটির টুকরা।

răm-i-fi-cā′-tion, *n.* **1.** Act, or process, of ramifying or branching ; mode of arrangement of branches ; also, the branches of a tree ; শাখাবিন্যাস (সাঃ পঃ) ; শাখাবিন্যাসরীতি ; শাখাসমূহ। **2.** (*Fig.*) A small branch or offshoot from a main stock or channel ; as, the *ramifications* of a river, society, trade, plot, etc. ; (লক্ষণায়) শাখাপ্রশাখা।

răm′-i-fȳ, *v. i.* & *t.* **1.** To shoot out in branches ; to branch out ; শাখায়িত হওয়া ; শাখাবিস্তার হওয়া। **2.** (*Fig.*) To be subdivided ; to send out or have offshoots or branches ; (লক্ষণায়) বিভিন্ন শাখায় বিভক্ত হওয়া ; শাখাপ্রশাখা বিস্তার করা। ***Verb t.*** (Usu. *passive*) To cause to branch out or spread out into branches ; as, railways were *ramified* over the country ; শাখায়িত করা, শাখাবিস্তার করা।

răm′-mish (-ĭsh), *adj.* **1.** Like a ram ; মেষবৎ। **2.** Rank-smelling ; উগ্রগন্ধ। **3.** Lewd ; লম্পট, কামুক।

rā′-mōse, *adj.* Branched ; full of branches ; branching ; শাখান্বিত ; শাখাবহুল ; শাখাবিস্তারী।

rămp, *n.* **1.** A slope ; (esp. in *fortific.*) an inclined road in a

slavery ; উচ্ছেদের অনুকুল মত বা উপায় সমূহ, বিশেষতঃ দাসত্ব-প্রথার উচ্ছেদসাধনের অনুকুল মত বা উপায় সমূহ। **—ist,** *n.* One who favours abolition, esp. of negro slavery ; বিলোপবাদী , বিশেষতঃ দাসত্ব-প্রথার উচ্ছেদ-সাধন-মতাবলম্বী।
(স্থপতিবিজ্ঞান) অসমতোরণের পরস্পর-বিপরীত স্তম্ভদ্বয়ের উচ্চতার প্রভেদ। **3.** A bend or slope usually in the vertical plane where a hand-rail, coping, etc. change their direction ; প্রাকারশীর্ষ, সোপান পংক্তির পার্শ্বস্থ গরাদে, প্রভৃতি যে প্রবণ বা আনত স্থলে দিক্ পরিবর্ত্তন করে। **On the ramp** — Wild ; excited ; অদম্য ; উত্তেজিত, উন্মত্ত।

rămp, *v. i.* & *t.* **1.** (Of a lion etc.) To stand with forelegs raised as in anger or excitement ; to be in, or assume, a threatening posture ; ক্রুদ্ধ বা উত্তেজিত হইয়া সম্মুখের পদদ্বয় উত্তোলনপূর্ব্বক দণ্ডায়মান হওয়া, উদ্ধৃতাগ্রপাদভাবে দণ্ডায়মান হওয়া ; ভীষণমূর্ত্তি ধারণ করা, ভয়ঙ্কর ভাব ধারণ করা। **2.** (*Now usu. facet.*) To move or act furiously ; to rage or storm ; প্রচণ্ডবেগে অগ্রসর হওয়া, ক্রোধান্বিত হইয়া কার্য্য করা ; তর্জ্জনগর্জ্জন করা। **3.** (*Arch.*) To ascend or descend to a different level as a wall ; (প্রাচীরাদি) বিভিন্ন তলে উঠা বা নামা। ***Verb t.*** (*Fortif.*) To furnish with a ramp or sloping way ; (দুর্গ) তির্য্যগ্‌বর্ত্ম সমন্বিত করা।

rămp'-age (-āj), *n.* & *v. i.* A state of passion or excitement ; violent conduct ; ক্রোধোন্মত্ততা, উন্মত্ততা ; উগ্র আচরণ। ***Verb i.*** **(ram-page')** **1.** To behave violently ; to rage or storm ; উগ্র আচরণ করা ; তর্জ্জনগর্জ্জন করা। **2.** To act or move wildly or excitedly ; অদম্যভাবে বা উত্তেজিতভাবে কার্য্য করা বা সঞ্চরণ করা। **Ram-pa'-geous,** *adj.* **Ram-pa'-geous-ly,** *adv.* **Ram-pa'-geous-ness,** *n.* **To be on the rampage**—To be in an excited or drunken state ; উত্তেজিত অবস্থায় থাকা, মাতাল অবস্থায় থাকা।

rămp'-ănt, *adj.* **1.** Ramping or standing on hind legs as lion, esp. in hearaldry ; as, lion *rampant* ; উদ্ধৃতাগ্রপদ (বিশেষভাবে কুলবিদ্যায় সিংহসম্বন্ধে), উন্নতচরণ (হিতঃ)। **2.** Violent or extravagant in action, manner or opinion ; unchecked ; aggressive ; as, a *rampant* theorist ; prevailing ; as, superstition is *rampant* among them ; অদম্য, অনিয়ন্ত্রিত, উদগ্র, উৎসিক্ত ; নিরবগ্রহ ; আক্রমণশীল ; প্রচলিত। **3.** Rank in growth as plants ; অতিবর্দ্ধনশীল। **4.** (Of arch etc.) With one abutment higher than the other ; (তোরণাদি সম্বন্ধ) একটী অবলম্বনস্তম্ভ অপরটী অপেক্ষা উচ্চতর। **—an-cy,** *n.*

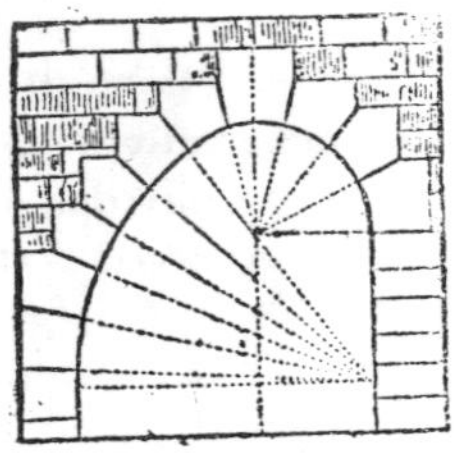

Rampantarch.

—ant-ly, *adv.* **Rampant arch**—যে তোরণের এক অবলম্বনস্তম্ভ অপর স্তম্ভ অপেক্ষা উচ্চতর, অসমতোরণ।

răm'-pârt, *n.* & *v. t.* **1.** A mound of earth around a place to resist canon-shot ; প্রাকার, বপ্র, [Syn. বরণ, শাল, চক্রগ্রহণী, চয়, ধূলি-কুট্টিম, ধূলি-কেদার, প্রগণ্ডী (মঃ ভাঃ)]। **2.** (*Fig.*) A defence ; (লক্ষণায়) আশ্রয়প্রাকার, আশ্রয়দুর্গ। ***Verb t.*** **1.** To protect, or fortify, with or as with a rampart ; বপ্র বা প্রাকার দ্বারা রক্ষা করা।

răm'-pi-ŏn, *n.* A kind of b[illegible] flower with edible tuber[illegible] roots ; একপ্রকার ঘণ্টাকৃতি পুষ্প।

răm-pīre, *n.* & *v. t.* (*Archa*[illegible] Same as RAMPART (which see).

răm'-shăck-le (-l), *adj.* D[illegible] jointed ; in a crazy state ; rickety ; as, a *ramshackle* house or carriage ; সন্ধিচ্যুত ; ভগ্নাবস্থ ; নড়বড়ে।

răm'-sŏn, *n.* A species of garlic ; এক জাতীয় লশুন।

răn. *Past tense* of RUN.

răn, *n.* A certain length of twine ; নির্দ্দিষ্ট দৈর্ঘ্যের সুতলী।

rance (răns), *n.* A kind of fine stone or marble ; একপ্রকার সুচিক্কণ মর্ম্মর পাষাণ বা অন্য প্রকার প্রস্তর।

rănch, *n.* & *v. i.* **1.** An establishment for rearing cattle, horse[illegible] etc. ; গোষ্ঠ, ব্রজ। **2.** A large farm[illegible] as, a fruit-*ranch* ; সুবিস্তীর্ণ কৃষিক্ষেত্র[illegible] ***Verb i.*** To conduct a ranc[illegible] গোষ্ঠ বা বিস্তীর্ণ কৃষিক্ষেত্র পরিচালনা কর[illegible]

răn'-cid, *adj.* Having a ra[illegible] smell or taste ; as, *rancid* butte[illegible] গুমসা, বিস্বাদ, কড়ুয়া, বেসেড়া, উগ্রগ[illegible] উগ্রগন্ধি। **—cid'-i-ty, —ness,** *ns.*

ran'-cour (răng-kêr), *n.* Malice[illegible] malignity ; inveterate hatred[illegible] বিদ্বেষ ; অসূয়া, হিংসা ; বদ্ধমূল বিদ্বে[illegible] **—cor-ous,** *adj.* Deeply mali[illegible]nant ; malicious ; spiteful ; hateful ; অতিদ্রোহী ; বিদ্বেষপরায়ণ বিদ্বে[illegible] অসূয়াপরবশ, বিদ্বেষকলুষিত ; হিংস্র[illegible] ঘৃণ্য। **—cor-ous-ly,** *adv.*

rănd, *n.* **1.** (*Dial.*) A bor[illegible] edge or margin ; (উপভা[illegible] প্রান্ত, কিনারা। **2.** (*Shoe-mak*[illegible]) A strip of leather put on be[illegible] the lifts of the heel ; a thin ir[illegible] sole for a sho[illegible] ; (জুতা তৈরি) [illegible] তলি এবং গোড়ালির মধ্যে যে চা[illegible] নিবিষ্ট করা হয় ; জুতার সুখত[illegible] **3.** (S. Africa) Highlands [illegible] either side of a river vall[illegible]

-দক্ষিণ আফ্রিকা) নদীতটের উভয় 'ধ্বরে উচ্চ ভূমি। **The Rand**—ohannesburg; জোহানেসবার্গ।

a'-dăn, *n.* A mode of rowing or three men; a boat propelled y such rowing; তিন ব্যক্তির দাঁড় ানিবার জন্য এক প্রকার প্রণালী; ঐরূপ প্রণালীতে দাঁড় টানা।

răn'-dŏm, *adv.* & *n.* With three horses harnessed to a vehicle tandem; অগ্রপশ্চাৎক্রমে সংযোজিত অশ্বত্রয়বিশিষ্ট। *Noun.* A carriage or team so driven; অগ্রপশ্চাৎক্রমে সংযোজিত অশ্বত্রয়দ্বারা বাহিত শকট, ঐরূপে সংযোজিত অশ্বত্রয়।

răn'-dom (-dŭm), *n.* & *adj.* A haphazard course or progress; caprice, (esp. in the phrase *at random*); যদৃচ্ছ আচরণ অগড়বগড়, অনিয়ত (হিঃ কোঃ); খেয়াল। *Adj.* 1. Acting, done, or made, without definite direction, aim or purpose; haphazard; left to chance; যদৃচ্ছাক্রমে কৃত বা ়সাধিত; উদ্দেশ্যবিহীন; দৈবকৃত, ৴বন্যস্ত। 2. (*Masonry*) With ɜones of irregular size and hape; (ইমারত কাজে) অসম ৰারতনের প্রস্তর রচিত। **—ly,** *adv.* Rare). **At random**—Without lefinite direction, rule or me-hod; at haphazard; without any aim or purpose; heedlessly; ৃচ্ছাক্রমে; উদ্দেশ্যবিহীনভাবে; লক্ষ্যহীন-ভাবে; অসতর্কভাবে।

n'-dy, *adj.* 1. (*Scot.*) Boister-ɜs; lusty; (স্কটলণ্ড) প্রচণ্ড, প্রবল; ৰান। 2. (*Dial.*, of cattle etc.) borderly; wild; উচ্ছৃঙ্খল; অদম্য। Lustful; কামুক, লম্পট। **—di-ɪs,** *n.*

ra

v

a

rɛ

, *p. t.* of RING.

ge (rānj), *v. t.* & *i.* 1. To ce in regular lines or ranks; বদ্ধভাবে সজ্জিত করা, সারি সারি া সাজান। 2. To dispose tematically; to class; সুবিন্যস্ত করা; শ্রেণীবদ্ধ করা। 3. To place as an individual among others esp. by way of espousing a cause, joining a party, etc., (usu. *reflex.* or *passive*); as, they *ranged* themselves on each side; পক্ষভুক্ত করা, শ্রেণীভুক্ত করা, দলভুক্ত করা। 4. To rove over or through; as, to *range* the fields; পরিভ্রমণ করা, পর্য্যটন করা। 5. To sail along or about (a coast, sea); পাইল তুলিয়া অগ্রসর হওয়া বা পরিক্রম করা। 6. To determine the elevation necessary for (a gun) for throwing a projectile at a given distance; কোন নির্দ্দিষ্ট দূরত্বে গোলা নিক্ষেপের জন্য (কামান) কতটা উচ্চে স্থাপিত করিতে হইবে তাহা নির্ণয় করা। 7. To train as a telescope; দূরদর্শন-যন্ত্র ঠিক করিয়া বসান। *Verb i.* 1. To wander; to roam; পর্য্যটন করা; পরিভ্রমণ করা। 2. To run about as a hunting dog seeking game; (শিকারী কুকুর প্রভৃতির পক্ষে) শিকারের অন্বেষণে ইতস্ততঃ ধাবিত হওয়া। 3. To pass or extend in a certain direction; as, to *range* east and west; to vary from point to point; as, the temperature *ranged* through 7° F.; নির্দ্দিষ্টদিকে চলা বা প্রসারিত হওয়া; উঠা নামা করা। 4. (*Gunnery*) To have range; to traverse; as, the projectile *ranged* over 7 miles; পাল্লা থাকা; অতিক্রম করা। 5. To be placed in order; to be ranked or class-ed; to rank; to admit of classi-fication; as, he *ranges* with the great waiters; শ্রেণীবদ্ধভাবে বিন্যস্ত হওয়া; শ্রেণীবদ্ধ হওয়া; পদমর্য্যাদানুসারে অবস্থিত হওয়া; শ্রেণীবিভাগযোগ্য হওয়া। **Ranging fancy**—অস্থির প্রণয়। **To range oneself**—To settle down *e.g.* by marry-ing; to take up a definite posi-tion in society; বিবাহের পর গার্হস্থ্য-জীবন আরম্ভ করা; সমাজে নির্দ্দিষ্ট স্থান গ্রহণ করা।

range (rānj), *n.* 1. A series of things in a line; a row; as, a *range* of buildings or moun-tains; শ্রেণী, রাজি; পংক্তি, সারি। 2. Direction; as, he kept the buoys in *range* with the light-house; দিক্। 3. An excursion; a ramble; পরিভ্রমণ; পর্য্যটন। 4. A region in which cattle or sheep may pasture; a stretch of hunting ground; গোচারণভূমি, গোষ্ঠ; মৃগয়াভূমি। 5. A piece of ground with targets for shoot-ing; চাঁদমারির স্থান। 6. The extent of country over which an animal or plant is distributed or found; an area concerned with something; যে স্থানের মধ্যে কোন জন্তু বা উদ্ভিদ্ পাওয়া যায়; ক্ষেত্র। 7. Reach; scope; sphere; as, *range* of voice, topics or thought; সীমা, গোচরতা, আয়ত্তি; প্রসর, আশয়; ক্ষেত্র। 8. Limits of variation; as, the *range* of the barometer readings is about 2 inches; উত্থানপতনের সীমা। 9. The distance to which a shot or other projectile is, or may be, thrown;

Range.

as, the *range* of a gun or pro-jectile; the space between a gun etc. and the objective; পাল্লা, বিষ

(সৌমিত্রেরপি পত্রিণামবিষয়ে—উত্তরঃ) ; কামান প্রভৃতি ও ইহাদের লক্ষ্যস্থলের মধ্যবর্ত্তী স্থান। 10. A kitchen grate and cooking apparatus ; উনানের ঝাঁঝরি এবং চুল্লি। **Range-finder**—যে বস্তুর উপর গুলি করিতে হইবে তাহার দূরত্ব নির্ণয়ের জন্য যন্ত্রবিশেষ। **Range of sight**—দৃষ্টিপথ।

rāng′-ėr, *n.* 1. One who ranges ; পর্য্যটক। 2. The keeper of a royal park or forest ; রাজোদ্যান-রক্ষক, রাজকীয় বনরক্ষক, অরণ্যপাল, বনপাল। 3. (*Pl.*) A body of mounted troops, (esp. the Connaught Rangers—the name of a British regiment) ; অশ্বারোহী সৈন্যদল। **—ship**, *n.*

rank (răngk), *n.* 1. A row ; a line ; শ্রেণী, সারি ; পংক্তি। 2. A line of soldiers ; সৈন্যপংক্তি। 3. Array ; order ; as, to keep *rank* ; ব্যূহ ; শৃঙ্খল। 4. A social class ; as, men of all *ranks* ; শ্রেণী। 5. Degree of dignity, eminence or excellence ; grade ; as, a poet of the first *rank* ; মর্য্যাদা, সমুন্নতি বা উৎকর্ষের মাত্রা ; শ্রেণী। 6. Grade of official position ; as, the *rank* of captain or general ; পদবী, পদ। 7. High grade or degree ; distinction ; high social position ; as, a man of *rank* ; উচ্চ শ্রেণী · খ্যাতি ; উচ্চ সামাজিক মর্য্যাদা, আভিজাত্য। 8. A place in a scale ; as, the first *rank* must be given to the rose; স্থান। **In the ranks**—Serving as a common soldier ; সাধারণ সৈনিকরূপে নিযুক্ত। **Persons of rank**—Members of the nobility ; সম্ভ্রান্তশ্রেণীর লোকগণ। **Rank and fashion** — High society ; সম্ভ্রান্তসমাজ, উচ্চশ্রেণী। **The ranks, The rank and file**—Common soldiers including corporals ; সাধারণ সৈন্যগণ। Lower classes or ordinary undistinguished people ; নিম্নশ্রেণী, সাধারণশ্রেণী। **To break rank**—To fail to keep in line ; শ্রেণীভঙ্গ হওয়া। **To keep rank**—To remain in line ; শ্রেণীবদ্ধভাবে থাকা। **To rise from the ranks**—To get promotion to the commissioned ranks from the position of a common soldier or sergeant ; সাধারণ সৈনিকের পদ হইতে সৈনিককর্ম্মচারীর পদে উন্নীত হওয়া। To become a self-made man ; স্বকীয় চেষ্টা দ্বারা বিদ্যা, বিত্ত ও যশোলাভ করা।

rank (răngk), *v. t.* & *i.* 1. To place or arrange in a line as soldiers, etc. ; সারিসারি করিয়া স্থাপন করা। 2. To class or classify ; to range ; শ্রেণীবিভাগ করা ; শ্রেণীবদ্ধ করা। ***Verb i.*** 1. To have rank or place ; as, Japan *ranks* among the great powers ; স্থান থাকা, (কোন কিছু বা কাহারো সহিত) শ্রেণীভুক্ত হওয়া। 2. (*Mil.*) To march ; (সামরিক-শাস্ত্র) যুদ্ধযাত্রা করা।

rank (răngk), *adj.* 1. Luxuriant or coarse in growth ; over productive ; choked with, or apt to produce, weeds ; প্রচুর বর্দ্ধনশীল ; অতিবর্দ্ধনশীল, অতিবর্দ্ধিষ্ণু, অতি উৎপাদনশীল ; আগাছা দ্বারা আচ্ছাদিত, আগাছা উৎপাদনশীল। 2. Rancid ; foul-smelling ; গুমসা ; দুর্গন্ধ। 3. Foul ; loathsome ; corrupt ; দুষ্ট ; ঘৃণ্য, ন্যক্কারজনক ; দূষিত। 4. Extreme ; flagrant ; gross ; virulent ; as, *rank* pedantry, treason, nonsense, poison, etc. ; নিতান্ত ; জলন্ত ; উৎকট ; ঘোর, উগ্র। **Rank′-ly**, *adv.* **Rank′-ness**, *n.*

rank′-ėr (răngk-), *n.* A soldier in the ranks ; esp. a commissioned officer promoted from the ranks ; সাধারণ সৈন্য ; সাধারণ সৈনিকের পদ হইতে সৈনিককর্ম্মচারীর পদে উন্নীত ব্যক্তি।

ran′-kle (răng-kl), *v. i.* 1. To fester as a sore or wound (*archaic*) ; জ্বালাকর হওয়া, যন্ত্রণাদায়ক হওয়া (অপ্রচ)। 2. To be bitter or painful, as envy, disappointment, etc. or their cause ; যন্ত্রণাদায়ক হওয়া, ক্লেশকর হওয়া। **To rankle in one's bosom** or **mind**—বেদনাজনক স্মৃতি মনে জাগা।

răn′-săck, *v. t.* 1. To search thoroughly ; as, to *ransack* a place, one's pocket, one's conscience, etc. ; তন্ন তন্ন করিয়া অনুসন্ধান করা, পুঙ্খানুপুঙ্খরূপে তল্লাস করা, পাঁতি পাঁতি করিয়া খুঁজা। 2. To pillage or plunder ; লুণ্ঠন করা, লুঠ করা, লুঠপাট করা, লুঠতরাজ করা।

răn′-som (-sŭm), *n.* & *v. t.* 1. Release from captivity by payment ; money or value paid for release from captivity or bondage ; অর্থপ্রদানে বন্ধনদশা হইতে মুক্তি ; নিষ্ক্রয় (cf. দদৌ দত্তং সমুদ্রেণ পীতেনেবাত্মনিষ্ক্রয়ং—রঘুবংশ)। 2. A blackmail ; a sum, etc. exacted in return for privilege or immunity ; as, graduated income-tax etc. are no more than a fair *ransom* paid by the rich ; ভয় প্রদর্শনে গৃহীত অর্থ ; কোনরূপ সুবিধা, অধিকার প্রদান বা দায় হইতে অব্যাহতি দেওয়ার জন্য যে অর্থ আদায় করা হয়। ***Verb t.*** 1. To deliver or release by paying a price ; to buy liberty ; অর্থপ্রদানে উদ্ধার করা ; অর্থদ্বারা স্বাধীনতা ক্রয় করা। 2. To release on payment of ransom ; to hold at ransom ; to exact ransom from ; নিষ্ক্রয় প্রদানে মুক্ত করা ; নিষ্ক্রয় আদায়ের জন্য আটক রাখা ; নিষ্ক্রয় আদায় করা। 3. (*Rare*) To expiate ; (ক্বচিদ্ব্যবহৃত) প্রায়শ্চিত্ত করা। **—less**, *adj.* **Ransom-bill, —bond**—নিষ্ক্রয় প্রদানের জন্য দায়িত্বগ্রহণ, বিশেষতঃ বন্দীকৃত জাহাজের নিষ্ক্রয় প্রদানের দায়িত্বগ্রহণ। **To hold one to or at ransom**—To be willing to release for a ransom ; নিষ্ক্রয় পাইলে মুক্তি প্রদানে ইচ্ছুক থাকা।

răn̄t, *v. i., t.* & *n.* **1.** To talk, speak or declaim in extravagant or bombastic language ; to recite or declaim theatrically ; বাগাড়ম্বরপূর্ণ ভাষায় কথা বলা, বাগাড়ম্বরপূর্ণ ভাষায় বক্তৃতা করা ; অভিনেতার মত ভঙ্গীতে আবৃত্তি বা বক্তৃতা করা। **2.** To preach noisily ; উচ্চৈঃস্বরে ধর্ম্মপ্রচার করা। ***Noun.*** A ranting or bombastic speech ; vehement language ; empty turgid talk ; বাগাড়ম্বরপূর্ণ বক্তৃতা ; তীব্রভাষা ; বাগাড়ম্বর, শব্দাড়ম্বর।

ră-nŭn′-cŭ-lŭs, *n.* A genus of flowering plants; পুষ্পতরুর গণবিশেষ।

ranz-des-vaches, (*F.*), *n.* A melody played by Swiss herdsmen ; সুইজরলণ্ডের গোপগীতি।

răp, *n., v. t.* & *i.* **1.** A light smart blow ; a knock ; ঠুকনি; ঘা, ঠক্‌ঠক্। **2.** A sound like that of knocking ascribed to mediumistic agencies as at spiritualistic seances ; একপ্রকার ঠক্‌ঠক্ বা খট্‌খট্ শব্দ—যাহা প্রেততাত্ত্বিকদিগের অধিবেশনে প্রেতাত্মাদ্বারা কৃত বলিয়া মনে করা হয়। ***Verb t.*** **1.** To strike smartly as one's knuckles ; কাহারো মুষ্টিবদ্ধ অঙ্গুলির সন্ধি প্রভৃতিতে ঠক করিয়া আঘাত করা। **2.** To utter abruptly or impetuously, (with *out*) ; as, to *rap out* an oath or pun ; সহসা বা আবেগের সহিত উচ্চারণ করা। **3.** (Of spirits) To express as a message, word, etc., by raps, (with *out*) ; (প্রেতাত্মাসম্বন্ধে) খট্‌খট্ শব্দদ্বারা কোন বার্ত্তা বা শব্দ প্রকাশ করা। ***Verb i.*** To knock ; to make or produce a sound called a rap ; ঘা দেওয়া; ঠক্‌ঠক্ করা। **To rap out**—See RAP, *v. t.*, 2 & 3. **To rap over the knuckles**—To strike smartly over the knuckles of a boy etc. by way of punishment ; (*fig.*) to censure sharply ; অঙ্গুলী সন্ধির উপর ঠক করিয়া ঘা দেওয়া; তীব্র তিরস্কার করা।

răp, *v. t.* **1.** To snatch away ; to take by force or violence ; কাড়িয়া নেওয়া ; বলপূর্ব্বক গ্রহণ করা। **2.** To transport out of oneself ; to affect with ecstasy or rapture ; as, *rapt* into admiration ; আত্মহারা করা ; হর্ষোন্মত্ত করা, আনন্দবিহ্বল করা। **To rap and ren, To rap and rend**—To seize and plunder ; to snatch by violence ; আক্রমণ করিয়া লুঠপাট করা ; বলপূর্ব্বক কাড়িয়া লওয়া। To get together by fair means or foul ; to procure at any cost ; সদুপায়েই হউক বা অসদুপায়েই হউক একত্র করা ; যে কোন উপায়েই হউক সংগ্রহ করা।

răp, *n.* A skein of yarn containing about 120 yards ; ১২০ গজ সূতার লুটী।

răp, *n.* An atom ; the least bit ; as, he does not care a *rap* for it ; পরমাণু ; তিল, অণু, কণা।

ră-pā′-cious (-shŭs), *adj.* Greedy of plunder ; grasping ; extortionate ; avaricious ; লুব্ধ, লুব্ধক ; গ্রাহী ; পীড়নাত্মক ; গৃধ্নু। **–ly,** *adv.* **–pac′-i-ty,** *n.* The quality of being rapacious ; greediness ; dispositions to plundering ; লুব্ধতা ; গৃধ্নুতা ; লুণ্ঠন প্রবণতা।

rāpe, *v. t.* & *n.* **1.** (*Poet.*) To take away by force ; (কবিতায়) হরণ করা। **2.** To ravish or violate as a woman ; বলাৎকার করা, ধর্ষণ করা, সতীত্ব নষ্ট করা, স্ত্রীলোকের ধর্ম্মনষ্ট করা। ***Noun.*** **1.** (*Poet.*) Act of carrying away by force ; "The *Rape* of the lock" ; (কবিতায়) হরণ। **2.** Carnal knowledge of a woman against her will ; বলাৎকার, ধর্ষণ, সতীত্বনাশ।

rāpe, *n.* Any of the six administrative divisions of Sussex ; ইংলণ্ডের অন্তঃপাতী Sussex প্রদেশের বিভাগবিশেষ।

rāpe, *n.* **1.** A kind of plant grown as food for sheep ; শ্বেতসর্ষপ, রাইসর্ষপ। **2.** A plant from the seeds of which oil is made ; সর্ষপ গাছ। **Rape-cake**—সরিষার খইল। **Rape-oil**—সর্ষপ তৈল, সরিষার তৈল। **Wild rape**—বন সরিষা।

rāpe, *n.* The pomace of grapes left after wine-making, used esp. in vinegar-making ; মদ্য নিষ্পীড়নের পর আঙ্গুরের যে ছোবড়া থাকে—ইহা বিশেষভাবে সির্কা প্রস্তুতে ব্যবহৃত হয়।

Răph-ă-ĕl-esque′ (-ĕsk), **Răff–,** *adjs.* In the style of Raphael ; ইতালীর সুপ্রসিদ্ধ চিত্রকর র‍্যাফেলপ্রবর্ত্তিত চিত্রাঙ্কণধারানুযায়ী।

Raphanus sativus—মূলা (বেলঃ)।

răp′-id, *adj.* & *n.* **1.** Swift ; quick ; fast ; as, a *rapid* brook ; ক্ষিপ্র, শীঘ্র ; ত্বরিত, তূর্ণ, ত্বরান্বিত ; দ্রুত, দ্রুতগামী, শীঘ্রগ, বেগমান, বেগবতী। **2.** Acting, happening or done, quickly ; শীঘ্রকারী, শীঘ্রসংঘটিত বা সম্পাদিত। **3.** Descending steeply as a slope ; পাতুক। ***Noun.*** A sudden or steep descent in a river-bed, where the current is swift ; নদীর যে অংশে অতিদ্রুতবেগে স্রোতঃ বহিতে থাকে, নদীপ্রপাত (সাঃ পঃ)।

ră′-pĭ-ĕr, *n.* A small sword used only for thrusting ; কিরিচ, [Syn. নিস্ত্রিংশ]। **Rapier-thrust**—The thrust of a rapier ; esp. (*fig.*) a delicate or witty repartee ; কিরিচের খোঁচা; (বিশেষতঃ লক্ষণায়) চটুল রহস্য, সরস উক্তি।

răp′-īne, *n.* Plundering ; pillage ; robbery ; লুণ্ঠন ; লুঠপাট, লুঠতরাজ ; দস্যুবৃত্তি।

răp-pa-ree′ (-ă-rē), *n.* An Irish irregular soldier or freebooter esp. of the 17th century ; আইরিশ জাতীয় অনিয়মিত সৈন্য বা লুঠেরা।

răp-pee′ (-pē), *n.* A coarse kind of snuff ; একপ্রকার অপকৃষ্ট নস্য।

răp-pōrt′, *n.* Relationship ; connexion ; as, to be in *rapport* with ; সম্পর্ক ; সম্বন্ধ, যোগ, সাযুজ্য (হিঃ কোঃ)।

rapprochement, (*F.*), *n.* Coming or being drawn near or together; re-establishment or recommencement of cordial relations esp. between States; সমীপাগমন, সন্নিকর্ষ, সন্নিকর্ষণ; পুনরায় সখ্য বা প্রীতিস্থাপন, বিশেষতঃ রাষ্ট্রসমূহের মধ্যে পুনরায় মৈত্রীস্থাপন, পুনর্মৈত্রীপ্রতিষ্ঠা।

ră-scăl'-lion (-yŭn), *n.* A rascal; a rogue; লুচ্চা, পাজী, বদমায়েস; দুর্ব্বৃত্ত।

răpt, *p. p.* & *adj.* **1.** Carried away bodily or in spirit from the earth, from life, etc.; সশরীরে নীত, লোকান্তরিত। **2.** Transported with love, delight, etc.; enraptured; আত্মহারা; হর্ষোন্মত্ত, আনন্দবিহ্বল। **3.** Absorbed; intent; as, he listened with *rapt* attention; অভিনিবিষ্ট; একাগ্রচিত্ত, সমাহিত।

Răp-tō'-rēs, *n.* The order of birds of prey; শিকারী পক্ষীর শ্রেণী।

răp-tō'-ri-ăl, *adj.* & *n.* Of, or relating to, the Raptores; living on prey as birds of prey; adapted to seize prey, as legs etc.; শিকারী জন্তুসম্বন্ধীয়; শিকারজীবী, শিকারী; শিকারোপযোগী। ***Noun.*** A bird of prey; শিকারী পক্ষী।

răp'-tūre, *n.* **1.** Extreme delight; ecstasy; transport; enthusiasm; পরমানন্দ, পরমহর্ষ, পরমসুখ, পরমপ্রমোদ (উজ্জ্বলঃ), প্রহর্ষ, রসোন্মত্ততা (রবীঃ), সংরাধন (বেদান্তঃ), হর্ষোন্মাদ, দিব্যোন্মাদ; সুখোন্মাদনা, হর্ষসম্মোহ, আনন্দাবেশ, হর্ষবিহ্বলতা; প্রহর্ষ, উল্লাস, মহোল্লাস; উন্মাদনা। **2.** An expression of ecstasy; a rhapsody; পরমানন্দপ্রকাশ; প্রেমধ্বনি। **–tur-ous,** *adj.* Feeling, or expressing, rapture; ecstatic; হর্ষাকুল, আনন্দবিহ্বল; রসোন্মত্ত। **–tur-ous-ly,** *adv.* **Raptures**—Vehement pleasure or the expression of it; পরমানন্দ, পরমানন্দ প্রকাশ। **To be in or go into raptures**—To be enthusiastic; to talk enthusiastically: পরমোৎসাহী হওয়া; পরম উৎসাহের সহিত বলা।

răp'-tūred, *adj.* Transported; enraptured; in ecstasy; আত্মহারা; আনন্দবিহ্বল; হর্ষোন্মত্ত, প্রহৃষ্ট, হর্ষাকুল, রসোন্মত্ত।

rā'-ră—ā'-vis, *n.* A rarity; an extraordinary or unusually excellent person or thing; দুষ্প্রাপ্য বস্তু, আজব জিনিষ; অসাধারণ বস্তু, অসাধারণ লোক।

rāre, *adj.* **1.** Not dense or thick; as, the *rare* atmosphere of mountain tops; বিরল, অঘন, অগাঢ়। **2.** (*Rare*) Thinly scattered; (ক্বচিদ্ ব্যবহৃত) বিরল। **3.** Seldom found or occurring; unusual; uncommon; অল্পপ্রয়োগ, দুর্ল্লভ, দুষ্প্রাপ্য, দুর্ঘট; বিরল; অসাধারণ। **4.** Unusually excellent; remarkably good; very amusing; অপূর্ব্ব; চমৎকার; অতি আমোদজনক। **Rare'-ly,** *adv.* **Rare'-ness,** *n.*

rāre'-bit, *n.* Same as WELSH RABBIT.

rar'-ee-show (-ē-shō), *n.* A show carried about in a box; a peep-show; any show or spectacle; বাক্সের ভিতর যে সব ছবি প্রভৃতি প্রদর্শনের জন্য নেওয়া হয়; একপ্রকার বাক্স—যাহার ক্ষুদ্র ছিদ্রের ভিতর দিয়া ছবি প্রভৃতি দেখিতে হয়; দৃশ্য।

răr'-ē-fȳ, *v. t.* & *i.* **1.** To make rare or less dense as air etc.; বিরলতাপাদন করা, তনুতাপাদন করা। **2.** To purify or refine as one's nature etc.; to make subtle as an idea etc.; বিশোধিত করা, পরিষ্কার করা। ***Verb i.*** To become less thick or dense; বিরল হওয়া, অঘন হওয়া। **–fac'-tion, –fi-ca'-tion,** *ns.* Act of rarifying; state of being rarified; বিরলীকরণ, বিরলতাপাদন, তনুকরণ; বিরলতা। **–fac'-tive,** *adj.*

răr'-i-tȳ, *n.* **1.** State of being rare; thinness; বিরলতা; তনুতা। **2.** State of being uncommon or unusually excellent; অপূর্ব্বতা, দুর্লভতা, চমৎকারিত্ব। **3.** A rare or uncommon thing; something valued as being rare; দুর্লভ বস্তু, অপূর্ব্ব বস্তু; অসাধারণ বস্তু।

Rasbora elanga—এলঙ্গ (গুপ্তঃ)।

răs'-căl, *n.* & *adj.* A scoundrel; a rogue; a knave (*often jocularly to a child etc.*); as, "You, lucky *rascal*!"; দুর্বৃত্ত, দুরাত্মা, নচ্ছার, দুষ্টু (*colloq.*); ধূর্ত্ত, শঠ; প্রবঞ্চক। ***Adj.*** Of, or relating to, the rabble; low; mean; ইতরজন সম্বন্ধীয়; ইতর; নীচ। **–cal'-i-ty, –dom, –ism,** *ns.* **–ly,** *adv.* **The rascal rout**—The common people; সাধারণ লোক।

rase (rāz), *v. t.* See RAZE.

răsh, *n.* An eruption on the skin with little or no elevation; ব্রণ, কণ্ডু, চুলকণা, পীড়কা।

răsh, *adj.* Hasty; overbold; reckless; acting, or done, without deliberation or caution; হঠকারী; ডাঙ্গপেটা (*colloq.*); অবিমৃশ্যকারী, অসমীক্ষ্যকারী, অপরিণামদর্শী, দুঃসাহসিক, গোঁয়াড়; অগ্রপশ্চাৎ বিবেচনা না করিয়া কৃত। **Rash'-ly,** *adv.* Hastily; recklessly; without deliberation or caution; অবিমৃশ্যকারিতার সহিত; বেপরোয়াভাবে; অগ্রপশ্চাৎ না ভাবিয়া। **Rash'-ness,** *n.*

răsh'-ēr, *n.* A thin slice of bacon or ham; শূকর মাংসের ফালি।

Ră-sō'-rēs, *n., pl.* Gallinae; ঘর্ষকপদী (প্রঃ বাঃ)।

ră-sō'-ri-ăl, *adj.* Belonging to an order of birds which scrapes the ground, for their food, as hen; ঘর্ষকপদিসম্পর্কীয়।

răsp, *v. t., i.* & *n.* **1.** To file with a rasp; to scrape roughly; মোটা দানাদার উখাদ্বারা মসৃণ করা; চাঁচা। **2.** (*Fig.*) To grate harshly upon; to offend or irritate; as, to *rasp* a person or his temper or feelings; (লক্ষণায়) কড়কড় করা; রুষ্ট করা, বিরক্ত করা, জ্বালাতন করা। 3. To remove by scraping, (with *off, away*); চাঁচিয়া ফেলা। ***Verb i.*** To rub or grate; to make a grating sound; ঘষা, ঘষিয়া পালিশ করা; কড়কড় শব্দ করা। ***Noun.*** A coarse species of file with separate teeth; একপ্রকার মোটা দানাদার উখা।

răs'-pă-tō-rŷ, *adj.* A rasp esp. for scraping bones in surgery; একপ্রকার উখা, বিশেষতঃ হাড় চাঁচিবার জন্য ডাক্তারদিগের একপ্রকার উখা।

rasp'-ber-ry (răz-bĕr-ĭ), *n.* The fruit of a plant allied to the bramble, this plant; বিলাতী গৌরী ফল, বিলাতী গৌরী ফলের গাছ। [French *Framboise*; Germ. *Himbeere*; Ital. *Mora di rovo*; Russ. *Malina*; Turk. *Aghaj-chileghi.*] **Indian raspberry**—(*Rubus lasiocarpus*); গৌরীফল, পুকুনা (হিন্দী), পাকানিয়া (Kaghan), আখি [Himalayan raspberry—(*Rubus purpureus*) (of Kulu)] [নীলগিরি মহীশূর, সিংহল ও হিমালয়ে পাওয়া যায়।] **Raspberry vinegar**—একপ্রকার পানক। **As plentiful as raspberry**—হাটে মাঠে পাওয়া যায়।

rasse (răs), *n.* A kind of civet cat; একপ্রকার গন্ধগোকুলা।

răt, *n.* & *v. i.* 1. rodent; ইঁদুর, ইন্দুর, মূষিক। [Syn. মূষীক, মূষিকা, মূষীকা, মুষ্ক, মুষ্কা, মূষী, মুষ [ঋক্ cf. Gk. μῦς (mus), Lat. *Mus*; Russ. *Mysh'*; Germ. *Mûs*; Eng. *Mouse*; Pers. موش (*mush*)]; উন্দুর, বজ্রদন্ত, আখু, ধান্যারি, ভিত্তিখাতন, ভিত্তিপাতন, বজ্রদংশন, উন্দুরু (সুশ্রুঃ), উন্দুরু, বিলেশয়, বিলকারী, বিলবাস, বিলবাসী, তুটুম, মহিষ্কিক, আখনিক, খনক।] 2. (*Polit.*) One who deserts his party esp. in adversity; a turncoat; স্বদলত্যাগী ব্যক্তি, বিশেষতঃ যে ব্যক্তি দুঃসময়ে নিজ দল ত্যাগ করে; স্বপক্ষত্যাগী ব্যক্তি। 3. A workman who declines to join strike, works in a striker's place and accepts less than trade-union wages; ধর্ম্মঘটে যোগদানে অনিচ্ছুক শ্রমজীবি, যে মজুর কোন ধর্ম্মঘটকারীর স্থলবর্ত্তী হইয়া কাজ করে, যে ব্যক্তি শ্রমজীবি-সম্মিলনী কর্ত্তৃক নির্দ্দিষ্ট বেতন অপেক্ষা অল্প বেতনে কাজ করে। ***Verb i.*** 1. To catch, hunt or kill, rats; ইঁদুর ধরা, ইঁদুর শিকার করা, ইঁদুর বধ করা। 2. To play the rat in politics; স্বপক্ষ ত্যাগ করা। **Rat'-ter**, *n.* 1. One who rats, or deserts his party, in adversity; যে ব্যক্তি দুঃসময়ে নিজের দল ত্যাগ করে। 2. A person or dog that catches rats; যে ব্যক্তি বা কুকুর ইঁদুর ধরিয়া থাকে। **Rat-ty**, *adj.* Characteristic of rat; abounding in rats; মূষিকসুলভ; মূষিকপূর্ণ। **Rat-catcher**—যে ব্যক্তি লোকের বাটীর ইঁদুর ধরিয়া জীবিকা নির্ব্বাহ করে। **Rats!**—(*Slang*) Nonsense! incredible! etc.; (ইতর ভাষায়) পাগল আর কি! **Ratsbane**—A poison for rats; ইঁদুর মারার জন্য একপ্রকার বিষ। **Rat's tail**—The tail of a rat; something shaped like a rat's tail *e. g.* a kind of file; মূষিকের লাঙ্গুল; মূষিকের লাঙ্গুলের আকার যন্ত্রাদি। **Rat-tail**—A hairless horse's tail; a horse with such a tail; নির্লোম অশ্বপুচ্ছ; লোমহীনলাঙ্গুলবিশিষ্ট অশ্ব। **Rat-tailed**, *adj.* Having a long tapering tail like that of a rat; মূষিকবৎ লাঙ্গুলবিশিষ্ট। **Rat'-tailed larva**—একপ্রকার কৃমি। **Rat-tailed spoon**—একপ্রকার চামচে—যাহার হাতল লাঙ্গুলের মত উহার পিঠের দিকে প্রলম্বিত থাকে। **Rat-trap**—*n.* & *adj.* A trap for rats; ইঁদুর-ধরা কল। A cycle pedal made of two parallel iron-plates with teeth; দ্বিচক্রযানের একপ্রকার পাদানি। *Adj.* (Of a cycle-pedal) Made of two parallel iron-plates with teeth; (দ্বিচক্রযানের পাদানি-সম্পর্কে) দন্তুরিত সমান্তরাল লৌহপট্টদ্বয়বিশিষ্ট। **Like a drowned rat**—Said of a person wet through; সর্ব্বাঙ্গসিক্ত। **Rats desert the sinking ship**—লক্ষ্মীর বরযাত্রী। **To smell a rat**—To have suspicions; to scent a plot or intrigue; সন্দেহ করা; কোনরূপ চক্রান্ত বা ষড়যন্ত্রের আভাস পাওয়া।

răt, *v. t.* (*3rd. pers. sing. pres. subj.*) = DRAT, (*vulg.*)

râ'-tă, *n.* A large handsome New-Zealand tree with crimson flowers and hard red wood; নিউজিলেণ্ডের একপ্রকার রক্তকাষ্ঠ ও লোহিত পুষ্পপ্রসূ সুবৃহৎ বৃক্ষ।

rāt'-ă-ble (-bl), *adj.* 1. (*Archaic*) Proportional; (কচিদ্‌ব্যবহৃত) আনুপাতিক, হারাহারিক। 2. Liable to taxation or payment of rates; as, one's *ratable* estate; করনির্দ্ধারণ-যোগ্য। **-bil'-i-ty**, *n.* **-bly**, *adv.*

răt-ă-fi'-ă (-fē-), **-fee-** (-fē-), *ns.* 1. A fine spirituous liquor flavoured with fruit or kernels of fruits; specifically a liquor of this character from Dantzig; একপ্রকার সুমিষ্ট সুরা, বিশেষভাবে Dantzig হইতে সমানীত সুমিষ্ট সুরা। 2. A kind of biscuit similarly flavoured; একপ্রকার সুবাসবাসিত বিস্কুট। 3. A kind of cherry; একপ্রকার চেরী-ফল।

rāt'-ăl, *n.* Amount on which rates are assessed; যে আয়ের উপর করনির্দ্ধারণ করা হয়।

ră-tăn', *n.* Same as RATTAN (which see.)

răt-ă-plăn', *n., v. t.* & *i.* The iterative sound of beating a drum or of a galloping horse; দুন্দুভিধ্বনি, অশ্বখুরধ্বনি। ***Verb t. & i.*** To play as on a drum; দুন্দুভি-নিনাদ করা।

ratch'-ĕt (răch-), **ratch** (răch), *n.* & *v. t.* 1. A bar containing angular teeth into which a pawl or catch drops to prevent machines from running back ; ত্রিকোণাকৃতি দন্তবিশিষ্ট দণ্ড-বিশেষ—যাহার উপর একটী আঁকড়া পতিত হইয়া উক্ত দণ্ডের পশ্চাদ্‌বর্ত্তন নিবারণ করে, সদন্তদণ্ড। 2. A wheel having angular teeth with which a reciprocating pawl engages to turn the wheel forward, or a stationary pawl to hold it from turning backward, (also *ratchet-wheel*) ; ত্রিকোণদন্তসমন্বিত চক্রবিশেষ—যাহার দন্তের সহিত পর্য্যায়ক্রমে অগ্রপশ্চাদ্‌গতিশীল একটী আঁকড়া জড়িত হইয়া ঐ চক্রকে সম্মুখদিকে ও স্থিতিশীল অপর আঁকড়া উহাকে পশ্চাদ্দিকে চালিত করে। **Ratchet-wheel**—See RATCHET, *n.* 2.

rāte, *n.* 1. The proportion or standard by which quantity or value is adjusted ; specifically quantity or amount measured per unit of time ; as, a rapid *rate* of travel ; নিরিখ ; হার, পরিমাণ। 2. Price fixed or stated ; tariff charge ; উক্ত বা নির্দ্ধারিত মূল্য ; আমদানী বা রপ্তানী মালের উপর গৃহীত শুল্ক। 3. (Usu. *pl.*) Tax ; as, parish *rates* ; কর। 4. Rank ; class ; kind ; (*archaic except in first-rate, third-rate,* etc.) ; as, I am a spirit of no common *rate* ; পদবী ; শ্রেণী ; জাতি। 5. Manner ; style ; "Thus sat they all around in securely *rate*" ; রীতি ; পদ্ধতি, প্রণালী। 6. (*Naut.*) The order or class of a ship according to its magnitude or force ; (নৌ-বিদ্যা) আয়তন বা শক্তি অনুসারে জাহাজের শ্রেণী। **Rate-payer**—করদাতা। **At any rate**—In any case ; whatever may be the circumstances ; যাহাই হউক না কেন ; যে কোন অবস্থায়।

rāte, *v. t.* & *i.* 1. To settle or fix the value, rank or degree of ; to estimate ; as, I do not *rate* his merits high ; মূল্য নির্দ্ধারণ করা ; নির্দ্ধারণ করা। 2. To assign fixed value to (coin, metals, etc.) in relation to monetary standard ; মুদ্রা, ধাতু, প্রভৃতির স্থির মূল্য নির্দ্দেশ করা। 3. To consider ; to reckon ; as, I *rate* him among my friends ; গণ্য করা ; গণনা করা। 4. (*Usu. in passive*) To subject to payment of a local rate ; as, houses *rated* at a sum smaller than the rent ; স্থানীয় কর প্রভৃতি বসান। 5. (*Naut.*) To class under a certain rating ; (নৌ-বিদ্যা) কোন নির্দ্দিষ্ট শ্রেণীভুক্ত করা। **To rate up**—(বীমায়) যে শ্রেণীর বীমাতে বর্দ্ধিত হারে কিস্তির টাকা দিতে হয়—তৎশ্রেণী ভুক্ত করা। [যথা জীবন বীমায় বীমাকারীর বয়সের সঙ্গে কতিপয় বৎসর যোগ করত কোন অতিরিক্ত আশঙ্কার (risk) কারণজনিত সম্ভাবিত ক্ষতি হইতে রক্ষা পাওয়ার ব্যবস্থা করা।] ***Verb i.*** To be set or considered in a class ; to make an estimate ; শ্রেণীতে স্থাপিত হওয়া, শ্রেণীহিসাবে বিবেচিত হওয়া ; আনুমানিক ব্যয় নির্দ্ধারণ করা।

rāte, *v. t.* & *i.* To chide ; তিরস্কার করা, ভৎর্সনা করা।

rā'-tĕl, *n.* A South-African quadruped ; দক্ষিণ আফ্রিকার চতুষ্পদ জন্তুবিশেষ।

rāt'-ĕr, *n.* 1. One who rates (*rare*) ; মূল্যনির্দ্ধারক, করনির্দ্ধারক (কচিদ্‌ব্যবহৃত)। 2. A vessel of a particular class ; কোন বিশেষ শ্রেণীর পোত।

răth, *n.* (Ireland) A prehistoric hill-fort ; (আয়র্লণ্ড) প্রাগৈতিহাসিক যুগের গিরিদুর্গ।

răth, *adv.* (*Obs.*) Soon ; quickly ; (অপ্রঃ) শীঘ্র ; ত্বরা।

rathe (răth), *adj.* & *n.* (*Poet.*) Early ; (কবিতায়) শীঘ্রাগত, শীঘ্রপক্ব। ***Noun.*** An early variety of apple, pea, etc. , মরশুমের প্রথমভাগে পক্ব সেওফল, মটর, প্রভৃতি।

răth'-ĕr, *adv.* 1. With preference or choice ; বরং, বরঞ্চ। 2. On the contrary ; "Was nothing bettered, but *rather* grew worse" ; পক্ষান্তরে। 3. More correctly speaking ; প্রত্যুত। 4. Somewhat ; as, he is *rather* better today ; কতকটা, কিয়ৎপরিমাণ, কিঞ্চিৎ, কথঞ্চিৎ। 5. (*Colloq.*) Used ironically as a strong affirmative ; as, have you been here before ? *rather* ! ; রহস্যচ্ছলে দৃঢ় নিশ্চয়ার্থে ব্যবহৃত হয়। **Had rather**—See under HAVE. **Rather of the ratherest**—A phrase colloquially applied to anything slightly in excess or deficit ; বরং কতকটা কম বা বেশী, ঈষৎ অল্প বা অধিক। **The rather**—Especially ; for better reason ; বিশেষতঃ ; বরং।

răt'-ĭ-fȳ, *v. t.* 1. To confirm ; দৃঢ় করা, বলবৎ করা। 2. To make valid ; to sanction ; সিদ্ধ করা ; মঞ্জুর করা। **—fi-ca'-tion,** *n.* The act of ratifying ; sanction ; বলবৎ করণ, দৃঢ়ীকরণ, সত্যাপন (অঃ), স্থিরীকরণ ; মঞ্জুর।

rāt'-ing, *n.* 1. Estimating ; assesment ; আনুমানিক মূল্য নির্দ্ধারণ ; করনির্দ্ধারণ। 2. The act of fixing the rank of ; rank ; as, the *rating* of men in the navy : the *rating* of ships ; গতি, শক্তি, পদবী, প্রভৃতি অনুসারে শ্রেণীবিভাগ ; পদবী, শ্রেণী।

rāt'-ing, *n.* Chiding ; তিরস্কার, ভৎসনা, গঞ্জনা।

rā'-ti-ō (-shĭ-), *n.* The ralation or proportion of one thing, such as quantity, to another ; rate ; অনুপাত, নিষ্পত্তি (হিঃ কোঃ), মানতারতম্য (হিঃ কোঃ), সম্বন্ধ (ঐ), আন্তর্য্য (ঐ) ; হার। **Compound ratio**—যোগনিষ্পত্তি (হিঃ কোঃ) [অর্থাৎ যদি কোন সংখ্যা অপর দুই সংখ্যার সহিত এইরূপ ভাবে সম্বন্ধান্বিত থাকে যে, প্রথমোক্ত সংখ্যা বৃদ্ধি বা হ্রাস করিলে অপর দুই সংখ্যার গুণফল

একই অনুপাতে বৃদ্ধি ও হ্রাস পায় তবে ঐ প্রথমোক্ত সংখ্যা অপর সংখ্যাদ্বয়ের সহিত মিশ্রনিষ্পত্তিতে (in compound ratio) আছে বলা হয়।] **Ratio of exchange**—বিনিময়ের অনুপাত, বিনিময় নিষ্পত্তি (হিঃ কোঃ) [অর্থাৎ যে অনুপাতে কোন জিনিষ অপর জিনিষের বিনিময়ে পাওয়া যাইতে পারে।] **Ratio sufficiency**—বিনিগমক (ব্রজঃ হিন্দু)।

ră-ti-ŏc'-i-nāte (-shĭ-), *v. i.* To reason formally; যথারীতি তর্ক করা, তর্কবিজ্ঞানসম্মত যুক্তিপ্রণালী অবলম্বনে তর্ক করা, যুক্তিযুক্ত বা সহেতুক বিচার করা। **—na'-tion,** *n.* The act or process of reasoning, esp. of reasoning deductively; যুক্তিযুক্ত বিচার, তর্ক (শ্রীঃ), অনুমান (হিঃ কোঃ), সম্বন্ধান্বেষণ (ঐ), যুক্তিযুক্ত বিচারপ্রণালী। **—na-tive,** *adj.*

ră'-tion, *n.* & *v. t.* **1.** A portion or fixed allowance of provision, drink and forage to each person in the military or naval service; provision; রসদ; খাদ্যসম্ভার। **2.** Allowance; ভাতা। ***Verb t.*** To supply with ration; রসদ জোগান।

ră'-tion-ăl, *adj.* & *n.* **1.** Endowed with reason; বিবেকবুদ্ধিসম্পন্ন, প্রজ্ঞাবান, ব্যুৎপন্নচিত্ত (বেদান্ত)। **2.** Agreeable to reason; as, *rational* conduct; sensible; wise; moderate; judicious; যুক্তিযুক্ত, যুক্তিসঙ্গত, সঙ্গত, যুক্তিসিদ্ধ, যুক্তিগর্ভ, সহেতুক (হিঃ কোঃ); সবিবেক, সজ্ঞান; জ্ঞানগর্ভ, ব্যুৎপন্নচিত্ত; পরিমিত; বিচারবুদ্ধিসম্পন্ন। **3.** (*Math.*) Expressible without radical signs; as, *rational* function; (গণিত-শাস্ত্র) অকরণীগত (হিঃ কোঃ)। ***Noun.*** **1.** A rational being; বিবেকবুদ্ধিসম্পন্ন জীব। **2.** A quantity expressible without radical signs; অকরণীগত সংখ্যা, অকরণী। **Rational Christians** — ক্রিয়াবাদী খৃষ্টানগণ। **Rational dress** (or **costume**)—স্ত্রীলোকদিগের জন্য একপ্রকার সঙ্গত বা সমীচীন পরিচ্ছদ, বর্ত্তমানে সাধারণতঃ দ্বিচক্রযানাদি আরোহণে ঘাগরার পরিবর্ত্তে জাঙ্গিয়ার প্রচলন বুঝায়। **Rational function**—অকরণীগত ফল (হিঃ কোঃ)।

ră-tion-ā'-lē, *n.* **1.** A statement of reasons; যুক্তিবিবৃতি। **2.** An account or elucidation of the principle of some of opinion, action, hypothesis, phenomenon, etc.; কোন মত, কার্য্য, কল্পনা, জগদ্ব্যাপার, প্রভৃতির মূল তত্ত্বের বিবৃতি বা ব্যাখ্যান।

ră'-tion-ăl-ĭsm, *n.* (*Metaph.*) **1.** The doctrine which finds in all knowledge a certain contribution of the pure reason; হেতুবাদ (হিঃ কোঃ), বুদ্ধিস্বাতন্ত্র্যবাদ (ঐ), যুক্তিবাদ। **2.** (*Theol.*) A system of opinions deduced from reason, as distinct from inspiration, or opposed to it; যে ধর্ম্মমত কোন প্রকার অতীন্দ্রিয় জ্ঞান বা প্রত্যক্ষ নিরপেক্ষভাবে কেবল মাত্র মানবীয় প্রজ্ঞা হইতে সমুদ্ভূত হইয়া থাকে, হেতুমূলকধর্ম্মবাদ, সহেতুক ধর্ম্মবাদ (হিঃ কোঃ)।

ră'-tion-ăl-ĭst, *n.* **1.** One that proceeds in scientific or philosophic inquiry solely on reason; যুক্তিপন্থী, হেতুবাদী (হিঃ কোঃ), বুদ্ধিস্বাতন্ত্র্যবাদী (ঐ), হৈতুক (মঃ সং)। **2.** One that makes a sole test of truth in religion; যে ব্যক্তি ধর্ম্মসংক্রান্ত ব্যাপারে কোনরূপ অতীন্দ্রিয় প্রত্যক্ষের উপর নির্ভর না করিয়া কেবল মাত্র যুক্তি দ্বারা চালিত হয়, সহেতুক ধর্ম্মবাদী (হিঃ কোঃ), যুক্তিবাদী।

ră-tion-ăl'-i-tȳ, *n.* **1.** The quality of being rational; the power of reasoning; বিবেকবুদ্ধিসম্পন্নতা, প্রজ্ঞাবত্তা (হিঃ দঃ); তর্কশক্তি, বিচারশক্তি। **2.** Reasonableness; যুক্তিযুক্ততা, যুক্তিসিদ্ধতা।

ră'-tion-ăl-īze, *v. t.* & *i.* **1.** To convert to rationalism; যুক্তিপন্থী করা। **2.** To interpret as a rationalist; যুক্তিবাদীর মত ব্যাখ্যা করা, যুক্তিমূলক ব্যাখ্যা করা। **3.** To perceive or understand the reason of; হেতু বা কারণ বুঝিতে পারা। **4.** (*Math.*) To clear from irrational expressions; (গণিত শাস্ত্র) অকরণীগত করা। ***Verb i.*** To be, or act as, a rationalist; যুক্তিবাদী হওয়া, যুক্তিবাদীর মত কার্য্য করা।

ră-tōōn', *n.* & *v. i.* A new shoot or sprout springing up from the root of the sugarcane after it has been cropped; কাটার পর ইক্ষুর মূল হইতে যে নবাঙ্কুর বা প্ররোহ উদ্গত হয়। ***Verb i.*** (Of sugarcane) To sprout or spring up from the root after being cropped; (ইক্ষু সম্পর্কে) কাটার পর নূতন অঙ্কুর বা প্ররোহ গজান।

răts'-bāne, *n.* Poison for rats; ইন্দুরনাশক বিষ; সেঁকো বিষ।

răt-tăt', **răt-ă-tat',** **răt--tăt-tat',** *ns.* Rapping sound; খট্ খট্ শব্দ, ঠক্ ঠক্ শব্দ।

răt-tăn', *n.* **1.** A genus of palm having smooth root-like stem; বেত, বেত্র, বেতস, বঞ্জুল (গীতঃ), বানীর (ঐ), [Syn. রথ, বিদুল, অভ্রপুষ্প, শীত, মৃদুপর্ব্ব, মৃদুপর্ব্বক।] [Malay *Rotan.*; Jav. *Panjalin*, *Kowasunda* (hence our সুঁন্দি বেত)]। **2.** A cane or walking stick formed of a rattan; বেত, বেতের ছড়ি।

răt'-tĕn, *v. t.* To maliciously destroy or take away the property or tools of non-unionists; শ্রমজীবিসম্মিলনীর সভ্যসমাজের বহির্ভূত লোকের জিনিষপত্র, যন্ত্রপাতি, প্রভৃতি নষ্ট করা বা গোপনে সরাইয়া নেওয়া।

răt'-tle (-l), *v. i.* & *t.* **1.** To clatter; ; ঠক্ ঠক্ করা, খট্ খট্ করা। **2.** To chatter; বক বক করা, ঘেনর ঘেনর করা। **3.** To move with a rattling noise; ঘড় ঘড় করিয়া চলা। ***Verb t.*** **1.** To cause to make a rattling sound; খট্ খট্ করা, ঠক্ ঠক্ করা। **2.** To rouse; উত্তেজিত করা। **3.** To make to move quickly; as, to *rattle* a fox; দ্রুত তাড়িত করা।

răt'-tle (-l), *n.* **1.** A clatter; খট্ খট্ শব্দ, ঠক্ ঠক্ শব্দ, ঝন ঝন্ শব্দ, শিঞ্জা,

ঝুমঝুমি, হুড়মুড় শব্দ। 2. Loud rapid talk; ঘেনর ঘেনর, বক বক, পচাল। 3. A jabberer; বকবক্‌কারী। 4. Roar; bustle; চীৎকার, সোরগোল, হল্লা; দৌড়ধাপ, তাড়াহুড়া। 5. An instrument or child's toy with which a clattering sound is made; ঝুনঝুনি। 6. The sound-producing organ on a rattle-snake's tail; ঘর্ঘরসর্পের লাঙ্গুলের ধ্বনিউৎপাদক অংশ। 7. A common meadow weed; একপ্রকার গুল্ম। 8. Same as DEATH-RATTLE (under death) **Rattle-bag, —box, —bladder**—যে থলি প্রভৃতি নাড়িলে ঘর্ঘর শব্দ নির্গত হয়। **Rattle-brained, Rattle-headed, Rattle-pated**—হীনমস্তিষ্ক ব্যক্তি বুদ্ধিহীন ব্যক্তি। **Rattle-snake**—আমেরিকাদেশীয় বিষধর সর্পবিশেষ — ইহাদের লাঙ্গুলে কতিপয়

Rattle-snake.

অস্থিবলয় থাকাতে চলার সময় একপ্রকার ঘর্ঘর শব্দ হয়, ঘর্ঘরসর্প। **Rattle-trap**—তুচ্ছ জিনিষ, ফটকী নাটকী; টলটলে, নড়বড়ে (যথা গাড়ী)।

răt'-tler (-lêr), *n.* 1. One that rattles; ঘর্ঘরনাদী, বকবককারী। 2. A smart heavy blow; খুব এক ঘা। 3. A remarkable specimen of anything; উমদা জিনিষ, সেরা জিনিষ।

rau'-cous (rä-cŭs), *adj.* Hoarse; কর্কশ, শ্রুতিকটু। **—ly,** *adv.*

rauque (räk), *adj.* (*Rare*) Same as RAUCOUS.

răv'-age (-āj), *v. t., i. & n.* To lay waste; to devastate; to spoil; to plunder; উচ্ছন্ন করা, উৎসন্ন করা; ছারখার করা; বিধ্বংস করা; লুণ্ঠন করা, লুঠপাট করা। ***Verb i.*** To commit havoc or destruction; উৎসন্ন করা, বিধ্বংস করা। ***Noun.*** 1. Devastation; উচ্ছেদ, ধ্বংস, উৎসাদন, অভিমর্দ্দন। 2. (*Pl.*) The destructive action or effects *of* disease etc.; as, the *ravages of* cholera; ধ্বংসজনকক্রিয়া বা পরিণাম, উপপ্লব উপদ্রব।

rāve, *n.* One of the upper side-pieces of a waggon-body frame or of a sleigh; শকট বা হিমানীশকটের কাঠামের ঊর্দ্ধভাগের পার্শ্ব-সংযুক্ত অংশ (যাহাতে অতিরিক্ত মাল প্রভৃতি রাখা হয়)।

rāve, *v. i., t. & n.* 1. (*Obs.*) To be mad; to talk irrationally; to be wild or furious; (অপ্রঃ) পাগল হওয়া, উন্মত্ত হওয়া; পাগলের মত প্রলাপ করা, বিড়বিড় করিয়া বকা; ক্রোধোন্মত্ত হওয়া। 2. To talk with unreasonable enthusiasm; "The hallowed scene which others *rave* of..."; উৎকট উত্তেজনাপূর্ণ স্বরে বলা, উন্মাদনাপূর্ণ স্বরে বলা। 3. To rage; "Where the dark sea with angry billows *rave*"; to dash; গর্জ্জন করা; প্রচণ্ডবেগে ধাবিত হওয়া। ***Verb t.*** To utter in a frenzied tone; উন্মাদনাপূর্ণ কণ্ঠে উচ্চারণ করা। ***Noun.*** 1. Act of raving; প্রলাপ। 2. Raving sound; গর্জ্জন।

răv'-ĕl, *v. t., i. & n.* 1. To disentangle; মোচন করা, পাক খোলা, গাঁইট খোলা। 2. (*Lit. & fig.*) To entangle; to twist together; to complicate; (শব্দানুযায়ী ও লক্ষণায়) জড়িত করা, জড়ান; একত্র পাকান; জটিল করা। ***Verb i.*** 1. To become entangled; জড়িত হওয়া। 2. To fray out (also *verb t.*); কাপড়ের সূতা বাহির করা। ***Noun.*** 1. Entanglement; complication; জড়িতাবস্থা; জটিলতা। 2. A broken thread; a loose end; ছিন্ন সূত্র; কাপড়ের যে প্রান্তের সূতা খোলা হইয়াছে তাহা। **—ment,** *n.*

rave'-lin (răv-), *n.* A detached work with two salient angles at the front, and open at the rear; উপদুর্গবিশেষ—যাহার সম্মুখভাগে দুইটী বহির্বিলম্বী কোণ এবং পশ্চাদ্‌ভাগ উন্মুক্ত থাকে।

rāv'-en (-n), *n. & adj.* 1. A large bird of a black colour, of the crow family; দাঁড়কাক [Syn. দ্রোণকাক, বনকাক, বনবাসী, মৃত্যুবঞ্চন, দণ্ডকাক, দগ্ধকাক, বৃদ্ধকাক, কাকোল, কাকাল, কাকল, অরণ্যবায়স, মহাপ্রাণ, পর্ব্বতকাক, দরা, দরী, ক্রূরবাচী, ক্রূরকারী, পললপ্রিয়, পললপ্রিয়, বনাশ্রয়।] 2. (*Fig.*) A prophet of evil; (লক্ষণায়) অশুভ সূচনাকারী। 3. The figure of raven on the flag of the Danish vikings or the flag itself; ডেনমার্কের প্রাচীন সাগর-দস্যুগণের পতাকার উপরি অঙ্কিত দাঁড়কাক বা উক্ত দস্যুদের দণ্ডকাকাঙ্কিত পতাকা। ***Adj.*** Glossy black; jet-black; as, *raven* locks; স্নিগ্ধকৃষ্ণ; ভ্রমরকৃষ্ণ (কুন্তল গুচ্ছ), মিসমিসে কালো। **Raven's luck**—একপ্রকার পাইলের কাপড়। **Raven-stone**—বধ্য শিলা। **Ravens were once as white as swans**—গ্রীক পুরাণানুসারে দাঁড়কাক পূর্ব্বে রাজহংসের মত বৃহৎ এবং শুভ্র বর্ণ ছিল। এক দিবস এক দাঁড়কাক Apollo দেবের নিকট তদীয় প্রণয়িনী Coronis এর ব্যভিচারের কথা বলায় তিনি Coronisকে বধ করেন এবং দাঁড়কাককে পরচর্চ্চার অপরাধে কৃষ্ণবর্ণ করিয়া দেন।

răv'-ĕn, *v. i. & t.* To prey with rapacity; to be greedy; লুব্ধভাবে শিকার করা; লুব্ধ হওয়া, লোলুপ হওয়া। ***Verb t.*** 1. To plunder; লুণ্ঠন করা। 2. To devour greedily; লুব্ধভাবে উদরসাৎ করা।

răv'-ĕn-ous (-ŭs), *adj.* 1. Voracious; as, *ravenous* hunger; উদরসর্ব্বস্ব, সর্ব্বগ্রাসী (ক্ষুধা), ঔদরিক। 2. Rapacious; লুব্ধ, হিংস্র। 3. Extremely hungry; অতিক্ষুধিত, অতিক্ষুধার্ত্ত, বুভুক্ষিত। **—ly,** *adv.* **—ness,** *n.*

răv'-in, *n.* 1. (*Poet.* or *Rhet.*) Robbery; দস্যুবৃত্তি। 2. Food got by violence; লুণ্ঠিত খাদ্য।

ră-vine' (-vēn), *n.* A deep or narrow hollow worn by a stream or torrent of water; a deep hollow pass between mountains ; নদী-স্রোতোদ্বারা খনিত গভীর অথবা অপ্রশস্ত খাত ; সঙ্কীর্ণ গিরিবর্ত্ম, পর্ব্বত মধ্যস্থ গভীর অপ্রশস্ত পথ, দরী (সাঃ পঃ), কন্দর।

răv′-ish, *v. t.* **1.** To seize and carry away by violence (now *rare*); বলপূর্ব্বক লইয়া যাওয়া (বর্ত্তমানে কচিদ্‌ব্যবহৃত)। **2.** To abduct a woman; হরণ করা, ধর্ষণ করা। **3.** To violate; বলাৎকার করা, সতীত্ব নষ্ট করা, ধর্ম্মনষ্ট করা। **4.** To charm; to enrapture; as, I have been *ravished*; মোহিত করা, বিমোহিত করা, বিমুগ্ধ করা; আনন্দ-বিহ্বল করা, হর্ষাবিষ্ট করা। **–er,** *n.* One who ravishes; স্ত্রীলোকের ধর্ম্মনষ্টকারী, রতিতস্কর। **–ing,** *adj.* Ecstatic; delighting to rapture; "Oh! what a *ravishing* comfort is the fellowship of the saints"; পরমানন্দজনক; পরম সুখদ। **–ment,** *n.*

raw (rä), *adj., n. & v. t.* **1.** Uncooked; as, *raw* eggs; অরন্ধিত, অসিদ্ধ, কাঁচা, আম। **2.** Not manufactured; in the natural state; কাঁচা; স্বাভাবিক অবস্থাপন্ন, অসংস্কৃত। **3.** Unburnt; as, *raw* bricks; অদগ্ধ, আপোড়া। **4.** (*Obs.*) Not distilled; as, *raw* water; (অপ্রচলিত) অপরিস্রুত। **5.** Not tanned; as, *raw* hide; অসংস্কৃত, অবিশোধিত, কাঁচা। **6.** Not diluted; as, *raw* brandy; অজলমিশ্রিত, নির্জ্জলা। **7.** Unripe; immature; hence, inexperienced; as, a *raw* recruit; কাঁচা, অপক; অপরিপক; (অতএব) অপরিণত-বুদ্ধি, অপক্কবুদ্ধি, অনভিজ্ঞ, কাঁচা, অর্ব্বাচীন। **8.** Crude; as, *raw* conception; স্থূল। **9.** Galled; as, a *raw* sore; কাঁচা। **10.** Bleak; cold and damp; as, the *raw* evening air; কনকনে ঠাণ্ডা, ঠাণ্ডা এবং স্যাঁতসেঁতে। ***Noun.*** **1.** A sore place; ক্ষত স্থান, রগড়াইয়া লুণছাল তোলা হইয়াছে—এরূপ স্থান। **2.** A sensitive spot; as, to touch one on the *raw* (আঁতে ঘা দেওয়া); মর্ম্ম, আঁত। ***Verb t.*** To excoriate; রগড়াইয়া লুণছাল তোলা। **Raw′-ness,** *n.* **Raw-boned**—কঙ্কালসার, অস্থিচর্ম্মসার **Raw-cloth**—কোরা কাপড়। **Raw-grain**—জলে ডুবাইয়া যে শস্য অঙ্কুরিত করা হয় নাই। **Raw material**—কাঁচা মাল, অবিশোধিত উপাদান, মূল উপাদান। **Raw head and bloody bones**—জুজু।

ray (rā), *n.* **1.** A line of light, or the right line supposed to be described by a particle of light; কিরণ, রশ্মি, অংশু, কর, মরীচি, দীধিতি, ময়ূখ [Syn. গভস্তি, অভীশু, অভীষু, অর্চিঃ, ঘৃণি, পাদ, উস্র, রুচি, পৃশ্নি, স্তোন, স্যুম, উপধৃতি, শিপি, পৃষ্টি, বীচি, ভানু।] **2.** A beam of moral intellectual light; "Bright reason's *ray*"; perception; apprehension; ধীরশ্মি, পুণ্যজ্যোতি, প্রতিভাপ্রভা; অনুভূতি; উপলব্ধি। **3.** Light; (*poet.*) glance; "All eyes directed their *rays* on him"; দ্যুতি, আলো, ত্বিষি; (কবিতায়) দৃষ্টি। **4.** A particle (*rare*); as, a *ray* of hope; কণা, কণিকা, লেশ, ক্ষীণরশ্মি। **5.** (*Bot.*) The radiating part of a flower or plant; (উদ্ভিদ্‌বিদ্যা) কোন পুষ্প বা বৃক্ষের কেন্দ্রবিসর্পী অংশ, অংশ (সাঃ পঃ)। **6.** Radius (*rare*); one of the lines or radii diverging from a centre; (কচিদ্ ব্যবহৃত) ব্যাসার্দ্ধ; কেন্দ্র হইতে বিকীর্ণ রেখা বা ব্যাসার্দ্ধসমূহের অন্যতম। **7.** Radial division of a star-fish; চাঁদা মাছের ব্যাসার্দ্ধবৎ বিভাগ। **Becquerel rays**—See RADIO-ACTIVE. **Infra red rays**—বর্ণচ্ছত্রের দক্ষিণ-সীমান্তবর্ত্তী রক্তবর্ণের পরবর্ত্তী অদৃশ্য, বর্ণরাজি। **Obliteration of ray**—অংশুবিমর্দ্দ (সূর্য্য বাঃ)। **Röntgen or X rays**—একপ্রকার কিরণ—যাহা সাধারণ আলোক দ্বারা অভেদ্য বস্তু সমূহ ভেদ করিতে পারে, রঞ্জনরশ্মি। [অধ্যাপক C. W. Röntgen ১৮৯৫ খৃঃ অব্দে এই রশ্মি আবিষ্কার করেন। এই রশ্মির সাহায্যে দেহের অভ্যন্তরস্থ অস্থি প্রভৃতি কঠিন পদার্থের আলোক-চিত্র তোলা যায়। **Ultra violet rays**—বর্ণচ্ছত্রের বাম সীমান্তবর্ত্তী অতি-নীলারুণ (বেগুণে বর্ণের পরবর্ত্তী) অদৃশ্য বর্ণমালা।

ray (rā), *v. i. & t.* **1.** To emit ray; to issue as rays; কিরণ বিকীর্ণ করা; কিরণচ্ছটাবৎ নির্গত হওয়া। **2.** To radiate; বিকীর্ণ হওয়া। ***Verb t.*** To shoot forth or emit; to cause to shine out; বিকীর্ণ করা; দীপ্তিমান করা।

ray (-rā), *n.* A genus of sea-fishes; একজাতীয় সামুদ্রিক মৎস্য, চাঁদা মাছ (সাঃ পঃ), অংশুকায় মৎস্য।

Rayah, *n.* A non-Mohammedan Turkish subject; তুরস্ক সম্রাটের অ-মোসলমান প্রজা।

raze, rāse, *v. t.* **1.** (*Rare*) To graze; (কচিদ্ ব্যবহৃত) ঘষড়াইয়া যাওয়া, ঈষৎ স্পর্শ করিয়া যাওয়া। **2.** To erase (*rare, except in the fig.*); (লক্ষণায় ব্যতীত কচিদ্ ব্যবহৃত) ঘষিয়া উঠান, অপহ্নব করা, লোপ করা। **3.** To demolish; as, to *raze* a city; ধ্বংস করা, নাশ করা, ভূমিসাৎ করা।

rā-zee′ (-zē), *n. & v. t.* A ship of war cut down to a lower size; পাটাতন বা পাটাতন সমূহ কাটিয়া ফেলিয়া যে রণপোতের আয়তন অল্প করা হইয়াছে। ***Verb t.*** To turn into a razee; ঐরূপ পোতে পরিণত করা।

rā′-zŏr, *n. & v. t.* **1.** A keen-edged knife used for shaving; ক্ষুর [Syn. ক্ষুরযন্ত্র, ক্ষৌর, বুদ্ধিপত্র, ক্ষৌরিক যন্ত্র।] **2.** A tusk of a wild boar; বন্যবরাহের দন্ত। ***Verb t.*** (*Rare*) To shave; to cut down; (কচিদ্ ব্যবহৃত) ক্ষৌর কার্য্য করা; কাটিয়া ফেলা। **Razor-back**—ক্ষুর-ধার পৃষ্ঠ; একপ্রকার তিমি মৎস্য; ক্ষুরাকৃতি গিরিপৃষ্ঠ। **Razor-backed**—ক্ষুরপৃষ্ঠ। **Razor-bill**—ক্ষুরাকৃতি চঞ্চু-বিশিষ্ট বিভিন্নপ্রকার পক্ষীর সাধারণ নাম। **Razor-billed**—ক্ষুরাকৃতি চঞ্চুবিশিষ্ট।

Razor-case — ক্ষুরভাণ্ড, ক্ষুরাধান, ক্ষুরাধার, ভাণ্ডি, কাতা (প্রাঃ সাঃ)। **Razor-edge**—ক্ষুরধার; (লক্ষণায়) পদরক্ষার সঙ্কীর্ণ স্থান; সঙ্কটাপন্ন অবস্থা। **Razor-grinder**—যে ব্যক্তি ক্ষুরে ধার দেয়; বিভিন্নপ্রকার পক্ষীর সাধারণ নাম। **Razor-strop, —strap**—চামাতি, ক্ষুরতেজনী, ক্ষুরতেজন চর্ম্ম। **Razor wit**—ক্ষুরধার বুদ্ধি (cf. *Razor-wit* for want of use grows rusty—*Boswell*). **To be on razor-edge** or **razor's edge**—To be in great peril; মহাসঙ্কটে পতিত হওয়া।

răz'-zi-ă, *n.* (From *Arab.* غازية). An incursion by military into an enemy's country for the purpose of carrying off cattle, destroying standing crops, etc.; গোধন হরণ, শস্যক্ষেত্র লুণ্ঠন, প্রভৃতির উদ্দেশ্যে সৈন্যগণকর্ত্তৃক শত্রুরাজ্য আক্রমণ।

răz'-zle-daz'-zle (-l-dăz-l), *n.* (*Slang*) Excitement; bustle; spree; (ইতর ভাষায়) উত্তেজনা; হল্লা; মাতালের কোলাহল।

rē, *n.* (*Mus.*) The second note of the diatonic scale; (সঙ্গীত-শাস্ত্র) রে।

rē–, *Pref.* A prefix from the Latin, denoting iteration, return, repetition, retrogression, etc.; পুনরুক্তি, প্রত্যাবর্ত্তন, পশ্চাদ্বর্ত্তনসূচক উপসর্গ। [In words beginning with a vowel *red* is used instead of *re*; as, *red*-eem, *red*-olent, etc. In some words *re* has lost its original significance; as, in *re*joice, *re*commend, etc.]

rē, (Ablative of Lat. *res*, thing). In the matter of; সম্পর্কে, বিষয়ে। The Latin phrase *in re* is similary used. **Re-infecta**—বিষয়টী অসম্পন্ন রাখিয়া।

reach (rēch), *v. t.* & *i.* **1.** To stretch or hold forth; "*Reach out* dead hands to comfort me"; বাড়াইয়া দেওয়া, প্রসারিত করা। **2.** To deliver with the hand by extending the arm; as, to *reach* one a blow; to hand to; as, I *reached* him the letter; হাত বাড়াইয়া দেওয়া; হাতে দেওয়া। **3.** To strike from a distance; as, to *reach* an object with an arrow; দূর হইতে আঘাত করা। **4.** To attain or obtain by stretching forth the hand; লাগাইল পাওয়া। **5.** To arrive at; as, the ship *reached* her port in safety; পৌঁছা, আসা। **6.** To extend influence; to impress; as, men are *reached* by kindness than by force; to penetrate; প্রভাব বিস্তার করা; হৃদয় স্পর্শ করা, ভেদ করিয়া প্রবেশ করা। **7.** To attain to by study, exertion or effort; চেষ্টা, উদ্যম বা অধ্যয়নের ফলে লাভ করা। **8.** (*Obs.*) To understand; (অপ্রঃ) বুঝা, হৃদয়ঙ্গম বা উপলব্ধি করা। ***Verb i.*** **1.** To stretch the hand in order to touch or attain a thing; কোন কিছু লাগাইল পাওয়ার জন্য হাত বাড়ান। **2.** (*Lit.* & *Fig.*) To grasp; (শব্দানুযায়ী এবং লক্ষণায়) ধরা, মর্ম্ম গ্রহণ করা। **3.** To amount to; মোট বা সমষ্টিতে হওয়া। **4.** To make effort to obtain or attain; "*Reaching* after a positive idea of infinity"; প্রাপ্তি বা লাভের জন্য চেষ্টা করা, যত্ন করা। **5.** (*Naut.*) To stand off and on; to sail by the wind upon any tack; (নৌবিদ্যা) একবার কূলের নিকট আবার কূল হইতে দূরে থাকা; যে কোন দিকে বাতাস বহেনা কেন পাইল খাটাইয়া চলা। **Reach'-less,** *adj.* **Reach-me-down,** *adj.* & *n.* (পোষাক সম্বন্ধে) তৈয়ারী; পুরাতন। (*Noun*) তৈয়ারী পোষাক, কাটা কাপড়; পুরাতন পোষাক। **To reach after** or **at**—To endeavour to obtain; পাইবার জন্য চেষ্টা করা, লাভ করার জন্য চেষ্টা করা।

reach (rēch), *n.* **1.** The act of reaching; the distance to which one can reach; কিছু ধরার জন্য হস্ত প্রসারণ; লাগাইল। **2.** Capacity; range; extent or limit of human faculty or attainment; শক্তি; সীমা, গোচর, গম্যতা, লভ্যতা, আয়ত্তি, গ্রাহ্যতা; মনুষ্য বুদ্ধির গোচরতা। **3.** Stretch; expanse; প্রসার; বিস্তার। **4.** A stretch of water; জলরাশি। **5.** A strait or channel; an arm of the sea; "The rocky *reaches*"; প্রণালী; সাগরশাখা। **6.** The straight course of a river between two bendings; নদীর দুই বাঁকের মধ্যবর্ত্তী স্থান যাহা একবারে দৃষ্টিগম্য হয়, বাঁক। **Within reach**—Near; নিকটে, কাছে।

rē-ăct', *v. t.* & *i.* To do over again; পুনরায় করা। ***Verb i.*** **1.** To excercise a reciprocal or reverse effect; প্রতিক্রিয়া করা। **2.** To undergo change by some influence; কোন কিছুর প্রভাব দ্বারা বিকার বা রূপান্তর প্রাপ্ত হওয়া। **3.** To act or move in opposition; to tend to return towards a previous condition; as, the public opinion soon *reacted* in his favour; বিপরীত দিকে ক্রিয়া করা বা চলা; পুর্ব্বাবস্থায় আসার দিকে উন্মুখ হওয়া। **—ac'-tion,** *n.* **1.** Counter tendency or movement; প্রতিক্রিয়া। **2.** Action in the contrary, specially backward direction; বিরুদ্ধক্রিয়া, পশ্চাদ্দিকে ক্রিয়া, প্রতিঘাত। **3.** (*Chem.*) The action of one chemical agent upon another; chemical change; (রসায়ন শাস্ত্র) রাসায়নিক দ্রব্যদ্বয়ের পরস্পরের উপর ক্রিয়া, প্রতিক্রিয়া (হিঃ কোঃ); রাসায়নিক পরিবর্ত্তন। **4.** Backward tendency from revolution, reform or progress; "From that day began a *reaction* in favour of monarchy"; বিপ্লব, শাসনসংস্কার বা উন্নতির পর অপেক্ষাকৃত অনুন্নত অবস্থায় প্রত্যাবর্ত্তনে

উন্মুখতা, প্রতিক্রিয়া। 5. (*Pathol.*) (*a*) The action of an organ which reflects upon another the irritation previously transmitted to itself ; (নিদান শাস্ত্র) কোন যন্ত্রে উপদাহ প্রভৃতি জন্মিয়া সেই উপদাহ প্রভৃতির অন্যযন্ত্রে গতি, প্রতিক্ষিপ্ত উপদাহ (হঃ চঃ)। (*b*) The response made by an organ to an external stimulus ; বাহিরের উত্তেজনার উপর কোন শারীরিক যন্ত্রের প্রতিক্রিয়া, প্রতিঘাত (হঃ চঃ)। (*c*) Depression of vital force consequent on over-exertion ; গুরুতর পরিশ্রমের পর শারীরিক অবসাদ। (*d*) The increased impetus which succeeds asphyxia, torpor, etc. ; স্নায়ুমণ্ডলে কোন কারণে অবসন্নতা জন্মিয়া তৎপরে উহার উত্তেজনা বা কার্য্যশীলতা, প্রতিক্রিয়া (হঃ চঃ), বিপাক (সুশ্রুঃ)। **—ac′-tion-ar-y,** *adj.* & *n.* Tending towards, or favouring, reaction ; প্রতিক্রিয়াত্মক, প্রতিক্রিয়াজনক, পশ্চাদ্‌গমনোন্মুখ, অনুন্নতশাসননীতি অবলম্বনে উন্মুখ। ***Noun.*** One who favours or promotes reaction ; esp. one who tries to check, undo or reverse political progress ; যে ব্যক্তি রাজনীতিক উন্নতিরোধের চেষ্টা করে ; বিশেষতঃ যে ব্যক্তি উন্নততর শাসননীতি পরিত্যাগ পূর্ব্বক অনুন্নত শাসননীতি গ্রহণের জন্য চেষ্টা করে, সংস্কারপরাঙ্মুখ, শাসনোন্নতিরোধক। **—ac′-tion-ist,** *n.* & *adj.*

read (rēd), *v. t., i.* & *n.* **1.** To peruse ; পাঠ করা, পড়া। **2.** To study by reading ; অধ্যয়ন করা। **3.** To interpret a dream, riddle, etc. ; (সমস্যা) পূরণ করা, ধাঁধার উত্তর দেওয়া, (স্বপ্নের) ফল বলা। **4.** To foretell ; as, to *read* one's fortune : to *read* a person's hand ; ভাগ্যফল বলা, (হাত) দেখা। **5.** To discern the thoughts and feelings of ; "Who can *read* a woman" ; কাহারো মনের ভাব বা চিন্তা ঠাওরান। **6.** To interpret (statement, action, etc.) in certain sense ; as, to *read* a statement as an insult ; (কোন উক্তি, কার্য্য, প্রভৃতি) কোন নির্দ্দিষ্ট ভাবে নেওয়া, ব্যাখ্যা করা। **7.** To indicate ; to register ; as, the thermometer *reads* 105° ; সূচনা করা ; উঠা। ***Verb i.*** **1.** To perform the act of reading ; পাঠ করা। **2.** To study ; to study books for a particular purpose ; as, to *read* for the bar ; অধ্যয়ন করা ; কোন বিশেষ উদ্দেশ্যে অধ্যয়ন করা। **3.** To stand written or printed ; as, the passage *reads* thus ; (এইরূপ) লিখিত বা মুদ্রিত থাকা। **4.** To bear construction or import ; (এইরূপ) অর্থ বা মর্ম্ম হওয়া। ***Noun.*** Perusal ; as, a long *read* ; পাঠ। **To read between the lines**—To perceive or appreciate the real motive and meaning of a writing or work ; লেখকের লিখিত বিষয়ের বা লেখকের গূঢ় উদ্দেশ্য বা অন্তর্নিহিত অর্থ বুঝা, কোন লিখার গূঢ় তাৎপর্য্য হৃদয়ঙ্গম করা। **To read music**—To understand musical notation ; স্বরলিপি পাঠ করিতে পারা। **To read off**—তাপমানযন্ত্র প্রভৃতির তাপমাত্রা প্রভৃতি টুকিয়া রাখা। To impress on ; মুদ্রিত করা (কাপড় প্রভৃতি)। **To read on**—To look on and read ; চাহিয়া পড়া (বর্ত্তমানে বিশেষতঃ চলিত ভাষায়)। **To read one a lecture or lesson**—To rebuke one vigorously ; কাহাকে তীব্র তিরস্কার করা, খুব এক চোট গাল দেওয়া। **To read oneself in**—নবনিযুক্ত যাজক কর্ত্তৃক ধর্ম্মসম্বন্ধীয় ৩৯টী ধারা পাঠান্তে বিধিনির্দ্দিষ্ট সম্মতিঘোষণা (Declaration of Assent) আবৃত্তি করা। **To read out of**—To expell from society etc. by reading out a declaration ; ঘোষণাপত্র পাঠপূর্ব্বক কোন ব্যক্তিকে কোন সমিতি প্রভৃতি হইতে বহিষ্কৃত করা। **To read right**—(*Obs.*) To have or take a correct view ; (অপ্রঃ) ঠিকভাবে বুঝা, ঠিকভাবে গ্রহণ করা। **To read through**—To peruse form beginning to end ; আদ্যোপান্ত পাঠ করা, আগাগোড়া পড়িয়া শেষ করা। **To read up**—To make a special study of ; বিশেষভাবে অনুশীলন করা।

read′-a-ble (rēd-ă-bl), *adj.* **1.** (*Rare*) Legible ; (ক্বচিদ্ ব্যবহৃত) সুখপাঠ্য। **2.** Worth reading ; interestingly written ; পাঠযোগ্য, পাঠ্য, পঠনীয় ; সুলিখিত। **—bil′-i-ty,** *n.* **—bly,** *adv.* **—ness,** *n.*

rē-ăd-drĕss′, *v. t.* To change the address of, as a letter ; কোন চিঠির ঠিকানা পরিবর্ত্তন করা।

read′-êr (rēd-), *n.* **1.** One who reads ; পাঠক, পাঠিকা (fem.)। **2.** One appointed to read the lessons, prayers, etc. in a place of worship ; যে ব্যক্তি ধর্ম্মমন্দিরাদিতে ধর্ম্মোপদেশ, প্রার্থনা, প্রভৃতি পাঠ করে। **3.** One employed to read and examine the merits of manuscripts for publication ; যে ব্যক্তি পুস্তকাদি প্রকাশের পূর্ব্বে পাঠপূর্ব্বক গুণাগুণ পরীক্ষা করে, গ্রন্থপরীক্ষক। **4.** A proof reader in a printing press ; মুদ্রাযন্ত্রের প্রুফ সংশোধক। **5.** A lecturer in some universities etc. ; কোন কোন বিশ্ববিদ্যালয়ের অধ্যাপক। **6.** An elementary book for instruction and practice in reading ; পাঠশিক্ষার্থ পুস্তক, পাঠ। **—ship,** *n.*

read′-i-ly̆ (rĕd-), *adv.* **1.** In a ready manner ; quickly ; promptly ; without difficulty ; as, it can be *readily* ascertained ; তৎপরতার সহিত ; ঝটিতি ; অচিরে ; অনায়াসে, অক্লেশে। **2.** Willingly ; "I accepted the offer very *readily*" ; ইচ্ছাপূর্ব্বক।

read′-i-nĕss, (rĕd-) *n.* **1.** State of being ready ; promptness ; willingness ; তৎপরতা ; সত্বরতা, ক্ষিপ্রকারতা ; ইচ্ছাপরতা। **2.** Facility of performance ; prompt resourcefulness ; সুকরতা ; প্রত্যুৎপন্নমতিত্ব।

read'-ing (rĕd-), *n.* **1.** Act of one who reads ; পঠন, পাঠ । **2.** Study of books ; scholarship ; as, a man of vast *reading* ; অধ্যয়ন ; পাণ্ডিত্য, বিদ্যাবত্তা, বৈদুষ্য । **3.** A public recital or lection ; "The Jews had their weekly *readings* of the law" ; যে সভা বা সম্মিলনীতে শ্রোতৃবৃন্দের নিকট কোন গ্রন্থ হইতে পাঠ করা হয়, পাঠসভা, পাঠ-গোষ্ঠী, পাঠ (যথা পুরাণ পাঠ) । **4.** A version or particular rendering of a text or passage ; পাঠান্তর, পাঠভেদ । **5.** Matter intended to be read esp. with reference to its quality or kind ; as, an interesting *reading* ; পঠনীয় বিষয়, পঠিতব্য বিষয় । **6.** That which is indicated, as on the scale of a graduated instrument ; as, 20° difference between day and night *readings* ; তাপমান যন্ত্র প্রভৃতির ক্রমাঙ্কিত গাত্রে যে মাত্রা সূচিত হয়, মাত্রা । **7.** The interpretation one attaches to anything or the view one takes of it ; as his *reading* of the facts was unfavourable ; the mode of rendering ; as, his *reading* of Iago was generally condemned ; কোন বিষয় সম্বন্ধে ব্যক্তিবিশেষের ব্যাখ্যা বা মত ; ভূমিকা প্রভৃতি অভিনয় । **Reading-desk** — পাঠ কালে পুস্তক রাখার জন্য এক-প্রকার টেবিল মেজ । **Reading-glass** — পুস্তকাদি পাঠে ব্যবহৃত গোলাকৃতি বিবর্দ্ধক কাচ । **Reading-room** — পাঠকক্ষ, পাঠপ্রকোষ্ঠ, পাঠাগার । **First, second and third reading**—কোন প্রস্তাবিত আইনের পাণ্ডুলিপি পার্লেমেন্টের উভয় গৃহে, প্রথম, দ্বিতীয় এবং তৃতীয় বার পাঠ ।

Reading-glass.

rē-ăd-jŭst', *v. t.* To adjust or put in order again ; পুনরায় যথাযথভাবে সন্নিবিষ্ট করা, পুনরায় ঠিকঠাক করিয়া লাগান ।

read'-y (rĕd-), *adj., adv., n. & v. t.* **1.** Prepared ; in a fit state ; as, *ready* for the journey ; প্রস্তুত ; সজ্জিত । **2.** Willing ; disposed ; apt ; as, *ready* to do it ; ইচ্ছুক ; প্রবৃত্ত, উন্মুখ ; প্রবণ । **3.** Quick ; prompt ; as, *ready* wit : *ready* answer ; dexterous ; ক্ষিপ্র, ত্বরিত, তরন্ত ; উপস্থিত, প্রত্যুৎপন্ন (মতি) ; দক্ষ, ক্ষিপ্রহস্ত, কুশল, নিপুণ । **4.** Immediately at hand ; as, *ready* assets, money, etc. ; রোক, নগদ । **5.** Not deferred ; as, *ready* payment ; নগদ । ***Adv.*** **1.** In a state of preparation ; as, packed *ready* : *ready*-made clothes ; প্রস্তুত, তৈয়ারী । **2.** (*Rare*) Quickly ; (কচিদ্ ব্যবহৃত) ত্বরা, ঝটিতি, তৎক্ষণাৎ । ***Noun.*** 1. (*Mil.*) A position in holding arms at which the piece is cocked or otherwise prepared for instant firing ; a command to hold arms in this position ; (সামরিক শাস্ত্র) সৈনিকের অবস্থান বিশেষ—যাহাতে তৎক্ষণাৎ আওয়াজ করার জন্য ঘোড়া উঠাইয়া বা অন্য কোন প্রকারে বন্দুক প্রস্তুত রাখা হয় ; ঐরূপ ভাবে অবস্থিত হওয়ার জন্য আদেশ । 2. (*Slang*) Ready money ; (ইতর ভাষায়) নগদ টাকা, রোক টাকা । ***Verb t.*** **1.** To make ready ; প্রস্তুত করা । **2.** (*Racing slang*) To prevent as one's horse from winning in order to secure a handicap in another race ; (ঘোড়দৌড়ের ইতর ভাষায়) অপর দৌড়ে সুবিধা পাওয়ার জন্য কোন দৌড়ে নিজের ঘোড়া যাহাতে জয় লাভ না করিতে পারে সেরূপ করা । **Ready money** — Actual coin ; payment on the spot ; রোক টাকা, নগদ টাকা ; নগদ প্রদান । **Ready-made**—Made and ready for use ; connected with articles ready-made ; as, a *ready-made*, shop ; তৈয়ারী (পোষাক) কাটা (কাপড়) ; তৈয়ারী পোষাকের (দোকান), কাটা কাপড়ের (দোকান) । **Ready reckoner**—যে পুস্তকের সাহায্যে বিনা গণনায় মূল্য প্রভৃতি জানা যায়, সহজগণক । **Ready wit**—See READY, *adj.* 3. **Ready-witted**—উপস্থিতবুদ্ধিসম্পন্ন, প্রত্যুৎপন্নমতি । **Good value for ready money**—চোখা কড়ি, চোখা মাল ।

rē-ăf-firm' (-fĕrm), *v. t.* To affirm again ; পুনরায় নিশ্চিত রূপে বলা ।

rē-ăf-fŏr'-ĕst, *v. t.* To convert anew into a forest ; পুনরায় বনে পরিণত করা ।

rē-ā'-gĕn-cy̆, *n.* Reactive power or operation ; প্রতিক্রিয়া-শক্তি, প্রতিক্রিয়া ।

rē-ā'-gĕnt, *n.* **1.** (*Chem.*) A substance employed to detect the presence of another ; (রসায়নশাস্ত্র) যে রাসায়নিক পদার্থের সাহায্যে অন্য কোন রাসায়নিক পদার্থের স্থিতি নির্ণয় করা হয়, প্রতিকারক (হিঃ কোঃ), পরীক্ষক (ঐ) । **2.** A reactive substance, force, etc. ; প্রতিক্রিয়া-সাধক পদার্থ, শক্তি, প্রভৃতি ।

rē-ăl', *n.* **1.** A small Spanish coin of silver worth $2\frac{1}{2}$*d.* ; স্পেন দেশীয় ২॥ পেন্স মূল্যের ক্ষুদ্র রৌপ্য মুদ্রা বিশেষ । **2.** A money of account, formerly the unit of Spanish monetary system ; স্পেনদেশীয় এক-প্রকার কল্পিত মুদ্রা—যাহা কেবল হিসাবে ধরা হয় ।

rē'-ăl, *adj.* **1.** Actually existing ; objective ; as, a *real* thing ; বাস্তবিক বিদ্যমান, সৎ, সাত্ত্বিক ; মূর্ত্ত, মূর্ত্তিমন্ত, বস্তুতন্ত্র । **2.** Genuine ; not fictitious or artificial ; not apparent, nominal or pretended ; natural ; as, *real* life ; sincere ; as, *real* and paper roses : *real* doubt : a *real* man ; প্রকৃত ; আসল ; বাস্তবিক, সত্য ; যথার্থ, বাস্তব ; স্বভাবজাত, নৈসর্গিক ; সরল

অকৃত্রিম, অকপট, খাঁটি। 3. Representing reality; as, *real* ideas, বাস্তবতাবাচক। 4. (*Philos.*) Having an absolute and necessary existence; (দর্শনশাস্ত্র) সৎস্বরূপ। 5. (*Law*) Pertaining to things fixed, permanent or immovable; as, *real* estate; (আইন) স্থাবর। **Real issue**—আসল কথা। **Real life**—বাস্তব জীবন। **Real man**—Unaffected or sincere man; also, a man worthy of the name; খাঁটি লোক, প্রকৃত মনুষ্য; যথার্থ মানুষ **Real money**—Coin; cash; মুদ্রা; নগদ টাকা। **Real property**—স্থাবর সম্পত্তি। **The real presence**—খৃষ্টের অন্তিমভোজনস্মারক অনুষ্ঠানের রুটি ও মদিরায় তদীয় মাংস ও রক্তের অবস্থিতি—যাহা খৃষ্টীয় শাস্ত্রবিদ্‌গণের বিবাদের বিষয়ীভূত ছিল। **The real thing**—Not a makeshift or inferior article; আসল জিনিষ।

rē′-ăl, *n.* 1. (With *the*) That which is real—(opposed to the *ideal*); বাস্তব বস্তু। 2. (Usu. *pl.*) Something real; as, to deal only with *reals* (*rare*); বাস্তব বিষয় (কচিদ্ ব্যবহৃত)। 3. (*Pl.*) The ultimate beings composing the world, each being of a simple indefinable quality; গুণ (ব্রজঃ হিন্দু)। **Real idealism**—প্রত্যয়জাত্যৈক্যবাদ (হিঃ কোঃ)।

rē-ăl′-găr, *n.* Red sulphuret of arsenic; মনঃশিলা, মনছাল [Syn. কুনটী (সাঃ পঃ), শিলা (ঐ), শৃঙ্গী (ধাঃ প্রঃ), শোণিতশিলা (ঐ), রক্তধাতু। Also see RED ARSENIC].

rē′-ăl-ĭsm, *n.* 1. (*Metaph.*) The doctrine that there is an immediate or intuitive cognition of external objects (opposed to *idealism*); আমরা বহির্জগতের বস্তুসমূহ সম্বন্ধে অব্যবহিত ও অপরোক্ষ জ্ঞানলাভ করিয়া থাকি—এইরূপ মতবাদ, বস্তুস্বাতন্ত্র্যবাদ (হিঃ কোঃ), অস্তিত্ববাদ (বিশ্বঃ), সত্তাবাদ (ঐ)। 2. The scholastic doctrine that general terms represent real existences; (মধ্যযুগের দর্শনে) সামান্যবাচক পদসমূহ বাস্তব পদার্থের প্রতিরূপ—এইরূপ মতবাদ। [(১) দেশ, কাল ও ইহাদের গুণসমূহের বাস্তব সত্তা আছে—সর্ব্বাতীতবস্তুস্বাতন্ত্র্যবাদ (Transcendental realism); (২) আমাদের সংবিৎ (consciousness) এবং সমবধারণ (conception) নিরপেক্ষ প্রপঞ্চের (phenomenon) সত্তা আছে—অনুভবমূলক স্বাতন্ত্র্যবাদ (Empirical realism)], জাতিবাস্তবত্ববাদ (হিঃ কোঃ), জাতিস্বাতন্ত্র্যবাদ (ঐ)। 3. Fidelity to nature or real life in representation (opposed to *idealism*); নাটক, উপন্যাস ও চিত্রকলাদিতে বাস্তবজীবন যথাযথ বর্ণন বা চিত্রণের প্রতি নিষ্ঠা, নিসর্গনিষ্ঠা, বস্তুতন্ত্রতা। [Zola, Dostoievsky, প্রভৃতি নিসর্গনিষ্ঠ লেখক।] বস্ত্বনুকরণ কলাবাদ (হিঃ কোঃ)। 4. Tendency to regard things as they really are; practical views and policy; স্বাভাবিকতা; কার্য্যকরী মত বা নীতি।

rē′-ăl-ĭst, *n.* & *adj.* 1. An advocate or supporter of realism; বস্তুস্বাতন্ত্র্যবাদী, জাতিবাস্তবত্ববাদী (হিঃ কোঃ), জাতিস্বাতন্ত্র্যবাদী (ঐ), গুণাতিরিক্তদ্রব্যবাদী (ঐ)। 2. (*Arts & literature*) (সাহিত্য ও ললিতকলা) নিসর্গনিষ্ঠশিল্পী, বস্ত্বনুকরণকলাবাদী (হিঃ কোঃ), বাস্তবদর্শী, বস্তুতান্ত্রিক। *Adj.* Same as REALISTIC.

rē-ăl-ĭs′-tĭc, *adj.* 1. Of, relating to, or characteristic of, the realists; বস্তুস্বাতন্ত্র্যবাদিসম্বন্ধীয়, নিসর্গনিষ্ঠ শিল্পী বা লেখকসম্বন্ধীয়। 2. Like reality; life-like; বাস্তববৎ; স্বভাবসঙ্গত, নিসর্গনিষ্ঠ। **–ti-cal-ly**, *adv.*

rē-ăl′-ĭ-tȳ, *n.* 1. State or quality of being real; বাস্তবিকতা, বাস্তবতা, বস্তুত্ব, যথার্থতা, সত্যতা। 2. That which is real; real existence; বাস্তববস্তু, তত্ত্ব, সারবস্তু, সদ্‌বস্তু, প্রকৃত বস্তু, সত্ত্ব, সারাৎসার, সত্য (ডিউসেন); বাস্তবসত্তা। 3. Something having objective existence; বাস্তব পদার্থ। 4. Likeness or resemblance to the original; as, reproduced with amazing *reality*; মূলের সহিত সৌসাদৃশ্য। 5. (*Law*) Real estate; (আইন) স্থাবর সম্পত্তি। **In reality**—Really; in fact; বাস্তবিক পক্ষে; প্রকৃত পক্ষে, বস্তুতঃ।

rē′-ăl-īze, *v. t.* 1. To make real; to convert into fact, as a hope, plan, etc.; as, a *realized* hope; বাস্তব করা; বাস্তব ঘটনায় পরিণত করা, সিদ্ধ করা। 2. To impress upon the mind as actual; to apprehend clearly; বাস্তব বলিয়া ধারণা জন্মান; স্পষ্টরূপে উপলব্ধি করা, হৃদয়ঙ্গম করা, হৃদ্‌বোধ করা, হৃদ্গত করা, তত্ত্বসাক্ষাৎকার করা। 3. To make realistic; নিসর্গনিষ্ঠ করা। 4. To convert into actual money as assets, securities, etc.; টাকায় পরিণত করা। 5. To gain as profits; to amass as a fortune; লাভস্বরূপ প্রাপ্ত হওয়া; বহু অর্থ সঞ্চয় করা। 6. To bring by sale or investment; as, the property sold *realized* a fair price; আদায় করা, উশুল করা। **–iz′-a-ble**, *adj.* **–i-za′-tion**, *n.* 1. The act of realizing; the action of forming a distinct concept; "His faith stood simply on a vivid *realization* of the person of Christ"; the concept thus formed; কার্য্যে পরিণত করণ, সাধন; তত্ত্বোপলব্ধি, হৃদয়ঙ্গম, তত্ত্বসাক্ষাৎকার (বেদান্ত), তত্ত্বজ্ঞান (এভেলন); উপলব্ধি। 2. The action of obtaining or acquiring (a sum etc.); আদায়, উশুল। **Eternally realised**—অনাদিসিদ্ধ (নারায়ণ), নিত্যসিদ্ধ (ঐ)।

rē′-ăl-lȳ, *adv.* 1. Actually; প্রকৃত পক্ষে, বাস্তবিকই, বস্তুতঃ, তত্ত্বতঃ, যথার্থতঃ, পরমার্থতঃ। 2. Indeed; বাস্তবিক পক্ষে, বাস্তবিকই, ঠিকই।

realm (rĕlm), *n.* 1. A kingdom; রাজ্য, রাষ্ট্র, জনপদ। 2. Province; region; প্রদেশ; অঞ্চল।

rē′-ăl-tȳ, *n.* Real estate; স্থাবর সম্পত্তি।

ream (rēm), *n.* A package of paper consisting of twenty quires ; এক রীম কাগজ (৪৮০ তা, সাধারণত: অপচয় প্রভৃতি পূরণের জন্য প্রতি রীমে ৫০০ তা থাকে)। **Printers' ream**—৫১৬ তা'র রীম।

ream (rēm), *v. t.* **1.** To enlarge or bevel out, as a hole in metal ; ধাতুর ছিদ্র বড় করা বা ছিদ্রের ভিতরের দিকে টের্চ্চা করিয়া কাটা। **2.** To open for caulking ; আলকাতরা ও পুরাতন কাছির শণের সাহায্যে ফাঁক রোধ করার জন্য জাহাজের তক্তার জোড় খোলা।

ream'-êr (rēm-), *n.* One who, or that which, reams ; an instrument for enlarging a hole ; ছিদ্রবিস্তারকারী; ছিদ্রবর্দ্ধকযন্ত্র, ছিদ্রবিস্তারক।

rē-ăn'-i-māte, *v. t.* & *i.* To revive ; to resuscitate ; পুনর্জীবিত করা ; পুনরুজ্জীবিত করা। ***Verb i.*** To become re-animated ; পুনর্জীবিত হওয়া, পুনরুজ্জীবিত হওয়া। **—ma'-tion** *n.*

reap (rēp), *v. t.* & *i.* **1.** To cut down with a sickle, scythe or reaping-machine ; to cut down and gather when ripe and ready ; কাস্তে বা শস্যচ্ছেদক যন্ত্র দ্বারা ছেদন করা ; শস্য কাটা। **2.** To receive as a reward, or as the fruit of labour or exertions ; "The greatest blessing you have *reaped* from wealth" ; চেষ্টা বা পরিশ্রমের ফল কিম্বা পুরস্কারস্বরূপ প্রাপ্ত হওয়া। ***Verb i.*** **1.** To gather harvest ; শস্যচ্ছেদন করা, শস্য কাটা। **2.** To receive the fruit of labour or exertions ; চেষ্টা বা পরিশ্রমের ফল প্রাপ্ত হওয়া। **Reap'-er,** *n.* One that reaps ; a machine for cutting down grain ; শস্যচ্ছেদক ; শস্যচ্ছেদক যন্ত্র, লবিত্র। **Reap'-ing,** *n.* **Reaping-hook**—কাস্তে, শস্য-কর্ত্তরিকা। **Reaping-machine**—শস্যচ্ছেদক যন্ত্র। **As you sow so you will reap**—তুমি কর্ম্মানুসারে ফল ভোগ করিবে। **To reap a harvest**—To receive as the fruit of one's labour ; পরিশ্রমের ফলস্বরূপ লাভ করা। **To reap the fruits of**—To take the consequence of one's action ; স্বকার্য্যের ফল ভোগ করা। **To reap where one has not sown**—To enjoy the fruits of other men's labour ; অন্যের পরিশ্রমের ফল ভোগ করা।

rē-ăp-pear' (-pēr), *v. i.* To appear again ; পুনরাবির্ভূত হওয়া, পুনরাগত হওয়া, পুনরায় উপস্থিত হওয়া। **—ance,** *n.*

rē-ăp-plȳ', *v. t.* & *i.* To apply afresh ; পুনরায় প্রয়োগ করা, পুনরায় লাগান। **—pli-ca'-tion,** *n.*

rē-ăp-point' (-poynt), *v. t.* To appoint again ; পুনরায় নিযুক্ত করা, পুনর্নিয়োগ করা। **—ment,** *n.*

rear (rēr), *n.* & *adj.* **1.** The back or hindmost part ; পশ্চাদ্‌ভাগ, পৃষ্ঠদেশ। **2.** The part of an army or of a fleet which is behind the rest, (opposed to *van* or *front*) ; সৈন্যদলের পশ্চাদ্‌ভাগ, পার্ষ্ণিদেশ, পৃষ্ঠ, রণপোতবহরের পশ্চাদ্‌ভাগ। ***Adj.*** Being at the back, or in the hindmost part ; hindmost ; পশ্চাদ্‌বর্ত্তী ; সর্ব্বপশ্চাদ্‌বর্ত্তী। **Rear-admiral**—নৌ-বিভাগের উচ্চপদস্থ কর্ম্মচারিবিশেষ। **Rear-arch** — পশ্চাদ্‌বর্ত্তী দ্বার বা বাতায়নের বহির্দ্দিকের তোরণ হইতে ভিন্নাকৃতি বা ভিন্নায়তনের তোরণ। **Rear-front** — সৈন্যদলের সর্ব্বপশ্চাৎ শ্রেণী। **Rear-guard** — প্রধান সৈন্যদলের পশ্চাদ্‌ভাগরক্ষক সৈন্য, পার্ষ্ণিরক্ষক, জঘন (মঃ ভাঃ)। **Rear-guard action**—পার্ষ্ণিরক্ষকদের সহিত শত্রুসৈন্যের যুদ্ধ। **Rear-line, —rank**—সৈন্যদলের পশ্চাদ্‌ভাগস্থ সৈন্যশ্রেণী। **Rear-vault**—তোরণাকৃতি বাতায়ন বা দ্বারশীর্ষ এবং প্রাচীরের ভিতরের দিকের তোরণের মধ্যবর্ত্তী খিলানবিশিষ্ট স্থান। **Rearward,** *adj., adv.* & *n.* At or toward the rear ; পশ্চাদ্‌ভাগে, পশ্চাদভিমুখে, পশ্চাদভিমুখীন। •(*Noun*) The rear guard ; rear ; সৈন্যদলের পশ্চাদ্‌বর্ত্তী রক্ষিসৈন্য ; পশ্চাদ্‌ভাগ, পৃষ্ঠদেশ, পার্ষ্ণিদেশ। **To rear one's steps**—(*Rare*) To ascend ; (ক্বচিদ্‌-ব্যবহৃত) আরোহণ করা, উপরে উঠা। **To bring up or close the rear**—To come last or latest ; সর্ব্বশেষে আগত হওয়া, সকলের পশ্চাতে আসা। **To get rear of**—To get behind ; পশ্চাতে যাওয়া। **To hang on one's rear** — To follow closely with a view to attack when opportunity offers ; সুবিধা মত আক্রমণ করার উদ্দেশ্যে অনুসরণ করা। **To take an enemy in the rear**—To attack him from the rear ; পশ্চাদ্‌ভাগ হইতে শত্রুকে আক্রমণ করা।

rear (rēr), *v. t.* & *i.* **1.** To set upright ; to raise ; খাড়া করা ; উত্তোলন করা, তোলা। **2.** To construct ; as, to *rear* an edifice ; নির্ম্মাণ করা, গড়িয়া তোলা। **3.** To breed, as cattle etc. ; to grow, as crops ; গবাদি পালন করা ; উৎপাদন করা, চাষ করা। **4.** To foster ; as, to *rear* a child ; লালন পালন করা, প্রতিপালন করা। **5.** To utter a (cry) ; (ক্বচিদ্‌ব্যবহৃত) চীৎকার করা। ***Verb i.*** To rise on the hind legs, as a horse ; (*rarely reflexive*) to assume an erect posture ; পশ্চাতের পদদ্বয়ের উপর ভর দিয়া দণ্ডায়মান হওয়া ; খাড়া হওয়া।

rē-ar-range' (-ā-rānj), *v. t.* To arrange anew or afresh ; পুনর্বিন্যস্ত করা, পুনরায় সাজান।

rea'-son (rē-zn), *n.* **1.** A ground, cause or motive acting upon the mind ; a statement of fact, as an argument in justification or condemnation of some act ; কারণ, উদ্দেশ্য, নিমিত্ত ; হেতুবর্ণন, হেতু (স্ত্রীঃ)। **2.** An efficient cause ; a final cause ; নিমিত্ত কারণ ; পরম কারণ। **3.** The faculty that draws inferences from facts and premises, apprehends the relation between causes and effects and devises means towards ends ;

intelligence ; প্রজ্ঞা, বিবেক, বিচার (cf. বিচারমূঢ়) ; বুদ্ধি। 4. (*Eng. Phil.*) Higher cognitive faculties, such as conception, judgment, reasoning, intelligence ; (ইংলণ্ডীয় দর্শন) বুদ্ধি-শক্তি, বুদ্ধিবৃত্তি, বোধশক্তি, বিচারবুদ্ধি। 5. (*Kantian Phil.*) The powers by which first principles are grasped *a priori* ; (ক্যান্টের দর্শন) যে শক্তিদ্বারা দেশ, কাল, নিমিত্ত, প্রভৃতি মূলতত্ত্বসমূহ স্বতঃসিদ্ধবৎ উপলব্ধ হয়, (তত্ত্ববোধিনী বৃত্তি)। [কান্তের দর্শনে বুদ্ধিবৃত্তি (understanding) ও reason এতদুভয়ের মধ্যে পার্থক্য করা হইয়াছে। কান্তের মতে বুদ্ধিবৃত্তির রাজ্য ইন্দ্রিয়-প্রত্যক্ষ জগতের সহিত অভিন্ন ; কিন্তু তত্ত্ববোধিনী বৃত্তি ইন্দ্রিয়াতীত রাজ্যের উপর স্বীয় অধিকার বিস্তার করে। বুদ্ধি (understanding) দ্বারা যে জ্ঞান লাভ হয় তাহা অব্যাপক ও অনিত্য ; পরন্তু প্রজ্ঞাপ্রসূত জ্ঞান নিত্য এবং ব্যাপক।] 6. Sanity ; reasonableness ; "So now my *reason* was restored to me" ; প্রকৃতিস্থতা ; ন্যায্যতা। 7. Due exercise of reasoning faculty ; right judgment ; ratiocination ; বুদ্ধিশক্তির যথোচিত পরিচালনা ; যথার্থ নির্ণয় ; তর্ক, বিচার। 8. Moderation ; moderate demands ; "The most probable way of bringing France to *reason* would be by making an attempt on the West Indies" ; পরিমিতত্ব, পরিমিততা ; পরিমিতদাবী, সঙ্গতদাবী। 9. (*Log.*) A premise, esp. a minor premise ; (তর্কবিজ্ঞান) হেত্ববয়ব, বিশেষতঃ অবান্তর বাক্য, উপনয়। **Discursive** or **logical reason**—ন্যায়বাক্য অনুমান-সিদ্ধান্ত করার বৃত্তি। **Intuitive reason** — Same as REASON, 5. **Practical reason** — যে প্রজ্ঞার সাহায্যে ইচ্ছামূলক কার্য্য সমূহের হেতু বা বিশ্বজনীনসূত্র নির্ণয় করা হয়—কৃত্যবুদ্ধি (হিঃ কোঃ)। **Pure reason**—অনুভবমূলক জ্ঞানসংস্পর্শশূন্য প্রজ্ঞা, শুদ্ধ প্রজ্ঞা, অন্বয়জ্ঞান (অর্থাৎ যে প্রজ্ঞায় অনুভবমূলক জ্ঞানের সংস্পর্শ নাই।) [In Kantian sense, *Pure* = অন্বয়)] **Speculative reason** — ইন্দ্রিয়ের অতীত বিষয় উপলব্ধির বৃত্তি। **A woman's reason**—স্ত্রীলোকের যুক্তি (অর্থাৎ স্ত্রীলোকেরা কখন কখন বলিয়া থাকেন যে আমরা এই জিনিষটিকে ভালবাসি বা বিশ্বাস করি—ইহাই আমাদের ভালবাসা, বা বিশ্বাসের যুক্তি)। **By reason of**—On account of ; হেতু, নিবন্ধন, দরুণ, বশতঃ, কারণ, জন্য। **In reason** or **in all reason**—In justice ; ন্যায়তঃ। **Reason of State**—রাজ্যের মঙ্গলের জন্য কোন (নীতি বিরুদ্ধ) কার্য্য করা হইয়াছে বলিয়া উহার ন্যায্যতাপাদন, রাষ্ট্রীয় হেতু। **To bring to reason**—To persuade to desist from resistance ; নিস্ফল চেষ্টা হইতে বিরত করার জন্য প্ররোচিত করা। **To have reason**—To be right ; ন্যায়তঃ কার্য্য করা।

rea'-son (rē-zn), *v. i.* & *t.* 1. To ratiocinate ; তর্ক করা, বিচার করা। 2. To discuss ; to debate ; আলোচনা করা ; তর্কবিতর্ক করা, বাদানুবাদ করা। ***Verb t.*** 1. To debate or discourse ; বাদানুবাদ করা, আলোচনা করা। 2. To support with reasons ; যুক্তিদ্বারা সমর্থন করা। 3. To persuade by reasoning or argument ; as, to *reason* one out of an opinion ; যুক্তিদ্বারা প্ররোচিত করা।

rea'-son-a-ble (rē-zn-ă-bl), *adj.* 1. Endowed with reason ; বিচারশক্তিসম্পন্ন, প্রজ্ঞাবিশিষ্ট, প্রজ্ঞাবান। 2. Agreeable to reason ; not unreasonable or extravagant ; যুক্তিসঙ্গত, যুক্তিযুক্ত, যুক্তিসিদ্ধ ; ন্যায্য, ন্যায়সঙ্গত। 3. Not excessive ; moderate ; proper ; অনতিরিক্ত ; পরিমিত ; সঙ্গত। **–bly,** *adv.* In a reasonable manner ; যুক্তি-সঙ্গতরূপে, যুক্তিযুক্তরূপে ন্যায়সঙ্গতরূপে, ন্যায্যরূপে, সঙ্গতরূপে, উচিতমত, ন্যায়মত। **–ness,** *n.*

rea'-son-êr (rē-zn-), *n.* One who reasons or argues ; যুক্তিপ্রদর্শনকারী, বাদানুবাদকারী, তার্কিক, তর্ককারী।

rea'-son-ing (rē-zn-), *n.* 1. The act of one who reasons ; argumentation ; তার্কিক ; বাদানুবাদ, বিতর্কণ, যুক্তিপ্রণালী। 2. The arguments employed ; course of argument ; the proofs or arguments relied on by a disputant ; প্রদর্শিত যুক্তিসমূহ ; যুক্তিতর্ক, যুক্তিপরম্পরা ; কোন বিবাদকারী যে যুক্তিপ্রমাণের উপর নির্ভর করে। **Reasoning in a circle**—চক্রক (মঃ উঃ) [Also see CIRCLE]।

rē-ăs-sĕm'-ble (-bl), *v. t.* & *i.* To assemble afresh ; পুনরায় জড় বা সংগ্রহ করা কিম্বা হওয়া।

rē-ăs-sêrt', *v. t.* To assert again ; পুনরায় দৃঢ়রূপে বলা।

rē-ăs-sĕss', *v. t.* To assess afresh ; পুনরায় কর ধার্য্য করা। **–ment,** *n.*

rē-ăs-sign' (-sīn), *v. t.* To assign back ; পুনরায় নির্দ্দেশ করা, পুনরায় হস্তান্তরিত করা।

rē-ăs-sūme', *v. t.* To assume again ; to resume ; পুনর্গ্রহণ করা ; পুনরায় গ্রহণ করা। **–sump'-tion,** *n.*

rē-as-sūre (-ă-), *v. t.* 1. To assure anew ; to free from fear or alarm ; পুনরায় নিশ্চিত করা ; ভয় বা ত্রাস দূর করা, ভরসা দেওয়া, আশ্বস্ত করা। 2. To reinsure ; পুনরায় বীমা করা। **–sur'-ance,** *n.* **–sur'-ing,** *adj.* That which reassures ; আশ্বাসজনক।

Rē-au-mūr' (-ä-), *adj.* & *n.* Pertaining to the French physicist René Antoine Ferchault de Réaumur (1683—1757) ; ফরাসী বৈজ্ঞানিক Reaumur সম্বন্ধীয়। **Reaumur's scale** — তাপমানযন্ত্রের রেখাঙ্কিত ক্রমবিশেষ—যাহার তুষারাঙ্ক ০ দ্বারা ও স্ফুটনাঙ্ক ৮০° দ্বারা সূচিত হইয়া থাকে।

reave (rēv), **reive** (rēv), *v. t.* & *i.* (*Archaic*) To rob ; to snatch ; (অপ্রঃ) কাড়িয়া লওয়া; ছিনাইয়া নেওয়া। ***Verb i.*** To plunder; লুঠিয়া নেওয়া।

rē-băp-tīze′, *v. t.* To baptize a second time ; পুনর্দীক্ষিত করা। **–bap′-tism,** *n.*

rē-bâr′-bâ-rīze, *v. t.* To barbarize again ; পুনরায় বর্ব্বরে পরিণত করা। **–ri-za′-tion,** *n.*

rē-bāte′, *v. t.* **1.** (*Archaic*) To diminish ; (অপ্রঃ) হ্রাস করা, কমান। **2.** To blunt ; ভোঁতা করা।

rē-bāte′, *n.* & *v. t.* Same as RABBET (which see).

rē-bāte′, *n.* Abatement in price ; reduction ; মূল্যহ্রাস ; বাটা, ধরাট।

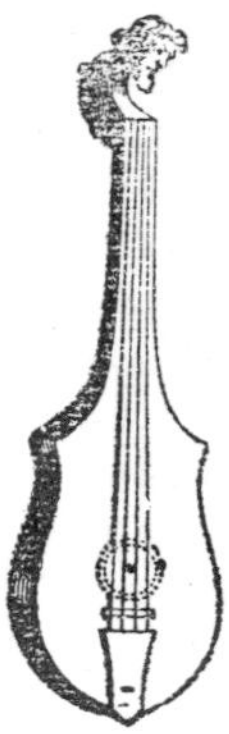

Rebec.

rĕ′-bĕc, re′-bĕck, *ns.* A stringed instrument somewhat similar to the violin ; রবাব।

rĕb′-ĕl, *n.* **1.** One who defies and seeks to overthrow the authority to which he is lawfully subject ; রাজদ্রোহী, বিদ্রোহী প্রজা। **2.** One who refuses to obey a superior ; বিদ্রোহী, বিদ্রোহভাবাপন্ন ব্যক্তি, গুরুদ্রোহী।

rē-bĕl′, *v. i.* **1.** To act as a rebel ; বিদ্রোহী হওয়া। **2.** To refuse to obey a superior ; গুরু ব্যক্তিকে অমান্য করা, গুরু ব্যক্তির আদেশ লঙ্ঘন করা, দ্রোহভাবাপন্ন হওয়া, বিদ্রোহাচরণ করা, অবাধ্য হওয়া। **3.** To conceive a loathing for ; as, my stomach *rebels* against nauseous food ; বিতৃষ্ণা বা বিরোগ প্রদর্শন করা।

rĕb′-ĕl, *adj.* Rebellious; as, *rebel* angles ; বিদ্রোহী।

rē-bĕl′-lion (-yŏn), *n.* **1.** Open and avowed renunciation of the authority of the government to which one owes his allegiance ; বিদ্রোহ। **2.** Open resistance to, or defiance of, any authority ; "Perhaps some *rebellion* against his destiny accounts for his atheism" ; কোনরূপ প্রভুশক্তির প্রতি প্রকাশ্যে বাধা প্রদান বা অমান্যতা-প্রদর্শন, বিদ্রোহাচরণ। **The Great Rebellion**—১৬৪২ হইতে ১৬৬০ খৃষ্টাব্দ পর্য্যন্ত পার্লেমেন্টের সহিত ১ম ও ২য় চার্লসের সংগ্রাম।

rē-bĕl′-li-ous (-yŭs), *adj.* **1.** In rebellion; disposed to rebel; বিদ্রোহী; বিদ্রোহপ্রবণ। **2.** (Of disease) Difficult to cure ; as, a *rebellious* ulcer; (of things) resisting operation ; as, *rebellious* gold ores ; refractory ; দুরারোগ্য, দুঃসাধ্য, দুশ্চিকিৎস্য ; ক্রিয়ারোধক ; অদ্রাব্য, অগলনীয়, দুর্দ্রবনীয়। **–ly,** *adv.* **–ness,** *n.*

rē-bīnd′, *v. t.* To bind again ; পুনরায় বাঁধা।

rē-birth′ (-bêrth), *n.* Reincarnation ; পুনর্জন্ম।

rē-bīt′-ing, *n.* The act or process for deepening the lines on engraved plates ; ক্ষোদিত ফলকের উপর রেখাসমূহ গভীরকরণ বা গভীর করার প্রণালীবিশেষ।

rĕb′-ō-ănt, *adj.* (*Poet.*) Loudly resounding ; (কবিতায়) নির্ঘোষকারী, গর্জ্জনকারী।

rē-bound′ (-bownd), *v. i.* **1.** To fly back by elastic force after impact with another body ; ঠিকরান, প্রতিক্ষিপ্ত হওয়া, প্রতিহত হইয়া আসা, উৎপতিত হওয়া। **2.** (*Now rare*) To re-echo ; (বর্ত্তমানে ক্বচিদ্ ব্যবহৃত) প্রতিধ্বনি করা।

rē-bound′ (-bownd), *n.* **1.** Act of rebounding ; প্রতিক্ষেপ, উৎপতন। **2.** Reaction after emotion ; আবেগ, উচ্ছ্বাস, প্রভৃতির পর প্রতিক্রিয়া। **To take at, by, from** or **upon rebound**—(*Obs.*) To try to persuade one to do something against his inclination at the time of one's reaction; (অপ্রঃ) কোন ব্যক্তিকে তাহার ইচ্ছার বিপরীত কোন কার্য্যে প্ররোচিত করার জন্য তাহার অবসাদ বা প্রতিক্রিয়ার অবস্থায় চেষ্টা করা।

rē-bŭff′, *n.* & *v. t.* A sudden check ; a defeat ; a repulse ; a snub ; আকস্মিক বাধা ; পরাভব ; ধাক্কা ; মুখঝামটা (*colloq.*)। ***Verb t.*** To give a rebuff to ; সহসা বাধা দেওয়া, ধাক্কা দেওয়া, দাবানি দেওয়া।

rē-build′ (-bĭld), *v. t.* To build again ; পুনরায় নির্ম্মাণ করা পুনর্নির্ম্মাণ করা।

rē-būke′, *v. t.* & *n.* To chide ; তিরস্কার করা, ভৎর্সনা করা, ধমকান। ***Noun.*** **1.** The act of rebuking ; a reproof or reprimand ; তিরস্কার করণ ; তিরস্কার, ভৎর্সনা, গঞ্জনা, ধমকানি। **To be without rebuke**—To be blameless ; নিষ্কলঙ্ক জীবন যাপন করা।

rē′-bŭs, *n.* An enigmatical representation of words by figures ; a kind of riddle or puzzle made up of such figures or pictures ; চিত্রাদির সাহায্যে শব্দ প্রকাশ, চিত্রলিপি [যথা একটী পর্ব্বত, চন্দ্র ও সিংহের ছবি দ্বারা নগেন্দ্র চন্দ্র সিংহ এই নাম লিখন।] ; ঐরূপ চিত্রাদির সাহায্যে রচিত ধাঁধা, চিত্রপ্রহেলিকা (আঃ বঃ)।

Rebus of the Abbot Islip, West-Minister Abbey.

rē-bŭt′, *v. t.* & *i.* **1.** To repell ; to drive back ; প্রতিহত করা ; প্রতিক্ষেপ করা, ফিরান। **2.** (*Law*) To refute ; (আইন) খণ্ডন করা। ***Verb i.*** **1.** (*Obs.*) To retire ; (অপ্রঃ) হটিয়া যাওয়া। **2.** (*Law*) To make an answer ; জবাব দেওয়া, উত্তর দেওয়া, প্রত্যুত্তর করা। **–tal, –ment, –ter,** *ns.*

rē-căl′-cĭ-trănt, *adj.* & *n.* Refractory ; দুর্দ্দান্ত, দুর্দ্দম, অবশ্য, অদম্য, অবাধ্য। ***Noun.*** A refractory person ; দুর্দ্দান্ত ব্যক্তি, অদম্য লোক।

rĕ-căl'-cĭ-trāte, *v. i.* To be refractory; অবাধ্য হওয়া, অদম্য হওয়া। **–tra'-tion,** *n.*

rĕ-că-lesce' (-lĕs), *v. t.* **1.** To grow hot again; পুনরায় উষ্ণ হওয়া (বিশেষতঃ লৌহ প্রভৃতি ধাতু চরম মাত্রায় উত্তপ্ত করার পর ঠাণ্ডা করিতে দিলে এক সময়ে উহা হঠাৎ কিয়ৎকালের জন্য উষ্ণ হইয়া উঠা)। **–les'-cence,** *n.*

rĕ-call', *v. t.* **1.** To call back; ফিরাইয়া আনা, ডাকিয়া ফিরান পুনরাহ্বান করা। **2.** To resuscitate; "Their eyes, their lips...*recall* my love"; পুনর্জ্জীবিত করা, সঞ্জীবিত করা। **3.** To revoke; as, to *recall* a decree; রদ করা, বাতিল করা। **4.** To remember; to revive in memory; স্মরণ করা, মনে করা; স্মৃতি জাগরূক করা। **5.** To call or summon back from a place or mission; as, to *recall* an ambassador from a foreign court; কোন কার্য্য বা কার্য্যস্থল হইতে পুনরাহ্বান করা। **6.** To call back; as, to *recall* a gift; ফিরাইয়া নেওয়া, প্রতিগ্রহণ করা।

rĕ-call', *n.* **1.** The act of calling back; summons to returns, প্রত্যানয়ন; প্রত্যাবর্ত্তনের জন্য আহ্বান, পুনরাহ্বান। **2.** The power or possibility of recalling; as, beyond *recall*; খণ্ডন বা প্রত্যাগমনের ক্ষমতা বা সম্ভাবনা। **3.** A signal sounded on drum etc. to call back soldiers; সৈন্যদিগকে শিবিরে বা স্ব স্ব পংক্তিতে প্রত্যাবর্ত্তনের জন্য দুন্দুভি প্রভৃতির সঙ্কেতধ্বনি। **4.** (*Naut.*) A signal calling a ship etc. to return; (নৌ-বিদ্যা) জাহাজ প্রভৃতিকে স্বস্থানে প্রত্যাবর্ত্তনের জন্য সঙ্কেত।

rĕ-cănt', *v. t. & i.* To retract; to abjure; প্রত্যাহার করা; শপথপূর্ব্বক ধর্ম্মমত প্রভৃতি পরিত্যাগ করা। ***Verb i.*** To renounce or disavow publicly an opinion or principle formerly held; পূর্ব্ব মত বা বিশ্বাস প্রকাশ্যে পরিত্যাগ বা প্রত্যাখ্যান করা। **–can-ta'-tion,** *n.*

rĕ-că-pit'-ū-lāte, *v. t. & i.* To give a summary of the principal facts, points or arguments of; to restate briefly; বক্তৃতা প্রভৃতির প্রধান প্রধান বিষয়ের সারাংশ প্রদান করা; পুনরায় সংক্ষেপে বলা। ***Verb i.*** To repeat in brief what has been said before; পূর্ব্বকথিত বিষয় সংক্ষেপে পুনরায় বলা। **–la'-tion,** *n.* **1.** The act of recapitulating; বক্তৃতাদির প্রধান প্রধান বিষয় সংক্ষেপে পুনর্ব্বর্ণন, সংক্ষেপে পুনরুক্তি। **2.** A summary of an essay etc.; (বক্তৃতাদির) স্থূলমর্ম্ম, সারমর্ম্ম। **3.** (*Biol.*) Repetition in an individual of phylogenetic development; (জীববিজ্ঞান) ব্যষ্টি জীবে জাতিগত অভিব্যক্তির পুনরাবর্ত্তন। **–la-to-ry,** *adj.*

rĕ-căp'-tūre, *v. t. & n.* To capure again; to retake from an enemy a ship, town, goods, etc. that had previously been taken; পুনরায় ধৃত করা, পুনরায় বন্দী করা; বিশেষতঃ শত্রুকর্ত্তৃক গৃহীত জাহাজ, নগর, বা দ্রব্যসমূহ পুনরায় অধিকার করা। ***Noun.*** **1.** The act of recapturing; পুনরায় বন্দীকরণ, বিশেষতঃ শত্রুকর্ত্তৃক গৃহীত জাহাজাদি পুনরায় অধিকার করণ। **2.** That which is recaptured; a prize retaken; পুনরায় বন্দীকৃত বস্তু; শত্রুর নিকট হইতে পুনরধিকৃত পোত, নগর, প্রভৃতি।

rĕ-căr'-rȳ, *v. t.* To carry back; পুনরায় বহন করা।

rĕ-căst', *v. t.* **1.** To cast or found again; পুনরায় ঢালাই করা। **2.** To remould; as, to *recast* literary work; পুনরায় গড়া, নূতন ছাঁচে গড়া। **3.** To compute a second time; পুনর্গণনা করা।

rĕ-cede' (-sēd), *v.i. & t.* **1.** To move back; to retreat; পশ্চাতে সরা, পশ্চাদ্-অপসৃত হওয়া; হটিয়া যাওয়া। **2.** To become more distant; ক্রমশঃ পশ্চাতে সরা। **3.** To withdraw from a claim or pretension; as, to *recede* a demand; to desist; কোনরূপ দাবী হইতে প্রতিনিবৃত্ত হওয়া; নিরস্ত হওয়া, বিরত হওয়া। ***Verb t.*** (*Rare*) To cede back again; (ক্বচিদ্ ব্যবহৃত) পুনরায় ভুক্ত করা।

rĕ-ceipt' (-sēt), *n. & v. t.* **1.** The act of receiving or taking; প্রাপ্তি, আদান, গ্রহণ। **2.** A recipe; ঔষধের ব্যবস্থাপত্র। **3.** That which is received; as, his *receipts* were found Rs. 50/- a day; drawings; প্রাপ্ত জিনিষ, প্রাপ্ত অর্থ; জমা, আয়। **4.** A written acknowledgment or account of something; প্রতিগ্রহপত্র (আঃ বঃ), রসিদ। ***Verb t.*** To give a receipt for; to write an acknowledgment of receipt on a bill; রসিদ দেওয়া; বিলের উপর প্রাপ্তি স্বীকার করা। **Receipt-book**—রসিদ-বহি। **Receipt-stamp**—রসিদ ষ্ট্যাম্প।

rĕ-ceive' (-sēv), *v. t.* **1.** To get or obtain; to take a proffered thing; প্রাপ্ত হওয়া; গ্রহণ করা। **2.** To take or admit into the mind; to gain the knowledge of; মনের মধ্যে গ্রহণ করা; জ্ঞান লাভ করা। **3.** To give admittance to; to welcome; as, to *receive* a guest; প্রবেশ করিতে দেওয়া; অভ্যর্থনা করা, সম্বর্দ্ধনা করা, সাদর সম্ভাষণ করা, বরণ করা (গীতাঞ্জঃ)। **4.** To meet with resistance; as, to *receive* an enemy's attack; প্রতিরোধ করা। **5.** To suffer; to undergo; "He had undoubtedly *received* much real provocation; ভোগ করা; সহা, সহ্য করা। **6.** To contain; "The brozen altar...was too little to *receive* the burnt offerings"; ধরা। **7.** To reset stolen goods; চোরাই মাল রাখা। **–ceiv'-a-ble,** *adj.*

rĕ-ceiv'-ĕr (-sēv-), *n.* **1.** One who receives; গ্রহণকারী, গ্রাহক, প্রাপক। **2.** An officer appointed to receive public money; esp. a person appointed by a court to hold and manage property of a bankrupt or property which is the subject of a litigation; সাধারণের অর্থ গ্রহণের জন্য নিযুক্ত কর্ম্মচারী, দাউলিয়ার সম্পত্তি কিম্বা মোকদ্দমাধীন সম্পত্তির রক্ষা ও পরিচালনের জন্য আদালতকর্তৃক নিযুক্ত কর্ম্মচারী; রিসীভর। 3. One that takes stolen goods, knowing them to be stolen; যে ব্যক্তি জানিয়া শুনিয়া চোরাই মাল রাখে, থানকীদার। 4. (*Chem.*) A vessel for receiving the products of distillation; পরিস্রুত পদার্থ যে ভাণ্ডে সঞ্চিত হয়, ঘটগ্রাহক (হিঃ কোঃ)। 5. A vessel for containing gas; বাষ্পভাণ্ড। 6. The bell-glass on the table of an air-pump; বায়ুনিষ্কাশন যন্ত্রের মেজের উপরিস্থ ঘণ্টাকৃতি কাচাবরণ। 7. The receiving part of a telegraph, telephone, etc.; তাড়িতবার্ত্তাবহ, দূরশ্রবণ যন্ত্র, প্রভৃতির যে অংশে তাড়িতপ্রবাহ দর্শনযোগ্য বা শ্রবণযোগ্য সঙ্কেতে পরিণত হয়, গ্রাহকযন্ত্র (সাঃ পঃ), শব্দগ্রাহক (প্রবাসী—১৩১৯)। **–ceiv′-ing,** *adj.* Adopted to receive; গ্রহণক্ষম। **Receiving-box**—চিঠি রাখার বাক্স। **Receiving-house**—যে কার্য্যালয়ে পুলিন্দা, চিঠি, প্রভৃতি প্রেরণের জন্য গ্রহণ করা হয়। **Receiving-instrument** — Same as RECEIVER, 7. **Receiving-office**—যে ক্ষুদ্র ডাকঘরে প্রেরণের জন্য চিঠি, পুলিন্দা, প্রভৃতি গ্রহণ করা হয়, কিন্তু যথা হইতে চিঠি পত্রাদি বিলি হয় না। **Receiving-ship**—যে জাহাজে থাকিয়া নৌবিভাগের শিক্ষানবীসগণ নাবিকের কার্য্য শিক্ষা করিয়া থাকে।

rē-cĕn′-sion, *n.* 1. (*Now rare*) The act of reviewing or revising; (বর্ত্তমানে কচিদ্‌ব্যবহৃত) সমালোচন, সংশোধন। 2. A text established by a critical editor; কোন পুস্তকের সংশোধিত সংস্করণ, প্রতিসংস্করণ, পাঠপ্রণালী (কৌষীতকী উপনিষৎ—টীকা)। **–ist,** *n.*

rē′-cĕnt, *adj.* 1. Of late origin, existence or occurrence; অচিরজাত, অচিরসংঘটিত, অচিরগত। 2. Fresh; as, *recent* news; টাট্‌কা, নূতন। 3. Modern; আধুনিক, ইদানীন্তন, অধুনাতন। **–ly,** *adv.* Lately; সম্প্রতি, ইদানীং, অধুনা।

rē-cĕp′-tă-cle (-cl), *adj.* 1. A repository; আধার, ভাণ্ড, আশয়, স্থালী, পাত্র, ভাজন, অধিশ্রয় (সুশ্রুঃ কুষ্ঠঃ), অধিকরণ, নিধি (*fig.*), নিধান (ঐ)। 2. (*Bot.*) That part of a flower upon which carpels are situated; (উদ্ভিদ্‌বিদ্যা) পুষ্পের যে অংশে কিঞ্জল্কসমূহ অবস্থিত থাকে, পুষ্পধী।

rē-cĕp′-tion, *n.* 1. The act of receiving; state of being received; গ্রহণ, গ্রহ; প্রাপ্তি। 2. Welcome; formal occasion or ceremony of receiving a guest; অভ্যর্থনা; সম্ভাষণ, সম্বর্দ্ধনা, সাদর সম্ভাষণ। 3. Admission; as, the *reception* of food into the stomach; প্রবেশন। 4. Acceptance, as of an opinion or doctrine; approbation; কোন মত বা সিদ্ধান্ত গ্রহণ; অনুমোদন। 5. (*Astrol.*) The fact of each of two planets being received into the other's house, exaltation or other dignity; গ্রহদ্বয়ের পরস্পরের ক্ষেত্র, তুঙ্গ, মূলত্রিকোণ, ইত্যাদিতে অবস্থান। **Reception-day**—অভ্যর্থনা দিবস। **Reception-committee**—অভ্যর্থনা সমিতি, সম্বর্দ্ধনা-সমিতি। **Reception order**—ক্ষিপ্ত ব্যক্তিকে উন্মাদাগারে গ্রহণ করার জন্য আদেশপত্র। **Reception room**—অভ্যর্থনা কক্ষ, বৈঠকখানা। **Warm reception**—Enthusiastic welcome; furious opposition; উৎসাহপূর্ণ অভ্যর্থনা; প্রচণ্ড প্রতিরোধ।

rē-cĕp′-tive (-tĭv), *adj.* Having the quality of grasping ideas; as, a *receptive* mind; able to hold or contain; গ্রহণশীল, গ্রহণক্ষম, ভাবগ্রহণশীল, ভাবগ্রহণক্ষম; ধারণক্ষম। **–tiv′-i-ty,** *n.* The quality or state of being receptive; গ্রহণশীলতা, গ্রহণক্ষমতা, ধারণক্ষমতা।

rē-cĕss′, *n.* & *v. t.* 1. A withdrawing or receding; as, the *recess* of the tides; পশ্চাদপসরণ, সরণ। 2. Temporary suspension of business; a short intermission, as of a legislative body, court or school; "The *recess* of the English Parliament lasted for six weeks"; অল্পকালের জন্য কার্য্য বিশ্রান্তি; ব্যবস্থাপক-সভা, বিদ্যালয়, আদালত, প্রভৃতির সাময়িক কার্য্যবিশ্রান্তি কাল, অবকাশ। 3. A place of retirement or secrecy; as, the inmost *recesses* of the Himalays; গোপন স্থান, নিভৃত স্থান, অন্তরতম প্রদেশ। 4. A receding part of a coast, range of hills, etc.; উপকূল, গিরিমালা, প্রভৃতির পশ্চাদপসৃত অংশ, বাঁক। 5. A niche; কুলুঙ্গী, দেওয়ালের খোঁদল। 6. (*Anat.* & *Bot.*) A sinus or an indentation; (শারীরসংস্থানবিদ্যা) গহ্বরনালী, (উদ্ভিদ্‌বিদ্যা) খাঁজ। ***Verb t.*** 1. To make into a recess; to make a recess in; as, to *recess* a wall; খোঁদল বা কুলুঙ্গীতে পরিণত করা; কুলুঙ্গী করা। 2. To seclude; বিবিক্ত করা, লোক-সমাজ হইতে দূরে রাখা, নিভৃত রাখা।

rē-ces′-sion (-sŏ-), *n.* The act of receding or withdrawal from a place; পশ্চাদপসরণ, সরণ।

rē-ces′-sion (-sĕ-), *n.* Restoration; as, the *recession* of a conquered territory; প্রত্যর্পণ।

rē-ces′-sion-ăl (-sŏ-), *adj.* & *n.* Pertaining to, or done in, interval; কার্য্যবিশ্রান্তিকালেকৃত, অবকাশকালে সম্পাদিত। ***Noun.*** Same as RECESSIONAL HYMN. **Recessional hymn**—উপাসনান্তে যাজক ও গায়কমণ্ডলীর কক্ষান্তরে গমনকালে যে গীত গাওয়া হয়।

Rĕch′-ăb-īte, *n.* 1. A teetotaller (See *Jer.* xxxv. 6.); মাদকদ্রব্য-পরিবর্জ্জনকারী। 2. A dweller in tent; শিবিরবাসী ব্যক্তি।

rē-charge′ (-chârj), *v. t.* **1.** To re-accuse ; পুনরায় অভিযুক্ত করা। **2.** To attack anew ; পুনরায় আক্রমণ করা।

rechauffe, (*F.*), *n.* **1.** A warmed-up dish ; পুনরায় গরম করা হইয়াছে এরূপ খাদ্যপূর্ণ স্থালী, পুনরুষ্ণীকৃত ব্যঞ্জন। **2.** Anything hashed up anew ; পুরাতন উপাদান দ্বারা প্রস্তুত কোন কিছু।

recherche, (*F.*), *adj.* Choice ; out of common ; exquisite ; as, a *recherche* stock of feather and ribbons ; উৎকৃষ্ট ; অসাধারণ ; চমৎকার।

rē-čid-i-vist, *n.* One who has been convicted a second time ; দাগী। **—vism, —va′-tion,** *ns.*

rĕč′-i-pē, *n.* **1.** A medical prescription (*abbr.* R) ; ঔষধের ব্যবস্থাপত্র। **2.** A receipt for preparing a dish etc. ; ব্যঞ্জনাদি প্রস্তুতের জন্য ফর্দ্দ। **3.** A means prescribed for attaining something ; "This corporation has one *recipe* for all difficulties—organization" ; কোন উদ্দেশ্য সাধনের জন্য উপায় বা ব্যবস্থা।

rē-čip′-i-ĕnt, *n.* & *adj.* A person who receives something ; গ্রহণকারী, গ্রাহক, গ্রহীতা, প্রাপক। ***Adj.*** Receiving ; গ্রহণকারী, গ্রহণশীল।

rē-čip′-rō-căl, *adj.* & *n.* **1.** Moving backwards and forwards ; অগ্রপশ্চাদ্গামী। **2.** Mutual ; as, *reciprocal* aid ; পারস্পরিক, অন্যোন্য, অন্যোন্যানুবন্ধী, অন্যোন্যগত (বিরুঃ), ইতরেতর, ইতরেতরাশ্রয়, পরস্পর। **3.** Mutually interchangeable ; corresponding ; complementary ; "These two rules will render a definition *reciprocal* with the thing defined" ; পরস্পরের সহিত পরস্পর বিনিময়যোগ্য ; পরস্পর অনুরূপ, পরস্পরানুসারী, পরস্পরানুবর্ত্তী ; অন্যোন্যপূরক, পুরণাত্মক। **4.** Of the nature of return ; as, to receive a *reciprocal* benefit ; প্রতিদানাত্মক, প্রতিদানস্বরূপ। **5.** (*Gram.*) (Formerly) Expressing mutual relation or action ; eflexive ; (ব্যাকরণ—পূর্ব্বে) অন্যোন্যসম্বন্ধ বা ক্রিয়াবাচক ; স্বয়মর্থক। **6.** (*Math.*) Denoting different kinds of mutual relations ; (গণিতশাস্ত্র) বিভিন্নপ্রকার অন্যোন্যসম্বন্ধবাচক। ***Noun.*** **1.** That which is reciprocal to another thing ; a counterpart ; অপর বস্তুর সহিত অন্যোন্যসম্বন্ধবিশিষ্ট বস্তু ; অনুরূপ অংশ। **2.** (*Math.*) The quotient of unity divided by any quantity ; কোন সংখ্যাদ্বারা এককে ভাগ করিলে যে ভাগফল লব্ধ হয়, ব্যুৎক্রম (হিঃ কোঃ)। **—ly,** *adv.* In a reciprocal manner ; অন্যোন্যসম্বন্ধবাচক ভাবে, অঙ্গাঙ্গি ভাবে। **Reciprocal-cross**—কোন এক জাতীয় জন্তুর পুরুষের এবং ভিন্ন জাতীয় জন্তুর স্ত্রীর সংসর্গে উৎপাদিত সঙ্কর এবং তৎপর দ্বিতীয় জন্তুর পুরুষ ও প্রথম জন্তুর স্ত্রীর সংসর্গে উৎপন্ন সঙ্কর, পারস্পরিক সঙ্কর। **Reciprocal demand**—(অর্থনীতি শাস্ত্র) দুই ব্যক্তি বা সম্প্রদায়ের পরস্পর উৎপন্ন দ্রব্যের জন্য গ্রাহকতা (চাহিদা)। **Reciprocal-equation**—অজ্ঞাত রাশির পরিবর্ত্তে উহার ব্যুৎক্রম (reciprocal) বসাইলে যে সমীকরণের রূপের কোন প্রকার পরিবর্ত্তন হয় না। **Reciprocally proportional**—ব্যুৎক্রম-যুগ্ম-নিষ্পত্তি সম্বন্ধী (হিঃ কোঃ)। **Reciprocal quantities**—যে দুই রাশি পরস্পর গুণ করিলে গুণফল ১ হয়। **Reciprocal ratio**—দুই রাশির ব্যুৎক্রম দ্বয়ের মধ্যে নিষ্পত্তি (ratio), পারস্পরিক (reciprocals) নিষ্পত্তি (যথা ২ : ৩এর পারস্পরিক নিষ্পত্তি — ½ : ⅓)। **Reciprocal terms**—সমার্থক পদসমূহ (অর্থাৎ যে পদ সমূহ পরস্পরের পরিবর্ত্তে প্রয়োগ করা যাইতে পারে), পরস্পরানুবর্ত্তী সংজ্ঞা (হিঃ কোঃ)।

rē-čip′-rō-cāte, *v. i.* & *t.* (*Now only in Mech*) To move with alternate motion ; (বর্ত্তমানে কেবল যন্ত্রবিজ্ঞানে ব্যবহৃত হয়) পর্য্যায়ক্রমে অগ্রপশ্চাতে চলা। ***Verb t.*** **1.** To cause to move backwards and forwards ; পর্য্যায়ক্রমে অগ্রপশ্চাদ্দিকে চালান। **2.** To interchange ; to return ; as, to *reciprocate* favours ; বিনিময় করা ; প্রতিদান করা, পরিশোধ করা। **—cat-ing,** *adj.* Backwards and forwards alternately ; পর্য্যায়ক্রমে অগ্রপশ্চাদ্গামী। **—ca′-tion,** *n.* The act of reciprocating ; ব্যুৎক্রমীভবন (হিঃ কোঃ)। **Reciprocating-engine** — (বাষ্পীয় যন্ত্র) যে কলের চাপদণ্ড (piston-rod) পর্য্যায়ক্রমে অগ্রপশ্চাতে চালিত হয়। **Reciprocating-motion** — কোন যন্ত্রের এক অংশ হইতে অপর অংশে যন্ত্রবলসঞ্চালনের প্রক্রিয়াবিশেষ। কোন মধ্যবিন্দু বা অক্ষের উপর একটী সুদৃঢ় দণ্ড দোলায়িত করা হয় এবং অক্ষের উভয় পার্শ্ববর্ত্তী যন্ত্রাংশসমূহ পর্য্যায়ক্রমে পরস্পরের স্থান অধিকার করিয়া থাকে। **Reciprocating proposition**—(তর্ক-বিজ্ঞান) যে বাক্য বা প্রতিজ্ঞা দ্বারা বিষয়ী এবং বিষয় পরিমাণে তুল্য ও অভিন্ন বলিয়া কথিত হয়, পরস্পরানুবর্ত্তী প্রতিজ্ঞা।

rĕč-i-prŏč′-i-tў, *n.* **1.** The quality or state of being reciprocal ; reciprocal action ; পারস্পরিকতা, অন্যোন্যানুবন্ধিতা, পরস্পরত্ব, পরস্পরতা, পরস্পরভাব, অন্যোন্যভাব, অন্যোন্যত্ব, অঙ্গাঙ্গি ভাব, অঙ্গাঙ্গিতা, ব্যতিকর (cf. ব্যতিকর সুখং—শকুন্তলা) ; পারস্পরিক কার্য্য। **2.** Reciprocation ; আদান-প্রদান। **3.** (*International trade*) Equal facilities or advantages by abolition of prohibitive or protective duties, or by equalizing the rates in each country ; (আন্তর্জাতিক বাণিজ্যে) প্রতিষেধাত্মক বা রক্ষণাত্মক শুল্ক উঠাইয়া দিয়া কিম্বা প্রতি দেশের শুল্কের হার সমান করিয়া সর্ব্বদেশের লোককে তুল্য সুবিধা বা সুযোগপ্রদান, পরস্পরপরিবর্ত্তন (হিঃ কোঃ)। **4.** (Kant.) Mutual action or reaction ; (কান্টের দর্শন) অন্যোন্যের উপর ক্রিয়া প্রতিক্রিয়া। **Reciprocity of exchange** — পরস্পরবিনিময় (হিঃ কোঃ)।

rē-čīt′-ăl, *n.* **1.** The act of reciting ; আবৃত্তি, পঠন, জপবাচন (হিঃ কোঃ)

2. A narrative ; as, the *recital* of one's adventures ; বর্ণনা। 3. A musical entertainment given by a single performer; একমাত্র গায়ককর্ত্তৃক গীতবাদ্যদ্বারা বিনোদন। 4. (*Law*) The part of a document stating facts ; দলীলের যে অংশে মূল বৃত্তান্ত উল্লিখিত থাকে।

rĕc-i-tā'-tion, *n.* 1. Recital; আবৃত্তি। 2. (*U. S.*) The repetition of a lesson by pupils before their teacher ; (মার্কিন যুক্তরাজ্যে) ছাত্রগণ কর্ত্তৃক শিক্ষকের নিকট পাঠ আবৃত্তি। 3. The composition or matter delivered or recited ; যে রচনা বা বিষয় আবৃত্তি করা হইয়াছে।

rē-cīte', *v. t.* & *i.* 1. To repeat, as something already prepared, written down, committed to memory, or the like ; আবৃত্তি করা, আওড়ান। 2. To narrate ; বর্ণনা করা। 3. To mention in order ; ক্রমানুসারে উল্লেখ করা। 4. (*Law*) To state in a document some fact bearing closely upon the matter in hand ; (আইন) কোন দলিলে মূলবিষয়ের সহিত সম্বন্ধবিশিষ্ট কোন বিষয়ের উল্লেখ করা।

rē-cīt'-ēr, *n.* 1. One who recites ; আবৃত্তিকারী। 2. Book containing passage for recitation ; আবৃত্তির উপযোগী কবিতাদি সম্বলিত পুস্তক।

rĕck, *v. i.* & *t.* 1. To care ; to heed ; ভাবা ; গ্রাহ্য করা। ***Verb t.*** To heed ; to regard ; গ্রাহ্য করা ; গণ্য করা।

rĕck'-lĕss, *adj.* Careless ; heedless of consequences ; হিতাহিত জ্ঞানশূন্য, অবিমৃষ্যকারী ; প্রমত্ত, ডাঙ্গপিটে (*colloq.*), অপরিণামদর্শী, বেপরওয়া (*colloq.*), প্রমাদী। **—ly,** *adv.* In a reckless manner ; বেপরওয়াভাবে, অগ্রপশ্চাৎ না ভাবিয়া। **—ness,** *n.* **Reckless youth makes rueful age**—আগে না বুঝিলে বাছা যৌবনের ঘোরে, পশ্চাতে কাঁদিতে হবে নয়নের লোরে।

rĕck'-on (-n), *v. t.* & *i.* 1. To count ; গণনা করা, গণা, সংখ্যা করা। 2. To esteem ; গণ্য করা। ***Verb i.*** 1. To make computation ; গণনা করা। 2. To settle accounts ; হিসাব বুঝাইয়া দেওয়া, হিসাব মিটান। 3. To depend or rely on ; "He could *reckon* no support within England itself" ; নির্ভর করা। 4. (*Dial.*) To think ; to guess ; (উপভাষায়) ভাবা ; অনুমান করা, আন্দাজ করা। **To reckon on** or **upon**—To rely on ; কোন কিছুর উপর নির্ভর করা বা ভরসা বাঁধা। **To reckon with**—To take into consideration ; to be prepared for ; গণনায় আনা ; প্রস্তুত থাকা। To call to account ; to exact penalty ; জবাবদীহি করা ; শাস্তি দেওয়া। **To reckon without one's host**—To ignore in an arrangement some essential consideration ; to enter upon an enterprise without knowing the cost ; কোন ব্যবস্থায় আসল বিষয় বাদ দেওয়া ; কি পরিমাণ ক্ষতি স্বীকার করিতে হইবে তাহা না ভাবিয়া কোন ব্যাপারে প্রবৃত্ত হওয়া।

rĕck'-on-ēr (-n-), *n.* 1. One who reckons ; গণনাকারী। 2. Same as READY RECKONER. **Ready-reckoner**—See READY.

rĕck'-on-ing (-n-), *n.* 1. Calculation ; গণনা। 2. The charge by the landlord of an inn etc. ; হোটেল স্বামীর পাওনার হিসাব। **Day of reckoning**—হিসাব মিটাইবার দিন ; প্রায়শ্চিত্ত দিবস, প্রতিশোধ নেওয়ার দিন। **Out in one's reckoning**—Mistaken in calculation or expectation ; গণনায় ভ্রান্ত, বৃথা আশা দ্বারা বিড়ম্বিত।

rē-claim' (-klām), *v. t.*, *i.* & *n.* 1. To claim back ; পুনরায় দাবী করা। 2. To tame ; as, to *reclaim* a hawk ; পোষ মানান। 3. To recall or bring back from evil course ; to reform ; সৎপথে ফিরাইয়া আনা ; সংশোধন করা। 4. To bring waste land under cultivation ; পতিত জমি আবাদ করা। ***Verb i.*** 1. To reform ; সংশোধন করা, চরিত্র-শোধন করা। 2. (*Obs.*) To cry out ; (অপ্রঃ) চীৎকার করা। ***Noun.*** (*Rare*) Reclaiming ; (ক্বচিদ্‌ব্যবহৃত) চরিত্র-সংশোধন, সংশোধন। **—cla-ma'-tion,** *n.*

reclame, (*F.*), *n.* Art or practice by which notoriety is secured ; যে কার্য্য দ্বারা অপকীর্ত্তি হয়।

rĕc'-li-nāte, *adj.* (*Bot.*) Bending downwards ; (উদ্ভিদ্‌বিদ্যা) নিম্নাভিমুখে আনত।

rē-clīne', *v. t.* & *i.* To lean back ; to lean sideways ; হেলান দিয়া রাখা, ঠেস দিয়া রাখা ; পাশের দিকে হেলান। ***Verb i.*** To lean ; to rest in a reclining position ; হেলা ; হেলিয়া থাকা, অর্দ্ধনিলীন ভাবে থাকা।

rē-clothe' (-clōth), *v. t.* To clothe again ; পুনরায় পরিধান করান।

rē-cluse' (-clūs), *n.* & *adj.* One who lives shut up apart from the world ; a hermit ; an anchorite ; সংসার-বিবিক্ত ব্যক্তি, একান্তবাসী, একান্তসেবী, বিজনবাসী ; যতী ; সন্ন্যাসী, তাপস, উদাসীন। ***Adj.*** 1. Living shut up or apart from the world ; সংসারবিবিক্ত। 2. (*Now rare*) Secluded ; as, *recluse* retreats ; (বর্ত্তমানে ক্বচিদ্ ব্যবহৃত) নিভৃত, নির্জ্জন, বিজন।

rĕc-ŏg-ni'-tion, *n.* 1. The act of recognizing ; the state of being recognized ; স্বীকার ; স্বীকৃতি। 2. The act of acknowledging as true or valid ; সত্য বা প্রামাণিক বলিয়া স্বীকার। 3. The act of apprehending a thing as having certain character; প্রত্যভিজ্ঞান (ভক্তিঃ), প্রত্যভিজ্ঞা (সাংখ্য)। 4. Perception of identity as already known in fact or description ; পরিচয়, অভিজ্ঞান, পরিজ্ঞাপ্তি, অনুস্মৃতি (শ্রীঃ)। 5. Special notice or attention ; as, his claim to the service had received *recognition* ;

বিশেষ লক্ষ্য, দৃষ্টি বা মনোযোগ, সবিশেষ অনুধান। 6. Acknowledgment of kindness, merit, etc.; as, a reward in *recognition* of one's merit; গুণ, উপকার, প্রভৃতি স্বীকার।

rē-cŏg′-nĭ-zance (-zăns), *n.* 1. Avowal; স্বীকার। 2. (*Law*) An obligation of record which a man enters into before some court of record or magistrate duly authorised with condition to do some particular act, as to keep the peace, to pay a debt, etc.; মুচলেকা, দর্শনাঙ্গীকার (আঃ বঃ)।

rĕc-ŏg-nīze, —nīse, *v. t.* 1. To perceive the identity of, with a person or thing formerly known; চিনিতে পারা, পরিচয় করা। 2. To acknowledge formally; যথারীতি স্বীকার করা। 3. To show appreciation of; as, to *recognize* merit; গুণগ্রহণ করা, স্বীকার করা, মর্য্যাদা করা। 4. To acknowledge acquaintance with, by bowing, raising the hat, etc.; as, he passed me without *recognizing* me; অভিবাদন, টুপি উত্তোলন, প্রভৃতি দ্বারা কাহারো সহিত পরিচয় স্বীকার করা। 5. To realize; "Kepler first *recognized* the fact that the eye is a camera"; হৃদয়ঙ্গম করা, উপলব্ধি করা। **—niz-a-ble,** *adj.* That can be recognized; অভিজ্ঞেয়, সংবেদ্য, সংবেদনীয়।

rē-coil′ (-koyl), *v. i.* & *n.* 1. To rebound; ঠিকরাইয়া আসা, পরাবর্ত্তিত হওয়া, প্রতিক্ষিপ্ত হওয়া। 2. To start or shrink back, as from something repulsive, distressing or alarming; বিরক্তিকর, কষ্টপ্রদ বা ভয়জনক কোন কিছু দেখিয়া চমকিয়া বা সঙ্কুচিত হইয়া আসা, ভয়াদি হেতু পশ্চাতে সরা বা পরাঙ্মুখ হওয়া, চমকিয়া পিছাই আসা। *Noun.* 1. A rebound; প্রতিক্ষেপ, পশ্চাদ্দিকে ধাক্কা, পশ্চাদ্ধাক্কা, পরাবর্তন, পরাবৃত্তি, ব্যপবৃত্তি, ব্যপবর্তন। 2. The reaction of fire-arms when discharged; আওয়াজ করার পর বন্দুকাদির পশ্চাদ্দিকে ধাক্কা, লাথি। **To recoil into**—To return into; প্রত্যাবৃত্ত হওয়া। **To recoil on** or **upon**—To fall back upon; পালটিয়া আসিয়া পড়া, উলটিয়া আসিয়া পড়া।

rē-coin′ (coyn), *v. t.* To coin again; পুনরায় মুদ্রা প্রস্তুত করা।

rē-cŏl-lĕct′, *v. t.* To collect again; পুনঃ সংগ্রহ করা, পুনরায় একত্র করা।

rĕc-ŏl-lĕct′, *v. t.* 1. To recall to the mind or memory; স্মরণ করা, স্মৃতিপথে আনা, মনে করা। 2. To recover composure of mind; পুনরায় মানসিক স্থৈর্য্যলাভ করা। **—lec′-tive,** *adj.*

rĕc-ŏl-lĕc′-tion, *n.* 1. The act of recollecting; স্মরণ। 2. The power of bringing back to the mind; স্মৃতি, স্মৃতিশক্তি। 3. That which is recollected; স্মৃতিপথে আগত বিষয়। 4. Memory; the period over which one's memory extends; as, an event within my *recollection*; স্মৃতি; স্মরণকাল। 5. Concentration; "He performs the sacred office with great *recollection* and division"; একাগ্রতা, নিবিষ্টতা। 6. (*Rare*) Composure; (ক্বচিদ্-ব্যবহৃত) মানসিক স্থৈর্য্য।

rē-cŏl′-ŏ-nize, *v. t.* To colonize a second time; পুনর্ব্বার উপনিবেশ স্থাপন করা।

rē-cŏm-bine′, *v. t.* To combine again; পুনরায় সংযুক্ত করা।

rē-com′-fort (-cŭm-fērt), *v. t.* To console anew; পুনরায় সান্ত্বনা দেওয়া।

rē-cŏm-mence′ (-mĕns), *v. t.* To begin anew; পুনরায় আরম্ভ করা।

rĕc-ŏm-mĕnd′, *v. t.* 1. To commend to the favourable notice of another; to praise or put forward as likely to be of service or advantage; সুপারিশ করা; কাহারো পক্ষে কার্য্যকর বা সুবিধাজনক হইবে বলিয়া সুখ্যাতি বা উপস্থাপিত করা। 2. To counsel; as, I would strongly *recommend* you to take sea-bath; পরামর্শ দেওয়া। 3. To commit to the care of; কাহারো হস্তে সমর্পণ করা। 4. To make acceptable; to attract favour to; "That man has little enough to *recommend* him whom women dislike"; গ্রহণীয় করা; প্রীতি আকর্ষণ করা। **—mĕn-da′-tion,** *n.* 1. (*Obs.*) The act of recommending or of commending; (অপ্রঃ) সুপারিশকরণ, প্রশংসাকরণ। 2. That which procures a favourable reception; লোকসমাজে সমাদর লাভ করার উপযোগী গুণ প্রভৃতি। 3. A letter of recommendation; সুপারিশ চিঠি, অনুরোধপত্র। 4. Exhortation; উপদেশ, পরামর্শ। **—men-da-to-ry,** *adj.*

rē-cŏm′-mĭt, *v. t.* 1. To commit again; as, to *recommit* a person to prison; পুনরায় প্রেরণ করা। 2. To refer again to a committee; মতামতের জন্য পুনরায় আলোচনা সভায় দেওয়া।

rĕc′-ŏm-pense (-pĕns), *v. t.* & *n.* 1. To requite; to reward; to compensate; শোধ করা, প্রতিদান দেওয়া, প্রতিফল দেওয়া; পুরস্কার দেওয়া; ক্ষতিপূরণ করা। *Noun.* Requital; reward; compensation; প্রতিদান, প্রতিশোধ, প্রতিফল; পুরস্কার, পারিতোষিক; ক্ষতিপূরণ।

rĕc′-ŏn-cile (-sīl), *v.t.* 1. To restore to union and friendship after estrangement; পুনর্মিলন করা, পুনরায় বন্ধুত্ব স্থাপন করা, পুনঃ সখ্যস্থাপন করা। 2. To harmonize; "The only means of *reconciling* the different accounts"; সঙ্গতিবিশিষ্ট করা, সামঞ্জস্যবিধান করা, মিল করা, ঐক্যস্থাপন করা। 3. To bring to acquiescence, content, or quiet submission; as, to *reconcile* one's self to affliction; নীরবে সহ্য করা, কোন কিছুতে সম্মত বা সন্তুষ্ট থাকিতে বাধ্য করা। 4. To settle ; as, to *reconcile* differences ; মীমাংসা করা । 5. To purify after pollution ; শুদ্ধ করা, শুদ্ধিবিধান করা । **–cil-i-a'-tion,** *n.* 1. Renewal of friendship after disagreement or enmity ; পুনর্মিলন, পুনঃসখ্যস্থাপন । 2. Harmony ; সঙ্গতি, মিল, সমন্বয় (হিঃ কোঃ), সৌসামঞ্জস্য । **–ment,** *n.*

rĕc'-ŏn-dīte, *adj.* 1. Abstruse ; "The *recondite* principles of philosophy ; profound ; জটিল, গহন, দুর্জ্ঞেয়, দুর্ব্বোধ ; দুরধিগম্য, গূঢ়, গভীর, দুরবগাহ । 2. Dealing with things abstruse ; as, *recondite* studies ; দুর্জ্ঞেয়বিষয়পূর্ণ । 3. (*Bot.* & *Entom.*) Concealed ; (উদ্ভিদ্‌বিদ্যা ও কীটতত্ত্ব) লুক্কায়িত, গুপ্ত । **–ly,** *adv.* **–ness,** *n.*

rē-cŏn-dŭct', *v. t.* To conduct again ; পুনরায় পথ দেখাইয়া নেওয়া ।

rē-cŏn-dŭc'-tion, *n.* A renewal of a lease ; নূতন করিয়া পাট্টা লওন ।

rē-cŏn'-nais-sance (-nās-săns), *n.* (Older spelling *reconnoissance.*) 1. Preliminary examination of a region by a detachment of troops to direct military operations or for the location of enemy ; শত্রুসৈন্যের অবস্থিতিনির্ণয় বা সামরিককার্য্য পরিচালনের জন্য কোন ভূখণ্ড সৈন্যদলের অংশবিশেষ দ্বারা পূর্ব্বে পরীক্ষণ, প্রাক্‌পরীক্ষণ । 2. (*Geol.*) preliminary examination or survey of a region in reference to its general geological character ; (ভূ-বিদ্যা) ভূমির সাধারণ অবস্থা বা স্বভাব জানিবার জন্য কোন স্থান পূর্ব্বে পরিদর্শন । 3. A preliminary survey made by any one for engineering operation etc. ; পূর্ত্তকার্য্যাদির জন্য (জরীপের) পূর্ব্বে ভূমি পরিদর্শন । 4. A body of troops sent to reconnoitre ; শত্রুসৈন্যের অবস্থিতি নির্ণয়ের জন্য অথবা সামরিক কার্য্যের নিমিত্ত কোন ভূমি পরীক্ষার্থ প্রেরিত ক্ষুদ্র সৈন্যদল । **Reconnaissance in force** — শত্রুসৈন্যের অবস্থান বা বলাবল অবগতির জন্য বহু সৈন্য কর্তৃক আক্রমণ বা আক্রমণের ভঙ্গি প্রদর্শন ।

rĕc-ŏn-noi'-trĕ (-noy-têr), **–têr,** *v. t.* & *i.* 1. To examine by the eye ; to examine or survey a tract or region for engineering, geological or military purpose ; চক্ষু দ্বারা পরীক্ষা করা ; পূর্ত্তকার্য্য, ভূপরীক্ষা বা সামরিক কার্য্যের জন্য কোন ভূখণ্ড পরীক্ষা বা জরীপ করা । 2. To spy and watch, as the position, movements, force, etc. of an enemy ; শত্রুসৈন্যের অবস্থান, গতিবিধি, চলাচল, প্রভৃতি নির্ণয়ের জন্য গোপনে অনুসন্ধান করা বা পর্য্যবেক্ষণ করা । ***Verb i.*** To make reconnaissance ; সামরিক কার্য্য প্রভৃতির জন্য কোন ভূখণ্ড পরীক্ষা করা ।

rē-con'-qer (-kŏng-kêr), *v. t.* To conquer again ; to recover by conquest ; পুনরায় জয় করা ; পুনরুদ্ধার করা ।

rē-cŏn-sid'-êr, *v. t.* To consider again ; পুনর্ব্বিবেচনা করা, পর্য্যালোচনা করা । **–a'-tion,** *n.* Act of reconsidering ; পুনর্বিবেচনা ।

rē-cŏn-stit'-ū-ĕnt, *adj.* & *n.* 1. Building up again, as a medical remedy ; পুনঃপুষ্টিবর্দ্ধক । ***Noun.*** A rebuilding medicine ; পুনঃপুষ্টিবর্দ্ধক ঔষধ ।

rē-cŏn-sti-tūte', *v. t.* 1. To constitute again ; পুনর্গঠন করা । 2. To place together past events into an intelligible whole ; অতীত ঘটনাসমূহ বোধগম্যরূপে একত্র সন্নিবেশ করা । **–tu'-tion,** *n.*

rē-cŏn'-strŭct, *v. t.* To rebuild ; পুনর্নির্ম্মাণ করা । **–struc'-tion,** *n.* The act of reconstructing ; পুনর্নির্ম্মাণ, পুনর্গঠন ।

rē-cŏn-vêrt', *v. t.* To convert again ; পুনর্দীক্ষিত করা ।

rē-cŏn-vey' (-vā), *v. t.* To convey back to the former place ; পুনরায় পূর্ব্বস্থানে লইয়া যাওয়া ।

rē-cŏrd', *v. t.* & *i.* 1. To write anything formally ; to set down in some permanent form ; "Sometimes the Morse signals are indicated to the ear or eye without being *recorded*" ; লিপিবদ্ধ করা ; স্থায়িভাবে চিহ্নিত করা । 2. To imprint deeply in the heart ; মনোমধ্যে গভীরভাবে মুদ্রিত করা । 3. (Of birds) To practise by singing in an undertone ; (পক্ষিসম্বন্ধে) অনুচ্চস্বরে গাহিয়া (সুর প্রভৃতি) অভ্যাস করা । ***Verb i.*** To sing or repeat a tune ; গান করা, গুণ গুণ করিয়া গাওয়া ।

rĕc'-ŏrd, *n.* 1. Act of recording ; state of being recorded ; register ; লিপিবদ্ধকরণ ; লিপিবদ্ধ অবস্থা ; লিপি, লেখ (শুক্রঃ বিনয়), লেখ্য । 2. An authentic official copy of a document entered in a book ; সরকারী খাতায় রক্ষিত দলীলাদির নকল । 3. Copy of pleadings etc. constituting a case to be decided by a court ; as, to travel out of *record* ; মোকদ্দমার কাগজপত্র, নথি, মিসিল । 4. (*Pl.*) Public documents kept in a recognized repository ; মহাফেজ খানায় রক্ষিত কাগজপত্র । 5. An account of some fact or event preserved in writing or other permanent form ; a monument ; লিখন বা মুদ্রণ দ্বারা বা অন্য কোনরূপ স্থায়ী উপায়ে রক্ষিত কোন ঘটনার বিবরণ ; স্মরণীয় দৃষ্টান্ত । 6. The list of known facts in a person's life ; as, he has an honourable *record* of service ; personal history ; কোন ব্যক্তির গত জীবনের জ্ঞাত ঘটনাসমূহ, প্রাগ্‌বৃত্ত ; ব্যক্তিগত ইতিহাস । 7. The cylinder or disc of hard wax, rubber, etc., used to reproduce sounds in instruments of the phonograph class ; ধ্বনিযন্ত্র, শব্দযন্ত্র, প্রভৃতিতে ধ্বনিউৎপাদনের জন্য রবর, কঠিন মোম, প্রভৃতি দ্বারা প্রস্তুত চক্র বা চোঙ্গ । 8. Highest results attained in athletic contests etc. ; (মল্লক্রীড়া, ব্যোমপর্য্যটন, প্রভৃতিতে) গতিনৈপুণ্য, সহিষ্ণুতা, ক্রিয়া প্রভৃতির সর্ব্বোচ্চ দৃষ্টান্ত । **Public records** — সরকারী দলীল

দপ্তাবেজ। **Record breaker**—মল্ল ক্রীড়া, ধাবন ব্যোমপর্য্যটন, প্রভৃতিতে পূর্ব্বের সকলকে অতিক্রমকারী। **Recording angel**—যে দেবদূত মানুষের পাপ-পুণ্যের বিবরণ খাতায় লিখিয়া রাখেন [cf. our চিত্রগুপ্ত]। **Record-keeper**—মহাফেজ। **Record-office**—মহাফেজখানা, দপ্তরখানা। **Court of records**—যে আদালতের কার্য্যাবলী লিপিবদ্ধ হইয়া থাকে। **To beat or break the record**—To outdo all previous performance; যাহা এপর্য্যন্ত কেহই করিতে পারে নাই—তাহা সমাধা করা। **To be on record**—লিপিবদ্ধ থাকা। **To keep to the record**—To refrain from introducing irrelevant matter; অপ্রাসঙ্গিক বিষয় অবতারণা করিতে বিরত হওয়া। **To put on record**—লিপিবদ্ধ করা, লিখিয়া রাখা। **To travel out of record**—To introduce irrelevant matter; অপ্রাসঙ্গিক বিষয়ের অবতারণা করা।

rĕ-cŏrd'-ĕr, *n.* 1. One who records; লিপিবদ্ধকারী। 2. The chief of a borough or city; পার্লেমেণ্টে সভ্যপ্রদানের ক্ষমতা প্রাপ্ত নগর কিম্বা কোন মহানগরীর প্রধান বিচারক, প্রাড়্‌বিবাক। 3. A recording apparatus in an instrument; কোন যন্ত্রমধ্যস্থ যে ক্ষুদ্র কলে কোন বিষয় লিপিবদ্ধ বা চিহ্নিত হয়। 4. An obsolete kind of flageolet; প্রাচীনকালে ব্যবহৃত বংশী বিশেষ।

rĕ-count' (-cownt), *v. t.* To relate in detail; সবিস্তারে বর্ণনা করা, বিবৃত করা।

rē-count' (-cownt), *v. t.* & *n.* To count again; পুনর্ব্বার গণনা করা। ***Noun.*** A second calculation (esp. of votes); পুনর্গণনা।

rē-coup' (-cōp), *v. t.* & *n.* 1. (*Law*) To keep back as a set-off or discount; to diminish by keeping back a part; (আইন) বাট্টাস্বরূপ বা ক্ষতিপূরণ স্বরূপ রাখা; কতকাংশ রাখিয়া হ্রাস করা। 2. To indemnify; ক্ষতিপূরণ করা। 3. To get a compensation for; ক্ষতিপূরণ পাওয়া। ***Noun.*** The act of recouping; ক্ষতিপূরণ। **—ment,** *n.* **To recoup oneself**—To recover what one has expended or lost; ক্ষতিপূরণ করা।

rĕ-course' (-kōrs), *n.* 1. A going to, as for help, succour or protection; আশ্রয় গ্রহণ, শরণ। 2. The person or thing resorted to; যাহার নিকট আশ্রয় লওয়া হয়, আশ্রয়, শরণ, সংশ্রয়, গতি। **To have recourse to**—To resort to for help, etc.; আশ্রয় লওয়া, শরণ লওয়া, আশ্রয় গ্রহণ করা।

rĕ-cov'-ĕr (-cŭv-), *v. t., i.* & *n.* 1. To regain; as, to *recover* a town; পুনঃপ্রাপ্ত হওয়া, পুনরুদ্ধার করা। 2. To cure; as, to *recover* a man from fever; আরোগ্য করা, আরাম করা, রোগমুক্ত করা 3. (*Obs.*) To rescue; (অপ্রঃ) উদ্ধার করা। 4. To make up for; as, to *recover* a loss; to atone for; ক্ষতিপূরণ করা; প্রায়শ্চিত্ত করা। 4. To restore or bring back to life or consciousness; পুনর্জীবিত করা, চৈতন্যসম্পাদন করা, সংজ্ঞাসম্পাদন করা। 5. (*Reflex.*) To regain one's natural position or balance; হোঁচট প্রভৃতি সামলাইয়া দাঁড়ান। 6. (*Law*) To gain as compensation; to obtain title to in a court of law; (আইন) ক্ষতিপূরণ স্বরূপ পাওয়া, খেসারত স্বরূপ পাওয়া; আদালতের বিচারে স্বত্ব ফিরাইয়া পাওয়া। ***Verb i.*** 1. To regain former state or condition, as after shock, misfortune, depression of mind, etc., (usu. followed by *of* or *from*); as, to *recover from* agitation; দুর্ভাগ্য, মানসিক গ্লানি, চমক, প্রভৃতির পর পুনরায় স্বাভাবিক অবস্থা প্রাপ্ত হওয়া, কাটাইয়া উঠা। 2. To regain health after sickness; রোগমুক্ত হওয়া, আরাম হওয়া, সারিয়া উঠা। 3. To be successful in a law-suit; মোকদ্দমায় জয়ী হওয়া। 4. (*Fencing* etc.) To regain the position of guard after thrusting etc.; (অসি ক্রীড়া প্রভৃতিতে) আঘাতাদি করার পর পুনরায় পূর্ব্বাবস্থায় অবস্থিত হওয়া। 5. To make up a loss again; পুনরায় ক্ষতিপূরণ করা। ***Noun.*** (*Fencing* etc.) The act of regaining the position of guard after thrusting etc.; অসি-ক্রীড়া প্রভৃতিতে আঘাতাদির পর পুনরায় পূর্ব্বাবস্থায় স্থিত হওন। **—a-ble,** *adj.* 1. That can be recovered; পুনঃপ্রাপ্য, পুনর্লভ্য, উদ্ধরণীয়, প্রতিলভ্য, আদায়নীয়, প্রাপ্য। 2. Obtainable from a debtor; আদায়যোগ্য।

rē'-cov-ĕr (-cŭv-), *v. t.* To cover again or anew; as, to *re-cover* an umbrella; পুনরায় আবৃত করা, পুনরায় ছাওয়া। **—y,** *n.*

rĕ-cov'-ĕr-ȳ (-cŭv-), *n.* 1. The act of recovering or regaining; পুনঃপ্রাপ্তি, পুনরুদ্ধার, পুনর্লাভ, লাভ। 2. Restoration from sickness or faintness; restoration from depression or misfortune; আরোগ্য-লাভ, রোগমুক্তি, রোগনিরসন, রোগ-নিবারণ, স্বাস্থ্যলাভ, সংজ্ঞাপ্রাপ্তি; মানসিক স্থৈর্য্য লাভ। 3. (*Fencing* etc.) Same as RECOVER, *n.* above. 4. (*Law*) The obtaining of right or title to something by a verdict or judgment of court from an opposite party in a suit; as, the *recovery* of damages; মোকদ্দমায় আদালতের রায় দ্বারা প্রতিপক্ষ হইতে কোন কিছুতে স্বত্ব বা অধিকার প্রাপ্তি।

rĕc'-rē-ănt, *adj.* & *n.* 1. Craven; coward; কাপুরুষ, কাকরুক (পক্ষ তঃ); ভীরু, দুর্ব্বলহৃদয়, পুরুষত্বহীন, পৌরুষবিহীন, নির্ব্বীর্য্য। 2. Apostate; স্বধর্ম্মত্যাগী স্বমতত্যাগী, স্বপক্ষদ্রোহী, ধর্ম্মভ্রষ্ট, ক্রিয়াভ্রষ্ট, ভ্রষ্টসংকল্প। ***Noun.*** 1. One who yields in combat and cries craven; a cowardly wretch; "You are all *recreants* and dastards"; যে ব্যক্তি যুদ্ধে পরাজিত

হইয়া শত্রুর নিকট কৃপা ভিক্ষা করে; কাপুরুষ, নরাধম। 2. An apostate; স্বধর্ম্মত্যাগী ব্যক্তি, স্বজনদ্রোহী ব্যক্তি, স্বধর্ম্মভ্রষ্ট ব্যক্তি। **—an-cy,** *n.*

rĕc'-rē-āte, *v. t.* & *i.* To revive the exhausted strength or languid spirits of; to divert; "The mind should be *recreated* and refreshed with a variety in our studies; গ্লানি ও শান্তি অপনোদন পূর্ব্বক পুনরায় সতেজ করা; বিনোদন করা, আমোদিত করা। ***Verb i.*** To take recreation; বিশ্রাম করা। **—a'-tion,** *n.* The act of refreshing the strength, spirits, etc. after toil or exerion; diversion; pastime; শ্রান্তি বা গ্লানি অপনোদনপূর্ব্বক সতেজ করণ; বিনোদন; প্রমোদ, ক্রীড়াকৌতুক।

rē-crē-āte', *v. t.* 1. To create or form anew; পুনঃ সৃষ্টি করা, পুনর্গঠন করা। **—a'-tion,** *n.*

rĕc'-rē-mĕnt, *n.* (*Rare*) Refuse; dross; (কচিদ্ ব্যবহৃত) জঞ্জাল; ধাতুমল, খাইদ। 2. (*Med.*) A fluid, which after being separated from the blood is again absorbed into it; যে তরল পদার্থ রক্ত হইতে বিভিন্ন বা নিঃসৃত হইয়া পুনরায় উহাতে মিশ্রিত হয় (যথা পিত্ত, নিষ্ঠীবন, প্রভৃতি)। **—men-ti'-tious,** *adj.*

rē-crim'-in-āte, *v. i.* To accuse in return; to charge back fault or crime on accuser; প্রত্যভিযোগ করা; অভিযোগকারীর উপর পাল্টা দোষ বা অপরাধ চাপান। **—i-na'-tion,** *n.* 1. The act of recriminating; প্রত্যভিযোগ করণ। 2. A counter-charge; প্রত্যভিযোগ, প্রত্যারোপ, প্রত্যাপবাদ, পালটা মোকদ্দমা।

re-crū-desce' (-dĕs), *v. i.* To breathe out again; to come into renewed vigour, activity, etc.; পুনরায় প্রাদুর্ভাব হওয়া; পুনরায় প্রকোপ বাড়া। **—des'-cence,** *n.* 1. The state of being recrudescent; পুনঃপ্রাদুর্ভাব। 2. (*Med.*) Increased severity of a disease after a temporary remission; (ভৈষজ্য-শাস্ত্র) অল্পকাল নিবৃত্তির পর রোগের প্রকোপ-বৃদ্ধি বা পুনঃ প্রকোপ বৃদ্ধি। **—des'-cent,** *adj.*

rē-cruit' (-crōt), *n.* 1. (*Obs.*) The supply of anything wasted; (অপ্রঃ) ক্ষয়পূরণ। 2. A newly enlisted soldier; নূতন সৈনিক, নূতন সিপাহী। 3. One who has newly joined a society, association, etc.; কোন সমিতি, পরিষৎ, প্রভৃতিতে নবপ্রবিষ্ট ব্যক্তি, নূতন সভ্য। 4. Renewal of strength or vigour; পুনরায় শক্তি বা বল লাভ।

rē'-cruit' (-crôt), *v. t.* & *i.* 1. To supply with new men; to enlist, as in an army; নূতন লোক জোগান; সৈন্যদল প্রভৃতিতে ভুক্ত করা, ভর্ত্তি করা। 2. (*Now rare*) To rapair by fresh supplies, as anything wasted; to replenish; (বর্ত্তমানে কচিদ্ ব্যবহৃত) নূতন কিছুদ্বারা ক্ষয় পূরণ করা; পুনঃ পূরণ করা। 3. To restore the wasted vigour of; as, to *recruit* one's health; to reinvigorate; নষ্টশক্তি পুনরায় লাভ করা; পুনরায় সতেজ করা, পুনরায় সবল করা, পুনরায় পুষ্টিসাধন করা। ***Verb i.*** 1. To raise new supplies of men; esp. to raise or enlist new soldiers; নূতন লোক সংগ্রহ করা; বিশেষতঃ নূতন সৈন্য সংগ্রহ বা ভর্ত্তি করা। 2. To recover vigour or health; as, lean cattle *recruit* in fresh pastures; to go to the country to recruit; স্বাস্থ্য বা তেজঃ পুনরায় লাভ করা; স্বাস্থ্যলাভের জন্য নগর ছাড়িয়া স্বাস্থ্যজনক স্থানে যাওয়া। **—al, —ment,** *n.* 1. Enlistment of men for an army etc.; সৈন্যসংগ্রহ, লোকসংগ্রহ। 2. Renewal of bodily health; পুনঃস্বাস্থ্যলাভ। **—er,** *n.* One who recruits; সৈন্যসংগ্রাহক, নূতন লোক সংগ্রাহক, আড়কাঠী (esp. a cooly-recruiter)। **Recruiting-sergeant** — সৈন্যসংগ্রাহক কর্ম্মচারি-বিশেষ।

rĕc'-tăl, *adj.* Of, or pertaining to, the rectum; সারলান্ত্রিক (হঃ চঃ), মলাশয়সম্বন্ধীয়।

rĕc'-tan-gle (-tāng-gl), *n.* A right-angled parallelogram; যে সমানান্তর চতুর্ভুজের যে কোন একটী কোণ সমকোণ থাকে, আয়তক্ষেত্র, আয়ত (হিঃ কোঃ), চতুর্ভুজ (ঐ), সমকোণী-চতুর্ভুজ। **—gu-lar'-i-ty,** *n.* **—tan'-gu-lar,** *adj.* Right-angled; সমকোণী, সমচতুরস্র, জাত্য (সাঃ পঃ), সমকোণ। **Rectangular co-ordinates** — পরস্পরের সহিত সমকোণ উৎপাদনকারী ভুজ-যুগ্ম। **Rectangular solid**—যে ঘনের অক্ষ উহার ভূমির লম্বস্বরূপ অবস্থিত থাকে।

rĕc'-ti-fȳ, *v. t.* 1. To make right; to amend; সংশোধন করা; শোধরান। 2. To put or set a thing right; ঠিক করা। 3. To correct or reform; as, to *rectify* the heart; সংশোধন করা, শোধরান, শুদ্ধিবিধান করা। 4. (*Chem.*) To refine by repeated distillation or sublimation; as, to *rectify* spirit or wine; (রসায়ন শাস্ত্র) বিশোধিত করা, শোধিত করা। 5. To set right; as, to *rectify* a timepiece; ঠিক করা। 6. (*Geom.*) To find a straight line equal to a (curve); (বক্রের) সমান সরল রেখা অঙ্কিত করা। 7. (*Elect.*) To transform an alternating current into a continuous one; (তাড়িতবিদ্যা) পর্য্যায়গামী অবচ্ছিন্ন প্রবাহে পরিবর্ত্তিত করা। **—fi-a-ble,** *adj.* That can be rectified; সংশোধনীয়। **—fi-ca'-tion,** *n.* The act of rectifying; শোধন, প্রতিশোধন (হিঃ কোঃ)। **Rectification of the globe**—গোল সংশোধন (হিঃ কোঃ)। **To rectify the globe**—গোলের ক্রান্তিবৃত্তস্থ সূর্য্যের অবস্থিতি স্থান পিত্তল-নির্ম্মিত যাম্যোত্তরে আনা অথবা কোন প্রস্তাবিত সমস্যা সমাধানের জন্য প্রস্তুত করণার্থ উহা (গোল) ঠিকঠাক করা, গোল সংশোধন করা।

rĕc'-ti-lin'-ē-ăl, *adj.* Same as RECTILINEAR.

rĕc-ti-lin'-ē-âr, *adj.* **1.** Moving in a straight line; সরলগামী। **2.** Bounded by a straight line; characterized by a straight line; consisting of straight lines; সরলরেখাবেষ্টিত; সরলরেখাত্মক, ঋজুরেখ; সরলরেখাময়। **–ly**, *adv.* **Rectilinear motion**—সরলগতি (হিঃ কোঃ)।

rĕc'-ti-tūde, *n.* **1.** Moral uprightness; righteousness; সাধুতা; ন্যায়পরায়ণতা, সত্যশীলতা, আর্জ্জব, ধর্ম্মপ্রাণতা, ধার্ম্মিকতা, শুচিতা। **2.** (*Rare*) Correctness; (কচিদ্ ব্যবহৃত) শুদ্ধতা।

rĕc'-tō, *n.* The right-hand page (opp. to *verso*); পুস্তকের ডাহিন দিকের পৃষ্ঠা।

rĕc'-tor (-tēr), *n.* **1.** The parson of a parish whose tithes are not impropriate; যে যাজকপল্লীর ধর্ম্মশুল্কের আদায় ও ব্যয়ের ভার যাজকের উপর ন্যস্ত থাকে—ঐরূপ পল্লীর যাজক, গ্রামাচার্য্য, পল্লীযাজক। **2.** (Scotland) The head master of an academy or important public school; (স্কটলণ্ড) কোন বিদ্যালয় বা বিশিষ্ট সরকারী বিদ্যালয়ের প্রধান শিক্ষক। **3.** (Esp. abroad) The head of a university, college, school or religious institution; (বিশেষতঃ গ্রেটব্রিটেন ব্যতিরিক্ত দেশসমূহে) কোন বিশ্ববিদ্যালয়, মহাবিদ্যালয়, বিদ্যালয় বা মঠের অধ্যক্ষ। **4.** (In England) The heads of Exeter and Lincoln Colleges, Oxford; (ইংলণ্ডে) অক্সফোর্ডের এক্সিটার এবং লিঙ্কলন মহাবিদ্যালয়দ্বয়ের অধ্যক্ষ। **–ess**, *n.* (*Fem.*) **–ship**, *n.*, **–to'-ri-al**, *adj.*

rĕc'-tŏ-ry, *n.* **1.** A rector's benefice; পল্লীযাজকের যাজকীয় বৃত্তি। **2.** A rector's mansion; পল্লীযাজকনিবাস, পল্লীযাজকভবন।

rĕc-tō-văg'-i-năl, *adj.* Pertaining to the rectum and vagina; সরলান্ত্র ও যোনিসংক্রান্ত।

rĕc-tō-vĕs'-i-căl, *adj.* Pertaining to the rectum and bladder; সরলান্ত্র ও মূত্রাশয়সংক্রান্ত।

rĕc'-tŭm, *n.* The third and last part of the large intestine terminating at the anus; বৃহদন্ত্রের তৃতীয় বা শেষ অংশ, সরলান্ত্র (বৃহদন্ত্রের এই অংশ সরল বলিয়া প্রাচীন শারীরসংস্থানবিদ্‌গণের ভ্রান্তবিশ্বাস ছিল—এই হেতু এই নাম), মলাশয়, গুদ।

rē-cŭm'-bĕnt, *adj.* Leaning; reclining; হেলান (সূর্য্য বিঃ); অর্দ্ধশয়ান, অর্দ্ধনিলীন, অর্দ্ধশায়িত, শয়ান (রাঃ রাঃ)। **–ben-cy**, *n.*

rē-cū'-pêr-āte, *v. t. & i.* To recover; to regain; as, to *recuperate* health; to restore to health; পুনরায় লাভ করা; পুনঃ প্রাপ্ত হওয়া; পুনরায় স্বাস্থ্য প্রদান করা। ***Verb i.*** To recover from ill-health, weakness, pecuniary loss, etc.; পুনরায় স্বাস্থ্য লাভ করা, পুনরায় সবল ও সতেজ হওয়া, আর্থিক ক্ষতিগ্রস্ত হওয়ার পর পুনরায় অবস্থার উন্নতি করা। **–a'-tion**, *n.* **–a-tive**, *adj.*

rē-cûr', *v. i.* **1.** To return to the mind; পুনরায় মনে উদয় হওয়া, পুনরায় মনে উঠা, পুনরায় মনে পড়া, পুনরায় স্মরণ হওয়া। **2.** To occur again; পুনরায় ঘটা, পুনঃসংঘটিত হওয়া। **3.** (*Math.—Cf figures in a decimal fraction*) To come again and again in the same order; (গণিত-শাস্ত্রে—পৌনঃপুনিক দশমিকের অঙ্ক সম্পর্কে) পুনঃ পুনঃ আসা। **–rence, –ren-cy**, *ns.* **1.** The act of recurring or the state of being recurred; প্রত্যাবর্ত্তন, প্রত্যাবৃত্তি। **2.** Returning to the mind; (মনে) পুনরুদয়, পুনরাবির্ভাব। **–ring**, *adj.* **Recurring curve**—যে বক্র আপনাতে প্রত্যাবৃত্ত হয় (যথা—বৃত্ত)। **Recurring decimal**—পৌনঃপুনিক দশমিক।

rē-cûr'-rĕnt, *adj. & n.* **1.** Returning from time to time; as, *recurrent* fever (পালাজ্বর); পুনঃ পুনঃ প্রকাশশীল, পুনরাবর্ত্তী, প্রত্যাবর্ত্তক, পুনঃপুনরাগামী। **2.** Having a reflex course; as, *recurrent* nerves; পুনরাগামী (ধমনী বা স্নায়ুর যে সকল শাখা যে স্থান হইতে উৎপন্ন হইয়াছে পুনরায় তৎস্থানাভিমুখে আসিলে তাহাদিগকে recurrent বা পুনরাগামী বলে)। ***Noun.*** A recurrent artery or nerve; esp. one of the two recurrent laryngeal nerves; মূল স্থানের দিকে পুনরাবর্ত্তী ধমনী বা স্নায়ু; বিশেষতঃ কণ্ঠনালীর ঊর্দ্ধভাগের পুনরাবর্ত্তী শিরাদ্বয়ের অন্যতর। **–ly**, *adv.*

rē-cûr'-vāte, *adj.* Bent backward; পশ্চাদ্দিকে বক্রীভূত, পুনঃ বক্রীভূত। **–va-ture**, *n.*

rē-curve' (-kêrv), *v. t. & i.* To bend backward; পশ্চাদ্দিকে বক্র করা বা হওয়া।

rĕc'-ū-sănt, *n. & adj.* **1.** One obstinate in refusing; পুনঃ পুনঃ অসম্মতি প্রদর্শনকারী। **2.** (*Hist.*) One who refused to attend divine service in the established Church; (ইতিহাস) রাজবিধিদ্বারা প্রতিষ্ঠিত ধর্ম্মসংঘের উপাসনায় যোগদানে অসম্মত ব্যক্তি। ***Adj.*** Obstinate in refusal; (*Hist.*) refusing to acknowledge the supremacy of the king in matter of religion or to conform to the rites of the established Church; মগরা; (ইতিহাস) ধর্ম্মসংক্রান্ত ব্যাপারে রাজার প্রাধান্য স্বীকারে এবং রাজবিধিদ্বারা প্রতিষ্ঠিত ধর্ম্মসংঘের অনুমোদিত আচার-পদ্ধতি অনুসরণে অসম্মত ব্যক্তি।

rĕd, *adj. & n.* **1.** Of a bright warm colour resembling blood; রক্ত, রাঙা, লাল, লোহিত, শোণ, অরুণ, রাতুল, কষায়, সিন্দুর-বর্ণ, কুঙ্কুমারুণ, রকত (*poet.*), হিঙ্গুলবরণ, ডগমগে, টুকটুকে (dark red), টকটকে (*ib.*), ডুগডুগে (*ib.*), রগরগে (dark red or orange), রাতা (পদাবলী সাহিত্যে—যথা "রাতা উৎপল অধর যুগল"—পদকল্পতরু)। [ইংরাজীতে লোহিত বলিতে সিন্দূরের লালবর্ণ হইতে আরম্ভ করিয়া কমলালেবুর রঙ্গ পর্য্যন্ত সকল আভার বর্ণ বুঝায়; বিশেষভাবে রক্ত, রামধনুর রক্তিমা, যুবতীর অধরের

অরুণাভা, সান্ধ্যমেঘ, প্রভাতরবি, জলন্ত অঙ্গার, প্রবাল, পদ্মরাগ, প্রভৃতির বর্ণ বুঝায়। আমাদের দেশীয় মতে—মঙ্গলগ্রহ, প্রভাতরবি, সন্ধ্যাংশুমালী, তাম্র, কুঙ্কুম, গুঞ্জাফল, গজরক্ত, নেত্রকোণ, অধর, জিহ্বা, রক্ত, মাংস, সিন্দূর, গৈরিক, কুক্কুটশিখা, পদ্মরাগমণি, হংসের চঞ্চু এবং চরণ, শুক এবং মর্কটের মুখ, চকোর, কোকিল, পারাবত প্রভৃতির নেত্র, অশোক, কিংশুক, কুসুম্ভ, বন্ধুক, পদ্ম, জবা, প্রভৃতি পুষ্প, বিম্বফল, দাড়িম্ব পুষ্প, তাম্বূলরাগ, নবপল্লব, মঞ্জিষ্ঠা, অলক্তক, রক্তচন্দন, নখক্ষত, প্রভৃতি রক্তবর্ণ বস্তু বলিয়া পরিগণিত হয়। [সংস্কৃত কাদম্বরী প্রভৃতি কাব্যে রক্তবর্ণের বিভিন্ন আভার অতি মনোরম বর্ণনা পাওয়া যায়—যথা "প্রভাতসন্ধ্যারাগলোহিতে গগনতলে কমলিনীমধুরক্তপক্ষসম্পুটে বৃদ্ধহংস ইব * * * চন্দ্রমসিপরিণতরঙ্কুরোমপাণ্ডুনি ব্রজতি বিশালতামাশাচক্রবালে গজরুধিররক্তহরিসটালোমলোহিনীভিরাতপ্তলাক্ষিকতন্তুপাটলাভিরাযামিনীভিরশিশিরকিরণদীধিতিভিঃ পদ্মরাগরশ্মিশলাকাসম্মার্জ্জনীভিরিব সমুৎসার্য্যমাণে।" "রক্তচন্দনাঙ্গরাগং রবিরুদ্বহৎ"..."পারাবতচরণপাটলরাগো রবিরম্বরতলাদলম্বত"... "বিদ্রুমলতেবাপাটলা সন্ধ্যা সমদৃশ্যত।" ... "সন্ধ্যারাগারুণা ইব সিন্দুরমণিকুট্টিমেষু।" "সান্ধ্যং তেজঃ প্রতিনবজবাপুষ্পরক্তং দধানঃ" মেঘদূত।] 2. (*Magnet.*) Pertaining to, or designating, the north pole of a magnet; (চৌম্বকবিদ্যা) চুম্বকের উত্তরধ্রুব সম্বন্ধীয় বা তৎসূচক। *Noun.* **1.** A colour resembling that of arterial blood; redness; রক্তবর্ণ, লোহিতবর্ণ, অরুণ বর্ণ; রক্তিমা, অরুণিমা। **2.** A red pigment; রক্তবর্ণ রঞ্জক পদার্থ। 3. A radical, republican or anarchist; "My father was a *Red*—an Anarchist"; চরমপন্থী, গরমদলের লোক, গণতান্ত্রিক, বিপ্লববাদী। **4.** A stuff, cloth, wine, etc. of red colour; as, he was clothed in *red*; রক্তবস্ত্র, রক্তবর্ণ দ্রব্য, রক্তবর্ণ সুরা, প্রভৃতি। 5. (*Obs.*) Menses; (অপ্রঃ) স্ত্রীলোকের ঋতু। **Red'-den,** *v. t.* & *i.* To make or become red; to blush; রক্তবর্ণে রঞ্জিত করা, রক্তবর্ণ ধারণ করা; লজ্জায় লাল হওয়া, লজ্জায় গণ্ডস্থল অরুণাভ হওয়া। **Red'-dish,** *adj.* Somewhat red; রক্তাভ, লালাভ, ঈষদ্‌রাঙ্গা, রাঙ্গাটে, লাল্‌চে, আরক্ত, ঈষদ্‌রক্ত, আলোহিত, অরুণাভ। **Red'-ness,** *n.* The quality of being red; red colour; অরুণতা, অরুণত্ব, শোণতা, রক্তিমা, লৌহিত্য, অরুণিমা, শোণিমা; অরুণাভা, লালরঙ, রক্তবর্ণ, রাঙারঙ, রক্তরাগ, রাগ। **Dark red**—ঘোর রক্তবর্ণ, অতিরক্ত, ঘনারুণ, গাঢ় রক্তবর্ণ, টুক্‌টুকে লাল, টক্‌টকে লাল, ডগ্‌ডগে লাল, রগ্‌রগে লাল, লাল টকটক্, ডগমগ লাল, কড়ালাল, ঘোর লাল, সুরক্ত। (*A dark red pigment*—গাঢ় রক্তবর্ণ রঞ্জকপদার্থ বিশেষ, খুনখারাপি, খুনখারাবি।) **Red admiral**—একপ্রকার সুন্দর প্রজাপতি (এইরূপ প্রজাপতির সামনের পাখায় কমনীয় কমলাবর্ণের রেখা থাকে।) **Red ant**—লাল পিঁপড়া। **Red arsenic**—রসনেত্রিকা, মনঃশিলা, মনছাল, শোণিতশিলা (রঃ প্রঃ), শৃঙ্গী (ধাঃ প্রঃ), রোচনী, নাগমাতা (অঃ), দীপ্ত (মঃ উঃ), কুনটী, মনোজ্ঞা, নাগজিহ্বিকা, নৈপাল (সুশ্রুঃ), শিলা (ঐ), মনোহ্বা (রাজ নিঃ), রোগশিলা (ঐ), নেপালিকা (ঐ), মনোগুপ্তা (ঐ), কল্যাণিকা (ঐ), গোলা (ভাব প্রঃ), দিব্যৌষধি (ঐ)। **Red astrachan**—একপ্রকার পীতাভ সেওফল। **Red-bark**—একপ্রকার রক্তবর্ণের সিঙ্কোনা বল্কল। **Red bat**—উত্তর আমেরিকাবাসী রক্তবর্ণ বাদুড়। **Red-beaked**—রক্ততুণ্ডক। **Red-belley, -bellied**—রক্তোদর। **Red-belley**—একপ্রকার কূর্ম্ম; স্থামনজাতীয় একপ্রকার ক্ষুদ্র মৎস্য। **Red-belted** — রক্তকটিবন্ধ বিশিষ্ট। **Red-billed**—রক্তচঞ্চু। **Red-billed teal**—দক্ষিণ আফ্রিকার মরালবিশেষ। **Red-blind**—রক্তবর্ণ দর্শনে অন্ধ। **Red book**—লাল-মলাটের বই; বিশেষতঃ (cap.) সরকারী কার্য্যে নিযুক্ত, বা পেন্‌সনপ্রাপ্ত, সরকারী কর্ম্মচারিগণের নামসম্বলিত সরকারী পুস্তক (যাহা পূর্ব্বে প্রকাশিত হইত)। **Red box**—অষ্ট্রেলিয়া দেশীয় বৃক্ষ-বিশেষ; যে লাল রঙ্গের বাক্সে মন্ত্রিগণ কাগজপত্র রাখেন। **Red-breast**—বিলাতের রবিন্ পাখী। **Red bud**—আমেরিকার বৃক্ষবিশেষ। **Red-button** — সর্ব্বোচ্চ শ্রেণীর সৈনিক কর্ম্মচারী (ইহাদের টুপিতে লাল বোতাম থাকিত বলিয়া এই নাম)। **Red-cabbage**—একপ্রকার লাল রঙের বাঁধা কপি। **Red cent**—তামার সেণ্ট মুদ্রা (যাহা পূর্ব্বে আমেরিকার যুক্তরাজ্যে প্রস্তুত হইত)। Same as BRASS FARTHING (*fig.*); কাণা কড়ি। **Red chalk**—লোহিতমৃত্তিকা, রক্তধাতু (নিঃ প্রঃ), রক্তকন্দল (ঐ), রক্তোপল, তাম্রধাতু, রক্তকন্দ (অঃ)। **Red-coat** — যে ব্যক্তি লালকোর্ত্তা পরিয়া থাকে, বিশেষতঃ ইংরেজ সৈনিক। **Red-coral** — রক্তপ্রবাল, বিদ্রুম। **Red corpuscle**—রক্তের লোহিতবর্ণ কণিকা (কণিকাগুলি পৃথগ্‌ভাবে দেখিতে রক্তপীতবর্ণ—কিন্তু কণিকাসমষ্টি গাঢ় রক্তবর্ণ দেখায়)। **Red cross**—(ইংলণ্ডের জাতীয় চিহ্নস্বরূপ) সিদ্ধপুরুষ জর্জ্জের ক্রুশ; সাদা জমির উপর লাল রঙের ক্রুশ (যাহা যুদ্ধাদিকালে আরোগ্যশালা এবং আহত ও রুগ্ন-ব্যক্তিবাহী পোতে প্রদর্শিত হয়); যুদ্ধাদির কালে রুগ্ন বা আহত ব্যক্তিগণের সেবার জন্য, কিম্বা ঝটিকা, ভূমিকম্প, প্রভৃতি দৈব উৎপাতে ক্ষতিগ্রস্ত ব্যক্তিগণের সাহায্যার্থ সমিতিবিশেষ; ঐরূপ সমিতির সভ্য বা সেবক। **Red cross knight**—স্পেনসারের Faery Queen নামক কাব্যগ্রন্থোক্ত মহাবীর। **Red curlew** — একপ্রকার পক্ষী। **Red deer**—রক্ত হরিণ, লাল হরিণ, তাম্র মৃগ। **Red dog, Red dog flour**—নিকৃষ্ট ময়দা। **Red dressing**—জলমিশ্রিত বল্কলচূর্ণ—যাহাতে প্রথমে চামড়া ডুবান হয়। **Red-eye**—একপ্রকার মৎস্য। **Red-fire**—একপ্রকার বারুদ—যাহা জ্বালাইলে লোহিতবর্ণের আলোক প্রকাশ পায়, লাল বারুদ। **Red-fish**—ডিমওয়ালা স্থামন মাছ; স্থামন মাছ। **Red flag**—রক্তবর্ণ পতাকা, লাল নিশান, বিশেষতঃ (পূর্ব্বে) বিপ্লববাদিগণের পতাকা; বর্ত্তমানে সাম্যবাদিগণের রক্তপতাকা; রণপতাকা; রেলওয়ে,—চাঁদমারীর মাঠ প্রভৃতির বিপৎসঙ্কেতসূচক পতাকা।

Red flowering—রক্তপুষ্পপ্রসূ (cf. রক্তাশোক)। **Red gum**—শিশুদিগের দন্তোদ্গমের সময়ে জাত একপ্রকার রক্তবর্ণ উদ্ভেদ ; রক্তবর্ণ নির্য্যাসপ্রদ বৃক্ষবিশেষ। **Red-hand**—রক্তরঞ্জিত হস্ত, শোণিত-শোণ পাণি (আঃ বঃ)। **Red-handed**—In the very act ; হাতে নাতে। **Red hard**—অত্যধিক উষ্ণ অবস্থায় লোহিতবর্ণ হইলে কাঠিন্যপ্রাপ্ত। **Red hat**—রোমের পোপের সভাসদ (cardinals) গণের লোহিতবর্ণ টুপি। **Red-head**—রক্তকেশ ব্যক্তি ; কয়েক প্রকার রক্তশীর্ষ পক্ষীর সাধারণ নাম। **Red-heat**—তাপের যে মাত্রায় পদার্থ সমূহ লাল হইয়া উঠে (প্রায় 930°—1630° F.)। **Red herring**—আস্তে আস্তে ধোঁয়ায় শুকাইয়া যে হেরীং মাছ লালবর্ণ করা হইয়াছে ; মূল প্রশ্ন হইতে চিত্তবিক্ষেপ করার জন্য যে অবান্তর বিষয় উত্থাপিত করা হয়। **Red-horse** — আমেরিকাদেশীয় মৎস্যবিশেষ। **Red-hot** — তাপরক্ত ; (লক্ষণায়) অত্যুত্তেজিত। **Red-hot poker**—অগ্নিশিখাবৎ পুষ্পপ্রসূ উদ্যান-রোপিত গুল্মবিশেষ। **Red Indian**

Red Indians.

(or Red)—আমেরিকার আদিম অধিবাসী। **Red jasmine**—আমেরিকার উষ্ণমণ্ডলজাত রক্তপুষ্পপ্রসূ গুল্মবিশেষ। **Red kettle** — সোনার টেঁক-ঘড়ী (বর্ত্তমানে) টেঁক-ঘড়ী। **Red-lac**—লা, লাক্ষা, অলক্ত (red juice), যাবক (*ib.*), রক্তক্রিমিজ, রক্তদ্রুমাময়, রক্তক্ষতোঘ্নী, রঙ্গমাতা, রক্তবর্গ। **Red laced jacket**—(সৈনিকদিগের ইতর ভাষায়) বেত্রাঘাত ; শুঁড়িখানার আলাপ। **Red lamp**—ঔষধের দোকান প্রভৃতিতে রাত্রিকালে যে রক্তবর্ণ জলপূর্ণ কাচগোলক ইত্যাদি প্রদর্শিত হয়। **Red-lane**—(ইতর ভাষায়) গলনালী। **Red lead**—সিঁদূর, সিন্দূর, (হ্যাভেঃ) নাগসম্ভব, সীসজ (অঃ), নাগজ, নাগরক্ত, নাগরেণু, রক্তরেণু, রক্তসীমন্তক, নাগগর্ভ, শোণ, শৃঙ্গার, শৃঙ্গারক, শৃঙ্গার-ভূষণ, সন্ধ্যারাগ, সৌভাগ্য, অরুণ, মঙ্গল, বীররজ, গণেশভূষণ, চীনপিষ্ট। **Red-legs**—বিভিন্ন প্রকার পক্ষীর সাধারণ নাম ; একপ্রকার গুল্ম। **Red-letter**, *adj. & v. t.* Of a day marked with red letters in calendar as saint's day or festival ; (hence) happily memorable ; পঞ্জিকায় সিদ্ধপুরুষদের দিবস বা পর্ব্বদিবস বলিয়া রক্তাক্ষরে মুদ্রিত ; (অতএব) আনন্দের দিন বলিয়া স্মরণীয়। (*Verb t.*) To record as memorable for joy ; উৎসবানন্দের জন্য স্মরণীয় বলিয়া চিহ্নিত করা। **Red-letter day**—সিদ্ধপুরুষের দিবস বা পর্ব্বদিবস—যাহা পঞ্জিকায় রক্ত অক্ষরদ্বারা চিহ্নিত করা হয় ; আনন্দের দিন, স্মরণীয় দিন, সুখের দিন, শুভদিন। **Red lotus**—লালপদ্ম, রক্তপদ্ম, রাঙা শতদল (রবীঃ), অরুণকমল, প্রবালপদ্ম, (সুশ্রুঃ) রক্তসরোরুহ, শোণিতোৎপল (মঃ উঃ), লোহিতশতপত্র (ভাগঃ), অরুণসরোরুহ, শোণপদ্ম (গীতঃ), রক্তমণ্ডল (মঃ উঃ), রক্তকমল, রক্তকোকনদ, রক্তরাজীব, রক্তকহ্লার, রক্তসংকোচক, শোণরাজীব (কালিকাঃপুঃ), কৃষ্ণকন্দ (অঃ), রক্তবারিজ, রাতাউৎপল (*poet.*), রক্তাম্ভোজ, কোকনদ, রক্তোৎপল, রবিপ্রিয়, লক্ষ্মীগৃহ, লক্ষ্মীবেশ্ম। **Red man**—আমেরিকার আদিম অধিবাসী। **Red meat**—গরু, ভেড়া, প্রভৃতির মাংস [বাছুর, শূকর, কুক্কুট, প্রভৃতির মাংসের নাম শ্বেতমাংস (white meat]। **Red-metal**—তাম্রমিশ্র ধাতুবিশেষ। **Red-mica**—রক্তাভ্র (সাঃ পঃ)। **Red-necked**—রক্তকণ্ঠ। **Red-nose** — রক্ত নাসিকা। **Red-nosed** — রক্তনাসিক। **Red-oak** — একপ্রকার ওকবৃক্ষ (ইহার কাষ্ঠ আরক্তবর্ণ এবং ঐ কাঠের রং বহুকাল স্থায়ী হইয়া থাকে)। **Red ochre, ocher**—গিরিমাটী, রক্তধাতু, গিরিধাতু, গবেধুক, ধাতু, সুরঙ্গ ধাতু, গিরিসম্ভব, বনালক্ত, গবেরুক, লোহিতমৃত্তিকা, সুরক্তক, সন্ধ্যাভ্র, গৈরিক (রঃ রঃ সঃ প্রঃ), পাষাণ গৈরিক (ঐ), রক্তগৈরিক, স্বর্ণগৈরিক, গিরিমৃত্তিকা। **Red pepper**—লঙ্কা মরিচ। **Red plague (or red pestilence)** — একপ্রকার মহামারী — যাহাতে সর্ব্বাঙ্গে রক্তবর্ণ দাগ বা ক্ষত উৎপন্ন হয়। **Red pimple** — রক্তপিণ্ড। **Red-pine**—

Red-pine.

রক্তবল্কল সরল বৃক্ষ। **Red-plum**—রক্তবর্ণ আলুবোখারা। **Red-poll**—চটক, তুতী, প্রভৃতি কয়েক প্রকার পাখীর সাধারণ নাম। One of the RED-POLLED CATTLE. **Red-polled cattle**—ইংলণ্ডের একজাতীয় শৃঙ্গহীন রক্তবর্ণ গো। **Red race**—আমেরিকার আদিম নিবাসী জাতি। **Red rag**—ক্রোধোদ্দীপক বস্তু (যেমন লাল ন্যাকড়া দেখিলে বৃষ ক্ষিপ্ত হইয়া উঠে) ; (ইতর ভাষায়) জিহ্বা ; গোধূমের রোগবিশেষ—যাহাতে শস্যে মরিচার মত দাগ পড়ে। **Red rain**—রক্তবৃষ্টি (উল্কাধূলির cobalt chloride দ্বারা রক্তবর্ণে রঞ্জিত বৃষ্টিজল)। **Red raspberry** — একপ্রকার লাল রঙের বিলাতী গৌরীফল। **Red Republican** — ফরাসীদেশের উৎকট গণতান্ত্রিক (এইরূপ গণতান্ত্রিকগণ লাল টুপি পরিত) ; চরমপন্থী, আমূল সংস্কারের পক্ষপাতী ব্যক্তি। **Red ribbon**—ইংলণ্ডের বাথ নামক অভিজাত সম্প্রদায়ের চিহ্নস্বরূপ রক্তবর্ণ ফিতা ; উক্ত অভিজাত সম্প্রদায় বা উহার সভ্যপদ। **Red rot**—ওক প্রভৃতি বৃক্ষের একপ্রকার

রোগ—যাহাতে বৃক্ষগাত্রে স্থানে স্থানে লাল দাগ উৎপন্ন হয়। **Red sanders, Red sandal wood**—রক্তচন্দন, লালচন্দন, লোহিতচন্দন, প্রবালফল (ভাবঃ প্রঃ), রক্তসার, শোণিত-চন্দন, তাম্রভ্রু (নিঃ প্রঃ), তাম্রাভ, রুধিরচন্দন (রঃ), কুচন্দন, অর্কচন্দন, পত্রাঙ্গ, কুঙ্কুমাগুরু, রঞ্জন, তিলপর্ণ, তিলপর্ণিক, তিলপর্ণিক, তাম্রবৃক্ষ, তাম্রসার, তাম্রসারক, লোহিত, শোণিত, চন্দন, ক্ষুদ্রচন্দন, রক্তাঙ্গ, পত্বগ, পত্তঙ্গ, পত্তুর (ভাবপ্রঃ), রক্তবীজ। **Red-shank**—একপ্রকার পক্ষী; রক্তচরণ মানব; বিশেষতঃ স্কটলণ্ডদেশের উত্তরভাগস্থ পার্ব্বত্য অঞ্চল এবং আয়র্লণ্ডবাসী কেল্টজাতীয় লোক। **Red Sea**—লোহিত সাগর। **Red shirt**—বিপ্লববাদী, বিপ্লব-পন্থী। **Red-short**—তপ্তাবস্থায় লোহিতবর্ণ ধারণ করিলে ভঙ্গপ্রবণ (লৌহ)। **Redskin**—আমেরিকার প্রাচীন অধিবাসী। **Red-snapper**—একপ্রকার মৎস্য। **Red snow**—শৈবালবিশেষদ্বারা স্থানে স্থানে রক্তবর্ণে রঞ্জিত মেরুসন্নিহিত প্রদেশের এবং আল্পস্ পর্ব্বতের তুষার, রক্ততুষার। **Red soldier**—শূকরের জ্বররোগবিশেষ—যাহাতে চর্ম্ম রক্তবর্ণ ধারণ করে; উক্ত রোগাক্রান্ত শূকর। **Red-spider**—একপ্রকার কীট—যাহা শীতপ্রধান দেশের কাচসমাচ্ছাদিত উদ্যানের বৃক্ষলতাদি নষ্ট করে বা গাছ ধ্বংসকারী একপ্রকার রক্তবর্ণ কীটাণু। **Red squadron**—পূর্ব্বে যে শ্রেণীত্রয়ে রাজকীয় রণপোতসমূহ বিভক্ত হইত—তাহার অন্যতম। **Red-squirrel**—আমেরিকার

Redstart.

কাঠ বিড়াল। **Redstart**—ইয়ুরোপ দেশীয় রক্তপুচ্ছ গায়কপক্ষিবিশেষ। **Red stone**—রক্তপ্রস্তর, লাল পাথর, রক্তপাষাণ। **Red-streak**—একপ্রকার সেওফল—ইহাতে রক্ত ও পীতবর্ণের ডোরা থাকে। **Red tape**—আফিসের কাগজ বাঁধিবার লাল ফিতা; সরকারী কার্য্যালয়ের রীতিনীতি, কায়দা কানুন ও দীর্ঘসূত্রতা। (*Red tapery, Red tapism*—সাধারণ বিচারবুদ্ধি বিসর্জ্জন পূর্ব্বক আফিসের কায়দা কানুন ও দস্তুরের বশবর্ত্তিতা। *Red-tapist, n.*) **Red-tincture**—রসেন্দ্র (কুলার্ণব) [অর্থাৎ যদ্দারা অপকৃষ্ট ধাতু স্বর্ণে পরিবর্ত্তিত করা যায় বলিয়া কল্পিত হইত।] **Red turtle dove**—রামঘুঘু, রাজঘুঘু। **Red-water**—গোমহিষ ও মেষাদির একপ্রকার রোগ—যাহাতে উহাদের মূত্র রক্তবর্ণ ধারণ করে। **Red-weed**—শস্যক্ষেত্রে জাত একপ্রকার আগাছা। **Red-wing**—বিভিন্ন প্রকার পক্ষীর সাধারণ নাম, দামা। **Red wood**—বিভিন্ন প্রকার রক্তকাষ্ঠবিশিষ্ট বৃক্ষের সাধারণ নাম। **Red-wood**—অতিরুহা (দ্রব্যগুণ)। **Red worm**—বড়শীর টোপে ব্যবহৃত একপ্রকার কীট, রক্তকীট। **Red all over**—লালে লাল (রবীঃ)। **The red cock will crow in his house**—(*Scott*—Guy Mannering, chap. III) His house will be set on fire; তাহার বাড়ীতে লাল ঘোড়া দৌড়িবে (অর্থাৎ আগুন লাগান হইবে)। **The red laws**—প্রাচীন রোমের দেওয়ানি আইন। **To be caught red-handed**—To be caught in the very act; হাতে হাতে ধরা পড়া, বমাল শুদ্ধ ধরা পড়া [cf. Sans. রূপাভিগ্রাহিত (আপ্তেঃ)]। **To draw a red herring across the track**—To divert from the main subject; মূল বিষয় হইতে মন বিক্ষিপ্ত করা। **To shoot or sport the red**—To develop the red colouring to the face and wattles; (কুক্কুটাদি সম্পর্কে) মুখে ও গলার নীচে লোহিতবর্ণ বিকাশ পাওয়া।

rĕd, *v. t. & i.* (*Scot.*) To counsel; (স্কটলণ্ড) পরামর্শ দেওয়া। ***Verb i.*** (*Scot.*) To conjecture; (স্কটলণ্ডে) আন্দাজ করা।

rĕd, rĕdd, *v. t.* **1.** To put in order; ঠিক করা। **2.** To take out of danger; বিপদ্ হইতে মুক্ত করা। **To red one's feet**—To free one's self from entanglement; ঝঞ্ঝাট হইতে মুক্ত করা, দায় এড়ান।

rē-dăct′, *v. t.* To give a presentable literary form to; to edit; প্রতিসংস্করণ করা; সম্পাদন করা। **—dac′-tion**, *n.* The act of redacting; a new edition; প্রতিসংস্করণ; নূতনসংস্করণ, নবসংস্করণ।

rē-dăn′, *n.* A field fortification composed of two faces, forming an angle toward the enemy and without any covering to the rear; যুদ্ধক্ষেত্রস্থ কোণাকৃতি উপদুর্গবিশেষ, ইহার কোণ শত্রুর অভিমুখে থাকে এবং পশ্চাদ্দিকে কোনরূপ আবরণ থাকে না।

rĕd′-dle (-l), *n. & v. t.* Red ochre; রক্ত গৈরিক। ***Verb t.*** To colour with red ochre; রক্ত গৈরিক দ্বারা রঞ্জিত করা, গিরিমাটিদ্বারা রঙ্গান।

rede (rēd), *n.* (*Obs.*) Counsel; (অপ্রঃ) পরামর্শ।

rede (rēd), *v. t.* **1.** To counsel; পরামর্শ দেওয়া। **2.** To interpret; ব্যাখ্যা করা, (স্বপ্নাদির) ফল বলা।

rē-deem′ (-dēm), *v. t.* **1.** To repurchase; পুনরায় ক্রয় করা। **2.** To make amends for; as, to *redeem* an error; ক্ষতিপূরণ করা, প্রায়শ্চিত্ত করা। **3.** To ransom; নিষ্ক্রয়প্রদানে মুক্ত করা। **4.** To deliver; "*Redeem* Israel, O Lord, out of all his troubles" উদ্ধার করা। **5.** (*Theol.*) To deliver from the bondage of sin and its penalties; "God manifested in the flesh, sent from heaven, to *redeem* a lost world"; মুক্তিদ্বারা পরিত্রাণ করা। **6.** To perform, as a promise; প্রতিজ্ঞা বা প্রতিশ্রুতি পালন, পূরণ বা সম্পাদন করা। **7.** (*Law*) To regain as mortgaged property by payment of what is due according to the terms of the mortgage; বন্ধকের সর্ত্ত অনুসারে দেয় টাকা প্রভৃতি প্রদানে বন্ধকী সম্পত্তি খালাস করা। **8.** To buy off, take up, or remove the obligation of, by payment or rendering of some consideration; টাকা দ্বারা বা অন্য কোন প্রকারে কিনিয়া ফেলা বা কোনরূপ বাধ্যবাধকতা হইতে রেহাই পাওয়া। **9.** To save a person or thing from some defect or fault; "A blank ceiling is not to be *redeemed* by a decorated ventilator"; কোনরূপ দোষ বা খুঁত শোধন করা। **--a-ble,** *adj.* That can be redeemed; উদ্ধার্য্য, মোচনীয়, শোধনীয়। **–er,** *n.* One who redeems; spec. Jesus Christ; উদ্ধারকর্ত্তা, মোচয়িতা, মুক্তিদাতা, মোক্ষদাতা; বিশেষতঃ পবিত্রাত্মা যীশুখৃষ্ট। **–ing,** *adj.* **Redeeming feature**—দোষ, খুঁত বা ত্রুটিশোধক গুণ, বিশেষত্ব বা লক্ষণ। **To redeem the time**—To make the best use of it; সময়ের সদ্ব্যবহার করা।

rē-demp'-tion (-dĕm-), *n.* **1.** Repurchase; ransom; rescue; পুনঃক্রয়, পরিক্রয়, পরিক্রয়ণ; নিষ্ক্রয়প্রদানে উদ্ধারসাধন; উদ্ধার। **2.** Deliverance from the bondage or consequence of sin; salvation; পাপবন্ধনমুক্তি, পাপনিষ্কৃতি, পাপমোচন, মোক্ষণ, পাপপরিণামমুক্তি; মুক্তি, উদ্ধার, মোক্ষ। **3.** (*Law*) The liberation of an estate from a mortgagee; বন্ধকী সম্পত্তি উদ্ধার। **4.** (*Commer.*) Repurchase by an issuer of notes, bills, etc. by paying their value in money to the holder; দাবীর টাকা প্রদানপূর্ব্বক উত্তমর্ণ হইতে হুণ্ডী, খত, প্রভৃতি পুনঃক্রয়। **5.** Atonement · প্রায়শ্চিত্ত। **6.** That which redeems; a redeeming feature; উদ্ধারসাধক বস্তু; দোষ বা ত্রুটিশোধক বিষয়। **–tive,** *adj.* **The year of our redemption**—Same as ANNO DOMINI (which see).

rē-dē-scend' (-sĕnd), *v. t.* To descend again; পুনরায় অবতরণ করা।

redif, *n.* (Arab. ردف) Turkish military reserve; a soldier of the Turkish military reserve; তুরস্কদেশের রিজার্ভ সৈন্য; ঐ সৈন্যদলের সৈনিক।

rĕd'-in-gōte (-ĭng-), *n.* A woman's long double-breasted outside coat; স্ত্রীলোকদিগের একপ্রকার জামা।

rē-dĭn'-tē-grāte, *v. t.* To restore to a perfect state; পুনরায় সর্ব্বাঙ্গসম্পন্ন করা, পুনরায় পূর্ণতাসাধন করা, অংশ যোজনপূর্ব্বক পুনরায় সর্ব্বাঙ্গসম্পন্ন করা। **–gra'-tion,** *n.* **1.** Restoration to a whole or sound state; renovation; পুনরখণ্ডতাপাদন, পুনঃসর্ব্বাবয়বতা সম্পাদন; নবীকরণ। **2.** (*Psychol.*) Revival of the whole of a previous mental state when part of it recurs; (মনোবিজ্ঞান) কোন পূর্ব্ববর্ত্তী মানসিক অবস্থার অংশবিশেষ মনে আসিলে ইহার সমস্ত অংশের স্মৃতি উদ্দীপন, প্রত্যর্পণ (হিঃ কোঃ), পুনস্ফুরণ (ঐ)।

rē-dī-rĕct', *v. t.* To readdress; পুনরায় শিরোনামা লিখা, নূতন ঠিকানা লিখিয়া দেওয়া।

rē-dĭs-cov'-ĕr (-cŭv-), *v. t.* To discover again; পুনরাবিষ্কার করা।

rē-dĭs-trĭb'-ūte, *v. t.* To distribute again; পুনরায় বিতরণ করা, পুনর্বণ্টন করা। **–tri-bu'-tion,** *n.* The act of redistributing; পুনর্বণ্টন।

rē-dī-vīde', *v. t.* To divide again; পুনরায় বিভাগ করা।

rĕd'-ō-lĕnt, *adj.* **1.** (*Now rare*) Sweet-smelling; (বর্ত্তমানে কচিদ্-ব্যবহৃত) সুগন্ধি, সুরভি। **2.** (Of smell etc.) Pleasant; sweet; (গন্ধসম্বন্ধে) মনোরম; মধুর। **3.** Full of the scent of; as, *redolent* with fragrant perfumes; গন্ধে ভরপুর, মসগুল। **4.** (*Fig.*) Strongly suggestive of, or impregnated with; "It is a strain *redolent* of bridegroom's joy"; (লক্ষণায়) অভিব্যঞ্জক, ভরপুর। **–lence,** *n.*

rē-dou'-ble (-dŭ-bl), *v. t.* & *i.* To intensify or to be intensified; দ্বিগুণিত করা, দ্বিগুণিত হওয়া, তীব্রতর করা, তীব্রতর হওয়া, প্রখরতর করা, প্রখরতর হওয়া।

rē-doubt' (-dowt), *n.* An outer-work usually of a square or polygonal shape without any flanking defence in fortification; পার্শ্বভাগে অরক্ষিত (সাধারণতঃ) চতুরস্র বা পঞ্চভুজাকৃতি উপদুর্গবিশেষ, মোরচ (ফাঃ হিঃ)।

Redoubt.

rē-doubt'-a-ble (-dowt-ă-bl), *adj.* Formidable; terrible; দুর্দ্ধর্ষ, অপ্রধৃষ্য; ভীমপ্রতাপ, ভীম, ভীষণদর্শন, মহাবলপরাক্রান্ত।

rē-doubt'-ĕd (-dowt-), *adj.* (*Archaic*) Dreaded; (অপ্রঃ) দুর্দ্ধর্ষ, ভীষণদর্শন।

rē-dound' (-downd), *v. i.* **1.** To return; to rebound; প্রত্যাবৃত্ত হওয়া; প্রতিক্ষিপ্ত হওয়া। **2.** To resound; প্রতিধ্বনিত হওয়া, নিনাদিত হওয়া। **3.** To conduce; to contribute; "I think it *redounds* to their praise"; to result; কোনরূপ ফলোৎপাদনে সহায়তা করা; ফলস্বরূপ আগত হওয়া; পরিণত হওয়া।

rē-drĕss', *v. t.* & *n.* **1.** To remedy or put to right; as, to *redress* a grievance; to make amends; প্রতীকার করা; ক্ষতিপূরণ করা। **2.** To readjust; পুনরায় ঠিক করা, পুনরায় সমঞ্জস করা। ***Noun.*** Reparation of a wrong; amends for a loss; প্রতীকার; ক্ষতিপূরণ। **To redress the balance**—To restore equality; পুনরায় সাম্য প্রতিষ্ঠা করা।

rē-dūce' (-dūs), *v. t.* **1.** To bring to a former state; পূর্ব্বাবস্থায় আনা। **2.** To bring to any state or condition, good or bad; as, to *reduce* to poverty; ভাল বা মন্দ যে

কোন অবস্থায় আনা, পরিণত করা। 3. To bring into subjection; অধীন করা, বশীভূত করা। 4. To lower in dignity; মর্য্যাদা হানি করা, গৌরব হ্রাস করা, গর্ব্ব খর্ব্ব করা। 5. To diminish in length, breadth, size, quantity or the like; দৈর্ঘ্য, প্রস্থ, আয়তন, সংখ্যা প্রভৃতি হ্রাস করা, কমান, ন্যূন করা। 6. (*Arith.*) To change (numbers) from one denomination to another without changing the value; as, to *reduce* pence to pound; মূল্য পরিবর্ত্তন না করিয়া এক নামীয় সংখ্যাকে অপর নামীয় সংখ্যাতে পরিণত করা। 7. (*Geom.*) To construct a figure similar to and smaller than (a given figure); (কোনও প্রদত্ত ক্ষেত্রের) সদৃশ ক্ষুদ্রতর ক্ষেত্র অঙ্কিত করা। 8. To bring into class, order, genus, etc.; শ্রেণী, বর্গ, গণ, প্রভৃতিতে ভুক্ত করা। 9. (*Surg.*) To restore to its proper place or state, as fractured or dislocated bone; ভগ্ন অথবা সন্ধিচ্যুত অস্থি পুনরায় যথাস্থানে নিবিষ্ট করা। 10. (*Log.*) To change a syllogism from an imperfect to a perfect mode; কোন সাবয়ব বাক্য অসম্পূর্ণ পদ্ধতি হইতে সম্পূর্ণ পদ্ধতিতে পরিবর্ত্তন করা। 11. To bring into action; কার্য্যে পরিণত করা। 12. To break down; to crush; to powder; ভাঙ্গা; ছেঁচা; চূর্ণ করা, পেষা। 13. (*Chem.*) To decompose; যৌগিক পদার্থ বিশ্লেষণ করা। 14. (*Photog.*) To render less dense; গাঢ়তা কমান। **To reduce a figure, draught**—নক্সা প্রভৃতি ক্ষুদ্র স্কেলে অঙ্কন করা, ক্ষুদ্র আয়তনে অঙ্কন করা। **To reduce a square**—চতুষ্কাকারে সজ্জিত সৈন্যসমূহ পংক্তিবদ্ধভাবে রচনা করা। **To reduce establishment**—ব্যয় হ্রাসের জন্য কর্ম্মচারিবর্গের সংখ্যা কমান। **To reduce to the ranks**—To degrade as a sergeant and corporal to the rank of a private; অচিহ্নিত (non-commissioned) সৈনিক কর্ম্মচারীকে সাধারণ সৈনিকে অবনীত করা।

Reductio ad absurdum, (*L.*), *n.* অসঙ্গতিপ্রদর্শন (হিঃ কোঃ), ব্যাহতিপ্রদর্শন।

rē-dŭc′-tion, *n.* 1. The act of reducing to any state or condition; সংহৃতি, সংস্কারক্রিয়া (হিঃ কোঃ), রূপান্তরীকরণ পরিবর্ত্তন, পরিণমন। 2. Conquest; subjection; জয়, বিজয়; আয়ত্তীকরণ, অধীনীকরণ। 3. Reduced copy of a picture, map, etc.; ছবি, মানচিত্র, প্রভৃতির ক্ষুদ্র আকারে অঙ্কিত প্রতিলিপি। 4. Diminution; হ্রাস, কমতি, ন্যূনতা। **Reduction to the absurd** or **to absurdity**—Same as REDUCTIO AD ABSURDUM.

rĕd′-uit (-wē), *n.* A keep for garrison to retire and hold when outworks are taken; বাহিরের উপদুর্গ প্রভৃতি শত্রুহস্তগত হইলে দুর্গবাসিসৈন্যগণ দুর্গাভ্যন্তরস্থ যে সুদৃঢ় স্থানে আশ্রয় গ্রহণপূর্ব্বক দুর্গ রক্ষা করে।

rē-dŭn′-dănt, *adj.* 1. Superfluous; superabundant; অতিরিক্ত, উদ্রিক্ত; সমধিক, অত্যধিক। **–dance, –dancy**, *ns.* **–ly**, *adv.*

rē-dū′-pli-cāte, *v. t.* 1. To double again; to repeat; পুনর্দ্বিগুণিত করা; দ্বিরুক্তি করা, পুনরুক্তি করা। 2. (*Philol.*) To repeat as the initial syllable or the rest of a word, as for the purpose of marking past time; (ভাষাবিজ্ঞান) অতীত কাল প্রভৃতি সূচনার জন্য কোন শব্দের আদ্যশব্দাংশ বা ধাতু দ্বিত্ব করা, অভ্যস্ত করা (the word অভ্যস্ত has been used for *reduplicate* in নিরুক্ত)। **–ca′-tion**, *n.* 1. The act of reduplicating; a part folded back on itself; পুনর্দ্বিগুণন, আম্রেড়ন; আপনাতে পুনরাবর্ত্তিত বস্তু। 2. (*Philol.*) The act of repeating the initial syllable or the root of a word; the part so repeated; (ভাষাবিজ্ঞান) অভ্যাস (নিরুক্ত); অভ্যস্ত অংশ।

rē-dye′ (-dī), *v. t.* To dye again; পুনরায় রঞ্জিত করা।

rē-ĕch-ō, *v. t.* & *i.* To echo again; প্রতিধ্বনিত করা। ***Verb i.*** To resound; প্রতিধ্বনিত হওয়া।

reed (rēd), *n.* & *v. t.* 1. One of a large family of plants with hollow jointed stems, such as the common reed, bamboo, etc.; নল, খাগড়া, শর [Syn. মৃদুপত্র, মৃদুপর্ব্ব, মৃদুপর্ব্বক, ধমন, নাড়ী, নাল, তৃণধ্বজ, তৃণকেতু, কীচক, পোটগল, খেখীরক, ছিদ্রান্ত, কুক্ষিরন্ধ্র, ত্বক্সার, শতপর্ব্বা, মস্কর, বিভীষণ, মৃদুচ্ছদ, বংশপত্র, শূন্যমধ্য, দীর্ঘবংশ, নড়, নালবংশ।] 2. (*Dial.*) Straw prepared for thatching; (উপভাষায়) ছন, খড়। 3. An arrow; "As whistles from the bow the *reed*"; বাণ, শর, তীর, সায়ক। 4. A pastoral pipe; as, the pastoral *reed* of Hermes; pastoral poetry; বংশী, বেণু, মুরলী, গোপবেণু; গোপকবিতা। 5. A weavers' instrument for separating the threads of the warp and for beating the weft up to the web; তাঁতের শাণা। 6. (*Mus.*) A little tube through which a bassoon, clarionet or other instrument is blown; শানাই প্রভৃতির মুখনল। 7. (*Mus.*) A thin elastic plate whose vibrations produce the notes of an organ, harmonium, etc.; যে পাতলা স্থিতিস্থাপক ফলকের স্পন্দন দ্বারা অর্গেন, হারমনিয়াম, প্রভৃতি বাদ্যযন্ত্রে ধ্বনি উৎপাদিত হয়, স্পন্দনশীল ফলক। 8. (*Arch.*) A smnll convex moulding; (স্থপতিবিদ্যা) একপ্রকার ক্ষুদ্র বহির্বর্ত্তুল ভূষা। ***Verb t.*** 1. To thatch with reeds; ছন দ্বারা ছাওয়া। 2. (*Arch.*) To decorate with reeds; (স্থপতিবিদ্যা) ক্ষুদ্র বহির্বর্ত্তুল ভূষা দ্বারা শোভিত করা। **Reed-babbler, Reed-warbler, Reed-wren** — একজাতীয় পক্ষী।

Reed-bunting or **reed-sparrow**—একপ্রকার পক্ষী। **Reed-mace**—একপ্রকার পক্ষী। **Reed-organ**—যে বাদ্যযন্ত্রের বায়ু ধাতুনির্ম্মিত মুক্ত স্পন্দনফলক শ্রেণীর উপর ক্রিয়া করে। **Reed-pheasant**—একজাতীয় পক্ষী। **Reed-pipe**—বংশী; অর্গেন যন্ত্রের যে নালীতে ধ্বনি উৎপাদনের জন্য স্পন্দনশীলফলক সংযুক্ত থাকে। **Reed-stop**—অর্গেন যন্ত্রের স্পন্দনশীল ফলক-বিশিষ্ট নালীসমূহ—যাহা একমাত্র রোধক পিণ্ড (stop knob) দ্বারা নিয়মিত হয়। **A broken reed**—A weak support; ভগ্ন যষ্টি, দুর্ব্বল আশ্রয়। **To lean on a reed**—To rely on an weak person or thing; দুর্ব্বল ব্যক্তি বা ভগ্নপ্রবণ বস্তুর উপর নির্ভর করা।

rē–ĕd′-i-fȳ, *v. t.* To rebuild; পুনর্নির্ম্মাণ করা, পুনর্গঠন করা।

rē–ĕd′-it, *v. t.* To edit anew; পুনরায় সম্পাদন করা, পুনঃসম্পাদন করা।

reed′-ling (rēd-), *n.* Bearded Titmouse; একপ্রকার পক্ষী।

reed′-ȳ (rēd-), *adj.* 1. Abounding with reeds; শরবহুল, নলময়, শরময়। 2. Made of reed; শরনির্ম্মিত, নলরচিত। 3. Applied to a voice or musical instrument characterised by a thin harsh tone, like the vibration of a reed; বাদ্যযন্ত্রের স্পন্দনশীল ফলকের স্পন্দনধ্বনিবৎ।

reef (rēf), *n.* 1. A chain, mass or range of rocks, in various parts of ocean, lying at or near the surface; সাগরপৃষ্ঠস্থ বা সাগর তলস্থ শৈলমালা। 2. (*Gold mining*) Gold-bearing quartz vein; (পাষাণাদির মধ্যস্থ) স্বর্ণগর্ভ কাচমণির শিরা। **A coral reef**—প্রবাল প্রাচীর (সাঃ পঃ)।

reef (rēf), *n.* & *v. t.* 1. The part of a sail which may be taken in or let out according to the force of the wind; বায়ুর বলানুসারে পাইলের যে অংশ গুটান বা ছাড়া যাইতে পারে। ***Verb t.*** To reduce the extent (of sail) by rolling or folding; গুটাইয়া পাইলের বিস্তার কমান। **To take**

Reefing of sail.

in a reef—To proceed cautiously; সাবধানে অগ্রসর হওয়া।

reef′-ēr (rēf-), *n.* 1. One who reefs sails; a midshipman; যে ব্যক্তি পাইলের কতকাংশ গুটাইয়া বা জড়াইয়া উহার বিস্তার কমায়; জাহাজের অধস্তন কর্ম্মচারিবিশেষ। 2. A close double-breasted stout jacket; একপ্রকার আঁট সাঁট কোর্ত্তা।

reek (rēk), *n., v.i.* & *t.* 1. Smoke; vapour; ধূম, ধূঁয়া, ভাপ; বাষ্প। 2. Foul odour; দুর্গন্ধ। ***Verb i.*** 1. To smoke; ধূঁয়া উঠা। 2. To emit vapour; ধূঁয়া বা বাষ্প নির্গত হওয়া, ভাপ উঠা। 3. To smell strongly and unpleasantly; as, *reeking* with the smell of bitter almonds; উগ্র দুর্গন্ধ করা। ***Verb t.*** To subject to the action of smoke; ধূঁয়া লাগান। **Reek′-y,** *adj.*

reel (rēl), *n., v. t.* & *i.* 1. A frame on which yarn, thread, lines, etc. are wound; a bobbin for thread; নাটাই, চরকী; কাঠিম। 2. A cylinder turning on an axis on which seamen wind the log-lines, and anglers their fishing-line; জাহাজের গতিমাপক ভাসমান যন্ত্র যে সূতায় বাঁধা থাকে—তাহা জড়াইবার জন্য, বড়শীর সূতা জড়াইবার চাকাযুক্ত সংলগ্ন কাঠিম। ***Verb t.*** 1. To wind upon reel as, yarn, thread, etc.; চরকায় জড়ান, কাঠিমে জড়ান। 2. To draw by reeling a line; as, to *reel* a fish; সূতা বড়শীর কাঠিমে গুটাইয়া তোলা। 3. To tell a story rapidly and fluently; গলগল করিয়া গল্প বলিয়া যাওয়া। ***Verb i.*** (Of grasshoppers etc.) To make a noise like a revolving reel; (ফড়িঙ প্রভৃতি সম্পর্কে) ঘূর্ণনশীল চরকার মত শব্দ করা, ফড় ফড় করা। **Off the reel**—In rapid succession; গল গল করিয়া। **To reel off**—To rattle off without pause, as a story; গল গল করিয়া গল্প বলিয়া যাওয়া।

reel (rēl), *n.* & *v. t.* A lively dance, peculiar to Scotland in which the couples form the figure 8; স্কটলণ্ড দেশীয় একপ্রকার উল্লাসপূর্ণ নৃত্য—যাহাতে নর্ত্তকযুগল ইংরাজী ৮(৪) অক্ষরের অনুরূপ ক্ষেত্র রচনাপূর্ব্বক নৃত্য করে। ***Verb t.*** To perform the dance reel; উক্তরূপ নৃত্য করা।

reel (rēl), *v. i.* & *n.* 1. To stagger; to swing violently; টলা, টলমল করা; প্রবলভাবে দুলা, টলিতে থাকা। 2. To whirl; as, my brain *reeled*; ভ্রমি দেওয়া, পাক দেওয়া, ঘুরা। 3. To give way; to fall back, as a line in battle; ভাঙ্গিয়া পড়া; পেছিয়ে পড়া। ***Noun.*** Reeling motion; পাক, ভ্রমি, মস্তকঘূর্ণন, টলন।

rē–ē-lĕct′, *v. t.* To elect again; পুনর্নির্ব্বাচন করা। **–lec′-tion,** *n.* The act of re-electing; পুনর্নির্ব্বাচন।

rē–ĕm-bārk′, *v.i.* & *t.* To embark or go on board again; পুনরায় জাহাজে উঠা, পুনর্ব্বার জাহাজে উঠান। **–bar-ka′-tion,** *n.*

rē–ē-merge′ (-mērj), *v. i.* To emerge again; পুনরায় উত্থিত হওয়া, পুনরায় নিক্রান্ত হওয়া, পুনরায় নির্গত হওয়া।

rē–ĕn-ā′-ble (-bl), *v. t.* To enable again; পুনরায় সমর্থ করা।

rē–ĕn-ăct′, *v. t.* To enact again; পুনরায় বিধিবদ্ধ করা। **–ac′-tion, –ment,** *ns.*

rē–ĕn'-gine (-jĭn), *v. t.* To supply (ship etc.) with new engine ; (জাহাজ প্রভৃতিতে) নূতন এঞ্জিন বা কল লাগান।

rē–ĕn'-têr, *v. t.* & *i.* **1.** To enter again ; পুনঃ প্রবেশ করা। **2.** (*Engraving*) To cut deeper, as those incisions of the plate which the acid has bitten insufficiently ; (ক্ষোদাইকার্য্যে) ফলকের যে রেখা সকল দ্রাবক দ্বারা সম্যগ্‌রূপে উৎকীর্ণ হয় নাই—সেই সকলকে পুনরায় গভীর করিয়া কাটা।

rē–ĕn'-têr-ing, *adj.* Entering by return or backward movement ; পশ্চাদ্‌গতিদ্বারা প্রবেশকারী। **Re-entering angle** — অন্তর্মুখী কোণ, (দুর্গাদিতে) রক্ষিত স্থানের অভিমুখীন কোণ।

rē–ĕn'-trănt, *adj.* & *n.* Same as RE-ENTERING. ***Noun.*** Same as RE-ENTERING ANGLE which see.

rē–ĕs-tăb'-lish, *v. t.* To establish anew ; পুনঃ প্রতিষ্ঠা করা। **–ment,** *n.* The act of re-establishing ; restoration ; পুনঃপ্রতিষ্ঠাপন ; পুনঃপ্রতিষ্ঠা।

reeve (rēv), *n.* (*Hist.*) The chief magistrate of a town or district ; (ইতিহাস) কোন জেলা বা নগরের প্রধান শাসনকর্ত্তা।

reeve (rēv), *n.* A bird, the female of the ruff ; একপ্রকার পক্ষী।

reeve (rēv), *v. t.* & *i.* **1.** To pass the end of a rope through any hole in a block, thimble, etc. ; to pass a rope through ; রজ্জুর প্রান্ত ছিদ্রের ভিতর দিয়া চালিত করা ; ভিতর দিয়া রজ্জু চালান। **2.** (*Fig.*) To go cautiously through openings ; as, the ship *reeved* the ice-pack ; ফাঁকের মধ্য দিয়া অগ্রসর হওয়া। ***Verb i.*** To run or pass through such a hole ; এইরূপ ছিদ্রের ভিতর দিয়া চালিত হওয়া।

rē–ex-am'-ine (-ĕgz-ăm-ĭn), *v. t.* To examine again ; পুনরায় পরীক্ষা করা। **–i-na'-tion,** *n.* **1.** A renewed examination ; পুনঃ পরীক্ষা। **2.** (*Law*) The examination of a witness after he has been cross-examined ; (আইন) জেরার পর সাক্ষীর পুনরায় জবানবন্দী।

rē–ĕx-pōrt', *v.t.* To export again ; আমদানীর পর পুনরায় রপ্তানী করা।

rē-face' (-fās), *v. t.* To put a new facing on a building ; অট্টালিকার সম্মুখভাগ নূতন করা।

rē-făsh'-ion (-ŭn), *v. t.* To form or mould into shape again or anew ; পুনরায় গড়া, পুনর্গঠন করা।

rē-fĕc'-tion, *n.* **1.** Refreshment after hunger or fatigue ; জলযোগ, জলপান। **2.** A spare meal ; a meal sufficient only to maintain life ; লঘুভোজন ; জীবনধারণোপযোগী ভোজন।

rē-fĕc'-tō-rȳ, *n.* An eating room in monastaries etc. ; মঠ প্রভৃতির ভোজনকক্ষ, ভোগমন্দির (উড়িষ্যা), ভোগমণ্ডপ (ঐ)।

rē-fêr', *v. t.* & *i.* **1.** To assign, impute or attribute ; as, to *refer* man's success to his talents ; আরোপ করা, নির্দ্দেশ করা। **2.** To hand over or entrust for consideration and decision ; to deliver over, as to another person or authority for consideration, treatment, information, decision, etc. ; as, to *refer* a student to a book ; বিবেচনা, নিষ্পত্তি বা মীমাংসার জন্য ন্যস্ত বা অর্পণ করা ; অন্য কোন ব্যক্তি বা প্রামাণিক গ্রন্থাদির নিকট মীমাংসার জন্য সমর্পণ করা। **3.** To betake oneself to ; to appeal to ; "I do *refer* me to the oracle" ; কোন স্থানে বা কোন ব্যক্তির সন্নিকটে যাওয়া ; প্রার্থনা করা। **4.** To assign to a particular class, genus, order ; as, to *refer* barnacles to the molluscs ; বিশেষ শ্রেণী, বর্গ, গণ প্রভৃতিতে আরোপ বা নির্দ্দেশ করা। ***Verb i.*** **1.** To relate ; as, this passage *refers* to the peculiar customs of the savage tribes ; to apply to ; সম্পর্ক থাকা, সম্বন্ধ থাকা, সংশ্রব থাকা ; কোন কিছুর সম্পর্কে খাটা। **2.** To have recourse to ; to consult ; as, to *refer* to a dictionary ; আশ্রয় নেওয়া ; দেখা।

rĕf-ĕr-ee' (-ē), *n.* & *v. i.* One to whom a thing is referred ; an arbitrator, esp. in football ; যে ব্যক্তির নিকট বিষয় মীমাংসার্থ অর্পণ করা হয় ; মধ্যস্থ (বিশেষতঃ পাদগোলক ক্রীড়ায়)। ***Verb i.*** To act as a referee esp. in football ; মধ্যস্থতা করা (বিশেষতঃ পাদগোলক ক্রীড়ায়)।

rĕf'-ĕr-ence (-ĕns), *n.* & *v. t.* **1.** The act of submitting a matter to some person or authority for consideration or decision ; কোন বিষয় মীমাংসা বা বিবেচনার জন্য অপর কোন ব্যক্তি বা প্রামাণিক ব্যক্তির নিকট অর্পণ। **2.** Relation ; as, in *reference* to your letter ; সম্পর্ক, সম্বন্ধ। **3.** Assigning ; আরোপ, নির্দ্দেশ। **4.** Allusion ; as, he made no *reference* to the case which has been stated ; উল্লেখ। **5.** (*Law*) The act or process of assigning a cause depending in a court, or some particular point in a case for decision, to a person or persons appointed by the court ; কোন আদালতে বিচারাধীন কোন মোকদ্দমা বা তৎসংক্রান্ত কোন বিষয় মীমাংসার জন্য আদালত কর্ত্তৃক নিযুক্ত ব্যক্তি বা ব্যক্তিবর্গের নিকট অর্পণ। **6.** One of whom enquiries may be made in regard to a person's abilities or the like ; as, who are your *references* ? ; যে ব্যক্তির নিকট অপর কোন ব্যক্তির চরিত্র, কার্য্যক্ষমতা, প্রভৃতি সম্বন্ধে সন্ধান লওয়া যাইতে পারে। **7.** A written statement of the qualifications of an employee given by the employer to the employed, at the termination of service ; as, he brought excellent *references* ; চাকুরীর অবসানে নিয়োগকারী নিযুক্ত

ব্যক্তিকে তদীয় যোগ্যতা প্রভৃতি সম্বন্ধে যে পত্র প্রদান করেন, প্রশংসাপত্র, যোগ্যতা-পত্র, নিদর্শনপত্র। 8. A passage in a work to which the reader is referred from another passage ; কোন পুস্তকের যে অংশ দেখিবার জন্য পুস্তকের অপর কোন অংশে নির্দ্দেশ করা হয়। 9. An indication of the author, books, etc. to be looked, at ; যে গ্রন্থ বা গ্রন্থকার প্রভৃতির আশ্রয় লইতে হইবে বা দেখিতে হইবে তাহার উল্লেখ। *Verb t.* To supply with references ; as, to *reference* a book ; কোন পুস্তকের ভিন্ন ভিন্ন অংশে তৎ তৎ অংশের সহিত সম্পৃক্ত প্রামাণিক গ্রন্থ, গ্রন্থকার বা গ্রন্থাংশ সমূহের উল্লেখ করা। **Reference-bible**—যে বাইবেলের বিভিন্ন বিভিন্ন অংশের পার্শ্বে তৎ তৎ অংশের সহিত গ্রন্থের অন্যান্য যে যে অংশের সম্বন্ধ আছে তাহার উল্লেখ থাকে। **Reference library**—যে পুস্তকালয়ে বসিয়া কেবল পুস্তক পাঠ করা যাইতে পারে—কিন্তু বাটীতে নেওয়া যাইতে পারে না। **Reference marks**—যে চিহ্ন (* † ‡ ‖ §) দ্বারা পুস্তকের অপর অংশ—বিশেষতঃ পাদটীকার কোন অংশ দেখার জন্য পাঠককে নির্দ্দেশ করা হয়, নির্দ্দেশ-চিহ্ন। **Book of reference**—অভিধান, বিশ্বকোষ, প্রভৃতি। **In or with reference to**—With respect to ; সম্পর্কে, সম্বন্ধে। **Without reference to**—Without regard to ; বিবেচনায় না আনিয়া।

rĕf-ĕr-ĕn′-dă-rȳ, *n.* 1. One to whose decision anything is referred ; a referee ; যে ব্যক্তির নিকট মীমাংসার জন্য কোন বিষয় অর্পণ করা হয় ; মধ্যস্থ। 2. An ancient officer who delivered the royal answer to petition ; যে প্রাচীন কর্ম্মচারী আবেদনের উপর রাজার আদেশ লিখিতেন।

rĕf-ĕr-ĕn′-dŭm, *n.* The submission of a proposed political question to public vote ; কোন প্রস্তাবিত রাজনৈতিক প্রশ্ন মতামতের জন্য সর্ব্বসাধারণের নিকট উপস্থিত করণ।

rē-fĭll′, *v. t.* To fill again ; পুনরায় পূর্ণ করা, পুনরায় ভরা।

rē-fīne′, *v. t.* & *i.* 1. To purify ; as, to *refine* sugar ; শোধিত করা, পরিষ্কার করা, নির্ম্মল করা। 2. To reduce from the ore ; to free or separate from other metals or from dross, or alloy ; as, to *purify* gold or silver ; খনিজবিমিশ্র ধাতু হইতে বাহির করা ; অপর ধাতু বা ধাতুমল বা মিশ্র ধাতু হইতে পৃথক করা, বিশোধিত করা। 3. To purify from what is gross, vulgar, inelegant, coarse, low and the like ; as, to *refine* the minds of one's countrymen ; মার্জ্জিত করা, পরিমার্জ্জিত করা। 4. To change or remove by refining ; পরিমার্জ্জিত করিয়া দূর করা বা পরিবর্ত্তন করা। *Verb i.* 1. To become pure ; বিশুদ্ধ হওয়া, নির্ম্মল হওয়া, বিশোধিত হওয়া। 2. To improve in accuracy, delicacy or excellence in any kind ; "How the wit brightens ! How the style *refines* !" ; মার্জ্জিত করা, পরিমার্জ্জিত করা, (গ্রন্থাদি) শোধন করা। 3. To affect nicety or subtlety in thought or language ; "By *refining* upon words in defiance of intention" ; অতিশয় সূক্ষ্ম চিন্তার ভাব দেখান, অতি সূক্ষ্ম বা চুলচেরা বিচার করিয়া ভাষা প্রয়োগ করা। **–fined′,** *pp.* Purified ; polished ; বিশোধিত, সংশুদ্ধ, সংস্কৃত, সংস্কারপূত ; মার্জ্জিত, পরিমার্জ্জিত। **–fin′-er,** *n.*

rē-fīne′-mĕnt, *n.* 1. The act of refining or the state of being refined ; শোধন, বিশোধন, সংশোধন, শুদ্ধি, সংশোধিতত্ব, শোধিতত্ব। 2. Elegance of taste, manners, language, etc. ; as, he is a man of *refinement* ; culture ; polish ; purity of taste, mind or the like ; মার্জ্জিত রুচি, শিষ্টাচার, মার্জ্জিত ভাষা, পারিপাট্য ; সভ্যতা ; মার্জ্জিত ভাব ; সুরুচি, নির্ম্মলচিত্ততা। 3. A subtlety ; "*Refinements* unintelligible to the common people" ; সূক্ষ্মতর্ক, সূক্ষ্মবিচার, চুলচেরা বিচার, মুন্সীয়ানা (ভ্রাঃ বিঃ), ন্যায়ের কচকচি।

rē-fīn′-ēr-ȳ, *n.* The place and apparatus for refining metal, sugar and the like ; ধাতু, চিনি, প্রভৃতি পরিষ্কারের কারখানা বা কল, শোধনাগার, শোধনযন্ত্র।

rē-fĭt′, *v. t.* & *i.* To fit or prepare again ; to repair ; as, to *refit* ships after war ; পুনরায় সজ্জিত করা ; মেরামত করা, পুনরায় সংস্কার করা। *Verb i.* (Of ships) To repair damages ; (জাহাজ সম্পর্কে) মেরামত করা।

rē-flĕct′, *v. t.* & *i.* 1. (*Obs.* or *rare*) To turn back ; to cast back ; (অপ্রচলিত বা কচিদ্‌ব্যবহৃত) ফিরান ; প্রতিক্ষেপ করা। 2. To throw off as light or heat, after striking or falling on the surface ; পরাবর্ত্তিত করা, মূর্চ্ছিত করা। 3. To mirror ; "Nature is the glass which *reflects* God" ; প্রতিবিম্বিত করা, প্রতিফলিত করা। 4. To cast or bring ; as, this *reflects* great credit on him ; ফেলা, আনা। *Verb i.* 1. To contemplate ; "It is a melancholy subject to *reflect* on" ; চিন্তা করা, ভাবা, অনুধ্যান করা, বিবেচনা করা। 2. (*Rare*) To be mirrored ; (কচিদ্‌ব্যবহৃত) প্রতিবিম্বিত হওয়া। 3. To cast censure or blame ; to make disparaging remarks upon ; "The clergy were strictly charged not to *reflect* on the Roman Catholic religion" ; দোষ দেওয়া, তিরস্কার করা, দোষারোপ করা ; অবজ্ঞাসূচক মন্তব্য করা। 4. To return rays or beams ; কিরণ বিঘট্টিত করা, কিরণ মূর্চ্ছিত করা, রশ্মি পরাবর্ত্তিত করা। **–ing,** *adj.* **–ingly,** *adv.* **Reflecting circle**—উচ্চতা এবং কৌণিকদূরত্ব মাপনের জন্য যন্ত্রবিশেষ। **Reflecting galvanometer**—একপ্রকার বিদ্যুচ্ছক্তিমাপক—যাহাতে একটী মুকুর সম্বদ্ধ থাকে এবং

যদ্দারা সূচীসমূহের বিক্ষেপ পাঠ করা যাইতে পারে, পরাবর্তক বিদ্যুচ্ছক্তিমান। **Reflecting goniometer**—প্রতিফলমান, কোণমাপক, কোণ মাপার জন্য যন্ত্রবিশেষ। **Reflecting telescope**—See TELESCOPE.

rĕ-flĕc′-tion, —flex′-ion (-flĕk-shŭn), *ns.* **1.** The act of reflecting or throwing back as of ray of light, heat, etc.; প্রতিফলন, প্রতিক্ষেপ, পরাবর্তন, রশ্মিপরাবর্তন কিরণপরাবর্তন (জ্যোতিঃ জ্যোঃ), মূর্চ্ছন (সাঃ পঃ), কিরণমূর্চ্ছন (ঐ), রশ্মিবিঘট্টন (বাৎস্যঃ), পরাবৃত্তি, অনুপ্রবেশ (রঃ)। **2.** Reflected light or heat; পরাবর্তিত তাপ বা আলোক, প্রতিভা (সাঃ পঃ—of light), প্রতিজ্যোতিঃ। **3.** An image given back from a reflected surface; প্রতিবিম্ব, প্রতিচ্ছবি, প্রতিচ্ছায়া, আভাস, ছায়া (প্রঃ চিঃ), প্রতিকৃতি (সাঃ পঃ), প্রতিফল (ঐ)। **4.** The turning of the mind to that which has already occupied it; meditation; contemplation; পর্য্যালোচন, অনুচিন্তন, পরিচিন্তন, সংচিন্তন; ভাবনা; ধ্যান, চিন্তা নিদিধ্যাসন। **5.** The action of the mind by which it takes cognizance of its own operation; যে ক্রিয়াদ্বারা মন স্বীয় ক্রিয়া বা ব্যাপার সম্বন্ধে পরিজ্ঞাত হয়, মনন (শ্রীঃ)। **6.** (Hegelianism) The intensification of the individuality of any state subsequent to its being illustrated or proved by something other than itself which is shown to depend on it or to presuppose it (*Webster*); কোন অবস্থার উপর সমাশ্রিত বলিয়া প্রদর্শিত বা সেই অবস্থার পূর্ব্বানুমানকারী অবস্থান্তর দ্বারা উদাহৃত ও প্রমাণিত হওয়ার পর সেই অবস্থার স্বাতন্ত্র্য গাঢ়ীভবন। **7.** Censure; imputation of fault; a reflecting remark; তিরস্কার, গ্লানি; দোষারোপ; গ্লানিসূচক মন্তব্য, কটাক্ষ। **8.** (*Anat.*) The folding of a membrane upon itself; কোন ঝিল্লীর পরাবর্তন। **9.** (*Phys.*) Same as REFLEX ACTION. **10.** A remark made after reflection; কোন বিষয়ে সুচিন্তিত মন্তব্য। **—al, —less,** *adjs.* **Angle of reflection**—পরাবর্তিত কিরণ এবং পরাবর্তন ধরাতলের লম্বের সংযোগে উৎপন্ন কোণ, মূর্চ্ছন কোণ। **Total reflection**—পূর্ণপরাবর্তন, কোন আলোকরশ্মি তিরোবর্তক আধান পদার্থ (refracting medium) অতিক্রম করার কালে ঐ আধানপদার্থের উপরিভাগে সম্পূর্ণরূপে পরাবর্তিত হওয়ায় উহা তথা হইতে নির্গত না হইলে এরূপ অবস্থার নাম রশ্মির পূর্ণপরাবর্তন।

rĕ-flĕc′-tive (-tĭv), *adj.* **1.** Throwing back or reflecting, as rays of light, heat, etc.; পরাবর্তক। **2.** (Of light, etc.) Reflected (*rare*); (আলোক, প্রভৃতি সম্পর্কে) পরাবর্তিত (কচিদ্‌ব্যবহৃত)। **3.** Deliberative; thoughtful; taking cognizance of the operations of mind; concerned with ideas; চিন্তাশীল; ভাবনাশীল, ভাবনাত্মক; ভাবুক; মননশীল। **4.** (*Gram.*) Same as REFLEXIVE. **—ly,** *adv.* **—ness,** *n.*

rĕ-flĕc-tŏm′-ĕ-têr, *n.* An instrument for measuring the extent to which a substance reflects light; পরাবর্তমাপক।

rĕ-flĕc′-tor (-têr), *n.* **1.** A polished, surface for reflecting light, heat, or sound in any required direction; তাপ, ধ্বনি, আলোক, প্রভৃতি ঈপ্সিতদিকে পরাবর্তনের জন্য মসৃণতল বস্তু, পরাবর্তক (হিঃ কোঃ)। **2.** Same as A REFLECTING TELESCOPE, MICROSCOPE, etc. **3.** An apparatus for reflecting images; প্রতিবিম্বপরাবর্তক যন্ত্র। **4.** That which gives or affords conscious or unconscious representation (of prejudices, habits, etc.); যাহা জ্ঞাতসারে বা অজ্ঞাতসারে কোনরূপ সংস্কার, অভ্যাস, প্রভৃতির প্রতিচ্ছায়া প্রদর্শন করে।

reflet, (*F.*), *n.* Lustre (esp. on pottery); দীপ্তি, দ্যুতি, চাকচিক্য।

rē′-flĕx, *adj.* **1.** Reflected; পরাবর্তিত, প্রতিবিম্বিত। **2.** (*Rare*) Recurved; (কচিদ্ ব্যবহৃত) পুনর্বক্রীভূত। **3.** Introspective; as, *reflex* thought; reactive; অন্তর্মুখী; প্রতিক্রিয়াত্মক। **4.** (*Physiol.*) Of the nature of, or marked by, reflex action; (শারীরবিজ্ঞান) অনিচ্ছাপ্রসূত ক্রিয়াসম্বন্ধীয়। **5.** (*Painting*) Illuminated by light reflected from another part of the same picture; একই চিত্রের অপর অংশ হইতে পরাবর্তিত আলোক দ্বারা দীপ্তিমান। **Reflex action**—যে ক্রিয়া কোনরূপ ইচ্ছার অপেক্ষা রাখেনা কেবল স্নায়ুমূলের উত্তেজনা বশতঃ সম্পাদিত হইয়া থাকে, প্রতিক্ষিপ্তক্রিয়া (হঃ চঃ)।

rĕ-flĕx′, *n.* **1.** A reflection; reflected light or colour; an image produced by reflection; পরাবর্তন; পরাবর্তনজনিত আলোক বা বর্ণ; প্রতিবিম্ব, প্রতিচ্ছবি, প্রতিচ্ছায়া। **2.** Light reflected from an enlightened surface to one in shade; (*painting*) the illumination of one body or a part of it by light reflected from another body represented in the same piece; দীপ্ত স্থান হইতে ছায়াবৃত স্থানে পরাবর্তিত আলোক; (চিত্রণ) কোন চিত্র বা চিত্রের অংশবিশেষ একই পটে অঙ্কিত অপর চিত্র বা চিত্রাংশ হইতে পরাবর্তিত আলোক দ্বারা প্রকাশন। **3.** (*Physiol.*) A REFLEX ACTION (see above). **4.** Something which reproduces certain essential features of another thing; যে বস্তু দ্বারা কোন বস্তুর কতিপয় মৌলিক বিশেষত্ব পুনরুৎপাদিত হয়।

rĕ-flexed′ (-flĕkst), *adj.* (*Bot.*) Curved back; as, a *reflexed* petal; (উদ্ভিদ্ বিদ্যা) পুনর্বক্রীভূত।

rĕ-flĕx′-ĭ-ble (-bl), *adj.* Capable of being reflected; পরাবর্তনীয়।

rĕ-flex′-ion (-flĕc-shŭn), *n.* Same as REFLECTION (which see).

rĕ-flĕx'-ive (-ĭv), *adj.* **1.** Bending or turning backward; পশ্চাদানত, পশ্চাদ্‌মুখ। **2.** (*Gram.*) Implying agent's action upon himself; (ব্যাকরণ) স্বয়মর্থক। **3.** (*Gram., of verbs*) Having for its direct object a pronoun which stands for the agent or subject; (ব্যাকরণ) কর্তৃপদ ও কর্ম্মপদ দ্বারা একই ব্যক্তি-সূচক। **Reflexive pronoun**—স্বয়মর্থক সর্ব্বনাম, যথা myself, himself, etc.। **Reflexive verb**—যে ক্রিয়ার মুখ্য কর্ম্ম স্বরূপ এরূপ একটী সর্ব্বনাম থাকে—যাহা ঐ ক্রিয়ার কর্তার স্থানবর্ত্তী হইয়া থাকে।

rē-float' (-flōt), *v. t.* To float again; পুনরায় ভাসান।

rĕf'-lū-ĕnt, *adj.* Flowing back; as, *refluent* tide; ebbing; পরাবর্ত্তী, পশ্চাৎপ্রবাহী; বেলাপরাঙ্মুখ, বেলাপবর্ত্তী। **--ence,** *n.*

rē'-flŭx, *n.* A flowing back; পশ্চাদ্‌বর্ত্তন, পশ্চাৎপ্রবহণ।

rē-fŏŏt', *v. t.* To put a new foot in; as, to *refoot* a boot; নূতন পা লাগান।

rē-fŏr'-ĕst, *v. t. & i.* To cover again with forest; পুনরায় বনদ্বারা আচ্ছাদিত করা। **-a'-tion,** *n.*

rē-fŏrm', *v. t. & i.* To introduce improvement in; to bring from a bad to a good state; as to *reform* a profligate man; সংস্কার করা, উৎকর্ষ সম্পাদন করা; সংশোধন করা; ***Verb i.*** To abandon that which is evil and return to good; শোধরান। **--a-ble,** *adj.* **--formed',** *p. p.* **Reformed church**—(সাধারণ অর্থে) রোমান ক্যাথলিক ধর্ম্মসংঘ হইতে বিচ্ছিন্ন খৃষ্টোপাসকমণ্ডলী; (বিশেষ অর্থে) যে সকল খৃষ্টীয় সম্প্রদায় লুথার প্রবর্ত্তিত প্রোটেষ্টান্ট সম্প্রদায়ের মত এবং আচার অনুষ্ঠানের অনুসরণ করেন না।

rē-fŏrm', *n.* The amendment or reformation of that which is corrupt, vicious, defective or the like, esp. of a corrupt or oppressive political institution; as administrative *refrom*; (রাজনৈতিক) সংস্কারসংসাধন। **Reform Act** or **Bill**—পার্লেমেণ্টে সভ্যপ্রেরণ রীতির সংস্কারসাধনের জন্য ১৮৩২ খৃষ্টাব্দে বিধিবদ্ধ আইন। **Reform-school**—Same as REFORMATORY (used in America.)

rē-fŏrm', *v. t. & i.* To form or arrange again; পুনরায় সজ্জিত করা বা হওয়া, পুনরায় বিন্যাস করা। **--for-ma'-tion,** *n.*

rĕf-ŏr-mā'-tion, *n.* The act of reforming; correction or removal of evil or error; সংস্কার, সংস্কারসাধন; সংশোধন, দোষসংশোধন, ভ্রমসংশোধন। **The Reformation**—ষোড়শ শতাব্দীতে জর্ম্মাণ দেশে মার্টিন লুথর কর্তৃক আরব্ধ ধর্ম্মবিপ্লব—যাহার ফলে প্রতীচ্য ধর্ম্মসংঘ (Western Church) রোমানক্যাথলিক ও প্রোটেষ্ট্যাণ্ট এই দুই শাখায় বিভক্ত হয়।

rē-fŏrm'-ā-tive (-tĭv), *adj.* Same as REFORMATORY, *adj.*

rē-fŏrm'-ā-tō-rȳ, *adj.* & *n.* Tending to produce reformation; সংশোধনী, সংস্কারাত্মক, সংস্কারজনক। ***Noun.*** An institution for the reception and reclaiming of juvenile offenders; চরিত্রসংশোধনাগার, সংশোধনী কারাগার।

rē-fŏrm'-ĕr, *n.* **1.** One who effects reformation or amendment; সংস্কারক, সংশোধক, সংস্কর্ত্তা। **2.** One of those who took a prominent part in the reformation of religion in the sixteenth century; ষোড়শ শতাব্দীর ধর্ম্মসংস্কারের অন্যতম নেতা। **3.** One who promotes or favours political reforms; রাজনৈতিক সংস্কারক, রাজনৈতিক সংস্কারের পক্ষপাতী ব্যক্তি।

rē-frăct', *v. t.* **1.** To deflect (light) at certain angle passing from one medium to another of different density; বিভিন্ন গাঢ়ত্ববিশিষ্ট এক আধান পদার্থ হইতে অপর আধান পদার্থের ভিতর দিয়া গমন কালে কোন নির্দ্দিষ্ট কোণ উৎপাদনপূর্ব্বক (কিরণ) বিক্ষেপ করা, (কিরণ) বিবর্ত্তন করা। **2.** (*Chem.*) To analyse (nitre) with a view to finding out percentage of impurities; (রসায়নশাস্ত্র) শতকরা কতভাগ ময়লা আছে তাহা নির্ণয়ের জন্য (সোরা) বিশ্লেষণ করা। **--frac'-tion,** *n.* **1.** The act of refracting; কিরণ-বিবর্ত্তন (জ্যোতিঃ জ্যোঃ), তির্য্যগ্‌গমন (ব্রজঃ হিন্দু), বক্রীভবন (ঐ), তিরোবর্ত্তন, তির্য্যগ্‌বর্ত্তন (সাঃ পঃ), বিস্ফারণ (ঐ)। **2.** (*Astron.*) The deflection of the rays of light in their passage through the earth's atmosphere in consequence of which the heavenly bodies appear higher than they really are; ভূবায়ুর ভিতর দিয়া গমনকালে জ্যোতিষ্ক সমূহ হইতে আগত কিরণের বিবর্ত্তন—যাহার ফলে উহারা বাস্তবপক্ষে যথায় আছে তদপেক্ষা উচ্চে রহিয়াছে বলিয়া প্রতিভাত হয়, বায়ুবলন (ভারতবর্ষ)। **3.** (*Chem.*) The process of ascertaining the percentage of impurities in a sample of nitre; the sum of the impurities thus ascertained; (রসায়নশাস্ত্র) সোরার মধ্যে শতকরা কি পরিমাণ অবিশুদ্ধ পদার্থ আছে—তাহা নির্ণয়ের প্রণালী; উক্ত প্রকারে নির্ণীত অবিশুদ্ধ পদার্থের পরিমাণ। **--frac-tive,** *adj.* **--frac'-tive-ness,** *n.* **Astronomical** or **atmospheric refraction**—See REFRACTION, 2.

rē-frăc-tŏm'-ē-ter, *n.* An instrument for measuring the refraction of light; তিরোবর্ত্তমাপক, তিরোবর্ত্তমান।

rē-frăc'-tor (-têr), *n.* Same as REFRACTING TELESCOPE (under TELESCOPE.)

rē-frăc'-tŏ-rȳ, *adj.* **1.** Obstinate; unmanageable; as, a *refractory* child; rebellious; একগুঁয়ে, মগরা; দুর্দ্দান্ত, অদম্য, অবশীভূত; বিদ্রোহী। **2.** Resisting ordinary treatment; difficult of fusion, reduction or the like; "The most *refractory* substances such as carbon, may be made to appear as gases ; দুঃসাধ্য ; দুর্দ্রবণীয়। 3. (*Med.*) Not yielding to treatment ; as, a *refractory* sore ; (ভৈষজ্যশাস্ত্র) কঠিন। 4. (*Med.*) Able to resist disease ; not susceptible to disease ; (ভৈষজ্যশাস্ত্র) রোগরোধক ; আরোগ্যপ্রবণ। **–ri-ly,** *adv.* **–ri-ness,** *n.*

rĕ-frăc'-tŏ-rŷ, *n.* 1. An obstinate person ; মগরা লোক, অদম্য ব্যক্তি, একগুঁয়ে লোক। 2. (*Pottery*) A piece of ware covered with vapourable flux and placed in a kiln to communicate a glaze to other articles ; (মৃৎ-শিল্প) বাষ্পীভবন-যোগ্য দ্রবতাসাধক চূর্ণ দ্বারা আচ্ছাদিত ভাণ্ডখণ্ড—যদ্দ্বারা অপর ভাণ্ড সমূহের চাকচিক্য সম্পাদিত হয়।

rē-frain' (-frān), *n.* The burden of a song ; গানের ধুঁয়া, ধ্রুপদ।

re-frain' (-frān), *v. t.* & *i.* To hold back ; to curb ; to restrain ; নিবৃত্ত করা, ক্ষান্ত করা, বিরত করা ; নিরোধ করা ; সংযত করা। ***Verb i.*** To forbear ; বিরত হওয়া, নিবৃত্ত হওয়া, ক্ষান্ত হওয়া, নিরস্ত হওয়া।

rē-frăn'-gĭ-ble (-bl), *adj.* Capable of being refracted ; (কিরণ সম্বন্ধে) বিবর্তনীয়, তির্য্যগ্‌বর্তনীয়। **–gib'-il-i-ty,** *n.*

rē-frĕsh', *v. t.* & *i.* 1. To make fresh by wetting or cooling ; ঠাণ্ডা বা আর্দ্র করিয়া সরস বা নবীন করা। 2. To make fresh or vigorous again ; to give new strength to ; to relieve from fatigue or exhaustion ; to reanimate ; পুনরায় সতেজ করা, পুনঃ সবল করা ; নববল প্রদান করা ; শ্রান্তি বারণ করা, শ্রমাপনোদন করা, গতক্লম করা ; পুনরুজ্জীবিত করা, সঞ্জীবিত করা। 3. To freshen up memory ; স্মৃতিশক্তি পুনরায় সতেজ করা। 4. To furnish with refreshment ; জলযোগ করান। 5. To make (a surface) fresh esp. by cutting ; as, to *refresh* the edges of a wound by blister ; (উপরিভাগ) কাটিয়া বা চাঁচিয়া তাজা রাখা। 6. To lay in stock of fresh provisions ; নূতন খাদ্যদ্রব্য সম্ভার ভাণ্ডারজাত করা। ***Verb i.*** 1. To give or supply refreshment ; জলযোগ করান, জলযোগ যোগান। 2. To take refreshment ; জলযোগ করা। **–ing,** *adj.* **–ing-ly,** *adv.*

rē-frĕsh'-ĕr, *n.* 1. One that refreshes ; ক্লান্তিবারক, শ্রমাপহারক, শ্রান্তিবারক, আরামপ্রদায়ক, আরামদায়ক। 2. A refreshment ; (*colloq.*) drink ; জলযোগ ; (চলিত ভাষায়) পানীয়। 3. (*Law*) An additional fee paid to a counsel when the case continues for sometime ; মোকদ্দমা দীর্ঘকাল চলিলে কৌঁসুলিকে যে অতিরিক্ত পারিশ্রমিক (fees) দেওয়া হয়।

rē-frĕsh'-mĕnt, *n.* 1. The act of refreshing ; শ্রমাপনোদন, ক্লান্ত্যপহার, ক্লান্তিবারণ, প্রহ্লাদন, সঞ্জীবন। 2. That which refreshes ; (usu. *pl.*) food and drink, that refreshes ; as, he took some *refreshments* ; ক্লান্তিবারক বস্তু ; জলযোগ, পানীয়, জলপান। **Refreshment room**—রেলওয়ে ষ্টেশনের জলযোগাগার। **Refreshment car**—বাষ্পীয় শকট শ্রেণীর যে শকটে জলযোগের বন্দোবস্ত থাকে।

rē-frĭg'-ĕr-ănt, *adj.* & *n.* Cooling ; allaying heat ; শৈত্যজনক, শৈত্যকারক ; তাপপ্রশামক, শীতলকর (সাঃ পঃ)। ***Noun.*** 1. A cooling medicine ; শৈত্যজনক ঔষধ, তাপনিবারক ঔষধ। 2. A cooling drink ; শৈত্যজনক পানীয়, তাপনিবারক পানীয়। 3. Any substance which reduces temperature below freezing point ; as, liquid air is a *refrigerant* ; যে বস্তুদ্বারা তাপ তুষারাঙ্কে নীত হয়। 4. Anything which cools or allays ; as, this may serve as a *refrigerant* for their ardour ; তাপপ্রশামক দ্রব্য, শৈত্যজনক বস্তু।

rē-frĭg'-ĕr-āte, *v. t.* 1. To make cool ; ঠাণ্ডা করা, শীতল করা, তাপ নিবারণ করা। 2. To freeze or chill food for preservation ; টাটকা রাখার জন্য খাদ্যদ্রব্য শীতে জমান বা ঠাণ্ডা করা। **–a'-tion,** *n.* **–a-tive,** *adj.* **–a-tor,** *n.* 1. That which makes cool ; শৈত্যজনক বস্তু। 2. A vessel, room or apparatus, for keeping food or other articles cold ; খাদ্য বা অন্য পদার্থ শীতল রাখার জন্য ভাণ্ড, কক্ষ বা যন্ত্র। **Refrigeration of the globe**—এই পৃথিবী পূর্ব্বে তাপপ্রদীপ্ত ছিল এবং বহু লক্ষ বৎসর ব্যাপিয়া ক্রমশঃ শীতল হইয়া বর্তমান অবস্থা প্রাপ্ত হইয়াছে এবং পৃথিবীর এই তাপহ্রাসক্রিয়া এখনও চলিতেছে—এই মত বা অনুমান।

rē-frĭg'-ĕr-ā-tŏ-rŷ, *n.* & *adj.* 1. That which refrigerates ; শৈত্যজনক বস্তু। 2. The chamber or tank in which ice is formed in an ice-machine ; বরফের কলে যে কক্ষ বা কুণ্ডে বরফ হয়। 3. A vessel filled with cold water attached to a still for condensing vapour ; সুরাবীর্য্যের বাষ্প ঘনীকরণের জন্য মদের ভাঁটিতে সম্বদ্ধ শীতলজলপূর্ণ ভাণ্ড। 4. Same as REFRIGERATOR 2. ***Adj.*** Refrigerating ; শৈত্যজনক, তাপনিবারক।

rĕf'-ūge, *n., v. t.* & *i.* 1. Shelter or protection from danger or distress ; as, to seek *refuge* in flight ; শরণ, আশ্রয়, গতি, সমাশ্রয়, অবলম্বন। 2. That which shelters or protects from danger, calamity, etc. ; a place of shelter or security ; an asylum ; আশ্রয়দাতা, আশ্রয়স্থল ; আশ্রয় স্থান ; আশ্রয় কুটীর। 3. Excuse ; plea ; device ; "Patriotism is the last *refuge* of a scoundrel" ; ছল, অছিলা; ফন্দী ; কৌশল। 4. A raised piece in the middle of a busy road for securing the safety of foot-passengers ; পাদচারিগণের নির্ব্বিঘ্নতার জন্য বহু লোকজন, গাড়ীঘোড়া চলাচল

করে—এইরূপ রাস্তার মধ্যস্থলে রচিত উচ্চ স্থান। ***Verb t.*** To shelter or protect ; আশ্রয় দান করা, রক্ষা করা। ***Verb i.*** (*Rare*) To take refuge ; (কচিদ্‌ব্যবহৃত) আশ্রয় গ্রহণ করা। **City of refuge**—বাইবেলের প্রাচীন নিয়ম গ্রন্থে উক্ত যে ছয় নগরীতে নরহত্যাকারিগণ আশ্রয় গ্রহণ করিতে পারিত। **House of refuge**—নিঃস্ব এবং গৃহহীন ব্যক্তিগণের আশ্রয়ের জন্য প্রতিষ্ঠানবিশেষ, আশ্রয়নিকেতন। **To take refuge**—To take shelter ; আশ্রয় গ্রহণ করা।

rĕf-ū-gee' (-jē), *n.* 1. One who flies to a shelter or place of safety ; শরণাগত ব্যক্তি, আশ্রিত জন। 2. One that flies to a far country from religious or political persecution ; ধর্ম্মসংক্রান্ত বা রাজনীতিক নির্যাতন হইতে রক্ষা পাওয়ার জন্য বিদেশে পলায়িত ব্যক্তি।

rē-fŭl'-gĕnt, *adj.* Emitting a bright light ; shining brightly ; সমুজ্জ্বল ; ভাস্বর, জ্যোতির্ম্ময়, দীপ্তিমান। **-gence,** *n.* Splendour or brilliance ; দীপ্তি, দ্যুতি, প্রভা, ঔজ্জ্বল্য, উজ্জ্বলতা।

rē-fŭnd', *v. t., i.* & *n.* 1. To pay back ; (টাকা, পয়সা) ফিরাইয়া দেওয়া, প্রত্যর্পণ করা, পরিশোধ করা। 2. To resupply with funds ; পুনরায় খরচের টাকা যোগান। ***Verb i.*** To make repayment ; পুনরায় টাকা প্রভৃতি প্রদান করা। ***Noun.*** The act of refunding or that which is refunded ; (টাকা) প্রত্যর্পণ, প্রত্যর্পিত অর্থ। **-er,** *n.*

rē-fur'-bish (-fêr-), *v. t.* To furbish a second time ; দ্বিতীয়বার ঘষিয়া মাজিয়া চকচকে করা।

rē-fur'-nish (-fêr-), *v. t.* To furnish again ; পুনরায় সজ্জিত করা।

rē-fūs'-ăl, *n.* 1. The act of refusing ; a denial or rejection of something ; অস্বীকার, অস্বীকৃতি ; প্রত্যাখান, অপরিগ্রহ। 2. The choice of taking or refusing ; as, to give one the *refusal* of a land ; pre-emption ; অপরের পূর্ব্বে গ্রহণ বা প্রত্যাখ্যানের সুবিধা বা অধিকার ; পূর্ব্বক্রয়াধিকার। 3. The resistance to further driving offered by a pile ; খোঁটা আর বসাইতে গেলে যে বাধা পাওয়া যায়। **He will take no refusal**—He is persistent ; সে (কোন কিছু পাইবার জন্য) জেদ করিয়া বসিয়া আছে, সে না কথা শুনিবে না। **To have the refusal of a thing**—অপর সকলের আগে কোন বস্তু গ্রহণ, অপরিগ্রহ বা ক্রয়ের সুবিধা বা অধিকার থাকা।

rē-fūse', *v. t.* & *i.* 1. To decline to accept ; গ্রহণ করিতে অস্বীকার করা, প্রত্যাখ্যান করা। 2. To deny the request of ; কাহারো অনুরোধ রক্ষা করিতে অস্বীকার করা, অস্বীকার করা। 3. (Of a horse) To decline to jump or leap over a fence etc. ; (অশ্ব সম্পর্কে) বৃতি প্রভৃতি উল্লঙ্ঘন করিতে না চাওয়া। 4. (*Card game*) Not to follow suit ; (তাস খেলায়) পাশ দেওয়া। ***Verb i.*** 1. To decline to accept ; গ্রহণ করিতে অস্বীকার করা, প্রত্যাখ্যান করা। 2. (Of a pile) To resist further driving ; (খোঁটা সম্পর্কে) আর বসিতে না চাওয়া।

rĕf'-ūse, *adj.* & *n.* Refused ; rejected ; hence, worthless ; প্রত্যাখ্যাত ; পরিত্যক্ত ; অসার, হেয়, অকিঞ্চিৎকর। ***Noun.*** Worthless part ; অসার অংশ, আবর্জ্জনা, জঞ্জাল, উচ্ছিষ্ট, উঁচা।

rē-fūse', *v. t.* To fuse again ; পুনরায় দ্রবীভূত করা, পুনরায় গালান।

rē-fūs'-ēr, *n.* 1. One who refuses ; প্রত্যাখ্যানকারী, অস্বীকারকারী। 2. A recusant ; ইংলণ্ডের রাজবিধিদ্বারা প্রতিষ্ঠিত ধর্ম্মসংঘের আচার অনুষ্ঠান পালনে অসম্মত ব্যক্তি। 3. A horse that refuses to leap over a fence etc. ; বৃতি প্রভৃতি উল্লঘনে পরাঙ্মুখ অশ্ব।

rē-fūte', *v. t.* To disprove and overthrow by argument ; to prove to be false or erroneous ; খণ্ডন করা, নিরাকরণ করা, নিরাস করা ; অলীক বা ভ্রান্ত বলিয়া প্রমাণ করা। **-fut'-a-ble,** *adj.* **-fut'-al,** *n.*

rĕf-ū-tā'-tion, *n.* The act of refuting ; খণ্ডন, নিরাকরণ, প্রত্যাখ্যান, নিরসন, দূষণ।

rē-gain' (-gān), *v. t.* 1. To gain anew ; পুনরায় প্রাপ্ত হওয়া। 2. To arrive at again ; as, they *regained* the shore ; পুনরায় পৌঁছা।

rē'-găl, *adj.* Pertaining to a king ; fit for a king ; রাজকীয় ; রাজোচিত। **-ly,** *adv.*

rē-gāle', *n.* 1. A sumptuous repast or banquet ; ভোজ। 2. A dainty ; রসনাতৃপ্তিকর খাদ্য। 3. Refreshment ; বিনোদন।

rē-gāle', *v. t.* & *i.* To entertain sumptuously ; to gratify ; to refresh ; as, to *regale* one's eyes or taste ; ভোজ দেওয়া ; আপ্যায়িত করা ; রঞ্জন করা, বিনোদন করা। ***Verb i.*** To feast ; ভোজ খাওয়া। **-ment,** *n.*

rē-gā'-li-ā, *n.* 1. (*Rare*) Royal prerogatives ; (কচিদ্‌ ব্যবহৃত) রাজার বিশেষ অধিকারসমূহ। [সাধারণতঃ রাজার এই ছয়টী বিষয়ের উপর বিশেষ অধিকার আছে বলিয়া কথিত হয়—(১) দণ্ডনীতিপয়োগ (২) জীবন মরণ (৩) যুদ্ধ এবং শান্তি (৪) অস্বামিক ধন (৫) কর নির্দ্ধারণ (৬) মুদ্রা প্রস্তুত]। 2. Insignia of royalty ; রাজচিহ্ন, অভিষেককালে ব্যবহৃত দণ্ড, মুকুট, প্রভৃতি রাজচিহ্ন, রাজোপকরণ, রাজাভরণ (বঃ উঃ), রাজলিঙ্গ। **Regalia of the Church**—ইংলণ্ডের রাজবিধিদ্বারা প্রতিষ্ঠিত ধর্ম্মসংঘের রাজপ্রদত্ত বিশেষ অধিকারসমূহ।

rē-gā'-li-ā, *n.* A large kind of cigar ; বড় আকারের চুরট।

rē'-găl-ism, *n.* The doctrine or principle of royal supremacy in ecclesiastical matters ; যাজকীয় ব্যাপারে রাজার প্রাধান্যসম্বন্ধীয় নীতি বা মত।

rē-găl′-ĭ-tў, *n.* **1.** Royalty ; রাজত্ব, নরেন্দ্রত্ব, নৃপত্ব। **2.** An ensign or badge of royalty ; রাজচিহ্ন। **3.** Royal privilege ; রাজার বিশেষ অধিকার। **4.** A country or territory subjected to royal jurisdiction ; রাজ্য।

rē-gârd′, *v. t.* & *i.* **1.** To gaze upon ; "Thou *regardest* them all with an impartial eye" ; দেখা। **2.** To observe attentively ; to take notice of ; মনোযোগপূর্ব্বক দেখা ; অবধান করা, গ্রাহ্য করা। **3.** To honour ; to reverence ; সম্মান করা, শ্রদ্ধা করা, মান্য করা ; ভক্তি করা। **4.** To consider ; as, I *regard* him as a friend ; মনে করা, বিবেচনা করা, ভাবা, গণ্য করা। **5.** To have a relation to ; সম্পর্ক থাকা। ***Verb i.*** **1.** (*Rare*) To look ; দেখা। **2.** To pay attention to ; মনোযোগ দেওয়া, লক্ষ্য করা, অবধান করা। **As regards**—With respect to ; সম্পর্কে। **It does not regard me in the least**—It does not concern me in the least ; এই বিষয়ের সহিত আমার অণুমাত্রও সম্পর্ক নাই।

rē-gârd′, *n.* **1.** A look ; দৃষ্টি, চাহনি। **2.** Heed ; care or concern ; "With some *regard* to what is just or right" ; মনোযোগ, অবধান ; যত্ন, তত্ত্বাবধান। **3.** Respect ; reverence ; as, I have great *regard* for him ; esteem ; শ্রদ্ধা ; ভক্তি ; সমাদর। **4.** Relation (*rare*) ; সম্পর্ক, সংশ্রব, সম্বন্ধ (কচিদ্ ব্যবহৃত)। **5.** Matter ; "*Regards* that stand aloof from the main point" ; condition ; motive ; বিষয় ; অবস্থা ; উদ্দেশ্য। **6.** (*Pl.*) Respects ; compliments ; as, tender my best *regards* to your mother ; শ্রদ্ধা ; নমস্কার, অভিনন্দন। **–ful**, *adj.* **1.** Heedful ; মনোযোগী, অবধানপর, অবহিত। **2.** Respectful ; ভক্তিপূর্ণ, শ্রদ্ধাসম্পন্ন। **–ful′-ly**, *adv.* **–less**, *adj.* **1.** Heedless ; অমনোযোগী, দৃক্‌পাতশূন্য। **2.** Slighted ; not meriting regard ; অনাদৃত ; অশ্রদ্ধেয়। **–less-ly**, *adv.* **As regards**—About ; বিষয়ে, সম্পর্কে। **In one's regard**—With respect to one ; কাহারো সম্পর্কে। **In regard of** or **to**—With respect or reference to ; সম্বন্ধে, সম্পর্কে। **Out of regard for**—খাতিরে। **Without regard to**—Without reference to ; সম্পর্ক না রাখিয়া। **With regard to**—Touching about ; সম্পর্কে।

rē-gârd′-ănt, *adj.* (*Herald.*) Looking backward ; (কুলবিদ্যা) পশ্চাদবেক্ষী।

rē-găt′-tă, *n.* A rowing or sailing race ; বাইচ, নৌকাদৌড়।

rē-gē′-late, *v.i.* (*Phys.*) To freeze together again ; (পদার্থ বিজ্ঞান) পুনরায় একত্র জমাট বাঁধা। **–a′-tion**, *n.*

rē′-gĕn-cў, *n.* **1.** (*Rare*) Rule ; (কাচিদ্‌ব্যবহৃত) শাসন। **2.** The office or jurisdiction of a regent ; প্রতিনিধিনৃপতিত্ব, প্রতিনিধিনৃপতির এলাকা। **3.** The time during which a government is carried on by a regent ; প্রতিনিধিনৃপতির শাসনকাল। **4.** A body of men appointed to rule the kingdom during the absence, minority, illness, insanity of a king ; রাজার অনুপস্থিতি, নাবালকত্ব, অসুস্থতা বা উন্মাদাবস্থারকালে নিযুক্ত প্রতিনিধিবর্গ।

rē-gĕn′-êr-āte, *v. t.* & *i.* **1.** To reproduce ; পুনরুৎপাদন করা। **2.** (*Theol.*) To cause to be spiritually born again ; (খৃষ্টীয়-ধর্ম্মশাস্ত্র) নবজীবন প্রদান করা। ***Verb i.*** **1.** To form again ; পুনর্গঠন করা। **2.** To reform one's self ; আত্মসংশোধন করা।

rē-gĕn′-êr-āte, *adj.* **1.** Reproduced ; পুনরুৎপাদিত, পুনর্জাত। **2.** (*Theol.*) Born anew ; (খৃষ্টীয়ধর্ম্মশাস্ত্র) নবজীবনপ্রাপ্ত (cf. our দ্বিজত্ব প্রাপ্ত)। **–a′-tion**, *n.* **1.** The act of regenerating ; পুনর্জনন, পুনরুৎপাদন, পুনর্জীবন (কৃষ্ণ), পুনরুদ্ভব, পুনরুৎপত্তি। **2.** (*Theol.*) The fact of being born again in a spiritual sense ; (খৃষ্টীয়ধর্ম্মশাস্ত্র) নবজন্মপ্রাপ্তি (cf. our দ্বিজত্ব প্রাপ্তি)। **3.** (*Biol.*) Reproduction of a part which has been destroyed ; (জীববিজ্ঞান) নষ্টদেহাংশের পুনরুৎপাদন।

rē-gĕn′-êr-ā-tor (-têr), *n.* **1.** One who regenerates ; পুনরুৎপাদক, নবজীবনপ্রদায়ক। **2.** A fuel-saving device attached to a furnace ; চুল্লীতে সংবদ্ধ জ্বালানি কাঠ বাঁচাইবার জন্য একপ্রকার কল।

rē-gĕn′-ē sis, *n.* The state of being renewed or reproduced ; নবজন্ম, নবজীবনপ্রাপ্তি।

rē′-gĕnt, *n.* & *adj.* **1.** One who governs a kingdom during the minority, absence, or disability of a king ; যে ব্যক্তি রাজার নাবালকত্ব, অনুপস্থিতি এবং অক্ষমতার কালে রাজ্য শাসন করেন, প্রতিনিধিনৃপ। **2.** (*Pl.*) A state board of school-superiendence in New York ; বিদ্যালয়, পুস্তকাগার প্রভৃতির পরিদর্শন ও তত্ত্বাবধানের জন্য নিউইয়র্ক নগরে প্রতিষ্ঠিত সভাবিশেষের সভ্য বৃন্দ। ***Adj.*** Acting as a regent ; প্রতিনিধিস্থলীয়। **Regent-bird** — অষ্ট্রেলিয়া দেশীয় একপ্রকার সুন্দর পক্ষী। **Regent diamond**—উৎকৃষ্ট হীরকবিশেষ—ইহার ওজন প্রায় ১৩৭ ক্যারাট। এই হীরক ১৭১৭ খৃঃ অব্দে মান্দ্রাজের শাসনকর্তা Pitt সাহেবের নিকট হইতে ফরাসীদেশের প্রতিনিধিনৃপ Duke of Orleans ক্রয় করেন। এই হীরকের অপর নাম Pitt-diamond।

rē-gêr′-mĭ-nāte, *v. i.* To germinate again ; পুনরঙ্কুরিত হওয়া, পুনরায় গজান।

rĕg′-ĭ-cīde, *n.* **1.** A king-killer ; রাজঘাতক, রাজহন্তা। **2.** The killing or murder of a king; রাজহনন, রাজবধ, রাজঘাত, নৃপঘাত, নৃপহিংসা, রাজহত্যা। **—cid'-al,** *adj.* **The regicides** — ইংলণ্ডাধিপতি, প্রথম চার্লসের বিচার ও শিরশ্ছেদ ব্যাপারে সংসৃষ্ট ব্যক্তিগণ; ফরাসীরাজ ষোড়শ লুইএর মুণ্ডচ্ছেদন ব্যাপারে সংসৃষ্ট ব্যক্তিগণ।

regie, *n.* Any kind of Government monopoly (esp. in tobacco, salt, etc.); কোন জিনিষে সরকার বাহাদুরের একচেটিয়া অধিকার।

rē-gild', *v. t.* To gild anew; নূতন করিয়া গিল্টি করা।

re-gime', (rā-zhēm), *n.* Mode of government; administration; শাসনপ্রণালী, রাজ্যশাসন পদ্ধতি; শাসন, রাজ্যশাসন। **Ancien regime**—১৭৮৯ খৃষ্টাব্দের রাজ্যবিপ্লবের পূর্ব্ববর্ত্তী ফরাসীদেশের শাসনপ্রণালী।

rĕg'-i-mĕn, *n.* 1. Orderly government; rule; সুব্যবস্থিত শাসনতন্ত্র; শাসন। 2. (*Med.*) The systematic management of food and drink, exercise, etc.; (ভৈষজ্যশাস্ত্র) পথ্যাপথ্যবিধি, অন্নপানবিধি (আঃ বঃ)। 3. (*Gram.*) A relation of syntax between words; (ব্যাকরণ) শব্দসমূহের মধ্যে পদান্বয়ঘটিত সম্বন্ধ।

rĕg'-i-mĕnt, *n.* & *v. t.* 1. A body of troops consisting usually of two battalions of infantry or several squadrons of cavalry under the command of a colonel; পল্টন, সেনাপল্টন। 2. (*Obs.*) Rule; (অপ্রঃ) শাসন। 3. A multitude; "A *regiment* of old vellum-bound books"; বহুসংখ্যক ব্যক্তি বা বস্তু, সংঘ, সমূহ, কদম্ব, শ্রেণী। ***Verb t.*** 1. To form into regiment or regiments; সেনাপল্টন বা সেনাপল্টনসমূহ গঠন করা। 2. To oraganize; to systematize; as, the people are *regimented* into bodies; ব্যূহবদ্ধ করা; সংঘবদ্ধ করা, শৃঙ্খলাবদ্ধ করা, প্রণালীবদ্ধ করা। **—men-ta'-tion,** *n.*

rĕg-i-mĕn'-tăl, *adj.* & *n.* Belonging to a regiment; সেনাপল্টনসম্বন্ধীয়, পল্টনের। ***Noun.*** (*Pl.*) Military uniform; সামরিক পরিচ্ছদ।

Rē-gī'-nă, *n.* (*Abbr. R.*) The reigning queen; রাজ্ঞী।

rē-gī'-năl, *adj.* (*Rare*) Of, or pertaining to, a queen; queenly; রাজ্ঞীসম্বন্ধীয়; রাজ্ঞ্যুচিত।

rē'-gion (-jŭn), *n.* 1. A tract of land of large but indefinite extent; a country; a province; বিস্তৃত ভূখণ্ড; দেশ; প্রদেশ। 2. (Usu. *pl.*) Separate part of the world or universe; as, the lower *regions* (অধোলোক); পৃথিবী বা বিশ্বের বিভিন্ন অংশ, লোক, ভবন। 3. A part or division of the body or a part of it; দেহের বা দেহাংশের অংশ, স্থান, মণ্ডল (as স্তনমণ্ডল)। 4. Sphere; ক্ষেত্র, মণ্ডল, রাজ্য। 5. (*Zoo Geography*) A division of the earth with respect to the geographical distribution of animals; জন্তু সমূহের ভৌগোলিক সংস্থানসম্পর্কে পৃথিবীর বিভাগ। **—al,** *adj.* 1. Of, or pertaining to, a particular region or district; বিশেষ অঞ্চল বা জেলা সম্বন্ধীয়। **Antarctic regions** — দক্ষিণ প্রদেশ (হিঃ কোঃ)। **Arctic regions**—উত্তর প্রদেশ (হিঃ কোঃ)। **Botanical regions** — উদ্ভিদ্ বিশেষের প্রদেশ, উদ্ভিদ্ প্রদেশ (হিঃ কোঃ)। **Ethiopean region** — ইথিপিয়স্থ প্রদেশ। **Lower regions**—অধোলোক, নরক। **Neoarctic regions**—নব সুমেরু প্রদেশ (সাঃ পঃ), নবোদীচ্যবর্ষ (ঐ)। **Neotropical regions**—নব অয়নান্ত প্রদেশ (সাঃ পঃ), নব্যোষ্ণ প্রদেশ (ঐ)। **Oriental region**—পূর্ব্বপ্রদেশ (হিঃ কোঃ), প্রাচ্য প্রদেশ। **Palearctic regions**—প্রত্ন সুমেরু প্রদেশ (ঐ)। **Rainless regions**—নির্বর্ষ দেশ, নির্বর্ষণ প্রদেশ (হিঃ কোঃ)। **Tropical regions**—অয়নান্ত প্রদেশ (হিঃ কোঃ)। **Upper regions**—ঊর্দ্ধলোক, আকাশ, স্বর্গ। **Zoological regions**—প্রাণিবিশেষের প্রদেশ, পশুপ্রদেশ (হিঃ কোঃ)। **Regions of constant calm**—নিয়তবাহী বায়ুমণ্ডল। **Regions of constant precipitation**—সন্ততবর্ষস্থান, নিয়ত বর্ষ দেশ, প্রবর্ষ প্রদেশ (হিঃ কোঃ)। **Regions of constant winds**—নিয়তবাহী পবন-মণ্ডল (হিঃ কোঃ)। **Regions of the variable wind**—অনিয়মবাহী বায়ুমণ্ডল, অনিয়তবাহী পবনমণ্ডল (হিঃ কোঃ), অস্থির বায়ুমণ্ডল।

rĕg'-is-tĕr, *n.* 1. A written account or record; লিখিত হিসাব বা বিবরণ। 2. A book containing such record; খাতা। 3. The officer or persons whose business it is to keep a register; খাতা-রক্ষক কর্ম্মচারী। 4. An official document issued as evidence of a ship's nationality; কোন জাহাজ কোন জাতির তাহার প্রমাণস্বরূপ সরকারী-পত্র। 5. A device for indicating the revolutions made, or amount of work done, by a machinery; যে যন্ত্রদ্বারা কোন যন্ত্রের আবর্ত্তনের সংখ্যা এবং কার্য্যের পরিমাণ সূচিত হয়, সূচকযন্ত্র। 6. (*Print.*) Exact adjustment of position in the press-work of books printed on both sides; উভয় দিকে মুদ্রিত কাগজের উভয় দিকের পৃষ্ঠা, স্তম্ভ, পংক্তি প্রভৃতির পরস্পরের সহিত যথাযথ সঙ্গতি। 7. A lid or sliding piece in a furnace, stove, etc. to regulate the admission of air and the heat of the fire; যে ডালা বা স্রংসনশীল অংশদ্বারা চুল্লী প্রভৃতিতে বায়ু প্রবেশ বা চুল্লী প্রভৃতির অগ্নির উত্তাপ নিয়মিত হয়, নিয়ামক। 8. The compass of a voice or instrument; কোন স্বর বা বংশী প্রভৃতির ধ্বনির চরম সীমা। 9. A portion of the compass of a voice; as, the upper or middle *register*; ধ্বনির চরম সীমার অংশবিশেষ। 10. The stop of an organ; অর্গেন যন্ত্রের যে নালীশ্রেণী দ্বারা বিশিষ্ট নাদসমূহ উৎপাদিত হয়। 11. The knob by which any stop is put in or out of action;

যে চাবি প্রভৃতি দ্বারা উক্ত নালীসমূহের কোন একটী ক্রিয়াশীল বা নিষ্ক্রিয় করা হয়। **12.** The inner part of the mould in which printing types are cast; অক্ষর ঢালার ছাঁচের অভ্যন্তর ভাগ। **13.** (*Phot.*) Correspondence of focussing screen with the sensitive plate or film; (আলোক-চিত্রবিদ্যা) যে পর্দ্দাদ্বারা রশ্মিসমূহ কেন্দ্রীভূত হয়—তাহার সহিত বিকারশীল রাসায়নিক দ্রব্যলিপ্ত ফলকের অবস্থান-সামঞ্জস্য। **Lloyd's Register of British and foreign shipping**—ব্রিটিশ এবং বৈদেশিক সমুদ্রগামী পোতের বিবরণ এবং আয়তনাদি অনুসারে শ্রেণী বিভাগ প্রভৃতি সম্বলিত বিবরণী—যাহা প্রতিবর্ষে Lloyd সমিতি কর্ত্তৃক প্রকাশিত হয়।

rĕg'-is-têr, *v. t. & i.* **1.** To enter in a register or record; খাতায় তোলা। **2.** To record automatically; as, the thermometer *registered* 105°; সূচনা করা, নির্দ্দেশ করা। **3.** (*Print.*) To make to correspond exactly; (মুদ্রণ) মুদ্রিত তায়ের উভয় দিকের পংক্তিতে পংক্তিতে এবং স্তম্ভে স্তম্ভে সামঞ্জস্য রাখা। **4.** To secure special protection of by prepayment of an additional fee; as, to *register* a letter; চিঠি প্রভৃতি রেজেষ্টরী করা। **5.** To twist as yarns into strand; গুণ পাকান। ***Verb i.*** To correspond exactly as columns or lines of printed matter on both sides of a printed sheet; উভয়দিকে মুদ্রিত কাগজের স্তম্ভে স্তম্ভে বা পংক্তিতে পংক্তিতে মিল বা সমাঞ্জস্য হওয়া। **-tra-ble,** *adj.* **-tra'-tion,** *n.*

reg'-is-trâr *n.* **1.** An official reorder; যে কর্ম্মচারী দলীল প্রভৃতি সরকারী খাতায় লিপিবদ্ধ করেন, রেজিষ্ট্রার। **2.** (*Indian Universities*) The head of the ministerial establishment of a university; (ভারতবর্ষ) বিশ্ববিদ্যালয়ের দপ্তরের প্রধান কর্ম্মচারী, রেজিষ্ট্রার। **-ship,** *n.*

rĕg-is-tră-rȳ, *n.* The registrar of the Cambridge University; কেম্ব্রিজ বিশ্ববিদ্যালয়ের দপ্তরের প্রধান কর্ম্মচারী।

Rē'-gĭ-ŭs, *adj.* Royal; appointed by a king; রাজকীয়; রাজনিযুক্ত। **Regius professors**—ইংলণ্ডীয় বিশ্ব-বিদ্যালয় সমূহের যে সকল অধ্যাপকের আসন অষ্টম হেনরী কর্ত্তৃক প্রতিষ্ঠিত হইয়াছিল; (স্কটলণ্ডে) নৃপতিকর্ত্তৃক প্রতিষ্ঠিত অধ্যাপকের আসন।

rē'-năl, *adj.* Pertaining to a reign, kingdom or king; রাজত্ব-সম্বন্ধীয়, রাজ্যসম্বন্ধীয়, নৃপতিসম্বন্ধীয়। **Regnal day** — রাজ্যারোহণের সাম্বৎসরিক উৎসব। **Regnal year**—রাজার সিংহাসনারোহণের সাম্বৎসরিক দিবস হইতে গণিত বৎসর। **Regnal years**—কোন রাজার রাজ্যকাল।

rĕg'-nănt, *adj.* **1.** Reigning; রাজত্ব-কারী, রাজপদে প্রতিষ্ঠিত, রাজ্যাভিষিক্ত। **2.** Predominant; "A traitor to the vices *regnant*"; প্রভুত্বকারী, প্রবল, প্রধান, বলবৎ। **Queen Regnant**—যে রাজ্ঞী স্বাধিকার বলে রাজ্য-শাসন করেন—রাজার পত্নী বলিয়া নহে।

rē-gorge' (-gŏrj), *v. t. & i.* **1.** To vomit up; উদ্বমিত করা। **2.** To swallow again; পুনরায় গ্রাস বা গলাধঃকরণ করা। ***Verb i.*** To gush or flow back again; পুনরায় ছুটা বা প্রবাহিত হওয়া।

rē-grāte', *v. t.* To buy provision to sell them at a profit again in the same or neighbouring market or fair; খাদ্যদ্রব্য ক্রয়পূর্ব্বক উহা সেই বাজারে বা নিকটবর্ত্তী বাজারে বা মেলায় পুনরায়অধিক মূল্যে বিক্রয় করা [এইরূপ কার্য্য পূর্ব্বে অপরাধ স্বরূপ গণ্য হইত]। **-grat'-er, -gra'-tor,** *ns.*

rē-grĕss', *n.* **1.** Passage back; প্রত্যাবর্ত্তন, পশ্চাদপসরণ। **2.** Retrogression; অবনতি, পতন। **3.** (*Astron.*) Retrogradation; (জ্যোতির্বিজ্ঞান) বক্রগতি।

rē-grĕss', *v. i.* To go back (esp. in *Astron.*); পশ্চাদ্‌গামী হওয়া, বক্রী হওয়া (বিশেষতঃ জ্যোতির্বিজ্ঞানে)।

rē-gres'-sion (-grĕ-), *n.* Retrogression; return; পশ্চাদ্‌গমন, অপসর্পণ, অপসরণ, বক্রগতি (জ্যোতির্বিজ্ঞান); প্রত্যাবর্ত্তন। **Regression of the moon's nodes**—রাশিচক্রের উপর রাহু ও কেতুর প্রতিলোম গতি।

rē-grĕt', *v. t. & n.* To lament; to grieve at; খেদ করা, দুঃখ করা; পরিতাপ করা, আক্ষেপ করা, আপশোষ করা, পস্তান (*colloq.*)। ***Noun.*** **1.** Grief or sorrow for the loss or want of something; দুঃখ, খেদ (গীতাঞ্জঃ), শোক, পরিদেবন। **2.** Pain or regret at something done or undone; পরিতাপ, আপশোস, পশ্চাত্তাপ, অনুশোচনা। **-ful, -ta-ble,** *adjs.* To be regretted; শোচনীয়। **-ful-ly,** *adv.*

rē-group' (-grôp), *v. t.* To group again; পুনরায় শ্রেণীবদ্ধ করা।

rĕg'-ū-lă-ble (-bl-), *adj.* Capable of being regulated; নিয়মানুবর্ত্তনীয়, নিয়মসহ।

rĕg'-ū-lar (-lĕr), *adj. & n.* **1.** Conforming to a rule, law or principle; নিয়মানুযায়ী, নিয়মানুবর্ত্তী, নিয়মপরায়ণ, নিয়মনিষ্ঠ, নিয়মানুসারী, যথাপদ্ধতি, যথাবিহিত। **2.** Orderly; methodical; as, *regular* exercise; নিয়মিত; প্রণালীবদ্ধ, প্রণালীসঙ্গত, সুব্যবস্থিত। **3.** (*Geom.*) With sides and angles equal; (জ্যামিতি) সমভুজী এবং সমকোণী। **4.** Returning at stated intervals; নির্দ্দিষ্ট সময়ান্তে আগমনশীল; **5.** (*Mil.*) Belonging to a standing or permanent army; (সামরিক-শাস্ত্র) স্থায়ী সৈন্যদলভুক্ত। **6.** (*Colloq.*) Thorough; as, he is a *regular* humbug; পাকা, পুরা, ডাহা, দস্তুরমত। **7.** Duly authorised or constituted; as, a *regular* meeting; properly qualified or trained; উপযুক্ত ক্ষমতা-প্রাপ্ত, যথারীতি গঠিত; উপযুক্ত গুণসম্পন্ন, উপযুক্তরূপে শিক্ষিত। **8.** Belonging to religious or monastic order; সন্ন্যাসি-সম্প্রদায়ভুক্ত, যাজক সম্প্রদায়ভুক্ত।

9. Symmetrical ; সমপরিমিত, সুসমঞ্জস, সৌষ্ঠবসম্পন্ন, সমসঙ্গতাবয়ব। 10. Habitual ; constant ; "The revolving globe is maintained in its *regular* orbit" ; অভ্যাসসিদ্ধ ; রীতিসিদ্ধ; চিরন্তন, নিয়ত। 11. Well-ordered; well-behaved ; steady ; as, to lead a *regular* life ; সুব্যবস্থিত, সুনিয়মিত ; শিষ্ট ; শান্ত, স্থির, স্থিরচিত্ত, স্থিরমতি, অবিক্ষুব্ধ। 12. (*Gram.*) Declined or inflected according to the common or ordinary form ; (ব্যাকরণ) সাধারণ নিয়মে বিভক্তিযুক্ত বা রূপান্তরিত, নিয়মিত। 13. (*Bot.*) Applied to parts of plants when symmetrical in their figure, size and proportion of their parts ; নিয়মিক (সাঃ পঃ)। ***Noun.*** 1. A monk who has taken the vows in some order recognised by the Church ; ধর্ম্ম-সংঘকর্ত্তৃক স্বীকৃত কোন সম্প্রদায়ভুক্ত সন্ন্যাসী, যতী। 2. A soldier belonging to the permanent army ; স্থায়ী সৈন্যদলভুক্ত সৈনিক। 3. (*Colloq.*) A person permanently employed ; (চলিত ভাষায়) স্থায়ী কর্ম্মচারী। **–i-za′-tion,** *n.* **–ize,** *v. t.* **–lar′-i-ty,** *n.* The state or quality of being regular ; নিয়মানুবর্ত্তিতা, নিয়মনিষ্ঠা, সৌসামঞ্জস্য, নিয়মিতত্ব। **–ly,** *adv.* In a regular manner ; নিয়মিতরূপে, নিয়মিতভাবে, বিধিপূর্ব্বক। **Regular flower**—নিয়মিত-পুষ্প (সাঃ পঃ)। **Regular verbs**—যে সকল ক্রিয়ার অতীতকালে *d, t* বা *ed* যুক্ত হয়।

rĕg′-ü-lāte, *v. t.* 1. To adjust by rule, method or established mode ; নিয়মিত করা, নিয়ন্ত্রিত করা। 2. To put or keep in good order ; as, to *regulate* a clock ; ঠিক রাখা, সুব্যবস্থিত করা। **–lat′-ing,** *adj.* 1. Tending to regulate ; নিয়ামক। **Regulating Act**—ইষ্টইণ্ডিয়া কোম্পানীর ভারতশাসন-ক্ষমতা নিয়ন্ত্রিত করার উদ্দেশ্যে ১৭৭৩ খৃঃ অব্দে পার্লেমেণ্টে যে আইন বিধিবদ্ধ হয়। **Regulating box**—তাড়িতযন্ত্রের চুম্বকের তারকুণ্ডলীতে প্রবহমাণ তাড়িত-প্রবাহ নিয়মিত করার জন্য আধারবিশেষ।

rĕg-ü-lā′-tion, *n.* & *adj.* 1. Act of regulating or the state of being regulated ; নিয়মিতকরণ, ব্যবস্থাপন, সুব্যবস্থা। 2. A rule or order prescribed by a superior or competent authority, regulating the action of those under his control ; a governing direction, precept or law ; as, police *regulations* ; বিধি, নিয়ম, আইন ; ব্যবস্থা, বিধান। ***Adj.*** Prescribed ; as, *regulation* uniform ; ordinary ; common ; as, the *regulation* mode of cutting the hair ; *regulation* sword ; বিধিনির্দ্দিষ্ট ; সাধারণ, সাচরাচরিক; চলিতরকম। **Regulation provinces**—কোম্পানীর আমলের বঙ্গ, মাদ্রাজ ও বোম্বে এবং উত্তর-পশ্চিম প্রদেশ।

rĕg′-ü-lā-tive (-tĭv), *adj.* 1. Regulating ; নিয়ামক, ব্যবস্থাপক। 2. (*Metaph.*) Assumed by the mind as the basis and condition of all other knowledge ; determining or regulating by external force or influence ; অপর সর্ব্বপ্রকার জ্ঞানের ভিত্তি বা নিয়ত নিমিত্ত (condition) বলিয়া মন কর্ত্তৃক পরিগৃহীত ; বহির্মুখ শক্তি বা প্রভাবদ্বারা নিশ্চায়ক বা নিয়ামক।

rĕg′-ü-lā-tor (-tẽr), *n.* 1. One who regulates ; নিয়ামক, ব্যবস্থাপক। 2. The lever of a watch ; টেঁকঘড়ীর কলের দণ্ডযন্ত্র। 3. A mechanical contrivance for regulating or equalizing motion ; গতিসাম্যকারক বা গতিনিয়ামক যান্ত্রিক কৌশলবিশেষ। 4. A device for regulating the passage of air, electricity, gas, water, etc. ; বায়ু, বিদ্যুত, বাষ্প, জল, প্রভৃতির আগম নির্গম নিয়ামক কৌশলবিশেষ। 5. A device for adjusting the balance of a clock or watch ; ঘড়ী বা টেঁকঘড়ীর স্পন্দননিয়ামক যন্ত্র ঠিক করার জন্য যান্ত্রিক কৌশলবিশেষ। 6. A lever in a watch for determining the length of the hair-spring ; টেঁকঘড়ীর কেশবৎ সূক্ষ্ম তারের দমের দৈর্ঘ্য নিয়মনের জন্য দণ্ড-যন্ত্রবিশেষ। 7. A clock keeping accurate time ; যে ঘড়ী ঠিক সময় রাখে।

rĕg′-ü-lŭs, *n.* 1. (*Cap.*) A bright star in the constellation Leo ; মঘা নক্ষত্র। 2. The pure metal which in smelting ores falls to the bottom of the crucible or furnace ; a still impure product of smelting ; খনিজ বিমিশ্র ধাতু গালাইবার সময় যে বিশুদ্ধ ধাতু মুচী বা চুল্লীর নীচে পড়ে ; খনিজবিমিশ্র ধাতু গালাইবার পর যে অবিশুদ্ধ অবস্থার ধাতু পাওয়া যায়। 3. A golden-crested wren (*Regulus cristalus*) ; ইংলণ্ডদেশীয় পক্ষিবিশেষ। 4. A petty king or ruler; ক্ষুদ্র রাজা বা শাসনকর্ত্তা। 5. (*Math.*) A simply infinite system of lines where the consecutive lines do not intersect ; অন্তহীন সরল রেখাশ্রেণী—যাহাতে ক্রমিক রেখাদ্বয় পরস্পরকে ছেদন করেনা।

rē-gur′-gi-tāte (-gẽr-), *v. t.* & *i.* To throw or pour back in great quantity ; পুনরায় ঢালা বা নিঃসৃত করা। ***Verb i.*** To be poured back ; পুনরায় নিঃসৃত হওয়া। **–ta′-tion,** *n.*

rē-hă-bĭl′-i-tāte, *v.t.* 1 To reinstate ; পুনরায় স্বপদে বা স্বাধিকারে প্রতিষ্ঠিত করা, পুনঃ প্রতিষ্ঠিত করা, পূর্ব্বাধিকার প্রদান করা। 2. To restore to public esteem or respect ; as, to *rehabilitate* a bad man ; to re-establish the character and reputation ; পুনরায় জনসাধারণের শ্রদ্ধা বা সমাদরভাজন করা ; কাহারো চরিত্র বা সুনামের পুনঃপ্রতিষ্ঠা করা। **–ta′-tion,** *n.*

rē-hăn′-dle (-dl), *v. t.* To handle again ; পুনরায় হাত দেওয়া, পুনরায় আলোচনা করা, পুনরায় ব্যবহার করা।

rē-hăng′, *v. t.* To hang again ; পুনরায় টাঙ্গান।

rĕ-hăsh′, *v. t.* & *n.* To work up old materials in a new form ; to restate in new language ; পুরাতন উপাদানদ্বারা নূতনভাবে গড়া ; পুনরায় নূতন ভাষায় বলা। ***Noun.*** Something made of materials formerly used; পুরাতন উপাদানে নূতনভাবে গঠিত জিনিষ।

rĕ-hear′ (-hër), *v. t.* To hear again ; to try a second time ; পুনরায় শোনা ; পুনরায় বিচার করা।

rĕ-hears′-ăl (-hêrs-), *n.* **1.** The repetition of the words of another; recital ; আবৃত্তি ; বর্ণনা। **2.** A trial performance of a drama etc. before public exhibition ; as, the *rehearsal* of a drama ; মহালা, মহাড়া, তালিম, পূর্ব্বাভিনয়, ঘরানা অভিনয় (সত্যমিথ্যা—বিপিন)।

rĕ-hearse′ (-hêrs), *v. t.* & *i.* **1.** To recite ; আবৃত্তি করা, আওড়ান। **2.** To relate ; বর্ণনা করা, বিবৃত করা। **3.** To recite or perform in private for experiment before exhibition to the public ; তালিম দেওয়া, মহালা দেওয়া, মহাড়া দেওয়া, পূর্ব্বাভিনয় করা, প্রয়োগ করা (cf. ভরতস্তমপ্সরোভিঃ প্রযোজয়িষ্যতি — উত্তররাম চরিত)। ***Verb i.*** **1.** To recite ; আবৃত্তি করা। **2.** To engage in rehearsal ; মহাড়া দেওয়া।

rĕ-house′ (-hows). *v. t.* To place in a new house ; নূতন বাটীতে স্থাপন করা।

rĕ-hü′-măn-īze, *v. t.* To humanize again ; পুনরায় মানবত্ব প্রদান করা, পুনরায় মানবদেহ গ্রহণ করা।

reichsrat(h), *n.* The imperial parliament of the Austrian Empire ; অষ্ট্রিয় সাম্রাজ্যের পার্লেমেন্ট বা ব্যবস্থাপক-সভা।

reichstag, *n.* The imperial parliament of the German Empire ; জর্ম্মণ সাম্রাজ্যের পার্লেমেন্ট বা ব্যবস্থাপক সভা।

rĕ′-ĭ-fȳ, *v. t.* To materialise ; জড় বস্তুতে পরিণত করা, জড়ধর্ম্মান্বিত করা, মূর্ত্ত করা। **—fi-ca′-tion,** *n.*

reign (rān), *n.* **1.** Sovereignty ; rule ; royal authority ; রাজত্ব ; শাসন, রাজ্যশাসন ; রাজক্ষমতা। **2.** The time during which a sovereign reigns ; রাজত্বকাল, রাজত্ব। **3.** Power ; influence ; "Every season's *reign*" ; শক্তি ; প্রভাব, অধিকার, রাজত্ব। **4.** (*Rare*) Empire ; kingdom ; (কচিদ্ ব্যবহৃত) সাম্রাজ্য ; রাজ্য।

reign (rān), *v. i.* **1.** To rule as a sovereign ; রাজ্য করা, রাজত্ব করা, রাজ্যশাসন করা। **2.** To prevail; as, a disease which commonly *reigns* in summer ; প্রাদুর্ভাব হওয়া। **3.** To rule ; to have predominance ; শাসন করা, রাজত্ব করা ; প্রভাব বা প্রাধান্য থাকা। **Reigning sovereign** — সাম্প্রতাধিপ (মার্কঃপুঃ)। **Reign of Terror** — ফরাসী রাষ্ট্রবিপ্লবকালীন ঘোর অরাজকতার কাল। **The reigning beauty**—তৎকালীন সর্ব্বশ্রেষ্ঠা সুন্দরী বা সুন্দরীশিরোমণি।

rĕ-ĭg-nīte′, *v. t.* To rekindle ; পুনঃ প্রজ্বালিত করা।

rĕ-ĭm-burse′ (-bêrs), *v. t.* **1.** To replace in a treasury, purse, or coffer as an equivalent for what has been taken, expended or lost ; as, to *reimburse* the expenses of a war ; to refund ; ধনভাণ্ডার, ধনভস্ত্রিকা বা সিন্দুক হইতে যাহা নেওয়া হইয়াছে, কিম্বা খরচ করা বা হারান গিয়াছে তাহা পূরণ করিয়া রাখা, টাকা পূরণ করিয়া রাখা ; পুনরায় ফিরাইয়া দেওয়া। **2.** To pay back ; to repay ; প্রতিদান করা ; পরিশোধ করা। **—ment,** *n.* The act of reimbursing ; পরিশোধ, পূরণ।

rĕ-ĭm-pōrt′, *v. t.* To import again what has been exported ; রপ্তানীমাল পুনরায় আমদানী করা। **—pōr-ta′-tion,** *n.*

rĕ-ĭm-pōse′, *v. t.* **1.** To levy anew ; পুনরায় বসান। **2.** (*Rare*) To tax again ; (কচিদ্ ব্যবহৃত) পুনরায় কর বসান।

rein (rān), *n.* & *v. t.* **1.** The strap of bridle ; লাগাম, বল্গা, রশ্মি, অশ্বরশ্মি। [Syn. অভীষু (শকুঃ), অভীশু, অবক্ষেপণী, দন্তালিকা, কুশা, প্রগ্রহ, প্রগ্রাহ, বস্থ, বাগা, কষা (শিশুঃ)।] **2.** A means of checking or guiding or governing ; restraint ; government ; নিরোধ, সংযমন বা পরিচালনের উপায় ; সংযমন, সংযম ; শাসন। ***Verb t.*** **1.** To check with rein ; রশ্মিদ্বারা সংযত করা। **2.** To restrain ; to control ; সংযত করা ; দমন করা, নিরোধ করা। **Rein′-less,** *adj.* Unrestrained ; অসংযত। **To drop the reins**—To give up control or guidance ; কর্ত্তৃত্ব বা শাসনভার ত্যাগ করা। **To give the rein or the reins** — To give license ; রশ্মি ছাড়িয়া দেওয়া, যথেচ্ছভাবে চলিতে দেওয়া, রাশ আল্‌গা করা। **To take the reins**—To assume the guidance or direction ; শাসনভার গ্রহণ করা, নেতৃত্ব গ্রহণ করা।

rĕ-ĭn-căr′-nāte, *v. t.* & *i.* To incarnate again ; পুনরবতীর্ণ করা, পুনরবতীর্ণ হওয়া। **—na′-tion,** *n.* The act of reincarnating ; পুনরবতরণ, পুনরায় নরকলেবর ধারণ, পুনঃলীলাবিগ্রহ ধারণ, পুনরায় লীলা মনুষ্যবিগ্রহ ধারণ, পুনরায় লীলা তনু ধারণ।

rĕ-ĭn-cŏr′-pŏ-rāte, *v. t.* & *i.* To incorporate anew ; পুনরঙ্গীভূত করা।

rein′-deer (rān-dër), *n.* A species of deer inhabiting the Arctic

Reindeer.

regions, which has been domesticated and rendered in many ways serviceable to man ;

বল্গা হরিণ। Reindeer-moss—একপ্রকার শৈবাল।

Reindeer-moss.

rē-in-force′ (-fōrs), *v.t.* & *n.* **1.** To strengthen by new assistance or support ; অতিরিক্ত সৈন্য প্রভৃতিদ্বারা বলীয়ান করা। **2.** (*Rare*) To enforce again ; (কচিদ্ব্যবহৃত) পুনরায় আমলে আনা। ***Noun.*** **1.** A stregthening patch ; কোন কিছু শক্ত করার জন্য যে তালি বা পট্টি লাগান হয়। **2.** That part of a cannon nearest to the breech, which is made tronger to resist the explosive force of the powder ; বারুদের বিস্ফোরণশক্তি প্রতিরোধের জন্য কামানের পশ্চাদ্ভাগের নিকটতম যে অংশ অতিরিক্ত লৌহবেষ্টনী প্রভৃতি দ্বারা দৃঢ় করা হয়।

rē-in-force′-mĕnt (-fōrs-), *n.* **1.** The act of reinforcing ; বলসংযোজন। **2.** Fresh assistance ; esp. an additional supply of men, ships, to augment the strength of an army or fleet ; নূতন সাহায্য ; কোন সৈন্যদল বা রণপোতবহরের বলবৃদ্ধির জন্য প্রেরিত অতিরিক্ত সৈন্য, যুদ্ধজাহাজ, প্রভৃতি। **3.** (*Now rare*) The act of enforcing anew , (কচিদ্ব্যবহৃত) পুনঃপ্রবর্ত্তন।

rē-in-grā′-ti-āte (-shi-), *v. t.* To ingratiate again ; পুনরায় অনুগ্রহভাজন করা।

rē-ink′ (-ingk), *v. t.* To ink again ; পুনরায় কালি লাগান।

reins (rānz), *n.* (*Archaic*) The kidneys ; the loins ; (অপ্রঃ) মূত্রাশয় ; কটি, শ্রোণি।

rē-in-sĕrt′, *v. t.* To insert a second time ; পুনরায় অন্তর্নিবিষ্ট করা। **—ser′-tion,** *n.*

rē-in-spīre′, *v. t.* To inspire anew ; পুনরায় অনুপ্রাণিত করা।

rē-in-stall′, *v. t.* To instal anew ; পুনরায় অভিষিক্ত করা, পুনরায় রাজপটে বা রাজতক্তে বসান।

rē-in-state′, *v. t.* **1.** To restore to a state from which one has been removed ; পুনরায় স্বপদে প্রতিষ্ঠিত করা, পুনঃ প্রতিষ্ঠিত করা, বাহাল করা। **2.** To restore to health or proper order ; পুনরায় স্বাস্থ্য প্রদান করা, পুনরায় সুসন্নিবিষ্ট করা। **—ment,** *n.* The act of reinstating ; প্রতিষ্ঠাপন, পুনঃপ্রতিষ্ঠা।

rē-in-sūre′, *v. t.* To insure again ; পুনরায় বীমা করা।

rē-in-têr′, *v. t.* To inter again ; পুনরায় সমাহিত করা, পুনরায় ভূগর্ভে প্রোথিত করা।

rē-in-vĕst′, *v. t.* **1.** To invest anew ; পুনরায় সমন্বিত করা। **2.** To invest money again ; পুনরায় টাকা ফেলা।

rē-in-vig′-ŏr-āte, *v. t.* To revive vigour in ; to reanimate ; পুনরায় সতেজ করা ; নব বলে বলীয়ান করা, নবশক্তি সঞ্চার করা, নববল প্রদান করা, পুনরুজ্জীবিত করা।

reis, *n.* A head ; chief ; leader ; সর্দ্দার ; প্রধান ব্যক্তি ; নায়ক, নেতা। **Reis Effendi** — তুরস্কের প্রাচীন পররাষ্ট্রসচিব এবং রাজস্বসচিব।

reis, *n.*, *pl.* A Portuguese money of account ; পর্ত্তুগাল দেশের হিসাবে ব্যবহৃত ক্ষুদ্র মুদ্রাবিশেষ। [প্রায় $\frac{1}{২০}$ পেন্সের সমান, ব্রাজিলে $\frac{1}{৪০}$ পেন্সের সমান]।

rē-is-sue′ (-ish-ü), *v. t., i.* & *n.* To issue a second time ; পুনরায় বাহির করা, পুনঃ প্রচার করা। ***Verb i.*** To issue or go forth again ; পুনরায় বাহির হওয়া, পুনরায় নিঃসৃত হওয়া। ***Noun.*** A second issue ; পুনরায় বাহির, পুনঃ প্রচার।

rē-it′-ĕr-āte, *v. t.* To say or do repeatedly ; to repeat ; বার বার বলা, পুনঃ পুনঃ করা ; পুনরাবৃত্তি করা। **—a′-tion,** *n.* The act of reiterating ; পুনরাবৃত্তি, সমভিহার।

rē-jĕct′, *v. t.* **1.** To cast out ; to discard ; ফেলিয়া দেওয়া ; অগ্রাহ্য করা, নামঞ্জুর করা। **2.** To refuse to receive ; to slight ; গ্রহণ করিতে অস্বীকার করা, প্রত্যাখ্যান করা ; অবজ্ঞা করা, তাচ্ছিল্য করা। **3.** To vomit ; as, to *reject* food ; উদ্বমন করা, বমি করিয়া ফেলা। **—a-ble,** *adj.* **—jec′-tion,** *n.*

rē-jĕc-tā-mĕn′-tă, *n.* **1.** Refuse ; waste matter ; আবর্জ্জনা, জঞ্জাল ; পরিত্যক্ত জিনিষ, বাজে জিনিষ। **2.** Excremental matter ; মল।

rē-joice′ (-jōys), *v. i.* & *t.* To feel great joy or pleasure ; to exult ; আনন্দ ভোগ করা, হর্ষোৎফুল্ল হওয়া ; উল্লসিত হওয়া, আনন্দে পূর্ণ হওয়া, আনন্দে মাতোয়ারা হওয়া, আহ্লাদিত হওয়া, হর্ষোচ্ছ্বাসিত হওয়া। ***Verb t.*** To make joyful ; to exhilarate ; আনন্দিত করা, হর্ষোৎফুল্ল করা ; উল্লসিত করা, হৃষ্ট করা। **—joic′-ing,** *n.* The act of expressing joy ; festivity ; আনন্দ-প্রকাশ, সুখোচ্ছ্বাস, আনন্দোচ্ছ্বাস ; আনন্দোৎসব। **—joic′-ing-ly,** *adv.* **To rejoice in**—To have ; থাকা।

rē–join′ (-jōyn), *v. t.* & *i.* **1.** To unite again after separation ; পুনর্মিলিত করা। **2.** To ioin a person or a company again ; পুনরায় কোন দলে বা কোন লোকের সহিত যোগ দেওয়া। ***Verb i.*** To unite again ; পুনর্ম্মিলিত হওয়া।

rē-join′ (-jōyn), *v. t.* & *i.* To answer ; to say in reply ; উত্তর দেওয়া ; প্রত্যুত্তরে বলা। ***Verb i.*** To answer to a reply ; (*law*) to answer as the defendant to the plaintiff's recrimination ; কোন কিছুর প্রত্যুত্তরে উত্তর দেওয়া ; (আইন) পাল্টা জবাব দেওয়া।

rē-join′-dĕr (-jōyn-), *n.* **1.** An answer ; a retort ; প্রত্যুক্তি, প্রত্যুত্তর, কথার পৃষ্ঠে কথা ; কড়া জবাব।

2. (*Law*) The defendant's answer to the plaintiff; replication; (আইন) পাল্টা জওয়াব; দ্বন্দ্বজওয়াব।

rē-jü'-vē-nāte, -nize, *v. t.* & *i.* To restore to youth; নবযৌবন প্রদান করা, পুনর্যৌবন প্রদান করা। *Verb i.* To become young again; নবযৌবন প্রাপ্ত হওয়া, পুনর্যৌবন প্রাপ্ত হওয়া। **-na'-tion**, *n.*

rē-jü-vē-nĕs'-cence (-ĕns), *n.* A renewing of youth; the state of becoming young again; নবযৌবন-প্রদান, পুনর্যৌবনপ্রদান; নবযৌবন লাভ, পুনর্যৌবন প্রাপ্তি, নবতারুণ্য প্রাপ্তি।

rē-jü-vē-nĕs'-cent (-ĕnt), *adj.* Becoming young again; rejuvenating; নবযৌবনপ্রাপী; নবযৌবন প্রদায়ক, রসায়ন (ঠাকুর)।

rē-kin'-dle (-dl), *v. t.* & *i.* 1. To kindle again; পুনঃ প্রজ্বালিত করা, পুনঃপ্রদীপ্ত করা। 2. To inflame again; পুনরুদ্দীপ্ত করা, পুনরুত্তেজিত করা। *Verb i.* To take fire again; পুনঃপ্রজ্বালিত হওয়া, পুনরায় জ্বলা।

rē-lā-bel (-bl), *v. t.* পুনরায় অঙ্কপত্র (label) লাগান।

rē-lapse' (-lăps), *v. i.* & *n.* 1. To fall or slip back into a former bad state or practice; as, to *relapse* into vice; পুনরায় পতিত হওয়া। 2. To fall back into an illness after recovery or from a state of convalescence; আরোগ্যোন্মুখ অবস্থায় বা তাহার অল্প পরে রোগের পুনরাবৃত্তি হওয়া। *Noun.* 1. Sliding or falling particularly to a former bad state; পুনরায় পূর্ব্বাবস্থা প্রাপ্তি, পুনরায় অধঃপতন। 2. The falling back again into illness after partial recovery; আরোগ্যোন্মুখ অবস্থায় বা তাহার অল্প পরে রোগের পুনরাবৃত্তি।

rē-lāte', *v. t.* & *i.* 1. To tell or narrate; বলা, বর্ণনা করা, বিবৃত করা। 2. To bring into relation between; উভয়ের মধ্যে সম্বন্ধ স্থাপন করা, সম্বন্ধান্বিত করা। *Verb i.* To have reference or respect; সম্পর্ক থাকা, সম্বন্ধ থাকা। **-lat'-ed**, *pp.* 1. Recited; কথিত, বর্ণিত। 2. Allied; সম্বন্ধান্বিত, সম্বন্ধবিশিষ্ট। **-lat'-ed-ness**, *n.*

rē-lā'-tion, *n.* 1. The act of relating or telling; narration; বর্ণন; কথন। 2. A narrative; বৃত্তান্ত, আখ্যান। 3. Respect; reference; as, in *relation* to; সম্বন্ধ; সম্পর্ক। 4. Connection perceived or imagined between things; the condition of being such or such in respect to something else; সম্বন্ধ; সম্পর্ক। 5. Connection by birth or marriage; kinship; সম্বন্ধ, সম্পর্ক, কুটুম্বিতা; গোত্রসম্বন্ধ, সগোত্রত্ব, জ্ঞাতিত্ব। [মিতাক্ষরায় এই কয় শ্রেণীতে কুটুম্বগণ বিভক্ত হইয়াছে। (১) সপিণ্ড (সপ্তম-পুরুষ পর্য্যন্ত জ্ঞাতি); (২) সমানোদক (অষ্টম হইতে চতুর্দ্দশ পুরুষ পর্য্যন্ত); (৩) সগোত্র বা গোত্রজ (এক গোত্র বিশিষ্ট); (৪) বন্ধু বা বান্ধব (স্ত্রীলোক সম্পর্কীয় কুটুম্ব); (৫) সনাভি (রক্ত-গতসম্পর্কীয় কুটুম্ব; (৬) সকুল্য (এক কুল বা পর্য্যায়ভুক্ত); (৭) জ্ঞাতি (=সনাভি)।] 6. Relative; as, he is no *relation* of mine; kinsman; (*pl.*) relatives; কুটুম্ব, জ্ঞাতি; আত্মীয় কুটুম্ব; জ্ঞাতিবর্গ, স্বজনবর্গ। 7. (*Law*) The referring of an act to a prior date as the time of its taking effect; (আইন) কোন কার্য্য প্রকৃতপক্ষে যে কালে ঘটিয়াছে তদপেক্ষা পূর্ব্ববর্ত্তী কাল হইতে উহা আমলে আনার জন্য তৎসময়ের সহিত উহা অন্বিত করণ। 8. (*Law*) Laying of information before Attorney-General for him to take action upon: কোন বিষয়ে মোকদ্দমা প্রভৃতি স্থাপনের জন্য তৎসম্পর্কীয় সংবাদ এটর্নিজেনেরেলের গোচর করণ। 9. (*Math.*) Ratio; proportion; (গণিতবিদ্যা) নিষ্পত্তি; অনুপাত। **-al**, *adj.* **-ship**, *n.* The state of being related by kindred affinity or other alliance; সম্বন্ধ সম্পর্ক, কুটুম্বিতা, আত্মীয়তা। **Inseparable relation** or **cause** — সমবায়িকারণ (কেণ্ডিঃ)। **Intimate relation**—সমবায় (শ্রীঃ), সমবায় সম্বন্ধ, নিত্য সম্বন্ধ। **In** or **with relation**—With respect to; সম্বন্ধে, সম্পর্কে, বিষয়ে। **Relation of causality**—কার্য্যকারণ ভাব (ব্রজঃ হিন্দুঃ)। **Relation of space**—দিগ্‌দেশ সম্বন্ধ (ব্রজঃ হিন্দুঃ)। **Relation of time**—কালিক সম্বন্ধ (ব্রজঃ হিন্দুঃ)। **To have** or **make relation**—To have or make reference to something; কোন বিষয়ের সহিত সম্পর্ক থাকা, কোন বিষয়ের সম্পর্কে উল্লেখ করা।

rĕl'-ā-tive (-tĭv), *adj.* & *n.* 1. (*Gram.*) Introducing a dependent clause qualifying an expressed or implied antecedent; (ব্যাকরণ) সম্বন্ধবাচক, সম্বন্ধদ্যোতক। 2. Having relation or bearing to something else; relevant; "All *relative* matter, not absolutely essential to the subject"; সম্বন্ধ-বিশিষ্ট, সম্পৃক্ত, সম্বন্ধান্বিত; প্রাসঙ্গিক, প্রসঙ্গানুকূল। 3. Having reciprocal relationship; corresponding; অন্যোন্যসম্বন্ধবিশিষ্ট, অন্যোন্যসম্বন্ধী, পরস্পরানুবন্ধী, অন্যোন্যাত্মক, অন্যোন্যাপেক্ষ, পরস্পরাপেক্ষ; অনুবন্ধী। 4. Not absolute or independent; আপেক্ষিক, সাপেক্ষ। 5. Comparative; তুলনামূলক, তুলনাত্মক। 6. Offered or paid indirectly by means of or through an image; as, *relative* worship; (প্রতীকোপাসনা) প্রতীকাত্মক। *Noun.* 1. A person connected by blood or affinity; a kinsman or kinswoman; কুটুম্ব, আত্মীয়, স্বজনবর্গ (*pl.*), পরিজন (উজ্জ্বলঃ); জ্ঞাতি। 2. (*Gram.*) A relative pronoun; সম্বন্ধবাচক সর্ব্বনাম। 3. (*Log.*) A relative term; সাপেক্ষপদ, সম্বন্ধিপদ, (যথা স্বামী, স্ত্রী; প্রভু, ভৃত্য)। **-ly**, *adv.* **-ness**, *n.* **-tiv'-i-ty**, *n.*

Relative term—সাপেক্ষপদ (হিঃ কোঃ), সম্বন্ধিপদ (ঐ)।

rĕl′-ă-tiv-ĭsm, *n.* (*Philos.*) The doctrine that knowledge is only of relation; (দর্শন-শাস্ত্র) আমাদের সর্ব্বপ্রকার জ্ঞান কেবল সম্বন্ধেরই জ্ঞান—এই মত বা তত্ত্ব, সম্বন্ধবাদ।

rē-lā′-tor (-têr), *n.* **1.** (*Rare*) A relater; (ক্বচিদ্‌ব্যবহৃত) বর্ণনকারী, কথক, আখ্যায়ক। **2.** (*Law*) A maker of relation; (আইন) যে ব্যক্তি এটর্নি জেনেরেলের নিকট কোন সংবাদ প্রদান করে (এবং যে সংবাদের উপর নির্ভর করিয়া তিনি মোকদ্দমা প্রভৃতি রুজু করেন)।

rē-lăx′, *v. t.* & *i.* **1.** To slacken; শিথিল করা, শ্লথ করা, ঢিলা করা। **2.** To make less severe or rigorous; to tone down; as, to *relax* a rule; শিথিল করা; উপশম করা, কঠোরতা হ্রাস করা। **3.** To abate; to diminish; হ্রাস করা, লাঘব করা; কমান। **4.** To afford relaxation to; "They *relaxed* themselves by conversation"; বিনোদন করা। **5.** To relieve from constipation; (কোষ্ঠ) খোলাসা করা। ***Verb i.*** **1.** To abate in severity or tension; হ্রাস হওয়া, কমা, লাঘব হওয়া। **2.** To grow milder; মৃদু হওয়া, উপশম হওয়া। **3.** To remit in close attention; শিথিলপ্রযত্ন হওয়া, শ্লথোদ্যম হওয়া।

rē-lăx-ā′-tion, *n.* **1.** Diminution of tension, closeness or firmness; শিথিলীকরণ, শৈথিল্য, শিথিলতা, বিস্রংসন (বাৎস্যঃ)। **2.** Partial remission of penalty etc.; দণ্ড প্রভৃতির আংশিক মাপ। **3.** The act of refreshing or recreating; recreation; শ্রমাপনোদন; বিনোদন, বিনোদ। **4.** Diminution of severity, intensity, vigour, etc.; উপশম, হ্রাস, লাঘব। **5.** (*Path.*) Laxity; (নিদান) বিরেচন, বিরেচকতা।

rē-lay′ (-lā), *n., v. t.* & *i.* **1.** A set of fresh horses placed at certain stages on the road in readiness to relieve others to expedite travel; ঘোড়ার ডাক। **2.** A squad of men to take turn of work at stated intervals; যে লোকের দল নির্দ্দিষ্ট সময়ান্তে অপর দলের স্থলবর্ত্তী হইয়া কার্য্য করে। **3.** (*Telegraph*) A device for enabling telegraphic message to be sent over long distances; তাড়িতবার্ত্তা বহুদূরবর্ত্তী স্থানে প্রেরণের জন্য যান্ত্রিক কৌশলবিশেষ। [সমস্ত তারপথ (line) কতিপয় বিভাগে বিভক্ত হয়। প্রত্যেক বিভাগের প্রান্তে একটী বিদ্যুচ্চুম্বক (Electro-magnet) সংবদ্ধ থাকে। প্রথম বিভাগ অতিক্রমের পর তাড়িতপ্রবাহ ক্ষীণশক্তি হইলে উহা ঐ বিভাগের প্রান্তস্থ বিদ্যুচ্চুম্বক হইতে নবশক্তি আহরণ করিয়া অগ্রসর হয়।] ***Verb t.*** To provide with, or replace by, fresh relays; ডাক বসান, শ্রান্ত অশ্বাদির স্থানে নূতন অশ্বাদি যোগান। ***Verb i.*** To get a fresh relay; ক্লান্ত অশ্বাদির স্থানে নূতন অশ্বাদি প্রাপ্ত হওয়া।

rē-lay′ (-lā), *v. t.* To lay again; পুনরায় বসান, পুনরায় বিছান।

rē-lease′ (-lēs), *v. t.* **1.** To set free; to unfasten; মুক্ত করা, ছাড়িয়া দেওয়া, খালাস দেওয়া; বন্ধন মুক্ত করা। **2.** To give up; to surrender; as, to *release* a claim; ছাড়িয়া দেওয়া; সমর্পণ করা। **—leas′-a-ble,** *adj.* **—leas-ee′, —lea′-sor,** *ns.*

rē-lease′ (-lēs), *n.* **1.** Liberation; মুক্তি, খালাস। **2.** Dicharge from obligation or responsibility; অব্যাহতি, রেহাই। **3.** (*Law*) The act of making over an estate to another; the document effecting this; (আইন) সমর্পণ, হস্তান্তর; মুক্তিপত্র। **4.** A receipt; a written dicharge or aquittance; প্রাপ্তি-স্বীকারপত্র, রসীদ; ইনফসলী, দাখিলা। **5.** (*Mech.*) A device adapted to release part of a machine etc.; যে কলদ্বারা কোন যন্ত্রাদির কোন অংশ মুক্ত করা যায়।

rĕl′-ĕ-gāte, *v. t.* **1.** To banish; নির্ব্বাসিত করা, বিবাসিত করা। **2.** To consign to some obscure position or sphere; "We have not *relegated* religion to obscure municipalities"; কোন অপকৃষ্ট স্থান বা অবস্থায় প্রেরণ করা বা ফেলা। **3.** To put in a special category; to send or submit as for decision, information; কোন বিশেষ শ্রেণীতে ভুক্ত করা; নিষ্পত্তির জন্য বা কোন বিবরণ জানিবার নিমিত্ত প্রেরণ বা উপস্থাপিত করা। **—ga-ble,** *adj.* **—ga′-tion,** *n.*

rē-lĕnt′, *v. i.* To soften in temper; to become less severe or more tender; নরম হওয়া, কোমল হওয়া; একটু গলা, রোষাদি কিঞ্চিৎ প্রশমিত হওয়া, ঈষৎ দ্রবচিত্ত হওয়া। **—ing-ly,** *adv.* **—less,** *adj.* Cruel; নিষ্করুণ, নির্দ্দয়, নিষ্ঠুর, ক্রুর, নিঠুর (*poet.*), নিদয় (*ib.*)। **—less-ly,** *adv.* **—less-ness,** *n.*

rĕl′-ē-vănt, *adj.* Pertinent; প্রাসঙ্গিক, প্রসঙ্গানুকূল। **—vance, —van-cy,** *ns.* The state of being relevant; প্রাসঙ্গিকতা, প্রসঙ্গানুকূলতা, প্রসঙ্গসঙ্গতি।

releve, *n.* A fresh course of dish at dinner etc.; অপরাহ্ণ ভোজনাদিতে নূতন পরিবেষিত ব্যঞ্জন।

rē-lī′-ă-ble (-bl), *adj.* Trustworthy; বিশ্বাসযোগ্য, বিশ্বাসভাজন, বিশ্বস্ত, বিশ্বসনীয়। **—bil′-i-ty, —ness,** *ns.* **From reliable source**—From a trustworthy person; বিশ্বস্তসূত্রে।

rē-lī′-ance (-ăns), *n.* **1.** Confidence; trust; dependence; বিশ্বাস, আস্থা; প্রত্যয়, ভরসা, নির্ভরতা। **2.** That on which one depends; as, he is our chief *reliance*; ground of trust; নির্ভরের বস্তু নির্ভর; বিশ্বাসভূমি।

rĕl′-ic, *n.* **1.** The remains of saints or martyrs or parts of them, or of their belongings ; মহাপুরুষদিগের দেহাবশেষ, দন্ত, কেশ, প্রভৃতি, অথবা তাঁহাদিগের পরিচ্ছদ প্রভৃতির অংশ—যাহা পরম শ্রদ্ধার সহিত সংরক্ষিত হয়, মহাপুরুষের চিহ্ন। **2.** Memento ; "Some lost, some stolen, some as *relics* kept" ; স্মৃতিচিহ্ন। **3.** (*Now rare, Pl.*) A corpse ; "The bleeding *relics* of men who had been the captains of armies" ; remains ; (বর্ত্তমানে কচিদ্‌ব্যবহৃত) মৃতদেহ, শব ; দেহাবশেষ। **4.** Remnant ; "The *relics* of lost innocence" ; অবশেষ, ধ্বংসাবশেষ।

rĕ-lict′, *n.* A widow ; বিধবা।

rē-lief′ (-lēf), *n.* **1.** Alleviation of pain, anxiety, etc. ; উপশম, লাঘব, শান্তি, আরাম, আসান, সোয়াস্তি, দুঃখশমন। **2.** Assistance ; esp. assistance given under the Poor-Law to a pauper ; সাহায্য ; বিশেষতঃ দরিদ্রআইনের বিধান মতে দরিদ্রকে যে সাহায্য প্রদান করা হয়। **3.** Redress of a grievance ; প্রতীকার। **4.** Release from some occupation or post of duty ; esp. the release of a sentry from his post which is taken by another soldier ; বদলী দেওন ; প্রহরীদিগের বদলী ; **5.** A feature etc. that diversifies monotony ; বৈচিত্র্যসাধক বিষয়,—যদ্দ্বারা একটানা বা একঘেঁয়ে ভাব দূরীকৃত হয়। **6.** A relieving force ; as, the *relief* came in time ; সাহায্যার্থ প্রেরিত সৈন্য। **Relief works**—দুর্ভিক্ষ, অন্নকষ্ট, প্রভৃতির কালে দুঃস্থ ব্যক্তিগণের সাহায্যকল্পে (রাস্তা নির্ম্মাণ, খালখনন প্রভৃতি) যে সকল পূর্ত্তকার্য্য আরব্ধ হয়।

rē-lief′ (-lēf), *n.* **1.** A prominence in sculpture, beyond the ground or plane on which it is formed ; ভাস্কর্য্য প্রভৃতিতে উদ্গত কারুকার্য্য, উদ্গত কার্য্য, প্রাচীরাদির গাত্রে উৎকীর্ণ খোদকারী কাজ। **2.** (*Painting*) Appearance of projection and solidity in represented objects ; (চিত্রবিদ্যা) উদ্গত কার্য্যের অনুকরণে চিত্রিত আলেখ্য। **3.** The undulations or surface elevation of a country ; কোন দেশের উচ্চাবচতা। **4.** Prominence or distinction given to anything by contrast ; vividness ; as, to bring out the facts in full *relief* ; বৈপরীত্য প্রদর্শন দ্বারা যে স্পষ্টতা প্রদান করা হয় ; স্পষ্টতা, প্রকট ভাব।

High relief.

5. The total height of a parapet above the bottom of ditch ; পরিখার নিম্ন হইতে প্রাচীরের উচ্চতা। **High relief**—Same as

Low relief.

ALTO-RILIEVO. **Low-relief**—Same as BASSO-RILIEVO. **Relief map**—দেশের উচ্চাবচতা নির্দ্দেশক মানচিত্র, বন্ধুর মানচিত্র।

rē-lieve′ (-lēv), *v.t.* **1.** To free from any burden ; to mitigate ; to alleviate ; মুক্ত করা, উদ্ধার করা ; উপশম করা, প্রশমিত করা ; লাঘব করা। **2.** To give ease, comfort or consolation ; to give succour ; আরাম দেওয়া, সান্ত্বনা দেওয়া, শান্তি দেওয়া ; দুঃসময়ে সাহায্য করা। **3.** To release from a post, station, task or duty by substituting another person or part ; as, to *relieve* a guard ; বদলি দেওয়া। **4.** To prevent from being tiresome, tedious, or monotonous by the introduction of some variety ; "The large black eyes which agreeably *relieved* a face...somewhat shy and sullen" ; বৈচিত্র্যজনক কোন কিছু দ্বারা কোনরূপ পীড়াজনক বা অবসাদজনক একঘেঁয়ে ভাব দূর করা, অবসাদ বা গ্লানিমার উপর দীপ্তি বিস্তার করা বা মাধুর্য্যের আভা ফুটান। **5.** To raise, or cause to be raised, in relief ; উদ্গত করা। **6.** To help in poverty or necessity ; as, to *relieve* the needy ; সাহায্য করা। **7.** To render prominent or distinct ; "The twilight *relieving* in purple masses the foliage on the island" ; সুস্পষ্ট করা, সুপ্রকট করা। **—liev′-ing,** *adj.* & *n.* **Relieving arch**—প্রাচীর হইতে উদ্গত তোরণ। **Relieving officer**—পল্লীর দরিদ্রদিগকে অর্থ সাহায্য করার জন্য নিযুক্ত কর্ম্মচারী। **To feel relieved**—হাঁপ ছেড়ে বাঁচা। **To relieve guard**—পাহারা বদলী দেওয়া। **To relieve nature**—To evacuate the bladder or bowels ; প্রস্রাব করা, মলত্যাগ করা।

rē-lie′-vō (-lē-), *n.* (An erroneous spelling of *rilievo.*) Relief (*in sculpture*) ; উদ্গত কারুকার্য্য।

rē-li′-gion (-jŏn) *n.* **1.** An acknowledgment of our obligation to God accompanied by a feeling of reverence and love ; ধর্ম্ম। **2.** Any system of faith and worship ; as, the Hindu *religion* ; ধর্ম্ম। **3.** (*R. C. Ch.*) A monastic or religious order (*rare*) ; a monastic condition ; (কচিদ্‌ব্যবহৃত) সন্ন্যাসি-সম্প্রদায়, যাজকসম্প্রদায় ; সন্ন্যাস-জীবন। **4.** Devotion or fidelity to a principle or practices ; as, these practices are still continued with much *religion* ;

নিষ্ঠা। **Natural religion**—See NATURAL. **Religion of humanity**—Same as POSITIVISM (which see). **Revealed religion**—প্রত্যাদেশ, লব্ধধর্ম্ম, প্রত্যাদিষ্ট ধর্ম্ম। **To get religion**—(ইতর ভাষায়) কোন ধর্ম্মে দীক্ষিত হওয়া। **To make a religion of**—To be scrupulously careful to do something; ধর্ম্মস্বরূপ মনে করা, অলঙ্ঘ্য কর্ত্তব্যস্বরূপ মনে করা।

rē-lĭ′-gion-ēr (-jŏn-), *n.* **1.** A member of a monastic order; কোন সন্ন্যাসিসম্প্রদায়ভুক্ত ব্যক্তি। **2.** A religious bigot; ধর্ম্মান্ধ ব্যক্তি।

rē-lĭ′-gion-ĭsm (-jŏn-), *n.* The outward practice of religion; affectation or pretence of religion; বাহ্যধর্ম্মানুষ্ঠান, বাহ্যানুষ্ঠান; কপট ধর্ম্মভাব, ভণ্ডামি। **—ist,** *n.* **1.** A religious enthusiast; a religious bigot or pretender; ধর্ম্মোৎসাহী ব্যক্তি; গোঁড়া, ভণ্ড, ধর্ম্মধ্বজ।

rē-lĭ′-gion-īze (-jŏn-), *v. t.* & *i.* To render religious; ধর্ম্মনিষ্ঠ করা, ধর্ম্মপরায়ণ করা। ***Verb i.*** To exhibit bigotry or religious zeal; ধর্ম্মান্ধতা প্রদর্শন করা, গোঁড়ামি দেখান।

rē-lĭ-ġĭ-ōse′, *adj.* Fervidly religious; উৎকট ধর্ম্মপ্রবণ, অতিরিক্ত ধর্ম্মপ্রবণ।

rē-lĭġ′-ĭ-ŏs′-ĭ-tỹ, *n.* **1.** Religious feeling or sentiment; ধর্ম্মভাব। **2.** Quality of being fervidly religious; affected religiousness; ধর্ম্মপ্রাণতা; ধর্ম্মধ্বজিতা।

rē-lĭ′-gious (-jŭs), *adj.* & *n.* **1.** Pertaining to religion; ধর্ম্মসম্বন্ধীয়, ধর্ম্মবিষয়ক। **2.** Pious; devout; ধার্ম্মিক, ধর্ম্মশীল; ধর্ম্মনিষ্ঠ, ধর্ম্মপরায়ণ, ধর্ম্মিষ্ঠ। **3.** Characterised by religion or piety; ধর্ম্মাত্মক। **4.** Engaged by vows to a monastic life; "The superintendence of all the houses of *religious* women in his kingdom"; belonging to a religious order; সন্ন্যাসব্রতাবলম্বী, সন্ন্যাসি সম্প্রদায়ভুক্ত, ভিক্ষুণীসংঘভুক্ত; সন্ন্যাসিসম্প্রদায়ের অধিকৃত। **5.** Scrupulously faithful or exact; as, to do one's duty with *religious* care; conscientious; কর্ত্তব্যাদি পালনে অতি সূক্ষ্মভাবে নিষ্ঠ, পরমনিষ্ঠাসহকৃত, সূক্ষ্মরূপে সম্পাদিত; ধর্ম্মবুদ্ধিসম্পন্ন। ***Noun.*** A monk; a nun; সন্ন্যাসী; সন্ন্যাসিনী, ভিক্ষুণী। **—ly,** *adv.* **—ness,** *n.* The state of being religious; ধার্ম্মিকতা, ধর্ম্মিষ্ঠতা, ধর্ম্মশীলতা, ধর্ম্মপরায়ণতা। **Religious Tract Society**—ধর্ম্ম-পুস্তিকা প্রচারসমিতি। [এই সমিতি ১৭৯৯ খৃঃ অব্দে ধর্ম্মপুস্তিকা, ধর্ম্মগ্রন্থ প্রভৃতি প্রচারের উদ্দেশ্যে প্রতিষ্ঠিত হয়।]

rē-līne′, *v. t.* To provide with new lining; নূতন আস্তর দেওয়া।

rē-lin′-quish (-lĭng-), *v. t.* **1.** To give up; to abandon; ছাড়িয়া দেওয়া, পরিত্যাগ করা, পরিহার করা; ত্যাগ করা। **2.** To renounce a claim; as, to *relinquish* a debt; দাবী ছাড়িয়া দেওয়া, ইস্তফা দেওয়া। **3.** To loose hold of; মুঠা ছাড়িয়া দেওয়া। **—ment,** *n.* The act of quitting; the renouncing a claim to; ত্যাগ, পরিত্যাগ; দাবীত্যাগ, ইস্তফা (আদালতে), তগির (ঐ), দস্তবরদারী।

rĕl′-ĭ-quă-rỹ, *n.* A casket in which relics are kept; সাধু মহাপুরুষদিগের দেহাবশেষ প্রভৃতি রাখার জন্য পেটক বা আধার।

rē-liq-ui-ae (-lĭk-wĭ-ē), *n.* **1.** Remains; ধ্বংসাবশেষ, দেহাবশেষ। **2.** The fossil remains of plants and animals; বৃক্ষ এবং জন্তুর শিলীভূত অবশেষ। **3.** (*Bot.*) The withered remains of leaves decaying on stem; কাণ্ডের উপর ক্ষীয়মাণ শুষ্কপত্রাবশেষ।

rĕl′-ĭsh, *n.* **1.** Savour; taste; esp. a pleasing taste; রস; আস্বাদ, স্বাদ, তার; সুস্বাদ, সুতার। **2.** Liking; taste; inclination; as, he has great *relish* for music; অনুরাগ; রুচি, অভিরুচি, পসন্দ, সখ; আসক্তি। **3** An admixture; a tincture; "Without a shadow, a *relish*, a smutch, a tinge anything, the slightest that can be imagined of anger"; আভাস, আমেজ; লেশ, নাম গন্ধ। **4.** Something taken with food to increase the pleasure of eating; খাদ্যের সহিত গৃহীত রুচিবর্দ্ধক বস্তু, আচার, চাটনী, রাইবাটা, প্রভৃতি।

rĕl′-ĭsh, *v. i.* & *t.* **1.** To have a pleasing taste; to give gratification; সুস্বাদ হওয়া, সুতার হওয়া, প্রীতিপ্রদ হওয়া; মনোরঞ্জন করা। **2.** To have flavour; রস থাকা। **3.** To smack of; কোন কিছুর আভাস বা আমেজ থাকা। ***Verb t.*** **1.** To like the taste or flavour of; to taste or eat with pleasure; খাইতে ভাল লাগা; স্বাদ গ্রহণ করা, রসাস্বাদন করা, রুচির সহিত আহার করা। **2.** To give a relish or agreeable flavour or taste to; স্বাদু করা, সুস্বাদু করা, সুতার করা, রুচিজনক করা। **3.** To take pleasure or delight in; "Now I begin to *relish* your advice"; আনন্দ পাওয়া, সুখ পাওয়া, মজা লাগা, রসসম্ভোগ করা, ভাল লাগা।

rē-live′ (-lĭv), *v. i.* & *t.* To revive; পুনর্জীবিত হওয়া বা করা।

rē-load′ (-lōd), *v.t.* To load again, as a gun; বন্দুকাদিতে পুনরায় গুলি বারুদ ভরা।

rē-lū′-cĕnt, *adj.* (*Rare*) Shining; (কচিদ্ ব্যবহৃত) উজ্জ্বল, জ্যোতির্ম্ময়, সপ্রভ।

rē-lŭct′, *v. i.* **1.** To offer opposition; বাধাপ্রদান করা। **2.** To show reluctance; অসম্মতি প্রদর্শন করা।

rē-lŭc′-tănt, *adj.* **1.** (*Rare*) Struggling or resisting violently; (কচিদ্ ব্যবহৃত) প্রবলপ্রতিরোধকারী, সংগ্রামে রত। **2.** Unwilling; averse; অনিচ্ছুক, অনভিলাষী; নারাজ, অসম্মত। **3.** Proceeding from an unwilling mind; done or granted unwillingly; অনিচ্ছাপ্রসূত; অনিচ্ছাকৃত, অনিচ্ছাপ্রদত্ত। **—ly,** *adv.* **—tance,** *n.* Unwillingness; অনিচ্ছা, অনভিপ্রায়, অমত, অসম্মতি।

rē-lūme′, *v. t.* 1. To light anew ; পুনরায় আলোকিত করা, পুনরায় প্রকাশিত করা।

rē-lȳ′, *v. i.* To rest on ; to have confidence in ; নির্ভর করা ; বিশ্বাস থাকা, ভরসা থাকা।

rē-main′ (-mān), *v. i.* 1. To continue in a place or state ; থাকা, অবস্থান করা, রহা। 2. To stay or be left behind after others have gone ; to be left after a number or quantity has been removed or taken away ; অপর সকলে চলিয়া গেলে থাকা ; অবশিষ্ট থাকা, বাকী থাকা।

rē-main′ (-mān), *n.* 1. (Usu. *pl.*) Remainder ; remnant ; অবশিষ্ট, অবশিষ্টাংশ ; অবশেষ। 2. Relics ; ধ্বংসাবশেষ, স্মৃতিচিহ্ন। 3. A dead body ; মৃতদেহ, শব, দেহাবশেষ। 4. The literary works of dead author ; posthumous works; "The *remains* of Clement and Polycarp" ; পরলোকগতগ্রন্থকারের গ্রন্থসমূহ ; গ্রন্থকারের মৃত্যুর পর প্রকাশিত গ্রন্থ সমুহ।

rē-main′-dêr (-mān-), *n.* & *adj.* 1. That which remains ; অবশেষ, অবশিষ্টাংশ, শেষ ভাগ, অনুশয় (শ্রীঃ)। 2. (*Arith.*) The quantity left after subtraction ; (পাটীগণিত) অবশিষ্ট, বিয়োগশেষ, অন্তর (সাঃ পঃ), উত্তর (ঐ) শেষ (ঐ)। 3. (*Law*) An estate limited to take effect after another estate is determined ; (আইন) যে সম্পত্তি নির্দ্দিষ্ট কাল পর্য্যন্ত কোন ব্যক্তির ভোগে থাকার পরে অপর ব্যক্তির অধিকারে আসে, ভোগাবশেষ। [যদি কোন সম্পত্তির মালীক ঐ সম্পত্তি উইল বা দানপত্র দ্বারা ক কে যাবজ্জীবন ভোগের জন্য দেন এবং ক এর মৃত্যুর পর উক্ত সম্পত্তি চিরকালের জন্য খ এবং তাহার উত্তরাধিকারিগণের অধিকারে আসিবে এইরূপ ব্যবস্থা করেন তবে ঐ সম্পত্তিতে খ এর যে স্বার্থ তাহাকে ভোগাবশেষ (Remainder) বলা যায়।] 4. An edition the sale of which has practically ceased and which is cleared by the trader at a reduced price ; পুস্তকের যে সংস্করণের বিক্রয় কার্যতঃ প্রায় বন্ধ হইয়া আসিয়াছে এবং যাহা অল্প মূল্যে বিক্রয় পূর্ব্বক গুদাম সাবাড় করা হইয়া থাকে। ***Adj.*** Remaining ; অবশিষ্ট, বাকী, বক্রী। **Contingent remainder**—কোন সম্পত্তির মালীক যদি তদীয় উইল বা দানপত্রদ্বারা কোন ব্যক্তিবিশেষকে নির্দ্দিষ্ট কালের জন্য কোন সম্পত্তির ভোগদখলের অধিকার প্রদান করেন—এবং ঐ কালের পর বা ঐকালের পর সংঘটিত কোন অনিশ্চিত ঘটনার পর (যথা কোন ব্যক্তি বিদেশ হইতে আসিলে) অপর কোন অজ্ঞাত বা অনির্দ্দিষ্ট ব্যক্তি ঐ সম্পত্তি পাইবে এইরূপ ব্যবস্থা করেন—তবে ইহাকে অনিশ্চিত ভোগাবশেষ (contingent remainder) কহে। **Cross remainder**—যদি কোন সম্পত্তিতে দুই ব্যক্তির প্রত্যেকের পরস্পরের অংশে ভোগাবশেষ অধিকার থাকে (যথা এক ব্যক্তি নিঃসন্তান হইলে তাহার সম্পত্তির ভোগাবশেষ অপর ব্যক্তির অধিকারে আসিবে)—তবে ইহাকে ব্যত্যস্ত ভোগাবশেষ (cross remainder) কহে। **Remainder man** — কোন সম্পত্তির ভোগাবশেষের অধিকারী ব্যক্তি।

rē-make′, *v. t.* To make again ; পুনরায় গড়া, নূতন করিয়া গড়া।

rē-măn′, *v. t.* 1. To equip with fresh man ; নূতন লোক দ্বারা সজ্জিত করা। 2. To restore to courage ; পুনরায় সাহস প্রদান করা।

rē-mănd′, *v. t.* & *n.* 1. (*Rare*) To send back ; (ক্বচিদ্ব্যবহৃত) পুনরায় প্রেরণ করা। 2. To send back to jail as an accused party, in order to give time to collect more evidence against him ; হাজতে দেওয়া। ***Noun.*** Recommittal to custody ; হাজতে প্রেরণ।

rĕm′-ă-nĕnt, *adj.* 1. Remnant ; অবশিষ্ট, অবশেষ। 2. A parliamentary bill left over for another session ; পার্লেমেণ্ট মহাসভার পুনরধিবেশন কালে বিবেচিত হইবার জন্য যে প্রস্তাবিত আইন স্থগিত রাখা হয়।

rē-mär′-gĭn, *v. t.* 1. To furnish a book with a new margin ; পুস্তকের কিনারায় নূতন কিনারা লাগান।

rē-märk′, *v. t., i.* & *n.* 1. To observe ; লক্ষ্য করা, দৃষ্টি করা। 2. To mark by way of remark, comment or observation ; মন্তব্য করা। ***Verb i.*** To make comment upon ; মন্তব্য প্রকাশ করা। ***Noun.*** 1. Notice ; লক্ষ্যকরণ, লক্ষ্য। 2. Comment ; মন্তব্য।

rē-märk′-ă-ble (-bl), *adj.* 1. Worthy of notice ; দ্রষ্টব্য, প্রণিধানযোগ্য। 2. Extraordinary ; wonderful ; conspicuous ; distinguished ; অসাধারণ ; আশ্চর্য্য, অদ্ভুত, অপূর্ব্ব ; জাজ্বল্যমান ; প্রখ্যাত, বিখ্যাত, প্রসিদ্ধ। **—bly**, *adv.* **—ness**, *n.*

remarque, (*F.*), *n.* A mark, usu. a marginal sketch, indicating a certain state of the engraving plate ; চিহ্ন, সাধারণতঃ ক্ষোদিত ফলকের পার্শ্বে উৎকীর্ণ উহার কোন বিশেষ অবস্থাসূচক ক্ষুদ্র বিবরণ।

rē-măr′-ry (-ĭ), *v. t.* & *i.* To marry again ; পুনরায় বিবাহ করা, পুনরায় দারপরিগ্রহ করা। ***Verb i.*** To be married again ; পুনরায় বিবাহ হওয়া। **—ri-age**, *n.* Any marriage after the first ; পুনর্ব্বার দারপরিগ্রহ পুনর্ব্বিবাহ।

rē-mâst′, *v. t.* To furnish with a second mast or set of masts ; নূতন মাস্তুল বা মাস্তুলশ্রেণী লাগান।

rē-mē′-dĭ-ăl, *adj.* Affording a remedy ; প্রতীকারজনক, প্রতীকারক।

rĕm′-ē-dy, *n.* & *v. t.* 1. That which cures a disease ; রোগনাশক ঔষধ, রোগের প্রতীকারক ঔষধ। 2. Relief ; redress ; reparation ; কিনারা, চারা, উপায় ; প্রতীকার, প্রতিবিধান ; ক্ষতিপূরণ। ***Verb t.*** 1. (*Rare*) To cure ; (ক্বচিদ্ব্যবহৃত) আরাম করা, আরোগ্য করা। 2. To redress ; to make good ; প্রতীকার করা, প্রতিবিধান করা ; ক্ষতিপূরণ করা। **Re-me′-di-a-ble**, *adj.* That can be remedied ; প্রতীকার্য্য প্রতীকারশক্য।

rĕ-mĕm'-bĕr, *v. t.* **1.** To recollect ; to keep or bear in mind ; স্মরণ করা, মনে আনা ; স্মৃতিপথে জাগরূক রাখা, মনে রাখা। **2.** To bear in mind with gratitude, regard or reverence ; শ্রদ্ধা, ভক্তি বা কৃতজ্ঞতার সহিত স্মরণ রাখা। **3.** To convey greetings from one person to another ; as, *remember* me to your father ; সাদরসম্ভাষণ বা নমস্কার জানান। **4.** To keep in mind as entitled to a reward ; as, he *remembered* me in his will ; to reward ; to tip ; "He assured the hostler that he would *remember* him the next day" ; পুরস্কৃত করার যোগ্য বলিয়া মনে রাখা ; পুরস্কার দেওয়া ; বকশিশ দেওয়া। **5.** (*Rare*) To think of ; to consider , (কচিদ্-ব্যবহৃত) চিন্তা করা ; বিবেচনা করা। **6.** To mention in one's prayers ; প্রার্থনার সময় উল্লেখ করা। **–a-ble,** *adj.* Worthy of remembrance ; স্মরণীয়, স্মরণযোগ্য।

rĕ-mĕm'-brance (-brăns), *n.* **1.** The act of remembering ; memory ; স্মরণ ; স্মৃতি। **2.** The power or faculty of remembering ; স্মরণশক্তি, স্মৃতিশক্তি। **3.** The time over which memory extends ; as, it happened within my *remembrance* ; স্মরণকাল। **4.** A memento ; a souvenir ; "I desire your acceptance of a ring, a small *remembrance* of my father" ; স্মৃতিচিহ্ন, স্মরণচিহ্ন ; অভিজ্ঞান। **5.** (Usu. *pl.*) Greetings conveyed through a third person ; তৃতীয় ব্যক্তির দ্বারা জ্ঞাপিত অভিবাদনাদি, সাদরসম্ভাষণ, নমস্কার।

rĕ-mĕm'-branc'-ĕr, (-brăns-) *n.* **1.** One who, or that which, reminds ; স্মারক। **2** A memento ; স্মৃতিচিহ্ন। **3.** An officer of the Court of Exchequer ; ইংলণ্ডের উচ্চতম আদালতের কর্ম্মচারিবিশেষ। **City Remembrancer**—পার্লেমেণ্ট মহাসভায় লণ্ডন নগরের নাগরিক সমিতির প্রতিনিধি। **King's** or **Queen's Remembrancer**—যে কর্ম্মচারী রাজা বা রাণীর প্রাপ্য টাকা উশুল করেন। **Legal remembrancer** (or **Remembrancer of legal affairs)** — (ভারতবর্ষ) যে কর্ম্মচারী সরকার পক্ষে মোকদ্দমা স্থাপন করেন।

rĕ-mī'-grāte, *v. i.* To return to a former place or state ; পূর্ব্বস্থানে বা পূর্ব্বাবস্থায় প্রত্যাবৃত্ত হওয়া। **--gra'-tion,** *n.*

rĕ-mīnd', *v. t.* To put in mind ; স্মরণ করাইয়া দেওয়া, মনে করাইয়া দেওয়া।

rĕ-mīnd'-ĕr, *n.* **1.** One who, or that which, calls into the mind or designed to do so ; স্মারক, স্মারকলিপি, স্মারকপত্র, তাগিদ, তাগিদ চিঠি। **2.** (*Pl., Path.*) Secondary syphilitic symptoms ; (নিদানশাস্ত্র) উপদংশের দ্বিতীয় অবস্থার লক্ষণসমূহ।

rĕ-mīnd'-fûl, *adj.* **1.** Tending, or adapted to, remind ; স্মৃতিজনক, স্মৃতিজননশীল, স্মৃতিজননোপযোগী। **2.** Mindful ; মনোযোগী।

rĕm-i-nis'-cence (-sĕns), *n.* **1.** The act or power of remembering ; memory ; স্মরণ, স্মৃতিশক্তি ; স্মৃতি। **2.** A narration or relation of recollections ; as, the *reminiscences* of an octogenerian ; (*pl.*) the collective events remembered by one put into literary form ; স্মৃত ঘটনা সমূহের বর্ণন ; স্মৃতিকাহিনী। **3.** A feature, fact, etc. that reminds other thing ; as, there is a *reminiscence* of the Saturnalia in the modern carnival ; অন্য কোন বিষয়ের স্মৃতি উদ্দীপক বিষয়, লক্ষণ, ঘটনা, প্রভৃতি।

rĕm'-i-nis'-cĕnt, *adj.* & *n.* **1.** Having remembrance ; pertaining to, or characterized by, reminiscence ; স্মৃতিসমন্বিত ; স্মৃতিসম্বন্ধীয়, স্মৃত্যাত্মক। **2.** Reminding one of something else ; (কোন বিষয়ের) স্মৃতি উদ্দীপক, স্মৃতি উদ্বোধক। ***Noun.*** One who reminds or records past events ; যে ব্যক্তি অতীত ঘটনার স্মৃতি জাগরিত করে, যে ব্যক্তি অতীত ঘটনার স্মৃতি লিপিবদ্ধ করে, স্মৃতি-কাহিনী লেখক।

rĕ-mint', *v. t.* To mint again ; পুনরায় মুদ্রায় পরিণত করা।

rĕ-mise' (-mēz), *n.* & *v. t.* **1.** A surrender as of a claim ; মকুফ, ত্যাগ। **2.** (*Fencing*) A second thrust made after the first has missed ; (অসিক্রীড়া) প্রথম আঘাত না লাগিলে দ্বিতীয়বার যে আঘাত করা হয়। ***Verb t.*** To make over or surrender by a deed ; দলীল দ্বারা দান করা বা কোন বিষয়ের উপর দাবী ছাড়িয়া দেওয়া।

rĕ-miss', *adj.* **1.** Careless in the performance of duty or business ; negligent ; কর্ত্তব্যকার্য্যে অমনোযোগী ; অসাবধান, অনবহিত, অবহেলাকারী। **2.** Lacking force or energy ; slow ; as, a *remiss* pulse ; নিস্তেজ, শিথিল, শক্তিহীন, মৃদু, ঢিলা ; শিথিল। **–ly,** *adv.* **–ness,** *n.* The quality of being remiss ; অমনোযোগিতা, অনবধানতা, শৈথিল্য, ঢিলামি।

rĕ-mis'-si-ble (-ĭ-bl), *adj.* Capable of being remitted ; মার্জ্জনীয়, রেয়াৎ করার যোগ্য, মকুফ করার যোগ্য।

rĕ-mis'-sion (-mĭ-), *n.* **1.** Abatement ; উপশম, লাঘব, হ্রাস। **2.** The act of remitting or forgiving ; forgiveness ; ক্ষমা করণ ; ক্ষমা, মার্জ্জনা। **3.** Discharge or relinquishment of a debt, charge, claim, right, etc. ; মকুফ, রেয়াত, রেহাই, মাফ। **4.** Remittance ; টাকা প্রেরণ। **5.** (*Path.*) A temporary subsidence of the violence of a disease ; (নিদান) রোগের প্রাবল্যের ক্ষণিক হ্রাস বা বিরাম (হ: চ:)। **–sive,** *adj.*

rĕ-mit', *v. t.* & *i.* **1.** To relax in intensity ; মন্দীভূত করা, হ্রাস করা, ন্যূন করা। **2.** To refrain from exacting, enforcing or inflicting ; to relinquish ; মকুফ করা, রেয়াত করা, রেহাই দেওয়া, মাফ করা ; ছাড়িয়া দেওয়া। **3.** To forgive ; মার্জ্জনা করা, ক্ষমা করা। **4.** (*Rare*) To give or deliver up ; (ক্বচিদ্-ব্যবহৃত) ত্যাগ করা, ছাড়িয়া দেওয়া। **5.** To transmit money, etc. ; টাকা প্রভৃতি প্রেরণ করা। **6.** To postpone ; স্থগিত করা, মুলতবী করা। **7.** To refer ; to send to an inferior court ; কোন প্রামাণিক ব্যক্তি বা ব্যক্তি সমূহের নিকট অভিমতের জন্য প্রেরণ করা ; নিম্নতম আদালতে প্রেরণ করা। **8.** To put back into a previous state ; পূর্ব্বাবস্থায় স্থাপন করা। ***Verb i.*** **1.** To abate ; হ্রাস পাওয়া, মন্দীভূত হওয়া, প্রশমিত হওয়া। **2.** (*Med.*) To abate in violence for a time without intermission ; (ভৈষজ্য শাস্ত্র) স্বল্পকালের জন্য বিরাম হওয়া। **3.** To transmit money etc. ; টাকা প্রভৃতি প্রেরণ করা। **–tal,** *n.* **–tee′, –ter,** *ns.* **1.** One who remits ; প্রেরণকারী। **2.** One who sends a remittance · টাকা প্রভৃতি প্রেরণকারী, প্রেরক।

rē-mit-tance (-ăns), *n.* **1.** The act of transmitting money, bills, etc. ; টাকা, হুণ্ডী, প্রভৃতি প্রেরণ, অর্থ প্রেরণ। **2.** Money, bills, etc. sent to a person ; প্রেরিত অর্থ, হুণ্ডী প্রভৃতি। **Remittance-man** — যে নবাগত ঔপনিবেশিক মাতৃভূমি হইতে প্রেরিত অর্থ দ্বারা জীবিকা নির্ব্বাহ করে।

rē-mit′-tent (-ĕnt-), *adj.* & *n.* **1.** Temporarily ceasing ; স্বল্পকালের জন্য বিরামশীল, স্বল্পবিরাম। ***Noun.*** Same as REMITTENT FEVER. **Remittent-fever**—যে জ্বর একবারে ছাড়ে না, কিন্তু মগ্নাবস্থায় থাকিয়া পুনরায় প্রকাশ পায় (ডাক্তার হরিপ্রসাদ চক্রবর্ত্তী), বিষমজ্বর, অবিরামজ্বর (বোঃ), একজ্বর।

rē-mit′-ter (-ĕr), *n.* **1.** Remitting of a case to other court ; কোন মোকদ্দমা অপর আদালতে বিচারার্থ প্রেরণ। **2.** (*Law*) The restitution of one that obtains possession of a property under a defective title to his rights under a more valid title ; কোন ব্যক্তি কোন দোষযুক্ত স্বত্বের বলে কোন সম্পত্তির অধিকার পাইলে তাহাকে পুনরায় অধিকতর বিধিসিদ্ধ স্বত্বের বলে ঐ সম্পত্তির অধিকারে স্থাপন। **3.** (*Rare*) Restoration to rights ; (ক্বচিদ্ ব্যবহৃত) পুনরায় অধিকার প্রদান।

rĕm′-nănt, *n.* & *adj.* **1.** That which is left after the separation, removal or destruction of a part ; অবশিষ্ট, অবশিষ্টাংশ। **2.** A scrap ; a fragment ; টুকরা, টুকরা-টাকরা ; ক্ষুদ্র অংশ। **3.** A trace ; as, Ojein has no *remnants* of her former greatness ; লেশ, চিহ্ন। **4.** An end of a cloth etc. left after the main portion has been sold ; টুকরা কাপড়, কাপড়ের টুকরা। ***Adj.*** Remaining ; অবশিষ্ট, বাকী।

rē-mŏd′-ĕl, *v. t.* To model again ; to reconstruct ; নূতন আদর্শানুযায়ী গঠন বা নির্ম্মাণ করা ; পুনর্গঠন করা।

rē-mŏn′-ē-tīze, *v. t.* To restore to use as legal tender ; as, to *remonetize* gold ; পুনরায় মুদ্রাস্বরূপ প্রচলন করা। **–ti-za′-tion,** *n.*

rē-mŏn′-strance (-străns), *n.* **1.** Strong representation of reasons against a measure ; কোন ব্যবস্থার বিরুদ্ধে প্রবল হেতুপ্রদর্শন। **2.** Protest ; expostulation ; প্রতিবাদ ; অনুযোগ, আপত্তি। **The Grand Remonstrance** — প্রথম চার্লসের যথেচ্ছাচারমূলক আচরণের বিরুদ্ধে তীব্র প্রতিবাদপত্র — যাহা ১৬৪১ খৃঃ অব্দে পার্লেমেন্টের প্রাকৃতসভাকর্ত্তৃক রাজার নিকট প্রেরিত হয়।

rē-mŏn′-strate, *v. i.* & *t.* To expostulate ; to make an urgent appeal in opposition ; to urge strong reasons against ; as, his friends *remonstrated* regarding his habits ; অনুযোগ দেওয়া ; তীব্র প্রতিবাদ করা ; কোন কিছুর বিরুদ্ধে প্রবল যুক্তি প্রদর্শন করা। ***Verb t.*** To show clearly ; to protest against ; স্পষ্টরূপে দেখাইয়া দেওয়া ; প্রতিবাদ করা। **–strant,** *adj.* **–strant-ly,** *adv.* **–stra-tive,** *adj.* **–stra-tor,** *n.*

rē-mŏn′-tănt, *adj.* Flowering again ; পুনর্বিকাশী [বৎসরে একাধিক বার বিকাশমান গোলাপ সম্বন্ধে উক্ত হয়।]

rĕm′-ō-ră, *n.* **1.** The sucking-fish ; চোষক মৎস্য। [প্রাচীনকালে লোকের

Remora.

বিশ্বাস ছিল এই মৎস্য জাহাজের তলায় লাগিয়া উহার গতি স্থগিত করিতে পারিত।] **2.** (*Rare*) Obstacle ; (ক্বচিদ্ ব্যবহৃত) বাধা, প্রতিবন্ধক। **3.** (*Surg.*) An instrument to retain parts in place ; (ক্বচিদ্‌ব্যবহৃত) একপ্রকার যন্ত্র—যদ্দ্বারা ভগ্নঅস্থি প্রভৃতি স্বস্থানে রক্ষিত হয়।

rē-morse′ (-mŏrs), *n.* **1.** Bitter repentance ; compunction ; অনুশোচনা, অনুতাপ, পশ্চাত্তাপ, সন্তাপ, অনুশোক ; আত্মগ্লানি। **2.** (*Rare*) Sympathetic sorrow ; (ক্বচিদ্‌ব্যবহৃত) দরদ, সমবেদনা। **–ful,** *adj.* **–ful-ly,** *adv.* **–ful-ness,** *n.* **–less,** *adj.* Without remorse ; pitiless ; cruel ; আত্মগ্লানিশূন্য ; নির্দ্দয় ; নিষ্ঠুর, নিষ্করুণ।

rē-mōte′, *adj.* **1.** Distant in place or time ; সুদূর, দূরস্থ, অনাসন্ন, দূরস্থিত, দূরসংস্থ, অসন্নিহিত। **2.** Alien or distant in kind ; ভিন্নজাতীয়, ভিন্নরূপ। **3.** Distant in affinity or consanguinity ; as, a *remote* kinsman ; দূরসম্পর্কীয়। **4.** Retired ; secluded ; as, a *remote* village ; বিজন, নিভৃত ; নির্জ্জন। **5.** Slight ; as, there is a *remote* resemblance between them ; ঈষৎ,

সামান্য, অণুমাত্র। 6. Not directly producing an effect; as, the *remote* cause of a disease; পরোক্ষ, গৌণ। 7. (*Philos.*) Separate; abstracted; "Wherever the mind places itself by any thought either amongst, or *remote* from, all bodies"; নিঃসঙ্গ; প্রত্যাহৃত, বিবিক্ত, ব্যবহিত। **–ly,** *adv.* **–ness,** *n.*

rē-mould' (-mōld), *v. t.* To shape again or anew; পুনরায় গঠন করা, পুনরায় গড়া।

rē-mount' (-mownt), *n.* A supply of fresh horses for regiment etc.; a fresh horse; সেনাপল্টন প্রভৃতির জন্য নূতন অশ্ব সরবরাহ; নূতন অশ্ব।

rē-mount' (-mownt), *v. t. & i.* To mount again; পুনরায় আরোহণ করান, পুনরায় উঠান, পুনরায় চড়ান। ***Verb i.*** 1. To reascend; পুনরায় আরোহণ করা, পুনরায় চড়া। 2. To go back as in time or researches; "The shortest and the surest method of arriving at real knowledge...is to *remount* to first principles"; পশ্চাতে যাওয়া, গবেষণায় বা তত্ত্বানুসন্ধানে আদিতে বা মূলে যাওয়া।

rē-môv'-ā-ble (-bl), *adj. & n.* 1. Capable of being removed; স্থানান্তরকরণীয়, অপসার্য্য, অপনেয়, অপনয়নীয়, নিরসনীয়, বহিষ্কার্য্য। 2. Admitting of being removed from an office or station; কোন পদ হইতে রাজা কিম্বা কর্তৃপক্ষের ইচ্ছানুসারে অপসারণীয়। ***Noun.*** Same as REMOVABLE MAGISTRATE. **–bil'-i-ty,** *n.* **Removable Magistrate**—আয়র্লণ্ডের যে দণ্ডনায়ক রাজা কিম্বা কর্তৃপক্ষের ইচ্ছামাত্র কার্য্য হইতে অপসৃত হইতে পারেন।

rē-môv'-āl, *n.* 1. The act of taking away; change of place; অপসারণ, দূরীকরণ, স্থানান্তরনয়ন, উচ্ছিত্তি (সাংখ্য), অপনোদন; স্থানান্তর গমন। 2. The act of displacing from an office; পদচ্যুতকরণ। 3. Murder; সরান (cf. আপনি যদি হুকুম করেন তবে লোকটাকে সরাইয়া দিতে আর কতক্ষণ?)।

rē-môve', *v. t. & i.* 1. To cause to change place; স্থানান্তরিত করা, স্থানচ্যুত করা। 2. To displace from an office; as, to *remove* a clerk; কর্ম্মচ্যুত করা, পদচ্যুত করা, জবাব দেওয়া, ছাড়াইয়া দেওয়া (*colloq.*)। 3. To cause to leave or cease to be; to take off; তাড়ান, দূর করা, সরান; নিরাকৃত করা, ঘুচান অপনোদন করা, অপনীত করা। 4. To kill; as, to *remove* a man by poison; নিকাশ করা, সরান। 5. (*Law*) To carry from one court to another; (আইন) মোকদ্দমা অন্য আদালতে উঠাইয়া নেওয়া। ***Verb i.*** To move from one place to another; to change the place of residence; as, to *remove* from Calcutta to Dacca; স্থানান্তরিত হওয়া, একস্থান হইতে অন্য স্থানে যাওয়া, স্থান ত্যাগ করা; বাসস্থান পরিবর্ত্তন করা। **–moved',** *p. p.* 1. Remote; দূরবর্ত্তী। 2. Distant in relationship by a certain degree of descent; সম্পর্কে নির্দ্দিষ্টসংখ্যক পুরুষ অন্তর। 3. Displaced; কর্ম্মচ্যুত, পদচ্যুত। 4. Changed in place; স্থানান্তরিত, স্থানচ্যুত। **A first cousin once removed**—খুড়তত ভাই, পিসতত ভাই, প্রভৃতির সন্তান, অথবা পিতা বা মাতার খুড়তত ভাই, পিসতত ভাই বা ভগ্নী প্রভৃতি। **A first cousin twice removed**—খুড়তত ভাই, পিসতত ভাই বা ভগ্নী প্রভৃতির নাতি বা নাতিনী, অথবা পিতামহ বা মাতামহ প্রভৃতির খুড়তত, পিসতত ভাই, ভগ্নী, প্রভৃতি।

rē-môve', *n.* 1. A class in certain schools; "He is placed by the headmaster in some class, division or *remove*"; কোন কোন বিদ্যালয়ের শ্রেণী। 2. Promotion from one class to another; বিদ্যালয়ের একশ্রেণী হইতে অন্য শ্রেণীতে উন্নয়ন। 3. A dish removed from table to make room for another; অপর স্থালীর স্থান করার জন্য মেজ হইতে যে ব্যঞ্জন-পাত্র সরান হয়। 4. A step or degree in any scale of gradation; as, a cousin in the first *remove*: "A postertity that lies many *removes* from us"; পুরুষ, ধাপ, সিঁড়ি, ক্রম। 5. (*Rare*) Change of residence; removal; (ক্বচিদ্ব্যবহৃত) বাসস্থানপরিবর্ত্তন; স্থানান্তরগমন। 6. (*Rare*) Distance; (ক্বচিদ্ব্যবহৃত) দূরত্ব। 7. The act of resetting a horse's shoe; ঘোড়ার নাল খুলিয়া খুর পরিষ্কার করার পর উহা পুনরায় লাগানি।

rē-mū'-nēr-āte, *v. t.* 1. To reward; পুরস্কার দেওয়া, পারিতোষিক দেওয়া, পুরস্কৃত করা। 2. To requite; প্রতিদান দেওয়া। **–a'-tion,** *n.* 1. The act of remunerating; পুরস্কার-প্রদান, প্রতিদান। 2. Recompense; reward; পুরস্কার; পারিতোষিক। **–a-tive,** *adj.* Lucrative; লাভজনক, আয়জনক। **–a-tive-ly,** *adv.* **–a-tive-ness,** *n.*

rēn-ais-sance' (-ās-sâns), *n.* 1. The revival of art and literature in Europe under the influence of classical models which began in Italy in the 14th century and spread in the 16th century to France and Northern Europe; গ্রীক ও রোমান আদর্শের প্রভাবে ইয়ুরোপের সাহিত্য ও শিল্পজগতে নবযুগের অভ্যুদয়, ইয়ুরোপের নবজাগরণ, নবীন ইয়ুরোপের জন্ম, রেনেশাঁস [ইয়ুরোপে যখন একদিন মানুষের হৃদয়প্রবৃত্তিকে অত্যন্ত সংযত ও পীড়িত করার দিন ঘুচিয়া গিয়া তাহার প্রবল প্রতিক্রিয়াস্বরূপ রেনেশাঁসের যুগ আসিয়াছিল সেক্সপিয়ারের সমসাময়িক কালের নাট্যসাহিত্য সেই বিপ্লবের দিনেরই নৃত্যলীলা—জীবনস্মৃতি (রবীন্দ্রনাথ)।] [মধ্যযুগের কুসংস্কারতমসাচ্ছন্ন ইয়ুরোপে সাহিত্য, ললিতকলা, ধর্ম্ম, রাজনীতি, নীতিবিজ্ঞান, প্রভৃতির নব অভ্যুদয়কে Renaissance বা নবযুগারম্ভ কহে।

ইতালীদেশে সাহিত্যে Petrarch, Boccaccio, প্রভৃতি; ললিতকলায় Raphael, Michael Angelo, প্রভৃতি, এই নবযুগের প্রবর্ত্তন করেন। এই নবজাগরণের প্রভাব ক্রমে ফ্রান্স, ইংলণ্ড, জর্ম্মণী, প্রভৃতি দেশে বিস্তার লাভ করে। "মানবাত্মা চিরমুক্ত" এই মহাবাণীর গম্ভীর মন্দ্রে এই সময়ে ইয়ুরোপীয় জাতিসংঘ যুগব্যাপী মহানিদ্রা হইতে প্রবুদ্ধ হইয়া উঠে। জনৈক প্রসিদ্ধ লেখকের মতে নবযুগারম্ভের প্রকৃত অর্থ—স্বাধীনতার নবজন্ম। এই সময়ে মানবাত্মা ললিতকলার ভিতর দিয়া মানবদেহের ও বহির্জগতের সৌন্দর্য্য আস্বাদন করে। বিজ্ঞানে প্রজ্ঞার এবং ধর্ম্মে ধর্ম্মবুদ্ধির অবাধ প্রভাব প্রতিষ্ঠিত হয়। রাজনৈতিক স্বাধীনতার বীজ এই সময়েই উপ্ত হয়। গ্রীক ও রোমান সাহিত্য ও ললিতকলার প্রভাবেই এই নবযুগের অভ্যুদয়; এবং এই কালে কি শিল্পে, কি সাহিত্যে, কি ভাস্কর্য্যে প্রাচীন ও নবীনের সমন্বয়ে অপূর্ব্ব মূর্ত্তি, অপূর্ব্ব সৌধ ও অপূর্ব্ব গ্রন্থনিচয় সৃষ্ট ও রচিত হইয়া মানবমণ্ডলীকে এক নবজগতের পরমাশ্চর্য্য শোভা ও সম্পদের অধিকারী করে। [See J. A. Symond's *Italian Renaissance*; J. D. Symon's and Bensusan's *The Renaissance and its Makers.*] 2. Any revival of art, literature; as, *renaissance* of the Bengali literature; সাহিত্য, শিল্প, প্রভৃতির নব-অভ্যুদয়, নবজাগরণ, নবযুগারম্ভ, নবযুগ, প্রতিভাপুনঃপ্রদীপ্তি (আর্য্যাবর্ত্ত), নবজনন (হিঃ কোঃ)। **–sant,** *adj.* **Renaissance architecture**—গ্রীক ও রোমান স্থাপত্যরিতীর প্রভাবে ইতালীদেশে পঞ্চদশ শতাব্দীর প্রথমভাগে প্রবর্ত্তিত স্থাপত্যশিল্পের নূতন ধারা।

rē′-năl, *adj.* Of, or pertaining to, the kidneys; মূত্রাশয়সম্পর্কীয়।

rē-nāme′, *v. t.* To give a new name to; নূতন নাম দেওয়া, পুনর্নামকরণ করা।

rĕn′-ărd, *n.* A fox (a name used in fables); খেঁকশেয়াল, শেয়াল মামা।

rē-năs-cence′ (-sĕns), *n.* 1. Rebirth; নবজীবন। 2. Same as RENAISSANCE (which see).

rĕn-coun′-têr (-cown), **–cŏn′-tre** (-têr), *ns.* 1. Encounter; duel; a collision; সম্মুখ যুদ্ধ; দ্বন্দ্বযুদ্ধ; সংঘর্ষ, সম্মর্দ। 2. An unexpected meeting; হঠাৎ দেখা, অপ্রত্যাশিত মিলন।

rĕnd, *v. t.* & *i.* 1. To tear asunder; to split; চিরিয়া ফেলা, ছিঁড়া; বিদীর্ণ করা, বিদারণ করা, ভেদ করা, বিপাটিত করা, ফাঁড়া। 2. To convert wood into lath; চেলা করা। ***Verb i.*** To be rent or torn asunder; বিদীর্ণ হওয়া, ফাটা। **To rend the heart**—To break the heart; হৃদয় বিদীর্ণ করা, বুক ফাটান।

rĕn′-dêr, *v. t., i.* & *n.* 1. To pay or give back; to give in return; to give back by reflection; প্রতিদান করা; প্রত্যর্পণ করা, ফিরাইয়া দেওয়া; প্রতিবিম্বিত করা। 2. To afford; to give; as, to *render* thanks; দেওয়া; প্রদান করা। 3. To translate, as from one language to another; অনুবাদ করা, অনূদিত করা, ভাষান্তরিত করা, তর্জ্জমা করা। 4. To give up; to surrender; পরিত্যাগ করা; সমর্পণ করা। 5. To reproduce, represent or depict esp. by painting, music, or the like; as, to *render* a scene felicitously; সঙ্গীত, চিত্রশিল্প, প্রভৃতির সাহায্যে বর্ণিত বা চিত্রিত করা। 6. To exhibit the meaning, force or spirit of; তাৎপর্য্য, মর্ম্ম বা অন্তর্নিহিত ভাব প্রদর্শন করা। 7. To submit to for approval or consideration; to send in account etc.; অনুমোদন বা বিবেচনার জন্য পেশ করা; হিসাব প্রেরণ করা। 8. To invest with qualities; কোনরূপ গুণসম্পন্ন করা, সমন্বিত করা। 9. To cause to be; as, to *render* one old; to convert; সংঘটন করা; পরিণত করা। 10. To melt; as, to *render* fat; to boil down and clarify; as, to *render* oil; গালান; সিদ্ধ করিয়া পরিস্কার করা। 11. To recover with a first coat; to plaster; প্রথম পোঁচড়া দেওয়া; আস্তর করা। ***Verb i.*** Same as TO REEVE (which see.) ***Noun.*** A coat of plaster; আস্তর। **–ing,** *n*

rĕn′-dêr-sĕt, *v. t., adj.* & *n.* To plaster with two coats; দুই পোঁচ আস্তর দেওয়া। ***Adj.*** Designating work in which there are only two coats; দুই পোঁচ আস্তরের কাজসূচক। ***Noun.*** Plastering of two coats; দুই পোঁচ আস্তর।

rĕn′-dez-vous (-dĕ-vô), *n., v. i.* & *t.* A place appointed for meeting; a place at which persons customarily meet; esp. a place where troops or ships of war assemble to join company; মিলনস্থলী, সম্মিলনস্থান, সমাগমস্থলী, সঙ্কেতস্থান; আড্ডা; সৈন্য, রণপোতশ্রেণী, প্রভৃতির সমাগম স্থান। ***Verb i. & t.*** To assemble or meet together at a place, esp. by appointment; সঙ্কেতানুসারে মিলা, কোন স্থানে মিলিত হওয়া বা মিলিত করা, আড্ডায় একত্র হওয়া।

rĕn-dĭ′-tion, *n.* 1. (*Rare*) Surrender of a fort etc.; (ক্বচিদ্ব্যবহৃত) শত্রুহস্তে দুর্গ প্রভৃতি সমর্পণ, আত্মসমর্পণ। 2. (*U. S.*) Translation; (মার্কিণ যুক্তরাজ্যে) অনুবাদ, তর্জ্জমা। 3. (*U. S.*) The art of reproducing artistically; (মার্কিণ যুক্তরাজ্যে) সঙ্গীত, শিল্পকলা, প্রভৃতির সাহায্যে প্রদর্শন।

rĕn′-ē-gāde, *n.* & *v. i.* 1. An apostate from a religious faith; ধর্ম্মত্যাগী ব্যক্তি, স্বধর্ম্মত্যাগী, স্বধর্ম্মভ্রষ্ট ব্যক্তি। 2. One who deserts a party and joins another; যে ব্যক্তি স্বদল ত্যাগ করিয়া অপর দলে যোগপ্রদান করে, স্বপক্ষত্যাগী ব্যক্তি। ***Verb i.*** To turn renegade; স্বধর্ম্মত্যাগ করা, স্বপক্ষ ত্যাগ করা।

rē-new′ (-nü), *v. t.* & *i.* 1. To make new or fresh again; to revive; পুনরায় নবীন করা, পুনরায় সতেজ করা, পুনর্নবীভূত করা; পুনরুজ্জীবিত করা। 2. To make again;

to grant again ; as, to *renew* a treaty or lease ; পুনরায় নূতন করিয়া করা ; পুনরায় দেওয়া । 3. To recommence ; as, to *renew* the fight ; পুনরায় আরম্ভ করা । 4. To repeat ; "The birds their notes, *renew*" ; পুনরাবৃত্তি করা, পাল্টাইয়া বলা বা গাওয়া, সুর ভাঁজা । 5. To regenerate spiritually ; নবজীবন প্রদান করা, দ্বিজত্বপ্রদান করা । 6. To restore or re-establish ; "Man *renews* himself at the same time as the spirit *renews* him ; প্রত্যর্পণ করা, পুনঃ প্রতিষ্ঠা করা । ***Verb i.*** 1. (*Rare*) To grow new again ; (ক্বচিদ্ ব্যবহৃত) পুনরায় নবীন হওয়া । 2. To begin again ; পুনরায় আরম্ভ করা । **—a-ble,** *adj.* **—al,** *n.*

rĕn'-i-fôrm, *adj.* Kidney-shaped ; as, a *reniform* leaf ; মূত্রাশয়াকৃতি, বৃক্কাকার ।

rĕn'-nĕt *n.* 1. A mass of curdled milk found in the stomach of an unweaned calf used in making cheese ; the inner membrane of the fourth stomach of the calf or an infusion or preparation from it used for coagulating milk ; দুগ্ধপায়ী বৎসের পাকস্থলীতে প্রাপ্ত দধির মত পদার্থ—যাহা পনীর প্রস্তুতে ব্যবহৃত হয় ; গোবৎসের চতুর্থ পাকস্থলীর অন্তর্ঝিল্লী বা উহার কাথ বা উহা হইতে প্রস্তুত কোন পদার্থ—যদ্দারা দুগ্ধ জমান হয় । 2. Anything used in curdling milk ; দুগ্ধ জমাইবার জন্য ব্যবহৃত কোন বস্তু, সাঁচ ।

rĕn'-nĕt *n.* Kinds of dessert apple ; বিভিন্নপ্রকার সেওফল — যাহা ভোজনের পর আহার করা হয় ।

rĕn'-nin (-ĭn), *n.* (*Chem.* & *Physiol.*) A milk curdling ferment found in the gastric juice of men and other higher animals; মনুষ্য এবং অন্যান্য উচ্চ শ্রেণীর জীবের পাচকরসে প্রাপ্ত একপ্রকার পদার্থ—যাহার স্পর্শে দুগ্ধ জমিয়া যায় ।

rē-nounce' (-nowns), *v. t., i.* & *n.* 1. To disown ; to disclaim ; অস্বীকার করা ; (দাবী) পরিত্যাগ করা । 2. To forsake ; to cast off ; to disclaim relationship ; as, to *renounce* a son ; পরিত্যাগ করা, ত্যাজ্য করা ; বর্জ্জন করা, ত্যাগ করা ; সম্বন্ধচ্ছিন্ন করা । 3. (*Card-playing*) To play a card of different suit from that which has been led ; (তাস খেলায়) পাশ দেওয়া । ***Verb i.*** (*Card playing*) Not to follow suit ; (তাস খেলায়) পাশ দেওয়া । ***Noun.*** (*Card playing*) A revoke ; a chance of renouncing ; (তাস খেলায়) পাশ দেওন ; পাশ দেওয়ার সুযোগ । **—ment,** *n.* **To renounce the world**—To withdraw from worldly interest in order to lead the life of an ascetic ; সংসার ত্যাগ করা, সন্ন্যাস গ্রহণ করা ।

rĕn'-ō-vāte, *v. t.* 1. To renew ; to restore to freshness ; to repair ; নূতন করা, নবীভূত করা ; নবীন করা ; মেরামত করা, জীর্ণসংস্কার করা । 2. To refresh ; পুনরায় সতেজ করা । **—va'-tion,** *n.* 1. The act of renovating or the state of being renovated ; নবীকরণ, নবতা, নবীনতা । 2. Spiritual regeneration ; "External reformation is nothing without internal *renovation*" ; নবজীবন প্রদান । **—va-tor,** *n.*

rē-nown', *n.* Fame ; celebrity ; খ্যাতি, যশঃ ; কীর্ত্তি, প্রসিদ্ধি ।

rē-nowned' (-nownd), *adj.* Famous ; বিখ্যাত, প্রসিদ্ধ, কীর্ত্তিমান, প্রতিষ্ঠাবান, লব্ধপ্রতিষ্ঠ, প্রখ্যাতনামা, নামজাদা ।

rĕnt, *pt.* & *pp.* of REND (which see.)

rĕnt, *n.* 1. An opening made by rending or tearing ; a fissure ; a cleft ; ফাঁক, ফাটা, চির ; ফাটল ; ছিন্ন স্থান, টুটা (কাপড়ের) । 2. A schism ; as, a *rent* in the church ; ভেদ, বিচ্ছেদ, দলাদলি ।

rĕnt, *n., v.t.* & *i.* 1. Money or anything valuable payable periodically for use or occupation of lands, houses, property of any kind or tenements ; খাজানা, জমা । 2. A fixed annual return, usually, but not necessarily in money, issuing out of lands or tenements corporeal ; ভূমির বার্ষিক আয় । 3. Payment for hire of machinery etc. ; কল প্রভৃতির ভাড়া বাবত যে টাকা দেওয়া হয় । ***Verb t.*** 1. To take or occupy for rent ; খাজানা দিয়া গ্রহণ করা, খাজানা দিয়া ভোগ করা । 2. To grant the possession and enjoyment of for rent ; খাজানা লইয়া পত্তন করা, ভোগ দখল করিতে দেওয়া । ***Verb i.*** To be let or leased for rent ; খাজানা লইয়া প্রজাবিলী করা বা ভোগ দখল করিতে দেওয়া । **Rent'-a-ble,** *adj.* **Rent-arrear**—বাকী খাজানা । **Rent-charge**—ভূমির আয়ের যে অংশ দানপত্রাদি দ্বারা মালিক ভিন্ন অন্য কোন ব্যক্তির নামে লিখিয়া দেওয়া হয় । **Rent-day**—খাজানা আদায়ের দিন, পুণ্যাহ । **Rent-free**—লাখেরাজ । **Rent-receipt** — দাখিলা । **Rent-roll** — খাজানার তালিকা, জমাবন্দী, তৌজী । **Rent service**—খাজানার পরিবর্ত্তে কাজ করিয়া দিবে এই সর্ত্তে ভূমি গ্রহণের প্রথা, চাকরাণ জমি গ্রহণের প্রথা ।

rĕnt'-ăl, *n.* 1. A rent-roll ; তৌজী, জমাবন্দী । 2. Income from rents ; খাজানার আয় । 3. Rent ; খাজানা । **Rental-right**—অতি অল্প খাজানায় ভূমি বন্দোবস্ত দেওয়ার রীতি ।

rente, (*F.*), *n.* 1. French Government stock ; ফরাসীদেশের কোম্পানীর কাগজ । 2. Annual income from annuities, dividends, etc. ; বার্ষিক বৃত্তি, লভ্যাংশ, কোম্পানীর কাগজের সুদ, প্রভৃতি হইতে বার্ষিক আয় ।

rentier, (*F.*), *n.* One who has fixed income as from lands, stock, etc.; যে ব্যক্তির ভূমি, কোম্পানীর কাগজ, প্রভৃতি হইতে স্থায়ী আয় আছে।

rē-nŭm′-bêr, *v. t.* To number again, to change numbers of series etc.; পুনরায় একাদিক্রমে সংখ্যা দেওয়া; ক্রমবিন্যস্ত বস্তু সমূহের ক্রমিক সংখ্যার পরিবর্তন করা।

rē-nŭn-ĉi-ā′-tion, *n.* **1.** Disclaiming; rejection; দাবীত্যাগ; পরিত্যাগ, পরিবর্জন, নিরাকৃতি। **2.** The act of renouncing the world, passions, etc.; self-denial; ত্যাগ, বৈরাগ্য (বেদান্ত), ন্যাস (ডিউসেন), সন্ন্যাসগ্রহণ, সংসারত্যাগ; আত্মত্যাগ। **—nun′-ci-a-tive, —nun′-ci-a-to-ry**, *adjs.*

rē-ŏc′-cū-pȳ, *v. t.* To occupy again; পুনরায় অধিকার করা।

rē-ō′-pĕn, *v. t.* **1.** To open again; পুনরায় খোলা। **2.** To resume the discussion of something; কোন বিষয় পুনরায় আলোচনা করা। **3.** To begin firing again; পুনরায় গোলাগুলি বর্ষণ করিতে আরম্ভ করা।

rē-ŏr-dain′ (-dān), *v. t.* To ordain again; পুনরায় দীক্ষিত করা। **—di-na′-tion**, *n.*

rē-ŏr′-găn-īze, *v. t.* To reduce again to an organized condition; পুনরায় বৃ্যহবদ্ধ করা, পুনরায় ব্যবস্থাবদ্ধ করা। **—i-za′-tion**, *n.* The act of reorganizing; as, the *reorganization* of the army; পুনরায় বৃ্যহবদ্ধ করণ, পুনরায় ব্যবস্থাবদ্ধকরণ।

rĕp rĕpp, rĕps, *ns.* A dress fabric having a ribbed or corded appearance, the ribs being transverse; পোষাক তৈরীর জন্য একপ্রকার শিরাল কাপড়।

rĕp, *n.* (*School slang*) Verse, etc. learnt by heart (*Abbr.* of *repetition*); (বিদ্যালয়ের ইতরভাষায়) যে কবিতা প্রভৃতি কণ্ঠস্থ করা হয়।

rĕp, *n.* (*Slang*) A man of loose character; (ইতর ভাষায়) লোচ্চা।

rē-pāĉe′, *v. t.* To pace back or again; পশ্চাতে যাওয়া।

rē-păck′, *v. t.* To pack a second time; পুনরায় প্যাক করা, পুনরায় বস্তাবন্দী করা।

rē-pā′-găn-īze, *v. t.* & *i.* To make or become pagan again; পুনরায় পৌত্তলিক করা বা হওয়া। **—i-za′-tion**, *n.*

rē-paint′ (-pānt), *v. t.* & *n.* To paint again; পুনরায় চিত্রিত করা, পুনরায় রঙ দেওয়া। ***Noun.*** A substance used in repainting; দ্বিতীয়বার রঙ দিতে যে পদার্থ ব্যবহৃত হয়।

rē-pair′ (-pār), *v. t.* **1.** To restore to a sound or good state after decay, injury, dilapidation or partial ruin; মেরামত করা, জীর্ণসংস্কার করা। **2.** To compensate; as, to *repair* a loss; to remedy; ক্ষতিপূরণ করা; প্রতিবিধান করা, প্রতীকার করা। **—a-ble**, *adj.*

rē-pair′ (-pār), *n.* **1.** The act of repairing; restoration to a sound or good state after decay, dilapidation, etc.; মেরামতকরণ; মেরামত, জীর্ণসংস্কার, জীর্ণোদ্ধার। **2.** State or condition as regards want of repairing; as, the house is in bad *repair*; মেরামত। **Out of repairs**—বে-মেরামত।

rē-pair′ (-pār), *v. i.* & *n.* To go to some particular place; to betake oneself; as, to *repair* to a sanctuary for protection; কোন নির্দ্দিষ্ট স্থানে গমন করা; আশ্রয় নেওয়া। ***Noun.*** Haunt; আড্ডা, সমাগমস্থান।

rē-pănd′, *adj.* (*Bot.* & *Zool.*) With undulating margin; as, *repand* leaf; undulating; (উদ্ভিদ্‌বিদ্যা এবং জন্তুবিদ্যা), তরঙ্গায়িতপ্রান্তবিশিষ্ট, বক্রপ্রান্ত (সাঃ পঃ); তরঙ্গায়িত।

rē-pa′-pêr (-pĕ-), *v. i.* To paper again; পুনরায় কাগজ দ্বারা আচ্ছাদন করা।

rĕp′-ă-ră-ble (-bl), *adj.* Capable of being made good; as, a *reparable* loss; পূরণীয়, পূরণযোগ্য।

rĕp-ă-rā′-tion, *n.* **1.** The act of repairing; repair; মেরামতকরণ; মেরামত। **2.** Amends; as, *reparation* for a wrong or injury; প্রতিবিধান।

rĕp-ăr-tee′ (-tē), *n.* & *v. i.* A smart, ready and witty reply; সরস উত্তর, চটুল উত্তর, ফষ্টি, চটপট উত্তর, বাক্‌কেলী (দশকুঃ)। ***Verb i.*** (*Rare*) To make a repartee; (কচিদ্ ব্যবহৃত) চটুল উত্তর দেওয়া, সরস এবং উপস্থিত প্রত্যুত্তর দেওয়া, চটপট উত্তর দেওয়া।

rē-păr-tĭ′-tion, *n.* A division into smaller parts; a fresh partition; অবান্তর বিভাগ; পুনর্বিভাগ।

rē-păss′, *v. t.* & *i.* **1.** To pass, or go past again; পুনরায় অতিক্রম করা। **2.** To recross; পুনরায় পার হওয়া। **3.** To pass (a bill, resolution, etc.) again; পুনরায় বিধিবদ্ধ করা। **4.** To cause to pass again; পুনরায় প্রবেশ করান। ***Verb i.*** To pass or go back; পুনরায় অতিক্রম করা।

rē-păst′, *n.* **1.** The act of taking food; আহার, ভোজন। **2.** Food; খাদ্য, আহার্য্য।

rē-pā′-trĭ-āte, *v. t.* & *i.* To restore to one's country; স্বদেশে পুনঃ প্রেরণ করা। ***Verb i.*** To return to one's native land; স্বদেশে প্রত্যাবর্তন করা, মাতৃভূমিতে প্রত্যাগমন করা। **—a′-tion**, *n.* Return or restoration to one's own country; "The Porte could not afford the outlay for the *repatriation* of the refugee"; পুনরায় স্বদেশে প্রেরণ, স্বদেশে প্রত্যাগমন।

rē-pay′ (-pā), *v. t.* & *i.* **1.** To pay back; পরিশোধ করা। **2.** To return; to retaliate; as, to *repay* an injury; প্রতিদান দেওয়া; প্রতিশোধ দেওয়া, প্রতিফল দেওয়া, দাদ তোলা (*colloq.*)। ***Verb i.*** To make repayment or return ; to requite either good or evil ; "Vengeance is mine ; I will *repay*, saith the Lord" ; পরিশোধ করা; প্রতিদান দেওয়া, প্রতিশোধ লওয়া। **—ment,** *n.*

rē-peal' (-pēl), *v. t.* & *n.* To revoke ; to annul ; রদ করা ; রহিত করা, বাতিল করা। ***Noun.*** Abrogation; as the *repeal* of the Arms Act ; বাতিল, খণ্ডন, রদ। **—er,** *n.* One who repeals ; esp. one who agitates for a repeal of the Union between Ireland and England ; রদকারী ; বিশেষতঃ গ্রেটব্রিটেনের সহিত আয়র্লণ্ডের সংযোগ ছেদনের জন্য আন্দোলনকারী ব্যক্তি। **Repeal of the Union**—গ্রেটব্রিটেনের সহিত আয়র্লণ্ডের সংযোগ বিচ্ছিন্ন করার জন্য ১৮১০ খৃঃ অব্দে যে আন্দোলনের সূত্রপাত হয়।

rē-peat' (-pēt), *v. t., i.* & *n.* **1.** To do or perform a second time ; পুনরায় করা, আবার করা। **2.** To recite ; to say again ; to relate ; পুনরাবৃত্তি করা, আওড়ান ; ফের বলা, পুনরুক্তি করা ; বিবৃত করা। **3.** (*Scotch Law*) To restore ; to refund ; (স্কটলণ্ডের আইন) প্রত্যর্পণ করা ; টাকা ফিরাইয়া দেওয়া। **4.** To reproduce the signal made by an admiral ; রণপোতাধ্যক্ষকর্তৃক প্রদর্শিত সঙ্কেত পুনরায় প্রদর্শন করা। **5.** To cause to occur or appear ; সংঘটন করা, পুনরায় আনা। ***Verb i.*** **1.** To say or do again ; পুনরায় করা, পুনরায় বলা, পুনরুক্তি করা। **2.** To recur ; পুনরাগত হওয়া, পুনঃ পুনঃ আসা। **3.** To strike the hours ; as, a *repeating* timepiece ; (ঘড়ী সম্বন্ধে) ঘণ্টায় ঘণ্টায় বাজা। **4.** (Of a fire-arm) To fire several shots without reloading ; as, a *repeating* rifle ; (বন্দুক, পিস্তলাদি সম্বন্ধে) একবার গুলিবারুদ ভরিলে কয়েকবার আওয়াজ হওয়া। ***Noun.*** **1.** Repetition ; পুনরুক্তি, পুনঃকথন, পুনঃসম্পাদন। **2.** That which is repeated ; পুনরুক্ত, পুনঃকথিত বা পুনঃসম্পাদিত বিষয়। **3.** (*Mus.*) A passage to be repeated ; a sign that a movement or a part of movement is to be twice performed ; পুনর্ব্বার গেয় অংশ ; যে কোন চাল বা চালের অংশ দোহারা করিতে হইবে—তাহা নির্দ্দেশ করার জন্য চিহ্ন। **4.** A duplicate of something ; কোন বস্তুর প্রতিরূপ, প্রতিলিপি। **5.** (*Commer.*) A second or fresh supply of goods similar to one previously supplied ; an order for such a supply ; পূর্ব্বের জিনিষের অনুরূপ জিনিষ দ্বিতীয়বার যোগানি ; ঐরূপ যোগানির জন্য ফরমায়েস। **6.** The repetition of a figure in a design on cloth, paper, etc. ; কাপড় কাগজ, প্রভৃতির উপর যে কোন এক নমুনা সর্ব্বত্র অঙ্কিত থাকে। **—a-ble,** *adj.* **—ed-ly,** *adv.* Again and again ; পুনঃ পুনঃ, বারম্বার, বারবার, ভুয়োভূয়ঃ, ফিরিয়া ফিরিয়া, মুহুর্মুহুঃ, ঘড়ি ঘড়ি (*colloq.*)। **—er,** *n.* **1.** One who repeats ; a reciter ; পুনরুক্তিকারী, পুনঃসম্পাদনকারী; পুনরায় আবৃত্তিকারী। **2.** A watch that strikes the time upon pressure of a spring ; যে টেঁকঘড়ীর কোন দমে চাপ দিলে ঘণ্টা প্রভৃতি বাজে। **3.** (America) A fraudulent voter ; আমেরিকার প্রতারক ভোটদাতা। **4.** (*Arith.*) An indeterminate decimal in which the same figure continually recurs ; (পাটীগণিত) পৌনঃপুনিক দশমিক। **5.** A fire-arm that may be discharged several times in quick succession without reloading ; একবার বারুদ গুলি ভরিয়া যে আগ্নেয়াস্ত্র প্রভৃতি উপর্য্যুপরি কয়েক বার আওয়াজ করা যায়। **6.** (*Teleg.*) A device for retransmitting messages ; (তাড়িতবার্ত্তা) সংবাদ পুনঃ প্রেরণের জন্য কৌশল-বিশেষ। **7.** A ship which repeats a signal ; যে জাহাজ অপর জাহাজ হইতে প্রদর্শিত সঙ্কেত পুনরায় প্রদর্শন করে। **To repeat one's self**—To say or do over again ; পুনরুক্তি করা, পুনরায় করা।

rē-pĕl', *v. t.* **1.** To drive back ; to repulse ; পশ্চাত্তাড়িত করা, হটাইয়া দেওয়া, ঠেলিয়া দেওয়া ; প্রতিহত করা, দূরে ঠেলা (জিঃ)। **2.** To oppose ; to resist ; বাধা দেওয়া ; প্রতিরোধ করা। **3.** To cause aversion in ; "Such extravagances *repel* minds that have a sense of truth" ; বিতৃষ্ণা জন্মান, বিরাগ জন্মান। **—lent,** *adj.* & *n.* **1.** Having the effect of repelling ; repulsive ; as, a *repellent* mien ; প্রতিহতিজনক, প্রতিরোধকারী, নিবারক, নিরোধক ; বিকৃত, দুর্মন, বিদ্ঘুটে, ন্যক্কারজনক, বীভৎস, বিরাগজনক। **2.** (*Med.*) (*Rare*) Checking the development of tumours, eruptions, or the like ; ব্রণ, অর্ব্বুদ, উদ্ভেদ, প্রভৃতি রোধক, স্তম্ভনকর (সাঃ পঃ)। (*Noun*) **1.** A repelling power or influence ; প্রতিরোধজনক শক্তি বা প্রভাব। **2.** A repellent medicine ; যে ঔষধ প্রয়োগে শরীরের উপরিভাগের অর্ব্বুদ, স্ফোটক, প্রভৃতি সারিয়া যায়।

rē'-pĕnt, *adj.* (*Bot.*) Creeping ; (উদ্ভিদ্‌বিদ্যা) পরিসর্পক (সাঃ পঃ)।

rē-pĕnt', *v.t.* & *i.* To remember with self-reproach or sorrow ; অনুতাপ করা, অনুশোচনা করা, পশ্চাত্তাপ করা, পস্তান (*colloq.*)। ***Verb i.*** To feel pain, sorrow or regret for something done or left undone by oneself ; অনুতপ্ত হওয়া অনুশোচনা ভোগ করা। **—ance,** *n.* The act of repenting ; sorrow for what we have done or said amiss ; sorrow for sin ; অনুতাপকরণ ; অনুশোচনা, পশ্চাত্তাপ (গোপালঃ), অনুশয় (শকুঃ) ; অনুতাপ। **—ant,** *adj.* & *n.* Experiencing repentance ; অনুতপ্ত। ***Noun.*** One who repents ; অনুতপ্ত ব্যক্তি।

rē-peo'-ple (-pē-pl), *v. t.* To people anew ; পুনরায় লোকপূর্ণ করা।

rē-pêr-cus′-sion (-cŭsh-ŭn), *n.* Reverberation ; প্রতিধ্বনি, প্রতিনিনাদ।

rĕp′-êr-toire (-twâr-), *n.* A list of operas, dramas, pieces, parts, etc. which can be readily performed by a person, dramatic or operatic company ; যে সকল নাট্য, গীতিনাট্য, ভূমিকা, প্রভৃতি কোন নাট্যসম্প্রদায় বা গীতিনাট্যসম্প্রদায় বা ব্যক্তি দ্বারা তৎক্ষণাৎ অভিনীত হইতে পারে—তাহার তালিকা।

rĕp′-êr-tō-rȳ, *n.* A storehouse or repository ; ভাণ্ডার, গুদাম, মালঘর, গোলা, মালখানা।

rē-pē-rūse′, *v. t.* To peruse again ; পুনরায় পাঠ করা।

rĕp-ē-tĕnd′, *n.* (*Arith.*) The part of a repeating decimal which recurs continually, *ad infinitum* ; পৌনঃপুনিক দশমিকের যে অংশ পুনঃ পুনঃ আগত হয়।

rĕp-ē-ti′-tion, *n.* **1.** The act of doing or uttering a second time ; reiteration ; পুনরুক্তি, পুনরুল্লেখ, পুনঃসম্পাদন, পুনঃকথন, আম্রেড়ন, অনুবৃত্তি, পুনঃকরণ ; পৌনঃপুন্য। **2.** An instance of repetition ; পুনরুক্ত বিষয়, পুনরুক্ত (ন্যায় সূত্র), অভ্যাস (শ্রীঃ)। **3.** A recital ; narration ; আবৃত্তি ; বর্ণন। **4.** A piece set to be learnt by heart ; মুখস্থ করার জন্য নির্বাচিত বিষয়। **5.** A copy, a replica ; প্রতিলিপি ; চিত্রের প্রতিলিপি। **6.** (*Rhet.*) Repetition of the same word or the same sense in diffierent words to make deeper impression ; (অলঙ্কার-শাস্ত্র), ভাবের গাঢ়তা বৃদ্ধির জন্য একই শব্দের বা বিভিন্ন শব্দে একই ভাবের পুনরুক্তি, পুনরুক্তবদাভাস (সাঃ দঃ)। **—al, —a-ry, —tious, Re-pet′-i-tive,** *adjs.*

rē-piece′ (-pēs), *v. t.* To piece together again ; খণ্ডসমূহ পুনরায় যথাস্থানে সন্নিবিষ্ট করা।

rē-pīne′, *v. i.* To feel discontent ; to complain ; to murmur ; দুঃখবোধ করা, অসন্তুষ্ট হওয়া ; অভিযোগ করা ; খিট্‌খিট্ করা, কিট্‌কিট্ করা, গজ্‌গজ্ করা, গসগস করা। **—pin′-ing,** *adj.* **—pin′-ing-ly,** *adv.*

rē-pique′ (-pēk), *n., v. t.* & *i.* The winning of thirty or more points at piquet before an opponent has scored at all ; প্রতিদ্বন্দ্বী কোন ক্রীড়াঙ্ক লাভের পূর্ব্বে ৩০ বা তদধিক ক্রীড়াঙ্ক লাভ। *Verb t.* To score a repique against an opponent ; প্রতিদ্বন্দ্বী কোন ক্রীড়াঙ্ক লাভের পূর্ব্বে ত্রিশ বা তদধিক ক্রীড়াঙ্ক লাভ করা। *Verb i.* To win a repique ; প্রতিদ্বন্দ্বী কোন ক্রীড়াঙ্ক লাভের পূর্ব্বে ত্রিশ বা তদধিক ক্রীড়াঙ্ক লাভ করা।

rē-place′ (-plās), *v. t.* **1.** To put again in a former place ; as, to *replace* a sum stolen or spent ; পুনরায় পূর্ব্বস্থানে রাখা, পূরণ করিয়া রাখা। **2.** To put in a new place ; নূতন স্থানে স্থাপিত করা। **3.** To repay ; to refund ; পরিশোধ করা ; টাকা ফিরাইয়া দেওয়া। **4.** To supply an equivalent for ; to fill the place of ; as, they talked of *replacing* buildings of bricks with buildings of stone ; কোন কিছুর পরিবর্ত্তে সমতুল্য কিছু দেওয়া ; কাহারো স্থান পূরণ করা, কোন কিছুর স্থানে বসান বা স্থাপিত করা। **5.** To take the place of ; to be substituted for ; স্থান গ্রহণ করা ; স্থলবর্ত্তী হওয়া, স্থলে প্রদত্ত হওয়া। **—a-ble,** *adj.* **—ment,** *n.*

rē-plănt′, *v. t.* **1.** To plant again ; পুনরায় রোপণ করা। **2.** To reinstate ; পূর্ব্বস্থানে কিম্বা পূর্ব্ব পদে পুনঃ প্রতিষ্ঠিত করা।

rē-plĕn′-ish, *v. t.* To fill up again after having been emptied or diminished ; to fill completely ; পুনরায় পূর্ণ করা ; পরিপূর্ণ করা। **—ment,** *n.*

rē-plete′ (-plēt), *adj.* Filled ; charged ; পরিপূর্ণ, ভরা, ছাপাছাপি ; সম্পূরিত। **—ple′-tion,** *n.*

rē-plĕv′-in, *n.* **1.** The restoration to, or recovery by a person of goods and chattels distrained or taken from him on condition to restore the property if the action goes against him ; মোকদ্দমা বিরুদ্ধে নিষ্পত্তি হইলে ফিরাইয়া দেওয়া হইবে এই সর্ত্তে কোন ব্যক্তির নিকট হইতে ক্রোক করা জিনিষপত্র বা জায়দাদ পুনরুদ্ধার বা তৎকর্ত্তৃক প্রত্যর্পণ। **2.** A case arising out of a matter in which goods have been restrained and subsequently replevied ; ক্রোক করা সম্পত্তি পুনরুদ্ধার করা বা প্রত্যর্পিত হইলে তৎসম্পর্কে যে মোকদ্দমা রুজু করা হয়। **3.** A writ granting replevin ; ক্রোকী মাল উদ্ধার বা প্রত্যর্পণের পরওয়ানা। **—i-sa-ble,** *adj.*

rē-plev′-ȳ, *v. t.* To recover by replevin ; মোকদ্দমায় হারিলে ফিরাইয়া দেওয়া হইবে এই সর্ত্তে বন্ধকী মাল পুনরুদ্ধার করা।

rĕp′-li-că, *n.* **1.** A copy of a work by the author of the original ; মূল চিত্রাদির অঙ্কনকারীর স্বহস্তকৃত প্রতিলিপি। **2.** A facsimile ; "Each house was a *replica* of the rest" ; প্রতিরূপ, অবিকল নকল।

rĕp′-li-cănt, *n.* One who makes a reply ; উত্তরকারী।

rĕp′-li-cāte, —cāt-ĕd, *adjs.* Folded back upon itself ; পুনরাবর্ত্তিত, মোড়ান।

rĕp′-li-cāte, *v. t.* **1.** (*Rare*) To Repeat ; (ক্বচিদ্ ব্যবহৃত) পুনরায় বলা। **2.** To fold back ; মোড়া, জড়ান। **3.** To make a replica of ; প্রতিরূপ বা অবিকল নকল প্রস্তুত করা।

rĕp-li-cā′-tion, *n.* **1.** (*Rare*) A folding back ; (ক্বচিদ্ ব্যবহৃত) মোড়ান। **2.** An echo ; প্রতিধ্বনি, প্রতিনিনাদ। **3.** A copy ; প্রতিরূপ, নকল, প্রতিলিপি। **4.** A reply ; (*law*) the reply of the plaintiff in matters of fact to the defendant's plea ; প্রত্যুত্তর, জবাব ; (আইন) জওয়াব (রঃ অঃ), দর জওয়াব (ঐ)।

rē-ply̆′, *v. t., i. & n.* To return an answer; প্রত্যুত্তর দেওয়া। *Verb i.* 1. To answer or respond; উত্তর দেওয়া, জবাব দেওয়া, উত্তর করা। 2. (*Law*) To answer a defendant's plea; (আইন) জবাব দেওয়া। 3. To do or give something in return for something else; as, the enemy *replied* to our fire; কোন কিছুর প্রতিদানে বা প্রত্যুত্তরে পাল্টা কোন কিছু করা বা দেওয়া। *Noun.* 1. An answer; উত্তর, প্রত্যুত্তর, প্রতিবচন (বাংস্কৃ:)। 2. (*Law*) A replication; (আইন) জবাব। 3. Something given or done in return for something else; কোন কিছুর পরিবর্ত্তে কৃত বা প্রদত্ত বস্তু।

rē-point′ (-point), *v. t.* To point a wall etc. again; পুনরায় চুণ সুরকি দ্বারা জোড়া বন্ধ করা।

rē-pŏl′-ish, *v. t.* To polish again; পুনরায় পালিশ করা।

repondez s'il vous plait, (*F.*), *n.* (*Abbr. R. S. V. P.*) A formula appended to invitation or other letter; নিমন্ত্রণ পত্র, বা অপর পত্রাদির শেষে সংযোজিত শব্দ বা উহার আদ্যক্ষর চতুষ্টয় (ইহার অর্থ—অনুগ্রহপূর্ব্বক উত্তর দিবেন।)

rē-pŏp′-ū-lāte, *v. t.* Same as REPEOPLE (which see.)

rē-pōrt′, *v. t. & i.* 1. To bear or bring back, as an answer; to relate, as what has been discovered by a person sent to examine, explore or investigate; প্রত্যুত্তর আনা; কোন বিষয়ে মন্তব্য বা মতামত প্রকাশ করা, অনুসন্ধান প্রভৃতির ফল জ্ঞাপন করা। 2. To relate; to recite; বর্ণনা করা; বিবৃত করা। 3. To give an official or formal account or statement; সরকারী কর্ম্মচারিরূপে কোন বিষয়ের বিবরণ দেওয়া। 4. To make minutes of a speech or of the proceedings of a public assembly; কোন বক্তৃতার বিবরণ বা সভা প্রভৃতির কার্য্য-বিবরণী লিপিবদ্ধ করা। 5. To mention as having failed in duty, obedience, etc.: কাহারো কর্ত্তব্যকার্য্যে ত্রুটি, অবাধ্যতা প্রভৃতির বিষয় কর্ত্তৃপক্ষের কর্ণগোচর করা, এত্তেলা করা, উল্লেখ করা। *Verb i.* 1. To furnish in writing an account of a speech, or the proceedings of a public assembly; কোন বক্তৃতার বিবরণ বা সভার কার্য্যবিবরণী লিপিবদ্ধ করা। 2. To act as a reporter to the press; সংবাদপত্রের সংবাদদাতার কাজ করা। 3. To betake one's self as to a superior officer, and to be in readiness for orders and to do service; ঊর্দ্ধতন কর্ম্মচারীর নিকট উপস্থিত হইয়া কার্য্যের জন্য বা আদেশ পালনের জন্য প্রস্তুত থাকা। **-a-ble**, *adj.* **-er**, *n.* 1. (*Rare*) One who reports or relates; (কচিদ্‌ব্যবহৃত) জ্ঞাপক, বর্ণনকারী। 2. One who reports the proceedings of meeting, etc. esp. for newspaper; সংবাদদাতা। **It is reported**—It is generally said; এইরূপ কথিত হয়। **To report one's self**—Same as REPORT, *v. i.*, 3.

rē-pōrt′, *n.* 1. A statement of the result of an investigation, examination, etc. in reply to an enquiry; কোন বিষয়ের পরীক্ষা, অনুসন্ধান প্রভৃতির প্রদত্ত বিবরণী প্রতিবেদন (পালি সহিত্য), বিজ্ঞাপনী। 2. An account; relation; বিবরণ, সমাচার বৃত্তান্ত, বার্ত্তা; বর্ণনা। 3. Rumour; জনরব, গুজব। 4. Repute; reputation; খ্যাতি; গৌরব। 5. Sound; noise; as, the *report* of a gun; শব্দ, ধ্বনি; আওয়াজ। 6. A detailed account of cases, readings, and decisions in law-courts; মোকদ্দমার বিবরণী। 7. An account published in the newspapers of the proceedings, debates etc. of a legislative assembly; an epitome or fully written account of a speech or meeting; সংবাদপত্রে প্রকাশিত ব্যবস্থাপক সভা প্রভৃতির কার্য্যবিবরণী; কোন সভার কার্য্যবিবরণী বা কার্য্যবিবরণীর সারমর্ম্ম, কোন বক্তৃতার সারমর্ম্ম বা পূর্ণ বিবৃতি। 8. An official statement of facts written or verbal; লিখিত বা মৌখিক সরকারী বিবরণ।

rē-pōse′, *v. t.* To place hope, trust, etc.; (আশা, বিশ্বাস) প্রভৃতি ন্যস্ত বা স্থাপন করা।

rē-pōse′, *v. t., i. & n.* To lay at rest; আরাম করিয়া শোয়ান। *Verb i.* To lie at rest; to sleep; শুইয়া আরাম করা; শোয়া, নিদ্রা যাওয়া। *Noun.* 1. Rest; বিশ্রাম, বিরাম, বিশ্রান্তি, শান্তি, জিরেন। 2. Rest of mind; শান্তি, প্রশান্তভাব, শান্তভাব, প্রশান্তি। 3. Composure; ease of manner; স্থৈর্য্য; স্বচ্ছন্দভাব। 4. (*Art.*) That quality in a work of art which gives it entire dependance on its inherent ability and does not appeal by gaudiness of colour or exaggeration of attitude to a false estimate of ability; an avoidance of obtrusive tints and striking actions in figures; (কলাবিদ্যা) চিত্রাদির গুণবিশেষ—যদ্দ্বারা উহা স্বীয় অন্তর্নিহিত শক্তির উপর সর্ব্বতোভাবে নির্ভর করে এবং বর্ণের চটক কিম্বা মূর্ত্তিসমূহের ঢংএর বাহুল্যেরদ্বারা উহার কলাশক্তি সম্পর্কে ভ্রান্ত ধারণা জন্মায় না; মূর্ত্তি প্রভৃতিতে অতিরিক্ত বর্ণোচ্ছ্বাস বা আতপ্রকট অঙ্গসংস্থানভঙ্গী পরিহার। **Angle of repose** — বিশ্রামকোণ (হিঃ কোঃ)।

rē-pŏs′-i-tŏ-ry̆, *n.* A receptacle; a storehouse; ভাণ্ড; ভাণ্ডার কোষ, নিধি (আঃ বঃ) (as জ্ঞাননিধি), গুদাম, মালখানা।

rē-pŏs-sĕss′ *v. t.* To possess again; পুনরায় অধিকার করা।

rē-pōst′, *n. & v. i.* Same as RIPOSTE (which see)

rē-pŏt′, *v.t.* To put plants into fresh pot; নূতন টবে ফুলগাছ রোপণ করা।

rĕpp, Same as REP (which see.)

rĕp-rē-hĕnd', *v. t.* To rebuke; to blame; তিরস্কার করা, তর্ৎসনা করা; দোষারোপ করা, গালিমন্দ করা। **—hen'-si-ble,** *adj.* **—hen'-sion,** *n.*

rĕp-rē-sĕnt', *v. t.* **1.** To present again or in place of something else; to exhibit the image or counterpart of; to typify; পুনরায় উপস্থাপিত করা, অন্য কিছুর স্থলে উপস্থাপিত করা; প্রতিমূর্ত্তি বা প্রতিরূপ প্রদর্শন করা; চিহ্ন বা আদর্শ দ্বারা প্রদর্শন করা। **2.** To bring clearly and distinctly before the mind; to call up in one's mind by an act of imagination; as, we cannot *represent* eternity to ourselves; স্পষ্টভাবে মনোমধ্যে উপস্থিত করা; কল্পনা দ্বারা মনোমধ্যে আনা, ধারণা করা। **3.** To portray or depict by pictorial or plastic art; to delineate; as, to *represent* an object faithfully; চিত্রকলা, মূর্ত্তিশিল্প, প্রভৃতির সাহায্যে চিত্রিত বা নির্ম্মিত করা, চিত্রিত করা; অঙ্কিত করা। **4.** To act the part or character of; to personate; কোন ভূমিকার অভিনয় করা; অপর কোন ব্যক্তিরূপে কার্য্য করা। **5.** To exhibit to another mind in language; to show by arguments, reasoning or statement; to describe; ভাষার সাহায্যে অন্যের নিকট ব্যক্ত করা; যুক্তি, তর্ক, বা উক্তি দ্বারা প্রদর্শন করা; বর্ণনা করা। **6.** To fill the place of; to be a substitute or agent for; as, he *represents* his master; to act on behalf of; কাহারও স্থান পূর্ণ করা; কাহারও প্রতিনিধি বা স্থলবর্ত্তী হওয়া, স্থলাভিষিক্ত হওয়া; কাহারো হইয়া কার্য্য করা, কাহারো পক্ষে কার্য্য করা। **7.** To serve as a sign or symbol of; as, words *represent* ideas; চিহ্ন বা নিদর্শনস্বরূপ হওয়া। **8.** To serve as a specimen or example of; "Both English and Danish blood was *represented* in the assembly"; to serve as an embodiment of; to indicate; নমুনা, দৃষ্টান্ত বা উদাহরণ স্বরূপ হওয়া; মূর্ত্তিমান বিগ্রহ স্বরূপ হওয়া; সূচনা করা। **9.** (*Metaph.*) To image or picture in consciousness; জাগ্রৎ চৈতন্যের নিকট প্রতিবিম্বিত বা অঙ্কিত করা। **10.** To be equivalent to; to correspond to; as, the *puma* of the New World was held to *represent* the lion and the tiger of the Old World; তুল্য হওয়া; অনুরূপ হওয়া। **—a-ble,** *adj.* **—sen-ta'-tion,** *n.* **1.** The act of representing, describing, depicting or exhibiting; প্রতিরূপপ্রদর্শন, বর্ণন, চিত্রণ, প্রদর্শন, প্রতিস্মরণ (হিঃ কোঃ)। **2.** An image or likeness; a facsimile; প্রতিমূর্ত্তি, প্রতিকৃতি; প্রতিরূপ। **3.** A dramatic performance; অভিনয়, প্রয়োগ (মৃচ্ছঃ)। **4.** A statement of arguments, fact, etc. made with a view to effecting some change etc.; remonstrance; protest; as, *representation* was made to the Viceroy; কোন বিষয়ে পরিবর্ত্তনসাধনের জন্য যুক্তি, উপপত্তি, প্রভৃতি প্রদর্শন; অনুযোগ; আপত্তি, প্রতিবাদ। **5.** The part performed by a representative, agent or a delegate; the function of a representative in a legislative assembly; the principle or system according to which communities, districts are represented in such assemblies; "The reform in *representation* he uniformly opposed"; প্রতিনিধি বা কার্য্যকারকের কার্য্য; ব্যবস্থাপক সভা প্রভৃতিতে নির্ব্বাচিত প্রতিনিধির কার্য্য; যে মূলনীতি বা পদ্ধতি অনুযায়ী ব্যবস্থাপক সভায় প্রতিনিধি প্রেরণ করা হয়। **6.** A body of representatives; প্রতিনিধিবর্গ। **7.** (*Law*) A standing in the place of another; স্থলবর্ত্তিত্ব। **8.** (*Philos.*) The act or process by which the mind forms an image or concept of an object; an image or concept thus formed; (দর্শনশাস্ত্র) মনের যে ক্রিয়া দ্বারা মনে কোন বস্তুর ধারণা বা মানসিক প্রতিরূপ সঞ্জাত হয়; মানসিক প্রতিরূপ বা ধারণা, অবভাস (মঃ উঃ)। **9.** (*Philos.*) Recurrent presentation; প্রতিস্মরণ (হিঃ কোঃ)। **10.** (*Insurance*) A collateral statement of facts relating to the proposed adventure, not inserted in the policy, as are necessary to enable the insurer to form a just estimate of the risk; (বীমা) বীমাপত্রে লিখিত হয় নাই এরূপ কতিপয় আনুষঙ্গিক বিষয়ের উক্তি—যাহা হইতে বীমাগ্রহীতা তাহার দায়ের পরিমাণ আন্দাজ করিতে পারে। **—sen-ta'-tion-al,** *adj.* **Proportional representation**—See under PROPORTIONAL.

rĕp-rē-sĕnt'-ā-tive (-tiv), *adj.* & *n.* **1.** Exhibiting likeness or similitude; fit to represent; প্রতিরূপপ্রদর্শক, প্রতিকৃতিপ্রদর্শক, সাদৃশ্যপ্রদর্শক; সাদৃশ্যপ্রদর্শনযোগ্য। **2.** Acting as a substitute; as, a *representative* assembly; প্রতিনিধিস্বরূপ, প্রতিনিধিস্থানীয়, স্থলবর্ত্তী, স্থলাভিষিক্ত। **3.** Conducted by delegates; প্রতিনিধিবর্গ দ্বারা নির্ব্বাহিত। **4.** Typical of a class; কোন জাতির আদর্শস্বরূপ। **5.** (*Metaph.*) Giving a transcript of what was once presentative knowledge; as, *representative* faculty: *representative* knowledge; পূর্ব্বে যাহা মনের নিকট প্রত্যক্ষভাবে উপস্থিত হইয়াছিল তাহার প্রতিরূপপ্রদায়ক বা প্রতিরূপস্বরূপ বর্ত্তমান, স্মরণাত্মক (হিঃ কোঃ), প্রতিরূপক (ঐ), প্রদর্শক (ঐ)। ***Noun.*** **1.** One who, or that which exhibits likeness of another; সাদৃশ্য বা প্রতিরূপপ্রদর্শক। **2.** An agent, deputy or substitute; কার্য্যকর্ত্তা, প্রতিনিধি, গোমস্তা, স্থলবর্ত্তী ব্যক্তি। **3.** (*Law*) One who stands in the place of another as heir; উত্তরাধিকারিরূপে

স্থলবর্ত্তী। 4. Specimen; embodiment of; "Krishna is the great *representative* of our religious life"; দৃষ্টান্ত, নমুনা; মূর্ত্তিমান বিগ্রহ। —ly, *adv.* —ness, *n.* **House of Representatives**—মাকিণ রাষ্ট্রমণ্ডলের সাধারণ বা নিম্নতর বিভাগ। [এই বিভাগে প্রতি রাষ্ট্র হইতে দুই বৎসরের জন্য অন্ততঃ একজন প্রতিনিধি নির্ব্বাচিত হয়]। **Personal representative** — অছি। **Real representative**—উত্তরাধিকারী। **Representative species**—যে জাতিতে অপেক্ষাকৃত আধুনিক রূপান্তর পরিলক্ষিত হয় এবং উহা যে স্থানে দৃষ্ট হয় তন্নিকটবর্ত্তী কোন স্থান উহার উৎপত্তিস্থল হইয়া থাকে।

rē-prĕss', *v. t.* To crush; to put down; to check; to subdue; দলন করা; দমন করা; নিরোধ করা; বশীভূত করা, নিয়ন্ত্রিত করা। **—pres'-sion**, *n.* 1. The act of repressing, checking or subduing; দলন, দমন, নিরোধ। **—pres'-sive**, *adj.* Having the nature of, or tending to subdue or restrain; as, *repressive* measures; দমনাত্মক, দলনাত্মক, নিরোধক, পীড়নাত্মক, তাড়নাত্মক।

rē-prieve' (-prēv), *n.* & *v. t.* 1. The suspension of the execution of a criminal's sentence, esp. of the sentence of death; কোন অপরাধী ব্যক্তির দণ্ড, বিশেষতঃ প্রাণদণ্ড সাময়িক ভাবে স্থগিত করণ। [এইরূপ দণ্ড যে যে অবস্থায় স্থগিত থাকিতে পারে তাহা এই:— (১) রাজার আদেশে। (২) আদালতের আদেশে (দণ্ডপ্রদানের পূর্ব্বে অথবা পরে) দণ্ড স্থগিত রাখা আদালতের ইচ্ছাধীন; কিন্তু এই দুই ক্ষেত্রে আদালত দণ্ড স্থগিত রাখিতে বাধ্য—(১) মৃত্যুদণ্ডে দণ্ডিতা স্ত্রীলোক গর্ভবতী হইলে। (২) দণ্ডাজ্ঞা প্রচারের পর বন্দী উন্মত্ত হইলে]। 2. A warrant for suspension, remission or commutation of capital sentence; প্রাণদণ্ড স্থগিত, রহিত বা পরিবর্ত্তিত করার জন্য পরোয়ানা। 3. A respite from a calamity; কোনরূপ বিপদ হইতে সাময়িক নিবৃত্তি, বিরাম। ***Verb t.*** 1. To suspend or delay the execution of for a time; কিছুকালের জন্য প্রাণদণ্ড স্থগিত রাখা। 2. To relieve for a time; সাময়িক ভাবে বিশ্রাম দেওয়া, কিছুকালের জন্য বিরাম দেওয়া।

rĕp'-ri-mănd, *v. t.* & *n.* To reprove severely; to reprove publicly or officially by way of sentence; তিরস্কার করা, ভর্ৎসনা করা, তম্বী করা, তাড়া দেওয়া; অধস্তন কর্ম্মচারীর কোনরূপ ত্রুটীর দরুণ তাহাকে তিরস্কার করা। ***Noun.*** 1. Severe reproof; official reproof; তিরস্কার, ভর্ৎসনা; বাগ্‌দণ্ড, শব্দতাড়ন বিগ্‌দণ্ড, ধমক, তম্বী, তাড়া।

rē-print', *v. t.* To print again; পুনর্মুদ্রিত করা।

rē-print', *n.* A second or new edition of a printed work; a new impression; কোন মুদ্রিত পুস্তকের দ্বিতীয় সংস্করণ; পুনর্মুদ্রণ।

rē-prīs'-ăl, *n.* 1. (*Hist.*) The seizure of anything from an enemy by way of retaliation or indemnification; (ইতিহাস) প্রতিহিংসাসাধন মানসে বা ক্ষতিপূরণের জন্য শত্রুর নিকট হইতে কোন কিছু বলপূর্ব্বক গ্রহণ। 2. An act of severity done in retaliation; esp. in times of war the infliction of similar or severer punishment on the enemy, *e. g.* the infliction of suffering or death on a prisoner taken from him; প্রতিহিংসামূলক কার্য্য, প্রত্যপকার, প্রত্যপহার (আঃ বঃ); বিশেষতঃ যুদ্ধকালে তদনুরূপ বা তদপেক্ষা গুরুতর শাস্তি দ্বারা শত্রুর কৃত অত্যাচার প্রভৃতির প্রতিশোধ লওন।

rē-prīse', *n.* 1. Rent-charge or other payments to be made yearly from an estate; কোন সম্পত্তির আয় হইতে বৎসর বৎসর যে রাজস্ব প্রভৃতি দিতে হয়। 2. A ship recaptured from an enemy or pirate; শত্রু বা জলদস্যু হইতে পুনরায় ধৃত পোত।

rē-proach' (-prōch), *v. t.* & *n.* 1. To scold; তিরস্কার করা, ভর্ৎসনা করা, গঞ্জনা দেওয়া। 2. To find fault with; কাহারো দোষ ধরা। 3. To bring into reproach or discredit; কলঙ্কিত করা, দুর্নামগ্রস্ত করা। ***Noun.*** 1. The act of reproaching; censure; তিরস্কারকরণ; তিরস্কার, ভর্ৎসনা, গঞ্জনা। 2. An object of censure or scorn; the thing that brings disgrace or discredit; as, this road is a *reproach* to this town; তিরস্কারের পাত্র, নিন্দার পাত্র, অবজ্ঞার পাত্র, ঘৃণার পাত্র; কলঙ্কের বিষয়, কলঙ্কের কথা, দুর্নামের বিষয়, লজ্জার বিষয়, অখ্যাতির বিষয়। 3. Shame; disgrace; as, this casts a *reproach* on him; লজ্জা; কলঙ্ক। **—ful**, *adj.* **—ful-ly**, *adv.* **—ful-ness**, *n.* **The Reproaches**—(রোমানক্যাথলিক ভজনালয়ে) গুডফ্রাইডে দিবসে যীশুখৃষ্টের জনসমাজকে ভর্ৎসনা সম্বন্ধে যে সঙ্গীতাদি গীত হয়।

rĕp'-rō-bāte, *v. t.* 1. To condemn strongly; তীব্র তিরস্কার করা। 2. To abandon; to exclude from salvation; পরিত্যাগ করা, বর্জ্জন করা; মুক্তি হইতে বঞ্চিত করা। 3. To reject; "Every scheme ··· recommended by one of them was *reprobated* by the other"; অগ্রাহ্য করা।

rĕp'-rō-bāte, *adj.* & *n.* Abandoned in sin; morally abandoned; profligate; পাপপঙ্কে নিক্ষিপ্ত; নীতিবর্জ্জিত, দেবত্যক্ত, ধর্ম্মভ্রষ্ট; দুরাচার, দুর্বৃত্ত, ভ্রষ্টচরিত্র। ***Noun.*** A person cast off by God; a morally depraved man; a depraved wretch; ঈশ্বরত্যক্ত ব্যক্তি; ভ্রষ্টচরিত্র ব্যক্তি; নরাধম, নারকী। **—ba'-tion**, *n.* **—ba-tive**, *adj.*

rē-prō-dūce' (-dūs), *v. t.* & *i.* 1. To renew the production of; to generate as offspring;

পুনরুৎপাদন করা ; সন্তান উৎপাদন করা, প্রজনন করা। 2. To portray; to bring to the imagination; অঙ্কিত করা, চিত্রিত করা; মানসপটে অঙ্কিত করা। 3. To present or exhibit again; পুনরায় উপস্থাপিত করা, পুনরায় প্রদর্শন করা। *Verb i.* To multiply by generation; বংশবৃদ্ধি পাওয়া। **—duc'-tion,** *n.* 1. The act or process of reproducing; পুনরুৎপাদন, পুনরুদ্ভাবন (হিঃ কোঃ), প্রজনন (ঐ), পুনর্জনন, পুনরুৎপত্তি। 2. The process by which new individuals are generated, and the perpetuation of species insured; the process by which organisms are reproduced from those already existing; প্রজননক্রিয়া, বংশরক্ষাপ্রণালী; যে ক্রিয়া-দ্বারা কোন অঙ্গী হইতে অপর অঙ্গী উৎপন্ন হয়। 3. (*Philos.*) The process of bringing again into the mind in the same form; (দর্শন) পূর্ব্বদৃষ্ট রূপ মনোমধ্যে পুনরুৎপাদন, পুনর্জন্ম। 4. That which is reproduced; পুনরুৎপন্ন বস্তু। **—duc'-tive,** *adj.* Pertaining to reproduction; উৎপত্তিক (সাঃ পঃ), বংশরক্ষক (ঐ), পুনরুৎপাদক (হিঃ কোঃ)।

rē-proof', *n.* Blame spoken to the faces; rebuke; তিরস্কারবাক্য, নিন্দাবাক্য; তিরস্কার, ভৎর্সনা, গঞ্জনা, বাক্যগঞ্জনা।

rē-prove' (-prōv), *v. t.* To rebuke; to censure; তিরস্কার করা, ভৎর্সনা করা; গঞ্জনা দেওয়া।

rē-prō-vi'-sion (-zŭn), *v. t.* To supply with fresh provision; পুনরায় খাদ্যসম্ভার সরবরাহ করা।

reps, *n.* See REP.

rĕp'-tănt, *adj.* (*Zool.*) Creeping; (জন্তুবিদ্যা) বিসর্পী, উরোগামী।

rĕp'-tile, *adj.* & *n.* 1. Moving on the belly, or with short legs; বিসর্পী, উরোগামী। 2. Low; mean; vulgar; as, a *reptile* race; হীন; নীচ, অধম; ইতরজনোচিত। *Noun.* 1. A creeping animal; সরীসৃপ, উরগ। 2. A mean vulgar person; হীন ব্যক্তি, নীচ ব্যক্তি, অধম লোক। **—til'-i-an,** *adj.* & *n.* **—ti-lif'-er-ous, —til-i-form,** *adjs.*

rĕp-til'-i-a, *n.* A class of the animal kingdom embracing the tortoise, lizard, serpent and crocodiles; সরীসৃপবর্গ।

rē-pŭb'-lic, *n.* 1. A commonwealth; a state or political community in which the supreme power is vested either in certain privileged members or in the whole community; সাধারণতন্ত্র; গণতন্ত্র, প্রজাতন্ত্র শাসন, সর্ব্বতন্ত্র, প্রজাতন্ত্র রাষ্ট্র, প্রজাতন্ত্ররাজ্য (হিঃ কোঃ)। 2. (*Fig.*) A society of person or animals with equality between members; (লক্ষণায়) যে ব্যক্তি বা জন্তুর সম্প্রদায়ে সকলের তুল্য ক্ষমতা থাকে। **The republic of letters**—সাহিত্যিক মণ্ডলী, সাহিত্যিক সমাজ, সাহিত্য-ক্ষেত্র।

rē-pŭb'-lic-ăn, *adj.* & *n.* 1. Of, or pertaining to, a republic; গণতন্ত্র সম্বন্ধীয়, গণতান্ত্রিক। 2. Consonant to the principles of a republic; as, *republican* manners; গণতন্ত্রনীতির অনুসারী, গণতন্ত্রানুগ। 3. (*U. S., Cap.*) Distinguishing a special party, its principles, etc.; (মাকিন যুক্তরাজ্য) রাজনৈতিক দলবিশেষ এবং ঐ দলের মত প্রভৃতি সূচক। 4. (Of birds) Living in large communities; as, *republican* swallow; (পক্ষিসম্পর্কে) বহুসংখ্যায় একত্রবাসকারী, গণচারী। *Noun.* 1. One who favours or prefers a republican form of government; গণতান্ত্রিক। 2. The name of a political party in the United States of America; আমেরিকার যুক্তরাজ্যের রাজনৈতিক দলবিশেষ। **—ism,** *n.*

rē-pŭb'-lish, *v. t.* 1 To publish again or anew; পুনরায় প্রচার করা। 2. To publish a new edition; নূতন সংস্করণ প্রকাশিত করা। **—li-ca'-tion,** *n.*

rē-pū'-di-āte, *v. t.* 1. To reject; to disavow; to refuse dealings with; পরিত্যাগ করা, বর্জ্জন করা; অস্বীকার করা, প্রত্যাখ্যান করা; কোন প্রকার সংশ্রব রাখিতে অস্বীকার করা। 2. To refuse to acknowledge and pay, as debt; ঋণ প্রভৃতি স্বীকার বা পরিশোধ করিতে অস্বীকার করা। 3. To divorce a wife; পত্নী ত্যাগ করা। **—a'-tion,** *n.* The act of repudiating; নিরাকরণ (হিঃ কোঃ), প্রত্যাখ্যান, অস্বীকার।

rē-pugn' (-pūn), *v. i.* & *t.* (*Rare*) To oppose; (ক্কচিদ্ব্যবহৃত) বাধা দেওয়া। *Verb t.* 1. (*Rare*) To resist; to withstand; (ক্কচিদ্ব্যবহৃত) বাধা দেওয়া; যুদ্ধার্থ সম্মুখীন হওয়া। 2. To be repugnant to; অসঙ্গতি বিশিষ্ট হওয়া।

re-pŭg'-nance (-năns), *n.* 1. (*Rare*) Resistance; (ক্কচিদ্ব্যবহৃত) বাধা। 2. Unwillingness; aversion; antipathy; অনিচ্ছা; বিদ্বেষ; ঘৃণা, বিরাগ। 3. Inconsistency; অসঙ্গতি, পূর্ব্বাপরবিরোধ, অসামঞ্জস্য, অনৈক্য।

re-pŭg'-nant, *adj.* 1. Inconsistent; contradictory to; as, if there be anything *repugnant to* the text; অসঙ্গতিবিশিষ্ট, অসমঞ্জস; বিরোধী, প্রতিকূল, বিরুদ্ধ। 2. (*Poet.*) Disobedient; refractory; (কবিতায়) অবাধ্য; ঠেঁটা। 3. Offensive; as, such a behaviour is most *repugnant* to me; বিরক্তিকর, অপ্রীতিকর।

rē-pŭl'-lū-late, *v. i.* 1. To bud again; পুনরায় অঙ্কুরিত হওয়া, পুনরায় মুকুলিত হওয়া। 2. (Of disease) To recur; (রোগ সম্পর্কে) পুনরায় দেখা দেওয়া, পুনরায় আসা। **—la'-tion,** *n.*

rē-pulse' (-pŭls), *v. t.* & *n.* 1. To repel; as, to *repulse* an enemy; প্রতিহত করা, হটাইয়া দেওয়া। 2. To reject; to refuse; to rebuff; অগ্রাহ্য করা; অস্বীকার করা; প্রতিহত

করা। *Noun.* 1. The condition of being checked in advancing, or driven back by force ; প্রতিহতি, হঠন। 2. Refusal ; rebuff ; অস্বীকৃতি ; ধাক্কা, পরাভব, দাবানি, মুখঝামটা (*colloq.*)।

rĕ-pŭl′-sion, *n.* 1. (*Rare*) The act of repulsing ; (কচিদ্‌ব্যবহৃত) হঠন, প্রতিক্ষেপণ, নিরাকরণ (হিঃ কোঃ)। 2. Dislike; aversion ; অপ্রীতি, বিদ্বেষ দ্বেষ ; ঘৃণা, বিরাগ, বিতৃষ্ণা। 3. (*Phys.*) That power by which bodies or particles of bodies are made to recede from each other ; (পদার্থ-বিদ্যা) যে শক্তিদ্বারা পদার্থসমূহ বা পদার্থের কণাসকল পরস্পর হইতে বিপ্রকৃষ্ট হয়, বিপ্রকর্ষণ, বিকর্ষণ, প্রতিসারকশক্তি (কেণ্ডিঃ)।

rĕ-pŭl′-sive (-sĭv), *adj.* 1. (*Phys.*) Exerting repulsion ; (পদার্থ-বিজ্ঞান) বিপ্রকর্ষক, প্রতিসারক, নিবারক। 2. (*Rare*) Cold : forbidding ; as, *repulsive* manner ; অনুরাগশূন্য, প্রীতিশূন্য ; অপ্রীতিজনক। 3. Loathsome ; disgusting ; as, *repulsive*-looking woman ; ঘৃণনীয়, ঘৃণাজনক, জঘন্য ; ন্যক্কারজনক, বীভৎস, বিকট, বিদ্‌ঘুটে, বিতিকিচ্ছে, বিকৃত, দুশমন। **–ly,** *adv.* **–ness,** *n.*

rĕ-pŭr′-chase, *v. t.* & *n.* To buy back again ; পুনরায় ক্রয় করা। *Noun.* The act of purchasing again ; পুনঃ ক্রয়।

rĕ-pū′-rĭ-fȳ, *v. t.* To purify again ; পুনরায় বিশুদ্ধ করা।

rĕp′-ū-tă-ble (-bl), *adj.* Having good repute ; held in great esteem ; খ্যাতনামা, লব্ধপ্রতিষ্ঠ ; প্রথিতনামা, যশস্বী, শ্রদ্ধাভাজন, সর্ব্বজনমান্য। **–bly,** *adv.*

rĕp-ū-tā′-tion, *n.* Distinction ; good name ; credit ; খ্যাতি ; সুনাম, সুখ্যাতি, কীর্ত্তি ; খাতির, সম্ভ্রম, মানমর্য্যাদা, প্রতিষ্ঠা, গৌরব।

rĕ-pūte′, *n.* & *v. t.* Reputation ; credit ; honour ; খ্যাতি ; সম্ভ্রম ; মানমর্য্যাদা। *Verb t.* To hold ; to regard ; মনে করা ; গণ্য করা, বিবেচনা করা। **–put′-ed,** *p. p.* Generally considered or regarded as, or supposed ; as the *reputed* father of the bastard child ; সাধারণতঃ বিবেচিত বা পরিগণিত, অনুমিত, কল্পিত। **–put′-ed-ly,** *adv.*

rĕ-quĕst′, *n.* & *v. t.* 1. An entreaty ; solicitation ; অনুরোধ ; প্রার্থনা, মিনতি। 2. The thing asked for ; প্রার্থিত বিষয়। 3. A state of being desired, or esteemed desirable ; "Knowledge and fame were in as great *request* as wealth among us now" ; demand ; vogue ; কাম্যতা, স্পৃহনীয়তা, বাঞ্ছনীয়তা ; চাহিদা ; চল, চলতি। 4. (India) A small debt-court composed of military officers ; (ভারতবর্ষ) সেনানিবাসের ক্ষুদ্র আদালত—যাহাতে সৈনিক কর্ম্মচারিগণ ঋণের মোকদ্দমার বিচার করেন। *Verb t.* To make a request for ; to ask permission ; to solicit ; অনুরোধ করা ; অনুমতি চাওয়া ; প্রার্থনা করা, মিনতি করা, যাচ্‌ঞা করা।

rĕ-quĭck′-en (-n), *v. t.* To reanimate ; to revive ; পুনরুজ্জীবিত করা, সঞ্জীবিত করা ; পুনঃপ্রাণসঞ্চার করা, মৃতদেহে প্রাণসঞ্চার করা।

rē′-quĭ-ĕm, *n.* 1. A hymn sung for the repose of the soul of the dead ; মৃত ব্যক্তির আত্মার শান্তির জন্য গীত সঙ্গীত, মৃতাত্মবিরাম গীতি। 2. A special service or mass for the repose of the soul of the dead ; মৃত ব্যক্তির আত্মার বিরামের জন্য বিশেষ উপাসনা বা সুরারুটিকা শোধনানুষ্ঠান। 3 A grand musical composition performed in honour of some deceased person ; মৃত ব্যক্তির সম্মানার্থ (গীতবাদ্য)।

req-uĭ-ĕs′-căt (-rĕk-wĭ-), *n.* A prayer for the repose of a dead person ; মৃত ব্যক্তির পারলৌকিক শান্তি কামনায় প্রার্থনা। **Requiescat in pace**—(*Abbr.* R. I. P.) তাহার আত্মা শান্তি লাভ করুক (রোমানক্যাথলিকদিগের সমাধিফলকে এই শব্দগুলি উৎকীর্ণ হইয়া থাকে)।

rĕ-quīre′, *v. t.* & *i.* 1. To demand ; to insist on having by right or by authority ; "I will *require* my flock at thy hand" ; দাবী করা, দাওয়া করা ; পাওয়ার জন্য জেদ করা। 2. To need ; "Great acts *require* great means of enterprise" ; to want ; আবশ্যক করা, দরকার করা ; চাওয়া। 3. To compel one to do something ; as, to *require* a boy to attend school ; বাধ্য করা। *Verb i.* 1. To need ; to be obliged to ; as, the fact *requires* to be stated ; আবশ্যক হওয়া ; বাধ্য হওয়া। 2. To make a request or demand ; প্রার্থনা করা, দাবী করা। **–ment,** *n.* 1. Demand ; দাবী। 2. Something necessary ; a need ; আবশ্যক বস্তু ; আবশ্যক, প্রয়োজন। 3. An essential condition ; মূল সর্ত্ত।

req′-uĭ-site (rĕk-wĭ-zĭt), *adj.* & *n.* Necessary ; আবশ্যক, প্রয়োজনীয়। *Noun.* That which is necessary ; আবশ্যক বস্তু, প্রয়োজনীয় বস্তু, সাধন (হিঃ কোঃ), করণ (ঐ), দ্রব্য সম্ভার, লওয়াজিমা। **–ness,** *n.*

req-uĭ-sĭ′-tion (rĕk-wĭ-), *n.* & *v.t.* 1. The act of requiring ; a demand ; দাবীকরণ ; দাবী। 2. That which is required ; আবশ্যক বস্তু। 3. (*International Law*) The demand made by one state upon another for the extradition of a fugitive from justice ; (আন্তর্জাতিক আইন) পলায়িত অপরাধীকে প্রত্যর্পণ করার জন্য এক রাজ্য কর্ত্তৃক অপর রাজ্যের উপর দাবী। 4. A demand or order made upon a town, district, etc. to furnish or supply anything for military purpose ; সামরিক উদ্দেশ্য সাধনোপযোগী কোন দ্রব্য যোগাইবার জন্য কোন নগর, জেলা,

প্রভৃতির উপর দাবী বা আদেশ, রণদ্রব্য সরবরাহের দাবী বা আদেশ। 5. (*Rare*) A written call or invitation; as, the *requisition* for a public meeting; (কচিদ্ ব্যবহৃত) লিখিত অনুরোধ বা আহ্বান। 6. The state of being called or put into service; as, to put one in or into *requisition*; কোন কার্য্য সম্পাদনের জন্য আহূত বা নিযুক্ত হওয়ার অবস্থা। ***Verb t.*** 1. To make a requisition or demand upon for military purpose; সামরিক উদ্দেশ্য সাধনের জন্য দাবী বা দাওয়া করা। 2. To demand military supplies from a town, district, etc.; কোন নগর, জেলা, প্রভৃতি হইতে সামরিক দ্রব্যসম্ভারের দাবী করা। 3. To call upon; to press into service; আহ্বান করা; জোর করিয়া কাজে লাগান।

rē-quīte', *v. t.* 1. To repay; to reward; পরিশোধ করা; পুরস্কার দেওয়া। 2. To avenge; প্রতিশোধ লওয়া, প্রতিহিংসা লওয়া। 3. To compensate; ক্ষতিপূরণ করা। **—quit'-al**, *n.* 1. Return; compensation; reward; প্রতিদান, প্রতিফল, প্রতিক্রিয়া; ক্ষতিপূরণ; পুরস্কার। 2. Retaliation; প্রতিশোধ, প্রতিহিংসা।

rē-read' (-rĕd), *v. t.* To read again; পুনরায় পাঠ করা।

rere'-dŏs (rēr-), *n.* 1. The screen at the back of an altar; বেদীর পশ্চাদ্দিকস্থ পর্দ্দা। 2. The back of a fireplace; গৃহমধ্যস্থ অগ্নিসেবনকুণ্ডের পশ্চাদ্দেশ।

rēs, *n.* A matter; a point; বিষয়; দফা। **Res angusta domi**—দারিদ্র্য, অস্বচ্ছলতা। **Res gestæ** — সম্পন্ন বিষয়। **Res judicata**—যে বিষয়ের পূর্ব্বেই বিচার হইয়া গিয়াছে।

rē-săd'-dle (-l), *v. t.* To saddle again; পুনরায় জীন বাঁধা।

rē-sāle', *n.* The act of selling again; (ক্রীতবস্তু) পুনর্বিক্রয়।

rē-scind' (-sĭnd), *v. t.* 1. (*Fig.*) To cut off; কাটিয়া ফেলা, ছিন্ন করা। 2. To abrogate; to annul; বাতিল করা, খণ্ডন করা; রদ করা, নাকচ করা। **—scis'-sion**, *n.* The act of abrogating or annulling; রদকরণ, নাকচকরণ, খণ্ডন।

rē'-script, *n.* 1. An edict or decree of the Pope in reply to a knotty question on canon law or morals; পোপের পাঁতি বা ব্যবস্থা। 2. The written reply of a Roman emperor to a reference on a question of law made by a magistrate or some other person; রোম সম্রাটের নিকট কোন দণ্ডনায়ক বা অন্য কোন ব্যক্তি আইন সম্পর্কীয় কোন সন্দিগ্ধ বিষয় মীমাংসার জন্য অর্পণ করিলে তিনি তাহার যে লিখিত উত্তর দিতেন। 3. A decree; an edict; ব্যবস্থা; অনুশাসন। 4. (*Rare*) Act of rewriting or that which is written; (কচিদ্ ব্যবহৃত) পুনর্লিখন, পুনর্লিখিত বিষয়।

rĕs'-cue (-cū), *v. t.* & *n.* 1. To free from any confinement, danger or evil; মুক্ত করা, উদ্ধার করা, রক্ষা করা। 2. (*Law*) To liberate by forced or illegal means from lawful custody; as, to *rescue* a prisoner from the custody of a constable; to forcibly recover property; (আইন) বলপূর্ব্বক বা অবৈধরূপে মুক্ত করা; বলপূর্ব্বক সম্পত্তি পুনরুদ্ধার করা। ***Noun.*** 1. The act of delivering; deliverance; উদ্ধারকরণ; মুক্তি, উদ্ধার। 2. (*Law*) Forcible and illegal release from the custody of law; forcible recovery; (আইন) বলপূর্ব্বক এবং অবৈধভাবে উদ্ধার করণ; বলপূর্ব্বক পুনরুদ্ধার। **—cu-er**, *n.*

rē-search' (-sĕrch), *v. t.*, *i.* & *n.* 1. (*Now rare*) To search; to examine or study with diligence and care; (বর্ত্তমানে কচিদ্ব্যবহৃত) অনুসন্ধান করা; তত্ত্বানুসন্ধান করা। 2. To search again; পুনরায় অন্বেষণ করা। ***Verb i.*** To make researc or investigations; গবেষণা করা, তত্ত্বানুসন্ধান করা। ***Noun.*** 1. Laborious and continued search after truth; গবেষণা, তত্ত্বানুসন্ধান। 2. Capacity for, or habit of, research; as, he is a man of great *research*; তত্ত্বানুসন্ধানের ক্ষমতা, গবেষণাশীলতা।

rē-seat' (-sēt), *v. t.* 1. To seat again; পুনরায় বসান, পুনরায় পূর্ব্ব স্থানে প্রতিষ্ঠিত করা। 2. To provide with new seat or seats; as, to *reseat* a theatre; নূতন আসন বা আসনশ্রেণী সমন্বিত করা।

rē-sĕct', *v. t.* To cut off; কাটিয়া ফেলা, ছেদন করা।

rē-sē'-dă, *n.* 1. A genus of herbs; একজাতীয় গুল্ম। 2. A pale green colour; একপ্রকার ম্লান সবুজ রং।

rē-seek' (-sēk), *v.t.* To seek again; পুনরায় অন্বেষণ করা, পুনরায় খুঁজা।

rē-seize' (-sēz), *v. t.* To seize again; to take possession of again; পুনরায় ধৃত করা; পুনরায় অধিকার করা।

rē-sĕll', *v. t.* To sell again; পুনরায় বিক্রয় করা।

rē-sĕm'-ble (-bl), *v. t.* To have similarity to, in form, figure or qualities; সদৃশ হওয়া, অনুরূপ হওয়া, গুণগত সাদৃশ্য থাকা। **—blance**, *n.* 1. The quality or state of resembling; likeness; সাদৃশ্য, সারূপ্য, সাম্য; অনুরূপতা, একরূপতা। 2. (*Now rare*) Alikeness; (বর্ত্তমানে কচিদ্ ব্যবহৃত) প্রতিকৃতি, প্রতিরূপ।

rē-sĕnt', *v. t.* To consider as an injury or affront; to show or feel indignation at; as, to *resent* one's insult; ঔদ্ধত্য বা বেআদবী বলিয়া মনে করা; রাগ হওয়া, রাগ দেখান, রুষ্ট হওয়া, রাগান্বিত হওয়া, রোষমিশ্রিত অসন্তোষের ভাব দেখান। **—ful**, *adj.* **—ful-ly**, *adv.* **—ment**, *n.* A strong feeling of ill-will and anger against the author of an affront, insult or the like; উদ্ধত ব্যবহার, বেআদবি, অপমান, প্রভৃতির দরুণ সঞ্জাত

রোষ, অমর্ষ, আক্রোশ, মন্যু, ক্ষোভ। **To resent one's self**—To revenge one's self in resentment ; আক্রোশ মিটাইবার জন্য প্রতিশোধ লওয়া।

rĕs-ĕr-vā'-tion, *n.* **1.** The act of reserving or keeping back ; concealment ; that which is kept back or concealed ; কতকটা প্রকাশ না করণ, কিয়দংশ রাখিয়া দেওন ; সংগোপন, গোপন ; ভবিষ্যতের ব্যবহারের জন্য রক্ষিত বস্তু। **2.** A limiting condition ; as, he is to be believed with some *reservation* ; বাদসাদ। **3.** (*Eccl.*) The act of reserving as tithes ; যাজকদিগের প্রাপ্য দশমাংশ ভবিষ্যতের ব্যবহারের জন্য সংরক্ষণ। **4.** The state of being treasured up or kept in store ; সঞ্চিতাবস্থা, ভাণ্ডারজাতাবস্থা। **5.** (*Law*) A clause by which something is reserved ; a proviso : (আইন) দানপত্র প্রভৃতির যে প্রকরণ বা দফাদ্বারা কোন বিষয় বর্জ্জিত হয় ; বর্জ্জিত বিষয়, বর্জ্জিত কথা। **6.** (America) A tract of public land reserved for schools, the use of Indians, etc. ; (আমেরিকায়) বিদ্যালয়, লালইণ্ডিয়ান, প্রভৃতির ব্যবহারের জন্য রক্ষিত সরকারী জমি। **7.** The right reserved to pope to vacant benefice ; যাজকের শূন্যপদে নিয়োগের পোপের বিশিষ্ট ক্ষমতা। **8.** Act of reserving, specially to one's self ; নিজের অনন্যসাধারণ ভোগ বা ব্যবহারের জন্য সংরক্ষণ। **Mental reservation**—যাহা প্রকাশ করিলে কোন উক্তি, প্রতিশ্রুতির অর্থ, প্রভৃতি ভিন্নরূপ হইয়া দাঁড়ায়—ইচ্ছা পূর্ব্বক এমন কোন কথা উল্লেখ না করণ, সত্যাভাস [cf. 'অশ্বত্থামা হত ইতি গজঃ।]

rĕ-serve' (-zĕrv), *v. t.* **1.** To keep back ; to keep in store for future or other use ; to withhold from present use ; রাখিয়া দেওয়া ; ভবিষ্যতের ব্যবহারের জন্য বা অন্যরূপ ব্যবহারের নিমিত্ত রাখিয়া দেওয়া ; বর্ত্তমানে ব্যবহার না করা। **2.** To retain as one's own ; as, to *reserve* seats in a train ; একান্তভাবে নিজের ব্যবহারের জন্য রাখা, নিজের অনন্যসাধারণ ব্যবহারের জন্য সংরক্ষিত করা। **3.** To set apart ; to destine for some use or fate ; "*Reserved* and destined for eternal woe" ; পৃথক করিয়া রাখা ; কোনরূপ ব্যবহারের জন্য বা অদৃষ্টের কোনরূপ ফলভোগের জন্য পূর্ব্ব হইতে নির্দ্ধারিত করা।

rĕ-serve' (-zĕrv), *n.* **1.** The act of reserving, keeping back or withholding; ভবিষ্যতের ব্যবহারের জন্য পৃথক করিয়া রাখন, সংরক্ষণ। **2.** That which is reserved or kept for future or other use ; a store ; ভবিষ্যতের ব্যবহারের জন্য সংরক্ষিত বস্তু ; ভাণ্ডার। **3.** Something in the mind withheld from disclosure ; মনের এমন কোন কথা—যাহা ইচ্ছা পূর্ব্বক প্রকাশ করা হয় নাই **4.** Modest diffidence ; self-restraint ; reticence ; avoidance of too much familiarity ; lack of cordiality ; "On the whole, they made just allowance for his habits of distant *reserve*" ; লজ্জাজনিত কুণ্ঠা ; আত্মসংযম ; বাক্‌সংযম, তুষ্ণীম্ভাব ; অতিরিক্ত অন্তরঙ্গতার ভাব পরিহার, মাখামাখি না করণ ; অন্তরঙ্গতার অভাব। **5.** Restriction ; qualification ; as, to accept a statement without *reserve* ; limitation ; as, an auction without *reserve* [অর্থাৎ কোন নির্দ্দিষ্ট সীমায় ডাক উঠিলে বিক্রীত হইবে এই রীতির অনুসরণ না করিয়া যাহাই ডাক উঠুক না কেন তাহাতেই বিক্রয় করণ].; সংকোচ ; ইতরবিশেষ, বাদসাদ ; সীমা। **6.** (*Mil.*) A part of an army or fleet reserved to assist those engaged in action ; a force to fall back upon when the regulars have failed or are not equal to the emergency ; as, naval *reserves* ; any supply of stores which is located between the army and its base of operations ; যুদ্ধে নিযুক্ত সৈন্য বা রণপোতশ্রেণীর সাহায্যের জন্য রক্ষিত সৈন্য বা রণপোতবহর ; দেশের স্থায়ী সৈন্য যুদ্ধে পরাভূত হইলে বা যুদ্ধের জন্য অপ্রচুর হইলে যে সৈন্যের আশ্রয় লওয়া হয়, সংরক্ষিত সেনা ; যুদ্ধে নিরত সৈন্যদল এবং উহাদের মূল স্থানের মধ্যবর্ত্তী সামরিক দ্রব্যভাণ্ডার। **7.** A tract of land, esp. public land set apart for a particular purpose ; as, forest *reserves* ; কোন বিশেষ উদ্দেশ্যে পৃথগ্‌ভাবে রক্ষিত ভূখণ্ড, বিশেষতঃ সরকারী ভূমি, সংরক্ষিত ভূমি। **8.** (*Law*) Same as RESERVATION, *n.* 5. **9.** (*Banking*) That portion of a capital which is retained in order to meet average liabilities and which is therefore not employed in discounts or loans ; (ব্যাঙ্কিং) উদ্বৃত্ত অর্থ। **10.** Extra men kept in case substitute is needed ; অন্য লোকের স্থানপূরণের জন্য সংরক্ষিত অতিরিক্ত লোকসমূহ। **11.** (*Calico-printing*) Same as RESIST (which see.) **12.** (*Exhibition*) A distinction indicating that an exhibit will get prize in the event of another being disqualified ; যে চিহ্ন দ্বারা ইহা বুঝায় যে, অন্য কোন প্রদর্শিত বস্তু পুরস্কারপ্রাপ্তির অযোগ্য বিবেচিত হইলে কোন নির্দ্দিষ্ট প্রদর্শিত বস্তু পুরস্কার পাইবে। **Reserve price**—কোন জিনিষের সর্ব্বনিম্ন দর—যাহা কোন জিনিষের বিক্রেতা হাতে রাখে। **In reserve**—In keeping for other or future use ; ভবিষ্যতের ব্যবহারের জন্য, অপর কার্য্যে ব্যবহারের জন্য।

rĕ-served' (-zĕrvd), *p. p.* **1.** Kept for another or future use ; ভবিষ্যতের ব্যবহারের জন্য পৃথগ্‌ভাবে সংরক্ষিত বা অন্য কোনরূপ ব্যবহারের জন্য রক্ষিত। **2.** Not free or frank in words, actions, or social intercourse ; অনালাপী,

অমিশুক, রহঃশীল, মৌনী, সংযতবাক্, অনালাপী, সংকোচশীল, আলাপপরাঙ্মুখ। **Reserved seat**—রঙ্গালয় প্রভৃতিতে যে সমস্ত আসন পূর্ব্ব হইতে বিশেষভাবে নিজের বা আত্মীয়বন্ধুবর্গের উপবেশনের জন্য বন্দোবস্ত করিয়া রাখা হয়।

rĕ-šĕrv′-ist, *n.* One who belongs to, or serves in, the reserve forces; রক্ষিত সৈন্যদলভুক্ত সৈনিক, সংরক্ষিতসৈনিক।

rĕš′-ĕr-voir (-vwär), *n.* & *v.t.* **1.** A place where anything is kept for store; an artificial lake or pond from which pipes convey water to a town; structures for storing large quantities of water for the supply of towns etc.; ভাণ্ডার; যে কৃত্রিম হ্রদ বা পুষ্করিণী হইতে নলসহযোগে নগরে জল সরবরাহ করা হয়; নগর প্রভৃতিতে জল সরবরাহের জন্য বহু পরিমাণ জল সঞ্চয়ের জন্য মৃত্তিকা বা ইষ্টকাদি নির্ম্মিত কুণ্ড, উদকাধার, বারিধানী (কথাঃ সঃ), তোয়াধার। **2.** A part of an apparatus in which a liquid is held; কোন যন্ত্রের যে অংশে কোন তরলপদার্থ সঞ্চিত থাকে। **3.** A store; ভাণ্ডার। ***Verb t.*** To store in a reservoir; ভাণ্ডারে বা জলকুণ্ডে সঞ্চিত করা। **Reservoir-pen**—মসীকুণ্ডসমন্বিত লেখনী।

rê-sĕt′, *v. t.* To receive stolen goods; to harbour a criminal; চোরাই মাল গ্রহণ করা; অপরাধীকে আশ্রয় দেওয়া।

rē-sĕt′, *v. t.* To set again; পুনরায় বসান।

rē-sĕt′-tle (-l), *v. t.* **1.** To re-establish; পুনঃ প্রতিষ্ঠিত করা। **2.** To settle over again; পুনরায় বাসস্থান স্থাপন করা। **3.** To bring into order again; পুনরায় শৃঙ্খলাস্থাপন করা।

rē-shape′, *v. t.* To shape anew; পুনরায় গড়া।

rē-ship′, *v. t.* & *i.* **1.** To put on board of a ship again; পুনরায় জাহাজে তোলা। **2.** To transfer to another ship; অপর জাহাজে স্থানান্তরিত করা। ***Verb i.*** To take ship again; পুনরায় জাহাজে উঠা। **—ment**, *n.*

rē shŭf′-fle (-l), *v. t.* To shuffle cards again; পুনর্ব্বার তাস ভেস্তান।

rē-šide′, *v. i.* **1.** To continue in a place as an inhabitant permanently or for a length of time; বাস করা, বসবাস করা, সংসার পাতিয়া বাস করা। **2.** To inhere; অন্তর্নিহিত থাকা, প্রকৃতিগত হওয়া। **3.** To be vested in person etc.; কোন ব্যক্তির উপর ন্যস্ত বা অর্পিত থাকা।

rĕš′-i-dence (-dĕns), *n.* **1.** The act of abiding or dwelling in a place; বাস, স্থিতি, সংস্থিতি, অবস্থিতি, বাস্তব্য, প্রতিষ্ঠা, অধিষ্ঠান, অবিস্থিতি। **2.** Residing where one's duties are; নিজের কার্য্যস্থানে বাস। **3.** A place where one dwells; বাসস্থান, নিবাস, আবাসস্থলী, বসতিস্থান, ঘর, নিকেতন। **4.** A dwelling house esp. one of a superior kind; a mansion; আবাসবাটী, আবাসভবন; প্রাসাদ।

rĕš′-i-dĕn-cy̆, *n.* **1.** (*Obs.*) Residence; (অপ্রঃ) বাস, নিবাস। **2.** Official residence of the representative of the Viceroy in the court of native prince in India; ভারতবর্ষের দেশীয় রাজদরবারে প্রেরিত বড়লাটের প্রতিনিধির সরকারী আবাসভবন।

rĕš′-i-dĕnt, *n.* & *adj.* **1.** One who resides or dwells in a place for some time; বাসী, নিবাসী, অধিবাসী, বাসিন্দা। **2.** Viceroy's political agent residing at the court of a native prince in India; a diplomatic agent sitting at a foreign court; ভারতবর্ষের দেশীয় রাজার রাজদরবারের বড়লাটের প্রতিনিধি; বৈদেশিক রাজদরবারে প্রেরিত কূটরাজনীতিজ্ঞ প্রতিনিধি। ***Adj.*** **1.** Residing; বাসকারী। **2.** (Of birds) Non-migratory; অদেশান্তরগামী, অপ্রব্রজনশীল। **3.** Inherent; অন্তর্নিহিত, প্রকৃতিগত। **4.** Having quarters on the spot; as, a *resident* physician; কার্য্যস্থানে বাসকারী।

rĕš-i-dĕn′-tial (-shăl), *adj.* **1.** Relating to a residence; আবাসবাটী-সম্পর্কীয়। **2.** Suitable, used for, or containing a residence; as, *residential* university; আবাসভবনোপযোগী, আবাসভবনরূপে ব্যবহৃত, আবাসসমন্বিত, সছাত্রাবাস, সাশ্রম (প্রবাসী ১৩১৯)।

rĕš-i-dĕn′-tia-ry̆ (-shê-), *adj.* & *n.* **1.** Having residence; residing; আবাসসমন্বিত; বাসকারী। **2.** Pertaining to residence; আবাসভবন-সম্পর্কীয়। ***Noun.*** **1.** A resident; বাসিন্দা। **2.** An ecclesiastic that keeps a certain residence; নির্দ্দিষ্ট ভবনে বাসকারী যাজক।

rē-šĭd′-ū-ăl, *adj.* & *n.* **1.** (*Math.*) Resulting from subtraction; ব্যবকলনজনিত, অবশিষ্ট (হিঃ কোঃ)। **2.** Remaining after a part is taken, or as residue; অবশিষ্ট, অবশেষ স্বরূপ। **3.** Remaining to be explained or corrected; "Leaving as it were, a *residual* phenomenon to be explained"; অনির্ণীত, অসংশোধিত। ***Noun.*** The expression which gives the remainder of a subtraction; ব্যবকলিত সংখ্যা। **2.** A remainder; অবশিষ্ট বা অবশেষ।

rē-šid′-ū-ā-ry̆, *n.* Pertaining to, or of the nature of, a residue or part remaining; অবশিষ্টসম্পর্কীয়, অবশিষ্টাত্মক। **Residuary legatee**—উইলের নির্দ্ধারণানুসারে সম্পত্তি বাঁটিয়া দেওয়ার পর যে ব্যক্তি অবশিষ্ট পাইয়া থাকে, অবশিষ্টভোগী।

rĕš′-i-due (-dü), *n.* **1.** Remainder; অবশিষ্ট, বাকী, অবশেষ, শেষ। **2.** (*Law*) That which remains of a testator's estate after all charges, bequest, etc. have been paid; (আইন) উইলের নির্দ্ধারণানুসারে ঋণ প্রভৃতি আদায় এবং উত্তরাধিকারিগণকে দেওয়ার পর উইল সম্পাদনকারীর সম্পত্তির

যে অংশ অবশিষ্ট থাকে। 3. (*Chem.*) Same as RESIDUUM.

rē-ṡid′ ū-ŭm, *n.* 1. Residue; অবশিষ্টাংশ, অবশেষ, পরিশেষ 2. (*Law*) Same as RESIDUE, 2. 3. The substance left after combustion or evaporation; জ্বলন বা বাষ্পীকরণের পর যে অংশ অবশিষ্ট থাকে, অবশেষ (হিঃ কোঃ), সংস্কার (হিঃ কোঃ), সংস্কারশেষ (ঐ)। 4. The scums or dregs of society; সমাজের হীনতম শ্রেণীর লোক।

rē-sign′ (-sīn), *v. t.* To sign again; পুনরায় সহি করা।

rē-sign′ (-zīn), *v. t.* 1. To give up; to give back as an office or commission; ত্যাগ করা, ছাড়িয়া দেওয়া, পরিত্যাগ করা; কার্য্যত্যাগ করা, ইস্তফা দেওয়া। 2. To give oneself or one's mind up to some condition, emotion, etc.; as, they *resigned* themselves up to a solitary life; গা ছাড়িয়া দেওয়া, গা ঢালিয়া দেওয়া, আত্মসমর্পণ করা। **—ed,** *adj.* **—ed-ly,** *adv.*

rěṡ-ĭg-nā′-tion, *n.* 1. The act of resigning; ত্যাগ, পরিত্যাগ, পদত্যাগ, উৎসর্গ, উৎসর্জন। 2. Submission; quiet submission or acquiescence; as, *resignation* to the will of providence; সমর্পণ, আত্মসমর্পণ; নীরবে আত্মসমর্পণ।

rē-ṡīle′, *v. i.* To start back; to recede or draw back from a purpose or engagement; to retract; প্রতিক্ষিপ্ত হওয়া, ঠিকরান; কোনরূপ উদ্দেশ্যসাধন বা প্রতিশ্রুতি পালনে পশ্চাৎপদ হওয়া; প্রত্যাহার করা। **—sil′-i-en-cy,** *n.* **—sil′-i-ent,** *adj.*

rěṡ′-in, *n.* A solid inflammable substance obtained from trees either by exudation or extraction; রজন, ধুনা। [Syn. সর্জ্জরস, সালনির্যাস, সালরস, যক্ষধূপ, ধূনক বৃক্ষধূপ, সর্জ্জমণি, ললন, সুরধূপ, দেবেষ্ট, রাল, বহ্নিবল্লভ, শীতল, অগ্নিবল্লভ, তীক্ষ্ণতৈল, বহুরূপ, মহারূপ, ধূপন, রসাহ্ব, দাধি, বৃক্ষনির্যাস, সাল, কনকোদ্ভব, সর্জ্জনির্য্যাসক, সুরভি, বল, কবলক। **—a′-ce-ous, —ous, —if′-er-ous,** *adjs* **—ate,** *v. t.* **—i-fy,** *v. t. & i.* **—ize,** *v. t.*

rěs i pis′-cence (-sěns), *n.* (*Rare*) Change of mind; reformation; repentance; recognition of error; মানসিক পরিবর্তন; সংশোধন; অনুতাপ; ভ্রমস্বীকৃতি।

rē-ṡist′, *v. t. & i.* To stand against; to oppose; বিরুদ্ধে দণ্ডায়মান হওয়া; বাধা দেওয়া, প্রতিরোধ করা, নিরোধ করা, নিবারণ করা, সম্বরণ করা, ঠেকাইয়া রাখা। *Verb i.* To offer resistance; বাধা প্রদান করা। **—er,** *n.* **—i-ble,** *adj.* That can be resisted; প্রতিরোধনীয়, নিবার্য্য। **—less,** *adj.* 1. Irresistible; অপ্রতিরোধনীয়, অপ্রতিরোধ্য, প্রতীকারাশক্য। 2. Having no power to resist; অপ্রতিরোধনক্ষম। **—less-ly,** *adv.* **—sis′-tive** *adj.* **—sis-tiv′-i-ty,** *n.* The quality of resisting; রোধশীলতা (সাঃ পঃ)।

rē-ṡist′, *n.* 1. (*Obs.*) Opposition; (অপ্রঃ) বাধা। 2. A substance to preserve the parts white in calico-printing; যে বস্তুর সাহায্যে ছিটের কাপড়ের যে সকল অংশ শাদা রাখার দরকার তাহা শাদা রাখা যায়। **Resist work**—নীল জমির উপর শাদা রঙ্গের ফুটকী বা দাগবিশিষ্ট ছিটের কাপড়।

rē-ṡist′-ance (-ăns), *n.* 1. The act of resisting; opposition; বাধাপ্রদান; বাধা, প্রতিবন্ধ, রোধ, প্রতিরোধ, নিবারণ। 2. (*Phys.*) The opposition offered by any body to the pressure or movement of another; (পদার্থ-বিজ্ঞান) প্রতিরোধকারী বল, প্রতিরোধ (হিঃ কোঃ), স্থানাবরোধকতা। 3. (*Electr., Magnet. & Heat*) Non-conductivity; (তাপ, তাড়িত ও চুম্বক বিদ্যা) অচালকতা, অপরিচালকতা, রোধ (সাঃ পঃ), প্রতিরোধ (ঐ)। 4. (*Elect.*) A part of an electric apparatus offering resistance to a current; তাড়িতযন্ত্রের অংশবিশেষ—যদ্দ্বারা তাড়িত-প্রবাহ বাধাপ্রাপ্ত হয়। **Mechanical resistance**—ঘর্ষণ (সাঃ পঃ), বিঘর্ষণ (ঐ), বাধা (ঐ)। **Passive resistance**—শারীরিক বল প্রকাশ না করিয়া কোনরূপ অন্যায় আদেশ বা আইন মান্য করিতে অস্বীকার, নিষ্ক্রিয় প্রতিরোধ, নিরস্ত্র প্রতিরোধ। **Resistance-box**—এক বা ততোধিক তারকুণ্ডলীসমন্বিত পেটক। **Resistance-coil**—প্রতিরোধ বৃদ্ধি করার জন্য তাড়িত প্রবাহের পথে নিবিষ্ট তারকুণ্ডলী, বাধককুণ্ডলী। **Resisting medium**—অবরোধক মধ্যস্থ (হিঃ কোঃ)।

rē-ṡist-i-bil′-i-ty̆, *n.* 1. The quality or state of being resistible; প্রতিরোধ্যতা। 2. The power of offering resistance; প্রতিরোধকতা।

rē-sōle′, *v. t.* To furnish with a new sole; নূতন তলি লাগান।

rěṡ′-ō-lū-ble (-bl), *adj.* Capable of being again melted or dissolved; পুনর্দ্রবণীয়, পুনর্দ্রাব্য, পুনর্গালনীয়।

rěṡ′-ō-lūte, *adj.* Determined; firm; decided; bold; বদ্ধসংকল্প; দৃঢ়প্রতিজ্ঞ, স্থিরমতি, স্থিরচিত্ত, স্থিরপ্রতিজ্ঞ, স্থিরনিশ্চয়; দৃঢ়সংকল্প, কৃতনিশ্চয়; সাহসী, নির্ভীক। **—ly,** *adv.*

rěṡ-ō-lū′-tion, *n.* 1. The act or process of resolving or separating the parts of anything; transformation; বিশ্লেষণ; রূপান্তর। 2. Dissolution; বিদ্রাবণ। 3. Firmness of purpose; constancy; দৃঢ়সংকল্প, স্থিরসংকল্প, দৃঢ়প্রতিজ্ঞা; সংকল্প (সাংখ্য), ব্যবসায় (হিঃ ক্রোঃ), অধ্যবসায় (ঐ)। 4. A formal determination or expression of opinion of a legislative or other body; a proposition put before a meeting to discuss and decide; as, the *resolution* of a meeting; ব্যবস্থাপক সভা প্রভৃতির নির্দ্ধারণ; প্রস্তাব। 5. (*Med.*) The disappearance of inflammation without suppuration; (ভৈষজ্য-শাস্ত্র) ফোঁড়া প্রভৃতি বসিয়া যাওন। 6. (*Mech.*) The act of resolving a force into two or more, which would have the same effect ; কোন বলকে দুই বা তদধিক তুল্য শক্তিসম্পন্ন বলে পরিণত করণ। 7. Substitution of two short syllables for one long ; (ছন্দঃশাস্ত্র) একটী গুরু শব্দাংশের পরিবর্ত্তে দুইটী লঘু শব্দাংশ ব্যবহার। 8. Solution ; answer ; as, the *resolution* of a riddle ; সমাধান ; উত্তর।

rĕs'-ō-lū-tive (-tĭv), *adj.* & *n.* (*Rare*) Resolving ; (কচিদ্ ব্যবহৃত) বিদ্রাবক। ***Noun.*** A resolutive drug ; যে ঔষধ প্রয়োগে ফোঁড়া প্রভৃতি বসিয়া যায়। **Resolutive-condition**—যে সর্তমতে কাজ করা হইলে চুক্তি প্রভৃতির অবসান হয়।

rē-solve' (-zŏlv), *v.t.*, *i.* & *n.* **1.** To reduce to component elements ; বিশ্লেষণ করা। 2. To determine ; to decide ; স্থির করা ; সংকল্প করা। **3.** (*Mech.*) To split up a force in two or more equivalent forces ; (যন্ত্র-বিজ্ঞান) কোন বলকে দুই বা ততোধিক তুল্যশক্তিক বলে পরিণত করা। **4.** To declare or decide by a formal vote ; ভোট দ্বারা প্রকাশ বা স্থির করা। 5. To solve ; to unravel ; সমাধান করা ; উদ্‌ঘাটন করা। 6. To explain ; to make clear ; to dispel ; as, *resolve* me this doubt ; ব্যাখ্যা করা ; সুখবোধ্য করা, বিশদ করা ; সংশয়াদি নিরাস করা। 7. To disperse as an inflammation or tumour ; ফোঁড়া প্রভৃতি বসাইয়া দেওয়া। 8. To convert or transform ; রূপান্তরিত করা। ***Verb i.*** 1. To disintegrate ; বিশ্লিষ্ট হওয়া। 2. To determine by vote ; ভোট দ্বারা স্থির করা। 3. To determine ; স্থির করা, সংকল্প করা। **4.** (*Law.*) To become void ; to lapse ; (আইন) অসিদ্ধ হওয়া, বাতিল হওয়া; খেলাপ হওয়া। ***Noun.*** A fixed or firm determination ; স্থিরপ্রতিজ্ঞা, স্থিরসঙ্কল্প, দৃঢ়সঙ্কল্প। **—solv'-a-ble,** *adj.*

rē-sŏlv'-ĕnt, *adj.* & *n.* Causing solution; বিদ্রাবক। ***Noun.*** (*Med.*) That which has the power of dispersing as an inflammation or a tumour ; যে ঔষধের সাহায্যে ফোঁড়া প্রভৃতি বসিয়া যায়।

rĕs'-ō-nance (-năns), *n.* **1.** The act of resounding ; অনুনাদ (সাঃ পঃ), অনুরণন (ঐ)। 2. (*Phys.*) The prolongation of sound by reflection or by the production of vibrations in other bodies ; (পদার্থ-বিদ্যা) পরাবর্ত্তন, অপর বস্তুতে কম্পন উৎপাদনদ্বারা ধ্বনি দীর্ঘীকরণ, প্রতিকম্পন (সাঃ পঃ), অনুকম্পন (ঐ), অনুজ্ঞাপন (ঐ)। 3. (*Med.*) An ausculatory sound ; (ভৈষজ্য-শাস্ত্র) আকর্ণন-যন্ত্র (stethescope) সংযোগে বক্ষঃস্থল, হৃৎপিণ্ড, প্রভৃতি হইতে যে ধ্বনি শ্রুত হয়, অনুনাদ (হঃ চঃ), প্রতিধ্বনি (ঐ)। **Resonance-box**—বাদ্যযন্ত্রের কোষ্ঠ-বিশেষ—যাহার সাহায্যে উহার ধ্বনি বৃদ্ধিপ্রাপ্ত হয়, অনুনাদীপেটী (হিঃ কোঃ)।

rĕs'-ō-nănt, *adj.* 1. Returning sound ; অনুনাদী, প্রতিশব্দায়মান, অনুরণক। 2. Resounding with ; মুখরিত, মুখর। 3. Characterised by resonance in the nasal passage ; অনুনাসিক। 4. (*Phys.*) Tending to prolong sound by vibration ; (পদার্থ-বিদ্যা) কম্পনদ্বারা ধ্বনির স্থায়িত্ব বর্দ্ধক, অনুকম্পক। **—ly,** *adv.*

rĕs'-ō-nā-tor (-têr), *n.* **1.** An instrument for facilitating the analysis of compound sounds ; মিশ্রধ্বনি বিশ্লেষণের জন্য যন্ত্রবিশেষ। 2. An appliance for increasing sound by resonance ; পরিবর্তন বা কম্পন-প্রবাহদ্বারা ধ্বনিবৃদ্ধি করার জন্য যন্ত্রবিশেষ, অনুরণক (সাঃ পঃ)। 3. (*In wireless Teleg.*) An apparatus for detecting electric waves ; (অতারতাড়িত-বার্তা) তাড়িতোর্ম্মির সত্তা নির্ণয়ের জন্য যন্ত্রবিশেষ, অনুজ্ঞাপক (সাঃ পঃ)।

rē-sŏrb', *v. t.* To absorb again ; পুনরায় শুষিয়া লওয়া। **—ence,** *n.* **—ent,** *adj.*

rĕs-ŏr'-cin (-sĭn), *n.* (*Chem.*) A dye-stuff produced by the action of potash on galbanum ; (রসায়ন-শাস্ত্র) গন্ধবিরজার উপর ক্ষারের ক্রিয়াদ্বারা উৎপন্ন রাগদ্রব্যবিশেষ।

rē-sŏrp'-tion, *n.* The act of resorbing ; পুনঃশোষণ।

rē-sŏrt', *v. i.* **1.** To have recourse ; as, I was compelled to *resort* to force ; আশ্রয় লওয়া, শরণ লওয়া, আশ্রয় গ্রহণ করা। 2. To go ; to repair ; যাওয়া ; গমন করা।

rē-sŏrt', *n.* 1. A resource or refuge ; আশ্রয়, শরণ, গতি, আশ্রয়-স্থল, সদন। 2. The act or habit of frequenting or going in numbers ; বহুসংখ্যায় গমন। 3. A place much frequented (esp. for rest, recreation, health, etc.) ; বহুলোকের গমনস্থল, বৈঠক। 4. (*Rare*) Crowd ; (কচিদ্ ব্যবহৃত) জনতা, ভিড়। **Last resort**—শেষ আশ্রয়স্থল।

rē-sŏrt', *v. t.* To sort again ; পুনরায় শ্রেণীবিভাগ করা, পুনরায় কিসিম করা।

rē-sound' (-zownd), *v.t.* & *i.* **1.** To send back sound ; প্রতিধ্বনিত করা, অনুরণিত করা। 2. (*Rare*) To extol with sound ; (কচিদ্‌ব্যবহৃত) বাদ্যভাণ্ড প্রভৃতির সাহায্যে যশোকীর্ত্তন করা। ***Verb i.*** 1. To re-echo ; প্রতিধ্বনিত হওয়া, অনুরণিত হওয়া। 2. To ring with some sound ; মুখরিত হওয়া, নিনাদিত হওয়া। 3. To be renowned ; "Milton, a name to *resound* for ages" ; to be celebrated ; কীর্ত্তিমান হওয়া ; কীর্ত্তিত হওয়া। **—ing-ly,** *adv.*

rē-source' (-sōrs), *n.* **1.** Any source of help, support or safety ; expedient ; আশ্রয়স্থল, গতি ; উপায়, কৌশল, ফন্দী। 2. (*Pl.*) Pecuniary means ; সঙ্গতি, সম্বল, সংস্থান। 3. The collective means possessed by any country for its own support or defence ; কোন দেশের রক্ষা ও পোষণের উপযোগী সঙ্গতি। 4. Capability of meeting a situation ; as, a man of *resource*; উপায়জ্ঞতা। **—ful,** *adj.* 1. Clever in finding out expedient; উপায়জ্ঞ, উপায়োদ্ভাবনক্ষম। 2. Rich; সঙ্গতিশালী, সঙ্গতিসম্পন্ন। **—ful-ness,** *n.* **—less,** *adj.* Destitute of resources; সঙ্গতিহীন, সঙ্গতিশূন্য। **Having no other resources**—অনন্যগতি হইয়া, অনন্যোপায় হইয়া। **Last resource**—শেষ উপায়, অন্তিম উপায়।

rĕ-spĕct', *n.* 1. Reference; সম্পর্ক, সম্বন্ধ। 2. Regard; reverence; credit; মান, সম্মান, শ্রদ্ধা, মান্যতা, সম্ভ্রম; আদর, সমাদর, খাতির, কদর, ইজ্জত। 3. An expression of regard; as, give him my *respects*; অভিবাদন, নমস্কার। 4. A particular; as, in all *respects*; an aspect; বিষয়; দিক্‌, বিভাগ। 5. Partiality or favour in regard of persons or things; as, judges should never show *respect* of persons; পক্ষপাতিত্ব, ভেদবুদ্ধি, ভেদদৃষ্টি, অনুগ্রহ। 6. (*Obs.*) Consideration; interests; (অপ্রঃ) বিবেচনা; স্বার্থ, মনোযোগ। 7. Heed; regard; মনোযোগ; প্রণিধান। **As respects**—With regard to; সম্পর্কে। **In all respects, In every respect**—সর্ব্বাংশে। **In respect (of)**—With reference to; সম্পর্কে। Considering; since; বিবেচনা করিতে গেলে; যেহেতু, কেননা। **In this respect**—এই হিসাবে। **To have respect to**—To have relation to; সম্পর্ক থাকা, সম্বন্ধ থাকা। To give attention to; মন দেওয়া, প্রণিধান করা। **To pay one's respect**—To show respects by making a call; কোন সম্ভ্রান্ত লোকের বাটীতে যাইয়া নমস্কার জানান। **With due respect**—যথাবিহিত সম্মানপুরঃসর। **Without respect**—Without regard to; বিবেচনা না করিয়া, গণনায় না আনিয়া, বিচার না করিয়া। **With respect to**—With reference to; সম্পর্কে, সম্বন্ধে।

rĕ-spĕct', *v. t.* 1. To be concerned with; সম্পর্কীয় হওয়া, সংক্রান্ত হওয়া, বিষয়ক হওয়া, সম্পর্ক থাকা, সংস্রব থাকা। 2. To look up to with reverence or respect; সম্মান করা, শ্রদ্ধা করা, ভক্তি করা, মান্য করা। 3. (*Obs.*) To regard; (অপ্রঃ) গণ্য করা, বিবেচনা করা। 4. To avoid obtruding or interfering with; to spare; as, to *respect* one's privacy; to *respect* one's feelings; অনাহূতভাবে প্রবেশ না করা; হস্তক্ষেপ না করা, রক্ষা করা, সমীহা করা। **To respect oneself**—To have self-respect; আত্মমর্য্যাদা বোধ থাকা, আত্মসম্মান বোধ থাকা। **To respect one's silence**—To let one remain silent; কাহারো নীরবতা ভঙ্গ না করা। **To respect the person** or **persons**—To show undue favour or bias towards—কাহারো প্রতি অনুচিত পক্ষপাত বা অনুগ্রহ প্রদর্শন করা।

rĕ-spĕct-ă-bil'-i-tў, *n.* 1. The state or quality of being respectable; মান্যতা, সম্মানসম্পন্নতা, সামাজিক মর্য্যাদা, সম্ভ্রম। 2. A respectable person or thing; "Smooth shaven *respectabilities* not a few one finds, that are not good for much"—*Carlyle*; সম্ভ্রান্তপরিবারের ব্যক্তি, শ্রদ্ধাজনক বস্তু, সামাজিক সম্ভ্রমশালী ব্যক্তি।

rĕ-spĕct'-ă-ble (-bl), *adj.* & *n.* 1. Worthy of respect; মান্য, সম্মানার্হ, শ্রদ্ধেয়, মাননীয়। 2. Belonging to a fairly good position in society; as, a *respectable* citizen; ভদ্র (মিলনে), সামাজিকপদমর্য্যাদাসম্পন্ন। 3. Befitting a respectable person; as, *respectable* cloth; ভদ্রোচিত। 4. Considerable in size or number; as, a *respectable* hill; moderate; mediocre; passable; tolerable; "It is at best a *respectable* production"; বিপুলায়তন, বিশাল, বহুল; মাঝারিগোছের; একরকম, চলনসই; বড় মন্দ নয়। *Noun.* A respectable person; মান্যগণ্য লোক, মান্য ব্যক্তি।

rĕ-spĕct'-ĕr, *n.* One who respects; শ্রদ্ধাপ্রদর্শনকারী। **Respecter of persons**—One who regards or judges with partiality; পক্ষপাত প্রদর্শনকারী, ভেদবুদ্ধিসম্পন্ন ব্যক্তি।

rĕ-spĕct'-fŭl, *adj.* Full of, marked by, or showing, respect; ভক্তিমান, শ্রদ্ধাপূর্ণ, ভক্তিপূর্ণ, সম্ভ্রমপূর্ণ, সম্ভ্রমসূচক, শ্রদ্ধাসম্পন্ন, শ্রদ্ধাশীল, শ্রদ্ধাপ্রদর্শক। **—ly,** *adv.* In a respectful manner; ভক্তিপূর্ব্বক, শ্রদ্ধাসহকারে, সসম্ভ্রমে, সম্ভ্রমভরে।

rĕ-spĕc'-tive (-tĭv), *adj.* Relating or pertaining severally each to each; নিজ নিজ, আপন আপন, স্ব স্ব। **—ly,** *adv.* Each to each; severally; ইতরেতর; যথাক্রমে।

rē-spĕll', *v. t.* To spell again; পুনরায় বর্ণবিন্যাস করা, পুনরায় বানান করা।

rĕ-spīr'-ă-ble (-bl), *adj.* Suitable for respiration; capable of being breathed; শ্বসনযোগ্য; শ্বসনীয়।

rĕs-pĭ-rā'-tion, *n.* 1. The act of breathing; the function of breathing; শ্বসন; শ্বাসপ্রশ্বাসক্রিয়া, শ্বাসকর্ম্ম (সাঃ পঃ), শ্বাসোচ্ছ্বাস (হিঃ কোঃ)। [Syn. প্রাণ (সুর্থাঃ বাঃ), অসু (ঐ)।] 2. (Of plants) The absorption of oxygen from the air, and the emission of carbonic acid; (বৃক্ষাদি সম্পর্কে) বায়ু হইতে অম্লজান বাষ্প গ্রহণ এবং অঙ্গারাম্লমোচন।

rĕs'-pĭ-rā'-tor (-tĕr), *n.* 1. A contrivance of network which covers the mouth, and protects the lungs from the sudden inspiration of cold or impure air; নিঃশ্বাসবায়ু উষ্ণীকরণের জন্য অথবা শোধনের নিমিত্ত মুখের উপর যে জালের আবরণ পরা হয়, শ্বাসজালি।

rĕ-spīre', *v. i.* & *t.* 1. To breathe in and out; শ্বাসপ্রশ্বাসক্রিয়া সম্পন্ন করা। 2. To breathe again after distress, trouble, etc.; হাঁপছাড়া। 3. (*Obs.*) To take rest or refreshment

(অপ্রঃ) বিশ্রাম করা, শ্রমাপনোদন করা। *Verb t.* 1. To inhale and exhale; শ্বাসপ্রশ্বাসক্রিয়া সম্পন্ন করা। 2. (*Rare*) To exhale; (ক্বচিদ্ব্যবহৃত) বাষ্পাকারে নিঃসৃত করা। **–spir'-a-to-ry,** *adj.*

rĕs'-pīte, *n.* & *v. t.* 1. Extension of time granted or asked; মাহালত। 2. Interval of rest; pause; অবকাশ, অবসর; বিরাম। 3. Temporary suspension of the execution of a criminal; প্রাণদণ্ডে দণ্ডিত ব্যক্তির ফাঁসি কিছুদিনের জন্য স্থগিত রাখন। *Verb t.* 1. To give or grant a respite; সময় দেওয়া, মাহালত দেওয়া। 2. To reprieve; প্রাণদণ্ডে দণ্ডিত ব্যক্তির ফাঁসি প্রভৃতি কিছুদিনের জন্য স্থগিত রাখা। 3. To put off; as, the case was *respited* sine die; স্থগিত রাখা। 4. (*Mil.*) To withhold pay; (সামরিক-শাস্ত্র) বেতন দেওয়া স্থগিত রাখা, বেতন আটকান।

rĕs-plĕnd'-ĕnt, *adj.* Brilliant; vividly or dazzlingly bright; সমুজ্জ্বল, অর্চ্চিষ্মান, মহোজ্জ্বল, প্রোজ্জ্বল; দ্যুতিমান, মহাপ্রভ, তীব্রোজ্জ্বল, আলো-ঝলমল (রবীঃ)। **–ence, –en-cy,** *ns.*

rē-spŏnd', *v. i.* 1. To answer; উত্তর দেওয়া। 2. To exhibit some action or effect in reply to a force or stimulus; "To every theme *responds* thy various lay"; সাড়া দেওয়া। 3. (*U. S.*) To be answerable for payment; টাকা প্রভৃতি প্রদানের জন্য দায়ী হওয়া। 4. (*Obs.*) To correspond; (অপ্রঃ) অনুসারী হওয়া। **–ence, –en-cy,** *ns.* 1. Correspondence; সামঞ্জস্য, ঐক্য। 2. Response to a stimlus; সাড়া।

rē-spŏnd', *n.* 1. A reply; উত্তর। 2. A short anthem chanted in the interval of reading a chapter in a religions service; উপাসনাকালে বাইবেলের কোন অধ্যায় পাঠের অবকাশ-কালে গীত ক্ষুদ্র ভজনসংগীত। 3. (*Arch.*) A half pillar or pilaster attached to a wall to support an arch; প্রাচীরগাত্র হইতে অর্দ্ধ বা ঈষদুদ্গত তোরণধারক স্তম্ভবিশেষ।

rē-spŏnd'-ĕnt, *adj.*, & *n.* 1. Answering; উত্তরদাতা, উত্তরকারী। 2. Responsive to some stimulus; সাড়া প্রদায়ক। *Noun.* 1. One who answers; one who maintains a thesis in reply; উত্তরদাতা; যে ব্যক্তি কোন নিবন্ধের স্বপক্ষে উত্তর প্রদান করে। 2. A defendant; esp. a defendant in a divorce suit; প্রতিবাদী, প্রতিপক্ষ, উত্তরপক্ষ; বিশেষতঃ বিবাহ-বিচ্ছেদের মোকদ্দমার প্রতিবাদী।

rē-sponse' (-spŏns), *n.* 1. The act of replying; a reply; উত্তরপ্রদান; উত্তর, প্রতিবাক্য, জবাব। 2. A responsive act or feeling; সাড়া, প্রতিস্পন্দন (ব্রহ্মবিদ্যা)। 3. An oracular answer; কোন প্রশ্নের উত্তরে দেবতার বা দেবাশ্রিত পুরোহিত বা যাজিকার উত্তর, দেববাণী, প্রশ্ন (হিঃ কোঃ), শাকুন (ঐ)। 4. (*R. C. Church*) A kind of anthem sung after the morning lesson; একপ্রকার প্রাভাতিক ভজনসঙ্গীত।

rē-spŏn-si-bil'-i-tȳ, *n.* 1. The state of being responsible; দায়িত্ব, জবাবদাতৃতা (হিঃ কোঃ), জবাবদিহী (ঐ)। 2. A care or trust for which one is responsible; দায়, ঝুঁকি, অনুযোজ্যতা (হিঃ কোঃ), জিম্মাদারী (ঐ)।

rē-spŏns-i-ble (-bl), *adj.* 1. Accountable; answerable; দায়ী; জবাবদীহি। 2. Reliable; trustworthy; as, the delivery of parcels must be undertaken by one *responsible* person; respectable; নির্ভরযোগ্য, দায়িত্বসম্পন্ন, দায়িত্ববোধ-সম্পন্ন; বিশ্বাসযোগ্য; পদস্থ, প্রতিপত্তিশালী। 3. Involving responsibility; as, a *responsible* office; দায়িত্বপূর্ণ।

rē-spŏn'-sion, *n.* Same as LITTLE GO (which see)

rē-spŏn'-sive (-sĭv), *n.* 1. Answering; উত্তরদায়ক। 2. Responding readily to some influences; sympathetic; ত্বরা সাড়াপ্রদায়ক; সমবেদনা-সম্পন্ন, দরদী। **–ly,** *adv.* **–ness,** *n.*

rē-spŏn'-sō-rȳ, *n.* The answer of the people to the priest in church service; গির্জ্জার উপাসনায় যাজকের প্রশ্নে উপাসকগণ যে উত্তর প্রদান করে।

rĕst, *v. i.* & *t.* 1. To lay at rest; as, to *rest* on a bed; শুইয়া আরাম করা, শুইয়া বিশ্রাম করা। 2. To be dead; as his brother *rests* in the churchyard; চিরবিরাম ভোগ করা, অনন্তনিদ্রায় শায়িত হওয়া। 3. To take repose; to be still; as, the waves that never *rest*; বিশ্রাম করা, বিরাম করা, জিরান; শান্ত থাকা, প্রশান্ত থাকা। 4. To abide; to remain; "The spirit of the Lord shall *rest* upon him"; বাস করা; থাকা, অবস্থান করা। 5. To be supported; as, the roof *rests* on pillars; অবলম্বিত হওয়া, ধৃত হওয়া। 6. To have quiet of mind; মানসিক শান্তি থাকা। 7. To rely on or upon; as, to *rest on* a man's promise; to put trust; to be satisfied; "To *rest* in heaven's determination"; নির্ভর করা; বিশ্বাসস্থাপন করা; সন্তুষ্ট থাকা। 8. To stand; as, I will tell you how the matter *rests*; দাঁড়ান। *Verb t.* 1. To give rest or repose to; to keep undisturbed; বিশ্রাম দেওয়া, বিরাম দেওয়া; শান্ত রাখা। 2. To place as on a support; "Her weary head upon your bosom *rest*"; অবলম্বিত রাখা, সমুদ্ধৃত রাখা। **Land was allowed to rest**—জমি পতিত রাখা হইয়াছিল। **The last resting place**—সমাধি, কবর। **The matter cannot rest here**—It has to be further examined, investigated or discussed; এই বিষয়টী আরও অনুসন্ধান বা আলোচনা করিতে হইবে। **To rest one's self**—To take rest; বিশ্রাম করা। **To rest on the oars**—See OAR. **To rest with**—To depend upon; নির্ভর করা।

rĕst, *n.* 1. A cessation from labour; বিশ্রাম, বিরাম, বিশ্রান্তি,

কর্ম্মবিরাম, জিরেন। 2. Peace ; tranquillity ; as, *rest* of body or mind ; শান্তি ; প্রশান্তভাব, নিরুদ্বেগ। 3. Slumber ; as, to retire to *rest* ; নিদ্রা, শয়ন। 4. (*Poet.*) Death ; (কবিতায়) চিরনিদ্রা, অনন্তনিদ্রা, চিরবিরাম। 5. (*Phys.*) Continuance in the same position or place ; (পদার্থবিদ্যা) একই স্থানে বা একই অবস্থায় স্থিতি, গতিহীনতা, নিশ্চলতা, নিষ্ক্রিয়তা (হিঃ কোঃ), গতিরোধ (ঐ), স্থিতি (ঐ)। 6. That on which anything rests or leans for support ; নির্ভর, অবলম্বন, আশ্রয়। 7. Lodging-place or shelter provided for sailors, cabmen, etc. ; নাবিক, শকটচালক, প্রভৃতির জন্য আশ্রয়কুটীর। 8. (*Pros.*) Caesura ; (ছন্দঃ শাস্ত্র) যতি। 9. (*Mus.*) An interval between tones ; also its marks ; (সঙ্গীতশাস্ত্র) বিরাম (মিউজিক) ; বিরামচিহ্ন। **Rest-balk**—লাঙ্গলপদ্ধতির মধ্যে মধ্যে যে আল রাখা হয়। **Rest-cure** — কিছুকালের জন্য রোগীকে বিছানায় বিশ্রাম করাইয়া রোগের চিকিৎসা। **Rest-day** — বিশ্রাম দিবস ; (বিরল প্রয়োগ) রবিবার। **Rest-house**—ডাকবাংলা, বিশ্রামবাটিকা, বিশ্রামশালা। **To set at a rest**—To decide finally ; চূড়ান্ত নিষ্পত্তি করা।

rĕst, *v. i.* To remain ; to be left ; থাকা ; বাকী থাকা, অবশিষ্ট থাকা।

rĕst, *n.* 1. Remainder ; remaining parts or individuals ; অবশিষ্ট, পরিশেষ; অবশিষ্ট অংশ, অবশিষ্ট লোকগণ। 2. The reserve fund of a bank ; ধনাগার প্রভৃতির অসময়ের জন্য সংরক্ষিত অর্থ। **And the rest**—এবং অন্যান্য, গয়রহ। **For the rest**—As regards all other matters or points ; অন্য সকল ব্যাপার বা বিষয় সম্পর্কে।

rĕst, *n.* (*Hist.*) A contrivance attached to the cuirass to receive the butt end of the lance ; as, to keep one's lance at *rest* ; (ইতিহাস) আক্রমণকালে বর্শার বাঁট রক্ষার জন্য বর্ম্মসংলগ্ন কলবিশেষ।

rē-stămp′, *v. t.* To stamp again ; পুনরায় ছাপ দেওয়া, পুনরায় মোহর দেওয়া।

rē-stârt′, *v. i.* To start again ; পুনরায় যাত্রা করা।

rē-stāte′, *v.t.* To state over again ; পুনরায় ব্যক্ত করা।

rĕs′-tau-rănt (-tö-), *n.* A house where liquors and cooked food are sold ; an eating house ; জলযোগাগার, জলযোগালয় ; ভোজনাগার।

restaurateur, (*F.*), *n.* One who keeps a restaurant ; জলযোগালয়ের মালীক, ভোজনগারের অধিকারী।

rĕst′-fụl, *adj.* Full of rest ; soothing ; quiet ; বিরামপূর্ণ ; আরামজনক ; শান্ত, প্রশান্ত, অচঞ্চল। **—ly**, *adv.* **—ness**, *n.*

rĕst′-hăr-row (-ō), *n.* A British shrub ; ব্রিটিশদ্বীপজাত গুল্মবিশেষ।

rĕs′-tiff, *n.* Same as RESTIVE (which see.)

rĕs′-ti-tūte, *v. t.* & *i.* (*Rare*) To restore to a former state to be restored to a former state ; (ক্বচিদ্‌ব্যবহৃত) পূর্ব্বাবস্থায় আনা ; পূর্ব্বাবস্থায় আনীত হওয়া।

rĕs′-ti-tū′-tion, *n.* 1. The act of restoring anything to its rightful owner, or giving an equivalent for any loss, damage, or injury ; as, the *restitution* of conjugal right ; প্রত্যর্পণ, প্রত্যানয়ন (হিঃ কোঃ), পুনঃপ্রদান, ক্ষতিপূরণ। 2. (*Phys.*) Recovering of a former state ; tendency to resume a previous state ; as, the *restitution* of an elastic body ; (পদার্থবিদ্যা) পূর্ব্বাবস্থাপ্রাপ্তি ; পূর্ব্বাবস্থাপ্রাপণশীলতা।

rĕs′-tive (-tĭv), *adj.* Unruly unwilling to go on ; as, a *restive* horse ; unmangeable ; অদম্য ; অগ্রগমনে অনিচ্ছুক ; দুর্দ্দান্ত, অবাধ্য, নগরা। **—ly**, *adv.* **—ness**, *n.*

rĕst′-lĕss, *adj.* 1. Not resting ; not quiet ; uneasy ; অবিরাম ; অশান্ত, চঞ্চল, অব্যবস্থিতচিত্ত, ব্যগ্রচিত্ত, লীলালোল (*poet.*), বিহ্বল ; অস্থির, ছটফটে, ব্যাকুল, উতালা, উতরোল। 2. Unsettled in disposition ; অস্থিরমতি, চঞ্চলমতি, দুরন্ত। 3. Sleepless ; "My nights are very *restless* and tiresome" ; বিনিদ্র, নিদ্রাহীন, নিদ্রাত্যক্ত, অনাগতনিদ্র। 4. Never ceasing or pausing ; as, *restless* eyes ; লোল, চটুল, বিলোল, অবিশ্রান্ত, অবিরাম। **—ness**, *n.* 1. The state of being restless ; চাঞ্চল্য। 2. Uneasiness or unquietness of mind ; অশান্তি, অস্থিরতা, আইঢাই, ছটফটানি, ব্যাকুলতা।

rē-stŏck′, *v. t.* To stock again or anew ; পুনরায় ভাণ্ডারজাত করা।

rĕs-tōr-ā′-tion, *n.* 1. The act of replacing in a former state or postion ; পুনঃস্থাপন, পুনঃপ্রতিষ্ঠাপন। 2. Renewal ; revival ; re-establishment ; as, the *restoration* of commerce ; নবীকরণ ; পুনরুজ্জীবন ; পুনঃপ্রতিষ্ঠা। 3. Recovery, as of health ; স্বাস্থ্যলাভ। 4. Repairing injuries suffered by works of art, buildings, etc. ; as, the *restoration* of an ancient monument ; ভগ্ন বা নষ্ট প্রাসাদ, শিল্পদ্রব্য প্রভৃতির সংস্কার, জীর্ণোদ্ধার, নষ্টোদ্ধার, নষ্টোদ্ধরণ, পুনঃসংস্কার (বাপীকূপ তড়াগেষু দেবতায়তনেষু চ পুনঃসংস্কারকর্ত্তারং লভতে মৌলিকং ফলং—বিষ্ণুস্মৃতি, ৯১ অধ্যায়)। 4. A model or drawing representing the original form of an extinct animal, ruined buildings, etc. ; অধুনালুপ্ত জন্তু বা ধ্বংসপ্রাপ্ত প্রাসাদ প্রভৃতির পূর্ব্বরূপের প্রতিরূপস্বরূপ চিত্র, আদর্শ, প্রভৃতি। 5. The re-establishment of monarchy by the return of Charles II. in 1660 ; ২য় চার্লসের প্রত্যাবর্ত্তনের ফলে ১৬৬০ খৃঃ অব্দে ইংলণ্ডে পুনঃ রাজতন্ত্র শাসনের প্রতিষ্ঠা।

rĕs-tōr-ā′-tion-ĭsm, *n.* Belief in a final restoration of all to the favour and presence of God ; চরমে সকলেই ঈশ্বরের অনুগ্রহ ও তাঁহার সহিত সালোক্য লাভ করিবে—এই বিশ্বাস।

rĕs-tōr′-ā-tive (-tĭv), *adj.* & *n.* Restoring strength or vigour; শক্তিপ্রদ; বলদ, জীবনীশক্তিপ্রতিষ্ঠাপক (হঃ চঃ), বলবর্দ্ধক, তেজস্কর। *Noun.* A medicine that has power to restore health or strength; বলবর্দ্ধক ঔষধ, বল্য, সঞ্জীব-স্থাপন (ঠাকুর), বৃংহণ (সুশ্রঃ কুঞ্জঃ)।

rĕ-stōre′, *v. t.* 1. To give back; প্রত্যর্পণ করা, প্রতিদান করা। 2. To put a thing or person into former place or position; পূর্ব্বাবস্থায় প্রতিষ্ঠিত করা, পূর্ব্বপদে প্রতিষ্ঠিত করা। 3. To heal; to cure; আরাম করা; আরোগ্য করা। 4. To bring to life; to revive; as, to *restore* to life; পুনর্জীবিত করা; সঞ্জীবিত করা। 5. To re-establish; as, to *restore* friendship; পুনঃ প্রতিষ্ঠা করা। 6. To bring back from a state of decay or injury, as near as may be, to its primitive state, by a correct imitation of the original work of the author; as, to *restore* a picture; সংস্কার, সংশোধন, কিম্বা পুনঃ চিত্রাদিদ্বারা প্রাসাদ, চিত্র, গ্রন্থ, প্রভৃতি প্রায় পূর্ব্বের মত করা, পূর্ব্বানুরূপ করা। 7. To orm a picture or model of the original form, as of something lost, extinct or mutilated; নষ্ট, অধুনালুপ্ত বা অঙ্গহীন কোন বস্তুর আদিমরূপের প্রতিরূপস্বরূপ চিত্র বা আদর্শ প্রস্তুত করা, পূর্ব্বরূপ প্রদান করা, পূর্ব্বাকৃতি প্রদান করা। **–stor′-a-ble**, *adj.* **–stor′-er**, *n.*

rĕ-strain′ (-strān), *v. t.* 1. To repress; to curb; দমন করা, নিরোধ করা, সংযত করা; বাধা দেওয়া, নিবারণ করা, সামলান, সম্বরণ করা, সংহরণ করা, দমাইয়া রাখা। 2. To confine; as, one of them had been *restrained* for two months; আটক করা, কয়েদ করা। **–a-ble**, *adj.* **–ed-ly**, *adv.*

rĕ-strain′ (-strān), *v. t.* To strain again; পুনরায় ছাঁকা।

rĕ–straint′ (-strānt), *n.* 1. The act of restraining; সংযমন, নিরোধ, দমন, নিবারণ, নিগ্রহণ, নিবন্ধন, নিয়ন্ত্রণ, সংরোধন, নিগ্রহ (হিঃ কোঃ) নিয়মন (ঐ), দমন (ঐ)। 2. Restraining action or influence; self-restraint; সংযম, যম; আত্মসংযম। 3. Detention; as, to be under *restraint*; আটক, অবরোধ, কয়েদ। 4. (*Rare*) Reserve; (কচিদ্ব্যবহৃত) রহঃশীলতা। **Restraint of princes**—Same as EMBARGO (which see). **Without restraint**—Freely; মুক্তভাবে, অবাধে।

rĕ-strict′, *v. t.* To keep within bounds; to limit; সীমার ভিতর রাখা; সীমাবদ্ধ করা, সঙ্কোচ করা। **–stric′-tion**, *n.* 1. Confinement within bound; সঙ্কোচ, সীমাবন্ধন। 2. A restraint; আটক, বাধা। **–stric′-tive**, *adj.* That which restricts; প্রতিবন্ধজনক, প্রতিবন্ধকর, প্রতিবন্ধক।

rĕ-stŭff′, *v. t.* To stuff again or anew; পুনরায় ঠাসিয়া ভরা।

rĕ-ŝŭlt′, *n.* & *v. i.* 1. Consequence; effect; ফল; পরিণাম। 2. The quantity, formula, etc. obtained by calculation; ফল, উত্তর। *Verb i.* To follow as a result or consequence; to end; ফলস্বরূপ আগত হওয়া, ফলে হওয়া; পরিণামে হওয়া, পরিণামে দাঁড়ান, পরিণত হওয়া। **–ful, –less**, *adjs.* **Undue result**—অতিপ্রসঙ্গ (সাংখ্য)। **Without result**—Fruitless; নিষ্ফল, নিরর্থক।

rĕ-ŝŭlt′-ănt, *adj.* & *n.* Arising or following; resulting from the combination of two agents; ফলস্বরূপ, পরিণামস্বরূপ; যোগোদ্ভূত, সমবায়োৎপন্ন, লব্ধ (হিঃ কোঃ), বলজ (ঐ)। *Noun.* 1. That which results or follows from; পরিণামস্বরূপ আগত বিষয়। 2. (*Mech.*) A force which is the joint effect of two or more forces; দুই বা ততোধিক বলের যোগোদ্ভূত ফলস্বরূপ বল, সংঘাতবল, সামঞ্জস্যফল (অভিঃ), লব্ধবল (হিঃ কোঃ)।

rĕ-ŝūme′, *v. t.* & *i.* 1. To take up again after interruption; as, to *resume* a speech; পুনরায় আরম্ভ করা। 2. To summarise; চুম্বক করা, সারোদ্ধার করা। 3. To take again; as, to *resume* a gift; to recover; as, to *resume* one's courage; to reoccupy; পুনরায় গ্রহণ করা, পুনরায় পরিগ্রহ করা, দত্তাপহরণ করা; পুনরুদ্ধার করা; পুনরায় অধিকার করা। *Verb i.* To recommence after interruption; পুনরায় আরম্ভ করা, পুনরায় প্রবৃত্ত হওয়া। **–sum′-a-ble**, *adj.*

resume, (*F.*), *n.* A summary; epitome; সারমর্ম; সারকথা, সারসংগ্রহ।

rĕ-sŭm′-mons (ŏnz), *n.* Renewed summons; নূতন শমন।

rĕ-sump′-tion (-zum-), *n.* The act of taking back or taking up again; পুনরারম্ভ, পুনর্গ্রহণ, দত্তাপহরণ, পুনরাদান। **–tive**, *adj.* **–tive-ly**, *adv.*

rĕ-sū′-pi-nāte, *adj.* 1. Inverted; বিপর্য্যস্ত। 2. (*Bot.*) Turned or twisted upwards; (উদ্ভিদ্‌বিদ্যা) উর্দ্ধাভিমুখীন, উর্দ্ধ্বব্যবর্ত্তিত, উর্দ্ধাকুঞ্চিত। **–na′-tion**, *n.*

rĕ-surge′ (-sêrj), *v. t.* To rise again, as from the dead; পুনরুত্থিত হওয়া। **–sur′-gent**, *adj.* & *n.* Rising again or tending to rise; as, *resurgent* Italy; পুনরুত্থায়ী, পুনরুত্থানোন্মুখ, পুনরুত্থানশীল। *Noun.* One who, or that which, rises again; পুনরুত্থানশীল মানব বা বস্তু। **–sur′-gence**, *n.*

rĕŝ-ur-rĕct′(-êr-), *v. t.* 1. To exhume; কবর হইতে উত্তোলিত করা। 2. To restore to life; to reanimate; পুনর্জীবিত করা; পুনরুজ্জীবিত করা, সঞ্জীবিত করা।

rĕŝ-ur-rĕc′-tion (-êr-), *n.* 1. The act of rising again (esp. from the dead); পুনরুত্থান, বিশেষতঃ সমাধি-গর্ত্ত হইতে পুনরুত্থান, মৃতোত্থান (আঃ বঃ)। 2. A revival; as, a moral *resurrection*; পুনরুদ্ভব (সাংখ্য), পুনরুজ্জীবন, নবজীবন। 3. The state of being risen from the dead; the future; "In the *resurrection* they neither marry nor are given in marriage" (*Math.* xxii. 30.); সমাধি হইতে পুনরুত্থানের অবস্থা; পরলোক। 4. The rising again of men at the last day ; অন্তিম বিচার দিবসে (কেয়ামতের দিনে) সমাধি হইতে মানবগণের পুনরুত্থান। 5. A disinterred corpse ; উৎখাতিত শব। 6. A festival in commemoration of Christ's resurrection ; যীশুখৃষ্টের পুনরুত্থানস্মারক পর্ব্ব, পুনরুত্থানোৎসব। **–al**, *adj.* **–ist**, *n.* A grave-robber; যে ব্যক্তি শবব্যবচ্ছেদকগণের নিকট বিক্রয়ের জন্য সমাধি হইতে শব উৎখাতিত করে, শবাপহারক। **Resurrection-man** — Same as RESURRECTIONIST, *n.* **Resurrection pie**—পূর্ব্বদিনের খাদ্যাবশেষ হইতে প্রস্তুত পিষ্টক। **Resurrection-plant, Resurrection flower**—(১) একপ্রকার শৈবাল—যাহা শুষ্ক হওয়ার পর আর্দ্র করিলে পুনরায় পূর্ব্বাবস্থা প্রাপ্ত হয়; (২) জেরুজেলম, আরব, মিসর, প্রভৃতি দেশে জাত বৃক্ষবিশেষ, কাফ মরিয়ম (আরবী নাম)। [এই গাছ গ্রীষ্মের রৌদ্রে শুকাইয়া পিণ্ডাকৃতি ধারণ করে এবং নববর্ষার নবজলধারাস্পর্শে পুনরায় সঞ্জীবিত হইয়া উঠে। জনপ্রবাদ এইরূপ যে, স্ত্রীলোকের প্রসববেদনার প্রারম্ভে কাফমরিয়মের পিণ্ডীভূত শুষ্ককাণ্ড জলে ডুবাইয়া রাখিলে শিশু ভূমিষ্ঠ হওয়া মাত্র উহা পুনরায় বিকাশপ্রাপ্ত হয়। স্ত্রীলোকের পদাঘাত, বদনমদিরাক্ষেপ, নৃত্যগীত এবং হাস্যাদিতে বিভিন্ন বৃক্ষ কুসুমিত হয় আমাদের দেশেও এইরূপ কবিপ্রসিদ্ধি আছে। যথা—(পাদাঘাতাদশোকস্তিলককুরবকৌ বীক্ষণালিঙ্গনাভ্যাং স্ত্রীণাং স্পর্শাৎ প্রিয়ঙ্গুর্বিকসতি বকুলঃ শীধুগণ্ডূষসেকাৎ। মন্দারো নর্ম্মবাক্যাৎ পটুমৃদুহসনাচ্চম্পকো, বক্ত্রবাতাৎ চূতো গীতান্নমেরুর্বিকসতি চ পুরো নর্ত্তনাৎকর্ণিকারঃ)। কেহ কেহ বলিয়া থাকেন পবিত্রাত্মা যীশুখৃষ্টকে অভিবাদনের জন্য তদীয় জন্মের পূর্ব্ব দিবস কাফমরিয়মের প্রথম পুষ্পোদ্গম হয় এবং খৃষ্টের পুনরুত্থানের প্রতি শ্রদ্ধা প্রদর্শনের জন্য ঈষ্টার পর্য্যন্ত ইহা বিকশিত ছিল]।

rĕ-sur'-vey (-sĕr-vā), *n.* A new survey ; নূতন জরীপ।

rē-sur-vey' (-sĕr-vā), *v. t.* **1.** To review ; পুনরায় আলোচনা করা। **2.** To survey (land etc.) again ; পুনরায় জরীপ করা।

rē-sŭs'-ci-tāte (-ĭ-), *v. t.* & *i.* To revivify ; to revive ; পুনর্জীবিত কর ; পুনরুজ্জীবিত করা, সঞ্জীবিত কর। ***Verb i.*** To revive ; পুনর্জীবিত হওয়া, বাঁচিয়া উঠা। **–ta'-tion**, *n.* Revival ; revivification ; পুনরুজ্জীবন, সঞ্জীবন ; পুনর্জীবন প্রদান, পুনর্জন্মদান। **–ta'-tive**, *adj.* **–ta-tor**, *n.*

rĕt, rāte, rait (-rāt), *v. t.* & *i.* **1.** To expose to moisture as flax in order to render easier the extraction of fibre ; আঁশ বাহির করার সুবিধার জন্য শণ প্রভৃতি জলে ডুবান। **2.** To spoil by rot or moisture; পচাইয়া বা ভিজাইয়া নষ্ট করা। ***Verb i.*** To be spoilt by wet or rot ; পচিয়া বা ভিজিয়া নষ্ট হওয়া।

rē-ta'-ble (-bl), *n.* Same as SUPERALTAR (which see).

rē'-tail (-tāl), *n.* & *adj.* Selling of articles in small quantities ; খুচরা বিক্রী। ***Adj.*** Selling in small quantities ; খুচরা বিক্রীত।

rē-tail' (-tāl), *v. t.* & *i.* **1.** To sell in small quantities; খুচরা বিক্রী করা। **2.** To relate in detail ; as, to *retail* an adventure ; সবিস্তারে বর্ণনা করা, বিবৃত করা, ফাঁদা (*colloq.*)। ***Verb i.*** To be sold by retail ; খুচরা বিক্রীত হওয়া। **–er**, *n.* One who retails ; খুচরা জিনিষের দোকানদার।

rē-tain' (-tān), *v. t.* **1.** To detain ; to keep ; to hold back ; আটক করা ; রাখা ; ধরিয়া রাখা, ছাড়িয়া না দেওয়া। **2.** To engage by the payment of a preliminary fee ; as, to *retain* a barrister ; পূর্ব্ব হইতেই ফিস দিয়া নিযুক্ত করিয়া রাখা। **3.** To remember ; স্মরণ রাখা, মনে রাখা। **–a-ble**, *adj.* **Retaining fee**—Same as RETAINER. **Retaining force**—যে সৈন্যদল শত্রুসৈন্যগণকে নিষ্ক্রিয় রাখে। **Retaining wall**—জলের পার্শ্বিকচাপ নিরোধার্থ প্রাচীর।

rē-tain'-ĕr (-tān-), *n.* **1.** A fee paid to retain the services of a lawyer ; ব্যারিষ্টার, উকীল, প্রভৃতিকে কোন মোকদ্দমার পূর্ব্ব হইতে নিযুক্ত করিয়া রাখার জন্য যে দক্ষিণা দেওয়া হয়। [Retainer দ্বিবিধ (1) General retain—কোন ব্যক্তি যে কোন মোকদ্দমাই করুক না কেন সেই মোকদ্দমাতেই উপস্থিত হইতে হইবে এই সর্ত্তে ব্যারিষ্টার প্রভৃতিকে যে দক্ষিণা দিয়া পূর্ব্ব হইতে নিযুক্ত রাখা হয় তাহাকে General retainer কহে। (2) Special retainer—কোন বিশেষ মোকদ্দমার জন্য যে দক্ষিণা দ্বারা ব্যারিষ্টার প্রভৃতিকে পূর্ব্ব হইতেই নিযুক্ত করিয়া রাখা হয় তাহাকে Special retainer কহে]। **2.** The act by which a client engages the services of a lawyer ; কোন মোকদ্দমায় কোন ব্যারিষ্টারকে দক্ষিণা দিয়া পূর্ব্ব হইতে নিযুক্ত করণ। **3.** The withholding of what one has in his hands by virtue of some right ; কোন অধিকার বলে হস্তগত বস্তু সংরক্ষণ। **3.** An authorization given to an attorney to act in a case ; কোন মোকদ্দমার কাজ করার জন্য কোন এটর্নিকে যে ক্ষমতাপত্র দেওয়া হয়। **4.** One who, or that which, retains ; a preserver ; ধারক; রক্ষক। **5.** An attendant of a person of note ; সম্ভ্রান্ত ব্যক্তির অনুচর, অনুযায়ী, অনুচারী, সেবক, পার্শ্বগ, পার্শ্বচর।

rē-take', *v. t.* **1.** To take again ; পুনরায় গ্রহণ করা। **2.** To recapture ; পুনরায় ধৃত করা।

rē-tăl'-i-āte, *v. t.* & *i.* To repay by an act of the same kind as has been received ; প্রতিশোধ নেওয়া, শোধ নেওয়া, প্রতিফল দেওয়া। ***Verb i.*** To requite ; প্রতিশোধ দেওয়া। **–a'-tion**, *n.* The act of retaliating ; requital of evil ; reprisal ; প্রতিশোধগ্রহণ ; প্রতিশোধ ; প্রতিফল। **–a-tivĕ, –a-to-ry**, *adjs.*

rē-târd', *v. t., i.* & *n.* To prevent from progress ; to impede ; to delay ; অগ্রগতি রোধ করা ; গতিরোধ করা ; বিলম্ব করা, গৌণ করা, দেরী করা। ***Verb i.*** To be delayed ; বিলম্বে আসা, দেরীতে আসা ***Noun.*** Same as RETARDATION

—a′-tion, *n.* The act of abating velocity of motion; the act of delaying; delay; গতিবেগরোধ; বিলম্বসাধন; বিলম্ব। **—ment**, *n.* **Retardation of the tide**—1. Same as RETARD OF THE TIDE. 2. সাবনদিনের অতিরিক্ত যে কাল জোয়ার বর্তমান থাকে। **Retard of the tide or high water**—চন্দ্রের যাম্যোত্তর গমন এবং তৎপরবর্তী জোয়ার আরম্ভের মধ্যবর্তী কাল।

rē-tāste′, *v. t.* To taste again; পুনরায় আস্বাদ করা।

retch (rĕch), *v. i. & n.* To make an effort to vomit; বমনের চেষ্টা করা। *Noun.* Such motion or sound of it; বমনচেষ্টা, ওয়াক ওয়াক।

rē-tĕll′, *v. t.* 1. To tell again; পুনরায় বলা। 2. To relate anew; পুনরায় বিবৃত করা। 3. To count afresh; পুনরায় গণনা করা।

rē-tĕn′-tion, *n.* 1. The act of retaining; রক্ষণ, ধারণ। 2. The power of retaining; memory; ধারণাশক্তি; স্মৃতিশক্তি, মেধা। 3. (*Med.*) A failure to evacuate urine or other secretion; as, *retention* of urine; মলমূত্রাদির অবরোধ, স্তম্ভন (হঃ চঃ)। **Retention of breath**—কুম্ভক।

rē-tĕn′-tive (-tĭv), *adj.* 1. Having the power to retain; as, *retentive* memory; ধারণক্ষম, ধারণাশক্তিবিশিষ্ট, ধারয়িষ্ণু। 2. (*Surg.*) Serving to retain in place; (অস্ত্রোপচারবিদ্যা) ধারক। **—ly**, *adv.* **—ness**, *n.* **Retentive faculty**—মেধা (হিঃ কোঃ), ধৃতি (ঐ), উপস্থিতি (ঐ), ধারণাশক্তি।

retenue, (*F.*), *n.* Self-control; reserve; আত্মসংযম; রহঃশীলতা।

rē′-ti-ā-ry (-shĭ-), *n. & adj.* A spider which weaves a net to catch its prey; জালবুননকারী মাকড়, ঊর্ণনাভ। *Adj.* 1. Pertaining to the weaving of nets; জালরচনাসম্বন্ধীয়। 2. Armed with a net; জালায়ুধ।

rĕt′-i-cence (-sĕns), *n.* Refraining from speaking freely; মৌন, তুষ্ণীম্ভাব, নির্ব্বাকতা। **—cent**, *adj.* Having disposition to be silent, মৌনস্বভাব, মৌনাবলম্বী, তুষ্ণীম্ভূত।

rĕt′-i-cle (-cl), *n.* 1. A small net; ক্ষুদ্র জাল। 2. Same as RETICULE, 2.

rē-tĭc′-ū-lar (-lẽr) *adj.* Having the form of net or network; জালাকৃতি, জালিদার।

rē-tĭc′-ū-late, *v. t. & i.* To divide or mark in such a way as to form or resemble a network; জালাঙ্কিত করা, জালবৎ বিভক্ত করা, জালাঙ্কিত হওয়া, জালবৎ অঙ্কিত বা বিভক্ত হওয়া। **—la′-tion**, *n.*

rē-tĭc′-ū-lāte, —lāt-ĕd, *adjs.* (*Bot.*) Having distinct lines or veins forming a net-work; জালাঙ্কিত (সাঃ পঃ), জালবৎ রেখা বা শিরাবিশিষ্ট, জালাকৃতি (বিঃ)।

rĕt′-i-cūle, *n.* 1. A lady's bag of network; a lady's hand bag; মহিলাদিগের জালের থলি; স্ত্রীলোকদিগের হাত ব্যাগ। 2. A network of fine lines in the object-glass of a telescope for measuring small celestial distances; দূরদর্শন যন্ত্রের পদার্থতালে (object-glass) অঙ্কিত সূক্ষ্মরেখাসমূহ—যৎসাহায্যে আকাশমণ্ডলের অতি ক্ষুদ্র দূরত্ব পরিমাপ করা যায়। 3. A Southern constellation; দক্ষিণাকাশের নক্ষত্র বিশেষ।

rē-tĭc′-ū-lŭm, *n.* 1. The honeycomb bag or second stomach of the ruminants; রোমন্থনকারী জন্তুগণের দ্বিতীয় পাকস্থলী, মৌচাক (সাঃ পঃ), দ্বিতীয় কোষ্ঠ (ঐ)। 2. Net-like structure; জালবৎ বস্তু।

rē′-ti-fōrm, *n.* Net-like; জালবৎ, জালাকৃতি, জালী।

rĕt′-i-nă, *n.* The interior membrane of the eye, consisting of a network of nerves connected with the optic nerve; চক্ষুর অভ্যন্তরস্থ অর্দ্ধস্বচ্ছ জালবৎ-আবরণ—ইহাতে প্রতিবিম্ব গৃহীত হইয়া দৃষ্টিজ্ঞান জন্মে, চিত্রপত্র (ডাঃ হরিপ্রসাদ চক্রবর্তী), নেত্রদর্পণ (কেণ্ডিঃ), অক্ষিপট (হিঃ কোঃ), **—nal**, *adj.* **—ni′-tis**, *n.* Inflammation of the retina; চিত্রপত্রপ্রদাহ।

rĕt′-i-nue (-nü), *n.* A body of attendants; a suite; অনুচরবর্গ, অনুযাত্রিবর্গ, পারিষদবর্গ; পারিপার্শ্ব।

rē-tīre′, *v. i., t. & n.* 1. To retreat; হটিয়া যাওয়া, পশ্চাতে সরা। 2. To go to bed; নিদ্রা যাওয়া, শয়ন করা। 3. To withdraw from business, office, or public life; কার্য্য হইতে অবসর গ্রহণ করা। 4. To recede; as, the shores *retire* to form a bay; পশ্চাদ্দিকে সরিয়া আসা। 5. To go from company or from a public place to privacy; নির্জ্জনে যাওয়া। *Verb t.* 1. To withdraw from circulation, or from the market; to take up and pay a bill when due; as, to *retire* a note; প্রচলন বন্ধ করা; হুণ্ডী প্রভৃতির টাকা শোধ করা। 2. To cause to retire; অবসর দেওয়া। *Noun.* 1. (*Rare*) Withdrawal from society or world; (ক্বচিদ্-ব্যবহৃত) লোকসঙ্গত্যাগ, সংসারত্যাগ। 2. (*Rare*) A place to which one retires; বিশ্রামস্থান, নির্জ্জনস্থান। 3. (*Mil.*) A signal to troops to retire; সৈন্যগণকে শয়নার্থ গমনের জন্য সঙ্কেত। **—tired′**, *pp.* 1. Withdrawn from business or active life; অবসরপ্রাপ্ত, কর্ম্মনিরস্ত, বিষয়নিরত, বিরাগী। 2. Secluded; as, a *retired* life; বিজন, নির্জ্জন, নিঃসঙ্গ। **—tir′-ing**, *adj.* **—tir′-ing-ly**, *adv.* **Retired list**—অবসরপ্রাপ্ত কর্ম্মচারিগণের তালিকা। **Retired-pay**—পেন্সন। **To retire from the world**—To renounce the world; সংসার ত্যাগ করা, সন্ন্যাস গ্রহণ করা। **To retire into oneself**—To be reserved; অনালাপী হওয়া, লোকসঙ্গপরাঙ্মুখ হওয়া।

rē-tīre′-mĕnt, *n.* 1. Withdrawing from society or public life; লোকসঙ্গত্যাগ, নির্জ্জনবাস, বিজনবাস, অবসরগ্রহণ। 2. State of being retired or withdrawn; নিবৃত্তি, নিঃসঙ্গতা, বিবিক্ততা, কর্ম্মাপসৃতি। 3. The place to which one retires; secluded place ; a retired abode ; বিরাম-স্থান ; নির্জ্জনস্থান, বিজনস্থলী, নিভৃত স্থান ; বিজনবাস। 4. Seclusion ; privacy ; নির্জ্জনতা ; নিভৃতত্ব, বিজনতা।

rĕ-tôrt′, *v.t., i.* & *n.* **1.** To return : to requite ; প্রতিদান দেওয়া ; প্রতিশোধ লওয়া। **2.** To give a ready and smart answer ; পটু করিয়া জবাব দেওয়া। **3.** To bend or curve back ; বাঁকান। **4.** To hurl back ; প্রতিক্ষেপ করা। **5.** To reflect ; পরাবর্ত্তিত করা। ***Verb i.*** **1.** To return an argument or charge ; পাল্টা যুক্তি দেওয়া, পাল্টা অভিযোগ আনা। **2.** To make a ready and smart reply ; পটু করিয়া জবাব দেওয়া, টাট্‌কা জবাব দেওয়া। ***Noun.*** **1.** A reply in return to an argument, charge or incivility ; a sharp reply ; কাটা জবাব, টাট্‌কা জবাব, বক্রোক্তি। **2.** Retaliation ; শোধ, প্রতিশোধ। **–ed,** *p.p.* Curved backwards ; বক্রীভূত।

rĕ-tôrt′, *n.* & *v. t.* A chemical vessel for distilling with a long, bent neck, to which a receiver may be fixed ; বক্র এবং দীর্ঘ গল-

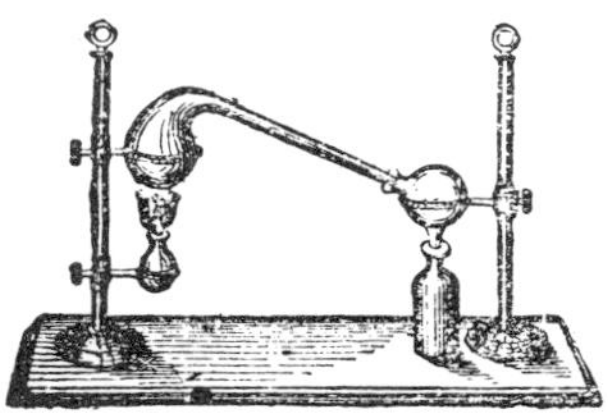

Retort.

বিশিষ্ট চোয়ানপাত্র, বকযন্ত্র, পাতনযন্ত্র (সাঃ পঃ), কুপ (ভাবঃ প্রঃ), কুপক (রঃ প্রঃ সুঃ প্রঃ)। ***Verb t.*** To purify mercury by heating in a retort ; পাতনযন্ত্রে উত্তপ্ত করতঃ পারদ শোধন করা।

rĕ-tôr′-tion, *n.* **1.** The act of bending or turning backwards ; পশ্চাদপসরণ, বক্রীভবন। **2.** (*Inter. Law*) Retaliation by one State upon the subjects of another ; (আন্তর্জাতিক আইন) কোন রাষ্ট্র অপর রাষ্ট্রের প্রজাবর্গের উপর (অনুরূপ আচরণ-দ্বারা) যে প্রতিশোধ লয়, প্রত্যপকার।

rĕ-touch′ (-tŭch), *v. t.* & *n.* To improve by new touches, as a picture or an essay ; পুনরায় তুলিকা-পাত (চিত্রাদির পক্ষে) বা সংশোধন (রচনাদির পক্ষে) দ্বারা উৎকর্ষ সাধন করা, চানকান দেওয়া। ***Noun.*** A revisal ; (esp. in *fine arts*) the reapplication of an artist's hand to a work which he had before considered in a finished state ; সংশোধন, শোধন ; বিশেষতঃ (ললিত-কলায়) সম্পন্ন চিত্রাদিতে উৎকর্ষসাধনের জন্য পুনরায় তুলিকাপাত, চানকান।

rĕ-trace′ (-trās), *v.t.* **1.** To go over again in a reversed direction ; পুনরায় পশ্চাদ্দিক গমন করা, প্রত্যাবর্ত্তন করা। **2.** To look over again with care or close attention ; পর্য্যালোচনা করা, বিশেষ মনোযোগ সহকারে বা অতি সতর্কতার সহিত পুনরায় দেখা। **3.** To recall ; পুনরায় মনে আনা।

rĕ-trace′ (-trās), *v. t.* To renew the outline of, as a drawing ; চিত্রাদির অস্পষ্ট বাহ্য রেখা পুনরায় সুস্পষ্ট করিয়া আঁকা।

rĕ-trăct′, *v. t.* & *i.* **1.** To draw back in ; as, a cat can *retract* its claws ; ভিতরের দিকে আকর্ষণ করা। **2.** To withdraw ; to take back ; to revoke ; as, to *retract* a statement ; প্রত্যাহার করা ; ফিরাইয়া নেওয়া, উঠাইয়া নেওয়া ; রদ করা, অন্যথা করা। ***Verb i.*** **1.** To undergo retraction ; ভিতরের দিকে আকৃষ্ট হওয়া। **2.** To take back a statement ; to withdraw a concession or declaration ; প্রত্যাহার করা ; উঠাইয়া নেওয়া, অন্যথা করা। **–a-ble, –i-ble, –trac′-tile,** *adjs.* Capable of being drawn back or in ; প্রত্যাকর্ষণযোগ্য, পশ্চাদাকর্ষণযোগ্য। **–trac′-tion,** *n.* **1.** Recantation ; revocation ; প্রত্যাহার ; উঠাইয়া লওন, অন্যথাকরণ। **2.** The act of drawing back or in ; ভিতরের দিকে আকর্ষণ, প্রত্যাকর্ষণ। **–trac′-tive,** *adj.* Serving to retract ; প্রত্যাহারসাধক। **–trac′-tor,** *n.* **1.** One who or that which, retracts ; প্রত্যাকর্ষক। **2.** A muscle for drawing back ; পশ্চাদ্দিকে আকর্ষক পেশী। **3.** (*Surg.*) A surgical instrument used in amputation to protect the soft parts ; (অস্ত্রোপচারবিদ্যা) অঙ্গচ্ছেদন-কালে কোমল অংশসমূহ রক্ষার জন্য ব্যবহৃত যন্ত্রবিশেষ। **4.** (*Surg.*) An instrument used to hold apart the edges of a wound in amputation ; (অস্ত্রোপচার-বিদ্যা) অঙ্গচ্ছেদনকালে আহত স্থানের প্রান্তদ্বয় ফাঁক করিয়া রাখার জন্য যন্ত্রবিশেষ।

rē′-trăl, *adj.* Hinder ; পশ্চাদ্বর্ত্তী।

rē-trăns-fêr′, *v. t.* & *n.* To transfer again ; পুনরায় স্থানান্তরিত করা। ***Noun.*** (-trans′-) The act of retransfering ; পুনঃ স্থানান্তর।

rē-trăns-fôrm′, *v. t.* To change back again ; পুনরায় রূপান্তরিত করা। **–for-ma′-tion,** *n.*

rē-trăns-lāte′, *v. t.* To translate again into the original language ; পুনরায় পূর্ব্বের ভাষায় অনুবাদ করা। **–la′-tion,** *n.*

rē-tread′ (-trĕd), *v. t.* To tread again ; পুনরায় পূর্ব্বস্থানে পাদচারণ করা।

rē-treat′ (-trēt), *v. i., t.* & *n.* To withdraw ; to retire ; as, the enemy *retreated* before our superior force ; পশ্চাদ্দিকে সরা, পশ্চাদ্বর্ত্তী হওয়া ; হটিয়া যাওয়া, পিছু হটা। ***Verb t.*** **1.** To draw or lead back ; to remove ; পশ্চাদ্দিকে টানা, পশ্চাদ্দিকে চালনা করা ; সরান, স্থানান্তরিত করা। **2.** (*Chess*) To move (a piece) back ; (সতরঞ্চ) পশ্চাদ্দিকে (গুটি) চালা। ***Noun.*** **1.** The act of retiring or withdrawing oneself ; লোকসঙ্গ-বর্জ্জন, অবসরগ্রহণ। **2.** Temporary retirement for religious exercises; সাধনভজনের জন্য কিছুকালের জন্য নির্জ্জনে স্থিতি, বিবিক্তবাস। 3. The retiring of troops before superior force; হটন, হটিয়া যাওন। 4. A secluded place; a refuge; an asylum for lunatics, etc.; "O joy to him in this *retreat*, Immantled in ambrosial dark"; নির্জ্জন স্থান, বিজন স্থান, নিভৃত-স্থলী; আশ্রয়স্থল; বাতুলাশ্রম, প্রভৃতি। 5. A signal to the troops to retire; as, to sound the *retreat*; সৈন্যগণকে হটিবার জন্য যে সঙ্কেত দেওয়া হয়।

rĕ-trĕnch′, *v.t.* & *i.* 1. To reduce; to curtail; as, to *retrench* expenses; কমান, হ্রাস করা; ব্যয়সঙ্কোচ করা। 2. To excise; as, to *retrench* a portion of a book; কাটাছাঁটা। 3. To furnish with a retrenchment or retrenchments; অন্তঃপ্রাকার, অন্তঃপরিখা বা অন্তপ্রাকার বা পরিখাশ্রেণী সমন্বিত করা। ***Verb i.*** To cut down expenses; ব্যয় হ্রাস করা, ব্যয় কমান। **—ment**, *n.* 1. The cutting down of expenses; ব্যয়হ্রাস, ব্যয়সংক্ষেপ। 2. The act of excising; কাটনছাঁটন। 3. An inner line of defence usually consisting of a trench or parapet; অন্তর্ব্বর্ত্তী প্রাকার বা পরিখাশ্রেণী।

rĕ-trī′-ăl, *n.* A second trial; পুনর্ব্বিচার।

rĕt-ri-bū′-tion, *n.* 1. The act of requiting; প্রতিকার, পরিশোধ, প্রতিশোধ, প্রতিফল। 2. Distribution of reward and punishment in a future life; পরজীবনে পাপপুণ্যের জন্য দণ্ড পুরস্কার। **Re-trib′-u-tive, Re-trib′-u-to-ry**, *adjs.* Involving retribution or recompense; as, *retributive* justice; প্রতিকারী, প্রতিকারক, প্রতিফলাত্মক, প্রতিফলপ্রদ, পরিশোধক।

rĕ-trieve′ (-trēv), *v. t., i.* & *n.* 1. To find again and bring in (killed or wounded game); নিহত বা আহত জন্তু খুঁজিয়া আনা। 2. To regain; to re-establish; to recover; পুনঃপ্রাপ্ত হওয়া; পুনঃপ্রতিষ্ঠা করা; পুনরুদ্ধার করা। 3. To make good; ক্ষতিপূরণ করা। ***Verb i.*** To find and bring back game which has been killed or wounded; নিহত বা আহত জন্তু পাইয়া আনা। ***Noun.*** Possibility of recovery; পুনরুদ্ধারের সম্ভাবনা। **—triev′-al**, *adj.* **—triev′-er**, *n.*

rĕ-trim′, *v. t.* To trim again; পুনরায় উসকান, পুনরায় চুমরান (দাড়ী), পুনরায় ঠিকঠাক করা, পুনরায় সাজান।

rĕ′-trō- (*or* rĕ-), *pref.* A prefix signifying backward or back; পশ্চাদ্দিকসূচক উপসর্গ।

rĕ-trō-ăct′ (*or* rĕ-), *v. i.* To act backward; to be retrospective; পশ্চাদ্দিকে ক্রিয়া করা; গতকাল হইতে কার্য্যকরী হওয়া। **—ac′-tion**, *n.* **—ac′-tive**, *adj.* **—ac′-tive-ly**, *adv.*

rĕt′-rō-cede (*or* rĕ-trō-sēd), *v. i.* 1. To go back; to recede; পশ্চাদ্‌গামী হওয়া; পশ্চাদপসৃত হওয়া। 2. (Of gout) To go to the interior; (গেঁটে বাত সম্পর্কে) ভিতরের দিকে যাওয়া। **Re-tro-ced′-ent**, *adj.*

rĕ-trō-cede′ (*or* rĕ-trō-sēd), *v. t.* To cede territory back again; কোন রাজ্য পুনরায় ভুক্ত করা।

rĕ-trō-ces′-sion (-sĕ-), *n.* 1. The act of moving backward; পশ্চাদ্‌গমন, পশ্চাদপসরণ। 2. The act of giving back; পুনঃপ্রদান। 3. (*Astron.*) Same as PRECESSION OF THE EQUINOXES (which see). **—sive**, *adj.*

rĕ′-trō-choir (-kwīr), *n.* An extension of church behind the high altar; প্রধান বেদীর পশ্চাদ্‌বর্ত্তী গির্জ্জার অংশ।

rĕ′-trō-flĕct-ĕd, **rĕ′-trō-flĕx**, **rĕ′-trō-flexed** (-flĕkst), *adjs.* (*Bot.*) Bent or turned backward; (উদ্ভিদ্‌বিদ্যা) পশ্চাদানত, পশ্চাদাবর্ত্তিত।

rĕt-rō-grā-dā′-tion, *n.* 1. The act of retrograding; পশ্চাদ্‌গমন। 2. (*Astron.*) The apparent motion of a planet from east to west or contrary to the order of the signs; (গ্রহগণের) বক্রগমন, বক্রগতি। **Retrogradation of arc**—চাপবক্রত্ব (হিঃ কোঃ)।

rĕt′-rō-grāde (*or* rēt-), *adj., n.* & *v. i.* 1. Going or moving backwards; পশ্চাদ্‌গামী। 2. (*Astron.*) Apparently or really moving in a direction contrary to the order of the signs; as, *retrograde* venus (বক্রী শুক্র); (জ্যোতির্ব্বিজ্ঞান) বক্রী, বক্রগামী, প্রতিগত (সাঃ পঃ)। 3. Declining; অধঃপতনশীল। 4. Reversed; প্রতীপ। ***Noun.*** 1. A degenerate person; অধঃপতিত ব্যক্তি। 2. (*Rare*) Backward tendency; (ক্বচিদ্‌-ব্যবহৃত) অনুন্নতিপ্রবণতা, অপকর্ষপ্রবণতা। ***Verb i.*** 1. To go or move backward; পশ্চাদ্দিকে গমন করা, পশ্চদ্‌গামী হওয়া, বক্রগামী হওয়া। 2. To decline; অধঃপতন হওয়া। **Retrograde evolution** — যে প্রকার ক্রমোন্নতিতে উচ্চতর বা স্ফুটতর স্বাতন্ত্র্য-বিশিষ্ট অঙ্গিসমূহের (organisms) উৎপাদনের পরিবর্ত্তে ক্রমাবনতিশীল ও অধিকতর ব্যাপকধর্ম্মী (generalised) অঙ্গিসমূহ উৎপাদিত হয়। **Retrograde motion**—বক্রগতি (শুঃ সিঃ)।

rĕ′-trō-grĕss (*or* rĕ-), *v. i.* 1. To move back or backwards; পশ্চাৎচলা, পশ্চাদ্দিগে চলা। 2. To degenerate; অধঃপতিত হওয়া, অনুন্নত হওয়া, অপকর্ষপ্রাপ্ত হওয়া। **—gres′-sive**, *adj.* **—gres′-sive-ly**, *adv.*

rĕ-trō-gres′-sion (*or* rĕ-trō-grĕ-), *n.* 1. (*Astron.*) Same as RETROGRADATION. 2. The act of going backward; পশ্চাদ্‌গমন, প্রতীপগমন। 3. (*Biol.*) Backward development; deterioration; (জীববিজ্ঞান) (আকার, গঠন, বৈশিষ্ট্য, প্রভৃতি সম্পর্কে) ক্রমাবনতি, বৃদ্ধির সঙ্গে সঙ্গে অপকর্ষতা প্রাপ্তি; অপকর্ষ।

rĕ′-trō-jĕct, *v. t.* To throw or cast back; প্রতিক্ষেপ করা।

rē-trŏ-pŭl′-sion (*or* rĕ-), *n.* (*Pathol.*) Transference of an external disease to some internal part or organ ; (নিদান) কোন বাহ্যিক রোগ অভ্যন্তরস্থ অঙ্গে স্থানান্তর।

rē-trörse′, *adj.* Turned backwards or downwards ; পশ্চাদ্দিকে আনত, নিম্নাভিমুখে আনত।

rĕt′-rŏ-spĕct (*or* rēt-), *n.*, *v. i.* & *t.* 1. View or contemplation of something past ; পশ্চাদ্‌দৃষ্টি, পশ্চাদ্দর্শন, গতবিষয়ের চিন্তা বা আলোচনা, পুনরালোচনা। 2. A regard or reference to something past ; গত কোন বিষয়ের সম্বন্ধ বা সম্পর্ক। ***Verb i.*** To look back ; to refer to ; to reflect on ; "To *retrospect* with shame and remorse on a life so basely spent ; পশ্চাৎদৃষ্টি করা ; উল্লেখ করা ; চিন্তা করা। ***Verb t.*** To think retrospectively ; গত বিষয়ের চিন্তা করা, গত বিষয় সম্বন্ধে ভাবা।

rĕt-rŏ-spĕc′-tion (*or* rēt-), *n.* 1. The act of looking back on things past ; a survey of past time or event ; পশ্চাদ্‌দৃষ্টি (হিঃ কোঃ), পশ্চাদ্দর্শন, গত বিষয় বা কালের উপর দৃষ্টিপাত ; অতীতকাল বা ঘটনা সমূহ পর্য্যালোচন। 2. The faculty of looking back on things past ; পশ্চাদ্দর্শিনী বৃত্তি।

rĕt-rŏ-spĕc′-tive (*or* rēt-rŏ-spĕc-tĭv), *adj.* 1. Looking back on past time or events ; পশ্চাদ্‌দর্শী, গতাবলোকনকারী। 2. Having reference to things past ; operative with regard to past time ; "Statutes creating new crimes...ought not to be *retrospective*" ; গত কালের সহিত সম্পর্কবিশিষ্ট ; গতকাল হইতে কার্য্যকর। 3. Backward ; as, *retrospective* view ; পশ্চাদ্‌বর্ত্তী, পশ্চাদ্দেশস্থ। **–ly,** *adv.*

retrousse, (*F.*), *n.* Turned up (said esp. of the nose) ; উপরের দিকে আবর্ত্তিত।

rē-trŏ-ū′-tĕr-ĭne, *adj.* Situated behind the uterus or womb ; জরায়ুর পশ্চাদ্দিকে অবস্থিত।

rē′-trŏ-vērt (*or* rĕ-), *v. t.* To turn backward or downward ; পশ্চাদ্দিকে বা নিম্নদিকে আনত করা। **–ed,** *p.p.* **–ver′-sion,** *n.* 1. (*Path.*) Displacement in a backward and downward direction ; as, the *retroversion* of the uterus ; জরায়ু প্রভৃতি কোন যন্ত্রের উর্দ্ধাংশের পশ্চাদ্দিকে ও নিম্নদিকে অবনতি এবং নিম্নাংশের উপরের দিকে এবং সম্মুখের দিকে উন্নতিবিশিষ্ট অবস্থানবিচ্যুতি (ডাঃ হরিপ্রসাদ চক্রবর্ত্তী)। 2. The act of turning and looking back ; পশ্চাদ্‌বীক্ষণ, পশ্চাদ্দর্শন। 3. Retranslation into the original language ; অনুবাদিত বিষয়ের পুনরায় পূর্ব্বের ভাষায় অনুবাদ, পুনরায় ভাষান্তর।

rē-trȳ′, *v. t.* To try again (in various senses of the verb) ; পুনরায় চেষ্টা করা, পুনরায় বিচার করা।

rĕt′-ter-ȳ (-ĕr-), *n.* A place where flax is retted ; যে স্থানে শণ ভিজান হয়।

rē-turf′ (-tērf), *v. t.* To lay again with new turf ; পুনরায় চাপড়া বসান।

rē-turn′ (-tērn), *v. t.* & *i.* 1. To give back ; to give back in requital ; ফিরাইয়া দেওয়া, প্রত্যর্পণ করা ; প্রতিদান স্বরূপ দেওয়া, প্রতিদান দেওয়া। 2. To repay ; as, to *return* one's money ; to give back in reply ; পরিশোধ করা ; প্রত্যুত্তরে বলা। 3. To answer ; উত্তর দেওয়া, প্রত্যুত্তরে বলা। 4. To report officially ; to render an account to a superior ; সরকারী কর্ম্মচারিরূপে গোচর করা ; উর্দ্ধতন কর্ম্মচারীর নিকট হিসাব দেওয়া। 5. To elect, as a member of a legislative assembly ; ব্যবস্থাপক সভা প্রভৃতির সভ্যরূপে নির্ব্বাচন করা। 6. To send ; to convey ; to transmit ; "He should levy money and *return* the same to the treasurer" ; প্রেরণ করা ; বহন করা ; পাঠান। 7. To make a return of, as a writ ; পরওয়ানা প্রভৃতির জারি হওয়ার লিখিত বিবরণ আদালত প্রভৃতিতে প্রেরণ করা। 8. To report ; to make known ; "Moses *returned* the words of the Lord to the people" ; গোচর করা ; জ্ঞাত করা। 9. To yield ; প্রদান করা, উৎপাদন করা। 10. (*Cricket* etc.) To play or throw back ; as, to *return* a ball to the bowler ; প্রতিক্ষেপণ করা, পাল্টাইয়া দেওয়া। 11. (*Card playing*) To play a card of the same suit as played by one's partner before ; ক্রীড়কের সহযোগী যে তাস খেলিয়াছে সেই জাতের তাস খেলা। ***Verb i.*** 1. To come or go back ; প্রত্যাবর্ত্তন করা, ফিরিয়া আসা, পুনরাগমন করা, ফিরিয়া যাওয়া, প্রতিবর্ত্তন করা। 2. To come or go back to the same state ; পূর্ব্বাবস্থা প্রাপ্ত হওয়া। 3. To reply ; "He said, and thus the queen of Heaven *returned*" ; উত্তর দেওয়া, প্রত্যুত্তর করা। 4. To revert ; as, to *return* to my subject ; প্রত্যাবৃত্ত হওয়া। **–a-ble,** *adj.* Legally requiring to be returned ; আইনমতে প্রত্যর্পণীয়, (পরওয়ানা প্রভৃতি সম্পর্কে) জারির লিখিত বিবরণসহ প্রত্যর্পণীয়। **–ing,** *adj.* & *n.* **Returned empties**—পুনরায় প্রেরিত প্যাকিংএর বাক্স প্রভৃতি। **To return to oneself**—To regain consciousness ; সংজ্ঞালাভ করা। **To return to one's muttons**—To return to one's topic or subject of discussion ; মূল বিষয়ে প্রত্যাবৃত্ত হওয়া।

rē-turn′ (-tērn), *n.* 1. The act or fact of coming or going back ; প্রত্যাবর্ত্তন, প্রত্যাবৃত্তি, প্রতিগমন, প্রত্যাগমন, পুনরাগমন, পুনর্গমন। 2. One who, or that which, is sent back ; প্রত্যর্পিত বস্তু বা পুনঃপ্রেরিত ব্যক্তি। 3. Repayment ; requital ; restoration ; পরিশোধ ; প্রতিদান ; প্রত্যর্পণ। 4. A reply ; প্রত্যুত্তর, জবাব। 5. A periodical coming back ; নির্দ্দিষ্ট সময়ান্তে প্রত্যাগমন। 6. Proceeds of an undertaking ; gain or profit on investment ; as, the *returns* were considerable ; কোন ব্যবসায় প্রভৃতি হইতে যে অর্থাগম হয়; আয়, লাভ, উৎপন্ন। 7. A report or account esp. official ; কার্য্য বিবরণী, কার্য্যের হিসাব (বিশেষতঃ সরকারী কার্য্যের)। 8. The rendering back of a writ to the proper office or tribunal ; উপযুক্ত আদালত বা কার্যালয়ে পরওয়ানা প্রভৃতি জারীর লিখিত বিবরণ পেশকরণ। 9. (*Electr.*) A line or conductor which carries the current back to the starting point after it has traversed a circuit ; তাড়িত-প্রবাহের শক্তি ব্যবহারে লাগাইবার পর উহা যে তার বা পরিচালক দ্বারা যে স্থান হইতে প্রথম প্রবাহিত হইয়াছিল তথায় পুনরায় বাহিত হয়। 10. (*Arch.*) The continuation in a different direction of the face of a building, colonnade, etc. ; অট্টালিকার সম্মুখভাগ অথবা স্তম্ভশ্রেণী প্রভৃতির ভিন্নদিকে অপসরণ। 11. (*Pl.*) A kind of mild pipe-tobacco; ধূম্রপানের উপযোগী একপ্রকার তামাক। 12. A candidate's election as a member of a legislative assembly; কোন সভ্যপদপ্রার্থীর ব্যবস্থাপক সভা প্রভৃতির সভ্যরূপে নির্ব্বাচন নির্ব্বাচন। 13. The act of returning a ball to an opponent or to another player ; প্রতিপক্ষ বা অন্য ক্রীড়কের নিকট কন্দুক প্রতিক্ষেপণ। 14. Same as RETURN-TICKET (below). **Return-case**—আরোগ্যশালা হইতে গৃহে প্রত্যাগমনের পর কোন ব্যক্তির যে সংক্রামক রোগ হয়। **Return-match, Return game**—পাল্টা ম্যাচ, পাল্টা খেলা। **Return-officer**—নির্ব্বাচনের তত্ত্বাবধানকালজ্ঞাপনকারী কর্ম্মচারী। **Return-ticket**—যে টিকিটে একবার আসা যাওয়া যায়। **In return**—In exchange ; পরিবর্ত্তে, পাল্টা। **In return for**—In requital of ; প্রতিদানে। **Many happy returns** or **returns of the day**—(জন্মদিন প্রভৃতি সম্পর্কে) বহুবার ফিরিয়া আসুক (অর্থাৎ দীর্ঘকাল জীবিত থাকার শুভাকাঙ্ক্ষা)।

rĕ-tūse′, *adj.* (*Bot.*) Terminating in a round end, the centre of which is depressed ; (উদ্ভিদ্‌বিদ্যা) মধ্যভাগে আনত গোলপ্রান্তবিশিষ্ট, গোলপ্রান্ত।

rē-ūn′-i-ŏn, *n.* 1. A union after separation ; পুনর্ম্মিলন, পুনর্যোগ, পুনঃসংযোগ, পুনঃসমাগম। 2. A social gathering ; প্রীতিসম্মিলনী।

rē-ū-nīte′, *v. t.* & *i.* To unite again ; to join again ; পুনর্মিলিত করা ; পুনঃসংযোগ করা। *Verb i.* To become united agin ; পুনর্মিলিত হওয়া, পুনরায় সংযুক্ত হওয়া, পুনরায় একত্র হওয়া।

rē-urge′ (-ērj), *v. t.* To urge again ; পুনরায় নির্ব্বন্ধাতিশয়ের সহিত বলা, পুনরায় সনির্ব্বন্ধ অনুরোধ করা।

rē-văc′-cĭ-nāte, *v. t.* To vaccinate again or a second time ; পুনরায় টীকা দেওয়া। **—na′-tion**, *n.*

rĕv-ā-lĕn′-tā, *n.* A food prepared from lentil or barley-flour ; বার্লি এবং মসুর ডাইলের মিশ্রণে প্রস্তুত খাদ্যবিশেষ।

rē-văl′-ue (-ū), *v. t.* To value again or anew ; পুনরায় মূল্য নির্দ্ধারণ করা।

rē-veal′ (-vēl), *v. t.* 1. To disclose ; to divulge; as, to *reveal* a secret ; প্রকাশ করা, প্রকটন করা ; ব্যক্ত করা, উদ্ঘাটন করা, উদ্ভেদ করা, ভেদ করা। 2. To display ; to make to appear ; প্রদর্শন করা ; প্রতিভাত করা। 3. To make known something unknown or concealed in a supernatural manner ; অলৌকিক উপায়ে প্রকাশিত করা, প্রত্যাদেশ দ্বারা জ্ঞাত করা। **—a-ble**, *adj.* **Revealed religion**—ঈশ্বরাদিষ্ট ধর্ম্ম (হিঃ কোঃ)।

rē-veal′ (-vēl), *n.* (*Arch.*) The vertical side of an aperture between the front of the wall and of the window or door-frame ; প্রাচীরের উপরিভাগ (outer surface) এবং (দ্বার বা বাতায়নের) চৌকাঠের মধ্যবর্ত্তী দরজা বা জানালার ফাঁকের খাড়া পার্শ্ব।

rē-veil′-le (-văl-yā), *n.* Beat of drum, bugle sound or other signal given about break of day to awaken soldiers ; অরুণোদয়কালে সৈন্যদিগকে শয্যাত্যাগের জন্য বংশীধ্বনি, দুন্দুভিনাদ প্রভৃতি যে সঙ্কেত দেওয়া হয়।

rĕv′-ĕl, *v. i., t.* & *n.* 1. To feast with boisterous merriment ; to carouse ; প্রমোদকোলাহলের সহিত পানভোজন করা ; ইয়ারের বৈঠকে বসিয়া মদ খাইয়া কোলাহল করা। 2. To take great delight in ; as, his mind *revels* in poetry ; অতিশয় আনন্দ পাওয়া, পরম আনন্দ পাওয়া, আনন্দে মত্ত হওয়া। *Verb t.* To waste time or money in revelry ; কোলাহলপূর্ণ আমোদপ্রমোদে সময় বা অর্থ ব্যয় করা। *Noun.* A feast with noisy jollity ; a Bacchanalian orgy ; কোলাহলপূর্ণ উৎসব ; মদ্যপানোৎসব। **—er, —ry**, *ns.* **Revel rout**—কোলাহলপূর্ণ প্রমোদ-ভোজ ; মদ্যোপানোৎসব ; মদ্যপানকারীর দল। **Master of the revels**—Same as the LORD OF MISRULE (which see.)

rĕv-ē-lā′-tion, *n.* 1. The act of revealing ; প্রকাশন, প্রকটন, উদ্ভেদ, উদ্ঘাটন। 2. The act of revealing or communicating divine truth ; তত্ত্বপ্রকটন, ঐশ্বরিক প্রত্যাদেশপ্রদান। 3. That which is disclosed by God or any supernatural agency to men ; ঐশ্বরিক প্রত্যাদেশ (বিশ্বঃ), শব্দ (বেদান্ত), আপ্তবচন, আপ্তবাক্য, ঈশ্বরাদেশ (হিঃ কোঃ), শ্রুতি (ঐ), আগম (সাংখ্য)। 4. Striking disclosure ; as, it was a *revelation* to me ; বিস্ময়জনক রহস্যোদ্ঘাটন।

5. (*Cap.*) The last Book of the New Testament; বাইবেলের নূতন নিয়মের সর্ব্বশেষ প্রকাশিত পুস্তক। (Bengali New Testament—আপ্তবাণী, আগমগ্রন্থ)। **—al,** *adj.*

rĕv-ē-lā'-tion-ist, *n.* **1.** One who makes a revelation; the author of the Apocalypse; প্রত্যাদেশ-প্রকাশক, আগমকার; বাইবেল গ্রন্থের নব নিয়মের অন্তর্গত প্রত্যাদেশ পুস্তকের গ্রন্থকার। **2.** A believer in revelation; প্রত্যাদেশে বিশ্বাসী ব্যক্তি, আপ্তবাক্যে আস্থাবান ব্যক্তি।

revenant, (*F.*), *n.* One who returns, after a long exile or death; দীর্ঘ নির্ব্বাসনান্তে প্রত্যাগত ব্যক্তি, যমলোক হইতে প্রত্যাগত ব্যক্তি।

rē-vĕn'-dī-cā'-tion, *n.* The act of demanding the restoration of anything taken away or retained illegally; অবৈধভাবে গৃহীত বা রক্ষিত কোন বস্তু প্রত্যর্পণের জন্য দাবীকরণ।

ē-venge' (-vĕnj), *v.t., i.* & *n.* **1.** To return an injury for injury; প্রতিহিংসা নেওয়া, প্রতিশোধ লওয়া, বৈরনির্যাতন করা, বৈরশুদ্ধি করা, প্রত্যপকার করা, দাদ তোলা (*colloq.*)। ***Verb i.*** To take vengeance; প্রতিহিংসা লওয়া। ***Noun.*** **1.** The act of revenging; প্রতিহিংসাগ্রহণ, বৈর-নির্য্যাতন (বাংস্থঃ)। **2.** Vengeance; প্রতিহিংসা, প্রতিশোধ, প্রতিদ্রোহ (হিঃ কোঃ), বৈরশুদ্ধি, বৈরপ্রতিক্রিয়া, বৈরোদ্ধার, প্রত্যপকার। **3.** Desire or disposition to revenge; জিঘাংসা, প্রতিহিংসা প্রবণতা। **4.** (*Game*) A chance given for retrieving one's self; (ক্রীড়ায়) হারিয়া গেলে পুনরায় জয়লাভের যে সুবিধা দেওয়া হয়। **-ful,** *adj.* Disposed to take vengeance; প্রতিহিংসাপরায়ণ, প্রতি-হিংসাগ্রহণশীল, প্রত্যুপচিকীর্ষু। **—ful-ly,** *adv.* **—ful-ness,** *n.* **To be revenged**—To revenge one's self; প্রতিশোধ লওয়া, প্রতিহিংসা বৃত্তি চরিতার্থ করা। **To give one his revenge**--To give one an opportunity of retrieving one's self by a return game; প্রতিযোগিতার ক্রীড়ায় হারিয়া গেলে পুনরায় ক্রীড়ার সুবিধা দেওয়া।

rĕv'-ē-nue (-nū), *n.* **1.** The annual rents, returns or profits from any kind of property; জমা, মালগুজারী। **2.** The annual income of an estate derived from the taxation, customs dues, excise or other sources, from which public expenses are met; রাজস্ব, ভাগ (Land revenue শুক্রঃ বিষয়ঃ)। **Revenue cutter**—নিষিদ্ধ পণ্য দ্রব্য আমদানী ও রপ্তানী প্রভৃতি নিবারণের কার্য্যে নিযুক্ত রণপোত। **Revenue-department** — রাজস্ববিভাগ। **Revenue officer** — নিষিদ্ধ দ্রব্য আমদানী ও রপ্তানী বারণের জন্য নিযুক্ত কর্ম্মচারী।

rē-vêr'-bêr-āte, *v. t.* & *i.* To echo; to reflect; as, to *reverberate* heat; প্রতিধ্বনিত করা, প্রতিশব্দ করা; প্রতিফলিত করা, পরাবর্ত্তিত করা। ***Verb i.*** **1.** To rebound; ঠিকরান, প্রতিক্ষিপ্ত হওয়া, উৎক্ষিপ্ত হওয়া। **2.** To resound; প্রতিধ্বনিত হওয়া, প্রতিনিনাদিত হওয়া। **—a'-tion,** *n.* **1.** The act of reflecting or throwing back light, heat or sound; প্রতিফলন, পরাবর্ত্তন, প্রতিধ্বনিজনন। **2.** A sound reverberated or re-echoed; প্রতিধ্বনি, প্রতিনিনাদ, প্রতি-গর্জ্জন, প্রতিনাদ। **3.** A reflected light or colour; পরাবর্ত্তিত আলোক বা বর্ণ। **—a-tive, —a-to-ry,** *adjs.* **Reverberating furnace**—একপ্রকার পোয়ান—যাহাতে অগ্নিশিখা ছাদ হইতে অভ্যন্তরস্থ বস্তুর উপর প্রতিক্ষিপ্ত হয়, প্রতিক্ষেপক চুল্লী।

rē-vêr'-bêr-ā-tor (-têr), *n.* **1** One who, or that which, reverberates; প্রতিক্ষেপক, পরাবর্ত্তক। **2.** A reflecting lamp; পরাবর্ত্তক প্রদীপ।

rē-vere' (-vēr), *v. t.* To regard with veneration; to venerate; ভক্তির চক্ষে দেখা; ভক্তি করা, গভীর শ্রদ্ধা করা, সম্মান করা, মান্য করা।

rĕv'-ēr-ence (-ĕns), *n.* & *v. t.* **1.** Veneration; ভক্তি, মান্যতা, গভীর শ্রদ্ধা। **2.** A title of the clergy; as, your *reverence*; যাজকদিগের নামের পূর্ব্বে ব্যবহৃত উপাধি বিশেষ, ঠাকুর। ***Verb t.*** To regard with veneration; to venerate; ভক্তির চক্ষে দেখা; ভক্তি করা, গভীর শ্রদ্ধা করা, মান্য করা। **—enc-er,** *n.* **—en'-ti-al,** *adj.* **—en'-ti-al-ly,** *adv.* With reverence; ভক্তিপূর্ব্বক, ভক্তিপুরঃসর।

rĕv'-ēr-ĕnd, *adj.* & *n.* Worthy of reverence; মাননীয়, মান্য, শ্রদ্ধেয়, পূজ্য, পূজনীয়, অর্চ্চনীয়, পূজার্হ, সমর্চ্চনীয়। ***Noun.*** **1.** A title of respect given to clergymen; যাজকদিগের নামের পূর্ব্বে ব্যবহৃত সম্মানসূচক উপাধি বিশেষ। **2.** (*Pl.*) Clergymen; "We are not so meddlesome as your *reverends* are"; যাজকবর্গ। **Right Reverend, Very Reverend, Most Reverend** — এই শব্দত্রয় যথাক্রমে বিশপ, ডিন ও আর্কবিশপের নামের পূর্ব্বে ব্যবহৃত হয়। **The reverend gentleman**—ধর্ম্মযাজক।

rĕv'-ēr-ĕnt, *adj.* **1.** Expressing reverence; deeply respectful; ভক্তিসূচক; ভক্তিমান। **—ly,** *adv.*

rĕv'-ēr-ie (-ī), *n.* **1.** A day-dream; a fit of deep musing or mental abstraction; a loose irregular train of thought occurring in musing or meditation; as, she was lost in *reverie*; দিবাস্বপ্ন, জাগ্রৎস্বপ্ন; ধ্যান, চিন্তা (হিঃ কোঃ), বিচিন্তা (ঐ), অনুধ্যান; অসংলগ্ন চিন্তা-প্রবাহ। **2.** A wild or loose conceit of the fancy or imagination; উদ্ভট কল্পনা।

revers, *n.* (*Pl. the same*) A part turned to show the lining; আস্তর দেখাইবার জন্য কোর্ত্তা প্রভৃতির যে অংশ উল্টাইয়া দেওয়া হয়।

rē-verse' (-vêrs), *adj.* Opposite; contrary; turned back; বিপরীত, উল্টা, বিরুদ্ধ; বিপর্য্যস্ত, ব্যত্যস্ত, পরাবৃত্ত, বিলোম, বাম, প্রতীপ। **—ly,** *adv*

Reverse battery, Reverse-fire, etc. — শত্রুসৈন্যের পার্ষ্ণিদেশে স্থাপিত কামানশ্রেণী, পশ্চাদ্দিক হইতে শত্রু-সৈন্যের উপর গোলাবৃষ্টি। **Reverse order**—বিলোম। **Reverse side**—উল্টা পিঠ।

rĕ-verse' (-vêrs), *v. t.* & *i.* To turn upside down; বিপর্য্যস্ত করা। **2.** To annul; as, to *reverse* a decree; রদ করা, রহিত করা, বাতিল করা, নাকচ করা। **3.** To undo; কৃতকর্ম্ম নষ্ট করা। **4.** To transpose; উল্টান, ক্রমবিপর্য্যয় করা। **5.** To cause to go or move in an opposite direction; as, to *reverse* an engine; বিপরীতদিকে চালান। **6.** To hold or carry in a position contrary to that in which it is generally held or carried; as, to *reverse* arms; সাধারণতঃ যে স্থানে ধরা হয়—তাহার বিপরীত দিকে ধরা বা ধরিয়া নেওয়া। ***Verb i.*** (*Dancing*) To move or turn in an opposite direction; (নৃত্যে) বিপরীত দিকে চলা বা ঘুরা। **—ver'-sal,** *n.* **1.** The act of moving or causing to move in an opposite direction; বিপরীত দিকে আবর্ত্তন, বিপরীত দিকে সঞ্চালন, বিপর্য্যস্ত করণ, পরাবৃত্তি, বিপর্য্যাস। **2.** Annulment; রদ, নাকচ, বাতিল, খণ্ডন। **—vers-i-bil'-i-ty,** *n.* **—vers'-i-ble,** *adj.* That can be reversed; পরাবর্ত্তনীয়, পরাবর্ত্ত্য। **Reversible coat**—যে কোর্ত্তা উল্টাদিকেও গায়ে দেওয়া যাইতে পারে।

rĕ-verse' (-vêrs), *n.* **1.** The contray; বিপরীত। **2.** Disaster; defeat; as, the enemy suffers a *reverse*; ভাগ্যবিপর্য্যয়, বিপর্য্যয়, (সঃ সঃ), দুর্ঘটনা, অনিষ্টপাত, কার্য্যবিপত্তি, দুর্ভাগ্য, দুর্দ্দৈব; পরাজয়, পরাভব। **3.** The second or back surface; as, the *reverse* of a medal; উল্টা দিক, উল্টা পিঠ (অর্থাৎ যে দিকে রাজা রাণীর মাথা বা মুল বিষয় উৎকীর্ণ থাকে না)। **In reverse of the enemy**—In the rear of the enemy; শত্রুসৈন্যের পার্ষ্ণি দেশে।

reversi, (*F.*), *n.* A game played by two men on a draught-board with sixty-four counters; একপ্রকার শতরঞ্চ খেলা।

rĕ-vêr'-sion, *n.* **1.** (*Law*) The return of an estate to the grantor or his heirs at the end of the period for which the grant was made; an estate which returns to the grantor; the estate that remains to the grantor where he grants away an estate smaller than that which he has himself; (আইন) ভুমির কোন বিশেষ পাট্টার মিয়াদ ফুরাইয়া গেলে প্রকৃত মালিক কিম্বা তাহার উত্তরাধিকারীর সেই ভুমিতে দখল পাওন; উক্তরূপে মালীকের অধিকারে প্রত্যাবৃত্ত সম্পত্তি; পত্তনি প্রভৃতি দেওয়ার পর সম্পত্তির যে অবশিষ্ট অংশ মালীকের দখলে থাকে। **2.** The act of returning to a certain condition; পুর্ব্বাবস্থাপ্রাপ্তি, নিবর্ত্তন (হিঃ কোঃ), প্রত্যাবর্ত্তন (সাঃ পঃ)। **3.** (*Biol.*) A return towards some ancestral type or character; (জীববিজ্ঞান) পুর্ব্বপুরুষের আকৃতি বা প্রকৃতিপ্রাপ্তি, পুর্ব্বানুবৃত্তি (সাঃ পঃ)। **4.** A right or hope of future possession or enjoyment; ভবিষ্যতে ভোগদখলের আশা বা অধিকার, ভাবিভোগাধিকার। **5.** A sum payable on a person's death esp. by way of life-insurance; কোন ব্যক্তির মরণান্তে দেয় টাকা। **—a-ry,** *adj.* **—er,** *n.* **1.** One who has reversion; কোন পাট্টা প্রভৃতির নির্দ্দিষ্ট মিয়াদ ফুরাইয়া গেলে যে ব্যক্তির দখলে ঐ সম্পত্তি পুনরায় আসে। **2.** Any one having a vested right to a future estate; যে ব্যক্তির কোন সম্পত্তির উপর ভাবি অধিকার আছে, শেষাধিকারী (আঃ বঃ)। **Reversion duty**—পাট্টাদ্বারা কোন ভুমি হস্তান্তরিত হইলে—ঐ ভুমির মুল্য হইতে, যে টাকা লইয়া পুর্ব্ববর্ত্তী ব্যক্তিকে ঐ ভুমির পাট্টা দেওয়া হইয়াছিল তাহা বাদ দিলে, যত টাকা অবশিষ্ট থাকে তাহার উপর যে শুল্ক গ্রহণ করা হয়। **Reversionary interest or right**—শেষভোগাধিকার (আঃ বঃ)।

rĕ-vêrt', *v.i., t.* & *n.* **1.** To return; ফিরিয়া আসা, প্রত্যাবৃত্ত হওয়া, পুনরাগমন করা। **2.** To return to a former state; পুর্ব্বাবস্থা প্রাপ্ত হওয়া, পুনরায় পুর্ব্বস্থানে আসা। **3.** To go back to former subject of discourse; পুনরায় মূল বিষয়ে আসা। **4.** (*Law*) To return to the proprietor after the termination of a particular estate; পাট্টার মিয়াদ ফুরাইয়া গেলে পর পুনঃ মালীকের দখলে আসা। ***Verb t.*** To cause to come to a former state; পুর্ব্বাবস্থায় আনা। ***Noun.*** **1.** Return; readoption; প্রত্যাবর্ত্তন; পুনর্গ্রহণ। **2.** One who returns to his previous faith; স্বধর্ম্মে বা স্বসমাজে পুনঃপ্রবিষ্ট ব্যক্তি।

rĕ-vêrt'-i-ble (-bl), *adj.* (Of property) Subject to reversion; (সম্পত্তি সম্পর্কে) পুনরায় পুর্ব্বাধিকারীর অধিকারে প্রত্যাবর্ত্তনীয়, বিপর্য্যাসযোগ্য (হিঃ কোঃ)।

rĕ-vĕt'-mĕnt, *n.* A retaining or breast-wall; a lining or facing (of stone etc.) to a wall, bank, parapet; আবক্ষ উচ্চ প্রাচীর; প্রাচীর, বাঁধ, আবক্ষ উচ্চ প্রাচীর, প্রভৃতির প্রস্তর-খণ্ডাদি রচিত আচ্ছাদন।

rĕ-vict'-ual (-vĭt-l), *v. t.* To furnish again with provisions; পুনরায় খাদ্যসম্ভার যোগান বা সরবরাহ করা।

rĕ-view' (-vü), *n.* **1.** A re-examination; a retrospective survey পুনরালোচনা, পর্য্যালোচনা; পুর্ব্ববর্ত্তী বিষয়ের আলোচনা। **2.** A criticism সমালোচনা, গুণদোষবিচার। **3.** A periodical publication containing essays and criticisms সমালোচনা পত্র, সমালোচনী। **4.** An examination or inspection o troops under arms; সৈন্য পরিদর্শন **5.** A judicial re-examination of as of the proceedings of a lowe court by a higher ; ছানি, ছানি বিচার। **Under review**—Under examination ; পরীক্ষাধীন।

rē-view′ (-vü), *v. t.* & *i.* **1.** To view or examine again ; পুনরালোচনা করা, পর্য্যালোচনা করা। **2.** To survey ; পরিদর্শন করা। **3.** To write a critical notice of ; as, to *review* a book ; সমালোচনা করা। **4.** To inspect troops ; সৈন্য পরিদর্শন করা। **5.** To subject to legal revision ; ছানিবিচার করা। *Verb i.* To write reviews ; সমালোচনামূলক প্রবন্ধ লিখা। **–a-ble,** *adj.* **–al, –er,** *ns.*

rē-vīle′, *v. t.* & *i.* **1.** To reproach abusively ; গালি দেওয়া, গালিগালাজ করা, গালিমন্দ করা, গালি পাড়া। *Verb i.* To abuse ; গালি দেওয়া। **–vil′-er,** *n.* **–vil′-ing,** *n.* **–vil′-ing-ly,** *adv.*

rē-vīse′, *v. t.* & *n.* To go or read over for correction ; to amend faults, errors, etc. ; সংশোধনের জন্য পুনরায় পাঠ করা ; সংশোধন করা, শোধন করা। *Noun.* **1.** A re-examination for correction ; সংশোধন। **2.** A proof sheet taken after the first correction ; প্রথমবার সংশোধনের পর যে মুদ্রণীপত্র গৃহীত হয়।

rē-vi′-sion (-zhŏn), *n.* **1.** Re-examination or going over again for correction ; revisal ; সংশোধনের জন্য পুনঃ-পরীক্ষণ বা পুনঃপাঠ ; সংশোধন, গ্রন্থ সংশোধন, গ্রন্থশোধন। **2.** That which is revised ; a revised version ; সংশোধিত পুস্তকাদি ; সংশোধিত সংস্করণ। **3.** A retrospective survey ; পুনরালোচনা, পুনঃপরিদর্শন। **–a-ry, –al,** *adjs.*

rē-vĭs′-it, *v. t.* To visit again ; পুনরায় দর্শন করা।

rē-vī′-tăl-īze, *v. t.* To restore vitality to ; নবশক্তি সঞ্চার করা, নবজীবন প্রদান করা।

rē-vīv′-ăl, *n.* **1.** Act of reviving ; the state of being revived ; নবজীবনপ্রদান ; নবজীবনপ্রাপ্তি, পুনরুজ্জীবন (হিঃ কোঃ)। **2.** Return or recall to life from death or apparent death ; পুনর্জন্মপ্রাপ্তি, পুনর্জন্মদান। **3.** Return from a state of langour or depression ; নবজাগরণ, পুনরোদ্বোধন, পুনরুদ্দীপন, সঞ্জীবন। **4.** Renewed interest in religion after indifference and decline ; ধর্ম্ম-জগতে নবজাগরণ। **5.** (*Arch.*) The reintroduction of Gothic architecture in the 19th century ; (স্থপতি বিজ্ঞান) উনবিংশ শতাব্দীতে গথিক স্থাপত্যধারার পুনঃপ্রবর্ত্তন। **6.** (*Theatre*) The reproduction after a lapse for sometime of a play etc. ; কিছুকাল বন্ধ থাকার পর কোন নাটকের পুনরাভিনয়। **8.** Republication of an old literary work ; কোন অপ্রচলিত গ্রন্থের পুনঃ প্রকাশ। **8.** (*Law*) Restoration of force, validity or effect to, as a law ; (আইন) পুনরায় বলবৎ বা বিধিসিদ্ধকরণ। **–ism,** *n.* The form of religious activity which manifests itself in revivals ; ধর্ম্মের নবজাগরণ কালে ধর্ম্মান্দোলনের ধারা। **–ist,** *n.* One who takes an active part in revivals of religion ; নব জাগ্রৎ ধর্ম্মপ্রচারে সাহায্যকারী। **Revival of learning or letters**—সাহিত্যজগতে নবযুগারম্ভ।

rē-vīve′, *v. i.* & *t.* **1.** To return to consciousness ; সংজ্ঞা লাভ করা, চৈতন্য লাভ করা, হুঁস হওয়া (*colloq.*), চেতনা লাভ করা। **2.** To return to life ; পুনর্জীবিত হওয়া, পুনরায় বাঁচিয়া উঠা। **3.** To recover from a state of neglect or depression ; পুনরুজ্জীবিত হওয়া, পুনরুদ্বুদ্ধ হওয়া, সঞ্জীবিত হওয়া, নবজীবন সঞ্চার হওয়া, নবশক্তিলাভ করা, নবজাগরণ হওয়া। **4.** (*Chem.*) To return to the metallic state ; (রসায়ন-শাস্ত্র) পুনরায় ধাতব অবস্থা প্রাপ্ত হওয়া। *Verb t.* **1.** To bring to consciousness again ; চৈতন্য সম্পাদন করা, সংজ্ঞা-সম্পাদন করা। **2.** To bring to life again ; পুনর্জীবন প্রদান করা, পুনরায় বাঁচান, পুনরায় জীবন দান করা। **3.** To raise from langour, depression or disappointment ; to reanimate ; to quicken ; to reinvigorate ; সঞ্জীবিত করা, নবপ্রবুদ্ধ করা ; পুনরুজ্জীবিত করা, পুনরাশ্বাসিত করা ; নবজীবন সঞ্চার করা ; নূতন প্রাণসঞ্চার করা, পুনরায় সতেজ করা, নবশক্তি সঞ্চার করা। **4.** (*Chem.*) To restore to metallic state ; as, to *revive* a metal after calcination ; (রসায়ন-শাস্ত্র) পুনরায় ধাতব অবস্থায় আনা। **5.** To bring to recollection ; to reawaken ; পুনরায় স্মৃতি উদ্দীপ্ত করা ; পুনঃ জাগরিত করা। **6.** To bring again into notice ; to bring again into vogue ; as, to *revive* a drama ; to bring again into validity ; পুনরায় জনসাধারণের গোচরে আনা ; পুনঃ প্রচলন করা, পুনঃ প্রবর্ত্তিত করা ; পুনরায় বিধিসিদ্ধ করা। **–viv′-a-ble,** *adj.*

rē-vīv′-ẽr, *n.* **1.** One who, or that which, revives ; উদ্বোধনকারী, সংজ্ঞাসম্পাদনকারী, নবশক্তিসঞ্চারক। **2.** (*Slang*) A stimulating drink ; (ইতর ভাষায়) উত্তেজক পানীয়। **3.** A preparation for restoring colour, polish or the like ; রং, পালিশ, প্রভৃতি পুনরায় চকচকে করার জন্য একপ্রকার বস্তু।

rē-vīv′-i-fȳ, *v. t.* **1.** To cause to revive ; পুনর্জীবিত করা। **2.** To reanimate ; to reinvigorate ; পুনরুজ্জীবিত করা, সঞ্জীবিত করা ; পুনরায় সতেজ করা, নবশক্তি সঞ্চার করা।

rĕv-i-vĭs′-cence (-sĕns), *n.* Restoration to life, vigour, or the like ; নবজীবনপ্রদান, নবজীবনসঞ্চার। **–cent,** *adj.*

rē-vī′-vŏr, *n.* Revival of a suit which is abated ; কোন মোকদ্দমা পুনরুত্থাপন।

rĕv′-ō-că-ble (-bl), *adj.* Capable of being revoked ; রদযোগ্য, খণ্ডনযোগ্য, খণ্ডনীয়।

rĕv-ō-cā′-tion, *n.* **1.** (*Rare*) Recall ; (কচিদ্ব্যবহৃত) পুনরাহ্বান

2. The act of annulling ; খণ্ডন, রদ।

rĕ-vōke', *v. t., i. & n.* 1. (*Now rare*) To call back to mind ; (বর্ত্তমানে কচিদ্‌ব্যবহৃত) মনে আনা, স্মৃতিপথে আনা। 2. To cancel ; to make void ; as, to *revoke* a decree ; রদ করা, খণ্ডন করা ; বাতিল করা, রহিত করা। ***Verb i.*** 1. To make revocation ; খণ্ডন করা। 2. (*Card playing*) To renounce or neglect to follow suit, though able to do so ; (তাস খেলায়) হাতে জাত থাকা স্বত্বেও পাশ দেওয়া। ***Noun.*** (*Card playing*) A failure to follow suit, though able in violation of the rule of the game ; (তাস খেলায়) জাত ছাপাইয়া পাশ দেওন।

rĕ-vōlt', *v. i., t. & n.* 1. To rebel ; বিদ্রোহী হওয়া। 2. To feel nausea or disgust ; as, my stomach *revolts* at such bad food ; to rise in repugnance against something ; as, her conscience *revolted* against the crime ; বিরাগ বা বিতৃষ্ণা বোধ করা ; ঘৃণা বা বিরক্তিতে বিদ্রোহী হইয়া উঠা। ***Verb t.*** To cause to shrink and turn away in abhorrence ; to nauseate ; ঘৃণা বা বিরক্তিতে সঙ্কুচিত করা ; ঘৃণা বা বিরাগ উৎপাদন করা। ***Noun.*** Rebellion; an insurrection against any authority whether personal or moral ; as, a *revolt* against art ; বিদ্রোহ ; কোনরূপ কর্ত্তৃত্বশক্তির বিরুদ্ধে বিদ্রোহ। **–ing**, *adj.* Causing abhorrence or extreme disgust ; as, *revolting* crime ; বীভৎস।

rĕv'-ō-lūte, *adj.* (*Bot.* etc.) Rolled or curved backward or downward ; (উদ্ভিদ্‌বিদ্যা প্রভৃতি) পশ্চাদ্দিকে বা নিম্নদিকে আনত বা আবর্ত্তিত, বিদ্বিবর্ত্তিক (সাঃ পঃ)।

rĕv'-ō-lūte, *v. i.* (*Slang*) To engage in revolution ; (ইতর ভাষায়) বিদ্রোহে প্রবৃত্ত হওয়া।

rĕv-ō-lū'-tion, *n.* 1. A turning round on a centre ; প্রদক্ষিণ, আবর্ত্তন, বিবর্ত্তন, আবৃত্তি, বিবর্ত্ত, সংভ্রম, ঘূর্ণন, পাক, পরিবৃত্তি, পরিক্রম (হিঃ কোঃ)। 2. (*Astron.*) The movement of a heavenly body in an elliptical course ; the time taken by a heavenly body in completing a full circuit ; ভ্রম (সাঃ পঃ), ভগম (ঐ), ভগণ (ঐ), পরিবর্ত্ত (ঐ), গতি (সাঃ পঃ), ভ্রম (ঐ), ভ্রমণ (ঐ), পর্য্যায় (ঐ), পরিবর্ত্তন (সূঃ সিঃ), ভূভ্রমণ (of the earth) ; একবার কক্ষা-ভ্রমণে গ্রহাদির যে কাল লাগে, ভগণকাল। 3. The return or recurrence of a point or period of time ; দিন, মাস প্রভৃতির আবর্ত্তন বা পরাবৃত্তি। 4. A total or radical change ; as, moral *revolution* ; বিপ্লব। 5. A total or radical change in the Government and constitution of a country ; রাজ্যবিপ্লব, রাষ্ট্রবিপ্লব। **–a-ry**, *adj. & n.* 1. Pertaining to revolution ; বিপ্লব-সম্বন্ধীয়। 2. Producing or tending to produce, a revolution ; as, *revolutionary* changes in the Government ; বিপ্লবসাধক, রাষ্ট্রবিপ্লব-জনক, রাজ্যপরিবর্ত্তন বিষয়ক। (*Noun*) One engaged in a revolution ; a revolutionist ; রাষ্ট্রবিপ্লবপ্রবর্ত্তক ; বিপ্লব-পন্থী, বিপ্লববাদী। **–ism, –ist**, *ns.* A favourer of revolution ; বিপ্লব-পন্থী, বিপ্লববাদী, রাজ্য-পরিবর্ত্তনব্রতী (আঃ বঃ)। **–ize**, *v. t. & i.* To effect a radical change in anything ; as, to *revolutionize* industry ; বিপ্লব আনয়ন করা, যুগান্তর আনয়ন করা। (*Verb i.*) To engage in revolution ; রাষ্ট্রবিপ্লবে প্রবৃত্ত হওয়া। **Period of revolution**—ভগণ কাল (হিঃ কোঃ)। **Sidereal revolution** — নক্ষত্রভগণ (হিঃ কোঃ), নক্ষত্রপরিক্রমণ (ঐ)। **Revolutionary calendar**—প্রথম ফরাসীগণতন্ত্রের পঞ্জিকা—এই পঞ্জিকায় ফরাসীগণতন্ত্রের প্রতিষ্ঠাদিবস ১৭৯২ খৃঃ অব্দের ২২শে সেপ্টেম্বর হইতে বৎসর গণিত হইত। এই পঞ্জিকায় দ্বাদশ মাসের নিম্নোক্তরূপ নামাকরণ হইয়াছে। (১) Vendémiaire (দ্রাক্ষাসংগ্রহ-কাল) ; (২) Brumaire (কুজ্‌ঝটিকা) ; (৩) Frimaire (শিলাবৃষ্টি) ; (৪) Nivôse (হিমশিলা) ; (৫) Pluvôise (বৃষ্টি) ; (৬) Ventôse (অনিল) ; (৭) Germinal (বীজ) ; (৮) Floréal (কুসুম) ; (৯) Prairial (পশু-চারণ) ; (১০) Messidor (শস্য-সংগ্রহ) ; (১১) Thermidor or Feidor (তাপ) ; (১২) Fructidor ; (ফল)। **The American Revolution** — ১৭৭৫—৮৩ খৃষ্টাব্দব্যাপী আমেরিকার রাষ্ট্রবিপ্লব—যাহার ফলে মার্কিণ যুক্তরাজ্যের অধিবাসিগণ ইংলণ্ডের অধীনতাপাশ ছেদন করেন। **The English Revolution**—১৬৮৮—১৬৮৯ খৃষ্টাব্দব্যাপী ইংলণ্ডের রাষ্ট্রবিপ্লব—যাহার ফলে দ্বিতীয় Jamesএর স্থানে William of Orange এবং মেরী ইংলণ্ডের সিংহাসনে অধিষ্ঠিত হন। **The French Revolution**—(১৭৮৯ খৃষ্টাব্দের) ফরাসী রাষ্ট্রবিপ্লব।

rĕ-vŏlve', *v. t. & i.* 1. To rotate ; আবর্ত্তিত করা, ঘুরান, পুনরাবর্ত্তন করা। 2. To ponder over ; to reflect repeatedly ; as, to *revolve* a problem in the mind ; তোলাপাড়া করা, মনে মনে আন্দোলন করা ; পুনঃ পুনঃ চিন্তা করা, বার বার ভাবা। ***Verb i.*** 1. To move round a centre; আবর্ত্তিত হওয়া, ঘূরা, পাক খাওয়া, প্রদিক্ষণ করা। 2. To recur ; ঘুরিয়া ঘুরিয়া আসা, পুনঃ পুনঃ আসা। **–volv'-ing**, *adj.* Turning or moving round ; ঘূর্ণ্যমান, ঘূর্ণায়মান।

rĕ-vŏlv'-ĕr, *n.* A firearm (commonly a pistol) with loading chambers so arranged as to revolve on an axis and be discharged in succession by the same lock for firing after each discharge ; একপ্রকার আগ্নেয়াস্ত্র (সাধারণতঃ পিস্তল) যাহাতে একবার কার্ত্তুজ ভরিলেই পর পর কয়েকবার

আওয়াজ করা যায়, ঘূর্ণচক্র (সাঃ পঃ)। **Policy of the big revolver**—অনুরূপ শুল্ক নির্দ্ধারণদ্বারা প্রতিশোধ লওয়া হইবে—বৈদেশিক রাজ্যকে এইরূপ ভয় প্রদর্শন।

rē-vŭl′-sion, *n.* **1.** (*Med.*) The act of turning any disease from one part of the body to another; counter-irritation; (ভৈষজ্য শাস্ত্র) শরীরের একাংশ হইতে অপরাংশে রোগ স্থানান্তরীকরণ; ঔষধ দ্বারা শরীরের একস্থানে উপদাহ জন্মাইয়া অন্যস্থানের উপদাহ দূর করণ, প্রত্যুপদাহ (হঃ চঃ), প্রত্যুত্তেজনা (ঐ)। **2.** (*Rare*) Drawing; withdrawl; as, the *revulsion* of capital from other trades; (কচিদ্ব্যবহৃত) উঠাইয়া নেওন; তুলিয়া নেওন। **3.** A sudden and violent change esp. of feeling; "A violent *revulsion* of feeling"; আকস্মিক উগ্র পরিবর্তন, প্রবল এবং আকস্মিক ভাবপরিবর্ত্তন, চিত্তবিপ্লব।

rē-vŭl′-sive (-sĭv), *adj.* & *n.* Producing revulsion; আকস্মিক উগ্র পরিবর্ত্তনজনক, (প্রলেপ প্রভৃতি সম্পর্কে) প্রত্যুপদাহজনক। ***Noun.*** Counter-irritant application; প্রত্যুপদাহজনক প্রলেপ প্রভৃতি।

rē-ward′, *n.* & *v. t.* **1.** Recompense; পুরস্কার, পারিতোষিক, ইনাম (*colloq.*)। **2.** Retribution; ফল (এভেলন), প্রতিফল। **3.** A (sum of) money offered for the detection of a criminal or for recovery of something; কোন আসামীকে ধরার জন্য বা কোন হারানো জিনিষ বাহির করিয়া দেওয়ার জন্য যে পুরস্কার দেওয়া হয়, পুরস্কার। ***Verb t.*** **1.** To recompense; পুরস্কার দেওয়া, পারিতোষিক দেওয়া। **2.** To requite; প্রতিশোধ করা, শোধ করা। **3.** To punish; "They were *rewarded* with the loss of their heads"; প্রতিশোধ লওয়া, প্রতিফল দেওয়া, সাজা দেওয়া। **—less,** *adj.*

rē-win′, *v. t.* To recover; পুনরুদ্ধার করা।

rē-word′ (-wê.d), *v. t.* **1.** To repeat; পুনরুক্তি করা। **2.** To restate in other words; অন্য ভাষায় বলা।

rē-write′ (-rīt), *v. t.* **1.** To write again; পুনরায় লিখা, পুনর্লিখিত করা। **2.** To write in reply; প্রত্যুত্তরে লিখা।

Rĕx, *n.* (*Abbr.* R) A king; রাজা।

Rey′-nârd (rā-), *n.* Same as RENARD (which see).

rhab′-dō-măn-çy̆ (răb-), *n.* Divination by means of a rod or wand; esp. the art of discovering the locality of minerals, springs, etc., underground by means of a divining-rod; যষ্টি বা দণ্ডের সাহায্যে অলৌকিক উপায়ে অনুমান; বিশেষতঃ মায়াযষ্টির সাহায্যে ভূগর্ভস্থ ধাতু, নির্ঝর, প্রভৃতির অবস্থানস্থল আবিষ্কার।

Rhad′-ă-măn′-thŭs (răd-), *n.* **1.** A son of Jupiter and one of the judges of the lower world; জুপিটারের পুত্র এবং পরলোকগত মানবের অন্যতম বিচারক। [ইঁহার মাতার নাম Europa। পৃথিবীতে ইনি অতি ন্যায়নিষ্ঠ বিচারক বলিয়া প্রখ্যাত ছিলেন। এই হেতু ইঁহার দেহত্যাগের পর জুপিটার ইঁহাকে অধোলোকের অন্যতম বিচারকের পদে প্রতিষ্ঠিত করেন।] **2.** (*Fig.*) A scrupulously honest and upright judge; যে বিচারক ন্যায়ের তুলাদণ্ড ধারণপূর্ব্বক বিচার করেন, ধর্ম্মরাজ। **—thine,** *adj.*

Rhæ′-ti-ăn (rē-shĭ-), *adj.* & *n.* Pertaining to a part of the Alps comprising the country of Tyrol and the Grisons; আল্‌প্‌স্ পর্ব্বতের অংশবিশেষ সম্পর্কীয় (প্রাচীনকালে এই স্থানকে *Rhætia* কহিত)। ***Noun.*** A native or inhabitant of Rhætia; প্রাচীন Rhætiaর অধিবাসী। **3.** Rhæto-Romanic; সুইজরলণ্ডের দক্ষিণপূর্ব্বাঞ্চলের লোকের ভাষা।

Rhæ′-tic (rē-), *adj.* & *n.* (*Geol.*) Pertaining to the set of strata intermediate between lias and trias extensively developed in the Rhætiam Alps; (ভূবিদ্যা) স্তরবিশেষ সম্বন্ধীয়। ***Noun*** Rhætic formation; (ভূবিদ্য) লণ্ডের দক্ষিণপূর্ব্বাঞ্চলে প্রাপ্ত স্তরা...

Rhæ-tō–Rō-măn′-ic (rē-..., **–mance** (-măns), *adjs.* & *ns.* Of the Romance dialect spoken in the South-Eastern Switzerland, সুইজরলণ্ডের দক্ষিণ-পূর্ব্বাঞ্চলে প্রচলিত উপভাষাসম্বন্ধীয়। ***Noun.*** Same as RHÆTIAN, *n.* 3.

rhap′-sōde (răp-), *n.* An ancient Greek ministrel or a reciter of epic poems; প্রাচীন গ্রীসের চারণ বা বন্দী, পুরাণকথক, সূত।

rhap′-sō-dist (răp-), *n.* **1.** Same as RHAPSODE (which see). **2.** One who recites or sings verses for livelihood; চারণ, বন্দী, কথক। **3.** One who writes or speaks disconnectedly with great excitement or exuberance of feeling; যে ব্যক্তি উৎকট উচ্ছ্বাসপূর্ণ ভাষায় অসংলগ্ন রচনা করে বা কথা বলিয়া থাকে।

rhap′-sō-dīze (răp-), *v. t.* & *i.* **1.** To utter or recite as a rhapsodist; কথকতা করা। ***Verb i.*** To talk or write rhapsodies; অসংলগ্ন এবং অতিরিক্ত উচ্ছ্বাসপূর্ণ ভাষায় লিখা বা কথা বলা।

rhap′-sō-dy̆ (răp-), *n.* **1.** An epic or a portion of an epic, recited by a rhapsodist at one time; কথকতার উপযোগী মহাকাব্য বা মহাকাব্যের অংশ **2.** (*Rare*) A recitation or chanting of epic poetry; (কচিদ্ব্যবহৃত) মহাকাব্যের অংশবিশেষের আবৃত্তি বা গান, কথকতা। **3.** An outburst of extravagant sentiment; a rambling composition or talk characterised by excessive emotionalism; "After some wild and vehement *rhapsodies*...he was easily persuaded to retire"; উৎকট ভাবোচ্ছ্বাস; অসংলগ্ন এবং উৎকট ভাবোচ্ছ্বাসপূর্ণ রচনা বা আলাপ। **—sod′ic, —sod′-i-cal,** *adjs.* **—sod′-i-cal-ly,** *adv.*

..y (răt-), *n.* The root of ..uth-American shrub with ..tringent and tonic properties; the extract of this root used in adulterating port; দক্ষিণ আমেরিকার কষায়স্বাদ এবং বলজনক মূলবিশেষ; এই মূলের ক্বাথ — যদ্দারা পোর্ট মদিরায় ভেজাল দেওয়া হয়।

rhe'-ă (rē-), *n.* (*Assam.*) Ramie or its fibre; আসামদেশজাত একপ্রকার গাছ—ইহার বল্কল হইতে সূত্র প্রস্তুত হয়, ঐ গাছের আঁশ, কঙ্কুরা, কাণখুরা। [Burm. *Goon*; Malay *Rami*; Nepal *Pohu*; Chin. *Chuma*, *Tchuma.*]

Rhe'-ă' (rē-), *n.* **1.** (*Astron.*) One of the satellites of Saturn; (জ্যোতির্বিজ্ঞান) শনৈশ্চরের উপগ্রহবিশেষ। **2.** (*Class. Mythol.*) The daughter of Uranus and Ge and wife of Saturn; (গ্রীক পুরাণ) Uranus এবং Geর কন্যা এবং শনৈশ্চরের জননী। [ইনি Zeus, Hades, Poseidon, Hera, Hestia এবং Demeterএর জননী। এইজন্য ইনি দেবমাতা বলিয়া অভিহিতা হইয়া থাকেন।] **3.** (*Orinth.*, *l. c.*) The three-toed ostrich of South America; দক্ষিণ আমেরিকার একজাতীয় উটপাখী।

Rhe'-mish (rē-), *adj.* Of, or pertaining to, Rheims in France; ফরাসীদেশের Rheims নগরীয়। **Rhemish Bible, Rhemish Testament, Rhemish version, Rhemish translation**—১৫৮২ খৃঃ অব্দে প্রকাশিত Rheims নগরীর ইংরাজ রোমান ক্যাথলিকগণকর্তৃক বাইবেলের নবনিয়মগ্রন্থের অনুবাদ।

Rhen'-ish (rĕn-), *adj.* & *n.* Of, or pertaining to, the river Rhine or the districts adjoining it; রাইননদী সম্পর্কীয়, রাইন নদীর তীরবর্ত্তী প্রদেশসমূহ সম্পর্কীয়। ***Noun.*** (*Rare*) Same as RHINE-WINE.

rhe-ŏm'-ĕ-tėr (rē-), *n.* **1.** Same as GALVANOMETER (which see.) **2.** An instrument for measuring currents; বিজলীপ্রবাহ মাপক, প্রবাহমাপক (হিঃ কোঃ)।

rhe'-ō-scōpe (rē-), *n.* An instrument for detecting electric current; তাড়িত প্রবাহদর্শক, প্রবাহদর্শক (হিঃ কোঃ)।

rhe'-ō-stăt (rē-), *n.* An instrument for regulating the strength of an electric current; তাড়িত প্রবাহের শক্তি নিয়ামক যন্ত্র, তাড়িদ্ নিয়ামক (হিঃ কোঃ)। **—stat'-ic,** *adj.*

rhe'-ō-tōme (rē-), *n.* A device for interrupting current; তাড়িতপ্রবাহ রোধক কৌশল, প্রবাহবাধক, তাড়িতপ্রবাহপরিবর্ত্তক (হিঃ কোঃ)।

rhe'-ō-trōpe (rē-), *n.* An instrument which periodically inverts a current; তাড়িতপ্রবাহ পরিবর্ত্তক (হিঃ কোঃ)।

rhe'-tŏr (rē-), *n.* **1.** An ancient Greek or Roman professor of rhetoric; প্রাচীন গ্রীক বা রোমান অলঙ্কারশাস্ত্রের অধ্যাপক। **2.** (*Rare*) An orator; a mere talker; (ক্বচিদ্ব্যবহৃত) বাগ্মী; বাক্যবাগীশ।

rhet'-ō-ric (rĕt-), *n.* **1.** The science or art of persuasive speech; অলঙ্কার শাস্ত্র, অলঙ্কার। **2.** A treatise on rhetoric; অলঙ্কারশাস্ত্র সম্বন্ধীয় পুস্তক, অলঙ্কার গ্রন্থ। **3.** Persuasiveness; influence; as, the *rhetoric* of the eyes; প্রবৃত্তিজনকতা; প্রণোদনা, আকর্ষণ, প্রভাব। **4.** Showy oratory; আলঙ্কারিক বক্তৃতা।

rhe-tŏr'-i-căl (rĕ-), *adj.* Pertaining to rhetoric; oratorical; অলঙ্কারশাস্ত্র সম্বন্ধীয়; আলঙ্কারিক বাগ্মিতাপূর্ণ, প্রবচনপটু (হিঃ কোঃ)। **—ly,** *adv.* **Rhetorical question** — যে প্রশ্ন কোনরূপ উত্তর পাওয়ার জন্য করা হয় না, কেবল বাক্যের অলঙ্কারস্বরূপ ব্যবহৃত হইয়া থাকে [যথা Who does not like a fair woman?]

rhet-o-ri'-cian (rĕt-ŏ-rĭ-shăn), *n.* **1.** Same as RHETOR (which see.) **2.** A rhetorical speaker or writer; অলঙ্কারশাস্ত্রজ্ঞ, আলঙ্কারিক।

rheum (rūm), *n.* **1.** A thin serous fluid secreted by the mucou glands; cold; শ্লেষ্মা, সিক্নি; সর্দ্দি। **2.** (*Pl.*) Rheumatic pains; বাতের বেদনা।

rheu-măt'-ic (rū-), *adj.* & *n.* Pertaining to rheumatism; produced by rheumatism; suffering from rheumatism; বাতসম্বন্ধীয়; বাতজনিত; বাতরোগগ্রস্ত। ***Noun.*** **1.** (*Pl.*) Rheumatic patient; বাতরোগী। **2.** (*Colloq.*) Rheumatism; (চলিত ভাষায়) বাতরোগ। **—i-cal,** *adj.*

rheu'-mă-tism (rū-), *n.* A painful disorder of the muscles and joints; বাত, বাতরোগ, আমবাত, ধনুর্বাত, গ্রন্থিবাত, বাতব্যাধি। **Acute rheumatism**—বাতরক্ত (কেঃডিঃ), ধাতুগুল্ম (ঐ)।

rheum'-y (rūm-), *adj.* **1.** (*Archaic*) Consisting of rheum; শ্লেষ্মাপূর্ণ। **2.** Damp; as, *rheumy* air; আর্দ্র, ভিজা, স্যাৎস্যেতে।

rhi'-năl (rī-), *adj.* Of, or pertaining to, the nose or nostril; নাসাসম্বন্ধীয়, নাসারন্ধ্র সম্বন্ধীয়।

Rhine (rīn), *n.* A river of Germany; জর্ম্মনীর নদী বিশেষ। **Rhinestone**—একপ্রকার নকল হীরা; একপ্রকার স্ফটিক। **Rhine-wine**—রাইন নদীর তীরবর্ত্তী দ্রাক্ষাক্ষেত্রজাত দ্রাক্ষা হইতে প্রস্তুত মদিরা।

rhi'-nō (rī-), *n.* (*Slang*) Money; (ইতর ভাষায়) টাকা পয়সা।

rhi-nō- (rī-), *n.* Combining form of Greek *rhinos* (nose); নাসাবাচক পূর্ব্বপদ।

rhi'-nō (rī-), *n.* (*Slang*) Rhinoceros; গণ্ডার।

rhi-nŏc'-ĕr-ŏs (rī-), *n.* A large

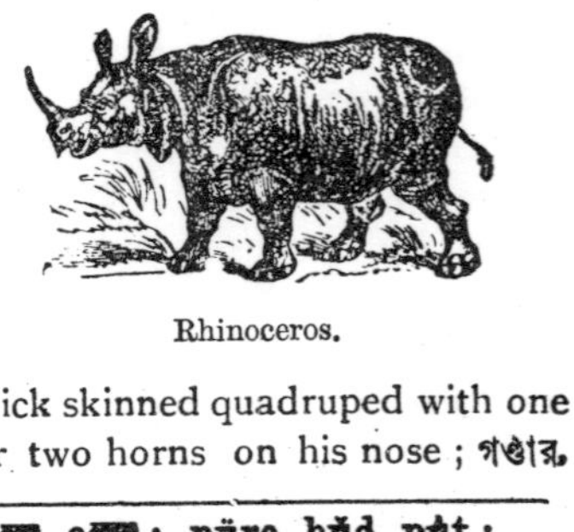

Rhinoceros.

thick skinned quadruped with one or two horns on his nose; গণ্ডার.

[Syn. খড়্গী, খড়্গবিষাণ, রণোৎসাহ, তুঙ্গমুখ, খড়্গমৃগ, ক্রোড়ামুখ, বলী, বাধ্রীনস, গণোৎসাহ, খড়্গিধেনু (she-rhinoceros), তৈতিল, বজ্রচর্ম্মা, একশৃঙ্গ, গণ্ড, গণ্ডক, গণ্ডাঙ্গ, একচর] **—ot′-ic,** *adj.* **Rhinoceros-bill** — মালয় দ্বীপের ধনেশ পাখী।

rhi′-nö-lith (rī-), *n.* A concretion formed in the nostril ; নাসাশিলা।

rhi-nö-phăr-ŷn-gī′-tis (rī-), *n.* Inflammation of the mucous membrane of the nose and pharynx ; নাসা এবং গলকোষের শ্লেষ্মার প্রদাহ। **—yn′-ge-al,** *adj.*

rhi′-nö-plăs-tŷ (rē-), *adj.* Plastic surgery of the nose ; নিকটস্থ স্থান হইতে চর্ম্ম আকর্ষণ পূর্ব্বক নব নাসিকা প্রস্তুত প্রক্রিয়া। **—plas′-tic,** *adj.*

rhi-nor-rhe′-a (rī-nŏr-ē-ă), *n.* Mucous discharge from the nose ; নাসিকা হইতে শ্লেষ্মাস্রাব। **—al,** *adj.*

rhi′-nö-scōpe (rī-), *n.* A small mirror for inspection of the passages of the nose ; নাসাভ্যন্তর দর্শনার্থ ক্ষুদ্র দর্পণ, নাসাবীক্ষণ। **—nos′-co-py,** *n.*

rhi′-zö– (-rī-), Combining form of root ; মূলবাচক পূর্ব্বপদ।

rhi′-zōme (rī-), *n.* (*Bot.*) A species of creeping stem which grows under ground spreading out shoots above and roots below ; (উদ্ভিদ্‌-বিদ্যা) কন্দ, মূলাকার কাণ্ড (বিশ্বঃ), ব্রধ্নাকারকাণ্ড (সাঃ পঃ), সংশ্লিষ্ট নিরাট কন্দ (ঐ)।

Rhi-zŏp′-ō-dă (rī-), *n.* A class of simple animal organism of gelatinous structure and moving by processes ; ভূজপদী (সাঃ পঃ), অস্থায়ী পদী (ঐ)।

Rho′-di-ăn (rō-), *adj.* & *n.* Of Rhodes ; রোড্‌স্‌ দ্বীপসম্পর্কীয়। ***Noun.*** A native of Rhodes ; রোডস্‌ দ্বীপের অধিবাসী।

rho′-di-ŭm (rō-), *n.* (Also *Rhodium-wood*) The fragrant wood of convolvulus floridus and Convolvulus scoparius ; একপ্রকার সুগন্ধি কাঠ। **Oil of Rhodium**— উক্ত কাঠ হইতে প্রাপ্ত সুরভি তৈল।

rho′-di-ŭm (rō-), *n.* A hard white metal of the platinum group ; প্লাটিন্যাম জাতীয় শ্বেতবর্ণ কঠিন ধাতু বিশেষ। [এই ধাতু ১৮০৩ খৃষ্টাব্দে Wollaston কর্ত্তৃক আবিষ্কৃত হয়।] **Rhodium pen**—যে কলমের কাপের (nib) মুখে রোডিয়াম ধাতুর একটু কণা লাগানো থাকে। **—dic, —dous,** *adjs.*

rho′-dō– (rō-), Combining form of Greek word for rose ; গোলাপবাচক পূর্ব্বপদ।

rho-dŏ-dĕn′-drŏn (rō-), *n.* A genus of shrubs with evergreen leaves and large rose-like flowers ; একজাতীয় বৃহৎ গোলাপ তুল্য পুষ্পপ্রসূ চিরশ্যামল গুল্ম।

rhomb (rŏm), *n.* 1. Same as RHOMBUS. 2. Same as RHOMBO-HEDRON. 3. A lozenge shaped object ; বরফির আকার জিনিষ।

Rhomb.

rhom-bö-hē′-drŏn (rŏm-), *n.* A solid bounded by six equal rhombuses ; ছয় সমায়তন সমচতুর্ভুজ দ্বারা পরিবেষ্টিত ঘন।

rhom′-boid (rŏm-boyd), *adj.* & *n.* Having the shape of a rhomb ; বরফির আকার, সমচতুর্ভুজক্ষেত্রাকৃতি। ***Noun.*** 1. A quadrilateral figure, whose opposite sides and angles are equal, but which is neither equilateral or equiangular ; আজাত্যায়ত (হিঃ কোঃ), বিষম সমচতুর্ভুজ (ঐ), বিষমায়ত (আঃ বঃ)। 2. A rhomboid muscle ; সমচতুর্ভুজাকৃতি পেশী। **Rhomboid muscle**—Same as RHOMBOID, *n.* 2.

rhom-boi′-dăl (rŏm-boy-), *adj.* Having the shape of a rhomboid ; বিষম সমচতুর্ভুজাকৃতি। **—ly,** *adv.*

rhom′-bŭs (rŏm), *n.* 1. A parallelogram having its four sides equal, but with two opposite angles acute and two obtuse ; সমবাহু অসমকোণী চতুর্ভুজ, অসমচতুরস্র, সমচতুর্ভুজ, তুল্যচতুর্ভুজ (লীলাঃ)। 2. A genus of flat fish comprising the turbot, brill, etc. ; একজাতীয় চ্যাপ্টা মৎস্য।

rho′-tă-cĭsm (rō-), **rho tă-cĭs′-mŭs** (rō-), *ns.* 1. Excessive use or mispronunciation of the letter *r* ; ইংরাজী *r* অক্ষরের অতিরিক্ত ব্যবহার বা অশুদ্ধ উচ্চারণ। 2. The tendency to convert other sounds into *r* ; অন্যধ্বনি ইংরাজী *r* এর ধ্বনিতে রূপান্তরের প্রবণতা। **—cize,** *v. i.*

rhu′-bârb (rô-), *n.* 1. A well-known plant, the acid leaf-stalks of which are used in cooking ; একপ্রকার গুল্ম—যাহার অম্ল পত্রবৃন্ত সমূহ ব্যঞ্জনাদিতে ব্যবহৃত হয়। [ইহার অপর নাম English Rhubarb বা French Rhubarb। ইহার পাতাগুলি পানের আকৃতি।] 2. The root of a Chinese and Tibetan plant used as a cathartic and astringent ; রেউচিনি, গন্ধিনী, পীতমূলী। "গন্ধিনী পীতমূলী চ বল্যা সা মৃদুরেচনী। হন্ত্যাজীর্ণমতিসারং বহ্নিমান্দ্যমরোচকম্‌। বিট্‌সঙ্গং শীতপিত্তঞ্চ দুষ্টব্রণবিরোহিণী।"—বৈদ্যকশব্দসিন্ধু—উমেশচন্দ্র কবিরত্ন]। [Arab. *Khgai* (Rheum palmatum) ; Chin. *Ta-hwang, hwang-liang, ho-san* ; Russ. *Rewen* (Rheum radix).] [*Syn.* Marhatti রেবন, রেবাচিনি।] [পূর্ব্বে চীনদেশীয় রেউচিনি তুরস্ক ও রুশ দেশ হইতে ইংলণ্ডে আমদানী হইত বলিয়া ইহা Russian ও Turkish Rhubarb নামে অভিহিত হইত। ১৮৬০ খৃঃ অব্দ হইতে এই ভেষজ সাক্ষাৎভাবে চীন হইতে আমদানী হইতেছে। ডাক্তারদিগের মধ্যে ইহা Turkey Rhubarb or Russian Rhubarb নামে পরিচিত। কিন্তু সওদাগরদিগের মধ্যে East Indian ও Chinese Rhubarb এই দুই নামের সমধিক প্রচলন।

rhumb (rŭm), *n.* 1. (*Naut.*) A line which makes any given angle with the meridian; (নৌবিদ্যা) দ্রাঘিমার সহিত নির্দ্দিষ্ট কোণউৎপাদক রেখা। 2. Any of the points of the mariner's compass; মৎস্য-যন্ত্রের দিক সমূহের অন্যতম। 3. The track of a ship sailing on the same point of the compass (also *rhumb-line*); ক্রমাগত একই দিকে গমনশীল পোত কর্ত্তৃক অনুসৃত পথ। 4. The angular distance of the two successive points of the compass; দিক্‌দর্শন যন্ত্রের ক্রমিক দিকদ্বয়ের কৌণিক দূরত্ব (=১১°–১৫')।

rhyme (rīm), **rīme**, *ns.* **1.** Similarity of sounds at the ends of two or more words at the end of successive or alternate lines of certain kinds of poetry; metrical lines; কবিতার মিল, শব্দমিল, মিত্রাক্ষরতা, যমক; মিলবিশিষ্ট কবিতার পংক্তিসমূহ। **2.** Poetry; verse; "Things unattempted yet in prose or *rime*"; পদ্য; কবিতার কলি। **3.** A word which rhymes with another; যে শব্দ অন্য শব্দের সহিত মিল হয়। **Neither rhyme nor reason**—Neither sense nor reason; না মিল না অর্থ। **Without rhyme or reason**—Without reasonable and sensible grounds; অকারণে, অনর্থক, কোনরূপ যুক্তিতর্কের ধার না ধারিয়া।

rhyme (rīm), **rīme**, *v. i.* & *t.* **1.** To accord or correspond in the final syllables; মিল থাকা, মিল হওয়া। **2.** To make verses; "He *rhymed* out sonnets in her praise; কবিতা লিখা। ***Verb t.*** **1.** To put into rhyme; as, to *rhyme* a story; কবিতায় রূপান্তরিত করা। **2.** To influence or bring into certain state by rhyme; as, to *rhyme* to death; কবিতার দ্বারা প্রভাবিত করা বা কোন অবস্থায় আনা। **3.** To compose rimed verses; মিত্রাক্ষর ছন্দে কবিতা লিখা। To while away time in rhyming; কবিতা লিখিয়া কাল কাটাইয়া দেওয়া।

Rhym'-er, Rhym'-es-ter, *ns.*

Rhynchobdella aculeata—তারাবাইম (গুপ্তঃ)।

rhythm, (rĭthm), *n.* **1.** Regularity of accents in verse or music; তাল, লয়। **2.** Rhyme; metre; poetry; কবিতায় শব্দের মিল; ছন্দ; কবিতা। **3.** (*Art.*) Harmonious correlation of parts; (কলাবিদ্যা) বিভিন্ন অংশের সুসঙ্গতি, সুসঙ্গতি, সৌসামঞ্জস্য। **4.** Regularity of recurrence; পুনরাবৃত্তির নিয়মিতত্ব, পৌনঃপুনিকতা। **5.** (*Physiol.*) The order of proportion as to time between the different movements of an organ; an intermittent or remittent disease, etc. at successive periods; (শারীর বিজ্ঞান) কোন শারীরিক যন্ত্রের বিভিন্ন অংশের সঞ্চলন বা স্পন্দন; কোন অবিরাম বা সবিরাম রোগ প্রভৃতির বিভিন্ন প্রকোপের মধ্যে কালসম্পর্কীয় অনুপাতের ধারা বা পরম্পরা, অনুপাত, তাল (হঃ চঃ), সাময়িকতা।

Rhyth'-mic, Rhyth'-mi-cal, *adjs.* Harmonical; তালবদ্ধ, তালানুগত।

Rhyth'-mi-cal-ly, *adv.*

Rī-ăl'-tō, *n.* **1.** A bridge over the Grand Canal at Venice; ভেনিস্ নগরীর সেতু বিশেষ [এই স্থানে নগরীর শ্রেষ্ঠি-সমাগম ভবন অবস্থিত ছিল।] **2.** (*l. c.*) An exchange mart; শ্রেষ্ঠিসমাগম ভবন, হট্ট-স্থান, বাণিজ্যকেন্দ্র।

rī'-ănt, *adj.* Smiling; cheerful; সস্মিত, স্মের; উৎফুল্ল, হর্ষোৎফুল্ল, সানন্দ।

—an-cy, *n.*

rib, *n.* & *v. t.* **1.** A side-bone of animal bodies; পাঁজর, পঞ্জরাস্থি, পর্শুকা, পার্শ্বাস্থি। [পঞ্জরাস্থি এক এক পার্শ্বে বার খানা মেরুদণ্ড হইতে উৎপন্ন হইয়া বক্ষঃস্থলের দিকে আসিয়াছে; এই বার খানার সাত খান বক্ষঃস্থলের অস্থির সহিত সংলগ্ন। ইহাদিগকে প্রকৃত পর্শুকা (*true ribs* বা *sternal ribs*) কহে; অবশিষ্ট যে পাঁচখানি বুকাস্থির সহিত সংলগ্ন নহে উহাদিগকে কৃত্রিম পর্শুকা (*false ribs*), *floating ribs, asternal ribs* বা *short ribs*) কহে।] **2.** A person's wife; woman; "Punch and his *rib* Joan"; স্ত্রী (আদমের পঞ্জরাস্থি হইতে তদীয় পত্নী ইভ সৃষ্ট হইয়াছিল—বাইবেলের এই উক্তি মূলক); স্ত্রীলোক। **3.** A piece of flesh containing one or more rib bones; এক বা ততোধিক পঞ্জরাস্থি সংলগ্ন মাংসখণ্ড। **4.** A piece of timber which forms or strengthens the side of a ship; পোতপার্শ্ব কাষ্ঠ, জাহাজের পার্শ্বস্থ যে কাষ্ঠখণ্ড দ্বারা জাহাজের পার্শ্ব দৃঢ় করা হয়। **5.** Anything small and narrow; a strip; as, a *rib* of land; ক্ষুদ্র এবং স্বল্প পরিসর বস্তু; চিলট। **6.** The continuation of the petiole along the leaf; পত্রের শিরা, পর্শুকা (সাঃ পঃ)। **7.** A prominent line or ridge in knitted goods; মোজা প্রভৃতির শিরা। **8.** A bar or rod of iron or wood serving to strengthen or support a structure; কোন কিছু সমুদ্ধৃত বা দৃঢ়ীভূত করার জন্য লৌহ বা কাষ্ঠ নির্ম্মিত দণ্ড বা ফলক, বাতা, পট্টি। **9.** (*Bookbinding*) One of the ridges on the back of a book which serves as a covering for the cords and for ornaments; (পুস্তক বাঁধাই) বাঁধান পুস্তকের পিঠের উপর যে শির তোলা হয়। **10.** One of the strips of stout metal wire forming the framework of an umbrella; ছাতার শিক। **11.** An arch-formed piece of timber for supporting the lath and plaster work of a vault; খিলানের কাঠ ও চুণসুর্কি সমুদ্ধৃত করার জন্য তোরণাকৃতি কাষ্ঠখণ্ড। **12.** A vein of ore; পাষাণাদির মধ্যস্থ ধাতু প্রভৃতির শিরা। **13.** A wave mark on sand; সৈকতোপরি তরঙ্গাভিঘাত চিহ্ন। ***Verb t.*** **1.** To furnish with ribs; বাতা লাগান, ডাঁসা লাগান, শিক লাগান। **2.** (*Knitting*) To purl;

(বুনন) শির তোলা। **3.** To shut in; বন্ধ করা। **4.** To form or shape into ridges; আলবিশিষ্ট করা। **5.** To plough with ribs between the furrows; লাঙ্গলপদ্ধতির মধ্যে মধ্যে আল রাখিয়া কর্ষণ করা। **Ribbed,** *pp.* Formed like, or with, ribs; শিরওয়ালা, শিরাল, শিকওয়ালা। **Rib-grass, Rib-wort**—(*Plantago lanceolat*) ইংলণ্ডদেশের একপ্রকার কলাগাছ—ইহার পাতা দীর্ঘ, অপ্রশস্ত ও শিরাল হইয়া থাকে। **Rib-roasting,** *n.* A sound beating; বেদম প্রহার। **To poke in the rib**—To draw one's attention; খোঁচা দিয়া কাহারো মনোযোগ আকর্ষণ করা।

rib′-ăld, *n.* & *adj.* One who uses obscene or irreverent language; অশ্লীলভাষী ব্যক্তি, অপভাষী ব্যক্তি, দেবনিন্দক। ***Adj.*** Obscene; scurrilous; obscenely licentious; blasphemous; অশ্লীল; কুরুচিপূর্ণ; জঘন্য; দেবনিন্দক। **—ry,** *n.* Low, base, or mean speech or writing; অশ্লীল কথাবার্ত্তা, অশ্লীল রচনা, খেউড়, জঘন্য কথাবার্ত্তা। **—rous,** *adj.*

rib′-ănd, *n.* Same as RIBBON (which see.) **—ed,** *adj.*

rib′-bon (-ŏn), *n., v. t.* & *i.* **1.** A fillet or silkband used as a trimming for some part of a lady's attire: ফিতা, পট্টবন্ধ। **2.** A strip or shred; ফালি, চিল্টা। **3.** The badge of an order of knighthood; সম্ভ্রান্ত সম্প্রদায়ের চিহ্নস্বরূপ ফিতা। **4.** (*Colloq.*) Reins for driving; গাড়ীর ঘোড়ার লাগাম। ***Verb t.*** **1.** To adorn with ribbons; to furnish with stripes resembling ribbons; ফিতা দ্বারা শোভিত করা; ফিতার মত ডোরা কাটা। **2.** To tear into ribbons; ছিঁড়িয়া ফালি ফালি করা। ***Verb i.*** To form into a ribbon or ribbons; ফিতার আকার ধারণ করা। **—ed,** *adj.* **—ism,** *n.* The principles of Ribbon Society; পট্টবন্ধসমিতির মত। **—y,** *adj.* **Blue-ribbon**—গার্টার নামক সম্ভ্রান্তসম্প্রদায় (এই সম্প্রদায়ের পরিচায়ক পদক নীল ফিতাদ্বারা ঝুলান হয়)। **Ribbon-fish** — রূপপাতিয়া (গুপ্তঃ)। **Ribbon-grass**—একপ্রকার খড়। **Ribbon-man**—পট্টবন্ধসমিতির সভ্য। **Ribbon-Society** — ঊনবিংশ শতাব্দীর প্রথমভাগে আয়র্লণ্ডদেশে গঠিত রোমান ক্যাথলিকগণের গুপ্তসমিতিবিশেষ, পট্টবন্ধসমিতি। **Ribbon-weaver**—ফিতা বুননকারী। **The red ribbon**—বাথ নামক সম্প্রদায় (এই সম্প্রদায়ের পরিচায়ক পদক লালবর্ণের ফিতা দ্বারা ঝুলান হয়)। **To handle** or **take the ribbons**—To drive; গাড়ী চালান।

rī′-bēs, *n.* (*Bot.*) A genus of plants comprising currants or gooseberry; (উদ্ভিদ্ বিদ্যা) টেপারী জাতীয় ফল।

Rib′-stŏn-pĭp-pin (-ĭn), *n.* A variety of apple; একপ্রকার সেওফল। [Yorkshireএর অন্তর্গত Ribston নামক স্থানে Sir Henry Goodrickএর উদ্যানে সর্ব্ব প্রথম উৎপন্ন হয় বলিয়া এই নাম।]

Rĭ-cār′-dĭ-ăn, *adj.* & *n.* Of, or pertaining to, the English political economist Ricardo; ইংরেজ অর্থনীতিবিদ্ রিকার্ডো সম্বন্ধীয়। ***Noun.*** A follower of Ricardo; রিকার্ডো-পন্থী।

rice (rīs), *n.* A plant cultivated in all warm countries and its seed used as an article of food (Lat. *Oryza Sativa*); ধান-গাছ; চাউল, তণ্ডুল। [আইনী আকবরীতে এই কয়েক প্রকার চাউলের উল্লেখ দৃষ্ট হয়। যথা:—খঞ্জন চাউল, দেওয়ানপ্রসাদ চাউল, দওজেরা চাউল, মিছরী চাউল, সংজেরা চাউল, সুখদোষ চাউল, ষাঠি চাউল, দেকের চাউল। প্রাচীন বাংলা গ্রন্থসমূহে বহুপ্রকার চাউলের নাম দৃষ্ট হয়। যথা:—আজান, আন্ধারকুলি, আমপাবন, আমলো, আলোচিত, আসতির, আসঅঙ্গ, উড়াসালী, ককাচি, কনকঅচুর, কাঁওদ, কামদা, কালাকাত্তিক, কালাযুগর, কুসুমমালী, কোটা, খীরকম্বা, খেজুরছড়ি, খেমরাজ, গঅাবালী, গন্ধতুলসী, গন্ধমালতী, গুজুরা, গোতমপল্লাল, গোপালভোগ, চন্দনসালি, জলারাঙ্গি, জেঠ, জোলি, ঝিঙ্গাস টাঙ্গন, তসরা, তিলসাগরি, তুলানধান তুলসালি, তোজনা, দলাগুরি, দাড়, দুধরাজ, নাগরজুগান, পলাল, পর্ব্বতজিরা, পাঙ্গুসিয়া, পাতল, পাথরা, ফেফেরি, বককড়ি, বঙ্কি, বালি, বিন্ধসালী, বুখি, বুড়ামাত্তা, ভজনা, ভাদোলী, ভান্দমুখি, মইপাল (মহীপাল?), মাধবলতা, মুক্তাহার, মুলা-মুক্তাহার, মৌকলস, রক্তশাল, রাঅগড়, রাজদল, লতামৌ, লাউসলী, লালকামিনি, বাঁকই, বাঁকচুর, বাঁকসাল, বাগনবিচি, বাঁসকটা, বাঁজগজা, বাঁসমতী, বোআলী, সনাখড়কি, সালছাটী, সীতাসালী, সোলপনা, হরি, হরিকালি, হাতিপাঙ্গর, হুকুলী—"শূন্যপুরাণ"। কটকী, কনকচূর, কনকলতা, কল্মীলতা, কপোতকণ্ঠিকা, কয়াকচ্চা, কালিন্দী, কামোদ, কালিয়া, কার্ত্তিকা, কাশীফুল, কুসুমশালী, কৃষ্ণশালী, কেলেকানু, কেলেজিরা, কোঙরভোগ, কোঙরপুণিমা, দুধরাজ, দুর্গাভোগ, পর্দ্দেশী, ধুস্তুর, খেজুরথুপী, খয়েরশালি, ক্ষেম, গঙ্গাজল, গয়াবলি, গন্ধমালতী, গোপালভোগ, গৌরীকাজল, গুয়াথুপী, গুণাকর, চামরঢালি, চন্দনশালি, ছত্রশালি, জটাশালি, জগন্নাথভোগ, জামাইলাড়ু, জলারাঙ্গী, ছিঙ্গাশালি, বলাইভোগ, ধুল্যা, নিমুই, নন্দনশালি, রূপনারায়ণ, পাতসাভোগ, পায়রারস, পিপীড়াবাঁক, তিলসাগরী, বাঁকশালি, বাকোই, বুয়ালী, দাড়ুবঙ্গী, বাঁকচূর, বুড়ামাত্রা, রামশালি, রাঙ্গী, রাঙ্গামেট্যা, রামগড়, রঙ্গয়কড়ি, পুণ্যবতী, নছীপ্রিয়, লাউশালি, লক্ষ্মীকাজল, ভোজনা, ভবানীভোগ, সীতাশালি, শঙ্করশালি, শঙ্করজটা, হরিশঙ্কর, হাতিপাঙ্গর, হুড়া, হরকুলি, হাতিপাদ, হিঙ্গী, হলুদগুঁড়া—"শিবায়ন"। সমগ্র ভারতবর্ষে প্রায় ৫.৬ হাজার রকমের চাউল পাওয়া যায়। গবর্ণমেণ্ট কর্ত্তৃক প্রকাশিত The Agricultural Ledger 1910—Nos. 1 & 2 Oryza Sativa নামক পুস্তক হইতে নিম্নলিখিত নামগুলি সঙ্কলিত হইল। যথা:—অচিন, অচমিতা, অচমিত্রা, অগ্নিসাইল, অমর্ত্তসাল, অমর্ত্তমণ্ডি, অমৃতভোগ, অমৃতসাগর, আবরসাইল, আবিলকল্মা, আবছাইয়া, আচারভোগ, আচর,

দাশালি, আগুনবাণ, আগুনিয়া, আকাশমণি, আলমভোগ, আলাপশি, আল্লাদকুড়ি, আমনখাসা, আমারি, আমনলতা, আমির পসন্দ, আমঝুঁকি, আনারকলি, আন্দারকুলী, আউনবাঁশী, আর্য্যরাজ, আশার গাজিয়া, আশিন, আশিনা, আশিনাবারা, আশমাগাহি, আশকারাম, আশামটা, আউশ গুড়গুড়ি, আউশ কাজল, ইন্দ্রসাইল (বঙ্গীয় কৃষিবিভাগের মতে এই ধানের ফলন সাধারণ ধানের দ্বিগুণ হইয়া থাকে), ঈশ্বরভোগ, উখনীভোগ, উখনী মধু, উকাইবা রাবণ, উরি ধান, কবির মালিক, কাচারি সালি, কদলিয়া চম্পা, কালা ভোমরা, কালা চম্পা, কালা চিনি, কালাডোম, কালাকচু, কালামাণিক, কালি বাজাল, কালিগৌরী, কালিজিরা, কালিফুল, কমলভোগ, কামরাং, কামিনীসরু, কানাইবাঁশী, কানাইলাল, কনকচুর, কাঁচননী, কাশীফুল, কাশ্মিরী বাঁশমতি, কস্তুরী, কাঁটালভোগ, কাটারীভোগ, কায়াবাদলী, কাজলমেথী, কেশমুক্তী, কেশরী, কাবুলীভোগ, কোচমঙ্গল, কচিকুমারী, কৈসেড়, কলাথোড়, কলা আমন, কলাসাগর, কলুভোগ, কমাল, কমলভোগ, কুমড়া, কুমারী, কুমড়ীভাজা, কুসুমফুল, কৈমাগুর, কৃষ্ণচুড়া, কৃষ্ণজিরা, কৃষ্ণকালা, কৃষ্ণমণি, কৃষ্ণপ্রসাদ, কুমারভোগ, কুমড়ি বাজাল, কুসুমশালী, খাচামাহি, খয়ের গুঁড়ি, খৈচুর, খৈরাজ, খৈয়া মুড়কী, খেজুর হাঁড়ী, খালী শোওয়ার, খলসী পুঁটী, খামতি বোকা, খরাই পিঁপড়া, খড়্গনাকি, খড়িকা জবা, খাসা, খাসাগন্ধি, খাসাদুধসাইল, খাসিয়া পরাণ, খাটখেমিয়া, খেজুর ছড়ী, খেজুর কাঁদী, খেসারী, খিরসা, খোরকা মাটী, খোস্‌কীনোনা, খুদী ধান, খুদী খাস, খৈয়া মুরগী, খুরমা, গোবরাশনি, গজমুক্তা, গজপতি, গন্ধমালতী, গন্ধ কস্তুরী, গঙ্গাবালি, গঙ্গাজল, গঙ্গাজলখাসা, গঙ্গাসাগর, গাজীভোগ (Aman rice of Faridpur. The name means a food for the brave), গোবিন্দভোগ, গোকুলসর, গোপালভোগ, গৌরাঙ্গসাল, গৃহস্থপাগল, গুড়গুড়ি, ঘাড়ভাঙ্গা, ঘি কৈ, ঘৃতকাঞ্চন, চামার মণি, চম্পা, চম্পাকুশী, চন্দনচুর, চন্দ্রভোগ, চেতীচিকন, চন্দ্রহার, চন্দ্রমণি, চাঁপাকলি, চপলা, চাপলাস, চৌদ্দ খোপা, চিকন সাইল, চিনি আলো, চিনি সক্কর, চিনিভোগ, চিনি সাগর, চিনি সরকার, চিন শক্কর, চিন্তামণি, ছাগলবকরী, ছাইতন ডোমরা, ছোট চম্পা, জগন্নাথভোগ, জামাইভোগ, জিরা, টিয়াকাটী, ঠাকুরভোগ, ঠাকুর প্রসাদ, ডুমুর ফুল, ঢাকি, ঢাকেশ্বরী, ঢালা মাণিক, ঢোল, ঢোলী দুধরাজ, তাকুরভাগা, তালমুগুর, তাংগ্রাই, তারাবালি, তারামণ্ডল, তারাক, তিলাই, তিলবাদল, তিলবাজালি, তিলকাকুড়, তিলকাফুর, তিলকস্তুরী, তিলাকস্তুরী, তিলকাঞ্চন, ত্রিপুরামসাল, তুলাসাল, তুলসী মুকুল, তুলসীফুল, তুলসীরস, তুলসী, তুলসীভোগ, তোতারাম, তুলামণি, তুলাপঞ্জি, তুলসীমালা, তুলসীজবা, থামেট্‌-মি (Burma. The name signifies "So delicious that a mother-in-law will forget her daughter's husband"), থুবড়ী, দাদখানি, দেওয়ানভোগ, দোদানা, দুধবিলাস, দুধরাজ, দুধসর, দুধসাইল, দুর্গাপ্রসাদ, দুধকলমা, দুধকুমার, দুধলুচি, দুধমণি, দুধেরসর, দুধিসরু, নয়নাকাজল, নাকা, ননীভোগ, নারাঙ্গি, নারি পারিজাত, নারিকেল ঝুঁকি, নারিকেল ঝোঁপা, নারিকেল জিরা, নারিকেল ফুল, নীলকানাই, নীলকুমার, নৃপতিভোগ, পদ্মদাম, পদ্মলাল, পাদশাভোগ, পাখীরাজ ("King of birds"—Mymensigh, Pabna, Dacca, Bakarganj), পক্ষিরাজ, পলাশ ফুল, পানিপাট, পংখীরাজ, পানমৌরি, পরমান্ন সাইল, পর্ব্বত জিরা, পারিজাত, পরমান্নভোগ, পরমান্নমুক্তা, পাটেশ্বরী, পতিরাজ, পিয়ারমণি, পেশওয়ারী (considered very superior—24 Pergs.), পেটপাকা, পিলরাজ, পিঁপড়া বালাম, পিত্তরাজ, পিঁপড়া লেজ, পদ্মখোসা, পলাশ, প্রসাদভোগ, পুরবী খাসা, পুরবী, ফুলঝরি, ফুলকুমারী, বাবুরাম, বাচ্চা, বদরংগি, বাদশা ভোগ, বাদশা পসন্দ, বাদশাই ভোগ, বাগা ঝুল (Aman rice in Cooch-Behar. Eaten uncooked and only requires to be steeped in cold water for a short time to soften it. cf. বোকা চাউল of Assam), বাঘরাজ, বাবা (ফরিদপুর—Having some properties of the tiger, probably the colour), বাগুনবিচি, বাঘনখী, বহুরাণী, বাঁকতুলসী (Scented rice), বয়রা চাপলাস, বলরামভোগ, বল্লম, বালুপ্রমাণ, বামনভোগ, বান্দরপাতা, বঙ্গল বকরী, বনগাউজল, বানিয়া ভাতার, বাঁশগোপাল, বাঁশফুল, বাঁশকাটা, বংশীকলম, বংশীরাজ, বাঁশমতি, বাঁশপাতা, বর সোহাগমণি, বড় চোঙ্গা, বড় ধান চাউল, বড় কুমড়া, বাঁশিরাজ, বাসুদেবভোগ, বাতাসা, বাতাসফেনী, বাতাসাভোগ, বীরপোলা, বেণাফুল, বেঙ্গী, বেঙ্গী লালপাট্‌নী, বেণীভোগ, বেতাক, বিভীষণশাল, বীরমালী, বোয়ালঝুপী, বহুমালী, বোকা (Goalpara—Eaten uncooked being only steeped in water), বোরবালাম, বোরো, বউ পাগলা (Scented rice—So called as the daughter-in-law who is supposed to cook it becomes intoxicated or maddened by the fumes arising from the process of boiling), বসন্তমালতী, বুড়া বিন্নি, বুড়া হরিণ, বুড়া পাগলিনী, বুড়া মুলা, বুড়ী, বৃন্দাবনী, বোরো, বর্ষা বাহাদুর, ভৈসা চণ্ডী, ভেড়ফুল, ভিজাকাঁথা, ভোগ জিরা, ভোগলস্কর, ভুতশালি, ভুতনন্দী, মাছরাঙ্গা, মাছিয়া, মধু ভাকুন, মাগুরসাইল, মাগুরী, মহাশোল, মহেশভোগ, মহিষকান্দি, মাইচিকন, মাইডল, মাইঢোলী, মাইদুল, মাইটোপ, ময়নাগুড়ি, মালতী, মালভোগ, মালিকা, মাণিকচোর, মতিচুর, মতিহারি, মধু সাইল, মোহনভোগ, মোহনমালা, মহিষবাহন, মুক্তাহার, মুলুক আঁধার, মরিচসুতা, মোক্তার, মুরলী, মুরগী ভোমরা, মুসুরীমুখী, যাত্রামুকুট, রাবণ, রাধাকৃষ্ণভোগ, রাধারাণী, রাধাতিলক, রাধাবৈষ্ণব, রাঁধুনী পাগল (Nadia, Burdwan, Murshidabad, "That which maddens the cook and implies that cooks cannot restrain themselves from eating up so fragrant a dish), রঘুনাথভোগ, রাইভোগ, রাইমণি, রাইমাণিক, রাইমুখী, রাজভোগ, রাজমোহন, রামচন্দ্রভোগ, রামফুল, রামপ্রসাদ, রংমহল, রংএর গুড়া,

রাণী কাজল, রাণী পাগল, রাস, রসকদম্ব, রসালভোগ, রম্বুলভোগ, রাতাজংলী, রতনচুরী, রতনগোপ, রুক্মিণীভোগ, রূপনারায়ণ, রুক্মিণীকান্ত, রংমোহন, রূপরাজ, রূপেসা পৈরী, রূপেশ্বর, লক্ষ্মীবিলাস, লক্ষ্মীনারায়ণপ্রিয়া (Balasore—Coarse, red, unwholesome grain), লক্ষ্মীপারিজাত, লালবাতি, লালমতি, লম্বা কলা, লামা, লাঙ্গল, লাউবুকা, লাউডুম, লেমা, লেপা (Faridpur, Bakarganj, also a race of aus rice in Murshidabad. Can be grown in water up to 18 feet), লেপাধোলা, লছমি দিঘা, লোহাচুর, লছমনভোগ, শ্যামসুন্দর, শ্যামাকান্ত, শঙ্করভোগ, শঙ্করচিনি, শঙ্করমুখী, শঙ্খবড়ী, শঙ্খরেখা, শান্‌কী, শানমুলগী, শান্তি বোকা, শীতলচিনি, শীতলজিরা, শাক জিরা, শাল গোজা, শাল ঝাটী, শাল কুটী, শালি ভাদই, শ্যামরস, শানাজিরা, শামলিতি, শানমুক্তা, শ্যামজিরা, শাঁকচুর, শীলকুমার, শসা ফুল, শ্যামরস, শীলকাতুর, শশার ধান, শসাবিচি, শ্রীহট্টী, শ্রীকমল, শূদ্রশালী, শ্যামরাজ, শ্যামসুন্দর, সফেদ বাঁশমতি, সফেদা, সাগরচিনি, সাহারা, সাইল থাজুরী, সাজানথালি, সাক্করথোরা, সাকরচিনি, সালভোট্‌কা, সালবুড়া, সালকুমার, সালিবরণ আমন, সালিভট্ট, সমুদ্রবালি, সমুদ্রফেনা, সন্ধ্যামণি, সোনাভাতা, সান্তনিভোগ, সাউবাজ, সফাবিনি, সফরি, সরিষাবাটী আউস, সরু সফরিভোগ, শা পছন্দ, শা জিরা, সাইল চাপলাস, সাইল চিকন, সাইল চিকলাল, সাইলকালা, সাইলথাসা, স্নাকরচিনি, সাকের থোরাক, সাকোর থারো, সা পাহাড়, সরবতি, সরকলা, স্বর্ণলতা, সিন্ধুকাটী, সিঁদুর কটুয়া, শিঙ্গারবিলাস, সিঙ্গাড়া কচু, সীতাভোগ, সীতিপাটনাই, সালিভাদই, সোনামুখী, সোনামুক্তা, সোনা উজল, সোনার গাই, স্বর্ণ জিরা, সূর্য্যমণি, সরিষাবুটী, সুজনী, সুক্তি আউস, সুলকুমার, সুলতানভোগ, সূর্য্যমণি, সূর্য্যমুখী, সরুবান বুলি, সীমাঘট, সিকী সিঁদুরী, সিঁদুরকান্ত, সিঙ্গা, সিঙ্গাড়া, সীতাহার, সীতা লক্ষ্মীয়া, সীতা নবমী, সীতা মালতী, সীতা চিনি, সোহাগমতি, সোমরাজ, সোনখরিকা, সোনাখিল, সোনামুগুর, সোনারগাই, সোনার চম্পা, সোহাগমণিশালী, সুন্দর সাইল, সৌদামিনী, সৌলকুমার, সুয়া পংখী, স্বর্ণ খড়্গা, সুখদর্শন, সুখমায়া, সুখবিলাস, সুখ দাস, সুলতানবাস, সুলতানভোগ, সুলতান চম্পা, সুরদাস, হলদিগুড়ী, হংস, হংসরাজ, হাসথাল, হনুমান ঘাতা, হরিদাসী, হরিদাস, হরিমুদী, হরিনারায়ণ, হরিশঙ্কর, হরিদ্রা রং, হরিণ কাজলিয়া, হরমুক্তা, হাতী দাঁত, হাতিকানী, হীরা কলমা, হলদি কোটা, হরিণ কাজলা, হুগলী, হুরাপাট্‌নী, ক্ষীরচাঁচি, ক্ষেপা ঝিঙ্গা, ক্ষিরাইজালী, ক্ষিরসাভোগ, ক্ষিরসাপাট, কুঙ্কুমাকৃতি। (Gallon's Sans. Dic.), মহাশালী (সুশ্রুঃ), মহাবুশ (A sort of rice which takes a year to ripen)। এতদ্ভিন্ন শিলচরে নিম্নলিখিত তিনটী প্রসিদ্ধ চাউল পাওয়া যায়। যথা:—ভেড়াপাওয়া, সাহেব সাইল (Silchar. Called ঠাকুর-ভোগ in Sylhet), হরিনারায়ণ। **Rice-bird**—একপ্রকার পক্ষী। **Rice-bug**—গাঁধি পোকা (যোঃ)। **Rice-flour**—চাউলের গুঁড়া, তণ্ডুলচূর্ণ। **Rice-milk**—পায়স, পরমান্ন (cf. সিতকান্তিগন্ধি পরমান্নং—গোপাল চম্পূ), ক্ষারিকা (ভাব প্রঃ)। [cf. শুদ্ধেঽর্দ্ধপক্বে দুগ্ধে তু ঘৃতাক্তাংস্তণ্ডুলান্ ক্ষিপেৎ। তে সিদ্ধাঃ ক্ষীরিকা খ্যাতা সা সিতাজ্যযুতোত্তমা—ভাবপ্রকাশঃ।] **Rice-paper**—একপ্রকার কাগজ—যাহাতে চীনারা ছবি আঁকে। **Rice-weevil** — চাউলের পোকা। **Sunned rice**—আতপতণ্ডুল। **Wild rice**—নীবার (শ্রীঃ)।

rich, *adj.* 1. Wealthy; ধনী, ধনশালী, ধনবান, ধনাঢ্য, বিত্তশালী, বিভবশালী, বিভবসম্পন্ন। 2. Costly; precious; as, *rich* gloves and boots; মূল্যবান; মহার্ঘ্য, দামী। 3. Abundant; as, a *rich* harvest; প্রচুর, প্রভূত, ভূয়িষ্ঠ, বহুল। 4. (Of countries, soil, etc.) Abounding in natural resources; fertile; as, *rich* land; fruitful; উর্ব্বর; ফলশালী। 5. Abounding in agreeable or nutritive qualities; as, *rich* wine; containing large proportion of fat, oil, spice, etc. highly seasoned; সুরুচির, সুরস; রসাল, গুরুপাক প্রচুর ঘৃতাদি সংযুক্ত, মসল্লাদার। 6. Splendid; sumptuous; luxurious; as, *rich* repast; জাঁকালো; জমকালো; বিলাসিতাপূর্ণ। 7. Abounding in beauty; as, a *rich* landscape; শোভাসমুজ্জ্বল। 8. (Of colours) Strong; deep; vivid; as, a *rich* colour; (বর্ণসম্বন্ধে) গাঢ়; ঘন; উজ্জ্বল, দীপ্ত। 9. (Of odours) Full of fragrance; (গন্ধ সম্বন্ধে) সৌরভপূর্ণ, আঢ্য, গন্ধাঢ্য, আমোদাঢ্য [cf. কদম্বামোদাঢ্যা বিপিনপবনাঃ — ছন্দোমঞ্জরী]। 10. Sweet; mellow; soft; as, *rich* tone; মধুর; কান্ত; কোমল। 11. Abounding in humour or wit; highly amusing; funny; as, a *rich* idea; রসিকতাপূর্ণ; অতিশয় আমোদজনক; মজার। **Rich'-en,** *v.t.* & *i.* **Rich'-ness,** *n.* **The rich**—ধনিসম্প্রদায়, ধনবানসম্প্রদায়।

Rich'-ărd, *n.* The name of a person; কোন ব্যক্তির নাম। **Richard Roe**—উচ্ছেদের মোকদ্দমার বিবাদী; **Poor Richard's Sayings**—বেঞ্জামিন ফ্রাঙ্কলিন কর্ত্তৃক প্রকাশিত পঞ্জিকা হইতে গৃহীত নীতিবচনমালা।

rich'-ĕs, *n.* (Usu. *pl.*) Wealth; ধন, ধনসম্পত্তি, দৌলত, সম্পত্তি, বিত্ত, ঐশ্বর্য্য, সমৃদ্ধি।

rich'-ly, *adv.* 1. In a rich manner; ধনীর মত, ধনরত্নসমন্বিতভাবে, সম্পন্নভাবে। 2. Splendidly; জাঁকালোভাবে, জমকালোভাবে, সমৃদ্ধভাবে। 3. Thoroughly; as, he *richly* deserves the punishment; fully; সম্পূর্ণরূপে; পুরাপুরি। 4. Abundantly; প্রচুররূপে, প্রভূতরূপে।

ric'-i-nŭs, *n.* A genus of plant of which the type is castor oil plants; ভেরেণ্ডা [Syn. ব্যাঘ্রপুচ্ছ, কান্ত, তরুণ, শুক্র, বাতারি, দীর্ঘপত্রক (also see PALMA CHRISTI)]।

rick, *n.* & *v. t.* A large pile or stock of hay, corn, etc.; শুষ্ক ঘাস, খড়, প্রভৃতির গাদা, পালই, পালা। **Rick-stand**—খড় প্রভৃতির গাদার

মাচা। *Verb t.* To heap in ricks etc.; খড় প্রভৃতি গাদা করা।

rick, *v. t.* & *n.* Same as WRICK (which see)

rick'-ĕts, *n.* A disease that affects children, and is characterised by bulky and softened bones; অস্থির কোমলতা, বিবর্দ্ধন, বিকৃতি ও শীর্ণতাদি লক্ষণবিশিষ্ট শিশুরোগবিশেষ, বালাস্থি-বিকৃতিরোগ।

rick'-ĕt-ȳ, *adj.* 1. Affected with rickets; বালাস্থিবিকৃতিরোগবিশিষ্ট। 2. Tottering; shaky; as, a *rickety* chair; weak; টলমলে; নড়বড়ে; দুর্ব্বল।

rick'-shaw (-shä), **–shä,** *n.* Same as JINRICKSHA (which see.)

ric'-ō-chĕt', *n., v. t.* & *i.* A rebounding or skipping as of a stone along water or a cannon-ball or bullet along water or the ground; the motion known as ducks and drakes; জলের উপর প্রস্তাদির অথবা কামান বা বন্দুকের গুলির জল বা স্থলের উপর ঠিকরাইয়া বা ছিনিমিনি খেলিয়া চলন; ছিনিমিনি। *Verb t.* To skip or glance with a rebound or series of rebounds; ঠিকরাইয়া যাওয়া, ঠিকরাইয়া ঠিকরাইয়া চলা, ছিনিমিনি খেলিয়া চলা, বারবার উৎপতিত হইয়া চলা। *Verb i.* To hit with ricochet shots; ঠিকরাইয়া চলে এরূপ গুলিদ্বারা আঘাত করা। **Ricochet-fire**—গোলা বারম্বার উৎপতিত হইয়া চলে এরূপ ভাবে কামান দাগন।

ric'-tŭs, *n.* 1. The gape of a man's mouth; হাঁ। 2. The gape of the mouth of a fish or bird; পক্ষীর বা মাছের মুখের হাঁ। 3. (*Bot.*) The gape of a bilabiate corolla; দ্বি-ওষ্ঠ গর্ভদলের বিস্তার।

rid, *v. t.* To deliver; to disencumber; উদ্ধার করা, ত্রাণ করা, নিষ্কৃতি দেওয়া, খালাস দেওয়া, মুক্ত করা; ঝঞ্ঝাট হইতে মুক্তি দেওয়া। **Rid'-dance,** *n.* 1. Act of ridding; উদ্ধারকরণ, খালাসকরণ। 2. Escape; নিষ্কৃতি, উদ্ধার, নিস্তার, মুক্তি, অব্যাহতি। **To be rid of, To get rid of**—To be deliverd from; নিষ্কৃতি পাওয়া, নিস্তার পাওয়া, উদ্ধার পাওয়া, অব্যাহতি লাভ করা।

rid'-den (-n), *p. p.* Of RIDE (which see.)

rid'-dle (-l), *n.* & *v. t.* 1. A puzzle in words; ধাঁধা, প্রহেলিকা, হেঁয়ালী, কূটপ্রশ্ন, প্রবহ্লিকা (গোপালঃ)। 2. Anything puzzling; হেঁয়ালী, জটিল বিষয়, সমস্যা। *Verb t.* To speak ambiguously; হেঁয়ালীর ছন্দে কথা বলা। **To solve a riddle**—ধাঁধার উত্তর দেওয়া, সমস্যা পূরণ করা।

rid'-dle (-l), *n.* & *v. t.* A large sieve with meshes for separating grosser materials from finer; একপ্রকার মোটাচালুনী, ঝাঁঝরা। *Verb t.* 1. To pass through or separate with a riddle; মোটাচালুনি দ্বারা চালা। 2. To sift; পুঙ্খানুপুঙ্খরূপে পরীক্ষা করা। 3. To perforate with balls and shots so as to make like a riddle; to pierce with many holes; as, a ship *riddled* with bullets; বন্দুকের গুলি দ্বারা চালুনীর মত ছিদ্রসমাকীর্ণ করা; ছিদ্রবহুল করা। 4. To pelt with questions; প্রশ্নের উপর প্রশ্ন করা।

ride, *v. i.* & *t.* 1. To be borne along on the back of an animal, esp. a horse; কোন জন্তুর পৃষ্ঠে আরোহণ করিয়া চলা, বিশেষতঃ অশ্বপৃষ্ঠে আরোহণ করিয়া চলা, ঘোড়ায় চড়িয়া চলা। 2. To be borne in a vehicle; গাড়ী প্রভৃতিতে চড়া। 3. To float; ভাসা। 4. (Of a vessel) To ride at anchor; নোঙ্গর ফেলিয়া থাকা। 5. To be borne along; বাহিত হওয়া। 6. (Of moon etc.) To seem to float in space; শূন্যে ভাসিতেছে বলিয়া বোধ হওয়া। 7. To overlap; একটীর কিনারা অপরটীর উপর থাকা। *Verb t.* 1. To mount and manage; to sit on; চড়া; আরোহণ করা। 2. To go over or traverse in riding; চড়িয়া অতিক্রম করা, অশ্বাদি আরোহণে অতিক্রম করা। 3. To domineer over; to oppress; "Grim fear *rode* him day and night"; কর্তৃত্ব ফলান, প্রভুত্ব করা; অত্যাচার করা, নির্যাতন করা, পীড়িত করা, সম্পীড়িত করা। 4. To do or execute by riding; অশ্বাদি আরোহণে সম্পাদন করা। 5. To cause to ride; চড়ান, পিঠে উঠান। 6. To overlap; একটীর কিনারা অপরটীর উপর থাকা। *Noun.* 1. An excursion on a horse-back or in a vehicle; অশ্বারোহণে ভ্রমণ, গাড়ী প্রভৃতিতে ভ্রমণ। 2. A road cut in a wood for riding in; অশ্বারোহণের জন্য জঙ্গল কাটিয়া যে রাস্তা বাহির করা হইয়াছে। 3. A band of mounted recruits; যুদ্ধের জন্য সেনাবিভাগে নূতন গৃহীত অশ্বারোহিদল। 4. A saddle horse; চড়িবার ঘোড়া, আরোহণোপযোগী অশ্ব। 5. The side of a log on which it rests when being dragged; টানিয়া নেওয়ার সময় কাঠখণ্ডের যে পার্শ্ব ভূমিতে থাকে। 6. One of the certain districts into which a coast is divided for excise purpose; আবগারী কার্য্যের জন্য সাগরের উপকূল যে বিভিন্ন বিভাগে বিভক্ত হয়—তাহার অন্যতম। **Rid'-a-ble,** *adj.* **To ride a hobby**—To take part in or talk constantly of some favourite pursuit or pastime; কোনরূপ খেয়ালে মাতিয়া থাকা, কোনরূপ সখ বা খেয়ালের কথা সর্ব্বদা বলা। **To ride and tie**—To take turns with another in labour and rest; অপর কোন ব্যক্তির সহিত পালাক্রমে কাজ ও বিশ্রাম করা। [মূল অর্থ:—দুইজন পথিকের মধ্যে একটী অশ্ব থাকিলে একজন কতকদূর যাইয়া দ্বিতীয় ব্যক্তির জন্য অশ্ব বাঁধিয়া রাখিয়া অগ্রসর হয় এবং দ্বিতীয় ব্যক্তি ঐ অশ্বে আরোহণপূর্ব্বক প্রথমোক্ত ব্যক্তির নিকট যাইয়া তাহাকে অশ্ব দিয়া পুনরায় পদব্রজে গমন করে—এরূপভাবে পথ চলন।] **To ride**

down—To overthrow or trample over in riding ; অশ্বপদদলিত করা, উপর দিয়া অশ্ব ছুটাইয়া যাওয়া। To pursue on horseback and take ; অশ্বারোহণে পশ্চাদ্ধাবনপূর্ব্বক ধরা। (*Naut.*) To bend or bear-down by main strength or weight ; (নৌবিদ্যা) সবলে বা ভারদ্বারা নত করা। To exhaust a horse by over-riding ; অতিরিক্ত চড়িয়া অশ্বকে পরিক্লান্ত করা। **To ride easy**—(Of a vessel) To pitch lightly ; (জাহাজ সম্পর্কে) মৃদু আন্দোলিত হওয়া। **To ride fast and long**—অতিবেগে বহুদূর ভ্রমণ করা। **To ride for a fall**—To act recklessly ; বেপরোয়াভাবে কাজ করা। **To ride hard**—(Of a ship) To pitch violently ; (জাহাজ সম্পর্কে) প্রবলভাবে আন্দোলিত হওয়া। **To ride out**—To sustain a gale without great damage or dragging anchor ; ঝড় কাটাইয়া উঠা। **To ride over**—To treat despotically or harshly ; অত্যাচার করা, পীড়ন করা, দলন করা, কঠোর ব্যবহার করা। **To ride roughshod**—To tyrannise over a person regardless of the loss or distress it may cause ; কাহারও ক্ষতি ও কষ্টের দিকে দৃক্‌পাত না করিয়া তাহার উপর পীড়ন করা। **To ride the horse**—To assume grand or arrogant airs ; গর্ব্বিত বা উদ্ধত ভাব ধারণ করা, টঙ্গে চড়া। **To ride the shanks' mare**—(*Slang*) To walk ; (ইতর ভাষায়) পায়ে হাঁটা। **To ride the wild mare**—(*Obs.*) To play at see-saw ; (অপ্রঃ) কোন কিছুর উপর দোদুল্যমান তক্তার দুই প্রান্তে বসিয়া উঠা নামা করা। **To ride to hounds**—To hunt fox with hounds ; কুকুর লইয়া খেঁকশিয়াল শিকার করা। **To ride up**—(কোটের কলার প্রভৃতি সম্পর্কে) স্বস্থান হইতে উপরে উঠা।

rid'-er, *n.* **1.** One that rides ; আরোহী, সওয়ার। **2.** An addition to a manuscript or drawing made after ; কোন দলীল প্রভৃতির পাণ্ডুলিপিতে বা চিত্রে পরবর্ত্তী কালে সংযোজিত বিষয়। **3.** (*Geom.*) An exercise on some book-problem or theorem ; (জ্যামিতি) কোন প্রতিজ্ঞার সহিত সংসৃষ্ট অনুশীলনী। **4.** (*Naut., pl.*) Additional set of timbers or iron plates strengthening a ship's frame ; জাহাজের খোল যে অতিরিক্ত কাষ্ঠ ফলক বা লৌহ-পট্টশ্রেণীদ্বারা দৃঢ়ীকৃত করা হয়।

ridge (rij), *n., v.t. & i.* **1.** The line of junction in which two sloping surfaces meet ; দুইটি ঢালু জিনিষের সংযোগরেখা, টের্চ্চা চালদ্বয়ের সংযোগ-স্থল। **2.** A range of hills or mountains or the back of such a range ; গিরিশ্রেণী, গিরিমালা, গিরিপৃষ্ঠ। **3.** A strip thrown by a plough ; চষা ক্ষেতের লাঙ্গলপদ্ধতির মধ্যে যে আল থাকে তাহার একটী। ***Verb t.*** **1.** To form into a ridge ; to furnish with ridge ; আল বাঁধা ; আলসমন্বিত করা। **2.** To plant in ridges ; আলের উপর রোপণ করা। ***Verb i.*** To rise in ridges ; গিরিপৃষ্ঠাকারে উত্থিত হওয়া, আলের মত হইয়া উঠা। **Ridg'-y,** *adj.*

rid'-i-cūle, *n. & v. t.* **1.** Raillery ; বিদ্রূপ, ঠাট্টা, উপহাস, ব্যঙ্গ, পরিহাস। **2.** A laughing-stock ; as, to make one a *ridicule* to a company ; a laughing matter ; উপহাসের পাত্র ; উপহাসের বিষয়। **3.** Ridiculousness ; বিদ্রূপজনকতা। ***Verb t.*** To subject to ridicule ; বিদ্রূপ করা, ব্যঙ্গ করা, ঠাট্টা করা, উপহাস করা। **To turn to ridicule, To turn into ridicule**—To make ridiculous ; উপহাসজনক করা, উপহাসভাজন করা।

ri-dic'-ū-lous (-lŭs), *adj.* Exciting derisive laughter ; laughable ; উপহাসজনক, হাস্যোদ্দীপক ; হাস্যকর, অবহাস্য। **—ly,** *adv.* **—ness,** *n.*

rid'-ing, *n. & adj.* **1.** The act of one that rides ; অশ্বারোহণ, যানাদি-আরোহণ। **2.** A road cut through a wood for riding purpose ; বনমধ্যে রচিত অশ্বারোহণবর্ত্ম। ***Adj.*** Suitable for riding ; আরোহণোপযোগী। **Riding-coat** — অশ্বারোহণকালে পরিহিত কোর্ত্তা ; বিশেষতঃ অশ্বারোহণকালে বৃষ্টির জল হইতে দেহরক্ষার্থ একপ্রকার লম্বা কোর্ত্তা ; **Riding-habit**—মহিলাদিগের অশ্বারোহণোপযোগী পরিচ্ছদ।

rid'-ing, *n.* **1.** One of the three administrative divisions of Yorkshire ; ইয়র্কসায়ারের শাসনসম্পর্কীয় বিভাগত্রয়ের অন্যতম। **2.** A similar division of other counties in the United Kingdom or its colonies ; গ্রেটব্রিটেন বা আয়র্লণ্ডের বা তদধীন কোন উপনিবেশের উক্তরূপ বিভাগ।

rifacimento, *n.* An adaptation of a literary work ; কোন সাহিত্য-গ্রন্থের দেশকালের উপযোগী সংস্করণ।

rife, *adj.* Abounding ; current ; prevailing ; as, the rumour was *rife* ; সঙ্কুল ; প্রচলিত ; খুব প্রচলিত।

riff'-raff, *n.* **1.** Sweeping ; আবর্জ্জনা, জঞ্জাল। **2.** The rabble ; the mob ; সমাজের আবর্জ্জনা ; ইতর লোকের ভিড়।

ri'-fle (-fl), *v. t. & i.* **1.** To snatch-away ; কাড়িয়া নেওয়া, ছিনাইয়া নেওয়া। **2.** To plunder ; to strip ; লুণ্ঠন করা, লুঠপাট করা ; বিহীন করা, চ্যুত করা, বিরহিত করা। ***Verb i.*** To rob ; to pillage ; লুণ্ঠন করা ; লুঠতরাজ করা।

ri'-fle (-fl), *v. t.* **1.** To groove internally with spiral channels ; as, to *rifle* a gun-barrel ; ভিতরে পেঁচের মত খাঁজ কাটা। **2.** (Also *Verb i.*) To shoot with a rifle ; বন্দুক দ্বারা গুলি করা। **3.** To whet with a rifle ; শিরীষ প্রভৃতি দ্বারা আচ্ছাদিত কাষ্ঠখণ্ডে শাণ দেওয়া।

ri'-fle (-fl), *n.* **1.** One of the grooves made in rifling a gun ; বন্দুকের ভিতরে কাটা খাঁজ। **2.** A musket whose barrel is spirally grooved ; যে বন্দুকের নালীতে পেঁচের মত খাঁজ কাটা থাকে, বন্দুক, রাইফেল। **3.** A body of troops armed with rifles; "Some 500 *rifles*, of which about 10 per cent. are sick"; রাইফেল-বন্দুকধারী সৈন্য। **4.** A piece of wood covered with emery or similar material for sharpening scythes; কাস্তে ধার করার জন্য শিরীষ বা তদ্বৎ কোন জিনিষ দ্বারা আবৃত কাষ্ঠ-খণ্ড। **Rifle-bird**—অষ্ট্রেলিয়া মহাদ্বীপের একপ্রকার গাঢ় সবুজবর্ণ পক্ষী। **Rifle brigade**—ব্রিটিশ সৈন্যদলের কোন কোন পল্টনের দল। **Rifle green**—(*Noun*) রাইফেল বন্দুকধারী সৈনিকের পরিচ্ছদের মত সবুজ রং। **Rifle-green**—(*Adj.*) উক্ত পরিচ্ছদের মত হরিদ্বর্ণের। **Rifle-man**—রাইফেল বন্দুকধারী সৈনিক। **Rifle-pit**—শত্রুর উপর গুলি করার কালে রাইফেলধারী সৈনিক যে গর্ত্তে আশ্রয় লয়। **Rifle-range**—রাইফেল বন্দুকের পাল্লা, রাইফেল বন্দুক অভ্যাসের স্থান। **Rifle-shot**—রাইফেল বন্দুকের গুলি; রাইফেল বন্দুক দ্বারা লক্ষ্যভেদনিপুণ ব্যক্তি; রাইফেল বন্দুকের পাল্লা।

rift, *n.* & *v. t.* A cleft; ছেঁদা, ফুটা, ফাটোল, ফাইট, ফাঁক। ***Verb t.*** To rend apart; to cleave; ছেঁদা করা, ফুটা করা, বিদারণ করা; ফাঁক করা, ফাটান। **Rift′-less**, *adj.* **Rift′-y**, *adj.* **Rift-valley**—ভূপৃষ্ঠস্থ সুদীর্ঘ নিম্ন স্থান। **A little rift within the lute**—Any defect which if not remedied in time will eventually mar the whole thing; তানপুরার সামান্য ফাঁক, (লক্ষণায়) কোন বিষয়ে সামান্য ত্রুটি বা খুঁত—যাহা সময়ে না সারিয়া নিলে পরিণামে বিষম হইয়া দাঁড়ায়।

rig, *v. t.*, *i.* & *n.* **1.** (*Naut.*) To fit the shrouds, stays, brace, etc. to their respective masts and yards; to fit with tackling; as, to *rig* a ship; (নৌ-বিদ্যা) জাহাজের দড়াদড়ী, মাস্তুলের পাইল যথাস্থানে খাটান; দড়াদড়ী খাটান। **2.** To equip; to fit up; সজ্জিত করা, ঠিকঠাক করা; দড়াদড়ী-লাগান। **3.** To dress; পোষাক পরা, সাজগোজ পরা। ***Verb i.*** To prepare a ship for sea by fitting with necessary tackle; আবশ্যক দড়াদড়ী প্রভৃতি লাগাইয়া জাহাজ সমুদ্রগমনোপযোগী করা। ***Noun.*** **1.** The peculiar style in which the masts and sails of a ship are fitted; জাহাজের পাইল ও মাস্তুল সন্নিবেশ করার বিশিষ্ট ধারা। **2.** Dress; পোষাক, সাজসজ্জা। **Rig′-ging**, *n.* The cordage of a ship for supporting the mast and extending the sails; জাহাজের মাস্তুল ও পাইলের দড়াদড়ী। **To rig in a boom**—To draw it in from its situation upon the end of a yard or bowsprit; জাহাজের যে দণ্ডের উপর পাইল ছড়ান হয় তাহা স্বস্থান হইতে পাইলদণ্ড বা পোতাগ্র হইতে প্রলম্বিত পাইলের টানাদড়ী বাঁধিবার দণ্ডের প্রান্তে টানিয়া নেওয়া। **To rig out a boom or spar**—To thrust out a pole or spar upon the end of a yard or bowsprit, in order to extend the foot of a sail; পাইলের পাদ-দেশ বিস্তারের জন্য মাস্তুলসংলগ্ন টের্চ্ছা পাইলদণ্ডের প্রান্তে বা পোতাগ্র হইতে প্রলম্বিত যে দণ্ডে পাইলের টানা দড়ী বাঁধা থাকে—তাহার প্রান্তে কোন দণ্ড প্রলম্বিত করা।

rig, *n.* & *v. t.* **1.** Trick; dodge; চাতুরী; ফন্দী, ফিকির। **2.** Same as CORNER *n.* 6 (which see). ***Verb t.*** **1.** To hoax; ধোঁকা দেওয়া। **2.** To raise or lower the market prices by some fraud or trick; জুয়াচুরী বা চাতুরী করিয়া বাজারদর বাড়ান বা কমান। **To rig the market**—Same as RIG, *v. t.* 2.

Rig′-a, *n.* A city and port of European Russia; রুশিয়ার নগর এবং বন্দরবিশেষ। **Riga balsam**—স্থায়ী বা উদ্বায়ী তৈলবিশিষ্ট একপ্রকার ধূনা। [*Pinus Cembrá* নামক সরল গাছ হইতে পাওয়া যায়]।

ri-ges′-cent(-ent), *adj.* Growing stiff or rigid; কাঠিন্যপ্রাপী। **—cence**, *n.*

rig′-ger (-er). *n.* **1.** One who rigs; যে ব্যক্তি জাহাজের পাইল ও মাস্তুলের দড়াদড়ী খাটায়। **2.** (*Mech.*) A cylindrical pulley; a band-wheel; চোঙ্গাকার কপিকল; যে চক্র দোয়ালি সংযোগে অন্য চক্রদ্বারা ঘূর্ণিত হয়।

right (rīt), *adj.*, *v. t.*, *i.*, *n.* & *adv.* **1.** Straight; as, a *right* line; সরল, সোজা, ঋজু। **2.** Fit; suitable; as, *right* conduct; becoming; উপযুক্ত; সঙ্গত, সমীচীন, সমুচিত; শোভন, ন্যায্য, বৈধ, ন্যায়সঙ্গত। **3.** Correct; as, the sum is not *right*; শুদ্ধ, নির্ভুল। **4.** Real; actual; true; just; lawful; as, the *right* heir; প্রকৃত; বাস্তব; যথার্থ; ঠিক; আইনসঙ্গত। **5.** Not mistaken or wrong; অভ্রান্ত। **6.** Opposite to left; as, *right* hand; দক্ষিণ, ডাহিন, বামেতর। **7.** (*Math.*) Rising perpendicularly; having a perpendicular axis; as, a *right* cone; (গণিত-শাস্ত্র) লম্বস্বরূপ, খাড়া; লম্ব অক্ষ-বিশিষ্ট। **8.** (*Math.*) Formed by one line or direction perpendicular to another; as, *right* angle; (গণিত-শাস্ত্র) সম (হিঃ কোঃ)। **9.** Well-placed or adjusted; orderly; as, I shall never get them *right* again; সুবিন্যস্ত, ঠিকঠাক; সুশৃঙ্খল। **10.** (*Rare*) Upright; (কচিদ্ব্যবহৃত) সাধু, সৎ। **11.** Sound in body or mind; as, I am all *right* now; whole; সুস্থ; নিরাময়। **12.** Genuine; as, the *right* Virginian tobacco; খাঁটি, সাচ্চা। **13.** Chief or ornamental side; as, the *right* side of a rug; প্রধান বা নক্সাদার দিক। **14.** Most favourable or convenient; as, the balance is on the *right* side; অনুকূল বা সুবিধাজনক। ***Verb t.*** **1.** To restore to the natural position; যথাস্থানে সন্নিবিষ্ট করা। **2.** To adjust; to correct; ঠিকঠাক করা; শুদ্ধ করা। **3.** To do justice to; to relieve from wrong; as, to *right* the oppressed; ন্যায়বিচার করা; অন্যায় উৎপীড়ন হইতে

রক্ষা করা। *Verb i.* To resume an upright or vertical position; পুনরায় খাড়া হওয়া। *Noun.* 1. That which is right or correct; শুদ্ধ বিষয়। 2. Justice: integrity; ন্যায়; ন্যায়নিষ্ঠা। 3. A just claim; ন্যায্য দাবী। 4. Legal power or authority; বৈধ ক্ষমতা বা অধিকার, অধিকার (হিঃ কোঃ), স্বত্ব (ঐ)। 5. Right condition; ঠিক অবস্থা। 6. Right hand; ডাহিনদিক, ডাহিন। 7. The most finished and outward surface, as of a piece of cloth; কাপড়, কম্বল, প্রভৃতির বাহিরের দিক বা মসৃণ-দিক্। 8. (In France etc.) Conservative or monarchist members of a legislative assembly; ব্যবস্থাপকসভার রক্ষণশীল বা রাজ-পক্ষভুক্ত সভ্যগণ। *Adv.* 1. Justly; according to the will of God; ন্যায্যভাবে; ঈশ্বরানুমোদিতভাবে। 2. Correctly; শুদ্ধরূপে। 3. Truly; correctly; সত্যরূপে, যথার্থরূপে; সঠিকভাবে। 4. Very; extremely; as, the *right* honourable; মহা; নিরতিশয়। **Right'-a-ble,** *adj.* **Right'-er,** *n.* **Right'-ly, Right'-ward,** *advs.* **Individual right**—স্বকীয় স্বত্ব (হিঃ কোঃ)। **Miss Right**—নিরূপিতা পত্নী। **Mr. Right**—নিরূপিত পতি। **Proprietory right**—স্বামিত্ব, অধিকার (হিঃ কোঃ), হক্ মালিকানা (ঐ)। **Right-about**—Same as RIGHT-ABOUT TURN. **Right-angle**—সমকোণ। **Right-angled**—সমকোণী। **Right-angled triangle**—জাত্যত্রিভুজ। **Right ascension**—বিষুবাংশ (হিঃ কোঃ)। **Right-down**—Downright; পুরা, পাকা, বিলকুল। **Right down**—(*Colloq.*) Plainly; (চলিতভাষায়) সোজাভাবে। **Right-drawn**—ন্যায়সঙ্গত ব্যাপারে নিষ্কোষিত (অসি)। **Right enough**—ভালরকম, বেশ। **Right heir**—প্রকৃত উত্তরাধিকারী, আইনসঙ্গত উত্তরাধিকারী। **Right-honourable**—মহামান্য। **Right line**—সরল রেখা। **Right-meaning**—সদিচ্ছাকারী। **Right-minded**—সাধুমনাঃ, সাধুচিত্ত, সদন্তঃকরণ। **Right prism**—খাড়াভাবে স্থিত ত্রিপার্শ্বকাচ (So *right cone, right cylinder,* etc.)। **Right pyramid**—যে পিরামিডের ভুমি সমকোণী বহুভুজক্ষেত্র হইয়া থাকে, এবং যাহার চূড়া হইতে ভুমিতে কোন রেখা টানিলে ঐ ভুমির মধ্যবিন্দু অতিক্রম করে। **Right-saddling**—সোজা উত্তর, দক্ষিণ, পুর্ব্ব বা পশ্চিমদিকে গোতচালন। **Right smart**—(American) Considerable; বহু। **Right sphere**—এরূপভাবে স্থাপিত গোলক—যাহাতে উহার বিষুবরেখা বা কোন দ্রাঘিমা দিক্‌চক্রবালের সহিত সমান্তরাল থাকে, সমগোল (সূর্য্যঃ বিঃ)। **Right tool**—ডাহিন হাত দ্বারা কাজ করার উপযোগী যন্ত্র। **Right turn**—পুর্ব্বস্থানের সহিত সমকোণে আবর্ত্তন। **Right whale**—একপ্রকার তিমি মাছ—যাহার পিঠের পাখনা থাকেনা। **All right**—বেশ, তাই হবে। **A right-hand man**—দক্ষিণহস্তস্বরূপ ব্যক্তি, দক্ষিণহস্ত, কাহারো প্রধান অবলম্বন। **At right angles**—লম্বস্বরূপ। **At or on the right hand**—দক্ষিণ পার্শ্বে স্থিত (সম্মানার্থে)। **By right, By rights**—Rightly; ঠিকভাবে, সঙ্গতভাবে, ন্যায্য ভাবে। **Declaration or Bill of Rights**—১৬৮৯ খৃষ্টাব্দে ১৩ই ফেব্রুয়ারী তারিখে পার্লেমেণ্টের উভয় গৃহের সভ্যগণ কর্তৃক Prince of Orangeএর প্রজাধিকারস্বত্ব ও অধিকার সম্বন্ধে যে ঘোষণাপত্র অর্পিত হইয়াছিল। **His heart is in the right place**—He is faithful and right-minded; তিনি খুব বিশ্বস্ত এবং সদন্তঃকরণ। **In one's right mind**—Sane; প্রকৃতিস্থ। **In right of, By right of**—By virtue of a title; কোন স্বত্ব বা অধিকার মতে। **Of right**—Rightly; ন্যায়সঙ্গতরূপে, ন্যায়মত। **Out of one's right mind**—Insane; উন্মাদ, অপ্রকৃতিস্থ। **Right-about turn or face**—এরূপভাবে ঘূর্ণন যাহাতে পূর্ব্বে যে দিকে মুখ ছিল সেই দিকে পৃষ্ঠ থাকে। **Right and left**—On both or all sides; উভয়দিকে, সর্ব্বত্র, চারিদিকে। All whom one meets; এলোপাতাড়ি, যাকে তাকে। **Right-and-left-screw**—যে স্ক্রুপের উভয় প্রান্তে বিপরীত রকমের পেঁচ থাকে। **Right and wrong**—ন্যায় অন্যায়। **Right as a trivet**—খুব সুস্থ এবং নিরাপদ। **Right away, Right off**—At once; অমনি, তৎক্ষণাৎ। **Right-handed blow**—দক্ষিণ হস্তের আঘাত। **Rightly served**—যেম্নি কর্ম্ম তেম্নি ফল, বেশ আক্কেল হয়েছে। **Right of action**—মোকদ্দমা করার অধিকার। **Right of search**—জাহাজাদি তল্লাস করিয়া দেখার অধিকার। **Right of support**—একজনের বাড়ীর কড়িকাঠ প্রভৃতি প্রতিবেশীর বাড়ীর প্রাচীরের উপর লাগাইবার অধিকার। **Right of way**—বহুকাল ধরিয়া গমনাগমন করা হেতু কোন রাস্তায় চলাচলের যে অধিকার জন্মে, অন্যের জায়গার উপর দিয়া চলাচলের অধিকার। **Right shoulder arms**—ঘাড়ের উপর টের্চ্ছাভাবে বন্দুক ধারণ। **The right**—ন্যায়, পুণ্য, ধর্ম্মনিষ্ঠা। **The right man in the right place**—উপযুক্ত স্থানে উপযুক্ত. লোকই নিযুক্ত হইয়াছে। **The right side of 50**—এখনও পঞ্চাশ বৎসর বয়স হয় নাই। **To be in the right**—To have justice, reason and fact on one's side; ন্যায়পথে থাকা। **To put to or set to right**—To adjust; to put into good order; ঠিক করা; দোরস্ত করা, শোধরাইয়া নেওয়া। **To right a ship**—(নৌ-বিদ্যা) জাহাজ খাড়া করিয়া রাখা। **To right the helm**—To put it in line with the keel; হাইল ঘুরাইয়া পানিতরাসের সহিত সমরেখায় আনা। **To send to the right-about**—To dismiss without ceremony; কোনরূপ শিষ্টাচার না দেখাইয়া বিদায় করা। **To set one right**—To correct one ; সংশোধন করা। To clear one's character ; অপবাদ মোচন করা, কলঙ্ক হইতে মুক্ত করা। **To set to right**—To cure ; নিরাময় করা। **Woman's rights**—ভোট প্রদানের ক্ষমতা এবং অন্যান্য যে সকল অধিকার-প্রাপ্তির জন্য বিলাতের মহিলাগণ আন্দোলন করেন।

right'-eous (rī-chŭs), *adj.* **1.** Upright ; virtuous ; সাধু, সৎ ; ধর্ম্মপরায়ণ, ধর্ম্মাশ্রিত, ধর্ম্ম্য, ধার্ম্মিক, ধর্ম্মনিষ্ঠ, ধর্ম্মাত্মা, ন্যায়পরায়ণ, ধর্ম্মপ্রাণ। **2.** Just ; as, a *righteous* cause ; ন্যায্য, ন্যায়সঙ্গত। **—ly,** *adv.* **—ness,** *n.* Virtue ; purity of life ; ধর্ম্ম ; ধার্ম্মিকতা, ধর্ম্মপ্রাণতা, পুণ্যতা।

right'-fûl (rīt-), *adj.* **1.** Just ; ন্যায্য, ন্যায়সঙ্গত। **2.** Legal ; lawful ; as, a *rightful* heir ; বৈধ ; বিধিসঙ্গত। **3.** Appropriate ; as, a *rightful* reception ; যথোচিত, সমুচিত। **—ly,** *adv.* **—ness,** *n.*

right'-ly̆ (rīt-), *adv.* **1.** Honestly ; সাধুভাবে, ধর্ম্মসঙ্গতরূপে। **2.** Properly ; fitly ; সঙ্গতরূপে, সমীচীনরূপে ; সমুচিতরূপে। **3.** Correctly ; অভ্রান্তরূপে, নিভুর্লরূপে।

rig'-id, *adj.* **1.** Not flexible ; stiff ; hard ; অনমনীয় ; আড়ষ্ট ; দৃঢ়, কঠিন। **2.** Strict ; stern ; as, *rigid* discipline ; কড়া ; কঠোর। **3.** Punctilious ; as, *rigid* observance of law ; সূক্ষ্মভাবে পালিত। **—ly,** *adv.* **Ri-gid'-i-ty, —ness,** *ns.* **1.** Want of pliability ; অনমনীয়তা, কাঠিন্য। **2.** Want of ease or airy elegance ; অস্বচ্ছন্দতা, আড়ষ্টতা আড়ষ্টভাব।

rig'-mă-rōle, *n.* & *adj.* A long confused silly discourse ; a succession of incoherent or foolish statement ; an incoherent and long-worded harangue ; balderdash ; "A long *rigmarole* was told how the journalist's hat had fallen into the Seine" ; পূর্ব্বাপর সঙ্গতিহীন সুদীর্ঘ আলোচনা ; পূর্ব্বাপর সঙ্গতিহীন বা অর্থশূন্য উক্তি পরম্পরা, বারমাসী (*colloq.*), পাঁচালী (*ib.*) ; অসম্বদ্ধ বাক্‌প্রপঞ্চ, অর্থশূন্যবাগ্‌-বিস্তার। ***Adj.*** Long-winded ; nonsensical ; সুদীর্ঘ ; অর্থহীন।

rigor, *n.* (*Path.*) A sudden chill with shivering before fever etc. ; (নিদান শাস্ত্র) জ্বরাদির পূর্ব্বে সহসা শীতানুভব ও কম্প। ***Rigor mortis***—Stiffening of body after death ; মৃত্যুর পর দেহের আড়ষ্টতা।

rig'-our (-ŏr), *n.* **1.** Stiffness ; rigidity ; আড়ষ্টতা, অসাড়তা ; কঠিনতা। **2.** Strictness ; কঠোরতা, কড়াকড়ি। **3.** Austerity ; কঠোরনিয়মনিষ্ঠা, ব্রতনিয়মাদি পালনে কঠোরতা। **4.** Severity of weather, climate, cold, etc. ; দুর্য্যোগ, শীত প্রভৃতির প্রাবল্য। **4.** Sternness ; cruelty ; কঠোরতা ; নিষ্ঠুরতা। **5.** Exactitude ; strict accuracy ; সূক্ষ্মতা ; সঠিকতা। **6.** Harsh measures ; কঠোর উপায়-সমূহ। **7.** Extreme distress ; as, they experienced the utmost *rigours* of famine ; অশেষ দুর্গতি, দুর্গতির একশেষ, দুর্গতির পরাকাষ্ঠা। **—ism,** *n.* **1.** Austerity ; কঠোরতা, কঠোরনিয়মনিষ্ঠা। **2.** Severity of style, writing, etc. ; অলঙ্কারবিহীনতা, স্বল্পাক্ষরতা, অল্পাক্ষরবিশিষ্টতা। **3.** Strictness in the observance of moral laws ; কঠোর নৈতিকতা। **4.** (*Kant.*) The principle of observing one's duty without any hope of future reward ; নিষ্কাম কর্ত্তব্যসাধন নীতি, তপোবাদ (হিঃ কোঃ), নিষ্কাম কর্ম্মতত্ত্ব। **—ist,** *n.* **—ous,** *adj.* **1.** Severe ; strict ; কঠোর ; কড়া। **2.** Harsh ; as, *rigorous* treatment ; কঠোর, কর্কশ। **3.** (Of climate) Severe ; extremely cold ; (জলবায়ু সম্পর্কে) দুর্য্যোগপূর্ণ ; অতি শীতল, কনকনে। **4.** (India) Attended with hard labour ; as, *rigorous* imprisonment ; কঠোর পরিশ্রম সহকৃত, সশ্রম।

Riksdag, *n.* The Swedish parliament ; সুইডেনদেশের পার্লেমেন্ট।

rīle, *v. t.* (*Slang*) To make cross or angry ; to irritate ; ক্রুদ্ধ করা, বিরক্ত করা ; চটান।

rilievo, *n.* Same as RELIEF (which see.)

rĭll, *n.* & *v. i.* A rivulet ; runnel ; ক্ষুদ্র নদী ; নালা, কুল্যা। ***Verb i.*** To issue or flow as a rill ; ক্ষুদ্রনদী বা নালার মত প্রবাহিত হওয়া।

rille (rĭl), *n.* (*Astron.*) A trench or narrow valley seen on the moon's surface through a telescope ; (জ্যোতির্বিজ্ঞান) দূরদর্শনযন্ত্রযোগে চন্দ্রবিম্বোপরি দৃষ্ট ক্ষুদ্র নালা বা প্রশস্ত উপত্যকা।

rĭll'-ĕt, *n.* A small rill ; ক্ষুদ্র নালা।

rĭll'-ĕtts, —ettes (-ĕts), *ns.* A tinned preparation of minced ham, chicken, fat, etc. ; কুচি কুচি করিয়া কাটা শূকরমাংস, কুক্কুটমাংস, চর্ব্বি, প্রভৃতি দ্বারা প্রস্তুত টিনের কৌটায় ভরা খাদ্য।

rĭm, *n.* & *v. t.* **1.** The circular wooden portion forming the periphery of a wheel ; চক্রপ্রান্ত, নেমি (Syn. প্রধী, নেমী)। **2.** The border or margin of anything ; প্রান্ত, কিনারা, ধার। **3.** The outer frame of a sieve ; চালুনির প্রান্তবেষ্টনী। **4.** Surface of water ; as, under the *rim* of water ; জলের উপরিভাগ। **5.** A circular object ; গোলাকৃতি বস্তু, চক্র, বলয়। ***Verb t.*** **1.** To furnish with rim ; to border ; to encircle ; নেমি-সমন্বিত করা ; কিনারা লাগান ; বেষ্টিত করা, বলয়িত করান। **2.** (*Amer.*) To gash the side of a mackeral to make it appear fatter ; মোটা দেখাইবার জন্য মেকারিল মাছের পার্শ্ব হাঁসান। **Rim'-less,** *adj.* **Rim'-med,** *p. p.* **Golden rim**—স্বর্ণমুকুট, কনককিরীট, কনকমুকুট। **Rim-brake**—যে চক্রগতিরোধকযন্ত্র নেমির উপর ক্রিয়া করে।

rim, *n.* (*Rare*) The lower part of the belly ; (কচিৎ ব্যবহৃত) উদরের নিম্নাংশ।

rime, *n.* & *v. t.* Same as RHYME (which see).

rime, *n.* & *v. t.* Hoar-frost ; তুষার-পুষ্প, তুষারবিন্দু, ঘন-নীহার (আঃ বঃ)। ***Verb t.*** To cover with rime ; তুষারবিন্দু দ্বারা আচ্ছাদিত করা। **Rim'-y,** *adj.*

rime, *n.* A rung or round of ladder ; মইএর ধাপ বা কোয়া।

rī'-mōse, –mous (-mŭs), *ns.* Full of cracks or chink ; ছিদ্রবহুল, সচ্ছিদ্র।

rind, *n.* & *v. t.* **1.** The bark of tree or plant ; বল্কল, ছাল, বৃক্ষত্বক। **2.** The outer coat of fruits or vegetables ; বাকল, ত্বক, খোসা, চোকলা। **3.** Skin ; skin of bacon ; চামড়া ; শূকর মাংসের পরদা। **4.** The outer crust of cheese etc. ; পনীর প্রভৃতির কঠিন বহিরাবরণ। **5.** (*Fig.*) External aspect of anything ; (লক্ষণায়) কোন বস্তুর বাহ্য ভাব। ***Verb t.*** To strip the rind from ; বাকল উঠান, খোসা ছাড়ান, ছোলা। **Rind'-ed,** *p.p.*

rin'-dêr-pĕst, *n.* A malignant infectious disease of cattle ; গবাদি পশুর একপ্রকার মড়ক রোগ, গোবসন্ত। (বোঃ)।

ring, *n., v. t.* & *i.* **1.** A circle or hoop of gold or other material worn on the fingers, nose, or other parts of body as ornament ; আংটী, অঙ্গুরী, অঙ্গুরীয়ক, বালি (nose-ring), বলয়, কঙ্কণ (arm-ring), অনন্ত, ইয়ারাং (ear-ring)। **2.** A hoop of metal or other materials used for great variety of purposes ; লৌহাদির বলয়, চক্র, পিপার হালি প্রভৃতি। **3.** A circular band or circlet ; বলয়, চক্র, মেখলা, বেষ্টনী, মণ্ডল, কুণ্ডলী। **4.** A race-course, usually circular ; ঘোড়দৌড়ের চক্র, দৌড়চক্র। **5.** An inclosed space for wrestling, boxing, etc. ; মল্লযুদ্ধ এবং মুষ্টিযুদ্ধের জন্য বেষ্টিত অঙ্গন। **6.** The betting arena in a race-course ; hence (*fig.*) the book-makers ; ঘোড়দৌড়ের মাঠের যে স্থানে লোকে বাজী ধরে ; যাহারা ঘোড়দৌড়ে ঘোড়ার উপর বাজী রাখে। **7.** The inclosed space in which horses etc. are exhibited or exercised in a cattle-show or market ; হট্টস্থান বা পশুপ্রদর্শনীর যে বেষ্টিতস্থানে অশ্ব প্রভৃতি প্রদর্শিত হয় বা অশ্বাদির অঙ্গচালনা করান হয়। **8.** Circular or spiral course ; চক্রবৎগতি, কুণ্ডলিত গতি। **9.** A combination of persons to control for their own advantage the production or sale of particular articles or to control local affairs or politics ; ব্যবসায়িগণের জোট, রাজনীতিকগণের জোট। **10.** (*Chem.*) An arrangement of atoms graphically represented as a ring ; পরমাণু সমূহের অঙ্গুরীয়াকারে সন্নিবেশ। **11.** (*Anat.*) Anything resembling a ring ; (শারীরসংস্থানবিদ্যা) অঙ্গুরীয়াকৃতি অস্থি প্রভৃতি। **12.** (*Geom.*) The space between two concentric circles ; (জ্যামিতি) এককেন্দ্রিক বৃত্তদ্বয়ের মধ্যবর্ত্তী স্থান। ***Verb t.*** **1.** To provide with a ring ; অঙ্গুরীয়সমন্বিত করা। **2.** To encircle ; বেষ্টিত করা, বলয়িত করা। **3.** To cut a ring of bark from ; বৃক্ষ হইতে বলয়াকারে বল্কল কাটিয়া নেওয়া। **4.** To exhibit or exercise in a ring ; বেষ্টিতঅঙ্গনে পশু প্রভৃতি প্রদর্শন করা বা উহাদের অঙ্গচালনা করান। **5.** To cut onions etc. in rings ; পেঁয়াজ প্রভৃতি গোল গোল বা চাক চাক করিয়া কাটা। ***Verb i.*** (Of a hawk) To rise in the air spirally ; ঘুরিয়া ঘুরিয়া আকাশে উঠা। **Ring-bark**—*v. t.* গাছ নষ্ট করার জন্য বা উহার বৃদ্ধি রোধ করার উদ্দেশ্যে গাছের বাকলের উপর অঙ্গুরীয় কাটা। **Ring-bolt** — রজ্জু প্রভৃতি বাঁধার জন্য আংটাওয়ালা শঙ্কু। **Ring-bone** — অশ্বের পাদরোগ বিশেষ। **Ring-dove** — বনকপোত, ঝুঁটিদার পায়রা। **Ring-fence**—বৃত্তাকৃতি বৃতি। **Ring-finger** — অনামিকা, অনামা (cf. অনামা-মূলমারভ্য কনিষ্ঠাদিত এব চ-রুদ্রযামল), উপমধ্যমা (আপঃ শ্রৌঃ)। **Ring-goal**—একপ্রকার খেলা—যাহাতে পিপার হালি যষ্টির আঘাতে লক্ষ্যস্থলে নিক্ষিপ্ত হয়। **Ring-hunt**—একপ্রকার মৃগয়া — যাহাতে অগ্নিময় বেষ্টনী দ্বারা পশুদিগকে ভিতরের দিকে তাড়িত করা হয়। **Ring-leader**—দলের সর্দ্দার, দলপতি, নায়ক (হিঃ কোঃ), চাঁই। **Ring-maker**—See BOOK-MAKER. **Ring-master**—সার্কাসের অধ্যক্ষ। **Ring-neck**—একপ্রকার হংস বা তিত্তির পক্ষী (Plover) যাহার গলায় রঙ্গীন চক্র থাকে। **Ring-net**—স্যামন মাছের জাল। **Ring-ouzel**—একপ্রকার পক্ষী। **Ring-snake** — ইয়ুরোপ দেশীয় সর্প বিশেষ (সচরাচর কুণ্ডলী পাকাইয়া থাকে বলিয়া এই নাম)। **Ringworm**—দদ্রুরোগ, দদ্রু, দাদ, দদ্রুক। **Ring of saturn**—শনির কৃষ্ণ উপবীত (জ্যোতি জ্যোঃ), মেখলা (সাঃ পঃ)। **To form a ring**—See RING 9. **To make rings round**—To go, or perform a thing, more quickly ; দ্রুততরগমন বা সম্পাদন করা। **To ring a quoit**—To throw it so as to encircle the pin ; এরূপ ভাবে চাকা ফেলান যাহাতে উহা খোঁটা বেড়িয়া পড়ে। **To ring off**—(মানসমূর্ত্তি প্রভৃতি সম্পর্কে)—বলয়াকারে পরিণত হইয়া মিলাইয়া যাওয়া। **To ring the bull**—এক প্রাচারাদিতে নিবদ্ধ আঁকড়াতে বলয় নিক্ষেপ করা বা ঝুলাইয়া দেওয়া।

ring, *v. t., i.* & *n.* **1.** To cause to sound, esp. by striking metallic body ; ঘণ্টা প্রভৃতি বাজান, বাদন করা, নিনাদিত করা। **2.** To attend or celebrate, proclaim or usher in by means of ringing ; as, to *ring* in the new year ; ঘণ্টাদি বাদনপূর্ব্বক কাহারো সঙ্গে অনুগমন করা, কোন উৎসবাদির অনুষ্ঠান করা বা কাহারো আগমন বিজ্ঞাপিত করা। **3.** To sound ; নিনাদিত করা। **4.** To repeat often loudly or earnestly ; as, to *ring* one's praises ;

উচ্চকণ্ঠে বারম্বার বলা, বিঘোষিত করা। *Verb i.* 1. To sound as a bell ; (ঘণ্টা প্রভৃতি) বাদিত হওয়া, নিনাদিত হওয়া। 2. To cause to sound a bell ; as, to *ring* for a servant ; ঘণ্টা বাজান। 3. To sound ; to resound; নিনাদিত হওয়া; প্রতিধ্বনিত হওয়া। 4. To have the sensation of some continued sound ; to tingle ; as, my ears *ring* with the noise ; ক্রমাগত বাজিতে থাকা ; ঝিন ঝিন করা, ঝিঁ ঝিঁ করা। 5. To fill with talk or tune ; as, the whole country *rings* with his praise ; কোন কথা দেশ-শুদ্ধ বা সহরময় প্রচার হওয়া, সুখ্যাতিতে পূর্ণ হওয়া। *Noun.* 1. The sound of a bell etc. ; act of ringing a bell ; ঘণ্টা প্রভৃতির ধ্বনি, ঘণ্টাধ্বনি ; ঘণ্টা প্রভৃতি বাদন। 2. A chime or set of bells harmonically tuned ; ধ্বনির ক্রম মিল অনুসারে সজ্জিত ঘণ্টা শ্রেণী। 3. Any loud sound or sound continued, repeated or reverberated ; as, the *ring* of applause ; নিনাদ, নিক্কণ, প্রতিধ্বনি, রণন, রণরণি, ধ্বনিপ্রবাহ। 4. Particular character when uttered ; as, he had a *ring* of sincerity in his tone ; বিশিষ্ট ধ্বনি, সুর। **To ring changes upon, To ring the changes**—See CHANGE. **To ring down**—To conclude ; সমাপন করা। To give the signal to lower the curtain down ; যবনিকা ফেলিবার জন্য ঘণ্টা দেওয়া। **To ring off**—To finish telephonic-interview ; টেলিফোঁ-যোগে কথাবার্ত্তা শেষ করা। **To ring out**—To sound vigorously ; জোরে বাজান। **To ring the bells backward**—To sound the chimes in reverse order ; সজ্জিত ঘণ্টাশ্রেণী বিপর্য্যস্ত ক্রমে বাজান। **To ring the knell**—To announce the death or abolition of ; মৃত্যু বা বিলোপ ঘোষণা করা। **To ring up**—To give the signal to raise the curtain ; যবনিকা উঠাইবার জন্য ঘণ্টা দেওয়া। **To ring up on telephone**—To get or seek communication with ; কাহারো সহিত টেলিফোঁতে কথোপকথনের ব্যবস্থা করা বা কথাবার্ত্তা বলার জন্য চেষ্টা করা।

rin'-gĕnt, *adj.* 1. (*Obs.*) Gaping ; (অপ্রঃ) ব্যাদিত। 2. (*Bot.*) Applied to the corolla of plants when the petals are irregular and gaping ; (উদ্ভিদ্ বিদ্যা) মুক্তমুখ (সাঃ পঃ)।

ring'-ĕr, *n.* 1. A bell-ringer ; ঘণ্টাবাদক। 2. A quoit that falls so as to surround the pin ; যে আংটা খোটা বেড়িয়া পড়ে। 3. A crow-bar ; ভারি জিনিষ চাড়া দিয়া তোলার জন্য দণ্ড, উত্তোলন দণ্ড, ঠেকো। 4. A device for ringing the bell ; ঘণ্টা বাজাইবার জন্য হাতুড় প্রভৃতি। 5. A fox etc. which runs in a ring when hunted ; শিকারী দ্বারা তাড়িত হইয়া মৃগয়াচক্রের ভিতর ধাবিত শৃগাল প্রভৃতি। 6. A swindle operating in false coining (Australia) ; অষ্ট্রেলিয়ায় যে ব্যক্তি মেকি টাকা চালাইয়া লোককে ঠকায়। 7. A man who shears the highest number of sheep per day ; যে ব্যক্তি প্রতিদিন অধিকতম সংখ্যক মেষের রোমচ্ছেদন করে। 8. A horse entered in a game under a false name ; a man who closely resembles another man ; যে অশ্বকে মিথ্যা নাম দিয়া দৌড়ের জন্য ভর্ত্তি করা হয় ; অপর ব্যক্তির সহিত সৌসাদৃশ্য বিশিষ্ট ব্যক্তি।

ring'-lĕt, *n.* 1. (*Rare*) A small ring ; (কচিদ্ব্যবহৃত) ক্ষুদ্র অঙ্গুরী, অঙ্গুরীয়ক। 2. (*Rare*) A fairy-ring ; (কচিদ্ব্যবহৃত) দুর্ব্বাদলোপরি পরিবালিকাদের নৃত্যচক্র। 3. A curl of hair ; কুঞ্চিত কুন্তলগুচ্ছ, অলকগুচ্ছ, চূর্ণ কুন্তলগুচ্ছ। **-ed, -y,** *adjs.*

rink (rĭngk), *n.* & *v. i.* 1. A sheet of ice measured off for the game of curling ; ক্রীড়াবিশেষের জন্য তুষারক্ষেত্র। 2. A sheet of ice usually under cover for skating on ; a building containing such a sheet of ice ; সচক্র কাষ্ঠপাদুকা দ্বারা ক্রীড়াচ্ছলে বিচরণের জন্য (সচরাচর আচ্ছাদিত) হিমানীক্ষেত্র ; ঐরূপ ক্রীড়ার গৃহ। *Verb i.* To skate in a rink ; সচক্র কাষ্ঠপাদুকার সাহায্যে ক্রীড়াচ্ছলে তুষারাঙ্গণোপরি বিচরণ করা। **Rink'-er,** *n.*

rinse (rĭns), *v. t.* & *n.* 1. To cleanse lightly with clean water ; ধৌত করা, প্রক্ষালন করা, পরিষ্কার জলদ্বারা ধৌত করা। 2. To wash by filling with water etc. and shaking and emptying ; ঝাঁকড়াইয়া ধোয়া। *Noun.* The act of rinsing ; ঝাঁকড়াইয়া ধৌতকরণ, ধৌতকরণ।

rī'-ŏt, *n., v. i.* & *t.* 1. Uproar ; tumult ; সোর গোল, হট্টগোল ; হল্লা। 2. Wild and loose festivity ; revelry ; "Luxury and *riot*, feast and dance" ; তাণ্ডবলীলা ; মদ্যপানকোলাহল। 3. (*Law*) A tumultuous disturbance of the peace by three or more persons ; (আইন) হাঙ্গামা। 4. A brilliant display of colour ; as, a *riot* of scarlet on gold ; সমুজ্জ্বল বর্ণচ্ছটা, রঙের খেলা। *Verb i.* 1. To go to excess in feasting, drinking or other dissipation ; to act in an unrestrained and wanton manner ; পানভোজন প্রভৃতি অমিতাচারে প্রবৃত্ত হওয়া ; উচ্ছৃঙ্খলের মত কাজ করা, তাণ্ডবলীলা করা। 2. To join in riot ; হাঙ্গামায় যোগ দেওয়া। *Verb t.* To spare money or waste time in riot or luxury ; বিলাসব্যসনে সময় বা অর্থ নষ্ট করা। **-ous,** *adj.* Indulging in riot or luxury ; wanton ; profligate ; হাঙ্গামাকারী, হল্লাকারী ; উচ্ছৃঙ্খল, স্বেচ্ছাচারী ; লম্পট, বিলাসোন্মত্ত। **To read the Riot Act**—To read a proclamation before ordering police or military to fire on a riotous assembly ; হাঙ্গামাকারিগণের

উপর গুলি চালাইবার জন্য পুলিশ বা সৈনিকগণকে আদেশ দেওয়ার পূর্ব্বে ঘোষণাপত্র পাঠ করা। [ঘোষণাটী এই :—Our Sovereign Lady the Queen chargeth and commandeth all persons, being assembled, immediately to disperse themselves, and peaceably to depart to their habitations or to their lawful business, upon the pains contained in the Act made in the first year of King George for preventing tumults and riotous assemblies.] (*Fig.*) To give warning before taking extreme measures; to reprimand strongly; চূড়ান্ত উপায় অবলম্বনের পূর্ব্বে সাবধান করা; তীব্র তিরস্কার করা। **To run riot**—To act without restraint; অসংযত ভাবে কার্য্য করা, উচ্ছৃঙ্খল ভাবে কার্য্য করা, যথেচ্ছাচার করা। To grow luxuriantly or wildly; অতি প্রচুর পরিমাণে জন্মা, বুনো হইয়া যাওয়া, অতিরিক্ত পরিমাণে বাড়িয়া উঠা।

rip, *n.* 1. An old worn out horse; অকর্ম্মণ্য বৃদ্ধ অশ্ব। 2. A scamp; a rake; ধূর্ত্ত, শঠ; লম্পট।

rip, *v. t., i.* & *n.* To cut or tear asunder, open or away; ছিঁড়া, ফাঁড়া, ছেঁড়া, বিদীর্ণ করা। ***Verb i.*** 1. To become torn apart; বিদারিত হওয়া, ছিঁড়া, ফাঁড়িয়া যাওয়া। 2. To slash; হাঁসান। 3. To rush along with great speed; প্রচণ্ড বেগে ধাবিত হওয়া। 4. To disclose; "They *ripped* up all that had been done from the beginning of the rebellion"; to open up wounds or sores; (*fig.*) to recall old difficulties; as, to *rip up* an old sore; খুলিয়া বাহির করা, উদ্ঘাটন করা; ফোঁড়া বা ঘায়ের মুখ আবার খোলা; (লক্ষণায়) পুরাতন কলহ বা বিবাদ বিসম্বাদের কথা পুনরায় উত্থাপন করা, পুরাতন কাসুন্দী ঘাঁটা। ***Noun.*** A rent made by ripping; ফাটা, চির। **Rip'-ping,** *adj.* Splendid; খাসা, চমৎকার, বাহারের, তোফা, সেরা।

rip, *n.* A wicker basket to carry fish in; মাছের ঝুড়ী, খালুই।

ri-pā'-ri-ăl, *adj.* 1. Same as RIPARIAN. 2. (*Zool.*) Living on, or frequenting, banks of rivers, lakes, etc.; নদীতীরবাসী, নদীতীর চর।

ri-pā'-ri-ăn, *adj.* & *n.* Pertaining to the banks of a river; situated on the banks of a river; নদীতীরসম্বন্ধীয়; নদীতীরবর্ত্তী। ***Noun.*** A riparian proprietor; নদীতীরবর্ত্তী ভূমির মালীক। **Riparian nations**—নদীর পরস্পর বিপরীত তীরবর্ত্তী ভূমির বা এক তীরের বিভিন্ন অংশের অধিকারী জাতি সমূহ। **Riparian rights**—যে ভূস্বামীর অধিকৃত ভূখণ্ডের মধ্যে হ্রদ, নদী প্রভৃতি থাকে—তাঁহার ঐ নদী, হ্রদ প্রভৃতির, তীর, গর্ত্ত, ও জলে অধিকার।

rīpe, *adj., v. t.* & *i.* 1. Ready for reaping or gathering; পাকা, পক্ব, পোক্ত, ঝুনা (esp. of a coccanut)। 2. Mature; as, a *ripe* scholar; পরিপক্ব, পরিণত (পরিণত কবিত্বশক্তি মঃ সং), পক্ববুদ্ধি, পক্বধী। 3. Advanced to the state of being fit for use; as, *ripe* cheese; *ripe* wine; ব্যবহারোপযোগী অবস্থাপ্রাপ্ত। 4. Ruddy and full as a red fruit; as, *ripe* lips; রক্তবর্ণ ফলের মত সরস, সুপুষ্ট এবং অরুণবর্ণ, পক্ব [cf. পক্ববিম্বাধরোষ্ঠী (মেঘ দূঃ)]। 5. Fully developed or perfectly suppurated; as, a *ripe* boil; পাকা। 6. Ready; suitable; as, the time is *ripe* for war; প্রস্তুত; উপযোগী। ***Verb t.*** To make ripe; পাকান, পরিণত করা। ***Verb i.*** To become ripe; পাকা। **Ripe'-ly,** *adv.* **Rip'-en,** *v. t.* & *i.* **Ripe'-ness,** *n.*

ri-pōst', —poste' (-pōst), *n.* & *v. i.* (*Fencing*) The thrust or blow with which one follows up a successful parry; a smart or witty reply; (অসিক্রীড়া) আঘাত বা খোঁচা আটকাইয়া পরে আঘাত বা খোঁচা দেওন; টাট্‌কা জবাব, সরস উত্তর। ***Verb i.*** To deliver a riposte; to retort smartly; খোঁচা বা আঘাত আটকাইয়া পুনরায় আঘাত করা বা খোঁচা দেওয়া; টাটকা জবাব দেওয়া।

rip'-per (-ĕr), *n.* 1. One who rips; বিদারক, ছেদনকারী। 2. A tool for ripping roof; ছাদের টালি প্রভৃতি খুলিবার জন্য যন্ত্র বিশেষ। 3. (*Slang*) A first-class person or thing; (ইতর ভাষায়) সেরা লোক, সেরা জিনিষ, বাহারের জিনিষ।

rip'-ple (-pl), *n.* & *v. t.* A large comb for cleaning away seeds from flax; শণ হইতে বীজ ছাড়াইবার জন্য একপ্রকার বৃহৎ চিরুনী। ***Verb t.*** To clear away seeds from flax; আঁচড়াইয়া শণ পরিষ্কার করা।

rip'-ple (-pl), *n., v. i.* & *t.* 1. The fretting of the surface of water; small wave or waves; জলের হিল্লোল; ক্ষুদ্রতরঙ্গ, বীচি, বীচিমালা, লহরী। 2. A sound as of rippling water; as, the *ripples* of laughter; কলরোল, কলতান, কলনাদ। ***Verb i.*** 1. To wear a ruffled surface; to be covered with small waves; হিল্লোলিত হওয়া; বীচিমালিনী হওয়া, লহরী সমাকুল হওয়া। 2. To make a sound resembling that of rippling water; কুলকুল নাদ করা, কলকল করা, কলরোল তোলা। ***Verb t.*** 1. To cover with wavelets; ক্ষুদ্রতরঙ্গময় করা, বীচিপূর্ণ করা। 2. To ruffle, as the surface of water; হিল্লোলিত করা। **—plet,** *n* **—ply,** *adj.*

Rip-ū-ā'-ri-ăn, *adj.* Of the ancient Franks, dwelling on the banks of Rhine near the present city of Cologne; বর্ত্তমান কলোন নগরীর সন্নিহিত রাইননদীর তীরবর্ত্তী প্রদেশবাসী প্রাচীন ফ্রাঙ্ক জাতির লোকগণ-সম্বন্ধীয়। **Ripuarian law**—উক্ত লোকগণের আইন।

Rip-văn-Win-kle (-wing-kl), *n.* A person of antiquated ideas; সেকেলে লোক, সাবেকি ধরণের লোক, মান্ধাতের আমলের লোক। [Washington Irvingকৃত "Rip van Winkle" নামক গল্পের নায়কের নাম। Kaatskill পর্ব্বতের উপত্যকায় Rip van Winkleএর সহিত এক অপরিচিত লোকের সাক্ষাৎ হয়। সে ঐ লোকের আবাসে এক চুমুক মদ্য পান করিয়া অজ্ঞান হইয়া পড়ে। বিশবৎসর পর সে জাগিয়া বাটীতে যাইয়া দেখে যে, তাহার স্ত্রী মারা গিয়াছে, কন্যা সকলের বিবাহ হইয়া গিয়াছে এবং তাহার স্বদেশ আমেরিকা স্বাধীনতা প্রাপ্ত হইয়াছে।]

rīse, *v. i.* & *t.* **1.** To mount up; to ascend; উঠা; উত্থিত হওয়া। **2.** To emerge above the eastern horizon; as, the sun *rises*; উদিত হওয়া, উঠা। **3.** To assume an upright position after a fall; as, to *rise* from a fall; খাড়া হওয়া, উঠিয়া দাঁড়ান। **4.** To grow up; as, the tree *rises*; বৃদ্ধি পাওয়া। **5.** To get out of bed; as, he *rises* at 5 A. M.; শয্যাত্যাগ করা, উঠা (cf. আমি রোজ পাঁচটার সময় উঠি)। **6.** To increase in price; as, sugar *rises*; দাম চড়া, মূল্য বাড়া। **7.** To ascend from the grave; as, the dead shall *rise*; কবর হইতে উত্থিত হওয়া। **8.** To rebel; to take up arms; "No more shall nations against nations *rise*"; বিদ্রোহী হওয়া; অস্ত্রধারণ করা। **9.** To close a session; "Parliament will *rise* on Friday next"; অধিবেশন বন্ধ হওয়া। **10.** To swell; as, the boil *rises*; ফুলিয়া উঠা, ফুলা, স্ফীত হওয়া, ফাঁপিয়া উঠা। **11.** To swell in the process of fermentation, as dough or the like; ফুলিয়া উঠা (যথা পাঁউরুটী প্রভৃতি)। **12.** To reach a higher level by increase of quantity; as, the tide *rises*; আয়তন বা পরিমাণ বৃদ্ধি হেতু উপরে উঠা। **13.** To slope upwards; as, the road *rises* up the mountain; উপরের দিকে প্রবণভাবে উঠা। **14.** To increase in force or intensity; as, the storm *rises*; শক্তি বা প্রবলতা বৃদ্ধি পাওয়া, প্রকোপ বৃদ্ধি পাওয়া। **15.** To increase in amount; as, his expense *rises* every month; বৃদ্ধি পাওয়া। **16.** To develop powers equal to; as, he *rose* to the occasion; কোন অবস্থার অনুরূপ শক্তি বিকাশ পাওয়া। **17.** To spring up; as, difficulties may *rise*; উদ্ভূত হওয়া, উপজাত হওয়া। **18.** To happen; as, a quarrel *rises* between them; ঘটা, সংঘটিত হওয়া। **19.** To become more buoyant or more cheerful; as, his spirit *rises*; উৎসাহ বা স্ফূর্ত্তি বৃদ্ধি হওয়া। **20.** To become apparent; to appear; to emerge into sight; as, colour *rose* in her cheeks; প্রতিভাত হওয়া; বোধ হওয়া; দৃষ্টিগোচর হওয়া। **21.** To attain to a higher position; as, to *rise* in society; to thrive; উচ্চতর পদ লাভ হওয়া, পদোন্নতি হওয়া, সামাজিক পদগৌরব বৃদ্ধি হওয়া, প্রতিষ্ঠা বৃদ্ধি হওয়া; উন্নতি লাভ করা। **22.** (*Mus.*) To rise from a lower tone to a higher; (সঙ্গীত-শাস্ত্র) উচ্চতর গ্রামে উঠা। **23.** To become audible; শ্রুতিগোচর হওয়া, শ্রবণযোগ্য হওয়া। **24.** To become more dignified or forcible; to increase in dignity, power, interest or impressiveness; "Horace always *rises* above himself when he has Homer in his view"; অধিকতর উন্নত ও শক্তিশালী হওয়া; অধিকতর হৃদয়গ্রাহী, আমোদজনক বা গুরুত্ব সম্পন্ন হওয়া, অধিকতর গাম্ভীর্য্যপূর্ণ হওয়া। **25.** To be excited; as, his anger *rose*; উত্তেজিত হওয়া। **26.** To be built or reared; "Beside the eternal Nile, the Pyramids have *risen*"; নির্ম্মিত হওয়া, গাঁথিয়া তোলা। **27.** To be circulated; as, a rumour *rose*; উঠা, প্রচারিত হওয়া। ***Verb t.*** **1.** To ascend; উঠা, উত্থিত হওয়া। **2.** To raise; উঠান, তোলা। **3.** (*Angling*) To cause a fish to come to the surface of water; as, the angler *rose* a fish; (বড়শী দ্বারা) মাছ উঠান। **The rising generation**—দেশের ভবিষ্যৎ আশাস্থল যুবকসমাজ। **To rise from table**—To leave table after meal; আহারের পর আসন ত্যাগ করা। **To rise to the occasion**—To acquit oneself worthily in difficult or unexpected circumstances; কোনরূপ সঙ্কটজনক বা অপ্রত্যাশিত অবস্থায় সমুচিতরূপে নির্দ্দিষ্ট কর্ত্তব্য সাধন করা।

rīse, *n.* **1.** Act of rising; উঠন, উত্থান, উদয়। **2.** The distance through which anything rises; as, the *rise* of the river is 5 feet; যে স্থান ব্যাপিয়া কোন কিছু উঠিয়া থাকে **3.** Elevation; as, the *rise* of a hill; উচ্চতা, উৎসেধ, উচ্ছ্রায়। **4.** A rising ground; as, the house stood on a *rise*; উচ্চভূমি, টিলা। **5.** Spring; source; as, the *rise* of river; উৎপত্তি, উদ্ভব; উৎপত্তিস্থল। **6.** Increase, as of price, value, rank, property, fame, etc.; advance; as, the *rise* of power; বৃদ্ধি; অভ্যুদয়, উন্নতি। **7.** Elevation or ascent of voice; চড়তি। **8.** Elevation of thought, style, language, etc.; চিন্তা, ভাষা, ভাব, রচনারীতি প্রভৃতির গুরুত্ব বা গাম্ভীর্য্য। **9.** The upward spring of a fish to seize food or bait; খাদ্য অথবা টোপ গিলার জন্য মৎস্যের উল্লম্ফন। **10.** Vertical height of step, arch, incline, etc.; সিঁড়ি, তোরণ, প্রবণভূমি, প্রভৃতির উলম্বী উচ্চতা। **To get or take a rise out of one**—To make sport of; কাহাকে উপহাস বা বিদ্রূপের পাত্র

করা। **To give rise to**—To produce; উৎপাদন করা। **To take one's rise**—To issue from; উৎপত্তি হওয়া।

ris'-ĕr, *n.* **1.** One who rises; উত্থানকারী। **2.** The upright part of steps; সিঁড়ির ধাপের খাড়া অংশ। **3.** (*Print.*) The block on which a plate is mounted; (মুদ্রণ) যে কাঠ-ফলকের উপর কোন চিত্রফলক সংবদ্ধ করা হয়। **4.** An opening through a mould into which metal rises as the mould fills; ছাঁচের ছিদ্র।

ris'-i-ble (-bl), *adj.* **1.** Prone to laugh; হাস্যপ্রবণ। **2.** (*Rare*) Exciting laughter; (কচিদ্‌ব্যবহৃত) হাস্যোদ্দীপক, হাস্যজনক। **3.** Of, or pertaining to, laughter; as, *risible* nerves; হাস্যসম্পর্কীয়।

ris'-ing, *adj.* & *n.* **1.** Appearing above horizon; উদীয়মান, উদ্যৎ (cf. উদ্যৎভাস্করসন্নিভং)। **2.** Growing; advancing; as, *rising* generation; উঠন্ত, বৃদ্ধিশীল, বর্দ্ধিষ্ণু; অভ্যুদয়শীল। ***Noun.*** **1.** Appearance above horizon; উদয়। **2.** The act of one who rises; উত্থান। **3.** Insurrection; as, to quell a *rising*; বিদ্রোহ, প্রজাবিক্ষোভ। **Empire** or **Land of the Rising Sun**—জাপান। **Order of the Rising Sun**—জাপানের সম্ভ্রান্তসম্প্রদায়বিশেষ। **Rising in the air**—যোগবলে শূন্যে উত্থান। [মধ্যযুগে ইয়ুরোপেও যোগবলে শূন্যে উঠিতে পারা যায় এই বিশ্বাস প্রবল ছিল। কথিত আছে St. Philip সাধনাবস্থায় কয়েক হস্ত ঊর্দ্ধে উঠিতে পারিতেন, কখনও ছাদ পর্য্যন্ত তাঁহার মাথা ঠেকিত। বিখ্যাত দার্শনিক Ignatius Loyola ঐ অবস্থায় ও কয়েক ফিট ঊর্দ্ধে উঠিতে পারিতেন। ঐ সময়ে তাঁহার দেহ এক অপূর্ব্ব দিব্য জ্যোতিতে উদ্ভাসিত হইয়া উঠিত। St. Robertও সাধনকালে ১৮ হইতে ২০ ইঞ্চি উপরে উঠিতেন। St. Dunstan মৃত্যুর অল্পকাল পূর্ব্বে শূন্যমার্গে দৃষ্ট হইয়াছিলেন। সাধু পুরুষ Savonarola সম্বন্ধে কথিত আছে যে, বধ্যমঞ্চে নীত হওয়ার অব্যবহিত পূর্ব্বে প্রার্থনাকালে তিনি শূন্যে উত্থান করেন এবং তদবস্থায় বহুক্ষণ পর্য্যন্ত অবস্থিত ছিলেন। সেন্ট-ফ্রান্সিসও সাধনাবস্থায় মধ্যে মধ্যে শূন্যে উত্থান করিতেন—সামসময়িকগ্রন্থে এইরূপ বর্ণনা পাওয়া যায়। (See *The Mystic Way* by Evelyn Underhill.)]

risk, *n.* & *v.t.* **1.** Hazard; danger; বিপদ্; সঙ্কট, আপদ্। **2.** Chances of loss; ঝুঁকি। ***Verb t.*** **1.** To expose to peril; বিপদাপন্ন করা, সঙ্কটাপন্ন করা। **2.** To take the chance of; ঝুঁকি নেওয়া। **Risk'-ful, Risk'-less,** *adjs.* **Risk-money**—বৈজ্ঞানিকপরীক্ষাগার প্রভৃতিতে কার্য্যকারী ছাত্রগণের নিকট হইতে যন্ত্রাদি ভাঙ্গিয়া গেলে ক্ষতিপূরণ আদায় করার জন্য যে টাকা জমা নেওয়া হয়।

risk'-ȳ, *adj.* **1.** Hazardous; বিপৎসঙ্কুল, সঙ্কটপূর্ণ। **2.** Suggesting something indecent or obscene; as, a *risky* story; কুরুচিব্যঞ্জক, অশ্লীলতাব্যঞ্জক। **—i-ly**, *adv.* **—i-ness**, *n.*

ris'-sole (-ōl), *adj.* A ball of minced meat or fish covered with bread crumbs etc.; কোপ্তা।

Rita buchanani—রিটা মাছ।

ritardando, *adv.* (*F.*), (*Mus.*) Slowly; (সঙ্গীতশাস্ত্র) মৃদুভাবে, আস্তে আস্তে।

rite, *n.* A religious ceremony; a ceremonial; a religious observance; শাস্ত্রোক্ত কর্ম্ম (হিঃ কোঃ); বিধি (ঐ), ক্রিয়া; ক্রিয়াকাণ্ড, আচার অনুষ্ঠান। **Burial** or **funeral rites**—অন্ত্যেষ্টি ক্রিয়া। **Conjugal** or **nuptial rite**—পতীপত্নীর সংসর্গ। **Rites of hospitality**—অতিথিকৃত্য।

rit'-ū-ăl, *adj.* & *n.* Pertaining to rites; ক্রিয়াসম্বন্ধীয়, ক্রিয়াকাণ্ডসম্পর্কীয়, আনুষ্ঠানিক, বিধিসম্বন্ধীয়। ***Noun.*** **1.** The manner of performing divine service; ক্রিয়াকাণ্ডপদ্ধতি, অনুষ্ঠানপদ্ধতি, ক্রিয়াপদ্ধতি। **2.** A book prescribing this; ক্রিয়াকাণ্ড-সম্পর্কীয় পুস্তক, ক্রিয়াকাণ্ডবারিধি। **3.** Ceremonial act; ক্রিয়াকাণ্ড, আচার অনুষ্ঠান। **—ism**, *n.* **—ist**, *n.* One versed in rituals; ক্রিয়াপদ্ধতিজ্ঞ, ক্রিয়াকাণ্ডজ্ঞ। **—is'-tic**, *adj.* Pertaining to the ritual; ক্রিয়াকাণ্ড-সম্বন্ধীয়, আনুষ্ঠানিক। **—ize**, *v. i.* & *t.* **Ritual gestures**—মুদ্রা (এভেলন)। **Ritual offering**—অর্ঘ্য (এভেলন)।

riv'-age (-āj), *n.* (*Poet.*) Coast; shore; (কবিতায়) উপকূল; সাগরতীর।

rī'-văl, *n.*, *adj.*, *v. t.* & *i.* One who competes with another in any pursuit or strife; a competitor; প্রতিদ্বন্দ্বী; প্রতিবাদী (হিঃ কোঃ), সপত্ন (ঐ), প্রতিযোগী। ***Adj.*** Holding the position of a rival; প্রতিদ্বন্দ্বীস্বরূপ, প্রতিদ্বন্দ্বী। ***Verb t.*** To stand in competition with; to strive to equal or excel; প্রতিদ্বন্দ্বিরূপে বা প্রতিযোগিরূপে দণ্ডায়মান হওয়া; প্রতিদ্বন্দ্বিতা করা, প্রতিযোগিতা করা। ***Verb i.*** To be a competitor; প্রতিদ্বন্দ্বী হওয়া, প্রতিযোগী হওয়া। **—ry**, *n.* **1.** Act of rivalling; প্রতিদ্বন্দ্বিতাকরণ। **2.** Endeavour to equal or excel another; competition; প্রতিদ্বন্দ্বিতা, প্রতিবাদিতা, টক্কর (*colloq.*); প্রতিযোগিতা। **—ship**, *n.* **Without rival**—অদ্বিতীয়, অপ্রতিম।

rive, *v. t.* & *i.* To rend asunder; বিদারণ করা, ফাঁড়া। ***Verb i.*** To be rent; to admit of being rent; বিদীর্ণ হওয়া; ফাঁড়ার যোগ্য হওয়া।

riv'-el (-l), *v. t.* (*Rare*) To shrivel; (কচিদ্‌ব্যবহৃত) কুঞ্চিত করা, কোঁকড়ান, কোঁচকান, মুষড়াইয়া দেওয়া।

riv'-en (-n), *p. p.* See RIVE.

riv'-ĕr, *n.* **1.** A large natural flowing stream of water; নদী, নদ, গাঙ (East Bengal)। [Masculine, of which the Sans. syns. are পুনর্ব্বহ, ভিদ্য, উদ্য, সরস্বান, as ব্রহ্মপুত্র নদ, নীলনদ (the Nile), সিন্ধুনদ, শোণনদ, দামোদর, ভৈরবনদ।] [Syn. সরিৎ, স্রোতস্বতী, স্রোতস্বিনী, নির্ঝরিণী, তটিনী,

তরঙ্গিণী, প্রবাহিণী, দ্বীপবতী, জলগা, তাবিষি, বেলবক্র, রোধোবতী, সিন্ধু, শৈবলিনী, শৈবালিনী, স্রোতোবহা, স্রোতোবহা, আপগা (cf. বিশ্বাপগোল্লাসিনী—মাধুর্য্যকাদম্বিনী — বিশ্বনাথ চক্রবর্ত্তী), নিম্নগা, স্রবন্তী, দ্রবন্তী, পয়স্বিনী, জলধিগা, সাগরগামিনী, সমুদ্রগা, কূলঙ্কষা, কূলবতী, ধুনী, কুনী, ধেনা, জম্বালিনী, নির্ঝরিণী, সমুদ্রদয়িতা, পর্ব্বতজা, সমুদ্রকান্তা, হ্রদিনী, হ্রাদিনী, সরস্বতী, কৃষ্ণা, বাহিনী। (নদী শব্দের বৈদিক পর্য্যায় যথা :—অবনয়, যব্যা, খা, সীরা, স্রোত্যা, এন্য, ধুনয়, রুজানা, বক্ষণা, স্বাদোঅর্ণা, রোধচক্রা, হরিত, সরিত, অগ্রুব, নভন্ব, বধ্ব, হিরণ্যবর্ণা, রোহিত, সস্রুত, অর্ণ, সিন্ধব, কুল্যা, বর্য্যা, উর্ব্বা, ইরাবত্য, পারবত্য, স্রবন্ত্য, উর্জ্জস্বত্য, পয়স্বত্য, সরস্বত্য, তরস্বত্য, হরস্বত্য, রোধস্বত্য, ভাস্বত্য, অজিনা, মাতর, নদ্য—বেদনিঘণ্টু)।] 2. The boundary between life and death; as, he has crossed the *river* (of life) on whose brink he had been so long waiting; জীবন মরণের সীমা বা সন্ধিস্থল। 3. A large stream; copious flow; as, *rivers* of blood [রক্তের নদী, রক্ত-গঙ্গা (more idiomatic)]; বৃহৎস্রোত, নদী, কুল্যা; স্রোত।] **River-bank**—নদীতট, সরিত্তট। **River-bed**—নদীগর্ভ। **River-craft**—নদীতে চলাচলের উপযোগী জাহাজ বা নৌকা। **River-dragon**—কুম্ভীর। **River-god**—জলদেবতা। **River-irrigated**—নদীমাতৃক। **River-horse**—সিন্ধুঘোটক। **Riverside**—*n.* নদীতট। **Riverside**—*adj.* নদীতীরবর্ত্তী। **River-tortoise**—কচ্ছপ। **River water**—নদীর জল। **River of Paradise**—সেণ্ট বানার্ড (১০৯১—১১৫৩ খৃষ্টাব্দ)। [পৃথিবীর কতিপয় প্রধান নদনদীর দৈর্ঘ্য:—

মিসিসিপি (আমেরিকা) ৪,২০০ মাইল।
এমাজন ,, ৪,০০০ মাইল।
ইয়েংসিকিয়াং (এসিয়ার মধ্যে সর্ব্বাপেক্ষা দীর্ঘ নদী) ৩,৫০০ মাইল।
ভল্গা (ইয়ুরোপের মধ্যে সর্ব্বাপেক্ষা দীর্ঘ নদী) ২,৩০০ মাইল। নীলনদ (আফ্রিকার মধ্যে সর্ব্বাপেক্ষা দীর্ঘ নদী) ৪,৩৭০ মাইল। গঙ্গা ১,৫০০ মাইল। ব্রহ্মপুত্র নদ ১,৮০০ সিন্ধুনদ ২,০০০ মাইল।]

riv'-ĕr-ine, *adj.* Belonging to a river; situated on a river; নদী সম্বন্ধীয়, নাদেয়; নদীতীরবর্ত্তী।

riv'-ĕt, *n.* & *v. t.* A bolt clinched at both ends by being hammered; রিপিট, প্রেক, জিনারী। *Verb t.* 1. To join or fasten with rivets; জিনারী দ্বারা বদ্ধ করা বা জোড়া দেওয়া। 2. To fasten firmly; to concentrate; as, to *rivet* one's attention; দৃঢ়রূপে নিবদ্ধ করা; একাগ্র করা, সমাহিত করা।

Rivet.

riviere, *n.* A gem necklace, esp. of more than one string; মণিহার, রত্নহার, রত্নমালা, মণিমালা (একাধিক লহর বা গুচ্ছবিশিষ্ট।)

riv'-ü-lĕt, *n.* A small brook or stream; ক্ষুদ্র নদী, ক্ষুদ্র তরঙ্গিণী, নালা।

rix-dŏl-lar (-ĕr), *n.* A silver coin of Germany, Holland, Denmark, and Sweden, ranging in value in different places from 2*s.* 6*d.* to 4*s.* 6*d.*; জর্ম্মণী, হলণ্ড, সুইডেন প্রভৃতি দেশের একপ্রকার রৌপ্য মুদ্রা।

roach (rōch), *n.* A common fresh-water fish of carp family; স্বাদুজলবাসী রোহিত জাতীয় মৎস্যবিশেষ। **As sound as roach**—Perfectly sound; খুব সুস্থ।

Roach.

roach (rōch), *n.* The upward curve of a sail; পাইলের পাদদেশের ঊর্দ্ধাভিমুখীন বক্রতা।

road (rōd), *n.* 1. An open way or public passage; রাস্তা, পথ, বর্ত্ম, রাজপথ, রাজমার্গ, বাট (*poet.*) (বিঘিনী বিতাড়িত বাট—বিদ্যাপতি। সারাদিন যেন পাখি ডাকা ছায়ায় ঢাকা তোমার পল্লীবাটে। তোমার ধানভরা আঙ্গিনাতে জীবনের দিন কাটে।), রথ্যা (high road), অধ্ব। 2. A place at some distance from the shore where a ship may ride at anchor; উপকূল হইতে অল্প দূরবর্ত্তী জাহাজ নোঙ্গর করার স্থান। 3. (*Fig.*) Way; (লক্ষণায়) পন্থা, পথ, মার্গ (cf. জ্ঞানমার্গ, কর্ম্মমার্গ।) **Road'-less**, *adj.* **Road'-worthy**, *adj.* 1. Fit to be used on the road; রাস্তায় ব্যবহারের উপযোগী। 2. (Of a man) Fit to travel; রাস্তায় চলার উপযুক্ত। **Paved road**—বাঁধা রাস্তা, পাকা রাস্তা। **Public road**—রাজপথ। **Road-agent** — রাহাজান, পন্থঘাতক (জাতক)। **Road-book**—কোন দেশের রাস্তাঘাট সম্বন্ধে জ্ঞাতব্য বিবরণপূর্ণ পুস্তক। **Road-cess**—পথকর, পথিদেয়। **Road-hog**—যে দ্বিচক্রযানারোহী বা হাওয়া-গাড়ীর চালক পথের লোকের বিপদের প্রতি ভ্রূক্ষেপ না করিয়া প্রচণ্ড বেগে যান চালায়। **Road-man** — রাস্তা নির্ম্মাণ বা মেরামতকারী। **Road-metal**—রাস্তা মেরামত করার জন্য খোয়া। **Road-side** — পথিপার্শ্ব (*noun*), পথিপার্শ্বস্থিত (*adj.*)। **Road-side tree**—মার্গবৃক্ষ (বিশ্বকর্ম্মা), পথতরু (পথতরু শাখে ধরেছে মুকুল—রবীন্দ্রনাথ—কথা), মার্গদ্রুম (কথা সঃ)। **Roadstead**—Same as ROAD 2. **Road surveyor** — পথপরিদর্শক। **Roadway**—রাস্তা, বর্ত্ম। **Royal road**—(লক্ষণায়) সোজা রাস্তা, প্রশস্ত পথ; কোন কিছুর প্রশস্ত উপায়। **By road**—By walking or riding along the way; রাস্তার উপর দিয়া পদব্রজে বা অশ্বারোহণে (ট্রেণে বা জাহাজে নয়)। **On the high road to**—In a fair way to attain; কোন কিছু পাওয়ার পথে অগ্রসর। **On the road** — Travelling;

পর্য্যটনরত। **Rule of the road**—বিপরীত দিক হইতে আগত অশ্ব বা শকট রাস্তার কোন পার্শ্বে চালবে তন্নিয়ামক বিধি। **To take the road**—To set out; রওয়ানা হওয়া, যাত্রা করা। **To take to the road**—To become a highway man; রাহাজান হওয়া। To tramp; টোঁ টোঁ করিয়া ঘুরা।

road'-stêr (röd-), *n.* 1. A ship at anchor in a roadstead; উপকূল হইতে অল্প দুরে নোঙ্গরবদ্ধ জাহাজ। 2. A horse for riding or driving; চড়িবার বা গাড়ী টানিবার ঘোড়া। 3. A bicycle or tricycle for ordinary use; সদাসর্ব্বদা ব্যবহারের জন্য দ্বিচক্রযান বা ত্রিচক্রযান।

roam (röm), *v. i., t.* & *n.* To wander; ঘূরিয়া বেড়ান, উদ্দেশ্যহীনভাবে ঘূরা। *Verb t.* To wander over; বিচরণ করা। *Noun.* A wandering; ইতস্তত: ভ্রমণ, বিচরণ।

roan (rön), *adj.* & *n.* 1. Of a mixed colour with a decided shade of red; কপিশ বর্ণ। 2. Made of roan leather; কপিশবর্ণ চর্ম্মে প্রস্তুত। *Noun.* 1. A roan colour; কপিশবর্ণ। 2. A horse or cow of a roan colour; কপিশ বর্ণের অশ্ব বা গাভী, কপিলা গাই। 3. A leather of sheep-skin stained to imitate ungrained morocco; পুস্তক বাঁধাই প্রভৃতির কাজে ব্যবহৃত অদানাদার মরক্কো চর্ম্মের অনুকরণে প্রস্তুত মেষ চর্ম্ম।

roar (rör), *v. i., t.* & *n.* 1. To cry with a full loud continued sound; to bellow; গর্জ্জন করা; চীৎকার করা, উচ্চ নাদ করা। 2. To make a loud, confused, and continued sound, as the waves, wind, etc.; গর্জ্জন করা। 3. To laugh out loudly and continuously; as, the boys *roared* at his jokes; হাসির রোল পড়া, হাসির গর্‌রা পড়া। 4. To make a loud noise in breathing, as, a diseased horse; (রুগ্ন অশ্বসম্পর্কে) নাসিকাগর্জ্জন করা। *Verb t.* To utter with a roar; to cry or proclaim aloud; গর্জ্জিয়া বলা; উচ্চৈঃস্বরে চীৎকার করা বা ঘোষণা করা। *Noun.* 1. Any loud continuous sound; গর্জ্জন, হুঙ্কার, নির্ঘোষ। 2. A loud cry of lion or other beast; সিংহনাদ, সিংহগর্জ্জন, গর্জ্জন। 3. The cry of a person in distress; চীৎকার। 4. A shout or outcry of mirth or laughter; as, to set the table in a *roar*; আনন্দধ্বনি, হাস্যকোলাহল, হাসির রোল। **Roar'-er**, *n.*

roar'-ing (rör-) *n.* & *adj.* 1. A loud, deep and prolonged sound; a shout of distress; রোল; গর্জ্জন, অভিগর্জ্জন, চীৎকার; আর্ত্তনাদ। 2. A disease in the air passage of horses accompanied with a singular noise in breathing; অশ্বের বায়ুকোষের রোগ বিশেষ—যাহাতে উহার শ্বাসে একরূপ বিশেষ ধ্বনি অনুভূত হয়। *Adj.* 1. Riotous; কোলাহলপূর্ণ, মদ্যপানকোলাহলপূর্ণ। 2. Very brisk; as, he drives a *roaring* trade; হুহু, খুব জোর। 3. Stentorian; as, a *roaring* voice; নির্ঘোষকারী, গর্জ্জনকারী। **Roaring boy** or **lad**—হাঙ্গামাকারী লোক, হল্লাকারী লোক। **Roaring drunk**—বদ্ধ মাতাল। **Roaring forties**—চত্বারিংশত্তম ও পঞ্চাশত্তম অক্ষাংশের মধ্যবর্ত্তী ঝটিকাবিক্ষুব্ধ সাগরাংশ। **Roaring game**—Same as CURLING. **Roaring health**—চমৎকার স্বাস্থ্য। **Roaring horsetails**—(অষ্ট্রেলেশিয়া) Aurora australis শব্দের অপভ্রংশ, (কুমেরু জ্যোতিঃ)। **Roaring Meg**—(অপ্র:) বৃহৎ কামান। **A roaring night**—ঝটিকাচ্ছন্ন রজনী; মদ্যপানোৎসবে যাপিত যামিনী।

roast (röst), *v.t.* & *i.* 1. To cook or prepare, as meat for the table by exposure to heat at or before a fire; ভর্জ্জিত করা, ঝলসান। 2. To dry or parch by exp[osure] to heat; as, to *roast* coffe[e] ভাজা। 3. To banter; as, t[o] *roast* a person mercilessly; to tease; বিদ্রূপ করা, ব্যঙ্গ করা; ক্ষ্যাপান, জ্বালাতন করা। 4. (*Metallurgy*) To expose ores etc. to a protracted fire in order to expel volatile matter; to calcine; (ধাতুবিদ্যা) খনিজ-বিমিশ্র ধাতু হইতে উদ্বায়ী পদার্থ দূরীভূত করার জন্য উহা দীর্ঘকাল ব্যাপিয়া উত্তপ্ত করা; জারিত করা। *Verb i.* To become roasted; ভর্জ্জিত হওয়া, ভাজা হওয়া। *Noun.* 1. That which is roasted; a piece of roast meat; that part of an animal which is reckoned fitter for roasting than for boiling or stewing; ভাজা; ভাজা মাংস, ভর্জ্জিত মাংস, শূল্য মাংস (শূল্যমাংসভূয়িষ্ঠ আহারে(:)শ্চতে—শকু:); ভাজা করার উপযোগী মাংসখণ্ড। 2. Severe banter or criticism; তীব্র বিদ্রূপ বা সমালোচনা। *Adj.* Roasted; as, *roast* beef; ভর্জ্জিত, ভাজা, শূল্য, ধাপিত (সা: প:), পুটিত (ঐ), ধ্মাত (ঐ), ভাবিত (ঐ)। **Roasting-jack**—মাংস ভাজারকালে শিক ঘূরাইবার জন্য যন্ত্র-বিশেষ। **Roasting pit**—পুটকুণ্ড (সা: প:), পুটগর্ত্ত (ঐ)। **To cry roast meat**—To proclaim one's good fortune; নিজের সৌভাগ্যের কথা প্রচার করা। **To rule the roast (or roost)**—To lord over; প্রভুত্ব করা, কর্ত্তৃত্ব ফলান।

roast'-êr (röst-), *n.* 1. One who roasts meat; মাংস ভর্জ্জনকারী। 2. A kind of oven for roasting; ভাজা করার জন্য একপ্রকার চুল্লী। 3. A pig, etc. for roasting; ভাজা করার জন্য শূকরশাবক প্রভৃতি। 4. A device for roasting coffee; কাফী ভাজিবার জন্য একপ্রকার চাটু। 5. A furnace used in roasting ore; খনিজ বিমিশ্র ধাতুর উদ্বায়ী পদার্থ নিষ্কাশনের জন্য ব্যবহৃত চুল্লী বিশেষ।

v. t. **1.** To seize and carry from by violence and with felonious intent ; to steal from ; লুঠিয়া নেওয়া ; চুরি করিয়া নেওয়া। 2. To plunder ; লুঠা, লুণ্ঠন করা। **3.** To deprive of ; as, to *rob* one of good name ; বিরহিত করা, বঞ্চিত করা। **4.** (*Mining*) To extract pillars previously left for support before the abandonment of mine ; (খনিজ বিদ্যা) খনির কাজ বন্ধ করার পূর্ব্বে স্তম্ভ সমূহ হইতে খনিজবিমিশ্র ধাতু বাহির করিয়া লওয়া। **Rob'-ber,** *n.* One who robs or steals from another ; দস্যু, লুণ্ঠনকারী, লুঠেরা। **Rob'-ber-y,** *n.* Taking away by violence ; plundering ; দস্যুবৃত্তি; লুণ্ঠন বৃত্তি। **Robbing Peter to pay Paul**—পরের গোয়ালে গোদান।

rŏb, *n.* The inspissated juice of ripe fruit mixed with honey or sugar to the consistence of a conserve ; ফলের সিরাপ। [From Arab. *robb* or *rub.*]

rōbe, *n., v. t.* & *i.* **1.** A kind of gown or outer garment worn as an indication of rank, position, etc. ; a dress of state or dignity, as, of princes, judges priests, etc. ; পদমর্য্যাদা, প্রভৃতি সূচক একপ্রকার দীর্ঘ গাউন বা বহিঃপরিচ্ছদ ; রাজা, পুরোহিত, বিচারক প্রভৃতির পদোচিত পরিচ্ছদ। **2.** A long flowing woman's dress ; স্ত্রীলোকদিগের পরিচ্ছদ, পোষাক। **3.** Dress ; দীর্ঘ ঢিলা পোষাক। **4.** (*Fig.*) A covering or vesture ; as, the *robe* of night ; আবরণ, আচ্ছাদন। **5.** A dressed buffalo skin ; শোধিত মহিষ চর্ম্ম। ***Verb t.*** To invest with robes ; to array ; পোষাক পরান ; সজ্জিত করা। ***Verb i.*** To put on robes ; পরিচ্ছদ পরা। **Robed,** *p. p.* **Rob'-ing,** *n.* **Long robe** — ব্যবহারজীবিগণের পোষাক, যাজকীয় পরিচ্ছদ। **Robe-col-lante**—একপ্রকার আঁটসাঁট পোষাক, স্ত্রীলোকদিগের একপ্রকার আঁটসাঁট পোষাক। **Robe-de-chambre** — একপ্রকার ঢিলা জামা। **Gentlemen of the robe** (or **of the long robe**) — ব্যবহারজীবী সমাজ। **Robe of honour**—খিলাত। **The robe**—আইন ব্যবসায়।

rŏb'-in, *n.* A well known bird with a red breast ; একপ্রকার লাল বুকওয়ালা পাখী। [খৃষ্টানদিগের মধ্যে এইরূপ প্রবাদ আছে যে যীশু বধ্যভূমির দিকে যাওয়ার পথে এই পাখী তাঁহার কাঁটার মুকুট হইতে চঞ্চু দ্বারা একটী কাঁটা

American Robin.

তুলিয়া লইলে প্রভুর ক্ষতস্থান হইতে উৎসরিত রক্ত দ্বারা ঐ পাখীর বুক লাল বর্ণে রঞ্জিত হয়।] **Robin Goodfellow**—কৌতুকপ্রিয় ভূত বিশেষ। এই ভূত রাত্রে আসিয়া গৃহস্থের বাটীর কোন কোন কাজ করিয়া যায়। **Robin Hood** — ত্রয়োদশ শতাব্দীতে বর্ত্তমান ইংলণ্ড দেশীয় দস্যুবিশেষ—এই দস্যু তাল্লিয়াতীলের মত ধনীর প্রাসাদ এবং বড় বড় ধর্ম্মমন্দির হইতে ধনরত্নাদি লুণ্ঠন পূর্ব্বক দরিদ্রদিগকে বিলাইয়া দিত। সে স্ত্রীলোকের উপর কোনরূপ অত্যাচার হইতে দিত না। এতদ্ভিন্ন সাহস, শিষ্ট-ব্যবহার এবং মহাপ্রাণতার জন্য সে তৎকালীন সাধারণ লোকের অতিশয় প্রিয় হইয়া উঠিয়াছিল। এই Robin Hood সম্বন্ধে প্রাচীন বহু গাথা আছে। **Robin Mutton** — হাবা। **Robin's-eye**—একপ্রকার গুল্ম। **Robin-run-the-hedge**—গুল্ম বিশেষ। **To go around Robin Hood's barn**—(*Colloq.*) To come to a conclusion in a roundabout way ; (চলিত ভাষায়) অনেক ঘুরিয়া ফিরিয়া কোন সিদ্ধান্তে উপনীত হওয়া। **To sell Robin Hood's pennyworth**—To sell goods at half their ; value ; অর্দ্ধ মূল্যে বিক্রয় করা।

rŏb'-ō-rănt, *adj.* Strengthening ; বলপ্রদ, শক্তিসঞ্চারক।

rŏb'-ō-rāte, *v. t.* To strengthen ; to corroborate ; বলপ্রদান করা, শক্তিসঞ্চার করা ; দৃঢ়তর করা। **—ra'-tion,** *n.*

Rŏb'-Roy (-roy̆), *n.* **1.** A nickname given to the famous Scottish outlaw Robert Macgregor ; স্কটলণ্ডের সুবিখ্যাত দস্যু Robert Macgregorএর উপনাম। এই দস্যু অনেকাংশে Robin Hoodএর অনুরূপ ছিল। **2.** A kind of canoe ; একপ্রকার সাল্‌তী নৌকা।

rō'-bur-ite (-bêr-), *n.* A powerful explosive substance having ammonium nitrate as its basis ; একপ্রকার শক্তিশালী বিস্ফোরক পদার্থ।

rō-bŭst', *adj.* **1.** Strong ; vigorous ; বলবান, সবল, দৃঢ়াঙ্গ ; সতেজ। **2.** Requiring vigour or strength ; invigorating ; as, *robust* work, employent or exercises ; বলসাপেক্ষ, শক্তিসাপেক্ষ ; বলজনক। **3.** (*Rare*) Rough ; (ক্বচিদ্ ব্যবহৃত) কর্কশ, রূঢ় **4.** (Of intellect etc.) Sensible ; straight-forward ; not confused by subtleties ; বিচারক্ষম ; সরল। সূক্ষ্ম তর্কাদিদ্বারা অবিহ্বল। **—ly,** *adv.* **—ness,** *n.*

rō-bŭst'-ious (-yŭs), *adj.* **1.** Robust ; সবল, শক্তিমান। **2.** Boisterous ; noisy ; গোলযোগকারী ; কোলাহলকারী।

rŏc, *n.* A large fabulous bird mentioned in Arabian Tales ; (আরব্য উপন্যাসে উক্ত) রকপক্ষী।

rŏc'-ăm-bōle, *n.* A kind of leek which grows in Denmark etc. ; ডেনমার্ক প্রভৃতি দেশে জাত একপ্রকার গন্ধ-পেঁয়াজ।

rŏch'-ĕt, *n.* A white linen garment worn by bishops or other dignitaries, resembling the surplice ; ধর্ম্মাধ্যক্ষ প্রভৃতির পরিধেয় শুভ্র ক্ষৌম বস্ত্রের বহির্ব্বাসবিশেষ।

rŏck, *n.* **1.** A large mass of stone; the stony matter which constitutes the earth's crust; পাষাণস্তূপ, শিলোচ্চয়; পৃথিবীর কঠিন বহিরাবরণস্বরূপ পাষাণময় পদার্থ। **2.** A peak or promontary or crag of rock; পাষাণময় গিরিশৃঙ্গ, পাষাণময় অন্তরীপ, পাষাণগিরি। **3.** Something which affords shelter or protection; "They remembered that God was their *rock*"; আশ্রয়স্থল, অবলম্বনস্থল, আশ্রয়শৈল। **4.** A cause or source of peril or disaster in allusion to shipwreck; as, this was the *rock* on which he split"; বিপদ বা দুর্দ্দৈবের কারণ বা হেতু। **5.** A firm or immovable foundation; সুদৃঢ় ভিত্তি। **6.** A kind of hard sweetmeat; একপ্রকার কঠিন মিঠাই। **7.** (*U. S. slang*) Coin; money; as, to pile up the *rocks*; (মার্কিণ যুক্তরাজ্যের ইতরভাষায়) মুদ্রা; টাকাকড়ি। **8.** (*Dial.*) A stone; (উপভাষায়) পাথর। **Rock'-er-y,** *n.* A mound of rock fragments filled in with earth and set with plants; পাষাণখণ্ডরাজি রচিত ক্ষুদ্র শৈলবিশেষ—যাহার ফাঁকে ফাঁকে মৃত্তিকা ভরিয়া উহাতে পর্ণাঙ্গ (fern) প্রভৃতি রোপিত হয়, পাষাণগুল্মবাটিকা, কৃত্রিম পর্ব্বত (প্রবোধ), লীলাগিরি, লীলাশৈল, লীলাচল। **Rock'-y,** *adj.* **Crystalline-rock**—স্ফটিক (সাঃ পঃ)। **Fossilised-rock**—শিলীভূত জীবজ (সাঃ পঃ)। **Metamorphic-rock**—পারিণামিক (সাঃ পঃ)। **Plutonic-rock**—বারুণ (সাঃ পঃ)। **Rock-basin**—পাষাণমধ্যস্থ জলপাত্রের আকৃতি গর্ত্ত। **Rock-bed**—পাষাণতল। **Rock-bird**—পক্ষিবিশেষ। **Rock-bottom**—নিম্নতম। **Rock-bound** — পাষাণশৈলবেষ্টিত। **Rock-butter**—মাখনের সহিত দ্বিগুণ পরিমাণ শর্করা মিশ্রণপূর্ব্বক প্রস্তুত খাদ্যবিশেষ। **Rock-cake**—কঠিন আবরণবিশিষ্ট ক্ষুদ্র পিষ্টকবিশেষ। **Rock-candy** — মিশ্রী, মৎস্যণ্ডিকা। **Rock-cork**—একপ্রকার শঙ্খপলিতা। **Rock-crystal**—স্ফটিক, ফটিক (বোঃ), [Syn. ভাস্বর, স্ফাটিক, সিতোপল, অমররত্ন, স্ফাটিকোপল, শালিপিষ্ট, ধৌতশিল, নির্ম্মলোপল, স্বচ্ছ, স্বচ্ছমণি, অমরমণি, অমররত্ন, নিস্তব রত্ন, শিবপ্রিয়, ভীষ্মরত্ন (বিশ্বঃ)]। **Rock-dove**—Same as ROCK-PIGEON. **Rock-drill**—পাষাণে রন্ধ্র করার জন্য একপ্রকার বেধন যন্ত্র। **Rock English**—জিব্রল্টারে প্রচলিত ভাঙ্গা ইংরাজী। **Rock fever**—জিব্রল্টারের একপ্রকার আন্ত্রিক জ্বর। **Rock-fire**—পোত, অট্টালিকা, প্রভৃতিতে অগ্নিসংযোগের জন্য একপ্রকার বারুদ। **Rock-fish**—বিভিন্ন প্রকারের মৎস্যের সাধারণ নাম। **Rock-garden**—যে উদ্যানে বৃহৎ বৃহৎ পাষাণস্তূপের ফাঁকে ফাঁকে মৃত্তিকার উপর পর্ণাঙ্গ (fern) প্রভৃতি রোপিত হয়, লীলাশৈলোদ্যান। **Rock-goat**—Same as IBEX. **Rock-hewn**—পাষাণস্তূপ হইতে কর্ত্তিত। **Rock-honey**—পাষাণস্তূপবাসী মক্ষিকাগণ কর্ত্তৃক প্রস্তুত মধু। **Rock-leather** — Same as ROCK-CORK. **Rock-oil** — গিরিতৈল, মেটে তৈল। **Rock-paper**—Same as ROCK-CORK. **Rock-pigeon**—একপ্রকার কপোত। **Rock-ribbed** — পশু কাকৃতি পাষাণবিশিষ্ট। **Rock-rose**—একপ্রকার পীত, পাটল বা কপিলবর্ণ পুষ্পপ্রসূ গুল্মশ্রেণী। **Rock-salt**—সৈন্ধব লবণ [Syn. মাণিমন্থ, শিতশিব, সিন্ধূপল, সিন্ধুমন্থজ, সিন্ধুভব, সিন্ধুজ, সিন্ধু লবণ, সিন্ধুজন্ম, নশির, সিন্ধুদেশজ, মাণিবন্ধ, নাদেয়, শিব, সিন্ধ, লবণোত্তম, শিবাত্মজ, পথ্য।] **Rock-shelter**—পাষাণস্তূপের যে স্বাভাবিক গর্ত্তে কোন কোন অসভ্য জাতির লোক বাস করে। **Rock-silk**—Same as ROCK-CORK. **Rock-snake**—পাহাড়ীয়া বোড়া সাপ। **Rock-sucker**—একপ্রকার বাইন মাছ। **Rock-tar**—কেরোসিন তৈল। **Rock-temple** — পাষাণস্তূপ কর্ত্তন পূর্ব্বক নির্ম্মিত দেবমন্দির। **Rock-water**—পাষাণস্তূপ হইতে নির্গত স্ফটিক-স্বচ্ছ বারি। **Rock-whistler** — আল্পস্ পর্ব্বতবাসী মূষিকজাতীয় জন্তুবিশেষ। **Rock-wood** — Same as ROCK-CORK. **Rock-work**—Same as ROCKERY. **Stratified rock**—স্তরীভূত পাষাণ (সাঃ পঃ)। **Submarine rock**—অন্তঃসমুদ্র। **On the rocks**—(*Slang*) Quite out of funds; (ইতরভাষায়) একবারে কপর্দ্দকশূন্য, রিক্তহস্ত। **Rock-bottom price**—(*U. S. slang*) The lowest possible price; (মার্কিণ যুক্তরাজ্যের ইতর ভাষায়) যতদূর সম্ভব অল্প মূল্য। **Rocks ahead**—Danger ahead; সম্মুখে বিপদ। **The Rock**—জিব্রল্টার।

rŏck, *v. t.* & *i.* **1.** To move backwards and forwards; দোলান, দোল দেওয়া, দোলায়িত করা। **2.** To move backwards and forwards in cradles, chairs, arms, etc.; as, to *rock* a child to sleep; দোলনা, চেয়ার বা বাহুর উপর রাখিয়া দোল দেওয়া। **3.** To put to sleep by rocking; to quiet; দোল দিয়া ঘুম পাড়ান; শান্ত করা। **4.** To abrade the surface of a copper or steel plate preparatory to scraping a mezzotint; বিন্দুফলক (See MEZZOTINTO) ক্ষোদনের পূর্ব্বে তাম্র বা ইস্পাতের ফলক উল্লেখন করা। ***Verb i.*** To move or swing from side to side; দোলা, দোল খাওয়া। **Rock'-ing,** *adj.* & *n.* Oscillating; দোলায়মান, দোদুল্যমান। (*Noun.*) Act of rocking; দোল দেওন। **Rocking-chair**—একপ্রকার চেয়ার—যাহার উপর বসিয়া দোল খাওয়া যায়। **Rocking-horse** — ছেলেদের একপ্রকার কাঠের ঘোড়া—যাহার উপর বসিয়া দোল খাওয়া যায়, দোলনাশ্ব।

rŏck'-ĕr, *n.* **1.** One who, or that which, rocks; দোলনকারী। **2.** One of the curved pieces of wood on which a cradle or chair rocks; যে বক্র কাষ্ঠ খণ্ডের উপর কুর্সি বা দোলনা দুলিয়া থাকে। **3.** A gold miner's cradle (See CRADLE 8.) **4.** A skate with a curved blade; বরফের উপর খেলার জন্য বক্রফলক সমন্বিত কাষ্ঠপাদুকা।

rŏck'-ĕt, *n.* A name given to various cruciferae ; একজাতীয় গুল্ম।

rŏck'-ĕt, *n.*, *v.t.* & *i.* A fire-work sent up high in the air, used for enjoyment or for making military or naval signals or for sending a rope to help ship-wrecked seamen ; একপ্রকার আতসবাজী—যাহা আমোদের জন্য উড়ান হয়, অথবা সামরিক বা নৌবিভাগীয় সঙ্কেতপ্রদানে বা জলমগ্ন জাহাজের নাবিকগণের সাহায্যার্থ রজ্জুক্ষেপের জন্য ব্যবহৃত হয়, হাউইবাজী, খধুপ, (উক্ষপ্রচক্রুর্নগরস্য মার্গান্ ধ্বজান্ ববন্ধু মুর্মুচুঃ খধূপান—ভট্টিকাব্য)। *Verb t.* To discharge rockets at ; কোন কিছুর উপর হাউই নিক্ষেপ করা। *Verb i.* **1.** (Of a horse) To dart like a rocket ; (অশ্বসম্পর্কে) হাউইবাজীর মত ছুটা। **2.** (Of pheasants) To fly up straight into the air when disturbed ; (তিত্তিরপক্ষিসম্পর্কে) উদ্বেজিত হইলে সোজা উপরের দিকে উঠা। **—er**, *n.*

rôck'-ȳ, *adj.* **1.** Resembling rock ; hence, hard ; পাষাণসম ; কঠিন। **2.** (*Fig.*) Obdurate ; unfeeling ; পাষাণ হৃদয় ; নির্ম্মম। **—i-ness**, *n.* **The Rocky Mountains**—উত্তর-আমেরিকার পর্ব্বতবিশেষ।

rŏck'-ȳ, *adj.* (*Rare*) Tottering ; (ক্বচিদ্ ব্যবহৃত) টলমলে।

rō-cō'-cō, *n.* & *adj.* A style of architecture or painting current in the 17th century noted for extravagance and tastelessness

Rococo.

of ornamentations ; bad taste in design or ornament ; সপ্তদশ শতাব্দীর একপ্রকার স্থাপত্য রীতি বা চিত্রাঙ্কণ-পদ্ধতি যাহাতে অলঙ্কারের আতিশয্য ও সুরুচিহীনতা পরিলক্ষিত হয় ; পরিকল্পনা ও অলঙ্করণে উৎকটতা বা সুরুচির অভাব। *Adj.* **1.** Excessively or tastelessly ornate ; অতিরিক্ত অলঙ্কৃত, রুচিহীনরূপে অলঙ্কৃত। **2.** Antiquated ; সেকেলে, মান্ধাতার আমলের। **3.** Fantastic ; কিম্ভূত কিমাকার।

rŏd, *n.* **1.** A long twig ; a wand ; লম্বা ডগা ; দণ্ড, যষ্টি, ছড়, ছড়ী। **2.** An instrument of chastisement ; (*fig.*) chastisement ; "Spare the *rod* and spoil the child" ; punishment ; বেত্র, বেত ; (লক্ষণায়) বেত্রাঘাত ; দণ্ড। **3.** A kind of sceptre or badge of office ; "The *rod*, and bird of peace" ; power ; tyranny ; রাজদণ্ড, একপ্রকার দণ্ড বা কোন কর্ম্মচারীর দণ্ড ; ক্ষমতা ; অত্যাচার। **4.** An enchanter's wand ; ঐন্দ্রজালিকের দণ্ড, মায়াদণ্ড, মায়াযষ্টি। **5.** A fish-pole ; ছিপ। **6.** An angler ; যে ব্যক্তি বড়শী দ্বারা মৎস্য ধরে। **7.** A unit of linear measure equal to $5\frac{1}{2}$ yards ; $৫\frac{১}{২}$ গজ পরিমিত রৈখিক মাপের একক। **8.** A measuring rod ; মাপ কাঠি। **9.** Any bar connecting parts of a machine ; যন্ত্রের বিভিন্ন অংশসংযোজক দণ্ড। **10.** (*Script.*) A sprout ; hence, a race or family ; (বাইবেল) অঙ্কুর ; (অতএব) বংশ, গোষ্ঠী, শাখা, পরিবার। **11.** A divining rod ; ভূগর্ভে ধাতু প্রভৃতি আছে কিনা তন্নির্ণয়ের জন্য অলৌকিক শক্তিসম্পন্ন দণ্ড। **12.** (*Anat.*) A rod-shaped structure ; দৈহিকযন্ত্রের দণ্ডাকৃতি অংশ। **Rodman, Rodster**—যে ব্যক্তি ছিপদ্বারা মাছ ধরে। **To have, or put a rod in pickle**—See PICKLE. **To kiss the rod**—See KISS. **To make a rod for one's back**—To prepare a punishment for one's-self ; নিজের জন্য শাস্তির যোগাড় করিয়া রাখা।

rōde, *p.p.* OF RIDE (which see.)

rō'-dĕnt, *adj.* & *n.* **1.** Belonging to the order rodentia ; দন্তুরজন্তুবর্গ-সম্পর্কীয়। **2.** Gnawing ; ছেদনকারী। *Noun.* An animal of the order of rodentia ; দন্তুর জন্তুবর্গ ভুক্ত জন্তু, তীক্ষ্ণদন্ত (হিঃ কোঃ)।

rō-dĕn'-ti-ȧ (-shi-), *n.* An extensive class of animals, so called from their habit of nibbling or gnawing food, as the rat, hare, beaver, etc. ; মুষিকাদিবর্গ, শশকবর্গ (মিউজিয়াম)।

rŏd-ō-mŏn-tāde', *n.*, *adj.* & *v. i.* Empty bluster ; empty boasting ; তর্জ্জন গর্জ্জন ; বড়াই, লম্বাচৌড়াই, গর্ব্বিত বাক্য, উদ্ধত বচন। [Ariosto-কৃত *Orlando Furioso* নামক গ্রন্থের সাহসী, দাম্ভিক এবং আত্মশ্লাঘাপরায়ণ নায়কের নাম হইতে গৃহীত।] *Adj.* (*Rare*) Boastful ; (ক্বচিদ্‌ব্যবহৃত) আত্মশ্লাঘাপরায়ণ, দম্ভোক্তিকারী, দম্ভপরায়ণ। *Verb i.* To talk boastingly ; বড়াই করা, আত্মশ্লাঘা করা, লম্বাই চওড়াই করা। **—ta'-der**, *n.*

roe (rō), *n.* **1.** A small species of deer elegant in shape and nimble of movement, frequenting hilly districts (also *roe-buck*) ; ক্ষুদ্রজাতীয় হরিণ বিশেষ। **2.** A female of the hart ; মৃগী, মৃগবধূ, হরিণী, মৃগাঙ্গনা, কুরঙ্গী।

roe (rō), *n.* **1.** The eggs or spawn of fish ; মাছের ডিম, মৎস্যাণ্ড, মীনাণ্ড, ঝষাণ্ড। **Hard roe**—স্ত্রীমৎস্যের ডিম্ব। **Roe-corn**—মাছের ডিমের একটী কণা বা রেণু। **Roe-stone**—Same as OOLITE (which see)। **Soft roe**—পুং মৎস্যের ডিম্ব।

rō-gā'-tion, *n. Pl.* **1.** Litany ; a supplication ; উপাসনাকালীন প্রার্থনা বিশেষ ; মিনতি। **2.** (*Rom. Antiq.*) A law proposed before the people by the consul or tribune ; (রোমীয় প্রত্নতত্ত্ব) প্রাচীন রোমনগরীর প্রধান দণ্ডনায়ক বা জনবন্ধু কর্ত্তৃক জনসাধারণের নিকট প্রস্তাবিত আইন। **Rogation-day** — স্বর্গারোহণ পর্ব্বের অব্যবহিত পূর্ব্ববর্ত্তী দিবসত্রয়ে অনুষ্ঠিত পর্ব্ব বিশেষ। **Rogation-flower**—একপ্রকার গুল্ম।

Rög'-ĕr, *n.* **1.** A black flag formerly used by pirates (also (*Jolly Roger*) ; জলদস্যুগণের কৃষ্ণপতাকা [এই পতাকাতে একটী শ্বেতবর্ণের নরকপাল এবং তন্নিম্নে কোণাকোণি ভাবে স্থাপিত ঊর্বস্থিযুগল থাকিত]। **Roger or Sir Roger de Coverley**—পল্লী নৃত্যবিশেষ।

rogue (rög), *n.* & *v. t.* **1.** A knave ; a swindler ; a rascal ; ধূর্ত্ত, দুর্বৃত্ত, পাজী, ডেকরা (*slang*) ; প্রবঞ্চক, জুয়াচ্চোর ; ধড়ীবাজ, ধাপ্পাবাজ। **2.** A familiar term of slight endearment ; "What a young *rogue* this is" ; দুষ্টু, বাঁদর, দুরন্ত ছেলে। **3.** (*Archaic*) A vagrant ; (অপ্র:) ভবঘুরে। **4.** A wild elephant or buffalo living apart from the herd and of savage temper ; যূথের অপর হস্তী বা মহিষ হইতে পৃথগ্‌ভাবে বাসকারী অদম্য হস্তী বা মহিষ। **5.** Inferior seedlings ; নিকৃষ্ট বীজপ্ররোহ সমূহ। ***Verb t.*** **1.** To cheat ; ধড়িবাজি করা, ধাপ্পাবাজি করা। **2.** To weed out inferior plants from seedlings ; নিকৃষ্ট বীজপ্ররোহ সমূহ নিড়াইয়া ফেলা। **Ro'-gu-ish,** *adj.* **Ro'-guish-ly,** *adv.* **Ro'-guish-ness,** *n.* **Rogue's gallery** — পুলিশের ব্যবহারের জন্য দুর্বৃত্তদিগের চিত্রসংগ্রহ। **Rogue's march**—জনসাধারণের বিরাগভাজন বা দণ্ডপ্রাপ্ত কোন ব্যক্তিকে বিতাড়নের কালে যে অবজ্ঞাসূচক বাদ্য বাদিত হয়।

rö'-guer-ÿ (-gĕr-), *n.* **1.** Cheating ; Dishonest practices ; ধড়িবাঁজি ; দুর্বৃত্ততা, শাঠ্য। **2.** Playful or mischievous tricks ; fun ; দুরন্তপনা, দুষ্টামী, নষ্টামি ; কৌতুক, মজা।

roinek, *n.* A British soldier ; ইংরেজ সৈনিক (দক্ষিণ আফ্রিকায় অবজ্ঞাচ্ছলে ব্যবহৃত হয়)।

roist'-ĕr (roÿst-), *v. i.* To bluster ; to swagger ; to bully ; তর্জ্জন করা ; দম্ভ করা, বড়াই করা ; শাসান, দাবান।

Rö'-lănd, *n.* A nephew of Charlemagne and defender of the Christians against the Saracens ; সার্লেমেনের ভ্রাতুষ্পুত্র মহাবীর রোলাণ্ড। [Ariosto কৃত Orlando Furioso কাব্যে এই বীরের নানা অবদানের কাহিনী বর্ণিত হইয়াছে। Rolandএর সহযোগী অপর মহাবীরের নাম Oliver.] **A Roland for an Oliver**—Tit for tat ; ইটের বদলে পাটকেল। **To die like Roland**—To die of starvation or thirst ; তৃষ্ণায় বা অনাহারে প্রাণত্যাগ করা। [কথিত আছে যে, Pyrenese পর্ব্বত অতিক্রম করার কালে Roland তৃষ্ণায় ও অনাহারে প্রাণত্যাগ করেন।]

röle, *n.* **1.** An actor's part ; অভিনেতার ভূমিকা। **2.** Any part or function played by any one ; ভূমিকা, নির্দ্দিষ্ট কার্য্য, করণীয় কার্য্য।

röll, *n.* **1.** The act of rolling ; as, the *roll* of a ship ; the state of being rolled ; বলন, আবর্ত্তন, নড়ন, আন্দোলন, দোল, রোল-নড়া [সেদিন ক্রীট হইতে সিসিলি পর্য্যন্ত আসিতে জাহাজের রোল-নড়া খাইয়াছি—(বর্ত্তমান জগৎ—বিনয় সরকার)] ; আবর্ত্তিতাবস্থা, দোলায়মানাবস্থা। **2.** Something formed by rolling ; that which can be rolled up ; চোঙ্গাকারে গুটানো জিনিষ ; যে জিনিষ চোঙ্গার আকারে গুটাইয়া রাখা যাইতে পারে। **3.** A quantity of cloth or paper wound up in a cylindrical form ; চোঙ্গাকারে গুটানো কাগজ বা কাপড়। **4.** Documents ; official records ; a catalogue ; as, the *roll* of saints ; দলীল দস্তাবেজ ; সরকারী কাগজপত্র ; তালিকা। **5.** A piece of dough rolled up into a cylindrical form before baking ; সেঁকিবার পূর্ব্বে চোঙ্গার আকারে বেলা ময়দা। **6.** A cylindrical twist of tobacco ; চোঙ্গার আকারে জড়ানো তামাকের পাতা। **7.** A roller ; cylinder ; ডল্‌না ; চোঙ্গ। **8.** A prolonged deep sound ; as, *rolls* of thunder ; the sound caused by continuous beating of drum or any resembling it ; গর্জ্জন, নির্ঘোষ ; প্রভৃতির নির্ঘোষ বা তদ্বৎধ্বনি। **9.** turned back edge of something ; কোন কিছুর উল্টানো কিনারা। **Roll-call**—নাম ডাকন।

röll, *v. t.* & *i.* **1.** To cause to revolve by turning over and over ; to whirl or wheel ; ঘুরান, ঘূর্ণিত করা, পাকান ; গড়াইয়া চালান। **2.** To wrap round upon itself or on something else ; বলা, পাকান। **3.** To convey in a carriage etc. ; গাড়ী প্রভৃতিতে নেওয়া। **4.** To form by rolling into a spherical or cylindrical body ; পাকাইয়া পিণ্ডাকৃতি বা চোঙ্গাকৃতি করা। **5.** To press or level with a roller ; ডলনা দিয়া চাপ দেওয়া বা সমান করা। **6.** To turn or revolve mentally ; "I came home *rolling* resentment in my mind" ; মনে মনে আন্দোলন করা, পর্য্যালোচন করা। **7.** To draw or impel forward with a sweeping easy motion ; as, river *rolls* its water to the sea ; গড়াইয়া নেওয়া। **8.** To inwrap ; জড়ান। **9.** To utter copiously ; to utter with deep sounds ; অনর্গল বলিয়া যাওয়া ; গম্ভীর মন্দ্রে উচ্চারণ করা। **10.** To beat rapidly as a drum ; দুন্দুভি প্রভৃতি দ্রুত নিনাদিত করা। **11.** To turn the eyes in different directions with a kind of circular motion ; চোক ঘূরান, চোক পাকান, বিলোল দৃষ্টিপাত করা। **13.** To pronounce with a quick vibration of the tongue ; জিহ্বা দ্রুত কম্পনপূর্ব্বক উচ্চারণ করা। ***Verb i.*** **1.** To turn like a wheel ; to turn on an axis ; to turn over and over ; ঘূরা, ঘূর্ণিত হওয়া ; পাক খাওয়া ; গড়াইয়া চলা। **2.** To move with rise and falls as waves and billows ; তরঙ্গবৎ পর্য্যায়ক্রমে উঠিয়া নামিয়া চলা। **3.** To sound with deep prolonged

.d as drum or thunder; .ধ্বনিত হওয়া, গর্জ্জা। 4. To be .ormed into a cylinder or ball; নলাকার বা পিণ্ডাকার হওয়া। 5. To be tossed from side to side; এক পার্শ্ব হইতে অপর পার্শ্বে আন্দোলিত হওয়া, টলা, নড়া, দুলা। 6. To perform periodical revolution; আবর্ত্তিত হওয়া। **Rolled**, *pp.* **Roll'-ing**, *adj.* & *n.* 1. Moving from side to side; revolving; বিলোল; ঘূর্ণিত, বিঘূর্ণমান। 2. Moving on wheels; চক্রের উপর গমনশীল। 3. Undulating; উচ্চাবচ, তরঙ্গবৎ, ঢেউখেলানিয়া। 4. Making a continuous sound; গুরুগুরু গর্জ্জনকারী, গুরুগম্ভীরনাদী। ***Noun.*** Revolution; ঘূর্ণন, দোলানি। **Rolled glass**—ডলনা দ্বারা ডলিয়া তৈরী একপ্রকার নিকৃষ্ট কাচ। **Rolled gold**—নিকৃষ্টতর ধাতুর উপর যে সোণার পাত ডলনা দ্বারা লাগান হয়। **Rolling-fire**—শ্রেণীবদ্ধভাবে সজ্জিত সৈন্যগণের পর পর অগ্নি বর্ষণ। **Rolling look**—বিলোল দৃষ্টি। **Rolling-mill**—উত্তপ্ত ধাতু ডলিয়া পাত প্রভৃতি করার জন্য যন্ত্রবিশেষ। **Rolling-pin** — বেলন, বেল্লনী। **Rolling-press**—তাম্রফলক হইতে চিত্র মুদ্রণের জন্য ঘূর্ণনশীল চোঙ্গবিশিষ্ট মুদ্রাযন্ত্রবিশেষ। **Rolling-stock**—লৌহবর্ত্মের উপর চালিত বাষ্পীয় যন্ত্র, শকট, প্রভৃতি। **Rolling stone**—যে ব্যক্তি বারবার বাসস্থান, ব্যবসায়, প্রভৃতি পরিবর্ত্তন করে। **Roll-top desk**—একপ্রকার মেজ—যাহার উপরের কাঠ বাঁকানো খাঁজের ভিতর ঠেলিয়া দেওয়া যায়। **A rolling stone gathers no moss**—See MOSS. **To roll up**—(*Colloq.*) To accumulate; (চলিত ভাষায়) রাশি রাশি ধন সঞ্চয় করা।

rōll'-ĕr, *n.* 1. One who, or that which, rolls; ঘূর্ণনকারী। 2. A cylinder of wood, stone or metal for rolling etc.; ডলনা, লোড়া, বেলন (for rolling flour). 3. (*Print.*) A cylinder coated with a composisition of glue and molasses for spreading over the types; ছাপাখানায় কালি দেওয়ার জন্য ডলনা, রোলার। 4. (*Surg.*) A long, broad bandage of cotton or linen; (অস্ত্রোপচার-বিদ্যা) একপ্রকার দীর্ঘ ক্ষতবন্ধনী। 5. A long, heavy, swelling wave; উত্তাল তরঙ্গ, পর্ব্বত-প্রমাণ ঢেউ। 6. A kind of bird which turns or somersaults in the air; একপ্রকার পক্ষী (ইহারা বাতাসে ডিগবাজী খাইয়া থাকে)।

rŏl'-lic, *v. i.* & *n.* To move in a careless swaggering air; to frolic; হেলিয়া দুলিয়া চলা; ক্রীড়াকৌতুক করা, ফষ্টিনষ্টি করা। ***Noun.*** 1. Frolic; ক্রীড়াকৌতুক, ফষ্টিনষ্টি, ফক্কুড়ি। 2. Exuberant gaiety; উল্লাস, বেজায় স্ফূর্ত্তি।

rŏ'-lȳ-pŏ'-lȳ, *n.* & *adj.* 1. A sheet of paste spread with jam and rolled into a pudding (also *rolly-polly*); ফলের চাটনি প্রভৃতির পুর দেওয়া একপ্রকার চোঙ্গা পিঠা। 2. A kind of game; একপ্রকার ক্রীড়া ***Adj.*** Plump; গোলগাল, নাদুসনুদুস্।

Rom, *n.* (*pl.* ROMA) A male gipsy; (*pl.*) gipsies; পুরুষ হাঘরিয়া; (বহুবচন) হাঘরিয়াগণ, যাযাবর সমাজ।

Rō-mā'-ic, *n.* & *adj.* Vernacular in modern Greece; আধুনিক গ্রীসের ভাষা। ***Adj.*** Relating to the language of modern Greece; বর্ত্তমানগ্রীসের ভাষাসম্বন্ধীয়।

Rō'-mă-i-kă, *n.* A modern Greek dance in which the dancers throw handkerchiefs at each other; গ্রীকদেশীয় আধুনিক নৃত্য বিশেষ—যাহাতে নর্ত্তকগণ পরস্পরের উপর রুমাল নিক্ষেপ করিয়া থাকে।

Rō'-măn, *n.* & *adj.* 1. A native or permanet resident of the city of Rome; রোমনগরীর অধিবাসী। 2. (*Pl.*) Christians in ancient Rome; as, Epistle to the *Romans*; প্রাচীন রোমনগরবাসী খৃষ্টধর্ম্মাবলম্বী জনগণ। 3. A Roman Catholic; রোমান ক্যাথলিক। 4. A Roman letter or type; খাড়া ছাঁদের অক্ষর বা হরফ। ***Adj.*** 1. Pertaining to Rome or the Romans; রোমনগরীসম্বন্ধীয়, রোমকপত্তনসম্বন্ধীয়, রোমকগণসম্বন্ধীয়। 2. Characteristic of the Roman people; noble; brave; patriotic; "Burke, in whose breast a *Roman* ardour glowed"; রোমকগণ সুলভ; উন্নত; শূর; দেশপ্রেমিক। 3. Pertaining to the Roman Catholics; রোমানক্যাথলিকগণসম্বন্ধীয়। 4. Designating Roman letters or types; খাড়াছাঁদের অক্ষর বা হরফ সূচক। **–ish,** *adj.* **–ism, –ist,** *ns.* **–i-za'-tion,** *n.* **–ize,** *v. t.* & *i.* 1. To fill with Latin words or idioms; ল্যাটিন শব্দ বা বাগ্‌ধারা দ্বারা পূর্ণ করা। 2. To use Roman letters or types; খাড়াছাঁদের অক্ষর বা হরফ ব্যবহার করা। 3. To convert into the Roman Catholic opinion; রোমানক্যাথলিক সম্প্রদায়ের মতে দীক্ষিত করা। ***Verb i.*** 1. To use Latin words or idioms; ল্যাটিন শব্দ বা বাগ্‌ধারা ব্যবহার করা। 2. To conform to Roman Catholic opinions; রোমান ক্যাথলিক মত বা রীতিনীতির অনুসারী হওয়া। **Roman candle**—একপ্রকার আতসবাজী—যাহা হইতে শাদা কিংবা নানা বর্ণের তারারাজি নির্গত হয়। **Roman Catholic**—যে সকল খৃষ্টানগণ আধ্যাত্মিক ব্যাপারে পোপের সর্ব্বময় কর্ত্তৃত্ব স্বীকার করিয়া থাকেন, রোমান্ ক্যাথলিক। **Roman cement**—Same as HYDRAULIC CEMENT (which see). **Roman Empire**—রোমসাম্রাজ্য, রোমক সাম্রাজ্য। [সম্রাট আগষ্টাস্ কর্ত্তৃক খৃঃ পূঃ ২৭ অব্দে প্রতিষ্ঠিত হয়। এই বৃহৎ সাম্রাজ্য ৩৯৪ খৃঃ অব্দে সম্রাট থিয়োডিসিয়াস কর্ত্তৃক পূর্ব্ব অথবা গ্রীক ও পশ্চিম অথবা ল্যাটিন সাম্রাজ্যে বিভক্ত হইয়াছিল। পূর্ব্ব সাম্রাজ্য ১৪৫৩ খৃঃ অব্দ পর্য্যন্ত স্থায়ী থাকে এবং পশ্চিম সাম্রাজ্য ৪৭৬ খৃঃ অব্দে একবার লুপ্ত হইয়া পুনরায় ৮০০ খৃঃ অব্দে সম্রাট সার্লেমেন কর্ত্তৃক পুনঃপ্রতিষ্ঠিত হইয়া পবিত্র

রোমসাম্রাজ্য (Holy Roman Empire) নামে ১৮০৬ খৃঃ অব্দ পর্য্যন্ত বর্ত্তমান ছিল।] **Roman fever**—একপ্রকার ম্যালেরিয়া জ্বর। [রোমনগরীতে এই জ্বরের প্রবল প্রাদুর্ভাব দৃষ্ট হয়।] **Roman law**—রোমক আইন। [বহু আধুনিক আইনের ভিত্তিস্বরূপ প্রাচীন রোমকদিগের আইন।] **Roman nose**—খগচঞ্চুবৎ নাসিকা, শুকনাস। **Roman numeral**—রোমীয় প্রণালীতে লিখিত সংখ্যা (যথা I=1; II=2; III=3; IV=4; V=5; X=10; L=50; C=100; D=500; M=1000.) **Roman pearl** — একপ্রকার ঝুঁটা মতি। **Roman school** — র‍্যাফেলপন্থী চিত্রকর-সম্প্রদায়। **Roman toga**—See TOGA.

rō-mance′ (-mans), *n., adj. & v. i.* **1.** A tale written in *Romance*, or 11th or 12th century French instead of in Latin; any fictitious or wonderful tale in prose or verse; খৃষ্টীয় একাদশ বা দ্বাদশ শতাব্দীর ফরাসীভাষায় লিখিত কথাগ্রন্থ; কথা, আখ্যান, আখ্যায়িকা। **2.** A kind of novel dealing not so much with everyday life as with surprising adventures and picturing almost an imaginary state of society; উপন্যাস, রমন্যাস, কল্পকথা। **3.** Romantic idea, character, quality, association or suggestion; "*Romance* gets out of a man's head when their hair gets gray"; ঔপন্যাসিকভাব, ঔপন্যাসিকতা, ঔপন্যাসিক ভাবোদ্দীপক দৃশ্য প্রভৃতি, ঔপন্যাসিক ভাবের ব্যঞ্জনা। **4.** Those languages of Southern Europe which grew out of the literary section of Rome and the ordinary spoken dialects of ancient Italy in the different provinces of Roman Europe (Italian, Spanish, Portuguese, Provencal, French, etc.); রোমের লেখ্য ল্যাটিন ভাষা এবং প্রাচীন ইতালীর কথ্যভাষার মিশ্রণে রোমাধিকৃত ইয়ুরোপের বিভিন্ন প্রদেশে উদ্ভূত ভাষাসমূহ, রোমক ভাষা শ্রেণী (বর্ত্তমান ইতালী, স্পেন, পর্ত্তুগাল, প্রোভেন্স, ফ্রান্স, প্রভৃতি দেশের ভাষা)। **5.** (*Mus.*) A song or short instrumental music in ballad style; গাথা বা তদুপযোগী বাদ্য। *Adj.* Belonging to the dialects called romance; রোমকভাষাশ্রেণী-সম্পর্কীয়। *Verb i.* To forge and tell fictitions stories; উপন্যাস রচনা করা, ঔপন্যাসিককাহিনী বিবৃত করা।

rō-mănc′-ĕr, *n.* **1.** A writer of romances; রমন্যাসকার। **2.** An inventor of picturesque falsehood; বিচিত্র মিথ্যাবচনরচনচতুর ব্যক্তি।

Romanes, *n.* Gipsy language; হাঘরিয়াদিগের ভাষা, যাযাবর ভাষা।

Rō-măn-esque′ (-ĕsk), *adj. & n.* **1.** Applied to the dialects of some southern districts of France; ফরাসীদেশের দক্ষিণ ভাগের কতিপয় উপভাষা সম্বন্ধে প্রযুক্ত। **2.** Pertaining to the debased style of architecture and ornament adopted in the later Roman Empire; পরবর্ত্তী রোমীয় সাম্রাজ্যে (৫০০—১১০০ খৃঃ অব্দ পর্য্যন্ত) গৃহীত অপকৃষ্ট স্থাপত্যরীতি বা মণ্ডনপদ্ধতি সম্বন্ধীয়। **3.** Of, or pertaining to, romance; রমন্যাসসম্পর্কীয়। *Noun.* The Romanesqe style of art or architecture; পরবর্ত্তীকালে রোমীয়সাম্রাজ্যে প্রচলিত অপকর্ষপ্রাপ্ত স্থাপত্যরীতি বা কলাপদ্ধতি। **Romanesque architecture** or **style**—রোমান স্থাপত্যরীতির বিলয় ও গথিক স্থাপত্যরীতি প্রবর্ত্তনের মধ্যবর্ত্তীকালে পশ্চিম ইয়ুরোপের বিভিন্ন অংশে যে স্থাপত্যরীতি প্রচলিত ছিল।

Rō-măn′-ic, *adj.* **1.** Pertaining to the Roman languages or dialects; রোমক ভাষা বা উপভাষাসমূহ সম্বন্ধীয়। **2.** Related to the Roman people by descent; রোমকবংশজ।

Rō-mănsh′, Rou′—, Ru′— (rō-), *adj. & n.* In the Rhaeto-Romanic tongue of the North-Western part of East Switzerland; পূর্ব্ব সুইজরলণ্ডের উত্তর-পশ্চিমাঞ্চলের ভাষায়। *Noun.* **1.** The Rhaeto-Romanic tongue of the North-Western part of East Switzerland; পূর্ব্ব সুইজরলণ্ডের উত্তর-পশ্চিমাঞ্চলের ভাষা। **2.** Same as RHAETO-ROMANIC.

rō-măn′-tic, *adj. & n.* **1.** Pertaining to romance; as, *romantic* literature (পরী সাহিত্য); fanciful; unreal; রমন্যাসসম্বন্ধীয়; কাল্পনিক, কল্পনাময়, পরীরাজ্যসুলভ; অবাস্তব। **2.** Given to extravagant or fanciful ideas; ঔপন্যাসিক, উৎকট কল্পনারসিক। **3.** Full of, or suggestive of, romance; as, it is a *romantic* spot (কল্পলোক); ভাবব্যঞ্জক, রসময় (হিঃ কোঃ), কল্পলোকোপম, পরীরাজ্যোপম, ঔপন্যাসিকতাময়, ঔপন্যাসিকতামাখা। **4.** Fantastic; dreamy; উদ্ভট; স্বপ্নজড়িত, স্বপ্নময়। **5.** Pertaining to the style of Christian or popular literature and art of the Middle Ages and uninfluenced by classical model; গ্রীক ও রোমীয় সাহিত্যের প্রভাববিমুক্ত মধ্যযুগের খৃষ্টীয় বা লোকসাহিত্যের ধারাসম্বন্ধীয়। *Noun.* **1.** A romantic feature or idea; ঔপন্যাসিকত্ব, ঔপন্যাসিক ভাব। **2.** A romantic person; ঔপন্যাসিক ভাবময় ব্যক্তি, কল্পলোকবাসী, স্বপ্নলোকবাসী, পরীরাজ্যবাসী। **Roma ic school**—কল্পতন্ত্র। (১) Novalis, Tiecks প্রভৃতি এবং Schlegel ভ্রাতৃদ্বয় কর্ত্তৃক ১৮০৮ খৃঃ অব্দে জর্ম্মণিদেশে প্রতিষ্ঠিত নব্য কবিতাতন্ত্র। (২) ডুমা, ভিক্তর হুগো, ল্যামারটাইন, প্রভৃতি কর্ত্তৃক ফরাসীদেশে প্রবর্ত্তিত সাহিত্যের নূতনধারা।

rō-măn′-ti-cĭsm, *n.* **1.** Romantic characteristic or principle; রমন্যাসকত্ব, ঔপন্যাসিকত্ব। **2.** The principle or the spirit of the movement in literature, art, etc. towards freedom in subject and treatment (opp. to *classicism*); সাহিত্য, শিল্প প্রভৃতির নূতন ধারা বিশেষের মূলতত্ত্ব বা অন্তর্নিহিতভাব, কল্পপন্থা। [এই নব আন্দোলনকে (Romantic movement) গ্রীক ও রোমীয় সাহিত্য এবং কলাপদ্ধতির অচলপ্রতিষ্ঠ নিয়মের বিরুদ্ধে বিদ্রোহ বলা যাইতে পারে। এই আন্দোলন খৃষ্টীয় অষ্টাদশ শতকের শেষভাগে জর্ম্মণ সাহিত্যক্ষেত্রে ল্যাসিং, শিলার, প্রভৃতি সাহিত্যরথিগণ কর্ত্তৃক আরব্ধ হয়; অচিরেই ইহা সমগ্র ইয়ুরোপের কলাক্ষেত্রে প্রভাব বিস্তার করে। Heineএর মতে "গ্রীক ও রোমান শিল্পীরা কেবল সাস্তেরই প্রকাশ করিতেন; সুতরাং শিল্পীর মানসচিত্র পটে বা পাথরে অবিকলরূপে ফুটাইতে পারিলেই তাহাদের পক্ষে যথেষ্ট হইত; কিন্তু রমন্যাস-শিল্পীকে অসীমের এবং পরমতত্ত্বের আভাস দিতে হইত—কাজেই প্রতীক বা লক্ষণার আশ্রয় গ্রহণ ভিন্ন তাহার উপায়ান্তর ছিল না।" স্নেহ, প্রেম, অনুরাগ, প্রভৃতি মানবচিত্তের সুকুমার ভাবসমূহ ফুটাইয়া তোলাই রমন্যাসশিল্পের প্রধান লক্ষ্য ছিল—বহির্জগতের রূপপ্রদর্শন ঐ শিল্পের উপ লক্ষ্য ছিল। ইংলণ্ডীয় সাহিত্যে Scott, Shelley, Byron, Wordsworth; ফরাসী সাহিত্যে Victor Hugo, de Musset, Georges Sand এবং Sainte-Beuve এবং জর্ম্মণ সাহিত্যে Goethe, Heine, Tiecks এবং Hoffmann প্রভৃতি এই নবসাহিত্যিক আন্দোলনের প্রধান নায়ক]।

Rŏm'-ā-ny̆, *n.* **1.** A gipsy; যাযবরিয়া। **2.** The gipsy language; যাযাবর-দিগের ভাষা।

rō-maunt' (-mänt), *n.* (*Rare*) A romance; a romantic ballad; (ক্বচিদ্ব্যবহৃত) নবন্যাস; গাথা।

Rōme, *n.* **1.** The city of Rome; রোমনগরী, রোমকপত্তন (লঙ্কা কুমধ্যে যমকোটিরস্যাঃ প্রাক্‌পশ্চিমে রোমকপত্তনঞ্চ — সিদ্ধান্ত শিরোমণি), রোমকপুরী (গোলঃ), রোমকপুর। **2.** The Roman empire; রোম-সাম্রাজ্য, রোমক বিষয় (আর্য্যঃ)। **3.** Applied to Constantinople, the capital of the Eastern Roman Empire; কনস্তান্তিনোপাল, রুম (as রুমের বাদসা—The Sultan of Turkey)। **4.** Roman Catholic Church; রোমান ক্যাথলিক ধর্ম্মসংঘ। **Rom'-ish,** *adj.* **Rome'-ward,** *adv.* **1.** Towards Rome; রোমের অভিমুখে। **2.** Towards the Roman Catholic Church; রোমান ক্যাথলিক ধর্ম্মসংঘের দিকে। **Rome was not built in a day**—রোম নগরী এক দিনে নির্ম্মিত হয় নাই, কোন বিরাট কার্য্যই অনায়াসে বা অল্প সময়ে সম্পন্ন হইতে পারে না। **When at Rome do as Roman or Pope does**—যস্মিন দেশে যদাচারঃ, যেখানে যেমন সেখানে তেমন।

rŏmp, *v. i.* & *n.* **1.** To leap or frisk about in play; to play boisterously; লাফালাফি করা, ছুটাছুটি করা; সোরগোল করিয়া খেলা। **2.** (*Racing slang*) To move easily and with great rapidity; (ঘোড়দৌড়ের ইতর ভাষায়) অনায়াসে ও অতি দ্রুত-বেগে ছুটা। ***Noun.*** **1.** A girl or child fond of romping; গেছো মেয়ে, দস্যি মেয়ে, যে শিশু বা বালিকা ছুটাছুটি ও লাফালাফি ভালবাসে। **2.** Boisterous play or frolic; দৌড়ধাবের খেলা, ছুটাছুটি লাফালাফির খেলা।

rŏn'-deau (-dö), *n.* A poem usually of thirteen or ten verses, divided into three parts, parts of which are repeated; একপ্রকার ত্রয়োদশপদী বা দশপদী কবিতা।

rŏn'-dĕl, *n.* A special kind of rondeau; একপ্রকার বিশিষ্টধরণের ত্রয়োদশপদী বা দশপদী কবিতা।

rondo, *n.* A piece of music having one principal subject, to which return is always made after the introduction of other matter; একরূপ সঙ্গীত—যাহার কোন মূল অংশ পুনঃ পুনঃ গাওয়া হয়।

rŏn'-düre, *n.* (*Poet.*) A circle; a round object; (কবিতায়) বৃত্ত; গোলাকার বস্তু।

Rönt'-gĕn rays, *n.* See RAY.

rōōd, *n.* **1.** The fourth part of on acre; এক একরের চতুর্থাংশ। **2.** A measure of $5\frac{1}{2}$ yards; $৫\frac{১}{২}$ গজ পরিমিত দৈর্ঘ্যের মাপ। **3.** A figure of Christ's cross, and often of the crucifix, esp. that placed at the entrance to the choir in mediaeval churches; যীশুখৃষ্টের ক্রুশের চিত্র, ক্রুশবিদ্ধ যীশুখৃষ্টের চিত্র, বিশেষতঃ মধ্যযুগের খৃষ্টীয় ধর্ম্মমন্দিরের ভজনচক্রের প্রবেশপথে স্থাপিত ক্রুশ। **Rood-arch**—খৃষ্টীয়ধর্ম্মমন্দিরের মধ্যস্থল এবং গায়কগণের উপবেশনস্থলীর মধ্যবর্ত্তী তোরণ। **Rood-beam**—গায়কমণ্ডলীর উপবেশনস্থলীর সম্মুখস্থ কাঠ বা পাথরের পর্দ্দার উপরিস্থ এড়ো কাঠ। **Rood-cloth**—লেণ্ট পর্ব্বকালে যে তিরস্করণী-দ্বারা খৃষ্টীয়ধর্ম্মমন্দিরের উপবেশনস্থলীর সম্মুখস্থ কাঠ বা পাথরের পর্দ্দা আচ্ছাদিত করা হয়। **Rood-loft**—খৃষ্টীয়ধর্ম্মমন্দিরের গায়কমণ্ডলীর উপবেশনস্থলীর সম্মুখস্থ কাঠ বা পাথরের পর্দ্দার উপরিস্থ মঞ্চ। **Rood-Screen**—খৃষ্টীয়ধর্ম্মমন্দিরের মধ্যভাগ এবং গায়কদিগের উপবেশনস্থলীর মধ্যবর্ত্তী কাঠ বা প্রস্তরের তিরস্করণী।

rōōf, *n.* & *v. t.* **1.** The covering of a house or building; ছাদ, ছাত (*colloq.*), চাল (thatched roof); **2.** That which corresponds with, or resembles, the covering of a house, as the top of a carriage, bŏat, car, etc.; গাড়ীর ছাদ, ছই, ছাপ্পর। **3.** Canopy; heaven; "Under the *roof* of the blue Ionian weather"; চন্দ্রাতপ, চাঁদোয়া; গগনপটল, আকাশপটল। **4.** A house; গৃহ, বাটী। **5.** The palate; তালু। ***Verb t.*** To cover with a roof; to be a roof; ছাদ দেওয়া; ছাদস্বরূপ হওয়া। **Roof'-ing** *n.* **1.** The act of covering with a roof; ছাদ দেওন। **2.** Material for a roof; ছাদের মাল মসলা। **3.** A roof; ছাদ। **Roof'-less,** *adj.* **Roof-tree**—মুদ্গম কাঠ, মধ্যম কাষ্ঠ, দোচালা খড়ের ঘরের দুই চালের সংযোগ-স্থলের কাঠ। **Under one's roof**—In one's house; কাহারো গৃহে।

rōōk, *n.* & *v. t.* **1.** A bird of the genus corvus; কাকজাতীয় পক্ষি-বিশেষ, রাজকাক। **2.** A sharper; জুয়াচোর। ***Verb t.*** To cheat;

"He was much *rooked* by gamesters ;" ঠকান। **Rook'-er,** *n.* A swindler ; জুয়াচোর। **Rook'-y,** *adj.* **Rook-pie**—রাজকাকশাবক হইতে প্রস্তুত পিষ্টক বিশেষ। **Rook-rifle**—রাজকাক মারিবার জন্য বন্দুক।

rook, *n.* (*Chess*) Castle ; (দাবা খেলায়) রথ বা নৌকা।

rook'-ĕr-y̆, *n.* **1.** Group of nests on trees occupied by rooks ; দাঁড়কাকের কুলায়শ্রেণী। **2.** A close assemblage of poor mean dwellings inhabited by the lowest poor ; নিম্নশ্রেণীর দরিদ্র লোকদিগের বাসের জন্য কুঁড়েশ্রেণী। **3.** A resort of thieves, swindlers, etc. ; চোর, জুয়াচোর, প্রভৃতির আড্ডা। **4.** A resort of seals, penguines, etc. ; সীল, পেঙ্গুইন, প্রভৃতির সমাগমস্থান।

room, *n.* **1.** An apartment in a house ; কোঠা, কক্ষ, কুঠরী, কামরা। **2.** Space ; as, there is plenty of *room* ; স্থান, জায়গা। **3.** Opportunity ; as, there is no *room* for dispute ; scope ; সুবিধা, সুযোগ ; অবকাশ, আশয়। **4.** The person assembled in a room ; as, the eyes of the whole *room* turned towards him ; কক্ষে সমবেত লোকবৃন্দ। **5.** Place or station once occupied by another; stead ; কোন ব্যক্তির অধিকৃত স্থান ; পরিবর্ত্ত, স্থল। **Room'-y,** *adj.* Spacious ; বিস্তৃত, প্রশস্ত, সুপরিসর, চওড়া। **To give room**—To withdraw ; স্থান ছাড়িয়া দেওয়া। To give space ; জায়গা দেওয়া। **To make a room**—To open a way or passage ; পথ খোলা। To open a space or place for anything ; স্থান করা। **To prefer another's room to his company**—To wish another to leave ; to like to avoid his society ; সে সম্মুখ হইতে চলিয়া যাউক এরূপ ইচ্ছা করা ; তাহারো সঙ্গ ভাল না লাগা।

roost, *n.*, *v. i.* & *t.* **1.** The pole or other support on which fowls rest at night ; পক্ষীদের বসিবার দণ্ডকাষ্ঠ, দাঁড়, বাসযষ্টি (মেঘদূঃ), যষ্টিনিবাস (রঃ) নিবাসযষ্টি, বাসদণ্ড। **2.** A collection of fowls roosting ; একত্র দাঁড়ে উপবিষ্ট কুক্কুটশ্রেণী। **3.** A resting place ; বিশ্রামস্থান, নিলয়নস্থান। ***Verb i.*** **1.** To occupy a roost ; দাঁড়ে বসা। **2.** (*Colloq.*) To sleep ; (চলিত ভাষায়) ঘুমান, নিদ্রা যাওয়া। ***Verb t.*** To provide with sleeping place ; ঘুমাইবার স্থান দেওয়া। **At roost**—দাঁড়ে বসা ; নিদ্রিত। **Curses come home to roost**—Curses recoil upon the curser ; অভিশাপ অভিশাপদাতার উপর ফিরিয়া পড়ে। **To go to roost**—To go to sleep ; ঘুমাইতে যাওয়া।

roost'-ĕr, *n.* A domestic cock ; গৃহপালিত কুক্কুট।

root, *n.*, *v. t.* & *i.* **1.** That part of a plant which fixes itself in the earth and draws nourishment from the soil ; মূল, শিকড়। **2.** An edible root ; যে সকল মূল আহার করা যায়। **3.** The origin, source or cause of anything ; as, he is the *root* of all evil ; কারণ, উৎপত্তি, মূল। **4.** The first ancestor or progenitor ; বংশের আদি পুরুষ, বীজ পুরুষ। **5.** (*Gram.*) That part of a word which conveys its essential meaning as distinguished from the formative part ; ধাতু। **6.** (*Math.*) The fraction of a quantity which multiplied by itself produces the quantity ; মূল (cf. বর্গমূল, ঘনমূল)। **7.** The bottom or base of anything ; as, the *root* of a hill ; কোন কিছুর ভূমি বা নিম্নদেশ। **8.** Foundation ; support ; ভিত্তি, বুনিয়াদ ; আশ্রয়। ***Verb t.*** **1.** To plant and fix in the ground by the root ; শিকড় সহিত রোপণ করা। **2.** To impress deeply and durably ; বদ্ধমূল করা। **3.** To uproot ; উপড়াইয়া ফেলা, উন্মূলিত করা। ***Verb i.*** **1.** To take root ; শিকড় বাঁধা। **2.** To be firmly fixed ; বদ্ধমূল হওয়া। **Root'-er,** *n.* **Root'-less,** *adj.* Without root ; অমূলক, অকারণ (সাংখ্য)। **Root'-let,** *n.* **Root'-y,** *adj.* **Root-crop**—মূলা, গাজর প্রভৃতি। **Root race** — মূলজাতি (হিঃ কোঃ)। **At the root of**—At bottom ; মূলে। **Root of a gem**—কোন রত্নের, বিশেষতঃ পান্নার নিষ্প্রভ অংশ—যদ্দারা উহা খনির প্রস্তরে সংলগ্ন ছিল। **Root of bitterness**—ভ্রান্তি, পাপ বা অশুভ। **The root of evil**—ধনাগমতৃষ্ণা। **The root of the matter**—সুগভীর ধর্ম্মবিশ্বাস। **To root out**—To exterminate ; সমূলে বিনাশ করা, উন্মূলিত করা। **To take or strike root**—To settle in a place ; কোন স্থানের স্থায়ী বাসিন্দা হওয়া।

root, rout (rowt), *v. i.* & *t.* **1.** To turn up the earth with the snout, as swine ; শূকরের মত মুখ দ্বারা মাটি খুঁড়িয়া তোলা। **2.** To rummage about ; চারিদিকে খোঁজা। ***Verb t.*** (Of swine) To dig or turn up the ground with the snout ; (শূকর সম্পর্কে) মুখ দ্বারা মাটি খুঁড়া বা উল্টান।

root'-ĕr-y̆, *n.* A pile of roots for plants being planted ; ফুলের গাছ প্রভৃতি রোপণের জন্য শিকড় স্তূপ।

root-le (-l), *v. t.* & *i.* Same as ROOT, *v. i.* & *t.*

rōpe, *n.*, *v. i.* & *t.* **1.** A thick cord of several strands twisted together ; দড়ী, রজ্জু, রশি। **2.** A row or string consisting of a number of things united ; as, a *rope* of onions ; লহর, সারি। ***Verb i.*** To draw out or extend into a string or thread by means of glutinous or adhesive quality ; আটালো হওয়ার দরুণ টানিলে রজ্জুর মত হওয়া। ***Verb t.*** **1.** To fasten with a rope ; রজ্জুদ্বারা বাঁধা। **2.** To draw as by a rope ; রজ্জু প্রভৃতি দ্বারা টানা। **3.** (In mountaineering) To attach persons to each other for safety by means of a rope ; (পর্ব্বতারোহণে) রজ্জুদ্বারা একের সহিত অপরকে বাঁধা। **4.** To catch by means of a rope ; রজ্জুদ্বারা ধরা। **5.** To restrain as a horse by its rider to prevent it from winning a race ; কোন ঘোড়া যেন দৌড়ে জিতিতে না পারে তজ্জন্য উহাকে রশ্মি দ্বারা সংযত করা। **Rop′-er-y,** *n.* A place where ropes are made ; রজ্জু প্রস্তুতের স্থান, রজ্জুনির্ম্মাণশালা। **Rop′-y,** *adj.* Glutinous ; adhesive ; চটচটে ; আটালো। **Rope-dancer** — রজ্জুনর্ত্তক, দড়াবাজিকর। [Syn. কলায়ন সূত্রায়ন।] **Rope-ladder** — দড়ির সিঁড়ী। **Rope-maker**—রজ্জু প্রস্তুতকারী। **Rope's-end**—যে ক্ষুদ্র রজ্জুখণ্ড দ্বারা আঘাত করিয়া নাবিকদিগকে শাস্তি দেওয়া হয়। **Rope-trick** — দড়ী খেলা (বাজীকরকে দৃঢ়রূপে রজ্জু দ্বারা বাঁধিলে সে যে কৌশলে নিজকে মুক্ত করে)। **Rope-walk**—রজ্জুনির্ম্মাণস্থলী। **Wire-rope**—তারের রজ্জু। **Give a rogue rope enough and he will hang himself**—A bad man will certainly bring about his ruin ; দুষ্ট লোক তাহার সর্ব্বনাশের পথ প্রস্তুত করিবেই ইহার অন্যথা হইবে না। **On the high ropes**—অত্যুল্লসিত, টঙ্গের উপর। **Rope of sand**—Tie or union easily broken ; বালির বাঁধ [cf. খলের পিরীতি বালির বাঁধ]। **The rope**—ফাঁসির দড়ী। **Throwing the rope after the bucket**—ঢাকী শুদ্ধ বিসর্জ্জন। **To come or run to the end of one's rope**—To be ultimately checked in evil-doing ; কুপথের শেষ সীমায় আসা। **To give one rope**—Not to check him ; রাশ ছাড়িয়া দেওয়া। **To give one rope enough**—To allow one liberty to do as he likes ; কাহাকে ইচ্ছামত চলিতে দেওয়া। **To know the ropes**—To know how to do something ; কোন কাজ কিরূপে করিতে হয় তাহা জানা। **To rope in**—To decoy ; ভুলাইয়া আনা। **With a rope round one's neck**—In imminent peril of losing one's life ; শিয়রে শমন, মৃত্যুমুখে।

Roque′-fort (rŏk-fŏr), *n.* A kind of cheese made from goats' and ewes' milk, at Roquefort, in the South West of France ; ফ্রান্সের দক্ষিণপশ্চিমাঞ্চলস্থ রকফর নামক স্থানে ছাগী ও মেষীর দুগ্ধ হইতে প্রস্তুত একপ্রকার পনীর।

roq′-ue-laure (rŏk-ō-lōr), *n.* A kind of short cloak much used in the earlier portion of the eighteenth century ; অষ্টাদশ শতকের প্রথমভাগে বহুল ব্যবহৃত একপ্রকার খাটো জামা।

rō′-quet (-kŏt), *v. t.* & *n.* (In croquet) To strike one ball with another ; এক কন্দুক দ্বারা অপর কন্দুকে আঘাত করা। ***Noun.*** The stroke so made ; ঐরূপ আঘাত।

Rorqual.

rŏr′-quăl, *n.* A large species of whale ; একজাতীয় বৃহৎকায় তিমি-মৎস্য, তিমিঙ্গিল।

rŏr′-tȳ, raugh′-tȳ (rä-), *adjs.* (*Slang*) Enjoyable ; আমোদপূর্ণ, মজার।

rosace, *n.* **1.** Same as ROSE-WINDOW. **2.** A rose-shaped ornament ; গোলাপপুষ্পাকৃতি ভূষা। **3.** An ornamental piece of plaster-work in the centre ceiling, in which a chandelier is placed ; ভিতরের ছাদের মধ্যস্থ শোভাসাধক কারুকার্য্যখচিত স্থানবিশেষ—যাহাতে ঝাড় বিলম্বিত করা হয়।

Rosa centifolia—কাঁটা গোলাপ (বেল:)।

rō-šā′-ceous (-shŭs), *adj.* Of the order of Rosaceae ; গোলাপবর্গভুক্ত।

Rosa Indica—কাঁটা গোলাপ, কাঠ-গোলাপ।

Rosa Indica var—গুজকাঁটা, গুঁজা গোলাপ।

rōs-ăn′-i-line, *n.* (Triamino-tolyldiphenyl carbinol $C_{20}H_{19}N_3$) An organic base forming salts of value in dyeing ; রঞ্জনকার্য্যে ব্যবহৃত বহু প্রয়োজনীয় রঙ্গের লবণ-উৎপাদক জৈব ভস্মবিশেষ। [ব্যবসায়িগণের নিকট ইহা chloride, fuchsine or magenta নামে পরিচিত]।

rō-šā-ri-ăn, *n.* A cultivator of roses ; গোলাপচাষকারী।

rō′-šā-rȳ, *n.* **1.** A rose-garden ; a bed of roses ; গোলাপের বাগান ; গোলাপের কেয়ারী। **2.** A chaplat ; a garland ; "Christ has now knit them into *rosaries* and coronets" ; মৌলিমাল্য ; মাল্য, মালিকা। **3.** A string of beads used in counting prayers ; জপমালা, জপামালিকা (তন্ত্র), অক্ষমালা, করমালা (fingers used as rosary), অক্ষমালিকা, অক্ষসূত্র। [খৃষ্টানদিগের জপমালায় ৫টী বা ১৫টী বিভাগ থাকে। প্রত্যেক বিভাগে ১০টী ক্ষুদ্র ও একটী বৃহৎ মালা থাকে। প্রত্যেক ক্ষুদ্র মালাতে "Ave Maria' ও প্রতি বৃহৎ মালাতে "Paternoster" জপ করিতে হয়।]

Rō′-sci-ăn (-shĭ-), *adj.* Like the famous Roman actor Roscius ; রোমনগরীর সুবিখ্যাত অভিনেতা Roscius সম্বন্ধীয়।

rōse, *n.* & *v. t.* **1.** A well-known and universally cultivated plant and flower of the genus Rosa, natural order Rosaceæ ; গোলাপ গাছ, গোলাপ, গোলাপফুল, গোলাব পুষ্প, সেবতী (Indian white rose), সেমন্তী (*ib.*), সেঁওতি (*ib.*),

গুলাব [Sanskritised form—cf. চতুর্ধা স্থলপদ্মানি সেবন্তি গুলদাবদী। নৈপালী চ গুলাবশ্চ বকুলশ্চ কদম্বকঃ॥ (অর্কপ্রকাশ -- শব্দকল্পদ্রুমোদ্ধৃত)]। [Syn. শতপত্রী, সুমনা, রাজতরুণী, তরুণী, চারুকেশরা, গন্ধাঢ্যা, কর্ণিকা, মহাকুমারী, লাক্ষা, কৃষ্ণা, শিববল্লভা, সৌম্যগন্ধা, শতদলা, সুবৃত্তা (রাজনির্ঘণ্ট)]। [(Pers. *Gul*; Arab. *Ward*; Chin. *Ying-shih, Tsiang-wei, Tsiang-mi*; Fr., Russ., Sp., It. *Rosa*, *Rosa*. Tam. *Gulaba-pu*; Teleg. *Roja-pu*; Greek. *Rodon*]। নিম্নে কয়েক প্রকার উৎকৃষ্ট গোলাপের নাম প্রদত্ত হইল:—Black Prince, (বর্ণ কৃষ্ণলোহিত বলিয়া এই নাম।) Blue Rose (বর্ণ খাঁটি নীল নহে—উহার বর্ণ নীলাভ লোহিত)। Green rose (দুষ্প্রাপ্য), Rosa verdiflora (সবুজ গোলাপ), Sappho, Champion of the world, Crimson Rambler, Paul Neron Marie Bauman, Senatiar Vaisse, Xavier Olibo, Monte Cristo, Her Majesty, Queen of Queens, Glory of Waltham, Mrs. Harkness, Aurora, The Bride, The Queen, Kaiserin Augusta Victoria, Richard Laxton, Reynold's hole, Donna Muria, Alba Damask, Charles Lawson, Paul Recant, Coup de Hebet, Charles Duval, Paul Perras, Persian yellow; Double yellow rose, Dwarf double yellow, Dundee Rambler, Queen of the Belgians, Ruga, Myrrh scented Rose, Splenden's Rose, Princess Marie, Princess Louise, Felicite perpetue, Madame Sancy De Parabire, Perpetual moss, Madame Ory, Perpetual Damask, Madame Bosanquet, Marechal Neil. **2.** A delicate red or pink colour; গোলাপী রঙ্গ। **3.** A knot of ribbon formed like a rose; গোলাব পুষ্পের আকারে গ্রথিত ফিতার গুচ্ছ। **4.** Full flush or bloom of the complexion; as, she has spoilt her natural *roses*; গণ্ডের গোলাবী আভা, গণ্ডের গোলাবী রাগ, গণ্ডের পাটল রাগ, গোলাপ। ("শ্রমে পদ্মপর্ণ কপোল যুগলে ভাসিছে গোলাপ সদাবিকশিত—কুরুক্ষেত্র।) **5.** Same as ERYSIPELAS. **6.** (*Arch.*) A rosette; (স্থপতিবিদ্যা) গোলাপপুষ্পাকৃতি ভূষা। **7.** (*Arch.*) Same as ROSE-WINDOW (below). **8.** A circular card with radiating lines; as, the *rose* of a mariner's compass; মধ্য বিন্দু হইতে বিকিরণশীল রেখাসমূহ সমন্বিত গোলাকার স্থূল কাগজখণ্ড। **9.** A woman of great beauty; "She called her *rose* of Sherwood"; সুন্দরীশিরোমণি। **10.** A perforated nozzle for spreading water in fine spray; সূক্ষ্মকণাকারে জল ছড়াইবার জন্য পাত্রাদির নলমুখে সংবদ্ধ সচ্ছিদ্র আবরণ। *Verb t.* **1.** To render rose-coloured; to cause to blush; গোলাপবর্ণে রঞ্জিত করা; গণ্ডস্থল সরমরক্তিম করা। **2.** To perfume as with rose; গোলাপ সুরভিত করা,

Dog rose.

গোলাবগন্ধ করা। **Dog rose**—জবঘণ্টী গোলাপ। **Red rose** — ইংলণ্ডের ল্যাঙ্কাষ্টার রাজপরিবারের চিহ্ন। **Rose aniline**—Same as ROSANILINE. **Rose-apple**—গোলাপজাম, জম্বু (also জম্বু)। **Rose-bud**—গোলাপকলিকা। **Rose-bug** — একপ্রকার গোবরে পোকা—ইহারা গোলাপের পাঁপড়ী আহার করিয়া থাকে। **Rose bush**—গোলাবগুল্ম। **Rose-camphor**—যে উদ্বায়ী তৈলদ্বয় হইতে আতর প্রস্তুত হয়—তাহার অন্যতর। **Rose-chafer**—Same as ROSE-BUG. **Rose-cheeked**—গোলাবগণ্ড। **Rose-coloured**—গোলাববর্ণ। Uncommonly beautiful; extremely pleasing; as, *rose-coloured* views; অতি সুন্দর; অতি মনোমদ। **Rose-cut**—যে মণির নিম্নভাগ সমতল রাখা হয় -- এবং উপরিভাগে ত্রিকোণাকার পল কাটা হইয়া থাকে তৎসম্বন্ধে উক্ত। **Rose-diamond**—প্রায় অর্দ্ধ বর্ত্তুলাকৃতি হীরকবিশেষ—যাহার মধ্যভাগস্থ ষট্‌কোণের চতুর্দ্দিকে চব্বিশটী ত্রিকোণাকৃতি পল কাটা হইয়া থাকে, কমল হীরা (এক গাছা হীরের কণ্ঠী দিয়েছে তার দাম বাবু বল্লেন ২৫ হাজারের কম হবে না—দিব্যি জিনিষটী। সব কমল হীরা—জ্যোতিঃহারা)। **Rose-drop**—গোলাবপুষ্পসার দ্বারা সুবাসিত লজঞ্জুস; অতিরিক্ত মদ্যপান হেতু নাসিকায় জাত রক্তবর্ণ ব্রণ। **Rose-engine**—কুন্দনযন্ত্রের সহিত সংযুক্ত উপযন্ত্র বিশেষ—যদ্দ্বারা ধাতু, কাষ্ঠ, প্রভৃতিতে বিভিন্ন প্রকার বক্ররেখা খোদিত হয়। **Rose-festivel**—৮ই জুন তারিখে ফরাসী দেশে অনুষ্ঠিত উৎসব বিশেষ—তিন জন গুণবতী মহিলার মধ্যে শ্রেষ্ঠতমা নারীকে নির্ব্বাচনপূর্ব্বক ভজনালয়ে নিয়া তথায় তাঁহাকে গোলাব পুষ্পদ্বারা ভূষিত করিয়া সম্মানের আসনে অধিষ্ঠিত করা হয়। **Rose-fever**—Same as HAY-FEVER. **Rose-fish**—নরওয়ে দেশের মৎস্য বিশেষ। **Rose-hued**—গোলাপবর্ণ, গোলাবি। **Rose-knot**—গোলাব পুষ্পাকারে গ্রথিত ফিতার গুচ্ছ। **Rose-lake**—লাক্ষা ও মঞ্জিষ্ঠা হইতে প্রস্তুত একপ্রকার উজ্জ্বল রক্তবর্ণ। **Rose-leaf**—গোলাপের পাঁপড়ী। **Rose lip**—গোলাবী অধর। **Rose-nail**—ত্রিকোণাকৃতি পলবিশিষ্ট গোল মাথাওয়ালা পেরেক। **Rose noble** — ইংলণ্ডের একপ্রকার প্রাচীন স্বর্ণ-মুদ্রা—ইহাতে একটী গোলাপের চিত্র মুদ্রিত থাকিত। **Rose-pink**—গোলাবী রং; ব্রাজিল কাষ্ঠের কাথ ও ফিটকারী দ্বারা খড়ি

রঞ্জনপূর্ব্বক প্রস্তুত একপ্রকার গোলাবী রঞ্জক পদার্থ। **Rose-quartz**—পাটলবর্ণ স্ফটিক প্রস্তর। **Rose-tinted**—গোলাব-বর্ণ। **Rose-vinegar**—সির্কায় গোলাব ডুবাইয়া প্রস্তুত ক্বাথবিশেষ। **Rose-water**—গোলাপ জল; গোলাপবারি। (*Adj.*) Affectedly fine, delicate or sentimental; "*Rose-water* philanthrophy"; কৃত্রিম কোমলতা বা সৌকুমার্য্যযুক্ত, কৃত্রিম ভাবপ্রবণ। **Rose-window**—একপ্রকার গোলাকার বাতায়ন—যাহাতে পুষ্পদলের মত নক্সাদার কাজ থাকে। **Rose-wood**—ব্র্যাজিল হইতে সমানীত গাঢ় রক্তবর্ণ কাষ্ঠ বিশেষ। [এই কাষ্ঠ হইতে অতি মূল্যবান আসবাব প্রস্তুত হয়; নুতন কাটা অবস্থায় ইহার গন্ধ কতকটা গোলাপের মত বলিয়া প্রতিভাত হয়]। **White-rose**—ইংলণ্ডের ইয়র্ক পরিবারের চিহ্ন; শুদ্ধ স্বভাবের চিহ্ন। **A bed of roses**—See BED. **Beneath the roses lies the serpent**—বিষকুম্ভ পয়োমুখম্। **Roses have thorns**—কণ্টক বিনা কমল নাই। **Rose of Sharon**—(*Hypericum calycinum*) একপ্রকার পীত পুষ্পপ্রসূ-গুল্ম। **To look through rose-coloured spectacles**—To take up a cheerful, highly favourable or optimistic view of a matter; কোন বিষয় খুব ভাল ভাবে দেখা, কোন বিষয় খুব আশাজনক ভাবে দেখা, প্রেমের অঞ্জন চোখে দিয়া দেখা। **Under the rose**—Secretly; গোপনে, নিভৃতে, রহসি। **Wars of the Roses**—পঞ্চদশ শতাব্দীতে ইংলণ্ডের ল্যাঙ্কেষ্টার ও ইয়র্ক পরিবার দ্বয়ের মধ্যে ভীষণ লোকক্ষয়কর যুদ্ধ।

rōse, *pp.* Of RISE.

rō'-sē-āte, *adj.* Rose-coloured; গোলাপী, পাটল, গোলাবী রংয়ের। **—ly,** *adv.*

rō-selle' (-zĕl), *n.* An East Indian rose-mallow; মেস্ত (ফার্সি), জবির (আরবি—খোরী), আকলি-উল্-জবি।

rōse'-ma-rȳ, *n.* An evergreen shrub cultivated for its flowers and leaves, from which oil of Rosemary is distilled in France and Spain; একপ্রকার চিরশ্যামল গুল্ম। ইহার পত্র ও পুষ্প হইতে স্পেন ও ফরাসী দেশে একপ্রকার তৈল বাহির করা হয়।

rō'-sē-ō-lă, *n.* A rose-coloured rash of several varieties; একপ্রকার গোলাবী রংয়ের কণ্ডুরোগ।

rō'-sĕt, *n.* A red colour used by painters; চিত্রকরগণকর্ত্তৃক ব্যবহৃত একপ্রকার গোলাবী রং।

Rō-sĕt'-ta-stōne (-ĕ-), *n.* A stone found near the Mussalman city on the Rosetta, a branch of the river Nile bearing inscriptions in hieroglyphics, demotic and Greek, by the aid of which a key was obtained to the hieroglyphics of Ancient Egypt; মিশরের Rosetta নদীর তীরবর্ত্তী নগর বিশেষে প্রাপ্ত শিলাখণ্ড বিশেষ—যাহার উপর উৎকীর্ণ লেখসমূহ হইতে প্রাচীন মিশরের চিত্রলিপির অর্থোদ্ধারের সঙ্কেত পাওয়া গিয়াছিল।

Rō-sĕt'-ta-wood (-ĕ-), *n.* A wood of a lively orange colour with dark veins used in cabinet-making; কৃষ্ণবর্ণের শিরাবিশিষ্ট একপ্রকার উজ্জ্বল কমলাবর্ণের কাষ্ঠ।

rō-sette' (-zĕt), *n.* **1.** An ornament of ribbon somewhat resembling a rose in shape; গোলাপপুষ্পাকৃতি ফিতা গুচ্ছ। **2.** Same as ROSE DIAMOND. **3.** (*Arch.*) An ornament resembling a rose; (স্থপতি-বিজ্ঞান) গোলাপপুষ্পাকৃতি ভূষা। **4.** A thin disc formed by cooling the surface of molten metal with water; গলিত ধাতুর উপরিভাগ জল দ্বারা শীতল করিয়া যে ধাতুর চাকতি গঠিত হয়। **Red rosette**—ফরাসী দেশের Legion of Honour নামক অভিজাত সম্প্রদায়ের চিহ্ন।

Rō-sī-cru'-ti-ăn (-krō-shĭ-), *n.* One of a fraternity, who, in the beginning of the 15th century affected an intimate acquaintance with the secrets of nature and claimed by the study of alchemy and other occult sciences to be possessed of wonder-working powers; খৃষ্টীয় পঞ্চদশ শতাব্দীর প্রথম ভাগে প্রাদুর্ভূত ইয়ুরোপীয় তান্ত্রিক সমাজবিশেষভুক্ত ব্যক্তি। [এই তান্ত্রিকসমাজ Christian Rosen-Kreuz নামক জনৈক জর্ম্মণদেশীয় সম্ভ্রান্ত পুরুষ কর্ত্তৃক ১৪৮৪ খৃষ্টাব্দে প্রতিষ্ঠিত হইয়াছিল বলিয়া উক্ত হয়। কথিত আছে Rosen বহুকাল প্রাচ্যদেশে বাসের পর এই সমস্ত তান্ত্রিকরহস্য বিদ্যায় সিদ্ধিলাভ করেন। এই তান্ত্রিকগণ নিকৃষ্ট ধাতুকে স্বর্ণে রূপান্তর এবং আয়ুষ্কালের পরিমাণ বৃদ্ধির রহস্য অবগত ছিল বলিয়া কথিত হয়। এতদ্ভিন্ন তাহারা নানারূপ যোগবলের অধিকারী ছিল বলিয়া লোকে বিশ্বাস করিত। (ইহাদের অপর নাম Brothers of the Rosy Cross, Rosy Cross Knights, Rosy Cross philosophers, etc.)—See Waite's *Real History of the Rosicrucians*; C. Murr, *True Origin of the Rosicrucians*; De Quincey's *Rosicrucians and Freemasons.*] **—ism,** *n.*

rŏs'-in, *n.* & *v. t.* The residuum of turpentine after the oil is distilled off; অপরিশোধিত তার্পিণ হইতে তার্পিণ তৈল চোয়াইবার কালে যে কঠিন অংশ অবশিষ্ট থাকে, রজন। ***Verb t.*** To rub over with rosin; রজনদ্বারা ঘষা, রজন মাখান। **—y,** *adj.*

Rŏs-ĭ-năn-tē, Rŏz—, *ns.* A worn-out or ill-conditioned horse; জরাগ্রস্ত অশ্ব, অকর্ম্মণ্য অশ্ব (Sp. *rocinante*)। [Don. Quixoteএর অশ্ব Rosinanteএর নাম হইতে গৃহীত।]

rō-so'-lĭō, *n.* **1.** A sweet cordial of the southern region of Europe made of brandy, sugar, raisins, etc.; ইয়ুরোপের দক্ষিণাঞ্চলে ব্রাণ্ডি, চিনি, কিসমিস, প্রভৃতি সহযোগে প্রস্তুত উত্তেজক পানীয়বিশেষ।

rŏs′-têr, *n.* **1.** A list of names of persons or corps, subject to military or other duties in succession ; পর্য্যায়ক্রমে কর্ত্তব্যপালনের জন্য নির্দ্দিষ্ট সৈনিক বা সৈন্যদল সমূহের নামের তালিকা। **2.** A roll or list ; তালিকা।

rŏs′-trăl, *adj.* **1.** Pertaining to a beak ; চঞ্চু-সম্পর্কীয়। **2.** Resembling the beak of ship ; পোতমুখ-তুল্য, পোতাগ্রনিভ। **3.** (Of column) Adorned with beaks of ships either actual or sculptured ; (স্তম্ভ-প্রভৃতি সম্বন্ধে) প্রকৃত বা ক্ষোদিত পোতমুখদ্বারা সমালঙ্কৃত।

rŏs′-trăt-ĕd, *adj.* **1.** Same as ROSTRAL 3. **2.** (*Zool.*) Having a rostrum ; (প্রাণিবিদ্যা) চঞ্চুবিশিষ্ট।

rŏs′-trŭm, *n.* **1.** (In ancient Rome) An erection for speaking in the

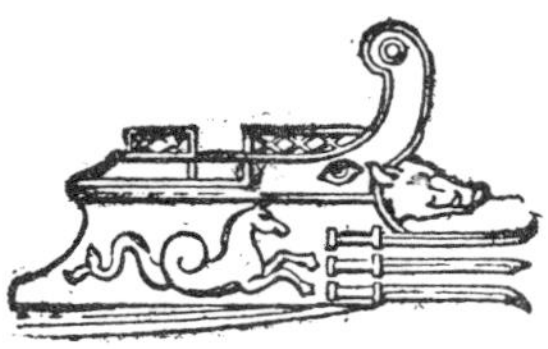

Prow armed with Rostrum.

forum ; প্রাচীন রোমের হট্টস্থানস্থিত বক্তৃতামঞ্চ। [এই মঞ্চ শত্রুপোত-সমূহের চঞ্চ্বাকৃতি মুখে পরিশোভিত থাকিত বলিয়া এই নাম।] **2.** A stage for public speaking ; বক্তৃতামঞ্চ, বক্তৃতা-পীঠ, বক্তৃতা বেদীকা। **3.** (*Rom. Antiq.*) The beak of a war galley ; রণতরীর মুখ। **4.** The beak or bill of a bird or anything resembling it ; চঞ্চুবৎ কোন কিছু।

rŏs′-ū-lāte, *adj.* **1.** (*Bot.*) Arranged in the form of rosettes ; (উদ্ভিদ্‌বিদ্যা) ক্ষুদ্রগোলাপবৎশিক্ষস্ত।

rōs′-ȳ, *adj.* **1.** Resembling a rose ; blooming ; blushing ; গোলাব তুল্য ; ফুটফুটে ; সরমরক্তিম, লজ্জারুণ। **2.** Rose-coloured; rose-red; গোলাবী রংএর ; গোলাবরক্ত। **3.** Rose-scented ; গোলাপগন্ধ, গোলাপসুরভিত। **4.** Strewn with roses ; গোলাপ-কুসুমাস্তৃত, গোলাপপুষ্পাস্তৃত। **5.** Bright; gladsome ; as, *rosy* hours ; উজ্জ্বল ; আনন্দজনক, প্রফুল্ল। **Rosy-bosomed**—গোলাপপুষ্পস্তনী। **Rosy cross**—খৃষ্টীয় তান্ত্রিক সম্প্রদায়, (Rosicrucian) দিগের চিহ্নস্বরূপ মণ্ডলমধ্যস্থ অথবা গোলাপপুষ্পভূষিতাগ্র ক্রুশ **Rosy drop**—Same as ROSE-DROP. **Rosy-fingered**—গোলাবাঙ্গুলীবিশিষ্ট। **Rosy-tinted**—গোলাপবর্ণ।

rŏt, *n.* & *interj.* **1.** Putrefaction ; decay ; পচন, পচা ; ক্ষয়। **2.** A fatal disease which attacks sheep and other animals ; মেষ প্রভৃতির রোগ বিশেষ। **3.** A disease of the potato ; আলুর রোগ বিশেষ। **4.** Nonsense ; twaddle ; as, do not talk *rot* ; ছাইভস্ম ; বাজে কথা। **5.** (*Cricket, war,* etc.) A series of rapid break down on one side ; কোন পক্ষে বার বার দ্রুত পরাজয়। ***Interj.*** Nonsense ; ছাইভস্ম ! মাথামুণ্ডু ! **Dry rot**—বায়ুশূন্য স্থানে থাকা হেতু ছত্রাকজনিত কাষ্ঠক্ষয় ; (লক্ষণায়) অজ্ঞাতসারে নৈতিক বা মানসিক অপকর্ষ।

rŏt, *v. i.* & *t.* **1.** To putrefy ; to become decomposed ; পচা ; গলিত হওয়া। **2.** (*Fig.*) To perish gradually ; ধীরে ধীরে ক্ষয়প্রাপ্ত হওয়া। **3.** (*Slang*) To spoil ; as, to *rot* all plan ; (ইতর ভাষায়) নষ্ট করা। **4.** (*Slang*) To mock severely ; (ইতর ভাষায়) তীব্র বিদ্রূপ করা। ***Verb t.*** To cause to rot ; পচান, গলিত করা। **Rot-gut**—(*Noun*) নিকৃষ্ট বীয়র বা অপর মদ্য। (*Adj.*) নিকৃষ্ট, পাকস্থলীর পক্ষে অনিষ্টকর।

rō′-tă, *n.* **1.** Same as ROSTER. **2.** A list of school-boys, soldiers, etc. ; বিদ্যালয়ের ছাত্র, সৈন্য, প্রভৃতির তালিকা। **3.** (*R. C. Ch.*) The supreme court of justice ; (also called *Rota Romana*) ; (রোমান ক্যাথলিক ধর্মসংঘ) সর্ব্বোচ্চ বিচারালয়।

rō′-tă-rȳ, *adj.* & *n.* Having a motion on its axis ; ঘূর্ণনশীল, ভ্রাম্যমাণ, চক্রাবর্ত্তী। ***Noun.*** A rotary machine ; ঘূর্ণনশীল যন্ত্র।

rō′-tāte, *adj.* (*Bot.*) Wheel-shaped ; (উদ্ভিদ্‌বিদ্যা) শকটচক্রাকৃতি।

rō′-tāte, *v. i.* & *t.* **1.** To turn or move round on a centre ; আবর্ত্তিত হওয়া, ভ্রাম্যমাণ হওয়া, ঘুরা। **2.** To do anything in rotation ; to leave office and be succeeded by another ; পর্য্যায়ক্রমে কোন কিছু করা ; কার্য্যত্যাগের পর অন্য লোকের সেই কার্য্যে নিযুক্ত হওয়া। ***Verb t.*** **1.** To cause to revolve on a centre or axis ; আবর্ত্তিত করা, ঘুরান, ঘূর্ণিত করা। **2.** To cause to take or change in turn ; as, to *rotate* men in office ; পর্য্যায়ক্রমে গ্রহণ বা পরিবর্ত্তন করান। **–ta-tive, –ta-to-ry, –tat′-a-ble,** *adjs.* **Rotatory motion**—ভ্রমণ (ব্রজঃ হিন্দু)।

rō-tā′-tion, *n.* **1.** The act of rotating ; ভ্রমণ, আবর্ত্তন (সাঃ পঃ), পরিভ্রমণ (হিঃ কোঃ), ঘূর্ণন, ব্যাসপরিভ্রমণ, চক্রাবর্ত্ত, চক্রভ্রমণ, চক্রাবর্ত্তন। **2.** Regular succession ; নির্দ্দিষ্ট কালের পর পুনঃ পুনঃ আগমন, পর্য্যায়ক্রমে আগমন, পর্য্যায়বৃত্তি। **3.** (*Agri.*) The cultivation of different kinds of crop each year for a certain period to prevent the exhaustion of soil (also *rotation of crop*) ; ভূমির উৎপাদিকা শক্তি অব্যাহত রাখার জন্য প্রতি-বর্ষে বিভিন্ন প্রকার শস্যের চাষ, শস্যাবর্ত্তন। **By rotation**—পর্য্যায়-ক্রমে। **Period of rotation**—পরিভ্রমণকাল (হিঃ কোঃ)।

rōt′-ă-tor (-têr), *n.* **1.** One that rotates ; আবর্ত্তক। **2.** (*Anat.*) A muscle which gives circular motion ; (শারীরসংস্থানবিদ্যা) চক্রগতি-বিধায়ক পেশী, আবর্ত্তকপেশী। **3.** A revolving apparatus or part ; আবর্ত্তক যন্ত্র বা যন্ত্রাংশ।

rotch (rŏch), **rotche** (rŏch), *ns.* The little auk ; উত্তরসাগরচর পক্ষিবিশেষ।

rōte, *n.* Unintelligent memory; অর্থ না বুঝিয়া মুখস্থ, তোতার মত মুখস্থ। **To learn by rote**—অর্থ না বুঝিয়া মুখস্থ করা, তোতার মত মুখস্থ করা।

rō'-ti-fêr, *n.* One of the wheel-animalcules; চক্রাবর্ত্তী কীটাণু।

rō-tif'-êr-ă, *n.* Wheel-animalcules; চক্রাবর্ত্তী কীটাণু, ঘূর্ণকীট (সাঃ পঃ)।

rō'-ti-fŏrm, *adj.* Shaped like a wheel; চক্রাকৃতি।

rō'-tŏr, *n.* The rotating or revolving part of a dynamo, motor, etc.; বিজলীজনক, গতিসঞ্চারক প্রভৃতি যন্ত্রের ঘূর্ণনশীল অংশ।

rŏt'-ten (-n), *adj.* **1.** Putrid; পচা, গলিত, সড়া। **2.** Defective through wear or exposure; as, *rotten* silk; জীর্ণ। **3.** Affected with rot; পচা-ধরা। **4.** (Of rocks etc.) Disintegrate; (প্রস্তরাদিসম্বন্ধে) বিশ্লিষ্ট, অসংহত, জীর্ণ। **5.** Weak; morally, socially or politically corrupt; "Something is *rotten* in the state of Denmark"; ক্ষীণ, শক্তিহীন; ভ্রষ্ট, নীতিভ্রষ্ট, সদাচার-ভ্রষ্ট, কলুষিত। **6.** Yielding below the feet; as, *rotten* moors; থসথসে। **7.** Rainy; as, *rotten* weather; বাদলা। **8.** (*Slang*) Beastly; abominable; as, a *rotten* team; (ইতর ভাষায়) পাশব; জঘন্য, পচা। **9.** Untrustworthy, অবিশ্বাস্য। **—ly,** *adv.* **—ness,** *n.* **Rotten borough**—See BOROUGH. **Rotten-stone**—একপ্রকার জীর্ণ চুণা পাথর—এই প্রস্তরের চূর্ণদ্বারা ধাতুনির্ম্মিত পাত্রাদি পালিশ করা হয়।

Rot'-ten-Row' (-n-rō), *n.* (Also *the Row*) A road in Hyde Park much used as a fashionable resort for driving and riding; লণ্ডনের হাইড পার্কের অন্তর্গত রথ্যা-বিশেষ। এই সুপ্রশস্ত রাজবর্ত্মে নগরীর ধনী বিলাসীরা অশ্ব ও শকটে পরিভ্রমণ করেন।

rŏt'-ter (-êr), *n.* **1.** A thing rotten with age; জীর্ণ বস্তু, জরাজীর্ণ ব্যক্তি। **2.** (*Slang*) A person who is disliked by some one; জঘন্য লোক।

rō-tŭnd', *adj.* **1.** Round; sphericial; গোলাকার; বর্ত্তুল। **2.** (*Bot.*) Circumscribed by one unbroken curve or without angles; as, a *rotund* leaf; (উদ্ভিদ-বিদ্যা) সুগোল। **3.** Plump; গোলগাল, নাদুসনুদুস। **4.** (Of mouth) Rounded while speaking; hence, grandiloquent; as, *rotund* oratory; (মুখ সম্বন্ধে) বাক্যোচ্চারণকালে গোলাকৃতিপ্রাপ্ত; অতএব, বাগাড়ম্বরপূর্ণ। **—tun'-di-ty,** *n.* The state of being rotund; বর্ত্তুলতা, পরিমণ্ডলতা, গোলত্ব, গোলাকারত্ব।

rō-tŭn'-dă, *n.* **1.** A round building; গোলাকার অট্টালিকা। (রোমনগরের Pantheon এই জাতীয় অট্টালিকা সমূহের মধ্যে সর্ব্বপ্রসিদ্ধ।) **2.** A circular apartment; গোলাকৃতি কক্ষ।

roturier, (*F.*), *n.* Plebeian; প্রাচীন রোমনগরের নিম্নশ্রেণীর লোক।

rou'-ble (rô-bl), *n.* A silver coin of Russia, worth about 2*s.* $1\frac{1}{2}$*d.*; রুশদেশে প্রচলিত রজত মুদ্রাবিশেষ—এই মুদ্রা প্রায় আমাদের দেশের ১ টাকা ।/১০ আনার সমান।

roucou, *n.* **1.** A West-Indian die-yielding tree (*Bixa Orellana*); পশ্চিমভারতীয় দ্বীপপুঞ্জে জাত রঞ্জক-পদার্থপ্রদ বৃক্ষবিশেষ। **2.** An orange dye obtained from an West-Indian tree; পশ্চিম ভারতীয় দ্বীপপুঞ্জে জাত বৃক্ষবিশেষ হইতে প্রাপ্ত কমলাবর্ণ রঞ্জক পদার্থ বিশেষ।

roue, (*F.*), *n.* A fashionable scoundrel; a rake; বিলাসী লম্পট; লম্পট।

rouge (rôzh), *n., v. t. & i.* **1.** A pigment of a red powder prepared from safflower for imparting an artificial bloom to the cheek or lips; মুখ এবং গণ্ডদেশ আরঞ্জিত করার জন্য কুসুমফুল হইতে প্রস্তুত পাটলবর্ণ চূর্ণ বিশেষ, রাগচূর্ণ। **2.** Red-oxide of iron used for polishing gold, silver, etc.; সোনা রূপা পালিশ করার জন্য প্রস্তুত একপ্রকার লোহিতবর্ণ চূর্ণ। ***Verb t. & i.*** To tint with rouge; রাগচূর্ণ দ্বারা গণ্ড, অধর, প্রভৃতি আরঞ্জিত করা বা হওয়া। **Rouge Croix**—ইংলণ্ডের প্রধান কুলাচার্য্যের অধীন কর্ম্মচারিবিশেষ [সেণ্টজর্জ্জের রক্তবর্ণ ক্রুশ হইতে এই নাম।] **Rouge Dragon**—ইংলণ্ডের প্রধান কুলাচার্য্যের অধীন কর্ম্মচারিবিশেষ [ব্রিটনদিগের শেষ রাজা Cadwaladyr এর পতাকায় অঙ্কিত রক্তবর্ণ বিকট জীব (dragon) হইতে এই নাম।] **Rouge et noir**—তাসের একপ্রকার ভাগ্য-পরীক্ষার খেলা। **Rouge-royal**—বেলজিয়ম দেশে প্রাপ্ত একপ্রকার আরক্ত মর্ম্মরপাষাণ।

rouge (rôj), *n.* **1.** (*Foot-ball*) Same as SCRUMMAGE (which see). **2.** When a ball passes behind the goal-line by a passage other than through the posts and is touched by one of the attacking sides a rouge is scored; কন্দুক স্তম্ভদ্বয়ের মধ্যবর্ত্তী পথ ব্যতিরিক্ত গমন সীমারেখা অতিক্রম করিলে যদি আক্রমণকারী দলের কেহ উহাকে স্পর্শ করে তবে যাহা হয়।

rough (rŭf), *adj., adv., n. & v. t.* **1.** Not smooth or plain; harsh to the touch; কর্কশ, আবড়োখাবড়ো, বিষম, অমসৃণ, খসখসে, খড়খড়ে; খরস্পর্শ। **2.** Not level; as, a *rough* ground; বন্ধুর, উচ্চাবচ। **3.** Violently agitated; as, a *rough* sea; বিক্ষুব্ধ, ঝটিকাবিক্ষুব্ধ; **4.** Harsh; violent; rude; কর্কশ; উগ্র; রূঢ়। **5.** Harsh to the taste; sour; as, *rough* wine; উগ্রস্বাদ; টক, অম্লস্বাদ। **6.** Harsh to the ear; discordant; শ্রুতিকটু; বিস্বর। **7.** Unfinished; as, a *rough* diamond; অপরিকর্ম্মীকৃত। **8.** Boisterous; tempestuous; as, *rough* weather; ঘোরারাবপূর্ণ; ঝটিকাময়, ঝটিকাসঙ্কুল। **9.** Wild; as, a *rough* colt ; বুনো, বন্য । 10. Not exact or precise ; as, *rough* estimate : মোটামুটি, স্থুল । 11. Shaggy ; ঝাকড়া মাকড়া, রোমশ। *Adv.* In a rough manner ; কর্কশভাবে, উগ্রভাবে, রূঢ়ভাবে, পরুষভাবে। *Noun.* 1. The quality or state of being rough : বন্ধুরতা, কর্কশতা, উচ্চাবচতা, খরস্পর্শতা, রুক্ষতা। 2. A rough ground ; বন্ধুর ভূমি 3. A rowdy ; a hooligan ; দুর্বৃত্ত ; গুণ্ডা । 4. The unfinished or the natural state ; অপরিকল্পীকৃত অবস্থা, নৈসর্গিক অবস্থা। *Verb t.* 1. To render rough ; বন্ধুর করা, আবড়ো খাবড়ো করা, খরস্পর্শ করা, খস্‌খসে করা। 2. To break in as horse ; ঘোড়া সায়েস্তা করা। **Rough'-en,** *v. t. & i.* **Rough-ly,** *adv.* 1. Unevenly ; আবড়োখাবড়োভাবে। 2. Rudely ; harshly ; রূঢ় ভাবে ; কর্কশ ভাবে। 3. Without exactness; as, *roughly* speaking মোটামুটিভাবে, স্থুল ভাবে। **Rough and ready**—কাটপোট্টা, চাঁচা ছোলা, কাটাছাঁটা ; সরাসরি। **Rough-and-tumble** — অসংযত, উচ্ছৃঙ্খল। **Rough diamond** — অপরিকল্পীকৃত হীরক ; যে ব্যক্তির বাহিরটা রুক্ষ কিন্তু অন্তরটা কোমল এবং মধুর। **Rough draft** — খসড়া। **Rough-draw**— স্থুলভাবে অঙ্কিত করা। **Rough-footed** — পালকাবৃতচরণ। **Rough-grained** — রূঢ় প্রকৃতি, রূঢ়স্বভাব। **Rough handling**—কঠোর ব্যবহার। **Rough leaf**—বীজদলের পর উৎপন্ন সর্ব্বপ্রথম পত্র। **Rough rice**—ধান্য। **Rough-rider** — যে ব্যক্তি ঘোড় সায়েস্তা করে। **Roughshod**—সকণ্টক নাল দ্বারা বাঁধা (অশ্ব)। **Rough-scuff** — অসভ্য লোক, ইতর লোক। **Rough-spoken**—রূঢ়ভাষী। **Rough work** — অত্যাচার, বলপ্রয়োগ। **A rough customer**—ক্রুরপ্রকৃতি ব্যক্তি, বে-আড়া লোক। **In the rough**—In the crude state; অসংস্কৃত অবস্থায়, অশোধিত অবস্থায়। **Rough-cast** (*Verb t.*) — খসড়া করা, প্রথম নক্সা করা ; চূণা এবং কঙ্কর দ্বারা আস্তর করা। (*Noun*) অপরিকল্পীকৃত আদর্শ ; চূণা ও কঙ্করের একপ্রকার আস্তর। **Rough-dry** — (*Verb t.*) ইস্ত্রী না করিয়া তাড়াতাড়ি শুষ্ক করা। **Rough on**—Hard on ; কষ্টকর, ক্লেশকর। **Rough-hew** — পালিশ না করিয়া কাটিয়া গড়া, স্থুলভাবে গঠন করা। **To give one a lick with the rough side of one's tongue**—To reproach one severely ; তীব্র তিরস্কার করা। **To have a rough time**—To suffer hardship ; দুর্দশা ভোগ করা, দুর্গতি ভোগ করা। **To rough it**—To put up with hardship ; দুঃখ দুর্গতি সহ্য করা। **To rough one up the wrong way**—To irritate him ; কাহাকে বিরক্ত বা জ্বালাতন করা। **To rough-shod**—To pursue a violent course regardless of consequence, pain or distress it may cause to another ; অপরের ক্ষতি, দুর্গতি বা মনঃকষ্টের দিকে দৃকপাত না করিয়া কঠোর আচরণ করা, দলন করিয়া যাওয়া। **To sketch in roughly**—মোটামুটি ভাবে নক্সা করা, স্থুলভাবে নক্সা করা।

roulade, (*F.*), *n.* (*Mus.*) Quick succession of notes rythmically equivalent to one ; (সঙ্গীত শাস্ত্র) সুরের দ্রুতগতি —যাহা একমাত্রা বলিয়া গৃহীত হয়।

rou-leau' (rô-lö), *n.* 1. A roll of coins in paper ; কাগজে মোড়া মুদ্রার তাক। 2. (In dress making) A large piping or fold ; (পোষাকের) চোঙ্গাকৃতি ভাঁজ।

rou-lette' (rô-lĕt), *n.* 1. A game of chance played with a revolving disc and ball ; একপ্রকার ক্রীড়া। 2. A tool used by engravers for producing dotted work ; ফুটকী ফুটকী কাজ করার জন্য খোদাইকারগণের একপ্রকার যন্ত্র। 3. A wheeled instrument for making a dotted line ; ক্ষুদ্র ক্ষুদ্র ছিদ্রবিশিষ্ট রেখা করার জন্য এক প্রকার চক্রযন্ত্র। 4. A cylindrical object for curling hair ; চুল কোঁকড়াইবার যন্ত্র বিশেষ। 5. (*Math.*) A curve generated by a point on a rolling curve ; কোন ঘূর্ণনশীল বক্ররেখার উপরিস্থ কোন বিন্দুদ্বারা রচিত বক্র রেখা।

Rou-mā'-ni-ăn (rô-), *adj.* 1 An inhabitant of Roumania ; রুমেনিয়ার অধিবাসী। 2. The language of Roumania ; রুমেনিয়ার ভাষা।

Rou-mē'-li-ōte (rô-), *n.* A native of Roumelia ; রুমেলিয়ার অধিবাসী।

roun'-ci-văl (rown-), *n.* (Also *rouncival pea*) A large variety of pea ; একপ্রকার বড় আকারের মটর।

round (rownd), *adj.* 1. Circluar ; spherical ; globular ; বৃত্তাকার, চক্রাকার ; গোলাকার, মণ্ডলাকার, গোলাকৃতি ; বর্ত্তুল। 2. Cylindrical ; as, the *round* barrel of a gun ; চোঙ্গাকার, নলাকৃতি। 3. Having a curved form ; as, a *round* arch ; বক্রাকৃতি বক্র। 4. Plump, corpulent ; well-shaped ; "They are *round*, ruddy and handsome" ; গোলগাল, মোটাসোটা, সুগোল ; মোটা, স্থুলকায় ; সুগঠিত। 5. Not fractional ; approximately in exact units, tens, hundreds, etc. ; as, in *round* numbers ; অখণ্ড ; পূর্ণাঙ্ক। 6. Large ; as, *round* sum ; বড়, মোটা। 7. Summary ; harsh ; as, *round* proceedings ; সরাসরি ; কঠোর। 8. Quick ; brisk ; as, a *round* trot ; সত্বর ; ক্ষিপ্র, চটুল। 9. Continuous, full and open in sound ; flowing ; as, a *round* voice ; উদাত্তগম্ভীর; অনর্গল 10. Outspoken ; plain-spoken ; as, a *round* answer ; স্পষ্ট, সোজাসুজি ; স্পষ্টবাদী, উচিতবক্তা। 11. Labial; ঔষ্ঠ্য। **Round'-ish,** *adj.* **Round'-ness,** *n.* The state of being round ; গোলত্ব, বৃত্তত্ব, বর্ত্তুলতা। **Round arch**—অর্দ্ধ বৃত্তাকার তোরণ। **Round dance** — মণ্ডলাকারে নৃত্য, মণ্ডলনৃত্য। **Round face**—সুগোল বদন। **Round game**—একপ্রকার

তাস খেলা — যাহাতে অনির্দ্দিষ্টসংখ্যক ব্যক্তি যোগদান করিতে পারে। **Round hand**—একপ্রকার লিখার ছাঁচ—যাহাতে অক্ষরগুলি প্রায় খাড়াভাবে ও প্রত্যেকটী পৃথগ্‌ভাবে স্পষ্ট করিয়া লিখা হয়। **Round-head** — সপ্তদশ শতাব্দীর অন্তর্বিগ্রহ-কালীন ইংলণ্ডের পার্লেমেন্টের সভ্য (ইহারা খাটো করিয়া চুল ছাঁটিত বলিয়া এই নাম)। **Round house**—(ইতিহাস) গারদ; (আমেরিকার রেলওয়ে) এঞ্জিন-ঘর; জাহাজের কক্ষ বিশেষ। **Round shot**—গোলাকার কামানের গোলা (বর্ত্তমানে ক্বচিদ্ ব্যবহৃত হয়)। **Round shoulders**—সম্মুখের দিকে এত আনত যে পৃষ্ঠদেশ ন্যুব্জাকৃতি দৃষ্ট হয়; আনতস্কন্ধ। **Round Table**—(ক) যে প্রকাণ্ড গোলাকৃতি মারবেল পাথরের মেজের চারিদিকে রাজা আর্থার ও তদীয় বীরগণ বসিতেন। (এইরূপ মেজে উপবেশন নিবন্ধন বীরগণের মধ্যে সম্মানের তারতম্য লক্ষিত হইত না)। (খ) ঐ মেজের চারিদিকে যে সকল বীর উপবেশন করিতেন। **Round table conference**—যে বৈঠকে সভ্যগণ গোলাকার মেজের চতুর্দ্দিকে উপবেশন করেন। [এইরূপভাবে উপবিষ্ট হওয়াতে সভ্যগণের উপবেশন সম্পর্কে সম্মানের কোনরূপ তারতম্য হয় না।] **Round-top**—মাস্তুলাগ্রস্থ মঞ্চ (পূর্ব্বে গোলাকার থাকিত)। **A round nothing**—শূন্য। **A round robin**—যে আবেদনপত্র প্রভৃতি—কে আগে স্বাক্ষর করিয়াছে তাহা যাহাতে বুঝিতে পারা না যায় তজ্জন্য স্বাক্ষরকারিগণ বৃত্তাকারে নাম স্বাক্ষরিত করিয়া থাকে। **At a round rate** — Rapidly; দ্রুতবেগে। **Round-arm** or **round-hand bowlling**—(ক্রীকেট ক্রীড়ায়) হাত ভূমির সহিত সমান্তরালভাবে ঘুরাইয়া আনিয়া কন্দুক ক্ষেপণ করা। **To be round with one**—(*Rare*) To speak in an outspoken manner to one; (ক্বচিদ্ ব্যবহৃত) কাহাকেও স্পষ্টাক্ষরে বলা।

round (rownd), *n.* **1.** That which is round, as a circle, a sphere or globe; গোলাকার বস্তু, চক্র-মণ্ডল। **2.** A circle; as, a *round* of politicians; মণ্ডলী। **3.** The act of going or passing round and round a circle or a company; as, the joke made the *round* of the table; ঘুরিয়া ঘুরিয়া সকলের কাছে যাওন, চক্রভ্রমণ। **4.** The aggregate of similar acts done successively by each of a number of persons, and coming back to where the series began: thus, the playing of a card each, by a company at table is a *round*; কতিপয় সংখ্যক লোকের প্রত্যেক কর্ত্তৃক পর পর কৃত সমরূপ কার্য্যের সমষ্টি—যে সকল কার্য্য পুনরায় ঘুরিয়া যে স্থান হইতে আরব্ধ হইয়াছিল তথায় প্রত্যাবৃত্ত হয়। **5.** A series of like events recurring in continuance; যে ঘটনাবলী পুনঃ পুনঃ ঘুরিয়া আসে। **6.** (Usu. *pl.*) A walk by a guard or officer to visit the posts, sentries, etc.; the beat of a policeman, watchman, etc.; রোঁদ, অটন (বাৎস্য); গমনচক্র। **7.** The rung of a ladder; মইয়ের ধাপ বা কোয়া। **8.** A general discharge of fire-arms by a body of troops in which each soldier fires once; ammunition for firing once; as, five *rounds* were served to each soldier; কোন সৈন্যদল কর্ত্তৃক এরূপ গোলাবর্ষণ—যাহাতে প্রতি সৈনিক একবার গুলি ছোড়ে; একবার আওয়াজের জন্য গোলাবারুদ। **9.** A round dance; মণ্ডলনৃত্য। **10.** A turn or bout followed by an intermission; as, the winners in the first *round*; বাজি, বার। **11.** Revolving motion; as, the yearly *round* of the earth; আবর্ত্তন। **12.** Bounds; extent; as, in all the *rounds* of nature; সীমা; বিস্তার। **Roundsman**—ব্যবসায়ীর যে কর্ম্মচারী স্থানে স্থানে ঘুরিয়া ক্রেতা সংগ্রহ করে। **In the round**—(ভাস্কর্য্যে) পূর্ণ আকৃতিতে ক্ষোদিত। **Round of beef**—গোলভাবে কর্ত্তিত গোমাংসখণ্ড, বিশেষতঃ গরুর নিতম্ব দেশ হইতে কর্ত্তিত অংশ খণ্ড। **To go the round**—To be circulated; to be carried to the different members of an association; প্রচারিত হওয়া; কোন সমিতির বিভিন্ন সভ্যের নিকট প্রেরিত হওয়া। **To make or go one's rounds**—To travel through the whole of one's jurisdiction for discharge of duty; রোঁদ ফিরা।

round (rownd), *adv.* & *prep.* **1.** On all sides; চতুর্দ্দিকে, চারিদিকে। **2.** Circularly; বৃত্তাকারে, চক্রাকারে। **3.** In circumference; বেড়ে, ঘেরে। **4.** By circuitous course; ঘুরা পথে। **5.** To each in turn; as, to hand *round* a glass; ঘুরাইয়া ঘুরাইয়া। *Prep.* **1.** Around; চতুর্দ্দিকে, চারিদিকে। **2.** In a circular course or all parts; as, to go *round* a city; প্রদক্ষিণ করিয়া, সর্ব্বত্র। **All round**—Over the whole place; in every direction; সর্ব্বত্র; চতুর্দ্দিকে। **An all-round man**—সর্ব্বতোমুখী প্রতিভাসম্পন্ন ব্যক্তি। **To bring one round**—To restore one to health, good spirits, consciousness, or the like; আরোগ্য করা, মনে স্ফূর্ত্তি সঞ্চার করা, সংজ্ঞাসম্পাদন করা। To make one change one's opinion, or to change from one party to another; কাহারো মত পরিবর্ত্তন করান, কাহাকে এক পক্ষ ত্যাগ করিয়া অপর পক্ষ অবলম্বন করান। **To come round**—To be restored to health, good spirits, consciousness or the like; আরোগ্য লাভ করা, সংজ্ঞা লাভ করা, পুনরায় মানসিক স্ফূর্ত্তি লাভ করা। **To come or get round one**—To gain advantage by flattery or deception; তোষামোদ করিয়া কিম্বা ফাঁকি দিয়া সুবিধা করিয়া লওয়া। **To turn round**—To change one's party; পক্ষ পরিবর্ত্তন করা।

round (rownd), *v. t.* & *i.* **1.** To make round or circular; গোলাকার করা, বৃত্তাকার করা। **2.** To pass, go, or travel round; প্রদক্ষিণ করা, পরিক্রম করা। **3.** To pass round so as to go to the opposite side of a place ; as, the ship *rounded* the cape of Good Hope ; কোন স্থানের বিপরীত দিকে যাইবার জন্য ঘুরিয়া চলা। **4.** To cause to turn round ; ঘুরান। **5.** To bring into completion ; as, to *round* a career ; সমাপ্ত করা, অবসান করা। ***Verb i.*** **1.** To walk or go about ; to go the rounds ; পরিক্রম করা ; রোঁদ ফিরা। **2.** To round ; গোলাকার হওয়া। **3.** To wheel about ; ঘূর্ণিত হওয়া। **To round in**—To pull upon a slack rope which passes through one or more blocks in a direction nearly horizontal ; এক বা ততোধিক কপিকলের ভিতর দিয়া প্রায় সমানভাবে প্রসারিত শ্লথ রজ্জু ধরিয়া টানা। **To round on**—(*Colloq.*) To assail, as with reproach ; কটূক্তি বর্ষণ করা। **To round off**—To make round by trimming edges or angles ; কিনারা বা কোণ কাটিয়া গোল করা। To complete an estate etc. by securing adjoining lands ; সন্নিহিত ভূমি অধিকারভুক্ত করিয়া কোন সম্পত্তি প্রভৃতি পূর্ণ করা। To finish gracefully, as a speech, with a well-rounded period ; বক্তৃতা প্রভৃতি সরস মধুর বাক্যাবলী দ্বারা পরিসমাপ্ত করা। **To round on a person**—To behave unfaithfully to him ; কাহারও সহিত বিশ্বাসঘাতকতা করা। **To round to**—To turn the head of a ship toward the wind বাতাসের দিকে জাহাজের মুখ ফিরান। **To round up**—To collect or gather up in a round mass ; পিণ্ডাকৃতি করা। To collect together cattle etc. ; চতুর্দ্দিকে বিক্ষিপ্ত গো-মহিষাদি একত্র করা।

round (rōwnd), *v. i.* & *t.* (*Rare*) To whisper ; (কচিদ্ ব্যবহৃত) কাণে কাণে ফিসফিস করিয়া বলা।

round'-a-bout (rōwnd-ā-bōwt), *adj.* & *n.* **1.** Not direct ; ঘুরানো। **2.** Comprehensive ; ব্যাপক। **3.** Plump ; মোটাসোটা। ***Noun.*** **1.** Circumlocution ; কথার মারপেঁচ। **2.** Same as MERRY-GO-ROUND. **3.** A scene of incessant changes ; সতত পরিবর্ত্তনশীল দৃশ্য। **4.** A tight-fitting jacket worn by sailors, boys, etc. ; বালক, নাবিক প্রভৃতির একপ্রকার আঁটসাট কোর্ত্তা। **A round-about chair**—যে হাতাযুক্ত কেদারার পৃষ্ঠ গোলাকৃতি হইয়া থাকে।

roun'-dĕl (rōwn-), *n.* **1.** A round form or figure ; গোল আকৃতি বা গোলাকার মূর্ত্তি। **2.** (*Poet.*) Same as ROUNDELAY. **3.** A little disc ; ক্ষুদ্র চাকতি। **4.** A small round shield ক্ষুদ্র গোলাকৃতি ঢাল।

roun'-de-lay (rōwn-dĕ-lā), *n.* **1.** A sort of ancient song in which certain parts are repeated ; একপ্রকার প্রাচীন সঙ্গীত—যাহার নির্দ্দিষ্ট অংশ সমূহ পুনঃ পুনঃ গীত হয়। **2.** A bird's song ; পক্ষীর কাকলী। **3.** A kind of circular dance ; একপ্রকার মণ্ডলনৃত্য।

round'-ĕr (rōwnd-), *n.* **1.** One who makes rounds ; one who travels in a round course ; যে ব্যক্তি রোঁদ ফিরে ; পরিক্রমকারী। **2.** A game played with a bat and a small soft ball ; একপ্রকার ক্রীড়া।

round'-lȳ (rōwnd-), *adv.* **1.** In a round form; বৃত্তাকারে, চক্রাকারে। **2.** Openly ; plainly ; খোলাখুলিভাবে ; স্পষ্টভাবে, স্পষ্টাক্ষরে, স্পষ্টাস্পষ্টি। **3.** In a thorough-going manner; সম্পূর্ণরূপে।

roup (rôp), *v. t.* & *n.* (*Scot.*) To sell by auction ; নীলামে বিক্রয় করা। ***Noun.*** Auction ; নীলাম।

roup (rôp), *n.* A disease in poultry ; গৃহপালিত কুক্কুটাদির রোগবিশেষ।

rouse (rôz), *n.* **1.** (*Archaic*) A bumper of liquor ; toast ; পরিপূর্ণ সুরাপাত্র; কাহারো মঙ্গলকামনায় পীত মদ্য। **2.** A carousal ; মাতালের কোলাহল।

rouse (rōwz), *v. t., i.* & *n.* **1.** To startle from a lair or lurking place ; বাসগহ্বর বা গোপন স্থান হইতে ভয় দেখাইয়া বাহির করা। **2.** To awake from sleep or repose ; জাগরিত করা, জাগান। **3.** To excite to thought or action from a state of idleness, langour, stupidity or inaction ; as, to *rouse* up a people ; উদ্বুদ্ধ করা, প্রবুদ্ধ করা। **4.** To excite to action ; উত্তেজিত করা, উদ্দীপিত করা, উদ্দীপ্ত করা, সন্ধুক্ষিত করা। **5.** To agitate ; as, to *rouse* the sea ; বিক্ষুব্ধ করা, আলোড়িত করা, বিক্ষোভিত করা। **6.** To stir beer etc. while brewing ; চুয়াইবার কালে বীয়র প্রভৃতি আলোড়িত করা। ***Verb i.*** **1.** To awake from sleep or repose ; জাগা, জাগরিত হওয়া। **2.** To be excited to thought or action from a state of indolence, sluggishness or langour ; উদ্বুদ্ধ হওয়া, প্রবুদ্ধ হওয়া, উত্তেজিত হওয়া। **Rous'-ing,** *n.* **1.** Act of rousing ; জাগরণ, উদ্বোধন। **2.** A signal or call to wake ; জাগরণের জন্য আহ্বান বা সঙ্কেতধ্বনি। **A rousing fire**—জ্বলন্ত অনল। **A rousing lie**—জ্বলন্ত মিথ্যা কথা। **To rouse one self**—To bestir one's self ; মহোদ্যমে প্রবৃত্ত হওয়া

rouse (rōwz), *v. t.* (*Naut.*) To haul vigorously in ; (নৌবিদ্যা) (কাছি) সবলে টানিয়া আনা বা তোলা।

rouse (rōwz), *v. t.* To sprinkle herring with salt in curing ; শুকাইবার কালে হেরীং প্রভৃতি মাছে লবণ ছড়ান।

rous'-ĕr (rōwz-), *n.* **1.** One who, or that which, rouses ; জাগরণকারী, উদ্বোধক। **2.** An implement for stirring beer etc. while brewing ; চোলাই করার কালে বীয়র প্রভৃতি আলোড়িত করার জন্য যন্ত্রবিশেষ। **3.** An outrageous lie ; জ্বলন্ত মিথ্যাকথা।

Rous-seau'-ĭsm (rô-sä-), *n.* The theories of the French writer Jean Jacques Rousseau (1712—1778) ; ফরাসীদেশীয় গ্রন্থকার রুশোর মতবাদ। [রুশো তাহার অভিনব মতবাদ দ্বারা শিক্ষা, ধর্ম্ম, রাজনীতি, প্রভৃতি ক্ষেত্রে

যুগান্তর আনয়ন করেন। রুশোর শিক্ষা-বিজ্ঞানসম্বন্ধীয় মত তদীয় Emile নামক গ্রন্থে এবং ধর্ম্ম ও রাজনীতি সম্বন্ধীয় মতবাদ Contrat Social নামক গ্রন্থে নিবদ্ধ হইয়াছে।] **–i-an, –ish, –esque,** *adjs.* **–ist,** *n.* **–ite** *n.* & *adj.*

Roussillon, (*F.*), *n.* A red wine; লালসুরা, লোহিত মদিরা। [ফরাসীদেশের প্রাচীন Roussillon প্রদেশের নাম হইতে গৃহীত।]

rout (rowt), *n.* & *v. t.* 1. A tumultuous clamorous crowd; the rabble; কোলাহলকারী জনসংঘ; ইতর শ্রেণী। 2. The utter defeat of an army or a body of troops; the confusion and disorder attended with a defeat; সম্পূর্ণ পরাজয়; ছত্রভঙ্গ। 3. (*Archaic*) A fashionable assembly or a large evening party; (অপ্রঃ) বিলাসী জনগণের সম্মিলনী, বিরাট সান্ধ্যসম্মিলনী। 4. An assemblage of three or more persons to do an unlawful act; কোন বেআইনী কার্য্য করার জন্য তিন বা ততোধিক ব্যক্তির সম্মিলন, বেআইনী-জনতা। 5. Riot; disturbance of the peace; tumult; হাঙ্গামা; শান্তি-ভঙ্গ; তুমুল কোলাহল। ***Verb t.*** To put to rout; সম্পূর্ণরূপে পরাজিত করা, ছত্রভঙ্গ করা। **Rout-cake**—বিরাট সান্ধ্যসম্মিলনীতে ভোজনের জন্য প্রস্তুত একপ্রকার সুমিষ্ট এবং উপাদেয় পিষ্টক। **Rout-seat**—বিরাট প্রীতিসম্মিলনীতে আগন্তুকগণের উপবেশনের জন্য একপ্রকার দীর্ঘ আসন।

rout (rowt), *v. i.* & *t.* To turn up with the snout; প্রলম্বিত মুখ দ্বারা উল্টান। ***Verb t.*** 1. To root up; উন্মূলিত করা, উপড়াইয়া ফেলা। 2. To scoop out; খুঁড়িয়া খুঁড়িয়া তুলিয়া ফেলা। **To rout out**—To discover; বাহির করা, আবিষ্কার করা। To turn or bring out by force; জোর করিয়া বাহির করা, টানিয়া আনা।

route (rôt), *n.* 1. A way; পথ, গমন-পথ। 2. (*Mil.*) A marching order; অভিযানের আদেশ। **To give, get the route**—To give or receive orders to march or to quit one station for another; যুদ্ধযাত্রার জন্য বা এক আড্ডা হইতে অন্য আড্ডায় যাইবার জন্য আদেশ দেওয়া বা পাওয়া।

rou-tine′ (rô-tēn), *n.* 1. The round or daily course of business or official duties; নিত্যকর্ম্ম, নিয়মিত কার্য্যের ব্যবস্থা। 2. Any regular practice or course of action adhered to from mere force of habit; অভ্যাসমূলক নিত্যক্রিয়া, গতানুগতিকতা। 3. (*Attrib.*) Of mechanical character; as, *routine* duties; নিত্যনৈমিত্তিক, গতানুগতিক।

roux, (*F.*), *n.* A material made of melted butter and flour for thickening soup; ঝোল প্রভৃতি গাঢ় করার জন্য ঘৃত ও ময়দার মিশ্র বিশেষ।

rōve, *v. i., t.* & *n.* 1. To wander over; ভ্রমণ করা, বিচরণ করা। 2. (*Angling*) To troll with live bait; জ্যান্ত টোপ নড়কাইয়া ছিপে মাছ ধরা। ***Verb t.*** 1. To wander over or through; ভ্রমণ করা, বিচরণ করা, পর্য্যটন করা। 2. To plough into ridges by turning one furrow upon another; আল তুলিয়া কর্ষণ করা। ***Noun.*** Wandering; ভ্রমণ, বিচরণ, পর্য্যটন।

rōve, *n.* & *v. t.* A roll of wool, cotton, etc. drawn out and slightly twisted; ঈষৎ পাকানো তুলা, পশম, প্রভৃতির লুটি। ***Verb t.*** To form into roves; তুলা, পশম, প্রভৃতি পিজিয়া সুতা কাটার উপযোগী অবস্থায় আনা।

rōv′-ēr, *n.* 1. A mark or target; লক্ষ্য, শরব্য। 2. A wanderer; পর্য্যটন-কারী, বিচরণকারী। 3. A pirate; জলদস্যু, বোম্বেটে। 4. (*Croquet*) A ball that has passed through all the hoops; (ক্রোকে খেলায়) যে কন্দুক সমস্ত চক্রের ভিতর দিয়া অতিক্রম করিয়াছে।

row (rō), *v. t., i.* & *n.* 1. To impel as a boat or vessel along the surface of water by oars; দাঁড়টানা। 2. To carry a person in a boat propelled by oars; দাঁড়ের নৌকায় নেওয়া। ***Verb i.*** 1. To labour with oars; দাঁড় টানা। 2. To be moved by oars; দাঁড়ে চলা, দাঁড় দ্বারা চালিত হওয়া। ***Noun.*** An excursion taken in a boat with oars; দাঁড়ের নৌকায় বিচরণ। **Row-boat**—দাঁড়ের নৌকা। **Row-ports**—ক্ষুদ্র পোতাদির জলসীমার নিকটবর্ত্তী কোটরসমূহ। **Rowed of all**—দাঁড় টানা বন্ধ করার জন্য আদেশ। **To row dry**—জল না ছিটকাইয়া দাঁড় টানা; শাস্তিস্বরূপ শূন্যে দাঁড় টানা।

row (rō), *n.* 1. A series of persons and things arranged in a continued line; সারি, শ্রেণী, পংক্তি, কাতার, রাজি। 2. A line of houses; গৃহপংক্তি, ভবনশ্রেণী। **A hard row to hoe**—(*U. S.*) A difficult task; (মার্কিণ যুক্তরাজ্যে) শক্ত কাজ। **A row of pins**—অকিঞ্চিৎকর বস্তু, নগণ্য জিনিষ।

row, *n.* & *v. t.* A riotous noisy disturbance; গোলমাল, হাঙ্গামা। ***Verb t.*** 1. To involve in a quarrel or disturbance; গোলমাল বাঁধান, হাঙ্গামা বাঁধান। 2. To scold abusively; as, he will *row* you well if you do not keep your word; ধমকান, তিরস্কার করা। **Row′-ing,** *n.* **To make or kick up a row**—To raise a noise; গোলমাল বাঁধান, হাঙ্গামা বাঁধান। **A row royal**—তুমুল কাণ্ড।

row′-ăn, *n.* The mountain ash or its scarlet berry; পার্ব্বত্য আঁশ বৃক্ষ বা উহার লাল ফল।

row′-dē-dow, *n.* Uproar; সোর-গোল, হল্লা।

row′-dy̆, *n.* & *adj.* A riotous turbulent fellow; হাঙ্গামাকারী লোক, ষণ্ডা, দাঙ্গাবাজ লোক। ***Adj.*** Riotous; হাঙ্গামাকারী, দাঙ্গাবাজ। **–ish,** *adj.* **–ism,** *n.*

row'-ĕl, *n.* & *v. t.* **1.** The little star like wheel of a spur ; অশ্বারোহীর পাদুকাসংলগ্ন কাঁটাতে সংবদ্ধ নক্ষত্রাকৃতি চক্র। **2.** A little ring or wheel on a horse's bit ; অশ্বের খলীনের উপরি ক্ষুদ্র আংটা বা চক্র। **3.** A roll of horse-hair or silk to pass through the flesh of horses to discharge humours answering to a seton in surgery ; পুষ প্রভৃতি বাহির করার জন্য অশ্বের মাংসের ভিতর প্রবিষ্ট অশ্ব লোম বা পশমের গুচ্ছ। *Verb t.* To pierce the skin of horses and insert a roll of horse-hair or silk ; অশ্বের চর্ম্ম ভেদ করিয়া মাংসের ভিতর অশ্ব লোম বা রেশমের গুচ্ছ প্রবিষ্ট করা।

row'-lock (rö-lŏk), *n.* A contrivance in the gunwale of a boat for resting and holding the oar when rowing; নৌকার পার্শ্বস্থ দাঁড় আটকাইবার খাঁজ বা শঙ্কুদ্বয়, দাঁড় বাঁধিবার কীলক।

Rŏx'-burghe (-bêrg), *n.* A style of book-binding in which the back is plain leather with gilt letters and sides of cloth or paper, the top gilt-edged and uncut front and bottom ; এক ধরণের পুস্তক বাঁধাই—যাহাতে পিঠে চামড়া থাকে এবং তদুপরি স্বর্ণাক্ষর অঙ্কিত থাকে এবং কাগজ বা কাপড়ের উপরের প্রান্ত স্বর্ণরঞ্জিত ও সম্মুখ ও নিম্ন প্রান্ত অকর্ত্তিত থাকে।

roy'-al, *adj.* & *n.* **1.** Pertaining to a king ; রাজকীয়। **2.** Becoming a king ; princely ; রাজসমুচিত ; রাজযোগ্য। **3.** Patronised or founded by royalty ; as, *Royal* Society ; রাজপ্রতিষ্ঠিত, রাজাকর্তৃক পৃষ্ঠপোষিত। **4.** Splendid ; as, *royal* reception ; big ; as, *royal* Bengal tiger ; জাঁকালো, জাঁকজমকশালী, রাজভোগ্য ; প্রকাণ্ড। ***Noun.*** **1.** (*Colloq.*) A member of royal familiy ; (চলিত ভাষায়) রাজপরিবারভুক্ত ব্যক্তি, রাজপরিবারের লোক। **2.** A large kind of paper (24″×19″ for writing and 25″×20″ for printing) ; একপ্রকার বৃহদায়তনের কাগজ। **3.** (*Naut.*) A square sail spread immediately above the top-gallant sail ; (নৌ-বিদ্যা) জাহাজের মাস্তুলের চতুর্থ বংশের উপর প্রসারিত পাইল। **4.** (*Pl.*) The first regiment of foot of the British army ; ব্রিটিশ সৈন্যদলের প্রথম পদাতিক সৈন্য। **5.** One of the shoots of a stag's horn ; হরিণ-শৃঙ্গের শাখা। **6.** A stag of eight years or more ; অষ্টবর্ষ বা তদধিক বয়স্ক হরিণ। **–ly,** *adv.* **Royal Academy**—১৭৬৮ খৃঃ অব্দে লণ্ডন নগরীতে চিত্র, ভাস্কর্য্য এবং ক্ষোদনশিল্পের উন্নতির জন্য প্রতিষ্ঠিত সমিতিবিশেষ। **Royal Academy of Music**—সঙ্গীতবিদ্যার উন্নতির জন্য লণ্ডন নগরীতে প্রতিষ্ঠিত সঙ্গীত-সংঘবিশেষ। **Royal-antler**—মৃগশৃঙ্গের তৃতীয় শাখা। **Royal Army Medical Corps**—ইংলণ্ডের সামরিক বৈদ্যসংঘ। **Royal assembly**—রাজসভা। **Royal assent**—See ASSENT. **Royal Asiatic Society**—এসিয়াখণ্ডের প্রাচীন সাহিত্য, পুরাতত্ত্ব সম্বন্ধীয় আলোচনার জন্য লণ্ডন নগরীতে প্রতিষ্ঠিত সম্প্রদায়বিশেষ। **Royal Astronomical Society**—১৮২০ খৃষ্টাব্দে লণ্ডন নগরীতে প্রতিষ্ঠিত জ্যোতিষিকতত্ত্বানুসন্ধানসমিতি। এই সমিতি ১৮৩১ খৃঃ অব্দে রাজসনন্দ প্রাপ্ত হয়। **Royal audience assembly** — রাজদরবার। **Royal-burgh** — রাজা হইতে সাক্ষাৎসম্বন্ধে সনন্দপ্রাপ্ত স্বায়ত্ত শাসনের অধিকারপ্রাপ্ত নগরী। **Royal-blue** — একপ্রকার সমুজ্জ্বল নীলবর্ণ রঞ্জকপদার্থ **Royal bounty**—যুদ্ধে নিহত বা সাংঘাতিকরূপে আহত সৈনিক কর্ম্মচারিগণের স্ত্রীগণের সাহায্যার্থ ভাণ্ডারবিশেষ। **Royal charter**—রাজকীয় সনন্দ। **Royal City**—রাজধানী। **Royal commission**—কোন গুরুতর রাজনৈতিক বা সামাজিক ব্যাপার সম্বন্ধে অনুসন্ধানের জন্য নৃপতি কর্তৃক মনোনীত বিশেষজ্ঞগণদ্বারা গঠিত সমিতিবিশেষ। এই বৈঠকের সভ্যগণের অনুসন্ধানফল অবলম্বনে তৎ তৎ বিষয়ে আইন বিধিবদ্ধ হইয়া থাকে। **Royal edict**—রাজশাসন, অনুশাসন, শাসনবাণী। **Royal Family**—ইংলণ্ডের রাজপরিবার। **Royal-glass**—বিচিত্র কাচ **Royal Hospital**—পীড়িত সৈনিকদিগের চিকিৎসার জন্য ইংলণ্ডের অন্তঃপাতী Chelsea নামক স্থানে ১৬৯৪ খৃঃ অব্দে প্রতিষ্ঠিত আরোগ্যশালা। **Royal household** — রাজপ্রাসাদের কর্ম্মচারিবর্গ। **Royal Mail Steam Packet Company**—পশ্চিম-ভারতীয় দ্বীপপুঞ্জে ডাক বহনের জন্য জাহাজ কোম্পানী। **Royal mast**—জাহাজের পাটাতন হইতে মাস্তুলের চতুর্থ বিভাগ। **Royal Naval Reserve**—বাণিজ্য জাহাজের কর্ম্মচারী এবং মাল্লাগণ কর্তৃক গঠিত নৌসেনাদল সম্প্রদায়বিশেষ। **Royal Oak**—১৪০-১৫০ টনের সুবৃহৎ ব্রিটিশ রণপোতবিশেষ। **Royal road**—রাজপথ ; প্রশস্ত উপায়, সোজা রাস্তা। **Royal Society, Royal Society of London for improving Natural Knowledge**—লণ্ডন নগরীর বিশ্ববিখ্যাত বৈজ্ঞানিক তত্ত্বানুসন্ধান-সমিতি। এই সমিতি ১৬৬২ খৃঃ অব্দে দ্বিতীয় চার্লস হইতে প্রথম সনন্দ প্রাপ্ত হন। এই সমিতির সভ্যগণের নামের শেষে F. R. S. উপাধি সংযোজিত হইয়া থাকে। মৌলিক বৈজ্ঞানিক তত্ত্বের আবিষ্কর্ত্তৃগণই কেবল এই পরমসম্মানজনক উপাধি লাভের অধিকারী। এই সমিতির সভ্য সংখ্যা ৪৫০। ব্রিটিশ গভর্ণমেণ্ট বৈজ্ঞানিক গবেষণার উন্নতিকল্পে সমিতির জন্য বার্ষিক ৬০,০০০ টাকা বৃত্তি মঞ্জুর করিয়াছেন। এই সমিতি হইতে প্রকাশিত পত্রিকার নাম Philosophical Transaction. সম্প্রতি রামানুজ নামক জনৈক ২৬ বর্ষীয় মান্দ্রাজী যুবক কেম্ব্রিজ বিশ্ববিদ্যালয়ের উচ্চ গণিতে অপূর্ব্ব কৃতিত্বের পরিচয় দিয়া ভারতবাসীদের মধ্যে প্রথম F. R. S. রূপ জয়টীকা ললাটে ধারণ করিয়াছেন। **Royal Society of Edinburgh**—১৭৪৪ খৃষ্টাব্দে এডিনবরা নগরীতে প্রতিষ্ঠিত পরিষদ্‌বিশেষ। এই পরিষদের দুইটী শাখা আছে। একটীতে সাহিত্য ও অপরটীতে বিজ্ঞান সম্বন্ধে আলোচনা ও গবেষণা হইয়া থাকে। **Royal symbol**—রাজচিহ্ন। **Royal**

yard — মাস্তুলের সহিত আড়ভাবেস্থিত পাইলদণ্ড। **The Royal Institution of Great Britain**—বিজ্ঞানের উন্নতি এবং বৈজ্ঞানিক শিক্ষার বিস্তারের জন্য ১৮০০ খৃঃ অব্দে লণ্ডন নগরীতে প্রতিষ্ঠিত বিজ্ঞান-পরিষদ্‌বিশেষ।

roy'-al-ist, *n.* **1.** An adherent to a king; a supporter of kingly government; রাজপক্ষভুক্ত ব্যক্তি; রাজতন্ত্রশাসনের পক্ষপাতী ব্যক্তি। **2.** (*Cap.*) One who supported king (Charles I.) in the Civil war (1642-1651); (১৬৪২-১৬৫১ খৃষ্টাব্দের) অন্তর্বিগ্রহকালে যে ব্যক্তি রাজার (প্রথম চার্লসের) পক্ষ সমর্থন করিয়াছিলেন। **3.** (*Cap.*) An adherent to the Bourbon family after the first French Revolution; প্রথম ফরাসী বিপ্লবের উত্তরকালে বুরবোঁ রাজপরিবারের পক্ষভুক্ত ব্যক্তি। **–ism,** *n.* **–is'-tic,** *adj.*

roy'-al-ty, *n.* **1.** The office or dignity or power of king and queen; রাজপদ, নরেন্দ্রত্ব, রাজগৌরব, রাজশক্তি। **2.** The person of a king; রাজা। **3.** Members, of a royal family; রাজপরিবারভুক্ত ব্যক্তিগণ, রাজার পরিবারবর্গ। **4.** Domain; "The *royalty* of the modern comic dramatists"; রাজ্য। **5.** (*Obs.*) An emblem of royalty; (অপ্রঃ) রাজচিহ্ন। **6.** Share or portion due to a king or to a superior, as to an inventor for the use of his patent, or to a landowner for privilege of working mines on his estate; the sum paid to a patentee for the use of his patent or to an author for each copy of his book sold; নজর, সেলামী; পেটেণ্ট ব্যবহারের জন্য পেটেণ্টের স্বত্বাধিকারীকে বা কোন গ্রন্থকারকে প্রতি খণ্ড পুস্তক বিক্রয়ের জন্য যে টাকা দেওয়া হয়।

roy'-ster-er, *n.* More correctly ROISTERER (which see.)

Roys'-ton-crow (-crō), *n.* A hooded crow; একপ্রকার ঝুঁটিওয়ালা কাক। [ইংলণ্ডের Royston নামক নগরের নাম হইতে গৃহীত।]

rub, *v. t., i.* & *n.* **1.** To move or pass along, or over the surface of with pressure or friction; ঘষান, বুলান, ঘর্ষণ করা। **2.** To scour or polish or brighten by rubbing; ঘষিয়া মাজিয়া পালিশ করা, ঘষিয়া মাজিয়া চক চকে করা। **3.** To smear; as, to *rub* anything with oil; মাখা, মালিস করা। **4.** To remove by rubbing; ঘষিয়া ফেলা। **5.** To irritate; to tease; জ্বালাতন করা; ক্ষেপান। **6.** To stimulate; to stir up; "You should *rub* him on the point for his recollection becomes misty"; চেতাইয়া দেওয়া, উস্‌কাইয়া দেওয়া; জাগাইয়া দেওয়া। ***Verb i.*** **1.** To move along the surface of a body with pressure; to grate; ঘসড়াইয়া যাওয়া; কড়কড় করা। **2.** To move or pass with difficulty; as, he can just manage to *rub* along; কষ্টে চলা। **3.** To admit of rubbing; ঘর্ষণসহ হওয়া। ***Noun.*** **1.** The act of rubbing; ঘর্ষণ, মালিস। **2.** Hindrance; pinch; as, the *rubs* and worries of life; বাধা, প্রতিবন্ধক, বিঘ্ন; অভাব, অর্থকষ্ট। **3.** An unevenness or inequality of surface, as of the ground in the game of bowls; a fault; ভূতলের অসমতা বা উচ্চাবচতা, বিশেষতঃ কন্দুক ক্রীড়ায় ভূমির উচ্চাবচতা; দোষ, খুঁত। **4.** Sarcasm; taunt; বিদ্রূপ; ব্যঙ্গ। **Rub-stone**—শাণ পাথর। **Rub of or on the green**—(গোলক ক্রীড়ায়) গতিশীল কন্দুকের বিরুদ্ধে আকস্মিক বাধা। **There is the rub, Here lies the rub**—That is the point which causes me trouble; এই জায়গায়ইতো গোল, এইতো মুস্কিল। **To rub down**—To comb or curry a horse; to clean by rubbing; ঘোড়ার শরীর আঁচড়ান, ঘোড়ার শরীর ডলা, খড়রা মরা; ঘষিয়া পরিষ্কার করা। (*Colloq.*) To search a person by passing the hand all over the body; (চলিত ভাষায়) শরীরের সকল স্থানে হাত বুলাইয়া তল্লাস করা। **To rub in**—(Of colours etc.) To apply by rubbing; ঘষিয়া শুষ্ক রঙ্গ প্রভৃতি লাগান। To draw a picture in this way; কোন কিছুতে শুষ্ক রঙ্গ ঘষিয়া ছবি আঁকা। To emphasize by repeating; পুনরায় বলিয়া কোন কথার উপর জোর দেওয়া। **To rub it**—To remove by rubbing; ঘষিয়া ফেলা। **To rub on or along**—To manage to get on somehow; কোনপ্রকারে চালান, কষ্টেসৃষ্টে চালান। **To rub out**—To erase; ঘষিয়া তোলা। **To rub shoulders with**—To associate with; কাহারো সহিত মিশা, কাহারও সহিত ঘনিষ্ঠ সংস্রবে আসা। **To rub the wrong way**—To irritate; জ্বালাতন করা, উত্ত্যক্ত করা। **To rub up**—To refresh; to revive; to stimulate; to recall to mind; সতেজ করা; পুনরায় জাগান; চেতান; পুনরায় মনে আনা। **To rub upon**—To tease or irrirate by sarcastic remark; ক্ষ্যাপান, চিড়ান।

rub'-a-dub, *n.* & *v. i.* The roll of a drum; দুন্দুভিধ্বনি। ***Verb i.*** To make the rolling sound of a drum; দুন্দুভিধ্বনি করা।

rub'-ber (-ėr), *n.* & *v. t.* **1.** One who, or that which, rubs; ঘর্ষণকারী, ঘর্ষক। **2.** An instrument used in rubbing; মার্জ্জনী, ঘর্ষণী। **3.** A whetstone; শাণ পাথর। **4.** A coarse file or the rough part of it; একপ্রকার মোটা দানাদার উখা বা উহার বন্ধুর অংশ। **5.** An eraser, esp. of caoutchouc; পেন্সিলের লেখা তোলার জন্য রবার খণ্ড। **6.** Caoutchouc or India-rubber; রবর। **7.** A Turkish-bath attendant; যে ব্যক্তি তুরস্ক স্নানাগারে স্নানার্থ আগত ব্যক্তিগণের শরীর ডলিয়া দেয়। **8.** (*Pl.*) Overshoes (esp.

of Indian-rubber); জুতার উপরে পরিবার আবরণ (বিশেষতঃ রবরের তৈরী)। **9.** A pair of light shoes with rubber soles; রবারের তলির হালকা জুতা। **10.** The cushion of an electric machine; তাড়িতযন্ত্রের গদি। **11.** (In gaming) Two games out of the three deciding the contest; (ক্রীড়ায়) যে তিনবার ক্রীড়া দ্বারা জয়পরাজয় নিশ্চিত হয় তন্মধ্যে দুইবারের খেলা। **12.** An uneven place in a bowling green; বল খেলার মাঠে উচ্চাবচ স্থান। **13.** Hence, impediment; difficulty; misfortune; অন্তরায়, কষ্ট, টানাটানি; অনটন; দুর্ভাগ্য। ***Verb t.*** To coat with rubber; রবার দ্বারা আচ্ছাদিত করা। **–ize,** *v. t.* **Rubber-cloth**—রবার দ্বারা আচ্ছাদিত কাপড়। **Rubber-plant, Rubber-tree** — রবার গাছ। **Rubber-stamp**—রবার ষ্ট্যাম্প, রবরের উপর ক্ষোদিত নামের মোহর।

rub'-bish(-ĭsh), *n.* & *interj.* **1.** The mixed materials of ruined or crumbling building; ভগ্ন বা জীর্ণ অট্টালিকার কাষ্ঠ, ইষ্টক, প্রভৃতি। **2.** Refuse; জঞ্জাল, আবর্জ্জনা, ওঁছলা। ***Interj.*** Nonsense; মাথামুণ্ড, ছাইভস্ম। **–ing, –y,** *adjs.* Trashy; অসার অকিঞ্চিৎকর। **A good riddance of a bad rubbish**—আপদ দুর হইল।

rŭb'-ble (-l), *n.* **1.** Water-worn or rough stones, broken bricks, etc. used in coarse masonry or as fill-in for walls; rubble-work; জল দ্বারা ক্ষত বা খরগাত্র প্রস্তর, ভগ্ন ইষ্টক খণ্ড, প্রভৃতি—যাহা মোটা গাঁথুনির কাজে ও দেওয়ালের ফোকর বন্ধ করার জন্য ব্যবহৃত হয়; ঐরূপ পাথরের গাঁথুনির কাজ। **2.** The upper fragmentary and decomposed portion of a mass of stone; পাষাণস্তূপের উপরিভাগস্থ খণ্ড খণ্ড প্রস্তরপূর্ণ বিশ্লিষ্ট অংশ। **3.** Water-worn stone; সলিলক্ষত প্রস্তর। **Rubble-stone** — Same as RUBBLE 1. **Rubble-work**—মশলা পাথরের গাঁথুনি; ফোকর প্রভৃতি বন্ধ করার জন্য চূণ বালির সহিত মিশ্রিত প্রস্তর খণ্ড। **–bly,** *adj.*

ru-be-fa'-ci-ĕnt (rō-bē-fā-shĭ-), *adj.* & *n.* Producing redness; লৌহিত্যজনক। ***Noun.*** A substance that causes redness of the skin not followed by blister; একপ্রকার পদার্থ—যাহা লাগাইলে চর্ম্ম লোহিত বর্ণ ধারণ করে, অথচ ফোস্কা পড়েনা, লোহিতক, কন্দুর (ঠাকুর)।

rŭ-bē-făc'-tion, *n.* The act of making the skin red; redness produced by a rubefacient; চর্ম্ম লোহিত করণ; লোহিতক প্রয়োগজনিত চর্ম্মের রক্তিমা।

rū'-bē-fȳ, *v. t.* Same as RUBIFY (which see.)

ru-bē'-ō-lă, *n.* Same as MEASLES (which see.)

Rubia Munjishta—মঞ্জিষ্ঠা (বেলঃ)।

rū'-bĭ-cĕll, –celle (-sĕl), *ns.* An orange-red precious stone; নারঙ্গবর্ণ মণিবিশেষ, নারঙ্গ রত্ন, কমলামণি।

Ru-bĭ-cŏn (rō-), *n.* A small river which separated Italy from Cisalpine Gaul; আল্পস্ পর্ব্বতের দক্ষিণদিগ্‌বর্ত্তী এবং প্রাচীন ইতালির অন্তর্ব্বর্ত্তী ক্ষুদ্র নদী। [আল্পস্ পর্ব্বতের দক্ষিণদিগ্‌বর্ত্তী গল প্রদেশ জুলিয়াস সীজরকে প্রদান করা হইয়াছিল। জুলিয়াস সীজার তাঁহার নির্দ্দিষ্ট দেশ হইতে Rubicon নদী অতিক্রম পুর্ব্বক ইতালীর ভুমিতে পদার্পণ করিলে পর তিনি ইতালীর আক্রমণকারী বলিয়া গণ্য হন।] **To cross** or **pass the Rubicon**—To take decisive step; এমন কোন কাজে প্রবৃত্ত হওয়া যাহা হইতে আর প্রত্যাবৃত্ত বা পশ্চাৎপদ হওয়ার জো নাই।

ru'-bĭ-cŭnd (rō-), *adj.* Inclining to redness; ruddy; আরক্তিম, আরক্ত, গোলাবী, রক্তাভ, রক্তিমাভ, অরুণাভ, লালাভ; লোহিত। **–cun'-di-ty,** *n.*

ru-bid'-ĭ-ŭm (rō-), *n.* A soft, silvery alkaline metal discovered by spectrum-analysis in 1860; ১৮৬০ খৃষ্টাব্দে বর্ণচ্ছত্রবিশ্লেষণের ফলে আবিষ্কৃত একপ্রকার কোমল রজতাভ ক্ষারধর্ম্মা ধাতু। [এই ধাতু Kirchhoff এবং Bunsen কর্ত্তৃক আবিষ্কৃত হয়। ইহার সাঙ্কেতিক নাম Rb.; আণবিক গুরুত্ব ৮৫·৪], রূপদক (সাঃ পঃ)।

ru-bied (rō-bĭd), *adj.* Red as a ruby; পদ্মরাগরক্ত।

ru'-bĭ-fȳ (rō-), *v. t.* To redden; লোহিতবর্ণ করা।

ru-big-ĭ-nous (rō-bĭj-ĭ-nŭs), *adj.* Rust-coloured; rusty; লৌহকলঙ্কবর্ণ, মস্তুরবর্ণ, মরচে পড়া।

ru-bi-ous (rō-bĭ-ŭs), *adj.* (*Poet.*) Resembling a ruby; ruby-coloured; পদ্মরাগনিভ; পদ্মরাগবর্ণ, পদ্মরাগরক্ত।

ru'-brĭc (rō-), *n.* **1.** Some parts of a manuscript, or printed matter, that is, or in former times usually was, printed in red; হস্তলিখিত বা মুদ্রিত পুস্তক দলিলাদির যে অংশ লাল কালীতে লিখিত বা মুদ্রিত হয় এবং পূর্ব্বকালে সচরাচর ঐবর্ণে মুদ্রিত হইত। **2.** The title or heading of a statute written in red; রক্তবর্ণ কালিতে লিখিত কোন বিধির শিরোনামা বা শীর্ষলিপি। **3.** The direction and rules for the conduct of church-service in the Prayer Book, formerly printed in red; ভজনালয়ের উপাসনার বিধি ও নিয়মনিচয়—যাহা পূর্ব্বে প্রার্থনাপুস্তকে লালবর্ণে মুদ্রিত হইত। **4.** Red; লালবর্ণ। **5.** An authoritative direction; "Let him your *rubric* and feast prescribe"; বিধান, ব্যবস্থা। **6.** (*Rare*) Red-letter entry in the calendar of saints; a calendar of saints; (কচিদ্ ব্যবহৃত) খৃষ্টীয় সিদ্ধপুরুষগণের নাম-পঞ্জীর লোহিত অক্ষরে মুদ্রিত অংশ; খৃষ্টীয় সিদ্ধপুরুষগণের নামপঞ্জী। **–bri-cal,** *adj.* **–bri-cal-ly,** *adv.*

ru-brĭ-cate, (rō-), *v. t.* To mark or distinguish with red; লোহিত বর্ণের অক্ষর দ্বারা চিহ্নিত করা বা পার্থক্য প্রদর্শন করা। **–ca'-tion, –ca-tor,** *ns.*

ru'-by̆ (rōō-), *n., adj.* & *v. t.* A beautiful and highly valued gem, a variety of corundum of various shades of red (Also called *true* or *Oriental ruby*); চুণি পাথর, পদ্মরাগ, পদ্মরাগ মণি, মাণিক (cf. মাণিক রচিত চন্দ্রসম নখপাঁতি—চণ্ডিদাসের কৃষ্ণকীর্ত্তন), লাল (হিন্দী)। [বুন্দেল হীরা রাশি আরাকানি লাল—অভ্র ও আবির (সত্যেন্দ্র নাথ দত্ত)।] [*Syn.* অরুণোপল, শোণমণি (সাঃ দঃ), শোণোপল, শোণরত্ন, রবিরত্ন, লক্ষ্মীপুষ্প, অরুণ, তরণিরত্ন, লোহিতক (শিশুঃ), সৌগন্ধিক, রঙ্গমাণিক্য, সিন্দুরমণি (কাদঃ), শোণিতোপল, পাটলোপল (শিশুঃ), অর্কোপল, সরোজরাগ (cf. পশ্চাচ্চ গারুত্মতনীলরত্নৈঃ সৌম্যেন বৈদূর্য্যসরোজরাগৈঃ—মৎস্যপুরাণ), লালরতন, লালমণি, অর্কোপল, ভাস্করপ্রিয়, কুরুবিন্দ মহামূল্য, লোহিত, কুরুবিন্দক, রত্নরাজ, রাগদৃক্, শোণাশ্ম, তাম্রাশ্ম (বৌদ্ধঃ), শৃঙ্গারী, তরুণ, রবিরত্নক (রাজ নিঃ), কুরুবিন্দ (cf. কুরুবিন্দারুণবর্ণাঃ—প্রপঞ্চঃ), মণিরাগ (a kind of) (cf. মণিরাগসমন্বিতাং সবস্ত্রাং মহিষীং দদ্যাৎ ইতি শতাতপোক্ত প্রায়শ্চিত্ত বিবরণ), রত্ননায়ক, রগযুক, রত্ন।] Arab. & Pers. *Yakut*; It. *Rubino*; Fr. *Rubis*; Dutch. *Robijin*: Germ. *Rubin*; Russ. *Rubim*; Sinhalese *Lanka-ratti*; Tam. *Kembu kallu*; Teg. *Kempu rai*]. [সংস্কৃত সাহিত্যে জবা, বন্ধুক, দাড়িম্ব-বীজ, কিংশুক, সিন্দুর, কুঙ্কুম, লাক্ষারস, গুঞ্জাফল, নাগরঙ্গ, প্রভৃতির তুল্য বর্ণ বিবিধ প্রকার পদ্মরাগ মণির উল্লেখ দৃষ্ট হয়। বর্ত্তমানকালে কপোতরক্ত-বর্ণের পদ্মরাগই সমধিক সমাদৃত হয়। যুক্তিকল্পতরুতে ব্রাহ্মণ, ক্ষত্রিয়, বৈশ্য এবং শূদ্রভেদে পদ্মরাগমণির চারি প্রকার বিভাগ করা হইয়াছে। যথা:—"মাণিক্যস্য প্রবক্ষ্যামি যথা জাতিচতুষ্টয়ম্। ব্রহ্মক্ষত্রিয়বৈশ্যাশ্চ শূদ্রশ্চাথ যথাক্রমম্॥ রক্তশ্বেতো ভবেদ্বিপ্রস্তু তিরক্তস্তু ক্ষত্রিয়ঃ। রক্তপীতো ভবেদ্বৈশ্যঃ রক্তনীলস্তথান্ত্যজ। শোণপদ্মসমাকারঃ খদিরাঙ্গারসপ্রভঃ। পদ্মরাগো দ্বিজঃ প্রোক্তশ্ছায়াভেদেন সর্ব্বদা। গুঞ্জাসিন্দূরবন্ধুকনাগরঙ্গসমপ্রভঃ। দাড়িমীকুসুমাভাসঃ কুরুবিন্দস্তু বাহুজঃ। হিঙ্গুলাভাশোকপুষ্পাভমীষৎ পীতলোহিতম্। জবালাক্ষারসপ্রায়ং বৈশ্যং সৌগন্ধিকং বি আরক্তঃকান্তিহীনশ্চ চিক্কণশ্চ বিশেষতঃ। মাংসখণ্ডসমাভাসোহন্ত্যজঃ পাপনাশনঃ॥ মাংসখণ্ডস্ত নীলগন্ধেঃ সংজ্ঞা। রত্নশাস্ত্রে শ্রেষ্ঠ পদ্মরাগের এই সকল লক্ষণ বর্ণিত হইয়াছে: যে পদ্মরাগ বালভানুর কিরণ-স্পর্শে লোহিতশিখা বমন করে—তাহা মহাগুণবান বলিয়া উক্ত হয়। যে পদ্মরাগ শতগুণ দুগ্ধে নিক্ষিপ্ত হইলে তাহাকে স্বর্বর্ণে রঞ্জিত করে—উহা অতি উৎকৃষ্ট। মহাঘোর অন্ধকারে ন্যস্ত হইলে যে পদ্মরাগ সূর্য্যের ন্যায় প্রকাশমান হয়—সেই পদ্মরাগ অতিশ্রেষ্ঠ। পদ্মকোরককে রক্ষিত হইলে যে পদ্মরাগ তৎক্ষণাৎ সেই পদ্মকলিকাকে বিকশিত করে—তাহা সর্ব্বশ্রেষ্ঠ এবং দেবগণেরও দুর্লভ। Professor Verneuil, এমোনিয়া এলাম ও ক্রোম এলাম হইতে কৃত্রিম পদ্মরাগমণি প্রস্তুতে সিদ্ধকাম হইয়াছেন। পদ্মরাগ, নীলকান্তমণি ও পুষ্পরাজ (পোখরাজ) দৃশ্যতঃ অনেকাংশে বিভিন্ন হইলেও প্রকৃতপক্ষে অভিন্ন রাসায়নিক পদার্থ। শ্যাম, ব্রহ্ম ভারতবর্ষ ও সিংহলে উৎকৃষ্ট পদ্মরাগমণি পাওয়া যায়। বোহেমিয়া-দেশে যে পদ্মরাগ পাওয়া যায়—তাহা অপেক্ষাকৃত নিকৃষ্ট।] 2. A carbuncle; a red pimple on the face; পদ্মরাগবর্ণ পৃষ্ঠাঘাত প্রভৃতি দূষিত ব্রণ; রক্তবর্ণ মুখ-ব্রণ। 3. A type smaller than nonpariel and larger than pearl; (মুদ্রণ) একপ্রকার অতি ক্ষুদ্র হরফ। 4. The colour of the ruby; redness; "And keep the natural *ruby* of your cheeks"; পদ্মরাগবর্ণ; রক্তিমা, শোণিমা। 5. (*Pl.*) The lips; অধরোষ্ঠ। 6. Red wine; লাল মদ। 7. A Brazilian bird, the males of which have a ruby-red neck; ব্রাজিলদেশীয় পক্ষিবিশেষ। [এই জাতীয় পক্ষীর কণ্ঠদেশ পদ্মরাগ তুল্য রক্তবর্ণ হইয়া থাকে।] 8. (*Pugilism*) Blood; (মল্লযুদ্ধ) রক্ত। ***Adj.*** Ruby-coloured; পদ্মরাগবর্ণ, পদ্মরাগরক্ত। ***Verb t.*** To tinge with ruby-red colour; পদ্মরাগবর্ণে রঞ্জিত করা, পদ্মরাগারুণ করা। **Ruby-and-topaz humming bird**—দক্ষিণ আমেরিকার উষ্ণাঞ্চলবাসী সুন্দর পক্ষি-বিশেষ। **Ruby-blende**—মনঃশিলা। **Ruby-glass**—রাসায়নিক প্রক্রিয়াবিশেষ দ্বারা গাঢ় লোহিতবর্ণে রঞ্জিত কাচ। **Ruby light**—আলোকচিত্রের কার্য্যে অন্ধকার কক্ষে রক্তবর্ণ কাচের ভিতর দিয়া যে আলোক পাতিত হয়। **Ruby silver**—রক্তবর্ণ খনিজবিমিশ্র রৌপ্য। **Ruby spinel** or **Spinel ruby**—একপ্রকার রক্তবর্ণ প্রস্তর—পদ্মরাগের পরিবর্ত্তে ব্যবহৃত হয়। এই প্রস্তর গোলাপপুষ্পবৎ পাটলবর্ণ হইলে ইহাকে Balas ruby, কমলালেবুর বর্ণ হইলে rubicelle এবং বেগুণি বর্ণের হইলে almandine নামে অভিহিত হয়। **Ruby-sulphur**—মনঃশিলা। **Ruby-throat**—একপ্রকার রক্তকণ্ঠ গায়ক পক্ষী; **Ruby-tail**—উদরের উপরেরদিকে উজ্জ্বল রক্তবর্ণ বিন্দুবিশিষ্ট একপ্রকার নীলাভ-হরিদ্বর্ণ কীট; বোলতা। **Ruby-tiger**—ইংলণ্ডদেশীয় সুন্দর প্রজাপতি-বিশেষ। **Ruby-wedding**—বিবাহের পঞ্চত্বারিংশৎ সাম্বৎসরিক বৎসর। **Ruby-wood** — রক্তচন্দন। **Above rubies**—Priceless; অমূল্য।

ruche, *n.* Quilted net, silk, lace or the like; পাখার ডাঁটার মত কোঁচানো জাল, রেসম, ফিতা, প্রভৃতি।

rŭck, *n.* & *v. t.* A wrinkle or plait; কোঁচ, চুনট। ***Verb t.*** To wrinkle; কোঁচান, চুনট করা।

rŭck, *n.* A common crowd or herd; লোকের ভিড়, জনতা।

rŭck'-le (-l), *n.* & *v. i.* The gargling sound esp. in the throat of dying person; ঘরঘর শব্দ, বিশেষতঃ মুমূর্ষু ব্যক্তির গলার ঘরঘর শব্দ। ***Verb i.*** To make such sound; ঐরূপ শব্দ করা।

rŭc'-tion, *n.* Disturbance; গোলমাল, হাঙ্গামা।

rŭdd, *n.* A fresh-water European fish; ইয়ুরোপদেশের নদী-জলচর মৎস্যবিশেষ।

rŭd'-der (-êr), *n.* **1.** The instrument by which a ship is steered; helm; জাহাজের হাইল; কর্ণ, অরিত্র। **2.** That which guides or governs the course; কর্ণধার, পথপরিদর্শক। **3.** (*Brewing*) A paddle for stirring malt in mash-tub; (মদ চোলাইর কার্য্যে) গামলায় জলমিশ্রিত অঙ্কুরিত যব আলোড়িত করার জন্য বৈঠা। **–less,** *adj.* **Rudder-fish**—যে সকল বিভিন্ন জাতীয় মৎস্য জাহাজের পশ্চাৎ পশ্চাৎ ছুটে।

rŭd'-dle (-l), *n.* & *v. t.* Red ochre, esp. a variety used for marking sheep; রক্তগৈরিক, বিশেষতঃ মেষের গায়ে অঙ্কনের জন্য একপ্রকার রক্তগৈরিক। ***Verb t.*** To mark or tinge with red ochre; রক্তগৈরিকদ্বারা চিহ্নিত বা রঞ্জিত করা।

rŭd'-doc (-ŏk), **–dock** (-ŏk), *ns.* The robin-redbreast; রক্তবক্ষোবিশিষ্ট ক্ষুদ্র পক্ষিবিশেষ। **Red ruddocks**—(ইতরভাষায়) স্বর্ণমুদ্রা।

rŭd'-dy (-ĭ), *adj., v. t.* & *i.* **1.** Red; reddish; লাল, রাঙ্গা; রক্তাভ, লালাভ, রক্তিম। **2.** Of a lively red or rose colour from health or from blushing; as, *ruddy* lips; লাল, লাল টুকটুকে, টুকটুকে, সরমরক্তিম, লজ্জারুণ, সরমরাগদীপ্ত, লজ্জারাগোজ্জ্বল, লজ্জাপাটল। **3.** Vivid; glowing; as, *ruddy* memories; জ্বলন্ত; জীবন্ত। ***Verb t.*** To make ruddy or red; রাঙ্গা করা, লোহিত করা। ***Verb i.*** (*Rare*) To turn red; (কচিদ্ ব্যবহৃত) লাল হইয়া উঠা। **–di-ly,** *adv.* **–di-ness,** *n.* **Ruddy goose**—চক্রবাক, চকাচকি [Syn. কোক, চক্র, রথাঙ্গাহ্বয়নামক, ভুরিপ্রেমা, দ্বন্দ্বচারী, সহায়, কান্তকামী, রাত্রিবিশ্লেষগামী, রামাবক্ষোজোপম, কামুক।]

rude (rôd), *adj.* **1.** Unformed by art, taste or skill; not nicely or delicately finished, smoothed, or polished; as, *rude* designs; *rude* sketches; শিল্পচাতুর্য্যবিহীন, অপরিষ্কৃত। **2.** Unlearned; unpolished; অশিক্ষিত; অমার্জ্জিত। **3.** Rough; impudent; uncivil; রূঢ়; ধৃষ্ট, দুর্বিনীত, গোঁয়ার; অশিষ্ট, অভদ্র, অভব্য। **4.** Unmanufactured; raw; as, the cotton in its *rude* state; স্বাভাবিক অবস্থার; কাঁচা। **5.** Sturdy; vigorous; as, *rude* health; বলিষ্ঠ, সবল, দৃঢ়িষ্ঠ; সতেজ। **6.** Insolent; as, *rude* remarks; উদ্ধত। **7.** Fierce; impetuous; as, the *rude* shock of armies; ভীষণ; প্রচণ্ড। **8.** Unpolished; inelegant; as, *rude* style; অমার্জ্জিত; অসুন্দর। **9.** Violent; rough; as, *rude* blast; প্রচণ্ড; ঝটিকাবিক্ষুব্ধ। **Rude'-ly,** *adv.* **Rude'-ness,** *n.* **Rud'-ish,** *adj.*

Ru'-des-hei-mêr (rô-dĕs-hī-), *n.* A white Rhine wine; রাইন নদীর সন্নিহিত প্রদেশে উৎপন্ন মদ্য।

ru'-dĭ-mĕnt (rô-), *n.* **1.** The beginning, foundation or first principles of anything; কোন বিষয়ের মূল, মুলতত্ত্ব, আদি বা বীজ, অঙ্কুর (হিঃ কোঃ)। **2.** (Usu. *pl.*) The elements or elementary notions of some branch of knowledge; কোন বিষয়ের প্রাথমিক পুস্তক, প্রাথমিক তত্ত্ব, প্রাথমিক সূত্র। **3.** (*Biol.*) An undeveloped organ; (জীববিজ্ঞান) অপরিণত অঙ্গ। **–men'-tal, –men'-ta-ry,** *adjs.*

rue (rô), *v. t.* & *n.* To grieve for; to repent; to lament; দুঃখ করা; অনুশোচনা করা; খেদ করা। ***Noun.*** (*Archaic*) Repentance; অনুতাপ, অনুশোচনা। **Rue'-ful,** *adj.* Causing to lament; mournful; খেদজনক, শোকজনক; বিষাদপূর্ণ, শোকপূর্ণ। **Rue'-ful-ly,** *adv.* **Rue'-ful-ness,** *n.*

rue (rô), *n.* An evergreen shrub with greenish yellow flowers; হরিদাভপীতপুষ্পপ্রসূ চিরশ্যামল গুল্মবিশেষ।

rŭ-fĕs'-cent (-ĕnt), *adj.* Reddish; রক্তাভ, লালাভ, রক্তিম।

rŭff, *n.* **1.** A kind of plaited collar or frill formerly worn round the neck by both sexes; একপ্রকার কুঁচি দেওয়া গলবেষ্টনী। **2.** A projecting or conspicuously coloured ring of feathers round bird's or beast's neck; পশু বা পক্ষীর উদ্গত এবং সমুজ্জ্বল বর্ণের পালক কিম্বা রোমের গলবেষ্টনী। **3.** A species of domestic pigeon having neck-feathers forming a ruff; একজাতীয় গৃহ কপোত।

rŭff, *n.* A bird allied to the wood-cock and sand-piper (the male has a tuft of feathers around the neck, during the breeding-season); একপ্রকার পক্ষী। [সঙ্গম ঋতুতে এই জাতীয় পুংপক্ষীর গলদেশের চতুর্দ্দিকে পালকগুচ্ছ উপজাত হয়।]

rŭff, *n.* A kind of fresh-water fish; একপ্রকার মিঠাজলের মাছ।

rŭff, *n., v. i.* & *t.* Trumping; তুরূপ করণ। ***Verb i. & t.*** To trump instead of following suit; তুরূপ করা। **To over-ruff**—তুরূপের উপর বড় তুরূপ দেওয়া।

rŭf'-fi-ăn (-ĭ-), *n.* A boisterous brutal fellow; গুণ্ডা, ষণ্ডা, গোঁয়ার। **–ism** *n.* **–ly,** *adj.*

rŭf'-fle (-fl), *v. t., i.* & *n.* **1.** To contract with plaits or folds; কোঁচান, চুনট করা। **2.** To furnish with ruffles; কুঁচি দেওয়া। **3.** To disturb the surface of; to agitate; তরঙ্গায়িত করা; আন্দোলিত করা। **4.** To disorder by disturbing a smooth or calm state; as, to *ruffle* one's heart; বিক্ষুব্ধ করা। **5.** To trouble; to irritate; উত্ত্যক্ত করা; জ্বালাতন করা। ***Verb i.*** **1.** To become irritated; উত্ত্যক্ত হওয়া, জ্বালাতন হওয়া, বিক্ষুব্ধ হওয়া। **2.** (Of wind etc.) To grow rough or turbulent; প্রচণ্ড হওয়া, ভীষণ গর্জ্জন করা। **3.** To swagger; গর্ব্বিত ভাব ধারণ করা, বুক ফুলাইয়া চলা। **3.** To act roughly; রূঢ় ব্যবহার করা ***Noun.*** **1.** A strip of plaited cambric or other fine cloth attached to one's dress ; কুঁচি-দেওয়া বা চুনট-করা বস্ত্রখণ্ড বা কামিজ প্রভৃতির বেল, কুঁচি। 2. (*Rare*) Disturbance ; commotion ; (কচিদ্-ব্যবহৃত) বিক্ষোভ ; চাঞ্চল্য। **—fler,** *n.* A bully ; a swaggerer ; গুণ্ডা ; দাম্ভিক লোক, আস্ফালনকারী ব্যক্তি। **To ruffle one's feathers** or **plumage**—(*Verb t.*) To irriate ; ক্ষুব্ধ করা, জ্বালাতন করা, উত্ত্যক্ত করা। (*Verb i.*) To get irritated ; ক্ষুব্ধ হওয়া, উত্ত্যক্ত হওয়া।

ru'-fous (rô-fŭs), *adj.* Reddish-brown ; yellowish ; কপিশবর্ণ ; পীতাভ রক্তবর্ণ।

rŭg, *n.* 1. A coarse, warm woollen cloth having a long shaggy nap used as a coverlet or as a wrap for protecting the leg against cold in driving, railway-travelling, etc. ; কম্বল। 2. A soft woolly mat or hearth rug ; একপ্রকার কোমল পশমী মাদুর বা গৃহ-মধ্যস্থ অগ্নিসেবনস্থলীর সম্মুখস্থ গালিচার উপর পাতার জন্য পশমের আস্তরণ।

Rŭg'-bȳ, *n.* Football as played under the rules of the Rugby Foot-ball Union (founded 1871), or as originally at Rugby school ; পাদগোলক ক্রীড়ার প্রকারবিশেষ।

rŭg'-ged (-ĕd), *adj.* 1. Uneven ; as, *rugged* ground ; বন্ধুর, উচ্চাবচ, বিষম, নতোন্নত। 2. Rough ; খসখসে, খরগাত্র, খরস্পর্শ। 3. Rough in temper ; unpolished ; রূক্ষস্বভাব ; অমার্জ্জিতস্বভাব। 4. Harsh in sound ; শ্রুতিকটু। **—ly,** *adv.* **—ness,** *n.*

ru'-gōse (rô-), *adj.* Wrinkled ; কুঞ্চিত।

ru'-in (rô-), *n., v. t.* & *i.* 1. Destruction ; ধ্বংস, নাশ, ক্ষয়, ভঙ্গ। 2. That which destroys ; ধ্বংসকারক বস্তু। 3. A building or anything in a state of decay or dilapidation ; as, a Gothic *ruin* ; a wreck ; ধ্বংসপ্রাপ্ত বা ক্ষয়প্রাপ্ত অট্টালিকা প্রভৃতি ; ধ্বংসাবশেষ। 4. (*Pl.*) The remains of a demolished city, house, fortress or the like ; ধ্বংসাবশেষ, লুপ্তাবশেষ, ক্ষয়াবশেষ। 5. The state of being destroyed; ধ্বংসপ্রাপ্ত অবস্থা। 6. Complete loss of property, rank or position ; সর্ব্বস্বান্ত অবস্থা, সামাজিক মৃত্যু। ***Verb t.*** 1. To bring to ruin ; to subvert ; ধ্বংস করা, নাশ করা, উচ্ছেদসাধন করা ; লোপ করা। 2. To reduce to a state of poverty with abundance of goods in his warehouse ; "A particular merchant may sometimes be *ruined* by not being able to sell them in time" ; সর্ব্বস্বান্ত করা। ***Verb i.*** 1. To fall into ruin ; ধ্বংসপ্রাপ্ত হওয়া, ধ্বংসোন্মুখ হওয়া। 2. (*Rare*) To be reduced to a state of poverty ; সর্ব্বস্বান্ত হওয়া। 3. To fall with a crash ; ভীষণ শব্দে ভাঙ্গিয়া পড়া, মড় মড় শব্দে ভাঙ্গিয়া পড়া। **To ruin a woman**—To violate her chastity ; স্ত্রীলোকের ধর্ম্ম নষ্ট করা, সতীত্ব লঙ্ঘন করা, স্ত্রীলোকের সর্ব্বনাশ করা। **—a-ble,** *adj.* **—ate,** *v. t.* **—a'-tion,** *n.*

ru-in'-ous (rô-ĭn-ŭs), *adj.* 1. In a state of ruin ; ধ্বংসাবস্থাপন্ন, ধ্বংস-প্রাপ্ত। 2. Destructive ; disastrous ; ধ্বংসজনক, বিলোপকর ; দুর্গতিজনক।

rule (rôl), *n., v.t.* & *i.* 1. An established or customary principle or mode of action in individual or social life ; precept ; নিয়ম ; বিধি, রীতি। 2. The body of regulations observed by a religious society, corporation, etc. ; ধর্ম্মসম্প্রদায় প্রভৃতি কর্ত্তৃক অনুসৃত বিধিসমূহ বা নিয়মনিচয়। 3. (*Gram.*) A statement by which some established order in the construction or use of words is expressed ; (ব্যাকরণ) নিয়ম। 4. (*Math.*) The method prescribed for performing any operation ; (গণিতশাস্ত্র) নিয়ম। 5. (*Obs.*) Behaviour ; (অপ্রঃ) আচরণ। 6. (*Pl.*) The body of regulations or orders regulating the practice and procedure of the courts superior and inferior ; an order made by a court in connection with a particular case ; নিম্ন এবং উচ্চ বিচারালয়ের কার্য্য-পদ্ধতি-নিয়ামক আদেশ বা নিয়মাবলী ; কোন বিশেষ মোকদ্দমা সম্পর্কে কোন আদালতের আদেশ। 7. Administration ; sway ; রাজ্যশাসন, শাসন ; প্রাধান্য, প্রভুত্ব। 8. An instrument by which straight lines are drawn ; যে দণ্ডের সাহায্যে সরল রেখা টানা হয়, রুল, রেখাঙ্কনদণ্ড। 9. A graduated bar of wood, ivory, etc. by which short lengths are measured ; রেখাঙ্কিত মানদণ্ড। 10. (*Print.*) A thin slip of brass etc. for separating headings, columns, etc ; (মুদ্রণ) বিন্যস্ত অক্ষরের স্তম্ভ, শীর্ষলিপি, প্রভৃতি পৃথক করার জন্য পিতলাদির সরুফলক, রুল। 11. (*Pl.*) A defined area in the vicinity of certain prisons within which certain kinds of prisoners were permitted to live on furnishing proper security ; কোন কোন কারাগারের সন্নিকটস্থ নির্দিষ্টসীমাবচ্ছিন্ন স্থান—যথায় উপযুক্ত জামিন প্রদানে কোন কোন শ্রেণীর বন্দী বাস করিতে পারিত। 12. A criterion ; a test ; "A knave when tried on honesty's plain *rule*" ; গুণাগুণ নির্ণয়ের আদর্শ ; পরীক্ষা। ***Verb t.*** 1. To govern ; to have dominion, control or authority over ; শাসন করা ; প্রভুত্ব থাকা, প্রাধান্য থাকা, কর্ত্তৃত্ব থাকা। 2. (*Rare*) To establish or settle by a rule ; (কচিদ্ ব্যবহৃত) কোন নিয়ম দ্বারা ব্যবস্থিত বা প্রতিষ্ঠাপিত করা। 3. (*Law*) To establish by a decree or decision ; (আইন) কোনরূপ বিধান বা ব্যবস্থা-দ্বারা প্রতিষ্ঠিত করা। 4. To determine ; to decree ; মীমাংসা করা ;

বিধান করা। 5. To mark with lines with a ruler or ruling instrument; রেখাঙ্কনদণ্ড বা যন্ত্রের সাহায্যে রেখাঙ্কিত করা। *Verb i.* 1. To have power or command; to govern; প্রভুত্ব থাকা, কর্তৃত্ব থাকা; শাসন করা। 2. (*Law*) To lay down judicially; (আইন) বিধান করা। 3.(*Commr.*) To be current; to stand or maintain a level; "Things *rule* at starvation prices here"; (বাণিজ্য) প্রচলিত থাকা; কোন নির্দ্দিষ্ট সীমার ভিতর থাকা। **As a rule**—On the whole; generally: মোটের উপর; সচরাচর,সাধারণতঃ। **As the rule**—As the usual practice; প্রচলিত বিধি অনুসারে। **Rule absolute**—কোন সাপেক্ষ আদেশের প্রতিকূলে সন্তোষজনক কারণ প্রদর্শিত না হইলে বিচারক যে আদেশ দ্বারা তাহার পূর্ব্ববর্ত্তী আদেশ চূড়ান্ত বা অবশ্যপালনীয় করিয়া থাকেন, চূড়ান্ত আদেশ। **Rule Britannia**—ইংরেজ কবি Thomson কৃত ইংলণ্ডের জাতীয়সঙ্গীত। **Ruled surface**—রেখাঙ্কিত পৃষ্ঠ (হিং কোঃ)। **Rule of the road**—Regulations framed to prevent collisions on the road; রাস্তায় গাড়ী প্রভৃতির সংঘর্ষ নিবারণের জন্য নিয়ম। (ইংলণ্ডের নিয়ম শকটচালক বা অশ্বারোহী রাস্তার অপর শকটচালক বা অশ্বারোহীর সম্মুখীন হইলে তাহার দক্ষিণ দিক দিয়া যাইবে। অপর অপর দেশের নিয়ম ইহার বিপরীত।) **Rule of three**—Rule of proportion; ত্রৈরাশিক। **Rule-of-thumb**—A rule or method derived from practice or experience; কেবল অভ্যাস বা অভিজ্ঞতালব্ধ নিয়ম বা পদ্ধতি (অর্থাৎ যাহার মূলে কোনরূপ বৈজ্ঞানিক জ্ঞান নাই)। (*Adj.*) অভ্যাস বা অভিজ্ঞতালব্ধ পদ্ধতিমূলক বা ঐরূপ পদ্ধতির অনুসরণকারী। **Rule to show cause, Rule nisi**—কোন উচ্চতর আদালত হইতে প্রাপ্ত সাপেক্ষ (conditional) আদেশ। এইরূপ আদেশ যে পক্ষের উপর জারি হয় সেই পক্ষ ইহার প্রতিকূলে সন্তোষজনক কারণ দর্শাইতে অসমর্থ হইলে ঐরূপ আদেশ চূড়ান্ত বা অবশ্যপালনীয় হইয়া থাকে। **Standing rule**—কোন সমবায়ের কার্য্যপ্রণালীনিয়ামক নিয়মনিচয়। **To rule out**—To pronounce irrelevent or ineligible; অপ্রাসঙ্গিক বা অযোগ্য বলিয়া প্রকাশ করা। **To rule the roast (or roost)**—To domineer; to be paramount; কর্তৃত্ব করা, প্রভুত্ব করা; সর্ব্বেসর্ব্বা হওয়া। **To rule with a rod of iron**—To govern tyrannically; কঠোর ভাবে শাসন করা, প্রজাপীড়ন করা।

rul'-êr (rôl-), *n.* 1. One who rules or governs; শাসনকর্ত্তা, রাজা, শাসক। 2. An instrument for drawing lines by; রেখাঙ্কনদণ্ড।

rul'-ing (rôl-), *adj.* & *n.* 1. Governing; prevalent; as, *ruling* passion; শাসনকারী, প্রভুত্বকারী; নিয়ামক, প্রবল, বলবৎ। 2. Used in marking lines; as, a *ruling* machine; রেখাঙ্কক। 3. Current; as, *ruling* prices; চলিত, বর্ত্তমান। ***Noun.*** A point settled by a judge or court; as, a *ruling* of the High Court; কোন বিচারক বা আদালতের নির্দ্ধারণ। **Ruling prince**—ভারতবর্ষের দেশীয় রাজা।

rŭm, *n.* Spirit distilled from cane juice or from treacle or molasses; ইক্ষুরস বা গুড় হইতে প্রস্তুত মদ্যবিশেষ, রম, শীধু, গোড়ী। **Rum-shrub**—রম, চিনি ও লেবুর রসের মিশ্রণে প্রস্তুত সুমিষ্ট আসব বিশেষ।

rŭm, rŭm'-my̆, *adjs.* (*Slang*) Odd; queer; (ইতরভাষায়) সৃষ্টিছাড়া, অদ্ভুত; কেমনতর, অপরূপ। **A rum start**—A strange condition of affair; উদ্ভট ব্যাপার, সৃষ্টিছাড়া ব্যাপার। **A rum customer**—A person difficult to deal with; শক্ত লোক।

rŭm'-ble (-bl), *v. i., t.* & *n.* To make a low, heavy, continued, sound, as of wheels, thunder, etc.; গুরু গুরু গর্জ্জন করা, ঘর্ঘর নাদ করা, ঘর ঘর করা, গুড় গুড় শব্দ করা। ***Verb t.*** To make continuous rolling noise; ঘর ঘর করা, গুরু গুরু শব্দ করা। ***Noun.*** 1. A low heavy continuous sound, as of distant thunder; গুরু গুরু গর্জ্জন, ঘর্ঘরনাদ, গুরুগম্ভীর শব্দ। 2. A seat behind a carriage for servants; গাড়ীর পশ্চাতে ভৃত্যদিগের বসিবার আসন। **Rum'-bling,** *n.* & *adj.* **Rumble-tumble**—ঘর্ঘরনাদী শকট, ঘর্ঘর শব্দে গমন। **Rumbling of bowels**—পেটের ঘড় ঘড় শব্দ, অন্ত্রকূজন, অন্ত্রবিকূজন।

rŭm-bŭs'-tious (-tŭs), *adj.* (*Colloq.*) Boisterous; (চলিত ভাষায়) তুমুল কোলাহলপূর্ণ।

rü'-mĕn, *n.* The upper first stomach of an animal which chews the cud; রোমন্থনকারী জন্তুর প্রথম পাকস্থলী।

rü'-mi-nănt, *n.* & *adj.* An animal that chews the cud; রোমন্থনকারী জন্তু, গিলিতচর্ব্বণকারী জন্তু। ***Adj.*** 1. Chewing the cud; রোমন্থনকারী। 2. Contemplative; চিন্তাশীল, অনুধ্যানশীল, ধ্যানপরায়ণ, চিন্তারত।

rü'-mi-nāte, *v. i.* & *t.* 1. To chew over again; রোমন্থন করা, গিলিতচর্ব্বণ করা, জাবর কাটা। 2. (*Fig.*) To muse; to reflect; as, to *ruminate* on misfortunes; (লক্ষণায়) চিন্তা করা, পুনঃ পুনঃ ভাবা; অনুধ্যান করা, সংচিন্তন। ***Verb t.*** To muse or meditate; "Mad with desire, she *ruminates* her sin"; চিন্তা করা, অনুধ্যান করা। **—na-tive,** *adj.* **—na-tive-ly,** *adv.* **—na-tor, —na'-tion,** *ns.*

rum'-mage (rôm-āj), *v. t., i.* & *n.* 1. To ransack; তন্ন তন্ন করিয়া অনুসন্ধান করা, পাতি পাতি করিয়া খুঁজা। 2. To discover by a thorough search; তন্ন তন্ন করিয়া খুঁজিয়া বাহির করা। ***Verb i.*** 1. To make a thorough search; তন্ন

তন্ন করিয়া খুঁজা। 2. To create confusion ; লণ্ডভণ্ড করা। *Noun.* 1. Miscellaneous articles ; rubbish ; টুকিটাকি জিনিষ ; জঞ্জাল, আবর্জ্জনা। 3. A thorough search ; তন্ন তন্ন করিয়া অনুসন্ধান, পাতি পাতি করিয়া তল্লাস। **Rummage-sale**—দানকার্য্যের অর্থসংস্থানের জন্য প্রদত্ত টুকিটাকি জিনিষ নীলামে বিক্রয়, রেলকোম্পানী, বন্ধকগ্রহীতা, পুলিশ প্রভৃতি কর্ত্তৃক বেওয়ারিশ মাল বিক্রয়।

rŭm'-mer (-êr), *n.* A large drinking glass ; বৃহৎ পানপাত্র।

rŭm'-my (-ĭ), *adj.* Same as RUM, *adj.* (which see).

ru'-mour (rô-mêr), *n.* & *v. t.* A popular report ; গুজব, জনরব, রটনা, জনপ্রবাদ, লোকপ্রবাদ, জনশ্রুতি। *Verb t.* To circulate by report ; গুজব প্রচার করা, জনরব প্রচার করা। **Every rumour has some truth at the bottom**—যা রটে তা বটে।

rŭmp, *n.* 1. The end of the backbone of an animal with the parts adjacent ; the buttocks ; জন্তুর শিরদাঁড়ার প্রান্ত এবং তৎসন্নিহিত অংশ ; পাছা। 2. The fag-end of something ; a small or contemptible part of a parliament or similar body ; কোন বস্তুর অকেজো অংশ ; পার্লেমেণ্ট বা অনুরূপ সভাসমিতির ক্ষুদ্র বা নগণ্য অংশ। **The Rump** or **Rump Parliament**—১৬৪৮ খৃঃ অব্দে Oliver Cromwell পার্লেমেণ্টের সভ্যদিগকে ১ম চার্লসের প্রাণদণ্ডের অনুমোদনে বাধ্য করার জন্য পার্লেমেণ্ট সভাগৃহে Colonel Purgeএর অধীন দুইটী সেনাপল্টন প্রেরণ করেন। এই সকল সৈন্য ৪১ জন সভ্যকে পার্লেমেণ্টের নিম্নতলের এক কুঠরীতে রুদ্ধ করে, ১৬০ জনকে বাটীতে যাওয়ার জন্য আদেশ দেয় এবং ক্রমওয়েলের পক্ষাবলম্বী ৬০ জন সভ্যকে মাত্র সভাগৃহে অবস্থান করিতে দেওয়া হইয়াছিল। এই ৬০ জন সভ্যই পরে পার্লেমেণ্ট সভার কার্য্য নির্ব্বাহ করেন। এই পার্লেমেণ্টকে Rump or Rump Parliament কহে।

rŭm'-ple (-pl), *v. t.* To wrinkle ; to crease ; কুঞ্চিত করা, কোঁকড়ান ; কোঁচান, কোঁচকান।

rŭm'-pŭs, *n.* (*Slang*) Disturbance ; row ; uproar ; (ইতর ভাষায়) গোলমাল ; হল্লা ; সোরগোল, কোলাহল।

rŭm'-pȳ, *n.* A tailless cat of the island of Man ; ম্যানদ্বীপের একপ্রকার লাঙ্গুলহীন মার্জ্জার।

rŭn, *v. i.* & *t.* 1. To move or pass swiftly on the ground with legs ; দৌড়া, ছুটা, বেগে ধাবিত হওয়া। 2. To move in a hurry ; তাড়াতাড়ি ছুটা। 3. To contend in a race ; ঘোড়দৌড় প্রভৃতিতে প্রতিযোগিতা করা। 4. To enter into a contest ; to offer oneself as a candidate for some office ; as, to *run* for an office ; কোনরূপ প্রতিযোগিতার ক্রীড়ায় প্রতিদ্বন্দ্বিশ্রেণীভুক্ত হওয়া ; কোন পদের প্রার্থী হওয়া। 5. To flee from ; পলায়ন করা। 6. To steal from ; গোপনে সরিয়া পড়া। 7. To make haste ; to be active ; as, the people *ran* almost from all places to assist his cause ; তাড়াতাড়ি করা, ছুটিয়া আসা ; তৎপর হওয়া। 8. To go back and forth from place to place, as a train, a packet or the like ; as, steamers *run* between Dacca and Goalundo ; (ট্রেণ, জাহাজ, প্রভৃতি সম্পর্কে) চলাফেরা করা, যাতায়াত করা, গমন করা। 9. To turn, as a wheel ; to move on wheels ; চাকা ঘূরা ; চাকার উপর চলা। 10. To spread or flow ; to spread and blend together ; as, colours *run* in washing ; ছড়ান ; ছড়াইয়া যাওয়া, ছড়াইয়া একত্র মিশ্রিত হওয়া। 11. To melt ; গলিত হওয়া, গলা। 12. (Of fish, ship, etc.) To go straight and fast ; (মৎস্য, জাহাজ প্রভৃতি সম্পর্কে) সোজাসোজি দ্রুত ধাবিত হওয়া। 13. To discharge pus ; as, an ulcer *runs* ; পূষ নিঃসৃত হওয়া। 14. To press for payments as upon a bank with numerous demands ; as, to *run* on a bank ; ব্যাঙ্ক হইতে ঘন ঘন টাকা তুলিয়া লওয়া। 15. To rush at a person with a view to attacking him ; to attack a person ; আক্রমণ করার উদ্দেশ্যে কাহারো দিকে ধাবিত হওয়া ; কাহাকে আক্রমণ করা। 16. To come aground ; জাহাজাদি চড়ায় লাগা। 17. To be widely current ; বহুল প্রচার হওয়া। 18. (Of milk etc.) To curdle ; (দুগ্ধাদি সম্বন্ধে) জমিয়া যাওয়া, ছিঁড়িয়া যাওয়া, নষ্ট হওয়া। 19. To continue ; চলিতে থাকা, ক্রমাগত চলিতে থাকা। 20. To grow exuberantly ; as, if the richness of the ground causees the turnips to *run* to leaves ; প্রচুর পরিমাণে জন্মা। 21. To pass from one state to another ; কোন অবস্থা হইতে অবস্থান্তর প্রাপ্ত হওয়া। 22. To have a certain tenor or purport ; to read ; as, the document *runs* thus ; কোনরূপ মর্ম্ম, তাৎপর্য্য বা ভাবের হওয়া ; কোনরূপ লিখিত বা মুদ্রিত থাকা। 23. To reach ; as, his memory does not *run* so far ; পৌঁছা। 24. (Of fish) To migrate ; এক অঞ্চল হইতে অন্য অঞ্চলে যাওয়া। 25. To have a certain course or line ; as, the road *runs* west ; কোন নির্দ্দিষ্ট দিকে যাওয়া। 26. To proceed ; to pass ; as, time *runs* ; অগ্রসর হওয়া ; চলা, অতিবাহিত হওয়া। 27. To rise ; as, the debate *ran* high ; উঠা। 28. To be or to continue in operation ; চলা, চলিতে থাকা। 29. To desert ; as, the sailor *ran* from his ship ; ত্যাগ করা। 30. To take recourse to ; as, he was forced to *run* to him for succour ; আশ্রয় লওয়া, শরণ লওয়া। 31. (Of a ship) To sail ; (জাহাজসম্পর্কে) সমুদ্রপথে যাওয়া। 32. To flow ; as, the river *ran* with flood ; to be wet with ; প্রবাহিত হওয়া ; সিক্ত

হওয়া, আর্দ্র হওয়া। **33.** To revolve as on an axle; অক্ষদণ্ড প্রভৃতির উপর ঘুরা। ***Verb t.*** **1.** To cause to run; দৌড়ান। **2.** To cause to ply; যাতায়াত করান। **3.** To melt; to pierce; to stab; গালান; ভেদ করা; ছুরি বসান। **4.** To break through; to evade; as, to *run* a blockade; ভেদ করিয়া যাওয়া; এড়ান। **5.** To smuggle; অবৈধভাবে মাল আমদানী বা রপ্তানী করা। **6.** To form in a mould by melting; to cast; as, to *run* bullet; গালাইয়া ছাঁচে গড়া; ঢালাই করা। **7.** To incur; to meet with; as, to *run* a risk; গ্রস্ত হওয়া, নিজের উপর আনা; সম্মুখীন হওয়া। **8.** To draw or cause to be drawn or marked; as, to *run* a picture; অঙ্কন করা, অঙ্কিত করা; চিহ্নিত করা। **9.** To pour forth in a stream; স্রোতঃ প্রবাহিত করা। **10.** To keep going on or in operation; as, to *run* a shop; চালান। **11.** To sew by passing the needle through and through in a continuous line; সোজা সেলাই করা। **12.** To cause to enter; প্রবেশ করান, ঢুকান, প্রবিষ্ট করা। **13.** To pursue; to hunt; অনুসরণ করা, পশ্চাদ্ধাবন করা; শিকার করা। **14.** *(Archaic)* To pursue in thought; to carry in contemplation; "To *run* the world back to its first original and view nature in its cradle"; (অপ্রঃ) চিন্তায় অনুসরণ করা; চিন্তায় নীত করা। **15.** To discharge; নির্গত করা, নিঃসৃত করা। **16.** To go upon (an errand); (সংবাদ) লইয়া যাওয়া। **17.** To introduce a person in society; কোন ব্যক্তিকে ভদ্রসমাজে পরিচিত করান। **18.** To prosecute a person; as, I shall *run* him for insulting me; কাহারো নামে নালিস করা, কাহারো বিরুদ্ধে অভিযোগ করা। **19.** To be charged with; as, the river *ran* blood; পূর্ণ হওয়া। **He that runs may read**—Even a careless observer may notice at once; বিশেষ মনোযোগের সহিত না দেখিলেও চোখে পড়ে। **Run ship run, Run my ship run**—ছেলেদের একপ্রকার ক্রীড়া—যাহাতে কয়েকটী ছেলে মেষ, একজন নেকড়ে বাঘ এবং অপর একজন মেষপালক সাজে। **The tub runs**—The tub leaks; চুয়ায়। **To be run after**—To be admired by all; সকলের প্রশংসা পাওয়া। **To be run down**—To become weak or ill; স্বাস্থ্যভগ্ন হওয়া। **To be run out of anything**—To have no more in stock; ভাণ্ডারে না থাকা, টান পড়া, অপ্রতুল হওয়া, বাড়ন্ত হওয়া (*euphem.*) [cf. কাল হইতে তাহার ভাণ্ডারে সমস্ত জিনিষ বাড়ন্ত হইয়া উঠিয়াছে—পণ্ডিত মশাই (শরৎ চট্টো)]। **To run**—To strike; লাগা। **To run across**—To meet with by chance; ঘটনাক্রমে দেখা হওয়া, হঠাৎ সাক্ষাৎ হওয়া। **To run after**—To pursue or follow; অনুসরণ করা। **To run against**—Same as TO RUN ACROSS. To operate against; কাহারো বিরুদ্ধে ক্রিয়া করা। To collide with; সংঘৃষ্ট হওয়া, ঠোকাঠুকি লাগা। **To run aground**—To strand; জাহাজ চড়ায় লাগা। **To run a mine**—To dig a part under the earth and fill it with some explosive material with a view to blow up something; কোন কিছু উড়াইয়া দিবার জন্য ভূগর্ভে গর্ত্ত খনন পূর্ব্বক তাহা বিস্ফোরক দ্রব্যদ্বারা পূর্ণ করা। **To run a race**—To contend in running; দৌড়ে প্রতিযোগিতা করা, ঘোড়দৌড়ে বাজি খেলা। To lead a certain kind of life; সৎ বা অসৎভাবে জীবনযাপন করা। **To run amuck**—See AMUCK. **To run at**—To attack; আক্রমণ করা। To rush upon; কাহারো দিকে প্রচণ্ডবেগে ধাবিত হওয়া। **To run away**—To elope; স্ত্রীলোককে ভাগাইয়া নেওয়া কোন স্ত্রীলোককে ফুসলাইয়া কুলের বাহির করা। **To run away with**—To bolt with; লইয়া চম্পট দেওয়া। To be carried by some wrong notion; কোনরূপ ভ্রান্ত ধারণা দ্বারা পরিচালিত হওয়া। To consume; ধ্বংস করা, নিঃশেষিত করা। To grow luxuriously; প্রচুর পরিমাণে জন্মা। **To run before**—To flee before; পলায়ন করা। To excel; to outstrip; উৎকর্ষে অতিক্রম করা। ছাড়াইয়া যাওয়া। **To run down**—To have the motive power exhausted, as a clock; গতিজনক শক্তি পর্য্যবসিত হওয়া। To chase to weariness; শিকারেতাড়া করিতে করিতে হয়রান করা। To crush; ধ্বংস করা; বিধ্বস্ত করা। To decrease; হ্রাস পাওয়া। To hunt down; যে পর্য্যন্ত ধরা বা বধ না করা যায় সেই পর্য্যন্ত শিকারের পশ্চাৎ পশ্চাৎ তাড়া করা। To overcome or overwhelm; পরাস্ত করা, অভিভূত করা। To melt; গালান। To vilify; অপবাদ করা, কলঙ্ক রটনা করা, কুৎসা প্রচার করা। **To run down a coast**—To sail along a coast; উপকূলের নিকট দিয়া জাহাজ চালান। **To run down a vessel**—To run against and sink her; কোন জাহাজের সহিত ঠোকাঠুকি লাগিয়া উহাকে ডুবাইয়া দেওয়া। **To run for it**—To flee away; ছুটিয়া পালান। **To run for office**—To try to secure some appointment; কোন চাকুরীর জন্য চেষ্টা করা। **To run foul of**—See under FOUL. **To run hard**—To press hard in a race or other competition; ঘোড়দৌড় প্রভৃতিতে খুব বেশী রকম চাপ দেওয়া। To press with ridicule—বিদ্রূপবাণ বর্ষণ করা। To urge with importunity; চাপিয়া ধরা। **To run high**—To rage furiously; প্রচণ্ড হইয়া উঠা, উত্তালতরঙ্গসঙ্কুলিত হইয়া উঠা। **To run in**—To fall in arrears; বাকী পড়া। To pay a short visit; অল্পকালের জন্য দেখা করা।

To insert ; ঢুকান। (*Slang*) To take into custody ; to lock up ; (ইতর ভাষায়) পাকড়ান ; গারদে পুরা, আটক করা। (*Print.*) To place the carriage with the forme, so as to obtain an impression ; ছাপার জন্য ফর্ম্মা ভিতরে ঠেলিয়া দেওয়া। **To run in the family**—To be hereditary ; বংশগত হওয়া, কৌলিক হওয়া। **To run in one's head**—To constantly recur to one's memory ; বার বার মনে উঠা। **To run into** — To incur ; to involve in ; নিজের উপর আনা ; গ্রস্ত হওয়া, জড়িত হওয়া। To fall into ; পতিত হওয়া। To blend into ; মিশিয়া যাওয়া। To reach ; as, the book *ran* into 5 editions ; প্রাপ্ত হওয়া। **To run in** or **into** — To enter ; to step in ; প্রবেশ করা, পদার্পণ করা। **To run in trust**—(*Obs.*) To run in debt ; (অপ্রঃ) ঋণগ্রস্ত হওয়া। To get credit ; ধারে পাওয়া। **To run in with** — To agree with ; একমত হওয়া, মিলা। (*Naut.*) To sail close ; নিকট দিয়া যাওয়া। **To run mad**—To become wild with excitement ; পাগল হইয়া উঠা, উন্মত্ত হইয়া উঠা। **To run mad after** — To follow an object with great infatuation ; পাগলের মত পাছু পাছু ছুটা। **To run off**—To flow away ; প্রবাহিত হওয়া। To diminish ; হ্রাস পাওয়া। To alter ; পরিবর্ত্তিত হওয়া। To remove ; স্থানান্তরিত হওয়া। To make off ; পিট্টান দেওয়া। **To run on**—To talk incessantly ; অনর্গল বকা। To keep on ; চালান। To be continued ; চলিতে থাকা। To continue a course ; কোন পথে চলা। (*Print.*) To continue in the same line without a break or new paragraph ; (মুদ্রণ) নূতন প্যারা আরম্ভ না করিয়া বা লাইন না ভাঙ্গিয়া ক্রমাগত চালাইয়া যাওয়া। To have the mind occupied with ; চিত্ত নিরত থাকা ; মন ব্যাপৃত থাকা। To continue ; চলিতে থাকা। To pass ; গত হওয়া। To talk much ; অতিশয় বকা। To relate to ; কোন কিছুর সম্বন্ধে বা সম্পর্কে হওয়া। **To run on all fours**—To crawl ; হামাগুড়ি দিয়া চলা। To be exactly similar to something else ; to agree ; অন্য কিছুর ঠিক অনুরূপ হওয়া ; মিলা। **To run out**—To come to an end ; শেষ হওয়া, ফুরাইয়া যাওয়া। To push out ; to extend ; ঠেলিয়া দেওয়া ; বিস্তার করা। To waste ; নষ্ট করা। To withdraw the carriage, with the forme of type after taking an impression ; (মুদ্রণ) ছাপ দেওয়ার পর ফর্ম্মা টানিয়া লওয়া। To sew up, by taking a series of stitches on the needle at the same time ; to repair temporarily by sewing ; একবারে সূচের কয়েকটি ফোঁড় দিয়া সেলাই করা ; উপস্থিত কাজ সারার মত সেলাই করা। To erect hastily ; তাড়াতাড়ি খাড়া করা, দ্রুত গাঁথিয়া তোলা। To expire, as lease ; মেয়াদ ফুরান। To leak ; চুয়ান। **To run over**—To run the eye hastily over ; তাড়াতাড়ি চোখ বুলাইয়া যাওয়া, উপর উপর দেখিয়া যাওয়া। To overflow ; উপচিয়া পড়া, উথলিয়া পড়া। To go over and examine ; আলোচনা ও পরীক্ষা করা। To drive or ride over ; উপর দিয়া গাড়ী বা ঘোড়া চালাইয়া যাওয়া। To think over ; ভাবা। To recite quickly ; দ্রুত আবৃত্তি করা, তাড়াতাড়ি আওড়ান। To pay a hurried visit ; অল্প সময়ের জন্য সাক্ষাৎ করা। **To run rampant**—To be widespread ; বহুদূর বিস্তৃত হওয়া। **To run riot**—See RIOT. **To run short**—To be out of stock ; ফুরাইয়া আসা, টান পড়া, ব্যস্তসমস্ত হওয়া (*Euphem.*), অকুলান হওয়া। **To run the gauntlet**—See GAUNTLET. **To run through**—To expend ; to waste ; ব্যয় করিয়া ফেলা ; উড়াইয়া দেওয়া। To go through hurriedly ; তাড়াতাড়ি পাঠ করা, তাড়াতাড়ি দেখা, চোখ বুলাইয়া যাওয়া। To pass through ; অতিক্রম করা। To pierce through ; ছুরিদ্বারা এফোঁড় ওফোঁড় করা। To strike out a line ; পংক্তি কাটিয়া ফেলা। **To run to**—To come to in number or quantity ; পরিমাণে বা সংখ্যায় হওয়া। **To run to earth**—To chase (fox, etc.) to its hole ; খেঁকশিয়াল প্রভৃতি তাড়া করিয়া গর্ত্তের আশ্রয় লইতে বাধ্য করা। To discover after search ; বহু অনুসন্ধানের ফলে আবিষ্কার করা। **To run together** — To mingle together একত্র মিশ্রিত হওয়া। To combine esp. in melted state ; একত্র মিশান, বিশেষতঃ গালানো অবস্থায় সংমিশ্রিত করা। **To run to seed** — (Of Plants) Rapidly to develop seed ; (*fig.*) to become impoverished, exhausted or worn out ; to lose vital force ; (বৃক্ষ সম্বন্ধে) দ্রুত বীজ উৎপাদন করা ; (লক্ষণায়) নিঃস্ব, অবসন্ন, অথবা পরিশ্রান্ত হওয়া ; জীবনীশক্তি হীন হওয়া। **To run up**—To increase ; বাড়া, বর্দ্ধিত হওয়া, বৃদ্ধি পাওয়া। To swell ; স্ফীত হওয়া। To increase in price etc. ; মূল্য প্রভৃতি বৃদ্ধি পাওয়া, চড়া। To add up hurriedly ; তাড়াতাড়ি ঠিক দেওয়া। To sew hurriedly ; তাড়াতাড়ি রিপু করা। **To run up a score**—To buy articles on credit ; ধারে জিনিষ কেনা। **To run upon**—To have a fancy for ; কোন কিছুর জন্য সখ হওয়া। To be occupied with ; লাগিয়া থাকা, ব্যাপৃত থাকা, নিরত থাকা। To fall into ; পতিত হওয়া। To make a butt of ; (মার্কিণ যুক্তরাজ্যে) উপহাসপাত্র করা, হাস্যাস্পদ করা। **To run wild**—To be allowed to go unrestrained ;

অসংযতভাবে চলিতে দেওয়া, উচ্ছৃঙ্খলভাবে চলিয়া যাইতে দেওয়া। To grow without culture or training; বুনো হইয়া যাওয়া। **To run with**—To go along with; সহগামী হওয়া। **To run with the hare and hold with the hound**—See HARE.

run, *n.* & *adj.* **1.** The act of running; a course run; দৌড়ান; দৌড়। **2.** A continued course; a long succession; as, a *run* of luck; প্রবাহ, ধারা; অবিচ্ছিন্ন প্রবাহ। **3.** Great demand; as, a *run* on Bankim's novels; খুব চাহিদা। **4.** Act of being repeated on the stage (said of a play); রঙ্গমঞ্চে পুনঃ পুনঃ অভিনয়। **5.** (*Colloq.*) Trip; as, to take a *run* to Shillong; প্রমোদভ্রমণ। **6.** Distance sailed by a ship; a voyage; জাহাজ কর্তৃক অতিক্রান্ত স্থান; নৌযাত্রা, জলযাত্রা। **7.** Clamour; as, a violent *run* against university education; গোলমাল, কোলাহল, কোন কিছুর বিরুদ্ধে চীৎকার। **8.** A rivulet; a brook; ক্ষুদ্রনদী; নালা। **9.** An uncommon pressure on a bank for payment; ব্যাঙ্ক হইতে টাকা তোলার জন্য হুড়াহুড়ি। **10.** Rapid fall; দ্রুত পতন। **11.** A place where animals may run; a large pasture ground; যে বিস্তীর্ণ ভূমিতে জন্তুগণ দৌড়িতে পারে; সুবিস্তৃত পশুচারণ ভূমি। **12.** Generality; as the common *run*; সাধারণ শ্রেণী। **13.** Character; as, he knew the *run* of the country; অবস্থা, স্বভাব, প্রকৃতি। **14.** A pair of mill-stones; একজোড়া জাঁতার পাথর। **15.** An assemblage of fishes which ascend the river for the purpose of spawning; ডিম ছাড়িবার জন্য নদীর স্রোতের বিপরীত দিগ্‌গামী মাছের ঝাঁক। **16.** (*Colloq.*) Freedom of movement; (চলিত ভাষায়) স্বচ্ছন্দগতি, অবাধগতি। **17.** Aft part of a ship's bottom; জাহাজের তলার যে অংশ পাছা গলুইয়ের দিকে ক্রমশঃ অগ্রসর হইয়া আসে। ***Adj.*** **1.** Melted; দ্রবীভূত। **2.** Smuggled; as, *run* goods; অবৈধভাবে আমদানী বা রপ্তানীকৃত। **Home run**—গৃহাভিমুখে প্রত্যাবর্তন। **A run upon a bank**—See RUN, *n.* 9. **By the run**—Suddenly; হঠাৎ, সহসা। **In the long run**—At length; অবশেষে। **On the run**—পলায়নপর। **The common run**—যাহা সচরাচর হয়। **The common run,** or **The run of mankind**—The generality; সাধারণ লোক। **The ordinary** or **common run**—সাধারণ ব্যাপার। **The run of one's teeth**—একজন লোক যতটা খাইতে পারে। **To get the run**—To bring into ridicule; উপহাসাস্পদ করা, বিদ্রূপভাজন করা।

rŭn'-ă-gāte, *n.* A vagabond; ভবঘুরে।

rŭn'-ă-way (-wā), *n.* & *adj.* One who flies from danger or restraint; deserter; যে ব্যক্তি সৈন্য-বিভাগের বা নৌ-বিভাগের কার্য্য পরিত্যাগ পূর্ব্বক পলায়ন করে; পলাতক। ***Adj.*** Effected by running or eloping; পলায়ন দ্বারা সাধিত, প্রণয়ীর সহিত পলায়ন পূর্ব্বক সম্পাদিত।

rŭn'-cĭn-āte, *adj.* (*Bot.*) Irregularly saw-toothed, with the tooth inclining backward; (উদ্ভিদ্‌বিদ্যা) অসমক্রকচপত্রী, অক্রকচপত্রবৎ (সাঃ পঃ)।

rŭn'-dāle, *n.* A system of holding land in single holdings made of detached pieces; একপ্রকার জোত—যাহাতে বিভিন্ন স্থানের জমি এক পর্য্যায় মধ্যে গৃহীত হয়।

rŭn'-dle (-dl), *n.* **1.** A rung; মইয়ের ধাপ। **2.** Something which revolves round an axis; যাহা কোন অক্ষের চতুর্দ্দিকে ঘূর্ণিত হয় (যথা চক্র)।

rūne, *n.* **1.** One of a set of alphabetic characters peculiar to the ancient northern nations of Europe; ইয়ুরোপের উত্তরাঞ্চলবাসী প্রাচীন জাতিসমূহের বর্ণমালার অক্ষর, রুণিক অক্ষর। **2.** (*pl.*) Words or characters in ancient Teutonic or Scandinavian characters inscribed on sepulchral stones; সমাধিশিলার উপর উৎকীর্ণ প্রাচীন টিউটনিক বা স্কেণ্ডেনিভীয় শব্দ বা অক্ষরসমূহ। **3.** (*pl.*) Rhymes or poetry or other matter in runic characters; ঐ অক্ষরে লিখিত কবিতা। **4.** Mystery connected with an invisible world; magic; অলৌকিক রহস্য; ইন্দ্রজাল। **Rune-staff**—রুণিক অক্ষর খচিত যাদুদণ্ড।

rŭng, *n.* **1.** The round or step of a ladder; মইএর ধাপ বা কোয়া। **2.** A cudgel; লগুড়। **Runged,** *p. p.* **Rung'-less,** *adj.*

rŭng, *p. p.* of RING (which see).

rū'-nĭc, *adj.* & *n.* **1.** Pertaining to the ancient Goths, their language or letters; inscribed with rune; প্রাচীন গথ জাতিসম্পর্কীয়, গথভাষা সম্পর্কীয়, গথঅক্ষরসম্পর্কীয়; রুণিক অক্ষর-ক্ষোদিত। **2.** (Of ornaments) Interlacing as runic monuments etc.; (ভূষা সম্পর্কে) রুণিক অক্ষর ক্ষোদিত স্মৃতিস্তম্ভ প্রভৃতির উপরিস্থি ভূষার মত সংগ্রথিত। ***Noun.*** **1.** Runic inscription; রুণিক শিলালেখ। **2.** A kind of type with thick face; একপ্রকার হরফ।

rŭn'-lĕt, *n.* A small barrel; ক্ষুদ্র পিপা।

rŭn'-lĕt, *n.* A small stream; ক্ষুদ্র স্রোতস্বিনী।

rŭn'-nel (-l), *n.* **1.** A rill; ক্ষুদ্র নদী। **2.** A gutter; নালা।

rŭn'-ner (-ėr), *n.* **1.** One who runs; ধাবনকারী, ধাবক। **2.** That on which something runs or slides; যাহার উপর কোন কিছু ছুটিয়া চলে বা গড়াইয়া যায়। **3.** A messenger; a letter-carrier; a tout; সংবাদবাহক; হরকরা; টর্নি। **4.** A detective or police officer; গোয়েন্দা, পুলিশ

কর্ম্মচারী। 5. (*Bot.*) A stem running along the ground and taking root ; (উদ্ভিদ্ বিদ্যা) লতানিয়া ডগা, ধাবক (সা৹ পঃ)। 6. The moving stone of a grain-mill ; শস্যপেষণ যন্ত্রের আবর্ত্তমান প্রস্তর। 7. A kind of fish ; একপ্রকার মৎস্য। 8. A ship which runs a blockade ; যে পোত বা পোতাধ্যক্ষ শত্রুর জাহাজের আগম ও নির্গমের পথ রোধ করিয়া অবস্থান করে। 9. (*American*) One whose business it is to solicit passengers for railways, steamboats, etc. ; যে ব্যক্তি রেলওয়ে, জাহাজ, প্রভৃতির জন্য যাত্রী জুটায়। 10. Any bird of the Cursores ; উট পক্ষী প্রভৃতি জাতীয় দ্রুতধাবনশীল পক্ষী। 11. The slider on the central rod of an umbrella ; যে পিতল প্রভৃতির চুঙ্গীতে ছাতির ডাঁশা সকল আটকান থাকে এবং যাহা ছাতা খোলা বা বন্ধ করার কালে বাঁটের উপর উঠিয়া নামিয়া থাকে। **Runner-up**—প্রতিযোগিতায় দ্বিতীয় পুরস্কার প্রাপ্ত শিকারী কুকুর; প্রতিযোগিতার ক্রীড়ায় যে ব্যক্তি বা যে দল দ্বিতীয় স্থান অধিকার করে।

rŭn'-ning (-ĭng), *n.* & *adj.* 1. The act of one who, or that which, runs ; দৌড়ন, ধাবন। 2. That which runs or flows ; যাহা ধাবিত বা প্রবাহিত হয়। 3. Discharge from a sore ; ক্ষতাদি হইতে নিঃসৃত স্রাব। *Adj.* 1. Moving with rapidity ; ধাবনশীল, ধাবমান। 2. Kept for the race ; as, a *running* horse ; ঘোড়দৌড়ের জন্য রক্ষিত, দৌড়ের। 3. Continuous ; in succession ; as, to visit four days *running* ; ক্রমাগত ; পরপর। 4. Discharging pus ; as, a *running* sore ; পূযস্রাবী। **Running-fire**—See FIRE. **Running powers**—কোন রেলওয়ে কোম্পানী কর্ত্তৃক ঐ কোম্পানীর লৌহবর্ত্মে অপর কোম্পানীকে বাষ্পীয় শকট চালাইবার যে অধিকার দেওয়া হয়। **Running-title**—পুস্তকের পৃষ্ঠার উপরিভাগে লিখিত নাম। **A running hand**—টানা লেখা। **In or not in the running**—Competing or not competing ; having chance or having no chance of winning ; দৌড় প্রভৃতিতে প্রতিযোগী বা প্রতিযোগী নয় ; জয়লাভের আশা আছে বা নাই। **To be in running**—To have a good chance of success among a number of competitors; বহু প্রতিযোগিগণের মধ্যে জয়ী হওয়ার বিশেষ আশা থাকা। **To be out of running**—To have no chance of success among a number of competitors ; কতিপয় প্রতিযোগিগণের মধ্যে জয়ী হওয়ার আশা না থাকা। **To make good one's running** — To run as well as one's rival ; প্রতিদ্বন্দ্বীর সহিত তুল্যবেগে দৌড়া। **To make the running**—To force the pace at the beginning of a race ; দৌড়ের প্রারম্ভে ঘোড়া বেগে চালান। **To take up the running**—To take the lead ; to take the most active part in any undertaking ; নেতৃত্ব গ্রহণ করা ; কোন কার্য্যের কর্ত্তৃত্বভার গ্রহণ করা।

rŭn'-rig, *n.*, (*Scot.*) Same as RUNDALE (which see).

ru-pee' (rô-pē), *n.* A silver coin the unit of value in British India, worth 1*s.* 4*d.* ; টাকা, তঙ্কা, টঙ্ক।

Rupert's drop, *n.* A drop of glass thrown in a liquid state into water, and hardening into a retort-like shape ; গলিত অবস্থায় জলে নিক্ষিপ্ত কাচবিন্দু—যাহা কঠিন হইয়া ক্ষুদ্র বকযন্ত্রের আকার প্রাপ্ত হয়।

rŭp'-türe, *n.*, *v. t.* & *i.* 1. The act of breaking or bursting ; বিদারণ, ভাঙ্গন, ভেদ। 2. Breach of peace or concord between individuals and nations ; breaking off of friendly relations ; মনোভঙ্গ, ভেদ, এক জাতির সহিত অপর জাতির বিচ্ছেদ ; বন্ধুত্বভঙ্গ, সুহৃদ্‌ভেদ। 3. (*Med.*) Same as HERNIA (which see). *Verb t.* 1. To cause rupture in ; ফাটান, ভগ্ন করা। 2. To cause a breach ; মনোভঙ্গ করা, সুহৃদ্‌ভেদ করা। *Verb i.* To suffer a breach or disruption ; ভঙ্গ হওয়া, মনোভঙ্গ হওয়া। **Rupture of the spleen**—প্লীহা ফাটন।

ru'-răl (rô-), *adj.* 1. Pastoral; rustic ; পল্লীসম্বন্ধীয়, পল্লীসুলভ ; গ্রাম্য, পাড়াগেঁয়ে, জানপদ, গ্রামীণ (হিঃ কোঃ)। 2. Agricultural ; কৃষিবিষয়ক। **–i-za'-tion,** *n.* **–ize,** *v. i.* & *t.* **–ral'-i-ty,** *n.* **Rural dean**—বিশপ এবং আর্কডীকনএর অধীন যাজকবিশেষ—যিনি জেলার যাজক ও সাধারণ লোকের ধর্ম্মসম্বন্ধীয় ব্যাপার তত্ত্বাবধান করেন।

ru'-să (rô-), *n.* A large East-Indian deer ; একজাতীয় বৃহৎ হরিণ।

ruse (rôz), *n.* A stratagem ; an artifice ; চাতুরী, কৌশল ; ফিকির, ফন্দী, ছল।

ruse, (*F.*), *adj.* (*Fem.* RUSEE) Sly ; cunning ; ধূর্ত্ত ; চতুর, চালাক, ফন্দীবাজ, কৌশলী।

rŭsh, *n.* & *v. t.* 1. A plant with long, ready stems ; নলখাগড়া। 2. Anything worthless or of little value ; অসার বস্তু, তুচ্ছ জিনিষ, নগণ্য বস্তু। *Verb t.* To supply a chair-bottom or straw floor with rush ; চেয়ারের তলায় খড় দেওয়া, মেজের উপর খড় বিছান। **Rush'-y,** *adj.* **Rush-bottomed** — খড়ের তৈরী তলার। **Rush-candle, Rush-light**—খড়ের পলিতাবিশিষ্ট চর্ব্বির বাতি, তৃণালোক (আঃ বঃ) ; (লক্ষণায়) ক্ষীণপ্রতিভা দীপ্তি, সামান্য জ্ঞান, প্রভৃতি।

rŭsh, *v. t.*, *i.* & *n.* 1. To hurry forward ; as, to *rush* a bill ; তাড়াতাড়ি অগ্রসর করা। 2. To charge; to take by assault ; as, to *rush* a trench ; to defeat or capture by assault ; প্রচণ্ডবেগে আক্রমণ করা ; প্রচণ্ডবেগে আক্রমণ পূর্ব্বক অধিকার করা ; আক্রমণপূর্ব্বক ধৃত বা পরাজিত করা। *Verb i.* 1. To move or drive forward with impetuosity ; ধাবিত

হওয়া, ধাবমান হওয়া, ছুটা, ঠেলিয়া অগ্রসর হওয়া। 2. To enter with eagerness or without due deliberation or preparation ; as, to *rush* into print ; বিশেষ না ভাবিয়া চিন্তিয়া বা ভালরূপে প্রস্তুত না হইয়া কোন কার্য্যে প্রবৃত্ত হওয়া। ***Noun.*** 1. A driving forward with eagerness and haste ; ধাবন। 2. An impetuous or violent onset ; প্রচণ্ডবেগে আক্রমণ। 3. An eager demand ; হুড়াহুড়ি। 4. A sudden migration of people to a cerain place, esp. gold-field ; কোনস্থানে বিশেষতঃ স্বর্ণক্ষেত্রে সহসা বহুলোকের গমন।

rŭsk, *n.* A bread like hard cake browned in the oven ; রুটির মত একপ্রকার হালকা কঠিন পিষ্টক—যাহা চুল্লীর মৃদু অগ্নিতে বাদামী রংয়ের করা হয়।

Rŭss, *n.* & *adj.* A Russian ; Russian language ; রুশিয়াবাসী ; রুশভাষা। ***Adj.*** Russian ; রুশিয়।

Rŭs'-sel (-l), *n.* A woollen cloth ; একপ্রকার পশমী কাপড়।

rŭs'-set (-ĕt), *adj.* & *n.* Of a reddish brown colour ; কপিশবর্ণ, গেরুয়া রংয়ের। ***Noun.*** 1. A reddish brown colour ; কপিশবর্ণ। 2. Homespun cloth of a reddish-brown colour formerly worn by peasants ; প্রাচীনকালে কৃষকগণকর্ত্তৃক ব্যবহৃত একপ্রকার কপিশবর্ণ বস্ত্র। 3. A kind of apple of a russet colour; একজাতীয় কপিশবর্ণ সেওফল।

Rus'-sia (rŭsh-yă), *n.* 1. The name of a country; রুশদেশ। 2. Same as RUSSIA-LEATHER. **Russia-duck**—একপ্রকার শুভ্র সুকোমল ক্যাম্বিস কাপড়। **Russia-leather**—একপ্রকার শোধিত চর্ম্ম। [এইরূপ চর্ম্ম পূর্ব্বে রুশদেশে প্রস্তুত হইত।]

Rus'-sian (rŭsh-yăn), *adj.* & *n.* Of, or pertaining to, Russia or its inhabitants ; রুশদেশীয়, রুশদেশবাসি-সম্পর্কীয়। ***Noun.*** A native of Russia ; language of Russia ; রুশদেশের লোক ; রুশদেশের ভাষা। **—ize**, *v. t.* **Russian Church**—রুশদেশে প্রতিষ্ঠিত ধর্ম্ম-সংঘ। ইহা গ্রীক ধর্ম্ম-সংঘের শাখাবিশেষ। গ্রীক ধর্ম্মপ্রচারকগণ রুশদেশবাসিগণকে খৃষ্টধর্ম্মে দীক্ষিত করে।]

Rŭss'-ni-ăk, *n.* 1. A member of a branch of Slavic race, inhabiting Galicia, Hungary, Podolia, Volhynia and Lithuania ; গ্যালিসিয়া, হাঙ্গারী, প্রভৃতি প্রদেশের স্লেভ জাতীয় লোক। 2. The language of that people ; ঐ জাতির ভাষা।

rŭst, *n.*, *v. t.* & *i.* 1. The red or orange-coloured coating formed on iron when exposed to moisture ; মরিচা, লোহমল, মণ্ডুর, অয়োমল, কলঙ্ক (যোঃ)। 2. A disease of some plants or flowers ; কোন কোন গাছ বা ফুলের একপ্রকার রোগ। 3. Loss of power or inactivity ; inaction ; "A life of *rust*" ; আলস্য হেতু শক্তি, ক্ষমতা, প্রভৃতির ক্ষয় ; নিষ্ক্রিয়তা, জড়তা। ***Verb t.*** 1. To cause to contract rust ; মরচে পড়ান, মরচে ধরান। 2. To impair by time and inactivity ; জড়তা বা নিষ্ক্রিয়তা দ্বারা, নষ্ট করা। ***Verb i.*** 1. To contract rust ; মরচে পড়া, মরচে ধরা। 2. To degenerate in idleness ; to become dull by inaction ; আলস্য হেতু ক্ষয় বা অকপর্ষ প্রাপ্ত হওয়া ; নিষ্ক্রিয়তা হেতু জড়তাপ্রাপ্ত হওয়া।

rŭs'-tic, *adj.* & *n.* 1. Of the country ; rural ; গ্রাম্য ; পাড়াগেঁয়ে। 2. Rude ; unpolished ; রূঢ়, অমার্জ্জিত, পাড়াগেঁয়ে, চাষাড়ে, চাষাড়িয়া। 3. Simple ; as, *rustic* dress ; সাদাসিধা, অনাড়ম্বর। 4. Honest ; artless ; সাধু ; সরল। **—tic'-i-ty**, *n.* A countryman; a peasant ; পাড়াগেঁয়ে লোক ; চাষা, কৃষাণ। **Rustic-work**—একপ্রকার পাথরের গাঁথুনির কাজ—যাহাতে পাথর গুলি এরূপ ভাবে কাটা হয় যাহাতে ইহারা স্বাভাবিক অবস্থার অনুরূপ বন্ধুর দেখায়; বন্ধুর শাখা প্রভৃতি দ্বারা নির্ম্মিত নিদাঘভবন বা নিদাঘভবনের গৃহসজ্জা।

rŭs'-ti-cāte, *v. i.* & *t.* To dwell or reside in the country ; পল্লীবাসী হওয়া, পল্লীগ্রামে বাস করা। ***Verb t.*** 1. To send into the country ; পল্লীগ্রামে প্রেরণ করা। 2. To banish from a university or college for sometime ; কিছুকালের জন্য কলেজ বা বিশ্ববিদ্যালয় হইতে বিতাড়িত করা। **—ca'-tion**, *n.* 1. The act of residing in a country ; পল্লীগ্রামে বাস করণ। 2. Temporary banishment from a university or college ; বিশ্ববিদ্যালয় বা কলেজ হইতে কিছুকালের জন্য বিতাড়ন।

rŭs-tle (-l), *v. i.*, *t.* & *n.* To give a slightly sibilant sound when shaken ; খস খস শব্দ হওয়া, সন্ সন শব্দ হওয়া, মর্ম্মরিত হওয়া। ***Verb t.*** To cause to make a rattling sound as the rubbing or movement of silk, leaves, ete. ; খস্ খস্ করান, সন সন করান, মর্ম্মরিত করান। ***Noun.*** A quick succession of low short sounds as of the rubbing of silk or dry leaves or of the movement of leaves, silk, etc. ; খস খস শব্দ, সন্ সন্ শব্দ, মর্ম্মর, মর্ম্মর রব, মর্ম্মর ধ্বনি।

rŭst'-ȳ, *adj.* 1. Affected with rust ; মরিচা-পড়া, মরিচা-ধরা। 2. Of the colour of rust ; লৌহমলবর্ণ, লৌহকলঙ্কবর্ণ। 3. Harsh ; as, a *rusty* voice ; কর্কশ। 4. Dull from inactivity ; নিষ্ক্রিয়তা হেতু জড়তাপ্রাপ্ত। **—i-ly**, *adv.* **—i-ness**, *n.*

rŭt, *n.* & *v. t.* 1. The track of wheel ; মাটীর উপর চাকার দাগ, চক্রাঙ্ক, ধারাপথ 2. Beaten track ; as, he got one of his usual *rut* ; চির আচরিত পন্থা। ***Verb t.*** To mark with ruts ; চক্রাঙ্ক দ্বারা চিহ্নিত করা।

rŭt, *n.* & *v. i.* The copulation or sexual desire in deer, reindeer and boar ; হরিণ এবং শূকরের সঙ্গমেচ্ছা বা মৈথুন। ***Verb i.*** To lust, as deer ; হরিণ প্রভৃতির সঙ্গমেচ্ছা হওয়া।

Ruta graveolens—সোমলতা (বেলঃ)। **ruth** (rôth), *n.* (*Archaic*) Pity; (অপ্রঃ) করুণা, দয়া, মমতা। **Ruth'-less,** *adj.* Cruel; নিষ্ঠুর, ক্রুর, করুণাশূন্য। **Ruth'-less-ly,** *adv.* **Ruth'-less-ness,** *n.*

rye (rī), *n.* A cereal plant and its seed; একপ্রকার রবি শস্য। [এই শস্য জর্ম্মনী ও রুশিয়ার প্রধান খাদ্য। Fr. *segala, seigle*; Germ. *rocken, roggen*; Ital. *segala.* Pers. *senteio, centeo.* Russ. *rosh, rozh, sel, jar.*]

rye'-grass (rī-), *n.* A kind of grass cultivated for cattle and horses; গবাদি পশুর খাদ্যোপযোগী তৃণবিশেষ।

rȳ'-ŏt, *n.* An Indian cultivator of the soil; রাইয়ত।

S

S, 1. The nineteenth letter of the English alphabet; ইংরাজী বর্ণমালার উনবিংশতিতম অক্ষর। 2. (*Chem.*) A symbol for the element sulphur; (রসায়নশাস্ত্র) গন্ধকের রাসায়নিক সঙ্কেত। 3. An S-shaped object; ইংরাজী S-অক্ষরাকৃতি বস্তু।

Să-bæ-ăn (-bē-), **-bē'-ăn,** *adj.* & *n.* Of ancient Yemen; প্রাচীন ইমেন প্রদেশসম্বন্ধীয়। ***Noun.*** A native of Yemen; আরবদেশের অন্তঃপাতী ইমেনের অধিবাসী। [Yemen এর প্রধান নগরীর নাম Saba. এই নগরীর সার্থবাহগণ ভারতবর্ষ হইতে নানাবিধ মসল্লা, সুগন্ধিদ্রব্য, মণিরত্ন, প্রভৃতি আমদানী করিয়া ইয়ুরোপে বিক্রয় করিত।]

Să'-bæ-ĭsm (-bē-), **-bă-ĭsm,** *ns.* Worship of the sun, moon and stars; star-worship; সূর্য্য, চন্দ্র ও নক্ষত্রের পূজা; নক্ষত্রার্চ্চনা, তারাপূজা।

Săb'-ă-ōth, *n.* Armies; "The Lord of *Sabaoth*"; সৈন্যদল। [এই শব্দটী বাইবেলে দুইবার মাত্র ব্যবহৃত হইয়াছে।]

săb'-bă-tă'-ri-ăn, *n.* & *adj.* A strict observer of sabbath; যে ব্যক্তি বাইবেলনির্দ্ধারিত বিশ্রামদিবসে সর্ব্বপ্রকার বিষয়কর্ম্ম হইতে নিবৃত্ত থাকে। [খৃষ্টিয়ানদের মধ্যে কেহ কেহ সপ্তাহের সপ্তমদিবস অর্থাৎ শনিবার বিশ্রামদিবস বলিয়া মানিয়া থাকে, অনেকে আবার রবিবার বিশ্রামদিবস পালন করে।] ***Adj.*** Of, or pertaining to, sabbatarian or their tenets; বিশ্রামদিবসপালনকারিগণ সম্বন্ধীয়, বিশ্রামদিবসপালনকারিগণের মত সম্বন্ধীয়।

săb'-băth, *n.* 1. The day of rest; Sunday; বিশ্রামবার, বিশ্রামদিবস; রবিবার। 2. Same as WITCHES' SABBATH (below). **Sabbath-breaker**—যে ব্যক্তি রবিবারে বিষয়কর্ম্ম করে, বিশ্রামদিবস ভঙ্গকারী। **Sabbath-day's journey**—অল্প স্থান ভ্রমণ [ইস্রায়েলাইটগণ বিশ্রামদিবসে কেবল মাত্র প্রায় ⅔ মাইল পরিমিত স্থান ভ্রমণ করিতে পারিত।] **Witches' sabbath** — ভূত, প্রেত, ডাকিনী পিশাচাদির বার্ষিক মধ্যনিশীথ উৎসব।

săb-băt'-ic, -i-căl, *adjs.* Pertaining to the sabbath; resembling sabbath; enjoying sabbath; বিশ্রামদিবস সম্বন্ধীয়; বিশ্রামদিবসবৎ; বিশ্রামদিবসোপভোগকারী। **Sabbatical year**—প্রতি সপ্তম বর্ষ—যাহাতে প্রাচীন ইহুদীগণকে ক্ষেত্র পতিত রাখিতে এবং অধমর্ণদিগকে ঋণদায় হইতে মুক্তি দান করিতে হইত।

săb'-bă-tize, *v. i.* & *t.* To keep the sabbath; বিশ্রামদিবস পালন করা। ***Verb t.*** 1. To make into sabbath; বিশ্রামদিবসে পরিণত করা। 2. To keep as a sabbath; বিশ্রামদিবসস্বরূপ পালন করা।

Să-bĕl'-li-ăn (-ī-), *n.* & *adj.* A follower of Sabellius, a philosopher in the third century, who taught that there is only one Person in the Godhead and that the Son and Holy Spirit are only different attributes, functions or emanation of God the Father; খৃষ্টীয় তৃতীয় শতকের দার্শনিক Sabellius সম্বন্ধীয়। [সেবিলিয়াসের মতানুসারে ঈশ্বর এক এবং অদ্বিতীয়। পুত্র এবং পবিত্রাত্মা পিতৃরূপী ঈশ্বরের বিভিন্ন গুণ, কার্য্য বা কায়ব্যূহস্বরূপ।] ***Adj.*** Pertaining to Sabellius or his doctrine; Sabellius বা তদীয় মত সম্বন্ধীয়। **-ism,** *n.*

Să'-bi-ăn, *n.* & *adj.* 1. A native of Yemen; ইমেনের অধিবাসী। ***Adj.*** Pertaining to Saba or its inhabitants; ইমেনের প্রধান নগরী Saba বা উক্ত নগরীর অধিবাসিসম্বন্ধীয়।

Să'-bi-ăn, *n.* 1. A star-worshipper; নক্ষত্রপূজক। 2. One of an early sect of Christians called also Christians of St. John; প্রাচীন খৃষ্টীয়সম্প্রদায়বিশেষভুক্ত ব্যক্তি।

Să'-bine, *adj.* & *n.* Pertaining to an ancient Italian race merged in the Roman; রোমানদিগের সহিত একীভূত ইতালি দেশবাসী প্রাচীন জাতিবিশেষ সম্বন্ধীয়। ***Noun.*** One of the Sabine people; স্যাবাইন জাতির লোক। [প্রাচীন রোমের প্রতিষ্ঠাতৃগণ উক্ত জাতির কন্যাগণকে বলপূর্ব্বক হরণ

করে। স্যাবাইনগণ এই অপমানের প্রতিশোধের জন্য রোমনগরী আক্রমণের উপক্রম করিলে ঐ সমস্ত স্ত্রীলোকগণ তাহাদের পতী ও পিতৃকুলের মধ্যে মধ্যস্থতা করিয়া উভয় জাতির মধ্যে শান্তির প্রতিষ্ঠা করে।]

sā'-ble (-bl), *n.* & *adj.* **1.** A small carnivorus quadruped of the weasel family, whose fur is highly

Sable.

valued ; নকুল জাতীয় ক্ষুদ্রকায় মাংসাশী জন্তুবিশেষ। **2.** Its skin or fur ; ঐ জন্তুর চর্ম্ম বা লোম। **3.** (*Pl.*) Mourning garments ; "The *sables* she wore were not solely for the dead earl" ; কৃষ্ণবর্ণ শোক-পরিচ্ছদ। **4.** A brush of the sable's hair ; উক্ত জন্তুর লোম হইতে প্রস্তুত বুরুশ। ***Adj.*** Black ; dusky ; কৃষ্ণবর্ণ, অসিতবর্ণ, ধূসর। **Sable-antelope**—একপ্রকার কৃষ্ণসার মৃগ।

sā'-bot (-bō), *n.* A wooden shoe worn by continental peasants ; একপ্রকার কাষ্ঠপাদুকা—যাহা ইয়ুরোপের বিভিন্ন দেশীয় কৃষকগণ পরিয়া থাকে।

sā'-bre (-bêr), *n.* & *v.t.* **1.** A sword with one edge ; অসি, তরবার, তলোয়ার, তরবারি, খাণ্ডা, খাঁড়া, বক্র খড়্গ [Syn. see SWORD]। **2.** (*Pl.*) Horse-soldiers ; as, 300 *sabres* ; অশ্বারোহী সৈন্য। **3.** A copper tool for skimming molten glass ; গলিত কাচের উপরের পর্দা উঠাইবার জন্য একপ্রকার তাম্র-নির্ম্মিত যন্ত্র। ***Verb t.*** To strike, cut, or kill with a sabre ; তরবারি দ্বারা আঘাত করা, অসিদ্বারা ছেদন করা, তরবারির আঘাতে বধ করা। **Sabre-bill, Sabre-wing**—বিভিন্ন জাতীয় পক্ষীর নাম। **Sabre-toothed lion, Sabre-toothed tiger**—অধুনালুপ্ত স্তন্যপায়ী চতুষ্পদ জন্তু। এই জন্তুর উপরের খদন্ত অসির আকৃতি ছিল বলিয়া এই নাম। **The sabre**—সামরিক শক্তি বা শাসন।

Sabre.

sā'-bre-tache (-bêr-tâsh), **-tasche** (-tâsh), *ns.* A leathern pocket worn by cavalry, suspended from the sword-belt ; অশ্বারোহী সৈনিকের কটিবন্ধ হইতে দোদুল্যমান চর্ম্মভস্ত্রিকা।

sabreur, *n.* A cavalryman with sabre ; অসিধারী অশ্বারোহী সৈনিক।

săb'-ū-lous (-lŭs), *adj.* Sandy ; gritty ; বালুকাময় ; কঙ্করময়।

sā-bŭr'-ra, *n.* Foul granular matter deposited in the stomach ; পাকস্থলীতে সঞ্চিত দূষিত দানাদার পদার্থ।

săb-ŭr-ra'-tion, *n.* The application of hot sand inclosed in a bag or bladder to any part of the body ; তপ্তবালির সেক।

săc, *n.* **1.** A bag or cyst ; a receptacle for liquid ; থলি, ছালা, কোষ ; তরলপদার্থ রাখার জন্য আধার।

săc-cate (-āt), *adj.* **1.** (*Bot.*) Having the form of a sack or pouch ; (উদ্ভিদ্‌বিদ্যা) থলিবৎ, থলির আকার, স্থলীবর্দ্ধিত (সাঃ পঃ)। **2.** Contained in a sack ; থলিস্থিত।

săc'-chă-rate, *n.* (*Chem.*) A salt of saccharic acid ; (রসায়ন-শাস্ত্র) শর্করাম্লের লবণ।

săc-chăr'-ic, *adj.* Contained in, or obtained from, sugar ; শর্করায় স্থিত, শর্করা হইতে প্রাপ্ত, শার্কর। **Saccharic acid**—($C_6 H_{10} O_8$) ; শর্করাম্ল।

săc-chă-rĭf'-êr-ous (-ŭs), *adj.* Producing sugar ; শর্করোৎপাদক, শর্করাগর্ভ।

săc-chăr'-ĭ-fȳ, *v.t.* To convert into sugar ; শর্করায় পরিণত করা।

săc-chă-rĭm'-ē-têr, *n.* Same as SACCHAROMETER.

săc-chă-rĭm'-ē-trȳ, *n.* Same as SACCHAROMETRY (which see).

săc'-chă-rĭn, *n.* An intensely sweet substance obtained from coal-tar ; আলকাতরা হইতে প্রাপ্ত একপ্রকার অতি সুমিষ্ট দ্রব্য, শর্করীণ, [ইহার মিষ্টতা চিনির প্রায় চারিশত গুণ।]

săc-chă-rine (-rĭn), *adj.* Pertaining to sugar ; having the qualities of sugar ; শর্করাসম্বন্ধীয় ; শর্করাসংক্রান্ত, শার্করিক, শর্করাধর্ম্মী।

săc'-chă-rīte, *n.* A finely-grained variety of felspar ; একপ্রকার স্ফটিকপ্রস্তর, শর্করাপাষাণ।

săc-chă-rŏm'-ē-têr, *n.* An instrument for measuring the quantity of sugary matter in a solution ; কোন জলীয় পদার্থে কি পরিমাণ শর্করা আছে—তন্নিরূপণার্থ যন্ত্রবিশেষ, শর্করামাপক।

săc-chă-rŏm-ē-trȳ, *n.* The operation of measuring the quantity of sugar in any solution ; শর্করামিতি।

săc'-chă-rōse, *n.* A chemical name for pure crystalline sugar ; দোবারা চিনি।

săc'-chă-rŭm, *n.* **1.** A genus of grasses ; মুঞ্জ প্রভৃতি তৃণ। **2.** Sugar ; চিনি, শর্করা।

Saccharum munja—মুঞ্জঘাস (আয়ু রসঃ)। [Syn. মৌঞ্জীতৃণাখ্য, ব্রাহ্মণ্য, তেজনাহ্বয়, বাণীরক, মুঞ্জনক, শীরী, দৃঢ়মূল, দৃঢ়তৃণ, দর্ভাহ্বয়, বহুপ্রজ, রঞ্জন, শক্রভঙ্গ।] [উপনয়নকালে ব্রাহ্মণসন্তানগণ মুঞ্জতৃণের মেখলা ধারণ করিয়া থাকে।]

Saccharum officinarum—আক (বেলঃ), ইক্ষু।

Saccharum sara—শরতৃণ, খাগ, খগড়া।

Saccharum semi-decumbens—খোরি (বেলঃ), খুরী (ঐ)।

Saccharum spontaneum—কাশ, কাশিয়া, কুশতৃণ।

săc'-cĭ-fôrm, *adj.* Sac-shaped ; থলিবৎ, কোষাকৃতি।

săc'-cule (-ūl), *n.* A small sack or cyst ; ক্ষুদ্র থলি, কোষ। **-cu-lar**, *adj*

—cu-late, —cu-lat-ed, *adjs.* **—cu-la′-tion,** *n.*

săc′-ēr-dō-tage, *n.* (*Joc.*) Subjection to priest craft ; (কৌতুকচ্ছলে) পুরোহিততন্ত্রাধীনতা।

săc-ēr-dō′-tăl, *adj.* Pertaining to the priests or priesthood ; as, *sacerdotal* class ; যাজকীয়, পৌরোহিত্য-সম্বন্ধীয়। **—ism,** *n.* **—ist,** *n.* The state of being sacerdotal ; যাজ্ঞিকতা (হিঃ কোঃ)। **—ize,** *v. t.*

sa′-chĕm, *n.* **1.** A chief among some of the American Indian tribes ; আমেরিকার আদিম অধিবাসিগণের মধ্যে কোন কোন জাতির সর্দ্দার, অসামরিক দলপতি (সাঃ পঃ)। **2.** A big-wig ; খাঞ্জা খাঁ।

sa-chet′ (-shā), *n.* **1.** A small bag for odoriferous substance ; সুগন্ধি দ্রব্য রাখার জন্য থলি। **2.** A perfumed pad or the like for laying among cloth etc. ; পোষাক প্রভৃতির মধ্যে রাখার জন্য সুরভিত পট্ট, গন্ধপট্ট।

săck, *n.* & *v. t.* **1.** A bag for flour, wool, etc. ; ছালা, বোরা। **2.** The quantity which a sack holds ; এক ছালা। **3.** A short loose coat or jacket ; একপ্রকার খাটো কোর্ত্তা। **4.** Dismissal ; as, to get the *sack* ; জবাব। ***Verb t.*** **1.** To put in a sack or bag ; ছালাজাত করা, ছালায় ভরা। **2.** To dismiss or discharge from employment ; কাজ হইতে জবাব দেওয়া, ছাড়াইয়া দেওয়া, বরখাস্ত করা। **Sack-cloth**—ছালার কাপড়, চট। শোক বা অনুতাপসূচক পরিচ্ছদ। **Sack-race**—ছালার ভিতর গলা পর্য্যন্ত পুরিয়া দৌড়। **In sack-cloth and ashes**—By wearing the customary garb of grief and penitence ; শোক এবং অনুতাপসূচক পরিচ্ছদে। In deep repentance ; গভীর অনুশোচনায়। **To get the sack**—To be dismissed ; জবাব হওয়া, বরখাস্ত হওয়া। **To give one the sack, To give the sack**—To dismiss from service ; জবাব দেওয়া, ছাড়াইয়া দেওয়া, বরখাস্ত করা, বরতরফ করা।

săck, *v. t.* & *n.* To plunder when taken by storm ; to plunder ; অধিকৃত নগর লুট করা ; লুণ্ঠন করা, লুটপাট করা, লুটতরাজ করা। ***Noun.*** The plunder or pillage of a town ; নগর ধ্বংস, নগর লুণ্ঠন, নগর-মোষ (দশঃ)।

săck, *n.* An old name for different sorts of dry wines ; শর্করাজাতীয় পদার্থপূর্ণ কয়েক প্রকার মদ্যের প্রাচীন নাম।

săck′-būt, *n.* A musical instrument of the trumpet or trombone kind ; এক প্রকার বংশী।

săck′-lĕss, *adj.* **1.** Innocent ; নির্দ্দোষ। **2.** Quiet ; শান্ত, সুধীর, সুশীল।

sacque (săk), *n.* A kind of loose gown ; একপ্রকার ঢিলা ঘাগরা।

sa′-crăl, *adj.* **1.** (*Anat.*) Pertaining to the sacrum ; (শারীরসংস্থান-বিদ্যা) ত্রিকাস্থি সম্পর্কীয়। **2.** (*Anthrop.*) Pertaining to sacred rites ; intended for sacred rites ; (নৃতত্ত্ব) পূজার্চ্চনাদি-সম্বন্ধীয় ; পূজার্চ্চনার জন্য অভিপ্রেত। **Pudic nerve of the sacral plexus to the left of the spinal cord** — কুহু (ব্রজঃ বিঃ)। **Sacral plexus**—স্বাধিষ্ঠানচক্র (ব্রজঃ হিন্দুঃ)। [লিঙ্গমূলস্থ বাদিলান্তবর্ণযুক্তহীরকসমপ্রভ-ষড়্‌দলপদ্ম]

săc′-ră-mĕnt, *n.* & *v. t.* **1.** An outward or visible sign of an inward or spiritual grace ; esp. a solemn religious ceremony or rite enjoined by Christ or the Church to be observed by Christians, as baptism or the Lord's supper ; (there being seven sacraments confirmation, the eucharist, penance, extreme unction, orders and matrimony in the Roman or Greek Church) ; আভ্যন্তরিক বা আধ্যাত্মিক দেবানুগ্রহের বহিঃদৃশ্য; সংস্কার। [হিন্দুশাস্ত্রানুসারে সংস্কার দশবিধ যথা :— গর্ভাধান, পুংসবন, সীমন্তোন্নয়ন, জাতকর্ম্ম, নামকরণ, অন্নপ্রাশন, চূড়াকরণ, উপনয়ন, সমাবর্ত্তন, গার্হস্থ্য আশ্রমে প্রবেশ] **2.** The Lord's supper ; the Host ; খৃষ্টের অন্তিমভোজনানুষ্ঠান, প্রভুভোজন (কেঃগুঃ) ; উক্ত ক্রিয়ায় ব্যবহৃত রোটিকা। **3.** A solemn pledge ; "Bound by no *sacrament* of military obedience to the state" ; প্রতিজ্ঞা, সত্য, দিব্য। **4.** (*Obs.*) Mystery ; (অপ্রঃ) রহস্য। **5.** Symbol ; "He then by a *sacrament* sent salvation to David" ; চিহ্ন, প্রতীক। ***Verb t.*** To bind by a sacrament ; প্রতিজ্ঞাপাশে বদ্ধ করা।

săc-ră-mĕn′-tăl, *adj.* & *n.* **1.** Of, or pertaining to, the sacraments ; সংস্কারসম্বন্ধীয়। **2.** Having the character of a sacrament ; সংস্কারাত্মক। ***Noun.*** **1.** The elements or the bread or wine used in the eucharist ; খৃষ্টের অন্তিম-ভোজনানুষ্ঠানে ব্যবহৃত মদ্য এবং রোটিকা। **2.** (*Pl.*) Rites which are of a sacramental character, but are not sacraments ; সংস্কারাত্মক অনুষ্ঠান। [যথা পবিত্র বারি ব্যবহার, অঙ্গুলীদ্বারা ক্রুশের অনুকরণ।] **—tal′-i-ty, —ism, —ist,** *ns.*

săc′-ră-mĕn-tā-ri-ăn, *adj.* & *n.* **1.** Pertaining to sacrament or sacraments ; সংস্কারসম্বন্ধীয়। **2.** (*Cap.*) One who holds the sacraments to be simply visible symbols ; যে ব্যক্তি সংস্কারসমূহকে কেবলমাত্র প্রতীক স্বরূপ মনে করে। [যথা, যে ব্যক্তি খৃষ্টের অন্তিমভোজনানুষ্ঠানে রুটি ও সুরাকে খৃষ্টের রক্ত ও মাংসের প্রতীক বলিয়া মনে করে কিন্তু খৃষ্টের প্রকৃত রক্ত বা মাংস বলিয়া স্বীকার করেনা।]

sa-cra′-ri-ŭm, *n.* **1.** (*Rom. Antiq.*) A domestic chapel devoted to some particular divinity ; the adytum ; (রোমীয় প্রত্নতত্ত্ব) গৃহস্থের বাটীর দেবমন্দির; প্রাচীন দেবমন্দিরের পবিত্রতম অংশ, গর্ভগৃহ (হাণ্ডেঃ)। **2.** A private chapel ; the chancel of a church ; কোন

বাটীর অন্তর্গত ক্ষুদ্র গির্জ্জা; গির্জ্জার যে অংশে যাজকবৃন্দ, গায়কগণ, প্রভৃতি উপবেশন করে।

să'-crĕd, *adj.* 1. Holy; পবিত্র, পূত, পুণ্য, মেধ্য। 2. Religious; as, *sacred* rites; ধর্ম্মবিষয়ক, ধর্ম্মসম্বন্ধীয়। 3. Venerable; মান্য, মাননীয়, পূজ্য। 4. Consecrated; as, a temple *sacred* to Jove; উৎসর্গীকৃত। 5. Inviolable; as, their persons will be held *sacred*; অলঙ্ঘনীয়, অলঙ্ঘ্য। **–ly,** *adv.* **–ness,** *n.* **Sacred ape**—Same as SACRED MONKEY. **Sacred bark**—Same as CASCARA SAGRADA (which see). **Sacred-bean**—পদ্মবীজ; পদ্ম। **Sacred-beetle**—Same as SCARAB. **Sacred-book**—ধর্ম্মগ্রন্থ। **Sacred fig**—অশ্বত্থ। **Sacred grove**—তপোবন। **Sacred Heart**—যীশুখৃষ্টের হৃৎপিণ্ড। [সপ্তদশ শতাব্দীতে Margaret Mary Alacoque নাম্নী জনৈক ফরাসীদেশীয়া সন্ন্যাসিনী খৃষ্টের হৃৎপিণ্ডের পূজা প্রবর্ত্তন করেন।] **Sacred malady**—Same as EPILEPSY. **Sacred monkey**—প্রাচীন মিসরবাসিগণ কর্ত্তৃক পূজিত বানর। **Sacred War**—ধর্ম্ম যুদ্ধ। বিশেষতঃ ডেল্‌ফী নগরীর দেবমন্দির রক্ষার্থ যুদ্ধ চতুষ্টয়ের অন্যতম। প্রথম, দ্বিতীয়, তৃতীয় ও চতুর্থ যুদ্ধ যথাক্রমে খৃঃ পূঃ ৬০০—৫০৯, খৃঃ পূঃ ৪৪৯, খৃঃ পূঃ ৩৫৬ (বা ৩৫৭)—৩৪৬ এবং খৃঃ পূঃ ৬৬৯—৩৩৮ অব্দে সংঘটিত হয়।] **Sacred Books of the East**—ইয়ুরোপের কতিপয় প্রথিতনামা প্রাচ্যবিদ্যাবিৎ কর্ত্তৃক ম্যাক্সমুলারের সম্পাদকতায় উনবিংশ শতাব্দীর শেষভাগ হইতে প্রকাশিত প্রাচ্যদেশীয় ধর্ম্মসম্বন্ধীয় গ্রন্থমালা। **The sacred college**—রোম নগরীস্থ ক্যাডিন্যাল সম্প্রদায়।

săc'-ri-fice (-fīs), *n., v. t. & i.* 1. The offering of anything to God; consecratory rite; ঈশ্বরের উদ্দেশ্যে কোন বস্তু প্রদান; বলিদান (হিঃ কোঃ), ক্রতু, আহুতি, যাগ, যজ্ঞ। 2. Anything consecrated or offered to a divinity; a victim; দেবোদ্দেশ্যে প্রদত্ত বস্তু, নৈবেদ্য, উপায়ন; বলি। 3. The giving up of something for the sake of others; as, the *sacrifice* of life; উৎসর্গ, বলিদান। 4. The selling or disposing of one's goods at a value under cost price; as, to sell one's goods at a *sacrifice*; ক্রয়মূল্যের অল্প দরে জিনিষ বিক্রয়, ক্ষতি স্বীকার করিয়া জিনিষ বিক্রয়। ***Verb t.*** 1. To make an offering, or sacrifice of; to consecrate or present by way of expiation or propitiation to some divinity; উপায়ন স্বরূপ প্রদান করা; বলিদান করা। 2. To give up in favour of a higher or more imperative duty or claim; উৎসর্গ করা, ত্যাগ করা, আহুতি প্রদান করা। 3. To kill; বধ করা, বিনাশ করা। 4. To sell or dispose of at a value under cost price; খরিদ মূল্য অপেক্ষা কম দরে বিক্রয় করা। ***Verb i.*** To offer up sacrifice to some deity; দেবতার নিকট বলি দেওয়া। **–fic-er,** *n.* One that sacrifices or immolates; a priest; বলিপ্রদানকারী, আত্মোৎসর্গকারী; পুরোহিত, ঋত্বিক। **–fi'-cial,** *adj.* Pertaining to sacrifice; performing sacrifice; বলিসম্পর্কীয়, যজ্ঞবিষয়ক, যজ্ঞীয়; বলিসম্পাদনকারী, যজ্ঞকর্ত্তা। **Fire for sacrifice**—হোমাগ্নি, যজ্ঞানল, যজ্ঞাগ্নি। **Human sacrifice**—নরমেধ, নরযজ্ঞ, নরবলি। **Pit for sacrifice**—যজ্ঞকুণ্ড। **Place of sacrifice**—যজ্ঞশালা। **Post of sacrifice**—যূপ। **Sacrificial knife**—খড়্গ।

săc'-ri-lege (-lĕj), *n.* 1. The act or crime of violating or profaning sacred things; পবিত্রবস্তু বা দেবস্থান দূষণ বা লঙ্ঘন, দেবস্থানে অত্যাচার, পবিত্র বস্তু বা দেবস্থান দূষণ বা লঙ্ঘনের অপরাধ। 2. The crime of stealing sacred things, esp. from churches; পবিত্র বস্তু হরণের অপরাধ, বিশেষতঃ ধর্ম্মমন্দির হইতে পবিত্রদ্রব্য হরণের অপরাধ, দেবস্বচৌর্য্য, দেবস্বাপহার।

să-cri-lĕ'-gious (-jŭs), *adj.* 1. Violating sacred things; guilty of sacrilege; দেবস্থানদূষণ, দেবস্থানলঙ্ঘনকারী; দেবস্বাপহারক। 2. Involving sacrilege; দেবস্থানলঙ্ঘনাত্মক, দেবস্বাপহরণাত্মক। 3. Impious; অসাধু, দেবদ্বেষী, পাষণ্ড। **–ly,** *adv.* **–ness,** *n.* **–sac'-ri-le-gist,** *n.*

sā'-cring, *n.* (*Archaic*) The act of consecrating; (অপ্রঃ) উৎসর্গীকরণ। **Sacring-bell** — (রোমানক্যাথলিক ও কোন কোন অ্যাংলিক্যান ধর্ম্মসংঘে) খৃষ্টের অন্তিমভোজনানুষ্ঠানের সুরা ও রোটিকা শোধনের বার্ত্তা ঘোষণার জন্য যে ঘণ্টা নিনাদিত হয়।

sā'-crist, *n.* A church official in charge of sacred vessels etc.; মন্দিরের তৈজসপত্র প্রভৃতি রক্ষক।

săc'-ris-tăn, *n.* 1. Same as SACRIST. 2. (*Archaic*) Same as SEXTON (which see).

săc'-ris-tȳ, *n.* An apartment in a church where the sacred utensils, vestments, etc. are kept; খৃষ্টীয় ধর্ম্মমন্দিরের যে কক্ষে তৈজসপত্র, রাজাদিগের পোষাক পরিচ্ছদ, প্রভৃতি রক্ষিত হয়।

Sacro coccygeal plexus—আধারচক্র (ব্রজঃ হিন্দু), মূলাধার [cf. মূলাধারে ত্রিকোণাখ্যে ইচ্ছাজ্ঞানক্রিয়াত্মকে। মধ্যে স্বয়ম্ভুলিঙ্গন্তু কোটীসূর্য্যসমপ্রভম্॥ তদূর্দ্ধে কাম বীজন্তু কলশান্তীন্দুনাদকম্। তদূর্দ্ধেতু শিখাকারং কুণ্ডলী ব্রহ্মবিগ্রহা॥ তদ্বাহ্যে হেমবর্ণাভং ব স বর্ণচতুর্দ্দলম্। দ্রুতহেমসমপ্রখ্যং পদ্মং তত্র বিভাবয়েৎ।

săc'-rō-sanct (-săngkt), *adj.* & *n.* Sacred; inviolable; পবিত্র, পূত; অলঙ্ঘ্য। ***Noun.*** That which is most holy; পবিত্রতম বস্তু।

sā'-crŭm, *n.* The compound bone which forms the inferior extremity of the vertebral column; মনুষ্যের মেরুদণ্ডের অন্ত্যভাগের ত্রিকোণ অস্থি, ত্রিকাস্থি (হঃ চঃ)।

săd, *adj.* 1. Sorrowful; mournful; melancholy; gloomy; বিষাদপূর্ণ; শোকপূর্ণ; বিষণ্ণ; ম্লান। 2. Expressive of sorrow; বিষাদসূচক, দুঃখসূচক।

3. Causing sadness ; lamentable ; as, the *sad* end of his career ; বিষাদজনক, দুঃখজনক ; শোচনীয়। 4. (Of colour) Dark ; as, the leaves are of a *sad* green ; (বর্ণ সম্বন্ধে) কৃষ্ণ, কাল, নিষ্প্রভ, মলিন। 5. (*Colloq.*) Wicked ; bad ; as, a *sad* old fellow ; shocking ; (চলিত ভাষায়) মন্দ ; খারাপ ; ভয়ানক। 6. (*Obs.*) Heavy ; as, a *sad* cake ; (অপ্রঃ) ভারি, অসম্যক স্ফীত। **Sad'-den,** *v. t.* & *i.* **Sad'-den-ing,** *adj.* Causing sadness : বিষাদজনক, অপ্রফুল্লকর। **Sad'-dish,** *adj.* **Sad'-ly,** *adv.* **Sad'-ness,** *n.* Sorrowfulness ; melancholy ; বিষণ্ণতা, শোকাকুলতা ; বিষাদ, ম্লানিমা। **Sad iron**—ইস্ত্রী। **A sad dog**—A merry fellow ; ফূর্ত্তিবাজ লোক, আমুদে লোক।

săd'-dle (-l), *n.,* & *v. t.* 1. A seat for a rider of a horse ; ঘোড়ার জীন। [Syn. পর্য্যাণ, পল্যয়ন, পর্য্যয়ণ, পল্যান।] 2. A seat for the rider of a bicycle etc. ; দ্বিচক্রযান প্রভৃতি আরোহীর আসন। 3. Something resembling a saddle in form, use, or the like ; পর্য্যাণের আকারগত, ব্যবহারগত বা অন্য কোন প্রকার সাদৃশ্য-বিশিষ্ট বস্তু। 4. Joint of mutton or of venison consisting of two loins ; কসাই কর্ত্তৃক কর্ত্তিত হরিণ বা মেষের মেরুদণ্ডের নিম্নভাগের উভয় দিগের মাংসখণ্ড। 5. (In bridges) A block on the top of a pier over which suspension cables pass or to which they are attached : (সেতুনির্ম্মাণে) পিল্লার উপরিস্থিত ইষ্টকাদি নির্ম্মিত স্তূপ—যাহার উপর দিয়া দোদুল্যমান সেতুর শৃঙ্খল নীত হয় অথবা যাহাতে উক্তরূপ শৃঙ্খল সংবদ্ধ থাকে। 6. A support on which a gun is placed for bouching ; নূতন মুখ কাটার জন্য যে অবলম্বনের উপর কামান রক্ষিত হয়। *Verb t.* 1. To put a saddle on ; জীন লাগান, জীন কষা (cf. একটা ভাল ঘোড়ায় জীন কষতে বল)। 2. To burden ; as, to *saddle* one with debts ; ভারচাপান, ভারাক্রান্ত করা। **–dler,** *n.* A maker of saddles or harness ; জীনপ্রস্তুতকারী, অশ্বসজ্জা-প্রস্তুতকারী। **–dler-y,** *n.* 1. The trade or employment of a saddler ; জীন-প্রস্তুতের কার্য্য, অশ্বসজ্জা প্রস্তুতের কার্য্য, জীন বা অশ্বসজ্জা প্রস্তুতের ব্যবসায়। 2. The articles usually manufactured or sold by a saddler ; অশ্বসজ্জা,—জীন, লাগাম, প্রভৃতি। 3. A place where saddles and other equipments for horses are sold ; অশ্বসজ্জা বিক্রয়ের স্থান, অশ্বসজ্জা-বিপণি। **Saddle-bow**—জীনের বক্রাকৃতি অগ্রভাগ। **Saddlehorse** — চড়িবার ঘোড়া। **Saddle-back**—জীনের আকৃতি গিরি বা গিরিচূড়া ; একপ্রকার শুক্তি ; বিভিন্ন প্রকার পক্ষী ও মৎস্যের নাম। **Saddle-backed**—ন্যুব্জাকৃতি,ন্যুব্জপৃষ্ঠ। **Saddle-bag** — জীনের পশ্চাদ্দিকের উভয় পার্শ্বে যে থলিদ্বয় ঝুলাইয়া নেওয়া হয়—উহাদের অন্যতর ; আরব প্রভৃতি দেশে উষ্ট্রের পৃষ্ঠে বাহিত থলিয়া বিশেষের আকারে প্রস্তুত গালিচা সূচনার্থে ব্যবহৃত। [এইরূপ গালিচা দ্বারা বর্ত্তমানে অল্পমূল্যের আসবাবপত্র মোড়া হইয়া থাকে।] **Saddle-cloth**—জীনপোষ। **Saddle-tree**—জীনের কাঠাম। **In the saddle** — In office ; কার্য্যে নিযুক্ত। Ready for work ; কার্য্যের জন্য প্রস্তুত। **To cast out of saddle**—To dismiss ; পদচ্যুত করা, বরখাস্ত করা। **To lay or set the saddle on right horse**—To lay blame on the right person ; প্রকৃত দোষী ব্যক্তির উপর দোষারোপ করা।

Săd'-dū-cee (-sē), *n.* One of a sect among the Jews who denied the resurrection and the existence of angels and spirits ; প্রাচীন ইহুদীদিগের সম্প্রদায়বিশেষভুক্ত ব্যক্তি। [এই সম্প্রদায়ের লোকগণ মৃত ব্যক্তির সমাধি হইতে পুনরুত্থান এবং দেবদূত প্রভৃতির অস্তিত্ব সম্বন্ধে অবিশ্বাস করিত।] **–ce'-an,** *adj.* **–ism,** *n.*

sā'-dism, *n.* Sexual pervresion attended with cruelty ; নিষ্ঠুরাচরণ সহকৃত অস্বাভাবিক অভিগমন। [Count de Sade (১৭৪০—১৮১৪) নামক জনৈক প্যারীনগরবাসী লেখকের নাম হইতে গৃহীত। এই Sade কোনরূপ অস্বাভাবিক অপরাধের জন্য প্রাণদণ্ডে দণ্ডিত হয়। Bastille কারাগারে রুদ্ধ থাকার কালে Sade কতিপয় অতি জঘন্য ও অশ্লীল নাটক ও উপন্যাস রচনা করে।]

sāfe, *n.* 1. A strong case for containing money, valuable documents, etc. ; লোহার সিন্দুক। 2. Same as MEAT-SAFE.

sāfe, *adj.* 1. Free from or not liable to langour of any kind ; নিরাপদ, নির্ব্বিঘ্ন। 2. Conferring safety ; as, a safe *harbour* ; নির্ব্বিঘ্নতাজনক, আপৎশূন্য। 3. Placed beyond the power of doing harm ; as, the mad man has been kept in a *safe* place ; অনিষ্টসাধনাক্ষম। 4. Uninjured ; অক্ষত। 5. Cautious ; moderate ; as, a *safe* critic ; সতর্ক ; মৃদু-প্রকৃতি। **Safe'-ly,** *adv.* 1. Without harm or injury ; নিরাপদে, নির্ব্বিঘ্নে। 2. Securely ; সুরক্ষিত ভাবে। **Safe-conduct**—বিদেশে শত্রুরাজ্যে নিরাপদে ভ্রমণের জন্য অনুমতিপত্র, অভয়পত্র ; ভ্রমণকারীর শরীররক্ষিবর্গ। **Safe-guard**—Same as SAFE-CONDUCT ; also রক্ষা, সতর্কতা। (*Verb t.*) রক্ষা করা, নিরাপদ করা। **Safe-keeping**—হেফাজত, জিম্মা। **Safe-lock**—লোহার সিন্দুকের তালা। **Safe and secure**—অক্ষত, অটুট। **Safe bind safe find**—যে বস্তু সাবধানপূর্ব্বক রাখা যায় তাহা অনায়াসেই আবশ্যককালে পাওয়া যায়।

sāfe'-tȳ, *n.* 1. Condition or state of being safe ; freedom from danger, নির্ব্বিঘ্নতা ; আপৎশূন্যতা, ক্ষেম, কুশলতা। 2. (*Rare*) Close custody ; (অপ্রঃ) সুরক্ষিত অবস্থা। **Safe-ty-belt**—সন্তরণকারিগণের ব্যবহারের জন্য একপ্রকার লঘুপদার্থে প্রস্তুত বা

বায়ুদ্বারা স্ফীতকরণোপযোগী কটিবন্ধ। **Safety-fuse**—যে দাহ্যপদার্থপূর্ণ নল বা পলিতা নির্দ্দিষ্ট হারে জ্বলিয়া থাকে। **Safety-lamp** — একপ্রকার লণ্ঠন—যাহার ভিতরের দীপশিখা সূক্ষ্ম তারের জালদ্বারা আবৃত থাকায় খনিমধ্যস্থ আশুজ্বলনশীল বাষ্পের সংস্পর্শে আসিতে পারেনা, রক্ষকদীপ (হিঃ কোঃ), সেফ্‌টী ল্যাম্প (ঐ)। **Safety-match**—যে দিয়াশলাইয়ের ফুস্ফুরক প্রভৃতি রাসায়নিকদ্রব্যলিপ্ত পার্শ্বদ্বয় ভিন্ন অন্যত্র শলাকাদ্বারা ঘর্ষণ করিলে অগ্নি উৎপাদিত হয়না, আপৎবারকদীপশলাকা, রক্ষক-দিয়াশলাই (হিঃ কোঃ), সেফ্‌টী দিয়াশলাই (ঐ)। **Safety pin**—একপ্রকার সূচী—ইহার সূক্ষ্মপ্রান্ত পার্শ্ববর্ত্তী অপর প্রান্তের কলে আটকান যায় বলিয়া সহসা ছুটিয়া আসে না বা ধারণকারীর শরীরে ফুটিতে পারেনা, রক্ষকসূচী। **Safety-tube**—রক্ষকনলিকা (হিঃ কোঃ), সেফ্‌টী নলিকা (ঐ)। **Safety-valve** —বাষ্পনিঃসরণ রন্ধ্র বা দ্বার, সংরক্ষক পিধান;

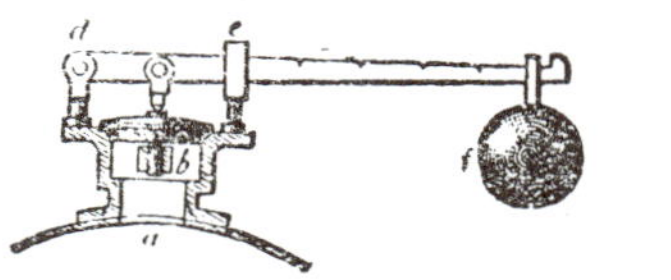

Safety valve.

(লক্ষণায়) কোনরূপ বিঘ্ন উৎপাদন বিনা উত্তেজনাদির বহিঃপ্রকাশের উপায়।

săf'-fi-ăn (-ĭ-), *n.* A brilliantly dyed leather made at Astracan and other parts of Asiatic Russia; আস্ত্রাকান এবং এসিয়ার অন্তর্গত রুশিয়ায় অন্যান্য স্থানে প্রস্তুত একপ্রকার উজ্জ্বলবর্ণে রঞ্জিত চর্ম্ম।

săf'-flow-ẽr, *n.* **1.** A composite plant of the genus carthamus (*Carthamus tinctorius*); কুসুম ফুলের গাছ [Syn. কুসুম্ভ, রজস্, কমলোত্তর, রক্তসংকোচ, অগ্নিশিখ, বহ্নিশিখ, বহ্নিশেখর, বহ্নিদীপক, রক্ত, লোহিত, রোহিত, পীত, মহারজন (cf. মহারজন রক্তেন পূর্ব্বমস্ত্রপদং যুতম্—তন্ত্রসার), মহারঞ্জন (মঃ ভাঃ), পাবক, বস্ত্ররঞ্জন, পদ্মোত্তর, কৌসুম্ভ (wild species)।] **2.** The dried petals of the flowers of the tree; কুসুম ফুলের শুষ্ক পাঁপড়ি। **3.** A colouring matter obtained from the dried flowers; কুসুম ফুলের রঙ্গ, কুসুম্ভরাগ।

săf'-frŏn, *n., adj. & v. t.* **1.** A bulbous plant, the stigmas of which are used as a colouring and flavouring ingredient in cookery and yield an orange-red extract used in dyeing and painting (*Crocus sativus*); কুঙ্কুম গাছ। **2.** A deep orange coloured substance consisting of the dried stigmas of the plant; কুঙ্কুম, কুমকুম (*poet.*) [cf. লোরে মিটায়ল পীন পয়োধর মৃগমদ কুমকুম রেখা—বৈষ্ণব পদাবলী।], জাফ্রান [Syn. কাশ্মীরজ, কেসর, ঘুসৃণ (cf. যত্র স্ত্রীণাং মসৃণঘুসৃণালেপনোঙ্ক কুচশ্রীঃ—বিক্রমাঙ্কদেবচরিত), লোহিতচন্দন, পীতচন্দন, বাহ্লীক, বাহ্লিক, বরবাহ্লীক, পীতক, পীতিকা, পীতন, রক্ত, রক্তসংজ্ঞ, কুচন্দন, ধীর, পিশুন, সঙ্কোচ, অগ্নিশিখ, বহ্নিশিখ, শোণিত, লোহিত, গৌর, সূর্য্যসংজ্ঞ, হরিচন্দন, চারু, শঠ, ঘোর, কান্ত, তরুণ, রুচির, অসৃক, অগ্নিশেখর, কাশ্মীরজ, কাশ্মীরজন্ম, কাশ্মীর (গীতঃ), কাশ্মীরসম্ভব, কালেয়ক, কুসুমাত্মক, পুষ্পরজ, তৃণকুঙ্কুম (Kashmir crocus), গন্ধাধিক (ibid), শোণিতাহ্বয়, রোহিত, খল, রজ, বর, দীপক, সৌরভ, চন্দন (অঃ), পীতহরিদ্রা, জাগুড়, দীপন, রক্তাঙ্গ, পীতকাবের, কেশরবর, রঞ্জনী, বর্ণ, বরেণ্য, রুধির (চঃ), পাটল, কাবের। দেশভেদে কুঙ্কুম ত্রিবিধ যথা :—কাশ্মীরদেশজে ক্ষেত্রে কুঙ্কুমং যদ্ভবেদ্ধিতৎ। সূক্ষ্মকেশরমারক্তং পদ্মগন্ধি তদুত্তমম্॥ বাহ্লীকদেশসঞ্জাতং কুঙ্কুমং পাণ্ডুরংভবেৎ। কেতকীগন্ধযুক্তং তন্মধ্যমং সূক্ষ্মকেশরম্॥ কুঙ্কুমং পারসীকেয়ং মধুগন্ধি তদীরিতম্। ঈষৎপাণ্ডরবর্ণং তদধমং স্থূলকেশরম্ (ভাবপ্রকাশ)। বৈদ্যকশাস্ত্রমতে কুঙ্কুমের গুণ — কাসবাতকফাকণ্ঠরোগমূর্দ্ধশূলবিষদোষনাশিত্বম্। রোচনত্বম্। তনুকান্তিকরত্বঞ্চ—রাজনির্ঘণ্ট। বিবর্ণতাকণ্ডুনাশিত্বঞ্চ (রাজবল্লভ)। ডাক্তারি মতে কুঙ্কুম বলকারক, হিক্কানিবারক, রজোনিঃসারক এবং কণ্ডুপ্রভৃতি নাশক ঔষধস্বরূপ ব্যবহৃত হয়। [Arab. *zaifran, karkam*; Sp. *azafran*; Burm. *tha n'wen*; Chin. *fan-hung-hwa*; Fr. *safran*; Pers. *abir, karkam, safran*; It. *zafferano*; Germ. *safra'n*]. **2.** A Saffron coloured dye; কুঙ্কুমবর্ণ রঞ্জকপদার্থ। ***Adj.*** Having the rich orange colour of saffron; কুঙ্কুমবর্ণ, জাফ্রাণবর্ণ, কুঙ্কুমারক্ত, কুঙ্কুমারুণ। ***Verb t.*** To colour with or like saffron; কুঙ্কুমরঞ্জিত করা, জাফ্রান দ্বারা রঙ্গান, কুঙ্কুমবর্ণে রঞ্জিত করা। **—y,** *adj.* **Bastad saffron**—কুসুমফুলের গাছ। **Indian saffron**—হলুদ। **Saffron-cake**—কুঙ্কুম দ্বারা রঞ্জিত পিষ্টক, কুঙ্কুমপিষ্টিকা।

săf'-ră-nin, *n.* **1.** The colouring matter of saffron; জাফ্রাণের রঞ্জকবস্তু। **2.** A saffron-like dye-stuff obtained from coal-tar; আলকাতরা হইতে প্রাপ্ত একপ্রকার কুঙ্কুমবর্ণ রঞ্জকপদার্থ, কুঙ্কুমীন।

săg, *v. i., t. & n.* **1.** To sink in the middle; মধ্যভাগ বসিয়া যাওয়া। **2.** To sink under care and difficulties; to fall as price; দমিয়া যাওয়া; মূল্য প্রভৃতি হঠাৎ নামা। ***Verb t.*** To cause to sag; বসান, কমান, দাবিয়া দেওয়া, দমাইয়া দেওয়া। ***Noun.*** **1.** The fact of sagging; দমিয়া যাওন। **2.** Decline in price; মূল্যহ্রাস। **3.** Tendency, as of a vessel leeward; নির্বাতপার্শ্বে জাহাজের গতিপ্রবণতা। **Sag'-gy,** *adj.*

sä'-gă, *n.* The heroic tales and myths of the nations of northern Europe; নরওয়ে, ডেনমার্ক, প্রভৃতি দেশের প্রাচীনকাহিনী, পৌরাণিকী কথা।

să-gā'-cious (-shŭs), *adj.* **1.** Keen-witted; discerning; তীক্ষ্ণবুদ্ধি, ধীমান, সূক্ষ্মধী, কুশাগ্রমতি; সূক্ষ্মদর্শী। **2.** Showing sagacity; সূক্ষ্মবুদ্ধির পরিচায়ক। **3.** (Of animals) Intelligent; (জন্তু সম্পর্কে) বুদ্ধিমান। **—gac'-i-ty,** *n.* **1.** Quickness of discernment; the quality of being sagacious; বুদ্ধিমত্তা; তীক্ষ্ণবুদ্ধিতা, সূক্ষ্মবুদ্ধিতা। **2.** (Of animals) Intelligence approching that of mankind; (জন্তু-সম্পর্কে) বুদ্ধিবৃত্তি। **—ly,** *adv.*

săg'-ă-mōre, *n.* Same as SACHEM I.

sāge, *n.* A garden herb largely used in cookery for seasoning; পুদিনার মত উদ্যানরোপিত গুল্ম বিশেষ। [ইহার পত্র ব্যঞ্জনাদি

Sage-plant.

সুরভিত করার জন্য ব্যবহৃত হয়।] **Sage-green**—সেজের পাতার মত ম্লান সবুজবর্ণ। **Sage tea** — সেজের পাতার নির্যাস — যাহা ঔষধস্বরূপ গ্রহণ করা হইয়া থাকে। **Sage and onions**—হাঁস, শূকর, প্রভৃতির ভিতর দিবার জন্য পেঁয়াজ ও সেজ পত্রের পুর।

sāge, *adj.* & *n.* **1.** Wise; prudent; জ্ঞানী, সদ্বিবেচক, সুবিজ্ঞ; প্রাজ্ঞ। **2.** Proceeding from prudence; shrewd; well-considered; সদ্বিবেচনাপ্রসূত; বুদ্ধির পরিচায়ক; সুবিবেচিত। *Noun.* **1.** A wise man; জ্ঞানী লোক। **2.** A grave philosopher; গভীর দার্শনিক। **3.** A man venerable for years and of sound judgment and prudence; প্রবীণ জ্ঞানী ব্যক্তি।

săg'-gar (-år), *n.* **1.** A clay pot used in making pottery ware; মৃদ্‌ভাণ্ডাদি নির্ম্মাণে ব্যবহৃত মৃৎপাত্রবিশেষ। **2.** A clay used in making saggars; উক্তরূপ ভাণ্ড নির্ম্মাণে ব্যবহৃত মৃত্তিকা।

să-gĭt'-ta (-ă), *n.* **1.** The typical genus of arrow worms; বাণকৃমি (সিউজিয়াম)। **2.** (*Geom.*) The versed sine of an arc; (জ্যামিতি) বৃত্তখণ্ডের উৎক্রম জ্যা। **3.** (*Arch.*) The keystone of an arch; (স্থপতি-বিদ্যা) খিলানের মধ্যপ্রস্তর। **4.** One of the otoliths of a fishe's ear; মৎস্যের কাণকোর মধ্যবর্ত্তী ক্ষুদ্র অস্থিসমূহের অন্যতম।

săg-it'-tăl (-ĭ-), *adj.* Pertaining to an arrow; resembling an arrow; বাণসম্বন্ধীয়; বাণসদৃশ।

Săg-it-tā'-rĭ-ŭs (-ĭ-), *n.* **1.** The ninth sign of the zodiac; ধনুরাশি [Syn. তৌক্ষিক, চাপ, কার্ম্মুক (cf. কার্ম্মুকেচ মহাহানিঃ—বিশ্বকর্ম্মাপ্রকাশ)] **2.** The constellation; পূর্ব্বাষাঢ়া (δ sagitarii), উত্তরাষাঢ়া (φ sagittarii). **3.** An ancient zodiacal constellation representing a centaur drawing a bow; ধনুর্দ্ধর (cf. পূর্ব্বার্দ্ধ মনুষ্যাকার শেষার্দ্ধাশ্বাকার ধনুর্দ্ধারী পুরুষঃ)।

săg'-it-tāte (-ĭ-), **—tā-tĕd,** *adjs.* Shaped like the head of an arrow; বাণাগ্রসদৃশ, বাণাগ্রবৎ।

sā'-gō, *n.* A starchy substance usually in the form of pearly grains obtained from the pith

Sago-palm.

of several palms; তালজাতীয় কয়েক প্রকার বৃক্ষের মজ্জা হইতে প্রাপ্ত একপ্রকার শ্বেতসারবহুল পদার্থ, সাগু, সাগুদানা।

Să-hâr'-ă, *n.* **1.** The great desert of Lybia; সাহারা মরুভূমি। **2.** A wilderness; মরুভূমি, মরুপ্রান্তর।

Sâ'-hib (-ĭb), *n.* A term of respect much the same as Mr. or Mrs.; সাহেব।

said (sĕd), *p. t.* & *p. p.* of SAY (which see).

sai'-gă (sā-), *n.* A ruminant resembling the antelope, but having the head peculiarly shaped, found

Saiga.

in the steppes of Russia; রুশিয়ার তরুহীন বিশাল প্রান্তরসমূহে প্রাপ্ত একজাতীয় হরিণ।

sail (sāl) *n.* **1.** A piece of cloth stretched to catch wind and so to move ship or boat; পাইল, বাদাম। [Syn. বাতবসন, মরুৎপট, বায়ুবসন, নৌকাপট, নৌবসন, নৌবস্ত্র, বাতবস্ত্র, বায়ুবস্ত্র, বায়ুপট।] **2.** A ship; a fleet; "A portly *sail* of ships make hitherward"; জাহাজ; জাহাজের বহর। **3.** The wing of a bird; পাখা। **4.** That part of the arm of a wind-mill which catches the wind; বাতযন্ত্রের যে অংশে বায়ু ধৃত হয়। **Sail-cloth**—পাইলের কাপড়; পোষাক তৈরীর উপযোগী একপ্রকার কাপড়। **Sail-fish**—একপ্রকার মৎস্য—ইহাদের পিঠের পাখনা অতি বৃহৎ। **Sail ho!**—ঐ জাহাজ। **Sail of line**—Men-of-war; রণপোতশ্রেণী। **To live at a low sail**—দীনভাবে বাস করা। **To make sail**—To start by spreading the sails; পাইল তুলিয়া রওয়ানা হওয়া। To start; যাত্রা করা।

To sail close to the wind—To go to the verge of impropriety or danger ; কোনরূপ অনুচিত আচরণ করিয়া ফেলা, প্রায় বিপদে পতিত হওয়া। **To set sail**—See SET. **To shorten sail**—To reduce sail by taking it in ; পাইল কমাইয়া দেওয়া। **To strike sail**—To lower the sails ; পাইল নামান। To be humble ; বিনীত হওয়া। **To take in sail**—To curbe one's ambition ; দুরাকাঙ্ক্ষা সংযত করা। **To take wind out of sails**—See WIND. **Under sail**—Having the sail set : পাইল বিস্তার করিয়া। **With full sail**—সকল পাইল বিস্তার করিয়া।

sail (sāl), *v. i., t.* & *n.* **1.** To be carried over the water by sails ; পাইল দ্বারা চালিত হওয়া, পাইলে চলা। **2.** To be moved or impelled by any mechanical power ; কোনরূপ যান্ত্রিকশক্তি দ্বারা পরিচালিত হওয়া। **3.** To be conveyed in a vessel on water ; জলোপরি জাহাজে নীত হওয়া। **4.** To set sail ; to start on a voyage ; পাইল তুলিয়া যাত্রা করা ; জলযাত্রা করা, সমুদ্রযাত্রা করা। **5.** To float ; as, the birds *sail* in the sky ; ভাসিয়া চলা। ***Verb t.*** **1.** To pass over by means of sails ; পাইল তুলিয়া চলা। **2.** To glide or fly through ; "On broad wings the buzzard slowly *sails* the sky" ; উড়িয়া চলা, ভাসিয়া চলা, অনায়াসে চলা। **3.** To direct or manage the motion ; as, to *sail* a ship ; (পোত) চালনা করা। **4.** (Of a woman ; sometimes of an animal) To move or walk in a stately manner ; "She *sailed* down upon Richard" ; গরবভরে চলা, বুক ফুলাইয়া চলা, গজেন্দ্রগমনে চলা, সাটোপে চলা, ঠমকের সহিত চলা। ***Noun.*** Voyage ; passage by a sailing vessel ; জলযাত্রা ; পাইলের জাহাজে ভ্রমণ। **Sail-boat**—যে নৌকা সচরাচর পাইল দ্বারা চালিত হয়। **To sail in**—(*Slang*) To rush in ; to begin boldly to do something ; হুড়মুড়িয়া প্রবেশ করা ; খুব সাহসের সহিত কোন কার্য্যে প্রবৃত্ত হওয়া।

sail'-êr (sāl-), *n.* A ship with reference to her power of sailing ; as, a fast *sailer* ; নির্দ্দিষ্ট গতিশক্তিবিশিষ্ট পোত।

sail'-ing (sāl-), *n.* & *adj.* **1.** Act of one, or that which, sails ; পাইল দ্বারা নৌচালন, ভাসিয়া চলন। **2.** The art or rules of navigation ; নৌচালনকলা, নৌচালননিয়ম। **3.** A voyage ; সমুদ্রযাত্রা। **4.** Departure of a ship from port ; বন্দর হইতে জাহাজের যাত্রা। ***Adj.*** Moved by sails ; পাইল দ্বারা চালিত। **Sailing-boat**—পাইল দ্বারা চালিত নৌকা। **Sailing-master**—জাহাজ (বিশেষতঃ প্রমোদতরণী) প্রভৃতির প্রধান চালক

sail'-or (sāl-êr), *n.* **1.** A seaman ; জাহাজের মাল্লা, নাবিক, সামুদ্র (যাত্রঃ), পোতবাহ, পোতবাহক, পোতপ্লব। **2.** Same as SAILOR-FISH. **3.** Same as SAILOR-HAT. **4.** One not much affected by sea-sickness ; as, she is a good *sailor* ; যে ব্যক্তি জাহাজে সামুদ্রিক পীড়া দ্বারা ততটা আক্রান্ত হয় না। **Sailor-fish**—Same as SAIL-FISH (which see). **Sailor-hat**—স্ত্রীলোকদিগের পরিধেয় একপ্রকার কিনারা ও মাথা চ্যাপ্টা খড়ের টুপি। **Sailor's home**—সমুদ্রতীরস্থ বাটীবিশেষ—যথায় নাবিকগণ অল্পব্যয়ে বাস করিতে পারে, নাবিকনিকেতন। **–ing,** *n.* **–ly,** *adj.*

sain'-foin (sān-fo͡yn), *n.* A kind of herb used as fodder ; গবাদির আহারোপযোগী একপ্রকার গুল্ম।

saint (sānt), *n.* & *v. t.* **1.** A person eminent for piety or virtue ; a godly or holy person ; সাধু ; মহাত্মা, জীবন্মুক্ত। **2.** One of the blessed in heaven ; স্বর্গধামপ্রাপ্ত, সিদ্ধ (হিঃ কোঃ), মহাপুরুষ (ঐ), সাধুসন্ত। **3.** A person canonised by the Roman Catholic Church ; রোমান ক্যাথলিক ধর্ম্মসংঘকর্তৃক খৃষ্টীয় সিদ্ধপুরুষশ্রেণীভুক্ত ব্যক্তি। ***Verb t.*** **1.** To canonise ; খৃষ্টীয় সিদ্ধপুরুষশ্রেণীভুক্ত করা। **2.** To regard as a saint ; সিদ্ধপুরুষরূপে গণ্য করা। **Saint'-dom, Saint'-hood, Saint'-ship,** *ns.* **Saint'-ed,** *p. p.* **1.** Canonised ; সিদ্ধপুরুষশ্রেণীভুক্ত। **2.** Holy ; "And, like a glory, the broad sun Hangs over *sainted* Lebanon" ; পবিত্র, পুণ্য, পূতঃ। **3.** Gone to heaven ; স্বর্গগত, স্বর্গপ্রাপ্ত, [illegible]। **Saint'-like, Saint'-ly,** *adjs.* **Saint'-li-ness,** *n.* **Latter-day saints**—Same as MORMON (which see). **St. Agnes's Eve**—২০শে জানুয়ারীর সায়াহ্ন। [ঐ দিবস রাত্রে কতকগুলি বিশেষ নিয়ম পালন করিলে কুমারীগণ ভাবী পতির মূর্ত্তি প্রত্যক্ষ করিতে পারে—এইরূপ বিশ্বাস ইংলণ্ডের স্বল্পশিক্ষিত নারীসমাজে অদ্যাপি বর্ত্তমান আছে।] **St. Agnes's-flower**—একপ্রকার শ্বেতবর্ণ পুষ্প (snow-flake). **St. Andrew's cross**—See CROSS. **St. Anthony's cross**—ইংরেজী T অক্ষরের আকৃতি ক্রুশ। **St. Anthony's fire**—See FIRE. **St. Bernard dog, St. Bernard**—একজাতীয় প্রকাণ্ডকায় কুকুর [আল্‌পস পর্ব্বতের মঠবাসী খৃষ্টীয় সন্ন্যাসিগণ এই কুকুরের সাহায্যে বিপন্ন এবং পথভ্রান্ত পথিকদিগকে উদ্ধার করিয়া আনিতেন। **St. Cuthbert's duck**—মেরুসাগরচর হংসবিশেষ (the eider duck). **St. Elmo's-fire**—See FIRE **St. Gobains glass**—ফরাসীদেশের অন্তঃপাতী St. Gobain নামক স্থানে প্রস্তুত একপ্রকার উৎকৃষ্ট কাচ। **St. Guy's dance**—ব্যাপক তাণ্ডব রোগ। **St. James's Palace**—তৃতীয় উইলিয়ম হইতে ভিক্টোরিয়ার সিংহাসনারোহণকাল পর্য্যন্ত লণ্ডননগরীস্থ রাজপ্রাসাদ। **St. Leger**—কর্ণেল St. Leger কর্তৃক ১৭৭৬ খৃঃ অব্দে প্রবর্ত্তিত ঘোড়দৌড়। এই দৌড়ে কেবল তিন বৎসর বয়স্ক ঘোটক বা ঘোটকী প্রতিযোগিতা করিতে পারে। **St. Lubbock's day**—Sir John Lubbock কর্তৃক ১৮৭১ খৃঃ অব্দে বিধিবদ্ধ আইনদ্বারা

নির্দ্ধারিত ব্যাঙ্কের ছুটির দিবস। **St. Martin's evil** — মাতলামি। **St. Michale's orange**—একপ্রকার কমলালেবু। ইহার খোসা অতি পাতলা এবং ইহাতে বীজ নাই। **St. Monday**—সোমবার। বহু শ্রমজীবী সোমবার দিবস ছুটীর দিন করিয়া লইয়াছে। **St. Nicholas's clerk** or **clergyman**—চোর, বাটপাড়, রাহাজান। **St. Partridge's Day**—১লা সেপ্টেম্বর। এই দিন হইতে ইংলণ্ডে তিত্তির পক্ষী শিকারের মরসুম আরব্ধ হয়। **St. Patrick's cross**—Same as ST. ANDREW'S CROSS. **St. Peter's Chains** — রোমান-ক্যাথলিকগণ কর্ত্তৃক ১লা আগষ্টে অনুষ্ঠিত খৃষ্টপার্ষদ পিতরের কারাবাসের স্মৃতি উৎসব। **St. Peter's Chair**—(১) খৃষ্টপার্ষদ পিতর কর্ত্তৃক Antioch নগরীতে বিশপের যে শ্রীপাট প্রতিষ্ঠিত হয় তৎস্মৃতিরক্ষণার্থ ২২শে ফেব্রুয়ারী দিবসে অনুষ্ঠিত উৎসব। (২) খৃষ্টপার্ষদ পিতর কর্ত্তৃক রোমনগরীতে পোপের শ্রীপাট প্রতিষ্ঠার স্মৃতিরক্ষণার্থ ১৮ই জানুয়ারী দিবসে অনুষ্ঠিত উৎসব। **Saints day**—বিভিন্ন খৃষ্টীয় মহাপুরুষের স্মৃতি উৎসব দিন। **St. Sylvester's Eve**—৩১ সে ডিসেম্বরের রজনী। **St. Valentine's Day**—খৃষ্টীয় তৃতীয় শতকে আবির্ভূত মহাপুরুষ St. Valentine এর স্মৃতি উৎসব দিবস (১৪ই ফেব্রুয়ারী।) এই দিবস হইতে পক্ষিগণের সঙ্গমঋতু আরব্ধ হয় বলিয়া অতি প্রাচীনকাল হইতে একটা বিশ্বাস চলিয়া আসিয়াছে। **St. Vitus's dance** — একপ্রকার স্নায়বিক রোগ। এই রোগে মুখমণ্ডল এবং দেহের অন্যান্য অংশের পেশীসমূহ হাস্যোদ্দীপক ভাবে আকুঞ্চিত ও সঞ্চালিত হয় বলিয়া ইহাকে তাণ্ডব বলে, তাণ্ডবরোগ (হঃ চঃ)। **Court of St. James's**—ব্রিটিশ রাজদরবার।

saith (sāth), 3rd person, singular, present, indicative of SAY.

Să-it'-ic, *adj.* Of, or pertaining to, Sais, an ancient city of the Nile delta ; নীল নদের ব-দ্বীপে অবস্থিত প্রাচীন Sais নগরীসম্বন্ধীয়।

sake, *n.* Account ; reason ; জন্য, হেতু, খাতির, দৌলত, কল্যাণ (cf. তোমার মেজবৌ এর কল্যাণে তোমার ঠাকুর পো'ও একটী হয়ে উঠবে—শরৎ চট্টোঃ) ; হেতু, নিমিত্ত, নিবন্ধন, অনুরোধ। **For sake's sake**—Due to previous acquaintance ; পূর্ব্ব পরিচয়ের দরুণ। **For the sake of**—জন্য, খাতিরে, দৌলতে, কল্যাণে।

sake, *n.* A Japanese rice beer ; জাপান দেশীয় সুরা বিশেষ।

săk'-êr, *n.* A species of hawk ; এক জাতীয় বাজপক্ষী (বিশেষতঃ স্ত্রীপক্ষী)। **—et,** *n.* The male of the saker ; উক্ত জাতীয় পুংপক্ষী।

săl, *n.* Salt ; লবণ। **Sal-ammoniac**—নিশাদল, চুলিকালবণ, নবসার। **Sal-volatile**—উদ্বায়িলবণ।

să-laam' (-lâm), *n.* & *v. t.* (In the East) A salutation ; সেলাম। ***Verb t.*** To salute ; সেলাম করা।

săl'-ă-ble (-bl), *adj.* Fit for sale ; বিক্রেয়। **Salable price**—বিক্রেয় মূল্য।

să-la'-cious (-shŭs), *adj.* Lustful ; lecherous ; কামুক ; লম্পট। **—lac'-i-ty, —ness,** *ns.* **—ly,** *adv.*

săl'-ăd, *n.* **1.** A dish of certain vegetables, as lettuce, cress, etc. dressed and eaten raw ; কাঁচা শাক-সব্জীর ঘণ্ট। **2.** Vegetables or herbs eaten raw ; যে সকল শাকসব্জী কাঁচা খাওয়া যায়। **Salad-days**—Immature years ; অপরিণত বয়স, কাঁচা বয়স। **Salad-dressing**—কাঁচা তরিতরকারীর সহিত যে তৈল, সির্কা, সর, প্রভৃতির মিশ্র খাওয়া হয়। **Salad-oil**—উৎকৃষ্ট জলপাইয়ের তৈল।

săl'-ă-măn-dêr, *n.* **1.** A kind of lizard formerly believed able to live in fire ; গিরগিটি (সাঃ পঃ)। **2.** The name of certain harmless amphibians allied to the newts ; গোধা জাতীয় কয়েকপ্রকার উভচর অনপকারী জন্তুর সাধারণ নাম। **3.** A kind of imaginary spirit living in fire ; একজাতীয় অগ্নিবাসী দৈত্য। **4.** A man able to endure great heat ; অতিমাত্রায় উত্তাপ সহনে সমর্থ ব্যক্তি। **5.** A soldier who fearlessly exposes him to enemy's fire ; "In battles a man who feared fire was of no use, and Mr. Gee was the soundest *salamander* he had ever known" ; যে সৈনিক শত্রুর গোলাবৃষ্টির মধ্যে নির্ভয়ে দণ্ডায়মান থাকে। **6.** A circular iron plate used in browning pudding etc. ; গোলাকার চাটু—যাহা উত্তপ্ত করিয়া উপরে স্থাপনপূর্ব্বক পিষ্টকাদি বাদামি করা হয়। **7.** A red-hot poker for igniting gun-powder etc. ; বারুদ প্রভৃতিতে অগ্নিসংযোগের জন্য তাপদীপ্ত লৌহদণ্ড। **8.** A fire-proof safe ; অগ্নিতেও যে লৌহসিন্দুকের অভ্যন্তরস্থিত বস্তু নষ্ট হয় না। **—man'-dri-an, —man'-drine,** *adjs.*

săl'-an-gāne (-ăng-), *n.* The species of swallow which builds edible nest prized by the Chinese; একজাতীয় বাবুই পাখী—ইহাদের কুলায় চীনদেশীয়গণের অতি প্রিয় খাদ্য।

săl'-ă-ry, *n.* & *v.t.* Wages ; বেতন, মাহিয়ানা, তলব (*slang*), দরমাহা (*slang*), মাইনে (*colloq.*), মুশহারা (*colloq.*), ভৃতি (শুক্রঃ বিনয়)। ***Verb t.*** To pay salary to ; বেতন দেওয়া। **—ried,** *p.p.* Getting salary ; বেতনভোগী, বৈতনিক, বেতনগ্রাহী।

sāle, *n.* **1.** The exchange of a commodity for money of equivalent value ; বিক্রয়। **2.** Market ; demand ; বিক্রী; চাহিদা। **3.** Auction ; নীলাম। **4.** A special disposal of goods esp. at the end of a season at a reduced rate with a view to their speedy disposal : as, the August *sale* of Whiteaway Laidlaw & Co. ; কোন দোকানের পুরাতন মাল বৎসরের শেষে অল্প মূল্যে বিক্রয়, সাবাড়ী বিক্রয়। **Sale-certificate**—বয়নামা। **Sale-price**—বিক্রেয় মূল্য ; নিলামের মূল্য। **Sale or return, Sale and return**—যে বন্দোবস্তদ্বারা খুচরা

as, the *sallies* of youth ; আমোদ-প্রমোদের উদ্দাম উচ্ছ্বাস, আমোদোচ্ছ্বাস। ***Verb i.*** 1. To rush out ; to rush out suddenly from a besieged place to attack the besiegers ; প্রচণ্ডবেগে বহির্গত হওয়া ; অবরোধকারিগণকে আক্রমণ করার জন্য অবরুদ্ধ স্থান হইতে প্রচণ্ডবেগে ধাবিত হওয়া। **2.** To go forth on a journey ; ভ্রমণে বাহির হওয়া। **Sally-port**—যে দ্বার বা সুড়ঙ্গপথে বহির্গত হইয়া দুর্গস্থিত সৈন্যগণ অবরোধকারিগণের উপর প্রচণ্ডবেগে আপতিত হয়, ধাবনদ্বার।

Săl′-lỹ-Lŭn, –Lŭnn, (Also *l. c.*) *ns.* A kind of sweet bun or tea-cake ; একপ্রকার মিষ্ট পিষ্টক। [অষ্টাদশ শতাব্দীর শেষভাগে Sally Lun নাম্নী জনৈকা যুবতী ইংলণ্ডের অন্তঃপাতী বাথ সহরে ঐরূপ পিষ্টক লইয়া ফেরি করিত।]

Salmalia Malabrica—রক্তশিমুল, শাল্মলী [*Syn.* স্থূলফল, দীর্ঘায়ু, দীর্ঘদ্রুম, যমদ্রুম, বহুবীর্য্য, রম্যপুষ্প, কণ্টকদ্রুম, রক্তোৎপল, মোচাখ্য, তুলবৃক্ষ, রক্তপুষ্পক, রক্তপুষ্পা, পিচ্ছিল, চিরজীবী, কণ্টকারী, মোচনী, কুক্কুটী, তুলিনী, দুরারোহা, শাল্মলিনী, মোচা, স্থিরায়ুঃ, পূরণী।]

săl′-mă-gŭn′-dĭ, –dỹ, *ns.* **1.** A dish of chopped meat, anchovies, eggs, cabbage, etc. ; থুরকুচি করা মাংস, এঙ্কোভি মাছ, ডিম, বাঁধাকপি, প্রভৃতির ঘণ্ট। **2.** A miscellany ; as, *salmagundy* of subjects ; জগাখিচুড়ী।

săl′-mi (-mē), *n.* A ragout esp. of game birds ; মাংসের কোর্ম্মা—বিশেষতঃ শিকারের পক্ষীর মাংসের কোর্ম্মা।

salm′-on (săm-ŭn), *n.* A silver-scaled sea-fish having reddish

Salmon.

flesh ; একপ্রকার সামুদ্রিক মৎস্য—ইহার আঁইশ রজতবর্ণ ও মাংস গোলাবী আভাবিশিষ্ট কমলালেবুর বর্ণের হইয়া থাকে। **Sal′-mon-oid,** *adj.* & *n.* Like salmon ; স্যামন মৎস্যের ন্যায়। **Salmon colour**—পাটলাভ কমলাবর্ণ। **Salmon-ladder, Salmon-stair, Salmon-pass, Salmon-leap**—বাঁধ প্রভৃতি অতিক্রম করিয়া নদীতে প্রবেশের জন্য স্যামন মাছের জন্য যে ধাপ প্রভৃতি প্রস্তুত করিয়া দেওয়া হয়। **Salmon-steak**—স্যামন মাছ ভাজা। **Salmon trout**—ইয়ুরোপের উত্তর ভাগে প্রাপ্ত স্যামন মাছের অনুরূপ মৎস্যবিশেষ।

Săl-ŏ-mŏn′-ĭc –mō′-nĭ-ăn, *adjs.* Of, or pertaining to, Solomon ; সলোমোনসম্বন্ধীয় সলোমানবৎ।

salon, (*F.*). *n.* **1.** A reception-room esp. in a palace ; ফরাসীদেশের রাজপ্রাসাদের বা ধনিগৃহের অভ্যর্থনাকক্ষ, সুসজ্জিত এবং সুবিশাল অভ্যর্থনা কক্ষ, রংমহাল। **2.** A fashionable gathering ; ধনী, সম্ভ্রান্ত এবং বিলাসিজনগণের সম্মিলনী। **3.** A reception-room of Parisian ladies ; প্যারীনগরীর-সম্ভ্রান্ত মহিলার অভ্যর্থনাকক্ষ। **The Salon**—প্যারী নগরীতে প্রতিবৎসর জীবিত চিত্রশিল্পিগণের চিত্রসমূহের যে বার্ষিক প্রদর্শনী হয়।

să-lōōn′, *n.* **1.** A spacious compartment for the reception of company, works of art, etc. ; বৈঠকখানা, রংমহাল, সুসজ্জিত এবং সুবিশাল অভ্যর্থনাকক্ষ, শিল্পদ্রব্যাদি প্রদর্শনের বিশাল কক্ষ। **2.** (On a passenger-ship) A large cabin for the use of first class passengers or all passengers ; (যাত্রী জাহাজ) প্রথম শ্রেণীর আরোহিগণের জন্য বা সকল আরোহীর ব্যবহারের জন্য বৃহৎ কামরা। **3.** Same as SALOON-CAR, SALOON-CARRIAGE. **4.** A hall for public entertainment or amusement ; সাধারণের আমোদ উৎসবের জন্য গৃহ, প্রমোদভবন। **5.** (*U. S.*) A place where wines etc. are sold ; (মার্কিণ যুক্তরাজ্যে) মদ্য বিক্রয়ের স্থান। **Saloon-car**—একপ্রকার বাষ্পীয় শকট—যাহা কেদারা, মেজ, প্রভৃতি দ্বারা বৈঠকখানার মত সুসজ্জিত করা হয় এবং যাহা ভিন্ন ভিন্ন প্রকোষ্ঠে বিভক্ত থাকে না। **Saloon-deck**—প্রথম শ্রেণীর যাত্রীদিগের ব্যবহারের জন্য উপরের পাটাতন।

să-lōōp′, *n.* **1.** Same as SALEP. **2.** A decoction prepared from the dried root of salep ; ছালে মিশ্রীর আসব।

Să-lō′-pĭ-ăn, *adj.* & *n.* Of, or pertaining to, Shropshire ; ইংলণ্ডের অন্তঃপাতী শ্রপশায়ারসম্বন্ধীয়। ***Noun.*** A native of Shropshire ; শ্রপশায়ারের অধিবাসী।

Săl-pĭ-glŏs′-sis (-ĭs), *n.* A herbaceous plant with showy flowers ; নানাসমুজ্জ্বলবর্ণ পুষ্পপ্রসূ গুল্মবিশেষ।

săl′-sĭ-fỹ, *n.* A meadow plant cultivated for its esculent root ; একপ্রকার গুল্ম—বিলাতের লোকেরা ইহার মূল আহার করিয়া থাকে।

salt, *n., adj.* & *v. t.* **1.** A substance (Sodium chloride) used for seasoning and preserving food ; লবণ, নুণ, নিমক (used esp. in compound as নিমক মহাল) [Syn. বসির, রুচক, ক্ষার।] **2.** (*Colloq.*) A sailor ; as, an old *salt* ; (চলিতভাষায়) নাবিক। **3.** Flavour ; স্বাদ, আস্বাদ। **4.** Wit ; as, Attic *salt* ; pungency ; piquancy ; রসিকতা ; ঝাল ; ঝাঁঝ। **5.** (*Chem.*) A term applied to a combination of acid with a metallic oxide ; (রসায়ন-শাস্ত্র) দগ্ধ ধাতু এবং দ্রাবকের মিশ্রণ, লবণক, লবণ। **6.** A salt-cellar ; নিমকদানি, লবণাধার, লবণপাত্র, লাবণিক। **7.** Allowance ; as, his statement must be taken with a grain of *salt* ; বাদসাদ। **8.** A salt marsh ; লোণা বিল। **9.** (*Pl.*) See SMELLING SALT. ***Adj.*** **1.** Having the taste of salt ; লবণস্বাদ, লোণা। **2.** Impregnated with salt ; লবণমিশ্রিত, লবণভাবিত। ***Verb t.*** **1.** To sprinkle, impregnate or season with salt ; to render salty ; লবণ মিশ্রিত করা, লবণভাবিত করা, নুনে জড়ান ; লবণাক্ত

as, the *sallies* of youth ; আমোদ-প্রমোদের উদ্দাম উচ্ছ্বাস, আমোদোচ্ছ্বাস। *Verb i.* 1. To rush out ; to rush out suddenly from a besieged place to attack the besiegers ; প্রচণ্ডবেগে বহির্গত হওয়া ; অবরোধকারিগণকে আক্রমণ করার জন্য অবরুদ্ধ স্থান হইতে প্রচণ্ডবেগে ধাবিত হওয়া। 2. To go forth on a journey ; ভ্রমণে বাহির হওয়া। **Sally-port**—যে দ্বার বা সুড়ঙ্গপথে বহির্গত হইয়া দুর্গস্থিত সৈন্যগণ অবরোধকারিগণের উপর প্রচণ্ডবেগে আপতিত হয়, ধাবনদ্বার।

Săl'-lȳ-Lŭn, –Lŭnn, (Also *l. c.*) *ns.* A kind of sweet bun or tea-cake ; একপ্রকার মিষ্ট পিষ্টক। [অষ্টাদশ শতাব্দীর শেষভাগে Sally Lun নাম্নী জনৈকা যুবতী ইংলণ্ডের অন্তঃপাতী বাথ সহরে ঐরূপ পিষ্টক লইয়া ফেরি করিত।]

Salmalia Malabrica—রক্তশিমুল, শাল্মলী [*Syn.* স্থূলফল, দীর্ঘায়ু, দীর্ঘদ্রুম, যমদ্রুম, বহুবীর্য্য, রম্যপুষ্প, কণ্টকদ্রুম, রক্তোৎপল, মোচাখ্য, তুলবৃক্ষ, রক্তপুষ্পক, রক্তপুষ্পা, পিচ্ছিল, চিরজীবী, কণ্টকারী, মোচনী, কুক্কুটী, তুলিনী, দুরারোহা, শাল্মলিনী, মোচা, স্থিরায়ুঃ, পুরণী।]

săl'-mă-gŭn'-dī, –dȳ, *ns.* 1. A dish of chopped meat, anchovies, eggs, cabbage, etc. ; খুরকুচি করা মাংস, এঙ্কোভি মাছ, ডিম, বাঁধাকপি, প্রভৃতির ঘণ্ট। 2. A miscellany ; as, *salmagundy* of subjects ; জগাখিচুড়ী।

sâl'-mi (-mē), *n.* A ragout esp. of game birds ; মাংসের কোর্ম্মা—বিশেষতঃ শিকারের পক্ষীর মাংসের কোর্ম্মা।

salm'-on (săm-ŭn), *n.* A silver-scaled sea-fish having reddish

Salmon.

flesh ; একপ্রকার সামুদ্রিক মৎস্য—ইহার আঁইশ রজতবর্ণ ও মাংস গোলাবী আভাবিশিষ্ট কমলালেবুর বর্ণের হইয়া থাকে। **Sal'-mon-oid,** *adj.* & *n.* Like salmon ; স্যামন মৎস্যের ন্যায়। **Salmon colour**—পাটলাভ কমলাবর্ণ। **Salmon-ladder, Salmon-stair, Salmon-pass, Salmon-leap**—বাঁধ প্রভৃতি অতিক্রম করিয়া নদীতে প্রবেশের জন্য স্যামন মাছের জন্য যে ধাপ প্রভৃতি প্রস্তুত করিয়া দেওয়া হয়। **Salmon-steak**—স্যামন মাছ ভাজা। **Salmon trout**—ইয়ুরোপের উত্তর ভাগে প্রাপ্ত স্যামন মাছের অনুরূপ মৎস্যবিশেষ।

Săl-ō-mŏn'-ic –mō'-nī-ăn, *adjs.* Of, or pertaining to, Solomon ; সলোমোনসম্বন্ধীয় সলোমানবৎ।

salon, (*F.*), *n.* 1. A reception-room esp. in a palace ; ফরাসীদেশের রাজপ্রাসাদের বা ধনিগৃহের অভ্যর্থনাকক্ষ, সুসজ্জিত এবং সুবিশাল অভ্যর্থনা কক্ষ, রংমহাল। 2. A fashionable gathering ; ধনী, সম্ভ্রান্ত এবং বিলাসিজনগণের সম্মিলনী। 3. A reception-room of Parisian ladies ; প্যারীনগরীর সম্ভ্রান্ত মহিলার অভ্যর্থনাকক্ষ। **The Salon**—প্যারী নগরীতে প্রতিবৎসর জীবিত চিত্রশিল্পিগণের চিত্রসমূহের যে বার্ষিক প্রদর্শনী হয়।

să-loon', *n.* 1. A spacious compartment for the reception of company, works of art, etc. ; বৈঠকখানা, রংমহাল, সুসজ্জিত এবং সুবিশাল অভ্যর্থনাকক্ষ, শিল্পদ্রব্যাদি প্রদর্শনের বিশাল কক্ষ। 2. (On a passenger-ship) A large cabin for the use of first class passengers or all passengers ; (যাত্রী জাহাজ) প্রথম শ্রেণীর আরোহিগণের জন্য বা সকল আরোহীর ব্যবহারের জন্য বৃহৎ কামরা। 3. Same as SALOON-CAR, SALOON-CARRIAGE. 4. A hall for public entertainment or amusement ; সাধারণের আমোদ উৎসবের জন্য গৃহ, প্রমোদভবন। 5. (*U. S.*) A place where wines etc. are sold ; (মার্কিণ যুক্তরাজ্যে) মদ্য বিক্রয়ের স্থান। **Saloon-car**—একপ্রকার বাষ্পীয় শকট—যাহা কেদারা, মেজ, প্রভৃতি দ্বারা বৈঠকখানার মত সুসজ্জিত করা হয় এবং যাহা ভিন্ন ভিন্ন প্রকোষ্ঠে বিভক্ত থাকে না। **Saloon-deck**—প্রথম শ্রেণীর যাত্রীদিগের ব্যবহারের জন্য উপরের পাটাতন।

să-loop', *n.* 1. Same as SALEP. 2. A decoction prepared from the dried root of salep ; ছালেমিশ্রীর আসব।

Să-lō'-pī-ăn, *adj.* & *n.* Of, or pertaining to, Shropshire ; ইংলণ্ডের অন্তঃপাতী স্রপশায়ারসম্বন্ধীয়। ***Noun.*** A native of Shropshire ; স্রপশায়ারের অধিবাসী।

Săl-pī-glŏs'-sis (-ĭs), *n.* A herbaceous plant with showy flowers ; নানাসমুজ্জ্বলবর্ণ পুষ্পপ্রসূ গুল্মবিশেষ।

săl'-sī-fȳ, *n.* A meadow plant cultivated for its esculent root ; একপ্রকার গুল্ম—বিলাতের লোকেরা ইহার মূল আহার করিয়া থাকে।

sâlt, *n., adj.* & *v. t.* 1. A substance (Sodium chloride) used for seasoning and preserving food ; লবণ, নুণ, নিমক (used esp. in compound as নিমক মহাল) [Syn. বসির, রুচক, ক্ষার।] 2. (*Colloq.*) A sailor ; as, an old *salt* ; (চলিতভাষায়) নাবিক। 3. Flavour ; স্বাদ, আস্বাদ। 4. Wit ; as, Attic *salt* ; pungency ; piquancy ; রসিকতা ; ঝাল ; ঝাঁঝ। 5. (*Chem.*) A term applied to a combination of acid with a metallic oxide ; (রসায়ন-শাস্ত্র) দগ্ধ ধাতু এবং দ্রাবকের মিশ্রণ, লবণক, লবণ। 6. A salt-cellar ; নিমকদানি, লবণাধার, লবণপাত্র, লাবণিক। 7. Allowance ; as, his statement must be taken with a grain of *salt* ; বাদসাদ। 8. A salt marsh ; লোণা বিল। 9. (*Pl.*) See SMELLING SALT. ***Adj.*** 1. Having the taste of salt ; লবণস্বাদ, লোণা। 2. Impregnated with salt ; লবণমিশ্রিত, লবণভাবিত। ***Verb t.*** 1. To sprinkle, impregnate or season with salt ; to render salty ; লবণ মিশ্রিত করা, লবণভাবিত করা, নুনে জড়ান ; লবণাক্ত

করা। 2. To fill with salt between the timbers and planks as a ship for the preservation of the timber; জাহাজ প্রভৃতির কাঠ রক্ষা করার জন্য তক্তার ফাঁক লবণ দ্বারা পূর্ণ করা। 3. To treat with a mixture or solution of salt; রাসায়নিক লবণজল বা লবণ-মিশ্রদ্বারা ধোতাদি করা। **Salt'-ing,** *n.* **Salt'-ish,** *adj.* **Attic salt**—রহস্য, রসিকতা। **Essential salt**—বনস্পতি (হিঃ কোঃ), বনস্পতিসত্ত (ঐ)। **Haloid salt**—সমুদ্রী খার (হিঃ কোঃ), সমুদ্রী লবণ (ঐ)। **Neutral salt**—উদাসীন লবণ (হিঃ কোঃ), শিথিল লবণ (ঐ)। **Permanent salt**—স্থির লবণ (হিঃ কোঃ), স্থায়ী লবণ (ঐ)। **Smelling salt**—See under SMELL. **Spilling salt**—দৈবাৎ কাহারো হাত প্রভৃতি লাগিয়া লবণ পড়িয়া গেলে বিশেষ অমঙ্গল ঘটিয়া থাকে,—প্রাচীন রোমানদিগের মধ্যে এই বিশ্বাস প্রচলিত ছিল। বর্ত্তমানে ইংলণ্ডের কোন কোন স্থানে এই কুসংস্কার প্রচলিত দেখা যায়। **Table-salt**—আহারের জন্য চূর্ণীকৃত লবণ। **White-salt**—শাদা লবণ। **Salt-block**—লবণমিশ্রিত জল হইতে বাষ্পীকরণের জন্য যন্ত্র-বিশেষ। **Salt-box**—লবণ রাখার জন্য কাঠের বাক্স। **Salt-butter**—লবণ-মিশ্রিত মাখন (লবণ মিশাইলে মাখন অনেক দিন তাজা থাকে)। **Salt-cake**—কাচ ও সাবান প্রস্তুতে ব্যবহৃত সোডিয়াম সালফেট। **Salt-cat** — চুণ, সাতু, মূত্র, প্রভৃতির মিশ্র—যদ্দারা প্রলুব্ধ করিয়া কপোত-দিগকে গৃহে রাখা হয়। **Salt-cellar**—নিমকদানি। **Salt-duty**—লবণ শুল্ক। **Salt-fish**—লোণা মাছ; লোণা জলের মাছ। **Salt-glazing**—চুল্লীতে লবণ ছড়াইয়া পাথরের বাসনে যে বর্ণক (glaze) দেওয়া হয়। **Salt-horse**—(*Naut., slang*) শুষ্ক এবং লবণাক্ত গোমাংস। **Salt-junk** — জাহাজে ভোজনের জন্য শুষ্ক লবণাক্ত গোমাংস। **Salt-lick**—যে সকল লবণনির্ঝরে যাইয়া জন্তুগণ লবণ চাটিয়া খায়। **Salt-marsh**—যে সাগরতীরবর্ত্তী পশুচারণ-ভূমি সময় সময় সমুদ্রজলদ্বারা প্লাবিত হয়। **Salt-mine**—লবণের খনি। **Salt-pan**—যে পাত্র বা কুণ্ড হইতে বাষ্পীকরণ-ক্রিয়াদ্বারা লবণ পাওয়া যায়। **Salt-pond**—সাগরজল বাষ্পকরণের জন্য কৃত্রিম বা নৈসর্গিক কুণ্ড। **Salt-spoon**—লবণ তোলার চামচ। **Salt-spring**—লবণ-প্রস্রবণ, লবণনির্ঝর। **Salt-water**—লোণাজল, সাগরবারি, লবণোদক, লবণাম্বু; অশ্রুজল। **Salt-well**—লবণকূপ **Salt-works**—লবণের কারখানা। **Salt-wort**—বিভিন্ন প্রকার গুল্মের সাধারণ নাম। **Above the salt**—In a position of honour; সমাজের উচ্চতরে অবস্থিত। **Below the salt**—In an inferior position; সমাজের নিম্নস্তরের। **He is true to his salt**—He is faithful to his master; সে নিমকের চাকর। **He wont earn salt for his porridge** — He wont earn money; সে টাকা পয়সা রোজগার করিবে না। **I am not made of salt**—আমি নুনের পুতুল নহি [অর্থাৎ বৃষ্টিতে বাহিরে গেলে গলিয়া যাইব না।] **Not worth one's salt**—Not worth the money spent for his maintenance; তাহার ভরণপোষণে যে ব্যয় হয় সে তাহার উপযুক্ত নয়। **Rather too salt**—The charge seems to be excessive; মূল্য বা দাবী অতিরিক্ত বোধ হইতেছে। **Salt of lemon** — আমরুলের দ্রাবক (Oxalic acid)। **Salt of soda**—কার্ব্বোনেট-অব-সোডা। **Salt of tartar**—কার্ব্বোনেট-অব-পটাশ। **Salt of vitriol**—জিঙ্ক সালফেট। **The salt of the earth**—The best men of the earth; পৃথিবীর শ্রেষ্ঠ লোকগণ। **To eat one's salt**—To be some one's guest or dependant; কাহারো অতিথি হওয়া, কাহারো নিমক খাওয়া। **To eat salt with**—To be the guest of some one; কাহারও অতিথি হওয়া। **To salt a mine**—To sprinkle some valuable ore on the mine to lead people to make a false estimate of its worth; কোন খনির মূল্য সম্বন্ধে লোকের ভ্রান্তধারণা জন্মাইবার জন্য উহাতে মূল্যবান খনিজ পদার্থের খণ্ড ছড়ান। **To salt an invoice, account etc.**—To put the extreme value upon each article; প্রতি জিনিষের উচ্চতম মূল্য ধরা। **To salt away, To salt down**—(*Slang*) To put by money; (ইতরভাষায়) টাকা জমান। **To take with a grain of salt**—To take with some allowance; কিছু বাদসাদ দিয়া গ্রহণ করা। **To throw salt on the tail**—To capture; to cheat; ধরা; ঠকান। **True to one's salt** — Faithful; বিশ্বস্ত, বিশ্বাসী [cf. নিমকহারাম (Not true to one's salt)]. **Worth one's salt**—Serviceable; কার্য্যকর।

saltarello, *n.* A kind of Italian and Spanish dance; স্পেন এবং ইতালী দেশীয় নৃত্য বিশেষ।

sal'-tănt, *adj.* Leaping; লম্ফনশীল, নর্ত্তনশীল। **–ta'-tion,** *n.* 1. The act of leaping; লম্ফন, উল্লম্ফন, অতিক্রান্তি (হিঃ কোঃ), পরিবর্ত্তাতিশয় (ঐ)। 2. Palpitation; স্পন্দন, ধুকধুকি। **–ta-to-ry, –ta-to'-ri-al,** *adjs.* 1. Pertaining to leaping; having the ability of leaping or actually doing so; লম্ফনসম্বন্ধীয়; উল্লম্ফনক্ষম, উল্লম্ফনশীল, উল্লম্ফী। 2. (*Fig.*) Proceeding by abrupt movement; "Her (Nature's) methods are *saltatory* and impulsive"; (লক্ষণায়) আকস্মিক গতিতে অগ্রসর, ক্ষণে দ্রুত ক্ষণে মৃদুগামী।

salt'-êr, *n.* 1. One who deals with salt; লবণ ব্যবসায়ী। 2. One who manufactures salt; লবণ প্রস্তুত-কারী। 3. Same as DRY-SALT (which see). 4. A person who salts fish etc.; যে ব্যক্তি মৎস্যাদি লবণভাবিত করে।

salt'-êrn, *n.* 1. A salt-work; লবণের কারখানা। 2. A place where salt is made; লবণ প্রস্তুতের স্থান। 3. A set of pools where the sea-water is admitted to be evaporated by the heat of the sun rays; যে নালাসমূহে সূর্য্যোত্তাপদ্বারা

বাষ্পীভূত করার জন্য সাগরজল প্রবিষ্ট করান হয়।

saltimbanco, (*It.*), *n.* Mountebank ; হাতুড়ে, গোবৈদ্য।

sal'-tire (-tẽr), **–tier** (-tẽr), *ns.* St. Andrew's Cross ; গুণন চিহ্নাকৃতি ক্রুশ।

salt-pē'-tre (-têr), **–têr**, *ns.* Nitre (Potassium nitrate, KNO_3) ; সোরা, যবক্ষার। [*Syn.* সৌবর্চ্চল (রঃ রঃ সঃ প্রঃ), স্বর্বর্চ্চিকা (রঃ প্রঃ), সোরক (সাঃ পঃ), গিরিমস্তক (রঃ প্রঃ), সোরক (রঃ কাঃ প্রঃ), যবশূক, তীক্ষ্ণরস, যবাগ্রজ, পাক্য, যবলাস, যাবশূক, সারক, রেচক, যবনালক, ক্ষার, তর্ক্ষ্য, যবনালজ, যবজ, যবশূকজ, যবাহ্ব, যবাপত্যম্।] [Arab. *ubkir* ; Fr. *salpetre* ; Pers. *shora* ; It. *nitro* ; Russ. *senitra* ; Germ. *salpeter.*] সোরা ভারতবর্ষের অযোধ্যা, বর্ম্মা, কটক, প্রভৃতি প্রদেশে প্রচুর পরিমাণে পাওয়া যায়। ইহা বারুদ, আতসবাজী, নাইট্রিক এসিড, প্রভৃতি প্রস্তুতে ব্যবহৃত হয়। **Saltpeter acid**—শোরাম্ল (হিঃ কোঃ), নেত্রিকাম্ল (ঐ)।

salts, *n., pl.* Epsom salt, or other salt used as a medicine ; ঔষধরূপে ব্যবহৃত কোন লবণ। **Smelling salts**—সর্দ্দি, মূর্চ্ছা প্রভৃতিতে আঘ্রাণ লইবার জন্য ল্যাভেণ্ডার প্রভৃতি সুরভি-দ্রব্য মিশ্রিত নিশাদল, গন্ধলবণ।

sal'-tŭs, *n.* Breach of continuity ; ক্রমভঙ্গ, অন্বয়ব লোপ (হিঃ কোঃ)।

să-lū'-bri-ous (-ŭs), *adj.* Healthy ; as, *salubrious* climate ; স্বাস্থ্যজনক, স্বাস্থ্যপূর্ণ। **–ness,** *n.* The state of being salubrious ; স্বাস্থ্যকরতা, নিরাময়তা। **–ty,** *n.*

săl'-ū-tă-rȳ, *adj.* 1. (*Now rare*) Wholesome ; promoting health ; (বর্ত্তমানে কচিদ্‌ব্যবহৃত) স্বাস্থ্যজনক, স্বাস্থ্যবর্দ্ধক। 2. Beneficial ; হিতকর, হিতজনক, কল্যাণকর, সুফলপ্রদ, ক্ষেমঙ্কর, কল্যাণজনক।

săl-ū-tā'-tion, *n.* **1.** The act of saluting ; অভিবাদন, নমস্কার, প্রণাম, বন্দনা। **2.** That which is uttered or done in saluting ; অভিবাদনকালে ব্যবহৃত বাক্য বা কৃত কার্য্য। **The Angelic Salutation**—Same as AVE MARIA

să-lūte', *v. t., i. & n.* **1.** To make a salutation to ; to greet ; প্রণাম করা, নমস্কার করা ; বন্দনা করা, অভিবাদন করা, তোপধ্বনি প্রভৃতি দ্বারা সম্মান করা। **2.** To greet with a kiss, bow or otherwise ; চুম্বন, প্রণতি, প্রভৃতি দ্বারা সম্ভাষণ করা। **3.** (In the army or navy) To honour by a discharge of fire-arms, striking the colours, by shouts etc. ; তোপ ধ্বনি করিয়া, পতাকা নামাইয়া, কিম্বা জয়ধ্বনি ইত্যাদি পূর্ব্বক সম্মানিত করা। **4.** (*Obs.*) To inflame ; (অপ্রঃ) উদ্দীপ্ত করা। ***Verb i.*** To perform a salutation or salute ; অভিবাদন করা। ***Noun.*** **1.** The expression of kind wishes or respect to any one present ; greeting ; অভিবাদন ; নমস্কার। **2.** A kiss ; "She was rewarded with a complimentary *salute* on the left cheek" ; চুম্বন। **3.** A discharge of cannon or small arms, lowering of colours, cheering, etc. in honour of some distinguished personage ; as, a *salute* of 21 guns was fired ; কোন রাজা বা তৎসদৃশ কোন ব্যক্তির প্রতি সম্মান প্রদর্শনার্থ তোপধ্বনি প্রভৃতি।

săl-ū-tif'-ēr-ous (-ŭs), *adj.* (*Rare*) Healthy ; (কচিদ্‌ব্যবহৃত) স্বাস্থ্যপ্রদ, স্বাস্থ্যজনক।

săl'-vāge, *n. & v. t.* **1.** The saving of property from fire etc. or of ship's cargo after shipwreck ; অগ্নিদাহ প্রভৃতি হইতে সম্পত্তি রক্ষণ অথবা জলমগ্ন জাহাজের দ্রব্যাদি উদ্ধার। **2.** That which is so saved ; অগ্নিদাহ বা জলমগ্ন জাহাজ প্রভৃতি হইতে যে দ্রব্য বা মাল উদ্ধার করা হইয়াছে। **3.** The allowance or compensation paid to those by whose exertion a ship or goods therein, have been saved from loss at sea (also *salvage money*) ; সাগরে মজ্জনোন্মুখ জাহাজ বা উহার মাল উদ্ধারকারী ব্যক্তিগণকে প্রদত্ত পারিতোষিক। ***Verb t.*** To save from wreck, fire, etc. ; অগ্নিদাহ এবং জলমগ্ন জাহাজ প্রভৃতি হইতে জিনিষপত্র রক্ষা করা।

salvarsan, *n.* A world-famous medicine of syphilis ; উপদংশ রোগের বিশ্ববিখ্যাত ঔষধ বিশেষ। [এই ঔষধ Dr. Ehrlich কর্ত্তৃক ১৯০৯ খৃঃ অব্দে আবিষ্কৃত হয়। ইহার রাসায়নিক নাম *Dioxydiamidoarsenobenzol.* Salvarsan ৬০৬ এই সংখ্যা দ্বারা পরিচিত। ইহার প্রকারান্তর Neo-salvarsan ৯১৪ সংখ্যা দ্বারা পরিজ্ঞাত হইয়া থাকে।]

săl-vā'-tion, *n.* **1.** Deliverance ; উদ্ধার, মুক্তিপ্রদান। **2.** The redemption of men from sin and death ; মুক্তি, পরিত্রাণ, পরমগতি, পরমপদ, পরাগতি, পরমমোক্ষ (final beatitude), তারণ, উদ্ধার, নিস্তার, অপবর্গ (হিঃ কোঃ), নিঃশ্রেয়স, মোক্ষ, অমৃতত্ব (গীতা), কৈবল্য, নির্ব্বাণ (According to the Buddhists), শ্রেয়ঃ, অমৃত। [নৈয়ায়িকদিগের মতে মুক্তি—আত্যন্তিক দুঃখনিবৃত্তি। বৈদান্তিকদিগের মতে মুক্তি—নিত্যসুখাবাপ্তি। বৈষ্ণবদিগের মতে মুক্তি পঞ্চবিধা যথা :—সার্ষ্টি (শ্রীভগবানের অনুরূপ ঐশ্বর্য্যলাভ), সালোক্য (শ্রীভগবানের সহিত এক লোকে বাস), সারূপ্য (শ্রীভগবানের তুল্য রূপ প্রাপ্তি), সামীপ্য (তৎসমীপে বাস), সাযুজ্য (শ্রীভগবানের সহিত যুক্ততা।) সালোক্যং ময়া সহ একস্মিন লোকে বাসম্। সার্ষ্টি সমানৈশ্বর্য্যম্। সামীপ্য নিকটবর্ত্তিত্বম্। সারূপ্যং সমানরূপতাম। সাযুজ্যম্ একতাম্।—ইতি শ্রীধরস্বামী।] **3.** That which saves ; পরিত্রাতা, উদ্ধারকারী, তারক। **- ist,** *n.* A member of the Salvation Army ; মুক্তিফৌজের সভ্য। **Salvation Army**—লোকসাধারণের সামাজিক ও ধর্ম্মবিষয়ক উন্নতিবিধানের উদ্দেশ্যে Rev. Booth কর্ত্তৃক ১৮৭৮ খৃষ্টাব্দে সেনাবিভাগের আদর্শে গঠিতা জনহিতসাধিনী সমিতিবিশেষ, মুক্তিফৌজ।

salve (sâv *or* sălv), *n.* & *v. t.* **1.** A healing ointment ; ঘায়ের মলম, প্রলেপ। **2.** That which heals, soothes or helps ; আরোগ্যজনক বস্তু, স্নিগ্ধকর বস্তু। ***Verb t.*** **1.** To apply salve to ; মলমপ্রয়োগ করা, প্রলেপ দেওয়া। **2.** To heal ; to soothe ; "To *salve* their wounded pride" ; আরোগ্য করা, আরাম করা ; সান্ত্বনা দেওয়া, প্রাণ জুড়ান। **3.** To harmonise ; to dispose of ; ঐক্য করা ; মিটান। **4.** To preserve ; রক্ষা করা। **To salve over**—To persuade by soothing speech ; প্রাণস্নিগ্ধকর বাক্যদ্বারা প্ররোচিত করা।

salve (sălv), *v. t.* Same as SALVAGE, *v. t.* (which see).

săl'-vē, (Also *Salve regina*), *n.* The first words of a prayer to Virgin Mary ; the prayer itself ; কুমারী মেরীর স্তববিশেষের প্রথম শব্দদ্বয় ; উক্ত স্তব।

săl'-vêr, *n.* A tray of gold, silver, brass, etc. on which letters, etc. are presented by servants ; যে সোনা, রূপা, পিত্তল, প্রভৃতির বারকোষে ভৃত্যগণ চিঠিপত্র, জলখাবার, প্রভৃতি প্রদান করিয়া থাকে, বারকোষ।

săl-vĭn'-ĭ-ă, *n.* A genus of heterosporous ferns ; ইন্দুর কানি, পাণা।

săl'-vō, *n.* **1.** A reservation ; বর্জ্জিত বিধি। **2.** Quibbling ; বাক্‌ছল, কুতর্ক।

săl'-vō, *n.* **1.** A general discharge of guns intended as a salute ; অভিবাদনের উদ্দেশ্যে যুগপৎ তোপদাগন। **2.** A shout of applause to welcome ; জয়ধ্বনি, জয়নাদ, জয়রব।

săl'-vō-lă'-tĭ-lē, *n.* See under SAL.

săl'-vŏr, *n.* One who renders salvage services ; a ship which assists in salvage ; যে ব্যক্তি অগ্নিদাহ হইতে বা নিমজ্জনোন্মুখ জাহাজ হইতে মালপত্র উদ্ধার করে ; নিমজ্জনোন্মুখ পোতের মাল উদ্ধারে নিযুক্ত জাহাজ।

Săm, *n.* **To stand Sam**—(*Slang*) To bear all expenses ; (ইতরভাষায়) সমস্ত ব্যয় নির্ব্বাহ করা।

săm'-ă-ră, *n.* An indehiscent superior fruit furnished with wings ; পক্ষক ফল (সাঃ পঃ)।

Samara of the common maple.

Să-măr'-ĭ-tăn, *adj.* & *n.* Relating to Samaria, a city of Israel ; এস্রায়েলের সামরিয়া নগরসম্বন্ধীয়। ***Noun.*** **1.** A native or inhabitant of Samaria ; স্যামরিয়ার অধিবাসী। **2.** The language of Samaria ; স্যামরিয়ার ভাষা। **3.** A charitable or benevolent person ; দানশীল লোক, পরোপকারী লোক। **A good Samaritan** — পরোপকারী লোক ; যে সদাশয় ব্যক্তি দুঃস্থ, আর্ত্ত এবং অভাবগ্রস্ত লোকদিগকে সাহায্য করে।

săm'-bō, *n.* The offspring of a Negro and Indian ; কাফ্রী এবং আমেরিকার প্রাচীন অধিবাসীর সহযোগে উৎপন্ন সন্তান।

sāme, *adj.* **1.** Identical ; সেই, অভিন্ন, অনন্য, সম (হিঃ কোঃ), এক (ঐ), স এব (ঐ)। **2.** Just mentioned or just about to be mentioned ; "A pound of the *same* merchant's flesh is thine" ; এই মাত্র উক্ত, এই মাত্র উক্ত হইবে—এরূপ। **3.** Being of the like kind ; as, *same* paper ; corresponding ; similar ; as, on the *same* day of the next year ; একজাতীয় ; একই ; সেই। **Same'-ness,** *n.* **1.** Identity ; অনন্যতা, অভিন্নতা, একতা, ঐক্য, সমতা। **2.** Similarity ; correspondence ; সমতা, সাম্য, তুল্যতা, সাদৃশ্য, সদৃশতা ; অনুরূপতা। **3.** Monotony ; "The scenery is *sameness* itself" ; একঘেয়ে ভাব, একটানাভাব, বৈচিত্র্যহীনতা। **All the same**—Identical ; অভিন্ন, একই। Nevertheless ; notwithstanding ; তবু, তথাপি ; তৎসত্ত্বেও। **Just the same**—Exactly similar ; ঠিক সেইরূপ, একই কথা, অভিন্ন। **One and the same**—অভিন্ন বস্তু। **The same**—Aforesaid person or thing ; পূর্ব্বোক্ত ব্যক্তি বা বস্তু।

săm'-ĕl, *adj.* (Of a brick etc.) Imperfectly burned ; (ইষ্টকাদিসম্বন্ধে) অসম্যগ্ দগ্ধ।

Să'-mĭ-ăn, *adj.* & *n.* Pertaining to the Grecian island of Samos ; গ্রীসদেশের অন্তঃপাতী শ্যামস্‌দ্বীপসম্বন্ধীয়। ***Noun.*** A native of Samos ; শ্যামস্‌দ্বীপের অধিবাসী। **Samian earth** — শ্যামস্‌দ্বীপ হইতে আনীত একপ্রকার মৃত্তিকা—ইহা পূর্ব্বে কোষ্ঠবদ্ধকর ঔষধস্বরূপ ব্যবহৃত হইত। **Samian letter**—Υ ; এই Υ অক্ষর গ্রীক দার্শনিক পিথাগোরাস পাপপুণ্যের বিভিন্নদিগ্‌গামিত্ব সূচনার্থ সাঙ্কেতিক চিহ্নস্বরূপ ব্যবহার করিতেন। **Samian Sage**—গ্রীক দার্শনিক পিথাগোরাস। **Samian-ware** — সেমিয়্যান মৃত্তিকায় প্রস্তুত বাসন ; প্রাচীন রোমের ধ্বংসাবশেষের মধ্যে প্রাপ্ত একপ্রকার রমোজ্জ্বল রক্তবর্ণের বাসন।

săm'-iel (-yŏl), *n.* Same as SIMOON (which see).

săm'-ĭ-sĕn, *n.* A Japanese three-stringed guitar ; জাপানী ত্রিতন্ত্রী বীণা বিশেষ।

să'-mīte, *n.* (*Arachic*) A richly embroidered silk fabric ; (অপ্রঃ) জরির কাজ-করা একপ্রকার বহুমূল্য রেশমী কাপড়।

săm'-lĕt, *n.* A young salmon ; স্যামন মাছের বাচ্চা।

Săm'-nīte, *n.* & *adj.* A people dwelling in ancient Samnium, a mountainous district in Italy ; ইতালীর অন্তঃপাতী প্রাচীন Samnium নামক পার্ব্বত্যপ্রদেশের অধিবাসী জাতিবিশেষ। [এই জাতি প্রাচীন রোমের গণতন্ত্রের সঙ্গে বহুকাল যাবৎ যুদ্ধে ব্যাপৃত ছিল।] ***Adj.*** Of the Samnites ; উক্ত জাতিসম্বন্ধীয়। **—nit'-ic,** *adj.*

Să-mō'-ăn, *adj.* & *n.* **1.** Of, or pertaining to, Samoa ; প্রশান্ত মহাসাগরের অন্তর্গত সেমোয়া দ্বীপপুঞ্জসম্বন্ধীয়। ***Noun.*** A native of Samoa ; the language of Samoa ; সেমোয়ার অধিবাসী ; সেমোয়ার ভাষা।

samovar, *n.* **1.** A copper urn with interior heat tube used in Russia for making tea ; চায়ের জল গরম করার জন্য অভ্যন্তরে উত্তাপসঞ্চারক নলযুক্ত ভাণ্ডবিশেষ। [উক্ত নলের ভিতর জ্বলন্ত কয়লা ভরিয়া জল উত্তপ্ত করা হয়।] **2.** A similar vessel for keeping soup heat ; সুপ গরম রাখার জন্য অনুরূপ পাত্র।

Săm-ō-yĕd′, —yede′ (-yĕd), *ns.* **1.** A Mongolian people living in the extreme north of European Russia ; ইয়ুরোপীয় রুশিয়ার উত্তর-প্রান্তবর্ত্তী প্রদেশবাসী মঙ্গোলীয় জাতি-বিশেষ। **2.** The language of this people ; উক্ত জাতির ভাষা।

Săm-ō-yĕd′-ic, *adj.* & *n.* Of, or belonging to, the Samoyeds ; সেমোইয়েড জাতিসম্পর্কীয়। ***Noun.*** The language of the Samoyeds ; সেমোইয়েড্ জাতির ভাষা।

săm′-păn, *n.* Any small boat of Chienese pattern ; চীনা ধরণের ক্ষুদ্র নৌকা, সাম্পান।

săm′-phire, *n.* The herbs of St. Peter, a marine plant whose saline and aromatic leaves are used in pickles ; সাগরতীরজাত গুল্মবিশেষ ; এই গুল্মের সুগন্ধি ও লবণাস্বাদপত্র আচার প্রস্তুতে ব্যবহৃত হয়।

săm′-ple (-pl), *n.* & *v. t.* **1.** A part shown as evidence of the quality of the whole (specimen) ; নমুনা। ***Verb t.*** **1.** To take a sample of ; to test the qualities of a thing by samples ; as, to *sample* treacle ; নমুনা স্বরূপ নেওয়া ; নমুনা দ্বারা কোন জিনিষের উৎকর্ষাপকর্ষ পরীক্ষা করা। **2.** To present specimens of ; নমুনাস্বরূপ দেওয়া, নমুনা দেওয়া।

săm′-plêr, *n.* **1.** (*Obs.*) Same as SAMPLE. **2.** A sample of needle-work ; সূচিকর্ম্মের নমুনা। **3.** A young tree that is left standing when the rest are cut down ; অপর সকল গাছ কাটিয়া ফেলার পর যে অপরিণত গাছটী রাখা হয়।

săm′-plêr, *n.* A man appointed to test the quality of goods ; জিনিষের উৎকর্ষ বা অপকর্ষ নির্দ্ধারণার্থ নিযুক্ত ব্যক্তি, গুণাগুণ পরীক্ষা।

săm′-shōō, *n.* An alcoholic liquor made in China ; চীনদেশীয় মদ্য।

Săm′-sŏn, Samp′—, (săm-), *ns.* Isralite mentioned in Bible noted for his superhuman strength ; জনৈক অমানুষিক বলশালী ইহুদী (See *Judges* XIII—XVI). **Sampson's post**—জাহাজের পাটাতনের অবলম্বন-স্বরূপ সুদৃঢ় কাষ্ঠফলক।

Samurai, *n.* **1.** The military class of Japan ; জাপানের প্রাচীন-কালের যুদ্ধব্যবসায়িসম্প্রদায়, জাপানের ক্ষত্রিয় সমাজ। **2.** A member of the military class of Japan ; জাপানের ক্ষত্রিয় সমাজ। **3.** A Japanese military officer ; জাপান-দেশীয় সামরিক কর্ম্মচারী। [এই শব্দের বহুবচনে কোন পরিবর্ত্তন হয় না]।

săn′-ă-tive (-tĭv), **—tŏ-rȳ,** *adjs.* Curing; tending to cure; concerned with health ; আরোগ্যজনক, স্বাস্থ্য-জনক, স্বাস্থ্যবিধায়ক, স্বাস্থ্যকর, স্বাস্থ্যপ্রদ ; স্বাস্থ্যজননপ্রবণ; স্বাস্থ্যসংক্রান্ত,স্বাস্থ্যবিষয়ক।

săn-ă-tō′-ri-ŭm, *n.* **1.** A place with good climate, etc. where people go to regain health ; as, Darjeeling is a *sanatorium* ; স্বাস্থ্যবাস, স্বাস্থ্যনিবাস, স্বাস্থ্যজনক স্থান, স্বাস্থ্যকর স্থান। **2.** An establishment for certain special forms of medical treatment or for the general treatment of convalescents ; রুগ্নব্যক্তিদিগের জন্য বিশেষতঃ ক্ষয়রোগ বা অন্য কোন বিশেষ রোগে আক্রান্ত ব্যক্তি-গণের নিমিত্ত আরোগ্যশালা, রোগিনিকেতন, স্বাস্থ্যমন্দির, আরোগ্যমন্দির, স্বাস্থ্যনিকেতন।

săn-bĕ-ni′-tō (-nē-), *n.* **1.** A sackcloth worn by penitents on their reconciliation to the church ; খৃষ্টীয় ধর্ম্মসংঘে পুনঃপ্রবেশ-কালে অনুতপ্ত ব্যক্তিগণ যে ছালার কোর্ত্তা পরিয়া থাকে। **2.** A kind of loose upper garment painted with flames, devils, etc. worn by heretics condemned to death by the Inquisition when led to the stake ; স্পেনদেশীয় যাজকীয় বিচারালয়ে দণ্ডিত প্রচলিত খৃষ্টধর্ম্মের বিরুদ্ধমতাবলম্বী ব্যক্তিগণ জীবন্ত দগ্ধ হওয়ার জন্য অগ্নিকুণ্ডে নীত হওয়ার কালে যে অগ্নিশিখা, প্রেতমূর্ত্তি, প্রভৃতি অঙ্কিত প্রাবরণ পরিধান করিত।

sanc′-ti-fȳ (săngk-), *v. t.* **1.** To consecrate or set apart for a religious use ; দেবকার্য্যের জন্য উৎসর্গীকৃত করা, দেবোদ্দেশ্যে পৃথক্ করিয়া রাখা। **2.** To make holy ; to free from sin ; পবিত্র করা, পূত করা শুদ্ধ করা ; পাপনির্ম্মুক্ত করা, পাপমুক্ত করা। **3.** To keep or observe as holy ; পবিত্র বলিয়া পালন করা। **4.** To render productive of holiness or piety ; "Sufferings are *sanctified* and made a means of reaching heaven" ; পবিত্রতা বা ভগবদ্ভক্তি উৎপাদন করা। **5.** To justify ; as, the end *sanctifies* the means ; ন্যায্যতাপাদন করা। **—fi-ca′-tion,** *n.* **1.** The act of consecrating or setting apart for a religious use ; দেবোদ্দেশ্যে উৎসর্গী-করণ, দেবকার্য্যের জন্য পৃথক করিয়া রাখন। **2.** The act of making holy ; পবিত্রীকরণ, পাবন, তীর্থীকরণ (ভাগঃ)।

sanc-ti-mo′-ni-ous (săngk-tĭ-mō-nĭ-ŭs), *adj.* **1.** (*Obs.*) Holy ; (অপ্রঃ) পবিত্র। **2.** hypocritically devout or pious ; কপটধার্ম্মিক, ছদ্মতাপস, ধর্ম্মধ্বজ (হিঃ কোঃ), দাম্ভিক (ঐ), ধর্ম্মধ্বজী, ভণ্ড, মর্কটবৈরাগ্যশীল।

sanc′-ti-mŏ-nȳ (săngk-), *n.* **1.** (*Obs.*) Holiness ; (অপ্রঃ) পবিত্রতা। **2.** Hypocritical devoutness ; ধর্ম্মধ্বজিতা, কপটধার্ম্মিকতা, দম্ভ (হিঃ কোঃ), ধর্ম্মাভিমান (ঐ), বকবৃত্তি (ঐ), মর্কট-বৈরাগ্য, [মর্কট-বৈরাগ্য না কর লোক দেখাইয়া যথাযোগ্য বিষয় ভুঞ্জ অনাসক্ত হৈয়া (শ্রীচৈতন্য চরিতামৃত)।]

sanc′-tion (săngk-), *n.* & *v. t.* **1.** Ratification ; approbation ; an that it goes over (an obstacle) ; গোল্‌ফের বলে আঘাত করা ; এরূপভাবে বলে আঘাত করা যাহাতে ইহা (কোন প্রতিবন্ধকের) উপর দিয়া যায়। 2. To keep (pigeons) in a loft ; পায়রা টংয়ে রাখা। **Loft'-er,** *n.* A golf-club for ofting ; কন্দুক উর্দ্ধে উৎক্ষেপের জন্য গোল্‌ফ্‌ ক্রীড়াদণ্ড। **On loft**—উপরে। **The cock of the loft**—পালের গোদা, দলের সর্দ্দার।

ift'-ỹ, *adj.* 1. Of great height ; towering ; soaring ; as, *lofty* mountain ; অত্যুচ্চ ; উত্তুঙ্গ ; উন্নত। 2. Haughty ; proud ; দাম্ভিক, দৃপ্ত ; সগর্ব্ব। 3. Exalted ; sublime ; elevated in character or sentiment ; high-flown ; majestic ; সমুন্নত ; মহান্‌, সুমহান্‌ ; উন্নতচরিত্র, সমুন্নতভাবপূর্ণ, উন্নতমনাঃ ; শব্দাড়ম্বরভূয়িষ্ঠ, শব্দচ্ছটাযুক্ত ; মহিমান্বিত। **Loft'-i-ly,** *adv.* In a lofty position or manner ; proudly ; haughtily ; উচ্চস্থানে, উচ্চভাবে, উন্নতভাবে ; গর্ব্বিতভাবে ; দৃপ্তভাবে, উদ্ধতভাবে। **Loft'-i-ness,** *n.* State of being lofty ; height ; elevation ; grandeur ; haughtiness ; উচ্চাবস্থা ; উচ্চতা ; সমুন্নতি, উন্নতভাব ; মহিমা, গরিমা ; ঔদ্ধত্য।

ŏg, *n.* & *v. t.* 1. A bulky piece of wood unhewed ; স্থূল কাষ্ঠখণ্ড, কাঠের কুঁদা। 2. A floating contrivance, attached to a line for measuring the speed of a ship ; other apparatus for the same purpose ; জাহাজের গতিবেগমাপক যন্ত্রবিশেষ ; ঐরূপ উদ্দেশ্যসাধক অন্যান্য যন্ত্র। 3. Same as LOG-BOOK. ***Verb t.*** 1. To cut as timber into logs ; গাছ খণ্ড খণ্ড করা। 2. To enter in a ship's log-book, as the distance run ; নৌবিবরণী পুস্তকে লিপিবদ্ধ করা।

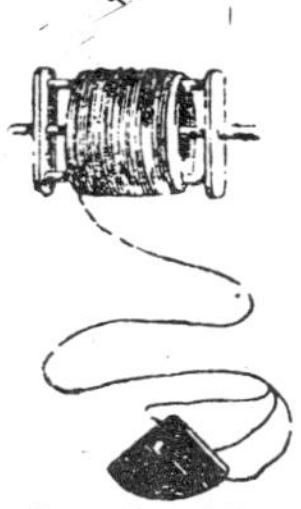
Log of a ship.

4. Right of affording such protection or shelter ; ঐরূপ আশ্রয় প্রদানের অধিকার। [পূর্ব্বে ইংলণ্ড প্রভৃতি দেশের কোন বিশেষ বিশেষ দেবমন্দিরে অপরাধিগণ আশ্রয় লইলে পুলিসের লোক তাহাদিগকে গ্রেপ্তার করিতে পারিত না। কেবল রাজদ্রোহী এবং ধর্ম্মদ্রোহী ব্যক্তিগণ ঐরূপ আশ্রয় হইতে বঞ্চিত হইত]।

sanc'-tŭm (săngk-), *n.* 1. A sacred place ; পবিত্র স্থান। 2. (*Colloq.*) A private room ; as, an editor's *sanctum* ; (চলিত ভাষায়) খাসকামরা, নিভৃত কক্ষ। **Editorial sanctum**—সম্পাদকীয় পীঠস্থলী। **Sanctum sanctorum** — ইহুদীদিগের দেবমন্দিরের পবিত্রতম অংশ, গর্ভগৃহ, বিমান (উড়িষ্যা) ; খাসকামরা, নিভৃতকক্ষ, বিজন কক্ষ।

sanc'-tŭs (săngk-), *n.* A hymn beginning with the words *sanctus, sanctus, sanctus* ; স্তোত্রবিশেষ। **Sanctus bell**—খৃষ্টের অন্তিমভোজনস্মারক অনুষ্ঠানের কালে বাদিত ঘণ্টা।

sănd, *n.* & *v. t.* 1. Any mass of fine particles of silicious stone not strictly reduced to powder or dust ; বালি, বালুকা, সিকতা [Syn. সিক্তা, শীতলা, সূক্ষ্মশর্করা, মহাসূক্ষ্মা (রাজ নিঃ), প্রবাহী, সূক্ষ্মা, পানীয়চূর্ণিকা, কর্পরাশ, ইষ্টগন্ধ।] 2. (*Pl.*) Tracts of lands consisting of sand ; beach ; বালুকাভূমি ; সৈকতভূমি। 3. (*Slang*) Pluck ; সাহস বুকের পাটা। ***Verb t.*** 1. To sprinkle with sand ; esp. to sprinkle freshly painted surface in imitation of stone ; বালি ছড়ান ; পাথরের মত দেখাইবার জন্য নূতন চিত্রিত কাগজাদির উপরে বালি ছড়ান। 2. To bury under sand ; বালির নীচে প্রোথিত করা। 3. To adulterate sugar etc. by the admixture of sand বালি মিশাইয়া চিনি প্রভৃতি ভেজাল করা। **Sand-bag**—বালির বস্তা। **Sand-bank**—বালুকাতট, কচ্ছ। **Sand-bath**—উত্তপ্ত বালুকার স্বেদ, বালুকাস্বেদ ; ভাণ্ড প্রভৃতিতে সমরূপ তাপ প্রদানের জন্য উত্তপ্ত বালুকাপূর্ণ পাত্রবিশেষ, বালুর তাপযন্ত্র (হিঃ কোঃ)। **Sand-blast**—কাচ প্রভৃতি কঠিন পদার্থ কাটা বা খোদাই করাইবার প্রণালী বিশেষ—যাহাতে বায়ু, বা বাষ্পপ্রবাহের সাহায্যে বালুকাধারা সজোরে প্রক্ষিপ্ত হয় ; যে যন্ত্রদ্বারা উক্তরূপে বালুকাধারা প্রক্ষিপ্ত হয়। **Sand-blind**—কাণা, নকুলান্ধ (ভাব প্রঃ)। **Sand-box**—কাগজের কাঁচা কালির উপর বালি ছড়াইবার জন্য সচ্ছিদ্র ডালাওয়ালা বাক্স (এইরূপ বাক্স পূর্ব্বে শোষ কাগজের পরিবর্ত্তে ব্যবহৃত হইত) ; ঢালাই কাজে ব্যবহৃত বালির ছাঁচ ; লৌহবর্ত্মের পাতরেলের উপর বালি ছড়াইবার জন্য গতিশীল বাষ্পীয়যন্ত্রে সংলগ্ন ধূলিপূর্ণ আধার। **Sand-boy**—আমুদে লোক। **Sand-clock** — বালুকাঘড়ী, রেণুগর্ভ (সুশ্রুঃ বিঃ)। **Sand-corn**—বালুকণা। **Sand-crack** — ইষ্টক বা অশ্ব খুরের ফাটা। **Sand-eel**—একপ্রকার বাইন মৎস্য। **Sand-flood**—বালুকাস্রোত। **Sand-glass** — Same as HOUR-GLASS (which see). **Sand-grouse** — একজাতীয় মরুপ্রদেশবাসী উজ্জ্বলপক্ষ বিহঙ্গম। **Sand-hill**—বালুকাশৈল, বালুকগিরি, বালিয়াড়ি (কপালঃ), বালুকাচল। **Sand-jet** — Same as SAND BLAST. **Sand-martin**—একপ্রকার ক্ষুদ্রপক্ষী—যাহারা বালির নীচে গর্ত্ত করিয়া বাস করে। **Sand-paper**—শিরীষ কাগজ। **Sand-piper**—ব্রিটিশ দ্বীপের কয়েক প্রকার পক্ষীর সাধারণ নাম। **Sand-shoes**—বালিতে ব্যবহারের জন্য রবার বা শণের তলিওয়ালা কাষ্ঠনির্ম্মিত জুতা। **Sand-spout** — মরুভূমিতে উত্থিত বালুকাস্তম্ভ। **Sand-stone**—বেলে পাথর। **Sand-storm**—ধূলিবাত্যা। **A rope of sands**—বালির বাঁধ (cf. খলের পিরীতি বালির বাঁধ)। **The sand has run out**—The time of grace has expired নির্দ্দিষ্ট কাল অতীত হইয়া গিয়াছে।

săn'-dăl, *n.* & *v. t.* 1. A kind of shoe fastened to the foot by straps ; একপ্রকার জুতা—উহার তলি চামড়ার দোয়াল দ্বারা পায়ের সহিত বাঁধা হইয়া থাকে উপানৎ। 2. A tie or strap for fastening a sleeper or low shoe over the foot or round

Sandals.

the ankle ; চটী বা নীচু জুতা পায়ের সহিত বাঁধার জন্য দোয়ালি। ***Verb t.*** **1.** To put sandal on ; উপানৎ পায়ে পরান। **2.** To fasten a sleeper or a low shoe with straps ; দোয়ালি দ্বারা চটী বা নীচু জুতা বাঁধা।

săn'-dăl, –wood, *ns.* The fragrant wood of certain East Indian trees ; চন্দন, মলয়জ। [Syn. গন্ধসার, ভদ্রশ্রী, ভদ্রশ্রিয় (সুশ্রুঃ), ভদ্রশ্রয়, ভদ্রাশ্রয়, চন্দ্রদ্যুতি, চন্দ্রকান্ত, সর্পহৃদয় চন্দন (A kind of), তিলপর্ণ, পীতিকা (yellow), পীতকাষ্ঠ (*ib.*), পীতগন্ধ (*ib.*), হিত, শ্রীখণ্ড, মহার্হ, গোশীর্ষ, সারগন্ধ, সারঙ্গ, গন্ধরাজ, মালয় (tree), পীতসার (*ib.*), মঙ্গল্য, উৎপলগন্ধিকা (species of the colour of brass and very fragrant), মলয়োদ্ভব, সুগন্ধ, শীতল, গন্ধাঢ্য, ভোগিবল্লভ, হিম, সৌগন্ধিক, বর্ণকদারু, পাবন, শীতগন্ধ, তৈলপর্ণিক, শীতলপ্রদ, বর্ণক, পটীর, মলয়াগুরু, ভদ্র, সুরোত্তর, সুশীত (yellow), সেব্য (red), রৌহিণ, যাম্য, সর্পাবাস, সর্পেষ্ট, একাঙ্গ। [ভাবপ্রকাশ নামক বৈদ্যক গ্রন্থে শ্রেষ্ঠ চন্দনের এইরূপ লক্ষণ লিখিত আছে ঃ— স্বাদে তিক্তং কষে পীতং ছেদে রক্তং তনৌ সিতম্। গ্রন্থিকোটরসংযুক্তং চন্দনং শ্রেষ্ঠমুচ্যতে।] [Arab. *sandal-abiaz* ; Chin. *peh-chen-tan* ; Fr. *sandale, santal* ; Germ. *sandel-holz* ; It. *sandalo* ; Russ. *sandalœ dereos* ; Pers. *sandal safed*]। **Red-sandal**—See under RED. [তাম্রবৃক্ষ তাম্রবীজ, তাম্রদ্রু, তাম্রবৃন্ত, অরুণচন্দন, (cf. তথাপ্যর্য্যম্লেহরুণ-চন্দনঞ্চ—বাস্তুশাস্ত্র) For other synonyms See under RED.] **Sandal-oil**—চন্দন তৈল।

săn'-dă-răc, *n.* Gum sandarac ; বার্নিশ প্রভৃতি প্রস্তুতে ব্যবহৃত একপ্রকার রজন, চন্দরস (যোঃ), সন্দরস (হিঃ কোঃ), চন্দ্ররস।

săn'-dĕrs, saun– (sän-), *ns.* **1.** Same as SANDAL-WOOD (which see). **2.** Same as RED SANDAL.

săn'-dĭ-vĕr, –dĕ-vĕr, *ns.* The scum of glass-fusion used, when pulverized, as a polish substance ; গলিত কাচের গাদ—যাহা চূর্ণ করিয়া পালিশের কার্য্যে ব্যবহৃত হয়।

sănd'-wich, *n.* & *v. t.* **1.** Slices of bread with meat or something savoury between ; রুটি, মাংস, ডিম্ব, প্রভৃতির পুর দেওয়া রুটি খণ্ডদ্বয়। **2.** Same as SANDWICH MAN (below). ***Verb t.*** To insert a statement etc. between two of another character ; "Mr. Disraeli, *sandwiches* between sensible suggestions some of his very worst thoughts" ; দুইটী বিসদৃশ বিষয় বা উক্তির মধ্যে অপর কোন বিষয় প্রবিষ্ট করা। **Sandwich-board**—রাস্তায় ঘুরিয়া ঘুরিয়া বিজ্ঞাপন প্রদর্শনের জন্য কোন ব্যক্তির সম্মুখে ও পশ্চাতে যে বিজ্ঞাপনফলকদ্বয় ঝুলান থাকে তাহার অন্যতর। **Sandwich-boat**—বাইচে যে নৌকা দ্বিতীয় সারির অগ্রে আসা হেতু প্রথম সারির ঠিক পশ্চাতে চলিতে পারে। **Sandwich-boy, Sandwich-man**—যে ব্যক্তি সম্মুখে একটী ও পশ্চাতে একটী বিজ্ঞাপনফলক ঝুলাইয়া রাস্তায় রাস্তায় ঘুরে।

sănd'-ў, *adj.* **1.** Consisting, or composed of, sand ; abounding with sand ; বালুকাময়, বালুকারচিত, বেলে, পাংশুল, সিকতাময়, বালুকাকীর্ণ ; বালুকাবহুল। **2.** (Of hair) Yellowish red ; (কেশসম্পর্কে) কপিশবর্ণ, আপীত রক্তবর্ণ। **3.** Dry ; নীরস। **Sandy-loam**—দোয়াস (প্রবোধ)।

sāne, *adj.* **1.** Of sound mind ; স্থিরমতি, প্রকৃতিস্থ, অবিচলিত বুদ্ধি। **2.** (Of opinions etc.) Sensible, moderate ; সদ্বিবেচনাপ্রসূত ; ধীর। **Sane'-ly,** *adv.*

San'-gă (săng-), **–găr,** *ns.* **1.** (India) A breastwork ; আবক্ষ উচ্চ প্রাচীর। **2.** (In North-west Himalya and Afghanisthan) A stone parapet erected for defence ; আত্মরক্ষার্থ আবক্ষ উচ্চ প্রাচীর।

san-ga-ree' (săng-gă-rē), *n.* Wine and water sweetened and spiced and sometimes iced used as a refreshing drink in warm countries or warm weather ; গ্রীষ্মের দিনে বা গ্রীষ্মপ্রধান স্থানে শ্রান্তিবারক পানীয়রূপে ব্যবহৃত একপ্রকার মদ্য, জল, চিনি ও মসলা এবং সময় সময় বরফ সংযোগে প্রস্তুত সরবৎবিশেষ।

sang-de-bœuf, (*F.*), *n.* & *adj.* A deep red colour found in ancient Chinese porcelain ; প্রাচীনকালের চীনা বাসনে দৃষ্ট একপ্রকার গাঢ় রক্তবর্ণ। ***Adj.*** Of such colour ; উক্তরূপ বর্ণের।

sang-froid, (*F.*), *n.* Coolness ; calmness in agitating circumstances ; অবিক্ষুব্ধতা, প্রশান্তভাব, স্থৈর্য্য, ধীরতা।

săn-graal' (-grāl), **săn'-gre-ăl** (-grā-), **săn-grail'** (-grāl), *ns.* See GRAIL.

san-gui-fi-ca'-tion (săng-gwĭ-), *n.* The production of blood ; the conversion of chyle into blood ; রক্তজনন, শোণিতোৎপাদন ; অন্নরসের রক্তে রূপান্তর, রুধিরীকরণ।

san'-guin-ă-rў (săng-gwĭn-), *adj.* **1.** Abounding in blood ; consisting of blood ; full of blood ; রক্তবহুল, রক্তময়, রুধিরময় ; রক্তাত্মক ; রুধিরপূর্ণ। **2.** Attended with bloodshed ; bloody ; as, a *sanguinary* battle ; রক্তগঙ্গাপ্রবাহী ; রক্তস্রাবী, রুধিরস্রাবী। **3.** (Of Laws) Passing death-sentence freely ; (আইন সম্পর্কে) মৃত্যুদণ্ডপ্রদানতৎপর।

san'-guine (săng-gwĭn), *adj., n.* & *v. t.* **1.** Abounding with blood ; রক্তপূর্ণ, রুধিরপূর্ণ। **2.** Bloodthirsty ; murderous ; "Passions make us *sanguine*" ; রক্তপিপাসু, রুধিরলালস (মঃ ভাঃ) ; খুনী।

3. Of the temperament in which the blood predominates over the other humours; রক্তপ্রধান, বাতপ্রকৃতিক (হিঃ কোঃ), রক্তসার (বৃঃ সং), রুধিরসার (লঘুজাতক)। **4.** (*Now rare*) Pertaining to blood; as, *sanguine* substance; (বর্তমানে কচিদ্‌ব্যবহৃত) রক্তসম্বন্ধীয়, রৌধির [cf. পিবন্তীং রৌধিরীং ধারাং—ছিন্নমস্তাস্তোত্র।] **5.** Blood-red; রুধিরবর্ণ, রক্তবর্ণ। **6.** Warm; ardent; as, *sanguine* temper; *sanguine* of success; আবেগপূর্ণ, অনুরাগী, রাগবান, উদ্দীপনাপূর্ণ; আশাপূর্ণ, আশান্বিত। **7.** (Of complexion) Ruddy; লাল, লোহিত। ***Noun.*** **1.** Blood colour; রক্তবর্ণ। **2.** A kind of red crayon; একপ্রকার লোহিতবর্ণে রঞ্জিত চিত্রবর্ত্তিকা বা খড়ি। **3.** A drawing in red crayon; লাল খড়িদ্বারা অঙ্কিত চিত্র। ***Verb t.*** To tinge with blood; to colour with red colour; রক্তরঞ্জিত করা; লোহিতবর্ণে রঞ্জিত করা। **—ly,** *adv.* **—ness,** *n.*

san-guin'-e-ous (săng-gwĭn-ē-ŭs), *adj.* **1.** Pertaining to blood; bloody; রক্তসম্পর্কীয়; রক্তময়, রুধিররঞ্জিত। **2.** Blood-red; রক্তবর্ণ। **3.** (*Rare*) Plethoric; রক্তবহুল। **4.** Blood-thirsty; রক্তপিপাসু, জিঘাংসু। **5.** Hopeful; আশান্বিত, আশাপূর্ণ।

săn'-hĕ-drĭm, —drin, *ns.* The supreme court and legislative council among the Jews; প্রাচীন জেরুজালেম নগরীর সর্ব্বপ্রধান ধর্ম্মাধিকরণ এবং ব্যবস্থাপক সভা (এই সভার সভ্যসংখ্যা ৭১ জন ছিল।)

săn'-ĭ-cle (-kl), *n.* An umbelliferous plant of several species; একপ্রকার ছত্রপুষ্পী গুল্ম।

sā'-nĭ-ēs, *n.* A thin reddish discharge from wounds or sores; ক্ষতাদি হইতে নিঃসৃত পাতলা, লালাভ স্রাব, কলতানি, রসানি।

săn'-ĭ-fȳ, *v. t.* To make healthy; স্বাস্থ্যকর করা, স্বাস্থ্যজনক করা।

săn-ĭ-tā'-rĭ-ŭm, *n.* A health station; a sanatorium; স্বাস্থ্যজনকস্থান (হিঃ কোঃ); স্বাস্থ্যমন্দির।

săn'-ĭ-tā-rȳ, *adj.* **1.** Hygienic; relating to the preservation of health; স্বাস্থ্যসম্বন্ধীয়, স্বাস্থ্যরক্ষাবিষয়ক। **—ri-ness,** *n.* **—ta'-ri-an,** *adj.*

săn'-ĭ-tās, *n.* An antiseptic and disinfectant preparation; এক প্রকার পচননিবারক এবং সংক্রামকবীজাণুনাশক দ্রব্য।

săn'-ĭ-tāte, *v. t.* To make sanitary; to provide with sanitary appliances; স্বাস্থ্যজনক করা; স্বাস্থ্যবিধায়ক উপায়াদি সমন্বিত করা।

săn-ĭ-tā'-tion, *n.* **1.** Improvement of sanitary condition; the adoption of sanitary measures; স্বাস্থ্যোন্নতিবিধান; স্বাস্থ্যজনক ব্যবস্থার প্রয়োগ। **2.** Hygiene; স্বাস্থ্যবিজ্ঞান, স্বাস্থ্যতত্ত্ব। **—ist,** *n.*

săn'-ĭ-tȳ, *n.* The state of being sane; soundness of health; প্রকৃতিস্থতা, চিত্তসাবধানতা (হিঃ কোঃ), সাবধানচিত্ততা (ঐ); মানসিক সুস্থতা, মনের সুস্থতা, অপ্রমত্ততা, সুস্থতা।

sanjak, *n.* (In Turkey) A sub-division of a vilayet; (তুরুস্ক দেশে) জেলা।

sănk (săngk), *p. t.* Of SINK (which see.)

săns, *prep.* Without; ছাড়া, বিনা। **Sans ceremonie**—অশিষ্টভাবে, আদবকায়দার ধার না ধারিয়া। **Sans-culotte**—ফরাসীবিপ্লব কালের নীচ শ্রেণীর বিপ্লববাদী; চরমবিপ্লববাদী (শব্দানুযায়ী পাজামাহীন)। **Sans doute**—নিঃসন্দেহে। **Sans facon**—স্পষ্টাক্ষরে, স্পষ্টাস্পষ্টি। **Sans-gene**—স্বচ্ছন্দভাবে, অনাড়ষ্টভাবে, প্রাণখুলিয়া। **Sans peur et sans reproche**—নির্ভীক এবং নিষ্কলঙ্ক। **Sans phrase**—এক কথায়, ইতর বিশেষ না করিয়া, কোনরূপ পরিবর্ত্তন না করিয়া। **Sans-souci**—ভাবনাহীনতা, নিশ্চিন্তভাব।

săn'-sĕr-ĭf, *n.* & *adj.* A form of type without serifs; একপ্রকার মুদ্রাক্ষর। ***Adj.*** Of such type; ঐরূপ অক্ষর সম্বন্ধীয়।

Săn'-tă-Claus, Săn'-tă-c (-klăz), *n.* The imaginary personage who fills children's stockings with toys and other litttle presents on Christmas; যে কল্পিত ব্যক্তি রাত্রিকালে আসিয়া ছেলেদের মোজার ভিতর খেলানা, পুতুল, প্রভৃতি বড়দিনের উপহার রাখিয়া যায়।

săn'-tŏn, *n.* A Mohammedan ascetic; মুসলমান যোগী বা তাপস।

săn-tŏn'-ĭ-că, *n.* A kind of wormwood; একপ্রকার চিরতা।

săn'-tö-nĭn, *n.* An anthelmintic medicine ($C_{15}\ H_{18}\ O_3$) obtained from the seeds of southern wood (*artemisia santonica*); একপ্রকার ক্রিমিঘ্ন ঔষধ, সেন্টোনিন।

săp, *n.* & *v. t.* **1.** The juice or fluid which circulates in plants or trees; উদ্ভিদ্ রস। **2.** Same as SAP-WOOD. **3.** Vigour; essential element; তেজঃ; সারপদার্থ, সত্ত্ব। ***Verb t.*** **1.** To exhaust the sap of tree; বৃক্ষের রস নিঃশেষিত করা। **2.** To deprive of vigour; as, to *sap* one's constitution; তেজোবীর্য্য নষ্ট করা, নির্বীর্য্য করা। **Sap'-ful, Sap'-py,** *adjs.* **Sap'-pi-ness,** *n.* **Sap'-less,** *adj.* **Sap-green**—(*noun*) একপ্রকার ফিকে সবুজ রং। (*Adj.*) ঐ রংয়ের। **Sap-lath**—কোমল কাষ্ঠের বাতা; **Sap-wood**—অন্তর্ব্বল্কল ও কঠিন কাষ্ঠের মধ্যবর্ত্তী শ্বেতবর্ণ কাষ্ঠ, কোমল কাষ্ঠ (সাঃ পঃ), পলকা কাঠ (ঐ), অসার (ঐ)।

săp, *v. t., i.* & *n.* **1.** To undermine; অধঃখনন করা। **2.** To destroy or impair by some hidden or invisible process; গোপনে নষ্ট করা, গোপনে সর্ব্বনাশ করা। **3.** To unsettle; to weaken; ভিত্তিদেশে খনন করিয়া টলমলায়মান করা; দুর্ব্বল করা **3.** To approach a fortress with saps; to pierce ground with saps; পরিখা কাটিয়া দুর্গাভিমুখে অগ্রসর হওয়া; সুড়ঙ্গ কাটা। ***Verb i.*** **1.** To dig a covered destroy utterly ; to criticize severely ; বিধ্বংস করা ; কঠোর সমালোচনা করা। **To cut up rough**—To be disagreeable or quarrelsome about anything ; কোন বিষয় লইয়া অপ্রীতির সঞ্চার হওয়া, কোন বিষয় লইয়া কলহ করা। **To cut up**—To leave large fortune ; প্রচুর সম্পত্তি রাখিয়া যাওয়া।

cū-tā'-nē-ous (-ŭs), *adj.* Of the skin ; চর্ম্ম সম্বন্ধীয়, চার্ম্মিক।

cutch—কথ (বেলঃ)।

cūte, *adj.* (*Colloq.*) Clever ; (চলিত ভাষায়) চালাক। **Cute'-ly,** *adv.* **Cute'-ness,** *n.*

cū'-ti-cle, *n.* **1.** The epidermis or the scarf-skin ; বাহ্যত্বক, উপত্বক অবভাসিনী (মঃ ইঃ)। **2.** (*Bot.*) Superficial film of plants ; (উদ্ভিদ-বিদ্যা) বৃক্ষাদির বাহিরের পর্দ্দা, কৃত্তিক (সাঃ পঃ)। **—tic'-u-lar,** *adj.*

cū'-tis, *n.* The true skin under the cuticle ; বাহ্যত্বকের নিম্নবর্ত্তী প্রকৃত ত্বক, প্রকৃত-ত্বক (হঃ চঃ)।

cŭt'-lăss, *n.* A broad curving sword used by sailors ; নাবিক-দিগের দা বা কাটারি, কর্ত্তরিকা।

cŭt'-lêr, *n.* One who makes or deals in knives or other similar instruments ; ছুরি, কাঁচি প্রভৃতি নির্ম্মাতা বা বিক্রেতা।

cŭt'-lêr-ȳ, *n.* **1.** The business or trade of a cutler ; ছুরি, কাঁচির ব্যবসায়। **2.** Articles made or sold by a cutler ; ছুরি, কাঁচি প্রভৃতি।

cŭt'-lĕt, *n.* A small slice of meat (esp. mutton or veal) for cooking ; রাঁধিবার জন্য মাংসের ফালি (সাধারণতঃ পাঁজর এবং তৎসংলগ্ন মাংস), ভৃষ্ট-ফালিকা (আঃ বঃ)।

cŭt'-têr, *n.* **1.** A person or thing that cuts ; কর্ত্তক, কর্ত্তনকারী। **2.** A soft brick that can be cut to any shape ; এক প্রকার নরম ইট, যাহা যে কোন আকারে কাটা যাইতে পারে। **3.** A small boat used by ships of war ; রণপোত সমূহদ্বারা ব্যবহৃত ক্ষুদ্র নৌকা। **4.** A vessel with one mast and a straight running

Cutter.

bow-sprit, closely resembling sloop ; একপ্রকার এক মাস্তুলের জাহাজ

cŭt'-ting, *n.* Act of separating with a sharp-edged instrument ; কর্ত্তন, ছেদন। **Press cutting**—A paragraph etc. cut from a newspaper ; সংবাদপত্র হইতে কর্ত্তিত প্রবন্ধাংশ প্রভৃতি।

cŭt'-tle, *n.* A mollusc which ejects a black fluid to conceal itself (also *cuttle-fish*) ; এক প্রকার কম্বুজ—ইহার শরীর হইতে একরূপ কৃষ্ণ-বর্ণ তরল পদার্থ নির্গত হইয়া ইহাকে লুক্কায়িত করে, সমুদ্র-জিহ্বা (সাঃ পঃ), দশভুজা (আঃ বঃ)। **Cuttle-bone** — Its internal shell, used for polishing ; সমুদ্রফেন, সিন্ধুকফ, হিণ্ডীর।

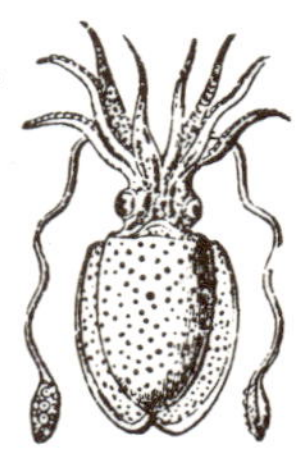

Cuttle-fish.

cŭt'-tȳ, *adj.* & *n.* Abnormally short ; অতি খাটো। ***Noun.*** A short tobacco-pipe ; ধূমপানের ক্ষুদ্র নল। **Cutty-stool** — স্কটলণ্ড দেশীয় ধর্ম্মমন্দিরের আসন বিশেষ — যাহাতে বসিয়া অসতী নারীগণ প্রকাশ্য তিরস্কার ভোগ করিত।

cŭt'-wa-têr, *n.* **1.** The forepart of a ship's prow that cuts the water.; পোতাগ্রদেশের সম্মুখ ভাগ,—যাহা জল কাটিয়া চলে, তরঙ্গভেদী অগ্রসরের জন্য পরিখাখননকারী সৈনিক। **2.** A private of Royal Engineers; সামরিক পূর্ত্তবিশারদ দলের সাধারণ কার্য্যকারক (বর্ত্তমানে সরকারী কাগজপত্রে এই অর্থে ব্যবহৃত হয় না।)

Sap'-phic (săf-), *adj.* & *n.* Of Sappho, the ancient Lesbian poetess who flourished in 600 B. C. ; প্রাচীন Lesbos নগরীর নারী কবি Sappho সম্বন্ধীয়। ***Noun.*** A metre used by Sappho ; a Sapphic verse ; Sappho কর্ত্তৃক প্রবর্ত্তিত ছন্দ ; Sappho কর্ত্তৃক রচিত কবিতা। **Sapphic vice** — রমণীতে রমণীতে অস্বাভাবিক রমণ।

sap'-phīre (săf-), *n.* & *adj.* **1.** A precious stone of very great hardness and of various shades of blue ; নীলা (cf. নানীরঙ্গের পেশোয়াজে মুক্তার ফুল, গোলাবী ওড়নায় সোণার পাড়, পান্নার চুড়ী, নীলার কণ্ঠী, হীরার চিক — রাজকাহিনী — অবনীন্দ্র-নাথ ঠাকুর।), নীলাপাথর [Syn. নীলকান্ত, নীলমণি, ইন্দ্রনীল, ইন্দীবর নীলোপল (শিশুঃ), মহানীল, নীল (cf. বৈদূর্য্যনীলঞ্চ যথা মরকতক্রমাৎ — যুক্তিকল্পদ্রুম), মহানীলমণি (cf. ব্রাহ্মণায় মহানীলমণিদ্বয়ং দদ্যাৎ), নীলম্ (হিঃ কোঃ), নীলরত্ন, নীলরত্নক, নীলাশ্ম (শিশুঃ), তৃণগ্রাহী (ঘর্ষণে তড়িজ্জননহেতু ইহা তৃণাদি আকর্ষণ করিয়া থাকে বলিয়া এই নাম), শিতিরত্ন, শনিপ্রিয় [শনি নীলমণির অধিষ্ঠাত্রী দেবতা বলিয়া এই নাম। ইয়ুরোপীয় জ্যোতিষেও নীলবর্ণ তুরুষ্ক মণি (Turquoise)এর অধিষ্ঠাত্রী দেবতা শনি। ফলিতজ্যোতিষ মতে এই মণি ধারণে বা গ্রহাচার্য্যকে দানে শনিগ্রহের অশুভ প্রভাব হইতে রক্ষা পাওয়া যায়। কোন কোন শব্দতত্ত্ববিৎ পণ্ডিতের অনুমান এই যে, "শনিপ্রিয়" শব্দ হইতে Jewish Aramic ভাষার *Sampirina* শব্দ এবং এই শেষোক্ত শব্দ হইতে Hebrew ভাষার *Sappir* শব্দ আসিয়াছে। এই *Sappir* শব্দ ইয়ুরোপের যাবতীয় ভাষার *Sapphire* শব্দের মূল বলিয়া অবধারিত হইয়াছে।] সৌরিরত্ন (রাজ নিঃ), সৌরিমণি, শক্রনীল (গোপালঃ), অভ্ররুহ,

নীলোৎপল (রঃ প্রঃ), সুনীলক, মসার। [Arab. *sufir* ; Fr. *saphir* ; Germ. *sapphir* ; It., Sp. *zaffiro* ; Russ. *jachant, sapfir*]. গরুড় পুরাণ মতে ইন্দ্রনীলমণির পরীক্ষা যথা :—যে নীলকান্ত মণির মধ্যে ইন্দ্রায়ুধের তুল্য প্রভা দৃষ্ট হয় তাহা—পৃথিবীতে দুর্ল্লভ। যে নীলমণি শত-গুণ দুগ্ধে রক্ষিত হইলে সমস্ত দুগ্ধকে নীল-বর্ণে রঞ্জিত করে—তাহার নাম মহানীল"। ইন্দ্রনীলমণি সিংহলদ্বীপে ও ব্রহ্মদেশের পদ্মরাগমণির আকরে এবং শ্যাম প্রভৃতি দেশে প্রচুর পরিমাণে পাওয়া যায়। প্যারী নগরীর প্রাকৃতিক ইতিহাসের চিত্রশালায় (Museum of Natural History) একটী ১০০ ক্যারেট ওজনের স্বচ্ছ ইন্দ্রনীলমণি আছে। এই মণিটী বঙ্গদেশ হইতে প্রায় ১০২০০০৲ টাকা মূল্যে ক্রীত হইয়াছিল।] **2.** The colour of a sapphire ; blue ; নীলকান্তমণির বর্ণ; নীলবর্ণ। **3.** Kinds of humming birds ; বিভিন্নপ্রকার নীল ও সবুজ বর্ণ পাখীর সাধারণ নাম। ***Adj.*** Of, or resembling, sapphire ; নীলমণিসম্বন্ধীয়, নীলকান্তবৎ।

sap′-phir-ine (săf-), *adj.* & *n.* Made of sapphire ; resembling sapphire ; নীলমণিময়, ইন্দ্রনীলমণি-বিরচিত ; নীলকান্তবৎ, নীলমণিসদৃশ। ***Noun.*** A mineral of a pale blue colour; ম্লান নীলবর্ণের খনিজ পদার্থবিশেষ।

Sap′-phism (săf-), *n.* Same as SAPPHIC VICE (under SAPPHIC.)

să-prae′-mi-ă (-prē-), **—prē′-**, *ns.* Septic-poisoning ; ক্ষতাদির মাংস-পচন হেতু রক্তদুষ্টি। **—prae′-mic,** (or **—pre′-mic**), *adjs.*

săp-rö-gĕn′-ic, *adj.* Causing putrefaction ; পচনজনক। **Sa-prog′-e-nous,** *adj.*

să-prŏph′-ă-gous (-gŭs), *adj.* Feeding on decomposed matter ; গলিতপদার্থভোজী, গলনজীবী (সাঃ পঃ)।

săp′-rö-phile, *adj.* & *n.* **1.** Inhabiting putrid matter ; গলিত-পদার্থে বাসকারী। **2.** A bacterium living in putrid matter ; গলিত পদার্থে বাসকারী জীবাণু বিশেষ।

săp′-rö-phȳte, *n.* A plant growing on decaying organic matter ; পচ্যমান জৈবপদার্থে জাত উদ্ভিদ্।

săr, *n.* An individual of the genus sargus ; একপ্রকার মৎস্য।

săr′-ă-bănd, *n.* **1.** A slow Spanish dance ; স্পেনদেশীয় মৃদুমন্দ নৃত্য বিশেষ। **2.** A piece of music adapted to the dance ; ঐ নৃত্যের উপযোগী সঙ্গীত।

Săr′-ă-cĕn, *n.* & *adj.* An Arabian of the early proselytizing period ; মধ্যযুগের আরব দেশীয় মুসলমান। ***Adj.*** Saracenic ; ঐ যুগের আরব দেশীয় মুসলমান সম্বন্ধীয়। **—cen′-ic,** *adj.* **Saracen-corn**—Same as BUCK-WHEAT.

Să-ră-tö-gă, (Also *Saratoga trunk*), *n.* A lady's large travelling trunk; ভ্রমণকালে সঙ্গে নেওয়ার উপযোগী স্ত্রীলোকদিগের বৃহৎ তোরঙ্গ। **Saratoga chips**—চর্ব্বিতে ভাজা আলুর পাতলা চাকতি।

săr′-căsm, *n.* A bitter cutting jest ; a satirical remark ; ব্যঙ্গ, বিদ্রূপ, ঠাট্টা ; ব্যঙ্গোক্তি। **—cas′-tic, —cas′-ti-cal,** *adjs.* Characterised by sarcasm ; taunting; expressing sarcasm ; satirical ; বিদ্রূপাত্মক, ব্যঙ্গাত্মক ; বিদ্রূপজনক, উপহাসজনক, ব্যঙ্গব্যঞ্জক ; বিদ্রূপসূচক ; বিদ্রূপপ্রিয়।

săr-cĕl-le′ (-ē), *n.* A teal ; পানা জাতীয় হংসের সাধারণ নাম।

sarce′-nĕt (sârs-), *n.* Same as SARSANET (which see).

săr′-cö-cele (-sēl), *n.* A fleshy tumour of a testicle ; অণ্ডকোষের মাংসল ও কঠিন স্ফীতি, মাংসজবৃদ্ধি।

săr′-cōde, *n.* Protoplasm ; জীব-পঙ্ক, প্রাণপঙ্ক।

săr-cŏl′-ö-ġȳ, *n.* That branch of anatomy which treats of flesh, fat, etc. ; শারীরসংস্থানবিদ্যার যে শাখায় মাংস, মেদ, পেশী, প্রভৃতির বিষয় আলোচিত হয়।

săr-cō′-mă, (*pl.* -MATA) *n.* A fleshy tumour ; বেদনা ও প্রদাহশূন্য দৃঢ় মাংসল অর্ব্বুদ, মাংসার্ব্বুদ, মাংস সংঘাত।

săr-cŏph′-ă-gŭs (*Pl.* -GUSES or -GI), *n.* **1.** A limestone used among the Greeks for making coffins believed to have the property of consuming bodies deposited in it within a few weeks ; একপ্রকার চূণা পাথর—প্রাচীন গ্রীকগণ, এই পাথর দ্বারা শবাধার নির্ম্মাণ করিত ; কথিত আছে এইরূপ শবাধারে মৃতদেহ রাখিলে কয়েক সপ্তাহের মধ্যেই ইহা ক্ষয়প্রাপ্ত হইত। **2.** A stone coffin in which the ancients deposited dead bodies ; একপ্রকার পাষাণময় শবাধার—যাহাতে কোন কোন প্রাচীন জাতির লোকগণ মৃতদেহ রক্ষা করিতেন। **3.** A kind of stone-chest generally more or less ornamented for receiving a dead body ; শবরক্ষার্থ অল্পাধিক কারুকার্য্যখচিত পাথরের সিন্দুক।

săr′-cö-plăsm, *n.* The outer fibrillose substance of muscles ; পেশীর বহির্ব্বর্ত্তী অংশুময় মধ্যবর্ত্তী পদার্থ।

săr′-cous (-kŭs), *adj.* Consisting of flesh or muscles; মাংস বা পেশীময়।

sărd, *n.* A variety of cornelian of a yellow or orange colour ; পীত বা কমলাবর্ণের রুধিরাক্ষ মণি।

Sâr-dă-nă-pa′-lŭs, *adj.* Like Sardanapalus, king of Nineveh ; নিনভেরাজ সার্ডেনেপ্যালাসসম্বন্ধীয়। [নিনভেরাজ সার্ডেনেপ্যালাস্ মহা বিলাসী ছিলেন। Media দেশের সৈন্য Sardanapalus এর রাজপ্রাসাদ আক্রমণ করিলে তিনি তদীয় উপপত্নীগণের সহিত অগ্নিকুণ্ডে প্রাণবিসর্জ্জন করেন। ইঁহার ঐতিহাসিক নাম Ashurbanipal।]

săr′-delle (-dĕl), *n.* A fish like sardine; স্যার্ডিন মাছের মত একপ্রকার মাছ।

săr′-dine (-dīn), *n.* Same as SARD (which see).

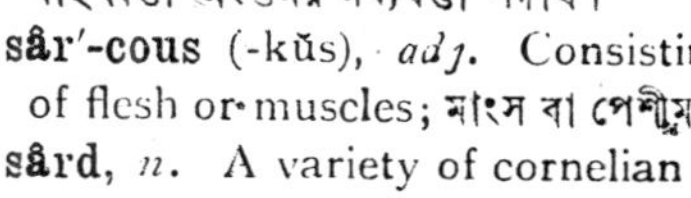

Sardine.

săr′-dine (-dīn), *n.* A small fish allied to the herring and pilchard caught in the Mediterranean, esp. of Sardinia ; হেরিং জাতীয় ক্ষুদ্র মৎস্যবিশেষ (এই মাছ টিনে পুরিয়া নানা দেশে রপ্তানি করা হয় ।) **Packed like sardines**—(Of crowded company) ঘিজিঘিজি (*colloq.*), তিল ধারণের স্থান শূন্য ।

Sâr-dĭn′-ĭ-ăn, *adj.* & *n.* Of, or pertaining to, the island, kingdom or people of Sardinia ; সার্ডিনিয়া দ্বীপ, রাজ্য বা বাসিসম্বন্ধীয় । ***Noun.*** An inhabitant of the island or kingdom of Sardinia ; সার্ডিনিয়া-দ্বীপ বা সার্ডিনিয়ারাজ্যের অধিবাসী ।

sâr-dŏn′-ic, *adj.* **1.** Forced ; as, *sardonic* laughter ; কৃত্রিম, কাঠ (হাসি), দেঁতো (cf. দেঁতোহাসি) । **2.** (Of laughter) Scornful ; mocking ; (হাস্যসম্বন্ধে) অবজ্ঞাসূচক ; বিদ্রূপাত্মক । **Sardonic laughter**—(ভৈষজ্য-শাস্ত্র) আক্ষেপিক ও অনৈচ্ছিক হাস্য ।

sâr′-dŏ-nȳ, *n.* An agate with sard and white chalcedony in alternate layers ; একপ্রকার পালঙ্ক মণি । [এই মণিতে পর পর সীমমণি ও গোমেদ মণির এক এক স্তর থাকে ।]

sâr-găs′-so (-ö), *n.* Same as GULF-WEED (which see).

sâr′-ĭs-să, *n.* (*Greek Antiq.*) A long lance ; (গ্রীকপ্রত্নতত্ত্ব) দীর্ঘ বর্শা ।

sârk, *n.* (*Scot.*) Shirt ; chemise ; (স্কটলণ্ডে) জামা ; সেমিজ ।

Sâr-mā′-ti-ăn (-shĭ-), **–măt′-ic,** *adjs.* & *ns.* Of, or pertaining to, ancient Sarmatia ; (*poet.*) Polish ; রুশিয়া এবং পোলণ্ড সম্বন্ধীয় ; (কবিতায়) পোল জাতি সম্বন্ধীয় । ***Noun.*** An inhabitant of ancient Sarmatia ; রুশিয়া বা পোলণ্ডের অধিবাসী ।

sâr-mĕn′-tōse, –tous (-tŭs), *adjs.* (*Bot.*) Having runners ; (উদ্ভিদ্‌বিদ্যা) ধাবকসমন্বিত ।

sâr′-sȧ-pȧ-rĭl′-lȧ, *n.* **1.** A species of smilax whose root is valued in medicine ; মেক্সিকোদেশীয় গুল্মবিশেষ,—ইহার মূল ঔষধে ব্যবহৃত হয় । **2.** The dried cordlike root of this tree ; ঐ গাছের শুষ্ক মূল (ইহা হইতে একপ্রকার বলকারক ঔষধ প্রস্তুত হয়) । **Indian sarsaparilla**—অনন্তমূল ।

sâr′-sĕn, *n.* Blocks of sandstone lying on Wiltshire downs ; উইল্টসায়ারের বৃক্ষহীন উচ্চভূমিতে প্রাপ্ত বেলেপাথরের বৃহৎ বৃহৎ খণ্ড ।

sarse′-nĕt (särs-), *n.* A species of fine, thin, woven silk used for ribbons, linings, etc. ; পিরাণের আস্তর, ফিতা, প্রভৃতির জন্য একপ্রকার মিহি রেশমী কাপড় ।

sâr-tō′-rĭ-ăl, *adj.* Of or pertaining to, a tailor or tailoring ; দর্জ্জীসম্বন্ধীয়, দর্জ্জীর কাজ সম্বন্ধীয়, সৌচিকসম্বন্ধীয়, সূচিকর্ম্মসম্বন্ধীয় ।

Sā′-rŭm, *n.* Salisbury ; সেলিসব্যারী । **Sarum-use**—Salisburyর বিশপকর্ত্তৃক ১০৭৮ খৃঃ অব্দে প্রবর্ত্তিত ভজন-পদ্ধতিবিশেষ ।

săsh, *n.* A long band or scarf worn over the shoulders usually as a part of uniform or round the waist by women or children ; সামরিক পরিচ্ছদের উপর উপবীতাকারে পরিধেয় উত্তরীয় বিশেষ, স্ত্রীলোক ও শিশুদিগের কটিবন্ধস্বরূপ পরিধেয় বস্ত্রখণ্ড ।

săsh, *n.* The frame of a window etc. ; জানালা প্রভৃতির কাচ বসাইবার ফ্রেম বা কাঠাম, কাচাবার (আঃ বঃ) ।

Sasin or Indian antelope.

sâ′-sĭn, *n.* The common Indian antelope [*Antilope cervicapra*] ; কৃষ্ণসার ।

săs′-sa-bȳ (-ā-), *n.* A large South-African antelope ; দক্ষিণ আফ্রিকার বৃহৎকায় কৃষ্ণসারবিশেষ ।

săs′-să-frăs, *n.* A kind of laurel, the bark of which has medicinal virtues ; ভেষজগুণসম্পন্ন বল্কলবিশিষ্ট লরেল বৃক্ষ বিশেষ ।

Săs-sā′-nĭ-an, –nĭd, *adjs.* & *ns.* Of, or pertaining to, Sassanidae ; পারস্যদেশীয় রাজবংশবিশেষ সম্বন্ধীয় । ***Noun.*** One of the Sassanidae ; উক্তবংশীয় রাজা । [সাসানীয় বংশীয় সম্রাট্‌গণ ২২৪ খৃঃ অব্দ হইতে ৬৫১ খৃঃ অব্দ পর্য্যন্ত পারস্য সাম্রাজ্যের একচ্ছত্র অধীশ্বর ছিলেন । ইঁহাদের রাজধানী Ctesiphon নগরে প্রতিষ্ঠিত ছিল । ইহারা রোমানদিগের সহিত নিয়ত সংগ্রামে নিরত ছিল । Ardashir বা Artaxerxes এই বংশের প্রতিষ্ঠাতা । ইনি Parthia এবং Media জয় করিয়া "রাজরাজেশ্বর" উপাধি গ্রহণ করেন ।]

Săs′-sĕn-ach, *n.* A Celtic name for Saxon ; an Englishman ; সেক্সন জাতীয় লোক [কেল্টজাতীয় লোকগণ কর্ত্তৃক প্রদত্ত নাম)] ; ইংরেজ ।

săt, *p. t.* of SIT (which see).

Sā′-tăn, *n.* **1.** The grand adversary of men ; বাইবেল গ্রন্থে উক্ত দেবদ্বেষী দানব, শয়তান । [বাইবেল অনুসারে শয়তান বা Lucifer পূর্ব্বে স্বর্গরাজ্যে ঈশ্বরের অতি প্রিয় দেবদূত ছিল । পরে ঈশ্বরের সহিত বিদ্রোহাচরণ করায় সে স্বর্গরাজ্য হইতে চ্যুত হয়], মার (Among the Buddhists) ।

Sā-tăn′-ic, –ĭ-căl, *adjs.* **1.** Having the qualities of Satan ; শয়তানের মত প্রকৃতিবিশিষ্ট । **2.** Infernal ; fiendish ; নারকীয় ; পৈশাচিক, শয়তানী, দানবীয় ।

Sā′-tăn-ĭsm, *n.* **1.** The evil and malicious spirit of Satan ; diabolic spirit ; শয়তানী প্রকৃতি ; দানবীয়তা, দানবতা । **2.** Worship of Satan ; শয়তানপূজা । **–ize,** *v. t.*

Sā-tăn-ŏl′-ŏ-gȳ, *n.* The knowledge relating to Satan ; শয়তানতত্ত্ব ।

Săt′-ā-ra, *n.* A kind of ribbed broadcloth made at Satara ; ভারতবর্ষের অন্তর্গত সেতারা নগরীতে প্রস্তুত একপ্রকার শিরাল বনাত ।

satch′-ĕl (săch-), *n.* A bag for a school boy's books esp. for carrying to and from school ; ছেলেদের পুস্তক রাখিবার ক্ষুদ্র ব্যাগ, বিশেষতঃ চামড়ার ফিতা দ্বারা ঝুলানো যে ক্ষুদ্র ব্যাগে করিয়া ছেলেরা পুস্তক বহিয়া নেয়। **–elled,** *p. p.*

sate (săt *or* sāt), *v.t.* **1.** To gratify ; তৃপ্ত করা, চরিতার্থ করা। **2.** To cloy ; ভোগ-বিতৃষ্ণ করা, ভোগাবসন্ন করা, অপরিমিত তৃপ্তি দ্বারা বিরক্তি বা বিতৃষ্ণা জন্মান। **Sate′-less,** *adj.* Insatiable ; অতৃপ্ত।

să-teen′ (-tēn), *adj.* A kind of glossy woollen or cotton fabric resembling satin ; সাটিনের মত এক প্রকার চকচকে সূতা বা পশমের কাপড়।

săt′-ĕl-līte, *n.* **1.** A small planet which attends on or rolls round a large one ; যে ক্ষুদ্র গ্রহ কোন বৃহৎ গ্রহের চতুর্দ্দিকে ঘুরিয়া থাকে, উপগ্রহ (যথা চন্দ্র)। **2.** An obsequious dependent ; পারিপার্শ্বিক, পারিষদ, মোসাহেব, পোঁধরা (*slang*), কাছাধরা (*ib.*), ধামাধরা (*ib.*)।

sat′-i (sŭt-ē), *n.* Same as SUTTEE (which see).

să-ti-āte′ (-shi-), *v.t.* & *adj.* **1.** To satisfy the appetite or desire of ; পরিতৃপ্ত করা, চরিতার্থ করা। **2.** To surfeit ; to cloy ; অপরিমিত মাত্রায় ভোগ করা ; ভোগবিতৃষ্ণ করা, ভোগাবসন্ন করা, অপরিমিত ভোগ দ্বারা বিতৃষ্ণা বা বিরাগ উৎপাদন করা। ***Adj.*** Sated ; পরিতৃপ্ত, সন্তৃপ্ত, ভোগক্লান্ত, ভোগাবসন্ন, ভোগবিতৃষ্ণ। **–a-bil′-i-ty,** *n.* **–a-ble,** *adj.* **–a′-tion,** *n.*

să-tī′-ĕ-tȳ, *n.* Fulness of gratification of any appetite or any sensual desire ; the disgust or weariness arising from excess of enjoyment ; পরিতৃপ্তি, পরিতোষ, সন্তৃপ্তি ; ভোগবিতৃষ্ণা, ভোগাবসন্নতা, ভোগবিরাগ, ভোগক্লান্তি, ভোগশ্রান্তি।

săt′-in, *n., adj.* & *v. t.* A closely woven glossy silk cloth ; একপ্রকার ঠাসাবুনা চকচকে রেশমী কাপড়, সাটিন, চীন, চীনাংশুক। ***Adj.*** Made of satin ; সাটিনের তৈরী। ***Verb t.*** To impart a satin-like glossiness to ; as, to *satin* wall-paper; সাটিনের মত চকচকে করা। **Denmark satin**—মহিলাদিগের জুতার জন্য একপ্রকার মসৃণ পশমী কাপড়। **Satin beauty**—একপ্রকার রেশপসো বা তসরে পোকা। **Satin-bird, Satin bower-bird**—একপ্রকার পক্ষী—ইহার কৃষ্ণবর্ণ পালকসমূহ সাটিনের মত চকচকে বলিয়া এই নাম। **Satin-carpet** — একপ্রকার রেশপসো বা তসরে পোকা। **Satin cloth**—সাটিনের মত পালিশ একপ্রকার পশমী কাপড়। **Satin-de-laine**—একপ্রকার টের্চা বুনা পশমী কাপড়; Silesiaতে প্রস্তুত একপ্রকার কালো রঙ্গের কাশ্মীরী কাপড়। **Satin finish**—ধাতুর বুরুশ দ্বারা রূপার উপরে একপ্রকার পালিশের কাজ। **Satin-flower**—একপ্রকার গুল্ম। **Satin-glass**—সাটিনের মত চকচকে একপ্রকার কাচ। **Satin gypsum**—মুক্তার ন্যায় দীপ্তিবিশিষ্ট একপ্রকার খড়িমাটী। **Satin-lisse**—ফরাসীদেশে প্রস্তুত একপ্রকার সাটিনের মত কার্পাস বস্ত্র। **Satin-paper**—একপ্রকার পালিশ ও মোলায়েম কাগজ। **Satin pug, Satin pygmy**—বিভিন্ন প্রকার তসরে বা রেশপসো পোকা। **Satin sheeting**—জীর্ণ রেশম ও কার্পাস হইতে প্রস্তুত একপ্রকার বস্ত্র। **Satin-spar**—একপ্রকার কার্ব্বোনেট অব লাইম—যাহা পালিশ করিলে সাটিনের ন্যায় চকচকে হয়। **Satin-stitch**—সমান্তরাল রেখায় এক প্রকার সূচের কাজ—যাহা সাটিনের মত চকচকে দেখায়। **Satin-stone** — Same as SATIN-GYPSUM. **Satin-straw**—টুপি তৈরীর জন্য একপ্রকার কোমল নমনীয় খড়। **Satin sultan**—একপ্রকার রেশমী কাপড়—ইহার উপরিভাগ সাটিনের মত। **Satin-white**—কৃত্রিম সলফেট অব লাইম। **Satin-wood**—ভেরু (Indian — সোঃ)। **White satin**—একপ্রকার গুল্ম; একপ্রকার শাদা প্রজাপতি।

săt-i-nette′ (-nĕt), *n.* **1.** A thin satin ; একপ্রকার পাতলা সাটিন।

authoritative summary of the articles of Christian faith, (also *the creed*) ; খৃষ্টধর্ম্মের মত বা বিশ্বাসের সংক্ষিপ্ত এবং প্রামাণিক সারমর্ম্ম। **2.** A system of religious belief ; ধর্ম্মবিশ্বাসের প্রণালীবদ্ধ ব্যবস্থাসমূহ। **3.** Any solemn profession of principles or opinions ; অচলপ্রতিষ্ঠ মত বা বিশ্বাস গম্ভীরভাবে বিঘোষণ।

creek (crēk), *n.* **1.** A small inlet, bay or cove ; খাড়ি। **2.** A small port or harbour ; ক্ষুদ্র বন্দর বা পোতাশ্রয়-স্থলী। **3.** Short arm of a river ; নদীর ক্ষুদ্র শাখা। **3.** (*U. S.*) A rivulet ; a stream ; (মার্কিণ-যুক্তরাজ্য) ক্ষুদ্রনদী ; স্রোতস্বতী। **4.** A narrow plain between mountains ; পর্ব্বতসমূহের মধ্যবর্ত্তী সঙ্কীর্ণ উপত্যকা।

creel (crēl), *n.* An osier basket, esp. a fisher's ; angler's fishing basket ; ঝুড়ি, চাঙ্গারি, বিশেষতঃ ধীবরদিগের মৎস্যের ঝুড়ি; মৎস্যবেধকগণের ঝুড়ি।

creep (crēp), *v. i.* & *n.* **1.** To move on the belly as a worm ; সরীসৃপের মত বুকে হাঁটিয়া চলা। **2.** To advance slowly, timorously or [illegible]

săt′-i-rīze, *v. t.* To attack with a satire ; to make an object of ridicule ; to write satire upon ; to describe in a satircal manner ; বিদ্রূপবাণবর্ষণ করা ; বিদ্রূপভাজন করা, কোন বিষয় অবলম্বনে ব্যঙ্গকবিতাদি লিখা ; বিদ্রূপাত্মক ভাবে বর্ণনা করা।

satis, (*L.*), *adv.* & *n.* Enough ; প্রচুর, যথেষ্ট। **Satis superque**—প্রচুর এবং অতিরিক্ত।

săt-is-făc′-tion, *n.* **1.** The act of contenting ; gratification ; তুষ্টিসাধন, তুষ্টিবিধান, সন্তোষণ, প্রীণন, সন্তর্পণ, পরিতোষণ, প্রতোষণ (গোপালচঃ), প্রসাদন, হৃদ্‌রঞ্জন ; সন্তোষ, পরিতোষ, তুষ্টি, প্রসাদ, তৃপ্তি। **2.** Settlement of a claim or demand ; as, the *satisfaction* of a debt ; indemnification ; পরিশোধ, শোধ,

নির্দ্ধারিত ব্যাঙ্কের ছুটির দিবস। **St. Martin's evil** — মাতলামি। **St. Mi-hale's orange**—একপ্রকার কমলালেবু। ইহার খোসা অতি পাতলা এবং ইহাতে বীজ নাই। **St. Monday**—সোমবার। বহু শ্রমজীবী সোমবার দিবস ছুটীর দিন করিয়া লইয়াছে। **St. Nicholas's clerk** or **clergyman**—চোর, বাটপাড়, রাহাজান। **St. Partridge's Day**—১লা সেপ্টেম্বর। এই দিন হইতে ইংলণ্ডে তিত্তির পক্ষী শিকারের মরসুম আরব্ধ হয়। **St. Patrick's cross**—Same as ST. ANDREW'S CROSS. **St. Peter's Chains** — রোমান-ক্যাথলিকগণ কর্তৃক ১লা আগষ্টে অনুষ্ঠিত খৃষ্টপার্ষদ পিতরের কারাবাসের স্মৃতি উৎসব। **St. Peter's Chair**—(১) খৃষ্টপার্ষদ পিতর কর্তৃক Antioch নগরীতে বিশপের যে শ্রীপাট প্রতিষ্ঠিত হয় তৎস্মৃতিরক্ষণার্থ ২২শে ফেব্রুয়ারী দিবসে অনুষ্ঠিত উৎসব। (২) খৃষ্টপার্ষদ পিতর কর্তৃক রোমনগরীতে পোপের শ্রীপাট প্রতিষ্ঠার স্মৃতিরক্ষণার্থ ১৮ই জানুয়ারী দিবসে অনুষ্ঠিত উৎসব। **Saints day**—বিভিন্ন খৃষ্টীয় মহাপুরুষের স্মৃতি উৎসব দিন। **St. Sylvester's Eve**—৩১ সে ডিসেম্বরের রজনী। **St. Valentine's Day**—খৃষ্টীয় তৃতীয় শতকে আবির্ভূত মহাপুরুষ St. Valentine এর স্মৃতি উৎসব দিবস (১৪ই ফেব্রুয়ারী।) ঐ দিবস হইতে পক্ষিগণের সঙ্গমঋতু আরব্ধ হয় বলিয়া অতি প্রাচীনকাল হইতে একটা বিশ্বাস চলিয়া আসিয়াছে। **St. Vitus's dance** — একপ্রকার স্নায়বিক রোগ। এই রোগে মুখমণ্ডল এবং দেহের অন্যান্য অংশের পেশীসমূহ হাস্যোদ্দীপক ভাবে আকুঞ্চিত ও সঞ্চালিত হয় বলিয়া ইহাকে তাণ্ডব বলে, তাণ্ডবরোগ (হঃ চঃ)। **Court of St. James's**—ব্রিটিশ রাজদরবার।

saith (sāth), 3rd person, singular, present, indicative of SAY.

Sā-it′-ic, *adj.* Of, or pertaining to, Sais, an ancient city of the Nile delta; নীল নদের ব-দ্বীপে অবস্থিত প্রাচীন Sais নগরীসম্বন্ধীয়।

sāke, *n.* Account; reason; জন্য, হেতু, খাতির, দৌলত, কল্যাণ (cf.

Săt′-sü-mà, —ware (-wār), *n.* A kind of Japanese pottery; একপ্রকার ঈষৎ পীতবর্ণ জাপানী মৃদ্‌ভাণ্ড।

săt′-ü-rāte, *v. t.* **1.** To cause to be completely impregnated or soaked: পরিপূরিত করা, সম্পূরিত করা, পূর্ণ সিক্ত করা, অনুবিদ্ধ করা, ব্যাপ্ত করা। **2.** (*Chem. & Phys.*) To impregnate or unite till no more can be received; সম্পূর্ণরূপে অনুসিক্ত বা সম্পূরিত করা। **—ra′-tion**, *n.* **1.** The act of impregnating completely; পরিপূরণ, সম্পূরণ, অতিপূরণ (কেঃিঃ), পরিষেক (সাঃ পঃ)। **2.** The state of being completely impregnated, charged, soaked or penetrated; সম্পূরণ, পরিষেক বা আচ্ছন্নতার অবস্থা।—যাহাতে যে পরিমাণ দ্রব্য মিশ্রিত আছে, যে পরিমাণ বস্তুদ্বারা পরিষিক্ত বা আচ্ছন্ন রহিয়াছে — তদপেক্ষা অণুমাত্রও অধিক গৃহীত হইতে পারে না, পূর্ণসিক্তাবস্থা পূর্ণসিক্ততা, সম্পৃক্ততা (হিঃ কোঃ)।

Săt′-ur-day (-ėr-dā), *n.* The seventh or last day of the week; শনিবার। **Saturday Review**—১৮৬৬ খৃষ্টাব্দ হইতে প্রকাশিত সুপ্রসিদ্ধ সাপ্তাহিক পত্র।

Săt′-urn (-ėrn), *n.* **1.** (*Gk. Myth.*), One of the oldest and principal deities, father of Zeus; (রোমক পুরাণ মতে) দেবরাজ জীয়ানের পিতা। ইনি সত্যযুগে রাজত্ব করিতেন। **2.** (*Astron.*) One of the planets next in magnitude to Jupiter; (জ্যোতির্বিজ্ঞান) শনি [Syn. শনৈশ্চর, মন্দ, ভাস্করি, ভানুজ, পাতঙ্গি, মার্ত্তণ্ডি, সৌরি, অর্কনন্দন, আদিত্য-সূনু, রবিসূনু, অর্কজ (বৃঃ সং), সূর্য্যসুত, সূর্য্যপুত্র, সূর্য্যনন্দন, রেবতীভব, ছায়াত্মজ, ছায়াপুত্র, ছায়াতনয়, ছায়াসুত, সহস্রাংশুজ (বৃঃ সং), নীলবাস, নীলাম্বর, অসিতাম্বর, অসিত, অর্কি, পঙ্গু, ক্রূরাত্মা, আর, কোণ (from Gk. *Cronos*), গ্রহনায়ক, ক্রোড়, বক্র, কোল, সপ্তার্চ্চি, সপ্তাংশু-পুঙ্গব (বোধ হয় প্রাচীন হিন্দুগণ শনির সাতটী উপগ্রহের বিষয় পরিজ্ঞাত ছিলেন বলিয়া এই নাম), কাস, ক্রূরলোচন, ব্রহ্মণ্য, ব্রাহ্মণ্য, ক্রূরদৃক্। [এই পর্য্যন্ত শনির ১০টী উপগ্রহ আবিষ্কৃত হইয়াছে। ইহাদের নাম *Mimas, Enceladus, Tethys, Dione, Rhea, Titan, Hyperion, Japetus, Phoebe* (১৮৯৮ খৃঃ অব্দে আবিষ্কৃত), *Themis* (১৯০৫ খৃঃ অব্দে আবিষ্কৃত)।

The planet Saturn.

প্রাচীনগণ শনিকে দূরতম গ্রহ বলিয়া জানিতেন; বর্ত্তমানে Uranus ও Neptune নামক দূরতরবর্ত্তী গ্রহদ্বয় আবিষ্কৃত হওয়াতে গ্রহদিগের মধ্যে শনি সূর্য্য হইতে দূরত্ব হিসাবে তৃতীয়স্থান প্রাপ্ত হইয়াছে। শনিগ্রহ সূর্য্য হইতে গড়ে প্রায় ৮৮৪,০০০,০০০ মাইল দূরে থাকে। শনি ১০ ঘণ্টা ১৪ মিনিটে একবার স্বীয় কক্ষে আবর্ত্তন করে। অতএব শনির দিন প্রায় আমাদের দিনের অর্দ্ধেক। কিন্তু একবার সূর্য্যকে প্রদক্ষিণ করিতে শনির ২৯½ বৎসর লাগে বলিয়া ঐ গ্রহের এক বৎসর আমাদের ২৯½ বৎসরের সমান। শনিগ্রহের চতুর্দ্দিকে জ্যোতির্বলয়শ্রেণী দৃষ্ট হয়। শনির গাঢ়তা পৃথিবীর গাঢ়তার প্রায় অষ্টমাংশ। **3.** (*Old Chem.*) Lead; (প্রাচীন রসায়ন-শাস্ত্র) সীসক [সংস্কৃতে শনির এক নাম অসিত, কৃষ্ণ ও অসিত উভয় শব্দই সংস্কৃতে কৃষ্ণবর্ণ বুঝায়। 'কৃষ্ণ' সংস্কৃতে সীসক শব্দেরও অন্যতর প্রতিশব্দ।] সম্ভবতঃ শনির বর্ণ কৃষ্ণবর্ণ বলিয়া বর্ণ-সামঞ্জস্যহেতু সীসক ও শনি প্রাচীন রসায়নে একার্থে ব্যবহৃত হইয়াছে।] **Saturn's ring**—শনিবলয় (হিঃ কোঃ)।

săt-ur-nā′-li-à (-ėr-), *n.* **1.** Among the Romans, the festival of Saturn, celebrated in December as a period of unrestrained license and merriment for all classes, even slaves; প্রাচীন রোমের কৃষি-দেবতার উৎসব—ঐ সময়ে আমাদের দেশের হোলির মত লোকসকল অসংযত আমোদ-প্রমোদে মত্ত হইয়া নানারূপ বীভৎস

আচরণ করিত। 2. Similar revelry ; কোলাহলপূর্ণ উৎসব, হোলি। **—an,** *adj.* 1. Pertaining to Saturnalia ; রোমানদিগের হোলিউৎসব-সম্বন্ধীয়। 2. Riotously merry ; dissolute ; উচ্ছৃঙ্খল আমোদপ্রমোদে রত ; লম্পট।

Să-tur′-ni-ăn (-têr-), *adj.* & *n.* 1. Pertaining to the god Saturn ; pertaining to, or resembling, the Golden age ; as, *Saturnian* era ; গ্রীকপুরাণোক্ত শনিদেব-সম্বন্ধীয়; সত্যযুগবৎ, সত্যযুগের। 2. Pertaining to the planet Saturn ; শনিগ্রহসম্বন্ধীয়। 3. (*Rare*) Leaden ; dull ; (কচিৎ-ব্যবহৃত) সীসকময় ; মলিন, নিষ্প্রভ, অনুজ্জ্বল। ***Noun.*** An inhabitant of Saturn ; শনিগ্রহের অধিবাসী। **Saturnian verse**—প্রাচীন ইতালীয়-গণের প্রাচীনতম স্বদেশীয় কবিতা।

Să-tur′-nic, (-têr-), *adj.* Affected with lead-poisoning ; শরীরে সীসক গ্রহণ হেতু বিষক্রিয়াদ্বারা পীড়িত। **Sat′-ur-nism,** *n.*

Săt′-ur-nīne (-êr-), *adj.* 1. Supposed to be under the influence of the planet Saturn ; শনিগ্রহদ্বারা প্রভাবিত। 2. Morose ; dull ; phlegmatic ; বিষণ্ণ ; স্ফূর্তিহীন ; জড়, অলস। 3. Pertaining to lead ; like lead ; সীসকসম্বন্ধীয় ; সীসকবৎ।

săt′-yr (-êr), *n.* 1 A sylvan deity of the ancient Greeks and Romans part man and part goat, and extremly wanton ; ছাগদেব [প্রাচীন গ্রীক ও রোমানদিগের বনদেবতাবিশেষ। ইহার অর্দ্ধশরীর ছাগাকৃতি ও অপরার্দ্ধ মানবাকৃতি এবং ইহার কামপ্রবৃত্তি অতিশয় প্রবল।] 2. A lascivious man ; লম্পট ব্যক্তি, অতিশয় কামার্ত্ত লোক। 3. Orang-outang ; বনমানুষ।

Satyr.

să-tўr′-ic, *adj.* Pertaining to satyrs ; গ্রীক ও রোমানদের ছাগদেব সম্বন্ধীয়। **Satyric drama**—একপ্রকার গ্রীক নাট্য। এই নাট্যে ছাগদেবগণ নৃত্য ও সঙ্গীত করিয়া থাকে।

sauce (säs), *n.* & *v. t.* 1. A preparation usually liquid to be eaten as a condiment or seasoning for food ; চাটনী, আচার। 2. (In America) Any vegetable eaten with meat or fish ; (আমেরিকায়) মৎস্য মাংসের সহিত যে তরিতরকারী খাওয়া হয়। 3. (*Colloq.*) Pertness ; insolent language ; as, none of your *sauce* ; প্রগল্‌ভতা ; প্রগল্‌ভ বাক্য। ***Verb t.*** 1. To season with sauces ; চাটনী প্রভৃতি মিশান। 2. To render pungent or sharp ; ঝাঁঝাল করা। 3. (*Colloq.*) To be impudent to ; (চলিত ভাষায়) ধৃষ্টতা করা। 4. (*Obs.*) To carve ; as, to *sauce* a foul ; (অপ্রঃ) কুটা। **Sauce-boat**—আচারদান। **Sauce-box**—ধৃষ্ট যুবক। ***Sauce hollandaise***—হলণ্ড দেশীয় চাটনী (মাখন, গালা ঘি, ডিমের কুসুম ও লেবুর রসদ্বারা প্রস্তুত করা হয়।) **Saucepan**—লম্বা হাতলওয়ালা পাকপাত্র বিশেষ, কন্দু (শুক্রঃ)। **Sauce piquante**—ঝাঁঝাল চাটনী। **Sauce-tureen**—আচারদান। **Hunger is the best sauce**—See HUNGER. **Poor man's sauce**—ক্ষুধা। **The saucepan should not call a kettle black**—ওল বলেন মানকচু ভাই তুমি নাকি বড় লাগ। (See also under POT). **To serve one with the same sauce**—(*Colloq.*) To retaliate one injury with another ; অনুরূপ ব্যবহার দ্বারা প্রতিশোধ লওয়া। **What is sauce for the goose is sauce for the gander**—See GANDER.

sau′-cer (sä-), *n.* 1. A piece of china etc. on which a tea-cup, etc. is set ; যে ক্ষুদ্র চীনা মাটী প্রভৃতির ক্ষুদ্র রেকাবীতে চার পেয়ালা প্রভৃতি রাখা হয়, পিরীচ। 2. A vessel placed under a flower-pot to prevent water running away at once ; যাহাতে জল তৎক্ষণাৎ সরিয়া না যায়, তজ্জন্য ফুলের টবের নীচে যে পাত্র রক্ষিত হয়। 3. Anything resembling a saucer, as the socket of iron for the pivot of a capstan ; পিরীচের আকৃতি কোন কিছু—যথা নোঙ্গর উত্তোলনযন্ত্রের ঘূর্ণন-দণ্ডের জন্য লৌহময় কোটর। **Sauce-eye**—পিরীচের মত গোল এবং বৃহৎ চক্ষু (সাধারণতঃ ভূত-প্রেতের অক্ষি সম্পর্কে ব্যবহৃত হয়)।

sau′-cy̆ (sä-), *adj.* 1. Impudent ; rude ; ধৃষ্ট, প্রগল্‌ভ, বে-আদব ; রূঢ়। 2. (*Slang*) Stylish ; smart ; (ইতর-ভাষায়) চটকদার ; চোস্ত। 2. Wanton ; উচ্ছৃঙ্খল। **—ci-ness,** *n.* **—ci-ly,** *adv.*

sauerkraut, *n.* A German dish of pickled cabbage ; জর্ম্মাণ দেশীয় বাঁধা কপির আচার।

saun′-dêrs (sän-), *n.* Same as SANDERS (which see).

saun′-têr (sän-), *v. i.* & *n.* To stroll ; to wander idly ; ইতস্ততঃ ভ্রমণ করা, উদ্দেশ্যবিহীনভাবে ঘুরা ; টো টো করিয়া ঘুরা। ***Noun.*** 1. A sauntering ; ইতস্ততঃ ভ্রমণ, টো টো করিয়া ঘুরণ। 2. A place for sauntering ; উদ্দেশ্যহীনভাবে ভ্রমণের স্থান, পাদচারণ স্থান। **—er,** *n.* **—ing-ly,** *adv.*

sau′-ri-ăn (sä-), *adj.* & *n.* Pertaining to the Sauria or lizards ; কৃকলাসবর্গসম্বন্ধীয়। ***Noun.*** A lizard or lizard-like animal ; কৃকলাস বা তদ্বৎ জন্তু।

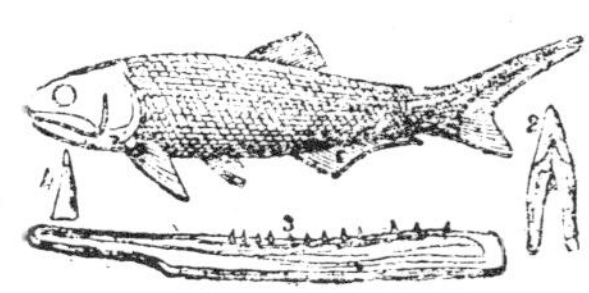

Sauroid fish (fossil)
1. Pygopterus ; 2 and 4, teeth (enlarged) ; 3, Jaw with teeth.

sau′-roid (sä-roÿd), *n.* A kind of fossil fish ; একপ্রকার শিলীভূত মীন।

sau'-sâge (sä-), *n.* The gut of an animal prepared and stuffed with minced meat seasoned; কুচি কুচি করিয়া কাটা এবং মসলা মিশানো মাংস পশুর নাড়ীর ভিতর পুরিয়া যে একপ্রকার কাবাব প্রস্তুত করা হয়, নাড়ীকাবাব। **Bologna sausage**—শূকর,গোবৎস, প্রভৃতির মাংসদ্বারা যে বৃহৎ আকারের নাড়ীকাবাব প্রস্তুত করা হয়। **Sausage-machine** — নাড়ীকাবাবের জন্য খুব কুচি কুচি করিয়া মাংস কাটার জন্য একপ্রকার যন্ত্র। **Sausage-meat**—নাড়ীকাবাবের জন্য কুচিকুচি করিয়া কাটা এবং মসলা মিশ্রিত মাংস। **Sausage-poisoning** — নাড়ীকাবাবে সময় সময় যে একপ্রকার বিষ জাত হয়। **Sausage-roll**—কুচি কুচি করিয়া কাটা এবং মসলা মিশানো মাংস রেশমের লম্বা আবরণে ভরিয়া যে নাড়ীকাবাব রাঁধা হয়।

Sau-terne' (sö-têrn), *n.* A species of white French wine; একপ্রকার ফরাসী দেশীয় পীতবর্ণ মদিরা (ফরাসী দেশের অন্তঃপাতী Sauterne নামক স্থানের নাম হইতে গৃহীত)।

sauve-qui-peut, *n.* A complete route and flight in varions directions; ছত্রভঙ্গ হইয়া নানাদিকে পলায়ন।

săv'-āge, *adj., n. & v. t.* **1.** Wild; as, *savage* beast; বন্য, জঙ্গলী। **2.** Beastly; পাশবিক। **3.** Uncivilized: barbarous; cruel; অসভ্য; বর্ব্বর; নিষ্ঠুর, ক্রুর। **4.** (*Colloq.*) Furiously angry; as, you need not look so *savage*; অগ্নিশর্ম্মা, চণ্ড। ***Noun.*** **1.** An uncivilized man; a barbarous man; অসভ্য লোক; বর্ব্বর। **2.** One of a brutal unfeeling disposition; পাশব প্রকৃতির লোক, নরপশু, চোয়াড়। ***Verb t.*** **1.** (*Rare*) To make barbarous or cruel; (কচিদ্‌ব্যবহৃত) অসভ্য করা, ক্রুর করা, নিষ্ঠুরোচিত করা। **2.** (Of a horse) To attack, bite or crush under foot; "A dangerous horse was *savaging* him"; (অশ্ব-সম্পর্কে) আক্রমণ, দংশন বা পদদলিত করা। **–ly,** *adv.* **–ness, –ry,** *ns.*

să-văn'-nă, –nah (-nă), *ns.* The name given by the Spanish settlers to the great plains or prairies of North American continet; উত্তর আমেরিকার দিগন্তব্যাপী নিবৃর্ক্ষ প্রান্তর, নিবৃর্ক্ষ প্রান্তর।

să'-vant (-văng), *n.* A man of great learning; a distinguished scientist; পণ্ডিত, সুবিদ্বান ব্যক্তি, ভট্ট; সুবিখ্যাত বৈজ্ঞানিক পণ্ডিত, বিজ্ঞানশাস্ত্র পারদর্শী পণ্ডিত।

savate, *n.* A kind of French boxing in which feet and head are also used; ফরাসী দেশে প্রচলিত একপ্রকার মুষ্টিযুদ্ধ—যাহাতে মস্তক এবং পদও ব্যবহৃত হয়।

sāve, *v. t., i. & n.* **1.** To preserve from injury, destruction or evil of any kind; রক্ষা করা, উদ্ধার করা, ত্রাণ করা, নিস্তার করা, তরান। **2.** To deliver a person from spiritual ruin and eternal death; মুক্তি দেওয়া, পরিত্রাণ করা, মোক্ষ প্রদান করা। **3.** To lay up; to spare; জমান; বাঁচান। **4.** To obviate or prevent the need or use of; as, a stitch in time *saves* nine; যাহাতে কোন কিছুর দরকার না হয় বা কোন কিছু ব্যবহার করিতে না হয় তাহার বিধান করা। **5.** To prevent the occurrence of; as, to *save* a lady's blush; কোন কিছু হইতে বা ঘটিতে না দেওয়া, বারণ করা। **6.** To take advantage of; to catch; as, to *save* the mail; সুযোগ গ্রহণ করা; ধরা। **7.** To separate gold from quartz; স্ফটিক হইতে স্বর্ণ পৃথক করা। **8.** (*Football*) To prevent opponents from scoring; প্রতিপক্ষকে ক্রীড়াঙ্ক লাভে বাধা প্রদান করা। ***Verb i.*** **1.** To be economical; মিতব্যয়ী হওয়া। **2.** To last; as, food that will *save*; টিকা, স্থায়ী হওয়া। ***Noun.*** (*Football*) Prevention of opponents from scoring; as, a clever *save*; প্রতিপক্ষের ক্রীড়াঙ্ক প্রাপ্তিতে বাধা প্রদান। **Sav'-a-ble,** *adj.* **Sa'-ver,** *n.* **Save-all**—(১) ক্ষতি নিবারণের উপায়। (২) শামাদান। (৩) কাগজের কলে অপচয় নিবারণের জন্য ভাণ্ডবিশেষ। (৪) মিতব্যয়ী লোক। (৫) চাঁদা প্রভৃতির টাকা রাখার জন্য বাক্স। (৬) (*Adj.*) কৃপণ, কঞ্জুষ। **To save appearances**—To do something to obviate or prevent exposure or embarrassment; বাহিরের ঠাট বজায় রাখা, লোকের নিকট মুখ রক্ষা করা। **To save one's face**—To conceal one's disgrace, humiliation, loss of prestige, etc. by some pretence; মুখ রক্ষা করা। **To save one's pocket**—To save money; টাকা বাঁচান। **To save one's skin**—To escape unhurt; অক্ষত দেহে রক্ষা পাওয়া। **To save the situation**—To find out some means of getting out of danger; বিপদ হইতে রক্ষা পাওয়ার কোনরূপ উপায় বাহির করা।

sāve, *prep. & conj.* Except; বিনা, ছাড়া, ব্যতিরেকে, ব্যতীত। ***Conj.*** (*Archaic*) Except; unless; (অপ্রঃ) বিনা, ছাড়া; যদি না।

săv'-ĕ-loy, *n.* A highly seasoned dry sausage; একপ্রকার প্রচুর মসলাদার নাড়ীকাবাব।

săv'-in, *n.* An evergreen tree which yields a volatile oil of medicinal value; চিরহরিৎ গুল্মবিশেষ—যাহা হইতে একপ্রকার ভেষজগুণসম্পন্ন উদ্বায়ী তৈল পাওয়া যায়।

sāv'-ing, *n., adj. & prep.* **1.** Preserving from loss or destruction; রক্ষণ, পরিত্রাণ। **2.** (*Pl.*) Money put by; সঞ্চিত অর্থ, জমা টাকা। ***Adj.*** **1.** Frugal; মিতব্যয়ী। **2.** Reserving; (দলীলের দফাসম্বন্ধে) সর্ত্তের বহির্ভূতকারী। ***Prep.*** Excepting; ব্যতীত, ছাড়া। **Saving clause**—যে দফা দ্বারা কোন বিষয় দলীলের সর্ত্তের বহির্ভূত করা হয়, প্রতিপ্রসব। **Savings bank**—নির্দ্দিষ্ট পরিমাণ সঞ্চিত অর্থ জমা রাখিবার জন্য

অভিজ্ঞান পত্র (মঃ ইঃ) (শব্দানুযায়ী এবং লক্ষণায়)।

crĕd′-i-ble, *adj.* Worthy of credit or belief; প্রত্যয়যোগ্য, বিশ্বাস্য, বিশ্বাসার্হ, বিশ্বসনীয়, শ্রদ্ধেয়। **—bil′-i-ty,** *n.* **—bly,** *adv.*

crĕd′-it, *n.* **1.** Belief; faith; trust; প্রত্যয়; শ্রদ্ধা; বিশ্বাস, বিশ্রম্ভ (মঃ ইঃ)। **2.** Reputation; good name; honour; "A citizen of *credit* and renown;" মান, পশার; সুনাম; কীর্ত্তি, খ্যাতি, প্রতিষ্ঠা, ইজ্জত, ভরম, সম্ভ্রম। **3.** Power derived from reputation etc.; প্রতিপত্তি। **4.** Honour; acknowledgment of merit; as, to get *credit* for a meritorious act; a source of honour; as, to be a *credit* to one's family; সম্মান; গুণের সম্মান; সম্মানের হেতু। **5.** (*Comm.*) Sale on trust; mercantile reputation entitling one to be trusted; the time given for payment of goods sold on trust; as, a long *credit*; (বাণিজ্য) ধার; বাজার সম্ভ্রম; ধারে বিক্রীত জিনিষের মূল্য প্রদানের জন্য নির্দ্দিষ্ট সময়, ম্যাদ, মুদ্দত। **6.** (*Book-keeping*) The acknowledgment of payment by entry in an account; হিসাবে জমা করিয়া টাকার প্রাপ্তি-স্বীকার। **7.** (*Book-keeping*) The side of an account in which payment is entered, (opposed to *debit*); the sum on the credit side of an account; হিসাবের জমার দিক; জমার দিকের টাকার অঙ্ক। **8.** A sum that a person can get from a bank; কোন লোক ধনাগার হইতে যত টাকা পাইতে পারে, তাহার সংখ্যা। **9.** A sum which the administration is empowered by vote of Parliament to borrow and expend in anticipation of the amount voted in the Annual Estimates; বার্ষিক আয়ব্যয় নির্দ্ধারণের সময় মঞ্জুর হইবে আশায় যে টাকা কর্জ্জ করিয়া খরচ করার জন্য পার্লেমেণ্টমহাসভা

ব্যঞ্জন—বিশেষতঃ ক্ষুধা বা পরিপাকশক্তি বৃদ্ধির জন্য ভোজনের প্রথমে বা শেষে যে ব্যঞ্জনাদি আহার করা হয়, শুক্ত, অম্বল। **—i-ly,** *adv.* **—i-ness,** *n.*

sā-voy′, *n.* A kind of cabbage with curled leaves; একপ্রকার বাঁধাকপি—যাহার পাতাগুলি কোকড়ানো থাকে।

Sā-voy′-ârd, *n.* & *adj.* A native of Savoy; ফরাসী রাজ্যের অন্তর্ভুক্ত সেভয় নামক জেলার অধিবাসী। ***Adj.*** Of, or pertaining to, Savoy; সেভয়সম্বন্ধীয়।

saw (sä), *n.*, *v. t.* & *i.* A cutting instrument of steel with a toothed edge; করাত [Syn. কদর, করপত্র, ক্রকচ।] ***Verb t.*** **1.** To cut with a saw; করাত দ্বারা চিরা। **2.** To form by cutting with a saw; as, to *saw* planks; করাত দ্বারা চিরিয়া গঠন করা। **3.** To move through, or make motions, as in sawing; "Do not *saw* the air too much with your hands"; করাতীর মত অঙ্গচালনা করা। ***Verb i.*** **1.** To use a saw; করাত ব্যবহার করা। **2.** To admit of being cut with a saw; to be cut with the saw; as, the timber *saws* easily; করাতদ্বারা চিরার উপযোগী হওয়া; করাতে কাটা। **3.** To cut with a saw; করাতদ্বারা চিরা। **Saw-back**—ক্রকচ-পৃষ্ঠ; ক্রকচদন্তবৎশিখরশ্রেণীসমন্বিত। **Saw-bill**—বিভিন্ন প্রকার ক্রকচচঞ্চু পক্ষীর সাধারণ নাম। **Saw-bones**—(ইতর ভাষায়) বদ্দী, ডাক্তার। **Sawdust**—

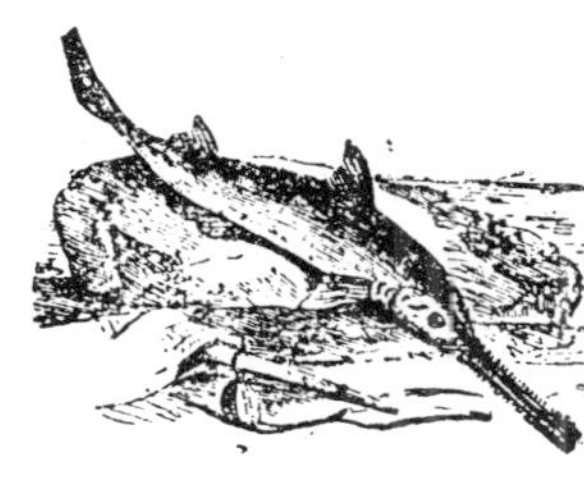

Saw-fish.

করাতের গুঁড়া। **Saw-fish**—একপ্রকার হাঙ্গর মাছ—ইহার লম্বিত মুখের অভ্যন্তরে করাতের মত কাঁটা থাকে, ক্রকচমৎস্য, ক্রকচমুখ। **Saw-fly** — বৃক্ষগুল্মাদির অনিষ্টকর কয়েকপ্রকার কীটের সাধারণ নাম। **Saw-horse**—চিরার কালে যে অবলম্বনের উপর বৃক্ষাদি রক্ষিত হয়। **Saw-mill**—করাতের কল। **Saw-pit**—যে গর্ত্তের নীচে করাতী দাঁড়াইয়া থাকে। **Saw-set**—করাতের দাঁত পর্য্যায়ক্রমে দক্ষিণে ও বামে হেলাইবার জন্য যন্ত্রবিশেষ। **Saw-wort**—একপ্রকার গুল্ম। **Saw-wrest**—Same as SAW-SET. **Back-saw**—Same as TENON SAW. **Band-saw**—বক্র জিনিষ চিরিবার জন্য একপ্রকার করাত। **Circular-saw**—বৃক্ষের কাণ্ড খণ্ড খণ্ড করিয়া কাটিবার জন্য একপ্রকার গোলাকার করাত। **Cross-cut saw**—উভয়দিকে হাতলবিশিষ্ট একপ্রকার করাত—যদ্দ্বারা বৃহৎ বৃক্ষের কাণ্ড কর্ত্তন করা হয়। **Endless-saw**—Same as BAND-SAW. **Grooving-saw**—খাঁজ কাটার জন্য একপ্রকার গোল করাত। **Hand-saw**—হাত করাত। **Jig-saw**—ফ্রেমে আঁটা [illegible] ততোধিক সরু ফলকবিশিষ্ট যন্ত্র[illegible]াত। **Rip-saw**—[illegible]ভাবে কাঠ চিরিবার জন্য একপ্রকার বড় দাঁতওয়ালা করাত। **Ten-on-saw** — ক্ষুদ্র ক্ষুদ্র কাঠের কাজে লম্বলম্বি ভাবে কাটার জন্য একপ্রকার সরু ফলার করাত। **To let sawdust out of**—To expose the hollowness of; অন্তঃসারশূন্যতা প্রদর্শন করা, অসারতা প্রদর্শন করা।

saw (sä), *p. t.* of SEE (which see).

saw (sä), *n.* A proverb; a maxim; প্রবচন; নীতিবাক্য।

saw′-dēr (sä-), *n.* Flattery; তোষামোদ। **Soft sawder**—চাটুবাক্য, তোষামোদ, তৈল (cf. তৈল মর্দ্দন)।

Saw′-ney (sä-nĭ), **—nȳ,** *ns.* **1.** Scotchman; স্কটলণ্ডের লোক। **2.** (*Slang*) A fool; বেকুব।

saw′-yēr (sä-), *n.* **1.** One who saws timber; করাতী, ক্রাকচিক। **2.** (*U. S.*) A tree in the river where branches sway up and down with the current; (মার্কিণ যুক্তরাজ্য) নদীজলে

প্রবমান বৃক্ষ—যাহার শাখাসমূহ স্রোতোবেগে পর্য্যায়ক্রমে উত্থিত ও পতিত হইয়া থাকে। **3.** Different kinds of larva which bore holes in timber ; বিভিন্ন জাতীয় কীট—যাহারা কাষ্ঠে ছিদ্র করিয়া থাকে।

săx, *n.* A slate-cutter's hammer ; শ্লেটপ্রস্তর ছেদনকারীদিগের হাতুড়ী।

săx′-a-tīle, *adj.* Living among rocks ; growing on rocks ; পাষাণ পর্ব্বত মধ্যে বাসকারী, পাষাণাদ্রিবাসী ; পাষাণজাত।

saxe (săx), *n.* A kind of photographic paper ; আলোকচিত্রে ব্যবহৃত একপ্রকার কাগজ।

săx′-hŏrn, *n.* A musical instrument of the trumpet class invented

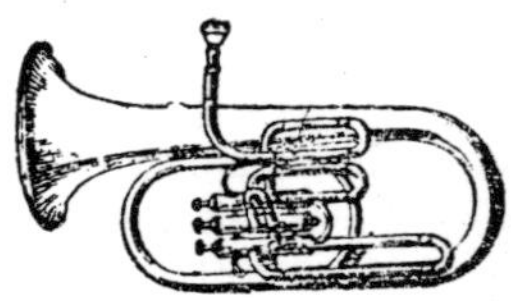

Saxhorn.

by Ado… in 1840 ; একপ্রকার বাঁশী।

săx-ĭc′-ō-līne, –lous (-lŭs), *adjs.* Same as SAXATILE.

săx′-ĭ-frāge, *n.* A popular name of various plants, which grow mostly on rocks ; পাষাণপর্ব্বতোপরি জাত বিভিন্ন প্রকার গুল্মের সাধারণ নাম।

Săx′-ŏn, *adj.* & *n.* **1.** Pertaining to Saxons, their country or to their language ; স্যাক্সন জাতি, দেশ বা ভাষাসম্বন্ধীয়। **2.** Relating to modern Saxony or its inhabitants ; আধুনিক স্যাক্সনি প্রদেশ বা ঐ প্রদেশের অধিবাসিগণসম্পর্কীয়। ***Noun.*** **1.** An Anglo-Saxon ; প্রাচীন এংলোস্যাক্সন জাতির লোক। **2.** Anglo-Saxon language ; এংলো-স্যাক্সন ভাষা। **3.** One of English race ; ইংরেজ। **4.** A native of Saxony ; স্যাক্সনি প্রদেশের অধিবাসী। **Saxon-architecture** — ইংলণ্ডের স্বদেশীয় স্থাপত্যশিল্পের প্রাচীনতম ধারা। ইংলণ্ডবাসিগণের খৃষ্টধর্ম্মের পরিগ্রহণের সময় হইতে নরম্যান বিজয় পর্য্যন্ত এই স্থাপত্যধারার কাল। **Saxon-blue**—গন্ধকদ্রাবকে নীল গুলিয়া যে একপ্রকার রঞ্জক-পদার্থ প্রস্তুত করা হয়।

săx′-ō-nȳ, *n.* **1.** A fine kind of wool and cloth made from it ; একপ্রকার মিহি পশম, ঐ পশমের কাপড়। **2.** A kind of fine flannel ; একপ্রকার মিহি ফ্লানেল। **3.** A kind of Berlin wool (also called *Saxon-yarn*) ; একপ্রকার উলসূতা। **Saxony-blue**—Same as SAXON-BLUE.

săx′-ō-phōne, *n.* A brass wind-instrument invented by Adolphe

Saxophone.

Sax ; এডলফ্ সেক্স নামক জনৈক বেলজিয়ামবাসী কর্তৃক উদ্ভাবিত সুষির যন্ত্রবিশেষ।

săx′-tū-bă, *n.* A large saxhorn ; একপ্রকার বৃহৎ বংশী।

say (sā), *v. t., i* & *n.* **1.** To utter or express in words ; বলা, কহা। **2.** To repeat ; as, to *say* one's prayers ; আবৃত্তি করা। **3.** To suppose; as, he has, *say*, 1000 Rs. ; অনুমান করা, আন্দাজ করা, ধরা। ***Verb i.*** To speak ; বলা, কহা। ***Noun.*** **1.** Opportunity of saying ; বলার সুবিধা। **2.** What one has to say ; as, say your *say* ; an expression of opinion ; a statement ; বক্তব্য ; মতপ্রকাশ ; উক্তি। **3.** A maxim ; প্রবচন, নীতিবাক্য। **Easier said than done**—বলা যত সহজ করা তত সহজ নয়, বলা সহজ করা কঠিন। **It is said, They say**—এইরূপ বলা হইয়া থাকে, লোকে বলে। **It says**—It is said ; এইরূপ কথিত আছে। **Not to say**—That need not be mentioned ; সে কথা না বলিলেও চলে, সে কথার উল্লেখ নিষ্প্রয়োজন। **Say the word**—Give the order ; আদেশ দিন। **That is to say**—That is ;

sa-lā′-cious (-shŭs), *adj.* Lustful ; lecherous ; কামুক ; লম্পট। **–lac′-i-ty, –ness,** *ns.* **–ly,** *adv.*

săl′-ăd, *n.* **1.** A dish of certain vegetables, as lettuce, cress, etc. dressed and eaten raw ; কাঁচা শাক-সব্জীর ঘণ্ট। **2.** Vegetables or herbs eaten raw ; যে সকল শাকসব্জী কাঁচা খাওয়া যায়। **Salad-days**—Immature years ; অপরিণত বয়স, কাঁচা বয়স। **Salad-dressing**—কাঁচা তরিতরকারীর সহিত যে তৈল, সির্কা, সর, প্রভৃতির মিশ্র খাওয়া হয়। **Salad-oil**—উৎকৃষ্ট জলপাইয়ের তৈল।

săl′-ă-măn-dêr, *n.* **1.** A kind of lizard formerly believed able to live in fire ; গিরগিটি (সাঃ পঃ)। **2.** The name of certain harmless amphibians allied to the newts ; গোধা জাতীয় কয়েকপ্রকার উভচর অনপকারী জন্তুর সাধারণ নাম। **3.** A kind of imaginary spirit living in fire ; একজাতীয় অগ্নিবাসী দৈত্য। **4.** A man able to endure great heat ; অতিমাত্রায় উত্তাপ সহনে সমর্থ

3. A contagious disease in sheep ; মেষের সংক্রামক রোগ বিশেষ। **4.** (*Archaic*) A mean shabby fellow ; (অপ্রঃ) জঘন্য নোংরা লোক, দুরাত্মা। **5.** A workman who refuses to join in a strike or labour union ; ধর্ম্মঘটে বা কর্ম্মিকসম্মিলনীতে যোগদানে অসম্মত শ্রমজীবী। ***Verb i.*** To form a scab over ; ক্ষতাদির উপরে মামড়ী পড়া। **Scab′-bed,** *p. p.* **Scab′-bi-ly,** *adv.* **Scab′-bi-ness,** *n.* **Scab′-by,** *adj.* **Scab-wort**—একপ্রকার গুল্ম। ইহার পত্র ও মূল তিক্তাস্বাদ এবং উগ্র সুরভিযুক্ত।

scăb′-bard (-ârd), *n.* The sheath of a sword or other similar weapon ; তরবারির খাপ, কোষ, পিধান, খড়্গাকোষ, দ্রুণহ (অঃ)। **Scabbard-fish**—খড়্গাকৃতি রজতশ্বেত মৎস্যবিশেষ।

scā′-bĭ-ēs, *n.* The itch ; কণ্ডু, বিচর্চ্চিকা।

scă′-bi-ous (-ŭs), *adj.* & *n.* Scabby; মামড়ি-পড়া, বিচর্চ্চিকারোগাক্রান্ত। *Noun.* A genus of herbaceous plants so called as deemed efficacious in scaly eruptions; কণ্ডু প্রভৃতি রোগে হিতকর বলিয়া বিবেচিত এক জাতীয় গুল্ম।

scā′-brous (-brŭs), *adj.* **1.** Rough; rugged; কর্কশ; আবড়োখাবড়ো, খরসম্পর্শ, রূক্ষতল (সাঃ পঃ)। **2.** (Of verse etc.) Harsh; unpolished; (কবিতাদি সম্পর্কে) শ্রুতিকটু; অমার্জ্জিত। **3.** Almost indelicate; as, *scabrous* novels; কুরুচির আভাসযুক্ত।

scăd, *n.* **1.** A kind of fish; একপ্রকার মৎস্য।

scăf′-fold (-öld), *n.* & *v. t.* **1.** A temporary structure to support workmen in the erection of a building; মাচান, মাচা, ভারা। **2.** An elevated platform for the execution of a criminal; বধমঞ্চ। ***Verb t.*** To furnish with a scaffold; মাচান বাঁধা, ভারা বাঁধা। **–ing,** *n.* **1.** A structure for support of workmen in building; ভারা, মাচান। **2.** A supporting framework; কোন কিছুর অবলম্বন স্বরূপ কাঠাম।

scaglia, n. A reddish Italian limestone; ইতালী দেশীয় আরক্তবর্ণ চূর্ণপ্রস্তর।

scagl′-io-lă (skăl-yö-), *n.* A hard, polished plaster, coloured in imitation of marble; মার্ব্বেল পাথরের অনুকরণে রঞ্জিত কঠিন এবং মসৃণীকৃত প্যারী প্লাস্তার।

scāl′-ă-ble (-bl), *adj.* See under SCALE.

scă-lăr′-i-fôrm, *adj.* Shaped like a ladder; resembling a ladder; মইয়ের আকৃতি; মইয়ের সদৃশ, অধিরোহিণীবৎ।

scăl′-ă-wăg, *n.* A scamp; a good-for-nothing fellow; পাজীলোক, নচ্ছার; নিষ্কর্ম্মা লোক।

scăld, *v. t.* & *n.* **1.** To burn or injure with hot liquor; উষ্ণ-জল প্রভৃতি দ্বারা দগ্ধ করা। **2.** To wash or cleanse with hot water; উষ্ণজল দ্বারা ধৌত বা পরিষ্কার করা। **3.** To expose to burning heat over fire or in liquid; জ্বাল দেওয়া, উষ্ণ তরল পদার্থের মধ্যে রাখা। ***Noun.*** A burn or injury by hot liquor or vapour; উষ্ণ জল প্রভৃতি দ্বারা চর্ম্মদাহ। **Scalded cream**—জ্বাল দেওয়া দুধ হইতে যে সর তোলা হয়। **Scalding tears**—তপ্ত অশ্রুজল।

scăld, *n.* An ancient Scandinavian poet or bard; প্রাচীন স্কেণ্ডিনেভিয়ার কবি বা চারণ।

scăld′-head, (-hĕd) *n.* A scalp disease of children; শিশুদিগের শিরস্ত্বকের রোগবিশেষ।

scaldino, n. A small earthen brazier used in Italy for warming the hands etc.; হস্তপদ উষ্ণ করার জন্য ইতালীদেশে ব্যবহৃত একপ্রকার ক্ষুদ্র অঙ্গারধানিকা।

scāle, *n., v. t.* & *i.* **1.** One of the thin overlapping plates on the skin of many fishes and reptiles; আঁইশ, পাঁতি। [*Syn.* শল্কল, বল্ক, পত্র, পটল, মীনবল্ক, মৎস্যবল্ক, শল্ক (তৈত্তিরীয় সংহিতা—cf. Old Teutonic *skala*).] **2.** Anything resembling the scale of a fish; মৎস্যের শল্কসদৃশ কোন বস্তু। **3.** A film; ছিল্কা, চিল্টা, চল্টা। **4.** A hard incrustation deposited inside of a vessel in which water is habitually heated, as a steam-boiler, kettle, etc.; যে পাত্রে সদা-সর্ব্বদা জল উত্তপ্ত করা হয়—তাহাতে যে কঠিন আচ্ছাদন পতিত হয়। **5.** The tartar on teeth; দন্তশর্করা, দাঁতের পাথরি। **6.** The thin metallic lining on the handle of a pocket-knife; ছুরির বাঁটের উপর ধাতুর পাতলা আস্তর। ***Verb t.*** **1.** To strip or clear of scales; আঁশ ছাড়ান। **2.** (*Obs.*) To clean the inside of a cannon by exploding a little powder; (অপ্রঃ) অল্প পরিমাণ বারুদ স্ফুটিত করিয়া কামানের অভ্যন্তরভাগ পরিষ্কার করা। **3.** To spread manure; সার ছড়ান। **4.** To pare off the surface; উপরের আবরণ চাঁচিয়া ফেলা। **5.** To form scales on; as, leprosy *scales* one's skin; উপরে আঁইশের মত গঠন করা। **6.** To remove tartar from the teeth; দাঁত হইতে পাথরি চাঁচিয়া ফেলা। **7.** (*Obs.*) To disperse; as, to *scale* a crowd (used only in Scotland and North of England); (অপ্রঃ) তাড়ান। ***Verb i.*** To come off in scales or thin layers; শল্কের আকারে উঠিয়া আসা, চিল্টা চিল্টা হইয়া উঠিয়া আসা। **Scal′-y,** *adj.* Having scales; covered with scales; শল্কলী, সশল্ক; শল্কলাবৃত। **Scale-armour**—যে বর্ম্মে বস্ত্র বা চর্ম্মের উপর মৎস্যের শল্কের মত ক্ষুদ্র ক্ষুদ্র ধাতুখণ্ড সমূহ গ্রথিত হইয়া থাকে, শল্কচর্ম্ম। **Scale-bark**—শল্কপতৎবল্ক (সাঃ পঃ)। **Scale-board**—ছবি, আয়না, প্রভৃতির পশ্চাদ্‌ভাগে দিবার জন্য অতি পাতলা ফলক। **Scale-fern** — একপ্রকার পর্ণাঙ্গ। **Scale-insect** — একশ্রেণীর শল্ককল্প কীট—যাহারা বৃক্ষের বল্কলে দৃঢ়রূপে সংসক্ত থাকে। আঁইষ-পোকা (যোঃ)। **Scale-moss**—ক্ষুদ্র ক্ষুদ্র শল্কের মত পত্রবিশিষ্ট একপ্রকার পরগাছা। **Scale-work** — মৎস্যাদির শল্কবিন্যাসের অনুরূপ শিল্পকার্য্য। **To remove the scales from one's eyes**—To make him see clearly; কাহারো চক্ষুর ঘোর কাটাইয়া দেওয়া, চোখের পর্দ্দা সরাইয়া দেওয়া, কাহারো চক্ষুর ঝাপসাভাব দূর করা।

Scales.

scāle, *n., v. t.* & *i.* **1.** The dish of a balance; the balance itself (also *a pair of scales*) ; তুলাদণ্ডের পাত্র, তুলাঘট ; তুলাদণ্ড, নিক্তি, তৌল, মানদণ্ড, দাঁড়িপাল্লা, তরাজু, শলাকা (হিঃ কোঃ), কাঁটা (esp. large ones)। **2.** (*Pl.*) (*Astrol.*) The sign of the balance or libra, in the zodiac ; (ফলিতজ্যোতিষ) তুলারাশি [Syn.- জূক, বণিক, সপ্তম, তৌলী, তুলাভৃত, যূক, যুক, ধট]। *Verb t.* **1.** (*Rare*) To weigh in scales ; (কচিদ্ ব্যবহৃত) নিক্তিতে ওজন করা। **2.** To weigh so much ; ওজন হওয়া। **To hold the scales even** — To judge impartially ; ন্যায়ের তুলাদণ্ড ধরিয়া বিচার করা, নিরপেক্ষ ভাবে বিচার করা। **To throw one's weight into the scale**— To exercise one's influence in one's favour ; কাহারো সাহায্যের জন্য নিজের প্রভাব বা ক্ষমতা প্রয়োগ করা।

scale, *n., v. t. & i.* **1.** Anything graduated, esp. when used as a measure or rule, as a slip of wood, ivory, etc. with spaces marked and numbered, for measuring ; ক্রমাঙ্কিত মানফলক, ক্রমাঙ্কিত মানদণ্ড, মাপনদণ্ড (হিঃ কোঃ), পরিমাণদণ্ড। **2.** A series of steps or ranks ; ধাপ, শ্রেণী, ক্রম, শ্রেঢ়ী (কেঙিঃ), সোপানপদ্ধতি। **3.** (*Mus.*) A gamut consisting of a graduated scale of musical notes ; (সঙ্গীত শাস্ত্র) স্বরগ্রাম। **4.** Relative dimension of a map or drawing ; as, a map on a *scale* of an inch to the mile ; চিত্র বা মানচিত্রের আপেক্ষিক আয়তন, স্কেল। *Verb t.* **1.** To climb by a ladder or get over a wall or the like ; to clamber up ; to ascend ; as, to *scale* the walls of a fort ; মইয়ের সাহায্যে আরোহণ করা, উল্লঙ্ঘন করা ; অতি কষ্টে আরোহণ করা ; আরোহণ করা। **2.** To measure or regulate by scale ; মানদণ্ডের সাহায্যে মাপা বা নিয়মিত করা। **3.** (Usu. wth *down*) To reduce according to a fixed scale or standard ; as, to *scale down* a man's income ; নির্দ্ধারিত ক্রম বা আদর্শের অনুযায়ী সঙ্কোচ করা। *Verb i.* To climb or ascend by, or as by, a ladder ; অধিরোহিণীর সাহায্যে আরোহণ করা। **Scaling ladder**— দুর্গপ্রাচীর উল্লঙ্ঘনের উপযোগী আরোহিণী। **Chromatic scale** — ক্রোমীয় মাপদণ্ড (হিঃ কোঃ)। **Decimal scale**—দাশমিক ক্রম (হিঃ কোঃ)। **Graduated scale**— রেখাঙ্কিত ক্রম (হিঃ কোঃ)। **Notation scale**—সংখ্যাত্মকক্রম (হিঃ কোঃ)।

scă-lene' (-lēn), *adj. & n.* (Of a triangle) Having three unequal sides ; (ত্রিভুজসম্পর্কে) বিষম বাহু, অসমবাহু। *Noun.* **1.** A triangle whose sides are all unequal ; অসমবাহু ত্রিভুজ, বিষম বাহু ত্রিভুজ (সাঃ পঃ), বিষম (ঐ)। **2.** Same as SCALENE MUSCLE. **Scalene cone, scalene cylinder**— যে সূচীক্ষেত্র বা যষ্টি ঘনক্ষেত্রের অক্ষভূমির লম্বস্বরূপ নহে। **Scalene muscle**—পঞ্জরাস্থি ও মেরুদণ্ডসংযোজক পেশীসমূহের অন্যতম।

scall, *n.* (*Archaic*) Scurf ; (অপ্রঃ) খোস, বিচর্চ্চিকা।

scăl'-lă-wăg, *n.* Same as SCALAWAG (which see).

scăl'-lion (-yŭn), *n.* A kind of onion or shallot ; একজাতীয় পেঁয়াজ বা গন্ধ-পেঁয়াজ।

scăl'-lŏp (*or* scŏl-), *n. & v. t.* **1.** An edible bivalve of the oyster family ; একপ্রকার খাদ্য ঝিনুক [প্যালেষ্টাইনদেশের সাগরোপকূলে প্রাপ্ত একপ্রকার ঝিনুক। এক সময়ে প্যালেষ্টাইন হইতে প্রত্যাগত যাত্রিগণ এই জাতীয় ঝিনুক তীর্থযাত্রার চিহ্নস্বরূপ মস্তকে ধারণ করিত।] **2.** A kind of dish for cooking oysters in ; শুক্তি পাক করার জন্য একপ্রকার ক্ষুদ্র চাটু। **3.** A curving of the edge of anything like the segment of a circle ; পোষাক প্রভৃতির প্রান্তে কর্ত্তিত ক্ষুদ্র ক্ষুদ্র বৃত্তখণ্ডসমূহের অন্যতম। *Verb t.* **1.** To mark or cut on the edge in segments of circles ; পোষাক প্রভৃতির প্রান্ত ক্ষুদ্র ক্ষুদ্র বৃত্তখণ্ডে কাটা বা চিহ্নিত করা। **2.** To cook as oysters in a shell of scallop ; বড় ঝিনুকের খোলে শুক্তি প্রভৃতি পাক করা। **—loped,** *adj.* Cut into segment of circles ; প্রান্তে ক্ষুদ্র ক্ষুদ্র বৃত্ত কর্ত্তিত, চাঁদ-কাটা।

scăl'-lȳ-wăg, *n.* Same as SCALAWAG (which see).

scălp, *n. & v. t.* **1.** Top of the head ; মাথার চাঁদি। **2.** The skin on the top of the head with the hair on it ; মস্তকের কেশযুক্ত ত্বক, শিরস্তক (আমেরিকার প্রাচীন অধিবাসিগণ শত্রুর সকেশ শিরস্ত্বক উন্মোচন করিয়া নিত)। **2.** A whale's head without lower jaw ; নিম্নের হনুবিহীন তিমি মস্তক। **3.** (*Colloq., Finance*) A small profit taken in a quick transaction ; তাড়াতাড়ি মাল বিক্রয় করিলে যে অল্প লাভ হয়। **4.** A bare peak ; নগ্ন চূড়া। *Verb t.* **1.** To deprive of the scalp ; শিরস্ত্বক উন্মোচন করা। **2.** To cut or tear the scalp from the head of ; মস্তকের সকেশত্বক উন্মোচন করা। **3.** To criticize severely ; তীব্র সমালোচনা করা। **4.** To destroy the political influence of ; রাজনীতিক প্রভাব বিনষ্ট করা। **5.** (*Colloq.*) To buy at a small rate so as to sell at less than official rate ; সরকার কর্তৃক নির্দ্দিষ্ট দর অপেক্ষা অল্প দরে বিক্রয়ের জন্য অল্প দরে কোন জিনিষ ক্রয় করা। **Scalp-lock** — ছিন্ন করার সুযোগ প্রদানের উদ্দেশ্যে লাল ইণ্ডিয়ানগণকর্তৃক মুণ্ডিত-মস্তকে রক্ষিত একমাত্র কেশগুচ্ছ।

scăl'-pĕl, *n.* A small knife used in operations and dissection ; শরীরের কোমলাংশ ছেদনার্থ একপ্রকার ছুরিকা, ডাক্তারের ছুরি।

scăl-pĕl-lĭ-fôrm, *adj.* Shaped like the blade of pen-knife ; ছুরির ফলার আকৃতি।

scălp'-ĭng-ī-ron (-ərn), *n.* A surgeon's instrument for scraping;

রূপ অস্থি চাঁচিবার জন্য অস্ত্রচিকিৎসকদিগের যন্ত্রবিশেষ।

scăm-mŏ'-nў, *n.* **1.** A plant of the genus convolvulousgrowing abundantly in Syria ; মহামুদা (ওয়াট)। **2.** A tensively as an ingredient in purgum-resin obtained from the tuberous roots of *convolvulus scammonia* used a strong purgative ; মহামুদার কন্দজ মূল হইতে প্রাপ্ত একপ্রকার তীব্র বিরেচক পদার্থ। [Arab. *sukmoonia*; Fr. *scammonee*; Germ. *skammonien*; It. *scammonea*; Russ. *pessya smert* ; Sp. *escamonea*].

scămp, *n.* A rascal ; a rogue ; a good-for-nothing fellow ; a knave ; পাজী, দুষ্ট, বিটল; নিষ্কর্ম্মা লোক ; ধূর্ত্ত।

scămp, *v. t.* To do or execute something in a perfunctory manner ; অসম্পূর্ণভাবে কোন কায করা, যেমন তেমন করিয়া কায সারা।

scăm'-pêr, *v. i.* & *n.* To run away hastily ; to hurry away ; দৌড়িয়া পালান ; ছুটিয়া চলা। *Noun.* **1.** A hasty flight or escape ; দ্রুত পলায়ন। **2.** A hasty excursion ; দ্রুত পর্য্যটন। **3.** A rapid course of reading ; দ্রুত পঠন।

scăn, *v. t.* & *i.* **1.** To divide lines of poetry into "feet" and mark the places of the accented syllables ; to read or recite so as to indicate the metrical structure ; কবিতার পংক্তি বিভিন্ন ভাগে বিভাগ করা এবং মাত্রা দ্বারা চিহ্নিত করা, ছন্দোমাত্রাগনণ (কেণ্ডিঃ) ; যথাস্থানে জোর দিয়া এবং ছন্দঃ রক্ষা করিয়া পাঠ করা। **2.** To examine carefully ; পুঙ্খানুপুঙ্খরূপে পরীক্ষা করা। *Verb i.* To follow or agree with the rules of metre ; ছন্দঃশাস্ত্রের নিয়মানুযায়ী হওয়া।

scăn'-dăl, *n.* **1.** Something uttered injurious to the reputation of others which is either wholly or partially untrue ; কুৎসা, অপবাদ, কলঙ্ক, পরিবাদ, পরীবাদ। **2.** Something notoriously reprehensible ; কেলেঙ্কারি, ঢলানি, ঢলাঢলি [cf. দুদিন আগে আপনি আলিপুর আসিলে এ ঢলাঢলিটা হইত না (আমার জীবন—নবীন সেন)], কলঙ্কজনক বিষয়। **–ous,** *adj.* Disgraceful to reputation ; shameful ; কলঙ্কজনক, কুৎসাজনক ; লজ্জাজনক, লজ্জাকর। **Scandal-monger**—কুৎসাব্যবসায়ী, কলঙ্করটনাকারী।

scăn'-dăl-ize, *v. t.* **1.** To offend by some action ceemed wrong or disgraceful ; to bring shame, disgrace or reproach upon ; to shock the moral feelings of ; কলঙ্কজনক কার্য্য দ্বারা ব্যথিত করা, ঢলান ; লজ্জা, কলঙ্ক বা গ্লানি আনয়ন করা ; বীভৎস আচরণ দ্বারা স্তম্ভিত করা। **2.** To disgrace ; কলঙ্কিত করা। **3.** (*Obs.*) To defame ; (অপ্রঃ) মানহানি করা। **4.** To reduce sail on (a mizzenmast) when before the wind, so that the sails on the main mast may have the full force of the wind ; প্রধান মাস্তুলের পাইলসকল যাহাতে বাতাসের পূর্ণ জোর পাইতে পারে তজ্জন্য ত্রিমাস্তুল পোতের সর্ব্বাপশ্চাদ্‌বর্ত্তী মাস্তুলের পশ্চাদ্দিকে টাঙ্গানো পাইল হ্রস্ব করা।

Scandalum magnatum (*L.*), *n.* The offence of defaming the great personages of the realm ; রাজ্যের শীর্ষস্থানীয় লোকদিগের মানহানির অপরাধ।

Scăn-di-nā'-vi-ăn, *adj.* & *n.* Relating to Norway, Sweden, Denmark and Iceland ; নরওয়ে, সুইডেন, ডেনমার্ক এবং অ ইসল্যাণ্ড-সম্বন্ধীয়। *Noun.* A native of one of these countries ; নরওয়ে, সুইডেন, ডেনমার্ক এবং আইসল্যাণ্ডের অধিবাসী।

scăn-sō'-rēs, *n.*, *pl.* An order of birds, popularly known as climbing birds, having the feet provided with four toes of which two are turned backwards and two forwards ; পক্ষীর বর্গবিশেষ। এই বর্গভুক্ত পক্ষীর পদে চারিটী পদাঙ্গুলী থাকে, তন্মধ্যে দুইটী পশ্চাদ্দিকে এবং অপর দুইটী সম্মুখদিকে আবর্ত্তিত থাকে (টিয়া কোকিল, কাঠঠোকরা, প্রভৃতি পক্ষী এই বর্গভুক্ত), কাণ্ডচারী (প্রঃ বাঃ), বৃক্ষারোহী (সাঃ পঃ)।

scănt, *adj.* & *v. t.* Barelv sufficient ; as, *scant* courtesy ; অপ্রচুর, অপ্রতুল, অল্প, সামান্য, যৎসামান্য, স্বল্প। *Verb t.* To curtail ; to abridge ; "She *scans* me of my rights" ; সংকোচ করা ; কমাইয়া দেওয়া।

scănt'-ling, *n.* **1.** (*Rare*) A sample ; (অপ্রঃ) নমুনা। **2.** A rough draft ; খসড়া। **3.** A modicum ; a small amount ; যৎসামান্য ; সামান্য পরিমাণ, একরতি। **4.** A kind of trestle or horse for supporting a cask ; পিপা রাখার জন্য কাঠাম। **5.** Timber sawed or cut into pieces less than five inches square ; ৫ বর্গ ইঞ্চির কম পুরু ও চওড়া তক্তা।

scănt'-ў, *adj.* **1.** Small ; narrow ; "His dominions were very narrow and *scanty*" ; ক্ষুদ্র ; সংকীর্ণ, অল্পবিস্তৃত। **2.** Barely sufficient ; স্বল্প, অপ্রচুর, অপর্য্যাপ্ত, অল্প, সামান্য। **–i-ly,** *adv.* **–i-ness,** *n.*

scāpe, *n.* **1.** (*Bot.*) A stem rising directly from a root ; (উদ্ভিদ-বিদ্যা) মূল হইতে উদ্গত দীর্ঘ পুষ্পদণ্ড, ভৌমপুষ্পদণ্ড (সাঃ পঃ)। **2.** (*Arch.*) The shaft of a column ; the spring of a column with a curve from the base ; (স্থপতিবিদ্যা) স্তম্ভদণ্ড, স্তম্ভবপু ; অধিষ্ঠানভূমি হইতে বক্রোৎপাদন পূর্ব্বক স্তম্ভের অভ্যুত্থান। **3.** The shaft of a feather ; পালকবৃন্ত। **4.** (*Entom.*) The basal joint of an insect's antenna ; কীটের শুঁয়ার মূলভাগের সন্ধিস্থল।

scāpe'-goat (-gōt), *n.* **1.** A goat upon whose head the Jewish priests symbolically placed the sins of the people, then turning him into the wilderness ; ইহুদীদিগের প্রধান পুরোহিত যে ছাগের স্কন্ধে সকল লোকের পাপের বোঝা চাপাইয়া ছাড়িয়া দিতেন, মুক্তিছাগ (ভ্রাঃ বিঃ)। **2.** One made to bear blame due to others ; যে ব্যক্তি অপরের দুষ্কর্ম্মের জন্য নিন্দার ভাগী হয়।

scăpe′-grāce, *n.* A careless hare-brained fellow ; a graceless fellow ; নচ্ছার লোক, বেপরওয়া লোক, লক্ষ্মীছাড়া লোক, হতভাগা লোক, অলপ্পেয়ে (*slang*), আবাগের বেটা ভূত (*slang*) ; অভব্য লোক।

scāpe′-mĕnt, *n.* Same as ESCAPEMENT (which see).

scăph′-oid (-ōyd), *adj.* & *n.* Boat-shaped ; নাবাকার, নৌকাকার। ***Noun.*** Same as SCAPHOID-BONE. **Scaphoid bone**—নৌকাকৃতি অস্থি, নৌকাস্থি।

scă-phŏp′-ō-dă, *n.* A small class of marine mollusca ; দন্তসংখ্যশ্রেণী—উহার কোমল আবরণ এবং দেহপদ লম্বা। ঐ আবরণ দেহপদকে চোঙ্গের ন্যায় ঢাকিয়া রাখে। ইহার চাড়া লম্বা ও গোল এবং অনেকটা সরু, অনেকটা লম্বা গোল দাঁতের মত (মিউজিয়াম)।

scăp′-ū-lă, *n.* Shoulder blade ; অংসফলক।

scăp′-ū-lar (-lėr), *adj.* & *n.* Pertaining to the shoulder, or to the scapula ; স্কন্ধসম্পর্কীয়, স্কন্ধাস্থিসম্পর্কীয়। ***Noun.*** 1. A bandage for shoulder-blade ; স্কন্ধাস্থির জন্য বস্ত্রবন্ধনী। 2. A monastic garment resting on the shoulders with a flap hanging down in front and another behind ; খৃষ্টীয় সন্ন্যাসিগণের পরিচ্ছদবিশেষ—যাহার একটী প্রলম্বিত অংশ সম্মুখে এবং অপর অংশ পশ্চাদ্দিকে দোলায়মান থাকে। 3. Same as SCAPULAR FEATHERS. **Scapular feathers**—পক্ষের সন্ধিস্থলে উদ্গত পালকগুচ্ছ।

scăp′-ū-lō–, Combining form of *scapula* ; as, *scapulo*-radial, *scapulo*-ulna.

scăr, *n., v. t.* & *i.* 1. The mark of a wound or of an ulcer remaining after healing ; ক্ষতচিহ্ন, ক্ষতাঙ্কিণ। 2. A mark left on a stem or a branch by the fall of a leaf ; পত্রপতনহেতু শাখা-কাণ্ডে যে চিহ্ন থাকে। ***Verb t.*** To mark with a scar or scars ; ক্ষতচিহ্নিত করা। ***Verb i.*** 1. To be covered with scars ; ক্ষতচিহ্নিত হওয়া। 2. To form scars ; (ক্ষতসম্পর্কে) শুষ্ক হইয়া চিহ্ন মাত্র থাকা।

scăr, scaur (skär), *ns.* A cliff ; a bare and rugged part of a mountain-side ; খাড়া পাহাড় ; দুরারোহ গিরিপার্শ্ব, গিরিপার্শ্বের নগ্ন এবং বন্ধুর অংশ।

scăr′-ăb, *n.* 1. A dung-beetle ; গোবরে পোকা। [প্রাচীন মিসরবাসিগণ এই কীটকে অতিশয় সম্মানের চক্ষে দেখিত।] 2. A gem cut in the form of a beetle ; গোবরে পোকার আকারে কর্ত্তিত মণি।

scăr′-ă-bae′-id (-bē-), *n.* A member of the scarabaeidae beetles ; গোবরে পোকা জাতীয় কীট।

scăr-ă-bae′-oid (-bē-ōyd), *adj.* & *n.* Like a scarab or scarabaeid ; গোবরে পোকার মত, গোবরে পোকা জাতীয় কীটের মত। ***Noun.*** A false scarab gem ; গোবরে পোকার আকারে কর্ত্তিত ঝুঁটা পাথর।

scăr-ăb′-oid (-ōyd), *n.* 1. A scarabaeid beetle ; গোবরে পোকা জাতীয় কীট। 2. A scarab-shaped gem ; গোবরে পোকার আকারে কর্ত্তিত মণি।

scăr′-ă-mouch (-mowch), *n.* 1. A personage in Italian comedy characterised by great poltroonery and boastfulness ; ইতালীদেশীয় মিলনান্ত নাটকের বিদূষক। 2. A buffoon ; a poltroon or braggadocio ; ভাঁড় ; কাপুরুষ, আস্ফালনকারী, লম্ফঝম্পকারী।

scarce (scārs), *adj.* & *adv.* 1. Not plentiful or abundant ; scanty or in small quantity in proportion to need or demand ; স্বল্প, অপ্রচুর ; দুষ্প্রাপ্য, দুর্ল্লভ। ***Adv.*** Scarcely ; কদাচিৎ। **To make oneself scarce**—To take to heels; গা ঢাকা দেওয়া, সরিয়া পড়া, চম্পট দেওয়া। **Scarce′-ness,** *n.*

scarce′-lȳ (scārs-), *adv.* 1. Rarely ; কদাচিৎ, কচিৎ, কালেভদ্রে। 2. Only just ; barely ; সবে মাত্র, সবে ; প্রায়। **Scarcely had he gone, done, etc.**—সে যাইতে না যাইতে, করিতে না করিতে, ইত্যাদি।

scār′-ci-tȳ, *n.* Smallness of quantity or smallness in proportion to the wants or demands ; rareness ; deficiency of things necessary to subsistence of men ; অপ্রচুরতা, স্বল্পতা ; দুষ্প্রাপ্যতা ; অন্নকষ্ট, আকাল, অনটন, টানাটানি।

scāre, *v. t.* & *n.* 1. To strike with sudden fright or terror ; to terrify ; to frighten ; ভয়চকিত করা, ভয়সন্ত্রস্ত করা, আতঙ্কিত করা ; ভয়ার্ত্ত করা ; ভয় দেখান। 2. To keep birds away from sown lands etc. ; ক্ষেত্র প্রভৃতি হইতে পাখী তাড়ান। ***Noun.*** A sudden fright or panic ; ত্রাস, আতঙ্ক। **Scare-crow**—পক্ষী প্রভৃতি তাড়াইবার জন্য শস্যক্ষেত্রে যে বিকটমূর্ত্তি স্থাপিত করা হয়, চঞ্চাপুরুষ, কাকতাড়ানো ; বিকটমূর্ত্তি ; অস্থিচর্ম্মসার ব্যক্তি, তালপাতার সিপাহী ; জুজু। **To scare away**—To drive off by frightening ; ভয় দেখাইয়া তাড়ান। **To scare up**—To bring into the open as game by beating ; জঙ্গল ঠেঙ্গাইয়া শিকার বাহির করা। To find out ; বাহির করা।

scārf, *n.* A light article of dress worn round the neck etc. ; a man's neck-tie ; উত্তরীয়, উপবস্ত্র (কেঃ), ওড়না, চাদর ; পুরুষের গলবন্ধ। **Scarf-pin**—গলবন্ধের উভয় অংশ একত্র সংযোজনের জন্য স্বর্ণাদি নির্ম্মিত সূচী। **Scarf-skin**—উপরের ত্বক, উপত্বক, বাহ্যত্বক্। **Scarf-loom** — স্বল্পপরিসর বস্ত্রাদি তৈরীর জন্য তাঁত। **Scarf-wise**—উপবীতাকারে।

scārf, *v. t.* & *n.* 1. To unite two pieces of timber by letting the end of one into the end of other ; টের্চ্চাভাবে কাটিয়া বা খাঁজ কাটিয়া একটী কাঠের প্রান্ত অপর কাঠের

প্রান্তের উপর রাখিয়া জোড়া দেওয়া। 2. To cut off the skin and blubber of whale; তিমি মৎস্যের চর্ম্ম এবং মেদ কাটিয়া ফেলা। ***Noun.*** The joint by which the ends of two pieces of timbers are united so as to form a continuous piece; যেরূপ জোড় দ্বারা দুই খণ্ড কাঠ এইরূপভাবে সংযুক্ত করা হয়—যাহাতে উভয়ে সংযুক্ত অবস্থায় একই ফলক বলিয়া প্রতিভাত হয়।

scăr′-i-fi-că-tor (-têr), *n.* An instrument used in scarification; চর্ম্মের উপর এক সময়ে একাধিক স্থান কর্ত্তনের জন্য একপ্রকার যন্ত্র (এই যন্ত্রের টিপ-কলে টিপ দিলে কয়েকটী ছুরিকাগ্র বহির্গত হয়), দ্বাদশকূর্চ্চাস্ত্র [after ত্রিকূর্চ্চক (সুশ্রুত)]।

scăr′-i-fī-êr, *n.* **1.** The person who scarifies; প্রচ্ছানক্রিয়াকারী। 2. Same as SCARIFICATOR. 3. An agricultural instrument with prongs for stirring the soil; ভূমি আঁচড়াইবার জন্য কৃষিযন্ত্রবিশেষ।

scăr′-i-fȳ, *v. t.* **1.** (*Surg.*) To make small superficial incisions in the skin so as to draw blood without opening a large vein; বৃহৎ শিরা ছেদন বিনা রক্তমোক্ষণের জন্য চর্ম্মের কোন স্থান একাধিক বার কাটা, প্রচ্ছানক্রিয়া করা। 2. To stir the soil as with a scarifier; উল্লেখনযন্ত্রদ্বারা ভূমি আলোড়িত করা; 3. To remove the flesh about a tooth; দন্তের চতুর্দ্দিকের মাংস অপসারিত করা। **–fi-ca′-tion,** *n.* **1.** The act of making small superficial incisions in the skin; দ্বাদশকূর্চ্চাস্ত্র দ্বারা চর্ম্মের উপর এক সময়ে একাধিক স্থান কর্ত্তন, প্রচ্ছান (সুশ্রুঃ)। 2. The act of removing the flesh about tooth; দন্তের চতুর্দ্দিকের মাংস অপসারণ।

scă′-ri-ous (-ŭs), *adj.* (*Bot.*) Membranous and dry; (উদ্ভিদ্ বিদ্যা) শুষ্ক এবং ঝিল্লীরহুল।

scăr-lă-ti′-nă (-tē-), *n.* Same as SCARLET-FEVER.

scâr′-lĕt, *n.* & *adj.* **1.** A bright red colour; উজ্জ্বল লোহিতবর্ণ। 2. A cloth or robe of that colour; as, clothed in *scarlet*; উজ্জ্বল লোহিতবর্ণের বস্ত্র বা পরিচ্ছদ। ***Adj.*** Of a bright red colonr; উজ্জ্বল লোহিতবর্ণের। **Scarlet admiral**—একপ্রকার প্রজাপতি। **Scarlet bean**—Same as SCARLET RUNNER. **Scarlet fever**—একপ্রকার সংক্রামক-জ্বর—যাহাতে সর্ব্বাঙ্গে গাঢ় রক্তবর্ণের পীড়কা উৎপন্ন হয়, আরক্তজ্বর, উদর্দ্দ (সাঃ পঃ); সৈনিক পুরুষের প্রতি ইংরেজ রমণীগণের বিশেষ অনুরাগ, লালকোর্ত্তাওয়ালাদিগের প্রতি অনুরাগ। **Scarlet-grain**—একপ্রকার কীট—যাহা হইতে রুশিয়া এবং তুরস্কদেশে একপ্রকার লাল রং প্রস্তুত করা হয়। **Scarlet hat**—কার্ডিন্যালগণের টুপি; কার্ডিন্যালগণের পদ। **Scarlet rash**—Same as ROSEOLA. **Scarlet runner**—একপ্রকার উদ্যানলতিকা। **Scarlet woman, Scarlet whore**—রোমান ক্যাথলিক ধর্ম্মসংঘ; রোমান ক্যাথলিকদিগের মতে লণ্ডননগরী। **Though your sins be as scarlet as blood they shall be as white as snow**—তোমার পাপ যতই রক্তবর্ণ হউক না কেন তাহা তুষারের মত শুভ্র হইবে (যীশুখৃষ্টের উক্তি)।

scă′-roid (-rȳd), *n.* & *adj.* A fish of scarus genus; একজাতীয় মৎস্য। ***Adj.*** Resembling scarus; ঐ জাতীয় মৎস্যসদৃশ।

scârp, *n.* & *v. t.* **1.** The interior slope of the ditch of a fortification at the foot of the rampart; দুর্গপ্রাচীরপাদস্থ পরিখার আভ্যন্তরিক ঢালু। 2. Any steep slope; দুরারোহ প্রবণভূমি। ***Verb t.*** To cut down like a scarp; to cut down perpendicularly or nearly so; দুর্গপ্রাচীরপাদের পরিখার আভ্যন্তরিক ঢালুর আকারে কাটা; খাড়া করিয়া কাটা, প্রায় খাড়া করিয়া কাটা।

scă′-rŭs, *n.* A genus of Labridæ with ten species; একজাতীয় মৎস্য। [এই জাতীয় মৎস্যের চোয়াল খুব শক্ত এবং আঁইশ বৃহৎ। ইহাদের হনুদেশের আকৃতি শুকচঞ্চুবৎ ও দেহের বর্ণ অতি সমুজ্জ্বল বলিয়া উহাদিগকে শুকমীন (Parrot-fish) বলা হইয়া থাকে।]

scāthe, scāth, *v. t.* & *n.* To hurt; to injure; ক্ষতি করা; অনিষ্ট করা, হানি করা। ***Noun.*** Hurt; injury; অনিষ্ট, ক্ষতি; হানি। **Scath′-ing,** *adj.* **1.** Hurtful; হানিজনক, অনিষ্টকর। 2. Very bitter or severe; as, *scathing* sarcasm; তীব্র, কঠোর। **Scathe′-less,** *adj.* Unharmed; অক্ষত। **Scathe′-less-ly,** *adv.* **One doth the scath and another has the scorn**—উদোর পিণ্ডি বুধোর ঘাড়ে।

scă-tŏl′-ŏ-ġȳ, *n.* Study of excrement; পুরীষ-তত্ত্ব।

scă-tŏph′-ă-gous (-gŭs), *adj.* Feeding on excrements; পুরীষভোজী।

Scatophagus argus—রূপচাঁদা (গুপ্তঃ)।

scăt′-têr, *v. t.* & *i.* **1.** To strew; ছড়ান, আস্তৃত করা, বিক্ষিপ্ত করা। 2. To disperse; "*Scattered* the clouds away"; ইতস্ততঃ বিক্ষিপ্ত করা, ছিন্নভিন্ন করা, ছত্রভঙ্গ করা। 3. To dissipate and frustrate; as, to *scatter* hopes; বিদূরিত করা, বিতাড়িত করা, বিফল করা, ব্যর্থ করা। ***Verb i.*** **1.** To be dispersed or dissipated; ইতস্ততঃ বিক্ষিপ্ত হওয়া, ছিন্নভিন্ন হওয়া। **–tered,** *pp.* **1.** Dispersed; বিক্ষিপ্ত। 2. Separated by wide intervals; as, *scattered* houses; খুব ফাঁক ফাঁক, খুব দূরে দূরে অবস্থিত। 3. Disconnected; as, *scattered* thoughts; অসংলগ্ন। 4 (*Bot.*) Having an irregular arrangement; (উদ্ভিদবিদ্যা) অসমবিন্যস্ত। **Scatter-brain, –brains**—ক্ষীণমস্তিষ্ক ব্যক্তি, চিন্তাশক্তিহীন ব্যক্তি, বিক্ষিপ্তমতি ব্যক্তি, বিক্ষিপ্তবুদ্ধি ব্যক্তি। **Scattered light**—চতুর্দ্দিকে বিক্ষিপ্ত পরাবর্ত্তিত আলোক।

scaup (skăp), **scaup′-dŭck** (skăp-), *ns.* A species of duck, the *Fuligola marila*; একজাতীয়

হংস [এই জাতীয় হংসের বর্ণ ধূসর; গায়ে কালো কালো ডোরা। মাথা ও গলা কালো। সময় সময় ঐ রং বদলাইয়া সবুজ রং ধরে। ঠোঁটের রং সীসার মত। উদর শাদা এবং পাখার ফুট ফুট শাদা দাগ থাকে।]

scaup′-ėr (skăp-), *n.* A tool used by engravers; খোদাইকারদিগের যন্ত্রবিশেষ।

scaur (skär), *n.* Same as SCAR (which see.)

scăv′-ĕn-gêr, *n.* **1.** A person whose employment is to clean the streets of a city; যে ব্যক্তি রাস্তা ঝাঁট দেয়, ঝাড়ুদার, বর্ত্মসম্মার্জ্জক। **2.** An animal that feeds on carrion; গলিতজীবদেহভোজী জন্তু। **3.** A writer of obscene books etc.; অশ্লীল পুস্তকাদির লেখক। **–enge,** *v. t.* & *i.* **–y,** *n.*

scā′-zŏn, *n.* An iambic trimeter with a spondee or trochee in the last foot; একপ্রকার ছন্দঃ।

scena, *n.* **1.** A scene of an opera গীতিনাট্যের দৃশ্য। **2.** A solo for a single voice in which various dramatic emotions are displayed; এক ব্যক্তি কর্ত্তৃক গেয় সঙ্গীতবিশেষ—যাহাতে বিভিন্নপ্রকার নাট্যসমুচিত ভাবাঙ্গ প্রকটিত হয়।

scenario, (*It.*), *n.* An outline of a play or of an opera giving particulars of the scenes and showing the entrance and exits of the actors; কোন নাটক বা গীতিনাট্যের বিভিন্ন দৃশ্যের সারমর্ম্ম এবং নটনটীগণের প্রবেশ ও প্রস্থানাদির বিবরণ-সমন্বিত পুস্তিকা।

scene (sēn), *n.* **1.** (*Archaic*) The stage of a theatre; (অপ্রঃ) রঙ্গমঞ্চ। **2.** A division of an act; নাটকের দৃশ্য। **3.** The place of action or occurrence; the imaginary place in which the actions of a play or the events set forth in a book are supposed to occur; as, the *scenes* are laid in France; কোন ঘটনা বা কার্য্যের স্থান, ঘটনা-স্থল; যে কল্পিত স্থানে কোন নাট্য বা উপন্যাসোক্ত ঘটনাবলী ঘটিয়াছে বলিয়া মনে করা হয়, দৃশ্য। **4.** One of the painted devices used to give an appearance of reality to an acted play; দৃশ্যপট, রঙ্গপট। **5.** An exhibition of strong feelings between two persons; as, do not make *scene*; display of emotion; কাণ্ড, বিশ্রীকাণ্ড; উচ্ছ্বাস, আবেগ প্রকাশ। **5.** A spectacle; দৃশ্য। **Scene-man, Scene-shifter**—যে ব্যক্তি রঙ্গমঞ্চের দৃশ্যপটসমূহ সঞ্চালিত করে, দৃশ্যপট-সঞ্চালক। **Scene-painter**—দৃশ্যপটচিত্রকর। **Behind the scenes**—যবনিকার অন্তরালে, নেপথ্যে; (লক্ষণায়) ভিতরের কথা জ্ঞাতসার। **To quit the scene**—To leave the stage; (*fig.*) to die; রঙ্গমঞ্চ হইতে প্রস্থান করা; ভবলীলার অবসান হওয়া, সংসার রঙ্গমঞ্চ হইতে বিদায় গ্রহণ করা, ভবনাট্যলীলার অবসান হওয়া।

scen′-ėr-y̆ (sēn-), *n.* **1.** The representation of a place of action or occurrence; the paintings representing the scenes of a play put on the stage; theatre scenes with their accessories; ঘটনাস্থানের চিত্র; নাটকীয় ঘটনাসমূহের চিত্র; নাটকীয় দৃশ্যপটসমূহ এবং তদানুষঙ্গিক সাজসজ্জা। **2.** Landscape characteristic; নৈসর্গিক দৃশ্য, প্রাকৃতিক দৃশ্য।

sce′-nĭc (sē-), **scen′-ĭ-căl** (sēn-), *adjs.* **1.** Pertaining to the stage; dramatic; রঙ্গমঞ্চসম্বন্ধীয়; নাটকীয়। **2.** Of, or pertaining to, scenery; affording beautiful scenery; as, the *scenic* railway; দৃশ্যসম্বন্ধীয়; দৃশ্যপ্রদর্শক, মনোরম দৃশ্যপ্রদর্শক। **3.** Put on; as, *scenic* love; কৃত্রিম, ছদ্ম। **Scenic railway**—যে ক্ষুদ্র বাষ্পীয় শকটে যাত্রিগণ বিচিত্র দৃশ্যরাজির চিত্র-পরম্পরার মধ্য দিয়া নীত হয়।

sce-nŏg′-ră-phy̆ (sē-), *n.* The representations of buildings etc. according to the rules of perspective; পরিপ্রেক্ষিতের নিয়মানুসারে অট্টালিকাদি চিত্রণ। **Scen′-o-graph,** *n.* **Scen-o-graph′-ic,** *adj.* **Scen-o-graph′-i-cal-ly,** *adv.*

scent (sĕnt), *v. t., i.* & *n.* **1.** To smell; গন্ধ পাওয়া, আঘ্রাণ করা। **2.** To perfume; সুরভিত করা, সুগন্ধি করা, সুবাসিত করা। **3.** To have an inkling of; আভাস পাওয়া, টের পাওয়া, সন্ধান পাওয়া। ***Verb i.*** **1.** To have a smell; গন্ধ করা। **2.** To hunt animals by the scent; গন্ধ দ্বারা শিকার অনুসরণ করা। ***Noun.*** **1.** Perfume; smell; সুগন্ধ, সুবাস, সৌরভ, খোসবো; বাস, গন্ধ। **2.** A perfume; গন্ধদ্রব্য। **3.** Sense of smell; as, to delight one's *scent*; ঘ্রাণশক্তি, ঘ্রাণেন্দ্রিয়। **4.** Odour left on the ground enabling an animal's track to be followed; পলায়িত জন্তু গমনপথে যে গন্ধ রাখিয়া যায়। **5.** (*Rare*) An inkling; টের, আভাস, খেই, সুলুক, সন্ধান, পাত্তা। **Scent-bag**—জন্তুদিগের দেহের যে থলিতে সুগন্ধি পদার্থ থাকে, গন্ধপুট, গন্ধকোষ। **Scent-bottle**—পুষ্পসার প্রভৃতি রাখার জন্য শিশি। **Scent-gland** — জন্তু-দেহের যে গ্রন্থি হইতে সুগন্ধি দ্রব্য নিঃসৃত হয়। **Scent-spray**—ক্ষুদ্র ক্ষুদ্র কণাকারে তরল সুগন্ধি দ্রব্য ছড়াইবার জন্য একপ্রকার শিশি। **To be on the scent**—To get an inkling; সন্ধান পাওয়া, টের পাওয়া। **To follow up the scent**—To get some clue and follow it; কোনরূপ সুলুক সন্ধান পাইয়া তাহার অনুসরণ করা। **To lose the scent**—To lose the clue; কোনরূপ সূত্র পাইয়া তাহা হারান, খেই হারান। **To put one off the scent**—To put on the wrong track; অনুসরণকারীকে ফাঁকি দিবার উদ্দেশ্যে যে পথে গেলে ধৃত হইবার সম্ভাবনা সেই পথে না গিয়া অন্য পথে যাওয়া। **To put one on the wrong scent**—To misdirect one;

যাহাতে সন্ধান না পাইতে পারে তজ্জন্য কাহাকে ভ্রান্তপথে চালিত করা।

scep'-sis (skĕp-), *n.* Scepticism; sceptic philosophy; অজ্ঞেয়তাবাদ, সন্দেহবাদ; অজ্ঞেয়তাবাদমূলক দর্শন।

scep'-tic (sĕp-), *n.* **1.** A philosophic doubter, specially one who denies or anyhow doubts the trustworthiness of the senses as media of absolute truth; an agnostic; যে ব্যক্তি পরমতত্ত্ব-সম্বন্ধীয় জ্ঞানলাভবিষয়ে ইন্দ্রিয়গণের কোনরূপ মধ্যস্থতা আছে বলিয়া অস্বীকার বা সন্দেহ প্রকাশ করে, সন্দেহবাদী, অবিশ্বাসী (হিঃ কোঃ), সংশায়াত্মা (ঐ), অশ্রদ্ধালু (ঐ), সংশয়বাদী (ঐ); অজ্ঞেয়তাবাদী। **2.** One who doubts or disbelieves in Christianity; খৃষ্টধর্ম্মে অবিশ্বাসী বা সন্দেহকারী। **3.** An atheist; নাস্তিক। **4.** An unbeliever; অবিশ্বাসী।

scep'-tic (skĕp-), **–ti-căl,** *adjs.* Pertaining to a sceptic; characteristic of a sceptic; doubting everything; অজ্ঞেয়তাবাদি-সম্বন্ধীয়; অজ্ঞেয়তাবাদিসুলভ; সন্দেহকারী, সংশয়াপন্নমানস, সংশয়াত্মা (কেণ্ডিঃ)।

scep'-ti-cĭsm, (skĕp-), *n.* **1.** The doctrine of a sceptic; doubt; disbelief; অজ্ঞেয়তাবাদ, সন্দেহবাদ; সন্দেহ, সংশয়; অবিশ্বাস। **2.** The principle of universal doubt, or at least doubt with regard to the validity of all judgments respecting that which lies beyond the range of experience; সর্ব্ববিষয়ে সন্দেহ, অথবা অন্ততঃ অতীন্দ্রিয় বিষয়ের সত্তা সম্বন্ধে সন্দেহ, সন্দেহবাদ, বেদাবিশ্বাসবাদ (হিঃ কোঃ), ঈশ্বরাবিশ্বাসবাদ (ঐ), অনাগ্রহবাদ (ঐ)।

scep'-tre (sĕp-tẽr), *n.* **1.** A staff of a sovereign borne as an authority; রাজদণ্ড, দণ্ড। **2.** Royal power or authority; রাজশক্তি, রাজক্ষমতা। **–tred,** *adj.*

sched'-üle (shĕd-, *or* sĕd-), *n.* & *v. t.* A list or inventory annexed to a large document, as a will, lease or the like; a list; তফশিল, ফিরিস্তি; ফর্দ্দ, তালিকা। ***Verb t.*** To make a schedule of; to insert in a schedule; ফিরিস্তি করা, তফশিল করা; ফিরিস্তি বা তালিকায় ভুক্ত করা। **Scheduled time**—রেলগাড়ী প্রভৃতি আসিবার ছাড়িবার নির্দ্ধারিত সময়।

schē'-mă, *n.* **1.** Plan; outline; diagram; পরিকল্পনা; আদরা; ক্ষেত্র। **2.** (*Log.*) Syllogistic figure; ন্যায়-বিজ্ঞান, ন্যায়শৃঙ্খল। **3.** (*Rhet.*) Figure of speech; অলঙ্কার। **4.** (*Kantian Philos.*) Any form of the transcendental imagination through which general thinking is enabled to apply its categories to phenomena; (কাণ্টের দর্শন) অতীন্দ্রিয় কল্পনার রূপ বিশেষ — যদ্দ্বারা সাধারণ মনন উহার পদার্থসমূহ প্রপঞ্চগত বিষয়ে প্রয়োগ করিতে পারে, মূলরূপ। [মূলরূপ (schema) স্বরূপতঃ কল্পনাসম্ভূত এবং বিষয় ভিন্ন আর কিছুই নহে। কিন্তু যেহেতু কল্পনার সংশ্লেষণের (synthesis) লক্ষ্য কেবল একটীমাত্র বোধি (intuition) নহে কিন্তু ইন্দ্রিয় চেতনা নিশ্চয়ী করণের জন্য একত্ব মাত্র (determination of sensibility) সুতরাং প্রতিরূপ (image) এবং মূলরূপ এতদুভয়ের মধ্যে যে পার্থক্য রহিয়াছে তাহা স্পষ্টতঃই বোধগম্য। অতএব যদি আমি পর পর ◦ ◦ ◦ ◦ ◦ পাঁচটী বিন্দু স্থাপন করি তবে, ইহাকে ৫ এই সংখ্যার প্রতিরূপ বলা যাইতে পারে। পক্ষান্তরে যদি আমি কেবল একটী সাধারণ সংখ্যা ভাবি—যে সংখ্যা ৫ কিম্বা ১০০ উভয়ই হইতে পারে—তবে এইরূপ মনন (বস্তুর) প্রতিরূপ না হইয়া বরং এরূপ কোন উপায়ের প্রতিরূপ হইয়া দাঁড়ায় যাহা কোনরূপ বিভাবনের অনুযায়ী কোন সংখ্যা (যথা, ১,০০০) প্রদর্শন করে। এই উপায়ে প্রতিরূপ দর্শনযোগ্য করা কিম্বা উক্ত বিভাবনের সহিত তুলনা করা সুকঠিন। এক্ষণে কোনরূপ বিভাবনের প্রতিরূপ উপস্থাপনের জন্য (to present image) কল্পনার কোন সাধারণ ক্রিয়া-পদ্ধতির যে এবম্প্রকার প্রতিরূপ (representation) তাহাকেই আমি ঐ বিভাবনের মূলরূপ বলিয়া আখ্যা প্রদান করি।—ক্যাণ্টের অনুবাদ।] **5.** (In Leibnitz's monadology) The principle which is essential to each monad, and constitutes its peculiar characteristic; (লেইবনিজের জীবতত্ত্বে) প্রতি জীবের (monad) সারতত্ত্ব।

schē-măt'-ic, *adj.* Pertaining to a schema; পরিকল্পনাসম্বন্ধীয়, মূলরূপ সম্বন্ধীয়। **–ism,** *n.*

scheme (skēm), *n., v. t.* & *i.* **1.** Design; system; purpose; পরিকল্পনা, যুক্তি; প্রকার (হিঃ কোঃ), সূত্র (ঐ), অনুসন্ধি (ঐ), ব্যবস্থা; উদ্দেশ্য। **2.** An outline; as, to draw a *scheme* of Calcutta; নক্সা, আদরা। **3.** A contrivance; artful or underhand design; কৌশল; ফন্দি, ফিকির, উপায়, চাতুরী, চক্রান্ত। **4.** (*Astrol.*) A representation or diagram of the aspects of celestial bodies at a given time; রাশি-চক্র। ***Verb t.*** **1.** To plan; to contrive; to plot; to design; কল্পনা করা; কৌশল পূর্ব্বক উদ্ভাবন করা; চক্রান্ত করা; পরিকল্পনা করা। **2.** To play truant from school; to go on the spree; স্কুল হইতে পালান; মদ্যপানোৎসবে মত্ত হওয়া। ***Verb i.*** To form a plan; ফন্দী আঁটা, উপায় উদ্ভাবন করা। **Schem'-er,** *n.* **Schem'-ing,** *adj.* **1.** Planning; উপায় উদ্ভাবনকারী। **2.** Artful; intriguing; চালাক, কৌশলী, ফন্দীবাজ; চক্রান্তকারী, কুমন্ত্রণাকারী। **Scheme-arch**—অর্দ্ধবৃত্তাপেক্ষা অল্প আয়তনের তোরণ। **Scheme of colours**—কোন বিশেষ চিত্রকরের বা চিত্রকলা-পদ্ধতির অনুযায়ী বর্ণনির্ব্বাচন বা বর্ণবিন্যাস রীতি। **Wild cut scheme**—যে ব্যবস্থা অনুযায়ী সফলতা লাভ অসম্ভব।

scherzando, (*It.*), *adv.* (*Mus.*) In a lively manner; স্ফূর্ত্তির সহিত, সলীলভাবে।

Schie-dăm′ (skë-), *n.* Gin imported from Holland ; হলণ্ড হইতে সমানীত মদ্য।

schip′-per-kē (-ēr-), *n.* A kind of lapdog ; একপ্রকার ক্ষুদ্র কুক্কুর।

schism (sĭzm), *n.* **1.** A division or separation ; ভেদ, দলাদলি। **2.** A breach of unity among people of the same religious faith ; সমধর্ম্মাবলম্বিগণের মধ্যে বিচ্ছেদ বা মতভেদ, ধর্ম্মভেদ (হিঃ কোঃ)।

schis-măt′-ic (sĭz-), **–i-căl,** *adj.* & *n.* Pertaining to schism ; implying schism ; ধর্ম্মভেদসম্বন্ধীয় ; ধর্ম্মভেদসূচক। ***Noun.*** One who separates from an established church or religion ; one who partakes in a schism ; বিধিপ্রতিষ্ঠিত ধর্ম্মসংঘ বা ধর্ম্মত্যাগী ব্যক্তি ; ধর্ম্মভেদে যোগদানকারী।

schist (shĭst), *n.* A rock of slaty structure ; শ্লেট পাথরের স্তরবিশিষ্ট পাষাণবিশেষ।

schiz-ăn′-thŭs (shĭz-), *n.* A genus of annual plants, with dainty white, violet or crimson flowers ; পুষ্পবৃক্ষের "গণ" বিশেষ। এই গণের অন্তর্ভুক্ত বিভিন্নজাতীয় তরুতে শ্বেত, বেগুণে ও লোহিতবর্ণের পুষ্প প্রস্ফুটিত হইয়া থাকে।

schiz-o-car′-pous (shĭz-ö-câr-pŭs), *n.* A dry fruit which splits at maturity into several closed one-seeded portions ; যে শুষ্ক ফল পক্বাবস্থায় বিদীর্ণ হইয়া কতিপয় রুদ্ধ এক বীজযুক্ত অংশে পরিণত হয়, ভেদকফল (সাঃ পঃ)।

schi-zŏg′-ă-mȳ (shĭ-), *n.* Reproduction by division of the body into a sexual and asexual individual ; দেহ, সলিঙ্গ এবং অলিঙ্গ অংশে বিভাজনদ্বারা প্রজনন ; উদ্ভিজ্জতা (হিঃ কোঃ)।

schi-zog′-e-nous (shĭ-zŏg-ĕ-nŭs), *adj.* (*Bot.*) Formed by fission ; (উদ্ভিদ্‌বিদ্যা) বিভিন্ন খণ্ডের বিদারণ ফলে গঠিত, ভেদজনিত (সাঃ পঃ)।

schiz-ō-mȳ-cē′-tēs (shĭz-), *n.* Same as SCHIZOPHYTA (which see).

schi-zŏph′-ȳ-tă (shĭ-), *n.* A subdivision of the Thallophytes embracing the group of minute organisms familiarly known as Bacteria and sometimes designated Schizomycetes or splitting fungi ; ভেদছত্রিকা (সাঃ পঃ), ভেদোদ্ভিদ্ (ঐ)।

schi-zŏp′-ŏ-dă (shĭ-), *n.* A tribe of long-tailed decapod crustaceans; সামুদ্রিক চিংড়ী মৎস্যের শ্রেণী বিশেষ।

schmelze (shmĕls), *n.* Various kinds of coloured glass ; বিভিন্ন প্রকার রঙ্গীন কাচ।

schnap(p)s (shnăps), *n.* Holland gin ; হলণ্ড দেশীয় মদ্য বিশেষ।

schŏl′-ar (-ĕr), *n.* **1.** (*Archaic*) A pupil ; ছাত্র, অন্তেবাসী, শিষ্য। **2.** A learned man ; পণ্ডিত, বিদ্বান, বিদ্বজ্জন, বিবুধ, সুধী, বিদ্যানিধান, সুরী, ভট্ট। **3.** One that learns anything ; যে ব্যক্তি কোন বিষয় শিক্ষা করে, শিক্ষার্থী। **4.** One who holds a scholarship ; বৃত্তিধারী ছাত্র। **–ly,** *adj.* Exhibiting scholarship ; পাণ্ডিত্যপূর্ণ। **–ship,** *n.* **1.** Erudition ; attainments in science or literature ; বিদ্যাবত্তা ; পাণ্ডিত্য। **2.** An allowance to a student to aid him in the prosecution of his studies ; বৃত্তি, ছাত্রবৃত্তি, জলপানি (*colloq*)।

schō-lăs′-tic, *adj.* & *n.* **1.** Pertaining to a scholar or school ; scholar like ; ছাত্রসম্বন্ধীয়, বিদ্যালয়সম্বন্ধীয়, বিদ্যালয়সংক্রান্ত, বিদ্যালয়বিষয়ক ; পাণ্ডিত্যোচিত, পণ্ডিতী (হিঃ কোঃ)। **2.** Pedantic ; subtle ; as, *scholastic* precision ; পাণ্ডিত্যাভিমানী, বিদ্যাভিমানসূচক ; সূক্ষ্ম, চুলচেরা, পণ্ডিতী। **3.** Pertaining to scholastic philosophy ; মধ্যযুগের দার্শনিকবাদবিশেষসম্বন্ধীয়। ***Noun.*** An adherent of scholastic philosophy ; মধ্যযুগের দার্শনিক। **–ti-cism,** *n.* Scholastic philosophy ; মধ্যযুগের খৃষ্টীয় ধর্ম্মশাস্ত্র ও দার্শনিক মত, পণ্ডিতী বিচার (হিঃ কোঃ)। [এই ধর্ম্মমত ও দার্শনিক মত প্রধানতঃ খৃষ্টীয় ধর্ম্মের আদিমাচার্য্যগণ এবং আরিস্তোতল ও তদীয় টীকাকারগণের মতবাদের উপর প্রতিষ্ঠিত।]

schō′-li-ăst, *n.* **1.** A writer of the scholium ; পার্শ্বটীপ্পনীলেখক। **2.** A name given to the old critics or grammarians who annotated the classics ; টীকাকার, ভাষ্যকার, বৃত্তিকার।

schō-li-ŭm, *n.* **1.** A marginal note, annotation or remark ; a comment esp. on the text of a classic by an old grammarian ; পার্শ্বটীকা, পার্শ্বটীপ্পনী ; ভাষ্য, টীকা, বৃত্তি।

schōōl, *n., adj.* & *v. t.* **1.** A place for the instruction of pupils and students ; স্কুল, বিদ্যালয়, বিদ্যামন্দির, শিক্ষাগৃহ, শিক্ষালয়, শিক্ষামন্দির, অধ্যয়নাগার, চতুষ্পাঠী (for Sanskrit students)। **2.** A college in the middle ages for instructing in the various branches of speculative knowledge ; মধ্যযুগে ন্যায়দর্শন প্রভৃতি শিক্ষার্থ মহাবিদ্যালয়। **3.** The system of a master; as, the Italian *school* ; বৈজ্ঞানিক, দার্শনিক, চিত্রকর প্রভৃতির বিশেষ তন্ত্র বা সম্প্রদায়, সম্প্রদায় (ব্রজঃ বৈষ্ণঃ)। **4.** A system or state of matter prevalent at certain time, a body of persons united by a general similarity of principles or methods ; as, a painter of New *school* ; কোন নির্দ্দিষ্ট কালের পদ্ধতি বা ব্যবস্থা, তন্ত্র (নব্যতন্ত্র), শাখা। **5.** The persons instructed ; as, to teach a *school* ; school hours ; "Where between *schools* the children play with flowers" ; ছাত্রবৃন্দ ; যে নির্দ্দিষ্ট কয়েক ঘণ্টা বিদ্যালয়ে পাঠ করিতে হয়। **6.** A training-ground ; শিক্ষাস্থল, শিক্ষাস্থান। **7.** The room or hall in English universities where examinations for honours or degrees are held ; ইংলণ্ডীয় বিশ্ববিদ্যালয়ের যে কক্ষে বা দালানে উপাধি বা অনার্স পরীক্ষা গৃহীত হয়

8. The B. A. Examination of Oxford; one of the subjects for B. A. Examination in Oxford; অক্সফোর্ড বিশ্ববিদ্যালয়ের বি, এ পরীক্ষা; ঐ পরীক্ষার জন্য পঠনীয় কোন বিষয়। *Adj.* 1. Pertaining to a school; বিদ্যালয়সম্বন্ধীয়। 2. Of, or pertaining to, schoolmen; মধ্যযুগের খৃষ্টীয়শাস্ত্রবিদ্ দার্শনিকগণসম্বন্ধীয়। *Verb t.* 1. To teach; শিক্ষা দেওয়া। 2. To train; শিক্ষিত করা। 3. (*Rare*) To rebuke; (কচিদ্-ব্যবহৃত) তিরস্কার করা, ভর্ৎসনা করা। **School'-ing,** *n.* 1. Teaching; শিক্ষাপ্রদান। 2. Reproof; as, to give one a severe *schooling*; তিরস্কার, ভর্ৎসনা। 3. Money paid for instructions given; ছাত্রবেতন। **School-board**—স্থানীয় শিক্ষাসংক্রান্ত-ব্যাপারের ভারপ্রাপ্ত সমিতি, শিক্ষাসমিতি [ইংলণ্ডে (১৮৭০ হইতে ১৯০৩ খৃঃ অব্দ পর্য্যন্ত) স্থানীয় বালকদিগের প্রাথমিক শিক্ষার তত্ত্বাবধানের জন্য করদাতৃগণ কর্ত্তৃক নির্ব্বাচিত ব্যক্তিবর্গ। উক্ত ব্যক্তিবর্গ ঐ স্থানের প্রত্যেক বালকের প্রাথমিক শিক্ষার জন্য ব্যবস্থা করিয়া থাকেন এবং আবশ্যক বোধ করিলে প্রাথমিক শিক্ষার সুব্যবস্থার জন্য ইঁহারা অতিরিক্ত কর বসাইতে পারেন। স্কটলণ্ডে অদ্যাপি উক্তরূপ ব্যবস্থা প্রচলিত আছে।] **School-book**—বিদ্যালয়ের পাঠ্যপুস্তক। **Schoolboy**—বিদ্যালয়ের ছাত্র। **School-days**—পঠদ্দশা, ছাত্রজীবন। **School fee, School-fees**—ছাত্রবেতন। **School-fellow, School-mate**—সহপাঠী, সহাধ্যায়ী, সতীর্থ। **School-girl**—বিদ্যালয়ের ছাত্রী। **School-going**—বিদ্যালয়গমন (*Noun*); বিদ্যালয়গামী (*Adj.*)। **School-house**—বিদ্যালয় গৃহ। **School-Inspector**—বিদ্যালয়-পরিদর্শক কর্ম্মচারিবিশেষ। **School-man**—মধ্যযুগের দার্শনিক এবং খৃষ্টীয় পণ্ডিত। [St. Thomas Aquinas, Anselm, Duns Scotus, Alexander of Hales, প্রভৃতি।] **School-master**—শিক্ষক। **School-mistress**—শিক্ষয়িত্রী। **School-room**—বিদ্যালয়ের অধ্যাপনাকক্ষ। **School-teacher**—Same as SCHOOL MASTER. **Commercial school**—ব্যবসায়বাণিজ্য সংক্রান্ত কার্য্যশিক্ষার জন্য বিদ্যালয়, বাণিজ্য-বিদ্যালয়। **Continuation school**—কোন ব্যক্তি পাঠশালা পরিত্যাগের পর কোন ব্যবসায় অবলম্বন করিতে বাধ্য হইলে সে অবসরকালে (সাধারণতঃ) রাত্রিকালে যে বিদ্যালয়ে পাঠ করে, ক্রমিক বিদ্যালয়। **Free school**—অবৈতনিক বিদ্যালয়। **Night-school**—নৈশবিদ্যালয়। **Primary school**—প্রাথমিক বিদ্যালয়। **Secondary school**—প্রাথমিক বিদ্যালয় (পাঠশালা প্রভৃতি) এবং কলেজ প্রভৃতির মধ্যবর্ত্তী বিদ্যালয়, মাধ্যমিক বিদ্যালয় (যথা প্রবেশিকা বিদ্যালয়।) **Technical school**—শিল্পবিদ্যালয়। **School of Mathematics**—গণিতসম্প্রদায় (হিঃ কোঃ)। **The school master is abroad**—See under ABROAD. **To tell tales out of school**—To let the cat out of the bag; হাটে হাঁড়ি ভাঙ্গা, গুপ্তকথা প্রকাশ করা।

sc͟hōōl, *n.* & *v. i.* A shoal of fish; মাছের ঝাঁক। *Verb i.* To form a shoal; ঝাঁক বাঁধা। **School-fish**—যে সকল মাছ ঝাক বাঁধিয়া থাকে, সংঘচারী মৎস্য।

sc͟hōōl'-ȧ-ble (-bl), *adj.* Liable to go to school; বিদ্যালয়গমনার্হ।

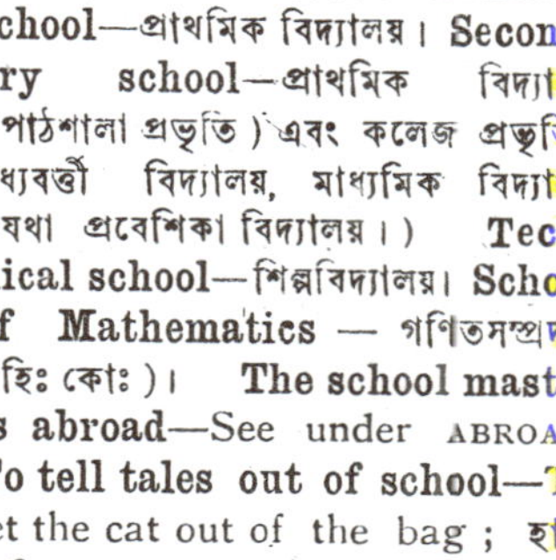

Topsail schooner.

sc͟hōōn'-ẽr, *n.* A small two-masted vessel; একপ্রকার ক্ষুদ্র দ্বিমাস্তুল পোত।

s͟chorl (shŏrl), *n.* A variety of tourmaline; একপ্রকার তুর্ম্মলীন।

schot'-tische (shŏt-tĭsh), **-tish,** *ns.* A kind of polka; music for it; একপ্রকার নৃত্য; ঐ নৃত্যের উপযোগী সঙ্গীত।

sci-ăg'-ră-phy̆ (sī-), *n.* 1. The art of delineating shadows; ছায়াচিত্রণ কলা। 2. Photography by Rontgen rays; রঞ্জনআলোর সাহায্যে আলোকচিত্র গ্রহণ। 3. The profile or vertical section of a building to exhibit its interior structure; হর্ম্ম্যের অভ্যন্তরভাগ প্রদর্শনের জন্য উহার পার্শ্বচিত্র বা লম্বচ্ছেদ। 4. The art of dialling; শঙ্কু-বিজ্ঞান, সূর্য্য-ঘড়ীনির্ম্মাণকলা, ছায়াযন্ত্রনির্ম্মাণকলা। **-raph-er,** *n.* **-raph-ic,** *adj.* **-raph-i-cal-ly,** *adv.* **Sci'-a-graph,** *n.* & *v. t.*

sci-ăm'-ȧ-c͟hy̆ (sī-), *n.* A fighting with a shadow; an imaginary or futile combat; ছায়ার সহিত যুদ্ধ; নিষ্ফল যুদ্ধ, কল্পিত যুদ্ধ।

sci-ăm'-ĕt-ry̆ (sī-), *n.* Theory of eclipses; গ্রহণতত্ত্ব।

sci-ā-thẽr'-ic (sī-), *adj.* Of, or pertaining to, a sundial; সূর্য্যঘড়ী-সম্বন্ধীয়, ছায়াযান্ত্রিক।

sci-ăt'-ic (sī-), *adj.* 1. Of, or pertaining to, the hip; শ্রোণিসম্বন্ধীয়। 2. Affecting the hip; শ্রোণিসংক্রান্ত। **Sciatic nerve**—কটি-স্নায়ু।

sci-ăt'-ĭ-ca (sī-), *n.* Neuralgia or inflammation of the sciatic nerve or great nerve of the thigh; কটিস্নায়ুর অনুগামী একপ্রকার বেদনা বা বাত, গৃধ্রসী (সাঃ পঃ), কটিশূল, কটিবাত, বস্তিশূল (ভাবপ্রকাশ), শ্রোণিবেদনা, শ্রোণিশিরাবেদনা।

sci'-ence (sī-ĕns), *n.* 1. Knowledge; জ্ঞান। 2. Knowledge duly arranged and systematized; বিজ্ঞান-বিদ্যা (হিঃ কোঃ), শাস্ত্র (শ্রীঃ), শাসন (ঐ), অনুশাসন (ঐ)। **Natural** or **Physical science**—পদার্থবিজ্ঞান। **Pure science**—স্বতঃসিদ্ধ সত্যসমূহের উপর প্রতিষ্ঠিত

বিজ্ঞান, যথা গণিতশাস্ত্র, ন্যায়শাস্ত্র প্রভৃতি। **Science of medicine**—বৈদ্যবিদ্যা (সাঃ পঃ)। **Science of surgery**—শস্ত্রবিদ্যা (ঐ)। **The dismal science**—অর্থনীতিশাস্ত্র। **The science**—(ইতর ভাষায়) মুষ্টিযুদ্ধ।

sci-ĕn′-têr (sī-), *adv.* (*Legal*) Knowingly; (আইন) জ্ঞানপূর্ব্বক।

sci-ĕn-tif′-ic (sī-), *adj.* **1.** Pertaining to science; বৈজ্ঞানিক, বিজ্ঞানসম্পৃক্ত (জিঃ), শাস্ত্রীয় (হিঃ কোঃ)। **2.** According to the rules of science; বিজ্ঞানসম্মত, বিদ্যাসূত্রানুযায়ী। **Scientific apparatus** — বৈজ্ঞানিক যন্ত্র (হিঃ কোঃ)। **Scientific chemist**—বৈজ্ঞানিক রসায়ন (ঐ)। **Scientific method**—বৈজ্ঞানিক রীতি।

sci′-ĕn-tist (sī-), *n.* One versed in science, esp. natural science; বৈজ্ঞানিক, বিজ্ঞানবিৎ।

scil′-i-cĕt (sĭl-), *adv.* That is to say; অর্থাৎ।

scim′-i-tar (sĭm-ĭ-têr), *n.* A short curved oriental sword; ভোজালী, তরবার, বক্র খড়্গ, কৃপাণ।

scin-til′-lă (sĭn-), *n.* **1.** A spark; স্ফুলিঙ্গ, অগ্নিকণা, আগুনের ফুলকি। **2.** An atom; কণা, তিল। **–lant,** *adj.*

scin′-til-lāte (sĭn-), *v. i.* **1.** To emit spark; স্ফুলিঙ্গ নির্গত করা। **2.** To sparkle; to twinkle, as the fixed stars; ঝিক্‌মিক্ করা, ঝক্‌মক্ করা; মিট মিট করা। **–la′-tion,** *n.* **1.** The act of scintillating; স্ফুলিঙ্গ নির্গম। **2.** A spark; স্ফুলিঙ্গ। **3.** A flash or brilliant display (of wit etc.); বুদ্ধি প্রভৃতির চমক, দীপ্তি। **Scintillation of stars**—নক্ষত্রোন্মীলন (হিঃ কোঃ)।

sci′-ŏ-list (sī-), *n.* **1.** A smatterer, or one who knows many things superficially; পল্লবগ্রাহী, পণ্ডিতম্মন্য। **–lism,** *n.* A show of learning without substantial foundation; পল্লবগ্রাহিতা। **–lis′-tic,** *adj.*

sciolto, (*It.*), (*Mus.*) In free manner; স্বচ্ছন্দভাবে।

sci-ŏm′-ă-chy̆ (sī-), *n.* Same as SCIAMACHY (which see).

sci′-ŏn (sī-), *n.* **1.** A shoot of plant esp. for the purpose of being grafted; কলমের ডাল, পল্লব, প্রশাখা, পরবৃক্ষাঙ্গ। **2.** A descendant (esp. of a noble family); বংশধর (বিশেষতঃ সম্ভ্রান্ত বংশের)।

sci-ŏp′-t(r)ics, (sī-), *n.* The science of exhibiting images of external objects received through a double convex glass into a darkened room; অন্ধকার গৃহে দ্বিবহির্বর্ত্তুল কাচের ভিতর দিয়া গৃহীত বহির্ব্বর্ত্তী বস্তুর প্রতিচ্ছায়া প্রদর্শনসংক্রান্ত বিজ্ঞান। **–t(r)ic,** *adj.*

Sci′-ōte (sī-) **–ŏt,** *ns.* An inhabitant of Scio, the ancient Chios; Scio নামক স্থানের অধিবাসী।

sci-re–fa′-ci-ăs (sī-rē—fā-shi-), (Abbr. *Sci. fa*) *n.* A writ to enforce, quash or annul judgments, patent, etc.; রায়, প্যাটেন্ট, প্রভৃতি আমলে আনা বা রদ করার জন্য পরোয়ানাবিশেষ।

sci-rŏc′-cŏ (sī-), *n.* Same as SIROCCO (which see).

scir′-rhus (-rŭs), *n.* A hard tumour on any part of the body; কঠিন অর্ব্বুদ। **–rhoid, –rhous,** *adjs.*

scis′-sĕl (sĭs-), *n.* **1.** Clippings of metal made in various mechanical operations; ধাতুর ছাঁট। **2.** The slips of metals from which discs have been cut for the purpose of coinage; যে ধাতুখণ্ডসমূহ হইতে মুদ্রার জন্য চাকতি প্রস্তুত করা হয়।

scis′-sile (sĭs-sĭl), *adj.* Capable of being cut easily; অনায়াসচ্ছেদ্য।

scis′-sion (sĭ-), *n.* Act of cutting or splitting; ছেদন, বিদারণ, ভেদন।

scis′-sor (sĭ-zêr), *v. t.* To cut with scissors; to prepare with the help of scissors; কাঁচিদ্বারা কাটা; কাঁচির সাহায্যে প্রস্তুত করা।

scis′-sors (sĭz-ĕrz), *n.* A cutting instrument consisting of two blades which meet and cut an object placed between them; কাঁচি, খণ্ডধার (মঃ উঃ), ক্রীবী, কর্ত্তরিকা, পট্ট সন্দংশ, শরালী মুখ (সুশ্রুঃ কুঞ্জঃ)। **Scissor′-wise,** *adv.* In the manner of scissors; কাঁচির মত। **Scissor-bird, Scissor-tail** — একপ্রকার পক্ষী—ইহাদের পুচ্ছ দেখিতে অনেকটা কাঁচির মত বলিয়া এই নাম। **Scissor-tooth**—মাংসাশী জন্তুদিগের দন্তবিশেষ। **Scissor and paste**—অপর ব্যক্তির রচনার অংশসমূহ কাঁচি দিয়া কাটিয়া পুস্তকসংকলন।

sci′-ū-rīne (sī-), *adj.* Pertaining to the squirrel tribe; squirrel-like; কাষ্ঠমার্জ্জারজাতিসম্বন্ধীয়; কাষ্ঠবিড়ালবৎ, কাষ্ঠমার্জ্জারবৎ।

Sclăv, Sclăv-ŏn-ic, See SLAV, SLAVONIC.

sclĕ′-ră, *n.* Same as SCLEROTIC (which see.)

sclere (sklēr), *n.* A spicule esp. of a sponge; সূচিকাবৎ অংশ—বিশেষতঃ স্পঞ্জের সূচ্যাকার অংশ।

sclĕ-rē′-mă, *n.* Same as SCLEROMA (which see.)

sclĕ-rĕn′-chy̆-mă, *n.* **1.** The calcareous tissue of which a coral is composed; যে চূর্ণময় বিধানতন্ত্র হইতে প্রবাল রচিত হয়। **2.** (*Bot.*) A tissue forming the hard parts of plants such as nutshell; (উদ্ভিদ্-বিদ্যা) যে বিধান-তন্তুদ্বারা উদ্ভিদের কঠিন অংশ গঠিত হয়।

sclĕ′-rī-ă-sis, *n.* Any hard tumour or induration; কঠিন অর্ব্বুদ।

sclĕ-rī′-tis, *n.* Same as SCLEROTITIS (which see.)

sclĕ′-rŏ-blăst, *n.* One of the cells of a sponge by which a sclere is formed; স্পঞ্জের যে অণুকোষদ্বারা সূচ্যাকার অংশ গঠিত হয়, দৃষকোষ (সাঃ পঃ)।

sclĕ-rŏ-dêr′-mă, –tă, *ns.* A family of fishes or reptiles having skins covered with hard scales; কঠিন শল্কাবৃত মৎস্যশ্রেণী,

কঠিনশল্কী, দৃঢ়চর্ম্মী, চর্ম্মাখ্য (সাঃ পঃ)। **—mous, —tous,** *adjs.*

sclē′-rō-gĕn, *n.* The hard matter deposited on the inner surface of the cells of plants; উদ্ভিদের কোষাভ্যন্তরে সঞ্চিত কঠিন পদার্থ।

sclē′-roid (-roȳd), *adj.* (*Bot.* & *Zool.*) Having a hard structure; কঠিনগঠন বিশিষ্ট।

sclē-rō′-mă, —rē′-mă, *ns.* (*Med.*) Induration of cellular tissue; (ভৈষজ্য শাস্ত্র) কৌষিক ঝিল্লীর দার্ঢ্য।

sclē-rō′-sĭs, *n.* **1.** Same as SCLEROMA. **2.** Induration of the nervous system; স্নায়ুমণ্ডলের দার্ঢ্য। [এই দৃঢ়তা মস্তিষ্কে জন্মিলে তাহাকে সেরিব্রাল স্ক্লিরোসিস্, পৃষ্ঠবংশীয় মজ্জায় স্পাইনেল স্ক্লিরোসিস্, স্নায়ুমণ্ডলের স্থানে স্থানে অথবা বিবিধ স্নায়ুতে হইলে মাল্টিপেল স্ক্লিরোসিস্ কহে।] **Sclerosis of the brain, Cerebral sclerosis**—মস্তিষ্কের দৃঢ়তা।

sclē-rō-skĕl′-ē-tŏn, *n.* The hardened or ossified fibrous and tendinous tissues which enclose organs; শারীরযন্ত্রসমূহের আবরক কঠিনীভূত বা অস্থিতে পরিণত অংশুল এবং কণ্ডরাধর্ম্ম বিধানতন্তুসমূহ।

sclē-rŏt′-ic, *adj.* & *n.* Hard; firm; কঠিন; দৃঢ়। ***Noun.*** The dense outer membrane of the eye-ball; অক্ষিগোলকের শুভ্রাংশ নির্ম্মাণকর দৃঢ়, শুভ্র, অস্বচ্ছ, তন্তুময় বিধান; শুভ্রপটল (সাঃ পঃ), শুভ্রমণ্ডল।

sclē-rō-tī′-tis, *n.* Inflammation of the sclerotic coat; তারকামণ্ডলের চতুর্দ্দিকস্থ আবরকচর্ম্মের প্রদাহ, শুভ্রমণ্ডলপ্রদাহ।

sclē-rŏt′-ō-mȳ, *n.* Incision of the sclera; চক্ষুর বহির্ঝিল্লীচ্ছেদন।

sclē′-rous (-rŭs), *adj.* Hard, bony; কঠিন; অস্থিময়।

scŏbs, *n.* Sawdust; dross of metals etc.; raspings of metals, ivory, etc.; করাতের গুঁড়া; ধাতুমল প্রভৃতি; ধাতু, গজদন্ত, প্রভৃতির ছাঁট। **Scob′-i-form,** *adj.*

scŏff, *n., v. i.* & *t.* **1.** An expression of scorn or contempt; taunt; বিদ্রূপোক্তি; বিদ্রূপ, শ্লেষ, উপহাস, অবহাস। **2.** An object of derision; a laughing-stock; উপহাসের পাত্র; বিদ্রূপের পাত্র। ***Verb i.*** To utter scoffs and contemptuous language; বিদ্রূপ করা, শ্লেষ করা, ব্যঙ্গ করা। ***Verb t.*** To treat with scorn; to mock at; অবজ্ঞার সহিত ব্যবহার করা; বিদ্রূপ করা। **Scoff′-er,** *n.* **Scoff′-ing-ly,** *adv.*

scōld, *v. i., t.* & *n.* **1.** To find fault or rail with rude clamour; বকুনি দেওয়া, গালি দেওয়া, মুখ করা। ***Verb t.*** To rebuke; তিরস্কার করা, ভর্ৎসনা করা, গঞ্জনা করা। ***Noun.*** A railing woman; as, the *scold* of a wife; দুর্ম্মুখা স্ত্রীলোক, কটুভাষিণী স্ত্রীলোক।

scō′-lĕx, *n.* The larva of the tape-worm; ফিতা ক্রিমির পোকা।

scō-li-ō′-sĭs, *n.* A distortion of the spine to one side; মেরুদণ্ডের পার্শ্বিক বক্রতা।

scŏl′-lop (-ŏp), *n.* & *v. t.* Same as SCALLOP (which see).

scŏl-ō-pā′-ceous (-shŭs), **scŏl-ō-pā′-cīne, scŏl-ō-pā′-coid** (-coȳd), *adjs.* Pertaining to the snipes; like snipes; কাদাখোঁচাসম্বন্ধীয়; কাদাখোঁচার মত।

scŏl-ō-pĕn′-dră, *n.* A centipede; শতপদী। **—drine,** *adj.*

scŏl-ō-pĕn′-dri-ŭm, *n.* A general name for various kinds of ferns; বিবিধপ্রকার পর্ণাঙ্গের সাধারণ নাম।

scŏm′-bêr, *n.* Mackerel; সামুদ্রিক মৎস্যবিশেষ।

scŏn, *n.* Same as SCONE (which see).

sconce (skŏns), *n.* & *v. t.* **1.** (*Archaic*) A protection; a screen; (কচিদ্ ব্যবহৃত) আশ্রয়; পর্দ্দা। **2.** A case or tube for a candle; a hanging candlestick or one fixed on a wall; শামাদান; দোলায়মান বা প্রাচীরসংবদ্ধ মোমবাতির শামাদান। **3.** A small fort or redoubt; ক্ষুদ্র দুর্গ বা উপদুর্গ। **4.** (In the university of Oxford etc.) Fine; জরিমানা। **5.** A cover or protection for a light; a lantern for a candle; a dark lantern; আলোর আবরণ; মোমবাতির লণ্ঠন; চোরা লণ্ঠন। **6.** Helmet; শিরস্ত্রাণ। **7.** (*Colloq.*) The head; skull; (চলিত ভাষায়) মাথা; করোটী। **8.** A fragment of an ice-floe; প্রবমান হিমানীস্তরের খণ্ড। ***Verb t.*** (In Oxford univ. etc.) **1.** To fine; জরিমানা করা। **2.** To imprison; কারারুদ্ধ করা।

scŏn, scōne, *ns.* A kind of thin cake; একপ্রকার রুটি।

scoop, *n.* & *v. t.* **1.** An implement of the nature of a shovel or ladle for lifting things; জিনিষ তোলার জন্য হাতা বা জলসেচনীর ন্যায় পাত্রবিশেষ। **2.** A vessel with a long handle used to raise, throw out, water or other fluid; জলসেচন বা জলোত্তলনার্থ লম্বা হাতলওয়ালা পাত্রবিশেষ, জলসেচনী। **3.** An instrument for hollowing out; কোন কিছু খোঁড়ার জন্য যন্ত্রবিশেষ। **4.** A spoon-shaped vessel used to extract certain foreign bodies; অস্ত্র চিকিৎসদিগের চমসাকার (চামচের আকার) যন্ত্রবিশেষ। **5.** A place hollowed out; খনিত স্থান। **6.** A coal-scuttle; কয়লার ঝুড়ি। **7.** (A cant term on the Stock Exchange) Sudden breaking down of prices for the purpose of buying stocks at cheaper rates, followed by a rise; সস্তাদরে কোম্পানীর কাগজ ক্রয়ের জন্য হঠাৎ মূল্য হ্রাস করণ। ***Verb t.*** **1.** To take out with, or as with, a scoop; to bale out; to gather in; তক্ষণী দ্বারা খুদিয়া বাহির করা, তক্ষণীবৎ কোন কিছু দ্বারা খুদিয়া বাহির করা; নৌকাদি হইতে জলসেচন করা; কুড়াইয়া আনা। **2.** To empty by lading; as, to *scoop* a boat dry; সেচিয়া খালি করা। 3. To excavate; to dig out; to make hollow; ক্ষোদন করা, খুঁড়া; ক্ষুদিয়া তুলিয়া ফেলা; ক্ষুদিয়া শূন্যগর্ভ করা। 4. (*Slang*) To secure large profit etc. by sudden action or stroke of luck; (ইতর ভাষায়) হঠাৎ কোন কার্য্য করিয়া বা দৈববশে অনেক টাকা লাভ প্রভৃতি করা। **Scoop-net**—বেড়াজাল। **Scoop-wheel**—নদী প্রভৃতির তলকর্ষণের জন্য চক্র এবং দ্রোণিশ্রেণী রচিত কৌশলবিশেষ।

scoop'-ẽr, *n.* 1. One who, or that which, scoops; a small chisel with a scoop-like blade used by engravers; ক্ষোদক; তক্ষণী, ক্ষোদন-যন্ত্র। 2. A kind of avocet; ইয়ুরোপের দীর্ঘচঞ্চু পক্ষিবিশেষ।

scoot, *v. i.* (*Slang*) To dart off; to rush; (ইতর ভাষায়) ছুটিয়া পালান; ভোঁ দৌড় দেওয়া।

scō'-pă, *n.* (*Entom.*) The pollen brush of a bee; (কীটতত্ত্ব) মৌমাছির পাদের সূক্ষ্মরোমগুচ্ছ—যদ্দারা উহারা পুষ্প হইতে পরাগ সংগ্রহ করে। **–pate**, **–pi-form**, *adjs.*

scōpe, *n.* 1. (*Now rare*) The object or end aimed at; (বর্ত্তমানে কচিদ্‌ব্যবহৃত) লক্ষ্য। 2. Intention; drift; as, the *scope* of a law; উদ্দেশ্য, অভিপ্রায়; আশয়। 3. Free or wide outlook or aim; as, a mind of wide *scope*; reach or range of mental activity; দৃষ্টি বা লক্ষ্যের অবাধ প্রসার; প্রসর, সীমা, গোচর, বিস্তার (হিঃ কোঃ), বিষয় (ঐ)। 4. Room or field for free observation or action; vent; as, to seek *scope* for one's energies; ক্রিয়াক্ষেত্র, কার্য্যক্ষেত্র, দৃষ্টিক্ষেত্র, কার্য্যের প্রসর; ক্রিয়ার অবকাশ।

scŏr-bū'-tic, *adj.* & *n.* Pertaining to, resembling, or affected with, scurvy; শীতাদরোগসম্পর্কীয়, শীতাদরোগসদৃশ, শীতাদরোগাক্রান্ত। ***Noun.*** A person affected with scurvy; শীতাদরোগাক্রান্ত।

scŏrch, *v. t., i.* & *n.* 1. To burn superficially; উপরিভাগ পোড়াইয়া দেওয়া, ঝলসান। 2. To affect painfully with heat; দগ্ধ করা। ***Verb i.*** 1. To be burnt on the surface; to be parched or dried up; ছেঁচকি পোড়া হওয়া, দগ্ধীভূত হওয়া; বিশুষ্ক হওয়া। 2. (Of a cyclist etc. *slang*) To drive or ride at a furious speed; নক্ষত্রবেগে ছুটা। ***Noun.*** (In the above sense.) **Scorch'-ing**, *adj.* 1. Burning; as, the *scorching* sun; অগ্নিবর্ষী, জ্বালামালাসঙ্কুল, প্রচণ্ড (cf. প্রচণ্ডসূর্য্যঃ—ঋতুসংহার। 2. Causing a burning sensation; জ্বালাকর। 3. Bitingly sarcastic; তীব্র বিদ্রূপাত্মক।

scŏrch'-ẽr, *n.* 1. That which scorches; দাহক। 2. (*Slang*) Anything finest of its kind; (ইতরভাষায়) সেরা জিনিষ, উমদা জিনিষ। 3. (*Slang*) One who rides or drives furiously; (ইতর ভাষায়) যে ব্যক্তি প্রচণ্ডবেগে অশ্ব, দ্বিচক্রযান, প্রভৃতি চালনা করে।

scōre, *n., v. t.* & *i.* 1. A notch or incision; খাঁজ। 2. The number twenty, as having been represented by a notch; কুড়ি। 3. (*Pl.*) A large number; বহুসংখ্যা। 4. long line or scratch; দীর্ঘরেখা বা আঁচড়। 5. An account; হিসাব। 6. Bill; debt; হোটেল প্রভৃতির পাওনার হিসাব; দেনা। 7. Runs, points, or hits, etc. made in game; ক্রীড়াঙ্ক। 8. (*Obs.*) Reason; motive; (অপ্রঃ) হেতু; উদ্দেশ্য। 9. (*Mus.*) Draft of a musical composition in which all the parts are brought together in two or more staves; স্বরলিপি। 10. Sake; দৌলত, কল্যাণ, খাতির। 11. Good fortune; as, what a *score*!; সৌভাগ্য। ***Verb t.*** 1. To make scores or scratches on; to mark with furrows, notches or incisions; লম্বা রেখা কাটা, উল্লেখন করা, মাছ প্রভৃতি আজা (East Bengal), কেঁচিয়া দেওয়া, দাগিয়া দেওয়া; খাঁজ কাটা। 2. To cause to be registered on one's account; as points, hils, in a game; ক্রীড়াঙ্ক। 3. To set down in an account; হিসাবে তোলা। 4. To incur debt; ধার করা। 5. To win; as to *score* a triumph; লাভ করা। 6. To write down music in proper order or arrangement; সঙ্গীতের স্বরলিপি লিখা। ***Verb i.*** 1. To make points in a game; ক্রীড়াঙ্ক লাভ করা। 2. To gain success; as, they are sure to *score*; কৃতকার্য্যতা লাভ করা, সিদ্ধিলাভ করা, সফলকাম হওয়া। **Scor'-er**, *n.* **Scor'-ing**, *n.* **Score-card, Scoring-card**—যে স্থূল কাগজের উপর ক্রীড়াঙ্ক প্রভৃতি লিখিত হয়। **In score**—(*Mus.*) Having the parts in proper order and methodically arranged; বিভিন্ন অংশ যথাক্রমে এবং প্রণালীবদ্ধভাবে সন্নিবিষ্ট ভাবে। **On the score of**—For the sake of; খাতিরে, কল্যাণে, দরুণ, দৌলতে। **To get the score**—To get the highest number of runs; সর্ব্বোচ্চ ক্রীড়াঙ্ক লাভ করা। **To go off, or set off at score**—(Of a horse) To run at a furious speed; (অশ্বসম্পর্কে) প্রচণ্ডবেগে ধাবিত হওয়া, নক্ষত্রবেগে ছুটা। To break out suddenly into an uncontrolled speech or action; সহসা উদ্দাম ভাবে বক্তৃতা দেওয়া বা আচরণ করা। **To pay off old scores**—To repay old grudges; প্রতিশোধ লওয়া, দাদ তোলা। **To quit score**—To clear off accounts; হিসাব চুকান, দেনা পাওনা মিটান। **To run up a score**—To buy things on credit; ধারে জিনিষ কেনা। To contract debt; ধার করা। **To score down**—To make with lines or scratches; দাগ কাটা। **To score off**—(*Slang*) To worst in argument or repartee ; to humiliate ; তর্কে পরাস্ত করা, ব্যঙ্গোক্তি দ্বারা পরাভূত করা ; মুখ চুণ করা। **To score out**—To cancel ; as, to *score out* some words; কাটিয়া ফেলা।

scō'-ri-ā, *n.* 1. Dross ; ধাতুমল। 2. (*Pl.*) Volcanic ashes ; আগ্নেয়গিরি হইতে নিঃসৃত ভস্ম। **—a'-ce-ous**, *adj.*

scō'-ri-fȳ, *v. t.* To reduce to dross ; to separate the dross from the valuable metals ; ধাতুমলে পরিণত করা ; স্বর্ণরৌপ্যাদি মূল্যবান ধাতু হইতে খাদ বাহির করা। **—fi-ca'-tion**, *n.* **—fi-er**, *n.* A small cup used in assaying ; পরখের উদ্দেশ্যে ধাতু গালাইবার জন্য ক্ষুদ্র পাত্র।

scŏrn, *n.* & *v. t.* 1. Extreme disdain ; derision ; দারুণ ঘৃণা, বিজাতীয় ঘৃণা ; অবজ্ঞা, অশ্রদ্ধা। 2. An object of extreme disdain ; দারুণ ঘৃণার পাত্র। ***Verb t.*** To despise exceedingly ; যৎপরোনাস্তি ঘৃণা করা, দারুণ অবজ্ঞা করা। **Scorn'-ful**, *adj.* Expressing extreme disdain ; disdainful ; অবজ্ঞাসূচক, অবজ্ঞাব্যঞ্জক ; ঘৃণাপূর্ণ, অবজ্ঞাপূর্ণ। **To laugh to scorn**—To mock ; to ridicule ; বিদ্রূপ করা ; উপহাস করা। **To think scorn of**—To despise ; অবজ্ঞা করা।

Scŏr'-pi-ō, *n.* 1. (*Astron.*) The eighth sign of the zodiac ; (জ্যোতির্বিজ্ঞান) বৃশ্চিক রাশি, অলি (সাঃ পঃ), বিছা (ঐ), বৃশ্চিক (ঐ)। 2. A zodiacal constellation ; তারাপুঞ্জবিশেষ (জ্যেষ্ঠা, অনুরাধা ও পূর্ব্বাষাঢ়া)।

scŏr'-pi-oid (-ōyd), *adj.* & *n.* (*Bot.*) Curved at the end like a scorpion's tail ; কাঁকড়া বিছার পুচ্ছের মত অগ্রভাগে বক্র। ***Noun.*** An inflorescence curled up at the end like a scorpion's tail ; কাঁকড়া-বিছার পুচ্ছের মত অন্তভাগে বক্র পুষ্পমঞ্জরী।

scŏr'-pi-ŏn, *n.* 1. An animal of the class arachnida, with a jointed tail terminating with a venomous sting ; বিছু ; কাঁকড়া বিছা। 2. (*Cap.*, *Astron.*) Same

Scorpion.

as SCORPIO. 3. A whip armed with iron points ; লৌহশঙ্কুবিদ্ধ বেত্র। **Scorpion-fish**—শিঙ্গি মাছ। **Scorpion-plant**—যবদ্বীপে জাত একপ্রকার পরগাছা—ইহার শাদা ফুলগুলি অনেকটা মাকড়সার মত দেখায়। An ancient military engine for throwing stones ; প্রাচীনকালে ব্যবহৃত একপ্রকার শিলাবর্ষী যন্ত্র, যন্ত্রপাষাণ। **Scorpion-shell**—একপ্রকার কড়ি,—ইহার বহির্দেশ হইতে কয়েকটী বক্র অংশ উদ্গত হইয়া থাকে। **Scorpionis**—পূর্ব্বাষাঢ়া (বৃঃ সং)। α **Scorpionis**—জ্যেষ্ঠা (বৃঃ সং)। δ, β **Scorpionis**—অনুরাধা (বৃঃ সং)। **Scorpion's heart**—বৃশ্চিকমধ্যতারা (হিঃ কোঃ)।

scŏt, *n.* (*Hist.*) A tax ; (ইতিহাস) কর। **Scot-free** — Unharmed ; as, to go *scot-free* ; অক্ষত, নির্ব্বিঘ্ন। **To pay scot and lot**—To pay tax according to one's means ; সাধ্যানুসারে কর প্রদান করা।

Scŏt, *n.* 1. A native of Scotland ; স্কটলণ্ডের অধিবাসী। 2. A Gaelic people from Ireland who settled in Scotland in about the 5th century ; খৃষ্টীয় ৫ম শতকে যে গেলিক জাতীয় লোক আয়র্লণ্ড হইতে আসিয়া স্কটলণ্ডে বসবাস স্থাপন করে।

Scotch (skŏch), *adj.* & *n.* Pertaining to Scotland or its inhabitants; স্কটলণ্ড বা তদ্দেশবাসিগণসম্পর্কীয়। ***Noun.*** 1. The dialect or dialects of English spoken in Scotland; স্কটলণ্ডে প্রচলিত ইংরাজী উপভাষা। 2. The people of Scotland ; স্কটলণ্ডবাসী। **Scotch cap**—হাইলেণ্ডারের টুপি। **Scotch collops** — See under SCOTCH below. **Scotch-man** (also **Scots-man**) — স্কটলণ্ডবাসী। **Scotch-marriage**—সমাজ-বিরুদ্ধ বিবাহ। **Scotch-mist**—টিপ্ টিপ্ বৃষ্টি। **Scotch pebble**—একপ্রকার গোমেদ মণি। **Scotch-terrier** — একপ্রকার ক্ষুদ্র জাতীয় কুকুর। **Scotch whisky** — ধোঁয়ার মত গন্ধবিশিষ্ট একপ্রকার হুইস্কী ; সর্ব্বপ্রথম Scotlandএ প্রস্তুত হয়। **Scotch-woman** (also **Scots-woman**) — স্কটলণ্ডবাসিনী। **Flying Scotchman**—স্কটলণ্ডাভিমুখগামী ডাকগাড়ী। **I did not scotch my mind**—I said plainly ; আমি স্পষ্টাস্পষ্টি বলিয়াছিলাম। **Out of all scotch**—Extreme ; নিরতিশয়।

scotch (skŏch), *n.* & *v. t.* (*Archaic*) An incision ; খাঁজ। ***Verb t.*** To cut with a narrow incision ; to wound slightly ; খাঁজ কাটা, দাগ কাট ; সামান্য আহত করা, সামান্য জখম করা ; **Scotched collops**—(Wrongly *Scotch scollops*) ; পলাণ্ডু, মসলা প্রভৃতির সংযোগে প্রস্তুত ক্ষুদ্র ক্ষুদ্র গোমাংস খণ্ডের ব্যঞ্জন।

scō'-tĕr, *n.* A large sea-duck ; বিশালকায় সাগরচর হংস।

scō'-ti-ā (-shi-), *n.* A concave moulding at the base of a column ; স্তম্ভপাদদেশের মধ্যোন্নত ভূষা।

Scō'-tĭsm, *n.* The philosophical doctrines of Duns Scotus ; ডানস্ স্কটাস নামক মধ্যযুগীয় দার্শনিকের মতবাদ।

Scŏt'-lănd, *n.* A country in Great Britain ; স্কটলণ্ড দেশ। **Scotland yard**—লণ্ডন নগরীর পুলিসের প্রধান কেন্দ্র, বিশেষতঃ লণ্ডনীয় গোয়েন্দা পুলিশের প্রধান আড্ডা।

scŏt-ō-dĭn'-ĭ-ă, *n.* Giddiness ; ঘূর্ণিরোগ।

scŏt-ō-grăph, *n.* An instrument for writing in the dark or for aiding the blind to write ; অন্ধকারে লিখিবার

জন্য বা অন্ধদিগকে লিখন কার্য্যে সহায়তা করার নিমিত্ত যন্ত্রবিশেষ, অন্ধলেখনী।

Scōts, *n.* See SCOTCH.

Scŏt'-ti-cĭsm, *n.* An idiom, phrase or expression peculiar to the natives of Scotland ; স্কটলণ্ড দেশের ভাষার বিশেষত্বসূচক বাক্য, উক্তি বা রীতিসিদ্ধ প্রয়োগ।

Scŏt-ti-cīze, *v. t.* & *i.* To render Scottish in character ; স্কটীয় ভাবাপন্ন করা। ***Verb i.*** To imitate the Scotch in idioms or habits ; স্কটলণ্ডবাসিগণের রীতিনীতি, ভাব বা বিশেষ বাগ্ধারার অনুসরণ করা।

scoun'-drĕl (skown-), *n.* A villain; a rascal ; দুর্বৃত্ত, দুরাত্মা ; বদমায়েস, পাজীলোক, নরাধম, বদ্‌জাত, দুর্জ্জন। **–dom,** *n.* **–ism,** *n.* **–ly,** *adj.*

scour (skowr), *v. t.* & *n.* 1. To make clean and bright by friction ; ঘষিয়া মাজিয়া পরিষ্কার করা, ঘষিয়া মাজিয়া চক্‌চকে করা, ঘষামাজা। 2. To flush ; জলধারা প্রবাহিত করিয়া পরিষ্কার করা। 3. To purge ; (কোষ্ঠাদি) পরিষ্কার করা, খোলসা করা। ***Noun.*** 1. The clearing action of a strong swift current ; প্রবল খরস্রোতের পরিষ্করণ ক্রিয়া। 4. Diarrohea or dysentery in cattle ; (অশ্বগবাদির) উদরাময় বা আমাশয়। 5. A cleansing agent ; যে সমস্ত বস্তুদ্বারা কাগজ প্রভৃতি পরিষ্কার করা হয়।

scour (skowr), *v. i.* & *t.* To pass swiftly over ; দ্রুত অতিক্রম করা, দ্রুত ভ্রমণ করা, দ্রুত পর্য্যটন করা। ***Verb t.*** To run over ; দ্রুত বিচরণ করা।

scourge (skērj), *n.* & *v. t.* 1. (*Archaic*) A whip ; (অপ্রঃ) বেত, চাবুক। 2. A means of inflicting punishment or vengeance ; punishment ; শাস্তি-প্রদান বা প্রতিহিংসা সাধনের উপায় ; দণ্ড। 3. One who afflicts or harasses ; কষ্টপ্রদানকারী, অত্যাচারী। ***Verb t.*** 1. (*Archaic*) To lash ; (অপ্রঃ) চাবকান, বেত্রাঘাত করা। 2. To chastise ; to oppress ; to afflict ; শাস্তি দেওয়া ; অত্যাচার-জর্জ্জরিত করা ; পীড়িত করা। **Scourge of God**—হূণাধিপতি এটিলা (Attila)। **Scourge of Princes**—ইতালীদেশীর ব্যঙ্গ কবি এরেটিনো (Aretino)।

scout (scowt), *n.* & *v. i.* 1. A person sent out to obtain and bring in information; esp. one employed to observe the motions and obtain intelligence regarding an enemy ; চর; শত্রুর গতিবিধি সম্বন্ধে সংবাদ সংগ্রহের জন্য প্রেরিত চর, সামরিক চর। 2. A college servant at Oxford ; অক্সফোর্ড বিদ্যালয়ের ভৃত্য। 3. Act of obtaining information, esp. military information ; সংবাদসংগ্রহ, সামরিক সংবাদ সংগ্রহ। 4. The common guillemot; একপ্রকার পক্ষী। ***Verb i.*** To act as a scout ; চরের কার্য্য করা, সামরিক চরের কার্য্য করা।

scout (skowt), *v. t.* To treat with disdain or contempt ; to reject with scorn ; অবজ্ঞার সহিত ব্যবহার করা ; অবজ্ঞার সহিত অগ্রাহ্য করা।

scow, *n.* A large flat-bottomed boat ; একপ্রকার বৃহৎ চ্যাপ্টা-তলা নৌকা।

scowl, *v. i., t.* & *n.* To wrinkle the brow in displeasure ; to look sullen, severe or angry ; ভ্রূকুটি-করা, ভ্রূকুঞ্চিত করা ; মুখভার দেখান, ক্রুদ্ধ দেখান। ***Verb t.*** To drive with a scowl or frown; ভ্রূকুটি করিয়া তাড়ান, সরোষকটাক্ষ দ্বারা বিতাড়িত করা। ***Noun.*** An angry frown ; an expression of sourness, sullenness, anger or discomfort ; সরোষকটাক্ষ, ভ্রূকুটি, ভ্রূভঙ্গী, রোষকুটিল কটাক্ষ ; ভ্রূকুটিকুটিল মুখভঙ্গী। **Scowl'-ing,** *n.*

scrăb'-ble (-l), *v. i.* & *t.* 1. To scrawl; to scribble ; আঁচড়পাঁচড় করা ; হিজিবিজি লিখা, কাকের ছাঁ বকের ছাঁ লিখা। 2. To grope about for something ; to gather hastily something ; কোন জিনিষ হাতড়ান; তাড়াতাড়ি কুড়াইয়া লওয়া। ***Verb t.*** 1. To scribble ; হিজিবিজি লিখা। 2. To obtain by scratching or digging about ; আঁচড়াইয়া বা খুঁড়িয়া তোলা।

scrăg, *n.* & *v. t.* 1. A lean, thin person, plant or animal ; অস্থি-চর্ম্মসার ব্যক্তি, তালপাতার সিপাহী, ক্ষীণ বৃক্ষ বা জন্তু। 2. The bony part of the neck of a sheep ; (*slang*) neck ; ভেড়ার ঘাড়ের অস্থিময় অংশ ; (ইতর ভাষায়) ঘাড়। ***Verb t.*** 1. (*Colloq.*) To kill by hanging ; (চলিত ভাষায়) ফাঁসী দেওয়া। 2. To wring the neck of ; ঘাড় মোচড়াইয়া দেওয়া। 3. (*Fooball*) To screw an opponent's neck under the arm in order to induce him to drop the ball ; (পাদগোলক ক্রীড়ায়) প্রতিদ্বন্দ্বীকে কন্দুক ফেলিয়া দিতে বাধ্য করার জন্য বাহু দ্বারা বেষ্টন করিয়া তাহার ঘাড় মোচড়াইয়া দেওয়া। **Scrag'-gi-ly,** *adv.* **Scrag'-gi-ness,** *n.* **Scrag'-gy,** *adj.* Lean ; bony ; rough ; কাহিল ; অস্থিচর্ম্মসার ; কর্কশ, বন্ধুর, আবড়োথাবড়ো।

scrăm'-ble (-bl), *v. i., t.* & *n.* 1. To move or climb with the heads and feet ; হস্তপদের সাহায্যে চলা বা আরোহণ করা, হামাগুড়ি দিয়া চলা বা উঠা। 2. To snatch or catch eagerly at anything before another ; as, to *scramble* for seats ; কোন জিনিষ পাইবার জন্য হুড়াহুড়ি বা কাড়াকাড়ি করা। 3. To break eggs into a pan and fry with butter, salt, milk, pepper, etc. ; as, *scrambled* eggs ; পাত্রে ডিম ভাঙ্গিয়া তাহাতে মাখন, দুগ্ধ, লবণ, গোলমরিচ প্রভৃতি সংযোগপূর্ব্বক ভর্জ্জিত করা। 4. To throw coins etc. to be scrambled for ; কাড়াকাড়ি করিয়া নেওয়ার জন্য টাকা পয়সা ফেলা। ***Verb t.*** 1. To collect hurriedly ; তাড়াতাড়ি কুড়ান। ***Noun.*** 1. Act of jostling or pushing to get something before all others ; সকলের আগে কোন জিনিষ পাইবার জন্য হুড়াহুড়ি বা কাড়াকাড়ি। 2. A rude, eager struggle for something ; টানা হেঁচড়া। 3. Climbing on all fours or clambering ; হস্তপদের সাহায্যে কষ্টে আরোহণ, হাঁচড়পাঁচড় (*colloq.*)।

scrăn'-nel (-ĕl), *adj.* (*Archaic*) Thin; weak; unmelodious; "Grate on their *scrannel* pipes of wretched straw" ; কৃশ ; ক্ষীণ ; শ্রুতিকটু।

scrăp, *n.* & *v. t.* **1.** A small piece ; ক্ষুদ্র টুকরা। **2.** A fragment of something written or printed ; চিরকুট। **3.** A short extract ; সংক্ষিপ্ত উদ্ধৃত অংশ। **4.** A small picture ; ক্ষুদ্র চিত্র। **5.** The crisp substance that remains after frying or melting animal fat ; জন্তুর চর্ব্বি গালাইবার পর যে মচমচে জিনিষ অবশিষ্ট থাকে। 6. Old iron or old machinery, broken up; পুরাতন লোহ বা পুরাতন যন্ত্রাদির ভগ্ন অংশ, লোহার ছাঁট (প্রবাসী ১৩১৯)। ***Verb t.*** To make into scrap or scraps ; to discard as refuse ; ক্ষুদ্র টুকরা করা, চিরকুট করা, ছাঁটে পরিণত করা ; আবর্জ্জনাস্বরূপ বর্জ্জন করা। **Scrap'-py,** *adj.* Incomplete ; disjointed ; অসম্পূর্ণ ; অসম্বদ্ধ। **Scrap-book**—যে শাদা বহিতে ছবি, সংবাদপত্রাদির কাটছাঁট প্রভৃতি জুড়িয়া রাখা হয়। **Scrap-metal**—ধাতুর ছাঁট। **To go to the scrap**—ধ্বংস প্রাপ্ত হওয়া।

scrăp, *n.* (*Slang*) Scrimmage ; (ইতর ভাষায়) মারামারি, হাঙ্গামা।

scrāpe, *v. t, i.* & *n.* **1.** To rub the surface of with a rough or a sharp instrument or with something hard ; ঘষা, মাজা, চাঁচা। **2.** To remove or take off by rubbing ; চাঁচিয়া বা ঘষিয়া ফেলা। **3.** To gather by laborious effort ; to save or get together penuriously (commonly followded by *together* or *up*) ; as, to *scrape* *together* money ; বহুকষ্টে প্রদান করিয়া অতি কষ্টে জমান। **4.** To f credit— তুলিয়া ফেলা। **5.** To ট হইতে টাকা approbation of, or **n** or **upon** drown the voice o**the credit** meetings, by drawircurity of ; along the floor ; গ্‌**c carry to** দ্বারা কোন বক্তার বক্তৃতা**redit to)**— প্রকাশ করা কিম্বা তedit side of শ্রুতির অযোগ্য করা।র জমার দিকে 1. To roughen o**edit to**—To surface by rubb**To give one** ফেলা, চাঁচিয়া আবদ্ধer as a sum 2. To make a hাহারও হিসাবের sound ; ঘর্ষর শব্দ লখা। (*Fig.*) To make an awkward bow ; বিসদৃশ ভাবে অভিবাদন করা। **4.** To play a violin etc. unskilfully ; আনাড়ীর মত বেহালা প্রভৃতি বাজান। ***Noun.*** 1. Act of rubbing or scraping ; ঘর্ষণ, চাঁচন। **2.** The effect of scraping or rubbing ; ঘষা বা চাঁচার ফল। 3. An awkward predicament or position ; as, to get into a *scrape* ; সঙ্কট, লেঠা, কৃচ্ছ্র, মুস্কিল, ফাঁপর, দায়, বিভ্রাট, পেঁচ, হাঙ্গামা, গোল, ফ্যাসাদ। **4.** An awkward bow in which the foot is drawn backward on the ground ; পদ পশ্চাদ্দিকে প্রত্যাকর্ষণপূর্ব্বক বিসদৃশভাবে অভিবাদন। 5. (*Jocularly*) A shave ; (রঙ্গচ্ছলে) খেউরী। **Scrape of pen**—তাড়াতাড়ি হিজিবিজি করিয়া লিখা দুই এক কথা, কলমের আঁচড়। **To get into a scrape**—To fall in difficulty ; পেঁচে পড়া, সঙ্কটে পড়া, দায়ে পড়া, ফেরে পড়া, ফ্যাসাদে পড়া। **To scrape acquaintance with anyone**—To make one's self acquainted ; to insinuate oneself into intimacy with some one ; স্বয়ং প্রবৃত্ত হইয়া কাহারো সহিত পরিচয় করা ; পায়ে পা ঠেকাইয়া আলাপ করা (মিল্‌নে), গায়ে পড়িয়া বন্ধুত্ব করা।

scrāp'-ẽr, *n.* **1.** An instrument for scraping ; চাঁচিবার যন্ত্র, উল্লেখন-যন্ত্র, ঘর্ষণী, উল্লেখনী। **2.** The of an ahe foot drawn over হিসাবের ডা; মেঝের উপর পায়ের 3. (*Rom.* **3.** One who scrapes a contrac money laboriously ; যুক্তির প্রতিবহু কষ্টে টাকা পয়সা জমা **crē-dō,** 4. A poor or vile fiddler ; of belie বেহালাবাদক। **5.** A metal **crĕd'-ŭ**t the door on which mud readyiped off from boots ; দ্বারদেশে বিশ্বাস যে ধাতুফলকে বুট জুতার মাটী কানা ফেলা হয়।

2. **tch** (skrăch), *v. t., i., n.* & *adj.* cr To rub with something rough or sharp ; আঁচড়ান, উল্লেখন করা। **2.** To rub or scrape with nails ; নখদ্বারা আঁচড়ান। **3.** To withdraw from the list of competitors ; প্রতিদ্বন্দ্বীর তালিকা হইতে নাম উঠাইয়া লওয়া। **4.** To dig or excavate with claws ; নখদ্বারা খুঁড়া। ***Verb i.*** To use the nails, claws or the like in tearing a surface or in digging ; উল্লেখন করা, নখদ্বারা আঁচড়ান, আঁচড়াইয়া গর্ত্ত করা। ***Noun.*** 1. A mark made by scratching ; a slight incision with nails ; উল্লেখন ; আঁচড়। 2. A kind of wig covering only a part of the head ; একপ্রকার পরচুলা—যদ্দ্বারা মস্তকের অংশ মাত্র ঢাকা যায়। **3.** A line drawn across the prize ring up to which boxers are brought when they join in fight ; মুষ্টিযোদ্ধৃগণ যুদ্ধারম্ভে রঙ্গক্ষেত্রের যে রেখা পর্য্যন্ত আনীত হয়। **4.** The starting point, or the time of starting for those competitors who are not allowed any advantage at the start ; a competitor allowded no advantage, যে সকল প্রতিদ্বন্দ্বীকে কোনরূপ সুবিধা দেওয়া হয়না—তাহার যাত্রার কাল বা স্থান; দৌড়ে যে প্রতিদ্বন্দ্বী কোনরূপ সুবিধা প্রাপ্ত হয় নাই। ***Adj.*** Chosen by chance; hastily collected; যথেচ্ছভাবে নির্ব্বাচিত ; তাড়াতাড়ি সংগৃহীত। **Scratch-back**—একপ্রকার খেলনা—ইহা মানুষের পিঠের উপর দিয়া টানিয়া দিলে

কাপড় ছিঁড়ার মত শব্দ হয়; পূর্ব্বকালে ব্যবহৃত মহিলাদিগের পৃষ্ঠকণ্ডূয়নের জন্য হস্তাকৃতি যন্ত্রবিশেষ। **Scratch-brush**—উঁখা প্রভৃতি পরিষ্কার করার জন্য তারের একপ্রকার বুরুশ। **Scratch race**—যে ঘোড়দৌড়ে সকল প্রতিযোগী সমান সুযোগ পাইয়া থাকে। **Scratch-wig**—Same as SCRATCH *Noun* 2. **Scratch-work**—Same as GRAFFITO 2. **Old Scratch**—শয়তান। **To bring one to the scratch** — To bring one to form a decision; কাহাকে স্থির সিদ্ধান্তে উপনীত করান। **To come to the scratch**—To come to a decision; কোন বিষয়ে স্থির সিদ্ধান্তে উপনীত হওয়া।

scratch'-ĕr (scrăch-), *n.* **1.** One who, or that which, scratches; উল্লেখক। **2.** One of the Rasores; কুক্কুট প্রভৃতি পক্ষী—যাহারা নখদ্বারা আঁচড়াইয়া খাদ্য বাহির করিয়া থাকে, ঘর্ষণপদী।

scrawl (skräl), *v. i., t.* & *n.* To write hastily or irregularly; হিজিবিজি লিখা, আঁচড়াইয়া লিখা। ***Verb t.*** To write awkwardly; হিজিবিজি করিয়া লিখা। ***Noun.*** A piece of bad or hasty writing; হিজিবিজি, কাকের ছাঁ বকের ছাঁ, কালির আঁচড়।

scream (skrēm), *v. i.* & *n.* **1.** To shriek; চেঁচান, চীৎকার করা, চেঁচাইয়া উঠা। **2.** To laugh immoderately; অট্টহাস্য করা। ***Noun.*** A sharp shrill cry; চীৎকার।

scream'-ĕr (skrēm-), *n.* **1.** One that screams; চীৎকারকারী। **2.** A kind of American bird; আমেরিকা-দেশীয় পক্ষিবিশেষ। **3.** Something very great, excellent or exciting; a tale etc. that raises screams of laughter; সেরা জিনিষ, তোফা জিনিষ; বেজায় হাসির গল্প।

scree (skrē), *n.* An accumulation of loose stones at the base of a cliff or precipice; উচ্চ সরলোন্নত গিরির পাদদেশে সঞ্চিত শিলারাশি।

screech (skrēch), *v. i.* & *n.* To cry out with a sharp shrill voice; কেকারব করা, পেচকের মত চীৎকার করা। ***Noun.*** A sharp, shrill cry, such as is uttered in acute pain or sudden fright; কাল-পেচকের মত চীৎকার, কেকারব। **Screech-owl**—কাল-পেচক।

screen (skrēn), *n.* & *v. t.* **1.** Something movable used to intercept, heat or cold; পর্দ্দা, তিরস্করণী, যবনিকা, ব্যবধান (মঃ উঃ)। **2.** Anything that shelters or affords concealment; যদ্দ্বারা কোন কিছু আশ্রিত, রক্ষিত বা লুক্কায়িত হয়। **3.** A kind of riddle or sieve; একপ্রকার বৃহৎ চালুনী। ***Verb t.*** **1.** To shelter or protect from inconvenience, injury or danger; as, to *screen* one from danger; to cover; to conceal; বিপদ্‌, অসুবিধা বা অনিষ্ট হইতে রক্ষা করা; ঢাকিয়া রাখা; আড়ালে রাখা। **2.** To sift or riddle by passing through a screen; বৃহৎ চালুনি দ্বারা চালা।

screw (skrō), *n., v.t.* & *i.* **1.** A cylinder of wood or metal grooved spirally; পেঁচ, স্ক্রু, কর্ষণী (হিঃ কোঃ)।

Screw-propeller.

2. A screw-propeller; বাষ্পীয়পোত চালাইবার জন্য একপ্রকার পেঁচকল। **3.** A niggardly person; কৃপণ, কঞ্জুষ। **4.** (*Slang*) Wages; (ইতর ভাষায়) বেতন, মাইনে, মুষহারা। **5.** An importunate fellow; an extortioner; নাছোড়বান্দা লোক; পীড়নপূর্ব্বক অর্থ আদায়কারী, অর্থশোষক। ***Verb t.*** **1.** To turn or apply a screw to; to fasten by a screw; পেঁচ ঘুরান, পেঁচ লাগান, ইস্ক্রুপ লাগান, ইস্ক্রুপ আঁটা; ইস্ক্রুপদ্বারা আঁটা। **2.** To press; পীড়ন করা। **3.** To extort money; পীড়নপূর্ব্বক অর্থ আদায় করা। **4.** To distort; অর্থ-বিকৃতি করা। ***Verb i.*** **1.** To be propelled by means of screw; পেঁচকলদ্বারা চালিত হওয়া। **2.** To practise extortion, oppression, or the like; পীড়ন করা, অর্থ শোষণ করা, পেষণ করা। **Female** or **Interior screw**—যে স্ক্রুপের পেঁচ ভিতরের দিকে থাকে। **Male** or **Exterior screw**—যে স্ক্রুপের পেঁচ বাহিরের দিকে থাকে। **Screw-driver**—পেঁচ বসাইবার যন্ত্র। **Screw-jack**—ভারোত্তলন যন্ত্রবিশেষ। **Screw-key, Screw-pine**—কেতকী, কেওড়া, কেয়া। [Syn. সূচীপুষ্প, হলীন, জম্বুল, ক্রকচচ্ছদ, কেতক, সূচিকাপুষ্প, জম্বুক, তীক্ষ্ণপুষ্পা, বিফলা, ধূলিপুষ্পিক, মেধ্যা, কণ্টদলা, নৃপপ্রিয়া, দীর্ঘপত্রা, গন্ধপুষ্পা, ইন্দুকলিকা, দলপুষ্পা, পাংশুলা, স্বর্ণকেতকী (of golden colour), হেমকেতকী (*ib.*), কনকপ্রসবা (*ib.*), হৈমী (*ib.*), স্বর্ণপুষ্পি (*ib.*), ছিন্নরুহা (*ib.*), বিষ্টারুহ (*ib.*), কামখড়্গদলা, (*ib.*), কৈতক, ক্রকচা, স্থিরগন্ধা (রাজনিঃ), পুষ্পচামর, শিবদ্বিষ্টা (রাজ নিঃ)।] **Screw-propeller**—ইস্ক্রুপের পেঁচের মত ঘূরানোভাবে সজ্জিত দাঁড়শ্রেণীবিশিষ্ট চক্র—যদ্দ্বারা এক শ্রেণীর জাহাজ চালিত হয়। **Screw-steamer**—উক্ত প্রকার চক্রের সাহায্যে চালিত পোত। **Screw-wrench** — পেঁচটানা যন্ত্র, ইস্ক্রুপ বসাইবার জন্য পাক-সাঁড়াশী। **An old screw** — A stingy man; কঞ্জুষ লোক, হাতকষা লোক। **A screw loose**—Something wrong somewhere; কোথায় কোন গোল। **Not to put on the screw**—Not to take great risk in a trade; ব্যবসায়ে বেশী ঝুঁকি না লওয়া। **To draw one's screw**—To get one's pay; বেতন পাওয়া। **To put the screw on**—To extort money;

পীড়নপূর্ব্বক টাকা আদায় করা। **To put under the screw**—To compel ; বাধ্য করা। **To screw one's courage to the sticking place**—To decide to do something ; কোন কার্য্য করার জন্য সংকল্প করা। **To screw up courage**—To take heart ; সাহসে বুক বাঁধা।

screw (scrô), *n.* A vicious or worn-out horse ; দুষ্ট অশ্ব, পরিক্লান্ত অশ্ব।

screwed (scrôd), *adj.* (*Slang*) Drunken ; (ইতর ভাষায়) মাতাল।

scrib'-ble (-l), *v. t., i.* & *n.* **1.** To write with haste or without care or regard to correctness or elegance ; হিজিবিজি লিখা। **2.** To cover or fill with careless, hasty or illegible writing ; হিজিবিজি লিখিয়া পূর্ণ করা। ***Verb i.*** To scrawl ; হিজিবিজি লিখা। ***Noun.*** A scrawl ; হিজিবিজি, কাকের ছাঁ বকের ছাঁ। **—bler,** *n.* **1.** One who scribbles or writes hastily or carelessly ; যে ব্যক্তি হিজিবিজি করিয়া লিখে। **2.** A petty writer ; নগণ্য লেখক।

scrib'-ble (-l), *v. t.* To card or tear wool or cotton coarsely with a wire-comb ; পশম বা তুলা তারের চিরুণী দ্বারা মোটাভাবে আঁচড়ান। **—bler,** *n.* A machine for scribbling wool ; পশম আঁচড়াইবার জন্য যন্ত্র।

scribe, *n.* **1.** A writer ; লেখক, লিপিকর। **2.** An amanuensis ; a copyist ; শ্রুতিলেখক, প্রতিলিপিকারক ; নকলনবীশ। **3.** (Amongst the ancient Jews) An expounder of the law and a copyist of the same ; প্রাচীন ইহুদীগণের মধ্যে শাস্ত্রব্যাখ্যাতা এবং শাস্ত্রগ্রন্থের লিপিকর।

scrim'-mage (-āj), **scrŭm'—,** *ns.* A skirmish ; a tussle ; হাঙ্গামা ; মারামারি, হুড়াহুড়ি, ধ্বস্তাধ্বস্তি।

scrimp, *v. t.* & *i.* Same as SKIMP (which see).

scrim'-shaw (-shä), *v.t., i.* & *n.* To adorn shells, ivory, etc. by engraving etc. ; ক্ষোদনাদি দ্বারা শঙ্খ, শুক্তি, গজদন্ত, প্রভৃতি মণ্ডিত করা। ***Noun.*** A piece of such work ; উক্তরূপ শিল্পকার্য্য।

scri'-ni-ŭm, *n.* (*Roman antiq.*) A box for books, paper, etc. ; (রোমক প্রত্নতত্ত্ব) পুস্তক কাগজ প্রভৃতি রাখার বাক্স।

scrip, *n.* (*Archaic*) A small bag or wallet ; (অপ্রঃ) ঝুলি।

scrip, *n.* **1.** A small piece of paper ; চিরকুট। **2.** A provisional certificate of stock subscribed to a bank or other company, or of a share of other joint property ; ব্যাঙ্ক কিম্বা কোন যৌথকারবারে প্রদত্ত টাকার কাঁচা রসিদ।

script, *n.* **1.** (*Law*) Original document ; (আইন) আসল দলীল, মূল দলীল। **2.** Written character ; হাতের লিখা। **3.** A type in the form of written letter ; হাতের লিখার অনুরূপ মুদ্রাক্ষর (*This is printed in script*).

scrip-tō'-ri-ŭm, *n.* **1.** The room in a monastery set apart for the writing or copying of manuscripts ; খৃষ্টীয় মঠের যে কক্ষে গ্রন্থাদি লিখা বা নকল করা হইত, লিপিকক্ষ। **2.** A room set apart for writing ; লিখনগৃহ।

scrip'-tūr-ăl, *adj.* Contained in, or according to, the scripture ; founded on scriptures ; বাইবেল গ্রন্থে লিখিত, বাইবেল গ্রন্থানুযায়ী ; বাইবেলগ্রন্থ মূলক। **—ism, —ist,** *ns.* **—ly,** *adv.* **—ness,** *n.*

scrip'-tūre, *n.* **1.** The Bible ; বাইবেল। **2.** Sacred writings or records ; as, the Hindu *scriptures* ; ধর্ম্মগ্রন্থ, ধর্ম্মশাস্ত্র, শাস্ত্র (এভেলন), শ্রুতিস্মৃতি (হিঃ কোঃ)। [বিভিন্ন জাতি ও ধর্ম্মাবলম্বিগণের প্রধান ধর্ম্মগ্রন্থের নাম :—খৃষ্টান (বাইবেল) ; হিন্দু (বেদ) ; বৌদ্ধ (ত্রিপিটক) ; শিখ (গ্রন্থ সাহেব) ; চৈনিক (পঞ্চরাজা—Five kings) ; পারসীক (জেন্দাবেস্ত) ; মুসলমান (কোরাণ) ; প্রাচীন স্কেণ্ডিনেভিয়ান (ইদ্দাস — Eddas)]। **Scripture-reader**—যে ব্যক্তি দরিদ্রগণের বাটীতে যাইয়া বাইবেল পাঠ করিয়া থাকে।

scrive'-nĕr (skriv-), *n.* **1.** A scribe ; one who draws up contract or other writing ; লিপিকর ; যে ব্যক্তি দলিল প্রভৃতি মুসাবিদা করে। **2.** (*Obs.*) A money broker or money-lender ; (অপ্রঃ) দালাল, কুসীদজীবি। **3.** A poor author ; দরিদ্র গ্রন্থকার। **Scrivener's-palsy**—Same as WRITER'S CRAMP.

scrō-bic'-ū-lāte, —lāt-ĕd, *adjs.* (*Bot.* & *Zool.*) Pitted ; (উদ্ভিদ্-বিদ্যা এবং জন্তুবিদ্যা) রন্ধ্রপূর্ণ।

scrŏf'-ū-lă, *n.* A defect of constitution tending to the formation of, and deposition of, tubercles in the tissues and organs of the body ; গণ্ডমালা, কণ্ঠমালা, গলগণ্ড। **—lous,** *adj.* **—lous-ly,** *adv.* **—lous-ness,** *n.*

scrōll, *n., v. t.* & *i.* **1.** A roll of paper or manuscript ; আবর্ত্তিত বা গুটানো কাগজ কিম্বা পাণ্ডুলিপি, কাগজের তাড়া। **2.** A list ; a schedule ; ফর্দ্দ, তালিকা ; তফশিল। **3.** A flourish added to a man's name in signature ; নাম স্বাক্ষরের উপর টানটোন। **4.** An ornament of a somewhat spiral form ; আবর্ত্তিত ভূষা বা অলঙ্কার। **5.** The curved head of the instruments of the violin family ; বেহালাজাতীয় বাদ্যযন্ত্রের বক্র অগ্রভাগ। ***Verb t.*** **1.** To adorn with scrolls ; কোঁচানো ভূষা দ্বারা বিশোভিত করা। **2.** To record ; to draft ; লিপিবদ্ধ করা ; মুসাবিদা করা। ***Verb i.*** To curl up like a scroll ; গুটাইয়া যাওয়া। **Scroll-work**— কুণ্ডলিত রেখাদ্বারা রচিত ভূষা, জালি (উড়িষ্যা)।

scrō-ti'-tis, *n.* (*Med.*) Inflammation of the scrotum ; অণ্ডকোষের স্ফীতি।

scrō'-tō-cele (-sēl), *n.* A scrotal hernia ; অণ্ডকোষের অন্ত্রবৃদ্ধি।

scrō'-tŭm, *n.* The bag which contains the testicles ; অণ্ডকোষ, মুষ্কত্বক্। **–tal**, *adj.*

scrŭb, *v. t*, *i.* & *n.* To rub hard with a brush or with something coarse or rough, for the purpose of clearing scouring or making bright ; ঘষামাজা করা, ঘষিয়া মাজিয়া পরিষ্কার করা, রগড়াইয়া পরিষ্কার করা। ***Verb i.*** To work hard ; to be diligent and penurious ; কঠোর পরিশ্রম করা ; কঠোর পরিশ্রম করিয়া হীনভাবে বাস করা। ***Noun.*** **1.** One that labours hard and lives meanly ; কঠোর পরিশ্রমী, হীনভাবে জীবনযাপনকারী। **2.** Something small and mean ; তুচ্ছ পদার্থ, হীন পদার্থ। **3.** A worn-out brush ; ক্ষয়প্রাপ্ত বুরুশ। **4.** A kind of broom or scrubbing brush ; সম্মার্জ্জনী, ঘষামাজার জন্য একপ্রকার শক্ত বুরুশ। **5.** An apparatus for freeing coal-gas from impurities ; এমোনিয়া এবং অন্যান্য অবিশুদ্ধ দ্রব্য নিষ্কাশনপূর্ব্বক কয়লার বাষ্প শোধন করার জন্য যন্ত্রবিশেষ। **Scrub'-by**, *adj.* **1.** Small and mean ; ক্ষুদ্র এবং হীন। **2.** Stunted in growth ; বেঁটে, খাটো।

scrŭff, *n.* The back of the neck ; ঘাড়।

scrŭm'-mage (-āj), *n.* Same as SCRIMMAGE (which see).

scrŭmp'-tious (-shŭs), *adj.* (*Slang*) Delicious ; first-rate ; মজাদার ; সেরা, উমদা।

scrŭnch, *v. t.*, *i.* & *n.* **1.** To crush with the teeth ; চর্ব্বণ করা। **2.** (*Colloq.* & *Dial.*) To squeeze ; to crush ; নিষ্পীড়ন করা ; গুঁড়া করা। ***Noun.*** Act or sound of scrunching ; চর্ব্বণ, চর্ব্বণের শব্দ।

scru'-ple (scrô-pl), *n.*, *v. i.* & *t.* **1.** A weight of 20 grains ; ২০ গ্রেণ ওজন। **2.** A very small quantity ; অতি সামান্য পরিমাণ। **3.** Hesitation, esp. from conscientious motive ; as, he is a man of no *scruple* ; দ্বিধা, কুণ্ঠা, সংশয়, সঙ্কোচ, আশঙ্কা। ***Verb i.*** To doubt ; সংশয় করা। ***Verb t.*** To hesitate about doing anything ; কোন কিছু করিতে সংশয় বা দ্বিধা করা, ইতস্ততঃ করা।

scru'-pu-lous (scrô-pū-lŭs), *adj.* Full of scruples ; cautious ; punctilious ; rigourous ; as, *scrupulous* care ; কুণ্ঠাযুক্ত ; সতর্ক ; সূক্ষ্মবিষয়ে মনোযোগী, সূক্ষ্মবিষয়ে মনোযোগাত্মক, সূক্ষ্মানুসন্ধায়ী ; কঠোরকর্ত্তব্যপরায়ণ। **–los'-i-ty**, *n.* **–ly**, *adv.* **–ness**, *n.*

scru-ta'-tor (scrô-tā-têr), *n.* A close examiner or enquirer ; সূক্ষ্মদর্শী, সূক্ষ্মানুসন্ধায়ী।

scrutin, scrutin de liste, (*F.*), *ns.* Voting for a group of candidates for the same kind of office on one ticket or ballot ; একবারে একই টিকেটের সাহায্যে একসঙ্গে কতিপয় ব্যক্তির জন্য ভোট দেওয়া।

scru-ti-neer' (scrô-tĭ-nēr), *n.* **1.** One who scrutinizes ; সূক্ষ্মানুসন্ধায়ী, সূক্ষ্ম পরিদর্শক। **2.** One who acts as an examiner of rolls to see if they are valid ; যে ব্যক্তি নির্ব্বাচনকালে ভোট পরীক্ষা করিয়া থাকে, ভোটপরীক্ষক।

scru'-ti-nize (scrô-), *v. t.* & *i.* **1.** To examine closely or minutely ; to investigate or inquire into critically ; পুঙ্খানুপুঙ্খরূপে অনুসন্ধান করা ; সূক্ষ্মভাবে পরীক্ষা করা। ***Verb i.*** To make scrutiny ; সূক্ষ্মভাবে পরীক্ষা করা। **–niz-ing-ly**, *adv.*

scru'-ti-ny̆ (skrô-), *n.* **1.** Close examination or inquiry ; সূক্ষ্মভাবে অনুসন্ধান, সূক্ষ্মপরীক্ষা, সূক্ষ্মানুসন্ধান, সূক্ষ্মপরিদর্শন, সূক্ষ্মনিরূপণ, পুঙ্খানুপুঙ্খরূপে পরীক্ষা। **2.** Examination of votes given at an election ; নির্ব্বাচনকালে প্রদত্ত ভোট পরীক্ষণ।

scŭd, *v. t.*, *i.* & *n.* To run with haste or alacrity ; দ্রুতবেগে ছুটা, ছুটিয়া চলা। ***Verb i.*** **1.** To move swiftly ; দ্রুতবেগে ছুটা। **2.** (*Naut.*) To be driven swiftly by the wind ; (নৌ-বিদ্যা) বায়ুদ্বারা দ্রুতবেগে ধাবিত হওয়া, বাত্যাতাড়িত হওয়া। ***Noun.*** **1.** Act of scudding ; দ্রুতবেগে ধাবন, ছুটন। **2.** Loose, vapoury clouds driven swiftly by the wind ; বাত্যাতাড়িত লঘু মেঘমালা। **3.** (*Scot.*) Slap ; (স্কটলণ্ড) চপেটাঘাত।

scu'-dō (skô-), *n.* An old Italian silver coin ; প্রাচীন ইতালীয় রজতমুদ্রাবিশেষ।

scŭff, *v. i.* To walk without raising the feet from the ground or floor ; পা না তুলিয়া চলা, পা মাটীতে ঘষড়াইয়া কষ্টে চলা।

scŭf'-fle (-l), *n.* & *v. i.* A confused contest at close quarters; ধ্বস্তাধ্বস্তি, হাঙ্গামা, হুড়াহুড়ি, হাতাহাতি, জাপটাজাপটি, মারামারি, ধ্বস্তাধ্বস্তি। ***Verb i.*** To strive or struggle with a close grapple ; জাপটাজাপটি করা, ধ্বস্তাধ্বস্তি করা, হাতাহাতি করা, হুড়াহুড়ি করা।

scŭll, *n.*, *v. t.* & *i.* **1.** A small row boat ; ক্ষুদ্র নৌকা, ডিঙ্গি। **2.** An oar so short that one man can manage two ; ক্ষুদ্র দাঁড়—যাহার এক জোড়া এক ব্যক্তি টানিতে পারে। **3.** An oar used to propel a boat by being worked over the stern ; নৌকার পাছা গলুইর উপর দিয়া যে দাঁড় টানা হয়। ***Verb t.*** To propel a boat with a scull or sculls ; উক্ত উভয় প্রকারে দাঁড় টানিয়া নৌকা চালান। ***Verb i.*** To scull a boat ; দাঁড় টানিয়া নৌকা চালান।

scŭll'-ēr *n.* **1.** One who uses sculls ; যে ব্যক্তি ক্ষুদ্র দাঁড়দ্বারা নৌকা টানে। **2.** A boat rowed by one man with two sculls ; যে ক্ষুদ্র ডিঙ্গি এক ব্যক্তি কর্ত্তৃক দুইটী ক্ষুদ্র দাঁড়ের সাহায্যে চালিত হয়।

scŭl'-ler-y̆ (-êr-), *n.* **1.** A place where dishes, kettles, etc. are kept ; যে স্থানে থালা, কেটলী, প্রভৃতি রাখা হয়। **2.** A place where culinary utensils are cleaned and kept ; থালা, বাটী, ডেগচী, প্রভৃতি মাজিবার স্থান।

scŭl′-lion (-yŏn), *n.* A servant that does menial services in the kitchen; a worthless fellow; বাসন-মাজা চাকর, ভাণ্ডমার্জ্জক, ডেগচী-মাজা চাকর; অপদার্থ।

scŭl′-pin, *n.* A kind of small sea-fish; একপ্রকার ক্ষুদ্র সামুদ্রিক-মৎস্য।

sculpsit, sculpserunt, *v.* (*Abbr. sc.* or *sculps.*) So-&-so sculptured or engraved it; অমুকের দ্বারা ইহা ক্ষোদিত বা তক্ষিত হইয়াছে।

scŭlp′-tŏr, *n.* (*Fem.* SCULPTRESS), One who works in sculpture or whose occupation is to carve or hew figures; ভাস্কর, মূর্ত্তিরচক, রূপকার (কথাঃ সঃ), মূর্ত্তিশিল্পী, শিলাশিল্পী (বিশ্বকর্ম্মা)।

scŭlp′-türe, *n., v. t.* & *i.* 1. The art of carving wood, stone or other materials into images; ভাস্কর্য্য, মূর্ত্তিশিল্প, শিলাশিল্প। 2. Carved work in wood, stone, metal, etc.; ক্ষোদিত মূর্ত্তি প্রভৃতি। 3. (*Zool.* & *Bot.*) Raised or impressed markings on shells etc.; শুক্তি, শম্বুকাদির উপর ক্ষোদকারী কাচের মত চিহ্নসমূহ। ***Verb t.*** To form with the chisel on stone, wood or metal; to engrave; ক্ষোদিত করা; তক্ষিত করা। ***Verb i.*** To be a sculptor; ভাস্করের কার্য্য করা। **–tur-al-ly,** *adv.* **–tur-esque′,** *adj.*

scŭm, *n., v. t.* & *i.* 1. Extraneous matter or impurities which rise to the surface of liquors in boiling or fermentation; মণ্ড মাড়, গাঁদ, গাঙ্গ। 2. Refuse; vile people; জঞ্জাল, আবর্জ্জনা; সমাজের আবর্জ্জনা হীনব্যক্তিগণ, ইতরসমাজ। ***Verb t.*** To skim; গাদকাটা, গাদ কাটিয়া তোলা, মাড় গালা। ***Verb i.*** To form a scum; to be covered with scum; গাদ পড়া; গাদদ্বারা আবৃত হওয়া।

scŭm′-ble (-bl), *v. t.* & *n.* (In painting) To cover with a semi-transparent tinge to soften or tone down too bright a colour; (চিত্রণে) বর্ণের অতি দীপ্তি প্রশমিত বা মন্দীভূত করার জন্য (চিত্রাদি) অর্দ্ধস্বচ্ছ বর্ণদ্বারা আচ্ছাদিত করা। ***Noun.*** The toning down of a picture by covering with semi-transparent colours; অর্দ্ধস্বচ্ছবর্ণদ্বারা আচ্ছাদন পূর্ব্বক চিত্রের বর্ণের অতিদীপ্তি প্রশমন।

scŭn′-cheon (-chŭn), *n.* Stones or arches across angles of square tower supporting alternate sides of ocatagonal spire; অষ্টকোণ চূড়ার একান্তরিত ভুজসমূহ বিধৃত করার জন্য চতুষ্কোণ বুরুজের কোণসমূহে যে শিলাখণ্ড বা তোরণসমূহ স্থাপিত করা হয়।

scŭp′-per (-ĕr), *n.* A hole for carrying off water from the deck of a ship; জাহাজের পাটাতনের জলনির্গম ছিদ্র।

scurf (skêrf), *n.* 1. Dry scales or flakes on the skin; মরামাস, খুস্কী, শুষ্ক চর্ম্ম। 2. A layer of matter adhering to a surface; কোন বস্তুতে সংলগ্ন কোন পদার্থের স্তর।

scŭr′-ril-ous (-ŭs), *adj.* 1. Grossly coarse or abusive; full of low buffoonery; অতিশয় অশ্লীল, কুরুচিপূর্ণ, জঘন্য; নীচ, ভাঁড়ামিপূর্ণ। **–ril′-i-ty,** *n.* 1. The quality or state of being scurrilous; অশ্লীলতা, জঘন্য অশ্লীলতা। 2. Scurrilous language; a scurrilous remark or act; অশ্লীল ভাষা, অপভাষা, জঘন্য ভাষা, বাক্‌পারুষ্য; জঘন্য ভাঁড়ামি, খেউর, অশ্লীল উক্তি বা কার্য্য।

scŭr′-rȳ, *v. i.* & *n.* To hasten away along; তাড়াতাড়ি ছুটা। ***Noun.*** Haste; তাড়াতাড়ি, ত্বরা, তাড়াহুড়া।

scur′-vȳ (skêr-), *n.* & *adj.* A disease characterised by livid spots, bleeding gums, etc. and bodily prostration affecting persons deprived of a due quantity of vegetable food and sucessfully treated by lime or lemon-juice; দন্তমূলের কোমলতা, রক্তস্রাবশীলতা এবং চর্ম্মে বেগুনি রংএর পীড়কা ও কালিমা লক্ষণবিশিষ্ট একপ্রকার রোগ, [সরস উদ্ভিজ্জাদি আহারের অভাবে এই রোগ জন্মে।], শীতাদ (সাঃ গঃ)। ***Adj.*** Low; mean; discourteous; worthless; as, *scurry* friendship; নীচ, হীন; অধম, ইতর; অভদ্র; অসার।

scŭt, *n.* Short tail; খর্ব্ব লাঙ্গুল, খাটো লেজ।

scü′-tage (-tāj), *n.* A tax on feudal tenants; সামন্ততন্ত্রাধীন জায়গীরদারগণের প্রদেয় শুল্ক।

scutch (skŭch), *v. t.* & *n.* To dress fibrous material by beating; পুনঃ পুনঃ আঘাত করিয়া পাইট করা। ***Noun.*** An instrument used in scutching flax and hemp; শণ পাইট করার জন্য যন্ত্র। **Scutch′-er,** *n.*

scutch′-eon (skŭch-ŏn), *n.* 1. Same as ESCUTCHEON. 2. The ornamental bit of brass plate on a keyhole; (তালার) কুঞ্চিকা-প্রবেশরন্ধ্রের আবরণস্বরূপ শোভাসাধক পিত্তলফলকখণ্ড, তালার ছিদ্রের পিত্তল-নির্ম্মিত আবরণ। 3. A name-plate on a coffin, pocket-knife, or other object; শবাধার, ছুরিকা প্রভৃতির উপরিস্থ নামপট্ট।

scüte, *n.* Same as SCUTUM.

scü-tĕl′-lum (-ŭm), *n.* A little shield or shield-shaped scale, as on plants or animals; ক্ষুদ্র ঢাল, জন্তু বা উদ্ভিজ্জাদির উপরিস্থ ক্ষুদ্র ঢালাকৃতি শল্ক। **–late, –lar, Scu′-tel-lat-ed,** *adjs.* **–la′-tion,** *n.*

scŭt-ter (-ĕr), *v. i.* Same as SCURRY (which see).

scŭt′-tle (-l), *n.* & *v. t.* 1. A square hole in a roof with a lid; ছাদের উপরের ঢাকনিযুক্ত সমচতুষ্কোণ ছিদ্র। 2. A small hatchway or opening in a deck, provided with a lid to cover it; জাহাজের পাটাতনে ঢাকনি-যুক্ত ছিদ্রবিশেষ। 3. A hole in the side or bottom of a ship; জাহাজের পার্শ্বে বা তলদেশে ছিদ্র। ***Verb t.*** To make hole or holes in a ship, esp. for the purpose of sinking ; জাহাজে ছিদ্র করা, বিশেষতঃ ডুবাইবার উদ্দেশ্যে জাহাজে ছিদ্র করা।

scŭt'-tle (-l), *v. i.* & *n.* To hurry along ; to fly from danger or difficulty ; ছুটিয়া চলা ; পলায়ন করা, চম্পট দেওয়া, ছুটিয়া পালান। ***Noun.*** A quick pace or short run ; দ্রুতধাবন, দৌড়।

scŭt'-tle (-l), *n.* A metal pan or pail for holding coal (also *coal-scuttle*) ; কয়লার ঝুড়ি, কয়লার পাত্র, কয়লার ভাণ্ড।

scü'-tŭm, *n.* **1.** A shield belonging to the heavy armed Roman legionaries; প্রাচীন গুরুভার অস্ত্র ও বর্ম্মধারী রোমকসৈনিকগণের ঢাল। [এইরূপ ঢাল সাধারণতঃ অণ্ডাকৃতি হইত।] **2.** (*Anat.*) The knee-pan; (শারীর-সংস্থানবিদ্যা) মালাইচাকী। **3.** (*Zool.*) A shield-like dermal plate or scale; ঢালের আকার খোল বা শল্ক। **–tal, –tate, –ti-form,** *adjs.*

Scyl-lă (sĭl-), *n.* See CHARYBDIS.

scy̆'-phŭs, *n.* **1.** A kind of large drinking glass used by the ancient Greeks ; প্রাচীন গ্রীকগণ-কর্ত্তৃক ব্যবহৃত একপ্রকার বৃহৎ পানপাত্র। **2.** (*Bot.*) A cup-shaped appendage to a flower ; (উদ্ভিদ্‌বিদ্যা) পুষ্পের পেয়ালার আকার উপাঙ্গ। **–phose, –phi-form,** *adjs.*

scythe (sīth), *n.* & *v. t.* An implement for mowing grass or cutting grain, having long carved blade ; একপ্রকার বড় কাস্তে, শস্যকর্ত্তরিকা। ***Verb t.*** To cut with a scythe ; কাস্তেদ্বারা কাটা। **Scythed,** *p.p.*

Scyth'-i-ăn (sĭth-), *adj.* & *n.* Of ancient Scythia ; উত্তর এসিয়াবাসী যাযাবর জাতিবিশেষসম্পর্কীয়, শকগণ সম্পর্কীয়। ***Noun.*** **1.** A native of Scythia; সিথিয়ার অধিবাসী, শাকদ্বীপের অধিবাসী। **2.** The language of Scythia ; সিথিয়ার ভাষা। **Scythian-disease** — শিশ্নজাড্য, লিঙ্গস্তম্ভ। [এই রোগগ্রস্ত ব্যক্তিগণের পুরুষোচিত স্বার্থসমূহ লোপ পায়]। **Scythian insanity** — সিথিয় মস্তিষ্কবিকৃতি। [এই রোগাক্রান্ত পুরুষগণের পুরুষোচিত ধর্ম্মসমূহ লোপ পায় এবং তাহারা স্ত্রীজনোচিত হাবভাব ও বেশভুষা ধারণ করিয়া থাকে।]

'sdeath (sdĕth), *Interj.* (Abbr. for *God's death*), (*Archaic*) An expression of anger, surprise, etc. ; ক্রোধ, বিস্ময়, প্রভৃতি, সূচক অব্যয়।

sea (sē), *n.* **1.** The mass of salt-water covering most of the earth ; সমুদ্র, সাগর, দরিয়া (*poet.*), পাথার (*poet.* যথা "রূপের পাথার," "রসের পাথার"—বৈষ্ণব পদাবলী), কালাপাণি (*slang*), [Syn. জলধি, অর্ণব, পারাবার, সিন্ধু, বারিধি, উদধি, অম্বুধি, জলনিধি, নীলাম্বুরাশি, নীরধি, অব্ধি, অকূপার, উদন্বান, সরস্বান, অপাংপতি, মহাকচ্ছ, নদীকান্ত, জলেন্দ্র, দ্বীপবান্, তরীষ, মকরালয়, ক্ষৌণীপ্রাচীর, মস্থির, নীরনিধি, সরিৎপতি, পাথোনিধি, পাথোধি, ইন্দুজনক, যাদপতি, নদীন, তিমিকোষ, বারিনিধি, বার্দ্ধি, তোয়নিধি (কুমারঃ), কীলালধি, ধরণীপুর, বাঙ্ক, কচঙ্গল, পেরু, মিতদ্রু, বাহিনীপতি, তিমি, দারদ, গঙ্গাধর, প্রাণভাস্বান, উর্ম্মিমালী, মহাশয়, অম্ভোরাশি, শৈলশিবির, মহী-প্রাচীর, পয়োধি, সরিন্নাথ, সরিদধিপতি, সরিদভর্ত্তা, সলিলনিধি, সরিন্নাথ, সলিলরাশি (শিশু), সলিলাকর (রাঃ তঃ), ধুনীনাথ, বারিরাশি, অম্ভোনিধি, নিত্য, কব্ধি, অপাংনাথ, মীনালয়, অম্বুরাশি (cf. যথা বিশ্বাধরারমা অম্বুরাশিতলে—মেঘনাদবধ), তরিষ, কুলঙ্কষ, তারিষ, বারিনাথ, বারীশ, অম্বুনাথ, অম্বুনিধি, অম্বুপতি (বৃঃ সং), অম্বুরাজ (নলঃ), তোয়ধি (সুঃ সিঃ), তোয়ালয়, তোয়রাশি (কাদঃ), নীররাশি (শিশুঃ), সলিলার্ণব (রঃ), লবণজল (মঃ ভাঃ), লবণজলধি (ভাগঃ), লবণজলনিধি (রঃ), লবণবারি (শারঙ্গঃ পঃ), লবণসমুদ্র, লবণসিন্ধু (শিশুঃ টীকা), লবণাম্বুধি (মার্কঃ পুঃ), লবণার্ণব (ভাগঃ), রত্নাকর, লবণোদক (বৌদ্ধঃ), লবণোদ (মঃ উঃ), লবণোদধি (রঃ), উদকার্ণব (রঃ), তরঙ্গমালী, তরঙ্গিণীনাথ (বাল রাঃ), তরঙ্গিণীভর্ত্তা (বুদ্ধঃ), বীচিমালী (অঃ), নদীনাথ, নদীপতি, যাদসাম্পতি। **2.** The ocean ; মহাসাগর, মহোদধি সিন্ধুনাথ (শিশুঃ)। **3.** A name of certain lakes when large ; কতিপয় বৃহৎ হ্রদের নাম। **4.** Any large quantity ; as, *sea* of grief ; সাগর (cf. দুঃখসাগর, অমিয় সাগর, অশ্রুসাগর)। **5.** The swell of the ocean ; "They had continued fine weather and no *sea*" ; a large wave ; "A heavy *sea* broke over our quarter" ; সাগরের কল্লোলান্বিত অবস্থা ; কল্লোল। **6.** A large basin or cistern which Solomon made in the temple of Jerusalem ; জেরুজেলেমের মন্দিরে সলোমনকর্ত্তৃক নির্ম্মিত বৃহৎ জলকুণ্ড বা জলাধার। [ইহাতে ৬০০০ গেলন জল ধরিত বলিয়া কথিত আছে।] **Sea-acorn**—Same as BARNACLE. **Sea-anchor**—ঝটিকা-বিক্ষুব্ধ সমুদ্রে ব্যবহৃত একপ্রকার প্লবমান নোঙ্গর। **Sea-anemones**—সাগরোপকূলস্থ পাষাণেপ্রাপ্ত একপ্রকার শ্লিষ্ট জীবপুঞ্জ। **Sea-bank**—বালীয়াড়ী। **Sea-bat**—উড়ুক্কু মৎস্য। **Sea-bath**—সাগরস্নান; সাগরস্নানের স্থান। **Sea-beach**—সাগরতট, সাগরসৈকত। **Sea-bird**—সাগরচরপক্ষী, সামুদ্রিক পক্ষী। **Sea-bloom, sea-blossom** — সামুদ্রিক উদ্ভিদের পুষ্প, সাগর-কুসুম। **Sea-blubber**—Same as JELLY-FISH. **Sea-blue**—সাগরনীল। **Seaboard**—সিন্ধুতট, সমুদ্রতট। **Sea-born**—সাগরজাত, সমুদ্রভব। **Sea-borne**—সমুদ্রগামী অর্ণবপোতে নীত, সমুদ্রের উপর বাহিত, সামুদ্রিক। **Sea-bow**—সাগর শীকরে দৃষ্ট রামধনু, সাগরধনু। **Sea-breeze**—See BREEZE; সাগরানিল, সমুদ্রানিল, সমুদ্রসমীর (সাঃ পঃ)। **Sea-calf**—মাংসাশী এবং স্তন্যদায়ী জলজন্তু বিশেষ, শীলমৎস্য। **Sea-canary**—শ্বেত-তিমি। **Sea-captain** — সমুদ্রগামী পোতের অধ্যক্ষ, সাগরপোতাধ্যক্ষ, বিশেষতঃ বাণিজ্যপোতাধ্যক্ষ। **Sea-cloth**—সাগরতীরের দৃশ্যপট। **Sea-coast**—সাগরোপকূল। **Sea-colour**—সাগর-বর্ণ। **Sea-conny, Sea-cunny,**

Sea-connie, Secony — সুখানী, কর্ণধার। [পারস্য ভাষার سکانی শব্দের ইংরাজী অপভ্রংশ।] **Sea cow**—একপ্রকার স্তন্যপায়ী সামুদ্রিক প্রাণী—পশ্চাদ্দিগের পদবিহীন এবং অল্প অল্প লোমবিশিষ্ট, সিন্ধুঘোটক। **Sea-craft**—পোতচালন নৈপুণ্য। **Sea-crow**—বিভিন্ন প্রকার পক্ষীর সাধারণ নাম। **Sea-deity** — সাগরদেবতা। **Sea-devil**—বিভিন্ন প্রকার কদাকার মৎস্যের সাধারণ নাম। **Sea-dog**—একজাতীয় ক্ষুদ্র হাঙ্গর মৎস্য; শীলমৎস্য; প্রবীণ নাবিক, পাকা নাবিক। **Sea-duck** — একপ্রকার সাগরচর হংস; একপ্রকার মৎস্য (called also *Bombay duck*). **Sea-ear**—একপ্রকার শম্বুক। **Sea-elephant**— অতিকায়, স্তন্যদায়ী জলজন্তুবিশেষ, জলমাতঙ্গ। **Sea-encircled**—সাগরবেষ্টিত, সাগর-বলয়িত। **Sea-fare**—জাহাজে যে খাদ্য আহার করা হয়। **Sea-farer**—নাবিক, সাগরযাত্রী, সমুদ্রযাত্রী। **Sea-faring** — সমুদ্রগ (বুঃ সং), সমুদ্রগামী। **Sea-fight**—জলযুদ্ধ, সাগরযুদ্ধ, সাগররণ। **Sea-fish**—সামুদ্রিক মৎস্য। **Sea-fowl**—Same as SEA-BIRD; সাগরোপকূলবাসী বিহঙ্গ। **Sea-foam**—সাগরফেণ, সমুদ্রফেণ, সমুদ্র কফ। **Sea front**—অট্টালিকা প্রভৃতির সাগরাভিমুখীন অংশ। **Sea-gauge**—জাহাজের প্রধান তলকাষ্ঠ যে পরিমাণ নিমজ্জিত হয়; সমুদ্রের গভীরতামাপক যন্ত্রবিশেষ। **Sea-girt**—সাগরবেষ্টিত, সাগরবলয়িত, সাগরমেখল। **Sea-girt Isle**—ইংলণ্ড। **Sea god**—সাগরদেবতা, বরুণদেব। **Sea-going** — সমুদ্রগামী (পোত), সমুদ্রগ। **Sea-grape**—সমুদ্রজিভ মৎস্যের (cuttle fish) ডিম্বগুচ্ছ; একপ্রকার গুল্ম। **Sea-green** — সাগরবারিতুল্য, আনীলহরিদ্বর্ণ, সামুদ্রসবুজ, সাগরশ্যামল, সমুদ্র-

Sea-gull.

শ্যামল, জলধিশ্যামল। **Sea-gull** — সাগরবলাকা। Same as GULLY.

Sea-hare—একপ্রকার শম্বুক, সমুদ্রশশক। **Sea-hog**—শিশুমার, শুশুক, ঘড়াল। **Sea-horizon**—সাগরচক্রবাল, সাগরদিগন্ত, সাগরক্ষিতিজ। **Sea-horse**—সিন্ধুঘোটক। **Sea-horses**—সাগরোপকূলে প্রতিহত ফেনশুভ্র তরঙ্গ। **Sea-island cotton**—জর্জ্জিয়া এবং দক্ষিণ কেরোলিনার নিকটবর্ত্তী সাগরের দ্বীপসমূহে জাত একপ্রকার সূক্ষ্ম কার্পাস। **Sea-ivory**—বৃহৎকায় সামুদ্রিক জন্তুসমূহের দন্ত। **Sea-king**—খৃষ্টীয় অষ্টম ও দশম শতাব্দীর নোর্সজাতীয় জলদস্যুদলপতি। **Sea-lawyer** — ছিদ্রান্বেষী ব্যক্তি (নাবিকদিগের মধ্যে ব্যবহৃত। **Sea-level** — সাগরপৃষ্ঠ, (সাঃ পঃ), সিন্ধুধরাতল (হিঃ কোঃ)। **Sea-lilies**—সামুদ্রিক পদ্মতারাশ্রেণী (মিউজিয়াম) ইহাদের বাহ্যাকৃতি ঠুনকো তারামাছের ন্যায়। মধ্যস্থানের গোল চাক অনেকটা বাটার মত। **Sea-lion** — বহিঃকর্ণবিশিষ্ট শীলমৎস্যবিশেষ, নক্রসিংহ। [এই

Sea-lion.

জন্তুর গর্জ্জন সিংহের মত এবং নরদিগের সিংহের মত কেশর থাকে।] **Seaman** — নাবিক; নৌচালননিপুণ ব্যক্তি। **Sea-manship**—পোতচালনবিদ্যা, পোতচালননৈপুণ্য। **Sea-mark**—নাবিকদিগের পথপ্রদর্শক চিহ্ন। **Sea-mew**—গাং চিল। **Sea-mile**—প্রায় ৬০৮০ ফিট বা ১ ১/৭ মাইল। **Sea-music**—সাগরসঙ্গীত। **Sea-needle**—একপ্রকার মৎস্য। **Sea-nymph**—জলপরী, সাগরপরী। **Sea-painter**—সাগরচিত্রকর। **Sea-pen**—একজাতীয় সামুদ্রিক প্রাণী—ইহাদের মুখের কতক অংশ উল্টিয়া ভিতরে ঢুকিয়া প্রকৃত গলনালীর সৃষ্টি করিয়াছে এবং ইহাদের অন্ত্রনালী ঝিল্লীদ্বারা অনেকভাগে বিভক্ত। ইহা আকার অনেকটা কলমের ন্যায়, সামুদ্রিক

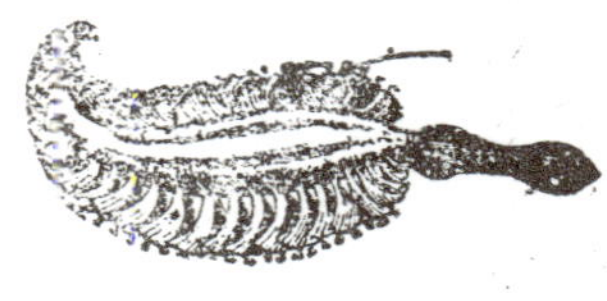

Sea-pen.

কলম (মিউজিয়াম), সামুদ্রিকলেখনী। **Sea-pie**—মাংস এবং শাকসব্জীর খাদ্য বিশেষ। **Seaport**—বন্দর, পত্তন। **Sea-robber** — জলদস্যু, সাগর-দস্যু বোম্বেটিয়া। **Sea-room**—পোতচালনার পক্ষে যথেষ্ট স্থান। **Sea-rover**—সাগরদস্যু। **Sea-salt** — সাগরোত্থ, সমুদ্রলবণ, জলরস (অঃ)। **Sea-scape**—সাগরচিত্র, সাগরদৃশ্য। **Sea-serpent**—সাগরবাসী প্রকাণ্ড নাগবিশেষ, সমুদ্রনাগ, সাগরনাগ, সমুদ্রসাপ (সাঃ পঃ), সমুদ্রভুজঙ্গ। **Sea-service** — নাবিকের কাজ, বিশেষতঃ রণপোতে কার্য্য। **Sea-shell**—সাগরশুক্তি। **Sea-shore**—সাগরতীর, সাগরান্ত (রঃ), সমুদ্রকুক্ষি। **Seasick** — পোতান্দোলনজনিত বমনপীড়াদ্বারা আক্রান্ত, সাগরপীড়াক্রান্ত। **Sea-sickness**—সাগরবক্ষে পোতান্দোলনজনিত বমনপীড়া, সমুদ্রপীড়া। **Sea-side**—সমুদ্রের কিনারা, সাগরতট, সাগরপার্শ্ব। **Sea-tale**—সাগরের কথা, সাগরকথা, সাগরকাহিনী। **Sea-unicorn**—একজাতীয় সামুদ্রিক প্রাণী, নারওয়াল—ইহাদের সমস্ত দাঁত লোপ পাইয়া উপরের চোয়ালে মাত্র ১ জোড়া গজদন্তের তুল্য দাঁত অবশিষ্ট রহিয়াছে। **Sea-urchin**—সুগোল এবং কণ্টকাবৃত জলজন্তুবিশেষ; সামুদ্রিক ডিম্বের শ্রেণী (মিউজিয়াম), সাগরাণ্ড। [এই শ্রেণীর কণ্টকচর্ম্মীদের উপর খড়ীর একটী কঠিন আবরণ আছে।] **Sea-voice**—সাগরোদ্ভূত নিঃস্বন, সাগরবাণী। **Sea-voyage** — সাগরযাত্রা, সমুদ্রযানযাত্রা (দিব্যাবদান)। **Sea-wall**—সাগরজলরোধের জন্য বাঁধ, সাগরপ্রাচীর। **Sea-ward**—সাগরাভিমুখে। **Sea-way**—জাহাজের গতিবেগের হার; পোতচালনার পক্ষে যথেষ্ট স্থান। **Sea-weed**—সামুদ্রিক

...দ্। **Sea-wolf** — গ্রেটব্রিটনের চতুষ্পার্শ্ববর্ত্তী সাগর-বাসী হিংস্র এবং বৃহৎকায় মৎস্যবিশেষ; জলদস্যু। **Sea-worthy** — (পোতসম্পর্কে) সাগর-গমনোপযোগী, সমুদ্রগমনোপযোগী। **A heavy sea** — উত্তালতরঙ্গসঙ্কুল সমুদ্র, ঝটিকাবিক্ষুব্ধ সিন্ধু। **At full sea**—At full tide; পূর্ণ জোয়ারে। **At sea**—On the ocean; astray; in a state of perplexity; সাগরে; বিপথে; কিংকর্ত্তব্যবিমূঢ় অবস্থায়, অকূল পাথারে। Employed as a sailor; নাবিকের কার্য্যে নিযুক্ত। **Beyond seas**—সাগরের অপর পারে। **By sea, By the sea**—On or over the sea; সাগরোপরি, সাগরপথে। **Inland Sea** — স্থলগর্ভিত সাগর (সাঃ পঃ)। **Half seas over**—See HALF. **Main sea**—মহাসাগর। **On the other side of the sea** — সাগরের অপর পারে। **On or upon the sea** — At sea; on ship-board; সাগরে; জাহাজের উপরি। **Over sea, Over the sea** — Across the sea; সাগরের উপর দিয়া। **The four seas**—গ্রেট-ব্রিটেনের চতুষ্পার্শ্ববর্ত্তী সাগর। **The high seas**—The open ocean; বাহির দরিয়া। **The molten sea**—See SEA, 6. **The son of a sea-cook**—জাহাজের মাল্লাদিগের মধ্যে এক প্রকার গালি। **To follow the sea**—To become a sailor; নাবিক হওয়া। **To get one's sea-legs on**—To be able to walk on ship-board without reeling; তরঙ্গান্দোলিত পোতে না টলিয়া চলিতে সমর্থ হওয়া। **To go to sea**—To proceed to sea; সমুদ্রে যাওয়া, সমুদ্রে চলা। To become a sailor; নাবিকবৃত্তি অবলম্বন করা। **To put to sea**—To sail; জাহাজ ছাড়িয়া দেওয়া। **To take to the sea**—To become a sailor; নাবিকবৃত্তি অবলম্বন করা। To go to a foreign land in a ship; জাহাজে বিদেশে গমন করা।

seal (sōl), *n.* & *v. i.* An aquatic carnivorous mammal, valuable for its skin and oil; সীল মৎস্য। *Verb i.* To hunt seals; সীল মৎস্য

Seal.

শিকার করা। **Seal-skin**—সীল মৎস্যের চর্ম্ম; সীল মৎস্যের সলোম চর্ম্ম; সীল মৎস্যের চর্ম্মের স্ত্রীলোকদিগের অঙ্গরক্ষা।

seal (sēl), *n.* & *v. t.* 1. A hard substance bearing some device, used to make impressions; মুদ্রা, মোহর, নামমুদ্রা, মুদ্রিকা (cf. সৌবর্ণীং রাজতীং তাম্রীমায়সীং বা সুশোভিতাম্ সলিলেন সকুদ্ধৌতাং প্রক্ষিপেৎ তত্র মুদ্রিকাং॥ —মিতাক্ষরা—ব্যবহারাধ্যায়), শীলমোহর। 2. The wax attached to a writing and impressed or stamped with a seal; শীলমোহরাঙ্কিত গালা। 3. Assurance; any act of confirmation; "It gives the *seal*, to all experimental knowledge"; that which confirms or modifies; নিশ্চয়তা; দৃঢ়তাবিধায়ক কার্য্য; যদ্দ্বারা কোন কিছু স্থিরীকৃত বা রূপান্তরিত হয়। *Verb t.* 1. To set or affix a seal to as a mark of a authenticity; শীলমোহরাঙ্কিত করা, মুদ্রাঙ্কিত করা, গালামোহর করা। 2. To ratify; to confirm; to decide irrevocably; as, to *seal* one's fate; দৃঢ় করা; পাকা করা; চিরদিনের জন্য নির্দ্দিষ্ট করা। 3. To close hermetically; দৃঢ়রুদ্ধ করা। **Sealing-wax**—মোহর করার গালা। **Seal of love**—চুম্বন, সন্তানের জন্ম, প্রভৃতি।

seal'-ėr (sēl-), *n.* 1. One who seals; যে ব্যক্তি শীলমোহর দেয়। 2. A ship or man engaged in seal-hunting; সীলমৎস্য শিকারে নিযুক্ত পোত বা লোক।

seam (sēm), *n.* & *v. t.* 1. The line of junction formed by the sewing or stitching of two different pieces of cloth etc.; সেলাইর সন্ধিরেখা বা জোড়মুখ, সীবনসন্ধিরেখা। 2. (*Anat.*) Suture; (শারীরসংস্থান-বিদ্যা) সীবনীসন্ধি, সীবনী। 3. A cicatrix or scar; শুষ্ক ক্ষত, শুষ্ক ব্রণ। 4. The juncture of planks in a ship's side or deck; জাহাজের পার্শ্ব বা পাটাতনের কাষ্ঠফলকসন্ধি। 5. A vein or stratum of metal, ore, coal and the like; ধাতু, খনিজ-বিমিশ্রধাতু, কয়লা, প্রভৃতির শিরা। *Verb t.* 1. To unite by seam; to form a seam on; সেলাই করিয়া জোড়া দেওয়া; সীবনসন্ধিরেখা রচনা করা। 2. To scar; (ক্ষতাদি) শুষ্ক করা। 3. (*Knitting*) To make ridges in stockings etc.; মোজা প্রভৃতির উপর শির তোলা। **Seam'-less**, *adj.* Without seam; অনসেলাই। **Seam-presser**—লাঙ্গলকৃষ্ট-ভূমি চৌরস করার জন্য কৃষিযন্ত্রবিশেষ।

seam'-strĕss (sĕm-), **sĕmp'–**, *ns.* A woman whose occupation is sewing; মেয়ে দর্জ্জী, সীবনকারিণী, সূচিকর্ম্মনিপুণা নারী।

seam'-ȳ (sēm-), *adj.* Having a seam; showing a seam; সীবন-সন্ধিরেখাযুক্ত; সীবনসন্ধিরেখাপ্রদর্শী, সেলাইএর রেখা দেখানিয়া। **Seamy side**—কাপড়ের যেদিকে সেলাইর জোড়মুখ দেখা যায়; (লক্ষণায়) কোন কিছুর নিকৃষ্ট দিক, ভাব বা অবস্থা।

seance, *n.* 1. Session, as of some public body; বৈঠক। 2. A meeting of spiritualists; as, the phenomena of the *seance-room*; প্রেততাত্ত্বিকগণের বৈঠক, প্রেত-তত্ত্বানুশীলনের জন্য অধিবেশন, প্রেত-তত্ত্বানুশীলনসভা।

sear (sēr), *adj.* & *v. t.* Withered; শুষ্ক, বিশুষ্ক, শুক্‌না। *Verb t.* 1. To wither; শুষ্ক করা, বিশুষ্ক করা। 2. To cauterise; to burn; to scorch; দাহক পদার্থ দ্বারা বা তপ্ত লৌহ দ্বারা শরীরের কোন স্থান দগ্ধ করা; পোড়ান, দগ্ধ করা; ছেঁকা। 3. To make callous or insensible ; as, to *sear* one's conscience ; অসাড় করা, সাড়াহীন করা, সংবেদনশূন্য করা। **The sear and yellow leaf**—Old age ; বার্দ্ধক্য।

sear (sēr), *n.* Same as SERE (which see).

search (sêrch), *v. t., i.* & *n.* **1.** To look over or through for the purpose of finding something ; তল্লাস করা, খুঁজা, অনুসন্ধান করা, অন্বেষণ করা। **2.** To probe ; as, to *search* a wound ; to pierce ; শলাকা দ্বারা ক্ষতের গভীরতা প্রভৃতি পরীক্ষা করা ; ভেদ করা। **3.** To examine ; to try ; "*Search* me, O God, and know my heart" ; পরীক্ষা করা ; পরীক্ষা করিয়া দেখা। ***Verb i.*** **1.** To seek ; খুঁজা, অন্বেষণ করা। **2.** To investigate ; অনুসন্ধান করা। ***Noun.*** **1.** The act of seeking or looking for something ; তালাস, খোঁজন, অন্বেষণ, এষণা (হিঃ কোঃ)। **2.** Investigation ; অনুসন্ধান। **Search′-a-ble,** *adj.* That can be searched ; অনুসন্ধাতব্য, অনুসন্ধেয়, অন্বেষ্য। **Search′-ing,** *adj.* & *n.* Scrutinizing penetrating ; keen ; as, a *searching* wound ; পুঙ্খানুপুঙ্খ, তন্ন তন্ন, সূক্ষ্মানুসন্ধায়ী ; তীক্ষ্ণ ; তীব্র, দারুণ। ***Noun.*** The act of searching ; অন্বেষণ। **House-search** — খানাতল্লাস। **Search-light**—শত্রুপক্ষীয় পোত প্রভৃতির গতিবিধি পর্য্যবেক্ষণের জন্য তীব্র বৈদ্যুতিক আলো, তল্লাসী আলো, অন্বেষক আলোক। **Search-party** — খানাতল্লাসকারীর দল। **Search-warrant**—খানাতল্লাসির পরোয়ানা। **Right of search**—(আন্তর্জাতিক আইন) কোনরূপ নিষিদ্ধ পণ্যদ্রব্য আছে কিনা পরীক্ষার জন্য যুধ্যমান জাতিকর্তৃক নির্লিপ্ত জাতির জাহাজ তল্লাসের অধিকার। **Searchings of hearts**—পাপাদির জন্য মনের সংশয় বা খটকা।

sea′-son (sē-zn), *n., v. t.* & *i.* **1.** One of the four divisions of a year ; ঋতু। [ইংরাজেরা প্রতিবর্ষ Spring, Summer, Autumn, Winter এই চারিটী ঋতুতে বিভক্ত করেন। হিন্দুরা ছয়টী ঋতু গণনা করিয়া থাকেন। যথা, গ্রীষ্ম (বৈশাখ, জ্যৈষ্ঠ), বর্ষা (আষাঢ় শ্রাবণ), শরৎ (ভাদ্র, আশ্বিন), হেমন্ত (কার্ত্তিক, অগ্রহায়ণ), শীত (পৌষ, মাঘ), বসন্ত (ফাল্গুন, চৈত্র)।] **2.** A fit, convenient or suitable time ; as, a word in *season* ; উপযুক্ত সময়, উপযুক্তকাল, সুযোগ। **3.** The time of the year when a particular locality is most frequented by visitors or shows most bustling activity ; as, the London *season* ; that time of the year when a profession or business is in the greatest state of activity ; as, the publishing *season* যে সময় কোন স্থান বহু দর্শনার্থী লোকে পরিপূর্ণ হয় এবং খুব সরগরম হইয়া উঠে ; বৎসরের মধ্যে যে কয়েক মাস কোন ব্যবসায়ে খুব জাঁকিয়া উঠে, মরসুম। **4.** The time of year when a plant blooms or bears fruits or any particular edible is fit for production ; as, mango is out of *season* : oysters are in *season* ; মরসুম, বন্দ (কৃষিসম্পদ)। **5.** Awhile ; "Thou shalt be blind not seeing the sun for a *season*" ; কিছুকাল, কতক সময়। ***Verb t.*** **1.** (*Obs.*) To render fit ; to prepare ; (অপ্রঃ) উপযোগী করা ; প্রস্তুত করা। **2.** To inure ; অভ্যস্ত করা। **3.** To give a zest or relish to ; to spice ; to render palatable ; রসাল করা ; মসলাদি মিশ্রিত করা ; সুস্বাদু করা, মুখরোচক করা। **4.** To render less severe ; as, to *season* justice with mercy ; উগ্রতা হ্রাস করা, তীব্রতা মন্দীভূত করা, কঠোরতা হ্রাস করা। **5.** To dry and harden ; as, to *season* wood ; শুষ্ক এবং কঠিন করা, পচান। **6.** To imbue ; "Mind thoroughly *seasoned* with religion ;" অনুরঞ্জিত করা, অনুপ্রাণিত করা। ***Verb i.*** **1.** To become mature ; to grow fit for use ; to become adapted to a climate ; পরিপক্ব হওয়া, ব্যবহারের উপযোগী হওয়া ; কোনরূপ আবহাওয়ার উপযোগী হওয়া। **2.** To become dry and hard, as timber ; শুষ্ক এবং কঠিন হওয়া। **–a-ble,** *adj.* Opportune ; কালোচিত, সময়োচিত, প্রাসঙ্গিক, সাম্প্রত (সর্ব্বদঃ), কালিক (সঃ ভাঃ)। **–a-ble-ness,** *n.* **–a-bly,** *adv.* Opportunely ; সময়োচিতভাবে। **–al,** *adj.* **–er,** *n.* **–ing,** *n.* **1.** That which is added to a food to give it a higher relish ; লবণ, মসলা প্রভৃতি, উপস্কর (আঃ বঃ)। **–soned,** *p. p.* **Season-flower**—মরসুমী ফুল, ঋতুবাহার। **Season-ticket**—ছয় মাস, এক বৎসর কিম্বা অপর কোন নির্দ্দিষ্টকালের জন্য বাষ্পীয়শকট প্রভৃতিতে যাতায়াত বা রঙ্গালয় প্রভৃতিতে গমনের জন্য যে যে প্রবেশপত্র দেওয়া হয়। **Breeding season** — জননঋতু (মিউজিয়াম)। **In season**—In proper time ; যথাসময়ে, যথাকালে। **In season and out of season**—At all time ; অনুদিন, কালে অকালে, কালাকাল বিচার না করিয়া, যখন তখন, সব সময়, অষ্টপ্রহর। **Out of season**—Inopportune ; অসময়োচিত। **Not in season** ; মরসুম নয়। **The dry season and the rainy season**—গ্রীষ্ম ও বর্ষা ঋতু [উষ্ণমণ্ডলে বৎসর কেবল মাত্র এই দুইটী ঋতুতে বিভক্ত হইয়া থাকে। আমাদের শাস্ত্রাদিতেও এইরূপ ঋতুবিভাগ দৃষ্ট হয়। যথা—"কার্ত্তিকাদিষণ্মাসাঃ শীতঃ বৈশাখাদি ষণ্মাসাঃ গ্রীষ্মঃ—শব্দকল্পদ্রুমধৃত স্মৃতিবচন। **To be in season**—To be opportune ; সময়োপযোগী হওয়া, কালোপযোগী হওয়া। (Of a plant or animal) To be in a state of eating or in a flourishing state ; খাদ্যোপযোগী হওয়া, মরসুম হওয়া।

seat (sēt), *n.* & *v. t.* **1.** The place or thing upon which a person sits ; a chair ; a bench ; আসন, পীঠিকা ; কেদারা, কুর্সি ; দীর্ঘ আসন।

2. That part of a chair etc. on which a person sits ; কেদারা প্রভৃতির যে অংশে কেহ উপবেশন করে। 3. Place of abode ; a country mansion ; as, a gentleman's country *seat* ; বাসস্থান, বাসস্থলী ; পল্লী-প্রাসাদ, পল্লীবাটিকা। 4. The buttocks (also jocularly *seat of honour*) নিতম্ব। 5. The place where anything is situated, fixed, settled or established or on which anything rests, resides or abides; স্থলী, স্থান, নিকেতন। 6. A right to seat ; উপবেশনের অধিকার, বসিবার অধিকার। 7. A part or surface on which the base of something rests ; অধিষ্ঠানভূমি। 8. Posture ; as, a rider has a firm *seat* ; উপবেশনভঙ্গী। *Verb t.* 1. To place on a seat ; to cause to sit down ; আসনস্থ করা ; উপবিষ্ট করান, বসান। 2. To fit up seats in ; as, to *seat* a church ; আসনসমূহ সজ্জিত করা। 3. To put into a seat of parliament etc. ; পার্লেমেণ্ট প্রভৃতির সভ্যপদে অধিষ্ঠিত করা। 4. (*Rare*) To settle or establish ; (কচিদ্ব্যবহৃত) স্থাপিত করা, প্রতিষ্ঠিত করা। 5. To repair seats of chairs, trousers, etc. ; কেদারার উপবেশনস্থান, পাজামা প্রভৃতির নিতম্বদেশাবরক অংশ মেরামত করা। **Seat of honour**—গৌরবাসন (রবীঃ)। **To seat a candidate**—To elect him as a member of parliament ; কোন ব্যক্তিকে পার্লেমেণ্টের সভ্যপদে নির্ব্বাচিত করা।

sē-bā′-ceous (-shŭs), *adj.* Pertaining to fat ; made of fat ; secreting fatty matter ; মেদসম্বন্ধীয় ; মেদময় ; মেদস্রাবী।

sē-bĕs′-tĕn, —tăn, *ns.* 1. An East-Indian tree ; the fruit of this tree ; বহুয়ারী গাছ ; ঐ গাছের ফল। [Arab. *sabastan* ; Pers. *sapistan* ; F. *sebeste* ; Sp. *sebasta, sebesten* ; It. *sebesten* ; Portug. *sebeste* ; Hind. *lasura, goudni*].

sec, (*F.*), *adj.* (Of wine) dry ; (মদ্য-সম্পর্কে), মিষ্টতা এবং ফলগন্ধ পরিশূন্য।

sē′-cănt, *adj.* & *n.* 1. Cutting ; dividing in two parts; ছেদক; দ্বিখণ্ডকারী। *Noun.* 1. (*Geom.*) A line that cuts another ; অবচ্ছেদক। 2. (*Trigon.*) A straight line from the centre of a circle cutting the circumference and meeting a tangent to the same circle ; (ত্রিকোণমিতি) বৃত্তের কেন্দ্র হইতে অঙ্কিত রেখা বিশেষ — যাহা পরিধি ভেদপূর্ব্বক ঐ বৃত্তের স্পর্শজ্যাকে স্পর্শ করিয়া থাকে ; ছেদনরেখা (হিঃ কোঃ)।

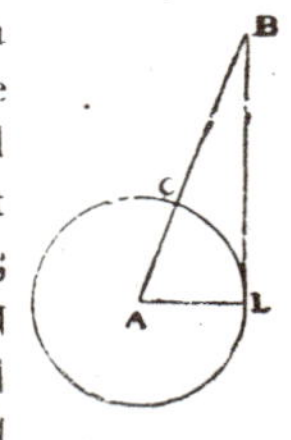

A, B, C secant.

secco, (*It.*), *adj.* & *n.* Dry ; শুষ্ক। *Noun.* Same as SECCO-PAINTING. **Secco-painting**—শুষ্ক আস্তরের উপর অঙ্কিত চিত্র, শুষ্কচিত্র।

sē-cede′ (-sēd), *v. i.* 1. To withdraw from fellowship, communion or association ; কোন সমাজ বা সম্প্রদায়ের সহিত সম্পর্ক বিচ্ছিন্ন করা। 2. To separate one's self ; বিচ্ছিন্ন করা, সংস্রব ত্যাগ করা, সম্বন্ধ ছিন্ন করা। **—ced′-er,** *n.* 1. One who secedes ; ভিন্নমতগ্রাহী, মতান্তরাশ্রিত। 2. A body who seceded from the established Church of Scotland in 1733 ; স্কটলণ্ডের রাজবিধিদ্বারা প্রতিষ্ঠিত ধর্ম্মসংঘ হইতে ১৭৩৩ খৃষ্টাব্দে বিচ্ছিন্ন ব্যক্তিগণ।

sē-cĕrn′-ĕnt, *adj.* & *n.* Secretory; স্রাবী, স্রাবণশীল, ক্ষরণশীল। *Noun.* That which promotes secretion ; a secretory vessel ; স্রাববর্দ্ধক ; স্রাবনিঃসারকগ্রন্থি।

sē-ces′-sion (-sĕ-), *n.* 1. The act of seceding ; কোন সমাজ বা সম্প্রদায়ের সহিত সম্বন্ধচ্ছেদ। 2. The act of withdrawing from a political or religious organization ; রাজনীতিক বা ধর্ম্মসম্বন্ধীয় প্রতিষ্ঠানের সহিত সম্বন্ধচ্ছেদ, সম্প্রদায়ত্যাগ। 3. Departure; প্রস্থান। **—ism,** *n.* **—ist,** *n.* **War of Secession**—১৮৬১—৬৫ খৃঃ অব্দের আমেরিকার অন্তর্যুদ্ধ।

sē-clūde′, *v. t.* To shut up apart ; to separate, as from society or company ; to set apart ; নির্জ্জনে রাখা, বিজনে রাখা ; লোক সমাজ হইতে দূরে রাখা ; পৃথক করিয়া রাখা। **—clud′-ed, —clud′-ed-ly,** *adv.*

sē-clū′-sion (-zhŭn), *n.* 1. The act of secluding or the state of being secluded ; retirement ; privacy ; নির্জ্জনে অবস্থান ; নির্জ্জনবাস, নিভৃতবাস, বিজনবাস ; নির্জ্জনতা, বিজনতা, নিঃসঙ্গতা। 2. Secluded place ; নির্জ্জন স্থান, বিজনালয়, বিজনস্থান, বিজনপ্রদেশ।

sĕc′-ond (-ŭnd), *adj., n.* & *v. t.* 1. The next following the first in order of place or time ; দ্বিতীয়। 2. Inferior ; "They are *second* to none in the Christian world" ; নিকৃষ্ট, অপকৃষ্ট, হীন, ন্যূন। 3. Secondary ; গৌণ (সূর্য্য বাঃ), ভাক্ত (শ্রীঃ), অপর (ঐ)। 4. Prototype ; "A *second* Daniel ; দ্বিতীয়। *Noun.* 1. One or that next the first ; দ্বিতীয় ব্যক্তি, দ্বিতীয় বস্তু, দোসর। 2. A person who aids, abets or supports another ; সহায়ক, সাহায্যকারী, সমর্থক, দ্বিতীয়ক (সাঃ প্রঃ)। 3. One who attends another in a duel ; দ্বন্দ্বযুদ্ধে সহায় বা সহায়ক, দ্বন্দ্বযুদ্ধে সঙ্গী। 4. The sixtieth part of a minute of time or that of a degree, being the second division next to the hour or degree ; একমিনিটের ১/৬০ অংশ, এক সেকেণ্ড, এক ডিগ্রীর ৬০ ভাগের এক ভাগ, ২॥ অনুপল, অর্দ্ধকাষ্ঠ, বিপল (সাঃ পঃ)। 5. (*Pl.*) Goods of second quality, esp. coarse flour or bread made from it; দ্বিতীয় শ্রেণীর জিনিষ, বিশেষতঃ মোটা আটা বা মোটা আটার রুটি। 6. Same as SECOND IN

COMMAND. ***Verb t.*** **1.** To follow or attend; অনুগমন করা, অনুসরণ করা। **2.** To support; to encourage: "So well he was *seconded* by the multitude of labourers at his command"; সাহায্য করা; উৎসাহিত করা। **3.** To join with in proposing a measure; as, to *second* a proposal; সমর্থন করা, অনুমোদন করা। **4.** (*Mil.*) To remove an officer temporarily from an appointment with a view to appoint him to staff or extraregimental post; (সামরিক-শাস্ত্র) কোন কর্ম্মচারিকে সাময়িকভাবে স্থানান্তরিত করিয়া প্রধান সেনাপতির সহায়করূপে বিম্বা পল্টনের বহির্ভূত কোন পদে নিযুক্ত করা। **—er,** *n.* **1.** One that supports what another attempts; সাহায্যকারী, সহায়ক। **2.** One who supports a motion in a public meeting; সমর্থক, অনুমোদক। **Second Advent**—যীশুখৃষ্টের পুনরবতরণ, বিশেষতঃ যীশুখৃষ্টের দ্বিতীয়বার ধরাধামে অবতরণ। **Second Adventist**—পৃথিবীতে যীশুখৃষ্টের আশু আবির্ভাব সম্বন্ধে বিশ্বাসবান ব্যক্তিগণ [এই মতাবলম্বী ব্যক্তিগণের ৬টী বিভিন্ন সম্প্রদায় আছে যথা—(1) The Evangelical Adventist, (2) The Advent Christians, (3) The Life and Advent Union; (4) The Age-to-Come Adventist, (5) Th Seventh day Adventist, (6) The Church of God. William Muller এই মতের আদি প্রবর্ত্তক। মুলার ঘোষণা করেন ১৮৪০ খৃঃ অব্দে প্রলয় সংঘটিত হইবে এবং তৎসময়ে খৃষ্ট দ্বিতীয়বার অবতার গ্রহণ করিবেন। এই ভবিষ্যদ্বাণী বিফল হওয়া সত্ত্বেও মূলারের মতাবলম্বিগণ অদ্যাপি খৃষ্টের আশু আবির্ভাব সম্বন্ধে গভীর বিশ্বাসের সহিত প্রতীক্ষা করিতেছেন।—See W. C. Long's *End of the Ungodly*, 1882.] **Second-best**—দ্বিতীয়শ্রেণীর, দ্বিতীয়স্থানীয়; পরাস্ত, পর্যু্যদস্ত। **Second chamber**—পার্লেমেন্টের লর্ড সভা, ইংলণ্ড ব্যতিরিক্ত অপর দেশের ব্যবস্থাপক সভার অনুরূপ উচ্চতর শাখা। **Second childhood**—বার্দ্ধক্য। **Second coming**—Same as SECOND ADVENT. **Second cousin**—সাক্ষাৎ খুড়তাত, মামাত, প্রভৃতি ভাই ভগিনীর ছেলে। **Second distance**—চিত্রের পুরোভূমি এবং পশ্চাদ্‌ভূমির মধ্যবর্ত্তী অংশ। **Second floor**—ত্রিতল। **Second-hand**—অন্যকর্তৃক ব্যবহৃত, পুরাতন, অন্যভুক্ত। (*Noun*) পূর্ব্বাধিকারী হইতে প্রাপ্ত বস্তু; ঘড়ীর সেকেণ্ডের কাঁটা। **Second nature**—অর্জ্জিত প্রবৃত্তি। **Second Person**—খৃষ্টীয় ত্রিপুরুষের মধ্যে দ্বিতীয় পুরুষ, যীশুখৃষ্ট। **Second price**—রঙ্গালয়ে দ্বিতীয় শ্রেণীর আসনের মূল্য। **Second-rate**—দ্বিতীয় শ্রেণীর, মধ্যবিত্ত। **Second-self**—দ্বিতীয় আত্মা, অভিন্নাত্মা, অভিন্নদেহ। **Second-sight**—দিব্যদৃষ্টি, দিব্যচক্ষুঃ [স্কটলণ্ড এবং আয়র্লণ্ডের কেল্ট জাতীয় বহু লোক এইরূপ অতীন্দ্রিয় দৃষ্টিসম্পন্ন বলিয়া গণ্য হয়।] **Second thought**—পুনর্বিবেচনা। **Second in command**—প্রধান সেনাপতির অব্যবহিত নিম্নপদস্থ কর্ম্মচারী। **Second of an arc**—বিকলা (সাঃ পঃ)। **To come in second, To finish second**—To be in second in race; ঘোড়দৌড় প্রভৃতিতে দ্বিতীয় স্থান অধিকার করা। **To come off second-best**—To be defeated; হারিয়া আসা, পরাস্ত হইয়া আসা। **To play second fiddle**—See FIDDLE. $\frac{1}{35750}$ **of a second**—ত্রুটি (সাঃ পঃ)। $\frac{2}{675}$ **of a second**—তৎপর (সাঃ পঃ)। $\frac{4}{45}$ **of a second**—নিমেষ। **2 seconds**—কাষ্ঠা (সাঃ পঃ)। **4 seconds**—প্রাণ (সাঃ পঃ), অনু (সাঃ পঃ)। **24 seconds**—বিনাড়ী (সাঃ সঃ)।

sĕc'-ond-ā-rȳ (-ŭnd-), *adj.* & *n.* **1.** Of second place, origin, rank or importance; subordinate; দ্বিতীয় স্থানীয়, দ্বিতীয়শ্রেণীর; অপ্রধান, গৌণ, দ্বিতীয়কোটিস্থ (হিঃ কোঃ), অমুখ্য (ঐ)। **2.** (*Geol.*) Same as MESOZOIC. ***Noun.*** **1.** One who acts in subordination to another; a deputy; দ্বিতীয়স্থানীয় ব্যক্তি, অধীন ব্যক্তি; প্রতিনিধি। **2.** (*Pl.*) Secondary symptoms of syphilis; উপদংশ রোগের দ্বিতীয় অবস্থা। **3.** One of the feathers growing on the second bone of a bird's wing; পক্ষীর ডানার দ্বিতীয় অস্থিতে জাত পালক। **4.** Same as SECONDARY CIRCLE. **5.** Same as SECONDARY PLANET. **6.** (*Miner.*) A secondary strata; দ্বিতীয়ক (সাঃ পঃ)। **8.** A cathedral dignity of second rank; মহাধর্ম্মমন্দিরের দ্বিতীয় শ্রেণীর যাজক। **—rily,** *adv.* In the second place; দ্বিতীয়তঃ। **Secondary action**—গৌণক্রিয়া (হিঃ কোঃ)। **Secondary amputation**—পুযসঞ্চার রুদ্ধ হওয়ায় অঙ্গচ্ছেদন। **Secondary axis**—গৌণাক্ষ (হিঃ কোঃ)। **Secondary battery** — বিদ্যুৎসঞ্চারক ঘটমালা (হিঃ কোঃ), গৌণ ব্যাটারী (ঐ)। **Secondary bow** or **Secondary rainbow**—মূল রামধনুর সহিত সমান্তরাল ম্লান এবং বহির্বর্ত্তী দ্বিতীয় ধনু। **Secondary cause** — গৌণ কারণ। **Secondary circle**—যে বৃহদ্‌বৃত্ত উহার ধরাতলের লম্বস্বরূপ অপর বৃহদ্‌বৃত্তের মেরুদ্বয় ছেদন করিয়া যায়, গৌণবৃত্ত। **Secondary circuit**—গৌণবিদ্যুন্মণ্ডল (হিঃ কোঃ)। **Secondary coil**—গৌণবিদ্যুৎবেষ্টন (হিঃ কোঃ)। **Secondary colour**—See COLOUR. **Secondary education** or **instruction**—প্রাথমিক শিক্ষা এবং বিশ্ববিদ্যালয়ের (কলেজের) শিক্ষার মধ্যবর্ত্তী শিক্ষা, মাধ্যমিক শিক্ষা। **Secondary haemorrhage**—আঘাত বা অস্ত্রোপচারের কতিপয় দিবস অন্তে রক্তস্রাব। **Secondary planet**—গৌণগ্রহ (হিঃ কোঃ)। See PLANET. **Secondary Property**—গৌণ গুণ (হিঃ কোঃ)। **Secondary school**—See SCHOOL. **Secondary wing**—কীটের পশ্চাদ্দিকের পক্ষ।

sĕ-con'-dĕ (-cŭn-) *n.* A fencing position ; অসিক্রীড়ার ভঙ্গিবিশেষ।

sē'-crĕ-cȳ, *n.* Concealment ; the quality of keeping secret ; গোপনতা (গীতাঞ্জঃ), সংগুপ্তি, গূঢ়তা, গুপ্তি, গোপনীয়তা, গুহ্যতা, নিভৃতত্ব, পরম গোপন ; আড়াল আবডাল (*colloq.*), ঢাক ঢাক গুড় গুড় (*colloq.*) ; সংগোপনশীলতা, মন্ত্রগুপ্তি । **In secrecy**—Secretly ; গোপনে, সংগোপনে ।

sē'-crĕt, *adj.* & *n.* 1. Concealed ; private ; অপ্রকাশিত, লুক্কায়িত, প্রচ্ছন্ন ; গোপন, একান্ত । 2. Occult ; as, *secret* doctrine ; inscrutable ; গুপ্ত, রহস্যপূর্ণ, রহস্যাচ্ছন্ন, গুহ্য, গূঢ়, নিগূঢ় ; দুজ্ঞের্য়, দুরধিগম্য । 3. Being in retirement or seclusion ; নির্জ্জনবাসী, বিবিক্ত । 4. Secluded ; নির্জ্জন, নিভৃত, নিরিবিলি । *Noun.* 1. A mystery ; রহস্য, গুপ্তরহস্য, নিগূঢ় রহস্য, ভিতরের কথা । 2. Something carefully kept or concealed ; গোপনীয় বিষয়, অপ্রকাশিত বিষয়, গুহ্যবিষয়, গোপন কথা (রবীঃ), নিগূঢ়তত্ত্ব, ভেদ (আগমপুরাণ cf. বেদ না জানে তোমার ভেদ), গুপ্ততত্ত্ব, গুপ্তকথা । 3. (*Pl.*) The private parts ; গোপনীয় অঙ্গ । 4. The true but not generally known cause ; as, the *secrets* of health ; প্রকৃত, কিন্তু সর্ব্বজনপরিজ্ঞাত নয়—এইরূপ কারণ । **–ly,** *adv.* In a secret manner ; গোপনে, সংগোপনে, রহসি । **Secret marriage**—গুপ্তবিবাহ, চোরিকা বিবাহ । **Secret-service** — সরকারের জন্য গোপনীয় কার্য্য । [এই সব কার্য্যের বিষয় জনসাধারণে প্রকাশ করা যায় না । ইহার ব্যয় গুপ্তকোষ (Secret-service fund, Secret-service money) হইতে নির্ব্বাহিত হয় ।] **Secret-society**—গুপ্তসমিতি । **In secret**—Secretly ; গোপনে, সংগোপনে, অপ্রকাশ্যে । **Open secret** — যে গোপনীয় কথা—যে ইচ্ছা করে সেই জানিতে পারে, উদ্ভিন্ন রহস্য । **To keep a secret, To keep the secret**—Not to reveal a secret ; গুপ্তকথা ব্যক্ত না করা । **To make no secret of**—Not to keep secret ; গোপন না রাখা ।

Secretaire, *n.* Same as ESCRITOIRE (which see.)

sĕc-rē-tā'-ri-ăt, –ate, *ns.* 1. The office of a secretary ; সম্পাদকের কার্য্য, সাচিব্য । 2. The place where a secretary transacts business ; দপ্তরখানা, সরকারী দপ্তরখানা, রাজসেরেস্তা (রবীঃ) । **Military Secretariat**—সামরিক দপ্তরখানা ।

sĕc'-rē-tă-rȳ, *n.* 1. A person employed to write orders, letters, despatches, or the like according to instructions received ; উপদেশানুসারে পত্র, আদেশ, দ্রুত প্রেরিতব্য সরকারী পত্র, প্রভৃতি লিখিয়া কোন বিভাগের প্রধান কর্ম্মচারী প্রভৃতিকে সাহায্য করিবার জন্য নিযুক্ত ব্যক্তি । 2. One who conducts the affairs of a public body ; সম্পাদক । 3. A public officer whose business it is to superintend and manage the affairs of a particular department ; কোন বিশেষ বিভাগের কার্য্যনির্ব্বাহক কর্ম্মচারী, সরকারী দপ্তরখানার প্রধান কর্ম্মচারী, সচিব । 4. Same as a SECRETAIRE. 5. (*Print.*) A kind of script type ; একপ্রকার হস্তাক্ষরের অনুরূপ হরফ । 6. Same as SECRETARY-BIRD. **–ta'-ri-al,** *adj.* **Secretary-bird** — আফ্রিকা-

Secretary-bird.

দেশীয় সর্পভোজী পক্ষিবিশেষ, কেরানী পাখী [এই পাখী প্রায় ৪ ফিট উচ্চ । বর্ণ ধূসরাভ নীল । কণ্ঠ শ্বেত, পদদ্বয় ও পক্ষপালক কৃষ্ণবর্ণ । পুচ্ছ সুদীর্ঘ এবং মাথার উপর দীর্ঘ পালকগুচ্ছ বিরাজিত । ঐ পালকগুচ্ছের পক্ষের সহিত লেখনীর কল্পিত সাদৃশ্য হইতে ইহার নাম কেরানীপাখী ।] **Foreign Secretary**—পররাষ্ট্রসচিব । **Home Secretary**—স্বরাষ্ট্রসচিব । **War Secretary**—সমরসচিব । **Secretary of State for India**—ভারতসচিব । **Secretary of State for the Colonies**—ঔপনিবেশিক মন্ত্রী ।

sē-crete' (-crēt), *v.t.* 1. To conceal ; লুকান, গুপ্তস্থানে রাখা, লুক্কায়িত রাখা । 2. To produce by means of secretion ; to emit as a secretion ; ক্ষরণ দ্বারা উৎপাদিত করা ; ক্ষরিত করা, স্রাব নির্গত করা । **–cre'-tor,** *n.* **–cre'-to-ry,** *adj.*

sē-crē'-tion, *n.* 1. Act of secreting ; সংগোপন, প্রচ্ছাদন । 2. The physiological process by which various products or substances are separated from the blood of animals or the sap of plants ; যে দৈহিক ক্রিয়াদ্বারা জন্তুর রক্ত হইতে এবং উদ্ভিদের রস হইতে বিভিন্ন প্রকার পদার্থ (যথা, মূত্র, লালা, পিত্ত, রস) পৃথগ্‌ভূত হয়, নিঃসরণক্রিয়া, ক্ষরণক্রিয়া, নিঃসরণ । 3. A substance formed by certain specialized cells from materials furnished by the fluid substance of the organism ; স্রাব, (সাঃ পঃ), রস (ঐ), দূষিকা (ঐ) ।

sē-crē'-tive (-tĭv), *adj.* 1. Given to secrecy ; uncommunicative ; রহঃশীল ; অনালাপী, অমিশুক । 2. Producing secretion ; মূত্রলালাদি উৎপাদক, স্রাবী, নিঃসরণশীল । **–ly,** *adv.* **–ness,** *n.*

sĕct, *n.* A body or number of persons united in tenets, or who follow some teacher or leader ; ধর্ম্মসম্প্রদায়, সম্প্রদায়, শাখা, পক্ষ (কেণ্ডিঃ) ।

sĕc-tā'-ri-ăn, *adj.* & *n.* Of, or pertaining to, a sect ; সাম্প্রদায়িক । *Noun.* A bigoted adherent of a sect ; সাম্প্রদায়িক ব্যক্তি, শাখামার্গী (কেন্ডিঃ), শাখাশ্রয়ী (ঐ), একদেশিমার্গাবলম্বী (ঐ)। **--ism,** *n.* The tendency to form sects ; bigotry ; সাম্প্রদায়িকতা ; ধর্ম্মান্ধতা, গোঁড়ামি, সম্প্রদায়াগ্রহ (হিঃ কোঃ), মতাভিনিবেশ (ঐ)। **—ize** *v. t.*

sĕc'-tā-rȳ, *n.* (*Archaic*) A sectarian ; one who separates himself from an established church ; (অপ্রঃ) সাম্প্রদায়িক ; বিধিপ্রতিষ্ঠিত ধর্ম্মসংঘ হইতে বিচ্ছিন্ন ব্যক্তি।

sĕc'-tile (-tĭl), *adj.* Capable of being cut (esp. of mica, talc, etc.); ছেদ্য, ছেদনীয়।

sĕc'-tion, *n.* & *v. t.* **1.** The act of cutting or dividing ; ছেদন, ভেদন। **2.** A part cut off or separated ; a slice ; বিচ্ছিন্ন অংশ, ছিন্নাংশ ; খণ্ড। **3.** A distinct part or portion of a book or writing ; a division or subdivision of a chapter ; the division of a law ; hence, the character (§) often used to denote such a division ; পুস্তকের খণ্ড, কোন রচনার বিভাগ, পটল, প্রকরণ, পর্ব্ব, বর্গ, কাণ্ড, খণ্ড, স্কন্ধ, ভাগ, বিভাগ, শাখা, পরিচ্ছেদ, বিচ্ছেদ, অধিকরণ (বেদান্ত), উল্লাস (যথা কাব্যপ্রকাশে), উচ্ছ্বাস (যথা দশকুমারচরিতে), সর্গ, উদ্ঘাত, অধ্যায়, অঙ্ক (esp. of a drama), পরিবর্ত্ত, স্থান, আহ্নিক (যথা মহাভাষ্যে), গ্রন্থসন্ধি, আশ্বাস, লম্বক (যথা কথাসরিৎসাগরে), তরঙ্গ (a section of literary works that contain in their names a word like sea, river, etc. ; (*e. g.* রাজতরঙ্গিনী), পাদ, স্তবক (a section or chapter in such books as contain in their names words লতা, মঞ্জরী, etc.), উদ্যত, তন্ত্র [(esp. the section of a scientific work)—cf. তন্ত্রৈঃ পঞ্চভিরেতচ্চকার সুমনোহরং শাস্ত্রং—পঞ্চতন্ত্র]; কোন অধ্যায়ের বিভাগ বা অবান্তর বিভাগ ; আইনের ধারা ; ঐরূপ বিভাগসূচক চিহ্ন §। **4.** A distinct part of a city, country, people or the like ; দেশ, জাতি, নগর, প্রভৃতির বিভাগ, সমাজ, সম্প্রদায়। **5.** A drawing showing the interior of the object represented ; অঙ্কিত বস্তুর অন্তর্ভাগপ্রদর্শক রেখাচিত্র। **6.** The cutting of a solid by a plane ; the plane figure formed by such a cutting ; ধরাতলদ্বারা ঘনক্ষেত্র ছেদন, ছেদন (সাঃ পঃ) ; ঐরূপ ছেদনজনিত ক্ষেত্র, ছেদ (সাঃ পঃ)। **7.** (*Nat. Hist.*) The subdivision of a genus ; (প্রাকৃতিক ইতিহাস) গণের অবান্তর বিভাগ। ***Verb t.*** To cut or separate in sections ; বিভিন্ন অংশে ছিন্ন বা বিভক্ত করা, খণ্ডিত করা। **–al,** *adj.* **1.** Of, or pertaining to, a section ; local ; partial ; খণ্ডাত্মক, অংশাত্মক ; স্থানীয়, স্থানিক ; আংশিক। **2.** Composed of several sections ; as, *sectional* boats ; খণ্ডসমুচ্চয়রচিত, ফলকসমূহ রচিত। **–al-ism** *n.* **Longitudinal section**—ঊর্দ্ধাধঃ অনুলম্ব (সাঃ পঃ)। **Microscopic section**—আণুবীক্ষণিক পরীক্ষার জন্য কোন বস্তু হইতে কর্ত্তিত শল্কবৎ অংশ। **Tangential-section**—পার্শ্বিক (সাঃ পঃ)। **Transeverse section** — তির্য্যক্ (সাঃ পঃ), অনুপ্রস্থ (ঐ)। **Vertical section**—লম্বচ্ছেদ (সূত্যঃ বিঃ)।

sĕc'-tŏr, *n.* **1.** The part of a circle comprehended between two radii and the intercepted arc ; ব্যাসার্দ্ধদ্বয়ের মধ্যবর্ত্তী বৃত্তখণ্ড, বৃত্তখণ্ড (সাঃ পঃ), বৃত্তাংশ (কেন্ডিঃ)। **2.** A mathematical instrument marked with lines of chords, sines, secants, tangents, etc. and used in making plans, diagrams, sections, etc. ; গণিতিক যন্ত্রবিশেষ, বিচ্ছেদক (কেন্ডিঃ)। **—al,** *adj.* **—to'-ri-al,** *adj.* & *n.* Adapted to, or intended for, cutting ; carnassial ; কৃন্তনোপযোগী ; আমিষচ্ছেদনোপযোগী। ***Noun.*** A carnassial tooth ; আমিষচ্ছেদনোপযোগী দন্ত।

sĕc'-troid (-troyd), *n.* A term applied to the surface of two adjacent groins in a vault ; বৃত্তখণ্ডাভাস (হিঃ কোঃ)।

sĕc'-ū-lar (-lêr), *adj.* & *n.* **1.** Pertaining to the present world or to things not spiritual, sacred or holy ; ঐহিক, লৌকিক, বৈষয়িক, সাংসারিক, প্রাপঞ্চিক (কেন্ডিঃ), ব্যাবহারিক (ঐ), অনাধ্যাত্মিক, অযাজকীয়। **2.** (Of a priest) Not under a monk's vow ; (পুরোহিত সম্পর্কে) অগৃহীতসন্ন্যাস, গৃহবাসী, গৃহী। **3.** Coming, or observed, once in an age or century ; "The rare and *secular* phenomena of siege, fire and plague" ; aged; as, a *secular* banian tree ; শতাব্দ বা বহু বর্ষ অন্তে আগমনশীল বা সংঘটিত, যুগান্তে অনুষ্ঠিত ; প্রাচীন, অক্ষয় (cf. অক্ষয়বট)। ***Noun.*** **1.** A Roman Catholic ecclesiastic not bound by monastic laws ; মঠসম্বন্ধীয় প্রতিজ্ঞায় অনাবদ্ধ, গৃহবাসীযাজক, অগৃহীতসন্ন্যাস যাজক। **2.** A layman ; সাংসারিক লোক, বৈষয়িক লোক। **3.** A church official whose functions are confined to the vocal departments of the choir ; খৃষ্টীয় ধর্ম্মমন্দিরের ভজনসঙ্গীতের তত্ত্বাবধায়ক। **–ism,** *n.* **1.** The theory that education should be purely secular ; ধর্ম্মবিবর্জ্জিতশিক্ষাবাদ, ধর্ম্মসংস্রবহীন শিক্ষাবাদ। **2.** A system of ethical principles, which aims to substitute the piety of usefulness for the usefulness of piety ; একপ্রকার নীতিতত্ত্ব—যাহাতে ধর্ম্মভাবের হিতজনকত্ব স্থলে যাহা হিতজনক তাহাই ধর্ম্ম বলিয়া গৃহীত হয়। [G. J. Holyoke ১৮৪৬ খৃঃ অব্দে এই মত প্রবর্ত্তন করেন। এই মতানুসারে যাহা বর্ত্তমান জীবনে মানবের মঙ্গলকর তাঁহাই সন্নীতি। নীতির সহিত ঈশ্বরের কোন সংস্রব নাই] ঐহিকবাদ (হিঃ কোঃ)। **—ist,** *n.* **—i-za'-tion,** *n.* **–ize,** *v. t.* **1.** To convert from religious, sacred or ecclesiastical to secular use ; ঐহিক কার্য্যে নিয়োগ

করা, সংসারিক কার্য্যে নিয়োগ করা, অযাজকীয় কার্য্যে নিযোগ করা, দেবোত্তর সম্পত্তি সাধারণ সম্পত্তিতে পরিণত করা। **2.** To make worldly or unspiritual; ঐহিক করা, ইহকালপরতন্ত্র করা, বিষয়াসক্ত করা, বিষয়নিষ্ঠ করা, বৈষয়িক করা, অনাধ্যাত্মিক করা। **—lar′-i-ty,** *n.* The state of being secular; ঐহিকতা, সাংসারিকতা, লৌকিকতা। **Secular acceleration** — জ্যোতিষ্কের মৃদু গতিবৃদ্ধি। **Secular change**—মৃদু অথচ নিরবচ্ছিন্ন পরিবর্ত্তন। **Secular cooling or refrigeration** — বাষ্পাবস্থা হইতে পৃথিবীর ক্রমশঃ শীতলতাপ্রাপ্তি। **Secular fame**—কল্পান্তস্থায়ীকীর্ত্তি, চিরস্থায়ী কীর্ত্তি। **Secular equation**—শতাব্দিক সমীকরণ (হিঃ কোঃ)। **Secular games**—(রোমক প্রত্নতত্ত্ব) সাম্রাজ্যের মঙ্গলের জন্য অনুষ্ঠিত ত্রি অহোরাত্র ব্যাপী নৃত্যগীতোৎসব, যুগক্রীড়োৎসব, মঙ্গলোৎসব। **Secular-poem or hymn**—(রোম নগরীতে) যুগক্রীড়োৎসব উপলক্ষে রচিত কবিতা বা স্তোত্র। **Secular variation**—ভৌমিক বিকার (হিঃ কোঃ)। **The secular bird**—Same as PHOENIX (which see).

sĕ′-cŭnd, *adj.* (*Bot. & Zool.*) Arranged on one side only; কেবল এক পার্শ্বে বিন্যস্ত, একপার্শ্ববিন্যস্ত, একপার্শ্বিক। ***Secundi adjacentis*** — ক্রিয়া-কর্ত্তব্যাত্মক বাক্য (হিঃ কোঃ), নির্বিধেয় প্রতিজ্ঞা (ঐ)।

sĕc′-ŭn-dīne, *n.* Afterbirth; গর্ভপরিস্রব, গর্ভের ফুল।

secundum, (*Lat.*), *prep.* According to; অনুসারে। ***Secundum artem*** — অনৈসর্গিকরূপে, নিপুণভাবে, বিজ্ঞানসম্মতরূপে। ***Secundum naturam***—স্বাভাবিকভাবে, নৈসর্গিকভাবে। ***Secundum quid***—কতকাংশে, ব্যাপকভাবে নয়, আপেক্ষিকভাবে, আন্তর্য্যেণ (হিঃ কোঃ)।

sĕ-cūre′, *adj.* & *v.t.* **1.** Free from fear or apprehension; easy in mind; ভয়মুক্ত, ভয়শূন্য, বীতভয়, নিশ্চিন্ত, ভয়শঙ্কারহিত, নিঃশঙ্ক, নির্বিশঙ্ক; নিরুদ্বিগ্ন, উদ্বেগশূন্য, ভাবনাহীন, খাতিরজমা (*colloq.*)। **2.** Confident; depending; বিশ্বাসবান, কৃতনিশ্চয়, স্থিরনিশ্চিত, স্থিরচিত্ত; নির্ভরশীল। **3.** In a state of safety; safe; নির্বিঘ্ন; নিরাপদ। **4.** (*Rare*) Careless; over-confident; "They were *secure* where they ought to have been wary"; (ক্বচিদ্ব্যবহৃত) অসাবধান; অতিরিক্ত নিশ্চিত। **5.** Sure; নিশ্চিত। **6.** In safe custody or possession; নিরাপদভাবে রক্ষিত। ***Verb t.*** **1.** To free from care or fear; to make safe; নিঃশঙ্ক করা, ভয়শূন্য করা; নিরাপদ করা, নির্বিঘ্ন করা। **2.** To make certain; স্থিরনিশ্চিত করা। **3.** To make fast or secure; to fasten; as, to *secure* a door; বন্ধ করা; রুদ্ধ করা। **4.** To make certain of payment; as, to *secure* a debt by mortgage; to assure against loss; পরিশোধ সম্বন্ধে নিশ্চিত করা; বীমা করা। **5.** To shut up; to seize and confine; to imprison; as, to *secure* a prisoner; বন্ধ করা; ধরিয়া বন্ধ করা; কারারুদ্ধ করা। **6.** To get possession of something; to obtain; as, he *secured* the prize; অধিকার করা, অধিগত করা, হস্তগত করা; প্রাপ্ত হওয়া, লাভ করা। **To secure arms**—To hold a rifle or musket with the muzzle down and lock well up under the arm, the object being to guard the weapon from rain; মুখ নীচের দিকে এবং কল বাহুর উপরে রাখিয়া বন্দুক ধরা।

sĕ-cū′-rĭ-fōrm, *adj.* Axe-shaped; কুঠারাকৃতি, পরশ্বাকৃতি।

sĕ-cū′-rĭ-tȳ, *n.* **1.** Freedom from care, anxiety, or apprehension; confidence of safety; নিঃশঙ্কতা, নির্ব্বিঘ্নতা, নির্বিশঙ্কতা, নিরুপদ্রবতা, নিরুদ্বেগ, নির্ভাবনা; অকুতোভয়তা, অভয়। **2.** Certainty; assurance; নিশ্চয়তা; দৃঢ়প্রত্যয়, স্থিরবিশ্বাস। **3.** Something which makes safe; a protection; নিরাপদজনক বিষয়; আশ্রয়। **4.** An evidence of debt, stock, shares, etc.; as, government *securities*; a pledge; খত, ঋণপত্র, কোম্পানীর কাগজ, অংশ, প্রভৃতি; বন্ধক। **5.** Something given or done to secure peace or good behaviour; জামিন, জামানত, প্রতিভূ। **6.** A surety; জামিনদাতা। **Security for appearance**—দর্শনপ্রতিভূ, দর্শন প্রতিভাব্য।

sĕ-dăn′, sĕ-dăn′ chair (-chăr), *ns.* A kind of covered chair

Sedan-chair.

or box for carrying a single person, borne on poles carried by two men; শিবিকাবিশেষ, জম্পান, দোলা।

sĕ-date′, *adj.* Composed; calm; unruffled by passions; স্থৈর্য্যসম্পন্ন, আত্মসংস্থ, স্থিরবুদ্ধি; প্রশান্ত, প্রশান্ত-গম্ভীর; ধীর, স্থির, অপ্রমত্ত, অক্ষুব্ধ, নিরুদ্বিগ্ন, অচঞ্চল, অচপল। **—ly,** *adv.* **—ness,** *n.*

sĕd′-a-tive (-tĭv), *adj.* & *n.* **1.** Tending to sooth; উপশামক, শান্তিকর, বেদনাপ্রশামক, শান্তিপ্রদ। ***Noun.*** A medicine which allays irritability and assuages pain; যে ঔষধদ্বারা জীবনীশক্তির জড়তা, অতিক্রিয়ার হ্রস্বতা, উপদাহের সান্ত্বনা এবং বেদনার ন্যূনতা জন্মে, অবসাদন (প্রঃ), প্রহ্লাদন (সাঃ পঃ)।

se defendendo, (*F.*), *adv.* In self-defence; আত্মরক্ষার্থ।

sĕd′-ĕn-tā-rȳ, *adj.* & *n.* **1.** Accustomed to sit much; বহুক্ষণ

উপবেশনে অভ্যস্ত। 2. Requiring much sitting; as, *sedentary* occupation; বহুক্ষণব্যাপী উপবেশনসাপেক্ষ। 3. (*Rare*) Inactive; sluggish; (কচিদ্‌ব্যবহৃত) জড়, নিষ্ক্রিয়, নিশ্চেষ্ট, নিরুদ্যম, নিরুদ্যোগ; অলস। 4. (*Zool.*) Not migratory; (জন্তুবিদ্যা) একস্থানসংসক্ত। ***Noun.*** 1. A sedentary person; দীর্ঘকালব্যাপী উপবেশনে অভ্যস্ত ব্যক্তি। 2. Same as SEDENTARY SPIDER. **–ri-ly,** *adv.* **–ri-ness,** *n.* **Sedentary spider**—যে মাকড়সা শিকার জালে না পড়া পর্য্যন্ত ওঁৎ পাতিয়া থাকে।

sĕ-dē'-rŭnt, (*L.*), *n.* A sitting of a deliberative body; অধিবেশন।

sedge (sĕj), *n.* The popular name of a many grass-like plants growing in marshes or swamps; জলা ও বিলজাত ঘাস, বাদার ঘাস। **Sedg'-y,** *adj.* **Sedge-warbler, Sedge-wren**—একপ্রকার পাখী।

sĕ-dil'-ĭ-ă, *n.* The stone seats on the south side of the altar in catholic churches; রোমান ক্যাথলিক-দিগের গির্জ্জায় বেদীর দক্ষিণদিকে স্থিত শিলাসনশ্রেণী।

sĕd'-ĭ-mĕnt, *n.* That which settles on the bottom of liquors; lees; তলানি, তলছাট; গাদ, কাইট, শিটা, কিট্ট, পলি (সাঃ পঃ), পলল (ঐ), ক্লেদ (ঐ), অদ্রবণীয় পদার্থ (জাহিঃ), কলঙ্ক।

sĕ-dĭ'-tion, *n.* Offences against the state, such as writing, publishing or uttering words that might bring about or excite to treason or an insurrection; রাজদ্রোহ। **–tious,** *adj.* 1. Tending to excite sedition; রাজদ্রোহকর, রাজদ্রোহজনক। 2. Guilty of sedition; রাজদ্রোহী, রাজদ্রোহাপরাধে অভিযুক্ত। **–tious-ly,** *adv.* **–tious-ness,** *n.*

sĕ-dūce', *v. t.* 1. To lead aside or astray; to tempt and lead to wrong; বিপথে চালিত করা, কুপথগামী করা; ফুসলাইয়া পাপকর্ম্মে নিয়োজিত করা। 2. To entice to a surrender of chastity; স্ত্রীলোককে ফুসলাইয়া নিয়া তাহার সতীত্ব নষ্ট করা, স্ত্রীলোককে প্রলুব্ধ করিয়া ব্যভিচারিণী করা। **–duc'-er,** *n.* **–duc'-i-ble,** *adj.* **–duc'-ing-ly,** *adv.* **–duc'-tion,** *n.* 1. Act of leading astray; the state of being led astray; বিপথে পরিচালন, কুপথগামিকরণ; সৎপথচ্যুতি। 2. The persuading of a female to surrender her chastity; "*Seduction* is seldom employed without fraud"; সতীত্ববিসর্জ্জনের জন্য স্ত্রীলোককে প্রলুব্ধ করণ, স্ত্রীসংগ্রহণ (মঃ সং), কন্যাদূষণ (মিতঃ টীকা)। 3. Allurement; "Aimd every temptation and *seduction*": *seductions* of art; প্রলোভন, আকর্ষণ, বিলোভন। **–duc'-tive,** *adj.* Alluring; "*Seductive* charms of poetry"; winning; প্রলোভনজনক, লোভনীয়, চিত্তবিমোহন; মোহকর, মোহন, মনোহারী, প্রাণমনভুলানো, প্রাণমাতানো। **–duc'-tive-ly,** *adv.* **–duc'-tive-ness,** *n.*

sĕd'-ū-lous (-lŭs), *adj.* Industrious, diligent and laborious; constant, steady and persevering in any pursuit; persistent; as, *sedulous* attention; পরিশ্রমী, শ্রমশীল; উদ্যোগী, অধ্যবসায়ী, উদ্যমী, একনিষ্ঠকর্ম্মী; একাগ্র। **–ly,** *adv.* **–ness,** *n.*

see (sē), *v. i.* & *t.* 1. To have the power of sight; to behold; দেখিতে পারা, দৃষ্টিশক্তি থাকা; দেখা। 2. To discern; to understand; as, to *see* through a plan; ঠাওরান, ঠাহর করা; বুঝা। 3. To be attentive; to take care; as, to *see* to the house; দেখা, দেখাশোনা; তত্ত্বাবধান করা। 4. To examine; to enquire; as, you must *see* into it; পরীক্ষা করা; অনুসন্ধান নেওয়া, খবর নেওয়া, দেখা। ***Verb t.*** 1. To perceive by the eye; to behold; দেখা; দর্শন করা, নিরীক্ষণ করা, নয়নগোচর করা, অবলোকন করা, হেরা (*poet.*), নেহারা (*poet.*)। 2. To understand; to comprehend; বুঝা; উপলব্ধি করা। 3. (*Now rare*) To suffer; to feel; to undergo; as, he had *seen* better days; to experience; (বর্ত্তমানে কচিদ্‌ব্যবহৃত) ভোগ করা; অনুভব করা, বোধ করা; সহা; অভিজ্ঞতা থাকা। 4. To escort; as, to a *see* a lady home; অনুগমন করা, শরীর রক্ষার্থ অনুগমন করা। 5. To ascertain; নির্ণয় করা, ঠিক করা। 6. To learn by reading; "Did you *see* her death in the newspaper?"; পড়িয়া দেখা, পাঠ করিয়া জানা। 7. (*Colloq.*) To take care; "If you get your letters ready early in the day, I will *see* and get them franked; to give attention to; (চলিত ভাষায়) সাবধান হওয়া; মনোযোগী হওয়া, দৃষ্টি রাখা, মনোযোগ দেওয়া। 8. (*Colloq.*) To interview or consult in order to influence, esp. improperly, as in order to bribe (Webster); "The president of a great railway road...must have adroit agents at the state capitals...ready to *see* leading legislators"; কোনরূপে, বিশেষতঃ কোনপ্রকার অসঙ্গত উপায়ে প্রভাবিত করার জন্য সাক্ষাৎ করা। 9. To call on a visit; to receive; as, to *see* visitors; দেখা করিতে যাওয়া; দেখা করা। 10. (*Mil.*) To dominate a position; "An interior intrenchment formed so as to *see* the principal streets"; (সামরিক শাস্ত্র) উপর হইতে আধিপত্য করা। **See'-ing,** *n.* & *conj.* Sight; দর্শন, অবলোকন, নিরীক্ষণ। ***Conj.*** Considering; inasmuch as; বিবেচনায়; যেহেতু। **See-bright**—একপ্রকার গুল্ম। **Seeing-stone**—(অপ্রঃ) দর্পন; ভৌতিক আয়না। **Let me see**—Wait a bit; দাঁড়াও, রসো, ভাবিয়া দেখি। **None is so blind as will not see**—চক্ষু থাকিতে কাণা।

Seeing is believing—জুয়াচোরের বাড়ীর ফলার না আঁচালে বিশ্বাস নাই, দেখতে পেলে শুনতে চায়না। **To have seen better days**—To have been in better circumstances ; একদিন ভাল অবস্থা থাকা। **To see**—To look over ; তত্ত্বাবধান করা। **To see about a thing**—To pay some attention to it ; to consider it ; কোন বিষয়ে একটু মনোযোগী হওয়া ; কোন বিষয় ভাবিয়া দেখা। **To see after**—To look after ; দেখা শোনা। **To see a person at York first**—To be extremely unwilling to do something ; কোন কার্য্য করিতে একান্ত অনিচ্ছুক হওয়া। **To see at a glance**—To see at once ; দৃষ্টিমাত্রই বুঝিতে পারা। **To see a thing done** — To supervise over it ; কোন কার্য্য পরিদর্শন করা। **To see double**—To be drunk ; মাতাল হওয়া, নেশায় বিভোর হওয়া। **To see eye to eye**—To be of identical opinion ; একমত হওয়া, অভিন্নমত হওয়া। **To see fit**—To think fit ; সঙ্গত মনে করা। **To see good**—To consider right or expedient ; সঙ্গত বা যুক্তিযুক্ত মনে করা। **To see into**—To investigate ; to examine , অনুসন্ধান করা ; পরীক্ষা করা। **To see into millstone, To see through brick wall**—To have the most acute intellect ; অলৌকিকধীশক্তিসম্পন্ন হওয়া, কুশাগ্রবুদ্ধি হওয়া। **To see life**—To have experience of worldly life ; সাংসারিক জীবনের অভিজ্ঞতা থাকা, দুনিয়া কিরূপ জিনিষ তাহা জানা থাকা, সংসারের চালচলন বা ধরণ ধারণ সম্বন্ধে অভিজ্ঞতা থাকা। **To see of**—To observe ; ভাল করিয়া দেখা। **To see off**—To be present at the time of departure ; বিদায়ের সময় উপস্থিত থাকা। **To see one's way**—To find means of doing something ; কোন কিছু করার জন্য উপায় করা। **To see out**—To survive ; কোন ব্যক্তি অপেক্ষা অধিক দিন জীবিত থাকা, কাহারো পরে মরা। To see to the end ; শেষ পর্য্যন্ত দেখা। **To see service**—To be in active military service ; হাতে হাতিয়ারে যুদ্ধ করা। To be put to hard use or wear ; কঠোর অভিজ্ঞতার ভিতর দিয়া অতিক্রম করা। **To see stars**—To see flashes of light as from a blow on the head ; চক্ষে সরিষার ফুল দেখা। **To see the back**—To get rid of ; রেহাই পাওয়া। **To see the world**—Same as TO SEE LIFE (above). **To see through**—To understand another's thoughts or purposes ; অপরের উদ্দেশ্য বা অভিসন্ধি বুঝিতে পারা। To undertake to do ; কোন কার্য্যের ভার গ্রহণ করা। To penetrate ; ভেদ করা। **To see through and through**—To see minutely ; পুঙ্খানুপুঙ্খরূপে দেখা, তন্ন তন্ন করিয়া দেখা। **To see to**—To attend to ; to look after ; মনোযোগ দেওয়া ; দেখাশোনা, তত্ত্বাবধান করা। **To see to anything**—To attend to anything ; কোন বিষয়ে মনোযোগী হওয়া। **To see wolf**—To lose one's voice ; বাক্‌শক্তি লোপ পাওয়া। [ইংলণ্ডে এক-সময়ে এইরূপ প্রবাদ ছিল যে কোন লোক নেকড়ে বাঘ দ্বারা দৃষ্ট হওয়ার পূর্ব্বে ঐ নেকড়ে বাঘকে দেখিলে অন্ততঃ কিছুকালের জন্য তাহার বাক্‌শক্তি লোপ পাইত।]

see (sē), *n.* **1.** The seat of an episcopal power ; the jurisdiction of a bishop or archbishop ; খৃষ্টীয় ধর্ম্মাধ্যক্ষের আসন বা পাট, শ্রীপাট ; ধর্ম্মাধ্যক্ষ বা মহাধর্ম্মাধ্যক্ষের এলেকা। **2.** The authority of the Pope ; the Papal Court ; পোপের ক্ষমতা ; পোপের দরবার। **Holy see, See of Rome**—পোপের শ্রীপাট, পোপের দরবার।

seed (sēd), *n., v. i.* & *t.* **1.** The embryo with its envelope, or the matured ovule, which gives origin to a new plant ; বীজ, বীচি, আঁটি। **2.** (*Now rare*) The generative fluid of the male ; sperm ; (বর্ত্তমানে ক্বচিদ্‌ব্যবহৃত) বীর্য্য, শুক্র, ধাতু, বীজ ; শুক্রকীট, রেতঃ। **3.** First principle ; বীজ, আদি, মূল, বীজতত্ত্ব, মূলতত্ত্ব। **4.** Offsprings ; as, the *seeds* of Abraham ; সন্তানসন্ততি, বংশধর। **5.** (*Pl.*) Land sown with corn ; grasses raised from seed ; "Yet it is those who have had *seeds* to cut that have come off best this haysel" ; শস্যক্ষেত্র ; বীজ হইতে উৎপন্ন ঘাস। **6.** The ova of the lobster and of the silkworm-moth ; গল্‌দাচিংড়ীর ডিম, রেশমপোকার প্রজাপতির ডিম। ***Verb i.*** **1.** To sow seed ; বীজ বপন করা, বীজ বুনা। **2.** To grow to maturity, so as to produce seed ; পাকিয়া বীজ হওয়া। **3.** To shed the seed ; বীজ ত্যাগ করা। ***Verb t.*** **1.** To sow ; to sprinkle seed ; বীজ বপন করা ; বীজ ছড়ান। **2.** To ornament with seed-like decoration ; বীজাকৃতি ভূষাদ্বারা শোভিত করা। **Seed'-ling,** *n.* বীজের চারা (কলমের নয়), চারা (যোঃ), বীজাঙ্কুর, বীজপ্ররোহ। **Seed-bed**—বীজ জমি। **Seed-cake**—শা-জিরাদ্বারা সুবাসিত পিষ্টক। **Seed-coral**—বীজাকৃতি প্রবাল। **Seed-corn**—বীজ-শস্য। **Seed-drill**—যে যন্ত্র দ্বারা এক সঙ্গে নালা কর্ত্তন, বীজবপন এবং বীজ আচ্ছাদনের কার্য্য সাধিত হয়। **Seed-eater**—একপ্রকার পক্ষী। **Seed-fish**—ডিমওয়ালা মাছ। **Seeding-machine** — বপনযন্ত্র। **Seeding-plough**—একপ্রকার লাঙ্গল যাহাতে কর্ষণকালে লাঙ্গলপদ্ধতির উপর বীজ উপ্ত হয়। **Seed-leaf**—বীজপত্র।

Section of seed. *r r* radicle, *c c* cotyledon.

Seed-lobe—বৃক্ষের প্রথমোদ্গত পত্র, ভ্রূণ-পত্র। **Seed-oil** — বীজ হইতে নিষ্পীড়িত তৈল। **Seed-pearl**—বীজাকার মুক্তা, মুক্তাফল, সুবর্ত্তুল, মুক্তা, সুবৃত্ত (সর্ব্বতো বর্ত্তুলং যচ্চ সুবৃত্তং তন্নিগদ্যতে—গরুড় পুরাণ)। **Seed-plant**—বীজজাত বৃক্ষ। **Seed-plot**—বীজভূমি; (রাজদ্রোহ প্রভৃতির) ক্ষেত্র। **Seed-pot**—বীজজাত বৃক্ষ যে গামলায় জন্মান হয়। **Seedsman**—বীজ-ব্যবসায়ী, বীজবিক্রয়ী। **Seed-time**—বীজ বপনের কাল, বপনকাল। **Seed-vessel** — বীজকোষ। **Seed-wool** — বীজযুক্ত কাঁচা কার্পাস। **The seed of the woman shall bruise the serpent's head**—যীশুখৃষ্ট শয়তানের মস্তক চূর্ণ করিবেন। **To run to seed**—See RUN.

seed'-ėr (sēd-), *n.* **1.** One who plants or sows seeds; বীজবপনকারী। **2.** A machine for removing seeds from fruit; a seed-drill; ফলের বীজ ছাড়াইবার জন্য একপ্রকার যন্ত্র; যে যন্ত্রে একসঙ্গে নালা কাটা, বীজবুনা এবং বীজ ঢাকার কার্য্য সাধিত হয়। **3.** A spawning fish; ডিমওয়ালা মাছ।

seed'-ȳ (sēd-), *adj.* **1.** Full of seed; running to seed; বীজপূর্ণ, বীচি-গজগজে; পক্কাবস্থায় বীজধারী। **2.** Shabbily dressed; worn out; as, a *seedy* coat; looking miserable; জীর্ণবস্ত্রপরিহিত; জীর্ণ; খিন্ন। **3.** (Of brandy) Having the flavour of weeds growing among vines; (ব্রাণ্ডি সম্পর্কে) দ্রাক্ষাক্ষেত্রে জাত আগাছার গন্ধবিশিষ্ট। **—i-ly,** *adv.* **—i-ness,** *n.*

seek (sēk), *v. t. & i.* **1.** To search for; তল্লাস করা, খুঁজা, অনুসন্ধান করা। **2.** To ask for; to beseech; "Others tempting him *sought* of him a sign"; চাওয়া; প্রার্থনা করা। **3.** To try to gain; to try for; as, to *seek* wealth; পাইতে চেষ্টা করা; কোন কিছুর জন্য চেষ্টা করা। **4.** (*Obs.*) To search; "Have I *sought* every country far and near"; (অপ্রঃ) অনুসন্ধান করা, খোঁজা। ***Verb i.*** **1.** To search; অনুসন্ধান করা, তল্লাস করা, খুঁজা, অন্বেষণ করা। **2.** To endeavour; "They *sought* to lay hands upon him"; চেষ্টা করা। **3.** To solicit; "*Seek* and ye shall find"; প্রার্থনা করা। **Seek'-er,** *n.* **1.** One who seeks; অন্বেষণকারী, অন্বেষ্টা। **2.** An inquirer; অনুসন্ধানকারী। **3.** An instrument for seeking; অন্বেষণ করার জন্য যন্ত্রবিশেষ, অন্বেষক। **Sought-after**—সর্ব্বজন-বাঞ্ছিত, সর্ব্বজনপ্রার্থিত। **To seek, Much to seek**—Wanting; অভাব-বিশিষ্ট, বিরহিত। **To seek after**—To search; অনুসন্ধান করা। To court; বিবাহার্থ হৃদয় পরাজয়ের চেষ্টা করা। **To seek for**—To look for; অনুসন্ধান করা, তল্লাস করা। **To seek to**—(*Archaic*) To resort; to have recourse to; (অপ্রঃ) বহুলোক এক সঙ্গে গমন করা; আশ্রয় নেওয়া।

seel (sēl), *v. t.* **1** (*Archaic*) To close the eye of a hawk with a thread; সূতা দ্বারা বাজ পক্ষীর চক্ষু বন্ধ করা। **2.** (*fig.*) To hoodwink; (লক্ষণায়) চোখে ঠুলি দেওয়া, চোখে ধূলি দেওয়া।

seem (sēm), *v. i.* To appear; বোধ হওয়া, মনে হওয়া, প্রতিভাত হওয়া। প্রতীয়মান হওয়া। **It seems** — It appears; এইরূপ প্রতিভাত হয়। **To seem well** — ভাল ঠেকা (cf. শোভাবতীর ছেলের ··· উদ্দেশ্য থাকাতে আমার ভাল ঠেকেনা—চরিত্রহীন—শরৎ চট্টো।)

seem'-ĭng (sēm-), *adj. & n.* Apparent; আপাতপ্রতীয়মান, আপাত প্রতিভাত, আপাতদৃষ্ট, আপাতবোধ, প্রাতীতিক (cf. স প্রাতীতিক এব ন বাস্তবঃ—মাধুর্য্য-কাদম্বিনী—বিশ্বনাথচক্রবর্ত্তী)। ***Noun.*** **1.** Aspect; outward look; ভাব, বিভাব; বাহ্যদৃশ্য, বাহ্যরূপ, মায়িকরূপ। **2.** Illusion; hypocrisy; মায়া, বিসদৃশ প্রতীতি, প্রতিভাস (বেদান্ত), প্রতিভাসন (সাঃ দঃ), অবভাস, অনুভবাভাস; কপটতা।

seem'-lȳ (sēm-), *adj.* Decorous becoming; শোভন, সমীচীন, ভদ্রতাসঙ্গত, সমুচিত, যোগ্য; সঙ্গত। **—li-ness,** *n.* Decorousness; ঔচিত্য, শোভনতা, সমীচীনতা।

seen (sēn), *p. p.* Of SEE (which see).

sē'-ėr (*or* sēr), *n.* **1.** One who sees; দ্রষ্টা। **2.** One gifted with special spiritual prophetic vision or insight; দিব্যদৃষ্টিসম্পন্ন মহাপুরুষ, ঋষি, বিপশ্চিৎ (ডিউসেন), মুনি, সত্যদর্শী।

seer (sēr), *n.* A measure used in all retail dealings which varies all over India but in Bengal is equivalent to the wieght of eighty rupees; একসের।

seer'-hănd (sēr-), *n.* A kind of muslin; একপ্রকার মসলিন কাপড়।

seer'-paw, *n.* (From Pers. *sir*=head, *pa*=foot.) A complete set presented as a dress of honour by a sovereign or his representative; শিরোপা, খিলাত।

seer'-sŭck-ėr (sēr-), *n.* A thin linen or cotton fabric originally made in India; শণ বা কার্পাসের সূতার একপ্রকার মিহি কাপড়।

see'-saw (sē-sä), *adj., n. & v. i.* Moving up and down or to and fro; পর্য্যায়ক্রমে উত্থানপতনশীল। ***Noun.*** **1.** A swinging movement up and down; পর্য্যায়ক্রমে উত্থান ও পতন। **2.** A game in which children swing up and down on the two ends of a balanced piece of timber; একপ্রকার ক্রীড়া—যাহাতে শিশুগণ দোলায়িত কাষ্ঠফলকের উভয় প্রান্তে পর্য্যায়ক্রমে উঠা নামা করিয়া থাকে। **3.** A board or plank adjusted for such purpose; উক্তরূপ তক্তা, ঢেঁকিকল। ***Verb i.*** **1.** To move as in the game of see-saw; to move up and down; ঢেঁকি কলে উঠা-নামা করা; পর্য্যায়ক্রমে উঠা নামা করা। **2.** To vascillate; সন্দেহদোলায় দোলায়মান হওয়া।

seethe (sēth), *v.t.* & *i.* **1.** (*Archaic*) To boil ; (অপ্রঃ) সিদ্ধ করা। **2.** To soak in liquor ; ভিজান, অনুসিক্ত করা। ***Verb i.*** To be in a state of ebullition ; to be agitatead ; as, the country was *seething* with discontent ; টগবগ করিয়া ফুটা ; বিক্ষোভিত হওয়া।

seeth'-ing (sēth-), *adj.* **1.** Intensely heated ; অত্যুত্তপ্ত। **2.** Ebullient ; as, *seething* waves : *seething* discontent ; tumultuous ; অন্তঃক্ষোভজনক ফেনিল, ফেনায়মান ; তুমুল।

sĕ-gâr', *n.* (Wrongly used for) CIGAR (which see).

sĕg'-mĕnt, *n.*, *v. i.* & *t.* **1.** A part cut off ; ছিন্নাংশ, খণ্ড। **2.** (*Geom.*) A part cut off from a figure by a line or plane ; (জ্যামিতি) রেখার ধরাতল দ্বারা কোন ক্ষেত্র হইতে কর্ত্তিত অংশ, খণ্ডমণ্ডল (of a circle), অবধা (হিঃ কেঃ), চাপক্ষেত্র। **3.** A section ; পর্ব্ব, খণ্ড, গ্রন্থি। ***Verb i.*** To divide into segments ; খণ্ডক্ষেত্রে বিভক্ত হওয়া। ***Verb t.*** **1.** To separate in segments ; বিভিন্ন খণ্ডে বিভক্ত করা। **2.** To subject to the process of multiplication of cells ; কোষসংখ্যা বৃদ্ধিকরার জন্য কোন বিশেষ প্রক্রিয়ার অধীন করা। **–ed,** *adj.* Divided or marked off into segments ; গ্রন্থিশরীর (হিঃ কোঃ)। **–men-ta'-tion,** *n.* Act or process of dividing into segments ; প্রভেদন (হিঃ কোঃ)। **Segment-saw**—ধনুকাকৃতি বা বৃত্তাকার করপত্র। **Segment-shell** — একপ্রকার দীর্ঘাকৃতি গোল্ম—ইহা কতিপয় লৌহ সমবায়ে গঠিত এবং সীসক দ্বারা আচ্ছাদিত হইয়া থাকে। ইহার চোঙ্গাকৃতি অংশের ভিতরে বিস্ফোরক দ্রব্য ভরা হয়।

sĕg'-rĕ-gāte, *v. t.* & *i.* To separate ; পৃথক করা, স্বতন্ত্র করা, বিচ্ছিন্ন করা। ***Verb i.*** To be separated ; পৃথক হওয়া, বিচ্ছিন্ন হওয়া। **–ga'-tion,** *n.* The act of segregating ; বিশ্লেষণ। **–ga-tive,** *adj.*

sĕg'-rĕ-gāte, *adj.* **1.** (*Archaic*) Set apart ; পৃথকীকৃত। **2.** (*Zool.*) Simple ; (জন্তুবিদ্যা) অমিশ্র। **Segregate polygamy**—(*Bot.*) যে সকল বিভিন্ন পুষ্পপরিধিবিশিষ্ট পুষ্পকগুচ্ছ একই পুষ্পচ্ছদের অন্তর্ভুক্ত থাকে।

Seid'-litz–pow-dêr (sĭd-lĭts-), *n.* An aperient powder containing bicarbonate and potass and tartarate of soda and tartaric acid ; একপ্রকার মৃদু বিরেচক চূর্ণ। [Rochelle salt এবং Bicarbonate একটী পুরিয়ায় রাখা হয়, অপর পুরিয়ায় Tartaric acid থাকে। এই উভয় পুরিয়ায় চূর্ণ স্বতন্ত্রভাবে জলে গুলিয়া একত্র মিশাইবামাত্র ফুস ফুস শব্দে ফেনাইয়া উঠিলে সেবনীয়। Bohemia দেশের অন্তঃপাতী Seidlitz নামক গ্রামের নির্ঝরবারির তুল্য ভেষজগুণসম্পন্ন বলিয়া এই নাম।]

seign'-eur (sĕn-yêr), **–ior** (-yêr), *ns.* **1.** The lord of a manor ; সম্ভ্রান্ত ভূম্যধিকারী। **2.** A title of honour ; সম্মানসূচক উপাধিবিশেষ। **Grand Seigneur**—তুরুস্ক সুলতানের উপাধি, রোমের বাদশাহ; মহাসম্ভ্রান্ত ব্যক্তি।

seign'-or-āge (sĕn-yêr-), **–ior-āge** (-yêr-), *ns.* **1.** Something claimed by a sovereign or by a superior as a prerogative ; রাজা বা জমিদারকর্ত্তৃক বিশেষ অধিকারস্বরূপ যাহা দাবী করা হয়, সেলামী। **2.** A species of tax on bullion forming a part of the royal revenue ; টঙ্কশালায় মুদ্রা প্রস্তুতের জন্য আনীত স্বর্ণ ও রৌপ্যের যে অংশ রাজার প্রাপ্য ছিল, মুদ্রাশুল্ক। **3.** The profit derived from issuing coins at a rate above their intrinsic value ; প্রস্তুতের ব্যয় ও ধাতুর মূল্য বাদে মুদ্রার উপর যে লাভ ধরিয়া উহা প্রচার করা হয়। **4.** Royalty payable to authors etc.; গ্রন্থাদির মূল্যস্বরূপ গ্রন্থকার প্রভৃতিকে যে অর্থ দেওয়া হয়।

seign'-ior-ȳ, –or-ȳ. (sĕn-yêr-) *ns.* Power or authority as sovereign or lord ; রাজা বা উপরিতন ভূম্যধিকারিস্বরূপ ক্ষমতা বা কর্ত্তৃত্ব।

seine (sēn), *n.*, *v. t.* & *i.* A large fishing-net for encircling, buoyed up by floats ; বেড়জাল। ***Verb t.* & *i.*** To catch (fish) with seine ; বেড়জাল দ্বারা (মাছ) ধরা। **Seine-boat** — বেড়জালের নৌকা। **Seine-gang**—যে জনসমূহ বেড়জাল দ্বারা মৎস্য ধৃত করে। **Seine-needle**—বেড়জাল বুনিবার জন্য সূচী।

seis'-mic (sĭs-), **–măl**, *adjs.* (*Rare*) Pertaining to earthquake ; (কচিদ্‌ব্যবহৃত) ভূমিকম্পসম্বন্ধীয়।

seis'-mō-grăph (sĭs-), *n.* An electro-magnetic instrument for registering the shocks of earthquake ; ভূমিকম্পের স্পন্দনমাপক যন্ত্র, ভূস্পন্দনমানযন্ত্র (সাঃ পঃ), ভূস্পন্দনলেখ (ঐ), স্পন্দনমানযন্ত্র (ঐ)।

seis-mŏg'-ră-phȳ (sĭs-), *n.* An account of earthquakes ; ভূকম্পবর্ণন, ভূস্পন্দন বর্ণনা।

seis-mŏl'-ŏ-ġȳ (sĭs-), *n.* The science of earthquakes ; ভূস্পন্দনবিদ্যা (সাঃ পঃ)।

seis-mŏm'-ĕ-têr (sĭs-), *n.* An instrument for measuring the direction and force of earthquakes ; ভূমিকম্পের দিক্ এবং শক্তিমাপক যন্ত্র, ভূস্পন্দনমান।

seis'-mō-scōpe (sĭs-), *n.* Same as SEISMOMETER.

seize (sēz), *v. t.* & *i.* **1.** To put in legal possession (also *seise*) ; আইনসঙ্গত অধিকার দেওয়া। **2.** To take possession of by force ; বলপূর্ব্বক অধিকার করা, দখল করা। **3.** (*Law*) To take possession by warrant or legal authority ; (আইন) ক্রোক করা। **4.** To take hold of ; to clutch ; as, to *seize* one's hand ; ধারণ করা, ধরা ; সাপটিয়া ধরা। **5.** To comprehend ; ধারণা করা, উপলব্ধি করা। **6.** (*Naut*) To bind or fasten together, as ropes ; রজ্জু প্রভৃতি একত্র বাঁধা। ***Verb i.*** To grasp ; to take possession of ; ধরা, ধারণ করা ; অধিকার করা।

To seize up—To fasten a man by the waist to the shrouds for flogging ; বেত্রাঘাত করার জন্য কোন ব্যক্তির কটিদেশ মাস্তুলের রজ্জুর সহিত বাঁধা।

sei'-zin (sē-), **sei'-sin** (sē-), *ns.* 1. Possession of an estate of freehold ; সম্পত্তির অধিকার। 2. The act of taking possession ; অধিকার করণ। 3. What is so held ; অধিকৃত সম্পত্তি।

sei'-zūre (sē-), *n.* 1. The act of taking possession ; অধিকার করণ। 2. The act of taking possession by legal warrant etc. ; ক্রোককরণ। 3. Sudden attack of apoplexy etc. ; মৃগী, সন্ন্যাস, প্রভৃতি রোগের আকস্মিক আক্রমণ।

sē-jănt, *adj.* (*Herald.*) Sitting with the forelegs upright ; (কুলবিদ্যা) উদ্যদগ্রপদদ্বয় অবস্থায় উপবিষ্ট।

sĕj'-ū-gous (-gŭs), *adj.* (*Bot.*) Having six pairs of leaflets ; যুগ্মষট্পত্রকসমন্বিত।

sē-junc'-tion (-jŭngk-), *n.* (*Archaic*) Disuniting ; (অপ্রঃ) পৃথকীকরণ, বিয়োজন।

sē'-kŏs, *n.* A sacred enclosure ; প্রাচীন দেবমন্দিরাদির চতুঃপার্শ্ববর্তী বৃতিবেষ্টিত স্থান।

sĕl'-ă-chē, *n.* A genus of sharks ; একজাতীয় হাঙ্গর।

sĕl-ă-gĭ-nĕl'-lă, *n.* A genus of heterosporous cryptogams, allied to club-moss ; পাথরনুড়, পাষাণভেদী (যোঃ)।

sē-lăg-ĭ-nĕl-lă', **-cē-ae** (-ē), *ns.* A family of terrestrial mosslike plants of the order Lycopodiales ; হাতামুল্লাদি (সাঃ পঃ)।

sē'-lah (-lă), *n.* A musical direction indicating pause ; থামিবার জন্য সঙ্কেত। (বাইবেলে দৃষ্ট হিব্রু শব্দ)।

selamlik, *n.* The part of a Mohammedan home reserved for the men ; তুরুষ্কদেশে মুসলমানদিগের গৃহের পুরুষগণের জন্য নির্দ্দিষ্ট অংশ।

sĕl'-dŏm, *adv.* Rarely ; কচিৎ, কদাচিৎ, কালেভদ্রে, দৈবাৎ, কদাচ।

sē-lĕct', *adj. & v. t.* Choice ; বাছা, উৎকৃষ্ট। ***Verb t.*** To take by preference from among others ; নির্ব্বাচন করা, মনোনীত করা, বাছিয়া নেওয়া, পছন্দ করা, বাছাই করা, চুনা (*colloq.*)। **—lec'-tion,** *n.* 1. The act of selecting ; নির্ব্বাচন, বাছাই, বাছনি, চয়ন, উদ্ধরণ। 2. What is selected ; নির্ব্বাচিত বা মনোনীত বিষয়াবলী। **—lec'-tive,** *adj.* Pertaining to, or characterised by, selection ; চয়নাত্মক (হিঃ কোঃ)। **—lec'-tor,** *n.* **Select committee**—কোন প্রস্তাবিত আইন সম্বন্ধে পরামর্শ দেওয়ার জন্য বা বিশেষ ভাবে বিবেচনা করার নিমিত্ত ব্যবস্থাপক সভার কতিপয় (বিশেষজ্ঞ) সভ্যদ্বারা গঠিত সমিতি। **Natural selection**—প্রাকৃতিক গ্রহণ (হিঃ কোঃ), প্রাকৃতিক নির্ব্বাচন, নৈসর্গিক নির্ব্বাচন। **Sexual selection**—যৌননির্ব্বাচন, দাম্পতিক-নির্ব্বাচন।

sē-lĕc'-tance (-tăns), *n.* (*Electr.*) The action or quality of responding only to certain vibrations ; কতকগুলি নির্দ্দিষ্ট স্পন্দনে সাড়া প্রদান বা তদ্ধর্ম্ম।

sĕl'-ē-nīte, *n.* A crystallized variety of gypsum ; একপ্রকার স্ফটীকীভূত খটিক।

sē-lē'-nĭ-ŭm, *n.* An element related to sulphur and tellurium ; গন্ধকধর্ম্মা মূলপদার্থবিশেষ সলিলীন (মনীন্দ্র), সোমক (সাঃ পঃ)। [পারমাণবিক গুরুত্ব 79·2, সাঙ্কেতিক নাম Se. এই মূলপদার্থ Berzelius কর্ত্তৃক ১৮১৮ খৃঃ অব্দে আবিষ্কৃত হয়।]

sē-lē-nō-cĕn'-tric, *adj.* 1. Pertaining to the centre of the moon ; চন্দ্রকৈন্দ্রিক। 2. As seen or measured from the centre of the moon ; চন্দ্রের কেন্দ্র হইতে দৃষ্ট বা পরিমিত।

sē-lē'-nō-dŏnt, *adj.* Having molars with crescent ridges ; অর্দ্ধচন্দ্রাকৃতি বেষ্টনীর উপর বিন্যস্ত পেষণ-দন্তরাজিবিশিষ্ট।

sē-lē'-nō-grăph, *n.* A delineation or picture of the surface o the moon or a part of it ; চন্দ্রবর্ণন, চন্দ্রের চিত্র।

sĕl-ē-nŏl'-ŏ-gy̆, *n.* The branch of the astronomical science which treats of the moon ; চন্দ্রতত্ত্ব, চন্দ্রবিজ্ঞান।

Sē-leu'-cĭd (-lū-), *n.* (*Pl.* -CIDS, -CIDAE) One belonging to the dynasty founded by Seleucus Nicator in 312 B. C.; সেলুকাস কর্ত্তৃক খৃঃ পুঃ ৩১২ অব্দে প্রতিষ্ঠিত রাজবংশভুক্ত ব্যক্তি।

sĕlf, *n.* 1. The individual as object of his own consciousness ; one's individual person ; ব্যক্তি, আত্মা (শ্রী) ; স্ব, স্বয়ং, নিজ, পুরুষ (এভেলন)। 2. One's personal interest ; as, he cares for nothing but *self* ; স্বার্থ। 3. A flower or blossom of uniform colour ; একরঙ্গা ফুল, একবর্ণ কুসুম। **Highest self**—পরমাত্মা (শ্রীঃ), প্রাজ্ঞ (ঐ)। **Individual self**—স্বরাট (এভেলন)। **Inner self**—অন্তরাত্মা, আত্মাপুরুষ। **Second self**—অভিন্নহৃদয় বন্ধু। **Self-preservation is the first law of nature**—আগে আপন সামাল কর, চাচা আপন প্রাণ বাঁচা।

sĕlf–, *pref.* **Self'-hood,** *n.* (*Rare*) Personality ; (কচিদ্ব্যবহৃত) ব্যক্তিত্ব, পুরুষবিধত্ব। **Self-abuse**—হস্তমৈথুন ; আত্মনিন্দা, আত্মকুৎসা। **Self-accomplished**—স্বয়ংসিদ্ধ। **Self-acquired**—স্বোপার্জ্জিত, স্বার্জ্জিত, স্বয়মধিগত (বৃঃ সং), স্বয়মর্জ্জিত। **Self-acting**—স্বয়ংবহ, স্বয়ংক্রিয়, স্বয়ঞ্চল। **Self-action**—স্বাধীন ক্রিয়া। **Self-admiration**—আত্মপ্রশংসা, আত্মগুণানুকীর্ত্তন, আত্মশ্লাঘা। **Self-admirer**—স্বগুণ-প্রকাশক, আত্মশ্লাঘী। **Self-advantage**—আত্মহিত, আত্মসিদ্ধি, আত্মবিবৃদ্ধি। **Self-affairs**—স্বকার্য্য, স্বকর্ম্ম। **Self-aggrandizement** — স্বমহত্ত্ববৃদ্ধি। **Self-applause**—আত্মপ্রশংসা, আত্মগুণখ্যাপন, স্বগুণখ্যাপন, আত্মস্তুতি, আত্মশ্লাঘা। **Self-assertion**—স্বমতখ্যাপন,

আত্মপ্রকাশ **Self-assumption**—আত্মগর্ব। **Self-assurance**—Same as SELF-CONFIDENCE. **Self-begotten**—অনন্যজ, স্বয়ংজাত, স্বজ, স্বজাত। **Self-beguiled** — আত্মপ্রতারিত, স্ববঞ্চিত, স্বপ্রতারিত। **Self-black**—স্বভাবসিদ্ধ কৃষ্ণবর্ণের। **Self-born**—আত্মভু, স্বয়ভু, আত্মজনিত, স্বোৎপন্ন, স্বজ, আত্মসম্ভব, আত্মভূত। **Self-centred**—স্বনিষ্ঠ। **Self-collected**—স্থৈর্য্যসম্পন্ন, আত্মবশ, খাতিরজমা (*colloq.*)। **Self-collectedness**—স্বস্থতা। **Self-coloured**—একরঙ্গা, একবর্ণ (বিশ্বকর্ম্মা)। **Self-command**—আত্মসংযম, আত্মনিরোধ, দম। **Self-complacence**—আত্মপ্রসাদ, আত্মতৃপ্তি। **Self-complacent**—আত্মতৃপ্ত, আত্মারাম। **Self-conceit** — আত্মাভিমান, অভিমান, স্বাভিমান, অহম্মান, অহম্মতি, অহমহমিকা, আত্মগর্ব্ব, আত্মগরিমা, আত্মসম্ভাবনা, (কাদঃ)। **Self-conditioned**—স্বতন্ত্র, স্বচ্ছন্দ (হিঃ কোঃ)। **Self-confidence** — আত্মপ্রত্যয়, আত্মবিশ্বাস, স্বমতনিষ্ঠা, স্ববুদ্ধিনিষ্ঠা, আত্মসম্ভাবিত ভাব। **Self-confident**—আত্মপ্রত্যয়ী, আত্মবিশ্বাসী। **Self-congratulation**—আত্মাভিনন্দন। **Self-conjugate**—স্বসহচরিত (হিঃ কোঃ), মিথোবদ্ধ (ঐ)। **Self-consciousness** — অহঙ্কার (ডিউসেন), অহম্প্রত্যয় (বেদান্ত), আত্মজ্ঞান (বিশ্বঃ), স্বানুভূতি, স্বানুভব, জীবচৈতন্য (মাধুর্য্যকাদম্বিনী—বিশ্বনাথ চক্রবর্ত্তী), অন্তর্ব্বোধ (হিঃ কোঃ), নিজবোধ (ঐ)' স্বসংবেদন (ঐ), অহং-প্রত্যয় (বেদান্ত), আত্মচৈতন্য। **Self-consecration**—আত্মার্পণ। **Self-contempt**—আত্মজুগুপ্সা। **Self-contented**—আত্মারাম, আত্মতৃপ্ত। **Self-contradiction**—স্ববিরোধ। **Self-contradictory**—স্ববিরোধী, আত্মবিরোধী, ব্যাহত (হিঃ কোঃ)। **Self-control**—আত্মসংযম, যম, আত্মনিয়ম, আত্মবশ, আত্মবশতা, বশিতা (হিঃ কোঃ)। **Self-created**—স্বয়ংসৃষ্ট, স্বয়ম্ভু, আত্মভু, স্বয়ংকৃত, স্বজ, স্বোৎপন্ন, স্বভু (অঃ)। **Self-culture**—আত্মোৎকর্ষ, আত্মানুশীলন। **Self-deception**—আত্মপ্রতারণা, আত্মবঞ্চনা, আত্মপ্রবঞ্চনা (জিঃ)। **Self-defence**—আত্মপক্ষসমর্থন, আত্মরক্ষণ। **Self-delight**—আত্মানন্দ। **Self-deluded**—আত্মপ্রতারিত, আত্মপ্রবঞ্চিত। **Self-denyal** — আত্মত্যাগ, স্বার্থত্যাগ, স্বার্থহোম (হিঃ কোঃ), সংযম, আত্মনিয়ম, আত্মনিরোধ। **Self-denying**—আত্মত্যাগী, আত্মত্যাগমূলক, আত্মনিয়ামক, আত্মনিরোধী। **Self-denying ordinance**—(ইংলণ্ডের ইতিহাস) লংপার্লেমেণ্ট কর্ত্তৃক ১৬৪৫ খৃঃ অব্দে গৃহীত প্রস্তাব বিশেষ। [প্রস্তাবটী এই—"পার্লেমেণ্টে লর্ড বা কমনস্ সভার কোন সভ্য যুদ্ধ স্থিতিকাল পর্য্যন্ত কোনপ্রকার সামরিক বা অসামরিক পদে অধিষ্ঠিত থাকিতে পারিবেন না।"]; (লক্ষণায়) স্বার্থত্যাগমূলক কার্য্য, আত্মত্যাগমূলক কার্য্য। **Self-dependence** — আত্মাশ্রয় আত্মনির্ভর (কেভিঃ), স্বতন্ত্রতা। **Self-dependent**—স্বাশ্রয়, স্বাশ্রিত, স্বতন্ত্র, আত্মাধীন, আত্মাশ্রয়, আত্মাধার, আত্মনির্ভরশীল, স্বাধীন, স্বপ্রধান, স্বাশ্রিত, স্ববশ (রঃ), স্বাবলম্বী, স্বালম্ব (cf. আমরা এমন শিক্ষা চাই যাহাতে স্বতন্ত্র, স্বালম্ব, স্বনিষ্ঠ, স্বাধীন, সামাজিক প্রস্তুত হইবে—হীরেন্দ্রনাথ দত্ত)। **Self-destruction**—আত্মহত্যা, আত্মনাশ, আত্মহনন, স্বনাশ, স্ববিনাশ। **Self-destroyer**—আত্মঘাতী। **Self-determination**—স্বতন্ত্রতা (হিঃ কোঃ), স্বনির্দ্ধারণ। **Self-determined** — স্বনির্দ্ধারিত, স্বাবধারিত, স্বনির্ণীত। **Self-devised**—স্বকল্পিত, স্বযোজিত, স্বপ্রকল্পিত। **Self-devotion**—আত্মসমর্পণ, আত্মার্পণ, আত্মনিবেদন, আত্মোৎসর্গ। **Self-educated**—আত্মশিক্ষিত। **Self-enjoyment**—আত্মসুখ। **Self-esteem**—আত্মাদর, অহম্মান, অহম্মতি। **Self-evidence**—স্বতঃপ্রমাণতা, স্বতঃসিদ্ধি। **Self-evident**—স্বতঃপ্রমাণ, স্বয়ংপ্রমাণ, স্বতঃসিদ্ধ, স্বতঃস্পষ্ট, স্বপ্রকাশ। **Self-examination** — আত্মপরীক্ষা, আত্মপৃচ্ছা (কেভিঃ), আত্মবিচারণ, আত্মবিভাবন। **Self-executed**—আত্মকৃত, আত্মসম্পাদিত। **Self-exhibition**—আত্মপ্রদর্শন। **Self-exile** — আত্মনির্ব্বাসন। **Self-existence** — স্বতঃসিদ্ধি (ন্যায়সূত্র), স্বতঃসিদ্ধি (কেভিঃ), স্বত্ব (ঐ), স্বয়ংজাতত্ব (ঐ)। **Self-existent**—আপনাআপনি অবস্থিত, আত্মাবস্থিত, আত্মাবস্থিতি, স্বয়ম্ভু, নিরাধার (মহাঃ নিঃ), আত্মভু, স্বভু, নিজমূর্ত্তি। **Self-experience**—স্বাভিজ্ঞতা। **Self-feeling**—অহংভাব। **Self-fertilization**—স্বনিষেক (সাঃ পঃ)। **Self-forgetful**—আত্মবিস্মৃত। **Self-formed**—আত্মচেষ্টায় দরিদ্র দশা হইতে উন্নতিপ্রাপ্ত, আত্মরচিত, আপনগড়া, (গীতাঞ্জঃ)। **Self-gained**—স্বোপার্জ্জিত। **Self-given** — আত্মদত্ত। **Self-good**—স্বহিত, আত্মহিত, আত্মশ্রেয়ঃ। **Self-government** — স্বায়ত্তশাসন, স্বরাজ, আত্মশাসন, আত্ম-নিয়মন। **Self-growing**—স্বরুহ, স্বয়ংবর্দ্ধী। **Self-help**—আত্মসাহায্য। **Self-ignorance**—আত্মাজ্ঞান, অবিদ্যা। **Self-immolation**—আত্মাহুতি, আত্মোৎসর্গ। **Self-improvement** — আত্মোন্নতি। **Self-interest**—স্বার্থ, আত্মহিত (শুক্রঃ বিনয়)। **Self-invited** — আত্মাহূত, আত্মনিমন্ত্রিত। **Self-knowledge**—আত্মজ্ঞান, আত্মবিদ্যা, আত্মবোধ, আত্মবেদন, আত্মানুভব। **Self-less**—নিঃস্বার্থ, স্বার্থহীন। **Slef-love**—আত্মপ্রীতি, আত্মানুরাগ, স্বানুরাগ অহংমমতা, আত্মকাম। **Self-luminous**—স্বয়ংপ্রকাশ, স্বপ্রকাশ, স্বতোদীপ্ত, স্বতোজ্জ্বল, স্বভানু (ঋক্), স্বশ্চন্দ্র (ঋক্), স্বরুচি, স্বয়মুজ্জ্বল (বৃঃ সং), স্বয়ম্প্রভ। **Self-made**—আত্মচেষ্টায় দরিদ্রদশা হইতে উন্নতিপ্রাপ্ত, আত্মরচিত, আপনগড়া (গীতাঞ্জঃ)। **Self-manifest**—স্বপ্রকাশ। **Self-moved**—স্বয়ঞ্চালিত, স্ববহিত, স্বয়ংবহ। **Self-moving**—স্বয়ংচল (ঋক্)। **Self-murder**—আত্মহত্যা, আত্মহনন, আত্মহিংসা, আত্মঘাত। **Self-murderer**—আত্মঘাতী, আত্মহন্তা, স্বহন্তা, আত্মঘাতক। **Self-offence**—আত্মাপরাধ। **Self-opinion**—আত্মগর্ব্ব, আত্মগরিমা। **Self-opinionated**—স্বাভিমানী (কেভিঃ), স্বমতগ্রাহী, স্বমতাভিমানী, অহম্মন্য, আত্মদৃপ্ত, আত্মগর্ব্বিত, হামবড়া (*colloq.*)। **Self-pity**—আত্মমমতা। **Self-pleased**—স্বয়ংতৃপ্ত। **Self-pollution**—আত্মকলুষণ,

হস্তমৈথুন। **Self-possessed**—স্বস্থ, ধীরচেতা, সংযত, আত্মস্থ, ধৃতাত্মা। **Self-praise** — আত্মপ্রশংসা, আত্মশ্লাঘা, আত্মস্তুতি, আত্মস্তব (রঃ), স্বশ্লাঘা (আঃ)। **Self-preservation** — আত্মরক্ষণ, স্বরক্ষণ, স্বত্রাণ, আত্মরক্ষা। **Self-proved**—স্বতঃসিদ্ধ, স্বয়ংপ্রমাণিত। **Self-purification**—আত্মশুদ্ধি। **Self-realisation**—আত্মানুভূতি, স্বানুভূতি, আত্মসংভাব (হিঃ কোঃ), আত্মোপলব্ধি, আত্মজ্ঞান। **Self-renunciation** — আত্মত্যাগ। **Self-repression**—আত্মপীড়ন। **Self-reproach**—আত্মগ্লানি। **Self-repugnant** — আত্মবিরোধী। **Self-respect** — মর্য্যাদাবোধ, আত্মমর্য্যাদা, স্বাভিমান (কেঙিঃ), আত্মমান (ঐ), আত্মসম্মান, আত্মসম্ভাবিততা (হিঃ কোঃ), আত্মসম্ভাবনা (ঐ)। **Self-restrained** — আত্মসংবৃত, আত্মসংযত (কেঙিঃ), আত্মনিয়ন্ত্রিত, আত্মনিরুদ্ধ। **Self-restraint**—যম, দম (এভেলন), চিত্তসংযম, মিতসংযম, আত্মসংযম, আত্মনিগ্রহ, আত্মনিয়মন। **Self-righteousness** — পবিত্রমন্যতা। **Self-revolving**—স্বয়ম্ভ্রমী। **Self-sacrifice**—স্বার্থত্যাগ, আত্মোৎসর্গ, আত্মত্যাগ, স্বার্থহোম (হিঃ কোঃ) **Self-same**—অনন্য, ঠিক সেই, অভিন্ন। **Self-satisfaction** — আত্মপ্রসাদ, আত্মতুষ্টি। **Self-satisfied**—আত্মারাম (ভক্তিঃ), আত্মতৃপ্ত, আত্মসন্তুষ্ট, আত্মতুষ্ট। **Self-seeker**—স্বার্থনিষ্ঠ (কেঙিঃ), স্বার্থপর। **Self-seeking**—স্বার্থদৃষ্টি (কেঙিঃ), স্বার্থনিষ্ঠা, স্বহিতেচ্ছা, আত্মসুখপরায়ণ (ভস্মঃ) আত্মম্ভরী। **Self-slaughter** — আত্মবিনাশ, আত্মহনন। **Self-subdued**—সংযতাত্মা, জিতাত্মা, জিতেন্দ্রিয়। **Self-sufficient** — স্বপর্য্যাপ্ত, স্বয়ংসিদ্ধ, আপ্তকাম, স্বনিষ্ঠ, স্বাভিমানী। **Self-supported** — নিরালম্ব, নিরাধার। **Self-surrender**—আত্মসমর্পণ। **Self-undertaken**—স্বারব্ধ। **Self-will**—ঠেঁটামি, একগুঁয়েমি, স্বৈরিত।

sĕlf'-ish, *adj.* Caring only, or chiefly, for self; actuated by, or proceeding from, a regard to private advantage; স্বার্থপর, স্বার্থপরায়ণ, আত্মপরায়ণ (বঃ বিষ); স্বার্থপ্রণোদিত। **–ly**, *adv.* **–ness**, *n.* The quality of being selfish; স্বার্থপরতা, স্বার্থপরায়ণতা।

Sĕl-juk' (-jook), *n.* A member of a Turkish family which, under Togrul Beg, grandson of a chief named Seljuk, overthrew the Abbasside Caliphs of Bagdad about 1050; তুর্কিজাতিবিশেষের লোক। এই জাতীয় তুর্কিগণ অনুমান ১০৫০ খৃঃ অব্দে সেলজুক নামক সর্দ্দারের পৌত্র তগ্রুল বেগএর অধিনায়কত্বে বাগদাদের আবাসাইড খলিফাগণের সিংহাসন অধিকার করিয়াছিল।

sĕll, *v. t., i. & n.* **1.** To dispose of for money or other consideration; বিক্রয় করা, বেচা। **2.** To betray; "You would have *sold* your king to slaughter"; গোপনে কাহারো বিরুদ্ধে সংবাদ দেওয়া বা কাহাকে শত্রুহস্তে সমর্পণ করা। **3.** (*Slang*) To cheat; as, to *sell* another man; (ইতরভাষায়) ঠকান, চোখে ধূলি দেওয়া। ***Verb i.*** **1.** To dispose of commodities or property; বিক্রয় করা। **2.** To be sold; as, the book *sells* well; বিক্রীত হওয়া। ***Noun.*** **1.** An act of betraying; বিশ্বাসঘাতকতা পূর্ব্বক শত্রুহস্তে অর্পণ। **2.** A hoax; a trick; ধোকা; চাতুরী। **Sell'-er**, *n.* One who sells; বিক্রেতা, বিক্রয়ী। **Sell away**—Go on selling; বিক্রয় করিতে থাক। **To sell for, To sell at**—To fetch a price; নির্দ্দিষ্ট মূল্যে বিক্রীত হওয়া। **To sell off**—To dispose of the whole; সমস্তট বেচিয়া ফেলা। **To sell one's life dearly**—To cause great loss to those who are taking or seeking one's life; শত্রুপক্ষের গুরুতর ক্ষতি করার পর প্রাণ বিসর্জ্জন করা। **To sell one's self**—To enslave one's self; আত্মবিক্রয় করা। **To sell one up**—To sell a person's goods for the discharge of his debt; ঋণ পরিশোধের জন্য মালপত্র বিক্রয় করা। **To sell out**—To dispose of solely or entirely; সবটা বিক্রয় করা। To distribute by sale; বিক্রয় করিয়া বিতরণ করা। To dispose of one's shares in company; কাহারো কোম্পানীর অংশ বিক্রয় করা। (Formerly) To sell one's commission in the army and retire from the service; (পূর্ব্বে) সেনাবিভাগের কর্ম্মচারীর পদ বিক্রয় করতঃ অবসর গ্রহণ করা [পূর্ব্বে অর্থ দ্বারা সৈনিককর্ম্মচারীর পদ ক্রয় কর হইত এবং আবশ্যক হইলে এই পদ অন্যের নিকট বিক্রয় করা চলিত। ১৮৬৯ খৃঃ অব্দে এই প্রথা রহিত হইয়াছে]। **To sell over**—To clear out stock; গুদাম সাবাড় করা। To transfer by sale; বিক্রয় দ্বারা হস্তান্তর করা।

sĕl'-lăn-dêrs, *n.* See SALLENDERS.

Sĕl'-êrs-wâ-têr, (Less correctly SELTZER-) *n.* A medicinal mineral water from Selters, in Germany; জর্ম্মণীর অন্তঃপাতী Selters নামক স্থানে প্রাপ্ত একপ্রকার ভেষজগুণসম্পন্ন খনিজপদার্থবিমিশ্রজল।

sĕl'-zō-gene (-jĕn), *n.* Same as GAZOGENE (which see).

sĕl-vāge, –vedge (-vĕj), *ns.* **1.** The edge of a cloth where it is closed by complicating the threads; কাপড়ের ছিলা [Syn. দশা, বস্তী]। **2.** Border; as, the *selvedge* of a wood; ধার, কিনারা, প্রান্ত। **3.** (Only *selvage*) The edge-plate of a lock through which the bolt shoots; তালার প্রান্তফলক।

selves (sĕlvz), *n. Pl.* Of SELF (which see).

sĕm'-ă-phōre, *n.* সংবাদপ্রেরণের জন্য যন্ত্র, বার্ত্তাপ্রেরক। **–phor'-ic**, *adj.* **–phor'-i-cal-ly**, *adv.*

sĕ-măt'-ic, *adj.* (Of colours of animals) Serving for warning or attracting; (জন্তুর বর্ণ সম্বন্ধে) সাবধানকারী বা আকর্ষক [যথা কোন কোন বিষাক্ত কিম্বা হিংস্র জন্তুর উজ্জ্বল বর্ণ।]

sĕm'-blance (-blăns), *n.* **1.** Likeness; resemblance; প্রতিকৃতি,

প্রতিরূপ ; সাদৃশ্য, সদৃশতা, স্বরূপতা, অনুরূপতা। 2. Show ; আভাস, অবভাস।

sĕ-mei-ŏl′-ŏ-ğȳ (-mĭ-), **–ŏt′-ics,** *ns.* See SEMI-.

sē′-mĕn, *n.* The seed or fecundating fluid of male animal; বীর্য্য, শুক্র, রেতঃ, ধাতু [Syn. ধাতুরাজক, দৈত্যগুরু (*joc.*), বীজ, পুংস্ত্ব, পৌরুষং, তেজ, রম্য, ইন্দ্রিয়, অন্নবিকার, বল, রোহণ, মজ্জারস, বৃষ (মঃ উঃ), বস্তু (In the mystical language of some Vaisnaba sects), ধন (ঐ), চন্দ্র (ঐ), হীল (ঐ), আনন্দজ (ঐ), আনন্দপ্রভব (ঐ)।]

sē-mĕs′-têr, *n.* A term of six months in German or other universities; জর্ম্মন বা অপর বিশ্ববিদ্যালয়ে ছয়মাসব্যাপী অধ্যয়নকাল।

sĕm′-ĭ-, *pref.* Half; অর্দ্ধ, আধ, অংশিক। **Semi-animate**—অর্দ্ধচেতন, মৃতকল্প, মৃতপ্রায়। **Semi-axis**—অক্ষার্দ্ধ। **Semi-barbarian**—অর্দ্ধবর্ব্বর। **Semi-breve**—অর্দ্ধস্বর, দীর্ঘস্বর (কেণ্ডিঃ)। **Semi-castrate**—(*Verb t.*) আংশিকভাবে মুষ্ক ছিন্ন করা। **Semi-circle**—অর্দ্ধবৃত্ত, বৃত্তার্দ্ধ (হিঃ কোঃ), অর্দ্ধবর্ত্তুল। **Semi-circular**—অর্দ্ধবৃত্তাকার (সূর্য্যঃ বিঃ), অর্দ্ধবৃত্তাকৃতি বৃত্তার্দ্ধাকৃতি। **Semi-colon**—সেমিকোলন, অর্দ্ধচ্ছেদ। **Semi-crystalline**—অর্দ্ধস্ফাটিক। **Semi-detached**—এক পার্শ্বে সংলগ্ন, অংশতঃ বিশ্লিষ্ট। **Semi-diameter**—ব্যাসার্দ্ধ, অর্দ্ধব্যাস, ত্রিজ্যা, (হিঃ কোঃ)। **Semi-demi**—চতুর্থাংশ। **Semi-diurnal motion**—অহোরাত্র বৃত্তার্দ্ধভ্রমণ (হিঃ কোঃ)। **Semi-feral** — অর্দ্ধবন্য। **Semi-fluid**—অর্দ্ধ তরল। **Semi-god**—অর্দ্ধ দেবতা। **Semi-globe** — গোলার্দ্ধ। **Semi-logical fallacies** — মিশ্র-হেত্বাভাস (হিঃ কোঃ)। **Semi-lunar**—অর্দ্ধচন্দ্রাকার। **Semi-metal**—পারদ, দস্তা, প্রভৃতি আঘাতসহ ধাতু। **Semi-metallic**—অর্দ্ধধাতব। **Semi-nude**—অর্দ্ধনগ্ন। **Semi-official**—অর্দ্ধসরকারী। **Semi-tone**—অর্দ্ধস্বর, মূর্চ্ছনা (কেণ্ডিঃ)। **Semi-vowel**—অর্দ্ধস্বর ও অর্দ্ধহল, অন্তঃস্বর্ণ (সংস্কৃতে), (ইংরাজী বর্ণমালার) w and y দুই বর্ণ।

sĕm′-ĭ-năl, *adj.* 1. Pertaining to seed or semen; as, *seminal* weakness; বীর্য্যসম্বন্ধীয়, শুক্রসম্বন্ধীয়। 2. Rudimentary; মৌলিক, বৈজিক। **Seminal calculus** — শুক্রাশ্মরী (সুশ্রুঃ)। **Seminal duct**—রেতঃপ্রণালী, রেতোমার্গ। **Seminal forces** — প্রকৃতিবীর্য্য (হিঃ কোঃ), প্রকৃতিপ্রভাব (ঐ)। **Seminal-secretion**—ধাতুবিকার।

sĕm′-ĭ-nă-rȳ, *n.* 1. A place of education; শিক্ষাগার, বিদ্যালয়, শিক্ষালয়। 2. (*R. C. C.*) A school for training persons for priesthood; (রোমান-ক্যাথলিক ধর্ম্মসংঘ) যাজকীয় বিদ্যালয়। 3. A seed-bed; বীজভূমি।

sĕm-ĭ-nā′-tion *n.* (*Rare*) The act of sowing; dissemination; বপন; বিকিরণ, ব্যাপন।

sĕm-ĭ-nĭf′-êr-ous (-ŭs), *adj.* 1. Bearing or producing seed; বীজপ্রসূ, বীজোৎপাদী। 2. Bearing or producing semen; conveying semen; শুক্রজনক, বীর্য্যজনক; বীর্য্যবাহী, রেতোবাহী।

sĕ-mĭ-ŏl′-ŏ ğȳ, –ŏt′-ics, *ns.* (*Med.*) The doctrine of symptoms; (ভৈষজ্যশাস্ত্র) লক্ষণতত্ত্ব (হঃ চঃ)।

Sĕm′-īte, *n.* & *adj.* A member of the Semitic race; সেমিটিক জাতির লোক। ***Adj.*** Pertaining to the Semitic race; সেমেটিক জাতিসম্বন্ধীয়।

Sĕm-ĭt′-ic, *adj.* & *n.* 1. Pertaining to the descendants of Shem and the countries peopled by them; সেমের বংশধরগণ এবং তাহাদের দ্বারা অধ্যুষিত দেশসমূহসম্বন্ধীয় (See *Gen.* x)। 2. Pertaining to the Hebrew race or any others kindred to it, esp. Phoenicians, Arabs and Assyrians; হিব্রুজাতি বা তাহাদের নিকট সম্পর্কীয় কোন জাতি সম্পর্কীয়, বিশেষতঃ ফিনিসিয়ান, আরব এবং এসিরীয় জাতি-সম্পর্কীয়। ***Noun.*** The Semitic family of languages; সেমেটিক ভাষাসমূহ (হিব্রু, আরবী, পারসীক, ফিনিসিয়ান, প্রভৃতি)। **Sem′-i-tism, Sem′-i-tist,** *ns.* **Sem′-i-tize,** *v. t.*

sĕm-ō-lĭ′-nă, sĕm′-ō-lâ, *ns.* Granules of the floury part of wheat; সুজি।

sĕm-pi-têr′-năl, *adj.* Eternal; "We have discovered the elixir of *sempiternal* juvenility"; নিত্য, অনন্ত, শাশ্বত, সনাতন, অনাদি (হিঃ কোঃ)।

semplice, (*It.*), *adj.* Simple; সাদাসিধা, সরল।

sempre, (*It.*), *adj.* (*Mus. direction*) Throughout; আদ্যন্ত।

sĕmp′-strĕss, *n.* Same as SEAMSTRESS (which see).

sĕn, *n.* A Japanese copper-coin in value $\frac{1}{100}$th part of a yen; জাপানদেশীয় তাম্রমুদ্রা বিশেষ, ইহার মূল্য $\frac{1}{100}$ ইয়েন।

sĕ-nā′-rĭ-ŭs, *n.* (*Latin prosody*) A verse of six feet; (ল্যাটিন ছন্দঃশাস্ত্র) ষট্‌চরণবিশিষ্ট কবিতা পংক্তি।

sĕn′-ă-rȳ, *adj.* Belonging to six; containing six; on the basis of six; ষট্‌সম্বন্ধীয়; ষড়াত্মক; ষন্মূলক।

sĕn′-āte, *n.* 1. An assembly or council of citizens distinguished by birth, dignities, wealth, influence, etc. and invested with a share in the Government in ancient Rome; প্রাচীন রোমের পৌরপরিষৎ। [Tarquinus Priscus এর সময়ে সেনেটের সভ্যসংখ্যা ৩০০ শত ছিল। দেশনায়ক Sullaর সময়ে সভ্যসংখ্যা বৃদ্ধিপ্রাপ্ত হইয়া ৬০০তে পরিণত হয়। জুলিয়াস সীজারের সময় পৌরপরিষদের সভ্যসংখ্যা ৯০০ পর্য্যন্ত হইয়াছিল। সম্রাট্‌ আগষ্টাস পুনরায় ঐ সংখ্যা হ্রাস করিয়া ৬০০ শত করেন। রোমক গণতন্ত্রের অবসানকালে সম্ভবতঃ পৌরপরিষদে প্রবেশের বৎসর অন্যূন ২৭ বৎসর নির্দ্ধারিত হইয়াছিল। পূর্ব্বে সম্ভ্রান্তবংশীয়গণ ব্যতিরেকে কেহই পৌরপরিষদের সভ্য নির্ব্বাচিত হইতে পারিতেন না। পরবর্ত্তীকালে সাধারণ প্রজাগণ ও, (plebeians) পৌরপরিষদে প্রবেশ করিতে পারিতেন। প্রথম প্রথম পৌরপরিষৎ

রাজ্যশাসনব্যবস্থা সম্বন্ধে পরামর্শ মাত্র দিতে পারিতেন। ক্রমে ক্রমে পরিষদ্‌সংক্রান্ত বিধিব্যবস্থা প্রণয়নের অধিকার প্রাপ্ত হন।] 2. Council of ancient Athens or Sparta ; প্রাচীন এথেন্স ও স্পার্টার শাসনপরিষৎ। 3. The upper branch of legislature in various countries, as in France, United States, etc. ; বিভিন্ন দেশের ব্যবস্থাপকসভার উচ্চতর বিভাগ, যথা—মার্কিণ যুক্ত রাজ্যে। [মার্কিণ যুক্তরাজ্যে প্রতি রাষ্ট্র হইতে সেই রাষ্ট্রের ব্যবস্থাপক সভাকর্তৃক ২ জন সভ্য ৬ বৎসরের জন্য নির্ব্বাচিত হন। সভ্যদের বয়স অনূন ত্রিশ হওয়া আবশ্যক।] 4. A legislative assembly ; "An eloquent orator in the British *Senate*" ; ব্যবস্থাপকসভা। 5. The governing body of a university ; বিশ্ববিদ্যালয়ের পরিচালকসভা। 6. (*U. S.*) A council composed of the members of the faculty and elect students to watch the discipline etc. of students ; (মার্কিণ যুক্তরাজ্য) ছাত্রদিগের শাসন এবং তত্ত্বাবধানের জন্য নির্ব্বাচিত ছাত্র ও অধ্যাপকগণের সভা। **Senate-house**—ব্যবস্থাপক সভাগৃহ ; বিশ্ববিদ্যালয়ের সভামণ্ডপ।

sĕn'-ā-tŏr, *n.* A member of a senate ; প্রাচীন রোমের পৌরপরিষৎ, মার্কিণ যুক্তরাজ্য প্রভৃতির এবং বিশ্ববিদ্যালয়ের পরিচালক সভার সভ্য বা সদস্য। **–ship,** *n.* **–to'-ri-al,** *adj.* Befitting a senator ; সেনেটসভার সদস্যসমুচিত। **–to'-ri-al-ly,** *adv.*

senatus,n. The senate of anceint Rome ; প্রাচীন রোমের পৌরপরিষৎ। ***Senatus consult, Senatus consultum***—প্রাচীন রোমের পৌরপরিষদের বিধান। ***Senatus populusque Romanus*** — (*Abbr.* S. P. Q. R.) ; রোমের পৌরপরিষৎ এবং রোমবাসিগণ।

sĕnd, *v. t., i. & n.* **1.** To cause to go or pass from one place for another ; পাঠান, প্রেরণ করা। **2.** To throw ; to hurl ; as, this gun *sends* a ball 5,000 miles ; নিক্ষেপ করা ; ছোঁড়া। **3.** To make ; as, to *send* one mad ; করা। **4.** To refer to some author or authority "Writers who have *sent* us to the laws of the Christian empire ;" কোন গ্রন্থকার বা প্রামাণিক গ্রন্থ প্রভৃতির উল্লেখ করা। **5.** To impel ; to drive ; "They *sent* the rebels flying in all directions" ; ঠেলিয়া দেওয়া ; তাড়ান। **6.** To cause a thing to be conveyed or transmitted ; বহন করা, প্রেরণ করা। **7.** To cause food to be handed to a guest ; "You eat nothing, Let Mr. Rodney *send* you some lamb" ; নিমন্ত্রিত ব্যক্তির হস্তে খাদ্য প্রদান করা। **8.** To serve food ; as, to *send up* supper ; পরিবেষণ করা। **9.** To cause to take place ; to inflict ; "The Lord shall *send* upon thee cursing, vexation and rebuke"; ঘটান ; (দণ্ড প্রভৃতি) বিধান করা। ***Verb i.*** **1.** To despatch a messenger or a message ; দূত প্রেরণ করা, সংবাদ প্রেরণ করা। **2.** To pitch forward as a ship (*in this senss the past participle is used*) ; "She *sended* forward heavily and sickly on the long swell" ; সম্মুখভাগ এবং পশ্চাদ্‌ভাগ পর্য্যায়ক্রমে উঠানামা করা। ***Noun.*** **1.** (*Obs.*) A message ; সংবাদ। **2.** A gift ; উপহার। **3.** The impulse of a wave ; তরঙ্গাভিঘাত। **To be sent into the world**—To be born ; পৃথিবীতে জন্মগ্রহণ করা। **To send abroad**—To publish ; প্রচার করা। **To send along**—To cause to walk rapidly ; তাড়াতাড়ি ছুটান। To hasten the growth of ; দ্রুত বৃদ্ধি করা। **To send away**—To despatch ; প্রেরণ করা। **To send down** — To send from higher authority to a lower or from larger town to a smaller ; অধস্তন কর্ম্মচারী প্রভৃতির নিকট বা ক্ষুদ্রতর নগর প্রভৃতিতে প্রেরণ করা। To rusticate ; বিশ্ববিদ্যালয় হইতে বিতাড়িত করা। **To send for**—To require by message to be brought ; কাহারো জন্য লোক পাঠান, ডাকিয়া পাঠান : **To send forth**—To publish ; প্রকাশ করা। To export ; রপ্তানী করা। **To send forth, To send out**—To produce ; উৎপাদন করা। To emit ; নির্গত করা, নিঃসৃত করা। **To send in**—To give one's card or name to a servant when visiting some one ; কাহারো সহিত সাক্ষাৎ করার কালে ভৃত্যের কাছে নাম বা কার্ড প্রদান করা। To render an account or bill ; পাওনা টাকার বিল (হিসাব) দেওয়া। To cause a thing to be delivered at the proper place or to the proper person ; প্রকৃত ব্যক্তির নিকট বা প্রকৃত স্থানে প্রেরণ করা। **To send off** — To be present at the time of the departure of a person ; কোন ব্যক্তির বিদায়কালে উপস্থিত থাকা। **To send on** — To despatch beforehand ; পূর্ব্বে প্রেরণ করা, আগে পাঠান। To cause to go onward ; অগ্রসর করা। **To send one about one's business**—See BUSINESS. **To send round**—To circulate ; প্রচার করা। **To send to Coventry**—See COVENTRY. **To send to prison**—জেলে দেওয়া, কারাগারে প্রেরণ করা। To be made over by the police to a court for trial ; চালান দেওয়া। **To send up**—To shoot upwards ; to emit ; উদ্গত হওয়া, ঠেলিয়া উঠা; অঙ্কুরিত হওয়া, নির্গত করা। To send upstairs ; উপরে পাঠান। To serve up a meal ; পরিবেষণ করা। **To send word to**—To despatch a message or information ; সংবাদ দেওয়া, খবর পাঠান।

sĕn'-dăl, *n.* A kind of rich silk used in the Middle Ages ; মধ্যযুগে ব্যবহৃত একপ্রকার মূল্যবান পট্টবস্ত্র। [সংস্কৃত সিন্ধু শব্দের গ্রীক রূপ *Sindon* হইতে এই শব্দটী উপজাত হইয়াছে ।]

sĕnd'-ĕr, *n.* **1.** One who sends ; প্রেরক। **2.** (*Teleg.*) The instrument by which a message is transmitted ; (তাড়িতবার্ত্তাবহ) প্রেরক-যন্ত্র (সাঃ পঃ)।

sĕnd'-off(-ŏf), *n.* A demonstration of goodwill at, or before, a person's departure, at the opening of a shop etc. ; কোন লোকের যাত্রাকালে বা যাত্রার পূর্ব্বে বা কোন দোকান প্রভৃতি খোলার কালে প্রীতি বা বন্ধুভাব প্রদর্শন, বিদায়সম্ভাষণ, প্রীতি উৎসব।

sĕn'-ĕ-kă, —gă, *ns.* A drug consisting of the root of a plant of the United States, used in cough-mixtures ; মার্কিণ যুক্তরাজ্যের গুল্মবিশেষের মূল হইতে প্রস্তুত কফঘ্ন ঔষধ বিশেষ।

sĕn'-ē-găl, *n.* A small crimson bird of Africa ; আফ্রিকাদেশীয় রক্তবর্ণ ক্ষুদ্র পক্ষিবিশেষ।

sē-nĕs'-cĕnt, *adj.* Beginning to grow old ; বৃদ্ধপ্রায়। **—cence,** *n.* The state of being senescent ; জরত্ব (হিঃ কোঃ), জীর্ণমানতা (ঐ)।

sĕn'-ĕs-chal(-shăl), *n.* A steward ; ধনী ব্যক্তির বাটীর কর্ম্মাধ্যক্ষ বা দেওয়ান।

sĕn'-green (-grēn), *n.* House-leek ; একপ্রকার গন্ধপেঁয়াজ।

senhor, *n.* A Portugese title of courtesy corresponding to the English Mr. ; পর্ত্তুগিজদিগের ইংরাজী মিষ্টার শব্দের অনুরূপ উপাধি।

sē'-nīle, *adj.* **1.** Pertaining to old age ; proceeding from old age ; বার্দ্ধক্যসম্বন্ধীয়; বার্দ্ধক্যজনিত। **—nil'-i-ty,** *n.* Quality or state of being senile ; old age or its infirmity ; বার্দ্ধক্য ; বৃদ্ধবয়স, জরা, বৃদ্ধাবস্থা, বৃদ্ধভাব।

sē'-ni-or (-ēr), *adj.* & *n.* **1.** Older; বয়োজ্যেষ্ঠ। **2.** Older in office ; অফিসের কার্য্যে অধিকতর অভিজ্ঞ, কর্ম্ম-প্রবীণ, কর্ম্মজ্যেষ্ঠ। ***Noun.*** **1.** One older than the other ; বয়োজ্যেষ্ঠ ব্যক্তি। **2.** One who is older in office ; কর্ম্মপ্রবীণ ব্যক্তি। **3.** An aged person ; বৃদ্ধলোক। **—or'-i-ty,** *n.* Priority of birth, office, or service ; বয়োজ্যেষ্ঠতা, কর্ম্মজ্যেষ্ঠতা, কর্ম্মপ্রবীণতা। **Senior wrangler**—See WRANGLER.

seniores priores—(Latin sentence) জ্যেষ্ঠের দাবী অগ্রগণ্য।

sĕn'-nă, *n.* The dried leaves of certain plants of the genus Cassia, used as a purgative ;

Senna Plant.

সোণামুখী, রঙ্গলতা, দাদমারী, দদ্রুঘ্ন, শণপাট (খোরী) [Arab. *sanai, suna* ; Fr. *sene* ; Germ. *sennablater, senespflanze* ; Russ. *aleksandruskii* ; Sp. *sen.*]

sĕn-nĕt, *n.* A signal call on trumpet or cornet (used as a stage-direction in Elizabethan plays) ; রাজ্ঞী এলিজেবেথের সময়ের নাট্য রঙ্গমঞ্চে আদেশপ্রদানের জন্য বংশী প্রভৃতির সাহায্যে প্রদত্ত সংকেতধ্বনি।

sĕn'-night (-nīt), *n.* (*Archaic*) Seven nights and days ; a week ; (অপ্রঃ) অহোরাত্র; সপ্তাহ, সপ্তা।

sĕn'-nit, sin'-net (-ĕt), *ns.* A flat braided cord ; একপ্রকার চ্যাপ্টা-বিনান রজ্জু।

senor, *n.* (*Fem. senora, senorita*) A spanish title of courtesy corresponding to English Mr. ; ইংরাজী মিষ্টার উপাধির অনুরূপ স্পেন-দেশীয় ভদ্রলোকদিগের উপাধি।

Sē-nou'-si (-nōō-), **Sē-nous'-si** (-nōō-), *ns.* Same as SENUSSI (which see). **—an,** *adj.*

sĕn-sā'-tion *n.* **1.** An impression made upon the sensorium through the medium of the senses ; ইন্দ্রিয়সমূহের মধ্যবর্ত্তিতায় স্নায়ুচক্রে যে অনুভূতি উৎপাদিত হয় অনুভব (বেদান্ত), চেতনা, ইন্দ্রিয় চেতনা, নির্ব্বিকল্পপ্রত্যক্ষ (হিঃ কোঃ), সংবেদন (ঐ), শংসন (ঐ), উপলব্ধি (ঐ), জ্ঞান (ঐ), বোধ (ঐ), ঐন্দ্রিয়জ্ঞান (ঐ)। **2.** Feeling ; as, a *sensation* of cold ; অনুভূতি, বোধ। **3.** A state of excited interest or feeling ; as, the murder caused a great *sensation* in the town ; উত্তেজনা, হুলস্থুল, তোলপাড়, হৈচৈকাণ্ড, হুজুক ; **4.** That which produces excited interest or feeling ; as, it is the greatest *sensation* of the day; উত্তেজনাসঞ্চারক বিষয়, যে বিষয় নিয়া তোলপাড় হয়। **5.** Faculty of perceiving by the senses; ইন্দ্রিয়ানুভূতির বৃত্তি। **6.** (*Slang*) Trace ; as a *sensation* of sherry ; (ইতরভাষায়) লেশ, বিন্দু। **—al,** *adj.* **1.** Pertaining to sensation; dependent on sensation; সংবেদনসম্বন্ধীয়; সংবেদনসাপেক্ষ। **2.** Violently exciting ; as, *sensational* novels ; উত্তেজনাজনক, উত্তেজনাপূর্ণ।

sĕn-sā'-tion-ăl-ĭsm, *n.* **1.** The dictrine that our ideas originate solely in sensation, and consist of sensations transformed ; আমাদের ধারণাসমূহ কেবল সংবেদন হইতে উদ্ভূত এবং সংবেদনেরই রূপান্তর মাত্র—এই মত, সংবেদনবাদ, সংবেদন-বিজ্ঞানবাদ, ঐন্দ্রিয়মূলকতাবাদ। **2.** Love of sensational art or literature ; সাহিত্য বা ললিতকলায় উত্তেজনাসঞ্চারক এবং চমকপ্রদ বিষয়ের প্রতি অনুরাগ, চমৎকারপ্রিয়তা (হিঃ কোঃ)। **—ist,** *n.* An upholder of sensationalism ; সংবেদনবিজ্ঞানবাদী, ঐন্দ্রিয়মূলকতাবাদী,

প্রত্যক্ষবাদী, অনুভববাদী, প্রত্যয়বাদী (জিঃ)।

sense (sĕns), *n. & v. t.* **1.** One of the faculties by which men and the higher animals perceive external objects by means of impression made on certain organs of body ; ইন্দ্রিয়, জ্ঞানেন্দ্রিয়, বহিরিন্দ্রিয়, বাহেন্দ্রিয়। [Syn. অক্ষ, কারণ, গ্রহণ] [এতদ্দেশীয় পণ্ডিতগণের মতে ইন্দ্রিয় ত্রিবিধ :—জ্ঞানেন্দ্রিয় (organs of sense, কর্ণ, ত্বক্, চক্ষুঃ, জিহ্বা, নাসিকা) ; (২) কর্ম্মেন্দ্রিয়, (organs of action, বাক্, পাণি, পায়ু, উপস্থ) ; (৩) অন্তরেন্দ্রিয় (মন, বুদ্ধি, অহঙ্কার, চিত্ত)। মন সকল ইন্দ্রিয়ের নিয়ামক। চতুর্দ্দশ দেবতা চতুর্দ্দশ ইন্দ্রিয়ের নিয়ামক। কর্ণের দিক্, বায়ু ত্বকের, বরুণ রসনার, অশ্বিনীকুমারদ্বয় ঘ্রাণের, অগ্নি বাক্যের, ইন্দ্র হস্তের, বিষ্ণু পদের, পায়ুর মিত্র, উপস্থের প্রজাপতি, মনের চন্দ্র, বুদ্ধির চতুর্ম্মুখ, অহঙ্কারের শঙ্কর এবং অচ্যুত চিত্তের অধিষ্ঠাত্রী দেবতা। ন্যায়শাস্ত্র মতে পৃথিবীর ঘ্রাণ, জলের জিহ্বা, তেজের চক্ষুঃ, ত্বকের বায়ু এবং কর্ণ আকাশের ইন্দ্রিয়। প্রতীচ্য দার্শনিকগণ পৈশিক অনুভূতি (muscular sense) নামে একটী ষষ্ঠ ইন্দ্রিয় স্বীকার করেন। এই শেষোক্ত ইন্দ্রিয়ের সাহায্যে ইচ্ছাবাহী পেশী দ্বারা চালিত বিভিন্ন প্রত্যঙ্গ বা দেহাংশের দিক এবং অবস্থানসম্বন্ধে জ্ঞানলাভ হয়।] **2.** Sensation ; সংবেদন। **3.** Perception through the senses ; ইন্দ্রিয়ানুভূতি, অনুভূতি। **4.** Perception by the intellect ; discernment ; apprehension ; জ্ঞান ; বিচারণা শক্তি ; উপলব্ধি। **5.** One's reasons or will ; sanity ; as, he seems to be a man of *sense* ; বিদ্যাবুদ্ধি, জ্ঞানবুদ্ধি, বিচারবুদ্ধি ; প্রকৃতিস্থতা। **6.** Moral perception ; as, *sense* of right ; বোধ, জ্ঞান। **7.** Meaning or import ; gist ; অর্থ, তাৎপর্য্য, অভিপ্রায় ; মর্ম্ম, সার। **8.** Consciousness ; সংজ্ঞা, চেতনা, হুঁস। **9.** Opinion ; as, to take the *sense* of a meeting ; notion ; মত, মতামত ; ধারণা। *Verb t.* To perceive by the senses ; ইন্দ্রিয়দ্বারা অনুভব করা। **Sense′-less**, *adj.* **1.** Insensible ; অচেতন, সংজ্ঞাহীন, বেহুঁস, গতচেতন, বিচেতন। **2.** Foolish ; nonsensical ; as, *senseless* talk ; অজ্ঞান, নির্ব্বোধ ; অসার, অর্থহীন, অর্থশূন্য। **Sense-organs**—জ্ঞানেন্দ্রিয়, অধিপতি (শ্রীঃ), ইন্দ্রিয়নিবন্ধন (সাঃ পঃ), ইন্দ্রিয় গ্রাম। **Sense-perception**—ইন্দ্রিয়ানুভূতি, অনুভূতি। **Common-sense**—See COMMON. **Spiritual sense**—দিব্যবোধ (হিঃ কোঃ), মানসেন্দ্রিয় (ঐ)। **A man of sense** — A sagacious person ; বুদ্ধিমান লোক। **Object of sense**—ইন্দ্রিয় বিষয়। **Out of his senses**—Destitute of normal judgment and reasoning power ; insane ; বুদ্ধিভ্রষ্ট ; বিকৃতমস্তিষ্ক। **Sense of separateness**—ভেদবুদ্ধি (হিঃ কোঃ)। **To bring one to his senses**—To make one feel that he has done something foolish or improper ; কাহারো চৈতন্যোদয় করিয়া দেওয়া। **To give, make or have sense**—To be intelligible ; বোধগম্য হওয়া। **To make sense of**—To find the meaning of ; অর্থগ্রহণ করা।

sĕns-i-bil′-i-ty, *n.* **1.** The state or quality of being sensible ; অনুভূতি, সংবেতৃত্ব, সংবেদনশীলতা, প্রত্যক্ষগ্রাহকতা। **2.** Susceptibility of impressions upon the organs of sense ; impressibility ; delicacy of feeling ; quick emotion or sympathy ; অনুভবপ্রবণতা, সংবেদনপ্রবণতা, জ্ঞানগ্রহণসামর্থ্য (হিঃ কোঃ), বিষয়গ্রহণক্ষমতা, ইন্দ্রিয়চেতনা ; ভাবগ্রহণপ্রবণতা ; সূক্ষ্মঅনুভবসম্পন্নতা ; আবেগ, তীব্র আবেগ বা সমবেদনা। **3.** That quality of an instrument which makes it indicate very slight changes ; যন্ত্রের গুণবিশেষ — যদ্দ্বারা উহাতে অতি সূক্ষ্ম পরিবর্ত্তনও সূচিত হয়।

sĕn′-si-ble (-bl), *adj.* **1.** Perceptible by the senses ; as, *sensible* man ; ইন্দ্রিয়গ্রাহ্য, ইন্দ্রিয়জ্ঞেয়, ইন্দ্রিয়গোচর, সংবেদ্য (মাধুর্য্য)। **2.** Intelligent reasonable ; judicious ; as, *sensible* advice ; বুদ্ধিমান ; সদ্বিবেচক, সুধী, ধীমান ; যুক্তিযুক্ত, যুক্তিগর্ভ, যুক্তিসঙ্গত। **3.** Aware ; as, he was *sensible* of danger ; জ্ঞাতসার, বিদিত। **4.** Readily moved or affected by natural agents ; as, *sensible* thermometer ; আশুচঞ্চল, আশুবিকারী। **5.** Readily affected ; sensitive ; সহজে অভিভূত ; সংবেদনশীল। **Sensible heat**—জ্ঞেয়তাপ (হিঃ কোঃ), অনুভূত উষ্ণতা (সাঃ পঃ)

sĕn′-si-tive (-tiv), *adj. & n.* **1.** Having sense or feeling, or the capacity of receiving impressions from external objects ; অনুভূতিসম্পন্ন, চেতন, অনুভবশক্তিসম্পন্ন, সচেতন, চেতনাবান, ইন্দ্রিয়বিশিষ্ট (হিঃ কোঃ), সংচেত্য (ঐ), সংক্ষোভ্য (ঐ) সংবেদনশীল। **2.** Highly susceptible ; having feelings easily hurt ; shrinking from the touch ; তীব্রসংবেদনসম্পন্ন ; আশুক্ষুব্ধ ; স্পর্শকাতর, স্পর্শভীরু, স্পর্শসঙ্কুচিত। **3.** Rapidly fluctuating ; as, a *sensitive* market ; (বাজারের সম্বন্ধে) দ্রুতহ্রাসবৃদ্ধিশীল, অল্পপরিবর্ত্তী। **4.** Easily affected by hypnotic influence ; as, a *sensitive* medium ; সম্মোহনজনক প্রভাবদ্বারা সহজে অভিভূত। **5.** Readily affected by the action of appropriate agents ; as, a *sensitive* plate ; easily affected or moved ; delicate ; as, *sensitive* balance ; রাসায়নিক ক্রিয়াদ্বারা আশুবিকারশীল, সুগ্রাহক (হিঃ কোঃ), শীঘ্রগ্রাহক (ঐ) ; সহজে পরিবর্ত্তিত বা সঞ্চালিত ; সূক্ষ্ম। **6.** Pertaining to the senses or sensation ; ইন্দ্রিয়সম্বন্ধীয়, ইন্দ্রিয়ানুভূতিসম্বন্ধীয়। *Noun.* **1.** A sensitive person ; আশুবিচলিত ব্যক্তি। **2.** A person readily affected by hypnotic influence ; সম্মোহনক্রিয়ার প্রভাবদ্বারা

সহজে অভিভূত ও আচ্ছন্ন ব্যক্তি। **—ly,** *adv.* **—tiv'-i-ty,** *n.* **Sensitive-flame**—সুগ্রাহক জ্বালা (হিঃ কোঃ)। **Sensitive market**—যে বাজারে মূল্যের হ্রাসবৃদ্ধি হইয়া থাকে। **Sensitive paper** — আলোকের রাসায়নিক ক্রিয়া দ্বারা বিকার্য্য আলোকচিত্রে ব্যবহৃত রাসায়নিকদ্রব্যলিপ্ত কাগজ, সুগ্রাহক কাগজ (হিঃ কোঃ)। **Sensitive plant**—লজ্জাবতী, লজ্জালু। [Syn. রক্তপাদী, শমীপত্রা, স্পৃক্কা, খদিরপত্রিকা, খদিরপত্রী, সঙ্কোচিনী, নমস্কারী, প্রসারিণী, সপ্তপর্ণী, খদিরী, খদির, গণ্ডমালিকা, লজ্জা, স্বগুপ্তা, লজ্জরী, লজ্জিনী, লজ্জিরী, স্পর্শলজ্জা, রক্তমূলা, অশ্রখদির, অশ্ররোধিনী, লজ্জাকারিকা, মহাভীতা, গণ্ডকারী, গণ্ডকালী, সমঙ্গা, এলাপর্ণী, সুবহা, যুক্তরসা, রাস্না (*mimosa octandra*), তাম্রমূলা, সুতপ্তা, মহৌষধি, বাশনী, (*mimosa suma*), অঞ্জলিকারিকা, অলম্বুষ (a species of sensitive-plant), বৈপরীত্যা (*ib.*), বৈপরীত্যা লজ্জালু (*ib.*), মেদোগলা। [Burm. *nte-kayung*; Tam. *tota vadi*; Teleg. *attapatti.*] **Sensitive plate**—যে রসায়নদ্রব্যদ্বারা অনুলিপ্ত আলোকচিত্রের ফলক আলোকের রাসায়নিক ক্রিয়াদ্বারা বিকারপ্রাপ্ত হয়।

sĕn'-si-tīze, *v. t.* **1.** (*Phot.*) To make a plate sensitive to the chemical action of light; আলোকচিত্রের ফলক প্রভৃতি আলোকের রাসায়নিক ক্রিয়া দ্বারা বিকার্য্য করা। **2.** To make sensitive; আশুবিচলিত করা, সহজে ক্ষুব্ধ হয় এরূপ প্রকৃতিসম্পন্ন করা, শীঘ্রগ্রাহী করা, আশুবিকারী করা। **—ti-za'-tion, —tiz'-er,** *ns.*

sĕn-sō'-ri-ŭm, *n.* **1.** The centre of a sensation; brain; অনুভূতির কেন্দ্র, প্রত্যক্ষব্যূহ (হিঃ কোঃ), চেতনাস্পদ (ঐ), চেতনাশয় (কেণ্ডি), জ্ঞানাগার, ঐন্দ্রিয় জ্ঞানের মূলস্থান, মনশ্চক্র (ব্রজঃ বিঃ); মস্তিষ্ক। **2.** Brain or spinal cord or the grey matter of these; মস্তিষ্ক বা কশেরুকা কিম্বা উহাদের ধূসরবর্ণ পদার্থ।

sĕn'-sŏ-rŷ, *adj.* Pertaining to the sensorium or sensation or the senses; carrying sensation; মনশ্চক্রসম্বন্ধীয়, ইন্দ্রিয়ানুভূতিসম্বন্ধীয়, জ্ঞানেন্দ্রিয়সম্বন্ধী (হিঃ কোঃ), ঐন্দ্রিয়জ্ঞান সম্বন্ধী (ঐ), ঐন্দ্রিয়; চেতনাবাহী, চৈতন্যবাহী, (বাহ্য বস্তুর), জ্ঞানবাহী। **Sensory circle**—ঐন্দ্রিয় পরিখা (হিঃ কোঃ)। **Sensory element**—প্রাত্যক্ষ অংশ (হিঃ কোঃ)। **Sensory-motor** — প্রত্যক্ষপ্রেরিত (হিঃ কোঃ)। **Sensory nerve**—সংজ্ঞানাড়ী, অন্তর্মুখী স্নায়ু, চৈতন্যবাহিনী (সুশ্রুঃ কুঞ্জঃ)।

sĕn'-sū-ăl, *adj.* **1.** Pertaining to the senses; ইন্দ্রিয়সম্বন্ধীয়, ঐন্দ্রিয়িক। **2.** Not spiritual; carnal; অনাত্ম, ঐহিক, বৈষয়িক, বিষয়াত্মক, বিষয়াসক্ত; ইন্দ্রিয়জ, কামজ, পাশবিক। **3.** Devoted to the gratification of the senses; voluptuous; lewd; ইন্দ্রিয়পরায়ণ, ইন্দ্রিয়ারাম, ইন্দ্রিয়সুখপরতন্ত্র, ভোগবিলাসপরায়ণ, বিষয়াসক্ত, বিষয়ী, বিষয়পরায়ণ, কামোপভোগ নিরত; কামুক; লম্পট। **—ism,** *n.* **1.** Sensuality; ইন্দ্রিয়পরতন্ত্রতা, বিষয়াসক্ত ইন্দ্রিয়াসক্তি, ইন্দ্রিয়দোষ, ইন্দ্রিয়প্রসঙ্গ। **2.** The doctrine that knowledge is the outcome of sensation; আমাদের সর্ব্বপ্রকার জ্ঞানের মূল ইন্দ্রিয়জ অনুভূতি—এইরূপ মতবাদ, বিষয়প্রাধান্যবাদ (হিঃ কোঃ), প্রত্যক্ষপ্রাধান্যবাদ (ঐ), সংবেদনপ্রাধান্যবাদ (ঐ), ঐন্দ্রিয়প্রাধান্যবাদ (ঐ)। **3.** (*Ethics*) The doctrine that the gratification of the senses is the highest good; (নীতিবিজ্ঞান) ইন্দ্রিয়ের চারিতার্থই পরম শ্রেয়—এইমত। **—al'-i-ty,** *n.* The state of being sensual; ইন্দ্রিয়পরতা, ইন্দ্রিয়পরায়ণতা, বিষয়াসক্তি, বিষয়সুখাসক্তি। **—ist,** *n.* **1.** A person given to the indulgence of the appetites or senses; ইন্দ্রিয়সুখপরতন্ত্র ব্যক্তি, ইন্দ্রিয়সেবী, শিশ্নোদরপরায়ণ (cf. শিশ্নোদরপরায়ণ কৃষ্ণে নাহি পায়—শ্রীচৈতন্যচরিতামৃত), কেলিনাগর। **2.** One who holds to a doctrine of sensualism; প্রত্যক্ষপ্রাধান্যবাদী, বিষয়াসক্তিবাদী (হিঃ কোঃ)। **—i-za'-tion,** *n.* **—ize,** *v. t.* **Sensual enjoyment**—ইন্দ্রিয়সেবা, ইন্দ্রিয়সেবন।

sĕn'-sū-ous (-ŭs), *adj.* **1.** Relating to the senses or the objects perceived by them; ইন্দ্রিয়সম্বন্ধীয়, ঐন্দ্রিয়িক, ঐন্দ্রিয়ক, ঐন্দ্রিয়, ইন্দ্রিয়ানুভূতবিষয়সম্বন্ধীয়, ইন্দ্রিয়জ। **2.** Readily affected through the senses; keenly alive to the pleasures of the senses; as, *sensuous* face and expression; indicating a temperament highly susceptible to the senses; তীক্ষ্ণইন্দ্রিয়বৃত্তিসম্পন্ন; ইন্দ্রিয়সুখানুরাগী, ইন্দ্রিয়সুখপরতন্ত্র, ইন্দ্রিয়রাগাত্মক, ইন্দ্রিয়রাগোদ্দীপ্ত, ইন্দ্রিয়ানুরাগসূচক; রাগবান।

sĕnt, *v. t.* (*p. p.* and *pt.* of SEND which see.)

sĕn'-tence (-tĕns), *n.* & *v. t.* **1.** (*Archaic*) An opinion; as, my *sentence* is for war; judgment; মত, মতামত; বিবেচনা। **2.** A maxim; নীতিবাক্য, নীতিবচন। **3.** A judgment of a court of law; punishment; রায়, দণ্ডাজ্ঞা; দণ্ড। **3.** (*Gram.*) A number of words containing complete sense; (ব্যাকরণ) বাক্য। *Verb t.* To pronounce judgment on; to doom; দণ্ডাজ্ঞা প্রদান করা, শাস্তি প্রদান করা; ভাগ্যে নির্দ্দিষ্ট করা। **—ten'-ti-al,** *adj.* **Simple sentence**—যে বাক্যে একটী মাত্র উদ্দেশ্য (subject) এবং বিধেয় (predicate) থাকে, সরল বাক্য (as, I see the moon). **Complex sentence**—যে বাক্যে একটী প্রধান বাক্যের অন্তর্গত এক বা তদধিক অপ্রধান বাক্য থাকে, মিশ্রবাক্য, মহাবাক্য (সাঃ দঃ)। (as, The rose we saw was red). **Compound sentence**—যে বাক্যে উদ্দেশ্য কিম্বা বিধেয় বা উভয়ই দুই বা ততোধিক থাকে, যৌগিক বাক্য। (as, What the logicians call a proposition, the grammarians call a sentence).

sĕn-tĕn'-tious (-shŭs), *adj.* Abounding with sentences, axioms and maxims ; নীতিগর্ভ, সারগর্ভ। **—ly,** *adv.* **—ness,** *n.*

sĕn'-ti-ĕnt (-shĭ-), *adj.* Having sensation or the capacity of sensation ; সচেতন, চেতন, জ্ঞানগ্রহণশীল, সংবেদনক্ষম, বিষয়গ্রহণক্ষম, ইন্দ্রিয়জ্ঞান-বিশিষ্ট, চিচ্ছক্তিসম্পন্ন, চৈতন্যযুক্ত। **—ence,** *n.* The state of being sentient ; প্রত্যক্ষগ্রাহকতা (হিঃ কোঃ), সংবেত্তৃতা (ঐ)। **—ly,** *adv.*

sĕn'-ti-mĕnt, *n.* **1.** A thought prompted by passion or feeling ; ভাব, স্থায়িভাব। **2.** Feeling ; sensibility ; emotion ; মনোধর্ম্ম, মনোবৃত্তি, চিত্তবৃত্তি, হৃদ্গতভাব ; অনুভবপ্রবণতা ; আবেগ, হৃদয়াবেগ, হৃদয়োচ্ছ্বাস। **3.** Thought ; opinion ; as, to express one's *sentiment* on a subject ; ভাব ; মত, অভিমত। **4.** A thought or reflection coloured by, or proceeded from, emotion ; চিত্তরাগদ্বারা অনুরঞ্জিত মত, আবেগপ্রসূত মত। **5.** (*Phren.*) Faculties including self-esteem veneration, benevolence ascribed to the upper portion of the cranium ; (মস্তিষ্কসামুদ্রিক) করোটীর ঊর্দ্ধভাগের সহিত সংশ্লিষ্ট বৃত্তিসমূহ (যথা, আত্মাদর, ভক্তি, পরোপকার, প্রভৃতি বৃত্তি)। **6.** The leading idea which has governed the general conception of a work of art, or which makes itself visible to the eye and the mind of a spectator through the work of the artist ; কোন গ্রন্থ বা শিল্পকার্য্যের প্রধান ভাব, রস [These are nine—শৃঙ্গার বা রতি, উৎসাহ বা হাস্য, কারুণ্য, রৌদ্র বা ক্রোধ, বিস্ময় বা অদ্ভুত, ভয়, বীভৎস, শান্ত and বাৎসল্য।] **—men'-tal,** *adj.* **1.** Apt to be swayed by emotional feeling ; artificially or affectedly tender ; ভাবপ্রধান, ভাবরসপ্রবণ, ভাবুক, রসপ্রধান (হিঃ কোঃ), রাগবান, সরাগ ; কৃত্রিমভাবপ্রদর্শনকারী। **2.** Appealing to sentiment or feeling rather than to reason ; expressive of tender emotion ; as, *sentimental* music ; রসপ্রধান, ভাবপূর্ণ, অনুরাগময় ; মর্ম্মোচ্ছ্বাসসূচক। **—men'-tal-ism,** *n.* Affectation of excessive sensibility ; ভাবুকতা, ভাবকালি, ভাবোন্মাদ। **—men'-tal-ist,** *n.* **—men'-tal-ize,** *v.t.* **—men'-tal-ly,** *adv.*

sĕn'-ti-nĕl, *n.* & *v. t.* **1.** A soldier on guard ; শাস্ত্রী, প্রহরী, রক্ষী। **2.** Same as SENTINEL-CRAB. ***Verb t.*** To keep guard over ; পাহারা দেওয়া, রক্ষা করা। **Sentinel-crab** — ভারতমহাসাগরে প্রাপ্ত কর্কটবিশেষ।

sĕn'-trȳ, *n.* A sentinel ; a guard ; শাস্ত্রী ; প্রহরী। **Sentry-box**—শাস্ত্রী যে কাষ্ঠনির্ম্মিত ক্ষুদ্র কক্ষে দাঁড়াইয়া পাহারা দেয়, প্রহরিমণ্ডপ, প্রহরিমন্দির।

sē'-păl, *n.* A leaf or division of the green outer covering of a flower ; পুষ্পের সবুজবর্ণ বহিশ্ছদের দল বা বিভাগ, বৃতি (সাঃ পঃ), ছদ (ঐ), বহিশ্ছদ।

S. S. S.
Sepals.

sĕp'-ă-loid (-lŏyd), *adj.* Like a sepal ; ছদবৎ।

sĕp'-ă-rāte, *v.t.* & *i.* 1. To divide ; to disunite ; to sever ; বিভাগ করা ; পৃথক করা, স্বতন্ত্র করা ; বিচ্ছিন্ন করা। 2. To keep apart by an intervening space ; as, the Mediterranean sea *separates* Europe from Africa ; মধ্যবর্ত্তী স্থানদ্বারা বিচ্ছিন্ন বা পৃথক করা, তফাৎ করা, তফায়েৎ করা, আলাহিদা করা। **3.** To set apart ; "*Separate* the Barnabas and Gaul for the work whereunto I have called them" ; আলাহিদা করিয়া রাখা, পৃথক করিয়া রাখা। ***Verb i.*** **1.** To be disunited ; to be disconnected ; পৃথক হওয়া, স্বতন্ত্র হওয়া, বিচ্ছিন্ন হওয়া ; বিযুক্ত হওয়া, বিশ্লিষ্ট হওয়া। **2.** To come apart ; বিচ্ছিন্ন হইয়া আসা, পৃথক হইয়া আসা। **—ra-ble,** *adj.* Capable of being separated ; পৃথক্করণযোগ্য, বিভাজ্য, বিয়োজনীয়, বিশ্লেষ্য। **Separable accident**—ভেদ্য উপাধি (হিঃ কোঃ), পরিবর্ত্তনীয় উপাধি (ঐ)।

sĕp'-ă-rāte, *adj.* & *n.* **1.** Disjoined ; disconnected ; পৃথগ্‌ভূত, বিচ্ছিন্ন ; পৃথক্, পৃথক্, বিশ্লিষ্ট, বিযুক্ত। **2.** Unconnected ; বিযুক্ত, স্বতন্ত্র, পৃথক। **3.** Disembodied ; as, a *separate* spirit ; অদেহাশ্রিত, দেহমুক্ত, বিদেহী। **4.** Solitary ; বিবিক্ত, নিঃসঙ্গ। ***Noun.*** A copy of a single article etc. reprinted from the magazine of a society for distribution ; কোন পরিষদের পত্রিকা হইতে বিতরণের জন্য পুনর্মুদ্রিত প্রবন্ধ। **Separate estate**—বিবাহিতা স্ত্রীর নিজস্ব সম্পত্তি। **Separate land**—খারিজা জমি, স্বতন্ত্র জমি। **Separate-maintenance**—স্বামী হইতে বিচ্ছিন্না স্ত্রীর ভরণপোষণের জন্য স্বামী যে অর্থ প্রদান করে।

sĕp-ă-rā'-tion, *n.* **1.** The act of separating, disjoining or disuniting ; বিয়োজন, পৃথক্করণ, বিশ্লেষণ। **2.** The state of being separate ; disunion ; পৃথগ্‌ভাব, স্বাতন্ত্র্য, ব্যবধান (সাংখ্যঃ), পার্থক্য, বিপ্রয়োগ ; বিচ্ছেদ, বিরহ (of lovers), ছাড়াছাড়ি। **3.** The disunion of married persons ; বিবাহিতা স্বামী স্ত্রীর পরস্পর হইতে পৃথগ্‌ভাবে বাস।

sĕp'-ă-rā-tism, *n.* Cessation from a church on separatist principle ; কোন সংঘের সহিত সম্বন্ধচ্ছেদ।

sĕp'-ă-rā-tist, *n.* One who upholds or advocates separation ; a dissenter ; যে ব্যক্তি ধর্ম্মসংঘের সহিত সম্বন্ধচ্ছেদ সমর্থন করে ; ধর্ম্মসংঘের সহিত সম্বন্ধচ্ছেদনকারী।

sĕp'-ă-rā-tor (-tĕr), *n.* **1.** One who, or that which, separates ; পৃথক্কারী, বিয়োজক। **2.** A machine for separating cream from milk ;

দুগ্ধ হইতে সর পৃথক করার জন্য যন্ত্রবিশেষ, মন্থনযন্ত্র। **—to-ry,** *n.*

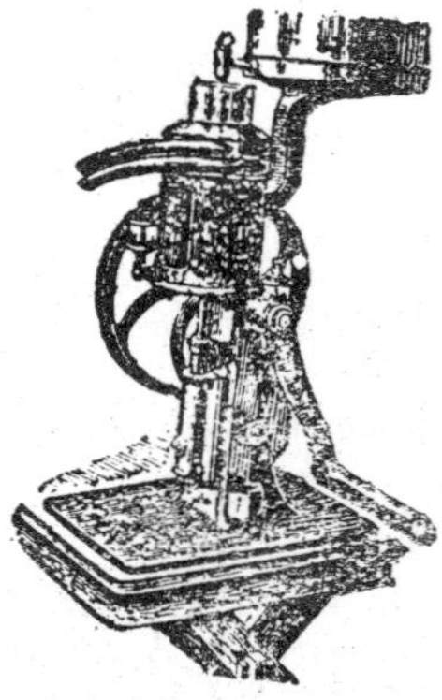

Separator.

sĕp-ă-rā′-tŭm, *n.* Same as SEPARATE, *n.*

sē′-pi-ă, *n.* & *adj.* **1.** The cuttle-fish ; সমুদ্রজিভ্ মৎস্য। **2.** A dark brown pigment prepared from the black secretion of this fish ; উক্ত মৎস্যের দেহ হইতে প্রাপ্ত কৃষ্ণবর্ণ পদার্থবিশেষ হইতে প্রস্তুত গাঢ় কপিশবর্ণ রঞ্জকপদার্থ। **3.** A dark reddish brown colour ; একপ্রকার গাঢ় কপিশ বর্ণ। ***Adj.*** **1.** Of the colour of sepia ; গাঢ় কপিশ বর্ণের। **2.** Done in sepia ; গাঢ় কপিশবর্ণের রঞ্জকপদার্থদ্বারা চিত্রিত।

sē′-pōy, *n.* An Indian serving as a soldier in the army of Britain ; সিপাহী। **Sepoy mutiny**—সিপাহী-বিদ্রোহ (১৮৫৭ খৃঃ অব্দে সংঘটিত হয়।)

sĕps, *n.* A genus of saurian reptiles ; গোধা, গোসাপ, প্রভৃতি জাতীয় জন্তুগণ।

sĕp′-sis, *n.* (*Med.*) Poisoning of the system by the introduction of putrescent material or pathogenic organisms in blood ; blood-poisoning; (ভৈষজ্য-শাস্ত্র) রক্তে পচনশীল পদার্থ বা রোগজনক কাটাণু প্রবিষ্ট হওয়ার দরুণ দৈহিক বিকৃতি ; রক্তদুষ্টি।

sĕpt, *n.* A clan, esp. in Ireland ; গোষ্ঠী (সাঃ পঃ)।

sĕpt, *n.* A railing ; গরাদ।

sĕp′-tă, *n.* Plural of SEPTUM (which see.)

sĕp′-tăl, *adj.* Of, or belonging to, SEPTUM (which see.)

sĕp′-tan-gle (-tăng-gl), *n.* A heptagon ; সপ্তাস্র ক্ষেত্র, সপ্তভুজ ক্ষেত্র।

sĕp-tan′-gu-lar (-tăng-gü-lêr), *adj.* Having seven angles ; সপ্তকোণী, সপ্তাস্র।

Sĕp-tĕm′-bêr, *n.* The ninth month of the year, so called as the seventh from March ; সেপ্টেম্বর মাস।

Sĕp-tĕm′-brist, *n.* One of the agents engaged in the massacre in Paris on September 2nd and 3rd 1792 ; ১৭৯২ খৃষ্টাব্দের সেপ্টেম্বর মাসের ২রা এবং ৩রা তারিখে প্যারী নগরীতে অনুষ্ঠিত ভীষণ হত্যাকাণ্ডে সংসৃষ্ট ব্যক্তি।

sĕp-tĕm-pâr′-tīte, *adj.* Divided into seven parts ; সপ্তধাবিভক্ত, সপ্তাংশিত।

sĕp-tĕm′-vir (-vêr), *n.* One of seven men joined in any office or commission ; কোন পদে নিযুক্ত সপ্তব্যক্তির অন্যতম।

sĕp′-tē-nă-rȳ, *adj.* **1.** Consisting of, or relating to, seven ; সপ্তাত্মক, সপ্তসম্বন্ধীয়, সাপ্ত। **2.** Lasting seven years ; occurring after seven years ; সপ্তবর্ষস্থায়ী ; সপ্তবর্ষান্তে সংঘটিত।

sĕp′-tē-nāte, *adj.* (*Bot.*) Having seven parts ; (উদ্ভিদ্‌বিদ্যা) সপ্তাংশবিশিষ্ট, সপ্তাঙ্গুল্যাকার (সাঃ পঃ)।

sĕp-tĕn′-ni-ăl, *adj.* **1.** Lasting seven years ; as, *septennial* parliament ; সপ্তবর্ষস্থায়ী, সপ্তবার্ষিক, সপ্তাব্দিক। **2.** Happening or returning once in seven years ; প্রতি সপ্তবর্ষান্তে সংঘটিত, প্রতি সপ্তবর্ষান্তে পুনরাগমনশীল।

Sĕp-tĕn′-tri-ō, *n.* (*Astron.*) The Great Bear ; সপ্তর্ষিমণ্ডল।

sĕp-tĕn′-tri-ŏn, *n.* & *adj.* The north or northern regions ; উত্তরদিক, উত্তরাঞ্চল। ***Adj.*** (*Rare*) Northern ; উদীচ্য।

sĕpt-foil (-fȳl), *n.* **1.** A plant of the genus Tormentilla ; একপ্রকার গুল্ম। **2.** A figure of seven equal segments of a circle used as a symbol of the seven sacraments ; খৃষ্টীয় সপ্ত সংস্কারের চিহ্নস্বরূপ ব্যবহৃত সপ্তসমায়তন বৃত্তখণ্ডের চিত্র।

sĕp′-tic, —ti-căl, *adjs.* & *ns.* Causing putrefaction ; পচনকারক, পচনজনক। ***Noun.*** (Only *septic*) A substance having the power to promote putrefaction ; পচনজনক পদার্থ, পচনকারক পদার্থ। **Septic poison**—জীবজ বিষ, জৈব বিষ। **Septic tank**—জীবাণুর সাহায্যে জৈব পদার্থ বিয়োজনের যে পুষ্করণীতে নর্দ্দমা প্রভৃতির ময়লা সঞ্চিত করা হয়।

sĕp-ti-cae′-mi-a (-sē-), *n.* Blood-poisoning by putrid matter ; পচনজনক পদার্থদ্বারা রক্তদুষ্টি।

sĕp′-ti-cīd-ăl, *adj.* (*Bot.*) Applied to seed-vessels which open by dividing through the septa or partitions of the ovary ; (উদ্ভিদ্‌বিদ্যা) ব্যবধানভেদী (সাঃ পঃ)

sĕp-tic′-i-tȳ, *n.* Tendency to promote putrefaction ; পচনজনকতা।

sĕp-tif′-rā-găl, *adj.* (*Bot.*) Applied to a mode of dehiscence in which the backs of the carpels separate from the dissepiments whether formed by the sides or by expansions of placenta (as, *convolvulus*) ; ছিন্নব্যবধানিক (সাঃ পঃ)।

sĕp-ti-lăt′-êr-ăl, *adj.* Consisting of seven sides; সপ্তভুজী, সপ্তাস্র।

sĕp-til′-li-ŏn, *n.* **1.** (England) A number consisting of a unit followed by forty-two ciphers ; ১এর ডাহিনে ৪২টী শূন্য বসাইলে যে সংখ্যা হয়। **2.** (In France and Italy) A unit followed by twenty-eight ciphers ; ১এর ডাহিনে ২৮টী শূন্য বসাইলে যে সংখ্যা হয়।

sĕp′-ti-sȳl-la-ble (-ă-bl), *n.* A word of seven syllables ; সপ্তাক্ষর শব্দ।

sĕp′-tĭ-măl, *adj.* Of the number seven ; সপ্তসম্বন্ধীয়।

sĕp′-tīme, *n.* A fencing position ; অসিক্রীড়ায় ভঙ্গিবিশেষ।

sĕp-tū-ă-gĕ-nā′-rĭ-ăn, *n.* & *adj.* A person seventy years of age ; a person between 69 and 80 years of age ; সপ্ততিবর্ষ বয়স্ক ব্যক্তি ; ঊনষষ্ঠি হইতে অশীতি বর্ষের মধ্যবর্ত্তী বয়স্ক ব্যক্তি। ***Adj.*** Of seventy years of age ; between 69 and 80 years of age ; সপ্ততিবর্ষ-বয়স্ক ; ঊনষষ্ঠি হইতে অশীতিবর্ষের মধ্যবর্ত্তী বয়স্ক।

sĕp-tū-ăg′-ē-nă-rȳ, *n.* Same as SEPTUAGENARIAN.

sĕp-tū-ă-gĕs′-ĭ-mă, *n.* The third Sunday before lent so called because it is about 70 days before Easter ; লেণ্ট পর্ব্বের পূর্ব্ববর্ত্তী তৃতীয় সপ্তাহ।

Sĕp′-tū-ă-gĭnt, *n.* Greek version of the Old Testament, executed at Alexendria by, it is said, seventy translators, about 270 B. C. ; খৃঃ পূঃ ২৭০ অব্দে আলেকজেন্দ্রিয়া (যবনপুর) নগরীতে সপ্ততিজন অনুবাদক কর্তৃক বাইবেলের প্রাচীন নিয়মের গ্রীক ভাষায় অনুবাদ।

sĕp′-tŭm, *n.* (*Pl.* SEPTA) **1.** A partition ; বিভাগ। **2.** (*Bot.*) A partition separating a fruit into two or more cells in the direction of its length ; যে পর্দ্দা দ্বারা কোন ফল লম্বার দিকে দুই বা তিন বিভাগে বিভক্ত হয়। **3.** (*Anat.*) The partition separating the nostrils ; the membrane separating the ventricles of the heart ; নাসারন্ধ্র-ব্যবধায়ক ঝিল্লী ; হৃৎকোষ্ঠ ব্যবধায়ক অস্থিখণ্ড। **4.** The partition in a chambered shell, some corals, etc. ; প্রবাল, কোষ্ঠ বিশিষ্ট শম্বুক প্রভৃতির বিভাজক। **Septum of scrotum**—মহাবীজা (সাঃ পঃ)।

sē-pŭl′-chrăl, *adj.* **1.** Pertaining to a tomb or to burial ; সমাধিমন্দির সম্বন্ধীয়, সমাধি-সম্বন্ধীয়। **2.** Suggestive of the tomb ; gloomy ; deep-toned ; as, *sepulchral* darkness ; শ্মশানভাবব্যঞ্জকপূর্ণ ; বিষাদপূর্ণ ; গম্ভীরনাদী।

sĕp′-ŭl-chre (-kêr), *n.* & *v. t.* A place of interment ; a tomb ; কবর ; সমাধিমন্দির, শবমন্দির প্রেতমন্দির, প্রেতাবাস। ***Verb t.*** To lay in a sepulchre ; সমাধিগর্ভে স্থাপন করা, কবরস্থ করা। **The Holy Sepulchre**—যীশুখৃষ্টের সমাধিমন্দির। **Whited sepulchre**—ভণ্ড ব্যক্তি, কপট ব্যক্তি।

sĕp′-ŭl-tūre, *n.* **1.** Burial ; interment ; সমাধি ; কবরস্থকরণ, গোর দেওন। **2.** Grave ; কবর, সমাধি।

sē-quā′-cious (-shŭs), *adj.* **1.** (*Obs.*) Inclined to follow a leader ; servile ; (অপ্রঃ) নেতার অনুগামী ; দাসবৎ অনুগামী। **2.** Logically consistent ; সুসম্বদ্ধ, সুসংলগ্ন, সুসঙ্গতিবিশিষ্ট। **–ly,** *adv.* **–quac′-i-ty,** *n.*

sē′-quĕl, *n.* **1.** A succeeding part ; continuation of a story etc. ; পরবর্ত্তী অংশ, পরবর্ত্তী বিষয় ; উত্তরভাগ, শেষভাগ, উত্তরার্দ্ধ। **2.** Consequence ; "Every phenomenon in the moral or material world was the *sequel* of a natural cause" ; ফল, পরিণাম, শেষফল। **3.** (*Rare*) Conclusion , inference ; (কচিদ্ ব্যবহৃত) সিদ্ধান্ত ; অনুমান।

sequela, *n.* **1.** An adherent or band of adherents ; অনুগামী, অনুগামিবৃন্দ। **2.** (*Path.*) What results from a disease ; (নিদান শাস্ত্র) কোন রোগের অন্তে যে রোগজনক অবস্থা বা রোগলক্ষণ প্রকাশ পায়, রোগের পরিণামোপসর্গ।

sē′-quence (-kwĕns), *n.* **1.** Series of things ; an order of succession ; consecutiveness ; বস্তুপরম্পরা ; অনুক্রম, অন্বয় (হিঃ কোঃ), ক্রমপর্য্যায়, পারম্পর্য্য ; পৌর্ব্বাপর্য্য, আনন্তর্য্য (শ্রীঃ), আনুপূর্ব্ব্য। **2.** (Card-playing) Three or more cards of the same suit in order ; (তাস খেলা) বিন্তী, পঞ্চাশ, প্রভৃতি ডাক, ডাক। **3.** (*R. C. C.*) A hymn introduced into the Mass after the gradual or introit ; (রোমান-ক্যাথলিক ধর্ম্মসংঘ) খৃষ্টের অন্তিম ভোজনানুষ্ঠান ক্রিয়োপলক্ষে গীত স্তোত্রবিশেষ। **4.** A subsequent event ; result ; পরবর্ত্তী ঘটনা ; ফল, পরিণাম। **–quen′-ti-al,** *adj.* **–quen-ti-al′-i-ty,** *n.* **Historic sequence** — ঐতিহাসিক পৌর্ব্বাপর্য্য।

sequentes, sequentia, (*Abbr. seq.* or *seqq.*) The following ; নিম্নলিখিত পংক্তি প্রভৃতি।

sē-quĕs′-têr, *v. t.* & *i.* **1.** To separate from other things ; to seclude ; পৃথক করা, স্বতন্ত্র করা ; নির্জ্জনে রাখা, বিবিক্ত করা। **2.** (*Law*) To set apart a debtor's property for the payment of creditors ; to put disputed property for a time into the possession of an indifferent person ; (আইন) দায়িকের সম্পত্তি অস্থায়িভাবে আটক করা, জব্দ করা ; কোন বিরোধীয় সম্পত্তি কিছুকালের জন্য কোন ব্যক্তির হাতে রাখা। ***Verb i.*** To renounce or disclaim as any concern with the estate of her deceased husband ; (বিধবার পক্ষে) মৃত স্বামীর সম্পত্তির উপর সর্ব্বপ্রকার হস্তক্ষেপের অধিকার ত্যাগ করা। **–ed,** *adj.* Solitary ; বিজন, নির্জ্জন, জনহীন।

sē-quĕs′-trāte, *v. t.* Same as SEQUESTER(*Law*). **Se′-ques-tra-tor, –tra′-tion,** *ns.* **–tra-ble,** *adj.*

sē-quĕs′-trŭm, *n.* The dead portion of a bone which separates from a sound part ; অস্থির সুস্থ অংশ হইতে বিশ্লিষ্ট মৃত অংশ। **–tral,** *adj.* **–trot′-o-my,** *n.*

sē′-quĭn, *n.* **1.** (*Hist.*) A Venetian gold coin, worth about 9*s.* 4*d.* ; প্রাচীন ভিনিস নগরীর মুদ্রা-বিশেষ (মূল্য প্রায় ৯ শিলিং ৪ পেন্স)।

2. A small metal disc used in the ornamentation of dress etc. ; পোষাক প্রভৃতির চুমকী।

sĕ-quoi'-ă (-koy-), *n.* A genus of coniferous tree ; দেবদারুজাতীয় বৃক্ষের গণবিশেষ।

sĕ-răc', *n.* The name for the cuboidal masses into which a glacier breaks when passing down a steep incline ; খাড়া স্থান অতিক্রম করার কালে তুষারনদীর তুষার রাশি ভাঙ্গিয়া যে চতুষ্ক খণ্ডসমূহে পরিণত হয়।

sĕ-ragl-io (-râl-yŏ), *n.* 1. The palace of the Sultan at Constantinople ; তুরষ্ক সুলতানের কনস্তান্তিনোপল নগরীস্থ রাজপ্রাসাদ। 2. A harem ; অন্তঃপুর, অবরোধ, জেনানামহাল, স্ত্রীমহাল, ভোগগৃহ (সায়ণ), ভোগাবাস (অ), শুদ্ধান্ত, অন্তর্মন্দির।

sĕ-rai' (-rā), *n.* In the East, a place for the accommodation of travellers ; সরাই, পান্থশালা।

sĕr'-ăph, *n.* (*Pl.* SERAPHIM, SERAPHS.) An angel of the highest rank ; সর্ব্বোচ্চশ্রেণীর দেবদূত। **Se-raph'-ic, Se-raph'-i-cal,** *adjs.* 1. Pertaining to a seraph ; angelic ; সর্ব্বোচ্চশ্রেণীর দেবদূতসম্বন্ধীয় ; দেবদূতপ্রতিম। 2. Pure ; পবিত্র, শুদ্ধ। **The Seraphic Doctor** — সেণ্টবোনাভেন্‌টিউরা (St. Bonaventura) বা সেণ্ট টেরেসা (St. Teresa).

sĕr-ă-phi'-nă, sĕr'-ă-phine (-(fēn), *ns.* A musical wind-instrument resembling a harmonium of which it was a precursor ; হার্ম্মিনোয়াম প্রচলনের পূর্ব্বে ব্যবহৃত তদ্বৎ বাদ্যযন্ত্র বিশেষ।

seraskier, *n.* A Turkish commander-in-chief or minister of war ; তুর্কি দেশীয় মহাসেনাপতি বা সমরসচিব।

Sêrb, *adj.* & *n.* Same as SERVIAN (which see.)

Sêr-bŏ'-ni-ăn--bŏg, *n.* 1. A marshy tract in Egypt covered with shifting sand; "A gulf profound as that *Serbonian bog,* Betwixt Damatia and mount Cassius old, Where armies whole have sunk" ; মিসর দেশস্থ চোরাবালি দ্বারা আচ্ছাদিত অনুপ ভূমি। প্রবাদ এইরূপ যে, এই স্থান অতিক্রম করিতে গিয়া সময় সময় বিরাট বাহিনী সমুহ ইহার কুক্ষিগত হইয়াছে। 2. A difficult or complicated situation ; সঙ্কটজনক অবস্থা, সঙ্কটস্থল।

sēre, *n.*. Catch of gunlock holding hammer at half or full lock ; বন্দুকের কলের ছিটকিনী, যদ্দ্বারা উহার ঘোড়া আটকাইরা রাখা হয়।

serein, *n.* A fine rain which falls in tropical climates from a cloudless sky ; গ্রীষ্মমণ্ডলে নির্ম্মেঘ গগন হইতে যে কুজ্‌ঝটিকার মত বৃষ্টি পতিত হয়।

sĕr-ĕ-nāde', *n.* & *v. t.* 1. A music played at night under the windows of a lady-love by her lover ; প্রেমিকার মনোরঞ্জনার্থ তদীয় গবাক্ষতলে প্রেমিক নিশাকালে যে গীতবাদ্য করিয়া থাকে। 2. A piece of music suitable for such performance ; ঐরূপ সঙ্গীতের উপযোগী বাদ্য। ***Verb t.*** To entertain with a serenade or nocturnal music ; প্রেমিকার বাতায়ননিম্নে নৈশসঙ্গীত গাহিয়া বা বাদ্য বাদন করিয়া তদীয় চিত্তবিনোদন করা। **–nad'-er,** *n.*

sĕ-rene' (-rēn), *adj., n.* & *v. t.* 1. (Of the sky) Cloudless ; as, the *serene* sky ; (আকাশ সম্পর্কে) মেঘমুক্ত, নির্ম্মেঘ। 2. Calm ; placid ; unruffled ; শান্ত, প্রশান্ত ; প্রসন্ন, অনুদ্বিগ্ন, অবিক্ষুব্ধ, নিরাকুল (মহানিঃ) ; সৌম্য, স্থির, ধীর, প্রশান্তগম্ভীর, স্থিরচিত্ত। ***Noun.*** 1. Serene expanse of clear sky, calm sea, etc. ; "Not a cloud obscured the deep *serene*" ; প্রশান্ত গগন বা নিস্তরঙ্গ সাগরের বিস্তার, শান্তনীলিমা, স্বচ্ছনীলিমা। 2. Serenity ; প্রশান্তি, সৌম্যতা, প্রসাদ। 3. Calm brightness ; "With moonlight patches...or fragments of the day's intense *serene* ;" শান্তোজ্জ্বলপ্রভা, প্রশান্ত দীপ্তি। ***Verb t.*** To make clear ; to quiet ; স্বচ্ছ করা ; প্রশান্ত করা, শান্ত করা। **–ly,** *adv.* **–ren'-i-ty,** *n.* 1. Clearness ; স্বচ্ছতা, নির্ম্মলতা। 2. Calmness ; প্রশান্তি। 3. Calmness of mind : unruffled state ; শান্তি, প্রশান্তি, নীরবতা, নিঃস্তব্ধতা ; প্রশান্তভাব, স্থিরচিত্ততা, মনঃপ্রসাদ, সম্প্রসাদ (শ্রীঃ)। **His serene Highness**—জর্ম্মণ সাম্রাজ্যের সামন্তরাজগণের উপাধি।

sêrf, *n.* A slave, in some cases the personal property of his master, in others attached to the soil, and transferable along with it ; গোলাম, নফর, চিরদাস-ক্ষেত্রদাস (কেভিঃ)। **Serf-age, Serf'-dom, Serf-hood,** *ns.*

serge (sĕrj), *n.* A kind of durable twilled worsted cloth ; একপ্রকার শক্ত টের্চ্চা-বুনা পশমী কাপড়, সার্জ্জ।

ser'-geant, –jeant (sâr-jănt), *ns.* 1. A non-commissioned officer in an army, in rank next above a corporal ; নায়কের (corporal) অব্যবহিত উর্দ্ধতন নিম্নশ্রেণীর সামরিক কর্ম্মচারিবিশেষ, সার্জ্জেণ্ট্। 2. A lawyer of the highest rank in England and Ireland ; ইংলণ্ড ও আয়র্লণ্ডের উচ্চশ্রেণীর ব্যবহারজীবি বিশেষ। 3. A police officer ranking between an inspector and constable ; (ইংলণ্ডে) ইনস্পেক্টর ও কনষ্টবলের মধ্যবর্ত্তী পুলিশ কর্ম্মচারী, পুলিস সার্জ্জেণ্ট। **–ship,** *n.* **Sergeant-at-arms** — পার্লেমেণ্টের কর্ম্মচারিবিশেষ, শান্তিরক্ষা এবং অপরাধিগণকে শাস্তি প্রদান ইঁহার কার্য্য। **Sergeant-fish**—একপ্রকার সামুদ্রিক মৎস্য **Sergeant-major**—নিম্নশ্রেণীর সামরিক কর্ম্মচারীদের মধ্যে সর্ব্বোচ্চ কর্ম্মচারী। **Colour sergeant** — সেনাপল্টনের সার্জ্জেণ্ট চতুষ্টয়ের মধ্যে প্রবীণতম ব্যক্তি। **Common sergeant**—লণ্ডন নগরীর মিউনিসিপাল কর্ম্মচারিবিশেষ।

sêrg-ette' (-ĕt), *n.* Thin serge ; একপ্রকার পাতলা সার্জ্জ কাপড়।

sē′-rĭ-ăl, *adj.* & *n.* Consisting of series; as, *serial* number; ধারাবাহিক, ক্রমিক, ক্রমবদ্ধ, আনুক্রমিক। ***Noun.*** 1. (*Rare*) A periodical publication; মাসিক, সাপ্তাহিক, প্রভৃতি। 2. An article issued in successive portion; ক্রমপ্রকাশ্যপ্রবন্ধ, ক্রমশঃ প্রকাশিত প্রবন্ধ, ধারাবাহিক প্রবন্ধ। **—ly**, *adv.* In regular order; ধারাবাহিকরূপে, একাদিক্রমে, যথাক্রমে।

sē′-rĭ-āte, —āt-ĕd, *adjs.* & *v. t.* Arranged in a series or succession; ক্রমবদ্ধ, যথানুক্রমিক, ক্রমনিবদ্ধ, ধারাবাহিক। ***Verb t.*** (Only *seriate*) To arrange in succession; ক্রমনিবদ্ধ করা, ক্রমবিন্যস্ত করা। **—a′-tion**, *n.*

sē-rĭ-ā′-tĭm, *adv.* In regular order; one after another; ক্রমবদ্ধভাবে, যথাক্রমে, আনুপূর্ব্বিকভাবে, যথানুক্রমে; একে একে।

Sēr′-ĭc, *adj.* 1. (*Rhet.*) Chinese; (আলঙ্কারিক ভাষায়) চীনদেশীয়, চৈন। 2. Silken; as, the manufacture of *seric* stuffs; পট্ট, রেশমী।

sĕr′-ĭ-cāte, —cāt-ĕd, sē-rĭ′-ceous, (-shŭs), *adj.* 1. Silky; রেশমী, পট্ট। 2. (*Bot.*) Covered with very soft hairs; কোমলরোমাবৃত।

sĕr′-ĭ-cĭ-cŭl-türe, *n.* Same as SERICULTURE.

sĕr′-ĭ-cŭl-türe, *n.* The culture of silkworms; গুটিপোকাপালন, রেশমকীট পালন। **—cul′-tu-ral**, *adj.* **—cul′-tur-ist**, *n.*

sĕr-ĭ-ē′-mȧ, *n.* A Brazilian bird of the size of a heron preying on serpents; ব্র্যাজিল দেশীয় সর্পভুক্ পক্ষিবিশেষ।

sē′-ries (-rēz *or* sē-rĭ-ēz), *n.* 1. A succession of things related to one another; order; অনুক্রম, শ্রেণী, পরম্পরা; শৃঙ্খলতা, পর্য্যায়, ধারা। 2. Row; set; শ্রেণী, পংক্তি; মালা, আবলি, হার। 3. (*Arith.* & *Algeb.*) A number of terms in succession increasing or diminishing in a certain ratio; (পাটীগণিত এবং বীজগণিত) শ্রেণী, শ্রেঢ়ী। 4. (*Chem.*) A group of compound each containing the same radical; a set of elements with common properties; (রসায়নশাস্ত্র) একই মূলকাত্মক যৌগিকপদার্থশ্রেণী; সমধর্ম্মা মূলপদার্থ শ্রেণী। 5. (*Nat. Hist.*) An order or subdivision of some classes of natural bodies; প্রাকৃতিক পদার্থ নিচয়ের বর্গ বা অবান্তর বিভাগ। 6. (*Electr.*) A number of wires of different metals each connected with the preceding; (তাড়িত শাস্ত্র) বিভিন্ন প্রকার ধাতুর তারসমূহ—যাহার প্রত্যেকটীর প্রান্ত পূর্ব্ববর্ত্তী তারের সহিত সংযুক্ত থাকে। 7. (*Geol.*) A set of strata with common characteristics; as, the greensand *series*; (ভূবিদ্যা) এক লক্ষণাক্রান্ত স্তরশ্রেণী। 8. A set of works or periodicals issued in succession; a set of works under a common name and edited by the same editor in chief; as, the Clarendon Press *series*; গ্রন্থমালা, মাসিক পত্রাদির পর্যায় (cf. বঙ্গদর্শন নবপর্য্যায়), মালা, পর্য্যায়; একই প্রধান সম্পাদক কর্ত্তৃক সম্পাদিত সাধারণ নামবিশিষ্ট গ্রন্থমালা। 9. (*Commr.*) A parcel of rough diamonds of assorted qualities; বিভিন্ন প্রকারের অমার্জ্জিত হীরক। **Infinite series**—(*In Arithmetic*) অনন্ত শ্রেণী (কেণ্ডিঃ); (*In Algebra*) বল্লী (কেণ্ডিঃ)। **In series**—(তাড়িত বিদ্যা—তার সমূহ সম্পর্কে) এরূপ ভাবে সংযুক্ত যাহাতে বিজলীপ্রবাহ ইহাদের মধ্য দিয়া পর পর অতিক্রম করে।

sĕr′-ĭf, *n.* A fine line in a letter esp. at the top or bottom of capitals; অক্ষরের নীচ বা উপরে যে সূক্ষ্ম টান দেওয়া হয়।

sĕr′-ĭn, *n.* A song-bird of the finch family; তুতিজাতীয় গায়কপক্ষিবিশেষ।

sĕr-ĭ-nette′(-nĕt),*n.* An instrument for training song-birds; গায়কপক্ষিগণের শিক্ষাদানের জন্য বাদ্যযন্ত্রবিশেষ

sē-rin-gȧ (-rĭng-), *n.* A South-American name for caoutchouc tree; দক্ষিণ আমেরিকার খদির বৃক্ষ।

sē-rĭ-ō—cŏm′-ĭc, *adj.* Blending serious and comic elements; একাধারে গাম্ভীর্য্য ও পরিহাসাত্মক।

serioso, (*It.*), *adv.* (*Mus.*) With solemnity; গাম্ভীর্য্যসহকারে।

sē′-rĭ-ous (-ŭs), *adj.* 1. Grave; thoughtful; গম্ভীর; চিন্তাশীল। 2. Important; weighty; গুরুতর; গুরুত্বপূর্ণ। 3. Dangerous; as, a *serious* matter; বিপজ্জনক, সঙ্গীন, গুরুতর বিষম, সঙ্কটজনক। 4. Being in earnest; not ironical or jesting; সত্যি সত্যি ইচ্ছুক; সত্যিকার, বাস্তবিক। 5. Concerned with religion or ethics; not secular; as, *serious* subject; ধর্ম্মসংক্রান্ত, নীতিসংক্রান্ত; অধ্যাত্ম। **—ly**, *adv.* **—ness**, *n.*

sĕr′-ĭph, *n.* Same as CERIPH.

ser′-jeant (sär-jănt), *n.* Same as SERGENT (which see.)

sêr′-mŏn, *n.* & *v. t.* 1. A religious discourse by a clergyman; ধর্ম্মোপদেশ। 2. A set exhortation or reproof; homily; "I will not repay your confidence with a *sermon*"; উপদেশাবলী, তিরস্কার, গঞ্জনা, অবসাদজনক নৈতিক উপদেশ। ***Verb t.*** To preach a sermon to; ধর্ম্মোপদেশ দেওয়া, অবসাদজনক নৈতিক উপদেশ দেওয়া। **—ize**, *v.t.* & *i.* **—izer**, *n.* **Sermon on the Mount**—মথিলিখিত সুসমাচারের ৫ম—৭ম অধ্যায়ে বর্ণিত যীশুখৃষ্টের সুবিখ্যাত ধর্ম্মোপদেশ।

sē′-rō-cyst, *n.* A cyst containing serum; লসিকার থলি।

sē-rō-pū′-rū-lĕnt, *n.* Consisting of pus and serum; পুঁষ এবং লসিকাপূর্ণ।

sē-rō-san-guin′-ō-lĕnt, (-săng-gwĭn-), *adj.* Pertaining to bloody serum; consisting of bloody serum; সরক্তলসিকাসম্বন্ধীয়; সরক্তলসিকাত্মক।

sĕr′-ō-tĭne, *n.* A kind of bat; একপ্রকার বাদুড়।

sē-rŏt'-i-nŭs, *adj.* Appearing late in season ; মরসুমের শেষভাগে আগত।

sē'-rous (-rŭs), *adj.* **1.** Of, or like, serum ; লসিকাসম্বন্ধীয়, লসিকাবৎ। **2.** Whey-like ; watery ; ছানার জলের মত ; জলীয়। **–ros'-i-ty,** *n.*

sêr'-pĕnt, *n.* **1.** Snake ; নাগ (for synonyms see SNAKE.) **2.** A malicious person ; সর্পপ্রকৃতির লোক, খল। **3.** A wind instrument now seldom used ; একপ্রকার সর্পাকৃতি সুষির যন্ত্র। **4.** (*Cap.*) The southern constellation Hydra ; অশ্লেষা নক্ষত্র, সার্প (বৃঃ সং), সর্প (আপ্তেঃ), নাগ। **5.** A kind of fire-work having a serpentine motion ; একপ্রকার আতসবাজী, সাপবাজী। **Serpent-bitten** — সর্পদষ্ট। **Serpent-charmer** — মালবৈদ্য, সাপুড়িয়া, অহিতুণ্ডিক। **Serpent-deity** — সর্পদেবতা। **Serpent-eater** — কেরাণী-পাখী। **Serpent force** — কুণ্ডলিনী শক্তি (এভেলন) [cf. মূলাধারপদ্মে সর্পাকার সার্দ্ধত্রিতয়বেষ্টনবিশিষ্টা বিদ্যুৎ-সমূহরূপা কুলকুণ্ডলিনী তিষ্ঠতি—পূর্ণানন্দকৃত ষট্‌চক্রপ্রকাশ (টীকা)]। **Serpent-gem**—সর্পমণি, সর্পের মাথার মণি, সর্পফণিজ, নাগরত্ন। **Serpent gourd**—চিচিঙ্গা। **Serpent-god**—Same as SERPENT-DEITY. **Serpent-grass** — একপ্রকার গুল্ম। **Serpent-stone** — সর্পমণি। [Chin. *Shi-hwang* or *Bez-oar*)—Tavernier এর মতে এই প্রস্তর প্রায় অণ্ডাকার। অনেকের ভ্রান্ত বিশ্বাস যে এই প্রস্তর সর্পের মাথায় জন্মিয়া থাকে। সে যাহা-হউক এই মণি যে সর্প-দষ্ট ব্যক্তির বিষ দূরীকরণে বিশেষ ফলপ্রদ ইহা সর্ব্ববাদিসম্মত। দষ্টস্থানে এই প্রস্তর সংলগ্ন করিলে যে পর্য্যন্ত সমস্ত বিষ শুষিয়া না লয় সে পর্য্যন্ত উহা পতিত হয় না। এই মণি পরিষ্কার করিতে হইলে ইহা বার ঘণ্টা পর্য্যন্ত স্ত্রীলোকের দুগ্ধে এবং তদভাবে গোদুগ্ধে নিমজ্জিত করিয়া রাখিতে হয়। **Serpent-wand** — Same as CADUCEUS (which see). **Serpent-wood**—(*Ophioxylon serpentinum*), চন্দ্র, চন্দ্রক কুচিলালতা (খোরী)। **Serpent-worship** — সর্পপূজা, নাগপূজা। [সর্পপূজা পৃথিবীর ভিন্ন ভিন্ন দেশে প্রাচীন জাতিদিগের মধ্যে প্রচলিত দেখা যায়। Fergussonএর মতে বাইবেলে বর্ণিত সর্পরূপী শয়তানের কাহিনীতে পবিত্রতর এবং উচ্চতর জিহোভার পূজা প্রচলন দ্বারা প্রাচীনতর নাগপূজামূলক ধর্ম্মের বিলোপসাধনের আভাস পাওয়া যায়। Kingsleyর মতে বাইবেলের Genesis গ্রন্থে উক্ত সর্পরূপী শয়তান সর্পপূজক কৃষ্ণকায় জাতির লোক ভিন্ন আর কেহই নহে। আমাদের হরি-বংশেও সর্প নামক ম্লেচ্ছজাতিবিশেষের উল্লেখ আছে। যথা, কোলিসর্পা মাহিষকা দার্ব্বাশ্চোলাঃ সকেরলাঃ। সর্ব্বে তে ক্ষত্রিয়াস্তাত ধর্ম্মস্তেষাং নিরাকৃতঃ। বশিষ্ঠ-বচনা রাজন্ সগরেণ মহাত্মনা—হরিবংশ ২৪ অধ্যায়।

কোন কোন পণ্ডিতের মতে সর্পপূজা পৃথিবীর প্রায় সর্ব্বত্রই প্রচলিত ছিল। এসিয়াখণ্ডের প্যালেষ্টাইন, বেবিলন, পারস্য, তিব্বত, সিংহল, ভারতবর্ষ, প্রভৃতি স্থানে এবং আফ্রিকার মিসর প্রভৃতি দেশে সর্পপূজা প্রচলিত থাকার প্রমাণ পাওয়া যায়। প্রায় খৃঃ পূঃ ২০০০ অব্দে ইহুদীদিগের মধ্যে সর্পপূজা প্রচলিত ছিল। Hezekiahর সময়ে এস্রায়েলের বংশধরগণ পিত্তলনির্ম্মিত সর্পের সম্মুখে ধূপাদি প্রজ্বালিত করিত। প্রাচীন প্রুসীয়গণও সর্পপূজক ছিল এবং তাহারা গৃহে প্রতিদিবস সর্পগণকে নৈবেদ্য প্রদান করিত। রোমনগরী হইতে ১৬ মাইল দূরবর্ত্তী Lanuviumএ Juno দেবীর কুঞ্জের নিকটবর্ত্তী কোন স্থানে একটী বৃহৎ সর্প পূজিত হইত। গ্রীক ধন্বন্তরি Esculapius সংগ্রথিত সর্পযুগলরচিত দণ্ড ধারণ করিতেন। গ্রীসের Epidausএর কুঞ্জ সর্পপূজার প্রধান কেন্দ্র ছিল। রোমনগরী প্রতিষ্ঠার ৪৬২তম বৎসরে রোমকপুরে ভীষণ মহামারীর প্রাদুর্ভাব হইলে রোমানগণ তথা হইতে বহু সমারোহের সহিত একটী সর্প রোমনগরীতে নিয়া পূজা করেন। মহাবীর অলীক-সন্দর নাগবংশসম্ভূত বলিয়া প্লুটার্ক উল্লেখ করিয়াছেন Thebesএর অধিবাসিগণ নাগবংশোদ্ভূত বলিয়া গর্ব্ব করিত। Scipio Africanus আপনাকে নাগপুত্র বলিয়া বিশ্বাস করিতেন। Aztecদিগের দেবতা Qetzalcoatlএর অঙ্গ সর্পমণ্ডিত ছিল। প্রাচীন মিসরবাসিগণ Apophis নামক নাগরাজের পূজা করিত। জুরাথাস্ত্রের শাস্ত্রে Azhi Dahaka নামক ভীষণ সর্পদেবতার উল্লেখ দৃষ্ট হয়। Tyreএ Ophites বা নাগপূজক নামে এক খৃষ্টীয় সম্প্রদায় গঠিত হয়। এবং ইহারা খৃষ্টার্চ্চনা অপেক্ষাও নাগপূজাতে সমধিক উৎসাহ প্রকাশ করিত। রোম সম্রাট্ আগষ্টাসের মাতা Atia তাহাকে কোন এক সর্প হইতে প্রাপ্ত হন বলিয়া প্রবাদ আছে। তুরাণ দেশে প্রচলিত বৌদ্ধধর্ম্মে শাক্যমুনির মূর্ত্তি তিন বা ততোধিক সর্পের ফণাতপতলে সমাসীন থাকে। পরবর্ত্তী কালে শিবের মস্তকে এবং শিবলিঙ্গোপরি এই প্রকার সর্পাভরণ দৃষ্ট হয়।

ভারতবর্ষে অতি প্রাচীনকাল হইতেই সর্পপূজা প্রচলিত ছিল। ঐতরেয় ব্রাহ্মণে সর্প নামক জনৈক ঋষির (অর্বুদ) উল্লেখ আছে। এই ঋষিই ঋগ্বেদের ১০ম মণ্ডলের কতিপয় সূক্তের রচয়িতা। ঋগ্বেদের দশম মণ্ডলের কতিপয় সূক্তের নাম সর্পরাজ্ঞী। এই সর্প ঋষি যে, অনার্য্যনাগকুলোদ্ভূত তদ্বিষয়ে কোন সন্দেহ নাই। সাঁচী এবং অমরাবতীর সুবিখ্যাত বুদ্ধস্তূপে নানাপ্রকার সর্পের ভূষা দৃষ্ট হয়। ভারতবর্ষের পুরাণাদিতে সর্পপূজার ভূরি ভূরি প্রমাণ পাওয়া যায়। কোন কোন পণ্ডিতের মতে মহাভারতে বর্ণিত জন্মেজয়ের সর্পযজ্ঞে বৈদিক-ধর্ম্মাবলম্বী আর্য্যগণকর্ত্তৃক নাগপূজক অনার্য্যজাতির ধ্যানের ইঙ্গিত পাওয়া যায়। আমরা নিম্নে বিভিন্ন পুরাণ হইতে নাগপূজা সম্বন্ধে কয়েকটী প্রমাণ উল্লেখ করিলাম।

পঞ্চম্যাং পূজয়েন্নাগাননন্তাদ্যান্ মহোরগান্।
ক্ষীরং সর্পিস্তু নৈবেদ্যং দেয়ং সর্ব্ববিষাপহম্॥
দেবীপুরাণ।

অনন্তং বাসুকিং শঙ্খং পদ্মং কম্বলমেব চ।
তথা কর্কোটকং নাগং ধৃতরাষ্ট্রঞ্চ শঙ্খকম্॥
কালিয়ং তক্ষকঞ্চাপি পিঙ্গলং মাসি মাসি চ।
যজেৎ তান্ নাগান দষ্টমুক্তোদিবং ব্রজেৎ॥
গরুড়পুরাণ।

পঞ্চম্যাং স্নাপয়ন্তীহ নাগান্ ক্ষীরেণ যে নরাঃ।
তেষাং কুলে প্রযচ্ছন্তি অভয়ং প্রাণদক্ষিণং॥
ভবিষ্যপুরাণ ৫মী কল্প।

যে চ হেলিমরীচিস্থা যেহন্তরিক্ষে দিবিস্থিতাঃ।
যে নদীষু মহানাগা যে সরস্বতিগামিনঃ॥
যে চ বাপী তড়াগেষু তেষু সর্ব্বেষু বৈ নমঃ।
নাগান্ বিপ্রাংশ্চ সম্পূজ্য বিসৃজ্যচ যথার্থতঃ॥
ভবিষ্যপুরাণ ৫মী কল্প।

ভূরি চন্দ্রময়ং নাগমথবা কলধৌতকম্।
কৃত্বা দারুময়ংবাপি অথবা মৃন্ময়ং নৃপ॥
পঞ্চম্যামর্চ্চয়েদ্ভক্ত্যা নাগং পঞ্চফণং নৃপ।
করবীরৈঃ শতপত্রৈর্জাতিপুষ্পৈশ্চ সুব্রত॥
তথা গন্ধপ্রধূপৈশ্চ পূজ্যং পন্নগমুত্তমম্।
ব্রাহ্মণং ভোজয়েৎ পশ্চাৎ ঘৃতপায়সমোদকৈঃ॥
ভবিষ্যৎপুরাণ ৫মী কল্পঃ।

কখনও কখনও নাগরাজ বাসুকী (অনন্ত) দেবাদিদেব বিষ্ণুর সহিত অভেদভাবে পূজিত হন। যথা—ওঁ দিব্যসিংহাসনাসীনং দেবেশং গরুড়ধ্বজম্।
শুক্লবর্ণং চতুর্ব্বাহুং নাগযজ্ঞোপবীতিনম্॥
শঙ্খচক্রগদাপদ্মধরং পীতাম্বরং বিভুং।
শ্রিয়াবাণ্যা চ সংশ্লিষ্টং কিরীটাদিসমুজ্জ্বলম্॥
ফণাশতসমাযুক্তং জগন্নাথং জগদ্গুরুং।
অনন্তং চিন্তয়েদ্দেবং নারদাদ্যৈরুপস্ততং॥
ইতি ভবিষ্যপুরাণ অনন্তব্রত॥

সর্প অনন্তের চিহ্নস্বরূপও ব্যবহৃত হয়। মিলিতপুচ্ছমুখ সর্পের চিত্র প্রাচীন কালে অনন্তের চিহ্নস্বরূপ ব্যবহৃত হইত। নারায়ণের অনন্তশয্যার অনন্তনাগ অনন্তেরই রূপক বলিয়া বোধ হয়। ভারতের নানাস্থানে নাগপঞ্চমী দিবসে নাগপূজা অনুষ্ঠিত হয়। নাগবেষ্টিতবিগ্রহা মনসাদেবী হিন্দুগণকর্ত্তৃক সর্পের অধিষ্ঠাত্রী দেবীরূপে সম্পূজিত হইয়া আসিতেছেন। শাস্ত্রে দুর্গামূর্ত্তির সহিত নাগের সংশ্রব দৃষ্ট হয়। যথা—অহিকলিত নীলকুঞ্চিতকুন্তল-বিলসৎ কিরীট শশিকলা। সর্পময়বলয়নূপুর-কাঞ্চী কেয়ূরহারসম্ভিন্না॥ —প্রপঞ্চসার তন্ত্র। মান্দ্রাজনগরের উপকণ্ঠস্থ Trivetoor, Washermanpetta and Perarmbore প্রভৃতি স্থানে কতিপয় নাগমন্দির অদ্যাপি বর্ত্তমান আছে। (See Cunningham's *India*; Taylor's *Hindu Myth*; Frere's *Antipodes*; *Darwinism in morals*; Fergusson's *Tree and Serpent Worship*; Lubbock's *Origin of Civilization*; Ward's *Hindus*; J. Bryant's *Ancient Mythology*; Taylor's *Primitive Culture.*] **Pharaoh's serpent**—See PHARAOH. **Their ears have been serpent licked**—They are gifted with the power of prophecy; তাহাদের ভবিষ্যৎকথনের ক্ষমতা আছে। **The Serpent**—শয়তান। **To cherish a serpent in one's bosom**—To show kindness to one who proves treacherous afterwards; দুধ কলা দিয়া সাপ পোষণ করা।

sêr'-pĕn-tīne, *adj. n.*, & *v.i.* **1.** Relating to, or like, a serpent; সর্পসম্বন্ধীয়, সার্প, ঔরগ, ভৌজঙ্গম, সর্পবৎ। **2.** Tortuous; meandering; as, a *serpentine* road; আঁকাবাঁকা, সর্পগতি; পেঁচালো। **3.** Crafty; খল, কুটিল। ***Noun.*** A mineral usually of mottled green, used for ornamental work; শিল্পদ্রব্যাদি নির্ম্মাণে ব্যবহৃত একপ্রকার খনিজ-পদার্থ, বিশেষতঃ একপ্রকার ফুট ফুট দাগবিশিষ্ট সবুজবর্ণের পাথর, সর্পপাষাণ, সর্পশিলা। ***Verb i.*** To move sinuously; বক্রগতিতে চলা, কুটিলগতিতে চলা। **Serpentine dance**—সর্পগতিতে নৃত্য। **Serpentine marble**—সর্পশিলার স্তূপ। **Serpentine powder**—অতি সূক্ষ্মরূপে চূর্ণীকৃত অগ্নিচূর্ণ। **Serpentine verse**—যে কবিতার পংক্তির আদ্য ও অন্ত শব্দ অভিন্ন হইয়া থাকে। **Serpentine wisdom**—গভীর জ্ঞান (See *Matthew* x. 16.) **The Serpentine**—হাইডপার্কের আঁকাবাঁকা খাল।

sêr-pĭg'-i-nous (-nŭs), *adj.* [Of skin disease) Creeping from one part of the body to another; (চর্ম্মরোগসম্পর্কে) দেহের এক অংশ হইতে অপর অংশে অপসর্পণশীল, অপসর্পী।

sêr-pī'-gō, *n.* (*Obs.*) Ringworm; (অপ্রঃ) দদ্রু।

sêr'-pü-lă, *n.* A genus of annelida inhabiting a calcareous tube secreted by them and attached to rocks etc.; একপ্রকার চক্রিত ক্রিমি—যাহারা স্বীয় দেহ নিঃসৃত চূর্ণময় নলের ভিতর বাস করিয়া থাকে।

sĕr'-ră, *n.* A saw or saw-like parts; করাত বা করাতের মত দেহাংশ।

sĕr-ră-dil'-lă, *n.* A plant *Ornithopus sativus*; একপ্রকার গুল্ম।

Serranus sonnerte—সোনভেটকী (গুপ্তঃ)।

sĕr'-rāte, -rāt'-ĕd, *adj.* & *v. t.* Notched on the edge like a saw; দন্তুরিত, ক্রকচদন্তী, অনুক্রকচ, করপত্রদন্তী, করপত্রনিভ। ***Verb t.*** (*-rate* only) To provide with a saw-like edge; ক্রকচবৎ প্রান্তসমন্বিত করা। **-ra'-tion**, *n.*

sĕr'-rĭ-cŏrn, *adj.* Having serrate antennae; (কীটসম্বন্ধে) দন্তুরিত শুঁয়াবিশিষ্ট।

sĕr'-rīed (-rĭd), *adj.* Compact; without gaps; as, *serried* trunk; ঘনবিন্যস্ত, ঘনসন্নিবিষ্ট; নিবিড়, সংহত।

sĕr-rĭf'-êr-ous (-ŭs), *adj.* Having saw-like organ; ক্রকচবৎ উপাঙ্গবিশিষ্ট।

sĕr'-rĭ-fŏrm, *adj.* Resembling a saw; ক্রকচাকৃতি, করপত্রনিভ।

sĕr-rĭ-rŏs'-trāte, *adj.* Saw-billed; ক্রকচচঞ্চু।

sĕr-rō-mö'-tŏr, *n.* See SERVO-MOTOR.

sĕr'-rŭ-lāte, -lāt-ĕd, *adj.* Finely serrate; সূক্ষ্মক্রকচদন্তী (সাঃ পঃ)।

sē'-rŭm, *n.* **1.** The thin part of blood etc.; রক্তের জলবৎ পাতলা ক্ষারময় অংশ, লসিকা। (সুশ্রুঃ কুঞ্জঃ), রক্তাম্বু, অসৃক্কর (সাঃ পঃ), কলতানি, চর্ম্মসার, চর্ম্মজল, রক্তদ্রব (কেশিঃ)। **2.** Whey; ছানার জল। **3.** Chyle; অন্নরস। **Serum-treatment**—রোগজনক জীবাণুর প্রভাব নষ্ট করার জন্য লসিকাদ্বারা টীকা দেওন। **Serum of the flesh**—মাংসজ (সাঃপঃ), মাংসসার (ঐ)।

Serval.

sĕr'-văl, *n.* African tiger-cat; দক্ষিণ-আফ্রিকার বন্য মার্জ্জারবিশেষ।

sėrv'-ănt, *n.* 1. An attendant in a household; one who is in the service of another; চাকর, ভৃত্য, পরিচারক, দাস, সেবক, কিঙ্কর, ভৃতিভুক্, বান্দা (among Mahommedans); কর্ম্মচারী, বেতনোপজীবী। 2. A devoted follower; as, a *servant* of God; দাস, ভক্ত। **Public servants**—সরকারী কর্ম্মচারী। **Servant of servants**—দাসানুদাস। **Servant of servants of God** (Lat. *servus servorum Dei*—ঈশ্বরের দাসানুদাস (রোমের পোপের উপাধি বিশেষ)। **Your humble obedient servant** — আপনার অনুগত বা বিনয়াবনত ভৃত্য, আপনার আজ্ঞাবহ ভৃত্য (শিষ্টাচারের অনুরোধে পত্রের নীচে লিখিতে হয়।)

serve (sêrv), *v. t., i.* & *n.* 1. To work for; to be in the employment of; কায করা; কাহারো অধীনে চাকরী করা। 2. To render spiritual obedience and worship to; as, to *serve* God; সেবা করা, অর্চ্চনা করা। 3. To supply with goods or articles in a shop or the like; as, to *serve* a customer; ক্রেতাকে জিনিষ পত্র দেওয়া। 4. To attend upon; পরিচর্য্যা করা। 5. To present food as on plate, china, etc.; to distribute food in portions; "*Serve* him with venison and he chooses fish"; খাদ্যদ্রব্য টেবিলের উপর সাজান; পরিবেষণ করা। 6. To make legal delivery of (a process or writ); as, to *serve* a notice; জারি করা। 7. To perform the service of; to perform the duties required in or for; as, a curate may *serve* two churches; কায করা; কর্ত্তব্যকার্য্য সম্পাদন করা। 8. To be sufficient for; to answer the purpose of; as, this will *serve* my purpose; প্রয়োজনানুরূপ হওয়া, যথেষ্ট হওয়া; কাজ চলা, চলা। 9. To handle or manipulate; as, to *serve* a gun; চালান। 10. To undergo; to go through, as punishment; as, to *serve* one's terms of imprisonment; ভোগ করা; কারাবাস প্রভৃতির নির্দ্ধারিত কাল কাটান। 11. To treat; to deal with; to requite; as, to *serve* one right; ব্যবহার করা; আচরণ করা; শোধ লওয়া, প্রতিফল দেওয়া। 12. To content; to satisfy; "Nothing will *serve* me but going on pilgrimage"; সন্তুষ্ট করা; প্রীতিবিধান করা। 13. To promote; to conduce; as, to *serve* one's interest; উদ্দেশ্য সাধনে অগ্রসর করা; সিদ্ধিলাভে অগ্রসর করা। 14. (Of male animal) To copulate with the female animal; সঙ্গম করা। 15. To wrap or wind up cord, canvas, etc., round an object; কোন কিছুর চতুর্দ্দিকে দড়ী, ক্যাম্বিস, প্রভৃতি জড়ান। ***Verb i.*** 1. To be a servant or slave; to perform menial service; চাকর হওয়া, ক্রীতদাস হওয়া; চাকুরী করা, দাস্যবৃত্তি করা। 2. To wait; পরিচর্য্যা করা। 3. To suit; to be convenient; as, when occasion *serves*; উপযোগী হওয়া; সুবিধাজনক হওয়া। 4. To suffice; to answer a purpose; যথেষ্ট হওয়া, প্রচুর হওয়া; কোন কিছুর কাজ চলা। 5. (*Tennis*) To start play by striking the ball into the opposite court বিপরীতদিকের অঙ্গনে কন্দুকতাড়নপূর্ব্বক ক্রীড়া আরম্ভ করা। ***Noun.*** (*Tennis*) First stroke; (টেনিস খেলায়) প্রথম আঘাত। **First come first served**—যে আগে আসে সে পাইবে। **To serve an attachment**—To levy it on the person or goods by seizure; ক্রোকী পরওয়ানা জারি করত ক্রোক করা। **To serve an office**—To discharge the duties incident to an office; কোন পদসংক্রান্ত কর্ত্তব্য সম্পাদন করা। **To serve a person out** — To wreak vengeance on him; প্রতিফল দেওয়া, প্রতিশোধ লওয়া, শিক্ষা দেওয়া। **To serve a warrant**—To read it, and to seize the person against whom it is issued; গ্রেপ্তারী পরওয়ানা পাঠপূর্ব্বক কোন ব্যক্তিকে গ্রেপ্তার করা। **To serve in**—To belong to, or do duty in army or navy; সেনাবিভাগে বা নৌ-বিভাগে কাজ করা। **To serve one a bad turn**—To do him an injury; কাহারো কোনরূপ অনিষ্ট করা। **To serve one a trick**—To play a trick on one; কাহারো সহিত চাতুরী করা। **To serve one right** — To treat one as he deserves; সমুচিত প্রতিফল দেওয়া, সমুচিত শাস্তি দেওয়া, উপযুক্ত শিক্ষা দেওয়া। **To serve one's country**—স্বদেশের সেবা করা। **To serve one's turn**—To serve one's purpose; নিজের উদ্দেশ্য সাধন করা। **To serve the rent**—To close the rent of a muzzle-loading gun while it is being loaded; বারুদ ভরার কালে কামানের রঞ্জকঘরা বন্ধ করা। **To serve out**—To distribute in portions; বাঁটিয়া দেওয়া, পরিবেষণ করা। **To serve up**—To prepare and present at table; ব্যঞ্জনাদির পাত্র সমূহ মেজের উপর সাজান। **To serve with the same sauce** — To retaliate in the same kind; অনুরূপ কার্য্যদ্বারা প্রতিশোধ লওয়া।

sêrv'-êr, *n.* 1. One who serves food, etc.; পরিবেষক। 2. One who assists the priest at the celebration of the eucharist; খৃষ্টের অন্তিম ভোজনানুষ্ঠানকালে যে ব্যক্তি পুরোহিতের কার্য্য করে। 3. A small tray; ক্ষুদ্র বারকোষ। 4. (*Pl.*) A spoon and fork for serving salad; সিদ্ধ মূলা প্রভৃতি তরকারী পরিবেষণের জন্য কাঁটা এবং চামচ।

Sêr'-vi-ăn, *n.* & *adj.* 1. A native of Servia; সার্ভিয়ার অধিবাসী। 2. The language of Servia, Bosnia, Herzegovina, Montenegro, etc.;

সার্ভিয়া, বোসনিয়া, হার্জিগোভেনা, মনটেনিগ্রো, প্রভৃতি দেশের ভাষা। *Adj.* Of, or pertaining to, Servia, its people or language ; সার্ভিয়াসম্বন্ধীয়, সার্ভিয়াবাসিসম্বন্ধীয়, সার্ভিয়ার ভাষাসম্বন্ধীয়।

Sėr′-vi-ăn, *adj.* Of Servius Tullius, sixth king of Rome ; রোমনগরীর ষষ্ঠ নৃপতি সার্ভিয়াস টুলিয়াস-সম্বন্ধীয়। **Servian wall**—রোমের রাজা সার্ভিয়াস্‌কর্তৃক নির্ম্মিত প্রাচীর—যাহার ধ্বংসাবশেষ অদ্যাবধি বর্ত্তমান আছে।

sėrv′-ice (-ĭs), *n.* **1.** Condition or occupation of a servant ; চাকুরী, দাসত্ব। **2.** Spiritual obedience, reverence and love ; as, the *service* of God ; ভগবৎসেবা, সেবা, প্রেমভক্তি। **3.** Public religious worship or ceremony ; an office of devotion ; religious rites appropriate to any event or ceremonial ; as, marriage *service* ; প্রকাশ্য উপাসনা, পূজোপচার (কেভিঃ) ; উপাসনা ; কোন ঘটনা বা অনুষ্ঠানের উপযোগী ক্রিয়া, অনুষ্ঠান। **4.** A musical composition for devotional purpose ; উপাসনাগীতি, স্তবসংগীত, ভজনসঙ্গীত। **5.** A set of vehicles or vessels affording accommodation for regular transit between two places ; as, the steamer *service* ; দুই স্থানের মধ্যে রীতিমত যাতায়াতকারী শকট বা পোতশ্রেণী। **6.** Labour done for another ; assistance ; as, this will be *service* to you ; good offices ; benefit ; পরের সাহায্যার্থ কৃত পরিশ্রম ; সাহায্য ; উপকার, হিতজনক কার্য্য ; হিত। **7.** The duty of a soldier or sailor ; as, to see much *service* abroad ; actual participation in war (usu. *active service*) ; সৈনিক বা নাবিক সেনার কার্য্য, যুদ্ধকার্য্য ; প্রকৃতপক্ষে যুদ্ধ ব্যাপারে যোগদান। **8.** An expedition or engagement ; অভিযান, যুদ্ধ। **9.** Distribution of food ; পরিবেষণ। **10.** (*Rare*) The food set before a person ; (কচিদ্-ব্যবহৃত) কোন ব্যক্তির সম্মুখে স্থাপিত খাদ্য। **11.** A set of dishes or vessels for the table ; as, tea *service* ; an assortment of table linen ; এক প্রস্থ থালা, বাটী, কাঁটা, চামচ, প্রভৃতি ; ভোজনের মেজের রকমারী চাদর, গামছা, প্রভৃতি। **12.** The supply of gas, water or the like to a building ; also the pipes by which such gas, water, etc. are supplied (also *service-pipe*) ; কোন বাড়ীতে গ্যাস, জল, প্রভৃতি সরবরাহ ; যে নলসমূহ দ্বারা গ্যাস, জল প্রভৃতি সরবরাহ করা হয়। **13.** The act of serving the ball in tennis etc. ; টেনিস প্রভৃতি ক্রীড়ায় কন্দুকে আঘাত। **14.** The materials used for serving a rope etc., as spun yarn ; রজ্জু প্রভৃতির চতুর্দ্দিকে যে বস্তু পেঁচানো হয়। **15.** Act of covering ; (পুং পশুর পক্ষে) স্ত্রীপশুর সহিত সঙ্গম। **16.** A branch of public employment, or a body of public servants connected with some particular department ; as, the consular *service* ; সরকারী কার্য্যের কোন বিশেষ বিভাগসংক্রান্ত শাখাবিশেষ, কোন বিশেষ বিভাগসংক্রান্ত কার্য্যে নিযুক্ত কর্ম্মচারিবর্গ। **17.** (*Law*) The execution of any writ or process ; (আইন) শমন প্রভৃতি জারি করণ। **Senior service**—রাজকীয় নৌসেনা (Royal Navy)। **Service-ammunition rifle**—সেনাবিভাগের বা নৌবিভাগের কার্য্যে ব্যবহৃত গোলাগুলি বা বন্দুক, যুদ্ধে ব্যবহারের জন্য গোলাগুলি বা বন্দুক। **Service-book** — উপাসনাপদ্ধতিবিষয়ক পুস্তক ; সরকারী কর্ম্মচারিগণের কার্য্যবিবরণী পুস্তক। **Service-pipe**—যে প্রধান নল হইতে জল সমানীত হয়, উপনল। **Service-reservoir**—যে বৃহৎ জলাধার হইতে সাগরের জল সরবরাহ হয়। **Service-room**—খাদ্যপরিবেষণগৃহ। **Service uniform** — যুদ্ধকালে পরিহিত পোষাক। **Service-wire**—প্রধান তার হইতে যে উপতারের সাহায্যে আলোক, উত্তাপ, বিদ্যুৎ, প্রভৃতির প্রবাহ বাহিত হয়। **Active service**—যুদ্ধকালে সৈনিকরূপে বা নাবিকসৈনিকরূপে কার্য্য ; যুদ্ধকালে ঐরূপ কার্য্যে নিযুক্ত কর্ম্মচারিবর্গ। **Military service** — সৈনিকবৃত্তি। **Personal service**—পরওয়ানা প্রভৃতির মর্ম্ম ব্যক্ত করিয়া তাহা কোন ব্যক্তির নিজ হস্তে জারি করণ। **At (a person's) service**—Ready to do one's bidding ; কাহারো আদেশপালনে প্রস্তুত। **At one's service**—At one's disposal ; কাহারো হাতে। **Of service**—Useful ; প্রয়োজনীয়, কার্য্যকর। **On His or Her Majesty's service**—(*Abbr. O. H. M. S.*) ; সম্রাট্ বা সম্রাজ্ঞীর কার্য্যে—সরকারী চিঠির খাম বা টিকিটের উপর (সংক্ষেপে) মুদ্রিত হইয়া থাকে। **Service of man**—নরসেবা, জনসেবা, মানবসেবা। **The service**—সেনাবিভাগ বা নৌসেনাবিভাগ। **To hold in service**—প্রজার নিকট পত্তন করিয়া রাখা। **To see service**—To have experience ; to have experience as a soldier or sailor ; কার্য্যে অভিজ্ঞতা থাকা ; সৈনিক বা নাবিকের কার্য্য করিয়া পাকা হওয়া। To have been much used ; বহুকাল যাবৎ ব্যবহৃত হওয়া। **To take service**—To enlist as a soldier or sailor ; সৈনিক বা নাবিকের কাজে ভর্ত্তি হওয়া।

sėrv′-ice (ĭs), *n.* A tree of the genus pyrus (also *service-tree*) ; একজাতীয় বৃক্ষ। **Service-berry** (or **Service**)—ঐ বৃক্ষের ফল।

sėrv′-ice-a-ble (-ĭs-ȧ-bl), *adj.* **1.** Useful ; beneficial ; প্রয়োজনীয়, কার্য্যকর, কার্য্যোপযোগী ; হিতকর, উপকারী, হিতজনক। **2.** Lasting ; as, *serviceable* boots ; টেঁকসই। **—bly,** *adv.* **—ness,** *n.* The state of being serviceable ; কার্য্যকারিকতা, উপকারিতা।

sėr-vi-ette′ (-ĕt), (*F.*), *n.* A table-napkin ; ভোজনকালে (প্রধানতঃ ভৃত্যাদি কর্ত্তৃক) ব্যবহৃত রুমাল।

sėr′-vile, *adj.* **1.** Slavish ; befitting a slave ; as, *servile* fear ;

mean; দাসবৎ; দাসোচিত; নীচ, হীন, হেয়। 2. Cringing; fawning; meanly submissive; as, *servile* flattery; পদলেহনাত্মক; হীনচাটুকারিতাপূর্ণ; হীনানুগত। 3. (*Gram.*) Not belonging to the original root; as, a *servile* letter; (ব্যাকরণ) মূলধাতুর বহির্ভূত। 4. (*Philol.*) Not itself sounded but serving to lengthen the sound of a preceding vowel (as, *e* in love); (ভাষাবিজ্ঞান) স্বয়ং অনুচ্চারিত থাকিয়া পূর্ব্ববর্ত্তী স্বরবর্ণের ধ্বনির দীর্ঘতা (গুরুতা) সাধক। **—ness,** *n.* **—vil'-i-ty,** *n.* **1.** Slavery; দাসত্ব, গোলামি। **2.** Slavish obsequiousness; দাসবৎ আনুগত্য, হীনানুগত্য, পদলেহনপ্রভৃতি। **Servile-war**—বিদ্রোহী ক্রীতদাসগণের সহিত প্রভুগণের যুদ্ধ। **Servile-work**—(রোমান ক্যাথালিক ধর্ম্মসংঘ) রবিবার দিবস যে সকল নীচ কাজ করা নিষিদ্ধ হইয়া থাকে।

sêr'-vi-tor (-têr), *n.* **1.** (*Archaic* or *Poet.*) Servant; attendant; (অপ্রচলিত বা কবিতায়) দাস, সেবক, ভৃত্য, কিঙ্কর; পরিচারক। **2.** An undergraduate who is partly supported out of the college funds and who had to perform menial duties in return; পূর্ব্বে অক্সফোর্ড বিশ্ববিদ্যালয়ে যে অনুপাধিপ্রাপ্ত ছাত্র ভৃত্যোচিত কার্য্যে সাহায্য করার জন্য কলেজ হইতে অর্থসাহায্য প্রাপ্ত হইত। **—ship,** *n.*

sêr'-vi-tūde, *n.* **1.** Slavery; involuntary subjection; দাসত্ব, ভৃত্যত্ব, সেবকত্ব; দাস্য, অধীনতা, পরাধীনতা, পরবশতা। **2.** Compulsory service or labour such as a criminal has to undergo as a punishment; as, penal *servitude*; কয়েদির শাস্তিস্বরূপ কঠোর পরিশ্রম। **3.** (*Law*) The right or title to the use of a thing for general or for a particular purpose, without having personal interest or property in it (such as, right of way, water, etc.); কোন সম্পত্তিতে কোনরূপ স্বত্বস্বামিত্ব না থাকা স্বত্বেও উহা সাধারণ ভাবে বা বিশেষভাবে ব্যবহারের অধিকার, ব্যবহার-স্বত্ব। **4.** The state of being under foreign yoke; "Liberty is better than quiet *servitude*"; অধীনতা।

Sêr'-vō–, *pref.* Combining form of Servian.

sĕs'-ă-mē, *n.* An annual herbaceous plant and its seeds from which an oil is expressed; তিল গাছ, তিল। [Syn. হোমধান্য (seed), স্বধাপ্রিয় (*ib.*), দৌহিত্র (*ib.*), পবিত্র (*ib.*), পিতৃতর্পণ (*ib.*), পূতধান্য (*ib.*), স্নেহফল, স্নেহরঙ্গ, স্নেহফলপূরফল, সারাল, সুবন্ধ, দলাঢ়ক]. [Arab. *jyljylau, duhu*; Pers. *kunjed*; Burm. *hnan*; Egypt. *semsem*; Tamil, *yelloo*; Teleg. *nuvu, nuvulu*; It. *sesamo*; Fr. *sesame*] [ভারতবর্ষে কৃষ্ণ, শ্বেত ও রক্ত ত্রিবিধ তিল উৎপন্ন হয়; তন্মধ্যে কৃষ্ণতিলই শ্রেষ্ঠ। যথা ভাবপ্রকাশে "কৃষ্ণঃ পথ্যতমঃ সিতোঽল্পগুণদঃ ক্ষীণাঃ কিলান্যে তিলাঃ। ইতি রাজনির্ঘণ্টঃ। "কৃষ্ণঃ শ্রেষ্ঠতমস্তেষু শুক্লো মধ্যমঃ সিতঃ। অন্যে হীনতরাঃ প্রোক্তাস্তজজ্ঞে রক্তাদয়স্তিলাঃ। ইতি ভাবপ্রকাশঃ]। **Open sesame**—আরব্যোপন্যাসোক্ত আলিবাবা ও চল্লিশ জন দস্যুর গল্পের "সিসেম দ্বার খোল" বাক্য—যাহা উচ্চারণ করিলে দস্যুদিগের গুপ্তদ্বার উন্মুক্ত হইত; কোন গহন বা দুষ্প্রবেশ্য বিষয়ে প্রবেশ লাভের গুপ্ত বা নিগূঢ় উপায়, উদ্ঘাটন মন্ত্র।

sĕs'-ă-moid (-moyd), *adj.* & *n.* Like sesame grain; nodular; তিলবৎ, তিলাকার, তিলাকৃতি; পিণ্ডাকার। ***Noun.*** Same as SESAMOID-BONES. **Sesamoid-bones**—তিলাকৃতি অস্থিসমূহ (যথা পদাঙ্গুলীর সন্ধিদেশের অস্থিসমূহ, বৃদ্ধাঙ্গুষ্ঠের সন্ধির অস্থিসমূহ)।

sĕs'-ă-mŭm, *n.* Same as SESAME above.

Sesbania Aegyptiaca — জয়ন্তি, জয়ন্তিকা (বেলঃ)

sĕs'-ĕ-li, *n.* A genus of umbelliferous plants; ছত্রপুষ্পী, পুষ্পসমূহের 'গণ' বিশেষ।

sĕs'-qui–, A prefix signifying one integer or whole and a half; সার্দ্ধসূচক অব্যয়।

sĕs-qui-ăl'-têr-ăl, *adj.* (*Math.*) One and a half more; (গণিতশাস্ত্র) সার্দ্ধ।

sĕs-qui-câr'-bō-nāte, *n.* A salt composed of $1\frac{1}{2}$ equivalents of carbonic acid and one equivalent of any base, or in the proportion of three of the one and two of the other; যে মিশ্র পদার্থে ৩ ভাগ অঙ্গারাম্ল এবং ২ ভাগ কোন প্রকার ভস্ম থাকে।

sĕs'-qui-cĕn-tĕn'-ni-ăl, *adj.* & *n.* Of, or pertaining to, a century and a half; সার্দ্ধশতবার্ষিক। ***Noun.*** One hundred and fiftieth anniversary; সার্দ্ধশতবার্ষিক উৎসব।

sĕs-qui-dŭ'-pli-cāte, *adj.* Denoting the ratio of two and a half to one; একের সহিত আড়াইএর অনুপাতজ্ঞাপক (যথা ২৫এর ১০)।

sĕs'-qui-ŏx'-īde, –id, *ns.* (*Chem.*) An oxide containing three atoms of oxygen and two of another element; (রসায়নশাস্ত্র) যে অম্লজানজারিত ধাতুতে অম্লজানের ৩ পরমাণু এবং অপর মূল পদার্থের ২ পরমাণু থাকে।

sĕs-qui-pē-dā'-li-ăn, *adj.* Measuring a foot and a half; দেড়-ফুট লম্বা (রহস্যচ্ছলে দীর্ঘশব্দ সম্বন্ধে প্রযুক্ত হয়)।

sĕs-quip'-li-cāte, *adj.* Designating the proportion one quantity or number has to another in the ratio of $1\frac{1}{2}$ to one; সার্দ্ধানুপাতসূচক।

sĕss, *n.* See CESS.

sĕs'-sīle, *adj.* **1.** (*Bot.*) Growing directly from the stem, without foot-stalk; অবৃন্ত, (সাঃ পঃ), অবৃন্তক (ঐ)। **2.** (*Zool.*) Permanently attached; (জন্তুবিদ্যা) নিত্যযুক্ত, নিত্যসম্বদ্ধ। **Sessile leaf**—অবৃন্তক পত্র (সাঃ পঃ)।

Sessile leaves.

ses'-sion (sĕ-), *n.* **1.** (*Rare*) The act of sitting ; the state of being seated ; (ক্বচিদ্‌ব্যবহৃত) উপবেশন ; উপবিষ্টাবস্থা। **2.** A continuous series of sittings of a court, council, legislature or the like for the transaction of business ; time or term for such sitting ; আদালত, ব্যবস্থাপক সভা, প্রভৃতির নিরবচ্ছিন্ন অধিবেশন ; ঐরূপ অধিবেশনের কাল। **3.** (*Law, pl.*) A sitting of justices in court upon commission ; দায়রা। **–al,** *adj.* **Court of Sessions**—(ভারতে) দায়রা আদালত ; (স্কটলণ্ডে) সর্ব্বোচ্চ দেওয়ানী আদালত। The period of time between the meeting and prorogation of parliament ; পার্লেমেণ্ট অধিবেশন এবং স্থগিত হওয়ার মধ্যবর্ত্তী কাল। **Petty-sessions**—ক্ষুদ্র ক্ষুদ্র অপরাধের সরাসরি বিচারের জন্য Justice of the peace সমূহের আদালতের অধিবেশন। **Quarter-sessions**—ইংলণ্ডের প্রতি জেলায় (county) জষ্টিস অব দি পিস ও স্বায়ত্ত শাসনাধিকারপ্রাপ্ত (boroughs) নগরীতে বৎসরে চারিবার রেকর্ডারগণের যে আদালত বসে। **To commit to the sessions**—সেসনে সোপর্দ্দ করা, দায়রায় সোপর্দ্দ করা।

sĕs'-terce (-têrs), **–têr-ti-ŭs** (-shĕ-), *ns.* Ancient Roman coin worth about 2*d.* ; প্রাচীন রোমের মুদ্রাবিশেষ।

sĕs-têr'-ti-ŭm (-shĭ-), *n.* (*Rom. Antiq.*) A money of account equal to 1000 sesterces ; (রোমক প্রত্নতত্ত্ব) প্রাচীন রোমনগরীর হিসাবে ব্যবহৃত মুদ্রাবিশেষ।

sĕt, *v. t.* & *i.* **1.** To cause to sit ; to fix ; to place ; উপবিষ্ট করা ; পোঁতা, বসান, গাড়া, লাগান, সন্নিবিষ্ট করা ; রাখা। **2.** To place a brooding fowl on a nest containing eggs ; মোরগকে ডিমের উপর বসান। **3.** To fix as precious stones on metal ; as, a diamond *set* in ring ; মণি প্রভৃতি বসান। **4.** To adorn with precious stones ; মণি-রত্নাদিদ্বারা খচিত করা, জড়িত করা, মুক্তাহীরকাদিদ্বারা খচিত করা, রত্ন-চিত্রিত করা (cf. কেবলং চন্দনেনৈব নির্ম্মিত রত্নচিত্রিতং — বিশ্বকর্ম্মাপ্রকাশ)। **5.** To propel a boat with a punting rod ; লগিদ্বারা (নৌকা) চালান। **6.** To plant ; রোপণ করা। **7.** To regulate or adjust ; as, to *set* a watch by the sun ; ঠিক করা। **8.** To point out by stretching out the tail ; as, a dog *sets* birds ; লাঙ্গুলপ্রসারণপূর্ব্বক নির্দ্দেশ করা। **9.** To fix beforehand ; to render stiff ; as, to *set* one's face ; to determine ; পূর্ব্বে স্থির করা ; শক্ত, অনমনীয় বা আড়ষ্ট করা ; স্থির করা, ধার্য্য করা। **10.** To fit to music ; সুরবাঁধা, সুর দেওয়া, সুর বসান। **11.** To reduce from a dislocated or fractured state, as a bone ; ভগ্ন বা সন্ধিচ্যুত অস্থি প্রভৃতি ঠিক করিয়া বসান। **12.** To give a fine edge ; ক্ষুর প্রভৃতি ধার দেওয়া, ধারাল করা, শাণিত করা। **13.** To spread as sails ; পাইল প্রভৃতি বিস্তার করা। **14.** To assign as a price ; মূল্য নির্দ্দেশ করা। **15.** To instigate, as a dog ; কুকুর প্রভৃতি লেলিয়ে দেওয়া, টোয়ান। **16.** To convert into curd ; (দুধ) টকিয়ে দেওয়া, বসান, জমান **17.** To embarrass or perplex ; "They are hard *set* to represent the bill as a grievance" ; হতবুদ্ধি করা, কিংকর্ত্তব্যবিমূঢ় করা, বিভ্রান্ত করা। **18.** (*Printing*) To compose ; as, to *set* types ; অক্ষর বিন্যাস করা, কম্পোজ করা। ***Verb i,*** **1.** To pass below the horizon ; অস্তমিত হওয়া, অস্ত যাওয়া, ডুবা, পাটে বসা (*colloq.* or *poet.*), অস্তাচলচূড়াবলম্বী হওয়া (about to set, *Rhet.*) অস্তগমন করা, অস্তমিত হওয়া, অস্তনিমগ্ন হওয়া (cf. বিড়ম্বয়ত্য-নিমগ্নসূর্য্যং — রঘুবংশ ১৬শ সর্গ), অস্তাবলম্বী হওয়া, (about to set) অস্তোন্মুখ হওয়া (*ib.*), অস্তশিখরাবলম্বী হওয়া (*rhet. ib.*), ঢলিয়া পড়া (about to set) । **2.** (*Fig.*) To decline ; "The glory of Egypt seemed to *set*" (মিসরের গৌরবরবি অস্তমিত বলিয়া প্রতিভাত হইল); to come to an end ; (লক্ষণায়) অস্তমিত হওয়া ; অবসানপ্রাপ্ত হওয়া, অবকাস প্রাপ্ত হওয়া। [cf. "আয়ুসূর্য্য অস্ত যায়"। "বিষয়িণঃ কস্যাপদোঽস্তং গতাঃ"—পঞ্চতন্ত্র। "ধৃতিরস্ত-মিতা"—রঘুবংশ। "অস্তমিতৈষা কথা"—কিরাতঃ। "শাপেনাস্তংগমিতমহিমা"—মেঘদূত।] **3.** To plant ; রোপণ করা। **4.** (*Colloq.*) To fit ; as, this suit *sets* well ; (চলিত ভাষায়) মানান, মানানসই হওয়া। **5.** To begin a journey, (always with *out*) ; রওয়ানা হওয়া, যাত্রা করা। **6.** To have a certain direction in motion ; to flow ; as, the current *sets* to the north ; কোন নির্দ্দিষ্ট দিকে উন্মুখ হওয়া ; প্রবাহিত হওয়া, বহা। **7.** To congeal or concrete ; জমিয়া যাওয়া, বসিয়া যাওয়া। **8.** To face one's partner in dancing ; নৃত্যকালে সহনর্ত্তকের সম্মুখীন হওয়া। **9.** To indicate the position of a game (said of a dog) ; (কুকুর সম্পর্কে) শিকারের অবস্থান নির্দ্দেশ করা। **10.** To become fixed or rigid ; to be fixed hard, closely or firmly ; "(It) maketh the teeth to *set* hard one against the other" ; কঠিন হওয়া, দৃঢ় হওয়া ; দৃঢ়ভাবে লাগা, কপাটি লাগা। **11.** To undertake earnestly ; to apply one's self ; as, to *set* to work ; সোৎসাহে প্রবৃত্ত হওয়া ; উঠিয়া পড়িয়া লাগা। **Set a beggar on horse-back he will ride to the devil**—আ-দ্যাখলার হ'লো ঘটী জল খেতে খেতে দাঁতকপাটী, অধমেন ধনং প্রাপ্য তৃণবৎ মন্যতে জগৎ। **Set with**—জড়িত, জড়ান (cf. হীরে জড়ান বালা), খচিত, চিত্রিত (See set *Verb t.* 4.) **Set with jewels**—পাথরবসানো, রত্ন-খচিত, রত্নানুবিদ্ধ, রত্নচিত্রিত। **To be hard set** — To be in great difficulty ; মহাসঙ্কটে পতিত হওয়া।

To be set—To be arranged ; বিন্যস্ত হওয়া । **To be set round** or **about with**—To be encircled with ; বেষ্টিত হওয়া, পরিবৃত হওয়া, বলয়িত হওয়া । **To be set with**—To be overgrown with ; উপরে জাত হওয়া । **To be sharp** or **keen set** — To be hungry ; ক্ষুধার্ত্ত হওয়া । **To be well set up, To be straight set up**—To have a close or compact body ; সুদৃঢ়দেহবিশিষ্ট হওয়া । To begin the use of ; ব্যবহার আরম্ভ করা । To restore to health ; স্বাস্থ্যপ্রদান করা । To put as a rival ; to incite ; প্রতিদ্বন্দ্বিস্বরূপ দাঁড় করা ; উত্তেজিত করা । **To set about** — To take in hand ; to begin ; হাতে নেওয়া ; আরম্ভ করা । To attack ; আক্রমণ করা । **To set abroach**—To tap and leave running ; পিপার মুখ খুলিয়া মদ্যাদি নিঃসৃত হইতে দেওয়া । To publish ; to spread ; প্রচার করা ; ছড়ান । **To set a butterfly**—To arrange a butterfly as an entomological specimen ; কীটবিদ্যানুশীলনের কাষ্ঠ প্রভৃতির ফলকে প্রজাপতি সাজাইয়া রাখা । **To set a clock**—To set it right ; ঘড়ী ঠিক করিয়া দেওয়া । **To set a colour**—To make a colour fast ; রং পাকা করা । **To set a fabric** — To fix the texture of a fabric ; কাপড়ের জমি কিরূপ করিতে হইবে তাহা ঠিক করা । **To set a face upon (a thing)**—To cause to put on a false appearance ; প্রকৃতভাব গোপন করতঃ কৃত্রিম ভাব ধারণ করা । **To set a fox to keep one's geese**—বাঘের হাতে ছাগল ভাগী দেওয়া । **To set against** — To oppose ; to attack ; বিরুদ্ধে দণ্ডায়মান হওয়া ; আক্রমণ করা । To compensate ; ক্ষতিপূরণ করা । To place in comparison ; তুলনার জন্য স্থাপিত করা । To move in an opposite direction ; বিপরীত দিকে চলা । **To set a-going**—To cause to move ; চালাইয়া দেওয়া । **To set a mark upon**—To mark with a special mark ; বিশেষ চিহ্নে চিহ্নিত করা । **To set an edge upon**—To give a keenness to ; ধারাল করা, শাণিত করা । **To set an example**—To do an act so that others may do the same ; দৃষ্টান্ত প্রদর্শন করা । **To set apart**—To separate for a special purpose ; বিশেষ উদ্দেশ্যে পৃথক করিয়া রাখা । **To set a person on the (or on his) way**—To put a person on the way leading to some place ; কোন স্থানে যাওয়ার পথে রাখিয়া আসা । **To set a picture**—To frame a picture ; ছবি বাঁধা । **To set a price on**—To fix a price ; মূল্য নির্দ্ধারণ করা । **To set a price on** or **upon one's head**—To offer a reward for taking one's life ; কাহাকে, বধ করার জন্য পুরস্কার ঘোষণা করা, কাহারো মাথা লওয়ার জন্য পুরস্কার ঘোষণা করা । **To set a sail**—To spread a sail ; পাইল খাটান । **To set a saw**—To bend every alternate tooth to one side, and the remainder to the other ; করাতের এক একটী অন্তর দাঁত একদিকে হেলান ও অবশিষ্ট দাঁত অপর দিকে হেলাইয়া দেওয়া । **To set aside**—To omit or pass over for the present ; ফেলিয়া রাখা । To abrogate ; to annul ; রদ করা ; রহিত করা, নাকচ করা, বাতিল করা, অন্যথা করা । To reject ; অগ্রাহ্য করা । To separate for a particular purpose; কোন বিশেষ উদ্দেশ্যের জন্য পৃথক করিয়া রাখা । (*Setting aside* — ব্যতীতও, ছাড়াও ব্যতিরেকেও) । **To set a stone**—To adorn an ornament with a stone or stones ; পাথর বসান । **To set at**—To attack ; আক্রমণ করা । **To set a table**—To spread a table with food ; মেজের উপর ব্যঞ্জনাদির পাত্র সাজান । **To set a task on**—To set an additional task on a boy by way of punishment ; শাস্তিস্বরূপ কোন বালকের উপর অতিরিক্ত কার্য্যভার চাপাইয়া দেওয়া । **To set at ease**—To keep in a peaceful state of mind ; খাতিরজমা রাখা । **To set at defiance**—To defy ; তুচ্ছ করা, উড়াইয়া দেওয়া । **To set at large**—To liberate ; মুক্তিপ্রদান করা, মুক্তি দেওয়া । **To set at liberty**—Same as TO SET AT LARGE. **To set at little**—To defy ; তুচ্ছ করা । **To set at naught**—See NAUGHT. **To set a trap** or **snare**—To place a trap to catch a bird etc. ; (*fig.*) to lay a plan of deceit in order to draw one into one's power ; ফাঁদ পাতা ; (লক্ষণায়) কাহারো জন্য ফাঁদ ফেলিবার চেষ্টা করা । **To set at rest**—To tranquilise ; সুস্থির করা, নিশ্চিন্ত করা, শান্ত করা । To settle ; মিটমাট করা, মিটাইয়া ফেলা, মীমাংসা করা, চুকাইয়া ফেলা । **To set at the least, To set at nothing, To set at no store, To set at no value, To set at a pease, To set at a pie's heel, To set at no price** -- To treat as of no account ; নগণ্য মনে করা, তুচ্ছ মনে করা, তৃণবৎ গণ্য করা । **To set at variance** — To bring into a state of disagreement ; বিরোধ জন্মান, অনৈক্য ঘটান । **To set at war** — To bring into a state of war ; যুদ্ধে প্রবৃত্ত করা । **To set at work**—To start on work ; কাজে লাগান । To engage in some work or show how to begin it ; কোন কার্য্যে নিযুক্ত করা, কোন কার্য্য ধরাইয়া দেওয়া । **To set away** — To lay up for future use ; তুলিয়া রাখা ।

To set back — To oppose ; প্রতিরোধ করা, বাধা দেওয়া। To put the hand of a clock to an earlier time ; ঘড়ীর কাঁটা পশ্চাদ্দিকে ঘুরাইয়া দেওয়া। To flow in a reverse direction ; উজান বহা। **To set before**—To hold before ; সম্মুখে স্থাপিত করা, উপস্থাপিত করা। **To set books**—To prescribe books ; পুস্তক নির্দ্দিষ্ট করা। **To set bounds to**—To fix a limit ; সীমা নির্দ্ধারণ করা। **To set by**—To lay up for future use ; তুলিয়া রাখা। (*Obs.*) To esteem ; (অপ্রঃ) সমাদর করা, শ্রদ্ধা করা। **To set by the ears**—See EAR. **To set down** — To snub ; to rebuke ; দাবান ; তিরস্কার করা। To attribute ; আরোপ করা। To put upon the ground ; মাটীতে বা মেঝের উপর রাখা। To put in writing ; to relate ; লিখিয়া রাখা ; বর্ণনা করা, বিবৃত করা। To fix ; নির্দ্ধারণ করা, প্রতিষ্ঠিত করা। To consider ; to rank ; গণ্য করা, বিবেচনা করা; এক শ্রেণীতে ফেলা। To situate ; অবস্থিত হওয়া। To cause to descend from a vehicle ; গাড়ী হইতে নামাইয়া দেওয়া। To be seated; বসা, উপবিষ্ট হওয়া। To begin ; to undertake ; আরম্ভ করা ; কোন কার্য্যে প্রবৃত্ত হওয়া। To have a direction toward ; কোন নির্দ্দিষ্ট দিকে উন্মুখ হওয়া। **To set down as for**—To consider to be ; কোন কিছু বলিয়া গণ্য বা বিবেচনা করা। **To set down to**—To attribute to ; আরোপ করা। **To set fire to**—To apply fire to ; to kindle ; অগ্নিসংযোগ করা ; জ্বালাইয়া দেওয়া। **To set free**—To liberate ; মুক্ত করা, মুক্তি দেওয়া। **To set foot on** or **in**—To place one's foot on or in ; পদার্পণ করা। **To set forth**—To lay out ; খাটান, (ব্যবসায়ে) টাকা ফেলা। To publish ; প্রচার করা, বাহির করা, প্রকাশিত করা। To arrange ; বিন্যাস করা। (*Verb t.*) To start ; রওনা হওয়া, যাত্রা করা। To express in details ; to narrate ; সবিস্তারে বলা ; বর্ণনা করা, বিবৃত করা। **To set forward**—To carry or thrust forward ; অগ্রে নেওয়া, ঠেলিয়া অগ্রসর করা। To put a clock's hands onward ; ঘড়ীর কাঁটা আগেরদিকে ঘুরাইয়া দেওয়া। **To set free**—To liberate ; মুক্ত করা, খালাস করা, ছাড়িয়া দেওয়া, মুক্তি দেওয়া। **To set hand to, To set one's hand to**—To undertake some work ; কোন কাজে হাত দেওয়া। To put one's signature ; স্বাক্ষর করা। **To set in**—To begin ; আরব্ধ হওয়া, সুরু হওয়া। To give a start to ; to put in ; আরম্ভ করা ; বরাইয়া দেওয়া, লাগাইয়া দেওয়া। To become settled in a particular state কোন বিশেষ অবস্থাতে স্থির হওয়া। **To set in action**—To cause to act ; চালাইয়া দেওয়া। To cause to move ; চালান। **To set in motion**—To start ; চালান। **To set in order**—To adjust or arrange ; to reduce to method ; ঠিকঠাক করা ; শৃঙ্খলাবদ্ধ করা। **To set milk**—To expose milk in open dishes at a certain temperature in order that the cream may rise to the surface ; সর ফেলার জন্য দুধ চুল্লীর উপরে উন্মুক্ত পাত্রে রাখা। To cause milk to be curdled, as by rennet ; দুধ জমান, ছানা করা, দুধ বসান। **To set much** or **little by**—To esteem highly ; অতিশয় সমাদর করা ; অল্প আদর করা। **To set off**—To place against, as an equivalent ; তুলনার জন্য তুল্য-বস্তুর বিরুদ্ধে দাঁড় করা। To adorn ; অলঙ্কৃত করা, মণ্ডিত করা, ভূষিত করা। To show off to the best advantage ; উৎকৃষ্টতমরূপে প্রদর্শন করা, যথাসম্ভব সুবিধাজনকরূপে প্রদর্শন করা। To form a contrast with ; বৈষম্য বা বৈপরীত্য প্রদর্শন করা। To commend ; প্রশংসা করা, গুণগান করা। To start ; রওনা হওয়া, যাত্রা করা। To compensate ; ক্ষতিপূরণ করা। To make conspicuous by contrast ; বৈপরীত্যপ্রদর্শনদ্বারা সুস্পষ্ট বা সুপ্রকট করা। To assign to a particular purpose ; কোন বিশেষ উদ্দেশ্য-সাধনের জন্য নির্দ্দিষ্ট করিয়া রাখা। **To set on**—To place upon ; কোন কিছুর উপর রাখা, স্থাপন করা। To urge as a dog etc. to attack ; লেলাইয়া দেওয়া, টোয়াইয়া দেওয়া। To incite ; উত্তেজিত করা, উস্কাইয়া দেওয়া, লেলাইয়া দেওয়া। To appoint a person to do something ; কোন লোককে কোন কার্য্য সম্পাদনের জন্য নিযুক্ত করা। To begin to work ; কার্য্য আরম্ভ করা। (*Verb i.*) To advance ; অগ্রসর হওয়া। To set a-going ; চালান। **To set on edge**—To incite ; উত্তেজিত করা। **To set one person against another**—To place in opposition ; একজনকে অপরের বিরুদ্ধে দাঁড় করা। **To set one's cap at**—See CAP. **To set one's eyes up**—To look upon ; দৃষ্টিপাত করা, দৃষ্টিনিবদ্ধ করা। **To set one's face against**—See FACE. **To set one's face** or **countenance**—To give a fixed expression to one's face ; মুখে একটা স্থির ভাব প্রকটিত করা। **To set one's face like a flint**—To be determined ; দৃঢ়প্রতিজ্ঞ হওয়া, স্থিরসংকল্প হওয়া। **To set one's hand to**—To undertake a work ; কোন কার্য্যে হাত দেওয়া। **To set one's heart at rest**—To remove one's anxiety ; কাহারো মন শান্ত করা। **To set one's heart** or **mind on**—To cause one's affections to be centred on ; মনঃপ্রাণ অর্পণ করা। **To set one's house in order** — To prepare for death by making one's will ; স্বীয় বিষয়সম্পত্তির শেষ বন্দোবস্ত করিয়া মৃত্যুর জন্য প্রস্তুত হওয়া। **To set one's self**

against—To place one's self determinedly in opposition; দৃঢ়ভাবে বিরুদ্ধে স্থাপন করা। **To set one's teeth** — To press one's teeth tightly together as a sign of strong determination; স্থিরপ্রতিজ্ঞতার চিহ্নস্বরূপ দন্তে দন্তে দৃঢ়ভাবে সংশ্লিষ্ট করা। **To set one's teeth on edge**—See EDGE. **To set one's wits to work**—To think upon a matter; কোন বিষয়ের চিন্তা করা। **To set on fire**—To kindle; জ্বালাইয়া দেওয়া। To communicate fire to; অগ্নিসংযোগ করা। To fill with disorder; লণ্ডভণ্ড করা। To inflame the passion of; কামানল বা ক্রোধানল প্রজ্বালিত করা। **To set on foot**—See FOOT. **To set on the rack**—To give extreme bodily or mental pain; নিরতিশয় শারীরিক বা মানসিক যন্ত্রণা দেওয়া। **To set out** — To start; রওয়ানা হওয়া, যাত্রা করা। To furnish; সমন্বিত করা, লাগান। To spread out; ছড়ান। To display; প্রদর্শন করা। To mark out; to mark out the boundary of; চিহ্নিত করা; সীমাচিহ্নিত করা। To adorn; মণ্ডিত করা, ভূষিত করা। To assign or allot; নির্দ্দিষ্ট করা, চিহ্নিত করিয়া দেওয়া। To arrange; বিন্যাস করা। To project; বহিরুদ্গত হওয়া, প্রলম্বিত হওয়া। To begin a course; কোন কার্য্য আরম্ভ করা, কোন প্রণালী মত বলিতে সুরু করা। To publish; প্রচার করা। **To set out for** — To start for; কোন স্থানে যাত্রা করা। **To set out in life**—To begin the world; সাংসারিক জীবনে প্রবেশ করা, সাংসারিক-জীবন আরম্ভ করা। **To set over**—To transfer; হস্তান্তরিত করা। To state at large; সবিস্তারে বর্ণনা করা। (*Verb i.*) To have a beginning; উদ্ভূত হওয়া। To appoint as a supervisor, inspector, governor or director; পরিদর্শক, পরিচালক বা শাসকের কার্য্যে নিযুক্ত করা। **To set pen to paper**—To write; লিখা, কালিকলমে এক করা। **To set questions**—To propound questions to be answered; প্রশ্ন করা। **To set right**—To adjust; ঠিক করা। To correct; ঠিক করা, শোধরান, দুরস্ত করা। **To set sail**—To start on a sea-voyage; সমুদ্রযাত্রা করা, জলযাত্রা করা। **To set spurs to**—To prick with spurs to cause to move faster; দ্রুততরবেগে ছুটাইবার জন্য পাদুকাসংলগ্ন লৌহশঙ্কু দ্বারা বিদ্ধ করা। **To set store by** or **on**—To value greatly; অতিশয় মূল্যবান জ্ঞানে সমাদর করা। **To set teeth** — To fix teeth; দাঁত বসান। **To set the axe to**—To apply an axe to; কুঠারাঘাত করা। **To set the face, To set one's face** — To put a settled expression to one's face; মুখে একটা স্থিরভাব প্রকটন করা। **To set the fashion**—To determine what shall be the leading fashion; ফ্যাসন নির্দ্ধারণ করা। **To set the fruit**—To develop as the result of fertilization; to cause a flower to develop into fruit; পরাগনিষেকদ্বারা বৃক্ষে ফল উৎপাদন করা; পুষ্পকে ফলে পরিণত করা। **To set the land** — To observe by the compass in what direction from the ship the land-lies; দিগ্‌দর্শন যন্ত্রের সাহায্যে জাহাজের কোনদিকে ভূমি আছে তাহা পর্য্যবেক্ষণ করা। **To set the pace** — To proceed at a rate of speed to be followed by another; এরূপ বেগে অগ্রসর হওয়া যাহাতে পশ্চাতের ব্যক্তি অনুসরণ করিতে পারে। **To set the sponge**—To leaven a mass of flour; ময়দার পিণ্ডে তাড়ির বীজ মিশান। **To set the table in a roar**—See ROAR (*Noun*)। **To set the teeth on edge** — To irritate; জ্বালাতন করা, চটান। **To set the Thames on fire**—See THAMES. **To set to** — To affix; লাগান, সংলগ্ন করা। To apply one's self to; কার্য্যে প্রবৃত্ত হওয়া, নিযুক্ত হওয়া, লাগা। To begin to fight; যুদ্ধ আরম্ভ করা। **To set together**—To prepare the milk for coagulation by adding the rennet; দুধ জমান। **To set to work**—To engage in some work; কোন কার্য্যে নিযুক্ত করা। To be engaged in some work; কোন কার্য্যে নিযুক্ত হওয়া। **To set up**—To erect; খাড়া করা, গাঁথিয়া তোলা। To raise; as, *to set up* a shout; তোলা। (*Print.*) To put in type; কম্পোজ করা, অক্ষরবিন্যাস করা। To post up notice; to advertize; বিজ্ঞাপন আঁটা; বিজ্ঞাপন দেওয়া। To place in an exalted position; to establish on a throne; উচ্চপদে প্রতিষ্ঠিত করা; সিংহাসনে প্রতিষ্ঠিত করা। To establish; প্রতিষ্ঠিত করা, প্রতিষ্ঠাপিত করা, প্রতিষ্ঠা করা। To lay claim to; দাবী করা। To advance or put forward; খাড়া করা, দাঁড় করা, উপস্থাপিত করা। (*Verb i.*) To begin business; ব্যবসায় আরম্ভ করা, ব্যবসায়ে প্রবৃত্ত হওয়া। (*Naut.*) To extend, as the shrouds, stays, etc.; মাস্তুলের দড়াদড়ি খাটান। To start in a new business; নূতন ব্যবসায়ে প্রতিষ্ঠিত করা, নূতন ব্যবসায়ে প্রবৃত্ত হওয়ার উপযোগী ব্যবস্থা করিয়া দেওয়া। To raise from depression; মানসিক অবসাদ দূর করা, উৎফুল্ল করা। To clear a certain route for the free passage of train; রেলগাড়ী চলার জন্য পথ পরিষ্কার করা। To be elated; to make elated; উৎফুল্ল হওয়া; উৎফুল্ল করা। To restore; to re-establish; প্রত্যর্পণ করা; পুনঃ প্রতিষ্ঠিত করা। **To set up**

for—To make pretensions to the character of ; কোন কিছু বলিয়া আপনাকে দাবী করা বা চালাইতে চেষ্টা করা। **To set up for oneself**—To start on a career on one's account ; স্বাধীনভাবে কোনরূপ জীবনব্যাপার আরম্ভ করা। **To set upon**—To attack ; আক্রমণ করা। **To set up one's back**—To excite one's anger ; কাহারো ক্রোধ উদ্দীপ্ত করা। **To set up one's bristles**—To be angry ; ক্রুদ্ধ হওয়া। **To set up one's comb or hair**—To be puffed up with pride ; গর্ব্বে ফুলিয়া উঠা। (*U. S.*) To treat to ; ভোজ্য, পেয়, প্রভৃতি দ্বারা আপ্যায়িত করা। To appoint ; নিযুক্ত করা। To put together the parts of a machine and cause it to stand in position ; যন্ত্রের বিভিন্ন অংশ সংযোজনপূর্ব্বক উহাকে দাঁড় করান। **Well set up**—সুগঠিত দৃঢ়কায়।

sĕt, *n.* & *adj.* **1.** The apparent descent of a heavenly body below the horizon ; অস্তগমন, অস্তপ্রয়াণ। **2.** (*Fig.*) Close ; termination; (লক্ষণায়) শেষ; অন্ত, অবসান। **3.** A collection of things of similar use ; প্রস্থ, সেট, দফা। **4.** A number of persons associated ; as, a *set* of men ; একদল লোক। **5.** A clique ; কুচক্রিদল। **6.** Attitude; build ; "Money in possession do give a *set* to the head and confidence to the voice" ; ভঙ্গী, ঢঙ্গ ; গঠন। **7.** A young plant for putting into the soil for growth ; রোপণের জন্য ক্ষুদ্র চারা। **8.** Direction or course ; as, the *set* of the tide ; দিক বা গমনপথ। **9.** (*Obs.*) A wager ; a game ; (অপ্রঃ) বাজী, পণ ; খেলা। **10.** Tendency ; as, the *set* of one's mind ; ঝোঁক, আসক্তি, প্রবণতা। **11.** Alternate deflection of saw-teeth ; করাতের দাঁত একটীর পর একটী করিয়া একদিকে এবং অবশিষ্ট গুলি একদিকে প্রবণ করণ। **12.** A potato or a portion of a potato used as seed ; বীজস্বরূপ ব্যবহৃত আলু বা আলুর অংশ। **13.** A square stone for paving ; রাস্তা প্রভৃতি বাঁধার জন্য সমচতুষ্কোণাকারে কর্ত্তিত প্রস্তর। **14.** A permanent change of figure caused by pressure ; চাপহেতু আকারের স্থায়ী পরিবর্ত্তন। *Adj.* **1.** Fixed ; as, a *set* countenance ; firm ; দৃঢ়সংবদ্ধ ; দৃঢ়। **2.** Established ; prescribed ; প্রতিষ্ঠিত ; নির্দ্দিষ্ট, বিহিত। **3.** Predetermined ; পূর্ব্বনির্দ্ধারিত। **4.** Regular ; নিয়মিত। **5.** (*Colloq.*) Conceited ; (চলিতভাবায়) গর্ব্বিত, দৃপ্ত। **Dead set**—বদ্ধ অবস্থা, নিশ্চল অবস্থা; মরিয়া ভাবে আক্রমণ, বিরুদ্ধাবস্থা; পুরুষের প্রণয় লাভের জন্য স্ত্রীলোকের প্রাণান্তকর চেষ্টা। **Dinner set**—Dinner service ; অপরাহ্নভোজনের জন্য এক প্রস্থ চীনবাসন, চামচ, কাঁটা প্রভৃতি। **Set-back**—বাধা, ভাগ্যবিপর্য্যয়; পরাভব; ধাক্কা। **Set-down** — রাস্তায় চলতি গাড়ীতে উঠিয়া কিছুপথ যাওয়ার সুযোগ ; তীব্র তিরস্কার, এক চোট গাল, মুখঝামটা ; দাবানি। **Set-fair**—বায়ুমান যন্ত্রের পারদস্তম্ভের সূচীর অগ্রভাগের বিপরীতদিকে অঙ্কিত শব্দ—যদ্দ্বারা বায়ুর অবস্থা ভালই আছে বলিয়া সূচিত হয়। **Set-in**—প্রারম্ভ। **Set-off**—যাত্রা, রওনা; পাল্টাদাবী, তুল্য মূল্য বস্তু ; অলঙ্কার, ভূষা, মণ্ডন। **Set-out**—নাট্য, প্রদর্শনী, নাচ গান, তামাসা, প্রীতিসম্মিলনী; দল; গোলমাল, গণ্ডগোল, হৈচৈ; সাজসজ্জা; প্রারম্ভ ; পোষাকপরিচ্ছদ:পরিধানের ধারা, পোষাক পরার রীতি বা ধরণ ; অশ্ব এবং অশ্বসজ্জাদিসমেত শকট ; আহারের জন্য মেজের উপর সজ্জিত খাদ্যদ্রব্য ; চীনাবাসন প্রভৃতির সেট, চীনাবাসন প্রভৃতি প্রদর্শন। **Set-piece, Set-scene**—কাঠামের উপর স্থাপিত দৃশ্যপট। **Set-speech**—পূর্ব্বে বাটীতে প্রস্তুত করিয়া আসিয়া সভাতে যে বক্তৃতা দেওয়া হয়, তৈরী বক্তৃতা। **Sharp-set**—ধারাল (করাত) ; ব্যগ্র, উৎকণ্ঠাকুল, উতলা ; প্রচণ্ড ক্রোধাবিষ্ট। **Set of day**—সূর্য্যাস্ত, দিনান্ত ; পশ্চিমদিক ; (লং জীবনের দিনান্ত, জীবনসন্ধ্যা। **Set to**—মুষ্টিযুদ্ধ ; যুদ্ধ, সংগ্রাম ; আক্রমণ **To make a dead set at**—To make a determined attack ; মরিয়া হইয়া আক্রমণ করা। To try her utmost to win the love of a man ; পুরুষের প্রণয়-লাভের জন্য প্রাণপণে চেষ্টা করা।

sē'-tă, *n.* (*Bot.*) Bristles when short and stiff ; অনুকণ্টক (সাঃ পঃ), শূক রোম (ঐ)।

sē-tā'-ceous (-shŭs), *adj.* **1.** Bristly; সকণ্টক। **2.** (*Bot.*) Pertaining to bristle ; having the form of a bristle ; অনুকণ্টকসম্বন্ধীয় ; অনুকণ্টকাকৃতি। **—ly,** *adv.*

sē-tĭf'-ēr-ous (-ŭs), *adj.* Having bristles ; কণ্টকযুক্ত।

sē'-tĭ-fôrm, *adj.* Having the form of a bristle ; অনুকণ্টকাকৃতি।

sē-tĭg'-ēr-ous (-ŭs), *adj.* Same as SETIFEROUS.

sē'-tŏn, *n.* (*Surg.*) A few horse hairs, or a twist of silk or fine linen, drawn through the skin by means of large needle, by which a small opening is made, and continued for the discharge of humours ; দীর্ঘ রেশম বা কার্পাস সূত্রের গুচ্ছ—যাহা বৃহৎ সূচী দ্বারা চর্ম্মের ভিতর দিয়া নীত হওয়ায় পূযাদি নির্গমনের জন্য ক্ষুদ্র রন্ধ্র গঠিত হয়।

sē'-tōse, *adj.* Same as SETIFEROUS.

sĕtt, *n.* *Var.* of SET.

sĕt-tee' (-tē), *n.* A long seat with a back ; a kind of arm-chair or short sofa for several persons to sit on at once ; উপবেশনের জন্য একপ্রকার দীর্ঘ আসন ; কয়েকজন লোকের একসময়ে বসিবার জন্য একপ্রকার আরামকেদারা বা ক্ষুদ্র সোফা, আরামখট্টা।

sĕt-tee' (-tē), *n.* A vessel with one deck, carrying two or three masts with lateen sails, used on the Mediterranean ; ভূমধ্যসাগরের দ্বি বা ত্রিমাস্তুল পোতবিশেষ।

tĕr, *n.* **1.** One who sets ; ব্যক্তি পাথর বসায়, অক্ষরবিন্যাসক, যে ব্যক্তি গানের সুর বাঁধে। **2.** A kind of long-haired dog for starting game, sitting or crouching when it perceives the scent ; একপ্রকার দীর্ঘরোমবিশিষ্ট শিকারী কুকুর—ইহারা শিকারের গন্ধ পাইবামাত্র গুঁড়ি মারিয়া বসে। **Setter-on**—প্ররোচক, উৎসাহদাতা।

sĕt′-ter-wôrt (-êr-), **sĕt′-ter-grăss** (-êr-), *ns.* The stinking Hellebore, or Bear's foot ; একপ্রকার গুল্ম।

sĕt′-ting (-ĭng), *n.* **1.** The act of one who sets ; বিন্যাস, সংস্থাপন, যোজনা, নিধান, সন্নিবেশ, রত্ন প্রভৃতি দ্বারা খচিত করণ, চিত্রণ, সংগ্রহণ [cf. কণকভূষণ সংগ্রহণোচিতঃ (মণিঃ—পঞ্চতন্ত্র)]। **2.** The apparent descent of a heavenly body below the horizon ; অস্তগমন, অস্তপ্রয়াণ। **3.** The mode of setting a jewel ; that in which something, as a jewel, is set ; as, the *setting* of a ring ; মণি প্রভৃতি বসাইবার প্রকার ; যে বস্তুতে কোন কিছু (যথা মণি প্রভৃতি) বসান হয়। **4.** The surroundings or environment of a person or thing ; "Mythology has a *setting* in geography and history" ; কোন বস্তুর চতুষ্পার্শ্ববর্ত্তী বস্তুরাজি, প্রতিবেশ, আবেষ্টন। **5.** The hardening of cement etc. ; চূণ বালি প্রভৃতির কাঠিন্যপ্রাপ্তি। **6.** The act of arranging or fitting words to music ; a musical arrangement of words ; সুর বাঁধন ; গত, ঠাট। **7.** Coagulation ; জমিয়া যাওন। **8.** The direction of a current ; প্রবাহের গতির দিক। **9.** The fixing of a stone in position in a wall ; প্রাচীরে শিলান্যাস। **10.** The way a play is put on the stage ; scenery, costumes, etc. ; রঙ্গমঞ্চে কোন নাট্য অবতারণের প্রণালী ; দৃশ্যপট, পোষাক প্রভৃতি। **Setting-board**—যে কাক (cork) দ্বারা আচ্ছাদিত ফলকের উপর কীটতত্ত্বানুশীলনের জন্য কীটসমূহ গাঁথিয়া রাখা হয়, কীটফলক। **Setting-box**—একপ্রকার বাক্স—যাহাতে দেরাজের মত কীটফলকশ্রেণী পরম্পরাক্রমে রক্ষিত হয়। **Setting-needle**—কীটফলকে কীট বসাইবার জন্য একপ্রকার সূচী, কীটসূচিকা। **Setting-rule**—Composing stick এ হরফ রাখিবার জন্য পিত্তল বা ইস্পাতের ফলকবিশেষ। **Setting-stick**—Same as COMPOSING STICK (for which see STICK).

sĕt′-tle (-l), *n.* A bench with a high back ; উঁচু পিঠওয়ালা দীর্ঘ আসন।

sĕt′-tle (-l), *v. t.* & *i.* **1.** To place in a fixed or permanent position ; to establish ; স্থায়ী পদে অধিষ্ঠিত করা ; প্রতিষ্ঠিত করা। **2.** To establish in business, life or like ; কোন ব্যবসায়ে বা সংসারিক জীবনে প্রতিষ্ঠিত করা। **3.** To decide ; as, to *settle* a question ; মীমাংসা করা, নিষ্পত্তি করা। **4.** To calm ; as, to let the excitement *settle* down ; স্থির করা, শান্ত করা। **5.** To adjust ; to clear off ; as, to *settle* a bill ; মিটান ; শোধ করা, পরিশোধ করা, চুকান। **6.** To put in order ; as, to *settle* a room ; to dispose of ; as, to *settle* an estate ; ঠিকঠাক করা, গুছান ; ব্যবস্থা করা। **7.** To cause to sink ; as, to *settle* the contents of a barrel by shaking it ; to render pure or clear ; থিতান ; নির্ম্মল বা বিশুদ্ধ করা। **8.** To people ; to colonize ; as, the French *settled* in Canada ; লোক বসান ; উপনিবেশ স্থাপন করা। **9.** To convey or secure by legal act or as pension, annuity ; বার্ষিক বৃত্তি প্রভৃতির ব্যবস্থা করিয়া দেওয়া। **10.** To free from uncertainty or wavering ; to determine ; সন্দেহ নিরাশ করা ; স্থির করা। **11.** (Of grounds, roads, etc.) To restore to a dry or passable state ; শুষ্ক বা গমনযোগ্য অবস্থায় আনা। **12.** (*Colloq.*) To give a finishing touch ; (চলিতভাষায়) শেষ চানকান দেওয়া। ***Verb i.*** **1.** To become fixed or permanent ; স্থায়ী হওয়া, সুপ্রতিষ্ঠিত হওয়া। **2.** To establish as a permanent residence ; স্থায়ী বসবাস স্থাপন করা। **3.** To descend and stop ; as, birds *settle* on trees ; অবতরণ করা। **4.** To sink down gradually ; (of the ground) to subside ; ধীরে ধীরে ডুবা ; বসিয়া যাওয়া। **5.** To sink to the bottom, as the dregs from a clarifying liquid ; to become clear and pure ; থিতাইয়া পড়া ; বিশুদ্ধ এবং নির্ম্মল হওয়া। **6.** To become calm ; শান্ত হওয়া। **7.** To marry and become established in life ; সংসারবাস আরম্ভ করা, গার্হস্থ্যাশ্রমে প্রবেশ করা। **8.** To decide ; as, to *settle* upon a plan ; স্থির করা। **9.** To adjust differences on account ; to come to an agreement ; মিটান, মিটমাট করা ; কোন বিষয়ে ঐক্য হওয়া। **–tled,** *p.p.* Fixed ; স্থিরীকৃত, অবধারিত, অটল, অচল। **Settled conviction**—স্থির বিশ্বাস, অটলবিশ্বাস। **That settles the matter**—আর কিছু বলিবার নাই। **To settle out of court**—মোকদ্দমা আপোষ করা।

sĕt′-tle-mĕnt (-l-), *n.* **1.** The act of settling, adjusting, accommodating or arranging ; বন্দোবস্ত, বিধি ব্যবস্থা, নির্দ্ধারণ, নিষ্পত্তি। **2.** Establishment in life, in business, or the like ; সংসারবাসে প্রতিষ্ঠা, ব্যবসায় প্রভৃতিতে প্রতিষ্ঠিত হওন। **3.** Ordination or installation as a pastor ; পল্লীযাজকপদে অভিষেক বা প্রতিষ্ঠা। **4.** Composure of doubts or differences ; মীমাংসা, কিনারা [cf. তার কিছু কিনারা করে যেতে পারলাম না—নবীনসন্ন্যাসী (প্রভাত)।] **5.** Colonization ; উপনিবেশস্থাপন। **6.** The act of settling down in a place ; কোন স্থানে বসবাস স্থাপন। **7.** Newly settled tract of country ; a colony ; নব উপনিবিষ্টপ্রদেশ ; উপনিবেশ। 8. The payment of an account ; হিসাব নিষ্পত্তি। 9. Bestowal by legal act ; a deed by which prosperty is settled ; দানপত্রাদিদ্বারা বৃত্তি প্রভৃতির ব্যবস্থা ; যে পত্র বা দলিল দ্বারা সম্পত্তি প্রভৃতির বিলিব্যবস্থা করা হয়। 10. The sum secured to a person, esp. a jointure made to a woman at her marriage ; কোন লোকের জন্য বৃত্তির ব্যবস্থা, বিশেষতঃ বিবাহকালে স্বামীর মৃত্যুর পর আজীবন ভোগের জন্য স্ত্রীকে যে সম্পত্তি বিলি ব্যবস্থা করিয়া দেওয়া হয়। 11. Subsidence of wall, house, etc. ; প্রাচীর প্রভৃতি বসিয়া যাওন। 12. (*India*) The act of arranging the terms and incidence of the land revenue over specified areas between the Government and the tenants ; (ভারতবর্ষে) সরকারকর্তৃক ভূমির জরিপ এবং বন্দোবস্ত, সেটেলমেণ্ট। **Settlement day**—হিসাব পরিষ্কারের দিন; (লণ্ডন নগরীর কোম্পানীর কাগজের বাজারে) হিসাব পরিষ্কারের শেষ দিন। **Act of Settlement**—১৭০২ খৃঃ অব্দে বিধিবদ্ধ আইনবিশেষ—যদ্দারা রাজ্ঞী এনের মৃত্যুর পর ১ম জেমসের পুত্রী হেনোভারের ইলেক্টরের পত্নী Sophia এবং তদীয় অঙ্গজাত Protestant মতাবলম্বী উত্তরাধিকারিগণ ইংলণ্ডের সিংহাসনে অধিরোহণ করিবে এইরূপ ব্যবস্থা করা হয়।

sĕt'-tler (-lêr), *n.* 1. One who settles in a colony ; ঔপনিবেশিক। 2. (*Colloq.*) A decisive blow, argument or the like ; "After the *settler* the man sat down" ; (চলিতভাষায়) চূড়ান্ত আঘাত, যুক্তি, প্রভৃতি, খতম ঘা। 3. A pan or vat in which something is allowed to settle ; যে পাত্রে কোন জিনিষ থিতান হয়।

sĕt'-wall, *n.* A species of valerian ; একপ্রকার লতা।

sĕv'-en (-n), *adj.* & *n.* One more than six ; সাত, সপ্ত। *Noun.* 1. The number greater than one by six ; সাত। 2. A playing card marked with seven tips ; তাসের সাতা। **-enth,** *adj.* সপ্তম। **-fold,** *adj.* সপ্তগুণ, সপ্তগুণিত। **-ti-eth,** *adj.* সপ্ততিতম। **-ty,** *adj.* & *n.* A **seven days' wonder**—যে বিষয় অল্পকাল জনসাধারণের বিস্ময় উৎপাদনের পর বিস্মৃতিগর্ভে নিমজ্জিত হয়। **Seven Bibles**—(১) খৃষ্টানদিগের বাইবেল গ্রন্থ ; (২) মুসলমানদিগের কোরাণ ; (৩) চিনাদিগের পঞ্চ কিং [পূর্ব্বে যে কাপড়ে উপর এই সমস্ত ধর্ম্মগ্রন্থ লিখিত হইত চীনাভাষায় তাহার নাম কিং]। (৪) বৌদ্ধদিগের ত্রিপিটক ; (৫) হিন্দুদিগের বেদ ; (৬) স্কাণ্ডিনিভিয়ানদিগের Eddas ; (৭) পারসীকদিগের জেন্দেবেস্ত (Zend-Avesta)। **Seven bishops** — Archbishop Sancroft, এবং Bishops Ken, Lake, Lloyd, Trelawney, Turner এবং White—যাঁহারা রাজা জেমসের Declaration of Indulgenceএর বিরুদ্ধে প্রতিবাদ করিয়াছিলেন। **Seven bodies in alchemy** — ইয়ুরোপীয় তান্ত্রিকদিগের সপ্তধাতু—রবি (=স্বর্ণ), চন্দ্র (=রৌপ্য), মঙ্গল (=লৌহ), বুধ (=পারদ), শনি (=সীসক), বৃহস্পতি (=রঙ্গ), শুক্র (=তাম্র)। **Seven champions of Christendom**—ইংলণ্ড, স্কটলণ্ড, ওয়েলেস, আয়র্লণ্ড, ফ্রান্স ও ইতালীদেশের রক্ষাকারী সপ্তমহাপুরুষ St. George, St. Andrew, St. David, St. Patrick, St. Denis, St. James এবং St. Anthony. **Seven deadly sins**—অহঙ্কার, ক্রোধ, মাৎসর্য্য, কাম, লোভ, ধনতৃষ্ণা, আলস্য। **Seven-hilled**—সপ্তশৈলের উপরি অবস্থিত (রোম নগরী)। **Seven joys of Mary**—খৃষ্টজননী মেরীর সপ্ত আনন্দ—(১) দেবদূত জেব্রিয়েলকর্তৃক খৃষ্টাবতরণ-ঘোষণা (The Annunciation) ; (২) John the Baptistএর জননী এলিজেবেথকে দর্শনপ্রদান ; কুমারী মেরীর আগমন (Visitation) ; (৩) প্রাচ্যদেশাগতজ্ঞানিগণকর্তৃক খৃষ্টার্চ্চনা (Adoration of the Magi) ; (৪) খৃষ্টজন্ম ; (৫) মন্দিরে আনয়ন (Presentation to the temple) ; (৬) পণ্ডিতগণের মধ্যে খৃষ্টকে দর্শন (Finding Christ among the Doctors) ; (৭) স্বর্গারোহণ (Assumption). **Seven league boots**—ছেলেদের উপকথায় উল্লিখিত বুটজুতা — যাহা পায়ে দিলে পবনবেগে বিচরণের ক্ষমতা জন্মিত। **Seven nights**—সপ্তরাত্র, একসপ্তাহ। **Seven Oceans**—উত্তর মহাসাগর, দক্ষিণ মহাসাগর, উত্তর এবং দক্ষিণ অতলান্তিক মহাসাগর, উত্তর এবং দক্ষিণ প্রশান্তমহাসাগর এবং ভারত মহাসাগর। **Seven sages** or **wise men**—প্রাচীন গ্রীসের সপ্তজ্ঞানী। (১) Athens নগরবাসী Solon (আপনাকে জান)। (২) Miletusএর Thales (জামিন হইলেই সর্ব্বনাশ)। (৩) Prieneএর Bias (বেশীর ভাগ লোকই মন্দ)। (৪) Lindusএর Cleobulus (শ্রেয়ঃ মধ্যপথ)। (৫) Spartaবাসী Chilo (অগ্রপশ্চাৎ ভাবিয়া কার্য্য করিও)। (৬) Corinthবাসী Periander (পরিশ্রমী লোকের অসাধ্য কিছুই নয়)। (৭) Myteleneবাসী Pittacus (সুযোগ বুঝিয়া কাজ করিবে)। উক্ত সপ্ত গ্রীক জ্ঞানীর নাম এবং তাঁহাদের উক্তি Delphi নগরীস্থ Appolo দেবের মন্দিরে উৎকীর্ণ ছিল। **Seven-sisters** — (অপ্রঃ) কৃত্তিকাপুঞ্জ। **Seven Sleepers**—Ephesus নগরবাসী যে সপ্তজন খৃষ্টীয় যুবক নির্যাতন হইতে রক্ষা পাওয়ার জন্য সিলিয়ন পর্ব্বতের গহ্বরে নিদ্রা যাইয়া ২৩০ বৎসর পর জাগরিত হইয়াছিল। **Seven-sisters rose, Seven-sister rose**—একজাতীয় লতা-গোলাপ — যাহাতে গুচ্ছে গুচ্ছে শ্বেত, রক্ত ও পাটলবর্ণের গোলাপ ধরিয়া থাকে। **Seven sorrows of virgin Mary** — Simeonএর ভবিষ্যদ্বাণী ; মিশরে পলায়ন ; খৃষ্টের সন্ধান অপ্রাপ্তি ; খৃষ্টের বন্ধন ; (খৃষ্টের) ক্রুশারোপণ ; ক্রুশ হইতে অবতারণ ; খৃষ্টের স্বর্গারোহণ।

Seven virtues — সপ্তগুণ—বিশ্বাস, আশা, বদান্যতা, বিজ্ঞতা, ন্যায়, সহিষ্ণুতা, মিতাচার। **Seven wonders of the world**—পৃথিবীর সপ্ত আশ্চর্য্য—(ক) প্রাচীন যুগের—(১) মিসরের পিরামিড; (২) বেবিলনের (প্রাচীন সংস্কৃত গ্রন্থোক্ত বভেরু বা বাভিরুশ নগরী) শূন্যোদ্যান; (৩) Caria রাজ Mausoleusএর সমাধিমণ্ডপ (তদীয় পত্নী Artemisia কর্তৃক খৃঃ পূঃ ৩৫৩ অব্দে Halicarnassus নামক স্থানে নির্মিত হয়; (৪) Ephesus নগরীস্থ Diana দেবীর মন্দির; Rhodes দ্বীপের কলোসাস্ নামক অতিকায় পিত্তল মূর্ত্তি; (৫) গ্রীসদেশীয় সুবিখ্যাত শিলাশিল্পী Phidias কর্তৃক ক্ষোদিত জুপিটারদেবের মূর্ত্তি; (৬) পারসীক সম্রাট Cyrusএর স্বর্ণমণ্ডিত রাজপ্রাসাদ বা আলেকজেণ্ড্রিয়া নগরীর (যবনপুরের) Pharos নামক রঙ্গমঞ্চ। (খ) মধ্যযুগের—(১) প্রাচীন রোমনগরীস্থ Coliseum নামক সুবিশাল রঙ্গভূমি; (২) আলেকজেণ্ড্রিয়া নগরীর বিরাট অন্তর্ভৌম সমাধিক্ষেত্র; (৩) চীনের প্রাচীর; (৪) ইংলণ্ডদেশের বিশাল-শিলাবেষ্টনী (Stonehenge); (৫) ইতালীর অন্তঃপাতী Pisa নগরীর হেলানো বুরুজ; (৬) Nankin নগরীর চীনামাটীর প্রাসাদ; (৭) কনস্তান্তিনোপল নগরীর St. Sophi মসজিদ্। **Seventy times seven**—অনির্দ্দেশ্য বৃহৎ সংখ্যা। **The seventies**—জীবনের বা শতাব্দীর ৬৯ এবং ৮০০ মধ্যবর্ত্তী বৎসর। **To be at sixes and seven**—See SIX.

sĕv'-ēr-ăl, *adj.* & *n.* **1.** Separate; distinct; পৃথক; স্বতন্ত্র। **2.** Separable; বিয়োজ্য, বিযুক্ত। **3.** Diverse; বিভিন্ন, বিবিধ, নানা। **4.** Consisting of a number more than two; কতিপয়, কয়েক, গোটাকয়েক। ***Noun.*** Persons or objects more than two but not many; কতিপয় লোক, কতিপয় বস্তু। **–ly,** *adv.* Separately; স্বতন্ত্রভাবে, পৃথক পৃথক ভাবে, একে একে, এক এক জন করিয়া, পৃথগ্ ভাবে। **–ty,** *n.* A holding by individual right; পৃথক জোত। **Joint and several bond**—যে খতে একাধিক ব্যক্তির স্বাক্ষর থাকে, এবং তাহাদের প্রত্যেকে খতের লিখিত সমস্ত টাকা পরিশোধের জন্য দায়ী থাকে।

sē-vēre', *adj.* **1.** Serious; গম্ভীর। **2.** Strict; কড়া। **3.** Rigourous; as, *severe* test: a *severe* examination; কঠোর, কঠিন। **4.** Violent; vehement; as, *severe* winter; দারুণ; প্রচণ্ড, চণ্ড। **5.** Not diffused or flowery; simple; as, a *severe* style; অনলঙ্কৃত, অপুষ্পিত; সাদাসিধা। **–ly,** *adv.* **–ver'-i-ty,** *n.* (Below).

sē-vĕr'-ĭ-tȳ, *n.* Gravity; গাম্ভীর্য্য। **2.** Rigour; কঠোরতা। **3.** A severe look or expression; as, the *severity* of her eyes; কঠোর দৃষ্টি বা ভাব। **4.** Severe rebuke or criticism; কঠোর সমালোচনা বা তিরস্কার। **5.** Austerity or chasteness in style; অলঙ্কারহীনতা, সাদাসিধাভাব। **6.** Inclemency; as, the *severity* of cold; violence; দারুণতা; প্রচণ্ডতা।

Se'-vres (sā-vr), *n.* A kind of porcelain manufactured at Sevres in France; ফরাসী দেশের অন্তঃপাতী Sevres নামক স্থানে প্রস্তুত একপ্রকার চীনামাটী।

sew (sō), *v. t.* & *i.* **1.** To unite or fasten together with a needle and thread; সেলাই করা, সীবন করা। ***Verb i.*** To practise sewing; to join things with stitches; সেলাই শিখা; সেলাই করিয়া জোড়া দেওয়া। **Sewing-machine**—সেলাইর কল, সীবনযন্ত্র। **Sewing-press — পুস্তক** সেলাই করার কল। **Sewn-up**—(ইতর ভাষায়) মাতাল। **To sew one up**—To utterly exhaust; অবসন্ন করা। **To sew up**—To inclose by sewing; সেলাই করিয়া বন্ধ করা। To inclose in anything sewed; সেলাই করিয়া কোন কিছুর ভিতর পুরা। To close or unite by sewing; সেলাই করিয়া জোড়া দেওয়া।

sew'-āge (sü-), *n.* & *v. t.* The filthy matter which passes through sewers; নর্দ্দমার ময়লা, নর্দ্দমার জল। ***Verb t.*** To manure with sewage; নর্দ্দমার ময়লা দ্বারা সার দেওয়া। **Sewage-farm**—যে কৃষিভূমিতে নর্দ্দমার ময়লা সারস্বরূপ ব্যবহৃত হয়। **Sewage-grass** — নর্দ্দমার ময়লাদ্বারা সার দেওয়া জমিতে জাত তৃণ।

sew'-ēr (sō-), *n.* (*Hist.*) A head or upper servant charged with the service of the table; (ইতিহাস) বড়লোকের বাটীতে ভোজনকালে যে ভৃত্য মেজে চাদর বিছাইত, অতিথিগণকে যথানির্দ্দিষ্ট স্থানে উপবিষ্ট করাইত এবং ভোজনপাত্রসমূহ স্থানান্তরিত করিত।

sew-ēr (sō-), *n.* One who sews; সেলাইকারী, সীবনকারী।

sew'-ēr (sü-), *n.* & *v. t.* A subterranean drain, as in a city, to carry off water, etc.; নগরীর রাজপথের নিম্নস্থ পয়ঃপ্রণালী, রাস্তার নীচের নর্দ্দমা, অন্তর্ভৌম পয়ঃপ্রণালী। ***Verb t.*** To provide with sewers; অন্তর্ভৌম পয়ঃপ্রণালীসমন্বিত করা। **–age,** *n.* **Sewar-gas**—রাস্তার নীচের নর্দ্দমার দূষিত বাষ্প। **Sewer-rat**—ইন্দুর।

sew'-in (sü-), **–ĕn**, *ns.* A variety of salmon-trout; একপ্রকার মৎস্য।

sewn (sün), *n.*, *pp.* of SEW (which see).

sĕx, *n.* The distinguishing peculiarity of male and female; স্ত্রী বা পুং চিহ্ন, লিঙ্গ। **Sex'-less,** *adj.* Without sex; neuter; লিঙ্গহীন; ক্লীব, নপুংসক। **Sex-character**—লিঙ্গলক্ষণ (হিঃ কোঃ)। **Sex-feeling** — লৈঙ্গিকসংবেদন (হিঃ কোঃ), কামভাব (ঐ)। **The fair, gentle, softer and weaker sex**—স্ত্রীজাতি, অবলাজাতি, ললনাসমাজ। **The sex**—স্ত্রীজাতি। **The sterner sex**—পুরুষ জাতি।

sĕx–, sĕx'-i–, Combining forms of Latin *sex* (six).

sĕx-ā-gē-na'-ri-ăn, *adj.* & *n.* Between 59 and 7০; ৫৯ এবং

১০ বৎসরে মধ্যবর্ত্তী। *Noun.* A person between 59 and 70 ; উনষট্টি এবং সত্তর বৎসরের মধ্যবর্ত্তী বয়সের লোক।

sĕx′-ăg′-ĕ-nā-rȳ, *adj.* Pertaining to, or designating, the number sixty; ষষ্টিসংখ্যা-সম্বন্ধীয়, ষষ্টিসংখ্যাবাচক।

sĕx-ā-gĕs′-i-măl, *adj.* Pertaining to, or founded on, number 60; ষষ্টিসংখ্যাসম্বন্ধীয়, ষষ্টিসংখ্যামূলক। **Sexagesimal Arithmetic**—ষষ্ট্যুত্তর গণনাপ্রণালী। **Sexagesimal fractions or numbers (or sexagesimals)** — যেসকল ভগ্নাংশের হর ৬০ বা ৬০এর কোন ঘাত (Power) হইয়া থাকে (যথা ১/৬০, ৩/৩৬০০ প্রভৃতি)।

sĕx′-an-gle (-ăng-gl), *n.* A figure having six angles; ষড়স্র ক্ষেত্র। **–gu-lar**, *adj.* **–gu-lar-ly**, *adv.*

sĕx-cĕn′-tĕ-nā-rȳ, *adj.* & *n.* Pertaining to the number 600; ষট্‌শতসম্বন্ধীয়। *Noun.* 600th anniversary; ষট্‌শতবার্ষিক উৎসব।

sĕx-ĕn′-ni-ăl, *adj.* 1. Lasting six years; ষড়বর্ষস্থায়ী। 2. Happening once in six years; ষড়বর্ষান্তে সংঘটিত, ষড়বার্ষিক, ষড়াব্দক।

sĕx′-i-fid, *adj.* (*Bot.*) Six-cleft; (উদ্ভিদ্‌বিদ্যা) ষড়ধা বিদীর্ণ।

sĕx-il′-lion (-yŭn), *n.* Same as SEXTILLION.

sĕx′-i-sȳl-la-ble (-ă-bl), *adj.* & *n.* Having six syllables; ছয় শব্দাংশবিশিষ্ট। *Noun.* A word of six syllables; ছয় শব্দাংশবিশিষ্ট শব্দ।

sĕx-i-vā′-lĕnt, *adj.* Same as SEXVALENT.

sĕx-pâr′-tite, *adj.* Divided into six parts; ষড়ংশিত।

sĕxt, sĕx′-te (-ti), *ns.* (*R. C. C.*) One of the canonical hours of prayer usually recited at noon; (রোমানক্যাথলিক ধর্ম্মসংঘ) মাধ্যাহ্নিক উপাসনার কাল।

sĕx′-tain (-tăn), *n.* A stanza of six lines; ষট্‌চরণাত্মক কবিতা।

sĕx′-tăn, *adj.* (Of fever) Recurring every sixth day; (জ্বরসম্বন্ধে) ষষ্ঠাহিক।

sĕx′-tănt, *n.* 1. The sixth part of a circle; বৃত্তের ষষ্ঠাংশ, বৃত্তষষ্ঠাংশ। 2. An instrument having an arc equal to the 6th part of a circle

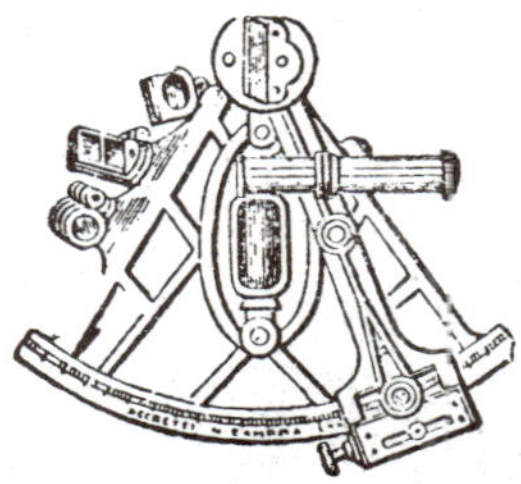

Sextant.

for measuring the angular distances of objects by reflection; কৌণিক দূরত্ব মাপের জন্য বৃত্তের ষষ্ঠাংশ পরিমিত কিরণ পরাবর্ত্তনদ্বারা চাপসমন্বিত যন্ত্রবিশেষ, ষষ্ঠাংশযন্ত্র (সাঃ পঃ), ষষ্ঠ্যংশযন্ত্র (ঐ)।

sĕx′-tile, *n.* বৃত্তষষ্ঠ্যংশান্তর (হিঃ কোঃ), ষষ্ঠভাগান্তর (ঐ)।

sĕx-til′-li-ŏn, *n.* A number consisting of 1 with 36 cyphers; একের ডাহিনে ৩৬টী শূন্য বসাইলে যে সংখ্যা হয়।

sĕx′-tō, *n.* A book with the leaf folded six times; ষষ্ঠাংশিত পুস্তক।

sĕx-tō-dĕc′-i-mō, *n.* The size of a book when each sheet makes sixteen leaves (usu. written 16 mo. and read *sixteenmo*); ষোড়শাংশিত পুস্তক।

sĕx′-tŏn, *n.* 1. An under-officer of a church who has charge of the vessels, vestry, etc.; খৃষ্টীয় ধর্ম্মমন্দিরের নিম্নশ্রেণীর কর্ম্মচারিবিশেষ (ইঁহার উপর মন্দিরের বাসনপত্র প্রভৃতি রক্ষার ভার থাকে)। **Sexton-beetle**—একপ্রকার গোবরে পোকা।

sĕx′-ū-ăl, *adj.* 1. Pertaining to sex or the sexes; স্ত্রীপুরুষসম্বন্ধীয়, যৌন, দাম্পত্য, ঔদ্বাহিক (প্রবাসী ১৩১৯), মৈথুনসম্বন্ধী। 2. Pertaining to the genital organs; as, *sexual disease*; জননেন্দ্রিয়সম্বন্ধীয়। 3. (*Biol.*) Having sex; (জীববিজ্ঞান) স্ত্রী বা পুংচিহ্নবিশিষ্ট। **Sexual affinity**—দাম্পত্যআকর্ষণ, যৌনআকর্ষণ। **Sexual appetite or desire** — রিরংসা, সঙ্গমেচ্ছা। **Sexual decoration**—যৌনসজ্জা, সঙ্গমঋতুতে পক্ষী প্রভৃতি শোভাজনক নব পালক প্রভৃতিতে ভূষিত হয়। **Sexual dimorphism**—স্ত্রীপুরুষ ভেদে ভিন্ন আকৃতি বিশিষ্টতা (মিউজিয়াম)। **Sexual enjoyment**—কামোপভোগ, সম্ভোগ। **Sexual intercourse, Sexual commerce** — সঙ্গম, সুরত [Syn. অধোপাসনা, হিঙন, ত্রিভদ্র, পশুক্রিয়া, রতিক্রিয়া, সংবেশন, রাসেরস, উপসৃষ্ট, ক্রীড়ারত্ন, মহাসুখ, ব্যবায়, গ্রাম্যধর্ম্ম, রত, নিধুবন, পঞ্চম (তন্ত্র), শৃঙ্গার, অভিমানিত, ধর্ষিত, সম্প্রয়োগ, অব্রহ্মচর্য্য, অনঙ্গপ্রসঙ্গ, মোহন, স্মরসমর (*Rhet.*), রতিরণ (*ib.*), ইন্দ্রিয়সেবা, রতিভোগ।] **Sexual organ**—জননেন্দ্রিয়। **Sexual power**—কামবল (ভাব প্রঃ)। **Sexual reproduction** — যোনিজনন, শুক্রশোণিতজনন, পিণ্ডজনন (হিঃ কোঃ)। **Sexual selection**—যে প্রাকৃতিক নির্ব্বাচনের ফলে কতিপয় বিশেষত্বের উদ্বর্ত্তন ও বিকাশ সাধিত হয়, [যথা পুংপক্ষীর সমুজ্জ্বল বর্ণ, মোহন কণ্ঠস্বর—যদ্দারা উহারা স্ত্রীপক্ষীদিগকে আকর্ষণ করে। এই ক্ষেত্রে যৌননির্ব্বাচনে দৈহিক পরিবর্ত্তন সাধিত হইয়াছে।], যৌননির্ব্বাচন, কাম্যনির্ব্বাচন (অভিঃ), লৈঙ্গিকবিচার (হিঃ কোঃ), কামিকবিচার (ঐ)। **Sexual system or method**—স্ত্রীপুরুষ ভেদে বৃক্ষাদির শ্রেণীবিভাগ।

sĕx′-ū-ăl-ist, *n.* An adherent of sexual system of botanical classification; যে ব্যক্তি স্ত্রীপুরুষভেদে বৃক্ষাদির শ্রেণীবিভাগ করিয়া থাকে, যৌনবাদী।

sĕx′-ū-ăl′-i-tȳ, *n.* The state of being distinguished by the sex; স্ত্রীপুরুষভেদে পরিচয়জনকতা।

sĕx′-ū-ăl-ize, *v. t.* To attribute to; স্ত্রী বা পুং চিহ্ন আরোপ করা। **–i-za′-tion**, *n.*

sĕx-văl′-ĕnt, (*Chem.*) Combining with six atoms of hydrogen ; (রসায়নশাস্ত্র) ছয় উদজান পরমাণু সহিত মিশ্রণশীল ।

sforzando, (*It.*), *n.* (*Mus.*) With sudden emphasis ; (সঙ্গীতশাস্ত্র) হঠাৎ জোরে ।

sfumato, (*It.*), *n.* (*Paint.*) With tints so blended that the outlines are scarcely perceptible ; (চিত্রবিদ্যা) অস্পষ্টবাহ্যরেখাবিশিষ্ট ।

shăb′-by (-ĭ), *adj.* **1.** Rugged ; ছিন্ন, জীর্ণ, ছেঁড়া, সূত্রমাত্রাবশিষ্ট । **2.** In a threadbare dress ; ছিন্নবস্ত্রপরিহিত । **3.** In bad repair ; জীর্ণশীর্ণ । **4.** Mean ; as, a *shabby* tact ; নীচ, হীন, হেয়, কদর্য্য । **–bi-ly,** *adv.* **–bi-ness,** *n.* **Shabby-genteel**—এক সময়ে বড় মানষির কতকটা চালচলন রাখিয়াছে—এরূপ ।

shăb′-răck, *n.* The cloth covering a cavalry officer's charger ; অশ্বারোহী সৈনিককর্ম্মচারীর জিনপোষ ।

shăck′-le (-l), *n.* & *v. t.* **1.** (*Pl.* A fetter ; handcuff ; পায়ের বেড়ী, নিগড়, পদশৃঙ্খল ; হাতকড়ি । **2.** That which obstructs or embarrasses free action ; ব্যাঘাত, অন্তরায়, বিঘ্ন, প্রতিবন্ধক । ***Verb t.*** **1.** To chain ; to fetter ; শৃঙ্খলিত করা, নিগড়িত করা ; পায়ে বেড়ী দেওয়া । **2.** To confine ; আটক করা । **3.** To trammel ; শৃঙ্খলিত করা ।

Shad.

shăd, *n.* A fish of the herring family ; ইলিশমৎস্য (Syn. বারিকপুর) ।

shăd′-dŏck, *n.* A tree and its fruit which is a large species of orange ; বাতাবি লেবুর গাছ, বাতাবি লেবু (From Batavia, capital of Java), জাম্বুরা [(East Bengal) । cf. Singhalese *Jamboola*] । [কাপ্তেন Shaddockকর্ত্তৃক খৃষ্টীয় অষ্টাদশ শতকে পশ্চিম ভারতীয়দ্বীপপুঞ্জে এই ফল প্রথম প্রবর্ত্তিত হয় বলিয়া এই নাম ।]

shade, *n.* & *v. t.* **1.** Interruption of rays of light, and consequent dimness and coolness ; ছায়া, অনাতপ, আভা (হিঃ কোঃ) । **2.** A shaded or obscure place ; a place sheltered from the sun's rays, as a grove or close wood ; hence, a secluded retreat ; নিভৃতস্থান ; ছায়াময় স্থান, ছায়াশীতল স্থান, ছায়াকুঞ্জ ; নিভৃতস্থলী । **3.** Something to intercept light or heat ; a screen ; আলো বা উত্তাপরোধক কোন কিছু ; পর্দ্দা । **4.** Darkness ; obscurity ; অন্ধকার ; অস্পষ্টালোক, ঘোর । **5.** A globe, bell or other form of more or lesss translucent material, as glass, porcelain, silk, paper, etc. to protect an artificial light from air-currents or soften its glare ; দীপালোকের তীব্রতা মন্দীভূত করার জন্য বা বায়ুপ্রবাহ হইতে দীপশিখা রক্ষার জন্য যে অর্দ্ধস্বচ্ছ কাচ, কাগজ বা চীনামাটীর আবরণ ব্যবহৃত হয়, ফানস । **6.** A figure of anything formed by interception of the rays of light ; কোন বস্তুর ছায়া, প্রতিবিম্ব । **7.** (*Pl.*) The soul. after its separation from the body ; spirit ; প্রেতাত্মা ; ছায়ামূর্ত্তি । **8.** (*Pl.*) The abode of departed spirits ; প্রেতলোক, পরলোক । **9.** A hollow glass-covering for protecting ornament etc. from dust ; অলঙ্কার প্রভৃতি ধূলি হইতে রক্ষা করার জন্য কাচের আবরণ । **10.** Degrees or gradations of light ; আলোকের ক্রম । **11.** A minute difference or variation of right meaning ; কোনরূপ ভাব, অর্থ, প্রভৃতির সূক্ষ্ম ভেদ বা বৈভিন্ন্য । **12.** A small or scarcely perceptible amount ; সামান্য পরিমাণ, লেশ, নামগন্ধ, ছায়া, আভাস, আমেজ । **13.** (*Paint.*) The dark or darker part of a picture ; চিত্রের অন্ধকার ভাগ বা অপেক্ষাকৃত অনুজ্জ্বল অংশ, ছায়া । **14.** Comparative obscurity ; as, to be thrown into *shade* ; অপেক্ষাকৃতি অপ্রসিদ্ধি । **15.** A variation of colour ; বর্ণবিভেদ, বর্ণভেদ, বর্ণবৈষম্য । ***Verb t.*** **1.** To screen from light ; ছায়াপ্রদান করা, ছায়াবৃত করা । **2.** To hide ; to shelter ; লুকান ; আশ্রয় দেওয়া । **3.** To obscure ; as, a sullen look *shaded* his face ; হীনপ্রভ করা, মন্দপ্রভ করা, অনুজ্জ্বল করা, ঘোরাল করা । **4.** To mark with gradation of light and colour ; বর্ণ বা ছায়ার ক্রম দ্বারা চিহ্নিত করা । **5.** To pass off by degrees into other colour or variety ; অন্য বর্ণে বা অন্য প্রকার কোন কিছুতে ক্রমশঃ বিলীয়মান হওয়া ।

shă-dōōf′, *n.* A contrivance used in Egypt and some other Eastern countries for raising water ; মিশর এবং অন্যান্য কতিপয় প্রাচ্যদেশে ব্যবহৃত জল উত্তোলনের যন্ত্রবিশেষ ।

shăd′-ow (-ō), *n.* **1.** Shade within defined limits, representing the form of a body that intercepts the rays of light ; ছায়া, অনাতপ । **2.** Shade representing the form of a body, which intercepts the light ; কোন বস্তুর ছায়া । **3.** Shelter ; cover ; আশ্রয় ; আবরণ । **4.** Anything unreal ; অবাস্তব বস্তু, অলীক বস্তু । **5.** A spirit ; a ghost ; প্রেতাত্মা ; ছায়ামূর্ত্তি । **6.** Inseparable companion ; that which follows likes a shadow ; নিত্যসহচর ; ছায়ার মতন অনুসরণকারী । **7.** A reflected image, as in a mirror or water ; hence, any image or portrait ; প্রতিবিম্ব, প্রতিচ্ছায়া ; প্রতিমূর্ত্তি, প্রতিকৃতি । **7.** A small degree ; shade ; ঈষৎ পরিমাণ ; ছায়া, আভাস, আমেজ, আঁচ । **8.** An uninvited guest introduced to a feast by one who is invited; নিমন্ত্রিত ব্যক্তির সহিত আগত অনিমন্ত্রিত অতিথি। 9. A kind of light sail used in fair wind; সুবাতাসের কালে ব্যবহৃত একপ্রকার হাল্‌কা পাইল। 10. A spy; "The refusal of the magistrate to allow a policeman to be asked whether he was a *shadow*"; পুলিসের গুপ্তচর। 11. Obscurity; privacy; অপ্রসিদ্ধি; নির্জ্জনতা। **–i-ness,** *n.* **–y,** *adj.* **Shadow-stitch**—একপ্রকার লেইসের কাজ। **Coming events cast their shadows before**—ভাবী ঘটনার আভাস পূর্ব্বেই পাওয়া যায়। **May your shadow never grow less!**—May you continue to be prosperous, তোমার সমৃদ্ধি যেন কখনও হ্রাসপ্রাপ্ত না হয়। **Shadow of death**—মৃত্যুর ছায়া। **Shadow of doubt**—সন্দেহের লেশ, সংশয়ের ছায়া। **To be afraid of one's shadow**—To be extremely timorous; নিজের ছায়া দেখে ভয় পাওয়া। **To start at one's shadow**—নিজের ছায়া দেখে আঁতকে উঠা।

shăd'-ow (-ö), *v. t.* 1. To overspread with shadow; ছায়াবৃত করা, ছায়াবিস্তার করা। 2. To cloud; to darken; to obscure; মলিন করা; অন্ধকার করা; ঘোরাল করা, অস্পষ্ট করা। 3. To set forth faintly, dimly or in outline; to adumbrate; আভাসে বলা, ইঙ্গিতে বলা, অস্পষ্টভাবে বলা; ছায়াপাত করা। 4. To dog or attend closely, esp. said of a detective who dogs the steps of a person under surveillance; as, he is *shadowed* by police; ছায়ার মতন অনুসরণ করা, অলক্ষিতে অনুসরণ করা। 5. To shelter or protect as with a wing; to shelter; পক্ষপুটের ছায়াতলে আশ্রয় দেওয়া; আশ্রয় দেওয়া। 6. To represent typically; আদর্শস্বরূপ প্রদর্শন করা।

shăd'-ÿ, *adj.* 1. Abounding with shade or shades; casting or causing shade; ছায়াবহুল, স্নিগ্ধচ্ছায়, সচ্ছায়; ছায়াপ্রদ, ছায়াবিস্তারী। 2. Disreputable; of doubtful morality; as, a *shady* business; গ্লানিজনক; নীতিসম্মত কিম্বা নীতিবিরুদ্ধ তৎসম্বন্ধে সংশয়জনক। **On the shady side of 40**—৪০ বৎসর অপেক্ষা অধিক বয়স্ক।

shăft, *n.* 1. A body of long cylindrical shape; চোঙ্গাকার দণ্ড। 2. The stem of an arrow; an arrow; বাণের বাঁট, বাণযষ্টি; সায়ক, বাণ, শর, বল্লম, বর্শা। 3. The stem of a feather; পক্ষবৃন্ত। 4. The pole of a carriage; গাড়ীর বোম, যুগন্ধর। 5. The spire of steeple; গির্জ্জার চূড়া। 6. The part of chimney which rises over the roof; ধূমনির্গমনলের যে অংশ ছাদের উপরে থাকে। 7. The cylindrical or column-shaped part of anything; কোন বস্তুর চোঙ্গাকার বা স্তম্ভাকৃতি অংশ। 8. The body of a column between the base and the capital; স্তম্ভের শীর্ষ এবং পাদদেশের মধ্যবর্ত্তী অংশ, স্তম্ভবপু (রাঃ রাঃ)। 9. A vertical or somewhat inclined well-like entrance into a mine; খনিতে প্রবেশের জন্য খাড়া বা ঈষৎ হেলানো কূপাকার সুড়ঙ্গ। 10. A ray of light; a streak of lightning; আলোকরশ্মি; বিদ্যুচ্ছটা। 11. The handle of a tool; হাতিয়ারের বাঁট। 12. (*Mech.*) A revolving bar or connected bars serving to convey the force which is generated in the engine or other prime mover to the different working machines; (যন্ত্রবিজ্ঞান) ঘূর্ণনশীল দণ্ড বা সংযুক্ত দণ্ডশ্রেণীর সাহায্যে যে কল বা প্রধান চালকযন্ত্র হইতে উপজাত শক্তি বিভিন্ন কার্য্যকরী যন্ত্রসমূহে সঞ্চারিত হয়, সঞ্চারকদণ্ড। 13. (*Mech.*) A large axle; (যন্ত্রবিজ্ঞান) বৃহৎ অক্ষদণ্ড। **Shaft-horse**—Placed opposite the front horse in tandem; গাড়ীর বোমে সংবদ্ধ অশ্ব। **To make a shaft or a bolt of a thing**—(*Prov.*) To take the risk; (ঝুঁকি) লওয়া।

shăg, *n.* 1. Coarse hair or rough woolly hair; ঝাঁকড়ামাকড়া চুল, ঝাঁকড়ামাকড়া রোম। 2. A cloth with a rough nap; ফুঁপিওয়ালা কাপড়। 3. A kind of tobacco cut into fine shreds; একপ্রকার মিহি করিয়া কাটা তামাক। 4. A shred; ফালি, টুকরা, ছিন্ন অংশ।

shăg, *n.* A species of cormorant; একজাতীয় অতিভোজী সামুদ্রিক পক্ষী।

shăg'-gy (-ĭ), *adj.* 1. Rough and rugged; ঝাঁকড়ামাকড়া। 2. Covered with long coarse or woolly hair; ঝাঁকড়ামাকড়াচুলবিশিষ্ট। 3. (Of hair) Rough and tangled; (চুলসম্পর্কে) ঝাঁকড়ামাকড়া। 4. (*Bot.*) Villous; (উদ্ভিদ্‌বিদ্যা) দীর্ঘ এবং কোমল লোমাবৃত। **–gi-ly,** *adv.* **–gi-ness,** *n.*

shă-green' (-grēn), *n.* A kind of grained leather prepared from the skins of the horse, ass, etc., also of sharks and seals; একপ্রকার সবুজবর্ণের দানাদার চামড়া।

Shah (shä), *n.* The monarch of Persia; পারস্যের শাহ।

shake, *v. t.* & *i.* 1. To cause to move with quick vibrations; to make to tremble or shiver; নাড়া, ঝাঁকুনি দেওয়া, আন্দোলিত করা, আলোড়িত করা, ঝাড়া; কম্পিত করা, কাঁপান, বিধূনিত করা, বেপথুমান করা, কম্পান্বিত করা, কম্পযুক্ত করা। 2. To move from firmness; to cause to waver, hesitate or doubt; as, to *shake* one's faith; to impair the resolution of; বিচলিত করা; সংশয়ান্বিত করা, কুণ্ঠান্বিত করা; টলান। 3. To move or remove by agitating; to throw off by a jolting, jerking or vibrating motion (usu. followded by *off*, *out* or *away*); "*Shake* the earth *away* from the roots; ঝাড়িয়া ফেলা, নাড়িয়া ফেলা; ঝাঁকড়াইয়া ফেলা।

4. To rid oneself off ; ঝাড়িয়া ফেলিয়া দেওয়া, কোনরূপ বন্ধন হইতে নিজকে মুক্ত করা। 5. (*Mus.*) To trill ; (সঙ্গীত-শাস্ত্র) স্বর কাঁপাইয়া গান করা, মুর্কি দেওয়া। 6. To rouse up with a shake ; নাড়া দিয়া জাগান। 7. To injure by a sudden shock ; as, he was very much *shaken* by the fall ; হঠাৎ ধাক্কা দিয়া আহত করা। ***Verb i.*** **1.** To be agitated with a waving or vibratory motion ; to tremble ; আলোড়িত হওয়া, আন্দোলিত হওয়া ; কম্পিত হওয়া, কাঁপা, আধূত হওয়া, বিধুনিত হওয়া, থরথর করিয়া কাঁপা, থরহরি কম্পিত হওয়া। 2. (*Dial.*) To loaf ; (প্রাদেশিক ভাষায়) টোঁ টোঁ করিয়া ঘুরা। **Shake-down** — উপস্থিত মত রচিত শয্যা, তৎকালোচিত শয্যা। **To occupy a shake-down** — উপস্থিত মত রচিত শয্যায় শায়িত হওয়া। **To rouse up with a shake**—To awake with a push ; নাড়া দিয়া জাগান। To restore a pillow etc. to shape by shaking ; ঝাঁকুনি দিয়া বালিস প্রভৃতির তুলা ঠিক করা। **To shake a leg**—To dance ; নাচা। To roam about ; ঘুরিয়া বেড়ান। **To shake a loose leg**—To wander aimlessly ; টোঁ টোঁ করিয়া ঘুরা। To live a roving, unsettled life ; ভবঘুরের মত জীবন যাপন করা। **To shake a person's hand, To shake a person by the hand**—করমর্দ্দন করা, করকম্পন করা। **To shake a vessel in the wind**—জাহাজের অগ্রভাগ বাতাসের প্রায় বিপরীতদিকে আনা—যাহাতে পাইল কম্পিত হইয়া থাকে। **To shake down**—To find a temporary accommodation ; অল্পকাল বাসের জন্য স্থান পাওয়া। **To shake down into**—To accommodate oneself to circumstances ; অবস্থার উপযোগী করা। **To shake hands**—To make an agreement or contract ; কোনরূপ চুক্তিতে বদ্ধ হওয়া। To take leave ; বিদায় গ্রহণ করা। **To shake in one's shoes**—To tremble in fright ; ভয়ে ঠক ঠক করিয়া কাঁপা, থরথর করিয়া কাঁপা। **To shake off**—To get rid of by shaking ; ঝাড়িয়া ফেলা। **To shake out**—To remove with a shake ; ঝাড়িয়া ফেলা, ঝাঁকড়াইয়া ফেলা। **To shake one's fist at**—To threaten to strike with the fist ; ঘুষি উঠান। **To shake one's head**—To move the head from side to side to express refusal, denial or disapproval ; অসম্মতি, অস্বীকৃতি, অননুমোদন প্রভৃতি প্রকাশার্থ, মস্তক সঞ্চালিত করা, মাথা নাড়া, ঘাড় নাড়া। **To shake one's side**—To laugh heartily ; হাসিয়া খুন হওয়া, হাসিতে হাসিতে পেট ফাটা। **To shake the elbow** — To gamble with dice ; দ্যূতক্রীড়া করা। **To shake the dust off one's feet**—To disclaim or renounce all connections, with a person or place ; কোন ব্যক্তি বা স্থানের সহিত সর্ব্বপ্রকার সম্বন্ধ ত্যাগ বা অস্বীকার করা। To cease travelling ; ভ্রমণে বিরত হওয়া। **To shake together**—To be on good terms ; ভাব থাকা, মিল থাকা, সদ্ভাব থাকা। **To shake up**—Same as TO SHAKE TOGETHER. (Also *slang*) To chide ; (ইতরভাষায়) তিরস্কার করা। To shake together for mixing ; ঝাঁকড়ান। To agitate ; বিচলিত করা, আলোড়িত করা, আন্দোলিত অরা।

shake, *n.* **1.** The act of shaking ; vacillating or wavering motion ; jerk ; trembling ; আলোড়ন, আন্দোলন, ঝাড়ন ; ঝাঁকি ; ঝাঁকুনি ; কম্পন, বিধুনন। 2. An instant ; "Wait a *shake* and I'll undo the side-gate" ; মুহূর্ত্ত, ক্ষণকাল। 3. (*Mus.*) Trill ; (সঙ্গীত-শাস্ত্র) মুর্কি। **4.** A fissure or rent in timber ; কাঠের ফাটল বা চির। 5. A shock ; ধাক্কা। **6.** A friendly clasp of hands ; করমর্দ্দন, করকম্পন। **No great shakes**—একটা অসাধারণ কিছু নয়, একটা মস্ত কিছু নয়, বিশেষ গণনীয় বিষয় নয়।

shāk'-ĕr, *n.* **1.** One who shakes ; আলোড়ক, কম্পনকারক। **2.** A member of the religious sect founded in Manchester and still existing in America ; খৃষ্টীয় অষ্টম শতকের মধ্যভাগে মাঞ্চেষ্টার নগরীতে প্রতিষ্ঠিত ধর্ম্মসম্প্রদায়বিশেষের সভ্য। [এই সম্প্রদায়ের নামান্তর "খৃষ্টের পুনরাবির্ভাবে বিশ্বাসী জনগণের মিলিতসম্প্রদায়" (United Society of Believers in Christ's Second Appearing)। James এবং Jane Wardleyকর্ত্তৃক অনুমান ১৭৪৭ খৃঃ অব্দে এই সম্প্রদায়ের প্রতিষ্ঠা হয়। কিছুকাল পরে মাঞ্চেষ্টার নগরবাসিনী Anna Lee এই সম্প্রদায়ে যোগদান করেন। Ann Lee কারাগারে একটা অলৌকিক দৃশ্য সন্দর্শন করার পর আপনাকেই যীশুখৃষ্টের দ্বিতীয় অবতার বলিয়া ঘোষণা করেন। ১৭৭৪ খৃঃ অব্দে এই সম্প্রদায় আমেরিকায় স্থানান্তরিত হয়। New Yorkএর অন্তঃপাতী লেবানন গিরি এই সম্প্রদায়ের প্রধান আড্ডা। এই সম্প্রদায়ভুক্ত নরনারীগণ ব্রহ্মচর্য্যব্রত অবলম্বনপূর্ব্বক ভ্রাতাভগিনীর মত বাস করে। নৃত্য ইহাদের ধর্ম্মের এক প্রধান অঙ্গ। ইহারা মাদক দ্রব্য ও শূকর মাংস বর্জ্জন করিয়া থাকে এবং নগর ছাড়িয়া পল্লীগ্রামে বাস করে। *See* Nordhoff's *Communistic Societies of the United States* ; W. H. Dixon's *New America*] **2.** A member of a religious sect founded in 1864 by Mrs. Mary Anne Girling who claimed to be an incarnation of God ; Mrs. Mary Anne Girlingকর্ত্তৃক প্রতিষ্ঠিত ধর্ম্মসম্প্রদায়বিশেষ। [এই গার্লিং আপনাকে অবতার বলিয়া প্রচার করিত এবং সে অমর বলিয়া শিষ্যগণের নিকট বলিত। কিন্তু ১৮৮৬ খৃঃ অব্দে Girlingএর মৃত্যু হওয়ায় এই সম্প্রদায়ের লোপ হয়।] **—ess,** (*n., fem.*)

Shak(e)′-spe(a)r-i-ăn (shăk-spēr-), *adj.* Pertaining to Shakespeare ; শেক্ষপীয়রীয়।

shăk′-ō, *n.* A soldier's peaked cap ; সৈনিকদিগের একপ্রকার সূক্ষ্মাগ্র টুপি।

shāk′-ў, *adj.* **1.** Tottering ; trembling ; weak ; liable to break down or give way ; as, a *shaky* chair ; টলমলে, টলটলায়মান; কম্পিত, কম্প্র, বেপথুমান; শীর্ণ, জীর্ণ, দুর্ব্বল ; টলমলে, নড়বড়ে। **2.** Unreliable ; as, a *shaky* story ; questionable ; as, a *shaky* business ; অবিশ্বাসযোগ্য ; সংশয়যোগ্য, সন্দিগ্ধ।

shāle, *n.* A fine-grained rock having a slaty structure ; শ্লেট-পাথরের মত একপ্রকার পাথর, শেইল পাথর। **Shale-oil**—শিলাজতুযুক্ত শেইল পাথর হইতে প্রাপ্ত একপ্রকার মেটেতৈল।

shăll, *v. aux.* Used to express futurity, compulsion, etc. ; ভবিষ্যৎকাল, বাধ্যতা প্রভৃতি সূচক সহকারী ক্রিয়াপদ। [উত্তম পুরুষে shall দ্বারা কেবল ভাবী বিষয় সূচিত হয়, কিম্বা কোন বিষয় ব্যক্ত হইয়া থাকে। মধ্যম পুরুষ (shalt) এবং প্রথম পুরুষ shall দ্বারা কোনরূপ প্রতিজ্ঞা বা সংকল্প সূচিত হয়। প্রশ্নে shall দ্বারা অনুমতি বা নিদেশ চাওয়া হয়।]

shăl-lōōn′, *n.* A certain kind of worsted stuff ; একপ্রকার পশমী কাপড়।

shăl′-lŏp, *n.* A light open boat ; একপ্রকার হাল্কা খোলা নৌকা।

shăl-(l)ot′ (-ŏt), *n.* A plant allied to the onion and like it, cultivated for its edible delicately flavoured bulbs (*Allium ascalonicum*) ; গন্ধ পেঁয়াজ, গদিনা (Chinese. *hi-ai, hi-ai-lu*).

shăl′-low (-lō), *adj., n., v.t.* & *i.* **1.** Not deep ; অগভীর। **2.** Not intellectually deep ; not penetrating deeply into abstruse matters ; "*Shallow* tops, who are governed by the eye, and admire everything that struts in vogue" ; superficial ; empty ; silly ; অগভীর-বুদ্ধি ; অমর্ম্মজ্ঞ, অমর্ম্মভেদী; পল্লবগ্রাহী ; শূন্যগর্ভ ; অল্পবুদ্ধি, অল্পমতি, মন্দধী, অল্পবিদ্য, অল্পমতি, অল্পজ্ঞ। **3.** (*Rare*) Not deep in tone ; (কচিদ্ব্যবহৃত) অগভীরস্বন। ***Noun.*** A place where the water is not deep ; a shoal ; অগভীর জলপূর্ণ স্থান ; জলমগ্ন চড়া। ***Verb t.*** To make shallow। অগভীর করা। ***Verb i.*** To become shallower ; অপেক্ষাকৃত অগভীর হওয়া। **—ness,** *n.* **Shallow-hearted, —brained** — সংকীর্ণচেতাঃ, অল্পমস্তিষ্ক, অল্পধী। **Shallow brooks are noisy**—বাহিরে চাকণচিকণ ভিতরে ঢন্ ঢন্।

shălt, *v. aux.* The second person singular of SHALL.

shăm, *n., adj., v. t.* & *i.* That which appears to be what it is not ; imposture ; humbug ; ভাণ, ছল, কপটতা ; ছলনা ; ফাঁকি, প্রতারণ। ***Adj.*** Feigned ; false ; counterfeit ; ছদ্ম ; কপট, কল্পিত ; জাল, কৃত্রিম। ***Verb t.*** To deceive ; to trick ; to feign ; প্রতারণা করা ; ছলনা করা, চাতুরী করা ; ভাণ করা। ***Verb i.*** To make false pretence ; ভাণ করা, ছদ্মভাব অবলম্বন করা। **Sham-fight** — কৃত্রিমযুদ্ধ, লীলারণ, লীলাকলহ, চিত্রযুদ্ধ (আঃ বঃ), কপটযুদ্ধ, মিথ্যাযুদ্ধ, ক্রীড়াযুদ্ধ। **Sham plea** — (আইন) মিথ্যা ওজর। **To sham Abraham (or Abram)**—To feign sickness ; পীড়ার ভাণ করা।

Shă′-măn, *n.* A priest of Shamanism ; পিশাচপূজক, ভূতের ওঝা।

Shă′-măn-ĭsm, *n.* A form of religion practised in Northern Asia, where the tribes believe that the government of the world is in the hands of deities whom it is necessary to propitiate by magic rites and spells ; উত্তর এসিয়া প্রভৃতি দেশের ধর্ম্মবিশেষ—এই ধর্ম্মাবলম্বিগণ ভূতপ্রেতের পূজা করিয়া থাকে, পিশাচ-পূজা (সাঃ পঃ), ভৌতিকবিশ্বাস (ঐ)।

shăm′-ble (-l), *v. i.* & *n.* To walk with an awkward, irregular and clumsy pace ; নেঙচাইয়া চলা। ***Noun.*** Walking unsteadily and with a shuffling gait ; নেঙচাইয়া চলন।

shăm′-bles (-bls), *n.* **1.** A place where butcher's meat is sold ; a slaughter-house ; মাংস বিক্রয়ের স্থান, কসাইখানা ; যে গৃহে কসাইগণ গবাদি জন্তু হত্যা করে, হত্যাগৃহ, বধশালা। **2.** (*Fig.*) A place of butchery ; as, the place became a *shambles* ; হত্যাকাণ্ডের স্থান, হত্যাভূমি।

shāme, *n., v. t.* & *i.* **1.** The uneasy sensation of mind produced by the consciousness of guilt or loss of reputation or by the exposure of that which nature or modesty prompts us to conceal ; susceptibility of such feeling or emotion ; লাজ, লজ্জা, সরম, ব্রীড়া [Syn. হ্রী, ত্রপা, শালীনতা, মন্দাস্য, মন্দাক্ষ] ; লজ্জাশীলতা। **2.** That which brings shame ; লজ্জাজনক বিষয়, লজ্জাকর বিষয়। **3.** Dishonour ; disgrace ; "Ye have borne the *shame* of the heathen" ; অপমান, অপবাদ, অপযশ ; কলঙ্ক, দুর্নাম। **4.** The part which modesty requires to be covered ; (*Is.* xlvii 3.) ; গোপনীয় অঙ্গ। ***Verb t.*** **1.** To make ashamed ; to cause to feel shame ; লজ্জিত করা ; লজ্জাবোধ করা। **2.** To disgrace ; to dishonour ; কলঙ্কিত করা, কলঙ্কলিপ্ত করা ; অপমানিত করা, অপদস্থ করা। ***Verb i.*** To be ashamed ; লজ্জিত হওয়া। **Shame′-ful,** *adj.* **1.** Disgraceful ; লজ্জাজনক, লজ্জাপ্রদ, লজ্জাবহ, কলঙ্কজনক, অপমানজনক, অখ্যাতিজনক। **2.** Indecent ; অশ্লীল। **Shame′-less,** *adj.* Destitute of shame ; audacious ; insensible to shame or disgrace ; লজ্জাহীন, নির্লজ্জ, বিগতলজ্জ ; ধৃষ্ট ; বেহায়া (*colloq.*), নাককাটা (*ib., slang*), কালামুখ (*ib.*)। **Shame-faced** — সলজ্জ, লজ্জাশীল ; মুখচোরা। **Shame on you** — তোমাকে ধিক্

To cry shame on or **upon**—To reproach for shameful conduct; ধিক্কার দেওয়া। **To have shame**—To feel shame; লজ্জাবোধ করা। **To put to shame**—To disgrace esp. by exhibiting superior qualities etc.; লজ্জিত করা, লাজ দেওয়া। **To think shame, To think it shame**—To be ashamed; লজ্জিত হওয়া।

shăm'-my (-ĭ), **shăm'-ōy**, Same as CHAMIOS (which see).

shăm-pōō', *v. t.* & *n.* **1.** To sqeeze or rub the body, usually in connection with the hotbath; অঙ্গ মর্দ্দন করা, গাত্রসংবাহন করা। **2.** To wash and rub thoroughly (head, hair, etc.) with soap and water; সাবানজলদ্বারা (মাথা, চুল, প্রভৃতি) ঘষিয়া ধৌত করা। ***Noun.*** The act of shampooing; a shampooing of the head; অঙ্গমর্দ্দন, সংবাহন; সাবানজলদ্বারা উত্তমরূপে কেশ ধৌত করণ।

shăm'-rŏck, *n.* A trefoil plant, the national emblem of Ireland; আয়র্লণ্ডের জাতীয়চিহ্নস্বরূপ ব্যবহৃত ত্রিপত্র ক্ষুপ বিশেষ।

shăn'-drȳ, shăn'-drȳ-dăn, *n.* **1.** A one horse Irish conveyance; আয়র্লণ্ড দেশে ব্যবহৃত একপ্রকার এক-ঘোড়ার গাড়ী। **2.** An old rickety vehicle; জীর্ণযান।

shăn'-dȳ-găff, *n.* A mixture of beer and ginger-beer or lemonade; বীয়র এবং আর্দ্রকবাসিত বীয়র মদ বা নিম্বুকপানকের মিশ্র।

shăng-hai' (-hī), *n.* **1.** A kind of domestic fowl; একপ্রকার গৃহকুক্কুট। **2.** (Australia) A catapult; (অষ্ট্রেলিয়ার) ফিঙ্গা বা ছিটকিনি কল।

shăng-hai' (-hī), *v. t.* To drug, and ship, on board a vessel while unconscious; "To be carried or forced on board of a ship in this manner is termed in sailor's parlance being *shanghied*"; মাল্লাকে ঔষধাদিদ্বারা অচেতন করিয়া জাহাজে তুলিয়া দেওয়া।

shank (shăngk), *n.* & *v. i.* **1.** Leg; পা, ঠ্যাঙ্গ (*colloq.*)। **2.** The part of the leg between knee and ankle; জানু হইতে গুল্‌ফ পর্য্যন্ত চরণের অংশ, পায়ের নলা। **3.** The shaft of a column; স্তম্ভবপু। **4.** The stem of an anchor; নঙ্গরের ডাঁটা। **5.** The stem of a key, spoon, etc.; চামচ, চাবি প্রভৃতির ডাঁটি। ***Verb i.*** To fall off, as flowers, leaf etc. due to the decay of stem; বৃন্তক্ষয়হেতু পুষ্প পত্র প্রভৃতি স্খলিত হইয়া পড়া। **To ride shank's mare**—To walk on foot; পদব্রজে গমন করা।

shȧn't, *v. aux.* Contraction of *shall not.*

shăn'-tȳ, *n.* A hut; a mean dwelling; কুড়ে ঘর; কুড়ে।

shāpe, *v. t., i.* & *n.* **1.** To give a form to; আকৃতি প্রদান করা, গড়া গঠন করা, গড়িয়া তোলা। **2.** To mould, cut or make into a particular form; বিশেষ আকারে কাটা বা গড়া। **3.** To adapt as to purpose; to regulate; to direct; "To the stream... he *shapes* his course"; কোন উদ্দেশ্যের উপযোগী করা; নিয়মিত করা; নির্দ্দেশ করা। **4.** To imagine; to image; to conceive; "My jealousy *shapes* faults that are not"; কল্পনা করা; মানসাকাশে প্রতিবিম্বিত করা; ধারণা করা। **5.** To develop from vagueness into something coherent; অস্পষ্ট অবস্থা হইতে সংহত বা সুসম্বদ্ধ অবস্থায় আনা। **6.** To design; to devise; to arrange; কল্পনা করা; ফন্দি আঁটা; শৃঙ্খলাবদ্ধ করা। ***Verb i.*** (*Rare*) To suit; (কচিদ্ব্যবহৃত) মানান। ***Noun.*** **1.** Figure; make; আকার, আকৃতি, ডৌল; গঠন, গড়ন। **2.** That which has form or figure; "The other *shape*, If *shape* it might be called That *shape* had none"; আকৃতিবিশিষ্ট বস্তু, মূর্ত্তি, ছায়ামূর্ত্তি। **3.** A pattern; a mould; as, the *shape* for a lady's dress; আদর্শ, নমুনা; ছাঁচ। **4.** Definite form; orderly arrangement; as, to get one's ideas into *shape*; সুস্পষ্টরূপ; সুশৃঙ্খলতা। **5.** (*Dial.*) Sexual organs; (প্রাদেশিক ভাষায়) যোনি বা লিঙ্গ। **6.** Kind; sort; as, in no *shape* or form; প্রকার; রকম। **7.** (*Colloq.*) Condition; as, the market is in bad *shape*; (চলিতভাষায়) অবস্থা। **8.** (*Cookery*) A dish of rice, jelly, or the like cast in a mould and turned out when it has grown firm; a mould for this purpose; ছাঁচে চাপ দিয়া কঠিনীকৃতি জেলি, ভাত, প্রভৃতি; ঐরূপ পিষ্টক প্রস্তুতের উপযোগী ছাঁচ। **Shap'-a-ble**, *adj.* **Shape'-less**, *adj.* Destitute of shape; wanting symmetry of dimensions; আকারহীন; কদাকার। **Shape'-li-ness**, *n.* **Shape'-ly**, *adj.* Well formed or proportioned; সুগঠিত, সুশ্রী, অঙ্গসৌষ্ঠবসম্পন্ন। **In no shape or form**—In no manmer at all; কোন প্রকারেই নয়। **To take shape**—To assume a definite form; কোনরূপ সুস্পষ্ট আকৃতি গ্রহণ করা। **To shape out**—To form out of some; কোন কিছু হইতে গঠিত করা। **To shape one's course**—To steer for a place; কোন স্থানের অভিমুখে জাহাজ চালান।

shāp'-ēr, *n.* **1.** One who, or that which, shapes or forms; আকৃতিদাতা, আকারপ্রদায়ক। **2.** Kinds of machine for turning, planing, stamping, moulding, etc.; কুন্দন, রেঁদাকরণ, মুদ্রণ বা ছাঁচে গড়নের জন্য বিভিন্ন প্রকার যন্ত্র।

shȧrd, shērd, *ns.* **1.** A fragment of an earthen vessel; ভাঙ্গা মাটীর বাসনের টুকরা। **2.** The wing-case of a beetle; গুটিপোকার পক্ষ-কোষ।

3. A shell or scale ; শামুক, ডিম, প্রভৃতির খোল, শল্ক।

shāre, *n., v. t.* & *i.* **1.** A part bestowed ; lot or portion ; ভাগ ; অংশ, হিস্যা, বখরা। **2.** (In a bank, company, etc.) One of the equal parts of capital invested ; (ব্যাঙ্ক, কোম্পানী, প্রভৃতির) অংশ। **3.** Same as PLOUGH-SHARE. ***Verb t.*** **1.** To divide in portions ; ভাগ করা, অংশ করা, বণ্টন করা। **2.** To partake of, enjoy or suffer in common with others ; as, to *share* one's joy ; একযোগে নেওয়া, সমভাগী হওয়া (cf. সমসুখদুঃখভাগী হওয়া)। ***Verb i.*** To receive a portion ; ভাগ পাওয়া, অংশ পাওয়া। **Share-holder** — যৌথকারবার প্রভৃতির অংশীদার, অংশীদার। **Share-list**— খনি, রেলওয়ে, ব্যাঙ্ক, প্রভৃতির অংশের মূল্যতালিকা। **Deferred shares**— যে সকল অংশের উপর কোন নির্দ্দিষ্ট তারিখ বা সম্ভাবিত ঘটনার পূর্ব্বে অপেক্ষাকৃত অল্পহারে লভ্যাংশ দেওয়া হয় কিম্বা ঐ তারিখ বা সময়ের পূর্ব্বে কোন লভ্যাংশই দেওয়া হয় না। **Preference or preferred shares**—See PREFERENCE. **Share and share alike**—সমান সমানভাগে। **To fall to one's share**—To fall to one's lot ; কাহারো ভাগ্যে ঘটা। **To go shares with**—To participate; অন্যের সহিত সমভাবে ভোগ করা।

shārk, *n., v. t.* & *i.* **1.** A fierce sea-fish ; হাঙ্গর, মকর (ব্রজঃ বিঃ),

Shark.

নক্ররাজ (কেণ্ডিঃ), গ্রাহ (ঐ) [Syn. জলাণ্টক (জাহিঃ), জলকিরাত, দৃঢ়দংশক।] **2.** A person who preys on others ; a sharper ; "The master of the lottery was, in truth, a mere *shark*" ; a greedy artful fellow ; a parasite ; পরপীড়ক ; জুয়াচোর, প্রতারক ; ধূর্ত্ত এবং লোভী ব্যক্তি; পরান্নভোজী। ***Verb t.*** To gather slyly or rapaciously in small quantities; শঠতাপূর্ব্বক বা লোলুপভাবে সংগ্রহ করা। ***Verb i.*** To practise fraud or trickery ; to live by cheating ; জুয়াচুরী করা, চাতুরী খেলান ; জুয়াচুরীদ্বারা জীবিকার্জ্জন করা। **Shark-moth** — একপ্রকার ধূসরবর্ণ কীট। **To live upon the shark**— To live by sharking ; জুয়াচুরীদ্বারা জীবনযাত্রা নির্ব্বাহ করা।

shārp, *adj., n.* & *adv.* **1.** Keen ; ধারাল, শাণিত, খর (cf. খর করবাল), খরধার, খরশাণ। **2.** Terminating in a point or edge ; সূক্ষ্মাগ্র, ধারালপ্রান্ত। **3.** Acute of mind ; of quick nice perceptions ; clever ; as, a *sharp* child ; সূক্ষ্মধী, তীক্ষ্ণধী, কুশাগ্রবুদ্ধি ; তীক্ষ্ণবুদ্ধি, প্রখর-বুদ্ধি, সূক্ষ্মদর্শী, তীক্ষ্ণদর্শী ; চালাক। **4.** Well-defined ; distinct ; as, a *sharp* negative ; সুপরিস্ফুট ; সুস্পষ্ট। **5.** Gritty ; as, *sharp* sand ; hard ; কঙ্করময় ; কঠিন। **6.** Emaciated ; "His face grows *sharp* and thin" ; ক্ষীণ, কৃশ, বিশীর্ণ, পরিক্ষীণ, কাহিল। **7.** Subtle ; witty ; marked by shrewdness or cleverness ; সূক্ষ্ম ; সরস, রসিকতাপূর্ণ ; সূক্ষ্মবুদ্ধির পরিচায়ক। **8.** Fierce ; violent ; fiery ; as, a *sharp* contest ; ভয়ঙ্কর ; প্রবল ; প্রচণ্ড, তুমুল। **9.** Vigorous ; brisk ; speedy ; as, to take a *sharp* walk ; সতেজ ; চটুল ; ত্বরিত, দ্রুত। **10.** Keen ; cutting ; as, a *sharp* look ; biting ; acrimonious ; harsh ; painful ; তীক্ষ্ণ ; মর্ম্মচ্ছেদী ; তীব্র ; কটু ; উগ্র ; যন্ত্রণাপ্রদ। **11.** Very attentive ; vigilant ; as, a *sharp* watch ; অতি অবহিত, কড়া ; সজাগ। **12.** Abrupt ; as, a *sharp* descent ; খাড়া, বিষম। **13.** Severe ; merciless ; as, a *sharp* judge : a *sharp* punishment ; কঠোর, কড়া ; নির্দ্দয়, করুণাশূন্য। **14.** (Of sight) Keen ; (দৃষ্টি সম্বন্ধে) তীক্ষ্ণ, প্রখর, খর। **15.** Artful ; dishonest ; as, *sharp* practices ; ধূর্ত্ত ; অসাধু। **16.** Shrill ; কর্কশ, শ্রুতিকটু। **17.** (*Mus.*) Above true pitch ; তীব্র (মিউজিক), পঞ্চম। **18.** Eager for prey ; hungry ; as, my stomach was *sharp* ; শিকারের জন্য আগ্রহান্বিত ; ক্ষুধিত। **19.** (Of winter or weather) Bitingly cold ; কনকনে। **20.** Pungent ; sour ; ঝাল ; টক। **21.** Dazzling; as, a *sharp* flash ; তীব্রোজ্জ্বল, চোখ-ঝলসানো। **22.** Careful of one's own interest ; স্বার্থপর। ***Noun.*** **1.** A cheat ; প্রতারক। **2.** (*Pl.*) The harder parts of ground wheat ; একবার পেষণের পর ময়দার যে কঠিন অংশ থাকে। **3.** (*Mus.*) A note raised by a semitone ; (সঙ্গীত-শাস্ত্র) কড়ি। **4.** A sewing needle of slender make ; একপ্রকার সূক্ষ্ম সূচ। **5.** (*Archaic*) A sharp weapon ; (অপ্রঃ) ধারাল অস্ত্র। ***Adv.*** **1.** sharply ; তীক্ষ্ণভাবে, তীব্রভাবে। **2.** Exactly ; punctually ; "Dinner had been ordered at *sharp* five" ; ঠিক ; কাঁটায় কাঁটায়। **3.** Suddenly ; সহসা, হঠাৎ। **Sharp′-ly,** *adv.* **Sharp′-ness,** *n.* The quality of being sharp ; প্রাখর্য্য, প্রখরতা। **Sharp-edged** — খরধার, তীক্ষ্ণধার, শিতধার। **Sharp-featured** — কৃশ, পরিক্ষীণ। **Sharp-ground**—শাণিত। **Sharp-looking**—ক্ষুধার্ত্ত, ক্ষুৎপীড়িত। **Sharp-pointed** — তীক্ষ্ণাগ্র, সূক্ষ্মাগ্র। **Sharp practice**—জুয়াচুরি, ধড়িবাজী ; যেরূপ আচরণ আইনতঃ দণ্ডনীয় না হইলেও লোকতঃ নিন্দনীয় হইয়া থাকে। **Sharp-set** — বুভুক্ষাপীড়িত, ক্ষুধার্ত্ত। **Sharp-shod**—(অশ্বাদি সম্বন্ধে) যাহাতে বরফের উপর পিছলাইয়া না পড়ে, তজ্জন্য প্রেকওয়ালা নাললাগানো। **Sharp-shooter**—অব্যর্থহস্ত ব্যক্তি,

অব্যর্থসন্ধানকারী, সুনিপুণলক্ষ্যভেদকারী, পাকা গুলিবাজ। **Sharp-sighted**—তীক্ষ্ণদর্শী, সূক্ষ্মদর্শী, তীব্রদৃষ্টি, তীক্ষ্ণদৃষ্টি। **Sharp-tongued**—কটুভাষী, ভুর্মুখ। **Sharp-witted**—তীক্ষ্ণবুদ্ধি, তীক্ষ্ণধী। **Sharp-work**—চট্ করিয়া যে কাজ সারা হয়; যুদ্ধ প্রভৃতি কার্য্য—যাহাতে কোন ব্যক্তির সমগ্রশক্তি প্রয়োগ করিতে হয়। **As sharp as a needle**—কুশাগ্রবুদ্ধি। **He was too sharp for me**—He cheated me; সে আমার উপর চালাকি করিয়াছিল। **To be sharp upon**—To be severe upon; কাহারো উপর কঠোর হওয়া (সাধারণতঃ সমালোচনাদি সম্পর্কে ব্যবহৃত হয়)। **To look sharp**—To be alert; সাবধান হওয়া, হুঁসিয়ার হওয়া।

shärp, *v. t.* & *i.* (*Archaic*) To whet; (কচিদ্‌ব্যবহৃত) ধার দেওয়া, শাণিত করা। ***Verb i.*** To swindle; জুয়াচুরি করা।

shärp'-en (-n), *v. t.* & *i.* **1.** To give a sharp or keen edge or point to; ধারাল করা, সূক্ষ্মাগ্র করা। **2.** To render more acute; তীব্রতর করা, প্রখরতর করা। **3.** To make more eager; কৌতূহল উদ্দীপ্ত করা। **4.** To make sour; টক করা, অম্লস্বাদ করা। **5.** To make thin; কৃশ করা, পরিক্ষীণ করা। **6.** To make biting or sarcastic; মর্ম্মচ্ছেদী করা, তীব্রবিদ্রূপাত্মক করা। ***Verb i.*** To become sharp; তীক্ষ্ণ হওয়া, তীব্র হওয়া, প্রখর হওয়া।

shärp'-ėr, *n.* A swindler; a cheat in bargaining or gaming; a tricking fellow; জুয়াচোর, প্রতারক, ঠক; যে ব্যক্তি ক্রীড়া অথবা ক্রয়বিক্রয়ে প্রতারণা করে; ধড়িবাজ।

shăt'-tėr, *v. t.*, *i.* & *n.* **1.** To break at once into pieces; খণ্ডবিখণ্ড করা, চূর্ণবিচূর্ণ করা, চুরমার করা। **2.** To derange; as, his mind was *shattered*; to overthrow; বিকৃত করা, বিকার উৎপাদন করা; ধ্বংস করা। ***Verb i.*** To be broken into fragments; খণ্ডবিখণ্ড হওয়া, চূর্ণবিচূর্ণ হওয়া। ***Noun.*** A fragment of anything shattered; ভগ্ন খণ্ড, টুকরা। **Shatter-brain**—বিক্ষিপ্তমতি। **Shatter-brained**—বিকৃতমস্তিষ্ক, বিক্ষিপ্তমতি, বিক্ষিপ্তবুদ্ধি।

shāve, *v. t.* & *i.* **1.** To cut or pare off with a razor or other edged instrument; ক্ষুর কিম্বা চাকু প্রভৃতি দ্বারা কাটিয়া ফেলা। **2.** To cut off close to the surface; to remove the growth of hair, from the chins etc. with a razor; to make smooth or bare by cutting or paring from the surface of; গোড়ায় লাগাইয়া কাটা; ক্ষৌরকর্ম্ম করা, খেউরী করা, কাটা; মুণ্ডন করা, মুড়া। **3.** To pare off surface of (wood etc.) with a plane; চাঁচা, ছোলা। **4.** To sweep by almost touching; to touch lightly in passing; "Now *shaves* with level wing the deep"; প্রায় লাগিয়া যাওয়া; প্রায় স্পর্শ করিয়া যাওয়া, ঘষড়াইয়া যাওয়া। **5.** To cut in thin slices; "Plants bruised or *shaven* in leaf or root"; পাতল পাতল চাক্ করিয়া কাটা। **6.** To plunder; to fleece; লুটিয়া নেওয়া; মাথায় হাত বুলান। ***Verb i.*** To use the razor; to remove the hair from the chin, head, etc. with a razor; ক্ষুর ব্যবহার করা; খেউরী করা, ক্ষৌরকার্য্য করা। **Shav'-ing**, *n.* **Shave-hook**—ধাতু চাঁচিবার অস্ত্রবিশেষ। **Shaving-brush**—কামাইবার আগে যে বুরুষদ্বারা চিবুকে সাবান-জল লাগান হয়। **Shaving-horse**—যে কাঠাধারের উপর রাখিয়া কাঠ চাঁচা হয়। **To shave a note**—ধার্য্য মূল্য অপেক্ষা অল্প মূল্যে নোট ক্রয় করা অথবা ঐ নোটের উপর আইনদ্বারা নির্দ্ধারিত সুদ অপেক্ষা বেশী হারে সুদ লওয়া।

shāve, *n.* **1.** Act of shaving, esp. the beard; ক্ষৌরকার্য্য, খেউরী, ক্ষৌরক্রিয়া, বিশেষতঃ দাঁড়ি কামানো। **2.** The act of passing closely as almost to strike or graze; a narrow escape; ঘষড়াইয়া যাওন, প্রায় স্পর্শ করিয়া যাওন; অল্পের জন্ত রক্ষা, চুলে চুলে রক্ষা। **3.** A tool with a long blade, and a handle at each end for shaving hoops etc.; পিপার হালি প্রভৃতি চাঁচিবার জন্ত লম্বা ফলা এবং উভয়প্রান্তে হাতলবিশিষ্ট অস্ত্রবিশেষ। **4.** A slice; চাক্‌তি। **5.** (*Slang*) A false report; a hoax; মিথ্যা গুজব; ধোকা, ফাঁকি, ধাপ্পা।

shāve'-grăss, *n.* A kind of plant employed for polishing wood, ivory and brass; পালিশের কাজে ব্যবহৃত গুল্মবিশেষ।

shāve'-ling, *n.* (*Archaic*) A man shaved; a monk; (অপ্রঃ) ক্ষৌরিত ব্যক্তি; সন্ন্যাসী, মুণ্ড (যাজঃ), মুণ্ডা (*fem.* অঃ)।

shāv'-ėr, *n.* **1.** A barber; ক্ষৌরকার, ক্ষৌরিক, নাপিত, নরসুন্দর। [ক্ষুরী, মুণ্ডী, দিবাকীর্ত্তি, অন্তাবসায়ী, বাৎসী, ছত্রী, সুত, গ্রামণী, নখকুট্ট, চন্দ্রিল, মুণ্ড, ভাণ্ডপুট।] **2.** (*Colloq.*) A lad; (চলিতভাষায়) বালক, ছোকরা। **3.** A sharp dealer; প্রবঞ্চক, জুয়াচোর, ধূর্ত্ত, শঠ। **4.** A droll fellow; মজার মানুষ। **5.** A pillager; লুণ্ঠনকারী, লুণ্ঠক।

shaw (shä), *n.* A small wood; a grove; বন, ঝোপ; কুঞ্জ।

shawl (shäl), *n.* An article of dress used generally as a loose covering for shoulder; শাল।

shawm (shäm), *n.* An obsolete musical instrument; একপ্রকার অপ্রচলিত বাদ্যযন্ত্র।

shay (shā), *n.* A vulgar corruption for CHAISE.

shē, *pron.*, *n.* & *adj.* The female before mentioned; তিনি [কেবল স্ত্রীলোক বা মানবধর্ম্মারোপিত পোত, বস্ত্র, বাষ্পীয়-শকট প্রভৃতি সম্পর্কে ব্যবহৃত হয়।] ***Noun.*** A woman; a female animal; "You are the cruelest *she* alive"; স্ত্রীলোক, নারী; স্ত্রী জন্তু। ***Adj.*** Female; as, a *she*-dog; স্ত্রী। **She-devil**—শয়তানী (দুষ্টা স্ত্রীসম্পর্কে)। **She-oak** — অষ্ট্রেলিয়ার একশ্রেণীর গুল্ম। **She-pine** — অষ্ট্রেলিয়াদেশীয়

দেবদারুজাতীয় বৃক্ষবিশেষ। She-world—পৃথিবী বা পৃথিবীর কোন অংশের নারীমণ্ডলী। The not impossible she—প্রণয়সাধ্যা রমণী।

shē'-ă, *n.* The tree yielding shea-butter (*Bassia butyracea*) ; আফ্রিকা এবং এসিয়াদেশের গ্রীষ্মমণ্ডলে জাত বৃক্ষবিশেষ, ফলওয়া (হিন্দী), ইয়েলপাতি (লেপ্চা ভাষায়), নবনীতরু। **Shea-butter**—(also called *Galam butter*) ; নবনীতরুর ফল হইতে প্রাপ্ত একপ্রকার উদ্ভিজ্জ মাখন। [এই বৃক্ষ আলমোরা পাহাড়ে ও কুমায়ুন অঞ্চলে জন্মে। ইহাতে ক্ষুদ্র ক্ষুদ্র শাদা ফুল হয়। গাছ ৬০ ফিটের অধিক উঁচু হয় না। এই বৃক্ষের বীজ-শস্য হইতে একপ্রকার মাখনের মত পদার্থ পাওয়া যায়।]

shead'-ing, (shĕd-), *n.* An administrative division of the Isle of Man; ম্যানদ্বীপের শাসনসংক্রান্ত বিভাগবিশেষ। [ম্যান দ্বীপ ৬টী সিডিং বা বিভাগে বিভক্ত।]

sheaf' (shēf), *n., v. t.* & *i.* 1. A bundle of new cut corn bound together ; শস্যের আঁটি। 2. A collection ; গুচ্ছ। ***Verb t.*** To make sheafs of ; আঁটি করা। ***Verb i.*** To bind sheaf ; আঁটি বাঁধা। **Sheaf'-y**, *adj.* Pertaining to, or consisting of, sheaves ; শস্যের আঁটিসম্বন্ধীয়, শস্যের আঁটি দ্বারা রচিত। **Sheaf-binder**—শস্যের আঁটি বাঁধিবার জন্য কল।

shear (shēr), *v. t.* & *i.* 1. To cut or clip with shears ; বড় কাঁচি দ্বারা কাটা বা ছাঁটা। 2. To fleece ; "In his speculation he had gone out to *shear*, and come home *shorn*" ; ঠকাইয়া লওয়া। ***Verb i.*** 1. To cut ; to penetrate ; কাটা ; ভেদ করা। 2. To deviate ; মূল পথ হইতে বিচ্যুত হওয়া। **Shear'-er**, *n.* **Shear'-ing**, *n.*

shear (shēr), *n.* (*Pl.*) 1. A cutting instrument of two blades which move on a pivot and act against each other ; বড় কাঁচি। 2. An engine for raising heavy weights ; গুরুভার দ্রব্য উত্তোলনের জন্য যন্ত্রবিশেষ। 3. Any of various machines for cutting metal esp. sheet-metal ; ধাতু, বিশেষতঃ ধাতুর চাদর কাটিবার জন্য বিভিন্ন প্রকার যন্ত্রের অন্যতম, কাতানী। **Shear-bill**—এক প্রকার পক্ষী। **Shear-grass**—একপ্রকার খরধার তৃণ। **Shear-machine**—লৌহ প্রভৃতির ধাতুর পাত বা দণ্ড কাটিবার জন্য যন্ত্র বিশেষ; কাপড়ের ফুঁপি প্রভৃতি কাটিবার জন্য যন্ত্রবিশেষ। **Shear-tail**—বড় কাঁচির ন্যায় পুচ্ছবিশিষ্ট একপ্রকার পক্ষী। **Shear-water**—একপ্রকার সামুদ্রিক পক্ষী।

shear'-ling (shēr-), *n.* Sheep once shorn ; যে মেষের রোম একবার মাত্র ছাঁটা হইয়াছে।

sheat'-fish (shēt-), *n.* A fish with a long slimy scaleless body and the back dusky like that of eel ; বোয়াল মাছ, বোদাল মৎস্য, পাঠীন মৎস্য [Syn. সহস্রদংষ্ট্র, সহস্রদংষ্ট্রী, বদালক]।

sheath (shēth), *n.* 1. A scabbard ; কোষ, খাপ, পিধান। 2. The wing-case of an insect ; কীটের পক্ষকোষ। 3. (*Bot.*) A petiole when it embraces the branch from which it springs ; (পত্রের) কোষ (সাঃ পঃ)।

sheave (shēv), *n.* A grooved wheel of a pulley on which a rope works ; কপিকলের খাঁজবিশিষ্ট চাকা।

sheave (shēv), *v. t.* Same as SHEAF *v. t.*

shē-been' (-bēn), *n.* 1. An Irish smuggler's hat; আয়র্লণ্ডদেশের শুল্কদস্যুগণের টুপি। 2. A house where excisable liquors are sold without licence ; যে দোকানে বিনা লাইসেন্সে মদ বিক্রীত হয়।

shĕd, *v. t.* 1. To cast or throw off ; as, to *shed* tears ; পাত করা (cf. অশ্রু বা রক্তপাত করা), ফেলা (cf. চোখের জল ফেলা), মোচন করা, (cf. (অশ্রুমোচন করা)। 2. To throw off as natural coverings ; as, to *shed* skin ; মোচন করা, ত্যাগ করা, ছাড়া (cf. খোলস ছাড়া)। 3. To diffuse ; as, flowers *shed* their fragrace ; বিকীর্ণ করা, ছড়ান, নিঃসৃত করা। **Shed'-der**, *n.*

shĕd, *n.* A slight or temporary erection built to shelter something ; a hut ; a hovel ; চালা ; কুঁড়েঘর ; ঝুপড়ি।

sheen (shēn), *n.* Lustre ; brightness ; দীপ্তি, প্রভা, দ্যুতি ; চাক্‌চিক্য, চিক্‌নাই, ঔজ্জ্বল্য।

sheep (shēp), *n.* 1. A ruminant animal valued for its wool and flesh ; ভেড়া, মেষ [Syn. অবি, মেঢ্র, উরভ্র, উরণ, ঊর্ণায়ু, বৃষ্ণি, এড়ক, ভেড়, হুড়, শৃঙ্গিণ, লোমশ, বলী]। 2. One who is foolishly modest and backward ; বেকুব লোক, নির্ব্বোধ লোক। 3. God's people with reference to the divine shepherd ; দেবমেষপালকরূপী যীশুখৃষ্টের রক্ষণাধীন মেষরূপীজনগণ, খৃষ্টের মেষ সকল (অর্থাৎ খৃষ্টবিশ্বাসীজনগণ)। 4. Sheepskin ; পুস্তক বাঁধাইবার জন্য শোধিত চর্ম্ম। **Sheep'-ish**, *adj.* Shy ; মেনিমুখো (মিলনে), মুখচোরা। **Black-sheep**—See under BLACK. **Sheep-berry**—একপ্রকার গুল্ম। **Sheep-cot, Sheep-cote, Sheep-pen**—মেষের খোঁয়াড়। **Sheep-dog**—মেষপালকের কুকুর, (ঘন লোমশদেহ ও খর্ব্বাকৃতি)। **Sheep-farmer, Sheep-master**—যে ব্যক্তি বিক্রয়ের জন্য মেষ পালন করে। **Sheep-headed** — নির্ব্বোধ, বুদ্ধিশূন্য। **Sheep-hook** — মেষপালকের বক্রাগ্র যষ্টি। **Sheep-kneed** — মেষের মত জানুবিশিষ্ট [যে অশ্বের অগ্রপদের জানুর নীচের অংশ কিঞ্চিৎ সম্মুখে উদ্গত থাকে—তৎসম্পর্কে উক্ত হয়]। **Sheep-louse, Sheep-tick**—মেষদেহে জাত উৎকুণ। **Sheepshanks**—রজ্জু খাটো করার জন্য গ্রন্থি। **Sheepskin** — শোধিত মেষচর্ম্মপট ; ঐরূপ পটে মুদ্রিত দলিল, প্রশংসাপত্র, প্রভৃতি; সলোম মেষচর্ম্ম হইতে প্রস্তুত পরিচ্ছদ বা কম্বল ; পুস্তক বাঁধাইবার কাযে ব্যবহৃত শোধিত মেষচর্ম্ম। **Sheep's wool**—মেষলোম, অবিলোম। **Sheep-walk**—মেষচারণভূমি। **Sheep-wash** — মেষের দেহের অনিষ্টকারী কীটনাশের জন্য ঔষধজল বিশেষ, **Broad** or **Thick tailed**

sheep — মেষ, মেষক (ভাব প্রঃ)

Broad tailed sheep.

To cast sheep's eye at — To cast side-long glances; কটাক্ষ-ক্ষেপ করা, নয়নবাণ হানা, চোক ঠারা।

sheer (shēr), *adj.* & *adv.* **1.** Mere; absolute; downright; শুদ্ধ, কেবল; পুরা, ডাহা; বিলকুল। **2.** Very thin; as, *sheer* muslin; অতি মিহি। **3.** Vertical; as, *sheer* descent; খাড়া। ***Adv.*** **1.** Quite; পুরা। **2.** Perpendicularly; খাড়া ভাবে।

sheer (shēr), *v. i.* (*Naut.*) To deviate from course; (নৌ-বিদ্যা) বিপথে যাওয়া। **To sheer alongside**—To come gently alongside an object; ধীরে ধীরে কোন বস্তুর পাশাপাশি আসা। **To sheer off**—To move off; to steer out; সরিয়া যাওয়া; সরিয়া পড়া। **To sheer up**—To turn or approach to a place or ship; কোন স্থান বা জাহাজের অভিমুখে ফিরা বা অগ্রসর হওয়া।

sheer (shēr), *n.* **1.** The longitudinal curve or line which a ship's deck or side presents to the eye; জাহাজের পাটাতন বা পার্শ্ব যে রেখা বা বক্ররেখারূপে চক্ষুর নিকট প্রতিভাত হয়। **2.** Deviation of a ship from its course; জাহাজের পথ-বিচ্যুতি।

sheer (shēr), *n.* (*Pl.*) A kind of hoisting-apparatus used in masting or dismasting, putting in, or taking out boilers, mounting or dismounting guns, etc.; জাহাজের মাস্তুল, বাষ্পকুণ্ড বা কামান উঠাইবার বা লাগাইবার জন্য একপ্রকার উত্তোলন যন্ত্র। **Sheer-hulk**—জাহাজের মাস্তুল উঠাইবার নামাইবার উত্তোলনযন্ত্রযুক্ত জীর্ণ পোত।

sheet (shēt), *n.* & *v. t.* **1.** A broad large piece of anything made thin, as paper, steel, etc.; কাগজের তা, ফর্দ্দ, লৌহ প্রভৃতির পাত বা চাদর। **2.** A broad piece of linen or cotton spread on a bed; বিছানার চাদর, শয্যোত্তরচ্ছদ (রঃ)। **3.** A book or pamphlet; "To this the following *sheets* are intended for a full and distinct answer"; a newspaper; as, a penny *sheet*; পুস্তক, পুস্তিকা; সংবাদপত্র। **4.** (*Poet.*) A sail; "Fierce Boreas drove against his flying sails, And rent the *sheets*"; (কবিতায়) পাইল। **5.** A rope fastened to the lower corner of a sail, to extend it in a particular situation; পাইল কোন বিশেষ দিকে ছড়াইবার জন্য উহার নিম্নকোণে যে রজ্জু সংবদ্ধ করা হয়। **6.** An expanse; as, a *sheet* of water; বিস্তার, রাশি। ***Verb t.*** **1.** To fold in a sheet; চাদর দ্বারা ঢাকা। **2.** To furnish with sheets; পাত প্রভৃতি দ্বারা মণ্ডিত করা। **3.** To cover as with a sheet; পাত, চাদর, প্রভৃতি দ্বারা আবৃত করা। **Sheet′-ing,** *n.* Cotton cloth for making bedsheets; বিছানার চাদরের কাপড়। **Sheet-anchor**—যে বৃহৎ নোঙ্গর কেবল বিপদের সময় ব্যবহৃত হয়; শেষ আশ্রয়, শেষ অবলম্বন শেষ নির্ভর, চরম আশ্রয়স্থল। **Sheet-glass**—কাচফলক। **Sheet-iron**—লোহার পাত, লোহার চাদর। **Sheet-lightning** — বিকীর্ণ বিদ্যুৎ, ব্যাপ্ত বিদ্যুৎ [সাধারণতঃ মেঘের প্রতিফলনে ব্যাপ্তভাবে পরিদৃষ্ট হয়।]. **A sheet in the wind, Three sheets in the wind**—(*Slang*) Slightly intoxicated; (ইতরভাষায়) আধমাতাল।

shĕk′-ĕl, *n.* **1.** An ancient Jewish weight, of about half an ounce, and silver coin worth about 2*s.* 7*d*; প্রাচীন ইহুদীদিগের ওজন-বিশেষ (প্রায় অর্দ্ধ আউন্স), প্রাচীন ইহুদীদিগের রজতমুদ্রা-বিশেষ (মূল্য প্রায় ২ শিঃ ৭ পেঃ)।

Shĕ-kī′-nah (-nă), **—chī-,** *ns.* The symbol of the divine presence which rested over the mercy-seat in the form of a cloud or glory; ইহুদীদিগের মন্দিরের করুণাসনের উপরি বিরাজিত ভগবজ্জ্যোতিঃ।

shĕl′-drāke, *n.* A genus of birds of the duck family; চক্রবাক জাতীয় পক্ষিবিশেষ। **Ruddy sheldrake**—Same as RUDDY GOOSE (which see.)

shĕlf, *n.* (*Pl.* SHELVES) **1.** A board fixed to a wall or almirah to support articles; তাক। **2.** A shoal or sand-bank in the sea; সাগরগর্ভস্থ পর্ব্বত বা বালুকাতট। **3.** A projecting layer of rock; উদ্গত পাষাণস্তর। **Shelf′-ful,** *adj.* **To lay** or **put on the shelf**—To put aside; ফেলিয়া রাখা।

shĕll, *n., v. t.* & *i.* **1.** The hard or stony covering of some fruits and seeds and of certain animals

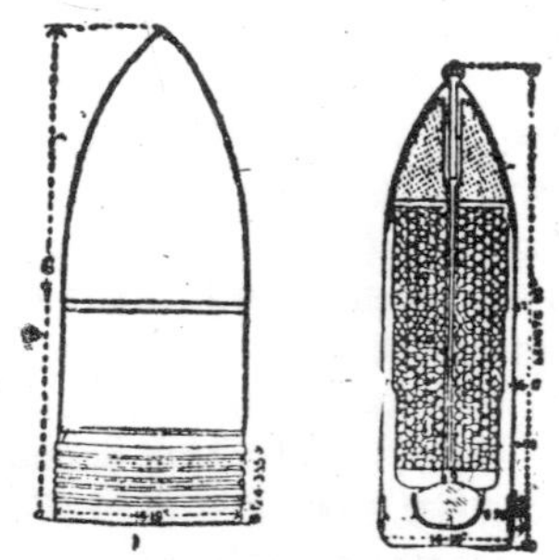

Shell for a 111-ton gun. 1, armor-piercing steel-shell; 2, shrapnel

as crabs, tortoise, etc., or an egg; খোলা, মালা (of cocoanut), চাড়া, কবচ, কঞ্চুক, খোসা। **2.** A shell-bearing mollusc; শুক্তি, শঙ্খ, কর্কট, কড়ি, প্রভৃতি। **3.** A projectile containing a bursting charge;

বিস্ফোরকদ্রব্যপূর্ণ গোলা, কামানের গোলা। **4.** A bomb-shell ; বোমা। **5.** A common coffin ; সাধারণ শবাধার। **6.** The outer part of a house unfinished ; অসম্পূর্ণ গৃহের বহির্ভাগ। **7.** An instrument of music, as a lyre ; বীণা প্রভৃতি বাদ্য যন্ত্র। **8.** A frame-work ; ঠাঁট, কাঠাম। **9.** A light racing-boat ; একপ্রকার হাল্‌কা বাইচের নৌকা। **10.** Handguard of a sword ; তরবারীর হস্তত্রাণ। **11.** An outward show ; a semblance ; বহির্দৃশ্য ; আভাস। ***Verb t.*** **1.** To stripe or break off the shell ; খোলা ভাঙ্গা, চাড়া ভাঙ্গা, খোসা ছাড়ান। **2.** To bombard ; গোলাবর্ষণ করা। ***Verb i.*** **1.** To cast the shell or outer covering ; খোলা ত্যাগ করা। **2.** (Of metals) To come off in scales ; (ধাতু সম্পর্কে) আঁইশের মত খসিয়া আসা। **Shell'-less, Shell'-y,** *adjs.* **Shell-back**—(ইতরভাষায়) বৃদ্ধ নাবিক। **Shell-bark** — একপ্রকার আখরোট-জাতীয় বৃক্ষ ও উহার বল্কল। **Shell-bit**—ছিদ্র করার জন্য বেধনী। **Shell-button**—কাপড়ের টুকরা প্রভৃতি আবৃত চাক্তিদ্বয় দ্বারা রচিত বোতাম। **Shell-fish**—শুক্তি, ঝিনুক, চিংড়ী, কর্কট, প্রভৃতি। **Shell-gun**—বিস্ফোরকদ্রব্যপূর্ণ গোলাবর্ষী কামান। **Shell-marble**—শিলীভূত শুক্তিশম্বুকাদিযুক্ত মর্ম্মর প্রস্তর। **Shell-proof** — গোলাদ্বারা অভেদ্য। **Shell-work**—কাঠ প্রভৃতির উপর ঝিনুকের কাজ। **An old shell**—বৃদ্ধমাল্লা। **To come out of the shell** — To throw off reserve ; সঙ্কোচ ত্যাগ করা। **To shell out**—(*Slang*) To pay up ; (ইতরভাষায়) পাওনা চুকাইয়া দেওয়া।

shĕl-lăc', *n.* & *v. t.* Lac melted and formed into thin cake ; লা বা গালার চাক্‌তি। ***Verb t.*** To varnish with shellac ; গালাদ্বারা বার্ণিশ করা।

shĕl'-tĕr, *n.* **1.** A protection ; আশ্রয়। **2.** An asylum ; আশ্রয়স্থল, আশ্রয়স্থান। **3.** One who shelters ; আশ্রয়দাতা। **To take or find shelter**—To take or find refuge ; আশ্রয় লওয়া, শরণ লওয়া।

shĕl'-tĕr, *v. t.* & *i.* **1.** To protect ; রক্ষা করা, আশ্রয় দেওয়া। **2.** To screen or cover from notice ; to disguise ; "In vain strove to check my growing flame ; And *shelter* passion under friendship's name" ; ঢাকিয়া রাখা, লুকাইয়া রাখা ; ছাপান। ***Verb i.*** To take shelter ; আশ্রয় নেওয়া, আশ্রয় গ্রহণ করা।

shĕl'-ty, —tie (-tĭ), *ns.* (*Scot.*) Shetland pony ; (স্কটলণ্ড) সেটলেণ্ডের টাট্টু ঘোড়া।

shĕl'-tỹ, *n.* A rude hut ; ঝুপড়ি, কুড়ে।

shelve (shĕlv), *v. t.* **1.** To place on a shelf or shelves ; তাকে রাখা। **2.** To put aside ; as, to *shelve* a question ; ফেলিয়া রাখা। **3.** To furnish with shelves ; তাক লাগান।

shelve (shĕlv), *v. i.* To slope gently ; মৃদু মৃদু প্রবণ হওয়া।

shelves (shĕlvs), *n., Pl* of SHELF (which see.)

Shĕ'-ŏl, *n.* (*Heb.*) Hades, or the abode of the dead ; (হিব্রুভাষায়) প্রেতলোক, নরক, যমপুরী।

shĕp'-herd (-ĕrd), *n.* & *v.t.* **1.** One who tends sheep ; মেষপাল, মেষপালক। **2.** A pastor ; পল্লীযাজক। ***Verb t.*** To tend sheep ; মেষচারণ করা, মেষ চরান। **—ess,** *n.* (*Fem.*) A woman who tends sheep ; a rural lass ; মেষপালিকা ; পল্লীবালিকা। **Shepherd-god** — বনদেবতা Panএর নামান্তর। **Shepherd Kings**—যে যাযাবর আরবজাতীয় লোকগণ খৃঃ পূঃ ২০০০ অব্দে মিসরদেশের নিম্নভাগ অধিকার করে—তাহাদের অধিনায়কবৃন্দ। **Shepherd's bag, Shepherd's-purse** — একপ্রকার গুল্ম। **Shepherd's crook**—মেষপালকদিগের বক্রাগ্র-যষ্টি। **Shepherd's-knot, —myrtle, —pouch, —rod, —staff**—বিভিন্ন প্রকার বৃক্ষের নাম। **The good Shepherd**—যীশুখৃষ্ট।

shĕp'-pỹ, *n.* A sheep-cote ; মেষশালা।

shĕr'-bĕt, *n.* An Eastern drink of water, the juice of fruits, and sugar ; শরবত, পানা (only used in reference to sugar and sugar-candy, cf. চিনির পানা), পানীয় (cf. মিষ্টদাড়িম্বপানীয়—পাকরাজেশ্বর), পানক।

shĕrd, *n.* Same as SHARD (which see).

Shĕ-reef' (-rēf), **—rif',** *ns.* **1.** A descendant of Mohammed through his daughter Fatima ; মহম্মদের কন্যা ফতিমার বংশধর। **2.** The chief magistrate of Mecca (Usu. called *Grand Shereef*) ; মক্কা নগরীর প্রধান শাসনকর্তা, শরীফ।

shĕr'-iff, *n.* **1.** The chief officer of crown in county or shire ; ইংলণ্ডের প্রধান প্রাদেশিক কর্ম্মচারী [ইঁহার উপর শান্তিরক্ষার ভার ন্যস্ত থাকে। আদালতের আদেশ এবং পরোয়ানা প্রভৃতি জারি ইনি করিয়া থাকেন। নির্ব্বাচনসভার সভাপতিত্বও ইঁহার অন্যতম কার্য্য।] **2.** The chief judge in Scotland ; স্কটলণ্ডের প্রধান বিচারপতি। **—dom, —ship, —alty,** *ns.* **Under-sheriff**—শেরিফের প্রতিনিধি।

shĕr'-rỹ, *n.* A wine of southern Spain ; স্পেনদেশের দক্ষিণাঞ্চলে প্রস্তুত মদিরাবিশেষ, শেরী। **Sherry-cobbler** — শেরীমদ্য, জল, লেবু বা কমলার রস, প্রভৃতির যোগে প্রস্তুত শ্রান্তিবারক পানীয়বিশেষ। **Sherry-glass**—যে মদের গেলাসে প্রায় ৪ টেবল চামচ মদ ধরে।

Shĕt'-lănd, *n.* A group of islands on the north of Scotland ; স্কটলণ্ডের উত্তরদিগ্‌বর্ত্তী দ্বীপপুঞ্জ। **Shetland lace**—একপ্রকার পশমী লেইস। **Shetland pony**—একপ্রকার শ্রমসহিষ্ণু অশ্ব। **Shetland-wool** — একপ্রকার উৎকৃষ্ট পশম।

shew (shō), *var.* of SHOW.

Shī'-ah (-ă), **Shī'-īte,** *ns.* A Mohammedan sect that regards the first successor of Mohammed and rejects the first three Sunni Caliphs ; মুসলমান সম্প্রদায়-বিশেষ—এই সম্প্রদায়ের লোকগণ আলীকে মহম্মদের প্রথম উত্তরাধিকারী বলিয়া গণ্য করে ও প্রথম তিন জন সুন্নী খলিফাকে অস্বীকার করিয়া থাকে।

shib'-bō-lĕth, *n.* 1. Watchword of a party ; that which distinguishes one party from another ; a pet phrase ; "But what comes Benthamism shorn of its *shibboleth*—a pet phrase, greatest happiness of greatest numbers" ; কোন দলের পরীক্ষাবাক্য বা সঙ্কেতবাক্য ; যদ্দ্বারা একদল হইতে অপর দলের বৈভিন্ন সূচিত হয় ; প্রিয়বাক্য [পুর্ব্বে ইহুদীদেশে কোন ব্যক্তি Gileadites কিম্বা Ephraimites জাতিভুক্ত তাহা নিরূপণের জন্য এই শব্দ ব্যবহৃত হইত। (শেষোক্ত জাতির লোক "*sh*" কে "*s*"এর মত উচ্চারণ করিত বলিয়া Shibbolethকে Sibbolethরূপে উচ্চারণ করিত (See *Judge.* XII. 6)।] 2. Old-fashioned doctrine ; সেকেলে মত।

shield (shēld), *n.* & *v. t.* 1. A broad piece of defensive armour ; ঢাল, চর্ম্ম, ফলক, খেটক (বুঃ সং)। 2. Anything that protects or defends ; রক্ষক। 3. A person that defends or protects ; "Fear not, Abraham, I am thy *shield* and thy exceeding great reward" ; রক্ষাকারী, রক্ষক। 4. (*Herald.*) Escutcheon ; (কুলবিদ্যা) কুলচিহ্নাঙ্কিত চর্ম্ম। ***Verb t.*** 1. To cover as with a shield ; ঢাল দ্বারা আবৃত করা। 2. To secure from danger ; to protect ; "A woman's shape doth *shield* thee" ; বিপদ্ হইতে রক্ষা করা ; রক্ষা করা। 3. (*Obs.*) To ward off ; (অপ্রঃ) রোধ করা, নিবারণ করা।

shi'-ĕr, —ĕst, Comparative and Superlative of SHY.

shift, *v. t.* & *i.* 1. To change in position ; as, to *shift* the ground ; স্থানান্তরিত করা, স্থান পরিবর্ত্তন করা। 2. To change ; as, to *shift* a shirt ; পরিবর্ত্তন করা, বদলান। 3. (*Obs.*) To evade ; to get rid of ; (অপ্রঃ) এড়ান ; রেহাই পাওয়া। ***Verb i.*** 1. To move ; to change place or position ; সরা ; স্থান পরিবর্ত্তিত হওয়া, দিক পরিবর্ত্তিত হওয়া, স্থানান্তরিত হওয়া ; 2. To resort to expedients ; to manage ; as, to *shift* for one's self (নিজের পথ দেখা) ; উপায় করা ; নির্ব্বাহ করা। 3. To fare ; to get along or make a livelihood ; চলা, চালান ; জীবিকার সংস্থান করা। **To shift about**—To vacillate ; ইতস্ততঃ করা, দ্বিধা করা। **To shift off**—To delay ; বিলম্ব করা। To disengage or disencumber one's self of ; মুক্ত করা, দায়িত্ব হইতে মুক্ত করা।

shift, *n.* 1. Change of place ; স্থানপরিবর্ত্তন। 2. Substitution of one thing for the other ; পরিবর্ত্তন, বদল। 3. Last resource ; artifice ; an evasion or subterfuge ; as, he tried many *shifts* ; শেষ উপায়, শেষ গতি ; চাতুরী ; ছল, ফন্দী, ফিকির। 4. (*Archaic*) A woman's chemise ; (অপ্রঃ) স্ত্রীলোকের সেমিজ। 5. (*Mining*) A dislocation of a seam or stratum ; (খনির কার্য্য) খনিজবিবিশ্র ধাতুর স্তরচ্যুতি। 6. A relay of workmen ; a turn of such work ; পর্য্যায়ক্রমে কার্য্যকারক শ্রমিকদল ; কাযের পালা। **Shift'-less,** *adj.* 1. Destitute of means ; unable to shift for one's self ; ফিকিরশূন্য, উপায়শূন্য ; নিজের জীবিকার সংস্থান করিতে অক্ষম। 2. Lazy ; inefficient ; অলস, কুড়ে ; অকর্ম্মণ্য, অক্ষম। **Shift'-y,** *adj.* Crafty, fertile in expedients ; well able to shift for one's self ; ধূর্ত্ত, চতুর ; উপায়জ্ঞ, কৌশলী ; সংস্থানক্ষম। **To make shift**—To manage by some artifice ; ফিকির খাটান, ফন্দী খাটান, পঞ্চাই ছক্কাই করা।

Shi'-ite, *n.* See SHIAH.

shil-lē'-lagh (-lā), **shil-lā'-lah** (-lā), **shil-lē'-lah** (-lā), **shil-lā'-li,** *ns.* (*Ireland*) An oaken cudgel ; ওক কাঠের যষ্টি।

shil-ling (-ing), *n.* A silver coin equal to twelve pence ; ইংলণ্ড দেশে প্রচলিত প্রায় বার আনা মূল্যের রৌপ্য-মুদ্রাবিশেষ, শিলিং। **To cut off one's heir etc. with a shilling**—To bequeath one's property ; চরমপত্র দ্বারা সম্পত্তি উত্তরাধিকারীকে দেওয়া। **To take King's** or **Queen's shilling**—To enlist in the army ; সৈন্যদলে ভর্ত্তি হওয়া। [পুর্ব্বে সৈন্যদলে ভর্ত্তি হওয়ার কালে রংরুটকে এক শিলিং দেওয়া হইত।]

shil-ly̆—shăl'-ly (-i), *n.* & *v. i.* Irresolution ; hesitation ; সংশয় ; দ্বিধা, গড়িমসি, টালমাটাল। ***Verb i.*** To act in an irresolute or undecided manner ; to vacillate ; টালমাটাল করা, গড়িমসি করা, ইতস্ততঃ করা, গয়ংগচ্ছ করা ; দ্বিধা করা।

shi'-ly̆, *adv.* Same as SHYLY under SHY.

shim, *n.* & *v. t.* A thin piece of metal placed between two parts to make a fit ; যন্ত্রাদির বিভিন্ন অংশ ঠিক করিয়া লাগাইবার জন্য উহাদের মধ্যে যে ধাতুর পাতল পাত প্রবিষ্ট করিয়া দেওয়া হয়। ***Verb t.*** To fit thus ; উক্ত প্রকার পাতের সাহায্যে যন্ত্রের অংশসমূহ ঠিক করিয়া লাগান।

shim'-mer (-ĕr), *v. i.* & *n.* To glisten ; to glimmer with a faint white light ; ঝক ঝক করা, ঝলমল করা, চিক চিক করা, ঝিলিমিলি করা, জ্বল জ্বল করা, ঝকমক করা, চিক্‌মিক্ করা, ঝিকমিক করা, ঝিকিমিকি করা ; ঝাঁ ঝাঁ করা, (মিলনে), ধু ধু করা (ঐ)। ***Noun.*** A tremulous light or gleam ; মিট মিট আলো, ঝিলিমিলি, ঝিকমিকি, চিকিমিকি, ধু ধু।

shim'-my (-i), *n.* (*Colloq.*) Chemise ; (চলিত ভাষায়) সেমিজ।

shin, *n.*, *v. i.* & *t.* The forepart of the leg esp. the human leg between the ankle and the knee ; জঙ্ঘার সম্মুখ অংশ, জঙ্ঘার অগ্রভাগ, জঙ্ঘাগ্রভাগ। *Verb i.* **1.** To kick on the shins ; জঙ্ঘার অগ্রভাগে পদাঘাত করা। **2.** To climb a tree by embracing with arms and legs ; হস্তপদের সাহায্যে বৃক্ষে আরোহণ করা। *Verb t.* **1.** To use the shins in climbing ; বৃক্ষাদি আরোহণে জঙ্ঘাগ্রাস্থি ব্যবহার করা। **2.** (*Slang*) To walk or run ; (ইতরভাষায়) হাঁটা, ছুটা। **3.**(In America) To borrow money ; (আমেরিকায়) টাকা ধার করা। **Shin-bone** — জঙ্ঘাস্থি। **Shin-guard**—(পাদগোলক ক্রীড়ায়) জঙ্ঘাগ্রভাগরক্ষক।

shin'-dy̆, *n.* A row ; brawl ; গোলমাল, হাঙ্গামা ; ঝগড়া।

shine, *v. i.* & *t.* **1.** To emit rays of lights ; আলোকরশ্মি নির্গত করা। **2.** To be bright ; দীপ্তিমান হওয়া, দীপ্ত হওয়া, উজ্জ্বল হওয়া। **3.** To be conspicuous or distinguished ; as, to *shine* in society ; সুপ্রকট হওয়া, গৌরবোজ্জ্বল হওয়া, প্রখ্যাত হওয়া। *Verb t.* (*Colloq.*) To make bright ; to polish ; as, to *shine* shoes ; (চলিত ভাষায়) উজ্জ্বল করা ; চক্‌চকে করা। **To cause the face to shine**—To be propitious ; (বাইবেল) সুপ্রসন্ন হওয়া, কল্যাণজনক হওয়া, মঙ্গলজনক হওয়া।

shine, *n.* **1.** Fair weather ; sunshine ; "Shower and *shine*" ; আকাশের প্রসন্নতা; রৌদ্র, সূর্য্যের আলো। **2.** Light ; brightness ; আলো ; দীপ্তি, প্রভা, ঔজ্জ্বল্য, দ্যুতি, উজ্জ্বলতা, চাকচিক্য, চিকনাই (*colloq.*)। **3.** (*Slang*) row ; (ইতর ভাষায়) গোলমাল। **4.** (In America) Fancy ; (আমেরিকায়) সখ। **To take the shine out of**—To cast into the shade ; to surpass ; মলিন করা ; অতিক্রম করা, ছাড়াইয়া যাওয়া।

shin'-ĕr, *n.* **1.** (*Slang*) Coin, esp. a bright one ; a sovereign ; (ইতর-ভাষায়) মুদ্রা, বিশেষতঃ চকচকে মুদ্রা ; সভারেণ। **2.** Money ; টাকা পয়সা। **3.** A kind of fish ; একপ্রকার মাছ।

shin'-gle (shing-gl), *n.* & *v. t.* A thin wooden plank used for roofing ; চাল ছাওয়ার জন্য কাঠের টালি। *Verb t.* To roof with shingle ; কাঠের টালিদ্বারা চাল ছাওয়া।

shin'-gle (shing-gl), *n.* Gravel and pebbles ; ক্ষুদ্রশিলাখণ্ড, নুড়ি, উপল।

shin'-gles (shing-glz), *n.* An eruptive disease which spreads round the body like a girdle ক্ষুদ্র ক্ষুদ্র পীড়কাবিশিষ্ট কটিবন্ধনীর চর্ম্মরোগ-বিশেষ, কীটদংষ্ট্র।

shin'-gly̆ (shing-), *adj.* Full of shingles ; উপলময়।

shin'-ing, *adj.* **1.** Bright ; উজ্জ্বল, উদ্ভাসমান, সমুজ্জ্বল, দীপ্ত। **2.** Illustrious ; as, a *shining* example ; সমুজ্জ্বল। **3.** (*Bot.*) Having most polished surface ; (উদ্ভিদ্‌বিদ্যা) মসৃণ এবং চক্‌চকে।

Shin'-tō, *n.* **1.** The religious belief of Japan prior to the introduction of Buddhism ; বৌদ্ধধর্ম্মের প্রবর্ত্তনের পূর্ব্ববর্ত্তী জাপানের ধর্ম [বৌদ্ধ-ধর্ম্ম ৫৫২ খৃঃ অব্দে কোরিয়া হইতে জাপানে প্রচারিত হয়]। **2.** A Shintoist ; সিণ্টোধর্ম্মাবলম্বী ব্যক্তি। **–ism**, *n.* The original religion of Japanese—a mixture of nature-worship and ancestor-worship ; প্রকৃতিপূজা ও পিতৃপুরুষার্চ্চনামূলক জাপানের প্রাচীন ধর্ম্ম [এই ধর্ম্মমতে মানবগণ দেববংশসম্ভূত এবং ধর্ম্মবুদ্ধিই মানবের প্রধান পরিচালক। সিণ্টো-ধর্ম্মাবলম্বিগণ বহু দেবদেবীর উপাসনা করিয়া থাকেন। সূর্য্যের অধিষ্ঠাত্রী Amatarasa দেবী ইহাদের সকল দেব-দেবীর মধ্যে প্রধানা। ইঁহার পীঠস্থান Ise নামক স্থানে বহুযাত্রীর সমাগম হইয়া থাকে।]

shin'-y̆, *adj.* **1.** Characterised by sun-light ; bright unclouded ; সূর্য্যকরোজ্জ্বল,রৌদ্রোজ্জ্বল; উজ্জ্বল প্রভাময়, দ্যুতিমান, ভাস্বর, সুপ্রভ, দীপ্তিমান; চাকচিক্যশালী ; মেঘমুক্ত। **2.** Glossy ; চকচকে, চিক্কণ।

ship, *n.*, *v. t.* & *i.* A large vessel adapted to navigation ; জাহাজ, পোত, অর্ণবযান, অর্ণবপোত [Syn. সমুদ্রবাহিকা, সমুদ্রকটক (বরাহমিহির—যোগযাত্রা — টীকা)]। *Verb t.* **1.** To put on board a ship ; to convey by water ; to receive in a ship ; to transport in a ship ; জাহাজে তোলা ; জলপথে বহন করা ; জাহাজে লওয়া ; জাহাজে চালান দেওয়া। **2** To engage for service on board a ship or other vessel ; as, to *ship* seamen ; জাহাজাদির কার্য্যে নিযুক্ত করা। **3.** (*Colloq.*) To get rid of ; (চলিত ভাষায়) রেহাই পাওয়া। **4.** To fix in its proper place ; as, to *ship* the oars ; যথাস্থানে রাখা। *Verb i.* **1.** To go on board a vessel ; জাহাজে উঠা। **2.** To be engaged to serve on board of a vessel ; জাহাজের কার্য্যে নিযুক্ত হওয়া। **Ship-biscuit**—জাহাজে ভোজনের জন্য একপ্রকার কঠিন বিস্কুট। **Ship-board**—জাহাজের পাটাতন, জাহাজের তক্তা ; জাহাজের পার্শ্ব। **Ship-boy**—জাহাজের কার্য্যে নিযুক্ত বালকভৃত্য, জাহাজের ছোকরা চাকর। **Ship-breaker**—যে ঠিকাদার পুরাতন এবং অব্যবহার্য্য জাহাজ ভাঙ্গিয়া থাকে। **Ship-broker**—জাহাজ বন্দরে আসিলে যে ব্যক্তি জাহাজের মালপত্রাদির বন্দোবস্ত করিয়া দেয় ; জাহাজ ক্রয়বিক্রয়ের দালাল ; যে ব্যক্তি জাহাজ বীমা করিয়া দেয়। **Ship-building** — পোতনির্ম্মাণকার্য্য, জাহাজ নির্ম্মাণের কায। **Ship-canal**—জাহাজ গমনা-গমনের উপযোগী খাল। **Ship-captain** — পোতাধ্যক্ষ। **Ship-chandler**—যে ব্যক্তি ক্যাম্বিস, দড়াদড়ী, এবং জাহাজের অন্যান্য সাজসজ্জা বিক্রয় করে। **Ship-fever**—একপ্রকার মোহ-জনক সান্নিপাতিক জ্বর। **Shipful**—জাহাজভরা, জাহাজবোঝাই। **Ship-holder**—জাহাজের মালিক। **Ship-letter** — ডাকের জাহাজ ছাড়ার জন্য জাহাজে নীত পত্র। **Shipload**—জাহাজ বোঝাই। **Shipmate** — সহনাবিক,

নাবিকের কার্য্যে সহযোগী। **Ship-money**—সরকারী নৌ-বিভাগের জাহাজ যোগাইবার জন্য যে কর বসান হয় [ইংলণ্ডের রাজা প্রথম চার্লস এই কর পুনরায় বসাইতে গেলে জনসাধারণের পক্ষ হইতে তীব্র আপত্তি উঠে এবং ইহারই ফলে ভীষণ রাজ্যবিপ্লব সংঘটিত হয়]। **Shipowner**—জাহাজের মালিক, জাহাজকোম্পানীর অংশীদার। **Ship-railway**—এক জলরাশি হইতে অপর জলরাশিতে জাহাজ নেওয়ার জন্য লৌহবর্ত্ম। **Shipshape**—ফিটফাট, ঠিকঠাক, সাজানো গোছান। **Ship's-husband**—জাহাজের দালাল (অর্থাৎ যে ব্যক্তি জাহাজের মালপত্রাদি জোগাড় করিয়া দেয়)। **Ship's papers**—জাহাজের মালিকের নাম, জাহাজ কোন জাতির ও ইহাতে কোন জাতীয় মালপত্র আছে—তাহা যে কাগজপত্র হইতে জানা যায়, জাহাজের কাগজ। **Ship-way**—যে হেলানো কাঠামের উপর জাহাজ নির্ম্মিত হয়। **Ship-worm**—জাহাজের কাঠে ছিদ্রকারী একপ্রকার শম্বুকজাতীয় প্রাণী। **Shipwreck**, *n.* & *v.t.* জাহাজ ডুবি, পোতভঙ্গ, বিপ্লব (হরিঃ), নৌব্যসন (শকুঃ), যানভঙ্গ (রত্নাবলী), প্রবহণভঙ্গ (ঐ), বহিত্রভঙ্গ (সাঃ দঃ), পোতসঙ্কট। (*Verb t.*) জাহাজ ভঙ্গ করা। **Ship-wright**—জাহাজ নির্ম্মাতা। **Ship-yard**—পোতনির্ম্মাণস্থলী। **Ship of the line**—বৃহৎ রণপোত। **The ship of the desert**—উষ্ট্র (*Lit.* মরুপোতক, cf. Sans. মরুদ্বীপ)। **To make shipwreck**—To be ruined ; ধ্বংসপ্রাপ্ত হওয়া। **To make or suffer shipwreck of one's hopes etc.**—To frustrate one's hopes or to be frustrated in one's hopes; কাহারো আশা ভঙ্গ করা, কাহারো আশা ভঙ্গ হওয়া। **To ship a sea**—To have the deck of a ship washed by a wave ; জাহাজের পাটাতনের উপর দিয়া ঢেউ বহিয়া যাওয়া। **To ship off**—To send away by water ; জলপথে প্রেরণ করা। **To take ship**—To embark ; জাহাজে উঠা। To take service in a ship ; জাহাজে কায নেওয়া। **When one's ship comes in, When one's ship comes home**—When one becomes rich ; যখন কেহ ধনী হইয়া উঠে।

ship'-mĕnt, *n.* **1.** Putting of goods etc. on board of a ship ; জাহাজে মাল বোঝাই করণ। **2.** Goods etc. shipped ; as, the merchants have made large *shipments* to Calcutta ; জাহাজে প্রেরিত মাল।

ship'-per (-êr), *n.* One who sends or gets goods by ship ; যে ব্যক্তি জাহাজে মাল প্রেরণ বা আনয়ন করে।

ship'-ping (-ĭng), *adj.* & *n.* Pertaining to ships ; জাহাজ সম্বন্ধীয়, পোতসম্বন্ধীয়। ***Noun.*** **1.** Ships or vessels of any kind for navigation in a port or a country ; the collective body of ships ; কোন বন্দর বা দেশের সমগ্র পোত সংখ্যা ; পোতশ্রেণী। **Shipping-agent**—কোন জাহাজ বা জাহাজ-কোম্পানীর প্রতিনিধি। **Shipping-articles**—(বেতনাদি সম্পর্কে) জাহাজের অধ্যক্ষ এবং মাল্লাদিগের মধ্যে চুক্তিপত্র। **Shipping-bill**—জাহাজে প্রেরিত মালের চালান। **Shipping-master**—যে কর্ম্মচারীর সম্মুখে জাহাজের প্রেরিত মালের চালান সহি এবং ভাড়া প্রভৃতি প্রদান করা হয় ; জাহাজের প্রতিনিধি। **Shipping-office**—জাহাজের গোমস্তা বা প্রতিনিধির কার্য্যালয়।

shi-râz' (shē-), *n.* A rich wine from Shiraz in Persia ; পারস্য দেশের সিরাজ নগরী হইতে আনীত একপ্রকার উৎকৃষ্ট সুরা, সিরাজী।

shīre, *n.* One of the divisions of Great Britain ; a county ; গ্রেটব্রিটেনের বিভাগবিশেষ ; জেলা। **Shire-horse**—লিঙ্কলন ও ক্যাম্ব্রিজ-সায়ার প্রভৃতি স্থানে প্রাপ্ত একপ্রকার বৃহৎকায় ভারবাহী অশ্ব। **Shire-town**—গ্রেটব্রিটেনের জেলার প্রধান নগর।

shirk (shêrk), *v. t.* & *n.* To avoid or get off from ; to slink away ; as, to *shirk* duty ; এড়ান, পরিহার করা ; কর্ত্তব্য এড়াইয়া চুপি চুপি সরিয়া পড়া। ***Noun.*** One who seeks to avoid duty, responsibily, fighting, danger, etc. ; যে ব্যক্তি কর্ত্তব্যকার্য্য, দায়িত্ব, বিপৎ, যুদ্ধ, প্রভৃতি এড়ায়, কর্ত্তব্যকার্য্যে পশ্চাৎপদ ব্যক্তি, কর্ত্তব্যপরাঙ্মুখব্যক্তি। **Shirk'-er**, *n.* Same as SHIRK, *n.*

shirr (shêr), *n.* & *v.t.* An insertion of cord (usu. elastic), in cloth or between two pieces of cloths ; the cord itself ; কোন বস্ত্র বা বস্ত্রখণ্ডদ্বয়ের মধ্যে রজ্জু (বিশেষতঃ স্থিতিস্থাপক রজ্জু) প্রবেশন ; ঐরূপ রজ্জু। ***Verb t.*** To pucker or draw up cloth by gathering threads ; সুতা টানিয়া বস্ত্র কুঞ্চিত করা। **Shirr'-ing**, *n.*

shirt (shêrt), *n.* A loose garment of cotton, linen, etc. worn next the skin by men and boys ; কামিজ, সার্ট, জামা। **Shirt'-ing**, *n.* Cloth for shirts ; সার্টের কাপড়। **Shirt-blouse, Shirt-waist**—স্ত্রীলোকদিগের একপ্রকার সাদাসিধাধরণের ব্লাউস—যাহার বোতাম সামনের দিকে থাকে। **Shirt-front**--জামার বুক, আল্লা বুক। **Oxford shirting**—জামার জন্য একপ্রকার শক্ত ডোরাদারর চৌখুপী কাপড়। **Red shirting**—সালু। **Near is my shirt, but nearer is my skin**—Self is the first consideration ; সকলের আগে নিজের কথা ভাবতে হয়। **Stripped to the shirt, In one's shirt-sleeves**—কেবলমত্র সার্ট জামা পরিহিত (কোট এবং ওয়েষ্ট-কোট বিহীন)।

shiv'-êr, *v. i., t.* & *n.* To quake ; to tremble ; কাঁপা, কম্পিত হওয়া ; শিহরা, শির শির করা, থর থর করা। ***Verb t.*** To cause to tremble ; কম্পিত করা, কাঁপান। ***Noun.*** **1.** A shaking with cold or fear ; কম্প, কাঁপুনি, কাঁপ, বেপথু, শিহরণ। **2.** (*Pl.*) A shaking fit ; ague ; কম্প, কম্পজ্বর।

shiv′-êr, *v. i., t.* & *n.* To fall at once into many small pieces or parts ; খণ্ডবিখণ্ড হওয়া, চূর্ণ বিচূর্ণ হওয়া। ***Verb t.*** To shatter ; to dash into pieces ; খণ্ডবিখণ্ড করা; চূর্ণ বিচূর্ণ করা। ***Noun.*** One of the small pieces or the pieces into which a thing is shattered ; ভগ্নখণ্ড, ভগ্নখণ্ডসমূহ। **—ing,** *n* **—y,** *adj.*

shoal (shōl), *adj., n.* & *v. i.* Shallow ; অগভীর। ***Noun.*** A sand-bank or bar ; নদ্যাদির যে স্থানে অল্প জল থাকে, কচ্ছ (সাঃ পঃ)। ***Verb i.*** To become more shallow ; অগভীরতর হওয়া।

shoal (shōl), *n.* & *v. i.* A crowd ; a throng (said esp. of fish) ; a great quantity ; as, *shoals* of letter ; দল, সমূহ ; ঝাঁক ; রাশিরাশি। ***Verb i.*** (Of fish) To form shoals ; (মৎস্যসম্পর্কে) ঝাঁক বাঁধা।

shŏck, *n.* **1.** A violent collision or concussion ; সংঘর্ষণ, সংঘাত, ধাক্কা, টক্কর। **2.** Anything which causes a sudden or violent impression or sensation ; as, the death of his father caused him a great *shock* ; মানসিক ধাক্কা, আঘাত। **3.** (*Electr.*) The effect on the animal-system of a discharge of electricity; (তাড়িতবিদ্যা) তড়িতস্পর্শজনিত স্নায়বিক ধাক্কা। **4.** (*Med.*) Any agitation or derangement of organic functions, and esp. of the nervous system ; শারীরিকযন্ত্রের,—বিশেষতঃ স্নায়ুচক্রের ক্রিয়ার বিক্ষোভ বা বিশৃঙ্খলতা, স্নায়বিকধাক্কা (ডাক্তারি)। **5.** (*Colloq.*) A sudden attack of paralysis ; পক্ষাঘাত রোগের আকস্মিক আক্রমণ। **Shock action**—অশ্বারোহী সৈন্যগণের প্রচণ্ড আক্রমণ। **Shock-battalion**—প্রচণ্ডভাবে শত্রুপক্ষের উপর আপতনের জন্য সৈন্যসমূহ। **Shock tactics**—ঘনসন্নিবিষ্ট অশ্বারোহী সৈনিকগণদ্বারা প্রচণ্ডভাবে আক্রমণের নীতি।

shŏck, *v. t.* & *i.* To strike with surprise, horror, terror or disgust ; to scandalise ; স্তম্ভিত করা, আপ্লুত করা, ঘৃণা বা বিরাগ উৎপাদন করা ; বীভৎস আচরণ দ্বারা স্তম্ভিত করা। ***Verb i.*** To meet with a shock ; to meet with a violent encounter ; ধাক্কা খাওয়া; প্রচণ্ডবেগে পরস্পরকে আক্রমণ করা। **Shock′-ing,** *adj.* Very obnoxious or repugnant ; বীভৎস, বিকট, উৎকট। **Shock′-ing-ly,** *adv.*

shŏck, *n.* & *v. t.* A pile of sheaves of wheat, rye, etc. ; শস্যের আঁটির স্তূপ। ***Verb t.*** To make up into shock or shocks ; শস্যের আঁটি সমূহ স্তূপাকারে রাখা।

shŏck, *adj.* & *n.* Shaggy ; having shaggy hair ; ঝাঁকড়ামাকড়া ; ঝাঁকড়ামাকড়াচুলবিশিষ্ট। ***Noun.*** **1.** A mass of shaggy hair ; ঝাঁকড়ামাকড়া চুল। **2.** A dog with shaggy hair ; ঝাঁকড়ামাকড়া চুলওয়ালা কুকুর। **Shock-dog**—Same as SHOCK, *n.* 2. **Shock-head, —headed**—ঝাঁকড়ামাকড়াচুলবিশিষ্ট।

shŏck′-êr, *n.* (*Colloq.*) A sensational novel or tale ; (চলিতভাষায়) উত্তেজনাপূর্ণ গল্প বা উপন্যাস, আক্কেলগুড়ুম।

shŏd, *pt.* & *p. p.* of SHOE (which see).

shŏd′-dy (-ĭ), *n.* & *adj.* **1.** (*Orig.*) Waste of wool in the manufacture of woollen goods ; (পূর্ব্বে) পশমী বস্ত্র প্রস্তুত করার কালে যে অব্যবহার্য্য এবং অপকৃষ্ট অংশ বাহির হয়। **2.** A fibre obtained from old woollen rags, torn up by machinery ; পুরাতন পশমী কাপড় হইতে কলের সাহায্যে যে অংশু বাহির করা হয়। **3.** The coarse inferior cloth made from this substance ; পুরাতন পশমী কাপড়ের তন্তু হইতে প্রস্তুত একপ্রকার স্থূল এবং নিকৃষ্ট বস্ত্র। **3.** Refuse or inferior articles of any kind ; কোনপ্রকার আবর্জ্জনা বা নিকৃষ্ট জিনিষ, জঞ্জাল। ***Adj.*** **1.** Made of shoddy; পুরাতন পশমী কাপড়ের সূতায় তৈরী। **2.** Trashy ; as, *shoddy* literature ; inferior ; sham ; বাজে, অসার ; নিকৃষ্ট ; ঝুঁটা।

shoe (shō), *n.* & *v. t.* **1.** A covering for the foot made of leather, canvas or rubber ; জুতা, পাদুকা, চর্ম্মপাদুকা [Syn. উপানৎ, বিনামা *colloq.* (used esp. by Mohamedans), পয়জার (*slang*), পন্নদ্ধা, পাদরক্ষিকা, প্রাণহিতা, পন্নদ্ধ্রী, কৌষী, পাদরথী।] [ব্রহ্মচারিণী মহাশ্বেতা নারিকেলত্বকের পাদুকা পরিধান করিতেন, কাদম্বরীতে উল্লেখ পাওয়া যায়। অগ্নিপুরাণে দেখা যায় জমদগ্নিমুনির পত্নী রেণুকা নিদাঘের তপ্তবালুকার উপর ভ্রমণে অতিশয় কাতরা হন। তদ্দর্শনে মুনিবর সূর্য্যের প্রতি কোপান্বিত হইয়া বাণদ্বারা তাঁহাকে সংহার করিতে উদ্যত হইলে তপনদেব ছত্র ও পাদুকা দান করিয়া ঋষির কোপ হইতে রক্ষা পান। এই স্থলেও ঋষিপত্নীর পাদুকাপরিধানের ইঙ্গিত আছে। প্রাচীনকালে রমণীগণের পাদুকা পরিধান সম্বন্ধে প্রাচীনশাস্ত্রে ও কাব্যাদিতে ভূরি ভূরি প্রমাণ আছে।] **2.** A plate of iron nailed to the hoof of an animal to defend it from injury ; ঘোড়া প্রভৃতির নাল। **3.** Anything more or less resembling a shoe in form or use ; ব্যবহারে বা আকারে পাদুকার অনুরূপ কোন বস্তু। **4.** An iron socket into which the end of a rafter is fitted ; যে লোহার কোঠরের মধ্যে গৃহের বর্গার প্রান্ত লাগান হয়। **5.** (*Electr.*) An apparatus which bears on the third rail in electric railway and conveys the current to the motor; (তড়িতবিদ্যা) তাড়িতশক্তিচালিত রেলগাড়ীর তৃতীয় রেলধারক যন্ত্রবিশেষ—যদ্দ্বারা সঞ্চালক যন্ত্রে তাড়িতপ্রবাহ সঞ্চারিত হয়। **6.** A notched piece on which something rests ; যে খাঁজকাটা বস্তুতে কোন কিছু বিধৃত থাকে। **7.** A small block of wood fastened to the fluke of an anchor, to prevent it from cutting the ship's side in hoisting etc. ; নোঙ্গর তোলানামার সময় যাহাতে জাহাজের পার্শ্ব না কাটিতে পারে—তজ্জন্য উহার হূল-ফলাতে যে ক্ষুদ্র কাষ্ঠখণ্ড লাগান হয়। 8. (*Railway*) That part of a brake which is brought in contact with the wheel ; (লৌহবর্ত্ম) চক্রগতি-রোধকযন্ত্রের যে অংশ চক্রের সহিত সংলগ্ন করা হয়। 9. The bend at the bottom of a water-pipe which discharges the water from a building ; দালানের জলনির্গমের চোঙ্গের অগ্রভাগে সংযুক্ত বক্রখণ্ড। 10. A kind of inclined trough ; একপ্রকার হেলানো কাঠের নালা। 11. A sort of drag placed under the wheel of a loaded vehicle on going down a steep part of a road ; রাস্তার খাড়া অংশে যাওয়ার কালে গাড়ীর গতি হ্রাস করার জন্য বোঝাই গাড়ীর চাকার নীচে যে কাষ্ঠ বা লৌহফলক লাগাইয়া দেওয়া হয়। 12. The step of a mast ; যে কোঠরের উপর মাস্তুল খাড়া করা হয়। ***Verb t.*** To fix with a shoe or shoes ; জুতালাগান, নাল লাগান। **Horse-shoe**—ঘোড়ার নাল। **Shoe-bill**—একপ্রকার পক্ষী। **Shoe-black**—যে ব্যক্তি রাস্তার লোকের জুতায় কালি দেয়। **Shoe-flower**—জবাফুল [Syn. ওড্রপুষ্প, ওড্রাখ্যা, রক্তপুষ্পী, অর্কপ্রিয়া, রাগপুষ্পী, প্রতিকা, হরিবল্লভা।] **Shoehorn, Shoeing-horn**—অক্লেশে জুতা পরিবার জন্য একপ্রকার শৃঙ্গ বা ধাতুর ফলক। **Shoe-lace, Shoe-string**—জুতার ফিতা। **Shoe-leather**—জুতার চামড়া। **Shoe-maker**—পাদুকা নির্ম্মাতা, পাদুকাকার, মোচিক (অঃ)। **As good a man as ever trod shoe-leather**—As good a man as ever lived ; অনন্যদশজনের মত একজন। **Quite a different pair of shoes**—Quite a different matter ; স্বতন্ত্র বিষয়, অন্যরূপ ব্যাপার, সে আর এক কথা। **This is where the shoe pinches**—See PINCH. **To be in another's shoes**—To be in o[illegible] ion or place ; কাহারো স্থা[illegible] স্থিত বা প্রতিষ্ঠিত হওয়া। **To die in one's shoes**—To die suddenly by violence ; to be hanged ; অপঘাত মৃত্যু হওয়া ; ফাঁসী হওয়া। **To put the shoe on the right foot**—To lay the blame on the right person ; প্রকৃত অপরাধীর ঘাড়ে দোষ ফেলা। **To shake in one's shoes**—To tremble in fear ; ভয়ে থরহরি কম্পমান হওয়া। **To tread the shoes straight**—To be righteous ; সৎপথে চলা। **To wait for another's shoes**—To wait for another's death ; কাহারো মৃত্যুর জন্য অপেক্ষা করা।

shō'-gŭn, *n.* Under the Japanese feudal system, the hereditary commander-in-chief of the Japanese army ; জাপান দেশীয় সামন্ত-তন্ত্রানুযায়ী জাপানের পুরুষানুক্রমিক সর্ব্ব-প্রধান সেনাপতি (১৮৬৮ খৃষ্টাব্দে এই পদের বিলোপ করা হয়)।

shone (shŏn), *p. p.* & *p. t.* of SHINE (which see.)

shōō, *Interj., v. t.* & *i.* Begone ; দূর হও ! যাও ! (পাখী তাড়াইতে ব্যবহৃত হয়)। ***Verb t.*** To scare away birds by crying shoo ; সু সু শব্দ করিয়া পাখী তাড়ান। ***Verb i.*** To cry shoos ; পাখী তাড়াইবার জন্য সু সু শব্দ করা।

shōōk, *p.t.* of SHAKE (which see).

shōōk, *n.* & *v. t.* A set of staves and headings sufficient to make one cask, or a set of boards sufficient to make a sugar-box, prepared or fitted for putting together ; এক পিপা নির্ম্মাণের উপযোগী কাষ্ঠফলক, মাথালী প্রভৃতি সরঞ্জাম, একটী চিনির বাক্স প্রস্তুতের উপযোগী কাষ্ঠফলক সমূহ। ***Verb t.*** To pack as staves in shooks ; একটী পিপা বা চিনির বাক্স নির্ম্মাণের উপযোগী কাষ্ঠফলক-সমূহ একত্র সংবদ্ধ করা।

shōōt, *v. i.* & *t.* 1. To perform the act of discharging a missile from a gun, fire-arm or bow, etc. ; to fire ; গুলি ছোড়া, বাণ নিক্ষেপ করা, বন্দুক ছোড়া ; বন্দুক আওয়াজ করা। 2. To germinate ; অঙ্কুরিত হওয়া, গজান। 3. To grow rapidly ; to avance to maturity ; দ্রুত বর্দ্ধিত হওয়া, তাড়াতাড়ি বাড়া ; পরিণতিরদিকে অগ্রসর হওয়া। 4. To feel a quick darting pain ; as, *shooting* pains ; টন্‌টনে বা কন্‌কনে ব্যথা করা। 5. To increase in value ; as, the price *shot up* ; মূল্য বৃদ্ধি পাওয়া, দাম চড়া। 6. To jut ; to project ; to push or be pushed out ; as, the tree *shot up* against the sky ; উদ্গত হওয়া ; প্রলম্বিত হওয়া; ঠেলিয়া উঠা বা ঠেলা খাইয়া উঠা। 7. To solidify ; ঘনীভূত হওয়া, জমাট বাঁধা। 8. To dart ; ছুটা, বেগে ধাবিত হওয়া। ***Verb t.*** 1. To let fly, or cause to be driven with force, as an arrow or bullet ; সবেগে নিক্ষেপ করা, ছোঁড়া। 2. To cast ; to emit ; to dart ; to throw ; as, they had just *shot* their nets ; নিক্ষেপ করা ; সবেগে নির্গত করা ; ছুটান ; ফেলা। 3. To kill or wound with a missile from a gun etc. ; গুলি করা, গুলি করিয়া মারা, বাণবিদ্ধ করা, শরবিদ্ধ করা। 4. To push or thrust forward ; বহির্গত করা, বাহির করা, প্রলম্বিত করা, ঠেলিয়া দেওয়া। 5. To pass rapidly through, under or over ; ছুটিয়া চলা, দ্রুতবেগে ছুটা। 6. To variegate as if by sprinkling and intermingling of different colours ; as, a piece of silk *shot* with green, purple and red ; to show different colours at different angles ; ধুপছায়া রঙ্গের করা ; বিভিন্ন কোণ হইতে বিভিন্ন বর্ণ প্রদর্শন করা। 7. To send forth new parts, as plants ; শাখাপল্লবাদি নির্গত করা, অঙ্কুরিত করা। 8. To plane straight or fit by planing ; রেঁদা করা, রেদা করিয়া লাগান।

9. To hunt over; শিকার করা। **Shoot´-ing,** *adj.* & *n.* **Shooting-box**—See BOX 8. **Shooting-coat, Shooting-jacket**—শিকারীর কোর্ত্তা বা জামা। **Shooting-iron**—(ইতর-ভাষায়) বন্দুকাদি। **Shooting pain**—টন্‌টনে ব্যথা, কন্‌কনে ব্যথা, কটকটে ব্যথা। **Shooting-range**—চাঁদমারির মাঠ। **Shooting star** — উল্কা। **I'll be shot**—যদি না হয় তবে আমাকে যা খুসী বলিও। **To shoot ahead**—To come quickly to the front of competitors etc.; প্রতিযোগী প্রভৃতির অগ্রে দ্রুত ছুটিয়া আসা। **To shoot Niagara**—(See NIAGARA.) **To shoot rubbish**—গাড়ী বা ভাণ্ড হইতে আবর্জ্জনা গড়াইয়া ফেলা। **To shoot the moon** —(*Slang*) To remove household goods by night to escape paying rent; ভাড়া দেওয়ার দায় হইতে অব্যাহতি পাওয়ার জন্য রাত্রে গোপনে জিনিষ পত্র সরান। **To shoot the pit**—To make oneself scarce without paying rent; জমিদারের খাজানা না দিয়া চম্পট দেওয়া। **To shoot the sun**—To measure the altitude of the sun; সূর্য্যের উচ্চতা পরিমাপ করা। **To shoot up**—(*Slang, U.S.*) To shoot hither and thither; (মার্কিণ যুক্তরাজ্যে—ইতর ভাষায়) এখানে ওখানে গুলি করা।

shoot, *n.* **1.** The act of shooting; গুলিকরণ, বাণক্ষেপণ। **2.** A match at a shooting party; গুলি ছোঁড়ার প্রতিদ্বন্দ্বিতা। **3.** A young branch issuing from the main stock; ডগা (সাঃ পঃ), পল্লব (ঐ), অঙ্কুর (ঐ), গজা (ঐ)। **4.** An inclined trough down which things may slide; যে হেলানো কাঠের নালার উপর দিয়া কোন কিছু গড়াইয়া পড়িতে পারে। **5.** A rapid; নদীর যে অংশে অতি বেগে স্রোত প্রবাহিত হয়।

shoot´-er, *n.* **1.** One who shoots; যে ব্যক্তি গুলি ছোঁড়ে, বাণক্ষেপকারী। **2.** An implement for shooting; a gun; গুলি প্রভৃতি ছোঁড়ার যন্ত্র, বন্দুক। **3.** (*Cricket*) A ball that rolls along the ground; ক্রীকেট ক্রীড়ায় যে কন্দুক ভূমিতে গড়াইয়া চলে।

shoot´-ing, *n.* **1.** The act of one who shoots; গুলিকরণ। **2.** Estate etc. rented to shoot over; গুলি ছোড়ার জন্য যে ভূমি খাজানা করিয়া লওয়া হয়। **3.** The right of shooting over any particular land; কোন বিশেষ ভূমিতে গুলি ছোড়ার অধিকার।

shŏp, *n.* & *v. i.* **1.** A place in which goods are sold by retail; দোকান, বিপণি, পণ্যশালা, আপণ, বিক্রয়শালা। **2.** A building where operatives work; as, a joiner's *shop*: an engineering *shop*; কর্ম্মশালা, কারখানা। **3.** (*Colloq.*) One's business or profession; "The *shop* sits heavy on him"; (চলিতভাষায়) কায, ব্যবসায়। **4.** (*Slang*) School; university; (ইতর ভাষায়) বিদ্যালয়; বিশ্ববিদ্যালয়। ***Verb i.*** To visit shops for the purpose of buying goods; বাজার করা, হাট করা। **Shop´-py,** *adj.* Pertaining to a shop or shops; বিপণিসংক্রান্ত, দোকান-সম্পর্কীয়। **Shop-boy, Shop-girl**—দোকানের কার্য্যে নিযুক্ত বালক বা বালিকা। **Shop-keeper**—দোকানদার, দোকানী [Syn. আপণিক, পণ্যাজীব]। **Shop-lifter**—যে ব্যক্তি জিনিষ ক্রয়ের ছলে কোন দোকানে যাইয়া জিনিষপত্র অপহরণ করে। **Shopwalker**—বড় দোকানে যে ব্যক্তি ক্রেতাদিগকে সাহায্য করে। **Shop-window** — দোকানের জানালা—যেখানে জিনিষ পত্র প্রদর্শিত হয়। **Shop-worn**—দোকানের লাট। **To shut up shop** — To cease doing something; কাজ বন্ধ করা, দোকানপাট বন্ধ করা। **To sink the shop**—To refrain from talking shop; to conceal one's occupation; কায কারবারের কথা বন্ধ কর; নিজের ব্যবসায়ের কথা গোপন রাখা। **To talk shop**—To make one's profession, business, etc. the subject of one's conversation; কেবল নিজের কাজ কারবারের কথা আলাপ করা।

shōre, *n.* The land bordering on a sea or a large mass of water; সাগরতীর, উপকূল, সমুদ্রতট, বেলা, বেলাভূমি। **2.** (*Law*) as FORESHORE. **Shore´-less,** *adj.* Having no shore or coast; অকূল, অপার, নিষ্পার, দুষ্পার (ষট্), বেলাবিহীন (বঃ বিঃ), কূলহারা।

shōre, *n.* & *v. t.* One of the props by which a ship is supported on dryland or by which

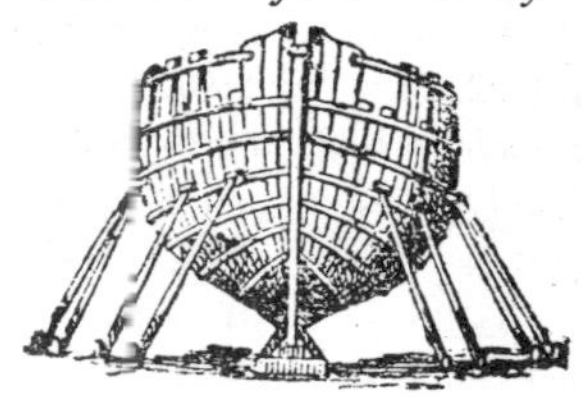

Shores supporting a vessel on the dock.

a wall or building is temporarily supported; চাড়া, ঠেকো। ***Verb t.*** To support with shore or shores; ঠেকো দেওয়া, চাড়া দেওয়া।

shŏrt, *adj.*, *n.* & *adv.* **1.** Not long; not having great length or linear extension; অদীর্ঘ; অল্পদীর্ঘ, খাটো, খর্ব্ব, হ্রস্ব, ছোট। **2.** Not of long duration; as, a *short* time; অল্প, অনতি, খানিক। **3.** Brief; concise; scanty; as, *short* account; অল্পাক্ষরগ্রথিত, সংক্ষিপ্ত; স্বল্পাক্ষর; অল্প, কম, স্তোক, অপ্রচুর। **4.** Curt; uncivil; as, a *short* answer; কাটা, রুখা; অভদ্র। **5.** Not coming up, as to a measure or standard; as, *short* of weight; নিরূপিত মান বা আদর্শ হইতে খাটো। **6.** Less than or inferior to; as, it is little *short* of a miracle; কোন কিছুর সহিত তুলনায় অল্প বা কম, কিঞ্চিদূন।

7. Pronounced with a less prolonged utterance ; (ছন্দঃশাস্ত্র) লঘু। 8. Brittle ; ভঙ্গপ্রবণ, ঠুন্‌কো। 9. Strong ; unmixed with water, as spirit ; কড়া ; নির্জ্জলা। 10. Crisp ; as, *short* pastry ; মচমচে, কড়কড়ে। 11. Unmixed ; as, *short* manure ; অমিশ্র। ***Noun.*** 1. Summary or concise account ; as, the long and *short* of it ; সংক্ষিপ্ত বিবরণ। 2. Whatever is deficient in number, quantity, etc. ; কমি, কমতি। 3. (*Pl.*) The bran and coarse part of meal in mixture ; ভুষি। 3. (*Slang*) Knee-breeches ; (ইতর ভাষায়) জাঙ্গিয়া। 4. A short syllable ; হ্রস্বস্বর। ***Adv.*** 1. Briefly ; সংক্ষেপে, অল্পকথায়। 2. Harshly ; কঠোর ভাবে। 3. Abruptly; অকস্মাৎ, সহসা। **Short'-age,** *n.* Deficiency ; amount of deficiency ; কমতি, কমি, অল্পতা ; কমতির পরিমাণ। **Short'-ly,** *adv.* **Short'-ness,** *n.* **Short-allowance**—(সৈন্য প্রভৃতিকে প্রদত্ত) নিয়মিত খাদ্যাদি অপেক্ষা অল্প খাদ্য। **Short-bread, Short-cake**—মচ্‌মচে রুটি, মচ্‌মচে পিঠা। **Short circuit**—(তাড়িতবিদ্যা) তাড়িতপ্রবাহের যে অংশে অপেক্ষাকৃত অল্প বাধা পাওয়া যায়। **Short clothes** or **coats**—জানু পর্য্যন্ত লম্বিত পাজামা এবং ফুল মোজা; শিশুদিগের পেনি। **Short-coat,** (*v. t.*) পেনি পরান। **Short commons**—অপ্রচুর খাদ্য। **Short cut**—একপ্রকার মিহি করিয়া কাটা তামাক ; (তামাক সম্পর্কে) মিহি করিয়া কাটা ; সোজারাস্তা। **Short-dated**—(হুণ্ডী প্রভৃতি সম্পর্কে) শীঘ্র প্রদেয়। **Short division**—সংক্ষিপ্ত ভাগহার। **Shorthand**—সাঙ্কেতিকলিপি, রেখাক্ষরবর্ণমালা, সংক্ষিপ্তলিপি। **Short-hander** — সাঙ্কেতিকলিখক, সঙ্কেত-লিপিকর। **Shorthorn**—একজাতীয় খর্ব্বশৃঙ্গবিশিষ্ট গো বা মহিষ। **Short-horned**—খর্ব্বশৃঙ্গী। **Short-legged**—খর্ব্বপাদ। **Short-lived**—অচিরস্থায়ী, মন্দায়ুঃ (ভাগঃ), ক্ষণস্থায়ী, ক্ষণভুক্ত। **Short rib**—Same as FALSE-. **Short shrift**—অনুতাপের অল্প সময় ; সঙ্গে সঙ্গে দণ্ডবিধান। **Short sight** — দৃষ্টিশক্তির ক্ষীণতা ; অপরিণামদর্শিতা, অদুরদর্শিতা। **Short-sighted**—ক্ষীণদৃষ্টি, অল্পচক্ষু (বৃঃ সং) ; অপরিণামদর্শী, অদূরদর্শী। **Short-spoken** — স্বল্পভাষী ; কাটা, রুখা। **Short-tempered**—অসহিষ্ণু, অসংযত। **Short-winded** — বহুক্ষণ শ্বাসরোধ করণে অসমর্থ, ক্ষীণশ্বাস ; অধিকক্ষণ দৌড়াইতে অক্ষম। **Short-witted**—অল্পবুদ্ধি, মূঢ়মতি। **In short**—In few words ; সংক্ষেপে, অল্প কথায়। **The long and the short of it** — The concise statement of a thing ; কোন বিষয়ের সার কথা, তাৎপর্য্য, মর্ম্ম। **To be short** — To be scantily supplied ; অপ্রচুর হওয়া, অপর্য্যাপ্ত হওয়া, টান পড়া, অভাব হওয়া। **To be taken short**—To have sudden calls of nature ; হঠাৎ বাহ্যপ্রস্রাবের পীড়া হওয়া। **To bring** or **pull up short**—To stop suddenly; হঠাৎ থামা। **To cut short**—To check or stop abruptly ; হঠাৎ বাধা দেওয়া, হঠাৎ থামান। To abridge ; সংক্ষেপ করা। **To come short** — To fall below one's expectation ; আশানুরূপ না হওয়া। **To fall short**—To be insufficient ; কম পড়া, ন্যূন হওয়া, অপ্রচুর হওয়া, টান পড়া, বাড়ন্ত, হওয়া (*euph.*)। **To make a short work of** — To destroy or dispose of quickly ; তাড়াতাড়ি শেষ করা, তাড়াতাড়ি নিকাশ করা। **To run short**—Same as TO RUN OUT. **To sell short**—To sell for future delivery what the seller does not at the time posseses but hopes to buy at a lower rate ; ভবিষ্যতে অল্পদরে যোগাইতে পারিবে ভরসায় বর্ত্তমানে নিজের কাছে নাই ঐরূপ জিনিষ বিক্রয় করা। **To stop short**—To stop ;at once ; হঠাৎ থামা, থমকিয়া দাঁড়ান। **To take short** — To reprimand ; ভৎর্সনা করা, তিরস্কার করা। **To turn short, To turn on the short**—যে স্থানে স্থিত ছিল তথায় থাকিয়া ঘুরা।

shŏrt'-en (-n), *v. t. & i.* 1. To make short ; to abridge ; to contract ; কমান, কম করা, ছোট করা, খাটো করা ; সংক্ষিপ্ত করা ; সঙ্কোচ করা। 2. To make short or friable ; মচ্‌মচে করা। 3. To diminish in extent as sail ; পাইল প্রভৃতি কমান। 4. To lop; to deprive ; ছেদন করা ; বিরহিত করা। ***Verb i.*** 1. To become short or shorter ; খাটো হওয়া, কমা, অল্প হওয়া। 2. To contract ; সঙ্কুচিত হওয়া, সঙ্কোচপ্রাপ্ত হওয়া।

shŏrt'-lȳ, *adv.* 1. Before long ; অচিরে, শীঘ্র, সত্বর, অবিলম্বে, অগৌণে, ত্বরা, অনতিবিলম্বে। 2. Briefly ; সংক্ষেপে, সংক্ষেপতঃ অল্প কথায়। 3. In an abrupt or curt manner ; as, he answered me *shortly* ; কড়াভাবে, কাটাভাবে, রুখাভাবে।

shŏt, *n. & v. t.* 1. Discharge of a firearm or other weapon from which a missile may be thrown ; as, several *shots* were fired ; গুলিকরণ, গুলিক্ষেপণ। 2. A missile, particularly a ball or bullet ; small balls of lead or iron for fowling-pieces ; ক্ষেপণীয় অস্ত্র, বিশেষতঃ গুলি ; ছররা, ছিটাগুলি। 3. A marksman ; as, he is a good *shot* ; লক্ষ্যভেদকারী, গুলিবাজ, তীরন্দাজ। 4. Range of shot ; (hence *fig.*) reach ; as, he is beyond ear-*shot* : গুলির পাল্লা ; পাল্লা, সীমা। 5. A cast of a net ; the whole sweep of nets thrown out at one time ; the draught of fishes made by a net ; জাল ফেলন ; একবারে যতটা জাল ফেলা হয় ; জালের একটানে যে পরিমাণ মাছ ধরা পড়ে। 6. A stroke or move in a play ;

ক্রীড়ায় আঘাত বা চাল। 7. (*Colloq.*) A conjecture; as, he made a bad *shot*; an attempt; (চলিতভাষায়) আন্দাজ, অনুমান; চেষ্টা। ***Verb t.*** To load with shot, as gun; বন্দুকাদিতে গুলি ভরা। **Bar-shot**—পূর্ব্বকালের কামানে ব্যবহৃত গোলাবিশেষ—উহা উভয় প্রান্তে কন্দুকবিশিষ্ট দণ্ডাকৃতি ছিল। **Case-shot** — See under CASE. **Chain-shot** — See under CHAIN. **Flying shot**—উড্ডীয়মান পক্ষী বা কোন প্রকার গতিশীল বস্তুর উপর যে গুলি ছোড়া হয়। **Grape-shot**—See GRAPE 4. **Parthian shot** — See PARTHIAN-SHAFT. **Shot-locker**—গুলি রাখার জন্য সুদৃঢ় ভাবে নির্ম্মিত পোত-কক্ষ। **Shot-metal**—একভাগ আর্সেনিক (সেঁকো বিষ) ও ৫৬ ভাগ সীসক দ্বারা প্রস্তুত গুলিপ্রস্তুতের উপযোগী মিশ্রধাতুবিশেষ। **Shot-silk**—ধূপছায়া রঙ্গের রেশম। **Shot-tower**—উচ্চ বুরুজবিশেষ—যাহার অগ্রভাগ হইতে চালুনির ভিতর দিয়া বিন্দু বিন্দু গলিত সীসক নিম্নস্থিত জল কিম্বা অপর কোনরূপ তরল পদার্থে পাতিত করিয়া ছোট ছোট গুলি প্রস্তুত করা হয়। **Shot-window**—প্রাচীর হইতে উদ্গত বাতায়ন। **A shot in the locker**—A remnant; last resource; অবশেষ; শেষ উপায়। **Like a shot**—Quickly; তীরবেগে, নক্ষত্রবেগে। **Not by a long shot**—(*Slang*) Not by much; (ইতর ভাষায়) বেশী কিছু দ্বারা নয়। **To make a bad shot**—To guess wrong; ভুল অনুমান করা। **Shot of a cable**—দুইটী কাছি একত্র পাকানো; একত্রপাকানো কাছিদ্বয়ের দৈর্ঘ্য।

shŏt, *p.t.* & *p.p.* of SHOOT (which see).

shŏt, *adj.* 1. Struck or killed by a shot; গুলি দ্বারা আহত বা নিহত। 2. Having a changeable colour, like that produced in weaving by all the warp-threads being of one colour and all the weft of another; intermingled; interspersed; ধূপছায়া রঙ্গের; বিমিশ্রিত; ব্যামিশ্র, সম্মিশ্র।

shŏt, *n.* A reckoning; proportional share of expenses incurred at a tavern; হিসাব; শুঁড়িখানায় মদ্যাদি পানে অংশমত দেয় টাকা।

should (shŭd), *v. aux.* See SHALL.

shoul'-dêr (shōl-), *n.*, *v. t.* & *i.* 1. The joint by which the arm or foreleg is connected with the body; কাঁধ, স্কন্ধ [Syn. অংস, ভুজাশির, শিখর (রাজ: নি:)]। 2. The upper joint of the foreleg of an animal cut for market; কসাই কর্ত্তৃক কাটা জন্তুর অগ্রপাদের উপরের সন্ধি। 3. (*Fig.*) The emblem of supporting strength; (লক্ষণায়) কাঁধ, স্কন্ধ, অবলম্বন। 4. (*Pl.*) The upper portion of the back; পৃষ্ঠের উপরিভাগ। 5. Anything resembling the shoulder; a prominence; a slope; স্কন্ধাকৃতি বস্তু; উন্নতস্থান; ঢালু জায়গা। 6. (*Fort.*) The angle formed by the junction of the face and flank; (দুর্গ) অগ্র ও পশ্চাৎ সংযোগজনিত কোণ। ***Verb t.*** 1. To push or thrust with the shoulder; কাঁধ দ্বারা ধাক্কা দেওয়া বা ঠেলিয়া দেওয়া। 2. To take upon the shoulder or shoulders; as, to *shoulder* a load; কাঁধে নেওয়া। ***Verb i.*** To force one's way forward; কাঁধ দিয়া ঠেলিয়া পথ করা। **Shoulder-belt**—সৈনিকদিগের উপবীতাকারে পরিধেয় চর্ম্মবন্ধনী প্রভৃতি। **Shoulder-blade**—স্কন্ধাস্থি, অংসফলক, পাখড়া (যোঃ)। **Shoulder-brace**—শিশু প্রভৃতির পৃষ্ঠের কুব্জতা দূর করার জন্য যন্ত্রবিশেষ। **Shoulder-joint**—অংস-সন্ধি। **Shoulder-knot** — বিলাতের তকমাপরা ভৃত্যগণ কাঁধের উপর যে ফিতার গুচ্ছ পরিয়া থাকে। **Shoulder-strap** — সৈনিকদিগের স্কন্ধদেশে পরিধেয় ফিতাবিশেষ—যাহাতে সেনাপল্টনের নাম, সংখ্যা, প্রভৃতি থাকে, স্কন্ধপট্ট, অংসপট্ট; স্কন্ধদেশে পরিধেয় সৈনিককর্ম্মচারীগণের পদপজ্ঞাপক ফিতা। **Shoulder-of-mutton sail**—একপ্রকার ত্রিকোণ পাইল। **Shoulder to shoulder**—With united effort; একযোগে, সমবেত চেষ্টায়। **To have an old head upon young shoulder**—To be wise like an old man though young; বয়স অল্প হইলেও জ্ঞানে প্রবীণ হওয়া। **To lay the blame on another's shoulder** — To impute blame upon another person; অপরের ঘাড়ে দোষ চাপান। **To put or set one's shoulder to the wheel**—To assist in bearing a burden or overcoming a difficulty; ভার বহনে সাহায্য করা, কোনরূপ সঙ্কটের অবস্থায় কাহাকে সাহায্য করা। **To rub shoulders with**—See RUB. **To shoulder arms**—To hold the gun in a vertical position over the shoulder; ঘাড়ের উপর বন্দুক সোজা করিয়া ধরা। **To turn or show or give the cold shoulder**—To treat coldly; অনুরাগশূন্য ভাব প্রদর্শন করা, প্রীতিশূন্যভাব প্রদর্শন করা। **With one shoulder**—With one consent; একমত হইয়া, একচিত্তে।

shout (showt), *v. i.*, *t.* & *n.* 1. To utter a loud sudden cry, as in triumph, exultation or to arrest attention of some one at a distance; চীৎকার করা, চেঁচান, উচ্চনাদ করা, উচ্চরব করা, ডাকাডাকি করা। 2. (*Slang*) To order drink for others by way of treat; (ইতরভাষায়) এক গ্লাস মদ্য দেওয়ার জন্য আদেশ করা, ইয়ারদিগকে আপ্যায়িত করার জন্য মদ্য যোগাইতে বলা। ***Verb t.*** To utter with a shout; চীৎকার করিয়া বলা, চেঁচাইয়া বলা। ***Noun.*** An outcry; চীৎকার, কলরব, হুঙ্কার, কোলাহল, উচ্চরব, উচ্চধ্বনি। **To shout at** — To mock with shouts; কোলাহল করিয়া বিদ্রূপ করা।

shove (shŭv), *v. t.*, *i.* & *n.* 1. To push before one; to thrust; ধাক্কা দিয়া অগ্রসর করা; ঠেলিয়া নেওয়া। 2. (*Colloq.*) To put; as, *shove* it in the drawer; (চলিত ভাষায়) রাখা।

Verb i. To push off; to drive forward; ঠেলিয়া চালান; ঠেলিয়া অগ্রসর করা। *Noun.* 1. Push; ধাক্কা, ঠেলা। 2. The central woody portion of the stem of flax; শণ গাছের কাণ্ডের কাষ্ঠময় মধ্য ভাগ। **To give one a shove off**—To assist one at the commencement of a work; কার্য্যারম্ভকালে কাহাকে সাহায্য করা। **To shove off**—To push off a boat with oar and punting rod; চোড় বা দাঁড়দ্বারা ঠেলিয়া নৌকা ভাসান।

shov'-ĕl (shŭv-), *n.* & *v. t.* An instrument with a broad shallow blade, for lifting earth etc.; মাটী, কয়লা প্রভৃতি তোলার জন্য একপ্রকার দণ্ডওয়ালা পাত্র, ক্ষেপণী। *Verb t.* To take up and throw with a shovel; to gather in great quantities; ক্ষেপণীর সাহায্যে লওয়া বা ফেলা; বহু পরিমাণে জড় করা। **Shovel-board, Shovel-groat**—একপ্রকার খেলা—যাহাতে ফলকের চিহ্নিত স্থানে চাক্তি সমূহ নিক্ষিপ্ত হয় (পূর্ব্বে চাকতির পরিবর্ত্তে মুদ্রা নিক্ষিপ্ত হইত)। **Shovel-hat**—এংলিকান যাজকদিগের চৌড়া কিনারাওয়ালা টুপি। **Shovel-head**—একপ্রকার মৎস্য। **To shovel food into one's mouth**—To eat like glutton; রাশি রাশি অন্ন আহার করা।

shov'-el-ler (shŭv-ĕl-êr), *n.* 1. One who shovels; যে ব্যক্তি ক্ষেপণীদ্বারা কয়লা প্রভৃতি তোলে বা নিক্ষেপ করে। 2. A genus of broad-billed ducks; একজাতীয় বিশালচঞ্চু হংস।

show (shō), **shew** (shō), *v. t.* & *i.* 1. To present to view; দেখান, প্রদর্শন করা। 2. To guide; as, will you *show* me to the school?; পথপ্রদর্শন করা। 3. To disclose; as, to *show* one's plans; প্রকাশ করা, প্রকটন করা, ব্যক্ত করা। 4. To prove; as, to *show* a person's mistake; to expound; প্রমাণ করা, প্রতিপাদন করা; ব্যাখ্যা করা, বিবৃত করা। 5. To inform; to instruct; as, *show* me how to work out this sum; জ্ঞাত করা, অবগত করা; উপদেশ দেওয়া, শিক্ষা দেওয়া। 6. To bestow; as, to *show* favour; প্রদান করা, অর্পণ করা। 7. To indicate; to point out; সূচনা করা; নির্দ্দেশ করা। *Verb i.* 1. (*Rare*) To become visible; (কচিদ্‌ব্যবহৃত) দৃষ্ট হওয়া। 2. To appear; to look; বোধ হওয়া, প্রতিভাত হওয়া; দেখান। 3. To become; মানান, শোভা পাওয়া। 4. To be present; উপস্থিত থাকা। 5. To be noticeable; as, does the spot *show*?; লক্ষ্য হওয়া, দৃষ্টিগোচর হওয়া। **Show-bill**—বৃহদক্ষরে মুদ্রিত বিজ্ঞাপন। **Show-case**—দ্রব্যাদি প্রদর্শনের জন্য কাচের ডালাওয়ালা বৃহৎ কাষ্ঠাধার, প্রদর্শনাধার। **Show-place** — দর্শনযোগ্য স্থান। **Show-room**—যে কক্ষে প্রদর্শনার্থ দ্রব্যাদি রক্ষিত হয়, প্রদর্শনকক্ষ। **Show-window**—যে জানালায় দ্রব্যাদি প্রদর্শিত হয়, প্রদর্শনবাতায়ন। **To show a clean pair of heels**—See under HEEL. **To show a person up**—to reaveal one's real character; কোন ব্যক্তির প্রকৃত চরিত্র লোকসমাজে ব্যক্ত করা। **To show forth**—To proclaim; to manifest; ঘোষণ করা; ব্যক্ত করা, প্রকটন করা। **To show in**—To conduct into a room; পথ দেখাইয়া কোন কক্ষে লইয়া যাওয়া। **To show off**—to exhibit in an ostentatious manner; জাঁকজমকের সহিত দেখান, বাহার দেখান, বাহার দেওয়া। **To show one's card** or **hand**—To disclose one's plans; কাহারো কার্য্যপ্রণালী প্রকাশ করা। **To show one's colour** or **colours**—See under COLOUR. **To show one's face**—To appear; উপস্থিত হওয়া। **To show the door**—See under DOOR. **To show the teeth**—To threaten by showing one's teeth; দাঁত খিঁচান, রাগে দাঁত কিড়িমিড়ি করা। **To show up**—To point out the way up; উপরের তালার পথ দেখাইয়া দেওয়া। (*Colloq.*) To appear; উপস্থিত হওয়া, দেখা দেওয়া। To hold up to ridicule; উপহাসাস্পদ করা।

show (shō), *n.* 1. The act of showing or exhibiting; as, *show* of goods; প্রদর্শন। 2. Pomp; জাঁকজমক, ধূম, সমারোহ, ঘটা। 3. An exhibition; a display; as, a flower-*show*: "His majestic *show* of luxury"; প্রদর্শনী; প্রদর্শন। 4. Pretext; "For a *show* make long prayers"; ছল, ভাণ। 6. Sign; চিহ্ন, লক্ষণ। 7. (*Slang*) The opportunity of acting or defending oneself etc.; as, give him a fair *show*; (ইতর ভাষায়) নিজে করার সুবিধা, নিজপক্ষ সমর্থনের সুযোগ। 8. (*Med.*) A mucous discharge streaked with blood which takes place one, two or three days before a woman falls into labour; প্রসবের এক, দুই বা তিন দিবস পূর্ব্বে স্ত্রীলোকের যোনি হইতে রক্তমিশ্রিত নির্গত শ্লেষ্মা। **Show'-i-ly,** *adv.* **Show'-i-ness,** *n.* **Show'-y,** *adj.* Gaudy; ostentatious; gay; জমকালো; জাঁকজমকপূর্ণ; বাহারের, চটকদার, সমুজ্জ্বল। **Showman**—পশুশালা বা পশুপ্রদর্শনীর অধ্যক্ষ। **A show of hands**—কোন সভায় মত (ভোট) প্রদানকালে হস্ত উত্তোলন। **Lord Mayor's Show**—লণ্ডননগরীতে প্রদর্শিত শোভাযাত্রাবিশেষ।

show'-ĕr, *n., v. t.* & *i.* 1. A fall of rain or hail of short duration; a copious and rapid fall; পসলা; বর্ষণ, ধারাবর্ষণ। 2. A fall of things in fast succession; as, a *shower* of flowers; বৃষ্টি, বর্ষণ, (cf. পুষ্পবৃষ্টি)। 3. A copious supply of anything; "A *shower* of beauty"; প্রাচুর্য্য, বৃষ্টি, ছড়াছড়ি। *Verb t.* 1. To water with a shower; বর্ষণসিক্ত করা। 2. To wet copiously with rain; to bestow liberally; বর্ষণ করা; (ধন প্রভৃতি) বৃষ্টি করা, ঢালিয়া দেওয়া, অজস্র প্রদান করা। ***Verb i.*** To rain in showers; to fall as a shower; বর্ষিত হওয়া; এক পসলা বৃষ্টি হওয়া। **–i-ness,** *n.* **–y,** *adj.* Raining in showers; abounding with frequent falls of rain; বর্ষা; প্রচুর বর্ষণশীল। **Shower-bath**—সচ্ছিদ্র ফলকের উপর হইতে বর্ষিত জলধারায় স্নান, ধারাস্নান; যে গৃহে উক্তরূপ স্নানের ব্যবস্থা থাকে, ধারাগৃহ (সুশ্রুঃ), জলযন্ত্রমন্দির (ঋতুঃ), ধারামণ্ডপ (ধারা মণ্ডপং/তোয়যন্ত্রৈঃ—বাস্তুশাস্ত্র), ধারাযন্ত্রগৃহ।

shrank (shrăngk), *p. p.* of SHRINK (which see).

shrăp'-nĕl, *n.* A spherical case filled with musket-balls, and containing a bursting-charge of powder, most destructive either to cavalry and infantry; ক্ষুদ্র ক্ষুদ্র গুলিপূর্ণ ধাতবগোলক—যাহা লক্ষ্যস্থানে পৌঁছিবার ঈষদ্‌পূর্ব্বে ফাটিয়া যায় এবং তদভ্যন্তরস্থ গুলি সমূহ বৃষ্টির ন্যায় শত্রু সৈন্যের উপর ছড়াইয়া পড়ে, বোমা-গুলি।

shrĕd, *n.* & *v. t.* **1.** Scrap; strip; টুকরা, ফালি; অংশ, খণ্ড। **2.** A fragment; as, there is not a *shred* of evidence; কণা, খণ্ড। ***Verb t.*** To tear into shreds; ছিঁড়িয়া টুকরা করা।

shrew (shrö), *n.* **1.** A peevish ill-tempered woman; a scolding woman; খিটখিটে ও কুঁদুলে স্ত্রীলোক; দুর্মুখা স্ত্রী। **2.** A harmless little animal, resembling a mouse; ছুঁচো। **Shrew'-ish,** *adj.* **Shrew'-ish-ly,** *adv.* **Shrew-mouse**—Same as SHREW 2.

shrewd (shrôd), *adj.* **1.** Vexatious; mischievous; malicious; বিরক্তিজনক; ক্ষতিজনক; ঈর্ষাপরায়ণ। **2.** Scolding; as, a *shrewd* wench; ভর্ৎসনাকারী, কোন্দলপ্রিয়। **3.** Wicked; swindling; দুষ্ট; জুয়াচোর, ধড়িবাজ। **4.** (Of pain, cold, etc. — *Archaic*) Biting; "*Shrewdest* pain"; (অপ্রঃ) কনকনে। **5.** Sagacious; as, a *shrewd* observer; judicious; discriminating; বুদ্ধিমান, বুদ্ধিশালী; বিচারবুদ্ধি-সম্পন্ন, বিজ্ঞ; কর্ত্তব্যাকর্ত্তব্য বিচারক্ষম। **6.** Artful; "These women are *shrewd* tempters with their tongues"; wily; cunning; চালাক; চতুর; শেয়ানা, বিদগ্ধ। **–ly,** *adv.*

shriek (shrēk), *v. i.* & *n.* **1.** To cry out shrilly; চীৎকার করা, চেঁচান, গোঙ্গান। **2.** To laugh immoderately; হাসিয়া খুন হওয়া। ***Noun.*** A shrill noise; চীৎকার, গোঙানি

shriev'-ăl-tȳ (shrēv-), *n.* **1.** The office or jurisdiction of a sheriff; শেরিফের পদ বা এলেকা।

shrift, *n.* (*Archaic*) Confession made to a priest; (অপ্রঃ) পুরোহিতের নিকট পাপস্বীকার। **Short shrift**—See SHORT.

shrīke, *n.* A genus of passerine birds which feed on insects, small

Shrike.

birds, etc.; একজাতীয় শিকারী পক্ষী—ইহারা ছোট পাখী, কীট প্রভৃতি শিকার করিয়া কাঁটায় বিঁধিয়া রাখে।

shrill, *adj., v. i.* & *t.* **1.** Piercing; high pitched in sound; কর্কশ; পরুষ, কর্ণকটু। **2.** (*Fig.*) Importunate; (লক্ষণায়) নির্ব্বন্ধাতিশয়যুক্ত। ***Verb i.*** To utter an acute piercing sound; কর্ণকটু শব্দ করা। ***Verb t.*** To utter in a shrill tone; শ্রুতিকটুকণ্ঠে উচ্চারণ করা।

shrimp, *n.* & *v.i.* **1.** A small shell-fish allied to the lobster; চিংড়ী মাছ, ইচা মাছ, ইঞ্চাক মৎস্য। **2.** An under-sized person; খর্ব্বকায় ব্যক্তি। ***Verb i.*** To go catching shrimps, চিংড়ী মাছ ধরিতে যাওয়া।

shrine *n.* & *v. t.* **1.** A reliquary; পবিত্র বস্তুর ধ্বংসাবশেষ রাখার স্থান। **2.** A sacred place; তীর্থস্থান, পীঠস্থান,

Portable shrine.

পীঠ (এভেলন)। ***Verb t.*** To place in a shrine; to enshrine; পবিত্র বস্তু রক্ষার স্থানে রাখা; মন্দিরে রক্ষা করা।

shrink (shrĭngk), *v. i., t.* & *n.* **1.** To contract spontaneously; to shrivel; কুঞ্চিত হওয়া; মুষড়াইয়া যাওয়া, পরিশুষ্ক হওয়া। **2.** To become of less dimension; as, the flannel *shrinks*; আয়তনে কমা, খাটো হওয়া। **3.** To withdraw; to retire; to recoil, as from danger; পশ্চাৎপদ হওয়া; হটিয়া আসা; পরাঙ্মুখ হওয়া। ***Verb t.*** To cause to shrink; সঙ্কুচিত করা। ***Noun.*** Shrinking; কুঞ্চন। **Shrink'-a-ble,** *adj.* **Shrink'-age,** *n.* **1.** A shrinking; আকুঞ্চন, সঙ্কোচন। **2.** Diminution in value; as, the *shrinkage* of an estate; মূল্যহ্রাস। **To shrink into one's self**—To become reserved; অনালাপী হওয়া, অমিশুক হওয়া। **To shrink on**—চাকার লৌহবেষ্টনী প্রভৃতি যে স্থানে লাগাইতে হইবে প্রথমতঃ তাহা অপেক্ষা ঈষৎ ক্ষুদ্রায়তন করিয়া পরে উত্তাপ প্রয়োগে উহার আয়তন বৃদ্ধিপূর্ব্বক

যথাস্থানে লাগাইয়া ঠাণ্ডা হইতে দিয়া উহা (ঐ লোহবেষ্টনী) দৃঢ়রূপে লাগান।

shrive, *v. t.* To hear the confession of; to confess; পাপস্বীকারোক্তি শ্রবণ করা; পাপস্বীকার করা।

shriv'-el, *v. i.* & *t.* To contract into wrinkles; সঙ্কুচিত হওয়া, কুঞ্চিত হওয়া, মুষড়িয়া যাওয়া, তুবড়ান। ***Verb t.*** To cause to contract into wrinkles; সঙ্কুচিত করা, কুঞ্চিত করা, কোঁচকান।

shroud (shrowd), *n.* & *v. t.* **1.** A winding sheet; garments of the dead; শবাচ্ছাদনবস্ত্র; শববস্ত্র।

Shroud.

2. That which clothes, covers or shelters; আচ্ছাদন, আবরণ। **3.** (*Pl.*) Large ropes in a ship supporting the mast; মাস্তুলের দড়াদড়ী। ***Verb t.*** **1.** To clothe corpse for burial; শবাচ্ছাদন করা। **2.** To shelter from danger; to conceal; to cover; বিপৎ হইতে আশ্রয় দেওয়া; ঢাকা, লুকান; আচ্ছাদিত করা, আবৃত করা।

Shrove'-Tues-day (shrōv-tūz-dā), *n.* The day immediately preceding the first day of Lent, or Ash Wednesday; খৃষ্টানদিগের পর্ব্বদিবসবিশেষ।

shrŭb, *n.* A plant with woody stems branching from the root, and of no great height; ক্ষুদ্র বৃক্ষ, ঝাড়, গুল্ম, গাছড়া, ক্ষুপ। **Shrub'-ber-y**, *n.* A plantation of shrubs; গুল্মবাড়ী, গুল্মবাটীকা। **Shrub'-bi-ness**, *n.* **Shrub'-by**, *adj.*

shrŭb, *n.* A beverage containing the root of fruits etc; ফলের রস প্রভৃতি হইতে প্রস্তুত শ্রান্তিবারক পানীয়বিশেষ।

shrŭg, *v. t.* & *n.* To draw up or to contract as shoulders; (ভয় বিরক্তি, প্রভৃতি সূচনার জন্য) কাঁধ ঈষৎ উপরের দিকে তোলা বা কুঞ্চিত করা। ***Noun.*** A drawing up of the shoulders; (ভয় বিরক্তি প্রভৃতি সূচনার জন্য) ঘাড় ঈষৎ উত্তোলন বা আকুঞ্চন।

shrunk (shrŭngk), **shrunk'-en** (shrŭngk-n), *p. p.* of SHRINK (which see).

shŭd'-der (-ėr), *v. i.* & *n.* **1.** To quake; to tremble; to shiver; কাঁপা; কম্পিত হওয়া; শিহরা, থর থর করিয়া কাঁপা, থরহরি কম্পমান হওয়া। ***Noun.*** A tremour; কম্প, কাঁপুনি, বেপথু, শিহরণ। **To give one a cold shudder**—To quake violently; থরহরি কাঁপা, গায়ে কাঁটা দেওয়া।

shŭff-le (-l), *v. t.*, *i.* & *n.* **1.** To shove one way and the other; to push from one to another; as, to *shuffle* money from hand to hand; একবার এদিকে আবার ওদিকে ঠেলিয়া দেওয়া; একের নিকট হইতে অপরের নিকট ঠেলিয়া দেওয়া। **2.** To change the relative position of, as of cards in a pack; to throw into disorder; তাস প্রভৃতি ভেস্তান; গোলমাল করিয়া দেওয়া। **3.** To remove or introduce with some artifical or fraudulent confusion; "It was contrived by your enemies and *shuffled* into the papers that were seized"; প্রতারণা বা কুঅভিসন্ধিপূর্ব্বক ঢুকাইয়া দেওয়া। ***Verb i.*** **1.** To change the relative position of cards in a pack; তাস ভেস্তান। **2.** To shift ground; to evade question; to equivocate; তর্কে বাক্‌ছল করা; প্রশ্ন এড়ান; কথার মারপেঁচ করা। **3.** To make shift; চালাকি করা, ফন্দী করা। **4.** To move with an irregular, slovenly or dragging gait; নেঙচাইয়া চলা। **5.** To scrap the floor with feet; মেঝে পা ঘষাণ। ***Noun.*** **1.** Act of shuffling; a thrusting out of order; the mixing up of cards in a pack before dealing; কুতর্ককরণ; তাড়াতাড়ি একত্র মিশাইয়া ফেলন; ভেস্তানি। **2.** A trick; an artifice; চাতুরী; ফন্দী। **To shuffle off**—To push off; to rid oneself off; ঠেলিয়া দেওয়া; রেহাই পাওয়া। **To shuffle off this mortal coil**—To die; দেহত্যাগ করা। **To shuffle up**—To throw up together in haste; to make up or form in confusion or with fraudulent disorder; তাড়াতাড়ি একত্র মিশাইয়া ফেলা; ভেস্তান।

shŭn, *v. t.* To aviod; to eschew; পরিহার করা; পরিত্যাগ করা। **Shun'-less**, *adj.* Inevitable; অপরিহার্য্য।

shŭnt, *v. t.*, *i.* & *n.* **1.** To turn off to one side; to shift; to move as a railway-carriage or train from the main line to a side-rail; এক পাশে ফিরান; পরিবর্ত্তন করা; বাষ্পীয় শকট বা শকটশ্রেণী প্রধান বর্ত্ম হইতে শাখাবর্ত্মে চালিত করা। **2.** To shift to another circuit, as an electric current; তাড়িতপ্রবাহ অন্য কুণ্ডলীতে স্থানান্তরিত করা। **3.** To get rid of; to put out of one's way; to free from something, as disagreeable; রেহাই পাওয়া; পথ হইতে সরান; কোন প্রকার অপ্রীতিকর ব্যাপার হইতে মুক্ত করা। ***Verb i.*** To go aside; to turn off; এক পাশে সরা; ভিন্ন দিকে চলা। ***Noun.*** A turning aside; (esp. *Railway*) turning off to a siding; একদিকে চালিত হওন, একপার্শ্বে সরণ; বিশেষতঃ লৌহবর্ত্মের প্রধান বর্ত্ম হইতে শাখাবর্ত্মে স্থানান্তরীকরণ। **Shunt'-er**, *n.* One who shunts; যে ব্যক্তি বাষ্পীয়শকট

বা শকটশ্রেণী প্রধান বর্ত্ম হইতে শাখাবর্ত্মে স্থানান্তরিত করে।

shŭt, *v. t.*, *i.* & *n.* 1. To close, as a door ; বন্ধ করা, রুদ্ধ করা, আটকান (*colloq.*)। 2. To forbid entrance into ; as, to *shut* a harbour ; to prohibit ; প্রবেশ নিষিদ্ধ করা ; নিষেধ করা। 3. To close by bringing the parts together ; অংশ সমূহ একত্র করিয়া বন্ধ করা। *Verb i.* To be closed ; as, flowers *shut* at night ; বন্ধ হওয়া, মুদিত হওয়া। *Noun.* 1. The act of shutting ; রুদ্ধকরণ। 2. The line of junction of two pieces of metals united by welding ; উত্তপ্ত অবস্থায় পিটিয়া জোড়া দেওয়া লৌহখণ্ডদ্বয়ের সংযোগরেখা। **Shut up**—Hold your tongue ; চুপ কর, চুপ রও, মুখ সামলাও। **To shut a person up**—To silence him ; কাহাকে চুপ করান। **To shut in**—To inclose ; বন্ধ করা। To intercept the view of ; দৃষ্টিরোধ করা। **To shut off**—To intercept ; as, to *shut off* supplies ; আটক করা, বন্ধ করা। **To shut out**—To bar entrance ; প্রবেশ করিতে না দেওয়া। **To shut the eyes**—Not to see or notice what passes before one's eyes ; চোখ বুজিয়া থাকা, দেখিয়া না দেখা। **To shut the stable door when the steed is stolen**—See LOCK. **To shut together**—To unite ; to close by welding ; একত্র জোড়া দেওয়া ; উত্তপ্ত অবস্থায় পিটিয়া জোড়া দেওয়া। **To shut up**—To obstruct ; (পথ) রোধ করা। To end ; অবসান হওয়া। To inclose ; আটক করা, বন্ধ করা। **To shut up shop**—To close business for the day or for good ; দোকান বন্ধ করা, কারবার গুটান, কারবার বন্ধ করা।

shŭt-ter (-ĕr), *n.* 1. One who shuts ; যে ব্যক্তি বন্ধ করে, অবরোধক। 2. A movable covering for a window or aperture ; খড়খড়ির পালি, ঝিলিমিলি।

shŭt′-tle (-l) *n.* An instrument used by weavers for shooting the thread of the woof through the warp ; মাকু, তুরী [Syn. সূত্রযন্ত্র, ত্রসর (বালরামায়ণ—৩—৮৫), সূত্রবেষ্টন, তসর, মল্লিক, নাড়ীচীর]। **Shut-tle-cock** — ব্যাডমিণ্টন প্রভৃতি ক্রীড়ায় ব্যবহৃত পক্ষযুক্ত কাক (cork) বিশেষ। Carrier of lower thread in lock-stitch sewing machine ; একপ্রকার সেলাইর কলে নীচের সুতা চালনার জন্য ব্যবস্থাবিশেষ।

Shuttle cock.

shȳ, *adj.* 1. Timid ; readily frightened ; as, a *shy* bird ; ভীরু ; সহজে চকিত। 2. Bashful ; coy ; সলজ্জ, লজ্জাশীল ; মুখচোরা, মেনিমুখো (*colloq.*)। 3. watchful ; cautious ; as, boatmen are very *shy* of rocks ; সাবহিত ; সতর্ক। 4. Suspicious ; jealous ; "Princes are by wisdom of state, somewhat *shy* of their successors" ; সন্দিগ্ধ ; ঈর্ষাপরায়ণ, দ্বেষী। **–ly**, *adv.*

shȳ *v. i.* & *n.* To start suddenly aside, used esp. of a horse ; as, the horse does not *shy* ; হঠাৎ চমকিয়া এক পাশে সরা, ভড়কান, আঁতকে উঠা। *Noun.* A sudden start aside made by a horse ; (অশ্বসম্পর্কে) সহসা চমকিয়া এক পাশে সরণ।

shȳ, *v. t.* & *i.* (*Colloq.*) To fling or throw stones ; "With a grievous 'clod' in his hand to *shy* at it" ; ঢিল ছোড়া, পাটকেল ছোড়া। *Verb i.* To throw stones ; ঢিল ছোড়া। *Noun.* The act of shying ; ঢিল ছোড়ন। **To have a shy at**—To try to hit with a missile ; ঢিল ছুড়িতে চেষ্টা করা। To jeer at ; বিদ্রূপ করা।

Shȳ′-lŏck, *n.* A heartless money-lender ; কঠোরহৃদয় মহাজন, নির্ম্মম মহাজন, শাইলক [শেক্সপীয়রের Merchant of Venice নামক নাটকের শাইলক নামক পাত্রের নাম হইতে গৃহীত।]

si (sē), *n.* (*Mus.*) The seventh note of the octave ; (সঙ্গীতশাস্ত্র) নি।

sī-ăl -ă-gouge (-gŏg), *n.* A medicine that promotes the salivary discharge ; লালাবর্দ্ধক ঔষধ, লালোৎপাদক (ঠাকুরঃ)।

sī′-ă-măng, *n.* The largest of the gibbons found in Sumatra and Malacca ; সুমাত্রা এবং মালাক্কা দ্বীপে প্রাপ্ত একপ্রকার বৃহৎকায় উল্লুক।

Sī′-ă-mese (-mēz), *adj.* & *n.* 1. Belonging to Siam ; শ্যামদেশীয়। *Noun.* 1. A native of Siam ; শ্যামদেশবাসী। 2. The language of Siam ; শ্যামদেশের ভাষা। **Siamese twins**—শ্যামদেশের যমজ শিশুদ্বয় ; শ্যামদেশে ১৮১১ খৃঃ অব্দে চেঙ্গ (Cheng) এবং এঙ্গ (Eng) নামক সংশ্লিষ্ট যমজ শিশু জাত হয়। ১৮৭৪ খৃঃ অব্দে ইহাদের মৃত্যু ঘটে] ; (লক্ষণায়) অভিন্নহৃদয় বন্ধু, হরিহর আত্মা।

sĭb, *adj.* (*Archaic, Scotch*) Related ; সম্পর্কীয়, সম্বন্ধান্বিত।

Sī-bē′-rĭ-ăn, *adj.* & *n.* Of, or pertaining to, Siberia ; সাইবিরিয়া দেশীয়। *Noun.* An inhabitant of Siberia ; সাইবিরিয়ার অধিবাসী। **Siberian dog**—একপ্রকার কুকুর—ইহাদের লোম দীর্ঘ এবং কর্ণ খাড়া হইয়া থাকে।

sĭb′-ĭ-lănt, *adj.* & *n.* Making a hissing sound ; হিস্ হিস্ শব্দকারী, হিস্ হিস্ উচ্চারণযুক্ত, উষ্ম (বর্ণ)। *Noun.* 1. A letter uttered with a hissing, as, *s* and *z* ; হিস্ উচ্চারণযুক্ত অক্ষর বা অক্ষরসমূহ।

sĭb′-ĭ-lāte, *v. t.* & *n.* To pronounce with a hissing sound ; হিস্ধ্বনি সহকারে উচ্চারণ করা। **–lance, –lan-cy, –la′-tion**, *ns.*

sĭb′-ĭl, *n.* A woman supposed to be endowed with a spirit of prophecy ; a prophetess ; প্রাচীন গ্রীস প্রভৃতি দেশে যে দেবমন্দিরবাসিনী

স্ত্রীলোকের উপর দেবতার ভর হইলে সে ভবিষ্যদ্বাণী করিত, সিদ্ধ (আঃ বঃ), যোগিনী; ভবিষ্যদ্বক্ত্রী।

sib'-y̆l-line, *adj.* **1.** Pertaining to the sibyls; প্রাচীন গ্রীসের ভবিষ্যদ্বক্ত্রীগণ সম্বন্ধীয়। **2.** Prophetical; occult; ভবিষ্যদ্বাণীসম্বন্ধীয়; গুহ্য, নিগূঢ়। **3.** Excessive; "My terms are *sibyline*"; অতিরিক্ত।

sic, (*L.*), *adv.* So written or printed; এইরূপ ভাবে লিখিত বা মুদ্রিত। [কোন বাক্য কিম্বা শব্দের যাথার্থ্য বা সঙ্গতিসম্বন্ধে সন্দেহ হইলে বাক্য বা শব্দটী যথাযথ লিখিয়া তাহার পার্শ্বে বন্ধনীর ভিতরে *Sic* শব্দটী লিখিত বা মুদ্রিত হইয়া থাকে।]

Si-că'-ni-ăn, *n.* & *adj.* An aboriginal inhabitant of Sicily; সিসিলি দ্বীপের আদিম অধিবাসী। ***Adj.*** Of, or pertaining to, the Sicanians; উক্ত জাতিসম্বন্ধীয়।

sic'-ca-tive (-ă-tĭv), *adj.* & *n.* Having drying property; শোষক। ***Noun.*** A substance having drying properties; শোষণধর্ম্ম বস্তু।

sīce, *n.* The six on dice; পাশার ছয়।

sīce, sȳce, *ns.* (*India*) Groom; (ভারতবর্ষ) সহিস।

Sic'-ĕl, Sik-ĕl, Si-cū'-li-ăn, *ns.* & *adjs.* A member of race that immigrated into Sicily; সিসিলীদ্বীপের অধিবাসী।

Si-cĭl'-i-ăn, *adj.* & *n.* Of the inhabitants of the island of Sicily; সিসিলীদ্বীপের অধিবাসিসম্বন্ধীয়। ***Noun.*** A native or inhabitant of Sicily; সিসিলীদ্বীপের অধিবাসী। **Sicilian Vespers**—১২৮২ খৃষ্টাব্দে সিসিলীদ্বীপে ফরাসীগণের হত্যা। সান্ধ্যকালীন ঘণ্টা-বাদন এই হত্যাকাণ্ড আরম্ভের সঙ্কেত ছিল বলিয়া এই নাম।

sick, *adj.* **1.** Ill; পীড়িত, কাতর, অসুস্থ, রুগ্ন। **2.** Tired; disgusted; as, to be *sick* of flattery ক্লান্ত; বিরক্ত, অবসাদগ্রস্ত। **3.** Inclined to vomit; বমনেচ্ছাযুক্ত। **4.** (*Stock Exchange*) Dull; (কোম্পানীর কাগজের বাজার) নরম। **5.** (Of wine) Muddy; (মদ্যসম্পর্কে) ঘোলা। **6.** Intended for sick people; as, a *sick-room*; রোগীর জন্য অভিপ্রেত। **Sick'-ish,** *adj.* **Sick-bed** — রোগশয্যা, রুগ্নশয্যা, রুগ্নাবস্থা। **Sick-brained**—বিকৃতমস্তিষ্ক (নিকোলাস ১৮৫৪ খৃঃ অব্দে ১৫ই জানুয়ারী এই শব্দ প্রথম প্রয়োগ করেন।) **Sick-call**—পীড়িত ব্যক্তিগণকে সমবেত হওয়ার জন্য রণবংশীবাদনে সঙ্কেতপ্রদান। **Sick-flag**—রুগ্ন ব্যক্তিদিগকে যে বাটীতে বা জাহাজে রাখা হয়—তথায় যে পীতবর্ণের পতাকা প্রদর্শিত হয়। **Sick-headache**—পিত্তজনিত শিরোবেদনা। **Sick-lay** — জাহাজের প্রধান পাটাতনের অংশবিশেষ—যাহা সাধারণতঃ রোগীদিগের জন্য পৃথক করিয়া রাখা হয়। **Sick-list**—রুগ্নব্যক্তিদিগের তালিকাবিশেষ; সেনাপল্টন, জাহাজ, প্রভৃতির রুগ্নব্যক্তিগণের তালিকা। **Sick Man**—তুরস্ক-সাম্রাজ্য। **Sick-room**—রোগীর কক্ষ। **On the sick-list**—Laid up; রোগে শয্যাগত। **Sick of love**—প্রেমকাতর, প্রেমার্ত্ত (গোপালঃ)। **The sick**—পীড়িত ব্যক্তিগণ। **To be or to feel sick** — To have a vomiting tendency; বমি বমি করা, গা মাটি মাটি করা। **To make sick**—To cause to vomit; বমি করান।

sick'-en (-n), *v. t.* & *i.* To make sick; কাতর করা, পীড়িত করা। **2.** To disgust; বিরক্ত করা, অবসাদগ্রস্ত করা। **3.** To make squeamish or qualmish; বমির ভাব জন্মান। ***Verb i.*** **1.** To be disgusted or nauseated; বিরক্তি বোধ করা, বিতৃষ্ণা বোধ করা। **3.** To decay; to languish; ক্ষয়প্রাপ্ত হওয়া, ক্ষীণ হওয়া; নিস্তেজ হওয়া। **—ing,** *n.* & *adj.*

sick'-le (-l), *n.* A reaping hook; কাস্তে, শস্যকর্ত্তরিকা, কর্ত্তনী (আঃ মঠ)। **Sickle-bill**—কাস্তের আকার চঞ্চুবিশিষ্ট বিভিন্ন প্রকার পক্ষী। **Sickle-feather**—কুকুটের পুচ্ছের মধ্যবর্ত্তী দীর্ঘপালক-সমূহের অন্যতম।

sick'-ly̆, *adj.* **1.** Apt to be ill; রোগা, রোগাটে (*colloq.*)। **2.** Faint; weak; languid; as, a *sickly* smile; ক্ষীণ; দুর্ব্বল; অবসাদগ্রস্ত। **3.** Causing ill health; রোগজনক। **4.** Mawkish; as, *sickly* sentimental; ভাবপ্রবণ।

sick'-nĕss, *n.* **1.** The state of being ill; কাতরতা। **2.** A disease; রোগ, পীড়া, ব্যারাম (*colloq.*), ব্যাধি, আময় (সাঃ পঃ)। **3.** A disordered state of the stomach, attended by nausea, retching or vomiting; বমি বমি ভাব, অরুচি।

Si-cū'-li-ăn, *n.* See SICEL.

sīde, *n.* **1.** The broad or long part or surface of a thing; পার্শ্ব, পাশ, বাজু (*colloq.* esp. of a bedstead)। **2.** One of the flat surfaces bounding an object; as, the cube has six *sides*; কোন বস্তুর তল বা পৃষ্ঠ, পার্শ্ব (cf. ত্রিপার্শ্ব কাচ)। **3.** Margin; কিনারা, প্রান্ত। **4.** Declivity; প্রবণতা, ঢালু। **5.** Vicinity; নৈকট্য, সামীপ্য। **6.** Any party, interest or opinion opposed to another; পক্ষ, তরফ। **7.** (*Geom.*) Any line which forms one of the boundaries of a right lined figure; (জ্যামিতি) ভুজ, বাহু। **Side'-long,** *adv.* & *adj.* Obliquely; তির্য্যগ্‌ভাবে, কুটিলভাবে। (*Adj.*) Oblique; টের্চ্ছা, বক্র, আড়। **Side-arms**—পার্শ্বদেশে বা কোমরবন্ধে যে অস্ত্র ধারণ করা হয়, যথা অসি, সঙ্গীন, প্রভৃতি। **Side-board** — পার্শ্বদ্বার, উপদ্বার, পক্ষদ্বার; অপরাহ্নভোজনের কক্ষে রক্ষিত ব্যঞ্জনাদির পাত্র রাখিবার জন্য দেরাজযুক্ত কাষ্ঠাধার বিশেষ; (ইতর ভাষায়) একপ্রকার খাড়া জামার কলার (অপ্রঃ); পার্শ্বের দাড়ি। **Side-bone**—শ্রোণির অস্থি। **Side-box**—রঙ্গালয়ের পার্শ্ববর্ত্তী আসনমঞ্চ। **Side-chain** — বাষ্পীয় শকটের কলের পার্শ্বের সহিত কয়লা ও জলবাহী শকটের পার্শ্ব যে শৃঙ্খলসমূহ দ্বারা যুক্ত হয়—তাহার অন্যতম। **Side-cut**—শাখাপথ, শাখাপ্রণালী; পরোক্ষ আঘাত বা আক্রমণ। **Side-dish**—অপরাহ্নভোজনের মেজের পার্শ্ববর্ত্তী মেজে রক্ষিত ব্যঞ্জনের থালা; অপ্রধান ব্যঞ্জন। **Sidelight**—পার্শ্বদেশ

হইতে আগত আলোক ; পোতপার্শ্বস্থ প্রদীপ ; গৌণভাবে প্রাপ্ত সংবাদ। **Side-line**—কোন ব্যক্তির ব্যবসায়ের অতিরিক্ত বিভাগ। **Side look, Side glance, Side-long glance**—কটাক্ষ, কুটিল-কটাক্ষ, লীলাবলোকন, দৃগঞ্চল (উজ্জ্বলঃ), দৃগ্‌ভঙ্গী (গোপালঃ); ভ্রূবিলাস (মেঘদূঃ), অপাঙ্গবিলাস (ঐ), অপাঙ্গচ্ছটা (ঐ), তেরছনয়ন, (প্রাঃ সাঃ), তেরছচাহনি (*ib.*), ভ্রূবিভ্রম, ভ্রূবিচেষ্টিত (রঃ), অপাঙ্গদর্শন, অপাঙ্গদৃষ্টি, তির্য্যক্‌প্রেক্ষণ, অপাঙ্গবীক্ষণ। **Side-niches**—কর্ণকুট। **Side-note**—পার্শ্বটীকা, পার্শ্বটিপ্পনী। **Side-piercing**—হৃদয়ভেদী। **Side-saddle**—স্ত্রীলোকের জিন। **Side-show** — অপ্রধান দৃশ্য, উপদৃশ্য। **Side-slip** — কোন যানের (বিশেষতঃ বাইসিকেল বা হাওয়াগাড়ীর চাকার) পথচ্যুতি, তির্য্যগ্‌গামী প্ররোহ ; জারজ সন্তান। **Sidesman**—খৃষ্টীয় ধর্ম্মমন্দিরে নিযুক্ত নিম্নশ্রেণীর কর্ম্মচারিবিশেষ ; ভজনালয়ে যে কর্ম্মচারী লোকদিগকে আসন প্রভৃতি প্রদর্শন করে। **Side-splitting**—পেটফাটা (হাসি)। **Side-stroke**—পার্শ্ব হইতে আঘাত, পার্শ্বের-দিকে আঘাত। **Side-table**—যে মেজ সাধারণতঃ প্রাচীরে ঠেস দিয়া রাখা হয়। **Side-track**—Same as SIDING. **Side-view**—এক পার্শ্ব হইতে দেখিলে যেরূপ দেখা যায় ; পার্শ্বদৃশ্য। **Side-walk**—পাদযাত্রীদিগের জন্য উচ্চ পথ। **Side-wind**—পার্শ্বদেশ হইতে প্রবাহিত বায়ু ; গৌণ ক্রিয়া বা প্রভাব। **Credit side**—জমার দিক। **Debit side**—খরচের দিক। **Off side**—ডাহিনদিক। **Wrong side**—উল্টাদিক। **By the side of** — Near ; নিকটে, পার্শ্বে। **From side to side**—Transversely ; অনুপার্শ্বে, আড়ে। **Side by side**—Placed near each other ; পাশাপাশি। **To choose sides**—To select parties for competition in exercise of any kind ; কোনরূপ প্রতিযোগিতার ক্রীড়ার জন্য উভয় পক্ষের লোক নির্ব্বাচন করা। **To put on side**—To treat insolently ; উদ্ধত ব্যবহার করা। **To shake one's sides**—See under SHAKE. **To take a side** — To join one party ; কোন পক্ষ অবলম্বন করা। **To take sides**—To range oneself with one or other of the contending parties ; পরস্পরবিরোধী পক্ষদ্বয়ের কোন এক পক্ষ অবলম্বন করা।

sī-dē'-rē-ăl, sĭd'-ĕr-ăl, *adjs.* 1. Pertaining to the stars ; নাক্ষত্র, নাক্ষত্রিক। 2. Measured or marked out by the apparent motion of the stars ; নক্ষত্রের স্ফুট গতিদ্বারা পরিমিত বা চিহ্নিত। **Sidereal day**—কোন স্থানের যাম্যোত্তরবৃত্তে কোন নক্ষত্র যে মুহূর্ত্তে দৃষ্ট হওয়ার পর যে মুহূর্ত্তে উহা তথায় পুনর্দৃষ্ট হয়—এতদুভয়ের মধ্যবর্ত্তী কাল, নাক্ষত্র অহোরাত্র (ইহার পরিমাণ প্রায় ২৩ ঘণ্টা ৫৬ মিনিট ৪'০৯ সেকেণ্ড)। **Sidereal magnetism** — জৈবচুম্বকে বিশ্বাসী ব্যক্তিগণের মতানুসারে রোগীর উপর নক্ষত্রের প্রভাব, নাক্ষত্রচুম্বক। **Sidereal system**—নক্ষত্রজগৎ [যেমন আমাদের পৃথিবী, শনি, বৃহস্পতি, প্রভৃতি এবং উহাদের উপগ্রহাদি আমাদের সৌরজগতের অন্তর্ভুক্ত তেমনি আমাদের সৌরজগৎ নাক্ষত্রজগতের অন্তর্ভুক্ত। এইরূপ এক একটী নক্ষত্রজগতে বহু সৌরজগৎ রহিয়াছে]। **Sidereal time**—নাক্ষত্র-দিবস অনুসারে গণিত সময়। **Sidereal year**—যে সময়ে অচল নক্ষত্র সমূহ কোন নির্দ্দিষ্ট স্থানে একবার দৃষ্ট হইবার পর পুনরায় সেই স্থানে দৃষ্ট হয়। [এক নাক্ষত্রবর্ষ প্রায় ৩৬৬ ২৫৬৩৬১২ নাক্ষত্রঅহোরাত্রের সমান।]

sĭd'-ĕr-īte, *n.* The loadstone ; the native iron protocarbonate ; চুম্বক প্রস্তর ; ব্যোমায়স (সাঃ পঃ)।

sĭd-ĕr-ŏg'-ră-phy̆, *n.* A process of engraving on steel ইস্পাত-ফলকের উপর ক্ষোদনের প্রণালীবিশেষ।

sĭd'-ĕr-ō-līte, *n.* A meteoric stone of iron ; ব্যোমায়সাশ্ম (সাঃ পঃ)।

sīde'-ward, -wards, *adv.* & *adj.* Laterally ; এক পার্শ্বে, পার্শ্বাভিমুখে। *Adj.* Lateral ; পার্শ্বিক, পার্শ্বাভিমুখীন।

sīde'-ways (-wāz), *adv.* & *adj.* Same as SIDEWARD (above).

sīd'-ĭng, *n.* 1. The attaching of one's self to a party ; পক্ষাবলম্বন। 2. A short additional line of rails for shunting ; লৌহবর্ত্মের পার্শ্বস্থিত উপবর্ত্ম।

sī'-dle (-l), *v. i.* To move to one side ; to go or move with one side foremost ; এক পার্শ্বে সরা ; তির্য্যগ্‌ভাবে চলা, কাতান।

Sī-dō'-nĭ-ăn, *adj.* & *n.* Of, or pertaining to, Sidon, an ancient seaport of Phoenicia ; প্রাচীন ফিনিশিয়ার সাইডন বন্দরসম্বন্ধীয়। ***Noun.*** An inhabitant of Sidon ; সাইডনের অধিবাসী।

siege (sēj), *n.* & *v.t.* 1. The setting of an army around or before a fortified place, for the purpose of compelling the garrison to surrender ; অবরোধ, সৈন্যবেষ্টন (কেঃ)। 2. Any continued attempt to persuade an unwilling person to do something ; "Love stood the *siege* and would not yield his breast" ; অনিচ্ছুক ব্যক্তিদ্বারা কোন কার্য্য করাইবার জন্য পুনঃ পুনঃ চেষ্টা, পীড়াপীড়ি। 3. The floor of a glass-furnace ; কাঁচচুল্লীর তলদেশ। ***Verb t.*** (*Archaic*) To besiege ; (অপ্রঃ) অবরোধ করা। **Siege-basket**—Same as GABION (which see). **Siege-gun**—অবরুদ্ধ দুর্গ ধ্বংস করার জন্য ব্যবহৃত কামান, দুর্গধ্বংস-কারী কামান। **Siege-train**—দুর্গ অবরোধে ব্যবহৃত কামান এবং অন্যান্য যন্ত্র। **Siege-works**—দুর্গাবরোধকারিগণের পরিখা, আশ্রয়স্থল, প্রভৃতি। **To lay siege to**—To besiege ; অবরোধ করা। **To push the siege** — To continue a siege vigorously ; প্রবল উদ্যমের সহিত অবরুদ্ধ দুর্গ অধিকারের চেষ্টা করা। **To raise the siege**—To abandon the attempt to take a fort ; দুর্গ অবরোধকার্য্য পরিত্যাগ করা।

Sieg'-fried (sēj-frēd), *n.* The hero of the first part of the Nibelungen-Lied ; Nibelungen-Lied গ্রন্থের

প্রথম অংশের নায়ক। ইনি Netherlandএর রাজা Siegmundএর পুত্র। ইঁহার মাতার নাম Sieglind। Siegfried Burgandyর রাজপুত্রী Guntherএর সহোদরা Kriemhildএর পাণিগ্রহণ করেন। Iceland হইতে Brunhild নাম্নী এক রূপবতী কন্যাকে হরণ করার জন্য Gunther ইঁহার সাহায্য চাহিলে Siegfried, বলপূর্ব্বক ঐ কন্যার এক মাদুলী লইয়া আসেন। এই মাদুলী দর্শনে Guntherএর কোপানল উদ্দীপ্ত হইলে তিনি Hagen নামক এক ডিনেমারকে Siegfriedকে বধের জন্য প্ররোচিত করেন। দেবতার বরে Siegrifiedএর স্কন্ধাস্থিদ্বয়ের মধ্যবর্ত্তী অংশ ভিন্ন দেহের অন্য অংশ অভেদ্য ছিল। Hagen ঐ স্থানে খড়্গাঘাত করিয়া Siegfriedকে হত্যা করেন।

Sieg′-mŭnd (sēj-), *n.* The father of Siegfried ; Siegfriedএর পিতা।

Sĭ′-ĕn-ese (-ēs), **–nese′** (-ēs), *adj.* & *n.* Of, or pertaining to, Sienna in Italy ; ইতালীর অন্তঃপাতী সায়েনা নামক স্থানসংক্রান্ত, সায়েনীয়। ***Noun.*** An inhabitant of Sienna ; সায়েনার অধিবাসী।

Sĭ′-ĕn-nă, –earth (-ērth), *ns.* An earthy pigment of a brownish-yellow colour when raw (*raw sienna*) and of a reddish-brown colour when burnt (*brown sienna*) (from Sienna in Italy) ; একপ্রকার গৈরিক, কপিলবর্ণ, রঞ্জকপদার্থবিশেষ, কপিল রঙ্গ, গেরুয়া রঙ্গ।

si′-er′-ră (sē-ĕr-ă), *n.* A chain of hills or mass of mountains with jagged or saw-like ridges ; ক্রকচদন্তবৎপৃষ্ঠবিশিষ্ট গিরিশ্রেণী, ক্রকচগিরি।

si′-ĕs′-tă (sē-), *n.* A short afternoon nap ; অপরাহ্নকালীন নিদ্রা, বৈকালিক নিদ্রা, অপরাহ্নতন্দ্রা।

sieve (sĭv), *n.* & *v. t.* **1.** A utensil generally in shape like the head of a drum, covered with hair or a material with open meshes, for separating flour from bran or the smaller particles of anything from the large ; ঝাঁঝরি, চালনী, রাঙ্গী। **2.** A kind of coarse basket ; একপ্রকার মোটা ঝুড়ি। **3.** A person who cannot keep a secret ; "The *sieve* of a patron let it out" ; যে ব্যক্তি কোন কথা গোপন রাখিতে পারেনা। ***Verb t.*** To put through sieve ; চালনীদ্বারা চালা। **Sieve-plate**—চালনীস্থালী।

sift, *v. t.* & *i.* **1.** To separate with, or as with, a sieve ; চালনিদ্বারা চালা। **2.** To examine closely ; as, to *sift* evidence ; পুঙ্খানুপুঙ্খরূপে অনুসন্ধান করা, তন্ন তন্ন করিয়া পরীক্ষা করা। **3.** To analyse the character of ; চরিত্র বিশ্লেষণ করা। ***Verb i.*** **1.** To pass through and through ; চালুনীদ্বারা চালা হওয়া। **2.** (*Fig.*) To make an enquiry ; to practise scrutiny ; (লক্ষণায়) অনুসন্ধান করা ; পুঙ্খানুপুঙ্খরূপে পরীক্ষা করা। **Sift′-er,** *n.*

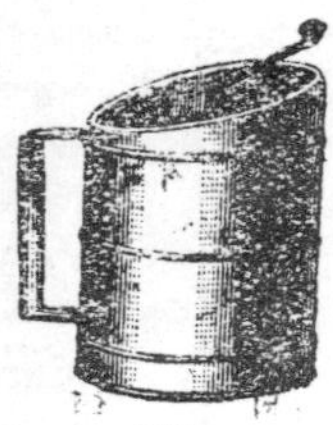
Sifter

sigh (sī), *v. i., t.* & *n.* **1.** To make a deep, single respiration, as the result of involuntary expression of grief, sorrow or the like ; hence, to grieve ; to mourn ; as, to *sigh* for past joys ; দীর্ঘ নিশ্বাস ফেলা ; দুঃখ করা ; শোক করা। **2.** To utter or give expression to a sound like, or suggestive of, a sigh ; "Whenever a March wind *sighs*" ; দীর্ঘনিঃশ্বাস পরিত্যাগ করা। ***Verb t.*** **1.** To lament ; to mourn ; বিলাপ করা ; শোক করা। **2.** To express by sighs ; as, to *sigh* out one's grief ; দীর্ঘ নিঃশ্বাস ফেলিয়া ব্যক্ত করা। ***Noun.*** A single deep respiration ; দীর্ঘনিঃশ্বাস। **A sigh of relief**—আরামের নিঃশ্বাস, স্বস্তিশ্বাস [cf. ধরণী স্বস্তিশ্বাস মোচন করিলেন—হীরেন্দ্রনাথ দত্ত।] **To sigh for**—To long or wish ardently for ; কামনা করা, প্রবল বাসনা করা।

sight (sīt), *n.* & *v. t.* **1.** The act of seeing ; view ; দর্শন ; দৃষ্টি, নজর। **2.** That which is seen ; a spectacle ; as, a sad *sight* ; দৃষ্টবস্তু ; দৃশ্য। **3.** Space within vision ; দৃষ্টিক্ষেত্র। **4.** Eye-sight ; দৃষ্টিশক্তি। **5.** Noteworthy features of a town etc. ; as, he went to see *sights* ; নগরাদির দর্শনীয় বস্তু। **6.** (*Obs.*) The eye ; (অপ্রঃ) চক্ষুঃ। **7.** Inspection ; examination ; notice ; as, this letter is intended for your *sight* only ; পরিদর্শন ; পরীক্ষা ; লক্ষ্য, গোচর। **8.** Opportunity for investigation ; opportunity ; অনুসন্ধানের সুবিধা ; সুবিধা, সুযোগ। **9.** (*Colloq.*) A great number or quantity ; "A *sight* of lawyers" ; বহুসংখ্যা, রাশি রাশি। **10.** A small aperture through which objects are to be seen, and by which the direction is settled or ascertained ; যে ক্ষুদ্র ছিদ্রের ভিতর দিয়া কোন বস্তু দর্শন করিতে হয় এবং যদ্দ্বারা সেই বস্তুর দিক নির্ণীত হইয়া থাকে। **11.** A piece of metal near the muzzle or the breech of a firearm to guide the eye in taking an aim ; বন্দুকাদির অগ্র বা পৃষ্ঠে নিবদ্ধ ধাতুখণ্ডবিশেষ—যদ্দ্বারা লক্ষ্য স্থির করা হয়, মাছি (রমাসুন্দরী—প্রভাত), তিলবিন্দু (শুক্রঃ)। [সাধারণতঃ অগ্রভাগে একটী এবং পৃষ্ঠে একটী — বন্দুকে এই দুইটী তিল বিন্দু থাকে। শেষোক্তটীতে একটী খাঁজ বা কোনরূপ ছিদ্র থাকে—যদ্দ্বারা প্রথমটী দৃষ্ট হইয়া থাকে।] **12.** An aim or observation taken by means of a sight or sights ; তিলবিন্দু বা জরীপের যন্ত্রাদির অংশবিশেষের সাহায্যে লক্ষ্য স্থির করণ। ***Verb t.*** **1.** To see ; দেখা, দর্শন করা। **2.** To look or examine through a sight ; বন্দুকের তিলবিন্দু সাহায্যে দর্শন করা, ক্ষুদ্র ছিদ্রের ভিতর দিয়া দর্শন করা।

3. To give proper elevation or direction to by means of sight ; তিলবিন্দু প্রভৃতির সাহায্যে আবশ্যকানুরূপ উচ্চে তোলা বা দিক্ নির্দ্দেশ করা। **Second sight**—অন্তর্দৃষ্টি; দিব্যদৃষ্টি। **Short sight**—See SHORT. Also (*fig.*) ; অদূরদর্শিতা। **Sighting line**—চাক্ষুষ-রেখা (হিঃ কোঃ), দৃষ্টিরেখা (ঐ)। **Sight-reader** — যে ব্যক্তি দেখিয়া (স্বরলিপি প্রভৃতি) পাঠ করিতে পারে। **Sight-seeing**—(*Adj.*) প্রাকৃতিক দৃশ্য-সমূহ দর্শনানুরাগী। (*Noun.*) প্রাকৃতিক দৃশ্যসমূহ দর্শনের অনুরাগ, নূতন এবং বিচিত্র বস্তুসমূহ দর্শনের কৌতুহল। **Sight-worthy**—দর্শনযোগ্য, দেখবার মত (*colloq.*), দর্শনীয়, দ্রষ্টব্য। **A bill at sight**—See BILL. **A sight for sore eyes**—A pleasant object ; নয়নরঞ্জন বস্তু, নেত্রপ্রীতিকর বস্তু, চোখ-জুড়ানো বস্তু। **At first sight**—At first appearance ; প্রথম দৃষ্টিতে, আপাতদৃষ্টিতে। **At or on sight**—The moment it is seen ; দর্শন মাত্র, দৃষ্টিমাত্র। **His face is a perfect sight**—It has been disfigured by sores, etc. ; অর্থাৎ তাহার মুখ ক্ষতাদি হেতু বিকৃত হইয়াছে। **Loss of sight** — দৃষ্টিশক্তি লোপ। **Out of sight !**—আমার সম্মুখ হইতে দুর হও। **Out of sight** — No longer seen ; দৃষ্টির বহির্ভূত, দৃষ্টি-পথের অন্তরাল। **Out of sight, Out of all sight**—Beyond all measure or comparison ; অপ্রমেয়রূপে, অতুলনীয়রূপে। **Out of sight out of mind**—চোখের আড়াল হইলেই মনের আড়াল। **To be in sight**—To be near at hand ; সন্নিকটবর্ত্তী হওয়া। **To catch sight of**—To begin to see ; দেখিতে পাওয়া, সন্দর্শন করা। **To get a sight of**—To manage to see ; দেখিতে পারা। **To know by sight** — To know by appearance ; মুখ দেখিয়া চিনিতে পারা। **To lose sight**—To disappear from sight ; দৃষ্টির অন্তরাল হওয়া। **To put out of sight**—To conceal ; to ignore ; গোপন করা, লুকান ; উপেক্ষা করা। **To sight** — To the eye ; চক্ষুর নিকট। **To take sight**—To take aim with a fire-arm ; বন্দুক প্রভৃতি নিশানা করা।

sight'-less (sīt-), *adj.* 1. Blind ; অন্ধ, দৃষ্টিহীন। 2. (*Poet*) Invisible ; "Upon the *sightless* couriers of the air" ; (কবিতায়) অদৃশ্য। **–ly**, *adv.* **–ness**, *n.*

sight'-ly (sīt-), *adj.* 1. Pleasing to the sight ; comely ; 'Many brave *sightly* horses" ; প্রিয়দর্শন, নেত্রপ্রীতিকর, নয়নরঞ্জন ; সুশ্রী সুন্দর। 2. (*U. S.*) Open to the view ; as, a *sightly* hill ; (মার্কিণ যুক্তরাজ্যে) মুক্ত, উন্মুক্ত। **–li-ness**, *n.*

sig-il-la'-ri-a, *n.* A genus of fossil trees some of which attain

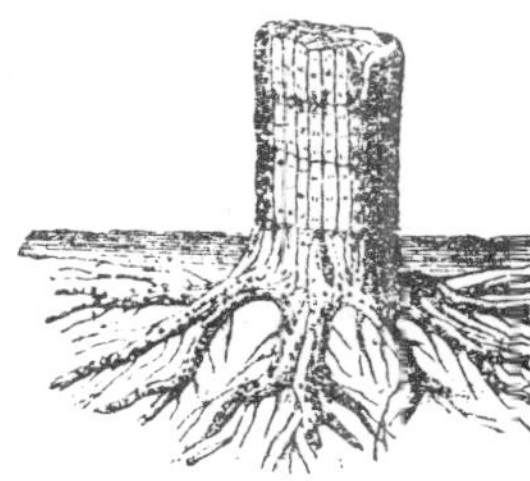

Sigillaria.

a height of nearly 100 ft. ; এক-জাতীয় শিলীভূত তরু।

sig'-il-late, *adj.* 1. (Of pottery) Impressed with seal ; (মৃন্ময়পাত্র সম্পর্কে) মুদ্রাঙ্কিত। 2. (*Bot.*) Having seal-like mark ; মুদ্রাবৎ চিহ্নিত।

sig'-ma, *n.* Greek letter (Σ, C) corresponding to English S ; ইংরাজী S অক্ষরের অনুরূপ গ্রীক অক্ষরবিশেষ।

sig'-mate, *adj.* 1. Shaped like the Greek letter sigma ; গ্রীকঅক্ষর সিগমার মত আকৃতিবিশিষ্ট। 2. S-shaped ; S অক্ষরাকৃতি।

sig'-mate, *v. t.* To increase by adding the letter sigma ; সিগ্মা অক্ষর সংযোগে বৃদ্ধি করা।

sig'-moid (-moyd), *adj.* Curved like the letter sigma or S ; (শারীরসংস্থানবিদ্যা) গ্রীক Sigma বা ইংরাজী S অক্ষরের তুল্য উভয়দিকে বক্র। **Sigmoid flexure**—স্থূলান্ত্রের শেষ বক্রাংশ।

sign (sīn), *n., v. t. & i.* 1. A mark ; a token ; an indication ; দাগ, চিহ্ন; অভিজ্ঞান ; লিঙ্গ (হিঃ কোঃ), লাঞ্ছন, নিদর্শন, সূচনা। 2. A gesture ; a proof ; ইঙ্গিত, ইসারা, সঙ্কেত ; প্রমাণ। 3. A wonder ; a miracle ; "Through mighty *signs* and wonders" : "Among His *signs* also are ships out at sea like mountains ; if such be His will He lulleth the wind and they lie motionless on the back of the waves" ; আশ্চর্য্য ব্যাপার ; অতি-প্রাকৃত ঘটনা, অলৌকিক ঘটনা। 4. A prodigy ; অতিপ্রাকৃত বস্তু। 5. An emblem ; a type ; as, the *sign* of cross ; আদর্শ ; প্রতীক। 6. Something set up on a house to show the tenant's occupation ; গৃহবাসীর ব্যবসায় সূচনার্থ যে বস্তু গৃহের সম্মুখে নিবদ্ধ করা হয়। 6. (*Astron.*) The twelfth part of the ecliptic ; (জ্যোতির্বিজ্ঞান) রাশি, ভ (সাঃ পঃ), ভবন (ঐ), গৃহ (ঐ)। 7. (*Math.*) Character or symbol, indicating the relation between ; (গণিত) যোগ, বিয়োগ প্রভৃতি (+, —) চিহ্ন। 8. (*Med.*) A symptom ; (ভৈষজ্যশাস্ত্র) লক্ষণ, রোগলক্ষণ। *Verb t.* 1. To mark with a sign ; চিহ্নাঙ্কিত করা। 2. To represent or make known by sign ; চিহ্ন দ্বারা প্রকাশ করা, চিহ্ন দ্বারা পরিজ্ঞাত করা। 3. To attach a signature to ; স্বাক্ষর করা, সহি করা। 3. To communicate by gestuers ; as, he *signed* me to come ; ইঙ্গিতে বলা, ইসারা দ্বারা বলা। *Verb i.* 1. To make a sign or signal ; ইঙ্গিত করা, ইসারা করা। 2. To converse in sign-language :

সাঙ্কেতিক ভাষায় কথা বলা, ঠারে কথা বলা। **Signboard**—যে কাষ্ঠফলকে দোকান প্রভৃতির নাম লিখা থাকে, নামপট্ট। **Sign manual** — স্বাক্ষর, সহি, বিশেষতঃ রাজার সহি। **Sign-post**—যে স্তম্ভে নামপট্ট টাঙ্গান হয়; পথনির্দ্দেশক স্তম্ভ। **Exalted sign**—তুঙ্গ (বৃঃ সং)। **Half of a sign**—হোরা (বৃঃ সং)। **Rising sign**—লগ্ন (বৃঃ সং)। **Sign-making function**—চিহ্নজনক বৃত্তি (হিঃ কোঃ)। **Third part of a sign**—দ্রেক্কাণ (বৃঃ সং)। **To sign off**—To relinquish one's claims; দাবি পরিত্যাগ করা।

sig'-năl, *adj.* Remarkable; extraordinary; as, a *signal* victory; অপূর্ব্ব, অসামান্য; অত্যাশ্চর্য্য, অসাধারণ, বিচিত্র। **–ly**, *adv.*

sig'-năl, *n., v. t.* & *i.* 1. A sign to give notice or communicate intelligence, orders, etc., at a distance, সঙ্কেত, ঠার। 2. The notice given; সাঙ্কেতিকবার্ত্তা। 3. A means of communication by audible signs between two distant points according to preconcerted system; পূর্ব্বনির্দ্ধারিত প্রণালী অনুসারে দূরবর্ত্তী স্থানদ্বয়ে সংবাদ আদান প্রদানের উপায়, সঙ্কেতযন্ত্র। ***Verb t.*** 1. To communicate by signal; সঙ্কেত দ্বারা সংবাদ দেওয়া বা বিজ্ঞাপিত করা। 2. To make signals to; সঙ্কেত করা, ইসারা করা। ***Verb i.*** 1. To give signals; সঙ্কেত করা। 2. To be a sign or omen; চিহ্নস্বরূপ হওয়া। **Signal-box, signal cabin**—লৌহবর্ত্মের পার্শ্বস্থিত কুটীরবিশেষ—যাহা হইতে সঙ্কেতযন্ত্র চালান হয়। **Signal-code**—গুপ্ত সাঙ্কেতিকবার্ত্তাপদ্ধতি। **Signal-fire** — সঙ্কেতসূচক অগ্নি। **Signal-man**—Same as SIGNALLER.

sig'-năl-ize, *v. t.* To make signal or eminent; to make distinguished from what is common; as, the soldier *signalised* himself; প্রতিষ্ঠাসম্পন্ন করা; প্রতিষ্ঠাভাজন করা, প্রখ্যাত করা, বিশ্রুত করা, প্রসিদ্ধ করা।

sig'-năl-lĕr, *n.* One who signals; especially one appointed to transmit signal; সঙ্কেতপ্রেরণকারী; সাঙ্কেতিকবার্ত্তাপ্রেরণকারী কর্ম্মচারী।

sig'-nă-tŏ-rȳ, *n.* One that is bound by signature to the terms of an agreement; (সন্ধিপত্র প্রভৃতি) স্বাক্ষরকারী।

sig'-nă-tūre, *n.* 1. The name of a person written or subscribed by himself; স্বাক্ষর, দস্তখত, সহি। 2. A letter or figure by which the sheet are distinguished and their order designated, as a direction to the binder, or the sheet so distinguished; ফরমার নম্বর, ঐরূপ নম্বরযুক্ত কাগজ। 3. (*Archaic*) Mark; (অপ্রঃ) চিহ্ন। 4. (*Mus.*) A sign indicating the key or numerals stating number and lengths of beats and measure; (সঙ্গীত-শাস্ত্র) চিহ্ন, মাত্রা।

sig'-nĕt, *n.* A seal, esp. the seal used by the sovereign in sealing private letters, and grants that pass by bill under the sign manual (called also *privy signet*); মোহর, মুদ্রা, ইংলণ্ডের রাজকীয় মোহর। **Signet-ring**—মুদ্রাযুক্ত অঙ্গুরীয়ক, মুদ্রা।

sig-nif'-i-cance (-kăns), *n.* 1. Meaning; import; অর্থ, তাৎপর্য্য; অভিপ্রায়, সার্থকতা, মূল্য (হিঃ কোঃ)। 2. Importance; গুরুত্ব।

sig-nif'-i-cănt, *adj.* 1. Bearing a meaning; অর্থযুক্ত। 2. Suggestive or containing some hidden meaning; as, a *suggestive* look; গূঢ়ার্থব্যঞ্জক, গূঢ়ার্থপ্রকাশক, সঙ্কেতগর্ভ, ইঙ্গিতময়, অর্থসূচক, স্বার্থক, অভিব্যঞ্জক, অভিদ্যোতক। 3. Momentous; গুরুত্ববিশিষ্ট। 4. Standing as a sign of something; "It was well said of Plotinus, that the stars were *significant*, but not efficient"; কোন কিছুর চিহ্নস্বরূপ ব্যবহৃত, প্রতীকস্বরূপ।

sig-ni-fi-cā'-tion, *n.* 1. (*Rare*) The act of signifying; (কচিদ্‌ব্যবহৃত) অর্থব্যঞ্জন। 2. Exact meaning or sense; প্রকৃত অর্থ বা তাৎপর্য্য, লক্ষণা (হিঃ কোঃ)।

sig-nif'-i-că-tive (-tiv), *adj.* 1. Betokening or representing by an external sign; অভিব্যঞ্জক। 2. Having meaning; অর্থপূর্ণ, অর্থযুক্ত।

sig'-ni-fȳ, *v. t.* & *i.* 1. To make known by a sign; কোনরূপ চিহ্ন বা লক্ষণদ্বারা প্রকাশ করা বা জ্ঞাত করা। 2. To imply; to mean; অর্থ প্রকাশ করা; বুঝান। ***Verb i.*** 1. To have a meaning; অর্থ থাকা। 2. To matter; as, it does not *signify* (এতে কিছু আসে যায় না); কোন কিছু আসা যাওয়া।

Signior, Signor, Signora, Signorina, *ns.* Italian title of respect corresponding to English Sir and Mr., Madam, Mrs. and Miss.; ইতালীদেশীয় ভদ্রলোক ও ভদ্রমহিলাগণের নামের পূর্ব্বে ব্যবহৃত শব্দ।

sī'-lage, *n.* & *v. t.* Same as ENSILAGE. ***Verb t.*** To put into a silo; গর্ত্তে বা বায়ুশূন্য কক্ষে গবাদির খাদ্যের জন্য কচি কচি ঘাস চাপা দিয়া রাখা।

sī'-lence (-lĕns), *n.* & *v.t.* 1. Quiet; stillness; নীরবতা, নিঃশব্দতা; মৌন, নিস্তব্ধতা, স্তব্ধতা, স্থিরতা। 2. Taciturnity; মৌন, তূষ্ণীম্ভাব, অননুভাষণ (ন্যায়শাস্ত্র)। 3. Forgetfulness; "What most merits fame in *silence* hid"; বিস্মৃতি। 4. Secrecy; গোপনতা। ***Verb t.*** 1. To cause to be still; নীরব করা, নিস্তব্ধ করা। 2. To cause an enemy to cease firing; as, to *silence* one's guns; শত্রুপক্ষের গোলাবর্ষণ বন্ধ করা। 3. To make silent by superior argument; as, to *silence* a speaker; প্রবলতর যুক্তিদ্বারা নিরুত্তর করা।

sī'-lĕnt, *adj.* 1. Free from sound or noise; নীরব, নিঃশব্দ, নিঝুম (*poet.*)। 2. Taciturn; speaking little; মৌনী, রুদ্ধবাক্, অল্পভাষী, স্বল্পভাষী,

সংযতবাক্। 3. Mute ; মূক, বোবা। 4. Not accompanied by any sound ; as, *silent* letter ; অনুচ্চারিত, অনুক্ত। **—ly,** *adv.* In a silent manner ; চুপি চুপি, নীরবে, নিঃশব্দে। **Silent partner** — যে অংশীদার ব্যবসায়ের পরিচালনা সম্বন্ধে কোনরূপ কর্তৃত্ব করিতে পারে না। **The silent system**—কারাগারের যে নিয়ম অনুসারে বন্দিগণ পরস্পরের সহিত কথাবার্তা বলিতে পারে না।

Si-le'-nus, *n.* 1. The foster father and teacher of Bacchus ; গ্রীকদেশীয় সুরাদেবতা ব্যাকাসের শিক্ষক এবং পালক পিতা। 2. A drunken old man ; বৃদ্ধ মাতাল লোক।

si-le'-si-a (-shi-), *n.* A species of linen cloth, originally made at Silesia ; একপ্রকার ক্ষৌমবস্ত্র—যাহা পূর্ব্বে সাইলিসিয়াতে প্রস্তুত হইত।

sil-hou-ette' (-ô-ĕt), *n.* & *v. t.* A representation of the outline of one object filled in with black or other uniform colour ; a profile or side-face represented as a solid black mass ; মসীলিপ্ত কৃষ্ণ বা অন্য কোন বর্ণে রঞ্জিত কোন বস্তুর রেখাচিত্র ; মসীলিপ্ত অর্দ্ধাস্য চিত্র বা মুখমণ্ডলের পার্শ্বচিত্র। ***Verb t.*** To represent or exhibit in silhouette; অর্দ্ধাস্য চিত্র করা। [Silhouette নামক জনৈক কৃপণ ফরাসী-দেশীয় রাজস্বসচিবের নাম হইতে গৃহীত।]

Silhouette.

sil'-i-ca, *n.* Oxide of silicon, the chief constituent of quartz, flint, etc. ; সিকতা, বালি (সাঃ পঃ), বালুকা (আয়ুঃ রসঃ)। **—cif'-er-ous,** *adj.* **Si-lic'-ic,** *adj.* **Si-li'-cious, Si-li'-ce-ous,** *adj.* **Silicic acid**—সিকতক দ্রাবক (সাঃ পঃ)।

sil'-i-cat-ed, *adj.* Combined with silica ; বালুকামিশ্রিত।

si-lic'-i-fy, *v. t.* & *i.* 1. To impregnate with the silica ; বালুকাময় করা। 2. To convert into silica ; বালুকায় পরিণত করা। ***Verb i.*** To turn into silica ; বালুকায় পরিণত হওয়া।

sil'-i-con, *n.* The non-metallic element of which silica is the oxide ; সিকতক, শিলাকণ (মনীঃ)।

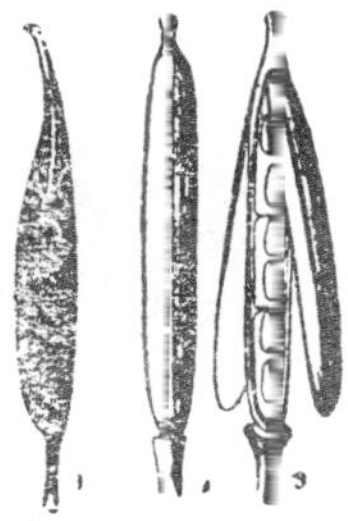

Siliqua or pod. 1, mustard ; 2, wall-flower ; 3, wallflower open to show arrangement.

sil'-i-qua, si-lique' (-lēk), (*Pl.* -QUÆ), *ns.* 1. Pod of plants of mustard family ; সর্ষপজাতীয় গুল্মের বীজকোষ। 2. Same as CARAT. **—quose,** *adj.*

silk, *n.* & *adj.* 1. The soft thread forming cocoon of the silk-worm moth; রেশম, পট্ট, পাট [(প্রাঃ সাঃ) cf. পাটের শাড়ী]। 2. The thread spun or the cloth woven from the abovenamed material ; "He caused the shore to be covered with Persian *silk* for him to tread upon" ; রেশমী সূতা, পট্টসূত্র, রেশমীকাপড়, পট্টবস্ত্র, চীনাংশুক (esp. of cloth from China-silk), কৌষেয় বস্ত্র, দুকূল। 3. A dress made of silk ; "She bethought her of faded *silk*" ; রেশমী পোষাক, পট্টপরিচ্ছদ। 4. A silk lustre seen in some rubies and sapphires and considered as defect ; চুনী ও নীলার মধ্যে যে একপ্রকার রেশমী আভা দেখায় এবং যাহা ঐ সকল মণির দোষ বলিয়া গণ্য হইয়া থাকে, পট্টকোষ। ***Adj.*** Made of silk ; রেশমী, কৌষিক, কৌষেয়, কৃমিকোষজ, কোষোদ্ভব, কৌশিক। **Silk'-en,** *adj.* **Chinese-silk** — চীনাংশুক। **Silk-cotton-tree**—শিমুলগাছ, শাল্মলীতরু [Syn. শাল্মলি, স্থিরায়ুঃ, পিচ্ছিলা, পূরণী, মোচা, দুরারোহা, শাল্মলিনী, শাল্মল, কুক্কুটী, তুলিনী, তুলবৃক্ষ, রক্তপুষ্পা, কণ্টকারী, মোচনী রক্তপুষ্পক, মোচাখ্য, কণ্টক-দ্রুম, রক্তোৎপল, রম্যপুষ্প, বহুবীর্য্য, যমদ্রুম, দীর্ঘদ্রুম, স্থূলফল, দীর্ঘায়ুঃ, কণ্টকাষ্ঠ (ভাবঃ প্রঃ)]। **Silk-fowl**—একপ্রকার কুক্কুট—যাহার পালক রেশমের মত চক চক করে। **Silk-gland** — রেশম-কীটের গ্রন্থি হইতে নিঃসৃত একপ্রকার তরল পদার্থ—যাহা রেশমে পরিণত হয়। **Silk-moth** — পাটপোকা। **Silk-thread**—রেশমী সূতা, পট্টসূত্র। **Silk-worm**—গুটিপোকা, পলু [Syn. তন্তুকীট,

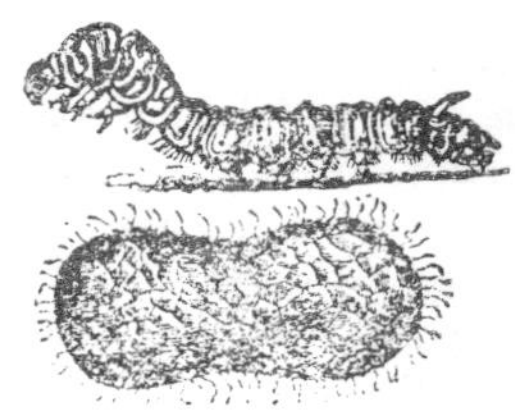

Cocoon and larvae.

কোষকার, তন্তুকৃমি, কোষবাসী, কোশস্থ, পুণ্ডরীক, পট্টকূল]। **The silken ties**—প্রেম ও প্রীতির বন্ধন। **To make a silk purse out of a sow's ear**—কদর্য্য বস্তু হইতে সুন্দর জিনিষ তৈয়ার করা, আমড়াগাছে আম ফলান, গাধা পিটিয়া ঘোড়া করা। **To take silk**—ইংলণ্ডের সরকারী উকীলের পদপ্রাপ্তি হেতু রেশমী পোষাক পরিধান করা (King's or Queen's counsel)।

silk'-y, *adj.* Like silk ; রেশমের মত, পট্টবৎ। **—i-ness,** *n.* **Silky manner**—কোমল ব্যবহার, মধুর ব্যবহার।

sill, *n.* The stone or timber at the bottom of a door or window-frame ; বাতায়ন বা দ্বারের নিম্নস্থ প্রস্তর বা কাষ্ঠফলক, শিলা, দেহলী, বাতায়নশিলা।

sil'-la-bub, *n.* A liquid food made by mixing wine etc. with milk ; দুগ্ধের সহিত সুরা প্রভৃতি মিশ্রণে প্রস্তুত করা খাদ্যবিশেষ।

sil'-ler (-êr), *n.* (*Scot.*) Silver coin ; (স্কটলণ্ড) রৌপ্য মুদ্রা।

sil-ler-ў (-êr), *n.* A high-class wine produced in and found in the village of Sillery in Champagne ; ফরাসীদেশের অন্তঃপাতী স্যম্পেনপ্রদেশের সিলারী গ্রাম এবং উক্ত গ্রামের নিকটবর্ত্তী গ্রামসমূহে প্রস্তুত একপ্রকার উৎকৃষ্ট মদিরা।

sil'-lў, *adj.,* & *n.* **1.** Foolish ; নির্ব্বোধ, বোকা, মন্দধী, অল্পবুদ্ধি, অল্পধী, বেকুব (*colloq.*), বোকা, দুর্ধী। **2.** Proceeding from folly ; characterised by folly ; unwise ; as, *silly* conduct; নির্ব্বুদ্ধিতাপ্রসূত ; নির্ব্বোধোচিত; বুদ্ধিহীন, জ্ঞানশূন্য। ***Noun.*** A fool ; as, do not be a *silly*, নির্ব্বোধ লোক, বোকা লোক । **—li-ly,** *adv.* **—li-ness,** *n.*

sī'-lō, *n.,* & *v. t.* The pit or airtight compartment in which green fodder is preserved in the method of ensilage ; যে গর্ত্ত বা বায়ুশূন্য কক্ষে গবাদির খাদ্যের জন্য কাঁচা ঘাস তাজা রাখা হয়। ***Verb t.*** To preserve thus ; গর্ত্তে বা বায়ুশূন্য কক্ষে গবাদির খাদ্যের জন্য কাঁচা ঘাস তাজা রাখা।

silt, *n., v. t.* & *i.* A deposit of fine earth from running or standing water ; পলি, ধোয়াট মাটী। ***Verb t.*** To choke with silt ; পলি দ্বারা রোধ করা। ***Verb i.*** To be choked with silt ; পলিদ্বারা রুদ্ধ হওয়া, পলি পড়িয়া বন্ধ হওয়া বা বুজিয়া যাওয়া, মজিয়া যাওয়া (cf. এই পুষ্করিণী এখন মজিয়া গিয়া সঙ্কীর্ণ আয়তন হইয়াছে।)।

Silundia Gangetica—সিলোন্দ-মাছ (গুপ্তঃ)।

Si-lü'-ri-ăn, *adj.,* & *n.* Applied to the lowest division of Palaeozoic strata ; ভূপঞ্জরের সর্ব্বনিম্নস্তরের অন্তর্বর্ত্তী নিম্নতম স্তরসম্বন্ধীয়, সিলিউরিক (রাখালঃ)। ***Noun.*** The Silurian period or system ; সিলিউরিক স্তর বা ঐ স্তরের যুগ। [দক্ষিণ ওয়েল্‌সের অন্তঃপাতী Siluria নামক স্থানে এই স্তর প্রথম পরীক্ষিত হইয়াছিল বলিয়া এই নাম।] **Silurian paper**—একপ্রকার ফুট ফুট, দাগবিশিষ্ট ধূসরবর্ণের কাগজ। **Lower Silurian formation**—পূর্ব্বসিলুরীয়স্তর। **Upper Silurian formation**—পরসিলুরীয়স্তর।

si-lü'-ri-dae (-dē), *n.* A family of fishes comprising the sheat-fish ; বোয়ালজাতীয় মৎস্যশ্রেণী, পাঠীনাদি।

silurus.

Silurus pelorius—Same as SHEAT-FISH (which see.)

sil'-văn, *adj.* See SYLVAN, *adj.*

sil'-vêr, *n., adj., v. t.* & *i.* **1.** A well-known metal of a peculiar white colour, having a brilliant lustre, malleable, ductile and soft when pure (Symbol Ag. ; Atom. weight 108.) ; রৌপ্য, রূপা, রজত [Syn. চন্দ্রলৌহ, চন্দ্রকান্তি, পাণ্ডুলোহ, মহাশুভ্র, চন্দ্রহাস, রূপ্য (সাঃ পঃ), তার (ঐ), শশি (ঐ), চন্দ্র (ঐ), তারক (ঐ), কলধৌত (also gold), ইন্দ্রলোহক, হংসাভিখ্য, শুভ্র, বসুশ্রেষ্ঠ, রুধির, শ্বেতক, তপ্তরূপক, চন্দ্রভূতি, সিত, কলধূত, ধৌত, সৌধ, খর্জ্জুর, দুর্ব্বর্ণ, শ্বেত, রঙ্গবীজ, রাজরঙ্গ, লোহরাজক, শুক্র, ব্রাহ্মপিঙ্গা, অকুপ্য, সিতপ্রভ।] **2.** Coin made of silver ; রৌপ্যমুদ্রা, রূপ্যমুদ্রা, রজতমুদ্রা। **3.** A plate etc. made of silver ; রৌপ্যনির্ম্মিত পাত্রাদি, রৌপ্যভাণ্ড, রৌপ্যপাত্র। **4.** A silvery lustre ; রজত আভা, রজতদ্যুতি, রজতপ্রভা। ***Adj.*** **1.** Made of silver ; রজতনির্ম্মিত, রৌপ্যনির্ম্মিত, রজতময়। **2.** Of, or pertaining to, silver ; রৌপ্যসম্বন্ধীয়, রাজত। **3.** White as silver ; রজতশুভ্র, রজতশ্বেত, রজতধবল। **4.** Bright and lustrous as silver ; "Spread o'er the *silver* waves thy golden hair" ; রজতোজ্জ্বল, রজতপ্রভ। **5.** (Of sound etc.) Sweet ; as, he has a *silver* tongue ; সুললিত, সুমধুর। **6.** (*Poet*) Soft ; as, *silver* slumber ; (পদ্যে) ধীর, শান্ত। ***Verb t.*** **1.** To coat with silver ; রৌপ্যমণ্ডিত করা, রূপার পাত দিয়া মোড়া। **2.** To cover or coat with tin-foil amalgamated with quicksilver ; as, to *silver* glass ; টীনের পাতল পাত এবং পারদের মিশ্র দ্বারা আবৃত করা। **3.** To adorn with a mild silvery lustre ; রজতাভ করা, রজতদীপ্তি প্রদান করা। **—vern, —y,** *adjs.* **Silver Age**—দ্বাপরযুগ ; রোমসম্রাট অগষ্টাসের পরবর্ত্তী ল্যাটিনসাহিত্যের যুগ। **Silver-bath**—ফটোগ্রাফের কার্য্যে ব্যবহৃত সিল্‌ভার নাইট্রেট্‌সলিউশন। **Silver-beater**—যে ব্যক্তি রৌপ্য পিটিয়া পাতলা পাত করে। **Silver fir**—See FIR. **Silver-fish** — বিভিন্ন প্রকার রজতবর্ণ মৎস্যের নাম ; বিশেষতঃ একজাতীয় বর্ণহীন স্বর্ণ মৎস্য। **Silver-fox**—একপ্রকার ধূসরাভ উজ্জ্বল কৃষ্ণবর্ণের খেঁকশিয়াল। **Silver-gilt**—রূপার গিল্‌টি। **Silver-grey** — রজতাভ ধূসরবর্ণ। **Silver-haired**—পক্ককেশ, শুক্লকেশ, শুভ্রকেশ। **Silver-leaf** — রূপার পাতা, রূপার তবক, তারপত্র (সাঃ পঃ)। **Silver-paper** — একপ্রকার অতি মিহি শাদা কাগজবৎ টিনের তবক। **Silver-print** — রৌপ্যের লবণক দ্বারা লিপ্ত কাগজের উপর মুদ্রিত আলোকচিত্র। **Silver-side**—গোমাংসের উৎকৃষ্ট খণ্ড। **Silver-side, —sides** — একজাতীয় ক্ষুদ্র মৎস্য—ইহাদের উভয় পার্শ্বে রজতবর্ণের রেখা থাকে। **Silversmith**—যে ব্যক্তি রূপার অলঙ্কার প্রস্তুত করে, রৌপ্যকার, রজতপাত্রনির্ম্মাতা। **Silver solder**—রূপা জোড়া দেওয়ার জন্য পান। **Silver standard** — রৌপ্যমুদ্রাব্যবহাররীতি। **Silver-stick** — রাজপ্রাসাদের কার্য্যে নিযুক্ত সৈনিককর্ম্মচারিবিশেষ। **Silver-tongued** —মিষ্টভাষী, মধুরভাষী, মঞ্জুভাষী, প্রিয়ম্বদ। **Silver-top**—তৃণরোগ বিশেষ। **Silver-weed** — ইংলণ্ডের পথিপার্শ্বে জাত গুল্মবিশেষ—যাহার পত্রের অপর পৃষ্ঠ রৌপ্যবর্ণ হইয়া

থাকে। Every cloud has a silver-lining — নিরাশার মেঘেও আশার আলো বিদ্যমান থাকে। Speech is silver(n), but silence is gold(en)—যত কম কওয়া যায় ততই ভাল। To be born with a silver-spoon in one's mouth—See SPOON.

sim'-i-ăn, *adj.* & *n.* 1. Pertaining to the monkey or ape genus; মর্কটজাতীয়। 2. Any monkey or ape, esp., anthropoid ape; বানর, মর্কট, বিশেষতঃ মনুষ্যপ্রকৃতি মর্কট।

sim'-i-lar, (-lêr) *adj.* & *n.* Resembling in many respects; তুল্য, সদৃশ, অনুরূপ, সঙ্কাশ, সমান, প্রতিম, সমতুল, সজাতীয় (হিঃ কোঃ), প্রতিভাস। ***Noun.*** That which is similar; সদৃশবস্তু, অনুরূপ বস্তু। **–lar'-i-ty**, *n.* Resemblance; তুল্যতা, সাদৃশ্য, অনুরূপতা, আনুরূপ্য, সদৃশতা। **–ly**, *adv.*

sim-i-lē, *n.* A common figure of speech, in which two things which have strong points of resemblance are compared; ব্যাক্যালঙ্কার-বিশেষ, উপমা, রূপক, উৎপ্রেক্ষা, দৃষ্টান্ত (হিঃ কোঃ)। [এতদ্দেশে সাধারণতঃ যে সকল উপমানবাচক শব্দের প্রয়োগ হয় সংস্কৃত কবিকল্পলতা নামক গ্রন্থে তাহার একটী সুন্দর সংগ্রহ আছে। যথা, "কেশপাশস্য চামরঃ, ময়ুরপুচ্ছঃ, (also সাপিনী—cf. জলের কান্ধারে কেশের আঁধারে সাপিনী লাগিল মোর—চণ্ডীদাস) (also আঁধার—cf. বদনকমলে ভ্রমরা বুলয়ে তিমির কেশের ধারা—চণ্ডীদাস)। ধর্ম্মিলস্য বিধুন্তুদঃ (রাহু), অন্ধকারঃ। সীমন্তস্য মেঘঃ, পন্থাঃ, দণ্ডঃ। ললাটস্য অষ্টমীচন্দ্রঃ (cf. শুভ্র ললাটে ইন্দু সমান ভাতিছে স্নিগ্ধ শান্তি — রবীন্দ্রনাথ), ফলকম্। কপোলস্য চন্দ্রঃ, মুকুরস্থলম্ [also গোলাব—যথা গোলাবগণ্ড (cf. শ্রমে পদ্মপর্ণ কপোলযুগল ভাসিছে গোলাপ সদ্য বিকসিত—নবীনচন্দ্র।] জ্রবোঃ খড়্গঃ, ধনুর্যষ্টিঃ, রেখা, পল্লবঃ, বল্লীঃ [also কালিন্দীহিল্লোল (cf. যাহা যাহা ভঙ্গুর ভাঙ্গ বিলোল। তাহা তাহা উছলহি কালিন্দীহিল্লোল—গোবিন্দদাস)।] (also কন্দর্পের ধনু — cf. কামধনু ভুরুর বলনি ইন্দ্রধনুকের আভা, (also চকোর cf.—নয়ন চকোর মোর পিতে করে উতরোল—চণ্ডীদাস), (also কালসর্প—(cf. শশীমুখি তব ভাতি ভঙ্গুর ভ্রূঃ যুবজনমোহনকরালকালসর্পী)। দৃশোঃ চকোরচক্ষুঃ, হরিণচক্ষুঃ মদিরা, খঞ্জনঃ, অঞ্জনং কুমুদং, নীলপদ্মং, প্রোষ্ঠিমৎস্যঃ। কর্ণস্য দোলা, পাশঃ। নাসায়াঃ বংশঃ, কেতকীপুষ্পকণ্টকঃ, অধোমুখতুণীরঃ, চঞ্চুঃ, তিলপুষ্পং, দণ্ডঃ। অধরস্য নবপল্লবং, বিম্বফলং (cf. বিম্বাধরমাধুরী—জয়দেব), প্রবালঃ [also তাম্র, বন্ধুক (বন্ধুজীবপুষ্প Beng. বাঁধুলি cf. বন্ধুজীবমধুরাধরপল্লবমুল্ল-সিতস্মিতশোভম্—গীতগোবিন্দঃ)], (also নবপল্লব—cf. অধরং নবপল্লবেন) দন্তানাং মুক্তাশ্রেণীঃ, কুন্দপুষ্পং, দাড়িম্ববীজং, (cf. দন্ত দ্বিজ দাড়িম্ববীজ—চণ্ডীদাস), হীরকম। স্মিতস্য জ্যোৎস্না, পীযূষম, কুন্দ-কুমুদ (cf. যাহা যাহা হেরিয়ে মধুরিম হাস, তাহা তাহা কুন্দকুমুদ পরকাশ)। শ্বাসস্য পদ্মগন্ধঃ, মুক্তাশীতলম্। জিহ্বায়াঃ জবাপুষ্পং, চঞ্চলবস্তু। বাণ্যাঃ কোকিলশব্দঃ, ভ্রমর-গুঞ্জনং, সুধা, মধু, বীণাবাদ্যম। মুখস্য চন্দ্রঃ (cf. বদন-চাঁদ কোন কুন্দারে কুন্দিল গো), পদ্মং, দর্পণম্ (also দাড়িম—cf. পাকারুণস্ফুটিতদাড়িমকান্তি-বক্ত্রং—মালতীমাধবঃ); কণ্ঠস্য শঙ্খঃ। চিবুকস্য দর্পণবৃন্তম। অংসস্য কুম্ভঃ, বাহ্বোঃ বল্লরী, মৃণালং, তরঙ্গঃ, শাখা, পাশঃ। হস্তস্য মৃণালাদয়ঃ। অঙ্গুল্যাঃ পল্লবং, পদ্মদলং, চম্পকপুষ্পং, নবদলং, দীপঃ। নখানাং রত্নং, তারাঃ, পুষ্পং, চন্দ্রঃ, (cf. অঙ্গুরীর আগে চাঁদ যে ঝলকে—চণ্ডীদাস), (also পদ্মরাগমণি—cf. মাণিক রাজি-সম নখচন্দ্র-পাঁতি—চণ্ডীদাস কৃষ্ণকীর্ত্তন)। স্তনয়োঃ পদ্মমুকুলং, ঘটঃ (cf. মনোভব মঙ্গলকলসসহোদরে — গীতগোবিন্দ)। হৃদয়ে কনক কলস আছে, মণিময় হার তাহার কাছে—চণ্ডীদাস), হস্তিকুম্ভঃ, গিরিঃ, চক্রবাকঃ, বিল্বযুগ্মম্—(cf. কনক বেলে জনু পড়ি গেও হিমা—বিদ্যাপতি), also কনকশম্ভু—(cf. কনকশম্ভুপরি ডারত সুরধুনী-ধারা — বিদ্যাপতি), (also দাড়িম—cf. সুন্দরস্ত্রী তিলযুক্তাননা কমলপত্রাক্ষী দাড়িমস্তনী গৌরাঙ্গী বিম্বোষ্ঠী মুক্তাহারকণ্ঠা কর্পূরচন্দনলিপ্তাঙ্গী সালঙ্কারা নায়কেন সহোপবিষ্টা হাবভাবকটাক্ষান্ কুর্ব্বতী—সঙ্গীতশাস্ত্রঃ), (also কনকের কটোরা—cf. কুচ যে মণ্ডলী কনক-কটোরী—চণ্ডীদাস), (also কনকমন্দির—cf. সোনার কটোরি কুচযুগগিরি কনকমন্দির লাগে, তাহার উপর চূড়াটী বনালে সে তার অধিক ভাগে—চণ্ডীদাস), (also স্বর্ণ-কন্দুক—cf. সই কে বলে কুচযুগ বেল। সোনার গুলি শোভিছে ভালি যুবক বধিবার শেল), (also আকাশ—cf. ঘটয়তিসঘনে কুচযুগগগনে—গীতগোবিন্দ), তাল (cf. তালফলাদপি গুরুমতিসরসম্—গীতগোবিন্দ। (also পুষ্পস্তবক — cf. পর্য্যাপ্তপুষ্প-স্তবকাবনম্রা সঞ্চারিণী পল্লবিনী লতেব—কুমার)। মধ্যস্য বরটক (বোলতা) মধ্যং, সিংহমধ্যং, বজ্রমধ্যং, ক্ষীণত্রব্যং, (also কলসীর গল—cf. যেমত কেশরী নিতম্ব মাঝারি ঘটের মুটকে পাই — চণ্ডীদাস), লোমশ্রেণ্যাঃ রেখা নীলকান্তমণিশিখা, শৈবাললতা, ধূমলতা, হস্তিশুণ্ডঃ, (also ভুজঙ্গী—cf. নাভির উপরে লোমলতাবলী সাপিনী আকার শোভা—চণ্ডীদাস)। নাভেঃ আবর্ত্তঃ, পদ্মং, হ্রদঃ, বিবরং, কূপঃ। ত্রিবল্যাঃ তরঙ্গঃ, সোপানং, নিশ্রেণী। জঘনস্য পুলিনং, পীঠঃ, ফলকম্। নিতম্বস্য স্থলং, পর্ব্বতঃ, পৃথিবী, স্থুলোপলং, মহদ্বস্তু, (also রথচক্র—cf. নিতম্ব বিমানচাক—চণ্ডীদাস), গজকুম্ভ (cf. গজকুম্ভ জিনি নিতম্বখানি—চণ্ডীদাস)। উর্ব্বোঃ কদলীকাণ্ডঃ, করিকরঃ। জঙ্ঘয়োঃ স্তম্ভঃ। পাদস্য পদ্মং, নবপল্লবম্। গতেঃ হংসগমনং, হস্তিগমনং, খঞ্জনগমনং। স্কন্ধস্য বৃষস্কন্ধঃ, বজ্রম্, অশ্বস্কন্ধঃ। বাহ্বোঃ-বৃহৎসর্পঃ, হস্তিশুণ্ডঃ (cf. ভুজ জিনিয়া করিশুণ্ড—চণ্ডীদাস। করিবরকর জিনি বাহুর বলনি গো — বৈষ্ণবপদাবলী), স্তম্ভঃ, অর্গলদণ্ডঃ। বক্ষসঃ শিলা, কবাটম্, (also দর্পণ—অতি সুশোভিত বক্ষ বিস্তারিত দেখিনু দর্পণাকার—চণ্ডীদাস)। গতেঃ প্রমত্তানুড়ুদ্গতিঃ। যশসঃ চন্দ্রকুন্দ-যূথিকাপ্রভৃতিশুক্লবর্ণপদার্থাঃ প্রতাপস্য অগ্নিঃ, বাড়বাগ্নিঃ, রবিঃ, রবিকিরণাদিঃ, জবাপদ্ম প্রভৃতিরক্তবর্ণপদার্থাঃ। পুণ্যস্য সংস্কারঃ, গৌঃ, বৃক্ষবীজম্, অঙ্কুরঃ, শুক্লবর্ণ-পদার্থাঃ। সামর্থ্যস্য মহদ্বস্তু, সিংহবিক্রমাদিঃ। নীতেঃ সাধ্বী স্ত্রী, প্রদীপজ্বালা, লতাদিঃ। আজ্ঞায়াঃ বেদবাক্যং গুরূপদেশঃ,

উৎকটেচ্ছাদিঃ। শাসনস্থ প্রারব্ধকর্ম্ম, স্থির-বস্তূনি। পাপস্থ কর্দ্দমঃ, কলঙ্কঃ, অকীর্ত্তিঃ, কৃষ্ণবর্ণকেশমসীপ্রভৃতিবস্তূনি, অন্ধকারঃ। অকীর্ত্তেঃ মালিন্যং, কৃষ্ণবর্ণবস্তূনি, অন্ধকারঃ। কস্তূরিকায়াঃ মেঘঃ, ভ্রমরঃ, নীলকান্তমণিঃ, কজ্জলং, সুগন্ধিদ্রব্যদাহজস্থ ধূমঃ, কৃষ্ণবর্ণপুষ্পপ্রভৃতিঃ, স্থলবিশেষে কন্দর্পাযশঃ, কামুকাযশঃ, কামিন্থযশশ্চ। কজ্জলস্থ মেঘাদীন্যেতানি। কর্পূরস্থ চন্দ্রঃ চন্দ্রকিরণঃ, কুন্দযূথিকাদিপুষ্পং, হিণ্ডীর-পিণ্ডঃ, বিরহিগণ্ডপ্রভৃতিঃ। মনোরথস্থ ফলপুষ্পাদিযুক্তবৃক্ষঃ, কবিবুদ্ধিরচনা। আনন্দস্থ সুধাসমুদ্রঃ, ব্রহ্মসাক্ষাৎকারাদিঃ। কামিন্থবলোকনস্থ নিত্যসুখসাক্ষাৎকারঃ, অমৃতরসঃ, পূর্ণচন্দ্রাদিসাক্ষাৎকারঃ, অতি-প্রিয়তমবস্তুপ্রাপ্তিঃ, ব্রহ্মসাক্ষাৎকারঃ। অমৃ-তস্থ কামিন্যধরাদিঃ, সৎকাব্যং, ব্রহ্মসাক্ষাৎ-কারঃ। বিষস্থ সাধ্বীস্ত্রীবিরহঃ, পাপং, মলিনবস্তু, দুঃখদবস্তু গ্রীষ্মাগ্নিঃ, শীত-কালীনশীতোদকং, ব্যভিচারিণী ভার্য্যা। বিরহস্থ অগ্নিঃ, আধিঃ, যাতনা, সমুদ্রঃ, তপ্তবস্তু, দুঃখদবস্তূনি। পুষ্পাণাং চন্দ্রাদিঃ, কামিনী, কর্পূরং, যশঃ। চন্দ্রস্থ প্রমদামুখম্, অতিশুভ্রবস্তু, যশঃপুণ্যাদি। সূর্য্যস্থ শিবনে-ত্রাগ্নিঃ, জবাপুষ্পং, বসন্তকালীনপলাশবৃক্ষঃ, কাঞ্চনবৃক্ষঃ, বাড়বাগ্নিঃ। পদ্মস্থ পাটল-পুষ্পং, কামিনীমুখাদিঃ, রক্তবর্ণদ্রব্যম্। ইন্দীবরস্থ নীলকান্তমণিঃ, কস্তূরী, কামিনী-নেত্রম্। কৈরবস্থ চন্দ্রঃ কুমুদাদি শুক্লবর্ণবস্তু। রাজ্ঞঃ ইন্দ্রঃ, কুবেরঃ, চন্দ্রঃ, সূর্য্যঃ, মান্ধাতৃভগীরথপ্রভৃতিপ্রসিদ্ধ-চক্রবর্ত্তিনঃ। মেঘস্থ কৃষ্ণঃ, কালী, নীলপদ্ম-সমূহঃ, ভ্রমরশ্রেণিঃ, ইন্দীবরবনং, দাতৃব্যক্তিঃ, কৃষ্ণবর্ণ বস্তু। শরন্মেঘস্থ চন্দ্রপ্রভৃতি-শুক্লবর্ণপদার্থঃ। কন্দর্পস্থ চন্দ্রঃ, পুরূরবাঃ, অশ্বিনীকুমারঃ, নলঃ। প্রদীপস্থ চম্পক-পুষ্পং, প্রতাপঃ, শাস্ত্রম্, ঋষিঃ। বায়োঃ শীঘ্রগপদার্থঃ। অশ্বস্থ বায়ুঃ, হরিণঃ, মনঃ। হস্তিনঃ পর্ব্বতঃ, মেঘঃ, তমালবৃক্ষঃ, অন্ধকারঃ। সৌধস্থ কৈলাসঃ, ঐরাবতঃ, উচ্চৈঃশ্রবাঃ, চন্দ্রঃ। শিবস্থ পূর্ব্বোক্তানি। শ্রীকৃষ্ণস্থ সজল-জলদঃ, তমালবৃক্ষঃ (cf. তমালনীলং—ভক্তিরসামৃতসিন্ধু), নীলমণিঃ (cf. যমুনার তটে রূপের হাটে বিকাত নীলকান্তমণি), ভ্রমরশ্রেণিঃ, নীলপদ্মম্, আকাশঃ। শ্রীরামস্থ পূর্ব্বকথিতাঃ, দূর্ব্বাদলং, বৃক্ষপল্লবম্। লক্ষ্ম্যাঃ পার্ব্বতী, চন্দ্রকান্তিঃ, রতিঃ, সীতা, দ্রৌপদী, পদ্মকান্তিঃ। সরস্বত্যাঃ চন্দ্রকলা, কৈলাসকান্তিঃ, শুক্লবর্ণপদার্থাঃ। বিপণেঃ সমুদ্রঃ, পণ্ডিতমনঃ, নারায়ণোদরং, ব্রহ্মাণ্ডম্। সমুদ্রস্থ মেঘাদিকৃষ্ণবর্ণবস্তু, বিদূর-ভূমি, মহাভারতম্, অপস্মারী। পুরস্থ স্বর্গঃ, কৈলাসঃ, মনোরমবৃহদ্বস্তু। রথস্থ পুষ্পকং বৈকুণ্ঠঃ, পুরী, পোতঃ, পৃথ্বী। কামিনী-মুখস্থ চন্দ্রঃ, পদ্মং, দর্পণঃ। কামিন্যাঃ তড়িৎ, তারা, স্বর্ণলতা, স্বর্ণবর্ণা কেতকী। নায়কস্থ চন্দ্রঃ, কন্দর্পঃ, ঐলঃ, অশ্বিনীকুমারঃ। সভায়াঃ সূর্য্যমণ্ডলং, সুধর্ম্মা, গণ্ডকীপর্ব্বতঃ, সুমেরুঃ, গঙ্গা। পণ্ডিতস্থ বৃহস্পতিঃ, শুক্রঃ, ঋষিঃ, সরস্বতী। বিরহিণঃ শ্রীরামঃ, শ্রীশিবঃ, অজঃ, দুঃখিব্যক্তিঃ, উন্মত্তব্যক্তিঃ, চন্দন-তরুঃ, শিবশিরশ্চন্দ্রঃ, বাড়বাগ্নিযুক্ত-সমুদ্রঃ, বল্মীকঃ, চন্দ্রশেখরপর্ব্বতঃ। দাতুঃ কর্ণঃ, উশীনরঃ, কল্পবৃক্ষঃ, কামধেনুঃ, রোহণঃ, সমুদ্রঃ, মেঘঃ, বলিঃ, জৈমিনিঃ, যুধিষ্ঠিরঃ। বসন্তঋতোঃ মলয়বায়ুঃ, মদ্যম্, উন্মাদরোগঃ। বিবহিণং প্রতি যমঃ, অগ্নিঃ, বিষং, সর্পঃ। গ্রীষ্মঋতোঃ অগ্নিঃ, বিরহঃ। বিরহিণীনিশ্বাসঃ সর্পনিশ্বাসঃ। বর্ষাঋতোঃ রাত্রিঃ, সমুদ্রঃ, গগনম্, নারায়ণঃ। শরদৃতোঃ কাশপুষ্পাদিরূপচামরৈরাবত-গজাঃ, চন্দ্রঃ। শীতঋতোঃ অপস্মারিব্যক্তিঃ, রাজ্যশূন্থরাজা। শিশিরঋতোঃ রাজাগমন-কালঃ। গুণিনঃ সমুদ্রঃ, পর্ব্বতঃ, পৃথিবী, মদনঃ, অশ্বিনৌ। সচিবস্থ বৃহস্পতিঃ। বাক্যস্থ কোকিলশব্দঃ, ভ্রমরগুঞ্জনং, বীণাবাদ্যম্—কবিকল্পলতা—৪ স্তবক—৪ কুসুম।

বাঙ্গালায় নিম্নলিখিত উপমার ব্যবহার দৃষ্ট হয় :—যৌবন—বনের পাখী (যৌবন বনের পাখী পিয়াসে মরয়ে গো—বৈষ্ণব পদাবলী), অনুরাগ—দধি (বৈষ্ণব-পদাবলী)। পদতল—স্থলপদ্ম (cf. স্থল-কমলগঞ্জনং মম হৃদয়রঞ্জনং — জয়দেব। যাহা যাহা অরুণ চরণে চলহৈ। তাহা তাহা থলকমল দল খলয়ে—গোবিন্দ-দাস)। লাবণ্য—বিজলী (cf. লাবণ্য বিজুরী বাঁটিয়া কেবা গাখানি মাজিল গো। চাঁদে মাখিল মু'খানি)।

বিদ্যাপতির নিম্নোদ্ধৃত কবিতায় এতদ্দেশীয় প্রাচীন ও নবীন কবিগণ সচরাচর রূপবর্ণনায় যে সকল উপমার প্রয়োগ করেন তাহার একটী সুন্দর তালিকা পাওয়া যায় :—

জিনি করিবর রাজহংসগতিগামিনী চললিহ সঙ্কেতগেহা। অমলতড়িত দণ্ড হেমমঞ্জরী জিনি অতি সুন্দর দেহা॥ জলধর চামর তিমির জিনি কুন্তল অলক ভৃঙ্গ শৈবালে। ভৌঁই (ভ্রূ) মদনধনু ভ্রমর ভুজঙ্গিনী জিনি আধ বিধুবর ভালে॥ নলিনী চকোর শফরী মধুকর মৃগী খঞ্জন জিনি আঁখি। নাসাতিলফুল গরুড় চঞ্চু জিনি গিধিনী শ্রবণ বিশেখী (বিশেষ করিয়া)॥ কনক মুকুর শশী কমল জিনিয়া মুখ জিনি বিম্ব অধর পবারে (প্রবালে)। দশন মুকুতা পাঁতি কুন্দ করগ (ডালিম) বীজ জিনি কম্বু কণ্ঠ আকারে॥ বেল তালযুগ কনয় (কনক) গিরি কটোরি জিনিয়া কুচ সাজা। বাহু মৃণালপাশ বল্লরী জিনি সিংহ ডমরু জিনি মাজা॥ (also রক্ত—কিংশুক, পলাশ, জবা—cf. যমুনার শ্যামসলিল যাঁহাদিগের শৌর্য্য-প্রভাবস্বরূপ শোণিতধারায় জবামাল্য-ভূষিতা রণরঙ্গিণী শ্যামার ন্যায় ভয়ঙ্কর-সৌন্দর্য্যে সুন্দর হইত, সেই পৌরব ও যাদব কৈ?—কালীপ্রসন্ন।) বাঙ্গলায় নিম্নলিখিত আশার উপমা ব্যববহৃত হয়। কুহকিনী, মায়াবিনী, মৃগতৃষ্ণিকা (cf. যে আশা মনুষ্যের মৃগচঞ্চলা মনোবৃত্তিকে মৃগতৃষ্ণিকায় উদ্‌ভ্রান্ত করিয়া দিগ্‌দিগন্তরে দেশদেশান্তরে ঘুরায়—কালীপ্রসন্ন ঘোষ)। (also সৌন্দর্য্যের—তাড়িত (cf. বসন ভেদিয়া রূপ উঠে গিয়া যেমন তাড়িত দেখি—চণ্ডীদাস)। কোমলতার, নবনীত, শিরীষ কুসুম—(cf. শিরীষ কুসুম জিনিয়া কোমল—চণ্ডীদাস)। নখক্ষতের—পলাশ, রক্ত উৎপল—(cf. দারুণ নখের ঘা হিয়াতে বিরাজে। রক্তোৎপল ভাসে যেন নীল সর মাঝে—চণ্ডীদাস)।

ইংরাজীতে সচরাচর নিম্নলিখিত উপমা ব্যবহৃত হয়। Bald as a coot. Bitter as gall, soot. Black as ink, coal, a crow. Blind as a bat, a beetle, a mole. Blunt as a hedge-hook. Brave as Alexander. Bright as silver. Brittle as glass. Brown as a berry. Busy as a bee. Chatter like a jay. Clear as crystal. Cold as ice, frog, charity. Cool as a cucumber. Cross as the tongs, two sticks. Dark as pitch. Dead as a door-nail. Deaf as a post. Dry as a bone. Fair as lily. False as hell.

Fat as a pig, a porpoise. Flat as a flounder, a pancake. Fleet as wind, a race-horse. Free as air. Gay as lark. Good as gold. Green as grass. Hard as iron, a flint. Harmless, as a dove. Heavy, as lead. Hoarse as a hog, a raven. Helpless as a babe. Hollow as a drum. Hot as fire. Hungry as a hunter. Light as feather, day. Loud as thunder. Limp as glove. Merry as a grig, a cricket. Mild as Moses, milk. Neat as wax, a new pin. Obstinate as a pig. Old as the hills, a Methuselah. Pale as a ghost. Patient as Job. Plain as pikestaff. Playful as a kitten. Plump as a partridge. Poor as a rat, a churchmouse, Job. Proud as Lucifer. Red as blood, a rose, a fox, a brick. Rough as a nutmeg-grater. Round as an orange, a ball. Rude as a bear. Safe as the bank (of England) or the stocks. Savage as a bear, a tiger, a bear with a sore head. Sick as a cat, a dog, a horse, a toad. Sharp as a needle. Sleep like a top. Slow as a snail, a tortoise. Sly as a fox, old boots. Soft as silk, velvet, soap. Sound as a roach, a bell. Sour as vinegar, verjuice. Stare like a stuck fig. Steady as old time. Stiff as a poker. Straight as an arrow. Strong as iron, a horse, brandy. Sure as a gun, fate, death and taxes. Surly as a bear. Sweet as sugar. Swift as lightning, the wind, an arrow. Thick as hops. Thin as a lath, a whipping post. Tight as a drum. Tough as leather. True as the Gospel. Vain as a pea-cock. Warm as a toast. Weak as water. Wet as a fish. White as driven snow, milk, a swan, a sheet, chalk. Wise as a serpent, Solomon. Yellow as a guinea, gold, saffron (*Brewer*).

ইংরাজীতে সাধারণতঃ রূপবর্ণনায় এই সমস্ত উপমার প্রয়োগ হইয়া থাকে :— কেশ (raven, coal) ; অধর (cherry, rose bud, coral) ; দন্ত (pearl) ; চক্ষুঃ (ফর্-গেট্-মি-নট্ পুষ্প)।

এতদ্ভিন্ন আরব্য ও পারস্য সাহিত্যে প্রায়শঃ নিম্নোক্ত উপমাসমূহ ব্যবহৃত হয় :— Love—water of life. Rain tears ; Misfortune, sorrow—cloud. Soul—wine. Body—flute. Spirit—the sound of a flute. Man—cup, magic lantern with a light therein. Dominion—breeze (due to its changeableness). Power—lightning (owing to its transitoriness). Reason—lamp. Anger—fire. Service of kings—sea-voyage (because at once profitable and fraught with peril). Upright man—A straight tree (for it spreads its root, whereas when it grows crooked it speedily pines away). Rough person—dog. Fool—ass. Veil of a woman—cloud. The face of a beautiful woman—sun. God—rose. Devotee—nightingale. Wine—love of God. Love—fire. Soul—fountain, mirror, bird, day. Ignorance—darkness. Heart of a good man—temple of Kabba. World—dream. Borrowing—scissors (of friendship). Cup-bearer—God. Death—flood. Hope—cloud (some of which drifts while others shed water). Life—Two-doored house. Fortune—wheel. Sin—dust. Righteousness—pearl. A worthy man—golden cup. Body—cage, night, dust, sepulchre. Anger—a flame that proceeds from Satan. Moral worth—musk. God—water. A man of worth—jewel. Worthless man—dust. Bodies of the righteous—pure soul [(cf. শ্রীচৈতন্য's remark about Rai Ramananda's body as being composed of ethereal substance (চিন্ময় দেহ) নির্ব্বিকার দেহ মন কাষ্ঠ পাষাণসম। আশ্চর্য্য তরুণী স্পর্শে নির্ব্বিকার মন॥ এক রামানন্দে হয় এই অধিকার। তাতে জানি অপ্রাকৃত দেহ তাহার॥ *** রাগানুগামার্গে জানি রায়ের ভজন। সিদ্ধ দেহ তুল্য তাতে প্রাকৃতে নহে মন॥] God—soul. World—body. A man of worth—pistachio. Love of God—magnet. Patience—key (of the treasury). Hope—horizon. Fortune—shining stars. Mankind—water-fowl. Soul—sea. Lust of wealth—chain. Body—garment. Fate—sword. Mankind—mould of clay. Affliction—clay. Kneading of clay—distress. Universe—lesson-book. Man—chessman. God—chess-player. Life—chess-board. Death—chess-box. Man—lute. Body—dervishe's party-coloured dress. Death of the poor—repose. Man—guest of God. Life—bubble of sea. Man—garden of sugar-cane. Lust—snake. God—lamp. Man—phantom. Pleasure—meteor in the sky. Nest of the soul—heaven. Aspiration and aim of a man—wings. God—purchaser. Man—sailor. Reason—ship. Fancy—bird. Conceit—curtain. Lust—house-dog. Advice to lovers—water in a sieve. Age—watch. Earth—a faithful trustee (gives back what we sow). Heart—mirror. Worthless man—onion (all coating and no kernel). Fools' company—empty pot. Princes' company—ocean full of risk and fear. Speech—pearl. Word of a king—king of words. Sky—blue canopy. Thought—arrow shot by God into the air (cf. So *thought* is an arrow shot by God into the air! How can you stay it in the air it returns to God). Ruby's colour—Its heart-blood (cf. None will be honoured till they suffer grief and toil and pain. The ruby must effuse its heart-blood ere it value gain—*Anwar-i-suheili*). Heart—lamp; Kabba (temple of Mecca). Happy-counsel—salve. Humility—embroidery of chief. Desire—steed. Mildness—sword (which conquers). Society of the uncongenial—grave. Man—dry valley. Body—perishable abode. Grace of God—rain. World—prison-house. Man—ruined city. God—architect. Childhood—morning. The redness of the morning—hue of the rose-garden. Deeds—writing. Good deeds—fair inscription. Pen—free will. Sinful man—unclean garment. God—washerman. Life—snow (in July's sun). Love—water of life. Heart—city. Spirit—pearl. Body—shell. World—camel. Mahammad—vase of rose. Saints—rose-buds. Death—torrent. Fortune—vicar. Death—ant. World—mother. Body—city. Soul—Sultan. Wisdom—Prime-minister. Earth—kitchen. Man—apprentice. Master—fate. World—light comrade. Pleasure — fire. Life — Bowl. Dregs—sorrow. Nature—a seller of vinegar and a crusher of unripened grapes. Kindness—branch. Joy—fruit. Soul—sun. Teaching—rain. God's grace—wine. Unalloyed happiness—sweet honey, sweet sherbet. Worldly happiness—honey with poison. Love—alchemist. Humble man—sparrow. The sigh of the oppressed—fire (that will set in flames both sea and land). World—ray (emanating from the sun of His face). People—root. King—tree. Man—worlds' eye. Beloved's (God's) tresses—grief. Joy derived from sorrow—musk which perfumes Beloved's tresses. A worthless man imitating a good man—dung perfumed with musk. Travel—tutor. Liberality—a remedy for all ill. Head (whose reason has fled)—tail. Man—pieces of steel. Heart of the believer—house of God. Drop—individual soul. Sea—God. Pearl-drop—soul. Sin—Thorn].

Similia similibus curantur—সমঃ সমেন সাম্যতি, বিষস্য বিষমৌষধম্, বিষে বিষক্ষয়। [সদৃশবিধান চিকিৎসাতন্ত্রের মূল সূত্র।]

sĭ-mĭl′-ĭ-tūde, *n.* Likeness; সজাতিত্ব (হিঃ কোঃ), সাজাত্য (ঐ), সাদৃশ্য, তুল্যতা, ঔপম্য।

sĭm′-ĭ-līze, *v. i.* **1.** To use a simile; উপমা প্রয়োগ করা। **2.** To compare; তুলনা করা।

sĭm′mer (-êr), *v. i., t.* & *n.* To boil gently or with a hissing; অল্প অল্প ফুটা, চড় চড় করিয়া ফুটা। ***Verb t.*** **1.** To cause to boil gently; মৃদু সিদ্ধ করা, ফুটান। **2.** To be in a state of suppressed anger, excitement, laughter; "The tribes of Afghanisthan were *simmering* to revolt"; অন্তর্নিরুদ্ধ ক্রোধ (উত্তেজনা, হাস্য প্রভৃতি) দ্বারা বিক্ষুব্ধ হওয়া। ***Noun.*** A slow heating; মৃদু উত্তাপে সিদ্ধকরণ।

sĭm′-nĕl-cāke, *n.* An ornamental cake offered as a gift at Christmas and Easter; খৃষ্টমাস এবং ইষ্টার পর্ব্বোপলক্ষে উপহারস্বরূপ প্রদত্ত একপ্রকার কারুকার্য্যশোভিত পিষ্টক।

sĭ-mō′-nĭ-ac, *n.* One who practises simony; যে ব্যক্তি অর্থের বিনিময়ে পদ গ্রহণ বা প্রদান করে।

sĭm-ō-nī′-ă-căl, *adj.* Relating to, or guilty of, simony; অর্থগ্রহণে যাজকীয় পদ প্রদান বা গ্রহণসম্বন্ধীয় বা উক্তরূপে কার্য্যের জন্য অপরাধী।

Sī′-mŏn-Pūre, *n.* & *adj.* (*Rare*) The real or genuine person or thing; প্রকৃত লোক, খাঁটি জিনিষ, সাঁচ্চা জিনিষ। ***Adj.*** Real; genuine; প্রকৃত; খাঁটি, সাঁচ্চা।

sĭm′-ŏ-nȳ, *n.* The crime of buying or selling church preferment; অর্থপ্রদানে বা গ্রহণে যাজকীয় পদ গ্রহণ বা প্রদানের অপরাধ। [Simon Magus নামক জনৈক ব্যক্তির নাম হইতে গৃহীত। See *Acts* viii. 18.]

sĭ-mōōm′ —moon′, (*incorrectly*), *n.* A hot dry wind that blows from the deserts of Northern Africa and Arabia; উত্তর আফ্রিকা এবং আরবদেশের মরুভূমি হইতে প্রবাহিত একপ্রকার শুষ্ক বা উষ্ণ বায়ু।

sĭm′-pêr, *v. i.* & *n.* **1.** To smile in a silly, affected, or conceited manner; ফিক ফিক করিয়া হাসা, মুচকিয়া হাস। **2.** To express by simpering; ফিক ফিক করিয়া হাসিয়া বলা। ***Noun.*** A silly affected smile; ফিক ফিক হাসি, মুচকি হাসি। **—er,** *n.* **—ing-ly,** *adv.*

sĭm′-ple (-pl), *adj.* & *n.* **1.** Not compound; as, a *simple* substance; অমিশ্র, অমিশ্রিত। **2.** (*Chem.*) Elementary; (রসায়নশাস্ত্র) মৌলিক। **3.** Easily done, or understood; সরল, সহজ, সোজা। **4.** Sincere; সরলচিত্ত, সরলপ্রকৃতি। **5.** Plain; as, a *simple* girl: *simple* diet; সাদাসিধা। **6.** Mere; as, it is *simple* madness; কেবল, শুদ্ধ, শুধু। **7.** Trifling; তুচ্ছ, নগণ্য। **8.** Weak in intellect; silly; "The *simple* believeth every word"; মন্দবুদ্ধি,

অল্পবুদ্ধি ; নির্ব্বোধ, বেকুব, বোকা। *Noun.* 1. Something unmixed or uncompounded ; অমিশ্রবস্তু। 2. A medicinal plant (so called because each vegetable is supposed to possess its particular virtue and constitute a single remedy) ; ভেষজ গুল্ম। **—ply,** *adv.* **Simple addition**—অমিশ্র যোগ। **Simple apprehension** — কেবল প্রতীতি (হিঃ কোঃ), প্রতীতিমাত্র (ঐ)। **Simple equation**—সরল সমীকরণ। **Simple-hearted**—সরলচিত্ত, সরলমনাঃ, অমায়িক। **Simple-minded**—সরলমতি, সরলমনাঃ। **Simple quantity**—অমিশ্র রাশি। **Pure and simple**—খাঁটি, নিছক, শুদ্ধ, নির্জ্জলা (*colloq.*)।

sĭm′-ple-tŏn (-pl-), *n.* A foolish person ; a silly person ; নির্ব্বোধ লোক ; বোকা, আহাম্মক, গোবেচারা, গোবরগণেশ, বেকুব।

sĭm-plĭ′-cĭ-tĕn, *adv.* Wholly ; absolutely ; সম্পূর্ণরূপে, সর্ব্বতোভাবে, পুরা ; নিরপেক্ষভাবে।

sĭm-plĭc′-ĭ-tȳ, *n.* 1. The state or quality of being unmixed ; অমিশ্রতা। 2. Sincerity; সরলতা, সারল্য, অকপটতা, আর্জ্জব। 3. Plainness ; সাদাসিধা ভাব, অলঙ্কারহীনতা। 4. Weakness of intellect ; বুদ্ধিহীনতা।

sĭm′-plĭ-fȳ, *v. t.* To make simple or easy ; সরল করা, সহজ করা, সরলতাপাদন করা।

sĭm-plĭ-fĭ-cā′-tion, *n.* The act or process of making simple ; সরলতাপাদন, বিশদীকরণ, সরলকর্ম্ম (হিঃ কোঃ)।

sĭm′-plĭsm, *n.* Affected simplicity ; কপট সরলতা, সরলতার ভাণ।

sĭm-ū-lā′-crŭm, *n.* 1. An image ; প্রতিমা। 2. A shadowy likeness ; a sham ; ছায়ামূর্ত্তি ; ভাণ, ছল।

sĭm′-ū-lāte, *v. t.* To feign ; to imitate; ভাণ করা, ছলনা করা; অনুকরণ করা। **—la′-ti′on,** *n.* 1. Counterfeiting; নকলকরণ। 2. Unconscious imitation ; অজ্ঞাতসারে অনুকরণ।

sĭ-mŭl-tā′-nē-ous (-ŭs), *adj.* Existing or performing at the same time ; সমকালীন, সমকালবর্ত্তী, এককালীন, যুগপৎ (হিঃ কোঃ), এককালবর্ত্তী, যৌগপদিক, সমকালিক, এককালিক। **—ly,** *adv.* At the same time ; একই সময়ে, যুগপৎ, এককালে, এক সঙ্গে, সমসময়ে। **—ne′-i-ty,** *n.* The state of being simultaneous ; সমকালীনতা, সমসময়বর্ত্তিতা, যৌগপদ্য। **Simultaneous differential equation** — সমকালিকচলনসমীকরণ (হিঃ কোঃ)। **Simultaneous equation**—সমকালীন সমীকরণ (হিঃ কোঃ)।

sĭ-mûrg′, *n.* A fabulous monstrous bird of Persian myth ; পারস্য দেশের প্রাচীন গ্রন্থসমূহে উক্ত এক বৃহৎকায় পক্ষী। [এই পক্ষীর সম্বন্ধে কথিত আছে যে, ইহা মনুষ্যের মত কথা কহিতে পারে এবং তিন বার পৃথিবীর প্রলয় দর্শন করিয়াছে।]

sĭn, *n.* & *v. i.* Trangression of the divine or moral laws ; পাপ, দুষ্কৃত, পাতক, কলুষ, কল্মষ, প্রত্যবায়। *Verb i.* 1. To violate divine law ; পাপ করা, পাতক করা। 2. To offend against ; as, to *sin* against propriety ; to transgress ; অপরাধ করা ; নিয়ম লঙ্ঘন করা। **Sin′-ner,** *n.* A sinful man ; পাপী, পাতকী, পাপাত্মা, পামর। **Sin′-ful,** *adj.* Full of sin; wicked ; characterised by sin ; পাপপূর্ণ; সপাপ; পাপাত্মক, অধর্ম্মাত্মক। **Sin′-less,** *adj.* Without sin ; পাপশূন্য, নিষ্পাপ, অপাপবিদ্ধ, অকলুষ, অকল্মষ। **Besetting sin** — মহাপাতক। **Sin-offering**—পাপের প্রায়শ্চিত্তস্বরূপ প্রদত্ত বলি প্রভৃতি। **The seven deadly sins**—See SEVEN.

Sĭ-nā-ĭt′-ĭc, *adj.* Of, or pertaining to, the mount Sinai or the peninsula of Sinai ; সিনাই পর্ব্বত সম্বন্ধীয়, সিনাই উপদ্বীপসম্বন্ধীয়।

Sinapis alba—সফেদ রাই (বেলঃ)। ***Sinapis dichotoma***—কালা সরিষা (বেলঃ)।

sĭn′-ă-pĭsm, *n.* Mustard-plaster ; সর্ষপচূর্ণের পুলটিস।

since (sĭns), *adv., prep. & conj.* In the time past; counting backward from the present ; ago ; হইতে ; অবধি, থেকে, আরম্ভ করিয়া ; অতীত হইল, পূর্ব্বে, আগে। *Prep.* After ; পরে, অনন্তর, তদনন্তর, ইহার পর। *Conj.* 1. From the time when ; অবধি, হইতে। 2. Seeing that ; because ; as, *since* you are unwilling to do this ; যেহেতু, কেন না ; কারণ।

sĭn-cēre′ (-sēr), *adj.* 1. (*Archaic*) Pure ; (অপ্রঃ) খাঁটি। 2. Frank ; honest ; সরল, অকপট, অমায়িক, আন্তরিক ; সৎ, সাধু, সহৃদয়। 3. True ; real ; as, a *sincere* desire প্রকৃত, সত্য ; ঠিক। **—ly,** *adv.*

sĭn-cĕr′-ĭ-tȳ, *n.* The state or quality of being sincere ; সরলতা, সত্যতা (হিঃ কোঃ), সারল্য, অকপটতা, আন্তরিকতা, অমায়িকতা।

sĭn′-cĭ-pŭt, *n.* The forepart of the head from the forehead to the coronal suture ; তালু, চাঁদি, মস্তকাগ্রভাগ।

sīne, *n.* (*Trigon.*) A straight line drawn from one extremity of the arc of a circle perpendicular to the diameter passing through the other extremity ; (ত্রিকোণমিতি) জ্যা (সুঃ সিঃ), মৌর্ব্বিকা (সাঃ পঃ), জীবা (ঐ)।

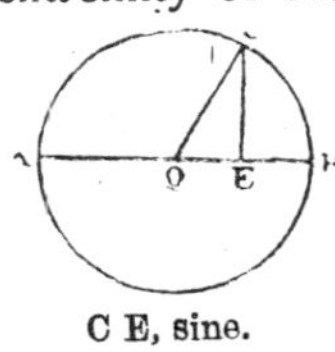

C E, sine.

Meridian sine—মধ্যজ্যা। **Orient sine**—উদয় (সূর্য্যঃ বাঃ)। **Sine of amplitude** — উদয়জ্যা (সূর্য্যঃ বাঃ)। **Sine of an arc**—ভুজজ্যা (কেণ্ডিঃ)। **Sine series**—জ্যাশ্রেণী (হিঃ কোঃ)। **Table of sines**—জ্যাপিণ্ড (সাঃ পঃ)। **Versed sine**—উৎক্রম জ্যা।

sine, (*L.*), *prep.* Without ; বিনা, ছাড়া। ***Sine die*** — অনির্দ্দিষ্ট দিবস পর্য্যন্ত। ***Sine quo***

ron — অপরিহার্য্য বিষয়, আবশ্যক (হিঃ কোঃ), পদভাবাদভাব (ঐ)।

si'-ne-cūre, *n.* & *v. t.* **1.** An ecclesiastical benefice without cure of souls ; যে যাজকীয় কার্য্যে বৃত্তি বা বেতন পাওয়া যায় কিন্তু তৎপরিবর্ত্তে কোনরূপ কার্য্য করিতে হয়না। **2.** An office which has an income attached to it, but little or no employment ; যে চাকুরীতে পরিশ্রম খুব অল্প বা মোটেই কোনরূপ পরিশ্রম করিতে হয় না, আরামের চাকুরী। ***Verb t.*** To put or place in a sinecure ; কর্ম্মহীন যাজকের পদ প্রদান করা, আরামের চাকুরী প্রদান করা। **—cur-ism, —cur-ist,** *ns.*

sin'-ew (-ū), *n.* & *v. t.* **1.** Tendon ; পেশীর প্রান্তসংলগ্ন রজ্জুবৎ পদার্থ, অস্থি-মাংসসংযোজক শিরা, কণ্ডরা, মহাশিরা (হঃ চঃ)। **2.** That which gives strength or vigour ; as, the *sinews* of war ; তেজ বা শক্তিসঞ্চারক বস্তু। **3.** Strength ; muscular power ; শক্তি, বল ; পৈশিক শক্তি। ***Verb t.*** To serve as sinews ; to strengthen ; to sustain ; কণ্ডরার কার্য্য করা ; শক্তিসম্পন্ন করা ; ধারণ করা। **—i-ness,** *n.* **—less, —y,** *adjs.*

sing *v. i., t.* & *n.* **1.** To utter sounds with melodious modulations of voice ; গান গাওয়া, গান করা। **2.** To utter sweet or melodious sound, as birds ; (পক্ষী প্রভৃতি সম্বন্ধে) গান করা। **3.** To relate in verse ; কবিতায় বর্ণনা করা। **4.** To make a humming sound (as a kettle when beginning to boil) ; শব্দ করা, চড় চড় শব্দ করা। ***Verb t.*** **1.** To utter with musical modulation ; গান করা। **2.** To celebrate in song ; কীর্ত্তন করা। ***Noun.*** **1.** The act of singing ; the power of singing ; গানকরণ ; সঙ্গীতশক্তি। **2.** The sound made by a bullet when in flight ; গুলির সোঁ সোঁ শব্দ। **Sing'-a-ble,** *adj.* **Sing'-er,** *n.* One who sings ; গায়ক। **Singing master**—যে গান শিক্ষা দেয়, সঙ্গীতশিক্ষক, সঙ্গীতাচার্য্য। **Sing-song** — একঘেয়ে সুর। **To sing another tune** — To change one's tone ; সুর বদলান। **To sing out**—To call loudly ; উচ্চৈঃস্বরে চীৎকার করিয়া ডাকা। **To sing small**—To take an humble attitude ; নরম সুরে কথা বলা, সুর নরম করা। **To sing sorrow**—To despond ; নিরাশ হওয়া। **To sing sorrow, woe** or **solfa**—To bemoan ; শোক করা। **To sing the same** or **one song**—To tell the same thing again and again ; একই কথা বার বার বলা, ঘ্যান ঘ্যান করা।

singe (sinj), *v. t.* & *n.* **1.** To burn slightly or superficially ; to burn the surface of ; ছেঁচকা পোড়া করা ; ঝলসান। **2.** (In calico printing) To remove the nap from ; to prepare the calico for dyeing or printing, by passing it over a red-hot roller ; ফুঁপি তুলিয়া লওয়া ; শ্বেতবর্ণ কার্পাসবস্ত্র তপ্তলোহিত ডলনার উপর দিয়া চালিত করিয়া উহাকে রঞ্জনের বা ছাপাইবার জন্য প্রস্তুত করা। ***Noun.*** (*Rare*) Superficial burn ; (কচিদ্‌ব্যবহৃত) ছেঁচকা পোড়া। **To singe a person's hair** — চুলের অগ্রভাগ ঈষৎ দগ্ধ করা। **To singe one's feather** or **wing**—To suffer some loss esp. in some venturous attempt ; কোন দুঃসাহসিক কার্য্যে প্রবৃত্ত হইয়া কিঞ্চিৎ ক্ষতি সহ্য করা। **To singe the king of Spain's beard**—স্পেন দেশের উপকূলে উপদ্রব করা।

sin'-gle (sing-gl), *adj.* & *n.* **1.** One only ; একমাত্র, এক (হিঃ কোঃ), অদ্বিতীয় (ঐ), একটী-মাত্র। **2.** Alone ; একাকী, একেলা। **3.** Individual ; ব্যক্তিগত। **4.** Unmarried ; অবিবাহিত, অনূঢ়। **5.** Not twisted, combined or doubled with others ; as, a *single* thread ; অন্য কোন কিছুর সহিত অপাকানো। **6.** Not compound ; অমিশ্র। **7.** Performed by one person only ; as, a *single* fight ; একজন লোক দ্বারা সম্পাদিত। ***Noun.*** A unit ; one ; একক ; এক। **—gly,** *adv.* **—ness,** *n.* Quality or state of being single ; একতা (হিঃ কোঃ), অদ্বিতীয়তা (ঐ)। **Single blessedness**—অনূঢ়াবস্থা। **Single combat**—দ্বন্দযুদ্ধ, দ্বৈরথ যুদ্ধ। **Single-entry** — See under ENTRY. **Single-eyed** — একপক্ষাবলম্বী, এক-চোখা। **Single-handed**—একাকী, একেলা। **Single hearted, Single minded**—ঐকান্তিক। **Single-heartedness** — ঐকান্তিকতা, অনন্যচিত্ততা, অনন্যতা (ভক্তিঃ)। **Single-stick**—অসিক্রীড়ায় ব্যবহৃত যষ্টিবিশেষ; অসিক্রীড়া।

sin'-gle (sing-gl), *v. t.* To select individually from among a number ; বাছিয়া পৃথক করা, বাছিয়া বাহির করা।

sing'-let (-glĕt), *n.* An under-shirt ; জামার নীচে পরিধেয় গঞ্জি প্রভৃতি।

sin'-gle-tŏn (sing-gl-), *n.* A single card of any suit held by a player ; কোন ক্রীড়কের হস্তস্থিত একজাতীয় একখান মাত্র তাস।

sing'-sŏng, *adj., n., v. i.* & *t.* Monotonous ; একঘেয়ে, একসুরা। ***Noun.*** A wearisome repetition of some words or tone ; একই কথা বা সুরের পুনঃ পুনঃ আবৃত্তি। ***Verb i. & t.*** To recite verse, or talk in a sing-song manner ; একটানা সুরে কবিতা প্রভৃতি আবৃত্তি করা বা একই কথা পুনঃ পুনঃ বলা।

sin'-gu-lar, (sing-gū-lėr), *adj.* **1.** (*Law*) Distinct ; অপ্রতিরূপ (হিঃ কোঃ), অন্যাসাধারণ (ঐ), বিশিষ্ট (ঐ), পৃথক, স্বতন্ত্র। **2.** (*Gram.*) Denoting only one person or thing ; (ব্যাকরণ) একবচনাত্মক। **3.** Queer ; কেমনতর, আধ-পাগলা, অদ্ভুতরকমের, সৃষ্টিছাড়া। **4.** (*Rare*) Remarkable ; (কচিদ্‌ব্যবহৃত) অপূর্ব্ব। **—ism,** *n.* Any philosophy which derives the universe from a single principle ; অদ্বৈতবাদ (হিঃ কোঃ)। **—ly,** *adv.*

Singular number — (ব্যাকরণ) একবচন। **Singular proposition**—অনন্যসামান্যপ্রতিজ্ঞা (হিঃ কোঃ), বিশেষ প্রতিজ্ঞা (ঐ)। **Singular term**—ব্যক্তিবাচক পদ, একবাচক পদ (হিঃ কোঃ)।

sin-gŭ-lăr'-i-tў (sĭng-), *n.* 1. The quality or state of being singular ; peculiarity ; অনন্যতা, স্বাতন্ত্র্য ; বিশিষ্টতা। 2. Strangeness ; uncommonness ; অপূর্ব্বতা ; অসাধারণতা।

sin'-gu-lar-ize (sĭng-gŭ-lẽr-), *v. t.* 1. To make singular or single ; অপূর্ব্ব করা, অসাধারণ করা, একমাত্র করা। 2. *(Gram.)* To give a singular form ; (ব্যাকরণ) একবচনান্ত করা।

sin'-is-tẽr, *adj.* 1. *(Obs.)* On the left hand ; বামদিকস্থ, বাম দিকের। 2. Unlucky; as, *sinister* influences; অশুভ, অমঙ্গলকারক। 3. Evil ; ill-looking ; wicked ; as, *sinister* aims ; মন্দ ; অশুভ ; অসাধু, দুষ্ট। **—ly,** *adv.*

sin'-is-trăl, *adj.* 1. Of, or pertaining to, the left hand ; বামহস্ত-সম্পর্কীয়। 2. (Of spiral shells) With whorle going to the left ; (শঙ্খসম্বন্ধে) বামাবর্ত্ত।

sin'-is-trō-, Combining form of SINISTER. **Sinistro-cerebral**—মস্তিষ্কের বাম গোলার্দ্ধসম্বন্ধীয়। **Sinistrorse**—বামাবর্ত্ত, বামদিগ্‌গামী।

sink (sĭngk), *v. t., i. & n.* 1. To immerse in a fluid ; ডুবান, নিমজ্জিত করা। 2. To bring from a higher to a lower level ; নামান। 3. To make by digging or delving ; as, to *sink* a well ; খনন করা। 3. To depress ; to lower ; দমান ; নত করা। 4. Not to take into account ; to suppress ; গণনার মধ্যে না আনা ; চাপিয়া রাখা। 5. To lower in value or amount ; as, to *sink* the price of goods ; দাম কমান, মূল্য হ্রাস করা। 6. To diminish or annihilate by payment ; ক্রমশঃ পরিশোধ করিয়া হ্রাস করা বা লোপ করা। 7. To invest, as money, more or less permanently in any undertaking or scheme for the sake of a profitable return, interest, or the like ; ব্যবসায়ে টাকা ফেলা। *Verb. i.* 1. To fall by the force of gravity ; to descend esp. in water ; পতিত হওয়া ; ডুবা। 2. To become hollow from loss of flesh (used esp. in *p.p.*) ; as, *sunken* cheeks ; বসিয়া যাওয়া। 3. To be impressed ; to enter deeply ; মনোমধ্যে মুদিত হওয়া, মনের মধ্যে বসিয়া যাওয়া ; গভীর ভাবে প্রবেশ করা। 4. To be overwhelmed or distressed ; অভিভূত হওয়া, কাতর হওয়া। 5. To fail in strength ; দুর্ব্বল হইয়া পড়া, শক্তিহীন হইয়া পড়া। 6. To fall off or decline in value estimation, or the like ; মূল্য বা আদর কমিয়া যাওয়া। 7. To fall to a lower level, as a river ; to subside ; (নদী প্রভৃতি সম্পর্কে) জল হ্রাস প্রাপ্ত হওয়া হেতু নামিয়া যাওয়া ; বসিয়া যাওয়া। *Noun.* 1. A cesspool ; নর্দ্দমা, নালা। 2. A basin or vessel connected with a drain for receiving filthy water ; ময়লা জল গ্রহণের জন্য নর্দ্দমার সহিত যে পাত্র সংযুক্ত রাখা হয়। 3. A place of filth ; আস্তাকুঁড়। 4. An opening in a stage through which scenes are raised or lowered ; রঙ্গমঞ্চের যে ফাঁকের ভিতর দিয়া দৃশ্যপটসমূহ উত্তোলিত বা অবনমিত করা হয়। **Sink'-a-ble,** *adj.* **Sink'-ing,** *n.* 1. A falling or settling down ; a subsidence ; নিমজ্জন ; বসিয়া যাওন 2. The digging of a vertical shaft from above downward ; (খনির কাজ) উপর হইতে সোজা নীচের দিকে সুড়ঙ্গ খনন। 3. A lowering of spirits ; অবসাদ, মানসিক গ্লানি। **Sinking-fund**—See FUND. **Leave him sink or swim**—Do not help him ; let him shift for himself ; তাহাকে সাহায্য করিওনা ; তাহাকে নিজের চেষ্টায় নিজের উন্নতি করিতে দাও। **To raid the sinking fund**—To devote such surplus in any year to any other purpose ; ঋণ পরিশোধের জন্য যে টাকা বৎসর বৎসর জমা করা হয় তাহা কোন এক বৎসরে অন্য উদ্দেশ্যে ব্যয় করা। **To sink beneath** or **under**—To go down ; ডুবিয়া যাওয়া, তলাইয়া যাওয়া। To be overwhelmed ; অভিভূত হওয়া। **To sink down**—To fail in strength ; শক্তিহীন হওয়া, অবসন্ন হইয়া পড়া। **To sink in**—To descend lower and lower in ; বসিয়া যাওয়া। **To sink into**—To enter deeply ; গভীরভাবে প্রবেশ করা, গভীররূপে মুদ্রিত হওয়া। **To sink to the level of**—To descend to the level of ; সমান অবস্থায় নামিয়া আসা। **To sink under**—To fail in strength under the pressure of ; কোন কিছুর চাপে অভিভূত হওয়া।

sin'-ō-logue (-lŏg), *n.* A person versed in sinology ; চীনদেশীয় ভাষা, ইতিহাস, প্রভৃতিতে ব্যুৎপন্ন ব্যক্তি।

si-nŏl'-ō-ġў, *n.* Knowledge of Chinese literature, laws, etc. ; চীন দেশের ভাষা, আইন, সাহিত্য, প্রভৃতিতে ব্যুৎপত্তি।

sin'-tẽr, *n.* A crystalline rock precipitated from mineral water ; নির্ঝরজল অধোক্ষিপ্ত স্ফাটিকপ্রস্তর।

sin'-ū-ate *adj.* (*Bot.*), Wavy edged ; (উদ্ভিদ্‌-বিদ্যা) তরঙ্গায়িত প্রান্ত, ঢেউতোলা কিনারাবিশিষ্ট। **—a'-tion,** *n.* **—ly,** *adv.*

sin'-ū-ous (-ŭs), *adj.* Winding ; আঁকাবাঁকা, সর্পবৎ বক্র, সর্পিল। **—os'-i-ty,** *n.*

sī'-nŭs, *n.* 1. A hollow ; গহ্বর। 2. A cavity in a bone or other part wider at the bottom than at the entrance ; অস্থি বা দেহের অপর অংশের গহ্বরবিশেষ—যাহার অগ্রভাগ অপেক্ষা পশ্চাদ্‌ভাগ প্রশস্ততর থাকে। 3. An elongated abscess with only a small orifice ; নালী ঘা। 4. (*Bot.*) A curve between lobes of leaf ; (উদ্ভিদ্‌বিদ্যা) অবটী (সাঃ পঃ)।

Sioux (sô *or* sï-ô), *n.* A tribe of North American Indians; উত্তর আমেরিকার প্রাচীন অধিবাসিগণের শাখাবিশেষ।

sī-phŏn, *n.* & *v. t.* **1.** A bent tube or pipe, with arms of unequal length, by which a liquid can be transferred from one vessel to another; অসম বাহুবিশিষ্ট বক্রনল—যাহার সাহায্যে তরলপদার্থ একপাত্র হইতে অপর পাত্রে স্থানান্তরিত করা যায়, বক্রনলিকা (হিঃ কোঃ)। **2.** A bottle for holding aerated waters (also *Siphon bottle*) ; সোডা, লেমনেড প্রভৃতি রাখার জন্য একপ্রকার বোতল। ***Verb t.*** To convey as water by means of a siphon ; to transmit or remove by a siphon ; বক্রনলিকাদ্বারা একপাত্র হইতে পাত্রান্তরে প্রবাহিত করা ; বক্রনলিকাদ্বারা সঞ্চালিত বা স্থানান্তরিত করা। **—al,** *adj.* **Siphon-barometer** — একপ্রকার বায়ুমান যন্ত্র—যাহার নল নিম্নদিকে বিপর্য্যস্ত S অক্ষরের মত বক্রভাবে থাকে।

sī'-phŏn-ĕt, *n.* one of the two tubes through which aphides exudes honey-dew ; উদ্ভিজ্জকীটবিশেষ যে নালীদ্বয়দ্বারা মধু নিঃসৃত করে তাহার অন্যতর।

sip'-pet (-ĕt), *n.* **1.** A small piece of bread served with soup etc. ; ঝোল প্রভৃতির সহিত যে ক্ষুদ্র রুটিকার টুকরা পরিবেষণ করা হয়। **2.** A small piece of bread etc. soaked in a liquid ; তরল পদার্থে ভিজানো ক্ষুদ্র রুটির টুকরা।

sir (sêr), *n.* **1.** A word of respect addressed to men ; মহাশয়। **2.** A title distinctive of knights and barons; নাইট এবং ব্যারণদিগের উপাধি, স্যর।

sir-dâr' (-sêr), *n.* **1.** (In India) A native chief ; a high military officer ; (ভারতবর্ষে) সর্দ্দার ; উচ্চ-সামরিক কর্ম্মচারী। **2.** (In Egypt) A commander-in-chief ; (মিশরদেশে) প্রধান সেনাপতি।

sīre, *n.* **1.** A father ; পিতা। **2.** The male parent of a beast (esp. of a horse) ; পশুর পালক (বিশেষতঃ অশ্বের)। **3.** A respectful word of address to a king ; রাজার প্রতি প্রযোজ্য সম্মানজনক শব্দ।

sī'-rĕn, *n.* & *adj.* **1.** One of a class of sea-nymphs who are fabled to lure the passing sailor to his ruin by the fascination of their music ; একশ্রেণীর সাগরদ্বীপবাসিনী—যাহারা নাবিকদিগকে মোহকর সঙ্গীতদ্বারা ভুলাইয়া আনিয়া পরে বধ করিত, সাগরগায়িকা, সাগরকন্যা, সাগরিকা। **2.** Sweet-singing woman ; সুগায়িকা। **3.** An enticing dangerous woman ; "Pleasure is a very *siren* attracting only to destroy" ; মোহিনী, কুহকিনী, মায়াবিনী। **4.** A kind of eel ; একপ্রকার বাইন মৎস্য। **5.** A large fog-horn ; কুজ্ঝটিকার কালে জাহাজ সতর্ক করার জন্য ব্যবহৃত একপ্রকার বৃহৎ বংশী। ***Adj.*** **1.** Pertaining to a siren ; সাগরকন্যা সম্পর্কীয়। **2.** Fascinating ; as, *siren* song ; মোহকর, মোহজনক, মোহন। **Siren song of sin**—পাপের আপাতমোহকর সঙ্গীত।

sī-rē'-ni-ăn, *n.* An order of fish ; একপ্রকার মৎস্যের "বর্গ"।

sir'-găng (sêr-), *n.* A bright green Asiatic bird ; এসিয়াদেশের উজ্জ্বল হরিদ্বর্ণ পক্ষিবিশেষ।

sī-rī'-ă-sis, *n.* **1.** Sunstroke ; সর্দ্দিগর্ম্মি। **2.** Exposure to a sun-bath ; সূর্য্যালোকে অবস্থান।

Sir'-i-ŭs, *n.* A large and bright star called the Dog-star, situated in the mouth of the constellation Canis Major ; মৃগব্যাধ (সাঃ পঃ), লুব্ধক (ঐ)।

sir'-loin (sêr-loyn), *n.* A loin of a beef ; বৃষের কটিদেশের মাংস খণ্ড।

sī-rŏc'-cō, sci— (sī-), *n.* An oppressive relaxing wind from the Libyan desert ; আফ্রিকার মরুভূমি হইতে ভূমধ্যসাগরের উপকূলে বিশেষতঃ ইতালী দেশে প্রবাহিত একপ্রকার ধূলিপূর্ণ উষ্ণ বায়ু।

sir'-rah (-ă), *n.* (*Archaic*) Sir ; (*in contempt*) fellow ; (অপ্রঃ) মহাশয় ; (অবজ্ঞাচ্ছলে) ওহে, মহাশয়।

sir'-ŭp, *n.* Same as SYRUP (which see).

sirvente, (*F.*), *n.* In the literature of the Middle ages a species of poem in common use usually satirical ; মধ্যযুগে প্রচলিত একপ্রকার ব্যঙ্গকবিতা।

Si-săl'-grăss, —hĕmp, *ns.* The prepared fibre of American aloe (so called from Sisal, a port in Yucatan) ; বিলাতী আনারসের আঁশ।

sis'-kin, *n.* A songbird ; একপ্রকার গায়কপক্ষী।

sis'-tĕr, *n.* **1.** A female whose parents are the same as that of another person ; ভগ্নী, ভগিনী, সহোদরা, স্বসা। **2.** A woman of the same faith ; সমধর্ম্মাবলম্বিনী স্ত্রীলোক, ধর্ম্মভগিনী। **3.** A female of the same society, convent, abbey, etc. ; একই সম্প্রদায়ভুক্তা নারী। **4.** One of the same kind or of the same condition ; as, *sister* fruits ; এক জাতীয় বা এক অবস্থাপন্ন বস্তু। **—hood,** *n.* **—li-ness,** *n.* **—ly,** *adj.* Like a sister ; becoming a sister ; ভগিনীবৎ, ভগিনীতুল্য ; ভগিনীসমুচিত। **Half-sister**—বৈপিত্রেয় বা বৈমাত্রেয় ভগিনী। **Sister-hook** — একপ্রকার ডবল আঁকড়া — যাহা রজ্জু প্রভৃতি আটকাইবার সময় খুলিয়া বন্ধ হইলে ইংরাজী ৮ (8) সংখ্যার মত দেখায়। **Sister-in-law** — শ্যালিকা, ননদিনী, ভ্রাতৃবধূ, প্রভৃতি। **Little Sisters of the poor**—ফরাসী দেশের রোম্যান ক্যাথলিক ভগিনীসম্প্রদায়। **Sister of charity, Sister of mercy**—See under CHARITY.

The Fatal Sisters or **Sisters three**—ভাগ্যদেবীত্রয় (see FATES).

sis'-têr-hood, *n.* **1.** The state of being a sister; ভগিনীত্ব। **2.** A society of sisters, or of women united in one faith; "The various works of charity which were chiefly carried by *sisterhoods*"; ভগিনীসম্প্রদায়, ভগিনীসমাজ। **3.** A group of things imagined as sisters; as, a *sisterhood* of churches; ভগিনীবৎ কল্পিত বস্তু শ্রেণী (In Sanskrit the word সহোদর is used in this sense—cf. পয়োধরে মনোভব মঙ্গল কলস সহোদরে—গীতঃ]।

Sis-tine (-tin), *adj.* Of, or pertaining to, Pope Sixtus V; পোপ পঞ্চম সিসট্যাস্‌সম্বন্ধীয়। **Sistine chapel**—রোমনগরীর সুবিখ্যাত ভ্যাটিকান প্রাসাদের দেবালয়। এই দেবালয়ের প্রাচীরে বিশ্ববিখ্যাত চিত্রশিল্পী মাইকেল এঞ্জেলোর অঙ্কিত বহু চিত্র বর্ত্তমান আছে। **Sistine Madonna**—র‍্যাফেল কর্ত্তৃক অঙ্কিত ম্যাডনার জগৎ-প্রসিদ্ধ চিত্র। এই চিত্র পূর্ব্বে ইতালীর অন্তঃপাতী Piacenza নগরীর St. Sixtus গির্জ্জায় বিদ্যমান ছিল। বর্ত্তমানে উহা Dresden নগরীর রাজকীয় চিত্রশালায় রক্ষিত আছে। এই চিত্রে দেবজননী মেরী শিশু যীশুকে অঙ্কে ধারণ পূর্ব্বক দেবশিশুগণের মুখরচিত মেঘপুঞ্জের উপরে অবস্থান করিতেছেন। তাঁহার দক্ষিণে St. Sixtus, বামে St. Berbera এবং নীচে দেবশিশুযুগল প্রণতজানু হইয়া উপবিষ্ট রহিয়াছে।

sis'-trŭm, *n.* A kind of jingling timbrel used by the Egyptians in the worship of Isis; প্রাচীন মিসরবাসিগণকর্ত্তৃক আইসিস দেবীর পুজায় ব্যবহৃত একপ্রকার ঝঞ্চন শব্দকারী বাদ্যযন্ত্র।

Sis-ў-phē'-ăn, *adj.* **1.** Relating to Sisyphus, a king of Corinth; করিন্থের রাজা সিসিফাস সম্বন্ধীয়। [পাপের শাস্তিস্বরূপ এই রাজাকে নরকে একখণ্ড প্রস্তর পাহাড়ের উপর তুলিতে হইত, পরে ঐ প্রস্তর গড়াইয়া নীচে পড়িলে পুনরায় তুলিতে হইত। এইরূপ কার্য্যে তাঁহার অনুক্ষণ ব্যাপৃত থাকিতে হইত।] **2.** Unceasing; as, *Sisyphean* labour; অবিশ্রান্ত, অবিরাম, বিরামবিহীন।

sit, *v. i.* & *t.* **1.** To rest upon the haunches; বসা, উপবেশন করা। **2.** (Of birds) To perch; (পক্ষি-সম্পর্কে) দাঁড়ে বসা। **3.** To cover or keep warm eggs for hatching; ডিমে তা দেওয়া। **4.** To be officially engaged in public business, as judges, legislators, or officers of any kind; (বিচারক প্রভৃতি সম্পর্কে) বসা। **5.** To meet or be convened as an assembly; সভা প্রভৃতির অধিবেশন হওয়া। **6.** To remain in a state of repose; to rest; শান্তভাবে অবস্থান করা; অবস্থান করা, থাকা। **7.** (*Obs.*) To become; (অপ্রঃ) শোভা পাওয়া, সাজা, মানান। **8.** To fit; as, a coat *sits* well; লাগা। **9.** To assume a position to have one's portrait taken, bust remodelled, or the like; as, to *sit* for a sculptor; চিত্র প্রভৃতি গ্রহণের জন্য বসা। ***Verb t.*** To sit upon; কোন কিছুর উপর বসিয়া থাকা। **2.** To seat; বসান, উপবিষ্ট করা। **3.** To become; শোভা পাওয়া। **Sitfast**—অশ্বপৃষ্ঠের কঠিন ক্ষত। **To make (one) sit up**—To subject him to hard work, pain, etc.; কাহাকে কঠোর পরিশ্রম করান, কাহাকে ব্যথা দেওয়া। To astonish him; কাহাকে অবাক করা, ভয় বিস্ময় প্রভৃতিতে বসাইয়া দেওয়া। **To seat at meat**—To be at table for eating; আহারে বসা। **To sit bodkin**—See BODKIN. **To sit down**—To place oneself on a chair or the like; উপবেশন করা। To settle; বসবাস করা। To begin siege; অবরোধ আরম্ভ করা। To come accidentally to the ground in a sitting posture; হঠাৎ বসিয়া পড়া। To rest content with; "A sober physician will not *sit down* with so short an account"; তৃপ্ত থাকা, সন্তুষ্ট থাকা। **To sit down with**—To accept something whether we like it or not; কোন জিনিষ ভালই লাগুক বা মন্দই লাগুক তাহাতে সন্তুষ্ট থাকিতে বাধ্য হওয়া। **To sit eggs**—To remain too long as a guest; কাহারো বাটীতে অতিথি হইয়া আর নড়িতে না চাওয়া। **To sit in**—To have a part as a player in a game; "We cannot all *sit in* at them"; কোন ক্রীড়ায় ক্রীড়কশ্রেণী ভুক্ত থাকা। To begin in earnest; "The squire *sat in* to his cups"—Tom Jones; উঠিয়া পড়িয়া লাগা। **To sit loose** or **loosely**—To be careless or indifferent; উদাসীন থাকা, অমনোযোগী হওয়া। **To sit on brood**—(*Shakes.*) To ponder; চিন্তা করা। **To sit on thorns**—To be in a bad plight; দুর্দ্দশায় পতিত হওয়া। **To sit on** or **upon**—To hold an official enquiry on any matter; "A coroner's jury has *sat on* the body, and returned a verdict of lunacy"; কোন বিষয়ে সরকারী অনুসন্ধানে প্রবৃত্ত হওয়া। **To sit out**—To be able to stay longer in one's sit than another person; অপর কোন লোক অপেক্ষা অধিকক্ষণ আসনে বসিয়া থাকিতে পারা। To sit apart from others; অপর সকল হইতে দূরে বসা। To sit in open air; খোলা বাতসেবসা, মুক্ত বায়ুতে উপবেশন করা। **To sit on**—To continue to sit; বসিয়া থাকা। **To sit out anything**—Not to take part in anything; কোন ব্যাপারে সংশ্রব না রাখা। **To sit over**—To be occupied with something while sitting; to read over; বসিয়া কোন কার্য্যে নিরত থাকা; পাঠ করা। **To sit tight**—To hold on; ধরিয়া থাকা। **To sit under**—To be accustomed to hear the preaching of ; কাহারো ধর্ম্মোপদেশ শ্রবণে অভ্যস্ত থাকা। **To sit under a clergyman** — To attend his church ; কোন ধর্ম্মযাজকের গির্জ্জায় যাওয়া। **To sit up**—To rise up from a recumbent posture ; উঠিয়া বসা। Not to go to bed ; জাগিয়া থাকা। To sit ; বসা। **To sit up for anyone**—To wait for one beyond the usual time for sleep ; কাহারো অপেক্ষায় রাত্রে জাগিয়া থাকা। **To sit upon a person**—To snub him ; কাহাকে মুখ ঝামটা দেওয়া।

site, *n.* **1.** A plot of ground for building on; বাস্তু, বাস্তুভূমি। **2.** The place where anything is set down; অবস্থান, অধিষ্ঠান। **3.** (*Rare*) Posture; (কচিদ্‌ব্যবহৃত) উপবেশনভঙ্গী।

sith, *conj.* (*Obs.*) Since ; (অপ্রঃ) যেহেতু।

sī-tŏl′-ō-ġȳ, sĭt-i-ŏl′-ō-ġȳ, *ns.* Dietetic ; পথ্যাপথ্যবিধি।

sī-tō′-phō′-bi-ă, sĭt-i-ō—, *ns.* A morbid aversion to food ; আহারে অরুচি।

sit′-ter (-ėr), *n.* **1.** One who sits ; উপবেশক, উপবেশনকারী। **2.** A person sitting for a portrait ; যে ব্যক্তি স্বীয় প্রতিকৃতি অঙ্কনার্থ চিত্রকরের সম্মুখে উপবিষ্ট হয়, উবেশক।

sit′-ting (-ĭng), *n.* **1.** The act of one who sits ; উপবেশন। **2.** The act of one who sits for the portrait; যে ব্যক্তি চিত্রঅঙ্কনার্থ চিত্রকরের সম্মুখে উপবিষ্ট হয়। **3.** A session ; a business meeting ; অধিবেশন ; সভা, বৈঠক। **4.** Incubation ; ডিমে তা দেওন। **Sitting-room**—বৈঠকখানা।

sit-ū-ā′-tion *n.* **1.** Circumstance ; অবস্থা। **2.** Location in respect to something else ; অবস্থান্। **3.** A post or employment ; as, a *situation* fell vacant ; চাকুরী, কায। **4.** A locality ; স্থান। **5.** Critical point or complication in a drama ; নাটকের অবস্থা-সঙ্কট। **6.** Temporary state or relation of affairs at a moment of action, as in dramatic sense ; "It is wildly melodramatic, and full of *situation* from end to end" ; (নাট্য) সম্বন্ধাবস্থান (প্রবাসী), ঘটনাসঙ্গতি (পাঃ)।

Sitz′-băth (sĭts-), *n.* A hip bath ; a tub adapted for such bath; আকটি-স্নান (ঐরূপ স্নানে পদ ও উরুদেশ জলপূর্ণ টবে নিমগ্ন রাখিতে হয়) ; ঐরূপ স্নানের উপযোগী গামলা।

six, *adj.* & *n.* Twice three ; ছয়, ষড়। ***Noun.*** **1.** The sum of three and three ; ছয় এই সংখ্যা। **2.** A card or die with six pips ; তাস বা পাশার ছয়। **Six-fingered** — ষড়াঙ্গুল। **Six-fold**—ষড়্‌গুণ। **Six-footed** — ষট্‌পদ। **Six-footer**—ছয় ফিট দীর্ঘ ব্যক্তি। **Six-penny**—ছয় পেনি মূল্যের। **Six-pounder**—যে কামানে ছয় পাউণ্ড ওজনের গোলা ব্যবহৃত হয়। **Six-shooter**—ছয়-নালা পিস্তল। **Six of one and half-a-dozen of the other**—যার নাম বার বুড়ি, তারই নাম তিন পণ। **To be at sixes and sevens**—To be in disorder or confusion ; এলেমেলো হইয়া যাওয়া, ছত্রহীন হয়ে পড়া, নয়ছয় হয়ে থাকা।

six′-ain (-ān), *n.* A six-line stanza ; যে কবিতার প্রতি কলিতে ছয়টী পংক্তি থাকে।

six′-ėr, *n.* A hit for six in cricket ; ক্রীকেট ক্রীড়ায় ছয় রণের জন্য দৌড়।

sixte (sĭxt), *n.* A position in fencing ; অসিক্রীড়ার অবস্থানবিশেষ।

six′-teen (-tēn), *adj.* & *n.* Six and ten ; ষোল, ষোড়শ। ***Noun.*** A symbol representing sixteen units ; ষোল সংখ্যা। **—teenth,** *adj.* Sixth after tenth ; ষোড়শতম।

sixth, *adj.* & *n.* Next in order after fifth ; ছয়ই, ষষ্ঠ। ***Noun.*** One of six equal parts ; ষষ্ঠাংশ। **—ly,** *adv.* In the sixth place ; ষষ্ঠতঃ।

six′-tȳ, *adj.* & *n.* Six times ten ; ষষ্ঠি, ষষ্ঠিসংখ্যক, ষাটি, ষাট। ***Noun.*** A symbol representing sixty units ; ষষ্ঠিসংখ্যা। **—ti-eth,** *adj.* & *n.*

sīz′-ă-ble (-bl), *adj.* Of a large size ; বৃহদাকার, বৃহদায়তন।

sīz′-ăr, *n.* The student at Cambridge and Dublin of a corresponding grade with a servitor at Oxford; ডবলিন এবং কেম্ব্রিজ বিশ্ববিদ্যালয়ের যে ছাত্র অল্প বেতনে পড়িতে পারে [পূর্ব্বে এইরূপ ছাত্রকে ভৃত্যের কার্য্যে সাহায্য করিতে হইত]। **—ship,** *n.*

sīze, *n., v. t.* & *i.* **1.** Extent of volume or surface ; আয়তন, পরিমাণ। **2.** A glutinous substance ; চিত্রকরগণকর্তৃক ব্যবহৃত একপ্রকার আঠালো পদার্থ। **3.** (In Cambridge University) Food from the college buttery ; (কেম্ব্রিজ বিশ্ববিদ্যালয়) কলেজের খাদ্যভাণ্ডার হইতে প্রেরিত খাদ্য। **3.** (*Obs.*) An instrument for measuring pearls ; (অপ্রঃ) মুক্তা-মাপের জন্য যন্ত্রবিশেষ। ***Verb t.*** **1.** To arrange according to size ; আয়তন অনুসারে সাজান। **2.** To increase the bulk of ; আয়তন বৃদ্ধি করা। **3.** To separate by a sieve ; (খনিজবিমিশ্র ধাতুসম্পর্কে) চালুনিদ্বারা চালিয়া পৃথক করা। ***Verb i.*** (In Cambridge University) To order food or drink from the buttery ; (কেম্ব্রিজ বিশ্ববিদ্যালয়ে) কলেজের খাদ্যভাণ্ডার হইতে খাদ্য বা পানীয় সরবরাহের জন্য আদেশ দেওয়া। **Size-stick**—পায়ের মাপ লওয়ার জন্য চর্ম্মকারদিগের কাঠিবিশেষ।

sīze, *n.* & *v. t.* A kind of weak soft glue used by painters ; a gummy varnish used by gilders, paper-makers and artists ; চিত্রকরগণকর্তৃক ব্যবহৃত একপ্রকার আঠালো পদার্থ ; শিল্পী, কাগজনির্ম্মাতা এবং গিল্টিকারগণকর্তৃক ব্যবহৃত একপ্রকার আঠালো পদার্থ। ***Verb t.*** To cover with size ; to prepare with size ; উক্তরূপ আঠালো জিনিষ দ্বারা

আবৃত করা; উক্তরূপ আঠালো জিনিষ ঘসিয়া প্রস্তুত করা।

siz'-zle (-l), *v. i.* & *n.* (*Colloq.*) To make a sound as in frying; (চলিত ভাষায়) চড় চড় শব্দ হওয়া। ***Noun.*** Such noise; চড়চড় শব্দ।

sjam'-bŏk (zăm-), *n.* & *v. t.* A short whip made of rhinoceros-hide; গণ্ডারের চর্ম্মে প্রস্তুত একপ্রকার চাবুক। ***Verb t.*** To beat with such a whip; গণ্ডারচর্ম্মের চাবুকদ্বারা আঘাত করা।

skāld, *v. t.* & *n.* Same as SCALD (which see).

skāte, *n.* A cartilaginous fish of the ray-kind; একপ্রকার মৎস্য।

skāte, *n., v. i.* & *t.* A wooden sole with a steel blade or set of rollers, fitted on the sole of a

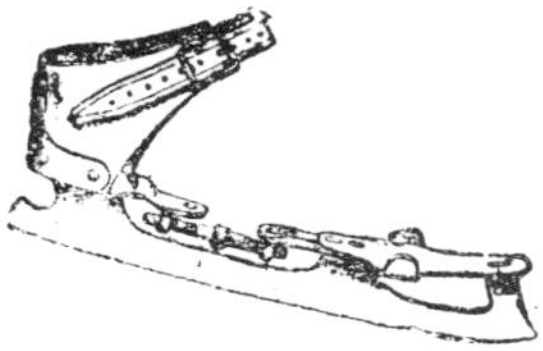

Skate.

boot used for moving rapidly along the surface of ice; বরফের উপর দ্রুতধাবনের জন্য ইস্পাতের পাত বা রোলার সংযুক্ত কাষ্ঠফলকবিশেষ—যাহা বুটের নীচে সংবদ্ধ করা হয়, তুষারপাদুকা। ***Verb i.*** **1.** To slide or move with skate; তুষারপাদুকার সাহায্যে পিছলাইয়া চলা বা বিচরণ করা। **2.** (*Slang*) To move quickly; (ইতরভাষায়) দ্রুত চলা। ***Verb t.*** **1.** To cause to slide on a smooth surface; কোন কিছুর মসৃণতলে পিছলাইতে দেওয়া। **2.** To compete by skating; তুষারপাদুকা দ্বারা দৌড়ে প্রতিযোগিতা করা। **Skat'-er,** *n.* One who skates; তুষারপাদুকাচারী। **To skate over thin ice**—To talk on a delicate subject; যে বিষয়ে কথা তুলিলে কাহারো মন ক্ষুণ্ণ হইতে পারে—তজ্জন্য সেইরূপ কোন বিষয়ে বিশেষ ভাবিয়া চিন্তিয়া কথা বলা।

skean (skēn), **skene** (skēn), **skain** (skān), *ns.* A long knife or short sword, used by the Irish and the Highlanders of Scotland; আয়র্লণ্ডবাসী এবং স্কটলণ্ডের পার্ব্বত্য-অঞ্চলের অধিবাসিগণ কর্তৃক ব্যবহৃত একপ্রকার দীর্ঘ ছুরিকা বা তরবারী।

skē-dăd'-dle (-l), *v. i.* & *n.* (*Slang*) To disperse in flight; (চলিতভাষায়) পলায়নকালে ছত্রভঙ্গ হওয়া। ***Noun.*** (*Colloq.*) Hurried flight or dispersal; (চলিতভাষায়) ছত্রভঙ্গ।

skee (skē-), *n.* Same as SKI (which see.)

skein (skān), *n.* **1.** A quantity of yarn from the reel; সূতার নুটি, সূতার দিস্তা, সূতার ফেটি। **2.** A flight of wild geese or swan; আকাশপথে উড্ডীয়মান বন্যহংসশ্রেণী। **3.** (*Fig.*) A tangle; cofusion; (লক্ষণায়) পাক, পেঁচ; গোলমাল।

skĕl'-ē-tŏn, *n.* **1.** The bones of any animal dried and retained in their natural position; কঙ্কাল, পঞ্জর, অস্থিপঞ্জর, অস্থিকঙ্কাল। **2.** A very thin person; কঙ্কালসার ব্যক্তি, তালপাতার সিপাহী (*colloq.*), অস্থিচর্ম্মসার ব্যক্তি। **3.** The outline or framework of anything; কাঠাম, আদরা, কঙ্কাল। **Skeleton key**—একপ্রকার খাঁজহীন চাবি—যাহাদ্বারা অনেক তালা খোলা যায়। **Skeleton regiment**—যে সেনাপল্টনে সৈনিকসমূহকে বিদায় দেওয়ার পরও ভবিষ্যতে পুনর্গঠনের জন্য কর্ম্মচারিসমূহ রক্ষিত হয়। **Skeleton screw**—একপ্রকার মৎস্য। **Skeleton suit**—একটী আঁট সাঁট খাটো কোর্ত্তা এবং পাজামা। উক্ত পাজামা বোতাম দ্বারা কোর্ত্তার সহিত আঁটা থাকে। **A skeleton at the feast**—আনন্দনাশক বস্তু। **A skeleton in the cupboard, house etc., A family skeleton**—পরিবারের কলঙ্কজনক কথা। **Mere skeleton**—তালপাতার সেপাই (রঃ প্রঃ)। **Skeleton-face type**—একপ্রকার মুদ্রণের হরফ—যাহার অক্ষরগুলি সূক্ষ্ম-ভাবে কাটা থাকে।

skĕl'-ē-tŏn-īze, *v. t.* **1.** To reduce to skeleton; অস্থিচর্ম্মসার করা। **2.** To sketch out; আদরা করা।

skene (skēn), *n.* Same as SKEAN (which see).

skĕp, *n.* **1.** A coarse sort of basket, wide at the top and narrow at the bottom; অগ্রভাগে প্রশস্ত এবং নিম্নভাগ সরু একপ্রকার ঝুড়ি। **2.** A bee-hive made of straw or wicker-work; খড় বা বাঁশবেতে তৈরী মৌমাছির বাসের জন্য ঝুড়ি।

skĕp'-sis, skĕp'-tic, *ns.* Same as SCEPSIS, SCEPTIC (which see).

sketch (skĕch), *n., v. t.* & *i.* **1.** An outline or general delineation of anything; a first or rough draft of a plan or design; নক্‌সা; আদরা, রেখান্যাস, পাতড়া, খসড়া, পাণ্ডুলেখ্য। **2.** A rough drawing; স্থুলচিত্র, রেখাচিত্র। ***Verb t.*** To give a sketch of; আদরা দেওয়া। ***Verb i.*** To make a sketch or sketches; আদরা করা, খসড়া করা। **Sketch'-er,** *n.* **Sketch'-i-ness,** *n* **Sketch'-i-ly,** *adv.* **Sketch'-y,** *adj.* **Sketch-book**—স্থুলচিত্র অঙ্কনের জন্য পুস্তক; স্থান বা ব্যক্তিসমূহের সংক্ষিপ্ত বর্ণনাসম্বলিত পুস্তক (as, Washington Irving's *Sketch Book*).

skew (skü-), *adj.* & *n.* Oblique; বাঁকা, টের্চ্ছা, টেরা, হেলানো, গড়ানিয়া। ***Noun.*** **1.** (*Dial.*) A piebald horse; (উপভাষায়) চকড়াপাকড়া ঘোড়া। **2.** The coping of a gable; an oblique arch; anything sloping from another at an obtuse angle; পাশকপালীর মাথাল বা কপিশীর্ষ; বক্রখিলান; যে বস্তু অন্য বস্তু হইতে স্থুল কোণ উৎপাদনপূর্ব্বক হেলানো থাকে। **3.** A sideward movement; পার্শ্বের দিকে গতি। **4.** An error; ভুল, ভ্রান্তি। **Skew-back**—যে প্রবণভূমিতে খিলানের অন্তর প্রান্ত অবলম্বিত

থাকে, যে ইষ্টক, লৌহপট্ট প্রভৃতি দ্বারা আচ্ছাদিত স্থানের উপর খিলানের পাদদেশ অবলম্বিত থাকে। **Skewbald** (অশ্ব-সম্বন্ধে) চকড়া পাকড়া। **Skew bridge**—যে সেতুর খিলান বা খিলানশ্রেণী তির্য্যগ্‌ভাবে স্থাপিত থাকে, তির্য্যক্‌সেতু। **Skew chisel**—যে বাঁটালির ধারাল প্রান্ত টের্চ্চা থাকে। **Skew-eyed**—টেরা।

skew'-ẽr (skū-), *n.* & *v.t.* **1.** A pin of wood or iron for holding meat compact while roasting; ভর্জ্জনকালে মাংস সংশ্লিষ্ট রাখার জন্য ব্যবহৃত একপ্রকার সূক্ষ্মাগ্র কাষ্ঠ বা লৌহশলাকা, শিক, শূল (Sans.)। **2.** (*Joc.*) Sword etc.; (রহস্যচ্ছলে) অসি প্রভৃতি। ***Verb t.*** To fasten with skewers; উক্তরূপ শলকাদ্বারা নিবদ্ধ করা।

ski, *n.* A kind of wooden shoe about 8ft. long, 4ft. broad for running or jumping on snow; বরফের উপর ধাবন বা লম্ফনের জন্য একপ্রকার ৮ ফিট লম্বা এবং ৪ ফিট প্রস্থ কাষ্ঠপাদুকা।

ski-ăg'-ră-phy̆, *n.* Same as SCIAGRAPHY (which see).

skid, *n., v. t.* & *i.* **1.** A piece of wood on which heavy weights are made to slide; যে কাষ্ঠখণ্ডের উপর গুরুভার দ্রব্য গড়াইয়া তোলা নামা করা হয়। **2.** A drag for the wheels of a vehicle; শকটচক্রের গতিরোধ করার জন্য কৌশলবিশেষ। **3.** (*Fig.*) A retarding influence; "It is for ever the function of Tories to be the *skid* and not the wheel"; প্রতিরোধজনক প্রভাব, বিঘ্ন, অন্তরায়। **4.** A curving timber to preserve a ship's side from injury; জাহাজে মাল উঠানামার কালে জাহাজের পার্শ্বে চোট না লাগে তজ্জন্য পোতপার্শ্বে যে বক্র কাষ্ঠফলক নিবদ্ধ করা হয়। **5.** A metal or timber support for a cannon; কামান স্থাপনের জন্য কাঠ বা ধাতুনির্ম্মিত আধার। ***Verb t.*** To protect with, or support in, a skid; বক্রকাষ্ঠফলকদ্বারা জাহাজের পার্শ্বদেশ রক্ষা করা, ধাতব বা কাষ্ঠময় আধারের উপর কামান স্থাপন করা। ***Verb i.*** To slip sideways as on a slippery road; পিচ্ছিল পথের একপার্শ্বে গড়াইয়া পড়া।

skiff, *n.* A small light boat; হালকা নৌকা, ডিঙ্গি, ডোঙ্গা।

skil'-fŭl, *adj.* Having skill; dexterous; বিচক্ষণ, বিশারদ, পটু, পটীয়ান, কৃতকর্ম্মা, নিপুণ, চতুর, কুশল, দক্ষ। **-ly,** *adv.* **-ness,** *n.* The quality of being skilful; পটুতা, নৈপুণ্য, চাতুর্য্য, পাটব (উজ্জ্বল:), পটিমা (ঐ), হিকমৎ (*colloq.*), বৈশারদ্য, বৈচক্ষণ্য।

skill, *n.* Knowledge, combined with dexterity; tact; নৈপুণ্য, কুশলতা, চাতুর্য্য, দক্ষতা; কর্ম্মকুশলতা, কার্য্যকুশলতা।

skilled (skĭld), *adj.* Having or showing, skill; as, *skilled* labour; চাতুর্য্যসম্পন্ন, কৌশলসম্পন্ন, সুদক্ষ, বিশারদ, সুনিপুণ।

skil'lĕss, *adj.* (*Rare*) Without skill; (কচিদ্‌ব্যবহৃত) চাতুর্য্যবিহীন, নৈপুণ্যশূন্য, অনিপুণ।

skil'-lĕt, *n.* A small vessel of metal with a long handle for heating water etc; জল প্রভৃতি উষ্ণ করার জন্য লম্বা হাতলবিশিষ্ট একপ্রকার ক্ষুদ্র পাত্র।

skills, *v. i.* 3rd person, sing., imper. **It skills not**—It makes no difference; এতে কিছু আসে যায় না।

skil'-ly (-ĭ), *n.* A thin soup, such as is served to prisoners or paupers; বন্দী ও দরিদ্রগণকে যে একপ্রকার পাতলা যূষ দেওয়া হয়।

skim, *v. t., i.* & *adj.* **1.** To take the scum; সর উঠান, সর তোলা। **2.** To take off by skimming; সর কাটিয়া তোলা। **3.** To touch lightly while passing; "On that day the sun, when lowest *skims* the horizon"; ঘষড়াইয়া যাওয়া। **4.** To glance over; "Where I just had been *skimming* a charming critique"; চোখ বুলাইয়া যাওয়া, উপর উপর দেখিয়া যাওয়া। ***Verb i.*** **1.** To pass lightly or hastily; ঘষড়াইয়া যাওয়া, মৃদুস্পর্শ করিয়া যাওয়া, দ্রুত অতিক্রম করা। **2.** To become coated with a film or scum; পর্দ্দা বা সর পড়া। **3.** To glance over; তাড়াতাড়ি চোখ বুলাইয়া যাওয়া। ***Adj.*** Skimmed; সরতোলা। **Skim milk**—সরতোলা দুধ।

skim'-mer (-ẽr), *n.* **1.** A ladle for skimming; সর কাটিবার জন্য একপ্রকার হাতা, উকড়ী। **2.** A general name for various kinds of water-birds; বিভিন্ন জাতীয় জলচরপক্ষীর সাধারণ নাম।

skimp, *v. t.* & *i.* **1.** To give in scanty measure; অল্প পরিমাণে দেওয়া। **2.** To do a thing imperfectly; অসম্পূর্ণভাবে কোন কার্য্য করা। ***Verb i.*** To be niggardly; কৃপণ হওয়া, ব্যয়কুণ্ঠ হওয়া। **Skimp'-y,** *adj.* **Skimp'-ing-ly,** *adv.*

skin, *n., v. t.* & *i.* **1.** The natural outer covering of an animal; চর্ম্ম, চামড়া, ত্বক্‌ [Syn. কৃত্তি (as in কৃত্তিবাস), অজিন (esp. deer's hide), অসৃগ্ধরা, রক্তাধার, রোমভূমি, শরীরাবরণ।] **2.** The exterior coat of fruits and plants; বৃক্ষের বল্কল, খোসা, ত্বক্‌। **3.** A vessel of skin, used for liquids; "Give me a *skin* of wine, a crust of bread, A pittance bare, a book of verse to read With thee O love, to share my solitude, I would not take the Sultan's realms instead"; তরলপদার্থ রাখার জন্য চর্ম্মপাত্র, মসক। ***Verb t.*** **1.** To strip the skin from; চর্ম্ম-উন্মোচন করা। **2.** To cover with skin; চর্ম্মদ্বারা আবৃত বা আচ্ছাদিত করা। **3.** To cover superficially; উপরের দিক আবৃত করা। **4.** (*Slang*) To fleece; "The emigration Trusts *skin* the emigrants"; ঠকাইয়া লওয়া। **5.** To abscond (with *out*); "You just gather up your traps and *skin out* of this"; চম্পট দেওয়া। 6. To glance over; "Each man *skinned* his cards"; চোখ বুলাইয়া যাওয়া। ***Verb i.*** To be covered with skin; to form skin; চর্ম্মদ্বারা আবৃত হওয়া; চামড়া হওয়া। **Skin'-ny,** *adj.* Wanting flesh; "The daughter of Herod is rather beautiful but too *skinny* and lean"; শীর্ণ। **Skin-bound** — অস্থিচর্ম্মসার, ছিপছিপে; চর্ম্মদ্বারা দৃঢ়বদ্ধ। **Skin-bound disease**—এরিওলার টিস্থর পুরাতন প্রদাহজনিত চর্ম্মের স্ফীত, শীতল, কঠিন, দৃঢ়বদ্ধ অবস্থা। **Skin deep**—Superficial; "The saying that beauty is but *skin-deep*, is but a *skin-deep* saying; not deep; ভাসা ভাসা; অগভীর। **Skin-flint**—কৃপণ, কঞ্জুষ, ঝামার বিষ্টা (*slang*)। **Skin-friction**—সমুদ্রগামী জাহাজ প্রভৃতির পার্শ্বিক বাধা। **Skin-grafting**—ক্ষতস্থানে দেহের অপর স্থান বা অন্য কোন জন্তু বা মনুষ্যের শরীর হইতে গৃহীত চর্ম্ম-সংযোগ। **Skin-tight**—চর্ম্ম দৃঢ়ভাবে বদ্ধ। **Skin-wool**—মেষের চর্ম্ম বা মৃতদেহ হইতে গৃহীত রোম। **Thick-skin**—গম্ভীরবেদী। **Thin skin**—যে ব্যক্তি সহজেই চটিয়া উঠে, আশুক্রোধী। **By** or **with the skin of one's teeth**—Barely; by a narrow margin; কষ্টেসৃষ্টে; অল্পের জন্য। **In** or **with the whole skin**—With impunity; অক্ষতদেহে। **To be only skin and bone**—To be a skeleton; অস্থিচর্ম্মসার হওয়া। **To keep one's eyes skinned**—(*Slang*) To be watchful; (ইতর ভাষায়) সতর্ক থাকা, সজাগ থাকা। **To skin a flint**—পিঁপড়ার পোঁদ টিপা (See also FLINT). **To skin up a sail in the Bunt**—To make the part of the canvas which covers the sails when furled, smooth and neat, by turning the sail well up on the yard; গুটানো পাইলের বাহিরের ভাঁজ মসৃণ করা।

To save one's skin—To escape without injury; অক্ষত দেহে রক্ষা করা, গা বাঁচান।

Skink.

skink (skĭngk), *n.* A kind of lizard; একপ্রকার গোধা।

skin'-ner (-ēr), *n.* 1. One who skins; যে চর্ম্ম উন্মোচন করে, চর্ম্ম-উন্মোচক। 2. One who deals in skins or hides; চর্ম্মব্যবসায়ী।

skip, *v. i., t.* & *n.* 1. To move with leaps and bounds; to leap lightly; লাফাইয়া চলা; লাফান। 2. To pass without notice (often followed by *over*); অলক্ষিতে চলিয়া যাওয়া। 3. (*Slang*) To leave hurriedly; তাড়াতাড়ি ছুটিয়া পালান। ***Verb t.*** 1. To leap lightly over; লাফাইয়া চলা। 2. To pass over; উপেক্ষা করা, ফেলিয়া যাওয়া। 3. To cause to ricochet; লাফাইয়া লাফাইয়া চালান, ছিনিমিনি খাওয়ান। 3. To leave hurriedly; তাড়াতাড়ি ফেলা। ***Noun.*** Skipping movements; লাফালাফি, মণ্ডূকগতি, প্লুতগতি। **Skip'-ping-ly,** *adv.* **Skipjack**—ছেলেদের

Skipjack.

একপ্রকার উল্লম্ফনকারী ক্রীড়নক; একপ্রকার গুবরে পোকা। **Skipping-rope**—বালিকাদিগের উল্লম্ফন-ক্রীড়ার জন্য কাষ্ঠের হাতলদ্বয়যুক্ত রজ্জু।

skip, *n.* A college-servant; কলেজের ভৃত্য।

skip, *n.* A leather-lined basket used in cotton-mills; সূতার কলে ব্যবহৃত একপ্রকার চর্ম্মাচ্ছাদিত চাঙ্গাড়ি।

skip'-per (-ēr), *n.* 1. The master of a trading or sailing vessel; বাণিজ্য জাহাজ বা পাইলের জাহাজের অধ্যক্ষ। 2. The larva of a cheese fly; পনীরকীটের পোকা। **Skipper's daughters**—উচ্চফেণচূড় তরঙ্গ।

skip'-pet (-ĕt), *n.* A circular box used for covering and protecting a seal; মোহর ঢাকিবার এবং রক্ষা করার জন্য একপ্রকার গোলাকার আবরণ।

skirl, *v. i.* & *n.* To scream shrilly; কর্কশভাবে চীৎকার করা। ***Noun.*** A shrill cry; কর্কশ চীৎকার।

skir'-mish (skêr-), *n.* & *v. i.* 1. A light combat between small parties; খণ্ডযুদ্ধ। 2. A light contest; সংঘর্ষ, মারামারি, হাঙ্গামা। ***Verb i.*** To fight slightly or in small parties; to be engaged in a skirmish; সংঘর্ষে প্রবৃত্ত হওয়া; খণ্ডযুদ্ধে প্রবৃত্ত হওয়া। **—er,** *n.*

skir'-ret (-ĕt), *n.* The water-parsnip; একপ্রকার জলজ গুল্ম।

skirt (skêrt), *n., v. t.* & *i.* 1. The lower and loose part of a coat or shirt that hangs below the waist; কোর্ত্তা এবং জামার যে অংশ শ্লথভাবে কটির নীচে ঝুলানো থাকে। 2. The edge of any part of a dress; অঞ্চল, আঁচল, আঁচলা, বস্ত্রাঞ্চল। 3. Border; margin; as, the *skirts* of a forest; extreme part; as, the *skirts* of Calcutta; প্রান্ত; কিনারা, ধার; সীমা। 4. A woman's garment like a petticoat; স্ত্রীলোকদিগের একপ্রকার নীচে পরিবার ঘাগরা। 5. (*Slang*) A girl or woman (ইতরভাষায়) ছুড়ী, ছুকরী, মেয়ে। 6. The diaphragm or midriff of animals; জন্তুর বক্ষোদরব্যবধায়ক পেশী। ***Verb t.*** 1. To surround; বেষ্টিত করা। 2. To border; to form the edge of; to move along the edge of; প্রান্তদেশে স্থিত হওয়া, প্রান্তদেশবর্ত্তী হওয়া; কিনারা বা প্রান্তস্থলীয় হওয়া; কিনারা দিয়া যাওয়া। ***Verb i.*** To be on the border;

to live on the border; to move along the edge; প্রান্তদেশবর্ত্তী হওয়া; প্রান্তদেশে বাস করা; কিনারা ধরিয়া চলা। **Skirt'-ing,** *n.* 1. The skirts collectively; material for skirts: অঞ্চল, নীচে পরার জন্য স্ত্রীলোকের ঘাগরাসমূহ; ঐ সকল প্রস্তুতের উপযোগী বস্ত্র। 2. Same as SKIRTING-BOARD. 3. Wool of an inferior quality: নিকৃষ্ট পশম। **Skirt'-less,** *adj.* **Divided skirt** — একপ্রকার ঢিলা পাজামা। **Skirt-dance**—একপ্রকার নৃত্য—যাহাতে নর্ত্তকী নৃত্যসময়ে লীলাচ্ছলে সুদীর্ঘ অঞ্চল হস্তদ্বারা নানা ভঙ্গীতে আন্দোলিত করে। **Skirting-board**—কক্ষপ্রাচীরের প্রান্তসংলগ্ন কাষ্ঠময় আচ্ছাদন। **To sit upon a man's skirts**—To meditate on revenge; প্রতিহিংসা সাধনের জন্য চিন্তা করা।

skit, *n.* 1. A frivolous woman; চপলা স্ত্রী। 2. Literary sqib; burlesque; "The British bull-dog has figured again and again in pictorial *skits*"; চুটকী; হাস্যোদ্দীপক অভিনয়, কৌতুকনাট্য, ব্যঙ্গজনক অনুকরণ। 3. A trick; a hoax; চতুরী; ধোকা। 4. A slight shower of rain; "It is blowing hard to-day with a dull grey sky and *skits* of rain"; ফিন ফিন বৃষ্টি।

skit-ter (-ĕr), *v. i.* 1. To skim lightly over; ঘষড়াইয়া যাওয়া, মৃদু স্পর্শ করিয়া চলিয়া যাওয়া। 2. To fish by drawing the baited hook along the surface of water; জলের উপরে টোপ টানিয়া ছিপে মাছ ধরা।

skit'-tish (-ĭsh), *adj.* 1. (Of horses) Nervous; timorous; (অশ্বসম্বন্ধে) সহজে ভীত, আশুচকিত; ভীরু। 2. Volatile; hasty; চঞ্চল, অস্থির-চিত্ত; ব্যস্তসমস্ত, উতলা, শশব্যস্ত। 3. Changeable; as, *skittish* fortune; পরিবর্ত্তনশীল। 4. Tricky; sportive; inconstant; coquettish; "Sobriety of dress must be enforced and *skittish* widows must be protected from their volatile tastes"; (স্ত্রীলোক-সম্পর্কে) চতুরা, ছলনানিপুণা, ছলাকলাপ্রিয়া; ক্রীড়াশীলা; চঞ্চলা, চপলা, সলীল, বিলাসবতী, বিভ্রমবতী, লীলাবিলাসবতী। **–ly,** *adv.* **–ness,** *n.*

skit'-tle (-l), *n., pl.* A game of nine pins in which a flattened ball or thick rounded disc is thrown to knock down the pins; একপ্রকার ক্রীড়া [এই ক্রীড়াতে শঙ্কুসমূহ স্থানচ্যুত করার জন্য একটী চ্যাপ্টা কন্দুক বা চাক্তি নিক্ষেপ করা হয়।

skīve, *n.* & *v. t.* The revolving table or wheel used by diamond-polishers in finishing the facets of a gem; মণির পলা পালিস করার জন্য একপ্রকার আবর্ত্তনশীল মেজ বা চক্র। ***Verb t.*** 1. To pare hide on the flesh-side; চর্ম্মের মাংসের দিক চাঁচা। 2. To polish the facets of gems; মণির পলা পালিস করা।

skīv'-ĕr, *n.* 1. A knife for skiving leather; চামড়ার মাংসের দিক চাঁচিবার জন্য ছুরি। 2. An inferior quality of leather made of split sheep-skin; চর্ম্মের মাংসের দিক চাঁচিয়া যে একপ্রকার পাতলা চামড়া প্রস্তুত হয়।

skü'-ă, *n.* A kind of gull; একপ্রকার সাগরবলাকা।

skûlk, *v. i.* To lurk; to get out of the way in a slinking, sneaking manner; "Should a common soldier *skulk* behind and thrust his general in the front of war"; মন্দ উদ্দেশ্যে লুকাইয়া থাকা; চুপে চুপে সরিয়া পড়া, বিপদের সময় গা বাচাইবার জন্য অলক্ষিতে বা গোপনে সরিয়া পড়া। **Skulk'-er,** *n.* **Skulk'-ing-ly,** *adv.*

skŭll, *n.* 1. The spherical bony covering of the brain, including the whole head except the lower part of the face; মাথার খুলি, করোটী, খর্পর, কপাল (স্ত্রীঃ) [Syn. নরকপাল, কর্পর, করঙ্ক]। 2. The head; "We have not an idea of our own in our *skulls*"; মস্তক। **Skull-cap** — একপ্রকার আঁটসাঁট মকমলের টুপি, আমাদের দেশের সাধারণ-শ্রেণীর মুসলমানগণের টুপি; একপ্রকার গাছ [এই গাছের ফুল দেখিতে অনেকটা টুপির মত।] **Skull and cross-bones** —See CROSS-BONES.

skŭnk (skŭngk), *n.* 1. A North-American carnivorous quadruped, nearly allied to the otter which defends when pursued, by the ejection of an offensively foul matter; উত্তর আমেরিকাদেশীয় নকুল-জাতীয় জন্তুবিশেষ, এই জন্তু তাড়িত হইলে মলদ্বার হইতে একপ্রকার দুর্গন্ধময় পদার্থ নির্গত করিয়া আত্মরক্ষা করে। 2. A contemptible fellow; ঘৃণিত লোক।

Skûp-shti-nă, *n.* The Parliament of Servia; সার্ভিয়া দেশের পার্লেমেণ্ট বা জাতীয় সমিতি। [এই সভার ¾ অংশ সভ্য জনসাধারণকর্ত্তৃক নির্ব্বাচিত এবং অবশিষ্ট ¼ অংশ নৃপতিকর্ত্তৃক মনোনীত হইয়া থাকে।]

skȳ, *n.* & *v. t.* 1. The apparent arch or vault of heaven; আকাশ, গগন, নভঃ, অম্বর, নভোমণ্ডল, আশমান (*colloq.*), [Syn. ব্যোম, খ, পুষ্কর, শূন্য, সুরবর্ত্ম, অন্তরীক্ষ, অনন্ত, বিয়ৎ, বিষ্ণুপদ, বিহায়, দিগন্তর, দিগন্তরাল, অভ্র, দেববর্ত্ম, মেঘবর্ত্ম, মেঘবেশ্ম, মরুৎপথ, মরুদ্বর্ত্ম, তারাপথ, নাক, ঘনপদবী, অন্তরীক্ষ, ঘনবীথি, নক্ষত্রবর্ত্ম, তারাবর্ত্ম]। 2. The heaven; স্বর্গ। 2. The abode of the gods; দেবভূমি, স্বর্গ। 4. The weather; climate; "I seek warmer *sky*"; আবহাওয়া; জলবায়ু। ***Verb t.*** 1. To hit a ball high up; আঘাত করিয়া কন্দুক উচ্চে তোলা। 2. (*Colloq.*) To hang high on a wall in an exhibition of paintings; as, his picture was *skied*; চিত্রপ্রদর্শনীতে কোন চিত্র প্রাচীরের উপরের দিকে টাঙ্গান। **Sky-blue**—আশমানী নীল। **Sky-born**—স্বর্গজাত। **Sky-clad**—(রঙ্গচ্ছলে) দিগম্বর, দিগ্বসন, দিগ্বাস। **Sky-colour**—আকাশবর্ণ, আসমানী। **Sky-high** — আকাশ-প্রমাণ উচ্চ; (লক্ষণায়) অত্যুল্লসিত। **Sky-kissing**—অম্বরচুম্বী, আকাশচুম্বী,

গগনচুম্বী, গগনস্পর্শী। **Skylark**—ভারুই পক্ষী, ভরতদ্বাজ পক্ষী। (*Verb i.*) ক্রীড়াচ্ছলে জাহাজের দড়াদড়ীর উপর দৌড়া, লাফালাফি ছুটাছুটি করা। **Skylight**—ছাদ, গুম্বজ বা জাহাজের পাটাতনস্থ বাতায়ন, নভোবাতায়ন। **Sky-line**—দিগন্তরেখা, দিক্‌চক্রবাল, দিগ্বলয়। **Sky-pilot**—(ইতরভাষায়) পুরোহিত। **Sky-rocket**—হাউই বাজী। **Sky-sail**—জাহাজের একপ্রকার হাল্‌কা পাইল। **Skyscape**—আকাশের চিত্র, গগনালেখ্য, আকাশ চিত্র, নভোচিত্র। **Sky-scraper**—(কৌতুকচ্ছলে) জাহাজের একপ্রকার হাল্‌কা পাইল। আমেরিকার নিউইয়র্ক প্রভৃতি নগরীর বহুতলবিশিষ্ট প্রাসাদ, অম্বরচুম্বী প্রাসাদ, অম্বর-চুম্বী হর্ম্ম্য [এই শ্রেণীর অট্টালিকার মধ্যে মিসসিপির পশ্চিমভাগে এম, সি, স্মিথের বাটী পৃথিবীর মধ্যে সর্ব্বাপেক্ষা উচ্চ। মূল বাড়ীটী একুশ তালা। তার উপর আর একটী ১২ তালা অত্যুচ্চ গুম্বজ। এতদ্ব্যতীত মৃত্তিকার নিম্নেও দুইটী তলা রহিয়াছে। ৫০ ফিট গভীর ভিত্তির উপর অট্টালিকাটী প্রতিষ্ঠিত আছে। ভিত্তি নির্ম্মাণে প্রায় ৪,০০০ পিপা বিলাতী মাটী এবং একসহস্র টনেরও অধিক ইস্পাত ব্যবহৃত হইয়াছে। এই ভিত্তির উপর ৭৬৫০ টন ওজনের অট্টালিকাটী স্থাপিত হইয়াছে।] **Sky-terrier**—স্কটলণ্ডদেশীয় একপ্রকার কুকুর। **Sky-tincture**—আকাশবর্ণ। **Skyward**—Toward the sky; আকাশাভিমুখে। **If the sky fall, we shall catch larks**—সাতমণ তেলও পুড়বেনা রাধাও নাচবেনা। **The skies** — দেবভূমি, স্বর্গ। **Under the open sky**—Out of doors; মুক্তাকাশতলে, মুক্তগগন তলে। **Was raised to the skies** — Was exceedingly praised; অতিশয় প্রশংসা করা হইয়াছিল, প্রশংসা করিয়া একবারে আকাশে তুলিয়া দেওয়া হইয়াছিল।

skye-(terrier) (skī-), *n.* See SKY-TERRIER under SKY.

slăb, *n.* & *v. t.* **1.** A thin flat piece of stone or other material; as, a *slab* of stone; পট্ট, পাট, শিলাপট্ট, শিলাফলক। **2.** An outside piece taken from a log in sawing it into boards or planks; কাঠের বাকলা। *Verb t.* **1.** To cut slabs or outside pieces from; শিলাপট্ট প্রভৃতি কর্ত্তন করা, কাঠের বাকলা কাটা। **2.** To cover with slabs; শিলাপট্টরাজিদ্বারা আচ্ছাদিত করা। **Slabbing-gang**—কাঠের বাকলা কাটার জন্য করাতশ্রেণী।

slăb, *adj.* (*Archaic*) Thick and slimy; (অপ্রঃ) আঠালো, চটচটে, পিচ্ছিল।

slăb'-ber (-ẽr), *v. i.* & *n.* Same as SLOBBER (which see).

slăck, *adj.*, *adv.*, *n.*, *v. t.* & *i.* **1.** Not tight or tense; as, a *slack* bandage; loose; as, *slack* cordage; ঢিলা, শ্লথ, শিথিল; আল্‌গা। **2.** Remiss; backward; as, *slack* in duty; not earnest or eager; "Some very great men have effected absolutely nothing not because their labour was *slack* but because their method was sterile"; শিথিল, ঢিলা; পশ্চাৎপদ; জড়, অলস, ঢিমা। **3.** Dull; as, *slack* business; মন্দা (*colloq.*), নরম। **4.** Weak; "From his *slack* hand the garland wreath'd for Eve Down dropped, and all the roses shed not holding tight"; দুর্ব্বল, শক্তিহীন, শিথিল। ***Adv.*** Insufficiently; slowly; as, *slack* dried; অসম্যক্‌রূপে; মৃদুভাবে। ***Noun.*** **1.** The slack part of a rope; রজ্জুর শিথিল অংশ। **2.** A quiet time; মন্দার সময়, মন্দার বাজার। **3.** Remission in work; কর্ম্মবিশ্রান্তি। ***Verb t.*** To relax; to loosen; শিথিল করা, শ্লথ করা; ঢিলা করা। **2.** To relieve; as, to *slacken* cares; উপশম করা। **3.** To abate; to make less intense; as, to *slacken* the heat of a fire; প্রশমিত করা; মন্দীভূত করা। **4.** To retard; প্রতিবন্ধকতা জন্মান, বাধা দেওয়া। ***Verb i.*** **1.** To be remiss or backward; "The kind physician will not *slack* to treat his patient"; ঢিলা হওয়া, শিথিলপ্রযত্ন হওয়া। **2.** To be made less tense, firm or rigid; শিথিল হওয়া, শ্লথ হওয়া, ঢিলা হওয়া। **3.** To abate; to become less violent; প্রশমিত হওয়া, হ্রাসপ্রাপ্ত হওয়া; মন্দীভূত হওয়া। **4.** To languish; to flag; to be indolent; দুর্ব্বল হওয়া; নিস্তেজ হওয়া, শিথিল হওয়া, অবসন্ন হওয়া; আলস্যপরায়ণ হওয়া। **Slack'-en,** *v. t.* & *i.* Same as SLACK. **Slack'-en-ing,** *n.* The act of one who slackens; বিশ্রংসন (বাৎস্যঃ)। **Slack'-ly,** *adv.* **Slack'-ness,** *n.* **Slack-baked**—অসম্যগ্‌ভাবে সেকা; স্রোতোহীন সাগরজলরাশি। **Slack in stays**—মৃদুগামী। **Slack-jaw**—(ইতরভাষায়) চড়া কথা। **Slack-water**—ভাঁটা। **To slack off**—To make less intense; মন্দীভূত করা, প্রশমিত করা। **To slack up**—To reduce the speed of train etc. before stopping; থামাইবার আগে রেলগাড়ী প্রভৃতির গতি কমান।

slăg, *n.* & *v. i.* **1.** Vitrified cinders from smelting furnace etc.; ধাতুমল, ঝামা, মণ্ডুর, খাইদ, লোহার গু (of iron only)। **2.** The scoria from a volcano; আগ্নেয়গিরির মুখ হইতে নিঃসৃত গৈরিক পদার্থ। **3.** Fused dross of metals; খাইদ। ***Verb i.*** **1.** To form slag; to be turned into slag; ধাতুমল গঠিত হওয়া; ধাতুমলে পরিণত হওয়া। **2.** To cohere into slag; সংশ্লিষ্ট হইয়া ধাতুমলে পরিণত হওয়া। **Slag'-gy,** *adj.*

slain (slān), *p. p.* of SLAY (which see).

slāke, *v. t.* **1.** To quench; "Here wild boars and deer *slake* their thirst in small lakes"; to satisfy; নিবৃত্তি করা, নিবারণ করা; চরিতার্থ করা। **2.** To mix with water as lime ; চূণের সহিত জল মিশান। **Slaked lime**—কলিচূণ।

slăm, *v. t., i* & *n.* 1. To shut with violence ; to bang ; ঝনাৎ করিয়া দ্বার প্রভৃতি বন্ধ করা ; সশব্দে বন্ধ করা। 2. To gain all the tricks in card-game ; তাসখেলায় সব পিঠ পাওয়া। ***Verb i.*** (Of doors etc.) To shut or strike against anything with violence and resounding noise ; ঝনাৎ করিয়া বন্ধ হওয়া। ***Noun.*** 1. A violent shutting of a door ; ঝনাৎ শব্দে দ্বার বন্ধ করণ। 2. The gaining of every trick in card-game ; তাসক্রীড়ায় সমস্ত পিঠ প্রাপ্তি।

slăn'-dêr, *n.* & *v. t.* 1. A false tale or report maliciously uttered and tending to injure the reputation of another ; অপবাদ, পরিবাদ, পরীবাদ, মিথ্যানিন্দা, দুর্নাম, অপযশ, কুৎসা, অখ্যাতি গ্লানি, পিশুনবাদ। 2. Defamation ; মানহানি। ***Verb t.*** 1. To injure by maliciously uttering a false report respecting one ; "You *slander* us in this point" ; অপবাদ করা, দুর্নাম করা, পরীবাদ করা। 2. To defame ; মানহানি করা। **—er,** *n.* **—ous,** *adj.* Calumnious ; পরিবাদগর্ভ, পরিবাদাত্মক, গ্লানিসূচক।

slăng, *n., v. t.* & *i.* 1. A class of expression not generally approved of, as being inelegant or undignified ; অবরভাষা, ইতরভাষা, নীচ ভাষা। 2. Cant ; as, racing *slang* ; কোন শ্রেণী বা সম্প্রদায়ের বিশেষভাষা। ***Verb t.*** To use abusive language to ; গালি দেওয়া। ***Verb i.*** To use slang ; অপভাষা প্রয়োগ করা, অবরভাষা প্রয়োগ করা, ইতর ভাষায় গালি দেওয়া।

slăng'-y, *adj.* Of the character of slang ; addicted to the use of slang ; অপভাষাত্মক ; অবরভাষা-প্রয়োগপ্রিয়।

slănt, *v. i., t., adj.* & *n* To slope ; to lie obliquely ; ঢালু হওয়া, প্রবণ হওয়া ; টের্চ্চাভাবে থাকা, হেলানোভাবে থাকা, হেলিয়া থাকা, কা'ৎ হইয়া থাকা। ***Verb t.*** To give a sloping or oblique direction to ; হেলান, টের্চ্চা করিয়া রাখা, কা'ত করিয়া রাখা, তির্য্যগ্‌ভাবে রাখা। ***Adj.*** Sloping ; oblique ; inclined from a direct line ; ঢালু, প্রবণ ; বক্র, তির্য্যক্ ; টের্চ্চা, হেলানিয়া, হেলানো, গড়ানিয়া, কা'ৎ, গড়ানো। ***Noun.*** 1. Slope ; oblique position ; ঢালু, প্রবণতা ; টের্চ্চাভাব, গড়ানিয়া ভাব, হেলানিয়া ভাব। 2. (*Colloq.*) Taunt ; "Whitwell felt an ironical *slant* in the words" ; বক্রোক্তি, ব্যঙ্গ। 3. (*Slang*) Opportunity ; as, the very first *slant* I had ; (ইতরভাষায়) সুযোগ। **Slant'-ing-ly,** *adv.* In a slanting manner ; কা'তভাবে, টের্চ্চাভাবে, হেলানো-ভাবে। **A slant of wind**—সুবাতাস, অনুকূল বায়ু।

slănt, *n.* A slight breeze or spell of wind; দমকা বাতাস।

slăp, *v. t., n.* & *adv.* 1. To strike with open hand; চড় মারা, চপেটাঘাত করা, চাপড় মারা, চট্‌কনা দেওয়া। 2. To rebuff ; মুখ ঝামটা দেওয়া। 3. To put with violence ; as, to *slap* one into jail ; to insult ; জোর করিয়া রাখা, পোরা ; অপমান করা। ***Noun.*** 1. A blow given with the open hand ; as, she gave her repeated *slaps* and blows" ; চড়, চাপড়, চট্‌কনা। 2. A gust of wind ; "A *slap* of wind carried nigh half the mast over the side" ; বাতাসের ঝাপটা। 3. Reproof ; rebuff ; insult ; তিরস্কার, ভৎর্সনা ; ধাক্কা ; অপমান। 4. Venture ; attempt ; সঙ্কটজনক কার্য্য ; চেষ্টা। ***Adv.*** With a sudden and violent blow ; plump ; পটাৎ করিয়া ; ধপ করিয়া, ধপাৎ করিয়া, ধুপ করিয়া। **Slap-bang**—সজোরে, হুড়মুড় করিয়া, উদ্দামবেগে, হুমড়ি খেয়ে। **Slap-dash**—প্রচণ্ডভাবে, দিগ্‌বিদিক্ শূন্যভাবে। (*Adj.*) প্রচণ্ড যদৃচ্ছগতি ; দৃক্‌পাতশূন্য, দিগ্‌বিদিগ্‌জ্ঞান-শূন্য। (*Noun.*) ঐরূপ কার্য্য। **Slap-up**—(ইতরভাষায়) সেরা, উৎকৃষ্ট ; হাল ফ্যাসনের। **At a slap**—At a time ; একবারে, এক সঙ্গে।

slăsh *v. t., i.* & *n.* 1. To cut by striking violently and at random ; যদৃচ্ছাক্রমে কোপান। 2. To cut with long incision ; হাসান। 3. To lash ; বেত্রাঘাত করা, কষাঘাত করা। 4. (*Mil.*) To fell trees ; (সামরিক-শাস্ত্র) গাছ কাটা, বৃক্ষ ছেদন করা। ***Verb i.*** To strike violently and at random with an edged instrument; ধারাল অস্ত্রদ্বারা যদৃচ্ছাক্রমে কোপান। ***Noun.*** 1. A long cut ; a cut given at random ; a wound made by a slashing cut ; লম্বা কাটা; যদৃচ্ছাক্রমিক কোপ ; হাসাইয়া কাটার দরুণ ক্ষত। 2. A large slit in the thigh and arms of old dresses ; প্রাচীনকালের পরিচ্ছদের উরু ও ভুজের নিম্নাংশে সুদীর্ঘ ছেদ।

slăsh, *v. i.* & *n.* To work in wet ; বৃষ্টিতে কায করা। ***Noun.*** A large quantity of watery food ; বহু পরিমাণ জলীয় খাদ্য। **Slash'-y,** *adj.* Dirty and muddy ; সেঁতসেঁতে।

slăt, *n.* A narrow slip of wood as in a venetian blind ; ঝিলমিলি।

slate, *n.* & *v. t.* 1. A rock which splits into thin plates ; শ্লেট পাথর। 2. A slab of slate stone for covering building ; ছাদের উপর দিবার শ্লেট পাথরের টালি। 3. A tablet for writing upon ; শ্লেট, লিখিবার জন্য শিলাফলক। ***Verb t.*** 1. To cover with slates ; শ্লেট পাথরের টালি দ্বারা ছাওয়া। 2. To put down one's name on a slate ; "He was *slated* for a month—that is his name was entered upon a slate in the porter's lodge which indicated that he was dangerosuly ill" ; কাহারো নাম শ্লেটে লিখা।

Slat'-er, *n.* Slat'-y, *adj.* **Slate club**—হিতসাধিনী সমিতিবিশেষ, যাহার সভ্যগণ্যকে প্রতি সপ্তাহে কিছু কিছু চাঁদা দিতে এবং পরস্পরকে সাহায্য করিতে হয়। **Slate-gray** — শ্লেট পাথরের মত ধূসরবর্ণ। **To clean the slate**—To renounce obligation ; বাধ্য-বাধকতাভাব পরিহার করা।

slāte, *v. t.* **1.** To thrash severely ; আচ্ছা করিয়া বেতান। **2.** (*Colloq.*) To criticise severely ; "When he wants to *slate* a good novel" ; to scold ; (চলিতভাষায়) তীব্র সমালোচনা করা, কঠোর সমালোচনা করা ; তিরস্কার করা। Slat'-ing, *n.*

slāte, *v. t.* To set on a dog ; I will *slate* my dog against thine; কুকুরকে লেলাইয়া দেওয়া।

slăt'-tern (-têrn), *n.* A woman who is negligent of her dress, or who suffers her clothes or furniture to be in disorder ; "The young girls were twadry *slatterns*" ; অপরিচ্ছন্না নারী, নোংরা স্ত্রীলোক। **—li-ness,** *n.* **—ly,** *adj.*

slaugh'-têr (slä-) *n.* & *v. t.* The act of slaying or killing ; massacre ; বধ, বিনাশ, হত্যা ; হত্যাকাণ্ড। ***Verb t.*** **1.** To kill ; to kill in masses ; বধ করা, হত্যা করা ; একসঙ্গে বহু লোক হত্যা করা। **2.** To kill for food ; to butcher ; আহারের জন্য বধ করা ; কাটা, জবাই করা। **—er,** *n.* One who slaughters ; a butcher ; হত্যাকারী ; কসাই। **Slaughter-house** — জবাইখানা, ঘাতনস্থান, আঘাত (মুচ্ছঃ কঃ), ঘাতস্থান। **Slaughter or massacre of the innocents**—শিশুমেধযজ্ঞ (বিশ্ববিদ্যালয়ের কর্তৃপক্ষগণ বহুসংখক পরীক্ষার্থীকে অনুত্তীর্ণ করিলে এই বাক্যের প্রয়োগ করা হয়)।

Slăv, *n.* & *adj.* One of a race of Eastern Europe, comprising the Russians, Poles, Bohemians, Bulgarians, etc. ; রুশ, পোল, বোহেমিয়ান, বুলগেরিয়ান, প্রভৃতি ইয়ুরোপের পূর্ব্ব অঞ্চলের অধিবাসী, শ্লেভ। ***Adj.*** Of the Slavs ; শ্লেভজাতি-সম্পর্কীয়, শ্লেভজাতীয়।

slāve, *n.* & *v. i.* **1.** A bond-servant ; ক্রীতদাস, গোলাম, নফর, চিরদাস। **2.** A drudge ; হীনকার্য্যে নিযুক্ত ব্যক্তি। **3.** A person wholly subject to the will of another ; one who has surrendered himself to any influence ; as, he is *slave* of passion : a *slave* to senses ; অপর ব্যক্তির ইচ্ছার সম্পূর্ণ বশীভূত ব্যক্তি; কোন প্রভাবের সম্পূর্ণ অধীন ব্যক্তি। ***Verb i.*** To work like a slave ; ক্রীতদাসের মত কাজ করা। **Slave-born**—জন্মদাস। **Slave-driver**—কার্য্যে নিযুক্ত ক্রীতদাসগণের পরিদর্শক ; কঠোর কার্য্যপরিদর্শক। **Slave-grown**—ক্রীতদাসগণের শ্রমপ্রসূত। **Slave-holder** — ক্রীতদাসগণের মালীক। **Slave-hunter** — বিক্রয়ার্থ কাফ্রী ক্রীতদাস সংগ্রহকার্য্যে নিযুক্ত ব্যক্তি। **Slave-labour**—গোলামের মেহনত (হিঃ কোঃ), দাসশ্রম। **Slave-ship**—দাসব্যবসায়ের কার্য্যে নিযুক্ত পোত। **Slave-States** — উত্তর আমেরিকার দক্ষিণাংশের রাষ্ট্রসমূহ—যথায় অন্তর্বিগ্রহের পূর্ব্বে দাসত্বপ্রথা প্রচলিত ছিল। **Slave-trade** — দাসব্যবসায়। **Slave-trader**—দাসব্যবসায়ী।

slāv'-êr, *n.* **1.** One who is engaged in slave-trade ; দাসব্যবসায়ে নিযুক্ত ব্যক্তি। **2.** A vessel engaged in slave-trade ; দাস ব্যবসায়ে নিযুক্ত পোত।

slăv'-êr, *v. i., t.* & *n.* **1.** To suffer the spittle to issue from the mouth ; লালা পড়া, লালা নিঃসৃত হওয়া। **2.** To fondle ; "He thought of his uncle how he had snubbed and then *slavered* over him" ; আদর করা, সোহাগ করা। **3.** To be besmeared with saliva ; নিষ্ঠীবনসিক্ত হওয়া, লালাসিক্ত হওয়া। ***Verb t.*** **1.** To smear with saliva ; নিষ্ঠীবনসিক্ত করা, লালাসিক্ত করা। **2.** (*Fig.*) To fondle ; "She wondered Mr. Runnington was not ashamed to be *slavering* such a girl" ; to flatter in a sycophantic manner ; (লক্ষণায়) অতিশয় আদর বা সোহাগ করা ; হীনচাটুকারিতা করা, পদলেহন করা। ***Noun.*** **1.** Saliva drivelling from the mouth ; মুখ-নিঃসৃত লালা। **2.** Fulsome flattery ; "A modest man to whom such *slaver* must be loathsome" ; nonsense ; "Some person may look upon this correspondence as a lot of squit and *slaver*" ; হীন চাটুকারিতা, পদলেহন ; অসার কথা। **—er,** *n.* A driveller ; an idiot ; যাহার মুখ হইতে অনবরত লালাস্রাব হয় ; জড়বুদ্ধি। **—y,** *adj.* Fondling ; fawing ; আদরপূর্ণ, সোহাগপূর্ণ ; পদলেহনকারী, পা-চাটা।

slāv'-êr-ȳ, *n.* **1.** Condition of a slave ; ক্রীতদাসত্ব, দাস্য, দাসত্ব, দাস্যবৃত্তি, গোলামী। **2.** Drudgery ; হাড়ভাঙ্গা খাটুনি। **3.** The institution of slave-holding ; দাসত্বপ্রথা। **Abolition of slavery** — দাসত্বপ্রথার বিলোপ।

slāv'-ey (-ĭ), *n.* (*Colloq.*) A maid-servant ; ঝি, দাসী, চাকরাণী।

Slăv'-ic, *adj.* & *n.* Same as SLAVONIC (which see).

slāv'-ish, *adj.* **1.** Pertaining to slaves ; ক্রীতদাসসম্বন্ধীয়। **2.** Servile ; mean ; as, *slavish* dependance ; দাসোচিৎ, দাসবৎ ; হীন, হেয়, নীচ। **—ness,** *n.*

slāv-ŏc'-rā-cȳ, *n.* A collective name for slave-owners ; ক্রীতদাসের প্রভুসম্প্রদায়, প্রভুতন্ত্র। **Slav'-o-crat,** *n.*

Slă-vō'-ni-ăn, *adj.* & *n.* Of the Slav race; শ্লেভজাতীয়। ***Noun.*** **1.** A member of the Slav race; শ্লেভজাতি-সমূহের লোক। **2.** The language of the Slavs ; শ্লেভজাতিসমূহের ভাষা।

Slă'-vŏn-ic, *adj.* & *n.* Pertaining to the Slavs or their language ; শ্লেভজাতি-সম্পর্কীয়, শ্লেভজাতিসমূহের

ভাষাসম্পর্কীয়। *Noun.* The language of the Slavs; শ্লেভজাতিসমূহের ভাষা।

Slăv′-ō-phile, -phil, *ns.* A lover of Slavs, their arts or institution; শ্লেভানুরাগী, শ্লেভদিগের শিল্পকলা বা প্রতিষ্ঠান সমূহের প্রতি অনুরাগবান ব্যক্তি।

Slă-vŏph′-ō-bist, *n.* One who dreads or dislikes the Slavs; শ্লেভাতঙ্কগ্রস্ত ব্যক্তি, শ্লেভবিদ্বেষী।

slay (slā), *v. t.* To kill; বধ করা, বিনাশ করা, সংহার করা, নিহত করা, নিধন করা, হত্যা করা। **Slay′-er,** *n.*

slea′-zy̆ (slē-), *adj.* Thin; wanting firmness of texture or substance; "Their one *sleazy* skirt giving little protection against the keen air"; পাতলা; পাতলা জমিনের।

slĕd, sledge (slĕj), **sleigh** (slā), *n., v. t.* & *i.* A carriage or vehicle, moved on runners for transporting loads over snow; বরফের উপর

Russian sledge.

চালাইবার জন্য একপ্রকার চক্রহীন শকট, তুষারযান, তুষারশকট। *Verb t.* To convey or transport on a sledge; তুষারযানোপরি বহন করা। *Verb i.* To ride or travel on a sledge; তুষারযানে আরোহণ করা, তুষারযানে ভ্রমণ করা। [আজকাল Sledge শব্দই সচরাচর "তুষারযান" অর্থে ব্যবহৃত হয়।]

sledge (slĕj), **sledge′-hăm-mēr** (slĕj-), *ns.* A large heavy hammer used chiefly by iron-smiths; as, *sledge-hammer* blows; কর্ম্মকারদিগের একপ্রকার বৃহৎ হাতুড়ী।

sleek (slēk), *adj.* & *v. t.* Smooth and glossy; as, a *sleek* or glossy skin; মসৃণ, স্নিগ্ধ, চিক্কণ, চিকণ (cf. চিকণ কালা)। *Verb t.* To make sleek; চিক্কণ করা, মসৃণ করা। **Sleek′-ly,** *adj.* **Sleek′-ness,** *n.* The quality of being sleek; চিক্কণতা, স্নৈগ্ধ্য, মসৃণতা।

sleep (slēp), *n.* The state of the body in which the voluntary exercise of the powers of body and mind is suspended; নিদ্রা, ঘুম, শয়ন [Syn. সুপ্তি, স্বাপ (ব্রজঃ হিন্দু); সংবেশ।] 2. (*Fig.*) Rest; repose; "The deep *sleep* of the landscape"; quiet; death; "They slept the *sleep* from which they shall not awake until the judgment day"; (লক্ষণায়) বিশ্রাম; বিশ্রান্তি, বিরাম; শান্তি, নিস্তব্ধতা; মৃত্যু, মহানিদ্রা, অনন্তনিদ্রা। **Sleep′-less,** *adj.* Without sleep; বিনিদ্র, নিদ্রাহীন, নিদ্রাশূন্য। **Sleep′-less-ly,** *adv.* **Sleep′-less-ness,** *n.* The state of being sleepless; নিদ্রাভাব, অনিদ্রা। **Sleep-walker**—স্বপ্নাটনকারী, যে ব্যক্তি নিদ্রিতাবস্থায় ইতস্ততঃ ভ্রমণ করে, স্বপ্নচর (হিঃ কোঃ), স্বপ্নসঞ্চরণকারী। **Sleep-walking**—স্বপ্নাটন, স্বপ্নসঞ্চরণ। **Anatomy of sleep**—নিদ্রার বিশ্লেষতত্ত্ব। **Dreamless sleep**—সুষুপ্তি (ব্রজঃ হিন্দু)। **Sleep that knows no breaking**—অনন্তনিদ্রা, মৃত্যু। **The sleep of the just**—সুনিদ্রা। **To go to sleep**—To fall asleep; নিদ্রা যাওয়া। To die; অনন্তনিদ্রায় শায়িত হওয়া।

sleep (slēp), *v. i.* & *t.* 1. To take rest by the suspension of the voluntary exercise of the bodily and mental powers; নিদ্রা যাওয়া, ঘুমান, শায়িত হওয়া। 2. To be careless or inattentive; "We *sleep* over our happiness"; দৃকপাতশূন্য হওয়া, ভাবনাশূন্য হওয়া, অমনোযোগী হওয়া। 3. To be dead; মৃত হওয়া। 4. To cohabit; as to *sleep* with another man's wife; সহবাস করা। 5. To be inactive or dormant; as, anger *sleeps*; সুপ্ত থাকা, নিষ্ক্রিয় থাকা, প্রচ্ছন্ন থাকা। *Verb t.* 1. To pass in sleeping; to get rid of by sleep; as, to *sleep* the pain off; নিদ্রায় কাটান, নিদ্রায় যাপন করা; ঘুমাইয়া নিস্তার পাওয়া। 2. (*Colloq.*) To furnish sleeping accommodation; (চলিতভাষায়) শয়নের স্থান প্রদান করা, ঘুমাইবার যায়গা দেওয়া। **Sleep′-ing,** *adj.* In a state of sleep; drowsy; ঘুমন্ত, শয়ান; নিদ্রালু। **Sleeping-bag**—মুক্তস্থানে নিদ্রা যাওয়ার জন্য একপ্রকার থলিয়া। **Sleeping-car, Sleeping-carriage** — শয্যাসমন্বিতবাষ্পীয়শকট। **Sleeping-draught** — অহিফেনাদি-গঠিত নিদ্রাজনক ঔষধ। **Sleeping-partner**—See PARTNER. **Sleeping sickness**—পশ্চিম আফ্রিকাদেশের রোগবিশেষ। [এই রোগে তন্দ্রা, শিরোবেদনা, শরীরের ক্ষীণতা প্রভৃতি জন্মে।] **Sleeping-suit**—শয়নকালে ব্যবহৃত পোষাক, শয়নবাস (ইয়ুরোপ-বাসীরা সচরাচর শয়নকালে ঢিলা পাজামা ও খাটো কোর্ত্তা পরিয়া থাকেন।) **Let the sleeping dogs lie**—Do not mention an unpleasant event; অপ্রীতিজনক ঘটনার উল্লেখ করিওনা। **The top sleeps**—It moves with such velocity and spins so smoothly, that its motion is imperceptible; লাটিমটী এরূপ দ্রুতভাবে এবং অবলীলাক্রমে ঘূর্ণিত হইতেছে—যেন বোধ হয় উহা এক স্থানেই স্থির রহিয়াছে। **To sleep away**—To get rid of by sleep; ঘুমাইয়া কাটান। **To sleep like a top**—To sleep soundly; গভীর নিদ্রা যাওয়া। **To sleep off**—To remove the effects of sleeping; "In the morning after he had *slept* his wine *off* he was very gay"; ঘুমাইয়া কোনরূপ কষ্ট বা যন্ত্রণার দায় হইতে রক্ষা পওয়া। **To sleep on, upon** or **over a question**—To defer its decision till to-morrow morning; "Colonel Goring *slept upon* his problem and woke the next morning resolute"; পরদিবস প্রভাত পর্য্যন্ত কোন বিষয়ের মীমাংসা স্থগিত রাখা। **To sleep one's last sleep**—To die; অনন্তনিদ্রায় নিদ্রিত হওয়া। **To sleep the clock round**—To sleep for twelve or twenty-four hours; বারো কি চব্বিশ ঘণ্টা ঘুমান। **To sleep upon anything**—To postpone taking any steps until next morning; পরদিন প্রভাত পর্য্যন্ত কোন কার্য্য স্থগিত রাখা।

sleep'-êr (slēp-), *n.* 1. One who sleeps; নিদ্রাকারী। 2. A wooden beam used as a support of rails etc.; যে কাষ্ঠ প্রভৃতি ফলকের উপর রেল প্রভৃতি পাতা হয়। 3. Same as SLEEPING-CAR.

sleep'-ў (slēp-), *adj.* 1. Drowsy; soporiferous; lazy; sluggish; তন্দ্রাবিষ্ট, নিদ্রালু; নিদ্রাজনক; অলস, জড়; ঢিমা। 2. Without bustle; as, a *sleepy* little town; নীরব, নিঝুম, নিস্তব্ধ। 3. Overdried; as, *sleepy* pear; beginning to rot; অতিরিক্ত শুষ্কীকৃত; অতিরিক্ত পক্কতা হেতু পচনোন্মুখ। **—i-ness,** *n.* The state of being sleepy; নিদ্রালুতা, সুপ্তা, সুপ্তি, সুপ্তত্ব। **Sleepy-cream**—ফেনার মত অবস্থা প্রাপ্ত সর। **Sleepy-headed** — নিদ্রালস ব্যক্তি, নিদ্রাতুর ব্যক্তি, তন্দ্রালস ব্যক্তি।

sleet (slēt), *n.* & *v. i.* Hail or snow falling mixed with rain and usually in fine particles; শিলাবৃষ্টি, তুষারকণা মিশ্রিত বৃষ্টি, হিমকণ (সাঃ পঃ), তুষারবর্ষ (হিঃ কোঃ)। ***Verb i.*** To snow or hail with a mixture of rain; শিলাবৃষ্টি হওয়া, তুষারকণার সহিত বৃষ্টি হওয়া। **Sleet'-i-ness,** *n.* **Sleet'-y,** *adj.*

sleeve (slēv), *n.* 1. The part of a garment that is fitted to cover the arm; আস্তীন, পোষাকের হাতা। 2. (*Rare*) A channel of water; (কচিদ্‌ব্যবহৃত) প্রণালী। 3. A tube surmounting a rod or another tube; যে নালী অপর নালী বা দণ্ডে প্রবিষ্ট করা হয়। **Sleeve'-less,** *adj.* Without sleeve; আস্তীনবিহীন, হাতকাটা। **Sleeve-buttons**—হাতের বোতাম। **Sleeve-fish** — একপ্রকার সমুদ্রজিত মৎস্য। **Sleeve-links**—জামার হাতায় একত্রগ্রথিত বোতামদ্বয়। **To laugh in one's sleeve**—To laugh privately or unperceived; "He had a dim impression that we might be *laughing in our sleeves*"; মুখ লুকাইয়া হাসা, গোপনে হাসা, অলক্ষিতে হাসা। **To have a card, plan etc. up one's sleeve**—To have it concealed; তাস প্রভৃতি গোপনে রাখা।

Sleigh.

sleigh (slā), *n.* Same as SLED.

sleight (slēt), *n.* Dexterity; চালাকি, কৌশল, চতুরতা, পটুতা। **Sleight of hand** — হাতের কৌশল, হাতের চালাকী, করকৌশল, হস্তলাঘব।

slĕn'-dêr, *adj.* 1. Slim; thin; কাহিল, ছিপছিপে; কৃশ, তন্বী (of woman), ক্ষীণ, সুভণ (চঃ)। 2. Moderate; trivial; সামান্য; নগণ্য। 3. Small; as, *slender* means; স্বল্প, অল্প, সামান্য। **—ly,** *adv.* **—ness,** *n.*

slĕpt, *p. p.* of SLEEP (which see).

slĕuth'-hound (slōth-hownd), *n.* A blood-hound; ডালকুত্তা।

slew (slū), **slue** (slū), *v. t.* To swing round; ঘুরান, পাকান।

slew (slū), *p.t.* of SLAY (which see).

slīce, *n., v. t.* & *i.* 1. A thin broad piece cut off; as, a *slice* of bread; ফালি, টুকরা। 2. That which is thin and broad, like a slice; চোকলা, ছিল্‌কা। 3. A broad thin piece of plaster; চুণ বালির পাতল এবং চৌড়া আস্তর। 4. A part; as, the *slice* of a town; অংশ, ভাগ। 5. (*Obs.*) A spatula; (অপ্রঃ) পলস্তরাদি প্রসারিত করিবার ও মলম প্রভৃতি নাড়িবার জন্য স্থূলমুখ প্রশস্ত ছুরিকার ন্যায় অস্ত্রবিশেষ। 6. A broad thin knife for taking up or serving fish; মাছ উঠাইবার জন্য বা পরিবেষণ করার জন্য একপ্রকার পাতলা ও চৌড়া ছুরি। 7. A trowel-like implement for turning up meat etc. when cooking in a pan; কটাহের মাংস প্রভৃতি উল্টাইবার জন্য রাজমিস্ত্রীদিগের কুনির আকার একপ্রকার ছেনি। 8. A spade-shaped tool used for cutting blubber form a whale; তিমিমাছের চর্ব্বি ছাড়াইবার জন্য একপ্রকার কোদালীর মত যন্ত্র। 9. A kind of implement with thin broad blade for clearing furnace bars of clinker; চুল্লীর শিকে সঞ্চিত ধাতুমল পরিষ্কার করার জন্য যন্ত্রবিশেষ। ***Verb t.*** 1. To cut into thin pieces or to cut off in thin broad pieces; ছিলকা ছিলকা করিয়া কাটা, ফালিফালি করিয়া কাটা, ছিলকা কাটিয়া নেওয়া। 2. To cut into parts; to divide; টুকরা টুকরা করিয়া কাটা; বিভাগ করা। 3. To clean by means of slice-bar; চুল্লীমার্জ্জকদ্বারা পরিষ্কার করা। ***Verb i.*** To cut cleanly or easily; পরিষ্কার করিয়া কাটা, সহজে কাটা। **Slic'-er,** *n.* **Slice-bar**—Same as SLICE, 9.

slick, *adj.* & *adv.* **1.** (*Slang*) Deft ; (চলিতভাষায়) চতুর, নিপুণ, কুশল। **2.** Excellent ; সেরা, চমৎকার, খাসা। **3.** Mere ; কেবল, শুদ্ধ। **4.** (*Dial.*) Sleek ; (উপভাষায়) মসৃণ, চিক্কণ। ***Adv.*** **1.** Exactly ; ঠিক। **2.** Deftly ; "They manage things there so *slick* that the college saves annually three thousand dollors"; নিপুণ ভাবে, চাতুর্য্যের সহিত।

slīde, *v. i.* & *t.* **1.** To move along the surface of anything by slipping ; পিছলাইয়া যাওয়া, গড়াইয়া যাওয়া, হড়কাইয়া যাওয়া, বিসর্পিত হওয়া। **2.** To move over the surface of the snow or ice with a smooth or uninterrupted motion ; বরফের উপর দিয়া গড়াইয়া যাওয়া। **3.** To pass unobserved ; to go quietly or secretly ; অলক্ষিতে চলিয়া যাওয়া ; চুপেচুপে সরিয়া পড়া, গোপনে সরিয়া পড়া। **4.** To move gently onward ; as, the boat *slides* through water ; ধীরে ধীরে অগ্রসর হওয়া ; মন্দমন্দ গতিতে অগ্রসর হওয়া। ***Verb t.*** To thrust smoothly along ; to thrust or push forward by slipping ; as, to *slide* along a log or piece of timber ; অনায়াসে সম্মুখের দিকে ঠেলিয়া দেওয়া ; পিছলাইয়া ঠেলিয়া দেওয়া। **Slid′-a-ble,** *adj.* **Slid′-er,** *n.* **Slid′-ing,** *adj.* & *n.* **Sliding-door, Slide-door**—যে দর্জ্জা খুলিবার সময় ফাঁকের ভিতর ঠেলিয়া দেওয়া যায়, অপসর্পী দ্বার। **Sliding-scale** — কর, শুল্ক প্রভৃতি মূল্যের হ্রাসবৃদ্ধির অনুপাতে হ্রাস এবং বৃদ্ধির হারবিশেষ ; শ্রমিকদিগের বেতনের হার বিশেষ — যাহাতে বেতন উৎপন্ন দ্রব্যের বিক্রেয় মূল্যের উপর নির্ভর করে। **Sliding-rule** (also **Sliding-scale)**—একপ্রকার ক্রমাঙ্কিত মানদণ্ড ইহাতে দুইটী ক্রমাঙ্কিত দণ্ড আছে—ইহার একটী অপরটীর উপর সংসর্পিত হয় এবং এরূপ বন্দোবস্ত থাকে যে খণ্ডদ্বয় যথাযথ ভাবে পরস্পরের সহিত সংশ্লিষ্ট করা হইলে কেবলমাত্র পরিদর্শনদ্বারা ইষ্টফল প্রাপ্ত হওয়া যায়। **Sliding-seat**—বাইচের সময় ব্যবহৃত একপ্রকার আসন—যাহা পর্য্যায়ক্রমে অগ্রে পশ্চাতে চালিত হওয়ায় দীর্ঘ দাঁড়ক্ষেপ করা যাইতে পারে। **To let things slide**—To be negligent ; অবহেলা করা।

slīde, *n.* **1.** Act of sliding ; গড়াইয়া চলন। **2.** (*Rare*) A smooth and easy passage ; (ক্বচিদ্‌ব্যবহৃত) সহজ পথ, সুগম পথ। **3.** A slope prepared of ice to slide on ; গড়াইয়া চলার জন্য বরফাবৃত প্রবণভূমি। **4.** The fall of a mass of earth or rock down a hill or mountain-side ; পর্ব্বতগাত্র হইতে পাষাণ বা মৃত্তিকা-রাশির স্খলন। **5.** An inclined plane for sending down heavy bodies ; গুরুভার দ্রব্য গড়াইয়া নীচে ফেলিবার জন্য প্রবণ ভূমি। **6.** The glass on which microscopic object is mounted ; the pictures shown by the stereoscope, magic lantern, etc. ; অণুবীক্ষণ প্রভৃতি দ্বারা পরীক্ষণীয় বস্তু যে কাচখণ্ডের উপর রক্ষিত হয় ; ঘনচিত্র-দর্শক, যাদুলণ্ঠন প্রভৃতির চিত্র যে কাচখণ্ড প্রভৃতির উপর চিত্রিত থাকে। **7.** The part of a machine or instrument that slides ; কোন কল বা যন্ত্রের যে অংশ সংসর্পিত হয়। **8.** A sliding piece that opens and closes an aperture ; যে সংসর্পিত কোন কিছু দ্বারা কোন ছিদ্র বন্ধ করা কিম্বা খোলা হয়। **9.** (*Mus.*) An embellishment of two notes sliding into each other ; (সঙ্গীত-শাস্ত্র) ঘর্ষণ (মিউজিক)।

slight (slīt), *n.* **1.** Slender ; কাহিল, কৃশ, ছিপছিপে। **2.** Small ; trifling ; ক্ষুদ্র, সামান্য ; যৎসামান্য, এতটুকু (*colloq.*—সে এতটুকুও হাঁপায় নাই), তুচ্ছ। **3.** Not severe or violent ; as, *slight* pain ; সামান্য, অল্প। **4.** Not firm or enduring ; as, a *slight* structure ; অদৃঢ়, অচিরস্থায়ী। **Slight′-ish,** *adj.* **Slight′-ly,** *adv.* **Slight′-ness,** *n.*

slight (slīt), *v. t.* & *n.* To neglect to disregard ; তাচ্ছিল্য করা অবহেলা করা, অনাদর করা, উপেক্ষা করা। ***Noun.*** A moderate degree of contempt, manifested by neglect ; উপেক্ষা, অনাদর, অবহেলা, তাচ্ছিল্য। **Slight′-ing-ly,** *adv.* **To put a slight upon**—To slight ; তাচ্ছিল্য করা।

slī′-ly̆, *adv.* See SLYLY.

slĭm, *adj.* **1.** Slender ; কাহিল, ছিপছিপে। **2.** Frail ; slight ; as, a *slim* chance ; দুর্ব্বল ; সামান্য, অল্প। **3.** (S. Africa) Crafty ; (দক্ষিণ আফ্রিকায়) ধূর্ত্ত, চালাক, ফন্দীবাজ। **Slim′-ly,** *adv.* **Slim′-mish,** *adj.* **Slim′-ness,** *n.*

slīme, *n., v. t.* & *i.* A soft, moist earth or clay having an adhesive quality ; কাদা, কর্দ্দম। **2.** Any dirty substance that is soft, moist and adhesive ; আঠালো জিনিষ, কাদাটে জিনিষ। **3.** A mucous viscous substance exuded from the bodies of certain animals ; মৎস্যাদির শরীর হইতে নিঃসৃত লালাবৎ পদার্থ, ক্লেদ, বিজল। ***Verb t.*** **1.** To cover with slime ; to make slimy ; ক্লেদাবৃত করা ; ক্লেদাক্ত করা। **2.** To remove slime from fish ; মৎস্যের ক্লেদ দূর করা (টিনে পুরিবার আগে)। **3.** To make one's way in a slimy fashion ; ঘৃণ্যভাবে অগ্রসর হওয়া। ***Verb i.*** To become slimy ; ক্লেদাক্ত হওয়া।

slīm′-y̆, *adj.* **1.** Viscous ; আঠালো, ক্লেদাক্ত, চটচটে, পিচ্ছিল। **2.** Covered with slime ; ক্লেদাক্ত। **3.** Morally defiled ; vile ; "I'll spoil his beauty, the *slimy* little liar" ; কলুষিত ; ঘৃণিত হেয়, জঘন্য।

slĭng, *v. t., i.* & *n.* **1.** To throw with a sling ; ফিঙ্গা দ্বারা নিক্ষেপ করা। **2.** To throw ; to hurl ; নিক্ষেপ কর ; ছোড়া। **3.** To hang ; ঝুলান। **4.** To put in ropes or suspend, as a cask, gun or the like ; রজ্জুর মধ্যে রাখা, পিপা, বন্দুক, প্রভৃতি ঝুলাইয়া রাখা। 5. To place in slings in order to hoist or lower ; কোন জিনিষ উঠান বা নামানের জন্য উহা রজ্জুর বন্ধনীতে স্থাপন করা। *Verb i.* 1. To be slung ; ফিঙ্গার দ্বারা নিক্ষিপ্ত হওয়া। 2. To move along with swinging steps ; to move with speed ; লাফাইয়া চলা ; সবেগে চলা। *Noun.* 1. An instrument for throwing stones ; ফিঙ্গা। 2. A bandage to support a wounded limb ; ভাঙ্গা হাত প্রভৃতি ঝুলাইয়া রাখার জন্য বন্ধনীবিশেষ। 3. A rope for raising or lowering heavy articles ; গুরুভার দ্রব্য উত্তোলন বা অবতারণের জন্য রজ্জু। **Sling-cart**—কামান প্রভৃতি বহনের জন্য শকট। এইপ্রকার শকটের চাকার আলে বাঁধা রজ্জুতে কামানাদি ঝুলাইয়া রাখা যায়। **Sling-dog**—মাল তোলার জন্য রজ্জুতে সংবদ্ধ আঁকড়াদ্বয়ের অন্যতর। **Sling-the-monkey**—একপ্রকার ক্রীড়া। **Slung-shot**—রজ্জু প্রভৃতি দ্বারা মণিবন্ধে সংবদ্ধ (প্রধানতঃ যুক্তরাজ্যে ব্যবহৃত) ধাতব গোলক—যাহা অস্ত্রস্বরূপ ব্যবহৃত হইয়া থাকে। **To sling ink**—(*Slang*) সম্পাদকতা করা, প্রবন্ধ প্রভৃতি লিখা। **To sling one's Daniel or hook**—(*Colloq.*) To make off ; (চলিত ভাষায়) চম্পট দেওয়া, পিট্টান দেওয়া।

sling, *n.* (*Chiefly U. S.*) A drink of equal parts of rum, gin, or spirit and water sweetened ; একপ্রকার আসব।

slink (slingk), *v. i.* To sneak ; to creep away meanly ; চুপি চুপি সরিয়া পড়া ; হীনভাবে, গুড়িসুড়ি মারিয়া সরিয়া পড়া।

slink (slingk) *v. t., i. & n.* To cast prematurely as a calf ; অসময়ে শাবক প্রসব করা, গর্ভপাত করা। *Verb i.* (Of animals) To miscarry ; (পশু সম্পর্কে) গর্ভপাত হওয়া, গাবরা ফেলা (*dial.*), বস্ পড়া (*dial.*)। *Noun.* Animal, esp. calf, so born ; its flesh ; অসময়ে প্রসূত শাবক ; ঐরূপ শাবকের মাংস।

slip, *v. i. & t.* 1. To slide or glide along ; পিছলাইয়া চলা, গড়াইয়া চলা। 2. To move out of place ; পিছলাইয়া পড়া, পদস্খলন হওয়া, হড়কান। 3. To pass unobserved or quickly ; as, time *slipped* by ; অলক্ষিতে চলিয়া যাওয়া, সরিয়া পড়া, দ্রুত অতিক্রম করা। 4. To pass unexpectedly or imperceptibly ; অপ্রত্যাশিত ভাবে বা অজ্ঞাতসারে অতিক্রম করা। 5. To enter by oversight ; as, some mistakes may have *slipped* into ; অনবধানতাবশতঃ ভুক্ত করা। 6. To commit some fault ; to err ; পদস্খলন হওয়া ; ভুল করা, ভুল চুক করা। *Verb t.* 1. To cause to slip ; to convey secretly ; to put quickly ; as, to *slip* a cartridge into a gun ; পিছলান, পদস্খলিত করা ; গোপনে প্রেরণ করা ; তাড়াতাড়ি ভরা। 2. To lose by negligence ; as, to *slip* an opportunity ; অবহেলা বশতঃ হারান। 3. To throw off ; as, the horse *slipped* his bridle ; হড়কাইয়া ফেলা। 4. (Of beasts) To make abortion ; (পশুসম্পর্কে) অকালে প্রসব করা, গর্ভপাত হওয়া। 5. (*Slang*) To let loose, as in pursuit of game ; as, to *slip* a hound ; ছাড়িয়া দেওয়া, বন্ধনমুক্ত করা। **To give the slip**—To avoid ; পাশ কাটান। **To let slip the dogs of war**—(*Slang*) To begin war ; (ইতরভাষায়) যুদ্ধে প্রবৃত্ত হওয়া। **To slip along**—(*Slang*) To go rapidly ; (ইতরভাষায়) বেগে চলা, দ্রুত চলা। **To slip into a man**—(*Slang*) To beat him severely ; (ইতরভাষায়) কাহাকে উত্তম মধ্যম দেওয়া, কাহাকে মারিয়া পাট পাট করা। **To slip off**—To take off quickly or quietly ; তাড়াতাড়ি খোলা, নিঃশব্দে খোলা। To depart imperceptibly ; চুপিচুপি সরিয়া পড়া। **To slip off the hooks**—Same as TO DROP OFF THE HOOKS (see under HOOK). **To slip on**—To put on hastily ; তাড়াতাড়ি পরা। **To slip one's breath or wind**—(*Slang*) To die ; (ইতরভাষায়) মরা, অক্কা পাওয়া, শিঙা ফুঁকান, পটল তোলা। **To slip one's cable**—To die ; মরা। **To slip out**—To slide out ; ফসকাইয়া যাওয়া। **To slip the collar**—To free oneself ; to disentangle oneself from difficulty ; মুক্ত করা ; ঝঞ্ঝাট হইতে মুক্ত করা। **To slip the leash**—To disengage one's self as from a leash or noose ; to free oneself from restraint ; পাশ হইতে মুক্ত করা ; মুক্ত করা। **To slip through one's fingers**—To die unexpectedly ; হঠাৎ মারা যাওয়া। To escape from one's grip ; কাহারো হাত হইতে ফসকাইয়া যাওয়া।

slip, *n.* 1. Act of slipping ; পিছলাইয়া যাওন। 2. An unintentional error ; a slight transgression ; ভুল চুক, ভ্রম, ভ্রমপ্রমাদ, স্খলিত ; পদস্খলন, কসুর। 3. A twig for grafting ; কলমের ডাল। 4. A scion ; "The girlish *slip* of Sicilian bride" ; বংশধর। 5. A leash ; কুক্কুরাদির চর্ম্ম-বন্ধনী। 6. A loose garment worn by a female ; a child's pinafore ; স্ত্রীলোকদিগের একপ্রকার শ্লথ পরিচ্ছদ ; শিশুদিগের জামার সম্মুখের অংশআবরক বস্ত্রখণ্ড। 7. A sloping plane on the bank of a river for ship-building ; a contrivance for raising vessel out of water for repairs ; পোতনির্ম্মাণের জন্য নদীতীরস্থ পাষাণাদিবদ্ধ প্রবণভূমি ; জীর্ণসংস্কারের উদ্দেশ্যে পোত উত্তোলনের জন্য কৌশলবিশেষ। 8. (*Print.*) A long galley-proof before being made up into pages ; (মুদ্রণ) পৃষ্ঠা বাঁধিবার পূর্ব্বে যে দীর্ঘাকৃতি কাগজখণ্ডে প্রুফ দেওয়া হয়। 9. An escape ; as, he gave me a *slip* ; a secret or unexpected desertion (usually with *give*); পলায়ন; গোপনে সরিয়া পড়ন। **10.** A long narrow piece; as, a *slip* of paper; ফালি, লম্বা টুকরা, চোতা। **11.** (*Cricket*) A fielder behind the wicket; the position of such a player; (ক্রীকেট ক্রীড়া) কন্দুক থামাইবার বা ফিরাইবার জন্য ত্রিদণ্ডের পশ্চাতে দণ্ডায়মান ক্রীড়ক; ঐরূপ ক্রীড়কের অবস্থান। **12.** A creamy mixture of ground flint etc. for making porcelain; চীনা মাটী তৈরীর জন্য চকমকি পাথর প্রভৃতির চূর্ণ দ্বারা প্রস্তুত সরের মত একপ্রকার মিশ্র। **13.** (*Theatre pl.*) The part from which scenes are slipped on; the part where actors stand before entering; (রঙ্গালয়) রঙ্গালয়ের যে অংশ হইতে দৃশ্যপট সমূহ ঠেলিয়া দেওয়া হয়; রঙ্গমঞ্চে প্রবেশ করার পুর্ব্বে রঙ্গালয়ের যে অংশে নটনটীগণ দণ্ডায়মান থাকে। **14.** (*Geol.*) A slight dislocation caused by the sinking of one section of the strata; স্তরের কোন অংশ বসিয়া যাওয়ার দরুণ ঈষৎ স্তরচ্যুতি। **15.** The slipping of earth from the side of hill; পর্ব্বতগাত্র হইতে মৃত্তিকাস্খলন। **16.** (*Book-binding*) A cord used in fastening the back of a book; পুস্তকের পিঠ বাঁধিবার জন্য ব্যবহৃত একপ্রকার শক্ত সূতা। **17.** A cylindrical iron-case in which wood for making gun-powder is charred; যে চোঙ্গাকার লৌহময় আধারে বারুদ প্রস্তুতের কাঠ অঙ্গারে পরিণত করা হয়। **Slip-carriage**—ডাকের গাড়ীতে সংযুক্ত শকটবিশেষ—যাহা ঐ গাড়ী চলন্ত অবস্থায় কোন ষ্টেশনে রাখিয়া যায়। **Slip-cover**—গৃহের অব্যবহৃত আসবাবপত্র ঢাকিয়া রাখার জন্য ছিটের আবরণ। **Slip-dock**—পাষাণবদ্ধভূমিবিশিষ্ট প্রবণ পোত-নির্ম্মাণস্থলী। **Slip-galley**—বিন্যস্ত অক্ষর রাখার জন্য দীর্ঘ কাষ্ঠাধার। **Slip-hook**—যে আঁকড়াতে এরূপ একটী কল থাকে—যদ্দারা উহা আবশ্যক হইলে তৎক্ষণাৎ খোলা যাইতে পারে। **Slip-knot**—পলাসী গেরো। **Slip-rope**—এরূপভাবে বদ্ধ রজ্জু—যাহা সহজে ও সত্বর খোলা যাইতে পারে। **Slip-shod**—নীচু গোড়ালিবিশিষ্ট পাদুকা পরিহিত; অপরিচ্ছন্ন, নোংরা; কাছাছাড়া (*slang*), কাছা খোলা (*ib.*), অসাবধান; অপ্রণালীবদ্ধ, বেবন্দোবস্তী। **Slip-slop**—নিস্তেজ সুরা; বাজে কথা, অসার কথা; আবেগপূর্ণ কথাবার্ত্তা। **Slip-way**—Same as SLIP-DOCK. **A mere slip of the tongue**—মুখ ফস্‌কে বেরিয়ে গেছে (মিল্‌নে)। **Slip of pen**—লিপিকরপ্রমাদ, কলমের ভুল। **There's many a slip 'twixt the cup and the lip**—Nothing is certain until it has happened; না আঁচালে বিশ্বাস নাই, শ্রেয়াংসি বহু বিঘ্নানি। **To give the slip**—To escape from; to evade; পলায়ন করা; পাশ কাটান, এড়ান, ফসকাইয়া যাওয়া।

slip'-per (-ẽr), *n.* & *v. t.* **1.** A loose easy shoe for indoor wear; চটিজুতা। **2.** A kind of iron brake or shoe for the wheel of a waggon; গাড়ীর চাকার গতিরোধ করার জন্য একপ্রকার লোহার কল। **3.** A person who slips greyhounds in coursing-match; শিকারের প্রতিযোগিতায় যে ব্যক্তি শিকারী কুকুর ছাড়িয়া দেয়। **4.** A kind of apron or pinafore for children; শিশুদিগের জামার সম্মুখভাগের আবরক বস্ত্রখণ্ড। **5.** Anything slipped on or over something; যাহা কোন কিছুর উপর পিছলাইয়া দেওয়া হয়। ***Verb t.*** To chastise with slipper; চটিজুতা দ্বারা প্রহার করা। **Slipper-bath**—চটিজুতার আকার আংশিক ভাবে আবৃত স্নানশালা। **Slipper-wort**—একপ্রকার গুল্ম।

slip'-per-ȳ (-ẽr-), *adj.* **1.** Not affording firm footing; as, a *slippery* road; পিচ্ছিল, পিছল। **2.** Difficult to hold in consequence of lubricity; as, a *slippery* eel; পিচ্ছিল। **3.** Untrustworthy; sly; as, *slippery* person; অবিশ্বাসযোগ্য; ধূর্ত্ত। **4.** (*Obs.*) Unchaste; (অপ্রঃ) অসতী। **5.** Changeable; পরিবর্ত্তনশীল। **—i-ly,** *adv.* **—i-ness,** *n.*

slip'-py (-ĭ), *adj.* (*Slang*) Same as SLIPPERY. **To look slippy**—(*Slang*) To make haste; to look sharp; (ইতরভাষায়) তাড়াতাড়ি করা; ত্বরান্বিত করা।

slit, *v. t.* & *n.* **1.** To cut lengthwise; to split; to cut into strips; লম্বালম্বি কাটা; চির করা; ফালি ফালি করিয়া কাটা। **2.** To cut; কাটা। ***Noun.*** A long cut or narrow opening; লম্বাচির, লম্বা ফাটোল।

slith'-ẽr, *v. i.* (*Colloq.*) To slide (চলিত ভাষায়) গড়াইয়া চলা, পিছলাইয়া যাওয়া।

sliv'-ẽr, *v. t., i.* & *n.* To cut or divide into long, thin pieces; "People delight to *sliver* lettuces into bowls"; to slice; চেরা, চেলা করা, ফালি করা; ছিলকা করা, ছিলকা করিয়া কাটা। ***Verb i.*** To split; চিরা। ***Noun.*** A long slender piece cut or rent off; ফালি, টুকরা।

slŏb'-ber (-ẽr), *v. i., t.* & *n.* Same as SLABBER (which see).

sloe (slō), *n.* A small, bitter, bluish-black plum-like fruit of the blackthorn; একপ্রকার আনীল কৃষ্ণবর্ণ ফল।

sloe'-wŏrm (slō-), *n.* Corruption of SLOW-WORM (which see).

slŏg, *v. i., t.* & *n.* To hit hard; জোরে মারা। ***Noun.*** A hard hit; জোরে আঘাত।

slō'-găn, *n.* The war cry of the Highlanders; হাইলেণ্ডারদিগের যুদ্ধকালীন হুঙ্কার বা সিংহনাদ।

sloid (sloyd), *n.* A system of manual training, esp. by means of wood-carving; বিদ্যালয়ের ছাত্রদিগের হাত ঠিক করিবার জন্য কাষ্ঠ প্রভৃতির ক্ষোদাই কার্য্য শিক্ষা দিবার প্রণালীবিশেষ।

sloop, *n.* A cutter-rigged vessel with one mast; একপ্রকার

Sloop.

একমাস্তুলের জাহাজ। **Sloop-rigged**—ঐরূপ জাহাজের মত দড়াদড়িবিশিষ্ট। **Sloop of war**—একপ্রকার ক্ষুদ্র রণপোত।

slŏp, *n., v. t. & i.* 1. (*Pl.*) Spilled water; a puddle; নিক্ষিপ্ত জল; ডোবা। 2. (*Pl.*) Liquid food; (*pl.*) dirty water; তরল খাদ্য; নোংরা জল, ময়লা জল। 3. (*Pl.*) The dirty water of house; বাড়ীর ময়লা জল। ***Verb t.*** To soil by letting liquid fall upon; অপরিষ্কার জল প্রভৃতি ফেলিয়া নোংরা করা। ***Verb i.*** To be spilled; to overflow, as a liquid by the motion of the vessel containing it; ছিটকাইয়া পড়া; ভাণ্ডের আন্দোলনহেতু জলপ্রভৃতি উপচিয়া পড়া। **Slop-basin**—ভোজনের পর পেয়ালার তরল সঞ্চিত মলিন বস্তু সংগ্রহের জন্য পাত্র। **Slop-pail**—ঘুমাইবার ঘরের ময়লা জল যে পাত্রে করিয়া সরান হয়। **To slop-over**—(*Fig.*) To be maudlin; (লক্ষণায়) দুর্ব্বল ভাবপ্রবণ হওয়া।

slŏp, *n.*, (*Pl.*) 1. (*Archaic*) Ready-made clothing; (অপ্রঃ) তৈরী পোষাক। 2. (*Navy*) The clothes and beddings of a solider; (নৌবিভাগ) নৌসৈন্যের পোষাক এবং বিছানাপত্র। 3. (*Pl.*) Wide breeches; চৌড়া পাজামা। 4. (*Slang*) A tailor; (ইতরভাষায়) দর্জ্জী। 5. A smock-frock; ক্ষেত্রের মজুরদিগের একপ্রকার উপরে পরিবার জামা। **Slop-room**—যে কক্ষ হইতে নৌসৈনিকদিগকে পোষাক এবং বিছানাপত্র যোগান হয়। **Slop-seller**—তৈরী-পোষাক বিক্রেতা। **Slop-shop**—তৈরী-পোষাকের দোকান, কাটা-কাপড়ের দোকান।

slōpe, *n., adj., v. t. & i.* 1. Obliquity; as, the piece of timber has a slight *slope* in it; বক্রতা। 2. Any ground whose surface forms an angle with the plane of the horizon; ক্রমনিম্নভূমি, উৎসর্পিণী বা অপসর্পিণী ভূমি, প্রবণ ভূমি, ঢালু। 3. Position of a soldier with rifle sloped; সৈনিকদিগের দাঁড়াইবার ভঙ্গীবিশেষ—যাহাতে উহারা বন্দুক টের্চ্চাভাব ধরিয়া থাকে। ***Adj.*** (*Rare*) Inclined; (ক্বচিদ্‌ব্যবহৃত) ঢালু, টের্চ্চা, গড়ানিয়া, প্রবণ। ***Verb t.*** To form with a slope; ঢালুসমন্বিত করা। ***Verb i.*** 1. To descend in a slanting direction; ঢালু হওয়া, প্রবণ হওয়া। 2. (*Slang*) To decamp; to saunter; (ইতরভাষায়) চম্পট দেওয়া; ইতস্ততঃ ঘুরা। **Slop′-ing**, *adj.* **Slope-arms**—স্ব স্ব স্কন্ধের উপর টের্চ্চাভাবে বন্দুক ধরার জন্য আদেশ।

slŏp′-py (-ĭ), *adj.* 1. (Of road) Muddy; splashy; কর্দ্দমাক্ত, কাদাটে; পচ্‌পচিয়া। 2. Slovenly; as, a *sloppy* piece of work; unsystematic; নোংরা, অপরিচ্ছন্ন; অপ্রণালীবদ্ধ। 3. Maudlin; দুর্ব্বলভাবপ্রবণ। **–pi-ly**, *adv.* **–pi-ness**, *n.*

slŏt, *n. & v. t.* 1. A groove, channel, slit or long aperture made in machines etc. to admit some other part; esp. a slit for penny or other coin that sets working a slot-machine; কোন যন্ত্রে অপর কোন অংশ প্রবিষ্ট করার জন্য যে খাঁজ, নালী বা সরু ছিদ্র করা হয়; বিশেষতঃ ক্রয়যন্ত্রের যে ছিদ্রের ভিতর দিয়া পয়সা, সিকি, দুয়ানি, প্রভৃতি ফেলিলে ঐ যন্ত্র ঘুরিয়া নির্দ্দিষ্ট মূল্যের জিনিষ বাহির করিয়া দেয়। 2. A trap-door in the stage of theatre; (রঙ্গালয়ে) রঙ্গমঞ্চের কুটদ্বার। ***Verb t.*** To cut slots in; যন্ত্রে ছিদ্র করা বা খাঁজ কাটা। **Slot-machine**—একপ্রকার যন্ত্র—যাহার ছিদ্রের ভিতর দিয়া পয়সা প্রভৃতি দিলে যন্ত্রের ভিতর হইতে ঐ দামের কোন জিনিষ বাহির হয় বা ঐ যন্ত্রের কাঁটা ঘুরিয়া কোন ব্যক্তির ওজন সূচিত হয়।

slŏt, *n.* The track of a deer; হরিণের পদচিহ্ন।

slōth, *n.* 1. Laziness; sluggishness; আলস্য, কুড়েমি; জড়তা, জাড্য। 2. A South American mammal;

Sloth.

দক্ষিণ আমেরিকার স্তন্যদায়ী জন্তুবিশেষ। **Sloth′-ful**, *adj.* Lazy; অলস, কুড়ে, জড়। **Sloth′-ful-ness**, *n.* **Sloth-bear**—কৃষ্ণ ভল্লুক। **Sloth-monkey**—একপ্রকার লাঙ্গুলহীন কপি।

slouch (slowch), *v. t., i. & n.* To depress; to cause to hang down; অবনমিত করা; ঝুলান। ***Verb i.*** 1. To hang down; ঝুলা। 2. To have a downcast clownish gait or manner; হেঁট হওয়া, ভাঁড়ের মত ভঙ্গী থাকা। ***Noun.*** A hanging down, as of the head or other part of the body; মস্তকাদির নতি। 3. An ungainly clownish-gait; ভাঁড়ের মত ভঙ্গী। 4. An awkward clownish fellow; বিদূষকের মত লোক। **Slouch-hat**—প্রশস্ত এবং নমনীয় কিনারাবিশিষ্ট একপ্রকার কোমল টুপি।

slough (slow), *n.* A place of deep mud or mire; গভীর কর্দ্দমপূর্ণ স্থান, পল্বল। **Slough′-y**, *adj.* **The Slough of Despond**—পাপপঙ্কে নিমজ্জনের অবস্থা।

slough (slŭf), *n., v. i.* & *t.* 1. The cast-off skin of a serpent, etc ; সাপের খোলস, সর্পাদির ত্বক, কঞ্চুক, নির্ম্মোক। 2. The dead flesh that separates from living parts in wound ; ক্ষতাদির কাঁচা অংশ হইতে যে মরা মাংস আলাহিদা হইয়া আসে, ক্ষতাদি হইতে যে অংশ পচিয়া পড়ে, পচলা। ***Verb i.*** 1. To separate from the sound flesh ; পচা অংশ আল্‌গা হইয়া আসা। 2. To shed ; মুক্ত হওয়া। ***Verb t.*** 1. To cast off, as the skin or dead tissue ; খোলস ছাড়া, নির্ম্মোক মোচন করা। 2. To discard ; ত্যাগ করা, পায়ে ঠেলা। **Sloughing ulcer**—দুষ্টব্রণ (সাঃ পঃ)। **To slough off**—To separate from the living part, as the dead part in mortification; ক্ষতাদি হইতে আলগা হইয়া আসা।

Slŏ-văk′ *n.* One of a Slavic race inhabiting North Hungary ; উত্তর হাঙ্গারী প্রদেশবাসী।

slov′-ĕn (slŭv-), *n.* A man careless of his dress or negligent ; a man habitually negligent of neatness and order ; অপরিচ্ছন্ন লোক, নোংরা লোক ; কাছাছাড়া লোক, কাছাঢিলা লোক। **—ly**, *adj.* Not neat or tidy ; habitually negligent of neatness or order ; অপরিচ্ছন্ন, নোংরা ; কাছাছাড়া, কাছাঢিলা। **—li-ness**, *n.*

Slŏ′-vene (-vēn), *n.* One of a Slavic people of Carinthia, Carniola and Styria in Austria Hungary ; শ্লেভজাতি বিশেষের লোক।

Slŏ-vē′-nī-ăn, *adj.* & *n.* Of, or pertaining to, Slovenes or their language ; শ্লভেনজাতি এবং উহাদের ভাষাসম্বন্ধীয়। ***Noun.*** Same as SLOVENE.

slow (slō), *adj., adv., v. i.* & *t.* 1. Not swift ; ধীরগামী, মন্দগামী (কপালঃ), মন্থর। 2. Not happening in a short time ; gradual ; as, *slow* progress ; ধীর, বিলম্বিত, মৃদুমন্দ ; ক্রমিক। 3. Not ready or prompt ; as, *slow* to believe ; অক্ষিপ্র, অত্বরিত। 4. Acting deliberately ; ধীর, ধীরপ্রকৃতি, ধীরমতি, ধীরস্বভাব। 5. Behind in time ; as, the watch is *slow* ; মৃদুগামী, ধীরগতি। 6. Inactive ; tardy ; sluggish ; জড়, নিষ্ক্রিয় ; চিরকারী, চিরক্রিয়, দীর্ঘসূত্র ; ঢিলা। 7. Stupid ; dull witted ; not brisk ; as, he was *slow* in company ; বোকা, নির্ব্বোধ ; জড়বুদ্ধি, মন্দবুদ্ধি; অচতুর, অচটুল, তন্দ্রিত। ***Adv.*** Slowly ; ধীরে ধীরে, আস্তে আস্তে, মন্দ মন্দ, মন্থরভাবে, শনৈঃ শনৈঃ। ***Verb i.*** To slacken speed ; as, the train *slows* ; গতি কমা। ***Verb t.*** To reduce the speed of ; গতি কমান, গতি হ্রাস করা। **Slow′-ly**, *adv.* In a slow manner ; মন্দ মন্দ, গজেন্দ্রগমনে (*rhet.*), ধীরেসুস্থে। **Slow′-ness**, *n.* The state of being slow ; মন্থরতা, ঢিলামি, আলস্য, মান্দ্য, মন্দতা। **Slow-match** — দাহ্যপদার্থদ্বারা প্রস্তুত মৃদুজ্বলনশীল পলিতাবিশেষ—যাহার সাহায্যে বারুদ প্রভৃতি প্রজ্বালিত করা হয়। **Slow-witted**—অল্পবুদ্ধি, অল্পমতি, অল্পধী। **Slow-worm**—কেঁচো, কেঁচুয়া। **A slow coach**—অলস ব্যক্তি, জড় ব্যক্তি, গদাই লস্কর (*colloq.*), অল্পবুদ্ধি ব্যক্তি।

slŭb, *n.* & *v. t.* A roll of wool slightly twisted ; ঈষৎ পাকানো পশমের গুচ্ছ। ***Verb t.*** To twist thus ; ঐরূপ ভাবে পাকান।

slŭb′-ber (-ēr), *v. t.* & *i.* 1. To do carelessly or imperfectly ; অসাবধানভাবে করা, অসম্পূর্ণভাবে করা। 2. To sully ; কলুষিত করা। ***Verb i.*** To move or act in a slovenly or hurried manner ; নোংরাভাবে করা, কাছাছাড়ার মত কায করা, এলোপাতাড়ি ভাবে করা।

sludge (slŭj), *n.* 1. Mire ; কর্দ্দম, কাদা। 2. Small floating piece of ice or snow ; জলে প্রবমান ক্ষুদ্র ক্ষুদ্র হিমশিলাখণ্ড। **Sludg′-y**, *adj.*

slue (slū), See SLEW.

slŭg, *n.* & *v. i.* 1. A cylindrical or oval piece of metal used for the charge of a gun ; এক প্রকার নলাকার বা ডিম্বাকার গুলি। 2. A kind of shell-less snail ; একপ্রকার কবচহীন শম্বুক, চাটা (মিউজিয়াম)। ***Verb i.*** To collect and destroy slugs in garden etc. ; বাগান প্রভৃতির চাটা জড় করিয়া ধ্বংস করা।

slŭg′-ă-bĕd, *n.* (*Archaic*) A person who lies late at bed ; (অপ্রঃ) যে ব্যক্তি অনেক বেলায় শয্যাত্যাগ করে।

slŭg′-gard (-ârd), *n.* & *adj.* A person habitually lazy ; অলস ব্যক্তি, কুড়ে লোক, ঢিলা লোক। ***Adj.*** Lazy ; অলস, কুড়ে, জড়, আঁলসে (*colloq.*)।

slŭg′-gĭsh (-ĭsh), *adj.* 1. Habitually idle and lazy ; অলস, কুড়ে, ঢিলা, জড়, নিস্তেজ, নিষ্ক্রিয়। 2. Slow-moving ; as, a *sluggish* stream মন্দগামী, মৃদুগামী, মন্থরগামী। **—ly,** *adv.* **—ness,** *n.* 1. The state of being sluggish ; জড়তা, আলস্য, মান্দ্য, জাড্য। 2. Slowness of motion ; মন্থরতা।

sluice (slūs), *n., v. t.* & *i.* 1. A water-gate ; a flood-gate ; জলনির্গম দ্বার ; স্রোতোদ্বার, কপাটকল। 2. A water-passage (also *sluice-way*) ; জলপ্রণালী। ***Verb t.*** 1. To provide with sluice or sluices ; স্রোতোদ্বার বা স্রোতোদ্বারসমূহ সমন্বিত করা। 2. To open a sluice or flood-gate upon ; to wet copiously, as by opening a sluice ; কোন কিছুর উপর স্রোতোদ্বার উন্মুক্ত করা ; স্রোতোদ্বার উন্মুক্ত করিয়া প্রচুর জলসিক্ত করা। 3. To cleanse by means of sluices ; as, to *sluice* earth in mining ; উন্মুক্ত স্রোতদ্বার হইতে নির্গত জলধারা দ্বারা ধৌত বা মাজ্জিত করা। ***Verb i.*** To pour as from a sluice ; কপাটকলের জলস্রোতের মত ঢালা। **Sluic′-y**, *adj.*

slŭm, *n.* & *v. i.* A low dirty street or district in a large city occupied by a poor dirty vicious class of people ; "There is little in the author's observations on *slums* and slum-life which has not been said before"; নগরের অপরিচ্ছন্ন রাস্তা বা মহল্লা, বস্তি। *Verb i.* To go about the slums to visit or examine the condition of inhabitants; বাসিন্দাদিগের অবস্থা পরিদর্শনের জন্য নগরের অপরিচ্ছন্ন রাস্তায় বা মহল্লায় যাওয়া। **Slum'-mer,** *n.*

slŭm'-bêr, *v. i., t. & n.* 1. To sleep lightly; তন্দ্রাবিষ্ট হওয়া, অল্প ঘুমান, ঘুমের আমেজ হওয়া। 2. To sleep; নিদ্রা যাওয়া, শয়ন করা, ঘুমান। 3. To be in a state of negligence, sloth, supineness or inactivity; to be dormant; as, public enthusiasm seemed to *slumber*; প্রসুপ্ত থাকা, সুপ্ত থাকা; নিদ্রিত থাকা, নিষ্ক্রিয় থাকা। *Verb t.* 1. (*Rare*) To lay to sleep; (কচিদ্ব্যবহৃত) নিদ্রিত করা, শোয়ান। 2. (*Rare*) To stupefy; (কচিদ্ব্যবহৃত) স্তম্ভিত করা। *Noun.* 1. Light sleep; অল্পনিদ্রা, তন্দ্রা, লঘুনিদ্রা [Sans. কাকনিদ্রা, শ্বাননিদ্রা।] 2. Sleep; repose; "Rest to my soul, and *slumber* to my eyes"; নিদ্রা, ঘুম; বিরাম, বিশ্রান্তি। **–brous, –ous,** *adjs.* **–brous-ly, –ous-ly,** *advs.*

slŭmp, *n. & v. i.* (*Colloq.*) A sudden or rapid fall in price, demand or interest; as, a *slump* in trade; (চলিতভাষায়) মূল্য, চাহিদা বা কৌতূহলের হঠাৎ দ্রুত হ্রাস, মন্দা, হঠাৎ নামিয়া যাওন। *Verb i.* (*Colloq.*) To undergo a sudden decline or falling; মূল্য প্রভৃতি হঠাৎ হ্রাস পাওয়া, হঠাৎ নামিয়া যাওয়া।

slŭng, *p. t. & p. p.* of SLING (which see).

slunk (slŭngk), *p. p.* of SLINK (which see).

slur (slêr) *v. t., i. & n.* 1. To pass with little notice; উপেক্ষা করিয়া যাওয়া, দেখিয়াও না দেখা। 2. To pronounce indistinctly; অস্পষ্ট ভাবে উচ্চারণ করা। 3. (*Mus.*) To sing or play in a gliding manner; to run notes into each other; (সঙ্গীতশাস্ত্র) সুরের উপর সুর অনায়াসে প্রবাহিত করিয়া গান গাওয়া বা যন্ত্রাদি বাদন করা; বিভিন্ন সুর একত্র মিশান। *Verb i.* To slip in making the impression, causing the printing to be blurred; মুদ্রণকালে পিছলাইয়া যাওয়া হেতু মুদ্রিত অক্ষর জুবড়াইয়া যাওয়া। *Noun.* 1. A stain; a slight reproach; কলঙ্ক; গ্লানি, অপবাদ। 2. (*Mus.*) A mark (⌒ or ⌣) connecting notes that are to be sung to the same syllable, or made in one continued breath; (সঙ্গীতশাস্ত্র) যে চিহ্ন দ্বারা যে সকল ধ্বনি একত্রে গাহিতে হইবে—তাহা সূচিত হয়। 3. (*Print.*) A blurred impression; মসীলিপ্ত ছাপ।

slŭsh, *n.* 1. Soft mud; নরম মাটী, কর্দ্দম, পঙ্ক। 2. Melting snow; গলিত বরফ। **Slush'-y,** *adj.*

slŭt, *n.* 1. A slovenly woman; নোংরা স্ত্রীলোক, পেতনী (*colloq.*)। 2. (*Joc.*) A girl; (রঙ্গচ্ছলে) ছুড়ী, পোঁটাচুন্নি (*slang*)। 3. (America) A bitch; কুক্কুরী। **Slut'-tish,** *adj.* **Slut'-tish-ly,** *adv.* **Slut'-tish-ness,** *n.*

slȳ, *adj.* 1. Cunning; shrewd; ধূর্ত্ত, চালাক, শঠ; চতুর, সেয়ানা। 2. Ironical; as, a *sly* remark; বিদ্রূপপূর্ণ, ব্যঙ্গাত্মক, চটুলপরিহাসাত্মক। **Sly'-ly,** *adv.* **Sly'-ness,** *n.* **Sly-boots**—চালাক লোক, সেয়ানা লোক। **On the sly**—Secretly; গোপনে, চুপি চুপি, চুপি সাড়ে।

slȳpe, *n.* A passage between two walls; প্রাচীরদ্বয়ের মধ্যবর্ত্তী স্থান।

smăck, *n., v. i., t. & adv.* 1. A slap; চড়, চপেটাঘাত। 2. The report caused by a quick or smart blow; the sound of the parting of lips; চাবুকের সপাংশব্দ, চড় চাপড়ের শব্দ; অধরোষ্ঠবিচ্ছেদ শব্দ, চপ চপ শব্দ (ওষ্ঠাধর সম্পর্কে)। 3. A loud kiss; "He kissed her face with such a clamorous *smack* that at the parting all the church did echoe"; সশব্দ চুম্বন, রভস চুম্বিত (আঃ বঃ)। *Verb i.* 1. To slap; চড় দেওয়া, চপেটাঘাত করা। 2. (Of lips) To part noisily in eager anticipation or enjoyment of food or other delight; সুস্বাদু খাদ্যাদি ভক্ষণের আশায় অধরোষ্ঠ ভিন্ন করত শব্দ করা (also *verb t.*)। 3. (Of whips) To crack; (চাবুক সম্বন্ধে) সপাং করিয়া শব্দ হওয়া বা করা (also *verb t.*)। *Adv.* (*Colloq.*) Outright; exactly; তৎক্ষণাৎ, ঝটিতি, চট্ করিয়া, পটাস করিয়া, সপাসপ; ঠিক। **To smack at**—To relish, as shown by the smacking of the lips; চপ চপ করিয়া খাওয়া।

smăck, *n. & v. i.* 1. A taste; a small tinge; আস্বাদ; আমেজ, আভাস, গন্ধ, লেশ। 2. A smattering; as, a *smack* of knowledge; পল্লবগ্রাহিতা, টটামটি। *Verb i.* (*Colloq.*) To taste slightly; ঈষৎ আস্বাদ থাকা, আমেজ থাকা।

smăck, *n.* A sloop, esp. for fishing; একপ্রকার ক্ষুদ্র এক মাস্তুলের জাহাজ, একপ্রকার এক মাস্তুলের জেলে-জাহাজ।

smăck'-êr, *n.* 1. Loud kiss; সশব্দ চুম্বন। 2. A remarkable specimen of anything; সেরা জিনিষ, সবার সেরা।

small, *adj., n. & adv.* 1. Little in size; ক্ষুদ্র, ছোট, স্তোক, দর (only in দরবিগলিত নেত্র)। 2. Little in duration; as, a *small* space of time; স্বল্পকালস্থায়ী, স্বল্প, অল্প। 3. Little in number; অল্পসংখ্যক। 4. Trifling; as, this is *small* matter; তুচ্ছ, সামান্য, ক্ষুদ্র, হেয়, অকিঞ্চিৎকর, নগণ্য। 5. Lesser; petty; as, *small* poets; ক্ষুদ্র; হীন। 6 Mean-hearted; as, *small* nature; ক্ষুদ্রমনাঃ, নীচাশয়, ক্ষুদ্রচিত্ত, হীনচেতাঃ। 7. Of little talent, worth or ability; undistinguished; poor; অল্পপ্রতিভাবান, হীনবুদ্ধি, হীন; অপ্রসিদ্ধ; দরিদ্র।

Noun. **1.** A small or little thing; ক্ষুদ্র জিনিষ। **2.** The small or slender part of anything; as, the *small* of the leg; কোন বস্তুর ক্ষুদ্র বা ক্ষীণ অংশ। **3.** (*Pl.*) Breeches; জাঙ্গিয়া। **4.** (*Pl.*) Same as RESPONSIONS. ***Adv.*** **1.** In a small extent, quantity or degree; সামান্যভাবে, সামান্য পরিমাণে, অল্প পরিমাণে, ক্ষুদ্রভাবে। **2.** Not loudly; faintly; অনুচ্চস্বরে, মৃদুস্বরে; মৃদুভাবে। **Small′-ish,** *adj.* **Small′-ness,** *n.* **Small-arms**—ক্ষুদ্র অস্ত্র, যথা পটিশ, বোমা, ধনু, তরবারী, বর্ষা, বন্দুক, পিস্তল, প্রভৃতি। **Small beer**—নিস্তেজ বীয়র। **Small capitals**—অপেক্ষাকৃত ক্ষুদ্র আকারের বড়হাতের হরফ। **Small cardamom**—ছোট এলাচ। [Syn. ক্ষুদ্রৈলা, উপকুঞ্চিকা, তুথা, কোরঙ্গী, ত্রিপুটা, ত্রুটি, বহুস্থা, তীক্ষ্ণগন্ধা, সূক্ষ্মৈলা, ত্রিপুটী।] **Small craft**—ক্ষুদ্র আকারের জাহাজ প্রভৃতি। **Small debt**—ক্ষুদ্র ঋণ। **Small minded**—ক্ষুদ্রমনাঃ, সংকীর্ণচিত্ত। **Small gross**—দশ ডজন। **Small hand**—সাধারণ লিখা। **Small hours**—See HOUR. **Small intestines**—গ্রহণী (সাঃ পঃ)। **Small pica**—একপ্রকার হরফ (This line is printed in small pica). **Small pox**—বসন্ত, মসূরক (সুশ্রুঃ), ইচ্ছাবসন্ত, শীতলা (also goddess of small-pox). **Small-talk**—সাধারণ কথাবার্ত্তা। **Small ware**—ঝালর, বোতাম, আঁকড়া, ফিতা, প্রভৃতি। **Great and small**—বড় ছোট সকলেই। **In a small way**—With a little capital; unpretentiously; স্বল্প মূলধনে; সামান্যভাবে। **Small-of the back**—কটিদেশের পশ্চাদ্ভাগ। **The beer is very small**—The beer is very weak; বীয়রটা মোটেই কড়া নয়। **The still small voice**—বিবেক, ধর্ম্মবুদ্ধি। **To chronicle small beer**—To talk of trifling matter as important; তুচ্ছ বিষয়কে অতিশয় গুরুত্বপূর্ণ করিয়া বর্ণনা করা। **To live in a small way**—To live unostentatiously; to live humbly; অনাড়ম্বরের সহিত জীবনযাপন করা; সাধারণ ভাবে জীবনযাপন করা। **To think no small beer of oneself**—To be conceited; আপনাকে বড় মনে করা।

small′-äge, *n.* Same as CELERY (which see).

smalt, *n.* **1.** A glass tinged with a fine blue; উজ্জ্বল নীলবর্ণে রঞ্জিত একপ্রকার কাচ। **2.** A pigment made by pulverizing this; উক্তরূপ কাচের চূর্ণ হইতে প্রস্তুত একপ্রকার নীলবর্ণ রঞ্জক পদার্থ।

smärt, *v. i.* & *n.* **1.** To feel sharp pain; টনটনে ব্যথা করা, জ্বলা, জ্বালা করা, যন্ত্রণা করা, চিনচিন করা, টন টন করা, টাটান। **2.** To be punished; to feel a pungent pain; as, to *smart* under difficulties; শাস্তি পাওয়া; তীব্র সন্তাপ ভোগ করা, মর্ম্মজ্বালা বোধ করা, তীব্র মানসিক যন্ত্রণা ভোগ করা। ***Noun.*** **1.** A sharp, quick, lively pain; টনটনানি, টাটানি, টনটনে ব্যথা। **2.** Sharp mental pain; তীব্র মানসিক সন্তাপ, তীব্র মনোবেদনা, মর্ম্মজ্বালা, মর্ম্মব্যথা, তীব্র মর্ম্মবেদনা। **Smart-money**—দণ্ড বা ক্ষতিপূরণস্বরূপপ্রদত্ত দণ্ড বা গৃহীত অর্থ। **To smart for**—To suffer consequences for; ফলভোগ করা, মজা টের পাওয়া।

smärt, *adj.* **1.** causing a keen local pain; টনটনেব্যথাজনক। **2.** Keen; severe; as, *smart* pain; তীব্র, প্রবল; গুরুতর। **3.** Quick; intelligent; clever; as, a *smart* man; চটপটে; বুদ্ধিমান; চতুর, চালাক, সেয়ানা। **4.** Vigorous; severe; as, *smart* skirmish; সতেজ; ঘোর। **5.** Brisk; active; not dull; চটুল, চটপটে; কর্ম্মতৎপর; প্রখর। **6.** Witty; as a *smart* saying; সরস, রসিকতাপূর্ণ। **7.** (*Now rare*) Spruce; elegantly dressed; as, *smart* clothes; (বর্ত্তমানে কচিদ্ব্যবহৃত) কায়দাদোরস্ত, বিলাসী; সুবেশ, জমকালো পোষাকে সজ্জিত। **8.** Brisk; fresh; as, a *smart* breeze; সতেজ; নির্ম্মল। **9.** Stylish; as, *smart* people; কায়দাদোরস্ত, চোস্ত। **Smart′-en,** *v. t.* **Smart′-ly,** *adv.* **1.** In a smart manner; প্রবলবেদনাজনকভাবে। **2.** Quickly; ত্বরিত, তাড়াতাড়ি, চটপট, ঝটপট, তূণ। **3.** Wittily; সরসভাবে, রসিকতার সহিত। **4.** Showily; জমকালোভাবে। **Smart′-ness,** *n.* **Smart dealing**—চালাকি।

smäsh, *v. t., i., n.* & *adj.* **1.** To break in pieces by violence; ভাঙ্গিয়া চুরমার করা, খণ্ড বিখণ্ড করা, চূর্ণ বিচূর্ণ করা। **2.** To crush; ধ্বংস করা। ***Verb i.*** **1.** To go to pieces; ভাঙ্গিয়া চুরমার হওয়া, খণ্ড বিখণ্ড হওয়া। **2.** To become bankrupt; দাউলিয়া হওয়া। **3.** To be propelled with great violence against something; as, the ship *smashed* against rocks; মহাবেগে কোন কিছুর উপর তাড়িত হইয়া পড়া, প্রবলবেগে ধাক্কা খাওয়া, প্রচণ্ডবেগে সংঘৃষ্ট হওয়া। **4.** (*Rare*) To utter a base coin; মেকি টাকা প্রভৃতি চালান। ***Noun.*** **1.** Breaking to pieces; বিমর্দ্দন, বিদলন, বিচূর্ণন। **2.** Ruin; bankruptcy; সর্ব্বনাশ; দাউলিয়া অবস্থা। **3.** (*Slang*) Ice and brandy water; (ইতরভাষায়) বরফ এবং ব্রাণ্ডিমিশ্রিত জল। **Smashing-machine**—পুস্তক বাঁধাইকারিগণের চাপযন্ত্র। **Smash-up**—সম্পূর্ণ ভঙ্গ। **All to smash**—All to pieces; ভাঙ্গিয়া চুরমার।

smäsh′-ėr, *n.* **1.** One who, or that which, smashes or breaks; খণ্ডবিখণ্ডকারী, চূর্ণবিচূর্ণকারী। **2.** One that passes a bad coin; যে ব্যক্তি মেকি টাকা চালায়। **3.** (*Slang*) Anything astounding, extraordinary, or very large or unusual; (ইতরভাষায়) আশ্চর্য্যজনক বস্তু, অসাধারণ বস্তু, অপূর্ব্ব বস্তু।

smăt'-ter-ing (-ĕr-), *n.* A slight superficial knowledge; as, he knows a *smattering* of English; ভাসাভাসা জ্ঞান, টটাটটি (*colloq.*)। **-er,** *n.*

smear (smër), *v. t.* & *n.* 1. To daub; লেপন করা, মাখা, ম্রক্ষণ করা, চর্চ্চিত করা। 2. To soil in any way; to contaminate; দূষিত করা; কলুষিত করা। ***Noun.*** A daub; a stain; লেপ; কলঙ্ক। **Smear'-y,** *adj.* **Smear dab**—এক প্রকার সামুদ্রিক মৎস্য।

smĕc'-tīte, *n.* A kind of whitish clay used for taking out grease from cloth etc.; কাপড় প্রভৃতি হইতে তৈল, চর্ব্বি ইত্যাদির দাগ তুলিবার জন্য একপ্রকার শাদাটে মাটী।

smĕg'-mă, *n.* A soaplike secretion (in fold of the skin); চর্ম্মের বলিতে প্রাপ্ত একপ্রকার চর্ব্বির মত পদার্থবিশেষ **-mat'-ic,** *adj.*

smĕll, *n., v. t.* & *i.* 1. The power or faculty of smelling; ঘ্রাণশক্তি। 2. Scent; গন্ধ, ঘ্রাণ, আঘ্রাণ, বাস। ***Verb t.*** 1. To obtain the scent of; গন্ধ লওয়া, ঘ্রাণ লওয়া, শুঁকা। 2. To scent out; গন্ধদ্বারা টের পাওয়া বা বাহির করা। ***Verb i.*** 1. To give an odour or perfume; গন্ধ দেওয়া। 2. To have a particular odour; কোন বিশেষ গন্ধ থাকা। 3. To smack of any quality; "Thy counsel *smells* of no cowardice"; কোন গুণের আভাস বা আমেজ থাকা। **Smell'-a-ble,** *adj.* **Smell'-ing,** *vb. n.* **Smell'-less,** *adj.* **Smelling-bottle**—সুগন্ধ দ্রব্যমিশ্রিত নিশাদলপূর্ণ শিশি। **Smell-ing-salt**—সর্দ্দি, প্রভৃতিতে ঘ্রাণ লওয়ার জন্য সুগন্ধিদ্রব্যমিশ্রিত নিশাদল, গন্ধনিশাদল। **To smell a rat**—See RAT.

smĕll'-ĕr, *n.* 1. One who smells; one who perceives by smell; যে ব্যক্তি গন্ধ গ্রহণ করে; যে ব্যক্তি গন্ধ দ্বারা অনুভব করে। 2. (*Slang*) The nose; (ইতরভাষায়) নাক। 3. A blow on the nose; নাকে আঘাত।

smĕlt, *v. t.* To melt, as ore, for the purpose of separating the metal; to extract metal from ore by melting; ধাতু পৃথক করার জন্য খনিজবিমিশ্র ধাতু গালান; গালাইয়া খনিজবিমিশ্র ধাতু হইতে ধাতু বাহির করা, ধাতু শোধন করা। **Smelt'-ing,** *n.* The act of one who smelts; ধাতু-শোধন (হিঃ কোঃ)। **Smelting-fur-ance**—খনিজবিমিশ্র ধাতু গালাইবার জন্য চুল্লী, ধাতুশোধন চুল্লী।

smĕlt, *n.* A small fish of the salmon family; স্যামনজাতীয় এক প্রকার ক্ষুদ্র মৎস্য।

smĕlt, *p. t.* & *p. p.* of SMELL (which see).

smew (smü), *n.* A diving bird; একপ্রকার জলচর পক্ষী।

smī'-lăx, *n.* A climbing plant, the root of several species of which yield sarsaparilla; এক-প্রকার লতা।

Smilax Chinensis — চোবচিনি (বেলঃ), রাস্না (ঐ), সুগন্ধমূল (ঐ)।

Smilax glabra—গুটীয়া শুকচিনা (বেলঃ), তোবচিনি, চোবচিনি।

Smilax lanceaefolia — হরিয়া শুকচিনা (বেলঃ)।

Smilax ovalifolia — কুমারিকা (বেলঃ)।

smīle, *v. i., t.* & *n.* 1. To express pleasure, love or kindness by the countenance, by contraction of the features of the face; ঈষৎ হাসা, মৃদুহাস্য করা, ঈষদ্ধাস্য করা। 2. To express slight contempt by a look implying sarcasm or pity; ঈষৎ অবজ্ঞা বা বিদ্রূপের হাসি হাসা। 3. To look gay and joyous; "The desert *smiled* And paradise was open'd in the wild"; স্মিতশোভা ধারণ করা, হাস্‌হাস্ করা। ***Verb t.*** 1. To express by a smile; ঈষদ্ধাস্য দ্বারা প্রকাশ করা। 2. To drive away with a smile; মৃদু হাসিয়া উড়াইয়া দেওয়া। ***Noun.*** 1. A slight contraction of the features of the face indicative of pleasure, amusement, kindness or approbation; ঈষদ্ধাস্য, অল্পহাস্য, মৃদুহাস্য, স্মিত, মন্দহাস্য, মন্দাস্মিত, মন্দহাস, মৃদুহসিত, মৃদুমন্দ হাস্য। 2. Gay or joyous appearance; as, the *smile* of spring; স্মিতশোভা। 3. Favour; propitiousness; as, the *smiles* of fortune; অনুগ্রহ; প্রসন্নতা। **Smile'-less,** *adj.* **Smil'-ing,** *n.* & *adj.* The act of one who smiles; মৃদু হাস্যকরণ। (*Adj.*) With a smile or look of pleasures; স্মের, সহাস্য, সাহাস্যমুখী, (*fem.*), চারু-হাসিনী (*fem.* Sweet smiling), স্মিত-মুখ, সহাস, সস্মিত। **Smil'-ing-ly,** *adv.* **Smiling face**—মৃদুহাস্যরঞ্জিত বদন, সস্মিত মুখ, স্মেরবদন। **Bland smile**—প্রসন্ন হাস্য।

smirch (smĕrch), *v. t.* & *n.* To soil; to stain; মলিন করা; কলঙ্কিত করা, দূষিত করা, কালিমালিপ্ত করা। ***Noun.*** Stain; spot; কলঙ্ক, কলঙ্ক-চিহ্ন, কলঙ্ককালিমা, কালোদাগ; চিহ্ন।

smirk (smĕrk), *v. i.* & *n.* To smile in an affected or conceited manner; to simper; কৃত্রিম হাস্য করা, কুটিল হাস্য করা; ফিক ফিক করিয়া হাসা। ***Noun.*** An affected smile; a simper; কৃত্রিম হাস্য, কপট হাস্য; ফিক ফিক হাসি।

smīte, *v. t.* & *i.* 1. To strike; "Whosoever shall *smite* thee on the right cheek, turn to him the other also"; আঘাত করা, প্রহার করা, মারা। 2. To kill; বধ করা, সংহার করা। 3. To blast; "And the flax and the barley were *smitten*"; বিনষ্ট করা, ধ্বংস করা, জীবনীশক্তি নষ্ট করা। 4. To strike or affect with passion as, love or fear; অভিভূত করা, বিহ্বল করা, জড়সড় করা, মদনবাণাহত করা, কামশর বিদ্ধ করা। ***Verb i.*** 1. To strike; আঘাত করা। 2. (*Archaic*) To collide; "And the knees *smite* together"; (অপ্রঃ) ঠুকাঠুকি লাগা। 3. To affect as by a stroke; to enter or penetrate with quickness or force; as, a glare of light *smote* on his eyes; আঘাত লাগা; সজোরে বা সত্বরতার সহিত প্রবেশ বা ভেদ করা, নক্ষত্রবেগে ভেদ করিয়া যাওয়া। ***Noun.*** Blow; আঘাত, ঘা। **To smite hip and thigh**—To defeat utterly; সম্পূর্ণরূপে পরাভূত করা। **To smite off**—To sever with one blow; এক কোপে কাটা।

smith, *n.* One who works in metals; one who forges iron; ধাতুদ্রব্যনির্ম্মাতা; কর্ম্মকার, কামার, লোহার।

smith-ĕr-eens' (-ēns), **smith'-ĕrs,** *ns.* Small fragments; powder; ক্ষুদ্র ক্ষুদ্র টুকরা; চূর্ণ।

smith'-ȳ, *n.* The workshop of a smith; কামারশালা, লৌহকারশালা।

smit'-ten (-n), *p. p.* of SMITE (which see).

smŏck, *n.* 1. (*Archaic*) Chemise; (অপ্রঃ) সেমিজ। 2. Same as SMOCK-FROCK (below). **Smock-faced**—মেয়েমুখো। **Smock-frock**—ক্ষেত্রের মজুরদিগের একপ্রকার লম্বা জামা; ঐরূপ জামা পরিহিত মনুষ্য। **Smock-marriage**—একপ্রকার বিবাহ-পদ্ধতি — যাহাতে স্বামী স্ত্রীর বিবাহের পূর্ব্ববর্ত্তী কালের ঋণদায় হইতে রেহাই পাইবে এইরূপ ভ্রান্ত বিশ্বাসের বশবর্ত্তী হইয়া বধূ কেবলমাত্র একখানি সেমিজ পরিধান করিতেন। **Smock-mill**—একপ্রকার বাতচক্র—যাহার কেবল মাত্র শীর্ষদেশ ঘূর্ণিত হয়। **Smock-race**—প্রাচীনকালে ইংলণ্ডের স্ত্রীলোকদিগের একপ্রকার দৌড়—যাহাতে জেত্রীকে একটী সেমিজ পুরস্কার দেওয়া হইত। **Smock-treason**—স্ত্রীলোকের রাজদ্রোহ।

smŏck'-ing, *n.* Honeycomb ornamentation on garments; পরিচ্ছদের উপর মৌচাকের মত কায।

smōke, *n.* 1. The sooty exhalation that escapes from burning materials; ধূম, ধূম্র, ধূয়া [Syn. অগ্নিসম্ভব, অগ্নিকেতু, অগ্নিবাহ।] 2. Vapour; বাষ্প। 3. Utter failure; as, it ended in *smoke*; vanity; idle talk; সম্পূর্ণ নিষ্ফলতা; বড়াই, দম্ভ; অসার কথা। 4. Act of smoking; as, you must have a *smoke*; ধূমপান। 5. (*Slang*) Cigar; (ইতরভাষায়) চুরুট। **Smok'-less,** *adj.* Free from smoke; as, *smokeless* powder; নির্ধূম, ধূমশূন্য, বিধূম (cf. বিধূমরোচিঃ)। **Smoke-ball**—একপ্রকার গোলা—যাহা হইতে ধূম বাহির হইয়া সৈন্যদিগের অবস্থান প্রভৃতি প্রচ্ছন্ন রাখে; হাঁপি প্রভৃতি রোগে নাসিকা দ্বারা ধোঁয়া প্রভৃতি গ্রহণের জন্য নানাপ্রকার কল। **Smoke-bell** — ভিতরের ছাদ যাহাতে ময়লা না হইতে পারে তজ্জন্য প্রদীপাদির উপর যে ঘণ্টাকৃতি আবরণ ঝুলাইয়া রাখা হয়। **Smoke-consumer**—চুল্লী, অগ্নিসেবনস্থলী, প্রভৃতির ধূম মুক্ত না করিয়া কার্য্যে লাগাইবার জন্য একপ্রকার কল। **Smoke-dried**—ধূম্রযোগে শুষ্কীকৃত (মাংসাদি সম্পর্কে)। **Smoke-hole**—কুটীরের ছাদের যে ছিদ্রপথে ধূম নির্গত হয়, ধূমনির্গম রন্ধ্র। **Smoke-jack** — ধূমনির্গমনালীর উষ্ণ ধূমপ্রবাহের সাহায্যে মাংস রোষ্ট করার শিক ঘুরাইবার যন্ত্রবিশেষ। **Smoke-plant, Smoke-tree**—একপ্রকার শোভাসাধক গুল্ম। **Smoke-rocket**—পয়োনালীর কোথায় ফুটা হইয়াছে তান্নির্ণয়ের নিমিত্ত উহার মধ্যে ধূমনিষেকের জন্য একপ্রকার যন্ত্র। **Smoke-stack**—জাহাজের ধূমনির্গমচোঙ্গ সমূহ। **Smoke-stone**—একপ্রকার পীত বা মদিরাবর্ণ মণি। **Like smoke**—(*Slang*) Very rapidly; (ইতরভাষায়) অতিশয় তাড়াতাড়ি। **No smoke without fire**—যেখানে ধূম সেখানেই আগুন (cf. পর্ব্বতো বহ্নিমান্ ধূমাৎ, বিনা বাতাসে নড়েনা।) **The smoke, The big** or **great smoke**—লণ্ডননগরী। **To end in smoke**—To come to nothing; নিষ্ফল হওয়া, ফুসফাস হওয়া, ধূমমাত্রে পর্য্যবসিত হওয়া, ধূম্রাবশেষ হওয়া। **To fall from smoke into smother**—To fall from one evil to another; ধোঁয়ার হাত এড়াইতে গিয়া আগুনে পড়া।

smōke, *v. i.* & *t.* 1. To emit smoke; ধূম নির্গত করা, ধোঁয়া উঠা, বাষ্পোদ্গিরণ করা, ধূমায়িত হওয়া, ধোঁয়াইয়া উঠা। 2. To burn; to rage; "His jealousy shall *smoke* against that man"; দগ্ধ হওয়া; ক্রোধোন্মত্ত হওয়া। 3. To raise a dust or smoke by rapid motion; to run at a furious speed; "*Smoking* along in his travelling chaise and four"; অতি দ্রুতগমনহেতু ধূলি বা ধূম্র উত্থিত হওয়া; প্রচণ্ডবেগে ধাবিত হওয়া। 4. (*Slang*) To blush; (ইতরভাষায়) লজ্জায় লাল হওয়া। 5. (*Colloq.*) To be punished; to suffer severely; "Some of you shall *smoke* for it in Rome"; (চলিতভাষায়) শাস্তি পাওয়া; গুরুতর কষ্ট ভোগ করা। 6. To use a pipe or cigar in the act of smoking; ধূমপান করা, ধূম্রপান করা। 7. (*Archaic*) To scent; (অপ্রঃ) সুরভিত করা। ***Verb t.*** 1. To apply smoke to; to hang in smoke; ধূমপ্রয়োগ করা; ধূমে ঝুলাইয়া রাখা। 2. To scent, medicate or dry by smoke; ধূমদ্বারা সুরভিত, ভেষজগুণসম্পন্ন বা শুষ্কীকৃত করা। 3. To draw smoke from into the mouth and expel it again; ধূমপান করা। 4. To drive out or expel by smoke (generally with *out*); ধূমদ্বারা বহির্গত করা। 5. To detect; বাহির করা। 6. (*Obs.*) To ridicule; (অপ্রঃ) ঠাট্টা করা, বিদ্রূপ করা। **Smok'-a-ble,** *adj.* **Smok'-ing,** *n.* & *adj.* **Smoke-dry**—ধোঁয়া লাগাইয়া শুকান। **Smoked glass**—ধূমদ্বারা ধূসরীকৃত কাচ। **Smoking-cap** or **smoking-jacket**—ধূমপানকালে ব্যবহৃত একপ্রকার কামদার টুপি বা কোর্ত্তা। **Smoking-carriage, Smoking-car** — বাষ্পীয়শকটে ধূমপানের জন্য গাড়ী। **Smoking-mixture**—ধূমপানের জন্য তৈয়ারী তামাক। **Smoking-room** — ধূমপানকক্ষ। **Smoking-tobacco** — ধূমপানের উপযোগী

তামাক। **Put that in your pipe and smoke it**—Reflect upon what has been said ; যাহা বলা হইল তাহা বেশ ভাল রকম ভাবিয়া দেখিও। **To smoke the calumet** or **pipe of peace**—See CALUMET.

smōk'-ėr, *n.* **1.** One that dries or preserves by smoke ; যে ধূম দ্বারা শুষ্ক করে বা তাজা রাখে, ধূমপ্রদাতা। **2.** One who habitually smokes tobacco ; ধূমপানকারী, ধূমপ, ধূমপায়ী, তামাকখোর, চুরটখোর। **3.** A smoking-car or compartment in a railway train ; বাষ্পীয়শকটের ধূমপানকক্ষ বা শকট।

smōk'-y̆, *adj.* **1.** Emitting smoke esp. in large quantity ; ধূমনির্গমকারী, প্রচুর ধূমনির্গমকারী। **2.** Filled with smoke ; ধূমপূর্ণ, সধূম, ধূমাবরুদ্ধ, ধূমবহুল। **3.** Having the appearance or nature of smoke ; ধূমবৎ, ধূমপ্রকৃতি। **4.** Tarnished ; with smoke ; of the colour of smoke ; ধূমমলিন, ধূমকজ্জলিত ; ধূম্রবর্ণ, ধূম্র (cf. ধূম্র-পাহাড়)। **5.** Subject to be soiled with smoke from a chimney ; ধূমনির্গমনালীর ধূমদ্বারা মলিনতা প্রাপনশীল।

smōōth, *adj.* **1.** Having an even or level surface ; sleek ; glossy ; মসৃণ, চিক্কণ, শ্লক্ষ্ণ (সাঃ পঃ), মেদুরিত (cf. নিসর্গ-সমাস্নিগ্ধ-নীলঃ) ; চিকণ (*Poet.* cf. চিকণ কালার গলায় মালা বাজন নূপুর পায়, চূড়ার ফুলে ভ্রমর বুলে তেরছ নয়নে চায়) ; তেলতলে ; স্নিগ্ধ, পালিশ, চকচকে। **2.** Evenly spread ; as, *smooth* hair ; সমভাবে বিস্তৃত, সুবিন্যস্ত। **3.** Gently flowing ; not ruffled, agitated, or undulating ; as, the *smooth* sea ; মৃদুপ্রবাহী ; নিস্তরঙ্গ, প্রশান্ত, অবিক্ষুব্ধ। **4.** Falling pleasantly on the ear ; "From her sweet lips *smooth* elocution flows" ; fluent ; শ্রুতিমধুর, ললিতমধুর, শ্রবণ-সুভগ ; অনর্গল। **5.** Equable ; 'unruffled' ; as, *smooth* temper ; প্রশান্ত ; ধীর। **6.** Soft and pleasing to the taste ; as, *smooth* ale ; সুস্বাদু, স্বাদু, সরস। **7.** Free from what is unpleasant ; as, *smooth* tidings ; মনোরম, সুখময়। **Smooth'-ly,** *adv.* **Smooth'-ness** *n.* The quality of being smooth ; মসৃণতা, চিক্কণতা, স্নিগ্ধত্ব (ব্রজঃ হিন্দুঃ), স্নৈগ্ধ্য। **Smooth-bore** — যে বন্দুকের নালীর ভিতরে খাঁজ কাটা থাকে না। **Smooth faced** — অজাতশ্মশ্রু, ক্ষৌরিতমুখ ; (বাক্য প্রভৃতি সম্বন্ধে) আপাতরম্য, আপাতসুখজনক ; মসৃণ ; কপটবন্ধুতাপ্রদর্শক। **Smooth-spoken**—মধুরভাষী, মঞ্জুবাক। **Smooth-tongued** —মিষ্টভাষী, প্রিয়ংবদ।

smōōth, smoothe (smōōth), *v. t.* & *n.* **1.** To make smooth ; মসৃণ করা, পালিশ করা, চিক্কণ করা। **2.** To free from obstruction ; to make easy ; "And *smooth* my passage to the realms of joy" ; বাধামুক্ত করা ; সহজ করা, অনায়াসলভ্য করা। **3.** To free from harshness ; শ্রুতিমধুর করা, শ্রোত্রমনোহর করা। **4.** To palliate ; "To *smooth* his fault I should have been more mild" ; দোষ লাঘব করা। **5.** To make calm ; to make agreeable ; শান্ত করা ; মনোরম করা, প্রীতিপ্রদ করা। ***Noun.*** **1.** The act of making smooth ; মসৃণীকরণ। **2.** That which is smooth ; the smooth part of anything ; মসৃণ বস্তু ; কোন বস্তুর মসৃণ অংশ। **3.** (*U. S.*) A grass-field ; (মার্কিণ যুক্তরাজ্য) ঘাসের ক্ষেত। **Smoothing-iron**—ইস্ত্রী। **Smoothing-plane**—শেষ পালিশ করার জন্য একপ্রকার রেঁদা।

smŏth'-ėr (smŭth-), *v. t.*, *i.* & *n.* **1.** To suffocate ; to kill by stopping breath ; শ্বাসরোধ করা ; শ্বাসরোধ করিয়া মারা। **2.** To suppress ; as, to *smother* one's anger ; দমন করা, চাপিয়া রাখা, রোধ করা। **3.** To cover closely up ; as, to *smother* a fire ; বেশ করিয়া

[illegible] ভ্রমণকালে যে ভাতা বা খাদ্যসামগ্রী প্রভৃতি দেওয়া হইত। **2.** (*Rom. Cath.*) The eucharist given to a dying person ; মুমূর্ষু ব্যক্তিকে খ্রীষ্টের অন্তিম-ভোজন স্মারক অনুষ্ঠানের সময় যে রুটি ও মদিরা প্রদান করা হইত। **3.** A portable altar ; বহনযোগ্য বেদী।

ri-brăc'-ū-lŭm (*pl.* -LA), *n.* One of the filamentous appendages of the cells of some of certain polyzoa ; কোন কোন বহুজৈবিকের অণুকোষের অংশুবৎ উপাঙ্গ, তন্তুক। **—lar,** *adj.*

vī-brate, *v. i.* & *t.* **1.** To move to and fro like pendulum ; to ward sign or indication ; as, a doubt still *smoulders* in his mind ; (লক্ষণায়) ধিকি ধিকি করিয়া জ্বলা, ভিতরে ভিতরে জ্বলা। ***Noun.*** Smouldering or slow combustion ; ধিকি ধিকি জ্বলন।

mudge (smŭj), **smutch,** (smŭch), *v. t.*, *i.* & *n.* **1.** (*Archaic*) To smear or stain with dirt or filth ; to blacken with smoke ; (অপ্রঃ) মলিন করা ; ধূমমলিন করা, ধূমকজ্জলিত করা। **2.** To blur or smear lines of writing or drawing ; চিত্র, অক্ষর প্রভৃতির রেখা জুবড়াইয়া ফেলা। ***Verb i.*** To become blurred ; জুবড়াইয়া যাওয়া, জুবড়ান। ***Noun.*** A stain ; blurred mark ; কলঙ্ক, দাগ ; জুবড়ানো দাগ। **Smudg'-i-ly,** *adv.* **Smudg'-i-ness,** *n.* **Smudg'-y,** *adj.*

smudge (smŭj), *n.* & *v. i.* (*U. S.*) A heap of damp combustibles, partially ignited, placed on the windward side of a house, tent, etc. so as to raise a dense smoke to keep off mosquitoes ; (মার্কিণ যুক্তরাজ্য) মশক নিবারণের জন্য গৃহ, তাঁবু, প্রভৃতির বাতাসের অভিমুখীন পার্শ্বে স্থাপিত ঈষৎ প্রজ্বালিত আশুজ্বলনশীল আর্দ্র বস্তুর স্তূপ। ***Verb i.*** To smoulder ; ধিকি ধিকি করিয়া জ্বলা। **Smudge coal**—একপ্রকার পাথুরিয়া কয়লা—বাহ

স্বভাবতই আংশিকরূপে কোক কয়লায় পরিণত হইয়াছে।

smŭg, *adj.* & *n.* **1.** Affectedly nice in dress; smart; ফিটফাট; চোস্ত (*colloq.*) **2.** Having a self-satisfied, conceited or conspicuously respectable air; as, a *smug* officer; কেতাদুরস্ত। **3.** Smooth; মসৃণ। ***Noun.*** (*Slang*) A student who is constantly engaged in study and does not take interest in any athletic pursuits; যে ছাত্র সর্ব্বদা পড়া নিয়া ব্যস্ত থাকে, এবং কোনপ্রকার ক্রীড়াদিতে যোগদান করেনা। **Smug′-ness,** *n.* **Smug-faced**—ফিটফাট চেহারা।

smŭg, *v. t.* To smarten up; ফিটফাট করা।

smŭg *v. t.* & *i.* To steal; চুরি করা। ***Verb i.*** **1.** To copy in an examination-hall; পরীক্ষায় নকল করা। **2.** To arrest; to imprison; গ্রেপ্তার করা; কয়েদ করা, জেলে দেওয়া। **Smug-boat**—চীনদেশের উপকূলে যে সকল নৌকায় অবৈধভাবে মাল আমদানী রপ্তানী করা হয়।

smŭg′-gle (-l), *v. t.* **1.** To import or export goods secretly without paying the custom-house duties; বিনা শুল্কে মাল আমদানী বা রপ্তানী করা, অবৈধভাবে মাল আমদানীরপ্তানী করা, ঘাট চুরি করা, মাশুল চুরি করা, ঘাট মারা। **2.** To convey or introduce clandestinely; "He never *smuggled* cigars into the dormitory"; গোপনে ঢুকাইয়া দেওয়া, গোপনে আনয়ন করা। **–gler,** *n.* One who smuggles; যে ব্যক্তি মাশুল ফাঁকি দিয়া অবৈধভাবে মাল আমদানী বা রপ্তানী করে, ঘাটমারনিয়া। **–gling,** *n.*

smŭt, *n.*, *v. t.* & *i.* **1.** A spot made with soot or coal; a particle of soot; কয়লা বা ঝুলের দাগ; ঝুলের গুঁড়া। **2.** Obscene language; "Spite, or *smut* or rhymes or blasphemes"; অশ্লীল ভাষা, কদর্য্য ভাষা। **3.** A parasitic fungus which forms in grain blasting it; শস্যের উপর জাত একপ্রকার ধ্বংসকারক ছত্রাক। ***Verb t.*** **1.** To stain or mark with smut; ঝুল, কয়লার গুঁড়া, প্রভৃতি দ্বারা মলিন করা। **2.** To taint with mildew; ছাতাধরান। **3.** To blacken; to tarnish; কালো করা; মলিন করা, কলঙ্কিত করা। ***Verb i.*** To gather smut; to give off smut; কয়লার গুঁড়া, ঝুল প্রভৃতি সঞ্চিত হওয়া; কয়লার গুঁড়া, ঝুল, প্রভৃতি নির্গত করা। **Smut′-ti-ly,** *adv.* **Smut′-ti-ness,** *n.* **Smut′-ty,** *adj.* **Smut-ball**—একজাতীয় ছত্রাক। **Smut-mill**—একপ্রকার যন্ত্র যদ্দারা শস্যের ছাতা ছাড়ান হয়।

smutch (smŭch), *v. t.*, *i.* & *n.* Same as SMUDGE (which see.)

Smyr′-na-ite (smêr-), **–ni-ŏt, –ni-ōte,** *adj.* & *n.* Of, or pertaining to, Smyrna; স্মির্ণা নগরীসম্বন্ধীয়। ***Noun.*** An inhabitant of Smyrna; স্মির্ণা নগরীর অধিবাসী।

snăck, *n.* **1.** A slight or hasty repast; সামান্য ভোজন, দ্রুত ভোজন। **2.** A share; অংশ, হিস্যা, ভাগ। **To go snack**—To go shares; ভাগাভাগি করা।

snăc′-ŏt, *n.* The great pipe-fish (*Syngnathus acus*); একপ্রকার মৎস্য।

snăf′-fle, (-l), *n.* A bridle, consisting of a slender bit mouth, with a single rein and without curb; একপ্রকার লাগাম, কজাই। **–fled,** *adj.*

snăg, *n.* & *v. t.* **1.** A short projecting stump; a knot; a protuberance; ছিন্নবৃক্ষের ভূমিলগ্ন উদ্গত অংশ; গাঁইট; স্ফীতি। **2.** A trunk or large branch of a tree imbedded in the bottom of a river at one end and rising at the other end to nearly to the surface and forming impediment to navigation; নদীগর্ভ প্রভৃতিতে প্রোথিত বৃক্ষকাণ্ড—যাহার সহিত সংস্পৃষ্ট হইয়া জাহাজ প্রভৃতি ধ্বংসপ্রাপ্ত হয়। **3.** (*Fig.*) Impediment; a projecting tooth; (লক্ষণায়) বাধা, বিঘ্ন, প্রতিবন্ধক; উদ্গত দন্ত। ***Verb t.*** **1.** To clear a river from snags; নদী হইতে প্রোথিত বৃক্ষকাণ্ড তুলিয়া ফেলা। **2.** To injure or destroy by running against the trunk or branches of a sunken tree; নিমগ্ন বৃক্ষকাণ্ডে বা শাখায় সংস্পৃষ্ট করিয়া ধ্বংস বা ক্ষতি করা। **Snag′-ged,** *adj.* **Snag′-gy,** *adj.*

snail (snāl), *n.*, *v. t.* & *i.* **1.** A slimy, slow-creeping, gasteropod mollusc; শম্বুক, শামুক, গুগ্‌লি [Syn. শাম্বুক, জলডিম্ব, জলশুক্তি, পঙ্কমণ্ডুক।] **2.** A lazy person; ঢিলা লোক, কুঁড়ে লোক। **3.** A piece of spiral machinery somewhat resembling a snail; একপ্রকার শম্বুকপ্রায়াকৃতি কুণ্ডলিত যন্ত্র। ***Verb t.*** To go very slowly; অতি মৃদুমন্দগতিতে গমন করা, অতি ধীরে ধীরে যাওয়া। ***Verb i.*** To clear of snails; to hunt for snails; শামুক বাছিয়া ফেলা; শম্বুক খুঁজা। **Snail-clover**—একপ্রকার গুল্ম। **Snail-fish**—একপ্রকার মৎস্য। **Snail-flower**—একপ্রকার পুষ্প। **Snail-like**—শম্বুকবৎ। **Snail-slow**—শম্বুকের মত মৃদুগামী, শম্বুকগতি। **Snail-trefoil**—একপ্রকার গুল্ম। **Snail-wheel**—ঘড়ীর শম্বুকপ্রায়াকৃতি দন্তুরিত চক্রবিশেষ—যদ্দারা বাদনের সংখ্যা নিয়মিত হয়। **At a snail's pace or gallop**—Lazily; ধীর গতিতে, মন্থর গতিতে।

snāke, *n.* **1.** A serpent; সাপ, সর্প, অহি, নাগ, ভোগী, ফণী, উরগ, ভুজঙ্গ, ভুজগ, বিষধর, পন্নগ [Syn. ব্যাল, দ্বিজিহ্ব, দ্বিরসন, ধ্বজী, দীর্ঘজিহ্ব, দংষ্ট্রী চক্রী, চক্ষুঃশ্রবা, আশীবিষ (cf. কি যাতনা বিষে বুঝিবে সে কিসে কভু আশীবিষে দংশেনি যারে), বিষাস্য, বিলাসী, গূঢ়পদ, গূঢ়পাদ, গূঢ়াঙিঘ্র, কুণ্ডলিনী, চক্রী, সরীসৃপ, কুণ্ডলী, কাকোদর, দর্ব্বীকর, দীর্ঘপৃষ্ঠ, দন্দশূক, তামস, বিলেশয়, জিহ্মগ,

পবনাশন, কুম্ভীনস, ভেকভুক, শ্বসনোৎসুক, ফণাধর, ফণধর, ফণাবান, ফণবান, ফণাকর, সমকোল, ব্যাড়, গোকর্ণ, উরঙ্গম, বিলবাসী, দর্ব্বিভৃৎ, হরি, প্রচলাকী, জলরুণ্ড, কঞ্চুকী, চিকুর, ভুজঙ্গম, উরঙ্গম, উরঃসর, অণ্ডজ, বিষানন, বিষায়ুধ, দীর্ঘরসন, দৃক্কর্ণ, লতাজিহ্ব, লতারসন, বায়ুভক্ষ, শ্বসনাশন, মণ্ডুকভুক্, কঞ্চুকালু, পৃদাকু, গহ্বর, তৃক্ষু, ভোগবান, ফণভৃত, কালিঙ্গ।] [সুশ্রুতের মতে সর্প অশীতি প্রকার। ইহারা পাঁচ শ্রেণীতে বিভক্ত। যথা :—(১) দর্ব্বীকর; (২) মণ্ডলী; (৩) রাজিমন্ত; (৪) নির্ব্বিষ সর্প; (৫) বৈকরঞ্জ। (For detailed information see Appendix)]. 2. A treacherous person; বিশ্বাসঘাতক লোক। **Snak'-y**, *adj.* 1. Abounding in snakes; সর্পবহুল। 2. Sly; deceitful; "Girded with *snaky* wiles"; ধূর্ত্ত; ছলনাপূর্ণ। 3. Covered with snakes; সর্পাবৃত। 4. Meandering; সর্পিল, আঁকা বাঁকা। **Snake-bird** — একপ্রকার মৎস্যভোজী পক্ষী। **Snake-catcher**—যে ব্যক্তি সর্প ধৃত করে, ব্যালগ্রাহী। **Snake-charmer**—সাপুড়িয়া, মালবৈদ্য, অহিতুণ্ডিক, তুবড়িওয়ালা [Syn. ফুল্লরীক, জাঙ্গুলী, জাঙ্গুলিক, বিষবৈদ্য।] **Snake-gourd**—চিচিঙ্গা, গোশিঙ্গা। **Snake-head**—শোল, গজার, প্রভৃতি মৎস্য। **Snake-lock**—সর্পকুন্তল। **Snakeshead**—একপ্রকার পুষ্প। **Snake-stone**—সর্পমণি নাগমণি, ফণামণি, সর্পফণজ। **Snake-wood** — (Indian) কুচিলা লতা। **Snake-worship** — Same as SERPENT-WORSHIP (which see). **Snake-worshipper** — নাগোপাসক, সর্পপূজক। **Snaky sisters**—Same as FURIES (which see). **A snake in the grass**—A hidden danger or secret enemy; অজ্ঞাতবিপদ, গুপ্তশত্রু (cf. ক্ষীরের ভিতর হীরের ছুরি)। **To raise or wake snakes**—To make disturbance; গোলমাল বাঁধান। **To see snakes**—(*Slang U. S.*) To have delirium tremens; (মার্কিণ যুক্তরাজ্যের ইতরভাষায়) মস্তিষ্ক বিকৃতি হেতু নানাপ্রকার বিকট দৃশ্য দেখা। **To warm or cherish a snake in one's bosom**—To maintain a traitor; to receive evil for good; দুধ কলা দিয়ে সাপ পোষা; উপকারীকে বাঘে খায়।

snap, *v. t.*, *i.* & *n.* 1. To break short; মটকাইয়া ভাঙ্গিয়া ফেলা। 2. To strike with a sharp sound; খট্ করিয়া আঘাত করা। 3. To shut with a sharp quick sound; খট্ করিয়া বন্ধ করা। 4. To bite or seize suddenly esp. with the teeth; কট্ করিয়া কামড় দেওয়া, কটাস করিয়া কামড়াইয়া ধরা। 5. To catch unexpectedly; খপ্ করিয়া ধরা। 6. To crack; as, to *snap* one's fingers; to crack a whip; মটকান, পটাস করিয়া ফুটান, তুড়িমারা; সপাং করিয়া মারা। 7. To twang; as, to *snap* the strings of a musical instrument; ঝঙ্কার দেওয়া। 8. To pick up hastity; টপ্ করিয়া তোলা। 9. To take an instantaneous photograph; চট্ করিয়া ফটোগ্রাফ তোলা। ***Verb i.*** 1. To try to catch something with the tooth; কামড়াইয়া ধরিতে চেষ্টা করা। 2. To crack; ফুটা, মট করিয়া উঠা, পটাস করিয়া উঠা, খট্ করিয়া উঠা। 3. To utter sharp, harsh, angry words (usually with *at*); as, to *snap at* a child; কড়া কথা বলা, চোখাচোখা বলা। 4. To catch eagerly at a proposal or offer; খপ্ করিয়া ধরা। ***Noun.*** 1. A sudden breaking or rupture of any substance; মট করিয়া ভাঙ্গন। 2. A sudden eager bite; খট করিয়া কামড়। 3. A sharp noise; মট শব্দ, খট খট, পটাস, সপাং। 4. A sudden sharp motion or blow as with the finger sprung from the thumb, or the thumb from the finger; তুড়ি, টোকা। 5. A kind of crisp biscuit; একপ্রকার মচমচে বিস্কুট। 6. A small catch or fastening, as of a bracelet; বালা প্রভৃতির আঁকড়া। 7. A sudden spell of cold weather; "A cold *sn*[ap] following eagerly on a thaw", হঠাৎ কিছুকালের জন্য শীতাগম। 8. An earing furnished with a catch; আঁকড়াকিশিষ্ট দুল। 9. A children's game of cards; ছেলেদের একপ্রকার তাসখেলা। 10. A glass moulder's iron rod; কাচদ্রব্যনির্ম্মাতার যন্ত্রবিশেষ। 11. A tool used in making rivets; নাচি প্রস্তুতের জন্য একপ্রকার যন্ত্র। 12. (*Colloq.*) Briskness; crispness; vigour; as, his style looks *snap*; (চলিতভাষায়) চটুলতা; ঝরঝরে ভাব; ওজস্বিতা। 13. (*Photog.*) Same as SNAPSHOT. 14. Same as SNAP-SHOT. 15. A scrap; টুকরা। 16. (*Theatre*) A short engagement as an actor; (রঙ্গালয়) অল্পকালের জন্য অভিনেতৃরূপে নিয়োগ। 17. A kind of beetle; একপ্রকার গোবরে পোকা। 18. (*Obs.*) A greedy fellow; (অপ্র:) লোভী ব্যক্তি। 19. (*Pl.*) Handcuffs; হাতকড়া। **Snap'-pish**, *adj.* 1. Eager to bite; দংশনোৎসুক। 2. Peevish; tart; খিট্‌খিটে; কড়া, রোখা। **Snap'-py**, *adj.* **Snap-dragon**—একপ্রকার উদ্যানজাত গুল্ম; একপ্রকার ক্রীড়া—যাহাতে জলন্ত ব্রাণ্ডিপূর্ণ পাত্র হইতে কিসমিস তুলিয়া খাওয়া হয়; কাচদ্রব্য প্রস্তুতকারিগণের একপ্রকার চিমটা। **Snaphance**—একপ্রকার সেকেলে বন্দুক। **Snap-lock**—একপ্রকার তালা—যাহা আঁকড়ার সাহায্যে বন্ধ করা হয়। **Snapshot**—যে ক্ষুদ্র ফটোগ্রাফযন্ত্রের সাহায্যে পট্ করিয়া ফটো তোলা হয়। **Snap-shot**—অনির্দ্দিষ্ট ভাবে নিক্ষিপ্ত গুলি; বিশেষরূপে নিশানা না করিয়া দ্রুত যে গুলি ছোড়া হয়। **To snap off**—To break suddenly; মটকাইয়া ভাঙ্গা। To bite off suddenly; হঠাৎ কামড়াইয়া দেওয়া। **To snap one's fingers**—To show contempt by cracking one's fingers; আঙ্গুল মটকাইয়া অবজ্ঞা প্রকাশ করা (cf. কলা

দেখান)। **To snap one up**—To treat with sharp words; কড়া কথা শুনাইয়া দেওয়া।

snare, *n.* & *v. t.* 1. Trap; ফাঁদ, পাশ, জাল, বাগুড়া, কুটযন্ত্র, পাখী-ধরা। 2. A noose; পাশ। 3. Anything by which one is entangled or brought into trouble; ফাঁদ। 4. One of the strings formed of twisted raw-hide stretched across the lower head of a drum; ঢক্কার দোয়ালী। 5. (*Surg.*) An instrument consisting of a wire noose for removing the tumours; স্ফোটকাদি অপসারণের জন্য একপ্রকার পাশযন্ত্র। ***Verb t.*** To catch with a snare; জালে বদ্ধ করা, পাশে বদ্ধ করা, ফাঁদে ফেলা, জালে আটকান। **Snar'-er,** *n.* **Snare drum**—একপ্রকার ঢক্কা—যাহার নীচের দিকের মাথার উপর দিয়া দোয়ালী প্রসারিত আছে।

snârl, *v. i.* & *n.* 1. To growl, as an angry dog; (কুকুর সম্বন্ধে) ভেউ ভেউ করিয়া ডাকা, ভুকা, খেঁকান, খেউ খেউ করা। 2. To speak roughly or crossly; খেউ খেউ করা। ***Noun.*** A sharp angry growl; খেউ খেউ শব্দ, খেঁকানি। **Snarl'-er,** *n.* **Snarl'-ing, Snarl'-y,** *adjs.* **Snarling iron** — ধাতুর চাদরের উপর ঢেউ তোলা বা টোপ তোলার জন্য একপ্রকার যন্ত্র। **Snarling letter**—ইংরাজী R অক্ষর। **To snarl out**—To utter in a snarling tone; ভেউ ভেউ করিয়া বলা।

snârl, *v. t.* & *n.* 1. (*Archaic*) To entangle; to complicate; (অপ্রঃ) জড়িত করা; গোলমাল করিয়া ফেলা। 2. To form raised work upon metal; ধাতুর উপর টোপ তোলার কার্য্য করা। ***Noun.*** (*Archaic*) Tangle; (অপ্রঃ) জট, গাঁইট।

snatch (snăch), *v. t., i.* & *n.* To seize hastily or abruptly; to seize or take without permission or ceremony; খপ করিয়া ধরা, কাড়িয়া নেওয়া, ছিনাইয়া নেওয়া। ***Verb i.*** To attempt to seize anything suddenly; to catch; কোন জিনিষ হঠাৎ ধরিতে চেষ্টা করা; ধরা ***Noun.*** 1. A hasty catching or seizing; খপ করিয়া ধরণ। 2. An attempt to seize anything; কোন জিনিষ ধরার জন্য চেষ্টা। 3. A short fit of vigorous action; a short fit or turn; as, he only works by *snatches*; একচোট; ক্ষণিক কার্য। 4. A small piece; as, *snatch* of a song; ক্ষুদ্র অংশ। **Snatch'-i-ly,** *adv.* **Snatch'-y,** *adj.* **To snatch at an offer**—To seize it eagerly; আগ্রহের সহিত গ্রহণ করা।

sneak (snēk), *v. i., t.* & *n.* 1. To creep or steal away privately; to slink; গোপনে সরিয়া পড়া, পাশ কাটান; চুপি চুপে সরিয়া পড়া। 2. To behave with meanness or servility; হীনজনোচিত ব্যবহার করা, নীচতা দেখান, নীচভাবে কায করা। ***Verb t.*** (*Slang*) To steal; (ইতরভাষায়) চুরি করা। ***Noun.*** 1. A mean, cowardly and treacherous fellow; হীনপ্রকৃতি লোক, নীচাশয় লোক। 2. (*School slang*) Informer; (ছেলেদের অবর-ভাষায়) যে ব্যক্তি গোপনে অন্য ছাত্রের বিরুদ্ধে লাগায়। 3. (*Cricket*) A ball bowled along the ground; (ক্রীকেট ক্রীড়া) ভূমিতে গড়াইয়া যে কন্দুক চালিত করা হয়। **Sneak'-ing,** *adj.* 1. Cowardly; furtive; underhand; ভীরু, কাপুরুষ; কুটিল; তলে তলে সাধিত। 2. Concealed; shamefaced; গুপ্ত; লজ্জাকর, লজ্জাজনক। **Sneak'-y,** *adj.* Same as SNEAKING above. **Sneak-boat**—পক্ষিশিকারীদের একপ্রকার চ্যাপ্টাতলা নৌকা। **Sneak-thief**—যে চোর দরজা জানালা খোলা পাইয়া চুরি করে। **To have a sneaking kindness for**—To have a secret sympathy for; গোপনে সহানুভূতি থাকা, তলে তলে সহানুভূতি থাকা।

snĕck, *n.* & *v. t.* Latch; খিল। ***Verb t.*** To fasten by a latch; খিল দেওয়া।

sneer (snēr), *v. i., t.* & *n.* 1. To show contempt by turning up the nose or by particular cast of countenance; মুখ ভঙ্গী করিয়া অবজ্ঞা প্রকাশ করা, নাক সিঁটকান, মুখ বাঁকান। 2. To speak derisively; অবজ্ঞা সহকারে কথা বলা, মুখ বাঁকাইয়া কথা বলা। 3. To scoff; বিদ্রূপ করা, অবজ্ঞা করা, উপহাস করা। ***Verb t.*** To utter with a sneer; অবজ্ঞার সহিত বলা, নাকসিঁটকাইয়া বলা। ***Noun.*** 1. Act of sneering; অবজ্ঞা প্রকাশকরণ। 2. An expression of contempt or derision; scoff; নাকসিঁটকানি, নাসিকাকুঞ্চন, মুখবাকানি; বিদ্রূপ, উপহাস, অবজ্ঞা, ব্যঙ্গোক্তি। **Sneer'-er,** *n.* **Sneer'-ing-ly,** *adv.* **Sneering accent**—টানা কথা, টান টান কথা।

sneeze (snēz), *v. i.* & *n.* To emit air through the nose, audibly and convulsively, in consequence of irritation in the inner membrane of the nose; হাঁচি দেওয়া। ***Noun.*** The act of sneezing; emission of wind audibly and violently through the nose; হাঁচি দেওন, ছিক্কন; হাঁচি, ছিক্কা। **Sneeze-wood**—নাকছিক্কানি (খোরী)। **Not to be sneezed at** — Not to be disregarded; উপক্ষেণীয় নয়। **To sneeze at a thing**—To despise; অবজ্ঞা করা, বিদ্রূপ করা, নাকসিঁটকান।

snĕll, *n.* 1. Pungent; ঝাঁঝাল। 2. Acrimonious; তীব্র, তীক্ষ্ণ।

snick, *v. t.* & *n.* 1. To cut slightly; ঈষৎ কাটা। 2. (*Cricket*) To hit a (ball) by a light glancing blow; ব্যাট হেলাইয়া আঘাত করা। ***Noun.*** 1. A slight notch or cut; খাঁজ। 2. (*Cricket*) A light glancing blow given to a cricket ball; ব্যাট হেলাইয়া মৃদু আঘাত।

snick'-ĕr, *v. i.* & *n.* To giggle; ফিক ফিক করিয়া হাসা। ***Noun.*** Giggle; ফিকফিক হাসি, খিল খিল হাসি।

snick'-ĕr-snee (-snē), *n.* A large knife; ছোরা।

Sni'-dėr, *n.* A kind of breech-loading rifle formerly in use; সাবেকীধরণের একপ্রকার রাইফেল বন্দুক। **Snider-rifle**—Same as SNIDER. [আবিষ্কারক Jacob Sniderএর নাম হইতে গৃহীত।]

sniff, *v. i., t.* & *n.* To draw air audibly up the nose; সশব্দে নিশ্বাস টানা, জোরে শ্বাস গ্রহণ করা। ***Verb t.*** 1. To draw in with the breath through the nose; নিশ্বাসের সহিত নাকের ভিতর টানিয়া লওয়া। 2. To perceive by sniffing; শুঁকিয়া অনুভব করা। ***Noun.*** 1. The act of sniffing; শুঁকন। 2. Smell; গন্ধ, বাস। 3. The sound of sniffing; জোরে শ্বাস টানার শব্দ। 4. That which is sniffed; as, a *sniff* of air; যাহা নাকে টানিয়া নেওয়া হয়। **To sniff at**—To try the smell of; গন্ধ পরীক্ষা করা। To show contempt for; নাক সিঁটকান।

sniff'-ÿ, *adj.* 1. (*Colloq.*) Disdainful; অবজ্ঞাপূর্ণ, ঘৃণাসূচক, অবজ্ঞাসূচক। 2. Supercilious; দৃপ্ত, উদ্ধত। 3. Slightly malodorous; ঈষদ্ দুর্গন্ধ।

snift'-ing-valve (-vălv), *n.* A valve in the cylinder of a steam-engine for the escape of air; বাষ্পীয়যন্ত্রের বায়ুনির্গমের জন্য কপাটকল।

snig'-ger (-ėr), *v. i.* & *n.* Same as SNICKER (which see).

snig'-gle (-l), *v. i.* & *t.* To fish for eels by thursting the bait into their hiding place; গর্তে টোপ ঢুকাইয়া বাইন মৎস্য শিকার করা। ***Verb t.*** To catch eels by this means; উক্ত উপায়ে বাইন মৎস্য ধরা।

snip, *v. t., i.* & *n.* To cut with scissors; কাঁচি দ্বারা কাটা, ছাঁটা। ***Verb i.*** To clip; কাঁচি দ্বারা কাটা। ***Noun.*** 1. A single cut with scissors; কাঁচি দ্বারা কাটন। 2. (*Slang*) A tailor; (ইতরভাষায়) দর্জ্জী।

snipe, *n., v. i.* & *t.* 1. A bird that frequents the banks of rivers and the borders of fens, distinguished by its long, slender and straight bill; কাদাখোঁচা পাখী, চাহাপাখী (হিউম্), কর্দ্দমখঞ্জনা (ষোঃ)। 2. (*Rare*) A fool; (কচিদ্‌ব্যবহৃত) বোকা। 3. A thin lean person; তালপাতার সিপাই। ***Verb i.*** 1. To hunt snipes; কাদাখোঁচা পাখী শিকার করা। 2. To shoot at detached men of an enemy's force, esp. when not in action (usually with *at*); সৈন্যদলের বিশেষ বিশেষ সৈন্যকে লক্ষ্য করিয়া গুলি করা (বিশেষতঃ যুদ্ধবিশ্রান্তি কালে) (also *verb t.*)। ***Verb t.*** To pick off person by shooting them at long range one at a time; শত্রুপক্ষের বিশেষ বিশেষ লোককে দূর হইতে গুলি করিয়া মারা।

snip'-ėr, *n.* One who snipes or shoots from concealment; যে ব্যক্তি শত্রুসৈন্যের বিশেষ বিশেষ লোককে বাছিয়া গুলি করে, যে ব্যক্তি লুকায়িত থাকিয়া গুলি করে।

snip'-pet (-ĕt), *n.* 1. A small piece cut off by snipping; কাটছাঁট। 2. Odds and ends; টুকিটাকি।

sniv'-ĕl, *v. i.* & *n.* 1. To run at the nose; নাক দিয়া ঝরা, নাসাপথে স্রাবিত হওয়া, শিকনি পড়া, নাক ঝরা। 2. To cry or whine as children; শিশুর মত কাঁদা, নাকে কাঁদা, গোঁ গোঁ করা। 3. To show maudlin emotion; ভাবোচ্ছ্বাস প্রদর্শন করা। ***Noun.*** 1. Mucous from the nose; সিংঘান, শিকনি। 2. The sound produced in the nostrils of animals from being stuffed with mucous; শ্লেষ্মাদ্বার রোধ হওয়া হেতু জন্তুর নাসারন্ধ্রে যে শব্দ নির্গত হয়। 3. Whining and weeping; ছিঁচকাঁদুনি। 4. Hypocricy; কপটতা, ভণ্ডামি, মায়া কান্না। **–er, –ing,** *ns.*

snŏb, *n.* 1. A vulgar person that apes gentility, or affect the intimacy of nobles and distinguished persons; সভ্যম্মন্যলোক, ফতোবাবু, ভদ্রম্মন্যব্যক্তি। 2. (*Univ. cant*) A townsman; (বিশ্ববিদ্যালয়ের ইতরভাষায়) নাগরিক। 3. (*Slang*) A shoe-maker; (ইতরভাষায়) মুচি। 4. Same as RAT. **Snob'-bish,** *adj.* **Snob'-bish-ness, Snob'-ber-y,** *ns.*

snōōd, *n.* (*Scot.*) A fillet to confine the hair; (স্কটল্যণ্ডে) স্ত্রীলোকদিগের কবরীবন্ধের জন্য ফিতা। **Snood'-ed,** *adj.*

snōōk, *n.* Kinds of fish; বিভিন্ন জাতীয় মৎস্যের সাধারণ নাম।

snooze (snôz), *v. i.* & *n.* To take a nap; to doze; অল্প নিদ্রা যাওয়া, ঈষৎ নিদ্রাবিষ্ট হওয়া, খানিক ঘুমান; ঝিমান। ***Noun.*** A short sleep; স্বল্প নিদ্রা, তন্দ্রা, ঝিমানি।

snōre, *v. i., t.* & *n.* To breathe through the open nose and open mouth in sleep with a rough hoarse noise; নিদ্রিত অবস্থায় নাক ডাকান বা নাসিকা গর্জ্জন করা। ***Verb t.*** To pass time in snoring (with *away*); নাক ডাকাইয়া কাল কাটান। ***Noun.*** 1. A hoarse breathing in sleep; নাক ডাকানি, নাসিকাগর্জ্জন, নাসিকাধ্বনি। 2 (*Pl.*) Same as SNIVEL 4 (which see). **Snor'-er,** *n.*

snŏrt, *v. i., t.* & *n.* 1. To force the air with violence through the nostrils like a horse; উচ্চ নাসিকাধ্বনি করা, নাকডাকা, নাসিকাগর্জ্জন করা। 2. (*Dial.*) To laugh loudly; (উপভাষায়) অট্টহাস্য করা। ***Verb t.*** 1. To utter with a snort; নাসিকাধ্বনিপূর্ব্বক উচ্চারণ করা। 2. (Of a railway engine etc.) To make a sound resembling a horse's snort; (বাষ্পীয়শকট সম্পর্কে) অশ্বের নাসিকাগর্জ্জনের মত শব্দ করা। 3. To express defiance by snorting; নাসিকাধ্বনি করিয়া অবজ্ঞা প্রকাশ করা। ***Noun.*** A forcible blowing of air through extended nostrils, as a horse; বিস্ফারিত নাসারন্ধ্রপথে সজোরে বায়ু নিঃসরণ, নাসিকাধ্বনি, নাসিকাশব্দ।

snŏrt′-ẽr, *n.* **1.** One who snorts ; নাসিকা গৰ্জ্জনকারী। **2.** A gale of wind ; ঝঞ্ঝা। **3.** (*Slang*) A blow on the nose ; নাসিকায় আঘাত। **4.** Any remarkable thing ; অসাধারণ বস্তু।

snŏt, *n.* **1.** (*Vulg.*) Mucus of the nose ; সিংঘান। **2.** A mean fellow ; হীন ব্যক্তি। **Snot-rag**—রুমাল।

snŏt′-ter (-ẽr), *n.* A Turkey-cock's wattles ; মোরগের গলার লতি।

snŏt′-ter (-ẽr), *v. i.* (*Scot.*) To go along lazily; (স্কটলণ্ড) অলস ভাবে চলা।

snŏt′-ty (-ĭ), *adj.* & *n.* Running with snot; foul with the mucus of the nose ; সিংঘানস্রাবী ; শ্লেষ্মাদূষিত। **–ti-ly,** *adv.* **–ti-ness,** *n.* (*Naut. slang*) Same as MIDSHIPMAN (which see).

snout (snowt), *n.* **1.** The projecting nose of a beast ; পশুর লম্বিত মুখাগ্র, তুণ্ড, ঘোণা (of a hog), পোত্র (কিরাঃ)। **2.** (*Contempt.*) The nose of a man ; (অবজ্ঞাচ্ছলে) মানুষের নাক। **3.** The pointed front of something ; nozzle ; কোন কিছুর সূক্ষ্মাগ্র মুখ ; নল প্রভৃতির অগ্রভাগ, উদ্গাত নল। **Snout′-ed,** *adj.* **Snout-beetle** — একজাতীয় গোবরে পোকা—ইহাদের মুখের অগ্রভাগ সূক্ষ্ম থাকে। **Snout-ring**—গাছ প্রভৃতি যাহাতে খুঁড়িয়া না তুলিতে পারে—তজ্জন্য শূকরের নাকে যে আংটা পরান হয়।

snow (snō) *n., v. i.* & *t.* **1.** The watery particles in the atmosphere frozen into small white crystalline flakes and falling to the earth or spread on it as a white layer ; বরফ, তুষার, হিমানী, হিমশিলা, হিম, তুহিন (cf. তুহিনসদৃশ—মৎস্যপুরাণ)। **2.** A fall of snow ; তুষারপাত, হিমানীপাত। **3.** Something which resembles snow ; as, her breast of *snow* ; তুষারবৎ কোনকিছু, তুষারশুভ্র বস্তু, হিমানীধবল বস্তু। **4.** (*pl.*) White breasts ; "Star-like eyes and heaving *snows*" ; তুষারশুভ্র কুচযুগল। **5.** A dish or confection resembling snow in apperance ; তুষারবৎ শুভ্র

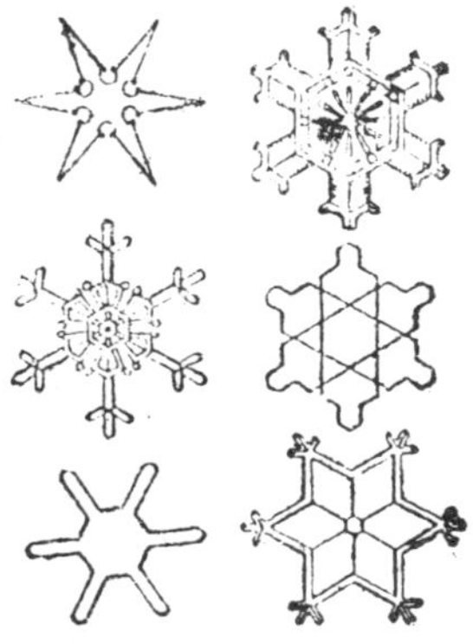

Formation of snow-crystals.

ব্যঞ্জন বা মিষ্টদ্রব্য। **6.** (*Poet.*) White marble ; (কবিতায়) শ্বেতমর্ম্মর। **7.** Whiteness as of snow ; ধবলিমা। **8.** (*Slang*) Those admitted to theatre on passes ; (ইতরভাষায়) যাহারা পাশ লইয়া থিয়েটারে যায়। ***Verb i.*** To fall in snow ; তুষারপাত হওয়া, হিমানীপাত হওয়া। ***Verb t.*** **1.** To scatter like snow ; তুষারের মত ছড়ান। **2.** To cover with snow ; তুষারাচ্ছাদিত করা। **Snow′-y,** *adj.* **Snowball**—বরফের পিণ্ড ; দানার্থ সংগৃহীত অর্থরাশি। **Snowball-tree** — একপ্রকার পুষ্পবৃক্ষ। **Snow-berry**—ক্ষুদ্র ক্ষুদ্র শ্বেতবর্ণ ফুলপ্রসূ একপ্রকার উদ্যানরোপিত গুল্ম। **Snow-bird**—বিভিন্ন জাতীয় শ্বেতবর্ণ তুতী পাখী। **Snow-blind**—তুষার হইতে প্রতিবিম্বিত আলোকদ্বারা নষ্টদৃষ্টি। **Snow-blink** — আকাশে হিমানী বা তুষারক্ষেত্রের প্রতিফলিত প্রভা। **Snow-boots**—বুটের উপর ধারণের উপযোগী রবার ও কাপড়ে তৈরী একপ্রকার পাদাবরণ। **Snow-bound**—তুষারমণ্ডিত, তুষারবদ্ধ। **Snow-cap** — একপ্রকার শ্বেতশীর্ষ পক্ষী। **Snow-capped**—তুষারশীর্ষ, তুষারচূড়, হিমচ্ছত্র (cf. হিমচ্ছত্রমহাশৃঙ্গং — মৎস্যপুরাণ), প্রালেয় (cf. প্রালেয়শীত — শিশুঃ ৪—৬৪)। **Snow-drift**—বায়ুচালিত তুষারস্তূপ, বায়ুদ্বারা সঞ্চালিত তুষার রাশি। **Snow-drop**—একপ্রকার ফুলগাছ। **Snow eyes**—তুষারপ্রভা দ্বারা যাহাতে অন্ধ না হইতে পারে—তজ্জন্য এস্কুইমোগণ যে একপ্রকার অতি লঘু কাষ্ঠনির্ম্মিত নেত্রাবরণ পরিয়া থাকে। **Snow-fall**—তুষারপাত, তুষারপতন, হিমানীপাত। **Snow-field**—তুষারক্ষেত্র (হিঃ কোঃ)। **Snow-flake** — তুষারকণা, তুষারতুল (হিঃ কোঃ)। **Snow-gague**—তুষারমানযন্ত্র। **Snow-goggles**—তুষারাচ্ছাদিত পৰ্ব্বতাদির উপর দিয়া চলার সময় তুষারের প্রতিফলিত প্রভাদ্বারা যাহাতে দৃষ্টিশক্তির হানি না হয়—তজ্জন্য যে একপ্রকার চসমা পরা হয়। **Snow-goose**—উত্তরমেরুবাসী একপ্রকার তুষারবর্ণ মরাল, তুষারমরাল। **Snow-grouse**—Same as PTARMIGAN (which see). **Snow-house, Snow-hut**—তুষারগৃহ, তুষার-কুটীর। **Snow-ice**—গলিত তুষার হইতে গঠিত অৰ্দ্ধস্বচ্ছ শ্বেত বরফ। **Snow-leopard**—Same as OUNCE 2. **Snow-line**—চিরতুষাররেখা, চিরনীহারসীমা, হিমরেখা (হিঃ কোঃ)। **Snow-on-the-mountain**—একজাতীয় শ্বেতপুষ্পপ্রসূ উদ্যানগুল্ম। **Snow-owl, Snowy-owl**—একজাতীয় শ্বেতবর্ণ পেচক। **Snow-plant, Red-snow**—বরফের উপর জাত একপ্রকার আণুবীক্ষণিক শৈবাল—যদ্দ্বারা তুষার রক্তবর্ণে রঞ্জিত হইয়া থাকে। **Snow-plough**—লৌহবর্ম্মের সম্মুখ হইতে হিমানীরাশি

Snow-shoe.

অপসারণের জন্য যন্ত্রবিশেষ। **Snow shoe**—বরফের উপর ভ্রমণ করার জন্য একপ্রকার পাদুকা। **Snow-shovel**—বরফ তোলার জন্য কাঠের বৃহৎ ফেওড়া বা বেলচা। **Snow-slip**—পৰ্ব্বতপার্শ্ব হইতে তুষারস্খলন, তুষারচ্যুতি। **Snow-storm**—তুষারপাত সহকৃত ঝঞ্ঝা, তুষারঝঞ্ঝা।

Snow-white — তুষারশুভ্র, তুষারশ্বেত, হিমগৌর (কিরাঃ), তুষারগৌর, তুষারধবল। **It snows** — Snow is falling; তুষারপাত হইতেছে। **Snowed up in**—তুষারবদ্ধ। **The snows of eighty years**—অশীতিপর বৃদ্ধের তুষারশুভ্র কেশরাশি। **To snow under**—To defeat by a large number of votes; বহুসংখ্যক ভোটদ্বারা পরাজিত করা।

snŭb, *v. t.* & *n.* **1.** To check, stop or rebuke with a tart sarcastic reply or remark; দাবান, দমাইয়া দেওয়া, থোতা মুখ ভোঁতা করা, মুখতাড়া দেওয়া। **2.** To check the way of (ship) esp. by rope wound round snubbing post; খোঁটায় দড়ী বাঁধিয়া জাহাজের গতি রোধ করা। ***Noun.*** Rebuff; মুখতাড়া, দাবানি। **To receive a snub**—থোঁতা মুখ ভোঁতা হওয়া। **To snub a cable**—To stop it suddenly when running out; জাহাজের কাছি ছাড়িতে ছাড়িতে হঠাৎ থামান।

snŭb, *adj.* & *n.* (Of nose) Short; (নাক সম্বন্ধে) থাঁদা। ***Noun.*** Snub nose; থাঁদ নাক। **Snub-nosed**—নাক থাঁদা, নত নাসিক।

snŭff, *v. i., t.* & *n.* **1.** To inhale forcibly through the nose; সজোরে নাকে টানিয়া লওয়া। **2.** To take snuff; নস্য গ্রহণ করা। ***Verb t.*** **1.** To draw in or inhale forcibly; সজোরে নিশ্বাসের সহিত টানিয়া লওয়া। **2.** To perceive by smelling; গন্ধদ্বারা টের পাওয়া। **3.** To sniff in order to find out; কোন কিছু বাহির করার জন্য শুঁকা। ***Noun.*** **1.** The act of inhaling by the nose; শ্বাস গ্রহণ। **2.** Smell; গন্ধ, বাস। **3.** Pulverised tobacco or other substance snuffed up or prepared to be snuffed up, by the nose; নস্য। **Snuff'-i-ness**, *n.* **Snuff'-y**, *adj.* **Snuff-box**—নস্যদান, নস্যের কৌটা, নস্যধানী, নস্যাধার। **Snuff-coloured**—নস্যবর্ণ। **Snuff-mill** — নস্য প্রস্তুতের যন্ত্র। **Snuff-spoon**—কৌটা হইতে নস্য লইবার জন্য ক্ষুদ্র চামচে। **To snuff pepper**—(*Archaic*) To get angry; (অপ্রঃ) রাগান্বিত হওয়া, চটা। **To take thing in snuff**—(*Archaic*) To take offence; (অপ্রঃ) দোষ লওয়া। **Up to snuff**—জ্ঞাতসার; সহজে ঠকিবার নয়, সেয়ানা।

snŭff, *v. t., i.* & *n.* To cut the snuff of as a candle; মোমবাতির শলিতা প্রভৃতির দগ্ধ অংশ কাটিয়া ফেলা। ***Verb i.*** (*Slang*) To die; (ইতরভাষায়) মরা। ***Noun.*** The charred part of a candle wick; প্রদীপের শলিতার দগ্ধ অংশ। **To snuff out**—To extinguish by snuffing; to annihilate; শলিতার দগ্ধ অংশ কাটিয়া ফেলিয়া দীপ নির্বাণ করা; ধ্বংস করা, নাশ করা।

snŭff'-ẽrs, *n.* An instrument for cropping the snuff of a candle; মোমবাতির শলিতার পোড়া অংশ কাটার জন্য একপ্রকার কাঁচি।

snŭf'-fle (-l), *n.* & *v. i.* **1.** A sound made by the passage of air through the nostrils; নাসাশব্দ, নাসাধ্বনি। **2.** An affected nasal twang; cant; নাকিসুর; ভণ্ডামি। ***Verb i.*** **1.** To breathe hard through the nose, esp. when obstructed by mucus; সশব্দে নিশ্বাস টানা। **2.** To speak through the nose; নাকিসুরে কথা বলা। **—fler**, *n.* **—fling**, *adv.*

snŭg, *adj.* **1.** Trim; cozy; as, a *snug* corner; পরিপাটী; আরামদায়ক, সুখদায়ক, আরামজনক। **2.** Concealed; "When you lay *snug*, to snap young Damon's goat"; লুক্কায়িত। **3.** Close-fitting; "The corsage of the gown should not be too *snug*"; আঁটসাট। **4.** Pleasant; as, *snug* climate; মনোরম, প্রীতিপ্রদ, রম্য। **5.** Substantial; as, *snug* income; সুখস্বাচ্ছন্দ্যজনক। **Snug'-ly**, *adv.* **Snug'-ness**, *n.*

snŭg'-ger-y̆ (-ẽr-), *n.* **1.** A snug place; a man's private room; আরামজনক স্থান, সুখময়স্থান; নিভৃত কক্ষ, নির্জ্জন কক্ষ, খাস কামরা।

snŭg'-gle (-l), *v. i.* & *t.* To move one way and another to get a snug, close place; to lie snug or close, esp. for warmth; উষ্ণ বা আরামজনক স্থানের জন্য এদিকে ওদিকে সঞ্চরণ করা; গরম হওয়ার জন্য আরামজনক স্থানে শায়িত হওয়া। ***Verb t.*** To draw close, as for comfort; to cuddle; আরামের জন্য কাছে টানিয়া আনা; বুকে চাপিয়া ধরা।

sō, *adv., conj.* & *interj.* **1.** In that manner; ঐরূপে, সেরূপে, এভাবে, সেভাবে। **2.** In like manner or degree; এমন, এমত, এরূপ, এপ্রকার, এত। **3.** (*Chiefly colloq.*) Very much; as, you are *so* good; এত, অতিশয়, অত্যন্ত। **4.** For this reason; therefore; "We leave at daybreak for Pekin, *so* I will wish you good-bye now"; এইহেতু, এই কারণে, এইজন্য, এজন্য; অতএব। **5.** Let it be as it is; "And if it please you, *so*; If not why *so*"; তাহাই হউক, তথাস্তু। **6.** In strong asseveration; as, *so* help me God!; নিশ্চিৎ বা দৃঢ় উক্তিতে। **7.** Such being the case; accordingly well; "And *so* farewell"; এরূপ অবস্থায়; অতএব; আচ্ছা। ***Conj.*** **1.** For this reason; therefore; এইহেতু; অতএব। **2.** Provided that; on condition that; "*So* the doctrine be but wholesome and edifying, though there should be a want of exactness in the manner of speaking or reasoning, it may be overlooked"; যদ্যপি যদি এইরূপ হয়; এই সর্ত্তে। ***Interj.*** Stop; that will do; থামো, রসো, দাঁড়াও; বস্। **In so far as** — To that extent; যতদূর, যে পরিমাণে, যতটা। **Is it so?**—Is it the fact?; বটে!, তাই নাকি, সত্যি নাকি। **Or so**—Or the like ; তেমন কিছু। Or thereabout; অথবা কাছাকাছি। **Quite so, Just so**—তাইতো। **So-and-so**—A certain person not mentioned by name ; অমুক অমুক ব্যক্তি অমুক লোক। **So as**—In such a manner as ; এরূপ ভাবে যে। Provided that ; যদি হয়, যদিস্যাৎ। **So called**—Generally called thus (*usu. imply contempt*) ; তথাকথিত। **So far as**—To such a degree or extent as ; এতদূর যে, ততদূর যে, ততটা যে। **So far forth**—(*Obs.*) To such a degree ; (অপ্র:) ততদূর। **So far so good**—এই পর্যন্ত বেশ হইয়াছে। **So forth, So on**—More of the same or similar kind ; এইরূপ, আরো, ইত্যাদি, প্রভৃতি, প্রমুখ। **So help me God**—A strong asseveration : পরমেশ্বরের দোহাই সত্য বলিতেছি। **So long**—For such a period of time ; এই পর্যান্ত, এতক্ষণ, এতকাল, এতদিন। **So long as**—For such time as ; যতক্ষণ—ততক্ষণ, যতকাল—ততকাল। **So much**—Such a quantity ; ততটুকু, এতটুকু, এই পরিমাণ, ততটা। To such a degree or extent ; এতদূর, এত অধিক। However much ; যতই হউক না কেন। So largely possessed of ; এত পরিমাণে অধিকারী। An equal sum or amount ; সমসংখ্যা বা পরিমাণ। Thus much ; এই পর্যান্ত। **So much as**—However much ; যতই হউক না কেন। Such a quantity as ; যতখানি—ততখানি, যতটুকু—ততটুকু। **So much so**—To such a degree or extent ; এতদূর, এই পরিমাণে। However much ; যতই হউক। **So much the better**—Better to that extent ; ততটা বেশ। **So much the worse**—Still worse ; আরো খারাপ। **So so**—Neither very good nor bad ; passable ; বড় ভালও নহে বড় মন্দও নহে ; একরূপ, একমত, অমনি একরকম। **So so**—well, well; আচ্ছা ! আচ্ছা, বেশ বেশ, ভাল ভাল। **So that**—In order that ; যেন, যাহাতে। In such a way that ; এত যে, এমন যে। **So then**—Therefore ; অতএব, সুতরাং। **So to say, So to speak**—To use such an expression ; বলিতে গেলে। **You do not say so ?**—An expression of surprise ; তাইকি ?

soak (sōk), *v. i., t. & n.* 1. To lie steeped in water or other liquid ; ভিজা, সিক্ত হওয়া, আর্দ্র হওয়া। 2. To enter into pores or interstices ; রন্ধ্রপথে প্রবেশ করা, ছিদ্রপথে প্রবেশ করা, শোষা। 3. To drink intemperately ; "You do nothing but *soak* with the guests all day long" ; বেজায় মদ খাওয়া। ***Verb t.*** 1. To steep ; ভিজান, সিক্ত করা। 2. To imbibe by the pores, as skin ; শুষিয়া নেওয়া। 3. To spend (money) in drink ; মদ খাইয়া (টাকা) উড়ান। 4. (*Slang*) To pawn ; (ইতরভাষায়) বাঁধা দেওয়া। 5. (*Dial.*) To bake thoroughly (উপভাষায়) উত্তমরূপে সেঁকা। 6. (*Slang*) To punish (ইতরভাষায়) সাজা দেওয়া। 7. To drink to excess ; অতিমাত্রায় মদ্যপান করা। ***Noun.*** 1. Soaking ; আর্দ্র হওন, সিক্ত হওন। 2. A liquid in which anything is soaked ; যে তরল-পদার্থে কোন কিছু ভিজান হয়। 3. Pawn ; বন্ধক। 4. A drinking bout ; মদ্যপান। 5. A drunkard ; মাতাল। 6. Cost ; মূল্য। **Soak'-ing, Soak'-age, Soak'-er,** *ns.* **To soak one's clay**—To drink excessively ; অতিমাত্রায় মদ্যপান করা।

soap (sōp), *n., v. t. & i.* 1. A compound of oil or fat with an alkali, used in washing ; সাবান, ফেনক (বাংস্তঃ)। 2. (*Slang*) Flattery ; (ইতরভাষায়) তোষামোদ, তেল, তৈল (cf. তৈল মর্দ্দন)। ***Verb t.*** 1. To rub or wash over with soap ; সাবান দেওয়া, সাবান লাগান, সাবান দ্বারা ধৌত করা। 2. (*Slang*) To flatter ; তোষামোদ করা, তৈল-মর্দ্দন করা। **Soap'-i-ly,** *adv.* **Soap'-i-ness,** *n.* **Soap'-less,** *adj.* **Soap'-y,** *adj.* 1. Like sope ; সাবানবৎ। 2. Flattering ; তোষামোদপূর্ণ। **Soap-boiler**—সাবান প্রস্তুতকারী। **Soap-bubble**—সাবানের জলের বুদ্বুদ। **Soap-suds**—ফেনাবিশিষ্ট সাবানজল। **Soap-factory**—সাবানের কারখানা। **Soap-maker**—সাবান প্রস্তুতকারী। **Soap nut, Soap-berry (tree)**—রীঠা, বড়, রীঠে, (বেলঃ), অরিষ্ট, ফেনিল, রীঠাকরঞ্জ। **Soap-stone**—মাটিয়াপাথর (যোঃ)।

soar (sōr), *v. i.* 1. To fly aloft ; উর্দ্ধে উড্ডীন হওয়া। 2. To tower mentally ; "He winged his upward flight and *soared* to fame" ; উচ্চ চিন্তা করা, উর্দ্ধলোকে বিচরণ করা, কল্পলোকে বিচরণ করা। **Soar'-ing-ly,** *adv.*

soave, soavemente, (*It.*), *adv.* (*Mus.*) With tenderness ; (সঙ্গীতশাস্ত্র) কোমলভাবে।

sŏb, *v. i., t. & n.* To weep with a convulsive catching of breath ; ফোঁপাইয়া কাঁদা। ***Verb t.*** To utter with a sob ; ফোঁপাইতে ফোঁপাইতে বলা, গদ্গদ্স্বরে বলা। ***Noun.*** A convulsive catching of the breath under the influence of grief ; ফোঁপানি। **Sob'-bing-ly,** *adv.* **To burst into sob**—To breathe with sobbing ; ফোঁপাইয়া ফোঁপাইয়া কাঁদা।

sō'-bĕr, *adj., v. t. & i.* 1. Not drunk ; as, she appealed from Philip drunk to Philip *sober* ; temperate ; অপানমত্ত, অপানপ্রসক্ত ; পরিমিতপানী, মিতপানী, পানসংযমী। 2. Self-controlled ; moderate ; sane ; not wild or visionary or heated with passion ; সংযমী ; মধ্যাবিধ, পরিমিত ; স্থিরমতি ; অপ্রমত্ত। 3. Solemn ; grave ; sedate ; গম্ভীর ; গম্ভীর ; ধীর, স্থির, প্রশান্ত। 4. Not bright, gay or showy ; "The *sober* tints of its feathers in winter"; অনুজ্জ্বল। 5. (*Dial.*) Not very well ; (উপভাষায়) বড় সুস্থ নয়। 6. Dull ; as, *sober* life ; নীরস। ***Verb t.*** 1. To make sober; পানদোষ দূর করা। 2. To make solemn, grave or sedate ; ধীর করা, শান্ত করা, গম্ভীর করা। 3. To become sober ; ধীর হওয়া, প্রশান্ত হওয়া, অপ্রমত্ত হওয়া, ধীর স্থির হওয়া, ধীর বুদ্ধি হওয়া। **—ly,** *adv.* **Sober-blood**—প্রশান্তচিত্ত। **Sober-minded**—ধীরচিত্ত, স্থিরমানস, প্রশান্তচিত্ত। **Sober-sides**—স্থিরবুদ্ধি ব্যক্তি, অপ্রমত্ত ব্যক্তি। **Sober-suited**—অনুজ্জ্বল বর্ণের পোষাকপরিহিত।

Sŏ-brăn′-jĕ, *n.* The national assembly of Bulgaria ; বুলগেরিয়ার জাতীয় মহাসভা। [দেশের সমস্ত প্রাপ্তবয়স্ক পুরুষগণ কর্তৃক প্রতি পাঁচ বৎসর অন্তর এই সমিতির সভ্যগণ নির্ব্বাচিত হইয়া থাকেন।]

sö-brī′-ĕ-tȳ, *n.* 1. Habitual temperance, especially in drinking spirituous liquors ; freedom from intoxication ; অপানপ্রসক্তি, মদ্যপানবিরতি, পানসংযম ; অমত্ততা। 2. Calmness ; seriousness ; প্রশান্তভাব, স্থৈর্য্য, অপ্রমত্ততা ; গাম্ভীর্য্য।

sŏ-bri-quet′ (-brē-kā), *n.* A nickname ; a derisive surname ; উপনাম ; কল্পিত নাম, ডাকনাম।

sŏc′-āge, sŏc′-cage (-āj), *ns.* A feudal tenure of land involving payment of rent or other service to superior ; মধ্যযুগের ভূম্যধিকারবিশেষ—যাহাতে উর্দ্ধতন ভূম্যধিকারীকে খাজানা প্রদান করিতে হইত অথবা তাহার বাটীতে কোনপ্রকার কার্য্য করিয়া দিতে হইত।

sŏc′-cer (-ĕr), *n.* Same as SOCKER (which see).

sŏ′-ci-ā-ble (-shĭ-ă-bl), *adj.* & *n.* 1. Companionable; affable; সঙ্গপ্রিয়, মিশুক ; অমায়িক, মধুরালাপী। 2. Affording opportunities for conversation and the enjoyment of the company of others ; as, a *sociable* party ; কথাবার্ত্তা বা মেলামেশার সুবিধাপ্রদায়ক। ***Noun.*** 1. A kind of phaeton with two seats facing each other ; একপ্রকার ফিটন গাড়ী—যাহাতে পরস্পরের সম্মুখীন দুইটী আসন থাকে। 2. A tricycle for two riders side by side ; দুইজন আরোহী পাশাপাশিভাবে চড়িতে পারে এইরূপ ত্রিচক্রযান। 3. An S-shaped coach for two persons who sit partially facing each other ; ইংরাজী S অক্ষরাকৃতি একপ্রকার গাড়ী—যাহাতে দুই ব্যক্তি পরস্পরেরদিকে কতকটা মুখ করিয়া বসিতে পারে। **—bil′-i-ty, —ness,** *ns.* The quality of being sociable ; জনসঙ্গপ্রীতি, সঙ্গপ্রিয়তা, সমাজপ্রিয়তা, সামাজিকতা। **—bly,** *adv.*

sö′-ci-ăl (-shĭ-), *adj.* 1. Pertaining to society ; সমাজসম্বন্ধীয়, সামাজিক। 2. Living in companies ; as, *social* animals ; সংঘচারী। 3. Companionable ; as, a *social* person ; মিশুক, সঙ্গপ্রিয়। 4. (*Bot.*) Growing thickly together ; একত্র প্রচুররূপে উৎপাদনশীল। **Social bees, —wasps**—যে সকল মৌমাছি, বোলতা, প্রভৃতি এক বাসায় বাস করে। **Social birds**—যে-সকল পক্ষী পরস্পরের সন্নিকটে নীড় নির্ম্মাণ করে। **Social compact, —contract**—আদিসমাজ সঙ্কেত (হিঃ কোঃ), আদিমর্য্যাদা (ঐ), সামাজিক সময়বন্ধ (ঐ)। **Social conference**—সামাজিক উন্নতিবিধানের জন্য সম্মিলনী, সামাজিকসম্মিলনী। **Social Contract (or Compact) or Contract social**—ফরাসীদেশীয় যুগপ্রবর্ত্তক রুশোর বিশ্ববিখ্যাত গ্রন্থের নাম ; এই গ্রন্থ ১৭৬২ খৃঃ অব্দে প্রকাশিত হয়। এই গ্রন্থে রুশো বলেন যে সকল মানুষই সমান অধিকার লইয়া জন্মগ্রহণ করিয়াছে। রাজা এবং প্রজা পরস্পরের সহিত চুক্তিতে বদ্ধ থাকিবে। প্রজার মত অনুসারে দেশের শাসনকার্য্য নির্ব্বাহিত হওয়া আবশ্যক। রুশোর মতে অসভ্য অবস্থাই মনুষ্যের স্বাভাবিক এবং প্রকৃত অবস্থা। এই অবস্থায় মানুষ পূর্ণ স্বাধীন। রুশোর মতে মানুষ স্বেচ্ছায় সকলের হিতার্থে নিজের স্বাধীনতার কিয়ৎ পরিমাণে সঙ্কোচ করিয়া সমাজবদ্ধ হইয়াছে। রুশোর এই সমস্ত মতের প্রচারই ফরাসী বিপ্লবের প্রধান কারণ। **Social consciousness** — অন্তর্জীবাস্তিত্বসংবিৎ (হিঃ কোঃ), সমাজসংবিৎ। **Social decay**—সামাজিক অবনতি (হিঃ কোঃ)। **Social Democrat**—পার্লেমেণ্ট প্রভৃতি সমাজতন্ত্রানুরাগী সভ্য। **Social dynamics** — সমাজপরিবর্ত্তনবিজ্ঞান (হিঃকোঃ), সমাজাভিবৃদ্ধিশাস্ত্র (হিঃ কোঃ)। **Social ethics** — সামাজিক আচার (হিঃ কোঃ)। **Social evil**—বেশ্যাসমাজ। **Social evolution**—সমাজাভিবৃদ্ধি (হিঃ কোঃ)। **Social force**—সমাজবল (হিঃ কোঃ)। **Social gathering**—সামাজিকসম্মিলনী, প্রীতিসম্মিলনী। **Social opposition**—সামাজিকবিরোধ (হিঃ কোঃ)। **Social organism**—সমাজব্যূহ (হিঃ কোঃ)। **Social Philosophy**—সমাজশাস্ত্র (হিঃ কোঃ), সমাজবিদ্যা (ঐ)। **Social process**—সামাজিক সংসৃতি (হিঃ কোঃ)। **Social progress**—সমাজোন্নতি, সমাজোপগতি। **Social retrogression**—সামাজিক অবনতি। **Social science**—সমাজবিজ্ঞান, সমাজসম্বন্ধীশাস্ত্র (হিঃ কোঃ), সমাজশাস্ত্র (ঐ)। [সামাজিক বা পারিবারিক স্বাস্থ্য, শিক্ষা, অপরাধীদিগের দণ্ড এবং সংশোধন, দারিদ্র্যনিবারণ প্রভৃতি বিষয় এই বিজ্ঞানের বিষয়ীভূত।] **Social statics**—সমাজস্থিতিশাস্ত্র (হিঃ কোঃ)। **Social status**—সামাজিকপ্রতিষ্ঠা (হিঃ কোঃ), সামাজিকপদ (ঐ)। **Social suppression, Social elimination**—সামাজিক পরিত্যাগ (হিঃ কোঃ), সামাজিক ভ্রংশন (ঐ)। **Social War**—(রোমের ইতিহাস) রোমানদিগের সহিত ইতালীয় মিত্রপক্ষগণের (খৃঃ পূঃ ৮৯—৯০) যুদ্ধ। (গ্রীসের ইতিহাসে) এথেন্সবাসিগণের সহিত তাহাদের মিত্রপক্ষীয়দিগের যুদ্ধ। **Social will**—সামাজিক ইচ্ছা (হিঃ কোঃ)।

sö′-ci-ăl-ĭsm (-shĭ-), *n.* That system which has for its object the reconstrucion of society on the basis of community of property and association, instead of competition in every branch of human industry ; পরস্পরের সহিত প্রতিযোগিতার পরিবর্ত্তে সমাজের সকল লোকের পরস্পরের সহিত সহযোগিতায় অর্থোপার্জ্জনের চেষ্টা করা সঙ্গত এবং উপার্জ্জিত অর্থ সকলের মধ্যে সমভাবে বিতরিত হওয়া উচিত—এইরূপ মতবাদ [আধুনিক সমাজতান্ত্রিকগণের মতে উৎপাদনের সহায়ক (অর্থাৎ ভূমি এবং মূলধনের স্বত্বস্বামিত্ব এবং বিতরণের ক্ষমতা) সর্ব্বজনের হিতার্থে রাষ্ট্রের হস্তে ন্যস্ত হইবে।], সমষ্টিবাদ (হিঃ কোঃ), সাধারণ-স্বত্ববাদ (ঐ), সমাজতন্ত্র, সমাজতান্ত্রিকতা। [Ferdinand Lassalle, Karl Marx প্রভৃতি সমাজতান্ত্রিকগণের মতে ধন এবং ভূমিতে ব্যক্তিবিশেষের স্বত্ব রহিত করিতে হইবে। সমস্ত "ধন" শ্রমিকগণ কর্ত্তৃক উৎপন্ন এবং উহা তাঁহাদেরই ন্যায্য প্রাপ্য। [See R. Blatchford, *Britain for the British* ; G. B. Shaw and others, The *Fabian Essays* ; H. G. Wells, *A Modern Utopia* ; J. Spargo, *Socialism* ; T. Kirkup, *Enquiry into Socialism* ; H. M. Hyndman, *Historical basis of Socialism in England*; R. Hunter, *Socialists at Work* ; R. C. Ensor, *Modern Socialism* ; W. S. Sanders, *The Socialist Movement in Germany* ; T. Kirkup, *History of Socialism* ; W. Sombart, *Socialism and the Social Movement* ; J. R. MacDonald, *Socialism and Society* ; J. Jaures, *Studies in Socialism*]. **–ist,** *n.* One who advocates socialism ; সমাজতান্ত্রিক, সমষ্টিবাদী (হিঃ কোঃ)। **–is′-tic,** *adj.* Pertaining to socialism or the socialists ; সমাজতন্ত্রসম্বন্ধীয়, সমাজতান্ত্রিক। **–is′-ti-cal-ly,** *adv.* **Christian socialism**—খৃষ্টধর্ম্মের উপদেশ অনুসারে সামাজিকজীবন গঠনের প্রয়াস। [Thomas Hughes, Charles Kingsley, F. D. Maurice প্রভৃতি এই মতের প্রচারক।] **Socialism of the chair** (*Germ.* **Katheder-socialismus**)—শ্রমজীবিসমাজের উন্নতিবিধানের জন্য সরকারী সাহায্য প্রদত্ত হওয়া উচিত—এই মতের প্রচারক জর্ম্মনদেশীয় রাজনীতিকবৃন্দ। ১৮৭২ সালে উক্ত সংঘকে বিদ্রূপচ্ছলে এই নাম প্রদান করা হয়।

sō′-ci-ăl-īze (-shĭ-), *v. t.* 1. To render social ; সামাজিক করা। 2. To form or regulate according to the principles of socialism ; সমাজতন্ত্রের মতানুসারে গঠিত বা নিয়মিত করা। **–i-za′-tion,**

sō-cī′-ĕ-tȳ, *n.* 1. Fellowship ; as, to leave the *society* of men ; সামাজিকতা, সঙ্গ, সংসর্গ। 2. A number of persons united in community ; "*Society* having ordained certain customs, men are bound to obey the laws of society and conform to its harmless orders......" সমাজ। 3. An association formed for the promotion of some object either literary, scientific, political, religious or the like ; as, a literary *society* ; সম্প্রদায়, সমাজ, সমিতি, পরিষৎ, সংঘ। 4. The more cultivated portion of any community; "Ovid is eminently the poet of *society*" ; শিক্ষিত সমাজ। **Society Islands**—প্রশান্ত মহাসাগরের দ্বীপপুঞ্জ বিশেষ। **Society journals, Society-newspapers** — যে সকল পত্রিকায় কেবল সভ্যসমাজের উপযোগী প্রবন্ধাদি বাহির হয়। **Society-verse** — একপ্রকার সরস এবং মার্জ্জিত গীতিকবিতা। **Society for ethical culture** — উন্নত নৈতিক-আদর্শ স্থাপনের উদ্দেশ্যে প্রতিষ্ঠিত পরিষৎবিশেষ। **Society for promoting Christian knowledge**—১৬৯৮ খৃঃ অব্দে প্রতিষ্ঠিত ধর্ম্মসংঘবিশেষ। এই সমিতি হইতে নানাপ্রকার ধর্ম্মগ্রন্থ প্রকাশিত হয়। এই সমিতির প্রধান কার্য্যালয় লণ্ডন নগরীর Northumberland Avenue নামক স্থানে অধিষ্ঠিত আছে। **Society of Friends** — Same as QUAKERS. **Society of Jesus**—Same as JESUIT. **To enjoy the society of**—সঙ্গসুখলাভ করা।

Sō-cin′-ĭ-ăn (-shĭn-), *adj.* & *n.* Pertaining to Laelius or Faustus Socinus ; সসিন্তাসসম্বন্ধীয়। ***Noun.*** One of the followers of Socinus ; সসিন্তাসের মতাবলম্বী ব্যক্তি। **–ism,** *n.* A form of Unitarianism founded by Laelius and Faustus Socinus ; Laelius এবং Faustus Socinus নামক ব্যক্তিদ্বয় কর্ত্তৃক প্রবর্ত্তিত একপ্রকার একেশ্বরবাদ। [এই সম্প্রদায় যীশুখৃষ্ট মানবজন্মগ্রহণের পূর্ব্বে দেবলোকে ঈশ্বরের পার্শ্বে বিরাজ করিতেন—এই কথা বিশ্বাস করেন না। ইঁহারা খৃষ্টের অলৌকিক জন্মে বিশ্বাসবান। ইঁহারা শয়তানের অস্তিত্ব অস্বীকার করিয়া থাকেন।]

sō-ci-ŏl′-ŏ-ġȳ, (-shĭ-) *n.* The science of the evolution and constitution of human society ; মানবসমাজের সংগঠন এবং ক্রমোন্নতি-সম্বন্ধীয় বিজ্ঞান, সমাজবিজ্ঞান, সমাজতত্ত্ব, সমাজশাস্ত্র (হিঃ কোঃ), সমাজবিদ্যা, (ঐ), ব্যবস্থাবিজ্ঞান (প্রবাসী ১৩২২)। **–gist,** *n.* **–o-log′-i-cal,** *adj.* **–o-log′-i-cal-ly,** *adv.* [See Spencer, *Principles of Sociology* ; Huxley, *Evolution and Ethics* ; Bluntschill, *The Theory of the State* ; Giddings, *Principles of Sociology* ; Marxs, *Kapital* (English Translation)].

sŏck, *n.* 1. A knit or woven covering for the foot, rather shorter than a stocking ; খাটো মোজা—যাহা হাঁটুর নীচ পর্য্যন্ত উঠিয়া থাকে, অনুপদীন। 2. The shoe of the ancient actors of comedy ; প্রাচীন মিলনান্ত নাটকের অভিনেতাদিগের জুতা।

sŏck, *v. t., n.* & *adv.* To fling ; নিক্ষেপ করা, ছোঁড়া। ***Noun.*** A blow inflicted by a missile ; ঢিল প্রভৃতির আঘাত। ***Adv.*** With such blow ; ঢিল প্রভৃতির আঘাতে।

sŏck, *n.* Ploughshare ; লাঙ্গলের ফাল।

sŏck-dŏl′-ă-ğĕr, *n.* **1.** A decisive blow, an argument or answer ; নিষ্পত্তিকারক আঘাত, যুক্তি বা উত্তর। **2.** (*Slang*, America) Something unusually large ; (আমেরিকার ইতরভাষায়) মস্ত জিনিষ।

sŏck′-ĕr, *n.* (*Slang*) Association football, form of football in which ball may not be touched with hand ; একপ্রকার পাদগোলক ক্রীড়া—যাহাতে কন্দুক হস্তদ্বারা স্পর্শ করা নিষিদ্ধ।

sŏck′-ĕt, *n.* Any hollow which receives and holds something else ; কোটর, আধার, ঘর, খোল, গর্ত্ত। **–ed,** *p. p.* **Socket-pipe**—যে নলের প্রান্তে অপর নল লাগাইবার জন্য প্রশস্ত থাকে। **Socket of the eye**—অক্ষিকোটর, অক্ষিকোষ।

sö′-cle (cl-), *n.* (*Archaic*) A plain block or plinth forming a low pedestal to a statue, column, etc. ; মূর্ত্তি, স্তম্ভ প্রভৃতির অধিষ্ঠানস্বরূপ অনুচ্চ পাষাণপীঠ।

Sō-crăt′-ic, –i-căl, *adjs.* Pertaining to the Greek philosopher Socrates ; গ্রীসদেশীয় দার্শনিক সক্রেতিস-সম্বন্ধীয়। **–i-cal-ly,** *adv.* **Soc′-ra-tism,** *n.* **Soc′-ra-tize,** *v. t.* **Socratic irony**—অপরকে তাহার বিদ্যাবুদ্ধি প্রকাশে প্ররোচিত করার জন্য অজ্ঞতার ভাণ। **Socratic method**—সক্রেতিসের তর্কপ্রণালী ; [কোন ব্যক্তিকে কোন তত্ত্ব স্বীকার করাইতে হইলে সক্রেতিস সেই বিষয়ে জিজ্ঞাসু হইয়া সেই ব্যক্তির নিকট গমন করতঃ তাহাকে প্রশ্ন করিতেন। ক্রমে প্রশ্নের উপর প্রশ্ন করিয়া তাহাকে এমন অবস্থায় আনিয়া ফেলিতেন যে শেষে সে নিজের মুখেই সক্রেতিসের উদ্দিষ্ট বিষয় স্বীকার করিতে বাধ্য হইত।], প্রশ্নোত্তর রীতি (হিঃ কোঃ)। **Socratic-Philosophy**—সক্রেতিস্ এবং তদীয় শিষ্যগণের দর্শন, বিশেষতঃ প্লেতো এবং আরিস্তোতলের দর্শন।

sŏd, *n.* & *v. t.* Turf ; ঘাসের চাপড়া। ***Verb t.*** To cover with sods ; ঘাসের চাপড়া বসান। **Sod′-dy,** *adj.* **Under the sod**—Under the grave ; সমাহিত, কবরস্থ।

sŏd, *v. t.* Same as SEETHE (which see).

sō′-dă, *n.* **1.** The protoxide of the metal sodium ; ক্ষার বিশেষ, সোডা। **2.** Same as SODA-WATER. **Soda alum**—সোডাফিটকিরী (হিঃ কোঃ)। **Soda ash**—সাজী (হিঃ কোঃ)। **Soda-fountain**—যে পাত্রে বিলাতি পানি চাপিয়া রাখা যায় এবং যাহা হইতে নলসহযোগে উহা বোতলে পুরা হইয়া থাকে। **Soda salt**—সোডা লবণ (হিঃ কোঃ)। **Soda-water**—সোডাওয়াটার, বিলাতিপানি [পূর্ব্বে বিলাতিপানি সোডা সংযোগে প্রস্তুত হইত বর্ত্তমানে অঙ্গারাম্ল বাষ্প সহযোগে প্রস্তুত হইয়া থাকে।]

sō-dăl′-i-tȳ, *n.* Fellowship or fraternity ; "A new confraternity was instituted in Spain, of the slaves of the Blessed Virgin, and this *sodality* established with large indulgencies" ; সম্প্রদায়, মণ্ডলী, ভ্রাতৃমণ্ডলী।

sŏd′-den (-n), *adj., v. t.* & *i.* **1.** Soaked ; সিক্ত, আর্দ্র। **2.** (Of bread) doughy, heavy or moist ; (রোটিকা সম্বন্ধে) অর্দ্ধ-পক্ব, কাঁচা। **3.** Pale and flaccid ; as, *sodden* features ; মলিন এবং ভস্‌কা। ***Verb t.*** **1.** To soak in ; সিক্ত করা, আর্দ্র করা। **2.** To deprive of freshness ; নবীনতা হীন করা। ***Verb i.*** To be seethed or soaked ; সিক্ত হওয়া, আর্দ্র হওয়া। **–ness,** *n.*

sō′-di-ŭm, *n.* The silver-white metallic base of the alkali soda ; কাচবৎশুভ্র রাসায়নিক মূলপদার্থ বিশেষ, লবণক, পত্রক (সাঃ পঃ)। [Sym. Na. At. Wt. 23. এই ধাতু উজ্জ্বল পীতবর্ণ শিখা বিস্তারে জ্বলিয়া থাকে এবং উষ্ণজলে প্রজ্বলিত হয়]। **Sodic carbonate**—অঙ্গারকীয় সর্জ্জিক (সাঃ পঃ)। **Sodic hypophosphite**—উপস্ফুরীয় সর্জ্জিক (সাঃ পঃ)। **Sodic phosphate**—স্ফুরীয় সর্জ্জিক (সাঃ পঃ)। **Sodium carbonate**—সর্জ্জিকা ক্ষার (সাঃ পঃ)। **Sodium caustic**—তীক্ষ্ণ ক্ষার (সাঃ পঃ)। **Sodium chloride**—সুশ্বেত (সাঃ পঃ)। **Sodium sulphate**—খাড়ী নুন।

Sŏd′-ŏm, *n.* **1.** The name of a city mentioned in the Old Testament ; বাইবেল গ্রন্থে উক্ত সোডম নগরী। [মরু সাগরের তীরে এই নগরী অবস্থিত ছিল। এই নগরের অধিবাসীদের পাপাচার এবং ইহার ধ্বংসের বিবরণ বাইবেলের Genesis গ্রন্থের ১৮-১৯ অধ্যায়ে বর্ণিত হইয়াছে।] **2.** An extremely corrupt place ; "Two, even in this military *Sodom* had the courage to proclaim Deyfus innocent" ; অতিশয় জঘন্য স্থান, পাপপুরী, নরক। **Sodom apple**—Same as APPLE OF SODOM (which see).

Sŏd′-ŏm-īte, *n.* **1.** An inhabitant of Sodom ; প্রাচীন Sodom নগরীর অধিবাসী। **2.** (*l. c.*) A person guilty of sodomy ; পুংমৈথুনকারী, লৌণ্ডাবাজ। **–it′-i-cal,** *adj.* **–it′-i-cal-ly,** *adv.*

sŏd′-ŏm-ȳ, *n.* Unnatural intercourse between male persons ; পুংমৈথুন, পুরুষমেহ (যাজ্ঞঃ), গুদমৈথুন (কুল্লূঃ)।

sō-ĕv′-ĕr, A suffix appended to such words as *who, which, whom, where*, etc. to render them more emphatic.

sō′-fă, *n.* A long seat with a stuffed bottom, back and ends ; একপ্রকার গদী-মোড়া দীর্ঘ আসন, সোফা।

sŏf′-fit, *n.* (*Arch.*) The lower surface of a vault, arch, archi-trave, balcony, etc. ; (স্থপতিবিদ্যা) খিলান, তোরণ, অধঃপ্রস্তর, অলিন্দ, প্রভৃতির নিম্নভাগ।

Architrave. S. soffit.

Sō′-fi, Sō′-fīsm, *ns.* See SUFI, SUFISM.

sŏft, *adj., n., adv.* & *interj.* **1.** Easily yielding to pressure ;

নরম, কোমল, পেলব, মৃদু, সুকুমার, মেদুর। **2.** Gentle ; tender ; as, *soft* voice ; mild; মৃদু, মৃদুল; কোমল; শান্ত, নম্র। **3.** (*Colloq.*) Easy ; idle ; as, a *soft* time; আরামপ্রিয় ; অলস। **4.** Low ; melodious ; "The *soft* rustle of a maiden's gown" ; অনুচ্চ, নম্র ; শ্রুতিমধুর, ললিত। **5.** Mild in nature ; tender-hearted ; নম্রপ্রকৃতি, শান্তপ্রকৃতি, শান্তস্বভাব ; কোমলচিত্ত, কোমলপ্রাণ। **6.** Weak ; effeminate ; "It looks so *soft* to say you wont fight" ; দুর্ব্বল ; মেয়েলী, স্ত্রীজনসুলভ। **7.** Pleasant to the touch ; as, *soft* velvet ; flexible ; not rough ; as, *soft* skin ; সুখস্পর্শ, সুকোমল ; নবনীয়; মোলায়েম। **8.** Rainy ; as, *soft* weather ; বাদলা। **9.** Foolish ; "He made fellows sharp *soft* melodies"; বোকা। **10.** Civil; courteous; as, a *soft* answer ; শিষ্ট ; ভদ্র। **11.** Not strong or glaring ; as, *soft* colour ; মিটমিটে, অনুজ্জ্বল, ম্লান, মেদুর (cf. মেদুররক্তিম), কোমল, মৃদু। **12.** Free from mineral substance ; as, *soft* water ; খনিজ লবণাদি বিহীন। **13.** Not sour, bitter or astringent ; অম্ল, তিক্ত বা কষায়-স্বাদ শূন্য। **14.** Not pronounced with a hard explosive utterance, but with more or less of a sibilant sound, as, *C* in "cinder" as opposed to *C* in "candle" ; অল্পাধিক 'ইস্' ধ্বনি সহকারে উচ্চারিত। **15.** Genial ; as, a *soft* day ; বৃষ্টি-বাত্যাহীন। **16.** Peaceful ; as, *soft* slumbers ; শান্তিপূর্ণ। ***Noun.*** **1.** A weak or foolish person ; দুর্ব্বল অথবা বুদ্ধিহীন ব্যক্তি। **2.** That which is soft ; কোমল বস্তু। ***Adv.*** Softly ; কোমলভাবে। ***Interj.*** Be gentle ; go gently ; stop ; শান্ত হও ; ধীরে যাও ; থাম। **Soft'-ish,** *adj.* **Soft'-ly,** *adv.* In a soft manner ; কোমলভাবে, মৃদুভাবে, মন্দ মন্দ, শনৈঃ শনৈঃ। **Soft'-ness,** *n.* **Soft coal**—শিলাজতু মিশ্রিত কয়লা। **Soft-conscienced** — চঞ্চলধর্ম্মবুদ্ধি-সম্পন্ন। **Soft goods** — বস্ত্রাদি। **Soft-headed**—ক্ষীণমস্তিষ্ক। **Soft-hearted**—কোমলহৃদয়, কোমলপ্রাণ, কোমলচিত্ত। **Soft money**—হুণ্ডী, নোট, প্রভৃতি। **Soft-nothings** — প্রেমালাপ। **Soft palate** — তালুর পশ্চাদ্ভাগ, কোমল তালু। **Soft roe**—পুং মৎস্যের ডিম্ব। **Soft snap**—লাভের কায, খুব লাভের ও আরামের চাকুরী। **Soft-sawder**—See SAWDER. **Soft soap**—(ইতর-ভাষায়) তোষামোদ; শিষ্টবাক্য। **Soft-spoken**—প্রিয়ংবদ, মধুরভাষী। **Soft sugar**—ভিজা চিনি। **Soft tack**—রুটি (জাহাজের মাল্লাগণ কর্তৃক ব্যবহৃত)। **Soft-water**—See SOFT *adj.* 12. **Soft as butter**—নবনীকোমল। **To be soft on** or **upon a person**—To be in love with him ; প্রেমানুরাগের সঞ্চার হওয়া, প্রণয়সঞ্চার হওয়া।

Sŏf'-tă, *n.* A Moslem student of sacred law and theological science ; মুসলমান ধর্ম্মশাস্ত্রাধ্যায়ী ছাত্র।

sŏf'-ten (-n), *v. t.* & *i.* To make soft ; কোমল করা, মৃদু করা, মন্দীভূত করা, লাঘব করা। ***Verb i.*** To become soft ; কোমল হওয়া, গলা, বিগলিত হওয়া, দয়ার্দ্রচিত্ত হওয়া। **Softening of the brain**—প্রদাহ, রক্তস্রাব বা পুষ্টিজনক খাদ্যাদির অভাব-হেতু মস্তিষ্কের কোমলতা প্রাপ্তি।

sŏg'-gy, *adj.* Saturated ; সিক্ত, আর্দ্র। **-gi-ness,** *n.*

sō-hō', *n.* A word used in calling from a distance ; a sportsman's halloo ; দূর হইতে কাহাকে ডাকিবার কালে ব্যবহৃত শব্দবিশেষ ; (কুক্কুরাদিকে উৎসাহিত করার জন্য) শিকারীর শব্দ।

soi'-bean (soy-bēn), *n.* A kind of grain grown in various parts of Bengal ; গড়িকালাই।

soi-disant, (*F.*), *adj.* Self-styled ; pretended ; স্ব-কথিত, স্ব-প্রদত্তনামা; কল্পিত

soil (soyl), *n.* **1.** The upper stratum of the earth ; ভূমির উপরের স্তর, মাটী, জমি, মৃত্তিকা। **2.** (*Rare*) Land ; country ; as, native *soil* ; (ক্বচিদ্ ব্যবহৃত) ভূমি ; দেশ। **Children of the soil**—Natives of the country ; দেশের লোক, দেশবাসিগণ, দেশমাতৃকার সন্তানগণ।

soil (soyl), *v. t., i.* & *n.* To make dirty ; to sully ; to tarnish ; মলিন করা, ময়লা করা ; অপরিষ্কার করা, নোংরা করা ; কলুষিত করা, মলদূষিত করা। ***Verb i.*** To take soil ; ময়লা হওয়া, মলিনতা প্রাপ্ত হওয়া। ***Noun.*** **1.** Any foul matter ; দূষিত পদার্থ। **2.** Stain; কলঙ্ক, দাগ। **3.** A marshy, wet or miry place ; কর্দ্দমপূর্ণ স্থান, পল্বল। **Soil-pipe** — শৌচাগারের ময়লাজল নিষ্কাশনের চুঙ্গী।

soil (soyl), *v. t.* To fatten cattle with green food ; কাঁচা ঘাস প্রভৃতি ভোজন করাইয়া গোমহিষাদিকে পুষ্ট করা।

soi-ree' (swä-rā), *n.* An evening party ; সান্ধ্যসম্মিলনী, সান্ধ্যপ্রীতিসম্মিলনী।

sō'-journ (-jĕrn), *v. i.* & *n.* To dwell for a time ; কিছুকালের জন্য অবস্থান করা। ***Noun.*** A temporary residence as that of a traveller in a foreign land ; as, during my short *sojourn* in America ; অল্পকাল বাস, অচিরপ্রবাস। **-er,** *n.*

Sŏl, *n.* (*Joc.*) The sun ; (কৌতুহলচ্ছলে) সূর্য্য।

sŏl, *n.* (*Mus.*) The fifth tone of the diatonic scale ; (সঙ্গীতশাস্ত্র) সপ্তকের পঞ্চম স্বর, পা।

sō'-lă, *n.* A plant of the genus Aeschynomene ; শোলা। **Sola-topi**—শোলার টুপি।

sŏl'-āce, *v. t.* & *n.* **1.** To comfort ; সান্ত্বনা দেওয়া, প্রবোধ দেওয়া, শোকাপনোদন করা। **2.** To allay ; "*Solace* our anguish and our wants relieve" ; হ্রাস করা, লাঘব করা, উপশম করা। ***Noun.*** **1.** Consolation ; alleviation ; সান্ত্বনা, প্রবোধ, শোকশান্তি ; শোকাপনোদন।

2. That which gives comfort ; সান্ত্বনাজনক বিষয়, সান্ত্বনাপ্রদ বিষয়।

sō'-lăn-(goose) (-gōōz), *ns.* Same as GANNET (which see).

sō-lā'-nŭm, *n.* An extensive genus of plants including the potato, egg-plant, nightshade ; বৃক্ষের গণবিশেষ—বিলাতী আলু, বেগুণ, কাকমারী, প্রভৃতি, উহার অন্তর্ভুক্ত। ***Solanum Indicum***—ব্যাকুড় (বেলঃ)। ***Solanum jacquini*** — কণ্টকারী (রেলঃ)। ***Solanum melongena*** — কুলি বেগুন (বেলঃ), হিঙ্গুলী, বার্ত্তাকু। [Syn. সিংহী, ভণ্টাকী, দুষ্প্রধর্ষিণী, বার্ত্তাকী, বার্ত্তা, বাতিঙ্গণ, বার্ত্তাক, শাকবিল্ব, রাজকুষ্মাণ্ড, বার্ত্তিক, বাতিগম, বৃন্তাক, বঙ্গণ, অঙ্গণ, কণ্টবৃন্তাকী, কণ্টালু, কণ্টপত্রিকা, নিদ্রালু, মাংসকফলা, বৃন্তাকী, মহোটিকা, চিত্রফলা, কণ্টকিনী, মহতী, কটুফলা, মিশ্রবর্ণফলা, নীলফলা, শাকশ্রেষ্ঠা, রক্তফলা, বৃত্তফলা, নৃপপ্রিয়ফলা, হিঙ্গীর, জুকুট, রক্তপাকী, বাতিগ, সিংহীলতা (ভাব প্রঃ)।] [Arab. *badangan* ; Burm. *kha-yan* ; Chin. *niu-sin-kia* (white variety), *kia* (purple), *kia-tsze* ; Lat. *mala insana* ; Pers. *budanjan*]. ***Solanum Nigrum*** — কাকমাচী, গুড়কামাই (বেলঃ)। [Syn. বায়সী, ধ্বাঙ্ক্ষমারী, বায়সাহ্বা, সর্ব্বতিক্তা, বহুফলা, কটুফলা, রসায়নী, গুচ্ছফলা, কাকমাতা, স্বাদুপাকা, সুন্দরী, তিক্তিকা, বহুতিক্তা।] ***Solanum rubrum***—গোরখী (বেলঃ)।

sō'-lar (-lėr), *adj.* **1.** Pertaining to the sun ; সৌর, ভানব, ভানব্য, সূর্য্যসম্বন্ধীয়। **2.** Measured by the progress of the sun ; as, the *solar* year ; সূর্য্যের গতিদ্বারা পরিমিত, সৌর, সাবন। **3.** Sunny ; as, *solar* shores ; সূর্য্যকরোজ্জ্বল, সৌরকরোজ্জ্বল। **4.** (*Astrol.*) Born under the predominant influence of the sun ; as, *solar* man ; (জ্যোতির্বিজ্ঞান), রবিতুঙ্গী, রবিকেন্দ্রী। **Solar cycle**—২৮ বৎসর পরিমিত-কাল—যে সময়ের অন্তে বার তারিখ প্রভৃতি একই দিনে পড়ে। **Solar day**—সৌর-দিবস। **Solar dynasty**—সূর্য্যবংশ। **Solar eclipse** — সূর্য্যগ্রহণ। **Solar engine, Solar motor**—যে যন্ত্রে অগ্নির পরিবর্ত্তে সূর্য্যালোক ব্যবহৃত হয়। **Solar flower**—যে সকল পুষ্প কেবল দিবাভাগে কতিপয় দণ্ড প্রস্ফুটিত থাকে। **Solar microscope**—একপ্রকার অণুবীক্ষণযন্ত্র—যাহাতে দর্শনীয় বস্তু কেন্দ্রীভূত সূর্য্যকিরণ দ্বারা বিভাসিত করা হইয়া থাকে। **Solar month**—সৌরমাস, সাবনমাস। **Solar-myth** — সৌর-ঘটনার রূপকস্বরূপ কোন পৌরাণিক কাহিনী প্রভৃতি। **Solar plexus**—কন্দ (ব্রজঃ বিঃ), ব্রহ্মগ্রন্থি (ঐ), ভানুভবন (ঐ)। **Solar print**—সূর্য্যালোকে মুদ্রিত আলোকচিত্র। **Solar sierra**—সৌরশিলা (হিঃ কোঃ)। **Solar spectrum**—সৌর বর্ণচ্ছত্র। **Solar spot**—সৌরকলঙ্ক। **Solar-system**—সৌর-জগৎ, সূর্য্যসম্প্রদায় (হিঃ কোঃ), সৌরপরিবার। [ভারতবাসিগণ প্রাচীন-কালে বিভিন্ন সৌরজগতের সত্তা-সম্বন্ধে পরিজ্ঞাত ছিলেন ; পুরাণাদিতে তাহার বহুল প্রমাণ প্রাপ্ত হওয়া যায়। আমরা "যোগবাশিষ্ঠ" হইতে এতৎসম্বন্ধে কিঞ্চিৎ উদ্ধৃত করিতেছি। "শুদ্ধ বোধস্বরূপ সেই চিদাকাশরূপ সমুদ্রে বহু ব্রহ্মাণ্ড নামক তরঙ্গমালা অনবরত উত্থিত হইতেছে এবং তাহাতেই বিলীন হইতেছে। সেই চিদাকাশ-সাগরের মধ্যে অনেক ব্রহ্মাণ্ড তরঙ্গ এখনও অনুৎপন্ন......যেমন জলসিক্ত বীজের কোষে শুভ্র অঙ্কুর জন্মে, সেইরূপ কোন কোন প্রথমারব্ধ ব্রহ্মাণ্ডের বিশুদ্ধ ভুবনে বিশুদ্ধ জীবসমূহের সৃষ্টি হইতেছে। যেমন তাপসংযোগে ঘনীভূত হিমবিন্দু গলিতে থাকে, সেইরূপ এই সময়ে কোন কোন ব্রহ্মাণ্ডে মহাপ্রলয় উপস্থিত হওয়ায় সূর্য্য, বিদ্যুৎ, পর্ব্বত প্রভৃতি (ভুবন দগ্ধ করিয়া) গলিতে আরম্ভ করিয়াছে। ...... যেমন ভীমান্ধকারপূর্ণ মহারণ্যে যক্ষগণ উন্মত্ত হইয়া নৃত্য করে, সেইরূপ বিতত এই মহাকাশের মধ্যে কতশত মহাজগৎ অদৃশ্যভাবে অবস্থিত (তৎসমুদায় বর্ণনাতীত।)—যোগবাশিষ্ঠ — বঙ্গবাসীর অনুবাদ। যস্য প্রভাপ্রভবতো জগ-দণ্ডকোটিকোটিষ্বশেষবসুধাদিবিভূতিভিন্নং। তদ্ব্রহ্ম নিষ্কল মনন্তমশেষভূতং গোবিন্দমাদি-পুরুষং ত্বমহং ভজামি।—ব্রহ্মাণ্ডপুরাণ। (See also Hirendra Nath Dutt's *Philosophy of the Gods*).] **Solar telegraph**—Same as HELIOGRAPH. **Solar-wheel** — ঘড়ির চক্রবিশেষ — যদ্দ্বারা সূর্য্যের স্ফুট আহ্নিকগতি সূচিত হইয়া থাকে। **Solar year**—সৌরবর্ষ, সাবনবর্ষ, সৌর সংবৎসর (মঃ উঃ)।

sō'-lår-iŝm, *n.* Belief in solar-myths as the chief source of mythology ; পৌরাণিক সমস্ত দেবদেবীর কাহিনী সূর্য্যরূপক মূলক—এইরূপ বিশ্বাস।

sō-lā'-rĭ-ŭm, *n.* **1.** A water-clock erected at Rome for the public by Scipio Nasica, B. C. 159 ; খৃঃ পূঃ ১৫৯ অব্দে Scipio Nasica কর্ত্তৃক রোমনগরীতে নির্ম্মিত জল-চালিত ঘটিকা-যন্ত্র। **2.** A sun-dial ; সূর্য্য-ঘড়ী। **3.** A room exposed to the rays of the sun for treating illness ; রুগ্ন ব্যক্তিগণের চিকিৎসার জন্য সূর্য্যকিরণোদ্ভাসিত কক্ষ।

sō'-lăr-īze, *v. i.* & *t.* (Of a photograph) To be injured by too long exposure to the sun's light ; বহুক্ষণ সূর্য্যালোকে উন্মুক্ত থাকার দরুণ নষ্ট হওয়া। ***Verb t.* 1.** To be exposed to sun's light ; সূর্য্যালোকে রক্ষিত হওয়া। **2.** (Of a photograph) To spoil by long exposure ; অধিকক্ষণ সূর্য্যালোকে উন্মুক্ত রাখিয়া নষ্ট করা। **—i-za'-tion,** *n.*

sō-lā'-tĭ-ŭm (-shĭ-), *n.* (*pl.* '-TIA). A compensation ; compensation for wounded feelings ; ক্ষতি-পূরণ ; মনোক্ষোভের ক্ষতিপূরণস্বরূপপ্রদত্ত অর্থ প্রভৃতি।

sōld, *p. t.* & *p. p.* of SELL (which see).

sŏl-dă-nĕl'-lă, *n.* A genus of Alpine plants ; আলপস্‌পর্ব্বতজাত বৃক্ষের 'গণ' বিশেষ।

sŏl'-dėr, *n.* & *v. t.* **1.** An easily soluble metallic cement ; পাইন, ঝালা, ধাতুলেপ। **2.** Anything which unites or cements; "Friendship mysterious cement of the soul, Sweet'ner of life! and *solder* of society!"—*Blair*, সংযোগসাধক বস্তু। ***Verb t.*** To unite two metallic surfaces by a fusible metallic cement; পাইন দেওয়া, ঝালা দেওয়া, ঝাইল দেওয়া। **Hard solder**—পাকা পাইন। **Soft solder**—কাঁচা পাইন।

sōl'-dier (-jêr), *n.* & *v. i.* **1.** A man engaged in military service; সৈন্য, সৈনিক, সিপাহী, যোদ্ধা, যোধ, শস্ত্রোপজীবী, ভট। **2.** A common soldier; সাধারণ সৈনিক। **3.** A man of much military experience or great valour; "So great a *soldier* taught us these, What long enduring hearts could do"; অতিশয় সাহসী ব্যক্তি, সামরিক, অভিজ্ঞতাসম্পন্ন ব্যক্তি, রণপণ্ডিত, যুদ্ধপ্রবীণ ব্যক্তি। **4.** Same as SOLDIER-BEETLE. **5.** Same as SOLDIER-CRAB. ***Verb i.*** **1.** To serve as soldier; সৈনিকের কায করা। **2.** (*Slang, Naut.*) To shirk work; (নাবিকদিগের ইতরভাষায়) কায এড়ান। **—ly**, *adj.* Befitting a solider; as, *soldierly* bearing; heroic; সৈনিক সমুচিত; বীরত্বসূচক, বীরজনোচিত, বীরোচিত। **—ship**, *n.* **Soldier-ant**—একজাতীয় যুদ্ধপ্রিয় পিপীলিকা। **Soldier-beetle**—একপ্রকার ঈষৎ রক্তবর্ণ কীট; একপ্রকার গোবরে পোকা। **Soldier-crab**—একজাতীয় কর্কট। **Soldier-hermit**—বড়শীতে ব্যবহৃত একপ্রকার কৃত্রিম মক্ষিকা। **Soldier-like**—সৈনিকোচিত। **Old soldier** — একবার বৈঠকে নিঃশেষিত বোতল; চুরুটের শেষ-টুকরা। **Soldier of fortune**—যে ব্যক্তি অর্থ লাভ বা আমোদের উদ্দেশ্যে নানাস্থানে বিশেষতঃ বিদেশে, ঘুরিয়া সৈনিকের কার্য্য করে, ভাগ্যান্বেষী সৈনিক। **Soldiers and sailors**—একপ্রকার গোবরেপোকা (শিশুগণ কর্ত্তৃক প্রদত্ত নাম)। **To come the old soldier over**—To claim to dictate to in virtue of greater experience; অধিকতর অভিজ্ঞতাসম্পন্ন বলিয়া কাহাকেও আদেশ দিবার দাবী করা।

sōl'-dier-ȳ (-jĕr-), *n.* Soldiers collectively; সৈনিকবৃন্দ, যোদ্ধৃবৃন্দ, সৈনিকসমূহ।

sōl'-dō, *n.* A small Italian coin worth about a half-penny; ইতালী দেশে ব্যবহৃত অর্দ্ধ পেনি মূল্যের মুদ্রাবিশেষ।

sōle, *n.* & *v. t.* **1.** The under or inner side of the foot; পায়ের তলা, পাদতল, চরণতল। **2.** (*Rare*) Foot; (কচিদ্ব্যবহৃত) পদ। **3.** The bottom of a boot or shoe; জুতার তলা। **4.** The bottom or lower part of anything or that on which anything rests; কোন বস্তুর নিম্নাংশ বা নিম্নতল, কোন বস্তুর অধিষ্ঠান। **5.** The bottom of a mine; খনির তলদেশ। **6.** The bottom of plane, plough, etc.; লাঙ্গল, রেঁদা, প্রভৃতির নিম্নাংশ। ***Verb t.*** To provide a shoe with sole; জুতার তলি লাগান। **Sole-channel**—বুট প্রভৃতির তলার ক্ষুদ্র নালী বিশেষ—যাহার ভিতরে শিলাই প্রচ্ছন্ন থাকে। **Sole-plate**—যন্ত্রাদির আধারফলক।

sōle, *n.* A kind of fish much esteemed for food; একপ্রকার সুখাদ্য মৎস্য।

sōle, *adj.* **1.** One and only; একমাত্র, কেবলমাত্র, শুদ্ধ। **2.** (*Law*) Unmarried; as, a male *sole*; (আইন) অবিবাহিত, অনূঢ়, অবিবাহিতা (*fem.*), অনূঢ়া (*ib.*)। **Sole'-ly**, *adv.*

sŏl'-ĕ-cism, *n.* **1.** Impropriety in language, or a gross deviation from the rules of syntax; an ungrammatical combination of words in a sentence; ব্যাকরণের নিয়ম প্রভৃতির ব্যতিক্রম, চ্যুতসংস্কৃতি (কাব্যাদর্শ), অপপ্রয়োগ, অশিষ্ট প্রয়োগ; ব্যাকরণের পদবিন্যাসের নিয়মলঙ্ঘনপূর্ব্বক কোন বাক্যের শব্দসংযোজন। **2.** A violation of the rules of society; সামাজিক নিয়মের ব্যতিক্রম, অশিষ্টাচার। **—cist**, *n.* **—cis'-tic**, *adj.*

sŏl'-emn (-ĕm), *adj.* **1.** (*Archaic*) Stately; (অপ্রঃ) জাঁকজমকপূর্ণ, সমারোহপূর্ণ। **2.** Sacred; পবিত্র, পূত, পুণ্য। **3.** Grave; গম্ভীর, গভীর, ভাবগম্ভীর, ধীরপ্রশান্ত। **4.** Awe inspiring; impressive; as, a *solemn* face; গম্ভীরভাবজনক; হৃদয়গ্রাহী। **5.** Dark; as, a suit of *solemn* black; sad; কৃষ্ণ; বিষাদসূচক, বিষাদব্যঞ্জক। **6.** Full of importance; as, *solemn* occasion; গুরুত্ববিশিষ্ট, গুরুত্বপূর্ণ। **7.** Serious; grave; as, *solemn* promise; গুরুত্বপূর্ণ; গভীর। **8.** Affectedly grave; as, a *solemn* face; কৃত্রিমগাম্ভীর্য্যপূর্ণ। **9.** Accompanied with all due forms or ceremonies; as, *solemn* war; made in form; যথানিয়ম বা যথাযোগ্যানুষ্ঠান সহকৃত; যথারীতিসম্পাদিত। **—ly**, *adv.* In a solemn manner; অনুষ্ঠান সহকারে, যথারীতি, গম্ভীরভাবে। **—ness**, *n.* **Solemn occasion**—গুরুত্বপূর্ণ কাল। **Solemn promise**—ঈশ্বরের নামে শপথ। **To put on a solemn face**—To look grave; মুখগম্ভীর করা।

sŏ-lĕm'-ni-tȳ, *n.* **1.** Gravity; impressiveness; seriousness; গাম্ভীর্য্য; গম্ভীরভাবজনকতা; গুরুত্ব, গুরুত্বপূর্ণতা। **2.** A religious ceremony; as, the *solemnities* of a funeral; any ceremony or celebration; a festival; ধর্ম্মকৃত্য, অনুষ্ঠান, পুণ্যক্রিয়া, ধর্ম্মক্রিয়া, দেবক্রিয়া; মঙ্গলকার্য্য, উৎসবাদির অনুষ্ঠান; উৎসব।

sŏl'-ĕm-nīze, *v. t.* **1.** To celebrate; অনুষ্ঠান করা। **2.** To perform duly; as, to *solemnize* one's marriage; যথারীতি সম্পাদন করা। **3.** To make grave, serious and reverential; as, to *solemnize* the mind for such high occasion; গাম্ভীর্য্যপূর্ণ করা, প্রশান্তগম্ভীর ভক্তিভাবোদ্দীপক করা। **—ni-za'-tion**, *n.*

sō'-lĕn, *n.* A genus of bivalve mollusc; একজাতীয় দ্বিপুটক শুক্তি প্রভৃতি।

sō'-lē-noid (-noyd), *n.* (*Electr.*) A helix of copper or other wire wound in the form of a cylinder ; (তাড়িতবিদ্যা) নলাকারে কুণ্ডলিত তাম্র বা অন্য ধাতুর তার, বেষ্টনী (সাঃ পঃ), তারকুণ্ডলী। [এইরূপ কুণ্ডলীর এক বা উভয় প্রান্ত কক্ষের সহিত সমরেখায় পুনরানীত হয়।]

sŏl–fä′, *v. i.* To pronounce the notes of the gamut, ascending or descending ; সা রে গা মা গাওয়া।

sŏl–fä′, *n.* 1. The gamut; স্বরগ্রাম। 2. Same as TONIC SOLFA.

solfatara, (*It.*), *n.* A volcanic vent which yields sulphurous gases ; গন্ধকধর্ম্মী বাষ্পনিঃসারক আগ্নেয়গিরিরন্ধ্র।

sŏl-feg′-gio (-jō), *n.* Arranging the scales by the names of *do, re, mi, fa, sol, la, si* ; সা রে গা মা পা ধা নি ইত্যাদি সপ্তকে বিন্যাস।

sŏl-fĕ-rī′-nō, *n.* A deep pink colour or dye; একপ্রকার ঘন পাটলবর্ণ রঙ্গ বা রঞ্জক পদার্থ। [১৮৫৯ খৃঃ অব্দে সংঘটিত, ইতালী দেশের Solferino নামক স্থানের যুদ্ধের বৎসর প্রথম প্রস্তুত হইয়াছিল বলিয়া এই নাম।]

sŏ-lĭc′-ĭt, *v. t.* & *i.* 1. To ask with eagerness ; কাতরভাবে প্রার্থনা করা, যাচ্ঞা করা, সকাতরে প্রার্থনা করা। 2. (*Rare*) To try to acquire ; পাইতে চেষ্টা করা। 2. To awake ; to invite ; to allure; "That fruit··· *solicited* her longing eye"; জাগরিত করা, উদ্বুদ্ধ করা ; আহ্বান করা ; প্রলুব্ধ করা। 3. To disquiet ; অস্থির করা, ব্যাকুল করা। 4. (Of a prostitute) To tempt a man in public places ; "She was arrested by a constable for *soliciting* a gentleman"; (বারাঙ্গনাসম্পর্কে) প্রকাশ্য স্থানে দাঁড়াইয়া লোককে প্রলুব্ধ করা। ***Verb i.*** To make solicitation ; যাচ্ঞা করা। **–i-ta′-tion,** *n.* 1. Earnest request ; সনির্ব্বন্ধ অনুরোধ, সাধ্যসাধনা, যাচ্ঞা। 2. Excitement ; allurement ; উত্তেজনা ; প্রলোভন।

sŏ-lĭc′-ĭ-tor (-têr), *n.* 1. (*Rare*) One who asks with earnestness ; (কচিদ্ব্যবহৃত) যাচক। 2. An attorney ; এটর্ণি। **Solicitor-General** — বিলাতে এডভোকেট জেনেরেলের অব্যবহিত নিম্নবর্ত্তী সরকারী কৌঁস্থলী।

sŏ-lĭc′-ĭt-ous (-ŭs), *adj.* Eagerly desirous ; as, he is very much *solicitous* for my welfare ; apprehensive ; troubled; anxious; উৎকণ্ঠিত, আগ্রহান্বিত ; সশঙ্কিত ; ব্যাকুল, ব্যগ্র ; উতলা, উৎসুক, উদ্বিগ্ন। **–ly,** *adv.* **–ness,** *n.*

sŏ-lĭc′-ĭ-tūde, *n.* Concern ; anxiety ; অসোয়াস্তি, ব্যাকুলতা ; উদ্বেগ, উৎকণ্ঠা।

sŏl′-ĭd, *adj.* & *n.* 1. Having its particles so close as to resist impression ; as, *solid* gold ; কঠিন, সংহত, সান্দ্র, ঘন। 2. Not hollow ; as, a *solid* tube ; ফাঁপা নয়, নিরেট। 3. Firm ; strong ; as, a *solid* structure ; দৃঢ় ; শক্ত, মজবুত। 4. (*Print.*) Unleaded ; as, *solid* compose ; ফাঁক বিহীন, লেড ছাড়া, ঠাসা। 5. Unanimous ; as, *solid* vote ; সর্ব্বসম্মত। 6. Solidified ; as, *solid* soup ; ঘনীভূত, পিণ্ডীভূত 7. Whole ; entire ; as, a *solid* hour ; পুরা ; অখণ্ড। 8. Entirely of the same substance; as, *solid* gold; অমিশ্রিত, বিশুদ্ধ, খাঁটি। 9. Trustworthy ; substantial ; weighty ; as, *solid* reasons ; satisfactory ; as, *solid* comfort ; বিশ্বাসযোগ্য ; সারবান, সারগর্ভ ; গুরুত্বপূর্ণ ; তুষ্টিজনক। 10. Financially sound or safe ; as, a *solid* scheme ; wealthy ; well-established ; সঙ্গতিসম্পন্ন ; ধনী, ধনবান ; সুপ্রতিষ্ঠিত। 11. (*Bot.*) Not hollow ; as, a *solid* stem ; (উদ্ভিদবিদ্যা) সারগর্ভ (সাঃ পঃ), নিরেট। 12. Concerned with solids ; as, *solid* geometry ; ঘনসংক্রান্ত, ঘন। 13. (Of colour) Uniform ; as, *solid* colour ; সর্ব্বত্র একরূপ। 14. Sober-minded ; ধীরচিত্ত, ধীরগম্ভীর। ***Noun.*** 1. A firm compact body ; কঠিন পদার্থ, নিরেট বস্তু। 2. (*Geom.*) A body with length, breadth and thickness ; (জ্যামিতি) ঘন, ঘনাবয়ব (সাঃ পঃ)। 3. (*Pl.*) The bones, flesh and vessels of animal bodies, as distinguished from the fluids ; জন্তুদেহের অস্থি, মাংস, নাড়ী প্রভৃতি কঠিন অংশ। **–ly,** *adv.* **So-lid-i-fi-ca′-tion,** *n.* The act of solidifying or being solidified ; সংহনন, ঘনীকরণ, ঘনীভবন। **So-lid′-i-fy,** *v. t.* & *i.* To make or become solid ; ঘনীভূত করা, সংহত করা, কঠিন করা, পিণ্ডীভূত করা, ঘনীভূত হওয়া, সংহত হওয়া। **So-lid′-i-ty,** *n.* The state of being solid ; ঘনতা (হিঃ কোঃ)। **Solid angle**—বিভিন্ন ধরাতলে অবস্থিত এবং এক বিন্দুতে সম্মিলিত তিন বা ততোধিক সরল কোণদ্বারা গঠিত কোণ ঘনকোণ। **Solid-hoofed**—অখণ্ডিতক্ষুর, একশফ। **Solid measure** — ঘনপরিমাণ। **Solid number**—তিন অদৃঢ় গুণাবয়ব সমন্বিত অখণ্ড সংখ্যা। **Solid problem**—যে সম্পাদ্য রেখা, বৃত্ত প্রভৃতির সাহায্যে গঠিত করিতে পারা যায় না এবং যাহা গঠন করিতে অবক্ষেত্র (Ellipse), পরবলয় (parabola), অতি পরবলয় (hyperbola), প্রভৃতির আবশ্যক হয়। **Solid square** — সমচতুষ্কোণাকারে সজ্জিত সৈন্যশ্রেণী ; যে ব্যূহে সৈন্যপংক্তি সমূহের সংখ্যা সম্মুখ ও পার্শ্বেরদিক হইতে গণনায় সমান হইয়া থাকে। **Regular solid** — সমান ধরাতল দ্বারা বেষ্টিত ঘন। **The solid**—কোন বস্তুর অংশ বা অঙ্গ। **The solid South** — মার্কিণ যুক্তরাজ্যের দক্ষিণঅংশের রাষ্ট্রসমূহ — যথাকার অধিবাসিগণ সর্ব্বদা গণতান্ত্রিকদিগের পক্ষে ভোট প্রদান করে। **To be, get,** or **make one's self solid with**—To gain the favour of ; কাহারো অনুগ্রহ লাভ করা। To wreak vengeance ; প্রতিশোধ লওয়া। **To go,** or **be, solid for**—To be united in favour of ; (কাহারো) পক্ষে ভোট প্রভৃতি দেওয়ার জন্য মিলিত হওয়া।

sŏl-ĭ-dăr′-ĭ-tў, *n.* 1. The state of being solid or perfect ; কঠিনতা, সংহতত্ব, পূর্ণাবয়বতা, পূর্ণাঙ্গতা । 2. Unity or community of interest and responsibilities ; সমস্বার্থভাগিতা, ঐক্যভাব (হিঃ কোঃ), সমূষ্টতা (ঐ), একসমাজতা ।

sŏl-ĭd-un′-gu-lar (-ŭng-gü-ler), **–lous** (-lŭs), **–late,** *adj.* & *n.* Not colven hoofed ; (পশু-সম্পর্কে) অখণ্ডিতক্ষুর, একশফ (রাজঃ সং) । ***Noun.*** (only *-late*) A solidungular animal ; একশফ জন্তু ।

sŏl′-ĭ-dŭs, *n.* (*Pl.* -DI) An ancient Roman golden coin introduced by Emperor Constantine ; রোমের স্বর্ণমুদ্রা বিশেষ । [১২ শিঃ ৫ পেন্সের সমান ।]

sŏl′-ĭ-fĭd′-ĭ-ăn, *n.* & *adj.* One who holds the doctrine that mere faith is sufficient for salvation ; কেবলমাত্র বিশ্বাসই মুক্তিলাভের পক্ষে যথেষ্ট এই মতে বিশ্বাসী ব্যক্তি । ***Adj.*** Of, or pertaining to, the above doctrine ; উক্ত মত সম্বন্ধীয় ।

sō-lĭl′-ō-quў, *n.* Talking to oneself ; "The interesting *soliloquy* was interrupted by a rustling noise in the hall" ; আত্মভাষণ, স্বগতবচন, স্বগতোক্তি, আকাশভাষিত । **–quist,** *n.* **–quize,** *v. t.*

sŏl′-ĭ-pĕd, *adj.* & *n.* Same as SOLIDUNGULATE (which see).

sŏl′-ĭp-sĭsm, *n.* The theory that the self is the only thing really existent ; "As long as we confine ourselves to the world given in experience...we must profess *solipsism*" ; অহম্বাদ (হিঃ কোঃ), মদৈকানুভববাদ, আত্মবাদ ।

sŏl-ĭ-sē′-quĭ-ous (-ŭs), *adj.* Following the sun, as the sunflower ; সূর্য্যানুগামী, সূর্য্যানুসারী ।

sŏl-ĭ-tairē′ (-târ), *n.* 1. A person who lives in solitude ; "There I could dwell a studious *solitaire*" ; a hermit ; নির্জ্জনস্থানবাসী ব্যক্তি ; যতি, মুনি । 2. A card-game for one person ; এক ব্যক্তির ক্রীড়াযোগ্য একপ্রকার তাস খেলা । 3. A game which a person can play alone on a round board ; একপ্রকার ক্রীড়া — যাহা কোন ব্যক্তি একাকী এক গোল মেজেতে খেলিতে পারে । 4. An ornament for the neck or ears ; an article of jewllery in which a single precious stone is set ; কণ্ঠভূষা, কর্ণভূষা, দুল, কুণ্ডল ; যে অলঙ্কারে কেবলমাত্র একটা রত্ন বসান হয় । 5. A species of thrush ; একজাতীয় দামা পাখী ।

sŏl′-ĭ-tā-rў, *adj.* & *n.* 1. Living alone without any companion ; "The *solitary* man is as speechless as the lower animals" ; inclined to be alone ; নির্জ্জনবাসী, সঙ্গিহীন, একেলা, একাকী, একক, নিঃসঙ্গ ; নির্জ্জনতাপ্রিয় । 2. Retired ; lonely ; as, *solitary* residence ; নিভৃত, নির্জ্জন, বিরল, নিরালা ; বিজন, জনমানবহীন, জনমানবশূন্য, জনহীন (আঃ মঠ) । 3. Sole ; as, *solitary* instance ; একমাত্র, অদ্বিতীয় । ***Noun.*** One who lives alone ; "The first meditation of a *solitary* is the behaviour of men in active life" ; a recluse ; নির্জ্জনবাসী ব্যক্তি ; যতি, সন্ন্যাসী । **–ri-ly,** *adv.* **–ri-ness,** *n.* The state of being solitary ; একাকিত্ব, বিজনতা, জনমানবহীনতা । **Solitary ants, bees, etc.**—যে সকল পিপীলিকা, মধুমক্ষিকা, প্রভৃতি দলবদ্ধ ভাবে বাস করে না । **Solitary confinement**—নির্জ্জন কারাবাস ।

sŏl′-ĭ-tūde, *n.* 1. The state of being alone ; নির্জ্জনতা, বিজনতা, নিঃসঙ্গতা, একাকিত্ব, নৈভৃত্য, জনশূন্যতা । 2. A solitary place ; "That busy scene was converted into a silent *solitude*" ; নির্জ্জন স্থান, নিভৃত স্থান, বিজন স্থান ।

sō-līve′ (-lēv), *n.* A joist or rafter of secondary importance ; অপ্রধান কড়িকাঠ বা বর্গা ।

sŏl-mĭ-za′-tion, *n.* (*Mus.*) A recital of the notes of the gamut ; (সঙ্গীতশাস্ত্র) সা রে গা মা প্রভৃতি সাধন ।

sō′-lō, *n.* 1. A musical piece performed by only one voice or instrument ; এক ব্যক্তি কর্ত্তৃক একমাত্র বাদ্যযন্ত্রের সাহায্যে গেয় সঙ্গীত । 2. A kind of card-game ; একপ্রকার তাসখেলা ।

Sŏl′-ō-mŏn, *n.* The king of Israel ; ইস্রায়েলের অধিপতি সলোমোন । [বাইবেলের প্রাচীননিয়ম গ্রন্থে ইঁহার বিবরণ বর্ণিত হইয়াছে । সলোমোন একজন আদর্শ জ্ঞানী ব্যক্তি ছিলেন । ইঁহার এক সহস্র পত্নী ও স্বর্ণ এবং দ্বিরদরদনির্ম্মিত প্রাসাদের বিচিত্র বর্ণনা বাইবেলগ্রন্থে পাঠ করা যায় ।] **–mon′-ic,** *adj.* **Solomon's Seal**—বিলাতী স্থলকুমুদের মত পুষ্পপ্রদ

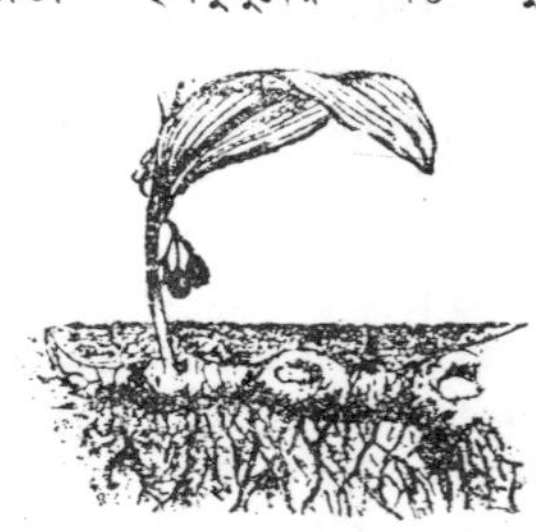

Solomon's Seal.

একজাতীয় গুল্ম ; দেহ এবং আত্মার সংযোগের প্রতীকস্বরূপ পরস্পর সংগ্রথিত ত্রিকোণদ্বয় । **The song of Solomon**—Same as THE SONG OF SONGS which see under SONG.

Sō′-lŏn, *n.* 1. The name of an Athenian lawgiver ; প্রাচীন এথেন্স নগরবাসী জনৈক আইন-কর্ত্তার নাম । 2. A wise man ; a legislator ; জ্ঞানী লোক ; ব্যবস্থাপক, ব্যবস্থা কর্ত্তা । **–lo′-ni-an, –lon′-ic,** *adjs.*

sō-long′ (-läng), *interj.* Good-bye till we meet ; এখন বিদায় হই, তবে এখন আসি ।

sŏl′-stice (-stĭs), *n.* 1. Either of the two points in the ecliptic at which the sun ceases to recede from the equator either north in summer or south in winter ; অয়নান্ত (সাঃ পঃ), অয়ন, সৌরস্থিতি (বঙ্গদর্শন), অয়নসন্ধি (হিঃ কোঃ)। 2. Either time at which the sun is furthest from the equator and appears to pause before returning ; যে দুই বিভিন্ন সময়ে সূর্য্য বিষুব বৃত্ত হইতে দূরতম স্থানে অবস্থিত থাকে এবং প্রত্যাবৃত্ত হওয়ার পূর্ব্বে স্থির বলিয়া প্রতিভাত হয়—তাহার অন্যতর, উত্তরায়ণ, দক্ষিণায়ণ। **–sti′-tial,** *adj.* Pertaining to the solstice ; অয়নান্ত-সম্বন্ধীয়, অয়নান্তকালিক। **Solstitial colure** — অয়নান্তবৃত্ত (সাঃ পঃ), অয়নপ্রোতবৃত্ত (ঐ)। **Solstitial points**—Same as SOLSTICE I. **Summer solstice**—উত্তরায়ণ, কর্কট-সংক্রান্তি। **Winter solstice**—দক্ষিণায়ন, মকরসংক্রান্তি।

sŏl′-ū-ble (-bl), *adj.* That can be dissolved in a fluid ; "It is probable that everything that affects the taste is in some degree *soluble* in the saliva" ; দ্রাব্য, দ্রবণীয়, ঘুলনশীল, গালনীয়, দ্রবণ্য, দ্রবণার্হ। **–bil′-i-ty,** *n.* The state of being soluble ; ঘুলনশীলতা, দ্রাব্যতা, দ্রবণীয়তা, বিলায়নীয়তা, গালনীয়তা, দ্রবণশীলতা।

sō′-lŭs, *adj.* Alone (used in stage-direction) ; (নাট্যালয়ে ব্যবহৃত হয়) একাকী, একক।

sö-lūte′, *adj.* & *n.* 1. (*Obs.*) Soluble ; (অপ্রঃ) দ্রাব্য। 2. (*Bot.*) Loose ; (উদ্ভিদ্‌বিদ্যা) পৃথক্ পৃথক্, আল্‌গা আল্‌গা। ***Noun.*** (*Chem.* & *Phys.*) A dissolved substance ; (রসায়নশাস্ত্র এবং পদার্থবিজ্ঞান) কোন কিছুতে বিদ্রাবিত পদার্থ।

sö-lū′-tion, *n.* 1. The act of solving a question, problem, etc. ; "A difficult problem of mixed law and fact for *solution* by the judges"; সমাধান, পূরণ, সাধন (হিঃ কোঃ), ভেদন (ঐ), উত্তর (ঐ)। 2. An explanation ; "These facts afford a rational *solution* of this curious problem" ; an answer ; decision ; "Expecting the *solution* of the judges in this point" ; ব্যাখ্যা, বিবরণ (হিঃ কোঃ) ; উত্তর ; মীমাংসা। 3. Separation ; "That Boer policy had not for its aim the *solution* of British supremacy in South Africa" ; dissolution ; breach ; "The easy and frequent *solutions* of conjugal society" ; পৃথকীকরণ ; বিশ্লেষণ ; ভঙ্গ। 4. The act of dissolving ; দ্রবণ, দ্রবীভবন, দ্রাবণ, বিদ্রাবণ, বিলায়ন, গালয়ন। 5. The preparation resulting from dissolving a solid in liquid ; "The *solution* of indigo in the sulphuric acid" ; দ্রব, দ্রাবক (হিঃ কোঃ), দ্রবপদার্থ (ঐ), কষায় (ঐ)। 6. The termination or crisis of a disease ; পীড়ার অবসান বা সঙ্কটকাল। 7. (*Law*) Payment ; 'It neither being by *solution* nor other transaction importing the consent of the creditor thereto" ; শোধ। **Chemical solution**—যে দ্রবে উপাদান পদার্থ-সমূহের রাসায়নিক ধর্ম্মের পরিবর্ত্তন সংঘটিত হয়, রাসায়নিক ঘোল (হিঃ কোঃ)। **Mechanical solution**—যে দ্রবে উপাদানবস্তুসমূহের রাসায়নিক ধর্ম্ম অবিকৃত থাকে, কৃত্রিম ঘোল (হিঃ কোঃ)। **Solution of continuity**—অস্থি প্রভৃতি বিদারণ, মাংসের ছিন্নভিন্ন অবস্থা।

solve (sŏlv), *v. t.* 1. To give or furnish a solution of ; "Any one who can *solve* a plane trigonometry will have no difficulty" ; সমাধান করা, পূরণ করা। 2. To dissolve ; ঘুলা, বিদ্রাবিত করা। **Solv′-a-bil′-i-ty,** *n.* **Solv′-a-ble,** *adj.*

sŏl′-vent, *adj.* & *n.* 1. Having the power or quality of solving ; দ্রাবণক্ষম, দ্রাবণধর্ম্মী, ঘোলক (হিঃ কোঃ)। 2. Able, or sufficient, to meet all liabilities ; as, a *solvent* merchant ; ঋণশোধক্ষম, ঋণাধিকধনসম্পন্ন, সাউকর। ***Noun.*** 1. A substance that dissolves another substance ; "Some of the acids frequently act as mere *solvents*" ; দ্রাবকপুট (সাঃ পঃ)। 2. Something which solves or settles ; "He was compelled to imply that universal *solvent* a cash payment" ; সমাধান-কারক বিষয়। 3. A laxative ; মৃদু বিরেচক ঔষধ। 4. A disintegrating influence ; "The great *solvent* of Indian caste prejudice is Western thought" ; বিলয়সাধকবস্তু, শক্তি-হ্রাসকর প্রভাব। **–ven-cy,** *n.* 1. The state of being soluble ; ঘুলনশীলতা। 2. The state of being solvent ; ঋণাধিকধনসম্পন্নতা, সাউকর।

sō-măt′-ĭc, *adj.* Corporeal ; শারীরিক, দৈহিক, ভৌতিক, স্থূল, জড়।

sō-mă-tō-gĕn′-ĭc, *adj.* Originative in the body ; দেহগত।

sō-mă-tŏl′-ō-ġȳ, *n.* The doctrine of bodies or material substance ; দেহতত্ত্ব, জড়তত্ত্ব, নরদেহ-বিদ্যা, শারীর-বিদ্যা, মনুষ্যবিদ্যা (হিঃ কোঃ), মানব-দেহতত্ত্ব, দেহবিজ্ঞান।

sŏm′-bre (–bêr), *adj.* 1. Dark ; gloomy ; "The city has a dark and *sombre* appearance" ; কৃষ্ণ ; মলিন, অন্ধকারাচ্ছন্ন ; তমসাবৃত, তমসাচ্ছন্ন। 2. Melancholy ; as, *sombre* mien ; dark and sullen ; বিষাদাচ্ছন্ন, বিষাদমলিন, বিষাদমাখা, বিষণ্ণ, নিরানন্দ ; অপ্রসন্ন, হাঁড়িপানা (*slang*)। **–brous,** *adj.* **–ly,** *adv.* **–ness,** *n.*

sŏm-brĕ′-rō, *n.* A broad-brimmed felt hat ; একপ্রকার চৌড়া কিনারা-ওয়ালা নেমদার টুপি।

some (sŭm), *adj., pron.* & *adv.* 1. Expressing certain quantity of a thing ; as, *some* milk ; কিছু, কতক। 2. Expressing a number of persons or things, greater or less, but indeterminate ; "I am going to ask him to put his care in *some* lawyer's hands" ; কতিপয়, গোটাকতক, কয়েকজন, কতক। 3. Indicating an unknown person or thing ; কেহ, কোন। 4. About ; as, *some* 600 men ; প্রায়। *Pron.* An indefinite part, quantity or number ; "*Some* (seeds) fell upon a rock, and it withered away" ; কতক, কিছু। *Adv.* 1. (*Dial.*) Somewhat ; "He hunted *some* fished *some*" ; (উপভাষায়) কতকটা, কিছুটা। 2. (*U. S.*) Very much ; (মার্কিণ যুক্তরাজ্যে) খুব। **Some-body**—কোন লোক, কোন ব্যক্তি; গণ্যমান্য ব্যক্তি (এই অর্থে বহুবচন *Somebodies*ও ব্যবহৃত হয়)। **Some few**—অল্প সংখ্যক। **Somehow** — কোন প্রকারে, কোন রকমে। **Something**—কোন বিষয়, কোন জিনিষ, কোন বস্তু; সত্য (as, there is *something* in what you say) ; কিছু অর্থ; একটা বিশেষ জিনিষ; বিশিষ্ট ব্যক্তি; কোন চাকুরী (as he is *something* in the District Judge's house) ; কতকটা সান্ত্বনার বিষয় (as, it is *something* to be safe in one's house)। **Sometime** — কিছুকাল ; কোন সময় ; (অপ্রঃ) ভূতপূর্ব্ব ; কখন। **Sometimes** — সময় সময়, মাঝে মাঝে, কখন কখন। **Someway** — কোন রকমে, কোন উপায়ে। **Somewhat**—বিশিষ্ট ব্যক্তি বা বস্তু; কতকটা। **Somewhere**—কোথায়ও। **Somehow or other** — One way or another ; যে কোনপ্রকারে, যে কোন উপায়ে। **Some of these days** — Ere long ; অল্প দিনের মধ্যেই, শীঘ্রই, এরই মধ্যে একদিন, অনতিকাল মধ্যেই, কিছুদিনের মধ্যেই। **Some one** — কোন লোক, কোন নির্দ্দিষ্ট ব্যক্তি। **Something dam or snork**—(ইতরভাষায়) পানীয়; সুরাসার। **Something is better than nothing** — নেই মামার চেয়ে কাণা মামা ভাল। **Something of a**—To a certain extent or degree; কিয়ৎ পরিমাণে, কতক পরিমাণে। **Something or other** — Either one thing or another ; কিছু, কিছুনা কিছু, একটা বা আরটা। **To make something of**—To improve in someway ; কোন উপায়ে উন্নতি বা উৎকর্ষ সাধন করা। **To take a drop of something**—To drink a little ; একটু মদ খাওয়া। **To take something**—To take some food or drink ; কিছুটা খাওয়া।

som'-er-sault (sŭm-ĕr-sălt), **–sĕt**, *n.* & *v. i.* A leap in which the heels turn over the head ; ডিগবাজি। *Verb i.* To turn somersault ; ডিগবাজি খাওয়া। **—er**, *n.* **Double somersault**—দুইবার ডিগবাজি খাওন, উর্দ্ধপাদ লম্ফন।

som'-ĕr-sĕt (sŭm-), *n.* A saddle padded before the knee and behind the thigh ; হাঁটুর অগ্রভাগে ও উরুর পশ্চাদ্‌ভাগে গদিবিশিষ্ট একপ্রকার জিন।

sō'-mite, *n.* A single segment in the body of an articulate animal ; গ্রন্থিবিশিষ্ট জন্তুর দেহের একটী পর্ব্ব। **—mit'-ic,** *adj.*

sŏm-năm'-bū-lĭsm, *n.* The act or practice of walking in sleep ; নিদ্রাটন, স্বপ্নচার (হিঃ কোঃ), নিদ্রাভ্রমণ (ঐ), স্বপ্নাটন, স্বপ্নপ্রয়াণ, স্বপ্নসঞ্চরণ, স্বপ্নপর্য্যটন, স্বপ্নপরিক্রম, নিদ্রাপরিক্রম। **—late,** *v. i.* & *t.* To walk during sleep; নিদ্রিতাবস্থায় বিচরণ করা, নিদ্রাটন করা, স্বপ্নসঞ্চরণ করা। **—list,** *n.* Sleep-walker ; স্বপ্নাটনকারী, নিদ্রাচর, নিদ্রাচারী। **—lis'-tic,** *adj.* **Artificial somnambulism**—Same as HYPNOTISM.

sŏm-nĭf'-ĕr-ous (-ŭs), *adj.* 1. Inducing sleep ; "The wine had exerted its *somniferous* influence"; নিদ্রাজনক, সুপ্তিজনক, স্বাপজনক, প্রস্বাপন। 2. Sleepy ; "Those respectable *somniferous* burghers" ; নিদ্রালু।

sŏm-nĭf'-ic, *adj.* Causing sleep ; "A *somnific* fit again overtook him, and in the next instant he was snoring in his chair" ; নিদ্রাজনক, সুপ্তিজনক, নিদ্রাকর, নিদ্রাকর্ষক, সুপ্তিকারক।

sŏm-nĭl'-ō-quence(-kwĕns), *n.* The act of talking in sleep ; নিদ্রাবস্থায় কথা বলন, নিদ্রাভাষণ, স্বপ্নপ্রলাপ, নিদ্রালাপ, স্বপ্নভাষণ। **—quize,** *v. i.*

sŏm-nĭp'-ă-thy̆ *n.* Hypnotic sleep ; যোগনিদ্রা, মায়ানিদ্রা। **—thist,** *n.* A person in a state of hypnotic sleep ; সম্মোহন ক্রিয়া দ্বারা মুগ্ধ ও আচ্ছন্ন ব্যক্তি, যোগনিদ্রাচ্ছন্ন ব্যক্তি।

sŏm'-nō-lĕnt, *adj.* 1. Inducing sleep or drowsiness ; "The noise made by the stream had a very pleasant *somnolent* effect" ; নিদ্রাজনক, নিদ্রাকর্ষক, তন্দ্রাজনক, তন্দ্রাকর্ষক, নিদ্রাপ্রবণ। 2. Sleepy ; drowsy ; "Fast and watching had made him more than usually *somnolent*" ; নিদ্রালু, নিদ্রাবিষ্ট; তন্দ্রালু, তন্দ্রাবিষ্ট, তন্দ্রাপ্রবণ। **—lence, —lency,** *ns.* The state of being somnolent ; তন্দ্রাবিষ্টতা, তন্দ্রাপ্রবণতা, নিদ্রাপ্রবণতা, স্বাপব্যসন, (মূর্চ্ছা), স্বাপপ্রবণতা। **—ly,** *adv.*

sŏm'-nō-lĭsm, *n.* Hypnotic sleep ; যোগনিদ্রা, মোহনিদ্রা, সম্মোহনসুপ্তি, যোগনিদ্রাচ্ছন্নতা।

son (sŭn), *n.* A male child ; পুত্র, ছেলে (*colloq.*) তনয়, আত্মজ, সূনু (cf. Anglo Sax. *sunu* ; Goth, *sunus*, Old High Germ. *sunu* ; Lithunian *sūnus*, Old Slav. *synŭ*, Zend. *hunu*), সুত (esp. in poet.), নন্দন (*ib.*), পুত (*slang*), বেটা (*dial*), ছেরা (*ib.*), পুঁয়া (*ib.*), ছাওয়াল (*ib.*)। [Syn. স্বজ, অঙ্গজ, তনুজ, তনূজ, তনুজাত, দারক, কুমার, আত্মসম্ভব, অপত্য, দায়াদ, কুলাধারক, আত্মজন্মা, দ্বিতীয়, প্রজা] [হিন্দুশাস্ত্রে দ্বাদশবিধ পুত্রের উল্লেখ আছে যথাঃ—ঔরসঃ ক্ষেত্রজশ্চৈব দত্তঃ কৃত্রিম এব চ। গূঢ়োৎপন্নোঽপবিদ্ধশ্চ দায়াদা বান্ধবাশ্চষট্‌॥ কানীনশ্চ সহোঢ়শ্চ ক্রীতঃ পৌনর্ভবস্তথা। স্বয়ন্দত্তশ্চ শৌদ্রশ্চ ষডদায়াদবান্ধবাঃ॥ ১। বিবাহ সংস্কারে সংস্কৃতা সবর্ণা পত্নীতে স্বয়ং উৎপাদিত সন্তানকে ঔরস পুত্র বলে। ২। অপুত্র মৃত ব্যক্তির, ক্লীবের অথবা

ব্যাধিগ্রস্তের পত্নীতে ধর্ম্মতঃ নিযুক্ত হইয়া যে দেবরাদি সপিণ্ড দ্বারা সন্তানোৎপাদন হয়, ঐ সন্তানকে ক্ষেত্রজ সন্তান বলে। ৩। পিতামাতা দুর্ভিক্ষাদি আপৎকালে অথবা প্রতিগ্রহীতার পুত্রাভাবাদি আপদে যে সমান জাতীয় পুত্রকে প্রীতিপূর্ব্বক জলগ্রহণ করিয়া প্রতিগ্রহীতাকে দান করেন, ঐ পুত্রকে দত্রিম বা দত্তক পুত্র বলে। ৪। গুণদোষবিচারক্ষম, পুত্রগুণযুক্ত অথচ স্বজাতীয় এমন বালককে পুত্রত্বে গ্রহণ করিলে কৃত্রিমপুত্র বলা হয়। ৫। আপনার ভার্য্যাতে স্বজাতীয় পুরুষ কর্তৃক উৎপন্ন কিন্তু কোন্ পুরুষ এমন নিশ্চয় জ্ঞান না থাকিলে ঐ পুত্রকে গূঢ়োৎপন্ন পুত্র বলে। ৬। পিতা মাতা কর্তৃক পরিত্যক্ত অথবা তাঁহাদের অন্যতর কর্তৃক যে পুত্র, উহাকে যে ব্যক্তি স্বীকার করে, উহা সেই প্রতিগ্রহীতার অপবিদ্ধ পুত্র বলিয়া কথিত হয়। ৭। পিতৃগৃহে থাকিয়া কন্যা গোপনভাবে সবর্ণপুরুষ দ্বারা যে পুত্র উৎপাদন করে, ঐ পুত্রকে কন্যাবিবাহকারীর কানীনপুত্র বলা যায়। ৮। জ্ঞাতগর্ভা বা অজ্ঞাতগর্ভা কন্যাকে বিবাহ করিয়া সেই গর্ভে যে পুত্র উৎপন্ন হয়, ঐ পুত্রকে বিবাহকারীর সহোঢ়পুত্র বলা যায়। ৯। পুত্রার্থ মাতাপিতার নিকট হইতে মূল্য দিয়া যে পুত্র ক্রয় করা যায়, ক্রেতার সবর্ণ হউক বা না হউক, তথাপি উহার ক্রীতক পুত্র হইবে। ১০। পতি কর্তৃক পরিত্যক্তা অথবা মৃত পতিকা বিধবা, স্বেচ্ছতঃ পুনর্ব্বার অন্যের ভার্য্যা হইয়া যে পুত্র উৎপাদন করে, ঐ পুত্রকে পৌনর্ভব পুত্র বলে। ১১। পিতৃমাতৃহীন অথবা তাহাদের কর্তৃক অকারণ পরিত্যক্ত পুত্র স্বয়ং যদি আপনাকে দান করে তবে উহা গ্রহীতার স্বয়ংদত্ত পুত্র হইবে। ১২। ব্রাহ্মণ কামবশতঃ শূদ্রাতে যে পুত্র উৎপন্ন করে ঐ পুত্রকে পারশব কহে।] **2.** A male descendant; as, the *sons* of Israel; বংশধর। **3.** One who inherits or displays the character of some persons, etc.; as, *sons* of Belial; কোন ব্যক্তি প্রভৃতির প্রকৃতি বা স্বভাবপ্রাপ্ত ব্যক্তি। **4.** A native of some specified place; as, *sons* of India; কোন দেশের অধিবাসী, সন্তান (as ভারতসন্তান)। **5.** The form of address used by an old man to a young one, by a priest or teacher to his disciple or the like; শিক্ষক, গুরু প্রভৃতি কর্তৃক শিষ্য এবং বৃদ্ধ কর্তৃক অপেক্ষাকৃত অল্পবয়স্ক ব্যক্তিগণের সম্বোধনে ব্যবহৃত শব্দ, পুত্র (cf. রে পুত্র!)। **6.** The second person of God; Jesus Christ; খৃষ্টীয় ত্রীশ্বরের দ্বিতীয় ঈশ্বর; যীশুখৃষ্ট **7.** An angel; দেবদূত। **Son′-less,** *adj.* **Son′-ship,** *n.* **Son-before-the-father**—বিভিন্নপ্রকার ক্ষুপের নাম। **Son-in-law**—জামাতা। **Son of Heaven**—চীন সম্রাট। **Son-of-the-sun**—একপ্রকার পক্ষী। **Sons of Liberty**—ষ্ট্যাম্প আইনের প্রতিরোধের জন্য আমেরিকায় ১৭৭৩—৭৪ বর্ষে প্রতিষ্ঠিত বিভিন্ন গুপ্ত সমিতি। **The Son of Man**—যীশুখৃষ্ট।

sŏ′-nănt, *adj.* & *n.* **1.** Sounding; নিনাদী। **2.** Applied to certain alphabetic sounds, as those of the vowels, semi-vowels, nasals and flat mutes, as *b, d, v, z, g* the sound of which is prolonged or uttered with some degree of resonance or intonation; কতিপয় স্বর অর্দ্ধস্বর, অনুনাসিক এবং *b, d, v, z, g* প্রভৃতির ধ্বনিসম্বন্ধে উক্ত, ঘোষী, ঘোষবাণ (পাণিনি—টীকা)। ***Noun.*** A sonant letter or sound; ঘোষবর্ণ (উইলসন্), বাদী (ঠাকুর)।

sō-nä′-tȧ, *n.* A musical composition of several movements for a solo voice; একব্যক্তি কর্তৃক গেয় কতিপয় তালবিশিষ্ট সঙ্গীত, স্বনতা।

sō-nă-tī′-nȧ, *n.* A short and simple sonata; সংক্ষিপ্তস্বনতা।

sŏng, *n.* **1.** That which is sung or uttered with musical modulation; সঙ্গীত, গান। **2.** A lay; a poem; "Our sweetest *songs* are those that tell of saddest thought"; গীতি, গীতিকা; কবিতা। **3.** Poetry; "Subjects for heroic-*song*"; কবিতা। **4.** A trifle; as, I bought it for a mere *song*; সামান্য, যৎকিঞ্চিৎ। **5.** A fuss or outcry for something "She had forborne likewise and no one made a *song* about it"; হল্লা, গোলমাল। **Song-bird**—গায়ক-পক্ষী। **An old song, A song**—তুচ্ছ জিনিষ, সামান্য জিনিষ **Indian Song of Songs**—স্যর এডুইন আর্ণল্ড কর্তৃক অনুদিত গীতগোবিন্দের নাম। **Song of Songs**—বাইবেলের প্রাচীন নিয়মগ্রন্থের অন্তর্গত সলোমোনের গীতি। [এই গীতিতে মেষপালক ও মেষপালিকাদিগের প্রেমকাহিনীর বর্ণনা অনেকটা বৃন্দাবনলীলার অনুরূপ।] [cf.

I am black, but comely,
O ye daughters of Jerusalem,
As the tents of Kedar,
As the curtains of Solomon.
(cf. চিকণ কালা, গলায় মালা, বাজন নুপুর পায়—গোবিন্দদাস।)

* * *

Look not upon me, because
I am swarthy,
Because the sun hath
scorched me.

* * *

Tell, me O thou whom my soul
loveth,
Where thou feedest thy flock,
where
Thou makest it to rest at noon:

* * *

(cf. তোমার নাগর, রাখাল খেয়াতি, সদা থাকে গোঠ মাঝে—জগদানন্দ। কোন্ বনে গিয়াছিলে ওরে রামকানু, আজি কেন চাঁদমুখের শুনি নাই বেণু—বলরাম দাস।)

* * *

My beloved is unto me as a
bundle of myrrh
That lieth betwixt my breasts.

* * *

I am a rose of Sharon,
A lily of the valleys.
As a lily among thorns
So is my love among the
daughters·

As the apple tree among the
trees of the wood
So is my beloved among
the sons.
* * *
Stay ye me with raisins, comfort
me with apples
For I am sick of love.
(cf. সবাই কহয়ে,পিরীতি কাহিনী; কে বলে পিরীতি ভাল। কানুর পিরীতি, ভাবিতে ভাবিতে, পাঁজর ধসিয়া গেল॥ জীবনে মরণে, পিরীতি বেয়াধি, হইল যাহার অঙ্গ। জ্ঞানদাস কহে, কানুর পিরীতি, নিতি নৌতুন রঙ্গ॥)
* * *
His left hand is under my head
And the right hand doth
embrace me.
* * *
Thy lips O my bride, drop
as the honeycomb
(cf. মধুরাধরপল্লব বিম্ব লিখি—গোবিন্দ দাস।)
Honey and milk are under
thy tongue;
And the smell of thy garments
is like the smell of Lebanon.
* * *
Thou art a fountain of gardens,
A well of living waters.
* * *
My beloved is gone down to his
garden, to the beds of spices,
To feed in the gardens and
to gather lilies.
(cf. গোধন সঙ্গে রঙ্গে যদুনন্দন বিহরই যমুনাতীর—গোবিন্দ দাস।)
I am my beloved's, and my
beloved is mine.
(cf. তুহু সে শ্যামের সরবস ধন, শ্যাম সে তোহারি প্রাণ—জ্ঞানদাস।)
* * *
There are threescore queens,
and fourscore concubines,
And virgins without number.
My dove, my undefiled,
is but one.
(cf. কোটী রমণী তুআ পায়ে নিরমঞ্ছিএ তুহুঁ মম জীবন রাই। তোমার নাম গুণ অবিরত জপি হাম, সদয় হৃদয় তুআ চাই—প্রেমদাস।)
* * *
For, lo, the winter is past,
The rain is over and gone;
The flowers appear on the earth;
The time of the singing *of*
birds is come,
And the voice of the turtle is
heard in our land;
The fig tree ripeneth her
green figs,
And the vines are in blossom,
They give forth their fragrance.
Arise, my love, my fair one,
and come away.
* * *
Thy two breasts are like
two fawns
(cf. কুচযুগ কোক,লোম ভুজঙ্গিনী ত্রিবলি। ত্রিবেণীবিলাস—রাধামোহন ঠাকুর।)
That are twins of a roe.
Thy neck is like the tower
of ivory.
* * *
And the hair of thine head
like purple
The king is held capture in
the tresses thereof
How fair and how pleasant
art thou,
(cf. মনোহর মধুর মুরতি নবকিশোর সদাই হিয়ার মাঝে জাগে—বসু রামানন্দ।)
O love, for delights!
This thy stature is like to a
palm tree
(cf. দুঁহু মুখ হেরইতে দুঁহু ভেল ধন্দ। রাই কহে তমাল মাধব কহে চন্দ॥)
And thy breasts to clusters
of grapes.
* * *
Let us get up early to the
vineyards;
Let us see whether the vine hath
Budded and its blossom be open
And the pomegranate be in flower
There will I give thee my love].
(cf. শাশুড়ী ননদে, বঞ্চনা করিয়া, আইলু গহন বনে। বড় সাধ মনে, এ রূপ যৌবনে, মিলিব বঁধুর সনে॥—চণ্ডীদাস।)
* * *
It is the voice of my beloved
that knocketh, *saying*,
Open to me, my sister, my
love, my dove, my undefiled:
For my head is filled with dew,
My locks with the drops of
the night.
(cf. আঙ্গিনার কোণে বঁধুয়া ভিজিছে দেখিয়া পরাণ ফাটে—চণ্ডীদাস।)

sŏng'-stêr, *n.* 1. A singer; "The peasant too...Himself a *songster* is as gay as he"; গায়ক। 2. A song-bird; "Haply some widowed *songster* pours his plaint"; কলকণ্ঠ পক্ষী, গায়কপক্ষী। **—stress**, *n.* 1. A female singer; a poetess; গায়িকা; স্ত্রী-কবি। 2. A female singing-bird; "Through the soft silence of the listening night, The sober-suited *songstress* trills her lay"; গায়িকা স্ত্রীপক্ষী।

sŏn'-i-fêr, *n.* An instrument for conveying sound to deaf persons; বধিরদিগের কর্ণে শব্দ প্রেরণের জন্য যন্ত্র-বিশেষ, স্বনবাহক।

sō-nif'-ĕr-ous (-ŭs), *adj.* Producing or conveying sound; শব্দজনক, ধ্বনিজনক, নাদজনক, শব্দবাহী, স্বনজনক।

sŏn'-nĕt (-ĕt), *n.* A short lyric poem of fourteen lines only, dealing with one idea; চতুর্দ্দশপদী কবিতা। **—eer'**, *n.* & *v. i.*

son'-ny (sŭn-i), *n.* A familiar term for addressing a son; "Yes, my dear *sonny*, that is exactly what I mean"; যাদু, বাছা, সোণা, যাদুমণি (*poet.*), সোণার যাদু (*ib.*), ধন।

sō-nŏm'-ĕ-tĕr, *n.* An instrument for tasting the hearing capacity of a patient or for measuring sound; রোগীর শ্রুতিশক্তি পরিমাপের

জন্য যন্ত্রবিশেষ, নাদমাপক (হিঃ কোঃ), শ্রুতিমান, ধ্বনিমান, স্বনমান।

sŏn-ō-rĕs'-cent (-ent), *adj.* (Of hard rubber etc.) Emitting sound under intermittent radiant heat or light; দীপ্ত তাপ বা আলোকের প্রভাবে স্বননশীল। **—cence,** *n.*

sŏ-nŏ-rif'-ic, *adj.* Producing sound; ধ্বনিজনক, শব্দজনক, নাদজনক।

sŏ-nō'-rous (-rŭs), *adj.* 1. Sounding when struck; resonant; "The first sound that welcomed us was his *sonorous* bray"; নিনাদী, মুখর; নাদজনক, বিরাবী। 2. Loud-sounding; giving a clear, loud or full-volumed sound; as, his *sonorous* voice; উচ্চনিনাদী; সুস্পষ্ট এবং শ্রুতিমধুর। 3. High-sounding; গুরুগম্ভীরনাদী। **—ly,** *adv.* **—ness,** *n.* **—nor'-i-ty,** *n.* **Sonorous figures**—(Also *acoustic figures, Chladin's figures*); ধূলিস্তর প্রভৃতির শব্দস্পন্দনদ্বারা জাত মূর্ত্তি, প্রভৃতি। **Sonorous rale** — অসুস্থ ফুসফুস হইতে উদ্ভূত শ্বাসপ্রশ্বাসের ধ্বনি ব্যতিরিক্ত নাদবিশেষ। **Sonorous tumour**—যে অর্ব্বুদে অঙ্গুলি দ্বারা আঘাত করিলে অনুনাদ উৎপন্ন হয়।

sōōn, *adv.* 1. Without delay; "The rout *soon* became general"; অবিলম্বে, শীঘ্র, অচিরে, ত্বরা, ঝটিতি, অচিরাৎ, আশু। 2. Quickly; সত্বর, দ্রুত, তূর্ণ, ক্ষিপ্র। 3. Easily; "Small lights are *soon* blown out"; সহজে, অনায়াসে। 4. Readily; willingly; as, I would as *soon* go as not; সত্বর; ইচ্ছাপূর্ব্বক। **As soon as**—As quickly as; যেই মুহূর্ত্তে, ঠিক যখন, যেইমাত্র, যেই। **It is sooner said than done**—It is easy to say but not so easy to do; বলা সহজ কিন্তু করা কঠিন। **Least said soon mended**—যত কম কথা বলা হয় ততই সহজে গোলমাল মিটিয়া যায়। **No sooner said than done**—Done as soon as it was uttered; বলামাত্রই করা হইল, মুখ হইতে বাহির হইতে না হইতেই সম্পন্ন হইল। **Sooner or later** — At sometime or other; দুদিন আগে বা দুদিন পাছে, আজ হউক বা কাল হউক। **So soon**—So quickly; এত সত্বর।

sōōt, *n.* & *v. t.* A black substance formed from burning matter; ঝুল, ভুষা, গৃহধূম, কজ্জল, দীপকিট্ট, দীপকজ্জল। ***Verb t.*** To cover or foul with soot; ঝুলমাখান, ভুষালিপ্ত করা। **Soot'-i-ness,** *n.* **Soot'-less,** *adj.* **Soot'-y,** *adj.* 1. Full of soot; as, a *sooty* chimney; soiled with soot; as, a *sooty* cap; কজ্জলময়; ধূমমলিন। 2. Having the colour of soot; as, *sooty* wings; কজ্জলবর্ণ, ধূম্রধূসর। **Soot-cancer**—ধূমনালীমার্জ্জকদিগের অণ্ডকোষে জাত একপ্রকার দুষ্ট ক্ষত।

sōōt'-ĕr-kin, *n.* 1. A kind of after-birth fabled to be produced by the Dutch women from sitting over their stoves; সন্তান জাত হওয়ার পর চুল্লীর উপর উপবেশন-দ্বারা ওলন্দাজ রমণীগণের যে গর্ভস্রাব হইত বলিয়া কথিত আছে। [There goes a report of the Holland women, that together with their children, they are delivered of a *sooterkin* not unlike to a rat, which some imagine to be the offspring of the stove.—*Cleveland*]. 2. An abortive proposal or scheme; নিষ্ফল প্রস্তাব বা কল্পনা।

sōōth, *n.* (*Archaic*) Truth; সত্য, প্রকৃত ব্যাপার। **In sooth, In good sooth**—Really; বাস্তবিক পক্ষে, প্রকৃতপক্ষে।

sōōthe (sōōth) *v. t.* 1. To calm; শান্ত করা। 2. To soften; to mollify; to mitigate; "—coffee which seems to have *soothed* his headache"; কোমল করা; জুড়ান; উপশম করা। 3. To flatter; to humour; "Is it good to *soothe* him in this contraries?"; মনোরঞ্জন করা, তুষ্ট করা, বিনোদন করা। **Sooth'-ing,** *adj.* That which soothes; প্রশামক, উপশমকর।

sōōth'-făst, *adj.* (*Archaic*) True; truthful; loyal; steadfast; (অপ্রঃ) সত্য; সত্যবাদী; নিষ্ঠ; অবিচলিত।

sōōth-say-ĕr (-sā-), *n.* A prognosticator: ভবিষ্যবাদী, ভবিষ্যকথক। **—ing,** *n.* Prediction; prophecy; ভবিষ্যকথন; ভবিষ্যদ্বাক্য, ভবিষ্যদ্বাণী।

sŏp, *n., v. t.* & *i.* 1. Something dipped in broth or liquid food; ঝোল প্রভৃতিতে ভিজানো রুটির টুকরা ইত্যাদি। 2. Anything given to pacify; "This lavish expenditure is intended as a *sop* to the disaffected"; কাহাকে শান্ত করার জন্য প্রদত্ত কোন কিছু। 3. Bribe; "I have got a *sop* to hold my tongue; ঘুষ, উৎকোচ। ***Verb t.*** 1. To dip in liquid; ঝোল প্রভৃতিতে ভিজান। 2. To bribe; ঘুষ দেওয়া। ***Verb i.*** To be soaked; ভিজা, সিক্ত হওয়া। **Sop'-py,** *adj.* **Sops in wine**—(অপ্রঃ) একপ্রকার লবঙ্গবর্ণ—যদ্দারা পূর্ব্বে সুরা রঞ্জিত করা হইত। **Sops of wine**—একপ্রকার গাঢ় রক্তবর্ণ সেওফল—যাহা নিদাঘশেষে পাকিয়া থাকে। **To throw a sop to Cerberus**—To pacify an enemy by bribing; অর্থ প্রদানে শত্রুর মুখ বন্ধ করা।

Sopherim, *n., (Pl.)* The scribes or teachers of Jewish law; ইহুদীদের শাস্ত্রকর্ত্তা।

sŏph-ĭsm, *n.* A specious but fallacious argument; "Others thought that the argument from revelation was a mere *sophism*"; ভ্রান্ত অথচ আপাতমোহকর যুক্তি, বাক্‌ছল, কুতর্ক, কূটতর্ক, হেত্বাভাস (হিঃ কোঃ), ছল (ঐ)।

sŏph'-ĭst, *n.* 1. One of a class leading public teachers in ancient Greece during the fifth and fourth centuries B. C.; খৃষ্ট পূর্ব্ব

চতুর্থ ও পঞ্চম শতাব্দীর প্রাচীন গ্রীসের তর্কশাস্ত্রবিদ্ অধ্যাপকগণের অন্যতম। 2. A captious or fallacious reasoner ; কুটতার্কিক, কুতার্কিক, অতিতার্কিক (হিঃ কোঃ), হেতুবাদী (হিঃ কোঃ), শাস্ত্রী (ঐ), হেত্বাভ সবাদী। **–ry,** *n.* The practice of sophists ; ratiocination ; কুটতার্কিকতা ; কুতর্ক, জল্প, সূক্ষ্মেষিকা (হিঃ কোঃ)। **So-phis′-tic, So-phis′-ti-cal,** *adjs.* **So-phis′-ti-cal-ly,** *adv.*

sŏph′-is-têr, *n.* A quibbling disputant ; a plausible fallacious reasoner ; কুতার্কিক, কুটতার্কিক ; জল্পকারী।

sŏ-phis′-ti-cāte *v. t.* & *i.* **1.** To pervert by sophistry ; কুতর্কদ্বারা দূষিত করা। **2.** To adulterate ; "If *sophisticated* with castor oil, the mixture soon becomes nearly colourless like white honey" ; to make spurious ; "Whom the manner and maxims of common world had *sophisticated*" ; ভেজাল দেওয়া ; কৃত্রিম করা। **3.** To corrupt ; to mislead ; as, to *sophisticate* ignorant people ; দূষিত করা ; ভ্রান্তপথে পরিচালিত করা। **4.** To tamper with a text etc. for the purpose of argument ; "They take the liberty of *sophisticating* Burke" ; অনুকূল যুক্তি প্রদানের উদ্দেশ্যে কোন গ্রন্থাদির মূল বাক্য পরিবর্তন করা। ***Verb i.*** To quibble ; কুতর্ক করা। **–ca′-tion,** *n.*

sŏph′-ō-mōre, *n.* In American colleges a second-year student ; আমেরিকার কলেজ সমূহের দ্বিতীয় বার্ষিক শ্রেণীর ছাত্র।

sō-pō-rif′-ic, *adj.* & *n.* Causing sleep ; নিদ্রাজনক, নিদ্রাকারক, নিদ্রাকারী, স্বাপজনক, স্বাপন, প্রস্বাপ। ***Noun.*** A narcotic ; নিদ্রাজনক ঔষধ। **–er-ous,** *adj.* **Soporific powder**—যোগচূর্ণ (সাঃ পঃ)।

sō-prâ′-nō, *n.* **1.** The highest kind of female voice ; বামাকণ্ঠের উচ্চতম স্বর। **2.** A singer with such a voice ; ঐরূপ স্বরে যে গান গায়। **–nist,** *n.*

sō′-ră, *n.* A small North American bird ; উত্তর আমেরিকার ক্ষুদ্র পক্ষিবিশেষ।

sŏrb, *n.* **1.** Same as SERVICE-TREE (which see) under SERVICE. **2.** The fruit of that tree ; ঐ বৃক্ষের ফল। **Sor′-bate, Sorb′-ic,** *adj.* & *n.*

sŏr-bĭ-fā′-ci-ĕnt (-shi-), *adj.* & *n.* (*Med.*) Causing absorption ; (ভৈষজ্যশাস্ত্র) শোষক। ***Noun.*** A medicine that causes absorption ; শোষণকারক ঔষধ।

sŏr′-bĕt, *n.* **1.** Water-ice flavoured with rum etc. ; রম প্রভৃতি দ্বারা সুবাসিত শর্করামিশ্রিত এবং তুষারীকৃত জল। **2.** Same as SHERBET.

Sŏr-bonne′ (-bŏn), *n.* The earliest and the most celebrated college in the University of Paris for the study of theology founded in 1253 by Robert of Sorbon ; Sorbonবাসী রবার্টকর্তৃক ১২৫৩ খৃষ্টাব্দে প্রতিষ্ঠিত খৃষ্টীয় ধর্মশাস্ত্রঅধ্যাপনার্থ মহাবিদ্যালয়।

sŏr′-cĕr-êr, *n.* A magician ; "This is the place where the *sorcerers* and soothsayers held their mystic and fearful rites" ; যাদুকর, ঐন্দ্রজালিক, মায়াবী, মায়াকার, মায়াজীবী, মায়াপটু। **–ess,** *n.* A female practising sorcery ; যাদুকরী, মায়াবিনী। **–y,** *n.* Witchcraft ; ঐন্দ্রজাল, ইন্দ্রজাল, যাদুবিদ্যা, যাদু (হিঃ কোঃ), অভিচার (ঐ), শাম্বরী, শাম্বরীবিদ্যা, শাম্বরশিল্প (নৈষঃ)।

sordamente, *adv.* (*Mus.*) In a muffled manner ; (সঙ্গীতশাস্ত্র) মন্দীভূত ভাবে।

sŏr′-dĕs, *n.* **1.** Foul matter ; দূষিত পদার্থ, ময়লা, ক্লেদ, মল। **2.** (*Med.*) The crusts that collect on the teeth in low fever etc. ; মৃদুজ্বর প্রভৃতিতে দন্ত এবং ওষ্ঠাধরে যে ময়লা সঞ্চিত হয়, দন্তশর্করা, দন্তপঙ্ক।

sŏr′-dĕt, *n.* Same as SORDINE (which see).

sŏr′-did, *n.* **1.** Mean ; হীন, নীচ, হেয়, ইতর। **2.** Covetous ; niggardly ; "Motives of avarice had prevailed upon the *sordid* mind of Judas" ; গৃধ্নু ; কঞ্জুষ, ব্যয়কুণ্ঠ, অর্থপিশাচ। **–ly,** *adv.* **–ness,** *n.*

sŏr′-dine (-dēn), **–dêt,** *ns.* Same as MUTE 6 (which see).

sōre, *adj.*, *n.* & *adv.* **1.** Painful ; as, the *sore* labour of child-birth ; sensitive ; ব্যথাজনক, বেদনাজনক ; সংবেদনসম্পন্ন। **2.** Distressing ; vexatious ; severe ; violent ; as, a *sore* trial ; কষ্টজনক ; বিরক্তিজনক ; গুরুতর, দারুণ ; প্রবল। **3.** Pained, grieved, or vexed ; মর্ম্মাহত, ব্যথিত। ***Noun.*** **1.** An ulcer ; a boil ; ক্ষত, ঘা ; স্ফোটক, ত্বক্‌কণ্ডুরা, ব্রণগ্রন্থি, কোথ (সুশ্রুঃ)। **2.** Grief ; affliction ; trouble ; দুঃখ ; দুর্দ্দশা ; কষ্ট। **Sore′-ly,** *adv.* **Sore′-ness,** *n.* **A sight for sore eyes**—A delightful person or thing ; আনন্দজনক ব্যক্তি বা বস্তু, নয়নানন্দজনক ব্যক্তি বা বস্তু। **To rap an old sore**—To revive a painful memory ; নিভান আগুন জ্বালান, পুরাতন কাসুন্দি ঘাঁটা।

sō-rē′-dĭ-ăl, –dĭ-ŭm, *ns.* (*Bot.*) One of the vegetative brood buds or gemmæ on the surface of the ; thallus or lichens জননপিণ্ড (সাঃ পঃ)।

sŏr′-ĕl, *n.* Same as SORREL.

sŏr′-ghum (-gŭm), *n.* A genus of grass etc. including millet ; চীনা, জোয়ার, যবনাল (*Sans.*), দেবধান্য (*ib.*), প্রভৃতি বস্তু।

Sorghum Vulgare.

Sorghum saccharatum—দেবধান্য (বেলঃ)। ***Sorghum vulgare***—চীনক, চীনা, কাককঙ্গু।

sŏr'-i-cīne, *adj.* Of, or pertaining to, the shrew mouse ; চিকাসম্বন্ধীয়, ছুচুন্দরীসম্বন্ধীয়।

sō-rī'-tēs, *n.* 1. A series of propositions, in which the predicate of each is the subject of the next, the conclusion being formed of the first subject and the last predicate (*Mansel*).

ARISTOTELIAN SORITIES.

Caius is a man
All men are finite beings
All finite beings are sentient
All sentient beings seek happiness
Therefore Caius seeks happiness.

GOCLENIAN SORITES.

All sentient beings seek happiness
All finite beings are sentient
All men are finite beings
Caius is a man
Therefore Caius seeks happiness.

ন্যায়শৃঙ্খল (সাঃ পঃ), ন্যায়াবলী, ন্যায়শৃঙ্খলা, মানশৃঙ্খলা (হিঃ কোঃ)। 2. A series or heap of things ; বস্তুপরম্পরা, বস্তুসমুচ্চয়।

sŏrn, *v. i.* 1. (*Scot.*) To obtrude oneself upon another for bed and board ; যে ব্যক্তি জোর করিয়া অপর কাহারো বাটীতে আহার শয়নের ব্যবস্থা করে। **Sorn'-er,** *n.*

sō-rō'-sis, *n.* (*Bot.*) A compound fleshy fruit, as a pineapple ; (উদ্ভিদ্‌বিদ্যা) আনারস প্রভৃতি মিশ্রফল, পনসি (স্যাঃ পঃ)।

sŏr'-rel (-ĕl), *n.* One of a several species of the genus rumex, allied to the dock, the leaves impregnated with oxalic acid (*oxalis corniculata*) ; চুকা পালং (প্রবোধ), থৈকল, (দ্রব্যগুণ), মেস্ত (*red*), (যোঃ), আমরুল (ওয়াট) [Syn. শতবেধী, অম্লবেধী, রসাম্ল, আম্লবেতস, বেতসাম্ল, অম্লসার, বেধক, ভীম, ভেদন, ভেদী, রাজাম্ল, অম্লভেদন, অম্লাঙ্কুশ, রক্তসার, ফলাম্ল, অম্লনায়ক, সহস্রবেধী, বীরাম্ল, গুল্মকেতু, বরাভিধা, শঙ্খদ্রাবী, মাংসদ্রাবী, বরাঙ্গী, চুক্র, দলাম্ল, শুক্তা, অম্লবেতস।]

Sorrel.

sŏr'-rĕl (-ĕl), *adj.* & *n.* Of a yellowish or reddish brown colour; গৈরিকবর্ণ, কপিলবর্ণ। ***Noun.*** 1. A reddish or yellowish brown colour ; গৈরিকবর্ণ, কপিলবর্ণ। 2. A buck of the third year ; তিন বৎসর বয়স্ক হরিণ।

sŏr'-row (-ō), *n.* & *v. i.* 1. Grief ; sadness ; mourning ; regret ; দুঃখ, সন্তাপ, কষ্ট ; বিষাদ, নিরানন্দ, মর্ম্মব্যথা (*Rhet.*), মর্ম্মজ্বালা (*ib.*), মর্ম্মবেদনা (ঐ), মর্ম্মযাতনা ; শোক, ক্লেশ, খেদ ; পরিতাপ, মনস্তাপ। 2. Lamentation ; as, his *sorrow* was loud and long ; বিলাপ, খেদ। ***Verb i.*** To feel pain of mind ; to grieve ; মনে কষ্ট পাওয়া, মর্ম্মবেদনা ভোগ করা ; শোক করা, দুঃখ করা। **—er,** *n.* **—ful,** *adj.* Full of sorrow ; sad ; as, his *sorrowful* countenance ; দুঃখপূর্ণ, বিষাদপূর্ণ ; বিষণ্ণ, বিরস, বিমর্ষ। **—ful-ness,** *n.* **—ing,** *adj.* **Sorrow-stricken**—দুঃখার্ত্ত, দুঃখ-পীড়িত, বিষাদ-খিন্ন, শোকার্ত্ত, সন্তপ্ত, দুঃখসন্তপ্ত।

sŏr'-rȳ (-i), *adj.* 1. Grieved ; melancholy; দুঃখিত, দুঃখসন্তপ্ত; বিষাদপূর্ণ। 2. Wretched ; as, a *sorry* horse ; worthless ; as, a *sorry* physician ; mean ; as, a *sorry* room ; a *sorry* breakfast; poor ; হতচ্ছাড়া ; নগণ্য, অসার ; হেয় ; হীন। **—ri-ly,** *adv.* **—ri-ness,** *n.*

sŏrt, *n.* 1. A kind or species ; রকম, প্রকার, শ্রেণী। 2. Nature ; as, people of evil *sort* ; প্রকৃতি, স্বভাব, ধরণ। 3. (*Print.*) Any letter, figure, point, space, etc. of a compositor's case ; (মুদ্রণ) অক্ষরবিন্যাসকের আধারের অক্ষর, অবকাশক (space), চতুষ্ক (quadrat), প্রভৃতি। 4. A considerable quantity ; বহুল পরিমাণ। 5. Way ; রকম, প্রকার, ধারা, রূপ, তর (cf. কেমনতর)। 6. Superiority in character, quality or position ; rank ; (now only in *plural*, with *of*) ; as, a dog *of sorts* ; চরিত্র, গুণ বা মর্য্যাদা সম্বন্ধে উৎকর্ষ বা শ্রেষ্ঠতা ; পদবী। **All sorts of things or persons**—Different kinds of things or persons ; নানারকমের মানুষ, হরেক রকমের জিনিষ। **A word of sort**—(*Rare*) An angry word ; চড়া কথা। **In a sort**—In an imperfect way ; একরকম ভাবে, কোন রকমে, যেমন তেমন করিয়া। **In a sort of way**—Not properly; একরকম ভাবে। **In some sort**—To a certain degree ; কিয়ৎ পরিমাণে, কতক পরিমাণে। **Nothing of the sort**—No such thing ; সেরকম কিছু নয়। **Of a sort**—(*Dial.*) Of the same kind ; এক রকম। **Of sorts** — (*Rare*) Of various kinds ; (ক্বচিদ্‌ব্যবহৃত) নানারকমের, হরেক রকমের। (*Disparagingly*) Of a sorry or poor kind ; as, an orator of *sorts* ; বড় বিশেষ ভাল নয়, একরকম। (*Print.*) Out of types of a particular kind ; কোন বিশেষ রকমের অক্ষরের টান পড়িয়াছে—এরূপ। **Out of sorts**—Not keeping good health ; অসুস্থ। Out of certain kinds of articles; কোন কোন রকমের জিনিষ ফুরাইয়া গিয়াছে—এইরূপ। **Something of the sort**—Something similar to that mentioned before ; সেইরকম কোন কিছু। **That is your sort**—(*Slang*) That is your way ; (ইতরভাষায়) এটাই তোমার ধারা। **To be hard on sorts**—To need various sorts of types ; নানা প্রকার অক্ষরের দরকার পড়া।

sŏrt, *v. t. & i.* To separate into classes ; to select ; রকম করা, কিছিম করা ; বাছনি করা। ***Verb i.*** 1. To associate : সঙ্গ করা। 2. To suit ; মানা, সাজা। **Sort'-er,** *n.* One who separates or arranges ; যে ব্যক্তি বাছাই করে, প্রকারকারক। **Sort'-a-ble,** *adj.*

sortes, *n.* A kind of divination by the chance selection of passages from the Bible, Homer, Virgil, etc. ; বাইবেল, হোমর বা ভার্জ্জিলের গ্রন্থাবলী প্রভৃতি হইতে যদৃচ্ছাক্রমে কোন অংশ নির্ব্বাচনপূর্ব্বক ভবিষ্যকথনের প্রকারবিশেষ।

sŏr'-tie (-tē), *n.* The issuing of troops from a besieged place ; অবরুদ্ধ স্থান হইতে বহির্গত হইয়া হঠাৎ শত্রুসৈন্যের উপর আপতন, অবস্কন্দ (মাল:)।

sŏr'-ti-lege (-lĕj), *n.* Divination by drawing lots : গুটিদ্বারা ভবিষ্যকথন

sō'-rŭs (*Pl.* SORI) *n.* (*Bot.*) Cluster of capsules on the fronds of ferns ; পর্ণাঙ্গের জন্মপত্রের উপরিস্থ বীজকোষগুচ্ছ।

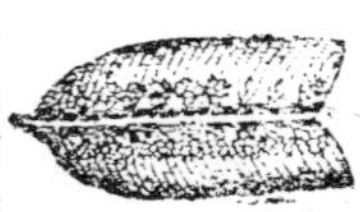

Frond with sori.

sō'-sō, *adj.* Not very good ; একপ্রকার, চলনসই, একরকম।

sostenuto, *n.* (*Mus.*) In a prolonged manner ; বিলম্বিতভাবে।

sŏt, *n. & v. i.* A habitual drunkard ; one stupefied by drinking ; মাতাল ; বদ্ধমাতাল। ***Verb i.*** To tipple ; মাতাল হওয়া। **Sot'-tish,** *adj.* **Sot'-tish-ly,** *adv.* **Sot'-tish-ness,** *n.*

Sō'-thic, *adj.* Pertaining to the dog-star ; সীরিয়াসসম্বন্ধীয়, মৃগব্যাধসম্বন্ধীয়। [মিসরদেশে Dog-starএর নাম Sothis]। **Sothic cycle** or **period**—১৪৬০ বৎসর পরিমিতকাল (এই কাল সাধারণ মিসরীয় বৎসরের ১৪৬১ বর্ষের সমান)। **Sothic year**—৩৬৫¼ দিবসাত্মক বৎসর।

sotto voce, *adv.* 1. In an undertone ; aside ; অস্ফুটস্বরে ; স্বগতঃ, জনান্তিকে। 2. Privately ; গোপনে, চুপে চুপে, চুপেসাড়ে।

sou (sö), *n.* A French money of account, and a copper coin in value the twentieth part of a franc ; ফরাসীদেশে প্রচলিত তাম্রমুদ্রাবিশেষ।

soubrette, *n.* A maid-servant or lady's maid ; পরিচারিকা, সখী।

sou'-chong (sô-shŏng) *n.* A kind of black tea of a fine quality ; একপ্রকার কালো রঙের উৎকৃষ্ট চা।

Sou-da-nese' (sô-dă-nēz), *adj. & n.* Of Soudan ; আফ্রিকার অন্তঃপাতী সুডানপ্রদেশসম্বন্ধীয়। ***Noun.*** An inhabitant of Soudan ; সুডানের অধিবাসী।

souf'-fle (sōōf-flā), *n.* (*Med.*) Low murmur heard in auscultation of various organs etc ; (ভৈষজ্যশাস্ত্র) সগর্ভ জরায়ু ও বক্ষঃস্থলাদির একপ্রকার আকর্ণন শব্দ।

soufflé, *n. & adj.* A light dish, consisting chiefly of the whites of eggs, whisked, spiced and baked ; ডিম্বের শ্বেতাংশ দ্বারা প্রস্তুত খাদ্যবিশেষ। ***Adj.*** 1. Made light and frothy ; লঘু এবং ফেনায়িত। 2. *(Ceramics)* Decorated with small drops or sprinkles of colour ; (মৃৎশিল্প) রঙ্গের ক্ষুদ্র ক্ষুদ্র বিন্দু বা ছিটা দ্বারা শোভিত।

sough (sŭf), *n. & v. i.* A low, continuous moaning sound as of the wind through an aperture ; শোঁ শোঁ শব্দ, সন্ সন্ শব্দ। ***Verb i.*** To emit such a sound ; শোঁ শোঁ শব্দ করা, সন্ সন্ শব্দ করা।

sought, (sät), *p. t. & p. p.* of SEEK (which see).

soul (sōl), *n.* 1. The spiritual, rational, and immortal part in man, which distinguishes him from brutes; আত্মা, জীবাত্মা, সচ্চিদংশ, চিৎকলা, অন্তরাত্মা, (বেদান্তঃ) পুরুষ (শ্রীঃ), প্রাণ (ঐ), জীব (ব্রজঃ বিঃ), কূটস্থ। 2. The world soul ; বিশ্বাত্মা, হিরণ্যগর্ভ। 3. Man's inner or spiritual nature ; অন্তঃপ্রকৃতি। 4. The vital or rational principle in man etc ; the animating or essential part ; the essence or quintessence ; as, he is the *soul* of nobleness ; জীবাত্মা ; জীবনীশক্তি ; প্রাণ। 5. Applied as a term of endearment; "Thou *soul* of my *soul*, I shall clasp thee again" ; প্রাণ, প্রাণ আমার। 6. The leader ; as, he is the *soul* of this movement ; the inspirer ; as, he is the *soul* of kindness ; পরিচালক ; জীবনসঞ্চারক, প্রাণ। 7. A disembodied spirit ; প্রেতাত্মা, বিদেহী আত্মা। 8. A human being ; as, a population of 600 *souls* ; মনুষ্য, লোক। 9. Spirit ; courage ; fire ; grandeur of the heart or other noble manifestation of heart or moral nature ; "And said by the *souls* only the nations shall be great and free;" intellectual or moral power ; I never saw so much *soul* in a woman's eyes, as hers ; উৎসাহ ; সাহস ; তেজঃ ; আত্মার মহিমা ; আধ্যাত্মিক বা মানসিক শক্তির প্রকাশ। **Soul'-ful,** *adj.* Full of deep emotion or sentiment ; উচ্ছ্বাসপূর্ণ, প্রবল আবেগপূর্ণ, ভাবোচ্ছ্বাসপূর্ণ। **Soul'-less,** *adj.* 1. Having no soul ; প্রাণশূন্য, নিষ্প্রাণ। 2. (Of the eyes) Dull; (চক্ষুসম্বন্ধে) নিষ্প্রভ, অনুজ্জ্বল। 3. Having no nobleness of mind ; প্রাণহীন, হৃদয়হীন, হৃদয়শূন্য। 4. (Of literature) Dull ; নীরস। **Soul'-less-ness,** *n.* **Cosmic soul**—সঙ্কর্ষণ (চৈঃ চঃ), কারণার্ণবশায়ী

(ঐ)। Individual soul—অদিতি (শ্রীঃ), জীব (ঐ), প্রত্যগাত্মা (ঐ), সঙ্কর্ষণ (ঐ), জীবাত্মা, ক্ষীরোদশায়ী (চৈঃ চঃ)। Non-soul—অজীব (শ্রীঃ)। Over soul—পরমাত্মা, ঋত, সত্য। Rational soul — চিদাত্মা। Soul-curer — ধর্ম্মোপদেষ্টা। Soul-stirring—প্রাণোন্মাদী। World soul—হিরণ্যগর্ভ (চৈঃ চঃ), অন্তর্যামী (ঐ), গর্ভোদকশায়ী (ঐ)। A soul of honour — A personification of honour; ধর্ম্মবুদ্ধি বা উন্নতনীতিজ্ঞানের মূর্ত্তিমান বিগ্রহ। Heart and soul—সর্ব্বান্তঃকরণ। Soul of the universe—ব্রহ্ম, পরমাত্মা। The aggregate soul—সমষ্টিপুরুষ (শ্রীঃ)।

sound (sōwnd), *adj.* & *adv.* 1. Healthy; as, a *sound* body; সুস্থ, নিরাময়, প্রকৃতিস্থ (of mind), স্বাস্থ্যপূর্ণ। 2. Firm; safe; trustworthy; solvent; as, a *sound* bank; দৃঢ়; নিরাপদ; বিশ্বাসযোগ্য; সাউকড়। 3. Unhurt; অক্ষত। 4. Free from imperfection, defect or decay; as, a *sound* wood; উৎকৃষ্ট, অক্ষত। 5. Free from error or fallacy; correct; অভ্রান্ত, টনটনে, ভ্রমশূন্য; শুদ্ধ, ঠিক। 6. Profound; as, *sound* sleep; গভীর, সু (cf. সুনিদ্রা)। 7. Valid; legal; as, a *sound* title; বৈধ; বিধিসিদ্ধ। 8. Severe; as, *sound* beating; গুরুতর। ***Adv.*** Fast; গভীরভাবে। **Sound-headed**—প্রকৃতিস্থ। **Sound-hearted**—সাধুস্বভাব; বিশ্বাসযোগ্য। **Sound as a bell or roach**—Quite sound; সম্পূর্ণ সুস্থ।

sound (sōwnd), *n.*, *v. i.* & *t.* 1. Anything perceived by the ear; ধ্বনি, শব্দ, নাদ, রব, স্বন (akin to *sound*), আওয়াজ, নির্ঘোষ। 2. Ear-shot; as, within *sound* of my voice; শ্রবণদূরত্ব, শ্রুতিসীমা। ***Verb i.*** 1. To make a noise; শব্দ হওয়া, ধ্বনিত হওয়া, নিনাদিত হওয়া। 2. To make a sound by blowing on a musical instrument; বাজান। 3. To be conveyed by sound; to be spread or published; "From you *sounded* out the word of the Lord"; শব্দদ্বারা নীত বা বাহিত হওয়া; ব্যাপ্ত হওয়া, প্রচারিত হওয়া। ***Verb t.*** 1. To play on; বাজান। 2. (*Now rare*) To express or pronounce; প্রকাশ করা, উচ্চারণ করা। 3. To declare; to announce; to celebrate; "Nations unborn your mighty names shall *sound*"; ঘোষণা করা; প্রচার করা; কীর্ত্তন করা। 4. To examine anything by auscultation; as, to *sound* lungs; আকর্ণন ধ্বনি দ্বারা কোনকিছু পরীক্ষা করা। **Sound'-ing,** *adj.* Resonant; শব্দিত, শব্দায়মান, মুখরিত, মুখর। **Sound'-less,** *adj.* **Sound-board** — Same as SOUNDING-BOARD (below). **Sound-bow**—ঘণ্টার যে অংশ নুড়নুড়িদ্বারা আহত হয়। **Sounding-board**—ধর্ম্ম প্রচারকের ধ্বনি শ্রোতৃবৃন্দের দিকে পরাবর্ত্তিত করার জন্য বেদীর পশ্চাতে স্থাপিত দারুময় তিরস্করণী; ধ্বনির মাত্রা বৃদ্ধির জন্য বাদ্যযন্ত্রে সংবদ্ধ অস্থূল পট্টবিশেষ। **Sound-shadow** — বৃহদ্‌বস্তু দ্বারা ধ্বনি রোধ। **Sound-wave**—স্বরতরঙ্গ, শব্দসন্তান। **To sound in damages**—To have the essential quality of damages; ক্ষতির মৌলিক লক্ষণ থাকা। [অনধিকার প্রবেশ প্রভৃতি দ্বারা যে ক্ষতি হয় তৎসম্পর্কে উক্ত হইয়া থাকে।]

sound (sōwnd), *v. t.*, *i.* & *n.* 1. To measure the depth of; গভীরতা মাপা। 2. To examine by means of a sound; এষণিশলাকা দ্বারা পরীক্ষা করা। 3. To cause to discover the opinion of; কাহারো মত প্রভৃতি তলাইয়া দেখা, পরীক্ষা করা। ***Verb i.*** To use the line and lead in order to ascertain the depth of water; জলের গভীরতা মাপার জন্য মানরজ্জু ব্যবহার করা। ***Noun.*** A surgeon's probe; এষণী (সুশ্রুঃ), এষণীশলাকা। **Sounding-line**—জলমানরেখা (সাঃ পঃ), জলমানসূত্র (ঐ)।

sound (sōwnd), *n.* A narrow passage of water; প্রণালী, সঙ্কীর্ণ জলডমরুমধ্য (হিঃ কোঃ)।

sound (sōwnd), *n.* 1. The air-bladder of a fish; মাছের টিকা। 2. Cut le-fish; সমুদ্রজিহ্ব মৎস্য।

sound'-ēr (sōwnd-), *n.* 1. That which sounds; নিনাদকারী, শব্দকারী। 2. An instrument for receiving a message which is read from the sound made by tapping lever; তাড়িতবার্ত্তাবহযন্ত্রের গ্রাহকযন্ত্র।

sound'-ēr (sōwnd-), *n.* An instrument for sounding; সাগর প্রভৃতির গভীরতামাপক যন্ত্র। **Flying-sounder**—একপ্রকার মানরজ্জু—যাহা জাহাজের গতি হ্রাস না করিয়া ব্যবহার করা যাইতে পারে।

soup (sōōp), *n.* A liquid food made generally from flesh and vegetables; ঝোল, যুষ, সুপ, রসা রসক।

soupcon, *n.* A dash; আভাস, ছিটা, ফোঁটা, গন্ধ, লেশ।

sour (sōwr), *adj.*, *v. i.* & *t.* 1. Of acid taste; অম্ল, টক, চুকা, খাট্টা (*slang*)। 2. Morose; sullen; harsh of temper; (ইতরভাষায়) বিষণ্ণ, নিরানন্দ; অপ্রসন্ন, মুখভার (*colloq.*); রূক্ষপ্রকৃতি, বদমেজাজী, খিটখিটে। ***Verb i.*** 1. To become sour or acid; টকিয়ে যাওয়া, চুকা হওয়া। 2. To become morose; বিষণ্ণ হওয়া। ***Verb t.*** 1. To make acid; অম্ল করা, টকিয়ে দেওয়া। 2. To make harsh in temper; রূক্ষপ্রকৃতি করা, খিটখিটে করা। **Sour'-ish,** *adj.* **Sour'-ly,** *adv.* **Sour'-ness,** *n.* The state of being sour; অম্লতা। **Sour-apple**—বিলাতী নোনা (ফার্ম্মিঃ)। **Sour-gruel**—কাঞ্জিক (সুশ্রুঃ কুঞ্জঃ)। **Grapes are sour**—আঙুর টক। [কোন অপ্রাপ্য বস্তুর প্রাপ্তির আশা করিয়া তদ্বিষয়ে হতাশ হইলে—এই কথা বলা হয়। ঈশপের শৃগাল ও দ্রাক্ষাগুচ্ছ নামক গল্প হইতে গৃহীত।]

source (sörs), *n.* **1.** That from which anything rises ; origin ; উৎপত্তিস্থল, মুল (হিঃ কোঃ), কারণ (ঐ) ; উৎপত্তি, উদ্গম, প্রভব, যোনি, আদিমূল, বীজ ; **2.** The spring etc. from which a stream proceeds ; নদী প্রভৃতির উৎপত্তিস্থল, সরিন্মুখ। **A source of income**—আয়ের সংস্থান, আয়ের পন্থা ।

sour-dine' (sôr-dēn), *n.* A stop in a harmonium ; হার্মোনিয়্যামের চাবি।

souse (sows), *n., v. t., i. & adv.* **1.** Pickle made with salt ; লবণ সহযোগে প্রস্তুত আচার। **2.** Anything steeped or preserved in pickle ; the ears, feet, etc. of swine pickled ; আচারে রক্ষিত কোনকিছু ; আচারে মিশ্রিত শূকরের কর্ণ, পদ প্রভৃতি। **3.** A dip or plunge in water ; জলে নিমজ্জন, ডুব। ***Verb t.*** **1.** To steep in pickle ; আচারে রাখা। **2.** To plunge into water ; জলে ডোবান, জলে নিমজ্জিত করা। **3.** To wet thoroughly ; সম্পূর্ণরূপে সিক্ত করা। ***Verb i.*** To strike ; আঘাত করা। ***Adv.*** Headlong ; হুমড়ি খেয়ে, উদ্দাম বেগে।

south (sowth), *adj., adv., n. & v. i.* Situated on the south ; proceeding from the south ; দক্ষিণদিগ্‌বর্ত্তী; দক্ষিণদিগ্ হইতে আগত। ***Adv.*** Towards the south ; দক্ষিণাভিমুখে। ***Noun.*** One of the four cardinal points of the compass, directly opposite to the north ; দক্ষিণ, অবাচী, যাম্য (cf. যাম্যাং যাতি যমদ্বারং—বিশ্বকর্ম্মাপ্রকাশ), প্রেতেশয় (cf. অগ্নিপ্রেতেশয়োর্মধ্যে আজ্যগেহং প্রশস্যতে—বিশ্বকর্ম্মা প্রকাশ)। ***Verb i.*** **1.** To move or turn towards the south ; দক্ষিণ দিকে ফিরা। **2.** (*Astron.*) To arrive at, or pass, the meridian of a place ; as, the moon *souths* at nine ; (জ্যোতির্বিজ্ঞান) কোন স্থানের যাম্যোত্তর রেখায় উপস্থিত হওয়া বা উহা অতিক্রম করা। **South'-ward,** *adj.* Lying or situated toward the south ; দক্ষিণদিগ্‌বর্ত্তী, দক্ষিণদিগাভিমুখীন। **South'-wards,** *adv.* Toward the south ; দক্ষিণাভিমুখে, দক্ষিণদিকে। **South-east**—অগ্নিকোণ, দক্ষিণপূর্ব্ব কোণ। (*Adj.*) অগ্নিকোণসম্বন্ধীয়। **Southdown**—একপ্রকার সুখাদ্য মেষ ; (*Adj.*) ঐরূপ মেষসম্বন্ধীয়। [এই জাতীয় মেষ সর্ব্বাগ্রে সাসেক্স এবং হ্যাম্পশায়ারে উৎপন্ন করা হইয়াছিল বলিয়া এই নাম।] **South Downs**—হ্যাম্পশায়ার ও সাসেক্সসম্বন্ধীয়। **Souther, South-easter**—দক্ষিণ দিগ্ বা অগ্নিকোণ হইতে প্রবাহিত বায়ু। **South-easterly**—*adj.* অগ্নিকোণের, অগ্নিকোণ হইতে প্রবাহিত। **South-eastern** — আগ্নেয়, অগ্নিকোণস্থিত, অগ্নিকোণবর্ত্তী,অগ্নিকোণাভিমুখী। **South-west**—নৈঋর্তকোণ, দক্ষিণপশ্চিম কোণ বা ঐ কোণীয়, যাম্য-পশ্চিম (বিশ্বকর্ম্মাঃ)। **South-wester**—*n.* **1.** A wind blowing from the south-west ; নৈঋর্ত কোণ হইতে প্রবাহিত বায়ু, নৈঋর্ত বায়ু। **2.** A waterproof hat with a flap hanging over the neck, worn in bad weather (usu. contracted into *Sou'wester*) ; বৃষ্টিবাত্যার কালে ব্যবহৃত ঘাড়ের উপর প্রলম্বিত লোলক (flap) বিশিষ্ট ক্যাম্বিস প্রভৃতির টুপি। **South-westerly**—নৈঋর্তকোণাভিমুখী, নৈঋর্তকোণস্থিত। **South Sea**—(ইতিহাস) প্রশান্ত মহাসাগর। **South Sea Bubble** — ১৭১০ খৃঃ অব্দে ইংলণ্ডে "দক্ষিণসাগরবাণিজ্যসম্প্রদায়" নামক এক কোম্পানী প্রশান্ত মহাসাগর ও দক্ষিণ আমেরিকার পূর্ব্বোপকূলে বাণিজ্য করার জন্য একাধিকার প্রাপ্ত হয়। এই কোম্পানীর ভবিষ্যৎ লোকের নিকট এমন আশাসমুজ্জ্বল বোধ হইয়াছিল যে, লক্ষ লক্ষ লোক সাগ্রহে ইহার অংশ ক্রয় করিতে আরম্ভ করে। ক্রমে ১০০ পাউণ্ডের অংশের দাম ১০০০ পাউণ্ডে উঠিয়াছিল। ১৭২০ খৃঃ অব্দে এই কোম্পানী দাউলিয়া হওয়ায় বহুলোক সর্ব্বস্বান্ত হয়।

south'-ėr-lў (sŭth-), *adj. & adv.* Pertaining to, situated in, and proceeding from the south ; দক্ষিণদিক্‌সম্বন্ধীয়, দক্ষিণদিক্‌স্থিত, দক্ষিণদিগ্ হইতে প্রবাহিত, দক্ষিণ (in compound)। ***Adv.*** Toward the south ; দক্ষিণদিকে, দক্ষিণদিকাভিমুখে। **–liness,** *n.*

south'-ėrn (sŭth-), *adj. & n.* **1.** Pertaining to the south ; দক্ষিণদিক্‌সম্পর্কীয়, দক্ষিণীয়, অবাচীন, যাম্য, অপাচীন, অবাচ্য। **2.** In the south ; দক্ষিণদিকস্থ। ***Noun.*** A native or inhabitant of a southern country or of a southern part of a country ; a native of the Southern States ; দক্ষিণদেশবাসী লোক, দক্ষিণাঞ্চলবাসী লোক ; মার্কিণ যুক্তরাজ্যের দক্ষিণাংশের রাষ্ট্রসমূহের অধিবাসী। **–er,** *n.* Same as SOUTHERN. **–most,** *adj.* **Southern cross**—দক্ষিণাকাশস্থিত ক্ষুদ্র যোগতারাবিশেষ [এই যোগতারার প্রধান নক্ষত্রগণ ক্রুশের আকারে অবস্থিত বলিয়া, এই নাম।], দক্ষিণীয় অনুস্পথ (হিঃ কোঃ)। **Southern fish** — দক্ষিণীয় মৎস্য (হিঃ কোঃ)। **Southern zone**—দক্ষিণকটিবন্ধ (হিঃ কোঃ)।

south'-ing (sowth-), *n.* **1.** The act of arriving or crossing the meridian of a place ; কোন স্থানের যাম্যোত্তর রেখায় আগমন বা ঐ রেখা অতিক্রম। **2.** The difference in latitude made by a ship in sailing south ; দক্ষিণ দিকে গমননিবন্ধন জাহাজের অক্ষাংশের যে ব্যতিক্রম হয়।

south'-rŏn (sŭth-), *adj. & n.* (*Archaic*) English ; (অপ্রঃ) ইংলণ্ডীয় (স্কটলণ্ডবাসিগণ কর্ত্তৃক ব্যবহৃত)। ***Noun.*** (*Archaic*) An Englishman ; (অপ্রঃ) ইংরাজ (স্কটলণ্ডবাসিগণ কর্ত্তৃক ব্যবহৃত।)

south'-wĕst-ėr (sowth-), *n.* See under SOUTH.

sou'-ve-nir (sô-vĕ-nēr), *n.* A remembrance ; a keepsake ; স্মরণচিহ্ন, স্মারকচিহ্ন ; স্মৃতিচিহ্ন।

sŏv'-ėr-eign (-ĭn), *adj. & n.* **1.** Supreme ; princely ; প্রধান, পরম, শ্রেষ্ঠ,

মুখ্য ; রাজোচিত। 2. Independent ; as, a *sovereign* state; স্বাধীন। ***Noun.*** 1. A supreme ruler ; a king, queen or emperor ; রাজচক্রবর্ত্তী, একচ্ছত্র নৃপতি, রাজাধিরাজ ; রাজা, রাণী, সম্রাট, অধিরাজ। 2. A gold coin, worth 20 shillings ; ২০ শিলিং মূল্যের স্বর্ণমুদ্রাবিশেষ। **—ty,** *n.*

sow (sō), *v. t. & i.* 1. To scatter, as seed upon the earth ; বপন করা, বুনা। 2. To propagate ; as, to *sow* dissension ; বিস্তার করা, ছড়ান। 3. To cover thickly with ; "A close-set robe of jasmine *sown* with stars" ; ঘনভাবে আচ্ছাদিত করা, আস্তৃত করা, আচ্ছন্ন করা, আস্তীর্ণ করা, সমাচ্ছাদিত করা, সমাচ্ছন্ন করা। ***Verb i.*** 1. To scatter seed to grow and produce crop ; বীজ বপন করা। **Sow'-er, Sow'-ing,** *ns.* **To sow one's wild oats**—(See OATS). **To sow the wind and reap the whirlwind**—To behave recklessly and suffer disastrous result ; অপরিণামদর্শীর মত কায করিয়া পরিণামে গুরুতর শাস্তি ভোগ করা, অর্ব্বাচীনের মত কার্য্য করিয়া পরিণামে তজ্জন্য গুরুতর ফল ভোগ করা।

sow, *n.* 1. The female of the swine ; শূকরী, বরাহী। 2. In smelting, the runner or main channel where the liquid metal first enters ; যে প্রধান নালীতে তরল ধাতু প্রথম প্রবিষ্ট হয়। 3. An oblong mass of metal ; আয়ত ধাতুখণ্ড। **Sow-back**—অনুচ্চ বালুকাশৈল প্রভৃতি। **Sow bread**—একজাতীয় ক্ষুপ, হাঠজোড়ি (হিন্দি—খোরী), বরাহমোদা। **Sow-drunk**—বদ্ধমাতাল। **Sow-thistle**—ক্ষুদ্র ক্ষুদ্র পীতবর্ণ পুষ্পপ্রসূ গুল্ম বিশেষ। **To have, take,** or **get the right** or **wrong sow by the ear**—To pitch upon the right (or wrong) person ; to come to the right or wrong conclusion ; ঠিক লোককে (বা অপ্রকৃত) লোককে ধরা ; ঠিক (বা ভ্রান্ত) সিদ্ধান্তে উপনীত হওয়া, প্রকৃত বা অপ্রকৃত সিদ্ধান্তে উপনীত হওয়া।

soy, *n.* 1. A kind of sauce for fish ; মাছের সহিত খাওয়ার জন্য এক প্রকার চাটনি। 2. Same as SOYBEAN (below). **Soy-bean**—গরি কালাই (যোঃ), ভাট কালাই (নৃত্যঃ)।

Soymidafebrifuga—পত্রাঙ্গ (বেলঃ)।

spa, *n.* Mineral spring ; a place where there is a mineral spring ; খনিজ পদার্থপূর্ণ প্রস্রবণ ; যে স্থানে খনিজ পদার্থপূর্ণ প্রস্রবণ আছে। [বেলজিয়মের অন্তঃপাতী Spa নামক স্থান হইতে গৃহীত।]

space, *n.* 1. (*Metaph.*) Extension considered in its own nature without regard to anything external or that which always remains the same and is infinite and immovable ; "Pure *space* is capable of neither resistance nor motion" ; (তত্ত্ববিদ্যা) দেশ (cf. দেশকাল নিমিত্ত আকাশ), (cf. নিষ্ক্রামণংপ্রবেশনমিত্যং আকাশস্য লিঙ্গং — বিক্রঃ)। [দেশের ধারণা বিশ্লেষণের কোনরূপ চেষ্টা না করিয়া যদি আমরা 'দেশ' এবং 'বস্তুধারণ শক্যতা' এই উভয়কে অভিন্ন বলিয়া অবগত থাকি তবেই আমাদের বর্ত্তমান উদ্দেশ্যের পক্ষে যথেষ্ট হইবে। দেশের এরূপ সংজ্ঞা যে অযৌক্তিক তাহা যে আমি পরিজ্ঞাত নহি এমন নহে ; কারণ 'বস্তু' এবং 'ধারণ' এই শব্দদ্বয় দ্বারাও দেশ সূচিত হইতেছে। অতএব এইরূপ সংজ্ঞার সহিত যে বিষয়ের সংজ্ঞা প্রদান করিতে হইবে তাহা জড়িত রহিয়াছে। দেশ এবং দেশে অবস্থিত বস্তু সমূহের ধারণা আমাদের যে কোন উপায়েই হউক না কেন, সে বিষয়ের আলোচনা অপ্রাসঙ্গিক বলিয়া পরিত্যাগ করতঃ যদি আমরা এরূপ বলি যে, "বস্তুরাজি এবং তৎসমূহের" ধারণশক্যতা, আমাদের ভাবনাতে ইন্দ্রিয়গ্রাহ্য অচিদ্বস্তু (জড়পদার্থ), এবং অনিন্দ্রিয়গ্রাহ্য অচিদ্বস্তু (দেশ) এতদুভয়ের বৈপরীত্য যথার্থরূপ প্রদর্শিত করে তবে ইহাতে কেহই আপত্তি করিবেন না—স্পেন্সার।] 2. Room ; as, there is only *space* for seven persons ; স্থান। 3. The interval between any two or more objects ; as, the *space* between two houses ; অবকাশ, ফাঁক। 4. A quantity of time ; as, a short *space* of time ; নির্দ্দিষ্ট কাল। 5. An interval between two spaces of time ; অবকাশ। 6. (*Print.*) A small piece of metal cast lower than a type, used to separate words or letters ; (মুদ্রণ) শব্দ বা অক্ষর পৃথক করার জন্য হরফ অপেক্ষা দৈর্ঘ্যে অল্প ক্ষুদ্র ধাতুখণ্ড, অবকাশক। 7. (*Astron.*) The immeasurable expanse in which the solar and stellar systems are situated ; (জ্যোতির্বিজ্ঞান) যে মহাকাশে সৌর এবং নাক্ষত্রজগৎ সমূহ অবস্থিত রহিয়াছে, মহাকাশ (যোগবাশিষ্ঠ), পরমাকাশ (ঐ), মহাব্যোম, দিগন্তর, অন্তরিক্ষ। [বশিষ্ঠ কহিলেন—তাঁহারা ক্ষণকাল মধ্যে...... প্রমাণবর্জ্জিত সেই পরমাকাশ দর্শন করিলেন এবং সেই পরমাকাশে এই বিশাল জগৎ এবং অণুপ্রমাণ অসংখ্য ব্রহ্মাণ্ড দর্শন করিলেন। যেমন আকাশে সূর্য্যাতপে কোটি ত্রসরেণু স্ফুরিত দেখা যায়, তদ্রূপ সেই ব্রহ্মাণ্ডসমূহে পূর্ব্বোক্ত প্রকার আবরণসমূহ দর্শন করিলেন, আরও দেখিলেন মহাকাশ-রূপ মহাসমুদ্রের মহাশূন্য, অবিদ্যারূপ জলে মহাচিতের দ্রবভাব হইতে সমুৎপন্ন অর্দ্ধবুদ্-প্রমাণ জলবুদ্বুদস্বরূপ অসংখ্য ব্রহ্মাণ্ডের কতক অধোদেশে পতিত হইতেছে, কতক ঊর্দ্ধদেশে গমন করিতেছে এবং কতক নিশ্চল হইয়া রহিয়াছে। "......এই ব্রহ্মাণ্ডসমূহে ব্যোমপূর্ণ অচলের ন্যায় একমাত্র আকাশেই অর্থাৎ শূন্যতায়ই অবস্থিত ; ফলতঃ ঐ সমুদয় বিস্তৃত এক মহাকাশ। বিষ্ণু প্রভৃতি দেবগণ আজীবন ধাবিত হইলেও ঐ মহাকাশের পরিমাণ করিতে পারেননা।" "......সেই পরমাকাশে কোন প্রকারেই আদি, মধ্য, অন্ত কল্পনা নাই, অর্থাৎ এই পরমাকাশ আদি মধ্য অন্তবিহীন। এই বিশাল শান্ত অনাদি, অন্তমধ্যবিহীন পরমাকাশ, মহান্ আত্মায় অবস্থিত ; উহাতে কোন প্রকার অবিদ্যাভ্রম নাই। অধিক কি যদি ঊর্দ্ধ

দেশ হইতে সেই স্থলে অতিবেগে কল্প পর্য্যন্ত শিলা পতিত হয় ; যদি অতিবেগে পতগরাজ তথায় উপস্থিত হয়, যদি আকল্প অতিবেগশালী মারুত প্রবাহিত হয়, তথাপি এই নির্ম্মল আকাশের সীমা প্রাপ্ত হয়না" (যোগবাশিষ্ঠ রামায়ণ—বঙ্গবাসীর অনুবাদ)।] **Space′-less,** *adj.* Infinite ; অসীম, সীমাহীন। **Space axis** — আকাশীয় অক্ষ (হিঃ কোঃ)। **Space-bar**—মুদ্রাক্ষরলিখকের (Typewriter) দণ্ডবিশেষ। **Space-perception** — দেশপ্রত্যক্ষ (হিঃ কোঃ)। **Space-sense** — দেশসংবিৎ (ঐ)। **Super sensuous space**—পরাকাশ, সূক্ষ্মাকাশ, চিদাকাশ পরব্যোম।

spāce, *v. t.* & *i.* (*Print.*) To put spaces between (esp. words letters, lines) ; শব্দ বা অক্ষর প্রভৃতির মধ্যে অবকাশক স্থাপন করা। ***Verb i.*** (*Obs.*) To roam about ; (অপ্রঃ) ইতস্ততঃ বিচরণ করা। **To space out** — (*Print.*) To put wider space between ; (মুদ্রণ) শব্দ প্রভৃতির মধ্যে আরো অধিক ফাঁক রাখা। **Spac′-er, Spac′-ing,** *ns.*

spā′-cious (-shŭs), *adj.* Extensive ; বিস্তীর্ণ, সুপরিসর, প্রশস্ত, বিশাল। **—ly,** *adv.* **—ness,** *n.* The quality of being spacious; বিশালতা, বিস্তীর্ণতা।

spă′-dăs-sin (-în), *n.* A swordsman ; a bully ; অসিধারী ; গুণ্ডা।

spāde, *n.* & *v. t.* **1.** An instrument for digging or cutting the ground ; কোদালী, খনিত্র। **2.** One of a suit of cards marked with a spade ; তাসের ইস্কাবন। **3.** A blubber-spade ; তিমিমৎস্যের চর্ব্বি বাহির করার জন্য যন্ত্র বিশেষ। ***Verb t.*** **1.** To dig with a spade ; কোদাল দ্বারা কাটা, কোদালী মারা। **2.** To cut blubbers from whales ; তিমিমৎস্যের শরীর হইতে চর্ব্বি বাহির করা। **Spade′-ful,** *adj.* **Spade-bayonet**—একপ্রকার চওড়া সঙ্গীন যাহা অস্ত্র এবং খননযন্ত্র উভয়রূপেই ব্যবহার করা যায়। **Spade-guinea**—তৃতীয় জর্জ্জের সময়ে ব্যবহৃত কোদালী অঙ্কিত গিনিমুদ্রা বিশেষ। **Spade-husbandry** — কোদালী দ্বারা গভীর ভাবে মৃত্তিকা কাটিয়া চাষ বা ভূমির উৎকর্ষসাধনের প্রণালীবিশেষ। **Spade-iron** — কোদালীর লৌহময় অংশ। **To call a spade a spade**—To say the right or proper thing without circumlocution ; সোজা কথায় বলা, স্পষ্ট ভাষায় বলা, ঢাক ঢাক গুড় গুড় না করিয়া বলা।

spāde, *n.* A gelded beast ; ছিন্নমুষ্ক জন্তু।

spadg′-ēr (spăj-), *n.* (*Slang*) A corrupt form of sparrow ; (ইতরভাষায়) Sparrow শব্দের অপভ্রংশ।

spă-dille′ (-dîl), **spă-dil′-lo** (-ō), *ns.* The ace of spades at ombre and quadrille ; ইস্কাবনের টেক্কা।

Spadix.

spā′-dix, *n.* (*Bot.*) A succulent spike with numerous flowers included in a spathe ; (উদ্ভিদ্‌বিদ্যা) মঞ্জরী, তালগুচ্ছ (সাঃ পঃ)। **—di′-ceous, —di-cose,** *adjs.*

spā′-dō, *n.* **1.** A castrated animal ; ছিন্নমুষ্ক জন্তু। **2.** An impotent person ; ক্লীব, নপুংসক।

spaghetti, *n.* A kind of macaroni ; ইতালীদেশীয় চোঙ্গাকার পিষ্টক বিশেষ।

spă′-hee, (-hî), **spă′-hi** *n.* **1.** One of the Turkish cavalry ; তুরস্কদেশীয় অশ্বারোহী সৈনিক। **2.** An Algerian cavalryman in the French army ; ফরাসীসৈন্যদলভুক্ত আলজেরিয়াবাসী অশ্বারোহী সৈনিক।

spāke, *p. t.* of SPEAK (which see).

spall, *n., v. t.* & *i.* Splinter ; chip ; চির, ফালি, চিল্‌তা ; চেলা। ***Verb t.*** **1.** To split ; চির করা, চেলা করা। **2.** To break, as ore, with hammer previous to sorting ; বাছাই করার জন্য খনিজবিমিশ্র ধাতু হাতুড়ী দ্বারা ভাঙ্গা। ***Verb i.*** To give off spall ; চেলা হওয়া।

spăl-peen (-pēn), *n.* (Ireland) A mean fellow ; (আয়র্লণ্ড) হীন লোক, ইতর লোক।

spalt, *n.* A whitish scaly mineral, used in the fusion of metals ; ধাতু গলাইবার কার্য্যে ব্যবহৃত একপ্রকার শ্বেতাভ শল্কাত্মক খনিজ পদার্থ।

spăn, *v. t.* & *i.* **1.** To measure by the hand with the fingers expanded ; বিঘত দ্বারা মাপা। **2.** To measure or reach from one side to the other ; as, a bridge *spans* a river ; এক পার্শ্ব হইতে অপর পার্শ্ব পর্য্যন্ত প্রসারিত হওয়া। **3.** To encompass ; বেষ্টন করা, বলয়িত করা। **4.** (*Dial.*) To hobble ; (উপভাষায়) ঘোড়ার একদিকের পদদ্বয় রজ্জুদ্বারা বাঁধিয়া দেওয়া। **5.** (*Naut.*) To confine with ropes ; (নৌবিদ্যা) রজ্জুদ্বারা বাঁধা। ***Verb i.*** **1.** (*U. S.*—of horse To match in colour ; to be well matched for ; (মার্কিণযুক্তরাজ্যে—অশ্বসম্পর্কে) বর্ণে সমতুল হওয়া; পরস্পরের অনুরূপ প্রতিদ্বন্দ্বি, হওয়া। **2.** To extend; "His thoughts span the descent" ; বিস্তৃত হওয়া।

spăn, *n.* **1.** The space from the end of the thumb to the end of the little finger when extended ; বিঘত, বিতস্তি, প্রাদেশ। **2.** The extent of an arch between its abutment ; পিল্লাদ্বয়ের মধ্যে তোরণের বিস্তার। **3.** (*U. S.*) A pair of horses or mules ; a pair of oxen ; (মার্কিণ যুক্তরাজ্যে) অশ্ব বা খচ্চরযুগল ; বৃষভযুগল। **4.** A small space of time ; as, "Life is but a *span*" ; অল্পকাল, সামান্যকাল। **5.** (*Naut.*) One or others of various ropes used in fastenings or a means of connection ; (নৌবিদ্যা) বন্ধনরজ্জু, সংযোগসাধকরজ্জু। **6.** A shackle ; নিগড়, বেড়ী। **Span-dogs**—আঁকড়াযুক্ত লৌহদণ্ডদ্বয় — যদ্দ্বারা কাষ্ঠফলক উত্তোলিত করা হয়। **Span-roof**—ঢালুপার্শ্বদ্বয়বিশিষ্ট ছাদ। **Span-worm**—একপ্রকার কীটের কৃমি।

spăn'-drĕl, *n.* The irregular triangular space between the curve of an arch and the rectangle

Arch of window : S, S, spandrels.

inclosing it ; তোরণের বক্রভাগ এবং তদ্বেষ্টক আয়তক্ষেত্রের মধ্যবর্ত্তী অনিয়ত ত্রিভুজাকৃতি অংশ।

span'-gle (spăng-gl), *n., v. t.* & *i.* 1. A small glittering metal ornament ; "The thousand *spangles* that deck the firmament" ; চুমকি, তারা, রজতপত্র (আঃ বঃ)। 2. A small sparkling object ; ঝলমল প্রভাময় ক্ষুদ্র বস্তু। 3. A spongy excrescence on the leaves and tender branches of the oak ; ওক বৃক্ষের পত্র এবং তরুণ শাখাসমূহে জাত শোথকবৎ অর্ব্বুদ। ***Verb t.*** To adorn with spangles ; চুমকি বসান, চুমকিদ্বারা ভূষিত করা। ***Verb i.*** 1. To adorn or set with spangle ; চুমকি বসান, চুম্‌কি দ্বারা ভূষিত করা। 2. To gleam with, or as with, spangles ; ঝলমল্ করা, চুমকি বসানো কোন কিছুর মত ঝকমক করা। **Spangle-work**—চুমকির কায। **–gly,** *adj.*

Spăn'-iard (-yĕrd), *n.* A native or inhabitant of Spain ; স্পেনদেশের অধিবাসী, স্পেনদেশবাসী।

spă'-ni-ĕl, *n.* 1. A dog used in sports of the field, remarkable for its sagacity, with pendulous ear and covered with long hair ; দীর্ঘ রোমবিশিষ্ট একপ্রকার নতকর্ণ কুকুর। 2. A cringy person ; "Have you nothing, *spaniel*, to complain in him" ; খোসামুদে লোক, পদলেহনকারী। **King Charles's spaniel**—একপ্রকার কৃষ্ণ এবং পিঙ্গলবর্ণের স্পেনিয়্যাল কুকুর।

Spăn'-ish, *adj.* & *n.* Of, or pertaining to, Spain ; স্পেনদেশীয়, হিস্পানীয়। ***Noun.*** The language of Spain ; স্পেনদেশের ভাষা। **Spanish Armada** — Same as ARMADA (which see.) **Spanish black**—দগ্ধীভূত কর্ক হইতে প্রস্তুত একপ্রকার কোমল কৃষ্ণবর্ণ রঞ্জকপদার্থ। **Spanish brown**—চিত্রকার্য্যে ব্যবহৃত একপ্রকার গাঢ় পিঙ্গলবর্ণ মৃত্তিকা। **Spanish castle** — গগননগর, আকাশ-কুসুম, খপুষ্প, গন্ধর্ব্বনগর, অভ্রপুষ্প (নৈঃ)। **Spanish fly**—ইয়ুরোপের দক্ষিণ অংশে প্রাপ্ত একপ্রকার উজ্জ্বল হরিদ্বর্ণ কীট [ফোস্‌কা উৎপাদন, বাজীকরণ, প্রভৃতিতে ব্যবহৃত হয়।] **Spanish-grass**—Same as ESPARTO GRASS. **Spanish main**—Orinoco হইতে Darien পর্য্যন্ত Caribbean সমুদ্রের উপকূল ; Caribbean সমুদ্র। **War of the Spanish succession**—স্পেন দেশের রাজা দ্বিতীয় চার্লসের নিঃসন্তান অবস্থায় মৃত্যু হইলে প্রুশিয়া প্রভৃতির সহিত ফ্রান্স এবং বেভেরিয়ার ১৭০১—১৭১৪ খৃঃ অব্দ পর্য্যন্ত যে যুদ্ধ সংঘটিত হয়।

spank (spăngk), *v. i, t.* & *n.* To move with quick pace ; to dash along ; দ্রুত ধাবিত হওয়া, ছুটিয়া চলা ; প্রচণ্ডবেগে ধাবিত হওয়া। ***Verb t.*** To slap on buttocks ; নিতম্বে চপেটাঘাত করা। ***Noun.*** A sounding blow with the hand ; চপেটাঘাত।

spank'-ĕr (spăngk-), *n.* 1. One who, or that which, spanks ; দ্রুতধাবনকারী, নিতম্বে চপেটাঘাতকারী। 2. A fast-going horse ; বেগগামী অশ্ব। 3. A tall person ; দীর্ঘকায় ব্যক্তি। 4. Anything larger than common ; অসাধারণ বৃহৎ বস্তু।

spank'-ing (spăngk-), *adj.* & *adv.* 1. Dashing ; বেগগামী। 2. (*Colloq.*) Striking ; large ; excellent ; as, a *spanking* time ; আশ্চর্য্য ; বৃহৎ, প্রকাণ্ড ; খাসা, চমৎকার। **A spanking breeze**—প্রবল বাত্যা।

spăn'-lĕss, *adj.* Immeasurable ; অপরিমেয়, অসীম, অপ্রমেয়, সীমাহীন।

spăn'-ner (-ĕr), *n.* 1. An instrument used in the manner of a lever for tightening or loosening the nuts on screws ; স্ক্রুপের ঢিবরি আঁটা বা ঢিল করার জন্য যন্ত্র বিশেষ। 2. A bar or lever for opening the valves of steam-engine ; বাষ্পীয়যন্ত্রের কপাটকল উন্মুক্ত করার জন্য দণ্ড বা দণ্ডযন্ত্র। 3. A connecting rod in the parallel motion of engine ; যন্ত্রের সমান্তরাল গতিতে সংযোগসাধক দণ্ড।

spâr, *n.* & *v. t.* 1. A long piece of timber ; a general term for masts, yards, booms and gaffs ; দীর্ঘ কাষ্ঠদণ্ড ; জাহাজের মাস্তুল প্রভৃতি কাষ্ঠদণ্ড। 2. The bar of a door ; দ্বাররোধক কাষ্ঠফলক। ***Verb t.*** To furnish with spar ; মাস্তুলাদি সমন্বিত করা। **Spar-deck**—উপরের পাটাতন।

spâr, *n.* A crystalline mineral ; একপ্রকার স্ফটিকাকার আকরিক পদার্থ। **Calcareous spar**—দুগ্ধপাষাণ, দুগ্ধাশ্ম। **Derbyshire spar** — Same FLUOR SPAR. **Iceland spar**—একপ্রকার স্বচ্ছ পাথর—যাহা চসমা, দুরবীক্ষণ, প্রভৃতি নির্ম্মাণে ব্যবহৃত হয়।

spâr, *v. i.* & *n.* 1. To move or flourish the fist in front of the body, as in boxing ; to box ; মুষ্টিযোদ্ধার মত শরীরের সম্মুখে বদ্ধমুষ্টি আন্দোলিত করা ; মুষ্টিযুদ্ধ করা। 2. To bandy words ; বাগ্‌যুদ্ধ করা, বাক্‌কলহ করা, কথা কাটাকাটি করা। ***Noun.*** 1. A movement in which the boxer is prepared offensively or defensively ; মুষ্টিযুদ্ধের ভঙ্গিবিশেষ—যাহাতে মুষ্টিযোদ্ধা আত্মরক্ষার্থ বা প্রতিদ্বন্দ্বীকে আক্রমণের নিমিত্ত প্রস্তুত থাকে। 2. A boxing match ; মুষ্টিযুদ্ধ। 3. A cock-fight ; কুক্কুটযুদ্ধ, মোরগের লড়াই।

spâr´-ă-ble (-bl), *n.* A headless nail for soles and heels of boots ; বুটের গোড়ালী বা তলায় লাগাইবার জন্য একপ্রকার মাথাবিহীন প্রেক।

spāre, *adj.* 1. Scanty ; স্বল্প, অপ্রচুর। 2. Lean; as, a *spare* body; কৃশ, ক্ষীণ, কাহিল, ক্ষীণজীবী। 3. Superfluous ; as, a *spare* bed ; extra ; as, *spare* time ; উদ্বৃত্ত, প্রয়োজনাধিক ; অতিরিক্ত। **Spare´-ly,** *adv.* **Spare´-ness,** *n.*

spāre, *v. t.* & *i.* 1. To use frugally ; to forbear free use ; "*Spare* the rod and spoil the child" ; হিসাব করিয়া ব্যয় করা, পরিমিত ভাবে ব্যবহার করা ; কার্পণ্য করা। 2. To do without ; to dispense with ; as, I cannot *spare* you ; ছাড়িয়া দেওয়া ; রেহাই দেওয়া। 3. To use tenderly ; to treat with mercy ; to forbear to punish, afflict or destroy ; "*Spare* us O Lord !" ; কোমল ব্যবহার করা, করুণ ব্যবহার করা ; সদয় ব্যবহার করা ; রক্ষা করা, রেয়াত করা (cf. অন্যায় দেখিলে তিনি কাহাকে রেয়াৎ করেন না)। ***Verb i.*** 1. To be frugal ; মিতব্যয়ী হওয়া। 2. To use mercy or forbearance ; to forgive ; দয়া প্রদর্শন করা ; ক্ষমা করা। **Spare the rod and spoil the child**—বেত্রাঘাত প্রদানে কার্পণ্য করিলে ছেলে নষ্ট হয়, বেতরেয়াত করিলে ছেলে নষ্ট হয়। [cf. লালনে বহবো দোষাস্তাড়নে বহবো গুণাঃ।] **To spare no pains**—To try on'es utmost ; যথাসাধ্য চেষ্টা করা।

spâr´-gĕr, *n.* A sprinkler ; a vessel used in sprinkling ; সেচনভাণ্ড ; কোনকিছু ছিটাইবার জন্য যন্ত্রবিশেষ।

spâr´-gō-ris, *n.* Extreme distension of the breasts by milk ; স্তন্যোচ্ছ্বাস, দুগ্ধাধিক্য হেতু স্তনদ্বয়ের অত্যধিক স্ফীতি।

spār´-ing, *adj.* 1. Frugal ; মিতব্যয়ী। 2. Saving ; রক্ষাকারী, রক্ষক, রক্ষণশীল।

spârk, *n.* 1. A fiery particle thrown off from burning substance ; স্ফুলিঙ্গ, অগ্নিস্ফুলিঙ্গ, অগ্নিকণা, বিস্ফুলিঙ্গ, আগুণের ফুলকী, জ্বলনকন (মুদ্রাঃ)। 2. A small shining body or transient light ; esp. a small diamond ; as, a ring set with very small *sparks* ; ঝলমলে উজ্জ্বল ক্ষুদ্র বস্তু, ক্ষণিকদীপ্তি, জ্যোতিঃকণা ; ক্ষুদ্র হীরক। 3. A small fragment or atom of anything ; as, small *spark* of a letter ; কণা, রতি, লব। 4. A small portion of anything active or vivid ; কোন সজীব বা চঞ্চল বস্তুর কণা। 5. (*Electr.*) Luminous effect of certain disruptive discharge ; তাড়িতস্ফুলিঙ্গ, বিদ্যুৎস্ফুলিঙ্গ। 6. A bright emanation or gleam of light ; উজ্জ্বল আলোকস্ফুরণ, আলোকশিখা। 7. The vital principle in man ; as, the *spark* of life ; জীবনীশক্তি। **Spark´-less,** *adj.* **Spark´-let,** *n.* **Fairy-sparks**—গলিত উদ্ভিজ্জ পদার্থ প্রভৃতি হইতে নির্গত স্ফুরক জ্যোতিঃ। **Spark-arrester** — (তাড়িতবিদ্যা) বাষ্পীয়যন্ত্রের স্ফুলিঙ্গের নির্গমরোধের জন্য লৌহজাল প্রভৃতির আবরণ বিশেষ ; তাড়িতযন্ত্র হইতে নির্গত বিদ্যুৎস্ফুলিঙ্গজনিত অনিষ্ট নিবারণের জন্য কৌশলবিশেষ, স্ফুলিঙ্গরোধক। **A spark in one's throat**—অনুক্ষণ তৃষ্ণার্ত্ত। **To strike sparks out of a person**—To excite him to be brilliant and witty in conversation ; কাহাকে এরূপ উত্তেজিত করা যাহাতে তাহার মুখ হইতে সরস ও চটুল উক্তি সমূহ নির্গত হয়।

spârk, *v. i.* To emit sparks ; স্ফুলিঙ্গ নির্গত হওয়া, অগ্নিস্ফুলিঙ্গ নির্গত হওয়া, বিদ্যুৎস্ফুলিঙ্গ নির্গত হওয়া। **Spark´-ing,** *n.* **Sparking-plug**—মোটরযন্ত্রে বিস্ফোরকমিশ্র প্রজ্বালনের জন্য কৌশলবিশেষ।

spârk, *n.* & *v. i.* A gay man ; "The finest *sparks* and cleanest beaux" ; a lover ; নাগর, কেলিনাগর, রসিক, স্ফূর্ত্তিবাজ লোক ; প্রেমিক, প্রণয়ী। ***Verb i.*** To play the gallant ; নাগরালি করা। **Spark´-ish,** *adj.*

spâr´-kle, (-kl), *v. i.* & *n.* 1. To emit spark ; স্ফুলিঙ্গ নির্গত হওয়া। 2. To glitter ; to glisten ; ঝকমক করা, ঝিকমিক করা ; ঝলমল করা। 3. To effervesce ; as, the wine *sparkles* ; ফুসফুস শব্দে ফেনাইয়া উঠা, বুদ্বুদায়িত হওয়া। ***Noun.*** 1. A spark ; স্ফুলিঙ্গ, অগ্নিকণা, অগ্নিস্ফুলিঙ্গ। 2. Fiery glance ; অগ্নিবর্ষী কটাক্ষ। 3. A small portion of anything ; as, a *sparkle* of iron ; কণা, রতি। **–kler,** *n.*

spâr´-kling, *adj.* 1. Emitting sparks ; স্ফুলিঙ্গনিঃসারী, অগ্নিকণাবর্ষী। 2. A Glistening ; ঝকমক, ঝলমল, আলো ঝলমল (গীতাঞ্জঃ)। 3. Effervescing ; ফেনায়মান, ফেনিল, বুদ্বুদায়মান। **–ly,** *adv.*

spâr´-row (-ō), *n.* A bird of the finch family ; চটক জাতীয় পক্ষী। **House-sparrow**—চড়ুই পাখী, চটক পক্ষী। [Syn. কলবিঙ্ক, চিত্রপৃষ্ঠ, কলানুনাদী, গৃহনীড়, বৃষায়ণ, কামুক, কামী, নীলকণ্ঠক, কলাবিকল, গৃহবলিভুক্ (also *crow*)] **Sparrow-grass**—(*Slang*) Same as ASPARAGUS. **Sparrow-hawk**—চটক প্রভৃতি পক্ষীশিকারী একপ্রকার ক্ষুদ্র বাজপক্ষী।

spâr´-ry (-ĭ) *adj.* Pertaining to spar ; like spar ; rich in spar ; দুগ্ধপাষাণসম্বন্ধীয় ; দুগ্ধপাষাণবৎ ; দুগ্ধপাষাণবহুল, দুগ্ধাশ্মবহুল।

sparse (spârs), *adj.* Thinly scattered ; as, *sparse* population ; বিরলসন্নিবিষ্ট, স্বল্প, অপ্রচুর। **Sparse´-ly,** *adv.* **Sparse´-ness,** *n.*

Spâr´-tăn, *adj.* & *n.* Of Sparta ; প্রাচীন গ্রীসের অন্তঃপাতী স্পার্টা নগরীসম্বন্ধীয়। ***Noun.*** A native of Sparta ; স্পার্টা নগরীর অধিবাসী। **Spartan-dog**—একপ্রকার শিকারী কুকুর।

spâr´-tĕr-ie (-ĭ), *n.* A collective name for various kinds of articles manufactured from esparto-grass, as mats, nets, cordage, ropes, etc. ; স্পেনদেশে জাত তৃণবিশেষ হইতে প্রস্তুত মাদুর, জাল, কাছি, রজ্জু, প্রভৃতি বস্তুর সাধারণ নাম।

spăsm, *n.* **1.** A violent contraction of muscle ; খেঁচুনি, আক্ষেপ, পেশীসঙ্কোচ, অঙ্গগ্রহ, খিল, উদ্বেষ্টন (হিঃ কোঃ), অঙ্গবিক্ষেপ। **2.** A sudden, violent and generally fruitless effort ; a sudden emotion ; as, a *spasm* of repentance ; আকস্মিক কার্য ; আকস্মিক আবেগ বা উচ্ছ্বাস। **Functional spasm**—গ্রন্থকার প্রভৃতির স্নায়বিক বিকার।

spăs-mŏd'-ic, *adj.* & *n.* **1.** Of spasm ; caused by spasm ; অঙ্গগ্রহসম্বন্ধীয় ; অঙ্গগ্রহজনিত। **2.** Marked by strong effort, but brief in duration ; shortlived ; as, *spasmodic* effort ; প্রবল অথচ ক্ষণস্থায়ী চেষ্টাসহকৃত, সবিরাম ; ক্ষণিক। ***Noun.*** Spasmodic utterance ; আকস্মিক উক্তি। **–i-cal-ly**, *adv.*

spăs'-tic, *adj.* Same as SPASMODIC above.

spăt, *p. t.* & *p. p.* of SPIT (which see).

spăt, *n.*, *v. i.* & *t.* The spawn of oysters ; ঝিনুকের ডিম। ***Verb i.*** **1.** (Of oyster) To spawn ; (ঝিনুক সম্বন্ধে) ডিম হওয়া। ***Verb t.*** (Of oyster) To shed spawn ; ডিম পাড়া।

spăt, *n.* A short cloth, gaiter or legging worn over a shoe ; জুতার উপর পরিহিত একপ্রকার জঙ্ঘাত্রাণ বা পাদচ্ছদ।

spatch'-cŏck (spăch-), *n.* & *v. t.* A cock killed and cooked hastily খুব তাড়াতাড়ি জবাই করা বা রাঁধা কুক্কুট। ***Verb t.*** To thrust hastily some words in a written or telegraphic communication ; কোন চিঠি বা টেলিগ্রামে তাড়াতাড়ি কয়েকটী কথা ঢুকাইয়া দেওয়া।

spāte, *n.* A sudden flood, as in a stream after heavy rain ; বন্যা, বান।

spāthe, *n.* (*Bot.*) The calix of a spadix opening longitudinally ; (উদ্ভিদ্‌বিদ্যা) লম্বাকারে উন্মোচনশীল মঞ্জরী-আচ্ছাদক পত্র, মঞ্জরীআচ্ছাদক-পত্র, মঞ্জরীচ্ছদ, পিধান (সাঃ পঃ), অসিফলক (ঐ)।

a, spathe.

spăth'-ic, *adj.* Of spar ; like spar ; দুগ্ধপাষাণসম্বন্ধীয় ; দুগ্ধপাষাণবৎ, দুগ্ধাশ্মবৎ। **–i-form**, *adj.*

spā'-ti-ăl (-shi-), *adj.* Pertaining to space ; দেশসম্বন্ধীয়, মহাকাশসম্বন্ধীয়। **–al'-i-ty**, *n.* **–ly**, *adv.*

spăt'-tĕr, *v. t.*, *i.* & *n.* **1.** To sprinkle with a liquid or with any wet substance, as water, mud, or the like ; জল, কাদা প্রভৃতি ছিটান, ছিটাইয়া দেওয়া, ছিটাইয়া ফেলা। **2.** To asperse ; কলঙ্ক আরোপ করা, অখ্যাতি করা। ***Verb i.*** To throw out of the mouth in a scattered manner ; মুখ হইতে ছিটাইয়া ফেলা। ***Noun.*** **1.** The act of spattering ; small splash ; ছিটানি ; ছিটা। **2.** A quick succession of light sound ; ছল ছল শব্দ, পচ পচ শব্দ।

spăt'-tĕr-dăsh, *n.* A covering for the legs to protect them from the dust ; কর্দম হইতে পাদদেশ রক্ষার জন্য পাদচ্ছদ বিশেষ।

spăt'-ū-lă, *n.* A broad thin knife for spreading plasters, and working colour compounds ; রং প্রভৃতি মিশাইবার জন্য চওড়া পাতলা ও নমনীয় ফলকযুক্ত ছুরিকার ন্যায় যন্ত্রবিশেষ, মলম প্রভৃতি প্রস্তুতের বা পলস্ত্রাদি ছড়াইবার জন্য চৌড়া, ছুরিকাকার যন্ত্র বিশেষ। **–late**, *adj.* Shaped like a spatula ; নৌদণ্ডাকার।

spăt'-ūle, *n.* **1.** Same as SPATULA. **2.** (*Zool.*) A spatulate organ or part ; পলস্ত্রাদি ছড়াইবার ছুরীর আকার দেহাংশ।

spăv'-in, *n.* A swelling in some of the joints of a horse, producing lameness ; অশ্বের অস্থিসন্ধির স্ফীতিরোগ বিশেষ।

spawn (spăn), *n.*, *v. t.* & *i.* **1.** The eggs of fishes, frogs and toads ; মৎস্য, ভেক এবং সোনা ব্যাঙের ডিম, মৎস্যাণ্ড, মীনাণ্ড। **2.** Any product or offspring ; উৎপাদিত বস্তু, সন্তান। **3.** The buds or branches produced from underground stem ; নিম্নস্থ কাণ্ড হইতে জাত অঙ্কুর বা শাখা সমূহ। **4.** The mycelium of mushrooms or other fungi ; যে শ্বেতবর্ণ অংশুল পদার্থ হইতে ছত্রাক প্রভৃতি সঞ্জাত হয়। ***Verb t.*** **1.** To produce and deposit eggs ; ডিম্ব উৎপাদন করা। **2.** To produce ; উৎপাদন করা। ***Verb i.*** **1.** To deposit eggs ; ডিম ছাড়া, ডিম পাড়া। **2.** (*Contempt*) To issue as an offspring ; (অবজ্ঞাচ্ছলে) প্রসব হওয়া।

spay (spā), *v. t.* To castrate a female animal ; স্ত্রী পশুর ডিম্বাশয় নষ্ট বা নিষ্কাশিত করা।

speak (spēk) *v. i.* & *t.* **1.** To utter words or articulate sounds ; "To sounds make all your trumpets *speak*, give them all breath" ; কথা বলা। **2.** To utter a speech ; as, to *speak* on a subject ; বক্তৃতা দেওয়া। **3.** To communicate ideas in any manner ; "His countenance now *spoke* promisingly" ; যে কোন উপায়ে মনোভাব ব্যক্ত করা। ***Verb t.*** **1.** To utter articulate sound ; কথা বলা। **2.** To utter ; উচ্চারণ করা। **3.** To deliver a speech ; বক্তৃতা দেওয়া, বক্তৃতা প্রদান করা। **4.** To indicate ; to reveal ; "The solidity of the structure *speaks* the industry of the ages" ; সূচনা করা ; ব্যক্ত করা। **5.** To address ; সম্বোধন করা। **Speak'-a-ble**, *adj.* **Fair-spoken**—মিষ্টভাষী। **Plain-spoken**—স্পষ্টবাদী, উচিতবক্তা। **So to speak**—বলিতে গেলে। **To speak** — To talk with ; কাহারো সহিত কথা বলা। **To speak about**—To say something of ; কাহারো সম্বন্ধে কিছু বলা।

To speak against—To express opinion, or discourse, against ; কাহারো বিরুদ্ধে কিছু বলা বা মত প্রকাশ করা। **To speak by the card**—To be careful with one's words ; to speak to the point ; বিশেষ সাবধানতার সহিত কথা বলা ; প্রাসঙ্গিক ভাবে বলা। **To speak by the** or **like a book**—See BOOK. **To speak daggers**—To utter biting words ; মর্ম্মচ্ছেদী বাক্য উচ্চারণ করা। **To speak fair**—To use polite language ; শিষ্টবাক্য বলা। **To speak for**—To speak on behalf of ; কাহারো পক্ষে বলা। To ask for ; চাওয়া। To indicate ; সূচনা করা। To order ; to engage ; ফরমায়েস দেওয়া ; নিযুক্ত করা। **To speak for itself**—To be self-evident ; স্বতঃসিদ্ধবৎ হওয়া, আপনা-আপনি প্রকাশ পাওয়া। **To speak in one's ear**—To whisper ; কাণে কাণে বলা। **To speak of**—To mention or discourse upon ; কাহারো সম্বন্ধে বলা বা উল্লেখ করা, কোন বিষয়ে বলা। Worth mentioning ; উল্লেখযোগ্য। **To speak one's mind** — To speak without reserve ; মনের কথা খুলিয়া বলা। **To speak out**—To talk loudly ; উচ্চৈঃস্বরে বলা, চেঁচাইয়া বলা। To talk freely or without reserve ; অবাধে বলা, খুলিয়া বলা, স্পষ্ট করিয়া বলা। To appear ; to be evident ; প্রতিভাত হওয়া ; প্রত্যক্ষগোচর হওয়া, পরিস্ফুট হওয়া। **To speak to**—To address ; সম্বোধন করা। To converse with ; কাহারো সহিত কথা বলা। (*Colloq.*) To reprove ; তিরস্কার করা। **To speak together**—To confer ; এক সঙ্গে পরামর্শ করা। **To speak unto**—Same as TO SPEAK TO. **To speak up**—To speak strongly for ; কাহারো পক্ষে খুব জোরের সহিত বলা। To talk in a loud voice ; উঁচু গলায় বলা। To talk without reservation ; স্পষ্ট করিয়া বলা, খুলিয়া বলা। **To speak upon**—Same as TO SPEAK ABOUT. **To speak volumes**—To be full of meaning ; অর্থপূর্ণ হওয়া। **To speak volumes etc. for, To speak well for**—To be a favourable or commendatory sign ; to be abundant evidence of ; প্রশংসার লক্ষণ হওয়া, অনুকূল হওয়া ; যথেষ্ট প্রমাণস্বরূপ হওয়া। **To speak well of**—To praise ; প্রশংসা করা, সুখ্যাতি করা। **To speak with**—To converse with ; আলাপ করা, কথাবার্ত্তা বলা।

speak'-ĕr (spēk-). *n.* 1. One who speaks, esp. in public; যে ব্যক্তি কথা বলে, বিশেষতঃ বক্তা। 2. (*Cap.*) The president of a deliberative assembly esp. of House of Commons ; সভাপতি, বিশেষতঃ পার্লেমেন্টের প্রাকৃত সভার সভাপতি [সভার শৃঙ্খলারক্ষণ ইঁহার প্রধান কার্য্য, এতদ্ব্যতীত কোন বিষয়ে স্বপক্ষে ও বিপক্ষে মতসংখ্যা সমান হইলে ইনি কোন পক্ষে স্বীয় মত প্রদান দ্বারা উক্ত বিষয়ের মীমাংসা করিতে পারেন।] —**ship**, *n.*

speak'-ing (spēk-), *n.* The act of one who speaks ; কহন, কথন, ভাষণ। **Speaking acquaintance**—কথাবার্ত্তা বলা যায় এরূপ পরিচয়, যে লোকের সহিত আলাপ পরিচয় আছে। **Speaking-trumpet**—যে বাদ্যযন্ত্রের সাহায্যে মনুষ্যের শব্দ বহুদূরে নীত হয়। **Speaking-tube**—যে নলের সাহায্যে কণ্ঠস্বর এক কুঠরী হইতে অপর কুঠরীতে কিম্বা এক গৃহ হইতে অন্য গৃহে নেওয়া যাইতে পারে। **I am not in speaking terms with him**—তাহার সহিত আমার বাক্যালাপ নাই। **Properly speaking**—যথাযথভাবে বলিতে গেলে। **Roughly speaking**—মোটামুটী বলিতে গেলে। **Strictly speaking**—ঠিকভাবে বলিতে গেলে।

spear (spēr), *n., v. t. & i.* **1.** A long pointed weapon ; শূল, বর্শা, বল্লম, শক্তি, ভল্ল, সড়কি, শেল। 2. A sharp-pointed and barbed instrument for stabbing fish etc. ; টেঁটা। 3. (*Poet.*) Same as SPEARMAN. *Verb t.* To pierce, strike or kill with a spear ; বর্শাদ্বারা আঘাত

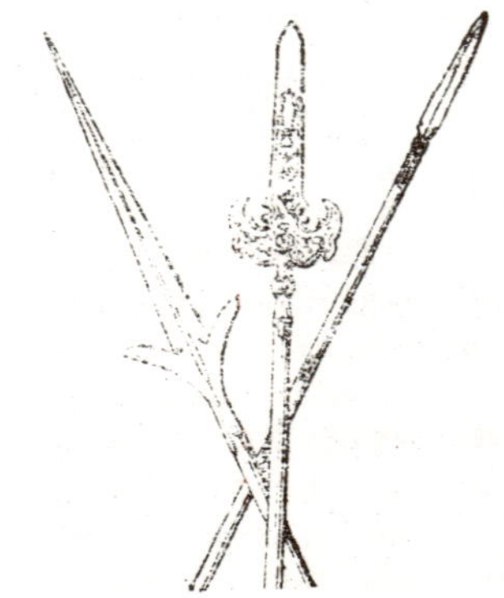

Ancient spears.

করা, বর্শাদ্বারা ভেদ করা, বর্শার আঘাতে বধ করা। *Verb i.* To shoot into a long stem ; লম্বা ডগা গজান। **Spear grass**—চোরকাঁটা। **Spear head**—বর্শার ফলা। **Spearman**—বর্শাধারী সৈনিক। **Spearmint** — পাহাড়ী পুদিনা (আর্য্য গৃহচিকিৎসা)। **Spear shaft**—বর্শার বাঁট। **Spear side**—কোন পরিবারের পুংশাখা। **Spearwort**—একজাতীয় গুল্ম।

spĕc, *n.* (*Colloq.*) Speculation ; (চলিতভাষায়) ঝুঁকিদার ব্যবসায়।

spĕ'-cial (-shăl), *adj.* & *n.* **1.** Particular ; extraordinary ; বিশিষ্ট ; অপ্রাকৃত, অসাধারণ, অসামান্য। 2. Designed for a particular purpose or occasion ; কোন বিশেষ উদ্দেশ্যের জন্য অভিপ্রেত, বিশেষ। 3. Confined to some particular branch or subject ; as, a *special* dictionary ; কোন বিশেষ বিষয়সম্বন্ধীয়। *Noun.* A train, a constable, a correspondent used for a special service or occasion ; an edition of newspaper containing the latest news etc. ; বিশেষ রেলগাড়ী, বিশেষ কনেষ্টবল, বিশিষ্ট সংবাদদাতা ; পত্রিকার বিশেষ সংস্করণ। —**ly**, *adv.* **Special anatomy**—শরীরের কোন বিশেষ দৈহিক

যক্সম্বন্ধীয় শারীরসংস্থানবিদ্যা। **Special appeal**—খাস আপীল। **Special case**—বিশেষ ঘটনা; মোকদ্দমায় কোন পক্ষ কর্তৃক যে বর্ণনাপত্র পেশ করা হয়। **Special constable**—হাঙ্গামা প্রভৃতির সম্ভাবনা হওয়ায় বিশেষ কনেষ্টবলরূপে নিযুক্ত ব্যক্তি। **Special correspondent**—পত্রিকার বিশেষ সংবাদদাতা। **Special hospital**—বিশেষ বিশেষ রোগে আক্রান্ত ব্যক্তিগণের জন্য আরোগ্যশালা। **Special jury**—সমাজের বিশিষ্ট ব্যক্তিগণ দ্বারা গঠিত জুরি [বিলাতে আইনতঃ esquire উপাধি গ্রহণের অধিকারী, ব্যাঙ্কার, সওদাগর নির্দিষ্ট মূল্যের বাটী, অট্টালিকা বা কৃষিক্ষেত্রের অধিকারী—এইরূপ লোকগণ বিশিষ্টজুরিরূপে নির্বাচিত হইয়া থাকেন।] **Special licence**—কোন বর ও কন্যাকে কোন বিশেষ স্থানে বা পূর্ব্ব ঘোষণা ব্যতিরেকে বিবাহিত করার জন্য যাজককে যে অনুমতিপত্র দেওয়া হয়। **Special logic**—কোন বিশেষ শ্রেণীর বস্তুসম্পর্কীয় ন্যায়শাস্ত্র। **Special pleading**—(আইন) কোন বিশেষ বা নূতন বিষয় আরোপ; আপাতরম্য যুক্তি। **Special sitting**—বিশেষ অধিবেশন। **Special creation theory**—আরম্ভবাদ (হিঃ কোঃ)।

spĕ'-cial-ist (-shăl-), *n.* One who has a special knowledge of a subject; কোন বিষয়ে বিশেষ ব্যুৎপন্ন ব্যক্তি, বিশেষজ্ঞ, বিশেষবিৎ।

spĕ-ci-ăl'-i-tȳ (-shi-), *n.* 1. A special feature or characteristic; বিশেষত্ব, বৈশিষ্ট্য (জিঃ)। 2. Special department; special pursuit; special skill; বিশেষ বিভাগ; বিশেষ ব্যবসায়; বিশেষ নৈপুণ্য। 3. A thing or article manufactured by a special firm or characteristic of a special place; "Most dealers control themselves with goods which are not *special* of their own"; কোন বিশেষ কারখানা কিম্বা কোন বিশেষ স্থান হইতে প্রস্তুত কোন দ্রব্য।

spĕ'-cial-ize (-shăl-), *v. t. & i.* 1. To mention specially; "I will not *specialize* few of these virtues"; বিশেষভাবে উল্লেখ করা। 2. To apply to special use; to devote or apply to a specific use or function; বিশেষ উদ্দেশ্যে প্রয়োগ করা; কোন বিশেষ কার্য্যসাধনে প্রয়োগ করা। 3. (*Biol.*) To develop (parts) by adaptation to surroundings; প্রতিবেশের উপযোগীকৃত করিয়া (অংশসমূহ) বিকাশ করা। ***Verb i.*** 1. To engage in the study of a particular subject; to be a specialist; কোন বিশেষ বিষয়ের অধ্যয়নে নিরত হওয়া; বিশেষজ্ঞ হওয়া। 3. To pursue a special mode of action or development; কোন বিশেষ কার্য্যপ্রণালী বা বিকাশের ধারার অনুবর্ত্তন করা। **—i-za'-tion,** *n.* The act of specialising; অসাধারণীকরণ (হিঃ কোঃ), বিশেষসম্পাদন (ঐ)।

spĕ-cial-tȳ (-shăl-), *n.* 1. A particular matter; বিশেষ বিষয়। 2. A special article in a contract; চুক্তিপত্রের বিশেষ দফা। 3. Special feature or characteristics; বিশেষত্ব, বৈশিষ্ট্য। 4. Same as SPECIALITY, 3. 5. (*Law*) A sealed contract or bond; শীলমোহরাঙ্কিত চুক্তিপত্র; তমঃসুক। **A specialty bond**—শীলমোহরাঙ্কিত তমঃসুক।

spē-cĭ-ā'-tion, *n.* (*Biol.*) The process by which species are formed; (জীববিজ্ঞান) যে প্রণালী দ্বারা জাতিসমূহ উৎপাদিত হয়, জাতিসংগঠন

spē'-cie (-shi), *n.* 1. A coin; মুদ্রা। 2. Copper, silver or gold used as a circulating medium; মুদ্রারূপে ব্যবহৃত তাম্র, রৌপ্য বা স্বর্ণ। **Paid in specie**—মুদ্রাদ্বারা প্রদত্ত [নোট, চেক, প্রভৃতি দ্বারা নহে।]

spē'-cies (-shēz), *n.* 1. A class of animals, plants, etc. which are essentially alike; জাতি, শ্রেণী, অপরজাতি (সাঃ পঃ)। 2. A kind; a sort; রকম, প্রকার; জাতি। 3. A mental image; "Wit... searches over all the memory for the *species* or ideas as of those things which it designs to represent"; মানসমূর্তি, মানসচিত্র। 4. (*Log.*) A conception subordinated to a generic conception or genus; (তর্কবিজ্ঞান) সামান্য (হিঃ কোঃ), অপরসামান্য (ঐ), উপজাতি (ঐ)। 5. A component part of a compound medicine; মিশ্র ঔষধের উপাদান। 6. A compound powder of any kind; মিশ্র চূর্ণ। 7. (*Law*) The form or shape given to materials; (আইন) কোন বিষয়কে যে আকার প্রদান করা হয়।

spē-cĭf-ic, *adj.* & *n.* 1. Pertaining to species; জাতিগত। 2. Definite; precise; peculiar; নির্দ্দিষ্ট, বৈশেষিক, বিশেষ; নিরূপিত, সঠিক, যথার্থ; অসাধারণ। 3. Infallible; অমোঘ। ***Noun.*** An infallible remedy; অমোঘ ঔষধ, অব্যর্থ ঔষধ, মহৌষধ (জাহিঃ)। **—i-cal-ly,** *adv.* **—ness, Spec-i-fic'-i-ty,** *ns.* **Specific cause**—কোন বিশেষ প্রকার রোগজনককারণ, কারণবিশেষ (সাঃ পঃ)। **Specific centre**—কোন জাতীয় জন্তু বা উদ্ভিদের মূল স্থান। **Specific character**—জাতিগত চরিত্র। **Specific difference**—জাতিগত পার্থক্য। **Specific gravity**—আপেক্ষিক গুরুত্ব, গুরুতা (হিঃ কোঃ), জাতিগত গুরুত্ব (হিঃ কোঃ), বিশিষ্ট গুরুত্ব (ঐ)। **Specific heat**—বিশিষ্ট তাপ (হিঃ কোঃ)। **Specific legacy**—উইল দ্বারা প্রদত্ত কোন বিশেষ বস্তু (আসবাব প্রভৃতি), বিশিষ্ট উত্তর দান। **Specific name**—জাতীয় নাম। **Specific resistance**—আপেক্ষিক রোধশীলতা (সাঃ পঃ), আপেক্ষিক প্রতিরোধ (ঐ)। **Specific weight**—বিশিষ্ট ভার (হিঃ কোঃ)।

spĕc-i-fi-ca'-tion, *n.* 1. The designation or statement of particulars; বিশেষ বিবরণ প্রদান, বিশেষ নির্দ্দেশ (হিঃ কোঃ), বিশেষোদ্দেশ (ঐ), বিশেষ ভাবে নির্দ্দেশ। 2. A particular or detailed account ; বিস্তৃত বিবরণ, বিস্তৃত বর্ণনা । 3. A written statement containing description or enumeration of particulars of an invention for patent ; কোন যন্ত্রাদি পেটেণ্ট করিতে হইলে উহার ব্যবহার ও নির্ম্মাণসম্বন্ধে যে লিখিত বিবরণ প্রদান করা হয় । 4. An article ; দফা । 5. (*Law*) The formation of new property from materials belonging to another ; (আইন) অপর সম্পত্তির উপাদান হইতে নূতন সম্পত্তি গঠন । 6. A detailed statement of the measurements of construction, workmanship, material, etc. of a work undertaken by an architect or contractor ; স্থপতি বা ঠিকাদার কর্তৃক গৃহীত কার্য্যের পরিমাপ, নির্ম্মাণ-প্রণালী, মাল মসলা, প্রভৃতির বিস্তৃত বিবরণ ।

spĕć'-ĭ-fȳ, *v. t.* 1. To name expressly ; to mention specially ; to relate in detail ; স্পষ্ট করিয়া নাম করা ; বিশেষভাবে উল্লেখ করা ; সবিস্তারে বর্ণনা করা । 2. To invest with a specific character ; বিশেষত্ব প্রদান করা ।

spĕć'-ĭ-mĕn, *n.* A part exhibited in order that the nature or quality of the body or substance may be known ; নমুনা । **Specimen page**—নমুনার পৃষ্ঠা । **What a specimen**—(*Colloq.*) What sort of a man ; (চলিতভাষায়) কি রকম লোক ।

spē'-ci-ŏl'-ō-ġȳ (-shĭ-), *n.* The science of species ; জাতিবিজ্ঞান । **—gi-cal,** *adj.*

spē'-cious (-shŭs), *adj.* Appearing well at first view ; plausible ; আপাতরম্য, আপাতন্যায্য ; দৃশ্যতঃ যুক্তিপূর্ণ, সত্যসঙ্কাশ (মঃ উঃ) । **—ci-os'-i-ty,** *n.* **—ly,** *adv.* **—ness,** *n.* The quality of being specious ; আপাতরম্যতা, আপাতন্যায্যতা ।

spĕck, *n.* & *v. t.* 1. A stain ; দাগ, কলঙ্ক । 2. A particle ; as, a *speck* of dust ; কণা । 3. A minute patch ; as a *speck* of cloud ; ক্ষুদ্র খণ্ড, তৎপর (সূর্য্যঃ বাঃ) । 4. A spot of rottenness in a fruit ; (ফলের) চিতি । *Verb t.* To mark with specks ; দাগ লাগান, দাগ বিশিষ্ট করা । **Speck'-less, Speck'-y,** *adjs.* **Specks of the eye**—পুষ্পক (সাঃ পঃ) ।

spĕck, *n.* Blubber, as of whales ; তিমি প্রভৃতির চর্ব্বি ।

spĕck-le (-l), *n.* & *v. t.* A speck or stain, esp. one occurring on the skin ; দাগ, চিহ্ন, তিল, তিলকালক, মেচক, নীল (সুশ্রুঃ) । *Verb t.* To mark with speckles ; তিলাঙ্কিত করা, তিল চিহ্নিত করা । **—led,** *adj.*

spĕck'-tion-eer (-ēr), *n.* (*Whaling*) Chief harpooner ; (তিমি শিকার) প্রধান শিকারী ।

spĕć'-tă-cle (-kl), *n.* 1. A public show ; সাধারণ প্রদর্শনী । 2. An unusual or contemptible person or thing exhibited before people ; সাধারণের সম্মুখে প্রদর্শিত, কৌতূহলোদ্দীপক বস্তু, আশ্চর্য্য বস্তু, অবজ্ঞার বস্তু । 3. A gazing stock ; সাধারণে প্রদর্শিত অদ্ভুত লোক । 4. A sight ; দৃশ্য । 5. (*Pl.*) A familiar optical instrument used to assist or correct some defect in the organs of vision ; চসমা, উপনেত্র, উপাক্ষ । 6. Something that adds the intellectual sight ; "Shakespeare...needed not the *spectacles* of books to read nature" ; জ্ঞাননেত্রের সাহায্যকারী বিষয় । **—cled,** *adj.* Wearing spectacles ; চসমা-আঁটা, চসমাধারী । **—cu-lar,** *adj.* 1. Worthy of being exhibited ; as, *spectacular* fight ; প্রদর্শনোপযোগী, প্রদর্শনযোগ্য । 2. Having markings on the face suggesting a pair of spectacles ; as, *spectacled* cobra ; মুখে চসমার-আকৃতি চিহ্নবিশিষ্ট । **Spectacle-case** — চসমার খাপ । **Spectacled-bear**—দক্ষিণ আমেরিকার একপ্রকার ভালুক—উহাদের চক্ষুর্দ্বয়ের চতুর্দ্দিকে ঠিক চসমার মত অপেক্ষাকৃত ফিকা রঙ্গের চক্র থাকে । **Spectacle-glass** — চসমার কাচ বা পাথর । **To see everything through rose-coloured spectacles**—To take cheerful or hopeful view of everything ; প্রত্যেক বিষয় আশা ও আনন্দের চক্ষে দেখা ।

spĕć'-tā'-tŏr, *n.* A looker on ; a beholder ; দর্শক ; দ্রষ্টা, প্রেক্ষক । **—tress,** *n.* (*Fem.*) **The Spectator**—ইংলণ্ডের সংবাদপত্র বিশেষ । বিখ্যাত সাহিত্যিক Addison এই সংবাদপত্রের একজন প্রধান লেখক ছিলেন ।

spĕć'-trăl, *adj.* 1. Pertaining to a spectre ; ghost like ; ভৌতিক ; ভূতবৎ । 2. Of spectrum ; বর্ণচ্ছত্র-সম্বন্ধীয়, সপ্তরঞ্জনসম্বন্ধীয় (হিঃ কোঃ) ।

spĕć'-tre (-têr), *n.* 1. An apparition ; a ghost ; a phantom ; অপচ্ছায়া ; ভূত, অপদেবতা, প্রেতযোনি ; ছায়ামূর্ত্তি । 2. (Epicurean school) One of the images or semblance supposed to emanate from corporeal things ; সূক্ষ্মদেহ, আতিবাহিক-দেহ, লিঙ্গদেহ, সূক্ষ্মশরীর । 3. A general name of thin animals ; as, *spectre*-bat ; ক্ষীণদেহ প্রাণীর সাধারণ নাম । **Spectre of the Brocken**—Brocken নামক স্থানে প্রথম পরিলক্ষিত গিরিচূড়ালগ্ননীহারিকা-মধ্যে প্রতিবিম্বিত স্বমূর্ত্তি ।

spĕć'-trō-grăm, *n.* A representation obtained by a spectrograph ; বর্ণচ্ছত্রাঙ্কক যন্ত্রের সাহায্যে গৃহীত চিত্র ।

spĕć'-trō-grăph, *n.* 1. An apparatus for photographing or mapping spectrum ; বর্ণচ্ছত্রের আলোকচিত্র গ্রহণের জন্য যন্ত্রবিশেষ, বর্ণচ্ছত্রাঙ্কক । 2. Same as SPECTROGRAM. **—graph'-ic,** *adj.* **—tro-gra-phy,** *n.*

spĕc-trŏl'-ō-ġȳ, *n.* The branch of science which determines the constituent elements and other conditions of bodies by examination of their spectra ; বিজ্ঞানের শাখা বিশেষ—যাহাতে কোন বস্তুর বর্ণচ্ছত্র-বিশ্লেষণ দ্বারা উহার উপাদান এবং অন্যান্য অবস্থা নির্ণয়ের উপায় বর্ণিত হইয়াছে,

বর্ণবিশ্লেষণবিদ্যা, সপ্তরঞ্জনবিদ্যা (হিঃ কোঃ), রশ্মিনির্ব্বাচনশাস্ত্র (ঐ), রশ্মিনির্ব্বাচকশাস্ত্র (ঐ) ।

spĕc-trŏm′-ĕ-tĕr, *n.* An instrument for measuring deviation of light-rays in passing through prism ; ত্রিপার্শ্বকাচের ভিতর দিয়া অতিক্রান্ত আলোকরশ্মির বিক্ষেপপরিমাপের জন্য যন্ত্রবিশেষ, বর্ণচ্ছত্রমান, সপ্তরঞ্জক তেজোমাপক (হিঃ কোঃ) ।

spĕc′-trŏ-phōne, *n.* A modification of spectroscope in which succession of sounds takes the place of the observation by the eye ; লেখাবীক্ষণযন্ত্রের প্রকারান্তর — যদ্দারা ধ্বনি পরম্পরা শ্রবণ করিয়া বস্তু পরিচয় করিতে হয়, লেখাকর্ণনযন্ত্র ।

spĕc′-trŏ-scōpe, *n.* One of the most important instruments of modern scientific research, in which the analysis of light coming from various bodies as light sources, is conducted by means of prisms, the object being to determine from the position of the spectral lines, the compostion of the bodies ; একপ্রকার যন্ত্র—যাহার সাহায্যে বস্তুর বর্ণচ্ছত্র উৎপাদন করিয়া ঐ বর্ণচ্ছত্রস্থিত রেখাসমূহের অবস্থান দৃষ্টে ঐ সমস্ত পদার্থ কি কি উপাদানে গঠিত তাহা নির্ণয় করা যায়, রশ্মিনির্ব্বাচনযন্ত্র, বর্ণবীক্ষণ যন্ত্র, বর্ণবিশ্লেষণযন্ত্র (হিঃ কোঃ), সপ্তরঞ্জনদর্শক (ঐ), রশ্মিদর্শন যন্ত্র (ঐ), রশ্মিবর্ণদর্শক (ঐ), স্পেক্‌ট্রোস্‌কোপ (ঐ), বর্ণবীক্ষণ (জ্যোতি জ্যোঃ), বর্ণরেখাবীক্ষণ (ঐ), লেখাবীক্ষণ (সা পঃ) । **–scop-ic**, *adj.*

spĕc′-trŭm, (*Pl.* -TRA), *n.* 1. An image seen after the eyes are closed and turned away ; কোন বস্তু হইতে চক্ষু ফিরাইয়া লইলে বা উহাতে দৃষ্টিপাতের পর চক্ষু মুদ্রিত করিলে ঐ বস্তুর যে আভাস দৃষ্ট হয়, অনুচিত্র । 2. A specially coloured band of light showing prismatic colours produced when light is subjected to analysis by a spectroscope ; বর্ণচ্ছত্র, রশ্মিবর্ণ (হিঃ কোঃ), স্পেক্‌ট্রাম (ঐ), সপ্তরঞ্জন (ঐ), ছটা (সাঃ পঃ), বর্ণলেখা (ঐ), বর্ণপট্টিকা (ঐ), লেখা (ঐ) । **Band spectrum** — বন্ধনীযুক্তবর্ণচ্ছত্র (প্রতিভা) । **Chemical spectrum**—রাসায়নিক রশ্মিবর্ণ (হিঃ কোঃ) । **Chromatic spectrum** — রশ্মিবর্ণ (হিঃ কোঃ) । **Continuous spectrum**—সরোতর রশ্মিবর্ণ (হিঃ কোঃ) । **Gaseous spectrum**—বাষ্পীয় রশ্মিবর্ণ (ঐ) । **High frequency spectrum**—দ্রুত কম্পমান বর্ণচ্ছত্র (প্রতিভা) । **Normal spectrum**—সাধারণ রশ্মিবর্ণ (হিঃ কোঃ) । **Ocular spectrum**—দৃশ্য রশ্মিবর্ণ (ঐ) । **Solar spectrum**—সূর্য্যরশ্মিসঞ্জাত (হিঃ কোঃ), সৌররশ্মিবর্ণ (ঐ) । **Spectrum absorption**—অপসর্পণ রশ্মিবর্ণ । **Spectrum analysis**—লৈখিক বিশ্লেষণ (সাঃ পঃ), রশ্মিবর্ণবিশ্লেষণ (হিঃ কোঃ) । [বিশেষতঃ বর্ণবীক্ষণযন্ত্রের সাহায্যে রাসায়নিক বিশ্লেষণ—এই অর্থে *Spectral analysis* শব্দও ব্যবহৃত হয় ।] **Thermal spectrum**—তাপরশ্মিবর্ণ (হিঃ কোঃ) ।

spĕc′-ū-lar (-lĕr), *adj.* 1. Pertaining to a speculum or mirror ; of the nature of a mirror ; মুকুরসম্বন্ধীয় ; মুকুরাত্মক । 2. Reflecting ; প্রতিবিম্বক । 3. (*Surg.*) Of a speculum ; conducted with the aid of a speculum ; (অস্ত্রোপচারবিদ্যা) প্রসারকযন্ত্র সম্বন্ধীয় ; প্রসারকযন্ত্র সাহায্যে কৃত ।

spĕc′-ū-lāte, *v. i.* & *t.* 1. To meditate ; to revolve in the mind ; চিন্তা করা, অনুধ্যান করা ; মনে মনে আলোচনা করা । 2. To purchase land, stock, goods, etc. in expectation of realising larger profits by their future sales ; as, to *speculate* in coffee ; ভবিষ্যতে প্রচুর লাভে বিক্রয়ের আশায় ভূমি, কোম্পানীর কাগজ, মাল প্রভৃতি ক্রয় করা, ঝুঁকিদার ব্যবসায়ে প্রবৃত্ত হওয়া । ***Verb t.*** To invest mony in a risky enterprise ; ঝুঁকিদার ব্যবসায়ে টাকা ফেলা । **–la′-tion**, *n.* 1. Mental view of anything in its various aspects and relations ; contemplation ; পরিচিন্তন, বিভাবন, অনুধ্যান । 2. Hazardous financial transactions ; ঝুঁকিদার ব্যবসায় । 3. The theory about a subject ; কোন বিষয়ক মতবাদ বা সিদ্ধান্ত (হিন্দুঃ) । 4. A kind of card game ; একপ্রকার তাস খেলা । **–la-tive**, *adj.* **–la-tive-ly**, *adv.* **–la-tive-ness**, *n.* **–lat′-or**, *n.* 1. A theorist ; উপপত্তিকারী । 2. One who engages in speculation ; ঝুঁকিদার ব্যবসায়ে প্রবৃত্ত ব্যক্তি ।

spĕc′-ū-lŭm, *n.* 1. An instrument for inspecting or dilating certain parts of the body that they may be attentively examined ; যোনি প্রভৃতি শরীরের কোন কোন অংশ পরিদর্শন ও প্রসারণের জন্য যন্ত্রবিশেষ, প্রসারক । 2. A mirror ; a mirror of polished metal ; মুকুর, দর্পণ ; ধাতুনির্ম্মিত দর্পণ । 3. (*Ornitho.*) A bright spot on animals, often iridescent, as upon the wing of a duck, tail of a pea-cock ; (পক্ষি-তত্ত্ব) পক্ষীর পক্ষ, পুচ্ছ, প্রভৃতির উপর নানাবর্ণদীপ্ত চিহ্ন, যথা ময়ূরের চন্দ্রক । **Speculum metal** — দর্পণ-ধাতু (হিঃ কোঃ), [একপ্রকার মিশ্র ধাতু যাহা অতি উত্তম রূপে পালিশ করা যাইতে পারে ।]

spĕd, *p. t.* & *p. p.* of SPEED. (which see).

speech (spēch), *n.* 1. The faculty of speaking ; বাক্‌শক্তি, বাক্ । 2. Language ; word ; ভাষা ; শব্দসমূহ । 3. That which is spoken ; talk ; conversation ; কথিত বাক্য ; বচন, উক্তি, বাক্য, বাণী ; আলাপ ; কথাবার্ত্তা । 4. A formal public discourse ; বক্তৃতা । 5. (*Mus.*) The sounding quality of organs etc. ; অর্গেন প্রভৃতি যন্ত্রের ধ্বনি উৎপাদিকা শক্তি । **Speech-day** — বিদ্যালয় প্রভৃতির পুরস্কার বিতরণের দিন । **Speech-reading**—বক্তার ওষ্ঠাধর সঞ্চালন দৃষ্টে মূকবধিরগণের বক্তৃতার অর্থবোধ ।

Set speech—পূর্ব্বে প্রস্তুত বক্তৃতা। King's or Queen's speech—রাজা বা রাণীর বক্তৃতা। [পার্লেমেণ্টের উদ্বোধনকালে রাজা বা রাণী স্বয়ং বা প্রতিনিধি দ্বারা মন্ত্রিবর্গ কর্ত্তৃক লিখিত স্বরাষ্ট্র ও পররাষ্ট্র বিষয় ব্যাপার সম্বন্ধে সংক্ষিপ্ত উক্তিবিশিষ্ট যে বক্তৃতা পাঠ করেন বা করাইয়া থাকেন।]

speech'-i-fȳ (spēch-), *v. i.* (*Contempt.*) To make a speech; to harangue; (অবজ্ঞাচ্ছলে) বক্তৃতা দেওয়া: গলাবাজি করা। **–fi-ca'-tion,** *n.* **–fi-er,** *n.*

speech'-lĕss (spēch-), *adj.* 1. Dumb; মূক, বোবা। 2. Unable to speak for a time; as, *speechless* with wonder; নিৰ্বাক, মৌন, নীরব, বাক্‌শূন্য। **–ly,** *adv.* **–ness,** *n.*

speed (spēd), *n.*, *v. i.* & *t.* 1. (*Archaic*) Success; prosperity; (অপ্রঃ) কৃতকার্য্যতা, সফলতা, সিদ্ধি, সাফল্য; উন্নতি, অভ্যুদয়। 2. Swiftness; rate of motion; দ্রুতত্ব, ক্ষিপ্রতা, সত্বরতা, সত্বরত্ব; গতিবেগ, বেগ। *Verb i.* 1. To hasten; ত্বরান্বিত করা, দ্রুত করা, ক্ষিপ্র করা। 2. To go fast; দ্রুতবেগে চলা। *Verb t.* 1. (*Archaic*) To make successful or prosperous; সফলকাম করা, সিদ্ধকাম করা, সমৃদ্ধ করা। 2. To dismiss with good wishes or friendly services; শুভ কামনা জ্ঞাপনপূর্ব্বক বিদায় দেওয়া। 3. To wish God-speed to; কাহারো কল্যাণ কামনা করা। **Speed indicator, Speed recorder**—চালমাপক (ইং কোঃ)। **God speed**—উন্নতি, অভ্যুদয়। **God speed you!**—ঈশ্বর তোমার কল্যাণ করুন।

speed'-ĕr (spēd-) *n.* 1. One who, or that which, speeds; দ্রুততা সাধক ব্যক্তি বা বস্তু। 2. Any of various devices for regulating or increasing the speed of a machinery; যন্ত্রের গতি নিয়মন বা বর্দ্ধনের জন্য বিভিন্ন প্রকার কৌশল।

speed'-ȳ (spēd-), *adj.* Quick; ক্ষিপ্র, দ্রুত, সত্বর, ত্বরান্বিত। **–i-ly,** *adv.* In a speedy manner; দ্রুত, তূর্ণ, শীঘ্র, সত্বরতা সহকারে। **–i-ness,** *n.*

speiss (spīs), *n.* The product first obtained when some lead ores are smelted; কোন কোন আকরোত্থিত সীসক গালাইয়া শোধন করার সময় যে লৌহ, তাল (arsenic), প্রভৃতির মিশ্র প্রাপ্ত হওয়া যায়।

spe-lae'-ăn (-lē-), *adj.* Of, or pertaining to, a cave or caves; dwelling in a cave or caves; গুহাসম্বন্ধীয়, গহ্বরসম্বন্ধীয়; গুহাবাসী, গহ্বরবাসী।

spĕl'-i-căn, *n.* Same as SPILLIKIN.

spĕll, *n.* An incantation; charm; যাদুমন্ত্র; যাদু, গুণ, তুক, করণ-প্রয়োগ, মন্ত্রতন্ত্র। **Spellbound**—মন্ত্রমুগ্ধ, মোহিত, বিমোহিত।

spĕll, *v. t.* 1. To tell the letter of a word, বানান করা, বর্ণবিন্যাস করা। 2. To read with labour or difficulty; বহুকষ্টে পড়া। 3. To make up a word; কোন শব্দ গঠন করা। 4. To signify; to constitute; as, this *spells* ruin for him; to involve; সূচনা করা; সংঘটন করা; সংসৃষ্ট করা। **To spell backward**—To repeat or write the letters of a word in reverse order; কোন শব্দের অক্ষরসমূহ উল্টাভাবে লিখা বা আবৃত্তি করা। To misinterpret; কদর্থ করা, অর্থ বিকৃত করা, অর্থ বিপর্য্যয় করা। **To spell baker**—To do a difficult task; কঠিন কার্য্য করা, কষ্টসাধ্য কার্য্য সম্পাদন করা।

spĕll, *n.* & *v. t.* 1. Turn of work; as, did a *spell* of carpentering; পালা, চোট। 2. A short period; as, wait for a *spell*; স্বল্পকাল। *Verb t.* (*Rare*) To relieve; (কচিদ্ ব্যবহৃত) কাহারো স্থান গ্রহণ করিয়া তাহাকে অবসর দেওয়া।

spĕll'-ĕr, *n.* 1. One who, or that which, spells; বর্ণবিন্যাসকারী। 2. Same as SPELLING-BOOK.

spĕll'-ing, *n.* The act of one who spells; বানান, বর্ণসংযোগ, বর্ণবিন্যাস। **Spelling-book**—বানান শিক্ষা দেওয়ার জন্য পুস্তক, বানানশিক্ষা।

spĕlt, *p. t.* & *p. p.* of SPELL (which see).

spĕlt, *n.* German wheat; একপ্রকার গোধূম—যাহা হইতে অতি উৎকৃষ্ট ময়দা প্রস্তুত হয়।

spĕl'-tĕr, *n.* (*Commerce*) Zinc; (বাণিজ্য) দস্তা।

spence (spĕns), **spense** (spĕns), *n. s.* (*Archaic*) A place where provisions are kept; a buttery; a larder; (অপ্রঃ) খাদ্যদ্রব্য রাখার স্থান; যে কক্ষে মদ্য প্রভৃতি পানীয় এবং খাদ্যদ্রব্য রক্ষিত হয়; মাংসাদি রাখার জন্য প্রকোষ্ঠ।

spĕn'-cĕr, *n.* (*Hist.*) A short over-jacket worn by man or woman; (ইতিহাস) একপ্রকার খাটো জামা। [Earl of Spencer এর নাম হইতে গৃহীত।]

spĕn'-cĕr, *n.* (*Naut.*) A trysail; (নৌবিদ্যা) একপ্রকার পাইল।

Spĕn'-cĕr-ism, *n.* The system advocated by Herbert Spencer (born 1820) in his works, the application of the principles of evolution to the phenomena of mind and society; হারবার্ট স্পেনসারের মতবাদ—অর্থাৎ মানসিক এবং সমাজ-সংক্রান্ত ব্যাপারের ক্রমবিকাশতত্ত্বের প্রয়োগ। **–ce'-ri-an,** *adj.* **–ce'-ri-an-ism,** *n.*

spĕnd, *v. t.* & *i.* 1. To expend; ব্যয় করা, খরচ করা, উড়াইয়া দেওয়া। 2. To waste; to squander; as, to *spend* one's estate in gaming; অপব্যয় করা; অপচয় করা, নষ্ট করা, উড়াইয়া দেওয়া। 3. To exhaust; to deprive of force; as, the storm is *spent*; অবসন্ন করা; শক্তিহীন করা। 4 To pass; as, to *spend* time; কাটান, যাপন করা, অতিবাহিত করা, ক্ষেপণ করা। *Verb i.* 1. To expend money; to consume; to waste; খরচ করা; নষ্ট করা; অপব্যয় করা, উড়াইয়া দেওয়া। 2. To lose force or strength; শক্তি লোপ পাওয়া, শক্তিহীন হওয়া। 3. To be consumed; ফুরাইয়া

যাওয়া। Spend′-a-ble, *adj.* Spend′-er, *n.* Spendthrift — অপব্যয়ী লোক, বেহিসাবী লোক, অতিব্যয়ী। Spent herring—ডিম ছাড়িয়াছে এরূপ হেরিং মাছ।

spense (spĕns), *n.* Same as SPENCE (which see.)

Spĕn-sē′-ri-ăn, *adj.* Of, or pertaining to, the English poet Spenser; ইংরাজকবি স্পেন্সার সম্বন্ধীয়।

spĕnt, *p. p.* & *p. t.* of SPEND (which see).

spêrm, *n.* Animal seed; বীর্য্য, শুক্র, রেতঃ, ধাতু (Also see SEMEN). **Sperm-cell**—শুক্রকণ (হিঃ কোঃ)।

spêrm, *n.* (Also *sperm-whale*) Same as CACHALOT (which see). **Sperm-oil** — তিমি বিশেষের খুলির অভ্যন্তরস্থ চর্ব্বিবৎ বস্তু হইতে প্রাপ্ত তৈল।

spĕr-mă-cē′-ti, *n.* A white fatty substance obtained chiefly from the cavities in the skull of sperm-whale; একজাতীয় তিমিমৎস্যের মস্তকের খুলির ভিতরে প্রাপ্ত একপ্রকার শ্বেতবর্ণ চর্ব্বিবৎ পদার্থ [এই পদার্থ মলম, মোমবাতি প্রভৃতি প্রস্তুতে ব্যবহৃত হয়।]

spêr′-mă-phōre, *n.* (*Bot.*) Same as PLACENTA.

spêr′-mă-rȳ, *n.* A sperm-gland; a testis; শুক্রকোষ, শুক্রাশয়, শুক্রাণ্বাশয়; অণ্ডকোষ।

spêr-măt′-ic, *adj.* 1. Consisting of sperm; seminal; শুক্রাত্মক; শুক্রসম্বন্ধীয়। 2. Pertaining to spermary; শুক্রকোষসম্বন্ধীয়। **Spermatic cord**—রেতঃরজ্জু, যে শিরা-গুচ্ছদ্বারা অণ্ড বিলম্বিত থাকে।

spêr′-mă′-tin, *n.* An organic substance resembling mucin and albumin found in the *vesiculoe seminales*; শুক্রস্থিত জৈবপদার্থবিশেষ।

spêr′-mă-tism, *n.* 1. Emission of semen; শুক্রপাত, শুক্রনির্গম। 2. The theory that germ in animals is produced by spermatic animalcules; পুরুষের শুক্র শুক্রকীটাণুদ্বারা উৎপাদিত হয়—এই মত, শুক্রকীটাণুবাদ। —tist, *n.* —tize, *v. i.*

spêr-mă′-ti-ŭm (-shi-), *n.* A minute spore within a spermogonium; নিষেককোষ (সাঃ পঃ)।

spêr′-mă-tō-blăst, *n.* Certain stalk-like filaments in the seminal ducts upon which the spermatozoa are developed; শুক্রবাহীশিরার বৃন্ত বা কেশরসমূহ—যাহাতে শুক্রকীট বিকাশ প্রাপ্ত হয়।

spêr′-măt-ō-cele (-sēl), *n.* A morbid distension of the epididymis and *vas deferens*; শুক্রবাহী শিরার রোগজনিত স্ফীতি।

spêr-mă-tō-gĕn′-ō-sis, *n.* Development of spermatozoa; শুক্রকীটের উৎপত্তি, শুক্রজনি (হিঃ কোঃ), শুক্রোৎপত্তি। —tog′-en ous, *adj.* —tog′-e-ny, *n.*

spĕr-mă-tŏl′-ō-ġȳ, *n.* The knowledge of sperm; শুক্রতত্ত্ব, বীর্য্যবিজ্ঞান —to-log′-i-cal, *adj.* —to-log′-ist, *n.*

spêr′-măt-ō-phōre, *n.* A case of albuminous matter in which the bundles of the spermatozoa are enclosed; যে কোষের ভিতর শুক্রকীটাণু আবদ্ধ থাকে, শুক্রকীটাণুকোষ।

spêr-mă-tōr-rhoe′-ă (-ē-), *n.* Emission of the semen without copulation; অনিচ্ছায় শুক্রস্রাব রোগ, শুক্রমেহ, ধাতুদৌর্ব্বল্য।

spêr-mă-tō-zō′-ŏn, (*Pl.* -ZOA) *n.* 1. A spermatic animalcula; শুক্রাণু, শুক্রকীট, শুক্রজীব (হিঃ কোঃ), শুক্রজন্তু (ঐ), কীটাণু, বীর্য্যাণু। 2. Similar element in lower plants; উদ্ভিজ্জাদির অনুরূপ বস্তু।

spêrm′-ism, *n.* Same as SPERMATISM. —ist, *n.*

spêr′-mō-blăst, *n.* Same as SPERMATOBLAST (which see).

spêr′-mō-dêrm, *n.* The whole integument of a seed; বীজাত্মক (সাঃ পঃ)।

spêr′-mō dŭct, *n.* A spermatic-duct; বীর্য্যবাহী শিরা।

spêr-mō-gō′-ni-ŭm, (*Pl.* SPERMOGONIA) *n.* The cysts containing spermatia in lichens; তন্তুকুণ্ড (সাঃ পঃ)।

spêr-mŏl′-ō-ġȳ, *n.* 1. Same as SPERMATOLOGY. 2. (*Bot.*) Study of seeds; (উদ্ভিদ্‌বিদ্যা) বীজতত্ত্ব, বীজবিদ্যা।

spêr-mō-phȳt′-ă, *n.* One of the four division of the vegetable-kingdom including flowering plants; বীজোদ্ভিদ্ (সাঃ পঃ)।

spew (-spü), **spue** (spü), *v. t.* & *i.* 1. To vomit; বমন করা। 2. To eject; নির্গতকরা, উদ্বমিত করা। *Verb i.* (Of a cannon) To droop as the muzzle on account of too rapid firing; (কামান সম্পর্কে) অতিদ্রুত গোলাবর্ষণহেতু অগ্রভাগ নত হইয়া পড়া।

sphăc′-ĕ-late, *v. t.* To affect with gangrene; পচাইতে আরম্ভ করা। —la′-tion, *n.*

sphaer′-(ō) (sfēr-)—In combination (Gk. *spharia* a ball); অন্য শব্দের সংযোগে গোলকার্থে ব্যবহৃত হয়।

sphĕn′-ō-, *pref.* Pertaining to wedge; resembling a wedge in shape; কাজলাসম্বন্ধীয়; কাজলার আকৃতি, কীলকাকৃতি।

sphĕn′-ō-grăm, *n.* A cuneiform character; কীলকাকৃতি অক্ষর, বাণাকৃতি অক্ষর, শরাকৃতি অক্ষর।

sphē′-noid (-nɔ̄yd), *adj.* & *n.* Wedge-shaped; কীলকাকৃতি। *Noun.* A wedge-shaped bone; করোটীর নিম্নস্থ কাজলার আকৃতি অস্থি, কীলকাকৃতি অস্থি।

sphere (sfēr), *n.* & *v. t.* 1. A body contained under a single surface, which, in every part, is equally distant from a point within, called the centre; globe; পরিমণ্ডল (ব্রজঃ হিন্দু), বর্ত্তুল, গোল (হিঃ কোঃ), মণ্ডল (ঐ); গোলক। 2. A heavenly body; জ্যোতিষ্ক, জ্যোতির্গোলক, পিণ্ড। 3. (*Astorn.*) The apparent surface of the heavens; ক্ষেত্র, প্রদেশ, আকাশমণ্ডল

গগনমণ্ডল, নভোমণ্ডল, অন্তরিক্ষমণ্ডল। **4.** (*Log., Rare*) Same as EXTENSION. **5.** Compass ; province ; as, the *sphere* of his activities ; field of action ; surroundings ; কার্য্যক্ষেত্র, বিষয় (হিঃ কোঃ) ; প্রকরণ (ঐ) ; অধিকার (ঐ), পরিধি, প্রসর ; পারিপার্শ্বিক-অবস্থা, প্রতিবেশ। **6.** Rank ; position in society ; পদবী ; সামাজিক পদ। **7.** A globe representing the earth or the apparent heavens ; গোলক। **8.** (*Poet.*) Atmosphere, heavens ; (কবিতায়) বায়ুমণ্ডল ; দ্যুলোক। ***Verb t.*** To enclose in a sphere ; গোলকে বদ্ধ করা। **Spher'-y,** *adj.* **Armillary sphere**—See ARMILLARY. **Oblique sphere**—যে স্থানের আহ্নিক-গতির বৃত্তসমূহ দিকচক্রবালের সহিত তির্য্যগ্‌ভাবে থাকে—তত্রত্য আকাশমণ্ডল [বিষুববৃত্ত ও মেরুমধ্যবর্ত্তী কোন স্থানে অবস্থিত দ্রষ্টার নিকট এইরূপ প্রতিভাত হইয়া থাকে।] **Parallel sphere**—যে স্থানে আহ্নিক-গতির বৃত্তসমূহ দিকচক্রবালের সহিত সমান্তরাল থাকে—তত্রত্য আকাশমণ্ডল। [মেরুদ্বয়ের অন্যতর কোন স্থানে অবস্থিত দ্রষ্টার নিকট এরূপ প্রতিভাত হইয়া থাকে।] **Right sphere** — See RIGHT. **Sphere geometry**—গোলীয় জ্যামিতি। **Sphere music** — Same as MUSIC OF THE SPHERES. **Doctrine of the spheres**—গোলীয় জ্যামিতি বা গোলীয় ত্রিকোণমিতি। **Harmony of the spheres**—Same as MUSIC OF THE SPHERES. **Sphere of influence** — (আন্তর্জাতিক আইন) প্রভাবক্ষেত্র। [যে ভূখণ্ডের ভিতর কোন জাতির রাজনীতিক প্রভাব বিস্তারে বা স্বার্থসাধনে অন্যান্য জাতিসমূহ বাধা প্রদান করেন না।] **To make sphere-shaped** — পরিমণ্ডলাকৃতি করা।

sphĕr'-ic, *adj.* & *n.* **1.** Pertaining to a sphere ; গোলক সম্বন্ধীয়। **2.** Planetary ; গ্রহসম্বন্ধীয়। **3.** Of the heavens ; স্বর্গীয়। **4.** Exhalted ; মহিমান্বিত, গৌরবান্বিত। ***Noun. (pl.)*** Geometry and Trigonometry of the sphere ; গোলীয় জ্যামিতি বা পরিমিতি, গোলাধ্যায় (সাঃ পঃ), গোল-গ্রন্থ, গোলপ্রবন্ধ।

sphêr'-i-căl, *adj.* **1.** Having the form of a sphere ; বর্ত্তুলাকৃতি, মণ্ডলাকৃতি, গোলাকার (সাঃ পঃ)। **2.** Pertaining to a sphere ; গোলকসম্বন্ধীয়, গোলীয় (হিঃ কোঃ)। **3.** Planetary ; গ্রহসম্বন্ধীয়। **—ly.** *adv.* **Spherical excess**—গোলীয় বৃদ্ধি (হিঃ কোঃ)। **Spherical geometry**—গোলীয় জ্যামিতি (হিঃ কোঃ), গোলীয় ভূমিতি (ঐ)। **Spherical harmonic** — গোলীয় হরাত্মক (হিঃ কোঃ)। **Spherical trigonometry** — গোলীয় ত্রিকোণমিতি (হিঃ কোঃ), গোলমিতি (সাঃ পঃ)। **Spherical triangle, polygon** — গোলকের বৃত্তের খণ্ডদ্বারা রচিত ত্রিভুজ, পঞ্চভুজ প্রভৃতি, চাপজাত্য ত্রিভুজ।

sphĕr'-ō-grăph, *n.* An instrument for the application of spherical geometry to navigation ; পোত চালনায় গোলীয় জ্যামিতি প্রয়োগের জন্য যন্ত্রবিশেষ।

sphē'-roid (-roid), *n.* A body or figure approaching to a sphere, but not perfectly spherical ; বর্ত্তুলপ্রায়, অণ্ডগোল (হিঃ কোঃ), গোলপ্রায় (ঐ), প্রগত উপবর্ত্তুল, গোলাভাস, মণ্ডলাভাস, বর্ত্তুলাভাস (সাঃ পঃ), উপবর্ত্তুল (সাঃ পঃ)। **—roi'-dal,** *adj.* **—roi-dal-ly,** *adv.* **—roi-dic'-i-ty,** *n.* **Oblate spheroid**—প্রথমাণ্ড গোল (হিঃ কোঃ). অভিগত উপবর্ত্তুল (সাঃ পঃ)। **Prolate spheroid**—দ্বিতীয়াণ্ড গোল (হিঃ কোঃ)।

sphē-rŏm'-ē-têr, *n.* An instrument for measuring the thickness of small bodies, finding radius of spheres, etc. ; ক্ষুদ্র বস্তুর বেধ, মণ্ডলের ব্যাসার্দ্ধ, প্রভৃতি পরিমাপের জন্য যন্ত্রবিশেষ, বর্ত্তুলমান, গোলমাপক (হিঃ কোঃ)।

sphêr'-ūle, *n.* A small sphere ; ক্ষুদ্র গোলক। **—u-lar, —u-late** *adjs.*

sphêr'-ū-līte, *n.* A vitreous globule as constituent of some rocks ; কোন কোনরূপ প্রস্তরের উপাদান-স্বরূপ একপ্রকার কাচধর্ম্মী গুলিকা। **—lit'-ic,** *adj.* **—lit-ize,** *v. t.*

sphinc'-têr (sfingk-), *n.* A muscle that contracts or shuts an orifice or opening which it surrounds ; মলদ্বার প্রভৃতি স্বাভাবিক রন্ধ্রের মুখরোধক গোলাকার পেশী, অন্তর্গুদবলয়। **—al, —i-al, —ic,** *adjs.*

sphinx (sfingks), *n.* **1.** A fabulous creature near Thebes that used to propose riddles to travellers, and tear to pieces those who could not solve them, usually represented as having the body of a lion and the face and breast of a young woman ; প্রাচীন গ্রীসের অন্তঃপাতী থিবস্ নগর-বাসিনী দানবী বিশেষ। ইহার বদন ও বক্ষঃস্থল যুবতীর মত এবং দেহ সিংহাকৃতি ছিল। এই দানবী পথিকদিগকে একটী সমস্যা পূরণ করিতে দিত। তাহারা উহা পূরণে অকৃতকার্য্য হইলে সে তাহাদিগকে খরনখরনিকরদ্বারা খণ্ড খণ্ড করিয়া ফেলিত,

Sphinx.

নারসিংহী। Oedipus নারসিংহীর সমস্যাপূরণে কৃতকার্য্য হইলে সে ভৃগুপাত-দ্বারা প্রাণত্যাগ করে। [Sphinxএর সমস্যাটী এই—এমন জীবের নাম কর যে প্রভাতে চারি পায়ে, মধ্যাহ্নে দুই পায়ে এবং অপরাহ্নে তিন পায়ে (অর্থাৎ বার্দ্ধক্যে যষ্টি ভর করিয়া) চলে (উত্তর—মনুষ্য)।] **2.** (*Egypt. Myth.*) A figure having the body of a lion, and a human (male or female) head ; (মিসরীয় প্রত্নতত্ত্ব)

সিংহের মত দেহ এবং মানুষ (নর বা নারীর মত) মুখবিশিষ্ট মূর্ত্তি, নারসিংহী। [Gizeh নগরীর পিরামিডের সন্নিকটে একটী বিরাট নারসিংহীর মূর্ত্তি আছে। ইহা উচ্চে ৬৬ ফিট এবং দৈর্ঘ্যে ১২২ ফিট। ইহার বক্ষের উপর অবলম্বিত করিয়া একটী ক্ষুদ্র মন্দির নির্ম্মিত হইয়াছে।] 3. Hawk-moth (also *sphinx-moth*); একপ্রকার তসরে পোকা। 4. A kind of baboon (also *sphinx baboon*); একজাতীয় মর্কট।

sphră-gĭs'-tĭcs, *n.* The science of seals, as bearing upon the age of documents to which they are attached; মোহরতত্ত্ব। [যে বিদ্যা দ্বারা কোন দলিলের মোহরাদি দর্শনে উহার সময় নির্ণয় করা যায়।]

sphy̆g'-mō-grăm, *n.* A record produced by sphygmograph; নাড়ীস্পন্দনলেখ কর্ত্তৃক অঙ্কিত লিপি।

sphy̆g'-mō-grăph, *n.* A contrivance for indicating and registering the state of the pulse; নাড়ীস্পন্দনলেখ।

sphy̆g-mŏm'-ĕ-tėr, *n.* An instrument for measuring pulsation; নাড়ীস্পন্দনমান।

sphy̆g-mō'-phōne, *n.* An instrument devised to enable a person to determine the rhythms etc. of the pulse at a distance by means of electric wire; বৈদ্যুতিক তারদ্বারা দূরবর্ত্তী ব্যক্তির নাড়ীস্পন্দন নির্ণয়ের জন্য যন্ত্রবিশেষ, দূরনাড়ীস্পন্দনলেখ।

sphy̆g-mō'-scōpe, *n.* An instrument for rendering the pulsation audible or visible; নাড়ীস্পন্দন দর্শনযোগ্য বা শ্রবণযোগ্য করার জন্য যন্ত্রবিশেষ, নাড়ীস্পন্দনবীক্ষণ।

sphy̆g'-mŭs, *n.* (*Physiol.*) Pulse; pulsation; (শারীরবিজ্ঞান) নাড়ী; নাড়ীস্পন্দন।

spī'-că, *n.* 1. (*Bot.*) A spike; (উদ্ভিদ্‌বিদ্যা) মঞ্জরী, চিত্রা (হিঃ কোঃ)। 2. (*Surg.*) A spiral bandage with reversed turns; একপ্রকার কুণ্ডলীবৎ বস্ত্রবন্ধনী। 3. A star of the first magnitude in the constellation virgo; চিত্রা (সাঃ পঃ)। **–ate, Spi-cat-ed,** *adjs.*

spīce, *n.* & *v. t.* 1. A vegetable-production aromatic to the smell, and pungent to the taste; সুগন্ধি মসলা, গরম মসলা, গন্ধদ্রব্য, কর্পূরাদি বর্গ (ভাবঃ প্রঃ)। 2. A small admixture; a flavour; as, there is a *spice* of conceit in him; লেশ; গন্ধ, আভাস, নামগন্ধ। *Verb t.* 1. To season with spice; গরম মসলা সংযোগ করা। 2. To embalm; মসলাদি দ্বারা সুবাসিত করা। 3. To smack; নামগন্ধ থাকা, আভাস থাকা। 4. To mix up with something which gives flavour or zest; "They will patronise a highly *spiced* sensational melodrama": রসাল করা, মজাদার করা। **Spice-bush**—আমেরিকাদেশীয় সুরভি গুল্মবিশেষ। **Spice mill**—মসলা পেষণের জন্য যাঁতা। **Spice-wood**—Same as SPICE-BUSH.

spĭck, *adj.* **Spick and span**—Brand-new; new and fresh; টাটকা নূতন, আনকোরা নূতন, ফিটফাট, চাকনচিকণ।

spĭc'-ūle, *n.* 1. A little sharp needle-shaped body; ছুঁচাল বস্তু। 2. One of the minute limy or flinty particles found in sponges; (প্রাণিবিদ্যা) শোষকের (স্পঞ্জ) ভিতরে প্রাপ্ত চূণা বা পাথরের কণার মত বস্তু। 3. (*Bot.*) A small or secondary spike; (উদ্ভিদ্‌বিদ্যা) ক্ষুদ্র মঞ্জরী, উপমঞ্জরী। **–u-lar, –u-late,** *adjs.*

spīc'-y̆, *adj.* 1. Pertaining to spice; flavoured with spice; গরমমসলাসম্বন্ধীয়; গরম মসলা দ্বারা সুবাসিত। 2. Pungent; smart; racy; as, a *spicy* story; ঝাঁঝাল; চোস্ত; তেজাল, সরস, রসাল। 2. Producing or abounding in spice; সুগন্ধি মসলা উৎপাদক, সুগন্ধিমসলাভূয়িষ্ঠ। **Spic'-i-ly,** *adv.* **Spic'-i-ness,** *n.*

spīd'-ėr, *n.* 1. An animal that spins webs for taking its prey; মাকড়সা, উর্ণনাভ [Syn. অষ্টপাদ, উর্ণায়ু, লূতা (cf. লূতাতন্তু), জালিক, তন্তুনাভ, তন্তুবায়, মর্কটক, নন্দ্যাবর্ত্ত (ব্রজঃ বিঃ), লূতিকা, শনক, তন্তুবায়।] 2. An iron pan with long handle used for frying food; ভাজা করার জন্য হাতলওয়ালা বড় চাটু। 3. A trivel; রন্ধনকালে যে লোহার ত্রিপদীর উপর পানপাত্র রাখা হয়। 4. A griddle; চাটু। **–like, –y,** *adjs.* **Spider-catcher**—বিভিন্নপ্রকার পক্ষীর নাম।

Spiders-crab.

Spider-crab—একপ্রকার লম্বা এবং সরু পা ওয়ালা কাঁকড়া। **Spider line**—অতি সূক্ষ্ম মাপের জন্য তুলাযন্ত্রে তারের পরিবর্ত্তে যে মাকড়সার জালের সূতা ব্যবহৃত হয়, সূক্ষ্মদ্রব্য বা দূরত্ব-মাপক যন্ত্রে যে মাকড়সার তন্তু ব্যবহৃত হয়। **Spider-monkey**—একপ্রকার দীর্ঘপদ এবং দীর্ঘলাঙ্গুল কপি। **Spider-wasp**—যে বোলতা শাবকদিগের আহারের জন্য চাকে মাকড়সা সঞ্চিত করিয়া রাখে। **Spider's thread**—মাকড়সার সূতা, উর্ণনাভ-তন্তু।

spie'-gel-ei-sen (spē-gėl-ē-zn), *n.* A kind of cast iron containing a large percentage of manganese and carbon; অঙ্গার, ম্যাঙ্গেনিজ, প্রভৃতি পূর্ণ ঢালা লৌহ।

spif(f)'-li-cāte, *v. t.* (*Slang*) To crush; to beat severely; (ইতর ভাষায়) ধ্বংস করা; বেদম মারা, মারিয়া পাট পাট করা।

spĭg'-ŏt, *n.* A small peg or plug; গোঁজ, ছিপি (পিপার ছিদ্র রোধ করার জন্য)।

incision into ; as, to *cut* one's finger ; কাটা ; ছেদন করা ; ক্ষত করা। **2.** To separate by cutting ; as, to *cut* a slice of meat ; কাটিয়া খণ্ড খণ্ড করা, কাটিয়া টুকরা টুকরা করা। **3.** To carve ; মাংসাদি খণ্ড খণ্ড করা কুটা। **4.** To trim or pare as hair or nail ; নখ, চুল প্রভৃতি কাটা। **5.** To fell as wood ; to hew as timber ; কাঠ প্রভৃতি কাটা ; কুঠার দ্বারা তক্তা প্রভৃতি ছেদন করা। **6.** To intersect ; as, lines *cut* one another ; ছেদন করা, কাটা। **7.** To fashion or shape by cutting ; as, to *cut* a coat or diamond ; to engrave as a plate, etc. ; to excavate, as a ditch etc. ; কাটিয়া গঠন করা ; ফলক প্রভৃতি খোদিত করা ; (খাল প্রভৃতি) কাটা। **8.** To wound the feelings of ; as, he was *cut* to the quick ; মর্ম্মাহত করা, মনে আঘাত দেওয়া। **9.** To perform ; as, to *cut* a caper, dash, or joke, etc. ; করা। **10.** To absent oneself from ; to avoid ; as, to *cut* a lecture ; অনুপস্থিত থাকা ; পরিহার করা। **11.** To abridge, as a drama ; নাটক প্রভৃতি সংক্ষেপ করা, কাটা ছাঁটা। **12.** To reduce in amount, as rates, prices, etc. ; মূল্য, প্রভৃতি হ্রাস করা। **13.** To divide in two or more parts as a pack of cards ; তাস কাটা। **14.** To mow or reap, as hay, corn, etc. ; ঘাস, শস্য প্রভৃতি কাটা। **15.** To strike, as with a whip, etc. ; চাবুক প্রভৃতি দ্বারা আঘাত করা। **16.** To decline to recognise ; না চিনা। **17.** To renounce, as, to *cut* a connexion ; ছিন্ন করা। ***Verb i.*** **1.** To do the work of an edge tool ; to make an incision ; ধারাল অস্ত্রের কাজ করা ; অস্ত্র বসাইয়া কাটা। **2.** To be divided as by a knife ; as, cheese *cuts* well ; ছুরি প্রভৃতি দ্বারা খণ্ডিত হওয়া। কাটা যাওয়া। **3.** To use a cutting instrument ; ধারাল অস্ত্র ব্যবহার করা। **4.** To pass (with *across, through,* etc..) ; অতিক্রম করা, চলিয়া যাওয়া। **5.** (*Slang*) To run away ; (ইতর ভাষায়) দৌড়িয়া যাওয়া। **6.** To strike with a whip etc. ; চাবুক প্রভৃতি দ্বারা আঘাত করা। **7.** To divide a pack of cards in two parts ; তাস কাটা। **Cut'-ting-ly,** *adv.* **Cut-glass**—Glass with a surface shaped or ornamented by grinding etc. ; বেলোয়ারি কাচ। **Cut-purse**—গাঁইট-কাটা। **Cut-throat**—হত্যাকারী ; গলা-কাটা। **Cut and come again**—Plenty or abundance, (a hospitable phrase) ; প্রাচুর্য্য, খাদ্য-পানীয়ের প্রাচুর্য্য। **To cut across**—To go or pass straight ; সোজা চলিয়া যাওয়া। **To cut a dash or figure**—To make a show ; to be conspicuous ; ভড়ক দেখান, জাঁক দেখান ; (নিজকে) জাহির করা, সুপ্রকট হওয়া। **To cut a joke**—To perform a joke ; ঠাট্টা করা। **To cut a tooth**—To have it appear through the gum as a child ; শিশুর দাঁত উঠান। **To cut capers**—To dance ; to frisk above ; নাচা কুঁদা ; লম্ফ ঝম্প দেওয়া। **To cut down**—To fell as a tree etc. ; গাছ প্রভৃতি কাটিয়া ফেলা। To curtail ; as, to *cut down* expenses ; সঙ্কোচ করা। **To cut in**—To enter abruptly ; হঠাৎ প্রবেশ করা। **To cut lots**—To determine lots by cutting cards ; তাস কাটিয়া ভাগ্য পরীক্ষা করা। **To cut off**—To sever ; to put an end to ; to intercept (communication etc.) ; ছেদন করা ; শেষ করা ; বাধা দেওয়া। **To cut off (a child) with a shilling**—To disinherit by bequeathing a shilling ; চরমপত্র দ্বারা এক শিলিং প্রদান করিয়া কাহাকেও উত্তরাধিকার হইতে বঞ্চিত করা, ত্যাজ্য সন্তান করা। **To cut one dead**—To decline to recognise an acquainted person in public ; কোন পরিচিত ব্যক্তিকে লোকসমাজে চিনিয়াও না চিনা। **To cut one lucky or one's stick**—To go ; যাওয়া। **To cut one's eye, teeth**—To become knowing or sharp ; চালাক বা জ্ঞাতসার হওয়া। **To cut one's way**—To force a passage through opposing forces ; ঠেলিয়া পথ করিয়া লওয়া। **To cut out**—To remove by cutting ; কাটিয়া ফেলা। To supplant ; কৌশলে স্থানচ্যুত করা। To shape (*lit.* & *fig.*) ; (শব্দানুযায়ী এবং লক্ষণায়) গড়া, গঠন করা। (*Naut.*) To seize and carry off (a vessel) from a harbour or from under the fires of an enemy ; (নৌ-বিদ্যা) পোতাশ্রয় হইতে অথবা শত্রুর গোলাবৃষ্টির মধ্যে হইতে (জাহাজ) ধরিয়া লইয়া যাওয়া। **To cut short**—To abridge ; সংক্ষেপ করা। **To cut the coat according to the cloth**—See under CLOTH. **To cut the (Gordian) knot**—To effect anything by short and strong measures ; কোন গোলমেলে বিষয় সোজাসুজি মীমাংসা করা। [ফ্রিজিয়া দেশের জনৈক কৃষক একটি গ্রন্থি বাঁধিয়া রাখে। এই গ্রন্থির বিষয় এই প্রবাদ প্রচলিত হয় যে ব্যক্তি উহা খুলিতে পারিবে সে সমগ্র এসিয়ার সাম্রাজ্য-লাভ করিবে। মহাবীর অলীকসুন্দর দিগ্বিজয় ব্যপদেশে ফ্রিজিয়ায় আসিলে পর তাহাকে এই গ্রন্থি প্রদর্শিত হয়। অলীকসুন্দর উহা তৎক্ষণাৎ তরবারি দ্বারা দ্বিখণ্ডিত করিয়া বলিলেন, "এই ভাবেই আমরা আমাদের গ্রন্থি ছেদন করিয়া থাকি।"] **To cut the ground from under one**—To leave an adversary no ground to stand on by disproving all his arguments ; প্রতিপক্ষের সমস্ত যুক্তি খণ্ডন করিয়া তাহাকে নিরুপায় করা। **To cut to the heart, To cut to the quick**—To wound the feelings of ; মর্ম্মে আঘাত করা, আঁতে ঘা দেওয়া। **To cut up, to cut in pieces**—To twisted and wound ; চরকার কাঠি, টাকু, টেকো, টক্র, টাকুর। [Syn. টক্র, তর্কু, তকুটী, সূত্রতর্কুটী, মেরুযন্ত্র।] 2. A slender-pointed rod or pin which turns round, or on which anything turns ; যে সূক্ষ্মাগ্রদণ্ড বা শলাকার উপর কোন কিছু ঘূর্ণিত হইয়া থাকে, ঘূর্ণনশীল সূক্ষ্মাগ্রযন্ত্র বা শলাকা। 3. Anything long or slender ; সরু বা দীর্ঘ বস্তু। 4. A ranging measure of length for yarn ; সুতার দৈর্ঘ্যের মাপবিশেষ। 5. The fusee of a watch ; টেঁক-ঘড়ীর মোচাকার চক্র। ***Verb i.*** To have or grow in a long or slender stalk or body ; সরু অথবা লম্বা ডগা থাকা, সরু অথবা লম্বা বৃন্ত উদ্গত হওয়া। **Spindle-legged, Spindle-shanked**—সরু সরু লম্বা পদবিশিষ্ট। **Spindle shanks** — ঐরূপ পদবিশিষ্ট ব্যক্তি। **Spindle-shaped**—টক্রাকৃতি। **Spindle-shell** — দীর্ঘ মোচাকার সামুদ্রিক শম্বুক। **Spindle-side**—কোন পরিবারের স্ত্রী-শাখা। **Spindle-tree**—টাকু প্রস্তুতের উপযোগী কঠিন কাষ্ঠপ্রদ তরু বা গুল্মবিশেষ। **Spindle-worm**—আমেরিকার তসরে পোকাবিশেষের কীড়া। **Dead spindle** — আবর্ত্তনহীন চক্র। **Live spindle**—আবর্ত্তনশীল চক্র।

spin′-drift, *n.* The spray of salt-water blown along the surface of the sea in heavy winds ; প্রবল ঝঞ্ঝার কালে সাগরপৃষ্ঠোপরি সঞ্চালিত লবণজলকণাসমূহ।

spine, *n.* **1.** The backbone of an animal ; মেরুদণ্ড, শিরদাঁড়া, ব্রহ্মদণ্ড (উত্তরগীতা)। **2.** A ridge of mountains ; গিরিপৃষ্ঠ। **3.** (*Bot.*) Any stiff sharp-pointed process distinguished from a thorn by the absence of vascular tissue ; (উদ্ভিদ্‌বিদ্যা) পত্রকণ্টক। **Spineback** — একজাতীয় মৎস্য—যাহাদের মেরুদণ্ড পিঠের পাখনা সমুহে বা পিঠের পাখনা সমুহের সম্মুখে থাকে। **Spined, Spi′-nose, Spi′-nous,** *adjs.* Having spines ; কণ্টী (সাঃ পঃ)। **Spi-nos′-i-ty,** *n.*

spin′-êl, *n.* **1.** A precious stone often of a red colour like the ruby, but less hard ; পদ্মরাগমণির মত সচরাচর লালবর্ণের কিন্তু অপেক্ষাকৃত কোমল একপ্রকার মূল্যবান প্রস্তর। **2.** A bleached yarn from which tape is made ; যে ধৌত শণসূত্র হইতে ফিতা প্রস্তুত হয়।

spine′-lĕss, *adj.* **1.** Invertebrate ; অমেরুদণ্ডী। **2.** Limp ; weak ; ঢিলা, নরম ; দুর্ব্বল।

spin′-ĕt, *n.* (*Hist.*) An old instrument of music resembling a harpsichord ; প্রাচীনকালের বাদ্যযন্ত্রবিশেষ

spin-i-cêr′-ê-brāte, *adj.* Having brain and spinal cord ; মস্তিষ্ক এবং মেরুদণ্ডবিশিষ্ট।

spi-nif′-êr-ous (-ŭs), *adj.* Having, or producing, spines ; মেরুদণ্ডবিশিষ্ট, মেরুদণ্ডোৎপাদী।

spin′-na-kêr (-ā-), *n.* A triangular sail carried by yachts on the opposite side to the main-sail in running before the wind ; অনুকূল বাতাসে প্রমোদতরীর প্রধান পাইলের বিপরীত পার্শ্বে যে ত্রিকোণ পাইল উড্ডীন করা হয়।

spin′-ner (-êr), *n.* **1.** One who spins ; সূত্রকর্ত্তনকারী। **2.** A spinning machine ; সুতার কল। **3.** A garden spider ; বাগানের মাকড়সা।

spin′-ner-ĕt (-êr-), *n.* An organ with which insects, such as silk-worms, form their silks or web ; যে যন্ত্রদ্বারা গুটিপোকা প্রভৃতি রেসম প্রস্তুত করিয়া থাকে, তন্তুপক (সাঃ পঃ)।

spin′-ney (-ī), *n.* A thicket ; ঝোপ, ঝাড়।

spin′-ning (-ĭng), *n.* The act of one, or that which, spins ; (সূত্রাদি) কর্ত্তন, কাটন। **Spinning gland**—সূতা কাটা থলী। **Spinning-house**—বারাঙ্গনাশোধনাগার। **Spinning-jenny**—এক সঙ্গে একাধিক সূতা কাটিবার জন্য কৌশলবিশেষ। **Spinning-machine**—সূতার কল **Spinning-wheel**—চরকা।

Spinning-wheel.

Spī-no′-zism, *n.* The system of philosophy of Baruch Spinoza who was born in Amsterdam in 1632 ; Spinoza কর্ত্তৃক প্রবর্ত্তিত দার্শনিকবাদ। [স্পিনোজার মতে সকল সত্তার মূলে এক পরম বস্তু বিদ্যমান রহিয়াছে। এই পরম পদার্থ 'জড়' ও 'চেতন', 'স্বাধীনতা' এবং 'অবশ্যম্ভাবিতা' প্রভৃতি পরস্পরাবরুদ্ধ বিষয়সমূহের আশ্রয়স্বরূপ। এই পরম বস্তুকেই স্পিনোজা 'ঈশ্বর' সংজ্ঞা প্রদান করিয়াছেন। স্পিনোজার মতে এই পরম পদার্থ অপর বস্তু নিরপেক্ষ, এবং ইহা ভিন্ন আর দ্বিতীয় বস্তু নাই। অনন্ত চিন্তা (চিদ্‌জ্ঞাপক) এবং অনন্তবিস্তার (জড়-জ্ঞাপক) এই পরম বস্তুর ধর্ম্ম। স্পিনোজার মতে সর্ব্বময় ঈশ্বর কেবলমাত্র অচল-প্রতিষ্ঠ পদ্ধতি অনুসারে কার্য্য করিতে সমর্থ নতুবা ঈশ্বরের প্রকৃতি পরিবর্ত্তনশীল হইয়া পড়ে ; এবং ঈশ্বর ব্যতিরিক্ত অপর কোনরূপ প্রকৃতির সত্তা স্বীকার করিতে হয়। 'চিৎ' এবং 'বিস্তার', 'জড়' ও 'চৈতন্য', 'সান্ত' ও 'অনন্ত', 'কারণ' এবং 'কার্য্য' 'সু' এবং 'কু', এই পরম পদার্থের ধর্ম্ম, এবং ইহার বিভিন্ন বিভাব মাত্র। স্পিনোজা এইরূপ সান্ত এবং অনন্তের সম্বন্ধ-বিষয়ক সমস্যা সমাধান করিয়াছেন। প্রত্যেক বস্তুই সেই পরম বস্তুর বিভিন্ন রূপ মাত্র। এই বস্তু একাধারে প্রকৃতি এবং প্রকৃতির অতীত। নির্ঝরের সহিত যেমন নির্ঝরিণীর কালের সহিত যেমন অনন্তকালের—পার্থক্য রহিয়াছে সেইরূপ প্রকৃতি এবং ঈশ্বরে বিভেদ বিদ্যমান আছে। স্পিনোজার, মতে ঈশ্বর পরা প্রকৃতি। ঈশ্বর শক্তি, প্রকৃতি তাঁহার ক্রিয়া। তাঁহার মতে মানব ঐশ্বরিক সত্তার একটী বিভাব মাত্র। তদীয় মন ঈশ্বর রূপ অগ্নির স্ফুলিঙ্গ, তাহার দেহ ঐশী সত্তার বিভাব মাত্র। স্পিনোজা বলেন যে, এই মায়িক বা অনিত্য জগতের অন্তরালে

একটী নিত্যজগৎ বিদ্যমান রহিয়াছে। এই শাশ্বতলোকের দিকে উন্মুখ হইলেই মানব ইন্দ্রিয়গ্রামের বন্ধন হইতে মুক্তিলাভ করিয়া আধ্যাত্মিক স্বাধীনতা—অর্থাৎ অমৃতত্ব লাভ করিতে পারে।] **Spin-o-zis'-tic,** *adj.* **—zist,** *n.*

spin'-stér, *n.* An unmarried elderly woman ; বর্ষীয়সী কুমারী। **—hood,** *n.*

spin-thâr'-i-scōpe, *n.* A small metal tube containing a speck of radium and rendering visible the tiny spark flying across the darkened end ; রেডিয়ামের কণাযুক্ত ধাতুর ক্ষুদ্র চোঙ্গবিশেষ—যাহাতে ঐ কণা হইতে নিক্ষিপ্ত ক্ষুদ্র ক্ষুদ্র আলোককণার চমক দৃষ্ট হয়, স্ফুলিঙ্গবীক্ষণ।

spi'-nūle, *adj.* (*Bot. & Zool.*) A small spine; ক্ষুদ্র পত্রকণ্টক ক্ষুদ্র মেরুদণ্ড। **Spin-u-lif'-er-ous, Spin'-u lose, Spin'-u-lous,** *adjs.*

spin'-ȳ, *adj.* **1.** Prickly ; কণ্টকময়, কণ্টকাকীর্ণ, কণ্টকবহুল। **2.** Troublesome ; "So difficult and *spiny* an affair" ; বিরক্তিজনক, কষ্টকর, গোলমেলে। **—i-ness,** *n.*

spir'-a-cle (-kl), *n.* Any aperture in animals for breathing ; শ্বাসরন্ধ্র। **Spi-rac'-u-lar, Spi-rac'-u-late,** *adjs.*

spi-rae'-ă (-rē-), *n.* A genus of plants bearing white or pink flowers : শ্বেত বা পাটলপুষ্পপ্রসূ বৃক্ষজাতিবিশেষ।

spi'-răl, *adj., n. & v. t.* Winding ; কুণ্ডলিত, পাকানো, চক্রাবর্ত্তী, পেঁচানো, ব্যবর্ত্তিত, সর্পিল (হিঃ কোঃ), ঘূর্ণাবর্ত্ত (সাঃ পঃ), আবর্ত্তিত (ঐ)। ***Noun.*** A curve which continually recedes from a centre round which it involves ; কুণ্ডলী, পেঁচানো পদার্থ। ***Verb t.*** To make spiral ; কুণ্ডলিত করা, পেঁচান। **—ly,** *adv.* **Spiral balance**—Same as SPRING BALANCE (which see). **Spiral energy**—কুণ্ডলিনী শক্তি। **Spiral vessel**—আবর্ত্তাঙ্কিত নাড়ীকা (সাঃ পঃ)। **Spiral wheel**—যে চক্রের দণ্ড অক্ষের সহিত কোণ উৎপাদনপূর্ব্বক কর্ত্তিত হয়। **Equiangular spiral** — সমকোণীয় সার্পিল (হিঃ কোঃ)। **Reciprocal spiral**—ব্যুৎক্রম সর্পিল (হিঃ কোঃ)।

spi'-rănt, *n. & adj.* A consonant sound uttered with perceptible expiration or emission of breath : ঈষৎ শ্বাসমোচনপূর্ব্বক উচ্চারিত ব্যঞ্জনবর্ণ। ***Adj.*** So uttered; উক্তরূপে উচ্চারিত।

spīre, *n., v. i. & t.* **1.** The tapering portion of a steeple rising along the tower ; মন্দির প্রভৃতির চূড়া, শিখর। **2.** The summit ; চূড়া, অগ্রভাগ। **3.** A sprout or shoot of a plant ; অঙ্কুর। **4.** (*Dial.*) Tall grass; reed; (উপভাষায়) দীর্ঘতৃণ ; শর। ***Verb i.*** To shoot forth or up ; অঙ্কুরিত হওয়া, গজাইয়া উঠা। ***Verb t.*** To furnish with spires ; চূড়াবিশিষ্ট করা, শিখরবিশিষ্ট করা। **Spir'-y,** *adj.*

spīre, *n.* A spiral cord ; কুণ্ডলী।

spir'-it, *n.* **1.** The soul as distinguished from the body which it occupies ; আত্মা, প্রাণ, জীবাত্মা, দেহী, জীব (হিঃ কোঃ), পুরুষ (ঐ), অন্তরাত্মা (সাংখ্য)। **2.** Life or principle of life considered independently of corporeal existence ; চিৎ (ব্রজঃ হিন্দু), চৈতন্য (opposed to জড়), প্রাণশক্তি। **3.** An apparition ; a spectre ; a ghost ; "Sent by some *spirits* to mortals good" ; অপচ্ছায়া, প্রতিবিম্বিত মূর্ত্তি (জাঃ অঃ), ছায়ামূর্ত্তি ; প্রেতাত্মা, দেবযোনি, দিব্যপুরুষ, দিব্যমানুষ ; ভূত। **4.** An individual ; as, the ruling *spirit* ; ব্যক্তি। **5.** Courage ; energy ; vivacity ; animation ; cheerfulness ; enthusiasm ; সাহস ; শক্তি ; সজীবতা ; স্ফূর্ত্তি ; উল্লাস, উৎসাহ। **6.** Temper or dispostion of the mind; mental condition ; tendency ; humour ; as, to be in low *spirits* ; প্রকৃতি ; মানসিক অবস্থা; আসক্তি, ঝোঁক, প্রবণতা; মেজাজ। **7.** Real meaning ; intent ; "The *spirit* of a passage" : "For the letter killeth while the *spirit* gives life" ; প্রকৃত অর্থ ; অন্তর্নিহিত অর্থ, তাৎপর্য্য, ভাবার্থ। **8.** The active, vital or essential part of a thing ; সত্ব, সার, বীর্য্য, নির্য্যাস। **9.** Any volatile inflammable liquid obtained by distillation, as brandy ; সুরাসার, সুরাবীর্য্য, মদ্যসার, স্পিরিট (হিঃ কোঃ), সার (ঐ)। **10.** (Hegelian philosophy) The complex of human institutions, family, society, state, church, and the productions in art, poetry, science and culture (*Geist*) ; (হেগেলের দর্শন) মানবীয় প্রতিষ্ঠান সমূহের সমবায়—যথা পরিবার, সমাজ, রাষ্ট্র, ধর্ম্মসংঘ, এবং কলাবস্তু, কবিতা, বিজ্ঞান ও সভ্যতা। **11.** Animating principle or influence ; mental or moral tendency ; as, the *spirit* of the age ; জীবনীশক্তি ; ধর্ম্ম। **Spirit-blue**—সুরাবীর্য্যে দ্রবণীয় একপ্রকার রাসায়নিক নীল। **Spirit body** — সূক্ষ্মশরীর, লিঙ্গশরীর, লিঙ্গদেহ, আতিবাহিক দেহ। **Spirit-circle**—Same as SEANCE (which see). **Spirit-duck** — একজাতীয় হংস—যাহারা বন্দুকের অগ্নিশিখা প্রভৃতি দর্শনে দ্রুত নিমজ্জিত হয়। **Spirit-hand** — একরূপ প্রেতাত্মার আবির্ভাব—যাহাতে পরলোকগত মানবের সূক্ষ্ম রকপ্রভহস্ত দৃষ্ট হইয়া থাকে। **Spirit-lamp**—(See LAMP) স্পিরিট ল্যাম্প (হিঃ কোঃ), মদ্যসার ল্যাম্প (ঐ)। **Spirit-level** — দিক্‌চক্রবালের সহিত সমান্তরাল রেখা বা সমতল নির্ণয় এবং দুই বা তদধিক স্থানের ভূমির আপেক্ষিক উচ্চতা নির্দ্ধারণের জন্য যন্ত্রবিশেষ, সমতলমান। [সুরাসারদ্বারা প্রায় পূর্ণ একটী কাচের চোঙ্গের উভয় প্রান্ত দৃঢ়রূপে রুদ্ধ করতঃ এই যন্ত্র নির্ম্মিত হয়। এইরূপ যন্ত্র সমতল স্থানে রাখিলে উহার অভ্যন্তরস্থ সুরাসারশূন্য স্থানের বায়ুবুদ্বুদ চোঙ্গের ঠিক মধ্যস্থলে থাকে।] **Spirit manifestations**—প্রেতাত্মার প্রকাশ বা আবির্ভাব **Spirit-merchant**—সুরাসার-বিক্রেতা।

Spirit-rapper — প্রেতাত্মা আনয়নে সমর্থ ব্যক্তি। **Spirit-rapping**—টেবিলের উপর ঠক্ ঠক্ শব্দ প্রভৃতি দ্বারা প্রেতাত্মা কর্তৃক তদীয় আবির্ভাব-সূচনা বা কোন প্রশ্নের উত্তর প্রদান। **Spirit-world**—প্রেতলোক। **Animal spirits**—সজীবতা, তেজস্বিতা। **God is spirit**—ঈশ্বর চিৎস্বরূপ। **Holy Spirit**—পবিত্রাত্মা। **Out of spirits**—বিষণ্ণ, স্ফূর্তিহীন, ম্রিয়মাণ, নিরুৎসাহ। **Poor or low spirits**—বিষাদ, নিরুৎসাহ। **Rectified spirit**—শুদ্ধ-মদ্যসার (হিঃ কোঃ)। **Spirit of the age or times**—যুগধর্ম্ম, কালধর্ম্ম। **Spirit of wine**—সুরাসার, সুরাবীর্য্য।

spir′-ĭt, *v. t.* **1.** To convey rapidly and secretly by, or as if by spirits ; "I felt as if I had been *spirited* into a castle of antiquity" ; ভূতাদি দ্বারা স্থানান্তরিত করা, ভৌতিক শক্তিবৎ কোন কিছু শক্তিদ্বারা নিমেষে বা অলক্ষিতে স্থানান্তরিত করা। **2.** To encourage ; to cheer up ; উৎসাহিত করা ; আশ্বাসিত করা।

spir′-ĭt-ĕd, *adj.* **1.** Full of spirit ; animated ; lively ; full of life and vigour ; as, a *spirited* answer ; তেজস্বী, সতেজ ; সজীব; জীবন্ত ; প্রাণবান, তেজোপূর্ণ, ওজঃপূর্ণ। **2.** Having a specified spirit ; বিশেষপ্রকৃতি-বিশিষ্ট। **—ly**, *adv.*

spir′-ĭt-ĭsm, *n.* Same as SPIRITUALISM. **—ist**, *n.*

spir′-ĭt-lĕss, *adj.* **1.** Destitute of spirit ; wanting in animation ; depressed ; নিস্তেজ ; স্ফূর্ত্তিহীন, প্রাণহীন; ম্রিয়মাণ। **2.** Destitute of vigour, life, courage and fire ; শক্তিহীন, তেজোহীন, সাহসহীন, নির্ব্বীর্য্য, হীনবীর্য্য।

spiritoso, *adv.* (*Mus. It.*) With spirit ; (সঙ্গীত-বিদ্যা) স্ফূর্তির সহিত, সতেজে।

spir′-ĭt-ū-ăl, *adj.* **1.** Incorporeal ; অমূর্ত্ত, অশরীরী, বিদেহী অরূপ, নিরাকার, চিদ্রূপ। **2.** Pertaining to the mind ; মানসী, মানসিক, চিন্ময়, চিদাত্মক, মনোময়, জ্ঞানময়। **3.** Pertaining to the moral feelings or the states of the soul ; pertaining to the soul or its affection as influenced by the spirit ; as, *spiritual* gift ; আধ্যাত্মিক ; আত্মিক। **4.** Proceeding from the holy spirit ; pure ; holy ; divine ; পবিত্রাত্মাসঞ্জাত ; শুদ্ধ, অপাপবিদ্ধ; পবিত্র ; দিব্য। **5.** Not temporal ; ecclesiastical ; as, the *spiritual* function of the clergy ; পারমার্থিক, পরমার্থবিষয়ক ; যাজকীয়। **—ly**, *adv.* **—ness**, *n.* **Spiritual court**—যাজকীয় বিচারালয়। **Spiritual man** — মানুষের অন্তঃপ্রকৃতি ; (বাইবেলে) নবজীবনপ্রাপ্ত মানব। **Spiritual minded** — পারমার্থিক চিন্তারত। **Spiritual peers**—Same as LORDS SPIRITUAL. **Spiritual wife** — আমেরিকায় বহুবিবাহকারী Mormon সম্প্রদায়ের লোকদিগের প্রথমা স্ত্রী ব্যতিরিক্তা স্ত্রী। **Lords spiritual**—বিশপ এবং আর্চবিশপগণ।

spir′-ĭt-ū-ăl-ĭsm, *n.* **1.** Belief in communication with the unseen world of the departed through the impressibility of certain media to so-called spiritual influences ; কোন মাধ্যমিক (medium) এর সাহায্যে কিম্বা জড়ীয়মূর্ত্তির পরিগ্রহণে মৃত ব্যক্তির আত্মার জীবিত ব্যক্তিদের সহিত সম্মিলন বা কথোপকথনসম্বন্ধীয় তত্ত্ব, প্রেতবিদ্যা। [See F. W. H Myers, *Human Personality* ; J. Maxwell, *Metapsychical Phenomena* ; G. G. Zerffi, *Spiritualism and Animal Magnetism* ; F. Podmore, *Mesmerism and Christian Science* ; *Light, Spiritual Magazine* (Published in Calcutta), etc. ; Edward Carpenter, *The Drama of Love and Death* ; Sir Oliver Lodge, *Raymond or Life and Death, The Survival of Man* ; Hereward Carrington, *Personal Experiences in Spiritualism* ; Lombroso (Cesare) *After Death—What ?*]. **2.** The state of being spiritual ; আধ্যাত্মিকতা। **3.** The doctrine in opposition to materialism which holds that mind is not a function of, but something distinct from, matter ; idealism ; জড় বাদের বিরোধী মতবিশেষ, যদনুসারে চিদ্বস্তু জড়ের বৃত্তি বা ক্রিয়াবিশেষ, কিন্তু জড় হইতে সম্পূর্ণ বিভিন্ন প্রকৃতির স্বতন্ত্র বস্তু বলিয়া পরিগৃহীত হইয়া থাকে ; অধ্যাত্মবাদ, পরমার্থবাদ, জীবাত্মবাদ,ব্রহ্মবাদ (হিঃ কোঃ)। **—ist**, *n.* **1.** One who believes in spiritualism ; প্রেততাত্ত্বিক, প্রেততত্ত্ববিৎ, প্রেতবাহক (হিঃ কোঃ), প্রেতবাদী (ঐ)। **2.** A believer in philosophical spiritualism ; an idealist ; অধ্যাত্মবাদী, পরমার্থবাদী, ব্রহ্মবাদী (হিঃ কোঃ) ; আত্মবাদী (ঐ), আস্তিক (ঐ)। **—is′-tic**, *adj.* **Spiritualistic philosophy**—জীবাত্মবিশিষ্ট দর্শনশাস্ত্র (হিঃ কোঃ)।

spir-ĭt-ū-ăl′-ĭ-tȳ, *n.* **1.** Spiritual quality ; অধ্যাত্মতা, আধ্যাত্মিকতা, পারমার্থিকতা, অমূর্ত্ততা। **2.** An ecclesiastical body or ecclesiastical bodies collectively ; যাজকবর্গ, যাজকসংঘসমূহ। **3.** That which belongs to the Church, or to a person, as an ecclesiastic, or to religion ; খৃষ্টীয় ধর্ম্মমন্দিরের বস্তু, ধর্ম্মসংঘের বা যাজকের অধিকৃত সম্পত্তি বা আয়।

spir′-ĭt-ū-ăl-īze, *v. t.* **1.** To refine intellectually or morally ; আধ্যাত্মিক ভাব দ্বারা অনুপ্রাণিত করা, চিন্ময় করা, চিদাত্মক করা। **2.** (*Rare*) To animate ; (কচিদ্ ব্যবহৃত) জীবনসঞ্চার করা, সঞ্জীবিত করা, অনুপ্রাণিত করা। **3.** To give a spiritual meaning to ; আধ্যাত্মিক ব্যাখ্যা করা। **4.** (*In old Chem.*) To extract spirit from ; to convert into spirit ; (প্রাচীন রসায়ন) সুরাসার বাহির করা ; সুরাসারে পরিণত করা। **—i-za′-tion**, *n.*

spĭ-rĭ-tū-ĕl′, —elle′ (-ĕl), *adjs.* Spiritual ; refined ; bright ; witty ; graceful ; as, a *spirituelle* woman ; আধ্যাত্মিকভাবসম্পন্ন; মার্জ্জিত ;

উজ্জ্বল ; রসিকতাপূর্ণ ; সুকুমার, মাধুর্য্যপূর্ণ ; মাধুর্য্যময়, ললিত।

spir′-it-ū-ous (-ŭs), *adj.* Containing much alcohol; as, a *spirituous* liquor ; সুরাসার বহুল। **—ness,** *n.*

spiritus, *n.* (*Greek Grammar*). ***Spiritus asper***—মহাপ্রাণ। ***Spiritus lenis***—অল্পপ্রাণ।

spi′-ri-valve (-vălv), *adj.* **1.** Having a spiral shell ; কুণ্ডলিত পুটকসম্পন্ন। **2.** (Of shell) Spiral ; (শঙ্খশম্বুকাদি সম্পর্কে) কুণ্ডলিত, পেঁচানো।

spirk′-ĕt (spêrk-), *n.* (*Naut.*) A space fore and aft between floor-timbers or futtocks of a ship's frame (নৌবিদ্যা) পোতের অংশবিশেষ।

spirk′-ĕt-ing (spêrk-), *n.* (*Naut.*) The planks from the water-ways to the port-sills ; (নৌবিদ্যা) পোতের অংশ বিশেষ।

spī′-rō-grăph, *n.* An instrument for marking out breathing movement ; শ্বাসমাপক।

spī-rŏm′-ĕ-têr, spī′-rō-scōpe, *ns.* An instrument for measuring the capacity of lungs ; ফুসফুসের ধারণ-শক্তি মাপিবার জন্য যন্ত্রবিশেষ, ফুস্ফুসস্থ বায়ুপরিমাণযন্ত্র, ফুসফুসমান, ফুসফুসবীক্ষণ, শ্বাসমাপক যন্ত্র (হিঃ কোঃ)। **—try,** *n.*

spī′-rō-phōre, *n.* An apparatus for inducing artificial respiration ; কৃত্রিম শ্বাসপ্রশ্বাস ক্রিয়া নির্ব্বাহের জন্য যন্ত্রবিশেষ, শ্বাসপ্রশ্বাসক।

spirt (spêrt), **spŭrt,** *v. i., t.* & *n.* To gush or issue out in a stream ; to rush from a confined place in a small jet or stream ; সবেগে ছুটা, উচ্ছলিত হওয়া ; ফিনকি দিয়া ছুটা। ***Verb t.*** To throw or force out in a jet or stream ; সজোরে নিক্ষেপ করা, ফিন্‌কি দিয়া ছুটান। ***Noun.*** Sudden gushing out; jet ; সবেগে নির্গম, উচ্ছলন ; ফিন্‌কি।

spir-ȳ, *adj.* Of a spiral form ; serpentine ; "Hid in the *spiry* volumes of the snake" ; কুণ্ডলিত ; সর্পিল।

spit, *n.* & *v. t.* **1.** An iron prong or bar pointed on which meat is roasted ; শিক, শলাকা, শূল, ছিঁচকা। **2.** A small point of land running into the sea ; সমুদ্রের উপর প্রলম্বিত ক্রমসূক্ষ্মাগ্র অন্তরীপ। ***Verb t.*** To thrust a spit through ; to put upon a spit ; (*fig.*) to pierce ; to transfix ; মাংসের ভিতর শিক পূরা ; শিকের মধ্যে মাংস নিবেশিত করা ; (লক্ষণায়) ভেদ করা ; এপিঠ ওপিঠ করিয়া ফোঁড় করা।

spit, *v. i.* & *t.* **1.** To eject saliva ; থুথু ফেলা, নিষ্ঠীবন ত্যাগ করা। **2.** To mizzle ; "It has been *spitting* with rain for the last half hour" ; টিপ টিপ বৃষ্টি হওয়া। ***Verb t.*** **1.** To thrust out as saliva or other matter from the mouth ; as, to *spit* blood ; মুখ হইতে নিষ্ঠীবন প্রভৃতি ত্যাগ করা, থুথু, কফ, প্রভৃতি ফেলা, ত্যাগ করা। **2.** To eject or throw out with violence ; to belch ; "To *spit* forth their iron indignation" ; সবেগে নিক্ষেপ করা, প্রচণ্ডবেগে নিক্ষেপ করা ; উদ্গিরণ করা। **Spitfire**—Person of fiery temper ; চণ্ডপ্রকৃতির লোক। Toy cone of wet gunpowder spitting when ignited ; ছেলেদের খেলার মোচাকার বাজী — যাহা হইতে ঝলকে ঝলকে অগ্নিকণা উত্থিত হয় (also *spitdevil*) **To spit cotton** or **sixpences**—শাদা সুতার মত থুথু নিক্ষেপ করা, অথবা মুদ্রার আকার শাদা থুথু ফেলা (ইহা দ্বারা তৃষ্ণা বুঝায়)। **To spit upon**—To treat with ignominy ; অবজ্ঞার সহিত ব্যবহার করা, অপমান করা।

spitch′-cŏck (spich-), *n.* & *v. t.* Eel split and broiled ; বিদারিত এবং ভর্জ্জিত বাইন মৎস্য। ***Verb t.*** To dress an eel with condiments etc. after splitting it lengthwise, then broiling it ; বাইন মাছ চিরিয়া তাহাতে মসলাদি মিশ্রণপূর্ব্বক ভাজা করা।

spīte, *n.* & *v. t.* Ill will ; malice ; hatred ; মনোমালিন্য ; বিদ্বেষ, হিংসা, অসূয়া, ঈর্ষা ; ঘৃণা। ***Verb t.*** **1.** To treat maliciously ; বিদ্বেষ করা, হিংসা করা, অসূয়া করা। **2.** To mortify ; to thwart maliciously ; to annoy ; মর্ম্মাহত করা ; দ্বেষপূর্ব্বক ব্যর্থ করা ; বিরক্ত করা, জ্বালাতন করা। **Spite′-ful,** *adj.* Having malicious disposition ; অসূয়াপরবশ, ঈর্ষাপরবশ, দ্বেষপূর্ণ। **Spite′-ful-ly,** *adv.* **Spite′-ful-ness,** *n.* **To cut off one's nose to spite one's face**—See NOSE.

spit′-tle (-l), *n.* Saliva ; থুথু, নিষ্ঠীবন, লালা।

spit-tōōn′, *n.* A box or earthenware vessel to receive discharges of saliva ; নিষ্ঠীবনপাত্র, পিক্‌দান, প্রতিগ্রাহ।

spitz, *n.* (Also *spitz-dog*) A Pomeranian ; একপ্রকার কুকুর।

splanch′-nic (splăngk-), *adj.* Pertaining or belonging to the bowels ; অন্ত্রসম্বন্ধীয়, আন্ত্রিক।

splanch-nŏl′-ō-ġȳ (splăngk-), *n.* A treatise or description of the viscera ; অন্তঃকোষ্ঠসম্বন্ধীয় পুস্তক, অন্তঃকোষ্ঠ বর্ণন।

splanch-nŏt′-ō-mȳ (splăngk-), *n.* The dissection of the viscera ; অন্তঃকোষ্ঠব্যবচ্ছেদ।

splăsh, *v.t., i.* & *n.* **1.** To bespatter person with water, mud, etc. ; জল, কর্দ্দম প্রভৃতি দ্বারা গায়ে ছিটা দেওয়া। **2.** To dash or spatter ; ছিটকান, ছিটকাইয়া দেওয়া। **3.** To decorate with patches of different colours ; ভিন্ন রংয়ের দাগ বা চিহ্নদ্বারা অলঙ্কৃত করা। ***Verb i.*** **1.** To dash about water or any liquid ; জল কিম্বা অন্য কোন তরলপদার্থ ছিটকাইয়া দেওয়া। **2.** (Of liquid) To fly about in drops or scattered portion ; ছিটকান, ছিটকাইয়া পড়া। **3.** To plunge into water splashing it ; ঝুপ করিয়া পড়া, ঝপ্ করে পড়া।

Noun. **1.** Water, or water and dirt, thrown upon anything ; ছিট, ছিটা । **2.** A noise, as from water or mud splashed about ; ছিটকানির শব্দ, ঝুপ্, পচ্ পচ্ । **3.** A blot ; a daub ; দাগ ; লেপ । **4.** A complexion powder used by ladies to whiten their necks and faces, generally the finest rice flour ; মুখে মাখিবার জন্য শ্বেতচূর্ণ । **4.** Patches of colour esp. on animal's skin ; রঙ্গীন দাগ, বিশেষতঃ জন্তুর চর্ম্মের উপর রঙ্গীন দাগ । **Splash-board, Splash-wing**—শকট প্রভৃতির সম্মুখস্থ কর্দ্দমরোধক কাষ্ঠ বা চর্ম্মফলকবিশেষ । **To make a splash**—To create sensation ; হুলস্থূল ব্যাপার করিয়া তোলা ।

splăsh'-ẽr, *n.* **1.** One who, or that which, splashes ; কর্দ্দমাদি নিক্ষেপকারী । **2.** A guard placed over the wheels of a locomotive engine to protect the machinery from dirt and wet ; বাষ্পীয়শকট প্রভৃতির সম্মুখস্থ কর্দ্দমনিবারক ফলক । **3.** A screen behind wash-stand to protect wall ; প্রাচীর রক্ষার জন্য হস্তপদপ্রক্ষালনপাত্রের পশ্চাতে স্থাপিত পর্দ্দা ।

splăt'-ter (-ẽr), *v. i.* & *t.* To splash ; to make splashing noise, as in water ; ছিটান, ছিটকান ; ঝুপঝাপ শব্দ করা । ***Verb t.*** To speak unintelligibly ; অস্পষ্টভাবে কথা বলা । **Splatter-dash** — গোলমাল, কলরব, কোলাহল, সোরগোল ।

splay (splā), *v. t.*, *n.* & *adj.* **1.** To dislocate or break a horse's shoulder-bone ; অশ্বের স্কন্ধাস্থি ভগ্ন বা সন্ধিচ্যুত করা । **2.** (*Arch.*) To slant ; (স্থপতিবিদ্যা) ঢালু হওয়া । ***Noun.*** **1.** Expansion ; বিস্তার । **2.** A slope ; ঢালু । ***Adj.*** Spreading out ; wide ; turned outward ; বহিঃপ্রসারিত ; ব্যাদিত ; বহির্গত । **Splay-foot**—প্রশস্ত পদ । **Splay-mouth**—ব্যাদিত মুখ ।

spleen (splēn), *n.* **1.** A vascular gland, situated on the left by hypochondriac region, and supposed by the ancients to be the seat of vexation, anger, and melancholy ; প্লীহা, পিলে, গুল্ম (*colloq.*) । **2.** Ill temper ; spite ; anger ; as, to vent one's *spleen* ; বদমেজাজ ; দ্বেষ ; ক্রোধ । **3.** Melancholy ; low spirits ; "We have long been characterised as a nation of a *spleen*, and our rivals on the continent as a land of levity" ; বিষাদ ; স্ফূর্ত্তিহীনতা, অপ্রসন্নতা, নিরুৎসাহ । **Spleen'-ful, Spleen'-ish, Spleen'-y,** *adjs.* **Spleen'-ful-ly, Spleen'-ish-ly,** *adv.* **Spleen'-less,** *adj.* **To vent one's spleen**—To vent one's spite or anger ; ঝালপাড়া ।

splē-năl'-gĭ-ă, *n.* Pain over the region of the spleen ; প্লীহাবেদনা । **-gic,** *adj.*

splĕn'-dĕnt, *adj.* Having bright metallic lustre ; দীপ্ত ধাতব প্রভাময়, ভাস্বর ।

splĕn'-dĭd, *adj.* **1.** Brilliant ; উজ্জ্বল, দীপ্ত, ভাস্বর, দীপ্তিশালী, সুরুচির, সমুজ্জ্বল, দ্যুতিমান, সপ্রভ, আলো ঝলমল (রবীঃ) । **2.** Illustrious ; grand ; heroic ; noble ; glorious ; as, *splendid* example of heroism ; magnificent : বিখ্যাত ; মহান ; শূর ; সমুন্নত ; গরিমাপূর্ণ, গৌরবোজ্জ্বল ; জমকালো । **3.** (*Colloq.*) Excellent ; as, a *splendid* fish ; খাসা, চমৎকার । **—ly,** *adv.*

splĕn-dĭf'-ẽr-ous (-ŭs), *adj.* Same as SPLENDID.

splĕn'-dour (-dẽr), *n.* **1.** Brilliancy ; দীপ্তি, ঔজ্জ্বল্য, দ্যুতি, প্রভা, ছটা, চটক । **2.** Magnificence ; grandeur ; pomp ; জাঁকজমক ; গরিমা, গৌরবশ্রী ; জাঁক, ঘটা, সমারোহ । **3.** (*Herald.*) Sun represented with human face and environed with rays ; (কুলবিদ্যা) ছটামণ্ডলমধ্যবর্ত্তী মানবমুখাকৃতি সূর্য্য ।

splē-nĕc'-tō-mȳ, *n.* Excision of the spleen ; প্লীহাচ্ছেদন ।

splē-nĕt'-ĭc, *adj.* & *n.* Peevish ; fretful ; খিটখিটে ; বদমেজাজী, ক্রোধশীল, কোপন । ***Noun.*** **1.** A person affected with spleen ; প্লীহারোগাক্রান্ত ব্যক্তি । **2.** A medicine for spleen ; প্লীহার ঔষধ । **—i-cal-ly,** *adv.*

splē'-nĭ-ăl, *adj.* (*Anat.*) Pertaining to splenius muscle ; (শারীরসংস্থানবিদ্যা) শিরঃসঞ্চালক পেশীসম্বন্ধীয় ।

splĕn'-ĭc, *adj.* Pertaining to the spleen ; প্লীহাসম্বন্ধীয় । **Sple'-noid,** *adj.* **Splenic apoplexy**—Same as SPLENIC FEVER. **Splenic fever**—Same as ANTHRAX (which see). **Splenic vein**—যে শিরা দ্বারা প্লীহা হইতে রক্ত বাহির হয় ।

splē-nī'-tĭs, *n.* Inflammation of the spleen ; প্লীহার প্রদাহ ।

splē'-nĭ-ŭs, *n. pl.* A strong muscle of the back of the neck serving to tilt the head backward ; ঘাড়ের কঠিন পেশীবিশেষ—যদ্দ্বারা মস্তক পশ্চাদ্দিকে হেলান যায়, শিরঃসঞ্চালক পেশী ।

splĕn-ĭ-zā'-tion, *n.* Conversion of lung into a substance resembling spleen ; ফুসফুস প্রদাহ রোগে ফুসফুসের প্লীহার ন্যায় অবস্থাপ্রাপ্তি ।

splē-nŏl'-ō-ğȳ, *n.* A treatise on the spleen ; প্লীহাতত্ত্ব ।

splē-nŏt'-ō-mȳ, *n.* Anatomical dissection of the spleen ; প্লীহাব্যবচ্ছেদ ।

splīce, *v. t.* & *n.* **1.** To unite the ends of two ropes by uniting the strands ; রজ্জু সমূহের প্রান্ত একত্র পাকাইয়া সংযুক্ত করা । **2.** To unite by lapping two ends together ; একটীর প্রান্তের উপর অপরটীর প্রান্ত রাখিয়া জোড়া দেওয়া । **3.** (*Colloq.*) To unite in marriage ; as, when did they get *spliced* ? ; (চলিত ভাষায়) বিবাহবন্ধনে বদ্ধ করা । ***Noun.*** **1.** The union of two ropes or pieces of wood by splicing ; একত্র পাকাইয়া রজ্জুর প্রান্ত কিম্বা একের প্রান্ত অপরের প্রান্তে রাখিয়া কাষ্ঠখণ্ড সংযুক্ত করা ।

2. Piece added to a rope by splicing ; কোন রজ্জুর প্রান্তে পাকাইয়া যে অংশ সংযুক্ত করা হয়। **To splice the main brace**—To give out an extra allowance of spirits after special exposure to cold or wet ; শীত বা বৃষ্টিতে অনাবৃত অবস্থায় থাকার দরুণ এক গ্লাস অতিরিক্ত মদ্য প্রদান করা।

spline, *n.* & *v. t.* 1. A rectangular piece or key fitting into a groove in the hub of a wheel, and a similar groove in a shaft, so that while the wheel may slide end-ways on the shaft, both must revolve together ; চক্রনাভির খাঁজে সংযোজনীয় চতুষ্কোণ চাবিবিশেষ। 2. A long flexible strip of wood or rubber used by draftsmen in laying out railway-curves etc. ; লৌহবর্ত্মের বক্র অঙ্কণে ব্যবহৃত নমনীয় কাষ্ঠ বা রবারের খণ্ড। ***Verb t.*** To fit with a spline; উক্তরূপ চাবি লাগান।

splint, *n.* & *v. t.* 1. A fragment or piece of wood split off ; কাঠের চেলা, চির,ফালি,চিল্‌তা, চেলা কাঠ। 2. A thin piece of wood or other substance, used to hold or confine a broken bone when set, or to maintain any part of the body in a fixed position : ভগ্ন অস্থি স্থিরভাবে রাখিবার জন্য দীর্ঘ ও পাতলা কাষ্ঠখণ্ড বা কোনরূপ বস্তু। ***Verb t.*** To confine broken limbs with splints; কাঠের চিলটা দ্বারা ভগ্ন অস্থি স্থিরভাবে রাখা। **Splint-bone**—অশ্বের জানুসন্ধি হইতে জঙ্ঘার পশ্চাদ্‌ভাগস্থ লোমগুচ্ছ পর্য্যন্ত বিস্তৃত অস্থিখণ্ডদ্বয়ের অন্যতর। **Splint-coal**—স্লেট পাথরের মত একপ্রকার কঠিন কয়লা।

splin-tĕr, *n., v. t.* & *i.* A thin piece of wood or other solid substance rent from the main body; as, the *splinters* of a wood; চিলটা, চির, চেলা কাঠ, টুকরা, খণ্ড। ***Verb t.*** To split into splinter ; চেলা করা, চিলতা করা। ***Verb i.*** To be split into splinters ; চেলা হওয়া, চিল্‌তা হওয়া। **Splinter-bar**—শকটের যে অনুপ্রস্থগামী দণ্ডে দম (spring) সমূহ অবলম্বিত থাকে অথবা যাহাতে ঘোড়ার মুখের উভয় পার্শ্বের চর্ম্মরজ্জু সংবদ্ধ থাকে। **Splinter-bone**— জঙ্ঘার দীর্ঘাস্থির সম্মুখস্থ সরু অস্থি। **Splinter-proof**—বিদীর্ণ গোলার খণ্ডসমূহদ্বারা অভেদ্য।

splin'-tĕr-ÿ, *adj.* 1. Pertaining to splinters ; চেলাকাঠ সম্বন্ধীয়। 2. Splinter-like ; চেলার মত। 3. Apt to splinter ; খণ্ডে খণ্ডে বিদারণশীল।

split, *v. t.* & *i.* 1. To divide longitudinally or lengthwise ; চেলা করা। 2. To tear asunder by violence ; to rend ; চিরা, ফাড়া ; বিদারণ করা। 3. To divide or break up into parts ; বিভিন্নভাগে বিভক্ত করা। ***Verb i.*** 1. To burst or part asunder ; to burst ; বিদীর্ণ হওয়া ; ফাটিয়া যাওয়া। 2. (*Colloq.*) To sever connection or relation with ; to disagree ; (চলিত ভাষায়) বিচ্ছেদ হওয়া, মনোভঙ্গ হওয়া, ভেদ হওয়া ; মতভেদ হওয়া, মতদ্বৈধ হওয়া, মতবৈষম্য হওয়া। 3. To burst with laughter ; হাসিয়া পেটফাটা। 4. (*Slang*) To betray confidence ; সহাপরাধীর গুপ্তঅপরাধের বিষয় প্রকাশ করিয়া দেওয়া। 5. (*Colloq.*) To run quickly ; ছুটা। **Split'-ter,** *n.* **Side-splitter**—পেটফাটা হাসি। **Split peas**—ভাঙ্গা মটর। **Split-tongue** — বিদীর্ণজিহ্ব। **A Splitting headache** — গুরুতর মাথাব্যথা। **To split a cause of action**—কোন দাবীর অংশ বিশেষের জন্য মোকদ্দমা করা। [এইরূপ মোকদ্দমার দাবীর অবশিষ্ট অংশের মোকদ্দমা প্রথম মোকদ্দমার ফলাফলের অপেক্ষায় স্থগিত রাখা হয়।] **To split hairs**—See HAIR. **To split on a rock**—To be unsuccessful ; বিফলপ্রযত্ন হওয়া, বিফলকাম হওয়া। **To split one's sides**—To laugh without moderation ; হাসিতে হাসিতে পেট ফাটা, হাসিয়া খুন হওয়া। **To split one's votes or vote**—To vote for each of opposed candidates ; প্রতিযোগী সভ্যপদপ্রার্থিদ্বয়ের প্রত্যেকের স্বপক্ষে ভোট দেওয়া। **To split the difference**—To divide the matter in dispute equally ; সমানভাবে ভাগ করিয়া দেওয়া।

split, *n.* 1. The act of splitting ; বিদারণ, ভঙ্গ। 2. A splinter ; চেলা, চিলটা, টুকরা। 3. Fissure ; crack ; ফাইট, ফাটোল ; ফাটা, চিড়। 4. A breach ; ভেদ, মনোভঙ্গ। 5. A small bottle of aerated water ; বিলাতি পানি প্রভৃতির ছোট বোতল। 6. (*Pl.*) An acrobat's trick of sitting on ground with legs spread out laterally ; পার্শ্বেরদিকে উভয়পদ প্রসারণপূর্ব্বক বাজীকরের উপবেশন। 7. (*Pl.*) Skins, hides or leather split into two layers by machine ; যন্ত্রের সাহায্যে দুই স্তরে বিপাটিত শোধিত বা অশোধিত চর্ম্ম। 8. Any of the dents of a reed ; তাঁতের শাণার শলা।

splotch (splŏch), **splodge** (splŏj), *ns.* Daub ; লেপ। **Splotch'-y,** *adj.*

splurge (splĕrj), *n.* & *v. i.* A bustle ; সোরগোল। ***Verb i.*** To make noise ; সোরগোল করা।

splŭt'-tĕr (-ĕr), *v. i., t.* & *n.* Same as SPLUTTER (which see). **-er,** *n.*

spŏf'-fish (-ĭsh), *adj.* (*Slang*) Bustling ; smart ; (ইতরভাষায়) গোলমালকারী ; চোস্ত।

spoil (spoyl), *n.* 1. That which is taken by violence ; লুণ্ঠিতদ্রব্য, লুঠের মাল। 2. The act of plundering ; লুণ্ঠন। 3. (*Obs.*) The slough of a serpent ; (অপ্রঃ) সাপের খোলস। 4. Profit ; advantage ; emolument ; লাভ ; সুবিধা ; বেতন। 5. The surplus excavated material which is laid down by the side of a railway, canal, or other work, at the mouth of a pit or mine to save expense of removal : স্থানান্তর করার ব্যয়সংক্ষেপ করিবার জন্য লৌহবর্ত্ম প্রভৃতির পার্শ্বে এবং খনির মুখ, প্রভৃতিতে যে অতিরিক্ত মৃত্তিকা, খনিজদ্রব্য প্রভৃতি স্তূপীকৃত করিয়া রাখা হয়। **Spoil-five**—একপ্রকার তাসখেলা। **Spoilsman** — নিম্নোক্তরূপ প্রথার পক্ষপাতী ব্যক্তি, নিম্নোক্তরূপ প্রথাদ্বারা স্বার্থসাধনে সচেষ্ট ব্যক্তি। **Spoils system**—(আমেরিকার যুক্তরাজ্যে) প্রবল জয়ীপক্ষের প্রতি অনুরক্ত লোকদিগকে সরকারী চাকুরী দেওয়ার প্রথা।

spoil (spoyl), *v. t.* & *i.* **1.** To plunder ; লুণ্ঠন করা, লুঠ করা। **2.** To injure ; to ruin ; as, to *spoil* a child ; নষ্ট করা, অনিষ্ট করা ; নাশ করা, সর্ব্বনাশ করা, মাথা খাওয়া (*Colloq.*)। ***Verb i.*** **1.** To practise plunder ; লুণ্ঠনবৃত্তি করা। **2.** To decay ; as, fruits will *spoil* in warm weather ; নষ্ট হওয়া, খারাপ হওয়া।

spoil'-āge (spoyl-), *n.* Paper spoilt in printing ; মুদ্রণে যে কাগজ নষ্ট হয়।

spōke, *n.* & *v. t.* **1.** The radius or ray of a wheel ; আরা, পাখি। **2.** The rung of ladder ; মইএর ধাপ বা কোয়া। **3.** A contrivance for fastening the wheel of a vehicle, to prevent it from turning in going down a hill ; পর্ব্বত হইতে নামিবার সময় যাহাতে উল্টাইয়া না যায়—তজ্জন্য যে কলদ্বারা শকটাদির চক্র রোধ করা হয়, চক্ররোধক। ***Verb t.*** **1.** To furnish with spokes ; আরা লাগান। **2.** To check wheels with a spoke ; চক্ররোধক দ্বারা শকটের চক্রের গতিরোধ করা। **Spoke-bone**—কনুই হইতে মণিবন্ধ পর্য্যন্ত প্রসারিত অস্থিদ্বয়ের মধ্যে ক্ষুদ্রতর অস্থি। **Spoking-machine**—যে যন্ত্রের সাহায্যে চাকার পাখিগুলি তুল্য রূপে হেলানোভাবে স্থাপন করা হয়। **To put a spoke in a person's wheel**—To thwart his purpose ; কাহারো উদ্দেশ্য ব্যর্থ করা।

spōke, spōk'-en (-n), *p. t.* & *p. p.* of SPEAK (which see).

spōkes'-măn (spōks-), *n.* One who speaks for others ; a representative ; মুখপাত্র ; প্রতিনিধি।

spolia opima, *n.* **1.** (*Rom. Antiq.*) The richest spoils ; the arms taken in the field by the victorious from the vanquished general ; (রোমীয় প্রত্নতত্ত্ব) সর্ব্বাপেক্ষা মূল্যবান লুণ্ঠিত দ্রব্য ; বিজয়ী সেনাপতি কর্ত্তৃক রণক্ষেত্রে পরাজিত সেনানায়কের নিকট হইতে যে অস্ত্রশস্ত্র নেওয়া হয়। **2.** (*Fig.*) Supreme achievement or distinction ; (লক্ষণায়) পরম অবদান বা খ্যাতি।

spō-li-ā'-tion *n.* **1.** Act of plundering ; লুণ্ঠন। **2.** The plundering of neutral vessels at sea by a belligerent ; সমুদ্রে যুধ্যমান কোন জাতিকর্ত্তৃক নির্লিপ্ত দেশের জাহাজ লুণ্ঠন। **3.** Extortion বলপূর্ব্বক আদায়। **4.** (*Law*) Destruction, mutilation, alteration of document to prevent its being used as evidence ; কোন দলিল যাহাতে প্রমাণস্বরূপ ব্যবহৃত না হইতে পারে তজ্জন্য উহার পরিবর্ত্তন, অঙ্গহানি সাধন বা নষ্টকরণ। **5.** An injury done by one clerk or incumbent to another in taking the fruits of his benifice without any right thereunto under a pretended title ; কল্পিত অধিকারের বলে এক যাজক কর্ত্তৃক অপর যাজকের যাজকোত্তর সম্পত্তির গ্রহণ দ্বারা শেষোক্ত ব্যক্তির ক্ষতিসাধন। **Writ of spoliation**—কল্পিত অধিকার বলে কোন যাজক অপর যাজকের সম্পত্তির ক্ষতি করিলে শেষোক্ত যাজক ঐ ক্ষতি পূরণের জন্য যাজকীয় আদালত হইতে যে পরোয়ানা বাহির করে। **Spo'-li-a-tor,** *n.* **Spo'-li-a-to-ry,** *adj.*

spŏn'-dā'-ic, *adj.* of SPONDEE (which see).

spŏn'-dee (dē-), *n.* A metrical foot of two long syllables ; যে কবিতার পদের উভয় অংশই গুরু (- -), দ্বিগুরু পদ।

Spondias mangifera—আম্রাতক, আমড়া, পীতন, কপীতন, বর্ষপাকী, পীতনক, পীনাস্ত, কপিচূড়া, অম্রশাটক, ভক্ষ্যফল, রসাঢ্য, তনুক্ষীর, কপিপ্রিয় অম্বরাতক, অমাবীর।

spŏn'-dўl, spŏn'-dyle (-dil), *ns.* A joint of the backbone ; a vertebra ; পৃষ্ঠাস্থির সন্ধি ; মেরুদণ্ডের অস্থিসমূহের অন্যতম।

sponge (spŭnj), *n.* **1.** A soft porous marine animal which readily imbibes water ; স্পঞ্জ, শোষক। **2.** A parasite ; পরভাগ্যানুজীবি, পরান্নভোজী, পরপিণ্ডাদ। **3.** An instrument for cleaning a cannon after discharge ; দাগিবার পর যে যন্ত্র দ্বারা কামান পরিষ্কার করা হয়। **4.** The extremity or point of a horseshoe answering to the heel ; ঘোড়ার নালের প্রান্ত বা গোড়ালী। **5.** A leavened dough before it is kneaded and formed ; তাড়ি মিশান ময়দার তাল। **6.** Iron or other metal in a soft or pasty condition কোমল বা মণ্ডবৎ অবস্থাপ্রাপ্ত লৌহ বা অন্যবিধ ধাতু। **Spon'-gi-form,** *adj.* **Spon-go'-lo-gist, Spon-go'-lo-gy,** *ns.* **Spong-cake** — স্পঞ্জের মত কোমল এবং হাল্কা পিষ্টক। **Sponge-cucumber, —gourd, Vegetable sponge**—স্নানকালে গাত্রমার্জ্জন করার জন্য একপ্রকার ঝিঙ্গা বা অলাবুজাতীয় ফলের শুষ্কীকৃত খোসা। **Sponge tent** — ক্ষতের মুখ উন্মুক্ত রাখার জন্য সন্নিবেশিত স্পঞ্জ প্রভৃতি। **Sponge-tree**—গ্রীষ্মমণ্ডলে জাত পীতবর্ণ পুষ্পপ্রসূ গুল্মবিশেষ। **To throw up the sponge**—To acknowledge defeat ; to give up the contest or struggle ; পরাজয় স্বীকার করা ; বিরোধ বা সংগ্রাম হইতে নিবৃত্ত হওয়া।

sponge (spŭnj), *v. t., i.* & *n.* **1.** To clean or wipe with a sponge ; স্পঞ্জ দ্বারা মুছা বা পরিষ্কার করা। **2.** To efface ; মুছিয়া ফেলা, বিলুপ্ত করা। **3.** To drain as, to *sponge* money ; শোষণ

করা। 4. To gain by sychophant means or arts; "To *sponge* a breakfast once a weak"; তোষামোদ দ্বারা বা ছল চাতুরী করিয়া লাভ করা। *Verb i.* 1. To suck in or imbibe as a sponge; স্পঞ্জের মত শোষণ করা। 2. To live upon others; to live by mean arts (with *on*); অন্যের গলগ্রহ হইয়া বাস করা; ছল-চাতুরী দ্বারা জীবনযাত্রা নির্ব্বাহ করা। 3. To gather sponges; স্পঞ্জ সংগ্রহ-করা। *Noun.* The act of sponging; স্পঞ্জ দ্বারা পরিষ্করণ বা জলশোষণ। **Spong'-er,** *n.*

spong'-ing (spŭnj-), *n.* The act of one who sponges; স্পঞ্জ দ্বারা পরিষ্করণ বা শুষ্কীকরণ। **Sponging-house**—(পূর্ব্বে) জেলে পুরিবার পূর্ব্বে আত্মীয়গণকে ঋণ-পরিশোধের সুযোগ দেওয়ার জন্য যে সরাইয়ে ২৪ ঘণ্টা কাল পর্য্যন্ত বেলিফকর্তৃক ঋণগ্রস্ত ব্যক্তিকে বন্দী করিয়া রাখা হইত।

spon'-ğī-ōle (spŭn-), *n.* (*Bot.*) The absorbent cellular tissue at the extremities of roots; (উদ্ভিদ্-বিদ্যা) শিকড়ের নিম্নস্থ শোষকধর্ম্মী বিধানতন্তু, সমষ্টিকোষ (সাঃ পঃ)।

spon-ğī-ō-pī'-līne (spŭn-), *n.* An absorbent of sponge and fibre on a waterproof backing used as a substitute for poultice; পুল্টিশের পরিবর্ত্তে স্পঞ্জ ও পশম স্তরেস্তরে মিশ্রিত এক পৃষ্ঠ রবারেআবৃত বস্ত্রবৎ পদার্থবিশেষ।

spon'-ğy (spŭn-), *adj.* 1. Like sponge; স্পঞ্জবৎ, শোষকবৎ। 2. Soft and full of cavities; কোমল এবং ছিদ্রবহুল।

spŏn'-sion, *n.* 1. Being surety for another; অন্যের প্রতিভূ হওন, প্রাতিভাব্য। 2. (*Inter. Law*) An act or engagement made on behalf of a State by a person not specially authorised; বিশিষ্ট ক্ষমতা প্রাপ্ত হয় নাই এরূপ ব্যক্তিকর্তৃক কোন রাষ্ট্রের পক্ষে কোনরূপ বাক্যদান।

spŏn'-sŏn, *n.* 1. The angular space before and abaft the paddle box against the ship's side; পোতচক্রের উপরিভাগের আবরণের সম্মুখ এবং পশ্চাদ্‌ভাগস্থ ত্রিকোণাকৃতি স্থান। 2. Projection from the side of a warship to enable a gun to be trained forward and aft; কামান সম্মুখ ও পশ্চাদ্দিকে সঞ্চালনের জন্য পোতপার্শ্ব হইতে উদ্গত স্থান।

spŏn'-sŏr, *n.* 1. A godfather or godmother; ধর্ম্মপিতা বা ধর্ম্মমাতা। 2. A surety; জামিন, প্রতিভূ। **—ship,** *n.* **—so'-ri-al,** *adj.*

spŏn-tā'-nĕ-ous (-ŭs), *adj.* 1. Proceeding from natural feeling, temperament, or disposition; স্বয়ংজাত, স্বয়ংকৃত, স্বতঃসিদ্ধ, অযত্নসম্ভূত, স্বতঃস্ফূর্ত্ত, স্বয়ংভূত, স্বাভাবিক, আপনা আপনি, অহৈতুকী, অহেতুক। 2. Voluntary; as, a *spontaneous* offer; ইচ্ছাকৃত। **—ly,** *adv.* In a spontaneous manner; স্বতঃএব, স্বচ্ছন্দতঃ। **—ne'-i-ty,** *n.* The quality or state of being spontaneous; স্বতোভাবিতা (হিঃ কোঃ), স্বতঃ-স্ফূর্ত্ততা, স্বচ্ছন্দতা। **—ness,** *n.* **Spontaneous combustion**—আভ্যন্তরিক তাপজননদ্বারা কোন বস্তু (যথা তৈলসিক্ত ন্যাকড়ার স্তূপ, জলসিক্ত কয়লা প্রভৃতি) প্রজ্বালন, স্বতঃপ্রজ্বালন, স্বতোদাহন। **Spontaneous generation**—অচেতন পদার্থ হইতে সচেতন পদার্থের উদ্ভব, স্বতঃসম্ভব, স্বতোজনি (হিঃ কোঃ), স্বতঃ-উৎপাদন। **Spontaneous suggestion**—স্বতঃস্ফূর্ত্ত ইঙ্গিত (যাহা ভাব সাহচর্য্য হইতে সঞ্জাত হয়—ইচ্ছাদ্বারা উৎপন্ন হয় না)। **Spontaneous variation**—স্বতোভেদন (হিঃ কোঃ)।

spŏn-toon', *n.* A kind of half-pike or halberd used by some British officers; ব্রিটিশ সামরিক কর্ম্মচারিগণ কর্তৃক ব্যবহৃত একপ্রকার টাঙ্গী।

spōōk, *n.* Ghost; ভূত। **Spook'-ish,** *adj.* **Spook'-y** *adj.*

spōōl, *n.* & *v. t.* A piece of cane or reed used by weavers for winding yarn; নাটাই, চরকী। *Verb t.* To wind on spool; নাটাইয়ে জড়ান, চরকীতে জড়ান।

spōōn, *n.*, *v. t.* & *i.* 1. A domestic utensil for taking up liquids etc. at table; চামচে, চমস। 2. A foolish fellow; বেকুব লোক, হাবা। 3. Same as SPOON-BAIT. *Verb t.* 1. To take up in a spoon; চামচেতে করিয়া নেওয়া। 2. (*Cricket*) To strike a ball feebly; (ক্রিকেট ক্রীড়ায়) দুর্ব্বল হস্তে কন্দুককে আঘাত করা। *Verb i.* To move rapidly through; দ্রুত চলা। **Spoon-bait** — একপ্রকার উজ্জ্বল ঘূর্ণনশীল, এবং চমসাকৃতি কৃত্রিম বড়শীর টোপ। **Spoon-bill**—ধনেশ পাখী। **Spoon-meat**—তরল খাদ্য, শিশু খাদ্য। **Spoon-net**—বড়শী দ্বারা মৎস্য শিকারকারিগণের ক্ষুদ্র জাল। **Dessert-spoon**—মধ্যম আকারের চাম্‌চে। **Gravy-spoon**—অতি বড় আকারের চাম্‌চে। **Marrow-spoon**—অস্থি মজ্জা বাহির করার জন্য চামচে। **Table-spoon**—বড় আকারের চাম্‌চে। **Tea-spoon**—ক্ষুদ্র আকারের চামচে, চার চাম্‌চে। **Wooden spoon** — কেম্ব্রিজ বিশ্ববিদ্যালয়ের গণিতের অনারে সর্ব্ব নিম্নস্থানপ্রাপ্ত ব্যক্তি। **It takes a long spoon to sup with him**—He is an evil spirit: সে ভূত বা প্রেতাত্মা। **To be born with a silver spoon in one's mouth** — See SILVER. **To be born with a golden spoon in one's mouth**—To be born in a rich family; বড় লোকের ঘরে জন্মগ্রহণ করা। **To be spoons on**—(*Slang*) To be in love with; প্রেমে পড়া। **To make a spoon or spoil a horn**—To succeed or utterly fail in an enterprize; কোন দুঃসাহসিক কার্য্যে সফলতা লাভ করা বা সম্পূর্ণরূপে অকৃতকার্য্য হওয়া।

Spōōn'-ĕr, —ĭsm, *ns.* Accidental transposition of initial letters etc. of two or more words; দুই বা ততোধিক শব্দের আদ্যক্ষর প্রভৃতির আকস্মিক বিপর্য্যয়।

spōōn'-y, spōōn'-ey (-ĭ), *adjs.* Soft; simple; silly; sentimental;

কোমল ; সরল ; বেকুব ; ভাবপ্রবণ। **—i-ly,** *adv.* **—i-ness,** *n.* **To be spooney on a girl**—To be foolishly fond of her ; নির্বোধের মত কোন বালিকার প্রতি অনুরক্ত হওয়া।

spŏ-răd'-ic, *adj.* Scattered; occurring only here and there : as, a *sporadic* case of disease; single; as, a *sporadic* individual of a species ; বিশ্লিষ্ট ; অব্যাপক, এখানে-সেখানে দৃষ্ট ; একমাত্র। **—i-cal,** *adj.* (*Rare*) **—i-cal-ness,** *n.*

spŏ-răn'-ğī-ŏ-phōre, *n.* A stalk or receptacle bearing sporangia ; রেণুস্থলীধর (সাঃ পঃ)।

spŏ-răn'-ğī-ŭm, (*Pl.* -A) *n.* (*Bot.*) The case in which spores are produced ; সূক্ষ্মবীজাধার, রেণুভাণ্ড, রেণুস্থলী।

spŏ-rā'-tion, *n.* Spore-formation ; সূক্ষ্মবীজগঠন।

spōre, *n.* **1.** That part of a flowerless plant which forms the function of the seed ; অপুষ্পক বৃক্ষের যে অংশ দ্বারা বীজের কার্য্য সাধিত হয়, রেণু (সাঃ পঃ), কোরককীটাণু। **2.** (*Biol.*) A germ of certain animal organism ; (জীববিজ্ঞান) কোন কোন জীবাবয়বের অঙ্কুর, জীবাঙ্কুর, সূক্ষ্মজীব। **3.** (*Fig.*) Seed or germ of anything ; বীজ, অঙ্কুর।

spō'-rō-cărp, *n.* A many-celled form of fruit produced in certain lower cryptogams in consequence of asexual act ; রেণুকুঠি (সাঃ পঃ)।

spŏ-rō-ğĕn'-ĕ-sis, *n.* Spore-formation ; সূক্ষ্মবীজজনন। **—rog'-e-nous,** *adj.*

spō'-rō-phōre, *n.* (*Bot.*) A spore-bearing branch or organ ; রেণুধর (সাঃ পঃ)।

spō'-rō-phȳl(l), *n.* (*Bot.*) A spore-bearing leaf ; রেণুপত্র (সাঃ পঃ)।

spō'-rō-phȳte, *n.* The spore-bearing stage in the life-cycle of a plant ; রেণুধরোদ্ভিদ (সাঃ পঃ)।

spŏr'-răn, *n.* The fur-pouch worn in front of the kilt by Highlanders; হাইলেণ্ডারগণ জাঙ্গিয়ার সম্মুখে যে সলোম চর্ম্মনির্ম্মিত থলি পরিধান করিয়া থাকে।

spōrt, *n.*, *v. t.* & *i.* **1.** Pastime ; amusement ; "It is as *sport* to a fool to do mischief" ; ক্রীড়াকৌতুক, লীলা, বিনোদ, কেলি ; আমোদ প্রমোদ। **2.** Fun ; diversion ; কৌতুক, রঙ্গ, তামাসা ; চিত্তবিনোদন। **3.** A comprehensive term embracing all sorts of athletic games of skill in which prizes are competed or money staked ; মল্লক্রীড়া। **4.** Diversions of the field such as hunting, fowling or fishing ; মৃগয়া, মৎস্য শিকার, প্রভৃতি আমোদজনক ব্যাপার। **5.** Mockery ; "Then make *sport* at me" ; mock ; ঠাট্টা বিদ্রূপ ; ব্যঙ্গ। **6.** (*Biol.*) A spontaneous division from the normal type ; (জীববিজ্ঞান) সাধারণ জাতিরূপে বিচ্যুতি বা ব্যভিচার, অপচয়। **7.** A plaything ; a helpless object of some force ; as, a *sport* of chance ; ক্রীড়নক ; কোন শক্তির ক্রীড়াসামগ্রী। **8.** (*Rare*) Amorous dallying ; (কচিদ্‌ব্যবহৃত) কেলি, রসক্রীড়া, কামকেলি, ললিত। *Verb t.* **1.** To divert oneself ; to make merry ; চিত্তবিনোদন করা ; রঙ্গ করা, আমোদপ্রমোদ করা, ক্রীড়াকৌতুক করা। **2.** (*Slang*) To exhibit or bring out in public ; "To *sport* silk and satin on the public race-course" ; (ইতরভাষায়) সাধারণের সমক্ষে প্রদর্শন করা। *Verb i.* **1.** To play ; to frolic ; ক্রীড়া করা, ক্রীড়া কৌতুক করা ; লীলাখেলা করা, আমোদ প্রমোদ করা। **2.** To trifle ; তুচ্ছ করা, হেলা করা। **3.** (*Biol.*) To assume a character different from the specific or varied type ; (জীববিজ্ঞান) কোন নির্দ্দিষ্ট জাতিরূপের ব্যভিচারী হওয়া। **Sport'-ful,** *adj.* **Sportsman** — ক্রীড়ক, খেলোয়াড়, শিকারী, মৎস্যশিকারী, মৃগয়াসেবী। **In sport**—Not seriously ; আমোদচ্ছলে, লীলাচ্ছলে, কৌতুকচ্ছলে। **To make a sport of**—To make ridiculous ; হাস্যাস্পদ করা, উপহাসাস্পদ করা। **To sport off**—To utter sportively ; to throw off with ease ; ক্রীড়াচ্ছলে বলা ; অনায়াসে নিক্ষেপ করা। **To sport one's oak**—See OAK.

spōr'-tive (-tiv), *adj.* **1.** Playful ; merry ; "Is it I that drive thee from the *sportive* court?"—*Shakes.* ; রঙ্গপ্রিয়, ক্রীড়াপ্রিয়, ব্যঙ্গপ্রিয়, লীলাপ্রিয়, সলীল, সখেল, কেলিপ্রিয়, কেলিপর ; আনন্দদায়ক, প্রফুল্ল, উৎফুল্ল। **2.** Amorous ; কামুক।

spŏr'-ūle, *n.* (*Bot.*) A small spore (উদ্ভিদ্‌বিদ্যা) অতি সূক্ষ্ম কোরককীটাণু।

spŏt, *n.* **1.** A mark ; a speck ; চিহ্ন ; দাগ। **2.** A blemish ; a flaw ; disgrace ; as, he is without a *spot* in his reputation ; খুঁত ; দোষ ; কলঙ্ক। **3.** A small extent of space ; a place ; ক্ষুদ্রস্থান ; স্থান, জায়গা। **4.** Kinds of fish and domestic pigeon ; নানাপ্রকার মৎস্য ও কপোতের সাধারণ নাম। **5.** A dark place on the disc of the sun or of a planet ; সূর্য্য বা কোন গ্রহের কলঙ্ক, সৌরকলঙ্ক। **6.** (*Pl.*) Commodities sold for cash ; নগদমূল্যে বিক্রীত বস্তু। **Spot'-less,** *adj.* Unblemished ; নিষ্কলঙ্ক, নির্ম্মল, অকলঙ্ক, অকল্মষ। **Spot'-less-ly,** *adv.* **Spot'-less-ness,** *n.* **Spot'-ti-ness.** *n.* **Spot'-ty,** *adj.* **Spot cotton**—বিক্রীত হওয়া মাত্র যে তুলা ক্রেতাকে সমর্পণ করিতে হইবে। **Spot prices**—তৎক্ষণাৎ দেয় মূল্য। **Spot-stroke**—বিলিয়াড ক্রীড়ায় আঘাত বিশেষ। **Spot wheat** — বিক্রীত হওয়া মাত্র যে গোধূম ক্রেতাকে বুঝাইয়া দিতে হয়। **In spot**—By intervals ; থাকিয়া থাকিয়া, মাঝে মাঝে, সময় সময়। **In** some respects ; কোন কোন অংশে। **On the spot** — Then and there ; as, to decide on the *spot* ; তন্মুহূর্ত্তে। On the alert ; সজাগ, হুঁসিয়ার।

spŏt, *v. t.* **1.** To make visible marks upon with some foreign matter ; as, to *spot* a cloth ; দাগ দেওয়া, চিহ্নিত করা। **2.** To stain ; কলঙ্কিত করা। **3.** To cover with small spots ; ফুট ফুট দাগবিশিষ্ট করা। **4.** (*Colloq.*) To recognise; to detect; as, I *spotted* him at once as an Indian ; (চলিত ভাষায়) চিনা, পরিচয় করা; ধরা। **5.** (*Colloq.*) To pick out beforehand the winner in a race or match : ঘোড়দৌড় বা প্রতিযোগিতার ক্রীড়ায় জয়ী অশ্ব, ব্যক্তি, প্রভৃতিকে পূর্ব্বেই বাছিয়া ঠিক করা। **Spot′-ted,** *p. p.* **1.** Marked with spots ; as, *spotted* leopard ; দাগবিশিষ্ট, চিত্রবিচিত্র, চকরা-পাকরা, ফোঁটা ফোঁটা, ফুট ফুট (*colloq.*)। **2.** Sullied ; as, *spotted* character ; কলঙ্কিত, কলুষিত। **Spotted fever**—একপ্রকার জ্বর—যাহাতে দেহে রক্তবর্ণ পীড়কা জাত হয়। **To spot a timber**—To cut it in preparation for hewing ; চেলা করার পূর্ব্বে কাঠছেদন করা, খণ্ড খণ্ড করা।

spous′-ăl (spowz-), *n.* & *adj.* (*usu. pl.*) Marriage; বিবাহ, পরিণয়, উদ্বাহ। ***Adj.*** Matrimonial ; বিবাহসম্বন্ধীয়, পরিণয়সংক্রান্ত, ঔদ্বাহিক, বৈবাহিক।

spouse (spowz), *n.* Husband or wife ; "I that lady to my *spouse* had won"; স্বামী কিম্বা স্ত্রী, বধূ, গৃহিণী।

spout (spowt), *n.*, *v. t.* & *i.* **1.** A nozzle, or projecting mouth of a vessel; চায়ের কেটলি প্রভৃতির মুখনল। **2.** A pipe for conducting water esp. from a roof ; নল, চোঙ্গ, বিশেষতঃ ছাদের নল। **3.** The column of spray sent up by a whale in breathing ; তিমিমৎস্য শ্বাসমোচনকালে যে জলকণাসমূহ উৎক্ষিপ্ত করে। **4.** Same as WATER-SPOUT. **5.** A kind of sloping trough for conveying coal, grain, etc. into a particular receptacle ; কয়লা-শস্য, প্রভৃতি কোন বিশেষ পাত্রে ঢালিবার জন্য একপ্রকার টের্চ্চা দীর্ঘপাত্র। **6.** The spout in a pawn-broker's shop ; a pawn-broker's shop ; বন্ধক-ব্যবসায়ীর দোকানের জিনিষ নীচে ফেলিবার জন্য গড়ানিয়া পাত্র ; বন্ধক ব্যবসায়ীর দোকান। ***Verb t.*** **1.** To throw out as liquid through a narrow orifice or pipe ; অপরিসর ছিদ্র বা নলের ভিতর দিয়া তরলপদার্থ পাতিত করা। **2.** To eject in a jet; ধারায় নির্গত করা। **3.** To throw out as words with affected gravity ; গুরুগম্ভীর ভাবে বলা। **4.** To pawn ; as to *spout* a watch ; বন্ধক দেওয়া। ***Verb i.*** **1.** To issue with violence or in a jet as liquid through a narrow orifice, or from a spout ; as, blood *spouts* from an wound; ফিন্‌কি দিয়া ছুটা, উচ্ছলিত হওয়া। **2.** To make a speech, esp. in a pompous manner ; বক্তৃতা করা, বাগাড়ম্বর পূর্ণ বক্তৃতা করা। **Spout-fish**—যে মৎস্য বা শম্বুকাদি জীব সবেগে জলধারা নির্গত করে। **Spout-hole**—জলধারা নির্গমের জন্য রন্ধ্র। **To be up the spout**—To be in difficulties ; to be compelled to pawn ; সঙ্কটে পড়া, দায়ে পড়া ; জিনিষ বন্ধক দিতে বাধ্য হওয়া। **To put up the spout**—To pawn ; বন্ধক দেওয়া। **Up the spout**—Pawned ; বন্ধকী।

sprăg, *n.* A stout bar of wood for checking the wheel of a cart ; শকটের চক্র প্রভৃতি রোধ করার জন্য কঠিন কাঠদণ্ড।

sprăg, *n.* (*Dial.*) A young salmon (উপভাষায়) স্যামন মাছের শাবক।

sprain (sprān), *v. t.* & *n.* To overstrain the muscles or ligaments of a joint so as to injure them ; (হাতের কব্জা, পায়ের গাঁইট, প্রভৃতি) মোচড়াইয়া দেওয়া, মচকান। ***Noun.*** A violent strain of a joint without dislocation ; মোচড়, মচকানি, খেঁচনা (যোঃ)।

spraints (sprānts), *n. pl.* Otter's dung ; উদ্বিড়ালের পুরীষ।

sprăng, *p. t.* of SPRING (which see)

sprăt, *n.* & *v. i.* A small fish of the herring family ; হেরিংজাতীয় ক্ষুদ্র মৎস্যবিশেষ। ***Verb i.*** To fish for sprat ; উক্ত মৎস্য শিকার করা। **Sprat′-ter,** *n.* **Sprat′-ting,** *n.* **Sprat-day**—৯ই নভেম্বর। [এই দিবস হইতে ইংলণ্ডে এই মৎস্য ধরার মরসুম সুরু হয়।]

spraŵl (sprāl), *v. i.*, *t.* & *n.* **1.** To lie ungracefully with the limbs stretched out or struggling ; কদর্য্যভাবে হাত পা ছড়াইয়া শায়িত হওয়া ; কদর্য্য ভাবে শুইয়া হাত পা আছড়ান। **2.** To spread irregularly, as vines, plants, or tree ; to spread ungracefully ; আঙ্গুরলতা, চারাগাছ প্রভৃতি এলোমেলোভাবে ছড়ান ; কদর্য্যভাবে ছড়ান। ***Verb t.*** To open out irregularly ; as, to *sprawl* a body of cavalry ; বিশৃঙ্খলভাবে প্রসারিত করা। ***Noun.*** The act or posture of sprawling ; কদর্য্যভাবে হস্তপদ প্রসারণপূর্ব্বক শায়িত হওন, কদর্য্যভাবে হস্তপদ প্রসারণের ভঙ্গী।

spray (sprā), *n.* **1.** A branch of tree with branchlet or flowers ; a small shoot or branch ; প্রশাখা-বিশিষ্ট শাখা, সপুষ্প শাখা ; প্রশাখা। **2.** A small branch of flowers, leaves, etc. worn by ladies in their hair or on the dress ; an ornament like a collection of twigs and flowers; as, a *spray* of brillants ; মহিলাগণের পরিচ্ছদে বা কুন্তলগুচ্ছে পরিহিত পুষ্পপল্লববিশিষ্ট ক্ষুদ্র-শাখা ; পুষ্পসমন্বিত ক্ষুদ্র শাখাকৃতি রত্ননির্ম্মিতভূষা, রত্নপল্লব, মণিমঞ্জরী। **Spray′-ey,** *adj.* **Spray-drain**—ক্ষেত্রমধ্যস্থ নালাবিশেষ—যাহা শাখাপ্রশাখা দ্বারা পূর্ণ করা হয়।

spray (sprā), *n.* & *v. t.* **1.** Water or any liquid flying in small drops or particles ; সূক্ষ্মকণাকারে উৎক্ষিপ্ত জল বা অন্য কোনরূপ তরল পদার্থ, শীকরধারা। **2.** The vapour from an atomizer ; শীকরপ্রক্ষেপক যন্ত্র

হইতে নির্গত বাষ্প। *Verb t.* 1. To scatter or let fall in the form of spray ; কণাকারে ছড়ান বা ফেলা, শীকরাকারে প্রক্ষেপ করা। 2. To throw spray upon ; to treat with a spray ; শীকর প্রক্ষেপ করা ; শীকরপ্রক্ষেপক যন্ত্রের বাষ্পদ্বারা প্রোক্ষিত করা। **Spray'-ey,** *adj.* **Spray-board**—তরঙ্গাদি হইতে উৎক্ষিপ্ত জলকণাসমূহ রোধ করার জন্য নৌকার ব্যবস্থাবিশেষ।

spread (sprĕd), *v. t.* & *i.* 1. To extend in length or breadth or in breadth only ; বিস্তার করা, প্রসারিত করা, ব্যাপ্ত করা, বিতত করা। 2. To unfurl ; as, to *spread* a sail ; ছড়ান, বিস্তারিত করা। 3. To overspread ; আবৃত করা, আচ্ছাদিত করা। 4. To publish ; as, to *spread* a report ; প্রচার করা, ছড়ান, রাষ্ট্র করা। 5. To propagate ; as, to *spread* a disease ; বিস্তার করা। 6. To set or furnish with provisions ; as, to *spread* a table ; খাদ্যদ্রব্য সজ্জিত করা। 7. To record ; as, to *spread* a resolution upon the minutes of a society ; লিপিবদ্ধ করা। *Verb i.* 1. To extend in all directions or in breadth only ; ছড়ান, বিস্তৃত হওয়া, বিস্তারিত হওয়া, ব্যাপ্ত হওয়া। 2. To be extended by drawing or beating ; টানিয়া বা পিটিয়া দীর্ঘ বা বিস্তৃত করা। 3. To be propagated ; পরিব্যাপ্ত হওয়া, ছড়াইয়া পড়া। 4. To be divulged ; প্রচারিত হওয়া, প্রকাশ হওয়া, প্রকাশ পাওয়া। **Spread'-ing,** *adj.*

spread (sprŏd), *p. p.* 1. Extended ; বিস্তারিত, প্রসারিত, প্রতানী (সাঃ পঃ), বিতত। 2. (Of a gun) Thin ; পুরু নয়, অস্থূল। **Spread eagle**—মার্কিণ যুক্তরাজ্যের জাতীয়চিহ্ন (ঊর্দ্ধে প্রসারিত পক্ষযুগল এবং প্রসারিত পদদ্বয়বিশিষ্ট উৎক্রোশ পক্ষী); ছত্রাকের সহিত পরিবেষিত বিদারিত এবং ভর্জিত কুক্কুট ; জাহাজের মাস্তুলের দড়াদড়িতে বাঁধিয়া যে নাবিককে বেত্রাঘাত করা হয়। (*Adj. spread-eagle*) বাগাড়ম্বরপূর্ণ ; বাগড়ম্বরপূর্ণ স্বাদেশিকতা-প্রদর্শনকারী। **Spread-eagleism**—মার্কিণযুক্তরাজ্যের অধিবাসিগণের দম্ভপূর্ণ স্বাদেশিকতা।

spread (sprĕd), *n.* 1. The act of spreading ; প্রসারণ। 2. Extent ; compass ; diffusion ; বিস্তার ; প্রসার ; ব্যাপ্তি। 3. (*Colloq.*) A meal or banquet ; as, had no end of a *spread* ; (চলিত ভাষায়) ভোজন ; ভোজ। 4. A cloth used as a cover for a bed or table ; আস্তরণ। 5. The privilege of demanding shares of stock at a certain price or of delivering shares of stock at another price, within a certain time agreed on ; নির্দ্দিষ্ট সময়ের মধ্যে নির্দ্দিষ্ট মূল্যে কোম্পানীর কাগজের অংশসমূহ দাবী করার কিম্বা অন্যরূপ দরে অংশসমূহ অর্পণ করার অধিকার।

spree (sprē), *n.* & *v. i.* A merry frolic ; esp. a drinking frolic : carousal ; ক্রীড়াকৌতুক, লীলাবিলাস ; পানোল্লাস ; পানকোলাহল। *Verb i.* To have a spree ; পানোল্লাস করা, পানকোলাহল করা।

sprĕnt, *adj.* (*Archaic*) Sprinkled ; (অপ্রঃ) সেচিত, প্রোক্ষিত।

sprig, *n.* & *v. t.* 1. A small shoot or twig ; ক্ষুদ্র শাখাপ্রশাখা, ছোট ডাল, ফেঁকড়ী। 2. The figure of a branch or spray in embroidery ; সূচীকর্ম্মে পুষ্পপল্লবসমন্বিত ক্ষুদ্র শাখা। 3. A small headless nail ; মাথাশূন্য ক্ষুদ্র প্রেক। 4. (*Humourously*) A lad ; (রহস্যচ্ছলে) ছোকরা। *Verb t.* To mark or adorn with the representation of small branches ; ক্ষুদ্র ক্ষুদ্র সপুষ্প শাখার ভূষাদ্বারা অঙ্কিত বা অলঙ্কৃত করা। **Sprig-tail**—সূক্ষ্মাগ্রপুচ্ছবিশিষ্ট বিভিন্ন জাতীয় হংস প্রভৃতি।

spright (sprīt), *n.* A spirit ; অপদেবতা, প্রেতাত্মা, দেবযোনি।

spright'-ly (sprīt-), *adj.* Vivacious ; lively ; gay ; জীবন্ত সজীব ; সতেজ ; উৎফুল্ল, স্ফূর্ত্তিব্যঞ্জক, আনন্দপূর্ণ, প্রফুল্ল। **—li-ness,** *n.*

spring, *v. i.* & *t.* 1. To leap ; লাফ দেওয়া, লম্ফ দেওয়া। 2. To shoot up, out or forth ; বেগে উত্থিত হওয়া, বেগে নির্গত হওয়া, বেগে ছুটা। 3. To come to light ; to emerge ; to come into existence ; প্রকাশিত হওয়া ; নির্গত হওয়া; উদ্ভূত হওয়া, উপজাত হওয়া, উৎপন্ন হওয়া। 4. To recoil; পশ্চাদ্দিকে ধাক্কা দেওয়া। 5. To start or rise suddenly from a covert ; আশ্রয় স্থান হইতে হঠাৎ চমকিয়া উঠা। 6. To bend from a straight direction or plane surface ; বাঁকিয়া যাওয়া। 7. (*Arch.*) To start from the impost bounding upward and outward (said of a vault or arch) ; (স্থপতিবিজ্ঞান) অধিষ্ঠান হইতে উদ্গত হওয়া। *Verb t.* 1. To start or rouse, as a game ; শিকারের পশুকে চমকিত করা বা জাগান। 2. To cause to explode ; as, to *spring* a mine ; ফুটান, সশব্দে বিদীর্ণ করা। 3. To cause to open, as, a leak ; ফুটা করা। 4. To crack ; to bend or strain so as to weaken ; ফাটান ; কঠিনতা হ্রাস করার জন্য নোয়ান বা চাপ দেওয়া। 5. To bend by force as something stiff or strong ; কোন শক্ত বা কঠিন বস্তু জোর করিয়া বাঁকান। 6. To cause to close suddenly, as a trap ; সহসা বন্ধ করা। 7. To throw off or set an arch from an abutment or pier ; পিল্পা হইতে খিলান বিচ্যুত করা। 8. To pass over by leaping ; লাফাইয়া পার হওয়া, ডিঙ্গান (*colloq.*), টপকান (*ib.*) 9. To produce or develop suddenly or unexpectedly ; as, to *spring* a theory ; সহসা বা অপ্রত্যাশিতভাবে উৎপাদন বা পরিস্ফুট করা। **To spring a butt**—To loosen the end of a plank by labouring in heavy sea ; প্রবল ঝটিকাবিক্ষুব্ধ সাগরের তরঙ্গাভিঘাতে জাহাজের তক্তা শ্লথ হওয়া। **To spring a leak**—To open the seams of a planking to the extent of becoming leaky ; ফুটা হওয়া, ছিদ্র হওয়া

To spring a mast—(Of a mast) To be bent or strained or to start from its fastenings; (মাস্তুল সম্পর্কে) বাঁকিয়া যাওয়া, বা আধার হইতে চ্যুত হওয়া। **To spring a rattle**—To make a rattling sound ; ঝুনঝুনি বাজান। **To spring at**—To leap towards ; কোন কিছুকে লক্ষ্য করিয়া লাফ দেওয়া। **To spring forth**—To leap out ; to rush out ; লাফ দিয়া বাহির হওয়া ; বেগে ধাবিত হওয়া। To spurt out ; বেগে নিঃসৃত হওয়া, ফিনকি দিয়া ছুটা। **To spring in** — To enter with a leap, or in haste ; লম্ফ প্রদানে প্রবেশ করা, লাফাইয়া ঢুকা, দ্রুত প্রবেশ করা। **To spring on or upon**—To rush on with haste or violence; to assault; লাফাইয়া উপরে পড়া ; আক্রমণ করা। **To spring to one's feet**—To rise suddenly with a leap ; হঠাৎ লাফাইয়া উঠা। **To spring the luff, To spring her luff**—To yield to helm and sail nearer to wind ; হাইলের দ্বারা চালিত হইয়া প্রায় বাতাসের বিপরীত দিকে চলা।

spring, *n.* **1.** Leap; "The prisoner with a *spring* from prison broke" ; লম্ফ, লাফ। **2.** The season of the year when plants begin to vegetate and grow—(usu. the months of March, April and May) ; বসন্ত, বসন্তকাল, বসন্তঋতু, মধুঋতু, ঋতুপতি (*poet.*) [Syn. পুষ্পসময়, ঋতুরাজ, সুরভি, মধু, মাধব, পিকানন্দ, কান্ত, কামসখ।] **3.** The resilience of a body recovering its former state by its elasticity ; as, the *spring* of a bow ; স্থিতিস্থাপকতা হেতু পূর্ব্বাকারপ্রাপ্তি বস্তুর পরাবৃত্তি। **4.** Elasticity ; as, his muscles have no *spring* in them ; স্থিতিস্থাপকতা। **5.** An elastic body, as a steel-rod, plate or coil ; স্থিতিস্থাপক গুণোপেত বস্তু, দম। **6.** A natural fountain ; as, a mineral *spring* ; নির্ঝর, উৎস, প্রস্রবণ, ঝরণা। **7.** The source from which a stream proceeds ; নদীর উৎপত্তি-স্থল। **8.** Any source of supply ; origin ; cause ; as, the *spring* of human action ; উৎপত্তি স্থান ; মূল, প্রভব ; কারণ, হেতু। **9.** Upward curve ; ঊর্দ্ধগামী বক্রতা। **10.** A crack or fissure ; ফাইট,

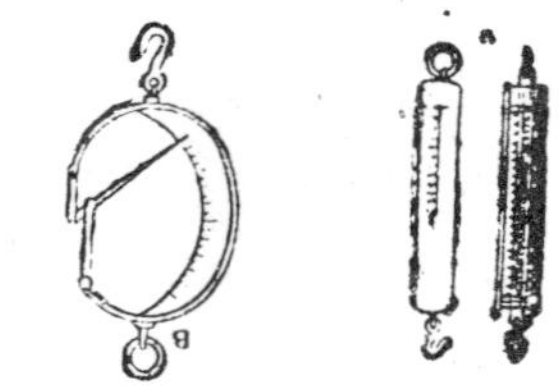

Spring balances.

ফাটোল। **Spring-balance**—দমের তুলাযন্ত্র। **Spring-beam**—একপ্রকার তুলাযন্ত্র যাহাতে দমের বিততি বা সঞ্চালনের ফলে শঙ্কুদ্বারা ক্রমাঙ্কিত ফলকে ওজন নির্দ্দিষ্ট হয়, দমের তুলাযন্ত্র। **Spring-bed**—দমের বিছানা। **Spring board**—যে স্থিতিস্থাপক ফলক হইতে লম্ফ প্রদান কালে, বা জলে নিমজ্জিত হওয়ার কালে বিশেষ বেগ পাওয়া যায়। **Spring-buck** — Same as SPRING-BOK. **Spring-carriage** — দমের গাড়ী। **Spring catarrh** — পর্ব্বণী, শুক্তিকা (সাঃ পঃ)। **Spring-gun**—কোন ব্যক্তি বা জন্তু হঠাৎ উপরে পতিত হইলে যে কামান আওয়াজ হয়। **Spring-mattress**—দমের গদি। **Springnight**—মধুযামিনী। **Spring-tide**—অমাবস্যা কিম্বা পূর্ণিমার পরে ভরা জোয়ার, ভরা কটাল। **Spring-time**—বসন্তকাল, মধু। **Spring-water**—নির্ঝর-বারি, ঝরণার জল।

spring'-al, -ald, *ns.* (*Archaic*) Youngster ; (অপ্রঃ) ছোকরা।

spring'-bŏk, *n.* A species of antelope inhabiting the plains of South Africa ; দক্ষিণ আফ্রিকার প্রান্তরবাসী কৃষ্ণসারমৃগবিশেষ।

springe (sprĭnj), A noose ; a snare ; পাশ ; ফাঁদ।

spring'-er (-ĕr), *n.* **1.** One who springs ; লম্ফপ্রদানকারী। **2.** The part of an arch where the curve begins ; the bottom stone of an arch ; তোরণের যে অংশে বক্রতা আরব্ধ হয় ; তোরণের নিম্নপ্রস্তর। **3.** A dog of the spaniel or setter kind ; একপ্রকার কুকুর। **4.** Same as GRAMPUS. **5.** Same as SPRING-BOK.

spring'-ȳ, *adj.* **1.** Elastic ; as *springy* movement ; সংকোচপ্রসারশীল, নমনীয়। **2.** Light ; হালকা, লঘু। **3.** Full of, or abounding with, springs ; wet ; spongy ; নির্ঝরপূর্ণ, নির্ঝরবহুল ; সিক্ত ; শোষকবৎ।

sprin'-kle (sprĭng-kl), *v. t., i.* & *n.* **1.** To scatter or disperse in small drops or particles, as watter, seed, etc. ; ছড়ান, ছিটান, সেচন করা, ছড়া দেওয়া (*colloq.*), আছড়া দেওয়া (*ib.*)। **2.** To cleanse with few drops or small quantity of water ; to purify ; কয়েক ফোঁটা বা সামান্য জল দ্বারা পরিষ্কার করা ; বিশুদ্ধ করা। ***Verb i.*** **1.** To perform the act of scattering a liquid, or any fine substance ; ছিটান, ছড়ান। **2.** To rain moderately or with drops falling now and then ; সামান্য বৃষ্টি হওয়া, থাকিয়া থাকিয়া বৃষ্টি হওয়া, ফোঁটা ফোঁটা বৃষ্টি হওয়া। ***Noun.*** **1.** A sprinkling ; ছড়া, ছিটা। **2.** Light shower of rain ; সামান্য বৃষ্টি। **—kling,** *n.*

sprint, *v. i., t.* & *n.* To run short distance with great speed ; অতিবেগে অল্পক্ষণ দৌড়া বা দৌড়ান। ***Noun.*** A short run at top speed ; অতি দ্রুতবেগে অল্পক্ষণ দৌড়ন।

sprit, *n.* A small spar which crosses a sail to extend or elevate it ; যে নাতিদীর্ঘ দণ্ড মাস্তুল হইতে কোণাকোণি ভাবে পাইলের ঊর্দ্ধকোণ পর্য্যন্ত প্রসারিত থাকে। **Spritsail**—উক্ত কাষ্ঠখণ্ডদ্বারা ছড়ানো পাইল।

sprite, *n.* Elf ; spirit ; goblin ; অপদেবতা ; প্রেতাত্মা ; দুষ্টভূত।

sprŏck'-ĕt, *n.* A projection on the periphery of a wheel or capstan for engaging a chain ; শিকল, কাছি প্রভৃতি আটকাইবার জন্য চক্রপ্রান্তের প্রলম্বক বা নোঙ্গর উত্তোলন যন্ত্রের উদ্গত অংশ। **Sprocket-wheel** — উদ্গত অংশসমূহ বিশিষ্ট চক্র।

sprout (sprowt), *v. i., t.* & *n.* 1. To shoot forth ; অঙ্কুরিত হওয়া, অঙ্কুরোদ্গত হওয়া, গজান (*colloq.*)। 2. To grow like the shoots of plants ; অঙ্কুরের মত উদ্গত হওয়া, উদ্গত হওয়া। ***Verb t.*** To cause to sprout ; as, rain *sprouts* seeds ; অঙ্কুরিত করা, অঙ্কুরোদ্গত করা। ***Noun.*** 1. Shoot of plants ; অঙ্কুর, প্ররোহ, কিসলয়, বিটপ। 2. Same as BRUSSELS SPROUTS.

spruce (sprôs), *adj.* & *v. t.* Neat without elegance or dignity ; "He is so *spruce* that he can never be genteel ;" dandified ; পরিপাটী, ফিটফাট, পরিচ্ছন্ন, ঝরঝরে ; বাবুয়ানীগোছের। ***Verb t.*** To dress with affected neatness or with affected finical neatness ; কৃত্রিম পরিপাটির সহিত পোষাক পরা, কৃত্রিম খুঁটিনাটির সহিত বেশভূষা করা। **Spruce'-ly,** *adv.* **Spruce'-ness,** *n.*

spruce, (sprôs), *n.* A pine tree yielding valuable timber (Also *spruce-fir*) ; একপ্রকার সরল বৃক্ষ। **Spruce-beer**—উক্ত বৃক্ষের পত্র এবং কোমল শাখা হইতে প্রস্তুত একপ্রকার সুরা। [ইহা শীতাদ রোগের (Scurvy) প্রতিষেধকস্বরূপ ব্যবহৃত হয়।]

sprue (sprô), *n.* 1. The passage of a mould through which metal is poured ; ছাঁচের যে রন্ধ্রে গলিত ধাতু ঢালা হয়। 2. The waste piece cast in the hole ; dross ; ঐ রন্ধ্রে নিক্ষিপ্ত অব্যবহার্য্য অংশ ; ধাতুমল।

sprŭng, *p. t.* & *p. p.* of SPRING (which see).

sprȳ, *adj.* Nimble ; active ; lively ; "She is as *spry* as a cricket" ; চটুল ; চটপটে ; উৎফুল্ল।

spŭd, *n.* & *v. t.* 1. A small spade for cutting the roots of weeds ; খন্তা। 2. Anything short and thick ; পুরু এবং খর্ব্ব বস্তু। 3. (*Colloq.*) Potato ; (চলিত ভাষায়) গোল আলু। ***Verb t.*** To dig or remove by means of spud ; খন্তাদ্বারা খুড়া বা সরান।

spue (spü), *v. t.* & *i.* Same as SPEW (which see).

spūme, *n.* & *v. i.* Froth ; ফেনা, ফেন। ***Verb i.*** To fume ; ফেনিল হওয়া, ফেনা উঠা, ফেনায়িত হওয়া। **Spu-mes'-cence, Spum'-i-ness,** *n.* **Spu'-mous, Spum'-y,** *adjs.*

spŭn, *p. t.* & *p. p.* of SPIN (which see).

spunge (spŭnj), *n.* (*Archaic*) Sponge ; (অপ্রঃ) স্পঞ্জ।

spunk (spŭngk), *n.* Courage ; as, a man of *spunk* ; mettle ; pluck ; সাহস ; তেজঃ, বীর্য্য ; বুকের পাটা। **Spunk'-y,** *adj.*

spur (spêr), *n., v. t.* & *i.* 1. An instrument having a little wheel with sharp points, worn on a horseman's heels to prick a horse in order to hasten its pace ; অশ্বকে দ্রুত গমনে উত্তেজিত করার জন্য অশ্বারোহীর পাদুকাসংলগ্ন সূক্ষ্মাগ্র কণ্টকবিশিষ্ট চক্র, অশ্বারোহীর পাদুকাসংলগ্ন কাঁটা, অশ্বতাড়নী। 2. Incitement ; "His ferocious temper needed no *spur*, yet a *spur* was applied" ; উত্তেজনা, প্রণোদনা, প্ররোচনা। 3. The largest or principal root of tree ; কোন বৃক্ষের প্রধানতম বা বৃহত্তম শিকড়। 4. The hard projection on a cock's leg ; কুক্কুটের পদের কঠিন উদ্গত অংশ। 5. A small range of mountains extending laterally from a larger range ; শৈলবাহু। 6. (*Bot.*) Any projecting appendage of a flower or blossom having the apperance of a spur ; (উদ্ভিদ্‌বিদ্যা) পুষ্প হইতে উদ্গত শঙ্কুবৎ অংশ, শঙ্কু (সাঃ পঃ)। 7. A morbid excrescence on rye ; রাইসরিষার একপ্রকার রোগদুষ্ট উদ্গত অংশ। 8. A spike in the boot-sole ; বুট্‌-জুতার তলিতে সংলগ্ন কাঁটা। 9. (*Med.*) The angle at which arteries leave a cavity ; (ভৈষজ্যশাস্ত্র) যে কোণ উৎপাদন পূর্ব্বক ধমনী সমূহ কোন কোষ্ঠ হইতে বহির্গত হয়। 10. A brace connecting or strengthening a post and some other part, as rafter or crossbeam ; যে ক্ষুদ্র কাষ্ঠখণ্ডদ্বারা খোঁটা প্রভৃতি শক্ত করা হয় কিম্বা বর্গা, আড়কাঠ প্রভৃতি শক্ত করা বা জোড়া দেওয়া হইয়া থাকে। 11. (*Fort.*) A wall crossing part of a rampart and joining it to interior work ; (দুর্গ) যে প্রাচীর বপ্রের অংশবিশেষ অতিক্রম করিয়া উহাকে অন্তর্দুর্গের প্রাচীরাদির সহিত সংযুক্ত করে। ***Verb t.*** 1. To prick with spurs ; পাদুকাসংলগ্ন লৌহকণ্টকদ্বারা বিদ্ধ করা। 2. To incite to a more hasty pace ; দ্রুতগমনের জন্য উত্তেজিত করা। 3. To put spurs on ; as, a *spurred* boot ; পাদুকায় অশ্বতাড়নী সংযুক্ত করা। ***Verb i.*** To ride hard ; "Now *spurs* the lated traveller" ; বেগে অশ্ব ছুটান। **Spur'-less,** *adj.* **Spur-royal**— প্রথম জেম্‌সের সময়ের মুদ্রাবিশেষ—ইহাতে ছটাবিশিষ্ট সূর্য্যের প্রতিকৃতি থাকিত। **Spur-wheel**—যে দন্তুর চক্রের দন্তসমূহ অক্ষের লম্ব স্বরূপে অবস্থিত থাকে। **Spurwort**—একপ্রকার গুল্ম। **On the spur of the moment** — At once ; তৎক্ষণাৎ, তন্মুহূর্ত্তে, ধাঁ করিয়া। **To set spurs to**—To prick with spurs ; জুতার কাঁটা দ্বারা খোঁচা দেওয়া। **To win spurs**—To gain knighthood ; to gain distinction; to make a name; নাইট হওয়া; খ্যাতিলাভ করা; নাম করা।

spurge (spêrj), *n.* A plant with an acrid milky juice powerfully purgative ; দুগ্ধধবল এবং অম্লস্বাদ বিরেচক নির্য্যাসবিশিষ্ট একপ্রকার বৃক্ষ, সুহ, সুহীবৃক্ষ, মনসাগাছ, মমজরিয়া (আরব খোরী), সীজগাছ, [Syn. সিহুণ্ড, সীহুণ্ড, শীহুণ্ড, স্নুক্, সমন্তদুগ্ধা, বজ্র,

বজ্রদ্রু, স্নুহা, গুড়ী, গুড়, বজ্রী, সুধা, বজ্রকণ্টক, কৃষ্ণসার]। **Spurge hawk-moth**—একপ্রকার প্রজাপাত। [সম্মুখের পক্ষদ্বয় ধূসর, মাঝে মাঝে জলপাইয়ের রঙ্গের দাগ থাকে। পশ্চাতের পক্ষদ্বয় পাটলবর্ণ, তাহাতে কালোবর্ণের দাগ এবং রেখা থাকে। কণ্ঠ এবং উদর জলপাইয়ের মত সবুজবর্ণ—তাহার উপর শাদা এবং কালো রঙ্গের ফুট ফুট বিন্দু এবং রেখামালা থাকে।]

spū'-ri-ous (-ŭs), *adj.* 1. Not genuine; counterfeit; false; অপ্রকৃত; নকল; কৃত্রিম, ঝুঁটা, মেকি। 2. Of illegitimate birth; bastard; বিজন্মা; জারজ। 3. (*Bot. & Zool.*) Superficially like but morphologically unlike; resembling an organ etc. but not having its function; as, *spurious* legs; (উদ্ভিদ্‌বিদ্যা ও জন্তুবিদ্যা) বহিরাকৃতিতে একরূপ কিন্তু অঙ্গবিন্যাসাদি সম্বন্ধে ভিন্নরূপ; কোন অঙ্গের সহিত আকারগত সাদৃশ্যবিশিষ্ট কিন্তু কার্য্য ও বৃত্তিতে সম্পূর্ণ বিভিন্ন। **—ly**, *adv.* **—ness**, *n.* **Spurious disease**—যে রোগ অপর কোন রোগ বলিয়া ভ্রান্তি জন্মে, কৃত্রিম রোগ। [যথা পশুর্কার মধ্য পেশীর বাতরোগ spurious pleurisy এই অপ্রকৃত নামে অভিহিত হয় কিন্তু ইহা pleurisy নহে।] **Spurious-rainbow** — মূল রামধনুর ধূমলবর্ণের অভ্যন্তরভাগের অতিসন্নিকটে অথবা গৌণ রামধনুর বহির্দ্দেশে অবস্থিত রামধনু, কৃত্রিম রামধনু। **Spurious-wing**—পক্ষের মধ্যভাগস্থ ক্ষুদ্রসন্ধিতে জাত ত্রি অথবা পঞ্চ সংখ্যক পালক, কৃত্রিম পক্ষ।

spur'-ling-line (spêr-) *n.* (*Naut.*) A line from the steering-wheel of a ship to the telltale in the cabin, made to show the position of the helm; (নৌবিদ্যা) হাইলের অবস্থান প্রদর্শনের জন্য হাইলের চাকা হইতে, জাহাজের কামরার প্রদর্শকসূচী পর্য্যন্ত প্রসারিত রজ্জু।

spurn (spêrn), *v. t., i. & n.* 1. To drive away as with the foot; as, to *spurn* a cur; পদাঘাতে তাড়িত করা, লাথি মারিয়া দূর করা। 2. To reject with the greatest disdain; as, to *spurn* an offer; (*colloq.*) to scorn; to despise; to treat with contempt; as, to *spurn* a beggar; অতিশয় ঘৃণার সহিত প্রত্যাখ্যান করা, পায়ে ঠেলা; অবজ্ঞা করা, তাচ্ছিল্য করা; ঘৃণা করা; অবজ্ঞার সহিত ব্যবহার করা। *Verb i.* To manifest disdain in rejecting anything; কোন কিছু অগ্রাহ্য করার কালে ঘৃণা প্রকাশ করা। *Noun.* 1. Disdainful rejection; অবজ্ঞার সহিত প্রত্যাখ্যান, ঘৃণার সহিত প্রত্যাখ্যান। 2. Contemptuous treatment; "The insolence of office and the *spurns*"; অবজ্ঞা, তাচ্ছিল্য, ঘৃণা।

spur'-ri-êr (spêr-), *n.* Spur-maker; অশ্ব-তাড়নী নির্ম্মাতা।

spur'-rÿ (spêr-ĭ), **—rey** (-ĭ) *ns.* A British plant found in corn-fields; ব্রিটিশ দ্বীপের শস্যক্ষেত্রে জাত একপ্রকার গুল্ম।

spurt (spêrt), *v. i., t. & n.* To spout forth; বেগে ছুটা, ফিন্‌কি দিয়া ছুটা, উচ্ছালত হওয়া (cf. দেবীগলোচ্ছলদ্‌ রক্তধারাপানং প্রকুর্ব্বন্তীম্—ছিন্নমস্তাস্তোত্র)। *Verb t.* To throw, drive or force out violently, as a stream from a pipe or small orifice; as, to *spurt* water from a syringe; বেগে ছুটান, উচ্ছলিত করা। *Noun.* 1. A gush of liquid; ফিন্‌কি, ধারা। 2. A sudden violent outbreak, as of feeling; as a *spurt* of rebellious fire; ঝটকা, চোট।

spurt, (spêrt), *v. i. & n.* To make a brief sudden violent effort; সহসা অল্পকালের জন্য প্রবল চেষ্টা করা। *Noun.* A sudden brief effort; as, a *spurt* in a race; অল্পকাল স্থায়ী আকস্মিক চেষ্টা, সহসা প্রবল উদ্যম, হঠোদ্যম।

spŭt'-ter (-ėr), *v. i., t. & n.* 1. To emit particles of saliva in speaking; কথা বলার সময় মুখ হইতে থুথুর কণা বাহির হওয়া। 2. To speak out hastily and indistinctly; তাড়াতাড়ি অস্পষ্টভাবে কথা বলা। *Verb t.* To utter rapidly and indistinctly; দ্রুত এবং অস্পষ্টভাবে কথা বলা। *Noun.* 1. Such speech; দ্রুত এবং অস্পষ্টভাবে উচ্চারিত বাক্য। 2. A moist matter thrown out in small particles; কণাকারে নিক্ষিপ্ত দ্রব বস্তু। **—er**, *n.* **—ing-ly**, *adv.*

spū'-tŭm, *n.* (*Pl.* SPUTA) 1. Saliva; থুথু, নিষ্ঠীবন। 2. The substance expectorated in bronchitis, pneumonia, and other chest affections; কফ।

spÿ, *n., v. t. & i.* 1. One who secretly watches on the actions and movements, etc. of others; গুপ্তচর, গোয়েন্দা, টিকটিকি (*colloq.*), [Syn. গূঢ়পুরুষ, গূঢ়চর, গূঢ়চার চারপুরুষ, অনিরুদ্ধচার (cf. চারচক্ষুর্মহিপতি — কুমারঃ), অপসর্প, প্রণিধি (মঃ সং)।] 2. A person sent into an enemy's camp to inspect their works secretly, ascertain their strength or their movements, and communicate intelligence to proper officer; চর, সামরিক চর। *Verb t.* 1. To gain sight of; to espy; দৃষ্টি করা; সন্দর্শন করা, অবলোকন করা। 2. To gain a knowledge by artifice; to discover by close search; "*Spy* what things are to be reformed in the church of England"; কৌশল বা চাতুরীপূর্ব্বক কোন বিষয় অবগত হওয়া; পুঙ্খানুপুঙ্খরূপে অনুসন্ধান করিয়া বাহির করা। 3. To view or inspect secretly; গোপনে পরিদর্শন করা। *Verb i.* 1. To search narrowly; পুঙ্খানুপুঙ্খরূপে অনুসন্ধান করা। 2. To play the spy (often with *on* or *upon*); as, to *spy upon* the enemy; to pry; গোয়েন্দাগিরি করা; গোপনে গতিবিধির উপর লক্ষ্য রাখা। **Spy-glass**—ক্ষুদ্র দূরবীণ। **Spy-hole**—উঁকি মারিবার ছিদ্র।

squab (sqwŏb), *adj., adv. & n.* Fat; plump; bulky; মোটা;

গোলগাল, নাদুসনুদুস; বৃহদায়তন। *Adv.* With a heavy fall; দুম করিয়া, ধপ করিয়া, ধড়াস করিয়া। *Noun.* **1.** A short fat person; "Like a fat *squab* upon a Chinese fan"; খাটো এবং মোটাসোটা মানুষ। **2.** A young pigeon or dove; কপোত বা ঘুঘু শাবক। **3.** A stuffed cushion; তুলা প্রভৃতি ভরা গদি। **Squab'-by,** *adj.* **Squab-chick**—অজাতপক্ষ পক্ষী। **Squab-pie** — কপোতের মাংসের পুর দেওয়া পিষ্টক, ভেড়ার মাংস, পেঁয়াজ এবং সেওফলের পুর দেওয়া পিষ্টক।

squab'-ble (skwŏb-l), *v. i., t. & n.* **1.** To quarrel noisily; to wrangle; কোন্দল করা; ঝগড়া করা, বিবাদ করা। **2.** To dispute; বাদানুবাদ করা, বাগ্‌বিতণ্ডা করা। *Verb t.* (*Print.*) To disarrange composed types; বিন্যস্ত অক্ষরসমূহ এলোমেলো করিয়া ফেলা। *Noun.* Petty or noisy quarrel; কলহ, ঝগড়া, বিবাদ, কোন্দল। **—bler,** *n.*

squăc'-co (-ö), *n.* A species of heron (*Ardea comata*); একজাতীয় বৃহৎ বক।

squad (skwŏd), *n.* **1.** A small party of men assembled for drill or inspection; কুচকাওয়াজ বা পরিদর্শনের জন্য সমবেত অল্পসংখ্যক সৈন্য। **2.** A small party of persons; as, a football *squad*; অল্পসংখ্যক লোক, ক্ষুদ্র দল। **Awkward squad**—যে সকল রংরুটগণ রীতিমত পল্টনে গৃহীত হইবার উপযুক্ত কুচকাওয়াজ শিক্ষা করে নাই; (লক্ষণায়) আনাড়ী লোকের দল।

squad'-rŏn (skwŏd-), *n. & v. t.* **1.** A body of cavalry comprising two companies of troops averaging from 120 to 200 men; সাদী সৈন্যের বিভাগ বিশেষ—যাহাতে ১২০—২০০ পর্য্যন্ত সৈন্য থাকে। **2.** A division of a fleet under a junior flag-officer employed on a particular occasion; কোন বিশেষ কার্য্যোপলক্ষে নিযুক্ত ক্ষুদ্র সমরপোতবহর। **3.** An orderly body of persons; সুব্যবস্থিত লোকশ্রেণী। *Verb t.* To form men into squadrons; অশ্বারোহী সৈন্যের ক্ষুদ্র দল গঠন করা। **Flying squadron**—দ্রুতগমনের জন্য সজ্জিত রণপোতশ্রেণী।

squail (skwāl), *n., pl.* A game with small wooden disks; কাঠের ক্ষুদ্র ক্ষুদ্র চাক্তিদ্বারা একপ্রকার ক্রীড়া।

squail'-ēr (skwāl-), *n.* A loaded stick used for throwing at animals such as squirrels etc.; কাঠবিড়াল প্রভৃতির উপর নিক্ষেপের জন্য একপ্রকার সীসকাবদ্ধ গুরুভার যষ্টি।

squal'-id (skwŏl-), *adj.* Dirty; foul; filthy; অপরিচ্ছন্ন, অপরিষ্কার, মলিন; ময়লা; কদর্য্য, সমল। **—ly,** *adv.* **—ness,** *n.* **—or,** *n.* **Squa-lid'-i-ty,** *n.*

squall, *v. i., t. & n.* To cry out; to scream violently; চীৎকার করা; চেঁচান। *Verb t.* To utter in a harsh screaming tone (usu. with *out*); as, she *squalled out* her complaints; চেঁচাইয়া বলা, চীৎকার করিয়া বলা। *Noun.* **1.** A loud cry or scream; চীৎকার। **2.** A sudden and violent gust of wind; ঝঞ্ঝা, ঝঞ্ঝাবাত্যা, ঝঞ্ঝানিল, ঝাপটা বাতাস, ঝটকা বাতাস, দমকা বাতাস। **Squall'-y,** *adj.* **Arched squall**—বিষুবমণ্ডলের নিকটবর্ত্তী স্থানের ঝঞ্ঝানিল, তোরণঝঞ্ঝা। [এইরূপ ঝঞ্ঝায় সহসা গগনমণ্ডলে তোরণাকার মেঘপটল দৃষ্ট হয় এবং সঙ্গে সঙ্গে বজ্রপাত হইতে থাকে]। **A black squall**—ঘনমেঘ সহকৃত ঝঞ্ঝা। **A thick squall** — শিলা, তুষারপাত, প্রভৃতি সহকৃত বাত্যা। **A white squall**—গ্রীষ্মমণ্ডলের বা তৎসন্নিহিত প্রদেশের ঝঞ্ঝা। **To look out for squalls**—(*Colloq.*) To be on one's guard; সাবধান থাকা, হুঁসিয়ার থাকা।

squā'-loid (-loyd), *adj.* Like a shark; হাঙ্গরবৎ।

squā'-mă, *n.* (*Bot. & Zool.*) Scale; a scale-like part of a bone; (উদ্ভিদ্‌বিদ্যা এবং জন্তুবিদ্যা) শল্ক; অস্থির শল্কাকৃতি অংশ। **—mous, —mose,** *adjs.* **Squam'-ule,** *n.* **Squamous bulb**—সপরিশল্ককন্দ (সাঃ পঃ)।

squan'-dêr (skwŏn-), *v. t.* To spend lavishly; as, to *squander* an estate; অপব্যয় করা, উড়ান, উড়াইয়া দেওয়া। **—er,** *n.* **—ing-ly,** *adv.*

square (skwār), *n., adj., adv., v. t. & i.* **1.** A figure having four equal sides and four right angles; বর্গক্ষেত্র, সমচতুষ্কোণ ক্ষেত্র, চতুষ্কোণ (সাঃ পঃ), চতুষ্টয় (ঐ), সমচতুরস্র (ঐ), সমচতুর্ভুজ (ঐ)। **2.** Any similar figures or area; উক্তরূপ ক্ষেত্র বা স্থান। **3.** A square piece, fragment, or surface; চতুষ্কোণ খণ্ড, চৌকা জিনিষ, ছক। **4.** An instrument having one edge at right angles to another; ইংরাজী L অথবা T অক্ষরাকৃতি সমকোণ পরিমাপক যন্ত্রবিশেষ, মাটাম যন্ত্র। **5.** A four-sided area with houses built round; চতুর্দ্দিকে ভবনশ্রেণীবিশিষ্ট সমচতুষ্কোণ স্থান, নগরচত্বর। **6.** A block of buildings bounded by four streets; রাজপথচতুষ্টয় দ্বারা বেষ্টিত ভবনশ্রেণী। **7.** A park; নগরোদ্যান, পুরোদ্যান। **8.** A body of infantry drawn up in rectangular form; সমচতুষ্কোণাকারে, সজ্জিত পদাতিকসৈন্যদল, চতুষ্কব্যূহ। **9.** (*Math.*) A product of a number multiplied by itself; (গণিতশাস্ত্র) বর্গ। **10.** Conformity; regularity; "I have not kept my *square*
but that to come
Shall all be done by the rule"; due proportion; justness in conduct or dealing; অনুরূপতা; নিয়মানুবর্ত্তিতা; যথোচিত অনুপাত; ন্যায়নিষ্ঠা, ন্যায়পরতা, ন্যায়মূলক আচরণ। **11.** Level; equality; "We live not on the *square*
with such as these
Such are our betters";
সমান অবস্থা; সাম্য। **12.** (*Printing*) A certain number of lines forming a portion of a column

nearly square ; (পত্রিকাদির) স্তম্ভের অংশস্বরূপ প্রায় সমচতুষ্কোণাকৃতি রেখাশ্রেণী। 13. (*Astrol.*) The position of planets distant 90 degrees from each other ; (ফলিত জ্যোতিষ) গ্রহগণের পরস্পর হইতে ৯০ ডিগ্রি দূরে অবস্থান। 14. (*Book-binding*) The projection of a board beyond the book-edge ; (পুস্তক বাঁধাই) পুস্তকের প্রান্তের বহির্ভূত মলাটের প্রলম্বিত অংশ। 15. A pane of glass ; জানালার কাচ, সাসী। 16. A quarrel ; বিবাদ, ঝগড়া। 17. (*Carp.*) 100 ft., that is 10×10 ; (সূতারের কাজ) ১০০ ফিট্। 18. A set of words arranged in a square so as to read alike across and downwards ; এরূপভাবে বিন্যস্ত শব্দসমূহ—যাহাতে উহাদিগকে পাশাপাশিভাবে বা নীচেরদিক হইতে পড়িলে একই রূপ হয়। (যথা—*cat ace ten*)। ***Adj.*** Having four equal sides and four right angles; সমচতুর্ভুজ বিশিষ্ট। 2. Forming a right angle ; সমকোণী। 3. Having a shape broad for the height ; stout ; প্রশস্তবক্ষ, ব্যূঢ়োরস্ক (রঃ); হৃষ্টপুষ্ট। 4. Fair ; as, *square* dealings ; just ; as, to be *square* with all men ; নিরপেক্ষ ; ন্যায়পরায়ণ, ন্যায়নিষ্ঠ। 5. Suitable ; উপযোগী। 6. Hearty ; complete ; satisfying ; as, a *square* meal ; তৃপ্তিজনক ; পূর্ণ ; তুষ্টিজনক। 7. Even ; leaving no balance ; জমা ও খরচ সমান; (জমাখরচ সম্বন্ধে) মিল। 8. Straightforward ; unequivocal ; সরল-প্রকৃতি ; সরল, অকপট। 9. Angular ; as, a *square* peg ; কোণবিশিষ্ট। 10. Thorough ; as, was met with a *square* refusal ; পুরা, সম্যক্। 11. In good order ; as, to get things *square* ; ঠিকঠাক, সাজানো গোছানো। ***Adv.*** 1. At right angles; সমকোণে। 2. (*Colloq.*) Fairly ; as, to play *square* ; সাধুভাবে, ন্যায়সঙ্গতরূপে। ***Verb t.*** 1. To make square ; সমচতুষ্কোণ করা। 2. To adjust ; to accommodate ; ঠিকঠাক করা ; উপযোগী করা। 3. To make even ; as, to *square* accounts ; জমা খরচ মিলান। 4. To multiply a number by itself ; বর্গ করা। 5. (*Astrol.*) To hold a quartile position respecting ; গ্রহদ্বয়ের পক্ষে পরস্পর হইতে ৯০ ডিগ্রী দূরে অবস্থান করা। 6. (*Slang*) To gain to one's side by bribe etc. ; উৎকোচাদি প্রদানে নিজের পক্ষে আনা। ***Verb i.*** 1. To suit ; to fit ; মানান, উপযোগী হওয়া ; লাগা। 2. (*Colloq.*) To take a boxing attitude ; মুষ্টিযুদ্ধের জন্য ভঙ্গিবিশেষে অবস্থান করা। **Square'-ly,** *adv.* **Square'-ness,** *n.* **Square built**—ব্যূঢ়োরস্ক, প্রশস্তবক্ষঃ, কপাট-বক্ষঃ। **Magic square**—See MAGIC. **Square-leg**—ক্রীকেট ক্রীড়ায় যে ক্রীড়ক কন্দুক থামাইবার জন্য ব্যাটধারীর বামে দণ্ডায়মান থাকে। **Square measure** — বর্গপরিমাণ। **Square number**—যে রাশির বর্গমূল নিষ্কর্ষণ করা যাইতে পারে (যথা, ৪, ৯)। **Square-rigged**—যে জাহাজের প্রধান পাইলসকল মাস্তুলের সহিত তির্য্যগ্‌ভাবে-স্থাপিত পাইল-দণ্ডে টাঙ্গান হয়—তৎসম্বন্ধে ব্যবহৃত। **Square root**—বর্গমূল। **Square-sail**—মাস্তুলের সহিত তির্য্যগ্‌-ভাবে স্থাপিত পাইলদণ্ডের উপর বিস্তারিত পাইল। **Square-shouldered** — উন্নত, বৃষস্কন্ধ, এবং প্রশস্তস্কন্ধ বিশিষ্ট। **Square-spot** — একপ্রকার তসরে পোকা। **Square-toed** — নৈষ্ঠিক, সূক্ষ্মনিয়মনিষ্ঠ; পিটপিটে (*colloq.*), খুঁতখুঁতে (*ib.*), সূক্ষ্মবিচারী। **Square-toes** — উৎকট নীতিপরায়ণ লোক। **All square**—বেশ, ভাল; অতিশয় আনন্দজনক। **A square peg in a round hole**—See HOLE. **By the square**—Honestly ; সাধুভাবে। **On square**—appropriatety; correctly; যথোচিতভাবে ; ঠিকভাবে। **On the or upon the square**—Worthy of respect—মাননীয়, সম্মানার্হ। At right angles ; সমকোণে। **Out of square**—Not at right angles—সমকোণে নয়। **Square of an anchor**—নোঙ্গরদণ্ডের ঊর্দ্ধাংশ। **To break no squares**—Not to blame ; not to make any difference ; দোষারোপ না করা ; কোনরূপ তারতম্য না করা। **To break squares**—To break any established rules ; কোন চিরপ্রচলিত নিয়ম ভঙ্গ করা। **To call it square**—To think anything as settled ; কোন বিষয় মীমাংসিত বলিয়া গণ্য করা। **To see how the squares go**—To see how matters are going ; ব্যাপার কিরূপ চলিতেছে দেখা। **To square anything to, with**—To make anything correspond with another thing ; অপর কোন বস্তুর সহিত সামঞ্জস্য করা। **To square the circle**—To attempt at impossibilities ; অসম্ভব সাধনে চেষ্টা করা। To construct a circle equal in area to a given square ; কোন নির্দ্দিষ্ট বর্গক্ষেত্রের আয়তনের বৃত্ত অঙ্কন করা। To determine the area of a circle in square measure ; বৃত্তের ক্ষেত্রফলের বর্গীয় পরিমাণ স্থির করা। **To square the yards**—To place at right angles with the mast; মাস্তুলের সহিত সমকোণে স্থাপন করা। **To square up or off**—মুষ্টিযুদ্ধের ভঙ্গিবিশেষে অবস্থান করা।

squar'-rose (-ōs), **-rous** (-ŭs), *adjs.* (*Bot. & Zool.*) Rough with projecting or deflexed scales ; (উদ্ভিদবিদ্যা এবং জন্তুবিদ্যা) বহির্বিলম্বী এবং নিম্নাভিমুখে আনত শল্কসমূহ দ্বারা বন্ধুর।

squar'-son (-sn), *n.* (*Facet.*) A clergyman who is also the land-owner in a parish; (রঙ্গচ্ছলে) যে ব্যক্তি কোন পল্লীর যাজক এবং ভূম্যধিকারী।

squash (skwŏsh), *v. t., i. & n.* 1. To beat or squeeze or crush into a flat mass or pulp ; পিটিয়া চিপিয়া, বা ছেঁচিয়া লেইয়ের মত করা, মণ্ডবৎ করা, শাঁসের মত করা, গুঁড়া করা। 2. To annul ; রদ করা। 3. To put an opponent to silence ; to humiliate ; প্রতিপক্ষকে চুপ করিয়া দেওয়া ;

হতগর্ব্ব করা। *Verb i.* (*Colloq.*) To fall heavily and helplessly ; (চলিতভাষায়) ধপ্ করিয়া পড়া। *Noun* 1. Something soft and easily crushed or pressed into a pulp ; something unripe and soft ; an unripe pod ; যে কোমল বস্তু সহজে পিটিয়া চূর্ণ বা মণ্ডবৎ করা যাইতে পারে ; কাঁচা এবং কোমল বস্তু ; কাঁচা শুঁটি। 2. A sudden fall of a heavy soft body ; the sound caused by the fall of such body ; "My fall was stopped by a terrible *squash* that sounded louder to my ears than the cataract of Niagara" ; কোমল এবং গুরুভার বস্তুর আকস্মিক পতন ; ঐরূপ বস্তুর পতনজনিত শব্দ, ধপ শব্দ। 3. A crushed mass ; মণ্ড, লেই। 4. A game played with racket and soft ball in fives court (also *squash-rackets*) ; একপ্রকার ক্রীড়া। **Squash'-y**, *adj.* Soft and wet ; pulpy ; muddy ; কোমল এবং আর্দ্র ; মণ্ডবৎ ; কর্দ্দমময়। **Lemon-squash**— See LEMON. **Squash-hat**—নেমদা (felt) প্রভৃতির কোমল টুপি। **Squash-squash**—পচ পচ শব্দ।

squash (skwŏsh), *n.* A species of gourd ; বিলাতী কুমড়া (প্রবোধ), একপ্রকার পেয়ারার আকৃতি তরকারী (খাসিয়া পাহাড়ে জন্মে)।

squat (skwŏt), *v. i., t., adj.* & *n.* 1. To sit down upon the hams or heels ; আসন করিয়া বসা, আসনপীড়ি হইয়া বসা। 2. To cower, as an animal ; গুটিসুটি মারা। 3. To settle on new lands ; নূতন জায়গায় বসবাস স্থাপন করা। *Verb t.* 1. To put on the hams or heels ; আসন করিয়া বসান। 2. To cause to cower or lie close to the ground ; গুটিসুটি মারান। *Adj.* 1. Sitting on the heels or hams ; আসন করা অবস্থায় উপবিষ্ট। 2. Cowering ; গুটিসুটি মারা অবস্থায়। 3. Short and thick ; "The body *squat* or tall" ; মোটা এবং খাটো। *Noun.* 1. The posture or position of one who sits on his ham or close to the ground ; আসন। 2. A person who squats ; যে ব্যক্তি আসন পাতিয়া বসে। 3 A mineral consisting of tin ore and spar ; খনিজবিমিশ্র বঙ্গ এবং দুগ্ধপাষাণ-পূর্ণ খনিজপদার্থ বিশেষ। 4. A small separate vein of ore ; খনিজবিমিশ্র ধাতুর ক্ষুদ্র এবং স্বতন্ত্র শিরা।

squat'-ter (skŏwt-êr), *n.* 1. Same as SQUAT *n.* 2. 2. One who settles on new land without title ; যে ব্যক্তি কোনরূপ স্বত্ব-স্বামিত্ব বিনা নূতন দেশে বসবাস স্থাপন করে। 3. (Australia) One who takes land as for sheep pasture on easy terms from government ; যে ব্যক্তি মেষচারণের জন্য সরকার হইতে অল্প খাজানায় ভূমির বন্দোবস্ত গ্রহণ করে।

squaw (skwä), *n.* American-Indian woman or wife ; প্রাচীন আমেরিকার লাল ইণ্ডিয়ান নারী বা স্ত্রী। **Squaw-man**—লাল ইণ্ডিয়ান নারীর শ্বেতাঙ্গ পতি।

squawk (skäwk), *v. i.* & *n.* To cry with a loud, harsh voice ; চীৎকার করা, চেঁচান। *Noun.* A loud harsh squeak or squall ; চীৎকার।

squeak (skwēk), *v. i., t.* & *n.* 1. To utter a sharp shrill sound ; to make a shrill noise, as an unoiled hinge, wheel, etc. ; চিঁ চিঁ করা, চেঁ চেঁ করা ; কেঁচর কেঁচর শব্দ করা। 2. (*Slang*) To confess ; to betray ; to turn an informer ; (ইতরভাষায়) দোষ স্বীকার করা, একরার করা ; বিশ্বাসঘাতকতাপূর্ব্বক ধরাইয়া দেওয়া ; পুলিশের সংবাদদাতা হওয়া। *Verb t.* 1. To cause to squeak ; চিঁ চিঁ করান, কেঁচর কেঁচর করান। 2. (*Rare*) To put out of order ; (কচিদ্ ব্যবহৃত) বিশৃঙ্খল করা। *Noun.* A short shrill sound ; চিঁ চিঁ শব্দ, কড় কড়, কিচির মিচির, কিচমিচ, কেঁচর কেঁচর শব্দ। **Squeak'-i-ly**, *adv.* **Squeak'-y**, *adj.* **A narrow** or **near squeak**—(*Colloq.*) A narrow escape ; অল্পের জন্য রক্ষা, চুলে চুলে রক্ষা।

squeak'-êr (skwēk-), *n.* 1. One who, or that which, squeaks ; চিঁ চিঁ শব্দকারী, কেঁচর কেঁচর শব্দকারী। 2. A young bird, esp. pigeon ; পাখীর ছানা, পায়রার ছানা।

squeal (skwēl), *v. i., t.* & *n.* 1. To cry with a sharp shrill voice ; কর্কশস্বরে চীৎকার করা। 2. (*Slang*) Same as SQUEAK, 2. *Noun.* A sharp shrill cry ; কর্কশস্বরে চীৎকার, চিঁ চিঁ।

squeal'-êr (skwēl-), *n.* 1. One who, or that which, squeals ; চিঁ চিঁ শব্দকারী। 2. Same as SQUEAKER, 2.

squeam'-ish (skwēm-), *adj.* 1. Having stomach easily turned ; সহজেই যাহার গা বমি বমি করে, বিবমিষু। 2. Fastidious ; over-nice ; over scrupulous in honesty ; "Quoth he, that honour's very *squeamish* That takes a basting for a blemish" ; উৎকটরুচি, দুষ্প্রসাদ ; পিটপেটে (*colloq.*), খুঁতখুঁতে (*ib.*) ; অতিরিক্ত সূক্ষ্মবিচারী। **—ly**, *adv.* **—ness**, *n.*

squee'-gee (skwē-jē), **squil'-gee** (-jē), *ns.* & *v. t.* 1. A plate of leather or India-rubber fixed to a handle for cleaning wet deck, road, etc. ; ভিজা পাটাতন, রাজপথ প্রভৃতি পরিষ্কার করার জন্য দণ্ডাগ্রসংবদ্ধ চর্ম্ম কিম্বা রবারের ফলক। 2. A similar instrument or roller of small size used by photographers ; আলোকচিত্রকর কর্ত্তৃক ব্যবহৃত অনুরূপ ক্ষুদ্রাকার যন্ত্র বা রবারের ডলনা। *Verb t.* To treat with squeegee ; উক্ত যন্ত্রদ্বারা ভিজা পাটাতন প্রভৃতি পরিষ্কার করা।

squeeze (skwēz), *v. t., i.* & *n.* 1. To subject to pressure ; to press closely ; চাপ দেওয়া, জোরে চাপ দেওয়া। 2. To clasp closely ; as, to *squeeze* one's hand ; চাপিয়া ধরা ; সজোরে চাপিয়া ধরা।

3. To oppress ; পীড়ন করা, নিষ্পেষণ করা, পেষণ করা। 4. To press so as to expel juice or moisture ; চিপা, নিংড়ান, নিষ্পীড়ন করা। 5. To force between close bodies ; ঘনসন্নিবিষ্ট বস্তুদ্বয়ের মধ্যে সজোরে ঠেলিয়া দেওয়া। 6. To constrain ; as, to *squeeze* the government to get a reform ; চাপ দেওয়া। 7. To take a copy or facsimile by pressing some soft material on to the thing of which a copy is to be made ; কোন বস্তুতে কোনরূপ কোমল বস্তুর চাপ দিয়া ঐ বস্তুর ছাপ তোলা। ***Verb i.*** 1. To force by pressing ; চাপ দিয়া ঢুকান। 2. To urge one's way by pressing ; as, to *squeeze* through a crowd ; ভিড় ঠেলিয়া অগ্রসর হওয়া। 3. To crowd ; ভিড় করা। ***Noun.*** 1. Application of pressure ; চাপপ্রয়োগ, সঙ্কাপন। 2. Crowd ; ভিড়, জনতা। 3. Impression of coin etc. taken by pressing some soft material on to these things ; কোনরূপ কোমল বস্তু দ্বারা চাপ দিয়া মুদ্রা প্রভৃতির যে ছাপ তোলা হয়। **Squeez-a-bil'-i-ty,** *n.* **Squeez'-a-ble,** *adj.* **Squeez'-ing,** *n.* The act of one who squeezes ; প্রপীড়ন, সম্পীড়ন, আপীড়ন, নিষ্পীড়ন। **Squeezed orange**—কোনও ব্যক্তি বা বস্তু—যাহা হইতে আর কিছুই পাওয়া যাইবে না, যাহা হইতে সমস্ত নিঃশেষে নিংড়াইয়া বাহির করা হইয়াছে। **To squeeze out**—To force out by pressure, as liquid ; নিংড়ান, নিংড়াইয়া ফেলা। **To squeeze through**—To pass through by pressing ; ভিড় ঠেলিয়া অতিক্রম করা।

squeez'-ër (skwēz-), *n.* 1. One who, or that which, squeezes; a device for squeezing ; as, a lemon *squeezer* ; সঙ্কাপক ; সঙ্কাপনযন্ত্র। 2. A contrivance like a large pair of pliers for shingling or squeezing the scoria from the puddled iron ; ঢালা লোহাকে পেটা লোহা করার কালে ধাতুমল প্রভৃতির বুদ্বুদ অপসারণ করার জন্য যন্ত্রবিশেষ, সঙ্কাপনযন্ত্র। 3. Playing-cards having the number spots marked at the upper right-hand corner of each ; যে তাসের প্রত্যেকটার উপরের ডাহিন দিকের কোণে ফোঁটাগুলি অঙ্কিত থাকে।

squëlch, *v. t.* & *n.* 1. To crush ; to destroy ; চূর্ণবিচূর্ণ করা ; ধ্বংস করা। 2. To discomfit ; to disconcert ; পরাভূত করা, পরাজিত করা ; ব্যর্থ করা, বিফল করা। ***Noun.*** 1. A flat heavy fall; ছুম শব্দে পতন। 2. A crushing blow or retort ; খতম ঘা, কাটা জবাব।

squë-teague'(-tēg),*n.* An American fish the *Labrus squeteague* ; আমেরিকাদেশীয় মৎস্যবিশেষ।

squib, *n., v. t.* & *i.* 1. A paper-tube filled with combustible matter which emits for a time a stream of sparks and then explodes with a crack ; ছুঁচাবাজী, পটকা। 2. A petty sarcastic writing or speech ; ব্যঙ্গব্যঞ্জক তুচ্ছ প্রবন্ধ বা বাক্য। 3. A head of asparagus ; শতমূলীর মাথা। 4. A cheap kind of candy ; এক-প্রকার নিকৃষ্ট মিশ্রি। ***Verb t.*** To write lampoon ; to attack with lampoon ; বিদ্রূপাত্মক প্রবন্ধ লিখা ; বিদ্রূপাত্মক বাক্য বা প্রবন্ধ দ্বারা আক্রমণ করা। ***Verb i.*** 1. To explode with a sharp crack ; "A Snider *squibbed* in the jungle" ; পট্ শব্দে ফুটা। 2. To publish squibs ; তুচ্ছ ব্যঙ্গব্যঞ্জক প্রবন্ধ প্রকাশ করা।

squid, *n.* & *v. i.* 1. A kind of cuttle-fish used as bait ; বড়শীর টোপস্বরূপ ব্যবহৃত একজাতীয় সমুদ্রজিত মৎস্য। 2. An artificial bait of metal, ivory, etc.; ধাতু, গজদন্ত, প্রভৃতি নির্ম্মিত কৃত্রিম টোপ। ***Verb i.*** To fish with a squid ; সমুদ্রজিত মৎস্য টোপস্বরূপ ব্যবহার করা, বড়শীতে কৃত্রিম টোপ ব্যবহার করা।

squil'-gee (-jē), *n.* & *v. t.* Same as SQUEEGEE (which see).

squill, *n.* 1. A lily-like plant having a bulbous root of acrid, emetic, diuretic and purgative properities ; বিলাতী স্থলকুমুদজাতীয় গুল্মবিশেষ—ইহার অম্লাস্বাদ কন্দ বমনজনক, মূত্রবর্দ্ধক এবং বিরেচক ঔষধস্বরূপ ব্যবহৃত হয়। 2. A species of shrimp (also *squill-fish*); একজাতীয় চিংড়ী মৎস্য। **Indian squill**—বন পেঁয়াজ, জঙ্গলী পেঁয়াজ।

squinch, *n.* A small arch across the interior angle of a square tower, to support the side of a superimposed octagon ; চতুষ্কোণ বুরুজের আভ্যন্তরিক কোণের অনুপ্রস্থগামী ক্ষুদ্র তোরণবিশেষ—যদ্দ্বারা উক্তরূপ বুরুজের উপরে স্থাপিত অষ্টকোণ চূড়া প্রভৃতির পার্শ্ব বিধৃত হয়।

squint, *v. i., t., n.* & *adj.* 1. To look obliquely or askance ; বক্রদৃষ্টি করা, তির্য্যগ্‌দৃষ্টি করা, টের্চ্ছাভাবে চাওয়া, আড়নয়নে দেখা। 2. To have the axes of the eyes not coincident ; টেরা হওয়া। 3. To have an indirect reference or bearing ; "In prudence too, you think my rhymes should never *squint* at courtier's crimes" ; ইঙ্গিত থাকা, পরোক্ষ সম্পর্ক থাকা। ***Verb t.*** 1. To turn the eye to an oblique position ; তির্য্যগ্‌ভাবে নেত্রপাত করা, আড়নয়নে চাওয়া। 2. To cause to look with a squint ; টেরাভাবে চাওয়ান। 3. (*Colloq.*) To close the eyes partly ; to close the eyes quickly ; (চলিতভাষায়) চক্ষু অর্দ্ধনিমীলিত করা ; তাড়াতাড়ি চোক বন্ধ করা। ***Noun.*** 1. The act of looking obliquely ; a sidelong look ; তির্য্যগ্‌নেত্রে দৃষ্টিপাত ; বক্রদৃষ্টি, টেরাচাহনি, আড় নজর। 2. Glance ; "After taking a prolonged *squint*, he called to me the object was a ship-boat" ; দৃষ্টি। 3. Inclination ; ঝোঁক, প্রবণতা।

4. A narrow aperture cut in the wall of a church affording a view of the altar from the transept; খৃষ্টীয় ধর্ম্মমন্দিরের প্রাচীরে কর্ত্তিত ক্ষুদ্র ছিদ্র—যাহার সাহায্যে ক্রুশাকৃতি গির্জ্জার পার্শ্বদেশ হইতে বেদী দৃষ্ট হইয়া থাকে। *Adj.* 1. Looking obliquely; বক্রদৃষ্টি, (*fig.*) বিদ্বেষ-পরায়ণ, পক্ষপাতদুষ্ট। 2. Not having the optic axes coincident; টেরা, টেগর, আড়চোখো, গজচক্ষুঃ। 3. Looking with suspicion; সন্দেহের নেত্রে দৃষ্টিকারী। **Squint′-er,** *n.* **Squint′-ing-ly,** *adv.* **Squint-eyed**—টেরা, গজচক্ষুঃ। **Squint-quoin**—বহিঃস্থ স্থূল কোণ।

squire, *n.* & *v. t.* 1. A knight's attendant; a knight's shield or armour-bearer; নাইটের সহচর; নাইটের ঢাল বা বর্ম্মবাহক। 2. A gentleman next in rank to a knight; নাইট উপাধিধারী ব্যক্তির অব্যবহিত নিম্ন পদবীর ভদ্রলোক। 3. A country gentleman; পল্লীবাসী ভদ্রলোক। 4. An attendant on a lady; a woman's escort or gallant; . স্ত্রীলোকের সহচর; রমণীরঞ্জক পুরুষ, নাগর। *Verb t.* 1. To attend as squire; অনুচররূপে নাইটের সঙ্গে অনুগমন করা। 2. To attend as a beau or gallant; নাগররূপে অনুগমন করা। **Squire′-ess,** *n.* (*Fem.*), **Squire′-hood, Squire′-let, Squire′-ling, Squire′-ship,** *ns.* **A squire of dames**—যে ব্যক্তি সর্ব্বদা স্ত্রীমহলে যাতায়াত করে এবং প্রমদাজনের মনোরঞ্জনের জন্য ব্যস্ত থাকে।

squire′-ărch-y̆, *n.* 1. The government by, or the political influence of, the squires; পল্লীবাসী ভদ্রলোকগণের দ্বারা দেশের শাসনকার্য্য পরিচালন, পল্লীবাসী ভদ্রলোকদিগের রাজনীতিক প্রভাব। 2. Country gentlemen collectively; পল্লীবাসী-ভদ্রলোকসমূহ।

squir-een′ (-ēn), *n.* A small landed proprietor esp. in Ireland; ক্ষুদ্র ভূম্যধিকারী, বিশেষতঃ আয়র্লণ্ড দেশের ক্ষুদ্র জমিদার।

squirm (skwĕrm), *v. i.* & *n.* 1. To wriggle; to writhe; কিলবিল করা, শরীর মোচড়ান, গা মোড়া দেওয়া। 2. (*Fig.*) To show or feel embarrassment; অপ্রতিভভাব দেখান বা বোধ করা। *Noun.* 1. A wriggling motion; মোচড়, কিলবিল। 2. (*Naut.*) A twist in a rope; দড়ীর মোচড়।

squir′-rĕl, *n.* A small rodent quadruped, with a long tufted tail, remarkable for its agility playfulness, grace and brightness; কাঠবিড়াল, কাষ্ঠমার্জ্জার [Syn পর্ণমৃগ, বৃক্ষমার্জ্জার, বৃক্ষবিড়াল, বৃক্ষমর্কটিকা।] **Barking squirrel**—Same as PRAIRIE-DOG. **Squirrel-fish**—তীক্ষ্ণ কণ্টকাবৃত মৎস্যজাতিবিশেষ **Squirrel-hawk**—একপ্রকার বৃহৎকায় কাষ্ঠমার্জ্জারশিকারী বাজপক্ষী। **Squirrel-monkey** — একজাতীয় ক্ষুদ্রকায় কপি। **Squirrel-tail** — কতিপয় যবজাতীয় তৃণের সাধারণ নাম।

squirt (skwĕrt), *v. t., i.* & *n.* To throw out in a stream from a narrow opening; (পিচকারী প্রভৃতি হইতে) ক্ষীণ ধারায় নির্গত করা *Verb i.* To be thrown out or ejected in a stream out of a narrow orifice; ক্ষীণ ধারায় নির্গত হওয়া, ফিন্‌কি দিয়া ছুটা। *Noun.* 1. An instrument for squirting; পিচকারী। 2. A jet; ফিন্‌কি, ধারা। 3. Same as SQUIRT-GUN (below). 4. (*Colloq.*, America) A foppish young fellow; (আমেরিকার চালত ভাষায়) ফুলবাবু। 5. An insignificant and self-assertive fellow; আত্মপ্রাধান্যখ্যাপনকারী তুচ্ছ লোক। **Squirt-gun**—শিশুদিগের ক্রীড়ার জন্য একপ্রকার পিচকারী।

stăb, *v. t., i.* & *n.* 1. To pierce with a pointed weapon; ছুরিকা প্রভৃতি দ্বারা বিদ্ধ করা, ছুরিকাঘাত করা। 2. To wound mortally with a stab; ছুরিকা দ্বারা সাংঘাতিকরূপে আঘাত করা, ছুরি মারা। 3. To injure secretly or by slander; to inflict keen and severe pain on; "*Stabbed* through the heart's affections"; গোপনে অনিষ্ট করা, মর্ম্মে আঘাত করা, অপবাদ করা; তীব্র যন্ত্রণা দেওয়া, তীব্র সন্তাপ দেওয়া। 4. To roughen the surface of a brick wall with a point for plastering; আস্তর লাগাইবার জন্য সূক্ষ্মাগ্র লৌহ দ্বারা প্রাচীর বন্ধুর করা। *Verb i.* 1. To give a wound with a pointed weapon; to aim a blow with pointed weapon; ছুরিকা প্রভৃতি দ্বারা আঘাত করা; ছুরিকা প্রভৃতি দ্বারা আঘাত করার জন্য নিশানা করা, ঘাইল করিতে চেষ্টা করা। 2. To give a mortal wound; সাংঘাতিক আঘাত করা। *Noun.* 1. The thrust of a pointed weapon; ছুরিকাঘাত। 2. An underhand injury; গোপনে সাধিত অনিষ্ট। **Stab-ber,** *n.* **To stab in the back**—To slander; পরোক্ষে অপবাদ করা, অসাক্ষাতে কলঙ্ক রটনা বা কুৎসা করা।

Stabat Mater, *n.* An old hymn on the crucifixion beginning with these words; খৃষ্টের ক্রুশারোহণ সম্বন্ধে প্রাচীন সঙ্গীতবিশেষ। *Stabat Mater* এই সঙ্গীতের প্রথম শব্দদ্বয়।

stă-bil′-ĭ-ty̆, *n.* 1. State or quality of being firm; firmness; দৃঢ়তা; স্থায়িত্ব (ঐ), অচলপ্রতিষ্ঠতা। 2. Firmness or steadiness of character; constancy; resolution; as, a man of little *stability*; স্বভাবের দৃঢ়তা, স্থিরতা, স্থৈর্য্য, স্থিতি; স্থিরচিত্ততা; দৃঢ়চিত্ততা। **Stability of value**—মূল্যের স্থিরতা (হিঃ কোঃ)।

stā′-ble (-bl), *adj.* 1. Firm; firmly established; as, a *stable* government; দৃঢ়স্থায়ী (হিঃ কোঃ); অচলপ্রতিষ্ঠ, অটল, স্থির। 2. Steady in purp ; firm in resolution; not fickle or vacillating; as, a man of *stable* character; স্থিরমনাঃ, স্থির-সংকল্প, স্থিরমতি; দৃঢ়প্রতিজ্ঞ, স্থিরপ্রতিজ্ঞ;

স্থিতপ্রজ্ঞ। **3.** Abiding ; not subject to change or destruction ; as, a *stable* position ; স্থায়ী ; অবিকার্য, অক্ষয়। **4.** (*Phys.*) Not easily moved from a state of equilibrium ; (পদার্থবিজ্ঞান) বলসামঞ্জস্যের অবস্থা হইতে সহজে বিচ্যুত হয়না—এইরূপ, স্থির। **—bly,** *adv.* **—ness, Stab-i-li za'-tion,** *ns.* **Stab'-i-lize,** *v. t.* **Stable, unstable equlibrium**—See under EQUILIBRIUM.

sta'-ble (-bl), *n., v. t. & i.* **1.** A house for horses etc. ; আস্তাবল, অশ্বশালা, বাজিশালা, ঘোড়াশালা (in folk-lore), মন্দুরা, তুরঙ্গশালা, বাহনকোষ্ঠ (কৌটিল্যঃ), অশ্বগোষ্ঠ, অশ্বালয় (বিশ্বকর্ম্মা), বাজীভবন, ঘোটকগৃহ। **2.** A race-horse of particular stable ; কোন বিশেষ আস্তাবলের দৌড়ের ঘোড়া। ***Verb t.*** To put or keep in a stable ; আস্তাবলে রাখা। ***Verb i.*** To be kept in a stable ; আস্তাবলে রক্ষিত হওয়া। **Augean stables**—See AUGEAN. **Stable boy, Stable-man**—আস্তাবলের কার্য্যে নিযুক্ত বালক বা পরিণতবয়স্ক ব্যক্তি। **Stable-call**—অশ্বকে খররা দিবার জন্য বা জল প্রদানের জন্য অশ্বারোহী সৈন্যপল্টনে ব্যবহৃত সঙ্কেতবিশেষ। **To lock or shut the stable-door when the steed is stolen**—See LOCK.

stab'-ling, *n.* **1.** The act of one who stables ; আস্তাবলে অশ্ব রাখন। **2.** A house, shed or room for horses or other beasts ; অশ্ব বা অন্য কোন পশুর বাসের জন্য গৃহ, চালা, কোঠা, প্রভৃতি।

stăb'-lish, *v. t.* (*Archaic*) To establish ; (অপ্রঃ) প্রতিষ্ঠাপিত করা।

staccato, *adj.* & *adv.* (*Mus.*) Disconnected ; distinct ; (সঙ্গীতশাস্ত্র) অসম্বদ্ধ ; পৃথক্, স্বতন্ত্র। ***Adv.*** To be played in an abrupt or detached manner ; আকস্মিক বা অসম্বদ্ধ ভাবে বাদনীয়।

stăck, *n.* & *v. t.* **1.** A pile (of hay, grain, etc.), খড়, শস্য, প্রভৃতির গাদা, স্তূপ, পুঞ্জ, পালই। **2.** A number of funnel or chimney standing together ; একত্রস্থিত ফুঁদেল এবং চিমনীর সমষ্টি। **3.** A single tall chimney ; সুদীর্ঘ ধূমনির্গমনালী। **4.** A pile of wood containing 108 cubic feet ; a pile of poles or wood of indefinite quantity ; ১০৮ ঘন ফুট কাঠের কাঁড়ি ; অনির্দ্দিষ্ট পরিমাণ খোঁটা বা কাঠের কাঁড়ি, কাষ্ঠস্তূপ। **5.** A pyramidical group of rifles ; esp. such a pile composed of three rifles ; ক্রমসূক্ষ্মাগ্র-স্তম্ভাকারে সজ্জিত বন্দুকপুঞ্জ ; বিশেষতঃ ত্রিকোণাকারে রক্ষিত বন্দুকত্রয়। **6.** (*Colloq.*) A large quantity ; as, *stack* of work ; (চলিতভাষায়) বহু পরিমাণ, রাশি রাশি। **7.** A high detached rock ; বিশ্লিষ্ট উচ্চ পাষাণস্তূপ। ***Verb t.*** To pile in stacks ; কাঁড়ি করিয়া রাখা, গাদা করিয়া রাখা। **Stack-funnel**—খড় প্রভৃতির গাদার ভিতর যাহাতে বাতাস ঢুকিতে পারে তজ্জন্য এই সকলের মধ্যস্থলে যে ক্রমসূক্ষ্মাগ্র ঠাট স্থাপিত করা হয়। **Stack-stand**—খড়ের পালইর মাচা। **Stack-yard**—খড় বা শস্যের পালই যে প্রাঙ্গণে স্থাপিত করা হয়। **To stack arms**—To place arms esp. three rifles in the form of a pyramid ; বন্দুক সমূহ ক্রমসূক্ষ্মাগ্র স্তম্ভের আকারে রাখা, বিশেষতঃ বন্দুকত্রয় ত্রিকোণাকারে রাখা। **To stack cards**—To arrange cards secretly for cheating ; প্রতারণা করার উদ্দেশ্যে গোপনে তাস ভাঁজ করা।

stăc'-tē, *n.* One of the spices used in making incense ; ধূনা প্রস্তুতে ব্যবহৃত একপ্রকার সুগন্ধি দ্রব্য।

stăc-tŏm'-ĕ-tĕr, *n.* An instrument for ascertaining the number of drops in equal bulks of different liquids ; সম আয়তনের বিভিন্ন প্রকার তরল পদার্থে কত বিন্দু আছে—তন্নির্ণয়ের জন্য যন্ত্র বিশেষ, বিন্দুমান।

stad'-hōld-ĕr, stadt'- (stăt-), *ns.* The chief magistrate of the United Provinces of Holland ; a governor or lieutenant-governor of a province ; হলণ্ডের যুক্তরাজ্যের প্রধান দণ্ডনায়ক ; প্রাদেশিক শাসনকর্ত্তা।

stā'-di-ŭm, *n.* **1.** A Greek measure equal to 606 feet 9 inches ; ৬০৬ গজ ৯ ইঞ্চির গ্রীসদেশীয় দৈর্ঘ্যের পরিমাণ বিশেষ। **2.** The course for foot-races at Olympia in Greece and elsewhere ; গ্রীসদেশের অন্তঃপাতী অলিম্পিয়া এবং অন্যান্য স্থানের দৌড়চক্র।

stăff, *n.* (*pl.* STAVES, STAFFS) **1.** A stick or rod ; দণ্ড, যষ্টি, লগুড়, লাঠি, ছড়ি। **2.** The handle of a tool or weapon or spear ; বর্শা প্রভৃতির আছাড়, বাঁট। **3.** A proper support ; "The boy was the very *staff* of my age" ; অবলম্বন, আশ্রয়, আশ্রয়যষ্টি। **4.** The round of a ladder ; মইএর ধাপ। **5.** A pole on which a flag is hoisted ; পতাকা-দণ্ড। **6.** (*Mus.*) The five parallel lines on which musical characters or lines are written ; (সঙ্গীতশাস্ত্র) যে পঞ্চ সমান্তরাল রেখার উপর সঙ্গীতের চিহ্ন লিখিত হয়। **7.** An ensign of authority ; আসাসোঁটা। **8.** A body of officers attached to an army, or to its commander, whose duty is to assist the commander in carrying his plans into execution, and in maintaining the army in a state of efficiency, যে সামরিক কর্ম্মচারিবৃন্দ প্রধান সেনাপতিকে সহায়তা করেন এবং যাঁহাদের উপর সেনাদলের এবং সেনাপল্টনের শাসন কার্য্যাদি পরিচালনের ভার ন্যস্ত থাকে। **9.** A body of officials connected with an office, schools, department ; কোন বিভাগের সহিত সম্পৃক্ত কর্ম্মচারিবর্গ, আফিসের কর্ম্মচারিবর্গ, বিদ্যালয় প্রভৃতির শিক্ষকবর্গ। **10.** (*Obs.*) A stanza ; (অপ্রঃ) কবিতার কলি। **11.** Kinds of instrument for taking altitude at sea ; সাগরের

উচ্চতা গ্রহণের জন্য বিভিন্ন প্রকার পরিমাণ যন্ত্র। 12. (*Surg.*) A surgeon's instrument used to guide the knife through the urethra into the bladder in the operation of lithotomy; (অস্ত্রোপচারবিদ্যা) মূত্রাশয় হইতে প্রস্তর নিষ্কর্ষণ করার কালে মূত্রনালীর ভিতর দিয়া মূত্রাধারে ছুরিকার পথ প্রদর্শনের জন্য অস্ত্রবিশেষ। **Staff-captain** — সমুদ্রগামী ব্রিটিশ নৌসৈন্যদলের অধ্যক্ষ। **Staff college**—যে সামরিক বিদ্যালয়ে প্রধান সেনাপতির সাহায্যকারী সৈনিক কর্ম্মচারিগণ শিক্ষিত হয়। **Staff-commander** — সমুদ্রগামী নৌসৈন্যদলের অধিনায়ক। **Staff-officer** — প্রধান সেনানায়কের সাহায্যকারী সামরিক কর্ম্মচারিগণের অন্যতম; আসাসোঁটাধারী চোপদার। **Staff-sergeant**—সেনানায়কের প্রধান কার্য্যালয়ে নিযুক্ত সার্জ্জেণ্ট। **Jacob's staff**—See JACOB. **Prime vertical staff**—সমমণ্ডল শঙ্কু (সূর্য্যবাঃ)। **The staff of life**—ভাত, রুটি, প্রভৃতি।

stäff, *n.* A mixture of plaster of Paris, cement, etc; প্যারী প্লাস্তার, বিলাতী মাটী, প্রভৃতির মিশ্র।

stăg, *n.* **1.** A male red deer; লাল হরিণ, রক্তকুরঙ্গ, কুরঙ্গ। **2.** A castrated bull; দামড়া, ছিন্নমুষ্ক বৃষ। **3.** (*Slang*) An irregular dealer in stocks; (ইতরভাষায়) কোম্পানীর কাগজের রীতিবিরুদ্ধ ব্যবসায়ী। **Stag-beetle** — একপ্রকার কীট — যাহার দংশনোষ্ঠ মৃগশৃঙ্গের মত বিভক্ত থাকে, মৃগকীট। **Stag-evil** — দাঁতকপাটি। **Stag-horn**—বিভিন্নজাতীয় শৈবাল এবং প্রবালের সাধারণ নাম। **Staghound**—যে কুক্কুর ঘ্রাণ বা দৃষ্টিদ্বারা হরিণ শিকার করিয়া থাকে।

stāge, *n.* **1.** A raised platform; মঞ্চ, মাঁচা। **2.** The platform on which theatrical performances are exhibited; theatre; drama as acted or exhibited; theatrical-profession; রঙ্গমঞ্চ, রঙ্গপীঠ, নাট্যবেদী (কথাঃ সঃ), আসর (গ্রাঃ বিঃ); রঙ্গালয়, নাট্যালয়, রঙ্গমণ্ডপ; অভিনয়; নটবৃত্তি। **3.** A place where anything is publicly exhibited; the scene of any noted action; যে স্থানে কোন কিছু প্রদর্শিত হয়, প্রদর্শনমঞ্চ; কোন বিরাট কার্য্যের ক্ষেত্র। **4.** A resting place on a journey; place appointed for the relay of horse; পথিপার্শ্বস্থ বিশ্রাম স্থান, চটী; যে স্থানে গাড়ী প্রভৃতির ঘোড়া বদলান হয়। **5.** Distance between two stopping places; বিরামস্থলদ্বয়ের মধ্যেবর্ত্তী স্থান। **6.** Same as STAGE-COACH. **7.** A landing quay or pier; অবতরণমঞ্চ, পোস্তা, ঘাট, উত্তরণমঞ্চ। **8.** Degree of progress or advance; degree of progression either in increase or decrease; as, the *stages* of a disease; point or period in development; উন্নতির অবস্থা; উন্নতি বা অবনতির ক্রম, গ্রাম; বিকাশ প্রভৃতির অবস্থা। **9.** The support on which an object is placed to be viewed by a microscope; অণুবীক্ষণদ্বারা দর্শনীয় বস্তু যে আধারে রক্ষিত হয়। **Hanging stage** — চিত্রকরদিগের ব্যবহারের জন্য রজ্জুর উপর অবলম্বিত মঞ্চ। **Landing-stage**—Same as STAGE 7. **Stage-coach**—যে শকট নিয়মিতরূপে সপ্তাহের নির্দ্দিষ্ট দিবসে একস্থান হইতে অপর স্থানে যাত্রী, ডাক, প্রভৃতি লইয়া গমন করে, অধ্বগযান (আঃ বঃ)। **Stage-coachman**—অধ্বযান চালক। **Stage-craft**—নাট্যবিরচনচাতুর্য্য, কোন নাটক সুন্দররূপে রঙ্গমঞ্চে স্থাপনার নিপুণ্য। **Stage-direction**—নাটকে অভিনেতা ও অভিনেত্রীগণের গতি, স্বর, অবস্থান, প্রভৃতি সম্বন্ধে যে লিখিত বা মুদ্রিত উপদেশ দেওয়া হয়। **Stage-door**—যে দ্বারে অভিনেতা ও অভিনেত্রী প্রভৃতি রঙ্গমঞ্চে প্রবেশ করে বা উহার পশ্চাদ্দেশে গমন করিয়া থাকে, রঙ্গদ্বার (ভাগঃ)। **Stage-driver**—Same as STAGE-COACHMAN. **Stage effect**—অভিনয়দর্শনজনিত ভাব; বাস্তবজীবনে উৎপাদিত কৃত্রিম বা নাটকীয় ভাব। **Stage-fever**—নটবৃত্তি অবলম্বনের জন্য উন্মত্ততা। **Stage-fright**—শ্রোতৃবৃন্দের সমক্ষে সর্ব্বপ্রথম উপস্থিত হওয়ার কালে যে চিত্তদৌর্ব্বল্য অনুভূত হয়। **Stage manager**—সূত্রধার (দশকুঃ)। **Stage-play**—নাট্যাভিনয়। **Stage-player**—অভিনেতা, নট, নটী (*Fem.*), অভিনেত্রী, রঙ্গচর, রঙ্গাজীব, রঙ্গাবতরক, রঙ্গোপজীবী (মৃঃ সং), কুশীলব, সর্ব্বতোভদ্রা (*fem.*), **Stage-right** — কোন বিশেষ নাটক অভিনীত করার একাধিকার। **Stage-struck** — নটবৃত্তি অবলম্বনের জন্য উন্মত্ত। **Stage whisper**—স্বগত উক্তি, জনান্তিক উক্তি।

stāge, *v. t.* & *i.* To put a play on the stage; রঙ্গমঞ্চে অভিনয় করা। ***Verb i.*** To be put on a stage; রঙ্গমঞ্চে অভিনীত হওয়া।

stāg'-ẽr, *n.* **1.** A horse employed in drawing a stage-coach; অধ্বযান টানিবার জন্য অশ্ব। **2.** An experienced man; অভিজ্ঞ লোক, পাকালোক। **Old-stager**—অভিজ্ঞ লোক, পাকা লোক।

stăg'-gard (-ärd), **-gart** (-ärt), *ns.* A stag four years old; চারি বৎসর বয়স্ক হরিণ।

stăg'-ger (-ẽr), *v. i.*, *t.* & *n.* **1.** To walk unsteadily; to reel; টলিয়া চলা; টলা। **2.** To fall; to cease to stand firm; পতিত হওয়া; টলমল করা। **3.** To hesitate: "He (Abraham) *staggered* not at the promise of God through unbelief"; সংশয় করা, সন্দেহদোলায় দোলায়মান হওয়া। ***Verb t.*** **1.** To cause to reel; টলান, টলমল করান। **2.** To cause to hesitate; সন্দেহদোলায় দোলায়মান করা, সংশয়াকুল করা, সংশয়াচ্ছন্ন করা, সংশয়ান্বিত করা। **3.** To set spokes in a hub on the respective sides of a median line; পর্য্যায়ক্রমে দক্ষিণে ও বামে হেলাইয়া চাকার আর স্থাপিত করা। ***Noun.*** **1.** Tottering movement; as, the *stagger* of drunkard; দোল, টলন, টলমল। **2.** (*Pl.*) Disease of horses and cattle attended with reeling or giddiness; অশ্ব এবং গবাদির শিরোরোগবিশেষ। **3.** (*Pl.*) Giddiness; ভ্রমি, শিরোঘূর্ণন।

stăg'-ger-êr (-êr-), *n.* 1. One who, or that which, staggers ; যে বা যাহা টলে বা টলমল করিয়া থাকে, টলমলকারী। 2. A blow etc. that causes one to stagger ; যে আঘাত প্রভৃতিতে মাথায় ভ্রমি জন্মে। 3. A statement or argument that staggers ; যে উক্তি বা যুক্তিতে কোন ব্যক্তি বিভ্রান্ত হয়।

stăg'-ing, *n.* 1. Scaffolding ; মঞ্চ, মাচা, ভারা। 2. The business of running, managing or of journeying in a stage-coach ; অশ্বযান চালান, অশ্বযানের কার্য্যনির্ব্বাহ, অশ্বযানে ভ্রমণ। 3. The act or art of putting a play on the stage ; কোন নাটক অভিনয়ের জন্য রঙ্গমঞ্চে উপস্থাপন, অভিনয়ের জন্য রঙ্গমঞ্চে নাট্য উপস্থাপনের শিল্পকলা, নাট্যোপস্থাপন কলা।

Stăg'-i-rite, *n.* **The Stagirite**—গ্রীক দার্শনিক আরিস্তোতল। [ম্যাসিডোনিয়ার অন্তঃপাতী Stageira আরিস্তোতলের জন্মভূমি ছিল বলিয়া এই নাম।]

stăg'-nate, *v. i.* 1. To cease to run or flow ; to have no current ; প্রবাহ বন্ধ হওয়া, গতিরুদ্ধ হওয়া ; স্রোত বন্ধ হওয়া, স্রোতোহীন হওয়া, জল আটকিয়া বা জমিয়া থাকা। 2. To cease to be brisk or active ; অচটুল হওয়া, স্ফূর্ত্তিহীন হওয়া, চাঞ্চল্যহীন হওয়া। **—nan-cy, —na'-tion,** *ns.* 1. The quality of being stagnant ; স্থৈর্য্য, স্থিরতা, স্থিরত্ব, নিশ্চলতা। 2. The state of being dull ; মান্দ্য, শ্লথতা, শিথিলতা। **—nant,** *adj.* 1. Not flowing in current or stream ; বদ্ধ, আটক। 2. Not active or brisk ; স্ফূর্ত্তিহীন, অচটুল। **—nant-ly,** *adv.*

stăg-nic'-ō-lous (-lŭs), *adj.* Living in stagnant water ; inhabiting swamps ; বদ্ধজলবাসী ; অনুপভূমিবাসী, বিলবাসী।

stăg'-ÿ, *adj.* Theatrical ; নাটকীয়, নাটুকে (*colloq.*)। **—i-ness,** *n.*

staid (stād), *adj.* Sober ; grave ; composed ; sedate ; ধীর, স্থির, গম্ভীর ; অপ্রমত্ত, স্থৈর্য্যসম্পন্ন ; প্রশান্ত, অক্ষুব্ধ। **Staid'-ly,** *adv.* **Staid'-ness,** *n.*

stain (stān), *v. t., i. & n.* 1. To discolour ; to make foul ; স্বাভাবিক বর্ণ বিকৃত করা, বদরঙ্গ করা, মলিন করা ; নোংরা করা। 2. To colour, as wood, glass, by means of chemical or other process ; রাসায়নিক বা অন্য উপায়ে কাঠ, কাচ, প্রভৃতি রঞ্জিত করা। 3. To dye ; রঞ্জিত করা। 4. To impress with figures or patterns in colours different from the ground ; জমির রঙ্গ হইতে ভিন্ন রঙ্গের পুষ্পপত্রাদিদ্বারা মুদ্রিত করা। 5. To render foul ; to tarnish ; দূষিত করা ; কলঙ্কিত করা। *Verb i.* 1. To cause a stain or discoloration ; দাগ লাগান, বিবর্ণ করা। 2. To become stained or soiled ; কলঙ্কিত হওয়া, দূষিত হওয়া, কলুষিত হওয়া। *Noun.* 1. A discoloration from foreign matter ; বিবর্ণ হওন। 2. A spot of a colour different from the ground ; জমিন হইতে ভিন্ন বর্ণের দাগ। 3. Blot ; blemish ; কলঙ্ক ; দোষ। 4. Cause of reproach ; shame ; disgrace ; কলঙ্কের হেতু ; লজ্জা ; অখ্যাতি, অপযশ। **Stain'-a-ble,** *adj.* **Stained,** *p. p.* **Stain'-er,** *n.* **Stain'-less,** *adj.* **Stain'-less-ly,** *adv.* **Stained glass**—জানালা প্রভৃতিতে ব্যবহৃত রঞ্জিত কাচ, নানাপ্রকার বর্ণের দাগ দ্বারা রঞ্জিত কাচ। **Without a stain on the character**—অকলঙ্ক চরিত্র। **Without stain** — দাগশূন্য ; নিষ্কলঙ্ক, অকলঙ্ক, নির্দ্দোষ, নিরঞ্জন, অপকলঙ্ক।

stair (stār), *n.* 1. One of a set of steps to go up or down by ; সিঁড়ি, সোপান, ধাপ। 2. (Usu. *Pl.*) A series of steps to ascend by ; সোপানশ্রেণী, সোপানাবলী, অধিরোহিণী, সোপানপংক্তি। **Stair-carpet** — সোপানাবলী আচ্ছাদনের জন্য গালিচা। **Staircase** — সোপানশ্রেণী, সিঁড়ি, সোপানপথ, সোপানপদ্ধতি। **Stair-rod** — সোপানদ্বয়ের মধ্যবর্ত্তী কোণে গালিচা টান করিয়া রাখার জন্য ধাতবদণ্ড বা অনুরূপ কার্য্যসাধক কোন বস্তু। **Stair-turret**—ঘুরাণো সিঁড়ির আবরণ-স্বরূপ বুরুজের আকৃতি গৃহ। **Stair-way** — Same as STAIR-CASE. **Back stairs**—See BACK. **Below-stairs** — In the basement of a house ; অট্টালিকাদির ভূনিম্নবর্ত্তী তলে (এইস্থানে সচরাচর ভৃত্যগণ অবস্থান করে)। **Corkscrew stair-case**—মধ্যবর্ত্তী স্তম্ভের চতুর্দ্দিকে আবর্ত্তিত সোপানাবলী। **Down stairs**—নীচের তালায়, নীচে। **Up stairs**—উপরের তালায়, উপরে।

stāke, *n. & v. t.* 1. A small piece of wood sharpened at one end set or to be set in the ground ; an upright bar to support a vine or a tree ; বেড়ার খুঁটি ; কোন বৃক্ষ বা আঙ্গুরলতার অবলম্বনস্বরূপ ভূপ্রোথিত দণ্ড, ঝাঁকা। 2. The piece of timber to which a person is bound while he is burning ; as, witches were burnt at the *stake* ; hence, death by fire ; জীবন্ত দগ্ধ করার কালে যে খোঁটায় কোন ব্যক্তিকে বন্ধন করা হইত ; অগ্নিদগ্ধাবস্থায় মৃত্যু। 3. That which is pledged or wagered ; বাজি, পণ। 4. A small anvil used by the smiths ; কর্ম্মকারগণের একপ্রকার ক্ষুদ্র নেয়াই। 5. The state of being put to hazard ; as, his honour is at *stake* ; সঙ্কটাপন্ন অবস্থায়। 6. An interest or property involved ; as, he has a *stake* in the country ; স্বার্থ বা সম্পত্তি। 7. Money to be counted for esp. in horse-race ; such race ; বাজীর টাকা, বিশেষতঃ ঘোড়দৌড়ে যে টাকা বাজী রাখা হয় ; টাকা বাজি রাখিয়া ঘোড়দৌড়। *Verb t.* 1. To set stakes in ; খোঁটা পোতা। 2. To mark the limit off by stake (now followed by *out*) ;

খোঁটা পুতিয়া সীমা চিহ্নিত করা। 3. To fasten, support or defend with stakes; খোঁটা দ্বারা রুদ্ধ, অবলম্বিত বা রক্ষা করা, ঠেকো দেওয়া। 4. To wager; বাজি ধরা, পণ করা। 5. To pierce with stakes; খোঁটা দ্বারা ভেদ করা। **Stake-boat** — নৌকাদৌড়ে গমনপথনির্দ্দেশের জন্য যে নৌকা নোঙ্গর করিয়া রাখা হয়। **Stake-net**—খোঁটা সমূহের উপর পাতা জাল। **At stake**—In question; risked; involved; বিষয়ীভূত; পণ (as in প্রাণপণ); জড়িত।

stă-lăc′-tīte, *n.* A mass of calcareous matter attached like an icicle to the roof of cavern;

Stalactites and Stalagmites.

গহ্বরের ছাদ হইতে তুষারকণাবৎ বিলম্বিত একপ্রকার চূর্ণময় পদার্থ। **—tic, —ti-form,** *adjs.*

stă-lăg′-mīte, *n.* A deposit of calcareous matter on the floors of cavern; গহ্বরের তলে সঞ্চিত চূর্ণময় পদার্থ। **—mit′-ic,** *adj.* **—mit′-i-cal-ly,** *adv.*

stāle, *adj., n., v. t.* & *i.* 1. Vapid or tasteless from age; as, *stale* beer; স্বাদহীন, ভব্‌কা, গুমসা। 2. Not freshly made; as, *stale* bread; পর্য্যুষিত, বাসি, পান্ত (esp. of boiled rice). 3. Having lost its novelty, or power of pleasing; as, *stale* jokes; পুরাণ, পুরাতন, নূতনত্বহীন, লোকোচ্ছিষ্ট (কেঙিঃ), বস্তাপচা (*colloq.*—cf. বস্তাপচা ঠাট্টা।) 5. Impaired in vigor or energy by prolonged activity; as, a *stale* athlete; বহুক্ষণ ধরিয়া দেহসঞ্চালনাদি হেতু নিস্তেজ। *Noun.* 1. That which is stale; পচা জিনিষ, বাসি জিনিষ। 2. (*Obs.*) A prostitute; (অপ্রঃ) বেশ্যা। 3. Urine of horses and cattle; অশ্ব এবং গবাদির মূত্র। *Verb t.* To make vapid, tasteless or worthless; to destroy the life, beauty or freshness of; গুমসা করা, স্বাদহীন করা; জীবনীশক্তি নষ্ট করা, সৌন্দর্য্য নষ্ট করা, নবীনতা নষ্ট করা। *Verb i.* 1. To grow stale; গুমসা হওয়া, স্বাদহীন হওয়া। 2. (Of horses) To discharge urine; (অশ্বসম্পর্কে) প্রস্রাব করা। **Stale′-ness,** *n.*

stāle, *n.* (*Archaic.*) Dupe; laughing stock; (অপ্রঃ) যে ব্যক্তি সহজে প্রতারিত হয়; উপহাসের পাত্র।

stāle′-māte, *n.* & *v. t.* (*Chess*) The position of the king, when, though not in check, he cannot move without being exposed to check, and when there is no other piece to move; (দাবাখেলায়) রাজার এইরূপ অবস্থা যে যখন উহার চাল বন্ধ হইয়া না থাকিলেও উহাকে যেখানেই চালা যায় উহার মাত হইতে পারে এবং যখন অন্য কোন গুটিও চালান যায় না। *Verb t.* 1. (*Chess*) To subject to stalemate; (দাবাখেলায়) উক্তরূপ অবস্থায় আনা। 2. To bring to a stand-still; to nonplus; গতিরোধ করা, চলৎশক্তি নষ্ট করা; কিংকর্ত্তব্যবিমূঢ় করা, হতবুদ্ধি করা।

stalk (stăk), *v. i., t.* & *n.* 1. To walk with high and proud steps; "With manly mien he *stalked* along the ground"; সাটোপে চলা, সদম্ভে চলা, সগর্ব্বে চলা। 2. To walk softly and warily; নিঃশব্দে এবং সন্তর্পণে চলা, চুপি চুপি চলা, পা টিপিয়া টিপিয়া চলা। 3. To walk behind something, as a screen for the purpose of taking a game; শিকার ধরার জন্য কোনরূপ পর্দ্দা প্রভৃতির পশ্চাতে চলা। *Verb t.* To pursue steathily; to watch and follow warily, as a game, for the purpose of killing; অলক্ষিতে অনুসরণ করা; শিকার নিহত করার উদ্দেশ্যে উহাকে লক্ষ্য করিয়া সন্তর্পণে অগ্রসর হওয়া। *Noun.* 1. A stately step or walk; সাটোপে চলন, সাটোপ গমন, সদম্ভপাদবিক্ষেপ। 2. The act of stalking wild animals; বন্য জন্তু নিহত করার উদ্দেশ্যে অতি সন্তর্পণে চলন। **Stalking-horse**—অশ্ব বা অশ্বাকৃতি কোন মূর্ত্তি—যাহার পশ্চাতে লুক্কায়িত থাকিয়া শিকারী হরিণ প্রভৃতি শিকার করিয়া থাকে; (লক্ষণায়) ছল, ব্যাজ, ছদ্মভান।

stalk (stāk), *n.* 1. The stem of a plant; ডগা, নাল, ডাঁটা। 2. The peduncle of a flower; বৃন্ত, বোঁটা, পুষ্পবৃন্ত, প্রসববন্ধ। 3. Anything resembling a stalk; বৃন্তাকার বস্তু। 4. The stem of a spoon; চামচের ডাঁটি। 5. A tall chimney; সুদীর্ঘ ধূমনির্গম চোঙ্গ। 6. Stem of wine-glass etc.; মদের গেলাসের ডাঁটি। 7. (*Arch.*) An ornament in the Corinthian capital which resembles the stalk of a plant; কোরিন্থিয়ান স্থাপত্যরীতি অনুযায়ী নির্ম্মিত স্তম্ভের বৃন্তাকার ভূষাবিশেষ। **Stalk′-less,** *adj.* **Stalk′-let,** *n.*

stall, *n., v. t.* & *i.* 1. A place where a horse or ox is kept and fed; গোশালা, অশ্বশালা, মন্দুরা, গোষ্ঠ। 2. Division of a stable for a single horse; এক একটী অশ্ব রক্ষার জন্য যে ক্ষুদ্র ক্ষুদ্র কক্ষে আস্তাবল বিভক্ত করা হইয়া থাকে — তাহার অন্যতর। 3. A bench or shed where anything is exposed to sale etc.; as, a book *stall*: a butcher's *stall*; হাটের চালা, মেলার টাট, যে মেজ কিম্বা চালায় বিক্রেয় দ্রব্যাদি প্রদর্শিত হয়, পণ্যবীথি, বীথি (শিষ্টঃ),

পণ্যবেশন (শুক্রঃ বিনম্র)। **4.** A high-class seat in a theatre; রঙ্গালয়ের উচ্চশ্রেণীর আসন। **5.** The seat of a church dignitary in a choir; খৃষ্টীয় ধর্ম্মমন্দিরের গীতমঞ্চে উচ্চশ্রেণীর যাজকদিগের আসন। **6.** Office, dignity, of a canon etc.; উচ্চশ্রেণীর যাজক প্রভৃতির পদ বা পদ-গৌরব। **7.** A covering or sheath for a finger or thumb; অঙ্গুষ্ঠ বা অঙ্গুলীর আবরণ, অঙ্গুষ্ঠত্রাণ, অঙ্গুলীত্রাণ। **8.** Working compartment in a coal-mine; কয়লায় খনির কর্ম্মকক্ষ। ***Verb t.*** **1.** To put into a stall; গোষ্ঠে বা আস্তাবলে রাখা। **2.** To furnish with stalls; গোষ্ঠসমন্বিত করা। **3.** To plunge into mire; to stop or check by causing to become fast in mud; as, to *stall* a cart by too heavy a load; পঙ্কে নিমগ্ন করা; পঙ্কে নিবদ্ধ করিয়া থামান বা গতিরোধ করা। ***Verb i.*** **1.** To live in a stall; গোষ্ঠে বা আস্তাবলে বাস করা। **2.** To be tired of eating, as cattle; ভোজনক্লান্ত হওয়া। **3.** To be set fast in mire; পঙ্কে নিবদ্ধ হওয়া। **Stall-fed**—অশ্বশালায় রাখিয়া যে অশ্বাদিগকে খাদ্য প্রদত্ত হয়—তৎসম্বন্ধে প্রযুক্ত। **Stall-man**—গোষ্ঠরক্ষক। **Stall-reader**—যে ব্যক্তি গ্রন্থবীথির সম্মুখে দাঁড়াইয়া পুস্তক পাঠ করে।

stall, *n.* A pick pocket's assistant; গাঁটকাটার সাহায্যকারী।

stall'-āge, *n.* **1.** The right of erecting stalls in fairs; মেলায় চালা বাঁধার অধিকার। **2.** The space for erecting stalls in fairs; মেলায় চালা বাঁধার জন্য যে স্থান দেওয়া হয়। **3.** The rent exacted for such privilege; ঐরূপ চালার জন্য দেয় শুল্ক।

stăl'-lion (-yŭn), *n.* A male horse, not castrated; অচ্ছিন্নমুষ্ক অশ্ব, জননাশ্ব, বীজাশ্ব (রাঃ তঃ), বাজী।

stal'-wart (-wêrt), *adj.* **1.** Brave; bold; redoubted; সাহসী; নির্ভীক; দুর্দ্ধর্ষ। **2.** Strong and tall; stout; big and strong in frame; বলিষ্ঠ এবং দীর্ঘকায়; শক্তিশালী; দৃঢ়কায় এবং বিপুলদেহ। **3.** Resolute; as, *stalwart* supporters; স্থির-প্রতিজ্ঞ, স্থিরসংকল্প, দৃঢ়প্রতিজ্ঞ, দৃঢ়-চিত্ত। **–ly,** *adv.* **–ness,** *n.*

Inside of a corolla, showing the stamens.

stā'-mĕn, *n.* **1.** The male organ of fructification in plants; পুষ্পের পরাগকেশর, পুংকেশর। **–min'-e-al, –min'-e-ous, Stam-i-nif'-er-ous,** *adjs.*

stăm'-i-nă, *n.* **1.** Innate vigour; that which constitutes the principal strength or support of a thing; staying power; তেজঃ, শক্তি; বল, সত্ব, ওজঃ; সহনশক্তি।

stăm'-i-năl, *adj.* Pertaining to stamens or stamina; পুংকেশর-সম্বন্ধীয়, ওজঃশক্তি সম্পর্কীয়।

stăm'-i-nāte, *n.* Furnished with stamens, but destitute of a pistil; পুংপুষ্প (যোঃ)।

stăm'-i-nōde, *n.* (*Bot.*) Same as STAMINODIUM.

stăm'-i-nō-di-ŭm, (*Pl.* -DIA), *n.* (*Bot.*) Bodies resembling stamens, and probably those organs in an abortive state found in certain plants; (উদ্ভিদ্‌বিদ্যা) উপপুমঙ্গ (সাঃ পঃ), বন্ধ্যাকেশর (ঐ)।

stăm'-mer (-ĕr), *v. i., t. & n.* To make involuntary breaks in utterance; তোতলান। ***Verb t.*** To utter or pronounce with hesitation or imperfectly (usu. with-*out*); তোৎলাইয়া বলা, সংশয়জড়িত কণ্ঠে বলা। ***Noun.*** A stutter; তোতলানি। **–er,** *n.* **–ing,** *adj* Apt to stammer; স্খলিতবাক্। **–ing-ly,** *adv.* In a stammering way; তোতলাইয়া।

stămp, *v. t., i. & n.* **1.** To strike with the sole of the foot by thrusting it downwards; as, to *stamp* the earth; পদদলিত করা, পদমর্দ্দিত করা, পদপিষ্ট করা। **2.** To impress with some mark or figure; as, to *stamp* a plate; মুদ্রিত করা, ছাপ দেওয়া। **3.** To impress; "God has *stamped* no original character on our minds"; to fix deeply; as, to *stamp* some virtues; মুদ্রিত করা; গভীরভাবে মুদ্রিত করা। **4.** To affix a postage stamp; ডাক টিকিট লাগান। **5.** To mark; চিহ্নিত করা। **6.** To put a stamp on; as, to *stamp* a letter; মোহর দেওয়া, মোহরমারা (*colloq.*)। **7.** To cut into various forms and figures with a stamp; ছেনি দ্বারা বিভিন্ন নমুনায় কাটা। **8.** To crush by the downward action of a heavy hammer; গুরুভার হাতুড়ী দ্বারা চূর্ণ করা। ***Verb i.*** **1.** To strike the foot forcibly downward; সজোরে পদক্ষেপ করা। **2.** To strike; to crush; আঘাত করা; চূর্ণ করা। ***Noun.*** **1.** An instrument for stamping pattern or mark; মোহর, ছাপ, মুদ্রা। **2.** A mark imprinted; মোহর, ছাপ। **3.** (*Fig.*) Characteristic mark; as, a *stamp* of dishonesty; (লক্ষণায়) বিশিষ্ট ছাপ, স্বভাবসিদ্ধ ছাপ। **4.** An official mark put on things chargeable with duty, as proof that the duty is paid; the impression of a public mark or seal made by the government or its officers upon a paper or parchment whereon private deeds or other legal instruments are written; paper or parchment with government stamps to write deeds on; শুল্ক-প্রদেয় দ্রব্যের উপর শুল্ক প্রদানের প্রমাণ-স্বরূপ যে মোহর দেওয়া হয়; কাগজ বা পার্চ্চমেণ্টের উপর যে সরকারী বা সরকারী কর্ম্মচারীর ছাপ দেওয়া হয়; রাজ-মোহরাঙ্কিত কাগজ, ষ্ট্যাম্প। **5.** A thing marked or stamped; a stamped or printed device or slip of paper, issued by the government, at fixed price ; a postage-stamp ; চিহ্নিত, ছাপযুক্ত বা মোহরাঙ্কিত বস্তু; ষ্ট্যাম্প কাগজ; ডাকটিকিট। 6. A kind of hammer or pestle for beating ores to powder ; খনিজ-বিমিশ্র ধাতু চূর্ণ করার জন্য একপ্রকার হাতুড়ী বা মুষল। 7. An instrument for cutting material into any required form by a blow or pressure ; চাপ বা আঘাত দ্বারা কোন বস্তু প্রয়োজনানুরূপ আকারে কর্ত্তিত করার জন্য একপ্রকার যন্ত্র, ছেনি। 8. (*Pl.*) Same as STAMP-DUTY (below). 9. (*Slang*) Money; esp. paper money ; (ইতরভাষায়) টাকা পয়সা; বিশেষতঃ নোট প্রভৃতি। 10. Make ; cast ; form ; character ; kind ; গঠন; ছাপ; আকৃতি; প্রকৃতি; জাতি। **Stamp Act**—ষ্ট্যাম্প আইন। (বিশেষতঃ) আমেরিকার উপনিবেশ সমূহে ব্যবহৃত সর্ব্বপ্রকার কাগজ, পার্চমেণ্ট প্রভৃতির উপর ব্রিটিশ পার্লেমেণ্ট কর্তৃক ১৭৬৫ খৃষ্টাব্দে বিধিবদ্ধ যে শুল্ক ধার্য্য করা হয়। এই বিধির প্রচারই আমেরিকার রাষ্ট্রবিপ্লবের প্রধান কারণ। **Stamp-collector**—যে ব্যক্তি সখ করিয়া নানা-দেশের ডাকটিকিট সংগ্রহ করে; ষ্ট্যাম্প-শুল্কসংগ্রাহক। **Stamp-duty**—বিশেষ বিশেষ দলিলের উপর যে মাশুল লওয়া হয়, ষ্ট্যাম্পশুল্ক। **Stamp-machine**—যে যন্ত্রে কাগজ প্রস্তুতের জন্য ছিন্ন বস্ত্র প্রভৃতি মণ্ডবৎ করা হয়। **Stamp-mill** — খনিজ-বিমিশ্র ধাতুর খণ্ডসমূহ চূর্ণ করার জন্য যন্ত্র, চূর্ণন-যন্ত্র। **Stamp-office**—যে কার্য্যালয় হইতে সরকারী ষ্ট্যাম্প বাহির করা হয় এবং যথায় ষ্ট্যাম্পশুল্ক জমা হইয়া থাকে। **Stamp-vendor**—ষ্ট্যাম্প কাগজ বিক্রেতা। **To stamp out**—To crush ; to destroy ; ধ্বংস করা, নাশ করা, বিনাশ করা; উৎসাদিত করা।

stăm-pede' (-pēd), *n.*, *v. i.* & *t.* 1. A sudden panic seizing a herd of animals and scattering them ; আকস্মিক ভীতিহেতু গবাদি পশুর সন্ত্রস্তভাবে চতুর্দ্দিকে পলায়ন। 2. Any sudden flight or hurried movement of soldiers due to panic ; আকস্মিক ভয়হেতু সৈন্যদিগের হঠাৎ পলায়ন বা ছত্রভঙ্গ, ছত্রভঙ্গ। 3. (*U. S.*) Any sudden movement of a number of persons under a common impulse ; as, a *stampede* to gold regions ; একই প্রেরণাবশে সহসা বহু লোকের কোন স্থানে অভিযান। ***Verb i.*** 1. To start off in panic or terror ; আকস্মিক ভয় বা ত্রাসে দ্রুতবেগে পলায়ন করা। 2. To take part in a stampede ; দ্রুত পলায়নে যোগদান করা। ***Verb t.*** To scamper off in panic ; আকস্মিক ভয়হেতু দ্রুত পলায়ন করা বা ছত্রভঙ্গ হওয়া।

stance (stăns), *n.* (*Golf.*, *Scot.*) Position ; (গোল্‌ফ ক্রীড়ায়, স্কটলণ্ডে) অবস্থান।

stanch, staunch (stânsh), *v. t.* To stop, as blood ; as, to *stanch* a cut ; রক্ত প্রভৃতির প্রবাহ রুদ্ধ করা, রক্তমোক্ষণ বন্ধ করা।

stăn'-chion (-shŭn), *n.* & *v. t.* 1. A proper support of wood or iron ; কাষ্ঠ বা লৌহের খোঁটা। 2. An upright support ; খোঁটা, খুঁটি, দণ্ড। ***Verb t.*** To fasten cattle to stanchion ; গবাদি পশু খোঁটায় বাঁধা।

stănd, *v. i.* & *t.* 1. To be stationary in an erect or upright position ; as, tell him to *stand* up ; to be set in an erect or upright position ; দণ্ডায়মান থাকা ; দণ্ডায়মান অবস্থায় থাকা, খাড়া থাকা। 2. To be situated ; as, Calcutta *stands* on the Ganges ; অবস্থিত থাকা। 3. To stop ; to pause ; থামা ; বিরত হওয়া। 4. To endure ; টিকা, স্থায়ী হওয়া। 5. (*Hist.* of a dog) To point ; (কুকুর সম্পর্কে) স্থিরদৃষ্টিপাতপূর্ব্বক নির্দ্দেশ করা বা শিকার বাহির করা। 6. To maintain one's ground or position ; as, has *stood* through worse storms ; নিজের কোট্ বজায় রাখা, স্থানচ্যুত না হওয়া, না হটা। 7. To be of interest or advantage ; as, *stood* it him to leave France for some months ; সুবিধাজনক হওয়া, স্বার্থের অনুকূল হওয়া। 8. To become a candidate for an office or the like ; কোন পদের প্রার্থী হওয়া। 9. To be consistent ; as, it *stands* to reason ; সঙ্গত হওয়া, সিদ্ধ হওয়া (cf. যুক্তিসিদ্ধ), যুক্ত হওয়া, (cf. যুক্তি-যুক্ত)। 10. Not to yield or give way ; to resist successfully ; না হটা, পশ্চাৎপদ না হওয়া ; সফল-ভাবে প্রতিরোধ করা। 11. To stagnate ; to be stagnant ; স্রোতোহীন হওয়া ; স্রোতঃ বন্ধ হওয়া। 12. To measure as from the feet to the head, or from bottom to top ; মাথা হইতে পা পর্য্যন্ত বা পা হইতে মাথা পর্য্যন্ত মাপে হওয়া। 13. To be in some particular state ; কোন বিশেষ অবস্থায় থাকা। 14. To hesitate ; as, he will not *stand* at murder ; দ্বিধা করা, কুণ্ঠা করা, সঙ্কোচ করা, ইতস্ততঃ করা। 15. (Of a ship) To keep a certain course ; (নৌবিদ্যা) কোন নির্দ্দিষ্ট পথে চলা। 16. To remain in force ; বলবৎ থাকা। 17. To persevere ; to persist ; দৃঢ়প্রযত্ন করা ; অধ্যবসায়ী হওয়া, জেদ করা। 18. To be pertinacious, unyielding or obstinate ; to insist ; as, to *stand* on ceremonies ; একগুঁয়ে হওয়া, একরোখা হওয়া ; নির্ব্বন্ধাতিশয় সহকারে প্রার্থনা করা। 19. To be in the place of anything ; to be equivalent ; "Their language being scanty had no words in it to *stand* for a thousand"; কোন কিছুর স্থলবর্ত্তী হওয়া, কোন কিছুর স্থানীয় হওয়া ; কোন কিছুর সমতুল্য হওয়া। 20. To depend ; to rest ; নির্ভর করা ; অবলম্বন করা। ***Verb t.*** 1. To cause to stand ; দাঁড় করা, দণ্ডায়মান করা। 2. To endure ; to be able to endure or meet ; সহা, ভোগ করা ; ভোগ করিতে বা সহ্য করিতে সমর্থ হওয়া। 3. (*Colloq.*) To pay for ; as, to *stand* treat ;

(চলিত ভাষায়) খরচ দেওয়া, ব্যয় বহন করা। **Stand-by** — অবলম্বন, আশ্রয়। **Stand-offish**—সংযতবাক্, অমিশুক, অনালাপী, অসামাজিক। (*Stand-offishness*), *n.* **Stand-still**—নিশ্চলভাবে দণ্ডায়মান। **Stand-up**—Tumultuous ; as, a *stand-up* fight ; তুমুল। **A stand of arms**—কামান, বন্দুক, এবং ইহাদের সরঞ্জাম। **Stand off**—Be off ; সরে যাও, তফাৎ যাও, ভাগো, দূর হও। **To make a stand**—To halt for the purpose of offering resistance to an enemy, or in a matter of duty or principle ; বাধা দিবার উদ্দেশ্যে দণ্ডায়মান হওয়া, কোনরূপ কর্ত্তব্য বা ধর্ম্মবুদ্ধিদ্বারা প্রণোদিত হইয়া দণ্ডায়মান হওয়া। **To put to stand**—To embarrass ; গোলে ফেলা, হতবুদ্ধি করা, কিংকর্ত্তব্যবিমূঢ় করা। **To stand a chance**—To have a chance ; সম্ভাবনা থাকা। **To stand against**—To oppose ; to resist ; প্রতিকূলে দণ্ডায়মান হওয়া ; প্রতিরোধ করা, বাধা দেওয়া। **To stand and deliver**—To halt and hand over ; থামিয়া হাতে দেওয়া। **To stand a test**—To go through trial successfully; পরীক্ষায় উৎরে যাওয়া,পরীক্ষায় টিকে-যাওয়া। **To stand at gaze**—To hesitate what to do; কি করিতে হইবে তদ্বিষয় ইতস্ততঃ করা। **To stand between**—To be a mediator ; মধ্যস্থ হওয়া। **To stand by** — To be near ; নিকটবর্ত্তী হওয়া। To support ; প্রতিপোষকতা করা। To be present ; উপস্থিত হওয়া। To be present without taking any active part ; নিষ্ক্রিয় অবস্থায় দণ্ডায়মান থাকা, দাঁড়াইয়া দেখা। To be set aside ; রহিত হওয়া, নাকচ হওয়া। To be neglected ; অবহেলা প্রাপ্ত হওয়া। To support ; সমর্থন করা। To rest in; স্থিত হওয়া, স্থাপিত হওয়া। **To stand by (or to) one's guns**—See GUN. **To stand fast**—To be unshaken; অটল থাকা, অবিচলিত থাকা ; স্থির থাকা। **To stand fire**—To receive enemy's fire without giving away ; পশ্চাৎপদ না হইয়া শত্রুর গোলাবর্ষণ সহ্য করা, অবিচলিত ভাবে শত্রুর গোলাবর্ষণ সহ্য করা। To remain firm ; দৃঢ় থাকা, অটল থাকা। **To stand for**—To offer one's self as a candidate ; কোন পদের জন্য আবেদন করা, কোন পদপ্রার্থী হওয়া। To side with ; পক্ষ অবলম্বন করা। To maintain ; সমর্থন করা। To be in the place of ; কাহারো স্থলবর্ত্তী হওয়া, স্থলাভিষিক্ত হওয়া। To sail towards ; কোন স্থানের অভিমুখে পোত চালনা করা। To guarantee ; জামিন হওয়া, প্রতিভূ হওয়া। **To stand from**—To sail away from ; কোন স্থান হইতে দূরে জাহাজ চালান। **To stand good**—See under GOOD. **To stand in**—To join in ; যোগদান করা। To cost ; খরচ লাগা, খরচ হওয়া। **To Stand in hand** — To serve one's interest ; কাহারো স্বার্থানুকুল হওয়া। **To stand in need of**—To require the help of ; কাহারো সাহায্যের আবশ্যক হওয়া। **To stand in one's light**—See LIGHT. **To stand in one's way (or in the way of)**—To thwart one ; বাধা দেওয়া, ব্যাঘাত করা, কাহারো পথ আগুলিয়া থাকা, ঠেকান (রবি-রাজা)। **To stand it**—To maintain one's ground ; নিজের কোট বজায় রাখা। To endure unswervingly ; অটলভাবে সহ্য করা। **To stand off**—To keep at distance ; কিছু দূরে থাকা। To keep at a distance in friendship or social intercourse ; দূরে রাখা, পায়ে ঠেলা। Not to comply ; অনুমোদন না করা। **To stand off and on**—To sail toward land and then from it, as a ship ; জাহাজ প্রথমতঃ, তীরের অভিমুখে চালাইয়া পরে তীর হইতে দূরে চালান। **To stand on** — To continue on the same tack or course ; (জাহাজ সম্বন্ধে) একই পথ ধরিয়া চলা। To observe scrupulously ; সূক্ষ্মভাবে পালন করা। **To stand on or upon**—To depend upon—নির্ভর করা। **To stand on ceremony**—To behave with a great show of civility ; to be very particular in the observance of etiquette ; অতিরিক্ত মাত্রায় বাহ্যিক শিষ্টাচার প্রদর্শন করা ; শিষ্টাচারের নিয়ম প্রভৃতি যাহাতে যথাযথরূপে পালিত হয় তদ্বিষয়ে সূক্ষ্ম দৃষ্টি রাখা। **To stand one**—To cost one—খরচ লাগা। **To stand (one) in good stead**—To be of great use or service to one ; কাহারো পক্ষে অতিশয় উপকারজনক, হিতজনক বা কার্য্যকর হওয়া, কাহারো বিশেষ কাযে লাগা। **To stand one's ground**—To maintain one's ground or position ; নিজের কোট বজায় রাখা। **To stand one's hand**—(*Slang*) To treat one to drink ; নিজের পয়সা খরচ করিয়া কাহাকে মদ খাওয়ান। **To stand on one's own bottom**—To stand on one's legs ; নিজের পায়ের উপর দাঁড়ান। **To stand on one's own leg or feet**—To depend on one's self ; নিজের পায়ের উপর দাঁড়ান। **To stand out**—To project, as from a wall ; প্রাচীরাদি হইতে উদ্গত হওয়া। To be prominent ; সুস্পষ্ট হওয়া, সুপ্রকট হওয়া। To persist ; জেদ করা, ধরিয়া থাকা। To resist ; প্রতিরোধ করা। To sail from land ; উপকূল হইতে দূরে পোত চালনা করা। **To stand over**—To be postponed ; আপাততঃ স্থগিত থাকা, মুলতবী থাকা। **To stand still**—To stand aghast ; স্তম্ভিত হওয়া। **To stand the racket of**—(*Colloq.*) To take the consequences of ; to take responsibility ; ফলভাগী হওয়া ; দায়িত্ব গ্রহণ করা। **To stand to** — To ply ; to persevere in using ; চালান ;

অধ্যবসায়ের সহিত ব্যবহার করা। To persevere ; দৃঢ়প্রযত্ন করা, পুনঃ পুনঃ চেষ্টা করা, লাগিয়া থাকা। To abide by ; মানিয়া চলা। To be consistent with ; সঙ্গত হওয়া, –যুক্ত হওয়া, –সিদ্ধ হওয়া। To apply oneself to ; নিয়োগ করা। **To stand together**—To be consistent ; to agree ; সঙ্গত হওয়া ; মিল হওয়া, ঐক্য থাকা, সামঞ্জস্য থাকা। **To stand to sea**—To direct the course from land ; ভূমি হইতে গতিপথ নির্দ্দেশ করা। To sail out to sea ; বাহির দরিয়ায় জাহাজ চালান। **To stand trial**—Not to give up without a trial ; পরীক্ষার ভিতর দিয়া যাওয়া। **To stand up**—To rise in opposition or resistance ; বিরুদ্ধে দণ্ডায়মান হওয়া, বাধা প্রদানের উদ্দেশ্যে দণ্ডায়মান হওয়া। To rise and stand on end ; খাড়া হইয়া উঠা, (কেশ সম্পর্কে) কণ্টকিত হওয়া, কাঁটাদিয়া উঠা। To rise from a standing position ; দাঁড়ান, দণ্ডায়মান হওয়া। **To stand up for**—To justify ; to support ; ন্যায্যতা প্রতিপাদন করা ; সমর্থন করা। **To stand upon**—To value ; to pride one's self on ; সমাদর করা ; গর্ব্ব করা। To be particular about ; কোন বিষয়ে বিশেষ খুঁটিনাটি ধরা। **To stand with**—To be consistent ; to agree with ; সঙ্গত হওয়া ; ঐক্য থাকা, সামঞ্জস্য থাকা। **To stand up to**—To confront or face boldly ; সাহসের সহিত সম্মুখীন হওয়া।

stănd, *n.* **1.** A cessation of progress ; as, to come to a *stand* ; stop ; স্থিতি ; গতিরোধ। **2.** Resistance ; বাধা, প্রতিরোধ। **3.** Station ; অবস্থানস্থল। **4.** A small table ; any frame on which vessels and utensils may stand ; ক্ষুদ্র মেজ ; মোমবাতি, ভাণ্ড, প্রভৃতি রাখার আধার, বৈঠক। **5.** A stall ; as, a cigar *stand* ; যে মঞ্চে বিক্রয়ের জন্য জিনিষ প্রদর্শিত হয়, প্রদর্শন-মঞ্চ। **6.** A place where vehicles await hiring ; ঠিকা গাড়ীর আড্ডা। **7.** Embarrassment ; "Make the ears a little longer then you begin to boggle ; make the face yet narrower, then you are at a *stand*" ; কিংকর্ত্তব্যবিমূঢ়তা। **8.** A young tree, usually reserved when others are cut ; অপর সকল বৃক্ষ ছেদনের পর সচরাচর যে তরুণ বৃক্ষ রক্ষিত হয়। **9.** (America) The place where a witness stands to give evidence in court ; (আমেরিকায়) সাক্ষীর কাঠগড়া। **10.** A weight of solid coal-tar from $2\frac{1}{2}$ cwt. to 3 cwt. ; $2\frac{1}{2}$ হন্দর হইতে ৩ হন্দর পর্য্যন্ত ওজনের ঘন আলকাতরা। **11.** An erection or raised station for spectators ; দর্শকদিগের জন্য মঞ্চ। **Stand-pipe**—বিভিন্ন উদ্দেশ্যসাধনের জন্য উর্দ্ধমুখী নল। **Stand-point**—নির্দ্দিষ্ট বিন্দু বা স্থান ; যে দিক্‌ হইতে কোন বিষয় বিবেচনা করা হয়, দৃষ্টির দিক্‌, দৃষ্টি (হিঃ কোঃ)। **Stand-rest**—চিত্রকর প্রভৃতির জন্য একপ্রকার হেলানো উচ্চ মেজ। **Stand-still**—গতিরোধ, স্থির বা নিশ্চল অবস্থা। **Stand of arms**—একজন লোকের জন্য একপ্রস্থ অস্ত্র।

stănd'-ărd, *n.* & *adj.* **1.** A figure adopted as an emblem by a nation ; as, the lion is the *standard* of Great Britain ; কোন জাতির চিহ্ন, জাতীয় চিহ্ন। **2.** A banner on a staff ; পতাকা, ধ্বজ, বৈজয়ন্তী, কেতু, কেতন। **3.** That which is established as a rule or model তুলনার মূল, মান (হিঃ কোঃ), পরিমাণ-চিহ্ন (ঐ), প্রতিমান (হিঃ কোঃ), নিরিখ (ঐ), উপমান, আদর্শ। **4.** That which is established by authority as a rule or measure of quantity ; hence, the original weight or measure sanctioned by government ; স্থাপিতমান, পরিমাণ (হিঃ কোঃ) ; সরকার কর্ত্তৃক নির্দ্দিষ্ট মান। **5.** A measure by which the regulated weight of recruits is ascertained ; যে মানদ্বারা রংরুটগণের নির্দ্দিষ্ট মাপ অবধারিত করা হয়। **6.** Thing recognised as a mode for imitation etc. ; as, the *standard* work on a subject ; আদর্শস্থানীয় বস্তু, আদর্শ। **7.** (*Coinage*) The proportion of weight of fine metal and alloy established by authority ; (মুদ্রাপ্রস্তুতে) কর্ত্তৃপক্ষগণ কর্ত্তৃক নির্দ্ধারিত বিশুদ্ধ ধাতু এবং মিশ্র ধাতুর (খাদের) অনুপাত। **8.** A standing tree or stem, as distinguished from a wall tree ; a shrub grafted on an upright stem ; দণ্ডায়মান বৃক্ষ বা কাণ্ড ; সরল কাণ্ডের উপর কোন গুল্মের জোড় কলম। **9.** An upright support ; খাড়া অবলম্বন। **10.** One of the ranks or grades of attainment according as pupils are classed and taught ; মান (cf. তৃতীয় মান)। **11.** (*Bot.*) Same as VEXILLUM. **12.** (*Naut.*) An inverted knee-timber placed upon the deck instead of beneath it ; জাহাজের পাটাতনের উপর স্থাপিত একপ্রকার বিপর্য্যস্ত দ্বিশাখ বক্র কাষ্ঠ বা লৌহফলক। *Adj.* **1.** Having a permanent quality ; fixed ; settled ; as, *standard* weight ; স্থায়িগুণসম্পন্ন ; নির্দ্ধারিত ; স্থাপিত। **2.** Not trained to a wall or support ; অনাশ্রিতভাবে দণ্ডায়মান। **3.** Of high excellence ; serving as a model ; as, the *standard* works on a subject ; উৎকৃষ্ট ; আদর্শীভূত। **Standard-bearer**—পতাকাবাহী, পতাকাধারী। **Standard-stars** — সর্ব্বাপেক্ষা অধিক অপরিচিত এবং পর্য্যবেক্ষণের বিশেষ উপযোগী তারাসমূহ। **Standard tree**—দাঁড়াগাছ (প্রবোধ)। **Battle of Standard**—ইয়র্কসায়ারের অন্তঃপাতী Northallerton নামক স্থানে ১১৩৮ খৃঃ অব্দে ইংরেজ ও স্কচগণের যে যুদ্ধ হয়। এই যুদ্ধে রাণী Matildaর পক্ষাবলম্বী

স্কটলণ্ডের নৃপতি David ইংলণ্ডাধিপতি Stephenএর সেনানায়ক Robert de Mowbrayর হস্তে পরাজিত হন। **Standard of rebellion**—বিদ্রোহ-পতাকা। **Standard of value**—মূল্যের পরিমাণ (হিঃ কোঃ)। **Standard of victory**—বিজয়বৈজয়ন্তী। **To flock to one's standard**—To gather in bands; দলে দলে আসিয়া কাহারো পতাকাতলে মিলিত হওয়া।

stănd'-ărd-ize, *v. t.* **1.** To adjust by, or to conform to, a standard; আদর্শদ্বারা ঠিক করা, আদর্শানুযায়ী করা, আদর্শানুরূপ করা। **2.** (*Chem.*) To obtain by analysis, specific value of (solution etc.); (রসায়ন শাস্ত্র) বিশ্লেষণ দ্বারা (দ্রাবণ প্রভৃতির) বিশিষ্টমান প্রাপ্ত হওয়া। **–i-za'-tion**, *n.*

stănd'-ing, *n.* **1.** The act of stopping or coming to a stand; দণ্ডায়মান হওন, থামন। **2.** Duration; as, a custom of long *standing*; স্থায়িত্ব। **3.** Station; অবস্থান স্থল। **4.** Rank; condition in society; as, a man of high *standing*; সামাজিক পদবী; সামাজিক পদমর্য্যাদা।

stănd'-ing, *adj.* **1.** Upright; erect; খাড়া; দণ্ডায়মান। **2.** Stagnant; স্রোতোহীন, বদ্ধ। **3.** Lasting; not liable to fade or vanish; স্থায়ী, চিরস্থায়ী; পাকা। **Standing army**—See ARMY. **Standing crop**—ক্ষেত্রস্থিত শস্য। **Standing jump**—পশ্চাদ্দিক হইতে না দৌড়িয়া যে লাফ দেওয়া হয়। **Standing orders**—পার্লেমেন্টের কার্য্যপরিচালন-সম্বন্ধীয় আদেশাবলী। **Standing water**—বদ্ধ জল। **A man of high standing**—সামাজিক পদমর্য্যাদাসম্পন্ন ব্যক্তি, অতি পদস্থ লোক। **Of long standing**—বহুদিনের, বহু পুরাতন।

stănd'-ish, *n.* (*Archaic*) Inkstand; (অপ্রঃ) কলম, দোয়াত রাখার জন্য আধার।

stăn'-hōpe, *n.* **1.** A light two or four-wheeled carriage without top; দুই বা চারিচাকার একপ্রকার খোলা এবং হালকা গাড়ী। **2.** Same as STANHOPE-PRESS. **Stanhope-lens**—বিষম বক্রসন্বিত মধ্যোন্নত তলদ্বয়-যুক্ত তাল। **Stanhope-press**—আর্ল অব ষ্টানহোপকর্তৃক ১৮০০ খৃষ্টাব্দে উদ্ভাবিত একপ্রকার মুদ্রাযন্ত্র।

stăn'-iel (-yĕl), *n.* Same as KESTREL (which see.)

stank (stăngk), *p. t.* of STINK (which see).

stăn'-na-rȳ (-ă-), *n.* & *adj.* **1.** Tin-mine; টিনের খনি। **2.** Tin-mining district; যে অঞ্চলে টিনের খনি আছে। ***Adj.*** Relating to tin-works; টিনের কারখানা সম্পর্কীয়। **Stannary court**—কর্ণওয়াল এবং ডিভনের টিনের খনিসমূহের জন্য বিচারালয়।

stăn'-nic (-ĭc), *adj.* (*Chem.*) Of tin; টিনসম্বন্ধীয়, বঙ্গসম্বন্ধীয়। **–nate, –nif'-er-ous, –nous**, *adjs.*

stăn'-ză, *n.* A combination or arrangement of lines of verse usually recurring whether like or unlike in measure; কবিতার কলি, শ্লোক।

stā'-ple (-pl), *n.*, *adj.* & *v. t.* **1.** An emporium; a town where certain commodities are chiefly taken for sale; বাজার, আড়ঙ্গ; গঞ্জ। **2.** Principle or important article of commerce; প্রধানবাণিজ্য দ্রব্য, প্রয়োজনীয় পণ্যদ্রব্য। **3.** The principle constituent in anything; কোন বস্তুর প্রধান উপাদান। **4.** Raw-material; কাঁচা মাল। **5.** The fibre of cotton, wool, etc.; as, long *stapled* cotton; কার্পাস, পশম, প্রভৃতির আঁশ। ***Adj.*** Principal; প্রধান, মুখ্য। ***Verb t.*** To sort or classify (cotton etc.) according to fibre; অংশুর সূক্ষ্মতা ও স্থূলত্বের তারতম্যানুসারে পশম, কার্পাস, প্রভৃতি কিসিম করা। **–pler**, *n.*

stā'-ple (-pl), *n.* & *v. t.* **1.** A loop of iron, or a bar of wire bent and formed with two points to be driven into wood to hold a hook, pin, bolt, etc.; খিল-ঘরা। **2.** A bent wire used in wire-stitching; বহি শেলাইর কার্য্যে ব্যবহৃত একপ্রকার বাঁকা তার। ***Verb t.*** To secure by staple; ঐরূপ বাঁকা তারদ্বারা আটকান। **Stapling-machine**—বাঁকা তারদ্বারা পুস্তক শেলাইর জন্য একপ্রকার যন্ত্র।

stâr, *n.* **1.** A luminous body in the heaven specially one that is self-luminous and fixed; তারা, তারকা, নক্ষত্র, [Syn. ঋক্ষ, উড়ু, তারক, ধিষ্ণ্য (জ্যোতি জ্যোঃ)।] **2.** An ornamental figure shaped like a star as a badge of knighthood; নাইট উপাধিধারিগণের সম্মানসূচক-পদক, নক্ষত্র (cf. ভারতনক্ষত্র বাঁধিয়া গলায়—হেমচন্দ্র)। **3.** An asterisk (thus *); তারকাচিহ্ন। **4.** A person of brilliant and attractive qualities; উজ্জ্বল নক্ষত্র (cf. তিনি দেশের একজন উজ্জ্বল নক্ষত্র)। **5.** A distinguished theatrical actor or the like; রঙ্গালয়ের সুবিখ্যাত অভিনেতা প্রভৃতি। **6.** White spot on the forehead of a horse etc.; অশ্ব প্রভৃতির ললাটের শ্বেতবর্ণ চিহ্ন, চাঁদ। **7.** Heavenly body, as influencing a person's fortune etc.; as, to born under a lucky *star*; গ্রহতারকাদি,—যাহা মানবের ভাগ্য নিয়ন্ত্রিত করিয়া থাকে। **Star'-less, Star'-like** *adjs.* **Star'-let**, *n.* **Star'-ry**, *adj.* Decked with stars; adorned with stars; নক্ষত্রাস্তৃত; তারকাখচিত, তারকা-শোভিত, নক্ষত্রখচিত। **Star-apple**—একপ্রকার বৃক্ষ, ঐ বৃক্ষের ফল। **Star-blind**—চক্ষুর ছানি প্রভৃতির জন্য অস্পষ্ট দৃষ্টি। **Star-chamber**—ইংলণ্ডের প্রাচীন বিচারালয়বিশেষ—এই বিচারালয়ে অভিযুক্ত ব্যক্তিকে অমানুষিক শাস্তি প্রদান করা হইত। **Star-chart**—তারাপত্র (জ্যোতি জ্যোঃ)। **Star-cluster, Star-groups**—তারাপুঞ্জ (হিঃ কোঃ), তারাসমূহ (ঐ), নক্ষত্রসমূহ, নক্ষত্র-পুঞ্জ। **Star-drift**—আকাশের কোন

বিশেষ স্থানের নক্ষত্রসমূহের অনুরূপ গতি। **Starfish** — সামুদ্রিক জন্তুবিশেষ; তারামাছ, তারা মৎস্য। [ইহাদের আকৃতি পাঁচ কোণা তারার ন্যায়, মাঝখানে চ্যাপটা গোলচাক, এই চাক হইতে পাঁচটী দেহ ক্রমশঃ সরু হইয়া পরিধির দিকে গিয়াছে, উপরের দিকে কাঁটায় জড়ানো পুরু চামড়া

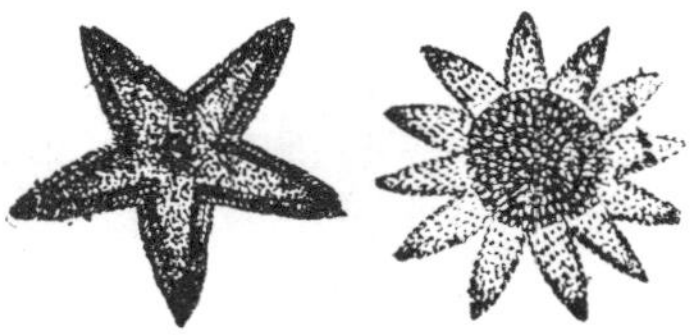

1. Sun Star-fish. 2, Butthorn Star-fish.

নীচের দিকে কেন্দ্রস্থানে পাঁচটী দেহভাগে পাঁচটী চুঙ্গী গিয়াছে। এই চুঙ্গী গুলির নীচে ছোট ছোট চাক্তির সারি। এই চাক্তির সাহায্যে প্রাণিগুলি পাঁচদিকের যে কোন দিকে অগ্রসর হইতে পারে (মিউজিয়াম)। **Star-gazer** — যে ব্যক্তি লক্ষ্যহীন এবং উদাসভাবে চতুর্দ্দিকে দৃষ্টিপাত করে; নক্ষত্রদর্শক (জ্যোতি জ্যোঃ), জ্যোতির্ব্বিদ্। **Star-light**—নক্ষত্রের আলো। **Star-lit**—নক্ষত্রালোকিত। **Star-ruby** — একপ্রকার লালমণি। **Star-shell**—একপ্রকার গোলা—যাহা অন্ধকারে বিদীর্ণ হইবামাত্র উহার অভ্যন্তর হইতে কতিপয় উজ্জ্বল তারকার মত পদার্থ নির্গত হইয়া শত্রুর অবস্থানস্থলী প্রভৃতি আলোকিত করে। **Star-shower** — উল্কাপাত (হিঃ কোঃ)। **Star-spangled**—তারকাখচিত, নক্ষত্রখচিত। **Star-stone**—একপ্রকার নীলকান্তমণি। **Star-turn**—সঙ্গীতশালায় সুবিখ্যাত গায়ককর্ত্তৃক গীত সঙ্গীত। **Binary star**— দ্বিতারা (সাঃ পঃ), যুগলতারা (ঐ)। **Daystar**—শুকতারা; সূর্য্য, দিনমণি। **Double star**—যুক্ততারা, দ্বিতারা। **Fixed stars**—স্থিরতারা, অচলতারা। **Good star**—শুভগ্রহ। **Ill-stared**—See ILL. **Multiple star**—৩ হইতে ৬টী পর্য্যন্ত তারকার পুঞ্জ। **Shooting star**—See SHOOT. **Variable stars**—পরিবর্ত্তক নক্ষত্র (হিঃ কোঃ), পরিবর্ত্তক তারা (হিঃ কোঃ)। **Conjunction of stars**—নক্ষত্রযুতি (হিঃ কোঃ)। **Constellation of stars** — নক্ষত্রপুঞ্জ (হিঃ কোঃ)। **His star is in the ascendant** — তাহার গ্রহ অতি সুপ্রসন্ন। **Proper motion of a star**—তারাগতি (হিঃ কোঃ)। **Star and stripes**—মার্কিণ রাষ্ট্রমণ্ডলের জাতীয় পতাকা। **Star of Bethlehem**—যে অলৌকিক তারকারদ্বারা প্রদর্শিত পথে পূর্ব্বদেশীয় জ্ঞানিগণ শিশু যীশুকে দর্শনের জন্য বেথলিয়মনগরে গমন করিয়াছিলেন; একপ্রকার নক্ষত্রাকৃতি স্থলকুমুদ। **Star of India**—রাজ্ঞী ভিক্টোরিয়া কর্ত্তৃক ভারতশাসনভারগ্রহণ স্মরণার্থ ১৮৬১ খৃঃ অব্দে যে নাইট-সংঘ প্রতিষ্ঠিত হয়। **The watery star**—চন্দ্র (সোক্ষপীয়র)।

stâr, *v. t.* & *i.* To set or adorn with star; তারকাখচিত করা, নক্ষত্রখচিত করা। ***Verb i.*** 1. To shine as a star; তারার মত আলোকিত করা। 2. To attract attention; মনোযোগ আকর্ষণ করা। 3. To appear as a star actor; প্রধান অভিনেতৃরূপে অবতীর্ণ হওয়া।

stâr'-blĭnd, *adj.* Partially blind; ছানি প্রভৃতির জন্য অস্পষ্ট দৃষ্টি।

stâr'-board (-bōrd), *n.*, *adj.* & *v.t.* The right-hand side of a ship to one looking at the bow; জাহাজের দক্ষিণ পার্শ্ব। ***Adj.*** Lying on the right side of a ship; পোতের দক্ষিণ পার্শ্ববর্ত্তী। ***Verb t.*** To put to the right side of a vessel; পোতের দক্ষিণপার্শ্বে রাখা।

stârch, *adj.*, *n.* & *v. t.* (*Rare*) Formal; prim; (কচিদ্ ব্যবহৃত) লেফাফা দুরস্ত; কেতা দুরস্ত। ***Noun.*** 1. A white farinaceous matter obtained from grain, potatoes and other vegetable substances used in the form of a jelly in stiffening articles of dress etc.; শ্বেতসার, পালো। 2. Formality; stiffness; লৌকিকতা; জড়তা, আড়ষ্টতা। ***Verb t.*** To stiffen with strach; শ্বেতসারের কলপ দ্বারা শক্ত করা। **Starch'-ed-ly**, *adv.* **Starch'-i-ness**, *n.* **Starch'-y**, *adj.* **Starch-grain**—পালোদানা।

stâre, *v. i.*, *t.* & *n.* 1. To look with fixed eyes as in horror, astonishment, admiration, etc.; হাঁ করিয়া একদৃষ্টে তাকান, সবিস্ময়ে দৃষ্টিপাত করা, স্থির দৃষ্টিতে অবলোকন করা, কটমট করিয়া তাকান। 2. To be very conspicuous on account of size, colour, etc.; as, *staring* colours; বর্ণ, আকার প্রভৃতির জন্য অতিশয় সুপ্রকট হওয়া। ***Verb t.*** To look earnestly or fixedly at; to gaze with a bold or fixedly vacant expression; to bring to a specified state by staring; স্থির নেত্রে দৃষ্টিপাত করা; উদাস দৃষ্টিতে চাওয়া; স্থির দৃষ্টিপাত দ্বারা কোন বিশিষ্ট অবস্থায় আনা। ***Noun.*** Staring gaze; স্থির দৃষ্টি, বদ্ধদৃষ্টি, কটমট চাহনি। **Star'-ing-ly**, *adv.* **To stare in the face**—To be before the eyes or imminent; সুপ্রকট হওয়া, সম্মুখবর্ত্তী হওয়া, আসন্ন হওয়া। To threaten; ভয়প্রদর্শন করা। To be ready to swallow or overwhelm; গ্রাস বা অভিভূত করিতে উদ্যত হওয়া।

stârk, *adj.* & *adv.* 1. Stiff; rigid; আড়ষ্ট; কঠিন। 2. Stout; powerful; "A *stark* moss trooping Scot was he"; বলিষ্ঠ; শক্তিশালী। 3. Mere; pure; as, *stark* nonsense; কেবল; শুদ্ধ, ডাহা, পুরা। ***Adv.*** Wholly; as, *stark* naked; সম্পূর্ণরূপে, পুরাপুরি, একেবারে। **Stark-naked**—সম্পূর্ণ উলঙ্গ, দিগ্‌বাস, গগনপরিধান (মঃ উঃ)।

stâr'-lĭng, *n.* A bird of the crow-kind, which can be taught to speak and sing; তেলিয়া ময়না (*Sturnus vulgaris*)।

stâr'-lĭng, *n.* A defence of piles driven round the piers of a bridge; সেতুর চতুর্দ্দিকে প্রোথিত খোঁটাসমূহ।

stârt, *v. i.* & *t.* 1. To move suddenly, as if by a twitch or an involuntary shrinking; as, to *start* aside; শিহরিয়া উঠা, আঁতকে উঠা, চমকাইয়া উঠা। 2. To set out ; যাত্রা করা, রওয়ানা হওয়া, বের হওয়া (*colloq.*—cf.—কবে বাড়ী থেকে বেরিয়েছিল — নবীন সন্ন্যাসী।) **3.** To become somewhat displaced and loosend ; as, the nail has *started* ; খসিয়া আসা, আলগা হইয়া আসা। **4.** (*Colloq.*) To begin ; as, to *start* in business ; (চলিতভাষায়) আরম্ভ করা, প্রবর্তন করা, ফাঁদা (*colloq.*)। ***Verb t.*** To cause to move suddenly ; as, to *start* an engine ; to rouse suddenly ; as, to *start* a hare ; সহসা চালিত করা ; বাসগুহা হইতে তাড়িত করা। **2.** To cause to be displaced or loosened ; as, to *start* a tooth ; to dislocate ; স্থানান্তরিত করা, শিথিল করা ; স্থানভ্রষ্ট করা, স্থানচ্যুত করা। **3.** (*Rare*) To startle ; to alarm ; (ক্বচিদ্‌ব্যবহৃত) চমকান ; ভীত করা। **4.** To begin ; as, to *start* a business ; আরম্ভ করা। **5.** (*Naut.*) To empty, as liquor from a cask ; (নৌবিদ্যা) ভিতর হইতে মদ ঢালিয়া পিপা খালি করা। **To start after**—To follow ; অনুসরণ করা। **To start against**—To set up as a candidate in opposition ; to oppose ; কোন পদপ্রার্থীকে বিরুদ্ধে দাঁড় করা ; বাধা দেওয়া, প্রতিরোধ করা। **To start an anchor**—To make it lose its hold of the ground ; মাটী হইতে নোঙ্গর আলগা করা। **To start a tack** (or **a sheet**) — To slack it off a little ; কতকটা শিথিল করা। **To start for**—To set out for ; যাত্রা করা, রওয়ানা হওয়া। To be a candidate for ; কোন পদপ্রার্থী হওয়া। To occur to the mind ; মনে উদয় হওয়া, মনে উঠা। To bring into motion ; চালাইয়া দেওয়া। **To start in**—(*Colloq.*) To begin ; (চলিত ভাষায়) আরম্ভ করা। **To start up**—To rise suddenly from a seat or coach ; to come suddenly into notice or importance ; হঠাৎ আসন বা খট্টা হইতে চমকাইয়া উঠা ; হঠাৎ লোকসাধারণের দৃষ্টির বিষয়ীভূত হওয়া, হঠাৎ লোকের নজরে পড়া। **To start with**—In the first place ; in the beginning ; প্রথমতঃ, প্রারম্ভে ; আদৌ।

stârt, *n.* **1.** A sudden motion or twitch from alarm ; শিহরণ, চমক, চমকানি, চকিত। **2.** A sudden voluntary movement, or change of place or position ; আকস্মিক গতি বা স্থানচ্যুতি। **3.** A spasmodic or brief effort or action ; "Nature does nothing by *starts* and leaps" ; আকস্মিক চেষ্টা বা উদ্যম, ক্ষণিক চেষ্টা বা উদ্যম। **3.** Beginning of journey, action or race ; যাত্রা কিম্বা ঘোড়দৌড় কিম্বা অপর কোন কার্য্যের প্রারম্ভ, কার্য্যারম্ভ। **4.** The outset ; as, a good *start* in life ; প্রারম্ভ। **5.** Advantage conceded in a race ; as, a *start* of ten yards ; দৌড়ে যে সুবিধা দেওয়া হয়। **6.** Advantage ; সুবিধা। **7.** A starting-post ; যাত্রাস্তম্ভ। **To get** or **have the start**—To have an advantage over, by starting first ; প্রথম যাত্রা করা হেতু অন্য কাহারো উপর সুবিধা প্রাপ্ত হওয়া।

stârt, *n.* (*Obs.*) The tail of an animal ; a plough-tail ; a handle ; (অপ্রঃ) জন্তুর লাঙ্গুল ; লাঙ্গলের মুষ্টি ; হাতল।

stârt'-ẽr, *n.* **1.** One who starts ; যাত্রাকারী। **2.** One who gives signal for the beginning of a race ; যে ব্যক্তি ঘোড়দৌড় আরম্ভের সঙ্কেত প্রদান করে। **3.** A dog that rouses game ; যে কুকুর বাসগহ্বর হইতে শিকার তাড়িত করে। **4.** One who shrinks from his purpose ; one who suddenly moves or suggests a question or an objection ; স্বীয় উদ্দেশ্য সাধনে সঙ্কুচিত ব্যক্তি ; যে ব্যক্তি সহসা কোন প্রশ্ন বা আপত্তি উত্থাপন করে। **5.** A horse or competitor starting in a race ; দৌড়ের ঘোড়া বা প্রতিযোগী। **6.** (*Slang*) Dried figs ; শুষ্ক আঞ্জীর (মৃদু বিরেচক বলিয়া এই নাম)।

stârt'-ing, *n.* The act of one who starts ; যাত্রা, রওনা। **Starting-point**—যাত্রাস্থলী, প্রস্থান (হিঃ কোঃ)। **Starting-post**—যে খুঁটি বা থাম হইতে দৌড়ের প্রতিযোগিগণ যাত্রা করে, যাত্রাস্তম্ভ। **Starting-prices**—যাত্রাকালে অশ্বের অনুকূলে বা প্রতিকূলে সুবিধা বা অসুবিধা।

stâr'-tle (-tl), *v.t.& i.* To excite, by sudden alarm, surprise or apprehension ; to shock ; চমকান ; সভয় চকিত করা ; স্তম্ভিত করা। ***Verb i.*** To move spasmodically and abruptly, as on feeling a sudden alarm ; শিহরিয়া উঠা, আঁতকে উঠা। **–tled,** *p. p.* Overcome by sudden fear ; ভয়চকিত, সঙ্কিত। **–tling,** *adj.* Surprising ; alarming ; আশ্চর্য্যজনক, চমকপ্রদ, বিস্ময়প্রদ, চমৎকারী, পরম চমৎকার (গোপালঃ) ; ভয়সঞ্চারক, ভয়জনক, ভীতিসঞ্চারক। **–tling-ly,** *adv.*

stâr-vā'-tion, *n.* Act of starving or the state of being starved ; অনশন, অনাহার। **Starvation-wages**—গ্রাসাচ্ছাদনের পক্ষে অপ্রচুর বেতন।

starve (stârv) *v. i.* & *t.* **1.** To perish with or suffer extremely from hunger ; to be very indigent ; অনশনে মৃত্যুমুখে পতিত হওয়া, বুভুক্ষাপীড়িত হওয়া ; অতিশয় দারিদ্র্যগ্রস্ত হওয়া, নিঃস্ব হওয়া। **2.** (*Colloq.*) To feel hungry ; (চলিত ভাষায়) ক্ষুধা বোধ করা। **3.** To suffer from cold ; শীতে কষ্ট ভোগ করা। **4.** To be in great want ; অতিশয় অভাব বোধ করা। ***Verb t.*** **1.** To kill with hunger ; অনশনে বিনাশ করা, অনাহারে মারা। **2.** To kill or afflict with cold ; শীতে মারা বা কষ্ট দেওয়া, শীতার্ত্ত করা, শীতপীড়িত করা। **3.** To destroy by want ; as, to *starve* plants by want of nutriment ; অভাব দ্বারা নষ্ট করা। **4.** To paralyse ; "The powers of their mind are *starved* by disease" ; আড়ষ্ট করা, অবসন্ন করা। 5. To compel to surrender by depriving of food ; as, to *starve* garrison to surrender ; খাদ্য বন্ধ করিয়া আত্মসমর্পণে বাধ্য করা।

starve'-ling (stârv-), *adj.* & *n.* Hungry ; lean ; ক্ষুধার্ত্ত ; অনশনশীর্ণ, অনাহারকৃশ। ***Noun.*** An animal or plant lean, thin and weak through want of nutriment ; অনশনক্লিষ্ট ব্যক্তি বা জন্তু, দুর্ভিক্ষপীড়িত ব্যক্তি, পুষ্টিজনক সার প্রভৃতির অভাবে শীর্ণ বৃক্ষ প্রভৃতি।

state, *n.* & *adj.* 1. Condition ; অবস্থা, দশা, গতি (হিঃ কোঃ)। 2. Rank ; সামাজিক পদবী, পদমর্য্যাদা। 3. (Often *Cap.*) The body politic ; রাষ্ট্র। 4. Dignity ; as, in a style befitting his *state* ; grandeur ; as, arrived in great *state* ; সম্ভ্রম ; জাঁকজমক, ঘটা, সমারোহ। 5. The civil power ; শাসনতন্ত্র। 6. (*Pl.*) Legislative body in Jersey and Gruernsey ; Jersey এবং Gruernsey দ্বীপের ব্যবস্থাপক সভা। ***Adj.*** Of, or concerned with, state ; রাষ্ট্রীয়, রাষ্ট্রসংক্রান্ত। **State-affairs**—রাষ্ট্রীয় ব্যাপার। **State-barge**—সরকারী বজরা। **State carriage**—রাজশকট, সরকারী গাড়ী। **State co-operation**—রাজসহকারিতা (হিঃ কোঃ)। **Statecraft**—রাষ্ট্রশাসনকৌশল, রাজ্যকৌশল। **States-General**—হলণ্ডের ব্যবস্থাপক সভা ; (১৭৮৯ খৃঃ অব্দের পূর্ব্বে) ফরাসীদেশের ব্যবস্থাপক সভা। **State industry**—সরকারী উদ্যম (হিঃ কোঃ)। **State-machinery**—রাষ্ট্রযন্ত্র। **State-prisoner** — রাজনীতিক অপরাধ হেতু ধৃত ব্যক্তি, রাজনীতিক বন্দী। **State rights**—(মার্কিণ যুক্তরাজ্যে) যে সকল ক্ষমতা মিলিতরাষ্ট্রসমূহে অর্পিত হয়না—কেবল বিশেষ বিশেষ রাষ্ট্রে সীমাবদ্ধ থাকে। **State-room**—দরবার গৃহ, দেওয়ান খানা ; জাহাজের শয়নপ্রকোষ্ঠ। **State rule**—রাজধর্ম্ম। **State socialism** — লোকসাধারণের হিতার্থ রেলওয়ে, শিল্পদ্রব্য, প্রভৃতির উপর রাষ্ট্রের অধিকারমূলক সাম্যবাদ, রাষ্ট্রসাম্যবাদ। **State-socialist** — রাষ্ট্রসাম্যবাদী। **State-trial**—রাজনীতিক অপরাধের বিচার। **State works**—সরকারী কার্য্যকল। **Free states**—আমেরিকার যে রাষ্ট্রসমূহে দাসত্ব প্রথা প্রচলিত ছিল না। **Slave States**—আমেরিকায় যে রাষ্ট্রসমূহে দাসত্ব প্রথা প্রচলিত ছিল। **He was in quite a state**—He was quite excited or anxious ; সে অত্যন্ত উৎকণ্ঠিত বা উত্তেজিত হইয়াছিল। **States of the Church, Papal States**—পূর্ব্বকালে প্রধানতঃ ইতালী দেশের মধ্যভাগে পোপের অধিকৃত যে বিস্তীর্ণ ভূখণ্ড ছিল। **To keep state**—To keep the dignity ; মর্য্যাদা অক্ষুণ্ণ রাখা, ঠাঁট বজায় রাখা।

state, *v. t.* 1. To express the particulars ; to set down in detail ; to narrate ; পুঙ্খানুপুঙ্খরূপে বলা ; সবিস্তারে বর্ণনা করা ; বর্ণনা করা, বিবৃত করা। **Stat'-ed,** (*p.p.*) Expressed in detail ; settled ; উক্ত ; নির্দ্দিষ্ট, নিরূপিত।

state'-ly, *adj.* 1. Gorgeous ; জাঁকজমকপূর্ণ, সমারোহপূর্ণ। 2. Elevated ; dignified ; as, *stately* style ; সমুন্নত ; মহিমান্বিত।

state'-mĕnt, *n.* 1. Expression of a narrative, fact or opinion ; "Admirable perspicuity of *statement*" ; a formal embodiment in language of facts or opinion ; as, the magistrate took down the *statement* of the witnesses ; উক্তি, বর্ণনা ; এজেহার, জবানবন্দী। 2. An abstract of an account showing the balance due ; হিসাবের চুম্বক—যাহাতে কত টাকা প্রাপ্য তাহা দেখান হয়।

stat'-ĕr, *n.* A standard coin of various cities and states of ancient Greece ; প্রাচীন গ্রীসের বিভিন্ন রাষ্ট্র এবং নগরীতে প্রচলিত মুদ্রাবিশেষ।

states'-măn, *n.* A man versed in the arts of government ; রাজনীতিজ্ঞ ব্যক্তি, রাজনীতিবিৎ পুরুষ, নয়বিৎ, নীতিজ্ঞ (হিঃ কোঃ)। **—ship,** *n.* The qualification of a statesman ; রাজনীতিজ্ঞতা, নয়নৈপুণ্য।

stăt'-ic, —i-cal, *adjs.* 1. Pertaining to the bodies at rest ; স্থিতিশীল বস্তুসম্পর্কীয়, স্থিতিসম্বন্ধী (হিঃ কোঃ), স্থিত্যাত্মক (হিঃ কোঃ), স্থিত্যাত্মকবস্তুসম্পর্কীয়। 2. Acting by mere weight ; শুদ্ধ ভারদ্বারা কার্য্যকারী। **Static energy**—যোগ্যতাশক্তি (হিঃ কোঃ)। **Static sensation**—শরীরসংস্থিতিসংবেদন।

stăt'-ics, *n.* That branch of mechanics which treats of the forces which keep bodies at rest or in equilibrium ; স্থিতিশীল পদার্থের গুরুত্ব কিম্বা বলসাম্যনির্ণায়ক বিজ্ঞানশাস্ত্র, স্থিতিবিদ্যা (হিঃ কোঃ), স্থিতিশাস্ত্র (ঐ), স্থিতিগণিত (ঐ), স্থিতিবিজ্ঞান।

stā'-tion, *n.* & *v. t.* 1. The place where anything stands ; post assigned ; অবস্থানস্থল, আড্ডা ; নির্দ্দিষ্ট স্থান। 2. A halting or starting place on a railway ; বাষ্পীয় শকটের বিরামস্থান,* বিরামস্থলী। 3. Position ; অবস্থান, সংস্থান (সাঃ পঃ)। 4. Position in life ; rank ; social position ; সামাজিক অবস্থা ; পদবী ; সামাজিক পদমর্য্যাদা। 5. A district or branch police office ; থানা, ফাঁড়ি। 6. (India) The place where group of military or civil officers reside ; (ভারতবর্ষ) সামরিক বা অসামরিক ইংরাজ কর্ম্মচারিগণ যে স্থানে বাস করে। 7. Employment ; occupation ; চাকুরী ; ব্যবসায়। 8. (*Survey*) The point from which measurements are made ; যে স্থান হইতে মাপ নেওয়া হয়। 9. (*Eccles.*) The fast of the fourth and sixth days of week Wednesday and Friday in commemoration of the council which condemned Christ, and of his passion ; যীশুর ক্রুশারোপণদণ্ড প্রাপ্তি হইতে সমাধি পর্য্যন্ত তদীয় চতুর্দ্দশ দুর্দ্দশা এবং তাঁহার প্রতি ক্রুশারোপণদণ্ডপ্রচারকারী সমিতি

স্মরণার্থ খৃষ্টীয় সম্প্রদায়ে সপ্তাহের চতুর্থ ও ষষ্ঠ (বুধ ও শুক্রবার) দিবসে অনুষ্ঠিত উৎসব বিশেষ। **10.** Same as STATION OF THE CROSS below. **11.** (*R. C. C.*) A church to which procession goes for devotions; যে খৃষ্টীয় ভজনালয়ে শোভাযাত্রা করিয়া যাজক-সংঘ উপাসনাদির উদ্দেশ্যে গমন করে। **12.** (*Bot. & Zool.*) The spot at which a given species is found; (উদ্ভিদ্‌বিদ্যা এবং জীববিজ্ঞান) যে স্থানে কোন বিশেষ জাতীয় বৃক্ষ বা পশু প্রভৃতি দৃষ্ট হয়। ***Verb t.*** To assign a station or position to; to place; স্থান নির্দ্দেশ করিয়া দেওয়া; স্থাপন করা। **Station-bill**—কোন জাহাজ কোম্পানীর নির্দ্দিষ্ট আড্ডাসমূহের তালিকা। **Station-calendar** — বাষ্পীয় শকটের বিরামস্থানে যে ফলকে প্রত্যেক প্লাটফর্ম্ম হইতে কোন সময় কোন ট্রেণ ছাড়িবে তাহা লিখিত থাকে। **Station-house**—থানা। **Station-master**—বাষ্পীয় শকটের বিরামস্থলের ভারপ্রাপ্ত কর্ম্মচারী, ষ্টেশনমাষ্টার। **Station-pointer** — নক্সায় কোন স্থান নির্দ্দেশের জন্য একপ্রকার ত্রিশাখ যন্ত্র। **Station of the cross**—ক্রুশারোপণ দণ্ডাজ্ঞাপ্রাপ্তি হইতে সমাধি পর্য্যন্ত যীশুখৃষ্টের চতুর্দ্দশ দুর্দ্দশার চিত্র বা প্রতিমূর্ত্তিসমূহ যাহা—রোমান ক্যাথলিক ভজনালয়ে বা ভজনালয়ের প্রবেশপথে যথাক্রমে স্থাপিত থাকে। [চিত্র বা প্রতিমূর্ত্তিগুলি এইরূপ :—(১) পিলাতকর্ত্তৃক প্রাণদণ্ডে দণ্ডিত খৃষ্ট। (২) খৃষ্টের ক্রুশপ্রাপ্তি। (৩) খৃষ্টের প্রথমবার পতন। (৪) মাতার সহিত সাক্ষাৎকার। (৫) Cyrenevাসী সাইমন কর্ত্তৃক যীশুর ক্রুশবহনে সাহায্য প্রদান। (৬) Veronica কর্ত্তৃক রুমালদ্বারা খৃষ্টের মুখ মার্জ্জন। (৭) খৃষ্টের দ্বিতীয়বার পতন। (৮) জেরুশেলেম নগরীর স্ত্রীগণের প্রতি খৃষ্টের উপদেশ। (৯) খৃষ্টের তৃতীয়বার পতন। (১০) খৃষ্টের বস্ত্র উন্মোচন। (১১) ক্রুশারোপণ। (১২) ক্রুশে যীশুর মৃত্যু। (১৩) ক্রুশ হইতে যীশুর দেহ অপসারণ। (১৪) যীশুর সমাধি।]

stā'-tion'-ă-ry̆, *adj.* & *n.* **1.** Remaining in one place; stable; নিশ্চল, স্থাবর; অচল, স্থির, গতিশূন্য, চলচ্ছক্তিহীন। **2.** Remaining in the same state or condition; not improving; একই অবস্থায় স্থিত; উন্নতিশূন্য। ***Noun.*** Stationary person; একই অবস্থায় স্থিত ব্যক্তি। **Stationary air**—যে বায়ু শ্বাসপ্রশ্বাস ক্রিয়ায় সাধারণতঃ ফুসফুস হইতে নির্গত হয় না। **Stationary engine** — স্থায়িভাবে প্রতিষ্ঠিত বাষ্পীয়যন্ত্র, স্থির বাষ্পীয় যন্ত্র। **Stationary diseases**—বায়ুমণ্ডলের অবস্থার পরিবর্ত্তনজনিত স্থানীয় রোগ—যাহা কিছুকাল পরে বিদূরিত হয়। **Stationary point**—(*Astron.*) স্থিরবিন্দু (হিঃ কোঃ), অচলস্থান (ঐ)।

stā'-tion-ėr, *n.* **1.** (*Obs.*) A bookseller; (অপ্রঃ) পুস্তকবিক্রেতা। **2.** One who sells paper, pens and other articles for writing; কালি, কলম, কাগজ, প্রভৃতি বিক্রেতা। **—y**, *n.* The articles retailed by stationers, such as, paper, pen, pencil, ink, etc.; কাগজ, কলম, কালি, প্রভৃতি দ্রব্য। **Stationer's Hall**—লণ্ডন নগরীস্থ যে কার্য্যালয়ে পুস্তকাদি রেজিষ্টরী করা হয়।

stăt'-ist, *n.* A dealer in statistics; নানা লৌকিক ও বৈষয়িক ব্যাপারের তথ্য সংগ্রাহক।

stā-tis'-tics, *n., pl.* **1.** A collection of facts respecting the state of a people, the domestic economy, health, longevity, wealth, etc.; the science which deals with these subjects; কোন দেশের লোকের অবস্থা, স্বাস্থ্য, ধন, আয়, ব্যয় প্রভৃতি সম্পর্কীয় তথ্যসংগ্রহ, নানা লৌকিক ও বৈষয়িক ব্যাপারের সাংখ্যিক বিবরণ সংগ্রহ; লোকতথ্য-বিদ্যা, গণনা (হিঃ কোঃ), হিসাব (ঐ)। **2.** That department of political science which classifies, arranges, and discusses, statistical facts; অর্থবিজ্ঞানের যে বিভাগে কোন দেশের লোকের স্বাস্থ্য, ধন, অবস্থা প্রভৃতি সম্পর্কে তথ্য সংগ্রহ করা হয়। **—tic, —ti-cal**, *adjs.* **—ti-cal-ly**, *adv.* **Stat-is-ti'-ci-an**, *n.* A person who is versed in statistics; one engaged in compiling statistics; লোকতথ্যবিদ্; লোকতথ্য সংগ্রাহক।

stăt'-ō-blăst, *n.* (*Biol.*) One of a number of peculiar internal buds developed in some of the Polyzoa, and liberated after the death of parent organism; (জীববিজ্ঞান) কোন কোন আদি জীবের দেহে সঞ্জাত বিশিষ্ট অন্তরঙ্কুরসমূহ এবং যাহা জনক অঙ্গীর মৃত্যুর পর বিমুক্ত হইয়া থাকে।

stăt'-ō-scōpe, *n.* **1.** An instrument for recording the rise and fall of a baloon or air-ship; ব্যোমপোতের উত্থান ও পতনসূচনার্থ যন্ত্রবিশেষ। **2.** An aneroid barometer for showing minute variations of pressure; একপ্রকার বায়ুচাপমানযন্ত্র।

stăt'-ū-ă-ry̆, *n.* & *adj.* **1.** The art of carving or sculpturing statues; মূর্ত্তিশিল্প। **2.** Statues regarded collectively; মূর্ত্তিসমূহ, মূর্ত্তিশ্রেণী। **3.** A carver of, or maker of, statues; মূর্ত্তিগঠনকারী, মূর্ত্তিকার, ভাস্কর, তক্ষক। ***Adj.*** Pertaining to statutary; মূর্ত্তি-শিল্পসম্বন্ধীয়। **Statutary bronze** — তাম্র, রঙ্গ, দস্তা এবং সীসকের মিশ্রবিশেষ। **Statutary-marble**—মূর্ত্তি নির্ম্মাণের জন্য একপ্রকার মিহি দানাদার শ্বেতমর্ম্মর প্রস্তর।

stăt'-ue (-ū), *n.* An image carved; প্রস্তরাদিনির্ম্মিত মূর্ত্তি, পাষাণমূর্ত্তি, ধাতবমূর্ত্তি, পাষাণপ্রতিমা। **—ued**, *adj.* **—ette'**, *n.* A small statue; ক্ষুদ্রমূর্ত্তি।

stăt-ū-esque' (-ĕsk), *adj.* **1.** Like a statue; প্রস্তরমূর্ত্তিবৎ। **2.** Having the dignity or pose of a statue; মূর্ত্তির মহিমা এবং অঙ্গবিন্যাস বিশিষ্ট। **—ly**, *adv.* **—ness**, *n.*

stăt'-ūre, *n.* The natural height of an animal; bodily height; জন্তুর দেহের স্বাভাবিক উচ্চতা; মানবদেহের উচ্চতা।

stā'-tŭs, *n.* **1.** Social position; rank; সামাজিক পদবী; পদবী,

পদমর্য্যাদা, অবস্থা (হিঃ কোঃ), পদ (ঐ)। **2.** Position of affairs ; কার্য্যের অবস্থা। **3.** State or condition of a person ; কোন ব্যক্তির অবস্থা। **4.** (*Law*) A person's relation to others as fixed by law ; (আইন) এক ব্যক্তির সহিত অপর ব্যক্তির বিধি-নির্দ্ধারিত সম্বন্ধ। ***Status quo***—অপরিবর্ত্তিত অবস্থা, পূর্ব্বে যে অবস্থায় ছিল সেই অবস্থা।

stăt'-ū-tā-ble (-bl), *adj.* Same as STATUTARY, *adj.*

stăt'-ūte, *n.* **1.** A law expressly enacted by the supreme legislature of a government ; ব্যবস্থা, বিধি। **2.** The act of corporation; as, the *statutes* of a University ; কোন সমবায়ের আইন। **3.** (*Bible*) A divine law ; (বাইবেল) ঐশ্বরিক বিধি। **Statute-book**—সর্ব্বোচ্চ ব্যবস্থাপক সভাকর্ত্তৃক বিধিবদ্ধ ব্যবস্থাসমূহ যে পুস্তকে অন্তর্ভুক্ত থাকে। **Statutes personal**—অস্থাবর সম্পত্তিসংক্রান্ত বিধানসমূহ। **Statute-real**—স্থাবর-সম্পত্তিসম্পর্কীয় বিধিসমূহ।

stăt'-ū-tō-rȳ, *adj.* Enacted by statute ; authorised by statute ; বিধিবদ্ধ; ব্যবস্থাসিদ্ধ, ব্যবস্থা-সম্মত। **Statutory provisions**—ব্যবস্থাবিধি।

staunch, stanch (stânsh), *adj.* Trustworthy ; loyal ; as, a *staunch* admirer ; steady ; বিশ্বস্ত, একনিষ্ঠ; অনুরক্ত, গোঁড়া ; অবিচলিত। **Staunch'-ly,** *adv.* **Staunch'-ness,** *n.*

stau'-rō-līte (stä-), *n.* A mineral crystallised in prisms often in the shape of a cross ; একপ্রকার খনিজ-পদার্থ—ইহা সাধারণতঃ ক্রুশের আকারে সজ্জিত ত্রিপার্শ্বসমূহে স্ফটিকীভূত হইয়া থাকে; ক্রুশপ্রস্তর।

stau'-rō-scōpe (stä-), *n.* An optical instrument for examining effects of polarised light on crystals ; স্ফটিকের উপর ধ্রুবতাপ্রাপ্ত আলোকের ক্রিয়া পরিবীক্ষণের নিমিত্ত যন্ত্রবিশেষ, ক্রুশবীক্ষণ।

stāve, *n.* **1.** A thin, narrow, piece of wood, of which casks are made ; পিপার কাঠ। **2.** Each of the boards forming the curve of a well or hollow cylinder ; কূয়ার পাট, যে সকল চাকা উপরি উপরি স্থাপনপূর্ব্বক চোঙ্গ নির্ম্মিত হয়—তাহার অন্যতম। **3.** The rung of a ladder ; মইএর ধাপ। **4.** A stanza ; a verse ; "Chant me now some wicked *stave*" ; কবিতার কলি ; কবিতার পংক্তি। **5.** (*Mus.*) The five lines and spaces on which music is written ; (সঙ্গীত-শাস্ত্র) যে পঞ্চরেখা ও অবকাশের মধ্যে সঙ্গীত লিখিত হয়।

stāve, *v. t.* **1.** To break a hole in ; to burst ; ভাঙ্গিয়া ছিদ্র করা ; বিদীর্ণ করা। **2.** To push as with a staff ; to put off ; to delay ; যষ্টি প্রভৃতি দ্বারা ঠেলিয়া দেওয়া ; স্থগিত করা ; বিলম্ব করা। **3.** To furnish with rundles ; মইএ কোয়া লাগান। **4.** To render metal firm or impervious by compression ; as, to *stave* lead ; চাপ প্রদানপূর্ব্বক ধাতু কঠিন বা নীরন্ধ্র করা। **To stave off**—To avert ; to ward off ; প্রতিনিবৃত্ত করা ; নিবারণ করা।

stāves'-ā-cre (-ker), *n.* Larkspur ; একপ্রকার গুল্ম। [ইহার বীজ কীটনাশক বিষরূপে ব্যবহৃত হইয়া থাকে।

stay (stā), *v. i., t.* & *n.* **1.** To remain in a place ; to dwell ; কোন স্থানে অবস্থান করা ; বাস করা। **2.** To remain ; থাকা। **3.** To wait ; অপেক্ষা করা। ***Verb t.*** **1.** To stop from falling; ধরিয়া রাখা। **2.** To stop ; to check ; to postpone as, to *stay* all further proceedings ; থামান ; রোধ করা ; স্থগিত করা। **3.** (*Slang*) To last through ; শেষ পর্য্যন্ত টিকা। ***Noun.*** **1.** Remaining ; abode for short time ; as, to make a short *stay* in a town ; অবস্থান ; অল্প সময়ের জন্য অবস্থিতি। **2.** (*Pl.*) Same as CORSET. **3.** A support ; "My only strength and *stay*" ; অবলম্বন। **4.** Check ; "Thy lust hath bounds and *stays*"; রোধ, আটক, প্রতিবন্ধ, প্রতিষ্টম্ভ। **5.** Corset ; স্ত্রীলোকের আঁটা জামাবিশেষ, কঞ্চুলিকা। **Stay-at-home,** *adj.* & *n.* গৃহবাসী, অপ্রবাসী। (*Noun*) অপ্রবাসী লোক। **Stay-bar, Stay-rod**—যন্ত্রের অবলম্বনদণ্ড। **Stay-lace**—স্ত্রীলোকের কঞ্চুলিকার লেইস। **To stay one's stomach**—To appease hunger for a time ; কিছুকালের জন্য ক্ষুধা নিবৃত্তি করা।

stay (stā), *n.* & *v. t.* A rope supporting mast or spar ; মাস্তুল-রজ্জু। ***Verb t.*** **1.** To support (mast etc.) with stays ; মাস্তুল-রজ্জুদ্বারা মাস্তুল প্রভৃতি খাড়া রাখা। **2.** To put hip on other tack ; জাহাজের গতির দিক্ পরিবর্ত্তন করা। **Stay-sail**—মাস্তুল-রজ্জুর উপর টাঙ্গানো পাইল। **In stays, Hove in stays**—একদিক ছাড়িয়া অন্য দিকে জাহাজের গতির দিক্ পরিবর্ত্তনশীল। **To miss stays**—To fail in endeavour to tack ; পাইলের রজ্জু বা স্থিতির পরিবর্ত্তন দ্বারা জাহাজের গতির দিক পরিবর্ত্তনে অকৃতকার্য্য হওয়া। **To stay a mast**—To incline it forward or aft or to one side, by the stays ; মাস্তুলরজ্জুর সাহায্যে জাহাজের মাস্তুল অগ্রে, পশ্চাতে বা পার্শ্বে হেলান।

stead (stĕd), *n.* Place or room which another had or might have ; স্থল, স্থান, জায়গা। **In one's stead, In stead of one**—স্থলে, স্থানে জায়গায়। **To stand in good stead**—See STAND.

stead'-fāst (stĕd-), *adj.* Constant ; firm ; resolute ; স্থির, স্থিরমনাঃ অচঞ্চল ; দৃঢ় ; অবিচলিত, একনিষ্ঠ। **-ly** *adv.* **-ness,** *n.* The state of being steadfast ; স্থৈর্য্য, স্থিরতা, একনিষ্ঠতা।

stead'-ȳ (stĕd-), *adj., n., v. t., i.* & *interj.* **1.** Firm in standing or position ; not shaking or tottering ; স্থির, দৃঢ়বদ্ধ ; অটল, অচল, নিশ্চল। **2.** Not fickle, changeable or wavering ; স্থিরমতি, স্থিরচিত্ত, স্থিরধী, স্থিরবুদ্ধি। 3. Regular ; as, the *steady* course of a sun ; constant ; uniform ; as, *steady* breeze ; নিয়মিত ; নিত্য ; নিয়ত একরূপ। 4. (*Colloq.*) Sober ; of industrious and temperate habits ; as, a *steady* man ; (চলিতভাষায়) অপ্রমত্ত ; পরিশ্রমী এবং মিতাচারী। ***Noun.*** Kinds of supports for hands or tools ; হস্ত বা যন্ত্রের বিবিধ প্রকার অবলম্বন। ***Verb t.*** To hold or keep from shaking, reeling or falling ; to support ; ঠিক রাখা, স্থির রাখা ; বিধৃত করা। ***Verb i.*** To become steady ; to regain or maintain an upright position ; স্থির হওয়া ; খাড়া থাকা, দণ্ডায়মান থাকা। ***Interj.*** An order to the steersman to keep the vessel's head pointing as it is ; পোতাগ্র যে দিকে আছে ঠিক সেই দিকে রাখিবার জন্য কর্ণধারকে যে আদেশ দেওয়া হয়। **–i-ly,** *adv.* **–i-ness,** *n.* **Steady-going**—Of steady or regular habits ; স্থির, ধীর, মিতাচারী।

steak (stāk), *n.* A slice of beef pork, venison, fish, etc. broiled or cut for broiling ; গোমাংস প্রভৃতির ফালি, ভর্জিত গোমাংস প্রভৃতির ফালি। **Hamburg steak** — আবৃত কটাহে ভর্জিত কুচিকুচি করিয়া কাটা মসলামিশ্রিত গোমাংস।

steal (stēl), *v. t., i. & n.* 1. To take clandestinely without right or leave, as the personal goods of another ; চুরি করা, অপহরণ করা, চক্ষুদান করা (*joc.*)। 2. To perform secretly ; as, to *steal* a look : to *steal* a kiss (চুরি করিয়া দেখা ; চুরি করিয়া চুমো খাওয়া) ; to appropriate to oneself secretly ; চুরি করিয়া করা, গোপনে সাধন করা ; গোপনে আত্মসাৎ করা। 3. To move stealthily ; গোপনে চালিত করা। 4. To go stealthily ; লুকাইয়া চলা, প্রচ্ছন্নভাবে চলা, চোরের মত চলা। ***Verb i.*** 1. To thieve ; চুরি করা। 2. To slip in or away secretly ; গোপনে ঢুকা, সরিয়া পড়া, সটকান দেওয়া (*colloq.*), অলক্ষিতে আসা বা চলিয়া যাওয়া। ***Noun.*** A successful long stroke in golf ; গোল্‌ফ ক্রীড়ায় দীর্ঘ সফল আঘাত। **Steal′-ing,** *n.* The act of one who steals ; তস্করতা। **To steal a march upon**—To march stealthily ; to gain an advantage secretly ; গোপনে অভিযান করা ; গোপনে বা অজ্ঞাতসারে কাহারো উপর সুবিধা করিয়া লওয়া।

stealth (stĕlth), *n.* A secret method of procedure ; a clandestine practice ; গোপনীয় কার্য্যপ্রণালী ; গুপ্তক্রিয়া। **Stealth′-y,** *adj.* Done by stealth ; unperceived ; secret ; গোপনে সাধিত ; অলক্ষিত ; গুপ্ত, গোপন, চোরা (cf. চোরা চাহনি)। **By stealth**—Surreptitiously ; গোপনে, তলে-তলে, লুকাইয়া, চোরের মত, ওতে-ঘাতে (*slang.*)

steam (stēm), *n.* 1. Aeriform fluid generated by the boiling of water ; বাষ্প, জলবাষ্প (হিঃ কোঃ), উষ্ণবাষ্প (সাঃ পঃ), ধূম। 2. Any exhalation ; ভাপ। 3. (*Colloq.*) Power ; as, his blow lacked *steam* ; energy ; শক্তি ; তেজঃ। **Steam′-i-ness,** *n.* **Steam′-y,** *adj.* **Steam-bath**—স্বেদনযন্ত্র (হিঃ কোঃ)। **Steam-boat**—বাষ্পীয়পোত, বাষ্পীয়তরণী, বাষ্পীয়নৌকা। **Steam-boiler**—বাষ্পীয়যন্ত্র চালাইবার জন্য যে লৌহময় বৃহৎ কুণ্ডে জ্বলন্ত কয়লার উত্তাপে জল বাষ্পীভূত করা হয়, বাষ্পজনক (হিঃ কোঃ)। **Steam-box, Steam-chest** — যে আধারের ভিতর দিয়া বাষ্প বাষ্পজনক হইতে বাষ্প-নলে চালিত হয়, বাষ্পপেটক। **Steam-car** — বাষ্পীয় শকট, বাষ্পীয় রথ। **Steam-colour**—ছিটের কাপড়ের উপর বাষ্প দ্বারা নিহিত বর্ণ। **Steam-cylinder**—যে নলের ভিতর বাষ্পীয়যন্ত্রের চাপদণ্ড উত্থিত ও পতিত হয়, বাষ্পনল। **Steam-engine**—বাষ্পীয় যন্ত্র, বাষ্পযন্ত্র (সাঃ পঃ)। **Steam-gas**—অতিরিক্ত উষ্ণীকৃত বাষ্প। **Steam-gauge**—বাষ্পের বল প্রদর্শনের

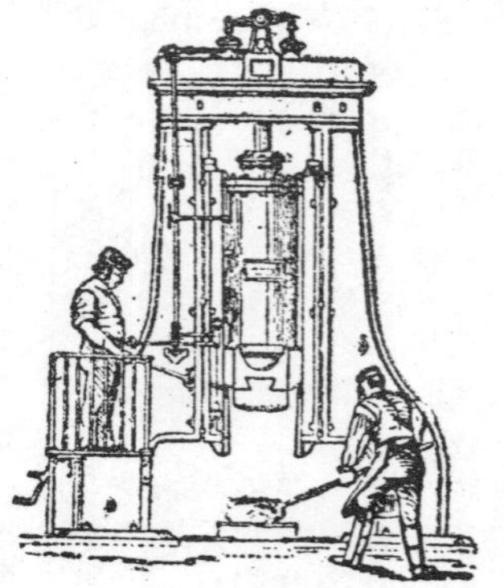

Steam-hammer.

জন্য বাষ্পজনকে স্থাপিত মানযন্ত্র। **Steam-hammer**—বাষ্পবলে চালিত হাতুড়ী। **Steam-heat**—তুষারাঙ্কের জল হইতে বাষ্প উৎপাদনের জন্য যে পরিমাণ উত্তাপের আবশ্যক হয় ; উত্তাপসঞ্চারক যন্ত্রাদির বাষ্প হইতে যে উত্তাপ প্রাপ্ত হওয়া যায়। **Steam-jacket**—চোঙ্গ প্রভৃতির আবরণ বিশেষ (এইরূপ আবরণ এবং চোঙ্গ প্রভৃতির মধ্যবর্ত্তী স্থান উষ্ণবাষ্প দ্বারা পূর্ণ করিতে হয়), ধূমকঞ্চুলিকা। **Steam-plough**—বাষ্পবলে চালিত লাঙ্গল, বাষ্পীয়লাঙ্গল। **Steam-port**—Each of two oblong passages from steam-chest into cylinder ; any passage for steam ; বাষ্পপেটক হইতে চোঙ্গ পর্য্যন্ত বিস্তৃত দীর্ঘ চতুরস্রাকৃতি পথদ্বয়ের অন্যতর, বাষ্পনির্গমরন্ধ্র। **Steam-power** — বাষ্পীয়শক্তি। **Steamship**—বাষ্পীয় পোত, বাষ্পীয়তরী। **Steam-tight**—বাষ্পনির্গম রোধনক্ষম, বাষ্পরুদ্ধ। **Steam tug**—অপর জাহাজ প্রভৃতিকে টানিবার জন্য বাষ্পীয় পোত। **Steam-whistle**—বাষ্পীয় যন্ত্রের বাষ্পজনক হইতে নির্গত বাষ্প দ্বারা বাদনীয় শিটি, বাষ্পবংশী। **To get up steam**—To accumulate energy for some special action ; কোন বিশেষ কার্য্য সাধনের শক্তি সঞ্চয় করা।

steam (stēm), *v. i. & t.* 1. To emit steam and vapour ; বাষ্প নির্গত

হওয়া, বাষ্পোদ্গম হওয়া। 2. To move or travel by the agency of steam ; বাষ্পীয় শক্তি দ্বারা পরিচালিত হওয়া। 3. To rise in vapour ; বাষ্পাকারে উত্থিত হওয়া। 4. To work vigorously ; to make great progress ; সতেজে কার্য্য করা ; অনেক দূর অগ্রসর হওয়া। *Verb t.* 1. To apply steam to for softening, dressing or preparing ; as, to *steam* wood ; বাষ্প দ্বারা কোমল, উত্তপ্ত, বা প্রস্তুত করা। 2. To cook food by steam ; বাষ্প দ্বারা রন্ধন করা। **Steam'-ing,** *n.* The act of emitting steam ; স্বেদন (ব্রজঃ হিন্দুঃ)।

steam'-êr (stēm-), *n.* 1. A steamboat ; বাষ্পীয় পোত। 2. A fire-engine with pumps worked by steam ; বাষ্পবলে চালিত অগ্নিনির্ব্বাপক যন্ত্র। 3. A vessel in which articles are subjected to the action of steam, as in washing or cookery ; যে পাত্রে বাষ্প দ্বারা কোন দ্রব্য পরিষ্কৃত হয়, যে পাত্রে বাষ্প দ্বারা রন্ধন করা হয়। 4. An automobile propelled by steam ; বাষ্পচালিত হাওয়া গাড়ী।

stē'-ă-rin, –rine (-rin), *ns.* The chief and harder ingredients of animal fat ; চর্ব্বির প্রধান এবং কঠিনতর অংশ। **-ar'-ic,** *adj.*

stē'-ă-tite, *n.* A compound of magnesia and silica of a very soapy feel ; একপ্রকার পিচ্ছিল খনিজ পদার্থ। **–tit'-ic,** *adj.*

stē-ă-tō-pȳ-gă, *n.* The name given to a remarkable accumulation of fat on the buttocks of certain Africans, especially of female Hottentots ; আফ্রিকানদিগের বিশেষতঃ হটেনটট রমণীদিগের নিতম্বদেশে অতিরিক্ত মেদসঞ্চয়, গুরুনিতম্ব।

steed (stēd), *n.* (*Poet.*) A horse ; war-horse ; (কবিতায়) তুরগ, হয় ; যুদ্ধাশ্ব, রণতুরঙ্গম।

steel (stēl), *n.* & *v. t.* 1. A very hard form of iron, produced by the addition of carbon ; ইস্পাত। [Syn. সারলৌহ, সংস্কৃতলৌহ, চীনজ, তীক্ষ্ণায়স।] 2. A sword, spear, or the like ; "Brave Macbeth with his brandished *steel*... carved out his passage" ; তলোয়ার, বর্শা, প্রভৃতি। 3. A kind of steel file for sharpening knife ; ছুরিতে ধার দিবার জন্য ইস্পাতের একপ্রকার উখা। 4. Anything of extreme hardness ; as, a heart of *steel* ; hardness ; অতিশয় কঠিন বস্তু ; কাঠিন্য, দৃঢ়তা, দার্ঢ্য। *Verb t.* To harden ; as, to *steel* one's heart ; কঠিন করা, দৃঢ় করা, শক্ত করা। **Steel'-i-fy,** *v. t.*

Steel-clad steamer.

Steel clad—লৌহবর্ম্মাবৃত। **Steel-engraving** — ক্ষোদিত লৌহফলক ; ঐরূপ ফলক হইতে গৃহীত চিত্র। **Steel-trap** — ইন্দুরমারা কল। **Steel-work** — ইস্পাতনির্ম্মিত দ্রব্যসমূহ। **Cast steel**—ঢালা ইস্পাত (হিঃ কোঃ)। **Cold steel**—তরবারি প্রভৃতি। **Mild steel**—নরম ইস্পাত (ঐ)।

steel'-ȳ (stēl-), *adj.* 1. Pertaining to steel ; hard as steel ; ইস্পাত-সম্পর্কীয় ; ইস্পাতের মত কঠিন। 2. Hard ; stern ; as, *steely* look ; দৃঢ়, কঠিন ; কঠোর।

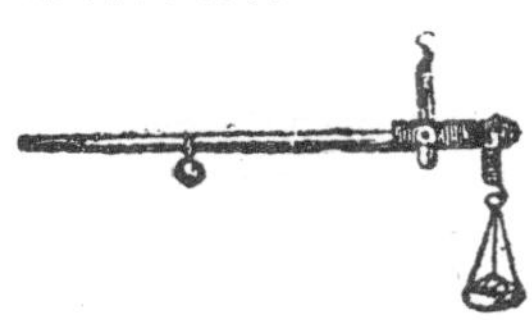

Steel-yard.

steel'-yărd (stēl-), *n.* A balance in which the weight is moved along a graduated rod ; একপ্রকার তুলাযন্ত্র—যাহাতে বাটখারা ক্রমাঙ্কিত দণ্ডের উপর দিয়া চালিত হয়, তুলাদণ্ড।

Steenbok, Steinbock, *ns.* Kind of small African antelope ; একপ্রকার আফ্রিকাদেশের বিভিন্নপ্রকার ক্ষুদ্রকায় কৃষ্ণসার মৃগ।

steen'-ing (stēn-), *n.* The brick lining of well or cesspool ; কূপ অথবা নর্দ্দমার ইষ্টক প্রস্তরময় আস্তর।

steen'-kirk (stēn-kêrk), *n.* (*Hist.*) Dress, wigs, powder, etc. named in allusion to the Battle of Steenkerke in Belgium in 1692 ; (ইতিহাস) বেলজিয়ামের Steenkerke যুদ্ধের নামানুসারে নামপ্রাপ্ত পোষাক, পরচুলা, অঙ্গরাগচূর্ণ, প্রভৃতি।

steep (stēp-), *adj.* & *n.* 1. Precipitous ; lofty ; খাড়া দুরারোহ, উৎসর্পী, সরলোন্নত ; উচ্চ, তুঙ্গ উন্নত। 2. Exorbitant ; unreasonable ; as, he seems a bit *steep* ; অতিরিক্ত, বেজায় ; অযৌক্তিক। ***Noun.*** A precipitous place ; a precipice ; দুরারোহ স্থান ; খাড়া পাহাড়। **Steep'-en,** *v. i.* **Steep'-ly,** *adv.* **Steep'-ness,** *n.* **Steep'-y,** *adj.*

steep (stēp), *v. t.* & *n.* To soak in liquid ; to imbue ; ভিজান ; সিক্ত করা। ***Noun.*** 1. Process of steeping ; সিক্তকরণ। 2. A liquid in which a thing is steeped ; যে তরল পদার্থে কোন দ্রব্য সিক্ত করা হয়। 3. A fertilizing liquid to quicken germination of seeds ; বীজের আশু অঙ্কুরোদ্গম করার জন্য একপ্রকার তরল পদার্থ।

steep'-êr (stēp-), *n.* A vessel or cistern in which anything is steeped ; যে ভাণ্ড বা কুণ্ডে কোন দ্রব্য সিক্ত করা হয়, মজ্জনপাত্র।

steeʹ-ple (stē-pl), A turret of a church tapering to a point; খৃষ্টীয় ভজনালয়ের সূক্ষ্মাগ্রচূড়া, শিখর, শৃঙ্গ। **–pled,** *p. p.* **–wise,** *adv.* **Steeple chase** —ঘোড়দৌড় বিশেষ—এইরূপ দৌড়ে অশ্বকে অনেকগুলি নালা প্রভৃতি অতিক্রম করিয়া যাইতে হয়। **Steeple-chaser** — উক্তরূপ দৌড়ের ঘোড়া, ঐরূপ ঘোড়ার আরোহী। **Steeple-crowned hat**—দীর্ঘ এবং ক্রমসূক্ষ্মাগ্র চূড়াবিশিষ্ট টুপি। **Steeple-jack**—যে ব্যক্তি জীর্ণসংস্কার প্রভৃতির উদ্দেশ্যে গির্জ্জার চূড়ায় আরোহণ করে। **Steeple-top** — মেরুপ্রদেশবাসী তিমি-বিশেষ—যাহার জল নিঃসারকরন্ধ্র মোচাকার হইয়া থাকে।

steer, (stër), *v. t.* & *i.* **1.** To direct with the helm; হাইল দ্বারা চালিত করা, বাওয়া। **2.** To guide; "That with staffs his feeble steps did *steer*"; to govern; পথপ্রদর্শন করা; নির্ব্বাহ করা, পরিচালনা করা। ***Verb i.*** **1.** To direct or govern the course of a ship or other vessels in its course by the movement of the helm; হাইল ঘুরাইয়া জাহাজ, নৌকা, প্রভৃতির গতি নিয়মিত করা। **2.** To take a direction or course; to be conducted; কোন পথে চলা; পরিচালিত হওয়া। **3.** (*Fig.*) To conduct one's self; to take or pursue a course or way; (লক্ষণায়) চলা; কোনরূপ পন্থা, অবলম্বন করা। **Steerʹ-a-ble,** *adj.* **Steerʹ-er,** *n.* **Steersman** — One who steers vessels; কর্ণধার, হাইলধারী, কাণ্ডারী। *Steersmanship n.* **Steer-ing-wheel** — জাহাজ প্রভৃতির হাইল ঘুরাইবার জন্য প্রান্তদেশে হাতল শ্রেণীবিশিষ্ট চক্র। **To steer clear of**—To avoid; পরিহার করা।

steer (stër), *n.* **1.** An ox; a castrated bullock from two to four years; ষাঁড়; ২ হইতে ৪ বৎসর বয়স্ক ষণ্ড, বৎসতর, অল্প বয়স্ক ষাঁড় বাছুর।

steerʹ-age (stër-), *n.* **1.** The act or practice of steering; হাইল চালন। **2.** The effect of a helm on a ship; জাহাজের উপর হাইলের কার্য্য। **3.** The part of a ship alloted to junior officers, clerks, etc. usually in the fore part; জাহাজের যে অংশ নিম্নশ্রেণীর কর্ম্মচারী, কেরাণী প্রভৃতির জন্য নির্দ্দিষ্ট থাকে। **4.** Part of ship alloted to inferior passengers; নিম্নশ্রেণীর যাত্রীদের জন্য নির্দ্দিষ্ট জাহাজের অংশ। **Steerage-way**—জাহাজ প্রভৃতি হাইলদ্বারা চালিত হওয়ার পক্ষে যে পরিমাণ গতিবেগের আবশ্যক হয়।

steeve (stēv-), *v. t., i.* & *n.* (Of the bowsprit) To give a certain angle of elevation to; নির্দ্দিষ্ট উচ্ছ্রায়ের কোণ প্রদান করা। ***Verb i.*** (Of the bowsprit) To project from the bows at an angle instead of horizontally; পোতাগ্র হইতে কোণ উৎপাদন পূর্ব্বক প্রলম্বিত হওয়া। ***Noun.*** Such an angle; ঐরূপ কোণ।

steeve (stēv-), *n.* & *v. t.* (*Naut.*) A long spar used in stowing cargo; (নৌ-বিদ্যা) জাহাজের মাল ঠাসিয়া বোঝাই করার জন্য ব্যবহৃত দীর্ঘ দণ্ড। ***Verb t.*** To stow with this; ঐরূপ দণ্ডদ্বারা জাহাজে মাল বোঝাই করা।

Steinʹ-bêrg-êr (stēn-), *n.* A white wine from grapes grown on the Rhine, near Wiesbaden, in Prussia; রাইন নদীর তীরবর্ত্তী ওয়াইজ-বেডেন নামক স্থানে দ্রাক্ষা হইতে প্রস্তুত একপ্রকার বাদামী বা স্বর্ণ বর্ণের মদিরা।

Steinbock, *n.* Same as STEENBOK (which see).

stēʹ-lē, –lǎ, *ns.* (*Gk. Archeol.*) An upright slab or pillar sometimes bearing more or less elaborate sculptures; (গ্রীসদেশীয় প্রত্নবিদ্যা) অল্পাধিক ক্ষোদিত ঋজু স্তম্ভ বা পাষাণফলক, স্তম্ভ (সাঃ পঃ), দারুস্তম্ভ (ঐ)।

stělʹ-lar (-lêr), *adj.* Of stars; নক্ষত্র সম্বন্ধীয়, নাক্ষত্র। **–lifʹ-er-ous,** *adj.* **–li-from,** *adj.* **Stellar sphere**—ভচক্র (সাঃ পঃ), নক্ষত্রলোক।

stělʹ-lāte, –lāt-ěd, *adjs.* Arranged in the form of stars; নক্ষত্রবৎ বিন্যস্ত, তারকাকৃতি (সাঃ পঃ)।

stělʹ-lu-lar (-ū-lêr), **–stělʹ-lu-lāte** (-ū-) *adjs.* **1.** Like stars; নক্ষত্রবৎ। **2.** Having marks like stars; তারকাবৎচিহ্নবিশিষ্ট, তারাঙ্কিত।

stěm, *n.* & *v. t.* **1.** The principle body of a tree, shrub, etc.; কাণ্ড, ডগা, ডাঁটা, স্কন্ধ। **2.** A stalk; বৃন্ত, বোঁটা। **3.** The stock of a family; "Which is one of the reasons that it hath continued these two ages and more in the *stem*, now so much spoken of"; কোন বংশের মূলকাণ্ড। **4.** Race; progeny; বংশ; সন্তানসন্ততি। **5.** Anything resembling the stalk of a plant; বৃক্ষের কাণ্ডবৎ কোনকিছু, ডাঁটি। **6.** The prow of a ship; a curved piece of timber at the prow to which the two sides are united; পোতাগ্র; পোতাগ্রস্থিত বক্র কাষ্ঠখণ্ড — যাহাতে জাহাজের উভয়পার্শ্ব সংযুক্ত থাকে। **7.** (*Fig.*) An advanced or leading position; (লক্ষণায়) অগ্রগণ্য স্থান। **8.** (*Mus.*) The upright or downright line added to the head of a note; (সঙ্গীতশাস্ত্র) ধ্বনির মাথায় যে উচ্চাভিমুখী বা নিম্নাভিমুখী রেখা সমূহ সংযোজিত করা হয়। **9.** (*Philol.*) That part of an inflected word which remains unchanged throughout a given inflection; (ভাষাবিজ্ঞান) বিভক্তিপ্রত্যয়াদিযুক্ত শব্দের যে অংশের কোনরূপ রূপান্তর হয়না, মূলশব্দ, ধাতু। **10.** (*Mining*) A day's work; (খনির কাষ) একদিনের কাষ। ***Verb t.*** To remove the stem of; বোঁটা ছিড়িয়া বা কাটিয়া ফেলা। **Stemʹ-less,** *adj.* **Stemʹ-let, Stemʹ-mer,** *ns.* **Stem-leaf** — বৃন্তপত্র। **From stem to stern** — From end to end; জাহাজের অগ্র হইতে পশ্চাদ্ভাগ পর্য্যন্ত।

stĕm, *v. t.* **1.** To dam up; to check; বাঁধ দিয়া রোধ করা; রোধ করা, গতিরোধ করা। **2.** To make headway against (adverse current etc.); to check the progress of; as, to *stem* the tide of public opinion; প্রতিকূল স্রোতঃ প্রভৃতির বিরুদ্ধে অগ্রসর হওয়া; গতিরোধ করা।

stĕm'-ma (-ă), (*Pl.* STEMMATA) *n.* **1.** A family tree or pedigree; বংশাবলী, কুলজী, গোত্রপট। **2.** (*Zool.*) One of the facets of a compound eye; a simple eye; (জন্তু-বিদ্যা) মিশ্র চক্ষুর অন্যতম পল; অমিশ্র চক্ষু।

stĕm'-ple (-pl), *n.* A cross-bar of wood in a mine-shaft constituting a support; খনিতে ব্যবহৃত অবলম্বন-স্বরূপ আড়কাঠ।

stĕnch, *n.* Offensive smell; দুর্গন্ধ, পূতিগন্ধ।

stĕn'-cil, *n.* & *v. t.* **1.** A thin plate with a pattern cut through it and brushed over with colour to mark a surface below; ধাতু প্রভৃতির পাতলা ফলক—যাহাতে কোনরূপ অক্ষর, চিত্রাদি কাটিয়া পরে উহাতে তুলিদ্বারা রঙ্গ লাগাইয়া ঐ চিত্রাদি নিম্নের কোন বস্তুতে তোলা হয়। **2.** A pattern produced by stencilling; উক্তরূপে যে চিত্রাদি অঙ্কিত করা হয়। ***Verb t.*** To paint or colour in figure with stencils; ঐরূপ চিত্রফলকের সাহায্যে চিত্রিত বা রঞ্জিত করা। **Stencil-plate**—Same as STENCIL *n.*

stĕn'-ō, (*Gk.*) (In combination) Narrow; সংকীর্ণ, স্বল্পপরিসর।

stĕn'-ŏch-rō'-mȳ, *n.* The art of printing in many colours at one impression; এক ছাপে বহুবর্ণে মুদ্রণের প্রণালী।

stĕn'-ō-grăph, *n.* **1.** Any writing in shorthand; সাঙ্কেতিকলিপি। **2.** A kind of type-writer; একপ্রকার সাঙ্কেতিক লিপিযন্ত্র। **3.** A character used in stenography; সাঙ্কেতিক লিপিতে ব্যবহৃত অক্ষরাদিবাচক চিহ্ন। **–graph'-ic,** *adj.* **Ste-nog'-ra-pher, Ste-nog'-ra-phist,** *ns.* One who is skilled in the art of shorthand writing; সাঙ্কেতিক-লিপিলেখক, সংকেতলিখক।

stĕ-nŏg'-ra-phȳ *n.* The art of writing in shorthand; short-hand; সংকেতলিপিবিদ্যা, রেখাঙ্কনবিদ্যা; সাঙ্কেতিক লিপি।

Stĕn'-tŏr, *n.* A person with powerful voice; গম্ভীর নাদী ব্যক্তি। [ট্রোজান যুদ্ধের সময়ের গ্রীকদূত Stentor এর নাম হইতে: এই ব্যক্তির কণ্ঠস্বর ৫০ জন ব্যক্তির সম্মিলিত কণ্ঠের সমান ছিল বলিয়া কথিত।] **–to'-ri-an, –to'-ri-ous,** *adjs.* Extremely loud; অত্যুচ্চ, বজ্রনাদী, গম্ভীরনাদী, ভীমনির্ঘোষকারী।

stĕp, *v. t.* & *i.* **1.** To set, as the foot; পদবিক্ষেপ করা, পদন্যাস করা, পা ফেলা। **2.** (*Naut.*) To fix the foot of, as a mast, in its step; (নৌবিদ্যা) মাস্তুল খাড়া করা। ***Verb i.*** **1.** To advance or recede by the movement of the feet; পদক্ষেপ করা। **2.** To go; to walk; to go a short distance; as, should not *step* too far; যাওয়া; হাঁটিয়া চলা, পদব্রজে চলা; অল্প দূর যাওয়া। **3.** To walk gravely, slowly or resolutely; "His flock before him *stepping* to the fold"; গম্ভীরভাবে চলা, ধীরপদবিক্ষেপে চলা, বদ্ধপরিকর হইয়া চলা। **Stepping-stone** — নদী বা বিলা জায়গায় স্থাপিত যে পাথরের উপর পা দিয়া পা না ভিজাইয়া, পায়ে কাদা না লাগাইয়া চলা যায়; উপায়, পন্থা। **Step this way**—এখানে আসুন, দুটী পায়ের ধূলো দিন। **To step aside**—To digress; মূল বিষয় ছাড়িয়া অবান্তর বিষয় ধরা। To move a little apart; একটু সরিয়া যাওয়া। **To step down**—(তাড়িত বিদ্যা) সম্ভাবনীয় (potential) হ্রাস হওয়া। **To step high**—To lift feet high; পা উপরে তোলা। **To step in**—To enter; প্রবেশ করা। (*Fig.*) To interfere; to help or check; (লক্ষণায়) হস্তক্ষেপ করা; বাধা দেওয়া, সাহায্য করা। **To step in or into**—To enter upon suddenly or easily; হঠাৎ প্রবেশ করা, অনায়াসে প্রবেশ করা। **To step out**—To go out; বাহির হওয়া। **To step short**—(*Mil.*) To diminish the length or rapidity of the step; পদবিক্ষেপের দ্রুততা হ্রাস করা। **To step up**—(তাড়িতবিদ্যা) সম্ভাবনীয় (potential) বৃদ্ধি পাওয়া।

stĕp, *n.* **1.** An advance or movement made by one removal of the foot; pace; পদক্ষেপ, পদগতি, পদবিক্ষেপ, পদন্যাস; এক পদ, এক পা। **2.** A stair; ধাপ, পৈঠা। **3.** The round of a ladder; মইএর ধাপ, কোয়া। **4.** A small space or distance; অল্পস্থান, অল্পদূর। **5.** Gradation; degree; পরম্পরা; ক্রম। **6.** A foot-print; পদাঙ্ক, পদচিহ্ন। **7.** Progress; অগ্রসর। **8.** (*Pl.*) The course which one follows; গমনপথ, অবলম্বিত পথ **9.** Gait; the sound of a step; গতিভঙ্গী, গমনভঙ্গী; পদশব্দ, পদধ্বনি। **10.** Measure; as, what *steps* do you propose to take; ব্যবস্থা, উপায়। **11.** A block or socket supporting the foot of a mast; যে কাষ্ঠখণ্ডের কোটরে মাস্তুলের পাদদেশ বিধৃত থাকে। **12.** (*Mus.*) An interval; (সঙ্গীতশাস্ত্র) অন্তরা। **13.** (*Mech.*) A portable framework of stairs; একপ্রকার মই। **14.** (*Mech.*) A lower socket or bearing for shaft; (যন্ত্রবিজ্ঞান) যন্ত্রের দণ্ডের নিম্নতর কোটর। **15.** (*Math.*) Same as VECTOR (which see.) **16.** Promotion; as, when did you get your *step*; পদোন্নতি। **Stepped,** *p. p.* **Step'-wise,** *adv.* **Step by step**—Gradually; in small degree; ক্রমে ক্রমে; অল্প অল্প করিয়া। **Step-by-step telegraph**—একপ্রকার তাড়িতবার্ত্তাবহ — যাহাতে সংবাদের প্রত্যেকটী অক্ষর একটী ফলকের উপর সূচি দ্বারা

নির্দ্দিষ্ট হইয়া থাকে। **Step-dance**—একপ্রকার নৃত্য—যাহাতে দেহের ভঙ্গী অপেক্ষা পদন্যাসের প্রতি অধিকতর মনোযোগ দেওয়া হয়। **Door-step**—পৈঠা। **At every step**—প্রতিপদে, পদে পদে। **In and out of step**—Stepping or not stepping in time with others or drum-beating etc.; অপরের সহিত বা ঢক্কানিনাদের সহিত তালে তালে পা ফেলিতেছে কিম্বা ফেলিতেছে না। **With hasty step**—দ্রুতপাদবিক্ষেপে।

stĕp, *pref.* A prefix to indicate that the person spoken of is a relative only by the marriage of a parent; বৈমাত্রেয়, বৈপিত্রেয়। **Step-brother or sister**—বৈমাত্রেয় কিম্বা বৈপিত্রেয় ভ্রাতা বা ভগিনী, অন্যপিতৃজ ভ্রাতা, অন্যপিতৃজ ভগিনী। **Step-father**—বিপিতা। **Step-mother**—বিমাতা, সৎমা। **Step-parent**—পিতা বা মাতার পরবর্ত্তী পত্নী বা পতি। **Step-son, Step-daughter**—সতিনী পুত্র, সতিনী কন্যা, সৎছেলে, সৎমেয়ে, (খৃষ্টীয়ান মুসলমান প্রভৃতি সমাজে) পত্যন্তরগ্রহিণী স্ত্রীর পুর্ব্ব পতির ঔরসজাত পুত্র বা কন্যা।

stĕph-ă-nō'-tis, *n.* A genus of shrubby twining plants of the milkweed family; একপ্রকার গুল্ম।

steppe (stĕp), *n.* An expanse of uncultivated, semi-barren treeless plains in S. E. of Europe and S. W. of Asia; ইয়ুরোপের উত্তর-পুর্ব্ব এবং এসিয়ার দক্ষিণ-পুর্ব্ব দিগ্‌বর্ত্তী অর্দ্ধ অনুর্ব্বর নির্বৃক্ষ প্রান্তর, ষ্টেপিজ (হিঃ কোঃ) উচ্চ তৃণভূমি (সাঃ পঃ), মালক্ষেত্র (cf. ক্ষেত্রমারুহ্যমালং—মেঘদূতঃ)।

stêr-cō-rā'-ceous (-shŭs), **stêr'-cō-răl**, *adjs.* Pertaining to dung or ordure; গোময়সম্বন্ধীয়, পুরীষসম্বন্ধীয়।

stêr'-ē-ō, *n.* (*Colloq.*) Same as STEREOTYPE.

stêr'-ē-ō-bāte, *n.* The substructure on which a building is based; অট্টালিকার অধিষ্ঠান।

stĕr-ē-ō-chĕm'-is-trў, *n.* That branch of chemistry dealing with the arrangement of the parts of a molecule in space; রসায়নশাস্ত্রের যে বিভাগে অণুর অংশ সমূহের দৈশিক-বিন্যাস সম্বন্ধে আলোচিত হইয়া থাকে, স্থিরসায়ন-বিদ্যা।

stêr'-ē-ō-chrō-mў, *n.* A method of wall-painting in which the colours are covered with a varnish of soluble glass; প্রাচীরচিত্রণের প্রণালী-বিশেষ—যাহাতে বর্ণরাজি দ্রাবণীয় কাচের সূক্ষ্ম স্তর দ্বারা আচ্ছাদিত করা হয়, স্থিররঞ্জন বিদ্যা।

stêr-ē-ō-ē-lĕc'-tric, *adj.* Of, or pertaining to, generation of electricity by means of solid bodies alone; ঘনজনন বৈদ্যুতিক (হিঃ কোঃ)।

stêr-ē-ŏg'-ră-phў, *n.* The art of delineating solid bodies on a plane; সমতল ভূমির উপর ঘন বস্তু চিত্রাঙ্কণের কলা, ঘনচিত্রাঙ্কণকলা। **—o-graph'-ic**, *adj.* **—o-graph'-i-cal-ly**, *adv.* **Ster'-e-o-gram, Ster'-e-o-graph**, *ns.*

stêr-ē-ŏm-ĕt'-êr, *n.* An instrument for measuring the specific gravities of various substances, solid as well as liquid; বিভিন্ন প্রকার ঘন ও তরল বস্তু পরিমাপের জন্য যন্ত্রবিশেষ, ঘনাধেয়মাপক (হিঃ কোঃ)। **—o-met'-ri-cal**, *adj.* **—o-met'-ri-cal-ly**, *adv.*

stêr-ē-ō-mŏn'-ō-scōpe, *n.* An instrument with two lenses for exhibiting on a screen of ground glass a single picture so as to give it an appearance of reality; পরকলাদ্বয় যুক্ত যন্ত্র বিশেষ—ইহার সাহায্যে ঘষাকাচের পর্দ্দায় পাতিত কোন চিত্রের প্রতিবিম্ব বাস্তববৎ প্রতিভাত হয়, ঘনৈকচিত্রদর্শক (হিঃ কোঃ)।

stêr'-ē-ō-scōpe, *n.* An optical instrument, illustrating the phenomena of binocular vision (two photographic pictures are viewed through two separate lenses, one for each eye, and adjusted to the angle of vision, so that only one image of the two pictures is impressed on the sensorium, and stands out in relief, and seemmingly solid); একপ্রকার বীক্ষণ-যন্ত্র—যাহার ভিতর দিয়া দৃষ্টি করিলে এক বস্তুর চিত্রদ্বয় একমাত্র চিত্ররূপে দৃষ্ট হয় এবং বাস্তব পদার্থের তুল্য উদ্গত এবং সংহত বলিয়া প্রতিভাত হইয়া থাকে, ঘনচিত্রদর্শক, ঘনচিত্রবীক্ষণ। **—os'-co-pist, —os'-co-py**, *ns.* **—scop'-ic**, *adj.*

stêr'-ē-ō-tўpe, *n.* & *v. t.* A solid metallic plate cast from a mould taken from a page of moveable types; কম্পোজ করা অক্ষরের পৃষ্ঠা হইতে গৃহীত ছাঁচ হইতে ঢালাই করা অক্ষরফলক, স্থিরাক্ষরফলক। ***Verb t.*** **1.** To make stereotypes of; স্থিরাক্ষরফলক প্রস্তুত করা। **2.** To print with a stereotype; স্থিরাক্ষরফলক দ্বারা মুদ্রিত করা। **3.** To fix or establish firmly or unalterably; অচলপ্রতিষ্ঠ করা, স্থিরনিবদ্ধ করা। **—typed**, *p. p.* **1.** Made or printed from stereotyped plates; স্থিরাক্ষরফলক হইতে প্রস্তুত বা মুদ্রিত। **2.** Fixed; unalterable; অচল; অচলপ্রতিষ্ঠ, অপরিবর্ত্তনীয়। **—typ-ist, —typ-y, —ty-pog'-ra-phy**, *ns.*

stē-rig'-mă, *n.* Filiform or pointed protuberances on special cells which develop into spores in fungals, the filaments forming the pedicels of the spermatia in fungals (*Tulasne*); জননতন্তু (সাঃ পঃ)।

stĕr'-ile, *adj.* **1.** Unproductive; barren; fruitless; অনুর্ব্বর; বন্ধ্যা (সাঃ পঃ), বাঁজা; নিষ্ফল। **2.** Free from living germs esp. bacilli or bacteria; জীবিত জীবাণু বা বীজাণুশূন্য। **3.** (Of composition etc.) Jejune; (রচনা প্রভৃতি সম্পর্কে) নীরস, রসহীন। **—i-li-za'-tion**, *n.* **—i-lize**, *v. t.* **1.** To make unproductive; অনুর্ব্বর করা, বন্ধ্যা করা। **2.** To deprive of fecundity or the power of reproducing ; জননশক্তি নষ্ট করা, প্রজননশক্তি নষ্ট করা, পুত্রকন্যোৎপাদন শক্তি নষ্ট করা। 3. To render free from living bacilli or bacteria ; সজীবজীবাণু বা বীজাণুশূন্য করা। **Ste-ril'-i-ty,** *n.* The state of being sterile ; বন্ধ্যাতা (হিঃ কোঃ), বন্ধ্যাত্ব (ঐ)।

stêr'-lĕt, *n.* A species of sturgeon found in the Caspian sea and Russian rivers ; কাস্পিয়ান সাগর এবং রুশদেশের নদী সমূহে প্রাপ্ত একপ্রকার মৎস্য।

stêr'-ling, *adj.* 1. Genuine ; pure ; of standard value or purity ; খাঁটী ; বিশুদ্ধ ; আদর্শানুরূপ মূল্য বা বিশুদ্ধিবিশিষ্ট। 2. Of excellent quality ; as, a work of *sterling* merit ; conforming to the highest standard ; শ্রেষ্ঠগুণসম্পন্ন, পরমোৎকৃষ্ট ; সর্ব্বোচ্চ আদর্শানুযায়ী।

stĕrn, *adj.* 1. Severe ; austere ; unrelenting ; as, *stern* measures ; দারুণ, কড়া, উগ্র ; কঠোর ; পরুষ, নির্ম্মম, নিষ্করুণ। 2. Resolute ; স্থিরপ্রতিজ্ঞ, স্থিরসংকল্প। **Stern'-ly,** *adv.* **Stern'-ness,** *n.* The quality of being stern ; কঠোরতা, উগ্রতা, দারুণতা, পারুষ্য।

stĕrn, *n.* 1. The after part of a vessel or boat ; জাহাজের পশ্চাদ্‌ভাগ,

Stern of a vessel

পাছাগলুই। 2. The tail of an animal, esp. of a dog ; লাঙ্গুল, বিশেষতঃ কুকুরের লাঙ্গুল। 3. Buttocks ; নিতম্ব, পাছা। **Stern'-ward,** *adj.* & *adv.* **Stern'-wards,** *adv.* **Stern-chase**—এক জাহাজকর্ত্তৃক অপর জাহাজের পশ্চাদ্ধাবন। **Stern-fast**—যে কাছি বা শিকল দ্বারা জাহাজ পোস্তা ঘাটের সহিত বাঁধা থাকে। **Stern-frame**—জাহাজের পশ্চাদ্ভাগের খোল। **Stern-post**—হাইল অবলম্বিত রাখার জন্য জাহাজের পানিতরাসের প্রান্তস্থ ঋজু কাষ্ঠখণ্ড। **Stern-sheets**—নৌকার পাছাগলুই এবং সর্ব্বপশ্চাদ্‌বর্ত্তী দাঁড়ীর আসনের মধ্যবর্ত্তী স্থান। **Stern-way** — (জাহাজের) পশ্চাদ্দিকে গতি। **Stern-wheeler**—যে জাহাজের পশ্চাদ্দিকে চাকা থাকে।

stêr'-năl, *adj.* See under STERNUM.

stêr-năl'-gĭ-ă, *n.* Pain in the breast ; বক্ষোবেদনা।

stĕr'-nō-clă-vic'-ū-lar (-lêr), *adj.* Connecting the sternum and clavicle ; বুকাস্থি এবং কণ্ঠাস্থি সংযোজক।

stêr'-nŭm, *n.* The breast-bone ; বক্ষঃস্থলের মধ্যভাগে অবস্থিত অপ্রশস্ত চেপ্টা অস্থি, বুকাস্থি, বুক। **—nal** *adj.* Pertaining to the sternum ; বুকাস্থি সম্বন্ধীয়, বৌক।

stĕr-nū-tā'-tion, *n.* The act of sneezing ; sneeze ; হাঁচন, ছিক্কন ; হাঁচি, ছিক্কা।

stêr-nū'-ta-tive (-tiv), *adj.* 1. Causing to sneeze ; ছিক্কাজনক, হাঁচিজনক, শিরোবিরেচক (সুশ্রু:)।

stêr-nū'-ta-tō-rȳ, *adj.* & *n.* Having the quality that provokes sneezing ; হিক্কাকারী (সাঃ পঃ), শিরোবিরেচক (সাঃ পঃ)। *Noun* A substance which has this quality ; snuff ; হিক্কাজনক বস্তু ; নস্য।

stêr'-tŏr-ous (-ŭs), *adj.* Making snore-like sound ; নাসিকাধ্বনিবৎ শব্দকারী, নাসিকাগর্জ্জনবৎ শব্দকারী। **-ly,** *adv.* **—ness,** *n.* **Stertorous breathing** — প্রতমকশ্বাস (সাঃ পঃ), নাসিকার ঘর ঘর শব্দ (আহিঃ)।

stĕt, In printing, a word written upon proof to signify that something which has been marked out is to remain ; মুদ্রণে যে "শব্দ" দ্বারা কোন কর্ত্তিত শব্দ প্রভৃতি পূর্ব্বে যেরূপ ছিল ঠিক সেইরূপই থাকিবে বুঝায়, পূর্ব্ববৎ।

stē-thŏm'-ē-tēr, *n.* An instrument for measuring the external movements of the chest during respiration ; শ্বাসপ্রশ্বাসচলাচলের সময়ে বক্ষের বহিশ্চলন পরিমাপের জন্য যন্ত্রবিশেষ।

stĕth'-ō-scōpe, *n.* A tube of light wood or guttapercha, with one end funnel-shaped, used by medical men for listening to the sounds produced in the chest or other cavities of the body ; বক্ষঃস্থলাদির ধ্বনিশ্রবণে রোগনিরূপণার্থ যন্ত্র-বিশেষ, বক্ষোবীক্ষণ-যন্ত্র, হৃদ্‌বীক্ষণ-যন্ত্র। **—scop'-ic, —scop'-i-cal,** *adjs.* **—scop'-i-cal-ly,** *adv.* **Ste-thos'-co-pist,** *n.*

stē'-vē-dōre, *n.* A man employed in loading and unloading ships ; যে ব্যক্তি জাহাজের মাল বোঝাই বা খালাস করে।

stew (stū), *n.* (*Archaic*) Brothel ; (অপ্রঃ) বেশ্যালয়, গণিকালয়।

stew (stū), *n.* 1. An artificial oyster-bed ; কৃত্রিম শুক্তিস্থান। 2. A fish-pond ; মাছ জিয়াইবার জন্য পুকুর।

stew (stū), *v. t., i.* & *n.* 1. To boil slowly or with simmering heat in closed vessel ; to cook by simmering in a small quantity of water ; মৃদু উত্তাপে সিদ্ধ করা ; স্বল্পজলে চড়চড় শব্দ উৎপাদন করিয়া পাক করা। 2. (*Colloq.*) To worry ; (চলিত ভাষায়) জ্বালাতন করা, ভাজা পোড়া করা (*slang*)। ***Verb i.*** 1. To be boiled or cooked in a slow or gentle manner ; মৃদু উত্তাপে সিদ্ধ বা পাক হওয়া, দমে পাক হওয়া। 2. To be oppressed by heat or moisture ; (গরমে) সিদ্ধ হওয়া, সিক্ত হওয়া। 3. (*Colloq.*) To be agitated ; (চলিত ভাষায়) বিক্ষুব্ধ হওয়া, বিচলিত হওয়া। ***Noun.*** 1. Meat slowly boiled in a closed vessel with but little water ; দমে পাক করা মাংস। 2. (*Colloq.*) A state of anxiety or confusion ; উৎকণ্ঠাকুলতা, বিক্ষোভ, হতবুদ্ধিতা। **Stew-pan**—মাংস দমে পাক করার জন্য পাত্র। **Irish stew**—দমে পাক করা মাংস এবং আলু ও পেঁয়াজের ব্যঞ্জন। **The tea is stewed**—অত্যধিককাল উষ্ণজলে সিক্ত করার দরুণ চা উগ্র বা তিক্তস্বাদ হইয়াছে।

stew'-ard (stü-ərd), *n.* 1. The manager of an estate, firm, institution, etc. ; দেওয়ান, কার্য্যাধ্যক্ষ, কর্ম্মকর্ত্তা, কর্ম্মাধ্যক্ষ। 2. One who regulates the domestic concerns of a great family ; বড়লোকের বাটীর গার্হস্থ্যব্যাপারের প্রধান পরিচালক, দেওয়ান। 3. An officer on a vessel who distributes the provision ; জাহাজের যে কর্ম্মচারী খাদ্যদ্রব্য বিতরণ করে। 4. A passenger's attendant and waiter on a ship ; জাহাজে যাত্রীদিগের পরিচারক বা পরিচর্য্যাকারী, জাহাজের ভাণ্ডারী। 5. An officer in a college who provides food for the students and superintends the concerns of the kitchen ; মহাবিদ্যালয়ের যে কর্ম্মচারী খাদ্যদ্রব্য সরবরাহ এবং রন্ধনশালার কার্য্য তত্ত্বাবধান করিয়া থাকেন। 6. A high officer of state ; উচ্চ রাজকর্ম্মচারিবিশেষ। 7. Any of the officials managing a race-meeting, ball, show, etc. ; বলনাচ, ঘোড়দৌড়, প্রভৃতির কার্য্যনির্ব্বাহক কর্ম্মচারিবর্গের অন্যতম। **–ess**, *n.* (*Fem.*) **–ship**, *n.* **Lord High Steward of England** — ইংলণ্ডের রাজকর্ম্মচারিবিশেষ। রাজার অভিষেকের আয়োজন, অভিজাতবংশীয়ব্যক্তির বিচার প্রভৃতি ইঁহার কার্য্য। **Lord Steward of the Household**—ইংলণ্ডে সর্ব্বোচ্চ আদালতের কর্ম্মচারিবিশেষ।

sthĕn'-ic, *adj.* (*Path.*) Attended with an unnatural and mordid increase of vital energy and strength of action in heart and arteries ; (নিদানশাস্ত্র) জীবনীশক্তি ধমনী এবং হৃৎপিণ্ডের ক্রিয়ার অস্বাভাবিক এবং রোগাত্মক বৃদ্ধিসহকৃত, জীবনীশক্তি, হৃৎপিণ্ড এবং ধমনীর ক্রিয়ার অস্বাভাবিক প্রাবল্যবিশিষ্ট, উত্তেজক (হিঃ কোঃ)।

stib'-i-ăl, *adj.* Pertaining to antimony ; like antimony ; রসাঞ্জন সম্বন্ধীয় ; রসাঞ্জনতুল্য। **–ism**, *n.* Antimonial intoxication or poisoning ; রসাঞ্জনগ্রহণজনিত মত্ততা বা বিষক্রিয়া।

stib'-i-ŭm, *n.* Antimony ; রসাঞ্জন।

stib'-nite, *n.* Trisulphide of antimony, consisting of 72.88 p. c. antimony and 27.12 sulpher ; সুরমা, স্রোতোঞ্জন (সাঃ পঃ), সৌবীর (ঐ), রসাঞ্জন (ঐ), পুষ্পাঞ্জন (ঐ), নীলাঞ্জন (ঐ), সৌবীরাঞ্জন (ঐ), [syn. সোরম, অঞ্জন, যামুন, কৃষ্ণ, নাদেয়, মেচক, স্রোতজ, দৃষ্পদ, নীল, সুবীরজ, চক্ষুষ্য, বারিসম্ভব, কপোত, কপোতক, কাপোতাঞ্জন, স্রোতোভব, স্রোতনদীভব, সাবীরসার, কপোতসার, বল্মীকশীর্ষ [Arab. *ismal*, *koh'l* ; Pers. *surma* ; Chin. *peh-lah* ; Burm. *tay-lak-youk* ; Malay. *kinang* ; Rus. *antimonia* ; ভাবপ্রকাশে সৌবীরাঞ্জনের শ্রেণী গুণসম্বন্ধে এইরূপ লিখিত আছে। স্রোতোঞ্জনং মতং শ্রেষ্ঠং বিশুদ্ধং সিন্ধুসম্ভবম্। দৃষ্টে কণ্ডুমলহরং দাহক্লেদরুজাপহম্॥ অক্ষোরূপাবহঞ্চৈব সহতে মারুতাতপৌ। নেত্ররোগা ন জায়ন্তে তস্মাদঞ্জনমাচরেৎ॥ স্রোতোঽঞ্জনং কৃষ্ণ সুরমা ইতি। শোধনং বিনাপি সিন্ধুনামপর্ব্বতসম্ভবম্॥ ইতি অথ সুরমা সৌবীর। অঞ্জনং যামুনঞ্চাপি কাপোতাঞ্জনমিত্যপি। তত্র স্রোতোঞ্জনং কৃষ্ণং সৌবীরং শ্বেতমীরিতম্॥ স্রোতোঞ্জন সমং জ্ঞেয়ং সৌবীরং তৎ তু পাণ্ডুরম্। স্রোতোঞ্জনং স্মৃতং স্বাদু চক্ষুষ্যং কফপিত্তনুৎ। কষায়ং লেখনং স্নিগ্ধং গ্রাহিচ্ছর্দ্দি বিষাপহম্। সিধ্মক্ষয়াস্রহৃচ্ছীতং সেবনীয়ং সদা বুধৈঃ॥ স্রোতোঞ্জনগুণাঃ সর্ব্বে সৌবীরেঽপি মতা বুধৈঃ। কিন্তু দ্বয়োরঞ্জনয়োঃ শ্রেষ্ঠং স্রোতোঞ্জনংস্মৃতং॥ ইতি ভাবপ্রকাশ।

stich'-ō-myth, **–myth'-i-ă**, *ns.* A dialogue in alternate lines of verse ; পর্য্যায়ক্রমে এক এক পংক্তি কবিতা বলিয়া কথোপকথন।

stick, *v. t., i. & n.* 1. To cause to enter, as a pointed instrument ; to pierce ; to stab ; as, to *stick* pigs ; ফুটান ; বিদ্ধ করা ; সূক্ষ্মাগ্র অস্ত্রদ্বারা আঘাত করা। 2. To thrust ; to poke ; ঢুকান, অনুবিদ্ধ করা ; খোঁচা দেওয়া। 3. To set ; লাগান, বসান। 4. To attach by causing to appear on the surface ; as, to *stick* a bill ; আঁটিয়া দেওয়া, আঠাদ্বারা লাগান, লাগান। 5. To fasten or attach by piercing or thrusting in ; as, to *stick* a flower in one's buttonhole ; গুঁজিয়া দেওয়া। 6. To fix on a pointed thing ; গাঁথিয়া রাখা। 7. (*Cant*) To compose or arrange in a composing stick ; (আরভাষায়) মুদ্রাক্ষর বিন্যস্ত করা। ***Verb i.*** 1. To adhere ; আঁটা, লাগিয়া যাওয়া। 2. To cleave ; সংলগ্ন থাকা, লাগিয়া থাকা। 3. To be fixed by thrusting in ; গুঁজিয়া থাকা। 4. To remain, abide or continue in a place ; কোন স্থানে অবস্থান করা বা ক্রমাগত বাস করা। 5. To adhere closely ; to hold fast ; লাগিয়া থাকা ; ধরিয়া থাকা। 6. To be hindered from proceeding ; অগ্রগমনে বাধাপ্রাপ্ত হওয়া। 7. To scruple ; to hesitate ; as, he will *stick* at nothing ; দ্বিধা করা ; ইতস্ততঃ করা। 8. To be brought to a standstill ; to be embarrassed or puzzled ; "They will *stick* long at part of demonstration for want of perceiving the connection between two ideas" ; একবারে থামিয়া যাওয়া ; হতবুদ্ধি হওয়া, কিংকর্ত্তব্যবিমূঢ় হওয়া। ***Noun.*** 1. A rod or wand ; a walking-stick ; দণ্ড ; ছড়ি, বেত্র, যষ্টি, লাঠি। 2. A stem or branch of any size cut for fuel or timber ; কাষ্ঠফলক, কাঠের চেলা, কাঠি। 3. An instrument of adjustable width, in which types are arranged in words and lines ;

মুদ্রাযন্ত্রে যে ফলকের উপর শব্দ বা পংক্তির আকারে হরফ সাজান হয়, অক্ষরধারণী। 4. (*Joc.*) A mast or spar; (রঙ্গচ্ছলে) মাস্তুল, মাস্তুলসংলগ্ন পাইল-দণ্ড। 5. (*Pl.*) Furniture; আসবাব। 6. (*Slang*) Pistol; (ইতর ভাষায়) পিস্তল। 7. Anything long or slender or more or less cylindrical; as, a *stick* of sealing wax; দণ্ড, কাঠি। 8. A rammer used in filling cartridges; কার্তুজ ভরিবার জন্য গাদন কাঠি। 9. A stab; খোঁচা, ঘা। 10. A stiff, stupidly obstinate person; স্থূলবুদ্ধি একরোখা লোক, গোঁয়াড়। **Stick'-ful,** *adj.* **Stick'-ing,** *n.* & *adj.* **Composing-stick**—যে ধাতুফলকে মুদ্রাক্ষর সন্নিবেশিত করা হয়, অক্ষরধারণী। **Mr. Stick-in-the-mud** — (ইতর ভাষায়) অমুক। **Sticking-piece**—বৃষের কণ্ঠ হইতে কর্ত্তিত মাংসখণ্ড। **Sticking-place, Sticking-point**—যে স্থান পর্য্যন্ত স্ক্রূপ ঘূরান যায়। **Sticking-plaster**—যে পলস্ত্রা ক্ষতস্থান প্রভৃতিতে লাগিয়া থাকে, ব্রণপট্টিকা (সাঃ পঃ)। **Stick-in-the-mud** — মন্দগতি, উন্নতিশূন্য। (*Noun*) মন্দগতি ব্যক্তি, উন্নতিশূন্য ব্যক্তি। **Stick-insect** — কাঁটাকীট। **Stick-up-collar**—খাড়া গলবেষ্টনী। **Stuck-up**—নাকউঁচু, গর্ব্বিত। **A poor stick**—চরিত্রহীন ব্যক্তি, তেজোবীর্য্যহীন ব্যক্তি। **A stick of eels**—২৫টী বাইন মৎস্য। **At a stick**—(*Dial.*) Confounded; (উপভাষায়) ভ্যাবাচ্যাকা। **Do not stick bills**—বিজ্ঞাপন আঁটিও না। **He wants the stick**—He should be whipped; তাহাকে বেত লাগান দরকার। **If you throw mud enough some will stick**—Even a person's absolute innocence cannot fully protect from the evil effects caused by false slander; সম্পূর্ণ নির্দ্দোষ কোন ব্যক্তির চরিত্রের উপর মিথ্যা দোষারোপ হইলে তাহাকে তাহার ফল কতকটা ভোগ করিতে হয়। **It sticks in one's gizzard**—It cannot be digested; ইহা পরিপাক হয় না, ইহা জীর্ণ করা যায় না। **Some money stuck in or to his fingers**—Some money was misappropriated by him; কতকটা টাকা সে তচ্ছুপ করিয়াছে। **Stick and stone**—Everything; সমস্ত, সর্ব্বস্ব। **To cut one's stick**—(*Slang*) To go off; (ইতর ভাষায়) চলিয়া যাওয়া। **To go to sticks and staves**—To fall in pieces; to go to ruin; খণ্ড খণ্ড হইয়া ভাঙ্গিয়া পড়া; ধ্বংসপ্রাপ্ত হওয়া। **To stick**—To stop in order to rob; to rob; টাকা পয়সা প্রভৃতি কাড়িয়া লইবার জন্য থামান; জোর করিয়া নেওয়া। **To stick at nothing**—To have no scruples; দ্বিধাশূন্য হওয়া, কোনরূপ কুণ্ঠা না করা। **To stick by**—To adhere closely; to be firm in supporting; সংসক্ত হওয়া; দৃঢ়ভাবে সমর্থন করা। To be troublesome by adhering; লাগিয়া থাকার দরুণ বিরক্তিজনক হওয়া। **To stick in**—To persevere; লাগিয়া থাকা, ধরিয়া থাকা। **To stick in the mud**—To be checked in advancement; উন্নতিরোধ হওয়া। **To stick on**—To overcharge; to deceive; অতিরিক্ত মূল্য ধরা; প্রতারণা করা। **To stick one's spoon in the wall**—(*Slang*) To die; (ইতর ভাষায়) শিঙ্গা ফুঁকা। **To stick out**—To refuse to surrender or comply; বশ্যতাস্বীকারে বা প্রার্থনা পূরণ করিতে অস্বীকার করা। **To stick out** or **up**—To protrude; to be erect; to make erect; বাড়াইয়া দেওয়া; খাড়া হইয়া উঠা; খাড়া করা। **To stick to**—To persist; লাগিয়া থাকা, ধরিয়া থাকা। **To stick up**—(*up* here as adverb) To become erect; খাড়া হইয়া উঠা। **To stick up**—(*up* here as preposition) To stop; to cause to fail; বন্ধ করা; (কারবারে) দেউলিয়া করা। **To stick up**—To maintain the cause of; to defend; পক্ষসমর্থন করা; সমর্থন করা। **To stick up a target**—To erect one; শরব্য দাঁড় করা। **To stick up for**—To vindicate an absent person; অনুপস্থিত ব্যক্তির পক্ষসমর্থন করা। **To stick up to**—To resist; বাধা দেওয়া। **To stick upon**—Not to give up; লাগিয়া থাকা, ধরিয়া থাকা। To dwell upon; কোন বিষয়ে বলা।

stick'-êr, *n.* 1. One who, or that which, sticks or causes to adhere; যে ব্যক্তি বিজ্ঞাপন প্রভৃতি আঁটিয়া দেয়। 2. One that adheres or clings to anything; যাহা কোনকিছুতে সংলগ্ন হয়। 3. An article of merchandize which sticks by the dealer and does not meet with a ready sale; যে পণ্য দ্রব্য বহু দিন দোকানে পড়িয়া থাকে। 4. One that sticks or stabs; যে ব্যক্তি বর্শা প্রভৃতি দ্বারা বিদ্ধ করে। 5. A batsman who is hard to get out; যে ব্যাটধারীকে সহজে আউট্‌ করা যায় না। 6. The arms of a crank-axis employed to change the plane and direction of a reciprocating motion; বকফেনির আকৃতি যন্ত্রাংশের যে ভুজ দ্বারা যন্ত্রের এক অংশ হইতে অপরাংশে সঞ্চালিত বলের গতির দিক ও তল পরিবর্ত্তিত হয়। 7. A sharp remark; কাটা জবাব।

stick'-le (-l), *v. i.* & *t.* 1. To altercate in a pertinacious manner on insufficient grounds; মিছামিছি তর্ক করা। 2. To play fast and loose; to take part with one side or other; নিতান্ত চঞ্চল মতি বা অব্যবস্থিতচিত্তের মত কার্য্য করা; এক পক্ষে বা অন্য পক্ষে যোগ দেওয়া। 3. To demur; ইতস্ততঃ করা। ***Verb t.*** (*Rare*) To intervene in; (কচিদ্‌ব্যবহৃত) হস্তক্ষেপ করা।

stick'-le-băck (-l-), *n.* A small British fish found in ponds and streams and remarkable for building nests; ইংলণ্ড দেশীয় মৎস্যবিশেষ।

stick'-lêr, *n.* An obstinate contender about anything, often about a thing of little consequence ; খুঁটিআখুরে।

stick′-ȳ, *adj.* Adhesive ; viscid ; আঠালো, সংশ্লেষক ; চটচটে। **–i-ly,** *adv.* **-i-ness,** *n.*

stiff, *adj.* & *n.* **1.** Not easily flexible, bent, or pliant ; rigid ; as, a *stiff* leg ; কঠিন, অনমনীয়, অনম্র, জড়, শক্ত ; আড়ষ্ট। **2.** Not liquid or fluid ; neither soft nor hard ; inspissated ; অতরল ; কঠিনও নয় কোমলও নয় ; গাঢ়। **3.** Taut ; কড়া, টান-টান। **4.** Not easily moved ; not working or moving easily ; আয়াসচালিত ; আয়াসে ক্রিয়াশীল। **5.** Constrained ; affected ; as, *stiff* style ; reserved ; as, *stiff* manners ; haughty ; unbending ; stubborn ; obstinate ; আড়ষ্ট ; কৃত্রিম ; অনালাপী ; উদ্ধত ; অনমনীয় ; অদম্য ; একরোখা। **6.** Difficult ; as, a *stiff* problem ; কঠিন। **7.** Not lowering in price ; as, a *stiff* market ; (মূল্য সম্বন্ধে) হ্রাসহীন। **8.** (Of price) High ; as, *stiff* price ; উচ্চ, চড়া। **9.** Violent ; as, a *stiff* gale ; প্রবল, ভীষণ। **10.** (Of wine etc.) Strong ; as, a *stiff* drink ; কড়া। ***Noun.*** (*Slang*) Negotiable paper ; (ইতরভাষায়) হস্তান্তর যোগ্য বা ক্রয়বিক্রয়যোগ্য কাগজ (যথা নোট, হুণ্ডী)। **Stiff′-en,** *v. t.* & *i.* **1.** To make unbending ; অনমনীয় করা। **2.** To benumb ; আড়ষ্ট করা। **3.** To inspissate ; গাঢ় করা, ঘনীভূত করা, লেইএর মত করা। ***Verb i.*** To become stiff ; অনমনীয় হওয়া, আড়ষ্ট হওয়া, লেইএর মত হওয়া। **Stiff′-en-er,** *n.* **Stiff′-ly,** *adv.* **Stiff′-ness,** *n.* The state or quality of being stiff ; জাড্য, স্তব্ধতা, স্তম্ভ, জড়তা, কঠোরতা, অবস্তব্ধতা, আড়ষ্টতা, অনমনীয়তা, কাঠিন্য ; অনালাপিতা, রহঃশীলতা। **Stiff-backed**—একগুঁয়ে। **Stiff-bit**—অশ্বের জোড়াবিহীন খলীন—যাহার প্রান্তে আংটা থাকে। **Stiff-neck**—স্কন্ধবাত, গ্রীবাস্তম্ভ। **Stiff-necked**—একগুঁয়ে, একরোখা, ঘাড়তেড়া (*Slang*)। **Stiff un**—পাকা খেলোয়াড়। **A stiff un**—(*Slang*) A dead body ; (ইতরভাষায়) শব। **Stiffness of the shoulder-joint**—অপবাহুক (সাঃ পঃ)। **To do a bit of stiff**— (*Slang*) To cash a bill ; (ইতরভাষায়) হুণ্ডী ভাঙ্গান। **To keep a stiff upper lip**—To show firmness of character ; চরিত্রের দৃঢ়তা প্রদর্শন করা।

stī′-fle (-fl), *v. t.* & *i.* Same as SMOTHER, *v.* **–fling,** *adj.* **–fling-ly,** *adv.*

stī′-fle (-fl), *n.* **1.** The knee-joint of a horse, ox, etc. ; অশ্ব, বৃষ, প্রভৃতির জানুসন্ধি। **2.** Disease of knee-joint ; জানুসন্ধির রোগ। **–fled,** *adj.* **Stifle-bone**—অশ্বের জানুসন্ধির সম্মুখস্থ ন্যুব্জাকৃতি অস্থি। **Stifle-shoe**—জানুসন্ধি রোগাক্রান্ত অশ্বের সুস্থপদের জন্য নালবিশেষ।

stig′-mȧ, *n.* **1.** A mark made with a burning iron ; a brand ; দাগ ; ছেঁকা। **2.** Stain ; কলঙ্ক, কলঙ্ক রেখা। **3.** (*Bot.*) A part of a flower-pistil which receives the pollen ; (উদ্ভিদ্‌-বিদ্যা) পুষ্পের গর্ভকেশরের যে অংশে রেণু থাকে, চিহ্ন (সাঃ পঃ), লক্ষণ (সাঃ পঃ), মুণ্ড (যোঃ), মস্তক। **4.** (*Pl.* STIGMATA) Marks said to have been supernaturally impressed upon the bodies of certain persons in imitation of the wounds on the crucified body of Christ ; as, the *stigmata* of St. Francis ; কোন কোন খৃষ্টীয় সাধকের দেহে অপ্রাকৃত উপায়ে ক্রুশবিদ্ধ খৃষ্টের দেহের যে সমস্ত বা কোন কোন ক্ষতচিহ্ন প্রভৃতি প্রকাশ পাইত। [নিম্নলিখিত খৃষ্টীয় সাধকগণের দেহে উক্তরূপ চিহ্ন প্রকাশ পাইত বলিয়া কথিত আছে।

Flower in section showing stigma, s.

(পুরুষ)

Angelo del Paz—সমস্ত চিহ্ন। Benedict of Reggio—কণ্টকমুকুট। Carlo di Saeta—বর্শার আঘাতজনিত ক্ষত। Dodo—সমস্ত চিহ্ন। Francis of Assisi—ঐ।

(স্ত্রী)

Bianca de Gazeran—কণ্টক মুকুট। St. Catharine of Sienna—ঐ। Catharine di Raconisco—ঐ। Cecilia di Nobili of Nocera—বর্শার-আঘাতজনিত ক্ষত। Clara di Pugny—ঐ। Estacia of Caldaro—সমস্ত চিহ্ন। Gabriella da Piezolo of Aquila—বর্শার আঘাতজনিত ক্ষত। Hieronyma Carvaglio—বর্শার আঘাত জনিত ক্ষত, এই ক্ষত হইতে প্রতি শুক্রবার রক্ত নির্গলিত হইত। Joanna Maria of the Cross—কণ্টকমুকুটের চিহ্ন। Maria Razzi of Chio—(ঐ)। Maria Villani—(ঐ)। Mary Magdalen di Pazzi—সমস্ত চিহ্ন। Mechtildis von Stanz—ঐ। Ursula of Valencia—ঐ। Veronica Guliani—ঐ। [এতদ্দেশীয় সাধক বিজয় কৃষ্ণ গোস্বামীর জীবনীতে উল্লিখিত আছে যে তাঁহার দেহে অনেক সময় "রাধা কৃষ্ণ" প্রভৃতি নাম ফুটিয়া উঠিত।] **5.** Similar mark or marks produced by hypnotic suggestion ; যোগনিদ্রাচ্ছন্ন ব্যক্তির দেহে সংকল্পাত্মক ইচ্ছার/ক্রিয়ার ফলে উৎপাদিত অনুরূপ চিহ্ন বা চিহ্নসমূহ। [Everyone has heard of the stigmata of the crucifixion appearing on the hands and feet of some religious devotee as in the celebrated case of Louise Lateau. Dr. Briggs of Lima once told a hypnotic that "a red cross would appear on her chest every Friday for a period of one month and obediently the mark appeared—*Drama of Love and Death, Edward Carpenter.*] **6.** A small red spot on a person's skin that bleeds periodically or under mental stimulus ; মনুষ্য-

দেহের রক্তবর্ণ ক্ষুদ্র চিহ্ন-বিশেষ—যাহা হইতে নিৰ্দ্দিষ্ট সময়ান্তে বা প্রবল মানসিক উত্তেজনার কালে রক্ত নির্গলিত হইয়া থাকে। **—mat′-ic,** *adj.* **—tist,** *n.* One on whom the marks of Christ's wounds are said to be supernaturally impressed ; যে ব্যক্তির দেহে খৃষ্টের ক্ষত চিহ্ন সমূহ অলৌকিক ভাবে ফুটিয়া উঠে, খৃষ্ট ক্ষতাঙ্কধারী। **—tose,** *adj.*

stig′-mă-tize, *v. t.* 1. To brand ; লোহা পুড়াইয়া দাগ দেওয়া। 2. To characterise by some opprobrious epithet ; কলঙ্কিত করা, কলঙ্ককালিমা লেপন করা। 3. To produce stigmata upon by hypontic suggestion etc. ; যোগনিদ্রা প্রভৃতি দ্বারা দেহে চিহ্ন প্রকটন করা। **—ti-za′-tion,** *n.*

stile, *n.* A step or set of steps for ascending and descending over a fence or a wall ; বৃতি, প্রাচীর প্রভৃতি ডিঙ্গাইবার জন্ম ধাপ বা সিঁড়ি।

sti-lĕt′-tō, *n.* & *v. i.* 1. A small strong dagger ; ছোরা, ছুরিকা। 2. A pointed instrument for making eyelet etc. ; যে সূক্ষ্মাগ্র যন্ত্রদ্বারা পাদুকা, টেলিগ্রামের ধাতুর ক্ষুদ্রনল বসাইবার জন্ম থাম প্রভৃতি ছিদ্র করা হয়। ***Verb i.*** 1. To stab with a stiletto ; ছোরাদ্বারা আঘাত করা, ছোরা বসান। 2. To pierce with a stiletto; সূক্ষ্মাগ্র যন্ত্রদ্বারা ক্ষুদ্র ছিদ্র করা।

still, *adj., n., v. t., i.* & *adv.* 1. Silent ; নীরব, নিঝুম, নিথর, নিঃশব্দ নিস্তব্ধ। 2. Quiet ; calm ; as, a *still* evening ; motionless ; as, to lie *still*; শান্ত; প্রশান্ত, নিশ্চল, স্তিমিত ; গতিশূন্য, নিষ্কম্প, স্থির। 3. Not effervescing ; অবুদ্বুদায়মান। ***Noun.*** Silence ; calm ; নীরবতা, নিস্তব্ধতা, নিঃশব্দতা ; শান্তভাব, প্রশান্তি। ***Verb t.*** 1. To silence ; নিস্তব্ধ করা। 2. To quiet ; শান্তকরা, প্রশান্তকরা। ***Verb i.*** (*Rare*) To be still or quiet ; to assuage ; (ক্বচিৎ ব্যবহৃত) শান্ত হওয়া, নিস্তব্ধ হওয়া, নীরব হওয়া ; প্রশমিত হওয়া। ***Adv.*** 1. To this time ; এই পর্য্যন্ত, অদ্যাবধি, অদ্যাপি, এযাবৎ। 2. (*Archaic*) Constantly ; continually ; uniformly ; "Still they dream that they shall still succeed and *still* they are disappointed" ; (অপ্র:) সতত ক্রমাগত ; সমরূপে। 3. After that; তারপর; তৎপর। 4. Even more: as *still* more: আরো, পূর্ব্বাপেক্ষা অধিক। 5. Yet ; তথাপি তবু। **Still′-ness,** *n.* The state of being still ; নীরবতা, নিস্তব্ধতা, স্তিমিতভা, নিঃশব্দতা, নিষ্কম্পতা, শান্তি প্রশান্তি। **Still-birth** — মৃত সন্তান-প্রসব। **Still-born**—মৃতাবস্থায় জাত, অন্তর্মৃত (সুশ্রু:), মৃতজাত (দশ:)। **Still-fish**—*v. i.* নোঙ্গরবদ্ধ নৌকা হইতে মৎস্য শিকার করা। **Still-life**—ফল, ফুল, আসবাব প্রভৃতি অচেতন পদার্থের চিত্র। **Still and anon**—প্রায়শ:, সর্ব্বদা। **Still small voice**—বিবেকের বাণী। **Still waters run deep**—সংযতবাক্ লোক সাধারণত: চিন্তাশীল হইয়া থাকেন।

still, *n.* & *v. t.* 1. A vessel or apparatus for distilling ; মদ্য

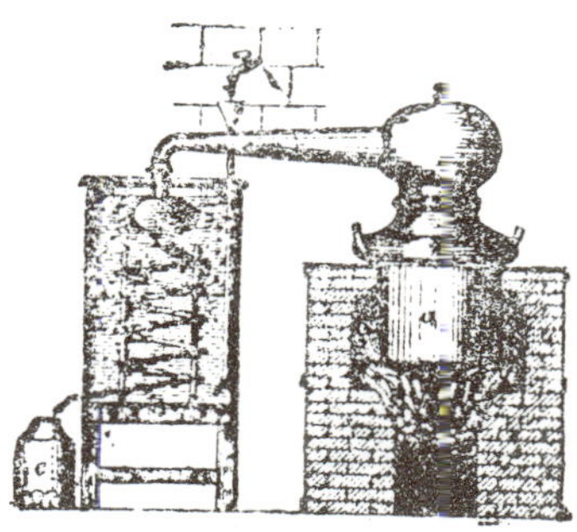

Simple form of a still.

চোলাই করার জন্ম পাত্র, ভগযন্ত্র (সাঃ পঃ), অধোযন্ত্র (উইলসন), মদ্যনিষ্কর্ষণ ভাণ্ড, বকযন্ত্র। 2. A distillery ; মদের ভাঁটি, খোলা ভাঁটি। ***Verb t.*** 1. (*Poet.*) To distill ; (কবিতায়) পরিস্রুত করা বা চুয়ান। 2. To expel spirit by heat and condense it in a refrigator ; উত্তাপদ্বারা সুরাসার বাহির করিয়া উহা শৈত্যজনক যন্ত্রে ঘনীভূত করা। **Still-room**—যে কোঠায় মদ্য, আচার, প্রভৃতি রক্ষিত হয় এবং যথায় চা, কাফি, প্রভৃতি প্রস্তুত করা হইয়া থাকে, ভাঁটি-ঘর।

stil′-lāge, *n.* A rack on which casks are placed ; যে তাকের উপর পিপাসমূহ রক্ষিত হয়।

Stilt.

stilt, *n.* & *v. t.* A pole of wood or bamboo with a rest for the foot in walking ; দীর্ঘ দণ্ড-বিশেষ—যাহার পাদস্থাপন স্থানে পদ রাখিয়া দীর্ঘপাদ-বিক্ষেপে ভ্রমণ করিতে পারা যায়, পাদযষ্টি, পাদদণ্ড। ***Verb t.*** To raise on stilts ; to elevate ; পাদযষ্টির উপর উত্তোলিত করা ; উন্নত করা। **Stilt-bird, Stilt-plover, Stilt-walker**—একপ্রকার দীর্ঘপাদ পক্ষী।

stilt′-ĕd. *adj.* 1. On stilts ; পাদযষ্টির উপরিস্থ। 2. Pompous ; bombastic ; জাঁকালো ; বাগাড়ম্বরপূর্ণ। **—ness,** *n.* **Stilted arch** — যে তোরণ অব্যবহিত ভাবে আধারস্তম্ভের শীর্ষ হইতে উত্থিত না হইয়া উহার উপরিস্থ চূণ সুর্কি নির্ম্মিত ক্ষুদ্র স্তম্ভ হইতে উত্থিত হইয়া থাকে।

Stil′-tŏn, *n.* A fine cheese, originally made at Stilton, in Huntingdonshire ; একপ্রকার উৎকৃষ্ট পনীর। [এই পনীর প্রথমতঃ Huntingdonshireএর অন্তর্গত Stilton নামক স্থানে প্রস্তুত হইত।]

stim′-ū-lănt, *adj.* & *n.* 1. Serving to stimulate ; উত্তেজক। 2. Producing increased vital action ; জীবনীশক্তির ক্রিয়াবর্দ্ধক, দীপন (cf. দীপনং রোচক ধান্যং—ভাব: প্র:)। ***Noun.*** That which stimulates ; উত্তেজক ঔষধ। **Never takes stimulants**—কখনও মদ্যপান করে না।

stim′-ū-lāte, *v. t.* 1. To incite ; to animate ; উত্তেজিত করা, উদ্দীপিত করা ; অনুপ্রাণিত করা। 2. To excite great vitality or keenness in ;

জীবনশক্তি বৃদ্ধি করা, প্রাখর্য্য বৃদ্ধি করা। **–lat-ing,** *n.* **–la'-tion,** *n.* The act of inciting or animating ; উত্তেজন (হিঃ কোঃ), প্রচোদন (ঐ), প্রণোদন (ঐ), প্রোৎসাহন (ঐ)। **–la-tive, –la-tor,** *ns.*

stim'-ū-lŭs, *n.* 1. A goad ; অঙ্কুশ। 2. Something which stimulates ; উত্তেজনা, অনুপ্রাণনা, প্রণোদনা, প্রচোদনা। 3. That which produces an increase of vital action ; জীবনীশক্তির ক্রিয়াবর্দ্ধক বস্তু। 4. A stimulant ; উত্তেজক ঔষধ। 5. (*Bot.*) A sting ; a prickle ; (উদ্ভিদ্‌বিদ্যা) দংশরোম ; কাঁটা **–lose,** *adj.* Stimulating ; উত্তেজক (হিঃ কোঃ), উদ্বোধক (ঐ), প্রোৎসাহক (ঐ)।

sting, *v. t., i. & n.* 1. To wound with sting ; হুল ফুটান, হুলদ্বারা দংশন করা। 2. To pain acutely ; তীব্র বেদনা সঞ্চার করা, মর্ম্মান্তিক যন্ত্রণা দেওয়া। 3. To stimulate ; উত্তেজিত করা। ***Verb i.*** 1. To use as a sting ; to wound with a sting ; to bite as a serpent ; হুল ফুটান ; হুলদ্বারা বিদ্ধ করা ; দংশন করা, ছোবল মারা। 2. To be acutely painful ; অতিশয় যন্ত্রণাপ্রদ হওয়া, তীব্র বেদনার সঞ্চার করা। ***Noun.*** 1. A goad ; অঙ্কুশ। 2. A sharp pointed weapon with which certain animals are armed for their defence ; হুল, দংশরোম (সাঃ পঃ), সর্পের বিষদাঁত, মশকের মস্তকের দংশনসূচী প্রভৃতি। 3. Infliction of wound with a sting ; wound so made ; a sharp pain ; keenness of vigour ; হুলদ্বারা বিদ্ধ করণ ; হুলের ক্ষত; দংশনযাতনা ; প্রখরতা, তেজঃ, শক্তি। 4. (*Bot.*) A stinging hair ; দংশরোম (সাঃ পঃ)। **Sting'-ing,** *adj.* **Sting'-ing-ly,** *adv.* **Sting'-less,** *adj.* **Sting-bull**—একপ্রকার মৎস্য। **Sting-nettle, Stinging-nettle**—বিছুটী গাছ। **Sting-ray**—নমনীয় এবং কন্টকাকৃত দীর্ঘপুচ্ছবিশিষ্ট একপ্রকার মৎস্য। **Sting-winkle**—একপ্রকার চঞ্চুবিশিষ্ট শঙ্খ—যাহারা অপর শঙ্খে ছিদ্র করিয়া থাকে।

sting-a-ree' (-gă-rē), *n.* Same as STING-RAY (which see).

sting'-er (-gêr), *n.* 1. One who, or that which, stings, vexes or gives pain ; দংশনকারী, যন্ত্রণা প্রদানকারী। 2. A sharp painful blow ; তীব্র যন্ত্রণাদায়ক আঘাত।

stin'-gō (sting-), *n.* (*Archaic*) Strong beer ; উগ্র বীয়র।

stin'-ġy̆, *adj.* Meanly avaricious ; very niggardly or close-fisted ; অর্থপিশাচ ; কঞ্জুষ, হাতকষা (*colloq.*)। **–gi-ly,** *adv.* **–gi-ness,** *n.* The quality of being stingy ; বদ্ধমুষ্টিতা।

stink (stingk), *v. i., t. & n.* 1. To emit a strong offensive smell ; দুর্গন্ধ নির্গত হওয়া, পুতিগন্ধ নিঃসৃত হওয়া। 2. To be in bad odour ; অপ্রীতিভাজন হওয়া। ***Verb t.*** To cause to stink ; দুর্গন্ধ নির্গত করা। ***Noun.*** 1. A strong offensive smell ; দুর্গন্ধ, পুতিগন্ধ। 2. (*Pl., Slang*) Chemistry ; natural science ; (ইতরভাষায়) রসায়নশাস্ত্র ; পদার্থবিদ্যা। **Stink'-ing,** *adj.* **Stink-alive**—একপ্রকার মৎস্য। [মৃত্যুর পর অতি দ্রুত গলিত হয় বলিয়া—ইহাদের এই নাম।] **Stink-ball**—Same as STINK-POT 2. **Stink-horn**—বিভিন্ন জাতীয় পুতিগন্ধ ছত্রাক। **Stink-pot**—(১) পচা জিনিষদ্বারা পূর্ণ ভাণ্ড। (২) দুর্গন্ধ বা শ্বাসরোধকর বস্তুপূর্ণ মৃদ্‌ভাণ্ড—যাহা পূর্ব্বে সময় সময় শত্রু-পোতের উপর নিক্ষিপ্ত হইত। **Stink-trap**—নর্দ্দমা উন্মুক্ত করিলে যাহাতে দূষিত বাষ্প নির্গত হইতে না পারে—তন্নিবারণার্থ যন্ত্রবিশেষ।

stink'-ărd, *n.* 1. A mean paltry fellow ; নীচাশয় লোক। 2. A quadruped found in Java and Sumatra, which like the skunk emits an offensive smell when irritated ; যব্‌ ও সুমাত্রা দ্বীপের জন্তুবিশেষ—উত্তেজিত হইলে ইহাদের শরীর হইতে একপ্রকার পুতিগন্ধ নির্গত হয়।

stink'-êr (stingk-), *n.* 1. Same as STINKARD. 2. Same as STINK-POT. 3. A kind of large petrel ; একপ্রকার বৃহৎকায় সামুদ্রিক পক্ষী।

stint, *v. t. & n.* 1. To restrict to a short or scanty allowance ; to limit ; খাদ্যাদির পরিমাণ হ্রাস করা ; সঙ্কোচ করা। 2. To supply niggardly or grudgingly ; কৃপণতার সহিত দেওয়া, অনিচ্ছার সহিত দেওয়া। ***Noun.*** 1. Limit or restraint set or observed ; restriction as to quantity ; সঙ্কোচ, ব্যয় প্রভৃতি সংকোচন ; পরিমাণ হ্রাস। 2. One of various sandpipers ; একপ্রকার পক্ষী। 3. Fixed or alloted amount of work ; "He lives very much like other men in the Household Brigade ; plays heavily, though not regularly : but he always has two *affaires de cœur,* at least, on hand at once ; that's his *stint*" ; নিরূপিত কার্য্য। **Stint'-ed,** *p. p.* **Stint'-less,** *adj.* **Without stint**—অকাতরে।

stī'-pāte, *adj.* (*Bot.*) Close-set ; ঘন-সন্নিবিষ্ট।

stīpe, stī'-pēs, *ns.* (*Bot.*) Stalk ; stem ; বৃন্ত ; ডগা, স্থাণু (সাঃ পঃ)।

stī'-pĕl, *n.* (*Bot.*) A secondary stipule at the base of leaflets of compound leaf ; (উদ্ভিদ্‌বিদ্যা) ক্ষুদ্র উপতৃণ (সাঃ পঃ), উপপত্রিকা (ঐ)।

stī'-pĕnd, *n.* 1. A settled pay for services ; yearly allowance ; বেতন ; বৃত্তি। 2. Clergyman's official income ; যাজকীয় বৃত্তি। **–pen'-di-a-ry,** *adj. & n.* Receiving stipend, wages or salary ; বেতনভোগী, বৃত্তিভোগী, বেতনগ্রাহী, বেতনজীবী, বৈতনিক, ভৃতিপোষিত (শুক্রঃ বিনয়ঃ), ভৃতক। ***Noun.*** 1. One who performs services for a settled payment, salary or allowance ; বেতনভোগী কর্ম্মচারী। 2. A paid magistrate in large town; বৃহৎ নগরীর বেতনভোগী ম্যাজিষ্ট্রেট।

sti'-pes, *n.* Same as STIPE (which see).

stip'-i-tate, *adj.* Furnished with a stipe; সোপতৃণক।

stip'-ple (-l), *v. t.* & *n.* 1. To engrave by means of dots in distinction from engraving in lines; অতি ক্ষুদ্র ক্ষুদ্র বিন্দু দ্বারা ক্ষোদিত করা। 2. To paint by means of small touches; ক্ষুদ্র ক্ষুদ্র তুলির স্পর্শদ্বারা চিত্রিত করা। ***Noun.*** A process of engraving by means of dots; ক্ষুদ্র ক্ষুদ্র বিন্দুর সাহায্যে ক্ষোদিত করণ। **—pler,** *n.* **—pling,** *n.* **Stipple-graver**—ক্ষুদ্র ক্ষুদ্র বিন্দুর সাহায্যে ক্ষোদাই করার জন্য যন্ত্রবিশেষ, বিন্দুক্ষোদক।

stip'-ü-late, *v. i.* & *t.* To make an agreement or covenant to do or forbear anything; to contract; কোন কার্য্য করার জন্য বা কোন কার্য্য হইতে নিবৃত্ত থাকিবার নিমিত্ত কাহারো সহিত চুক্তিতে আবদ্ধ হওয়া; চুক্তি করা। ***Verb t.*** To settle by agreement or covenant; চুক্তি দ্বারা স্থির করা। **—la'-tion,** *n.* 1. Act of stipulating; agreement; চুক্তি করণ; চুক্তি। 2. That which is stipulated or agreed upon; a contract or bargain; a particular item or condition in a contract or covenant; as, the *stipulations* of allied powers to furnish each his contingent of troops; চুক্তির বিষয়; চুক্তি, সময়, সংবাদ (কাঃ প্রোঃ); চুক্তির কোন বিশেষ দফা বা সর্ত্ত।

stip'-üle, *n.* A small leaf-like appendage to a leaf commonly situated at the base of the petiole in pairs; পত্রশল্ক (সাঃ পঃ)। **—u-lar, —u-la-ry, —u-li-form, —u-late,** *adjs.* Having stipules on it; শোবপত্রক। **—u-la'-tion,** *n.*

stir (stêr), *v. t., i.* & *n.* 1. To move; চালান, চালিত করা, সরান, স্থানান্তরিত করা, সঞ্চালিত করা। 2. To agitate; নাড়া, আলোড়িত করা, বিলোড়িত করা। 3. To incite; to rouse; to instigate; উত্তেজিত করা; উদ্বুদ্ধ করা; প্রণোদিত করা। ***Verb i.*** 1. To move one's self; to go or be carried in any manner; নড়া; চালিত হওয়া, স্থানান্তরে নীত হওয়া। 2. To be active or busy; ব্যস্ত হওয়া, কর্ম্মব্যস্ত হওয়া। 3. To rise in the morning; "If the gentlewoman that attends the general's wife be *stirring*, tell her, there's one Cassio entreats of her a little favour of speech'; প্রভাতে শয্যাত্যাগ করা। 4. To stir something; to be stirred; নাড়া; আলোড়িত হওয়া। ***Noun.*** 1. Public disturbance or commotion; আন্দোলন, বিক্ষোভ, সংক্ষোভ, নাড়াচাড়া, গোলমাল। 2. Agitation of thoughts; excitement; "Why all these words, this clamour and this *stir*?"; চিত্তবিক্ষোভ; মানসিক উত্তেজনা। 3. Slightest movement; সামান্য সঞ্চালন, ঈষৎ চাঞ্চল্য। **Stir'-ring,** *adj.* 1. Bustling; কর্ম্মকোলাহলপূর্ণ। 2. Inspiring; exciting; উদ্দীপনাপূর্ণ; উৎসাহসঞ্চারক, উত্তেজক, উত্তেজনাসঞ্চারক। **Stir'-ring-ly,** *adv.* **Stir-about**—(*Noun*) খইএর মণ্ড। (*Adj.*) কর্ম্ম কোলাহলপূর্ণ। **Stir your stumps**—Walk faster; তাড়াতাড়ি চল। **To stir up**—To mix by stirring; নাড়িয়া একত্র মিশান। To excite; to animate; উত্তেজিত করা; অনুপ্রাণিত করা। To enliven; উল্লসিত করা, উৎফুল্ল করা। To disturb; আলোড়িত করা। **To stir up one's bile**—পিত্ত জ্বলিয়া উঠা।

stir'-pi-cŭl-türe (stêr-) *n.* The breeding of special stocks or races; বিশেষ জাতি বা গোষ্ঠি পালন।

stirps (stêrps), *n.* The person from which a family is descended; race; family; কোন বংশের আদি পুরুষ, বীজপুরুষ; জাতি; বংশ, গোষ্ঠি, পরিবার।

stir'-rŭp (stêr-), *n.* 1. Either of two supports to receive the feet of a person when riding; জীনের রিকাব, পাদদান। 2. (*Naut.*) A rope with an eye at its end supporting a foot-rope; (নৌবিদ্যা) পাইলদণ্ডের অনুপ্রস্থগামী পাদস্থাপন রজ্জুধারক ফাঁসযুক্ত রজ্জু বিশেষ। **Stirrup-bar**—জীনের যে অংশে রিকাব সংবদ্ধ করা হয়। **Stirrup-bone**—মনুষ্য প্রভৃতির দেহের রিকাবের আকার অস্থি। **Stirrup-cup, Stirrup-glass**—অশ্বারোহীকে যাত্রার প্রাক্কালে যে সুরাপূর্ণ পাত্র পান করিতে দেওয়া হয়। **Stirrup-iron**—রিকাবের যে অংশে পদ স্থাপন করা হয়। **Stirrup-leather**—যে চর্ম্মরজ্জু দ্বারা রেকাব জীনের সহিত সংবদ্ধ করা হয়। **Stirrup-piece**—(ছুতার মিস্ত্রী প্রভৃতির) কার্য্যে দোলায়মান অবলম্বন।

stitch (stich), *n., v. t.* & *i.* 1. A sharp pain in one's side; পার্শ্বশূল। 2. A single pass of a needle in sewing; সূঁচের ফোঁড়, টাক। 3. A single turn of a thread round a needle in knitting; (মোজা প্রভৃতি শেলাইয়ের) ঘর। 4. (*Colloq.*) The smallest part of a dress; (চলিত ভাষায়) পোষাকের ক্ষুদ্রতম অংশ। 5. The space between the furrows; লাঙ্গলপদ্ধতির মধ্যবর্ত্তী স্থান। ***Verb t.*** 1. To sew in a continuous line; to unite by sewing; সেলাই করা; সেলাই করিয়া জোড়া দেওয়া, রিপু করা। 2. To form land into ridges; জমির মধ্যে মধ্যে আল করা। ***Verb i.*** To practise needle-work; to sew; সূচিকার্য্য শিক্ষা করা, সেলাই শিখা; সেলাই করা। **Stitching-horse**—অশ্বসজ্জা প্রস্তুতকারিগণ যে আঁকড়াতে আটকাইয়া জিনিষ প্রস্তুত করে। **Stitch-wheel**—অশ্বসজ্জা প্রস্তুতকারীদিগের বেধনযন্ত্রবিশেষ—যদ্দারা সেলাইএর ছিদ্র করা হয়। **Stitch-wort**—একপ্রকার গুল্ম। **To put a stitch or stitches**—To sew up wounds; ক্ষতস্থান সেলাই করা।

To stitch up—To mend by sewing ; রিপু করা।

stith'-ў, *n.* (*Archaic*) Smith's shop ; an anvil ; কামারশালা ; নেহাই, হাপর।

sti'-vêr, *n.* **1.** Dutch coin of small value ; হলণ্ড দেশের একপ্রকার অল্প মূল্যের মুদ্রা। **2.** A straw ; a fig ; একতিল ; অণুমাত্র।

stō'-ȧ, *n.* (*Pl.* STOÆ) A portico ; দ্বারমণ্ডপ, দ্বারপ্রকোষ্ঠ। **Stoa poikle**—চিত্রিত বারেন্দা (এপি:)।

stoat (stōt), *n.* **1.** The ermine in its summer coat ; গ্রীষ্মকালজ রোমরাজি-দ্বারা শোভিত নকুলজাতীয় জন্তুবিশেষ। **2.** The ermine and allied animals; নকুলজাতীয় জন্তু।

stŏck, *n.*, *v. t.* & *i.* **1.** A wooden post or stake ; a stump ; খুঁটি, স্থাণু; ছিন্নকাণ্ড বৃক্ষমূল। **2.** The main trunk of a tree ; বৃক্ষের কাণ্ড, স্কন্ধ (হিঃ কোঃ)। **3.** A block of wood ; কাষ্ঠখণ্ড। **4.** The butt-end of a gun ; বন্দুকের কুঁদো। **5.** A plant into which graft is inserted ; যে বৃক্ষে কলম করা হয়। **6.** A handle ; হাতল, বাঁট, ডাণ্ডা, ডাঁটি। **7.** The principal support for holding parts in certain implements or tools ; কোন কোন যন্ত্রের প্রধান অবলম্বন বা ধারক অংশ। **8.** The main race or line of a family ; lineage ; family ; the progenitor of a family and his direct descendants ; বংশ বা গোষ্ঠীর প্রধান শাখা ; বংশাবলী ; পরিবার ; কোন বংশের বীজপুরুষ এবং তদীয় পুত্র, পৌত্র, প্রভৃতি। **9.** (*Formerly*) The part of a tally struck in the exchequer, which was delivered to the persons that had lent the king money on account ; (পূর্ব্বে) রাজকোষ হইতে ঋণদাতাকে যে খাঁজ-কাটা নিদর্শন প্রদান করা হইত। **10.** The money or goods invested or employed in by a merchant, tradesman or company ; also the amount or value of goods on hand of a trader, manufacturer, etc. ; কোন সওদাগর, ব্যবসায়ী বা কোম্পানী ব্যবসায়ে যে অর্থ, মাল প্রভৃতি প্রয়োগ বা নিয়োগ করে, মূলধন, পুঁজি ; কোন ব্যবসায়ী, নির্ম্মাতা, প্রভৃতির বিপণি, শিল্পশালা প্রভৃতির মজুত মাল। **11.** Government securities ; a fund employed in the carrying of some business or enterprise, divided into shares and owned by individuals who jointly form a corporation ; shares ; as, railway *stock* ; কোম্পানীর কাগজ ; কোন যৌথকারবার প্রভৃতির মূলধন ; সমবায় প্রভৃতির অংশসমূহ। **12.** The beasts used or reared in farm ; কৃষিক্ষেত্রে ব্যবহৃত বা পালিত পশুসমূহ। **13.** Store ; accumulation ; ভাণ্ডার ; সঞ্চয়। **14.** An instrument of punishment confining the offender's ankles or wrists ; যে কাঠের কাঠামের ভিতর শাস্তিস্বরূপ অপরাধিগণের গুল্‌ফ বা মণিবন্ধ আবদ্ধ করা হইত, তুরুম (যো:)। **15.** (*Pl.*) Timbers on which a ship is supported while building or repairing ; যে কাষ্ঠফলক সমূহের উপর অবলম্বিত রাখিয়া জাহাজ নির্ম্মাণ বা মেরামত করা হয়। **16.** Raw material ; as, paper *stock* ; কাঁচা মাল। **17.** Production of plays, etc. by a stock company ; যৌথনাট্যসমাজ কর্ত্তৃক নাটক প্রভৃতির অভিনয়। **18.** The handle which contains a screw-cutting die ; স্ক্রু কাটিবার ছেনির বাঁট। **19.** That portion of a pack of cards which is not dealt out in certain games, but is allowed to remain on the table and may be drawn from as occasion requires ; কোন কোন রকম খেলায় যে সকল তাস বাঁটিয়া না দিয়া এক স্থানে রাখা হয়, এবং ক্রীড়কগণ যাহা হইতে আবশ্যকমত তাস গ্রহণ করিতে পারে। **20.** Red and gray bricks used in parti-coloured brick-works ; বিচিত্রবর্ণের গাঁথুনির কাজে ব্যবহৃত লোহিত এবং ধূসরবর্ণের ইষ্টক। **21.** The block of wood which constitutes the body of a plane and in which the cutting iron is fixed ; রেঁদার বাঁট। **22.** Something fixed, solid and senseless ; ঘন, স্থিরবদ্ধ এবং অচেতন জন্তু, জড়বস্তু। **23.** A stupid senseless person ; জড়ভরত, মাংসপিণ্ড। **24.** A bit-stock ; তুরপুণ, প্রভৃতি বেধনযন্ত্রের বাঁট। **25.** (*Book-keeping*) Same as STOCK-ACCOUNT. **26.** A plain soap before the addition of perfumery or colouring-matter ; সুগন্ধি-দ্রব্য এবং রঞ্জনবস্তু সংযোগের পূর্ব্বের সাবান। **27.** A cabbage ; বাঁধাকপি। **28.** Same as STOCK-GILLYFLOWER. **29.** The cross-piece of timber into which the shank of an anchor is inserted ; যে আড়কাঠে নোঙ্গরের হুল ফলা প্রবিষ্ট করা হয়। **30.** The liquid or jelly obtained by boiling meat or bones used for making foundation for soups ; সুপের জন্য মাংস, অস্থি জলে সিদ্ধ করিয়া যে কাথ প্রস্তুত করা হয়। **31.** A stiff band worn as a cravat ; একপ্রকার শক্ত গলবন্ধনী। **32.** Same as DEAD-STOCK. **33.** A race or group of generically and closely related individuals in a breed or species ; কোন জাতি বা গণভুক্ত নিকটসম্পর্কীয় জন্তুগণ। **34.** (*Zool.*) Aggregate organism ; (জন্তুবিদ্যা) সমষ্টিভূত অঙ্গী। ***Verb t*.** **1.** To lay up in store ; to store ; মজুত করা, গুদামজাত করা, ভাণ্ডারজাত করা ; সঞ্চিত করা। **2.** To provide or furnish with stock ; to supply with domestic animals ; আবশ্যক দ্রব্যজাত সরবরাহ করা, ভাণ্ডার জাত করা ; গৃহপালিত পশু যোগান। **3.** To provide with a stock ; বাঁট লাগান। **4.** To suffer, as cows, to retain their milk for twenty-four hours or more previous to being sold ; বিক্রয়ের পূর্ব্বে

২৪ ঘণ্টা বা তদধিক কাল গাভীর বাটে দুধ জমিতে দেওয়া। 5. To fill or cover with pasture-grass etc.; গোগ্রাসোপযোগী তৃণ প্রভৃতি দ্বারা আচ্ছাদিত করা। *Verb i.* 1. To take in, to provide, or procure supplies; ভাণ্ডারে মজুত করা, আবশ্যক দ্রব্যজাত যোগান বা সংগ্রহ করা। 2. To send out new shoots; নূতন অঙ্কুর গজান। 3. To swell; ফুলা। **Stock'-less,** *adj.* **Dead stock**—কৃষিযন্ত্র এবং উৎপন্ন কৃষিদ্রব্য। **Live stock**—See LIVE. **Stock-account, Stock-book** — ভাণ্ডারে মজুত মালের হিসাববহি; যে হিসাবে জমার দিকে মূলধন এবং পরবর্ত্তীকালে মূলধনের সহিত যুক্ত অর্থ এবং খরচের দিকে উঠানো টাকা বা ক্ষতির টাকা দেখান হইয়া থাকে। **Stock argument**—পুরাতন যুক্তি, বৈচিত্র্যহীন যুক্তি, সচরাচর ব্যবহৃত যুক্তি। (So *Stock remark, Stock joke,* etc.) **Stock-breeder**—যে ব্যক্তি গোমহিষাদি জন্তু পালন এবং পোষণ করে। **Stock-broker**—কোম্পানীর কাগজের দালাল, হুণ্ডীর দালাল। **Stock-car**—গো মহিষাদির জন্য খোলা গাড়ী। **Stockdove** — ইয়ুরোপীয় বন্যকপোত-বিশেষ। [এই কপোত হইতেই গৃহপালিত পারাবতের উদ্ভব হইয়াছে—এক সময়ে লোক এইরূপ বিশ্বাস করিত।] **Stock exchange**—কোম্পানীর কাগজের ক্রয়-বিক্রয় স্থল, কোম্পানীর কাগজের বাজার। **Stock-farm**—যে কৃষিক্ষেত্রে গৃহপালিত জন্তু উৎপাদন করা হয়। **Stock-farmer** — গৃহপালিত জন্তুর উৎপাদনের ব্যবসায়ে নিযুক্ত ব্যক্তি। **Stockfish** — লবণাক্ত এবং শুষ্কীকৃত মৎস্য; বিশেষতঃ রৌদ্রে শুষ্কীকৃত অলবণাক্ত কড মৎস্য। **Stock-gang**—একবারে অনেকগুলি তক্তা চিরিবার জন্য সাজ্জিত করাতশ্রেণী। **Stock-gilli flower**—পুষ্প গুল্মবিশেষ। **Stock-holder**—কোন কোম্পানীর অংশীদার। **Stock-in-trade** — কোন দোকানে মজুত বিক্রয়ের মাল; ব্যবসায়ের সরঞ্জাম। **Stock-jobber** — কোম্পানীর কাগজের ব্যবসায়ী। **Stock-list**—কোম্পানীর কাগজের মূল্যতালিকা। **Stock-lock**—একপ্রকার তালা। **Stock-man**—(অষ্ট্রেলিয়া) গোমহিষাদি জন্তুর রক্ষণাবেক্ষণে নিযুক্ত ব্যক্তি। **Stock-market**—Same as STOCK-EXCHANGE. **Stock-owl** — একপ্রকার বৃহদাকৃতি পেচক। **Stock-pot**—মাংসের ক্বাথ রাখার জন্য পাত্র। **Stock-rider**—(অষ্ট্রেলিয়া) গোমহিষাদির অশ্বারোহী পালক। **Stock-still** — স্থাণুবৎ, কাষ্ঠপুত্তলিকাবৎ। **Stock-taking**—নির্দ্দিষ্ট সময়ান্তে কোন দোকান প্রভৃতির মজুত মালাদির যে পরীক্ষা ও মূল্য নিরূপণ করা হয়। **Stock-whip**—রাখালদিগের একপ্রকার চাবুক (এইরূপ চাবুকের বাঁট ক্ষুদ্র থাকে)। **Stock-yard**—গোমহিষাদির জন্য প্রাঙ্গণ; বিশেষতঃ লৌহবর্ত্মের নিকটবর্ত্তী যে বৃতিবেষ্টিত প্রাঙ্গণে বিক্রয়ের, চালান দেওয়ার বা বধ করার পূর্ব্বে কিছুকালের জন্য গো, মহিষ, মেষ, শূকর, প্রভৃতি রক্ষিত হয়। **A laughing stock**—See LAUGH. **Lock, stock, and barrel**—Completely; সম্পূর্ণরূপে। **On the stocks**—Under construction; নির্ম্মাণাধীন। **Stocks and stones**—জড়পদার্থ সমূহ, অচেতন পদার্থ সমূহ। **Stock of anvil**—যে আধারের উপর নেয়াই স্থাপিত হয়, শূর্ম্মির অধিষ্ঠান। **The Stock Exchange** — লণ্ডন নগরীর কোম্পানীর কাগজের ব্যবসায়িগণের প্রধান কার্য্যালয়। **To make stock of**—To make gain from something; কোন কিছু হইতে লাভ করা। **To stock cards**—To arrange cards with a view to cheat an opponent; প্রতিপক্ষকে ঠকাইবার উদ্দেশ্যে তাস ভাঁজ করিয়া রাখা। **To stock down**—To sow as ploughed land with grass-seeds; কর্ষিত ক্ষেত্রে ঘাসের বীজ বপন করা। **To stock up**—(*Obs.*) To uproot; (অপ্রঃ) নির্ম্মূল করা, উৎপাটিত করা। **To take stock in**—To regard as valuable; to behave faithfully; মূল্যবান জ্ঞান করা; বিশ্বস্ততার সহিত ব্যবহার করা। **To take stock of**—To examine minutely; পুঙ্খানুপুঙ্খরূপে পরীক্ষা করা।

stŏck'-ade, *n.* & *v. t.* A defence or barrier constructed of trunks of trees or strong posts stuck in the ground, close to each other; an inclosure made with posts; সূক্ষ্মাগ্রকাষ্ঠনির্ম্মিত উচ্চ বৃতি, কাষ্ঠপ্রাচীর; খুঁটার প্রাচীর। *Verb t.* To surround or fortify with such barrier; উক্তরূপ বৃতি দ্বারা বেষ্টিত করা।

stŏck'-i-nĕt, *n.* An elastic, knit textile fabric of which stocking, under garments, etc. are made; গঞ্জি, মোজা, প্রভৃতির কাপড়।

stŏck'-ing, *n.* 1. A close-fitting knitted covering for the foot and leg; মোজা, পাদত্রাণ, পাদরক্ষক, অনুপদীনা, চরণাবরণ, চরণচ্ছদ। 2. A broad ring of colour on the lower part of the leg of a quadruped differently coloured from the rest of the body; চতুষ্পদ জন্তুর পদের নিম্নভাগে দেহের অপরাংশের বর্ণ হইতে ভিন্নবর্ণের প্রশস্ত বেষ্টনী। **—less,** *adj.* **Elastic stocking**—(অস্ত্রোপচারবিদ্যা) শিরার স্ফীতি, মাংসপেশীর মচকানি প্রভৃতির জন্য যে মোজার মত কাপড়ের তৈয়ারী আবরণ পরা হয়। **Stocking-frame** — মোজা, গঞ্জি প্রভৃতি বুনিবার তাঁত। **Stocking loam**—Same as STOCKING-FRAME. **Stocking-machine**—মোজার কল। **Stocking-weaver**—যে ব্যক্তি মোজা বুনে। **He stands six feet in his stockings** or **stocking feet**—জুতা ছাড়া মাপে ৬ ফুট হয়।

stŏck'-ȳ, stûg'-gȳ, *adjs.* (*Colloq.*) Stout; rather thick than tall or corpulent; (চলিত ভাষায়) হৃষ্টপুষ্ট; খর্ব্বকায় এবং হৃষ্টপুষ্ট। **Stock'-i-ly, Stug'-gi-ly,** *advs.* **Stock'-i-ness, Stug'-gi-ness,** *ns.*

stodge (stŏj) *v. i.* & *n.* 1. (*School slang*) To stuff with heavy food; to eat greedily; গুরুপাক দ্রব্যদ্বারা

উদরপূর্ণ করা ; পেটুকের মত খাওয়া। 2. To satiate ; পরিতৃপ্ত করা। *Noun.* 1. Heavy food ; গুরুপাক খাদ্য। 2. Full meal ; পূর্ণ ভোজন। 3. One who eats greedily ; যে ব্যক্তি পেটুকের মত আহার করে।

stodg'-ȳ (stŏj-), *adj.* 1. (Of food) Heavy ; গুরুপাক। 2. Muddy ; কাদাটে। 3. Short and thick ; খর্ব্বকায় এবং হৃষ্টপুষ্ট। 4. Stuffed ; গাদানো। 5. (Of book, style, etc.) Wanting in lightness ; (পুস্তক রচনা প্রভৃতি সম্পর্কে) লীলাপ্রবাহশূন্য, আড়ষ্ট। **—i-ness,** *n.*

stoep, *n.* (South Africa) A platform in front of a house ; (দক্ষিণ আফ্রিকা) গৃহের সম্মুখস্থ মঞ্চ।

Stō'-ĭc, *n.* & *adj.* 1. A disciple of the philosopher Zeno (342—270 B. C.) ; গ্রীক দার্শনিক জিনোর শিষ্য। [এই সম্প্রদায়ের দার্শনিকগণ সুখ দুঃখ সমজ্ঞান করিতেন। অতি দুঃখ কিম্বা অতি আনন্দেও ইঁহারা কখনও বিচলিত হইতেন না। ইঁহারা সর্ব্বেশ্বরবাদী ছিলেন। পরিণামে আত্মাও ধ্বংসপ্রাপ্ত হইবে, ইঁহারা এরূপ বিশ্বাস করিতেন। ইঁহারা অতি কঠোর নীতিমার্গ অনুসরণ করিতেন, তিতিক্ষাবাদী।] 2. A person not easily excited ; an apathetic person ; "A *Stoic* of the woods, a man without a tear" ; যে ব্যক্তি সহজে বিচলিত হয় না ; উদাসীন ব্যক্তি, উদাসীন, উদাসী। *Adj.* Pertaining to the Stoics or their teaching ; as, *Stoic* doctrine ; তিতিক্ষাবাদিসম্বন্ধীয়, তিতিক্ষাবাদসম্বন্ধীয়। **—i-cal,** *adj.* **—i-cal-ly,** *adv.* **—i-cism,** *n.* 1. The opinions and the maxims of the stoics ; তিতিক্ষাবাদ (হিঃ কোঃ)। 2. Impassiveness ; উদাসীনতা, ঔদাসীন্য, জিতেন্দ্রিয়তা, অক্ষুব্ধতা, নিস্পৃহতা, তিতিক্ষা, নিঃসঙ্গতা।

stōke, *v. t.* & *i.* To tend a fire, as with a stoker; to supply with fuel; আগুন উসকাইয়া দেওয়া ; কয়লা প্রভৃতি যোগান। *Verb i.* 1. To attend to and supply a furnace with fuel ; to act as a stoker ; চুল্লীতে কয়লা প্রভৃতি যোগান ; বাষ্পীয়যন্ত্র প্রভৃতির চুল্লীতে কয়লা দেওয়ার কার্য্য করা। 2. To take food hurriedly ; তাড়াতাড়ি আহার করা। **Stoke-hole**—জাহাজের চুল্লীকক্ষ।

stōk'-ēr, *n.* One that is employed to tend a furnace and to supply it with fuel ; যে ব্যক্তি জাহাজ প্রভৃতির চুল্লীকক্ষে কয়লা প্রদান করে। **Mechanical stoker**—জাহাজের চুল্লীকক্ষ প্রভৃতিতে কয়লা প্রদানের জন্য স্বয়ংবহযন্ত্র।

stō'-lă, *n.* A garment worn by a Roman woman over the tunic ; প্রাচীনকালের রোমক মহিলাগণের একপ্রকার প্রাবরণ।

stōle, *n.* 1. A long loose garment reaching to the feet worn by the matrons of ancient of Rome ; প্রাচীন রোমের গৃহিণীগণের পরিধেয় একপ্রকার আপাদলম্বী প্রাবরণ। 2. A long narrow scarf worn round the neck, with the ends hanging down, by clergymen of the Anglicans and Roman Catholic churches ; রোম্যান ক্যাথলিক এবং এংলিক্যান ধর্ম্মসংঘের যাজকগণ কর্ত্তৃক পরিহিত গলদেশ হইতে উভয় স্কন্ধের উপর দিয়া প্রায় জানু পর্য্যন্ত লম্বিত অপ্রশস্ত উত্তরীয় বিশেষ। [ডীকনগণ এইরূপ উত্তরীয় কেবল বামস্কন্ধের উপরে পরিধান করিয়া থাকেন।] **Stoled,** *adj.* **Groom of the stole**—See GROOM.

stōle, *n.* Same as STOLON (which see).

stōle, stōl'-en (-n), *p. p.* & *p. t.* of STEAL (which see).

stŏl'-ĭd, *adj.* Stupid ; impassive ; dull ; জড়বুদ্ধি ; উদাসীন, আবেগশূন্য ; ঢিমা। **Sto-lid'-i-ty,** *n.* **—ly,** *adv.* **—ness,** *n.*

stō'-lŏn, stōle, *ns.* 1. (*Bot.*) A creeping sucker which sends down roots ; জননশাখা (সাঃ পঃ)। 2. (*Zool.*) A rootlike-creeping growth ; (জন্তুবিদ্যা) শিকড়বৎ লতানিয়া অঙ্গ। **—ate,** *adj.* **—lo-nif'-er-ous,** *adj.*

stō'-mă, (*pl.* STOMATA) A breathing pore or orifice esp. in the epidermis of a leaf ; শ্বাসরন্ধ্র, বিশেষতঃ পত্রত্বকের শ্বাসরন্ধ্র, বায়ুকূপ (সাঃ পঃ), নাসারন্ধ্র (ঐ), তুণ্ডক (ঐ), শ্বাসরন্ধ্র (ঐ), পত্রকূপ (প্রবোধ)।

stŏm'-ăch, *n.* & *v. t.* 1. A membranous sac, serving as the principle organ of digestion ; পাকস্থালী, পকাশয় (সুশ্রুঃ), অন্নস্থালী, পক্বাধান, আমাশয়, (cf. তথৈবামাশয় গতং পশ্চাৎপিত্তাশয়ং ব্রজেৎ—প্রপঞ্চ-সারতন্ত্র—২য় পটল।) 2. Appetite ; as, he has good *stomach* for meat ; ক্ষুধা, বুভুক্ষা। 3. (*Erron.*) Belly ; abdomen ; উদর ; নিম্নোদর, তলপেট। 4. Taste ; readiness ; spirit ; as, he had no *stomach* for the fight ; রুচি ; তৎপরতা ; উৎসাহ। *Verb t.* 1. To put up with ; "English theatrical audiences, who will not *stomach* the uncompromising realism with which contemporary French dramatists set forth the workings of the deadlier sins" ; সহ্য করা, সহা। 2. To eat with relish ; রুচির সহিত আহার করা। **—less,** *adj.* **—ful,** *adj.* **Stomach'-al,** *adj.* **Stomach-ache**—উদরবেদনা। **Stomach-cough**—উদরের প্রদাহজনিত কাশি। **Stomach-pump**—পাকস্থলী শূন্য করার জন্য বা উহাতে তরলপদার্থ প্রবিষ্ট করার জন্য একপ্রকার পিচকারী। **Stomach-staggers**—পাকস্থলীর অবসন্নতাহেতু অশ্বের সন্ন্যাসরোগ। **Stomach-tooth**—শিশুদিগের শ্বাদন্তবিশেষ। **Stomach-tube**—একপ্রকার নল—যাহা কণ্ঠনালীর ভিতর দিয়া প্রবিষ্ট করিয়া পাকস্থলী ধৌত বা বায়ুশূন্য করা হয়। **Proud or high stomach**—উদ্ধত ভাব।

stŏm'-ăch-ēr, *n.* 1. (*Hist.*) An ornamental article of dress worn by women on the chest or breast;

(ইতিহাস) স্ত্রীলোকের বক্ষ বা স্তনোপরি পরিহিত কারুকার্য্যখচিত বস্ত্রখণ্ড। 2. A large brooch worn on the bodice of a woman ; স্ত্রীলোকের কঞ্চুলিকার উপর পরিহিত বৃহৎ বক্ষসূচি।

stō-măch′-ic, *adj.* & *n.* 1. Of, or pertaining to, the stomach ; পাকস্থালীসম্বন্ধীয়। 2. Strengthening the stomach ; promoting digestion or appetite ; অগ্নিবর্দ্ধক, অগ্নিদীপক, রুচিকর, দীপনীয় (ঠাকুরঃ) ; রুচিবর্দ্ধক, ক্ষুধাবর্দ্ধক, অগ্নিসন্দীপন, পাচক, পাচন, অগ্নিদীপন (সুশ্রুঃ), রবিদীপ্তিকর (রাজনিঃ), অনল-দীপন (মঃ উঃ)। *Noun.* A medicine which strengthens the stomach, and excites its action ; অগ্নিবর্দ্ধক ঔষধ, রুচিবর্দ্ধক ঔষধ, ক্ষুধাবর্দ্ধক ঔষধ।

stō-măp′-ō dă, *n.* An order of marine mala-costracous crustaceans, with six to eight pairs of legs near the mouth ; এক-জাতীয় খোলকী প্রাণী উহাদের মুখের কাছে ৬ কি ৮ জোড়া পদ থাকে, উদরপদী।

stŏm-ă-tī′-tis, *n.* Inflammation of the mouth ; মুখগহ্বরের প্রদাহ।

stŏm-ă-tō-găs′-tric, *adj.* Pertaining to the mouth and the stomach ; মুখগহ্বর এবং পাকস্থালীসম্বন্ধীয়।

stŏm′-ă-tŏl′-ō-ġy̆, *n.* Science of the mouth and its diseases; মুখ এবং মুখরোগসম্পর্কীয় বিজ্ঞান, মুখরোগ-বিজ্ঞান।

stŏm-ă-tō-plăs′-tic, *adj.* Pertaining to the formation of a mouth ; মুখগঠনসম্বন্ধীয়।

stŏm′-ă-tō-scōpe, *n.* An apparatus for examining the cavity of the mouth ; মুখগহ্বর পরিবীক্ষণের জন্য যন্ত্রবিশেষ, মুখবীক্ষণ।

stōne, *n.*, *adj.* & *v. t.* 1. Any loose mass of earthy matter of considerable hardness ; প্রস্তর, পাথর, পাষাণ, শিলা, অশ্ম [Syn. গ্রাবা, দৃষৎ, দৃষৎ, পারাক্ক, পারটীট, মৃন্ময়, কাচক, উপল।] 2. A gem ; পাথর, মূল্যবান প্রস্তর, মণি। 3. A concretion in the kidneys or bladder ; মূত্রাশয়ের পাথর, পাথরী, বৃহদশ্মরি (সাঃ পঃ), আশ্মরি (ঐ)। 4 The nut of a drupe or stone-fruit ; আঁটি, বিঁচি। 5. Testicle ; অণ্ডকোষ, বিঁচি (*colloq.*)। 6. A weight which is legally 14 lbs but in practice varies with the articles weighed ; ১৪ পাউণ্ড ওজন, বস্তুভেদে এই ওজনের তারতম্য হইয়া থাকে। 7. Pellet of hail; শিলা, করকা। 8. (*Obs.*) The glass of mirror ; a mirror ; (অপ্রঃ) আয়নার কাচ ; আয়না। 9. Symbol of hardness ; "He is a *stone*, a very pebble *stone*, and has no more piety in him than a dog" ; কঠিন বস্তু। 10. A grave stone ; সমাধিপ্রস্তর। 11. (*Print.*) A stand or table originally made of stone, now usually of metal, to impose types on ; মুদ্রাযন্ত্রে ব্যবহৃত শিলাদি রচিত অক্ষর-বিন্যাসফলক। *Adj.* Made of stone ; stone-like ; পাষাণনির্ম্মিত, পাষাণময় ; পাষাণবৎ। *Verb t.* 1. To pellet with stones ; প্রস্তরখণ্ড নিক্ষেপ করা। 2. To kill with stones ; শিলা বর্ষণে নিহত করা। 3. To free from stone ; as, to *stone* raisins ; বিচি ছাড়ান। 4. To pave with stones ; পাষাণাচ্ছাদিত করা, পাষাণ-বদ্ধ করা, পাথর দ্বারা বাঁধা। **Stone′-less**, *adj.* **Stone-axe**—প্রস্তর ছেদনের জন্য একপ্রকার স্থূলকোণী দ্বিধারবিশিষ্ট কুঠার। **Stone-blind**—সম্পূর্ণ অন্ধ। **Stone-blue**—শ্বেতসার কিম্বা খড়িচূর্ণের সহিত নীলের মিশ্রণ। **Stone-boiling**—কোন কোন অসভ্য জাতির মধ্যে প্রচলিত উত্তপ্ত প্রস্তরখণ্ডসমূহ জলে নিক্ষেপ পূর্ব্বক মাংস প্রভৃতি সিদ্ধ করার রীতি। **Stone-borer**—বিভিন্ন প্রকার শম্বুকাদি প্রাণীর নাম, পাষাণভেদক। **Stone-bread**—Same as SAXIFRAGE. **Stone-buck**—Same as STEENBOK. **Stone-butter**—একপ্রকার ফিটকিরি। **Stone-cast**—Same as A STONE'S CAST OR THROW (below). **Stone-chat** — ইয়ুরোপীয় গায়ক-পক্ষিবিশেষ। **Stone-coal**—Same as ANTHRACITE. **Stone-cold** — পাষাণশীতল। **Stonecrop** — প্রাচীর এবং পাষাণাদির উপরি জাত একপ্রকার বল্লরী। **Stone-curlew** — একপ্রকার তিত্তির পক্ষী। **Stone-cutter** — পাথর-কাটা মিস্ত্রী, প্রস্তরশিল্পী। **Stone-dead**—সম্পূর্ণ মৃত। **Stone-deaf**—সম্পূর্ণ বধির। **Stone-eater**—Same as STONE-BORER (above). **Stone-edifice**—পাষাণ-নির্ম্মিত সৌধ, মন্দির (cf. পাষাণৈ নির্ম্মিতং যত্তদ্ গৃহম্ মন্দিরং স্মৃতম্—বিশ্বকর্ম্মা-প্রকাশ। **Stone-fern**—পাষাণে জাত একপ্রকার গুল্ম। **Stone-fly**—বড়শীর টোপস্বরূপ ব্যবহৃত শিলাতলে প্রাপ্ত কীটবিশেষ। **Stone-fruit**—যে সকল ফলের বীজসমূহ কোমলফলশস্যসমাচ্ছাদিত কঠিন আবরণের ভিতর বদ্ধ থাকে ; যে সকল ফলের আঁঠি কোমল ফলশস্য দ্বারা আচ্ছাদিত থাকে। **Stone-gall**—বিচিত্র বালুকাপ্রস্তরে প্রাপ্ত কর্দ্দমপিণ্ড। **Stone-horse**—(অপ্রঃ) অচ্ছিন্নমুষ্ক অশ্ব, জননাশ্ব। **Stone-man** — Same as CAIRN (which see). **Stone-mason**—প্রস্তরশিল্পী, প্রস্তরস্থপতি, শিলা-শিল্পী। **Stone-parsley**—বৃতি রচনার উপযোগী গুল্মবিশেষ। **Stone-pine**—ইতালী দেশের দক্ষিণাংশে জাত একপ্রকার সরল বৃক্ষ—ইহার শাখারাজি ছত্রের মত প্রসারিত থাকে। **Stone-pit**—পাথরের খনি। **Stone-plover**—একপ্রকার তিত্তির পক্ষী। **Stone-rag**—একজাতীয় শৈবাল। **Stone-rue**—একপ্রকার পর্ণাঙ্গ। **Stone-saw**—বালুকার সাহায্যে পাষাণ ছেদনের জন্য করাতের কাঠামে স্থাপিত অদন্তরিত লৌহ-ফলক। **Stone-seed**—একপ্রকার গুল্ম। **Stone-snipe** — উত্তর আমেরিকার একপ্রকার বৃহৎজাতীয় কাদাখোচা পাখী। **Stone-throwing**—প্রতিবেশীর দোষ ধরণ, পরছিদ্রান্বেষণ। **Stone-walling**—(*Cricket*) Excessively cautious beating ; (ক্রীকেট ক্রীড়ায়) অতি সাবধানে ব্যাট চালনা। (*Austrl.*) Obstruction in parliamentay works ; (অষ্ট্রেলিয়া) নানা বাজে তর্কে সময় নষ্ট করিয়া পার্লেমেণ্টের কার্য্যে বাধা

প্রদান। **Stone-ware**—পাথরের জিনিষ। **Stone-weed**—Same as STONE-SEED. **Stone-work** — ভাস্কর্য্য, পাথরের কাজ, প্রস্তরশিল্প, শিলাশিল্প। **Stonewort**—বিভিন্ন প্রকার গুল্মের সাধারণ নাম। **A heart of stone** — পাষাণহৃদয়। **Artificial-stone**—চূণবালি এবং বিভিন্ন প্রকার প্রস্তরচূর্ণসহযোগে প্রস্তুত একপ্রকার কৃত্রিম প্রস্তর। **A stone's cast** or **throw**—A small distance ; অল্প দুর (একশত গজ কিম্বা তদপেক্ষা কিঞ্চিদধিক)। **Bristol stone**—একপ্রকার মূল্যবান রঙ্গীন বা অরঙ্গীণ স্ফটিক-প্রস্তর। **Meteoric stone** — উল্কাপ্রস্তর। **Philosophers' stone**—See under PHILOSOPHER. **Shower of stones** — প্রস্তরবৃষ্টি, শিলাবর্ষণ। **Stones for bread**—Something quite different from what was expected and which embitters one's mind instead of giving relief; রুটীর পরিবর্ত্তে প্রস্তরখণ্ড, প্রার্থিত বস্তুর পরিবর্ত্তে এমন কোন বস্তু যাহাতে অভাবের নিবৃত্তি করার পরিবর্ত্তে প্রাণে ব্যথা প্রদান করে। **Stones will cry out**—The wrong is deep enough to move even stones to pity ; পাষাণ পর্য্যন্ত বিগলিত হইবে, পাষাণ পর্য্যন্ত দ্রবীভূত হইবে। **The stone age**—মানবসভ্যতার যে যুগে প্রস্তরের অস্ত্রশস্ত্র ব্যবহৃত হইত, প্রস্তরযুগ। **Those who live in glass houses should not throw stones**—See under GLASS. **To break stones**—To earn one's livelihood by breaking stones for road-metalling ; রাস্তা বাঁধার জন্য পাথর ভাঙ্গিয়া জীবিকা অর্জ্জন করা। **To cast** or **throw a stone** or **stones at**—To slander ; নিন্দা করা, কুৎসা করা, অপবাদ করা। **To leave no stone unturned**—To spare no efforts ; কোন চেষ্টার ত্রুটি না করা, প্রাণপণ চেষ্টা করা।

stōn'-y̆, *adj.* & *adv.* **1.** Pertaining to, abounding in, or like stone ; প্রস্তরসম্বন্ধীয়, পাষাণবহুল, প্রস্তরবৎ, পাষাণবৎ। **2.** Inflexible ; pitiless ; as, a *stony* heart ; hard ; cold ; as, *stony* stare ; অনমনীয় ; নিষ্করুণ, পাষাণ হৃদয় ; কঠিন; আবেগশূন্য, আবেগহীন। **3.** Petrifying ; পাষাণকারী। ***Adv.*** Utterly (only in *Stony-broke*) ; সম্পূর্ণরূপে, পুরা। **–i-ly**, *adv.* **–i-ness**, *n.* **Stony heart**—Obdurate or unfeeling heart ; পাষাণেগড়া মন, পাষাণের মত হৃদয়, কঠিন মন। Hard case or interior ; কঠিন অভ্যন্তর ভাগ।

stōōd, *p. t.* & *p. p.* of STAND (which see).

stōōk, *n.* & *v. t.* (Same as STOCK in the sense of *corn-sheaves*).

stōōl, *n.* & *v. i.* **1.** A seat without back and with three or four legs, to be used by one person ; কাষ্ঠাসন, জলচৌকি। **2.** A bishop's seat or see ; বিশপের আসন, শ্রীপাট বা গদী। **3.** The seat used in evacuating the bowels ; যে আসনের উপর বসিয়া মলত্যাগ করিতে হয়। **4.** A discharge from the bowels ; faeces ; as, the doctor examined the patient's *stool* ; মলত্যাগ ; মল, বাহ্যি। **5.** The stump or root of a tree that throws shoots ; a cluster of roots arising out of a stump ; ছিন্নাগ্র বৃক্ষকাণ্ড হইতে উদ্গত অঙ্কুরগুচ্ছ ; যে ছিন্নাগ্র বৃক্ষকাণ্ড বা বৃক্ষ-শিকড় হইতে নবাঙ্কুরসমূহ উদ্গত হইয়া থাকে। **6.** A pole or a piece of wood to which a bird is attached to decoy other birds ; যে দণ্ড বা কাষ্ঠখণ্ডে অপর পক্ষীকে প্রলুব্ধ করিয়া আনার জন্য কোন পক্ষী স্থাপিত হইয়া থাকে। **7.** Window-sill ; জানালার দেহলী। ***Verb i.*** **1.** To evacuate the bowels ; মলত্যাগ করা, বাহ্যি করা। **2.** To throw up shoots from the stump root ; ছিন্নাগ্র বৃক্ষকাণ্ড বা শিকড় হইতে নবাঙ্কুর উদ্গত হওয়া। **3.** To decoy birds by a stool ; দণ্ড বা কাষ্ঠখণ্ডে পক্ষী রাখিয়া অপর পক্ষীকে প্রলুব্ধ করিয়া আনা। **Stool-ball**—ক্রীকেটের মত একপ্রকার খেলা—এইরূপ খেলা অদ্যাপি ইংলণ্ডের অন্তঃপাতী সাসেক্সের লোকেরা বিশেষতঃ বালিকারা খেলিয়া থাকে। **Stool-pigeon** — অন্য পক্ষীকে প্রলুব্ধ করিয়া আনার নিমিত্ত কপোত ; যে ব্যক্তি অন্য ব্যক্তিকে ভুলাইয়া আনে ; পুলিশের বেসরকারী গোয়েন্দা। **Stool of repentance** — স্কটলণ্ডদেশে ভজনালয়ের যে কাষ্ঠাসনে উপবিষ্ট করাইয়া পূর্ব্বে কুমারীদূষণকারী প্রভৃতিকে তিরস্কৃত করা হইত (বর্ত্তমানে লক্ষণায় ব্যবহৃত হয়)। **To fall beween two stools**—To fail through hesitating between two courses, দু নৌকায় পা দেওয়ার দরুণ পতিত হওয়া (cf. দুনৌকায় দুপা দিলে পড়ে যাবে অগাধ জলে)।

stōōp, *v. t., i.* & *n.* To lean or bend the body forward or downward ; নোওয়ান, ঝুঁকা, অবনত করা। ***Verb i.*** **1.** To bend forward or downwards ; ঝুঁকিয়া পড়া, নত করা, অবনত করা, হেঁট করা। **2.** To deign ; to lower one's self ; হীনতা স্বীকারপূর্ব্বক অনুগ্রহ করা ; অবনত করা। **3.** To submit ; বশীভূত হওয়া, বশ্যতা স্বীকার করা, মস্তক অবনত করা। **4.** To pounce ; আপতিত হওয়া, ছোঁ মারা। ***Noun.*** **1.** The act of stooping ; অবনমন। **2.** A habitual bending of the neck or shoulders ; মস্তক বা স্কন্ধের স্বাভাবিক নতি। **3.** Condescension ; humiliation ; হীনতাস্বীকার ; হেঁট, নতি স্বীকার। **4.** (*Archaic*) The fall of a bird on its prey ; ছোঁ। **Stoop'-ing**, *adj.* **Stoop'-ing-ly**, *adv.*

stōōp, *n.* Same as STOUP (which see).

stŏp, *v. i.* & *t.* **1.** To cease to go on ; থামা, বন্ধ হওয়া। **2.** (*Colloq.*) To stay ; to remain ; as, to *stop* in Calcutta ; (চলিত ভাষায়) অল্পদিবস অবস্থান করা, কিছুকাল বাস করা, থাকা। ***Verb t.*** **1.** To close by stuffing, filling, etc. ; কোনকিছু গুঁজিয়া বা ভরিয়া বন্ধ করা।

2. To impede; গতিরোধ করা। 3. To cause to cease working; as, to *stop* an engine; থামান, বন্ধ করা, রুদ্ধ করা, আটকান। 4. To suppress; to check; রোধ করা, বন্ধ করা; বাধা দেওয়া, প্রতিবন্ধক দেওয়া, প্রতিরোধ করা। 5. To discontinue; বিরত হওয়া। 6. (*Mus.*) To regulate the sound of, as musical strings, by pressing them against the finger-board; বাদ্যযন্ত্রের ধ্বনি নিয়মিত করা। 6. To parry; as, to *stop* a blow; আট্‌কান। 7. To cut off; as, to *stop* one's expense; to postpone; as, to *stop* a trial; সঙ্কোচ করা; স্থগিত করা। 8. To make fast; শক্ত করা, দৃঢ় করা। 9. To punctuate; কমা, সেমিকোলন প্রভৃতি দেওয়া। **Stop′-page**, *n.* 1. The act of stopping; গতিরোধ করণ। 2. The state of being stopped; গতিরুদ্ধাবস্থা। 3. Obstruction; বাধা, প্রতিবন্ধক, প্রতিরোধ। **Stop′-pered**—ঢাকনিদার। **Stop-thief!**—ঐ চোর ধর! **To stop down**—(*Photog.*) To obscure part of a lens with a diaphragm; পরকলার কতকাংশ পাতলা পর্দ্দাদ্বারা ঢাকিয়া ফেলা। **To stop a gap**—To repair a defect; কোনরূপ ছিদ্র মেরামত করা। To serve to meet a temporary end; তখনকার মত একটা ব্যবস্থা করা। **To stop a tooth**—To fill a cavity in the tooth with gold etc.; স্বর্ণ প্রভৃতি দ্বারা দন্তের ছিদ্র রোধ করা। **To stop off**—(*Moulding*) To fill in the part of a mould not necessary for present use with sand; (ছাঁচের কাজ) ছাঁচের উপস্থিত কার্য্যের জন্য অনাবশ্যক যে অংশ তাহা বালুকাদ্বারা পূর্ণ করা। To interrupt one's progress by a short stay in some place; কোন স্থানে অল্পকাল অবস্থান করিয়া গন্তব্যস্থানে পৌঁছিতে বিলম্ব করা। **To stop one's breath**—To kill one by strangling; কাহাকে গলা টিপিয়া মারা। **To stop one's ears**—To refuse to listen; কর্ণপাত করিতে অসম্মত হওয়া। **To stop out**—To cover parts of a block not meant to be acted upon by acid with a coating of something; চিত্রফলকের যে সকল অংশ দ্রাবকের ক্রিয়া হইতে রক্ষা করিতে হইবে তাহা কোন কিছুর লেপদ্বারা আচ্ছাদিত করা। (*Colloq.*) To pass the night away from one's house; (চলিত ভাষায়) বাহিরে কোনস্থানে রাত্রি কাটান। **To stop payment**—To be a bankrupt; দাওলিয়া হওয়া। **To stop short**—To cease suddenly; হঠাৎ থামা। **To stop the mouth**—To silence; to confound; মুখ বন্ধ করা; বিভ্রান্ত করা।

stŏp, *n.* 1. Act of stopping; check; থামান; বাধা, গতিরোধ, নিরোধ। 2. Obstacle; বাধা, প্রতিবন্ধক, বিঘ্ন, অন্তরায়। 3. (*Mus.*) A series of pipes in an organ giving sounds of a distinctive tone and quality; অর্গেনযন্ত্রের যে সকল নলশ্রেণী হইতে বিভিন্ন প্রকার ধ্বনি উৎপাদিত হয়, খুঁটি। 4. One of the vent holes of a musical instrument by the opening or closing of which musical sounds may be regulated and modified; the place in a stringed instrument pressed on for the production of musical sound; বাদ্যযন্ত্রের ছিদ্রবিশেষ—যাহা বন্ধ ও উন্মুক্ত করিয়া যন্ত্রের ধ্বনি পরিবর্ত্তিত ও নিয়মিত করা যাইতে পারে; তন্ত্রীবিশিষ্ট বাদ্যযন্ত্রের যে অংশে চাপ দিয়া ধ্বনি উৎপাদন করিতে হয়। 5. A point or mark in writing or for regulating the necessary pauses; বিরামচিহ্ন। 6. (*Fig.*) Manner of speech; (লক্ষণায়) বাগভঙ্গী। 7. (*Photog.*, *Opt.*) Diaphragm; (আলোকচিত্র এবং দৃষ্টি-বিজ্ঞান) পরকলা আচ্ছাদক লঘু আবরণ। 8. See MUTE, 3. **Stopcock**—জলের কলের চোঙ্গার মুখনল, ষ্টপ কক (হিঃ কোঃ)। **Stop-cylinder**—একপ্রকার মুদ্রাযন্ত্র। **Stop-gap**—সাময়িক উপায়। **Stop-motion**—যন্ত্র বিকল হইয়া গেলে, যে কলদ্বারা উহা আপনা আপনি বন্ধ হইয়া যায়। **Stop-order**—কোম্পানীর কাগজ কোন নির্দ্দিষ্ট মূল্যে ক্রয় বা বিক্রয় করার জন্য দালালের প্রতি আদেশ। **Stop-press**—মুদ্রণ কার্য্য আরব্ধ হইলে যে সকল সংবাদ পত্রস্থ করা হয়। **Stop-valve**—গুঁজ। **Stop-watch**—যে টেঁক ঘড়িতে এক সেকেণ্ডের ভগ্নাংশ পরিমিত সময় প্রদর্শিত হয় এবং প্রকৃত সময় সূচনার জন্য যাহার কাঁটা যে কোন মুহূর্ত্তে বন্ধ করা যাইতে পারে। **To come to a full stop**—To come to a standstill; বন্ধ হওয়া, থামা।

stŏp′-per (-ėr), *n.* & *v. t.* 1. One who, or that which, stops; রোধকারী, রোধক। 2. A cork or plug used for closing the mouth of a bottle; ছিপি। 3. A short piece of rope used for making fast; কোন কিছু শক্ত করিয়া বাঁধার জন্য খাটো দড়া। *Verb t.* To close or secure with a stopper; ছিপিদ্বারা বন্ধ করা। **Tobacco stopper**—কলিকায় তামাক সাজিবার জন্য একপ্রকার কল।

stŏp′-ple (-l), *n.* & *v. t.* That which stops or closes the mouth of a vessel; a stopper; ঢাকনি; ছিপি। *Verb t.* To close with a stopple; ঢাকনি দ্বারা ঢাকা, ছিপিদ্বারা বন্ধ করা।

stō′-răx, *n.* 1. An aromatic resinous substance resembling benzoin; শিলাকুসুম, শিলাপুষ্প, (ওয়াট), লোবান (খোরী), শিলাদদ্রু, শৈলাজ, গিরিপুষ্পক, শিলোদ্ভব, বৃদ্ধ, স্থাবর, পলিত, জীর্ণ, কালানুসার্য্যক, কালানুসারিত, কালানুসার্য্য, শিলোথ, শৈলাখ্য, শীতল, শৈল-নির্যাস, অশ্মপুষ্প, শিলাজ, শিলাভব, শীতপুষ্পক [Arab. *Mayah*; Chin. *Peh-kiau-hiang*, *fung-hiang-chi*, *su-hoh-yu*, *su-hoh-hiang*; Germ. *styrax-broom*; It. *storace*;

Sp. *azumber* (ওষাট্)]। **2.** The tree yielding this ; যে বৃক্ষ হইতে উক্ত প্রকার রজন নিঃসৃত হয়। **Liquid storax**—শিলারস, কপিতৈল (ভাবঃ প্রঃ)। [Malay, *rasa mala* ; Arab. *mayah, sailah*].

stōre, *n.* & *v. t.* **1.** A supply ; a hoard ; stock ; articles, especially of food, provided for some special purpose ; supplies, as of provisions, ammunition, arms, clothing, and the like for an army, ship, etc. ; সরবরাহ ; সঞ্চয় ; ভাণ্ডার ; কোন বিশেষ উদ্দেশ্যে যে সমস্ত জিনিষপত্র বিশেষতঃ খাদ্যদ্রব্য সরবরাহ করা হয় ; জাহাজ পল্টন ইত্যাদির জন্য খাদ্যসম্ভার, বারুদ, অস্ত্রশস্ত্র, পোষাক ইত্যাদির সরবরাহ। **2.** (*Obs.*) Abundance ; প্রাচুর্য্য, বাহুল্য, ভূয়িষ্ঠতা। **3.** A storehouse ; a warehouse ; a magazine ; ভাণ্ডারগৃহ ; গুদামঘর, মালখানা ; অস্ত্রাগার। **4.** A shop ; দোকান, বিপণি। **5.** A large shop where miscellaneous goods are sold ; as Army and Navy *stores* ; যে বৃহৎ বিপণিতে বিভিন্ন প্রকার জিনিষ বিক্রীত হয়, পণ্যভাণ্ডার। ***Verb t.*** **1.** To collect ; to accumulate ; to replenish ; সংগ্রহ করা ; সঞ্চিত করা ; পুনরায় পূর্ণ করা। **2.** To deposit in a store, warehouse, or other buildings for preservation ; ভাণ্ডারজাত করা, গুদামজাত করা। **3.** To contain ; ধারণ করা। **Stor′-a-ble,** *adj.* **Stor′-age,** *n.* **1.** The act of depositing in a store or warehouse for safe-keeping ; ভাণ্ডারজাত করণ, গুদামজাত করণ। **2.** The price for keeping of goods in store ; গুদাম ভাড়া। **4.** Space for the safe-keeping of goods; ভাণ্ডারে মাল রাখার স্থান। **Storage-battery**—তাড়িত সঞ্চায়ক বিদ্যুদ্‌বটমালা। **Store clothes** — Ready-made clothes ; কাটাকাপড়। **Store-house**—ভাণ্ডার, ভাণ্ডার গৃহ। **Store-keeper**—ভাণ্ডাররক্ষক ; (মার্কিন যুক্তরাজ্যে) দোকানদার, ভাণ্ডারী, ভাণ্ডারাধ্যক্ষ। **Store-room**—ভাণ্ডারগৃহ, ভাণ্ডার। **Store-ship**—Ships carrying stores for fleet, garrison, etc. ; সৈন্যদল, পোতবহর প্রভৃতির জন্য আবশ্যক দ্রব্যসম্ভারবাহী জাহাজ। **Marine stores**—পুরাতন জাহাজের উপাদানসমূহ। **In store**—Laid up in readiness ; as, I have a surprise *in store* for you ; about to come ; destined ; সঞ্চিত ; আসন্ন ; ভাগ্যে নির্দ্দিষ্ট। **To set store by** or **on**—To regard as valuable ; to give a high place ; মূল্যবান মনে করা ; উচ্চ স্থান দেওয়া।

stō′-rey (-rĭ), **—rȳ,** *ns.* **1.** Subdivision of the height of a house ; অট্টালিকা প্রভৃতির তল, তালা, ভূমি (cf. সপ্তভূমিক প্রাসাদ)। **Story-post**—An upright post supporting a beam on which rests a floor or wall ; ছাদের কড়িকাষ্ঠের অবলম্বনস্বরূপ কাষ্ঠখণ্ড। **Upper story**—উপরের তালা ; (লক্ষণায়) মস্তিষ্ক। **Wrong in the upper story**—Head-cracked ; মাথা পাগলা।

stōr′-gē, *n.* The strong instinctive affection which animals have for their parents ; পিতামাতার প্রতি অনুরাগ।

stō′-ri-at-ēd, *adj.* Decorated with ornamental and illustrative designs ; কারুকার্য্য খচিত, লতাপত্রপুষ্পাদির চিত্র দ্বারা পরিশোভিত।

stō′-ried (-rĭd), *adj.* **1.** Painted or adorned in any way with scene from stories or history ; "*Storied* urn" : "The trophied arches, *storied* halls, invade ;" নানাপ্রকার ঐতিহাসিক বা উপন্যাসিক আলেখ্য দ্বারা চিত্রিত। **2.** Furnished with, or having, stories ; গল্পসমন্বিত, গল্পবিশিষ্ট। **3.** Celebrated in legends ; উপকথায় প্রসিদ্ধ।

stō-ri-ette′ (-ĕt), *n.* A little story ; a short tale ; ক্ষুদ্র গল্প ; ক্ষুদ্র কাহিনী।

stŏrk, *n.* A large wading marsh-bird of passage, allied to the heron ; হাড়গিলা (*Leptoptilos argala* = Gigantic stork), চন্দনা (*Leptoptilos Javonica* = Crested stork),

White-stork.

মদনচূড় (*ib.*) মদনটাকি (*ib.*)। **King-Stork**—অত্যাচারী রাজা। **Stork's-bill**—একপ্রকার গুল্ম।

stŏrm, *n., v. i.* & *t.* **1.** A violent commotion or disturbance of the atmosphere with wind, rain, snow or hail, thunder and lightning ; ঝড়, ঝটিকা, তুফান, ঝঞ্ঝা, ঝঞ্ঝাবাত, চণ্ডবাত, প্রভঞ্জন। **2.** A civil, political, domestic tumult or commotion ; "Far more terrible to me than all the dangers of the *storm* itself" ; বিক্ষোভ, বিপ্লব, তুমুলকাণ্ড। **3.** A heavy shower or fall ; "Rattling *storms* of arrows barbed with fire" ; বৃষ্টি, বর্ষণ। **4.** A violent assault on a fortified place or strong position ; দুর্গাদি প্রচণ্ডবেগে আক্রমণ, প্রচণ্ড আক্রমণ। **5.** A great disaster or calamity ; "A brave man struggling in the *storms* of fate" ; মহাবিপদ, ঘোর দুর্ঘটনা। ***Verb i.*** **1.** To blow with violence ; to rain, hail, snow, and the like especially with violence ; প্রবলবেগে প্রবাহিত হওয়া ; ঝটিকা প্রবাহিত হওয়া, ঝড় বওয়া, তুফান ছুটা, প্রবলবেগে বৃষ্টি হওয়া, প্রবল শিলাপাত হওয়া। **2.** To rage ;

to be in a violent passion ; তর্জ্জন গর্জ্জন করা, ধমকান ; ক্রোধাবিষ্ট হওয়া, ক্রোধে আত্মহারা হওয়া। **3.** To rush about impetuously ; as, the mob *stormed* through the street ; প্রচণ্ডবেগে চতুর্দ্দিকে ধাবিত হওয়া। ***Verb t.*** To take by assault ; as, to *storm* a fort ; প্রচণ্ডবেগে আক্রমণপূর্ব্বক অধিকার করা। **Storm-beaten**—ঝটিকাসংক্ষুব্ধ, ঝঞ্ঝাহত। **Storm-bound** — ঝটিকা হেতু কোন স্থান ত্যাগ করিতে অসমর্থ, ঝটিকাবদ্ধ। **Storm-card**—যে নকসা দ্বারা পোতচালক ঝটিকার প্রভাবক্ষেত্রের কেন্দ্রস্থল নির্ণয়ে সাহায্য প্রাপ্ত হয়। **Storm-centre**—ঝটিকার প্রভাবক্ষেত্রের কেন্দ্রস্থল, ঘূর্ণিবাতে যে কেন্দ্রবিন্দুতে বায়ু কুণ্ডলিত ভাবে প্রবাহিত হয়; (লক্ষণায়) যুদ্ধ প্রভৃতির সঙ্কুলস্থান, আন্দোলনের প্রধান বিষয়। **Storm-cloud**—যে মেঘ হইতে ঝঞ্ঝা প্রবাহিত হয় ; (লক্ষণায়) যে অবস্থা হইতে তুমুলকাণ্ডের আশঙ্কা করা যায় (cf. প্রলয় মেঘ)। **Storm-cock**—এক জাতীয় পক্ষী। **Storm-cone**—প্রবল ঝটিকা সূচনার জন্য উত্তোলিত আলকাতরা মাখানো ক্যাম্বিস কাপড়ে তৈরী একপ্রকার মোচাকার চিহ্ন। [এইরূপ চিহ্ন খাড়া করিয়া দিলে উত্তর দিকে ও উল্টাইয়া দিলে দক্ষিণ দিক্ হইতে বাতাস বহিবে এইরূপ সূচিত হয়।] **Storm-door**—ঝটিকা বা প্রবল শীতের প্রকোপ হইতে রক্ষা পাওয়ার জন্য অতিরিক্ত বহির্ব্বর্ত্তী দ্বার। **Storm-drum**—প্রবল ঝটিকা সূচনার জন্য মোচাকৃতি ঝটিকাসূচকের সঙ্গে যে ঢোঙ্গাকার বস্তু সংযোজিত করা হয়। **Storm-finch**—Same as STORMY PETREL. **Storm-glass**—তরল পদার্থপূর্ণ কাচনলবিশেষ। এই নলের অভ্যন্তরস্থ পদার্থ আকাশের অবস্থার পরিবর্ত্তনের সঙ্গে সঙ্গে পরিবর্ত্তিত হয় বলিয়া অনুমিত হইত। **Storm-petrel**—Same as STORMY-PETREL. **Storm-sail**—ঝটিকার কালে ব্যবহৃত দৃঢ়বস্ত্রে নির্ম্মিত একপ্রকার অপেক্ষাকৃত ক্ষুদ্রাকৃতি পাইল। **Storm-signal**—আশুসম্ভাবিত ঝটিকা সূচনার্থ ঢোঙ্গাকার, মোচাকার বা অন্য কোন প্রকার চিহ্ন, ঝটিকাপ্রদর্শক। **Storm-tossed**—ঝটিকাবিক্ষুব্ধ, ঝটিকাসংক্ষুব্ধ। **Storm and stress**—অশান্তি, উত্তেজনা, ব্যাকুলতা ; ব্যক্তি বা জাতির জীবনের অশান্তি এবং বিক্ষোভের কাল।

stŏrm'-ȳ, *adj.* **1.** Characterised by storm : tempestuous ; ঝটিকাত্মক ; ঝটিকাবিক্ষুব্ধ। **2.** Violent ; as, a *stormy* sound ; turbulent ; প্রবল, প্রচণ্ড, উত্তাল ; তুমুল। **3.** Associated or threatened with storms ; ঝঞ্ঝাসহকৃত, ঝঞ্ঝাসূচক। **Storm'-i-ly,** *adv.* **Storm'-i-ness,** *n.* **Stormy petrel**—Same as PETREL (which see).

storthing, *n.* Norwegian Parliament ; নরওয়ে দেশের পার্লেমেণ্ট।

stō'-rȳ, *n.* **1.** (*Archaic*) History ; (অপ্রঃ) ইতিহাস। **2.** A narrative or an account of an incident or event ; কাহিনী, বৃত্তান্ত, বর্ণনা। **3.** A tale ; গল্প, কথা, উপাখ্যান, আখ্যান, আখ্যায়িকা। **4.** (*Colloq.*) A lie ; (চলিত ভাষায়) মিথ্যাকথা, মিছাকথা। **Story-book**—গল্পের বহি। **Story-teller**—গল্পকথক ; মিথ্যাবাদী। **It is quite another story now**—Things have changed now ; এখন সে সব চলিয়া গিয়াছে, সেই রামও নাই সেই অযোধ্যাও নাই। **The story goes**—It is said ; এইরূপ কথিত হয়। **To make a long story short**—To tell in a concise manner ; সংক্ষেপে বলিতে গেলে।

stoup (stôp), *n.* **1.** (*Archaic*) A vessel of liquor ; a flagon ; মদ্যপাত্র ; মদ্যভাণ্ড। **2.** A holy-water-basin ; পবিত্র জলের পাত্র।

stout (stowt), *adj.* & *n.* **1.** Strong ; vigorous ; robust ; বলবান ; তেজস্বী ; শক্তিশালী, বলিষ্ঠ। **2.** Bold ; brave ; valiant ; resolute ; সাহসী, অকুতোভয়, নির্ভীক ; শূর ; দৃঢ়প্রতিজ্ঞ, কৃতনিশ্চয়, স্থিরসংকল্প। **3.** Rather corpulent or fat and fleshy in proportion to size ; strongly built ; as, *stout* person ; হৃষ্টপুষ্ট, স্থূলকায় ; দৃঢ়কায়, দ্রঢ়িষ্ঠ। **4.** Firm ; enduring ; as, *stout* canvas ; দৃঢ়, শক্ত ; টেঁকসই, মজবুত। ***Noun.*** A kind of strong porter ; একপ্রকার কড়া মদ। **Stout'-ly,** *adv.* In a stout manner ; দৃঢ়ভাবে, জোরের সহিত, বলপূর্ব্বক, সাহসপূর্ব্বক। **Stout'-ness,** *n.* **Stout-hearted**—সাহসী, নির্ভীক।

stŏve, *n.* & *v. t.* **1.** (*Obs.*) A house or room artificially heated to a high temperature, and used for drying and other purposes; (অপ্রঃ) শস্যাদি শুষ্ককরণার্থ কৃত্রিম উপায়ে উত্তপ্ত গৃহ বা কক্ষ। **2.** An apparatus for warming a room, cooking, etc. ; চুল্লী, চুলা। **3.** A hot-house with artificial heat ; কৃত্রিম উপায়ে উষ্ণীকৃত উদ্যানের উষ্ণগৃহ। ***Verb t.*** To keep anything warm in a house or room by artificial heat ; গৃহে বা গৃহকক্ষে কৃত্রিম উপায়ে কোন বস্তু উষ্ণ রাখা। **Stove-pipe**—চুল্লীর ধূম ও বাষ্প নির্গমকারী নল। **Stove-pipe hat**—একপ্রকার দীর্ঘাকৃতি রেশমের টুপি।

stŏve *v. t.* See STAVE, *v. t.*

stow (stō), *v. t.* **1.** To put in a suitable place ; to lay up ; to pack ; যথা স্থানে রাখা ; রাখা ; ঠাসিয়া বোঝাই করা। **2.** To arrange anything compactly ; as, to *stow* hay in a mow ; to fill with articles completely arranged ; as, to *stow* a ship ; ঠাসিয়া রাখা ; জিনিস ঠাসিয়া রাখিয়া পূর্ণ করা। **3.** (*Slang*) To abstain from ; (ইতরভাষায়) বিরত থাকা, নিবৃত্ত থাকা। **Stow'-age,** *n.* **1.** Things stowed ; যে সকল জিনিষ ঠাসিয়া রাখা হয়। **2.** The state of being stowed ; ঠাসিয়া থাকার অবস্থা। **3.** The cost of stowing ; জাহাজ প্রভৃতিতে মালপত্র ঠাসিয়া বোঝাই করিতে যে ব্যয় পড়ে। **Stowaway**—One who conceals himself on a vessel or on a rail-road train, to obtain a free passage ; যে ব্যক্তি বিনা ভাড়ায়

জাহাজে উঠিয়া জাহাজ না ছাড়া পর্য্যন্ত লুকাইয়া থাকে। **Stow-wood**—জাহাজের খোপে রক্ষিত পিপাসকল স্থির-ভাবে রাখিবার জন্য কাষ্ঠখণ্ডসমূহ।

stră-bis'-mŭs, *n.* Squinting; তির্য্যগ্‌-দৃষ্টিরোগ, টেরারোগ। **–mal, –mic,** *adjs.* **Cross-eyed strabismus**—যেরূপ তির্য্যগ্‌দৃষ্টি রোগে এক চক্ষু বা উভয় চক্ষু ভিতরের দিকে উন্মুখ থাকে। **Wall-eyed strabismus**—যেরূপ তির্য্যগ্‌-দৃষ্টিরোগে চক্ষু বহির্দ্দিকে উন্মুখ থাকে।

stră-bŏt'-ŏ-mỹ, *n.* (*Surg.*) The operation for the cure of squinting by cutting the muscle or muscles that distort the eye; (অস্ত্রোপচার-বিদ্যা) তির্য্যগ্‌দৃষ্টিরোগ মোচনের জন্য চক্ষুর বৈরূপ্যজনক পেশী বা পেশীসমূহ ছেদন।

strad'-dle (-l), *v. t., i.* & *n.* To place the legs one on each side of; to stand or sit astride of; চড়িয়া বসান; চড়িয়া দাঁড় করা। ***Verb i.*** 1. To part the legs wide; to sit astride; পা ছড়ান; চড়িয়া বসা। 2. To vacillate; ইতস্ততঃ করা, দ্বিধা করা। ***Noun.*** 1. The act of standing or sitting with the legs far apart; চড়িয়া বসন, পা ছড়াইয়া দণ্ডায়মান হওন। 2. The distance between the legs and feet of one straddling; পা ছড়াইয়া দাঁড়াইলে বা বসিলে উভয় পদের মধ্যে যে ফাঁক থাকে। 3. A contract which gives the holder the privilege of calling for the stocks at a fixed price, or of delivering it at the same price to the party who signs the contract; একপ্রকার চুক্তি—যাহাতে চুক্তিগ্রহীতা নির্দ্দিষ্ট মূল্যে কোম্পানীর কাগজ ক্রয় করিতে বা চুক্তিস্বাক্ষরকারীকে উহা ক্রয়মূল্যে প্রদান করিতে অধিকারী হইয়া থাকে।

Străd-ĭ-vā'-rĭ-ŭs, Străd, *ns.* Violin or other stringed instrument made by Antonio Stradivari of Cremona (1644-1737); Cremona বাসী Antonio Stradivari কর্ত্তৃক উদ্ভাবিত বেহালা বা অনুরূপ তন্ত্রীবিশিষ্ট বাদ্যযন্ত্র।

străg'-gle (-l), *v. i.* 1. To wander apart from the direct course or companions; দল ছাড়িয়া যাওয়া, যূথভ্রষ্ট হওয়া। 2. To ramble; উদ্দেশ্যহীনভাবে ঘুরা। 3. To be scattered; to be isolated; to occur here and there; বিক্ষিপ্ত হওয়া; অনন্যসংলগ্নভাবে থাকা; এখানে সেখানে দেখিতে পাওয়া যাওয়া। **–gler,** *n.* 1. One who wanders from the regular line of march, or from his companions; a wanderer; যূথভ্রষ্ট ব্যক্তি, দলভ্রষ্ট ব্যক্তি; ভবঘুরে। 2. Something standing alone or apart from others; অন্য কোনকিছু হইতে পৃথগ্‌ভূত বা বিচ্ছিন্ন ব্যক্তি। **–gling-ly,** *adv.* **–gly,** *adj.* **Straggling-money**—সৈন্যদল প্রভৃতি পরিত্যাগী ব্যক্তিকে ধৃত করার জন্য যে পুরস্কার দেওয়া হয়; বিনা বিদায়ে অনুপস্থিত ব্যক্তির বেতন হইতে যে টাকা কাটা হয়।

straight (strāt), *adj., n.* & *adv.* 1. Not bent, curved or crooked; as, a *straight* pole; সরল, সোজা, সিধা, ঋজু। 2. Upright; as, a *straight* man of besiness; candid; as, *straight* dealing; সাধু, সৎ; সরল, অকপট। 3. Direct; plain; as, a *straight* answer; সোজা; স্পষ্ট। 4. In proper place; যথাস্থানে স্থিত। ***Noun.*** Straight part; straight direction; সরল অংশ; সোজাদিক। ***Adv.*** 1. Immediately; directly তৎক্ষণাৎ; সোজাভাবে। 2. Plainly; স্পষ্টভাবে, স্পষ্টাক্ষরে। **Straight'-en,** *v. t.* & *i.* To make straight; সোজা করা, সরল করা। (*Verb i.*) To become straight; সোজা হওয়া, সরল হওয়া। **Straight arch**—বিপর্য্যস্ত "V" অক্ষরের আকৃতি তোরণ। **Straight-forward**—সরল, সরল প্রকৃতি, স্পষ্টবাদী। **Straight hair** — অকুঞ্চিত কেশ। **Straight thinking**—যুক্তিমূলক চিন্তা (আবেগমূলক নহে)। **Straight tip**—ঘোড়দৌড় প্রভৃতিতে জয়ী হইতে পারিলে বা কোন ব্যাপারে ধন প্রয়োগ করিলে তাহ কিরূপলাভজনক হইবে তৎসম্বন্ধে প্রামাণিক ব্যক্তির নিকট হইতে প্রাপ্ত আভাস। **Straight off**—Without hesitation or deliberation; তৎক্ষণাৎ, ক্ষণমাত্রও চিন্তা বা দ্বিধা না করিয়া। **Straight-way** — (*Archaic*) Immediately; forthwith; (অপ্রঃ) তৎক্ষণাৎ; অব্যবহিত ভাবে। **The straight ticket** — (মার্কিণ-যুক্তরাজ্যে) কোন সম্প্রদায়ের অপরিবর্ত্তিত কার্য্যপ্রণালী।

strain (strān), *v. t.* & *i.* 1. To stretch; as, to *strain* a rope; to draw with force; প্রসারিত করা; সবলে টানা। 2. To exert to the utmost; as, they will *strain* themselves for relief; প্রাণপণ চেষ্টা করা। 3. To press; চাপ দেওয়া। 4. To purify and separate from extraneous matter by filtering; as, to *strain out* cofee grounds; ছাঁকা। 5. To harm by overexertion; as, to *strain* a horse by overloading; to sprain; as, to *strain* the wrist; অতিরিক্ত পরিশ্রম দ্বারা ক্ষতি করা; মোচড়াইয়া যাওয়া। 6. To wrest from true meaning; as, to *strain* the meaning of a passage; কদর্থ করা, কষ্টকল্পিত অর্থ করা। 7. To hug; (Now usually in the phrase *to strain to one's breast*); আলিঙ্গন করা। ***Verb i.*** 1. To make violent efforts; প্রাণপণ চেষ্টা করা। 2. To be filtered; to percolate; ছাঁকা হওয়া; চুয়ান। **Strain'-a-ble,** *adj.* **Strained,** *p. p.* **Strain'-er,** *n.* A device for straining; চালনী, ছাঁকনী, ঝাঁঝরী, ঝর্ঝর। **Strained relation**—মনোমালিন্য। **Straining-beam, Straining-piece**—যে কাষ্ঠ-ফলক দ্বারা অপর দুই খণ্ড ফলক পরস্পর হইতে পৃথক্‌ রাখা হয়। **To strain**—To try one's utmost; প্রাণপণ চেষ্টা করা। **To strain a point**—To break a rule; কোন নিয়ম ভঙ্গ করা। To exceed one's duty; to overstep one's commission; কর্ত্তব্যের অতিরিক্ত কার্য্য করা; কাহারো উপর অর্পিত কার্য্যের অতিরিক্ত কার্য্য করা। To make a special, and often inconvenient effort; to do something inconvenient or distasteful; বিশেষ চেষ্টা করা, অসুবিধাজনক চেষ্টা করা; কোনরূপ অসুবিধাজনক বা অপ্রীতিকর কার্য্য করা। **To strain at**—To be overscrupulous about; কোন বিষয়ে অতিরিক্ত সূক্ষ্মবিচারী হওয়া। **To strain at a gnat**—To make a fuss over a small matter; সামান্য বিষয় লইয়া গোলমাল করা। **To strain every nerve**—To try one's utmost; প্রাণপণ চেষ্টা করা, উঠিয়া পড়িয়া লাগা। **To strain one's authority**—আপনার অধিকারের বাহিরে প্রভুত্ব খাটান। **To strain one's eyes**—To see with expanded eyes; বিস্ফারিত নেত্রে দেখা।

strain (strān), *n.* **1.** A violent effort; an excessive stretching or exertion of the muscles, or of the mind; as, a *strain* on her strength; প্রবল চেষ্টা, প্রবল উদ্যম; প্রবল মানসিক চেষ্টা, অঙ্গের পেশীসমূহের অতিরিক্ত বিততি। **2.** The hurt or injury from excessive tension or use, as of the muscles, nerves, or an organ; অতিরিক্ত ব্যবহার বা প্রসারণজনিত ক্ষতি। **3.** A sprain; মচকানি, মোচড়। **4.** The subject or theme of a poem or discourse; কবিতা বা নিবন্ধের বিষয় বা সারমর্ম্ম। **5.** A trace; streak; as, he has a *strain* of melancholy; আভাস, লেশ; ছিট। **6.** A song; a poem; a lay; "All unworthy of thy nobler *strain*"; গীতিকা; কবিতা; গাথা। **7.** Hereditary character; "Intemperance...breeds diseases which...spoil the *strain* of a nation"; কৌলিক প্রকৃতি। **8.** Tendency; mood; temper; as, he was in a philosophizing *strain*; ঝোঁক, আসক্তি; ভাব; প্রকৃতি। **9.** Stress; thrust; force; চাপ, ভার; পার্শ্বের দিকে চাপ; বল। **10.** (*Mech.*) The force which acts on any material, and which tends to disarrange its component parts or destroy their cohesion; also, any definite alteration in the form or dimension of a given portion of matter; (যন্ত্র-বিজ্ঞান) যে বল কোন বস্তুর উপর ক্রিয়া করিয়া উহার উপাদানীভূত অংশ সমূহ বিশৃঙ্খল করিতে উন্মুখ করে অথবা উহাদের সংযোগ শীলতা নষ্ট করে; কোন জড় বস্তুর নির্দ্দিষ্ট অংশের আকার বা পরিমাণের সুস্পষ্ট পরিবর্ত্তন। **11.** Breed of animals; stock; as, he comes of a good *strain*; জন্তুর বংশ; বংশ, গোষ্ঠি। **12.** Sort; রকম, প্রকার। **13.** A snatch or spell of music or poetry; একচোট গান বা কবিতা, সঙ্গীতপ্রবাহ, কবিতাধারা। **14.** The tenor, tone, style of a song, speech, book, etc.; গান, বক্তৃতা পুস্তক প্রভৃতির ভাব, ধারা, পদ্ধতি বা আশয়।

strait (strāt), *adj.*, *n.* & *v. t.* **1.** Narrow; সংকীর্ণ, অপ্রশস্ত। **2.** Tight; শক্ত, আঁটসাট। **3.** Strict; rigorous; কঠোর; কঠিন। **4.** Difficult; distressful; কঠিন; কষ্টপূর্ণ, আর্ত্ত। ***Noun.*** **1.** A narrow stretch of water between continents or other portions of land; প্রণালী, জলডমরুমধ্য (হিঃ কোঃ)। **2.** A narrow mountain-pass; সংকীর্ণপার্ব্বত্যপথ, গিরিসঙ্কট। **3.** (*Usu. pl.*) Difficult position; distress; as, reduced to great *straits*; মুস্কিল, ঝঞ্ঝাট; দুর্দ্দশা, দুর্গতি। ***Verb t.*** **1.** To make strait; to confine; সঙ্কীর্ণ করা, অপ্রশস্ত করা; রুদ্ধ করা। **2.** To make tense or tight; আঁট করা, আঁটসাট করা। **3.** To distress; to put in pecuniary difficulty; দুর্গতিতে ফেলা, দুর্দ্দশাগ্রস্ত করা, বিপন্ন করা; অর্থকষ্টে ফেলা, অভাবে ফেলা। **Straitened circumstances**—Poverty; দুরবস্থা, অসচ্ছলতা, অর্থকৃচ্ছ্রতা। **Strait-jacket, Strait waistcoat**—A coat of strong matrial securing the body tightly or restraining violent maniacs etc.; আঁটসাঁট জামা, উন্মাদ ব্যক্তিদিগের পরিধেয় একপ্রকার জামা। **Strait-laced**—(*Fig.*) Strict in manner, morals or opinion, esp. in moral or religious views; "*Strait-laced* persons who deemed it scandalous to look on at *Hamlet* or *Othello*"; (লক্ষণায়) অতি কঠোর ধর্ম্মনিষ্ঠ, কঠোর নীতিমার্গাবলম্বী।

strake, *n.* A continous range of planks on the bottom or sides of a vessel; জাহাজের তলের বা পার্শ্বদেশের ক্রমপ্রসারিত কাষ্ঠফলকশ্রেণী।

stră-min'-ĕ-ous (-ŭs), *adj.* **1.** (*Archaic*) Strawy; (অপ্রঃ) খড়পূর্ণ। **2.** Coloured like straw; light as straw; খড়ের বর্ণ, পলবর্ণ; খড়ের মত লঘু।

stră-mō'-ni-ŭm, *n.* **1.** The thorn-apple (*Datura Stramonium*); ধুতুরা, ধুস্তুর, ধুস্তূর। [Syn. কিতব, উন্মত্ত, ধূর্ত্ত, কিতবাহ্বয়, মাতুল, মদন, ধর্ত্তূর, শঠ, মাতুলক, শ্যাম, শিবশেখর, খর্জ্জূঘ্ন, কাহলাপুষ্প, কণ্টফল, খল, মোহন, কলভ, মত্ত, শৈব, দেবিকা, তুরী, মহামোহী, শিবপ্রিয়, হিরণ্য, কনক (শুক্রঃ) কর্ব্বুর, কনকাহ্বয়।] [Arab. *masil, methel, jouz masil*]. **2.** A drug obtained from it, with properties similar to belladonna; ধুতুরার বীজ এবং পত্র হইতে প্রস্তুত শ্বাসকাশ প্রভৃতি রোগের ঔষধ।

strănd, *n.*, *v. i.* & *t.* Margin; beach; ধার, কিনারা; তট, কূল, তীর, বেলাভূমি, পুলিন; সৈকত। ***Verb i.*** To run aground; as, the ship *stranded* at high water; চড়ায় আটকান। ***Verb t.*** To drive or run aground on the sea-shore; as, to *strand* a ship; জাহাজ চড়ায় লাগান। **Strand'-ed,** *pp.* In difficulties; সঙ্কটে পতিত।

străñd, *n.* & *v. t.* A number of yarns or wires twisted together to form one of the parts of a rope ; রজ্জুর গুণ। ***Verb t.*** To break one of the strands of a rope ; রজ্জুর গুণ খোলা।

strānge, *n.* 1. Foreign ; বিদেশীয়, বৈদেশিক, পরকীয়। 2. Unacquainted ; bewildered ; অপরিচিত, অজানা, অচেনা ; বিভ্রান্ত, কিংকর্ত্তব্যবিমূঢ়। 3. Unaccustomed ; as, I am a *stranger to* the work ; inexperienced ; অনভ্যস্ত ; অনভিজ্ঞ। 4. Queer ; as, *strange* garments ; unnatural ; eccentric ; কেমন-একতর, অদ্ভুত ; অস্বাভাবিক ; ছিটগ্রস্ত। 5. Shy ; coy ; "She may be *strange* and shy at first" লজ্জিত, সরমিলা ; মুখচোরা, মেনিমুখো। 6. Novel ; wonderful ; unexpected ; নূতন ; বিচিত্র, আশ্চর্য্য, অপূর্ব্ব, অপরূপ, বিস্ময়জনক, আজগবি (*colloq.*), অনাসৃষ্টি (*ib.*), বিলক্ষণ (*ib.*) ; অপ্রত্যাশিত। **Strange'-ly,** *adv.* **Strange'-ness,** *n.* **A strange woman**—বারবনিতা। **Strange to say**—It is a matter of surprise ; আশ্চর্য্যের বিষয়। **To feel strange**—To feel out of one's element ; কেমন কেমন লাগা, কেমন একরকম বোধ করা। To feel dizzy ; মাথা ঘূরা।

strān'-gĕr, *n.* 1. Foreigner ; as, I was helped by a *stranger* ; বিদেশী, বিদেশবাসী, পরদেশী, বিদেশীয় ব্যক্তি, বৈদেশিক। 2. An unknown person ; অপরিচিত লোক, অজ্ঞাত ব্যক্তি, অজানা লোক, আগন্তুক, অজ্ঞাত-কুলশীল ব্যক্তি। 3. Unaccustomed as, I am a *stranger* to the custom ; অনভ্যস্ত। 4. (*Australia*) The rock whiting ; (অষ্ট্রেলিয়া) একপ্রকার মৎস্য। 5. (*Law*) One not privy or party to an act ; (আইন) কোন কার্য্যের সহিত অসংসৃষ্ট ব্যক্তি। **To make a stranger of**—To treat distantly ; আন্তরিকতা না দেখান। **To spy or see strangers**—বিলাতের কমন্স সভায় সভ্য এবং কর্ম্মচারিগণ ব্যতিরেকে অপর সকলকে বহিষ্কৃত করার জন্য দাবী করা।

stran'-gle (străng-gl), *v. t.* 1. To throttle ; শ্বাস রোধ করিয়া মারা, গলা টিপিয়া মারা। 2. (*Fig.*) To suppress ; "*Strangle* such thoughts" ; (লক্ষণায়) রোধ করা, দমন করা, চাপিয়া দেওয়া।

stran'-gles (străng-glz), *n., pl.* Tumour or swelling in a horse's throat ; অশ্বের কণ্ঠস্ফীতি রোগ।

stran'-gü-lāte (străng-), *v. t.* 1. (*Rare*) To strangle ; (কচিদ্-ব্যবহৃত) শ্বাস রোধ করিয়া হত্যা করা। 2. To stop circulation or vital action by compression ; চাপ দিয়া শিরা প্রভৃতির রক্ত চলাচল বন্ধ করা। **--la'-tion,** *n.* The act of strangulating ; রক্তাবরোধ।

stran'-gü-rȳ (străng-), *n.* 1. A disease in which there is pain in passing the urine which discharges drop by drop ; মূত্রকৃচ্ছ্র, মূত্রাঘাত। 2. A disease in plants produced by tight ligature ; দৃঢ়রূপে বন্ধন করার দরুণ বৃক্ষে উৎপাদিত রোগ বিশেষ। **—gu'-ri-ous,** *adj.*

străp, *n.* & *v. t.* 1. A long narrow slip of leather, cloth or other material ; চর্ম্ম, বস্ত্র প্রভৃতির ফালি, চর্ম্মবন্ধনী। 2. A plate, band or strip of metal to connect or hold parts together by screws or nails ; কোন বস্তুর অংশ দ্বয় স্ক্রুপ প্রভৃতির সাহায্যে সংযুক্ত করার জন্য ধাতুর পট্ট বা বন্ধনী। 3. A strip for sharpening razor ; ক্ষুর শাণ দিবার চামাতি, ক্ষুরতেজনী। 4. (*Bot.*) A ligule ; the blade or flat portion of a grass ; (উদ্ভিদ্‌বিদ্যা) বন্ধনী ; তৃণপত্র। ***Verb t.*** 1. To beat or chastise with a strap ; চর্ম্মের রজ্জু দ্বারা আঘাত করা। 2. To fasten or bind with a strap ; চর্ম্মের ফালি প্রভৃতি দ্বারা বন্ধন করা। 3. To strop ; চামতিতে ক্ষুর ধার দেওয়া। **Strap'-per,** *n.* Strap'-ping, *adj.* & *n.* Big : tall ; strong ; বড় ; দীর্ঘকায় ; বলবান, বলিষ্ঠ। ***Noun.*** 1. The act of fastening with a strap ; চর্ম্মের ফালি প্রভৃতি দ্বারা বন্ধন। 2. Materials for straps ; ফালি প্রভৃতি যে জিনিষে তৈরী হয়। 3. Thrashing ; বেত্রাঘাত। **Strap-laid**—(*Of rope*) Made by laying ropes side by side and joining them into a flat band ; গুণসকল পরস্পরের পার্শ্বে পাকাইয়া ফিতার মত (রজ্জু)। **Strap-oil**—(*Slang*) Beating given with a strap ; (ইতরভাষায়) খুব একচোট বেত্রাঘাত। **Strap-work** — বুনট করা ফিতার অনুরূপ কারুকার্য্য। **Strap-wort**—একপ্রকার শ্বেতপুষ্পপ্রসূ তৃণ।

străp-pa'-dō, *n.* & *v. t.* A punishment that consisted in having the hands of the offender tied behind his back, drawing him up to a certain elevation by rope and then suddenly letting him fall within a certain distance of the ground ; একপ্রকার দণ্ড—যাহাতে অপরাধী ব্যক্তির হস্ত পশ্চাদ্দিকে বন্ধন করিয়া রজ্জুর সাহায্যে তাহাকে উর্দ্ধে তোলার পর সহসা এরূপ ভাবে ছাড়িয়া দেওয়া হইত যে, তাহার পদদ্বয় ভূমি হইতে কিঞ্চিৎ উপরে ঝুলিতে থাকে। ***Verb t.*** To torture by strappado ; উক্তরূপে নির্যাতন করা।

strā'-tă, *n.* (*pl.*) See STRATUM.

străt'-ă-ğĕm, *n.* 1. A plan or trick for deceiving an enemy ; শত্রু সৈন্যকে প্রতারিত করার কৌশলবিশেষ, সমরোপায়, যুক্তি (শুক্রঃ বিনয়), রণচাতুরী। 2. A trick ; an artifice ; চাতুরী, কল, কৌশল ; ফন্দী, ফিকিরফন্দী, ফেরপেঁচ।

stră-tē'-ğic, —ğĭ-căl, *adjs.* Pertaining to strategy ; effected by strategy ; serving the ends of strategy ; রণকৌশলসম্বন্ধীয় ; কৌশল দ্বারা সাধিত ; রণচাতুরীর উদ্দেশ্যসাধক।

stră-tē'-gŭs, *n.* An Athenian military commander ; প্রাচীন এথেন্স নগরীর সেনানায়ক।

străt′-ĕ-ġў, *n.* 1. The science of directing great military movements ; সৈন্যপরিচালনবিদ্যা, সেনা-সন্নিবেশবিজ্ঞান, রণপরিচালনবিদ্যা । 2. The art of war ; যুদ্ধনীতি, রণনীতি, সমরনীতি । **–gist**, *n.*

străth, *n.* A broad mountain-valley ; সুবিস্তৃত গিরিউপত্যকা । **Strathspey** — স্কটলণ্ড দেশীয় নৃত্য-বিশেষ ; ঐরূপ নৃত্যের উপযোগী বাদ্য ।

stră-tic′-ū-late, *adj.* Arranged in thin layers ; স্তরবিন্যস্ত, স্তরনিবদ্ধ ।

străt′-ĭ-fŷ, *v. t.* To form in strata ; স্তরবিন্যস্ত করা, স্তরনিবদ্ধ করা, স্তরে স্তরে সজ্জিত করা । **–fi-ca′-tion** ; *n.* The act of stratifying; স্তরবিন্যাস, স্তরসঞ্চয়, স্তরীকরণ, স্তরীভবন । **–fied**, *adj.* Ranged in strata or layers ; as, *stratified* rocks ; স্তরীভূত, স্তরযুক্ত ।

strā′-tō–, Combining form of STRATUS.

stră-tŏc′-ră-ċў, *n.* Military government ; সামরিক শাসন, সৈন্যতন্ত্র, সামরিক তন্ত্র ।

strā′-tŭm, *n.* A layer of rock, sand or other mineral matter ; শিলা, বালুকা বা অপর কোন খনিজ পদার্থের স্তর । **–tal, Strat′-i-form**, *adjs.*

strā′-tŭs, *n.* A large and continuous sheet of cloud ; সুবৃহৎ এবং অবিচ্ছিন্ন জলদরেখা জলদমালা, স্তরীভূত মেঘ (সাঃ পঃ) ।

straw (strā), *n.* 1. The stalk of a corn-plant ; শস্যের নাল, পল । 2. A mass of the stalks of certain species of grain when cut, and after being thrashed ; খড়, পলাল, পল, বিচালী । 3. Something worthless ; অকিঞ্চিৎকর জিনিষ, তুচ্ছ পদার্থ, নগণ্য জিনিষ । **Straw′-y**, *adj.* **Straw-hat**—খড়ের টুপি । **Straw-mattress** ; খড়ের গদী । **Straw-stem**—একপ্রকার মদিরার গ্লাস—যাহার ডাঁটি পৃথক্‌ভাবে নির্ম্মাণ করিয়া গ্লাসের সহিত জোড়া দেওয়া হয় না । **Straw-worm**—Same as CADDIS. **A drowning man catches at a straw**—See DROWNING. **A man of straw**—See MAN. **A straw bid**—দাম চড়াইবার জন্য ডাক । **In the straw** (*Archaic*)—In childbed ; (অপ্রঃ) আঁতুড় শয্যায়। **My eyes draw straws**—I feel very sleepy ; আমার চোখ ঘুমে ঢুলু ঢুলু করিতেছে । **Not to care a straw or two straws**—Not to care a fig ; তৃণবৎ গণ্য করা (cf. তৃণগণনা, বুদ্ধচরিত—৬—২ ।) **The last straw**—A slight addition that makes a thing no longer tolerable ; যে সামান্য মাত্র কিছু সংযোগে কোন বিষয় দুর্ব্বহ এবং অসহনীয় হইয়া উঠে । **To draw straws**—To draw lot with straws of different length ; বিভিন্ন দৈর্ঘ্যের খড় দ্বারা স্ফূর্ত্তি খেলা ।

straw′-ber-rŷ (strā-bĕ-), *n.* A well-known pulpy berry; the plant bearing it ; সুমিষ্ট ফল বিশেষ; ঐ ফলের গাছ । **Strawberry-mark** — আরক্ত জড়ুল চিহ্ন। **Strawberry-pear** — পশ্চিম ভারতীয় দ্বীপপুঞ্জে জাত একপ্রকার গুল্ম ও ইহার ফল । **Strawberry-roan**—Same as ROAN (which see). **Strawberry-tree**—ষ্ট্রবেরীর মত ফলপ্রসূ একপ্রকার চিরহরিৎ বৃক্ষ । **Strawberry-tongue** — (ভৈষজ্যশাস্ত্র) অতিরিক্ত জ্বরাক্রান্ত ব্যক্তিদিগের ক্ষুদ্র ক্ষুদ্র কণ্টকবৎ মাংসোদ্ভেদ দ্বারা আচ্ছন্ন জিহ্বা । **Strawberry-vine**—ষ্ট্রবেরী গাছ । **Crushed-strawberry** – একপ্রকার মৃদুরক্তিম ষ্ট্রবেরী ফল । **The strawberry leaves**—Ducal rank, with reference to ornamentation of duke's coronet ; ডিউকের পদমর্য্যাদা (ডিউকদিগের মুকুটের উপরে ষ্ট্রবেরী পত্রের অনুরূপ কায থাকে বলিয়া এই নাম) ।

stray (strā), *v. t., n.* & *adj.* 1. To deviate ; "Thames among the wanton valleys *strays*" ; বিপথে যাওয়া, সরল পথ হইতে অপসৃত হওয়া । 2. To go astray ; as, a *straying* sheep ; দলভ্রষ্ট হওয়া, যূথভ্রষ্ট হওয়া । 3. To wander from the path of duty or rectitude ; "We have erred and *strayed* from Thy ways" ; সৎপথভ্রষ্ট হওয়া, সন্মার্গ-চ্যুত হওয়া । ***Noun.*** 1. Any domestic animal that wanders at large, and is lost ; যূথভ্রষ্ট পশু, দলভ্রষ্ট পশু ; 2. Property of deceased person escheating to crown in default of heirs ; উত্তরাধিকারীর অভাবে রাজসরকারেভুক্ত মৃত ব্যক্তির ত্যজ্য সম্পত্তি । ***Adj.*** 1. Having gone astray ; wandering ; দলভ্রষ্ট, যূথভ্রষ্ট ; পথভ্রান্ত । 2. Sporadic ; scattered ; as, *stray* instances ; কচিৎ দৃষ্ট ; ইতস্ততঃ বিক্ষিপ্ত ।

streak (strēk), *n.* & *v. t.* 1. A line or long mark ; a stripe ; জমি হইতে ভিন্ন রঙ্গের রেখা বা লম্বা দাগ, রেখা, লেখা ; ডোরা । 2. A layer ; ছিলকা । ***Verb t.*** To mark with streaks ; ডোরা কাটা, ডোরা টানা, ডোরা আঁকা । **Streaked**, *adj.* Marked or variegated with stripes. রেখাবিচিত্র, ডোরাকাটা, রেখাঙ্কিত । **Streak′-i-ly**, *adv.* **Streak′-i-ness**, *n.* **Streak′-y**, *adj.* **Streak of lightning**—বিদ্যুৎ লেখা, বিদ্যুচ্ছটা । **The silver streak**—ইংলিশ প্রণালী ;

stream (strēm), *n., v. t.* & *i.* 1. A river or brook ; নদী, ক্ষুদ্র নদী, স্রোতস্বিনী । 2. A flow of any fluid or melted substance, as of blood etc. ; ধারা, প্রবাহ, স্রোতঃ । 3. Current ; direction of flow ; স্রোতঃ, প্রবাহ ; প্রবাহের দিক । 4. Anything issuing or moving with continued succession of parts ; as, a *stream* of words ; প্রবাহ, স্রোতঃ । ***Verb t.*** 1. To send forth in a current or stream ; স্রোত বহান, স্রোত প্রবাহিত করা । 2. To cause to stream in the air, as a flag ; পত পত করিয়া উড়ান । ***Verb i.*** 1. To flow in stream ; প্রবাহিত হওয়া, বহা । 2. To pour out or emit abundant stream, as, of tears ; অশ্রুস্রোত প্রভৃতি প্রবাহিত

হওয়া। 3. To issue or streak out in rays or beams; আলোকচ্ছটা প্রভৃতি নির্গত হওয়া। **Stream'-let,** *n.* A small stream; নালা। **Stream-anchor**—একপ্রকার মধ্যমাকৃতির নোঙ্গর। **Against the stream** — স্রোতের প্রতিকূলে। **Stream of thought**—চিন্তনদী (হিঃ কোঃ), সংবিৎপ্রবাহ (ঐ), বিচার-প্রবাহ (ঐ), চিন্তাপ্রবাহ, চিন্তাস্রোত। **To go with the stream**—To do as others do; গড্ডলিকা প্রবাহের মত চলা। **To stream a buoy**—To let it drop into the water, previously to casting anchor; নোঙ্গর ফেলাইবার পূর্ব্বে জলে বয়া নিক্ষেপ করা।

stream'-êr (strēm-), *n.* 1. A long pennon; দীর্ঘ পতাকা, ধ্বজ, বৈজয়ন্তী। 2. A luminous beam or column shooting upward in aurora borealis; সুমেরু জ্যোতিঃ হইতে উৎক্ষিপ্ত আলোক ধারা। 3. A handsome British geometer moth; ব্রিটিশ দ্বীপপুঞ্জের প্রজাপতি বিশেষ।

street (strēt), *n.* & *v. t.* A road in a town or village; the roadway and houses together; রাজপথ, রথ্যা, বীথি, সড়ক, রাজমার্গ; উভয়-পার্শ্বে ভবনশ্রেণী সমন্বিত রাজপথ। **Street'-ed,** *adj.* **Street'-ward,** *adv.* **Street Arab**—See ARAB. **Street cries**—Cries of hawker; ফেরিওয়ালাদের ডাকহাঁক। **Street-door**—সদর দরজা, ফটক। **Street-orderly**—যে মালী রাস্তা ঝাঁট দেয়। **Street-sweeper**—রাজপথপরিমার্জ্জক, রাস্তার ঝাড়ুদার; রাজপথ পরিমার্জ্জনের জন্য যন্ত্রবিশেষ। **Streetwalker**—সাধারণ বেশ্যা, হট্টবিলাসিনী। **On the streets**—Living by whoredom; বেশ্যাবৃত্তিদ্বারা জীবিকানির্ব্বাহকারিণী। **To live in the street**—To live always outside one's house; অষ্ট প্রহর বাহিরে থাকা।

strĕngth, *n.* 1. Force; power; vigour; ক্ষমতা, সামর্থ্য, বীর্য্য; বল, পরাক্রম, শক্তি; ঊর্জ্জ, তেজঃ। 2. Vigour of style; as, he is a writer of great *strength*; ওজস্বিতা। 3. Vividness; intensity; brilliance; as, the *strength* of the colour; সজীবতা; প্রাখর্য্য, প্রাবল্য, প্রগাঢ়তা; দীপ্তি, দ্যুতি। 4. The quality or property of producing sensible effects on other bodies; ক্রিয়া করার ক্ষমতা, অপর কোন কিছুর ইন্দ্রিয়গ্রাহ্য ক্রিয়া করার ক্ষমতা। 5. Number of men in an army etc.; "To descry the *strength* of an enemy;" সৈন্যদল প্রভৃতির বল; লোকসংখ্যা। 6. What makes strong; a support; "My only *strength* and stay"; বল (cf. দুর্ব্বলের বল ভগবান); আশ্রয়। 7. Power of resisting attacks; "Our castle's *strength* will laugh a siege to scorn"; আক্রমণরোধ ক্ষমতা। 8. (*Art.*) Boldness of conception or treatment; "Caracci's *strength*, Correggio's softer line;" (ললিত কলা) চিত্রাদির বিভাবনে বা সম্পাদনে সাহসিকতা। **Strength'-less,** *adj.* **On the strength**—(সামরিকশাস্ত্র) তালিকাভুক্ত। **On the strength of**—On the faith of; in reliance on; কোন কিছুর উপর বিশ্বাস করিয়া; কোন কিছুর উপর নির্ভর করিয়া, কোন কিছুর বলে, কোন কিছুর উপর আস্থা স্থাপন করিয়া।

strĕngth'-ĕn, *v. t.* & *i.* To make or become stronger; শক্তি প্রদান করা, শক্তি সঞ্চার করা, সবল করা, শক্তিমান হওয়া, বলীয়ান করা। **—ing,** *adj.* Giving or increasing strength; বলজনক, শক্তিসঞ্চারক, বলপ্রদ, বলবর্দ্ধক, বলবর্দ্ধী।

strĕn'-ū-ous (-ŭs), *adj.* Zealous; ardent; energetic; persistent; উদ্যমশীল; উদ্যোগী, উদ্যমী; উৎসাহশীল, উৎসাহী, উৎসাহসম্পন্ন, অতন্দ্রিত; অবিচলিত। **—ly,** *adv.* **—ness,** *n.*

Strĕph'-ŏn, *n.* A sentimental lover; প্রণয়োন্মত্ত ব্যক্তি। [Sir Philip Sydneyর Arcadia নামক গ্রন্থের নায়ক Strephon নামক মেষপালকের নাম হইতে গৃহীত।]

strĕss, *n.* & *v. t.* 1. That which bears the force or weight; the force or weight itself; যাহা কোন-কিছুর শক্তি বা চাপ ধারণ করে; চাপ, গুরুত্ব, ভার, শক্তি। 2. Effort; demand upon energy; চেষ্টা, উদ্যম; শক্তির উপর চাপ। 3. A distress; goods taken under distress; ক্রোক; ক্রোকী মাল। 4. Emphasis; জোর। ***Verb t.*** 1. To narrow; to compress; সংকীর্ণ করা; চাপ দেওয়া, সঙ্কাপিত করা। 2. To emphasize; জোর দেওয়া। **Stress'-less,** *adj.*

stretch (strĕch), *v. t., i.* & *n.* 1. To draw out; to draw tight; to make tense; টানিয়া প্রসারিত করা; টান করা; টান টান করা। 2. To strain; কোনকিছুর উপর চাপ দেওয়া। 3. To hold out; as, he *stretched* his hand; বাড়াইয়া দেওয়া। 4. (*Colloq.*) To cause to lie at full length; মাটীর উপর শায়িত করা। ***Verb i.*** 1. To extend; বিস্তারিত হওয়া, প্রসারিত হওয়া। 2. To stretch one's limbs; গা টানা দেওয়া। ***Noun.*** 1. Extension in length or breadth; বিস্তার, প্রসার। 2. Reach; পাল্লা, নাগাল। 3. Effort; struggle; চেষ্টা, উদ্যম; সংগ্রাম। 4. An extended surface or portion; a spell; as, to work ten hours at a *stretch*; জল, ভূমি প্রভৃতির বিস্তার; চোট। 5. (*Naut.*) Distance covered on one tack; (নৌবিদ্যা) পার্শ্ববায়ুর দ্বারা চালিত হওয়ার দরুণ জাহাজের এক একবার দিক্ পরিবর্ত্তনে জাহাজ যে পরিমাণ স্থান অতিক্রম করে। 6. Direction; as, the *stretch* of seams of coal; বিস্তারের দিক্। **Stretch'-i-ness,** *n.* **Stretch'-ing,** *n.* **Stretch'-y,** *adj.* **At a stretch**—At one time continuously;

একক্রমে, একটানা, একচোটে। **Stretching of the limb**—অঙ্গমোটন। **To stretch a point**—See POINT. **To stretch one's self**—ঘুম হইতে উঠার পর গা মোড়া দেওয়া।

stretch'-êr (strŏch-), *n.* 1. One who, or that which, stretches; বিস্তারক, প্রসারক। 2. A brick or stone laid with its longer dimension in the line or direction of the wall; যে ইষ্টক বা প্রস্তরের দৈর্ঘ্যের দিক প্রাচীরের দৈর্ঘ্যের সহিত সমসূত্রে স্থাপিত করা হয়। 3. A contrivance for stretching things; কোন বস্তু প্রসারিত করিয়া রাখার জন্য কৌশলবিশেষ, প্রসারণযন্ত্র। 4. One of the rods in an umbrella attached at one end to one of the ribs and at the other to the tube sliding upon the handle; ছাতার ডাঁশা। 5. A litter or frame for carrying sick, wounded or dead persons; a canvas bed, as in camping; রুগ্ন, আহত বা মৃত ব্যক্তিগণকে বহনের জন্য খট্টা; ক্যাম্বিসের খাট। 6. (*Colloq.*) A statement which overstretches the truth; (চলিতভাষায়) সত্যের অপলাপ। **Stretcher-bond**—একপ্রকার গাঁথুনি যাহাতে ইষ্টক বা প্রস্তর সকল প্রাচীরের দৈর্ঘ্যের সহিত সমসূত্রে বিন্যস্ত করা হয়।

strew (strô *or* strō), *v. t.* 1. To scatter; ছড়ান, বিকীর্ণ করা, আস্তৃত করা, অবস্তীর্ণ করা। 2. To cover by scattering or spreading; কোনকিছু আস্তৃত করিয়া আচ্ছাদিত করা।

strī'-ā, *n.* (*Anat., Bot., Zool. & Geol.*) Small channels or thread-like lines in the shells of cockles and other substances; (শারীরসংস্থান-বিদ্যা, উদ্ভিদ্-বিদ্যা, জন্তু-বিদ্যা, ভূবিদ্যা) কড়ি, শম্বুক প্রভৃতির গাত্রে ক্ষুদ্র ক্ষুদ্র খাঁজ বা সূত্রাকার রেখাসমূহ। **–ate,** *adj.* **–ate,** *v. t.* **–at-ed,** *adj.* Streaked; marked with fine parallel or wavy lines; সূক্ষ্ম সমান্তরালতা বা তরঙ্গায়িত রেখা বিশিষ্ট; রেখাঙ্কিত (সাঃ পঃ), সরেখ (ঐ)। **–a'-tion, –ture,** *ns.*

strick'-en (-n), *p. p.* of STRIKE (which see).

strict, *adj.* 1. Exact; rigorously nice; ঠিক, যথার্থ; কঠোর। 2. Severe; rigorous; দারুণ কঠোর, কড়া, খাড়া (*Colloq.*, cf. খাড়া পাহারা), কড়াকড় (*colloq.*)। 3. Governed by exact rules; কঠোর নিয়মনিষ্ঠ। **Strict'-ness,** *n.* The quality of being strict; কঠোরতা, কড়াকড়ি, আঁটাআঁটি, আঁটুনি। **Strictly speaking**—If one is to use words in their strict sense; যথার্থভাবে বলিতে গেলে।

stric'-tūre, *n.* 1. Adverse criticism; critical remark; censure; প্রতিকূল সমালোচনা, বিরুদ্ধ সমালোচনা; সমালোচনা-মূলক মন্তব্য, মন্তব্য; তিরস্কার, গঞ্জনা। 2. A morbid or abnormal contraction of any canal or passage of the body; শরীরের কোন নালী বা দ্বারের অস্বাভাবিক আকুঞ্চন বা সংবৃতি। **Stricture of the urethra**—মূত্রস্রোত নিবন্ধ (সাঃ পঃ), নিরুদ্ধ-প্রকাশ (ঐ), মূত্রোৎসঙ্গ (ঐ)।

strīde, *v. i., t. & n.* 1. To walk or march with long steps; দীর্ঘপাদ-বিক্ষেপে চলা, লম্বা লম্বা পা ফেলিয়া চলা। 2. To step over; পদবিক্ষেপে অতিক্রম করা। *Verb t.* To bestride; "I mean to *stride* your steed"; চড়িয়া বসা। *Noun.* 1. A long often measured step; দীর্ঘপাদবিক্ষেপ। 2. The distance measured by a long step; একবার দীর্ঘপাদবিক্ষেপে যে পরিমাণ স্থান অতিক্রম করা যায়, পদক্ষেপপরিমিত স্থান। **To take obstacle in one's stride**—To clear it without changing one's step to jump; to get over with difficulty; দীর্ঘপাদবিক্ষেপে কোনরূপ বাধা অতিক্রম করা; (লক্ষণায়) অনায়াসে উত্তীর্ণ হওয়া।

strī'-dĕnt, *adj.* Loud and harsh in sound; ঘর্ঘরনাদী। **–ly** *adv.*

strī'-dŏr, *n.* A quick sharp sound; একপ্রকার কর্কশ শব্দ।

strid'-ū-lāte, *v. i.* (*Entom.*) To make a small, harsh or creaking noise, as some insects; (কীটতত্ত্ব) ঝিঁ ঝিঁ শব্দ করা, কট্ কট্ শব্দ করা। **–lant,** *adj.* **–la'-tion,** *n.* **–la-tor,** *n.*

strīfe, *n.* Contention; struggle; বিরোধ, দ্বন্দ্ব; সংগ্রাম, টক্কর (*colloq.*)।

strig'-il, *n.* A flesh-scraper; স্নানকালে চর্ম্ম চাঁচিবার জন্য প্রাচীন গ্রীক ও রোমের অধিবাসিগণ কর্তৃক ব্যবহৃত একপ্রকার ছুরিকাকার যন্ত্র।

strī'-gōse, strī'-gous (-gŭs), *adj.* (*Bot.*) Covered with little, upright, unequal stiff hairs; (উদ্ভিদ্ বিদ্যা) ক্ষুদ্র ক্ষুদ্র খাড়া অসম এবং কঠিন শূক-দ্বারা আচ্ছন্ন, কঠিন শূকাচ্ছন্ন।

strīke, *v. t., i. & n.* 1. To give a blow to; "who would be free themselves must *strike* the blow"; আঘাত করা। 2. To knock; ঘা দেওয়া। 3. To come into collision with; as, the ship *struck* a reef; to dash; as, *strike* one's head on a stone; সংঘৃষ্ট হওয়া; ধাক্কা লাগা। 4. To daub; লেপন করা, লিপ্ত করা। 5. To cause to ignite by striking, rubbing or the like; as, to *strike* a match; ঠোকা দিয়া, ঘষিয়া বা তদ্বৎ কোন কিছু করিয়া জ্বালান। 6. To lower; as, to *strike* a sail; নামান। 7. To impress; to coin; ছাপ দেওয়া; মুদ্রিত করা। 8. To occur to; as, that did not *strike* me; (মনে) উদয় হওয়া, ঠেকা। 9. To take down; to lower and pack up; উঠান; (শিবির) ভঙ্গ করা। 10. To give, deal or inflict (প্রহার) করা, (আঘাত) করা। 11. To erase; to efface; as, *strike out* this passage; কাটা; মুছিয়াফেলা, অপহৃত করা। 12. To thrust in; as, a tree *strikes* its roots; ভিতরে ঢুকান, ভিতরে ঠেলিয়া দেওয়া,

13. To impress strongly; as, he was *struck* with amazement: অভিভূত করা। **14.** To cause to sound by one or more beats; as, the clock *strikes* ten; বাজান, টং টং করিয়া বাজান। **15.** To take down as a flag, sail; নিশান পতাকা, প্রভৃতি নামান। **16.** To make, as a bargain; to ratify or confirm, as a treaty; চুক্তি করা; দৃঢ় করা, পাকা করা। **17.** To ground; চড়ায় আটকান। **18.** To hook a fish by a quick turn of wrist; হাতের কব্জা দ্রুত ঘুরাইয়া বড়শীতে মাছ আটকান। **19.** To propagate by cuttings; গাছের ডালা প্রভৃতি রোপণ করিয়া বৃক্ষের বংশ বিস্তার করা। **20.** To level, as, a measure of grain, salt, etc., by scraping off with a straight instrument what is above level of the top; শস্য, লবণ প্রভৃতির স্তূপের উপরিভাগ যন্ত্র বিশেষের সাহায্যে চাঁচিয়া সমতল করা। **21.** To lade into a cooler, as a liquor; মদ্য প্রভৃতি শৈত্যজনক পাত্রে রাখা। **22.** To borrow of; to urge for; কর্জ্জ করা; পীড়াপীড়ি করা। ***Verb i.*** **1.** To move or turn aside rapidly; to proceed; দ্রুত চলা, দ্রুত একদিকে সরা; অগ্রসর হওয়া। **2.** To light upon; as, my eye *struck* a strange word; কোন কিছুর উপর সহসা আপতিত হওয়া, সহসা দেখিতে পাওয়া। **3.** To make a blow; to hit; আঘাত করা; ঘা দেওয়া। **4.** To be stranded; চড়ায় লাগা, চড়ায় আটকান। **5.** To quit work to compel to better terms; ধর্ম্মঘট করা। **6.** To lower a flag or colours in token of respect, or to signify surrender to an enemy; সম্মান বা আত্মসমর্পণ সূচনার্থ পতাকা অবনমিত করা। **7.** To commence suddenly; হঠাৎ আরম্ভ করা। **8.** To collide; to clash; সংঘৃষ্ট হওয়া; ঠোকাঠুকি লাগা। **9.** To take root; শিকড় গজান। **10.** To make an attack; আক্রমণ করা। **11.** To deal blows; to fight; as, to *strike* for one's country; প্রহার করা; যুদ্ধ করা। **12.** (*Slang*) To steal, esp. money; চুরি করা, টাকা পয়সা চুরি করা। **13.** To sound by percussion, with blows or as with blows; বাজা। **14.** (*Rare*) To touch; to glance; (কৃচিদ্ ব্যবহৃত) স্পর্শ করা; কোন কিছুতে আহত হইয়া পিছলাইয়া যাওয়া। **15.** To pass quickly; to penetrate; "Till a dart *strikes* through his liver"; অতিক্রম করা; ভেদ করা। ***Noun.*** **1.** An instrument with a straight edge for levelling a measure of grain, salt, etc.; শস্য, লবণ, প্রভৃতির স্তূপ সমতল করার জন্য যন্ত্রবিশেষ। **2.** Act of workmen who quit work to force their employers to give better terms; ধর্ম্মঘট। **3.** A number of twenty-five eels; পঁচিশটী বাইন মৎস্য। **4.** Full measure; excellence of quality; "Three hogsheds of ale of the first *strike*;" পূর্ণ পরিমাণ; গুণোৎকর্ষ। **5.** (*Geol.*) The horizantal direction of the outcropping edges of tilted strata, it is always being at right angles to the dip; দিকচক্রবালের সহিত কোণ উৎপাদনপূর্ব্বক উচ্ছ্বসিত স্তর নিচয়ের অঙ্কুরিত প্রান্তসমূহের দিগ্‌বলয়ের সমান্তরাল দিগ্‌গামিতা, স্তরাঙ্কুরদিক্। **6.** A handful of flax that may be heckled at once; এক মুষ্টি শণ—যাহা একবার আঁচড়ান যায়। **7.** An imperfect matrix for type; অক্ষর তৈরীর অসম্পূর্ণ ছাঁচ। **8.** The crystalline appearance of hard soaps; কঠিন সাবানের স্ফাটিক আভা। **Strik'-er**, *n.* **Strik'-ing**, *adj.* Remarkable; surprising; আশ্চর্য্য; বিস্ময়জনক, বিস্ময়কর। **Staike-a-light** — অগ্নি উৎপাদনের জন্য প্রাচীন কালে ব্যবহৃত একপ্রকার পাষাণ উল্লেখনী। **Stricken hour**—Full one hour; পূর্ণ একঘণ্টা কাল। **Stricken in age**—Worn out with old age; জরাগ্রস্ত, জরাজীর্ণ। **Strike-pay**—শ্রমিকসম্মিলনী প্রভৃতি কর্ত্তৃক ধর্ম্মঘটকারিগণকে যে বেতন দেওয়া হয়। **Strike the iron while it is hot**—See IRON. **To strike a balance**—To compare the debit and credit sides of an account to find out which side exceeds the other and by what amount; জমাখরচের হিসাব দেখিয়া ফাজিল বা বাকী কাটা। **To strike a blow for**—To exert one's utmost to effect some purpose; কোন উদ্দেশ্য সাধনের জন্য প্রাণপণ চেষ্টা করা। **To strike a bold stroke**—To make a daring attempt; কোনরূপ অসমসাহসিক কার্য্যে প্রবৃত্ত হওয়া। **To strike across**—To dart across; কোন কিছুর উপর দিয়া দ্রুত ছুটা। **To strike all of a heap**—To strike with surprise; বিস্ময়াবিষ্ট করা, হতভম্ব করা, চক্ষুস্থির করা। **To strike a jury**—To form special jury by each party striking down a certain number of names from a prepared list of jurors so as to bring the number down to the limit prescribed by law; আদালতের আদেশানুযায়ী বিশেষ জুরি গঠন করা। **To strike a ledger or account**—To balance a ledger or an account; হিসাব ঠিক করিয়া জমা খরচ কাটা। **To strike a man dead**—To kill with a blow; কাহাকেও আঘাত করিয়া মারা। **To strike an attitude** — See ATTITUDE. **To strike a stroke** — To attack; আক্রমণ করা। **To strike at**—To try to hit; আঘাত করিতে চেষ্টা করা। **To strike at the root of**—To deal a death blow to; মূলদেশে আঘাত করা, মূলোচ্ছেদ করা। **To strike away**—To remove; স্থানান্তরিত করা, অপসারিত করা।

To strike back—To strike in return ; প্রতিপ্রহার করা। **To strike for** — To fight for something ; কোন কিছুর জন্য অস্ত্রধারণ করা, কোন কিছুর জন্য লড়া। **To strike hands** — To make a bargain ; to be a surety for any one's good behaviour; চুক্তি করা ; কাহারো সদাচরণের জন্য জামিন থাকা। **To strike hands with**—To shake hands with ; করমর্দ্দন করা। To bind oneself by some agreement ; কোনরূপ চুক্তিতে আবদ্ধ হওয়া। **To strike home** — To cut to the quick ; মর্ম্মস্থলে আঘাত করা, আঁতে ঘা দেওয়া। **To strike in**—To enter suddenly ; হঠাৎ প্রবেশ করা। To disappear ; ডুবিয়া যাওয়া, বিলীন হওয়া। To interpose ; মধ্যে পড়িয়া দুকথা বলা। **To strike into**—To dart into ; to penetrate ; সবেগে প্রবেশ করা ; ভেদ করা। **To strike in with**—To join with ; কাহারো সহিত যোগদান করা। To adapt one's self to ; উপযোগী করা। **To strike the keynote**—To enunciate the principle or idea ; মূলসূত্র নির্দ্দেশ করান **To strike note**—To cause a note to be sounded ; কোন বিশেষ স্বর বাজান। **To strike off**—To erase ; to deduct ; কাটিয়া ফেলা ; খারিজ করা, বাদ দেওয়া। To print; মুদ্রিত করা। **To strike off** or **into**—To turn abruptly to ; হঠাৎ কোনদিকে ফিরা। **To strike oil**—To find petroleum when boring for it ; ভূগর্ভে খুঁড়িতে খুঁড়িতে কেরোসিন তৈল প্রাপ্ত হওয়া। **To strike on** or **upon**—To dash against something ; কোন কিছুর সহিত ধাক্কা লাগা। **To strike one dumb** — To astonish ; হতভম্ব করা, অবাক করা, তাক লাগান, চক্ষুঃ স্থির করা। **To strike one's fancy**—To delight one ; কাহারো মনোরঞ্জন করা। **To strike one's head off**—To decapitate ; শিরশ্ছেদ করা। **To strike (one's name) off the rolls**—To erase one's name from a list ; তালিকা হইতে নাম কাটিয়া দেওয়া। **To strike one's tent**—To take to heels ; to depart ; চম্পট দেওয়া ; প্রস্থান করা। **To strike out**—To find out some means ; কোনরূপ উপায় উদ্ভাবন করা। **To strike out a plan**—To find out a plan ; কোনরূপ উপায় উদ্ভাবন করা। **To strike root**—To take root ; বদ্ধমূল হওয়া। **To strike the ball under the line**—To be frustrated in one's designs or attempts ; কাহারো উদ্দেশ্য বা চেষ্টা ব্যর্থ হওয়া। **To strike the ground**—To be stranded ; চড়ায় আটকান। **To strike up**—To begin ; আরম্ভ করা। To plan ; যুক্তি করা। To cause to sound ; বাজান। To begin to sound or play ; বাজাইতে আরম্ভ করা।

string, *n., v. t.* & *i.* **1.** A small rope, twine or cord ; রজ্জু, দড়ী, সুতলী, মোটাসুতা, ডোর। **2.** A ribbon ; ফিতা। **3.** The chord of a musical instrument ; তন্ত্রী, তার। **4.** A nerve or tendon of an animal body ; শিরা, পেশীর প্রান্তসংলগ্ন রজ্জুবৎ অস্থিমাংসসংযোজক শিরা, কণ্ডরা, মহাশিরা। **5.** The cord of a bow; জ্যা, ছিলা, মৌর্ব্বী, শিঞ্জিনী, গুণ। **6.** A strip, as of leather securing the covers of a book; পুস্তকের মলাট বাঁধিবার জন্য চামড়ার টুকরা। **7.** A series of things ; শ্রেণী, পরম্পরা। **8.** Stringed instruments ; সেতার, বেহালা, এস্রাজ, প্রভৃতি তন্ত্রীবিশিষ্ট বাদ্যযন্ত্র। ***Verb t.*** **1.** To furnish with rope ; রজ্জু বা রজ্জুশ্রেণী সমন্বিত করা, তার লাগান। **2.** To thread on a string ; as, to *string* bead ; গ্রন্থন করা, গাঁথা, গুম্ফিত করা। **3.** To deprive of strings ; as, to *string* beans ; আঁশ ছাড়ান। **4.** To make tense ; to impart vigour to ; টান দেওয়া ; সতেজ করা। ***Verb i.*** **1.** To form into a string or strings ; রজ্জুতে পরিণত হওয়া। **2.** To move in a string ; সারি বাঁধিয়া চলা। **3.** (*Billiard*) To make the preliminary strokes that decide which player shall begin ; কোন ক্রীড়ক প্রথম ক্রীড়া আরম্ভ করিবে তন্নির্ণয়ের জন্য প্রাথমিক আঘাত করা। **Stringed,** *p. p.* **Heart-strings**—হৃদয়তন্ত্রী, মর্ম্মতন্ত্রী। **String-alphabet**—অন্ধদিগের জন্য রজ্জুর উপর গ্রন্থি দ্বারা রচিত একপ্রকার বর্ণমালা। **Stringed instrument**—তন্ত্রীবিশিষ্ট বাদ্যযন্ত্র, তযন্ত্র। **To harp on the same-string** — See HARP. **To have one on a string**—To lord over some one ; কাহারো উপর প্রভুত্ব করা। **To have two strings (or a second string) to one's bow**—See under BOW. **To pull the strings** See under PULL. **To string up**—To kill by hanging ; ফাঁসি দিয়া মারা।

stringendo, (*It.*), (*Mus.*) With increased speed and loudness ; (সঙ্গীতবিদ্যা) দ্রুততরভাবে এবং উচ্চতর নাদে।

strin'-gĕnt, *adj.* **1.** Strict ; rigid ; কড়া ; কঠোর। **2.** (Of money-market) Tight ; (টাকার বাজার) শক্ত, কঠিন। **–gen-cy,** *n.* **–ly,** *adv.*

string'-ȳ, *adj.* **1.** Like string ; fibrous ; রজ্জুবৎ ; অংশুল, আঁশযুক্ত। **2.** Gluey ; আটালো, চটচটে। **–i-ness,** *n.*

strip, *v. t.* & *i.* **1.** To deprive ; to denude ; to skin ; to peel ; বর্জ্জিত করা, রহিত করা, বিরহিত করা, চ্যুত করা, বিহীন করা ; উলঙ্গ করা, নগ্ন করা ; চর্ম্ম উন্মোচন করা ; (খোসা) ছাড়ান, ছাড়ান। **2.** To plunder ; লুণ্ঠন করা, লুটিয়া নেওয়া। **3.** To milk dry ; as, to *strip* a cow ; এক ফোঁটাও দুগ্ধ না রাখিয়া গাভী দোহন করা। **4.** To unrig ; as, to *strip* a ship ; জাহাজের দড়াদাড়ি খুলিয়া লওয়া। ***Verb i.*** **1.** To uncover ;

to undress ; আবরণ উন্মোচিত হওয়া ; উলঙ্গ হওয়া। 2. (Of a screw) To lose thread ; (স্ক্রূপ সম্পর্কে) পেঁচ কাটিয়া যাওয়া। **Strip-leaf**—ডাঁটাছাড়ানো তামাকু পাতা। **To strip a tobacco**—To remove stems from ; তামাকের পাতার ডাঁটা ছিঁড়িয়া ফেলা। **To strip one to the skin** — To make one naked ; উলঙ্গ করা।

strip, *n.* A long narrow piece ; লম্বা সরু ফালি, চিলতা, দীর্ঘ এবং অপ্রশস্ত খণ্ড।

strīpe, *n.* 1. A streak ; ডোরা, রেখা। 2. (*Pl.*) Flogging ; বেত্রাঘাত। 3. A strip or long narrow piece attached to something of a different colour ; as, a *stripe* of silk sewed upon a garment ; বিভিন্ন বর্ণের কোন কিছুর উপর সংযুক্ত অপ্রশস্ত খণ্ড। 4. A discolouration caused by a blow or lash ; কালশিরা। **Striped**, *p. p.* Having stripes of different colours ; ডোরা কাটা, ডুরে, ডোরাদার। **Strip′-i-ness**, *n.* **Strip′-y**, *adj.*

strip′-ling, *n.* A tall slender youth ; ছোড়া, ছোকরা, কিশোর, বটু।

strīve, *v. i.* 1. To endeavour ; to struggle ; চেষ্টা করা ; সংগ্রাম করা। 2. To vie ; প্রতিদ্বন্দ্বিতা করা। 3. (*Obs.*) To quarrel ; (অপ্রঃ) কলহ করা, ঝগড়া করা, বিবাদ করা।

strŏb′-īle, *n.* (*Bot.*) A catkin the carpels of which are scale-like, as in the pines ; (উদ্ভিদ্‌বিদ্যা) শঙ্ক (সাঃ পঃ), মঞ্জরী (ঐ)।

strōde, *p. t.* of STRIDE (which see.)

strōke, *n.* 1. A blow ; আঘাত, প্রহার, ঘা, অভিঘাত। 2. Injury ; ক্ষত। 3. A throb ; স্পন্দন, ধুকধুকি। 4. A vigorous or energetic effort ; প্রবল উদ্যম, প্রবল চেষ্টা। 5. Any sudden attack of disease etc. ; as, a sun-*stroke* : a *stroke* of paralysis ; কোন রোগের আকস্মিক আক্রমণ। 6. A line or dash ; কলম, তুলি প্রভৃতির টান বা খোঁচা। 7. The sound of the clock ; ঘড়ীর টং টং শব্দ। 8. A sudden burst or flash ; as, a *stroke* of lightning ; উচ্ছ্বাস বা চমক। 9. Series of operations ; কার্য্য-পরম্পরা। 10. The sweep of an oar in rowing ; একবার দাঁড় ঘুরাণি। 11. The upward and downward motion of the piston of a steam-engine ; বাষ্পীয়যন্ত্রের নলদণ্ডের পর্য্যায়ক্রমে উর্দ্ধে উত্থান ও নিম্নে পতন। 12. Same as STROKE-OAR. **Finishing stroke**—শেষ তুলির রেখা, শেষ চানকান ; খতম ঘা। **Stroke-oar**—নৌকার গলুইএর দিকের সর্ব্বশেষ দাঁড় ; যে ব্যক্তি ঐ দাঁড় চালনা করে। **Strokesman**—Same as STROKE-OAR. **A stroke of genius**—প্রতিভার আশ্চর্য্য স্ফুরণ। **A stroke of policy**—ফিকির, ফন্দী। **A stroke of wit**—রঙ্গরসের উচ্ছ্বাস। **At one stroke**—এক আঘাতে, এক কোপে, এক চোটে, একদমে। **By a stroke of the pen**—কলমের এক খোঁচায়। **It is on the stroke of five**—পাঁচটা বাজিল বলিয়া। **On the stroke**—Punctually ; ঠিক সময় মত, একবারে ঘড়ীর কাঁটায় কাঁটায়। **Stroke of the sun**—সূর্য্যকিরণ (সাঃ পঃ)। **Stroke of the wind**—বাতাঘাত (সাঃ পঃ)।

strōke, *v. t.* & *n.* 1. To rub gently with the hand ; আদরে গা বুলান। 2. To make smooth ; মসৃণ করা। ***Noun.*** A stroking caress ; সোহাগে গা বুলানি। **Strok′-ing-ly**, *adv.* **To stroke the wrong way**—To ruffle ; বিক্ষুব্ধ করা।

strōll, *v. i.* & *n.* To rove; to saunter ; পরিভ্রমণ করা ; বেড়ান। ***Noun.*** A wandering on foot ; leisurely idle ramble ; পদব্রজে ভ্রমণ, পরিক্রম, পরিভ্রমণ, পর্য্যটন ; বৃথাটন। **Stroll′-er**, *n.*

strŏ′-mă, *n. Pl.* STROMATA. (*Biol.*) The spongy colourless frame-work of a red blood-corpuscle or cell ; (জীববিজ্ঞান) অণুকোষ বা রক্তের লোহিত কণিকার অবর্ণ এবং শোষকবৎ আধার। 2. (*Anat.*) The tissue which affords mechanical support ; (শারীরসংস্থানবিদ্যা) যান্ত্রিক আশ্রয় স্বরূপ বিধানতন্তু।

strŏng, *adj.* 1. Having power or force ; শক্তিমান, বলবান, বলিষ্ঠ, উর্জ্জস্বল, বলশালী, শক্তিশালী, শক্তি-সম্পন্ন, বীর্য্যবান। 2. Robust ; সুস্থ, সবল। 3. Violent ; প্রবল ; প্রচণ্ড। 4. Firm ; দৃঢ়, শক্ত। 5. Ardent ; zealous ; প্রবল, উৎসাহবান্। 6. Having virtues of great efficacy or having particular qualities in great degree ; as, *strong* tea : *strong* wine ; কড়া, উগ্র, তীব্র, টং (*colloq.* — cf. বেশী টং করিস্‌নে—নবীন সন্ন্যাসী)। 7. Containing a large proportion of alcohol ; অধিকমাত্রায় সুরাসারযুক্ত। 8. Glaring ; vivid ; as, *strong* light ; চোখ ঝলসানো ; তীব্র। 9. Powerful, mentally or morally ; as, a man of *strong* imagination ; দৃঢ়চিত্ত, মানসিকশক্তিসম্পন্ন। 10. Well-fortified ; দুর্গ প্রাকারাদি-দ্বারা সুরক্ষিত। 11. Firm ; well-established ; as, *strong* belief ; দৃঢ় ; অচলপ্রতিষ্ঠিত। 12. Rising ; as, a *strong* market ; চড়তি, চড়া। 13. Consisting of a specified number of men ; as, an army 10,000 *strong* ; নির্দ্দিষ্টপরিমাণে শক্তিসম্পন্ন। 14. (*Gram.*) Forming its tenses by vowel gradation ; (ব্যাকরণ) স্বরবর্ণের ক্রমপরিবর্ত্তন দ্বারা কালসাধক, সবল। 15. Nourishing ; solid ; পুষ্টিকর ; সারবান। 16. Well up ; as, he is very *strong* in English ; পাকা। **Strong′-ish**, *adj.* **Strong′-ly**, *adv.* **Strong-bodied, Strong-built**, *adj.* মাংসল, দৃঢ়াঙ্গ, দৃঢ়কায়। **Strong-box**—লৌহ প্রভৃতি নির্ম্মিত সুদৃঢ় সিন্দুক। **Strong drink, —waters**—তীব্র পানীয়, তীব্র

সুরা। **Stronghold**—দুর্গ, গিরিদুর্গ; আশ্রয়স্থল, কোট। **Strong language** — কড়া কথা, চড়া কথা। **Strong man**—শক্তিমান শাসনকর্ত্তা, প্রভাবসম্পন্ন শাসনকর্ত্তা। **Strong-minded** — দৃঢ়চিত্ত, স্থিরসংকল্প। **Strong-room**—চোর, অগ্নি, প্রভৃতি হইতে সুরক্ষিত দুর্ভেদ্য গৃহ। **Going strong**—(ইতর ভাষায়) পুরাদমে অগ্রসর; খুব সুস্থ সবল। **The strong hand**—শক্তি, বল, জোর। **To come** or **go it strong**—(*Slang*) To go to great length in something; কোন বিষয়ে অনেকদুর অগ্রসর হওরা।

strŏn′-ti-ă (-shĭ-), **–ti-ăn**(-shĭ-), *ns.* The oxide of strontium; একপ্রকার রাসায়নিক পদার্থ। [Nitrate of strontium এর সাহায্যে আতসবাজি প্রস্তুতকারিগণ লোহিত আলো উৎপাদন করে।]

strŏn′-ti-ŭm (-shĭ-) *n.* A dark yellow metal; একপ্রকার ঘন পীতবর্ণ ধাতু, ত্র্যংশক (সাঃ পঃ)।

strŏp, *n.* & *v. t.* A strip of leather or a strip of wood covered with leather used for sharpening razor; নাপিতের চামাতি, চর্ম্মপট, চর্ম্মঠ। ***Verb t.*** To sharpen on a strop; চামাতিতে ধার দেওয়া।

strō′-phē, *n.* **1.** The former of the two corresponding stanzas in an ode; গীতিকবিতার পরম্পরানুসারী কলিদ্বয়ের পূর্ব্ববর্ত্তী কলি। **2.** The movement of the chorus while turning from the right to the left of the orchestra; (প্রাচীন গ্রীসে) নর্ত্তনকালে নর্ত্তকগণের বাদ্যমঞ্চের দক্ষিণ হইতে বামে আবর্ত্তন, বামাবর্ত্তন।

strŏph′-ĭ-ōle, *n.* An aril-like appendage attached to the base of certain seeds; কোন কোন বীজের নিম্নে সংলগ্ন উপচ্ছদ তুল্য উপাঙ্গ বিশেষ, ত্বকোৎসেধ (সাঃ পঃ)।

strŏph′-ū-lous (-lŭs), *n.* A popular skin disease peculiar to infants and children; শিশুদিগের হামের ন্যায় পীড়কাবিশিষ্ট চর্ম্মরোগবিশেষ, অলজিকা (হঃ চঃ), বেলা (ঐ), অজগল্লিকা (সাঃপ ঃ)।

strōve, *Pt.* of STRIVE (which see.)

strow (strō), *v. t.* (*Archaic* For) STREW.

strŭck, *pt.* & *pp.* of STRIKE (which see.) **To be struck dumb**—To be astonished; অবাক হওয়া, চক্ষুঃ স্থির হওয়া, পেটের ভিতর হাত পা ঢুকা।

strŭc′-tūre, *n.* **1.** Something constructed or built, a bridge, dam, etc.; নির্ম্মিত বস্তু, সেতু, বাঁধ, প্রভৃতি, দেউল (উড়িষ্যা)। **2.** A building of any kind, but chiefly a building of some size or of magnificence; an edifice; "There stands a *structure* of a majestic frame"; অট্টালিকা; প্রাসাদ, হর্ম্ম্য। **3.** Manner of building; নির্ম্মাণপ্রণালী, গঠনপ্রণালী। **4.** Organization; অঙ্গবিন্যাস, অঙ্গসংস্থান, সংস্থান। **5.** Make; construction; গঠন, ডোল; নির্ম্মাণ, রচনা। **–less,** *adj.* Without structure; without organization; হীনবচন (সাঃ পঃ); অব্যবস্থান্ধ। **–tur-al,** *adj.* **–tur-al-ly,** *adv.*

strŭg′-gle (-l), *v. i.* & *n.* To make great efforts; to strive; প্রবল চেষ্টা করা, প্রাণপণ যত্ন করা, যথাসাধ্য চেষ্টা করা; সংগ্রাম করা, ধ্বস্তাধ্বস্তি করা, হুড়াহুড়ি করা। ***Noun.*** A violent effort of the body; contest; strife; প্রবল শারীরিক চেষ্টা; সংগ্রাম; দ্বন্দ্ব। **–gler,** *n.* **–gling-ly,** *adv.* **Struggle for existence** — জীবনসংগ্রাম, সত্তারক্ষার জন্য ধ্বস্তাধ্বস্তি, (দ্বিজেন্দ্রনাথ ঠাকুর), জীবনপ্রতিবাদিতা (হিঃ কেঃ), জীবনপ্রয়াস (ঐ)।

Strŭld′-brŭg, *n.* In Swift's Gulliver's Travels a class of men cursed with immortality; সুইফ্‌টের গালিভারের ভ্রমণকাহিনী বর্ণিত অমরত্ব দ্বারা অভিশপ্ত ব্যক্তিগণের অন্যতম।

strŭm, *v. i.* & *n.* To play badly and noisily on stringed instrument; বেহালা প্রভৃতি আনাড়ীর মত বাজান। ***Noun.*** A careless performance on a stringed instrument; আনাড়ীর মত বেহালা প্রভৃতি তন্ত্রীবিশিষ্ট বাদ্যযন্ত্র বাদন।

stru′-mă (strô-), *n.* **1.** Scrofula; গলগণ্ড, গণ্ডমালা। **2.** (*Bot.*) A swelling at the root of a leaf; পত্রমূলের স্ফীতি। **–mose,** *adj.*

strŭm′-pĕt, *n.* Prostitute; বেশ্যা, গণিকা। (See PROSTITUTE).

strŭng, *p. t.* & *p. p.* of STRING (which see).

strŭt, *v. i.* & *n.* To walk with a lofty proud gait and erect head; সাটোপে চলা, সগর্ব্বে চলা, সদর্পে পদক্ষেপ করা, বুক ফুলাইয়া চলা, ঠেকরিয়া চলা (*colloq.*)। ***Noun.*** A lofty proud step or walk, with the head erect; সাটোপে চলন, সগর্ব্বে চলন। **Strut′-ting-ly,** *adv.* In a strutting manner; সাটোপে।

strŭt, *n.* & *v. t.* A piece of timber obliquely placed from a king or queen-post to strengthen a rafter or a horizontal piece; গৃহের বর্গা বা অন্য কোন শয়ান কাষ্ঠাদির খণ্ড শক্ত করার জন্য ধন্নার উপরিস্থিত থাম হইতে তির্য্যগ্‌ভাবে প্রসারিত কাষ্ঠফলক, তির্য্যকফলক। ***Verb t.*** To brace with struts; তির্য্যকফলক দ্বারা শক্ত করা।

stru′-thi-ous (strō-thĭ-ŭs), *adj.* Pertaining to, or resembling, an ostrich; উটপক্ষি-সম্পর্কীয়, উটপক্ষিবৎ, উটপক্ষিসদৃশ।

strȳch′-nĭ-ă, –nin, –nine, *ns.* A vegetable alkaloid poison obtained from the seeds of nux-vomica; কুচিলার বীজ হইতে প্রাপ্ত একপ্রকার উদ্ভিজ্জ বিষ। [ইহা স্নায়বিক উত্তেজনা উৎপাদনের জন্য অতি অল্পমাত্রায় ব্যবহৃত হইয়া থাকে।]

Strychnos colubrina — (Snake wood) কুচিলা লতা (বেলঃ)।

Strychnos nuxvomica—কুচিলা (বেলঃ), বেশমুষ্টিবীজম্ (ঐ)।

stŭb, *n.* & *v. t.* **1.** The stump of a tree; ছিন্নকাণ্ড বৃক্ষের মূল, গাছের গুঁড়ি।

2. A remnant of anything; as, the *stub* of a candle, pencil, cigar, etc.; কোন বস্তুর ক্ষয়াবশেষ। 3. An old horse-shoe nail (also *stub-nail*); iron formed therefrom (also *stub-iron*); ঘোড়ার নালের পুরাতন প্রেক; ঐরূপ প্রেক হইতে গঠিত লোহ। ***Verb t.*** 1. To grub up by the roots; as to *stub* up root; উৎপাটিত করা, উন্মূলিত করা। 2. To remove stubs from; as, to *stub* land; (ভূমি হইতে) কাটাগাছের গুঁড়ি তুলিয়া ফেলা। **Stub'-by,** *adj.*

stŭb'-ble (-l), *n.* 1. The small stubs of grain left in the ground after reaping; শস্যচ্ছেদনের পর উহার যে অংশ ভূমির সহিত সংলগ্ন থাকে। 2. Cropped hair or beard; ছাঁটা দাড়ী, ছাঁটা চুল। **Stub'-bly,** *adj.*

stŭb'-born (-ŏrn), *adj.* 1. Obstinate; as, a *stubborn* child; intractable; obdurate; একগুঁয়ে, একরোখা; অদম্য; দুরাগ্রহ, দুর্দ্দম। 2. Not easily melted or worked; as, *stubborn* metal; দুর্দ্রবণীয়, যাহার উপরে সহজে কাজ করা চলে না—তদ্রূপ। **—ly,** *adv.* **—ness,** *n.*

stŭc'-cō, *n.* & *v. t.* A fine plaster used for internal decorations of rooms, as, cornices mouldings, etc. (In modern building *stucco* is generally an exterior coating in which cement is largely used); work made of stucco; একপ্রকার আস্তর—যদ্দারা অট্টালিকার ভিতরে নানাপ্রকার কারুকার্য্য করা হয়; ঐরূপ আস্তরের কায। ***Verb t.*** To overlay with fine plaster; মিহি আস্তরের লেপ দেওয়া।

Stŭck, Stŭck'-ŭp—See STICK.

stŭd, *n.* & *v. t.* 1. A kind of ornamental button or catch for shirt; কারুকার্য্যখচিত সার্টের বোতাম। 2. A nail with a large head, inserted in work chiefly for ornament; একপ্রকার প্রেক—যাহা প্রধানতঃ শোভার জন্য কোন জিনিষের মধ্যে প্রবিষ্ট করা হয়। 3. A small piece of timber or joist inserted in the sills and beams between the parts, to support the beams or other main timbers; কড়িকাঠ প্রভৃতির অবলম্বন-স্বরূপ কাষ্ঠফলক। ***Verb t.*** 1. To adorn with studs or ornamental nails; "Their harness *studded* all with gold and pearl;" শোভাসাধক প্রেকদ্বারা মণ্ডিত করা। 2. To set thickly, as with studs; আচ্ছন্ন করা, সংচ্ছন্ন করা (cf. অয়ঃকণ্টক-সংচ্ছন্ন)। 3. To be scattered over here and there; ইতস্ততঃ বিক্ষিপ্ত হওয়া।

stŭd, *n.* 1. A number of horses kept for certain purpose; অশ্বযূথ, অশ্বশ্রেণী। 2. The place where a stud is kept; যে স্থানে অশ্বযূথ রক্ষিত হয়। **Stud-book**—A book containing pedigree of horses; যে পুস্তকে অশ্বের বংশপরিচয় লিখিত থাকে। **Stud-farm**—Place where horses are bred; যে স্থানে অশ্ব উৎপাদন ও পালন করা হয়। **Stud-horse**—জননাশ্ব।

stŭd'-ding-sail (-ĭng-sāl), *n.* A narrow sail set at the side of a square-sail when the wind is light; মৃদু বায়ুতে চতুষ্কোণ পাইলের বহিঃপ্রান্তে যে অপরিসর পাইল টাঙ্গান হয়।

Studding sails.

stū'-dĕnt, *n.* 1. A person engaged in study; ছাত্র, বিদ্যার্থী (উজ্জ্বলঃ), শিক্ষার্থী। 2. A man devoted to books; অধ্যয়নশীল ব্যক্তি। 3. One who studies or examines, as, he is a *student* of chemistry; যে ব্যক্তি কোন বিষয় অধ্যয়ন বা পরীক্ষা করে। 4. The recipient of a scholarship; বৃত্তিধারী ছাত্র। **—ship,** *n.* 1. The state of being a student; ছাত্রত্ব। 2. Scholarship; বৃত্তি।

stū'-di-ō, *n.* The working-room of a painter, sculptor, etc.; চিত্রকর, শিলাশিল্পী প্রভৃতির কার্য্যশালা, কর্ম্মকক্ষ, শিল্পকক্ষ, শিল্পিশালা, কারুকক্ষ।

stū'-di-ous (-ŭs), *adj.* 1. Given to study; as, a *studious* man or life; fond of study or learning; devoted to the acquisition of knowledge; অধ্যয়ননিরত, অধ্যয়নশীল; অধ্যয়নপ্রিয়, অধ্যয়ন পরায়ণ; জ্ঞানার্জ্জনরত। 2. Earnest; mindful; as, he was *studious* of his affairs; diligent; আগ্রহবান; মনোযোগী; শ্রমশীল। 3. Devoted to, or spent in, study; অধ্যয়নে প্রযুক্ত, অধ্যয়নে ব্যয়িত। 4. Deliberate; "The frigid villany of *studious* lewdness"; zealous; anxious; as, *studious* care; চিন্তিত; উৎসাহসম্পন্ন; ব্যগ্র। **—ly,** *adv.* **—ness,** *n.*

stŭd'-ȳ, *n.* 1. Earnest mental endeavour; close attention; diligence; profound thought or meditation; প্রবল মানসিক চেষ্টা; গভীর মনোযোগ; পরিশ্রম; গভীর চিন্তা বা ধ্যান। 2. Application of mind to books, arts, science, etc. for the purpose of learning what was not before known; as the *study* of books: *study* of fishes; অধ্যয়ন, পাঠ। 3. Any particular branch of study; any subject of close consideration; as, the proper *study* of mankind is man; বিদ্যার কোন বিশেষ শাখা; গভীর অনুধ্যানের বিষয়। 4. A room devoted to study or literary pursuit; পাঠকক্ষ, পাঠপ্রকোষ্ঠ, অধ্যয়নশালা, বিদ্যাভ্যাসমন্দির

(বিশ্বকর্ম্মা)। 5. A work undertaken for improvement in the art and often left unfinished; শিল্পকলাকুশলতা লাভের জন্য শিল্পী যে চিত্রাদি অঙ্কন করে এবং যাহা সচরাচর অসম্পন্ন ভাবে রক্ষিত হইয়া থাকে। 6. A prefatory sketch from nature to be used in the composition of other larger and more finished works; বৃহত্তর এবং অধিকতর কলাসৌষ্ঠবসম্পন্ন আলেখ্য অঙ্কনের জন্য ব্যবহৃত নিসর্গ হইতে অঙ্কিত প্রাথমিক স্থূলচিত্র। 7. (*Theatre*) One who commits a part to memory; as, slow *study*; (রঙ্গালয়) যে ব্যক্তি কোন ভূমিকা মুখস্থ করে। 9. (*Mus.*) Composition designed to test or develop player's skill; বাদকের চাতুর্য্য পরীক্ষার জন্য বা বিকাশের উদ্দেশ্যে পরিকল্পিত সুর।

stŭd'-ȳ, *v. t.* & *i.* 1. To apply the mind to books or learning; পাঠ করা, অধ্যয়ন করা। 2. To endeavour diligently; প্রবল চেষ্টা করা। 3. To consider attentively; to examine minutely; "*Study* help for that which thou lamentest"; মনোযোগের সহিত বিবেচনা করা; পুঙ্খানুপুঙ্খরূপে পরীক্ষা করা। 4. To be solicitious for; as, to *study* one's own interest; ব্যগ্র হওয়া। ***Verb i.*** 1. To apply the mind to books or learning; পাঠ করা, অধ্যয়ন করা। 2. To endeavour diligently; "We beseech you...that ye *study* to be quiet, and to do your own business"; সবিশেষ চেষ্টা করা। 3. To meditale; ধ্যান করা, অনুধ্যান করা, গভীর চিন্তা করা। **–ied,** *pp.* Deliberate; false; as, *studied* courtesy; সুচিন্তিত, ইচ্ছাকৃত; কৃত্রিম। **–ied-ly,** *adv.* **To study one's part**—To try to commit it to memory; ভূমিকা মুখস্থ করিতে চেষ্টা করা।

stŭff, *n.*, *v. t.* & *i.* 1. Substance or matter indefinitely; বস্তু, জিনিষ, সামগ্রী, পদার্থ। 2. Essence; সার, মূল উপাদান। 3. (*Slang*) money; cash; (ইতরভাষায়) টাকা পয়সা; নগদ টাকা। 4. (*Comm.*) A general name for all kinds of fabrics of silk, cotton, wool, etc.; woollen cloth of slight texture, for linings and women's apparel; পশম, রেশম, কার্পাস প্রভৃতি বস্ত্রের সাধারণ নাম; আস্তর ও স্ত্রীলোকের পোষাকের জন্য একপ্রকার পাতলা ডুরে জমির পশমী কাপড়। 5. Refuse; worthless matter; "This is mere *stuff*"; জঞ্জাল, আবর্জ্জনা; অসার পদার্থ। 6. A medicine; a mixture; ঔষধ; মিশ্র। ***Verb t.*** 1. To fill by packing or crowding material into; as, to *stuff* a purse; to load to excess; ঠাসা, ঠাসিয়া ভরা; অতিরিক্ত বোঝাই করা। 2. To distend; স্ফীত করা, ফুলান। 3. To fill the skin of, as a dead animal, for presenting and preserving its form; as, to *stuff* a lion; অবয়ব অক্ষুণ্ণ রাখিবার জন্য মৃত জন্তুর চর্ম্ম কোন বস্তুদ্বারা পূর্ণ করা। 4. To fill with a seasoning composition; as, to *stuff* a turkey; রুটি, মাংস, মসলা, প্রভৃতির মিশ্র দ্বারা পূর্ণ করা, পুর দেওয়া। 5. To fill with cotton etc.; as, to *stuff* cushion; to furnish an yielding support; তুলা প্রভৃতি দ্বারা পুরা; নরম কোন জিনিষ ঠাসা। 6. To crowd; to pack closely with; গাদা করা; ঠাসাঠাসি করিয়া রাখা। 7. To crowd or fill with items of information, thoughts, ideas, emotions, etc.; as, who has been *stuffing* you; কোনরূপ বিবরণ, চিন্তা, আবেগ, প্রভৃতি দ্বারা পরিপুরিত করা। 8. To gull with lies; to hoax; মিথ্যা কথা বলিয়া প্রতারণা করা; ধোঁকা দেওয়া। ***Verb i.*** To feed gluttonously; অতিরিক্ত ভোজন করান। **Stŭff'-ing,** *n.* & *adj.* **Bread-stuff**—যে সকল জিনিষ হইতে ময়দা প্রস্তুত হয়। **Doctors' stuff**—ভেষজ দ্রব্য। **Food-stuff**—খাদ্যদ্রব্য। **Green stuff, Garden stuff**—শাকসব্জী। **Inch stuff**—এক ইঞ্চি পুরু কাষ্ঠফলক। **Stuff gown** — রাজা বা রাণীর কৌন্‌সলি (King's or Queen's counsel) হওয়ার কালে ব্যারিষ্টারগণ যে কার্পাসের গাউন পরিধান করিয়া থাকেন। **Stuffing-box**—কলের কোঠর বিশেষ—যাহার সমস্ত শূন্য স্থান তুলা নেকড়া প্রভৃতি দ্বারা পূর্ণ হওয়াতে দণ্ড চালিত হওয়ার কালে উহার ভিতরে বাতাস প্রবেশ করিতে পারে না। **Thick stuff**—৪ ইঞ্চি অপেক্ষা অধিক পুরু তক্তা।

stŭff'-ȳ, *adj.* Difficult to breathe in; close; stifling; শ্বাসগ্রহণে কষ্টকর; আবদ্ধ, রুদ্ধ; শ্বাসরোধকর।

stŭg'-gy (-ĭ), See STOCKY.

stŭl'-tĭ-fȳ, *v. t.* 1. To make foolish; নির্ব্বোধ প্রতিপন্ন করা, আহাম্মক করা, বোকা বানান। 2. (*Law*) To allege or prove to be insane for avoiding some act; কোন ক্রিয়া হইতে বিরত থাকার দরুণ উন্মাদ বলিয়া আরোপ বা ঘোষণা করা। 3. To render nugatory; to destroy the value of; অকার্য্যকর করা, ব্যর্থ করা; মূল্য নষ্ট করা। **–fi-ca'-tion,** *n.* **To stultify one's self**—To unsay, directly or by implication, what one has already said; to lay one's self open to an accusation of self-contradiction; প্রত্যক্ষভাবে বা প্রকারান্তরে পূর্ব্ব উক্তির বিরুদ্ধে কথা বলা; নিজের পূর্ব্ব উক্তির বিরুদ্ধে কথা বলার অভিযোগের অধীন হওয়া।

stŭm, *n.* & *v. t.* Unfermented grape-juice; অগাঁজান আঙ্গুর রস। ***Verb t.*** To prevent from fermenting; to secure against further fermentation in cask by the introduction of antiseptic; অন্তরুৎসেচন নিবারণ করা; পিপায় পচননিবারক বস্তুর সংযোগদ্বারা যাহাতে

দ্বিতীয়বার গাঁজিতে না পারে তাহার চেষ্টা করা।

stŭm'-ble (-bl), *v. i., t.* & *n.* **1.** To trip in moving ; হোঁচট খাওয়া, টক্কর খাওয়া। **2.** To walk in an unsteady manner ; "Instead of going they only *stumble* about their house" ; to perform anything blunderingly or confusedly ; টলিতে টলিতে চলা ; ভুল করিতে করিতে বা এলোমেলোভাবে কোন কিছু করা। **3.** To fall into error or crime ; ভ্রমে পতিত হওয়া, পাপে পতিত হওয়া। **4.** To fall by chance ; to come by chance (with *on, upon* or *against*) ; "Ovid *stumbled* by some inadvertence *upon* Livia in a Bath." ; দৈবক্রমে পড়িয়া যাওয়া; হঠাৎ আসিয়া পড়া। **5.** To feel scruples ; সঙ্কোচ বোধ করা। ***Verb t.*** **1.** To cause to stumble or trip ; হোঁচট খাওয়ান। **2.** To perplex ; বিভ্রান্ত করা, হতবুদ্ধি করা, কিংকর্ত্তব্যবিমূঢ় করা। ***Noun.*** **1.** The act of stumbling ; হোঁচট, টক্কর। **2.** Blunder ; ভুল, চুক, প্রমাদ, স্খলিত। **Stumbling-block**—Obstacle ; circumstances that causes difficulty or hesitation or scruples ; বাধা, বিঘ্ন ; প্রতিবন্ধক, অন্তরায়।

stŭmp, *n., v. i.* & *t.* **1.** The end remaining after something has been cut off ; ছিন্নাবশিষ্ট অংশ, ছিন্নাবশেষ। **2.** The remaining part of a branch of a tree after being cut down ; বৃক্ষের ছিন্নাবশিষ্ট শাখা। **3.** The part of limb, left after the rest is cut off or destroyed ; ছিন্নাবশিষ্ট অঙ্গ। **4.** (*Slang, pl.*) The legs ; as, to stir one's *stumps* ; (ইতর ভাষায়) পদদ্বয়। **5.** (*Cricket*) One of the three uprights of a wicket ; (ক্রীকেট ক্রীড়ায়) যে দণ্ডত্রয় ভূমিতে প্রোথিত করা হয়—তাহার অন্যতম। **6.** A short, thick roll of leather or paper, cut to a point, and used to shade or colour a crayon or pencil drawing ; পেন্সিল বা চিত্রবর্ত্তিকা দ্বারা অঙ্কিত চিত্র রঞ্জিত বা ছায়ান্বিত করার জন্য কাগজ বা চর্ম্ম গুটাইয়া খাটো পেন্সিলের আকারে প্রস্তুত তুলিকা। ***Verb i.*** **1.** To walk stiffly and noisily ; ঠকর ঠকর করিয়া চলা। **2.** To make speeches on the stump ; ছিন্নাবশিষ্ট বৃক্ষের উপর দাঁড়াইয়া বক্তৃতা করা। ***Verb t.*** **1.** To remove tree stumps ; ছিন্নাবশিষ্ট বৃক্ষের মূল অপসারিত করা। **2.** To travel over, delivering speeches for electioneering purposes ; to make stump speeches ; নির্ব্বাচনের জন্য বক্তৃতা প্রদানচ্ছলে পরিভ্রমণ করা ; গাছের গুঁড়ি বা তদ্বৎ কোন কিছুর উপর দাঁড়াইয়া বক্তৃতা করা। **3.** To put out of play a batsman who is not in his ground in cricket by knocking down a stump ; ব্যাটধারী স্বীয় নির্দ্দিষ্ট স্থানের বাহিরে থাকা অবস্থায়—তৎসন্নিহিত দণ্ডত্রয়ে কন্দুক নিক্ষেপ করিয়া তাহাকে আউট করা। **Stump-orator**—কোন প্রকার মঞ্চ হইতে উপস্থিত মত যে বক্তৃতা দেওয়া হয় ; বাগাড়ম্বরপূর্ণ রাজনৈতিক বক্তৃতা। **Stump oratory**—রাজনৈতিক বক্তৃতা (তুচ্ছার্থে)। **I am stumped**—I am at a loss ; আমি কিংকর্ত্তব্যবিমূঢ় হইয়াছি, আমি একবারে হতভম্ব হইয়াছি। **On the stump**—রাজনৈতিক বক্তৃতা প্রদান বা আন্দোলনে রত। **To stump up**—(*Slang*) To pay over ; (টাকা) চুকাইয়া দেওয়া।

stŭmp'-y̆, *adj.* **1.** Full of stumps ; ছিন্নবৃক্ষেরগুঁড়িদ্বারা আচ্ছন্ন। **2.** Short and thick ; খর্ব্ব এবং স্থূল, বজ্রবাঁটুলবৎ।

stŭn, *v. t.* **1.** To render senseless by a blow on the head ; মস্তক প্রভৃতিতে আঘাত করিয়া অচেতন করা। **2.** To overpower ; to stupefy ; অভিভূত করা ; স্তব্ধ করা, জড়ীভূত করা, স্তম্ভিত করা। **3.** To overcome ; esp. to overpower the sense of hearing ; অভিভূত করা ; বধির করা, কানে তালা লাগান, ঝালাপালা করা। **Stun'-ner,** *n.* **Stun'-ning,** *adj.* First-rate ; astonishingly fine, large or the like ; প্রথম শ্রেণীর ; চমৎকার। **Stun'-ning-ly,** *adv.*

Stŭn'-dĭsm, *n.* The belief of the Stundists ; রুশিয়াদেশের ধর্ম্মসম্প্রদায়-বিশেষের মত। **—dist,** *n.* A member of a dissenting religious sect of Russia that bases its practice on the Bible alone ; রুশদেশের ধর্ম্মসম্প্রদায় বিশেষ—এই সম্প্রদায়ভুক্ত ব্যক্তিগণের ধর্ম্মানুষ্ঠানপদ্ধতি কেবল মাত্র বাইবেলের উপর প্রতিষ্ঠিত।

stŭng, *p. t.* & *p. p.* of STING (which see).

stunk (stŭngk), *pt.* & *pp.* of STINK (which see).

stŭn'-sail (-săl), *n.* Same as STUDDING-SAIL (which see).

stŭnt, *v. t.* To stop the growth of ; to check ; to cramp ; বৃদ্ধি রোধ করা, বাড়িতে না দেওয়া ; বাধা দেওয়া ; প্রতিবন্ধক জন্মান। **Stunt'-ed,** *pp.* Hinderal from growth; খর্ব্বতাপ্রাপ্ত,খর্ব্বায়তন (বিঃ প্রঃ)।

stūpe, *n.* & *v. t.* Flannel, flax, etc. wrung out of hot water and applied to a sore ; সেক দিবার জন্য উষ্ণ জলে নিমজ্জিত করার পর নিংড়ানো ফ্লানেল প্রভৃতি। ***Verb t.*** To foment with a stupe ; শণ বা তদ্বৎ অন্য কোন বস্তু ঔষধমিশ্রিত উষ্ণ জলে ভিজাইবার পর নিংড়াইয়া লইয়া সেক দেওয়া।

stūpe, *n.* (*Slang*) Fool ; নির্ব্বোধ, বোকা।

stū'-pē-fȳ, *v. t.* To make stupid or torpid ; to deprive of sensibility ; to blunt the faculties or understanding of ; স্তব্ধ করা, স্তম্ভিত করা ; সংজ্ঞাশূন্য করা ; জড়ীভূত করা, আড়ষ্ট করা, নিস্পন্দ করা। **—fac'-tion,** *n.* The act of stupefying or the state of being stupefied ; বুদ্ধিনাশ, বুদ্ধিলোপ, আড়ষ্টতা, অচৈতন্য, স্তব্ধ, স্তব্ধতা, সংমোহ, জড়িমা।

stŭ-pĕn′-dous (-dŭs), *adj.* Astonishing; of astonishing magnitude or elevation; as, a *stupendous* pile; বিস্ময়কর, অসাধারণ, অদ্ভুত; বিপুল, বিরাট, বিশাল। **–ly,** *adv.* **–ness,** *n.*

stū′-pē-ous (-ŭs), *adj.* **1.** Like tow; শণসূত্রবৎ। **2.** (*Entom.*) Covered with long loose hairs or filaments like tow; (কীটতত্ত্ব) শণসূত্রবৎ সুদীর্ঘ শ্লথ লোম বা অংশুসমূহ দ্বারা আবৃত।

stū′-pĭd, *adj.* & *n.* **1.** Stupefied; insensible; in a state of stupor; স্তম্ভিত, জড়ীভূত; অচেতন; জড়তাপ্রাপ্ত। **2.** Silly; slow-witted; আহাম্মক, বেকুব, নির্ব্বোধ; জড়বুদ্ধি, মন্দমতি, মন্দধী, মন্দবুদ্ধি, স্থূলবুদ্ধি, স্থূলধী, মূর্খ অঘারাম (*slang*)। **3.** Characterised by, or resulting from, stupidity; as, a *stupid* suggestion; senseless; dull; as, a *stupid* book; নিবুর্দ্ধিতাসূচক, নির্ব্বুদ্ধিতাপ্রসূত; অর্থহীন, অর্থশূন্য; নীরস। ***Noun.*** A stupid person; নির্ব্বোধ লোক। **–ly,** *adv.* **–pid′-i-ty,** *n.*

stū′-pŏr, *n.* A condition in which the faculties are deadened; torpor; insensibility; জড়ভাব, জড়তা, জাড্য; স্তব্ধতা, আড়ষ্টতা, অসাড়তা, হতবুদ্ধিতা, বিহ্বলতা, অর্দ্ধচৈতন্যাবস্থা, অর্দ্ধবাহ্যাবস্থা; অচৈতন্য, সংজ্ঞাহীনতা, বুদ্ধিলোপ, ব্যামোহ (চিঃ কোঃ)। **–ous,** *adj.*

stū′-pōse, *adj.* (*Bot.* & *Zool.*) Having tuft of long hair like tow; (উদ্ভিদ্‌বিদ্যা এবং জন্তুবিদ্যা) শণাদির স্থূল অংশের মত দীর্ঘ কেশগুচ্ছবিশিষ্ট।

stur′-dȳ (stêr-), *adj.* **1.** Stout; strong; hardy; firm; robust; vigorous; as, *sturdy* blows; বলিষ্ঠ; হৃষ্টপুষ্ট, উর্জ্জস্বল, বলবান; শ্রমসহিষ্ণু; দৃঢ়; দৃঢ়াঙ্গ, দৃঢ়কায়, মাংসল; সতেজ। **2.** Stubborn; obdurate; as, *sturdy* sinner; একগুঁয়ে; কঠোর। **3.** Resolute; as, a *sturdy* patriot; দৃঢ়চিত্ত, দৃঢ়সংকল্প। **–di-ness,** *n.*

stur′-dȳ (stêr-), *n.* A disease affecting young sheep with staggering or stupor carried by a species of tapeworm in the brain; মেষের শিরোভ্রমিরোগবিশেষ। মস্তিষ্কেজাত একপ্রকার ফিতা ক্রিমি দ্বারা এই রোগ উৎপন্ন হয়।

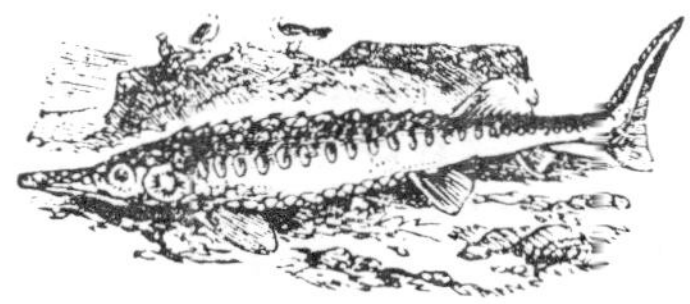

Sturgeon (*Acipenser sturio*)

stur′-geon (stêr-jŏn), *n.* A genus of large fishes having flesh valuable as food; একপ্রকার সুখাদ্য মৎস্য। ***Sturnus vulgaris***—তেলিয়া ময়না (বেলঃ)।

stŭt′-ter (-êr), *v. i., t.* & *n.* To stammer; তোতলান। ***Verb t.*** To utter in a stammering manner; তোতলাইয়া বলা। ***Noun.*** The act of stuttering; তোৎলামি। **–er,** *n.* One who stutters; তোৎলা। **–ing,** *n.* **–ing, ly,** *adv.*

stȳ, *n., v. t.* & *i.* **1.** An enclosure for swine; শূকরের খোঁয়াড়, শূকরশালা। **2.** Any filthy hovel or place; "A sensual *sty*"; নোংরা স্থান, শূয়র কুঁড়ো। ***Verb t. & i.*** To lodge in sty; শূকরের খোঁয়াড়ে বাস করা বা রাখা।

stȳ, stye (stī), *ns.* An inflamed tumour on the edge of the eyelid; চক্ষুর অঞ্জনী, অঞ্জনিকা (ভ বঃ প্রঃ) আঁজনি, উপনাহ (সুশ্রুঃ), কুম্ভীক (ঐ)।

Stȳg′-ĭ-ăn, *adj.* **1.** Pertaining to Styx, a fabled river of hell over which shades of the dead passed; গ্রীকপুরাণোক্ত যমলোকের বৈতরণীনদীসম্বন্ধীয়। **2.** Dark and gloomy; infernal; "At that so sudden blaze, the *Stygian* throng Bent their aspect"; deathly; "Upon those roseate lips a *Stygian* hue"; অন্ধতমসাবৃত; নারকীয়; মরণমলিন।

stȳle, *n.* & *v. t.* **1.** A pointed instrument used by the ancients for writing on wax tablets মোমের ফলকের উপর লিখিবার জন্য প্রাচীনগণ কর্ত্তৃক ব্যবহৃত একপ্রকার লৌহসূচী। **2.** A hard point for tracing, in manifold writing; লিখিবার জন্য লৌহ প্রভৃতির সূক্ষ্মাগ্র শলাকা। **3.** A pen; কলম, লেখনী। **4.** A pin of sundial; সূর্য্য ঘড়ীর শঙ্কু, ধ্রুবপট্ট। **5.** Manner of writing with regard to language; as, a terse or diffuse *style*; রচনারীতি, রচনাপদ্ধতি। **6.** Mode of presentation esp. in music or any of the arts; as, Renaissance *style*; কলারীতি, কলাপদ্ধতি, সঙ্গীতরীতি। **7.** (*Bot.*) The middle portion of the pistil; মধ্যভাগ, কর্ণিক (সাঃ পঃ) গর্ভতন্তু (ঐ), গ্রীব (যোঃ)। **8.** The peculiar manner or mode of action characteristic of the performance of an act; fashion; ধরণ, রীতি; চাল, ধাঁচ। **9.** A kind of blunt pointed surgical instrument; একপ্রকার অসূক্ষ্মাগ্র অস্ত্রোপচারোপযোগী অস্ত্র। **10.** Title; official designation; mode of address; উপাধি; আফিসের উপাধি; (রাজা প্রভৃতিকে) সম্বোধনের রীতি। **11.** A calendar; পঞ্জিকা। ***Verb t.*** To denominate; আখ্যাত করা, অভিহিত করা।

stȳle, *n.* Incorrect spelling for STILE.

stȳ′-lĕt, *n.* **1.** A slender pointed instrument; সূক্ষ্মাগ্র যন্ত্র। **2.** A probe; এষণী, শলাকা। **3.** A stiffening wire of catheter; মূত্রনিঃসারক, শলাকাযন্ত্রের অভ্যন্তরের শক্ত তার। **4.** A small poniard or dagger; ছুরিকা।

stȳl′-ĭsh, *adj.* Highly fashionable; as, *stylish* dress;

modish ; চটকদার ; কায়দাদুরস্ত, কেতাদুরস্ত, কায়দাবাজ ।

stȳl′-ist, *n.* One attentive to style ; one that is a master or model of (style) ; রচনারীতি-সম্বন্ধে বিশেষ মনোযোগী ব্যক্তি ; কোন-রূপ রচনারীতির আদর্শের প্রতিষ্ঠাতা, কোন রচনারীতিতে বিশেষ প্রাজ্ঞ ব্যক্তি । **Sty-lis′-tic,** *adj.* Pertaining to literary style ; রচনারীতিসম্পর্কীয় ।

stȳ′-lite, *n.* One of a sect of solitaries who lived on the tops of pillars in Syria ; মধ্যযুগের স্তম্ভ-শীর্ষোপরিবাসী সন্ন্যাসী ।

stȳ′-lō, *n.* (*Colloq. Abbr.*) STYLOGRAPH.

stȳ′-lō-bāte, *n.* A continuous pedestal on which a row of

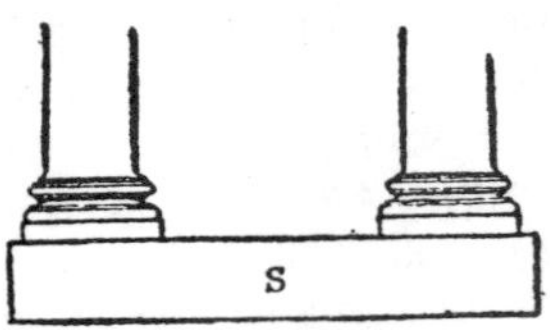

Columns on stylobate.

columns stand ; যে সুদীর্ঘ অধিষ্ঠানের উপর একস্তম্ভ পংক্তি অবস্থিত থাকে ।

stȳ-lō-glŏs′-sal (-ăl), *adj.* (*Anat.*) Connecting the styloid process and the tongue ; রসনা এবং ষ্টাইলয়েড প্রবর্দ্ধন সংযোগকারী ।

stȳ′-lō-grăph, *n.* A pointed fountain pen ; একপ্রকার নির্ঝরলেখনী—যাহার মুখে নিবের পরিবর্ত্তে একখণ্ড শক্ত তার থাকে । **—graph′-ic,** *adj.* **—graph′-i-cal-ly,** *adv.*

stȳ′-loid (-loyd), *adj.* & *n.* Pertaining to certain bony process ; কতিপয় অস্থিপ্রবর্দ্ধন সম্বন্ধীয় । ***Noun.*** Same as STYLOID PROCESS. **Styloid process**—শঙ্খাস্থির অধোদেশ হইতে মেরুদণ্ডের প্রবর্দ্ধন ।

stȳ-lō-pō′-di-ûm, *n.* The conical swelling or expansion at the base of the style ; স্তম্ভপদ (সাঃ পঃ) ।

stȳ′-lō-spōre, *n.* Tulsane's name for the naked spores in certain fungals ; স্তম্ভগ্রেরেণু (সাঃ পঃ) ।

stȳ′-mie (-mî), *n.* & *v. t.* Same as STIMY (which see).

stȳp′-tic, *adj.* & *n.* That stops blood ; রক্তরোধক, রক্তসঙ্কোচক, কষায়ান্বিত । ***Noun.*** An astringent agent applied to the bleeding part to stop the bleeding; রক্তরোধক ঔষধ, শোণিতস্থাপক (ঠাকুরঃ) ।

Styrax benzoin—লোবান (বেলঃ) ।

Stȳx, *n.* (*Gk. Myth.*) The principal river of the nether regions which had to be crossed in passing to the regions of the dead ; গ্রীকপুরাণোক্ত বৈতরণী নদী ।

Sua′-bi-ăn (swā-), *adj.* & *n.* Same as SWABIAN (which see).

sū′-ă-ble (-bl), *adj.* That can be sued ; মোকদ্দমাযোগ্য ।

suā′-sion (swā-), *n.* Persuasion ; প্ররোচন, প্রবর্ত্তনা, প্রণোদনা ।

suave (swāv), *adj.* Polite ; as, *suave* manners ; bland ; pleasant ; soothing ; শিষ্ট, ভদ্র ; কমনীয়, প্রসন্ন ; মনোরম, রমণীয় ; স্নিগ্ধ, শান্তিজনক, আরামদায়ক । **Suave′-ly,** *adv.* **Suav′-i-ty,** *n.* The quality of being suave ; স্নিগ্ধতা, মাধুর্য্য, কমনীয়তা, মনোজ্ঞতা, প্রসন্নতা, আরামদায়কতা । **Suavity of manners**—কমনীয় ব্যবহার, মধুর ব্যবহার ।

sŭb, *n.* (*Colloq.*) Same as SUBALTERN.

Sub, (*L.*), *prep.* Under ; নীচে, নিম্নে । ***Sub judice***—বিচারাধীন । ***Sub rosa***—গোপনে, বিরলে, চুপচুপে । ***Sub-silentio***—চুপিচুপি, গোপনে গোপনে, ঢাক ঢাক গুড় গুড় করিয়া । ***Sub voce*** — (Abbrev. *S. V.*) (অমুক) শব্দের নীচে ।

sŭb–, *pref.* Under ; নীচে, তলে ।

sŭb-ăb-dŏm′-i-năl, *adj.* In the lower part of the abdomen ; নিম্নোদরস্থ ।

sŭb-ăc′-id, *n.* A substance moderately acid ; ঈষন্মাত্র দ্রাবক ধর্ম্মাক্রান্ত বস্তু, উপদ্রাবক, উপাম্ল ।

sŭb-ă-cūte′, *adj.* Not much acute ; অনতিপ্রবল (হঃ চঃ) । **Sub-acute palpabral conjunctivitis**—প্রক্লিন্নবর্ত্ম (সাঃ পঃ) ।

sŭb-ā-ē′-ri-ăl, *adj.* **1.** Being, or lying, under the sky ; আকাশতলস্থ, আকাশনিম্নবর্ত্তী, গগনতলস্থ । **2.** (*Geol.*) Pertaining to, or taking place on, the land surface ; ভূতলসম্বন্ধীয়, ভূতলে সংঘটিত ।

sŭb-ā′-gĕnt, *n.* A depuy-agent ; উপপ্রতিনিধি । **—gen-cy,** *n.*

sŭb-ăl′-pīne, *adj.* Of, or belonging to, a region on lofty mountains immediately below the Alpine ; living in this region ; আল্পস্ পর্ব্বতের বৃক্ষ জননের শেষ সীমারেখার অব্যবহিত নিম্নতর সমুচ্চ পর্ব্বতের সন্নিহিত স্থান সম্বন্ধীয় ; উক্ত অঞ্চলবাসী ।

sŭb-al′-têrn, *adj.* & *n.* Below the rank of a captain ; সেনাবিভাগে কাপ্তেনের নিম্ন পদস্থ । ***Noun.*** **1.** A commissioned military officer below the rank of a captain ; কাপ্তেনের অব্যবহিত নিম্নপদস্থ সামরিক কর্ম্মচারি-বিশেষ । **2.** (*Log.*) Particular ; বিশেষ, অপ্রধান, অনুকূল (সাঃ পঃ), পরম্পরাধীন (হিঃ কোঃ) । **3.** (*Log.*) Same as SUBALTERNATE. **Subaltern genus**—(*Log.*) যে "গণ" (*Genus*) কোন উচ্চতর গণের "জাতি" (*Species*) হইয়া থাকে [যথা, চতুষ্পদ জন্তুগণ স্তন্যপায়ী জন্তুগণের জাতিভুক্ত], মধ্যম সামান্য (হিঃ কোঃ) ।

sŭb-ăl-têr′-nănt, *n.* A universal proposition ; ব্যাপ্তিপ্রতিজ্ঞা ।

sŭb-ăl-têr′-nāte, *adj.* & *n.* **1.** Succeeding by turns ; successive ; পরম্পরানুযায়ী, স্থানানুবর্ত্তী (হিঃ কোঃ) ; ক্রমিক । **2.** (*Rare*) Subordinate ; inferior ; (কচিদ্ব্যবহৃত) অপ্রধান ; নিম্নবর্ত্তী । ***Noun.*** (*Log.*) A particular as opposed to a universal proposition ; (তর্কবিজ্ঞান) ব্যাপ্যোদ্দেশকবাক্য ।

sŭb-ăl-tẽr-nā′-tion, *n.* **1.** Succession by turns ; পর্য্যায়ক্রমে অনুগমন, পর্য্যায়গমন । **2.** The relation of a particular proposition to the universal proposition having the same subject, predicate and quality ; অভিন্ন উদ্দেশ্য, বিধেয় এবং গুণবিশিষ্ট ব্যাপোদ্দেশক বাক্যের সহিত ব্যাপ্তি প্রতিজ্ঞার সম্বন্ধ ।

sŭb-ănt-ârc′-tic, *adj.* Pertaining to a region just outside the antarctic circle ; কুমেরুবৃত্তের অব্যবহিত বহির্বর্ত্তী অঞ্চলসম্বন্ধীয়, উপকুমেরুবৃত্তসম্বন্ধীয় ।

sŭb-ā-quăt′-ic, *adj.* **1.** Same as SUBAQUEOUS. **2.** (*Zool.*) Somewhat aquatic ; (জন্তুবিদ্যা) কথঞ্চিৎ জলীয়, ঈষজ্জলীয় ।

sŭb-ā′-quē-ous (-ŭs), *adj.* **1.** Being under or beneath the surface of water ; জলতলবর্ত্তী । **2.** Living under water ; জলতলবাসী ।

sŭb-ârc′-tic, *adj.* **1.** Applied to a region or climate next to the arctic ; সুমেরুর অব্যবহিত বহির্ব্বর্ত্তী অঞ্চল বা জলবায়ুসম্বন্ধীয় । **2.** Approximately arctic ; সুমেরুপ্রায় ।

sŭb-ăs′-trăl, *adj.* Beneath the stars ; terrestrial ; নক্ষত্রনিম্নবর্ত্তী ; পার্থিব ।

sŭb-ăs-trin′-ğĕnt, *adj.* Astringent in small degree ; অল্প কষায় ।

sŭb-ăt′-ŏm, *n.* (*Chem. & Phys.*) A component of an atom ; পরমাণুর উপাদান, পরম পরমাণু (হিঃ কোঃ), অতিপরমাণু । **—a-tom′-ic,** *adj.*

sŭb-au-dĭ′-tion (-ä-), *n.* **1.** The act of understanding something not expressed ; কোন উহ্য বা অনুক্ত বিষয় অবধারণ । **2.** That which is understood ; অনুক্ত বিষয়, উহ্য বিষয় ।

sŭb-ăx′-ĭl-lā-rȳ, *adj.* **1.** (*Bot.*) Placed under the axil or angle formed by the branch of a plant with the stem or by a leaf with the branch ; কাণ্ডের সহিত শাখার এবং শাখার সহিত পত্রের যে কোণ উৎপন্ন হয় তন্নিম্নে স্থিত, উপকাক্ষিক । **2.** Under the armpit ; কক্ষনিম্নবর্ত্তী ।

sŭb′-beā′-dle (-bē-dl), *n.* An inferior or under beadle ; খৃষ্টীয় ধর্ম্মমন্দিরের নিম্নতন কর্ম্মচারিবিশেষ ।

sŭb-cau′-dăl (-kä-), *adj.* Beneath the tail ; পুচ্ছনিম্নবর্ত্তী ।

sŭb-cĕ-lĕs′-tĭ-ăl, *adj.* **1.** Beneath the heavens ; স্বর্গনিম্নবর্ত্তী । **2.** (*Astron.*) Exactly beneath the zenith ; (জ্যোতির্বিজ্ঞান) খস্বস্তিকের অব্যবহিত নিম্নবর্ত্তী ।

sŭb-cĕn′-trăl, *adj.* Being under the centre ; somewhat central ; কেন্দ্রতলবর্ত্তী ; কথঞ্চিৎ মধ্যবর্ত্তী ।

sŭb′-clăss, *n.* A category below a class and above an order ; উপশ্রেণী ।

sŭb-clā′-vĭ-ăn, *adj.* Situated under the collar-bone ; কণ্ঠাস্থির নিম্নে অবস্থিত ।

sŭb-clā-vĭc′-ū-lar (-lẽr), *adj.* Same as SUBCLAVIAN (which see).

sŭb-cŏm-mĭt′-tee (-ē), *n.* An under committee ; অবান্তর সমিতি, উপসমিতি ।

sŭb-cŏn′-scious (-shŭs), *adj.* **1.** Partially or feebly conscious ; স্বল্পচেতনাবিশিষ্ট । **2.** Not clearly recognised in a present state of consciousness, but capable of developing afterwards into full consciousness ; মগ্নচৈতন্যসূচক, মগ্নচৈতন্যাত্মক, অনুদ্বুদ্ধ (হিঃ কোঃ), অনাবিষ্কৃত (ঐ), অনাবির্ভূত (ঐ), অনুদ্ভূত, অব্যক্ত । **—ness,** *n.* The state of being subconscious ; মগ্নচৈতন্যাবস্থা । **Subconscious world**—অব্যক্তচেতন লোক ।

sŭb-cŏn′-trăct, *n.* A contract under a previous contract ; কোন পূর্ব্ব চুক্তির অধীন চুক্তি, উপচুক্তি ।

sŭb-cŏn-stĕl-lā′-tion, *n.* (*Astron.*) A subordinate asterism or constellation ; অবান্তর তারাপুঞ্জ (হিঃ কোঃ)।

sŭb-cŏn-trăc′-tor (-tẽr), *n.* One who works under a principal contractor ; যে ব্যক্তি কোন ঠিকাদার হইতে ঠিকা লইয়া কার্য্য করে, অধীন ঠিকাদার ।

sŭb-cŏn′-trā-rȳ, *adj.* & *n.* **1.** Contrary in an inferior degree ; অপ্রধানরূপে বিপরীত, অনুবিরোধী (হিঃ কোঃ) । **2.** (*Log.*) Particular but differing in quality ; (তর্কবিজ্ঞান) অধীনবিপরীত (সাঃ পঃ) । **3.** (*Geom.*) Designating two similar triangles having a common angle, the opposite sides not being parallel ; একই কোণবিশিষ্ট ত্রিকোণদ্বয় যাহার পরস্পরের বিপরীত বাহুদ্বয় সমান্তরাল নহে—তৎসূচক । ***Noun.*** (*Log.*) A subcontrary proposition ; (তর্কবিজ্ঞান) অনুবিরোধী প্রতিজ্ঞা ।

sŭb-cŏr′-dāte, *adj.* Somewhat like a heart ; হৃৎপিণ্ডকল্প ।

sŭb-cŏs′-tăl, *adj.* & *n.* (*Anat.*) Situated under, or below, the ribs ; পঞ্জরাস্থিসমূহের নিম্নবর্ত্তী । ***Noun.*** Same as SUBCOSTAL MUSCLE. **Sub-costal muscles**—পর্শুকাসমূহের মধ্যবর্ত্তী পেশীসমূহ ।

sŭb-crȳs′-tăl-line (-ĭn), *adj.* Imperfectly crystallised ; অপূর্ণরূপে স্ফটিকীভূত, স্ফটিককল্প, উপস্ফাটিক ।

sŭb-cū-tā′-nē-ous (-ŭs), *adj.* Situated under the skin ; ত্বক্ বা চর্ম্মের নিম্নে স্থাপিত বা স্থিত, চর্ম্মনিম্নস্থ ।

sŭb-cū-tĭc′-ū-lar (-lẽr), *adj.* Being uuder the cuticle or scarf-skin ; উপরের চর্ম্মের নিম্নস্থ, ত্বকের নিম্নস্থ ।

sŭb-dea′-cŏn (-dē-), *n.* (*R. C. C.*) A deacon's assistant or an underdeacon ; (রোমানক্যাথলিক ধর্ম্মসংঘ) নিম্নশ্রেণীর যাজকবিশেষ । **—ry, —ship,** *ns.* The order and office of subdeacon in the Roman Catholic Church ; (রোমানক্যাথলিক ধর্ম্মসংঘে) উক্ত যাজকের পদ বা পদবী ।

sub′-dean (-dēn), *n.* An underdean ; a dean's substitute ; খৃষ্টীয় উপধর্ম্মাধ্যক্ষের নিম্নতর যাজক ; খৃষ্টীয় উপধর্ম্মাধ্যক্ষের প্রতিনিধি ।

—dean′-er-y, *n.* The office or rank of a subdean ; উপধর্ম্মাধ্যক্ষের নিম্নতর কর্ম্মচারীর পদ বা পদবী।

sŭb-dĕc′-ă-năl, *adj.* Relating to a subdean or subdeanery ; উপধর্ম্মাধ্যক্ষের নিম্নতর কর্ম্মচারিসম্বন্ধীয়, উক্ত কর্ম্মচারীর পদ বা পদবীসম্বন্ধীয়।

sŭb-dĕc′-ū-ple (-pl), *adj.* Containing one part of ten ; দশের এক অংশসমন্বিত।

sŭb-dĕnt′-ĕd, *adj.* Indented beneath ; নিম্নে খাঁজবিশিষ্ট, অধোদন্তুরিত।

sŭb-dē-pŏs′-ĭt, *n.* That which is deposited beneath something else ; যাহা অপর কোন পদার্থের নীচে সঞ্চিত হয়, তলসঞ্চয়, অধঃসঞ্চয়।

sŭb′-dē-rĭv′-ă-tive (-tĭv), *n.* A word derived from a derivative ; কোন ব্যুৎপন্ন শব্দ হইতে উদ্ভূত শব্দ। (যথা *Manly* হইতে *manliness*)।

sŭb-dī′-ăl, *adj.* (*Rare*) Of, or pertaining to, the open air ; being under the open sky ; (কচিদ্‌ব্যবহৃত) মুক্তবায়ুসম্পর্কীয় ; মুক্তাকাশতলস্থ।

sŭb′-dī′-ă-lĕct, *n.* An inferior or subordinate dialect ; অপকৃষ্ট বা অপ্রধান উপভাষা।

sŭb-dĭ-lāt′-ĕd, *adj.* Partially dilated ; আংশিক ভাবে বিস্ফারিত, অল্প বিস্ফারিত।

sŭb-dĭ-vêr′-sĭ-fȳ, *v. t.* (*Rare*) To diversify again what is already diversified ; (কচিদ্‌ ব্যবহৃত) পুনর্বৈচিত্র্য সম্পাদন করা।

sŭb-dĭ-vīde′, *v. t.* & *i.* To divide the parts of into more parts ; to divide again, as what has already been divided ; ক্ষুদ্রতর অংশ সমূহে বিভক্ত করা, অবান্তর বিভাগ করা, প্রবিভক্ত করা ; পুনর্বিভক্ত করা। ***Verb i.*** To be subdivided ; পুনর্বিভক্ত হওয়া। **—vĭ′-sion,** *n.* **1.** The act of subdividing or separating a part into smaller parts ; অবান্তর বিভাজন, প্রবিভাজন। **2.** Part of a thing made by sub-dividing ; অবান্তর ভেদ, উপাঙ্গ, প্রবিভাগ। **3.** (In India) A sub-district ; মহকুমা, উপবিভাগ।

sŭb′-dō-lous (-lŭs), *adj.* Sly ; cunning ; crafty ; deceitful ; ধূর্ত্ত ; চালাক ; ফন্দীবাজ ; ছলনাপূর্ণ।

sŭb-dŏm′-ĭ-nănt, *n.* (*Mus.*) The fourth tone above the tonic (so called as being under the dominant) ; (সঙ্গীতশাস্ত্র) চতুর্থস্বর, মধ্যম।

sŭb-dū′-ă-ble (-bl), *adj.* That may be subdued ; conquerable ; দম্য, বশ্য ; জেয়।

sŭb-dū′-ăl, *n.* The act of subduing ; দমন, বশীকরণ।

sŭb-dūce′, sŭb-dŭct′, *v. t.* **1.** (*Rare*) To withdraw ; to take away ; (কচিদ্‌ ব্যবহৃত) অপনয়ন করা ; প্রত্যাকর্ষণ করা। **2.** To subtract ; বিয়োগ করা, ব্যবকলন করা।

sŭb-dŭc′-tion, *n.* **1.** The act of taking away or withdrawing ; প্রত্যাকর্ষণ, অপনয়ন। **2.** Subtraction ; বিয়োগ, ব্যবকলন।

sŭb-due′ (-dū), *v. t.* **1.** To conquer and bring into subjection ; to conquer ; to vanquish ; পরাজিত করিয়া বশীভূত করা, করতলগত করা ; জয় করা ; পরাজিত করা, পরাস্ত করা। **2.** To bring under ; to tame ; বশীভূত করা ; দমন করা, বশ করা। **3.** To tone down ; to soften ; মৃদুপ্রভ করা, শান্তপ্রভ করা ; মৃদু করা, প্রশমিত করা। **dued,** *pp.* Softened ; mellowed ; tamed ; মৃদূকৃত ; শান্তোজ্জ্বল ; প্রশমিত, সুনম্য়ত। **—du′-er,** *n.* **—du′-ing,** *n.*

sŭb′-dū-ple (-pl), *n.* Containing one point of two ; দুইএর একাংশ সমন্বিত। **Subduple ratio**—১এর সহিত দুইএর অনুপাত। Thus 3 to 6 is a *subduple* ratio.

sŭb-dū′-plĭ-cāte, *adj.* (*Math.*) Expressed by the square root ; (গণিত শাস্ত্র) বর্গমূল দ্বারা ব্যক্ত। [Thus the *subduplicate ratio* of *a* to *b* is the ratio of $\sqrt{\ }$ to $\sqrt{b}$].

sŭb-dū′-răl, *adj.* (*Anat.*) Situated under the dura mater ; (শারীরসংস্থানবিদ্যা) মস্তিষ্কের বহিঃস্থ প্রথম পর্দ্দার নিম্নস্থ, দৃঢ়মাতৃকার নিম্নস্থ।

sŭb-ĕd′-ĭ-tor (-têr), *n.* An assistant editor ; (পত্রিকাদির) সহকারী সম্পাদক।

sŭb-ē-lŏng′-a-tĕd (-gā-), *adj.* Not fully elongated ; অসম্যগ্‌বর্দ্ধিত।

sŭb-ē-pĭ-dêr′-măl, *adj.* Lying immediately under the epidermis ; বহিশ্চর্ম্মের নিম্নবর্ত্তী।

sŭb-ē′-quăl, *adj.* Nearly equal ; প্রায় সমতুল, সমকল্প।

sū′-bêr-āte, *n.* A salt of suberic acid ($C_8\ H_{12}\ M_2\ O_4$) ; কর্কাম্লের, লবণ।

sū-bêr′-ĭc, *adj.* Pertaining to cork ; কর্ক বা কাকসম্বন্ধীয়। **Suberic acid** ($C_8\ H_{14}\ O_4$) — একপ্রকার অম্ল। কর্ক অথবা বিভিন্ন প্রকার বসাক্ত তৈলের উপর তাম্রদ্রাবের ক্রিয়ার ফলে এই দ্রাবক উৎপন্ন হয়, কর্কাম্ল।

sū′-bêr-ĭn, *n.* The cellular tissue of cork purified, constituting about seven-tenths of cork ; কর্কের বিশুদ্ধীকৃত কোষিক বিধানতন্তু—যাহাতে ১০ ভাগের ৭ ভাগ সাধারণ কর্ক থাকে।

sū′-bêr-ōse, —ous (-ŭs), *adjs.* **1.** Having a corky texture ; কর্কের অনুরূপ বুননবিশিষ্ট। **2.** Soft and elastic ; কোমল এবং স্থিতিস্থাপক। **Suberous layer**—কর্কস্তর (সাঃ পঃ)।

sū′-bêr-ōse, *adj.* (*Bot.*) Having the appearance of being gnawed ; (উদ্ভিদ্‌বিদ্যা) অনুক্রকচ।

sŭb-făm′-ĭ-lȳ, *n.* (*Nat. Hist.*) A subdivision of a family ; (প্রাকৃতিক ইতিহাস) জন্তুপরিবারের অবান্তর বিভাগ।

sŭb-flū′-vĭ-ăl, *adj.* **1.** Situated under a river ; নদীনিম্নস্থ।

sŭb-fī′-brous (-brŭs), *adj.* Slightly fibrous ; অংশুলপ্রায়।

sŭb-fŏs′-sĭl, *adj.* Applied to remains partially fossilised ; আংশিক ভাবে শিলীভূত জন্তুর দেহাবশেষ সম্বন্ধে প্রযুক্ত।

sŭb-gĕ-lăt'-ĭ-nous (-nŭs), *adj.* Imperfectly gelatinous ; অসম্যগ্‌রূপে শিরীষবৎ।

sŭb-gĕ-nĕr'-ĭc, *adj.* Pertaining to a subgenus ; উপগণসম্বন্ধীয়।

sŭb-gē'-nŭs, *n.* The subdivision of a genus, comprehending one or more species ; উপগণ।

sŭb-glā'-cial (-shăl), *adj.* Pertaining to the underside of a glacier ; under a glacier ; তুষারনদীর নিম্নভাগ-সম্বন্ধীয় ; তুষারনদীর নিম্নবর্ত্তী।

sŭb-glō'-bōse, *adj.* Not quite globose ; গোলপ্রায়, গোলকল্প।

sŭb-glŏb'-ū-lar (-lêr), *adj.* Almost spherical ; গোলপ্রায়, গোলকল্প।

sŭb-glū-mā'-ceous (-shŭs), *adj.* Somewhat glumaceous ; কিঞ্চিৎ তুষপত্রযুক্ত।

sŭb-grăn'-ū-lar (-lêr), *adj.* Somewhat granular ; অল্প দানাদার।

sŭb'-group (-grōp), *n.* The subdivision of a group ; উপশ্রেণী।

sŭb-hăs-tā'-tion, *n.* A sale by public auction ; প্রকাশ্য নীলামে বিক্রয়। [*Sub*=under ; *hasta*= spear ; রোমকগণ নীলামের স্থানে একটী বর্শা প্রোথিত করিত।]

sŭb-ĭn-dĭ-cā'-tion, *n.* The act of indicating by signs ; a slight indication ; চিহ্নদ্বারানির্দ্দেশ ; ইঙ্গিত, আভাস আঁচ।

sŭb-ĭn-feu-dā'-tion (-fū-), *n.* The process of feudal tenure, by which a feudatory granted parts of his lands to tenants or vassals under him ; যে প্রণালী অনুসারে সামন্ত তন্ত্রাধীন কোন ভূম্যধিকারী প্রজা বা অনুগত ব্যক্তিদিগকে ভূমি প্রদান করিতেন।

sŭb-ĭ-tā'-nĕ-ous (-ŭs), *adj.* Sudden ; hasty ; আকস্মিক ; ত্বরিত, হঠকারী।

subito, *n.* Quickly ; suddenly ; দ্রুত ; হঠাৎ।

sŭb-jā'-cĕnt, *adj.* Lying under or below ; being in a lower position though not directly below ; নিম্নস্থিত, অধঃস্থিত ; ঠিক অধোবর্ত্তী না হইলেও নিম্নাবস্থিত।

sŭb'-jĕct, *adj.* **1.** Being under the power and dominion of another ; অধীন, পরাধীন, পরতন্ত্র, পরবশ, বশবর্ত্তী। **2.** Exposed ; liable ; prone ; অধীন ; অর্হ ; প্রবণ। **3.** Being that on which anything operates ; মূলীভূত, বিষয়ীভূত। **4.** Conditional upon ; as, *subject* to the approval of the Government of India ; সাপেক্ষ। **5.** Obedient ; বাধ্য, অনুগত।

sŭb'-jĕct, *n.* **1.** One who owes allegiance to a sovereign, and is governed by him ; "The *subject* must obey his prince, because God commands it, and human laws require it" ; প্রজা, প্রকৃতি। **2.** One that is subjected, or submitted, to any physical operation or process ; a dead body for dissection ; কোন দৈহিক ক্রিয়া বা প্রক্রিয়ার অধীন ব্যক্তি ; ব্যবচ্ছেদের জন্য শব। **3.** The hero of a piece ; the person who is treated of ; the principal character ; নায়ক ; বিষয়ীভূত ব্যক্তি ; প্রধান চরিত্র। **4.** That which is spoken of, written of, thought of ; a theme ; কথিত, লিখিত বা আলোচ্য বিষয় ; বিষয়, প্রসঙ্গ, প্রস্তাব, বৃত্তান্ত। **5.** (*Log.*) That of which anything is predicated or denied ; (তর্কবিজ্ঞান) পক্ষ, পদ, উদ্দেশ্য (সাঃ পঃ), প্রকরণ, আধার, প্রস্তুত, আশয়। **6.** (*Philos.*) The active and immediate sentiment and thinking faculty which forms conceptions of ideas or objects ; "Accordingly, in their hands, the phrases conscious or thinking *subject* and *subject* means precisely the same thing" ; the ego ; বিষয়ী, অধিকরণ, জ্ঞাতা, প্রজ্ঞামাত্র (ঐ) ; অহম্, আত্মা। **7.** Substance ; substratum ; বস্তু, সার বস্তু ; আধার, আশ্রয়, অধিষ্ঠান। **8.** (*Gram.*) The nominative of a verb ; (ব্যাকরণ) কর্ত্তৃপদ। **9.** (*Fine arts*) The incident chosen by an artist ; the design of a composition or picture ; anything which constitutes the design or aim of any work of art ; শিল্পিকর্ত্তৃক নির্ব্বাচিত বিষয় ; কোন রচনা বা চিত্রের পরিকল্পনা ; কোন শিল্পদ্রব্যের লক্ষ্য বা পরিকল্পনার বিষয়। **10.** (*Mus.*) The principal melody or theme of a movement ; (সঙ্গীতশাস্ত্র) কোন চাল বা গতের প্রধান সুর বা বিষয়। **Subject-matter** — আলোচ্য বিষয়। **Subject object**—কোন বস্তু জ্ঞাতার নিকট যেরূপ প্রতিভাত হয় (অর্থাৎ উহা স্বরূপত যাহা তাহা নয়)।

sŭb-jĕct', *v. t.* **1.** To bring under the power or dominion of ; "Firmness of mind that *subjects* every gratification of sense to the rule of right reason" ; বশীভূত করা, বশে আনা, রাজ্যভুক্ত করা। **2.** To make liable ; as, credulity *subjects* a person to impositions ; অধীন করা। **3.** To expose ; as, to *subject* a substance to heat ; কোন কিছুর ক্রিয়ার অধীন করা। **—jec'-tion,** *n.* **1.** The act of bringing under the dominion ; অধীন করণ। **2.** The state of being under the control of another ; পরাধীনতা। **Sub'-ject-ist,** *n.* One versed in subjectivism ; বিষয়ীবিজ্ঞান-বাদী (হিঃ কোঃ), অহম্বাদী (ঐ), আত্মবাদী (ঐ)।

sŭb-jĕc'-tive (-tĭv), *adj.* **1.** Relating to the subject, as opposed to object ; বিষয়িসম্পর্কীয়, জ্ঞাতৃসম্পর্কীয়। **2.** (*Literature and art*) Applied to a production characterized by the prominence given to the individuality of the author or artist ; as, a *subjective* painter or writer ; modified by the individuality of a writer or artist ; যে রচনায় বা শিল্প-কার্য্যে শিল্পী বা গ্রন্থকারের ব্যক্তিত্ব

সুপরিস্ফুট হইয়াছে তৎসম্বন্ধে প্রযুক্ত; শিল্পী বা গ্রন্থকারের ব্যক্তিত্বদ্বারা অনুরঞ্জিত। **3.** Belonging to, or arising from, individual mind ; fanciful ; illusory ; as, *subjective* appearance ; ব্যক্তিবিশেষসম্বন্ধীয় বা তাহা হইতে উদ্ভূত, আত্মগত (হিঃ কোঃ) বিষয়িগত (ঐ), প্রত্যক্ (ঐ), অন্তর্মুখীন ; কল্পিত ; মায়িক। **4.** (*Gram.*) Of the subject ; (ব্যাকরণ) কর্তৃকারকসম্বন্ধীয়। **—ly,** *adv.* **—ness,** *n.* **—tiv'-i-ty,** *n.* **1.** The quality or state of being subjective ; বিষয়িনিষ্ঠতা। **2.** The belief that the test of religious truth is in the spirit rather than in revelation ; স্বানুভববাদ (হিঃ কোঃ)। **Subjective colours**—Same as ACCIDENTAL COLOURS (which see.) **Subjective idealism**—See IDEALISM. **Subjective sensation**—আভ্যন্তরিক কারণ হইতে ইন্দ্রিয় সমূহের স্নায়ুযন্ত্র উত্তেজিত হইলে যে সমস্ত সংবেদন জাত হয় তাহার অন্যতম, বিষয়িগতসংবেদন। (এইরূপ অবস্থায় মানুষ নানাপ্রকার অবাস্তব মূর্ত্তি দর্শন করে করিয়া থাকে)। **Subjective validity**—দ্রষ্টা, মন্তা এবং অনুভবকারীর মানসপ্রকৃতিসিদ্ধ প্রামাণিকতা, বিষয়িগত প্রামাণিকতা।

sŭb-jĕc'-tĭv-ĭsm, *n.* **1.** (*Metaph.*) The doctrine of Kant that all human knowledge is merely relative, or that we cannot prove it to be absolute ; the doctrine that we cannot prove that what appears true to us must in like manner appear true to all intelligible beings ; the doctrine which refers all knowledge to subjective states of impressions ; (তত্ত্ববিদ্যা) যাবতীয় মানবীয় জ্ঞানই আপেক্ষিক এবং উহার অনাপেক্ষিকত্ব প্রমাণে আমরা কদাচ সমর্থ নহি—ক্যাণ্টের এই মতবাদ সম্বন্ধে বিজ্ঞানবাদ ; আমাদের নিকট যাহা সত্য বলিয়া প্রতিভাত হয় তাহা অপর সকল বুদ্ধিমান জীবের নিকট অবশ্যই সত্য বলিয়া প্রতীয়মান হইবে, ইহা আমরা কখনও প্রমাণ করিতে পারি না—এই মত, বিষয়িবিজ্ঞানবাদ (হিঃ কোঃ) ; আমাদের যাবতীয় জ্ঞানই বিষয়িগত প্রতীতি সমূহের অবস্থা মাত্র—এই মত, বিজ্ঞানবাদ। **2.** A theory which attaches great or supreme importance to the subjective elements in experience ; অহম্বাদ (হিঃ কোঃ), বিষয়িপ্রাধান্য বাদ।

sŭb-join' (-joyn), *v. t.* To add at the end ; to add after something else has been said or written ; to affix ; অন্তে সংযোগ করা ; কোন কিছু উক্ত বা লিখিত হওয়ার পরে সংযোগ করা ; পরিশিষ্টরূপে সংযোগ করা।

sŭb'-jü-gāte, *v. t.* To subdue or bring under the yoke of power or dominion ; to conquer by force and compel to submit to the government of another ; বশীভূত করা ; অধীনতা স্বীকার করিতে বাধ্য করা। **—ga-ble,** *adj.* **—ga'-tion,** *n.* The act of one who subjugates ; the state of being subjugated ; বশীকরণ, নিগ্রহ ; বশিতা, দমন। **—ga-tor,** *n.*

sŭb-jŭnc'-tive (-tiv), *adj.* & *n.* (*Gram.*) Said of a mood of verbs that expresses condition, hypothesis or contingency ; (ব্যাকরণ) সংশয়ার্থক, আশংসাবাচক। ***Noun.*** (*Gram.*) Subjunctive mood ; সংশয়, সম্ভাবনা, প্রভৃতি সূচক ক্রিয়ার রূপবিশেষ। **—ly,** *adv.*

sŭb-lăp-să'-ri-ăn, *n.* One of a class of Calvinists who held that the fall of man was foreseen by God ; ক্যালভেনিষ্ট সম্প্রদায়বিশেষভুক্ত ব্যক্তি—ইঁহাদের মতে ঈশ্বর পূর্ব্ব হইতেই মানবের পতনের বিষয় অবগত ছিলেন।

sŭb'-lāte, *v. t.* (*Rare*) To remove ; (কচিদ্‌ব্যবহৃত) স্থানান্তরিত করা। **2.** (*Log.*) (*a*) To negate or deny ; (তর্কবিজ্ঞান) অস্বীকার করা। (*b*) To reduce to a subordinate element of a more comprehensive idea ; কোনরূপ ব্যাপকতর ভাবের অপ্রধান অঙ্গে পরিণত করা। **—lat'-ed,** *p. p.* In a state of sublation ; বাধিত (শ্রীঃ)। **—la'-tion,** *n.* **1.** (*Rare*) Removal ; (কচিদ্‌ব্যবহৃত) স্থানান্তরীকরণ, অপনয়ন (হিঃ কোঃ)। **2.** (*Hegalianism*) The reduction of an idea to a subordinate element of higher unity by adding to it what it needs or implies to make it intelligible (*W. T. Harris*) ; (হেগেলের দর্শন) বোধগম্য করার উদ্দেশ্যে আকাঙ্ক্ষিত বা উপলক্ষিত বিষয়ের সংযোগ দ্বারা কোন ভাবকে উচ্চতর ঐক্যের অপ্রধান অঙ্গরূপে পরিণত করণ, বাধ (শ্রীঃ), স্থানাপত্তি (হিঃ কোঃ)।

sŭb-lease', (-lēs), *n.* & *v. t.* A lease granted by one who is himself a lessee or tenant ; পাট্টাদার কর্ত্তৃক যে পাট্টা প্রদত্ত হয়, সিকিমী পাট্টা, পেটাও পাট্টা, কটকিনা, দরপাট্টা। ***Verb t.*** To sublet ; ভাড়াটিয়া কর্ত্তৃক ভাড়া দেওয়া, দর পাট্টা দেওয়া।

sŭb-lĕt', *v. t.* To underlet ; to lease, as a lessee to another person ; মালীকের নিকট হইতে গৃহাদি ভাড়া লইয়া অন্যের নিকট পুনরায় ভাড়া দেওয়া ; দর ইজারা দেওয়া, কোর্ফা বিলি করা।

sŭb-lē-va'-tion, *n.* **1.** The act of raising or uplifting ; উত্তোলন। **2.** (*Rare*) Insurrection ; (কচিদ্‌ ব্যবহৃত) বিদ্রোহ।

sŭb-lieu-tĕn'-ănt (-lĕf-), *n.* A second lieutenant ; দ্বিতীয় লেফটেনেন্ট।

sŭb'-lĭ-māte, *v. t.* **1.** To raise by heat, a solid substance, as camphor, sulphur, which on cooling returns again, to the solid state ; উত্তাপ দ্বারা কঠিন পদার্থকে (যথা, কর্পূর, গন্ধক) বাষ্পে পরিণত করা, ঊর্দ্ধপাতন করা। **2.** To refine ; to elevate ; "In words whose weight best suits a *sublimated* strain" ; বিশোধিত করা, নির্ম্মল করা ; উন্নয়ন করা। **—ma'-tion,** *n.*

1. The act of sublimating : **ঊর্দ্ধপাতন** (আয়ুঃ রসঃ)। **2.** The act of hightening or elevating ; "Religion is the perfection...and *sublimation* of morality" ; উন্নয়ন। **3.** That which is highly refined or purified ; অতিশয় নির্ম্মলীকৃত বা বিশুদ্ধীকৃত বস্তু। **Sublimation apparatus**—বিদ্যাধর যন্ত্র (রসরত্নসমুচ্চয়), উর্দ্ধপাতনযন্ত্র (ঐ), উর্দ্ধ পাতন (ঐ)।

sub′-li-mate, *adj.* & *n.* Sublimated; উর্দ্ধপাতিত। ***Noun.*** A sublimated substance ; উর্দ্ধপাতিত বস্তু, উর্দ্ধপাতনাবশেষ (হিঃ কোঃ)। **Sublimate of mercury**—রসকর্পূর। ভাবপ্রকাশে রসকর্পূর প্রস্তুতের এইরূপ বিধি লিখিত আছে। [শুদ্ধসূতসমং কুর্য্যাৎ প্রত্যেকং গৈরিকং সুধীঃ। ইষ্টিকাং খটিকাং তদ্বৎ স্ফটিকাং সিন্ধুজন্ম চ॥ বল্মীকক্ষারলবণংভাণ্ডরঙ্গকমৃত্তিকাম্। সর্ব্বাণ্যেতানি সংচূর্ণ্য বাসসা চাপি শোধয়েৎ॥ এভিশ্চূর্ণৈর্যুতং সূতং যাবদ্যামং বিমর্দ্দিতম। তচ্চূর্ণসহিতংসূতং স্থালীমধ্যে পরিক্ষিপেৎ॥ তস্যাঃ স্থাল্যামুখে স্থালীমপরাং ধাবয়েৎ সমাম্। সবস্ত্রকুট্টিতমৃদামুদ্রয়েদুভয়োর্মুখম্॥ সংশোষ্য মুদ্রয়েদ্ভূয়োভূয়ঃ সংশোষ্য মুদ্রয়েৎ। সম্যগ্ বিশোষ্য মুদ্রাং তাং স্থালীং চুল্লাং নিবারয়েৎ॥ অগ্নিং নিরন্তরং দদ্যাদ্যাবদ্দিনচতুষ্টয়ম্। অঙ্গারোপরি তদ্ যন্ত্রং রক্ষেদ্যত্নাদহর্নিশম॥ শনৈরুদ্ধারয়েদ্ যন্ত্রমূর্দ্ধস্থালীগতং রসং। কর্পূরবৎ সুবিমলং গৃহ্ণীয়াদ্গুণ বত্তরম॥~

sŭb-līme′, *adj.* & *n.* **1.** (*Obs.*) Lofty ; (অপ্রঃ) উচ্চ, তুঙ্গ উন্নত। **2.** Awakening or expressing the emotion of awe, adoration, veneration, etc. ; lofty ; grand ; **বিস্ময়রসজনক, গম্ভীরভাবজনক ; উন্নত, সমুন্নত** গৌরবান্বিত ; মহান **সুমহান,** মহিমান্বিত, প্রশান্তগম্ভীর, ভীমকান্ত, উদাত্ত (cf. উদাত্ত ভাব)। **3.** (*Anat.*) Not deep-sunk ; (শারীরসংস্থানবিদ্যা) অগভীর। ***Noun.*** The grand in the works of nature as distinguished from the beautiful ; **গম্ভীরভাবোদ্দীপক বিষয়,** গভীরভাবজনক **বিষয়,** বিস্ময়রস (cf. লোকোত্তরার্থ **বীক্ষাদেবিস্ময়বিস্তৃতি** — সাহিত্যদর্পণ)। [The passion caused by the great and sublime in nature when these causes operate most powerfully, is astonishment—*Burke.* Sublime is what is absolutely or beyond all comparison — great, that compared with which all else is small—*Kant.*] **—lim′-i-ty,** *n.* The state or quality of being sublime ; grandeur ; majesty ; something grand ; মহদ্ভাব, গম্ভীরভাবজনকতা, রসগাম্ভীর্য্য (প্রঃ চিঃ) ; মহিমা (রবীঃ) ; মহানভাব ; সুমহান বিষয়। **The Sublime Porte**— See PORTE.

sŭb-līme′, *v. t.* & *i.* **1.** sublimate ; উত্তাপ প্রয়োগে কঠিন পদার্থকে বাষ্পে পরিণত করা, উর্দ্ধপাতন করা। **2.** To purify ; বিশোধিত করা। ***Verb i.*** **1.** To be sublimated ; উবিয়া যাওয়া। **2.** To be purified ; বিশোধিত হওয়া।

sŭb-lim′-ĭ-nal, *adj.* Below the threshold of consciousness ; dormant ; অব্যক্তচেতনলোকস্থ, মগ্নচৈতন্যলোকস্থ ; প্রচ্ছন্ন, অব্যক্ত, অনুদ্ভূত। **Subliminal consciousness**—অব্যক্ত চৈতন্য, মগ্নচৈতন্য, অনুদ্ভূতচৈতন্য। **Subliminial self** — অব্যক্ত অহং, অনুদ্ভূত আত্মা।

sŭb-lin′-ē-ā′-tion, *n.* Mark of a line or lines under a word or words in a sentence ; কোন বাক্যের শব্দ বা শব্দসমূহের উপর কোন রেখা বা রেখা সকলের চিহ্ন।

sŭb-lin′-gü-ăl, (-lĭng-), *adj.* Situated under the tongue জিহ্বানিম্নবর্ত্তী।

sŭb-lĭ′-tion, *n.* (*Obs.*) The act or process of laying the ground ; (অপ্রঃ) আলেখ্যের ভূমি রঞ্জন।

sŭb-lü′-nar (-nêr), *adj.* Beneath the moon ; চন্দ্রতলস্থ।

sŭb′-lü-nă-rȳ, *adj.* **1.** Beneath the moon ; চন্দ্রতলবর্ত্তী। **2.** Terrestrial ; পার্থিব, সাংসারিক, লৌকিক, ঐহিক।

sŭb-lŭx-ā′-tion, *n.* A sprain ; মচকানি।

sŭb-mạ-rine′ (-rēn), *adj.* Situated, existing, growing, carried on, or exhibited at some depth in the sea ; সমুদ্রতলস্থ, সমুদ্রগর্ভস্থ, সাগরতলস্থ, সাগরমগ্ন, সিন্ধুগর্ভনিহিত, সাগরতলজ, সাগরতলে বাহিত বা প্রদর্শিত। **Submarine fire**—বাড়বাগ্নি, বাড়বানল। **Submarine rock**—মগ্নগিরি।

sŭb-mạ-rine′ (-rēn), *n.* A vessel so constructed that it can be propelled under water ; শত্রুপক্ষীয় রণতরী প্রভৃতি ধ্বংস করার জন্য সমুদ্রতলচর পোতবিশেষ, সাগরতলগামী পোত, সাগরতলচর পোত, অন্তর্জলী (প্রবাসী ১৩২২), মকরপোত (নায়ক), পানকৌড়ী (ঐ), ডুব জাহাজ (প্রবাসী), ডুবন্ত জাহাজ (ঐ), জলতলবিহারী।

sŭb-măx′-ĭl-lă-rȳ, *adj.* Situated under the lower jaw ; নিম্ন হনুর নীচস্থ।

sŭb-mē′-dĭ-ăl, —ăn, *adjs.* Lying under the middle ; মধ্যদেশের নিম্নবর্ত্তী।

sŭb-měn′-tăl, *adj.* Situated under the chin ; চিবুকনিম্নস্থ।

sŭb-merge′ (-mêrj), *v. t.* **1.** To put under water ; ডুবান, নিমজ্জিত করা, জলমগ্ন করা। **2.** To inundate ; প্লাবিত করা, পরিপ্লাবিত করা। **—mer′-gence, —mer′-sion,** *ns.* **Submerged leaf**—বিমগ্ন পত্র (সাঃ পঃ)। **The submerged tenth**—দেশের ঋণজালে জড়িত বা দুর্দ্দশাগ্রস্ত জনবৃন্দ।

sŭb-merse′ (-mêrs), *adj.* & *v. t.* (*Rare*) Being, or growing under water ; (কচিদ্ব্যবহৃত) জলতলবর্ত্তী, জলতলজ। ***Verb t.*** (*Rare*) To submerge ; (কচিদ্ব্যবহৃত) জলমগ্ন করা। **—mers′-i-ble,** *adj.*

sŭb-mis′-sion (-mĭ-), *n.* **1.** The act of submitting or the state of being submitted ; **বশ্যতাস্বীকার, বশ্যতা।** **2.** Obedience ; mildness ; বাধ্যতা, বশবর্ত্তিতা, আজ্ঞাবহতা, আনুগত্য ; বিনয়, নম্রতা। **—sive,** ***adj***

Inclined or ready to submit; obedient; compliant; meek; বশম্বদ, বাধ্য, অনুগত; আজ্ঞাশীল, আজ্ঞাসম্পদী (যাজ্ঞঃ) বচনগ্রাহী; বিনয়নম্র, বিনম্রস্বভাব, বিনয়ী, প্রণতিপ্রবণ (কিরাতঃ), বশ্য। **–sive-ly,** *adv.* **–sive-ness,** *n.*

sŭb-mit′, *v. t.* & *i.* **1.** To yield or surrender; আত্মসমর্পণ করা, বশ্যতা স্বীকার করা। **2.** To refer to the judgment of another; পেশ করা, দাখিল করা। ***Verb i.*** **1.** To yield; আত্মসমর্পণ করা, বশ্যতা স্বীকার করা। **2.** To acquiesce; "Our religion requires from us......to *submit* to pain, disgrace, and even death"; মানিয়া লওয়া, স্বীকার করা, সম্মত হওয়া, ঘাড় পেতে নেওয়া (*colloq.*)। **3.** To be submissive; বশম্বদ হওয়া, বচনগ্রাহী হওয়া, বিনয়নম্র হওয়া।

sŭb-mŏn′-tāne, *adj.* Situated at the foot of a mountain; গিরিনিম্নস্থ, গিরিপাদস্থ।

sŭb-mū′-cous (-cŭs), *adj.* Lying under a mucous membrane; ঝিল্লীনিম্নস্থ।

sŭb-mŭl′-tĭ-ple (-pl), *n.* A number or quality that divides another exactly; অবান্তরাপবর্ত্ত্য (হিঃ কোঃ), উপগুণনীয়ক।

sŭb-nŏr′-măl, *n.* (*Geom.*) That part of the axis of abscissa which is intercepted between the ordinate and the normal at any point of the curve; অবান্তর-মুখ্যলম্ব (হিঃ কোঃ)।

sŭb-nŏr′-măl, *adj.* Below the normal; উপনৈসর্গিক।

sŭb-ŏr′-dêr, *n.* A classification next below an order; উপবর্গ (সাঃ পঃ), অন্তবর্গ (ঐ)।

sŭb-ŏr′-dĭ-nāte, *adj.* & *n.* Inferior in rank, in nature, dignity, in power, importance, etc.; secondary; অধীন, আয়ত্ত, অধস্তন, নিম্নবর্ত্তী, নিম্নতন; অপ্রধান, গৌণ, উপ। ***Noun.*** A person working under another; অধীন কর্ম্মচারী, অধস্তন কর্ম্মচারী, অপ্রধান (হিঃ কোঃ)। **–ly,** *adv.* **Subordinate proposition**—অপ্রধান প্রতিজ্ঞা (হিঃ কোঃ), অধিষ্ঠান (ঐ)।

sŭb-ŏr′-dĭ-nāte, *v. t.* **1.** To place in a lower order or rank; নিম্নপদস্থ করা। **2.** To make subject; অধীন করা, বশীভূত করা। **–ly,** *adv.* **–ness,** *n.*

sŭb-ŏr-dĭ-nā′-tion, *n.* **1.** The act of subordinating; the state of being subordinate; অধীন করণ; অধীনতা। **2.** Inferiority in rank or dignity; পদমর্য্যাদায় হীনতা। **–ism,** *n.* (*Theol.*) The doctrine that the second and third persons of the Trinity are subordinate in order or essence to the first person; (খৃষ্টীয় ধর্ম্মশাস্ত্র) খৃষ্টীয় ত্রীশ্বরের দ্বিতীয় ও তৃতীয় পুরুষ ক্রমানুসারে ও স্বরূপতঃ প্রথম পুরুষ অপেক্ষা হীনতর—এই মতবাদ।

sŭb-ŏrn′, *v. t.* To bribe to commit perjury; to bribe to some wickedness; মিথ্যা সাক্ষ্য প্রদানের জন্য উৎকোচ প্রদান করা; উৎকোচ প্রদানে কোনরূপ অন্যায় কার্য্যে প্রবৃত্ত করা। **–or-na′-tion, –er,** *ns.*

sŭb-ō′-vāte, –vāt′-ĕd, *adjs.* Almost ovate; প্রায় ডিম্বাকার, অণ্ডকল্প।

sŭb-ŏx′-ide (-ĭd), *n.* (*Rare*) An oxide which contains less oxygen than normal oxide; (কচিদ্‌ব্যবহৃত) যে অম্লজানজারিত ধাতুতে সাধারণ অম্লজানজারিত ধাতু অপেক্ষা অল্প অম্লজান থাকে।

sŭb-pœ′-nă, (-pē-) *n.* & *v. t.* A writ commanding the attendance in court of a person, as witness; সাক্ষীর শমন, আহ্বান-পত্র, সফীনা। ***Verb t.*** To serve with a writ of subpœna; শমন-জারি করা।

sŭb-pō′-lar (-lêr), *adj.* Under or near the pole; মেরুনিম্নস্থ, মেরু-সন্নিহিত।

sŭb-pō′-tĕn-cy̆, *n.* (*Biol.*) Diminished potency in transmitting hereditary character; (জীব-বিজ্ঞান) কৌলিক স্বভাব সংক্রমণে ন্যূনীভূত শক্তি, দৌর্ব্বল্য (হিঃ কোঃ), আবল্য (ঐ), ন্যূনতা (ঐ)।

sŭb-quad′-rāte (-kwŏd-), *adj* Nearly square; সমচতুষ্কোণকল্প।

sŭb-quad′-ru-ple (-kwŏd-rō-pl) *adj.* Containing one part of four; চতুরংশাত্মক।

sŭb-quin′-tū-ple (-pl), *adj.* Containing one part of five; পঞ্চাংশাত্মক।

sŭb′-rāce, *n.* A subdivision of a race; অবান্তর জাতি (হিঃ কোঃ) উপজাতি (ঐ)।

sŭb-rā′-mous (-mŭs), *adj.* (*Bot.*) Having few branches; (উদ্ভিদ্‌-বিদ্যা) স্বল্পশাখ।

sŭb-rĕc′-tor (-têr), *n.* A rector's deputy or substitute; রেক্‌টরের প্রতিনিধি বা স্থলবর্ত্তী ব্যক্তি।

sŭb-rĕp′-tion, *n.* The act of obtaining a favour by surprise or unfair representation, that is by suppression or fraudulent concealment of fact; সত্যগোপনাদি দ্বারা অনুগ্রহলাভ।

sŭb-rŏt′-ŭnd, *adj.* Almost round or orbicular; গোলকল্প, গোলপ্রায়।

sŭb-scrībe′, *v. t.* & *i.* **1.** To append one's own signature to; to give consent to, as something written, or to bind one's self to the terms of, by writing one's name beneath; as, to *subscribe* a bond; স্বাক্ষর করা, নামসহি করা; নিম্নে নাম স্বাক্ষর করিয়া কোন বিষয়ে সম্মতি প্রদান করা বা কোনরূপ সর্ত্তে বদ্ধ হওয়া। **2.** To attest by writing one's name beneath; as, clerks *subscribe* copies of records; নিম্নে নাম স্বাক্ষর পূর্ব্বক সত্য বলিয়া নির্দ্দেশ করা। **3.** To promise to give by writing one's name; চাঁদা সহি করা। ***Verb i.*** **1.** To promise to give a certain sum by signing one's name to a paper ; চাঁদা স্বাক্ষর করা। 2. To assent ; "We will all *subscribe* to thy advice" ; স্বীকার করা, সম্মত করা। 3. To enter one's name, for a newspaper, a book, etc. ; পুস্তক, সংবাদপত্র প্রভৃতির গ্রাহক হওয়া।

sŭb-scrib'-ẽr, *n.* 1. One who signs an announcement, acknowledgment, etc. ; স্বাক্ষরকারী। 2. One who enters his name for a newspaper, periodical, book, or the like ; পুস্তক, পত্রিকা প্রভৃতির গ্রাহক গ্রাহক। 3. One that contributes to an undertaking by subscribing ; চাঁদাদাতা, চাঁদাস্বাক্ষরকারী।

sŭb'-script, *adj.* Written below ; নিম্নে লিখিত।

sŭb-scrip'-tion, *n.* 1. Act of subscribing ; চাঁদা স্বাক্ষর। 2. A sum subscribed ; চাঁদা, ভিক্ষা (cf. ভিক্ষা সংগ্রহ)। 3. Signature ; স্বাক্ষর। 4. Attestation ; স্বাক্ষর দ্বারা কোনকিছুর সত্যতা প্রতিপাদন।

sŭb-sĕc'-tion, *n.* The part or division of a section ; উপধারা।

sŭb-sĕl'-li-ŭm, *n.* (pl. -A), A low bench ; hence a bench or seat ; অনুচ্চ দীর্ঘাসন ; দীর্ঘাসন, আসন।

sŭb-sĕn'-si-ble (-bl), *adj.* Too profound for the senses to reach or grasp ; ইন্দ্রিয়াতিগ।

sŭb-sĕp'-tŭ-ple (-pl), *adj.* Containing one of seven parts ; সপ্তাংশত্মক।

sŭb'-sĕ-quĕnt, *adj.* Following in time ; posterior ; পরবর্ত্তী, পশ্চাদ্‌বর্ত্তী ; পশ্চাৎকালীন, উত্তর[illegible]। **-ly,** *adv.* **-quence,** *n.*

sŭb-serve' (-sẽrv), *v. t.* 1. To serve or be of service to ; কাযে লাগা, কার্য্যকর হওয়া। 2. To help on ; to promote ; "It is a greater credit to know the ways of captivating Nature and making her *subserve*, our purposes, than to have learned all the intrigues of policy" ; সহায়তা করা ; অগ্রসর করা, শ্রীবৃদ্ধি করা। **-ser'-vi-ence, -ser'-vi-en-cy,** *ns.* The state of being subservient ; পরতন্ত্রত্ব।

sŭb-sẽr'-vi-ĕnt, *adj.* 1. Serving to promote an object or end ; answering a purpose ; উদ্দেশ্যসাধনে সহায়ক, অভীষ্টসাধনে সহায়ক ; উদ্দেশ্যসাধক, অভীষ্টসাধক। 2. Cringing ; obsequious ; "These ranks of creatures are *subservient* each to another" ; হীন তোষামোদকারী ; হীনানুগত, পদলেহনকারী। **-ly,** *adv.*

sŭb-side', *v. i.* 1. To sink or fall to the bottom ; to settle, as lees ; তলে পড়া ; থিতাইয়া পড়া। 2. To fall into a state of calm or quiet ; শান্তিপূর্ণ হওয়া, বিরামলাভ করা। 3. To become lower ; to descend ; to sink ; to abate ; as, the fever has *subsided* ; নিম্নতর হওয়া ; নামিয়া আসা ; তলে পড়া ; প্রশমিত হওয়া, প্রকোপ হ্রাস পাওয়া। 4. (Of persons, usu. *joc.*) To sink into sitting or kneeling or lying posture ; as, to *subside* into an arm-chair ; (ব্যক্তি-সম্পর্কে-সাধারণতঃ রঙ্গচ্ছলে) বসিয়া পড়া, শুইয়া পড়া, প্রণতজানু হওয়া। **-sid'-ence,** *n.* 1. The act of sinking or falling to the bottom, as lees ; তলাইয়া পড়ন, থিতাইয়া পড়ন, অধোগমন (সাঃ পঃ)। 2. Act of sinking or gradually descending, as ground ; নিমজ্জন, ক্রমশঃ অধোগমন। 3. The state of becoming calm or quiet ; প্রশান্তি, শমতা।

sŭb-sid'-i-ă-ry, *adj.* & *n.* 1. Aiding ; assisting ; সহায়ক ; সাহায্যকারী। 2. Pertaining to subsidy ; উপগ্রহসম্বন্ধীয়। 3. Furnishing additional supplies ; অতিরিক্ত মাল প্রভৃতি সরবরাহকারী। *Noun.* An assistant ; an auxiliary ; সাহায্যকারী ; সহকারী, সহায়ক। **-ri-ly,** *adv.* **Subsidiary quantity or symbol** — যে রাশি বা সাঙ্কেতিক চিহ্ন মূলতঃ কোন সম্পাদ্যের অংশ নহে—কিন্তু যাহা উহার সমাধানের সাহায্যকরূপে গৃহীত হইয়া থাকে। **Subsidiary troops**—যুদ্ধাদির জন্য বেতনগ্রহণে অপর জাতির কার্য্যে নিযুক্ত সৈন্যগণ।

sŭb'-si-dīze, *v. t.* 1. To pay subsidy to ; to purchase the assistance of another by the payment of a subsidy to him ; আর্থিক সাহায্য প্রদান করা ; আর্থিক সাহায্য প্রদানে কাহারো নিকট হইতে সাহায্যতা লাভ করা। 2. To aid or promote, as a private enterprise with public money ; as, to *subsidize* a railway line ; কোনরূপ বেসকারী উদ্যোগে সরকারী অর্থ সাহায্য করা।

sŭb'-si-dȳ, *n.* 1. Pecuniary aid contributed by the State to the expenses of commercial undertakings, charitable institutions, etc. ; ব্যবসায় বাণিজ্য প্রভৃতি ব্যাপার, হিতকর প্রতিষ্ঠান প্রভৃতিতে সরকার কর্ত্তৃক যে অর্থসাহায্য প্রদত্ত হয়। 2. A sum of money paid by one nation to another for war ; যুদ্ধে সাহায্যতার জন্য এক জাতি কর্ত্তৃক অপর জাতিকে যে অর্থ সাহায্য প্রদত্ত হয়, আর্থিক সহায়তা (হিঃ কোঃ), উপগ্রহ (অর্থঃ)। 3. (*Hist.*) A sum of money granted by Parliament to the crown to meet urgent and pressing necessities ; (ইতিহাস) একান্ত প্রয়োজনীয় ব্যয়নির্ব্বাহের জন্য পার্লেমেণ্ট মহাসভা কর্ত্তৃক নৃপতিকে যে অর্থ মঞ্জুর করা হইত।

sŭb-sist', *v. i.* & *t.* 1. To exist ; থাকা, অবস্থান করা, বিদ্যমান থাকা, রহা। 2. To live ; as, to *subsist* on vegetables ; বাঁচিয়া থাকা, প্রাণধারণ করা, জীবণ ধারণ করা। 3. To hold or have being through the existence of something else (*Webster*) ; "Relations may *subsist*...but they cannot exist in the absence of the things to which they pertain" ; অন্য কিছুর সত্তা হইতে সত্তাবান হওয়া। ***Verb t.*** To feed ; to support with provisions ;

to maintain; ভোজন করা; খাদ্য দ্রব্যাদি প্রদানে পোষণ করা; প্রতিপালন করা।

sŭb-sist'-ence (-ĕns), *n.* 1. Inherency; অন্তর্নিহিতত্ব। 2. Means of support; livelihood; জীবিকার উপায়; উপজীবিকা, নির্ব্বাহমাত্র (হিঃ কোঃ), জীবিকা, বর্ত্তন (হিঃ কোঃ), জীবিকাবৃত্তি (ঐ), অনুবর্ত্তন (ঐ)। 2. Existence; সত্তা (এভেলন), অস্তিত্ব।

sub'-soil (-soyl), *n.* The bed or stratum of earth below the surface soil; নিম্নস্থ ভূমি, অন্তর্ভূমি (প্রবোধ), অধোভূমি (হিঃ কোঃ)। **Subsoil plough**—কর্ষিত জমির লাঙ্গলপদ্ধতির মাটী না উল্টাইয়া কয়েক ইঞ্চি গভীরভাবে মাটী ঝুরা করিবার জন্য যন্ত্রবিশেষ।

sŭb'-stance (-stăns), *n.* 1. Matter; material; জড়বস্তু, স্থূলভূত; বস্তু, দ্রব্য, পদার্থ। 2. The essence; as, the *substance* of a book; real meaning; সারভাগ, সত্ত্ব, সারমর্ম্ম; প্রকৃত অর্থ, তাৎপর্য্য। 3. Firmness; substantiality; দৃঢ়তা; সারবত্তা। 4. (*Philog.*) That which underlies outward manifestation; সদ্‌বস্তু, তত্ত্ব (হিঃ কোঃ), স্বরূপ। 5. Property; as, a man of *substance*; riches; resource; সম্পত্তি; ধন দৌলত; সঙ্গতি। 6. (*Theol.*) Essential nature; hypostasis; (খৃষ্টীয়ধর্ম্ম) মূলপ্রকৃতি; কায়ব্যূহ। **In substance** — Substantially; মূলতঃ। **Mixed substance** — মিলিত দ্রব্য (সাঃ পঃ), সংযুক্তভূতার্থ (ঐ)। **Transformation of substance** — দ্রব্যান্তরপরিণাম (সাঃ পঃ)। **Unctuous substance**—স্নেহ (সাঃ পঃ)। **Vegetable substance** — স্থাবর ভূত (সাঃ পঃ), উদ্ভিদ্ (ঐ)।

sŭb-stăn'-tial (-shăl), *adj.* 1. Real; actually existing; বাস্তব, মূর্ত্ত, বস্তুভূত; প্রকৃতপক্ষে বিদ্যমান। 2. Corporeal; material; দৈহিক; ভৌতিক। 3. Having firm or good substance; as, *substantial* meal; strong; as, *substantial* cloth; firm; সারবান, সদার; শক্ত; দৃঢ়, মজবুত। 4. Possessed of good estate; moderately wealthy; responsible; sound; সম্পত্তিশালী; সঙ্গতিশালী; দায়িত্বসম্পন্ন; সাউকড়। 5. Considerable; as, a *substantial* sum; প্রভূত, প্রচুর। 6. Virtual; practical; as, a *substantial* lie: *substantial* victory; কার্য্যতঃ; বস্তুতঃ। **—ly**, *adv.* Actually; esentially; materially; বাস্তব পক্ষে; মূলত; বস্তুতঃ। **—ti-al'-i-ty**, *n.* The quality or state of being substantial; দ্রব্যতা (হিঃ কোঃ), বস্তুতা (ঐ), দ্রব্যত্ব (সর্ব্বঃ)।

sŭb'-stăn-tial-ĭsm, (-shăl-), *n.* (*Philos.*) The doctrine that there exist substantial realities behind the phenomena; প্রপঞ্চের অন্তরালে সদ্বস্তু বিদ্যমান রহিয়াছে এই মতবাদ, বস্তুত্ববাদ (হিঃ কোঃ)।

sŭb-stăn'-tial-īze (-shăl-), *v. t.* 1. To render or become substantial; মূর্ত্ত করা, বাস্তবতা সম্পন্ন করা, সারবান করা, দৃঢ় করা।

sŭb-stăn'-ti-āte (-shĭ-), *v.t.* 1. To establish by proof; to verify; as, to *substantiate* a charge; প্রমাণ দ্বারা প্রতিপন্ন করা; সত্যতা প্রতিপাদন করা, সত্যতা প্রমাণ করা। 2. To embody; মূর্ত্তিমান করা, মূর্ত্ত করা। 3. To make real; বাস্তব করা। **—a'-tion**, *n.*

sŭb'-stăn-tive (-tĭv), *adj.* & *n.* 1. Expressing existence; সত্তাবাচক, সত্তাসূচক, দ্রব্যবাচক। 2. Independent; as, a *substantive* enactment; স্বতন্ত্র, স্বাধীন। 3. (*Rare*) solid; firm; (কচিদ্‌ব্যবহৃত) মজবুত; দৃঢ়। 4. Pertaining to, or constituting essential part or principle; মূল অংশ বা মূলতত্ত্ব সম্বন্ধীয়, মূলীভূত, সারভূত। ***Noun.*** Noun; বিশেষ্য পদ। **—ti'-val**, *adj.* **—ti'-val-ly**, *adv.* **Substantive colours**—যে সকল বর্ণ অন্য বস্তুর সাহায্য ব্যতিরেকে রঞ্জনকালে স্থায়ী বা পাকা হইয়া থাকে। **Substantive motion**—যে সংশোধিত প্রস্তাব গৃহীত হওয়ার পরে পরবর্ত্তী আলোচনার বিষয়ীভূত হইয়া থাকে। **Substantive punishment** — যে শাস্তির ফলে শারীরিক কষ্ট বা যন্ত্রণা ভোগ করিতে হয়। **Substantive verb**—*be* এই ক্রিয়া। **Substantive state of mind**—বস্তুবৃত্তি (হিঃ কোঃ)।

sŭb-stêr'-năl, *adj.* (*Anat.*) Situated below the sternum (শারীরসংস্থানবিদ্যা) বুকাস্থির নিম্নস্থ।

sŭb'-sti-tūte, *n.* & *v. t.* A person or thing put in the place of another; স্থলাভিষিক্ত ব্যক্তি, স্থলবর্ত্তী ব্যক্তি, প্রতিনিধি, অনুকল্প। ***Verb t.*** 1. To put in place of another; স্থলবর্ত্তী করা, স্থলাভিষিক্ত করা। 2. To put in exchange or interchange; পরিবর্ত্তে দেওয়া, বিনিময় করা। **—tu'-tion**, *n.* 1. Act of substituting or state of being substituted; অনুসংস্থাপন (হিঃ কোঃ), অনুসংস্থিতি। 2. (*Law*) A conditional appointment of an heir; (আইন) কোনরূপ সর্ত্তের অধীনে উত্তরাধিকারী নিয়োগ। 3. (*Chem.*) The replacement of one or more equivalents of a body by a like number of equivalents of another; (রসায়নশাস্ত্র) কোন বস্তুর এক বা তদধিক তুল্য শক্তিক স্থানে অপর বস্তুর সমসংখক তুলাশক্তিক সন্নিবেশ, প্রতিনিবেশন (হিঃ কোঃ), প্রতিনিধান (ঐ)। 4. (*Phil.*) A sound change consisting in the replacement of one vowel or consonant by another; (ভাষাবিজ্ঞান) এক স্বর বা ব্যঞ্জন বর্ণের স্থানে অপর স্বর বা ব্যঞ্জনের আদেশ, আদেশ। 5. (*Algeb.*) The replacement of one quantity by another which is equal to it but differently expressed; (বীজগণিত) কোন রাশির স্থলে তৎসম কিন্তু অন্য বিভিন্ন প্রকারে ব্যক্ত অপর রাশি সন্নিবেশন, স্থানাপন্ন

(হিঃ কোঃ)। **—tu′-tion-al, —tu′-tion-a-ry, —tu-tive,** *adjs.* **—tu′-tion-al-ly,** *adv.*

sŭb′-strā′-tŭm, *n.* 1. That which underlies or supports anything; আধার, অধিষ্ঠান, আশ্রয় (ব্রজঃ বিঃ), অধিকরণ, আধারক (সুশ্রুঃ)। 2. A layer or stratum lying under another; অধঃস্তর।

sŭb-strŭc′-tion, *n.* Foundation; ভিত্তি, বুনিয়াদ।

sŭb-strŭc′-tūre, *n.* An under-structure; foundation; অধোগৃহ; ভিত্তি, বুনিয়াদ।

sŭb′-stȳle, *n.* (*Dial.*) The line on which the style or gnomon stands; যে রেখার উপর সূর্য্যঘড়ীর শঙ্কু সন্নিবিষ্ট করা হয়।

sŭb-sūme′, *v. t.* To include under a more general class or category; ব্যাপকতর শ্রেণীর অন্তর্ভুক্ত করা। **—sump′-tion,** *n.* Act of subsuming or state of being subsumed; উপনয় (হিঃ কোঃ)।

sŭb-tăn′-gĕnt, *n.* (*Geom.*) The part of the axis contained between the ordinate and tangent drawn to the same point in the curve; (জ্যামিতি) উপস্পর্শিণী (সাঃ পঃ), অবান্তরস্পর্শরেখা (হিঃ কোঃ)।

sŭb-tĕn′-ănt, *n.* The tenant under a tenant; দর প্রজা, কোর্ফা প্রজা।

sŭb-tĕnd′, *v. i.* To extend under, or be opposite to; (জ্যামিতি—ত্রিভুজের বাহু সম্পর্কে) সম্মুখবর্ত্তী হওয়া, সম্মুখে অবস্থান করা, পরস্পরের বিপরীত দিকে অবস্থিত হওয়া।

sŭb-tense′ (-tĕns), *n.* A line subtending an arc or an angle; বৃত্তখণ্ড বা কোণের পার্দ্বিরেখা।

sŭb-tĕp′-ĭd, *adj.* Slightly tepid; ঈষদুষ্ণ, মন্দোষ্ণ।

sŭb′-tĕr—, (*prefix*) Under; নিম্নবর্ত্তী।

sŭb′-tĕr-fūge, *n.* A shift; an artifice; an evasion; ফন্দী, ফিকির; ফিকিরফন্দি, চাতুরী, কৌশল, ফাঁকিঝুঁকি, কলকৌশল; ছল।

sŭb′-tĕr-pō-sĭ′-tion, *n.* The state of lying or being situated under something else; নিম্নাবস্থান, নিম্নাবস্থিতি।

sŭb-tĕr-rā′-nē-ăn, *adj.* Situated within the earth or underground; ভুনিম্নস্থ, ভুনিম্নবর্ত্তী, অন্তর্ভৌম, ভুগর্ত্তস্থ, অধোভূমিক। **Subterranean river**—অন্তঃসলিলা নদী, অন্তঃসলিলবাহিনী নদী।

sŭb′-tīle, *adj.* 1. (*Archaic*) Subtle; (অপ্রঃ) সূক্ষ্ম। 2. Cunning; চালাক, কৌশলী। **—ly,** *adv.* **—til′-i-ty,** *n.* Extreme niceness or acuteness; cunning; সূক্ষ্মতা, কৌশল, চাতুরী; চালাকি। **Subtile vehicles of potential energy**—তন্মাত্র (ব্রজঃ হিন্দু), সূক্ষ্মভুত (ঐ)।

sub′-tle (sŭt-l), *adj.* 1. Not dense or gross; সূক্ষ্ম। 2. Artful; cunning; expert; চালাক, কৌশলী; চতুর, কুশল; নিপুণ, দক্ষ। 3. Skilfully devised; নিপুণভাবে কল্পিত। 4. Nicely discriminating; acute in intellect; characterised by niceness in drawing distinctions সূক্ষ্মবিচারী; সূক্ষ্ম, চুলচেরা; সূক্ষ্মবিশ্লেষণকারী। **—tly,** *adv.* **—ty,** *n.* The quality of being sly or subtle; craftiness; সূক্ষ্মবুদ্ধিতা, কুশাগ্রবুদ্ধিতা; চাতুর্য্য, নৈপুণ্য। 2. Nicety of discrimination; সূক্ষ্মবিচার, সূক্ষ্মবিশ্লেষণ। 3. A fine distinction; সূক্ষ্মভেদ, চুলচেরা ভাগ। **Subtle body**—সূক্ষ্মশরীর, লিঙ্গশরীর, আতিবাহিক দেহ। **Subtle element**—তন্মাত্র (শ্রীঃ)। **Subtle matter**—তন্মাত্র (শ্রীঃ)।

sŭb-trăct′, *v. t.* To withdraw or take apart from the rest; বিয়োগ করা, ব্যবকলন করা, বাদ দেওয়া। **—trac′-tion,** *n.* The act of subtracting; বিয়োগ, ব্যবকলন, পতন (ঐ), শোধন (ঐ)। **—trc′-tive,** *adj.*

sŭb′-trā-hĕnd, *n.* A sum or number to be subtracted from another; বিয়োজ্য রাশি, ঋণরাশি।

sŭb-trī′-ple (-pl), *n.* Containing a third or one part of three; ত্রয়াংশাত্মক।

sŭb-trĭp′-lĭ-cāte, *adj.* Expressed by the cube root; ঘনমূল দ্বারা প্রকাশিত, ঘনমূলীয়।

sŭb-trŏp′-ĭ-căl, *adj.* Belonging to the region near the tropics; গ্রীষ্মমণ্ডলের নিকটবর্ত্তী অঞ্চলসম্বন্ধীয়। **—ics,** *n.* The subtropical regions; গ্রীষ্মমণ্ডলের সন্নিহিত অঞ্চল।

sŭb-tū′-tŏr, *n.* An under-tutor; উপশিক্ষক।

sū′-bū-late, —lĭ-fŏrm, *adjs.* (*Bot.* & *Zool.*) Awl-shaped; (উদ্ভিদ্‌বিদ্যা এবং জন্তু বিদ্যা) এষণাকার, বেধনিকাকৃতি, আরাকার (সাঃ পঃ), ত্রপুণাকৃতি।

sū′-bū′-lĭ-cŏrns, *n.* (*pl.*) A family of insects with awl-shaped antennae; আরাকার শৃঙ্গ বা রেফবিশিষ্ট পতঙ্গ শ্রেণী।

sŭb-un′-gū-ăl (-ŭng-), *adj.* Under the nail; নখনিম্নস্থ।

sŭb′-ŭrb, *n.* An outlying part of a city or town; নগরোপকণ্ঠ, নগরোপান্ত, উপপুর (হিঃ কোঃ), শাখানগর (হরিবংশ), উপনগর, উপপুরী, সহরতলী।

sŭb-ŭr′-băn, *adj.* Pertaining to a suburb; inhabiting, or being in, the suburb of a city; নগরোপকণ্ঠসম্বন্ধীয়, ঔপনাগারিক (কপালঃ); নগরোপকণ্ঠবাসী, নগরোপকণ্ঠস্থ।

sŭb-vă-rī′-ĕ-tȳ, *n.* A subordinate variety; উপজাতি।

sŭb-vĕn′-tion, *n.* 1. The act of coming under; নিম্নে আগমন, অবতরণ। 2. Support; aid; আশ্রয়; সাহায্য। 3. A government grant or aid; pecuniary aid; সরকারী সাহায্য; আর্থিক সাহায্য।

sŭb-vĕrt′, *v. t.* To overturn; to upset; to ruin utterly; বিপর্য্যস্ত করা, উল্টাইয়া ফেলা; উৎপাতিত করা; উচ্ছেদসাধন করা, নাশ করা। **—ver′-sion,** *n.* The act of subverting; destruction; utter ruin

বিপর্য্যাস, বিপর্য্যয়; বিধ্বংস, ধ্বংস, উচ্ছেদ, উন্মূলন; বিলোপ, বিনাশ। **—ver′-sive,** *adj.*

sŭb′-way (-wā), *n.* An arched way underneath a street containing water-pipes, gas-pipes, telegraph-wires, etc., so that when these require repairs the street above need not be disturbed; রাজপথের নিম্নস্থ খিলানবিশিষ্ট পথ—যাহাতে জল ও গ্যাসের নল, টেলিগ্রাফের তার, প্রভৃতি থাকে।

sŭb-wŏrk′-ėr, *n.* A subordinate worker or helper; উপকার্য্যকারক, উপসহায়ক।

sŭc-cāde′, *n.* A sweetmeat or preserve in sugar; চিনির শিরায় ডুবানো মিষ্টদ্রব্য বা মোরব্বা।

sŭc-cē-dā′-nē-ous (-ŭs) *n.* Substitute; প্রতিনিধি, স্থলবর্ত্তী, গৌণকল্প, অনুকল্প।

sŭc-ceed′ (-sēd), *v.t.*& *i.* **1.** To take the place of; to be heir or successor to; স্থান গ্রহণ করা, স্থলবর্ত্তী হওয়া, স্থলাভিষিক্ত হওয়া; উত্তরাধিকারী হওয়া। **2.** To follow; to come after; অনুসরণ করা, অনুগামী হওয়া; পশ্চাদ্‌গামী হওয়া, পরে আসা, অনুবর্ত্তী হওয়া, অনুবর্ত্তন করা। ***Verb i.*** **1.** To follow in order; to come next or after; পর্য্যায়ক্রমে আসা, পর পর আসা; পরে আসা, অনুবর্ত্তন করা। **2.** To ascend the throne after the removal or death of the king; সিংহাসনে আরোহণ করা, সিংহাসনাধিরোহণ করা। **3.** To be successful; কৃতকার্য্য হওয়া, সফলকাম হওয়া, সিদ্ধকাম হওয়া।

sŭc-cĕn′-tŏr, *n.* One who sings the bass in a choir; খৃষ্টীয় ধর্ম্মমন্দিরের গায়কসম্প্রদায়ের যে ব্যক্তি খাদে গাহিয়া থাকে।

succès d'estime, *n.* A reception given to a performance out of respect rather than from appreciation; গুণগ্রহণের ভাব হইতে না করিয়া বরঞ্চ শ্রদ্ধা হইতে কোন অভিনয় প্রভৃতির উপর যে সমাদর প্রদর্শন করা হয়।

sŭc-cĕss′, *n.* **1.** (*Rare*) Issue of an act; as, good or bad *success*; পরিণাম, ফল। **2.** The prosperous termination of any attempt; কৃতকার্য্যতা, সিদ্ধি, সফলতা, সাফল্য, কার্য্যসিদ্ধি, সফলত্ব। **3.** A successful undertaking or attempt; সফল চেষ্টা। **4.** (*Colloq.*) A thing or person achieving success; as, the invention was a *success*; (চলিতভাষায়) সাফল্যপ্রাপ্ত বিষয়, কৃতকার্য্য ব্যক্তি, কৃতকর্ম্মা ব্যক্তি। **—ful,** *adj.* Gaining or having gained success; fortunate; prosperous; কৃতকার্য্য, সিদ্ধকাম, সফল, কৃতকৃত্য, প্রাপ্তকাম; ভাগ্যবান, সৌভাগ্যশালী; সমৃদ্ধ। **—ful-ly,** *adv.*

sŭc′-ces′-sion (-sŏ-), *n.* **1.** A following of things in order; পরম্পরা, অনুক্রম, আনুপূর্ব্ব (হিঃ কোঃ), পৌর্ব্বাপর্য্য, আনন্তর্য্য। **2.** The act of succeeding or coming in place of another; স্থলবর্ত্তী হওন, কোন ব্যক্তির স্থান অধিকার, উত্তরাধিকার, সিংহাসনাদি আরোহণ। **3.** Lineage; heirs; as, this was left to him and his *succession*; বংশাবলী; উত্তরাধিকারিবর্গ। **4.** (*Biol.*) Order of descent in development of species; (জীববিজ্ঞান) জাতির পরিণতিতে বংশানুক্রম। **—al,** *adj.* Consecutive; ক্রমিক। **Succession duties**—উত্তরাধিকারসূত্রে প্রাপ্ত সম্পত্তির উপর প্রদেয় শুল্ক। **Apostolic succession**—খৃষ্টের পার্ষদগণ হইতে আরম্ভ করিয়া ধর্ম্মাধ্যক্ষগণের (Bishops) দ্বারা অবিচ্ছিন্নভাবে পারমার্থিক ব্যাপার সম্বন্ধীয় ক্ষমতার সংক্রমণ। **Law of succession**—উত্তরাধিকারিবিষয়ক আইন। **Succession of crops**—Same as ROTATION OF CROPS (which see).

sŭc-cĕs′-sive (-ĭv) *adj.* Following one after another in a line or series; as, *successive* keys; consecutive; আনুক্রমিক, পারম্পরিক, পরম্পরাগত, পরম্পরীণ, ধারাবাহিক, ক্রমভাবী (ন্যায়দর্শন); ক্রমিক। **—ly** *adv.* In a successive manner; ধারাবাহিকরূপে, অনুক্রমে, পর্য্যায়ক্রমে, পরপর, পরম্পরাক্রমে।

sŭc-cĕs′-sor (-ŏr), *n.* A person or thing that succeeds another; উত্তরাধিকারী, পরবর্ত্তী লোক, উত্তরবর্ত্তী লোক, পশ্চাদাগত বস্তু।

sŭc-cinct′ (-sĭngkt), *adj.* Terse; concise; সংক্ষিপ্ত অথচ সারবান; স্বল্পাক্ষর, সংক্ষিপ্ত, অবিস্তীর্ণ, অল্পাক্ষরগ্রথিত, বাহুল্যদোষবর্জ্জিত, সামাসিক, অপল্লবিত। **—ly,** *adv.* **—ness,** *n.*

sŭc′-cō-rȳ, *n.* Same as CHICORY (which see).

sŭc′-cōse, *adj.* Sappy; সরস, রসাল, রসপূর্ণ।

sŭc′-cour (-ėr), *v. t.* & *n.* To give aid to; to relieve; সাহায্য করা, সহায়তা করা; উদ্ধার করা। ***Noun.*** **1.** Aid; সাহায্য, সহায়তা, আনুকূল্য। **2.** Troops serving as an aid or assistance or coming to the rescue; সাহায্যস্বরূপ প্রেরিত সৈন্য, উদ্ধারার্থ আগত সৈন্য। **—less,** *adj.*

sŭc′-cū-bȧ, —bŭs, *ns.* A female demon having sexual connection with men in sleep; এক জাতীয় দানবী—ইহারা নিদ্রিতাবস্থায় পুরুষের সহিত সংসর্গ করিয়া থাকে।

sŭc′-cū-lĕnt, *adj.* **1.** Juicy; রসাল, সরস, রসপূর্ণ। **2.** (*Bot.*) Having juicy or watery tissues; (উদ্ভিদ্‌বিদ্যা) সরস অথবা সজল বিধানতন্তুসম্পন্ন। **—lence,** *n.* **—ly,** *adv.* **Succulent stem**—নাল (সাঃ পঃ)।

sŭc-cumb′ (-cŭm), *v. i.* **1.** To submit; to give way; to die; as, to *succumb* to disease; পরাজয় স্বীকার করা; ভাঙ্গিয়া পড়া, অবসন্ন হওয়া; মরা।

sŭc-cur′-sȧl (-kêr-), *adj.* Auxiliary; subsidiary; as, *succursal* church or chapel of ease; সহায়ক; উপ।

sŭch, *adj.* & *pron.* **1.** Like; similar; এমন, এইরূপ, ঈদৃশ, এতাদৃশ

এবম্বিধ ; এমত, সেমত, তদ্রূপ, তদ্বৎ, সেইরূপ, তাদৃশ। 2. Certain ; অমুক, কোন এক। 3. So great ; as, *such* a fright ; এত বেশী, এত অধিক, এরূপ। ***Pron.*** 1. Such a person or thing ; এবম্প্রকার ব্যক্তি বা বস্তু। 2. (*Commerc.* & *vulg.*) The aforesaid thing or things ; (ইতরভাষায় বা বাণিজ্যে) উক্ত বস্তুসমূহ। **All such**—এইরূপ প্রকৃতির লোক সকল। **As such**—এইরূপে। **Such and such**—অমুক অমুক। **Such as**—যেমন, যথা ; এইরূপ, এই জাতীয় ; যাহারা (সাধারণতঃ কবিতায় ও বক্তৃতার ভাষায়)। **Such as it is**—যেমন আছে তেমনই। **Such like**—সেই প্রকার, তাদৃশ, এইরূপ, এইভাবের, এবম্ভূত। **Such master such servant**—যেমন মনীব তেমন ভৃত্য।

sŭck, *v. t.*, *i.* & *n.* 1. To draw with the mouth ; চুষিয়া নেওয়া। 2. To draw milk from the mother's breast etc. with mouth ; মাতৃস্তন প্রভৃতি হইতে দুগ্ধ পান করা। 3. To inhale ; to absorb ; শ্বাস লওয়া ; শুষিয়া নেওয়া। ***Verb i.*** To draw fluid with the mouth ; চুষিয়া নেওয়া। ***Noun.*** 1. The act of drawing with the mouth ; চোষণ, আচোষণ। 2. Milk drawn from the breast by sucking ; স্তন হইতে যে দুগ্ধ চুষিয়া নেওয়া হয়। 3. Small draught of ; ঢোক, চুমুক। 4. (*Slang.*, *pl.*) Sweets ; মিঠাই। 5. (*Slang*) Disappointment ; fiasco ; (ইতরভাষার) নৈরাশ্য ; হাস্যজনক বিফলতা। **Sucked orange**—See ORANGE. **To suck in**—To draw into the mouth ; টানিয়া নেওয়া, শুষিয়া নেওয়া। (*Slang*) To cheat ; ঠকান, চোখে ধূলি দেওয়া। To engulf ; কুক্ষিগত করা, গ্রাস করা। **To suck the monkey**—See under MONKEY. **To suck up**—To draw into the mouth ; চুষিয়া নেওয়া।

sŭck'-ĕr, *n.*, *v. t.* & *i.* 1. He who or that which, draws with the mouth ; চোষক, চোষণকারী, শোষক (সাঃ পঃ)। 2. The piston of a suction-pump; দমকলের নলদণ্ড। 3. A pipe or tube through which anything is drawn ; যে নলের ভিতর দিয়া কোন কিছু টানিয়া নেওয়া হয়। 4. The shoot of a plant from the roots or lower part of the stem ; কাণ্ডের মূল বা নিম্নাংশ হইতে নির্গত প্রশাখা, মৃন্মধ্যজা শাখা, গেঁড়। 5. A fish of the carp family ; রোহিত জাতীয় মৎস্য বিশেষ। ***Verb t.*** To stripe off the suckers from ; মৃন্মধ্যজা-শাখা শূন্য করা। ***Verb i.*** To produce suckers ; মৃন্মধ্যজা শাখা উৎপাদন করা।

sŭck'-ĕt, *n.* A sweetmeat that dissolves in the mouth ; একপ্রকার মিঠাই—যাহা মুখে মিলাইয়া যায়।

sŭck'-ing, *adj.* Drawing nourishment from the mother's breast ; স্তনন্ধয়, স্তন্যপায়ী। **Sucking-bottle**—বিলাতী মাই। **Sucking-pump**—Same as SUCTION-PUMP.

sŭck'-le (-l), *v. t.* To give suck to ; স্তন্যপান করান, মাই দেওয়া (*colloq.*)।

sŭck'-ling, *n.* A young child or animal nursed by the mother's milk ; স্তনন্ধয় শিশু, দুগ্ধপোষ্য শিশু, দুগ্ধপোষ্য শাবক, ক্ষীরকণ্ঠক, ক্ষীরাদ, বক্ষোজপানকৃত, দুধের ছেলে (*colloq.*), দুধের ছাওয়াল।

sū'-crōse, *n.* A name for the sugar identical with cane-sugar ; ইক্ষুজাত শর্করা, ইক্ষুজাত শর্করার মত ধর্ম্মবিশিষ্ট শর্করা।

sŭc'-tion, *n.* 1. Sucking ; চোষণ, আচোষণ। 2. The drawing up of a fluid by exhaustion of air ; বায়ু শূন্যীকৃত চুঙ্গী প্রভৃতি দ্বারা আকর্ষণ-পূর্ব্বক উত্তোলন। **Suction-fan**—শস্য হইতে তুষ ছাড়াইবার জন্য একপ্রকার ব্যজন-যন্ত্র। **Suction-plate**—কৃত্রিম দন্তপংক্তিবিশিষ্ট ফলক—যাহা বায়ুমণ্ডলের চাপদ্বারা যথাস্থানে স্থিত থাকে। **Suction-pump**—শোষণযন্ত্র, দমকল। **Suction root**—শোষক মূল।

sŭc-tō'-ri-ăl, *adj.* 1. Adapted to sucking ; শোষণক্ষম। 2. Living by sucking ; চোষণজীবী। 3. Capable of adhering by suction ; বায়ুর চাপদ্বারা সংলাগশীল। 3. Having suckers for eating ; আহারের উপযোগী চোষণফলকবিশিষ্ট।

sū-dăm'-i-nă, *n.* Vesicles resembling millet-seeds in form and magnitude, appearing in puerperal fever, typhus, etc. ; (নিদানশাস্ত্র) সান্নিপাতিক জ্বর প্রভৃতিতে উপজাত একপ্রকার পীড়কা।

Sū'-dă-nese' (-nēz), *adj.* Same as SOUDANESE (which see).

sū-dā'-ri-ŭm, *n.* 1. A cloth for wiping off sweat, esp. that of St. Veronica on which the features of Jesus and his way to the cross was miraculously impressed ; রুমাল, বিশেষতঃ, St. Veronicaর রুমাল—যাহাতে অলৌকিক উপায়ে যীশুখৃষ্টের ক্রুশগমনকালীন মূর্ত্তি চিহ্নিত হইয়াছিল। 2. Any miraculous portrait of Christ ; যীশুখৃষ্টের অলৌকিক চিত্র।

sū-dā'-tion, *n.* Sweating ; ঘর্ম্ম-নিঃসরণ, শ্রমজলক্ষরণ।

sū-dă-tō'-ri-ŭm, *n.* Hot-air bath for producing perspiration ; ঘর্ম্মজননের জন্য উষ্ণবায়ুতে স্নান।

sū'-dă-tō-rў, *adj* & *n.* Promoting perspiration ; ঘর্ম্মজনক, ঘর্ম্ম-বর্দ্ধক। ***Noun.*** A drug which promotes sweating ; ঘর্ম্মজনক ঔষধ।

sŭdd, *n.* A mass of floating water-plants, interlaced with trunks of trees etc. forming floating islands on the White Nile; নীল নদোপরি ভাসমান বৃক্ষকাণ্ডাদির সহিত সংগ্রথিত জলজ উদ্ভিদের পুঞ্জ।

sŭd'-den (-ĕn), *adj.* & *n.* 1. Happening without previous notice ; coming unexpectedly ; আকস্মিক, আচম্বিত, অচিন্তিত ; অপ্রত্যাশিতভাবে সংঘটিত। 2. Hastily prepared or done; quick ; rapid ; as, he is very *sudden* in his movements; দ্রুতসম্পাদিত, দ্রুতনির্ম্মিত; দ্রুত ; সত্বর, ক্ষিপ্র। ***Noun.*** (*Obs.*) An unexpected occurrence ; (অপ্রঃ) অপ্রত্যাশিত ঘটনা, আকস্মিক ঘটনা। **–ly,** *adv.* In a sudden or unexpected mannar ; হঠাৎ, সহসা, অকস্মাৎ, অপ্রত্যাশিতভাবে, আচমকা, দৈবাৎ। **–ness,** *n.* **Of a sudden, On a sudden**—Suddenly ; হঠাৎ, সহসা, আচমকা, (*colloq.*)।

sü-dŏr-ĭf'-ĕr-ous (-ŭs), *adj.* Producing or secreting perspiration ; ঘর্ম্মজনক, ঘর্ম্মক্ষরণশীল, ঘর্ম্মোৎপাদক, স্বেদজনক, স্বেদকারী (সাঃ পঃ)।

sü-dŏr-ĭf'-ĭc, *adj.* & *n.* Causing sweat ; স্বেদজনক, ঘর্ম্মজনক, ঘর্ম্মোৎপাদক। ***Noun.*** A medicine that produces sweat ; ঘর্ম্মজনক ঔষধ।

sŭds, *n.* Water impregnated with soap, and worked up into froths and bubbles ; সাবান জল।

sue (sü), *v. t.* & *i.* 1. To seek after ; to try to win ; to woo ; to seek in marriage ; অভিলাষ করা ; লাভ করিতে চেষ্টা করা ; প্রণয় যাচ্ঞা করা ; পাণিগ্রহণপ্রার্থী হওয়া। 2. To bring an action against ; মোকদ্দমা করা, নালিশ করা, মোকদ্দমা রুজু করা। ***Verb i.*** 1. To make request ; to entreat ; প্রার্থনা করা ; অনুরোধ করা, অনুনয় করা। 2. To woo ; বিবাহার্থ প্রেমোপাসনা করা। **To sue out**—To petition for and obtain ; as, *to sue out* a pardon ; আবেদন করিয়া প্রাপ্ত হওয়া।

suede (swād), *n.* Undressed kid ; অশোধিত ছাগচর্ম্ম।

sü'-ĕt, *n.* The harder fat of an animal about the kidneys and loins ; জন্তুর মূত্রাশয় এবং কটিদেশের সন্নিকটস্থ কঠিন মেদ।

sŭf'-fĕr, *v. t.* & *i.* 1. To endure ; to undergo ; to feel ; সহ্য করা, সহা ; (কষ্ট) ভোগ করা ; অনুভব করা। 2. To allow ; as, the king *suffered* the precious moments to pass away ; not to hinder ; to permit ; to tolerate ; চলিয়া যাইতে দেওয়া ; বাধা না দেওয়া ; কোন কিছু করিতে দেওয়া ; সহা। ***Verb i.*** 1. To feel or undergo pain of body or mind ; দুঃখ বা যন্ত্রণা সহ্য করা, কষ্টভোগ করা। 2. To undergo punishment ; শাস্তি ভোগ করা। 3. To sustain loss or damage ; as, your reputation will *suffer* ; ক্ষতিভোগ করা, হানি হওয়া। 4. (Of a condemned man) To be executed ; (প্রাণদণ্ডে দণ্ডিত ব্যক্তি সম্পর্কে), চরমদণ্ড ভোগ করা। **–a-ble,** *adj.* **–er,** *n.* **–ing,** *n.* 1. The bearing of pain ; যন্ত্রণাভোগ, কষ্টভোগ। 2. Pain endured ; distress ; ব্যথা, যন্ত্রণা, কষ্ট, ক্লেশ, যাতনা ; তাপ, দুর্দ্দশা।

sŭf'-fêr-ance (-ăns), *n.* 1. (*Archaic*) Submissiveness ; বশ্যতা। 2. Patient endurance ; সহিষ্ণুতা। 3. Permission ; অনুমতি অনুজ্ঞা। 4. A permission given for the shipment of goods ; জাহাজে মাল চালান দেওয়ার জন্য অনুমতিপত্র।

sŭf'-fete (-fēt), *n.* A chief magistrate of ancient Carthage ; প্রাচীন কার্থেজ নগরীর প্রধান দণ্ডনায়ক।

sŭf-fīce', *v. i.* & *t.* To be enough or sufficient ; as, this will *suffice* for me ; যথেষ্ট হওয়া, প্রচুর হওয়া। ***Verb t.*** To be sufficient for ; to meet the demands or requirements of ; প্রচুর হওয়া, যথেষ্ট হওয়া, যথোচিত হওয়া ; প্রয়োজনানুরূপ হওয়া, আবশ্যকানুরূপ হওয়া। **–fic'-ing-ly,** *adv.* **Suffice it to say that**—এই পর্য্যন্ত বলিলেই যথেষ্ট হইবে যে।

sŭf-fĭ'-cien-cy̆ (-shĕn-), *n.* 1. The state of being sufficient or adequate ; প্রাচুর্য্য। 2. Adequate substance or means ; যথোচিত দ্রব্য বা উপায়। 3. (*Archaic*) Competency ; (অপ্রঃ) উপযুক্ততা। 4. Conceit ; self-confidence ; self-sufficiency ; "*Sufficiency* is a compound of variety and ignorance" ; আত্মগর্ব্ব ; স্ববুদ্ধিনিষ্ঠা, স্বাভিমানতা।

sŭf-fĭ'-cient (-shĕnt), *adj.* & *n.* 1. Adequate to the wants ; enough ; যথোচিত ; যথেষ্ট, পর্য্যাপ্ত, প্রচুর। 2. Qualified ; fit ; যথোচিত গুণসম্পন্ন ; উপযুক্ত। **Sufficient reason**—হেতু পর্য্যাপ্ত (হিঃ কোঃ)।

sŭf'-fix', *v. t.* To add a letter or syllable to a word ; (শব্দে) বিভক্তি যোগ করা, (ধাতুতে) প্রত্যয় যোগ করা।

sŭf'-fix, *n.* A letter or syllable added to the end of a word ; বিভক্তি, প্রত্যয়।

sŭf'-fō-cāte, *v. t.* & *i.* 1. To choke or kill by stopping respiration ; to stifle ; শ্বাসরোধ করা ; দম আটকান। 2. To destroy ; বিনাশ করা। ***Verb i.*** To become choked or stifled ; শ্বাসরোধ হওয়া। **–ca'-tion,** *n.* 1. The act of suffocating, choking or smothering ; শ্বাসরোধ, শ্বাসাবরোধ। 2. Death caused by suffocation ; শ্বাসরোধজনিত মৃত্যু।

sŭf'-fră-găn, *adj.* & *n.* Assisting ; সহায়ক, সাহায্যকারী। ***Noun.*** A bishop considered as an assistant, or as subject, to his metropolitan ; অধীন ধর্ম্মাধ্যক্ষ। **–ship,** *n.*

sŭf'-frāge, *n.* 1. A vote ; approval or consent expressed by voting ; নির্ব্বাচন মত, ভোট ; ভোট দ্বারা ব্যক্ত সম্মতি বা অনুমোদন। 2. The right to vote ; ভোট প্রদানের অধিকার। 3. (*Eccles.*) An intercessory prayer or petition ; a short petition such as those after the Creed in Morning and Evening Prayer ; কোনরূপ বিপৎ প্রভৃতি হইতে রক্ষা পাওয়ার জন্য প্রার্থনা ; প্রাভাতিক বা সান্ধ্য উপাসনাকালে খৃষ্টধর্ম্মের মত বা বিশ্বাসের সংক্ষিপ্ত সারমর্ম্ম যে ক্ষুদ্র প্রার্থনায় ব্যক্ত করা হয়। **Manhood suffrage**—দেশের সমস্ত

প্রাপ্তবয়স্ক পুরুষের ভোট প্রদানের অধিকার। **Woman suffrage**—স্ত্রীলোকদিগের ভোট প্রদানের অধিকার। **Universal suffrage**—দেশের সমস্ত প্রাপ্ত বয়স্ক পুরুষ ও প্রাপ্তবয়স্কা স্ত্রীলোকের ভোট প্রদানের অধিকার।

sŭf-fră-gette′ (-jĕt), *n.* A woman agitating for the suffrage of women; নারীগণের ভোট প্রদানের অধিকার প্রাপ্তির জন্য আন্দোলনকারিণী স্ত্রী, সফরেগেট। **–get′-ism,** *n.*

sŭf′-fră-gist, *n.* **1.** A voter; ভোটদাতা, নির্ব্বাচনমত প্রদাতা। **2.** One who has certain opinions about suffrage; যে ব্যক্তি ভোট প্রদানের অধিকার সম্বন্ধে বিশেষ মত পোষণ করিয়া থাকেন।

sŭf-fūse′, *v. t.* To fill or overspread, as with something fluid; সিক্তকরা, আপ্লুত করা, পরিপ্লুত করা, ছলছল করা (সেধনী বিহনে তোমার আঁখি ছলছল—চণ্ডীদাস)। **–fu′-sion,** *n.*

sû′-fī, sō′-fī, *ns.* A Mohammedan mystic; মুসলমান ধর্ম্মাবলম্বী ধ্যান-রসিক, সুফী মরমী। [সুফী মত মুসলমানধর্ম্মের অন্তরঙ্গ সাধনা ও রহস্যমূলক। খৃষ্টীয় ৮ম শতাব্দীতে এই মত প্রথম প্রচারিত হয়। আরবীভাষায় সুফী শব্দের অর্থ পশম। এই মতাবলম্বী দরবেশগণ পশমের পোষাক পরিধান করিতেন বলিয়াই ইঁহাদিগকে সুফী বলা হইয়া থাকে, অনেকে এইরূপ অনুমান করেন। সুফী মতানুসারে ঈশ্বরই একমাত্র সৎস্বরূপ। তিনি অনন্ত সৌন্দর্য্য ও কল্যাণ-গুণের সমাশ্রয়। ভগবানের জীবের সহিত প্রেম, মিলন এবং জীবাত্মাতে পরমাত্মার লয় ইত্যাদি বিষয় সুফী ধর্ম্মের অঙ্গীভূত। সুফী সাধকগণ ঈশ্বর প্রেমে উন্মাদ। ইহা হাফেজ, জালালুদ্দিন রুমি, শাদী, প্রভৃতি সুফী কবিদিগের কবিতা হইতে সহজেই উপলব্ধ হইবে। এই মতানুসারে এই পরিদৃশ্যমান ব্রহ্মাণ্ড অদৃশ্য ঈশ্বরেরই বহিঃপ্রকাশ মাত্র। সর্ব্ব বস্তুতেই তিনি বিদ্যমান রহিয়াছেন। এই মত বাহ্যক্রিয়াকাণ্ড এবং আচারঅনুষ্ঠানের সম্পূর্ণ বিরোধী। ভগবানের সহিত অন্তরঙ্গসম্বন্ধ স্থাপনই এই ধর্ম্মের প্রধান লক্ষ্য। ইঁহারা বৈষ্ণব সাধকগণের মত শ্রীভগবানকে নিজ জন, প্রেমাস্পদ বা প্রেমপাত্রীরূপে ভাবিয়া থাকেন। নিম্নে প্রধান প্রধান সুফী কবিদের কয়েকটী কবিতার ইংরেজী অনুবাদ প্রদত্ত হইল। তাহা হইতে উপনিষদের ঋষি এবং কবীর, রামানন্দ, তুকারাম, তুলসীদাস, মীরাবাই, প্রভৃতি মরমীসাধক ও বঙ্গীয় ও তামিল বৈষ্ণবকবিদিগের সহিত পারস্যের সুফী কবিগণের সাধনার যে আশ্চর্য্য সাদৃশ্য রহিয়াছে তাহা সহজেই প্রতিপন্ন হইবে। (See *Malcolm's* Persia Vol. II., *Vaughan's* Persian Mystics in the Middle Ages):

The Sufi is as it were, the 'son of the season'
But the pure is exalted above season and state,
Religious raptures depend on feelings and will
But the pure one is regenerated by the breath of Jesus,
You are a lover of your own raptures, not of me,
You turn to me only in hope of experiencing raptures.
(*Jalaluddin Rumi—Whinfield*)

* * *

One day I was filled with longing
To behold in human form the splendours of the Friend,
To witness the ocean gathered up into a drop,
The sun compressed into a single atom. (*Ibid*).

* * *

The moon hath not the luminosity of Thy face,
In comparison with Thee the rose hath not the glory of grass.
The corner of Thy eye-brow is my soul's dwelling,
A happier corner than this the king hath not. (*Hafiz*)

* * *

The world is but a ray emanating from the Sun of his face
(*Jam-i-Kai-Khusro*)

Only in the night the moon shines,
Only in pain of heart seek the Beloved (*Jalaluddin Rumi*)

* * *

Love exalts our earthly bodies to heaven,
And makes the very hills to dance with joy!

* * *

Did my Beloved only touch me with his lips
I too, like the flute would burst out in melody
(*Jalaluddin Rumi—Whinfield*)

* * *

My life! I cannot keep myself far from thy door
I cannot be content with Paradise and the houris;
I lay my head at thy door for love not for hope of gain
And from that door I have not the patience to remove.
(*Jami—Beharistan*)

* * *

Love and mistress are both veiled and hidden
Impute not as a fault If I call him 'Bride.'
I would have kept silence from fear of my Beloved
If He had granted me but a moment's respite.
But He said, 'Speak on', 'tis no fault,
'Tis naught but the necessary result of the hidden decree
'Tis a fault only to him who only sees faults;
How can the Pure Hidden Spirit notice faults,
(*Jalaluddin Rumi—Whinfield*)

(বৈষ্ণব প্রেম-কবিতায় আমরা যে সমৃদ্ধ মধুরভাব দেখিতে পাই এখানে তাহার কি অপূর্ব্ব সূচনা!)

Love is that flame which, when it is kindled,
Devours everything except the Beloved.
(*Jalaluddin Rumi—Nicholson*)

* * *

I weighed thy beanty against that of the moon in the balance of my judgment :
The scale containing the moon flew up to heaven, and thou were left on the earth.
(*Rasikh—E. G. Browne*)

* * *

No lover ever seeks union with his beloved,
Without his beloved seeing him in turn.
(*Anawar-i-Suheili*)

* * *

O Thou, who art exempt from 'us' and 'we'
When man and woman become one, Thou art that one.
When their union is dissolved,
Lo Thou abidest.
(*Jalaluddin Rumi—Whinfield*)

* * *

Not till Thy secret beauty through the cheek
Of Laila smite, does she inflame Majnun,
And not till Thou have sugared Shirin's lip
The hearts of those two lovers fill with blood.
(*Jami—Fitzgerald*)

* * *

When seeking love, pay court to every heart,
When once admitted, seek the perfect heart.
A hundred ka'bas equal not one heart ;
Seek not the ka'ba, rather seek the heart.
(*Omar Khayyam—Whinfield*)

How well would it have been, if hell had been full of me,
Perhaps for others there might have been escape
(*Sadi's Bostan—Clarke*)

* * *

With thee hell would be a mansion of delight
With thee a prison would be a rose garden
(*Jalaluddin Rumi—Whinfield*)

* * *

Prize not at all life that has passed without love,
Love is the water of life : receive it in thy heart and soul.
(*Diwan-i-Shams-i-Tabriz—Nicholson.*)

* * *

I believe him whom I love without a mediator
And so I fall into such a state that I lose my way ;
He kindles a fire, then extinguishes it with a sprinkling,
For this reason thou seest me burnt and drowned.
(*Sadi's Guilstan—Platts.*)

* * *

Thirsty for my blood—He, and for His lip—I. So that when it happeneth,
My desire I will take from Him, or revenge He will take from me. (*Hafiz—Clarke.*)

* * *

Three be the ways of love : a knitting of heart to heart ; a pleasing of eyes and eyes ; a third love whose name is death. (*Anon.—C. J. Lyall*).] **–ism, –ist,** *ns.*

sug'-ar (shûg-êr), *n., v. t.* & *i.* **1.** A sweet substance manufactured chiefly from the expressed juice of the sugar-cane, beet, etc. ; চিনি, শর্করা। [Syn. সিতা, মিষ্ট, ইক্ষুসার, বালুকাত্মিকা, গুক্রোপলা, শুক্লা, গুড়োদ্ভবা, শ্বেতা, সুসিকতা।] 2. (*Obs. & Colloq.*) Honeyed or sweet words ; (অপ্রঃ বা উপভাষায়) মধুর কথা, মিষ্ট কথা। ***Verb t.*** **1.** To impregnate, season, cover, sprinkle or mix with sugar ; to sweeten ; শর্করাদ্বারা পরিপুরিত করা, শর্করা মিশ্রণে রসাল করা, শর্করাদ্বারা আবৃত করা ; সুমিষ্ট করা। **2.** (*Slang*) To work lazily ; (ইতরভাষায়) ঢিমা তেতালা ভাবে কায করা, মিঠা মিঠা জুইতে (ভাবে) কায করা (East Bengal). **3.** To disguise as something unpleasant or distasteful to render it acceptable ; গ্রহণযোগ্য করার জন্য কোনপ্রকার অপ্রীতিকর বা বিরক্তিজনক বিষয়ে মিষ্ট আবরণ দেওয়া। ***Verb i.*** To sweeten something ; কোনকিছু মিষ্ট করা। **–ared,** *p. p.* Sweet ; চিনিমাখা, সুমিষ্ট, মধুর, ধুমাখা। **–y,** *adj.* **Sugar-baker**—শর্করাশোধক। **Sugar-basin**—ভোজনের মেজে চিনি রাখার জন্য যে পাত্র ব্যবহৃত হয়। **Sugar-beet**—একপ্রকার বীট পালং — যাহা হইতে চিনি প্রস্তুত করা হয়। **Sugar-candy**—মিছরি [Syn. খণ্ড-শর্করা, মৎস্যণ্ডিকা (গোপালঃ), ঘন-রূপ]। **Sugar-cane**—ইক্ষু, আখ

Sugar-cane.

[Syn. দীর্ঘপর্ব্ব, মধুতৃণ, মধুতরু গুড়দারু, মহাক্ষীর কর্কোটক, কান্তার (a red variety) মৃত্যুপুষ্প।] **Sugar-gum**—অষ্ট্রেলিয়া দেশীয় মিষ্টস্বাদ পত্রবিশিষ্ট বৃক্ষবিশেষ। **Sugar-loaf**—পরিস্কৃত শর্করার মোচাকার খণ্ড ; উক্তরূপ শর্করা খণ্ডের আকৃতি টুপি ; উক্তরূপ আকারের পাহাড়। (*Adj.*) মোচাকৃতি। **Sugar-maple**—একপ্রকার বৃক্ষ—যাহার রস

হইতে চিনি প্রস্তুত করা হয়। **Sugar-mill**—আক্‌মাড়া কল, ইক্ষুপীড়নযন্ত্র, ইক্ষুযন্ত্র, (বিশ্বকর্ম্মাঃ) গুড়যন্ত্র (জাতক)। **Sugar-mite**—একপ্রকার ক্ষুদ্রকীট। **Sugar-orchard** — Sugar-maple নামক বৃক্ষের বাগান। **Sugar-plum**—চিনির লাড্ডু, কদমা; অতি রুচির বস্তু। **Suga-refinery** — শর্করাশোধনাগার, চিনি পরিষ্কারের কারখানা। **Sugar-tongs**—ভোজনের কালে পাত্র হইতে চিনির খণ্ড তুলিবার জন্য একপ্রকার ক্ষুদ্র চিমট। **Sugar of bamboo**—Same as BAMBOO-MANNA. **Sugar of milk**—Same as LACTOSE. **Sugar of lead**—মুদ্রাশঙ্খ (হিঃ কোঃ)।

sŭg-gest' (-ĕst, *or* sŭd-gĕst), *v. t.* **1.** To introduce indirectly to the thought; to hint; as, smoke *suggests* fire; কাহারো চিন্তায় পরোক্ষভাবে উপস্থিত করা; ইঙ্গিত করা, আভাস দেওয়া, সূচনা করা। **2.** To propose; as, he *suggested* a retreat; প্রস্তাব করা। •

sŭg-gest'-i-ble (-ĕst-ĭ-bl, *or* sŭd-gĕst-), *adj.* **1.** That may be suggested; ইঙ্গিতযোগ্য, আভাসযোগ্য। **2.** Prone to hypnotic suggestion; সম্মোহনজনক প্রেরণার অধীন।

Suggestio falsi, *n.* A misrepresentation of fact which though not a positive is yet a virtual lie; 'অশ্বত্থামা হত ইতি গজ' ধরণের মিথ্যা কথা।

sŭg-ges'-tion (-ĕs- *or* sŭd-jĕs-), *n.* **1.** The act of suggesting; a hint; পরোক্ষভাবে কাহাকে চিন্তায় উপস্থাপন; আভাস, ইঙ্গিত, ব্যঞ্জনা, দ্যোতনা, উপক্ষেপ, সূচনা (হিঃ কোঃ), আঁচ। **2.** Presentation of an idea or belief into the mind of hypnotic subjet; such belief or impulse; যোগনিদ্রাচ্ছন্ন ব্যক্তিকে প্রেরণা প্রদান; প্রেরণা। **3.** (*Metaph.*) Same as ASSOCIATION. **4.** Proposal; প্রস্তাব। **5.** (*Law*) An information without oath; (আইন) বিনা শপথে যে সংবাদ দেওয়া হয়।

sŭg-ges'-tive (-ĕs-tĭv, *or* sŭd-gĕs-tĭv), *adj.* **1.** Suggesting more than appears in the surface; as, this painting is full of *suggestion*; ব্যঞ্জনাত্মক, অভিব্যঞ্জনাপ্রবণ, ইঙ্গিতময়, ব্যঞ্জনাপূর্ণ, দ্যোতনাপূর্ণ। **2.** Suggesting something improper or indecent; কোনঅশ্লীল বা অসঙ্গত বিষয়ের অভিব্যঞ্জক। **3.** Of, or pertaining to hypnotic suggestion; সম্মোহণপ্রেরণা সম্বন্ধীয়। **—ly**, *adv.* **—ness**, *n.* **Suggestive medicine**—সম্মোহিত ব্যক্তিকে আদেশ বা প্রেরণাদ্বারা চিকিৎসা।

Sui generis—কোন বিশেষ শ্রেণী সম্পর্কীয় নয়, অনন্বয় (হিঃ কোঃ), অনন্য সামান্য, স্বসমান (ঐ)।

Sui juris—পূর্ণবয়স্ক, স্বাধীন।

sü'-i-cīde, *n.* **1.** Self-murder; আত্মঘাত, আত্মহত্যা, আত্মহনন। **2.** One guilty of self-murder; আত্মহত্যাকারী, আত্মঘাতক। **—cid-al**, *adj.* **1.** Pertaining to suicide; আত্মহত্যাসম্বন্ধীয়। **2.** Destructive of one's self-interest; as, a *suicidal* policy; স্বার্থহানিকর। **—cid-al-ly**, *adv.*

sü-il-līne, *adj.* Of, or pertaining to, the hog-family; শূকর-পরিবার-সম্পর্কীয়।

suit (süt), *n.*, *v. t.* & *i.* **1.** Wooing; courtship; "Since many a wooer doth commence his *suit*. To her he thinks not worthy"; বিহাহের উদ্দেশ্যে প্রেমকরণ; বিবাহার্থ প্রেমোপাসনা। **2.** A request; prayer; অনুরোধ, অনুনয়; প্রার্থনা। **3.** A set; series; প্রস্থ, শ্রেণী; আবলি। **4.** An action or process for the recovery of a right or claim; মামলা, মোকদ্দমা। **5.** A set of man's clothes; পুরুষের এক প্রস্থ পোষাক, বিশেষতঃ একরকম কাপড়ের তৈরী কোট, পাজামা এবং ওয়েষ্ট কোট। **6.** A company of attendants; সঙ্গিদল, অনুযায়িবৃন্দ, সহচরবৃন্দ। ***Verb t.*** **1.** To adapt; খাট্টান, উপযোগী করা। **2.** To fit; মানান, মানান সই করা। **3.** To be agreeable to; কাহারো পক্ষে প্রীতিকর হওয়া, পোষান। ***Verb i.*** **1.** To agree; to accord; মিলা; সঙ্গতি বিশিষ্ট হওয়া। **2.** To be fitting; খাপ খাওয়া, মানান। **—a-bil'-i-ty**, *n.* **Suit'-a-ble**, *adj.* Fitting; proper; উপযুক্ত, উপযোগী; যথাযোগ্য, সমুচিত। **Suit'-a-ble-ness**, *n.* The state of being suitable; উপযোগিতা। **Suit'a-bly**, *adv.* **To follow suit**—To follow one's example; দৃষ্টান্ত অনুসরণ করা, কাহারও দেখাদেখি কোন কাজ করা (as, *following* his *suit*; তাহার দেখাদেখি)। (*Card playing*) To play a card of the same suit; তাস খেলায় জাতে জাত দেওয়া।

suite (swēt) *n.* **1.** The retinue or attendants of a distinguished personage; as, a noble man and his *suite*; অনুচরবৃন্দ, সহচরবৃন্দ, পরিজন। **2.** A set of things; as, a *suite* of rooms; একপ্রস্থ জিনিষ, শ্রেণী, আবলি।

suit'-ŏr (süt-), *n.* **1.** A party to a law-suit or litigation; মোকদ্দমার পক্ষ। **2.** A man who asks a woman's hand in marriage; a wooer; পাণিগ্রহণার্থী ব্যক্তি, বিবাহার্থী ব্যক্তি; (বিবাহার্থ) প্রণয়ার্থী, প্রেমাকাঙ্ক্ষী। **3.** One who entreats; a petitioner; অর্থী, যাচক; আবেদনকারী।

sŭl'-cate, (*Bot.* & *Anat.*) Grooved; channelled; (উদ্ভিদ্‌বিদ্যা এবং জন্তুবিদ্যা) খাঁজকাটা; নালীবিশিষ্ট, সখাত।

sŭlk, *n.* & *v. i.* Sulky fit or mood; as, Radha in her *sulks*; মান, অভিমান। ***Verb i.*** To be sulky; মান করা।

sŭlk'-ȳ, *adj.* & *n.* **1.** Sullen; মানিনী (*fem.*)। **2.** A light two-wheeled carriage for one person; এক-ব্যক্তির উপযোগী দুই চাকার হালকা গাড়ী। **—i-ly**, *adv.* **—i-ness**, *n.*

Sŭl'-lan (-ăn), (*Rom. Hist.*) Of L. Cornelius Sulla; enacted by Cornelius Sulla; (রোমের ইতিহাস) কর্ণেলিয়াস সালা সম্পর্কীয়; কর্ণেলিয়াস সালাকর্ত্তৃক কৃত।

sŭl′-lėn (-ŏn) *adj.* & *n.* **1.** Ill humoured ; gloomy ; glum ; বদ্‌মেজাজী ; বিষণ্ণ, ম্রিয়মাণ, অপ্রসন্ন ; ম্লানগম্ভীর। **2.** Sluggish ; ঢিমা, ঢিলা, অলস। ***Noun.*** Sullen frame of mind ; অপ্রসন্নভাব, ম্লানগাম্ভীর্য্য। **–ly,** *adv.* **–ness,** *n.*

sŭl′-phāte, *n.* A salt of sulphuric acid ; গন্ধকদ্রাবকের লবণ। **Sulphate of copper**—তুঁতে, তুথ, তুথক [Syn. হেমতার, নীলাঞ্জন, হরিতাশ্ম, ময়ূরগ্রীব, ময়ূরগ্রীবক, অমৃতোদ্ভব, শিখিকণ্ঠ, নীল, তুথাঞ্জন, শিখিগ্রীব, বিতুন্নক, ময়ূরক, তুতক, মূষাতুথ, মৃতামদ হেমসার তাম্রগর্ভ, কৃত্রিম (মঃ উঃ)]। [For other synonyms see COPPER SULPHATE (under COPPER.)] [Chin. *shih-tun, tan-fan, tung-lo.*] **Sulphate of iron**—হীরাকস। [Syn. কেসর, কাশীশ, মলীমস, ধাতুশেখর, বিষদ, খেচর, ধাতুকাসীস, হংসলোমশ, শোধ, পাংশুকাসীস, শুভ্র, নয়নৌষধ] [also see IRON SULPHATE under IRON.] [Chin. *luh-fan, t'sing-fan* ; Pers. *tutiya subz, zunkur madni.*] **Sulphate of mercury**—কৃষ্ণভস্ম।

sŭl′-phīde, *n.* A compound of sulphur with a metal or other element ; কোন ধাতু বা অপর মূল পদার্থের সহিত গন্ধকের মিশ্র। **Cuprous sulphide**—পর্পটী তাম্র (ব্রজঃ হিন্দু)। **Sulphide of antimony**—নীলাঞ্জন (রঃ রঃ সঃ প্রঃ), সৌবীরাঞ্জন (ঐ)। **Sulphide of copper** — মারিততাম্র (আয়ু রসঃ)। **Sulphide of mercury**—রসামৃতচূর্ণ (ব্রজঃ হিন্দু), হিঙ্গুল (ঐ)।

sŭl′-phō-năl, *n.* A drug used as hypnotic, anaesthetic or soporific agent [$(CH_3)_2C(SO_2C_2H_5)_2$]; সম্মোহনজনক এবং সংবেদনলোপকর বা নিদ্রাকারক গুণোপেত ঔষধ বিশেষ। (মাত্রা—15—45 গ্রেণ)।

sŭl′-phur (-fėr), *n., adj.* & *v. t.* **1.** A simple mineral substance of a yellow colour which burns with a pale blue flame ; গন্ধক [Syn. ধাতুবৈরী, গন্ধপাষাণ, গন্ধ (রঃ প্রঃ), অরুণারি, শুকপুচ্ছ, পামাঘ্ন, পামারি, ধাতুমারী, শুল্বারি, কীটঘ্ন, কীটারি (গেলঃ), কুষ্ঠারি, ক্রূরগন্ধ, ক্রূরা, সুগন্ধক, দিব্যগন্ধ, গন্ধপিষ্টি (সাঃ পঃ), অতিগন্ধ, সৌগন্ধিক, গন্ধিক, সুগন্ধিক, গন্ধপাষাণ, গন্ধমোদন, পূতিগন্ধক, বর, সুগন্ধ রসগন্ধক, শরভূমিজ।] [Swed. *svafvel* ; Jav. *walerang* ; Malay *balirang* ; Dan. *svovl* ; Dutch. *zwavel* ; Tam. & Tel. *gendagum*; Turk. *kyukyurt* ; Arab. *kibreet* ; Pers. *gowgird* ; Fr. *soufre* ; Germ. *schwefel* ; It. *solfo, zolfo* ; Russ. *syera* ; Sp. *azufre* ; Portug. *enxofre* ; Burm. *kan* ; Chin. *shih liu-hwang.*] [রাজনির্ঘণ্ট গ্রন্থে গন্ধকের জাতি ও গুণ সম্বন্ধে এই প্রকার লিখিত আছে :—"শ্বেতো রক্তশ্চ পীতশ্চ নীলশ্চেতি চতুর্ব্বিধঃ। গন্ধকোবর্ণতো জ্ঞেয়ো ভিন্ন ভিন্ন গুণাশ্রয়ঃ। শ্বেতঃ কুষ্ঠাপহারী স্যাদ্রক্তো লোহপ্রয়োগকৃৎ। পীতোরসে প্রয়োগার্হো নীলো বর্ণান্তরোচিতঃ। অন্য গুণাঃ—কটুত্বম ; উষ্ণত্বম। তীব্রগন্ধত্বম। অতিবহ্নিকারিত্বম্। বিষকুষ্ঠকণ্ডূতি খর্জ্জূত্বগ্দোষ নাশিত্বঞ্চ।] **2.** Kinds of yellow butterfly ; নানাপ্রকার পীতবর্ণ প্রজাপতি। ***Adj.*** Of the hue of sulphur ; গন্ধকবর্ণ। ***Verb t.*** To apply sulphur to ; to fumigate with sulphur ; গন্ধক প্রয়োগ করা ; গন্ধকের ধূম প্রয়োগদ্বারা সংক্রামক রোগের বীজাণু নষ্ট করা। **–y,** *adj.* **Yellow sulphur** — পীতগন্ধক, গন্ধপাষাণ, পাষাণ। **Sulphur-ore**—Same as IRON-PYRITES (which see). **Sulphur-wort**—একপ্রকার পীতপুষ্পপ্রসূ ক্ষুপ—যাহা পূর্ব্বে ঔষধে ব্যবহৃত হইত। **Calcination of sulphur**—গন্ধক জারণ (সাঃ পঃ)। **Flowers of sulphur**—গন্ধক হইতে প্রাপ্ত একপ্রকার পীতচূর্ণ। **Milk of sulphur**—গন্ধক হইতে প্রাপ্ত একপ্রকার শ্বেতচূর্ণ।

sŭl′-phū-rāte, *v. t.* To impregnate with sulphur ; to fumigate with sulphur ; গন্ধকদ্বারা সম্পূরিত করা ; গন্ধকদ্বারা উপধূমিত করা। **–ra′-tion,** *n.* **–ra-tor,** *n.* **Sulphurate of iron**—ধাতুমাক্ষিক।

sŭl′-phū-rē-ous (-ŭs), *adj.* **1.** Impregnated with, or containing, sulphur; like sulphur ; গন্ধকপূর্ণ, গন্ধকসম্পূরিত ; গন্ধকবৎ। **2.** (*Bot.*) Sulphur-coloured ; (উদ্ভিদ্‌বিদ্যা) গন্ধকবর্ণ।

sŭl′-phū-rĕt-ted (-ĕd), *adj.* Having sulphur in combination ; containing or combined with sulphur ; গন্ধক সমন্বিত ; গন্ধকযুক্ত, গন্ধকমিশ্রিত, গন্ধক-সম্পৃক্ত। **Sulphuretted hydrogen**—একপ্রকার স্বচ্ছ, অবর্ণ এবং পূতিগন্ধ বাষ্প।

sŭl-phū′-ric, *adj.* (*Chem.*) Pertaining to sulphur ; obtained from sulphur ; গন্ধকসম্পর্কীয় ; গন্ধক হইতে প্রাপ্ত। **Sulphuric acid**—(H_2SO_4) গন্ধকদ্রাবক, তেজাব, গন্ধকাম্ল, তেজবার (আয়ু রসঃ), তুবরীসত্ত্ব (রঃ রঃ সঃ প্রঃ), সৌবীর সত্ত্ব (ঐ), দাহজল (ধাঃ প্রঃ), কাসীসসত্ত্ব (রঃ রঃ সঃ প্রঃ), সৌরাষ্ট্রী সত্ত্ব (রঃ প্রঃ)।

sŭl′-phur-īze (-fėr-), *v. t.* Same as SULPHURATE. **–i-za′-tion,** *n.*

sŭl′-phū-rous (-rŭs), *adj.* **1.** Same as SULPHUREOUS. **2.** Containing a small quantity of sulphur ; অল্প মাত্রায় গন্ধকবিশিষ্ট, গন্ধকাক্ত। **Sulphurous acid**—গন্ধকদ্রাবক (সাঃ পঃ)।

sŭl′-tăn, *n.* **1.** A Mohammedan sovereign ; the ruler of Turkey ; মুসলমান সুলতান, সুরতন (Sans. form found in inscription) ; তুরস্কের সুলতান। **2.** A small white variety of domestic fowl ; একপ্রকার ক্ষুদ্র জাতীয় শ্বেতবর্ণ গৃহকুক্কুট। **3.** Kinds of brillantly coloured birds (also *sultan-bird*) ; নানাপ্রকার উজ্জ্বলবর্ণ বিহঙ্গের সাধারণ নাম। **Sweet Sultan, –Yellow Sultan** — উদ্যানরোপিত বিভিন্ন প্রকার পুষ্পবৃক্ষ।

sŭl-tâ′-nă, *n.* **1.** The mother or wife of Sultan ; সুলতানের জননী

বা পত্নী। 2. The mistress of a great personage; বড়লোকের উপপত্নী। 3. A variety of seedless raisin; এক জাতীয় বীজবিহীন কিসমিস। 4. Same as SULTAN-BIRD above.

sŭl'-tăn-ĕss, *n.* Same as SULTANA I.

sŭl'-trȳ, *adj.* Very hot, oppressive or close; গরম, উষ্ণ, গুমটে। **–tri-ly,** *adv.* **–tri-ness,** *n.*

sŭm, *n., v. t.* & *i.* 1. Total; মোট, সমষ্টি, সর্ব্বসাকল্য। 2. An amount of money; as, a large *sum* of money; নির্দ্দিষ্ট পরিমাণ অর্থ। 3. An arithmetical question; as, this is a difficultt *sum*; অঙ্ক। 4. Substance; সার, সারকথা। ***Verb t.*** 1. To add into one whole; মোটদেওয়া, ঠিক দেওয়া। 2. To recapitulate briefly (with *up*); as, to *sum* up a debate; সংক্ষেপে পুনরায় বলা, সংক্ষেপ করা। ***Verb i.*** To recapitulate; সংক্ষেপে পুনরায় বলা। **To sum up**—To bring or collect into small compass; সংক্ষেপ করা। To make recapitulation of evidence or argument; যুক্তি বা প্রমাণ সমূহ পুনরায় সংক্ষেপে বর্ণনা করা।

sū'-măc,–măch, *ns.* 1. A shrub the leaves of which are used for tanning; একপ্রকার গুল্ম—যাহার পত্র চর্ম্মশোধন কার্য্যে ব্যবহৃত হয়। 2. The dried and chipped leaves and shoots of *Rhus coriaria* used in tanning; চর্ম্মশোধনকার্য্যে ব্যবহৃত গুল্মবিশেষের শুষ্কীকৃত পত্র এবং অঙ্কুর।

sŭm'-ma-rīze (-ă-), *v. t.* To make a summary of; to sum up; সংক্ষেপ করা; সংক্ষেপে বলা, সংক্ষেপে প্রকাশ করা, সংক্ষেপে ব্যক্ত করা। **–rist,** *n.*

sŭm'-ma-rȳ (-ă-), *adj.* & *n.* 1. Short; concise; সংক্ষিপ্ত; অল্পাক্ষরগ্রথিত, স্বল্পাক্ষর। 2. Rapidly performed; দ্রুত সম্পাদিত। 3. (*Law*) Said of proceedings specially intended to facilitate dispatch; as, a *summary* trial; (আইন) সরাসরি। ***Noun.*** That which contains the sum or substance of a fuller account; an abstract, abridgment or compendium; সংক্ষিপ্ত বর্ণনা; সংক্ষেপ, সারাংশ, চুম্বক, মর্ম্ম। **–ri-ly,** *adv.* In a summary manner; সংক্ষেপে সংক্ষিপ্তভাবে, সংক্ষেপতঃ; সরাসরিভাবে। **Summary trial**—সরাসরি বিচার।

sŭm-mā'-tion (-ā-), *n.* Addition; an aggregate; সংযোজন, সমাহার, সঙ্কলন, সমারোহণ, অধিরোহণ (হিঃ কোঃ); সমষ্টি।

sŭm'-mer (-ĕr), *n., v. i.* & *t.* 1. The warmest season of the year, which, north of the equator, may be said to comprise June July and August; গ্রীষ্মকাল, নিদাঘকাল। [Syn. উষ্ণক, উষ্ণাগম, উষ্ণোপগম, তপ, ঘর্ম্ম, তাপন, উষ্ণকাল।] 2. A whole year; as, a boy of ten *summers*; বৎসর। ***Verb i.*** To pass the summer at some place; কোন স্থানে গ্রীষ্ম যাপন করা। ***Verb t.*** 1. To keep or carry through summer; সারা গ্রীষ্মকাল রাখা বা চালান। 2. To feed during the summer; গ্রীষ্মকালে ভোজন করান। **–ly,** **–y,** **–less,** *adjs.* **Summer-friend** — সুসময়ের বন্ধু, সুদিনের বন্ধু। **Summer-house**—গ্রীষ্মবাটিকা, নিদাঘবাটিকা, উদ্যানস্থিত আরামবাটিকা। **Summer lightning**—দূরদৃষ্ট বিদ্যুৎশিখা। **Summer time**—গ্রীষ্মকাল, নিদাঘকাল। **Indian summer** — See INDIAN. **St. Luke's summer**—১৮ই অক্টোবরের কাছাকাছি যে ঝঞ্ঝামেঘবিমুক্তকালের আশা করা যায়।

sŭm'-mer (-ĕr), *n.* 1. (*Arch.*) The first stone laid over a column to make a cross vault; (স্থপতিবিজ্ঞান) খিলান প্রস্তুতকালে স্তম্ভের উপর প্রথম যে প্রস্তরখণ্ড উপস্থাপিত হয়। 2. A large timber supported on two strong posts, or a strong beam laid as a central floor timber; শক্ত খুঁটি বা পিল্লাদ্বয়ের উপর বিধৃত বৃহৎ কাষ্ঠফলক, গৃহতলের মধ্যভাগে স্থাপিত সুদৃঢ় কাষ্ঠফলক।

sŭm'-mer-sault (-ĕr-sălt), **–sŏt,** *ns.* Same as SOMERSAULT (which see).

sŭm'-mit (-ĭt) *n.* 1. The highest point; the top; as, the *summit* of a hill; উচ্চতমবিন্দু; শিখর, অগ্র, শীর্ষ, চূড়া, শৃঙ্গ, কূট, ককুভ (ঋক্)। 2. Highest degree; as, the *summit* of my ambition; উচ্চতম মাত্রা, শিখর (cf. উন্নতিশিখর)। **–less,** *adj.*

sŭm'-mon (-ŏn) *v. t.* 1. To call by authority to appear at a place specified; esp. to command to appear in a court of justice; as, to *summon* witness; আহ্বান করা; আদালতে উপস্থিত হওয়ার জন্য আহ্বান করা, শমন দেওয়া। 2. To send for; ডাকিয়া পাঠান, তলব দেওয়া। 3. To excite into action or exertion (usu. with *up*); as, to *summon up* one's courage; উদ্বুদ্ধ করা। 4. To call upon to surrender, as a fort; দুর্গাদি সমর্পণ করার জন্য আদেশ করা। **To summon up**—To gather; সংগ্রহ করা।

sŭm'-mons (-ŏnz), (*pl.* -MONSES), *n.* & *v. t.* 1. A call by authority or the command of a superior; আহ্বান, সমাহ্বান। 2. (*Law*) A citation to appear in court; আদালতে উপস্থিত হওয়ার জন্য আদেশ, শমন। 3. (*Law*) The written or printed document by which such a call is given; (আইন) শমন, আহ্বানপত্র (মুচ্ছঃ)। ***Verb t.*** To serve with summons; শমন জারী করা।

summum bonum, ***n.*** The chief good; পরম, শ্রেয়ঃ, ইষ্ট, নিঃশ্রেয়স (বেদান্ত), পরমপুরুষার্থ (হিঃ কোঃ), পরমার্থ।

summum genus—পরমসামান্ত (হিঃ কোঃ) পরসামান্ত (ঐ)।

sŭmp'-têr, *n.* & *adj.* A baggage-horse ; ভারবাহী অশ্ব। ***Adj.*** Carrying burden ; ভারবাহী।

sump'-tion (sŭm-) *n.* The major premise of a syllogism ; ব্যাপ্তি বাক্য।

sŭmp'-tü-ă-rŷ, *adj.* Regulating expenditure ; as, *sumptuary* allowance ; ব্যয়নিয়ামক। **Sumptuary law**—রাষ্ট্রের হিতের জন্য ব্যক্তিগত ব্যয়নিয়মনসম্বন্ধীয় আইন।

sŭmp'-tü-ous (-ŭs), *adj.* Very expensive or costly : splendid ; magnificient ; as, *sumptuous* table : *sumptuous* apparel ; বহু ব্যয়সাপেক্ষ, বহুমূল্য, মহার্ঘ, মহার্হ ; জমকালো ; জাঁকজমকপূর্ণ। **–ly,** *adv.* **–ness,** *n.*

sŭn, *n., v. t. & i.* The self-luminous orb which gives light and heat to all the planets ; আদিত্য, সূর্য্য, রবি, ভানু, তপন, অরুণ, অর্ক, সবিতা, দিবাকর, দিননাথ, দিবাকর, প্রভাকর, [Syn. সূর, অংশুধর, অংশুমান, অংশুহস্ত, অহস্কর (রাঃ তঃ), অর্হপতি, (রূঃ), অহর্বান্ধব, অহর্বন্ধু, অহর্মণি, অহঃপতি, অহোরত্ন, অহর্নাথ, অনূরুসারথি (শিশুঃ), অরুণকর (কাদঃ), অরুণসারথি, অরুণার্চ্চিঃ (rising sun), অহিমকর (cf. অহিমকর, করনিকর—কৃষ্ণঃকঃ অহিমকিরণ) (বৃঃ সং), অহিমত্বিষ্ (*ib.*), অহিমদীধিতি (শিশুঃ), অহিমময়ূখ (কিরাতঃ), অশিশিরকর, (কাদঃ), অহিমরশ্মি (শিশুঃ), অহিমরুচি, (*ib.*), অহিমাংশু (কিরাতঃ), অহিমতেজাঃ, অহিমদ্যুতি, অশিশিরকিরণ, (*ib.*), অশিশিররশ্মি (কিরাতঃ), অশীতকর, অশীতরশ্মি, অতুষাররশ্মি, অশীতরুচি, অব্জবান্ধব, অব্জহস্ত, অব্জিনীপতি (কথাঃ সঃ), অতুষারকর, অত্রি, অবি, অংশ, অরণি, অশ্ব, অম্বরমণি (সাঃ দঃ), অগ্র (অঃ), আদিতেয় (ঋক্), অজ, অম্বরীষ, অজয়, অগ্নি, অংশুপতি, অংশুমালী (morning sun), অব্জবন্ধু, আশুগ, অম্বুতস্কর, অগ্নির, অতুহিনধাম (বৃঃ সঃ), অতুহিনরশ্মি, অতুহিনরুচি, অঞ্জিষ্ঠ, অসুর, অহস্পতি, অহি, অরু, ইন (cf. ইনোদয়), ইন্দ্র, ঈশান, উষ্ণকিরণ (বৃঃসং), উষ্ণকর (কাদঃ), উষ্ণদীধিতি, উষ্ণাস, উষ্ণভৃত, উষ্ণরশ্মি (কুমারঃ), উষ্ণরুচি, উষ্ণাংশু, উস্র, (ঋক্), ঋত, একচক্ররথ, (গোপালঃ), কিরণপতি (বৃঃ সং), কিরণপাণি, কিরণমালী (কথাঃ সঃ), কমলবান্ধব (কাদঃ), কমলিনীকান্ত (কথাঃ সঃ), কমলিনীবন্ধু (ঐ), কোকবন্ধু, কিশোর, কঞ্জরা, কপিল (মঃ ভাঃ), কপিশ, কাশ্যপ, কণি, কলিঘ্ন, কুশেশয়কর, কশ্যপাত্মজ, কৌশিক, কলিকর্ত্তা, কালভর্ত্তা, কালিন্দীসূ, কলিন্দ, কঞ্জর, কবি, কীশ, কপি (cf. কপ্যাস্য), কিরণমালী, কামদ (মঃ ভাঃ), কাষ্ঠা (নিরুক্ত), কুতপ, কুপপ (মঃ ভাঃ), কুপপি (*ib.*), কুপপী (*ib.*), কুরম, খ, খচর, খতিলক, খদ্যোত (অঃ), খদ্যোতন, খাঙ্ক, খাধ্বলীন, খখোল্ক, খরময়ূখ, খরাংশু, খগ, গো, গভস্তি, গভস্তিপাণি, গভস্তিমান (রঃ), গভস্তিমালী (কাদঃ), গভস্তিহস্ত, গগনাধ্বগ, গোপতি (cf. গোপতি-তনয়াকুঞ্জ), গ্রহনায়ক (হর্ষ), গ্রহপতি, গ্রহরাজ (also moon and Jupiter), গ্রহেশ, গ্রহরাজ, গ্রহগ্রামণী, গ্রহনায়ক, (বালরামায়ণ), গ্রহপুষ, গ্রহপতি, গ্রহরাজ, ঘর্ম্মাংশু, ঘর্ম্ম, ঘুবত্র, ঘর্ম্মদীধিতি (রঃ), ঘর্ম্মদ্যুতি, ঘর্ম্মরশ্মি, (কিরাতঃ), ঘর্ম্মভানু, ঘৃতার্চ্চিঃ (a form of), ঘৃণিনিধি, চণ্ডকর, চণ্ডকিরণ, চণ্ডদীধিতি (কথাঃ সঃ), চণ্ডমরীচি, চণ্ডরশ্মি (হাস্যার্ণব), চণ্ডাংশু (ভাগঃ), চক্রবান্ধব, চক্রবাকবন্ধু, চিত্রভানু, ছন্দ, ছায়াভর্ত্ত জগৎসাক্ষী, জিষ্ণু, জ্যোতিঃ, জগদেকচক্ষু, জগৎপতি, জগৎস্বামী, জগচ্চক্ষুঃ, জগদ্দীপ (কথাঃ সঃ), জগন্নেত্র (also moon), জনচক্ষুঃ জিষ্ণু, জয় (মঃ ভাঃ), তাপন, তমোনুদ্, তিগ্মকর, তিগ্মদীধিতি, তিগ্মগু, তিগ্মতেজ (কথাঃ সঃ), তিগ্মদ্যুতি (শিশুঃ), তিগ্মময়ূখমালী (বরাহমিহির—যোগযাত্রা), খেটকেশ্বর, তিগ্মরশ্মি, তিগ্মরুচি, ত্বিষাম্পতি, ত্বিষামীশ, তিমিরচ্ছেদী, তপতাংপতি, তিগ্মাংশু, তীক্ষ্ণকর (কথাঃ সঃ), তীক্ষ্ণরশ্মি (হরিঃ), তীক্ষ্ণাংশু (বৃঃ সং), তীক্ষ্ণার্চ্চিঃ তিমিরনাশন, তিমিরনুৎ, তিমিরারি, তীব্রদ্যুতি, তমোহারী, তীব্রাংশু, তমিস্রহা, তিগ্মরোচি, তোদ (ঋক্), তমোঘ্ন, ত্বষ্টা, ত্বিট্‌পতি (গেলঃ), তার্ক্ষ্যবাহন, তরুণারুণ (morning sun), ত্রয়িতনু, ত্রিলোকেশ, দেবকৌস্তুভ, দেহকর্ত্তা, দিক্‌পতি, দিনকর্ত্তা, দিনকর, দিনপ্রাণ, দিনবন্ধু, দিনভর্ত্তা, দিনমণি, দিনরত্ন, দিনরাজ, দিনেশ্বর, দিবসকর, দিবসনাথ, দিবসভর্ত্তা, দিবসেশ্বর, দিবাপতি, দিবামণি, দিব্যাংশু, দিনপতি, দিনাধীশ, দিনেশ, দিনমুখ, দিবসপুষ্ট, দিব্যাংশু, দিনপ, দিবারত্ন, দিনবল্লভ, দিবিরত্ন, দীপ্তাংশু, দীধিতিমান (কুমারঃ), দীপ্তকিরণ (মৃচ্ছঃ), দীপ্তাংশু, দীপ্তাত্মা, দৈত্যহা, দ্যুপতি, দ্যুমণি (হর্ষঃ), দ্যুরত্ন, দুর্নিরীক্ষ্য, দ্যুবন, দৃশত, ধরণ, ধামকেশী, ধামনিধি, ধামাধিপ, ধর্ম্মাধর্ম্মপ্রকাশক, ধ্বান্তশত্রু, ধ্বান্তারাতি, ধ্বান্তারি, নাকন, নভোমণি, নিদাঘধাম (শিশুঃ), নিদাঘরুচি, নগ, পচত, পচেলিম, নভোনাবিক, নলিনীবান্ধব, নলিনীশ, নলিনীনাথ, নলিনীনায়ক, নলিনীকান্ত, নলিনীবন্ধু, নলিনীবধূবর পান্থ, পাপহর্ত্তা, পদ্মলাঞ্ছন, পদ্মিনীশ, পদ্মিনীনাথ, পদ্মিনীকান্ত, পদ্মবন্ধু, পদ্মবনবান্ধব, পদ্মিনীবল্লভ, পর্পরীক, পপী (also moon), পতঙ্গ, পুষ্পদন্ত (sun and moon—গৌড়োদয়ে পুষ্পদন্তৌ—শ্রীচৈতন্য চরিতামৃত, পুষ্কর, পূষা, প্রকাশকর্ত্তা, প্রকাশাত্মা, প্রজাপতি, প্রদ্যোতন, বচ, বণু, বসু, বহুরূপী, ব্রধ্ন, বালার্ক (morning sun), বালারুণ (*ib.*), বাসরকৃৎ, বাসরমণি, বাসরাধীশ (সাঃ দঃ), বাসরেশ (also moon and planet), বিশ্বাত্মা, বিভাকর, বিভাবসু, বিরোচন, বিশ্বকর্ম্মা, বিষ্ণুতেজ, বিশ্বরূপ, বিশ্বপা, বিশ্বকর্ত্তা, বিভস্বান, বিকর্ত্তন, বেদবিদ্য, বিয়ন্মধ্যহংস (দশঃ), ব্যোমরত্ন, বিভু, বীতিহোত্র, (হর্ষঃ), বৃষ (মার্কঃ পু), ব্রহ্ম, বিয়ন্মণি, ভগ (মঃ ভাঃ—also moon), ভয়নাশন, ভাস্বর, ভূতেশ, ভেন, (also moon), ভগ (মঃ ভাঃ), ভরণ্যু, ভল, ভসদ্, ভাকোষ, ভানুকেশর, ভানুমান, ভারত (sun shining on the south), ভাসু (অঃ), ভাসন্ত (also the moon and the stars), ভানেমি,

ভাতু, ভাস্কর, মণ্ডলী (অঃ), ময়ূখমালী, ময়ূখেশ, মার্ত্তণ্ড, মিত্র, মিহির (from Pers. *Mihr*), মরীচী, মরীচিমান (কথাঃ সঃ), মরীচিমালী, (কাদঃ), মাণিক্যমৌলি, যমুনাজনক, যজ্ঞেশ (মার্কঃ পুঃ), যমসূ, রাগ, রাজমণি, রাত্রিদ্বিষ, রাত্রিনাশন, রশি, রসাধার, রশ্মিবান্‌, রশ্মিমান, রশ্মিমালী, রশ্মিমৎ, রুচিধাম (শিশুঃ), রুচিধামা, রুচিকৃত, রোহিত, লোকসাক্ষী, লোকচক্ষুঃ, লোকবন্ধু, লোকনাথ, লোকবান্ধব, লোকলোচন, লোককৃত, লোকনায়ক, (হর্ষঃ), লোকপ্রকাশন, ললাটন্তপ, শাশ্বত, শুচি, শ্রীমান, সহস্রপাদ, সহস্ররশ্মি, সহস্রকর, সহস্রকিরণ, সহস্রগু, সহস্রভানু, (শিশুঃ), সহস্রমরীচি, সহস্ররুচ, সহস্রাংশু, সহস্রাঙ্ক, সহস্রার্চ্চিঃ, সহস্রদীধীতি, সহস্রধাম (মুদ্রাঃ), সপ্তহয়, সপ্তশক্তি, সপ্তরশ্মি, সপ্তাশ্ব, সপ্তাশ্ববাহন, সাম্বাদিত্য, সানু (অঃ), সরোজবান্ধব, সোমবন্ধু সৌম্য, সবিত্রা, সলিলজকান্তঃ, স্বীর, সৌরক, সুবর্ণ রেতাঃ, (poet.), সূরি, সূনু (অঃ), স্বর্ণভাজ্‌ (a particular sun), স্বর্ণরেতাঃ, স্বর্ণর (also সোম, প্রভৃতি), স্বর্ভানুসূদন (মঃ ভাঃ), স্বর্মণি (বালঃ), স্বর (ঋক্‌), হর্মুট, হর্ত্তা, হরিৎ, হরি (বৃঃ সং), হরিণ, হরিবাহন (also ইন্দ্র), হরিতাশ্ব, হরিদশ্ব, হেলিক, হেলি (বৃঃ জাঃ—From Greek *Helios*), হেমমালী (স যাতি পুরুষো বীর লোকান্‌ বৈ হেমমালিনঃ—ইতি তীর্থ্যাদিতত্ত্বম্‌), হুষু, ক্ষপাপহ (রামায়ণ), ক্ষিত্র ।] **2.** The sunshine ; as to dry in the *sun* ; সূর্য্যালোক, রৌদ্র। **3.** Revolution of the earth round the sun ; year ; পৃথিবীর সূর্য্য প্রদক্ষিণ ; বৎসর। **4.** Sunrise ; as, from *sun* to sunset ; সূর্যোদয়। ***Verb t.*** To expose in the sun ; to heat in sunshine ; রৌদ্র লাগান ; সূর্য্যালোকে উত্তপ্ত করা। ***Verb i.*** To bask in sunshine ; রৌদ্র পোহান। **Sun'-less,** *adj.* রৌদ্রশূন্য। **Sun'-less-ness,** *n.* **Sun'-like,** *adj.* **Sun'-ward, Sun'-wards,** *adv.*

Central sun—মহাসূর্য্য (হিঃ কোঃ)। **Mock-sun** — Same as PARHELION. **Sun-bath**—অনাবৃতদেহে রৌদ্রে অবস্থান, সৌরকর স্নান। **Sun-beam**—রবিকর, রবিকিরণ, রবিরশ্মি, সূর্য্যকিরণ, অহিমকরনিকর (কৃষ্ণঃ কঃ), রবিরশ্মিমালা (কপালঃ), সূর্য্যাংশু, মার্ত্তণ্ডময়ূখমালা, সৌরকররাশি। **Sun-bear**—মালয়দ্বীপের একপ্রকার ক্ষুদ্র জাতীয় ভল্লুক। **Sun-bird**—উজ্জ্বল পক্ষবিশিষ্ট ক্ষুদ্র পক্ষিবিশেষ, মধুপায়ী (যোঃ)। **Sun-bittern**—একপ্রকার পক্ষী। **Sun-blind**—জানালার পর্দ্দা। **Sun-burnt**—রৌদ্রদগ্ধ, রোদেপোড়া। **Sun-circle**—সূর্য্যমণ্ডল (এভেলন)। **Sun-cracks** — রৌদ্র বৃষ্টিতে অনাবৃত মৃত্তিকার উপরিস্ফোটন চিহ্ন। এইরূপ দাগ থাকিলে বুঝা যায় যে নূতন স্তরসঞ্চয়ের পর ঐ মৃত্তিকাস্তর সূর্য্যালোক দ্বারা শুষ্কীকৃত হইয়াছিল। **Sun-dance**—সূর্য্যার্চ্চনা কালে উত্তর-আমেরিকার প্রাচীন অধিবাসিগণের নৃত্য, সূর্য্যতাণ্ডব। **Sun-deed**—একপ্রকার বিলজাত গুল্ম। **Sun-dial**—সূর্য্যঘড়ী, ছায়াঘড়ী, ছায়াযন্ত্র (বৃঃ স), শঙ্কু (যোঃ)।

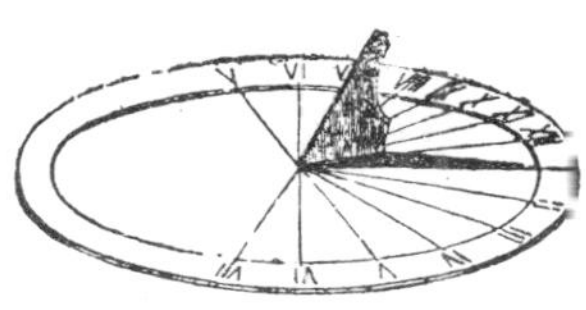

un-dail.

Sundown—সূর্য্যাস্ত, দিনান্ত। **Sun-dried**—রৌদ্রে শুষ্ক, রোদে শুখানো। **Sunfish** — বর্ত্তলাকৃতি মৎস্যবিশেষ।

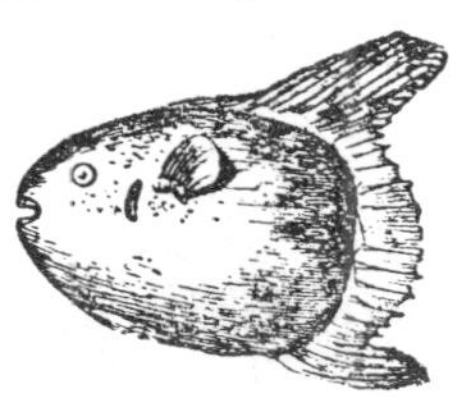

Short Sun fish.

Sun-flower—সূর্য্যমুখী ফুল, সূর্য্যকমল [Syn. শ্রীহস্তিনী, বেশদান, ভ্রামক, দিবাকর, জামাতা, বিধাত্রায়ু।] **Sun-myth**—Same as SOLAR-MYTH (which see). **Sun-picture**—আলোকচিত্র। **Sun-plant**—আকন্দ। **Sun-proof**—যাহা রৌদ্রদ্বারা নষ্ট হইবার নয়। **Sunrise**—সূর্য্যোদয়, অরুণোদয়। **Sunset**—সূর্য্যাস্ত, দিনান্ত, সন্ধ্যা, সূর্য্যাপায় (মেঘঃ দূঃ)। **Sunshade**—স্ত্রীলোকের ছোট ছাতা, চাঁদোয়া, শামিয়ানা, চন্দ্রাতপ। **Sunshine**—রৌদ্র, আতপ, সূর্য্যালোক ; সুদিন ; প্রফুল্লতা। **Sunshine recorder**—সূর্য্যালোক স্থিতিমান ; রৌদ্রমান। **Sun-spot**—সূর্য্যকলঙ্ক, সৌরকলঙ্ক। **Sun-stone**—সূর্য্যকান্ত, তপনোপল, তপনমণি, রবিমণি, অগ্নিমণি। **Sunstroke** — সর্দ্দিগর্ম্মি। **Sun-worship**—সূর্য্যার্চ্চনা, সূর্য্যোপাসনা, সূর্য্যপূজা [সূর্য্যপূজা অতি প্রাচীনকাল হইতে পৃথিবীর নানা দেশে প্রচলিত ছিল। প্রাচীন মিশরে Mu, Osiris, Ra নামে সূর্য্যদেব সম্পূজিত হইতেন। বেবিলোনিয়নদিগের সূর্য্যদেবতার নাম Samas. Heliopolis বা সূর্য্যপুর নগরীতে প্রাচীন এসিয়াবাসিগণ অতি সমারোহের সহিত সূর্য্য পূজা সম্পন্ন করিতেন। ইহাদের সূর্য্যদেবতার নাম ছিল Hadad. প্রাচীন গ্রীকগণের সূর্য্য দেবতা Apollo. উত্তর আমেরিকার Natchez নামক আদিম অধিবাসিগণও খুব ধুমধামের সহিত সূর্য্যপূজার অনুষ্ঠান করিত। ভারতবর্ষে অতি প্রাচীনকাল হইতে সূর্য্য পূজা চলিয়া আসিতেছে। ভবিষ্য পুরাণে লিখিত আছে যে শ্রীকৃষ্ণপুত্র সাম্ব পঞ্চনদ প্রদেশে এক সূর্য্যমন্দির প্রতিষ্ঠা করিয়াছিলেন। তিনি গরুড়পৃষ্ঠে আরোহণ করিয়া সূর্য্যপূজার জন্য শাক দ্বীপ হইতে মগস (Magi) নামক ব্রাহ্মণগণকে আনয়ন করেন উক্ত গ্রন্থে এইরূপ উল্লেখও দৃষ্ট হয়। অধুনাও ভারতবর্ষের নানাস্থানে সূর্য্যপূজা চলিতেছে। বঙ্গীয় নারীগণ মাঘ মাসের প্রতি রবিবারে সূর্য্যোদয় হইতে সূর্য্যাস্ত পর্য্যন্ত দণ্ডায়মান থাকিয়া সূর্য্যপূজা করিয়া থাকেন। রাজপুতনার উদয়পুর প্রভৃতি স্থানে সূর্য্যপূজার বিশেষ আড়ম্বর পরিলক্ষিত হয়। উদয়পুরের মহারাণার প্রাসাদের প্রধান কক্ষের নাম সূর্য্যমহল। সভাগৃহে সূর্য্যের এক বিপুল প্রতিমূর্ত্তি প্রতিষ্ঠিত আছে। ছোটনাগপুরের মুণ্ডা, হো, ওরেয়ন প্রভৃতি আদিম অধিবাসিগণও সূর্য্যপূজা

করিয়া থাকে। বরোদা নগরীতে একটী সূর্য্যমন্দির প্রতিষ্ঠিত আছে। ভারতের পারসীকগণও Mihr (মিহির) দেবতার অর্চ্চনা করিয়া থাকেন।] **Sun-worshipper**—সূর্য্যোপাসক। **Against the sun** - ঘড়ীর কাঁটার বিপরীত দিগ্‌গামী। **A place in the sun**—Favourable condition; অনুকুল অবস্থা। **His sun is set** — His days of glory are over; তাহার গৌরবরবি অস্তমিত হইয়াছে। **Holding a rush light before the sun**—ঢাকের কাছে টেমটেমি। **Order of the Rising Sun**—See under RISING. **Sine of the sun's anomaly**—রবিমন্দকেন্দ্রজ্যা (স্থঃ সিঃ)। **Sun and planet motion, wheels etc.**—একটী বৃহৎ চক্রের নাভি ও পরিধিতে স্থাপিত চক্রযুগল—সাধারণতঃ নাভিস্থ চক্রের (Sun-wheel) দন্তসমূহ অপর চক্রের দন্তে সংলগ্ন হইয়া উহাকে ঘূর্ণিত করে। **To be in the sunshine**—To be drunk; মাতাল হওয়া। **To hail** or **adore the rising sun**—To curry favour with the coming power; নবাভ্যুদয়শীল ব্যক্তিকে সম্বর্দ্ধনা করা। **To rise with the sun** — To rise early with sunrise; সূর্য্যোদয়ের সঙ্গে সঙ্গে শয্যাত্যাগ করা। **To take** or **shoot the sun**—See under SHOOT. **Under the sun**—On the face of the earth; পৃথ্বীতলে, ধরণীতলে, ভূমণ্ডলে। **With the sun**—ঘড়ীর কাঁটার গতির দিক অনুসারী।

Sŭn'-day (-dā) *n.* The first day of the week; রবিবার। **Sunday best**—রবিবারে ব্যবহারের জন্য রক্ষিত উৎকৃষ্ট পরিচ্ছদ। **Sunday letter**—Same as DOMINICAL LETTER (which see). **Sunday school**—রবিবাসরীয় নীতি বিদ্যালয়।

sŭn'-dêr, *v. t.* & *i.* To part; to separate; to disunite; ভাগ করা; পৃথক করা; বিযুক্ত করা। ***Verb i.*** (*Rare*) To separate; (কচিদ্‌ব্যবহৃত) বিযুক্ত হওয়া।

sŭn'-drȳ, *adj.* & *n.* Several; diverse; various; কতিপয়; নানা-প্রকার; বহুবিধ, নানাবিধ, বিবিধ, রকমারী। **All and sundry**—প্রত্যেকে স্বতন্ত্র স্বতন্ত্র এবং সকলে একযোগে।

sŭng, *p. p.* of SING (which see).

sunk (sŭngk), **sunk'-en** (sŭngk-n), *p. t.* & *p. p.* of SINK (which see).

sŭnn, sŭnn'-hĕmp, *ns.* An Indian leguminous plant cultivated for the fibre of its bark; মেস্তাপাট, শণ। [Syn. মাল্যপুষ্প, বমন, কটুতিক্তক, নিশাবন, দীর্ঘশাখ, ত্বক্‌সার, দীর্ঘপল্লবা।] [Lat. *crotalaria juncea*; Tam. *janapa, shanapa-nar*; Teleg. *janamoo.*]

Sûn'-na (-ă), **-nah** (-ă), *ns.* The traditionary part of the Moslem law, now collected into a volume; মুসলমানদিগের পরম্পরাগত স্মৃতি। [এই স্মৃতি মহম্মদ কর্ত্তৃক লিখিত না হইলেও তাঁহার কার্য্য এবং উপদেশই ইহার ভিত্তি। সুন্নি সম্প্রদায়ের মুসলমানগণ এই স্মৃতি মান্য করিয়া থাকে।]

Sûn'-nite (-īte), *n.* The name commonly given to orthodox Muslims, because in their rule of faith and manners the Sunna, or traditional teaching of the prophet is added to the Koran; সুন্নি সম্প্রদায়ভুক্ত মুসলমান।

sŭn'-ny (-ĭ), *adj.* **1.** Of, or pertaining to, the sun; like the sun; shining; bright; সূর্য্যসম্বন্ধীয়, সৌর, সূর্য্যবৎ; সূর্য্যকরোজ্জ্বল, রবিকরোজ্জ্বল; উজ্জ্বল, সমুজ্জ্বল। **2.** Exposed to the sun; as, the *sunny* side of the house; রৌদ্রে উন্মুক্ত। **3.** Cheerful; as a *sunny* smile; আনন্দোজ্জ্বল, হর্ষপ্রদীপ্ত, আনন্দদীপ্ত। **—ni-ly,** *adv.* **—ni-ness,** *n.*

sŭp, *v. t., i.* & *n.* To sip (also *Verb i.*) চুমুক দিয়া খাওয়া, একটু একটু করিয়া পান করা। ***Verb i.*** To take supper; নৈশভোজন করা। ***Noun.*** A sip; a hasty meal; চুমুক, ঢোক; তাড়াতাড়ি আহার। **To sup with Pluto**—To die; যমালয়ে গমন করা।

sū'-pêr, *n.* **1.** (*Slang*) A supernumerary character (ইতরভাষায়) অতিরিক্ত অভিনেতা। **2.** An object of unusual size or quality; অতিকায় বস্তু, লোকোত্তর গুণসম্পন্ন ব্যক্তি, অসাধারণ ব্যক্তি।

sū'-pêr-ā-ble (-bl), *adj.* Capable of being overcome, conquered or surmounted; অতিক্রমণীয়, পরাজেয়।

sū'-pêr-ā-bound (-bownd), *v. i.* To abound to excess; to be more than sufficient; অত্যধিক হওয়া, অতি প্রচুর হওয়া; অতিরিক্ত হওয়া।

sū'-pêr-ā-bŭn'-dănt, *adj.* Abounding to excess; অত্যধিক, অতিরিক্ত, অতিপ্রচুর, সমধিক, উপচিত। **—dance,** *n.* The state of being superabundant; অতিপ্রাচুর্য্য, বাহুল্য, আতিশয্য, আধিক্য (হিঃ কোঃ)। **—ly,** *adv.*

sū-pêr-ădd', *v. t.* To add over and above; to add to what has been added; অতিরিক্ত যোগ করা; যোগের উপর যোগ করা। **—ad-di'-tion,** *n.*

sū-pêr-ăn'-nū-āte, *v. t.* & *i.* To allow to retire on pension on account of old age, infirmity or invalidity; জরা, বার্দ্ধক্য বা রোগ-জীর্ণতার দরুণ পেনসন লইয়া চাকুরী হইতে অবসর গ্রহণ করিতে দেওয়া। ***Verb i.*** (*Obs.*) To last beyond a year; (অপ্রঃ) এক বৎসরের অধিককাল স্থায়ী হওয়া। **—at-ed,** *adj.* **—a'-tion,** *n.* **1.** Act of superannuating, or state of being superannuated; বার্দ্ধক্যাদির দরুণ পেন্সন লইয়া কার্য্য হইতে অবসর গ্রহণ, উক্তরূপ অবসর প্রাপ্তি। **2.** Retiring allowance; কার্য্য হইতে অবসর গ্রহণকালে যে পেন্সন বা বৃত্তি দেওয়া হয়, অবসরবৃত্তি।

sū-pêrb', *adj.* **1.** Rich; elegant; as, *superb* furniture or decorations; splendid; grand; as, a *superb* edifice; stately; সমুজ্জ্বল;

শোভন ; জমকালো, জাঁকালো, শোভাসম্পন্ন ; বিশাল, মহান ; সমুন্নত ; 2. First-rate ; উৎকৃষ্ট। **—ly,** *adv.* **—ness,** *n.* **Superb paradise bird**—হরিদ্বর্ণ ছায়াবিশিষ্ট গাঢ় ধূমল বা কৃষ্ণপ্রায় বর্ণের নন্দন পক্ষী। ইহাদের উভয় স্কন্ধে ব্যজনাকার পালকগুচ্ছযুগল শোভমান থাকে। **Superb wren**—অষ্ট্রেলিয়া দেশীয় নীলবর্ণ পক্ষিবিশেষ।

sü-pêr-câr′-gö, *n.* A person in a merchantship, appointed to manage the sales and superintend the commercial concerns of the voyage ; বাণিজ্যপোতের যে কর্ম্মচারী পণ্যদ্রব্যাদি বিক্রয়ের ব্যবস্থা ও বাণিজ্যসংক্রান্ত ব্যাপারের তত্ত্বাবধান করিয়া থাকেন।

sü-pêr-cē-lĕs′-tī-ȧl, *adj.* Situated above the firmament ; নভোমণ্ডলের উপরিস্থ।

sü-pêr-cĭl′-ī-ȧ-rȳ, *adj.* Pertaining to the eyebrows ; situated above the eyelid ; ভ্রূ সম্বন্ধীয় ; ভ্রূযুগলের উপরিস্থ।

sü-pêr-cĭl′-ī-ous (-ŭs), *adj.* Lofty with pride ; haughty ; overbearing ; assuming superiority ; গর্ব্বোদ্ধত ; দৃপ্ত ; দম্ভপূর্ণ ; আত্মপ্রাধান্যস্থাপক। **—ly,** *adv.* **—ness,** *n.*

sü-pêr-cŏ-lŭm-nī-ā′-tion, *n.* The placing of one order upon another ; একপ্রকার স্থাপত্যধারার উপর অপর প্রকার স্থাপত্যধারার বিন্যাস।

sü-pêr-cŏn′-scious (-shŭs), *adj.* Transcending human consciousness ; তুরীয়।

sü-pêr-ĕm′-ī-nĕnt, *adj.* Eminent in a superior degree ; অতিপ্রখ্যাত, অতিসমুন্নত।

sü-pêr-ĕr′-ö-gāte, *v. i.* To do more than is necessary or duty requires ; প্রয়োজনের অতিরিক্ত কার্য্য করা, কর্ত্তব্যের অতিরিক্ত কার্য্য করা। **—e-rog′-a-tor-y,** *adj.* **—ga′-tion,** *n.* Performance of more than duty or necessity demands ; কর্ত্তব্য বা প্রয়োজনের অতিরিক্ত কার্য্যকরণ। **Doctrine of supererogation** — সম্প্রদায়ভুক্ত প্রত্যেক ব্যক্তিই মণ্ডলীর কোন বিশেষ খৃষ্টানের সৎকর্ম্মের ফলভাগী হইয়া থাকেন—এই মত। **Works of supererogation**—(রোম্যান ক্যাথলিক ধর্ম্মসংঘ) একশ্রেণীর সৎকার্য্য—যাহা কোন ব্যক্তির মুক্তির পক্ষে একান্ত আবশ্যক নয়।

sü-pêr-ĕth′-ĭ-căl, *adj.* Transcending the ordinary rules of ethics ; নীতি বিজ্ঞানের সাধারণ নিয়মনিচয়ের অতীত, অতিনৈতিক।

sü-pêr-ĕx′-cĕl-lĕnt, *adj.* Excellent in an unusual degree ; অসাধারণ উৎকর্ষসম্পন্ন, অত্যুৎকৃষ্ট, অত্যুত্তম, পরমোত্তম। **—lence,** *n.*

sü-pêr-ĕx-cĭ-tā′-tion, *n.* Excitation in an unusual degree ; অত্যুত্তেজনা।

sü′-pêr-făm-ĭ-lȳ, *n.* A category of classification ranking next above a family ; অতিপরিবার।

sü-pêr-făt′-ted (-ĕd), *adj.* Exceedingly fatty ; অতিরিক্ত চর্ব্বিযুক্ত, অতিমেদস্বী।

sü-pêr-féc-ŭn-dā′-tion, *n.* The impregnation of any woman already pregnant ; একবার গর্ভসঞ্চারের পর পুনরায় গর্ভসঞ্চারণ, অতিরিক্ত গর্ভসঞ্চার।

sü-pêr-fē-tā′-tion, *n.* Same as SUPERFECUNDATION.

sü-pêr-fĭ′-cial (-shăl), *adj.* 1. Not penetrating the substance of thing ; not sinking deep বহিরঙ্গ ; বহিঃপৃষ্ঠব্যাপী। 2. Not deep or profound ; as, *superficial* knowledge ; shallow ; as, a *superficial* scholar ; অগভীর, ভাসা ভাসা ; পল্লবগ্রাহী। **—ci-al′-i-ty,** *n.* **—ly,** *adv.* **A superficial person**—পল্লবগ্রাহী ব্যক্তি। **Superficial contents of a figure**—পৃষ্ঠফল (সাঃ পঃ)।

sü-pêr-fĭ′-cies (-shēz), *n.* 1. The surface ; উপরিভাগ, উপরিতল, পৃষ্ঠ। 2. (*Law*) Everything on the surface of a piece of ground or of a building which is closely connected with it by art or nature, and constitute a part of the same, as houses, trees and the like ; particularly everything connected with another's ground, and especially a real right granted to a person (*Burrill*) ; (আইন) কোন বাটী বা ভূমির উপরিস্থ যাবতীয় বস্তু—যাহা শিল্পকার্য্যের ফলে নিসর্গতঃ উহার অংশরূপে পরিণত হইয়াছে, যথা বৃক্ষ, গৃহ প্রভৃতি ; বিশেষতঃ অপরের ভূমি সম্পর্কীয় যাবতীয় বস্তু এবং কোন ব্যক্তিকে অর্পিত কোন প্রকৃত স্বত্ব।

sü′-pêr-fīne, *adj.* 1. Very fine ; অতিসুন্দর। 2. Of a very fine texture ; as, *superfine* cloth ; অতি মিহি। 3. Oversubtle ; অতি সূক্ষ্মবিচারী। 4. Of extra quality ; অত্যুৎকৃষ্ট। **—ness,** *n.*

sü-pêr′-flü-ous (-ŭs), *adj.* Being more than what is intended ; rendered unnecessary by being in excess ; as, *superfluous* quantity of food ; more than sufficient ; প্রয়োজনাধিক ; উদ্বৃত্ত ; অতিরিক্ত, প্রয়োজনাতিরিক্ত। **—flu′-i-ty,** *n.* 1. Superabundance ; as, *superfluity* of wealth ; state of being superfluous ; a greater quantity than is wanted ; অতিপ্রাচুর্য্য ; অতিরিক্ততা, বাহুল্য ; প্রয়োজনাতিরিক্ত পরিমাণ। 2. Something that is superfluous ; thing not needed ; অতিরিক্ত অংশ ; অনাবশ্যক বস্তু। **—ly,** *adv.* **—ness,** *n.*

sü-pêr-heat′ (-hēt), *v. t.* 1. To heat to a temperature higher than that of boiling water ; ফুটন্ত জলের তাপমাত্রা অপেক্ষা উচ্চতর তাপমাত্রা পর্য্যন্ত উত্তপ্ত করা। 2. To heat steam apart from water until it resembles a perfect gas ; জল হইতে বিযুক্ত বাষ্পকে এরূপভাবে উত্তপ্ত করা যাহাতে ইহা নির্দ্দোষ গ্যাসের অবস্থাপ্রাপ্ত হয়।

sū'-pêr-hīve, *n.* A kind of upper story to a hive, removable at pleasure ; মধুমক্ষিকাগৃহের একপ্রকার উপরিতল—যাহা ইচ্ছামত স্থানান্তর করা যাইতে পারে।

sū-pêr-hū'-măn, *adj.* Above or beyond what is human ; divine ; as, *superhuman* wisdom ; অলৌকিক, অমানুষিক, অপৌরুষেয়, মানুষাতিগ (হিঃ কোঃ), অতিমানুষ (ঐ), লোকোত্তর, মানুষাতীত, জনাতিগ, অতিমর্ত্ত্য ; দৈব। **–ly,** *adv.* **Superhuman power**—অতিমানুষিক শক্তি, দৈবীশক্তি, ঐশীশক্তি।

sū-pêr-hū'-mêr-ăl, *n.* An archbishop's pallium ; an amice ; আর্কবিশপ দিগের প্রাবরণ ; রোম্যানক্যাথলিক পুরোহিতগণের গ্রীবা ও স্কন্ধদেশে পরিহিত চতুষ্কোণ শ্বেতক্ষৌমবস্ত্র।

sū-pêr-im-pōse', *v. t.* To lay or impose on something else ; অন্যকিছুর উপর স্থাপন বা বিন্যস্ত করা, সমারোপ করা, অধ্যারোপ করা। **–po-si'-tion,** *n.* The act of superimposing ; সমারোপ অধ্যারোপ, অধ্যাস (খ্রিঃ)।

sū-pêr-im-prĕg-nā'-tion, *n.* Same as SUPERFETATION (which see).

sū-pêr-in-cŭm'-bĕnt, *adj.* Lying or pressing upon something else ; উপরি সংস্থিত, উপরি ন্যস্ত, অধিশয়ান।

sū-pêr-in-dūce', *v. t.* To bring in or upon as an addition to something ; সংযুক্ত করা, সমাযুক্ত করা।

sū-pêr-in-tĕnd', *v. t.* To oversee with the power of direction ; পরিদর্শন করা, তত্ত্বাবধান করা। **–ence,** *n.* **–ent,** *n.* One who superintends ; পরিদর্শক, তত্ত্বাবধায়ক।

sū-pē'-ri-or (-êr), *adj.* & *n.* **1.** Higher in rank or office ; as, a *superior* officer ; উচ্চতর, ঊর্দ্ধ। **2.** Higher or greater in excellence ; as, a man of *superior* merit ; উৎকৃষ্টতর, প্রকৃষ্টতর, শ্রেষ্ঠতর। **3.** Being above, or beyond, the power or influence of (with *to*) ; "A great man *superior to* his sufferings" ; free from emotion or concern ; unaffected by ; কাহারো শক্তি বা প্রভাবের অতীত ; আবেগমুক্ত, ভাবনামুক্ত ; অবিকৃত। *Noun.* **1.** One that is more advanced in age ; as, the boys should respect their *superiors* ; জ্যেষ্ঠ, গুরুজন। **2.** One that is more elevated in rank or office ; কর্ম্মজ্যেষ্ঠ ব্যক্তি, কর্ম্মপ্রবীণ ব্যক্তি। **3.** The chief of a monastery, abbey or convent ; মঠাধ্যক্ষ, বিহারাধ্যক্ষ, মঠস্বামী। **4.** One superior in rank or in some respect ; শ্রেষ্ঠব্যক্তি, মান্যব্যক্তি। **–ly,** *adv.* **–or'-i-ty,** *n.* **Superior conjunction**—প্রধান যুতি (হিঃ কোঃ)। **Superior figures or letters**—পংক্তির উপর লিখিত পংক্তি বা অক্ষর। **Superior genus**—পরাজাতি। **Superior persons** — বিদ্যাবুদ্ধি প্রভৃতিতে উন্নতর ব্যক্তি ; বিদ্বন্মন্য। **Superior planet** — প্রধান গ্রহ (হিঃ কোঃ)। **To rise superior to**—Not to be affected by ; কোনকিছু দ্বারা প্রভাবিত না হওয়া, কোনকিছুর বহু উর্দ্ধে থাকা।

sū-pêr-jā'-cĕnt, *adj.* Same as SUPERINCUMBENT (which see).

sū-pêr'-lā-tive (-tiv), *adj.* & *n.* **1.** Highest in degree ; supreme ; সর্ব্বোৎকৃষ্ট, সর্ব্বোচ্চ, শ্রেষ্ঠ, বরিষ্ঠ, মুখ্য ; সর্ব্বাতিশায়ী, অতিশয়, অত্যন্ত, পরম। **2.** Absolute ; পরম। **3.** Applied to that form of an adjective or adverb which expresses the highest or utmost degree of the quality or manner denoted by the adjective or adverb ; (ব্যাকরণ) অতিশয়ার্থবাচক, পরমাবধিবাচক, আতিশয্যদ্যোতক। *Noun.* **1.** That which is of the highest or greatest degree or position ; "The *superlative* of hardiness and courage" ; পারম্য, মুখ্যতা, চরম অবস্থা। **2.** (*Gram.*) The superlative degree of an adjective or adverb ; (ব্যাকরণ) পরমাবধিবাচক ক্রম। **–ly,** *adv.* **–ness,** *n.* **The superlative degree**—পরমাবধিবাচক ক্রম।

sū-pêr-lū'-nar (-nêr), *adj.* Being above the moon ; চন্দ্রোপরিস্থ।

sū'-pêr-măn, *n.* An expected person of future possessing powers higher than present-day humanity ; জর্ম্মাণ দার্শনিক নিটসে (Nietzsche) কর্তৃক সূচিত অতিমানুষ, অতি মানুষ। (cf. যদি বঙ্গসাহিত্যের বিশ্ববিজয়ী সৌধ গড়িয়া তুলিতে হয়—তাহার জন্য কএক জন মানুষও চাই কএকজন অতিমানুষও চাই—হীরেন্দ্রদত্ত।) [নিটশে উজ্জ্বল ভাষায় মানবজাতির সম্মুখে অতিমানবের (*Uebermensch*) আগমন সম্বন্ধে আশাজনক মানসচিত্র অঙ্কিত করিয়াছেন। See Nietzsche's *Superman, Thus spake Zarathustra,* etc.]

sū-pêr-mŏl'-ē-cūle, *n.* A compound molecule, or combination of two molecules of different substances ; মিশ্র অণু, বিভিন্ন বস্তুর অণুদ্বয়ের সংযোগ।

sū-pêr-mŭn'-dāne, *adj.* Being above or superior to the world ; অতিপার্থিব, অতিসাংসারিক, অতিমর্ত্ত্য।

sū-pêr-năc'-ū-lar (-lêr), *adj.* First-rate ; প্রথম শ্রেণীর, অত্যুৎকৃষ্ট।

sū-pêr-năc'-ū-lŭm, *n.* Wine or other liquor of great excellence ; অতি উৎকৃষ্ট মদিরা, উৎকৃষ্ট পানীয়। **To drink supernaculum**—To drink to the lees ; নিঃশেষে পান করা। [পানীয়ের শেষ বিন্দু অঙ্গুষ্ঠের নখের উপর পতিত হয় বলিয়া।]

sū-pêr'-năl, *adj.* **1.** Being in a higher place or region ; ঊর্দ্ধস্থ, ঊর্দ্ধবর্ত্তী। **2.** Celestial ; স্বর্গস্থ, ঊর্দ্ধলোকস্থ।

sū-pêr-nā'-tănt, *adj,* Floating on the surface ; উপরে প্রবমান।

sū-pêr-năt'-ū-răl, *adj.* Being above or beyond nature; miraculous; অতিপ্রাকৃত, অপ্রাকৃত; লোকসীমাতীতবর্ত্তী (সাঃ দঃ), লোকাতিগ

(*ib*), লোকাতিশয় (*ib*), লোকাতীত (কাদঃ), লোকাতিশায়ী, লোকাধিক ; অতিপ্রাকৃত (হিঃ কোঃ), অতিদৈবিক, অলৌকিক **The supernatural** — অতিপ্রাকৃত ব্যাপার, অতিপ্রাকৃত ঘটনা। **—ism,** *n.* See SUPRANATURALISM ; অলৌকিকত্ববাদ (হিঃ কোঃ), অপৌরুষেয়বাদ (ঐ)। **—ist,** *n.*

sü-pêr-nü′-mĕr-ă-rȳ, *adj.* & *n.* Exceeding the stated number ; as, a *supernumerary* officer ; নির্দ্দিষ্ট সংখ্যার অতিরিক্ত, অতিরিক্ত। ***Noun.*** A person or thing beyond the stated or usual number extra person engaged for odd jobs; অতিরিক্ত ব্যক্তি বা বস্তু ; টুকিটাকি কায করার জন্য নিযুক্ত অতিরিক্ত ব্যক্তি।

sü-pêr-nü-trī′-tion, *n.* Excessive nutrition ; অতিপুষ্টিবিধান।

sü-pêr-ŏr′-di-nă-rȳ, *adj.* Above the ordinary ; অসাধারণ।

sü-pêr-ŏr-di-nā′-tion, *n.* The ordination of a person to fill an office still occupied ; কোন পদে অপর ব্যক্তি নিযুক্ত থাকা অবস্থায় কোন ব্যক্তিকে অভিষিক্ত করণ।

sü-pêr-ŏr-găn′-ic, *adj.* Above or beyond what is organic ; অঙ্গাতীত, অতিজৈব।

sü-pêr-ŏx′-īde, *n.* Same as PEROXIDE.

sü-pêr-phŏs′-phāte, *n.* A phosphate containing the greatest amount of phosphoric acid that can combine with a base ; যে ফস্‌ফেটে সর্ব্বোচ্চ পরিমাণে ফুসফুরক দ্রাবক থাকে।

sü-pêr-phȳs′-i-căl, *adj.* Incorporeal ; অশরীরী, অমূর্ত্ত, দৈব (এভেলন), অতিজরীয়।

sü-pêr-pōse′, *v. t.* To lay a thing upon another ; কোন বস্তু অপর বস্তুর উপর রাখা, অধ্যারোপ করা, অধিসন্নিবিষ্ট করা। **—po-si′-tion,** *n.* Act of superposing ; অধিসন্নিবেশ, আচ্ছাদন (হিঃ কোঃ)।

sü′-pêr-salt, *n.* An acid salt ; অম্লময় লবণ (হিঃ কোঃ)।

sü-pêr-săt′-ü-rāt-ĕd, *adj.* Saturated to excess ; অতিসম্পৃক্ত (হিঃ কোঃ), অতিসম্পৃক্ত (ঐ)।

sü-pêr-scrībe′, *v. t.* To write, inscribe, or engrave on the top or surface of a thing ; উপরে লিখা বা অঙ্কিত করা, উপরে ক্ষোদিত বা উৎকীর্ণ করা। **—script,** *adj.* **—scrip′-tion,** *n.* **1.** The act of superscribing ; উপরে অঙ্কিত বা উৎকীর্ণ করণ। **2.** That which is superscribed ; উপরে অঙ্কিত বা উৎকীর্ণ বিষয়। **3.** Address ; ঠিকানা। **4.** An impression of letters on coins ; মুদ্রার উপরি অক্ষরের ছাপ।

sü-pêr-sĕc′-ü-lar (-lêr), *adj.* Above secular things ; অতিবৈষয়িক, অতিসাংসারিক।

sü-pêr-sede′ (-sēd), *v. t.* **1.** To set aside ; রহিত করা। **2.** To take the place of ; to displace ; কাহারো স্থান অধিকার করা ; স্থানচ্যুত করা।

sü-pêr-sĕn′-sĭ-ble (-bl), *adj.* Above or beyond the reach of senses ; supernatural ; অতীন্দ্রিয়, ইন্দ্রিয়াতীত ; অতিপ্রাকৃত।

sü-pêr-sĕn′-sĭ-tive (-tĭv), *adj.* Excessively sensitive ; অতিশয় সংবেদনশীল।

sü-pêr-sĕn′-sü-ăl, *adj.* Above or beyond the reach of senses ; অতীন্দ্রিয়, ইন্দ্রিয়াতীত।

süpêr-sĕn′-sü-ous (-ŭs), *adj.* **1.** Excessively sensuous ; অতিশয় ইন্দ্রিয়াসক্ত। **2.** Supersensual ; অতীন্দ্রিয়, ইন্দ্রিয়াতীত।

sü-pêr-ses′-sion, (-sĕ-), *n.* The act of superseding ; the state of being superseded ; স্থলবর্ত্তীকরণ, কাহারো স্থানে নিযুক্ত করণ ; স্থলবর্ত্তিতা, স্থানচ্যুতি।

sü-pêr-sŏ′-lar (-lêr), *adj.* Above or beyond the sun ; অতিসৌর।

sü′-pêr-sŏl-ĭd, *n.* A solid of more than three dimensions ; তিনের অধিক পরিমাণ বিশিষ্ট ঘন, অতিঘন।

sü-pêr-spĭr′-ĭt-ü-ăl, *adj.* Over-spiritual ; অতিরিক্ত আধ্যাত্মিকতা সম্পন্ন, অত্যাধ্যাত্মিক।

sü-pêr-stĭ′-tion, *n.* A false misdirected religious belief ; কুসংস্কার, মিথ্যাধর্ম্ম (হিঃ কোঃ), অশাস্ত্রীয়ধর্ম্ম (ঐ), মূঢ়বিশ্বাস (ঐ)। **—tious,** *adj.* **1.** Addicted to superstition ; কুসংস্কারসম্পন্ন। **2.** Proceeding from, or manifesting, superstition ; কুসংস্কারজনিত ; কুসংস্কারপ্রসূত, কুসংস্কারসূচক। **—tious-ly,** *adv.* **—tious-ness,** *n.*

sü-pêr-strā′-tŭm, *n.* A stratum or layer above another ; এক স্তরের উপরি বিন্যস্ত অপর স্তর, উর্দ্ধস্তর।

sü-pêr-strŭc′-tion, *n.* Same as SUPERSTRUCTURE.

sü-pêr-strŭc′-türe, *n.* Any structure or edifice built on something else ; কোন কিছুর উপরি বিনির্ম্মিত অট্টালিকা প্রভৃতি। **—tur-al,** *adj.*

sü-pêr-sub′-tle (-sŭt-l), *adj.* Over subtle ; অতিসূক্ষ্ম।

sü-pêr-tĕm′-pŏ-răl, *adj.* **1.** Above the temples of the head ; শঙ্খাস্থির উপরিস্থ। **2.** Transcending time ; কালাতীত।

sü-pêr-ter′-rene (-tĕ-rēn), *adj.* Being above ground or above the earth ; ভূর্দ্ধস্থিত।

sü-pêr-ter-rĕs′-trĭ-ăl (-tĕ-), *adj.* Being above the earth or above what belongs to it ; অতিপার্থিব।

sü-pêr-vene′ (-vēn), *v. i.* **1.** To come as something extraneous ; to be added or joined ; অতিরিক্তভাবে যুক্ত হওয়া ; সংযুক্ত হওয়া। **2.** To occur ; "A tyranny immediately *supervened*" ; ঘটা, সংঘটিত হওয়া। **—ven′-tion,**

sü-pêr-vīse′ *v. t.* To superintend ; to inspect ; তত্ত্বাবধান করা ; তদারক করা, পরিদর্শন করা। **—vi′-sion,** *n.* The act of supervising ; তত্ত্বাবধান, পরিদর্শন, তদারক, নিরীক্ষণ (হিঃ কোঃ)। **—vi′-sor,** *n.* One who supervises ;

তত্ত্বাবধায়ক, পরিদর্শক, কার্য্যদর্শী, উপদ্রষ্টা (হিঃ কোঃ)।

sū-pīne', *adj.* **1.** Lying on the back ; উপর দিকে মুখ করিয়া শয়ান, চিৎ হইয়া শায়িত। **2.** Indolent ; without energy ; "He became pusillanimous and *supine,* and openly exposed to any temptation" ; জড়, অলস ; নিস্তেজ। **–ly.** *adv.* **–ness,** *n.*

sū'-pīne, *n.* (*L. Gram.*) A verbal noun with accusative ; ক্রিয়াবাচক বিশেষ্য।

sŭp'-per (-ẽr), *n.* The last meal of the day ; the evening meal ; দিবসের শেষ ভোজন ; নৈশভোজন, রজনীভোজন।

sŭp-plănt', *v. t.* To displace by stratagem ; to displace and take the place ; to undermine ; কৌশলে স্থানান্তরিত করা ; কৌশলে স্থানান্তরিত করিয়া তাহার স্থান গ্রহণ করা, অন্যায়রূপে বেদখল করা ; গোপনে খর্ব্ব করা।

sŭp'-ple (-l), *adj., v. t. & i.* **1.** Pliant ; flexible ; as, *supple* joints ; কোমল, নরম, মৃদু, সুকুমার, পেলব ; নমনীয়, সুনম্য, নমনশীল। **2.** Yielding and compliant ; বশ্য, আজ্ঞাকারী, বশবর্ত্তী। **3.** Fawning ; servile; "Cunning, *supple,* shameless, free from all prejudices and destitute of all principles" ; তোষামুদে ; দাসোচিত। ***Verb t. & i.*** To make or become soft ; কোমল করা বা হওয়া, নমনীয় করা বা হওয়া।

sŭp'-ple-mĕnt (-lē-), *n. & v.t.* **1.** An addition to anything by which its defects are supplied and it is made more comeplete ; something added to a book or paper to make good its deficiencies, or correct its errors ; পূরক, অনুপূরক ; (পুস্তকের) পরিশিষ্ট, (পত্রিকার) ক্রোড়পত্র। **2.** The quantity that must be added to an angle or an arc to make 180° ; যে কোণ অন্য_কোণের সহিত যোগ করিলে ২ সমকোণ (১৮০° ডিগ্রী) উৎপন্ন হয়। ***Verb t.*** To fill up or supply by additions to ; অনুপূরণ করা, কোনকিছুর যোগে পূরণ করা। **–men'-tal, –men'-ta-ry,** *adjs.* Added to supply what is wanted ; অনুপূরক, পূরক, পূরণকারী।

sŭp'-pli-ănt (-lĭ-), *adj. & n.* Asking earnestly and submissively ; entreating ; expressive of humble supplication ; মিনতিকারী ; যাচক, প্রার্থক ; মিনতিসূচক। ***Noun.*** A humble petitioner ; যাচ্ঞাকারী, অনুনয়কারী, প্রার্থনাকারী।

sŭp'-pli-cāte (-lĭ-), *v. t. & i.* To entreat for ; to beg humbly for ; to address in prayer ; as, to *supplicate* blessings ; প্রার্থনা করা ; যাচ্ঞা করা, ভিক্ষা করা, মিনতি করা, অনুনয় করা ; আবেদন করা। ***Verb i.*** To beg ; to petition ; to beseech ; প্রার্থনা করা, যাচ্ঞা করা ; আবেদন করা ; মিনতি করা, অনুনয় করা। **–ca'-tion,** *n.* **1.** The act of supplicating ; মিনতি করণ। **2.** An earnest or humble prayer ; অনুনয়, মিনতি, যাচ্ঞা, কাকুতিমিনতি। **–ca-to-ry,** *adj.*

sŭp-plȳ', *v.t. & n.* **1.** To provide ; to furnish ; as, to *supply* money ; যোগান ; সরবরাহ করা। **2.** To serve instead of ; পরিবর্ত্তে কার্য্য করা। **3.** To fill temporarily ; সাময়িক ভাবে কাহারো স্থান পূর্ণ করা। ***Noun (pl.)*** **1.** Sufficiency of things for use or want, esp. the food, etc. which meets the daily necessities of an army or any large body of men ; অভাবপূরণের পক্ষে প্রচুর বস্তু, বিশেষতঃ সৈন্যদলের রসদ প্রভৃতি। **2.** Stores or articles ; necessaries ; দ্রব্য সম্ভার ; প্রয়োজনীয় দ্রব্য। **3.** (Usu. *pl.*) A grant of money provided by a legislature for the expenses of government ; as, to vote *supplies* ; money allowance granted to a person ; দেশের শাসনব্যয় নির্ব্বাহের জন্য পার্লেমেণ্ট প্রভৃতি ব্যবস্থাপক সভাকর্তৃক যে অর্থ মঞ্জুর করা হয় ; অর্থসাহায্য, বৃত্তি। **4.** (*Econ.*) The quantity of any article offered at a given price ; (অর্থনীতিশাস্ত্র) নির্দ্দিষ্ট মূল্যে প্রদত্ত কোন দ্রব্যের পরিমাণ। **5.** A substitute ; কাহারো স্থানে নিযুক্ত ব্যক্তি, স্থলবর্ত্তী ব্যক্তি। **Commitee of supplies**—বিলাতের কমন্স সভার যে সমিতিতে রাজ্যশাসন সম্পর্কীয় অর্থ মঞ্জুর সম্বন্ধে সবিস্তারে আলোচনা হয়। **Supply Department**—যে বিভাগ হইতে সৈন্যগণের রসদ প্রভৃতি সরবরাহ হয়।

sŭp-pōrt', *n. & v. t.* **1.** To rest under and bear ; to prop ; অবলম্বিত করা, ধরিয়া রাখা ; বিধৃত করা। **2.** To endure ; সহ্য করা, সহা। **3.** To sustain ; as, to *support* one's courage ; রক্ষা করা। **4.** To maintain ; as, to *support* one's family ; পালন করা, প্রতিপালন করা, ভরণ পোষণ করা। **5.** To carry on ; চালান। **6.** To substantiate ; as, to *support* one's case ; সত্যতা প্রতিপাদন করা। **7.** To vindicate; as, to *support* one's own cause ; সমর্থন করা। **8.** To back up by being in readiness to come to the aid of ; as, to *support* a regiment ; সাহায্যের জন্য প্রস্তুত থাকিয়া পৃষ্ঠপোষণ করা। **9.** To act ; as, to *support* a character in a play ; to take the part of ; অভিনয় করা ; ভূমিকা গ্রহণ করা। **10.** To assist ; as, to *support* a party ; সাহায্য করা। **11.** To second or back up a resolution in a public meeting ; কোন প্রস্তাব পুনঃ সমর্থন করা। ***Noun.*** **1.** Act of supporting ; পালন, প্রতিপালন, ধারণ। **2.** A prop ; অবলম্বন, আলম্ব, আশ্রয়, অবষ্টম্ভ, ঠেস, ঠেকো। **3.** Advocay ; as, to speak in *support* of a bill ; patronage ; as, royal *support* ; সমর্থন ; পৃষ্ঠপোষকতা। **4.** Aid ; as the *support* of friends ; সাহায্য, সহায়তা। 5. One who, or that which, supports a person, family, etc. ; প্রতিপালক। 6. A line or detachment of troops immediately behind a skirmishing line to reinforce when necessary ; আবশ্যক মত সাহায্য করার জন্য কোন যুদ্ধে নিরত সৈন্য পংক্তির পশ্চাতে স্থাপিত সৈন্যশ্রেণী। 7. (*Theatre*) An actor playing a subordinate part with a star ; (রঙ্গালয়) যে অভিনেতা প্রধান অভিনেতার কোন উপভূমিকা অভিনয় করে। **–less,** *adj.* Having no support ; নিরাশ্রয় (হিঃ কোঃ), আশ্রয়হীন।

sŭp-pōrt′-ēr, *n.* 1. One who supports ; প্রতিপালক, পরিপোষক, সমর্থক। 2. A figure on each side of a heraldic shield ; কুলচিহ্নাঙ্কত চর্ম্মের অন্যতর পার্শ্বে স্থাপিত প্রতিমূর্ত্তি।

sŭp-pōse′, *v. t.* 1. To presume ; to assume tentatively ; অনুমান করা, বোধ করা, মনে করা ; মানিয়া লওয়া, ধরিয়া নেওয়া। 2. To imply ; সূচনা করা। **–pos′-a-ble,** *adj.* **–posed′,** *p. p.* Believed to exist ; কল্পিত। **–pos′-ed-ly,** *adv.* **–po-si′-tion,** *n.* 1. The act of supposing ; অনুমান, ভাবনা (হিঃ কোঃ), কল্পনা (ঐ), উপন্যাস (ঐ), সম্ভাবনা (ঐ), অভ্যুপগম (ঐ), 2. An hypothesis ; কল্পিত বিষয়, কল্পনা। 3. A surmise ; অনুমান, আন্দাজ। **–po-si′-tion-al,** *adj.* **–po-si′-tion-al-ly,** *adv.*

sŭp-pŏs-i-ti′-tious (-shŭs), *adj.* Not genuine ; as, *supposititious* writing ; counterfeit ; অপ্রকৃত, ঝুঁটা ; নকল। **–ly,** *adv.*

sŭp-pŏs′-i-tŏr-ȳ, *n.* A medical cone or cylinder introduced into the vagina, or rectum ; যোনি বা গুহ্যদেশে প্রয়োগার্থ আশুকার্যকর ঔষধ-মিশ্রিত মোচাগ্রাকৃতি বা নলাকৃতি দ্রব্য-বিশেষ, ফলবর্ত্তি।

sŭp′-prĕss′, *v. t.* 1. To cut down ; as, to *suppress* a rebellion ; দমন করা। 2. To conceal ; as, to *suppress* a fact ; গোপন করা। 3. To stop by medical means ; as, to *suppress* a hemorrhage ; ঔষধবর্ত্তি দ্বারা রোধ করা। **–i-ble,** *adj.* **–pres′-sion,** *n.* The act of suppressing ; রোধ, রোধন। **–pres′-sor,** *n.* **Suppression of urine**—নিবন্ধ (সাঃ পঃ)।

supressio veri, (*L*), *n.* Suppression of truth ; সত্য গোপন।

sŭp′-pū-rāte, *v. i.* To form or generate pus ; to fester ; পূয উৎপাদন করা ; পূয হওয়া, পাকা। **–ra′-tion,** *n.* The process or state of suppurating ; পূযোৎপত্তি, পূযসঞ্চার, পূযোৎপাদন। **–ra-tive,** *adj.* Tending to suppurate ; শোথপক্ককারী।

sū-prā-ā′-nāl, *adj.* Above the anus or the anal fin ; গুহ্যের উপরিস্থ, গুহ্যের পাখনার উপরিস্থ।

sū-prā-āx′-il-lā-rȳ, *adj.* Growing above the axil ; inserted above the axil ; কক্ষোর্দ্ধগত ; কক্ষোর্দ্ধপ্রবিষ্ট

sū-prā-cĭl′-i-ā-rȳ, *adj.* Situated above the eyebrow ; ভ্রূর্দ্ধগত।

sū-prā-clā-vic′-ū-lar (-lêr), *adj.* Above the clavicle ; কণ্ঠাস্থির উপরিস্থ।

sū-prā-crē-tā′-ceous (-shŭs), *adj.* Applied to rocks which lie above the chalk ; খটিকোর্দ্ধগত।

sū-prā-lăp′-sā′-ri-ăn, *adj.* & *n.* Of, or pertaining to, the supralapsarians or their doctrine ; পূর্ব্ববিধানবাদ সম্বন্ধীয়, পূর্ব্ব বিধানবাদ-সম্বন্ধীয়। *Noun.* One who maintains that God's decree of election as regards the eternal salvation of and eternal reprobation of others was a part of His original plan, and that the fall of Adam was predestined from all eternity ; পৃথিবীর কতকাংশ লোক মুক্তি প্রাপ্ত হইবে এবং অবশিষ্টাংশ চিরনরক ভোগ করিবে ঈশ্বর পূর্ব্ব হইতে এইরূপ বিধান করিয়াছিলেন — আদি মানব মানবীর পতনের সহিত এই বিধানের কোনরূপ সম্পর্ক নাই—যাহারা এইরূপ মত পোষণ করেন, পূর্ব্ববিধানবাদী।

sū-prā-lĭm′-i-nal, *adj.* Conscious or in consciousness ; সচেতন, চৈতন্যের মধ্যস্থ। **Supraliminal consciousness**—অতিব্যাপ্ত চৈতন্য।

sū-prā-mŭn′-dāne, *adj.* Being, or situated, above the world ; অতিপার্থিব।

sū-prā-ŏr′-bit-āl, *adj.* Above the eye socket ; অক্ষিকোটরের উপরিস্থ।

sū-prā-prō′-tĕst, *n.* An acceptance of bill by a third person after protest for non-acceptance by the drawer ; গ্রহীতাকর্ত্তৃক অগ্রহণের প্রতিবাদের পর তৃতীয় ব্যক্তি কর্ত্তৃক কোন হুণ্ডী গ্রহণ।

sū-prā-rē′-nāl, *adj.* Above the kidneys ; মূত্রাশয়ের উপরিস্থ।

sū-prĕm′-ā-cȳ, *n.* Highest authority ; as, the *supremacy* of a king ; আধিপত্য, প্রাধান্য, শ্রেষ্ঠত্ব। **Oath of supremacy**—(ইংলণ্ডের) খ্রীষ্টীয় ধর্ম্ম-সংঘে কেবল মাত্র রাজারই অধিকার-পোপের কোনরূপ আধিপত্য নাই—এই মর্ম্মে শপথ

sū-preme′ (-prēm) *adj.* 1. Highest ; সর্ব্বোচ্চ। 2. Absolute ; utmost ; অনন্যসাধারণ, পরম, মুখ্যতম ; সর্ব্বাতিশায়ী, সর্ব্বপ্রধান, চরম, প্রধান (হিঃ কোঃ), অতিসর্ব্ব। **–ly,** *adv.* **The Supreme Being** or **the Supreme**—পরমেশ্বর, পরব্রহ্ম, পরমাত্মা (হিঃ কোঃ), ব্রহ্ম (ঐ)।

su′-rā (sô-), **su′-rah** (sô-rā), *ns.* The chapter of a Koran ; মুসলমান-দিগের কোরাণ গ্রন্থের অধ্যায়, সুর।

su′-rah (sô-rā), *n.* A kind of soft twilled, usually, one-coloured silk ; একপ্রকার টের্চ্চা বুনা সাধারণতঃ একরঙ্গা, রেশমী কাপড়।

su-rāt′ (sô-), *n.* A coarse, short cotton, grown near Surat ; সুরাট অঞ্চলে উৎপন্ন একপ্রকার মোটা আঁশের তুলা।

sur-cease′ (sêr-sēs), *v. t.* & *n.* To stop ; to practise no longer ; বিরত হওয়া ; নিবৃত্ত থাকা। *Noun.* Cessation ; বিরতি।

sur·charge′ (sêr-chârj), *v. t.* & *n.* **1.** To overcharge ; to overload; as to *surcharge* a ship : *surcharged* with the fragrance of rose; অতিরিক্ত ভারাক্রান্ত করা ; পরিপূরিত করা। **2.** To put more cattle into, as a common, than the person has a right to do or more than the herbage will sustain ; যত সংখ্যক গো মহিষাদি রাথার অধিকার আছে বা যত সংখ্যক গো মহিষাদির উপযোগী ঘাস আছে তদপেক্ষা অধিক সংখ্যক রাথা। **3.** To show omission of credit in an account, for which a credit ought to have been given ; কোন হিসাবের খরচের দিকে কোন বিষয়ের বর্জ্জন প্রদর্শন করা। ***Noun.*** **1.** An extra charge or load ; অতি বোঝাই, অতিরিক্ত দাবী। **2.** An overstocking with cattle ; অতিরিক্ত পরিমাণ গো মহিষাদি রক্ষণ। **3.** Amount in official account not passed by auditor and having to be refunded by person responsible ; সরকারী হিসাবের যে টাকা অডিটার কর্ত্তৃক পাশ করা হয় নাই এবং যাহা ঐ টাকার জন্ম দায়ী ব্যক্তির প্রত্যর্পণ করিতে হয়। **4.** An extra charge made by assessors on such as neglect to make due return of the taxes to which they are liable ; করযোগ্য সম্পত্তির সঠিক বিবরণ না দিলে কোন ব্যক্তির যে অতিরিক্ত টেক্স ধার্য্য করা হয়।

sur′-cin-gle (sêr-sĭng-gl), *n.* & *v.t.* **1.** A belt, band, or girth which passes over a saddle or over anything on a horse's back to fasten it ; ঘোড়ার গদি বা অপর কোন কিছুর উপর দিয়া ফালি প্রভৃতি আঁটিবার জন্ম যে পেটী বাঁধা হয়। **2.** The girdle of a cassock ; এংলিক্যান যাজকদিগের জোব্বার মত পোষাক বাঁধিবার জন্ম কোমর বন্ধনী। ***Verb t.*** To surround with such ; ঐরূপ বেষ্টনী দ্বারা বেষ্টিত করা।

sur′-coat (sêr-kōt), *n.* **1.** A loose coat or robe worn over armour ; বর্ম্মের উপর পরিধেয় ঢিলা কোর্ত্তা। **2.** An outer garment from the thirteenth to fifteenth centuries worn by both sexes ; ত্রয়োদশ হইতে পঞ্চদশ শতাব্দী পর্য্যন্ত ইংলণ্ডে স্ত্রীপুরুষ নির্ব্বিশেষে পরিহিত একপ্রকার চাপকান।

Surcoat.

sur′-cu-lous (sêr-kū-lŭs), *n.* & *adj.* A shoot from a root stock; মূলধ্বজা শাখা। ***Adj.*** Producing suckers ; মূলধ্বজাশাখা উৎপাদক।

surd (sêrd), *adj.* & *n.* **1.** (*Math.*) Not capable of being expressed in rational numbers ; করণীগত। **2.** (*Philog.*) Produced by the action of the speech organs on the breath (not the voice), as the hard sounds *k, t, p, f, etc.* (ভাষাবিজ্ঞান) শ্বাসের উপর বাগ্‌যন্ত্রের ক্রিয়াদ্বারা উৎপন্ন। **2.** (*Obs.*) Deaf ; (অপ্রঃ) বধির। ***Noun.*** A quantity which cannot be expressed by rational numbers or exactly determined, as the square root of 2 or the cube root 3 ; করণীগত-রাশি, অরূপরাশি, করণী।

sure (shôr), *adj.* & *adv.* **1.** Perfectly confident or undoubting ; as, *sure* of success ; নিশ্চিত বিশ্বাসী, স্থিরবিশ্বাসী, নিশ্চিত, ধ্রুব, নিঃসন্দিগ্ধ, সংশয়শূন্য। **2.** Secure ; "Fetters *sure* and fast" ; সুদৃঢ়। **3.** Indisputable ; infallible ; as, *sure* remedy ; trusty ; অতর্ক্য, অখণ্ডনীয় ; অভ্রান্ত ; বিশ্বাসযোগ্য, বিশ্বস্ত। ***Adv.*** Certainty ; নিঃসন্দেহে, নিশ্চিতরূপে। **Sure′-ness,** *n.* **Sure card**—যে কল্পনা প্রভৃতির সফলতা সম্বন্ধে কোন সন্দেহ নাই। **Sure-footed**—অস্খলিত পদ। **As sure as a gun**—Colloquial form of asseveration ; আল্‌বৎ। **As sure shot**—A marksman who never misses; অব্যর্থসন্ধান ব্যক্তি। **To be sure** or **be sure**—Without doubt; certainly ; নিঃসন্দেহে ; নিশ্চিতরূপে, নিশ্চিতভাবে। **To make sure**—To ascertain undoubtedly that something is as expected ; কোন বিষয়ে নিশ্চিত হওয়া। **To make sure of**—To make certain or secure ; to secure so that there can be no possibility of disappointment ; নিশ্চিত করা, নিরাপদ করা ; সম্পূর্ণরূপে নিশ্চিত করা।

sure′-ly (shôr-), *adv.* **1.** With certainty or safety ; নিশ্চিতভাবে, অবশ্যম্ভাবিরূপে, অবশ্য, নিরাপদে, নির্ব্বিঘ্নে। **2.** (In answers) Certainly ; (প্রশ্নের উত্তরদানে) নিশ্চিতই, অবশ্যই।

sure′-ty (shôr-), *n.* One who must be responsible for another's payment of debt, attendance in court, etc. ; জামিন, জামিনদার, প্রতিভূ। **–ship,** *n.* The state of being surety ; প্রাতিভাব্য, প্রতিভূত্ব। **To stand surety**—To go bail for another ; কাহারো জন্ম প্রতিভূ বা জামিন হওয়া।

surf (sêrf), *n.* Waves breaking in rocks or shore ; তটে বা পাষাণ-স্তূপে প্রহত সাগরতরঙ্গ, কল্লোল। **Surf′-y,** *adj.* **Surf-bird**—সাগর-তটচর পক্ষিবিশেষ। **Surf-boat**—কল্লোলিত সাগরে চালাইবার জন্ম একপ্রকার হালকা নৌকা, কল্লোলতরী। **Surf-man**—কল্লোলতরীচালনায় সুনিপুণ ব্যক্তি।

sur′-face (sêr-), *n.* & *v. t.* **1.** The exterior part of anything which has length or breadth ; উপরিতল, পৃষ্ঠ, ধরাতল, পৃষ্ঠভূমি, পৃষ্ঠদেশ, বহির্ভাগ, বহিস্তল, তল, পৃষ্ঠ, মুখ (আর্য্যভট্ট—টীকা)। **2.** Outside apperance ; বহিঃদৃশ্য, বাহ্যাকার, বাহ্যাকৃতি। ***Verb t.*** **1.** To put a fine surface on ; to polish ;

উপরিতল মসৃণ করা ; মসৃণ করা, পালিশ করা। 2. To work over the surface of, as ground in searching for gold ; স্বর্ণের অনুসন্ধানে ভূমির উপরিতলে কার্য্য করা। **Surface-colour**—হরফ প্রভৃতি হইতে মুদ্রণে যে রঙ্গ ব্যবহৃত হয়। **Surface-man**—যে ব্যক্তি স্থায়ী লৌহবর্ত্ম ঠিক রাখে। **Surface-printing** — হরফ প্রভৃতি হইতে মুদ্রণ (অর্থাৎ উৎকীর্ণ - ফলক প্রভৃতি হইতে নয়)। **Surface-tension**—তরল পদার্থ যে ক্রিয়া দ্বারা বিন্দু বা বুদ্বুদে পরিণত হয়। **Surface-water**—যে জল ভূমির উপরে সঞ্চিত হইয়া সরিয়া পড়ে। **Developable surface**—যাহা বিচ্ছিন্ন বা বিশ্লিষ্ট না করিয়া কেবল খুলিলেই সমতলে পরিণত হয় (যথা সূচি ঘন বা চোঙ্গ)। **Plane surface**—সমতল, সমধরাতল।

sur′-feit (sêr-fĭt), *n., v. t. & i.* Excessive eating or drinking ; fulness and oppression of the system occasioned by excessive eating or drinking ; অতি পান-ভোজন ; অতি পানভোজনজনিত কষ্ট-বোধ বা বিতৃষ্ণা। ***Verb t.*** 1. To overfeed ; অতিরিক্ত ভোজন করান। 2. To satiate ; অতিরিক্ত পান ভোজন দ্বারা অরুচি জন্মান, আকণ্ঠ পানাহার প্রদানে অরুচি জন্মান। ***Verb i.*** To be fed till the system is oppressed and sickness and uneasiness ensues ; অতি ভোজনে অসোয়াস্তি বোধ হওয়া, অতি ভোজনে বিতৃষ্ণা বা বিরাগ জন্মা।

surge (sêrj), *n. & v. i.* 1. A great wave ; কল্লোল। 2. The act of heaving like a wave ; কল্লোলের মত উত্থান পতন। ***Verb i.*** To rise high and roll as waves ; তরঙ্গবৎ আন্দোলিত হওয়া, হিল্লোলিত হওয়া, তরঙ্গায়িত হওয়া।

sur′-geon (sêr-jŭn), *n.* 1. One who practises surgery ; অস্ত্র-চিকিৎসক, অস্ত্রবৈদ্য, শস্ত্রবৈদ্য (সাঃ পঃ)। 2. A medical practitioner having the Diploma of the Royal College of Surgeons but not the M. D. degree ; রয়েল কলেজ অব সার্জ্জনের ডিপ্লোমাপ্রাপ্ত (কিন্তু M. D. উপাধি অপ্রাপ্ত) চিকিৎসক। **Surgeon-apothecary**—অস্ত্র-চিকিৎসা ও ঔষধ বিক্রয় ব্যবসায়ী ব্যক্তি। **Surgeon-dentist**—দন্ত-চিকিৎসক, দন্তবৈদ্য। **Surgeon-fish**—একপ্রকার মৎস্য—ইহাদের পুচ্ছের উভয় পার্শ্বে ডাক্তারদিগের ছুরির আকার কাঁটা থাকে। **House surgeon**—সরকারী হাঁসপাতালের ভারপ্রাপ্ত চিকিৎসক, হাউস সার্জ্জন।

sur′-gĕr-y̆ (sêr-), *n.* 1. The science and art of a surgeon ; অস্ত্র-বিদ্যা, শস্ত্রবিদ্যা, অস্ত্র-চিকিৎসাবিদ্যা, অস্ত্রোপচারবিদ্যা, শল্যতন্ত্র (সুশ্রুঃ কুল্ল), আসুরী, শল্যবিদ্যা (ঠাকুরঃ), শরীর-চ্ছেদনবিদ্যা। 2. A surgeon's operating room ; অস্ত্র-চিকিৎসকের অস্ত্রোপচারকক্ষ। **Conservative surgery**—যে অস্ত্র চিকিৎসায় কোন অঙ্গ-চ্ছেদের আবশ্যক হয় না।

sur′-ğĭ-căl, (sêr-), *adj.* Pertaining to a surgeon or the science of surgery ; অস্ত্র-চিকিৎসাসম্বন্ধীয়, অস্ত্র-চিকিৎসক সম্বন্ধীয়। **Surgical fever**—অস্ত্রোপচারকালে দেহে ছুরিকাদি চালনা হেতু জাত জ্বর।

sŭ′-ri-cāte, *n.* A carnivorous African quadruped somewhat like ferret ; আফ্রিকাদেশীয় চতুষ্পদ জন্তুবিশেষ।

sur′-loin (sêr-loyn), *n.* Same as SIRLOIN (which see).

sur′-ly̆ (sêr-), *adj.* (*Collq.*) Gloomy ; morose ; uncivil ; rude ; sour ; হাঁড়ীমুখো ; বিষণ্ণ ; অশিষ্ট, অভদ্র ; অভব্য ; রূঢ়। **—li-ly,** *adv.* **—li-ness,** *n.*

sur′-mās-têr (sêr-), *n.* The second master in some schools ; কোন কোন বিদ্যালয়ের দ্বিতীয় শিক্ষক।

sur-mīse′ (sêr), *n., v. t. & i.* A guess ; a conjecture ; a supposition ; suspicion ; অনুমান, কল্পনা (হিঃ কোঃ) ; আন্দাজ ; ঠাহর, আঁচ ; সন্দেহ। ***Verb t.*** To guess ; to conjecture ; to imagine ; to suspect ; অনুমান করা ; আন্দাজ করা, আঁচ করা ; কল্পনা করা ; সন্দেহ করা। **—mis′-al,** *n.*

sur-mount′ (sêr-mownt), *v. t.* 1. To be in the top of ; কোন-কিছুর উপরে থাকা। 2. To get over by effort, as difficulties ; to overcome ; as, to *surmount* obstacles ; to get over ; উল্লঙ্ঘন করা, অতিক্রম করা ; জয় করা ; কাটাইয়া উঠা। **—a-ble,** *adj.* That can he surmounted ; অতিক্রমণীয়, লঙ্ঘনীয়, অতিক্রাম্য।

sur-mul′-let (sêr-mŭl-ĕt), *n.* The red mullet ; একপ্রকার মৎস্য।

sur′-name (sêr-), *n. & v. t.* 1. A name or appellation added to the baptismal or Christian name ; খৃষ্টীয় নামের সহিত সংযোজিত নাম। 2. An appellation added to the orignal name ; উপনাম। ***Verb t.*** To name or call by surname ; উপনাম করা, উপনাম ধরিয়া ডাকা।

sur-pāss′ (sĭr-), *v. t.* To outdo ; to excel ; অতিক্রম করা, ছাপাইয়া উঠা, ছাড়াইয়া যাওয়া ; গুণ বা উৎকর্ষে অতিক্রম করা। **—ing,** *adj.* Exceeding ; সর্ব্বাতিশায়ী, শ্রেষ্ঠ, গরিষ্ঠ, লোকোত্তর। **—ing-ly,** *adv.*

sur′-plice (sêr-plĭs), *n.* A white linen garment, worn over other dress by a clergy of the episcopal church during service, and by all who ministerially take part in it উপাসনা-কালে পরিধেয় যাজক-গণের শুভ্র আলখেল্লা-বিশেষ। **Surplice-choir**—শুভ্র আলখেল্লা পরিহিত ভজনগায়ক বৃন্দ। **Surplice-fee**—

Surplice.

দীক্ষা, 'অন্ত্যেষ্টি ক্রিয়া প্রভৃতি উপলক্ষে যাজকগণকে যে দক্ষিণা দেওয়া হয়।

sur′-plŭs (sêr-), *n.* & *adj.* **1.** That which remains when use or need is satisfied ; উদ্বৃত্ত অংশ, অতিরিক্ত অংশ, উদ্বর্ত্ত, অতিরেক, বাড়তি, ফাজিল। **2.** (*Law*) The residuum of an estate after the debts and legacies are paid ; ঋণ এবং উইলে লিখিত দানের টাকা প্রভৃতি প্রদানের পর সম্পত্তির যে অংশ অবশিষ্ট থাকে, অবশিষ্টাংশ। **–age,** *n.*

sur-prīse′ (sêr-), *n.* & *v.* t. **1.** The act of coming upon unawares, or of taking suddenly and without preparation ; as, the fort was taken by *surprise* ; অতর্কিত আক্রমণ, অতর্কিতভাবে আক্রমণ, পূর্ব্বক অধিকার। **2.** An emotion excited by something happening suddenly and unexpectedly ; বিস্ময়, আশ্চর্য্য, চমৎকৃতি। ***Verb t.*** **1.** To fall upon or capture, suddenly or unexpectedly ; অতর্কিতভাবে আক্রমণ করা, অতর্কিত ভাবে আক্রমণ করিয়া অধিকার করা। **2.** To strike with wonder or astonishment ; বিস্ময়ান্বিত করা, বিস্ময়-বিমুগ্ধকরা, আশ্চর্য্যান্বিত করা, বিস্ময়াভিভূত করা, তাক লাগান (*colloq.*), অবাক করা। **3.** To confound ; to perplex ; হতবুদ্ধি করা ; কিংকর্ত্তব্যবিমূঢ় করা। **4.** To bring one into some state in a sudden or unexpected way ; কোন লোককে অতর্কিত বা অপ্রত্যাশিতভাবে কোন অবস্থায় আনা। **–spris′-ing,** *adj.* Exciting surprise ; wonderful ; বিস্ময়োদ্দীপক, বিস্ময়জনক, আশ্চর্য্যজনক ; অদ্ভুত। **–pris′-ing-ly,** *adv.* **A surprise visit** — পূর্ব্বে কোনরূপ সংবাদ প্রদান না করিয়া হঠাৎ আগমন, হঠাৎ আগমন। **I have a surprise for you**—তোমাকে একটী নূতন সংবাদ দেওয়ার আছে, তোমাকে এমন একটী জিনিষ দিব যাহা তুমি কখনও আশা কর নাই। **To my great surprise**—বড়ই বিস্ময়ের বিষয়।

sur-rē-bŭt′ (sêr-), *v. i.* (*Law*) To reply, as a plaintiff, to a defendant's rebutter ; (আইন) বিবাদীর জবাবের উত্তর দেওয়া।

sur-rē-bŭt′-ēr (sêr-), *n.* The plaintiff's reply in pleading ; বাদীর জবাব।

sur-re-join′ (sêr-rē-jo͞yn), *v. t.* To reply, as a plaintiff to a defandant's rejoinder; বিবাদীর জবাবের উত্তর দেওয়া।

sur-re-join′-dêr (sêr-rē-jo͞yn-), *n.* (*Law*) The answer of a plaintiff to a defendant's rejoinder; বিবাদীর জবাবের উত্তরে জবাব, বাদীর পাল্টা জবাব।

sur-rĕn′-dêr (sêr-), *v. t., i.* & *n.* **1.** To deliver up ; to yield to the power of another ; সমর্পণ করা ; আত্মসমর্পণ করা। **2.** To resign in favour of another ; ত্যাগ করা, ইস্তফা দেওয়া। **3.** To relinquish ; ত্যাগ করা। **4.** To yield to any influence, emotion, or the like ; অভিভূত হওয়া। **5.** (*Law*) To yield ; to give up ; অর্পণ করা ; ত্যাগ করা। ***Verb i.*** To give up one's self to the power of another ; কাহারো নিকট আত্মসমর্পণ করা। ***Noun.*** The act of surrendering, yielding one's person or the possession of something into the power of another ; ত্যাগ, পরিত্যাগ, সমর্পণ, আত্মসমর্পণ। **Surrender-value**—জীবনবীমার টাকা কিছুকাল দেওয়ার পর বন্ধ করিয়া দিলে, প্রদত্ত টাকার যে কতকাংশ ফেরৎ পাওয়া যায়। **To surrender one's self at discretion**—বিনা সর্ত্তে আত্মসমর্পণ করা। **To surrender to one's bail**—জামিন খালাস হইয়া নির্দ্ধারিত দিবসে আদালতে উপস্থিত হওয়া।

sŭr-rĕp-tĭ′-tious (sêr-rĕp-tĭ-shŭs), *adj.* Done by stealth or without proper authority ; sceret ; accompanied by underhand dealing ; গোপনে সম্পাদিত ; চোরা ; গোপন। **–ly,** *adv,*

sŭr′-rō-gāte(sêr-), *n.* A deputy esp. of bishop ; a substitute ; প্রতিনিধি, উপধর্ম্মাধ্যক্ষ ; স্থলাভিষিক্ত ব্যক্তি।

sur-round′ (sêr-ro͞wnd), *v. t.* To inclose on all sides ; to enclose ; বেষ্টিত করা, পরিবেষ্টন করা, পরিবৃতকরা ; বলয়িত করা। **–ed,** *p. p.* **–ing,** *adj.* **Surrounding medium** — সমাবরণ (সাঃ পঃ)। **The surrounding country**—চতুঃপার্শ্ববর্ত্তী প্রদেশ।

sur-′round′-ings (sêr-ro͞wnd-), *n.* **1.** An encompassing ; বেষ্টন, পরিবেষ্টন। **2.** Environments ; পারিপার্শ্বিক অবস্থা, প্রতিবেশ।

sur′-tăx (sêr-), *v. t.* & *n.* To impose additional tax on ; অতিরিক্ত কর বসান। ***Noun.*** Additional tax ; অতিরিক্ত কর।

sur′-tout (sêr-tô), *n.* (*Now rare*) A man's coat to be worn over his other garments ; (ক্বচিদ্ ব্যবহৃত) একপ্রকার ঢিলা বড় কোট।

sur-veil′-lance (sêr-vāl-yăns), *n.* A keeping watch over ; নজর, নজরবন্দী। **Under surveillance**—নজরবন্দী।

sur-vey′ (sêr-vā), *v. t.* **1.** To inspect or take a view ; পরিদর্শন করা, পর্য্যবলোকন করা। **2.** To examine ; পরীক্ষা করা। **3.** To determine the boundaries, position, natural features or condition of ; জরীপ করা। **–ing,** *n.*

sur′-vey (sêr-vā), *n.* **1.** An attentive view ; পরিদর্শন। **2.** A particular view or examination of anything ; পরিবীক্ষণ। **3.** The determination of dimensions, boundaries and other topographical particulars of some part of the earth's surface ; জরীপ। **4.** A map or plan setting forth results of such survey ; নক্সা, মানচিত্র।

sur-vey′-or (sêr-vā-êr), *n.* **1.** An overseer ; পরিদর্শক। **2.** One that views or examines for the purpose of ascertaining the condition, quality or quantity of anything ; যে ব্যক্তি কোন কিছুর অবস্থা, গুণ বা পরিমাণ সম্বন্ধে পরীক্ষা বা পরিদর্শন করে, পরীক্ষক। 3. One that measures lands, or practises the art of surveying ; জরীপকারী, আমীন, ভূমাপক।

sur-vīv'-ăl (sêr-), *n.* 1. A living longer than, or beyond the life of, another person, thing or event ; অন্য কোন ব্যক্তি, বস্তু বা ঘটনা অপেক্ষা অধিককাল জীবিত বা বর্তমান থাকন, উদ্বর্তন। 2. (*Anthropol.*) Old habit, belief, opinion, etc. existing merely from custom ; (নৃতত্ত্ব) প্রাচীনকালের বিশ্বাস, মত প্রভৃতি। [The ordeal of the key and Bible, still in use, is a *survival*; the midsummer bonfire is a *survival* from sun and fire worship.] **Survival of the fittest** — যোগ্যতমের উদ্বর্তন, যোগ্যের জয় (যোঃ), যোগ্যতমাবশেষ (হিঃ কোঃ), শক্তাতিজীবন (ঐ)। (See NATURAL SELECTION.)

sur-vīve' (sêr-), *v. t.* & *i.* 1. To outlive ; as, the wife *survived* her husband ; অন্যের মৃত্যুর পর জীবিত থাকা, অন্য কেহ অপেক্ষা অধিক দিন জীবিত থাকা। 2. To outlast ; "His art *survived* the waters" ; কোনকিছু অপেক্ষা অপেক্ষাকৃত অধিক-কাল স্থায়ী থাকা। ***Verb i.*** To remain alive ; to exist ; to live after the death of another or anything else ; জীবিত থাকা ; বিদ্যমান থাকা, বর্ত্তমান থাকা ; কোন ব্যক্তি অপেক্ষা অধিকদিন জীবিত থাকা, অন্য কোন ঘটনার পর জীবিত থাকা, কাটাইয়া উঠা [cf. সকলেই জানিত কাশীনাথ এই আঘাত কাটাইয়া উঠিতে পারিবেনা—কাশীনাথ (শরৎ চট্টোপাধ্যায়)]। **—viv'-or,** *n.* 1. One who survives or outlives a person, event, etc. ; যে ব্যক্তি অপর কাহারো মৃত্যুর পর জীবিত থাকে, যে ব্যক্তি কোন ঘটনা প্রভৃতির পর জীবিত থাকে, অন্যোত্তর-জীবী। 2. (*Law*) The longer liver of two joint heirs, tenants, etc. ; দুইজন সহোত্তরাধিকারী, সহপ্রজা, প্রভৃতির মধ্যে যে ব্যক্তি অপরের মৃত্যুর পর জীবিত থাকে। **—viv'-or-ship,** *n*

sŭs-cĕp'-ti-ble (-bl), *adj.* 1. Admitting of ; as, *susceptible* of this interpretation ; capable of admitting any change or influence ; as, a body *susceptible* of colour ; impressible ; গ্রহণশক্য ; গ্রাহ্য ; বেদনসহ, সংবেদনীয়। 2. Impressionable ; sensitive ; as, children are *susceptible* to kindness ; easily made amorous ; as, a girl of *susceptible* heart ; সংক্ষোভ্য ; সংবেদনশীল, বেদনশীল ; কামপ্রবণ। **—bil'-i-ty,** *n.* 1. The state or quality of being susceptible ; অনুভবশীলতা, বেদনক্ষমতা (হিঃ কোঃ), বেদনসহতা, সংবেদনশীলতা, বেদনশীলতা, সংবেদনীয়তা, বেদনাগ্রাহকত্ব। 2. (*Pl.*) Susceptible points of one's nature ; as, to wound one's *susceptibilities* ; কোন ব্যক্তির প্রকৃতির সংবেদনপ্রবণ অংশ।

sŭs-cĕp'-tive (-tiv), *adj.* Capable of admitting ; readily admitting ; গ্রহণশীল ; সংবেদনশীল। **—tiv'-i-ty,** *n.* The state of being susceptive ; সংবেদনশীলতা, গ্রহণশীলতা, সংবেদনীয়তা।

sŭs-pĕct', *v. t.* 1. To have some belief or fear ; to mistrust ; to doubt ; অনুমান করা ; অবিশ্বাস করা ; সন্দেহ করা। 2. To have doubts of ; সন্দেহ থাকা।

sŭs-pĕct', *pred. adj.* & *n.* Suspected ; under suspicion ; সন্দিগ্ধ ; সন্দেহভাজন। ***Noun.*** A person suspected of a crime, offence, etc. ; as, a police *suspect* ; সন্দেহভাজন ব্যক্তি।

sŭs-pĕnd', *v. t.* 1. To hang up ; as, to *suspend* a ball by a thread ; ঝুলান, দোদুল্যমান করা। 2. To cause to cease for a time ; as, to *suspend* further operations ; স্থগিত করা। 3. To debar from the execution of any office, or from the enjoyment of an income ; অস্থায়িভাবে কর্ম্মচ্যুত করা, সাময়িকভাবে বাধা দেওয়া। **—pend'-ed,** *adj.* In a state of suspension ; দোলায়মান, দোলায়িত, নিম্নলম্বিত। **Suspended animation**—জলমগ্ন ব্যক্তি প্রভৃতির প্রাণবায়ু বহির্গত না হওয়া স্বত্ত্বেও মৃতবৎ অবস্থা। **To suspend payment**—দাউলিয়া বলিয়া স্বীকার কর।

sŭs-pĕnd'-êr, *n.* 1. That which suspends ; দোদুল্যমানকারী, দোলায়ক। 2. Straps for holding up pantaloons etc. ; পাজামা প্রভৃতি টানা দিয়া রাখার জন্য চৌড়া ফিতা।

sus'-pense (-pĕns), *n.* 1. A state of uncertainty, doubt, anxiety, with more or less apprehension ; as, to keep in *suspense* ; উৎকণ্ঠা, উদ্বেগ, অনিশ্চিতাবস্থা, অনিশ্চয়তা। 2. (*Law*) A temporary cessation of a man's right ; (আইন) সাময়িক ভাবে স্বত্ব বা অধিকার লোপ। **Suspense account**—কাঁচা জমাখরচ, খসড়া হিসাব।

sŭs-pĕn'-sion, *n.* 1. The act of hanging ; ঝুলাইয়া রাখন, বিলম্বন। 2. The postponement of judgment ; মতামত স্থগিতকরণ। 3. Temporary privation of power, authority or rights ; সাময়িকভাবে পদচ্যুত করণ, সাময়িকভাবে কোন ক্ষমতা লোপকরণ। 4. The state of floating undissolved in a liquid ; অমিশ্রিতভাবে কোন তরল পদার্থের উপর প্লবমান অবস্থা। 5. The ceasing to make payment ; (ব্যাঙ্ক প্রভৃতি সম্পর্কে) টাকা প্রদান বন্ধকরণ। **—sive,** *adj.* **—sive-ly,** *adv.* **Suspension-bridge**—দোলায়মান সেতু, ঝুলায়মান সেতু। **Suspension of arms**—উভয় পক্ষের সম্মতিক্রমে সাময়িক যুদ্ধ নিবৃত্তি। **Suspensive vote**—সাময়িকভাবে কার্য্যকারী ভোট।

suspensio per collum, ***n.*** (Abbrev. *Sus. per coll.*) Execution by hanging ; ফাঁসি দেওন।

sŭs-pĕn'-sŏr, *n.* 1. Something that suspends ; অবলম্বক। 2. A bag attached to a strap or belt, used to support the scrotum, as in hernia ; অন্ত্রবৃদ্ধি প্রভৃতি রোগে অণ্ডকোষ প্রভৃতি কোমরবন্ধে সংবদ্ধ যে থলিয়াতে অবলম্বিত থাকে। 3. (*Bot.*) A cellular cord by which the embryo of some plants is suspended from the foramen or the opening of a seed ; (উদ্ভিদ্‌বিদ্যা) অবলম্বন (সাঃ পঃ), ধারণকোষ (ঐ)।

sŭs-pĭ'-cion (-shŭn), *n.* & *v. t.* Act of suspecting ; feeling of one who suspects ; mistrust ; সন্দেহ করণ ; সন্দেহ, সংশয় ; অবিশ্বাস। ***Verb t.*** (*Slang*) To have suspicion that ; সন্দেহ থাকা। **—less,** *adj.* **Above suspicion**—সন্দেহের অতীত।

sŭs-pĭ'-cious (-shŭs), *adj.* 1. Given to suspicion ; সন্দেহপ্রবণ, সন্দিগ্ধচিত্ত। 2. Indicating suspicion ; causing suspicion ; suggesting suspicion ; সন্দেহসূচক ; সন্দেহজনক ; সন্দেহব্যঞ্জক। **—ly,** *adv.* **—ness,** *n.*

sŭs-pīre', *v. i.* (*Poet.*) To sigh ; (কবিতায়) দীর্ঘ নিঃশ্বাস ফেলা। **—pi-ra'-tion,** *n.*

sŭs-tain' (-tān), *v. t.* 1. To uphold ; as, to *sustain* a load ; ধারণ করা। 2. To hold suspended ; as, a rope *sustains* a weight ; ঝুলাইয়া রাখা। 3. To maintain ; as, to *sustain* one's family ; to nourish ; পালন করা ; পোষণ করা। 4. To establish by evidence ; to confirm ; as, to *sustain* a charge ; প্রমাণ দ্বারা প্রতিপন্ন করা ; দৃঢ় করা। 5. To endure or undergo without failing or yielding ; as, to *sustain* a defeat ; সহ্য করা ; ভোগ করা। 6. To allow the validity of ; to give decision in favour of ; to uphold ; as, to *sustain* one's objection ; বৈধতা স্বীকার করা ; কাহারো অনুকূলে নিষ্পত্তি করা ; বহাল রাখা। 7. (*Mus.*) To continue, as the sound of notes through their whole length ; (সঙ্গীতশাস্ত্র) একই ধ্বনি ক্রমাগত উৎপাদন করা। **—a-ble,** *adj.*

sŭs'-tē-nance (-năns), *n.* 1. (*Rare*) Nourishing ; maintaining ; support ; (কচিদ্ ব্যবহৃত) পুষ্টিসাধন, পুষ্টিবিধান ; প্রতিপালন ; ভরণপোষণ, লালনপালন। 2. That which supports life ; food ; পুষ্টিসাধক বস্তু ; খাদ্য।

sŭs-tĕn'-tā-tion, *n.* Support ; maintenance ; support of life ; লালনপালন ; ভরণপোষণ ; জীবনোপায়। **Sustentation fund**—দরিদ্র বালকদিগের ভরণপোষণের জন্য সংগৃহীত অর্থ।

sū-sur-ra'-tion (-sêr-), *n.* (*Rare*) A whisper ; a murmur ; (কচিদ্ ব্যবহৃত) অস্ফুট শব্দ ; মর্ম্মর ধ্বনি।

sŭt'-lêr, *n.* A person who follows an army and sells to the troop provisions, liquors, etc. ; সৈন্যদলের সহগামী খাদ্য, মদ্য প্রভৃতি বিক্রেতা।

sŭt-tee' (-tē), **să-tī',** *ns.* A Hindu woman who immolates herself in the funeral pyre of her husband ; সতী। **—ism,** *n.* The custom of Hindu women inmolating themselves in the funeral pyre of their husbands ; সতীদাহ প্রথা।

sū'-tūre, *n.* & *v. t.* 1. (*Anat.*) A seam or junction which unites the skulls ; (শারীরসংস্থানবিদ্যা) মস্তকাদির অস্থিসংযোজক ক্রকচদণ্ডবৎ ক্ষুদ্র ক্ষুদ্র সন্ধি, জোড় (সাঃ পঃ), সেবনী (ঐ), সেবনী সন্ধি। 2. (*Surg.*) The uniting of the lips or edge of a wound by stitching ; thread used for this ; সেলাই দ্বারা ক্ষতের প্রান্তদ্বয় সংযোজন ; ঐরূপ সেলাইয়ে ব্যবহৃত সূতা বা তার। 3. (*Bot.* & *Entom.*) Junction of parts ; অংশ সমূহের সন্ধি। ***Verb t.*** To unite thus ; সেলাই করিয়া ক্ষতের প্রান্তের মুখ জোড় দেওয়া। **—tur-al, —tur-al-ly,** *adv.* **—tu-ra'-tion,** *n.* **Sutural dehiscence**—সংযোজিত বিদারণ (সাঃ পঃ),

su'-ze-rain (sô-zĕ-rān), *n.* 1. The supreme or highest lord ; a feudal lord ; সম্রাট, সার্ব্বভৌম, অধিরাজ, রাজরাজেশ্বর, একচ্ছত্র নৃপতি ; ঊর্দ্ধতন ভূম্যধিকারী। 2. (*International law*) A state that exercises political control over another state ; যে রাষ্ট্র অপর রাষ্ট্রের উপর রাজনীতিক আধিপত্য করিয়া থাকে। **—ty,** *n.* The state of being a suzerain ; একাধিপত্য, সার্ব্বভৌমত্ব।

svelte, (*F.*), *adj.* Supple ; lissome ; সুকুমার ; মেদুর, পেলব।

swab (swŏb), *n.* & *v. t.* 1. A mop ; ঝাড়ু, সম্মার্জ্জনী। 2. (*Naut* & *slang*) An officer's epaulet ; নাবিক কর্ম্মচারীর স্কন্ধভূষা। 3. (*Naut. slang*) A clumsy fellow ; (নৌবিদ্যা—ইতর ভাষায়) আনাড়ী লোক। ***Verb t.*** To clean with a swab ; ঝাঁট দেওয়া, সম্মার্জ্জনী দ্বারা পরিষ্কার করা।

Swa'-bi-ăn, Sua'-bi-ăn (swā-), *ns.* An inhabitant of Swabia ; Swabiaর অধিবাসী। **Swabian emperors**—Hohenstaufens, (1138—1254).

swad'-dle (swŏd-l), *v. t.* To swathe ; to bind tight with clothes, as an infant ; বস্ত্র দ্বারা বেষ্টন করা, পরিচ্ছদাদি দ্বারা আচ্ছাদিত করা ; কাপড়চোপড় দিয়া জড়াইয়া রাখা। **Swaddling-bands, swaddling-clothes**—যে কাপড়চোপড় দ্বারা শিশুদিগকে জড়াইয়া রাখা হয় ; যে সকল কার্য্য দ্বারা চিন্তা বা স্বাধীনতা বাধা প্রাপ্ত হয়।

swăg, *n.* 1. (*Slang*) Something got by plunder ; লুণ্ঠিত বস্তু। 2. Gains made by political jobbery ; রাজনীতিক কৌশলদ্বারা অর্জ্জিত বস্তু।

swāge, *n.* & *v. t.* A tool having a face of given shape, the counterpart of which is imparted to the heated metal by forcible pressure as by hammering etc. ; একপ্রকার বিশেষ আকৃতিবিশিষ্ট যন্ত্র,—এই যন্ত্রের অনুরূপ অংশদ্বয়ের অন্তর

অংশ প্রতপ্ত ধাতুপটে সংলগ্ন করিয়া চাপ প্রয়োগে, যথা হাতুড়ী প্রভৃতি দ্বারা পিটাইয়া ঐ পট্টকে নানা আকারে গঠন করা হয় বা উহাতে বিভিন্ন প্রকার ছাপ অঙ্কিত করা হইয়া থাকে, পট্ট-সঙ্কালক। *Verb t.* To shape with swage ; পট্টসঙ্কালকের সাহায্যে গঠন বা সঙ্কালন করা। **Swage-block**—ঢালা লোহা বা ইস্পাতে তৈয়ারী এক-প্রকার সচ্ছিদ্র চতুষ্কোণ ধাতুখণ্ড—এইরূপ খণ্ডের চতুর্দ্দিকে খাঁজ কাটা থাকে। এই যন্ত্রের সাহায্যে বল্টু প্রভৃতির মাথা প্রস্তুত এবং লৌহপট্টে ছাপ প্রভৃতি মুদ্রিত করা হয়, চাপফলক।

swăg'-ger (-êr), *v. t.* & *n.* 1. To strut with a defiant or insolent air ; to hector ; গর্ব্বিতভাবে চলা, বুক ফুলাইয়া চলা, সদম্ভে চলা, নবাবী-ধরণে হাঁটা। 2. To boast or brag noisily ; "A rascal that *swaggered* with me last night" ; দম্ভ করিয়া চলা, লম্বাচৌড়াই করা। *Noun.* A piece of bluster ; boastfulness ; তর্জ্জন গর্জ্জন ; দর্প, দম্ভ। **—er,** *n.* One who swaggers ; blusterer ; bully ; আস্ফালনকারী ; দৃপ্তব্যক্তি, দাম্ভিক লোক ; তর্জ্জনগর্জ্জনকারী। **—ing-ly,** *adv.* **Swagger-cane**—একপ্রকার ছড়ি—যাহা সৈন্যগণ বেড়াইবার সময় লইয়া বাহির হয়।

swăg'-ger (-êr), *adj.* Smart ; fashionable ; চোস্ত ; কায়দাদুরস্ত।

swain (swān), *n.* 1. A young man dwelling in the country ; পল্লীবাসী যুবক। 2. A country gallant ; a lover ; a wooer ; "Blest *swains* whose nymphs in every grace excel" ; পল্লীবাসী প্রণয়ী ; প্রেমিক ; পরিণয়প্রার্থী ব্যক্তি।

swal'-low (swŏl-lō), *v. t., i.* & *n.* 1. To receive into the body through the mouth and the throat ; গ্রাস করা, গিলা, গলাধঃকরণ করা, উদরসাৎ করা। 2. To embrace or believe readily ; as, to *swallow* a doctrine ; নির্ব্বিচারে গ্রহণ করা। 3. To engulf ; to take up ; as, to *swallow* one's time ; to engross ; কুক্ষিগত করা ; নেওয়া ; ব্যাপৃত করা। 4. To recant ; as, to *swallow* one's remark ; প্রত্যাহার করা। 5. To put up with ; as, to *swallow* an insult ; সহ্য করা, সহা। *Verb i.* To perform the act of swallowing ; গ্রাস করা, গলাধঃকরণ করা। *Noun.* 1. Gullet ; গলনালী। 2. Voracity ; "There being nothing too gross for the *swallow* of political rancour" ; উদরিকতা। 3. (*Colloq.*) Taste ; liking ; (চলিতভাষায়) স্বাদ ; রুচি। 4. (*Colloq.*) The quantity swallowed at once ; as, a *swallow* of water ; (চলিতভাষায়) একেবারে যে পরিমাণে গলাধঃকরণ করা হয়, ঢোক। 5. A funnel-shaped cavity in limestone ; চূর্ণপ্রস্তরে কুপ্পীর আকার ছিদ্র। **To swallow a tavern token**—To be drunk ; মাতাল হওয়া।

swal-low (swŏl-lō), *n.* A name of certain small birds remarkable for length of wings and power of flight, living on insects ; তালচঞ্চুপক্ষী, বাবুই পাখী। **Swallow-fish**—একপ্রকার সামুদ্রিক মৎস্য। **Swallow-hawk, Swallow-plover, Swallow-shrike**—বিভিন্ন প্রকার পক্ষীর নাম। **Swallow-tailed** — (পক্ষী, প্রজাপতি প্রভৃতি সম্পর্কে) কাঁচির মত পুচ্ছবিশিষ্ট। **Swallow-tailed coat** — অপরাহ্ণ কালে পরিধেয় কোর্ত্তা বিশেষ—ইহার নিম্ন প্রান্ত কাটা থাকে। **Swallow-wort**—একজাতীয় গুল্ম। **One swallow does not make summer**—একটী মাত্র ঘটনা দেখিয়া কোনরূপ সিদ্ধান্তে উপনীত হওয়া যায়না।

swăm, *pt.* & *pp.* of SWIM (which see.)

swamp (swŏmp), *n.* & *v. t.* A piece of spongy land or ground filled with water ; বিল, জলাভূমি, অনূপ ভূমি। *Verb t.* 1. To plunge into inextricable difficulties ; ঘোর সঙ্কটে ফেলা। 2. To plunge or sink into a swamp ; বিলে ডুবান। 3. To cause to become filled, as a boat with water ; to sink boat by filling with water ; নৌকা জলদ্বারা পূর্ণ করা ; জলদ্বারা পূর্ণ করিয়া নৌকা ডুবান। 4. To submerge ; to overwhelm ; as, *swamped* with letters ; প্লাবিত করা ; অভিভূত করা। **Swamp'-y,** *adj.* **Swamp-ore**—বিলাভূমিতে প্রাপ্ত খনিজবিমিশ্র ধাতু।

swan (swŏn), *n.* 1. A large web-footed bird like goose, but handsome and more graceful and having also a longer

Swan.

beak, and being generally larger and stronger ; রাজহংস [Syn. অব্জাদ (বৃঃ সং), অতিসিতাঙ্গ বিহঙ্গ, অমলপক্ষ বিহঙ্গম (শিশুঃ)।] 2. A sweet singer or poet ; সুগায়ক, সুকবি। 3. (*Astron.*) The constellation Cygnus ; (জ্যোতিবিজ্ঞান) যোগতারাবিশেষ। **Swan'-like,** *adj.* **Swan'-ner-y,** *n.* **Swan-flower**—একপ্রকার অর্কিড্। **Swan-goose**—একপ্রকার দীর্ঘপদ চীনদেশীয় হংস। **Swan-herd**—যে রাজকর্ম্মচারী রাজহংসের চঞ্চুতে দাগ কাটিয়া থাকেন। **Swan-mark**—মালীকের পরিচয়ের জন্য রাজহংসের চঞ্চুর চর্ম্মে যে দাগ কাটিয়া দেওয়া হয়। **Swan-neck**—রাজহংসের সুদীর্ঘ এবং রমণীয় গ্রীবাদেশ, মরালগ্রীবা; রাজহংসের গ্রীবার মত বক্রপ্রান্ত ধূমপান-পাত্র। **Swan's-down** — রাজহংসের কোমলপক্ষ; একপ্রকার স্থূল কার্পাস বস্ত্র—যাহার একদিকে কোমল ফুঁপি থাকে। **Swan-skin**—একপ্রকার টের্চ্চা বুনা

মিহি ফ্লানেলের কাপড়। **Swan-song**—মৃত্যুসঙ্গীত; কোন গ্রন্থকারের শেষ পুস্তক প্রভৃতি। **Swan-upping**—টেমস্ নদীর রাজহংসগণের উপরের চঞ্চুতে পরিচয়ের জন্য প্রতিবৎসর যে দাগ কাটিয়া দেওয়া হয়। **All his geese are swans**—See GOOSE. **Swan of Avon**—শেক্ষপীয়র।

swank (swăngk), *v. i. & n.* To brag; বড়াই করা, আস্ফালন করা। ***Noun.*** (*Slang*) Bluff; brag; (ইতরভাষায়) হাঁকডাক, তর্জ্জনগর্জ্জন; আস্ফালন।

swap (swŏp), See SWOP.

swârd, *n.* A grassy surface of land; turf; তৃণভূমি, শাদ্বল, সতৃণ ভূমি; ঘাসের চাপড়া।

swâre, See SWEAR.

swârm, *n. & v. i.* **1.** A large number of small animals such as insects, birds, etc. in motion; ঝাঁক, শ্রেণী, দল, পাল, সংঘ, বৃন্দ। **2.** The cluster or great number of honey-bees which emigrate from a hive at once and seek new lodgings under direction of a queen; like bodies of bees united and settled permanently in a hive; পুরাতন মধুচক্র পরিত্যাগ করতঃ মক্ষীরাণী সহ নূতন মধুচক্রের সন্ধানে উড্ডীয়মান মধুপশ্রেণী; স্থায়ীভাবে কোন মধুচক্রে উপনিবিষ্ট উক্তরূপ মধুমক্ষিকার ঝাঁক। **3.** A great number or multitude; বহুসংখ্যা। ***Verb i.*** **1.** To depart from a hive in swarm; নূতন চাকের অনুসন্ধানে ঝাঁক বাঁধিয়া গমন করা। **2.** To crowd; জড় হওয়া, ভিড় করা, লোকারণ্য হওয়া।

swârm, *v. t. & i.* To climb a tree or pole by clasping it with arms and legs; হস্তপদের সাহায্যে আরোহণ করা।

swârt, *adj.* (*Archaic*) Dark-hued; (অপ্রঃ) শ্যামবর্ণ।

swârth'-ȳ, *adj.* Being of a dark hue or dark complexion; black or tawny; কৃষ্ণবর্ণ; কালো, মলিন, শ্যামবর্ণ।

swash (swŏsh), *n., v. t. & i.* **1.** A dash or splash of water; জলের ছলছল, জলের ছিটকানি। **2.** The sound caused by such dashing or splashing; তটাদিতে প্রহত জলরাশির কলকল ছল ছল শব্দ। **3.** A narrow channel of water lying within a sand-bank or between that and the shore; বলিয়াড়ীর মধ্যস্থ সংকীর্ণ প্রণালী, বলিয়াড়ী বা সাগরতীরের মধ্যবর্ত্তী সংকীর্ণ প্রণালী। ***Verb t.*** To splash water about; to dash about violently; জল ছিটকান; প্রচণ্ডবেগে ইতস্ততঃ ধাবিত হওয়া। ***Verb i.*** **1.** (*Archaic*) To strike forcibly; (অপ্রঃ) সজোরে আঘাত করা। **2.** To dash or splash noisily, as water; প্রচণ্ডবেগে ধাবিত হওয়া, কলকল ছলছল শব্দ করা। **Swash buckler** — গুণ্ডা, আস্ফালনকারী। **Swash-plate**—অক্ষ দণ্ডের উপর ঘূর্ণ্যমান হেলানো চাকতি যদ্দ্বারা উহার প্রান্তে সংলগ্ন দণ্ডে ঊর্দ্ধ ও নিম্নাভিমুখী গতি সঞ্চারিত হয়।

swas'-ti-kȧ (swŏs-), *n.* A curious religious symbol or talisman, believed to have originated in Judia or China and introduced into Europe in the 6th century (also called *Fylfot*); স্বস্তিক চিহ্ন। [এই চিহ্ন অধুনা চীন, ভারতবর্ষ এবং জাপানে বৌদ্ধ ও জৈনদিগের মধ্যে ব্যবহৃত হয়। আমেরিকার প্রাচীন অধিবাসিগণের মধ্যেও এই চিহ্নের প্রচলন আছে।]

Swastika.

swath, *n.* A line of grass or grain cut and thrown together by the scythe; the whole sweep of a scythe or the whole breadth from which grass or grain is cut by it; কাস্তে দ্বারা কাটা ঘাসের রেখা; কাস্তের প্রসর, ক্ষেত্রের যে পরিমাণ স্থান হইতে শস্য বা তৃণ প্রভৃতি কর্ত্তিত হয়—তাহার বিস্তার।

swāthe, *v. t. & n.* To bind with a band, bandage or bandages; to bind or wrap in swaddle; পটী জড়ান, পটী দ্বারা বাঁধন; শিশুকে কাপড়চোপড় দ্বারা জড়ান। ***Noun.*** (*Rare*) A bandage; পটী, বস্ত্রবন্ধনী।

sway (swā), *v. i., t. & n.* **1.** To swing backwards and forwards; দোলা। **2.** To lean; হেলা। **3.** To rule; শাসন করা। **4.** To wend one's course; কোন দিকে যাওয়া; **5.** To have weight or influence; গুরুত্ব থাকা, প্রভাব থাকা। ***Verb t.*** **1.** To move or wind with the hand; চালনা করা, পরিচালনা করা। **2.** To cause to lean or incline to one side; এক দিকে প্রবণ করা। **3.** To influence or direct by power, authority and moral force; "To *sway* the world, and land, and sea subdue"; ক্ষমতা বা নৈতিক বলদ্বারা পরিচালিত বা প্রভাব বিস্তার করা। **4.** (*Naut.*) To hoist; (নৌবিদ্যা) তোলা, উত্তোলন করা। ***Noun.*** **1.** A swaying motion; দোলন। **2.** Influence; প্রভাব। **3.** Government; control; শাসন; কর্ত্তৃত্ব। **Sway-backed**—(also *swayed*) (অশ্বসম্বন্ধে) পশ্চাদভাগ শক্তিহীন।

swear (swār), *v. i. & t.* **1.** To make or utter a solemn declaration with an appeal to God for its truth;; ঈশ্বরের নামে শপথ করা। **2.** To promise in a solemn manner; শপথ করা, প্রতিজ্ঞা করা, দিব্যি করা। **3.** To say emphatically (also *Verb t.*); জোরের সহিত বলা। **4.** To give evidence on oath; শপথ গ্রহণপূর্ব্বক সাক্ষ্য প্রদান করা, হলফ করিয়া সাক্ষ্য দেওয়া। **4.** To use profane language; to curse; অপভাষা প্রয়োগ করা; কুকথা বলিয়া গালি দেওয়া। ***Verb t.*** **1.** To utter or affirm with a solemn appeal to God for the truth of the declaration; ঈশ্বরের নামে শপথ করিয়া বলা। **2.** To vow; প্রতিজ্ঞা করা, শপথ

করা। **3.** To declare or charge upon oath ; as, he *swore* treason against his friend ; শপথগ্রহণপূর্ব্বক বলা বা অভিযুক্ত করা। **4.** (*Rare*) To utter in a profane manner, or by using the name or names of God irreverently ; (কচিদ্‌ব্যবহৃত) অপভাষায় বলা। **Sworn friends**—অন্তরঙ্গ বন্ধু। **To swear allegiance**—রাজভক্তি অক্ষুন্ন রাখিবে বলিয়া শপথ করা। **To swear at**—To curse ; অভিশাপ দেওয়া, কুৎসিত ভাষায় গালি দেওয়া। **To swear by**—To admire all his actions ; to have full confidence in ; কাহার সকল কার্য্য প্রশংসা করা ; কাহারো উপর সম্পূর্ণ বিশ্বাস থাকা। **To swear in**—To appoint men formally to the Government ; যথারীতি শপথ করাইয়া কোন ব্যক্তিকে সরকারী কার্য্যে গ্রহণ করা; উকীল, ব্যারিষ্টার, প্রভৃতিকে যথারীতি শপথ গ্রহণপূর্ব্বক হাইকোর্টের ব্যবহারজীবিসম্প্রদায়ভুক্ত করা। **To swear like a trooper**—To use profane language without any restraint ; অসংযতভাবে অশ্লীল বাক্য প্রয়োগ করা। **To swear of**—To give up ; পরিত্যাগ করা। **To swear out**—(*Archaic*) To renounce ; (অপ্রঃ) পরিত্যাগ করা। **To swear the peace against one**—কোন ব্যক্তিকে শান্তিরক্ষার মুচলেকায় আবদ্ধ করার পূর্ব্বে সেই ব্যক্তি হইতে কাহারো প্রাণহানি বা দৈহিক ক্ষতির সম্ভাবনা আছে—শপথ পূর্ব্বক এইরূপ উক্তি করা।

sweat (swĕt), *n.*, *v. i.* & *t.* **1.** The moisture which comes out upon the skin of an animal ; ঘর্ম্ম, ঘাম। [Syn. ঘর্ম্মবিন্দু, ঘর্ম্মবারি, ঘর্ম্মজল, ঘর্ম্মতোয়, (শিশুঃ), ঘর্ম্মপয়ঃ (ঐ), ঘর্ম্মাম্বু (সুশ্রুঃ), স্বেদ, শ্রমজল, শ্রমবারি, স্বেদলব (রঃ), স্বেদলেশ (শকুঃ), ঘর্ম্মাম্ভ (ঐ), ঘর্ম্মোদক (শকুঃ—টীকা), স্বেদবারি, স্বেদকণ, স্যন্দ, প্রস্বেদ, স্বেদকণিকা, স্বেদবিন্দু, স্বেদকণা, শ্রমাম্বু (উত্তরঃ), শ্রমবিন্দু, স্বেদাম্বু (গীতঃ), স্বেদাম্ভ (গীতঃ), শ্রমশীকর (ঐ).] **2.** Labour ; toil ; drudgery ; as, he cannot stand the *sweat* ; শ্রম ; পরিশ্রম, মেহনত ; খাটুনি। **3.** Moisture issuing from any substance ; as, the *sweat* of hay or grain ; কোন বস্তু হইতে নির্গত জলকণা। **4.** (*Colloq.*) A state of anxiety : (চলিত ভাষায়) উৎকণ্ঠাকুল অবস্থা। **5.** An exercise given a horse before a race ; দৌড়ের পূর্ব্বে অশ্বের অঙ্গচালনা। **6.** A febrile disease of ferrets ; অর্দ্ধবন্য গন্ধগোকুলাদিগের একপ্রকার জ্বর রোগ। ***Verb i.*** **1.** To perspire ঘর্ম্ম হওয়া, ঘর্ম্ম নিঃসৃত হওয়া। **2** To toil ; to drudge ; পরিশ্রম করা ; মাথার ঘাম পায়ে ফেলিয়া কাজ করা। **3.** To emit moisture as green plants in a heap ; কাঁচা গাছের স্তূপ হইতে জলকণা নিঃসৃত হওয়া। ***Verb t.*** **1.** To cause to execrate moisture from the skin ; ঘর্ম্ম নিঃসরণ করা। **2.** (*Slang*) To extort money ; (ইতরভাষায়) পীড়নপূর্ব্বক টাকা আদায় করা। **Bloody sweat**—রক্তমিশ্রিত ঘাম। **Cold sweat**—কাল ঘাম। **Sweat-band**—চর্ম্ম বা ফ্লানেলে তৈরী আস্তর। **Sweat-cloth**—অশ্বের জীনের বা গলার নীচের পাতলা কম্বল। **Sweat-duct**—ঘর্ম্মবাহীনালী, ঘর্ম্মনিঃসারক গ্রন্থি। **Sweat shop**—যে কারখানায় শ্রমজীবীদিগকে অত্যন্ত খাটিতে হয়। **Sweating-bath**—ঘর্ম্মনিঃসরণের জন্য স্নান। **Sweating-house**—পীড়াক্রান্ত ব্যক্তিদিগের ঘর্ম্মনিঃসারণের নিমিত্ত বা স্বাস্থ্যজনক স্নানের জন্য স্নানশালা। **Sweating-iron**—অশ্বের দেহের ঘর্ম্ম চাঁচিয়া ফেলিবার জন্য একপ্রকার যন্ত্র। **Sweating-room**—Same as TURKISH BATH. **Sweating-sickness**—পঞ্চদশ এবং ষোড়শ শতাব্দীর একপ্রকার ব্যাপক সংক্রামক জ্বর। **Sweating-system**—শ্রমজীবিগণের দারুণ অভাবের সুবিধা পাইয়া তাহাদিগকে অল্প বেতনে অতিরিক্ত পরিশ্রম করাইবার রীতি। **Under the sweat of on'es brow**—With hard labour ; মাথার ঘাম পায়ে ফেলিয়া

sweat'-ĕr (swĕt-) *n.* A knitted close-fitting jacket ; একপ্রকার আঁটসাঁট ফুল জামা, সুয়েট্যার।

Sweater.

Swede (swēd), *n.* **1.** A native of Sweden; সুইডেনের অধিবাসী। **2.** A Swedish turnip ; সুইডেনের শালগম

Swē-dĕn-bŏr'-gĭ-ăn, *adj.* & *n.* Of the Swedish Philosopher and mystic Swedenborg or his doctrine ; সুইজরলণ্ডের দার্শনিক এবং মরমী সুইডেনবর্গ বা তদীয় মতসম্বন্ধীয়। ***Noun.*** An adherent of Swedenborg ; সুইডেনবর্গের মতাবলম্বী ব্যক্তি। **–ism,** *n.* [Emmanuel Swedenborg ১৬৮৮ খৃঃ অব্দে সুইডেন দেশে জন্মগ্রহণ করেন। সুইডেনবার্গ ইয়ুরোপের একজন শ্রেষ্ঠ মরমী সাধক ছিলেন। শ্রমজীবনে তিনি নানা বিজ্ঞানে পারদর্শিতা লাভ করিয়া অবশেষে পরিণত বয়সে নিগূঢ় ধর্ম্ম সাধনায় মনোনিবেশ করেন। ইয়ুরোপের নানা স্থানে সুইডেনবার্গের মতাবলম্বী বহু ব্যক্তি রহিয়াছেন। সুইডেনবার্গের অমূল্য গ্রন্থ রাজি প্রচারের জন্য ১৯১০ খৃঃ অব্দে লণ্ডন নগরীতে Swedenborg Society নামক এক সমিতি প্রতিষ্ঠিত হইয়াছে। এই সমিতি হইতে সুইডেনবর্গের গ্রন্থাবলী হিন্দী, আরবী, জাপানী, প্রভৃতি অষ্টাদশটী ভাষায় প্রকাশিত হইয়াছে। সুইডেনবার্গ অসংখ্য ধর্ম্মগ্রন্থ রচনা করিয়াছেন। তন্মধ্যে Apocalypse Revealed, Heaven and Hell, Divine Love, Divine Providence, Conjugal Love True Christian Religion প্রভৃতি গ্রন্থ বিশেষ উল্লেখযোগ্য।]

sweep (swēp), *v. t.*, *i.* & *n.* **1.** To brush or rub over with a brush, broom or besom for removing loose dirt ; as, to *sweep* a chimney or a floor ; ঝাঁট দেওয়া, ঝাঁটান, ঝাড় দেওয়া, সম্মার্জ্জন করা। **2.** To drag ; to drag over ; as, to *sweep* the bottom of a river with a net ; টানা ; মাটির উপর দিয়া টানিয়া

নেওয়া, ছিঁচড়ান। 3. To carry off with celerity or violence ; উড়াইয়া নেওয়া, ভাসাইয়া নেওয়া। 4. To drive, destroy or carry off many at a stroke or with celerity and violence ; as, the pestilence *swept* off multitudes in a few days ; শমন সদনে প্রেরণ করা, ধ্বংস করা। 5. To graze ; "Whose garments *sweep* the ground" ; মৃদুস্পর্শ করিয়া যাওয়া, ঘসড়াইয়া যাওয়া। 6. To view with progressive rapidity ; as, to *sweep* the horizon ; দ্রুত দর্শন করা, ক্রমশঃ দ্রুততর ভাবে দেখিয়া যাওয়া। 7. To move swiftly over or along ; as, the ship *swept* the surface of the sea ; দ্রুত চলিয়া যাওয়া, সবেগে ধাবিত হওয়া। 8. To propel by means of a sweep or long oar ; দীর্ঘ দাঁড়ের সাহায্যে চালান। *Verb i.* 1. To pass with swiftness or violence, as something broad or brushing the surface of anything ; as, a *sweeping* flood ; দ্রুতবেগে ধাবিত হওয়া। 2. To pass over or brush along with celerity or force ; কোন কিছুর উপর দ্রুতবেগে যাওয়া, কোন কিছুকে মৃদু স্পর্শ করিয়া বেগে ধাবিত হওয়া। 3. To move with pomp or dignity ; as, he *swept* out of the room ; সগর্ব্বে চলা, সগর্ব্বে অতিক্রম করা। 4. To move with a long reach ; to move with a swinging motion ; as, a *sweeping* stroke ; পক্ষ প্রভৃতি অতি প্রসারিত করিয়া চলা, দীর্ঘ পাদবিক্ষেপে চলা ; দুলিয়া দুলিয়া চলা। *Noun.* 1. The act of sweeping ; a clearing out or away ; ঝাঁট দেওন ; ঝাঁটাইয়া দেওন, তাড়াইয়া দেওন। 2. Sweeping motion ; curve in road etc. ; ঘূর্ণিত গতি ; রাস্তার বক্রতা, বাঁক, মোড়। 3. The compass, range or reach of a continued motion or stroke ; as, a long *sweep* ; নিরবচ্ছিন্ন গতি বা অভিঘাতের পাল্লা, পরিসর, প্রসর বা সীমা। 4. Range ; পাল্লা, প্রসর। 5. A rapid survey with the eye ; অক্ষি দ্বারা দ্রুত পরিদর্শন। 6. (*Slang*) A low mean person ; (ইতরভাষায়) হীন ব্যক্তি, হীনচেতাঃ ব্যক্তি। 7. A long oar used to propel small vessels in a calm or light wind ; মৃদু বায়ুতে বা শান্ত সাগরাদিতে ক্ষুদ্র ক্ষুদ্র তরণী চালনার জন্য একপ্রকার দীর্ঘ দাঁড়। 8. A chimney-sweeper ; ধূমনালী পরিমার্জ্জক। 9. A pile or piece of timber moved on a fulcrum ; আলম্বের উপর সঞ্চালিত দণ্ড। 10. The winning of all the tricks in a hand ; এক হাতে সমস্ত পিঠ প্রাপ্তি। 11. A systematic search of the sky with the telescope ; দূরবীক্ষণ যন্ত্রের সাহায্যে নভোমণ্ডল পরিবীক্ষণ। **Sweep'-er,** *n.* One who sweeps ; ঝাড়ুদার। **Sweep'-ing,** *adj.* & *n.* 1. Wide ; comprehensive ; as, *sweeping* generalization ; ব্যাপক ; অতিব্যাপক। 2. Carrying everything before it ; সর্ব্বাভিভবকারী। *Noun.* 1. The act of one who sweeps ; সম্মার্জ্জক। 2. (*Pl.*) Things collected by sweeping ; আবর্জ্জনা, জঞ্জাল, ওঁচলা। **Sweep-net**—মাছ ধরিবার লম্বা জাল। **Sweep-stake**—একপ্রকার দ্যূতক্রীড়া — যাহাতে একজন ক্রীড়ক সমস্ত বাজির টাকা বা পুরস্কার জিতিয়া নেয়, যুক্তপণ দ্যূতক্রীড়া। **To make a clean sweep of**—To take or carry off the whole of anything ; সম্পূর্ণরূপে কাটাইয়া ফেলা, একদম সাফ করা। **To sweep away**—To clear out as if with a broom ; ঝাঁটাইয়া পরিষ্কার করা।

sweet (swēt), *adj.* & *n.* 1. Agreeable or grateful to the taste ; having the taste of honey or sugar ; মিষ্ট, মিঠা, সুরস, স্বাদু, সুস্বাদু ; মধুর, মধুময়। 2. Pleasing to the smell ; fragrant ; "Burn *sweet* wood to make the lodging *sweet*" ; সুগন্ধ, সুরভি ; মধুগন্ধি (cf. মধুরং মধুরং বপুরস্য বিভোর্মধুরং মধুরং বদনং মধুরং। মধুগন্ধিমৃদুস্মিতমেতদহো মধুরং মধুরং মধুরং — কৃষ্ণকর্ণামৃত)। 3. Pleasing to the ear ; as, *sweet* music ; মধুর, মধুরস্বন, শ্রবণসুভগ, সুশ্রাব্য, সুললিত, সুমধুর, শ্রোত্রাভিরাম, কলস্বন। 4. Pleasing to the eye ; beautiful ; "That *sweet* coral mouth" ; নয়নরঞ্জক, নেত্রপ্রীতিকর ; সুন্দর, সুশ্রী, সুভগ, সুদর্শন, মঞ্জু, মঞ্জুল, রমণীয়, মধুরিম (cf. মধুরিমহাস), মধুময়। 5. Dear ; as, my *sweet* sir ; প্রিয়। 6. Agreeable to the mind ; মনোমদ, মনোরম, প্রীতিপ্রদ। 7. Kind ; soft ; bland ; সদয় ; কোমল, সুকোমল ; প্রসন্ন। 8. Fresh ; not salted ; as, *sweet* water ; মিঠা, স্বাদু (cf. স্বাদুজল—রাজনির্ঘণ্ট) ; অলবণাক্ত। 9. Not sour ; অনম্ল। 10. Not stale ; as, *sweet* butter ; টাটকা। 11. Not rotten ; as, *sweet* fruit ; তাজা। 12. (Of wine) Containing sugar ; not dry ; (মদ্যসম্পর্কে) শর্করামিশ্রিত ; মিষ্টস্বাদ। *Noun.* 1. A substance sweet to the taste or smell ; মিষ্টদ্রব্য, সুগন্ধদ্রব্য। 2. A word of endearment ; আদরসূচকশব্দ। 3. Confectionery, preserve, etc. ; মিঠাই আচার, মোরব্বা, প্রভৃতি। 4. (*Usu. pl.*) Fragrance ; as, flowers diffusing their *sweet* ; সৌরভ। 5. Something pleasing or grateful to the mind ; pleasures ; আনন্দজনক বিষয়, মনোরম বস্তু ; সুখ। **Sweet'-en,** *v. t.* & *i.* 1. To make sweet or pleasant to the senses ; মিষ্ট করা, মধুর করা, মনোরম করা। 2. To make pleasant ; মনোরম করা, মঞ্জুল করা, রুচির করা, মাধুর্য্যসম্পন্ন করা। 3. To make soft or mild ; কোমল করা, মোলায়েম করা, শান্ত করা। 4. To make fertile ; as, to dry and *sweeten* soils ; উর্ব্বর করা। *Verb i.* To become sweet ; মিষ্ট হওয়া। **Sweet'-ness,** *n.* The state of being sweet ; মাধুর্য্য, মধুরতা, মধুবিমা, সুমিষ্টতা, স্বাদুতা, মাধুরী । **Sweet-apple** — আতা, নোনা। **Sweet-bread** (or *belly sweet-bread*)—ক্লোম (see PANCREAS) । **Sweet-brier**—একপ্রকার লতা। **Sweet-brier-rose**—Same as DOG-ROSE.

Sweetbrier-rose.

Sweet-flag—গোরাবচ,শ্বেতবচ ; [*Syn.* গোলোমী, শ্বেতবচা, শুক্লবচা, মেধ্যা, ষড়্‌গ্রন্থা, দীর্ঘপত্রিকা, তীক্ষ্ণগন্ধা, হৈমবতী, মঙ্গল্যা ।] বৈদ্যকশাস্ত্রে শ্বেতবচের গুণ এইরূপ লিখিত আছে :—"অতিগুণাঢ্যাত্বমা মতিমেধায়ুঃসমৃদ্ধিদত্বম । কফনাশিত্বঞ্চ, ইতি রাজনির্ঘণ্টঃ । ভাবপ্রকাশে পারস্য দেশীয় বচ সম্বন্ধে এইরূপ লিখিত আছে :—পারসীক বচা শুক্লা প্রোক্তা হৈমবতীতি সা। হৈমবত্যুদিতা তদ্বচ্ছুলং ইতি বিশেষতঃ ।] [Arab *ig'hir, waj, ikaroon* ; Chin. *shui-chang-pu* ; Fr. *acorus odorant* ; Pers. *vaj, vuj, ugir-turki* ; Tam. *vassambu* ; Telg. *vadaja, vassa, vasa, vudya.*] **Sweet-gale**—একপ্রকার জলজ গুল্ম। **Sweet going**—সুমসৃণ পথে অনায়াসগামী শকটে ভ্রমণকারী। **Sweet-heart**—প্রণয়িনী, প্রেয়সী, বল্লভ, দয়িত, দয়িতা, কান্ত, প্রেমিক, নায়ক, নায়িকা রমণ। **Sweet-john**—একপ্রকার পাটলপত্র গুল্ম। **Sweet melon** — খরমুজ, খর্ব্বুজ (ভাবঃ প্র), ষড়্‌ভুজা। **Sweet-meat**—মিঠাই, সন্দেশ, মিষ্টান্ন। **Sweet-oil** — জলপাইএর তৈল। **Sweet oleander** — শ্বেত বা রক্ত করবী। **Sweet one**—প্রিয়, দয়িত (সম্বোধনে)। **Sweet-pea** — একপ্রকার সুগন্ধ এবং উজ্জ্বলবর্ণ পুষ্পপ্রসূ উদ্যানরোপিত বর্ষজীবী গুল্ম। **Sweet-potato** — মিঠা আলু, শকরকন্দ আলু। **Sweet-rush** — Same as SWEET-FLAG. **Sweet-scented**—সুগন্ধি, সুরভি। **Sweet-sop** — আমেরিকার সমমণ্ডল প্রদেশে জাত একপ্রকার চিরহরিত বৃক্ষের ফল। **Sweet-stuff**—মিষ্টদ্রব্য, মিঠাই, খাবার (*colloq.*) (cf. খাবার দোকান)। **Sweet-tempered** — মিষ্টস্বভাব, মধুরপ্রকৃতি। **Sweet toil**—সখের খাটুনি। **Sweet tooth** — মিষ্টদ্রব্যপ্রিয়তা। **Sweet violet**—একপ্রকার সুগন্ধি ভায়োলেট পুষ্প (Opp. to DOG-VIOLET.) **Sweet water**—কাচাচ্ছাদিত উষ্ণ গৃহে রোপিত একপ্রকার শ্বেতবর্ণ আঙ্গুর। **Sweet-william** — একপ্রকার গুল্ম। **Sweet-willow**—Same as SWEET GALE. **One's sweet will**—One's pleasure ; সখ, মর্জ্জি, খেয়াল। **To be sweet on** or **upon**—To have attachment ; অনুরাগ থাকা, ভালবাসা থাকা। **Throat** or **neck sweet-bread**—উণ্ডুক গ্রন্থি। [ইহা শিশুকালে বড় থাকে কিন্তু যৌবনকালে থাকে না। [See THYMUS GLAND.]

sweet'-ing (swēt-), *n.* **1.** A kind of sweet apple ; একপ্রকার নোনা। **2.** (*Rere*) Darling ; প্রিয়তম।

swĕll, *v. i., t., n. & adj.* **1.** To grow larger by matter added within, or by expansion of the inclosed substance ; as, the leg *swells* ; ফুলা। **2.** To grow larger ; to dilate ; বৃদ্ধি পাওয়া ; স্ফীত হওয়া, ফাঁপিয়া উঠা। **3.** To increase in size or extent by any addition ; as, the river *swells* ; স্ফীত হওয়া, বিস্তৃত হওয়া। **4.** To bulge out ; ফুলিয়া উঠা। **5.** To be puffed up ; গর্ব্ব প্রভৃতিতে স্ফীত হওয়া, বুক ফুলিয়া উঠা। **6.** (*Colloq.*) To play the dandy ; বাবুগিরি করা। ***Verb t.*** **1.** To increase the size, bulk, volume or dimension of ; as, rains *swell* the river in spring ; wind *swells* the sail ; স্ফীত করা, ফুলান, ফাঁপান, বাড়ান। **2.** To raise to arrogance ; to puff up ; as, to be *swelled* with pride গর্ব্বোদ্ধত করা, দৃপ্ত করা ; গর্ব্বস্ফীত করা। **3.** To increase in number or quantity ; সংখ্যা বৃদ্ধি করা। **4.** (*Mus.*) To augment gradually as the sound of a note ; সুরের ধ্বনির মাত্রা ক্রমশঃ বৃদ্ধি করা। ***Noun.*** **1.** The act of swelling ; increase in bulk, quantity, etc. ; স্ফীত করণ ; আয়তন বৃদ্ধি, স্ফীতি। **2.** Increase of intensity or volume of sound ; ধ্বনির গাঢ়তা বৃদ্ধি। **3.** A gradual increase ; উত্তরোত্তর বৃদ্ধি। **4.** A gradual ascent or elevation of land ; ভূমির ক্রমিক উত্থান। **5.** A wave or billow, or rather a succession of waves ; as, a heavy *swell* is setting into the harbour ; ঢেউ, কল্লোল, কল্লোলশ্রেণী। **6.** A person of fashion ; "She found him very chatty, though a bit of a *swell*" ; a person of distinction or ability ; পোসপোষাকী বাবু, কেতাদুরস্ত লোক ; মস্ত লোক। ***Adj.*** **1.** Distinguished ; as, a *swell* painter ; বিখ্যাত, প্রসিদ্ধ, নামজাদা। **2.** Smart ; well-dressed ; চোস্ত ; সুবেশ। **Swell'-ing,** *n.* **1.** A rising or dilation ; স্ফীতি। **2.** A tumour or any morbid enlargement of the natural size ; স্ফীতি, শোথ (সাঃ পঃ)। **Swell'-ish,** *adj.* **Swell-mob, swell-mobsmen**—এক শ্রেণীর ভদ্রবেশী, গাঁট কাটা। **To swell the ranks of**—To increase the number of ; দল বাড়ান, দলপুষ্টি করা।

swĕl'-tĕr, *v. i. & n.* To be overcome and faint with heat or to be greatly oppressed by it ; গরমে দুর্ব্বল হওয়া, উত্তাপে গলদ্‌ঘর্ম্ম হওয়া, ঘামিয়া অস্থির হওয়া। ***Noun.*** Sweltering atmosphere ; গুমট, প্রচণ্ড গরম। **-ing,** *adj.* Sultry ; গরম, গুমসা, গুমটা।

swĕpt, *p. t. & p. p.* of SWEEP (which see).

swerve (swĕrv), *v. i. & t.* **1.** To turn aside ; to deviate ; [illegible]

যাওয়া; সরলপথ হইতে চ্যুত হওয়া। 2. To deviate from the path of rectitude, law, etc.; বিপথগামী হওয়া, উন্মার্গগামী হওয়া। *Verb t.* 1. To cause to turn aside; বিপথগামী করা। 2. (*Cricket*) To cause a ball to swerve in the air; কন্দুককে শূন্যে সরল পথ হইতে বিচ্যুত করা। *Noun.* Act of swerving; একপার্শ্বে গমন, বিপথগমন, উন্মার্গগমন।

swift, *adj.*, *adv.* & *n.* 1. Moving with great speed; fleet; দ্রুতগামী; দ্রুতগতি। 2. Quick; prompt; "Having so *swift* and excellent a wit"; সত্বর, ত্বরিত; তূর্ণ। *Adv.* Swiftly; দ্রুত, সত্বর। *Noun.* 1. The name of certain birds out-

Swift.

wardly resembling swallows, and so called from the rapidity of their flight; কয়েকপ্রকার দ্রুত-উড্ডয়নশীল পক্ষীর সাধারণ নাম। (এই জাতীয় ক্ষুদ্রাকৃতি পক্ষীরনাম Swiftlet)। 2. A frame forwinding yarn etc.; চরকা। 3. The common newt; গোধা, গোধিকা। 4. Kinds of moth; কয়েকপ্রকার তসরে পোকার সাধারণ নাম। 5. Kinds of pigeon; কয়েক জাতীয় কপোতের সাধারণ নাম। 5. (*Rare*) The current of a stream; (কচিদ্ব্যবহৃত) নদীর স্রোতঃ। **Swift'-ly**, *adv.* **Swift'-ness**, *n.* **Swift-footed**—দ্রুতগতি। **Swift-winged**—দ্রুত উড্ডয়নশীল।

swig, *v. t.*, *i.* & *n.* (*Slang*) To drink in large gulps; to drink off rapidly or greedily; (ইতরভাষায়) বড় বড় ঢোকে পান করা; দ্রুত পান করা, পেটুকের মত পান করা। *Verb i.* (*Colloq.*) To take a swig or a big draught; বড় এক ঢোক পান করা। *Noun.* The act of taking a draught of liquor; draught of liquor; এক ঢোকে পান করণ; এক ঢোক, চুমুক।

swill, *v. t.*, *i.* & *n.* 1. (*Obs.*) To wash; to rinse; (অপ্রঃ) ধৌত করা; প্রক্ষালিত করা। 2. To swallow in large draughts; ঢোকে ঢোকে পান করা, চুমুকে চুমুকে খাওয়া। *Verb i.* To drink grossly on greedily; "*Swilling* punch and cider"; পেটুকের মত পান করা, কদর্য্য ভাবে পান করা। *Noun.* 1. Large draught of liquor; বড় ঢোক। 2. Wash or liquid food given to swine; রন্ধনশালা প্রভৃতির অপরিষ্কার জল (যাহা শূকরগণকে ভোজনের জন্য দেওয়া হয়)। 3. (*Obs.*) Rinsing; (অপ্রঃ) প্রক্ষালন। 4. Inferior liquor; নিকৃষ্ট মদ্য।

swim, *v. i.*, *t.* & *n.* 1. To be supported in water or other liquid; ভাসা। 2. To move through water by the motion of the hands or feet or of fins; জলে ভাসা, সন্তরণ করা, সাঁতার দেওয়া, সাঁতার কাটা। 3. To glide along with a smooth motion or with a wavy motion; as, the ship *swims* to harbour; ভাসিয়া চলা, দুলিয়া দুলিয়া চলা, ঢেউ কাটিয়া চলা। 4. To abound; as, the river *swims* in fishes; প্রচুর পরিমাণে থাকা। 5. To be overflooded; "Sudden the ditches swell, the meadows *swim*"; বন্যাপ্লাবিত হওয়া। *Verb t.* 1. To pass or cross by swimming; সাঁতরাইয়া পার হওয়া। 2. To cause to swim or float; সন্তরণ করান, ভাসান। 3. To immerse in water so that the lighter parts may swim; as, to *swim* wheat for seed; এরূপভাবে ভিজান যাহাতে অপেক্ষাকৃত লঘু অংশ ভাসিতে পারে। *Noun.* 1. The act of swimming; সন্তরণ। 2. A smooth gliding motion; অনায়াস গতি, স্বচ্ছন্দগতি। 3. The sound of a fish; মাছের পটকা। 4. The part of a river etc. frequented by a fish; নদী প্রভৃতির যে অংশে মৎস্য বিচরণ করে। **Swim'-mer**, *n.* 1. One who swims; সন্তরণকারী। 2. (*Pl.*) An order of aquatic webfooted birds; একপ্রকার জলচর জালপদ পক্ষীর বর্গ। 3. A protuberance on the leg of a horse; অশ্বের পদের স্ফীতি। **Swim'-ming**, *n.* **Swimming-bath** — সন্তরণের উপযোগী স্নানকুণ্ড। **Swimming-belt**—সন্তরণ শিক্ষার্থিগণ যে কটিবন্ধনী পরিয়া ভাসিয়া থাকিতে পারে। **Swimming eyes**—অশ্রুপ্লাবিত নেত্র। **Swimming-pond**—সন্তরণ শিক্ষার জন্য পুষ্করিণী। **Swimming-stone** — শোষক (sponge)এর মত একপ্রকার স্ফটিক-প্রস্তর। **To be in the swim**—(*Colloq.*) To be acquainted with current events; সাময়িক ঘটনাসমূহের সহিত পরিচিত থাকা। **To swim with the stream**—To do as most people do; স্রোতে গা ভাসাইয়া দেওয়া, গড্ডালিকা প্রবাহের মত চলা।

swim, *v. i.* & *n.* To be dizzy or giddy; as, my head *swims*; মাথা ঘুরা, মাথায় পাক দেওয়া। *Noun.* A temporary dizziness; a swoon; মাথায় পাক, শিরোঘূর্ণন, ভ্রমি; মূর্চ্ছা।

swim'-mer-ĕt (-ĕr-), *n.* The swimming-foot in crustaceans; কর্কটাদির সন্তরণোপযোগী পদ।

swim'-ming-lȳ (-ĭng-), *adv.* Freely; easily; অবাধে; অনায়াসে, স্বচ্ছন্দে।

swin'-dle (-dl), *v. t.*, & *n.* To cheat and defraud grossly or with deliberate artifice; জুয়াচুরী করা, ঠকাইয়া নেওয়া, প্রবঞ্চনা করা।

Noun. 1. Act of defrauding ; জুয়াচুরী, প্রবঞ্চনা। 2. A cheat ; প্রতারক, ঠক, জুয়াচোর। **–dler,** *n.* One who swindles ; জুয়াচোর, ঠক, প্রতারক, প্রবঞ্চক। **–dling,** *n.* The act of one who swindles ; জুয়াচুরি। **–dling-ly,** *adv.*

swine, *n.* (*Plural* the same) 1. A well-known thick and bristly skinned quadruped fit for food ; শূকর, বরাহ, শূয়র। [Syn. রোমশঃ, স্তব্ধরোমা, কিরি, চক্রদংষ্ট্র, ক্রোড়, দন্তায়ুধ, বলী, পৃথুস্কন্ধ, পোত্রী, ঘোণী, ভেদন, কোল, পোত্রায়ুধ, শূর, বহুপত্য, রদায়ুধ।] 2. A greedy or beastly person ; পেটুক এবং পশুস্বভাব ব্যক্তি, ভোজনলম্পট (চৈঃ চঃ)। **swin'-er-y,** *n.* A place where swine are kept ; শূয়রের খোঁয়াড়। **Swin'-ish,** *adj.* **Swin'-ish-ly,** *adv.* **Swin'-ish-ness,** *n.* **Swine-bread** — চীনা-বাদাম। **Swine-fever**—Same as SWINE-PLAGUE. **Swine-herd**—শূকর-পালক, শূকররক্ষক। **Swine-plague**—শূকরের একপ্রকার সংক্রামক রোগ। **Swine-pox**—পানিবসন্ত, জলবসন্ত। **Swine's-snout**—কানফুল, ডুগাল।

swing, *v. i., t.* & *n.* 1. To move to and fro as a body suspended ; দোলা, ঝুলা, দোলায়মান হওয়া, দোদুল্যমান হওয়া। 2. To practise swinging ; দোল খাওয়া। 3. (*Naut.*) To turn around at anchor, as a ship ; নোঙ্গরবদ্ধ অবস্থায় ঘুরা। 4. (*Slang*) To be hanged ; as, he shall *swing* for it ; ফাঁসীকাঠে ঝুলা। 5. To advance with a free or waving movement ; স্বচ্ছন্দভাবে বা দোলায়িত গতিতে অগ্রসর হওয়া। *Verb t.* 1. To hang suspended ; ঝুলান। 2. To make to oscillate or play loosely ; to cause to wave or vibrate ; ঝুলান, দোলান ; দোল দেওয়া, দোলায়মান করা। 3. To whirl round in the air ; to flourish ; as, to *swing* arms ; ঘুরাণ ; চালনা করা। *Noun.* 1. Waving or vibratory motion ; oscillation ; দোল, আন্দোলন ; দোলন। 2. A swinging gait ; দোলায়িত গতি, হেলিয়া দুলিয়া চলন। 3. An apparatus suspended for persons to swing ; দোলা, দোলনা, হিন্দোল, বিলাসদোল, প্রেঙ্খা। 4. Free scope ; as, to give a full *swing* to one's activities ; unrestrained liberty or license ; as, the *swing* of propensities ; অবাধগতি ; সম্পূর্ণ স্বাধীনতা, যথেচ্ছাচারের ক্ষমতা। 5. Tendency : natural bent : আসক্তি, ঝোঁক ; স্বাভাবিক প্রবৃত্তি। 6. The tip or projection of a wheel outward from the vehicle ; যান হইতে চক্রের উদগতি। 7. Capacity of a turning lathe ; কুন্দন যন্ত্রের ঘূর্ণন-সীমা। **swing'-ing,** *n.* & *adj.* Moving to and fro ; দোলন, হিন্দোলন, প্রেঙ্খোলন। *Adj.* 1. Moving to and fro ; দোলায়মান, দোদুল্যমান। 2. (*Colloq.*) Very large ; প্রকাণ্ড। **Swing-boat** — কাঠামের উপর দোলায়মান নৌকাকৃতি শকট। **Swing-bridge**—ঝুলানো সেতু। **Swing-plough**—চক্রবিহীন বিলাতী লাঙ্গল। **A swinging chorus**—ছন্দের প্রবল দোলবিশিষ্ট বৃন্দসংগীত। **In full swing**—In full activity ; পুরা দমে। **To give full swing to**—To give indulgence ; to give full liberty ; প্রশ্রয় দেওয়া, আসকারা দেওয়া ; সম্পূর্ণ স্বাধীনতা দেওয়া। **To have full swing**—To be allowed full free exercise ; যথেচ্ছভাবে চলিতে পারা।

swinge (swinj), *v. t.* 1. To strike hard ; বেদম মারা, গুরুতর প্রহার করা। 2. To hammer ; হাতুড়ী দ্বারা পিটা। **swinge'-ing,** *adj.* Huge ; মস্ত, প্রকাণ্ড। **To swinge one's jacket**—To give one a beating ; পিটুনি দেওয়া।

swin'-gle, (swing-gl), *v. t.* & *n.* To clean, as flax by beating it with a wooden instrument like a large knife ; ছোরার আকৃতি কাষ্ঠখণ্ড দ্বারা আঁচড়াইয়া শণ পরিষ্কার করা। *Noun.* A wooden instrument like a large knife for crutching flax ; শণ আঁচড়াইবার জন্য ছোরার আকৃতি কাষ্ঠখণ্ড। **Swingle-tree**—যে আড়কাঠের সহিত গাড়ী, লাঙ্গল, প্রভৃতির জোত দড়ী দ্বারা বাঁধা হয়। **Swingling-tow**—শণের অসার অংশ।

swink (swingk), *v. i.* & *n.* (*Archaic*) To labour ; (অপ্রঃ) পরিশ্রম করা। *Noun.* Toil ; পরিশ্রম।

swipe, *v. i., t.* & *n.* To strike with a sweeping blow ; to strike or drive with great force ; হাত ঘুরাইয়া আঘাত করা ; সবলে আঘাত করা, অতি জোরে আঘাত করা, সবলে তাড়িত করা। *Noun.* A sweeping blow ; হাত ঘুরাইয়া আঘাত, হস্ত ঘূর্ণন পূর্ব্বক আঘাত। **Swip'-er,** *n.*

swipes, *n.* (*pl.*) A kind of small-beer ; একপ্রকার নিকৃষ্ট বীয়র মদ্য।

swirl (swêrl), *v. i., t.* & *n.* To move with an eddying or whirling motion ; আবর্ত্ত গতিতে অগ্রসর হওয়া, ঘূর্ণিত গতিতে অগ্রসর হওয়া, আবর্ত্তিত হওয়া, পাক খাওয়া, ঘূর্ণিত হওয়া। *Verb t.* To form eddies ; to whirl about ; আবর্ত্ত সৃষ্টি করা ; পাক খাওয়ান, ঘূর্ণিত করা, পাকান। *Noun.* 1. A whirling motion, as of wind or water ; an eddy ; আবর্ত্তগতি, পাক, ঘূর্ণি ; আবর্ত্ত। 2. A twist in the grain of a wood ; কাঠের আঁশে গ্রন্থি বা মোচড়। 3. The dart of the fish through water when hooked ; বড়শীতে বদ্ধ মৎস্যের জলে ছুটাছুটি।

swish, *v. t., i.* & *n.* 1. To wave or sway making the sound 'swish' ; as, her skirts *swished* ; সোঁসোঁ শব্দ করা। 2. (*Slang*) To flog ; "He has been known to argue with the headmaster as to whether he ought to be *swished*" ; (ইতরভাষায়) বেতমারা, বেতান, চাবকান। *Noun.* 1. A kind of rustling sound ; সোঁ সোঁ, ছপ ছপ

খস্, খস্। 2. A stroke of cane; বেত্রাঘাত।

Swiss, *adj.* & *n.* Of, or pertaining to, Switzerland or its people; সুইজরলণ্ডসম্বন্ধীয়, সুইজরলণ্ডবাসিসম্বন্ধীয়। ***Noun.*** 1. A native of Switzerland; সুইজরলণ্ডের অধিবাসী। 2. The language of Switzerland; সুইজরলণ্ডের ভাষা। **Swiss cambric**—একপ্রকার সাদা মলমল কাপড়। **Swiss embroidery**—শ্বেতবর্ণ বস্ত্রের উপর শ্বেতসূত্রের একপ্রকার কারুকার্য্য। **Swiss guards** — পূর্ব্বে ফ্রান্সদেশে এবং বর্ত্তমানে পোপের কার্য্যে নিযুক্ত সুইজরলণ্ডবাসী সৈনিকগণ, সুইস্‌রক্ষী সৈন্য। **Swiss muslin**—পর্দ্দা, পোষাক, প্রভৃতির জন্য একপ্রকার মোটা মলমল কাপড়। **Swiss roll** — আচার ও মাংসের পুর দেওয়া একপ্রকার পিষ্টক। **Swiss tea**—নানাপ্রকার ওষধির শুষ্ক পত্র হইতে প্রস্তুত চা।

switch (swich) *n., v. t.* & *i.* 1. A small flexible twig or rod; ক্ষুদ্র নমনীয় শাখা বা দণ্ড। 2. A tress of false hair; কৃত্রিম চুলের গোছা। 3. The end of the tail of some animals; as, the *switch* of a cow; কোন কোন জন্তুর পুচ্ছাগ্র। 4. A movable part of a rail for causing a railway train to shift from one line to another; পাতারেলের যে চালনযোগ্য অংশের সাহায্যে বাষ্পীয়শকট এক লৌহবর্ত্ম হইতে অপর লৌহবর্ত্মে স্থানান্তরিত করা হয়। 5. A device for changing the course of an electric current or for making or breaking a circuit; বিজলীপ্রবাহের গতিপথ পরিবর্ত্তনের জন্য অথবা সঞ্চরণপথ বিচ্ছিন্ন বা অবিচ্ছিন্ন করার নিমিত্ত একপ্রকার কল, বিজলীচালক। 6. A key for regulating the flow in some gas-burners; কোন কোন প্রকার গ্যাসের বাতিতে বাষ্পনিয়ামক চাবি। ***Verb t.*** 1. To strike with a small twig; to lash; ক্ষুদ্র শাখা দ্বারা আঘাত করা; বেত্রাঘাত করা। 2. To transfer from one line of rails to another; এক লৌহবর্ত্ম হইতে অপর লৌহবর্ত্মে স্থানান্তরিত করা। 3. (*Electr.*) To shift to another circuit by means of a switch; to turn electric light off or on; (তাড়িতবিদ্যা) তাড়িতপ্রবাহের গতিপথ পরিবর্ত্তন করা; বিজলীচালকে টিপ দিয়া বৈদ্যুতিক আলোক নির্ব্বাপিত বা প্রজ্বালিত করা। 4. To snatch suddenly; to swing round quickly; খপ্ করিয়া কাড়িয়া নেওয়া; দ্রুত ঘূর্ণিত করা। ***Verb i.*** (*Obs.*) To walk with a jerk; (অপ্রঃ) হেঁচকিয়া চলা। **Switch-back**—দুরারোহ পর্ব্বতগাত্রে উঠা নামার জন্য একপ্রকার আঁকা বাঁকা লৌহবর্ত্ম; মেলা প্রভৃতিতে যে গাড়ী আরোহিগণের আমোদের জন্য ক্রমনিম্ন এবং ক্রমোচ্চ পথে পর্য্যায়ক্রমে আরোহণ এবং অবরোহণ করিয়া থাকে (এইরূপ বাষ্পীয় শকট উচ্চস্থান হইতে প্রচণ্ড বেগে অবতরণের সময় যে শক্তি লাভ করে তদ্দ্বারা সম্মুখবর্ত্তী ক্রমোচ্চ ভূমিতে আরোহণ করিতে পারে)। **Switch-bar** — লৌহবর্ত্মের যে অংশ দ্বারা বাষ্পীয়শকট বর্ত্মান্তরিত হয় তাহার অংশবিশেষ; বিজলীচালকের অংশ বিশেষ। **Switch-board** — যে কলের সাহায্যে বিজলী প্রবাহসমূহের বিভিন্নরূপ সংযোগ সাধিত হয়। **Switch-signal**—লৌহবর্ত্মের সঙ্কেতস্তম্ভের স্থাননির্দ্দেশের জন্য পতাকা, লণ্ঠন, প্রভৃতি। **To switch off**—To cut off connection; তাড়িতপ্রবাহের সংযোগচ্ছেদ করা।

Swtiz'-êr, *n.* A Swiss; সুইজরলণ্ডবাসী।

swiv'-ĕl, *n., v.i.* & *t.* 1. A fastening or connection that allows the thing fastened to turn around freely; এরূপ বন্ধন বা সংযোগ যাহার উপর কোন বস্তু অবাধে ঘুরাইতে পারা যায়। 2. A link in a chain partly consisting of a pivot turning in a hole in the next link; একপ্রকার শিকলের কড়া। 3. A gun mounted on a pivot; বিবর্ত্তনকীলকের উপর স্থাপিত কামান (ঐরূপ কীলকের উপর থাকার দরুণ কামানটী যে দিকে ইচ্ছা ঘুরাইতে পারা যায়)। ***Verb i. & t.*** To turn or be turned on a swivel or pivot; বিবর্ত্তনকীলকের উপর ঘূর্ণিত করা বা হওয়া। **Swivel-eye**—টেরা চোখ।

swŏb, swŏb'-ber (-ẽr), Var. of (SWAB, SWABBER)

swŏll'-en (-n), **swōln,** (*Archaic*) *p. p.* of SWELL.

swōōn, *v. i.* & *n.* 1. To faint; মূর্চ্ছা যাওয়া, মূর্চ্ছিত হওয়া, সংজ্ঞালোপ হওয়া, অজ্ঞান হওয়া। 2. (*Music*) To die away gradually; (সঙ্গীতশাস্ত্র) ক্রমশঃ ক্ষীণ হইয়া বিলীন হওয়া। ***Noun.*** A fainting fit; মূর্চ্ছা, মোহ, চৈতন্য লোপ, সংজ্ঞালোপ। **Swoon'-ing-ly,** *adv.*

swoop (swôp), *v. t., i.* & *n.* 1. To fall on at once and seize; ছোঁ মারা। 2. To seize in a sweeping manner; "The physician looks with another eye on the medicinal herb than the grazing ox which *swoops* it in with the common grass"; ধরা। ***Verb i.*** 1. (*Obs.*) To pass with pomp; (অপ্রঃ) জাঁকজমকের সহিত চলা। 2. To descend upon a prey suddenly; ছোঁ মারা। ***Noun.*** 1. The sudden pouncing as of a rapacious bird on its prey; a sudden sweeping attack; ছোঁ; সহসা আক্রমণ, আপতন। 2. (*Colloq.*) Carrying off many things at once; as, to lose friends and fortune at one *swoop*; (চলিতভাষায়) একচোট।

swŏp, swăp, *v. t., i.* & *n.* (*Slang*) To barter; to exchange; "Would have *swoppd* youth for old age"; (ইতরভাষায়) বিনিময় করা; পরিবর্ত্তন করা, অদলবদল করা। ***Noun.*** (*Slang*) Barter; "He had made a foolish *swop*"; exchange; (ইতরভাষায়) বিনিময়; পরিবর্ত্তন,

অদলবদল। **Never swop horses while crossing the stream**—গোলমাল কাটিয়া না গেলে কোন নূতন কার্য্যে হস্তক্ষেপ করিও না।

sword (sōrd), *n.* **1.** A warlike offensive weapon consisting of a long steel blade and a handle or hilt used by hand either for thrusting or cutting; অসি, তরবারি, তলোয়ার, কৃপাণ, করবাল। [Syn. চন্দ্রহাস, নিস্ত্রিংশ, কৌক্ষেয়ক, ঋষ্টি, মণ্ডলাগ্র, করপাল।] **2.** The military profession; "It hath been told him that he hath no more authority over the *sword* than over the law"; সৈনিক-বৃত্তি। **3.** Military power; সামরিক শক্তি। **4.** (*Weaving*) One of the arms by which the lay of a loom is suspended; (বয়নবিদ্যা) যে ভুজদ্বয়ে তাঁতের দক্তি অবলম্বিত থাকে তাহার অন্যতর। **5.** War; "I came not to send peace, but a *sword*"; যুদ্ধ, লড়াই। **6.** The emblem of judicial punishment authority or power; ন্যায়ের দণ্ড। **Sword-arm** — দক্ষিণ হস্ত। **Sword-bayonet** — একপ্রকার তরবারি—যাহা সময় সময় সঙ্গীনের পরিবর্ত্তে ব্যবহৃত হয়। **Sword-bean**—মাখনা। [Syn. পদ্মবীজাভ, পানীয় ফল।] **Sword-bearer**—অভিষেকাদির কালে যে ব্যক্তি নৃপতির অগ্রে অগ্রে অসি বহন করে। **Sword-belt**—যে কোমরবন্ধনীতে তরবারির খাপ ঝুলানো হয়। **Sword-bill**—একপ্রকার দীর্ঘচঞ্চু পক্ষী। **Sword-blade** — তরবারির ফলক, অসিফলক, খড়্গলতা (মাঃ মাঃ), কৃপাণযষ্টি। **Sword-cane** — গুপ্তি। **Sword-cut**—অসির আঘাত। **Sword-dance**—অসিক্রীড়াপূর্ব্বক নৃত্য; হাইল্যাণ্ডারদিগের একপ্রকার নৃত্য, ইহাতে পরস্পরের সহিত আড়ভাবে দুইটি তরবারি ভূমিতে স্থাপিত হয়। ঐ তরবারি দ্বয়ের উপর দিয়া নর্ত্তক নর্ত্তকীগণ এরূপভাবে নৃত্য করে যাহাতে কোনপ্রকারে ঐ তরবারিযুগল তাহাদের পদদ্বারা স্পৃষ্ট না হয়। **Sword-fight**—অসি যুদ্ধ। **Sword-fish** — খড়্গা মাছ।

Sword-fish.

Sword-flighted—যে পক্ষীর পক্ষের পালক শরীরের অন্যস্থানের পালক হইতে ভিন্ন বর্ণের হইয়া থাকে এবং পক্ষ গুটাইলে উহা শ্রেণীবদ্ধ তরবারির মত দেখায়। **Sword-grass** — একপ্রকার অসিপত্র তৃণ বা জলজ গুল্ম। **Sword-guard** — তরবারির মুষ্টির হস্তরক্ষক অংশ। **Sword-knot**—অসির মুষ্টিতে সংবদ্ধ ফিতার গ্রন্থি বা থোপনা। **Sword-law** — সামরিক আধিপত্য। **Sword-lily**—একপ্রকার অসিপত্র গুল্ম। **Sword-play** — অসিক্রীড়া, তলোয়ার খেলা; (লক্ষণায়) কাটা জবাব। **Sword-proof**—তরবারিদ্বারা অভেদ্য। **Swords-draw**—See AT DAGGERS DRAWN under DAGGER. **Swordsman** — অসিযোদ্ধা, খড়্গিক, অসিযুদ্ধ-কুশল ব্যক্তি। **Swordsmanship**—অসিচালননৈপুণ্য। **Sword-stick** — গুপ্তি, কূট খড়্গ। **Cavalry sword**—খড়্গা। **Damocles' sword, Sword of Damocles** — See DAMOCLES. **Fire and sword**—বিজয়ী সৈন্যকর্ত্তৃক পরাজিত শত্রুর গৃহদাহ ও প্রাণবধ। **Sword of State** — অভিষেকাদির কালে নৃপতির সম্মুখে বাহিত তরবারি। **The sword**—যুদ্ধ; যুদ্ধ দ্বারা বিবাদ নিষ্পত্তি; সামরিকশক্তি; রাজশক্তি। **The sword of justice**—বিচারকের ক্ষমতা। **The sword of the spirit**—ভগবদ্বাক্য। **To cross or measure swords** — See CROSS. **To draw the sword**—To begin war; যুদ্ধে প্রবৃত্ত হওয়া। **To put to the sword**—To kill vanquished enemy etc.; পরাজিত শত্রু প্রভৃতিকে বধ করা। **To sheathe the sword**—To cease from war; যুদ্ধে নিবৃত্ত হওয়া। **To throw one's sword into the scale**—To assist with arms; কাহারো পক্ষ অবলম্বন করিয়া অস্ত্রধারণ করা।

swōre, swōrn, *adj., v. i. & p. p.* of SWEAR (which see.) **Sworn brothers**— বিশ্বস্ত বন্ধু।

swŏt. *v. i. & n.* (*School slang*) To labour hard esp. at books; হাড়ভাঙ্গা খাটা, সারাদিন ভূতের মত পড়া। ***Noun.*** **1.** Hard study; সারাদিন ভূতের মতন পড়ন। **2.** Hard labour; work that demands hard labour; হাড়ভাঙ্গা খাটুনি; হাড়ভাঙ্গা খাটুনির কাজ। **3.** A hard-working man; a man who studies hard; কঠোর পরিশ্রমী ব্যক্তি; যে লোক সারাদিন ভূতের মত পড়ে।

swŭm, *pt. & pp.* of SWIM (which see).

swŭng, *pt. & pp.* of SWING (which see).

sy̆b'-ă-rīte, *n. & adj.* A person devoted to luxury or pleasure; a voluptuary; "The hardy warrior of the mountains degenerated into a vulgar *sybarite.* His manliness became effeminacy; his piety a ritual of priests; himself a liar, a coward, a slave"; ভোগবিলাসপরায়ণ ব্যক্তি; কামোপভোগপরায়ণ ব্যক্তি। [দক্ষিণ ইতালীর অন্তর্গত Sybarite নামক গ্রীকনগরীর অধিবাসিগণ নিরতিশয় ভোগ-বিলাসপরায়ণ ছিল বলিয়া এই নাম।] ***Adj.*** Luxurious and effeminate; ভোগবিলাসী, কামোপভোগপরায়ণ, বিলাসবাসনাসক্ত। **—rit'-ic, —rit'-i-cal,** *adjs.* **—rit'-i-cal-ly,** *adv.* **—rit-ism,** *n.*

sȳ'-bil, *n.* Erroneous for SIBYL (which see).

sy̆c'-ă-mīne, *n.* (*Bible*) A tree mentioned in scripture and commonly supposed to be a species of mulberry ; বাইবেল গ্রন্থে উক্ত একপ্রকার তুঁত গাছ।

sўc'-ă-mōre, *n.* 1. A fruit tree of the fig family common in Palestine, Arabia and America ; আরব, প্যালেস্টাইন এবং আমেরিকার একপ্রকার আঞ্জীর জাতীয় বৃক্ষ। 2. A well-known British forest-tree belonging to the maple family, known by its five-lobed leaves and its profusion of flat-winged twin-fruits ; the plane tree ; ব্রিটিশদ্বীপপুঞ্জজাত এক জাতীয় বৃক্ষ ; সরল বৃক্ষ।

sўce, *n.* A groom in India ; সহিস।

sў-cee' (-sē), **—sĭl'-vėr,** *ns.* Silver in the shape of small half globes, used as currency in China ; চীনদেশের রাজমুদ্রাঙ্কিত অর্দ্ধ-গোলাকৃতি রৌপ্যখণ্ডসমূহ—যাহা ওজন হিসাবে টাকার পরিবর্ত্তে ব্যবহৃত হয়।

sўch-nō-cär'-pous (-pŭs), *adj.* (*Bot.*) Bearing fruits many times before perishing ; perennial ; মৃত্যুর পূর্ব্বে বহুবার ফলপ্রসবকারী ; বহুবর্ষজীবী।

sў-cō'-nĭ-ŭm, *n.* Same as SYCONUS (below.)

sў-cō'-nŭs, *n.* A fleshy hollow receptacle developing into multiple fruit as in fig ; মুদিতফল (সাঃ পঃ)।

sўc'-ō-phănt, *n.* A parasite ; a mean flatterer ; a toady ; চাটুকার ; খোসামুদে ; খয়েরখা (*colloq.*), ধামাধরা (*colloq.*), কাছাধরা (*slang*), চুরিখেকো (*ib.*)। **—phan-cy,** *n.* Obsequious flattery ; servility ; চাটুকারিতা, খোসামোদ ; পদসেবা। **—phan'-tic,** *adj.*

sў-cō'-sis, *n.* (*Med.*) A tubercular eruption upon the scalp or bearded part of the face ; (ভৈষজ্য-শাস্ত্র) মস্তকের চর্ম্ম বা মুখমণ্ডলের শ্মশ্রুল অংশের একপ্রকার মুখদুবিকা, ক্ষৌরকণ্ডু, মাষকদোষ।

sў'-ē-nīte, *n.* A grey crystalline rock composed of quartz, hornblende and mica ; একপ্রকার ধূসরবর্ণ স্ফটিক প্রস্তর। **—nit'-ic,** *adj.*

sўl'-lă-bă-rў, *n.* A catalogue of the syllables of a language ; কোন ভাষার মাত্রা সমূহের তালিকা।

sўl-lăb'-ĭc, *adj.* 1. Of, or pertaining to, syllables ; মাত্রাসম্বন্ধীয়। 2. Consisting of a syllable or syllables ; মাত্রা বা মাত্রা সমূহ সমন্বিত, মাত্রাত্মক। **—i-cal-ly,** *adv.*

sўl-lăb'-ĭ-cāte, sўl-lăb'-ĭ-fў, sўl'-lă-bīze, *v. t.* To divide into syllables ; to articulate in syllables ; মাত্রায় বিভক্ত করা ; মাত্রানুসারে উচ্চারণ করা। **—ca'-tion, —fi-ca'-tion,** *ns.*

sўl'-lă-ble (-bl), *n.* & *v. t.* 1. A sound or combination of sounds uttered with one effort and forming a word or part of a word ; একবারে উচ্চার্য্য ধ্বনি বা ধ্বনিসমূহ—যদ্দারা একটী শব্দ বা শব্দাংশ গঠিত হয়, পাঠ্যাংশ, শব্দাংশ, মাত্রা (রবী), অক্ষর (ছান্দোগ্য)। 2. A small part of a sentence or discourse ; "So many melancholy sports without one *syllable* of truth" ; a jot or tittle ; কোন বাক্য বা আলাপের অংশ ; বিন্দু বিসর্গ, অক্ষর। *Verb t.* 1. To pronounce by syllable ; to articulate distinctly ; মাত্রা অনুসারে উচ্চারণ করা ; স্পষ্টভাবে উচ্চারণ করা। 2. (*Poet.*) To utter ; (কবিতায়) উচ্চারণ করা।

sўl'-lab-bŭb (-lă-), *n.* A variation of SILLABUB (which see).

sўl'-lă-bŭs, *n.* 1. A compendium containing the heads of a discourse of a course of lectures etc. ; a course of teaching ; a table ; an abstract ; কোন প্রসঙ্গ, বক্তৃতা, প্রভৃতির প্রধান প্রধান বিষয়ের চুম্বক, শীর্ষসংগ্রহ, সারসংগ্রহ ; পাঠ্য-তালিকা, পাঠ্যবিধি ; নির্ঘণ্ট ; সার, চুম্বক। 2. (*R. C. C.*) A document issued by Pope Pius IX in 1864 in which eighty current doctrines, institutions, etc. were condemned as heresies ; ১৮৬৪ খৃঃ অব্দে পোপ নবম Pius কর্ত্তৃক প্রচারিত বিধান বিশেষ—যাহাতে অশীতিসংখ্যক প্রচলিত মত এবং প্রতিষ্ঠান অপধর্ম্মমূলক বলিয়া নিন্দিত হইয়াছিল [যথা সাম্যবাদ (Socialism), যুক্তিবাদ (Rationalism), বাইবেল প্রচার সমিতি (Bible Society), প্রভৃতি।]

sўl-lĕp'-sis, *n.* (*pl.* -SES) 1. (*Gram.*) A figure by which we conceive the sense of words otherwise than the words import, and construct them according to the intention of their author ; একপ্রকার অলঙ্কার—যদ্দারা কোন বাক্যের সাধারণ অর্থ পরিত্যাগ করিয়া গ্রন্থকারের উদ্দেশ্যের অনুরূপ বিভিন্ন অর্থ গ্রহণ করা হয়। 2. (*Gram.*) The agreement of a verb or adjective with one rather than another of two nouns, with either of which it might agree (*e. g.* neither you nor he knows) ; (ব্যাকরণ) কোন ক্রিয়া বা বিশেষণ কোন দুইটী বিশেষ্যের সহিত সমরূপে অন্বিত থাকিলে উভয়ের মধ্যে একতরের সহিত সঙ্গতি। **—ti-cal-ly,** *adv.*

sўl'-lō-gĭsm, *n.* 1. A form of reasoning or argument consisting of three propositions, of which the first two are called the major and minor premises and the last the conclusion, which necessarily follow from the premises ; যুক্তির প্রকারবিশেষ—যাহাতে ব্যাপ্তি বাক্য, ব্যাপ্যপূর্ব্ববাক্য এবং নিগমন এই তিনটী অবয়ব থাকে, ন্যায়বাক্য, ন্যায় (সাঃ পঃ), অবয়বঘটিত বাক্য, অবয়বোপেত বাক্য, মান (হিঃ কোঃ), অনুমানবাক্য, সাবয়ব বাক্য। যথা:—

Every virtue is laudable
Kindness is a virtue
Therefore kindness is laudable

[According to the Naya system a syllogism has five members

which are প্রতিজ্ঞা, হেতু, উদাহরণ, উপনয় and নিগমন। As পর্ব্বতোবহ্নিমানিতি—প্রতিজ্ঞা। ধূমবত্বাদিতি হেতুঃ। যো যো ধূমবান্ সঃ সঃ বহ্নিমান্ ইত্যুদাহরণং। তথাচায়মিত্যুপনয়ঃ তস্মাত্তথেতি—নিগমনং। ইতি পঞ্চাবয়বোপেতং বাক্যং। A syllogism according to the Mimansa system has only the three last members.] 2. Deductive reasoning ; নিগমনমূলক যুক্তি। **False syllogism**—যে ন্যায়ের অনুমানবাক্য যুক্তিযুক্ত নহে, ভ্রান্ত ন্যায়। **--gis-tic,** *adj.* **--gis'-ti-cal-ly,** *adv.*

sўl'-lō-gīze, *v. t.* & *i.* To express in syllogistic form ; ন্যায়বাক্যের মত ব্যক্ত করা। ***Verb i.*** To reason by syllogism ; ন্যায়বাক্যের সাহায্যে যুক্তি করা, ন্যায় বাক্যের সাহায্যে অনুমান করা (*also v. t.*).

sўlph, *n.* **1.** An imaginary being inhabiting the air and belonging to a class intermediate between those who have, and those who have not, a bodily frame, of any airy substance and a movement light and nimble ; দেবযোনি, বায়ুমণ্ডলবাসী অপদেবতা, যক্ষিণী, কিন্নরী, পরী। **2.** A slender and graceful woman ; as, she possesses, the form and hue of a wood-nymph with the beauty of a *sylph* ; তন্বী, তন্বঙ্গী। **3.** Kinds of long-tailed humming bird ; বিভিন্ন প্রকার দীর্ঘপুচ্ছ গুঞ্জনকারী পক্ষী।

sўl'-văn, *adj.* Same as SILVAN (which see).

sўm-bī-ō'-sis, *n.* (*Bot*) The living together in more or less intimate association or even close union of two dissimilar organisms ; (উদ্ভিদ্‌বিদ্যা) অন্যোন্যজীবিত্ব (সাঃ পঃ)।

sўm'-bŏl, *n.* A sign by which one knows or infers a thing ; a sign or representation of any moral thing by the images or proportion of a natural thing ; an emblem ; as, the cross is the *symbol* of Christianity ; সাঙ্কেতিক-চিহ্ন, সঙ্কেত (হিঃ কোঃ) ; লিঙ্গ, নিশান, প্রতীক ; প্রতিরূপ, বিগ্রহ, সংজ্ঞা, ব্যঞ্জন। **2.** A letter or character which is significant ; a sign ; সাঙ্কেতিক চিহ্ন ; চিহ্ন। **3.** A creed ; ধর্ম্মের প্রণালীবদ্ধ ব্যবস্থা। **--bol'-ic, --bol'-i-cal,** *adjs.* **1.** Serving as a symbol ; representative ; figurative ; লাক্ষণিক (হিঃ কোঃ), লক্ষণাত্মক, লক্ষণস্বরূপ ; নিদর্শনাত্মক, প্রতিরূপস্বরূপ, সাঙ্কেতিক ; সংকেতনী, বিগ্রহরূপী। **--bol'-i-cal-ly,** *adv.* **--bol'-i-cal-ness,** *n.* **Mathematical symbols** — গণিতের চিহ্ন (যোগ, বিয়োগ, পুরণ, ভাগ প্রভৃতির চিহ্ন)। **Symbolical books** — খৃষ্টধর্ম্মের মতসংগ্রহ। **Symbolical knowledge**—লাক্ষণিক জ্ঞান (হিঃ কোঃ), সাঙ্কেতিক জ্ঞান (ঐ)। **Symbolic function**—লাক্ষণিক বৃত্তি (হিঃ কোঃ), লক্ষণোৎপাদক বৃত্তি (ঐ), সঙ্কেতোৎপাদিক বৃত্তি (ঐ), সংকেতনীবৃত্তি।

sўm'-bŏl-ĭsm, *n.* **1.** The science of symbols ; চিহ্নবিদ্যা, প্রতীকবিদ্যা, সঙ্কেতসূত্র (হিঃ কোঃ), চিহ্নব্যাপার (ঐ)। **2.** The science of creeds ; ধর্ম্মসূত্র-বিজ্ঞান। **3.** The study of the symbol or mysterious rites of antiquity ; প্রাচীন তান্ত্রিকযন্ত্র এবং ক্রিয়াকলাপ সম্পর্কীয় বিদ্যা। **4.** The use of, or being represented by, symbols ; চিহ্নব্যবহার, চিহ্নদ্বারা প্রদর্শন। **5.** A system of symbols ; চিহ্নপদ্ধতি। **6.** The representation of any moral or spiritual thing by the images or properties of natural things or the assumption in external things of an inner spiritual meaning ; as, lamb is the *symbol* of meekness ; স্থূলজগতের কোনরূপ মূর্ত্তি বা গুণ দ্বারা কোন নৈতিক বা আধ্যাত্মিক বস্তুর দ্যোতন, অথবা বহির্জগতের বস্তুতে কোনরূপ গূঢ় আধ্যাত্মিক অর্থ রহিয়াছে এইরূপ অনুমান।

sўm'-bŏl-ĭst, *n.* **1.** One who employs symbols or symbolism ; চিহ্নপ্রয়োগকারী, সঙ্কেতপ্রয়োগকারী, লাক্ষণিক। **2.** One who holds the doctrine that poetry should translate the deepest secret of the soul by means of symbols connecting the physical with the spiritual world ; কবিতা জড় ও চিন্ময় জগতের সংযোগপূর্ব্বক সাঙ্কেতিক চিহ্ন-সমূহ দ্বারা আধ্যাত্মিক লোকের গভীর রহস্য ব্যক্ত করিবে এইরূপ মতাবলম্বী [Alfred de Vigny এই মতের প্রবর্ত্তক। Verlaine, Mallarme, Maeter-link, Kahn, Verhaeren, Laforgue, Viele, Griffin, প্রভৃতি এই মতের প্রধান প্রবক্তা।]

sўm'-bŏl-īze, *v. i.* & *t.* To have a typical resemblance ; প্রতিরূপ স্বরূপ হওয়া, প্রতীকস্বরূপ হওয়া। ***Verb t.*** To represent by symbols ; চিহ্ন দ্বারা প্রদর্শন করা।

sўm-mĕ'-trī-ăn, --trī'-cī-ăn (-shī-), **--trīst,** *ns.* (*Rare*) One eminently studious of proportion or symmetry in parts ; (কচিদ্ ব্যবহৃত) সৌষ্ঠববাদী।

sўm'-mĕ-trў, *n.* **1.** State or quality of having parts commensurate with, or proportional to, each other ; সুসঙ্গতি, সৌষ্ঠব, সমপরিমিতত্ব, সংমিতি (হিঃ কোঃ), সৌসামঞ্জস্য (সৌন্দর্য্য), অঙ্গসৌষ্ঠব। **2.** (*Rare*) Harmony ; (কচিদ্ ব্যবহৃত) সঙ্গতি। **3.** (*Bot.*) The orderly and familiar distribution of a certain number of parts in plants ; correspondence regarding numerical relationship between sepals, petals and stamens ; বৃক্ষের নির্দ্দিষ্ট অংশ সমূহের সুসমাবেশ ; পুষ্পের দল, বহিশ্চদ, পুংকেশরের সংখ্যাগত সম্বন্ধের সঙ্গতি, সৌষ্ঠব, সুসঙ্গতি, সমমাত্রা (সাঃ পঃ)। **--met'-ri-cal,** *adj.* **1.** Having parts mutually well proportioned ; regular ; সৌষ্ঠবসম্পন্ন, সুডৌল, সুঠাম, সুবিভক্ত ; সমপরিমিত,

সমসঙ্গতাবয়ব (হিঃ কোঃ)। 2. (*Bot.*) Having the number of parts of one series corresponding with that of other series ; (উদ্ভিদবিদ্যা) সঙ্গতিসম্পন্ন, সমমাত্রিক (সাঃ পঃ), সমাঙ্গ (ঐ)। **—met′-ri-cal-ly,** *adv.*

sỹm-păl′-mō-grăph, *n.* An apparatus for exhibiting sound-waves ; ধ্বনিতরঙ্গ প্রদর্শক।

sỹm-pă-thĕt′-ic, *adj.* & *n.* 1. Showing, or inclined to, sympathy ; produced by sympathy ; সহানুভূতি-সম্পন্ন, সহানুভূতিসূচক, সমব্যথী ; সহানুভূতিজনিত। 2. Compassionate ; সমবেদনাপূর্ণ, করুণাপূর্ণ, দরদী। 3. (*Physiol.* & *Path.*) Produced by sympathy ; সহানুভূতি-সম্ভূত, উপদাহসম্ভূত, ঔপসর্গিক (সুশ্রুঃ কুঞ্জঃ)। ***Noun.*** 1. Same as SYMPATHETIC NERVE or SYSTEM. 2. A person exceedingly sensitive to hypnotic influence; যে ব্যক্তি সহজে সম্মোহন বা যোগনিদ্রাজনক প্রভাবদ্বারা অভিভূত হয়। **Sympathetic ink**—অদৃশ্যকালি, গুপ্তমসী। **Sympathetic nerve** — অনুবেদনসম্পন্ন স্নায়ু, সহানুভৌতিক স্নায়ু। **Sympathetic pain**—সমবেদনা ; শরীরের এক অংশে কোন ব্যথা হইলে অপরপার্শ্বে যে অনুরূপ ব্যথা অনুভূত হয়, ঔপসর্গিক ব্যথা, অনুবেদনা। **Sympathetic sound, resonance, string**—স্পন্দনশীল বস্তু হইতে বায়ু অথবা অপর কোন মাধ্যমিক পদার্থের ভিতর দিয়া সঞ্চরিত স্পন্দনসমূহের দ্বারা সঞ্চারিত ধ্বনি। **Sympathetic system**—সমগ্র পৃষ্ঠবংশের উভয় পার্শ্বে প্রসারিত গ্রন্থিশৃঙ্খল হইতে উৎপন্ন সমবেদনাজনক স্নায়ুমণ্ডল।

sỹm′-pă-thīze, *v. i.* 1. To share commoner feeling ; একরূপ অনুভূতি-বিশিষ্ট হওয়া। 2. To feel or show sympathy ; সহানুভূতি করা, সহানুভূতি প্রকাশ করা, সহানুভূতি প্রদর্শন করা। 3. To share with another a feeling ; অন্যের অনুরূপ বোধ করা। 4. To harmonize ; সামঞ্জস্যবিশিষ্ট হওয়া, মিল থাকা, ঐক্য থাকা। **—thiz-er** *n.* One who sympathizes ; সহানুভূতিকারী।

sỹm′-pă-thỹ, *n.* 1. Feeling for another's distress ; pity ; সহানুভূতি, সমবেদনা, সমসুখদুঃখবোধ, প্রাণপরশ (cf. ঘটবটকে হোন হার সব প্রাণপরশ হোই জায়—দাদু), সহানুভব (হিঃ কোঃ), সহানুভূতি (ঐ), অনুকম্পা (ঐ); অনুতাপ (হিঃ কোঃ), করুণা। 2. An agreement of affections or inclinations or conformity of natural temperament ; ভাবসামঞ্জস্য, প্রকৃতি সামঞ্জস্য, রুচিসামঞ্জস্য, প্রকৃতি সাম্য, ভাবসাম্য। 3. Reciprocal influence exercised by the parts of the body on one another in affections or disorders of system ; শরীরের যে সম্বন্ধ বশতঃ একস্থানে ক্রিয়া বা উপদাহ জন্মিলে অন্যস্থানে তাহা অনুভূত হয় (যথা গর্ভাবস্থায় জরায়ুর উপদাহ বশতঃ আমাশয়ের ক্রিয়া জান্মিয়া বমন হয়)। 4. A tendency of things to unite or act on each other ; বস্তুসমূহের পরস্পরের উপর ক্রিয়া বা সংযোগের প্রবণতা।

sỹm-pĕl′-mous (-mŭs), *adj.* 1. (Of bird) Having tendons of toe-flexors united at a point ; সংযুক্ত চরণাঙ্গুলী অবনমনকারী পেশীর স্নায়ুরজ্জু এক বিন্দুতে সংযুক্ত।

sỹm-pĕt-ăl-ous (-ŭs), *adj.* Having petals united ; যুক্তদলী।

sỹm′-phō-nỹ, *n.* 1. (*Archaic*) Harmony; (অপ্রঃ) স্বরসঙ্গতি, ঐক্যতান। 2. (*Mus.*) A musical composition or a full orchestra, consisting of parts or movements ; (সঙ্গীত-শাস্ত্র) একপ্রকার সঙ্গীত। **—pho′-ni-ous, —phon′-ic,** *adjs.*

sỹm-phỹl′-lous (-lŭs), *adj.* Having leaves united ; যুগ্মপত্রী।

sỹm′-phỹ-sis, *n.* 1. (*Anat.*) The union of bones by cartilage (শারীরসংস্থান বিদ্যা) তরুণাস্থি দ্বারা অস্থি-সংযোগ। 2. A coalescence ; সংশ্লেষ। 3. Attachment of one part to another ; অংশসমূহের পরস্পরের সহিত সংযোগ। **—phys′-e-al,** *adj.*

sỹm-pi-ē-sŏm′-ē-tĕr, *n.* 1. A kind of barometer for measuring the weight of the atmosphere by the compression of a column of gas ; বাষ্পস্তম্ভের সঙ্কোচন দ্বারা বায়ুমণ্ডলের গুরুত্ব মাপনার্থ যন্ত্রবিশেষ, সঙ্কালমান। 2. An instrument for measuring the force of a current of water ; জলস্রোতের বলমাপনার্থ যন্ত্রবিশেষ, স্রোতোবলমান, জলবলমান।

Symplocos racemosa — লোধ্র, লোধ। [*Syn.* গালব, শাবর, তিল্ব, মার্জ্জন, তিরীট, রোধ্র, তিল্বক, ভিল্লতরু, কাণ্ডকীলক, লোধ্রকবৃক্ষ, শম্বর, হস্তিরোধ্রক, তিলক, কাণ্ডনীলক, হেমপুষ্পক, ভিল্লী, শাবরক।] [Tel. *lodduga, erra lodduga.*]

sỹm-pō′-di-ŭm, *n.* A stem made up of a series of superposed branches in a tree to imitate a simple axis ; যে কাণ্ডের পর্ব্বসমূহ প্রকৃতপক্ষে পরস্পরের পূর্ব্ববর্তী পর্ব্ব হইতে উদ্গত শাখামাত্র (যথা আঙ্গুরলতা), লগ্নদণ্ড (সাঃ পঃ)।

sỹm-pō′-si-ăc, *n.* A conference or conversation of philosophers at a banquet ; কোন ভোজে দার্শনিক-গণের বৈঠক বা সংলাপ।

sỹm-pō′-si-ărch, *n.* The president, director or a chairman of a feast ; কোন ভোজের প্রধান অধ্যক্ষ বা কর্ম্মকর্তা।

sỹm-pō′-si-ŭm, (*Pl.* -A) *n.* 1. An ancient-Greek after-dinner drinking-party, with music, dancing or conversation ; প্রাচীন গ্রীসে অপরাহ্ণ ভোজনের পরবর্তী পানগোষ্ঠী—যাহাতে নৃত্যগীত ও কথোপকথন হইয়া থাকে। 2. A banquet with philosophic discussion ; "In the *symposia* the pleasures of the table were improved by lively conversation" ; a drinking-party; যে ভোজে নানাপ্রকার দার্শনিক বিষয়ের আলোচনা হয় ; পানগোষ্ঠী। 3. Books describing the conversations of Plato ; গ্রীকদার্শনিক প্লেটোর কথোপকথনসম্বলিত

পুস্তক। 4. Conference ; general discussion ; বৈঠক ; আলোচনা। 5. A collection of short articles by several writers on a given topic ; কোন বিষয়ে কতিপয় লেখকের সংক্ষিপ্ত রচনাসংগ্রহ।

sŷmp'-tŏm (sĭm-), *n.* 1. Certain changes in the bodily processes of a patient which serve to indicate the nature and location of a disease ; রোগের লক্ষণ, উপসর্গ, আদিরোগ (মঃ উঃ), নিদান (হিঃ কোঃ), চিহ্ন (ঐ)। 2. A token or sign ; that which indicates the existence of something else ; লক্ষণ, চিহ্ন, প্রতীক ; ব্যঞ্জন। **–at'-ic**, *adj.* 1. Of, or pertaining to, symptoms ; লাক্ষণিক। 2. Indicating the existence of something else ; serving as a symptom ; চিহ্নস্বরূপ, দ্যোতক ; ব্যঞ্জক। 3. Made or arranged according to symptom ; লক্ষণ অনুসারে প্রস্তুত বা শ্রেণীবদ্ধ। **–at'-i-cal-ly**, *adv.* **Symptomatic disease** — শরীরের কোন স্থানের পূর্ব্বরোগ হইতে জাতরোগ, লাক্ষণিক রোগ, কান্তা (Wilson)। [যথা লাক্ষণিক জ্বর কোনরূপ স্থানিক আঘাত বা স্ফীতি হইতে উপজাত হইতে পারে।] **Objective symptom**—রোগের যে সকল লক্ষণ রোগী ভিন্ন অন্য লোকেও বুঝিতে পারে। **Subjective symptom**—রোগের যে সমস্ত লক্ষণ রোগী ভিন্ন অন্য কেহ জানিতে পারে না।

symp-tŏm-ă-tŏl'-ŏ-ğŷ (sĭm-), *n.* The science of the symptoms of diseases ; রোগলক্ষণতত্ত্ব, লক্ষণতত্ত্ব।

symp-tō'-sis (sĭm-), *n.* A concourse of vowels ; a hiatus ; স্বরবর্ণসমুচ্চয় ; সন্ধিবিশ্লেষণ।

sŷn-æ'-rĕ-sis (-ĕ-), *n.* The contraction of two syllables or vowels into one ; দ্বিমাত্রার সংযোগ, দ্ব্যক্ষরসংযোগ, দ্বিস্বরসংযোগ, সন্ধি।

sŷn-aes-the'-sĭ-ă (-ĕs-), *n.* An accompanying or secondary sensation, as the association of colour with sound ; সহগামী অনুভূতি, গৌণ অনুভূতি।

sŷn'-ă-gogue (-gŏg), *n.* 1. A congregation of Jews met for worship ; ইহুদীউপাসকমণ্ডলী। 2. A house appropriated to the religious worship of the Jews ; ইহুদীদিগের ভজনালয়। 3. (*Rare*) Any assembly ; "A *synagogue* of Jesuits" ; (ক্বচিদ্‌ব্যবহৃত) সমিতি পরিষৎ। **The great synagogue**—ইহুদী ভাববাদী Ezra কর্ত্তৃক প্রতিষ্ঠিত ধর্ম্মপরিষৎ। এই পরিষদের ১২০ জন সভ্য ছিল। প্রাচীনকালের শাস্ত্রগ্রন্থ সংগ্রহ ও সম্পাদনের ভার এই পরিষদের উপর ন্যস্ত হইয়াছিল।

sŷn-ă-lē'-phă, –loe'– (-lē-), *ns.* The contraction of two syllables into one by suppressing a vowel at the end of a word before another vowel ; অন্য স্বরবর্ণের পূর্ব্বস্থিত কোন পদের অন্তঃস্থিত স্বরবর্ণের লোপ দ্বারা দুই মাত্রাকে এক মাত্রায় সংকোচন, মাত্রাসংকোচন।

sŷn-ăl-lăg-măt'-ic, *adj.* Reciprocally binding ; as, a *synallagmatic* treaty ; পরস্পরপালনীয়, অন্যোন্যপালনীয়।

sŷn-ăn'-ği-ŭm, *n.* The boat shaped sorus of certain ferns ; যুক্তস্থলী (সাঃ পঃ)।

sŷn-ăn'-thêr-ous (-ŭs), *adj.* Having the anther growing together ; যুক্তপরাগকোষ (সাঃ পঃ)।

sŷn-ăn'-thous (-thŭs), *adj.* With flowers and leaves appearing simultaneously ; এককালে পত্র ও পুষ্পপ্রসূ, সমপত্রপুষ্পপ্রসূ।

sŷn-âr-thrō'-sis, *n.* Union of bones without motion ; close union as in suture ; গতি বিনা অস্থিসংযোগ, গতিশূন্য অস্থিসন্ধি ; দৃঢ়সংযোগ।

sŷn'-cârp, *n.* An aggregate fruit ; যুক্তফল। **–car'-pous**, *adj.* Having the carpel of a compound fruit completely united ; মিলিত ফলীয় (সাঃ পঃ), যুক্তকিঞ্জল্ক (ঐ)।

sŷn-căt-ĕ-gŏr-ĕ-măt'-ic, *adj.* & *n.* That can combine with, but cannot by itself constitute, a term ; অন্যের সহিত যুক্ত হইলে কোন পদ গঠিত করিতে পারে—স্বতন্ত্র নয়—এরূপ। *Noun.* A word of this description ; উক্তরূপ শব্দ। **Syncategorematic word** — পরতন্ত্রপদ (হিঃ কোঃ), অস্বাধীন পদ (ঐ), দ্যোতক পদ (ঐ)।

sŷn-c͟hŏn-drō'-sis, *n.* (*Anat.*) The connection of bones by means of cartilage ; (শারীরসংস্থানবিদ্যা) তরুণাস্থি দ্বারা অস্থিসংযোগ।

sŷn'-c͟hrŏ-nize, *v. i.* & *t.* To occur at the same time ; to show a uniform time ; একইকালে ঘটা, যুগপৎ সংঘটিত হওয়া ; একই সময় প্রদর্শন করা। *Verb t.* 1. To make to agree in time ; as, all clocks in the town were *synchronised* by the church clock ; একই সময় করিয়া দেওয়া, (ঘড়ি) মিলান। 2. To ascertain or set forth the correspondence in date of events ; ঘটনাসমূহের সংঘটনসাম্য নির্ণয় বা ব্যক্ত করা। **–nism, –ni-za'-tion**, *ns.* **–nous**, *adj.* Happening at the same time ; একইকালে সংঘটিত, সমকালীন, এককালিক। **–nous-ly**, *adv.*

sŷn-clăs'-tic, *adj.* Concave or convex all over ; সর্ব্বত্র নতপৃষ্ঠ বা উন্নতপৃষ্ঠ, একদিক্ বক্রী (হিঃ কোঃ)।

sŷn-clī'-năl, *adj.* (Of a strata) Inclined downwards from opposite directions ; inclining to a common plane ; বিপরীতদিক হইতে নিম্নাভিমুখে আনত ; একই ধরাতলে আনত।

sŷn'-clīne, *n.* Inclination downwards from opposite direction ; অবক্রম (সাঃ পঃ)।

sŷn'-cŏ-pāte, *v. t.* 1. To contract as a word by taking one or more letters or syllables from the middle ; মধ্য হইতে এক বা দুই অক্ষর বা মাত্রা অপসারণ করিয়া কোন শব্দের সঙ্কোচসাধন করা। 2. (*Mus.*) To prolong a note begun on the unaccented part of the next bar ; (সঙ্গীত-শাস্ত্র)

পদ্মবর্ত্তী দণ্ডের অস্বরিত অংশে আরব্ধ স্বর ক্রমাগত চালান। **–pa′-tion,** *n.*

sўn′-cō-pē, *n.* **1.** An elision or retrenchment of one or more letters or a syllable from the middle of a word ; কোন শব্দের মধ্য হইতে এক বা ততোধিক অক্ষর বা এক মাত্রার লোপ। **2.** A fainting or swooning ; মূর্চ্ছা, সংজ্ঞালোপ, নিঃসজ্ঞতা (হিঃ কোঃ)। **–cop′-ic, cop′-tic,** *adjs.*

sўn-cŏt-ў-lē′-dŏn-ous (-ŭs), *adj* With cotyledons united ; যুক্ত বীজদল (সাঃ পঃ)।

sўn-crē′-tism, *n.* An attempt to unite parties or principles at variance with each other ; পরস্পরের সহিত অনৈক্যবিশিষ্ট মত বা সম্প্রদায়ের সংযোগসাধনের চেষ্টা, সর্ব্বাঙ্গীকার (হিঃ কোঃ), সর্ব্বপক্ষতা (ঐ), সমন্বয়। **–cret′-ic,** *adj.* **–tist,** *n.* **–tis′tic,** *adjs.* **–tize,** *v. t.*

sўn-cў′-ti-ŭm, *n.* A mass of protoplasms with several nuclei but forming one cell ; কতিপয় বীজকেন্দ্র সমন্বিত কিন্তু একই অনুকোষে পরিণত জীবপঙ্কপুঞ্জ।

sўn-dăc′-tўl, –tўle, –tў-lous (-lŭs), *adjs.* Having the digits united as in webbed feet etc. ; যুক্তাঙ্গুলী। **–ism,** *n.*

sўn-dĕs-mō′-sis, *n.* The union of one bone with another by ligament ; বন্ধনী দ্বারা এক অস্থির সহিত অপর অস্থির সংযোগ। **–graph-y,** *n.* **–mol′-o-gy,** *n.* A treatise on ligaments ; বন্ধনীতত্ত্ব। **–mot′-ic,** *adj.*

sўn-dĕt′-ic, *adj.* Pertaining to conjunctions ; using conjunctions ; অব্যয়সম্বন্ধীয় ; অব্যয়ব্যবহারকারী।

sўn′-dic, *n.* **1.** An officer of Government invested with different powers in different countries ; magistrate ; বিভিন্ন প্রদেশে বিভিন্ন প্রকার ক্ষমতাবিশিষ্ট সরকারী কর্ম্মচারী বিশেষ ; দণ্ডনায়ক। **2.** A member of the syndicate of the Cambridge University ; ক্যামব্রিজ বিশ্ববিদ্যালয়ের সিণ্ডিকেটের সভ্য।

sўn′-di-cāte, *n.* & *v. t.* **1.** A body of syndics ; দণ্ডনায়কবর্গ। **2.** A body of Cambridge University syndics ; ক্যামব্রিজ বিশ্ববিদ্যালয়ের পরিচালক সভা, সিণ্ডিকেট। **3.** A body of persons associated to promote some enterprise, financial scheme or the like ; কোন নূতন ব্যবসায় প্রভৃতি স্থাপনের জন্য সভা। **–ca′-tion,** *n.*

syne, (Scot). Since ; as, auld lang *syne* ; বহু দিন হইল।

sўn-ĕc′-dŏ′-chē, *n.* A rhetorical figure by which the whole of a thing is put for a part, or a part for the whole ; বাক্যালঙ্কার বিশেষ, উপলক্ষণ (সাঃ দঃ)। [ইহাতে কোন বস্তুর অংশ বুঝাইতে সমগ্র বস্তু কিম্বা সমগ্র বস্তু বুঝাইতে সেই বস্তুর অংশ ব্যবহৃত হয়। (যথা, 30 *sails* for 30 *ships*)। **–doch′-i-cal,** *adj.*

sўn′-ē-chism, *n.* That tendency of philosophic thought insisting on the idea of continuity as of prime importance in philosophy and especially on the necessity of hypothesis involving true continuity.—*C. S. Pearce* ; অখণ্ডতাবাদ (হিঃ কোঃ), অবিচ্ছিন্নতাবাদ (ঐ)।

sўn-ĕch-phō-nē′-sis, *n.* The contraction of two syllables into one ; দুই মাত্রার সংযোগ।

sўn-ei-dē′-sis (-ē-), *n.* Consciousness ; সদসদ্বিচারশক্তি (হিঃ কোঃ), সজ্ঞানতা (ঐ)।

sўn-ē′-mă, *n.* (*Bot.*) That part of the column of an orchid which represents the filaments of the stamens ; (উদ্ভিদ্‌বিদ্যা) অর্কিডের স্তম্ভের যে অংশ পুংকেশরের অংশুর প্রতিরূপ স্বরূপ, অর্কিডকেশর।

sўn-ĕr′-gi-dă, *n.* (*Bot.*) An accessory cell ; (উদ্ভিদ্‌বিদ্যা) সহকারীকোষ (সাঃ পঃ)।

sўn′-ĕr-gism, *n.* The doctrine that divine grace requires a correspondent action of the will to make it effectual ; ঈশ্বরের প্রসাদ অহৈতুক নহে—ইহা প্রাপ্তির জন্য স্বাধীন ইচ্ছা দ্বারা প্রণোদিত হইয়া মানবের তৎসহায়ক কার্য্য করা আবশ্যক—এই মতবাদ, ঈশ্বরপ্রণিধানযোগবাদ (হিঃ কোঃ)। **–gy,** *n.* Combined action ; কৃতিসমাহার (হিঃ কোঃ) তন্ত্রসমাহার (ঐ)।

sўn′-ē-sis, *n.* Violation of grammatical rule due to influence exerted by the sense ; অর্থের অনুরোধে ব্যাকরণের নিয়ম ভঙ্গ।

sўn-gē-nē′-si-ă, *n.* The nineteenth class of the Linnaean system of Botany whose stamens are united into a cylindrical form by anthers ; একপত্রোৎপাদক (সাঃ পঃ)।

sўn-gĕn′-ē-sis, *n.* **1.** The production of the embryo both from the male or female element ; স্ত্রী পুরুষ উভয়ের সংযোগে ভ্রূণোৎপদন। **2.** Sexual reproduction; স্ত্রী পুরুষের সংযোগে ভ্রূণোৎপদন।

syng′-na-thous, *adj.* (sĭn-nă-thŭs), Pertaining to the family of fishes having an elongated tubular snout and lacking the ventral and first dorsal fins ; লম্বিত চোঙ্গাকারতুণ্ডবিশিষ্ট এবং উদর ও পৃষ্ঠের পাখনাবিহীন মৎস্যবর্গসম্পর্কীয়।

sўn′-i-zē-sis, *n.* **1.** The contraction of two syllables or two vowels into one ; স্বরবর্ণ দ্বয় কিম্বা মাত্রাদ্বয়ের সন্ধি, স্বরসন্ধি। **2.** An obliteration or contraction of the pupil of the eye ; চক্ষুর তারার সঙ্কোচ বা অপহ্নব।

sўn-ŏc-rē-āte, *adj.* (Of the stipules) Uniting together on the opposite side of the stem from the leaf, and inclosing it in a sheath ; বর্ত্তিলগ্ন (সাঃ পঃ)।

sўn′-ŏd, *n.* **1.** A council or meeting of the ecclesiastics ; যাজকসংসদ্। **2.** A meeting, convention or council ; as, the *synod* of Whitby ; সভা, সংসদ্, পরিষৎ। **3.** (*Astron.*) A conjunction of two or more heavenly bodies in the same optical part of the heaven ; (জ্যোতির্বিজ্ঞান) আকাশের একই দর্শনযোগ্য অংশে দুই বা ততোধিক জ্যোতিষ্কের সংযোগ, যুতি। **–al, –od′-ic, –od′-i-cal,** *adjs.* **–od′-i-cal-ly,** *adv.* **Synodical month**—চন্দ্রযুতি (সূর্য্যঃবিঃ)। **Synodical period**—রবিযুতিকাল। **Synodical time**—যুতিকাল (ঐ)। **Synodical year**—যুতিবর্ষ (হিঃ কোঃ)।

sўn-oe′-cious,(-ē-shŭs), *adj.* (*Bot.*) Having male and female flowers on the same head ; (উদ্ভিদ্ বিদ্যা) একই শীর্ষে পুং এবং স্ত্রীপুষ্পবিশিষ্ট।

sўn′-ō-nўm, *n.* A word having the same significations as another ; একার্থবোধক শব্দ, সমার্থবোধক শব্দ, সমনাম, প্রতিশব্দ, একার্থ শব্দ, সমানার্থক যুগ্মশব্দ, পর্য্যায় শব্দ, অপরপর্য্যায়। **–nym′-i-ty,** *n.* **–on′-y-mous,** *adj.* Having the same meaning ; একার্থবোধক, একার্থক, সমার্থক, একার্থবাচক, তুল্যার্থক, সমানার্থক, সহার্থ। **–on′-y-mous-ly,** *adv.*

sўn-ŏn′-ў-măt′-ic, –ō-nўm′-ic, *adjs.* Pertaining to synonyms ; using synonyms ; সমনামসম্বন্ধীয় ; সমনামব্যবহারকারী।

sўn-ŏn′-ў-mў, *n.* **1.** The quality of being synonymous ; সমনামতা, একার্থবোধকতা। **2.** Study of synonyms ; সমনামতত্ত্ব। **3.** Synonyms collectively ; সমনামসংগ্রহ, পর্য্যায়সংগ্রহ, পর্য্যায়মালা। **4.** A treatise on synonyms ; সমনামসম্বন্ধীয় পুস্তক, সমনামমালা, সমনামসংগ্রহ। **5.** A figure by which synonymous words are used to amplify a discourse ; একপ্রকার অলঙ্কার—যদ্দ্বারা কোন প্রসঙ্গ বিস্তারের জন্য সমানার্থক শব্দসমূহ ব্যবহৃত হয়।

sўn-ŏp′-sis, *n.* Summary ; brief statement of topics; সারসংগ্রহ, সংক্ষেপ, সংক্ষিপ্তসার ; চুম্বক, সংক্ষিপ্ত বিবরণ।

sўn-ŏp′-tic, *adj.* & *n.* **1.** Affording synopsis or general view ; সর্ব্বদিক প্রদর্শী, সর্ব্ববিষয়ের সারমর্ম্ম প্রদর্শী। **2.** Of the synoptic gospels ; মথি, মার্ক, এবং লুক লিখিত সুসমাচার সম্বন্ধীয়। *Noun.* A writer of a synoptic gospel ; মথি, মার্ক বা লুক। **–tist,** *n.* Same as SYNOPTIC. *n.* **Synoptic gospels**—মথি, মার্ক এবং লুক লিখিত সুসমাচার।

sўn-ŏs-tē-ŏl′-ō-ġў, *n.* **1.** The science of the joints of the body ; অস্থিসন্ধিবিজ্ঞান। **2.** A treatise upon the joints of the body ; অস্থিসন্ধিসম্বন্ধীয় পুস্তক।

sўn-ŏs-tē-ō′-sis, sўn-ŏs-tō′-sis, *ns.* Same as ANCHYLOSIS (which see).

sўn-ŏs′-tō-ŏt-ō-mў *n.* **1** The science of the joints ; অস্থিসন্ধিবিজ্ঞান। **2.** Dissection of the joints ; অস্থিসন্ধিব্যবচ্ছেদ।

sўn-ō′-vi-ȧ, *n.* A fluid secreted in the joints of the body, and resembling the white of an egg ; শরীরের অস্থিসন্ধি হইতে ক্ষরিত ডিম্বের শ্বেতাংশবৎ একপ্রকার পদার্থ। **–al,** *adj.*

sўn-tăc′-tic, –ti-cal, *adj.* & *n.* Of, or pertaining to, or according to, the rules of syntax ; বাক্যবিন্যাসসম্বন্ধীয়, পদবিন্যাসের নিয়মানুযায়ী। *Noun.* (Only *syntactic*) ; (*Math.*) The doctrine of the ways of combining things ; (গণিতশাস্ত্র) সংযোজনতত্ত্ব। **–ti-cal-ly,** *adv.* **Syntactical unity**—একবাক্যত্ব (শ্রীঃ)।

sўn′-tăx, *n.* The due arrangement of words in sentences according to established usage ; a set of rules governing this ; পদবিন্যাস, শব্দবিন্যাস, বাক্যরচনা, বাক্যযোজন, বাক্যবিন্যাস ; পদবিন্যাসের নিয়মনিচয়, পদবিন্যাসপদ্ধতি।

sўn-tĕr′-ē-sis, *n.* **1.** (*Med.*, *Obs.*) Prophylactic treatment ; (অপ্রঃ) প্রতিষেধক চিকিৎসা। **2.** Conscience, regarded as the internal repository of the right or wrong ; কর্ত্তব্যোপদেশক অন্তরাত্মা, কর্ত্তব্যাগার অন্তরাত্মা (হিঃ কোঃ)।

sўn′-thĕ-sis, *n.* **1.** Composition or putting of two or more things together ; সংশ্লেষণ, সংযোগ, সংমিশ্রণ, সংযোজন, সঙ্কলন (হিঃ কোঃ), একীকরণ। **2.** (*Chem.*) The uniting of elements to form compounds ; (রসায়নশাস্ত্র) যৌগিক পদার্থ প্রস্তুতের জন্য রূঢ় পদার্থ সমূহের সংযোগ, সংশ্লেষণ। **3.** (*Log.*) The combination of separate elements of thought into a whole, as of a simple into compound or complex conceptions, species into genera, individual proposition into a system, and the like ; চিন্তার বিভিন্ন মৌলিক অংশের সংশ্লেষণ, সামান্যাধিকরণ (হিঃ কোঃ), সমন্বয় (ঐ), গাঁথনক্রিয়া (দ্বিজেন্দ্র), সংযোজনক্রিয়া, সংকলনা। **4.** The operation by which divided parts are united ; (অস্ত্রোপচারবিদ্যা) বিযুক্ত অংশ সমূহের সংযোজন। **5.** (*Philol.*) Combination of radical or inflectional element into inflected words ; মূলধাতুর সহিত কৃৎ প্রত্যয়াদি সংযোজনে শব্দগঠন। **–thet′-ic, –thet′-i-cal,** *adjs.* **1.** Pertaining to synthesis ; consisting of synthesis ; সংশ্লেষণসম্বন্ধীয়, সংশ্লেষিক ; সংশ্লেষণাত্মক, সংযোগাত্মক, সংযোজক, উপবৃংহক (হিঃ কোঃ) সাংশ্লেষিক (ঐ)। **2.** (*Chem.*) Formed by artificial synthesis ; as, *synthetic* indigo ; কৃত্রিম সংশ্লেষণ দ্বারা গঠিত, কৃত্রিম উপায়ে প্রস্তুত। **Synthetic philosophy**—হার্ব্বার্ট স্পেনসরের দর্শন। [হার্ব্বার্ট স্পেন্সর তদীয় দর্শনে সকল বিজ্ঞানের সমন্বয়সাধনের প্রয়াস করিয়াছিলেন বলিয়া এই নাম।] **Synthetic-types**—যে সকল জীবশ্রেণীতে সমঞ্জসভাবে কতিপয় জীবশ্রেণীর বিশেষত্ব লক্ষিত হয়—এবং যাহারা কেবল পরবর্ত্তীকালে স্বতন্ত্র জীবরূপে পরিলক্ষিত হইয়া থাকে।

sўn-tō-ni-zā′-tŏr, *n.* (In wireless telegraphy) An apparatus which regulates the reception of messages and prevents the "tapping" of them ; (অতারতাড়িতযন্ত্র) সংবাদগ্রহণ

নিয়মনের নিমিত্ত এবং সংবাদ সমূহ যাহাতে অন্যায় রকমে অন্য যন্ত্র দ্বারা গৃহীত হইতে না পারে তন্নিবারণের জন্য যন্ত্রবিশেষ, বার্ত্তানিয়ামক।

sȳn'-tō-nīze, *v. t.* To adjust transmitter and receiver so that they may work together ; বার্ত্তা-প্রেরক ও বার্ত্তাগ্রাহক যন্ত্রদ্বয় একরূপভাবে সন্নিবিষ্ট করা যাহাতে তাহারা একযোগে কার্য্য করিতে পারে।

sȳn-tō-nȳ, *n.* The agreement or tuning between the sending and receiving apparatuses of wireless telegraphy ; অতারতাড়িতবার্ত্তা প্রেরক ও গ্রাহক যন্ত্রের উভয়ের মধ্যে সঙ্গতিসাধন।

sȳ'-phêr, *v. t.* To join planks with overlapping edges leaving a flush surface ; একটীর কিনারা অপরটীর উপর রাখিয়া যাহাতে উপরিভাগ সমতল থাকে সেরূপ ভাবে জোড়া দেওয়া। **Sypher-joint**—ঐরূপ জোড়া।

sȳph'-ĭ-lĭs, *n.* A chronic infectious disease generally contracted during sexual intercourse ; গর্ম্মির ব্যারাম,উপদংশরোগ,ফিরঙ্গরোগ(ভাবঃ প্রঃ), ফিরঙ্গাময় (*ib.*),ফিরঙ্গব্যাধি (*ib.*) [ফিরঙ্গ-সংজ্ঞকে দেশে বাহুল্যেনৈব যদ্ভবেৎ। তস্মাৎ ফিরঙ্গ ইত্যুক্তো ব্যাধির্ব্যাধিবিশারদৈঃ॥ তস্য বিপ্রকৃষ্টং নিদানমাহ। গন্ধরোগঃ ফিরঙ্গোঽয়ং জায়তে দেহিনাং ধ্রুবম্। ফিরঙ্গিণোঽতিসংসর্গাৎ ফিরঙ্গিণ্যাঃপ্রসঙ্গতঃ॥ ব্যাধিরাগরুজো হ্যেষ দোষাণামত্র সংক্রমঃ। ভবেৎ তাল ক্ষয়েৎ তেষাংলক্ষণৈর্ভিষজাংবরঃ। ফিরঙ্গিণ্যাঃ প্রসঙ্গত ইতি বিশেষার্থম্॥ রূপমাহ। ফিরঙ্গস্ত্রিবিধো জ্ঞেয়ো বাহ্যাভ্যান্তরতস্তথা। বহিরন্তর্ভবশ্চাপি তেষাং লিঙ্গানি চ ব্রুবে॥ তত্র বাহ্যঃ ফিরঙ্গঃ স্যাদ্বি-স্ফোটসদৃশোঽল্পরুক্। স্ফুটিতো ব্রণবদ্বেদ্যঃ সুখসাধ্যোঽপি স স্মৃতঃ॥ সন্ধেশ্চাভ্যেন্তরঃ স স্যাদ্ভয়োর্লক্ষণৈর্যুতঃ। কষ্টদোঽতি চির-স্থায়ী কষ্টসাধ্যতমশ্চ সঃ॥ উপদ্রবান্ আহ। কার্শ্যং বলক্ষয়ো নাসাভঙ্গো বহ্নেশ্চ মন্দতা। অস্থিশোষোঽস্থিবক্রত্বং ফিরঙ্গোপদ্রবা অমী॥ সাধ্যত্বাদিকমাহ। বহির্ভবো ভবেৎ সাধ্যো নূতনো নিরুপদ্রবঃ। আভ্যন্তরস্তু কষ্টেন সাধ্যঃ স্যাদয়মাময়ঃ॥ বহিরন্তভবোজীর্ণঃক্ষীণ, স্যোপদ্রবৈর্যুতঃ। ব্যোধ্যোব্যাধিরসাধ্যোঽয়-মিত্যুচুর্মুনয়ঃ পুরা। (ভাবপ্রকাশ) হিন্দুগণ উপদংশরোগে পারদের ব্যবহার অবগত ছিলেন :—ফিরঙ্গসংজ্ঞকং রোগঃ রসঃ কর্পূরসংজ্ঞকঃ। অবশ্যং নাশয়েদেতদূচুঃ পূর্ব্বে চিকিৎসকাঃ॥ লিখ্যতে রসকর্পূর প্রাশনে বিধিরুত্তমঃ। অনেন বিধিনাখাদন্মুখে শোথং ন বিন্দতি।

*   *   *   *

পারদষ্টঙ্কমানঃ স্যাৎ খদিরষ্টঙ্কসংমিতঃ। আকারকরভশ্চাপি গ্রাহ্যষ্টঙ্কদ্বয়োন্মিতঃ॥] [ইয়ুরোপীয় প্রণালীমতেও ফিরঙ্গ রোগের চিকিৎসায় পারদ এবং আইয়োডাইড ব্যবহৃত হইয়া থাকে। কিন্তু সম্প্রতি Dr. Ehrlich নামক Vienna বাসী জনৈক চিকিৎসক জাপানের টোকিয়ো নগরীর অধিবাসী ডাক্তার Hatar সহযোগিতায় Salvarsan নামক ফিরঙ্গরোগের এক অত্যাশ্চর্য্য ঔষধ আবিষ্কার করিয়াছেন। এই ঔষধের সাঙ্কেতিক নাম '606'। ১৯১৩ খৃষ্টাব্দে Lord Sydenham এর সভাপতিত্বে ফিরঙ্গরোগ সম্বন্ধে অনুসন্ধানের জন্য এক কমিটি বসে। এই কমিটির অনুসন্ধানের ফলে জানা যায় যে, কেবল লণ্ডন নগরীতেই 80,000 ফিরঙ্গরোগাক্রান্ত ব্যক্তির বাস। ফিরঙ্গ রোগের আদ্য, মধ্য ও অন্ত্য এই তিনটী অবস্থা দৃষ্ট হয়। আদ্য অবস্থায় (Primary syphilis) জননেন্দ্রিয়ে ক্ষতাঙ্কুর এবং উরু-সন্ধিতে বাঘি প্রকাশ পায়। মধ্য অবস্থায় (Secondary syphilis) শরীরের স্থানে স্থানে সপূয গুটিকা দৃষ্ট হয় এবং গলিত ক্ষত উৎপন্ন হয়। অন্ত্য অবস্থায় (Tertiary syphilis) এই রোগের প্রভাব মস্তিষ্ক, অস্থি ও শরীরের পেশীসমূহে লক্ষিত হইয়া থাকে। See McDonagh, *Salvarsan in Syphilis* ; *System of Syphilis* ; Martindale, *Salvarsan ('606')* ; Lambkin, *Syphilis* ; Hutchinson, *Syphilis* ; Beddœ, *Syphilis* ; Ehrlich and Wechselmann, *Salvarsan* ; Bayly, *Clinical Pathology of Syphilis and Parasyphilis* ; Browning and Mackenzie, *Recent Methods in the Diagnosis and Treatment of Syphilis* ; Dalton, *Venereal Generative Diseases* ; M'Intosh and Fildes, *Syphilis from the Modern Standpoint*] **—lit'-ic,** *adj.* Pertaining to, or of the nature of, syphilis ; infected with syphilis ; ফিরঙ্গরোগসম্বন্ধীয়, ফিরঙ্গরোগাত্মক ; ফিরঙ্গরোগাক্রান্ত। **—li-za'-tion,** *n.* **—lize,** *v. t.* To inocutale with syphilitic virus ; উপদংশের বীজদ্বারা টিকা দেওয়া। **—lol'-o-gy,** *n.* Medical knowledge of syphilis ; উপদংশতত্ত্ব, ফিরঙ্গ-রোগতত্ত্ব। **—lous, —loid,** *adjs.*

sȳ'-phŏn, *n.* Incorrect for SIPHON (which see).

Sȳr'-ĭ-ăc, *adj.* & *n.* Pertaining to ancient Syria or its language ; প্রাচীন সিরিয়াপ্রদেশ সম্বন্ধীয়, প্রাচীন সিরিয়া প্রদেশের ভাষাসম্বন্ধীয়, সিরীয়। ***Noun.*** The language of ancient Syria ; প্রাচীন সিরিয়ার ভাষা। **—a-cism,** *n.* **Syriac versions**—সিরীয়বাসীর ভাষায় বাইবেলের অনুবাদ। [সিরীয় ভাষায় খৃষ্টীয় পঞ্চম ও ষষ্ঠ শতাব্দীতে বাইবেলের অনুবাদ হয়।]

Sȳr'-ĭ-ăn, *adj.* & *n.* Of, or pertaining to, Syria ; সিরিয়া সম্বন্ধীয়। ***Noun.*** A native of Syria ; সিরিয়ার অধিবাসী।

sȳ-rĭn'-gȧ (-rĭng-) *n.* A flowering shrub ; একপ্রকার গুল্ম।

sȳr'-inge (-ĭnj), *n.* & *v. t.* An instrument consisting of a tube and bulb acting in the manner of a pump, and serving to draw in any fluid, and then to expel it with force ; পিচকিরি, বস্তি (সাঃ পঃ)। ***Verb t.*** To inject or cleanse by means of a syringe ; পিচকিরি দ্বারা চর্ম্মের ভিতরে ক্ষেপণ করা, পিচকিরি দ্বারা পরিষ্কার করা। **—ful,** *adj.* **Hypodermic syringe**—চর্ম্মের ভিতরে ঔষধাদি প্রবিষ্ট করার জন্য সূচ্চ পিচকিরি, সূচল পিচকিরি।

sȳr-ĭn-gī'-tĭs, *n.* Inflammation of the Eustachian tube ; বায়ু চলাচলের জন্য মুখের পশ্চাদ্ভাগ হইতে কর্ণপটহ পর্য্যন্ত প্রসারিত সূক্ষ্মনলের প্রদাহ।

sy̆r-in-gŏt′-ŏ-mȳ (-ing-), *n.* The operation of cutting for fistula ; ভগন্দরে অস্ত্র-প্রয়োগ।

sy̆r′-inx, (-ingks), *n.* **1.** The Pandean or Pan's Pipes ; প্যান দেবতার মুরলী। **2.** The organ of the voice in birds ; পক্ষীর স্বরযন্ত্র। **3.** (*Arch.*) Something tubular or cylindrical ; a tunnel-shaped rock-cut tomb of ancient Egypt ; নলাকার বস্তু; প্রাচীন মিসরের পাষাণে কর্ত্তিত সুড়ঙ্গাকার সমাধি। **4.** (*Anat.*) Eustachian tube from the throat to the drum of ear ; (শারীরসংস্থান-বিদ্যা) বায়ু চলাচলের জন্য মুখের পশ্চাদ্ ভাগ হইতে কর্ণপটহ পর্য্যন্ত প্রসারিত নালী। **5.** Fistula ; ভগন্দর। **Sy-rin′-ge-al,** *adj.*

Sȳ′-rō–, Combining form of SYRIAN ; as in *Syro*-Arabian.

syr′-tis (sêr-), *n.* Quicksand ; বালুকা, চোরাবালি।

sy̆r′-ŭp, *n.* **1.** A solution of sugar ; চিনির শিরা। **2.** The juice of fruits, boiled with syrup ; সিরাপ, আসব, পানক (ঠাকুরঃ), সরবত, পানা, প্রপানক (ভাবঃ প্রঃ)। **3.** Molasses ; treacle ; গুড়, ঝোলাগুড় ; মাতগুড়। **–y,** *adj.* **Golden syrup**—একপ্রকার অনুজ্জ্বল বর্ণের আসব।

sy̆s-sar-cŏs′-is (-âr-), *n.* The connection of one bone with another by intervening muscle ; মধ্যবর্ত্তী মাংস-পেশীর সাহায্যে অস্থিসংযোগ, পেশীসংযোগ।

sy̆s-si′-ti-ȧ, *n. pl.* (*Gk. Antiq.*) The ancient Spartan custom of eating together in public the chief meal of the day ; প্রাচীন স্পার্টানগরীর নগর-বাসিগণের একত্র মধ্যাহ্নভোজনের প্রথা।

sy̆s-tal′-tic, *adj.* Capable of alternately contracting or dilating; পর্য্যায়ক্রমে সংকোচন ও প্রসারণশীল।

sy̆s′-tĕm, *n.* **1.** Any combination or assemblage of things adjusted into regular and connected whole ; শ্রেণী, পর্য্যায়। **2.** An assemblage of parts or organs in an animal body which are composed of the same tissue or are essentially necessary to the performance of some functions ; as, the nervous *system* ; চক্র, শৃঙ্খলা। **3.** A regular method or order ; as, to have no *system* in one's study ; ধারা, ক্রম, রীতি, প্রণালী (হিঃকোঃ)। **4.** An arranged scheme ; as, a *system* of philosophy : *system* of government ; ব্যবস্থা, সংস্থিতি, সংস্থান। **5.** The universe ; বিশ্বব্রহ্মাণ্ড। **–less,** *adj.* **Mountain system**—পর্ব্বতশ্রেণী। **Nervous system** — স্নায়ুচক্র। **Planetry system** — গ্রহসম্প্রদায় (হিঃ কোঃ)। **Solar system**—সৌরজগৎ।

sy̆s-tĕm-ăt′-ic, *adj.* **1.** Pertaining to system ; পদ্ধতিসম্পর্কীয়। **2.** Methodical ; প্রণালীবদ্ধ, রীতিসঙ্গত, সুব্যবস্থিত, শৃঙ্খলাবদ্ধ, পদ্ধতিবদ্ধ। **3.** Proceeding, or formed, according to system or regular method; প্রণালীসঙ্গত, পদ্ধতির অনুযায়ী। **–a-ti-za′-tion,** *n.* **–i-cal-ly,** *adv.* In a systematic manner ; সুব্যবস্থিতভাবে, সুশৃঙ্খলার সহিত, ব্যবস্থাপূর্ব্বক, যথাপদ্ধতি। **Sys′-tem-a-tism, Sys′-tem-a-tiz-er,** *ns.*

sy̆s′-tĕm-ȧ-tize, *v.t.* To reduce to a system or regular method ; পদ্ধতিবদ্ধ করা, রীত্যনুযায়ী করা, প্রণালীসঙ্গত করা, ব্যবস্থান্বিত করা, শৃঙ্খলাবদ্ধ করা।

sy̆s-tĕm′-ic, *adj.* (*Physiol.*) Of the bodily system ; শরীরযন্ত্রসম্বন্ধীয়। **–i-cal-ly,** *adv.*

sy̆s′-tŏ-lē, *n.* (*Gram.*) **1.** The shortening of a long syllable ; (ব্যাকরণ) দীর্ঘ মাত্রার সঙ্কোচ। **2.** The contraction of the heart or arteries for driving onward the blood and carrying on the circulation ; রক্ত-সঞ্চালনক্রিয়া নিবারণের জন্য ধমনী ও হৃৎপণ্ডের সঙ্কোচ, সঙ্কোচ (সাঃ পঃ) **–tol′-ic,** *adj.*

sy̆s′-ty̆le, *n.* With columns comparatively close together ; অপেক্ষাকৃত ঘনসন্নিবিষ্ট স্তম্ভরাজিবিশিষ্ট।

sy̆s′-ty̆-lous (-lŭs), *adj.* (*Bot*). With styles united ; (উদ্ভিদ্‌বিদ্যা) যুক্তগর্ভ-তন্তুবিশিষ্ট।

sy̆z′-y̆-gy̆, *n.* The conjunction or opposition of a planet with the sun or any two of the heavenly bodies ; (জ্যোতির্বিজ্ঞান) কোন গ্রহের সূর্য্য কিম্বা অপর জ্যোতিষ্কদ্বয়ের সহিত সংযোগ বা বিরোধ, গ্রহযুতি (হিঃ কোঃ), ষড়ভান্তর (ঐ)।

THE MODERN ANGLO-BENGALI DICTIONARY

THE MODERN ANGLO BENGALI DICTIONARY

(In 6 Volumes)

(Volume-2)

CHARUCHANDRA GUHA

Publications

KALPAZ PUBLICATIONS

DELHI - 1100052

THE MODERN ANGLO- BENGALI DICTIONARY

ISBN : 81-7835 - 484 - 5 (Set)
ISBN : 81 - 7835 - 487 - X (Vol.3)

Rs. 4500 (Set)

CHURACHANDRA GUHA

Published in 2007 in India by
Kalpaz Publications
C - 30, Satyawati Nagar,
Delhi - 110052
E-mail : kalpaz@hotmail.com

Laser Typesetting at : Tact Computer, Delhi
Printed at : Mehra Offset Press, Delhi

Volume - II

D

D, **1.** The fourth letter of the English alphabet; as a numeral, equivalent to 500; ইংরাজি বর্ণমালার চতুর্থ অক্ষর; ৫০০ এই সংখ্যা। **2.** (*Mus.*) The second note of the natural major-scale; (সঙ্গীত-শাস্ত্র) মুদারার 'রে'।

dăb, *v. t.* & *n.* **1.** To strike lightly; to tap; to peck; মৃদু মৃদু আঘাত করা; চাপড়ান; ঠোকর মারা। **2.** To press but not rub (surface) with sponge etc.; শোষক (স্পঞ্জ) প্রভৃতি দ্বারা চাপ দেওয়া, থুপ্‌থুপিয়ে দেওয়া। ***Noun.*** **1.** A brief application of sponge, handkerchief, etc. to a surface without rubbing; শোষক, রুমাল, প্রভৃতির চাপ প্রয়োগ। **2.** A slight but sudden blow; a tap; a peck; মৃদু মৃদু আঘাত, লঘুঘাত (আঃ বঃ); চাপড়; ঠোকর। **3.** A small lump of anything moist or slimy; moisture or colour applied gently with some soft substance; ভিজা অথবা কাদাটিয়া বস্তুর ক্ষুদ্র পিণ্ড; কোন প্রকার কোমল বস্তুর সাহায্যে আস্তে আস্তে চাপ দিয়া যে রঙ্গ বা তরল পদার্থ লাগানো হয়। **4.** A small flat fish common on the sandy coast of Britain; ইংলণ্ড দেশীয় মৎস্য বিশেষ (চাঁদা মাছের মত)। **5.** (*Colloq.*) An adept; a skilful person; গুণী; ওস্তাদ।

dăb'-bĕr, *n.* **1.** One who or that which dabs; মৃদু মৃদু আঘাতকারী, যে ব্যক্তি কোমল বস্তুর উপর আস্তে আস্তে চাপ দিয়া রঙ্গ প্রভৃতি লাগায়। **2.** A sort of pad for dabbling ink used by printers, stereotypers, etc.; মুদ্রাকর প্রভৃতি যে ক্ষুদ্র নরম গদি দ্বারা কালি লাগায়।

dăb'-ble, *v. t.* & *i.* To wet slightly; to moisten; to sprinkle; অল্প ভিজান; ঈষৎ আর্দ্র করা; সিক্ত করা। ***Verb i.*** **1.** To play or splash about in water or mud; to move the hands and feet about in water; পঙ্কক্রীড়া করা, জলক্রীড়া করা; জল বা কাদা ছিটকান। **2.** (*Fig.*) To practise anything in superficial or amateur-like manner; to meddle; as, the old painter *dabbles* in poetry too; (লক্ষণায়) উপর উপর কায করা, সখ করিয়া কোন কায করা; অনধিকার চর্চ্চা করা। **—bler,** *n.* **1.** One who plays in water or mud; যে ব্যক্তি জল বা পঙ্কে ক্রীড়া করে। **2.** A superficial meddler; as, a *dabbler* in poetry; যে ব্যক্তি উপর উপর ভাবে কোন বিষয় অনধিকার চর্চ্চা করে, পল্লবগ্রাহী পণ্ডিত, শাস্ত্রগণ্ড (আঃ বঃ)।

dăb'-chick (-chĭk), *n.* **1.** A small swimming bird of the diver family; ডুবারী (যোঃ)। **2.** (*Fig.*) A childish person; শিশু-স্বভাব ব্যক্তি।

da capo, (*It.*) (*Mus.*) A direction to repeat from the beginning; (সঙ্গীত-শাস্ত্র) আরম্ভে প্রত্যাবর্ত্তন।

dāce. *n.* A small fresh-water (river) fish; ইংলণ্ডদেশীয় নদীজাত ক্ষুদ্র মৎস্য বিশেষ (কুরচীবাটা মাছের মত)।

dachshund, *n.* [Ger. badger-dog] A long-bodied short-legged dog; দীর্ঘকায় হ্রস্বপদ কুকুর বিশেষ।

dă-coit', dă-koit', (-coȳt), *n.* [Hind. *dakait* gang-robber]. One of a gang of armed robbers in India and Burmah; ডাকাইত, দস্যু। **—coi-ty, —koi-ty,** *n.* Gang-robbery; দস্যুবৃত্তি, ডাকাইতি।

dăc'-tȳl, *n.* [*Gr. finger.*] A poetical foot consisting of one long syllable followed by two short ones, as the joints of a finger; কবিতার চরণ বিশেষ, ইহার প্রথম বাক্যাংশ গুরু এবং তৎপরবর্ত্তী বাক্যাংশদ্বয় লঘু হইয়া থাকে, ভ গণ (মঃ ইঃ)। **—tyl'-ic,** *adj.* & *n.* Relating to or consisting chiefly of dactyls; উক্ত প্রকার কবিতার চরণ সম্বন্ধীয় বা বিশিষ্ট। (*Noun*) (usually *pl.*) Dactylic verses; উক্ত প্রকার চরণ-বিশিষ্ট কবিতা।

dăc-tȳl-ŏl'-ō-ġȳ, *n.* The art or science of the communication of ideas by means of motions of

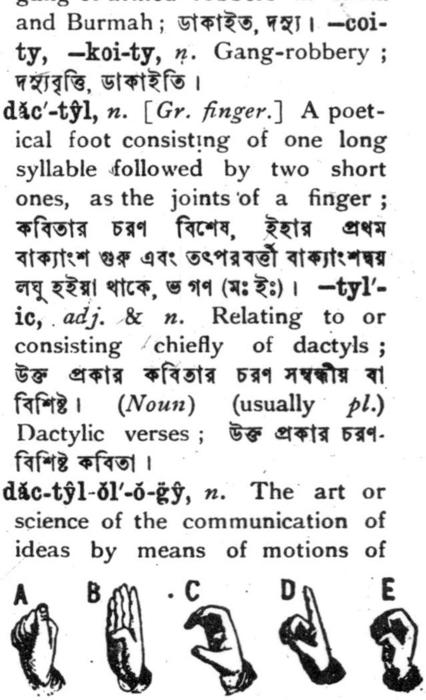

Dactylology.

the fingers or hands, like the deaf and dumb; করাঙ্গুলীর সাহায্যে মনোভাব প্রকাশের বিদ্যা, অঙ্গুলিভাষা (আঃ বঃ)।

dăd, dă, dă'-dă, dăd'-dȳ, *ns.* (*Colloq.*) A child's pet name for father; বাবা, তাত। **Daddy-long-legs** — The crane-fly; এক-শ্রেণীর কীট।

dăd'-dle, *v. t.* To walk in an unsteady manner, as a child or very old person; to toddle; শিশু

বা বৃদ্ধবৎ টলিয়া টলিয়া চলা ; দুর্ব্বলপদে টলিতে টলিতে চলা।

dā'-dō, *n.* **1.** (*Arch.*) That part of a pedestal between the base and the cornice ; (স্থপতি-বিজ্ঞান) তলপত্তন হইতে প্রস্তরাগ্রের (আলিসার) মধ্যবর্ত্তী উপপীঠের (স্তম্ভের পাদপীঠের) অংশ, কণ্ঠ (রাঃ রাঃ)। **2.** The lower few feet of the walls in rooms when faced with wood or coloured differently from the upper part ; কাষ্ঠফলকাচ্ছাদিত অথবা উপরিভাগ হইতে ভিন্নরূপে বিরঞ্জিত কক্ষ প্রাচীরের নিম্নভাগবর্ত্তী পাঁচ ছয় ফিট পরিমিত স্থান।

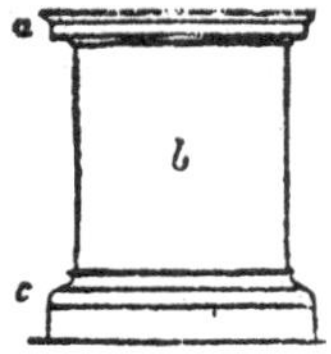

Dado

dæd'-āl (dĕd-), *adj.* **1.** Variegated ; curiously or ingeniously worked ; mazy ; বিচিত্র, চিত্রবিচিত্র ; বিচিত্র কারুকার্য্যখচিত ; গোলক ধাঁধাবৎ। **2.** Skilful ; ingenious ; inventive ; চতুর; প্রতিভাসম্পন্ন; উদ্ভাবনপটু। **3.** Manifold; complex ; বহু-গুণিত ; জটিল।

Dæ-dā'-li-ăn (dē-), *adj.* **1.** In the manner of Dædalus, the Greek artificer ; গ্রীকশিল্পী ডিডেলাসের অনুরূপ। [ডিডেলাস্ ক্রীট দ্বীপাধিপতি Minos এর জন্য সুবিখ্যাত গোলক-ধাঁধা রচনা করেন ; অবশেষে রাজকোপে পতিত হইয়া কৃত্রিম পক্ষের সাহায্যে আকাশপথে ইটালিদেশে পলায়ন করেন।] **2.** Intricate ; maze-like ; labyrinthine ; জটিল, গহন ; আঁকাবাঁকা ; গোলকধাঁধাবৎ।

dăff, *v. t* To put aside ; to waive ; এক পাশে ফেলিয়া রাখা ; দাবী ছাড়িয়া দেওয়া।

dăf'-fŏd-il, *n.* The popular name of a British plant with yellow bell-shaped flower, (also *daffodilly, daffadowndilly*) ; ইংলণ্ড-দেশীয় পীতবর্ণ পুষ্পবিশেষ।

dăft, *adj.* Foolish ; insane ; reckless ; crazy ; (applied to persons and things) ; as, he was a *daft* dog : let us think no more of this *daft* business ; অকাট-মূর্খ ; নির্ব্বোধ, মূঢ় ; বে-পরওয়া ; ক্ষেপা ; মাথা-পাগলা। **—ly,** *adv.* **—ness,** *n.*S

dăg'-ger (-êr), *n.* **1.** A short sharp-pointed two-edged weapon, used for stabbing ; ছোরা, ছুরিকা, কট্টারিকা (রাঃ তঃ), কৃপাণী (কাদঃ), অসিপুত্রিকা ; **2.** (*Print.*) A mark of reference in the form of a dagger, thus (†), the double dagger being another ; (মুদ্রণ) ছুরিকাচিহ্ন (†), দ্বিগুণিতছুরিকা-চিহ্ন (‡)। **Dagger-knife**—A weapon capable of being used either as a knife or as a dagger ; কাটারী। **To be at daggers drawn with each other**—To be on the point of fighting with each other ; to be on openly hostile terms ; পরস্পরের প্রতি খড়্গহস্ত হওয়া ;- আদাকাঁচকলা সম্বন্ধ হওয়া, পরস্পর দাকুমড়া সম্বন্ধ হওয়া। **To look, speak daggers**—To look, speak with great fierceness and animosity ; কটমট করিয়া চাওয়া, চোখা চোখা কথা বলা, বাক্যবাণে বিদ্ধ করা।

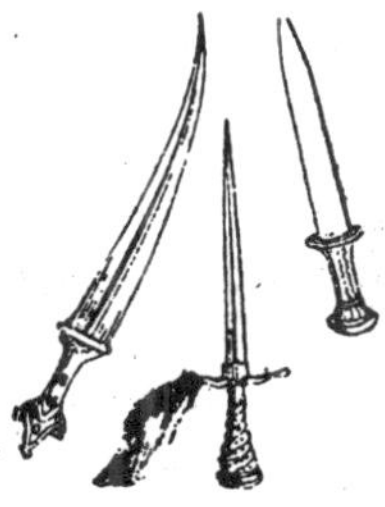

Dagger.

dăg'-gle, *v. t.* & *i.* To drag or trail in mud or wet grass ; to befoul ; to dirty (as the lower end of a garment) ; ভিজা ঘাস বা কাদার উপর টানিয়া নেওয়া ; মলিন করা, নোংড়া করা, ময়লা করা ; বস্ত্রাঞ্চল কর্দ্দম-লিপ্ত করা। *Verb i.* To run through wet or mire ; কাঁদা বা ভিজা জায়গার উপর দিয়া দৌড়িয়া চলা। **—gled,** *adj.* Having the lower ends of garment defiled with mud ; bemired ; কর্দ্দম-লিপ্তবস্ত্রাঞ্চল ; পঙ্ককলঙ্কিত।

dă'-gō-bă, *n.* A monumental structure containing relics of Buddha or some Buddhist saints ; (the word *Pagoda* appears to be a corruption of the term) ; বৌদ্ধস্তূপ।

Dā'-gŏn, *n.* The national god of the Philistines represented with upper part of a man and the tail of a fish ; পেলেষ্টাইন-বাসী ফিলিষ্টাইনগণের জাতীয় দেবতা,—এই দেবতার দেহের উপরিভাগ মানবাকার এবং নিম্নার্দ্ধ মৎস্যাকার ছিল (মৎস্যাবতারের অনুরূপ)।

dă-guer-rē'-ō-tȳpe (-jĕr), *n.* An early photographic process ; a portrait taken by that process ; আলোকচিত্র গ্রহণের প্রাচীন প্রণালীবিশেষ ; উক্ত উপায়ে গৃহীত আলোকচিত্র।

dă-hă-bi'-eh (bē-ā), *n.* A kind of boat in use on the Nile ; নীল নদে চলাচলের জন্য ব্যবহৃত তরণী বিশেষ। (Also DAHABEEAH, DAHABIYEH.)

dahl'-i-ă (dāl-), *n.* **1.** A genus of garden plants with large flowers ; বৃহৎ পুষ্পপ্রসূ উদ্যানজাত গুল্ম। **2.** A beautiful carmine ; a shade of red ; একপ্রকার সুদৃশ্য রক্তবর্ণ ; এক ছোব্ লালরঙ।

dail'-ȳ (dāl-), *adj., adv.* & *n.* Happening, appearing, recurring, done, every day ; necessary for each day ; as, *daily* labour : *daily* allowance : give us our *daily* bread ; দৈনিক, দৈবসিক, প্রাত্যহিক, আহ্নিক, নিত্যনৈমিত্তিক ; দৈনন্দিন। *Adv.* Every day ; day by day ; constantly ; often ; as, a thing happens *daily* ; প্রত্যহ, প্রতিদিন ; দিন দিন, রোজ রোজ, অহরহঃ ; সতত, সর্ব্বদা, অনুদিন ; প্রায়শঃ। *Noun.* A newspaper published daily ; (*pl. dailies*) ; দৈনিক পত্রিকা দৈনিক।

daim'-i-ō (dīm-), *n.* The official title of a class of feudal lords in Japan ; জাপানদেশীয় সামন্ত ভূস্বামি-গণের সরকারী উপাধি।

daint'-ŷ (dānt-), *adj.* & *n.* **1.** Delicious; of exquisite taste; as, *dainty* food; সুরস, সুস্বাদু; মুখরোচক, রসনাতৃপ্তিকর, উপাদেয়। **2.** Of delicate taste and sensibility; fastidious; as, a *dainty* taste: a *dainty* people; সুরুচি-সম্পন্ন; অতিরিক্ত সূক্ষ্মবিচারী। **3.** Pretty; of delicate beauty; tender; as, *dainty* hands or limbs: I would be a girdle about her *dainty* waist; চারু; রুচির, সুকুমার, ললিত, হৃদ্য; মেদুর, পেলব, কোমল। ***Noun.*** Something nice and delicate to the taste; that which is exquisitely delicious; অতিসুস্বাদু বস্তু, বিশিষ্টভোজন (আঃ বঃ), উপাদেয় খাদ্যসামগ্রী; পরম কমনীয় বস্তু, অতিরুচির বস্তু। **—i-ly,** *adv.* **—i-ness,** *n.* **1.** Delicacy; softness; elegance; লালিত্য; সৌকুমার্য্য; শোভা। **2.** Nicety in taste; fastidiousness; সূক্ষ্মরুচিতা; উৎকট-রুচিত্ব। **Dainty maketh dearth** — চোর বাছতে বাছতে গা উজাড়।

dair'-ŷ (dâr-), *n.* & *adj.* **1.** A room or building for keeping milk and cream and making butter etc.; দুগ্ধমন্থনশালা, দুগ্ধমন্থনালয়, গব্যাগৃহ (কেভিঃ), দুগ্ধশালা। **2.** A shop for milk, butter, etc.; দুগ্ধ, মাখন প্রভৃতির দোকান। **Dairy-farm** — যে কৃষিক্ষেত্রের অধিকাংশ গোচারণের জন্য রক্ষিত হয়, গোষ্ঠক্ষেত্র। **Dairy-maid**—গোয়ালিনী, আহিরিণী, গোপী, গোপিকা, বল্লবী, আভীরী। **Dairy-man**—গোষ্ঠক্ষেত্র-স্বামী; গোপ, গোয়াল, ঘোষ, দুগ্ধব্যবসায়ী।

dā'-is, *n.* **1.** A raised platform in any hall or room, on which the chief personages sit in any meeting; সভাস্থলে যে মঞ্চোপরি গণ্যমান্য ব্যক্তিগণ উপবেশন করেন, সভামঞ্চ। **2.** A raised floor at the upper end of the dining hall, where the high table stood; canopy with its seat at the high-table; মধ্যাহ্ন ভোজনকক্ষের অগ্রপ্রান্তস্থ উত্তোলিত গৃহতল—যদুপরি শ্রেষ্ঠব্যক্তিগণের উপবেশনের জন্য কাষ্ঠমঞ্চ স্থাপিত হইত; গণ্যমান্য ব্যক্তিগণের উপবেশন-মঞ্চের উপরিস্থ চন্দ্রাতপ এবং তন্নিম্নস্থ আসন।

dais'-ŷ (dāz-), *n.* **1.** A small European wild and garden flower; ইয়ুরোপদেশীয় পুষ্পবিশেষ। **2.** (*Slang*) A first-rate specimen of anything; (ইতরভাষায়) সেরা জিনিষ, উম্‌দা জিনিষ।

Flower of comon daisy.

Daisy-chain— উক্ত পুষ্পের মালা। **Daisy-cutter**—A trotting horse, *i. e.* one lifting feet very little; যে ঘোড়া কদমে চলে। (*Cricket*) A ball skimmed along the ground; (ক্রীকেট খেলায়) যে কন্দুক কেবলমাত্র ভূমি স্পর্শ করিয়া যায়।

dăk, *n.* See DAWK.

dalbergia latifolia — শ্বেতশাল (রেলঃ)।

dalbergia sissoo—শিশুগাছ।

dāle, *n.* A valley or low-lying place between two hills; উপত্যকা, দরী (মঃ ইঃ), কন্দর (ঐ)। **Dalesman** — উপত্যকাবাসী। (বিশেষভাবে ইংলণ্ডের উত্তরভাগস্থিত কতিপয় জেলাসম্পর্কে প্রযুক্ত হয়।)

dăl'-lŷ, *v. i.* **1.** To amuse oneself; to make sport; আত্মবিনোদন করা; ক্রীড়া কৌতুক করা, রঙ্গরস করা। **2.** To toy amorously (*with*); to exchange caresses with; to coquet with temptations, etc.; কেলি করা; চুম্বন, আলিঙ্গনাদি বিনিময় করা, কামক্রীড়া করা; হাবভাব বিলাসাদি প্রদর্শন করা। **3.** To be evasive with person or business; এড়ান, টালবাহানা করা। **4.** To idle; to loiter; to delay; আলস্যে কালক্ষেপ করা; হাসিয়া খেলিয়া সময় ক্ষেপ করা; গড়িমসি করা। **—liance,** *n.* **1.** The interchange of caresses; কামবিহার, স্মরকেলি (উজ্জ্বলঃ), কেলি (বাৎস্যঃ) কামকেলি, বিলাস (মঃ উঃ)। **2.** Conjugal conversation; sexual intercourse; প্রেমালাপ; রমণ, সুরত, বিহার। **3.** Delay; procrastination; as, my business cannot brook this *dalliance*; বিলম্ব, কালযাপন (মঃ ইঃ), কালক্ষয়; দীর্ঘসূত্রতা।

Dăl-mā'-tian (dog), (-shĭ-ăn), *n.* The spotted dog kept to run with carriages resembling the pointer in shape; এক প্রকার কুক্কুর। [From Dalmatia, a strip of Austrian territory along the Adriatic.]

dăl-măt'-ic, *n.* A wide-sleeved loose long vestment with slit sides worn by deacons and bishops on some occasions and by king and emperors especially at coronation; প্রশস্ত আস্তিনবিশিষ্ট পার্শ্বদেশে কর্ত্তিত শ্লথ পরিচ্ছদ বিশেষ,—যাহা খৃষ্টীয় ধর্ম্মাচার্য্য ও উপাচার্য্যগণ সময় সময় এবং রাজা ও সম্রাটগণ বিশেষভাবে অভিষেককালে পরিধান করিয়া থাকেন।

dal segno, [*It.* from the sign] (*Mus.*) A direction to repeat from the point indicated; (সঙ্গীত শাস্ত্র) নির্দ্দিষ্ট-স্থান হইতে আরম্ভ করিবার নির্দেশ।

dal'-tŏn-ism, *n.* Colour-blindness, esp. inability to distinguish green from red; [From Dalton, the chemist, so affected] বর্ণান্ধতা, বিশেষতঃ সবুজ এবং রক্তবর্ণ প্রভেদকরণে অসমর্থতা।

dăm, *n.* [A form of *dame*) A mother, used of beasts; মাতা, ধাড়ী।

dăm, *n.* & *v. t.* **1.** A barrier constructed to hold back water and raise its level, to form a reservoir, or to prevent flooding; a causeway; জলরোধার্থ বাঁধ বা আলি, সেতুবন্ধন, জলবন্ধক; জাঙ্গাল। **2.** A body of water so hemmed in; বাঁধ দ্বারা অবরুদ্ধ জলরাশি। ***Verb t.*** **1.** To furnish or confine with dam, (usu. *up*) ; বাঁধ দেওয়া, বাঁধ দ্বারা অবরুদ্ধ করা। 2. To block up ; to obstruct ; (*lit.* & *fig.*) ; আটক করা ; অবরোধ করা ; (শব্দানুযায়ী এবং লক্ষণায়)।

dăm'-āge, *n.* & *v. t.* 1. Any injury or harm to person, property or reputation ; mischief ; ক্ষতি, লোকসান ; অনিষ্ট, অপচয় (মঃ ইঃ), হানি, অপকার। 2. (*Law—pl.*) The sum of money claimed or adjudged in compensation for loss or injury ; (আইন) ক্ষতিপূরণ, খেসারৎ, উদয় (আঃ বঃ)। 3. (*Colloq.*) The cost of anything ; as, what is the *damage* ? (চলিত ভাষায়) দাম। ***Verb t.*** 1. To injure a thing so as to diminish its value ; ক্ষতি করা, হানি করা, অপকৃষ্ট বা খারাপ করা। 2. To detract from reputation of person etc. ; as, to *damage* the government : a *damaging* admission ; মানহানি করা, ক্ষতি বা সম্ভ্রম নষ্ট করা। **—a-ble,** *adj.*

dăm'-ăs-cēne, *v. t.* To ornament metal with inlaid gold and silver ; স্বর্ণ ও রজত পত্র দ্বারা লৌহ, ইস্পাত প্রভৃতি ধাতু খচিত করা (যেমন অসিফলক, পিস্তল প্রভৃতি করা হয়)।

dăm'-ăsk, *n., adj.* & *v. t.* 1. A silk stuff having some parts raised above the ground representing flowers and other figures ; বুটিদার রেশমী বস্ত্র, উন্নত পুষ্পাদি বা কারুকার্য্য খচিত চিত্রদুকূল বিশেষ। 2. A twilled table-linen with woven designs shown by reflection of light ; একপ্রকার টের্চ্চা-বুনা মেজ আচ্ছাদন বস্ত্র, — ইহাতে প্রতিবিম্বিত আলোক দ্বারা দর্শনীয় বিভিন্ন প্রকার নমুনা বুনট করা হয়। 3. The wavy pattern on the surface of Damascus steel ; ডামাস্কাস নগরীতে প্রস্তুত ইস্পাতের উপরিস্থ তরঙ্গাকার নমুনা। ***Adj.*** 1. Of the colour of the Damask-rose ; blush-coloured ; ডামাস্কাস গোলাবের বর্ণ ; লজ্জারুণ বর্ণ। 2. Made of or resembling the Damask silk, linen or steel ; ডামাস্কাসনগরীতে প্রস্তুত রেসম, ক্ষৌমবস্ত্র বা ইস্পাতের অনুরূপ বা তন্নির্ম্মিত ***Verb t.*** 1. To weave with richly figured design ; to ornament with variegated pattern as steel-work ; বস্ত্রাদিতে ফুল বা বুটি তোলা ; নানারূপ ধাতুময় কারুকার্য্য দ্বারা তরবারি প্রভৃতি খচিত করা। 2. To make (cheek etc.) red or blush-coloured ; as, Cathie's peach-like cheek was *damasked* by heat and laughter ; লজ্জারুণিত করা, সরমরক্তিম করা। **Damask plum**—একপ্রকার ক্ষুদ্র কাল জাম। **Damask-rose**—ডামাস্কাস নগরীজাত রক্তবর্ণ অতি-সুরভি সুবৃহৎ গোলাব, হেমপুষ্প (মঃ ইঃ)।

dăm'-as-keen, (-kēn), *v. t.* Same as DAMASCENE.

dāme, *n.* 1. A lady of rank ; সম্ভ্রান্ত মহিলা। 2. Mistress of a house ; গৃহকর্ত্রী, পুরন্ধ্রী, গৃহিণী। 3. An elderly woman ; বর্ষীয়সী স্ত্রী।

dăm'-mêr, *n.* An East Indian gum or resin ; ডামর (যোঃ) যক্ষ-ধূপ (বেলঃ), রাল (ঐ),।

dămn (dăm), *v. t.* 1. To condemn ; to censure ; দোষী করা ; নিন্দা করা। 2. To doom to hell ; to consign to perdition ; চিরনরকবাস নির্দ্দিষ্ট করা ; জাহান্নমে দেওয়া, অধঃপাতে দেওয়া, নরকে দেওয়া। 3. To condemn (a literary work, usually a play) as failure ; "A comedy by Mr. Hugh Kelly, which in the playhouse phrase, was *damned* ;" (কোন গ্রন্থ—সাধারণতঃ নাটক) অসার বলিয়া ধিক্কৃত করা।.

dăm'-nă-ble, *adj.* 1. Subject to, or deserving, damanation; অনন্ত নরক-বাস-যোগ্য। 2. Hateful; odious ; ঘৃণ্য, গর্হণীয় ; বীভৎস, নারকীয়। **—ness,** *n.*

dăm-nā'-tion, *n.* & *interj.* 1. Damning of play or literary work ; condemnation to everlasting punishment in the future state or the punishment itself ; কোন নাটক বা গ্রন্থ নিন্দন ; অনন্ত-নরক বাসের দণ্ডপ্রদান, অনন্ত নরকদণ্ড, অধোগতি, বিনিপাত (আঃ বঃ)। 2. A sin deserving of, or exposing one to, everlasting punishment ; অনন্ত নরকবাসাই পাপকার্য্য, মহাপাপ। ***Interj.*** May damnation take a person or a thing ; জাহান্নমে যাউক, অধঃপাতে যাউক।

dăm-nă-tŏ-rȳ, *adj.* Condemnatory ; as, *damnatory* invectives ; নিন্দাত্মক, তিরস্কারগর্ভ।

damned (dămd), *adj.* & *adv.* 1. Sentenced to everlasting punishment ; অনন্তনরকদণ্ডে দণ্ডিত। 2. Hateful ; infernal ; ঘৃণ্য, জুগুপ্সিত ; নারকীয়। 3. Used to express strong approbation or disapprobation and also as an intensive adverb = very; exceedingly (now usually printed d—d) ; as, *damned* fine ; a d—d lie : d—d hot (exceedingly hot) ; অতি প্রশংসা বা নিন্দাসূচনার্থ ব্যবহৃত হয় ; (ক্রিয়া-বিশেষণরূপে) অত্যন্ত ; নিতান্ত। **The damned** — The souls in hell ; নরকবাসিগণ।

dăm'-ni-fȳ, *v. t.* (*Legal*) To cause injury to ; (আইন) ক্ষতি করা **—fi-ca'-tion,** *n.*

damn'-ing (dăm-nĭng), *adj.* & *n.* **Damning evidence** —যে প্রমাণের বলে দণ্ড বিধান করা যাইতে পারে।

dam-no-sa-here-di-tas, [*L.*] *n.* Inheritance that brings more burden than profit ; যে পৈত্রিক সম্পত্তি লাভ-জনক না হইয়া ভারস্বরূপ হইয়া দাঁড়ায়।

Dăm'-ŏ-clēs, *n.* A flatterer in the court of Dionysius I. of Syracuse ; সিরাকোজরাজ ডাইও-নিসিয়াস্‌এর রাজসভাস্থ চাটুকার বিশেষ। **Damocles' sword, Sword of Damocles**—Imminent danger in the midst of prosperity ; সুখসমৃদ্ধির মধ্যে আসন্ন বিপদ। [চাটুকার ডেমোক্লিস

সিরাকোজ নৃপতির সুখসৌভাগ্যের উচ্চ প্রশংসা করাতে রাজা ডেমোক্লিজের সম্মুখে রাজ-ভোগ্য চর্ব্ব্য, চোষ্য, লেহ্য, পেয়াদি খাদ্যসামগ্রী স্থাপন করত, তদীয় মস্তকোপরি কেশ দ্বারা দোদুল্যমান একটি খড়্গ স্থাপন করেন। এই ঘটনা হইতে রাজ্যভোগ কিরূপ বিপজ্জনক এই শিক্ষা চিরদিনের তরে ডেমোক্লিজের মনোমধ্যে মুদ্রিত হইল।]

Dā'-mŏn & Fȳ'-thi'-ăs, *adj.* & *n.* As of devoted friends; হরিহর আত্মা। ***Noun.*** Inseparable friends; অন্তরঙ্গ বন্ধুযুগল। [ডেমন ও পাইথিয়াস্ নামক দুইজন অন্তরঙ্গ বন্ধু সিরাকোজ নগরে বাস করিতেন। সিরাকোজরাজ ডেমনকে কোন অপরাধে প্রাণদণ্ডে দণ্ডিত করেন। ডেমন তদীয় বন্ধু পাইথিয়াসকে প্রতিভূ রাখিয়া বৈষয়িক কার্য্যের বন্দোবস্তের জন্য গৃহে গমন করেন। ডেমনের প্রত্যাগমনে বিলম্ব হওয়ায় পাইথিয়াস্ বধ্যভূমিতে নীত হইয়াছেন, এমন সময়ে ডেমন ঊর্দ্ধশ্বাসে আসিয়া উপনীত হইলেন। রাজা এই অকপট বন্ধুত্বের দৃশ্যদর্শনে অতীব অভিভূত হইয়া ডেমনের অপরাধ মার্জ্জনা করিলেন।]

dămp, *adj., n., v. t.* & *i.* Slightly wet; humid; স্যাঁতসেঁতে; ঈষৎ আর্দ্র, সার্দ্র। ***Noun.*** 1. Moisture; humidity; ঈষৎ আর্দ্রতা; সজলতা। 2. Dejection; discouragement; "This news struck a *damp* into the hearts of the Castilians;" বিষাদ; মনোভঙ্গ, নিরুৎসাহ, চিত্তগ্লানি। ***Verb t.*** 1. To choke; to stifle; to extinguish; রোধ করা; চাপিয়া ফেলা; নির্ব্বাপিত করা। 2. (*Mus.*) To stop vibration of a string or the like; (সঙ্গীত-শাস্ত্র) বাদ্যযন্ত্রের তন্ত্রী প্রভৃতির কম্পন বন্ধ করা। 3. To depress; to deject; as, the failure of the enterprise *damped* the spirit of the soldiers; নিরুৎসাহ করা; বিষণ্ণ করা, দমিয়া দেওয়া। 4. To moisten; as, to *damp* cloth; আর্দ্র করা। ***Verb i.*** To become humid; আর্দ্র হওয়া। **Damp'-en,** *v. t.* & *i.* **Damp'-ish,** *adj.* **Damp'-ly,** *adv.* **Damp'-ness,** *n.* **To damp down a fire** or **furnace**—To cover with small coal, ashes, or coke, to prevent its going out; কয়লা, ছাই প্রভৃতি দ্বারা ঢাকিয়া চুল্লী বা আগুন জিয়াইয়া রাখা।

dămp'-er, *n.* 1. A person or thing that depresses; নিরুৎসাহকারী, অবসাদক। 2. A valve or movable plate in the flue or other part of a stove, furnace, etc. used to control combustion; চুল্লী, অগ্নিকুণ্ড প্রভৃতির জ্বলন-ক্রিয়া নিয়ামক গতিশীল ধাতুফলক বিশেষ। 3. (*Mus.*) A part of a pianoforte by which the sound is deadened; (সঙ্গীত-শাস্ত্র) পিয়ানোফোর্টের অংশ বিশেষ,—যদ্দ্বারা যন্ত্রের ধ্বনি মন্দীভূত হয়। 4. A contrivance for wetting paper, stamps, etc.; কাগজ, টিকেট, প্রভৃতি আর্দ্র করার জন্য যন্ত্র-বিশেষ।

dăm'-sĕl, *n.* A young unmarried woman; অনূঢ়া যুবতী, তরুণী, বালা, কন্যা, কুমারী।

dăm'-son (-zn), *n.* A small black plum; এক প্রকার ক্ষুদ্র কাল জাম।

dance (dăns), *n., v. t.* & *i.* 1. The movement of one or more persons with measured steps to music; নৃত্য, নাচ, নটন, লাস্য। 2. A ball; বল নাচ। 3. (*Mus.*) A tune by which a dancing is regulated; (সঙ্গীত-শাস্ত্র) নাচের সুর। 4. A dancing party; "When asked to a party, a *dance* or a dinner;" নৃত্যসম্মিলনী। ***Verb t.*** 1. To take part in as a dancer; as, to *dance* a polka; নৃত্য করা। 2. To dandle; "Many a time he *danced* thee on his knee; হাঁটুর উপর তুলিয়া নাচান। ***Verb i.*** To move with measured steps to music; নাচা, নৃত্য করা। **Dancing girl**— A professional dancer; নর্ত্তকী, দেবদাসী (বেলঃ), খেমটাওয়ালী। **Dancing hall**—নাটমন্দির। **Dancing master**—নৃত্যশিক্ষক, নৃত্যাচার্য্য। **Dance of Death** or **of Macabre**—ইয়ুরোপীয় মধ্যযুগের সর্ব্বধ্বংসী কালের চিত্র, মহাকালের তাণ্ডব নৃত্য। **St. Vitus's dance**—Disorder chiefly in children with convulsive involuntary movements; তাণ্ডবরোগ (হঃ চঃ)। **Wild dance**—তাণ্ডব। **To dance and pay the piper**—To take pains personally and contribute to the cost as well; কোন বিষয়ে নিজে খাটা, অধিকন্তু ব্যয়ভার বহন করা। **To dance attendance upon**—হাঁটাহাঁটি করা। **To dance on a rope, To dance upon nothing**—To be hanged; ফাঁসি-কাষ্ঠে ঝুলা। **To dance to one's tune** or **pipe**—To follow one's lead; কাহারও নেতৃত্বাধীনে চলা।

dănc'-ĕr, *n.* One who dances, esp. one who dances in public for money; নর্ত্তক, নর্ত্তয়িতা, লাসক। **Merry dancers**—Aurora borealis; মেরুজ্যোতিঃ।

dăn'-dē-lī-on (-ŭn), *n.* A common plant with a yellow flower and having leaves with jagged tooth-like edges; এক প্রকার পীত পুষ্প-প্রসূ বৃক্ষ, দুধাল (খোরী), কাণফুল (ঐ), সিংহতুণ্ড (আঃ বঃ), সিংহপর্ণী (মঃ ইঃ)।

dăn'-dêr, *n.* (*Colloq.* esp. in *U. S.*) Anger; indignation; (চলিতভাষায়, বিশেষতঃ মার্কিণযুক্তরাজ্যে) রাগ; গোসা। **To get one's dander up**—To grow angry; to make one angry; খাপ্পা হওয়া; খাপ্পা করা। **To raise a person's dander**—To put him in temper; কোন ব্যক্তিকে রাগাইয়া তোলা।

dăn'-dlē, *v. t.* To fondle or toss on the knee or in the arms as a baby; (শিশু প্রভৃতিকে) হাঁটুর উপর বা বাহুযুগলের মধ্যে তুলিয়া নাচান বা আদরসোহাগ করা।

dăn'-driff, dăn'-drŭff, *n.* A scarf on the head and beard that comes off in scales and particles ; মস্তকাদির এক প্রকার চর্ম্মরোগ, ইহাতে ক্ষুদ্র ক্ষুদ্র সাদা সাদা আঁইশ বা ভূষির ন্যায় উপত্বক উঠিয়া যায়, খুসকি, রুখি, দারুণ (আঃ বঃ), শিরোমল (মঃ ইঃ), মরামাস ।

dăn'-dȳ, *adj.* & *n.* Foppish ; সৌখীন, বাবুয়ানী । ***Noun.*** A person devoted to smartness, esp. of costumes ; a foppish person ; ফুলবাবু, সুবেশী (মঃ ইঃ) ; সৌখীন পুরুষ । **—di-fy,** *v. t.* To dress up as a dandy ; বাবুয়ানা করান । **—ish, —di-cal,** *adjs.* **—ism,** *n.* **Dandy-brush**—তিমি মাছের হাড় প্রভৃতি দ্বারা তৈয়ারী ঘোড়ার বুরুশ। **Dandy-cock**—এক প্রকার কুক্কুট ।

dăn'-dȳ, *n.* Same as DENGU. (which see.)

dăn-dȳ, *n.* A sloop-like vessel ; ক্ষুদ্র পোত বিশেষ ।

Dāne, *n.* A native of Denmark ; ডেন্‌মার্কের অধিবাসী । **Great Dane**—এক জাতীয় বলবান এবং হ্রস্বরোম কুক্কুর ।

dān'-gêr, *n.* **1.** Peril ; risk ; hazard ; exposure to any risk, injury or evil ; বিপদ্ ; আপদ্ ; দায়, সঙ্কট ; যেরূপ অরক্ষিত অবস্থায় অনায়াসে বিপৎপাত বা অনিষ্টাদি হইতে পারে । **2.** A thing that causes peril ; as, a *danger* to the peace of Europe ; বিপজ্জনক বিষয় । **—ous,** *adj.* **—ous-ly,** *adv.* **Danger-signal**—বিপৎ-সঙ্কেত ; বিশেষতঃ বাষ্পীয় শকটের সম্মুখে কোন প্রকার প্রতিবন্ধ আছে তৎসূচনার্থ রেলপথে যে সঙ্কেত ব্যবহৃত হয় । (সাধারণতঃ সঙ্কেতস্তম্ভের রক্তবর্ণে রঞ্জিত প্রসারিত বাহু বা লোহিতবর্ণ আলোক ।)

dan'-gle (dăngl), *v. t.* & *i.* **1.** To swing, as something suspended loosely ; ঝুলান, দোদুল্যমান করা, দোলান । **2.** To follow any one about ; কাহারো পাছে পাছে ঘুরিয়া বেড়ান । **3.** To hang (any one) on a gallows ; "This is evidence to *dangle* even an honester man than you ;" ফাঁসিকাঠে ঝুলান । ***Verb i.*** To be suspended and sway to and fro ; ঝুলা, দোদুল্যমান হওয়া, দোলায়িত হওয়া । **—gler,** *n.* One who dangles ; (applied particularly to men who hang about women) ; যে ব্যক্তি ঝুলে, স্ত্রীলোকের আঁচল-ধরা । **—gling,** *adj.* That dangles ; দোলায়মান, আঁচল-ধরা ।

Dăn'-iel (-yĕl), *n.* An upright judge ; a person of infallible wisdom ; ন্যায়নিষ্ঠ বিচারক ; অভ্রান্ত-বুদ্ধি ব্যক্তি । **A Daniel is come to judgement**—স্বয়ং ধর্ম্মরাজ বিচার করিতে আসিয়াছেন ।

Dān'-ish, *adj.* & *n.* Pertaining to Denmark or the Danes ; ডেন্‌মার্ক দেশ বা দিনেমার জাতি সম্বন্ধীয় । ***Noun.*** Language of Denmark ; দিনেমারদিগের ভাষা ।

dank (dăngk), *adj.* **1.** Oozy ; soaked ; আর্দ্র ; ভিজা । **2.** Unpleasantly or unwholesomely damp ; সেঁৎসেঁতে । **Dank'-ish,** *adj.* **Dank'-ish-ness,** *n.*

Dăn'-tē-ăn, *adj.* & *n.* Pertaining to the poet Dante or his writings ; ইতালির সুপ্রসিদ্ধ কবি দান্তে বা তদীয় রচনা সম্বন্ধীয় । ***Noun.*** A student of Dante ; কবি দান্তের গ্রন্থাধ্যায়ী ।

dăp, *n.*, *v. i.* & *t.* Bounce of a ball ; কন্দুকের লম্ফ । ***Verb i.*** **1.** (*Angling*) To fish by dropping the bait gently into the water ; আস্তে আস্তে টোপ ফেলিয়া মাছ ধরা । **2.** To bounce ; to skip ; লম্ফ দেওয়া (বল প্রভৃতি সম্পর্কে) ; লাফান । ***Verb t.*** To make a ball bounce ; বলকে লম্ফ প্রদান করান ।

Dăph'-nē, *n.* **1.** (*Gr. Myth*) One of the nymphs of Diana who was said to have been turned into a laurel tree ; (গ্রীকপুরাণ) ডায়েনা দেবীর সহচরী বিশেষ—ইনি লরেল বৃক্ষে রূপান্তরিতা হইয়াছিলেন । **2.** (*Bot.*) Kinds of flowering shrub ; কয়েক জাতীয় পুষ্পপ্রসূ গুল্মের সাধারণ নাম ।

dăp'-pêr, *adj.* Little and active ; neat ; neat in dress or appearance ; nimble ; ক্ষুদ্রকায় অথচ কর্ম্মঠ ; পরিপাটী, পরিচ্ছন্ন, ঝক্‌ঝকে ; ফিট্‌ফাট্ ; চটুল, চট্‌পটে ।

dăp'-ple, *adj.*, *v. t.* & *i.* Spotted ; variegated with spots of different colours ; as, *dapple* bay horse ; ফুট ফুট দাগ বিশিষ্ট, বিচিত্র বিন্দুযুক্ত ; কর্ব্বুরিত, চিত্র-বর্ণ । ***Verb t.*** To variegate with spots ; ফুটফুট চিহ্নে চিহ্নিত করা, কর্ব্বুরিত করা, বিচিত্রবর্ণ করা । ***Verb i.*** To become variegated with spots ; ফুট ফুট দাগবিশিষ্ট হওয়া । **Dapple grey**—ধূসরতর দাগ বিশিষ্ট ধূসরবর্ণ ।

dâr'-bies (-bēz), *n. pl.* (*slang*) Handcuffs ; (ইতরভাষায়) হাতকড়ি ।

Darby and Joan, *n.* Devoted old married couple ; পরস্পরের প্রতি অনুরক্ত বৃদ্ধ দম্পতী ।

dâre, *v. t.* **1.** To venture ; to have the courage or impudence to ; সাহস করা, হিম্মৎ করা (*Colloq.*) ; সাহস থাকা । **2.** To attempt ; to take the risk of ; as, to *dare* a leap ; চেষ্টা করা ; সঙ্কট বা আপদ্ ঘাড়ে নেওয়া । **3.** To defy ; to challenge ; তুচ্ছ করা, স্পর্দ্ধাপূর্ব্বক অগ্রাহ্য করা ; দ্বন্দার্থ আহ্বান করা **Dare-devil**—A reckless person ; অসমসাহসী ব্যক্তি, অকুতোভয় ব্যক্তি, বেপরওয়া লোক । **I dare say**—I am prepared to believe ; আমি বিশ্বাস করিতে প্রস্তুত আছি ।

dâre, *n.* The dace (which see).

dâr'-ing, *adj.* & *n.* Adventurous ; bold ; দুঃসাহসী ; বেপরওয়া, নির্ভীক । ***Noun.*** Adventurous courage ; অসম সাহস ।

dârk, *adj.* & *n.* **1.** Destitute, or partially destitute, of light ;

gloomy ; as, a *dark* room ; নিরালোক, নিষ্প্রভ, অন্ধকার, তমসাচ্ছন্ন, তমোময়, তিমিরাবৃত তামস ; নিরানন্দ। **2.** Wholly or partially black ; as, *dark* brown ; কৃষ্ণবর্ণ, কাল, ধূম্রবর্ণ, ধূসরবর্ণ, সধূম্র। **3.** Vile ; atrocious ; as, a *dark* deed ; জঘন্য ; ক্রূর, নিষ্ঠুর। **4.** Not fair, (of complexion) ; "My brother is a *dark* man of some six and twenty ;" (মুখের বর্ণ সম্বন্ধে) অগৌর। **5.** Cheerless ; as, a *dark* time in political affairs ; নিরানন্দ। **6.** Sad ; sullen ; as, a *dark* humour ; বিষণ্ণ, মলিন ; অপ্রসন্ন। **7.** Not enlightened with knowledge ; rude ; as, a *dark* age ; অজ্ঞানতমসাচ্ছন্ন ; অসভ্য। **8.** Secret ; mysterious ; obscure ; as, to keep a thing *dark* ; নিগূঢ়, গুহ্য ; রহস্যপূর্ণ; দুর্বোধ, জটিল, দুরধিগম্য। ***Noun.*** **1.** Absence of light ; "Here stood he in the *dark*, his sharp sword out ;" অন্ধকার, তিমির, তমিস্র, তমঃ, ধ্বান্ত। **2.** Night ; nightfall ; নিশি, রজনী, রাত্রি ; নিশাগম। **3.** Dark colour ; as, the lights and *darks* of a picture ; কৃষ্ণবর্ণ। **4.** Want of knowledge ; obscurity ; as, we are in the *dark* about it ; অজ্ঞানতা ; অস্পষ্টতা। **5.** Secrecy ; privacy ; as, things done in the *dark* ; গোপনতা ; নির্জ্জনতা। **Dark'-ly,** *adv.* In a dark manner ; গোপনে, নিভৃতে, অস্পষ্টভাবে। **Dark'-ness,** *n.* **1.** Absence of light ; অন্ধকার। **2.** Obscurity ; অস্পষ্টতা। **3.** Secrecy ; নির্জ্জনতা। **4.** Hell ; নরক। **5.** The quality or property of darkness ; as, the prince of *darkness* (শয়তান) ; তমোগুণ। **Dark ages**—কালেমেনের মৃত্যু এবং তদীয় বংশধরগণের রাজত্বের অবসান পর্য্যন্ত সময় (এই সময় সমগ্র ইউরোপ-খণ্ড অজ্ঞানতমসায় সমাচ্ছন্ন ছিল, ৫ম শতাব্দী হইতে পঞ্চদশ শতাব্দী পর্য্যন্ত), তিমিরযুগ। **Dark horse** — যে প্রতিযোগীর জয়লাভের সম্ভাবনা সম্বন্ধে কেহ কিছু অবগত নহে। **Dark lantern**—চোরা লণ্ঠন। **Dark room**—আলোকচিত্র পরিস্ফুটনের জন্য অন্ধকার কক্ষ। **In the dark** — In a state of ignorance ; অজ্ঞাত অবস্থায়। **Land of darkness** — Grave ; কবর। **The Dark Continent**—Africa ; আফ্রিকা মহাদেশ। **The power of darkness** — শয়তান ও তদীয় অনুচরগণ, দানবগণ। **To keep dark** — To keep secret ; গোপন রাখা। **To keep dark about anything** — To preserve secrecy about it ; কোন বিষয় প্রকাশ না করা।

dark'-en (dârkn), *v. t.* & *i.* **1.** To make dark ; অন্ধকারাচ্ছন্ন করা, নিষ্প্রভ করা। **2.** To obscure ; অস্পষ্ট করা। **3.** To render gloomy ; বিষণ্ণ করা। **4.** To render ignorant or stupid ; অজ্ঞ বা নির্ব্বোধ করা। **5.** To render less clear or intelligible ; to perplex ; অস্পষ্টতর বা দুর্বোধ করা ; জটিল করা। **6.** To sully ; কলুষিত করা। ***Verb i.*** To become dark ; অন্ধকার হওয়া। **To darken another's door** — To cross the threshold of his house ; কাহারও দ্বারে পদার্পণ করা। **To darken counsel** — To make perplexity worse ; গোলমাল বাড়াইয়া তোলা।

dârk'-ish, *adj.* **1.** Somewhat dark ; ঈষদন্ধকার। **2.** Dusky ; ধূসর।

darkle (dârkl), *v. i.* **1.** To be concealed ; লুকায়িত থাকা, গা ঢাকা দিয়া থাকা। **2.** To grow dark ; অন্ধকার হওয়া, আঁধার হইয়া আসা।

dârk'-ling, *adj.* & *adv.* Occurring in darkness ; characterized by darkness ; অন্ধকারে সংঘটিত ; অন্ধকারাত্মক। ***Adv.*** In the dark ; "As the wakeful bird sings *darkling* ;" অন্ধকারে।

dârk'-some (-sŭm), *adj.* Dark or darkish ; gloomy ; অন্ধকার, ঈষদন্ধকারাচ্ছন্ন ; অপ্রসন্ন।

dâr'-ling, *n.* & *adj.* One dearly beloved ; favourite ; আদরের ধন, যাদুমণি ; প্রিয়পাত্র, দয়িত, বল্লভ। ***Adj.*** Dearly beloved ; প্রিয়তম।

dârn, *v. t.* & *n.* To sew together with yarn or thread ; as, to *darn* stockings ; রিফু করা, সেলাই করা। ***Noun.*** A place mended by darning ; রিফু, বস্ত্র-সন্ধি (মঃ ইঃ)।

dâr'-nĕl, *n.* A kind of grass growing as weeds among corn ; শস্যক্ষেত্রের আগাছা বিশেষ।

Darnel.

dârt, *n.*, *v. t.* & *i.* **1.** A javelin ; a pointed missile intended to be thrown by hand ; শক্তি, শেল, বল্লম, পট্টিশ, শূল। **2.** Sting of an insect ; পতঙ্গের হুল। **3.** A sudden rapid motion ; আকস্মিক ক্ষিপ্রগতি। **4.** Act of throwing, or moving like a dart ; শেল-নিক্ষেপ বা শেলবৎ গতি। ***Verb t.*** To throw a pointed weapon with a sudden thrust ; to hurl or launch ; শেল প্রভৃতি সবলে নিক্ষেপ বা মোচন করা ; সবেগে নিক্ষেপ করা। **2.** To emit suddenly ; as, the sun *darts* forth his beams ; হঠাৎ নির্গত করা, ছুটান। ***Verb i.*** To start suddenly and run ; as, the deer *darted* from the thicket ; হঠাৎ কোন দিকে ধাবিত হওয়া, সহসা সবেগে ছুটা।

dârt'-ĕr, *n.* **1.** One who darts ; নিক্ষেপকারী। **2.** A web-footed bird of pelican tribe ; একপ্রকার জালপাদ পক্ষী। **3.** Kinds of fish ; কতিপয় বিভিন্ন জাতীয় মৎস্যের সাধারণ নাম।

dâr'-tre *n.* Any herpetic disease of the skin ; প্রদাহিত চর্ম্মের উপর রসপূর্ণ স্বতন্ত্র স্বতন্ত্র পীড়কার অসমস্তবকবিশিষ্ট চর্ম্মরোগ। **—trous,** *adj.*

Dăr-win′-ĭsm, *n.* The scientific teaching of Charles Darwin ; চার্লস্ ডারউইনের বৈজ্ঞানিক মত, জীবশ্রেণীর উৎপত্তি এবং অভিব্যক্তি বিষয়ক আলোচনা। **—ist,** *n.*

dăsh, *n., v. t. & i.* **1.** Violent striking together of two bodies ; collision ; সংঘট্ট, ঠক্কর, সংঘাত, সংমর্দ্দ (মঃ ইঃ) ; সংঘর্ষ। **2.** The splashing sound of water striking or being struck ; as, the *dash* of the waves ; জলের ছল ছল শব্দ। **3.** Infusion ; as, *dash* of good blood ; touch ; tinge ; ছিটা-ফোঁটা ; ছাট, ছিটা, আঁচ ; আমেজ, আভাস। **4.** Hasty pen-stroke ; "Fifty imperial towns have been erased from the list of independent states by one *dash* of pen ;" এক কলমের খোঁচা। **5.** A short line (—) occurring in a sentence to mark a more significant pause of movement than that indicated by a comma ; ড্যাস্ চিহ্ন। **6.** A rush ; a sudden vigorous attack ; as, a bold *dash* at the enemy ; প্রচণ্ড বেগে ধাবন ; প্রচণ্ডবেগে আক্রমণ। **7.** Showy appearance or behaviour, "Lived on his means cut no *dash* ;" জাঁক, ভড়ং, ভড়ক, বাহার। **8.** Animation ; promptness ; সজীবতা ; তৎপরতা। ***Verb t.*** **1.** To shatter to pieces ; as, a brave vessel *dashed* all to pieces ; চূর্ণবিচূর্ণ করা, চুরমার করা। **2.** To knock ; to drive, throw or thrust *away, off, out* or *down*, etc. ; as, to dash one's tears *away* ; ধাক্কা দেওয়া ; তাড়িত করা, নিক্ষেপ করা, ঠেলিয়া দেওয়া। **3.** To put to shame ; to abash ; as, he was *dashed* at the appearance of his judge ; লজ্জিত করা ; লজ্জা দেওয়া। **4.** To bespatter ; as, to *dash* colour on a canvas ; ছিটাইয়া দেওয়া। **5.** To dilute ; to qualify ; as, to *dash* water with spirit ; জল মিশাইয়া পাতলা করা ; মদ্যাদির তেজ প্রশমিত করা। **6.** To ruin ; to frustrate ; as, to *dash* one's hopes ; ধ্বংস করা ; বিফল করা। **7.** To write or sketch rapidly or carelessly, (often followed by *off*) ; as, to *dash off* a review ; তাড়াতাড়ি লিখা বা অসতর্কভাবে লিখা, তাড়াতাড়ি নক্সা করা। **8.** To erase or efface, (with *out*) ; মুছিয়া ফেলা, লোপ করা। **9.** To underline ; নিম্নরেখ করা। ***Verb i.*** **1.** To advance or move violently ; to rush ; as, the locomotive *dashed* forward ; প্রচণ্ডবেগে ধাবিত হওয়া ; প্রচণ্ডবেগে অগ্রসর হওয়া। **Dash-board** — অশ্বখুরনিক্ষিপ্ত জল, কর্দ্দম, প্রভৃতি যাহাতে আরোহিগণের শরীরে না লাগিতে পারে তজ্জন্য শকটের সম্মুখে যে কাষ্ঠ বা চর্ম্মময় তিরস্করণী (পর্দ্দা) সংবদ্ধ থাকে। **At a dash**—At one movement ; এক চোটে। **At first dash**—At once ; তৎক্ষণাৎ। **To cut a dash**—To make a brilliant show ; জাঁকজমক দেখান, বাহার দেখান। **To dash about**—To rush about ; প্রচণ্ডবেগে ধাবিত হওয়া। To show off ; আড়ম্বর প্রদর্শন করা। **To dash against**—To strike against in violent collision ; আছাড় মারা। **To dash along**—To rush violently on ; প্রচণ্ডবেগে ধাবিত হওয়া। **To dash at**—To make sudden attack or onset ; সহসা প্রচণ্ডবেগে আক্রমণ করা। **To dash off**—To form or sketch hastily ; তাড়াতাড়ি গঠন করা, তাড়াতাড়ি নক্সা করিয়া ফেলা। To rush away violently or excitedly ; প্রচণ্ডবেগে বা উত্তেজিতভাবে ধাবিত হওয়া।

dăsh′-ĕr, *n.* **1.** One who dashes ; যে ব্যক্তি জাঁকজমক প্রদর্শন করে। **2.** A contrivance for agitating cream in a churn ; মন্থনভাণ্ডস্থিত সর মন্থনের কৌশল বিশেষ।

dăsh′-ing, *pt. adj.* **1.** Driving or striking against ; সংঘট্টমান। **2.** Lively ; impetuous ; স্ফূর্ত্তিপূর্ণ ; তেজস্বী, প্রচণ্ড। **3.** Showy ; as, a *dashing* fashionable woman ; stylish ; as, *dashing* trousers ; পোষাক পরিচ্ছদের বাহার প্রদর্শনকারী ; জাঁকালো, চটকদার।

dăs′-tard (-tĕrd), *n.* A coward ; skulker ; ভীরু, কাপুরুষ ; ক্লীব (মঃ ইঃ)। **—ly,** *adj.* Cowardly ; base ; কাপুরুষোচিত ; হীন।

dăs′-y-ure (-yōōr), *n.* A small carnivorous quadruped of Australia and Tasmania ; অষ্ট্রেলিয়া ও ট্যাসমেনিয়াবাসী মাংসাশী জন্তুবিশেষ।

Dasyure.

dā′-tă, *n.* See DATUM.

dāte, *n.* **1.** The fruit of a palm constituting a staple food for the people of Northern Africa and Asia ; খর্জ্জুর ফল। **2.** The tree which yields this fruit ; খর্জ্জুর বৃক্ষ।

Date palm.

dāte, *n., v. t. & i.* **1.** That addition to a writing which specifies the year, month and day when it was executed ; দলিল প্রভৃতি সম্পাদনের সন, মাস, দিবস, প্রভৃতি। **2.** The point of time at which a transaction or event takes place or is appointed to take place ; তারিখ। **3.** Period ; duration ; as, when the *date* of youth is expired ; সময় ; স্থিতিকাল। ***Verb t.*** **1.** To mark the time of writing or executing; তারিখ দেওয়া। **2.** To ascertain, estimate or give the date of an event; as, to *date* the birth of Christ; কোন ঘটনার তারিখ নির্ণয়, অনুমান বা প্রদান করা। **3.** To reckon; as, a geological time is not *dated* by years; গণনা করা। ***Verb i.*** **1.** To have a date; as, the letter *dates* from home; তারিখ থাকা। **2.** To reckon chronologically; কালানুক্রমে গণনা করা। **3.** To have a beginning; as, the Batavian republic *dates* from the success of the French arms; আরম্ভ হওয়া। **Date'-less,** *adj.* **1.** Undated; তারিখশূন্য। **2.** Endless; "A *dateless* and hopeless eternity of horror;" অনন্ত। **3.** Immemorial; as, *dateless* usage; স্মরণাতীত। **Date line**—গ্রীণউইচ হইতে ১৮০° উত্তরদিগ্‌বর্ত্তী কল্পিত রেখা বিশেষ, উক্ত রেখার পূর্ব্বদিগ্‌বর্ত্তী স্থান সমূহের তারিখ পশ্চিম দিগ্‌বর্ত্তী স্থান সকলের তারিখ হইতে এক দিবস অধিকতর হইয়া থাকে। **From date**—From to-day; আজ হইতে, অদ্যাবধি। **To go out of date** — To become obsolete; অপ্রচলিত হওয়া। **Up to date**—Adapted or corrected to the present time; modern; বর্ত্তমানকালের উপযোগীকৃত, বর্ত্তমানকাল পর্য্যন্ত সংশোধিত; আধুনিক।

date plŭm, *n.* The fruit of Diospyros lotus; also the tree; আমলক ফল, (হিন্দী—বেলঃ); আমলক বৃক্ষ (ঐ)।

dā'-tive (-tĭv), *adj.* & *n.* The epithet applied to that case of a noun which follows a verb or other word expressive of giving, handing or passing over; সম্প্রদান-বাচক। ***Noun.*** The dative case; সম্প্রদান কারক।

dā'-tŭm, *n.* [*pl.* DATA] A thing known or granted; an assumption or premiss from which inferences may be drawn; স্বীকৃত সত্য; সামগ্রী (হিঃ কোঃ), নির্দ্দিষ্ট (ঐ)।

dă-tū'-ră, *n.* Kinds of poisonous plants including stramonium, yielding strong narcotic; ধুতুরা, প্রভৃতি বৃক্ষ। ***Datura alba***—সাদা ধুতুরা (বেলঃ), সফেদ ধুতুরা (ঐ)। ***Datura fastuosa***—কালা ধুতুরা (বেলঃ)।

daub (dăb), *n. v. t.* & *i.* A coarse painting; কদাকার চিত্র। ***Verb t.*** **1.** To coat with plaster, clay, etc.; লেপন করা, লেপ দেওয়া, মাখান। **2.** To paint inartistically; আনাড়ীর মত চিত্রিত করা। **3.** To soil, to stain; ময়লা করা; কলুষিত করা। ***Verb i.*** To apply plaster, paint or the like, unskilfully; আনাড়ীর মত চুণ, বালি বা রঙ্‌ লাগান। **Daub'-y,** *adj.*

daub'-stêr (dăb-), **—êr** *n.* **1.** A coarse painter; নিকৃষ্ট চিত্রকর, আনাড়ী পটুয়া।

daucus carota—গাজর (বেলঃ), গজ্জর (ঐ), গৃঞ্জন (ঐ)।

daugh'-têr (dä-), *n.* **1.** One's female child; কন্যা, সুতা, দুহিতা, পুত্রী, নন্দিনী, আত্মজা, তনয়া। **2.** A female descendant; a woman in relation to her native country or place; "Danced on the shores the *daughters* of the land;" কোন বিশেষ বংশোদ্ভূতা স্ত্রীলোক; জন্মভূমির সম্পর্কে কন্যা। **3.** A female member of a family; as, the *daughter* of Israel; পরিবারস্থ স্ত্রীলোক। **4.** A woman who is the spiritual or intellectual product of a person or a thing; as, a *daughter* of the church; অধ্যাত্ম বা মানস কন্যা। **—ly,** *adj.* Becoming a daughter; dutiful; কন্যোচিত; কর্ত্তব্যপালনশীলা। **Daughter-in-law**—পুত্রবধূ, স্নুষা। **Daughter of Eve**—স্ত্রীলোক।

daunt (dänt), *v. t.* & *n.* **1.** To discourage; to intimidate; নিরুৎসাহ করা, ভগ্নোৎসাহ করা; ভীত করা, ভয়াকুল করা, সন্ত্রস্ত করা। **2.** To press salted herrings into a barrel with a daunt; গোলাকৃতি কাষ্ঠখণ্ড দ্বারা চাপ প্রয়োগ করত পিপার ভিতরে লবণাক্ত হেরীং মৎস্য রাখা। ***Noun.*** A disc of wood for pressing the salted herrings down in a barrel; উক্ত কার্য্যোপযোগী গোলাকৃতি কাষ্ঠখণ্ড। **Daunt'-less,** *adj.* Intrepid; persevering; নির্ভীক, অকুতোভয়; অধ্যবসায়-সম্পন্ন।

dau'-phĭn (dä-), *n.* The title of the eldest son of the king of France; ফরাসী-রাজের জ্যেষ্ঠ পুত্রের উপাধি। **—ess, —phine,** *ns.* The title of the wife of the dauphin; তদীয় স্ত্রী।

dăv'-ĕn-pôrt, *n.* A kind of small writing-desk with drawers on each side; উভয় পার্শ্বে দেরাজ বিশিষ্ট লিখিবার ক্ষুদ্র মেজ।

dăv'-ĭt, *n.* **1.** A beam projecting from a ship's bow for the attachment of the tackle whereby the anchor-flake is lifted without dragging along the sides of the vessel; [the operation is termed '*fishing the anchor*']; রজ্জু-সংলগ্ন করার জন্য পোতাগ্র হইতে প্রলম্বিত কড়িকাঠের মত লৌহ বা কাষ্ঠ খণ্ড,—উক্ত রজ্জুদ্বারা জাহাজের পার্শ্বের সহিত সংঘৃষ্ট না করিয়া নোঙ্গরের নিম্নাংশ (হুল-দল) উপরে উত্তোলিত করা যায়। **2.** One of a pair of cranes for suspending or lowering ship's boat; জাহাজের ডিঙ্গী ঝুলান বা নামানের জন্য ভারোত্তলন স্তম্ভদ্বয়ের অন্যতর।

Davits with boat attached.

Da'-vȳ(lămp), *n.* Miner's wire-gauze safety lamp; খনির কার্য্যে নিযুক্ত ব্যক্তিদিগের প্রদীপ বিশেষ।

Davy Jones's locker, *n.* The deep; a watery grave in the sea ; গভীর সমুদ্র ; সলিল-সমাধি। **He has gone to Davy Jons's locker**—He is dead ; তিনি মরিয়া গিয়াছেন।

daw'-dle (dä-), *n., v. t.* & *i.* A trifler ; যে ব্যক্তি অকিঞ্চিৎকর আমোদ-প্রমোদে সময় নষ্ট করে, তুচ্ছকারী। ***Verb t.*** To waste by trifling ; as, to *dawdle* away a morning ; বাজে কাজে নষ্ট করা। ***Verb i.*** To trifle ; to dally ; অকিঞ্চিৎকর আমোদ-প্রমোদে মত্ত থাকা ; বৃথা আমোদে সময় নষ্ট করা।

dawk (däk), **dak,** *n.* **1.** Post or transport by relays of men or horses ; ডাক। **2.** Relay ; ঘোড়ার ডাক। **Dawk-bunglow**—ডাক বাংলা।

dawn (dän), *n.* & *v. i.* **1.** The break of day ; the first appearance of light in morning ; ভোর, উষাকাল ; অরুণোদয়, প্রভাত, প্রত্যূষ, দিবসমুখ (মঃ ইঃ)। **2.** First opening ; beginning "From the earliest *dawn* of history to the present day" উন্মেষ, প্রারম্ভ ; সূত্রপাত। ***Verb i.*** To begin to grow light in the morning ; উষা সমাগত হওয়া, ভোর হওয়া, অরুণোদয় হওয়া। **Dawn'-ing,** *adj.* & *n.* Opening ; extending ; উদীয়মান ; বিকাশী। ***Noun.*** Beginning ; উন্মেষ, নবোন্মেষ, আরম্ভ, উদয়।

day (dā), *n.* **1.** The time while the sun is above horizon ; দিবাভাগ। **2.** Date of specified festival, etc. ; as, the Christmas *day* ; দিন, দিবস, বাসর (আঃ বঃ)। **3.** Light ; sunshine ; "Let us walk honestly as in the *day* ;" আলোক ; সূর্য্যালোক, রৌদ্র, আতপ। **4.** The day of battle ; as, to carry the *day* ; যুদ্ধদিবস। **5.** Victory ; as, to win the *day* ; জয়। **6.** Period, (often *pl.*) ; as, in the *days* of old ; কাল, সময়। **7.** An appointed or fixed time ; "If my debtors do not keep their *day*"; নির্দ্দিষ্ট বা নিরূপিত সময়। **8.** (*Astron.*) The space of twenty-four hours ; as, solar *day* ; (জ্যোতির্বিজ্ঞান) অহোরাত্র। **All day**—সারাদিন। **All days**—সর্ব্বদা, চিরদিন। **Better day**—সুদিন। **Civil day**—পূর্ব্বদিন রাত্রি ১২টার পর হইতে আরম্ভ হইয়া পরদিন রাত্রি ১২টা পর্য্যন্ত। **Day-blindness** — দিনান্ধতা (সাঃ পঃ)। **Day-boarder** — যে ছাত্র বিদ্যালয়-সংসৃষ্ট ছাত্রাবাসে আহার করে, কিন্তু অন্যত্র শয়ন করিয়া থাকে। **Day-book**—মহাজনদিগের দৈনিক পুস্তক—যাহাতে দৈনিক ক্রয়বিক্রয়ের বৃত্তান্ত লিপিবদ্ধ হইয়া থাকে। **Day-boy** — যে ছাত্র বাটীতে আহার করে। **Day-dream**—আকাশ-কুসুম-কল্পনা, দিবাস্বপ্ন, খেয়ালী পোলাও। **Day-fly** — দিনজীবী কীট। **Day-labour**—দিনমজুরী। **Day-light**—The light of day ; as, broad *day-light* ; (স্পষ্ট দিবালোক) ; দিবালোক। Dawn ; ভোর। (*Slang or colloq.*) Publicity ; লোক-প্রকাশতা, রটনা। The visible interval as between boats in race, wine and glass-rim or rider and the saddle ; "After about a quarter of a mile *day-light* was visible between the two boats ;" নৌকাদৌড়ের নৌকাসকলের মধ্যে, মদ্যপাত্রের কাণা এবং পাত্রস্থ মদ্যের উপরিভাগের মধ্যে অথবা অশ্বারোহী এবং জিনের মধ্যে ফাঁক বা ব্যবধান। **Day-maid**—গোপী, গোয়ালিনী (শেক্ষপীয়রের গ্রন্থে ব্যবহৃত)। **Day-mare**—অনিদ্রা, দুঃস্বপ্ন (হিঃ কোঃ)। **Daysman**—মধ্যস্থ, শালিস। **Day-spring** — অরুণোদয়, উষাকাল। **Day-star**—শুক তারা ; দিনমণি, সূর্য্য। **Day-ticket**—যে টিকেট গ্রহণ করিলে সেই দিনই ফিরিয়া আসিতে হয়। **First day**—রবিবার। **Lunar day**—তিথি। **Natural day**—সূর্য্যোদয় হইতে সূর্য্যাস্ত পর্য্যন্ত কাল। **One's day** — জীবিত কাল। **Present day** — বর্ত্তমান, আধুনিক। **Sidereal day** — নাক্ষত্র অহোরাত্র। **Solar or astronomical day** — পূর্ব্বদিন মধ্যাহ্নকাল হইতে আরম্ভ হইয়া পরদিন মধ্যাহ্ন পর্য্যন্ত সময়, সৌর অহোরাত্র। **A day of the week**—বার। **As the day is long**—To the utmost extent ; চরমসীমা পর্য্যন্ত। Uninterruptedly ; অব্যাহতভাবে। **Day by day**—Every day ; দিন দিন, প্রতিদিন। **Day in, day out**—All day long ; সারাদিন। **Day of judgment**—অন্তিম বিচার দিবস। [খৃষ্টীয় ও মহম্মদীয় ধর্ম্মমতানুসারে যে দিবস ঈশ্বর কর্ম্মানুসারে মানবজাতির বিচার করিবেন।] **Days of grace**—বাদী কিম্বা প্রতিবাদীর প্রার্থনায় আদালত হইতে যে সময় দেওয়া হয়। **Every dog has his day**—No man is always unlucky ; কাহারও ভাগ্যদেবী চিরকাল অপ্রসন্না থাকেন না। **Every other day** — Every alternate day ; একদিন অন্তর এক দিন। **From day to day**—As time passes ; উত্তরোত্তর, দিনদিন। **His days are numbered**—He has only a shrot time to live ; তাহার দিন ফুরাইয়া আসিয়াছে। **Sufficient for the day is the evil thereof**—Do not anticipate trouble ; ভবিষ্যতে কি হইবে সেই ভাবনায় আকুল হইও না। **The day**—বর্ত্তমান কাল। **The day after the fair**—Too late or too early ; অতিবিলম্বে, অতি শীঘ্র। **The other day**—এই সেই দিন। **This day week**—গত বা আগামী সপ্তাহের এই দিন। **Time of the day**—Hour of the clock ; সময়। **To carry the day**—To be victorious ; বিজয়ী হওয়া, জয়লাভ করা। **To fall on evil days**—To fall in misfortune ; দুর্দ্দিনে পতিত হওয়া, দুঃসময়ে পড়া। **To keep the day** — To observe duly ; যথোচিতভাবে প্রতিপালন করা। To keep an appointment ; কথা রাখা, করার মত কার্য্য করা। **To name the day**—To fix the day of marriage ; বিবাহের দিবস ধার্য্য করা। **To win the day, To**

gain the day — To gain the battle ; to succeed in any enterprise : যুদ্ধে জয়লাভ করা ; কোন দুঃসাহসিক কার্য্যে কৃতকার্য্যতা লাভ করা।

dāze, *n.* & *v. t.* A state of being stupefied ; হতবুদ্ধিতা। ***Verb t.*** **1.** To stupefy ; হতবুদ্ধি করা ; **2.** To dazzle ; ঝলমল করা, ঝকমক করা।

dăz'-zle, *n.* & *v. t.* Glitter ; ঝলমল, ঝলক। ***Verb t.*** **1.** To overpower with light ; তীব্র আলোক দ্বারা ঝলসিয়া দেওয়া। **2.** To confound or surprise by brilliant display ; জাঁকজমক বা সমুজ্জ্বল শোভাসম্পদ দ্বারা হতবুদ্ধি বা বিস্ময়াভিভূত করা। **–zling,** *adj.* Bright to a degree that dazzles ; তীব্রোজ্জ্বল (কৃঃ), দুরালোক (ঐ), দুর্নিরীক্ষ্য, চোখ-ঝলসানো।

dea'-cŏn (dē-), *n.* **1.** (*Primitive church*) The appointed minister of charity ; (আদি যুগের খৃষ্টীয় সমাজে) দানকার্য্যনির্ব্বাহক যাজক। **2.** (*In the churches of Rome and England*) A spiritual officer ranking beneath the bishops and the priests ; (রোমানক্যাথলিক এবং ইংলণ্ডীয় ধর্ম্মসমাজে) প্রধান ধর্ম্মাধ্যক্ষ এবং পুরোহিতের নিম্নতর পদস্থ যাজক, উপপুরোহিত। **3.** (*Presbyterian church*) One of an order of officers attending to the secular affairs of a congregation ; (প্রিসবিটেরীয়ান ধর্ম্মসমাজে) যে যাজক-কর্ম্মচারী ধর্ম্মসমাজভুক্ত ব্যক্তি-মণ্ডলীর বৈষয়িক কার্য্য তত্ত্বাবধান করেন। **–ess,** *n. fem.* **–ship,** *n.*

dead (dĕd), *adj., adv.* & *n.* **1.** Deprived of life ; মৃত, জীবনশূন্য, প্রাণশূন্য, গতপ্রাণ, গতাসু, ত্যক্তজীবন। **2.** Disused ; obsolete ; as, a *dead* custom ; অনাচরিত ; অপ্রচলিত। **3.** Benumbed ; insensible ; as, a *dead* hand ; আড়ষ্ট, অসাড়, অবশ, স্তব্ধ ; বেদনাবোধশূন্য, অনুভবশক্তিহীন, স্তম্ভিত। **4.** Inanimate ; as, a *dead* fence ; জড়, অচেতন। **5.** Extinct ; dull ; lustreless ; as, *dead* coal ; নির্ব্বাপিত ; নিস্তেজ ; দীপ্তিহীন। **6.** Gloomy ; melancholy ; ম্লান ; বিষণ্ণ। **7.** Inactive ; motionless ; idle ; জড় ; নিশ্চল, নিস্পন্দ (মঃ ইঃ), অলস, নিশ্চেষ্ট। **8.** As good as dead in respect to (something) ; "He that is in monastery is *dead* to all worldly affairs ;" insensible to ; as, she is *dead* to love ; (কোন কিছুর পক্ষে) মৃতবৎ, মৃতকল্প (মঃ ইঃ) ; বোধশূন্য **9.** Abrupt ; complete ; as, to come to a *dead* stop ; আকস্মিক ; সম্পূর্ণ, পুরা। **10.** Empty ; শূন্য। **11.** Barren ; as, *dead* ground ; অনুর্ব্বর, ঊষর। **12.** Vapid ; নীরস। **13.** Unrelieved ; unbroken ; বৈচিত্র্যশূন্য, একঘেয়ে, একটানা ; অবিরাম। **14.** (*of* colour etc.) Without brightness ; as, drab is a *dead* colour, compared with crimson ; নিষ্প্রভ, অনুজ্জ্বল। **15.** (Of a sound) Dull or muffled ; as, a *dead* floor which obstructs the sound ; মন্দীভূত, শব্দ মন্দীভূত করার জন্য আচ্ছাদিত। **16.** Quite certain ; as, a *dead* shot ; exact ; direct ; স্থির-নিশ্চিত ; ঠিক ; সোজা। **17.** (*Law*) Deprived of all rights of citizenship ; (আইন) যাবতীয় নাগরিক অধিকার-বিচ্যুত। **18.** (*Theol.*) In a state of spiritual death ; "*Dead* in trespasses and sins ;" আধ্যাত্মিকভাবে মৃত। **19.** Useless ; as, *dead* steam ; অব্যবহার্য্য। **20.** Motionless ; the *dead* spindle of a lock ; নিশ্চল। **21.** Entire ; absolute ; "*Dead* calms are in the ocean ;" পরিপূর্ণ ; সম্পূর্ণ ; প্রশান্ত। ***Adv.*** Completely ; profoundly ; as, *dead* asleep ; সম্পূর্ণরূপে ; গভীরভাবে। ***Noun.*** One who is dead ; মৃত ব্যক্তি। **Dead-alive** — জীবন্মৃত, নিস্তেজ। **Dead beat** — সম্পূর্ণ ক্লান্ত। **Dead-born** — মৃত-প্রসূত, মৃত-জাত। **Dead certainty** — ধ্রুবনিশ্চয়। **Dead-colouring**—কোন চিত্রে উজ্জ্বল বর্ণরাজি সন্নিবিষ্ট করার পূর্ব্বে যে নিষ্প্রভ রঙ্গের লেপ দেওয়া হয়। **Dead-drunk**—ঘোর মাতাল। **Dead-eye** — (নৌ-বিদ্যা) মাস্তুলের রশারশি বিস্তারের জন্য চ্যাপ্টা এবং গোলাকার ত্রিছিদ্র বিশিষ্ট কাষ্ঠখণ্ড বিশেষ। **Dead-fence**—কাঠ প্রভৃতির বেড়া, (লৌহাদির নয়)। **Dead-fire** — মাস্তুলাগ্র প্রভৃতিতে দৃষ্ট বৈদ্যুতিক জ্যোতিঃ, (মৃত্যু সূচনা করে বলিয়া বিশ্বাস)। **Dead freight**—কোন মাল চালানের জন্য জাহাজ ভাড়া করিয়া মালদ্বারা জাহাজ সম্পূর্ণ বোঝাই করিতে অসমর্থ হইলে, জাহাজের খালি জায়গার জন্য যে ভাড়া দিতে হয়। **Dead-gold**—স্বর্ণ বা স্বর্ণপত্রের অমসৃণীকৃত উপরিভাগ। **Dead-heat** — যে দৌড়ে দুই বা ততোধিক প্রতিযোগী প্রায় সমকালে লক্ষ্যস্থলে আসিয়া পৌঁছাতে কে সর্ব্বপ্রথম পৌছিয়াছে মধ্যস্থ ব্যক্তি তাহা বলিতে অসমর্থ হয় ; অতএব তুল্য-প্রায়তা। **Dead horse** — যে কাজের জন্য আগাম টাকা দেওয়া হয়। **Dead-house** — শবব্যবচ্ছেদাগার। **Dead language** — অপ্রচলিত ভাষা, যথা সংস্কৃত, ল্যাটিন প্রভৃতি। **Dead letter**—যে চিঠি বিলি হয় নাই, অথবা যাহা কেহ দাবী করে নাই, অগৃহীত পত্র ; (লক্ষণায়) অপ্রচলিত বিষয়, অকার্য্যকর বিষয়। **Dead lift**—অত্যন্ত অসুবিধায় কোন বস্তু উত্তোলন ; অতএব অসাধ্য কর্ম্ম।

Dead-light.

Dead-light—(নৌ বিদ্যা) ঝড়ের সময় পোতকক্ষের জানালা বন্ধ করার জন্য আবরণ বিশেষ। **Dead-lock**—সম্পূর্ণ প্রতিবন্ধ। **Dead loss**—সম্পূর্ণ ক্ষতি। **Dead-march**—শ্মশান সঙ্গীত, বিশেষতঃ সৈন্যগণের অন্ত্যেষ্টি সঙ্গীত। **Dead men**—মদ্যপানোৎসবের পরে যে সমস্ত শূন্য বোতল থাকে। **Dead office**—প্রেতকৃত্য। **Dead-reckoning**—(নৌ বিদ্যা) নক্ষত্রাদি পর্য্যবেক্ষণদ্বারা জাহাজের অবস্থান নির্ণয় অসম্ভব হইলে গতিমাপক যন্ত্র, মৎস্য-যন্ত্র (compass), প্রভৃতি দ্বারা তাহা

নির্ণয় করণ। **Dead sea**—মরুসাগর। **Dead sea apple**—See APPLE OF SODOM. **Dead-set** — কোন ব্যক্তির বিরুদ্ধে পূর্ব্ব-কল্পিত ষড়যন্ত্র। **Dead-shot**—লক্ষ্যভেদে সিদ্ধহস্ত ব্যক্তি, অব্যর্থ-লক্ষ্যব্যক্তি। **Dead silence** — সম্পূর্ণ নিস্তব্ধতা। **Dead-smooth** — অতিশয় মসৃণ। **Dead sound**—প্রতিধ্বনিবিহীন শব্দ। **Dead-stand** — সুদৃঢ় বাঁধা। **Dead stock** — অব্যবহৃত মূলধন, যে মূলধন ব্যবসায়ে খটিতেছে না ; অবিক্রেয় জিনিষ। **Dead wall**—জানালা, দরজা প্রভৃতি বিহীন প্রাচীর, সাদা দেওয়াল। **Dead-weight**—অতিশয় ভারি বোঝা। **Dead-wind**—প্রতিকূল বায়ু। **Dead-wool**—মৃত বা নিহত মেষের শরীর হইতে যে পশম সংগৃহীত হয়। **Dead-work**—যে কার্য্য হইতে সাক্ষাৎ সম্বন্ধে কোনে লাভ হয় না, কিন্তু যদ্দারা লাভজনক কার্য্যের পথ হয়। **Dead-works**—জাহাজের যে অংশ জলোপরি ভাসমান থাকে। **Dead as a door nail**—Quite dead ; ডাহা মরা। **To wait for dead men's shoes**—To wait for a situation formerly held by a man now dead; কোন মৃত ব্যক্তির পদে প্রতিষ্ঠিত হইবার জন্য অপেক্ষা করা।

dead'-en (dĕdn), *v. t.* & *i*, **1.** To deprive of vitality, force, brightness, feeling, etc. ; নির্জীব করা, বলহীন করা, অনুজ্জ্বল করা, উদাসীন করা, নিস্তেজ করা, ম্লান করা, শিথিল করা। **2.** To make insensible to ; (কোন বিষয়ে) অনুভবশূন্য করা। **3.** To blunt ; কুণ্ঠিত করা, ভোঁতা করা। **4.** To retard ; as, to *deaden* a ship's headway ; দেরী করান। ***Verb i.*** To lose vitality, force, etc. ; শক্তিহীন হওয়া, বলহীন হওয়া, নিস্তেজ হওয়া।

dead'-lў (dĕd-), *adj.* & *adv.* **1.** Causing fatal injury ; mortal ; as, a *deadly* blow ; মারাত্মক ; সাংঘাতিক, মানুষ-মারা, প্রাণান্তকর, প্রাণান্তিক(আঃ বঃ)। **2.** Of poisonous nature ; as, a *deadly* nightshade (=বেলা-ডোনা) ; বিষাক্ত। **3.** Implacable ; অশাম্য, নিষ্করুণ। **4.** Death-like ; as, a *deadly* faintness ; মৃত্যুবৎ। **5.** Intense ; as, *deadly* haste ; অতীব। **6.** (*Theol.*) Productive of, or involving, spiritual death ; as, *deadly* sins ; (খৃষ্টীয় ধর্ম্মশাস্ত্র) আধ্যাত্মিক মৃত্যুজনক। ***Adv.*** **1.** As if dead ; as, *deadly* faint ; মৃতবৎ, শববৎ। **2.** Extremely ; as, *deadly* tired ; নিতান্ত। **Deadly sins**—প্রাচীন খৃষ্টীয় ধর্ম্মশাস্ত্রবেত্তাদিগের মতে অহঙ্কার, ধনলোভ, লালসা, ক্রোধ, ঔদরিকতা, হিংসা এবং আলস্য এই সপ্ত মহাপাতক।

dead'-nĕss (dĕd-), *n.* **1.** Want of natural life ; জীবনশূন্যতা। **2.** Want of animation ; dulness ; languor ; নির্জীবতা ; শৈথিল্য, নিস্তেজতা ; গ্লানি, অবসাদ, জড়তা।

deaf (dĕf), *adj.* **1.** Wholly or partly without hearing ; বধির, কালা। **2.** Inattentive ; not giving ear to ; as, he is *deaf* to reason ; অমনোযোগী ; অকর্ণপাতকারী, বধির। **Deaf'-ness,** *n.* **Deaf-nut**—শাসশূন্য বাদামাদি ফল। **Deaf-and-dumb alphabet** or **language**—যে সমস্ত সঙ্কেতের সাহায্যে বধিরেরা মনোভাব প্রকাশ করে অথবা অন্যের ভাব বুঝিতে পারে। **Deaf-and-dumb school**—মূক-বধির-বিদ্যালয়।

deaf'-en (dĕfn), *v. t.* **1.** To deprive of hearing by noise ; বধির করা। **2.** To drown by a louder sound ; উচ্চতর শব্দ দ্বারা অপেক্ষাকৃত মৃদু শব্দ অশ্রুত করা। **3.** (*Arch.*) To make a floor or wooden position impervious to sound ; (স্থপতি-বিদ্যা) (মৃত্তিকা, করাতের গুড়া, প্রভৃতির সাহায্যে) গৃহতল বা কাষ্ঠপ্রাচীরের শব্দসঞ্চার-পথ রুদ্ধ কর। **—ing,** *adj.* & *n.*

deal (dēl), *n.* A considerable amount ; as, a great *deal* ; বহুল পরিমাণ, প্রাচুর্য্য।

deal (dēl), *n., v. t.* & *i.* **1.** The act or system of sharing ; apportionment ; অংশনিরূপণ, অংশ নিরূপণ-পদ্ধতি ; অংশ-কল্পনা। **2.** Division or distribution of cards; তাস-বণ্টন। **3.** An act of buying or selling ; ক্রয়বিক্রয়। ***Verb t.*** **1.** To distribute ; to apportion ; (often with *out*) ; বণ্টন করা ; অংশ বিভাগ করা। **2.** To deliver ; to bestow ; "The nightly mallet *deals* resounding blows ; প্রদান করা ; দেওয়া। **3.** To distribute cards to players for a game ; তাস বাঁটা। ***Verb i.*** **1.** To be concerned with ; as, they *deal* in politics ; সংসৃষ্ট থাকা। **2.** To trade ; as, to *deal* in silk ; ব্যবসায় করা। **3.** To behave ; as, to *deal* honourably ; আচরণ করা, ব্যবহার করা। **To deal in**—To be engaged in ; to follow as a pursuit ; to practise ; রত হওয়া, ব্যাপৃত হওয়া ; কোন ব্যবসায় করা ; পরিচালন বা অনুশীলন করা। **To deal out**—To distribute ; বণ্টন করা, বাঁটা। **To deal with**—To have to do with ; সংস্রব থাকা।

deal, (dēl), *n.* **1.** A piece of sawn fir or pine-wood over 7 in. broad, 6 ft. long and not over 3 in. thick ; সরল বা তালীশ-পত্র প্রভৃতি কাঠের করাতে চিরা টুকরা। [৭ ইঞ্চির উপর প্রস্থ, ৬ ফিট লম্বা, এবং ৩ ইঞ্চি পর্য্যন্ত পুরু।] **2.** Pine or fir-wood ; as, a floor of *deal* ; সরল বা তালীশ-পত্র কাষ্ঠ, দেবদারু (মঃ ইঃ), ইন্দ্রদারু (ঐ)।

deal'-ĕr (dēl-), *n.* **1.** A trader ; ব্যবসায়ী। **2.** A player dealing at cards ; তাস বণ্টনকারী।

dē-ăm'-bū-lā-tō-rў, *adj.* Going about from place to place ; wandering ; পরিক্রমশীল ; পর্য্যটনশীল।

dean (dēn), *n.* **1.** A head over ten monks in a monastery ; দুশজন খৃষ্টীয় মঠবাসী সন্ন্যাসীর অধ্যক্ষ, দশপুরোহিতাধিপতি (মঃ ইঃ)। **2.** The head of the chapter or body of canons or prebendaries ; খৃষ্টীয় ধর্ম্মাচার্য্য, খৃষ্টীয় উপধর্ম্মাধ্যক্ষ, বৃত্তিভোগী যাজক সমূহের অধ্যক্ষ। 3. In the universities of Oxford and Cambridge the resident fellow with disciplinary and other functions ; অক্সফোর্ড এবং কেম্ব্রিজ বিশ্ববিদ্যালয়ের যে প্রতিনিধি কোন বিদ্যামন্দিরে বাস করিয়া ছাত্রদিগের শাসন ও তত্ত্বাবধান করেন, বিদ্যামন্দিরপাল। 4. The president in a faculty ; কোন বিশেষ বিষয়ের অধ্যাপক মণ্ডলীর সভাধ্যক্ষ বা সভাপতি।

dean'-êr-ŷ (dēn-), *n.* Office or residence of a dean ; খৃষ্টীয় ধর্ম্মাচার্য্যের পদ বা আবাস-ভবন।

dear (dēr), *adj., adv., n.* & *interj.* **1.** Beloved ; (often used also in forms of address ; as, *dear* sir etc.) ; প্রিয়, দয়িত, প্রেমাস্পদ, বল্লভ। 2. Costly ; of a high price ; মহার্ঘ, মহার্ঘ, দুর্ম্মূল্য, আক্রা ; বহুমূল্য। **3.** Marked by high prices ; as, a *dear* year (=দুর্বৎসর) : a *dear* shop ; দুর্ম্মূল্যের। ***Adv.*** **1.** Affectionately ; প্রগাঢ় স্নেহের সহিত, সপ্রেমে। 2. At a high price ; as, to sell *dear* ; দুর্ম্মূল্যে, অগ্নিমূল্যে। ***Noun.*** A dear one ; darling প্রেমপাত্র, প্রিয়জন ; আদরের ধন। ***Interj.*** Dear ! dear me! O dear, etc. used to express surprise, distress, sympathy, etc. ; ভাল আপদ্, আঃ কপাল, হরি ! হরি ! **Dear'-ly,** *adv.* **Dear'-ness,** *n.* The state of being dear ; দৌর্ম্মূল্য, দুর্ম্মূলতা। **Dear-bought**—বহুমূল্যে ক্রীত। **Dearest**—প্রিয়তম, প্রাণবল্লভ।

dearth (dêrth), *n.* **1.** Scarcity ; dearness of food ; দুষ্প্রাপ্যতা ; আকাল, দুর্ভিক্ষ। 2. Poor supply ; (with *of*) ; as, *dearth of* news ; অল্পতা।

dear'-ŷ (dēr-), **—ie** (-ĭ), *n.* Dear one ; যাদু, আদুরে গোপাল, দুলাল।

death (dĕth), *n.* **1.** Cessation of all vital functions without capability of resuscitation ; মৃত্যু, পঞ্চত্ব, মরণ, জীবলীলাবসান। **2.** Anything dreadful ; as, it was *death* to them to think of entertaining such doctrines ; মৃত্যুবৎ ভয়ঙ্কর বিষয়। **3.** End of social life; as, civil *death*; সামাজিক জীবনের অবসান, সামাজিক মৃত্যু। **4.** (Personified) The destroyer of life ; শমন, যম, অন্তক, কাল। **5.** (*Theol.*) Cessation of the spiritual life, (খৃষ্টীয় ধর্ম্মশাস্ত্র) আধ্যাত্মিক জীবনের অবসান, আধ্যাত্মিক মৃত্যু। 6. Cause or occasion of loss of life ; মৃত্যুর কারণ। **7.** Extinction ; destruction ; নির্ব্বাণ, লয়, বিনাশ ; ধ্বংস। **Death'-less,** *adj.* Without death ; অমর, অবিনাশী, অনশ্বর। **Death'-less-ly,** *adv.* **Death-less-ness,** *n.* **Death'-like,** *adj.* & *adv.* **Death'-ly,** *adj.* & *adv.* **1.** Fatal ; mortal; মারাত্মক ; সাংঘাতিক। **2.** Of the nature of death ; as, *deathly* silence ; মৃত্যুবৎ। (*Adv.*) Deadly ; as, *deathly* pale ; মৃতবৎ, শববৎ। **Death'-ward,** *adj.* & *adv.* **Black-Death** — See BLACK. **Civil-death**—See CIVIL. **Death-adder** — এক জাতীয় বিষধর সর্প। **Death-bed**—মৃত্যু-শয্যা। **Death blow**—সাংঘাতিক আঘাত, মৃত্যুজনক আঘাত, মরণ ঘা ; সর্ব্বনাশের হেতু। **Death-damp**—(মৃত্যুর পূর্ব্বের) কালঘাম। **Death-duties**—সম্পত্তি উত্তরাধিকারীর হস্তে হস্তান্তরিত হইবার পূর্ব্বে যে কর আদায় করা হয়। **Death feud**—মারাত্মক বিবাদ। **Death-head**—A human skull as an emblem of death; মৃত্যুর চিহ্ন স্বরূপ নরকপাল। A kind of moth ; একপ্রকার তসরে পোকা। **Death-rate**—কোন নগর বা দেশ প্রভৃতির লোক সংখ্যার অনুপাতে মৃত্যুর হার। **Death rattle**—মৃত্যুকালে কণ্ঠের ঘড় ঘড় শব্দ। **Death's man** — ঘাতক, জল্লাদ। **Death throe**—মৃত্যু যন্ত্রণা। **Death trap**—মৃত্যু-ফাঁদ। **Death-warrant**—(*Law*) ফাঁসির পরওয়ানা, প্রাণদণ্ডের আদেশ কার্য্যে পরিণত করার জন্য আজ্ঞাপত্র বধাদেশলেখ (আঃ বঃ) ; (লক্ষণায়) মৃত্যু বাণী। **Death-watch**—একপ্রকার কীট, যাহার শব্দ মৃত্যু সূচনা করিয়া থাকে, যম-কীট।

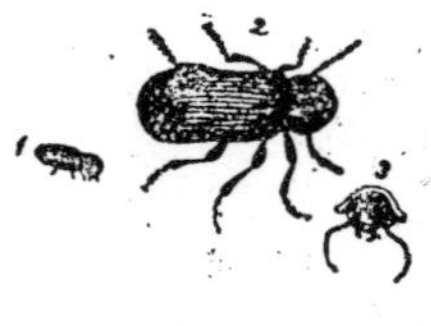

Death-watch.

At death's door—মৃত্যুমুখে, মৃত্যু-সন্নিকট। **Death on rats**—মূষিকের যম (যথা কুকুর)। **Gates** or **jaws of death**—মৃত্যুমুখ, কালগ্রাস, মৃত্যুগ্রাস। **Hold on like grim death**—মরণ কামড়ে ধরা। **Tired to death**—Utmost tired ; নিরতিশয় ক্লান্ত, নিতান্ত শ্রান্ত। **To be death on anything** — (*Hunting*) To be skilful in killing a game, or (*fig.*) at doing anything ; (মৃগয়া) শিকার বধ করণে চতুর হওয়া অথবা (লক্ষণায়) কোন কার্য্য-সম্পাদনে চতুর হওয়া। **To be in at the death**—(*Hunting*) To be up on the animal before the dog has killed it ; (মৃগয়ায়) কুকুর জন্তুকে নিহত করার পূর্ব্বে তৎসমীপে উপস্থিত হওয়া। (*Fig.*) To see an enterprise ended ; (লক্ষণায়) কোন দুঃসাহসিক কার্য্য সম্পাদিত হইয়াছে দেখা। **To be the death of**—যমস্বরূপ হওয়া। **To the death**—Fatally ; as, he was wounded *to the death* ; সাংঘাতিকরূপে।

debacle, *n.* (*F.*) **1.** Breaking up of ice in a stream ; স্রোতোজলে হিমশিলা ভঙ্গ। **2.** (*Geol.*) Sudden rush of water carrying along blocks of stone or other debris ; (ভূ-বিদ্যা) অকস্মাৎ উদ্দামবেগে ভগ্ন-পাষাণস্তূপবাহী জলরাশির প্রধাবন। **3.** (*Fig.*) A confused rout ; stampede ; ছত্রভঙ্গ ; (অশ্বাদির) সহসা ভয়ে যুগপৎ মহাবেগে পলায়ন।

dē-bâr', *v. t.* **1.** To cut off from entrance ; to exclude ; as, religion *debars* us from no pleasure; প্রবেশ করিতে না দেওয়া; বর্জ্জিত করা, বহির্ভূত করা, বহিষ্কৃত করা। **2.** To prevent; to stop (rare); নিষেধ করা, নিবারণ করা; থামান, (কচিৎ ব্যবহৃত)।

dē-bârk′, *v. t.* & *i.* To remove from on board a vessel; জাহাজ বা নৌকা হইতে স্থানান্তরিত করা। ***Verb i.*** To go ashore out of ship or boat; জাহাজ বা নৌকা হইতে তীরে যাওয়া। **—bar-ka′-tion,** *n.*

dē bāse′, *v. t.* **1.** To lower in quality, value or character; to vitiate; as, to *debase* style by vulgar words; অপভ্রংশ করা, হীন করা; দূষিত করা, বিকৃত করা। **2.** To adulterate; as, to *debase* a coin; খাইদ মিশান, ভেজাল দেওয়া। **—ment,** *n.*

dē-bāt′-ā-ble, *adj.* Disputable; subject to controversy; বিবদমান, তর্কস্থলীয়, অমীমাংসিত; বাদানুবাদ-যোগ্য। **Debatable ground** — যে ভূমি খণ্ডের জন্য দুই পক্ষ বিরোধ করিয়া থাকে, বিরোধীয় ভূমি; দুই দেশের মধ্যবর্ত্তী বিরোধীয় ভূমি, বিবাদ-ভূমি।

dē-bāte′, *n., v. t.* & *i.* Controversy; discussion; strife in argument; তর্কবিতর্ক; বাদানুবাদ, বাগ্‌বিতণ্ডা; তর্কযুদ্ধ, বাগ্‌যুদ্ধ। ***Verb t.*** **1.** To discuss; to argue; as, the question was *debated* till a late hour; আলোচনা করা; তর্ক বিতর্ক করা, বাদানুবাদ করা। **2.** To consider; to ponder; as, to *debate* a matter with one's self; বিবেচনা করা, বিচার করা; চিন্তা করা। **3.** To fight or contend for; "A well *debated* field;" কোন কিছুর জন্য যুদ্ধ বা বিরোধ করা। **4.** To engage in discussion or argument, esp. in a public assembly; আলোচনায় বা তর্কযুদ্ধে প্রবৃত্ত হওয়া, সভায় বাদানুবাদে প্রবৃত্ত হওয়া। **—bat′-er,** *n.* **Debating society**— বাদানুবাদ শিক্ষার্থ সভা, তর্ক-সভা।

dē-bauch′ (-bâch), *n.* & *v. t.* **1.** Bout or habit of sensual indulgence; lewdness; লাম্পট্য; ভ্রষ্টাচার, ব্যভিচার। **2.** An act of debauchery; as, a night's *debauch*; কুৎসিৎ আমোদ প্রমোদ। ***Verb t.*** To pervert from virtue or morality; to pollute; as, the seat of justice has been publicly *debauched*; to seduce a woman; to vitiate as taste or judgment; ভ্রষ্ট করা, সৎপথচ্যুত করা; কলুষিত করা; বিপথগামিনী করা, কলঙ্কিনী করা; বিকৃত করা। **—a-ble,** *adj.* **—er-y,** *n.* **1.** Intemperance; sexual immorality; অমিতাচার, পানাসক্তি; লাম্পট্য, ব্যভিচার। **2.** Corruption of fidelity, as of troops; সৈন্যদিগকে কর্ত্তব্যপরায়ণতা হইতে ভ্রষ্টকরণ।

dĕb-au-chee′ (-ō-shē), *n.* A libertine; a viciously sensual person; লম্পট; কামবৃত্ত (আঃ বঃ), ব্যসনী (মঃ ইঃ)।

dē-bĕn-tūre, *n.* **1.** A certificate signed by a public officer as evidence of a debt due to some person; সরকারী ঋণ-পত্র। **2.** A note acknowledging a debt; ঋণ-স্বীকার পত্র, দেয়-স্বীকার পত্র (আঃ বঃ)। **3.** A deed of mortgage given by a railway or other company for borrowed money; রেলওয়ে অথবা অন্য কোন ব্যবসায়ী সম্প্রদায় কর্ত্তৃক সম্পাদিত বন্ধকী তমঃসুক। **4.** (*Archaic* or *techn.*) Voucher given to a person supplying goods to Royal Household or Government Office entitling him to payment; রাজবাটী বা সরকারী কার্য্যালয় সমূহে কোন জিনিষ যোগাইবার জন্য সরবরাহকারী ব্যক্তিকে তাহার প্রাপ্য স্বীকার-সূচক যে প্রাপ্তিস্বীকার পত্র প্রদান করা হয়। **5.** A Custom-House certificate entitling an exporter of imported goods to a drawback of duties paid on their importation; শুল্কাগারের প্রত্যয়-পত্র—যাহার বলে কোন আমদানী মালের রপ্তানীকারী ঐ মাল আমদানীর সময় যে মাশুল প্রদত্ত হইয়াছিল তাহা ফেরৎ পাইবার অধিকারী হয়।

dē-bĭl′-ĭ-tāte, *v. t.* To weaken; to impair the strength of; to *debilitate* the constitution; দুর্ব্বল করা; শক্তিহীন করা।

dē-bĭl′-ĭ-tȳ, *n.* Feebleness; weakness; দুর্ব্বলতা, দৌর্ব্বল্য; শক্তিবৈকল্য, গ্লানি, অবসাদ (মঃ ইঃ)।

dĕb′-ĭt, *n.* & *v. t.* That which is entered in an account as debt; as, the *debit* exceeds the credit; the side of an account on which these entries are made; হিসাবের খরচের দিকের সংখ্যা; হিসাবের খরচের দিক, ঋণস্তম্ভ, খরচের জিল্লা, দেয়ধন-ভাগ (আঃ বঃ)। ***Verb t.*** **1.** To charge with debt; as, to *debit* a purchaser for goods sold; ঋণ চাপান, খরচ চাপান। **2.** To enter on the debit side of an account; to debit a sum against a person; হিসাবের ঋণের দিকে লিখা; কোন ব্যক্তির হিসাবের খরচের দিকে কোন টাকা লিখা। **Debit-side**—(In book-keeping) The left-hand side of an account, (opposed to *credit-side*); হিসাবের বাম দিক, হিসাবের খরচের দিক।

dĕb-ō-nair(e)′ (-nār), *adj.* (*Archaic.*) **1.** Genial; pleasant; (অপ্রচলিত) প্রীতিপদ; মনোরম। **2.** Courteous; affable; মার্জ্জিতাচার, শিষ্ট, ভদ্র, সুসভ্য, ভব্য; অমায়িকস্বভাব, প্রিয়বাদী (মঃ ইঃ)।

dē-boshed′ (-bŏshd), *adj.* Archaic for DEBAUCHED.

dē-bouch′ (-bŏsh), *v. i.* **1.** (*Mil.*) To march out from a wood, defile, etc., into open ground; (সামরিক শাস্ত্র) বন বা সঙ্কীর্ণ গিরি-সঙ্কট হইতে মুক্ত প্রান্তরে বহির্গত হওয়া। **2.** To emerge into a more open place; as, a tributary *debouches* into the main stream; অধিকতর উন্মুক্তস্থানে নিষ্ক্রান্ত হওয়া।

de-bris′ (dā-brē), *n.* **1.** Rubbish ; remains ; ভগ্নাবশেষ, রাবিস ; ধ্বংসাবশেষ । **2.** (*Geol.*) A mass of rocky fragments ; (ভূ-বিদ্যা) ভগ্ন-পাষাণস্তূপ ।

debt (dĕt), *n.* **1.** What one person owes to another ; liability ; ঋণ, কর্জ্জ, ধার ; দেনা, দায় । **2.** A state of obligation ; বাধ্যবাধকতা । **3.** A sin ; "Forgive us our *debts*" ; পাপ । **4.** An action for recovering a debt ; পাওনা টাকা আদায়ের জন্য মোকদ্দমা । **Debt of honour** — যে ঋণ পরিশোধের জন্য আইনতঃ কোন বাধ্যবাধকতা নাই, কিন্তু পরিশোধ না করিলে লোকসমাজে নিন্দনীয় হইতে হয়—যথা জুয়াখেলা অথবা বাজি রাখার দরুণ পণ । **Floating debt**—ঋণের যে অংশ চাওয়া মাত্র প্রদেয় । **Funded debt**—ঋণের যে অংশ মূলধনরূপে পরিণত করা হইয়াছে, এবং যাহার সুদ নিয়মমত প্রদেয় । **National debt**—জাতীয় ঋণ, রাজ্যঋণ (হিঃ কোঃ) । **To be in debt to** — To owe something to ; to remain under obligation to ; ঋণী থাকা ; কৃতজ্ঞতাপাশে বদ্ধ থাকা । **To be out of (one's) debt**—To be relieved of debt or obligation ; ঋণমুক্ত হওয়া, বাধ্যবাধকতা হইতে মুক্ত হওয়া । **To get into debt**—ঋণগ্রস্ত হওয়া । **To pay the debt of nature**—To die ; পঞ্চত্বপ্রাপ্ত হওয়া, মরা ।

debt′-or (dĕt-êr), *n.* **1.** One who owes a debt or obligation ; ঋণী, খাতক, অধমর্ণ, ঋণগ্রাহী, দেনাদার । **2.** (Book-keeping) The debit or left-hand side of an account or what is entered there, (abbr. Dr.) ; হিসাবের খরচের দিক বা ঐ দিকে লিখিত বিষয় ।

debut, (*F.*) *n.* Beginning ; hence first appearance in society or on stage etc. as a performer ; প্রারম্ভ ; অতএব সর্ব্বপ্রথম সমাজে বা জনসমাজে অবতীর্ণ হওন, অভিনেতা বা অভিনেত্রীর সর্ব্বপ্রথম রঙ্গমঞ্চে অবতরণ ।

debutant, (*F.*) *n.* One making first appearance before the public or in society ; যে ব্যক্তি সর্ব্বপ্রথম জনসমাজে বা রঙ্গমঞ্চাদিতে অবতীর্ণ হয় ।

dĕc′-ă, *n.* A prefix meaning ten and used in many technical words ; *deca*hedral ; দশ ।

dĕc′-ăd, –āde, *n.* **1.** A set of ten ; as, a *decade* of soldiers ; দশসমষ্টি । **2.** Ten years ; দশ বৎসর, দশাব্দ । **3.** Ten books ; দশসংখ্যক পুস্তক ।

dĕc′-ā-dăl, –dic, *adj.* Pertaining to ten ; দশ-সংখ্যা সম্বন্ধীয় ।

dĕc′-ā-dence (-dăns), **–dĕn-çÿ,** *ns.* Deterioration ; declension ; অবক্ষয় ; অবনতি, অধঃপতন । **–dent,** *adj.* & *n.* Decaying ; declining ; ক্ষীয়মাণ, ক্ষয়িষ্ণু, হ্রসমান ; বিশীর্য্যমাণ । (*Noun*) **1.** One who or that which is decaying or decayed ; ক্ষীয়মাণ বা ক্ষয়প্রাপ্ত ব্যক্তি বা বস্তু । **2.** A writer or artist affecting some vices and obscurities of style ; যে লেখক বা শিল্পীর রচনা অস্পষ্টতা-দোষযুক্ত এবং আড়ম্বরপূর্ণ ।

dĕc′-ă-gŏn, *n.* A plane figure with ten sides and angles ; দশভুজক্ষেত্র । **–al,** *adj.* **A regular decagon**—সমদশভুজ (হিঃ কোঃ) ।

dĕc′-ă-grăm, –gramme (-grăm), *n.* Ten grams ; ১০ গ্রাম ।

dĕc-ă-hē′-drŏn, *n.* A solid figure or body with ten sides ; দশভূজ ঘনক্ষেত্র ।

dē-căl′-cĭ-fÿ, *v. t.* To deprive of lime ; as, to *decalcify* a bone ; চূর্ণক বিরহিত করা । **–fi-ca′-tion,** *n.*

dec′-a-li-tre (dā-că-lē-têr), *n.* About $2\frac{1}{2}$ gallons ; প্রায় ২½ গ্যালন ।

dĕc′-ă-logue (-lŏg), *n.* The ten commandments given by God to Moses at mount Senai ; খৃষ্টীয় শাস্ত্রানুসারে ঈশ্বরের দশাদেশ, দশাজ্ঞাবলী, আজ্ঞাদশক, নিদেশদশক (আঃ বঃ) ।

Dĕ-căm′-ĕr-ŏn, *n.* A collection of 100 tales by Boccaccio, represented as related by a company in 10 days ; ইতালীয় কবি বোকাসিয়ো প্রণীত শতগল্প—উক্ত গল্প সমূহ দশদিবসে কথিত হইয়াছিল বলিয়া বর্ণিত হইয়াছে ।

dec′-a-me-tre (dā-că-mā-têr), *n.* Ten metres, or about 32 ft. 9 inches ; দশ মিটার (প্রায় ৩২ ফিট ৯ ইঞ্চি) ।

dē-cămp′, *v. i.* **1.** To break up or leave a camp ; শিবির ভঙ্গ করা, শিবির ত্যাগ করিয়া যাওয়া । **2.** To depart suddenly ; to run away ; to abscond ; সহসা প্রস্থান করা ; হঠাৎ গা ঢাকা দেওয়া, চম্পট দেওয়া, পলাইয়া যাওয়া ; পিঠটান দেওয়া, পলাতক হওয়া, ফেরার হওয়া । **–ment,** *n.*

dĕc′-ă-năl, *adj.* Pertaining to a dean or deanery ; খৃষ্টীয় ধর্ম্মাচার্য্য অথবা তদীয় পদ বা বাসস্থানসম্বন্ধীয় ।

dē-cănt′, *v. t.* **1.** To pour as a liquid by gradual inclination of the vessel without disturbing the sediment ; পাত্রটী ক্রমশঃ কা'ত করিয়া পাত্রস্থ তরল পদার্থ এমনভাবে আস্তে আস্তে ঢালা যাহাতে নীচের তলানি আলোড়িত না হয়, কা'ত করিয়া ঢালা । **2.** To pour from one vessel into another ; as, to *decant* wine ; এক পাত্র হইতে অন্য পাত্রে ঢালা । **–can-ta′-tion,** *n.* **–er,** *n.* **1.** A vessel used to decant liquors ; a stoppered glass-bottle for holding decanted liquors ; তলস্থ গাদ আলোড়িত না করিয়া মদ্যাদি ঢালিবার পাত্র ; তলানিশূন্য মদ ঢালিবার জন্য ছিপিযুক্ত কাচের বোতল । **2.** One who decants wine etc. ; যে ব্যক্তি তলানি আলোড়িত না করিয়া মদ্যাদি একপাত্র হইতে অন্য পাত্রে ঢালে ।

dē-căp′-ĭ-tāte, *v. t.* To behead ; to cut off the head of ; শিরশ্ছেদ করা ; ছিন্নশির করা, ছিন্নশীর্ষ করা, কতল করা (ফঃ হিঃ) । **–ta-ble,** *adj.* **–ta′-tion,** *n.* Beheading ; শিরশ্ছেদ ।

dĕc′-ă-pŏd, *n.* A ten-footed crustacean, as a crab, lobster, etc. ;

দশপদ খোলকী, যথা কাঁকড়া, চিংড়ী, প্রভৃতি।

dē-cär'-bŏn-īze, *v. t.* To deprive of carbon ; as, to *decarbonize* steel ; অঙ্গারকশূন্য করা, নিরঙ্গারক করা।

dĕc'-ă-stȳle, *n.* A portico with ten columns in front ; যে গাড়ী-বারাণ্ডা বা চাঁদনির সম্মুখদিকে দশটী স্তম্ভ থাকে।

dĕc-ă-sȳl-lăb'-ic, —syl'-la-ble, *adj.* & *n.* Having or containing ten syllables ; দশসংখ্যক শব্দাংশবিশিষ্ট। ***Noun.*** A line of ten syllables ; দশসংখ্যক শব্দাংশ-বিশিষ্ট পংক্তি।

dē-căth-ŏ'-lĭ-cīze, *v. t.* To divest of Catholic character ; ক্যাথলিক প্রকৃতি বিহীন করা।

dē-cay' (-cā), *n., v. t.* & *i.* **1.** Decline ; deterioration ; as, *decay* of the Roman empire : *decay* of the body ; decomposition ; rottenness ; অবনতি, ক্ষয়, পরিক্ষয়, ভ্রংশ, বিভ্রংশ; সংক্ষয় ; পচন ; গলিতাবস্থা। **2.** Ruinous state ; dilapidation ; ক্ষীণাবস্থা, ধ্বংসাবস্থা ; ধ্বংস। **3.** Break up of health ; disease, esp. phthisis ; স্বাস্থ্যভঙ্গ, স্বাস্থ্যহানি ; রোগ, বিশেষতঃ যক্ষ্মা। **4.** Rotten tissue ; as, to remove the *decay* ; গলিত বিধান-তন্তু। ***Verb t.*** **1.** To cause to deteriorate ; "Infirmity, that *decays* the wise,"—Shakes ; ক্ষয় করা, বিদীর্ণ করা। **2.** To rot ; পচান। ***Verb i.*** **1.** To deteriorate ; to waste or wither away ; ক্ষয়-প্রাপ্ত হওয়া ; জীর্ণ হওয়া, বিশীর্ণ হওয়া, বিলয় বা লয় হওয়া। **2.** To decline in health, strength, vigour or beauty ; স্বাস্থ্য, বল, তেজঃ বা সৌন্দর্য্য হ্রাস হওয়া। **3.** To rot ; পচিয়া যাওয়া।

dē-cease' (-sēs), *n.* & *v. i.* **1.** Departure from life ; death ; দেহত্যাগ, জীব-লীলার অবসান, ইহলোক-ত্যাগ, পরলোক-প্রাপ্তি, তনুত্যাগ (মঃ ইঃ) ; মৃত্যু, মরণ। ***Verb i.*** To die ; to depart this life ; মরা ; ইহলোক পরিত্যাগ করা, লোকান্তরিত হওয়া, পঞ্চত্ব প্রাপ্ত হওয়া, তনুত্যাগ করা, দেহত্যাগ করা। **—ceased,** *adj.* & *n.* Dead ; মৃত, পরলোকগত। *(Noun.)* The dead person (with *the* before it) ; মৃত ব্যক্তি, পরলোকগত ব্যক্তি।

dē-ceit' (-sēt), *n.* **1.** Misrepresentation, deception ; মিথ্যাবর্ণন ; প্রবঞ্চনা, ধোকা। **2.** Trick ; a wily device ; ফন্দি, ছল, ব্যাজ (মঃ উঃ), শাঠ্য, কপটতা, ফাঁকি ; চাতুরী। **—ful,** *adj.* Fraudulent ; cheating ; insincere ; ছলনাপর ; শঠ, প্রবঞ্চক, ধাপ্পা-বাজ ; চক্রবুদ্ধি, কুটিলমতি। **—ful-ly,** *adv.* **—ful-ness,** *n.*

dē-ceivê' (-sēt), *v. t.* & *i.* **1.** To lead into error ; to cheat ; ভ্রমে পাতিত করা ; প্রতারণ করা, ফাঁকি দেওয়া, ভোগা দেওয়া, ভাঁড়ান, ছলনা করা, ঠকান, বঞ্চনা করা, ধোকা দেওয়া। **2.** To disappoint ; to frustrate ; as, to *deceive* one's hopes ; হতাশ করা, নিরাশ করা ; বিফল করা। ***Verb i.*** To use deceit ; ছল প্রয়োগ করা। **—ceiv'-a-ble,** *adj.* **—ceiv'-er,** *n.* **To deceive oneself**—To juggle with one's own convictions ; আত্মপ্রতারণা করা। To be mistaken ; ভ্রান্ত হওয়া।

Dē-cĕm'-bêr, *n.* **1.** The twelfth month of the year ; ইংরাজী বর্ষের দ্বাদশ বা সর্ব্বশেষ মাস। **2.** *(Fig.)* The last period ; as, the *December* of his life ; (লক্ষণায়) শেষকাল।

dē-cĕm'-vir (-vêr), *n.* One of a body of ten magistrates in ancient Rome ; প্রাচীন রোম নগরীর দশজন শাসনকর্ত্তার অন্যতম। **2.** A member of any ruling body of ten, as at Venice ; দশজন শাসন-কর্ত্তার অন্যতম (যথা ভেনিস নগরীতে)। **—al,** *adj.* **—ate** *n.* **1.** A body of ten men in office ; দশ-কর্ম্মচারী সমবায়। **2.** The office or term of office of decemvirs in ancient Rome ; প্রাচীন রোমের দশজন শাসন-কর্ত্তার পদ, বা পদের স্থিতিকাল।

dē'-cĕn-cȳ, *n.* **1.** Proper formality ; propriety of conduct ; decorum ; সমুচিত-ব্যবহার ; সমীচীনতা, ঔচিত্য, শোভনতা ; শীলতা, ভব্যতা, শিষ্টতা। **2.** Modesty ; freedom from ribaldry or obscenity ; লজ্জাশীলতা, সরম, বিনয়, শালীনতা (আঃ বঃ), শীলতা ; সুরুচি-সম্পন্নতা। **3.** Respectability ; মান্যতা, সম্ভ্রম।

dē-cĕn'-nă-rȳ, *adj.* & *n.* Happening every ten years ; প্রতি দশবর্ষান্তে সংঘটিত, দশবার্ষিক। ***Noun.*** A period of ten years ; দশবর্ষ কাল।

dē-cĕn'-nĭ-ăd, —ŭm, *n.* A ten-year period ; দশবর্ষ কাল।

dē-cĕn'-nĭ-ăl, *adj.* **1.** Recurring in ten years ; দশবর্ষান্তে আগত। **2.** Pertaining to the period of ten years ; দশবর্ষকালিক, দশাব্দিক। **—ly,** *adv.*

dē'-cĕnt, *adj.* **1.** Seemly ; suitable ; becoming ; as, *decent* language or conduct ; সমুচিত ; যোগ্য ; শোভন। **2.** Modest ; not obscene ; সলজ্জ, সবিনয় ; সুরুচি-সম্পন্ন। **3.** Moderate ; fairly good ; reasonable ; as, a man of *decent* talents ; মধ্যবিধ ; একরূপ ; উপযুক্ত। **4.** Respectable ; as, *decent* parents ; সম্ভ্রান্ত। **—ish,** *adj.* Not severe or censorious ; অকঠোর, অদোষদর্শী। **—ly,** *adv.*

dē-cĕn'-trăl-īze, *v. t.* **1.** To cause to withdraw from the centre or the place of concentration ; বিকেন্দ্রীকৃত করা। **2.** To divide and distribute administration of public affairs ; দেশের শাসন-কার্য্য প্রধান কেন্দ্র হইতে অপসারিত করিয়া প্রদেশ, বিভাগ, জেলা, উপবিভাগ প্রভৃতি ভিন্ন ভিন্ন শাসন-কেন্দ্রে ন্যস্ত করা। **—tra-li-za'-tion,** *n.* Act of decentralizing; অধিকার বিচলন (হিঃ কোঃ)।

dē-cĕp'-tion, *n.* **1.** Deceiving ; state of being deceived or misled ;

প্রতারণা, প্রবঞ্চনা, ছলনা, প্রলম্ভ (মঃ ইঃ); প্রতারিতাবস্থা। 2. Artifice; as, the world is a *deception*; ছল, মায়া। **—tive,** *n.* Having the power to mislead; apt or tending to deceive; easily mistaken; ভ্রান্তিজনক; ছলনাপর; সহজে ভ্রান্ত। **—tive ly,** *adv.* **—tive-ness,** *n.*

dē-chrīs'-tiăn-īze, *v. t.* To turn from Christianity; খৃষ্ট-ধর্ম্ম হইতে বিচ্যুত করা। **—i-za'-tion,** *n.*

dĕc'-i—A prefix signifying tenth; দশম।

dē-cīde', *v. t.* & *v. i.* **1.** To determine; to settle: স্থির করা, নিশ্চয় করা, নির্দ্ধারণ করা, সাব্যস্ত করা; মীমাংসা করা, নিষ্পত্তি করা। **2.** To give judgment concerning; as, the court *decided* the case in favour of the plaintiff; বিচার নিষ্পত্তি করা। ***Verb i.*** To determine; "Who shall *decide* when doctors disagree;" to give judgment; to come to a conclusion; নির্ণয় করা; বিচার-মীমাংসা করা; কোন সিদ্ধান্তে উপনীত হওয়া। **—cid'-a-ble,** *adj.* **—cid'-ed,** *adj.* **1.** Definite; unquestionable; "*Decided* taste for science;" সুনিশ্চিত, স্পষ্ট, সুব্যক্ত; নিঃসন্দিগ্ধ, অবধারিত। **2.** Not vacillating; determined; দ্বিধাশূন্য; কৃতনিশ্চয়। **—cid'-ed-ly,** *adv.* **—cid'-ed-ness,** *n.*

dē-cīd'-êr, *n.* One who decides; মীমাংসাকারী, প্রমাণপুরুষ (মঃ ইঃ), নির্ণেতা (আঃ বঃ)।

dē-cĭd'-ū-ous (-ŭs), *adj.* **1.** (*Bot.*) Falling off or shedding leaves at maturity or at certain seasons; as, a *deciduous* tooth or horn; (উদ্ভিদ্-বিদ্যা) পরিণতাবস্থায় পতনশীল। (সাঃ পঃ)। **2.** (*Zool.*) Shedding wings after copulation, as an ant; (প্রাণি-বিজ্ঞান) সঙ্গমান্তে পক্ষত্যাগী। **3.** Ephemeral; ক্ষণস্থায়ী, ক্ষণভঙ্গুর, ক্ষণিক, অস্থায়ী।

dĕ-cĭl'-lion, (-yŏn) *n.* Tenth power of a million; (1 with 60 zeros annexed); ১এর ডাহিনে ৬০টী শূন্য বসাইলে যে সংখ্যা হয়। [ফ্রান্স্ এবং আমেরিকার সংখ্যালিখন প্রণালীতে, ১ এর ডাহিনে ৩৩টী শূন্য বসাইলে যে সংখ্যা হয়।] **—lionth,** *adj.* & *n.*

dec'-i-li-tre (dā-sī-lē-tre), *n.* A metric measure of volume containing 6·1024 cubic inches; আয়তনের পরিমাণ বিশেষ (৬.১০২৪ ঘন ইঞ্চি)।

dĕc'-i-mal, *adj.* & *n.* Numbered or proceeding by tens; দশমিক। ***Noun.*** A fraction having ten or some power of ten for its denominator, (also called *decimal fraction*); দশমিক ভগ্নাংশ, **—ist,** *n.* **—i-za'-tion,** *n.* **—ize,** *v. t.* **Decimal coinage** or **currency**—দশগুণোত্তর মুদ্রা প্রচলন রীতি (অর্থাৎ যে মুদ্রা প্রচলন ব্যবস্থায় কোন একশ্রেণীর মুদ্রা উহার অব্যবহিত পরবর্ত্তী মুদ্রার শ্রেণীর দশগুণ মূল্যের হইয়া থাকে।) **Decimal fraction**—যে ভগ্নাংশের হর বা ভাজক দশ বা দশগুণোত্তর সংখ্যা হইয়া থাকে। **Decimal notation** — দশমিক সংখ্যালিখন প্রণালী। **Decimal numeration** — একং দশং শতং ইত্যাদি প্রণালীতে গণন। **Decimal place**—দশমিক স্থান। **Decimal point**—দশমিক বিন্দু। **Decimal system**—দশমিক মান (যে মানের একক দশক বা দশের কোন ঘাত বা সামর্থ্য হইয়া থাকে)। **Recurring Decimal** — See under RECURRING.

dĕc'-i-māte, *v. t.* **1.** To take the tenth part of; দশমাংশ নেওয়া। **2.** To kill every tenth men of, as a punishment; as, to *decimate* a regiment for mutiny; শাস্তিস্বরূপ প্রতি দশজনের মধ্যে একজনকে নিহত করা। **3.** To destroy a considerable part of; as, plague *decimates* a people; অধিকাংশ ধ্বংস করা, বহুলোক-ক্ষয় করা। **—ma'-tion,** *n.* The act of decimating; দশমাংশ-গ্রহণ, বহুলোকক্ষয়।

dĕc'-i-mē-tre (-têr), *n.* A French measure of length $\frac{1}{10}$ of a metre or 3·9371 inches; ফরাসী দেশের দৈর্ঘ্যের পরিমাপ বিশেষ।

dē-cī'-pher, *n.* & *v. t.* A translation of a cipher document; সাঙ্কেতিক লিপির অনুবাদ। ***Verb t.*** **1.** To translate from secret characters or ciphers into intelligible terms; as, to *decipher* a letter; সাঙ্কেতিক লিপির রহস্যোদ্ভেদ করা, সাঙ্কেতিক লিপির অর্থ প্রকাশ করা। **2.** To make out the meaning of, as hieroglyphics, badly formed characters, or what is partially obliterated; to detect; to unfold; মিশরদেশীয় চিত্রাক্ষর, অথবা অস্পষ্ট বা আংশিকভাবে বিলুপ্ত লিপির অর্থনির্ণয় করা; উদ্ঘাটন করা; রহস্যোদ্ভেদ করা। **—a-ble,** *adj.* **—ment,** *n.*

dē-cī'-sion, *n.* **1.** Settlement (of question etc.); conclusion; নিষ্পত্তি, মীমাংসা, বিনিশ্চয়; সিদ্ধান্ত। **2.** Formal judgment as of a court; বিচারাজ্ঞা, রায়। **3.** Arbitration end, as of a struggle; as, the *decision* of a battle by arms; মীমাংসা, নিষ্পত্তি। **4.** Determination; firmness; decided character; "On the English face are combined *decision* and nerve"—Emerson; স্থির-প্রতিজ্ঞা, স্থিরসংকল্প; দৃঢ়তা, স্থৈর্য্য (আঃ বঃ); দৃঢ়-প্রতিজ্ঞা। **—sive,** *adj.* **1.** Deciding; conclusive; as, a *decisive* battle; নিশ্চায়ক, নিশ্চয়াত্মক নির্ণায়ক, সংশয়চ্ছেদী; চূড়ান্ত, চরম। **2.** Unmistakable; decided; as, *decisive* superiority of character; অসন্দিগ্ধ; অবধারিত, নিশ্চিত। **—sive-ly,** *adv.* **—sive-ness,** *n.*

dē-cĭv'-i-līze, *v. t.* To reduce from a civilized to a wild or savage state; অসভ্য করা, সভ্যতা-বিরহিত করা।

dĕck, *n.* & *v. t.* A platform of planks or wood-covered iron extending from side to side of a ship or a part of it; as, upper or lower *deck*; জাহাজের পাটাতন, পোতপৃষ্ঠ, পোতমঞ্চ, নৌকাস্তরণ (মঃ ইঃ)। ***Verb t.*** **1.** To furnish with, or cover as, a deck; পাটাতন বিশিষ্ট করা, পাটাতন দ্বারা আচ্ছাদিত করা। **2.** To embellish; to adorn; "Daisies *deck* the green;" অলঙ্কৃত করা; বিমণ্ডিত করা, বিভূষিত করা, বিশোভিত করা, সুসজ্জিত করা। **Deck-chair**—যাত্রি-জাহাজের আরাম-কেদারা। **Deck-house** or **room**—জাহাজের পাটাতনের উপরিস্থ গৃহ বা কক্ষ। **Fore-castle deck**—পোতাগ্রদেশস্থ ক্ষুদ্র মঞ্চ বা পাটাতন। **Orlop-deck** — নিম্নতর পাটাতনের নিম্নবর্ত্তী পাটাতন। **Poop-deck** — জাহাজের পশ্চাদ্‌ভাগস্থ ক্ষুদ্র মঞ্চ বা পাটাতন। **Quarter-deck**—জাহাজের মাস্তুল এবং পশ্চাদ্ভাগের মধ্যবর্ত্তী উচ্চতর পাটাতনের অংশ—যাহা উচ্চ নাবিক কর্ম্মচারিগণ ব্যবহার করেন। **Upper** or **spar deck**—জাহাজের একপ্রান্ত হইতে অপরপ্রান্ত বিস্তৃত প্রধান পাটাতনের উপরিস্থ পাটাতন। **To clear** or **sweep the decks**—To make open or void for passage or operation; যুদ্ধের জন্য অথবা গমনাগমনের জন্য অনাবশ্যক দ্রব্যাদি স্থানান্তরিত করত জাহাজের পাটাতন পরিষ্কার করা।

deck'-le (dĕkl), *n.* A contrivance in paper-making machine for limiting size of the sheet; কাগজের তাএর আয়তন পরিমিত করার জন্য কাগজের কলের মধ্যস্থিত ব্যবস্থাবিশেষ, আকার-নিয়ামক। **Deckle-edge**; উক্তরূপ কৌশলদ্বারা আবড়ো খাবড়ো ভাবে কাটা কাগজের কিনারা।

dē-claim' (-clām), *v. t. & i.* To utter rhetorically in public; অলঙ্কারিক ভাষায় প্রকাশ্য বক্তৃতা করা। ***Verb i.*** **1.** To speak rhetorically; to harangue; আলঙ্কারিক ভাষায় বক্তৃতা করা; সাধারণ্যে উত্তেজনাপূর্ণ বক্তৃতা করা, গলাবাজি করা। **2.** To deliver impassioned rather than reasoned speech; আবেগ-পূর্ণ বক্তৃতা করা, উচ্ছ্বাস-পূর্ণ বক্তৃতা করা। **—clam'-a-to-ry,** *adj.* Pretentiously rhetorical; বাগাড়ম্বরপূর্ণ।

dĕc-lă-mā'-tion, *n.* **1.** A harangue; an impassioned speech; শব্দাড়ম্বর-বহুল বক্তৃতা; উচ্ছ্বাসপূর্ণ বক্তৃতা, গলাবাজি। **2.** Act or art of declaiming; বাগাড়ম্বরপূর্ণ বক্তৃতা প্রদান, বাগাড়ম্বরপূর্ণ বক্তৃতা-প্রদান-কৌশল। **3.** Pretentious rhetorical display; কৃত্রিম বাগ্মিতা প্রদর্শন।

dē-clār'-ănt, *n.* One who makes a declaration in a legal action; ঘোষণাকারী, বিশেষতঃ মোকদ্দমায় ধর্ম্মতঃ প্রতিজ্ঞা-পূর্ব্বক ঘোষণাকারী।

dĕc-lă-rā'-tion, *n.* **1.** Act of declaring or announcing; proclamation; exposition; বিঘোষণ; ঘোষণা; খ্যাপন, প্রকাশন। **2.** Menifesto; formal expression; as, the *declaration* of independence; ঘোষণা-পত্র; প্রচার, উক্তি, বিজ্ঞাপন। **3.** (*Law*) Plaintiff's statement of claim in an action; (আইন) বাদীর আরজী। **4.** (*Law*) A solemn statement allowed to be made by witnesses etc. instead of the oath; (আইন) ধর্ম্মতঃ প্রতিজ্ঞা। **5.** (*Law*) A custom house statement; (আইন) শুল্কাগারে শুল্ক যোগ্য মাল সম্বন্ধে যে বর্ণনা-পত্র দাখিল করা হয়। **6.** (*Racing*) A formal withdrawal of a horse from a race in which it has been ntered; (ঘোড়দৌড়) ঘোড়দৌড়ের জন্য তালিকাভুক্ত অশ্বকে যথারীতি উঠাইয়া লওন। **Declaration of Independence** — ১৭৭৭ খৃষ্টাব্দের ৪ঠা জুলাই তারিখে উত্তর আমেরিকার ঔপনিবেশিকগণ কর্ত্তৃক স্বাধীনতা ঘোষণা। **Declaration of the polls, Declaration of rights**—১৬৮৯ খৃঃ অব্দে ব্রিটিশ পার্লেমেণ্ট কর্ত্তৃক ঘোষিত নাগরিক অধিকার সমূহ,—যাহা শাসনতন্ত্রকে মানিয়া চলিতে হয়। **Declaration of war**—যুদ্ধ-ঘোষণা, সমর-ঘোষণা।

dē-clāre', *v. t. & i.* **1.** To make known; to proclaim; "I will *declare* what he hath done for my soul;" ঘোষণা করা, বিদিত করা, রটনা করা; লোক-সমাজে প্রকাশ করা। **2.** To assert; to affirm; to pronounce to be something; as, he *declared* the man an enemy to human kind; দৃঢ়তাসহকারে বলা, খ্যাপন করা; নিশ্চয় ভাবে বলা; কোন কিছু বলিয়া ব্যক্ত করা। **3.** To make a full statement of, as of goods on which duties etc. are payable at a custom-house; যে সকল মালের উপর শুল্ক প্রদেয় তৎসম্বন্ধে সম্যক্ বর্ণনা করা। **4.** (*Racing*) To announce the withdrawal of a horse from a race in which it has been entered; (ঘোড়দৌড়) কোন ঘোড়দৌড়ের জন্য তালিকা ভুক্ত অশ্বের নাম তালিকা হইতে উঠাইয়া লওয়া হইয়াছে বলিয়া ঘোষণা করা। ***Verb i.*** **1.** To make an open avowal; দৃঢ়তার সহিত প্রকাশ্যে বলা। **2.** (*Law*) To make a statement of a claim as a plaintiff in a case; (আইন) (কোন বাদীকর্ত্তৃক) আরজী করা। **To declare against**—To proclaim one's self against; বিরুদ্ধে ঘোষণা করা। **To declare for**—To side with; পক্ষ অবলম্বন করা। **To declare one's self**—To avow intentions, (with *for* or *against*); অভিপ্রায় প্রকাশ করা। To reveal one's true character; প্রকৃত চরিত্র প্রকাশ করা। **To declare to**—To make an open and explicit avowal and declaration to; কাহারো নিকট অকপটে বা স্পষ্টাক্ষরে স্বীকার বা ঘোষণা করা।

dē-clăr'-ă-tive (-tĭv), *adj.* Explanatory; assertive; অর্থব্যঞ্জক, ব্যাখ্যাত্মক; খ্যাপক। **—a-to-ry,** *adj.* Expressive; affirmatory; as, a *declaratory* law; অর্থব্যঞ্জক, অর্থদ্যোতক; নিশ্চয়াত্মক, স্বীকারসূচক।

declasse, adj. (*F.*) That has lost caste or sunk in social scale ; জাতিচ্যুত, পতিত।

dĕ-clĕn'-sion, *n.* **1.** Deterioration ; decay ; as, the *declension* of science ; ক্ষয়, অপকর্ষ ; অবনতি, অধোগতি, পতন। **2.** Deviation from uprightness ; "The *declensions* of Israel ;" অধঃপতন। **3.** (*Gram.*) Act of declining a noun etc. ; one of the noun-classes distinguished by their different methods of case-inflection etc. ; (ব্যাকরণ) শব্দাদির রূপ করণ ; শব্দরূপ। **4.** Refusal (rare) ; অসম্মতি।

dĕc-li-nā'-tion, *n.* **1.** Downward bend ; obliquity ; অধোদিকে বক্রতা ; তির্য্যগ্ভাব। **2.** Deterioration ; decline ; "The *declination* of a monarchy ;" ক্ষয়, হ্রাস ; পতন, অধোগতি, অবনতি। **3.** (*Astron.*) Angular distance of a star etc. from the celestial equator ; celestial latitude ; (জ্যোতির্বিজ্ঞান) খগোলীয় নাড়ীমণ্ডল হইতে নক্ষত্রাদির কৌণিক দূরত্ব, খগোলীয় অক্ষাংশ ; ক্রান্তি (সাঃ পঃ), অপক্রান্তি (ঐ)। **4.** (*Compass*) Deviation of the needle from true North and South ; (দিগ্দর্শন যন্ত্র) দিগ্দর্শন যন্ত্রের সূচির প্রকৃত উত্তর বা দক্ষিণদিক হইতে চ্যুতি। **5.** Refusal, (rare) ; অসম্মতি, অস্বীকার। [illegible], *adj.* **Declination compass** — দিক্-পতন দর্শক (হিঃ কোঃ)। **Declination point**— উন্মণ্ডল (সাঃ পঃ)। **Circle of declination** — ক্রান্তিসূত্র (সাঃ পঃ)। **Declination of planets**—স্ফুটক্রান্তি (সাঃ পঃ)। **Declination of the sun**—অস্ফুট ক্রান্তি (সাঃ পঃ)। **Declination of a point in the ecliptic**— ক্রান্তিভাস (সাঃ পঃ)।

dĕ-clīne', *n.* **1.** Deterioration ; decay ; diminution ; as, the *decline* of the old Roman empire ; অবনতি ; ক্ষয়, অপচয় (মঃ ইঃ), ধ্বংস ; হ্রাস, ন্যূনতা। **2.** Setting ; last part of a course ; as, the *decline* of life ; অস্তগমন ; শেষভাগ। **3.** (*Med.*) Phthisis ; consumption ; as, to die of a *decline* ; (ভৈষজ্য-শাস্ত্র) রাজযক্ষ্মা ; ক্ষয়রোগ। **4.** A slope ; declivity ; (rare) ; ক্রমনিম্নতা ; ঢাল (ফঃ হিঃ)।

dĕ-clīne', *v. t.* & *i.* **1.** To bend downward ; "In melancholy deep, with head *declined*" : it *declines* its blossoms ; নিম্নদিকে আনত করা, ঝুঁকিয়া পড়া। **2.** To shun or avoid ; to refuse ; to reject ; as to *decline* an offer ; ত্যাগকরা, পরিহার করা, এড়ান ; অস্বীকার করা ; অগ্রাহ্য করা। **3.** (*Gram.*) To inflect or rehearse in order the changes of grammatical forms of ; as, to *decline* a noun ; শব্দাদির রূপ করা। ***Verb i.*** **1.** To lean downward ; as, the head *declines* towards the earth ; to slant or slope downward as a piece of land ; ঝুঁকিয়া পড়া, আনত হওয়া ; নিম্নদিকে ঢালু বা প্রবণ হওয়া। **2.** To sink morally ; অধঃপতন হওয়া, বিপথগামী হওয়া, পতন হওয়া। **3.** To draw to a close ; as, the day *declines* ; শেষ হইয়া আসা, অবসান হইয়া আসা। **4.** To decay ; as, the vigour of youth *declines* ; নষ্ট হওয়া, ক্ষয় হওয়া, হ্রাস হওয়া। **5.** To refuse ; অস্বীকার করা, প্রত্যাখ্যান করা (আঃ বঃ)। **—clin'-a-ble,** *adj.* Admitting of declension or inflexion ; বিভক্তিযোগে রূপান্তরসহ, নৈকরূপ (আঃ বঃ)। **To decline with thanks**—(*Iron.*) To refuse scornfully ; ধন্যবাদের সহিত (অর্থাৎ অবজ্ঞার সহিত) প্রত্যাখান করা (ব্যঙ্গচ্ছলে)।

dĕc-li-nŏm'-ĕ-têr, *n.* An instrument for measuring magnetic declination ; চুম্বকক্রান্তিমাপক যন্ত্র।

dĕ-clĭv'-i-tў, *n.* **1.** Inclination downward ; নিম্নাভিমুখে প্রবণতা। **2.** A sloping place ; উৎরাও, প্রবণ ভূমি (মঃ ইঃ), ঢালুস্থান, অবসর্পিণী ভূমি (আঃ বঃ), নতভূ (ঐ)।

dĕ-clī'-vous (-vŭs), *adj.* Sloping downward (esp. of a profile, in Zool.) ; নিম্নাভিমুখে প্রবণ।

dĕ-cŏct', *v. t.* To prepare by boiling ; to prepare a decoction of ; পাক করা, সিদ্ধ করা, ফুটাইয়া প্রস্তুত করা, ক্বাথ বাহির করা ; কোন জিনিষের ক্বাথ প্রস্তুত করা। **Decocted water**—ক্বথিত জল।

dĕ-cŏc'-tion, *n.* **1.** An extract of anything got by boiling ; কষায়, ক্বাথ, ফাণ্ট, আসব। **2.** An act or process of boiling so as to extract virtues of a thing ; ক্বাথ বাহির করণ।

dĕ-cŏl'-lāte, *v. t.* **1.** To behead ; to decapitate ; মস্তক ছেদন করা ; শিরশ্ছেদন করা। **2.** (*Conch.*) To break off the apex of as a shell ; (শঙ্খ-বিদ্যা) শঙ্খাদির চূড়া ভঙ্গ করা। **—lat-ed,** *adj.* **—la'-tion** *n.*

decollete, adj. (*F.*) **1.** Cut low in the neck or low-necked—said of dress ; (পোষাক-সম্বন্ধে) গলারদিকে নীচু করিয়া কাটা। **2.** Wearing a low-necked dress ; গলারদিকে নীচু করিয়া কাটা পোষাক-পরা।

dĕ-col'-o(u)r-īze (-cŭl-êr-), *v. t.* To deprive of colour ; বর্ণভ্রষ্ট করা, বর্ণহীন করা। **—i-za'-tion,** *n.* **—iz-er,** *n.*

dĕ-cŏm-plĕx', *adj.* Having complex parts ; জটিল অংশ বিশিষ্ট।

dĕ-cŏm-pōse', *v. t.* & *i.* **1.** To separate the constituent parts of ; as, to *decompose* light or a substance ; to analyse as a thought or motive ; বিশ্লেষণ করা ; চিন্তা বা উদ্দেশ্য বিশ্লেষণ করা। **2.** To rot ; পচান, গলিত করা। ***Verb i.*** To undergo dissolution ; to rot ; বিশ্লিষ্ট হওয়া ; পচা, গলিত হওয়া। **—pos'-a-ble,** *adj.* **—pos'-er,** *n.* **—po-si'-tion,** *n.* **1.** Decay ; dissolution ; অপক্ষয় ; বিঘটন, পৃথগ্ভবন, বিচ্ছেদন। **2.** Compounding of things already compound ;

বিশ্লেষণ, রাসায়নিক বিয়োগ, বিয়োজন। **Decomposition of forces**—(In Dynamics) Resolution of forces ; (গতি-বিজ্ঞান) বল-বিশ্লেষণ। **Decomposition of light** — আলোক-বিশ্লেষণ।

dē-cŏm-pound′ (-pownd), *adj.* & *n.* **1.** Compounded again ; পুনর্মিশ্রিত। **2.** (*Bot.*) Having divisions which are themselves compound ; (উদ্ভিদ-বিদ্যা) বহুভিন্ন (সাঃ পঃ)।

dē-cŏn′-sē-crāte, *v. t.* To secularize ; (পবিত্র দ্রব্যাদি) সাংসারিক ব্যবহারে আনা।

dĕc′-ō-rāte, *v. t.* **1.** To beautify ; to embellish ; as, to *decorate* a church with flowers ; শোভিত করা, বিভূষিত করা, অলঙ্কৃত করা ; মণ্ডিত করা। **2.** To invest with medal, order, etc. ; as, to *decorate* a hero ; সম্মানসূচক পদক, পদবী, প্রভৃতি প্রদান করা। **3.** To serve as adornment to ; অলঙ্কারস্বরূপ হওয়া। **Decorated style**—(*Arch.*) (স্থপতি-বিজ্ঞান) ইংলণ্ডের মধ্যযুগের স্থাপত্য-রীতিবিশেষ।

dĕc-ō-rā′-tion, *n.* **1.** Ornament ; embellishment ; ভূষা, অলঙ্কার ; মণ্ডন। **2.** Act of decorating ; বিভূষণ, প্রসাধন। **3.** A star, cross, medal, etc. worn as a mark of honour ; সম্মান-চিহ্নস্বরূপ পরিহিত তারা, ক্রুশ বা পদক প্রভৃতি। **4.** (*Pl.*) Wreaths, flags, etc. put up on an occasion of public rejoicing ; সাধারণের আনন্দোৎসব দিবসে বিন্যস্ত মাল্য, পতাকা, প্রভৃতি। **Decoration day**—৩০শে মে—যে দিবস আমেরিকার অন্তর্বিগ্রহে (১৮৬১-৬৫) নিহত সৈনিকগণের স্মৃতির প্রতি সম্মান প্রদর্শনার্থ তাহাদের সমাধি-মন্দির পুষ্পাদিদ্বারা অলঙ্কৃত করা হয় এবং বক্তৃতা প্রদান ও শোভাযাত্রাদির অনুষ্ঠান হইয়া থাকে।

dĕc′-ō-rā-tive (-tĭv), *adj.* Ornamental ; শোভাসাধক, প্রসাধক, আলঙ্কারিক। **Decorative art** — প্রসাধন-শিল্প।

dĕc′-ō-rā-tor (-têr), *n.* One who decorates, specif. an artist or artisan whose business is the decoration of houses, esp. of their interior ; মণ্ডনকারী, প্রসাধক, বিশেষতঃ যে শিল্পী বা চিত্রকর গৃহমণ্ডিত করে, বিশেষভাবে যাহারা গৃহের অভ্যন্তর-ভাগের মণ্ডনকার্য্য সম্পাদন করে।

dē-cō′-rous (-rŭs), *adj.* Dignified and decent ; seemly ; proper ; মর্য্যাদা-বোধসম্পন্ন ; ভদ্রোচিত ; সমীচীন। **—ly** *adv.*

dē-cō′-rŭm *n.* **1.** Seemliness ; etiquette ; as, a sense of *decorum* : decency or propriety of conduct ; শোভনতা ; ভদ্রতা, শীলতা, ভব্যতা ; সমীচীনতা, ঔচিত্য ; মর্য্যাদা (মঃ ইঃ)। **2.** An act required by social custom etc. ; শিষ্টাচার।

dē-coy′, *n.* & *v. t.* **1.** Anything intended to allure into a snare ; enticement ; লোভানি, যে জিনিষ দ্বারা প্রলুব্ধ করিয়া ফাঁদে ফেলান হয়, টোপ, আমিষ ; প্রলোভন। **2.** A place as a pond etc. where wild fowls are enticed and caught ; পুষ্করিণী প্রভৃতি স্থান,—যথায় বন্য পক্ষিগণকে প্রলুব্ধ করিয়া আনিয়া ধরা হয়। **3.** A bird etc., tamed and trained to entice others into a snare ; (also decoy duck) ; পক্ষী প্রভৃতি—যাহাদিগকে অপর বিহঙ্গাদিকে ভুলাইয়া ফাঁদে ফেলিবার জন্য শিক্ষিত করা হয়। **4.** (*Fig.*) One employed to allure others into a snare ; a tempter ; (লক্ষণায়) যে ব্যক্তি অপর ব্যক্তিগণকে ভুলাইয়া ফাঁদে ফেলিবার জন্য নিযুক্ত হয়, মায়াবী ; প্রলোভক। ***Verb t.*** To lure into a snare ; to entrap ; to entice ; নানা প্রলোভনে ভুলাইয়া ফাঁদে ফেলা ; ফাঁদে ফেলা ; প্রলুব্ধ করা।

dē-crease′ (-crēs), *n., v. t.* & *i.* Diminution ; lessening ; অপচয়, অবক্ষয়, ক্ষয় ; হ্রাস, উপশম। ***Verb t.*** to cause to grow less ; to diminish ; as, extravagance *decreases* one's means ; হ্রাস করা ; কমান। ***Verb i.*** To become less ; to be diminished gradually ; as, the days *decrease* in length from June to December ; লাঘব হওয়া, হ্রাস হওয়া ; ক্রমশঃ হ্রাসপ্রাপ্ত হওয়া।

dē-cree′ (-crē), *n.* & *v. t.* **1.** Ordinance or edict set forth by authority ; রাজাজ্ঞা, ফরমাণ (ফঃ হিঃ), শাসন, ব্যবস্থা। **2.** (*Law*) A judicial decision ; (আইন) নির্ণয়-পত্র ; নিস্পত্তি-পত্র, রায়, ফয়সলা। **3.** (*Theol.*) An eternal purpose of God foreordaining some event or condition ; (খৃষ্টীয় ধর্ম্মশাস্ত্র) বিধির বিধান, নিয়তি। ***Verb t.*** **1.** To ordain by decree ; বিধান করা। **2.** (*Law*) To order judicially by decree ; (আইন) রায় প্রদান করা, বিচারাদেশ প্রদান করা।

dĕc′-rē-mĕnt, *n.* **1.** Decrease ; diminution ; হ্রাস ; ন্যূনতা, অপচয়। **2.** The quantity lost by diminution or waste ; কমতি, ঘাট্‌তি।

dē-crĕp′-it, *adj.* Worn out by the infirmities of old age ; feeble ; as, a *decrepit* man or institution ; অবজীর্ণ, অতি বৃদ্ধ, খুড়্‌ খুড়ে জরাজীর্ণ, জরাগ্রস্ত, জরাতুর (আঃ বঃ)। **—i-tude,** *n.* Dotage ; জরা।

dē-crĕp′-i-tāte, *v. t.* & *i.* To roast or calcine so as to cause crackling ; as, to *decrepitate* salt ; চিড়্‌ চিড়্‌ শব্দে ভাজা বা দগ্ধ করা। ***Verb i.*** To crackle under heat ; অগ্নিতে নিক্ষিপ্ত লবণের মত চিড়্‌ চিড়্‌ শব্দ করা। **—ta′-tion,** *n.*

dē-crĕs′-cence (-sĕns), *n.* Act or process of decreasing ; ন্যূনীকরণ।

decrescendo, (*It.*) *adj.* & *adv.* (*Music*) With gradually diminishing volume ; with abatement of tone ; (সঙ্গীত-শাস্ত্র) ক্রমশঃ মন্দায়মান ; ক্রমশঃ মন্দায়মান ধ্বনি সহকারে।

dē-crĕs′-cĕnt, *adj.* Waning ; as, the *decrescent* moon ; ক্ষীয়মাণ।

dē-crē′-tăl, *adj.* Relating to a decree ; বিচারাজ্ঞাসম্বন্ধীয়।

dē-crē'-tăl, *n.* **1.** A papal decree ; রোমীয় ধর্ম্মসম্রাটের আদেশপত্র। **2.** (*Pl.*) Collection of papal decrees, forming part of canon law ; (বহুবচন) রোমীয় ধর্ম্মসম্রাটের আদেশপত্র সংগ্রহ। **3.** A decree ; বিধান।

decretum salutis—ঈশ্বরাধীন মুক্তি।

dē-crȳ', *v. t.* **1.** To condemn ; to cry down ; দোষী করা ; অপবাদ করা, অবগীত করা। **2.** To depreciate ; অনাদর করা, অমর্য্যাদা করা।

dĕc'-ū-măn, *adj.* Large ; as *decuman* waves ; বৃহৎ, প্রকাণ্ড।

dē-cŭm'-bĕnt, *adj.* **1.** Lying down ; prostrate ; শয়ান, শায়িত ; প্রণত। **2.** (*Bot.*) Declined or bending down, as a stem or shoot ; (উদ্ভিদ্-বিদ্যা) অগ্রোথিত (সাঃ পঃ)।

dĕc'-ū-ple, *n., adj., v. t.* & *i* Tenfold amount ; দশগুণিত সংখ্যা। ***Adj.*** Tenfold ; দশগুণিত। ***Verb t. & i.*** To multiply by ten ; দশ দ্বারা গুণন করা ; দশগুণিত হওয়া।

dē-cŭr'-rĕnt, *adj.* Running or extending downward ; অধোধাবক।

dē-cŭs'-sāte, *adj., v. t.* & *i.* **1.** X-shaped ; intersected ; ইংরেজী X অক্ষরের আকার ; পরস্পরের দ্বারা ছেদিত। **2.** (*Bot.*) Arranged in pairs each at right angles to the next pair above or below ; as, *decussate* leaves ; (উদ্ভিদ্-বিদ্যা) এরূপভাবে জোড়ায় জোড়ায় বিন্যস্ত যাহাতে প্রত্যেক জোড়া নীচের বা উপরের জোড়ার সহিত সমকোণ উৎপাদন করে, চতুষ্কোণী (সাঃ পঃ)। **3.** (*Rhet.*) Chiastic ; (অলঙ্কার-শাস্ত্র) যে শব্দালঙ্কারে প্রথম বাক্যাংশের শব্দের ক্রম পরবর্ত্তী বাক্যাংশে বিপর্য্যস্ত করা হয় তৎসম্বন্ধীয়। ***Verb t.*** To cut or divide in the forms of X ; X অক্ষরের আকারে কাটা বা বিভাগ করা। ***Verb i.*** To intersect ; as, the point where two lines *decussate* ; পরস্পরকে ছেদন করা।

dĕd'-i-cāte, *v. i.* To set apart or consecrate to God or to a sacred purpose ; as, to *dedicate* a temple to God ; উৎসর্গ করা, প্রতিষ্ঠা করা, নিবেদন করা (মঃ ইঃ)। **2.** To devote ; সমর্পণ করা। **3.** To give wholly and earnestly up to ; "To the face of peril myself I will *dedicate*" ; সম্পূর্ণরূপে আত্মসমর্পণ করা। **4.** To inscribe a book etc. to a patron or friend ; কোন বন্ধু বা প্রতিপালক-বড়লোকের নামে পুস্তকাদি উৎসর্গ করা। **—ca-tor, —ca-tee,** *ns.* **—ca-tive, —ca-to-ry,** *adjs.*

dĕd-i-cā'-tion, *n.* **1.** The act of dedicating ; উৎসর্গীকরণ। **2.** The act of devoting oneself etc. to the pursuit of a purpose etc. ; কোন রূপ উদ্দেশ্যাদি সাধনে আত্মসমর্পণ, আত্মোৎসর্গ। **3.** A dedicatory inscription on a book, building, etc. ; উৎসর্গপত্র, উৎসর্গ-লিপি।

dē-dūce', *v. t.* **1.** To draw a conclusion ; to infer, (with *from*) ; as, reasoning is nothing but the faculty of *deducing* unknown truths from principles already known ; সাধারণ তত্ত্ব হইতে বিশেষ-তত্ত্ব নির্ণয় করা, উপপাদন করা ; অনুমান করা, সিদ্ধান্ত করা। **2.** To trace descent of, (followed by *from*) ; উৎপত্তির অনুসরণ করা। **3.** To take the subject of, (with *from*) ; আকর্ষণ করা ; মূল বিষয় গ্রহণ করা। **—duc'-i-ble,** *adj.*

dē-dŭct' *v. t.* To take away ; to separate, (with *from* or *out of*) ; বাদ দেওয়া, বিয়োগ করা, কাটা, পৃথক করা। [In present usage *deduct* applies specifically to amounts or qualities, *subtract* to numbers.]

dē-dŭc'-tion, *n.* **1.** Act or process of deducing ; mediate inference in which the conclusion necessarily follows from a full understanding of given data or proposition ; নিগমন, নিগমন-প্রণালী ; অনুমান, নির্ণয়। **2.** Act of deducting or taking away ; subtraction ; কর্ত্তন ; বিয়োগ, ব্যবকলন। **3.** Amount deducted ; বাদ। **4.** A thing deduced or inferred ; a conclusion অনুমিত বিষয় ; সিদ্ধান্ত।

dē-dŭc'-tive (-tĭv), *adj.* Employing deduction in reasoning ; capable of being deduced from premises ; relating to deduction ; আনুমানিক (সাঃ পঃ), নিগমনাত্মক (হিঃ কোঃ) ; নিগমনসাধ্য, অনুমেয় ; অনুমান-সম্বন্ধীয়। **Deductive Logic**—নিগমন-বিদ্যা, নিগমনশাস্ত্র। **Deductive method**— (তর্কবিজ্ঞান) অবরোহ প্রণালী অর্থাৎ সাধারণ তত্ত্ব হইতে বিশেষ তত্ত্ব নির্ণয়।

dee (dē), *n.* **1.** The letter d or D ; D এই অক্ষর। **2.** D-shaped harness-ring ; D এই অক্ষরের আকার ঘোড়ার সাজের আংটি।

deed (dēd), *n.* **1.** A thing done intentionally ; কার্য্য, ক্রিয়া, কর্ম্ম, কৃত্য। **2.** Illustrious act ; achievement ; as, knightly *deeds* ; মহৎ-কার্য্য, মহৎকৃত্য ; অবদান, চরিত। **3.** Actual fact ; performance ; as, in words and *deeds* ; বাস্তবিক বিষয় ; সম্পাদন। **4.** (*Law*) An instrument on paper or parchment conveying real estate to a purchaser or donee ; (আইন) লেখ্য, দলীলনামা, নিদর্শনপত্র, কোবালা। **Deed of acquiescence given by a defendant**—সাফিনামা। **Deed of acquiescence given by a plaintiff**—রাজিনামা। **Deed of acquittance**—রাজিনামা, রিহাইনামা (ফঃ হিঃ)। **Deed of compromise**—সোলেনামা। **Deed of conditional sale**—কটকওয়ালা। **Deed of confirmation**—বহালী সনদ। **Deed of gift**—দানপত্র, হেবানামা। **Deed of sale** (public)—বয়নামা। **Deed of sale** (private)—কওয়ালা, কবালা।

deem (dēm), *v. t.* & *i.* To believe to consider ; as, it was, I *deemed,* time to go ; বোধ করা, ভাবা, মানা,

বিবেচনা করা। *Verb i.* To judge or think (of a person or thing); কোন ব্যক্তি বা বিষয় সম্বন্ধে বিবেচনা করা। **To deem highly**—To have a high opinion of; (কোন ব্যক্তি বা বিষয় সম্বন্ধে) উচ্চমত পোষণ করা।

deem′-stêr (dēm-), *n.* One of the two judges of the Isle of Man; ম্যান দ্বীপের অন্যতর বিচারক।

deep (dēp), *adj.* **1.** Descending far downward; profound; as, a *deep* hole; গভীর, গহন; প্রগাঢ়, ডুবগাহ। **2.** Going far in from surface or edge; as, a *deep* wound; গভীর, নিম্ন। **3.** Reaching back from the front; as, a company six *deep*; সম্মুখ হইতে পশ্চাৎ দিকে বিস্তৃত। **4.** Extreme; excessive; as, *deep* drinking; নিতান্ত; অতিরিক্ত। **5.** Not superficial; penetrating; as, *deep* bearing or insight; গভীর, অগাধ; সূক্ষ্ম, তীক্ষ্ণ। **6.** Engrossed; absorbed; "How *deep* am I in love;" নিবিষ্ট; নিমগ্ন। **7.** Unintelligible; দুর্জ্ঞেয়, দুর্বোধ। **8.** Heavy; "The *deep* thunder;" গুরুগম্ভীর। **9.** Intense; vivid; as, *deep* silence: *deep* colour; ঘন, গাঢ়, নিবিড়; সজীব। **10.** Obscure; secret; as, a *deep* plot; abstruse; অস্পষ্ট; জটিল; গূঢ়, নিগূঢ়। **11.** Heart-felt; affecting; as, a *deep* sigh; মর্ম্মস্পর্শী; করুণ। **Deep′-en,** *v. t.* & *i.* To make or become deep; গভীর বা নিবিড় করা বা হওয়া। **Deep′-ly,** *adv.* In a deep manner; গভীরভাবে, তলাইয়া। **Deep′-ness,** *n.* **Deep-mourning** — পূর্ণ শোকপরিচ্ছদ। **Deep-water** —(শব্দানুযায়ী) সাঁতার জল; (লক্ষণায়) বিষম বিপদ্ বা সঙ্কট। **A deep one**—(*Slang*) A cunning or secretive person; (ইতর ভাষায়) চালাক লোক, লুকোচুরিতে অভ্যস্ত ব্যক্তি। **A knee-deep**—এক হাঁটু। **Deep in debt**—Involved in debt; ঋণজালে জড়িত। **Deep in pursuit**—কোন বিষয়ে অভিনিবিষ্ট। **Deep in the human heart**—Fully versed in it; মানবহৃদয় গভীরভাবে পরিজ্ঞাত। **To be in deep water(s)**—To fall in distress; অগাধ বিপৎসাগরে পতিত হওয়া, দুঃখদুর্দ্দশায় পতিত হওয়া।

deep (dēp), *n.* **1.** The sea, (*poetry*); "Launch out into the *deep* and let down your nets;" সমুদ্র, সাগর, জলধি, পয়োনিধি, দরিয়া **2.** The middle or most intense part; as, the *deep* of winter; মধ্যভাগ, নিবিড়তম প্রদেশ। **3.** Abyss; pit; অতলস্পর্শ খাত; গর্ত্ত, গহ্বর। **4.** Mysterious region of thought or feeling; চিন্তা বা ভাবরাজ্যের রহস্যময় প্রদেশ। **5.** (*Pl.*) Deep parts of the sea; সাগরের গভীর অংশ সমূহ।

deep (dēp), *adv.* **1.** Deeply; as, to read *deep*; গভীরভাবে। **2.** Far on (in time); as, *deep* in the night; (সময় সম্পর্কে) গভীর। **Deep-drawn** (sighs)—Heart-felt; মর্ম্মস্পর্শী, করুণ। **Deep-laid**—Formed with profound skill or artifice; as, *deep-laid* plans; গভীর চাতুর্য্য ও কৌশল সহকারে কল্পিত, অতিশয় চাতুরীর সহিত উদ্ভাবিত। **Deep-mouthed**—Having a loud and sonorous voice; as, a *deep-mouthed* dog; গভীর-নিনাদী। **Deep-read** — মহা পণ্ডিত, বহুশ্রুত। **Deep-rooted**—Deeply implanted, usually said of feelings and opinions etc; বদ্ধমূল। **Deep-seated**—Having the seat far below the surface; গভীরতম প্রদেশে স্থিত। (*Fig.*) Hard to be removed; as, *deep-seated* prejudice; দৃঢ়বদ্ধ, বদ্ধমূল। **Still waters run deep**—Real feeling or knowledge is not showy; যাহাদের হৃদয়ের ভাব সুগভীর অথবা যাহাদের গভীর পাণ্ডিত্য আছে তাহারা কখনও বাহ্য আড়ম্বর প্রদর্শন করেন না।

deep′-ing (dēp-), *n.* A section, one fathom deep, of a fishing-net; মাছ ধরিবার জালের ৪ হাত গভীর অংশ।

deer (dēr), *n.* Kinds of ruminant quadrupeds with deciduous branching horns; হরিণ, মৃগ, কুরঙ্গ। **Deer-eyed woman**—মৃগাক্ষী, মৃগনেত্রা, মৃগনয়না, কুরঙ্গনেত্রা, হরিণনয়না, মৃগলোচনা। **Deer-forest** — হরিণ শিকারের জন্য রক্ষিত আরণ্যভূমি, মৃগবন। **Deer-hound** — একপ্রকার বৃহৎকায় শিকারী কুক্কুর। **Deer-lick**—লবণময় প্রস্রবণ বা সজল স্থান, যথায় হরিণগণ লেহন করিবার জন্য আসিয়া থাকে। **Deer-neck** — A thin ill-formed neck as of a horse; অশ্বাদির সরু এবং কুগঠিত গলদেশ। **Deer's foot** — এক প্রকার ঘাস। **Deer skin**—মৃগচর্ম্ম, মৃগাজিন, অজিন। **Deer-stalker**—যে ব্যক্তি অতর্কিতভাবে আক্রমণ করিয়া হরিণ শীকার করে। A low-crowned close-fitting cap; এক প্রকার আঁটসাট টুপি। **Deer-stalking** — অতর্কিতভাবে আক্রমণ করিয়া হরিণ শিকার।

dē-face′, *v. t.* **1.** To destroy the external appearance of; to disfigure; as, to *deface* a monument; বাহ্যাকার নষ্ট করা; বিরূপ করা, বিকৃত করা, শ্রীভ্রষ্ট করা, বিশ্রী করা, কদাকার করা। **2.** To discredit; অপযশ করা। **3.** To make illegible; to obliterate; as, the beginning of this letter irreparably *defaced*; অপাঠ্য করা; বিলুপ্ত করা, মুছিয়া ফেলা। **—a-ble,** *adj.* **—ment,** *n.*

de facto, (*L.*) *adj.* & *adv.* In fact; in reality; as, a *de facto* king; যথার্থতঃ; বস্তুতঃ, বস্তুগত্যা।

dē-fāl′-cāte, *v. i.* To embezzle or misappropriate money held in trust; গচ্ছিত অর্থ আত্মসাৎ করা, তহবিল তসরুফ করা, তহবিল ভাঙ্গা। **—ca′-tion,** *n.* **1.** Defection; shortcoming; খুঁত, কসুর; ত্রুটি। **2.** Misappropriation of money held in trust ; তহবিল তসরুফ করণ। **3.** Amount misappropriated ; তসরুফি টাকা। **—ca'-tor,** *n.*

dĕf-ă-mā'-tion, *n.* The act of defaming ; slander ; অখ্যাতিকরণ ; মানহানি, অপবাদ, কুৎসা, গ্লানি, পরিবাদ।

dē-fāme', *v. t.* To disgrace ; to speak ill of ; to calumniate ; মানহানি করা, অপযশ করা ; দুর্নাম করা, অপবাদ করা, অখ্যাতি করা, বদনাম করা ; কুৎসা প্রচার করা। **—fam'-a-to-ry,** *adj.*

dē-fault' (-fält), *n., v. t. & i.* **1.** Lack ; as, in *default* of ; অভাব। **2.** Neglect ; omission of what ought to be done ; as, this evil has happened through the Governor's *default* ; অবহেলা ; ত্রুটি, কসুর। **3.** Failure to pay ; পরিশোধ করণে ত্রুটি। **4.** (*Law*) A failure of appearance in court at a day assigned ; as, a judgment by *default* (a judgment given for the plaintiff on the defendant's failure to plead) ; (আইন) নিরূপিত দিবসে বিচারালয়ে উপস্থিতির ত্রুটি *Verb t.* **1.** To fail to perfrom or pay ; as, to *default* a dividend ; সম্পাদনে বা পরিশোধে অসমর্থ হওয়া। **2.** (*Law*) To give judgment against on account of failing to appear and answer ; (আইন) কোন ব্যক্তির উপস্থিতির ত্রুটিতে তাহার বিরুদ্ধে বিচারাদেশ প্রদান করা। *Verb i.* **1.** To fail in fulfilling a financial obligation ; অর্থ সংক্রান্ত অঙ্গীকার পালনে বিফল হওয়া। **2.** To fail to appear in court when called upon ; নিরূপিত দিবসে বিচারালয়ে উপস্থিত হইতে অসমর্থ হওয়া। **—er,** *n.* **1.** One who fails to appear in court when called ; আদালতে গরহাজির ব্যক্তি। **2.** One who fails to account for the public money entrusted to him ; যে ব্যক্তি তাহার নিকট গচ্ছিত সরকারী টাকার হিসাব দিতে পারে না। **3.** One who fails in payment ; বাকীদার। **A judgment by default**—কোন ব্যক্তির গরহাজিরের দরুণ তাহার বিরুদ্ধে মোকদ্দমা নিষ্পত্তি, একতর্ফা ডিক্রী। **In default**—অন্যথায়, অভাবে। **In default of**—Through the failure or lack of ; কোন কিছুর অভাবে, অন্যথাচরণে। **To make default**—To fail to act or appear ; অন্যথাচরণ করা, গরহাজির হওয়া।

dē-fea'-sance (-fē-zăns), *n.* Rendering null and void ; বাতিলকরণ, নাকচ করণ, বিপ্রতিপত্তি (মঃ ইঃ)।

dē-fea'-ṡi-ble (-fē-), *adj.* Capable of annulment ; liable to forfeiture ; as, a *defeasible* title ; রদকরণযোগ্য ; বাজেয়াপ্তকরণীয়, অনুশয়িতব্য। **—bil'-i-ty,** *n.*

dē-feat' (-fēt), *n. & v. t.* **1.** Frustration ; overthrow in a contest or battle ; বিফলীকরণ, বিঘাত (আঃ বঃ) ; পরাজয়, পরাভব, পরিভব, হার। **2.** (*Law*) Annulment ; রদ, বাতিল, নাকচ। ***Verb t.*** **1.** To frustrate ; as, our dearest hopes are often *defeated* : বিফল করা, ভঙ্গ করা, ব্যাহত করা, ব্যর্থ করা, পর্যুদস্ত করা। **2.** To overcome ; to disperse ; as, to *defeat* an army ; পরাভূত করা, পরাজিত করা, পরাহত করা ; ছিন্ন ভিন্ন করা। **3.** To render null and void ; as, to *defeat* a title to an estate ; নাকচ করা, বাতিল করা।

dē-fea'-tūre (-fē-), *v. t.* To make unrecognizable ; চিনিতে পারা না যায় এরূপ করা, অপরিচেয় করা।

dĕf'-ē-cāte, *v. t. & i.* **1.** To refine ; to purify ; (*lit. & fig*) ; নির্ম্মল করা, শোধিত করা ; বিশুদ্ধ করা। **2.** To remove as dregs, excrements, sin, etc. ; গাদ, ময়লা, পাপ প্রভৃতি দূর করা। *Verb i.* To void excrement ; মলত্যাগ করা। **—ca'-tion, —ca-tor,** *ns.*

dē-fĕct', *n.* **1.** Deficiency ; lack of something essential to completeness ; as, errors have been corrected and *defects* supplied ; অঙ্গহানি; ছিদ্র, খুঁত, ত্রুটি, অভাব; কমতি, ন্যূনতা, হীনতা, অসম্পূর্ণতা। **2.** Failing ; imperfection whether moral or physical ; as, a *defect* in the eye ; দোষ, কসুর ; খুঁত, অপূর্ণতা। **3.** The quantity or amount by which anything falls short ; কমি। **Defects of one's qualities**—Virtues carried to excess ; সদ্‌গুণের আতিশয্য—যাহা দোষের কারণ হয়। [Cf. "অতি-দানে বলীবর্দ্ধঃ" ; "গুণ হৈয়া দোষ হৈল বিদ্যার বিদ্যায়"।] **In defect of**—In default of ; for want of ; অন্যথায় ; অভাবে।

dē-fĕc'-tion, *n.* Desertion ; falling away from duty ; apostacy ; পরিত্যাগ ; কর্ত্তব্যচ্যুতি ; স্বপক্ষত্যাগ, স্বধর্ম্মত্যাগ।

dē-fĕc'-tive (-tĭv), *adj.* **1.** Incomplete ; faulty ; deficient ; as, a *defective* limb ; অসম্পূর্ণ, অসমগ্র, অঙ্গহীন ; দোষযুক্ত, সদোষ ; বিকল। **2.** (*Gram.*) Not having all the usual inflexions ; (defective verbs are can, could, ought, etc.) ; (ব্যাকরণ) অসম্পূর্ণ। **—ly,** *adv.* **—ness,** *n.*

dē-fence' (-fĕns), *n.* **1.** Defending from assault ; resistance against an attack ; state of being defended ; রক্ষণ, সংরক্ষণ ; রক্ষা, গুপ্তি (আঃ বঃ) ; রক্ষিতাবস্থা। **2.** Protection ; আশ্রয়, সংশ্রয়। **3.** Vindication ; "Men, brethren, father, hear ye my *defence* ;" পক্ষসমর্থন। **4.** (*Law*) A defendant's plea ; (আইন) জবাব। **5.** (*Mil. Pl.*) Fortification ; (সামরিক শাস্ত্র) দুর্গপ্রাকারাদি। **6.** (*Cricket*) Guarding of one's wicket ; also, batting, as opposed to bowling ; (ক্রীকেট ক্রীড়া) ব্যাট দ্বারা উইকেট রক্ষা করণ ; ব্যাট দ্বারা বল তাড়ন। **—less,** *adj.* Without defence ; অরক্ষিত। **—less-ly,** *adv.* **—less-ness,** *n.* **Best defence is offence**—Advantage goes with the initiative ; প্রথম

আক্রমণকারীই প্রকৃষ্ট সুবিধা লাভ করে। **Line of defence**—A continuous fortified line or succession of fortified points; দুর্গাদিদ্বারা সুরক্ষিত রেখা, উপদুর্গ বা বপ্রাদিদ্বারা রক্ষিত স্থলপরম্পরা। **Science or art of defence** — মুষ্টিযুদ্ধকৌশল, অসিচালনকৌশল। **To be in a posture of defence** — আত্মরক্ষার জন্য সম্পূর্ণ প্রস্তুত থাকা।

dĕ-fĕnd′, *v. t.* & *i.* **1.** To protect; to secure against attack; as, to *defend* a town; রক্ষা করা; দুর্গাদিদ্বারা শত্রুর আক্রমণ হইতে সুরক্ষিত করা। **2.** To support by repelling or denying a demand, charge or accusation; সমর্থন করা। **3.** To vindicate; to uphold by argument; as, to *defend* reputation; পক্ষ সমর্থন করা; যুক্তিদ্বারা সমর্থন করা। **4.** To forbid; as, God *defend* (ঈশ্বর না করুন); বারণ করা। ***Verb i.*** (*Law*) To enter or make a defence in an action or suit; (আইন) মোকদ্দমার জবাব দেওয়া, আত্মপক্ষ সমর্থন করা। **To defend one's self**—To conduct one's own defence in a law court; বিচারালয়ে আত্মপক্ষ সমর্থন করা।

dĕ-fĕnd′-ănt, *n.* A person accused or sued; প্রত্যর্থী, প্রতিবাদী, অভিযুক্ত-ব্যক্তি, আসামী, আত্মরক্ষক।

dĕ-fĕnd′-ẽr, *n.* One who defends; রক্ষক, সমর্থক। **Defender of the faith**—অষ্টম হেনরী হইতে আরম্ভ করিয়া ইংলণ্ডেশ্বরগণের উপাধি বিশেষ। (অষ্টম হেনরী মার্টিন লুথারের বিরুদ্ধে একটী নিবন্ধ লিখিয়া এই উপাধি লাভ করেন।)

dĕ-fĕn′-si-ble, *adj.* Capable of being defended; justifiable; রক্ষণীয়; সমর্থন-যোগ্য। **—bil′-i-ty**, *n.* **—bly**, *adv.*

dĕ-fĕn′-sive (-sĭv), *adj.* & *n.* **1.** Serving or proper for defence; as, *defensive* armour; রক্ষণ-সাধক, সংরক্ষক, রক্ষণোচিত। **2.** Not agressive; as, a *defensive* war; আত্মরক্ষাজনক। ***Noun.*** That which defends; রক্ষক, সমর্থক। **To be on the defensive, To stand on the defensive**—To be, or stand, in a state or posture of defence or resistance; আত্মরক্ষার্থ প্রস্তুত বা দণ্ডায়মান হওয়া।

dĕ-fêr′, *v. t.* & *i.* To put off; to postpone; স্থগিত করা; মুলতুবী রাখা। ***Verb i.*** To delay to act; to procrastinate; দেরী করা; দীর্ঘসূত্রী হওয়া। **—ment**, *n.* **Deferred pay**—বেতনের (বিশেষতঃ সৈনিকদিগের) যে অংশ মৃত্যুকালে বা কার্য্য হইতে অবসরগ্রহণকালে দেওয়ার জন্য গচ্ছিত রাখা হয়।

dĕ-fêr′, *v. i.* To yield or submit to the opinion or wishes of another, (with *to*); অন্যের মতানুবর্ত্তী হওয়া, অন্যের ইচ্ছার বশবর্ত্তী হওয়া।

dĕf′-ẽr-ence (-ĕns), *n.* **1.** Yielding in opinion; মতানুবর্ত্তিতা। **2.** Courteous regard; সম্ভ্রম, সম্মান, মান্যতা, সমাদর। **—en-tial**, *adj.* Expressing or given to deference; সম্ভ্রমসূচক, সম্ভ্রমশীল, মর্য্যাদাশীল, শ্রদ্ধাবান। **In deference to**—Out of regard for; মান্যতাহেতু, শ্রদ্ধাহেতু।

dĕf′-ẽr-ĕnt, *adj.* & *n.* (*Physiol.*) Conveying to a destination (of); (শারীর-বিজ্ঞান); গন্তব্য স্থানে বহনকারী। ***Noun.*** A vessel in the human body for the conveyance of fluids; মানবদেহস্থ তরলপদার্থবাহী নালী।

dĕ-fêr-vĕs′-cence (-ĕns), *n.* Abatement of heat; decrease of feverish symptoms; তাপোপশম; জ্বরোপশম।

dĕ-fī′-ance (-ăns), *n.* **1.** A challenge; a declaration of hostilities; যুদ্ধাহ্বান, যোধসংরাব, স্পর্দ্ধা (মঃ ইঃ), যুদ্ধঘোষণা। **2.** Open disobedience; setting at naught; প্রকাশ্যে অমান্যতা; অগ্রাহ্য। **In defiance** — Setting at naught; অগ্রাহ্য করিয়া, অবহেলা করিয়া। **To bid defiance, To set at defiance**—To defy; অগ্রাহ্য করা, অবহেলা করা, তুচ্ছ করা, তাচ্ছিল্য করা।

dĕ-fī′-ănt, *adj.* **1.** Bold; insolent; as, a *defiant* spirit or act; প্রগল্‌ভ, ধৃষ্ট; উদ্ধত। **2.** Suspicious; সন্দিগ্ধচিত্ত। **—ly**, *adv.*

dĕ-fĭ′-cien-cy̆ (-shĕn-), *n.* **1.** Inadequacy; a defect; an imperfection; lack; অসম্পূর্ণতা; খুঁত; কমতি; ন্যূনতা, কমি, ত্রুটি, অভাব। **2.** A thing wanting; কম্‌তি, ঘাট্‌তি। **3.** A deficit; (টাকার) কম্‌তি, ন্যূনতা।

dĕ-fĭ′-cient (-shĕnt), *adj.* **1.** Defective; imperfect; as, a *deficient* strength; হীন, ঊণ, ন্যূন; খুঁতবিশিষ্ট, অপূর্ণ। **2.** Lacking; inadequate; অভাববিশিষ্ট, অপ্রতুল; অসম্পূর্ণ, অপ্রচুর। **3.** Half-witted; অল্পবুদ্ধি, অল্পপ্রজ্ঞ (আঃ বঃ)। **—ly**, *adv.* **Deficient numbers**—(In *arith.*) (পাটীগণিত) ন্যূন সংখ্যা, অর্থাৎ যে সংখ্যার একাংশ সমূহের যোগফল, ঐ সংখ্যা অপেক্ষা কম হইয়া থাকে। যথা ৮ একটী ন্যূন সংখ্যা; কারণ ইহার একাংশ ১, ২, এবং ৪ এর যোগফল মাত্র ৭ হয়।

dĕf′-i-cĭt, *n.* **1.** The amount by which a sum of money is too small; a falling short, esp. of income; as, a *deficit* in taxes; (টাকার) কম্‌তি; (কোন কিছু অপেক্ষা) কম হওন, বিশেষতঃ আয়ের ন্যূনতা। **2.** Excess of liabilities over assets; মৃত ব্যক্তি বা ঋণ পরিশোধে অসমর্থ ব্যক্তির সম্পত্তির মূল্য অপেক্ষা ঋণের পরিমাণের অতিরিক্ততা।

de fide, (*L.*), *adj.* Required to be held as an article of faith; ধর্ম্মবিশ্বাসের অঙ্গরূপে গ্রহণীয়।

dĕf-i-lāde′, *v. t.* &. *n.* To secure (fortifications etc.) against enfilading fire; লম্বালম্বি ভাবে গোলা-বর্ষণ হইতে দুর্গবপ্রাদি নিরাপদ করা। ***Noun.*** The act or process of defilading;

লম্বালম্বি ভাবে গোলা বর্ষণ হইতে (দুর্গাবপ্রাদি) রক্ষার্থ উপদুর্গাদির সংস্থান।

dē-fīle′, *n.* & *v. i.* A narrow way through which troops can march only in files ; গিরি-সঙ্কট (সাঃ পঃ)। ***Verb i.*** To march off file by file ; সারিবন্দী হইয়া যাত্রা করা।

dē-fīle′, *v. t.* **1.** To make unclean ; to render foul or dirty ; "They that touch pitch will be *defiled* ;" to make impure ; মলিন করা ; অপরিষ্কার করা, নোংড়া করা। **2.** To make morally foul ; to corrupt ; কলুষিত করা ; দূষিত করা। **3.** To soil ; as, to *defile* reputation ; কলঙ্কিত করা। **4.** To make ceremonially unclean ; as, the food of even a low caste Hindu is *defiled* by the touch of a non-Hindu ; অশুচি করা, অপবিত্র করা। **5.** (*Rare*) To violate ; "The husband murdered and the wife *defiled* ;" সতীত্ব-লঙ্ঘন করা। **6.** To desecrate ; অপবিত্র করা। **—ment,** *n.* Act of defiling ; কলুষীকরণ, দূষণ, বিদূষণ, প্রদূষণ।

dē-fīne′, *v. t.* **1.** To mark the limits of ; as, to *define* the extent of a kingdom ; সীমা-নির্দ্দেশ করা। **2.** To make clear, esp. in outline ; as, a well-*defined* image ; সুপরিস্ফুট করা, সুপ্রকট করা। **3.** To explain ; to fix the exact meaning of ; as, to *define* a word ; ব্যাখ্যা করা ; প্রকৃত অর্থ নিরূপণ করা। **4.** To characterize ; to distinguish by special marks ; as, good manners *define* the gentleman ; সংজ্ঞা প্রদান করা ; বিশেষ লক্ষণদ্বারা নির্দ্দেশ করা। **—fin′-a-ble,** *adj.* **To define one's position**—To state it precisely ; স্বীয় মনোভাব সুস্পষ্টরূপে ব্যক্ত করা।

dĕf′-i-nite (-nĭt), *adj.* **1.** With exact limits ; bounded with precision ; as, a *definite* extent of land ; নির্দ্দিষ্ট, নিরূপিত, নিয়ত ; নির্দ্ধারিত, সীমাবচ্ছিন্ন। **2.** Distinct ; clear ; সুস্পষ্ট, ব্যক্ত; বিশদ। **—ly,** *adv.* **—ness,** *n.* **Past or preterite definite**—Past tense in French ; ফরাসী ব্যাকরণে অতীতকাল।

dĕf-i-nĭ′-tion, *n.* **1.** Act of making definite or clear ; as, the *definition* of a telescope ; স্পষ্টীকরণ, বিশদীকরণ। **2.** A brief and precise description of a thing by its properties ; statement of the precise meaning of a word or term ; লক্ষণ (হিঃ কোঃ), লক্ষণবচন (আঃ বঃ) ; সংজ্ঞা।

dē-fĭn′-i-tive (-tĭv), *adj.* **1.** Unconditional ; final ; as, a *definitive* answer, treaty or verdict ; অন্যথাসিদ্ধিশূন্য; চূড়ান্ত, চরম। **2.** Limiting ; determining ; as, a *definite* word ; নিয়ামক; নির্ণায়ক। **—ly,** *adv.*

dĕf′-lā-grāte, *v. t.* & *i.* To burn away with rapid flame ; as, to *deflagrate* spirit ; দপ্ করিয়া জ্বালাইয়া ফেলা। ***Verb i.*** To burn rapidly ; তাড়াতাড়ি জ্বলা, দপ্ করিয়া জ্বলিয়া উঠা। **—gra′-tion,** *n.* **—gra-tor,** *n.* (*Chem.*) A form of the voltaic battery producing rapid and powerful combustion ; একপ্রকার বিদ্যুদ্ঘটমালা,—যদ্দারা দ্রুত এবং সতেজ ভাবে জ্বলনকার্য্য সম্পন্ন হয়।

dē-flāte′, *v. t.* To reduce from an inflated state by releasing the inflating air or gas ; ভিতরের বায়ু বা বাষ্প বাহির করত ফাঁপা জিনিষের আয়তন কমান। **—fla-tion,** *n.*

dē-flĕct′, *v. t.* & *i.* To cause to turn or bend aside ; সরলরেখা হইতে বিচ্যুত করা। ***Verb i.*** To turn aside ; to deviate from a true course or right line ; to swerve ; "To *deflect* from the line of truth and reason ;" এক দিকে সরিয়া যাওয়া, পাশকাটান ; ন্যায় বা সত্য পথ হইতে ভ্রষ্ট হওয়া ; স্খলিত বা বিচ্যুত হওয়া, বিপথে যাওয়া। **—flec′-tion, —flex′-ion,** *ns.* **1.** Lateral or downward bend ; deviation ; পার্শ্ব-বিক্ষেপ, নিম্নাভিমুখে বক্রীভবন ; পথচ্যুতি, বিপথগমন, বিচলন, স্খলন, উৎক্রম (মঃ ইঃ), অপচার। **2.** (*Optics*) A bending of the rays of light from a straight line ; (দৃষ্টি-বিজ্ঞান) আলোক-রশ্মি সমূহের সরলরেখা হইতে বিক্ষেপ, রশ্মি-বিক্ষেপ। **3.** (*Electr.* & *Magn.*) Deviation of the needle from its zeros ; (তাড়িত ও চুম্বকবিদ্যা) ০ বিন্দু হইতে চুম্বক-সূচির বিক্ষেপ।

dĕf-lō-rā′-tion, *n.* Act of deflowering ; কৌমার্য্যহরণ, কৌমার্য্যভঙ্গ, কৌমার্য্যনাশ, কন্যাধর্ষণ।

dē-flow′-ẽr, *v. t.* **1.** To deprive of virginity ; to ravish ; to violate ; কৌমার্য্যহরণ করা, কৌমার্য্যভঙ্গ করা ; বলাৎকার করা; সতীত্ব-লঙ্ঘন করা। **2.** To rob of bloom and beauty ; to ravage ; সৌকুমার্য্য ও লাবণ্য নষ্ট করা ; বিধ্বস্ত করা। **3.** To strip of flowers ; পুষ্প-বিরহিত করা।

dĕf′-lū-ĕnt, *adj.* & *n.* Running down ; decurrent ; অধঃপ্রবাহী ; অধঃপ্রসারী। ***Noun.*** A down-flowing part, as the lower end of a glacier ; অধঃপ্রবাহী অংশ।

dē-flux′-ion (-flŭk-shŏn), *n.* **1.** Downflow ; নিঃসরণ, নিষ্যন্দ, নিঃস্রব, অধঃপ্রবাহ। **2.** (*Med.*) A flowing down of humours or fluid matter, as a copious discharge from the nose in catarrh ; (ভৈষজ্য শাস্ত্র) রক্ত, পুয, কফ, শ্লেষ্মাদির নিঃস্রব, ক্ষরণ। **3.** An inflammation of a part attended with increased secretion ; অতিশয় নিঃস্রব-স্রাবী প্রদাহ।

dē-fō-li-ā′-tion, *n.* The falling off of leaves ; পত্রপতন (সাঃ পঃ)।

dē-fŏr′-ĕst, *v. t.* To clear of forest ; বনশূন্য করা। **—a′-tion,** *n.*

dē-fŏrm′, *v. t.* **1.** To make ugly ; to deface ; as, to *deform* the person by an unbecoming dress ; বিকৃত করা ; বিরূপ করা। **2.** To misshape ; to disfigure ; as, a hump on the back *deforms* the body ; কদাকার করা ; শ্রীভ্রষ্ট করা, বিশ্রী করা। **—formed'**, *p.p.* Misshapen ; disfigured ; as, a *deformed* person ; বিকৃতাঙ্গ (উজ্জ্বলঃ), বেডৌল (ফঃ হিঃ), কুতনু ; বিরূপ, কুরূপ, অপরূপ।

dĕf-ŏr-mā'-tion, *n.* **1.** Disfigurement; অঙ্গবিকৃতি, বিকৃতাঙ্গতা, বৈরূপ্য। **2.** Transformation ; রূপান্তরীকরণ, আকারপরিবর্ত্তন। **3.** A word changed in form, as 'od for God ; রূপান্তরিত শব্দ। **4.** (*Phys.*) Altercation of form or shape ; (পদার্থবিদ্যা) রূপান্তর।

dē-fôrm'-i-tȳ, *n.* **1.** Ugliness ; disfigurement ; বিরূপতা, বৈরূপ্য ; বৈকল্য, বিকলাঙ্গতা, বিরূপাকারতা। **2.** Disproportion of limbs ; অঙ্গবিকৃতি।

dē-fraud' (-fräd), *v. t.* To cheat ; to overreach ; প্রবঞ্চিত করা, প্রতারিত করা ; ঠকান।

dē-fray' (-frā), *v. t.* To discharge by payment ; to meet ; (ব্যয়াদি) নির্ব্বাহ করা ; বহন করা। **—a-ble,** *adj,* **—al,** *n.*

dĕft, *adj.* Apt ; dexterous ; neat in action ; যোগ্য ; দক্ষ ; সাফ, নিপুণ, পটু, কৌশলময়।

dē-funct (-fŭngkt), *adj.* **1.** Dead ; deceased ; মৃত ; পরলোকগত, লোকান্তরিত, সংস্থিত (আঃ বঃ)। **2.** (*Fig.*) No longer existing ; as, it appeared some months ago, in a *defunct* periodical ; (লক্ষণায়) অধুনা অবর্ত্তমান।

dē-fȳ', *v. t.* **1.** To dare ; to challenge ; তুচ্ছ করা ; যুদ্ধার্থ আহ্বান করা। **2.** To resist successfully ; to set at nought ; as, to *defy* the arguments of an opponent ; সফলভাবে প্রতিরোধ করা ; অকিঞ্চিৎকর জ্ঞান করা, তাচ্ছিল্য করা, অবজ্ঞা করা। **3.** To present insuperable obstacles to ; as, to *defy* an attack ; দুরতিক্রম্য বাধা প্রদান করা। **To defy to**—To call to combat or strife ; যুদ্ধ বা সংগ্রামার্থ আহ্বান করা।

degage, (*F.*) *adj.* Easy ; free ; সহজ ; মুক্ত, অবাধ।

dē-gĕn'-ėr-āte, *adj., n.* & *v. i.* **1.** Deteriorated ; degraded ; অপকৃষ্টাবস্থাপ্রাপ্ত, হীনাবস্থাপ্রাপ্ত ; ভ্রষ্ট, পতিত, অধম। **2.** (*Biol.*) Having lost the good qualities of the species ; (জীব-বিজ্ঞান) জাতিগত সদ্গুণচ্যুত, মূলগুণভ্রষ্ট। ***Noun.*** A degenerate person or animal ; অপকৃষ্টাবস্থাপ্রাপ্ত ব্যক্তি বা বস্তু। ***Verb i.*** To deteriorate ; to grow worse ; অপকৃষ্টাবস্থা প্রাপ্ত হওয়া, অধঃপতিত হওয়া ; অপকৃষ্ট হওয়া, ক্রমশঃ হীন হওয়া। ***Verb i.*** **1.** To become lower in character ; অধঃপতন হওয়া। **2.** (*Biol.*) To degenerate ; (জীববিদ্যা) অপকৃষ্টাবস্থা প্রাপ্ত হওয়া। **3.** (Cambridge university) To put off entering the examination for a degree in honours a year beyond the usual time ; সসম্মান উপাধিলাভের জন্য নির্দিষ্ট সময় অপেক্ষা এক বৎসর পরে পরীক্ষা দেওয়া।

dē-gĕn-ėr-ā'-tion, *n.* **1.** Act or state of becoming degenerate ; deterioration ; অপকৃষ্টতা, নিকৃষ্টাবস্থা ; অপকর্ষ, ক্ষয়, হ্রাস, অপচয়, অধঃপতন। **2.** (*Path.*) The condition of a tissue of which the vitality has become diminished, perverted or impaired ; (নিদান-শাস্ত্র) কোন শারীরিক বিধানতন্তর বিকৃতি বা অপকর্ষপ্রাপ্তি, অপকর্ষ (হঃ চঃ)। **Fatty degeneration**—মেদাপকর্ষ অর্থাৎ দেহস্থ মেদের বিকৃতি বা অপকর্ষ।

dĕg-lū-ti'-tion, *n.* The act or power of swallowing ; গলাধঃকরণ, গিলন, গিলিবার শক্তি।

dĕg-ră-dā'-tion, *n.* **1.** Act of degrading ; পরিভবন, অধঃপতন, নিম্নপদারোপণ (আঃ বঃ)। **2.** State of being degraded ; debasement ; disgrace ; পাতিত্য ; অধঃপাত, অধোগতি, অবনতি, অপকর্ষ, হীনতাপাদন ; লাঞ্ছনা। **3.** Degeneration ; অপকৃষ্টতা।

dē-grāde', *v. t.* & *i.* **1.** To lower in rank ; to strip of honors ; as, to *degrade* a nobleman ; উচ্চতর পদ হইতে নিম্নতর পদে অবনত করা ; মর্য্যাদা নাশ করা। **2.** To debase : as, vice *degrades* a man ; অধঃপতিত করা, অধোগামী করা, হীন করা। **3.** (*Geol.*) To wear down by erosion as a rock ; (ভূ-বিদ্যা) ক্ষয়িত করা।

dē-grēe' (-grē), *n.* **1.** A step or station in any series ; a tier ; as, a high *degree* of efficiency ; ধাপ, সোপান, ক্রম (মঃ ইঃ), পদ (ঐ) ; শ্রেণী, সারি। **2.** Relative quantity or intensity ; as, tastes differ in kind as well as *degree* ; আপেক্ষিক পরিমাণ, মাত্রা বা প্রগাঢ়তা। **3.** A step in direct genealogical descent ; as, a relation in the third *degree* ; (বংশাবলী-সম্পর্কে) পুরুষ। **4.** Social rank or position ; as, a dame of high *degree* ; সামাজিক পদ বা শ্রেণী, প্রতিপত্তি (মঃ ইঃ)। **5.** Relative condition ; আপেক্ষিক অবস্থা। **6.** Extent ; as, to serve in a minor *degree* ; পরিমাণ, মাত্রা। **7.** (*Gram.*) One of the three grades—positive, comparative and superlative—in the comparison of an adjective and adverb ; (ব্যাকরণ) বিশেষণের ক্রম। **8.** (*Geom. etc.*) The 360th part of the circumference of a circle or the 90th part of a right angle ; (জ্যামিতি প্রভৃতি) বৃত্ত-পরিধির ৩৬০ অংশের এক অংশ, সমকোণের ৯০ ভাগের একভাগ, অংশ, লব, ভাগ, কলা (আঃ বঃ)। **9.** Academic rank conferred as guarantee of proficiency or on distinguished person; বিশ্ববিদ্যালয়ের উপাধি। **10.** (*Law*) Grade of crime ; অপরাধের গুরুতা বা লঘুতার পরিমাণ। **11.** (*Mus.*) Difference in elevation between two musical tones ; (সঙ্গীতশাস্ত্র) দুইটী সুরের

উচ্চতার মধ্যে বিভেদ। **12.** (*Therm.*) The unit of temperature in any scale; (তাপমান-যন্ত্র) তাপাঙ্ক, তাপাংশ (সাঃ পঃ)। **—less,** *adj.* **By degrees**—Gradually; ক্রমশঃ, ক্রমে ক্রমে, শনৈঃ শনৈঃ। **Prohibited (forbidden) degrees**—জ্ঞাতি বা অন্য কোন প্রকার নিকট সম্বন্ধ—যাহার ভিতর বিবাহ হইতে পারে না। **To a degree**—Extremely; as, proud *to a degree*; অতিশয়, নিতান্ত। **To the last degree** — To the utmost measure; চূড়ান্ত মাত্রায়।

de haut en bas, (*F.*) *adv.* By force; with authority; বলপ্রয়োগে; প্রভুত্ব-সহকারে।

dē-hisce′ (-hĭs), *v. t.* To gape; to burst open, as a seed vessel etc.; বিদারিত হওয়া, ফাটিয়া যাওয়া; বীজকোষাদি বিদারিত হওয়া। **—his′-cence,** *n.* Opening of pods and cells at maturity; বিদারণ, প্রস্ফোটন, পরাগকোষের বিদারণ। **—his′-cent,** *adj.*

dē-hŏr′-tā-tive (-tĭv), *adj.* & *n.* Dissuasive; নিবৃত্তিকর, নিবর্ত্তক। ***Noun.*** A thing meant to dissuade; নিবৃত্তিকারক বস্তু।

dē-hū′-măn-īze, *v. t.* To divest of human qualities, as pity, tenderness, etc.; মানবোচিত গুণ (করুণা, কোমলতা প্রভৃতি) বিহীন করা, অমানুষ করা, মনুষ্যত্বহীন করা।

dē-hȳ′-drāte, *v. t.* (*Chem.*) To render free from water; as, to *dehydrate* alcohol; নির্জ্জল করা।

dē-hȳp′-nō-tīze, *v. t.* To release from hypnotic state; সম্মোহিত অবস্থা হইতে মুক্ত করা।

dē′-ĭ-cīde, *n.* **1.** The killer or destroyer of a god, esp. one concerned in putting Christ to death; দেবহন্তা, বিশেষতঃ যীশুখৃষ্টের বধব্যাপারে সংসৃষ্ট ব্যক্তি। **2.** Act of killing a divine being, esp. the putting to death of Jesus Christ; দেবহনন, খৃষ্টহত্যা।

deic′-tic (dīc-), *adj.* (*Philol* & *Gram.*) Pointing; demonstrative; (ভাষাবিজ্ঞান ও ব্যাকরণ) নির্দ্দেশক; স্পষ্টপ্রদর্শী, উপপাদক।

dē′-ĭ-fŏrm, *adj.* God-like in form and nature; দেবাকৃতি, দেবপ্রকৃতিক।

dē′-ĭ-fȳ, *v. t.* **1.** To make a god of; to exalt to the rank of a deity; "Superstition......*deified* kings;" দেবত্ব আরোপ করা; দেবত্বে উন্নীত করা। **2.** To render god-like; "By our own spirits are we *deified*;" দেবপ্রতিম করা, দেবতুল্য করা। **3.** To praise or revere as a deity; to treat as an object of supreme regard; as, to *deify* money; দেবতার মত স্তুতি বা সম্মান করা; দেববৎ শ্রদ্ধা বা সম্মান করা। **—fi-ca′-tion,** *n.* The act of deifying; দেবত্বারোপন (হিঃ কোঃ), দেববৎ সম্মান-প্রদর্শন।

deign (dān), *v. i.* & *t.* To condescend; to think worthy; হীনতা স্বীকার করিয়া অনুগ্রহ করা; উপযুক্ত বলিয়া গণ্য করা। ***Verb t.*** To condescend to give; "The spirits stalks away, *deigning* no reply;" অনুগ্রহ পূর্ব্বক ন্যূনতা স্বীকার করিয়া কোন কিছু প্রদান করা।

dei gratia, (*L.*) *adv.* By God's grace; দেবানুগ্রহে।

de integro, (*L.*) *adv.* Afresh; anew; নূতনভাবে; নবভাবে, নূতন করিয়া।

dē′-ĭsm, *n.* **1.** Belief in existence of a personal God with disbelief in revealed religion; ঈশ্বরের ব্যক্তিগত অস্তিত্বে বিশ্বাস, কিন্তু ঈশ্বরাদিষ্ট ধর্ম্মে অবিশ্বাস। **2.** The doctrine that God exists as a being wholly distinct from the physical universe of which man is a part, God's operation upon the universe being purely mechanical; ঈশ্বর জগদ্‌ভেদবাদ, দ্বৈতবাদ।

dē′-ĭst, *n.* **1.** An adherent of deism or natural religion; ঈশ্বরের ব্যক্তিগত অস্তিত্বে বিশ্বাসী কিন্তু ঈশ্বরাদিষ্ট ধর্ম্মে অবিশ্বাসী ব্যক্তি, ঈশ্বর-জগদ্‌ভেদবাদী, দ্বৈতবাদী।

dē′-ĭ-tȳ, *n.* **1.** Divinity; দেবত্ব। **2.** A god or goddess; দেবতা, দেবী। **The deity** — God, the creator; ঈশ্বর, সৃষ্টিকর্ত্তা, দেবদেব (আঃ বঃ)।

dē-jĕct′, *v. t.* To dispirit; to discourage; (used in past participle;) as, a *dejected* look; বিরস করা; বিষণ্ণ করা, ম্লান করা, স্ফূর্ত্তিহীন করা, নিরুৎসাহ করা, উৎসাহ ভঙ্গ করা, মনোভঙ্গ করা, ভগ্নোদ্যম করা, দমাইয়া দেওয়া। **—ed′-ly,** *adv.*

dē-jĕc′-tā, *n.* Excrements; পুরীষ, বিষ্ঠা, মল।

dē-jĕc′-tion, *n.* **1.** Lowness of spirit; melancholy; বিষণ্ণতা, বিরসতা, স্ফূর্ত্তিহীনতা; বিষাদ, অবসাদ, ম্লানভাব, বিমর্ষভাব, বৈমনস্য (আঃ বঃ)। **2.** (*Med.*) Evacuation of bowels; (ভৈষজ্য-শাস্ত্র) মলত্যাগ-ক্রিয়া।

dejeuner, (*F.*) *n.* A breakfast; a lunch, esp. of a ceremonial kind; প্রাতরাশ; প্রাতরাশ ও অপরাহ্ণ ভোজনের মধ্যবর্ত্তী জলযোগ।

de jure, (*L.*) *adj.* & *adv.* Rightful; by right; ন্যায়সঙ্গত; ন্যায়তঃ।

dē-laine′ (-lān), *n.* A thin-figured muslin for lady's dresses; স্ত্রীলোকদিগের পোষাকের জন্য একপ্রকার মসলিন কাপড়।

dē-lāte′, *v. t.* **1.** To accuse; to impeach; অভিযুক্ত করা; কোন উচ্চপদস্থ কর্ম্মচারীর বিরুদ্ধে বিচারালয়ে অভিযোগ স্থাপন করা। **2.** To report (offence); (অপরাধ) জ্ঞাপন করা। **—la′-tion, —la′-tor,** *ns.*

dē-lay′ (-lā), *n., v. t.* & *i.* Lingering; procrastination; deferring or postponement; বিলম্ব, দেরী, গৌণ, কালবিলম্ব, গমনবিলম্ব (গীতঃ), কালহরণ; দীর্ঘসূত্রতা, ঢিলামি, শৈথিল্য; মুলতুবী। ***Verb t.*** **1.** To postpone; "My lord *delayeth* his coming"; স্থগিত রাখা। **2.** To retard ; to hinder for a time ; as, he was *delayed* by illness ; বিলম্বিত করা ; সাময়িকভাবে বাধা দেওয়া, গতিভঙ্গ করা, গতিরোধ করা। ***Verb i.*** To loiter ; বিলম্ব করা, দেরী করা, কালহরণ করা, কালক্ষেপ করা, গৌণ করা, দিরঙ্গ করা।

del credere, (*It.*) *adj., adv.* & *n.* (*Com.*) Under a selling agent's guarantee that the buyer is solvent ; (বাণিজ্য) ক্রেতা প্রাপ্য টাকা পরিশোধে সমর্থ, এই বিষয়ে গোমস্তার জামিনে। ***Noun.*** A guarantee which an agent or factor gives his principal regarding purchases ; ক্রেতার প্রাপ্য পরিশোধে সামর্থ্য সম্বন্ধে গোমস্তা মহাজনকে যে জামিন দিয়া থাকে।

dē′-lē, *v. t.* (*Print.*) Erase ; blot out, (abbr. *d.*) ; (মুদ্রণ) কাটিয়া ফেল ; মুছিয়া ফেল, উঠাইয়া ফেল।

dē-lĕc′-tā-ble, *adj.* Pleasing ; delightful ; আনন্দদায়ক ; অভিরাম (মঃ ইঃ), প্রীতিকর, আনন্দজনক, আহ্লাদ-জনক, রম্য (আঃ বঃ), মনোহর, সুভগ (মঃ ইঃ)।

dē-lĕc-tā′-tion, *n.* Enjoyment ; as, for one's *delectation* ; আনন্দ, হর্ষ।

dē-lĕc′-tŭs, *n.* A book of selected passages, esp. for learners of Greek and Latin ; সংগ্রহ-গ্রন্থ, বিশেষতঃ গ্রীক ও লাটিন ভাষাশিক্ষার্থি-গণের জন্য সংগ্রহ-গ্রন্থ।

dĕl′-ē-gā-cȳ, *n.* **1.** Appointment as delegate ; প্রতিনিধি নিয়োগ। **2.** System of delegating ; প্রতিনিধি-প্রেরণপদ্ধতি। **3.** A body of delegates ; প্রতিনিধিবর্গ।

dĕl′-ē-gate, *n.* An elected representative sent to a conference ; প্রতিনিধি, প্রতিপুরুষ।

dĕl′-ē-gāte, *v. t.* **1.** To depute ; to send as representative ; প্রতিনিধি নিয়োগ করা ; প্রতিনিধিরূপে প্রেরণ করা। **2.** To intrust to the care of another ; to assign ; as, to *delegate* authority to an envoy ; কোন ব্যক্তিকে ভারার্পণ করা ; নির্দ্দেশ করা।

dĕl-ē-gā′-tion, *n.* **1.** The appointment of a delegate ; প্রতিনিধি নিয়োগ। **2.** The charge or commission given to a delegate ; প্রতিনিধির উপর অর্পিত কার্য্যভার। **3.** A body of delegates ; প্রতিনিধিবর্গ। **The delegations** — সাম্রাজ্যসংক্রান্ত-প্রশ্ন একযোগে মীমাংসার জন্য অষ্ট্রিয়া ও হাঙ্গেরিয়ার পার্লেমেণ্টদ্বয়ের প্রতিনিধি-সভাদ্বয়।

dē-lēte′, *v. t.* To erase ; to obliterate ; (*lit.* & *fig.*) ; as, to *delete* a word etc. ; অপমার্জ্জনা করা (মঃ ইঃ), কাটিয়া ফেলা ; মুছিয়া ফেলা, উঠাইয়া ফেলা (শব্দানুযায়ী ও লক্ষণায়)। **—le′-tion,** *n.*

dĕl-ē-tē′-rĭ-ous (-ŭs), *adj.* Noxious ; pernicious ; বিষময় ; অনিষ্টকর, অপকারক। **—ly,** *adv.*

dĕlf, dĕlft, *n.* Glazed earthenware made at Delft in Holland ; হলণ্ডের অন্তঃপাতী ডেল্‌ফ্‌ নামক স্থানে নির্ম্মিত সূক্ষ্ম কাচস্তবকাচ্ছাদিত মৃৎপাত্র।

dē-lĭb-ēr-āte, *adj.* **1.** Intentional ; as, a *deliberate* murder (জ্ঞানকৃত নরহত্যা) ; carefully considered ; as, a *deliberete* opinion ; ইচ্ছ পূর্ব্বক কৃত, জ্ঞান-কৃত ; সুচিন্তিত, সুবিবেচিত। **2.** Circumspect ; cautious ; discreet ; as, a *deliberate* judge ; অবহিত-দৃষ্টি, চৌকস ; সতর্ক, ধীর (আঃ বঃ) ; বিচক্ষণ, বিমৃশ্যকারী, পাকা। **3.** Not hasty ; leisurely ; "He is very *deliberate* in his movements ; অব্যস্ত ; ঢিলা, অলস। **—ly,** *adv.* **—ness,** *n.*

dē-lĭb′-ēr-āte, *v. t.* & *i.* To ponder ; to consider maturely ; as, to *deliberate* a question ; চিন্তা করা ; সুবিবেচনা করা ***Verb i.*** **1.** To pause and consider ; as, a wise prince will *deliberate* before he wages war ; ভাবিয়া চিন্তিয়া দেখা, অনুধাবন করা **2.** To take counsel ; to hesitate ; পরামর্শ করা ; ইতস্ততঃ করা, দ্বিধা করা।

dē-lĭb-ēr-ā′-tion, *n.* **1.** Careful consideration ; mature reflection ; সুবিবেচনা, সুচিন্তা, অনুধাবন, চর্চ্চা ; বিচারণ, মন্ত্রণা। **2.** Debate ; discussing of reasons for and against ; as, the *deliberation* of a legislative body ; তর্কবিতর্ক, বাদবিতণ্ডা ; আলোচনা, আন্দোলন। **3.** Care ; avoidance of precipitation ; as, he spoke with great *deliberation* ; সতর্কতা ; অব্যস্ততা, ধীরত্ব। **4.** Leisureliness ; as, we saw the ice-berg roll over with utmost *deliberation* ; ঢিলামি, শৈথিল্য।

dē-lĭb′-ēr-ā-tive (-tĭv), *adj.* Pertaining to deliberation or debate ; deliberating ; as, a *deliberative* body ; বাদবিতণ্ডাঘটিত ; মন্ত্রণাঘটিত। **—ly,** *adv.*

dĕl′-ĭ-cā-cȳ, *n.* **1.** Fineness of texture, form or constitution ; tender beauty ; as, the *delicacy* of a fibre or hand ; বয়ন-সূক্ষ্মতা, গঠন-সূক্ষ্মতা ; সৌকুমার্য্য, লালিত্য, মাধুর্য্য, কমনীয়তা, লাবণ্য (মঃ ইঃ)। **2.** Nicety or subtle expressiveness of manipulation or touch ; as, the *delicacy* of a painter's stroke ; সূক্ষ্মতা, সূক্ষ্মদ্যোতনা। **3.** Anything that delights the taste ; as, the peach is a great *delicacy* ; রসনা-তৃপ্তিকর খাদ্য, মুখরোচক বস্তু। **4.** Tenderness ; scrupulousness ; as, *delicacy* of behaviour ; কোমলতা, মার্দব (আঃ বঃ) ; কুণ্ঠা, সঙ্কোচ, চক্ষুলজ্জা। **5.** Nice perception ; sensitiveness ; as, the *delicacy* of a balance ; সূক্ষ্ম অনুভূতি ; অনুভূতি-প্রবণতা। **6.** Weakliness ; susceptibility to disease etc. ; as, a *delicacy* of the constitution ; ক্ষীণতা ; রোগপ্রবণতা। **7.** A refinement ; a nicety ; "Ceremonious *delicacies*" ; মার্জ্জিতভাব ; খুঁতখুঁতে ভাব।

dĕl′-ĭ-cāte, *adj.* **1.** Pleasing to the taste or senses ;

রসনাতৃপ্তিকর, স্বাদু, সুরস, উপাদেয়; ইন্দ্রিয় তৃপ্তিকর। **2.** Exquisitely sensitive ; as, a *delicate* ear for music ; সূক্ষ্মসংবেদন-শক্তি-সম্পন্ন। **3.** Subtle ; "The most *delicate* differences ;" সূক্ষ্ম। **4.** Tenderly reared ; "A *delicate* and tender prince ;" frail ; susceptible to illness or injury ; as, a *delicate* health ; অতিশয় স্নেহের সহিত পালিত; ক্ষণ-ভঙ্গুর ; মৃদ্বঙ্গ (মঃ ইঃ), কোমলবপুঃ, প্রকৃতিদুর্ব্বল, রোগ-প্রবণ। **5.** Light or softly tinted ; as, a *delicate* colour ; মৃদুরঞ্জিত, মেদুররঞ্জিত। **6.** Slender ; fine of texture ; graceful ; fair ; as, a *delicate* fabric, figure or complexion ; সরু ; সূক্ষ্মভাবে বুনা ; সুকুমার, পেলব, পেশল, মাধুর্য্যময় ; ললিত, সুচারু। **7.** Deft ; as, a *delicate* touch ; নিপুণ। **8.** (Of instrument) Showing slight changes as a balance etc. ; (যন্ত্র-সম্বন্ধে) অতিসূক্ষ্ম পরিবর্ত্তন প্রদর্শনকারী। **9.** Refined ; modest ; as, a *delicate* behaviour ; মার্জ্জিত ; বিনীত, ভব্য। **10.** Considerate ; as, *delicate* actions ; বিবেচনাপূর্ণ, সুবিবেচিত। **11.** Showing subtle workmanship ; marked by ingenuity ; "*Delicate* machines ;" সূক্ষ্মকারুকার্য্যপূর্ণ ; কলাকৌশলপূর্ণ। **12.** Critical ; "Situation was *delicate* ;" গুরুতর। **13.** (*Poet*) Delightful ; (কবিতায়) আনন্দপূর্ণ, মনোহর, আহ্লাদজনক।

dē-lĭ'-cious(-shŭs), *adj.* Highly pleasing to the senses, esp. to the taste, smell or the sense of humour ; as, a *delicious* fruit or joke ; deligtful ; স্বাদু, সুরস, সুমিষ্ট, উপাদেয়, মধুর, রুচিকর, সরস ; রম্য, আনন্দজনক, সুখকর, সুখজনক, মনোমোহন। **—ly,** *adv.* **—ness,** *n.*

dē-lict', *n.* Violation of law ; offence ; আইনলঙ্ঘন ; অপরাধ।

dē-light' (-līt), *n., v. t. & i.* **1.** High pleasure ; joy ; আনন্দ, উল্লাস, প্রমোদ ; হর্ষ। **2.** Anything which gives great pleasure ; আনন্দজনক বস্তু। ***Verb t.*** To please highly ; as, a beautiful landscape *delights* the eye; আনন্দিত করা, উল্লসিত করা। ***Verb i.*** To be greatly pleased ; "I *delight* to do thy will, O my God ;" আনন্দিত হওয়া, উৎফুল্ল হওয়া, প্রহৃষ্ট হওয়া। **—ful, —some,** *adjs.* Full of delight ; আনন্দপূর্ণ, সুখাবহ, নর্ম্মদ, রম্য, রমণীয়।

Dē-lī'-lah (-lă), **Dā-,** *n.* The mistress of Samson who betrayed him ; hence a temptress ; a harlot ; পুরাতন বাইবেল গ্রন্থোক্ত Samson নামক বীরের উপপত্নী—যিনি বিশ্বাসঘাতকতাপূর্ব্বক উক্ত বীরকে শত্রুহস্তে সমর্পণ করিয়াছিলেন ; মোহিনী ; গণিকা।

dē-lĭm'-it, —lĭm'-i-tāte, *v. t.* To fix or mark the limit of ; সীমা-নির্দ্দেশ করা, সীমা-চিহ্নিত করা। **—i-ta'-tion,** *n.* Demarcation ; সীমানির্দ্দেশ।

dē-lĭn'-ē-āte, *v. t.* To sketch out ; to portray ; স্থূলভাবে অঙ্কিত করা, নক্সা করা ; চিত্রিত করা, বর্ণনা করা। **—a'-tion, —a-tor,** *ns.*

dē-lĭn'-quĕn-cy̆(-lĭng-), *n.* Neglect of duty ; a misdeed ; কর্ত্তব্যপালনে ত্রুটি, অবহেলা, ব্যতিক্রম, কসুর ; অকার্য্য, দুষ্কর্ম্ম, কুকার্য্য।

dē-lĭn'-quĕnt (-lĭng-), *adj. & n.* Failing in duty ; guilty ; কর্ত্তব্যভ্রষ্ট ; অপরাধী। ***Noun.*** An offender ; দোষী ব্যক্তি, অপরাধী।

dĕl-i-quesce' (-kwĕs-), *v. t.* **1.** To become liquid ; তরলপদার্থে পরিণত হওয়া। **2.** (*Fig.*) To melt away ; (লক্ষণায়) গলিয়া যাওয়া, দ্রব হইয়া যাওয়া, বসিয়া যাওয়া।

dē-lĭr'-i-ous (-ŭs), *adj.* Raving ; disordered in intellect ; insane ; ecstatic ; প্রলাপী ; মতিভ্রান্ত, বিকৃত-মস্তিষ্ক ; উন্মাদ ; আনন্দোন্মত্ত, রসোন্মত্ত। **—ly,** *adv.*

dē-lĭr'-i-ŭm, *n.* **1.** A temporary disordered state of mental faculties occurring during illness ; চিত্তবিভ্রম (হিঃ কোঃ), উন্মাদ (ঐ), বিকার (যোঃ), সন্নিপাত (ঐ), প্রলাপ, বুদ্ধিবিভ্রম, জ্ঞানভ্রংশ (মঃ ইঃ), বুদ্ধিবৈকল্য, জ্বর-মোহ, প্রজল্পাবস্থা, উন্মাদ বায়ু, কোন কোন রোগে মস্তিষ্কের ক্রিয়া বিকৃত হইয়া মনের যে বিশৃঙ্খল ও বাক্যের অসংলগ্ন অবস্থা জন্মে। **2.** Wild enthusiasm ; mad rapture ; ecstacy ; বিপুল উৎসাহ ; উন্মাদ আনন্দ ; রসোন্মাদ। **Delirium tremens**—অতিরিক্ত মাদক দ্রব্য সেবন অথবা উহার বিরতিহেতু অনিদ্রা ও কম্পসহকৃত প্রলাপ রোগ, পানাত্যয় (হঃ চঃ)।

dĕl-i-tĕs'-cence (-sĕns), *n.* **1.** Concealment ; seclusion ; গোপনতা ; নির্জ্জনতা, বিজনতা। **2.** (*Med.*) The sudden disappearance of inflammation or other symptoms of disease ; (ভৈষজ্য-শাস্ত্র) প্রদাহ এবং অন্যান্য রোগলক্ষণের আকস্মিক লোপ। **—cent,** *adj.* Latent ; অপ্রকট, অনুদ্ভূত।

dē-lĭv'-ēr, *v. t.* **1.** To rescue or save ; to release ; as, to *deliver* one from captivity ; উদ্ধার করা ; নিস্তার করা, পরিত্রাণ করা, মুক্ত করা, রেহাই দেওয়া (ফঃ হিঃ)। **2.** To disburden as woman of a child or young, (usually in the passive — *lit. & fig.*) ; গর্ভমোচন করা, প্রসব করান, খালাস করা, (শব্দানুযায়ী এবং লক্ষণায়)। **3.** To put into another's hand or power ; to distribute to owners ; as, to *deliver* letters etc. ; অন্য ব্যক্তির হস্তে সমর্পণ করা ; মালিকগণের হস্তে বাটিয়া দেওয়া। **4.** To discharge ; as, to *deliver* a blow ; ক্ষেপণ করা, মোচন করা, দেওয়া। **5.** To recite ; as, a well-*delivered* sermon ; আবৃত্তি করা। **6.** To surrender ; to resign ; as, to *deliver* a fortress to an enemy ; সমর্পণ করা ; ত্যাগ করা। **—a-ble,** *adj.* **To deliver to the wind**—To cast away ; to reject ;—অব্যবহার্য্য বোধে ফেলিয়া দেওয়া ; নিক্ষেপ করা, ফেলিয়া দেওয়া।

dĕ-liv′-êr-ance (-ăns-), *n.* **1.** Rescue ; release ; উদ্ধার, উদ্ধরণ, ত্রাণ, পরিত্রাণ ; বিমোচন, মুক্তি, নিস্তার। **2.** Emphatically or formally delivered opinion etc. ; সতেজে অথবা যথারীতি ব্যক্ত মত। **3.** A verdict ; অভিযুক্ত ব্যক্তি দোষী কি নির্দোষ তৎসম্বন্ধে জুরীগণের মত।

dĕ-liv′-êr-êr, *n.* **1.** One who delivers, esp. Saviour ; উদ্ধারকর্তা ; পরিত্রাতা, ত্রাণকর্তা, তারক। **2.** One who gives up or transfers as letters, goods, etc. ; পত্র-বণ্টক, মাল প্রভৃতি বণ্টনকারী।

dĕ-liv′-êr-ȳ, *n.* **1.** Rescue ; liberation ; উদ্ধার, নিস্তার ; মোচন। **2.** Surrender ; সমর্পণ। **3.** (*Law*) Formal handing over of property ; (আইন) যথারীতি সম্পত্তি সমর্পণ। **4.** Childbirth ; parturition ; গর্ভ-মোচন; প্রসব, খালাস (*colloq.*)। **5.** Style of utterance ; manner of speaking ; as, a good *delivery* ; act of uttering a speech ; as, its *delivery* took two hours ; বক্তৃতার ধারা বা রীতি ; বক্তৃতা প্রদান প্রণালী; বক্তৃতা-প্রদান। **6.** Delivering of letters ; পত্র-বণ্টন। **7.** Sending forth of missile, esp. of a cricket ball in bowling ; অস্ত্রক্ষেপণ, বিশেষতঃ ক্রিকেট ক্রীড়ায় কন্দুক ক্ষেপ।

dĕll, *n.* A small valley, usu. with tree-clad sides ; ক্ষুদ্র উপত্যকা, সাধারণতঃ তরুশোভিত-সানু উপত্যকা।

Dĕl′-lă-crŭs-căn, *adj.* & *n.* **1.** Pertaining to the style or methods of the Florentine Academy *Della Crusca,* (a society for purifying the Italian language, which issued an authoritative dictionary) ; ফ্লোরেন্স নগরীস্থ Della Crusca নামক বিদ্বজ্জনমণ্ডলীর অনুমোদিত ধারা বা পদ্ধতি-সম্বন্ধীয়। **2.** Of a group of sentimental English poets resident in Florence about 1784 ; (১৭৮৪ খৃঃ অব্দের কাছাকাছি) ফ্লোরেন্স নগরবাসী ইংলণ্ড-দেশীয় ভাবুক কবি-সম্প্রদায় সম্বন্ধীয়। *Noun.* A member of the Della Crusca Academy ; ডেলা ক্রুস্কা নামক পণ্ডিত মণ্ডলীর সভ্য। **—ism,** *n.*

Dĕl′-phi-ăn, Dĕl′-phic, *adjs.* **1.** Of or pertaining to the oracle of Delphi ; ডেলফী নগরীস্থ ভবিষ্যদ্বাণীর মন্দির সম্বন্ধীয়। **2.** Obscure ; ambiguous ; অস্পষ্টার্থ ; দ্ব্যর্থবোধক।

Dĕl′-phin, *adj.* Pertaining to the Dauphin, son of Louis XIV ; ফরাসীরাজ চতুর্দ্দশ লুইএর পুত্র সম্বন্ধীয়। **The Delphin classics**—ফরাসী রাজ চতুর্দ্দশ লুইএর পুত্রের জন্য উক্ত নৃপতির রাজত্বকালে প্রস্তুত প্রাচীন গ্রীক্ ও ল্যাটিন সাহিত্যিকগণের পুস্তকের সংস্করণ।

Delphini a Delphin—দ্রনিষ্ঠা (হিঃ কোঃ)।

dĕl′-phi-nine (-nîn), *n.* (*Chem.*) A poisonous alkaloid used medically ; (রসায়ন-শাস্ত্র) ঔষধরূপে ব্যবহৃত একপ্রকার বিষাক্ত ক্ষার পদার্থ।

dĕl′-tă, *n.* **1.** The fourth letter (Δ δ) of the Greek alphabet, corresponding to D. ; গ্রীক বর্ণমালার চতুর্থ অক্ষর — ইংরেজী ডী অক্ষরের অনুরূপ। **2.** A triangular alluvial tract at the mouth of a river enclosed or traversed by its diverging branches, esp. that of the Nile ; "ব" দ্বীপ (সাঃ পঃ), বিশেষতঃ নীল নদের "ব" দ্বীপ।

dĕl′-toid (toyd), *adj.* & *n.* **1.** Like the delta of a river ; "ব" দ্বীপাকার। **2.** Triangular ; as, a *deltoid* leaf ; ত্রিকোণাকৃতি। *Noun.* **1.** Deltoid muscle ; স্কন্ধের ত্রিকোণী পেশী। **2.** (*Zool.*) A deltoid moth ; (প্রাণি বিদ্যা) ত্রিকোণাকৃতি ধেপসো বা তসরে পোকা।

dĕ-lūde′, *v. t.* To impose on ; to deceive ; ভুলান, বিভ্রান্ত করা, ছলনা করা ; বঞ্চনা করা, ধোকা দেওয়া।

dĕl′-ūge, *n.* & *v. t.* **1.** A great flood ; জলপ্লাবন, মহাবন্যা, তোয়বিপ্লব, জলপ্লব, জলোচ্ছ্বাস(বং:ইঃ), সংপ্লব, একার্ণব। **2.** A heavy fall of rain ; প্রচুর বারি-বর্ষণ, ধারা-সম্পাত। **3.** (*Fig.*) Anything that overwhelms or causes great destruction ; as, a *deluge* of words ; (লক্ষণায়) প্রলয়ঙ্কর বিষয়। *Verb t.* **1.** To overflow with water ; to inundate ; জল-প্লাবিত করা ; আপ্লাবিত করা, ডুবাইয়া দেওয়া, নিমজ্জিত করা, ভাসাইয়া দেওয়া। **2.** (*Fig*) To overpower ; to submerge ; as, he was *deluged* with letters ; (লক্ষণায়) অভিভূত করা ; নিমগ্ন করা। **The Deluge**—Noah's flood ; (প্রাচীন বাইবেল গ্রন্থে বর্ণিত) নোয়ার সময়ের জলপ্লাবন।

dĕ-lū′-sion, *n.* **1.** Act of deluding ; ভ্রান্তি-উৎপাদন, প্রবঞ্চন। **2.** False belief ; error, esp. as a symptom of madness ; অবাস্তব বস্তু বা বিষয় বাস্তব বলিয়া জ্ঞান ; ভ্রান্তি, মোহ, ছল, মায়া, প্রপঞ্চ (মঃ ইঃ), ভ্রম। **—al,** *adj.*

dĕ-lū′-sive (-sîv), *adj.* Apt or tending to delude ; deceptive ; disappointing ; মায়াময়, ভ্রান্তিজনক ; ভ্রান্তিকর, মোহক, মোহজনক ; নৈরাশ্য-জনক। **—ly,** *adv.* **—ness,** *n.*

delve (dĕlv), *n., v. t.* & *i.* (*Archaic, poetic* or *dial.*) **1.** A cavity ; a pit ; গর্ত্ত ; বিবর, গহ্বর। **2.** A wrinkle ; সঙ্কোচ-রেখা। *Verb t.* & *i.* **1.** To dig ; খনন করা। **2.** To make research in documents etc. ; দলিল প্রভৃতিতে অনুসন্ধান করা। **3.** To make a sudden descent as a road etc. ; (রাস্তা প্রভৃতির পক্ষে) অকস্মাৎ নিম্নদিকে ধাবিত হওয়া।

dĕ-măg′-nĕt-ize, *v. t.* To deprive of magnetic quality ; চৌম্বক শক্তি নষ্ট করা। **—i-za′-tion,** *n.*

dĕm′-ă-gogue (-gŏg), *n.* **1.** A popular leader ; প্রাকৃতনায়ক (আঃ বঃ), জননায়ক। **2.** An unprincipled factious orator ; অব্যবস্থিতচিত্ত রাজদ্রোহী বক্তা। **—gog′-ic,** *adj.* **—gog-ism, —gog-y,** *ns.*

dĕ-mănd′, *n.* **1.** An asking with authority ; as, a note payable on *demand* ; দাবি। **2.** The asking or requiring of a price for goods offered for sale ; as, I cannot agree to his *demand* ; বিক্রেয় জিনিষের মূল্যের দাবি। **3.** An urgent claim ; as, many *demands* on my time ; দাবি। **4.** (*Law*) That which is claimed as due ; as, what are your *demands* on the estate ; (আইন) দাবি, দাওয়া, প্রাপ্য। **5.** (*Econ.*) Call of would-be purchasers for commodity ; as, laws of supply and *demand* ; গ্রাহকতা। **6.** (*Arith.*) The sum sought ; ইপ্সিত সংখ্যা, ইচ্ছক (সাঃ পঃ)। **In demand** — Sought after ; কাট্‌তি। **On demand**—As soon as the demand is made ; চাহিবামাত্র।

dē-mănd′, *v. t.* **1.** To call with authority ; as, the state *demands* loyalty ; দাবি করা। **2.** To ask or call for imperiously ; as, to *demand* surrender ; জোর করিয়া চাওয়া। **3.** To require ; as, the task *demands* skill ; আবশ্যক করা। **4.** To insist on being told ; "I could *demand* the cause ;" শুনিবার জন্য জেদ করা। **5.** To question ; "She *demanded* who we were ;" প্রশ্ন করা, জিজ্ঞাসা করা। **—a-ble,** *adj.* **—ant,** *n.*

dē-mâr-cā′-tion, *n.* **1.** Marking by boundary ; separation ; সীমা-নির্দ্দেশ ; পৃথকীকরণ। **3.** A fixed limit ; নির্দ্দিষ্ট সীমা। **—mar′-cate,** *v. t.*

de-mă-tē′-ri-ăl-īze, *v. t.* & *i.* To deprive of material qualities ; জড়ীয় গুণ নষ্ট করা, অশরীরী করা। ***Verb i.*** To be deprived of material qualities ; to be spiritual ; জড়ীয় গুণ বিরহিত হওয়া ; চিন্ময় সত্তা লাভ করা।

deme (dēm), *n.* **1.** (*Gr. Hist.*) Township of ancient Attica ; (গ্রীসের ইতিহাস) প্রাচীন এটিকার ক্ষুদ্র নগর। **2.** (*Biol.*) An undifferentiated aggregate of cells ; (জীব-বিজ্ঞান) অপৃথগ্‌ভূত কোষাণুপুঞ্জ।

dē-mean′ (-mēn), *v. t.* (usually *reflexive*) To conduct ; to comport ; "The troops were required to *demean* themselves with civility towards all classes ;" আচরণ করা, ব্যবহার করা ; চলা।

dē-mean′ (-mēn), *v. t.* To lower in dignity ; to degrade ; (with a reflexive pronoun) ; সম্ভ্রম নাশ করা, মর্য্যাদা-হীন করা ; অবনত করা, হীন করা।

dē-mean′-our (-mēn-êr), *n.* Bearing ; outward behaviour ; deportment ; চালচলন, আচরণ, আচার-ব্যবহার ; ঢং (ফঃ হিঃ), আকারপ্রকার, ভাবগতিক ; ভাবস্বভাব।

dē-mĕnt′, *v. t.* To drive crazy ; to render insane ; (used in past participle) ; ক্ষেপাইয়া দেওয়া ; পাগল করা, মস্তিষ্ক বিকৃত করা। **—ed-ly,** *adv.*

dementi, (*F.*), *n.* Official denial of remours etc. ; জনরব প্রভৃতির সরকারী প্রতিবাদ।

dē-mĕn′-ti-a (-shĭ-ă), *n.* (*Med.*) A form of insanity consisting in feebleness of mental powers ; মনোভ্রংশ, বুদ্ধি-বৈকল্য।

dē-mĕr′-it, *n.* **1.** Ill desert ; বৈগুণ, অপগুণ। **2.** Fault ; defect ; অধর্ম্ম ; দুর্গুণ।

dē-mĕr-i-tō′-ri-ous (-ŭs), *adj.* Lacking merit ; deserving blame ; ধর্ম্মশূন্য, অধর্ম্মজনক ; নিন্দার্হ। **—ly,** *adv.*

dē-mesne′ (-mān), *n.* **1.** (*Law*) Possession (of land) as one's own ; (আইন) নিজস্ব সম্পত্তি। **2.** An estate in land ; ভূ-সম্পত্তি। **3.** The land adjacent to a manor house kept in the proprietor's own hands ; খামার। **4.** A region ; a sphere ; অঞ্চল ; প্রদেশ। **5.** The territory or domain of a sovereign or state ; রাজা বা সরকারের নিজস্ব সম্পত্তি। **Royal demesne**—রাজা বা রাণীর নিজস্ব সম্পত্তি। **State demesne**—A land held by the state ; খাসমহাল।

dĕm′-i, *pref.* (Usually written with the hyphen, still used as prefix but more or less ousted by SEMI-) **1.** Half ; imperfect ; অর্দ্ধ ; অপূর্ণ, অসম্পূর্ণ। **2.** Partially ; partial ; অংশতঃ ; আংশিক।

dĕm′-i-gŏd, *n.* A partly divine being ; a godling ; দেবযোনি, অর্দ্ধদেব ; উপদেব, উপদেবতা।

dĕm′-i-john (-jŏn), *n.* A large glass vessel or bottle inclosed in wicker-work ; বংশবেত্রাদিনির্ম্মিত আবরণের ভিতর আবদ্ধ বৃহৎ কাচপাত্র বা বোতল।

dĕm′-i-lūne, *n.* **1.** A half moon or crescent ; অর্দ্ধচন্দ্র, চন্দ্রলেখা। **2.** (*Fort.*) An outwork of crescent shape protecting a bastion or curtain ; (দুর্গ) দুর্গের কোণে কোণে অবস্থিত গম্বুজ এবং গম্বুজদ্বয়ের মধ্যবর্ত্তী বপ্ররক্ষার্থ অর্দ্ধচন্দ্রাকৃতি উপদুর্গবিশেষ।

demimonde, (*F.*), *n.* Women of doubtful reputation, esp. kept women ; সন্দিগ্ধচরিত্রা স্ত্রীলোক, রক্ষিতা স্ত্রীলোক।

dĕm′-i-rĕp, *n.* A woman of suspected chastity ; সন্দিগ্ধচরিত্রা স্ত্রীলোক।

dē-mīse′, *n.* & *v. t.* **1.** Transfer of the crown or sovereignty to a successor, as by death or abdication ; কোন রাজার মৃত্যু বা রাজ্যত্যাগ হেতু উত্তরাধিকারীর সিংহাসন-প্রাপ্তি। **2.** The decease of a royal or princely person ; (grandiloquently) death ; রাজা বা রাজতুল্য ব্যক্তির মৃত্যু ; তিরোভাব, উপরম (আঃ বঃ)। **3.** (*Law*) Conveyance or grant of an estate by will or lease ; (আইন) চরমপত্র বা পাট্টা দ্বারা সম্পত্তি দান বা হস্তান্তর। ***Verb t.*** To convey, as an estate, by will or lease ; (আইন) চরমপত্র বা পাট্টা দ্বারা সম্পত্তি হস্তান্তর করা। **—mis′-a-ble,** *adj.*

dē-mis′-sion (-mĭ-), *n.* Relinquishment ; resignation or abdication ; পরিত্যাগ ; পদত্যাগ, সিংহাসনত্যাগ।

dē-mit′, *v. t.* & *i.* To resign (office etc.) ; পরিত্যাগ করা।

dĕm′-i-urge (-ẽrj), *n.* **1.** (*Philos.*) With Plato, the creator of the world ; (প্লাতোর দর্শনে) স্রষ্টা, বিধাতা। **2.** In some of the Peloponnesian states of ancient Greece, a magistrate or executive officer ; (প্রাচীন গ্রীস দেশের অন্তঃপাতী পিলোপনিশিয়্যান রাজ্যসমূহে) শাসন বিভাগীয় কর্ম্মচারি-বিশেষ।

dē-mō′-bi-līze, *v. t.* To release from mobilized state ; to disband (troops, ships, etc.) ; যুদ্ধার্থ প্রস্তুত সৈন্যদল ভঙ্গ করা ; (সৈন্য, পোত, প্রভৃতির) দল ভঙ্গ করা।

dē-mŏc′-ră-cȳ, *n.* **1.** Government by the people, direct or representative ; সাধারণতন্ত্র, গণতন্ত্র, প্রাকৃততন্ত্র, জনতাধীন-শাসন (হিঃ কোঃ), প্রজাতন্ত্র। **2.** A state practising this form of government ; যে রাজ্যে প্রজাতন্ত্র প্রতিষ্ঠিত আছে। **3.** The politically unprivileged class ; রাজনীতিক অধিকারশূন্য শ্রেণী।

dĕm′-ō-crăt, *n.* **1.** Adherent or advocate of democracy ; প্রজাতন্ত্রবাদী, প্রজাতন্ত্রশাসনানুরাগী। **2.** A member of the democratic party (*U. S.*) ; (মার্কিণযুক্ত রাজ্য) ব্যবসায়ি-সম্মিলন প্রভৃতির বিরোধী দলীয় ব্যক্তি। **De-moc′-ra-tion**, *n.*

dĕm-ō-crăt′-ic, *adj.* Pertaining to democracy ; favouring or based upon democracy ; প্রজাতন্ত্র-সংক্রান্ত ; প্রজাতন্ত্রমূলক, প্রজাতন্ত্রানুরাগী। **—i-cal-ly**, *adv.* **Democratic party**—মার্কিণযুক্ত রাজ্যে যে রাজনীতিক দল, সম্মিলন প্রভৃতি রাষ্ট্রীয়, স্থানীয় এবং ব্যক্তিগত স্বাধীনতার পক্ষ সমর্থন করে।

dē-mŏc′-ră-tīze, *v. t.* & *i.* To render or become democratic ; প্রজাতন্ত্রানুরাগী করা বা হওয়া। **—ti-za′-tion**, *n.*

Dē-mŏc-ri-tē′-ăn, *adj.* Of or relating to Democritus, his theory of atoms or his humour ; গ্রীক্ দার্শনিক ডিমক্রীতাস্, তদীয় পরমাণুবাদ বা পরিহাস-রসিকতা সম্বন্ধীয়।

Dē-mō-gŏr′-gŏn, *n.* A terrible infernal deity ; নরকবাসী ভীষণ দেবতা।

dē-mŏg′-ră-phȳ, *n.* Statistics of births, diseases, mortality, etc. showing conditions of communities ; জনসাধারণের জন্ম, মৃত্যু, রোগ প্রভৃতি সম্বন্ধীয় তথ্যাবলী, জনতাবর্ণন (হিঃ কোঃ), বসতিবর্ণন (ঐ)। **—mo-graph′-ic**, *adj.* **—pher**, *n.*

dem-oi-selle′ (dĕm-wä-zĕl′), *n.* **1.** The Numidian crane, so called from its gracefulness and symmetry of form ; নিউমিডিয়া দেশীয় ক্রৌঞ্চ পক্ষী। **2.** (*F.*) A damsel ; অবিবাহিতা তরুণী, বালা, কুমারী।

dē-mŏl′-ish, *v. t.* **1.** To throw or pull down ; to raze ; to destroy ; as, to *demolish* a building ; ভাঙ্গিয়া ফেলা ; ভূমিসাৎ করা ; ধ্বংস করা, উচ্ছন্ন করা, বিনাশ করা। **2.** To over-throw ; as, to *demolish* a theory ; বিপর্য্যস্ত করা, উল্টাইয়া ফেলা। **3.** (*Humorously*) To consume ; "They proceed to *demolish* the substantials ;" (কৌতুকচ্ছলে) খাইয়া ফেলা, ধ্বংস করা, (যথা অন্নধ্বংস করা)। **—li′-tion**, *n.* Destruction ; ধ্বংস, উচ্ছেদ, ভঙ্গ, উজাড়।

dē′-mŏn, *n.* **1.** A spirit or immaterial being holding a middle place between men and the celestial beings of the pagan ; দেবযোনি। **2.** An evil spirit ; a devil ; ভূত, পিশাচ, অপদেবতা ; দানব, অসুর, দৈত্য। **3.** An infuriated or fiend-like man ; অসুরপ্রকৃতি ব্যক্তি। **4.** Personified vice or passion ; মূর্ত্তিমান পাপ বা ক্রোধ।

dē-mŏn′-ē-tīze, *v. t.* To deprive of standard value as money ; as, to *demonetize* a metal ; কোনরূপ ধাতব মুদ্রার প্রচলন বন্ধ করা। **—ti-za′-tion**, *n.*

dē-mō′-ni-ăc, **dē-mō-nī′-ă-căl**, *adjs.* **1.** Influenced or produced by a demon ; possessed by an evil spirit ; relating to such possesion ; ভৌতিক ; ভূতগ্রস্ত, ভূতাবিষ্ট ; উক্তরূপ প্রভাব সম্পর্কীয়। **2.** Devellish ; characteristic of a demon ; fiercely energetic ; আসুর ; দানবোচিত, পৈশাচ ; প্রচণ্ডোৎসাহদীপ্ত।

dē-mō′-ni-ăc, *n.* A person possessed by an evil spirit ; ভূতগ্রস্ত ব্যক্তি, ভূতাবিষ্ট ব্যক্তি।

dē-mŏn′-ic, *adj.* **1.** Pertainig to, or of the nature of, a demon ; দানবীয়, অসুরপ্রকৃতিক, আসুরিক। **2.** Inspired ; of supernatural genius or impulses, "and call him a *demonic* man" ; আবিষ্ট ; অতিপ্রাকৃত প্রতিভাশালী বা আবেগপূর্ণ।

dē′-mŏn-ism, *n.* Belief in the power of demons ; ভূত-প্রেতাদির শক্তিতে বিশ্বাস।

dē-mŏn-ŏl′-ă-trȳ, *n.* Worship of spirits and demonic powers ; অসুর-পূজা।

dē-mŏn-ŏl′-ō-ġȳ, *n.* The branch of learning concerned with demons, or beliefs in demons ; ভূতবিদ্যা, ভূতবিজ্ঞান, অসুরবিদ্যা।

dē-mŏn-ō-mā′-ni-ă, *n.* A kind of mania in which the sufferer believes himself possessed by devils ; একপ্রকার উন্মাদ রোগ—যাহাতে রোগী আপনাকে ভূত-প্রেতাদির আশ্রিত মনে করে, আবিষ্টংমন্যতা (হিঃ কোঃ), অসুরাবেশ (ঐ), অসুরাবেশশঙ্কা (ঐ)।

dē-mŏn′-stră-ble, *adj.* Capable of being shown or logically proved ; সাধ্য (আঃ বঃ), প্রমাণযোগ্য, উপপাদনীয়। **—bly**, *adv.*

dĕm′-ŏn-strate, *v. t.* & *i.* **1.** To show or make evident by reasoning or proof ; to prove beyond possibility of doubt ; সপ্রমাণ করা, উপপাদন করা, প্রতিপাদন করা, সাধন করা ; নিঃসংশয়িতরূপে

প্রমাণ করা। 2. To describe and explain by specimens or experiments; as, to *demonstrate* anatomy or chemistry; আদর্শ প্রদর্শন বা বৈজ্ঞানিক পরীক্ষা দ্বারা বর্ণনা করা বা বুঝাইয়া দেওয়া। 3. To exhibit (feelings etc.) demonstratively; (মানসিক আবেগ প্রভৃতি) বাহ্যিক ভাব দ্বারা প্রদর্শন করা। 4. To show publicly the special value or merits of, with a view to its introduction or sale; as, to *demonstrate* a toilet article; কোন জিনিষ বিক্রীর বা চালাইবার জন্য সর্ব্বসমক্ষে উহার বিশিষ্ট গুণ বা কার্য্যকারিতা প্রদর্শন করা। 5. To be a proof of the existence of; কোন কিছুর সত্তার প্রমাণস্বরূপ হওয়া। ***Verb i.*** 1. To make a military demonstration; আক্রমণ করা হইবে এরূপ ভাব প্রদর্শন করিয়া সৈন্য চালনা করা। 2. To take part in a public demonstration; রাজনীতিক বা অন্যান্য বিষয়ে মত প্রকাশের জন্য অনুষ্ঠিত সভা, শোভাযাত্রা প্রভৃতিতে যোগদান করা। 3. To teach by demonstrations; আদর্শ প্রদর্শন দ্বারা বা বৈজ্ঞানিক পরীক্ষার সাহায্যে শিক্ষা প্রদান করা।

dĕm-ŏn-strā'-tion, *n.* 1. Exhibition of opinion on political and other question by public meeting or procession; সভা এবং শোভাযাত্রার সাহায্যে কোন রাজনীতিক বা অন্য বিষয়ে জনমত-প্রদর্শন, জনমত-প্রদর্শন। 2. A manifestation; an outward exhibition of feeling etc.; as, a *demonstration* of grief; বহিঃ-প্রকাশ; আবেগ প্রভৃতির বাহ্য প্রকাশ। 3. Demonstrating or proving logically; a thing serving as proof; a clear proof; প্রতিপাদন, উপপাদন; প্রতিপাদক বিষয়; স্পষ্ট প্রমাণ। 4. Exhibition and explanation of specimens or experiments by way of teaching; শিক্ষাদানের উদ্দেশ্যে কোন বস্তুর নমুনা বর্ণন ও প্রদর্শন কিম্বা বৈজ্ঞানিক পরীক্ষা করণ। 5. (*Mil.*) A movement of troops with a view to deceive; (সামরিক-শাস্ত্র) শত্রুকে প্রতারণা করার উদ্দেশ্যে সৈন্য সঞ্চালন, কপট-সঞ্চালন। 6. (*Math.*) A mode of proof by which any proposition is proved as a necessary consequence of assumed or already proved premises; উপপত্তি (সাঃ পঃ), প্রমাণ (ঐ), সাধন (ঐ), পরীক্ষা (ঐ)। **—al,** *adj.* **—ist,** *n.*

dē-mŏn'-strā-tive (-tĭv), *adj.* & *n.* Making evident; serving to exhibit; "*Demonstrative* figures;" proving conclusively; স্পষ্টদর্শী; প্রদর্শক; প্রতিপাদক। 2. Given to, or marked by, open expression of feeling; as, a *demonstrative* behaviour or person; আবেগ প্রদর্শনশীল, আবেগপ্রদর্শনাত্মক। 3. (*Gram.*) Serving to designate or point out the thing referred to or intended; as, a *demonstrative* pronoun; (ব্যাকরণ) উল্লিখিত বা অভিপ্রেত বস্তুনির্দ্দেশক, নির্দ্দেশক। 4. Giving proof of; উপপাদক (মঃ ইঃ), নির্ণায়ক (ঐ), প্রতিপাদক, প্রামাণিক। 5. Concerned with proof; as, Logic is a *demonstrative* science; প্রমাণাত্মক। ***Noun.*** (*Gram.*) A word having a demonstrative function; as, a *demonstrative* (pronoun); (ব্যাকরণ) নির্দ্দেশক শব্দ। **—ly,** *adv.* **—ness,** *n.*

dĕm'-ŏn-strā-tŏr (-têr), *n.* 1. One who demonstrates; প্রতিপাদক। 2. An assistant to a professor doing practical work with the students; অধ্যাপকের সহায়ক—যিনি ছাত্রদিগকে হাতে কলমে বৈজ্ঞানিক বিষয় শিক্ষা দিয়া থাকেন, পরীক্ষক। 3. One who exhibits parts when dissected; ব্যবচ্ছিন্ন শরীরাংশ প্রদর্শক। 4. A partaker in demonstration by public meeting; যে ব্যক্তি জনমত প্রকাশার্থ অনুষ্ঠিত সভা, শোভাযাত্রা, প্রভৃতিতে যোগদান করে।

dē-mŏr'-ăl-īze, *v. t.* 1. To pervert or deprave; to corrupt the morals of; সত্য বা ন্যায় পথ হইতে ভ্রষ্ট করা, ভ্রষ্ট করা; নীতিভ্রষ্ট করা, চরিত্র-ভ্রষ্ট করা, বিগড়াইয়া দেওয়া। 2. To deprive of courage, spirit, endurance and discipline; as, to *demoralize* troops; শৌর্য্য, সাহস, সহিষ্ণুতা এবং শাসনাধীনতা প্রভৃতি গুণ বিরহিত করা, সৈনিকোচিত গুণভ্রষ্ট করা। 2. To cast into disorder or confusion; বিশৃঙ্খল অবস্থায় পাতিত করা, ছত্রভঙ্গ করা। **—i-za'-tion,** *n.* Act of demoralizing or the state of being demoralized; নীতিভ্রষ্ট করণ, আচার-ভ্রংশ (হিঃ কোঃ), ভ্রষ্টতা, সৈনিকোচিত গুণ-ভ্রষ্টতা।

dē'-mŏs, *n.* The common people; the populace, esp. personified; the democracy; সাধারণ লোক; ইতরজনগণ; প্রজাতন্ত্র, সাধারণতন্ত্র।

Dĕm-ŏs-thĕn'-ic, *adj.* 1. Of or pertaining to the Athenian orator Demosthenes; like his oratory; প্রাচীন এথেন্স নগরীর সুবিখ্যাত বক্তা ডেমস্থিনিস সম্বন্ধীয়; ডেমস্থিনিসের বক্তৃতা-সদৃশ। 2. (*Fig.*) Eloquent; patriotic; denunciatory (of a speech); (লক্ষণায়) বাগ্মিতাপূর্ণ; স্বদেশপ্রেমিক; (বক্তৃতাসম্পর্ক) তিরস্কার-গর্ভ।

dē-mŏt'-ic, *adj.* 1. Pertaining to the people; vulgar; জনগণসম্বন্ধীয়; গ্রাম্য, ইতর। 2. (*Archaeol.*) Pertaining to the popular form of ancient Egyptian writing, (opposed to *hieratic*); (পুরাচিহ্ন-বিদ্যা) সাধারণের ব্যবহৃত প্রাচীন মিশরীয় লিপির প্রকার বিশেষ সম্বন্ধীয়।

dē-mŭl'-cĕnt, *adj.* & *n.* Soothing; assuasive; স্নিগ্ধকর, দাহঘ্ন (আঃ বঃ), শান্তিদ, উপশামক, উপশমকারী। ***Noun.*** (*Med.*) A substance capable of soothing an inflamed or abraded mucous membrane or protecting it from irritation; স্নিগ্ধকারক বা উপদাহ-প্রশামক ঔষধ, স্নেহোপজ (ঠাকুর)।

dë-mur′ (-mêr), *n.* & *v. i.* Objection ; scruple ; "After a little *demur* he accepted the offer ;" আপত্তি ; দ্বিধা, সঙ্কোচ, শঙ্কা, কুণ্ঠা, বিকল্প (মঃ ইঃ)। ***Verb i.*** **1.** To raise objections to ; to make scruples or difficulties ; আপত্তি করা ; দ্বিধা করা, সংশয় করা, টাল মাটাল করা। **2.** (*Law*) To interpose a demurrer ; (আইন) আইন-ঘটিত আপত্তি উপস্থাপিত করা। **—mur′-rant,** *n.*

dë-müre′, *adj.* **1.** Sober ; modest ; grave ; অপ্রমত্ত ; বিনয়ী ; গম্ভীর। **2.** Affectedly grave or coy ; কৃত্রিম গাম্ভীর্য্যপূর্ণ, কপটবিনয়ী, কপট লজ্জাপূর্ণ। **—ly,** *adv.* **—ness,** *n.*

dë-mŭr′-ra-ble (-ă-), *adj.* Open to objection, (esp. *legal.*) ; আপত্তি-যোগ্য (বিশেষতঃ আইনে)।

dë-mŭr′-räge, *n.* **1.** Detention of a vessel by the freighter beyond the time agreed upon ; মাল প্রেরক কর্ত্তৃক চুক্তির অতিরিক্ত কাল জাহাজ আটক রাখন, পোত-নিরোধ। **2.** Payment made to the owner of the vessel for the detention ; চুক্তির অতিরিক্তকাল জাহাজ আটক রাখার জন্য জাহাজের মালিককে যে টাকা দেওয়া হয়। **3.** Detention of railway wagons, etc. ; বাষ্পীয় শকট-শ্রেণী প্রভৃতির মালবাহী শকট অতিরিক্ত সময় আটক রাখন। **4.** A charge for detention of railway trucks ; রেলগাড়ীর মালবাহী শকট অতিরিক্ত সময় আটক রাখার দরুণ যে টাকা দিতে হয়। **5.** (India) A charge for failing to take delivery of goods by the consignee within specified time ; (ভারতবর্ষ) নির্দ্দিষ্ট সময়ের মধ্যে মাল খালাস না করার জন্য যে অতিরিক্ত ভাড়া দিতে হয়, বিলম্ব-দেয় (আঃ বঃ)। **6.** A charge ($1\frac{1}{2}$d. per oz) made by the bank of England for the exchange of notes or gold coins into bullion ; নোট বা স্বর্ণমুদ্রা স্বর্ণ বা রৌপ্যপিণ্ডে বিনিময় করিতে হইলে ব্যাঙ্ক অব্ ইংলণ্ডে যে মাশুল দিতে হয়।

dë-mur′-rêr (-mŭ-), *n.* **1.** (*Law*) A stop at some point in the pleadings and a resting on the decision of the cause on that point ; (আইন) মোকদ্দমায় নালিশপত্রের কি জাওয়াব প্রভৃতির কথার উপর আইন-ঘটিত আপত্তি, প্রতীপবাদ (আঃ বঃ)। **2.** Exception taken ; আপত্তি।

dë-mÿ′, *n.* A scholar on the foundation at Magdelan College, Oxford ; অক্সফোর্ড বিশ্ববিদ্যালয়ের বৃত্তিভোগী ছাত্র। **2.** A size of paper ; নির্দ্দিষ্ট আকারের কাগজ, ডিমাই কাগজ, (ছাপিবার ১৭″ × ২২″ ইঞ্চি, লিখিবার ১৫″ × ২০″)। **—ship,** *n.* A kind of scholarship at Magdelan College, Oxford ; অকসফোর্ডের মেগডেলেন কলেজের একপ্রকার ছাত্রবৃত্তি।

dĕn, *n.* **1.** A wild beast's lair ; বন্য জন্তুর গর্ত্ত, গুহা, বিবর, বিল। **2.** A squalid place of resort ; a wretched place of residence ; ইতর ব্যক্তিদিগের আড্ডা ; মলপূর্ণ বাসস্থান। **3.** A lurking place of thieves ; চোর প্রভৃতির লুকাইবার স্থান। **4.** A room in which a person secludes himself to work, etc. ; নির্জ্জন কক্ষ।

dë-nā′-ri-ŭs, *n.* An ancient Roman silver coin originally equivalent to about 8d. English money ; প্রাচীন রোম নগরীতে ব্যবহৃত রৌপমুদ্রা বিশেষ।

Denarius of Siberius Cæsar.

dĕn′-ă-rÿ, *adj.* Decimal ; ten-fold ; based on tens ; দশমিক ; দশগুণিত ; দশমূলক।

dë-nă′-tion-ăl-īze, *v. t.* To divest or deprive of national character or rights ; বিজাতীয় করা ; জাতীয়তা শূন্য করা ; জাতীয় অধিকার চ্যুত করা। **—i-za′-tion,** *n.*

dë-năt′-ü-răl-īze, *v. t. n.* **1.** To change the nature of ; to render unnatural ; প্রকৃতি পরিবর্ত্তন করা ; অস্বাভাবিক করা। **2.** To divest of the rights and duties of a citizen ; নাগরিক অধিকার বা কর্ত্তব্য হইতে বিচ্যুত করা। **—i-za′-tion,** *n.*

dë-nā′-tür-ănt, *n.* A denaturing agent ; যে দ্রব্য (বিশেষতঃ ভেজাল) মিশাইয়া কোন বস্তুর মৌলিক ধর্ম্মের পরিবর্ত্তন করা হয়।

dë-nā′-türe, *v. t.* To change the nature or essential qualities of, esp. by adulteration ; প্রকৃতি পরিবর্ত্তন করা, মৌলিক ধর্ম্ম পরিবর্ত্তন করা, (বিশেষতঃ ভেজাল মিশ্রিত করিয়া)।

dĕn′-drī-fórm, *adj.* Resembling a tree in structure or form ; বৃক্ষাকৃতি, দ্রুমাকার।

dĕn′-drīte, *n.* A mineral or stone with marks resembling plants or shrubs ; বৃক্ষ গুল্মাদির মত চিহ্ন বিশিষ্ট প্রস্তর বা খনিজ পদার্থ, দ্রুমাঙ্কিত প্রস্তর বা খনিজ পদার্থ। **—drit-ic,** *adj.*

dĕn′-droid (-droyd), **—droi′-dăl** (-drōy-), *adjs.* Like a tree in form ; বৃক্ষাকৃতি।

dĕn-drŏl′-ŏ-ġÿ, *n.* A natural history of trees or a discourse on them ; তরু গুল্মাদির প্রাকৃতিক ইতিহাস, দ্রুমবিজ্ঞান, পাদপতত্ত্ব। **—gist,** *n.*

dĕn-drŏm′-ë-têr, *n.* An instrument for measuring the height and diameter of trees ; বৃক্ষের উচ্চতা এবং ব্যাস পরিমাপক যন্ত্র।

dene (dēn), *n.* A sandy tract by the sea ; a low sand-hill ; বালিয়াড়ি ; অনুচ্চ বালুকাশৈল।

Dene bola—উত্তর ফাল্গুনী (হিঃ কোঃ)।

dĕn-ë-gā′-tion, *n.* (*Archaic*) Denial ; (অপ্রচলিত) অস্বীকৃতি।

dene′-hōle (dēn-), **dane-** (dān-), *n.* (*Archaeol.*) An artificial excavation in the chalk-formation ; খড়িময় ভূমিতে মনুষ্য হস্তখনিত গহ্বর বিশেষ।

den′-gue (dĕng-gā), *n.* Infectious eruptive fever with acute pain in joints ; আমবাতিক বেদনা ও পীড়কা বিশিষ্ট একপ্রকার বিশেষ ব্যাপক প্রবল জ্বর, ডেঙ্গুজ্বর।

dē-nī′-a-ble, *adj.* That may be denied ; অস্বীকার্য্য, প্রত্যাখ্যেয়, প্রতিবাদযোগ্য।

dē-nī′-ăl, *n.* **1.** Rufusal of a request ; অস্বীকৃতি, প্রত্যাখ্যান। **2.** Contradiction ; as, to meet a charge with flat *denial* ; প্রতিবাদ ; অপহার (আঃ বঃ)। **3.** Self-denial ; "The *denials* of obedience ;" আত্মত্যাগ। **4.** (*Law*) The opposing by the defendant of a claim or charge advanced against him ; (আইন) বিবাদীকর্ত্তৃক দাবী বা অভিযোগের প্রতিবাদ। **5.** Disavowal ; as, *denial* of God ; অস্বীকার।

dē-nī′-êr, *n.* One who denies ; অস্বীকারকারী।

dē-nī′-êr, *n.* An old French copper coin, the 12th part of a soy ; ফরাসীদেশীয় প্রাচীন তাম্রমুদ্রা বিশেষ।

dĕn′-i-grāte, *v. t.* To blacken ; to defame ; কালিমালিপ্ত করা, কলঙ্কিত করা ; মানহানি করা। **—gra′-tion, —gra-tor,** *ns.*

dē-nī′-trāte, *v. t.* To deprive of nitric acid, nitrates or oxides of nitrogen ; তাম্রদ্রাব প্রভৃতি হীন করা। **—tra′tion,**

dē-nī′-tri-fȳ, *v. t.* To denitrate ; তাম্রদ্রাব প্রভৃতি হীন করা। **—fi-ca′-tion,** *n.*

dĕn′-i-zen (-zn), *n.* & *v. t.* **1.** An inhabitant ; a dweller ; অধিবাসী, বাসিন্দা ; বাসী। **2.** One admitted to the rights of a citizen ; নাগরিক অধিকার প্রাপ্ত ব্যক্তি, কৃতপৌর (আঃ বঃ)। **3.** A naturalized foreign word, animal or plant ; কোন দেশের নিজস্বরূপে পরিণত বিদেশীয় শব্দ, জন্তু বা বৃক্ষ। ***Verb t.*** To admit to residence with certain rights and privileges ; "As soon as *denizened*, they domineer ;" নির্দ্দিষ্ট স্বত্ব বা অধিকার প্রদান করত বাস করিতে দেওয়া। **—ship,** *n.*

dē-nŏm′-i-nāte, *v. t.* **1.** To give a name to ; to call ; নাম প্রদান করা আখ্যা দেওয়া ; ডাকা, অভিহিত করা। **2.** To indicate ; to denote, (*obs.*) ; নির্দ্দেশ করা ; বুঝান, (অপ্রচলিত)।

dē-nŏm-i-nā′-tion, *n.* **1.** Name ; designation ; name for a class of like individuals ; নাম ; অভিধেয়, সংজ্ঞা ; লক্ষণ (মঃ ইঃ), একজাতীয় ব্যক্তি সমূহের সাধারণ নাম, শ্রেণী-নাম, উপাধি (মঃ ইঃ)। **2.** The act of denominating or naming ; নামকরণ। **3.** One of a series of related units or values denoted by special names ; পরস্পরের সহিত সম্বন্ধবিশিষ্ট এবং বিভিন্ন নাম দ্বারা সূচিত মূল্য বা একক শ্রেণীর একটী। **4.** A class, or society of individuals, called by the same name ; a sect ; একনামধারী শ্রেণী বা সম্প্রদায়গণ (আঃ বঃ) ; ধর্ম্ম-সম্প্রদায়। **—al,** *adj.* Of or pertaining to a denomination ; নাম-সম্বন্ধীয়, সাম্প্রদায়িক। **—al-ize,** *v.t.*

dē-nŏm′-i-nā-tive (-tĭv), *adj.* **1.** Conferring a name ; serving as a name ; সংজ্ঞাপক (হিঃ কোঃ) ; নামার্থক। **2.** (*Gram.*) Derived from a noun or adjective ; (ব্যাকরণ) বিশেষ্য বা বিশেষণ হইতে উৎপন্ন।

dē-nŏm′-i-nā-tor (-têr), *n.* **1.** The number below the line in a vulgar fraction ; ভাজক, হর, ছেদ (বৃঃ সং)। **2.** One who or that which denominates, (rare) ; নামদাতা (অপ্রচলিত)।

dē-nō-tā′-tion, *n.* **1.** The act of denoting ; marking off of anything ; নির্দ্দেশন ; চিহ্নীকরণ। **2.** Expression by symbols or marks ; সঙ্কেত বা চিহ্ন দ্বারা প্রকাশ। **3.** A sign ; an indication ; a name ; চিহ্ন ; লক্ষণ ; নাম। **4.** Meaning or significance of a term ; অর্থ, অভিপ্রায়। **5.** (*Log.*) The individuals or instances falling under any conception or term, and so, partly at least, definable by it ; extension ; (তর্কবিজ্ঞান) ব্যক্ত্যর্থ, (হিঃ কোঃ), ব্যক্তিবোধন (ঐ) ; বিশেষাভিধান (ঐ)।

dē-nōt′-ā-tive, *adj.* **1.** Indicative of ; designating ; নির্দ্দেশক ; প্রদর্শক **2.** (*Log.*) Merely designating ; implying no attributive ; (তর্কবিজ্ঞান) ব্যক্তি-নির্দ্দেশক ; ব্যক্তি-বোধক। **—ly,** *adv.*

dē-nōte′, *v. t.* **1.** To mark out ; to signify by a visible sign ; to indicate ; to point out ; to stand as a name for ; চিহ্নিত করা ; প্রদর্শন করা ; নির্দ্দেশ করা ; স্পষ্টরূপে নির্দ্দেশ করা, দেখাইয়া দেওয়া ; নাম-স্বরূপ হওয়া। **2.** To signify ; to mean ; অভিপ্রায় ব্যক্ত করা ; বুঝান। **—ment,** *n.*

dē-noue′-ment (dā-nô-mân), *n.* **1.** The unravelling or discovery of a plot, esp. of a drama etc. ; catastrophe ; রহস্যোদ্ঘাটন, নাটকাদির উপসংহার, কার্য্য (সাঃ দঃ) ; নিষ্ঠা (সাঃ দঃ), নির্ব্বহণ (ঐ)। **2.** The issue, or final solution, as of a situation, difficulty or mystery ; কোনরূপ অবস্থা, সঙ্কট বা রহস্যের চরম-সমাধান।

dē-nounce′ (-nowns), *v. t.* **1.** To inform against ; to accuse ; as, to *denounce* one for neglect of duty ; বিরুদ্ধে জ্ঞাপন করা ; অভিযুক্ত করা। **2.** To proclaim termination ; "The treaty was to continue from year to year unless *denounced* by either party." ; অবসান ঘোষণা করা। **3.** To prophesy ; to proclaim in a threatening manner ; "I *denounced* unto you this day that ye shall surely perish ;" ভবিষ্যদ্বাক্য কহা ; ভীতি-জনকভাবে বলা। **4.** To inveigh against openly ; প্রকাশ্যভাবে নিন্দা বা ভর্ৎসনা করা, ধমকান্। **—ment,** *n.*

de nouveau, (*F.*), *adv.* Afresh starting again ; নবভাবে ; পুনরায় আরম্ভ করিয়া।

de novo, (*L.*), *adv.* Same as DE NOUVEAU.

dense (dĕns), *adj.* **1.** Compact; thick ; সঘন, সান্দ্র; নিবিড়, গহন, ঘোর, পীবর (মঃ ইঃ)। **2.** Crowded together ; সঙ্কুলিত। **3.** Crass ; thick-headĕd ; স্থূল; স্থূলবুদ্ধি। **4.** (*Photo.*) Opaque, as a negative ; (আলোক-চিত্র) অস্বচ্ছ। **Dense′-ly,** *adv.* **Dense′-ness,** *n.*

dĕn′-si-tȳ, *n.* **1.** Closeness of substance ; state of being dense ; ঘনতা, নিবিড়তা ; সান্দ্রত্ব, সান্দ্রতা, গাঢ়তা। **2.** Stupidity ; মূর্খতা। **3.** (*Phys.*) The ratio of mass to bulk or volume ; (পদার্থ-বিদ্যা) মাত্রা ও আয়তনের অনুপাত, ঘনত্ব (সাঃ পঃ)। **4.** (*Photo.*) Degree of opacity ; (আলোক-চিত্র) অস্বচ্ছতার মাত্রা।

dĕnt, *n.* & *v.* t. An indentation ; a depression like that made by a blow, etc. ; খাঁজ ; ভগ্নমস্তকাদির অভ্যন্তর দিকে অবনতি, টোল। ***Verb t.*** To make a dent upon ; to indent ; as, a house *dented* with bullets ; খাঁজ-বিশিষ্ট করা ; তীক্ষ্ণ-দন্তিত করা।

dĕnt, *n.* (*Mach.*) A tooth in various technical uses ; (যন্ত্র-বিজ্ঞান) দন্ত।

dĕn′-tăl, *adj.* & *n.* **1.** Pertaining to the teeth or dentistry ; as, *dental* surgery ; দন্তসম্বন্ধীয় ; দন্ত-বিদ্যা-সম্বন্ধীয়। **2.** Articulated with the tip of the tongue against the upper front teeth ; as, a *dental* letter ; দন্ত্য। ***Noun.*** A letter made with tongue-tip against the upper front teeth or the front of the palate ; দন্ত্যবর্ণ। **—ize,** *v. t.*

dĕn′-tāte, *adj.* (*Bot.* & *Zool.*) Toothed ; with tooth-like notches ; দন্তিত ; তীক্ষ্ণদন্তিত (সাঃ পঃ), দন্তী (ঐ)। **—ta-tion,** *n.*

dĕn′-ti-cle, *n.* **1.** A small tooth or tooth-like projection ; ক্ষুদ্র দন্ত। **2.** (*Arch.*) A dentil ; (স্থপতি-বিজ্ঞান) আলিসার নিম্নস্থিত দন্তপংক্তিবৎ স্থাপত্য-ভূষা। **—tic′-u-lar,** *adj.* **—tic′-u-late, —lat-ĕd,** *adjs.* **—tic-u-la′-tion,** *n.*

dĕn′-ti-fôrm, *adj.* Tooth-shaped ; দন্তাকার।

dĕn′-ti-frice (-frîs), *n.* **1.** A powder or other substance used in cleaning the teeth ; দন্তমঞ্জনচূর্ণ, দন্তধাবনচূর্ণ, দন্তপাবন (আঃ বঃ), মিশি (ঐ), মাজন, মঞ্জন (ঠাকুর), প্রতিসরণ (সাঃ পঃ)।

dĕn-tĭg′-êr-ous (-us), *adj.* Bearing or carrying teeth ; দন্তধারী।

dĕn′-til, *n.* (*Arch.*) An ornament in cornices bearing some resemblance to teeth ; (স্থপতি-বিজ্ঞান) আলিসার নিম্নস্থিত দন্তপংক্তিবৎ স্থাপত্যভূষা।

dĕn′-tine (-tîn), *n.* The substance under the enamel of which the teeth are formed ; দন্তের মসৃণ বহিরাবরণের নিম্নস্থ পদার্থ বিশেষ, যাহা হইতে দন্ত গঠিত হয়, রদিন (সাঃ পঃ)।

dĕn′-tist, *n.* A dental surgeon ; দন্ত-চিকিৎসক, দন্ত-বৈদ্য, দাঁতবাঁধাইকার। **—ry,** *n.* The act or profession of a dentist ; দন্তচিকিৎসাবিদ্যা।

dĕn-ti′-tion, *n.* **1.** Teething ; দন্তোদ্ভেদ, দন্তনির্গম, দন্তোদ্গম। **2.** (*Zool.*) The characteristic arrangement of teeth in animals ; দন্তবিন্যাস, দন্তসংস্থান (সাঃ পঃ)।

dĕn-ū-dā′-tion, *n.* **1.** A making nude or bare ; নগ্নীকরণ। **2.** (*Geol.*) Erosion ; (ভূ-বিদ্যা) ক্ষয় (সাঃ পঃ)।

dē-nūde′, *v. t.* **1.** To make bare or naked ; to strip ; নগ্ন করা, উলঙ্গ করা ; দিগম্বর করা, বিবসন করা, বিবস্ত্র করা, অনাবৃত করা। **2.** (*Geol.*) To lay bare by erosion ; (ভূ-বিদ্যা) উপরিভাগের স্তর ক্ষয় হওয়ার দরুণ প্রকট হওয়া। **3.** To deprive (*of* any right, attribute, etc.) ; (গুণ, অধিকার, প্রভৃতি) বিরহিত করা।

dē-nŭn-ci-ā′-tion, *n.* **1.** Act of denouncing ; প্রকাশ্য ভৎ'সনা, গঞ্জনা। **2.** A public menace ; an arraignment ; as, a *denunciation* of war ; প্রকাশ্যে ভীতিপ্রদর্শন ; দোষপ্রদর্শন, বিদূষণ। **—nun′-ci-a-tive,** *adj.* **—nun′-ci-a-tor,** *n.* **—nun′-ci-a-to-ry,** *adj.*

dē-nȳ′, *v. t.* **1.** To gainsay ; to declare untrue ; as, to *deny* a charge ; প্রতিবাদ করা ; অসত্য বলিয়া প্রকাশ করা। **2.** To disavow ; অস্বীকার করা। **3.** To refuse to grant ; প্রদান করিতে অস্বীকার করা। **4.** To reject as unreal ; "To *deny* the resurrection of Christ ;" অবাস্তব বলিয়া অগ্রাহ্য করা। **5.** To refuse access to ; to report as not at home ; as, to *deny* oneself to a visitor ; প্রবেশানুমতি দিতে অস্বীকার করা ; বাটী হইতে অনুপস্থিত বলিয়া বলা। **To deny one's self** — To practise self-denial ; আত্মত্যাগ অনুষ্ঠান করা।

dē-ŏb′-strû-ĕnt, *adj.* (*Med.*) Removing obstruction ; (ভৈষজ্য-শাস্ত্র) শরীরের আভ্যন্তরীণ দ্বারাদির অবরোধক পদার্থ দূরকারক বস্তু, বন্দঘ্নী (সাঃ পঃ)।

dē′-ō-dănd, *n.* (*Hist.*) A thing which had been the immediate cause of the death of a person and for that reason forfeited to the crown, to be applied to pious uses ; (ইংলণ্ডের ইতিহাস) কোন ব্যক্তির মৃত্যুর অব্যবহিত কারণী-ভূত বস্তু, এবং তদ্ধেতু যাহা কোন সৎকার্য্যে ব্যবহৃত করার জন্য রাজভাণ্ডারভুক্ত করা হইয়া থাকে, দেবদেয় (আঃ বঃ)।

dē′-ō-dâr, *n.* A species of Indian cedar ; দেবদারু।

dē-ō′-dor-ize (-dêr-), *v. t.* To deprive of odour ; to disinfect ; as, charcoal *deodorizes* night-soil ; গন্ধহীন করা ; বীজাণু নষ্ট করা, পূতিগন্ধ দূর করা। **—i-za′-tion,** *n.* **—iz-er,** *n.*

dē-ŏn-tŏl′-ō-ġȳ, *n.* Science or ethics of duty ; কর্ত্তব্যবিজ্ঞান, শাস্ত্র-কৃত্য (হিঃ কোঃ)। **—gist,** *n.* **—to-log′-i-cal,** *adj.*

Deo volente, (*L.*) *adv.* (Abbr. D. V.) **1.** God willing ; ঈশ্বরেচ্ছা

থাকিলে। 2. If nothing occurs to prevent it; যদি বাধাজনক কিছু না ঘটে।

dē-ŏx'-i-dise, –dize, (-dīz) *v. t* To deprive of oxygen; অম্লজন বাষ্পশূন্য করা।

dē-pärt', *v. t. & i.* To retire from; as, to *depart* this life; অন্তরিত হওয়া। ***Verb i.*** 1. To set out; to start; যাত্রা করা; গমন করা, প্রস্থান করা, চলিয়া যাওয়া, রওনা হওয়া, বিদায় হওয়া। 2. To die; "Lord, lettest thou thy servant *depart* in peace;" ইহলোক ত্যাগ করা, পরলোক গমন করা। 3. To diverge; to deviate; as, to *depart* from a received custom; বিচ্যুত হওয়া; ভ্রষ্ট হওয়া। 4. (*Archaic*) To take one's leave; (অপ্রচলিত) বিদায়গ্রহণ করা।

dē-pärt'-ĕd, *adj. & n.* 1. Bygone; as, *departed* greatness; গত, অতীত, প্রয়াত, প্রস্থিত। 2. Deceased; মৃত, পরলোকগত, লোকান্তরিত। ***Noun.*** A dead man; পরলোকগত ব্যক্তি।

dē-pärt'-mĕnt, *n.* 1. A division, esp. of municipal or state administration; as, the Forest *department*; কাণ্ড, পরিচ্ছেদ, ভাগ, বিভাগ, অঙ্গ (মঃ ইঃ), প্রকরণ (ঐ), বিশেষতঃ শাসনতন্ত্রাদির বিভাগ, মণ্ডল (মঃ ইঃ)। 2. A sphere; a province; "Little progress has been made in this *department* of knowledge; ক্ষেত্র; রাজ্য। 3. A French administrative district; ফরাসী দেশের জিলা। **–men'-tal,** *adj.* 1. Pertaining to a division of a country; দেশের বিভাগ সম্বন্ধীয়। 2. Of or pertaining to a branch of state administration etc.; as, *departmental* punishment; শাসনতন্ত্রাদির বিভাগ সম্বন্ধীয়, বিভাগীয়। **–men'-tal-ly,** *adv.*

dē-pär'-türe, *n.* 1. Act of departing or going away; as, *departure* from London; starting or setting out, esp. of a railway train: গমন, প্রস্থান, প্রয়াণ; যাত্রা, বিশেষতঃ বেলগাড়ী ছাড়িয়া যাওন। 2. Deviation, as from a standard, rule or plan; abandonment, as of a purpose; বিচ্যুতি, ব্যতিক্রম (আঃ বঃ), ব্যভিচার, অপচার; পরিত্যাগ। 3. Death; decease; ইহলোক ত্যাগ, পরলোক গমন; মৃত্যু। 4. Setting out on a course of action or thought; as, the present act makes a fresh *departure* in Bankruptcy legislation; নূতন কার্য্যপ্রণালী বা চিন্তার অনুসরণ, অন্যথাচরণ। 5. (*Naut.*) The amount of a ship's change of longitude in sailing; (নৌ-বিদ্যা) জলপথগামী অর্ণবপোতের দ্রাঘিমান্তর।

dē-păs'-türe, *v. t. & i.* 1. To use for pasturage; "If Austria is forced to *depasture* the land with hordes of soldiers"; to graze upon; as, cattle *depasture* the land; গোচারণমাঠস্বরূপ ব্যবহৃত করা; চরান। 2. To put to graze; as, a right of *depasturing* cattle on the grounds of another; চরান, ঘাস খাওয়ান। ***Verb i.*** To graze; চরা। **–tur-age,** *n.*

dē-pau'-pĕr-āte (-pä-), *v.t.* 1. To make poor; to impoverish; দরিদ্র করা; নিঃস্ব করা। 2. To make degenerate; to reduce in vigour; অপকৃষ্ট করা; তেজোহানি করা। **–a'-tion,** *n.*

dē-pau'-pĕr-īze (-pä-), *v. t.* To free from pauperism; দৈন্যবিমুক্ত করা।

dē-pĕnd', *v. i.* 1. To rely for support, (with *on* or *upon*); to rest for maintenance, (with *on* or *upon*); নির্ভর করা, অবলম্বন করা; ভরণ-পোষণের জন্য নির্ভর করা। 2. To be in suspense; to be undermined; as, the suit is still *depending* in court; অমীমাংসিত থাকা; অনিশ্চিত অবস্থায় থাকা। 3. (*Poet. & Archaic*) To hang down; (কবিতায় ও অপ্রচলিত) দোদুল্যমান থাকা।

dē-pĕnd'-ă-ble, *adj.* That may be depended on; trustworthy; নির্ভরযোগ্য; বিশ্বাসযোগ্য। **–bly,** *adv.* **–ness,** *n.*

dē-pĕnd'-ănt (-ent), *n.* One who depends on another for support; a hanger on; a servant; পরাশ্রিত, আশ্রিত; গলগ্রহব্যক্তি; অনুচর।

dē-pĕnd'-ence (-ĕns), *n.* 1. Act or state of depending or hanging; টাঙ্গান, বিলম্বন, দোদুল্যমান করণ, দোদুল্যমানাবস্থা। 2. State of being conditional or subordinate; ঘটনাধীনতা, পরতন্ত্রতা, অধীনতা, পরাধীনতা। 3. The state of being dependent on another for support or maintenance; গলগ্রহভাব, পরাশ্রিতত্ব, পারতন্ত্র্য (মঃ ইঃ)। 4. Reliance; নির্ভর, অবলম্বন, আশ্রয়। 5. Mutual relation or connection; "*dependence* of ideas should be followed;" অন্যোন্য-সম্বন্ধ বা সংযোগ। 6. A thing relied on; as, he was her sole *dependence* নির্ভর। 7. Pendency, (chiefly in law); (প্রধানতঃ আইনে) অমীমাংসিত অবস্থা।

dē-pĕnd'-ĕn-cȳ, *n.* 1. State of being dependent; অধীনতা। 2. That which is attached to something else as its subordinate etc.; something dependent or subordinate, esp. a country or province controlled by another; as, England has its *dependencies* in Asia; পরাশ্রিত বা পরাধীন বস্তু; অধীন রাজ্য বা প্রদেশ।

dē-pĕnd'-ĕnt, *adj.* Contingent; subordinate, (with *on* or *upon*); depending on other for maintenance etc, (with *on* or *upon*); অনিশ্চিত; অধীন, সাপেক্ষ; পরাশ্রিত, অনুজীবী।

dē-phlĕg'-māte, *v. t.* To free form water; আর্দ্রতা নাশ করা।

—ma'-tion, *n.* The act of freeing from water ; আর্দ্রতা-নাশ।

dē-phŏs'-phŏr-īze, *v. t.* To remove phosphorus from ; ফুস্ফরক হীন করা। **—i-za'-tion,** *n.*

dē-pict', *v. t.* To delineate ; to represent in drawing or colours ; অঙ্কিত করা ; চিত্রিত করা। **2.** To describe ; কথায় ব্যক্ত করা, বর্ণনা করা। **—pic'-tion,** *n.* **—pic'-tive,** *adj.***—pic'-tor, —pic'-ter** *ns.*

dē-pic'-tūre, *v. t.* To depict ; to make a picture of ; চিত্রিত করা ; আলেখ্য অঙ্কিত করা।

dĕp'-i-lāte, *v. t.* To strip of hair ; নির্লোম করা। **—la'-tion,** *n.* Removal of hair ; লোমপাতন (সাঃ পঃ), লোমহরণ (আঃ বঃ)। **—la-tor,** *n.*

dē-pĭl'-ă-tō-rȳ, *adj.* & *n.* Having the quality or power of depilating ; লোমাপহারক, কেশহর। ***Noun.*** An agent used to remove hair ; লোমনাশক ঔষধ।

dē-plĕn'-ish, *v. t.* To deprive of stock or other contents ; শূন্য করা, খালি করা।

dē-plete' (-plēt), *v. t.* **1.** (*Med.*) To empty as the vessels of the human system by blood-letting or by purgation ; (ভৈষজ্যশাস্ত্র) রক্ত-মোক্ষণ অথবা বিরেচন দ্বারা শরীরের রক্তরসাদিবহা নাড়ী শূন্য করা। **2.** To empty out ; to exhaust ; শূন্য করা ; নিঃশেষিত করা। **—ple'-tion,** *n.* The act of depleting ; রিক্তকরণ, শূন্যকরণ। **—ple'-tive,** *adj.* & *n.* **—ple'-to-ry,** *adj.*

dē-plōre', *v. t.* To regret ; to lament ; to mourn ; গভীর আক্ষেপ করা ; আফসোস করা (ফঃ হিঃ), খেদ করা ; শোক করা। **—plor-a-bil'-i-ty,** *n.* **—plor'-a-ble,** *adj.* Lamentable ; শোচনীয়, খেদজনক, আক্ষেপজনক। **—plor'-a-ble-ness,** *n.* **—plor'-a-bly,** *adv.*

dē-ploy', *n., v. t.* & *i.* Act of deploying or extending from a column as of troops, etc. into a line ; the state of being deployed ; স্তম্ভাকারে সজ্জিত সৈন্যশ্রেণী প্রভৃতির বিস্তার ; সৈন্যস্তম্ভের প্রসারিতাবস্থা। ***Verb t. & i.*** To extend from column into line as a body of troops ; স্তম্ভাকারে সজ্জিত সৈন্যশ্রেণী প্রভৃতি বিস্তার করা, সৈন্যস্তম্ভ প্রসারিত করা। **—ment,** *n.*

dē-plume' (-ploōm), *v. t.* To strip of feathers ; পালকশূন্য করা, পালক তোলা।

dē-pō'-lar-īze (-lêr-), *v. t.* **1.** (*Optics*) To change direction of polarization of ; as, to *depolarize* a ray ; (দৃষ্টি-বিজ্ঞান) ধ্রুবাভিপতন করা। **2.** (*Electr. & magn.*) To divest of polarity ; (তাড়িত-বিদ্যা ও চৌম্বক-বিদ্যা) ধ্রুবত্বহীন করা। **3.** (*Fig.*) To disturb ; to shake loose ; as, to *depolarize* prejudices or conviction ; (লক্ষণায়) বিক্ষুব্ধ করা ; আলোড়িত করা। **—i-za'-tion,** *n.* **—iz-er,** *n.* **Depolarization of light**—ধ্রুবাভিপতন।

dē-pō'-nĕnt, *adj.* & *n.* (*L. & Gr. Gram.*) Passive in form but active in meaning ; (লাটিন্ ও গ্রীক্ ব্যাকরণ) আকারে কর্ম্মবাচ্যবৎ কিন্তু অর্থে কর্ত্তৃবাচ্যবৎ। ***Noun.*** **1.** A verb with this characteristic ; উক্ত প্রকৃতির ক্রিয়াপদ। **2.** A person who deposes under oath or gives written testimony for use in a court etc ; সাক্ষী।

dē-pŏp'-ū-lāte, *v. t.* & *i.* To deprive of inhabitants ; to lessen or eradicate the population of ; উজাড় করা, নির্জন করা ; লোকহীন করা, জনশূন্য করা, উচ্ছিন্ন করা, নির্মনুষ্য করা। ***Verb i.*** To decline in population ; লোকসংখ্যা হ্রাসপ্রাপ্ত হওয়া। **—la'-tion,** *n.*

dē-pōrt', *v. t.* **1.** To behave or conduct (one's self) ; আচরণ করা, চলা। **2.** To exile ; to send into banishment ; নির্ব্বাসিত করা ; বিবাসিত করা। **—por-ta'-tion,** *n.* The act of deporting ; নির্ব্বাসন, বিবাসন।

dē-pōrt'-mēnt, *n.* **1.** Demeanour ; manners ; ব্যবহার, আচরণ ; রকম-সকম, চালচলন, চাল। **2.** The way a thing behaves as a metal in chemical experiment ; কোন পদার্থ (বিশেষ অবস্থায়) যেরূপ ক্রিয়া প্রদর্শন করিয়া থাকে (যেমন কোন ধাতু রাসায়নিক পরীক্ষাকালে)।

dē-pōse', *v. t.* & *i.* **1.** To dethrone ; to remove from office or any high station ; সিংহাসন-চ্যুত করা, রাজপদচ্যুত করা, রাজপদভ্রষ্ট করা, সিংহাসন ভ্রষ্ট করা, রাজ্য ভ্রষ্ট করা ; উচ্চ পদ হইতে চ্যুত করা, স্থান-ভ্রষ্ট করা, স্থানচ্যুত করা, অধিকার-ভ্রষ্ট করা। **2.** To give testimony on oath ; ধর্ম্মপ্রতিজ্ঞা পূর্ব্বক সাক্ষ্য প্রদান করা। ***Verb i.*** To bear witness ; to give evidence ; সাক্ষ্য দেওয়া ; প্রমাণ করা।

dē-pŏs'-it, *n.* **1.** Something entrusted to the care of another ; গচ্ছিত দ্রব্য, ন্যাস, উপনিধি (সঃ ইঃ), আমানত (ফঃ হিঃ)। **2.** A sum placed in a bank usually at interest and not to be drawn on without notice ; ধনাগারে আমানতি টাকা, ধনাগারে গচ্ছিত অর্থ। **3.** Anything given as a pledge or security, as earnest money ; বন্ধকী জিনিষ, জামিনস্বরূপ প্রদত্ত জিনিষ, বায়না, ন্যস্ত দ্রব্য, নিক্ষেপ (আঃ বঃ)। **4.** Layer or preciptated matter ; natural accumulation ; "The rich brown *deposit* of the Nile ;" তলানি, কিট্ট ; তলছাট, জমাট, অধঃসঞ্চিত বস্তু।

dē-pŏs'-it, *v. t.* **1.** To commit to custody ; to entrust, esp. a sum at interest in a bank ; গচ্ছিত করা ; ধনাগারে গচ্ছিত করা, জমা রাখা, আমানত রাখা। **2.** To pay as pledge for fulfilment of contract or further payment ; জামিনস্বরূপ দেওয়া, বায়না স্বরূপ দেওয়া। **3.** To lay (eggs) ; as, these insects *deposit* in the ground a great number of eggs ; ডিম পাড়া।

dē-pŏs′-i-tȧ-rȳ, *n.* **1.** A person to whom a thing is commited ; a trustee ; যে ব্যক্তির নিকট কোন জিনিষ গচ্ছিত রাখা হয়, ন্যাস-রক্ষক ; নিক্ষেপগ্রাহক (আঃ বঃ)। **2.** A depository ; ভাণ্ডার।

dĕp-ö-ṡi′-tion, *n.* **1.** Removal from office, esp. dethronement ; সিংহাসনচ্যুতি, রাজ্যভ্রংশ ; পদচ্যুতি। **2.** Testimony under oath ; act of deposing or giving testimony; সাক্ষ্য, জবানবন্দী, ইজাহার; সাক্ষ্য-প্রদান। **3.** A statement ; উক্তি। **4.** Act of depositing ; precipitation ; তলানি ফেলন ; অবক্ষেপন (হিঃ কোঃ)। **5.** The taking down of Christ from the Cross ; a picture representing this ; যীশুখৃষ্টকে ক্রুশকাষ্ঠ হইতে নামান ; উক্ত বিষয়ক চিত্র। **6.** A thing deposited ; sediment ; alluvial matter ; তলানি ; তলছাট ; পলি।

dē-pŏṡ′-i-tor (-têr), *n.* **1.** A person who deposits money etc. ; আমানত-কারী, ন্যাসকর্ত্তা। **2.** An apparatus for depositing some substance ; কোন পদার্থের তলানি ফেলিবার জন্ম যন্ত্রবিশেষ।

dē-pŏṡ-i-tō-rȳ, *n.* **1.** A place where anything is deposited as for safe-keeping or for sale ; ভাণ্ডার, গুদাম, সঞ্চয়াগার। **2.** One with whom some thing is deposited ; যে ব্যক্তির নিকট কোন জিনিষ গচ্ছিত রাখা হয়, ন্যাস রক্ষক।

dĕ′-pot (-pō) *n.* **1.** A place of deposit ; an emporium ; storehouse ; আধার (ঐ), অধিশ্রয় (মঃ ইঃ) ; বাণিজ্যকেন্দ্র ; ভাণ্ডারগৃহ, মালগুদাম, তোষাখানা। **2.** A railway station (*U. S.*) ; (মার্কিণযুক্তরাজ্য) বাষ্পীয় শকটের বিরামস্থান। **3.** (*Mil.*) The place where men, horses and stores are mustered before distribution to army, regiment, etc. which stand in need of them ; (সামরিক-শাস্ত্র) যে স্থানে সৈন্য, অশ্ব, রসদ এবং অস্ত্রশস্ত্র রক্ষিত হয় এবং আবশ্যকমত সেনাপল্টন, বাহিনী প্রভৃতিতে প্রেরিত হয়। **4.** Headquarters of a regiment ; সেনা-পল্টনের সৈন্যদিগের অবস্থান-ভূমি। **5.** A recruit-drilling station ; নবনিযুক্ত সৈন্যগণের কুচ আওয়াজের আড্ডা। **6.** Part of regiment not on foreign service ; সেনাপল্টনের যে অংশ বৈদেশিক কার্য্যে নিযুক্ত নয়।

dē-prāve′, *v. t.* To make bad ; to corrupt ; to vitiate ; নষ্ট করা, বিগড়ান ; দূষিত করা, কলুষিত করা ; চরিত্রভ্রষ্ট করা। **—pra-va′-tion,** *n.*

dē-prăv′-i-tȳ, *n.* **1.** Corruption ; viciousness ; চরিত্রভ্রংশ ; ভ্রষ্টতা, নষ্টাচার। **2.** A corrupt act ; দূষিত কায।

dĕp′-rē-cāte, *v. t.* **1.** To express disapproval of ; as, to *deprecate* war ; বিরাগ-প্রকাশ করা, বিরক্তি-প্রকাশ করা। **2.** To plead against ; as, to *deprecate* one's anger (to request him not to be angry) ; কোন কিছুর বিরুদ্ধে অনুরোধ করা। **—cat-ing-ly,** *adv.* **—ca′-tion,** *n.* **—ca-tive, —ca-to-ry,** *adjs.*

dē-prē′-ci-āte (-shi-), *v. t.* & *i.* To lessen the price of ; as, to *depreciate* the currency ; to belittle ; to disparage ; মূল্য হ্রাস করা, মূল্যাপকর্ষ করা; তুচ্ছ করা, তাচ্ছিল্য করা ; অবজ্ঞা করা, লঘু মনে করা, অপকর্ষ করা, নিকৃষ্ট বস্তুর সহিত তুলনা করিয়া দর কমান, হতাদর করা, অপদস্থ করা। ***Verb i.*** To fall in value or esteem ; as, perishable goods *depreciate* rapidly ; মূল্যাপকর্ষ হওয়া, দর কমা, অনাদৃত হওয়া। **—at-ing-ly,** *adv.* **—a-to-ry,** *adj.*

dē-prē-ci-ā′-tion (-shí-), *n.* **1.** Act of depreciating or state of being depreciated ; falling in value ; "This *depreciation* of their funds ; অপকর্ষ-সাধন, অপকর্ষ ; মূল্যহ্রাস, মূল্যাপকর্ষ। **2.** The act of undervaluing in estimation ; the state of being undervalued ; as, given to *depreciation* of one's friends ; অনাদর, অগৌরব ; গৌরবহানি।

dĕp-rē-dā′-tion, *n.* (Usu. *pl.*) Spoliation ; ravages ; (সাধারণতঃ বহুবচনে) লুণ্ঠন ; লুঠপাট, অপহার (মঃ ইঃ), উপপ্লব (ঐ)।

dĕp′-rē-dā-tor (-têr), *n.* A spoiler; a robber ; লুণ্ঠনকারী, লুঠেরা ; দস্যু, ডাকাত।

dē-prĕss′, *v.t.* **1.** To press down ; to lower ; as, to *depress* the eyes ; অবনমিত করা ; অবনত করা, নীচু করা। **2.** To humble ; to bring low ; as, to *depress* pride ; হীন করা, লঘু করা ; খর্ব্ব করা। **3.** To reduce force, activity, etc. of ; to render languid ; as, to *depress* commerce ; মন্দীভূত করা ; মন্দা করা। **4.** To lower in pitch ; as, to *depress* voice ; ধ্বনির উচ্চতার মাত্রা হ্রাস করা। **5.** To deject ; to make sad ; as, to *depress* the mind ; বিষণ্ণ করা ; বিরস করা, দমাইয়া দেওয়া, খিন্ন করা, বিমর্ষ করা, মনোভঙ্গ করা।

dē-prĕss′-ănt, *adj.* & *n.* (*Med.*) Sedative ; (ভৈষজ্য-শাস্ত্র) অবসাদক। ***Noun.*** An agent that lowers functional or vital activity, as tobacco or aconite ; অবসাদক ঔষধ।

dē-pres′-sion (-prĕ-), *n.* **1.** Act of depressing ; state of being depressed ; degradation ; dejection ; অবনমন ; অপকর্ষ; মন্দা ; স্ফূর্তিহীনতা, উদাসভাব, বিষাদ, খেদ, অপ্রসন্নতা, বিমর্ষ। **2.** Reduction of vigour, pitch, vitality or spirits ; অবসাদন, স্বরের উচ্চতার মাত্রা হ্রাসকরণ, নিজীবকরণ। **3.** A hollow or sunk place on a surface ; কোন বস্তুর উপরিভাগস্থ গর্ত্ত বা অবনমিত স্থান। **4.** (*Astron.*) Angular distance of a celestical object below thehorizon ; (জ্যোতির্বিজ্ঞান)

দিক্‌চক্রবালের নিম্নে কোন জ্যোতিষ্কের কৌণিক দূরত্ব, অধরাংশ (হিঃ কোঃ)। 5. (*Meteorol.*) Lowering of barometer or atmospheric pressure ; (আবহ-বিদ্যা) বায়ুচাপমানযন্ত্রের বা বায়ুচাপের অবনমন। **Depressed fracture**—একপ্রকার ভঙ্গ (বিশেষতঃ করোটীর) যাহাতে ভগ্নাস্থিখণ্ডসমূহ বসিয়া যায়, পিচ্ছিত ভঙ্গ (সাঃ পঃ)।

dē-prĕs′-sor (-êr), *n.* (*Anat.*) A muscle that depresses or draws a part or organ ; যে পেশীর আকর্ষণে শরীরের কোন অংশ ভিতরেরদিকে আকৃষ্ট হয়।

dĕp-ri-vā′-tion, *n.* **1.** Act of depriving or state of being deprived ; loss ; bereavement ; বিরহিত করণ, বঞ্চিত করণ ; হানি, ক্ষতি, অপচয় ; প্রিয়জন-বিয়োগ। **2.** (*Eccle.*) A censure consisting in taking away from a clergyman his benefice or other spiritual promotion or dignity ; (যাজকীয়-শাস্ত্র) যাজকীয় বৃত্তি ও ক্ষমতা হরণ।

dē-prīve′, *v. t.* **1.** To strip ; to take from ; (followed by *of*) ; as, to *deprive* a man *of* strength ; বঞ্চিত করা ; বিরহিত করা, চ্যুত করা। **2.** (*Eccle.*) To depose from office ; (যাজকীয়-শাস্ত্র) পদচ্যুত করা। **—priv′-a-ble,** *adj.* **—priv′-al,** *n.*

de profundis, (*L.*), *adv.* & *n.* From the depths of sorrow, etc. ; গভীরতম বিষাদ হইতে। ***Noun.*** A cry from the depths of sorrow etc.; তীব্র সন্তাপ প্রভৃতি জনিত আর্ত্তনাদ।

dĕpth, *n.* **1.** Measurement from top down, from surface inwards or from front to back ; গভীরতা, বেধ। **2.** Profoundness ; as, *depth* of knowledge ; intensity ; as, the *depth* of colour etc. ; প্রগাঢ়তা ; ঘনত্ব। **3.** Immensity ; "The *depth* of some divine despair ;" বিশালতা। **4.** Lowness of pitch ; as, *depth* of sound ; সুরের নিম্নতা। **5.** Sagacity ; as, a man of extraordinary *depth* ; ধীশক্তির প্রখরতা। **6.** (*Log.*) The number of simple elements which an abstract conception or notion includes ; (তর্ক-বিজ্ঞান) অমূর্ত্ত বিভাবন বা প্রত্যয়ের অন্তর্ভুক্ত তত্ত্বসমূহ, ব্যাপ্তি (হিঃ কোঃ)। **7.** (*Pl.*) Deep water ; deep place ; abyss ; lowest or innest part ; গভীর জল ; গভীর স্থল ; অতলস্পর্শ খাত ; অন্তঃস্তর, অন্তরতম প্রদেশ, গভীরতম প্রদেশ। **8.** The middle, darkest or stillest part ; as, the *depth* of winter ; মধ্যভাগ, অন্ধতম বা প্রশান্ততম ভাগ। **9.** Deep or mysterious region of thought, feeling, etc. as, *depths* of degradation ; চিন্তা, ভাব প্রভৃতির গভীর রহস্যময় প্রদেশ **Out of one's depth**—In water too deep to stand in ; সাঁতার জলে। (*Fig.*) Engaged on too hard a subject or task ; (লক্ষণায়) অতি দুঃসাধ্য বিষয় সাধনে ব্যাপৃত।

dĕp′-ū-rāte, *v. t.* & *i.* To free from impurities ; নির্ম্মল করা। ***Verb i.*** To become free from impurities ; নির্ম্মল হওয়া। **—ra′-tion,** *n.* **—ra-tive,** *adj.* **—ra-tor,** *n.*

dĕp-ū-tā′-tion, *n.* **1.** Act of deputing ; the office of a deputy ; প্রতিনিধিনিয়োগ ; প্রতিনিধিত্ব। **2.** A body of persons appointed to represent others ; প্রেরিত প্রতিনিধিবর্গ।

dē-pūte′, *v. t.* **1.** To assign as to a deputy ; as, to *depute* authority ; প্রতিনিধির হস্তে অর্পণ করা। **2.** To delegate ; to appoint as a substitute ; প্রতিনিধি নিয়োগ করা ; স্থলবর্ত্তীরূপে নিয়োগ করা।

dĕp′-ū-tīze, *v. t.* To act as deputy, usually in reference to musical engagement ; প্রতিনিধিরূপে কাষ করা, বিশেষতঃ সঙ্গীতবাদ্যাদির অনুষ্ঠানে প্রতিনিধির কাষ করা।

dĕp′-ū-tȳ, *n.* **1.** One deputed or appointed to act for another ; প্রতিনিধি, প্রতিপুরুষ (মঃ ইঃ)। **2.** A member of deputation; কোন বিশেষ কার্য্য-সাধনে নিযুক্ত প্রতিনিধিবর্গের অন্যতম। **3.** A parliamentary representative ; পার্লেমেণ্টের প্রতিনিধি। **Deputy-collector** — প্রতিনিধি কর-নায়ক (আঃ বঃ)। **By deputy**—By proxy ; প্রতিনিধি দ্বারা। **Chamber of deputies**—The lower house in the French and other parliaments ; ফরাসী এবং অন্যান্য পার্লেমেণ্টের প্রাকৃত সভা।

dē-răc′-i-nāte, *v. t.* To pluck up by the roots ; উন্মূলিত করা, উচ্ছেদ করা।

dē-rail′ (-rāl), *v. t.* & *i.* To cause to leave the rails as trains etc. ; লৌহবর্ত্ম হইতে ভ্রষ্ট করা। ***Verb i.*** To leave the rails ; লৌহবর্ত্ম হইতে ভ্রষ্ট হওয়া, বর্ত্মচ্যুত হওয়া। **—ment,** *n.*

dē-rāngе′, *v. t.* **1.** To disarrange ; to throw into confusion ; বিশৃঙ্খল করা ; গোলমাল করা, উল্টাপাল্টা করা। **2.** To cause to act irregularly ; বিশৃঙ্খলভাবে কাষ করান। **3.** To disturb the action or functions of ; as, a sudden fall *deranges* some of our internal parts ; কার্য্য বা বৃত্তি বিশৃঙ্খল করা। **4.** To render insane, (usu. in *p. p.*) ; মতিভ্রংশ করা, বুদ্ধিভ্রংশ করা, চিত্ত-বিক্ষেপ করা। **5.** To disturb ; to interrupt ; বিক্ষুব্ধ করা ; বাধা দেওয়া। **—ment,** *n.*

Dêr′-bȳ, *n.* **1.** A race for three-year-old horses run annually at Epsom ; বিলাতের সুবিখ্যাত দৌড় **2.** A similar important race in other countries ; as, the French *Derby* ; অন্যান্য দেশের ডার্বির মত ঘোড়-দৌড়। **Derby cheese**—ইংলণ্ডদেশে প্রস্তুত মনোরম গন্ধবিশিষ্ট পনীর বিশেষ **Derby day**—ডার্ব্বি ঘোড়দৌড়ের দিন। **Derby dog** — ঘোড়দৌড়ের প্রাঙ্গণে যদৃচ্ছাভাবে-সঞ্চরণকারী কুকুর। (*Fig.*) **A** trivial untimely interruption ; (লক্ষণায়) অসময়োচিত তুচ্ছ বাধা।

Dêr′-bȳ-shire-nĕck (-shīr-), গলগণ্ড। [ইংলণ্ডের ডার্ব্বি সায়ার নামক প্রদেশ বিশেষে এই রোগের প্রাবল্য বশতঃ

এইরূপ নাম।] **Derby-shire-spar**—ডার্ব্বি প্রদেশে প্রাপ্ত খনিজ পদার্থ বিশেষ।

de regle, (*F.*) *pred. adj.* Customary ; proper ; প্রচলিত ; যথোচিত।

dĕr′-ē-lict, *adj.* & *n.* Ownerless ; forsaken ; as, a *derelict* vessel ; মালিকশূন্য ; পরিত্যক্ত, উৎসৃষ্ট, বর্জ্জিত। ***Noun.*** An abandoned property, esp. a ship ; পরিত্যক্ত সম্পত্তি, বিশেষতঃ জাহাজ।

dĕr-ē-lic′-tion, *n.* **1.** Act of abandoning ; utter forsaking ; উৎসর্জ্জন; পরিত্যাগ, পরিবর্জ্জন। **2.** State of being left or forsaken ; পরিত্যক্তাবস্থা। **3.** Failure in duty ; neglect as of duty ; কর্ত্তব্যকার্য্যে অবহেলা ; ত্রুটি, অবহেলা, কসুর।

dē-rīde′, *v. t.* To scorn ; to mock ; বিদ্রূপ করা ; উপহাস করা, অবহাস করা, চিরান (ফঃ হিঃ), ঠাট্টা করা।

de rigueur, (*F.*) *pred. adj.* Required by etiquette ; as, the evening dress is *de rigueur* ; শিষ্টাচারের নিয়মানুসারে প্রয়োজনীয়।

dē-rĭ′-sion, *n.* **1.** Mockery ; contempt manifested by laughter ; as, to hold one in *derision* ; বিদ্রূপ, ঠাট্টা ; উপহাস, অবহাস, পরিহাস। **2.** An object of derision ; a a laughing-stock ; বিদ্রূপের পাত্র ; উপহাসের পাত্র, উপহাসাস্পদ। **To be in derision**—To be laughed at ; উপহসিত হওয়া। **To have or hold in derision**—To mock at ; বিদ্রূপ করা।

dē-rī′-sive (-sĭv), **—rī′-sō-rȳ,** *adjs.* Expressing, or characterised by, derision ; scoffing ; বিদ্রূপসূচক, বিদ্রূপাত্মক ; বিদ্রূপকারী। **—ly,** *adv.* **Derisive cheers**—Ironical cheers ; বিদ্রূপসূচক উল্লাসধ্বনি।

dĕr-i-vā′-tion, *n.* **1.** Act of receiving from a source ; as, the *derivation* of an estate from ancestor ; প্রাপ্তি। **2.** Origin ; descent ; "The son was of God, showing his *derivation* ;" উৎপত্তি ; মূল (মঃ ইঃ), উদ্ভব (ঐ), জন্ম। **3.** (*Gram.*) The drawing or tracing of a word from its root or original ; the formation of a word from its original or radical elements ; (ব্যাকরণ) শব্দের মূলানুসন্ধান ; ব্যুৎপত্তি। **4.** Theory of evolution ; অভিব্যক্তিবাদ। **5.** (*Med.*) The drawing of the morbid humour etc. from a diseased part of the body ; (ভৈষজ্য-শাস্ত্র) রোগদুষ্ট দেহাংশ হইতে দূষিত রক্ত, রস প্রভৃতি আকর্ষণ।

dē-rĭv′-ă-tive (-tĭv), *adj.* & *n.* Derived from a source ; not original ; ব্যুৎপন্ন, উৎপন্ন, যৌগিক, ধাতুজ ; যোগজ, ব্যুৎপত্তি-লব্ধ। ***Noun.*** **1.** A thing of derived character ; অন্যবস্তু হইতে উদ্ভূত বস্তু। **2.** (*Gram.*) A word derived from another by some process of word-formation ; (ব্যাকরণ) যোগজশব্দ, কৃদন্ত শব্দ, বুৎপন্ন শব্দ। **3.** (*Chem.*) A substance obtained from another ; (রসায়ন শাস্ত্র) অন্য বস্তু হইতে প্রাপ্ত পদার্থ।

dē-rīve′, *v. t.* & *i.* **1.** To get ; to obtain ; (followed by *from*) ; প্রাপ্ত হওয়া ; লাভ করা। **2.** To draw, as from an origin ; as we *derive* idea from the senses ; উদ্ধার করা। **3.** To gather ; as, to *derive* knowledge ; সংগ্রহ করা। **4.** To trace the origin, descent or derivation of ; মূল বা উৎপত্তি নির্দ্দেশ করা, ব্যুৎপত্তি-নির্দ্দেশ করা, মূলানুসন্ধান করা। **5.** To be descended or have origin from ; (*pass.*) (কর্ম্মবাচ্যে) উদ্ভূত হওয়া, বহির্গত হওয়া, উৎপত্তি লাভ করা। **6.** (*Chem.*) To get (one substance) from another by actual or theoritical substitution ; (রসায়নশাস্ত্র) এক বস্তু হইতে অন্য বস্তু প্রাপ্ত হওয়া, নিষ্কর্ষণ করা। ***Verb i.*** To descend ; to originate ; to be deduced ; (with *from*) ; উদ্ভূত হওয়া ; উৎপত্তি লাভ করা ; উপপাদিত হওয়া। **—rīv′-a-ble,** *adj.*

dêrm, *n.* **1.** Skin ; চর্ম্ম, ত্বক্। **2.** The true skin or layer of tissue below epidermis ; অধস্ত্বক্।

dêr′-măl, dêr′-mĭc, *adjs.* Pertaining to skin ; ত্বক-সম্বন্ধীয়, চর্ম্ম-সম্বন্ধীয়।

dêr-mă-tŏl′-ō-ġȳ, *n.* The science which treats of the skin, its structure, functions, and diseases ; চর্ম্মবিদ্যা, চর্ম্মতত্ত্ব। **—gist,** *n.* One versed in dermatology ; a specialist in skin diseases ; চর্ম্মতত্ত্ববিৎ ; চর্ম্মরোগের বিশেষজ্ঞ।

dêrn, *v. t.* (*Slang*) To damn, (as an imprecation) ; (ইতর ভাষায়) অভিশাপ দেওয়া।

dernier ressort, (*F.*), *n.* Last resort ; desperate expedient ; শেষ উপায়, অন্তিম উপায় ; শ্মশান-চিকিৎসা।

dĕr′-ō-gāte, *v. i.* **1.** To detract ; to take away ; (usually with *from*) ; অপহরণ করা, হ্রাস করা, ন্যূন করা ; অপসারিত করা। **2.** To do something derogatory ; to degenerate ; হীনতাজনক কাজ করা ; হীন হওয়া।

dĕr′-ō-gā′-tion, *n.* **1.** The act of annulling or impairing a law, authority, dignity, etc. ; as, an act of parliament is passed in *derogation* of the King's prerogative ; হ্রাস করণ, খর্ব্বতাপাদন, হীনতাপাদন, মর্য্যাদাহানি। **2.** Deterioration ; অপকর্ষ।

dē-rŏg-ă-tō-rȳ, *adj.* **1.** Tending to lessen in value, authority, rank, influence or estimation ; detracting ; মূল্যাপকর্ষকর, ক্ষমতাহানিকর, অপযশকর (মঃ ইঃ); হীনতাপাদক। **2.** Unsuited to one's dignity or position ; depreciatory ; অগৌরবজনক, অপদোচিত ; মর্য্যাদাহানিকর, হীনতাজনক।

dĕr'-rĭck, *n.* An apparatus for hoisting heavy weights ; গুরুভার দ্রব্য উত্তোলনার্থ যন্ত্রবিশেষ, ভারোত্তলক।

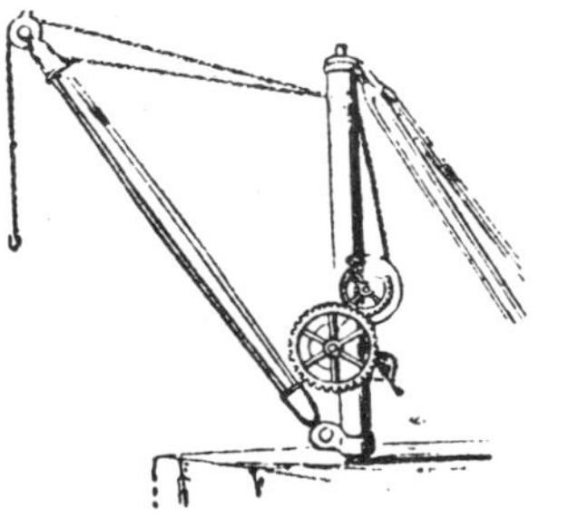

Derrick crane.

dĕr'-rĭng-dö, *n.* (A combination, meaning literally 'daring to do" but mistakenly used by Spenser and later writers as a substantive) Daring feats ; desperate courage ; সাহসিক কার্য্য ; মরিয়া অবস্থার সাহস।

dĕr'-rin-gêr, *n,* A small large-bore pistol ; বৃহৎ রন্ধ্রবিশিষ্ট ক্ষুদ্র পিস্তলবিশেষ।

dêr'-vĭsh, *n.* A Muhammadan priest or monk vowed to poverty and austerity ; দরবেশ।

Dervish.

dĕs'-cănt, *n.* **1.** (*Poet.*) Melody ; song ; (কবিতায়) সুর-মাধুর্য্য ; গান। **2.** A discourse ; a dissertation ; প্রসঙ্গ, আলোচনা ; ব্যাখ্যান।

dĕs'-cănt, *v. i.* To discourse at large ; to comment freely ; (with *upon* or *on*) ; সাধারণভাবে আলোচনা করা ; স্বাধীনভাবে সমালোচনা করা। **To descant upon the beauties of** — To speak highly of the beauties of ; কোন কিছুর সৌন্দর্য্যের উচ্চ প্রশংসা করা।

dē-scend (-sĕnd), *v. i.* & *t.* **1.** To fall ; to come or go down ; নামা পতিত হওয়া, পড়া। **2.** To incline or extend downward ; as, the road *descends* ; নিম্নদিকে প্রবণ হওয়া, নিম্নদিকে বিস্তৃত হওয়া। **3.** To fall violently ; "And on thy suitor let thy wrath *descend* ;" to make a sudden attack ; প্রচণ্ডভাবে পতিত হওয়া ; সহসা আক্রমণ করা। **4.** To condescend ; to stoop ; "*Descending* to play with little children ;" হীনতা স্বীকার করা ; অনুগ্রহ প্রকাশার্থ হীনতা স্বীকার করা। **5.** To lower or debase one's self ; as, he *descended* to mean pursuits ; অবনত করা, অধঃপতিত করা, হীন করা। **6.** To be derived ; to fall or pass by inheritance ; as, a crown *descends* to the heir ; উদ্ভূত হওয়া ; উত্তরাধিকারীর অধিকারগত হওয়া, উত্তরাধিকারীর হস্তে আসা। **7.** (*Astron.*) To move toward the south ; to approach the horizon ; (জ্যোতিবিজ্ঞান) দক্ষিণ দিকে অগ্রসর হওয়া ; দিক-চক্রবালের অভিমুখে অগ্রসর হওয়া। ***Verb t.*** To go down upon or along ; অবরোহণ করা, অবতরণ করা, অধোগমন করা, নামা। **—ing,** *adj.* Coming down ; অধোগামী, অবরোহণশীল, অবরোহী। **Descending scale**—রোহী। **Descending node**—কেতু।

dē-scend'-ance, —ence, (-sĕnd-ăns, -ĕns), *n.* Descent from a particular ancestor ; উদ্ভব, উৎপত্তি।

dē-scend'-ănt (-sĕnd-), *n.* A person or thing descended ; বংশধর, সন্তানসন্ততি, পরপুরুষ ; উদ্ভূত বস্তু।

dē-scend'-ĭ-ble, (-sĕnd-) **—ă-ble,** *adjs.* Transmissible by inheritance ; উত্তরাধিকারীর হস্তে হস্তান্তর করণীয়।

dē-scen'-sion (-sĕn-), *n.* The act of descending ; অধোগমন, অবরোহণ, পতন।

dē-scent' (-sĕnt), *n.* **1.** The act of descending ; change from higher to lower ; অধোগমন, অবতরণ ; অধঃপতন। **2.** Downward slope ; প্রবণ-ভূমি, গড়ানিয়া স্থান, উৎরাও। **3.** Way down ; গড়ানিয়া রাস্তা। **4.** Sudden attack ; আকস্মিক আক্রমণ, অতর্কিত আক্রমণ। **5.** Fall ; পতন। **6.** Derivation, as from an ancestor ; lineage ; উদ্ভব ; বংশ। **7.** Single generation ; as, lineal succession of four *descents* ; পুরুষ। **5.** Transmission by inheritance, as of property, title or quality ; বংশধরগণে সংক্রমণ, উত্তরাধিকারীর হস্তে হস্তান্তর।

dē-scrībe', *v. t.* & *i.* **1.** To set forth in words ; বর্ণনা করা, বিবৃত করা। **2.** To mark out ; as, to *describe* a circle ; অঙ্কন করা, টানা। ***Verb i.*** To give a description ; বর্ণনা প্রদান করা। **—scrib'-a-ble,** *adj.* That can be described ; বর্ণনীয়।

dē-scrĭp'-tion, *n.* **1.** Act of describing ; a verbal portraiture ; বর্ণন ; বর্ণনা। **2.** Kind ; class ; as, a tyrant of the worst *description* ; জাতি ; প্রকার, রকম, শ্রেণী। **A person or object answers to the description** — A person or object which has the qualities specified ; যে ব্যক্তি বা বস্তুর নির্দ্দিষ্ট গুণ সমূহ আছে।

dē-scrĭp'-tive (-tĭv), *adj.* Characterised by description ; fond of describing ; বর্ণনাত্মক ; বর্ণনশীল, বর্ণনপর। **—ly,** *adv.* **Descriptive Geometry**—চিত্র-জ্যামিতি।

dē-scrȳ', *v. t.* To espy ; to catch sight of ; (*fig.*) to detect ; to discover anything concealed ; দেখিতে পাওয়া ; হঠাৎ দর্শন লাভ করা ; (লক্ষণায়) সন্ধান করিয়া বাহির করা ; কোন গুপ্ত বিষয় বাহির করা।

dĕs'-ē-crāte, *v.t.* **1.** To violate the sanctity of ; to profane ; to divest of a sacred character ; "More plausibly might we *desecrate* sunday ; অপবিত্র করা ; কলুষিত করা ; পবিত্র ভাব নষ্ট করা। **2.** To dedicate to evil ; অসদুদ্দেশ্যে উৎসর্গীকৃত করা। **—cra'-tion,** *n.* **—cra-tor,** *n.*

dĕ-ṡêrt′, *n*. **1.** Merit or demerit; (*Pl.*) acts or qualities deserving good or bad recompense; "Accoding to their *deserts* will I judge them;" পাপপুণ্য, পুণ্যাপুণ্য গুণাগুণ ধর্ম্মাধর্ম্ম; (বহুবচন) দণ্ড বা পুরস্কারের যোগ্য কার্য্য সমূহ, কর্ম্ম। **2.** Excellence; worth; a worthy deed; "On the firm basis of *desert* they rise;" সদ্‌গুণ; যোগ্যতা; যোগ্যকায, উপযুক্ত কায। **3.** Reward or punishment merited; "He has got his *deserts*;" যোগ্য দণ্ড বা পুরস্কার। **4.** Deserving people; যোগ্য লোক সমূহ। **—less,** *adj*. Without merit; undeserving; গুণশূন্য, নির্গুণ; অযোগ্য।

dĕṡ′-êrt, *n*. & *adj*. **1.** A vast sandy, stony or rocky expanse almost destitute of moistnre and vegetation; মরু, মরুভূমি, বালুকার্ণব। **2.** (*Fig.*) An uninteresting subject, or period; (লক্ষণায়) নীরস বিষয়, বিচিত্র ঘটনা শূন্য কাল, নীরস কাল। ***Adj.*** **1.** Uninhabited; desolate; বশতিশূন্য; বিজন, জনমানবহীন, জনমানবশূন্য। **2.** Unproductive; barren; অনুর্ব্বর, অফলা; উৎপাদিকা-শক্তি হীন।

dĕ-ṡêrt′, *v. t.* & *i.* **1.** To leave; to give up; to forsake or abandon, as a friend, wife, etc.; to depart from, as a place etc.; ত্যাগ করা, (স্ত্রী, বন্ধু, প্রভৃতি) বর্জ্জন করা, পরিহার করা, পরিত্যাগ করা; প্রস্থান করা। **2.** To fail; বিফল হওয়া। **3.** (*Mil.*) To abscond from; to leave without permission; as, to *desert* the army, the colours or a ship; (সামরিক-শাস্ত্র) পলায়ন করা; বিনা অনুমতিতে ছাড়িয়া যাওয়া। ***Verb i.*** To run away; to quit a service, esp. military without permission; "The soldiers *deserted* in numbers;" পলায়ন করা; কর্ম্মত্যাগ করা, বিশেষতঃ বিনানুমতিতে সামরিক কার্য্য ত্যাগ করা। **—er,** *n*. One who deserts or quits a service without permission; যে ব্যক্তি বিনা অনুমতিতে কোন কার্য্য ত্যাগ করে, নিয়োগত্যাগী (আঃ বঃ)। **—ser-tion,** *n*. **1.** Act of deserting; ত্যাগ পরিত্যাগ। **2.** Quitting a service (esp. military) without permission; নিয়োগত্যাগ (আঃ বঃ)।

dĕ-serve′ (-zêrv), *v. t.* & *i.* To merit; to be entitled to, (something good or bad) by qualities or conduct; "Do you think that you *deserve* the favour;" যোগ্য হওয়া; উপযুক্ত হওয়া। ***Verb i.*** To be worthy of recompense, (usually with *ill* or *well*); as, he *deserves* well or ill of his neighbour; পুরস্কারের উপযুক্ত হওয়া।

dĕ-ṡêrv′-ĕd-lȳ, *adv*. Justly; সঙ্গতভাবে, সমীচীন ভাবে, যথাযোগ্য ভাবে, যোগ্য রূপে।

dĕ-ṡêrv′-ing, *adj*. Meritorious; worthy; উপযুক্ত; যোগ্য।

deshabille, (*F.*), *n*. The state of being undressed or not fully dressed; অসম্মতবসনতা, বিবসনতা।

dĕs′-ic-cāte *v. t.* & *v. i.* To dry up, (esp. milk etc. for preservation); শুষ্ক করা, নিরুদ করা। ***Verb i.*** To become dry; শুষ্ক হওয়া। **—ca′-tion,** *n*. The act of desiccating; the state of being desiccated; বিশোষণ, উচ্ছোষণ; শুষ্কীকরণ। **—ca-tive,** *adj*. Tending to desiccate; শোষণশীল। **—ca-tor,** *n*. **1.** One that desiccates; বিশোষক। **2.** (*Chem.*) A short glass-jar fitted with an air-tight cover and containing some desiccating agent; (রসায়ন-শাস্ত্র) বায়ুপ্রবেশ পথশূন্য ঢাকনি বিশিষ্ট, শোষক পদার্থ ধারক কাচ-নির্ম্মিত ঘট বিশেষ। **3.** An apparatus for drying milk, fruit, etc.; দুগ্ধ, ফল প্রভৃতির জলীয় অংশ শোষণার্থ যন্ত্রবিশেষ, শোষক-যন্ত্র।

dĕ-sid′-êr-āte, *v. t.* To feel the want of; to desire; "The great step which is now *desiderated* is education;" অভাব বোধ করা; কামনা করা, বাঞ্ছা করা, অভিলাষ করা।

dĕ-sid′-êr-ă-tive (-tîv), *adj.* & *n*. Having desire; expressing or denoting desire; as, a *desiderative* verb; অভিলাষী; কামনাসূচক, ইচ্ছাসূচক, (ব্যাকরণে) ইচ্ছাবাচক, সনন্ত। ***Noun.*** **1.** An object of desire; স্পৃহণীয় বস্তু, বাঞ্ছনীয় বস্তু, বাঞ্ছিত বস্তু। **2.** (*Gram.*) A verb formed from another verb and expressing the desire of doing the action implied in the primitive verb; (ব্যাকরণ) সনন্তক্রিয়া।

dĕ-sid-ĕ-rā′-tŭm, *n*. Anything desired; a want felt and recognised; বাঞ্ছিত বস্তু, কাম্য বিষয়, অভীষ্ট, ইষ্ট, অভাব।

dĕ-sign′ (-zīn), *n., v.t.* & *i.* **1.** Mental plan; purpose; intention; the end in view; কল্পনা; উদ্দেশ্য, আশয় (আঃ বঃ); অভিপ্রায়, মতলব, অভিসন্ধি। **2.** Evil intention; দুরভিসন্ধি। **3.** Contrivance; রচনা-কৌশল। **4.** Sketch; first idea represented by visible lines as in painting or architecture; a pattern; রেখাচিত্র, নক্‌সা; পরিকল্পনা; আদর্শ, নমুনা। **5.** An artistic device; as, it is the *design* that sells the cloth; কলা-কৌশল। **6.** Artistic invention; কলা-কৌশলপূর্ণ উদ্ভাবনা। ***Verb t.*** **1.** To plan; to project; to plot; to intend; to purpose; as, we *design* this ground for a garden; কল্পনা করা; ভাবিয়া স্থির করা; মতলব আঁটা; অভিপ্রায় করা; উদ্দেশ্য করা। **2.** To delineate; to sketch for a pattern or model; to draw out the plan of; অঙ্কন করা; পরিকল্পনা করা; নক্‌সা আঁকা। **3.** To set apart for a purpose; "What present I had *designed* for her;" কোন বিশেষ উদ্দেশ্যে পৃথক করিয়া রাখা। **4.** To destine as a person or thing *for* or *to* a purpose or service ; "He was *designed* to the study of law ;" নির্দ্দিষ্ট করা, নিরূপিত করা। ***Verb i.*** **1.** To make a design or designs ; পরিকল্পনা করা, অঙ্কিত করা, মতলব আঁটা। **2.** To be a designer ; পরিকল্পক বা নক্সাপ্রস্তুতকারক হওয়া। **—ed-ly,** *adv.* Purposely ; ইচ্ছাপূর্ব্বক। **Argument from design**—সৃষ্টির মধ্যে উদ্দেশ্য দর্শনে স্রষ্টার অস্তিত্ব প্রতিপাদনার্থ যুক্তিতর্ক, উদ্দেশ্যবাদ (হিঃ কোঃ)। **A school of design**—শ্রম-শিল্পসংক্রান্ত চিত্রাঙ্কণ শিক্ষাদানার্থ বিদ্যালয়।

dĕs'-ĭg-nāte, *adj.* & *v. t.* Appointed or chosen ; as, a bishop *designate* but not yet installed ; নিযুক্ত, নির্ব্বাচিত, মনোনীত। ***Verb t.*** **1.** To specify ; to particularize ; as, to *designate* the limits of the country ; বিশেষভাবে নির্দ্দেশ করা, নির্দ্ধারিত করা ; বিশেষ করিয়া বিবৃত করা। **2.** To call by a distinctive title ; to name ; to style ; বিশেষ নামে ডাকা ; আখ্যা দেওয়া ; নাম দেওয়া। **3.** To serve as a name of ; নাম স্বরূপ হওয়া। **4.** To appoint ; to assign ; (with *to* or *for*) ; নিযুক্ত করা ; নির্দ্দেশ করা। **5.** To form design ; মতলব আঁটা।

dĕs-ĭg-nā'-tion, *n.* **1.** Act of appointing, as to an office ; নিয়োগ। **2.** Act of designating ; a pointing out or indication ; নির্দ্দেশন ; উপলক্ষণ, লক্ষণ, সংজ্ঞা (মঃ ইঃ)। **3.** A distinguishing mark or name ; an appellation ; a title ; পার্থক্য-সূচক চিহ্ন বা নাম ; নাম, আখ্যা ; উপাধি।

dē-sign'-ēr (-zīn-), *n.* **1.** One who designs ; রচনাকারী, কল্পনাকারী। **2.** One who produces or creates original works of art or decoration ; যে ব্যক্তি মৌলিক শিল্পসামগ্রী বা ভুষা প্রভৃতি প্রস্তুত বা রচনা করে।

dē-sign'-ing (-zīn-), *adj.* **1.** Planning ; foreseeing ; as, a *designing* Providence ; কৌশলী ; দূরদর্শী। **2.** Artful ; intriguing ; চতুর, সেয়ানা, ধূর্ত্ত ; চক্রান্তকারী।

dē-sil'-vēr-īze, *v. t.* To extract the silver from, as lead etc. ; সীসা প্রভৃতি হইতে রৌপ্য বাহির করা।

dē-sip'-ĭ-ence (-ĕns), *n.* Folly ; নির্ব্বুদ্ধিতা, মূর্খতা।

dē-sīr'-ā-ble, *adj.* Worth wishing for ; agreeable ; বাঞ্ছনীয়, লোভনীয় ; স্পৃহনীয়, আকাঙ্ক্ষনীয়, প্রার্থনীয়, কাম্য ; কমনীয়। **—bil'-i-ty, —ness,** *ns* **—bly,** *adv.*

dē-sīre', *n.* **1.** Wish ; longing ; বাঞ্ছা, কাম, কামনা, ইচ্ছা ; অভীষ্ট, সাধ, রুচি, চিত্তরাগ, স্পৃহা, আকাঙ্ক্ষা, মনস্কামনা, মনোরথ, আশা, অভিলাষ। **2.** A prayer or request ; "He will fulfil the *desire* of them that fear him ; প্রার্থনা, অনুরোধ। **3.** An object of longing ; "The *desire* of all nations shall come ;" বাঞ্ছিত বস্তু, কাম্য বস্তু, অভিলাষের বিষয়। **4.** Lust ; appetite ; লালসা, লিপ্সা ; তৃষ্ণা।

dē-sīre', *v. t.* & *i.* **1.** To long for ; to wish ; to ask for ; বাসনা করা ; ইচ্ছা করা, কামনা করা, সাধ করা, স্পৃহা করা ; চাওয়া। **2.** To entreat ; to request ; to command ; as, to *desire* one to wait ; অনুনয় করা ; অনুরোধ করা ; অনুজ্ঞা করা। ***Verb i.*** To have or feel desire ; বাসনা হওয়া, কামনা হওয়া, অভিলাষ হওয়া।

dē-sīr'-ous (-ŭs), *adj.* Wishful ; solicitous ; eager ; covetous ; ইচ্ছুক, ইচ্ছান্বিত, অভিলাষী ; প্রার্থী ; উদ্বিগ্ন ; লালসাপর।

dē-sĭst', *v. t.* To cease ; (with *from*) ; নিরস্ত হওয়া, নিবৃত্ত হওয়া, ক্ষান্ত হওয়া, বিরত হওয়া।

dĕsk, *n.* An inclining table for the use of writers and readers often made with a box or drawer underneath ; একপ্রকার গড়ানিয়া মেজ, লিখনফলক (মঃ ইঃ), ডেস্ক। **Desk-ful,** *adj.* **The desk**—Clerical, office or literary work ; কেরাণীর কায, আফিসের কায, সাহিত্যিক কার্য্য।

Desmodium triflorum—কুদালিয়া (বেলঃ)।

dĕs'-ō-lāte, *adj.* & *v. t.* **1.** Left alone ; lonely ; forsaken ; disconsolate ; wretched ; "Voice of the poor and *desolate* ;" বিজন ; নির্জ্জন ; পরিত্যক্ত ; শোকার্ত্ত ; দুর্দ্দশাগ্রস্ত। **2.** Uninhabited ; বসতিশূন্য, জনহীন, জনশূন্য, জনমানবহীন, নির্মানুষ, মনুষ্যসমাগমশূন্য। **3.** Laid waste ; in a ruinous condition ; dreary ; as, *desolate* altars ; উচ্ছিন্ন, মরুময় ; ভগ্নদশাপ্রাপ্ত ; ঘোর। ***Verb t.*** **1.** To depopulate ; to make desolate ; as, the earth was nearly *desolated* by the flood ; লোকশূন্য করা ; জনহীন করা। **2.** To devastate ; to lay waste। ধ্বংস করা ; উৎসন্ন করা, উজাড় করা, ছারখার করা, বিধ্বস্ত করা। **3.** To make wretched ; দুর্দ্দশাগ্রস্ত করা। **4.** To leave alone ; to deprive of companions ; বিজন করা ; সঙ্গিহীন করা। **—ly,** *adv.* **—ness,** *n.* **—la-tor,** *n.*

dĕs-ō-lā'-tion, *n.* **1.** Destruction of inhabitants ; depopulation ; নির্জ্জনীকরণ ; নির্মানুষীকরণ। **2.** Ravage ; devastation ; gloominess ; উচ্ছেদ ; ধ্বংস, উজাড় ; বিষাদ। **3.** Loneliness ; state of being forsaken ; শূন্যতা ; নির্জ্জনতা, বিজনতা। **4.** A place or country wasted and forsaken ; জনমানবহীন দেশ, জনহীন স্থান, উৎসন্ন দেশ, পরিত্যক্ত স্থান।

dē-spair' (-spār), *n.* & *v. i.* **1.** Hopelessness ; নৈরাশ্য, আশাভঙ্গ। **2.** That of which there is no hope ; that which causes despair ; যাহার সম্বন্ধে কোন আশা নাই ; নৈরাশ্যজনক ব্যক্তি বা বিষয়। ***Verb i.*** To be without hope ; নিরাশ হওয়া। **—ing-ly,** *adv.* In a despairing manner ; হতাশভাবে।

dē-spatch' (-spăch), *n.* & *v.* Same as DISPATCH (which see).

dĕs-pêr-ā'-dō, *n.* A reckless criminal ; a wild ruffian ; হিতাহিতবোধশূন্য পাষণ্ড, আততায়ী, অত্যাহিতকর্ম্মা (মঃ ইঃ) ; গুণ্ডা, গোঁয়ার।

dĕs'-pêr-āte, *adj.* 1. Rash ; fearless of danger ; as, a *desperate* man ; হিতাহিতজ্ঞানশূন্য, কাণ্ডাকাণ্ডজ্ঞানহীন, গোঁয়ার ; বিপদ্‌ভয়শূন্য। 2. Without regard to danger or safety ; reckless ; as, a *desperate* effort ; জীবিতাশ-নিরপেক্ষ; মরিয়া। 3. Extremely bad ; as, a *desperate* storm ; নিতান্ত মন্দ। 4. Very great ; as, a *desperate* fool or fear ; অতি বড়, মহা। **—a'-tion,** *n.* **—ly,** *adv.* In a desperate manner ; জীবিতাশ-নিরপেক্ষ হইয়া। **—ness,** *n.*

dĕs'-pi-că-ble, *adj.* Contemptible ; vile ; অবজ্ঞেয় ; জঘন্য। **—bly,** *adv.*

dē-spīse', *v. t.* To look down upon ; to desdain ; অবজ্ঞা করা, অনাদর করা, উপেক্ষা করা, তাচ্ছিল্য করা ; হেয় জ্ঞান করা।

dē-spīte', *n.* & *prep.* 1. Malice ; malignity ; contemptuous hate ; offended pride ; বিদ্বেষ ; দ্রোহভাব, ঈর্ষা, মাৎসর্য্য ; অবজ্ঞামিশ্রিত ঘৃণা, উপেক্ষা, জুগুপ্সা (আঃ বঃ) ; অভিমান। 2. *(Archaic)* Outrage ; injury ; (অপ্রচলিত) অত্যাচার ; ক্ষতি। ***Prep.*** Notwithstanding ; সত্ত্বে। **—ful,** *adj.* **—ful-ly,** *adv.* **In despite of, despite of,** or **despite**—সত্ত্বেও। **In one's despite**—Inspite of one's own efforts, (archaic); কোন ব্যক্তির চেষ্টা সত্ত্বেও (অপ্রচলিত)।

dē-spoil' (-spoyl), *v. t.* To plunder ; to rob ; (often followed by *of*) "He could not *despoil* the slain man *of* his armour." লুণ্ঠন করা ; কাড়িয়া লওয়া। **-er,** *n.* **-ment, —spo-li-a'-tion,** *ns.*

dē-spŏnd', *v. t.* & *n.* To lose heart ; to be dejected ; হতাশ হওয়া, নিরাশ হওয়া, আশাত্যাগ করা ; বিমর্ষ হওয়া। ***Noun.*** *(Archaic)* Dejection ; (only in the phrase *the slough of despond*) (অপ্রচলিত) বিষাদ। **—ence, —en-cy,** *ns.* State of being without hope ; dejection ; নৈরাশ্য ; বিষাদ, নির্বেদ। **—ent, —ing,** *adjs.* Without courage or hope ; হতাশ্বাস, নিরাশ। **—ent-ly, —ing-ly,** *advs.*

dĕs'-pŏt, *n.* 1. An absolute ruler ; on autocrat ; যথেচ্ছাচারী রাজা, স্বৈরশাসক ; অবিসম্বাদ আধিপত্যকারী। 2. A tyrant ; an oppressor ; পীড়নকারী ; অত্যাচারী। **—pot'-ic, —pot'-i-cal,** *adjs.* **—pot'-i-cal-ly,** *adv.*

dĕs'-pŏt-ĭsm, *n.* 1. Arbitrary rule ; absolute control ; স্বৈরতন্ত্র, যথেচ্ছাচার, স্বৈরিতা ; প্রজাপীড়ন। 2. A state under a despot ; autocracy ; যথেচ্ছাচারী নৃপতির অধীন রাজ্য ; স্বৈর-রাজ্য। **—ist,** *n.*

des'-quā-māte, *v. i.* & *t.* To scale off ; to peel off ; "The cuticle now begins to *desquamate* ;" আঁইশ উঠিয়া যাওয়া ; চর্ম্ম উঠিয়া যাওয়া। ***Verb. t.*** To strip of scales ; আঁইশ ফেলান, শল্ক বৰ্জ্জিত করা। **—ma'-tion,** *n.* The separation of the cuticle of skin in scales ; ত্বক পরিপুটন (সুশ্রুঃ), উপত্বকপাতন। **De-squam'-a-tive, De-squam'-a-to-ry,** *adjs.*

des-sêrt' (dĕ-), *n.* A service of fruits and sweetmeats at the close of an entertainment ; ভোজের শেষকালে পরিবেষিত ফল এবং মিষ্টদ্রব্য, ভোজনোত্তর ফলাহার। **Dessert-spoon**—চার চামচ ও ভোজন কালে ব্যবহৃত সর্ব্ব বৃহৎ চামচের মঝামাঝি আকারের চামচা, ইহা ভোজের শেষে পরিবেষিত ফল, মিষ্টদ্রব্যাদি আহারে ব্যবহৃত হয়।

dĕs-ti-nā'-tion, *n.* 1. The place to which a thing is bound ; গম্যস্থান, গন্তব্য স্থান। 2. The act of destining or appointing ; নির্দ্দেশন, পুর্ব্বনিয়োজন, পুর্ব্বনিয়োগ।

dĕs'-tine (-tĭn), *v. t.* 1. To fore-ordain ; to predetermine ; as, the earth is *destined* to become a dead planet ; পূর্ব্ব হইতে নির্দ্দিষ্ট করা ; পূর্ব্বে নির্দ্ধারিত করা। 2. To appoint or design ; as, he was *destined* for the military ; নির্দ্দিষ্ট করা।

dĕs'-ti-nȳ, *n.* 1. Predetermined course of events ; "Who can turn the stream of *destiny* ?" ভবিতব্যতা। 2. Lot ; fate ; doom ; as, men are solicitous to know their future *destiny* ; ভাগ্য ; অদৃষ্ট ; নিয়তি, ললাটলিপি, বিধিলিপি, ভাগ্যলিপি। 3. Invincible necessity ; "The force of *destiny* ;" অবশ্যম্ভাবিত্ব। 4. The goddess of destiny ; (*Pl.*) the Fates ; নিয়তি দেবী ; (বহুবচন) গ্রীক পুরাণোক্ত ভাগ্য দেবীত্রয় (Clotho, Lachesis, Atropos).

dĕs'-ti-tūte, *adj.* 1. Without resources ; needy ; poor ; as, the family has been left *destitute* ; অকিঞ্চন, নিরাশ্রয় ; নিঃস্ব, দীন ; অনাথ। 2. Devoid ; deficient, (with *of*); as, a man *destitute* of virtue ; বিহীন, বিরহিত ; ন্যূন। **—tu'-tion,** *n.* State of being destitute ; deficiency ; extreme poverty ; অকিঞ্চনত্ব, নিরাশ্রয়ত্ব, অনাথাবস্থা ; রাহিত্য ; নিঃস্বতা।

dĕs'-tri-êr, *n.* A war-horse ; রণতুরঙ্গম, যুদ্ধাশ্ব।

dē-stroȳ', *v. t.* 1. To demolish ; to pull or tear down ; as, to *destroy* a fortification : ধ্বংস করা ; ভূমিসাৎ করা। 2. To ruin ; to annihilate ; ধ্বংস করা ; উচ্ছেদ করা, বিলোপ সাধন করা। 3. To counteract ; to nullify ; as, to *destroy* a theory ; প্রতিক্রিয়া করা ; নাকচ করা, বাতিল করা। 4. To kill ; "You shall *destroy* all his people ;" বিনাশ করা। **—a-ble,** *adj.*

dē-stroȳ'-êr, *n.* 1. One who or that which destroys ; বিনাশকারী, ধ্বংসকর্ত্তা, সংহারকর্ত্তা। 2. A torpedo-boat destroyer, (abbr. form) ;

জলতলচারী চুরটাকার গোলাবাহী দ্রুত-গামী জাহাজ ধ্বংসকারক-রণপোত বিশেষ।

dē-strŭct'-i-ble, *adj.* Liable to destruction; capaple of being destroyed; বিনাশ্য; নশ্বর (আঃ বঃ)। **—bil'-i-ty,** *n.*

dē-strŭc-tion, *n.* **1.** Act of destroying; demolition; ruin; devastation; বিধ্বংস, বিনাশ, বিপাটন; বিলোপন; উৎসাদন, নাশ; প্রধ্বংস, উচ্ছেদন, সাদন। **2.** State of being destroyed; বিনষ্টি (রবিঃ)। **3.** A cause of ruin; an agent that destroys; ধ্বংসের হেতু; ধ্বংসকারক বস্তু।

dē-strŭc'-tive (-tĭv), *adj.* & *n.* **1.** Ruinous; fatal; mischievous; ধ্বংসকর; সাংঘাতিক, মারাত্মক; অনিষ্টকর। **2.** Designed or tending to destroy or clear away, (opposed to *constructive*); as, a *destructive* criticism; ধ্বংসকর, বিনাশী। **3.** (*Log.*) Refuting without correcting; (তর্ক-বিজ্ঞান) খণ্ডনাত্মক, (হিঃ কোঃ), দূষণাত্মক (ঐ), নিষেধাত্মক। ***Noun.*** A person or thing that aims at, or effects, destruction; ধ্বংসকর্ত্তা, বিনাশক, সংহারকারী। **—ly,** *adv.* **—ness,** *n.* (*Chem.*) **Destructive distillation** — বদ্ধপাত্রে অস্থি, কয়লা প্রভৃতি উত্তাপযোগে বিশ্লিষ্ট করত উক্ত পদার্থ সমূহের উদ্বায়ী অংশ সংগ্রহের প্রণালী বিশেষ, অন্তর্ধূম-বিপক (সাঃ পঃ)।

dē-strŭc'-tor (-têr), *n.* A furnace for burning refuse; আবর্জ্জনা দগ্ধ করণার্থ চুল্লী বিশেষ।

dĕs-ū-dā'-tion, *n.* A profuse sweating; an eruption of small pimples on children; প্রচুর স্বেদ নির্গম; ঘামাচি।

dĕs'-ue-tūde (-wē-), *n.* Passing into disuse; a state of disuse; discontinuance of practice, custom or fashion; অপ্রচলন; অপ্রয়োগ (হিঃ কোঃ), অপ্রচার (ঐ); রীতি-নীতি আচার ব্যবহারের অপ্রচলন। **To fall into desuetude** — অপ্রচলিত হইয়া পড়া।

dē-sŭl'-phŭr-īze, *v. t.* To free from sulphur; গন্ধক শূন্য করা, নির্গন্ধক করা। **—i-za'-tion,** *n.*

dĕs'-ŭl-tō-rȳ, *adj.* **1.** Jumping or passing from one subject to another; disconnected; unsystematic; as, *desultory* conversation; বিষয় হইতে বিষয়ান্তরে লম্ফনাত্মক, বিশৃঙ্খল, শৃঙ্খলাশূন্য; অসংলগ্ন, অসম্বদ্ধ বেতাল, এলোমেলো, বিক্ষিপ্ত। **2.** Not connected with the subject; as, a *desultory* remark; অপ্রাসঙ্গিক **—ri-ly,** *adv.* **—ri-ness,** *n.*

dē-sȳn-ŏn'-ȳ-mīze, *v. t.* To differentiate in sense; (সমার্থব শব্দের) অর্থভেদ করা, অর্থ ব্যাবর্ত্তন করা

dē-tăch', *v. t.* **1.** To separate or disunite; to disengage; as, to *detach* a man from a party বিশ্লিষ্ট করা; বিযুক্ত করা, বিচ্ছিন্ন করা, পৃথক্ করা, মুক্ত করা, আল্গা করা, ভিন্ন করা, বিস্রস্ত করা। **2.** (*Mil.* & *Nav.*) To separate and send off ship, regiment, on special service; as, to *detach* a regiment from a brigade; (সামরিকশাস্ত্র ও নৌ-বিদ্যা) (জাহাজ বা পল্টন) মূলদল বা শ্রেণী হইতে বিচ্ছিন্ন করত বিশেষ কার্য্যে প্রেরণ করা। **—a-ble,** *adj.* **—ed-ly,** *adv.* **—ed-ness,** *n.* **Detached mind**—পক্ষপাত শূন্য মন। **Detached view**—পূর্ব্বসংস্কার-বিমুক্ত মত।

dē-tăch'-mĕnt, *n.* **1.** The act of detaching or the state of being detached; পৃথগ্‌করণ, বিয়োজন, বিশ্লেষ (আঃ বঃ), অবচ্ছেদ (মঃ ইঃ)। **2.** That which is detached as a part of a fleet or a body of troops; as, a *detachment* of troops; বিশ্লিষ্ট অংশ, মূল সৈন্যদল বা রণপোত বহর হইতে বিযুক্ত সৈন্য বা রণপোতশ্রেণী, বিচ্ছিন্নসেনা, বিচ্ছিন্ন রণপোত বহর। **3.** Standing aloof from, or unaffected by, surroundings, public opinion, etc.; abstraction from worldly objects; as, the *detachment* of a saint; independence of judgment; নিঃসঙ্গভাবে অবস্থান, নিঃসঙ্গভাব; বিষয়-বৈরাগ্য, উদাসীনতা, বিষয়বিবিক্ততা; বিচারে পক্ষপাতশূন্যতা।

dē-tail' (-tāl), *n.* **1.** A minute part; an item; a particular; as, the account is accurate in all its *details*; সূক্ষ্মাংশ; দফা; বিশেষ কথা বা বিষয়। **2.** A minute account; a narrative or report of particulars; as, he gave a *detail* of the transaction; পুঙ্খানুপুঙ্খ বর্ণনা; বিবরণ, বিস্তার। **3.** Detailed treatment; as, to go into *detail*; বিস্তৃত আলোচনা। **4.** (*Mil.*) A body of men detailed for particular service; the distribution of the daily orders to the officers; (সামরিক-শাস্ত্র) কোন বিশেষ কার্য্যের জন্য নিযুক্ত সৈন্যদল; সৈনিক কর্ম্মচারিদের দৈনিক আদেশ বিবরণ। **5.** (*Arch. etc.*) Minor decoration in a building, picture, etc.; the manner of treating this decoration; (স্থপতি-বিদ্যা প্রভৃতি) সৌধ, চিত্র প্রভৃতির উপভূষা; উক্ত ভূষা স্থাপন-পদ্ধতি। **In detail**—Part by part; item by item; সবিস্তারে; পুঙ্খানুপুঙ্খরূপে। **To go into detail**—To give the items separately; পুঙ্খানুপুঙ্খরূপে বিবৃত করা।

dē-tail' (-tāl), *v. t.* **1.** To relate minutely; to give the particulars of; পুঙ্খানুপুঙ্খরূপে বর্ণনা করা; সবিস্তারে বর্ণনা করা, বিবৃত করা। **2.** (*Mil.*) To detach or appoint for a particular service; (সামরিক শাস্ত্র) কোন বিশেষ কার্য্যের জন্য মূল সৈন্যদল হইতে বিযুক্ত করা বা বিযুক্ত করিয়া কোন বিশেষ কার্য্যে নিযুক্ত করা। **—tailed,** *adj.* Full of details; সবিস্তার, বিস্তারিত, সবিশেষ, দফাওয়ারী।

dē-tain' (-tān), *v. t.* **1.** To restrain or delay from proceeding; to stop; to check; as, we were *detained* by the rain; আটক

করা; থামান, বিলম্ব করান; নিরোধ করা। 2. To withhold; আটকাইয়া রাখা। 3. To hold or keep in confinement; কয়েদ করা, আটক করা।

dë-tain'-êr (-tān-), *n.* 1. One who detains; রোধকারী, আটককারী, প্রতিরোধক, নিরোধক। 2. (*Law*) The keeping or holding possession of what belongs to another; (আইন) অন্যের সম্পত্তি ভোগদখল করণ। 3. A writ authorising the keeper of a prison to continue to keep a person in custody; কারাগারে আটক রাখার পরওয়ানা, রক্ষাপত্র (আঃ বঃ)। 4. The keeping of a person in confinement; নিরোধন, কারারোধ।

dë-tĕct', *v. t.* 1. To discover; to bring to light; as, to *detect* a crime or error; বাহির করা, প্রকাশ করা; উদ্ঘাটিত করা। 2. To find out as a guilty person or one in committing a crime; (দোষী ব্যক্তিকে) ধরা, ধৃত করা। **—a-ble,** *adj.* **—tec'-tion,** *n.* **—tect'-or,** *n.*

dë-tĕct'-ive (-ĭv), *adj.* & *n.* Employed in or fitted for, detecting; as, a *detective* police; গোয়েন্দার কাজে নিযুক্ত, গোয়েন্দার কাজের উপযোগী। ***Noun.*** A police man whose business is to detect criminals or discover matters of secrecy; গুপ্তপুলিশ, গোয়েন্দা, টিক্‌টিকি (*Colloq.*) চর (আঃ বঃ)। **Amateur detective**—সখের গোয়েন্দা। **Private detective**—বেসরকারী গোয়েন্দা।

dë-tĕnt', *n.* (*Mech.*) A pin, stud or lever forming a check in a clock, watch, etc.; (যন্ত্র-বিজ্ঞান) ঘড়ি, টেক-ঘড়ি প্রভৃতির কলের আটক-স্বরূপ শঙ্কু প্রেক অথবা দন্তযন্ত্র।

detente, (*F.*) *n.* Cessation of friction or strained relations between states; রাষ্ট্র সমূহের মধ্যে সংঘর্ষ বা মনোমালিন্যের নিবৃত্তি।

dë-tĕn'-tion, *n.* 1. Act of detaining or withholding; আটক করণ, আবদ্ধকরণ, নিরোধন। 2. Confinement; custody; as, he was in *detention* at the court; অবরোধ; আটক। 3. Delay; as, the *detention* of the mail by bad roads; বিলম্ব, গৌণ। 4. (*At schools*) Keeping in as punishment; (বিদ্যালয়ে) কয়েদ। **House of detention**—A lock-up; হাজত-ঘর, হাজতখানা, গারদ-ঘর।

dë-têr', *v. t.* To discourage or frighten from any action; to hinder or prevent; নিবৃত্ত করা; বাধা দেওয়া, নিবারণ করা। **—rence, —ment,** *ns.* **—rent,** *adj.* & *n.* Serving to deter; as, deterrent punishment; প্রতিরোধক, নিবর্ত্তক। (*Noun*) That which deters; প্রতিরোধকারী বস্তু;

dë-têr'-gĕnt, *adj.* & *n.* Cleansing; purging; বিশোধক; মলাপহারক, পরিমার্জ্জক। ***Noun.*** A substance as soap etc having a cleansing power; a medicine to cleanse wounds, ulcers, etc.; মলাপহারক পদার্থ; বিস্রাবণ (সাঃ পঃ), ব্রণশুদ্ধিকর (ঐ)।

dë-tē'-ri-ö-rāte, *v. t.* & *i.* To make worse or inferior; to reduce in quality; as, to *deteriorate* the mind; হীন করা; অপকৃষ্ট করা। ***Verb i.*** To grow worse; to degenerate; অপকৃষ্ট হওয়া; হীনতাপ্রাপ্ত হওয়া। **—ra'-tion,** *n.* The act of deteriorating; ক্ষয়, অধোগতি, অপকর্ষ। **—ra-tive,** *adj.*

dë-têr'-mi-nănt, *adj.* & *n.* Serving or tending to determine; decisive; নিশ্চায়ক; চরম, চূড়ান্ত। ***Noun.*** 1. That which determines or causes determination; নিশ্চায়ক বস্তু। 2. (*Math.*) The sum of a series of products of several numbers, these products being formed according to certain specified laws; (গণিতশাস্ত্র) কতিপয় সংখ্যার গুণফলশ্রেণীর যোগফল। 3. (*Log.*) A mark or attribute added to the subject or predicate which narrows the extent of both, but renders them definite and precise; (তর্ক-বিজ্ঞান) উদ্দেশ্য ও বিধেয়ে সংযোজিত গুণ বা লক্ষণ,—যদ্দ্বারা উভয়ের প্রসারের সংকোচ হইলেও, ইহারা অধিকতর সুস্পষ্ট ও যথাযথ হয়, নির্দ্ধারক (হিঃ কোঃ), অধ্যবসায়ক (ঐ)।

dë-têr'-mi-nāte, *adj.* 1. Definite; fixed; limited or determined; সুস্পষ্ট; স্থিরীকৃত, নির্দ্ধারিত, সুনিশ্চিত; সীমাবদ্ধ, ব্যবস্থাপিত (মঃ ইঃ)। 2. Decisive; conclusive; নিশ্চায়ক; চূড়ান্ত, চরম। 3. Resolute; resolved; "Cool judgment and *determinate* character;" দৃঢ়-প্রতিজ্ঞ; কৃত-নিশ্চিত, ব্যবস্থাপিত (মঃ ইঃ)। 4. Decided; intended; "*determinate* voyage;" নিশ্চিত, নিরূপিত; অভিপ্রেত। **—ly,** *adv.* **—ness,** *n.*

dë-têr-mi-nā'-tion, *n.* 1. The act of determining, or the state of being determined; নির্ণয়, সংকল্প, অবধারণ, স্থিরসংকল্প, নির্দ্ধারণ। 2. (*Law*) Cessation of estate or interest; "*Determination* of the defendant's tenancy;" সম্পত্তি বা স্বার্থের অবসান। 3. (*Archaic*) Ending; অবসান। 4. A judicial decision; as, a speedy *determination* of causes promotes justice; মোকদ্দমা নিষ্পত্তি। 5. A direction or tendency to a certain end; কোন বিশেষ উদ্দেশ্য সাধনে উন্মুখতা, গতি (আঃ বঃ। 6. Resoluteness; adherence to aims or purposes; as, a man of *determination*; স্থিরপ্রতিজ্ঞতা; নিষ্ঠা। 7. The decision of a debate, etc.; তর্কাদির মীমাংসা। 8. Exact ascertainment of amount etc.; সংখ্যা প্রভৃতি সঠিক ভাবে নির্ণয়। 9. (*Med.*) A rapid flow; (ভৈষজ্য-শাস্ত্র) দ্রুতপ্রবাহ। 10. That which is determined or resolved upon; result of deliberation; as, they have acquainted me with their *determination* ; স্থিরীকৃত বিষয় ; মন্ত্রণার ফল। **11.** Definition ; delimitation ; সংজ্ঞা-প্রদান ; সীমা-নির্দ্ধারণ। **12.** Fixing of date etc. ; তারিখ স্থিরীকরণ। **13.** (*Log.*) The defining of a notion or concept by limiting it by the addition of differentia ; (তর্কবিজ্ঞান) ব্যবর্ত্তক (differentia) সংযোগ দ্বারা কোন বিভাবন সীমাবদ্ধকরণ, নির্ণয় (হিঃ কোঃ), অধ্যবসায় (ঐ), ব্যবসায় (ঐ)।

dē-têr′-mi-nā-tive (-tîv), *adj.* & *n.* **1.** Serving to determine ; conclusive ; নিশ্চায়ক ; নির্ণায়ক, অবধারক, নির্দ্ধারক। **2.** Serving to define or qualify ; as, a *determinative* mark or attribute ; সংজ্ঞাপ্রদায়ক, বিশেষক। ***Noun.*** **1.** (*Hierog.*) A sign prefixed or suffixed to a word for the purpose of determining its meaning ; (মিসরদেশীয় চিত্রাক্ষর) কোন শব্দের অর্থ স্থিরীকরণের জন্য ইহার পূর্ব্বে বা অন্তে যে চিহ্ন সংযোজিত করা হয়, অর্থাবধারক। **2.** (*Gram.*) A determinative or demonstrative word ; (ব্যাকরণ) নির্ণায়ক, নিশ্চায়ক বা প্রতিপাদক শব্দ।

dē-têr′-mine (-mîn), *v. t.* & *i.* **1.** To bring to an end as a controversy ; to settle judicially ; মীমাংসা করা ; বিচার দ্বারা মীমাংসা করা, নিষ্পত্তি করা। **2.** To decide ; to settle ; স্থির করা, নির্দ্ধারণ করা ; মীমাংসা করা, নিষ্পত্তি করা। **3.** To impel and direct, (followed usu. by *to*) ; as, another's will *determined* me to this course ; প্রণোদিত করা, চালিত করা। **4.** To resolve ; as, he *determined* to do this ; to lead ; as, this *determined* him to go immediately ; কৃতসংকল্প হওয়া, বদ্ধপরিকর হওয়া, স্থিরপ্রতিজ্ঞ হওয়া ; সংকল্প করা, চালিত করা। **5.** To ascertain definitely ; as, to *determine* an unknown plant or its name ; to settle ultimately ; as, this *determined* his fate ; নিশ্চয় করা ; নিরূপণ করা। **6.** To fix beforehand as a date etc. ; পূর্ব্বনির্দ্ধারিত করা। **7.** To limit ; to fix the boundaries of ; "God hath *determined* the time before appointed ;"—Acts XVII 26 ; সীমাবদ্ধ করা ; সীমানির্দ্ধারণ করা, সীমানির্দ্দেশ করা। **8.** To bound ; as, yonder hill *determines* our view ; সীমাবদ্ধ করা। **9.** To be the decisive factor in regard to ; as, demand *determines* supply ; নির্দ্ধারক হওয়া। **10.** To ascertain the amount etc. ; as, to *determine* nitrogen in the atmosphere ; সংখ্যা, পরিমাণ প্রভৃতি নির্ণয় করা। ***Verb i.*** **1.** To terminate ; to come to an end, esp. in law ; as, estates may *determine* on future contingencies ; অবসান হওয়া ; নিষ্পত্তি হওয়া (বিশেষতঃ আইন-সম্পর্কে)। **2.** To come to a decision or resolution ; as, he *determined* to remain ; (often with *on* ; as, to *determine on* a course or doing something ; স্থিরসংকল্প হওয়া, বদ্ধপরিকর হওয়া। **3.** To tend (*archaic*) ; "To these they will *determine* ;" উন্মুখ হওয়া। **—mi-na-ble,** *adj.* **—mined,** *adj.* **1.** Settled ; decided ; নিশ্চিত ; নিরূপিত। **2.** Firm in purpose ; resolute ; as, a *determined* foe ; বদ্ধপরিকর ; কৃতনিশ্চয়। **To be determined**—To have resolved ; বদ্ধপরিকর হওয়া, কৃতসংকল্প হওয়া।

dē-têr′-min-ĭsm, *n.* (*Metaph.*) The doctrine that the will is not free, but is invincibly determined by motives ; (তত্ত্ব-বিদ্যা) মানবের ইচ্ছা স্বাধীন নহে কিন্তু অভীষ্ট উদ্দেশ্য দ্বারা অলঙ্ঘ্যরূপে স্থিরীকৃত হইয়া থাকে—এইরূপ দার্শনিক মত, নিয়তিবাদ (হিঃ কোঃ)। **—ist,** *n.* & *adj.* (*Metaph.*) A believer in determinism ; নিয়তিবাদী। (*Adj.*) Relating to determinism ; as, *determinist* theories ; নিয়তিবাদ-সম্বন্ধীয়। **—ist′-ic,** *adj.*

dē-têr′-sive (-sîv), *adj.* & *n.* Cleansing ; বিশোধক। ***Noun.*** A cleansing agent or detergent ; মলাপহারক বস্তু, বিশোধক পদার্থ।

dē-tĕst′, *v. t.* To hate extremely ; as, to *detest* crimes or meanness ; নিরতিশয় ঘৃণা করা, বিজাতীয় ঘৃণা করা। **—a-ble,** *adj.* Worthy of being detested ; ঘৃণার্হ। **—a-ble-ness,** *n.* **—a-bly,** *adv.*

dĕt-ĕs-tā′-tion, *n.* **1.** A feeling of extreme hatred, (usually with *of*) ; "Our *detestation* of civil war ;" নিরতিশয় ঘৃণা, বিজাতীয় ঘৃণা, জুগুপ্সা। **2.** A detested person or thing ; অতিশয় ঘৃণার্হ ব্যক্তি বা বস্তু। **To have** or **hold in detestation**—To abhor ; নিরতিশয় ঘৃণা করা।

dē-thrōne′, *v. t.* To depose ; to divest of supreme authority or royal dignity ; "The right of subjects to *dethrone* bad princes ;" সিংহাসনচ্যুত করা ; অধিকারচ্যুত করা, রাজ্যচ্যুত করা। **—ment,** *n.*

dĕt′-i-nue (-nü). *n.* (*Law*) The unlawful detention of a personal chattel from another ; (আইন) অবৈধভাবে দ্রব্যাদি আটক রাখন। **Action of detinue**—অবৈধভাবে আটক-করা জিনিষের পুনরুদ্ধারের জন্য মোকদ্দমা।

dĕt′-ō-nāte, *v. i.* & *t.* To burn or explode with a sudden report ; as, niter *detonates* with sulphur ; সশব্দে বিদীর্ণ হওয়া, সশব্দে ফুটা। ***Verb t.*** To cause to explode with a loud report ; সশব্দে বিদীর্ণ করা, আস্ফুটিত হওয়া। **—na′-tion,** *n.* **—nat-ive,** *adj.* **—na-tor,** *n.* **1.** A detonating contrivance, as a percussion cap. ; বন্দুকে ব্যবহারের

জন্য বারুদলিপ্ত ধাতু-টোপর। 2. A case containing powder serving as a railway fog-signal; লৌহ-বর্ত্মের-কুজ্ঝটিকা সঙ্কেত স্বরূপ বারুদপূর্ণ আধার। **Detonating powder**—একপ্রকার বারুদ — যাহা উত্তপ্ত বা বিঘাতিত হইলে ভীষণ শব্দে বিদীর্ণ হয়।

dĕ-tour′ (-tōōr), *n.* A circuitous or round-about way; a deviation from a direct course; a turning; as, the *detours* of the Mississippi: to make a *detour* (to make a digression); আঁকা-বাঁকা পথ; সরলপথ হইতে ব্যতিক্রম; মোড়, বাঁক, পাক।

dĕ-trăct,′ *v. t.* & *i.* **1.** To take or draw away; লইয়া যাওয়া, অপসৃত করা। 2. To defame; to slander; মানহানি করা, কুৎসা করা, অপবাদ করা, অখ্যাতি করা। ***Verb i.*** To take away a part, especially from a person's reputation or good name, (often with *from*); "The fashion to *detract* from both the moral and literary character of Cicero;" অপসৃত করা, বিশেষতঃ কোন ব্যক্তির খ্যাতি বা সুনাম হ্রাস করা, মানক্ষয় করা। **—trac′-tion,** *n.* **—trac′-tor,** *n.* A slanderer; a defamer; অপবাদ-কারী; নিন্দক। **—ive,** *adj.*

dĕ-train′ (-trān), *v. t.* & *i.* To cause to alight from a railway train; as, to *detrain* troops; বাষ্পীয় শকট হইতে অবতরণ করান। ***Verb i.*** To come out of a railway train; বাষ্পীয় শকট হইতে অবতরণ করা।

dĕt′-ri-mĕnt, *n.* **1.** Damage; injury; that which causes harm or loss; ক্ষতি, লোকসান; অপচয়; অপায়; ক্ষতিজনক বস্তু বা বিষয়। 2. (*Her.*) The eclipse of the sun or moon; the moon nearly invisible in her change; (কুল-বিদ্যা) সূর্য্যগ্রহণ বা চন্দ্রগ্রহণ; প্রতিপচ্চন্দ্র।

dĕt-ri-mĕn′-tăl, *adj.* & *n.* Injurious; harmful; হানিকারক; ক্ষতিজনক। ***Noun.*** (*Slang*) One who pays great attention to a lady without serious intentions of marriage; the younger brother of the heir of an estate; (ইতর ভাষায়) যে ব্যক্তি প্রকৃতপক্ষে বিবাহ করিতে ইচ্ছুক না হইয়া কোন স্ত্রীলোকের ভজনা করে; কোন সম্পত্তির উত্তরাধিকারীর অনুজ।

dĕ-trĭt′-ĕd, *adj.* **1.** Worn down; ক্ষয়প্রাপ্ত। 2. (*Geol.*) Disintegrated; (ভূ-বিদ্যা) বিশ্লিষ্ট।

dĕ-trĭ′-tion, *n.* Wearing away by rubbing or by disintegration; ঘর্ষণ বা বিশ্লেষণজনিত ক্ষয়।

dĕ-trĭ′-tŭs, *n.* **1.** (*Geol.*) A mass of substances detached from solid bodies by attrition; (ভূ-বিদ্যা) সংহত পদার্থ হইতে বিশ্লিষ্ট পদার্থ-পিণ্ড। **2.** Disintegrated materials; "The mass of *detritus* of which modern languages are composed;" বিশ্লিষ্ট পদার্থ-পিণ্ড। **—tal,** *adj.*

de trop, (*F.*), *adj.* Not wanted; unwelcome; as, I found I was *de trop* and retired accordingly; অপ্রার্থিত, অবাঞ্ছিত; অপ্রীতিকর।

deuce (dūs), **1.** (*Gaming*) A card or die with two spots; as, the *deuce* of hearts; তাসের দুরি, পাশার দুই পো। 2. (*Tennis*) A term denoting that each side has gained three points; (আন্টালখেলা) আন্টালখেলায় ব্যবহৃত শব্দ বিশেষ — যদ্দ্বারা প্রত্যেক পক্ষ ৩ ক্রীড়াঙ্ক পাইয়াছে বুঝা যায়। **Deuce ace**—তিন পো।

deuce (dūs), *n.* Perdition; the devil; plague; as, go to the *deuce*: *deuce* take you; নিরয়, নরক; শয়তান, খন্নাস (ফঃ হিঃ); উৎপাত, বালাই। **Deuce a bit**—Not at all; মোটেই না। **Deuce take you** (The devil take you)—Get away; you annoy me; দূর হও; তুমি আমাকে বিরক্ত করিতেছ। **The deuce is in it if I cannot**—I certainly can; আমি নিশ্চয়ই করিতে পারি। **The deuce is in you**—You are a very demon; তুমি সাক্ষাৎ শয়তান। **The deuce to pay**—Trouble to be expected; উৎপাত হইবে আশা করা যায়। **To play the deuce with**—To ruin; to spoil; ধ্বংস করা; নষ্ট করা। **What the deuce is the matter**—What in the world is amiss: কি গোল ঘটেছে।

deu′-cĕd (dū-), *adj.* Devilish; extreme; as, in a *deuced* hurry; শয়তানী, পৈশাচিক; নিতান্ত, নিরতিশয়, ভীষণ। **—ly,** *adv.*

deus ex machina, (*L.*), *n.* A power or event that comes in the nick of time to solve difficulty; providential interposition, especially in a novel or play; যে শক্তি বা ঘটনা সময়মত কোন কঠিন বিষয়ের মীমাংসা করে; দেবতার মধ্যস্থতা, দৈব (বিশেষতঃ নাটক বা উপন্যাসে)।

deu-tĕr-ăg′-ō-nist (dū-), *n.* A person of next importance to a protagonist in a drama; গুরুত্ব-হিসাবে নায়কের অব্যবহিত নিম্নস্থানবর্ত্তী নাটকীয় পাত্র।

deu-tĕr-ŏg′-ă-mȳ (dū-), *n.* A second marriage; পুনর্বিবাহ।

deu-tĕr-ŏn′-ō-mȳ (dū-), *n.* The fifth book of the Pentateuch; বাইবেলের পুরাতন পুস্তকের অন্তর্গত পঞ্চম পুস্তক। **—mist,** *n.* The auothor or compiler or deuteronomy; উক্ত পুস্তকের প্রণেতা বা সংগ্রাহক। **—o-nom′-ic, —i-cal,** *adjs.*

deut′-zi-ă (dūt-sĭ-), *n.* White flowered shrubs; শ্বেতপুষ্পপ্রসূ গুল্মশ্রেণী বিশেষ।

deux-temps, (*F.*), *n.* A kind of waltz (a form of dance) more rapid than the trois-temps; একপ্রকার নৃত্য।

Devachan, *n.* Heaven, according to the Theosophists; (থিয়োসফিষ্ট-দিগের মতানুসারে) দেবস্থান, ভোগ-স্বর্গ

dē-vă-pō-rā′-tion, *n.* The change of vapour into water ; সলীলীভবন, বিবাষ্পীভবন।

dĕv′-ăs-tāte, *v. t.* To ravage ; to lay waste ; উৎসন্ন করা ; উজাড় করা, বিধ্বংস করা ; উচ্ছিন্ন করা। **—ta′-tion,** *n.* **1.** Act of devastating or the state of being devastated ; বিধ্বংস ; উচ্ছেদ, উৎসাদন, অমঙ্গল, উচ্ছিন্নাবস্থা। **2.** (*Law*) The waste of the goods of a deceased person by the executor or administrator ; (আইন) অছিকর্ত্তৃক মৃত ব্যক্তির সম্পত্তি ক্ষয়। **—ta-tor,** *n.*

dē-vĕl′-op (-ŭp), *v. t.* & *i.* **1.** To lay open ; to disclose ; to reveal ; to unfold ; as, to *develop* a plot or motive ; বিকাশ করা ; প্রকাশিত করা ; সুব্যক্ত করা ; উদ্ঘাটিত করা। **2.** To promote the growth of ; to further ; "To *develop* in our minds a sense of the......beauties of nature ;' ক্রমশঃ বিকাশ করা, পরিস্ফুট করা ; অগ্রসর করা। **3.** To form or expand by a process of growth ; as, sunshine and rain *develop* the bud into a flower ; ফুটাইয়া তোলা। **4.** (*Photo.*) To make visible the latent picture produced in the camera or under a negative ; (আলোকচিত্রণ) প্রচ্ছন্ন চিত্র পরিস্ফুট করা, চিত্র পরিস্ফুট করা। **5.** (*Math.*) To change the form of an (algebraic) expression, by executing certain indicated operations without changing the value ; (গণিতশাস্ত্র) বীজগণিতের রাশির মান পরিবর্ত্তন না করিয়া কতিপয় নির্দ্দিষ্ট ক্রিয়া সাধন করত উহার রূপ পরিবর্ত্তন করা, রূপ পরিবর্ত্তন করা। **6.** (*Mil.*) To open (as an attack) ; (সামরিক-শাস্ত্র) আরম্ভ করা (যথা, আক্রমণ)। ***Verb i.*** **1.** To progress from one stage to another ; to expand by a natural process ; as, the mind *develops* from year to year ; a blossom *develops* from a bud ; ক্রমশঃ বিকাশপ্রাপ্ত হওয়া ; স্বাভাবিকভাবে বিকাশপ্রাপ্ত হওয়া, বিকশিত হওয়া। **2.** To become visible or apparent ; to come to light ; as, a picture on sensitive paper *develops* on the application of heat : the plans of conspirators *develop* ; দৃষ্টিগোচর হওয়া, সুস্পষ্ট হওয়া, পরিস্ফুট হওয়া ; প্রকাশিত হওয়া, উদ্ঘাটিত হওয়া। **—a-ble,** *adj.* **—er,** *n.* **1.** One who or that which develops ; বিকাশকারী ব্যক্তি বা বস্তু। **2.** (*Photo.*) A reagent by the action of which the latent image upon a photographic plate is developed and made visible ; (আলোকচিত্রণ) এক প্রকার প্রতিক্রিয়া সাধক বস্তু—যদ্দারা আলোক-চিত্রের ফলকোপরিস্থ প্রচ্ছন্ন-চিত্র পরিস্ফুট ও দর্শনযোগ্য হয়, প্রকাশক।

dē-vĕl′-op-mĕnt (-ŭp-), **1.** The act of developing stage by stage ; a gradual unfolding ; a gradual growth ; a developed stage ; developing as of a photograph ; পরিণতি ; ব্যক্ততা, বিবৃতি (মঃ ইঃ) ; পরিস্ফুরণ, বিকাশ, পরিপুষ্টি ; পূর্ণতা ; স্ফুটতা। **2.** A more elaborate form ; স্ফুটতর রূপ। **3.** (*Bot.*) Evolution (of animal and plant races) ; (জীববিজ্ঞান) অভিব্যক্তি। **Doctrine of development**—অভিব্যক্তি বাদ।

dē-vĕl-op-mĕn′-tăl (-ŭp-), *adj.* Pertaining to development ; evolutionary ; বিকাশসম্বন্ধীয় ; ক্রমবিকাশী। **—ly,** *adv.* **Developmental diseases**—যে সমস্ত রোগ জীবনের বিশেষ বিশেষ কালে প্রকাশ হইয়া থাকে, এবং দৈহিক পরিবর্ত্তন দ্বারা সঞ্জাত হয়।

dē′-vi-āte, *v. i.* To turn aside from the common, or right way, course or line ; to go astray ; to digress ; as, to *deviate* from the common track : to *deviate* from the truth ; উন্মার্গ গমন করা, সৎপথ হইতে ভ্রষ্ট হওয়া, সন্মার্গচ্যুত হওয়া ; বিপথে চলা ; (মূলবিষয় বা পন্থা হইতে) বিচ্যুত হওয়া।

dē-vi-ā′-tion, *n.* **1.** Act of deviating ; wandering from the right course or path of duty ; ব্যত্যয়, ব্যভিচার, নড়চড়, উৎক্রম, অতিক্রম (আঃ বঃ) ; উন্মার্গগমন (ঐ), বিচলন (মঃ ইঃ), স্খলন। **2.** A transgression ; an error ; a sinful act ; পদস্খলন, অপরাধ, দোষ ; ভ্রান্তি ; পাপকার্য্য। **3.** Deflexion of the compass-needle by iron in a ship ; as, *deviation* of the campass ; পোতস্থ লৌহ দ্বারা দিগ্‌দর্শন যন্ত্রের সূচীর বিচলন, দিগ্‌দর্শক বিচলন (হিঃ কোঃ)। **Deviation from a type**—জাতিবৈলক্ষণ্য।

dē-vīce′, *n.* **1.** That which is devised or designed ; a scheme ; a project ; an artifice ; উপায়, ফিকির ; মন্ত্রণা, কল্পনা, যুক্তি, বুদ্ধি ; সংকল্প ; ফন্দি। **2.** Act or faculty of devising ; contrivance ; "Instruments of my own *device* ;" উদ্ভাবন, উদ্ভাবনীশক্তি ; কল, কৌশল। **3.** A drawing ; a figure ; রেখাচিত্র ; চিত্র। **4.** (*Her.*) The emblem borne upon a shield ; a motto ; (কুল-বিদ্যা) চর্ম্মফলকোপরিস্থ কুলচিহ্ন ; মূল-বাক্য, আদর্শবচন। **5.** (*Pl.*) Fancy ; will ; as, left to one's own *device* খেয়াল ; ইচ্ছা। **6.** (*Archaic*) Look ; make ; (অপ্রচলিত) আকার ; গঠন।

Device of Henry VII West Minister Abbey.

dĕv′-il, *n.* **1.** An evil spirit or being ; a fiend ; অপদেবতা ; ভূত, প্রেত, অসুর, পিশাচ, ইবলীস (ফঃ হিঃ) দেবদ্বেষী। **2.** Satan ; শয়তান, বেতাল, প্রেত, পিশাচ, কর্ণপিশাচ। **3.** A false or heathen god ; অলীক দেবতা, পৌত্তলিকদিগের দেবতা। **4.** A very wicked, cruel or hateful person ; a traitor ; নরপিশাচ, নরাধম, পাষণ্ড,

পাজি ; বিশ্বাসঘাতক। **5.** A wicked ; or wretched person ; "One of you is a *devil* ;" John VI 70 : a poor *devil* ; দুর্বৃত্ত ; দুর্ভাগালোক, পাপাত্মা। **6.** An expletive to express wonder or vexation ; "What the *devil* makes him cry ?" আশ্চর্য্য বা বিরক্তি বোধক বাক্য-পূরক শব্দ। **7.** A literary hack doing what his employer takes the credit and pay for ; ভাড়াটিয়া লেখক, সাহিত্যিকভৃত। **8.** A highly seasoned dish as a bone with some meat on it, broiled and excessively peppered ; প্রচুর মসলাযুক্ত ভর্জিত মাংস খণ্ড। **9.** A machine for cutting or tearing up rags ; একপ্রকার যন্ত্র, — যদ্দ্বারা ছিন্ন বস্ত্র খণ্ড কর্ত্তিত হয়। **10.** A ferocious animal of Tasmania ; টাস্‌মিনিয়া দ্বীপের ভয়ঙ্কর হিংস্র জন্তু বিশেষ। **11.** A junior legal counsel working for a pleader ; নূতন কৌঁসুলি—যিনি কোন প্রবীণ কৌঁসুলীর সহকারীরূপে কার্য্য করেন, নবীন কৌঁসুলী। **12.** Fighting spirit ; dashing energy in attack ; কলহ-প্রবৃত্তি ; আক্রমণে প্রচণ্ড তেজ। **13.** Printer's devil ; (see below.) **14.** Various kinds of animals, birds, implements or fire-works etc. ; also their names ; বিভিন্ন জাতীয় জন্তু, পক্ষী, যন্ত্র, আতস-বাজী, প্রভৃতি ; উক্ত জন্তু পক্ষী, প্রভৃতির নাম। **15.** (*Colloq. India*) A dust storm ; (চলিত ভাষায় — ভারতবর্ষে) ধূলিময় ঝঞ্ঝা। **16.** A seam in a ship's hull on or beneath the water-line ; জলের উপরে বা নীচে জাহাজের খোলে জোড়া। **—dom, —hood,** *ns.* **—ward(s)** *adv.* **Devil dodger**—A preacher ; a parson ; খৃষ্টীয় প্রচারক ; খৃষ্টীয় যাজক। **Devil fish**—কয়েক প্রকার বৃহৎ এবং কুৎসিত মৎস্যের সাধারণ নাম। **Devil's advocate**—(R. C. C.) রোমান ক্যাথলিক ধর্ম্ম সঙ্ঘ) যে ব্যক্তি সিদ্ধপুরুষের শ্রেণীভুক্তির প্রার্থীর বিরুদ্ধে আপত্তি উত্থাপন করে। **Devil's bed post**—চিড়তনের চৌকা। **Devil's bit** — এক প্রকার গুল্ম। **Devil's bones** — Dice ; পাশা। **Devil's books** — Cards ; তাস। **Devil's coach horse** — একপ্রকার গুব্‌রে পোকা। **Devil's cotton**—ওলট কম্বল। **Devil's dozen**—Thirteen ; (like *baker's dozen*) ; তের। **Devil's dung** — হিঙ্গ্‌। **Devil's dust**—পুরাতন পশমী কাপড়ের সূতা হইতে যে পশম পাওয়া যায়। **Devil's luck**—Very great good fotune ; মহা সৌভাগ্য। **Devil's own**—The 88th regiment of the Peninsular war ; (*also*) the Inns of court Volunteers ; পিনিনসুল্যার যুদ্ধের ৮৮ গণিত পল্টন ; ইংলণ্ডের ব্যবহারজীবীদিগের সমাজ চতুষ্টয়ের স্বেচ্ছাসেবকগণ। **Devil's snuff-box** — একপ্রকার ছত্রাক। **Devil's tattoo**—হস্ত বা পদ দ্বারা বাদন। **Devil a bit**—Not at all ; মোটেই না। **Devil may care**—Reckless ; rollicking ; দুঃসাহসী, বে-পরওয়া ; আমোদিয়া, দিলদরিয়া। **Printer's devil**—The youngest apprentice in a printing-office ; a printer's errand boy ; ছাপাখানার সর্ব্বাপেক্ষা অল্পবয়স্ক শিক্ষানবীশ, বাল-মুদ্রক (আঃ বঃ) ; ছাপাখানার সংবাদ-বাহক ছোকরা। **Tasmanian devil**—ট্যাস্‌মেনিয়া দ্বীপের মাংসাশী জন্তু বিশেষ। **The devil**—An exclamation of annoyance or surprise ; বিরক্তি বা বিস্ময়সূচক শব্দ বিশেষ। **The Devil**—শয়তান। **A devil of a temper**—A very bad temper ; অতিশয় বদমেজাজ। **Between the devil and the deep sea**—In a dilemma ; ডাঙ্গায় কুমীর জলে বাঘ। **Devil-in-the-bush** — A guarden-flower (also called love-in-a-mist) ; উদ্যানজাত পুষ্প বিশেষ। **Devil of a mess**—A very bad mess ; অতি কদর্য্য খাদ্য। **Devil on the neck**—প্রাচীন কালীন পীড়নযন্ত্র বিশেষ। **Devil on two sticks**—একপ্রকার ক্রীড়া। **Devil a one**—একজনও নয়। **Devil take the hindmost**—The man who is last must suffer ; সকলের শেষের লোককে কষ্টভোগ করিতে হইবে। **Devil to pay**—A serious trouble ahead ; সম্মুখে মহা বিপদ্। **Is the devil**—A great difficulty or nuisance ; মহাগোলমাল বা বিরক্তির বিষয়। **Like the devil**—With great energy etc. ; প্রচণ্ডতেজে। **Talk of the devil (and he will appear)**—কোন ব্যক্তির নাম করা মাত্র, ঠিক সেই সময় আসিয়া সে উপস্থিত হইল, এরূপ অবস্থায় এই বাক্য ব্যবহৃত হয়। **The devil among the tailors**—Row ; disturbance ; হাঙ্গামা ; গোলমাল। **The devil and all**—Every thing bad ; সবই খারাপ। [অনুবাদে :—লোকটা মন্দ বটে—তবে তাহার এই একটা গুণ আছে তাহা স্বীকার করিতেই হইবে।] **To give the devil his due**—To give justice to an evil or bad man ; to give him credit for any good there is in him ; মন্দলোকেরও ন্যায়তঃ যে প্রশংসা প্রাপ্য তাহা তাহাকে অর্পণ করা ; মন্দ লোকের মধ্যেও কোনরূপ সদ্‌গুণ থাকিলে তাহা স্বীকার করা। **To go to the devil**—To be ruined ; (*imperative*) to be off গোল্লায় যাওয়া, অধঃপাতে যাওয়া, জাহান্নমে যাওয়া ; তফাৎ হওয়া। **To play the devil with**—To bring to utter ruin ; সর্ব্বনাশ করা। **To whip the devil round the post** — To avoid rules or provisions etc. ; কোনরূপ নিয়ম, বিধি প্রভৃতি পালন কৌশলক্রমে পরিহার করা।

dĕv'-il, *v. t.* & *i.* **1.** To make devilish, or like a devil ; শয়তানের মত করা, শয়তানী করা। **2.** To season highly in cooking as with pepper ; "A *devilled* leg. of Turkey;" প্রচুর মসলা (গোল মরিচের চূর্ণ প্রভৃতি) সংযোগে রন্ধন করা। ***Verb i.*** To work as a lawyer's or author's devil ; কৌঁসুলির সহকারী রূপে কাজ করা, টাকা লইয়া কাহারো অধীনে পুস্তক লেখকের কার্য্য করা।

dĕv′-il-ish, *adj.* & *adv.* Pertaining to or resembling the devil ; diabolical ; malignant ; as, a *devilish* scheme ; শয়তানী ; ভূতুড়ে ; পৈশাচিক, আসুর। ***Adv.*** Very ; exceedingly ; ভারি ; নিতান্ত। **–ly, –ness,** *n.*

dĕv′-il-ism, *n.* **1.** An action, character or conduct like that of a devil ; শয়তানি। **2.** Worship of devils ; প্রেত বা পিশাচ পূজা।

dĕv′-il-mĕnt, *n.* **1.** Mischief ; roguery ; trickery ; নষ্টামি ; ধড়িবাজি ; চালাকি। **2.** A strange or devilish phenomenon ; ভূতুড়ে কাণ্ড।

dĕv′-il-(t)rȳ, **1.** The conduct suitable to the devil ; diabolical wickedness ; cruelty ; mischief ; শয়তানি ; পৈশাচিকতা, পৈশাচাচার, পৈশাচিক ব্যাপার ; ক্রূরতা ; নষ্টামি। **2.** Magic ; ইন্দ্রজাল। **3.** A body of evil spirits ; দানব সমাজ। **4.** Demonology ; প্রেত-তত্ত্ব।

dē′-vi-ous (-ŭs), *adj.* Out of the common way or track ; varying from directness ; as, a *devious* path ; [cf. বক্রঃ পন্থা যদপি ভবতঃ—মেঘঃ] বক্র ; কুটিল। **2.** Going astray ; erring ; as, a *devious* step ; উদ্ভ্রান্ত ; ভ্রান্ত। Sequestered ; remote ; "These *devious* and untrodden ice-fields ;" নির্জ্জন, বিজন ; বহুদূরবর্ত্তী। **–ly,** *adv.* **–ness,** *n.*

dē-vīse′, *v. t., i.* & *n.* **1.** (*Law*) To give or bequeath by will as a real estate ; (আইন) ইচ্ছাপত্র দ্বারা দান করা। **2.** To imagine ; to contrive ; to plan ; to invent ; to formulate by thought ; as, to *devise* an engine ; কল্পনা করা ; রচনা করা ; মতলব করা, মনে মনে আঁটা, ভাবিয়া ঠিক করা ; উদ্ভাবন করা ; চিন্তা করিয়া বাহির করা। ***Verb i.*** To lay a plan ; to contrive ; একটা মতলব স্থির করা ; বুদ্ধি কৌশলে স্থির করা। ***Noun.*** **1.** (*Law*) The act of bequeathing a land or real estate by will ; (আইন) ইচ্ছাপত্র দ্বারা উত্তরাধিকারীকে সম্পত্তি অর্পণ। **2.** A property given by will ; ইচ্ছাপত্রদ্বারা দত্ত সম্পত্তি। **3.** A will or a clause in it making a gift of real property ; ইচ্ছা-পত্র, ইচ্ছা পত্রের এক দফা,—যদ্দারা কোন সম্পত্তি অর্পিত হয়। **–vis′-a-ble,** *adj.* **–vi-see′,** *n.* One to whom a real estate is given by will ; উইল-ক্রমে সম্পত্তি-প্রাপ্ত ব্যক্তি। **–vis′-er, –vis′-or,** *ns.*

dē-vī′-tăl-īze, *v. t.* To make lifeless or effete ; নির্জ্জীব করা, নিষ্প্রাণ করা। **–i-za′-tion,** *n.*

dē-vĭt′-ri-fȳ, *v. t.* To deprive of the character or appearance of glass ; as, to *devitrify* glass ; কাচ-ধর্ম্ম নষ্ট করা। **–fi-ca′-tion,** *n.*

dē-void′ (-vŏyd), *adj.* Destitute ; not in possession ; (*with of*) ; as, *devoid* of common sense (কাণ্ডজ্ঞানহীন) ; রহিত ; বিরহিত, বিহীন, শূন্য, হীন, বিবর্জ্জিত।

dê-voir′ (-vwŏr), *n.* **1.** Duty ; service ; কর্ত্তব্য ; সেবা। **2.** (*Pl.*) respectful and courteous attentions ; শ্রদ্ধা, সমাদর।

dĕv′-ŏ-lūte, *v. t.* To transfer ; to devolve ; to depute as work ; পরিবর্ত্তন করা ; হস্তান্তরিত করা ; প্রতিনিধি নিয়োগ করা।

dĕv-ŏ-lū′-tion, *n.* **1.** Transference from one person to another ; a passing or falling upon a successor ; হস্তান্তর ; উত্তরাধিকারীতে সংক্রমণ। **2.** Deputing or delegation of work or power etc. (esp. by a house of Parliament to its committees) ; ক্ষমতার্পণ, ভারার্পণ, বিশেষতঃ পার্লেমেণ্ট মহাসভা কর্ত্তৃক কোন কার্য্য নির্ব্বাহক সমিতির হস্তে ক্ষমতা বা ভারার্পণ। **3.** A moving or passing on from one stage to another ; descent through a series of changes ; অবস্থা হইতে অবস্থান্তরে সংক্রমণ ; ক্রমাবনতি। **4.** (*Biol.*) Degradation of species ; (জীববিজ্ঞান) জাতির অবনতি।

dē-volve′ (-vŏlb), *v. t.* & *i.* **1.** To roll down ; to pass on ; "Eevery stream *devolves* its winding waters to the main ;" গড়াইয়া দেওয়া ; চলিতে থাকা, অগ্রসর হওয়া। **2.** To transfer, (with *upon*) ; "They *devolved* a considerable share of their power upon their favourite"—হস্তান্তরিত করা, সংক্রমিত করা। ***Verb i.*** To be handed down ; to fall or descend ; (generally with *on* or *upon* and sometimes with *to* or *into*) ; as, after the general fell, the command *devolved upon* or *on* the next officer in rank : "his estate *devoled to* Lord Somerville ;" হস্তান্তরিত হওয়া, সংক্রমিত হওয়া, অর্শান, বর্ত্তান।

Dē-vō′-ni-ăn, *adj.* & *n.* **1.** Of or pertaining to Devonshire in England ; ইংলণ্ডদেশের অন্তঃপাতী ডেবনসায়ার নামক প্রদেশ সম্বন্ধীয়। **2.** (*Geol*) Belonging to the old red sand-stone system as found in Devonshire ; (ভূ-বিদ্যা) ডেবন সায়ারে প্রাপ্ত প্রাচীন যুগের লাল বেলে পাথর সম্বন্ধীয়, ডিবনিক (সাঃ পঃ)। ***Noun.*** A native of Devon shire ; ডেবন সায়ারের অধিবাসী।

dē-vōte′, *v. t.* **1.** To dedicate ; to consecrate ; to doom ; সমর্পণ করা, সঁপা ; উৎসর্গ করা ; নির্দ্দিষ্ট করা। **2.** To give up wholly ; (generally with a reflexive) ; to addict ; as, to *devote* oneself to mirth : সম্পূর্ণরূপে আত্ম-নিয়োগ করা ; নিরত হওয়া। **–ment,** *n.*

dē-vōt′-ĕd, *adj.* Strongly attached ; zealous ; ardent ; as, a *devoted* friend ; নিষ্ঠ ; অনুরক্ত (আঃ বঃ), অত্যাসক্ত ; আগ্রহান্বিত তৎপর, পরায়ণ (in comp.), আসক্তচিত্ত, সমাহিত, নিরত। **2.** Consecrated or dedicated ; doomed; উৎসর্গীকৃত ; পূর্ব্ব হইতে নির্দ্দিষ্ট। **–ly,** *adv.*

dĕv-ō-tee′ (-tē), *n.* One who is zealously devoted ; especially one wholly given to religion ; a fanatic ; একনিষ্ঠ ব্যক্তি ; ভক্ত, তপস্বী, সাধু, ধর্ম্মনিষ্ঠ ব্যক্তি ; ধর্ম্মোন্মত্ত ব্যক্তি, গোঁড়া।

dĕ-vō′-tion, *n.* **1.** The act of devoting ; dedication ; consecration ; সমর্পণ ; উৎসর্গ ; প্রতিষ্ঠাপন। **2.** Devoutness ; addiction ; attachment ; zeal ; ভক্তি, ধ্যাননিষ্ঠা ; অত্যাসক্তি ; অনুরাগ ; একান্তিকতা। **3.** An act of worship ; (*pl.*) prayers ; as, he was at his *devotions* ; পূজার্চ্চনা ; আরাধনা ; (বহুবচন) প্রার্থনা, উপাসনা, সাধনভজন। **—al,** *adj.* Pertaining to, or fit for, devotion ; ভজনসম্বন্ধীয়, পূজার্চ্চনা-সম্বন্ধীয়, সাধনবিষয়ক ; ভজনোপযোগী। **—al-ly,** *adv.* **—al-ism, —ist,** *ns.*

dē-vour′ (-vowr), *v. t.* **1.** To eat up ravenously or greedily as a wild beast or a very hungryman ; উদরসাৎ করা, আত্মসাৎ করা, গলাধঃকরণ করা, গ্রাসকরা, উদরস্থ করা। **2.** To enjoy with avidity ; to gaze intently on ; to take in greedly with ears, eyes, etc. ; as, to *devour* a book, story, beauty or a beautiful person ; ব্যগ্রভাবে ভোগকরা ; সতৃষ্ণ নয়নে দৃষ্টিপাত করা, লোলুপ দৃষ্টিতে নিরীক্ষণ করা ; প্রবল আগ্রহের সহিত দর্শন, শ্রবণ বা পাঠ করা। **3.** To destroy ; to annihilate ; "Famine and pestilence shall *devour* him ;" ধ্বংস করা, নাশ করা ; কবলিত করা, কুক্ষিগত করা। **4.** To absorb the attention of ; নিবিষ্ট করা। **—ing-ly,** *adv.* **To devour the way etc.**—(In poetry) To go fast, especially as horses ; (কবিতায়) অতি দ্রুতবেগে চলা, নক্ষত্রবেগে ছুটা, তীরবেগে ধাবিত হওয়া।

dē-vout′ (-vowt), *adj.* **1.** Given up to religious thoughts and exercises ; pious ; reverent ; as, a *devout* man ; ধ্যাননিষ্ঠ ; ধর্ম্মনিষ্ঠ, ভজনশীল ; ভক্তিমান, ভক্তিপরায়ণ, ভক্তিপ্রবণ, ভক্তিনিষ্ঠ, দেবপরায়ণ, নিষ্ঠাবান, সাধু ; শ্রদ্ধালু, শ্রদ্ধাবান্। **2.** Hearty ; earnest ; genuine ; as, *devout* wishes for one's welfare ; আন্তরিক ; আগ্রহান্বিত ; অকৃত্রিম, অকপট। **3.** Expressive of devotion or piety ; "And eyes *devout*" — Milton ; ভক্তিব্যঞ্জক। **—ly,** *adv.* **—ness,** *n.*

dew (dū), *n.* **1.** Moisture condensed, especially at-night, upon the surface of certain cool bodies ; শিশির, নিহার, হিম, খজল, নিশাজল, রজনী-জল, নিশাপুষ্প (মঃ ইঃ)। **2.** (*Fig.*) Refreshing influence ; "The golden *dew* of sleep ;" (লক্ষণায়) আরামজনক প্রভাব, নবস্ফূর্ত্তি-সঞ্চারক প্রভাব। **3.** Early freshness ; fresh vigour ; "The *dew* of his youth" প্রভাতিক নবীনতা ; নবতেজ, নববল। **4.** Any beaded or glistening moisture as tears, sweat, etc. ; "*Dew* of lamentations" ; অশ্রুজল, স্বেদবিন্দু, প্রভৃতি। **Dew′-less, Dew′-y,** *adjs.* **Dew′-i-ly,** *adv.* **Dew-i-ness** *n.* **Dew-berry**—একপ্রকার আঁশ ফল। **Dew-claw**—কুকুরের পশ্চাদ্দিকের পদের অপরিণত মধ্যাঙ্গুলি। **Dew-drop**—শিশির-বিন্দু, নীহার-বিন্দু। **Dew-fall**—শিশির পাতের সময়, অর্থাৎ সায়াহ্ন ; শিশিরপাত, নীহারপাত। **Dew point**—বায়ুমণ্ডলের যেরূপ উষ্ণতায় শিশির বিন্দু উপজাত হয়, পরিবেকাঙ্ক (সাঃ পঃ) তুষারাঙ্ক (হিঃ কোঃ)। **Dew-rake**—একপ্রকার বিদা বা আঁচড়া। **Dew ret,** *v. t.* To rot away the gummy part of (hemp or flax) by exposure to dew and rain instead of steeping in water ; (শণ গাছ) শিশির বা বৃষ্টির জলে পচাইয়া (শণের) আটালোভোগ দুর করা। **Dew-worm** — The common earthworm ; কেঁচো। **Mountain-dew**—অবৈধভাবে প্রস্তুত হুইসকী।

dew (dū), *v. t.* & *i.* To wet with dew ; to moisten ; শিশিরসিক্ত করা ; সিক্ত করা, আর্দ্র করা। ***Verb i.*** To form or fall as dew ; as, it is beginning to *dew* ; শিশির গঠিত হওয়া, শিশির পড়া, ওস পড়া।

dew′-lăp (dū-), *n.* **1.** The pendulous skin under the throat of oxen, dogs, etc. ; গল-কম্বল, সাস্না (শিশুঃ)। **2.** The flesh of the human throat, that has become flaccid through age ; "On her withered *dewlap* pour the ale."—বার্দ্ধক্য হেতু লোলতাপ্রাপ্ত মনুষ্য-গল-চর্ম্ম। **—lap-ped,** *adj.*

dĕx′-têr, *adj.* Pertaining to, or situated on, the righthand side ; right, opposed to *left* ; দক্ষিণপার্শ্ব-সম্বন্ধীয়, দক্ষিণপার্শ্বে অবস্থিত ; দক্ষিণ, ডাহিন, অপসব্য (মঃ ইঃ)।

dĕx-têr′-i-tў, *n.* **1.** Physical adroitness or skill ; manual expertness ; করদক্ষতা, করকুশলতা, লঘুহস্ততা ; শিল্পাদি কার্য্যে নিপুণতা, পটুতা। **2.** Mental quickness or readiness ; skill in the management of a complicated affair ; tact ; as, the negotiation was conducted with *dexterity* ; তৎপরতা, সত্বর কার্য্যকারিতা ; কার্য্য-কুশলতা ; বিচক্ষণতা। **3.** Right-handedness ; দক্ষিণসাচিতা।

dĕx′-têr-ous (-ŭs), **—trous** (-trŭs), *adj.* Right-handed, (using the right hand by preference) ; skilful or clever in the use of hands etc. ; as, a *dexterous* workman ; দক্ষিণ-হস্ত কুশল ; করদক্ষ, কৃতহস্ত, লঘুহস্ত, দক্ষ। **2.** Done or managed with dexterity ; skilful ; "*Dexterous* of hands." দক্ষতার সহিত সম্পাদিত ; চাতুর্য্যপূর্ণ। **3.** Quick and ready in contrivance ; expert ; as, a *dexterous* manager ; ক্ষিপ্রহস্ত ; কার্য্যদক্ষ, কার্য্যকুশল। **—ly,** *adv.*

dĕx′-trin, *n.* (*Chem.*) Soluble gummy substance obtained from starch and used on adhesive stamps, etc. ; (রসায়ন শাস্ত্র) শ্বেতসার হইতে প্রাপ্ত তরল পদার্থে দ্রাব্য আঠালো জিনিষ,—ইহা ডাক টিকিট প্রভৃতিতে লাগান হয়।

dĕx′-trōse, *n.* A glucose sugar found in grapes etc., and manufactured from starch by means of sulphuric acid ; আঙ্গুরফল প্রভৃতিতে প্রাপ্ত শর্করা,—ইহা গন্ধক-দ্রাবক দ্বারা শ্বেতসার হইতে প্রস্তুত করা হয়।

-x′-trous, *adj.* Same as DEXTEROUS. **—ly,** *adv.*

-ey (dā), *n.* The governor of Algiers ; the ruler or pasha of Tunis or Tripoli ; এলজিয়ার্সের শাসনকর্ত্তা ; টিউনিস অথবা ত্রিপোলীর শাসনকর্ত্তা। [ষোড়শ শতাব্দীর পূর্ব্বে ফরাসীগণ দ্বারা অধিকৃত হওয়ার পূর্ব্ব পর্য্যন্ত।]

dhow (dow), **dow,** *ns.* A coasting vessel of Arabia, East Africa and the Indian ocean ; an Arab ship ; আরব, আফ্রিকা ও ভারতের উপকূলগামী জাহাজ ; আরবদেশবাসীদিগের জাহাজ।

-ī-ă-bē-tēs, *n.* A disease marked by a morbid and excessive discharge of urine ; বহুমূত্ররোগ, -তিসার, ইক্ষু-মেহ, মধুমেহ, সশর্কর মূত্র। **-bĕt′-ic,** *adj.* & *n.* Of or pertaining to diabetes ; বহুমূত্র-সংক্রান্ত, বহুমূত্রগ্রস্ত। ***Noun.*** A person suffering from diabetes ; বহুমূত্ররোগী।

-ī-â-′blĕ-rī, —blĕ-rie (-rī), *ns.* Devilry ; sorcery ; mischief ; love of devils ; wild recklessness ; শয়তানি ; যাদু, ভোজবিদ্যা, কুহক ; নষ্টামি ; পিশাচ-প্রীতি ; বেপরওয়া ভাব।

dī-ă-bŏl′-ic, —ĭ-căl, *adjs.* **1.** Pertaining to, or resembling, the devil ; concerned with, or proceeding from, the devil ; দানবীয়, পিশাচবৎ, অসুরবৎ, দানববৎ ; আসুরিক, ভৌতিক (মঃ ইঃ), বৈতালিক (ঐ)। **2.** Atrocious ; cruel ; outrageous ; as, a *diabolical* scheme ; পৈশাচিক ; ক্রূর, নৃশংস ; অমানুষিক। **—ly,** *adv.*

-ī-ăb′-ŏ-lĭsm, *n.* **1.** Devilish conduct or nature ; sorcery or black magic ; আসুরিক আচরণ বা স্বভাব, শয়তানি ; যাদু, প্রেতসিদ্ধি, পিশাচসিদ্ধি। **2.** The worship of, or belief in, the devil ; অসুর-পূজা, অসুরবিশ্বাস। **3.** Possession by the devil ; ভূতপ্রেতাদির আবেশ, ছাটা (*Colloq*), ভূতের দৃষ্টি।

dī-ăb′-ŏ-līze, *v. t.* To render devilish ; to make into a devil ; to represent as a devil ; আসুরিক করা ; দানব করিয়া তোলা ; দানবরূপে প্রদর্শন করা।

dī-ăb′-ŏ-lō, *n.* A game with two-headed top and sticks ; একপ্রকার ক্রীড়া।

dī-ăch′-ȳ-lŏn, —lŭm, —ăc′-ū-lŭm, *ns.* A common sticking-plaster ; বস্ত্রলিপ্ত মলম, পলস্তারা।

dī-ăc′-īd, *n.* দ্ব্যম্ল (হিঃ কোঃ)।

dī-ăc′-ŏ-năl, *adj.* Of or pertaining to a deacon ; খৃষ্টীয় উপাচার্য্য সম্বন্ধীয়।

dī′-ăc′-ŏ-nāte, *n.* The office of a deacon ; a body of deacons ; খৃষ্টীয় উপাচার্য্যের পদ, তদীয় পদের স্থিতি-কাল ; খৃষ্টীয় উপাচার্য্য সম্প্রদায়, খৃষ্টীয় উপাচার্য্যমণ্ডলী।

dī-ă-crit′-ĭ-căl, *adj.* **1.** Distinctive ; distinguishing ; as, *diacritical* signs ; প্রভেদজ্ঞাপক ; বিশেষক, বিভেদক। **2.** Capable of discerning distinctions ; "Where is his *diacritical* powers ; প্রভেদ-নিরাকরণক্ষম।

dī-ăc-tin′-ic, *adj.* Capable of transmitting the active or chemical rays of light ; আলোকের রাসায়নিক রশ্মিসঞ্চারণক্ষম। **Diactinic rays**—রাসায়নিক রশ্মি (হিঃ কোঃ)।

dī′-ă-dĕm, *n.* **1.** A band or fillet worn round the head as a badge of royalty ; a crown ; a wreath of leaves or flowers worn round the head ; রাজমুকুট, উষ্ণীষ, শেখর ; কিরীট, অবতংস ; পুষ্প রচিত শিরোমাল্য।

Diadem.

2. Sovereignty ; supreme power ; "Dandolo refused the *diadem* of all the Cæsars" ; রাজত্ব ; একাধিপত্য। **3.** Crowning glory or distinction ; সর্ব্বোচ্চ খ্যাতি বা গৌরব। **—ed,** *adj.* **Diadem spider**—একপ্রকার মাকড়সা।

dī-ær′-ĕ-sĭs, (-ĕr), **dī-ĕr′-,** *n.* **1.** (*Gram.*) Separation of one syllable into two ; (ব্যাকরণ) এক শব্দাংশকে দুইভাগে পৃথক্‌করণ। **2.** A mark (¨) placed over the second of two adjacent vowels to indicate that they should be separately pronounced, (as, aërated) ; পরস্পর-সংলগ্ন স্বরবর্ণদ্বয়ের দ্বিতীয়টীর উপর স্থাপিত (¨) চিহ্ন বিশেষ,—যদ্দ্বারা উভয়টী পৃথগ্‌ভাবে উচ্চারণ করিতে হইবে এই রূপ বুঝায়।

dī-ăg-nōse′, *v. t.* To determine from symptoms the nature of (a disease) ; লক্ষণ দৃষ্টে (রোগের) প্রকৃতি নির্ণয় করা।

dī-ăg-nō′-sĭs, *n.* **1.** The discrimination of diseases by their distinctive marks or symptoms ; a statement of this ; লক্ষণদৃষ্টে রোগ-নির্ণয়, রোগ-নির্ণয় (হিঃ কোঃ), রোগ-ভাবনা (কেণ্ডিঃ), নির্ণয়-তত্ত্ব (হঃচঃ) ; রোগ লক্ষণের বর্ণনা। **2.** Scientific determination of any kind ; assignment of species ; বৈজ্ঞানিক পন্থানুযায়ী নির্ণয় ; জাতি-নির্দ্দেশ। **3.** Critical perception of, or judgment concerning, motives or character ; "My *diagnosis* of his character proved correct ;" মানবের উদ্দেশ্য বা প্রকৃতি সম্বন্ধে সূক্ষ্ম অনুভূতি বা বিচার।

dī-ăg-nŏs′-tic, *adj.* & *n.* **1.** Pertaining to, or assisting, diagnosis ; রোগনির্ণয়-সম্বন্ধীয়, রোগনির্ণয়-সহায়ক। **2.** (*Med.*) Indicating the nature of a disease ; (ভৈষজ্য-শাস্ত্র) রোগ-লক্ষণ নির্দ্দেশক। **3.** (*Bot. & Zool.*) Distinguishing or determining the species ; (উদ্ভিদ-বিদ্যা এবং প্রাণি-বিদ্যা) জাতি-বিভেদক, জাতি-নির্ণায়ক।

Noun. A symptom ; রোগ-লক্ষণ। **–ti′-cian,** *n.* **–tics,** *n.* That branch of medicine to which the skill in noting and interpreting symptoms belongs ; ভৈষজ্য-শাস্ত্রের রোগ-লক্ষণ নির্ণয় বিষয়ক শাখা।

dī-ă-gŏm′-ĕ-têr, *n.* A form of electroscope for ascertaining conducting power ; বিদ্যুৎ-পরিচালনশক্তি-মাপক, বিদ্যুৎ-প্রবেশমাপক (হিঃ কোঃ)।

dī-ăg′-ō-năl, *adj.* & *n.* **1.** Joining two non-adjacent angles of a quadrilateral figure or multilateral figure and dividing it into two parts ; চতুর্ভুজ বা বহুভুজক্ষেত্রের পরস্পর বিপরীতদিগ্‌বর্ত্তী কোণদ্বয় সংযোজনকারী এবং উক্তরূপ ক্ষেত্রকে দ্বিবিভাগকারী, কর্ণ-স্বরূপ। **2.** Lying in an angular or oblique direction ; as, a *diagonal* row ; কোণাকুণি বা টের্চ্চাভাবে স্থিত, তির্য্যগ্‌গামী। **3.** Having diagonal parts or markings ; as, a *diagonal* cloth ; আড়কোণা। ***Noun.*** **1.** A straight line drawn between opposite angles of a figure of four or more sides and dividing it into two parts ; চতুর্ভুজ বা বহুভুজ ক্ষেত্রের পরস্পর বিপরীত দিগ্‌বর্ত্তী কোণদ্বয়-সংযোজক রেখা, কর্ণ (সাঃ পঃ) শ্রুতি (ঐ), কর্ণরেখা (যোঃ)। **2.** A diagonal cloth, (a kind of cloth having diagonal stripes, ridges, etc. made in the weaving) ; টের্চ্চাভাবে-বুনা ডোরা, শির প্রভৃতি বিশিষ্ট কাপড়। **–ly,** *adv.* **Diagonal scale**—একপ্রকার পরিমাণদণ্ড—ইহাতে এক সারি সমান্তরাল রেখা অপর এক সারি সমান্তরাল রেখাকে সমান সমান দূরে কর্ত্তিত করে,—এইরূপ পরিমাণ দণ্ডদ্বারা কোন পরিমাণের এককের ভগ্নাংশ নিরূপণ করা যায়।

Diagonal

dī′-ă-grăm, *n.* **1.** (*Geom.*) A figure or drawing for the purpose of demonstrating the properties of any definite figure, as a square, circle, etc. ; ক্ষেত্র (সাঃ পঃ), যন্ত্র। **2.** A sketch showing the features of an object needed for exposition ; symbolic representation, by lines, of force, process, etc. ; নক্‌সা, চিত্র ; রেখাদ্বারা বল, ক্রমিক গতি প্রভৃতির সাঙ্কেতিক প্রতিরূপ, পরিলেখ (হিঃ কোঃ)। **–gram′-mat-ize,** *v. t.* **–mat′-ic,** *adj.* **–mat′-i-cal-ly,** *adv.*

dī′-ă-grăph, *n.* An instrument for enabling unskilled persons to draw objects in outline ; একপ্রকার যন্ত্র,— ইহা দ্বারা আনাড়ী লোকেরা পদার্থ সমূহের রেখাচিত্র অঙ্কিত করিতে সমর্থ হয়, রেখা-চিত্রাঙ্কক।

dī′-ăl, *n.* & *v. t.* **1.** An instrument for showing the hour of the day by the sun's shadow upon a graduated plate, (usually called the *sundial*) ; সূর্য্যঘড়ী, প্রতোদ (মঃ ইঃ), ছায়াযন্ত্র (বৃঃ সং), শঙ্কু (যোঃ), শঙ্কু-যন্ত্র (আঃ বঃ) চক্রযন্ত্র (ঐ)। **2.** The graduated and numbered face-plate of a watch or clock, (also called *dial-plate*) ; ঘড়ী বা টেঁকঘড়ীর মুখপট্ট, ফলক (রবিঃ), শঙ্কুপট্ট, শঙ্কুবৃত্ত। **3.** A circular plate on which a moveable index shows the degree of pressure etc. ; as, the *dial* of a steam-gauge ; গোলাকৃতি ফলক-বিশেষ,—যদুপরি একটী সঞ্চরণশীল শঙ্কু চাপ প্রভৃতির পরিমাণ প্রদর্শন করে, যন্ত্রফলক। ***Verb t.*** To measure or indicate with, or as with, a dial ; "Hours of that true time which is *dialed* in heaven ;" সূর্য্যঘড়ীদ্বারা সময় নির্দ্দেশ বা পরিমাণ করা। **–a′-tion,** *n.* **Dial-plate**—See DIAL (2.)

dī′-ă-lĕct, *n.* **1.** Language ; "The universal *dialect* of the world ;" ভাষা। **2.** A form or subdivision of a language characterised by local peculiarities ; as, the York-shire *dialect* ; উপভাষা, প্রাদেশিক ভাষা, বুলি (*Colloq.*), দেশভাষা, প্রাকৃতভাষা। **3.** The cant or jargon of a class, profession, trade, etc. ; কোন বিশেষ শ্রেণী, সমাজ, ব্যবসায়ী প্রভৃতির সাম্প্রদায়িক ভাষা। **–lec′-tal,** *adj.* **–lec′-tal-ly,** *adv.* **–lec-tol′-o-gy,** *n.* That branch of philology which is devoted to the study of dialects ; ভাষাবিজ্ঞানের উপভাষা বিষয়ক শাখা, উপভাষাতত্ত্ব। **–lec-tol′-o-gist,** *n.*

dī-ă-lĕc′-tic, *n.* **1.** (*Modern Philos.*) Criticism dealing with metaphysical contradictions and their solution ; (আধুনিক দর্শনশাস্ত্র) তাত্ত্বিক বিরোধ এবং তৎসমন্বয়সংক্রান্ত সমালোচনা। **2.** (Often *pl.*) The art of reasoning or disputing ; that branch of logic which teaches the rules and modes of reasoning ; হেতুশাস্ত্র ; তর্কশাস্ত্র। **–ti′-cian** *n.* One versed in dialectics ; logician ; তর্কশাস্ত্রজ্ঞ ; তর্কশাস্ত্রি হেতুবিদ্যা বিশারদ (আঃ বঃ)।

dī-ă-lĕc′-tic, *adj.* & *n.* **1.** Pertaining to dialectics ; argumental ; logical ; addicted to the practice of dialectics ; তর্কপর, তর্কাশক্ত ; তর্ক-সম্বন্ধীয় ; তর্কাত্মক ; তর্কশাস্ত্রানুগত ; তর্ক-কুশল। **2.** Pertaining to a dialects ; উপভাষা সম্বন্ধীয়। ***Noun.*** A person addicted to the practice of dialectics ; তর্কপর ব্যক্তি, তর্কাশক্ত ব্যক্তি।

dī-ă-lĕc′-tĭ-căl, *adj.* Same as DIALECTIC (*adj.*) **–ly,** *adv.*

dī-ă-lŏg′-ic, *adj.* Of or relating to a dialogue ; in the form of a dialogue ; কথোপকথন-সম্বন্ধীয় ; কথোপকথনাত্মক।

dī-ăl′-ō-ġist, *n.* **1.** A speaker in a dialogue ; কথোপকথনকারী। **2.** A writer of dialogues ; কথোপকথনলেখক।

dī′-ă-logue (-lŏg), *n.* **1.** A conversation or discourse between two or more persons ; দ্বন্দালাপ, সংলাপ, উক্তি-প্রত্যুক্তি, কথোপকথন, সংবাদ, পরস্পর কথাবার্ত্তা। **2.** A composition in which two or more persons are represented as conversing on some topics ; as, the *dialogues* of Plato ; কথোপকথনাত্মক গ্রন্থ। **3.** The conversational part in a novel or drama ; নাটক বা উপন্যাসের কথোপকথনাত্মক অংশ। **—wise,** *adv.* In the form of a dialogue ; কথোপকথনাকারে।

dĭ-ăl′-ȳ-sĭs, *n.* **1.** (*Chem.*) The separation of the crystalloid elements of a body from the colloid by diffusion through a membranous septum or partition ; (রসায়ন-শাস্ত্র) কোন পদার্থের অ-দানাদার ভাগ হইতে দানাদার ভাগ পৃথকীকরণ, দ্বিবিশ্লেষণ-ক্রিয়া। **2.** (*Med.*) Debility ; dissolution of strength ; (ভৈষজ্যশাস্ত্র) দৌর্ব্বল্য ; শক্তিক্ষয়। **—a-lyt′-ic,** *adj.*

dĭ′-ă-lyse (-līz), *v. t.* To separate by dialysis ; দ্বিবিশ্লেষণ ক্রিয়াদ্বারা পৃথক্ করা।

dĭ-ă-măg-nĕt′-ic, *adj.* & *n.* Of or pertaining to diamagnetism ; আনুপ্রস্থিক চৌম্বকত্বসম্বন্ধীয়। [যে কাচ, বিষমদ (Bismuth) প্রভৃতির দণ্ড দোদুল্যমান অবস্থায় চৌম্বকশক্তি দ্বারা আক্রান্ত হইলে পূর্ব্ব পশ্চিমে অথবা চৌম্বক-কক্ষের সহিত অনুপ্রস্থে থাকিতে উন্মুখ হয়, তৎসম্বন্ধে উক্ত হইয়া থাকে।] ***Noun.*** A diamagnetic body or substance ; আনুপ্রস্থিক চৌম্বকত্বধর্ম্মা বস্তু বা পদার্থ, ব্যত্যস্ত-আকর্ষক। **—i-cal-ly,** *adv.* **—mag′-net-ize,** *v. t.*

dĭ-ă-măg′-nĕt-ĭsm, *n.* **1.** Diamagnetic tendency ; চৌম্বকশক্তি দ্বারা আক্রান্ত দোদুল্যমান কাচখণ্ড প্রভৃতির পূর্ব্ব-পশ্চিমে অথবা চৌম্বক-কক্ষের অনুপ্রস্থে স্থিতির উন্মুখতা, আনুপ্রস্থিক চৌম্বকত্ব। **2.** That branch of magnetism which treats of diamagnetic substances and phenomena ; চুম্বকবিজ্ঞানের আনুপ্রস্থিক চৌম্বকত্ববিষয়ক শাখা।

dĭ-ă-măn-tĭf′-êr-ous (-ĭs), *adj.* Yielding diamonds ; হীরকপ্রদ।

dĭ-ăm′-ē-têr, *n.* **1.** (*Geom.*) A straight line passing through the centre of a circle or other curvilinear figure, terminating each way in the circumference ; (জ্যামিতি) যে সরল রেখা বৃত্ত বা অন্যান্য বক্রাকার ক্ষেত্রের কেন্দ্রস্থল ভেদ করিয়া উভয় পার্শ্বে পরিধি স্পর্শ করে, ব্যাস, বিষ্কম্ভ (আঃ বঃ)।

Diameter

2. (*Arch.*) The measure across the lower part of the shaft of a column ; (স্থপতি-বিজ্ঞান) স্তম্ভ-দণ্ডের নিম্নাংশের ব্যাস। **3.** The unit of linear measurement of the magnifying power ; আয়তন-বৃদ্ধিকারিকা শক্তির রৈখিক পরিমাণের একক **—tral,** *adj.* **—tral-ly,** *adv.*

dĭ-ă-mĕt′-rĭ-căl, *adj.* **1.** Of or pertaining to a diameter ; ব্যাস-সম্বন্ধীয়। **2.** Directly adverse ; complete ; as, *diametrical* difference or opposition ; ঠিক বিপরীত ; পুরা। **—ly,** *adv.* In a diametrical manner ; directly ; completely ; as, *diametrically* opposite ; ব্যাসাভিমুখে ; সোজাভাবে ; সম্পূর্ণরূপে, পুরা।

dĭ′-ă-mŏnd, *n., adj.* & *v. t.* **1.** A precious stone of the most valuable kind, remarkable for its extreme hardness ; হীরক, হীরা, সূচীমুখ (মঃ ইঃ), ভার্গবপ্রিয় (ঐ), লোহজিৎ (ঐ), বজ্র। **2.** (*Geom.*) A figure of four equal sides with two obtuse and two acute angles ; a rhombus ; (জ্যামিতি) সমবাহুক চতুর্ভুজ,—যাহার দুইটী কোণ সূক্ষ্ম ও দুইটি কোণ স্থূল ; সমচতুর্ভুজ (হিঃ কোঃ)। **3.** A playing card bearing this figure ; রুহিতন। **4.** (*Print.*) Very small type used in English printing ; (মুদ্রণ) একপ্রকার অতিক্ষুদ্র ইংরাজী হরফ। **4.** (*Glazing*) A tool with a small diamond for cutting glass, (usually called *Glazier's* or *cutting diamond*) ; (কাচের কাজ) কাচ কর্ত্তনার্থ ক্ষুদ্র হীরকখণ্ড-সমন্বিত যন্ত্র বিশেষ, কাচকর্ত্তক। **5.** A glittering particle or point ; চাকচিক্যশালী কণা বা (যন্ত্রাদির) সূক্ষ্মাগ্র ভাগ। ***Adj.*** **1.** Made of or set with, a diamond or diamonds ; as, a *diamond* bracelet ; abounding in diamonds ; as, a *diamond* field ; হীরক-রচিত, হীরকনির্ম্মিত, হীরক-খচিত ; হীরকবহুল,। **2.** Shaped like a diamond or rhombus ; রুহিতনের আকৃতি। ***Verb t.*** To adorn with diamonds, dew-drops, etc. ; হীরক-ভূষিত করা, শিশিরবিন্দু-শোভিত করা। **—mon-dif′-er-ous,** *adj.* Yielding diamonds ; হীরকপ্রদ। **—wise,** *adv.* **Black diamond—**A dark coloured diamond ; কৃষ্ণবর্ণ হীরক, কৃষ্ণবজ্র। Coal ; কয়লা। **Bristol Diamond (cornish)** — হীরকসদৃশ মণিসকল। **Diamond-back**—Kinds of moth and turtle ; নানাজাতীয় তসরে পোকা এবং কূর্ম্ম। **Diamond-beetle** — একপ্রকার গোবরে পোকা। **Diamond-cement**—হীরক বসাইবার জন্য সংযোগসাধক পদার্থ বিশেষ। **Diamond-cutting** — হীরার পল কাটন। **Diamond-drill**—পাষাণাদিতে ছিদ্র করার জন্য বজ্র সূচী। **Diamond dust (powder)**—হীরকচূর্ণ। **Diamond-field**—যে অঞ্চলে হীরক পাওয়া যায়, হীরক-ক্ষেত্র। **Diamond jubille**—(সিংহাসনারোহণের) ষষ্ঠি বার্ষিক আনন্দোৎসব, হীরক জুবিলী। **Diamond-point** — A tool with a diamond shaped point used in engraving ; খোদাইর কাজে ব্যবহৃত হীরকাগ্র যন্ত্র। (Usually *pl.*) A place where two lines intersect obliquely ; (সাধারণতঃ বহুবচন) যে স্থানে দুইটী রেখা বা লৌহবর্ত্মের

পাতা রেল পরস্পরকে কোণাকুণি ভাবে ছেদন করে। **Diamond-snake**—অষ্ট্রেলিয়া ও তাসমেনিয়ার সর্পবিশেষ। **Diamond wedding** — The 60th anniversary ; ষষ্ঠি বাৎসরিক উৎসব। **Diamond wheel**—(বিবাহের) হীরক এবং অন্যান্য মূল্যবান প্রস্তর পালিশ করার জন্য হীরকচূর্ণ এবং তৈল দ্বারা মাখানো চক্র। **Glazier's or cutting diamond** — See DIAMOND (4). **Rough diamond** — An uncut diamond ; অকর্ত্তিতহীরক। A person of intrinsic worth but rough manners ; বাহ্য আচরণে রূঢ় গুণী ব্যক্তি। **Small diamond** — রুহিতনের ছোট তাস। **A diamond of the first water**—A man of the highest merit ; গুণিগণশ্রেষ্ঠ, মনুষ্য-রত্ন। **Diamond cut diamond** — সেয়ানে সেয়ানে কোলাকুলি।

Dī-ăn'-ă, *n.* (*L. myth.*) The daughter of Jupiter and Latona, the goddess of hunting and chastity, (later on identified with the Greek Artemis) ; (রোমীয় পুরাণ) মৃগয়া ও সতীত্বের অধিষ্ঠাত্রীদেবী, জুপিটার ইহার পিতা, লেটোনাদেবী ইহার মাতা।

dī-ăn'-drous (-drŭs), *adj.* Having two stamens ; দ্বিকেশরী (সাঃ পঃ)।

dī-ȧ-nō-ĕt'-ic, *adj.* Of or pertaining to reasoning ; প্রজ্ঞান-সম্বন্ধীয়।

dī-ȧ-pā'-sŏn, *n.* **1.** (*Greek music*) The interval or consonance of the octave ; (গ্রীসদেশীয় সঙ্গীতশাস্ত্র) স্বরগ্রামের স্বরসমূহের মধ্যে পরস্পর অবকাশ বা সামঞ্জস্য। **2.** Combination of notes or parts in a harmonious whole ; স্বরসমন্বয়। **3.** A fixed standard of musical pitch ; as, the French normal *diapason* ; সুরের নির্দ্দিষ্ট গ্রাম। **4.** Melody ; a grand swelling burst of harmony ; সুতান, সুস্বর ; একতানবাক্য বা সঙ্গীতের প্রবল উচ্ছ্বাস। **5.** The entire compass of the tones of a voice or of an instrument ; "The *diapason* closing full in man ;" পূর্ণস্বরগ্রাম, সপ্তক, স্বরাষ্টক। **6.** One of the two principal foundation stops of an organ, (*open* and *stopped* or *closed diapason*) ; অর্গেন নামক বাদ্য যন্ত্রের চাবিবিশেষ। **7.** Range ; "Those who run up to the topmost note of the *diapason* of dress ;" গ্রাম, প্রসর।

dī'-ȧ-pēr, *n.* & *v. t.* **1.** A linen or cotton cloth woven with a pattern of flowers or figures constantly repeated ; ফুল প্রভৃতি বুনা কাপড়। **2.** (*Fine arts*) An ornamental design of diamond reticulation for panels, walls, etc. ; (ললিত-কলা) দ্বার, দ্বার-প্রকোষ্ঠ প্রভৃতিতে রুহিতনের আকারে জালের কাজ। **3.** A towel or napkin for wiping the hands etc. ; হাত প্রভৃতি মুছিবার রুমাল বা তোয়ালে।

Diaper ornament.

4. A square piece of cloth for wrapping about the hips of a child ; শিশুর নিতম্ব দেশে জড়াইবার সমচতুষ্কোণ বস্ত্র-খণ্ড। ***Verb t.*** To decorate with figures etc. arranged in the pattern called diaper ; "And *diapered* with inwrought flowers" ; বুনার সময় কাপড়ের উপর ফুল প্রভৃতি তোলা।

dī-ȧ-phăn'-ō-scōpe, *n.* A dark box for exhibiting transparent pictures with or without a lens ; বিমলচিত্রসমীক্ষক (হিঃ কোঃ)।

dī-ăph'-ȧ-nous (-nŭs), *adj.* Transparent ; clear ; স্বচ্ছ ; বিমল, নির্ম্মল, পারদর্শক (হিঃ কোঃ), স্ফটিকপ্রভ (মঃ ইঃ)।

dī-ȧ-phō-rē'-sis, *n.* Perspiration ; ঘর্ম্ম, স্বেদ।

dī-ȧ-phō-rĕt'-ic, *adj.* & *n.* Having power to increase perspiration ; স্বেদোৎপাদক, ঘর্ম্মোৎপাদক, স্বেদবর্দ্ধক, ঘর্ম্মবর্দ্ধক। ***Noun.*** A diaphoretic agent ; স্বেদোপজ বস্তু, ঘর্ম্মবৃদ্ধিকারক ঔষধ।

dī'-ȧ-phōte, *n.* (*Elect.*) A telephote ; (তাড়িত-বিদ্যা) বিদ্যুৎ-চিত্র-লেখক যন্ত্র (হিঃ কোঃ)।

dī'-ȧ-phrăgm (-frăm), *n.* **1.** A muscle separating the chest or thorax from the abdomen, (the *midriff*) ; যে পেশীদ্বারা বক্ষ হইতে উদর পৃথকীকৃত হয়, বক্ষোদর-ব্যবধায়ক পেশী। **2.** A dividing membrane or thin partition ; ব্যবধায়ক ঝিল্লী। **3.** (*Opt.*) A metal plate with a central hole for cutting off side-rays in a camera, telescope, etc. ; (দৃষ্টি-বিজ্ঞান) মধ্যভাগে রন্ধ্র বিশিষ্ট ধাতু-ফলক বিশেষ,—ইহাদ্বারা আলোক-চিত্র গ্রাহক-যন্ত্র, দূরবীক্ষণ যন্ত্র প্রভৃতির পার্শ্বিক কিরণ সমূহ ছেদিত হইয়া থাকে, পার্শ্বাংশুচ্ছেদক। **4.** (*Zool.*) A calcareous plate which divides the cavity of certain shells into two parts ; (জন্তুবিদ্যা) যে চূর্ণকময় ফলকদ্বারা কোন কোন শম্বূক জাতীয় জন্তুর দেহগহ্বর দ্বিধা বিভক্ত হয়, ব্যবধায়ক। **5.** (*Bot.*) A transverse partition in a stem or leaf ; (উদ্ভিদ্-বিদ্যা) কাণ্ড বা পত্রের অনুপ্রস্থ-গামী বিভাজক, ব্যবধান (সাঃ পঃ)। **6.** (*Mach.*) A partition in any compartment for various purposes ; (যন্ত্র) যন্ত্রপ্রকোষ্ঠ-বিভাজক। **—phrag-mat'-ic**, *adj.*

dī'-ȧ-rist, *n.* One who keeps a diary ; দৈনন্দিন-লিপি লেখক, রোজ নামচা লেখক। **—ris'-tic**, *adj.*

dī'-ȧ-rīze, *v. i.* & *t.* To keep diary ; দৈনন্দিন লিপি লেখা, রোজ

নামা রাখা। *Verb t.* To enter in a diary; দৈনন্দিন লিপিতে বা রোজ নামচায় লিখা।

dī-ăr-rhœ'-ă (-rē-), **-rhe'-** (-rē-), *n.* Excessive purging or looseness of the bowels; উদরাময়, অতিসার (সাঃ পঃ), প্রবাহিকা (আঃ বঃ)। **—al, —rhœ'-ic,** *adjs.*

dī-âr-thrō'-sis, *n.* (*Anat.*) A form of articulation which admits of considerable motion; (শারীর-সংস্থান বিদ্যা) চল-সন্ধি, সচল অস্থি-সন্ধি (হঃ চঃ)।

dī'-ă-rȳ, *n.* A register of daily events or transactions; a calender with blank spaces for notes, memoranda, etc.; as, a physician's *diary*; a daily record; as, a *diary* of the weather; দৈনন্দিন-লিপি, দিন-বৃত্ত পত্র, রোজনামা, রোজনামচা; একপ্রকার পঞ্জিকা,—যাহাতে মন্তব্যাদি টুকিবার জন্য সাদা জায়গা থাকে; দৈনিক বিবৃতি, দৈনিক বিবরণী, দিনপত্রিকা (আঃ বঃ), দৈনিক পুস্তক (ঐ)। **—a'-ri-al,** *adj.*

dī'-ă stāse, *n.* (*Physiol.* & *chem.*) A nitrogenous substance produced during the malting of grain; জলে নিমজ্জিত শস্যাদির অঙ্কুরোদ্গম কালে যে যবক্ষার বাষ্পাত্মক পদার্থ উৎপন্ন হয়, শ্বেতসার-কিণ্ব (সাঃ পঃ)।

dī-ăs'-tă'-sis, *n.* A forcible separation of two bones previously in contact, or of the pieces of a fractured bone; ভগ্ন অস্থির সন্ধি-বিচ্যুতি (হঃ চঃ), বিসন্ধান (ঐ)।

dī-ăs'-tō-lē, *n.* **1.** (*Physiol.*) Dilation of the heart and arteries—(opposed to *systole* or contraction of the same); (শারীর-বিজ্ঞান) রক্ত-প্রবেশ বশতঃ হৃৎপিণ্ডের গহ্বর ও ধমনীর প্রসারণ, যুগ্ম-প্রসার, প্রসার (সাঃ পঃ)। **2.** (*Gr.* and *L. Prosody*) The protracting of a short syllable; a figure by which a syllable naturally short is made long; (গ্রীক ও ল্যাটিন ছন্দঃশাস্ত্র) শব্দাংশের প্রসার; যে চিহ্ন দ্বারা শব্দাংশ প্রসারিত হয়।

dī-ă-tĕs'-să-rŏn, *n.* **1.** A harmony of the four gospels; যীশুখৃষ্টের শিষ্যগণ কর্তৃক লিখিত সুসমাচার-চতুষ্টয়ের সমন্বয়, সমাচার-সমন্বয়। **2.** (*Old Med.*) A medicine made of four ingredients; (প্রাচীন ভৈষজ্য শাস্ত্র) চারি উপাদানের মিশ্রণে প্রস্তুত ঔষধ।

dī-ă-thêr'-măn-çȳ, *n.* The quality of transmitting radiant heat; উষ্ণতা-বাহিকা শক্তি। **—ma-nous, —mic,** *adjs.* Having the property of transmitting radiant heat; উষ্ণতাবাহী।

dī-ăth'-ē-sis, *n.* A particular condition of body; predisposition to certain diseases rather than to others; বিশেষ প্রকৃতি (হঃ চঃ); রোগবিশেষ প্রবণতা (হিঃ কোঃ)।

dī'-ă-tŏm, *n.* One of a natural order of microscopic vegetable organisms with siliceous coverings; আণুবীক্ষণিক উদ্ভিজ্জ বিশেষ, দ্বিদলঅণু (সাঃ পঃ)। **—a'-ceous,** *adj.*

dī-ă-tŏm'-ic, *adj.* (*Chem.*) Consisting of two atoms; (রসায়নশাস্ত্র) দ্বিপরমাণুক (হিঃ কোঃ)।

dī-ă-tŏn'-ic, *adj.* (*Mus.*) Proceeding by notes proper to a key without chromatic alteration; constructed from such a scale; as, *diatonic* harmonies or melodies; (সঙ্গীত-বিদ্যা) সপ্তক-সম্বন্ধীয়; সপ্তক হইতে গঠিত। **Diatonic scale**—সপ্তক।

dī'-ă-trībe, *n.* A bitter critical discussion; a strain of abusive languages; উত্তেজিত আলোচনা; গালাগালি বর্ষণ।

dib, *v. i.* Same as DAP which see.

dī-băs'-ic, *adj.* (*Chem.*) Having two atoms of hydrogen replaceable by basic atoms, in forming salts; (রসায়নশাস্ত্র) দ্বিভাস্মিক (হিঃ কোঃ)।

dib'-bêr, *n.* A pointed instrument used in gardening to make holes for planting seed etc., (also *dibble*); খুরপা, বীজাদি রোপণের গর্ত্ত করিবার জন্য সূক্ষ্মাগ্র খনিত্র।

dib'-ble, *n., v. t.* & *i.* A dibber; খুরপা। *Verb t.* To sow or plant with a dibble; to make holes in (soil) with a dibble for planting; to use as a dibble; খুরপা দ্বারা রোপণ করা; খুরপা দ্বারা গর্ত্ত করত বপন বা রোপণ করা; খুরপার মত ব্যবহার করা। *Verb i.* To dip or dib in angling; বড়শীর টোপ আস্তে আস্তে জলে ডোবান।

dibs, *n. pl.* **1.** Small bones in the knee of a sheep uniting the bones above and below the joints; (বহুবচন) মেষের অস্থি-সন্ধির ঊর্দ্ধ ও নিম্নস্থিত অস্থিদ্বয় সংযোজক ক্ষুদ্র অস্থিসমূহ। **2.** A child's game played by throwing up dib bones from the palm and catching them on the back of the hand; (বহুবচন) ক্রীড়া বিশেষ, উহাতে উক্ত প্রকার অস্থিখণ্ড সমূহ হাতের চেটো হইতে হাতের পিঠে ধরা হয়, গুট-খেলা। **3.** Counters at cards; একপ্রকার তাসের ক্রীড়ার হিসাব রাখিবার জন্য হাতীর দাঁত প্রভৃতির গুটি। **4.** (*Slang*) money; (ইতর ভাষায়) টাকা কড়ি।

dī'-căst, *n.* (*Gr. Antq.*) An officer of ancient Athens corresponding to the modern jury man, who gave both verdict and judgment; প্রাচীন এথেনস্ নগরীর জুরিগণের অন্যতম,—ইহারা অপরাধ সম্বন্ধে অভিমত ও দণ্ডাজ্ঞা উভয়ই প্রদান করিতেন। **—cas'-ter-y,** *n.*

dīçe, *n., v. i.* & *t.* (Pl. of die) A game played with die; পাশা খেলা, দ্যুত-ক্রীড়া, অক্ষ-ক্রীড়া। *Verb i.* To play at dice; "I *diced* not above seven times a week;" পাশা খেলা, অক্ষ ক্রীড়া করা।

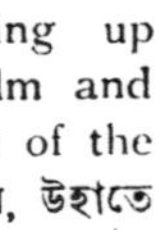

Dice.

Verb t. **1.** To gamble *away* at dice ; "Have I to *dice* my patrimony *away* ; পাশা খেলায় উড়াইয়া দেওয়া। **2.** To ornament or mark with squares etc. ; সমচতুষ্কোণ ক্ষেত্রাদিদ্বারা ভূষিত বা চিহ্নিত করা। **3.** To cut into dice or cubes as a bread ; পাউরুটী প্রভৃতি ঘনক্ষেত্রাকারে কাটা। **Di'-cer,** *n.* A player at dice ; অক্ষক্রীড়ক, দ্যূতকার। **Dice-box,** *n.* একপ্রকার বাক্স,—যাহা হইতে পাশা নিক্ষিপ্ত হয়। **Dice-box-insulator** — তাড়িত-বার্ত্তাবহের তার বাঁধার জন্য ঘণ্টাকৃতি চিনামাটীর খণ্ড। **Dice-coal**—এক প্রকার কয়লা যাহা ঘনক্ষেত্রাকার খণ্ডে খণ্ডে দ্রুতবিদীর্ণ হইয়া থাকে।

dī-c̲h̲lă-mȳd'-ē-ous, (-ŭs), *adj.* (*Bot.*) Having both a calyx and a corolla ; (উদ্ভিদ্-বিদ্যা) বহিরাবরণ ও অন্তরাবরণ বিশিষ্ট, দ্বিপরিচ্ছদ (সাঃ পঃ)।

dī-c̲h̲ŏg'-ă-mous (-mŭs), *adj.* (*Bot.*) Having stamens and pistils that ripens at different times so that self-fertilization is impossible ; (উদ্ভিদ্-বিদ্যা) ভিন্ন ভিন্ন সময়ে পরিপক্ব হয়—এরূপ স্ত্রী ও পুং-কেশরবিশিষ্ট (অতএব আত্মনিষেক অসম্ভব)।

dī-c̲h̲ŏt'-ŏ-mȳ, *n.* **1.** A division into two parts ; দ্বি-বিভাগ খণ্ডবিশ্লেষ। **2.** (*Log.*) The division of a class or genus into two sub-classes or genera opposed to each other by contradiction ; as, the division of the class "man"—into "white and not white" ; (তর্কবিজ্ঞান) কোন শ্রেণী বা গণকে পরস্পর বিরোধী উপশ্রেণী বা গণদ্বয়ে বিভাগ, দ্বৈরাজ্য (হিঃ কোঃ), দ্বৈরাজ্যকরণ (ঐ) **3.** (*Astron.*) That phase of the moon at which exactly half the disk appears illuminated ; (জ্যোতি-র্বিজ্ঞান) অষ্টমীর চন্দ্র, অর্দ্ধচন্দ্র (হিঃ কোঃ)। **4.** (*Bot.*) Repeated bifurcation into two uniformly developed branches ; (উদ্ভিদ্-বিদ্যা) সমপরিণতি-প্রাপ্ত শাখাদ্বয়ে পুনরায় বিভক্ত হওন, দ্ব্যন্তশাখোদ্গাম (সাঃ পঃ), দ্ব্যগ্রবর্দ্ধী। **–mist,** *n.* **–mize,** *v. t.* & *i.* To part into two divisions ; to cut into two ; দ্বিবিভক্ত করা ; দ্বিখণ্ডিত করা। (*Verb i*) To become dichotomous or separated into two parts ; দ্বি-বিভক্ত হওয়া, দ্বিখণ্ডিত হওয়া। **–mous,** *adj.* **–mous-ly,** *adv.* **–om'-ic,** *adj.*

dī-c̲h̲rō'-ic, *adj.* Showing different colours when viewed in different directions, as doubly refracting crystals ; বিভিন্নদিক হইতে দৃষ্ট হইলে বিভিন্ন বর্ণ-দর্শক, দ্বিরঙ্গ-দর্শক, দ্বিরাগ-দর্শক, দ্বিবর্ণ-দর্শক।

di'-c̲h̲rō-ism, *n.* A property possessed by several crystallized bodies of appearing under two distinct colours according to the direction in which light is transmitted to them ; কতিপয় স্ফটিকীভূত বস্তুর বিশেষ ধর্ম্ম,—যদ্দারা ইহারা বিভিন্ন দিগ্ হইতে আলোক-সঞ্চার হেতু বিভিন্ন বর্ণের বলিয়া প্রতিভাত হইয়া থাকে, দ্বিবর্ণ-প্রদর্শনকারিতা, দ্বিবর্ণ দৃষ্টি (হিঃ কোঃ), দ্বিরাগপ্রদর্শনকারিতা।

dī-c̲h̲rō-măt'-ic, *adj.* Having or exhibiting two colours, (esp. of animal species of which the individuals show different colourations) ; দ্বি-বর্ণ, দ্বিরঙ্গ-দর্শক।

dī-c̲h̲rō'-mic, *adj.* With only two colours, (esp. of defective vision seeing only two of the three primary colours) ; দ্বিবর্ণদর্শী, বিশেষতঃ দৃষ্টি-শক্তি বিকল হইলে যে অবস্থায় কেবল মাত্র দুইটী মূলবর্ণ দৃষ্ট হয়।

dī'-chrō-scōpe, *n.* An instrument for testing dichroism of crystals ; দ্বিবর্ণ-বীক্ষণ (সাঃ পঃ), দ্বিরাগ-দর্শক।

dĭck, *n.* **1.** (*Slang*) (Short for Richard) Hence fellow ; lad ; (ইতর ভাষায়) (রিচার্ড নামের সংক্ষেপ) লোক ; ছোকরা। **2.** A riding whip ; ঘোড়ার চাবুক। **3.** A leather apron ; দেহের সম্মুখভাগে পরিধেয় চর্ম্মনির্ম্মিত পরিচ্ছদ পরিরক্ষক। **To take one's dick**—(*Slang*) To swear ; to affirm; (ইতর ভাষায়) শপথ করা ; দৃঢ় করিয়া বলা। **Up to dick**—Excellent ; properly ; সাবাস, চমৎকার ; যথোচিতভাবে।

dĭck'-ĕns, *n.* (*Colloq.*) The devil, as in 'what the Dickens' ; (চলিত ভাষায়) শয়তান, ভূত। **To play the dickens**—To play the deuce or devil with ; to ruin or spoil ; ভুতুড়ে কাণ্ড করা ; লণ্ডভণ্ড করা।

dĭck'-ĕr, *n.* (*Com.*) The number ten of any commodity, esp. of hides ; as, a *dicker* of gloves ; (বাণিজ্য) কোন জিনিষের দশটী (বিশেষতঃ চামড়ার)।

dĭck'-ĕr, *v. i.* To barter ; to haggle (*U. S.*); দ্রব্য বিনিময় ব্যবসায় করা ; দর কষাকষি করা (মার্কিণ যুক্ত রাজ্যে)।

dĭck'-ȳ, *n.* **1.** A leathern apron ; দেহের সম্মুখভাগে পরিধেয় চর্ম্মনির্ম্মিত পরিচ্ছদ। **2.** A seat behind a carriage for a servant ; the driver's seat in a carriage ; গাড়ীর পশ্চাদ্ভাগে অনুচরের জন্য আসন ; গাড়ী-চালকের আসন। **3.** A false shirt front ; কামিজের কৃত্রিম বুক। **4.** (*Colloq.* & *Slang*) A donkey ; (চলিত বা ইতরভাষায়) ; গাধা। **5.** A small bird, (also *dicky-bird*) ; ক্ষুদ্র পক্ষী। **All dicky with any one**—A hopeless case for any one ; কাহারো পক্ষে সম্পূর্ণ নিরাশজনক বিষয়।

dĭck'-ȳ, *adj.* (*Slang*) Unsound ; shaky ; queer ; (ইতরভাষা) অসুস্থ ; নড়নড়ে; অপরূপ।

dī-cŏt-ȳ-lē'-don (-dŭn), *n.* A flowering plant having two cotyledons or seed leaves; দ্বিপর্ণিক, দ্বিপত্রী (সাঃ পঃ), দ্বি-বীজদল। **–led'-on-ous,** *adj.*

Dicta probantia—প্রমাণোক্তি (হিঃ কোঃ) ; বেদবাক্য (ঐ), আপ্ত বাক্য।

dĭc'-tāte, *v. t.* & *i.* **1.** To tell or read aloud (matter to be written down), as to a writer ; to compose ; inspire ; "Pages *dictated* by the Holy spirit" —(লিখিতব্য বিষয়) বলা বা উচ্চৈঃস্বরে পাঠ করা ; রচনা করা ; অনুপ্রাণিত করা। **2.** To lay down or prescribe authoritatively ; as, to *dictate* the terms of a treaty ; to impose ; to deliver to a subordinate ; as, a general *dictates* orders to his troops ; নির্দ্দেশ করা ; ব্যবস্থা করা, বিধান করা, নির্দ্ধারিত করা, ধার্য্য করা, স্থাপন করা ; অধীন কর্ম্মচারীর উপর জারী বা প্রচার করা। ***Verb i.*** **1.** To give orders ; to propose or impose terms ; আদেশ প্রদান করা ; কোন সর্ত্ত বা প্রস্তাব নির্দ্ধারণ করা। **2.** To say or recite something to be written or said by another ; অন্য কর্ত্তৃক বক্তব্য বা লিখিতব্য কোন বিষয় বলা বা আবৃত্তি করা। **—ta'-tion,** *n.* **1.** The act of dictating ; an authoritative or arbitrary command ; বক্তব্য বা লিখিতব্য বিষয় কথন বা উচ্চৈঃস্বরে আবৃত্তি করণ ; আদেশ, নিদেশ, হুকুম। **2.** That which is dictated ; শ্রুতলিপি, শ্রুতলিখন।

dic'-tāte, (*often in pl.*) *n.* An authoritative order or direction ; as, listen to the *dictates* of your conscience ; (*obs.*) a maxim ; আদেশ, নিদেশ ; (অপ্রচলিত) নীতিবাক্য, বিধি।

dic-tā'-tor (-tēr), *n.* **1.** One who dictates to a writer ; যে ব্যক্তি কোন লিখিতব্য বিষয় আবৃত্তি করে। **2.** One who prescribes rules etc. authoritatively for the direction of others ; "The *dictators* of behaviour, dress and politeness ;" আদেশ-কর্ত্তা, ব্যবস্থাকারী। **3.** One invested for a time with absolute authority ; a temporary absolute ruler of a state, esp. one who suppresses or succeeds a republican government ; যে ব্যক্তিকে সাময়িকভাবে অসীম ক্ষমতা প্রদত্ত হইয়া থাকে ; কোন রাজ্যের সাময়িক স্বৈর নৃপতি, বিশেষতঃ প্রজাতন্ত্রের উচ্ছেদসাধন, অথবা প্রজাতন্ত্রের বিলোপের পর যে ব্যক্তি শাসনভার গ্রহণ করে, অনিয়ন্ত্রিত শাসনকর্ত্তা, একাধিপতি। **—ship,** *n.* **—tress,** *n.* (*fem.*) ; A woman who dictates or commands ; "Earth's chief *dictatress*, ocean's mighty queen."—আদেশ-কর্ত্রী।

dic-tā-tö'-ri-ăl, *adj.* **1.** Of or pertaining to a dictator ; অনিয়ন্ত্রিত শাসক সম্বন্ধীয়। **2.** Overbearing ; imperious ; as, a *dictatorial* tone or manner ; প্রভুত্বকারী, অভিভবকারী ; দাম্ভিক, প্রভুত্বব্যঞ্জক, প্রভুত্বসূচক, প্রভুত্বপরায়ণ। **—ly,** *adv.*

dic'-tion, *n.* Style or mode of expression ; as, the *diction* of Chaucer's poems ; বাগ্‌বিন্যাস-প্রণালী, শব্দ বিন্যাসরীতি, রচনা-রীতি, বাগ্‌রীতি, বাগ্‌ব্যাপার, বাগ্‌ধারা।

dic'-tion-ă-ry, *n.* **1.** A book containing the words of any language in alphabetical order with their meanings, etymology, etc. ; অভিধান, কোষ, শব্দকোষ। **2.** Any work containing information on any department of knowledge, alphabetically arranged ; as, a *dictionary* of medicine or botany ; যে পুস্তকে কোন বিষয়ের জ্ঞাতব্য বিষয় সমূহ বর্ণানুক্রমে সজ্জিত হইয়া থাকে। **Dictionary catalogue**—যে তালিকা পুস্তকে বিষয় সমূহ বর্ণানুক্রমে লিখিত হয়। **Dictionary English** or **style**—অতি মাত্রায় শুদ্ধ ইংরেজী বা পাণ্ডিত্য-প্রদর্শী ভাষা। **Walking** or **living dictionary** — বহু বিষয়ে সুপণ্ডিত ব্যক্তি, সচল অভিধান।

dic'-tŭm, (*Pl.* -TUMS, -TA) **1** An authoritative statement ; "Critical *dicta* everywhere current ;" আদেশ, উক্তি, বাক্য, বচন। **2.** (*Law*) A judge's expression of opinion not having any legal validity ; (আইন) বিচারকের মত প্রকাশ (যাহা আইনতঃ বলবৎ নহে)। **3.** A maxim ; a current saying ; নীতিবাক্য ; প্রবচন। **Dictum de Omni et Nullo**—একটী শ্রেণীতে যাহা আছে তৎশ্রেণীভুক্ত প্রত্যেক বস্তুতেই তাহা আছে ; যদ্বর্গে তদেকস্মিন্ (হিঃ কোঃ)।

did, past tense of DO.

dĭ-dăc'-tic, *adj.* Adapted or fitted to teach ; instructive ; teaching some moral lesson ; as, *didactic* essays ; শিক্ষাদানোপযোগী ; উপদেশক, উপদেশাত্মক, উপদেশ-গর্ভ ; নীতিগর্ভবিষয় শিক্ষাদানকারী, সৌত্র। **—ti-cal-ly,** *adv.* **—ti-cism,** *n.*

dĭ-dăc'-tics, *n.* The art or science of teaching ; শিক্ষাশাস্ত্র (হিঃ কোঃ), শিক্ষানীতি, সূত্র।

dī'-dăp-pêr, *n.* A small diving water-fowl ; একপ্রকার ক্ষুদ্র ডুবুরী পক্ষী, প্লব পক্ষী।

did'-dle, *v. t.* To shake ; টলমল করা, লড়বড় করা, নড় নড় করা।

did'-dle, *v. t.* (*Slang*) To cheat ; (ইতর ভাষায়) ঠকান, ধোকা দেওয়া।

dī-dŷm'-i-ŭm, *n.* (*Chem.*) A rare metallic substance ; (রসায়ন-শাস্ত্র) দুষ্প্রাপ্য ধাতব পদার্থ বিশেষ, জিতুমক (সাঃ পঃ)।

did'-ŷ-mous (-mŭs), *adj.* Twin ; মিথুন।

die (dī), *n.* (*Pl.* DICE, DIES) **1.** A small cube with spots from one to six on its faces, used in gaming by being thrown from a box ; (*pl.* DICE) ; অক্ষ, পাশা, দেবল (মঃ উঃ), গুটিকা। **2.** Any small cubical body ; ক্ষুদ্র ঘনক্ষেত্রাকার বস্তু। **3.** Hazard ; chance ; "Such is the *die* of war ;" সঙ্কট ; দৈব। (In the following senses the *pl.* form is DIES)—**1.** A stamp for impressing coin, etc ; মুদ্রা প্রভৃতিতে ছাপ দিবার মোহর। **2.** (*Arch.*) The cubical part or dado of a pedestal ; (স্থপতি-বিজ্ঞান) পাদপীঠের ঘনক্ষেত্রাকার অংশ, কণ্ঠ (রাঃ রাঃ)।

Die-sinker — মোহর খোদাইকারী। **Die-work**—মোহর দ্বারা ধাতুফলকের উপর ছাপের কাজ। **False die**—কপট পাশা, কূটাক্ষ। **Upon the die**—At stake; পণ-স্বরূপ। **The die is cast** or **thrown** — The question is irrevocably decided; the decisive measure is taken; হাতের ঢিল ছোড়া হইয়াছে, কোন বিষয়ের চূড়ান্ত নিষ্পত্তি হইয়াছে; চরম উপায় অবলম্বন করা হইয়াছে।

die (dī), *v. i.* **1.** (Of animate beings and plants) To perish; to lose life; to expire; (often with *of, by, with, from,* etc.); as, to *die of* a disease; মরা; প্রাণত্যাগ করা; প্রাণবায়ু বহির্গত হওয়া, গতায়ু হওয়া, পঞ্চত্ব প্রাপ্ত হওয়া। **2.** (*Fig.*) To cease to exist; to become extinct or extinguished; as, my secrets shall *die* with me: (লক্ষণায়) অস্তিত্ব লুপ্ত হওয়া, লুপ্ত হওয়া; নির্ব্বাপিত হওয়া, নির্ব্বাণপ্রাপ্ত হওয়া। **3.** To sink; to languish with affection, weakness, etc.; "His heart *died* within him and he became as a stone": "They (young men) *died* for Rebecca;" অবসন্ন হওয়া, দমা; (স্নেহ, প্রেম, দৌর্ব্বল্য প্রভৃতি হেতু) খিন্ন হওয়া, ক্ষীণ হওয়া, বিশীর্ণ হওয়া, ম্রিয়মাণ হওয়া, নির্জীব হওয়া, নিস্তেজ হওয়া। **4.** To become gradually less distinct or perceptible; to vanish; (often with *away*); as, the sound *died away* in the distance; ক্রমশঃ অস্পষ্ট বা মন্দীভূত হওয়া; বিলীন হওয়া। **5.** To become insensible like one dead; as, to *die* to the world; জীবন্মৃত হওয়া। **6.** To suffer spiritual death; "Whosoever believeth in me shall never *die*"—John IX 26.; আধ্যাত্মিক মৃত্যু হওয়া। **7.** To endure sufferings like those of death; "I *die* daily;" মৃত্যু যন্ত্রণা ভোগ করা। **8.** To become spiritless and vapid as liquor; নিস্তেজ বা বিস্বাদ হওয়া (যথা মদ্য)। **Die-away,** *adj.* Languishing; ম্রিয়মাণ। **Die-hards,** ৫৭ সংখ্যক পদাতিক সৈনিক দল। **Never say die**—Do not give in; keep up courage; পরাভব স্বীকার করিও না; সাহস হারাইও না। **To be dying for** — To have great desire; "The young men are *dying for* her;" স্পৃহা বা বাসনা থাকা। **To die away** — To disappear by degrees; to become gradually inaudible; ক্রমশঃ বিলীন হওয়া, বিলীয়মান হওয়া; ক্রমশঃ শব্দ মন্দীভূত হওয়া। **To die game**—To keep up one's spirit to the last; শেষ পর্য্যন্ত উৎসাহ অক্ষুণ্ণ রাখা। **To die hard**—To die not without struggle; to be long in dying; জীবন রক্ষার জন্য শেষ মুহূর্ত্ত পর্য্যন্ত ধ্বস্তাধ্বস্তি করা; বহুক্ষণে মরা। **To die in one's bed**—To die of age or illness; বার্দ্ধক্য বা পীড়া হেতু মৃত্যুমুখে পতিত হওয়া। **To die in one's boots or shoes** — To die by violence; অপঘাত মৃত্যু হওয়া। **To die in harness**—To die while still at work; কার্য্যরত অবস্থায় মৃত্যু হওয়া। **To die in the last ditch**—To die desperately defending something; to fight till death; জীবনাশা ত্যাগ করিয়া কোন কিছু রক্ষা করিতে করিতে মরা; জীবনান্ত পর্য্যন্ত যুদ্ধ করা। **To die off**—To die quickly or in large numbers; অতি দ্রুত মৃত্যু হওয়া, বহু সংখ্যায় মৃত্যুমুখে পতিত হওয়া, মরিয়া উজাড় হওয়া। **To die of laughing**—To laugh to exhaustion; হাসিতে হাসিতে দম বন্ধ হওয়া, হাসিতে হাসিতে পেট ফাটিবার উপক্রম হওয়া। **To die out**—To become extinct; to disappear gradually; নির্ব্বাপিত হওয়া; ক্রমশঃ অন্তর্হিত হওয়া, বিলীয়মান হওয়া। **To die the death**—To suffer the penalty of death; মৃত্যুদণ্ড ভোগ করা। **To die unto (sin)**—To escape the thraldom of (sin); (পাপের) দাসত্ব হইতে মুক্তিলাভ করা।

dī-ē-lĕc′-tric, *adj.* & *n.* Transmitting electric effects without conducting; non-conductive; (তাড়িত-বিজ্ঞান) পরিচালন বিনা বৈদ্যুতিক ক্রিয়া সঞ্চারণকারী; অপরিচালক। ***Noun.*** A medium or substance through which electric force acts; a non-coductor; যে মধ্যস্থিত বস্তু বা পদার্থের ভিতর দিয়া বৈদ্যুতিক শক্তি ক্রিয়া করে; অপরিচালক পদার্থ, অচালক (হিঃ কোঃ), অপরিচালক।

dies irae, *n.* [*L.*] The day of judgment; the famous Latin hymn beginning with these words; (খৃষ্টীয় ও মহম্মদীয় ধর্ম্মানুসারে) অন্তিম বিচার দিবস; ল্যাটিন ভাষায় সুপ্রসিদ্ধ স্তোত্র,—যাহার আদিতে এই শব্দগুলি আছে।

dies non, *n.* [*L.*] (*Law*) A day when the courts do not sit, (as a sunday, a public holday, etc.); a day that does not count or can not be used; (আইন) আদালতের ছুটীর দিবস; যে দিন গণনার মধ্যে ধরা হয় না।

dī-ĕt, *n., v. t.* & *i.* **1.** A course of food prescribed or regulated by a physician; পথ্য। **2.** Way of feeding; আহার দান-প্রণালী। **3.** One's habitual food; victuals; "A change of *diet* confronts us;" কোন ব্যক্তি সচরাচর যে খাদ্য আহার করে, ভোজ্য খুরাক (ফঃ হিঃ); খাদ্যদ্রব্য। ***Verb t.*** To regulate the food of, as a person, oneself, etc., as a medical regimen or punishment; পথ্য বিধান করা, শাস্তিস্বরূপ খাদ্য নির্দ্দেশ করা। ***Verb i.*** To eat according to the rules prescribed; পথ্য গ্রহণ করা। **—a′-ri-an,** *n.* One who observes prescribed rules for diet; পথ্যগ্রহণকারী। **Diet-drink**—পথ্য পানীয় (মঃ উঃ), সিদ্ধজল (ঐ)।

dī′-ĕt, *n.* 1. A meeting of dignitaries or delegates for legislative or other purposes ; a legislative assembly in Germany, Poland, etc. ; a convention ; as, the *diet* of Worms, held in 1521 ; ব্যবস্থাদি প্রণয়নের জন্য সম্ভ্রান্ত ব্যক্তি বা প্রতিনিধিগণের সভা, ব্যবস্থাপক সভা ; জার্ম্মেনী, পোলণ্ড প্রভৃতি দেশের ব্যবস্থাপক সভা ; কোন বিশেষ বিষয় মীমাংসার জন্য আহূত সভা। 2. (*Scot.*) A session or sitting of a court or assembly ; (স্কটলেণ্ড্) বিচারাধিবেশন, সভাধিবেশন।

dī′-ĕt-ā-rȳ, *n.* & *adj.* A system or course of diet ; a book prescribing such a course ; a fixed allowance of food, as in a prison, hospital or workhouse ; নির্দ্দিষ্ট পথ্য-সমূহ ; পথ্য-সম্বন্ধীয় পুস্তক ; কারাগার, রুগ্নাবাস, শ্রমশালা প্রভৃতিতে নির্দ্দিষ্ট পরিমাণ খাদ্যের বরাদ্দ। ***Adj.*** Pertaining to diet or the rules of diet ; পথ্য-সংক্রান্ত, পথ্য-বিষয়ক, পথ্য-নিয়মাবলী-সংক্রান্ত।

dī-ĕ-tĕt′-ic, *adj.* Of or pertaining to diet or to the rules for regulating diet ; পথ্য-সম্বন্ধীয়, পথ্য-বিষয়ক নিয়মাবলী-সংক্রান্ত। **—tet′-ics,** *n.* Rules for regulating diet ; that branch of medicine which relates to the regulation of diet ; পথ্যের নিয়মাবলী ; ভৈষজ্য-শাস্ত্রের পথ্য-বিষয়ক শাখা। **—al-ly,** *adv.*

dif′-fêr, *v. i.* 1. To be dissimilar, distinct or unlike in condition, qualities or nature, (often followed by *from*) ; "Minds *differ* as rivers *differ* ;" প্রভেদ হওয়া, বিসদৃশ হওয়া, বিভিন্ন হওয়া, অমিল হওয়া। 2. To be at variance ; to dispute or contend ; বিসম্বাদ হওয়া ; তর্ক বিতর্ক করা, বাদ্‌বিতণ্ডা করা। 3. To be of a contrary or opposite opinion ; to disagree ; (often followed by *from* or *with*) ; "I *differ from* you or *with* you in that opinion ;" মতভেদ হওয়া, মতদ্বৈধ হওয়া, অনৈক্য হওয়া, গরমিল হওয়া। **To agree to differ**—To give up attempt to convince each other ; যুক্তি তর্কের সাহায্যে কোন বিষয়ে পরস্পরের প্রতীতি জন্মাইবার চেষ্টা পরিত্যাগ করা।

dif′-fêr-ence (-ĕns), *n.* & *v. t.* 1. The state of being different ; dissimilarity ; diversity ; as, there is a *difference* in nature between animals and plants ; বৈলক্ষণ্য, বিভেদ, ব্যতিক্রম তারতম্য (মঃ ইঃ) ; বৈসাদৃশ্য, প্রভেদ, তফাৎ, ইতরবিশেষ অনৈক্য ; বৈচিত্র। 2. Disagreement in opinion ; a dispute ; a quarrel ; as, there was a *difference* between him and his friend ; মতান্তর, মতদ্বৈধ ; বাদানুবাদ, বাগ্‌বিতণ্ডা ; বিবাদ। 3. Cause of dissention ; "Are you acquainted with the *difference* ;" মত-ভেদের কারণ, অনৈক্যের কারণ। 4. The quality which distinguishes one thing from another ; the marks of distinction ; বিভেদক গুণ ; প্রভেদের লক্ষণ-সমূহ। 5. (*Math.*) The quantity by which the amounts differ ; the remainder left after subtracting one quantity from another ; (গণিত-শাস্ত্র) অন্তর ; বিয়োগ ফল। 6. Change in the price of stocks etc. between certain dates ; as, to pay or meet the *difference* ; নির্দ্দিষ্ট তারিখ সকলের মধ্যে কোম্পানীর কাগজের মূল্যের পরিবর্ত্তন। 7. (*Log.*) An essential attribute belonging to some species and not found in the genus ; a differentia ; (তর্ক-বিজ্ঞান) কোন বিশেষ গুণ— যাহা জাতিতে দৃষ্ট হয়, কিন্তু পরা জাতিতে (*genus*) বর্ত্তমান থাকে না ; বিশেষ গুণ, ব্যবর্ত্তক গুণ, ব্যবর্ত্তক। 8. (*Her.*) A certain figure added to a coat of arms to distinguish the bearings of two persons which would otherwise be the same ; (কুল-বিদ্যা) দুই ব্যক্তির কুল-চিহ্ন একরূপ হইলে একটীতে যে প্রভেদ-চিহ্ন সংযোজিত করিয়া ঐ কুল-চিহ্নদ্বয়ের বৈভিন্ন্য সংসাধিত করা হয়। 9. Discrimination or distinction as in choice ; as, to make a *difference* ; প্রভেদকরণ। ***Verb t.*** 1. To make different ; to differentiate ; অন্যরূপ করা ; বিভিন্ন করা, প্রভেদ করা, পার্থক্য করা। 2. (*Her.*) To make a heraldic difference in ; (কুল-বিদ্যা) কুল-চিহ্নে প্রভেদ-জ্ঞাপক চিহ্ন সংযোজিত করা। **It makes a great difference**—It is important ; ইহা অতি গুরুতর। **To make a difference between**—To treat differently ; ইতর বিশেষ করা, প্রভেদ করা। **To split the difference**—To come to compromise ; মিট মাট হওয়া, কলহ নিষ্পত্তি হওয়া, বিবাদ-মিটিয়া যাওয়া।

dif′-fêr-ĕnt, *adj.* 1. Distinct ; not the same ; পৃথক, বিভিন্ন ; স্বতন্ত্র, অন্য, অন্যবিধ, অপর, ভিন্ন ; 2. Dissimilar ; unlike ; (followed by, *from, to* or *than*) ; অন্যরূপ, ভিন্নরূপ ; বিসদৃশ। **—ly,** *adv.*

dif-fêr ĕn′-ti-â (-shî-), *n.* The characteristic quality or attribute of a species ; কোন জাতির বিশেষ গুণ, [যথা, "ধর্ম্মাধর্ম্মবিবেক" মনুষ্যজাতির বিশেষ গুণ ; এই গুণ মনুষ্যের "পরাজাতি" "জন্তু"র মধ্যে দৃষ্ট হয় না।] জাতিগত গুণ, ব্যবর্ত্তক (হিঃ কোঃ)।

dif-fêr-ĕn′-tial (-shăl), *adj.* & *n.* 1. Relating to a difference ; distinguishing ; as, *differential* characteristic ; বৈভিন্ন্য-ঘটিত ; ভেদ-জনক, প্রভেদক, বৈশিষ্ট্য-সূচক। 2. Relating to specific differences : প্রভেদক, বৈভিন্ন্য সম্বন্ধীয়। 3. (*Math.*) Pertaining to a quantity or difference infinitely small ; as, *differential* calculus ; (গণিত শাস্ত্র) ক্ষুদ্রতম সংখ্যা বা অন্তর-সম্বন্ধীয়, চলন-সম্বন্ধীয়। 4. (*Mech.*) Concerning the difference of two or more motions, pressures, etc. ; দুই বা ততোধিক গতি, চাপ প্রভৃতির ভেদ-সম্বন্ধীয়।

Noun. (*Math.*) An infinitesimal difference between two states of a variable quantity ; পরিবর্ত্তন-সহ সংখ্যার ছুইটী বিভাবের মধ্যে নিতান্ত ক্ষুদ্র অন্তর বা ভেদ। **–ly,** *adv.* **Differential calculus**—See, CALCULUS. **Differential duties** — (*Comm.*) বিভিন্ন দেশজাত দ্রব্যের উপর বিভিন্ন হারে সংগৃহীত শুল্ক, সাপেক্ষিক কর (হিঃ কোঃ)। **Differential thermometer**—অতিসূক্ষ্ম তাপভেদ-নির্ণায়ক তাপমান যন্ত্র।

dif-fêr-ĕn'-ti-āte (-shi-), *v. t.* & *i.* **1.** To create a difference between ; to make difference; as, colour of skin *differentiates* the races of men ; to specialize (species, organs, synonyms, etc.) ; বৈভিন্ন্য করা ; পার্থক্য করা ; প্রভেদ করা। **2.** To discriminate ; to classify as different ; বিভেদ করা ; ভিন্ন শ্রেণী ভুক্ত করা। **3.** (*Biol.*) To make different in the process of developments, (chiefly in the passive) ; (জীব-বিজ্ঞান) বিকাশ-প্রণালী ভিন্ন প্রকার করা। *Verb i.* To acquire a distinct and separate character ; বিভিন্ন বা বিশিষ্ট প্রকৃতি প্রাপ্ত হওয়া। **–a'-tion,** *n.* **1.** The act of differentiating ; প্রভেদ করণ। **2.** (*Log.*) The act of describing a thing by giving its differentia ; বিভেদন (হিঃ কোঃ), ব্যাবর্ত্তন (ঐ), ব্যবচ্ছেদন (ঐ)। **3.** (*Biol.*) Modification of parts or organs of the body for special functions ; বিশেষ বিশেষ ক্রিয়া বা বৃত্তি পরিচালনের জন্য দেহের অংশ বা দৈহিক যন্ত্রাদির পরিবর্ত্তন। **4.** (*Math.*) The process or result of differentiating ; ব্যুৎপাদন, স্বগত-ভেদ (সাঃ পঃ), কলাগত ভেদ (ঐ), বিধানগত ভেদ (ঐ)। **Differentiated**—সবিকল্প (বেদান্ত)।

dif'-fi-cile (-sēl), *n.* (*F.*) *adj.* Difficult ; hard to deal with ; exigent ; কঠিন ; আয়াসসাধ্য ; ঘোরতর, দারুণ।

dif'-fi-cŭlt, (-ĭ-), *adj.* **1.** Hard to be made or done ; arduous ; requiring labour and pains ; as, a *difficult* task ; দুষ্কর, শক্ত ; দুরূহ, কৃচ্ছ্রসাধ্য, দুরধিগম্য ; প্রযত্নসাধ্য, কঠিন, বিষম, দুর্ঘট, আয়াসসাধ্য। **2.** Hard to be pleased ; not easily persuaded ; as, *difficult* man to deal with ; দুস্তোষ্য ; দুষ্প্ররোচনীয়।

dif'-fi-cŭl-tȳ (-ĭ-), *n.* **1.** The state of being difficult ; arduousness ; hardness ; as, the *difficulty* of an enterprise ; কঠিনতা ; শ্রমসাধ্যতা, দুষ্করতা, [illegible]। **2.** Anything difficult to be done or understood ; as, the *difficulty* of a science ; an obstacle ; an impediment ; দুষ্কর কার্য্য, দুর্ব্বোধ বিষয় ; বাধা, বিঘ্ন ; প্রতিবন্ধক। **3.** Perplexity ; trouble ; embarrassment of affairs, especially pecuniary affairs ; as, to be in *difficulties* ; ফাঁপর ; মুস্কিল, ফেসাদ ; ঝঞ্ঝাট, অর্থকৃচ্ছ্রতা, লেঠা, সঙ্কট। **4.** Reluctance ; demur ; objection ; "They never made any *difficulties* or demands ;" অসম্মতি ; দ্বিধা, ইতস্ততঃ ; আপত্তি। **5.** (*Colloq.*) A dispute ; a controversy ; a disagreement ; বাদানুবাদ ; তর্কবিতর্ক ; অনৈক্য। **With difficulty** — Not easily ; সহজে নয়। **To make difficulties** — To be unaccommodating ; নানারূপ বাধা বিঘ্ন উপস্থিত করা, অসুবিধা দেখান।

dif'-fi-dence (-dĕns), *n.* Want of self-confidence ; bashfulness ; modesty ; "it is good to speak in such question with *diffidence* ;" আত্ম-প্রত্যয়হীনতা, সঙ্কোচ ; লজ্জা, সরম ; বিনয়, ব্রীড়া।

dif'-fi-dĕnt, *adj.* **1.** Wanting in self-confidence ; bashful ; timid ; modest ; as, a *diffident* youth ; আত্মপ্রত্যয়হীন, সঙ্কোচপূর্ণ ; সলজ্জ ; সশঙ্ক ; বিনীত। **2.** (*Arhaic*) Distrustful, (with *of*) অবিশ্বাসী। **–ly,** *adv.* In a diffident manner ; সশঙ্কচিত্তে, সঙ্কুচিতভাবে।

dif'-flu-ence (-flōō-ĕns), *n.* A flowing or falling away on all sides ; fluidity ; চতুর্দ্দিকে প্রবহণ, চতুর্দ্দিকে পতন ; তরলতা, দ্রাব্যত্ব। **–ent,** *adj.*

dif-frăct', *v. t.* (Of the edge of an opaque body) To break or separate into parts, as a ray or beam of light ; ভাঙ্গিয়া যাওয়া, খণ্ডে খণ্ডে পৃথক হওয়া (যথা, আলোক রশ্মি), সাচিবর্ত্তন করা। **–frac'-tion,** *n.* (Optics) The peculiar modification which light undergoes when it passes by the edge of an opaque body by being deflected from its direct course ; (দৃষ্টি-বিজ্ঞান) আলোক-রশ্মি সমূহ সরল পথ হইতে বিক্ষিপ্ত হইয়া কোন অস্বচ্ছ বস্তুর প্রান্তদেশ দিয়া বহির্গত হইলে ইহার যে বিশেষ পরিবর্ত্তন হয়, সাচিবর্ত্তন (সাঃ পঃ), ব্যবর্ত্তন (ঐ)। **–frac'-tive,** *adj.* **–frac'-tive-ly,** *adv.*

dif-fūse', *adj.* **1.** Widely spread or dispersed ; not concise ; prolix ; as, a *diffuse* style or writer ; বিস্তৃত ; বাগ্‌বিস্তারপূর্ণ, বাগ্‌বাহুল্যবিশিষ্ট ; অতিবিস্তৃতিদোষ-যুক্ত। **2.** (*Bot.*) Spreading loosely, as a branch ; (উদ্ভিদ-বিদ্যা) বিসারী।

dif-fūse', *v. t.* & *i.* **1.** To spread ; to circulate ; to send forth or extend in all directions ; as, to *diffuse* light, particles, heat, geniality, knowledge, rumour, information, etc. ; পরিব্যাপ্ত করা ; বিস্তার করা ; বিকীর্ণ করা, ছড়ান। **2.** (*Phys.*) (Of gases or fluids) ; To intermingle by diffusion ; (পদার্থ-বিদ্যা) (বাষ্প এবং তরল পদার্থ-সম্পর্কে) ব্যাপ্তিহেতু মিশ্রিত হওয়া। *Verb i.* (*Phys.*) To spread ; বিস্তৃত হওয়া, বিকীর্ণ হওয়া, পরিব্যাপ্ত হওয়া। **–fus-i-bil'-i-ty,** *n.* **–fus'-i-ble,** *adj.* Capable of flowing in all directions; that may be dispersed; বিকিরণশীল; বিকীর্য্য। **–fu′-sion,** *n.* **1.** A spreading or scattering abroad; extension; বিস্তৃতি, ব্যাপ্তি, ব্যাপন; বিস্তার, বিততি। **2.** (*Phys.*) The passing of one gas into the space occupied by another; (পদার্থ-বিদ্যা) এক বাষ্প-দ্বারা অভিভূত স্থানে অপর বাষ্পের প্রবেশ, প্রবেশ (হিঃ কোঃ)। **–fu′-sive,** *adj.* **–fu′-sive-ly,** *adv.* **–fu′-sive-ness,** *n.* Verboseness; বাগ্‌বিস্তার। **Diffusion-tube** — বিভিন্ন প্রকার বাষ্পের প্রবেশের পরিমাণ নির্দ্ধারণার্থ যন্ত্র-বিশেষ, প্রবেশমান। **Diffusion theory of taxation**—কর-সম-ভার-বাদ (হিঃ কোঃ)।

dig, *v. t., i.* & *n.* **1.** To turn up or break up with a spade etc.; খুঁড়া, কোদাল দ্বারা কাটা। **2.** To excavate; to hollow out;" খনন করা; খোদা। **3.** To obtain by digging; as, to *dig* potatoes or coals; খুড়িয়া বাহির করা। **4.** To push or thrust in violently; to poke; as, to *dig* squares into a horse's side: to *dig* a person in the ribs; সজোরে ঠেলা বা সজোরে বসান; খোঁচা দেওয়া। ***Verb i.*** **1.** To work with a spade or other similar instrument; to do servile work; কোদালি প্রভৃতি দ্বারা কাজ করা; নীচ কাজ করা, হীন কর্ম্ম করা, ইতর জনোচিত কাজ করা। **2.** To make research; as, to *dig* for information; গবেষণা করা। **3.** (*U. S. Slang*) To study hard; (মার্কিণ যুক্তরাজ্যে ইতর ভাষায়) কঠোর অধ্যয়ন করা। ***Noun.*** **1.** A thrust; a poke; as, a *dig* in the ribs; (*fig.*) a remark; as, it is a *dig* at him; ধাক্কা; খোঁচা; (লক্ষণায়) মন্তব্য। **2.** An act of digging; খনন। **3.** (*U. S.*) A laborious student; (মার্কিণ যুক্ত রাজ্য) কঠোর পরিশ্রমী ছাত্র। **To dig down**—To undermine and cause to fall by digging; নিম্নস্থ মৃত্তিকা খনন করিয়া ভূমিসাৎ করা। **To dig in**—To cover by digging; as, to *dig in* manure; খুঁড়িয়া ঢাকিয়া ফেলা। To make an excavation in; কোন কিছুর ভিতর খোদা। **To dig from, out of,** or **out**—To get out or obtain by digging; খুঁড়িয়া বাহির করা, খুঁড়িয়া পাওয়া। **To dig up**—To get out by digging, as a tree; খুঁড়িয়া বাহির করা। **To dig through**—To open a passage through; to make an opening from one side to the other; কোন কিছুর মধ্য দিয়া পথ করা; একপার্শ্ব হইতে অপরপার্শ্ব পর্য্যন্ত খনন করা, সুড়ঙ্গ প্রস্তুত করা।

dĭ-găm′-mă, (*F.*), *n.* An obsolete letter of the Greek alphabet having the force of the letter w; গ্রীক বর্ণমালার অপ্রচলিত অক্ষর বিশেষ, ইংরেজী "w" অক্ষরের অনুরূপ উচ্চারণ বিশিষ্ট।

dig′-ă-mȳ, *n.* A second marriage; পুনর্ব্বিবাহ বা দ্বিতীয়বার দার-পরিগ্রহ। **–mist,** *n.* **–mous,** *adj.*

dī-găs′-tric, *adj.* & *n.* (*Anat.*) With two swelling ends; as, a *digastric* muscle; (শারীর-সংস্থান-বিদ্যা) মাংসল প্রান্তদ্বয়বিশিষ্ট, (নিম্নহনুর পেশী বিশেষের মত)। ***Noun.*** A muscle of the lower jaw; নিম্নহনুর পেশী বিশেষ।

dī′-gĕst, *n.* A summary of law; a methodically arranged body of laws; আইনের সারসংগ্রহ; সংহিতা। **The digest**—রোম সম্রাট জাস্টিনিয়ানের আদেশক্রমে সংকলিত রোমীয় বিধিসমূহ।

dī-gĕst′, *v. t.* & *i.* **1.** To arrange systematically; to classify; as, to *digest* the laws etc.; ব্যবস্থাবদ্ধ করা, শ্রেণীবদ্ধ করা; শৃঙ্খলাবদ্ধ করা। **2.** To separate, or dissolve in the stomach; to reduce into chyme; as, to *digest* food; জীর্ণ করা, পরিপাক করা; হজম করা। **3.** To draw out methodically in the mind; as, to *digest* a plan; মনে মনে আটা, মনোমধ্যে শৃঙ্খলাবদ্ধ করা। **4.** To brook; to be reconciled to; as, to *digest* an insult or opinion; সহা; মানিয়া লওয়া। **5.** To assimilate mentally or get mental nourishment from; হৃদয়ঙ্গম করা। **6.** To promote digestion of, as food, (said of drugs, wines etc.); পরিপাকশক্তি বৃদ্ধি করা, অগ্নিবৃদ্ধি করা। **7.** (*Chem.*) To soften by heat and moisture; (রসায়ন-শাস্ত্র) সিদ্ধ করিয়া কোমল করা, ভাবনা দেওয়া। **8.** To assimilate as a conquered territory; বিজিত দেশ প্রভৃতি অন্তর্ভুক্ত করা। ***Verb i.*** To admit of digestion; as, food *digests* well; পরিপাক হওয়া, জীর্ণ হওয়া। **–gest-i-bil′-i-ty,** *n.* **–gest′-i-ble,** *adj.* That can be easily digested; লঘুপাক, সুপাচ্য। **–gest′-i-bly,** *adv.*

dī-gĕst′-ĕr, *n.* **1.** One who digests; পরিপাককারী। **2.** A medicine etc., which promotes digestion of food; পরিপাকশক্তি-বর্দ্ধক ঔষধ, অগ্নিবর্দ্ধক ঔষধ, অগ্নিদীপক। **3.** (*Chem.*) A closed vessel in which to boil bony substances with a strong heat; (রসায়ন-শাস্ত্র) সুদৃঢ় বদ্ধ পাত্রবিশেষ—ইহাতে অস্থিময় পদার্থ প্রবল উত্তাপে সিদ্ধ করা হয়।

dī-gĕs′-tion, *n.* **1.** The act or process of digesting food; the act of digesting or obtaining mental nourishment from books etc.; পরিপাক ক্রিয়া, হজম, পচন ক্রিয়া; পুস্তক প্রভৃতির ভাব হৃদয়ঙ্গম করণ, পুস্তকাদি পাঠে মানসিক পুষ্টিসাধন। **2.** The power of digesting; as, a good or weak *digestion*; পরিপাক-শক্তি। **3.** Long steeping in hot fluid to extract essence; সার পদার্থ নিষ্কষিত করার জন্য দীর্ঘকাল উষ্ণ তরল পদার্থে নিমজ্জন, ভাবনা।

di-gĕs'-tive (-tĭv), *adj.* & *n.* Pertaining to, or promoting, digestion ; পরিপাক-ক্রিয়াসংক্রান্ত, পরিপাক-শক্তিবৃদ্ধিকর ; অগ্নিবর্দ্ধক, দীপনীয় (সুশ্রুঃ)। ***Noun.*** **1.** A substance which aids digestion ; পরিপাকশক্তি-বর্দ্ধক ঔষধ, হজমী। **2.** An ointment to promote suppuration ; পূযোৎপাদনের জন্য মলম বিশেষ। **—ly,** *adv.*

dig'-ger (-êr), *n.* **1.** One who, or that which, digs ; (also called a *gold digger*—one who digs or searches for gold in the gold fields) ; খনক। **2.** (Also called a *digger-wasp*) A division of Hymenopterous insects ; মক্ষিকাদি-বর্গের বিভাগ বিশেষ। **3.** A North American Indian living on roots ; উত্তর আমেরিকার কন্দভোজী আদিম অধিবাসী। **4.** The digging part of various machines ; বিভিন্ন প্রকার যন্ত্রের খননোপযোগী অংশ।

dig'-ging (-ĭng), *n.* **1.** The act of one who digs ; the place of excavating ; কোদাল দ্বারা মৃত্তিকা-ভেদন, খনন ; খননস্থান। **2.** (*Pl.*) A mine or gold-field ; খনি, স্বর্ণ-ক্ষেত্র, (অর্থাৎ যে স্থানে খনন করিলে সোণা পাওয়া যায়)। **3.** The materials dug out ; খনন দ্বারা উত্তোলিত পদার্থ। **4.** (*Pl.*) (*Colloq.*) Lodgings ; (চলিত ভাষায়) বাসগৃহ।

dight (dīt), *v. t.* **1.** (*Archaic & in poetry*) To adorn ; to array ; (অপ্রচলিত এবং কবিতায়) শোভিত করা, মণ্ডিত করা ; সজ্জিত করা। **2.** To make ready ; প্রস্তুত করা।

dĭg'-it, *n.* **1.** (*Zool.*) A finger or toe ; a finger's breadth or ¾ inch ; হাতের বা পায়ের আঙ্গুল ; এক অঙ্গুলী পরিসর প্রস্থ, ¾ ইঞ্চি, বুরুল। **2.** (*Astron.*) The twelfth part of the diameter of the sun or moon ; as, an eclipse of eight *digits* ; (জ্যোতির্বিজ্ঞান) সূর্য্য বা চন্দ্রের ব্যাসের দ্বাদশাংশ, (চন্দ্র-সম্পর্কে) ইন্দুকলা, শশি-লেখা, শশিকলা, ইন্দুরেখা, ইন্দুলেখা, ইন্দুদল, গ্রাস (হিঃ কোঃ)। **3.** (*Math.*) One of the ten figures, 0 to 9—they are so called from their being counted on the fingers) ; ১, ২, ৩, ৪ প্রভৃতি সংখ্যা, স্থানীয় সংখ্যা (হিঃ কোঃ), স্থানীয়াঙ্ক (ঐ), আদিসংখ্যা (আঃ বঃ), গুণনিকা (মঃ ইঃ)। **—al,** *adj.*

dĭg-i-tā'-lis, *n.* **1.** (*Bot.*) A genus of plants including the foxglove ; (উদ্ভিদ্-বিদ্যা) একজাতীয় গুল্ম। **2.** A medicine prepared from the foxglove ; উক্ত জাতীয় গুল্মের প্রকার বিশেষ হইতে প্রস্তুত ঔষধ বিশেষ।

dĭg'-i-t. te, —tāt-ĕd, *adj.* (*Zool.* & *Bot.*) Resembling a finger ; as, a *digitate* leaf ; (উদ্ভিদ্-বিদ্যা এবং জন্তু-বিদ্যা) অঙ্গুলি-সদৃশ, করাঙ্গুল্যাকার (সাঃ পঃ), করাঙ্গুলিবৎ বহুপত্র বিশিষ্ট। **—ta-tion,** *n.*

dĭg'-i-ti-grāde, *adj.* (*Zool.*) Walking on the toes, as a cat, lion, etc. ; (জন্তু-বিদ্যা) পদাঙ্গুল্যপরিচলনশীল।

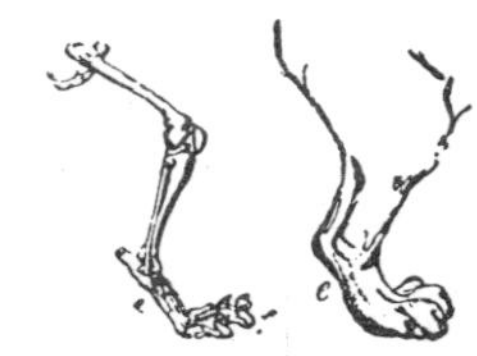

Digitigrade

dĭg'-ni-fȳ, *v. t.* **1.** To invest with honour or dignity ; to exalt ; to ennoble ; মর্য্যাদা-সম্পন্ন করা ; সম্ভ্রান্ত করা, সম্মানিত করা ; উন্নীত করা, অভ্যুত্থাপিত করা। **2.** To make stately ; (usually used as *p. p.*) ; মহিমান্বিত করা, গৌরবান্বিত করা। **—fied,** *p. p.* Marked with dignity; self-respecting ; stately ; as, a *dignified* judge ; সম্ভ্রান্ত ; আত্মমর্য্যাদা-সম্পন্ন, মর্য্যাদা-বোধসম্পন্ন ; মহিমান্বিত, গৌরবান্বিত।

dĭg'-ni-tă-rȳ, *n.* One in a dignified position or rank, especially in the church ; সম্ভ্রান্ত ব্যক্তি, সম্মানিত ব্যক্তি, উচ্চপদস্থ ব্যক্তি, (বিশেষতঃ খৃষ্টীয় ধর্ম্ম-সংঘে)।

dĭg'-ni-tȳ, *n.* **1.** Elevation in rank, place, etc. ; high office ; "Proud of such a *dignity* ;" degree of estimation ; গৌরব, মান, সম্ভ্রম, মর্য্যাদা, সম্মান, খ্যাতি, অনুভাব (রঃ) ; উচ্চপদ, সম্মানিত পদ। **2.** Grandeur ; stateliness ; "A *dignity* of dress adorns the guest ;" আড়ম্বর, জাঁক ; জমকালো ভাব। **3.** Elevation of manner ; গরিমা, মর্য্যাদাসম্পন্নতা ঔদার্য্য। **4.** A dignitary ; one holding a high office ; সম্ভ্রান্ত ব্যক্তি ; উচ্চপদস্থকর্ম্মচারী। **5.** (*Astrol.*) The location of a planet where its influence is enhanced either by its position in the zodiac or by its aspects with other planets ; (ফলিত-জ্যোতিষ) উচ্চস্থান। **Beneath one's dignity**—Unfit for one to do ; কোন ব্যক্তির পক্ষে অযোগ্য।

dī'-grăph, *n.* A union of two letters representing a single sound ; as, *ch* ; দুই বর্ণের সংযোগ—যদ্দ্বারা একটীমাত্র ধ্বনি সূচিত হয়।

di-grĕss', *v. i.* To deviate from the track ; to step aside from the main subject temporarily in speech or writing ; মূল পথ হইতে বিচলিত হওয়া ; মূল বিষয় ছাড়িয়া অবান্তর বিষয় ধরা। **—gres'-sion,** *n.* **1.** A going from the main point ; মূল বিষয় ছাড়িয়া বিষয়ান্তরে গমন, অবান্তর গমন। **2.** A part of a discourse deviating from the tenor or subject ; কোন বিষয়ের অপ্রাসঙ্গিক অংশ, অবান্তর অংশ। **3.** Transgression ; উন্মার্গগমন। **4.** (*Astron.*) The apparent distance of the inferior planets, Mercury and Venus, from the sun ; (জ্যোতির্বিজ্ঞান) বুধ ও শুক্র এই দুই লঘু গ্রহের সূর্য্য হইতে আপাতদৃশ্য দূরত্ব, লঘুগ্রহান্তরাংশ (হিঃ কোঃ)।

dĭg'-ȳ-nous, (-nŭs), *adj.* Having two pistils ; দ্বি-কেশরী, (সাঃ পঃ)।

dī-hĕx-ag'-ō-năl (-hĕk-săg), *adj.* Twelve-sided ; দ্বিষট্‌কোণিক (সাঃ পঃ)।

dīke, dȳke, *n.* & *v. t.* **1.** A ditch or artificial channel for water ; নালা,

পয়ঃপ্রণালী। **2.** A mound raised to prevent inundation ; বাঁধ, জলবন্ধ, হিতা, আধার (রঃ)। **3.** A low wall or fence of turf or stone ; পাথর বা ঘাসের চাপড়ার অনুচ্চ বেড়া। **4.** (*Geol.* & *mining*) A fissure in a stratum filled with deposited matter ; this matter ; (ভূ-বিদ্যা এবং খনিজ-বিদ্যা) সঞ্চিত পদার্থদ্বারা পূর্ণ প্রস্তরাদির স্তরের ফাটোল বিশেষ ; ঐরূপ সঞ্চিত পদার্থ । **5.** A causeway ; জাঙ্গাল। **6.** (*Fig.*) A barrier ; an obstacle ; a defence ; (লক্ষণায়) বাধা, প্রতিবন্ধক ; বিঘ্ন ; রক্ষা। ***Verb t.*** **1.** To surround or defend with a dike ; to provide with a dike ; বাঁধ দ্বারা বেষ্টিত করা, বাঁধ দ্বারা রক্ষা করা ; বাঁধ দেওয়া। **2.** To drain by a dike or ditch ; বাঁধ বা নালাদ্বারা জল নিঃসরণ করা। **Dike reeve**—জলাভূমিপূর্ণ প্রদেশের পয়ঃপ্রণালী, স্রোতোদ্বার, সাগরদ্বার প্রভৃতির ভার-প্রাপ্ত কর্ম্মচারী।

di-lăp'-i-dāte, *v. t.* & *i.* **1.** To bring into a state of disrepair or partial ruin ; to suffer to go to ruin ; ভগ্নাবস্থায় আনা, জীর্ণাবস্থায় আনা ; ধ্বংস করা, ধ্বংস হইতে দেওয়া। **2.** To waste ; "*Dilapidating* the revenues of the church ;" অপব্যয় করা, নষ্ট করা। ***Verb i.*** To get out of repair ; to fall into a state of decay or partial ruin ; জীর্ণ হওয়া ; ক্ষয়প্রাপ্ত হওয়া।

di-lăp-i-dā'-tion, *n.* **1.** The act of dilapidating ; the state of being dilapidated ; decay ; ruin ; ক্ষয়করণ ; জীর্ণাবস্থা, জীর্ণদশা ; ক্ষয় ; ধ্বংস। **2.** Impairing of church property during an incumbency ; the sum charged against the incumbent for the wear and tear during his tenancy ; যাজকীয় বৃত্তিভোগ কালে ধর্ম্মসংঘের সম্পত্তি নষ্ট করণ ; ধর্ম্মসংঘের সম্পত্তি নষ্ট করার দরুণ বৃত্তিভোগীর উপর যে ক্ষতিপূরণের টাকা দাবি করা হয়। **3.** The falling away of cliffs etc. ; debris resulting from it ; পর্ব্বত-পার্শ্বাদির পতন ; ভগ্ন-শৈলাবশেষ প্রভৃতি।

di-lāte', *v. t.* & *i.* To expand or swell out ; to distend ; প্রসারিত করা, স্ফীত করা, ফুলান ; বিস্ফারিত করা, বিস্তারিত করা। ***Verb i.*** **1.** To widen ; to swell or expand ; বিস্তৃত হওয়া ; স্ফীত হওয়া, প্রসারিত হওয়া। **2.** To speak at length ; to dwell on in narration ; (with *on* or *upon*) ; "But still they on their ancient joys *dilate* ;" বিস্তার পূর্ব্বক বলা, সবিস্তারে বর্ণনা করা ; কোন বিষয় বর্ণনা করা। **—lat'-a-ble,** *adj.* **—lat-a-bil'-i-ty, —la'-tion, —la-ta'-tion,** *ns.* The act of dilating or the state of being dilated ; expansion ; প্রসারণ ; প্রসার, বিস্তার।

di-lā'-tor (-têr), *n.* **1.** One who, or that which, dilates ; প্রসারক। **2.** (*Anat.*) A muscle that extends an organ ; (শারীর-সংস্থান বিদ্যা) প্রসারক পেশী। **3.** (*Surg.*) An instrument for expanding a part ; (অস্ত্রোপচারবিদ্যা) শরীরের স্বাভাবিক দ্বার বা ক্ষতাদির মুখ-প্রসারক যন্ত্রবিশেষ।

dil'-ă-tō-rȳ, *adj.* **1.** Tending or causing delay ; slow ; বিলম্বকারী, চিরকারী, ঢিলা, বিলম্বজনক ; ধীর, মন্থর। **2.** Given to procrastination as, *dilatory* messenger ; দীর্ঘসূত্রী। **—ri-ly,** *adv.* **—ri-ness,** *n.* The state of being dilatory ; দীর্ঘসূত্রতা, ঢিলামি, চিরকারিতা, শৈথিল্য।

di-lĕm'-mă, *n.* (*Log.*) **1.** An argument forcing the opponent to choose one of two alternatives both unfavourable to him ; (তর্ক-বিজ্ঞান) একপ্রকার যুক্তি—যাহাতে প্রতিপক্ষ দুইটী অপ্রীতিকর উপায়ের মধ্যে অন্যতরটী গ্রহণ করিতে বাধ্য হয়, উভয়-সঙ্কট, দ্বিকল্পন্যায় (সাঃ পঃ), বিকল্প (হিঃ কোঃ)। **2.** A position where each of two alternative courses is eminently undesirable ; a difficult choice or position ; উভয়-সঙ্কট ; দোটানা। **—mat'-ic,** *adj.* **The horns of a dilemma**—উভয়-সঙ্কট।

dĭl-ĕt-tăn'-te (-tā), *n.* & *adj.* A lover or admirer of the fine arts ; an amateur ; ললিত-কলানুরাগী ; যে ব্যক্তি সখ করিয়া কোনরূপ কলা-বিদ্যার আলোচনা করে। ***Adj.*** Trifling ; amateur ; not thorough ; অকিঞ্চিৎকর ; সখের ; পল্লবগ্রাহী। **—tish,** *adj.* **—tism,** *n.*

dĭl'-i-gence (-jĕns), *n.* Industry ; persevering effort ; assiduity in service ; steady application ; "The best of me is *diligence* ;" পরিশ্রম ; উদ্যোগ ; যত্নপরতা, আয়াস, শ্রমশীলতা, যত্ন ; অভিনিবেশ। **2.** Heedfulness ; care ; (the opposite of *negligence*); সতর্কতা ; সাবধানতা। **Diligence is the mother of good luck**—উদ্যোগিনং পুরুষসিংহমুপৈতি লক্ষ্মীঃ।

dĭl'-i-gence' (-jĕns), *n.* A French or continental stage-coach ; ফ্রান্স এবং ইয়ুরোপের অন্যান্য দেশের ডাকের গাড়ী।

dĭl'-i-gĕnt, *adj.* **1.** Constant and steady in application ; painstaking ; industrious ; যত্নবান, উদ্যোগী ; উদ্যমশীল ; পরিশ্রমী। **2.** Prosecuted with care and steady effort ; সযত্ন। **—ly,** *adv.* In a diligent manner ; সযত্নে, পরিশ্রমের সহিত।

dĭll, *n.* A plant resembling fennel but smaller ; শৌলফা।

Dillenia speciosa—চাল্‌তা (বেলঃ)

dĭl'-lȳ-dăl'-lȳ, *v. t.* (*Colloq.*) To vacillate ; (চলিত ভাষায়) গড়িমসি করা, টালমাটাল করা, নিড়ি বিড়ি করা।

dĭl'-ū-ĕnt, *adj.* & *n.* Diluting ; increasing the proportion of water in the blood, etc. ; জলীয়াংশ বৃদ্ধিকর ; রক্ত প্রভৃতির জলীয়ভাগ বৃদ্ধিকর। ***Noun.*** **1.** That which dilutes ; তরলতরকর পদার্থ। **2.** (*Med.*) A substance which increases the amount of water in the blood ; (ভৈষজ্য-শাস্ত্র) যে পদার্থদ্বারা শরীরের রক্ত-রসাদির জলীয়াংশ বৃদ্ধি প্রাপ্ত হয়।

di-lūte′, *adj.* Weakened by the addition of water ; faded as a colour ; (*Fig.*) watery or poor ; জল মিশ্রণ দ্বারা ক্ষীণীকৃত ; (বর্ণসম্বন্ধে) ম্লান, ক্ষীণ, পাতলা ; নিস্তেজ।

di-lūte′, *v. t.* **1.** To make thinner or more liquid by admixture ; তরলতর করা, অধিকতর হাল্কা করা, পাতলা করা। **2.** To weaken, as spirit etc. by an admixture of water ; to diminish the brilliance of, as, colour, by mixture ; জল মিশাইয়া সুরাসার প্রভৃতি নিস্তেজ করা ; জল মিশাইয়া বর্ণের ঔজ্জ্বল্য মন্দীভূত করা, রঙ্গ পাতলা করা। **3.** (*Fig.*) To weaken ; as, to *dilute* a zeal or doctrine ; (লক্ষণায়) নিস্তেজ করা। **—lu′-tion,** *n.* **1.** Act of diluting ; the state of being diluted ; তরলীকরণ, ক্ষীণীকরণ ; জলমিশ্রিতাবস্থা। **2.** That which is diluted ; জলমিশ্রিত পদার্থ। **3.** (*Homœo.*) A diluted medicine ; দ্রব ক্রম,—মূল ঔষধ ক্রমশঃ সুরাসারাদির (*Alcohol*) সহিত মিশ্রিত করিয়া প্রস্তুত ক্রম (dilution)।

di-lū′-vi-ăl, *adj.* **1.** Pertaining to a flood or deluge, esp. that in time of Noah ; বন্যা বা জল-প্লাবন সম্বন্ধীয়, জলপ্রলয় সম্পর্কীয় বিশেষতঃ নোয়ার সময়ের জলপ্লাবন-সম্পর্কীয়। **2.** (*Geol.*) Caused by, or resulting from, a deluge ; as *diluvial* changes ; (ভূ-বিদ্যা) জলপ্লাবন জনিত। **—ist,** *ns.* One who explains geological phenomena by the Noachian deluge ; যে ব্যক্তি ভূতত্ব সম্বন্ধীয় ব্যাপার সমূহ নোয়ার সময়ের জলপ্লাবনদ্বারা ব্যাখ্যা করে। **Diluvial-land**—শিকস্তী।

di-lū′-vi-ŭm, *n.* **1.** Inundation or flood ; প্লাবন, বন্যা। **2.** A deposit of sand, gravel, etc., caused by the extraordinary action of water ; জল প্লাবনের ফলে সঞ্চিত বালি, কাঁকর প্রভৃতির স্তূপ, শিকস্তী।

dĭm, *adj., v. i. & t.* **1.** Not bright or distinct ; obscure in lustre or sound ; dusky ; not clear or well-defined ; অনুজ্জ্বল, নিষ্প্রভ ; অস্পষ্ট, ন্যূনপ্রভ, ঝাপ্‌সা, অস্ফুট, স্তিমিত, মিট্‌মিটে ; ধূসর ; মন্দপ্রভ, অস্বচ্ছ, অপরিস্ফুট। **2.** Having the vision obscured and indistinct ; not seeing clearly ; as, *dim* eyes ; hence, dull of apprehension ; "The understanding is *dim* ;" ঘোরাল ; ক্ষীণ-দৃষ্টি ; হীন-বুদ্ধি। ***Verb i.*** To become dim ; নিষ্প্রভ হওয়া, অনুজ্জ্বল হওয়া। ***Verb t.*** **1.** To make dark or dim ; to obscure ; to make less bright ; to outshine ; "A king who *dims* all his attendants" ; অনুজ্জ্বল করা, নিষ্প্রভ করা ; ঝাপ্‌সা করা, অস্পষ্ট করা ; মন্দপ্রভ করা, হীনপ্রভ করা ; উজ্জ্বলতায় পরাস্ত করা। **2.** To impair the power of vision ; as, to *dim* the eye ; দৃষ্টিশক্তি ক্ষীণ করা। **Dim′-ly,** *adv.* **Dim′-ish** (or **dim′-mish),** *adj.* **Dim′-ness,** *n.*

dīme, (*U. S.*), *n.* A silver coin of the value of to cents ; the tenth part of a dollar ; (মার্কিণ-যুক্তরাজ্য) ১০ সেণ্ট মূল্যের রৌপ্য মুদ্রা ; এক ডলারের দশমাংশ। **Dime museum**—A cheap show ; সুলভ প্রদর্শনী। **Dime-novel**—সস্তা উপন্যাস, সুলভ উপন্যাস।

di-mĕn′-sion, *n.* **1.** A measurable extent of any kind, as length, breadth or thickness ; size ; "There are a few of greater *dimension* ;" পরিমাণ, দৈর্ঘ্য-প্রস্থ-বেধ ; আয়তন। **2.** (*Pl.*) Extent ; scope ; importance ; as, a project of large *dimensions* ; (বহুবচন) বিস্তার ; উদ্দেশ্য, অভিপ্রায় ; গুরুত্ব। **—al, —less,** *adjs.* **Dimension work**—Masonry in stones of specified size ; নির্দ্দিষ্ট আয়তনের প্রস্তর দ্বারা গাঁথুনি। **Fourth dimension** —বিন্দুর গতি হইতে রেখা, রেখার গতি হইতে সমতলক্ষেত্র, সমতলক্ষেত্রের গতি হইতে ঘনক্ষেত্র উপজাত হয় ; এইরূপে ঘনক্ষেত্রের গতি হইতে চতুরায়তন বিশিষ্ট ক্ষেত্রের উৎপত্তি কল্পনা করা হইয়া থাকে এবং এইরূপ বাস্তবরাজ্যের বহির্ভূত ক্ষেত্র সমূহ অবলম্বনে জ্যামিতির যে এক নূতন শাখার উদ্ভব হইয়াছে। **Of great dimensions**—Very large ; অতি প্রকাণ্ড, বিরাট, বিপুল। **The three dimensions** — [A point has no dimension ; a line one, a surface two, and a body three] ; দৈর্ঘ-প্রস্থ-বেধ।

dim′-êr-ous (Usually written *2-merous*) (-ŭs), *adj.* **1.** (*Bot.*) With two parts ; (উদ্ভিদ্‌-বিদ্যা) দ্ব্যংশক (সাঃ পঃ)। **2.** (*Entom.*) Having two-jointed tarsi ; (কীট-বিজ্ঞান) গ্রন্থিল জঙ্ঘা-বিশিষ্ট।

dim′-ĕ-têr, *n.* A verse of two measures ; দ্বিমাত্রাবিশিষ্ট কবিতা।

di-mid′-i-āte, *adj.* **1.** Divided into two equal parts ; দ্বিসমাংশে বিভক্ত। **2.** Having a shape that appears as if halved ; as, *dimidiate* leaf ; অর্দ্ধাঙ্গ (সাঃ পঃ)।

di-min′-ish, *v. t. & i.* **1.** To make smaller or less ; to lessen ; ন্যূন করা, হ্রাস করা ; কমান, অল্পতর করা। **2.** To degrade ; to impair ; to abase ; অবনত করা ; হানি করা, নষ্ট করা ; হীন করা, খর্ব্ব করা, খাট করা। **3.** (*Obs.*) To subtract ; (অপ্রচলিত) বিয়োগ করা। **4.** (*Mus.*) To lessen by a semitone ; as, a *diminished* seventh ; (সঙ্গীত-শাস্ত্র) অর্দ্ধস্বর (দুন) দ্বারা হ্রাস করা। **5.** (*Arch.*) To cause to taper ; "They (pillars) are all *diminished* from one-third part of the whole shaft ;" (স্থপতি-বিজ্ঞান) অগ্রভাগ ক্রমশঃ সূক্ষ্ম করা, মোচাগ্রবৎ করা। ***Verb i.*** **1.** To become actually, or in appearance less ; to subside ; কমা, অল্পতর হওয়া, ন্যূন হওয়া, হ্রাস পাওয়া ; শান্ত হওয়া।

2. (*Arch.*) To taper ; (স্থপতি-বিজ্ঞান) ক্রমশঃ সূক্ষ্ম হওয়া, মোচাগ্রবৎ হওয়া। **—a-ble,** *adj.* **—ing-ly,** *adv.*

di-min-ü-ĕn′-dō, *adv.* & *n.* (*Mus.* abbr. *dim.*—a direction to let the sound die away) With abatement of tone ; মন্দায়মান স্বরে। ***Noun.*** Gradual decrease ; a musical passage marked by it ; মন্দায়মানতা, ক্ষীয়মাণতা ; মন্দায়মান গীত বাদ্যাংশ।

dĭm-i-nū′-tion, *n.* **1.** The act of making or becoming less ; state of being diminished ; ন্যূনীকরণ, লঘূকরণ, ন্যূনীভবন, অল্পীভবন ; হ্রাস, ন্যূনতা, অল্পতা, কম্‌তি। **2.** (*Obs.*) Degradation ; deprivation of dignity ; (অপ্রচলিত) অবনতি ; গৌরব-হানি। **3.** (*Arch.*) Diminishing or tapering ; the amount of this (tapering) ; (স্থপতি-বিজ্ঞান) অগ্রভাগ ক্রমশঃ সূক্ষ্ম হওন ; ক্রমঃসূক্ষ্মতার পরিমাণ।

di-min′-ū-tive (-tĭv), *adj.* & *n.* **1.** (*Gram.*) Expressing a small thing of the kind denoted by corresponding primitive word ; as, a *diminutive* word ; অল্পতাবাচক, ক্ষুদ্রতাবাচক। **2.** Very small, little ; as, a *diminutive* thought ; অতি ক্ষুদ্র; ছোট। ***Noun.*** **1.** (*Gram.*) A word formed from another to express a little one of the kind denoted by the letter, as leaflet, hillock, etc. ; ক্ষুদ্রতাবাচক শব্দ বা পদ। **2.** Anything of a very small size ; অতি ক্ষুদ্রকায় ব্যক্তি, অতি ক্ষুদ্র জিনিষ। **—ness,** *n.* **—ti′-val,** *adj.* **—tive-ly,** *adv.*

dĭm′-is-sō-rȳ, *adj.* Sending away ; dismissing to another jurisdiction ; granting leave to depart ; স্থানান্তরে প্রেরণকারী ; অন্যাধিকারে প্রেরণকারী ; প্রস্থানার্থ অনুমতি-প্রদায়ী।

dĭm′-i-tȳ, *n.* A kind of white cotton fabric, ribbed or figured, used for hangings, etc. ; একপ্রকার শাদা শির-তোলা কার্পাস বস্ত্র, গিমটী (যোঃ)।

di-mŏr′-phic, —phous (-fŭs), *adjs.* (*Bot., Zoöl, Chem., Mineral.*) Exhibiting two distinct forms ; occurring in two different forms ; দ্বিরূপ-প্রদর্শক ; দ্বিরূপী (হিঃ কোঃ)। [যথা খনিজ জগতে carbon একটী দ্বিরূপী পদার্থ, হীরক ইহার একরূপ ও গ্রাফাইট্ অন্যতর রূপ ; দ্বিতীয়তঃ প্রাণিজগতে স্ত্রী-মধুমক্ষিকা একটী দ্বিরূপী প্রাণী ; রাণী মক্ষিকা ইহার একরূপ, কর্ম্মী মক্ষিকা অপর রূপ ; উদ্ভিজ্জ জগতে পদ্মপুষ্পের শ্বেত ও রক্ত এই দুইটী রূপ দৃষ্ট হয়।] **—phism,** *n.* The state of having two forms ; দ্বিরূপত্ব (সাঃ পঃ)।

dĭm′-ple, *n., v. t.* & *i.* **1.** A small natural depression in the cheek or other parts of the face ; গালের টোল, গণ্ডকূপ। **2.** A slight indentation on any surface ; কোন কিছুর উপরিভাগে ঈষৎ কুঞ্চন বা খাঁজ। ***Verb t.*** To mark with dimples ; গণ্ডকূপ উৎপাদন করা, ঈষৎ কুঞ্চিত করা। ***Verb i.*** To show dimples ; to form dimples ; গণ্ডকূপ প্রদর্শন করা ; গালে টোল পড়া। **—ply,** *adj.* Having dimples ; গণ্ডকূপ বিশিষ্ট, টোল-পড়া।

dĭn, *n., v. t.* & *i.* A loud continued noise ; roar ; clamour ; নির্ঘোষ ; গর্জ্জন, রোল ; কলরব। ***Verb t.*** **1.** To strike or stun with a loud continued noise ; to harass with noise ; মহানির্ঘোষে স্তব্ধ বা কর্ণতালি লাগান; কোলাহল করিয়া বিরক্ত করা। **2.** To utter with a noise ; to repeat noisily কলরব করিয়া বলা ; পুনঃ পুনঃ চেঁচাইয়া বলা। ***Verb i.*** To make a din ; রোল করা; মুখরিত করা। **To din into—** To impress on the mind of (another) by frequent and noisy repetitions ; উচ্চৈঃস্বরে পুনঃপুনঃ বলিয়া (কাহারও) মনোমধ্যে গাঢ়রূপে মুদ্রিত করা।

dīne, *v. i.* & *t.* To take dinner ; দিবসের প্রধান ভোজন করা। ***Verb t.*** **1.** To give a dinner to ; to entertain at dinner ; as, to *dine* a hundred man ; দিবসের প্রধান ভোজন প্রদান করা ; দিবসের প্রধান ভোজন প্রদানে আপ্যায়িত করা। **2.** To provide dining accommodation for (some number of men), as a room etc. "The saloon capable of *dining* 118 passengers ;" দিবসের প্রধান ভোজনের জন্য স্থান প্রদান করা। **Dining-hall, —room, —table—** ভোজন গৃহ, ভোজনশালা, ভোজন কক্ষ, ভোজনের মেজ। **To dine out—** To dine away from home ; বাটী হইতে অন্যত্র ভোজন করা। **To dine with Duke Humphrey**—To go without dinner ; (Like those who, unable to procure a dinner, loitered about Duke Humphrey's walk in St. Paul's) ; হরিবাসর করা, হরিমটর করিয়া থাকা।

dīn′-ĕr, *n.* **1.** One who dines ; a dinner-guest ; ভোজনকারী ; ভোজনের জন্য নিমন্ত্রিত ব্যক্তি। **2.** A railway dining-car ; রেলগাড়ীর ভোজন-শকট। **Diner out**—যে ব্যক্তি প্রায়শঃ ভোজের নিমন্ত্রণে গমন করে।

Ding an sich — স্বলক্ষণ বস্তু (হিঃ কোঃ)।

dĭng′-dŏng, *adv., n.* & *adj.* With alternating strokes as of two bells ; ঢং ঢং শব্দে। ***Noun.*** **1.** The sound of bell or bells ringing ; ঢং ঢং শব্দ। **2.** The jingle of rhyme ; মিত্রাক্ষরের ঝঙ্কার। ***Adj.*** **2.** Of or pertaining to the sound of bells etc. ; ঢং ঢং ধ্বনি সম্বন্ধীয়। **2.** Characterised by rapid succession ; as, *dingdong* blows ; vigorously contested ; উপর্য্যুপরি, পটাপট্; অনিশ্চিত জয়-পরাজয়। **Ding-dong-race**—যে দৌড়ে প্রতিযোগিগণ পর্য্যায়-ক্রমে পরস্পরকে পশ্চাতে ফেলিয়া যায়।

dĭn′-ghy, —gey (dĭng-gĭ), *n.* **1.** An extra small boat of a ship for common uses ; জাহাজের ডিঙ্গি ; **2.** (In India) a canoe ; ডিঙ্গি।

dĭn′-gle (dĭng-), *n.* A narrow valley ; সংকীর্ণ উপত্যকা।

din′-gō, *n.* A wild dog found in Australia ; অষ্ট্রেলিয়া মহাদ্বীপের আরণ্য কুক্কুরবিশেষ।

Dingo.

din′-gў, *adj.* Soiled ; of a dark colour; dirty; মলিন, ময়লা; অপরিচ্ছন্ন, অপরিষ্কার; নোংড়া। **—gi-ness,** *n.*

din′-nêr *n.* The chief meal of the day mostly eaten about midday ; a formal feast in honour of some person or event ; দিবসের প্রধান ভোজন, অপরাহ্ণ ভোজন ; ভোজ। **—less,** *adj.* **Dinner-set**—দিবসের প্রধান ভোজনের উপযোগী থালা, বাটী, চামচে প্রভৃতি। **Dinner-waggon**—ভোজনকক্ষে ব্যবহারার্থ তাকবিশিষ্ট ক্ষুদ্র মেজ।

dī′-nō-saur (-sör), *n.* An extinct gigantic reptile ; অধুনা লুপ্ত অতিকায় সর্প বিশেষ। **—sau′-ri-an,** *adj.* Pertaining to a dinosaur ; উক্ত জন্তু-সম্পর্কীয়।

dī′-nō-there (-thēr), *n.* An extinct animal of huge size with elephant like tusks and trunk, belonging to the genus dinotherium ; হস্তীর মত

Dinotherium Giganteum restored.

শুণ্ড এবং দন্ত বিশিষ্ট অতিকায় লুপ্ত জন্তুবিশেষ।

dint, *n.* & *v. t.* **1.** The mark made by a blow or pressure ; a dent ; আঘাতের চিহ্ন বা চাপের দাগ ; খাঁজ। **2.** Force ; power ; as, by *dint* of valour ; শক্তি, বল ; সামর্থ্য, প্রভাব। (মঃ ইঃ)। **3.** (*Archaic*) A blow ; a stroke : (অপ্রচলিত) আঘাত ; ঘা। ***Verb i.*** **1.** To make a mark on a substance by a blow or by pressure ; to dent ; আঘাত দ্বারা চিহ্ন রাখা, চাপ দ্বারা দাগ বসান ; খাঁজ কাটা। **By dint of**—By force or means of ; বলে, দ্বারা।

dī-ŏc′-ē-săn, *adj* & *n.* Pertaining to a diocese ; খৃষ্টীয় ধর্ম্মাধ্যক্ষের অধিকার সম্বন্ধীয়। ***Noun.*** **1.** A bishop in relation to his diocese ; খৃষ্টীয়-ধর্ম্মাধ্যক্ষ। **2.** One of the clergy or the people, of diocese ; খৃষ্টীয় ধর্ম্মাধ্যক্ষের অধীনস্থ যাজক বা তদধিকার-ভুক্ত স্থানবাসী লোক।

dī′-ō-cese (-sēs), *n.* **1.** The extent of a bishop's jurisdiction ; খৃষ্টীয় ধর্ম্মাধ্যক্ষের অধিকার-ভুক্ত স্থান। **2.** (*Hist.*) One of the provinces into which the Roman Empire was divided (*obs.*) ; (ইতিহাস) রোম সাম্রাজ্য যে সমস্ত প্রদেশে বিভক্ত হইয়াছিল তাহার অন্যতম (অপ্রচলিত)।

Dī-œ′-ci-ă (-ē-shî-), *n.* A class of plants having the stamens on one plant and the pistils on other ; একশ্রেণীর বৃক্ষ,—যাহাতে পুংকেশর একভাগে এবং স্ত্রীকেশর অপর ভাগে থাকে, ভিন্নাবাস-পুষ্প (হিঃ কোঃ)।

dī-œ′-cious (-ē-shŭs), *adj.* **1.** (*Bot.*) Having stamens on one plant and the pistils on another ; (উদ্ভিদ্-বিদ্যা) ভিন্নাবাস-পুষ্প সম্বন্ধীয়। **2.** (*Zool.*) Having the two sexes in separate individuals ; স্বতন্ত্র জন্তুতে পুং ও স্ত্রী চিহ্নবিশিষ্ট, অন্যতর-লিঙ্গক (হিঃ কোঃ)।

Dī-ō-nў′-sŭs, *n.* Same as BACCHUS (which see) [কেহ কেহ এই দেবতাকে দেবনহুশ ও পরশুরামের সহিত অভিন্ন বলিয়া মনে করেন।

dī ŏp′-trĭc, *adj.* & *n.* **1.** Of or pertaining to dioptrics ; refractive ; প্রকাশ-বর্ত্তন শাস্ত্র-সম্বন্ধীয় ; তির্য্যগ্‌বর্ত্তনকারী। **2.** Capable of being seen through ; as, a *dioptric* bee-hive ; স্বচ্ছ, পার-দর্শক। ***Noun.*** **1.** Unit of refractive power ; the power of a lens of which the local distance is one metre ; শক্তির একক ; যে তালের কিরণকেন্দ্রান্তর এক মিটার। **2.** (*Pl.*) The part of optics which treats of the transmission of light from one medium to another ; এক মধ্যবর্ত্তী পদার্থ হইতে অপর মধ্যবর্ত্তী পদার্থে আলোক-সঞ্চার বিষয়ক দৃষ্টিবিজ্ঞানের শাখা ; প্রকাশবর্ত্তক শাস্ত্র (হিঃ কোঃ)। **—trical-ly,** *adv.* **Dioptric system**—(আলোক-মন্দিরে) তাল-সমবায়ের সাহায্যে কাচমধ্যবর্ত্তী প্রদীপ হইতে আলোক সঞ্চারণ।

dī-ō-ră′-mă, *n.* **1.** An exhibition of pictures, illuminated and viewed through an opening in the wall of a darkened chamber ; অন্ধকারীকৃত কক্ষে ছিদ্র পথে প্রবিষ্ট আলোক রশ্মি দ্বারা প্রদীপ্ত ও পরিদৃষ্ট চিত্ররাজি-প্রদর্শন, দীপ্তালেখ্য প্রদর্শন। **2.** A building for such an exhibition ; দীপ্তালেখ্যপ্রদর্শন গৃহ। **—ram′-ic,** *adj.*

Dioscorea aculeata—মৌ আলু (বেলঃ)।

dī-ŏs′-môse, —mŏ′-sis, *ns.* The transmission of a liquid through a membrane ; ঝিল্লীর ভিতর দিয়া তরল-পদার্থের সঞ্চার।

Diospyros cordifolia—বন গাব (বেলঃ)।

dī-ox′-ide,(-ŏk-sīd), *n.* (*Chem.*) An oxide containing two equivalents of oxygen to one of a metal ; (রসায়ন-শাস্ত্র) যে অম্লজান-জারিত ধাতুতে দুই তুল্যশক্তিক অম্লজান এবং এক তুল্য-শক্তিক ধাতু আছে।

dip, *v. t.* & *i.* **1.** To plunge or immerse in any liquid for a short time ; to put into a fluid and withdraw ; "The priest shall *dip* his finger in the blood ; ডুবান, চুবকানি দেওয়া, চোবান ; ডুব দেওয়ান। **2.** To baptize by immersion ; জলাবগাহনান্তে খৃষ্টধর্ম্মে দীক্ষা প্রদান করা। **3.** To make (candles) by immersing wick in hot tallow ; উষ্ণ চর্ব্বিতে সলিতা ডুবাইয়া (চর্ব্বির বাতি) তৈয়ার করা। **4.** To lower and raise again ; as, to *dip* a flag or sail ; একবার নামাইয়া আবার উঠান। **5.** To take out with a ladle or other vessel by immersing it in a fluid ; as, to *dip* water from a boiler (often with *out*) ; হাতা বা অন্য পাত্র ডুবাইয়া কোনরূপ তরল পদার্থের কতক অংশ তুলিয়া লওয়া। **6.** To engage thoroughly in any affair ; কোন কার্য্যে সর্ব্ব-প্রযত্নে ব্যাপৃত হওয়া। **7.** (*Poet.*) To wet ; to moisten ; "Dew *dips* me all over ;" (কবিতায়) আর্দ্র করা, সিক্ত করা। **8.** To wash in vermin-killing liquid ; as, to *dip* sheep ; কীটনাশক তরল পদার্থে ধৌত করা। **9.** (*Colloq.*) To involve in debt ; "Never *dip* thy lands— ;" (চলিত-ভাষায়) ঋণজালে জড়িত করা। ***Verb i.*** **1.** To go under water or other liquid and emerge quickly ; ডুব দেওয়া, ডুবান। **2.** To sink ; ডুবা। **3.** To plunge a ladle etc., into water or other liquid for taking out a portion ; কোন তরল পদার্থের কতক অংশ তুলিয়া লওয়ার জন্য তাহাতে হাতা বা অন্য পাত্র ডুবান। **4.** To go deeply ; to penetrate ; গভীরভাবে প্রবেশ করা ; ভেদ করা। **5.** To read cursorily or here and there ; as, to *dip* into a book ; উপর উপর পড়া, চোক বুলাইয়া যাওয়া। **6.** To have a downward slope ; নিম্নদিকে ঢালু বা প্রবণ হওয়া। **Dipping-needle**—চুম্বকাবনতিমাপক সূচি।

dip, *n.* **1.** The action of dipping for a moment into a liquid ; ডুব দেওন, ডোবন। **2.** An inclination downwards ; slope ; প্রবণতা ; ঢালু। **3.** (*Geol.*) The angle a stratum of rock makes with a horizontal plane ; (ভূ-বিদ্যা) পাষাণস্তর ও ক্ষিতিজের সহিত সমান্তরাল ক্ষেত্রের সংযোগোৎপন্ন কোণ। **4.** (*Astron.*) Apparent depression of the horizon, due to the observer's elevation ; উন্নতস্থানে অবস্থান হেতু দ্রষ্টা দিকচক্রবালে যে অবনতি দর্শন করে, ক্ষিতিজাবকাশ (হিঃ কোঃ)। **5.** A candle made by dipping a wick in hot tallow ; উত্তপ্ত চর্ব্বিতে সলিতা ডুবাইয়া যে চর্ব্বির বাতি প্রস্তুত করা হয়। **6.** (*Colloq.*) A bath in the sea ; (চলিত ভাষায়) সাগর-স্নান। **7.** The quantity of liquid dipped up ; হাতা, কলম প্রভৃতি দ্বারা যে পরিমাণ তরল পদার্থ তোলা হয়। **8.** Depth of submergence, as of a vessel, paddle, etc. ; জাহাজ, দাঁড়, প্রভৃতির যে অংশ জলের নিম্নে থাকে। **9.** (*Magnetism*) The angle made by a magnetic needle with the horizon ; (চৌম্বক-বিদ্যা) চৌম্বকসূচি ও দিকচক্রবালের সংযোগে যে কোণ উৎপাদিত হয়, চুম্বকাবনতি (সাঃ পঃ)। **10.** A washing preparation for sheep etc. ; মেষ প্রভৃতি ধৌত করার জন্য কীটনাশক ঔষধ মিশ্রিত জল। **Dip needle**—চুম্বকাবনতি সূচি। **Dip net**—লম্বা হাতলবিশিষ্ট এক প্রকার ক্ষুদ্র জাল। **Dip of the horizon**—দ্রষ্টার উচ্চস্থানে অবস্থান হেতু প্রতিভাত দিকচক্রবালের অবনতি, অবপাত, (সাঃ পঃ), ক্ষিতিজাধরাংশ (হিঃ কোঃ)। **Dip** or **plunge of a paper-kite**—ঘুড়ীর গোতা। **Dipping the colours**—অভিবাদন বা প্রত্যভিবাদনের জন্য পতাকা অবনমিতকরত পুনরুত্তোলন।

dip-lei'-dō-scōpe (-lē-), *n.* An instrument for indicating the passage of the sun or of a star over the meridian ; সূর্য্য কিম্বা কোন নক্ষত্রের যাম্যোত্তর বৃত্ত অতিক্রম সূচনার্থ যন্ত্রবিশেষ, স্পষ্টমধ্যাহ্নবোধক যন্ত্র (হিঃ কোঃ)।

Dipterocarpus turbinatus—শ্বেত-গর্জ্জন (বেলঃ)।

diph-thē'-ri-ă, —rit-is, *ns.* An acute infectious disease of the throat which is accompanied by the formation of a false membrane ; কণ্ঠরোগ বিশেষ,—যাহাতে কণ্ঠদেশে একটী কৃত্রিম ঝিল্লি উপজাত হয়, আচ্ছাদন রোগ (হঃ চঃ), ঝিল্লিক প্রদাহ, রোহিণী রোগ। **—ther'-ic, —rit'-ic, Diph'-ther-oid,** *adjs.*

diph'-thŏng, *n.* **1.** Union of two vowels pronounced in one syllable ; দ্বিস্বর-সংযোজন। **2.** A vowel digraph ; as, in *people* ; দ্বিস্বর-যোগ, সন্ধি-স্বর, দ্বি-স্বর। **3.** A combination of two consonants in one syllable, as, *ch.* in chop ; এক শব্দাংশে দুই ব্যঞ্জনের সংযোগ। **—thon'-gal,** *adj.*

diph'-thŏng-īze, *v. t.* To form a simple vowel into a diphthong by affixing another vowel ; দ্বি-স্বর করা।

dip-lō-blăs'-tic, *adj.* (*Biol.*) Having two germinal layers ; (জীব-বিজ্ঞান) দ্বিজৈবনিক-বিশিষ্ট।

dip-lō-câr'-di-ăc, *adj.* (*Zool.*) With the right and left sides of the heart separate ; (জন্তু-বিদ্যা) পৃথগ্‌ভূত বাম ও দক্ষিণ হৃৎপিণ্ডবিশিষ্ট।

dip-lō-gĕn'-ĕ-sis, *n.* The production in duplicate of parts normally single ; যে সমস্ত অঙ্গ সচরাচর একটী থাকে—তাহার দুইটী উৎপাদন।

di-plō'-mă, *n.* **1.** A letter or writing conferring some power, privilege or honour ; esp. a university or college certificate of degree ; যোগ্যতা পত্র, ক্ষমতা-পত্র, সম্মান-পত্র, বিশেষতঃ বিশ্ববিদ্যালয়ের উপাধি পত্র। **2.** A state writing or official document ; a charter ; সরকারী দলিল পত্র ; সনন্দ, সনদ। **—less,** *adj.* **—maed,** *adj.*

di-plō'-mă-cy̆, *n.* **1.** The art or science of conducting negotiations between nations ; কূট-রাজনীতি।

2. Adroitness ; tact ; চাতুর্য্য ; কার্য্য-কুশলতা, কৌশল।

dip'-lō-măt, *n.* One skilled in diplomacy ; a diplomatist ; কূট-রাজনীতিবিৎ ; কূটরাজনীতিজ্ঞ।

dip-lō-măt'-ic, *adj.* & *n.* **1.** Of or pertaining to diplomacy ; relating to minister at a foreign court ; কূট রাজনীতি সংক্রান্ত ; বৈদেশিক প্রতিনিধি সম্বন্ধীয়। **2.** Of or pertaining to official documents, charters, etc. ; সরকারী কাগজপত্র, সনন্দাদি সম্বন্ধীয়। **3.** Skilled in diplomacy ; dexterous ; characterised by shrewdness ; as, *diplomatic* management ; কূটরাজনীতি বিশারদ; কৌশলী, দক্ষ ; বিচক্ষণ। ***Noun.*** A diplomatist ; কূটরাজনীতি বিশারদ ব্যক্তি। **–i-cal-ly,** *adv.* **Diplomatic body**—কোন রাজধানী বা রাজসভাস্থ বৈদেশিক মন্ত্রিবর্গ। **Diplomatic service**—বিদেশে প্রেরিত মন্ত্রী ও দূতগণ।

di-plō'-mă-tist, *n.* **1.** A person officially employed in diplomacy ; কূট রাজনীতি সংক্রান্ত কার্য্যে নিযুক্ত ব্যক্তি। **2.** A man who is artful or crafty in affairs ; চক্রী, কৌশলী।

di-plō'-mă-tīze, *v. i.* & *t.* To act as a diplomatist ; to practise diplomacy ; কূট রাজনীতি সংক্রান্ত কার্য্যে নিযুক্ত হওয়া ; কূট রাজনীতি প্রয়োগ করা।

dip-lō'-pi-ă, *n.* Double vision ; দ্বি-দর্শ, দ্বিত্ব দৃষ্টিরোগ (যে দৃষ্টি রোগ হেতু একটী বস্তু দুইটী দেখায়)।

Dip'-nō-i, *n.* (*Pl.*) An order of fishes having both gills and lungs ; যে মৎস্যশ্রেণীর কান্‌কো ও ফুসফুস্ উভয়ই রহিয়াছে, দ্বি-শ্বাসী (সাঃ পঃ) **–no-ous,** *adj.*

dip'-pêr, *n.* **1.** One who or that which dips in any liquid ; a ladle ; ডুবরী ; হাতা। **2.** A Baptist or Anabaptist ; a Dunker ; যে সমস্ত খ্রীষ্টানগণ দীক্ষাকালে জলে অবগাহন করেন, যে সমস্ত খৃষ্ট-ধর্ম্মাবলম্বীরা দ্বিতীয় বার জল-সংস্কার গ্রহণ করেন ; যে খৃষ্টীয় সম্প্রদায়বিশেষভুক্ত ব্যক্তিগণ তৃতীয় বার জল সংস্কার গ্রহণ করেন। **3.** A genus of birds of the thrush family that delight in water ; একজাতীয় জলচর পক্ষী। **3.** (*Photo.*) An apparatus for immersing negatives ; (আলোক-চিত্র) প্রচ্ছন্ন-চিত্র সমন্বিত কাচফলকসমূহ নিমজ্জনার্থ পাত্রবিশেষ। **4.** (*Astron.*) The seven principal stars in the constellation of the great Bear ; সপ্তর্ষি মণ্ডলের সপ্ত প্রধান তারা।

dip'-săs, *n.* A serpent whose bite was fabled to produce intense thirst ; একপ্রকার সর্প—এই সর্পদ্বারা দষ্ট ব্যক্তির প্রবল তৃষ্ণা উপজাত হইত বলিয়া প্রবাদ আছে।

dip-sō-mā'-ni-ă, *n.* A morbid craving for alcoholic stimulants ; মদ্যাদি পানের অদম্য ইচ্ছা, মদ্যোন্মাদ (হিঃ কোঃ)।

dip-sō'-sis, *n.* A morbid thirst ; তৃষ্ণাধিক্য (হঃ চঃ)।

dip'-têr-ăl, *adj.* **1.** (*Zool.*) Having two wings only ; (জন্তু-বিদ্যা) দ্বিপক্ষ-বিশিষ্ট। **2.** (*Ancient arch.*) Having a double range of columns on each of the flanks as well as in front and rear ; as, a *dipteral* temple ; (পুরাকালীন স্থপতি-বিদ্যা) প্রতিপার্শ্বে যুগলস্তম্ভশ্রেণী সমন্বিত।

dip'-têr-ous (-ŭs), *adj.* **1.** (*Zool.*) Having two wings (of insects with one pair of membraneous wings); belonging to this class of insects ; (জন্তু-বিজ্ঞান) দ্বিপক্ষ-সমন্বিত উক্তপ্রকার কীটশ্রেণীভুক্ত। **2.** (*Bot.*) With two wing-like appendages ; (উদ্ভিদ্-বিদ্যা) পক্ষবৎ উপাঙ্গ-যুগল সমন্বিত।

dip'-tych, *n.* **1.** A double folding writing-tablet ; দ্বিপাটবিশিষ্ট লিখিবার মেজ। **2.** A pair of pictures on two folding tablets ; দ্বিপাটিত ফলক-দ্বয়োপরি চিত্রযুগল। **3.** A register or list of bishops, saints, etc. ; খৃষ্টীয় ধর্ম্মাধ্যক্ষ, সিদ্ধপুরুষ, প্রভৃতির তালিকা।

dīre, *adj.* **1.** Calamitous ; dreadful ; dismal ; বিপৎপূর্ণ ; লোমহর্ষণ, ভয়ঙ্কর ; দারুণ, ঘোরতর। **2.** Ill-boding ; as, *dire* omens ; অশুভসূচক, অমঙ্গল-সূচক, দুর্নিমিত্তসূচক। **Dire'-ly,** *adv.*

di-rĕct', *v. t.* & *i.* **1.** To point or aim in a straight line towards a place or object ; as, to *direct* an arrow ; লক্ষ্যাভিমুখে সন্ধান করা। **2.** To address ; to superscribe (a letter, parcel, etc. to a person or place) ; শিরোনামা লিখা ; উপরি-ভাগে নামাদি লিখা বা অঙ্কিত করা। **3.** To cause to proceed ; to regulate ; to govern ; as, to *direct* the affairs of the state ; নিয়ন্ত্রিত করা ; পরিচালন করা, নির্ব্বাহ করা ; শাসন করা। **4.** To point out the proper course to ; to guide ; as, he *directed* me to the left-hand road ; প্রকৃত পথ নির্দ্দেশ করা ; পথ, প্রদর্শন করা। **5.** To utter or write to a person ; as, I *direct* my remarks to you ; কোন ব্যক্তিকে লক্ষ্য করিয়া বলা, কাহাকেও লিখা। **6.** To instruct as a superior ; to order ; as, to *direct* the servants ; উপদেশ দেওয়া ; আদেশ দেওয়া। ***Verb i.*** To act as a guide or director ; to give orders ; পরি-চালকের কার্য্য করা, পথ-প্রদর্শন করা ; আদেশ প্রদান করা। **–rec'-tive,** *adj.*

di-rĕct', *adj.* & *adv.* **1.** Quite straight ; leading by the shortest way to a point or end ; as, a *direct* line : a *direct* road to happiness ; right ; সোজা ; ঋজু ; বরাবর। **2.** Unambiguous ; plain ; not doubtful ; as, he made a *direct* acknowledgment ; সরল ; স্পষ্ট ; সাক্ষাৎ, প্রত্যক্ষ, অসন্দিগ্ধ। **3.** Sincere ; open ; straightforward ; as, *direct* dealing ; সরল, অকপট ; সোজাসুজি ; অকুটিল। **4.** In the line of descent from father to son—opposed to collateral, as, a descendant in a *direct* line ;

পিতৃপুত্রপরম্পরাগত। 5. (*Astron.*) Proceeding from east to west; not retrograde; (জ্যোতির্বিজ্ঞান) পূর্ব্ব হইতে পশ্চিমদিগ্‌গামী, মার্গী (সাঃ পঃ), সাক্ষাৎ; অবক্র। ৫. (*Mus.*) Not inverted; as, a *direct* interval or chord; not contrary, as motion; (সঙ্গীত-শাস্ত্র) অবিপর্য্যস্ত; অবিরোধী। 7. Diametrical; as, *direct* contradiction; ঠিক, সোজাসুজি। 8. (*Log.*) Following the uninterrupted chain of cause and effect etc.; as, a *direct* argument; (তর্ক-বিজ্ঞান) অবিচ্ছিন্ন, কার্য্যকারণপরম্পরানুসারী, অপরোক্ষ। 9. Personal; নিজ। ***Adv.*** 1. In a straight line; সরল রেখায়। 2. At once; immediately; তৎক্ষণাৎ; তন্মুহূর্ত্তে। 3. To the point; প্রাসঙ্গিকভাবে। 4. Personally; not by proxy; নিজে; প্রতিনিধি দ্বারা নহে। **—ness,** *n.* **Direct evidence**—সাক্ষাৎ প্রমাণ, প্রত্যক্ষ প্রমাণ। **Direct fire** — সৈন্যশ্রেণীর সম্মুখদিকে গোলা বর্ষণ। **Direct image**—সাক্ষাৎ বিম্ব (হিঃ কোঃ)। **Direct motion**—সাক্ষাৎ গতি (ঐ)। **Direct ray**—অপ্রতিবিম্বিত বা অপরাবর্ত্তিত রশ্মি। **Direct speech** or **oration**—(*Gram.*) উক্ত বাক্য। **Direct tax** — ভূমিকর প্রভৃতি (অর্থাৎ বাণিজ্যদ্রব্য ও আবকারী জিনিষের উপর স্থাপিত কর নয়), কর (হিঃ কোঃ)।

dī-rĕc′-tion, *n.* 1. The act of directing; aim at a certain point; management; guidance; অভিসন্ধান; সন্ধান; পরিচালন, নির্ব্বাহ; শাসন, পথ-প্রদর্শন। 2. Address; superscription; as, the *direction* of a letter; পত্রের শিরোনামাদি; পত্র বা খামের উপরিস্থ নাম বা ঠিকানা। 3. (Usually *pl.*) Instruction; order; command; guidance, whether verbal or written; as, he gave *directions* to the servants; (সাধারণতঃ বহুবচন) উপদেশ; আদেশ; নিদেশ, আজ্ঞা; পরিচালন। 4. The line or course in which anything moves; as, the different *directions* of London; দিক্। 5. The body of persons who guide or manage a matter; a board of directors; পরিচালকবর্গ; পরিচালকসভা। ৫. (*Gun.*) The direct line in which a gun is pointed; (কামান পরিচালন) যে সরল রেখায় কামান সন্ধান করা হয়। 7. Scope; sphere; subject; as, new *directions* of inquiry: improvement in many *directions*; উদ্দেশ্য; ক্ষেত্র; বিষয়। **In the direction of**—দিকে, পানে।

dī-rĕct′-lȳ, *adv.* 1. In a direct or straight course; সোজাসুজি। 2. By a direct process or means; সাক্ষাৎ-সম্বন্ধে, প্রত্যক্ষভাবে। 3. At once; immediately; তন্মুহূর্ত্তে, তৎক্ষণাৎ; অবিলম্বে। 4. In express terms; "And *directly* to condemn prayer;" completely; স্পষ্টাক্ষরে, সোজাসুজি; সম্পূর্ণরূপে। 5. Honestly; "I have dealt most *directly* in thy affair;" সরলভাবে, সাধুভাবে। 6. Exactly; ঠিক। 7. (*Colloq.*) As soon as; যেই মাত্র।

dī-rĕc′-tor (-têr), *n.* 1. One who directs; a manager; a superintendent; a guide; প্রযোক্তা; কর্ম্মকর্ত্তা, শাস্তা, নির্ব্বাহক; অধ্যক্ষ; পরিচালক। 2. A member of the managing board of a company or corporation; as, the *directors* of an insurance company; কোন সমবায়ের অন্যতম পরিচালক। 3. (*R. C. Church*) A priest acting as spiritual adviser; (রোমান ক্যাথলিক ধর্ম্মসংঘ) যে পুরোহিত আধ্যাত্মিক বিষয়ে উপদেশ প্রদান করেন। 4. (*Mech.*) A part of a machine or instrument which directs its motion or action; (যন্ত্র-বিজ্ঞান) কল বা যন্ত্রের যে অংশ দ্বারা উহার গতি বা ক্রিয়া পরিচালিত হয়। 5. (*Surg.*) A grooved instrument for guiding a bistoury; bullet extractor etc.; (অস্ত্রোপচার-বিদ্যা) নালীক্ষতাদি কাটার ছুরিকা, গুলি-উত্তোলক যন্ত্র, প্রভৃতির পথ নির্দ্দেশ করার জন্য খাঁজ-কাটা অস্ত্রবিশেষ; প্রদর্শক-যন্ত্র (হঃ চঃ)। 6. (*Fr. hist.*) A member of a directory; (ফরাসী ইতিহাস) ফরাসী বিপ্লবকালে প্রতিষ্ঠিত কার্য্য-নির্ব্বাহক সভার সভ্য। **—tô′-ri-al,** *adj.* **—ship,** *n.*

dī-rĕc′-tō-rāte, *n.* The office or position of a director; a body of directors; পরিচালকের কার্য্য বা পদ; পরিচালক-সভা।

dī-rĕc′-tō-rȳ, *adj.* Containing directions; directive; advisory; উপদেশগর্ভ; আদেশাত্মক; উপদেশক।

dī-rĕc′-tō-rȳ, *n.* 1. A book of directions for public worship; সাধারণ পূজার জন্য নিয়মাবলী, পুরোহিত দর্পণ। 2. A book containing the names and residences of the inhabitants of a place, their professions, business, etc.; কোন স্থানের অধিবাসিবৃন্দের নাম, ধাম, ব্যবসায় প্রভৃতি জ্ঞাতব্য বিবরণপূর্ণ পুস্তক, লোক-বিবরণী, জনবিবরণী, নাম-পঞ্জী, পঞ্জীগ্রন্থ (কেঃডিঃ)। 3. A body of directors; পরিচালকসভা। 4. (*Fr. hist.*) The revolutionary executive of five directors in power (1795—99); (ফরাসী দেশের ইতিহাস) ফরাসী বিপ্লব-কালে (১৭৯৫—৯৯) পঞ্চ সভ্য দ্বারা গঠিত কার্য্যনির্ব্বাহকসভা।

dī-rĕc′-trix, *n.* A directress; অনুশাসিনী, শাসিকা, অধিকারিণী।

dī-rĕc′-trix, *n.* (*Geom.*) A fixed line serving to describe a curve; (জ্যামিতি) বক্রাদি অঙ্কনে ব্যবহৃত স্থির রেখা, নিয়ত রেখা (হিঃ কোঃ)।

dīre′-fûl, *adj.* Dreadful; terrible; ভয়ঙ্কর; ভয়ানক। **—ly,** *adv.*

dirge (dêrj), *n.* A funeral song; শ্মশান-সঙ্গীত, অন্ত্যেষ্টি-সঙ্গীত, মরণগীতি।

dir′-i-gi-ble, *adj.* & *n.* Capable of being guided or steered; as, a *dirigible* baloon; চালনীয়, বাহনীয়। ***Noun.*** A dirgible baloon; যে ব্যোমযান ইচ্ছামত আকাশে চালাইতে পারা যায়।

dir′-i-mĕnt, *adj.* Rendering null and void ; nullifying ; নাকচকারী ; রাতিলকারক। **Diriment impediment**—যে বাধা বশতঃ বিবাহ প্রায়ই নাকচ হয়।

dirk (dêrk), *n.* & *v. t.* A kind of dagger or poniard ; একপ্রকার ছুরিকা, ছোরা। [এই প্রকার ছোরা পূর্ব্বে হাইল্যাণ্ড্‌বাসিগণ ব্যবহার করিত।] ***Verb t.*** To stab with a dirk ; ছুরি বসান, ছুরি মারা।

dirt (dêrt), *n.* **1.** Any foul or filthy substance as excrement, mud, etc. ; as, a cartload of *dirt* ; ময়লা, জঞ্জাল, কর্দ্দম, আবর্জ্জনা। **2.** A scornful name for land ; (অবজ্ঞার্থে) ভূমি। **3.** Soil ; মাটী। **4.** Dirtiness ; অপরিচ্ছন্নতা। **5.** Meanness ; sordidness ; নীচতা ; ক্ষুদ্রাশয়ত্ব, নীচাশয়ত্ব। **6.** A thing of little or no value ; তুচ্ছ জিনিষ, আবর্জ্জনা। **7.** Foul talk ; কুৎসিত আলাপ। **8.** (*Mining*) A term for the earth, gravel, stones, etc. before washing ; (খনির কাজ) অবিধৌত মাটী, কাঁকর, প্রভৃতি। **Dirt-bed**—কর্দ্দমস্তর। **Dirt-cheap**—Very cheap ; মাটীর দর, অতিসুলভ। **Dirt-eating**—এক প্রকার রোগ ইহাতে মাটী খাইবার জন্য প্রবল ইচ্ছা হয়। **Dirt-pie** — ছেলেদের তৈয়ারী মাটীর পিঠা। **Dirt rotten** — (Shakes.) wholly decayed ; অতিজীর্ণ। **Yellow dirt**—স্বর্ণ। **To fling dirt**—To talk slanderously or abusively ; কুৎসা করা, কলঙ্ক রটনা করা। **To eat dirt**—To put up with insult etc. ; নীরবে অপমান সহ্য করা, কিল খাইয়া কিল হজম করা। **To throw dirt at**—To abuse slanderously ; কুৎসা করা।

dirt′-ȳ (dêrt-), *adj., v. t.* & *i.* **1.** Foul ; filthy ; unclean ; soiled with dirt ; সরজ ; সমল, অপরিষ্কার ; নোংড়া ; মল-দূষিত। **2.** Mean ; base ; sordid ; as, a *dirty* fellow ; নীচ ; হীন ; নীচাশয়। **3.** Not pure or clear ; as, a *dirty* colour ; অবিশুদ্ধ, অস্বচ্ছ। **4.** Rough ; stormy ; as, a *dirty* weather ; বাত্যা-বিক্ষুব্ধ ; ঝটিকাময়। ***Verb t.*** **1.** To soil with dirt ; to make filthy ; to sully ; মলিন করা ; মল-দূষিত করা ; নোংড়া করা। **2.** To scandalize ; as, to *dirty* reputation or character ; কলঙ্কিত করা, কলঙ্ক-লিপ্ত করা। ***Verb i.*** To become dirty ; মলিন হওয়া নোংড়া হওয়া। **—i-ly,** *adv.* **—i-ness,** *n.* Foulness ; baseness ; sordidness ; মলিনতা, মলদূষিতত্ব ; নীচতা, হীনতা ; জঘন্যতা। **—y-ish,** *adj.* **Dirty shirts**—১০১ গণিত পদাতিক সৈন্য। [এই পল্টনের সৈন্যগণ অপরিষ্কার জামা পরিয়া দিল্লী নগরীতে যুদ্ধ করিয়াছিল।] **Dirty Allan**—একপ্রকার সামুদ্রিক পক্ষী, — ইহারা সামুদ্রিক বক প্রভৃতি পক্ষীর ভুক্ত খাদ্য উদ্গিরণ করাইয়া আহার করে।

dĭs-ă-bil′-i-tȳ, *n.* Want of physical, intellectual or moral ability or power ; want of legal qualification to do a thing ; অক্ষমতা, অপারগতা, অকর্ম্মণ্যতা ; আইনতঃ অযোগ্যতা।

dĭs-a′-ble, *v. t.* **1.** To deprive of power of acting ; to render unable ; to cripple ; to incapacitate ; শক্তিহীন করা ; অযোগ্য করা, অক্ষম করা, অসমর্থ করা ; পঙ্গু করা ; নির্ব্বল করা, অকর্ম্মণ্য করা, অশক্ত করা। **2.** To render legally incapable ; to disqualify legally ; আইনতঃ অযোগ্য করা ; অক্ষম করা। **—ment,** *n.*

dĭs-ă-būse′, *v. t.* To undeceive ; to free from error or illusion ; to set right ; as, to *disabuse* oneself of a false notion or prejudice ; ভ্রান্তি দূর করা, ভ্রান্তি অপনোদন করা ; ভ্রম-নির্ম্মুক্ত করা ; সংশোধন করা।

dĭs-ăc-cŏrd′, *n.* & *v. i.* Disagreement ; অনৈক্য, অমিল। ***Verb i.*** To disagree ; অমিল হওয়া, অনৈক্য হওয়া।

dĭs-ăd-văn′-tāge, *n.* **1.** Want of advantage ; a state or condition unfavourable to one's interest ; অসুবিধা ; প্রতিকূলাবস্থা। **2.** Loss ; injury ; as, to sell goods to *disadvantage* ; ক্ষতি ; অনিষ্ট।

dĭs-ăd-văn-ta′-geous (-jŭs), *adj.* **1.** Attended with disadvantage ; inconvenient ; ক্ষতিজনক, অনিষ্টজনক, প্রতিকূল, ইষ্টনাশক ; অসুবিধাজনক। **2.** Derogatory ; হীনতাজনক। **—ly,** *adv.*

dĭs-ăf-fĕct′-ĕd, *adj.* Having the affections alienated ; unfriendly ; disloyal ; as, *disaffected* subjects ; অসন্তুষ্ট ; বৈরভাবাপন্ন ; রাজভক্তিহীন।

dĭs-ăf-fĕc′-tion, *n.* State of being disaffected ; political discontent ; want of loyalty ; বিরাগ, অপ্রীতি ; রাজনৈতিক অসন্তোষ ; রাজভক্তিহীনতা।

dĭs-ăf-firm′ (-fêrm), *v. t.* **1.** To contradict or deny (what has been asserted or affirmed) ; প্রতিবাদ করা। **2.** (*Law*) To annul or reverse, as the decision of a lower court ; (আইন) বাতিল করা, নাকচ করা, রদ করা। **—fir-ma′-tion,** *n.*

dĭs-ăf-fŏr′-ĕst, *v. t.* To reduce from legal state of forest to ordinary land ; to bring (a forest) into the condition of a common land ; বন বিভাগের অধিকার হইতে বিমুক্ত করা ; (বন বিভাগের অধীন আরণ্য-ভূমি) সাধারণ ভূমির অবস্থায় আনা। **—es-ta′-tion,** *n.*

dĭs-ă-gree′ (-grē), *v. t.* **1.** Not to agree ; অসম্মত হওয়া। **2.** To hold opposite or contrary views ; to differ in opinion ; পরস্পরের বিরোধী মত পোষণ করা ; মত ভেদ হওয়া, অনৈক্য হওয়া। **3.** To prove unsuitable ; to have bad effects ; as, a food or climate *disagrees* with a person, his health or digestion, etc. ; অনুপযোগী হওয়া ; না সহা। **—ment,** *n.*

Want of agreement ; difference ; dispute ; discord ; discrepency ; অবনিবনাও, বিমত ; বিসংবাদ ; বিরোধ, অনৈক্য, মতানৈক্য ; গড়মিল।

dis-ă-gree′-ă-ble (-grē-), *adj.* & *n.* **1.** Discordant ; unsuitable ; প্রতিকূল ; অনুপযোগী। **2.** Unpleasant ; offensive ; অপ্রীতিকর ; বিরক্তিজনক। **3.** Unamiable ; bad-tempered; দুর্বিনীত; বদমেজাজী। ***Noun.*** (Usually *Pl.*) Troubles ; worries ; unpleasant experiences ; উৎপাত ; উপদ্রব, ঝঞ্ঝাট ; অপ্রীতিকর অভিজ্ঞতা। **—bly,** *adv.* **—ness,** *n.* Unpleasantness ; contrariety ; অপ্রিয়তা ; অনৈক্য, বৈপরীত্য, বিরুদ্ধতা, বিসংবাদিতা।

dis-ăl-lōw′, *v. t.* Not to allow ; to refuse to sanction ; to reject ; as, to *disallow* a claim ; অনুমতি না দেওয়া ; নামঞ্জুর করা ; অগ্রাহ্য করা।

dis-ăn-nŭl′, *v. t.* To make null and void ; to cancel ; নাকচ করা, বাতিল করা ; রহিত করা, রদ করা।

dis-ăp-pear′ (-pēr), *v. i.* **1.** To vanish from sight ; to cease to be perceived ; as, a ship *disappears* as she sails from port ; অদৃশ্য হওয়া ; অন্তর্হিত হওয়া, তিরোহিত হওয়া। **2.** To cease to exist ; অবসান হওয়া। **—ance,** *n.* Act of disappearing ; vanishing ; অন্তর্ধান ; তিরোধান, অদর্শন।

dis-ăp-point′ (-poynt), *v.t.* **1.** Not to fulfil the desire, hope or expectation of ; to hinder from the attainment of what has been expected ; নিরাশ করা, ভগ্নাশ করা, হতাশ করা ; আশাভঙ্গ করা, মনোভঙ্গ করা। **2.** To frustrate ; to defeat ; as, to *disappoint* one's efforts ; বিফল করা, নিষ্ফল করা ; পরাহত করা, বিমুখ করা। **—ed-ly,** *adv.* **—ing,** *adj.* Causing disappointment ; নৈরাশ্যজনক। **—ing-ly,** *adv.* **To be disappointed at**—কোনও কারণে আশাভঙ্গ হওয়া। **To be disappointed of one's hopes**—কোন কিছু ঘটাতে আশা ভঙ্গ হওয়া **To be disappointed of a thing**—কোন বস্তু না পাওয়াতে আশাভঙ্গ হওয়া। **To be disappointed in a thing**—কোন প্রাপ্ত বস্তু আশানুরূপ না হওয়ায় মনোভঙ্গ হওয়া। **—ment,** *n.*

dis-ăp-prō-bā′-tion, *n.* Disapproval ; অননুমোদন, বিরাগ, অশ্রদ্ধা, ঘৃণা। **—to-ry,** *adj.*

dis-ăp-prove′, (-proov), *v. t.* & *i.* **1.** To give an unfavourable opinion of ; to regard as blameworthy ; to dislike ; as, to *disapprove* the conduct of others ; অননুমোদন করা, দূষণীয় বলিয়া গণ্য করা ; ঘৃণা করা, অশ্রদ্ধা করা। **2.** To decline to sanction ; to reject ; মঞ্জুর করিতে অস্বীকার করা ; অগ্রাহ্য করা। ***Verb i.*** To express dislike ; (generally followed by *of*) ; বিরাগ প্রকাশ করা। **—ing-ly,** *adv.* **—pro′-val,** *n.*

dis-ârm′, *v. t.* & *i.* **1.** To deprive of arms ; to render defenceless ; নিরস্ত্র করা, শস্ত্রহীন করা, নিরায়ুধ করা ; অরক্ষিত অবস্থায় আনা। **2.** To deprive of the power to harm ; to make harmless ; as, to *disarm* a man's wrath ; অনিষ্টজনক প্রভাব নষ্ট করা ; অক্ষতিজনক করা। **3.** To pacify hostility or suspicions of ; "A tongue that every heart *disarms* ;" বিরুদ্ধভাব প্রশমিত করা, সন্দেহ ভঞ্জন করা, সংশয় ছেদন করা। **4.** To disband ; as, to *disarm* an army ; অতিরিক্ত সৈন্যাদি কমাইয়া শান্তির সময় যত সংখ্যক সৈন্য থাকে, তত সংখ্যক সৈন্যরাখা, সৈন্যদল ভঙ্গ করা। ***Verb i.*** **1.** To lay arms aside or down ; to divest oneself of arms ; অস্ত্র সমর্পণ করা ; অস্ত্রবিরহিত করা। **2.** To be reduced to a peace footing, as an army etc ; to disband troops ; অতিরিক্ত সৈন্য সংখ্যা হ্রাস করিয়া শান্তির সময়ের সংখ্যায় আনা ; সৈন্যদল ভঙ্গ করা। **—a-ment,** *n.*

dis-ăr-rānge′, *v. t.* To put out of order ; to disorganize ; বিশৃঙ্খল করা ; শৃঙ্খলাচ্যুত করা, শৃঙ্খলাভ্রষ্ট করা, উল্টাপাল্টা করা, লণ্ডভণ্ড করা।

dis-ăr-ray′ (-rā), *n.* & *v. t.* Disorder ; confusion ; বিশৃঙ্খলা ; গোলযোগ। ***Verb t.*** To throw into disorder ; (*poet.*) to take off the dress of ; to unclothe ; শৃঙ্খলাচ্যুত করা ; (কবিতায়) পরিচ্ছদ-বিরহিত করা ; বিবসন করা।

dis-âr-tic′-ū-lāte, *v. t.* To separate as the joints ; সন্ধিবিযুক্ত করা **—la′-tion,** *n.*

dis-ăs-sim-i-lā′-tion, *n.* (*Physiol.*) Same as KATABOLISM (which see).

dis-ăs′-têr, *n.* A calamity ; a sudden misfortune ; an adverse or unfortunate event ; a serious mishap ; বিপদ্, দুর্ঘটনা ; গ্রহ-বৈগুণ্য, বিপ্লব ; দৈবদুর্বিপাক, উপপ্লব, ব্যসন ; উৎপাত, অনর্থপাত। **—trous,** *adj.* Unlucky ; calamitous ; attended with suffering or misfortune ; দুর্দৈবপূর্ণ ; বিপৎপূর্ণ ; অনর্থপাতবহুল, দুর্বিপাকপূর্ণ, কষ্টবহুল, দুর্দশাজনক। **—trous-ly,** *adv.* **A record of disaster**—দুর্ভাগ্যকাহিনী।

dis-ă-vow′, *v. t.* **1.** To disclaim responsibility for ; to disclaim knowledge of ; as, to *disavow* a crime ; কোন কিছুর দায়িত্ব অস্বীকার করা ; কোন বিষয় জ্ঞাত থাকার কথা অস্বীকার করা। **2.** To deny; অস্বীকার করা। **—al,** *n.*

dis-bănd′, *v. t.* & *i.* To break up ; to disperse ; as, to *disband* an army ; দলভঙ্গ করা ; ছিন্নভিন্ন করা। ***Verb i.*** To separate ; to dissolve connection ; to disperse ; as, the army *disbands* at the close of the war ; পৃথক্ হওয়া ; সম্বন্ধচ্ছেদ হওয়া ; দলভঙ্গ হওয়া, ছিন্ন ভিন্ন হওয়া। **—ment,** *n.*

dis-bâr′, *v. t.* To expel as a barrister etc. from the bar ;

to deprive of the right to plead, as a barrister etc.; উকিল, ব্যারিষ্টার-দিগকে ব্যবহার-জীবিসমাজ হইতে বহিষ্কৃত করা; উকিল, ব্যারিষ্টারদিগকে অধিকার-চ্যুত করা। **—ment,** *n.*

dis-bĕ-lief′ (lēf), *n.* Denial of belief; অপ্রত্যয়, অবিশ্বাস, অশ্রদ্ধা।

dis-bĕ-lieve′ (-lēv), *v. t.* & *i.* To distrust; to have no faith in; অবিশ্বাস করা, অপ্রত্যয় করা; বিশ্বাস না থাকা। ***Verb i.*** To be without faith, (followed by *in*); to be sceptic; অবিশ্বাসী হওয়া, বিশ্বাস বিহীন হওয়া; নাস্তিক হওয়া।

dis-bĕnch′, *v. t.* (*Law*) To deprive (a bencher) of his status; (আইন) বিলাতের ব্যবহারজীবিসংঘের অধ্যক্ষকে পদচ্যুত করা।

dis-brănch′, *v. t.* To strip of branches; to tear off; শাখা বিহীন করা; ছিঁড়িয়া ফেলা।

dis-bŭd′, *v. t.* To cut away (esp. the superfluous) buds from; অতিরিক্ত চোক বা নবোদ্গত শাখা কাটিয়া ফেলা। **—ding,** *n.* The act of cutting away the excess of buds and shoots; শাখাপ্রশাখার শেষাগ্র-ভাগস্থিত ২।৩টী মাত্র চোক বা নবোদ্গত শাখা রাখিয়া অপরগুলিকে ভাঙ্গিয়া দেওন—ইহাতে শাখাগুলি তেজাল ও সুপুষ্ট হইতে পারে এবং পুষ্পসকল পূর্ণায়তন ও উজ্জ্বল বর্ণের হইয়া থাকে।

dis-bŭr-dĕn′, *v. t.* & *i.* **1.** To free or ease of a burden; to relieve; "The need she felt to *disburden* the mind;" বোঝা খালাস করা, ভার-মুক্ত করা, ভার-মোচন করা, ভার-লাঘব করা; লঘু করা, হাল্কা-করিয়া দেওয়া। **2.** To discharge; নিষ্কৃতি দেওয়া। ***Verb i.*** To relieve one's self of a burden; to get rid of one's burden; ভার লাঘব হওয়া; ভারমুক্ত হওয়া।

dis-burse′ (-bêrs), *v. t.* & *i.* To expend; to pay out; টাকা খরচ করা; টাকা প্রদান করা। ***Verb i.*** To pay money; টাকা বিলি করা। **—ment,** *n.* **1.** The act of disbursing; ব্যয়করণ, টাকা বিলিকরণ। **2.** That which is disbursed or paid out; ব্যয়িত অর্থ।

disc, *n.* **1.** A flat circular part or surface; গোলাকার বস্তুর উপরিভাগ, চক্র। **2.** (*Biol.*) A circular structure either in plants or in animals; (জীব-বিজ্ঞান) জীব বা উদ্ভিদের দেহস্থ চক্রাকার অংশ। **3.** (*Astron.*) The seemingly flat surface of a body; মণ্ডল (সাঃ পঃ), বিম্ব (ঐ), দৃশ্য (ঐ)। **Disc of the sun**—সূর্য্যমণ্ডল। **Disc of the moon**—ইন্দু মণ্ডল।

dis-căl′-cĕ-āte, *adj.* & *n.* Barefooted or only sandalled as a friar or nun; নগ্ন-পদ, অনাবৃত পদ, অথবা খৃষ্টীয় সন্ন্যাসী বা সন্ন্যাসিনিগণের মত উপানৎ পরিহিত। ***Noun.*** A friar or nun of the above description; উপানৎ পরিহিত খৃষ্টীয় সন্ন্যাসী বা সন্ন্যাসিনী। **—at-ed,** *adj.*

dis-calced′ (-kălst), *adj.* Same as DISCALCEATE.

dis-cârd′ *v. t., i.* & *n.* **1.** (*Cards*) To throw away or reject, as superfluous cards; (তাস খেলায়) অতিরিক্ত তাস ফেলিয়া দেওয়া বা অগ্রাহ্য করা। **2.** To cast off; to dismiss from service; "William was not the man to *discard* an old friend; দূরে নিক্ষেপ করা; পদচ্যুত করা, বিদায় দেওয়া, বরতরফ করা। **3.** To give up; to reject; as, to *discard* a prejudice, belief, habit, dress, etc.; পরিত্যাগ করা; অগ্রাহ্য করা। ***Verb i.*** (*Cards*) To throw certain cards out of the hand; (তাস খেলা) কতিপয় অতিরিক্ত তাস ফেলিয়া দেওয়া। ***Noun.*** The act of discarding; a discarded card; কতিপয় অতিরিক্ত তাস ফেলিয়া দেওন; পরিত্যক্ত তাস।

dis-cern′ (-zêrn), *v. t.* & *i.* **1.** (*Archaic*) To distinguish; প্রভেদ করা। **2.** To perceive with the eye or intellect; to see and recognise; as, to *discern* a difference; ঠাওরান, নির্ণয় করা; দেখা, পরিচয় করা। ***Verb i.*** **1.** To see or understand the difference; to make distinction; as, to *discern* between good and bad; প্রভেদ দর্শন করা বা বুঝিতে পারা; প্রভেদ করা, ইতরবিশেষ করা। **—i-ble,** *adj.* **—i-bly,** *adv.*

dis-cern′-ing (-zêrn-), *adj.* Having a true or quick insight; acute; penetrating; দূরদৃষ্টি সম্পন্ন; সূক্ষ্ম-দর্শী; তীক্ষ্ণ-বুদ্ধিসম্পন্ন।

dis-cern′-mĕnt (-zêrn-), *n.* The act of discerning; sagacity; insight; keenness of perception; সূক্ষ্মদর্শন; তীক্ষ্ণবুদ্ধিতা; দূরদৃষ্টি, অন্তর্দৃষ্টি; সূক্ষ্মদর্শিতা।

dis-cĕrp′-ti-ble, *adj.* Capable of being plucked apart or disunited; পৃথক্‌করণীয়, বিয়োজনীয়। **—bil′-i-ty,** *n.*

dis-cĕrp′-tion, *n.* **1.** Act of pulling to pieces; severance; a severed piece; খণ্ডবিখণ্ডীকরণ, পৃথকী-করণ; ব্যবচ্ছেদ (মঃ ইঃ), বিভেদ, বিভঙ্গ; ব্যবচ্ছিন্ন অংশ।

dis-charge′ (-chârj), *v. t.* & *i.* **1.** To free from a load or burden; to unload; as, to *discharge* a vessel; ভার-মুক্ত করা; মাল খালাস করা। **2.** To shoot; to fire off; as, to *discharge* a pistol etc.; (অস্ত্রাদি) মোচন করা, নিক্ষেপ করা, ছোড়া; বন্দুক আওয়াজ করা, কামান দাগা। **3.** To dismiss from any office or employment; কর্ম্মচ্যুত করা, পদচ্যুত করা, বিদায় দেওয়া। **4.** To free from an obligation, debt, duty; to acquit; বাধ্যবাধকতা হইতে রেহাই দেওয়া, ঋণদায় হইতে মুক্ত করা, কোন রূপ কর্ত্তব্য পালনের দায় হইতে মুক্ত করা, দায়মুক্ত করা; মুক্ত করা। **5.** To discharge electricity from; কোন বস্তু হইতে তাড়িৎ নিঃসৃত করা। **6.** To release from confinement or custody; কারামুক্ত করা,

খালাস দেওয়া। 7. To let fly; উড়ান, নিক্ষেপ করা। 8. To unload or remove; as, to *discharge* a cargo; বোঝাই মাল নামাইয়া লওয়া, খালাস করা, সরান। 9. To emit or send out; as, a pipe *discharges* water; to give vent to; as, to *discharge* a horrible oath; নির্গত করা, নিঃসৃত করা, পাত করা, ক্ষরিত করা; বাহির করা। 10. To perform or execute as a duty or office; to pay as a debt; কার্য্য সম্পাদন করা, কর্ত্তব্য সম্পাদন করা; ঋণ পরিশোধ করা। 11. To set aside; to dismiss; as, an order was *discharged* on appeal; রহিত করা, রদ করা; অগ্রাহ্য করা, নামঞ্জুর করা। ***Verb i.*** 1. To unload; to emit or send out liquid matter; বোঝাই খালাস হওয়া; তরল পদার্থ নির্গত বা নিঃসৃত হওয়া। 2. (*Dyeing*) To remove colour from a dyed fabric; (রঞ্জন-বিদ্যা) রঙ্গীন বস্ত্রাদি হইতে রঙ্গ উঠাইয়া লওয়া। **To discharge a bankrupt**—to relieve him of further liability; দাওলিয়াকে দায় হইতে নিষ্কৃতি দেওয়া।

dis-charge′ (-chârj), *n.* 1. Act of discharging; relieving of a charge or load; unloading; as, the *discharge* of a ship or of a cargo; বিসর্জ্জন, মোচন; ভার মোচন, দায় হইতে মুক্তি প্রদান; জাহাজাদির মাল নামাইয়া লওন। 2. Firing off; explosion; as, a *discharge* of artillery; আওয়াজ করণ; সশব্দ-স্ফোটন। 3. A dismissal from service or employment; কর্ম্মচ্যুতি, পদচ্যুতি, জবাব, পদভ্রংশ, (আঃ বঃ), কর্ম্মাপকর্ষ (ঐ)। 4. Acquittance or release from a charge or crime; as, the *discharge* of a debtor, নিষ্কৃতি, অব্যাহতি, রেহাই। 5. A performance; execution, or fulfilment, as of a duty, office or trust; payment as of a debt; সম্পাদন, নির্ব্বাহ (আঃ বঃ), অনুষ্ঠান (মঃ ইঃ): সাধন, প্রতিপালন; ঋণাদি পরিশোধ, ঋণসিদ্ধি (মঃ ইঃ)। 6. Emission as of a liquid, electricity or purulent matter; that which is emitted; নিঃসরণ, নির্গমন, ক্ষরণ, পতন, পাত; নিঃসৃত পদার্থ, নিঃস্রাব, স্রাব। 7. Liberation; release from confinement, etc.; as, the *discharge* of a prisoner; মুক্তি; খালাস। 8. Acquittal; অব্যাহতি। 9. Ransom or price paid for deliverence; a written document certifying to the discharge of a debt, duty or other obligation; বন্দীর উদ্ধারের জন্য যে অর্থ প্রদান করিতে হয়; ঋণ পরিশোধের রসিদ, ফারকত, দাবিত্যাগ পত্র প্রভৃতি। 10. (*Dyeing*) The act or process of discharging; a composition used in doing so; (রঞ্জন-বিদ্যা) অবর্ণীকরণ; বস্ত্রাদির রঙ্গ তুলিবার জন্য রাসায়নিক মিশ্র বিশেষ।

dis-charg′-er, *n.* One who or that which discharges; (*electr.*) an instrument for producing an electric discharge; নিক্ষেপকারী, সম্পাদক; (তাড়িত বিদ্যা) তাড়িত নিঃসরণ-কারক যন্ত্র, নিঃসারণ দণ্ড (আঃ বঃ)।

dis-ci′-ple, *n.* 1. One who receives instruction from another; শিষ্য, অন্তেবাসী, বিদ্যার্থী, চেলা। 2. One of the twelve followers of Christ; খৃষ্টের দ্বাদশ জন শিষ্যের অন্যতম। **—ship**, *n.*

dis-ci-plin-ā′-ri-ăn, *n.* One who maintains strict discipline; শাসন-কর্ত্তা, শাসিতা (আঃ বঃ), সুব্যবস্থাপক।

dis′-ci-plin-a-ry, *adj.* Of, relating to, or promoting, discipline; of the nature of mental training; নিয়মানুবর্ত্তিতা-সম্বন্ধীয়, নিয়মানুবর্ত্তিতা বিধায়ক; মানসিক শিক্ষা বা শাসন সম্বন্ধীয়।

dis′-ci-pline (-plin), *n.* 1. (*Archaic*) A branch of instruction or education; (অপ্রচলিত) শিক্ষা বা উপদেশের শাখা বিশেষ। 2. Mental and moral training; নৈতিক এবং মানসিক শিক্ষা, সুশিক্ষা। 3. Drill; a training to act according to certain established rules; as, military *dicipline*; trained condition or state; কস্রৎ; কতিপয় অচল-প্রতিষ্ঠনিয়মানুবর্ত্তী করার জন্য শিক্ষা, অনুশাসন (মঃ ইঃ); শিক্ষাপ্রাপ্তাবস্থা। 4. The practice of correcting or training by means of punishment or castigations; "Without giving her the *discipline* of the strap;" শাস্তি বা বেত্রাঘাত দ্বারা সংশোধন বা শিক্ষা প্রদান। 5. A system of rules for conduct; আচরণীয় নিয়মাবলী। 6. Subjection to control; habit of obedience; submission to order and rule; শাসনাধীনতা, বশবর্ত্তিতা, নিয়মানুবর্ত্তিতা; আদেশানু-বর্ত্তিতা; নিয়মনিষ্ঠা। 7. (*Eccl.*) An instrument of penance or punishment; mortification; (যাজকীয় শাস্ত্র) শাস্তি প্রদানের জন্য বা কৃত পাপের প্রায়শ্চিত্ত করার জন্য যন্ত্রবিশেষ।

dis′-ci-pline (-plin), *v. t.* 1. To train; as, to *discipline* a youth for a profession; শিক্ষা প্রদান করা। 2. To bring into state of discipline or order; to drill; to train to obedience and order; as, to *discipline* troops; শিক্ষিত করা; সামরিক শিক্ষা প্রদান করা; নিয়মাধীন করা, বশবর্ত্তী করা, নিয়মানুবর্ত্তী করা। 3. To chastise; to correct; শাস্তি প্রদান করা; শাসন করা, সংশোধন করা, শোধরান। 4. To inflict censures or punishments upon; কোন ব্যক্তিকে শাস্তি প্রদান বা তিরস্কার করা। **—plin-a-ble**, *adj.*

dis-claim′ (-clām), *v. t. & i.* 1. To give up all claims to; to reject as not belonging to one's self; to disown; to deny the responsibility for; সর্ব্বপ্রকার দাবি পরিত্যাগ করা; নিজের নয় বলিয়া অগ্রাহ্য করা; প্রত্যাখ্যান করা; দায়িত্ব গ্রহণ করিতে অসম্মত হওয়া। 2. (*Law*) To renounce legal claim to;

(আইন) দাবি পরিত্যাগ করা। 3. To refuse ; অস্বীকার করা। ***Verb i.*** To give up all claims or shares (with *in*) ; সর্ব্বপ্রকার দাবি বা অংশ ত্যাগ করা।

dis-claim'-êr (-clam-), *n.* **1.** One who disclaims ; প্রত্যাখ্যানকারী। **2.** (*Law*) A renunciation or disavowal, as of a claim, interest, etc. ; (আইন) দাবি পরিত্যাগ, দাবি অস্বীকার, স্বত্বত্যাগ, স্বত্ব অস্বীকার, প্রত্যাখ্যান (আঃ বঃ)।

dis-clōse', *v.t.* **1.** (*Obs.*) To open ; esp. of eggs ; (অপ্রচলিত) খোলা, ফুটান, বিশেষতঃ ডিম্ব সম্বন্ধে। **2.** To remove a cover from ; to lay open ; অনাবৃত করা ; আবরণ মুক্ত করা। **3.** To reveal, as that which has been kept secret ; to bring to light ; প্রকাশ করা ; ব্যক্ত করা, উদ্ভেদ করা, উদ্‌ঘাটন করা। **4.** To expose to view ; to cause to appear ; প্রদর্শন করা ; দৃশ্যমান করা।

dis-clō'-sure (-zhŭr), *n.* **1.** Act of disclosing ; exposure ; bringing to light ; প্রকাশন, প্রকটীকরণ ; উদ্ভেদ, বিবৃতি ; উদ্‌ঘাটন। **2.** A thing that has been disclosed ; প্রকাশিত বস্তু বা বিষয়।

dis-cŏb'-ŏ-lŭs, *n.* **1.** A thrower of the discus ; চক্রক্ষেপক। **2.** A statue of a disc-thrower in the act of throwing ; চক্রনিক্ষেপোদ্যত ব্যক্তির পাষাণমূর্ত্তি।

dis'-coid (-cōy̆d), *adj.* Having the shape of a disc ; চক্রাকার, বিম্বাকার, মণ্ডলাকার।

dis-col'-our (-cŭl-ŭr), *v. t.* & *i.* **1.** To change or spoil the natural colour of ; to stain ; as, silver is *discolured* by sea-water ; স্বাভাবিক বর্ণ বিকৃত করা ; বদ্‌ রং করা, রং খারাপ করা। **2.** To alter the appearance of ; to put a false hue upon ; "To *discolour* all your ideas ;" পরিবর্ত্তন করা ; মিথ্যাভাব প্রদান করা। **—our-, —or-a'-tion,** *n.* Act of discolouring or the state of being discoloured ; বর্ণান্তররঞ্জন, বিবর্ণীকরণ, বৈবর্ণ্য, বর্ণবিকার, বর্ণ বিকৃতি। **—ment,** *n.*

dis-com'-fit (-cŭm-), *v. t.* & *n.* **1.** To defeat ; to scatter in fight ; পরাভূত করা, পরাজিত করা ; ছত্রভঙ্গ করা, ছিন্নভিন্ন করা। **2.** Disconcert ; ব্যর্থ বা বিফল করা। ***Noun.*** (*Obs.*) Rout ; discomfiture ; as, such a *discomfit* as shall quite despoil him ; (অপ্রচলিত) পলায়ন ; পরাভব। **—fi-ture,** *n.* The state of being discomfited ; rout ; পরাভব ; পরাজয়, পলায়ন।

dis-com'-fort (-kŭm-fêrt), *v. t.* & *n.* **1.** (*Obs.*) To discourage ; to deject ; (অপ্রচলিত) নিরুৎসাহিত করা ; বিরস করা। **2.** To sadden ; to destroy the comfort of ; দুঃখিত করা ; সুখস্বাচ্ছন্দ্য নাশ করা, আরামহীন করা, অসুবিধা জন্মান। ***Noun.*** **1.** Uneasiness ; absence of comfort ; pain ; "Strive against all thy *discomforts* ;" উৎকণ্ঠা, উদ্বেগ, ব্যাকুলতা ; অস্বাচ্ছন্দ্য, অসুবিধা ; ব্যথা, কষ্ট, অসুখ, অনারাম, সুখাভাব। **2.** That which makes one uncomfortable ; inconvenience ; "The troops...had many *discomforts* to endure;" অসুখজনক বিষয় ; অসুবিধা। **—a-ble,** *adj.* Causing discomfort ; অসুবিধাজনক।

dis-cŏm-mĕnd', *v. t.* **1.** (*Rare*) To blame ; to disapprove ; (ক্বচিৎ ব্যবহৃত) দোষ দেওয়া ; অননুমোদন করা। **2.** To expose to censure or ill-favour (the opposite of recommend) ; নিগৃহীত করা, তিরস্কৃত করা। **—a-ble,** *adj.* **—men-da'-tion,** *n.*

dis-cŏm-mōde', *v. t.* To put to inconvenience ; অসুবিধায় ফেলা। **—mod'-i-ty,** *n.* **1.** Inconvenience ; অসুবিধা। **2.** (*Economy*) Anything that it is desired to avoid or get rid of ; (অর্থনীতি-শাস্ত্র) অসুবিধাজনক বিষয়।

dis-cŏm'-mon (-mŭn), *v. t.* **1.** To debar (tradesmen) to deal with undergraduates (at Oxford and Cambridge) ; অক্সফোর্ড ও কেমব্রিজে, বিশ্ববিদ্যালয়ের উপাধি অপ্রাপ্ত ছাত্রগণের সহিত কারবার করিতে (ব্যবসায়ীদিগকে) নিষেধ করা। **2.** To enclose, as commonland ; পশুচারণ ভূমি বৃতি বেষ্টিত করা।

dis-cŏm'-mons (-mŭns), *v. t.* **1.** To deprive of commons ; as, to *discommons* a member of a college ; নির্দ্দিষ্ট খাদ্য দ্রব্য হইতে বঞ্চিত করা **2.** To discommon, as a tradesman ; (ব্যবসায়ীকে) উপাধি অপ্রাপ্ত ব্যক্তিগণের সহিত কারবার করিতে নিষেধ করা।

dis-cŏm-mū'-ni-tȳ, *n.* A lack of common possessions, properties or relationship ; সাধারণ অধিকার, গুণ বা সম্বন্ধের অভাব, অসাম্য, অসাদৃশ্য।

dis-cŏm-plī'-ance (-ăns), *n.* (Rare) Failure or refusal to comply ; (ক্বচিৎব্যবহৃত) অবশবর্ত্তিতা, অবশ্যতা।

dis-cŏm-pōse', *v. t.* **1.** To agitate ; to ruffle ; আন্দোলিত করা ; আলোড়িত করা, বিক্ষুব্ধ করা, উদ্বিগ্ন করা, মনোভঙ্গ করা, শান্তিভঙ্গ করা, উত্তেজিত করা, ব্যাকুল করা। **2.** To disarrange ; to disorder ; বিশৃঙ্খল করা, গোলমাল করা, অবিন্যস্ত করা, এলোমেলো করা। **—pos'-ed-ly,** *adv.* **—po'-sure,** *n.* Disturbance ; perturbation ; আলোড়ন ; বিক্ষোভ, মানসিক উদ্বেগ, চাঞ্চল্য, বৈমনস্য, ক্ষোভ, অস্থিরতা, অশান্তি, ব্যাকুলতা।

dis-cŏn-cêrt, *n.* Want of concert ; disagreement, (*rare*) ; সঙ্গতি-শূন্যতা, মিলনাভাব ; বিসংবাদ, অমিল, অনৈক্য।

dis cŏn'-cêrt', *v. t.* **1.** To frustrate ; to upset ; as, the king *disconcerted* the plan of his enemy ; ব্যর্থ করা, বিফল করা, পণ্ড করা ; বিপর্য্যস্ত করা। **2.** To unsettle the mind of ;

to confuse the faculties of ; মানসিক স্থৈর্য্য নষ্ট করা ; বিচলিত করা, হতবুদ্ধি করা। **—cer'-tion, —ment,** *ns.* Perturbation ; বিক্ষোভ, মানসিক চাঞ্চল্য।

dĭs-cŏn-nĕct', *v. t.* To separate ; to disunite ; পৃথক করা ; বিযুক্ত করা, বিশ্লিষ্ট করা, সম্বন্ধচ্ছেদ করা, সম্বন্ধ ভঙ্গ করা। **—ed,** *adj.* Unconnected ; separate ; incoherent ; অবিযুক্ত ; পৃথগ্‌ভূত ; অসম্বদ্ধ। **—ed-ly,** *adv.* **—ed-ness,** *n.* **—nec'-tion,** *n.* Want of union ; separation (Also -NEXION) ; ভেদ (আঃ বঃ), সংযোগাভাব ; পৃথকীকরণ।

dĭs-cŏn'-sē-crāte, *v. t.* To deprive of sacredness *(rare)* ; পবিত্রতা নষ্ট করা (কচিৎ ব্যবহৃত)।

dĭs-cŏn'-sŏ-lāte, *adj.* **1.** Inconsolable ; deeply dejected ; unhappy ; disappointed ; "A poor *disconsolate* widow ; ম্রিয়মাণ, শান্তিশূন্য ; অতিশয় বিষণ্ণ ; অসুখী, দুঃখিত, সুখশূন্য ; খিন্ন, বিমনা, ভগ্নমনোরথ, হতাশ, ভগ্নাশ। **2.** Inspiring dejection ; cheerless ; as, the *disconsolate* darkness of the winter nights ; বিষাদজনক ; অপ্রফুল্লকর। **—ly,** *adv.* **—ness,** *n.*

dĭs-cŏn-tĕnt', *adj., n. & v. t.* Dissatisfied ; discontented ; অতুষ্ট ; অসন্তুষ্ট। ***Noun.*** Want of content ; inquietude of mind ; অসন্তোষ, অসন্তুষ্টি, অতুষ্টি ; অশান্তি। ***Verb t.*** To make discontented ; to dissatisfy ; অসন্তুষ্ট করা ; বিরক্ত করা। **—ed,** *adj.* Dissatisfied ; অসন্তুষ্ট, অতৃপ্ত, অতুষ্ট, অতৃপ্তমনস্ক। **—ed-ly,** *adv.* In a discontented manner ; অসন্তোষের সহিত। **—ed-ness, —ment,** *ns.* Uneasiness of mind ; মানসিক উদ্বেগ, অশান্তি।

dĭs-cŏn-tĭg'-ū-ous (-ŭs), *adj.* Not in contact ; not contiguous ; অসংযুক্ত ; অসংলগ্ন।

dĭs-cŏn-tĭn'-ue (-ū), *v. t. & i.* **1.** To interrupt the continuance of ; to give up ; as, to *discontinue* work or a habit etc. ; to cease ; স্থগিত করা ; পরিত্যাগ করা, ছাড়িয়া দেওয়া। **2.** *(Law)* To dismiss or abandon, as a suit ; (আইন) অগ্রাহ্য করা, পরিত্যাগ করা, ছাড়িয়া দেওয়া। **3.** To cease to take or pay ; as to *discontinue* a newspaper or subscription ; গ্রহণ করিতে বিরত হওয়া, মূল্যপ্রদানে বিরত হওয়া, বন্ধ করা। ***Verb i.*** To cease ; to stop ; "To *discontinue* a while from labour ;" নিবৃত্ত হওয়া, বিরত হওয়া ; থামা, স্থগিত হওয়া। **—ti-nu'-i-ty** *n.* Want of continuity ; as, *discontinuity* of surface ; বিচ্ছেদ, বিচ্ছিন্নতা, ব্যবধানতা, অসাতত্য। **—u-ance,** *n.* Want of continued connection or continuity of parts ; cessation ; as, a *discontinuance* of conversation ; বিচ্ছিন্নতা, বিচ্ছেদ, অন্তরায় (মঃ ইঃ) ক্রমভঙ্গ ; বিরতি, নিবৃত্তি, বিরাম, স্থগিতাবস্থা। **—u-a'-tion,** *n.* Interruption of continuity ; discontinuance ; ক্রমভঙ্গ, বিরতি।

dĭs-cŏn-tĭn'-ū-ous (-ŭs), *adj.* Not continuous in space or time ; intermittent ; broken off ; বিচ্ছিন্ন, সবিরাম ; সব্যবধান ; খণ্ডিত। **—ly,** *adv.*

dĭs-cŏph'-ŏ-ră, *n.* A sub-class of the Hydrozoa comprising sea-jellies, jelly-fishes, etc. ; সামুদ্রিক মৎস্যশ্রেণীবিশেষ, ছত্রক-দেহী।

dĭs'-cŏrd, *n.* **1.** Disagreement ; want of harmony ; strife ; অনৈক্য, বৈমত্য ; অসঙ্গতি ; বৈমনস্য, অসৌহার্দ্দ্য, ভিন্নভাব, দ্বন্দ্বভাব, বিবাদ। **2.** A harsh noise ; কর্কশস্বর, বিকৃতস্বর, বিস্বর (আঃ বঃ), অপরব (ঐ)। **3.** *(Mus.)* Dissonance ; (সঙ্গীত-বিদ্যা) স্বরবৈষম্য, স্বরমেলনাভাব। **4.** *(Mus.)* A single note which is discordant with another ; (সঙ্গীত-বিদ্যা) অন-মেল (ফঃ হিঃ)। **—ance, —an-cy,** *ns.* **1.** State of being discordant ; inconsistency ; অসঙ্গতি ; অনৈক্য, বৈষম্য। **2.** A discord of sounds ; স্বরানৈক্য, বৈস্বর্য্য। **—ant,** *adj.* **1.** Disagreeing ; incongruous ; quarrelsome ; "*Discordant* motives in one centre meet ;" অনৈক্যবিশিষ্ট ; প্রতিকূল অসমঞ্জস, বিষম (আঃ বঃ) ; কলহপ্রিয়। **2.** *(Mus.)* Not in harmony or musical concord ; harsh ; as, *discordant* notes ; (সঙ্গীত-বিদ্যা) বে-মিল, বে-তাল, বে-সুর, বদ্‌সুর, অপস্বর ; শ্রুতিকটু, কর্কশ। **3.** Opposite ; not coincident ; as, the *discordant* attractions of comets ; বিপরীত ; বিরুদ্ধ, অমিল। **—ant-ly,** *adv.* **Apple of discord**—See APPLE.

dĭs-cŏrd', *v. i.* To disagree ; to jar ; to clash ; (followed by *with, from*) ; as, one *discording with* the other ; অনৈক্য হওয়া, অসঙ্গতিবিশিষ্ট হওয়া ; পরস্পরের বিরোধী হওয়া, ঠুকাঠুকি লাগা।

dĭs'-count (-cownt), *n., v. t. & i.* **1.** A sum deducted for prompt and advanced payment ; ধরাট, বাট্টা, ব্যাজ, ছুট, ত্যাগ (আঃ বঃ)। **2.** The act of discounting ; বাটা ধরণ। **3.** *(In Banking)* A charge made for interest of money advanced on a bill or other document not presently due ; হুণ্ডী প্রভৃতির টাকা নিৰ্দ্দিষ্ট তারিখের পূর্ব্বে প্রদত্ত হইলে যে বাটা কাটিয়া রাখা হয়, মিতি (রঃ অঃ)। **4.** The rate of interest charged in discounting ; হুণ্ডী প্রভৃতির টাকা নিরূপিত দিবসের পূর্ব্বে দেওয়াতে যে হারে সুদ কাটিয়া রাখা হয়। **5.** Allowance for exaggeration in accepting a story ; অতিরঞ্জনের জন্য গল্পাদি হইতে যে বাদসাদ দেওয়া হয়। **6.** *(Billiards)* A deduction made from the score of one player for every point gained by his opponent ; (বিলিয়ার্ড) প্রতিপক্ষের অর্জ্জিত প্রত্যেক অঙ্কের জন্য কোন ক্রীড়কের অঙ্ক সমষ্টি হইতে যাহা বাদ দেওয়া হয়। ***Verb t.*** **1.** To deduct a certain sum or rate per cent from the principal sum; as, the merchant *discounts* 5 per cent for prompt payment; আসল টাকা হইতে শতকরা নির্দ্দিষ্ট সংখ্যক টাকা বাদ দেওয়া, ধরাট ধরিয়া দেওয়া। 2. To lend money upon deducting the discount or allowance for interest: as, the banks *discount* negotiable paper; সুদ বা বাট্টার টাকা বাদ দিয়া নির্দ্ধারিত কালের জন্য টাকা কর্জ্জ দেওয়া। 3. To estimate or take into account beforehand; to diminish or lessen by anticipation; as, to *discount* pleasure or pain; অগ্রে গণনা করা, অগ্রে বিবেচনা করা; অগ্র হইতে ভাবিয়া হ্রাস করা। 4. To leave out of account; to disregard; as, his application is to be *discounted* as irrelevant; গণনার মধ্যে না আনা; গণ্য না করা, অগ্রাহ্য করা। 5. To part with for immediate but smaller good; ভবিষ্যতে অধিক লাভের দিকে দৃষ্টি না করিয়া আশু অল্পলাভে ছাড়িয়া দেওয়া। 6. To make allowance for exaggeration in (stories etc.); অতিরঞ্জন হেতু (গল্পাদি হইতে) বাদসাদ দিয়া লওয়া। ***Verb i.*** To lend, or make a practice of, lending money, deducing the interest at the time of the loan; as, to *discount* for sixty or ninety days; সুদের টাকা কাটিয়া রাখিয়া নির্দ্ধারিত কালের জন্য টাকা কর্জ্জ দেওয়া। **—a-ble,** *adj.* **Bank discount**—হুণ্ডীর টাকা নির্দ্ধারিত দিবসের পূর্ব্বে দেওয়ার দরুণ, টাকা দেওয়ার তারিখ হইতে নির্দ্ধারিত দিবস পর্য্যন্ত সময়ের সুদ বাবত শতকরা নির্দ্দিষ্ট হারে যে বাট্টার টাকা, ব্যাঙ্ক কর্ত্তৃক হুণ্ডীর লিখিত টাকা হইতে কাটিয়া রাখা হয়। **Discount-broker**—যে দালাল বাট্টা দিয়া হুণ্ডী প্রভৃতি ভাঙ্গায়, হুণ্ডীর দালাল। **Discount day**—সপ্তাহের যে নিরূপিত দিবসে ব্যাঙ্ক হইতে বাট্টা কাটিয়া রাখিয়া হুণ্ডীর টাকা প্রদান করা হয়। **True discount**—যে সুদের টাকা মূলধনে যুক্ত হইলে পত্রলিখিত টাকার সমান হয়। **At a discount**—লিখিত বা প্রকৃত মূল্য অপেক্ষা কম দরে, বাজারদর অপেক্ষা কম মূল্যে; Deprecated; not in demand; "Personal merit is *at a* prodigious *discount* in the provinces;" অনাদৃত; কাটতিশূন্য, চাহিদাশূন্য।

dis-coun'-te-nance (-cown-tē-năns), *n.* & *v. t.* Disapprobation, (*archaic*); অননুমোদন (অপ্রচলিত)। ***Verb t.*** 1. To put out of countenance; to abash; লজ্জায় ফেলা, অপ্রতিভ করা; লজ্জিত করা। 2. To discourage; to refuse to give the support or approval to; to show disapproval of; as, a town meeting was convened to *discountenance* riot; নিরুৎসাহিত করা; সাহায্য বা অনুমোদন করিতে অস্বীকার করা; বিরাগ প্রদর্শন করা।

dis-cour'-age (-kŭr-), *v. t.* 1. To deprive of courage, confidence or energy, (opposite of *encourage*); সাহসহীন করা, নিরুৎসাহিত করা, ভগ্নোৎসাহ করা। 2. To deter from; to discountenance; as, they *discouraged* his efforts; নিবৃত্ত করা; দমাইয়া দেওয়া। **—ment,** *n.* 1. Act of discouraging or the state of being discouraged; dejection; নিরুৎসাহিত করণ, নিরুৎসাহ, উৎসাহভঙ্গ; বিষাদ। 2. Disapprobation; অননুমোদন। 3. That which discourages or disheartens; নিরুৎসাহকর বিষয়, নিবৃত্তিকর বিষয়। **—a-ging,** *adj.* Causing or indicating discouragement; নিরুৎসাহকর, নিরুৎসাহসূচক, উৎসাহক্ষয়ী (আঃ বঃ)। **—a-ging-ly,** *adv.*

dis-course' (-kôrs), *n.*, *v. t.* & *i.* 1. (*Archaic*) Conversation; talk; উক্তিপ্রত্যুক্তি; সংলাপ, কথাবার্ত্তা, আলাপ। 2. A formal dissertation; a treatise; a sermon; as, the preacher gave us a long *discourse* on duty; ব্যাখ্যান, বাদ; নিবন্ধ; ধর্ম্মোপদেশ। ***Verb t.*** To utter or give forth; as, it will *discourse* most eloquent music; রাগরাগিণী আলাপ করা। ***Verb i.*** 1. To expose one's views; to speak; to converse; মতপ্রদান করা; বলা; কথাবার্ত্তা বলা। 2. To treat of or discuss a subject in speech or writing; (লিখা বা বর্ত্তৃতায়) কোন বিষয় আলোচনা করা।

dis-cour'-te-ous (-kŭr-tē-ŭs), *adj.* Uncivil; rude; uncourteous; অশিষ্ট; অবিনীত, রূঢ়; অভদ্র, অদক্ষিণ (আঃ বঃ)। **—ly,** *adv.* **—sy,** *n.* Rudeness of behaviour or language; incivility; "Fierceness makes error a fault and truth *discourtesy*;" অসৌজন্য, অশিষ্টতা; অভদ্রতা।

dis-cov'-êr (-kŭv-), *v. t.* 1. To disclose; to lay open to view; প্রকাশিত করা, বাহির করা; উদ্ঘাটিত করা। 2. To obtain for the first time sight or knowledge of (something already existing); as, Columbus *discovered* America; আবিষ্কার করা। 3. To manifest; to show; to betray; as, his youth *discovered* his taste for sculpture; ব্যক্ত করা; প্রদর্শন করা; প্রকাশ করা। 4. To make known; জ্ঞাত করা। 5. To find out; to detect; সন্ধান পাওয়া, জ্ঞাত হওয়া, জানিতে পারা; ধরা। **—a-ble,** *adj.* Capable of being discovered; আবিষ্করণীয়। **—er,** *n.* One who discovers; আবিষ্কারক। **—er-y,** *n.* 1. The action of discovering; as, the *discovery* of the plot; আবিষ্করণ। 2. Disclosure; as, a bankrupt is bound to make a full *discovery* of his assets; উদ্ঘাটন, প্রকাশ। 3. The finding out something previously unknown or unrecognized; as, the *discovery* of new countries;

আবিষ্কার। 4. That which is discovered ; আবিষ্কৃতবিষয়, আবিষ্ক্রিয়া।

dis-cov'-ert (-kŭv-), *adj.* Unmarried ; widowed as a woman; অবিবাহিতা, অনূঢ়া ; বিধবা। **—erture,** *n.* (*Law*) Freedom of a woman from the coverture of a husband ; অনূঢ়াবস্থা, বৈধব্যদশা।

dis-crĕd'-it, *n.* & *v. t.* 1. Want or loss of reputation ; a thing involving loss of repute ; অখ্যাতি, কলঙ্ক, অপযশ ; অখ্যাতির বিষয়। 2. Disbelief ; "The effect of throwing *discredit* upon his evidence ;" অবিশ্বাস। 3. Lack of commercial credit ; বাজারসম্ভ্রম-হীনতা। ***Verb t.*** 1. To disbelieve ; অবিশ্বাস করা। 2. To deprive of good repute ; to disgrace ; সুনাম নষ্ট করা ; অপযশ করা, অখ্যাতি করা। **—a-ble,** *adj.* Injurious to reputation ; shameful ; অপযশজনক, অযশস্কর (আঃ বঃ), অখ্যাতিকর, কীর্ত্তি-নাশী (ঐ), কলঙ্কাবহ (ঐ) ; লজ্জাজনক। **—a-bly,** *adv.*

dis-creet' (-crēt), *adj.* Judicious ; prudent ; circumspect ; সদ্বিবেচক ; বিজ্ঞ ; বিমৃশ্যকারী, সমীক্ষ্যকারী, অবহিত। **—ly,** *adv.*

dis-crĕp'-ănt, *adj.* Discordant ; different ; inconsistent ; অমিল ; ভিন্ন, অনৈক্যবিশিষ্ট ; অসঙ্গতিপূর্ণ, সঙ্গতি-শূন্য। **—ance, —an-cy,** *ns.* Variance ; difference ; গড়মিল, অনৈক্য ; ভেদ।

dis-crete' (-crēt), *adj.* 1. Separate ; distinct ; বিভক্ত, ভিন্ন, বিশ্লিষ্ট ; পৃথগ্‌ভূত। 2. Disjunctive ; বিশ্লেষক, বিচ্ছেদক। 3. Consisting of distinct parts ; স্বতন্ত্র স্বতন্ত্র অংশবিশিষ্ট। 4. Discontinuous ; ছাড়া ছাড়া, বিচ্ছিন্ন, বিখণ্ডিত। 5. (*Metaphys.*) Abstract ; (তত্ত্ব-বিদ্যা) অমূর্ত্ত। 6. (*Log.*) Individually distinct but not different in kind ; as, the individual of a genus are mutually *discrete* ; (তর্ক-বিজ্ঞান) ব্যক্তিগতভাবে পৃথক্, কিন্তু জাতিগতভাবে নয়, ব্যক্ত (হিঃ কোঃ), বিভক্ত (ঐ)। **—ness,** *n.* **Discrete proportion**—একপ্রকার অনুপাত,—যাহাতে প্রথম ও দ্বিতীয় সংখ্যার অনুপাত, তৃতীয় ও চতুর্থ সংখ্যার অনুপাতের সমান। **Discrete quantity**—পৃথক্ পৃথক্ সংখ্যা।

dis-crĕ'-tion, *n.* 1. Cautious discernment, esp. as to matters of propriety and self-control ; as, the better part of valour is *discretion* ; সদ্বিবেচনা, সমীক্ষ্য-কারিতা (আঃ বঃ), বিবেক (ঐ), বিজ্ঞতা (ঐ)। 2. Freedom to act or decide according to one's own judgment ; ইচ্ছাধীনতা, স্বাতন্ত্র্য (মঃ ইঃ)। **—al, —a-ry,** *adjs.* Unrestricted ; as, the court is in certain cases invested with *discretionary* power ; অবারিত, যদৃচ্ছিক (মঃ ইঃ)। **At discretion**—Without conditions or stipulations ; as, a surrender *at discretion* ; বিনা সর্ত্তে। At one's own pleasure ; নিজের খুসী মত। **At the discretion of**—To be settled or disposed of by the will of ; কাহারও ইচ্ছামত মীমাংসনীয়। **Years** or **age of discretion**—The time of life when a man is fit to manage himself ; যে বয়সে কোন ব্যক্তি নিজের কার্য্যের দায়িত্ব গ্রহণ করিতে পারে। **Discretion is the better part of valour**—সদ্বিবেচনাই সাহসের উৎকৃষ্ট অংশ।

dis-crim'-i-nāte, *adj., v. t.* & *i.* 1. (*Archaic*) Distinct ; বিভিন্ন। 2. Marked by discrimination ; "*discriminate* perception ;" সূক্ষ্ম-ভেদাত্মক। ***Verb t.*** 1. To distinguish by discerning differences ; প্রভেদ করা। 2. To serve to distinguish ; to differentiate ; ভেদ প্রদর্শন করা ; পৃথক করা, স্বতন্ত্র করা। ***Verb i.*** To make a distinction ; to distinguish accurately ; প্রভেদ করা ; সূক্ষ্ম ভেদ করা। **—nated,** *adj.* **—na'-tion,** *n.* 1. The act of noting or marking differences ; সূক্ষ্মভেদকরণ, সূক্ষ্মভেদনির্দ্দেশ। 2. Faculty of nicely distinguishing ; as, a man of good *discrimination* ; বিবেক, বিবেচনা (হিঃ কোঃ)। **—na-tive,** *adj.* Distinctive ; characteristic ; as, that peculiar and *discriminative* form of life ; প্রভেদাত্মক, বিভেদক ; বিশেষত্ব-জ্ঞাপক। **—ness,** *n.* Distinctness ; বিভিন্নতা, স্বাতন্ত্র্য।

dis-crim'-i-nāt-ing, *adj.* Distinguishing ; discerning ; as, a *discriminating* critic ; সূক্ষ্মভেদ-কারী ; সূক্ষ্মদর্শী।

dis-crown', *v. t.* To take crown from ; to depose ; (*lit.* & *fig.*); মুকুট বিরহিত করা, বিমুকুটিত করা ; সিংহাসন-চ্যুত করা ; (শব্দানুযায়ী এবং লক্ষণায়)।

dis-cŭr'-sive (-sĭv), *adj.* 1. Passing from one thing to another ; desultory ; digressive ; বিষয় হইতে বিষয়ান্তরগামী ; নানাবিষয়ক (আঃ বঃ), শৃঙ্খলাহীন ; অবান্তরবিষয়গামী। 2. Proceeding by argument or reasoning ; not intuitive ; ব্যাখ্যানাত্মক ; আনুমানিক। **—ly,** *adv.* **—ness,** *n.*

dis'-cŭs, *n.* (*Fr.* & *Rom. Antiq.*) A quoit ; the exercise with the discus ; চক্রাস্ত্র ; উক্ত চক্রাস্ত্রচালনা।

dis-cŭss', *v. t.* 1. To examine by disputation ; to debate ; আলোচনা করা, বাদানুবাদ করা ; তর্কবিতর্ক করা। 2. (*Colloq.*) To try the quality of by eating or drinking ; to consume ; as, to *discuss* food, wine, etc. ; (চলিত ভাষায়) পানাহার দ্বারা (খাদ্যের) গুণাগুণ পরীক্ষা করা, চাকা ; নিঃশেষ করা। **—cuss-ive,** *adj.* & *n.* Able or tending to disperse tumours or coagulated matter ; অর্ব্বুদাদি-বিকিরণকর। (*Noun*) A medicine that disperses morbid humours ; একপ্রকার ঔষধ,—যদ্দারা শরীরস্থ বিকৃত তরল পদার্থ বিকীর্ণ হয়, শোথহর (ঠাকুর)। **—i-ble,** *adj.*

dis-cus'-sion (-kŭsh-ŭn), *n.* **1.** Dispersion, as of a tumour, (*rare*) ; অর্ব্বুদাদির বিকিরণ (কচিৎ ব্যবহৃত) । **2.** Examination by argument; debate ; বাদবিতণ্ডা, আলোচনা, বিচারণ ; বাদানুবাদ । **3.** Investigation of quality by eating and drinking (*colloq.*) : পানাহার দ্বারা খাদ্যের গুণাগুণ নিরূপণ, চাকন ।

dis-cū'-tient (-shĕnt), *adj.* & *n.* (*Med.*) Serving to disperse morbid matter ; শোথহর (ঠাকুর) । ***Noun.*** A discutient agent ; অর্ব্বুদাদি বিকিরণকর ঔষধ ।

dis-dain' (-dān), *n.* & *v. t.* A feeling of contempt and aversion ; scorn ; অনাদর; উপেক্ষা, অবজ্ঞা, ঘৃণা । ***Verb t.*** **1.** To deem unbecoming ; as, to *disdain* to do mean act ; অযোগ্য বলিয়া বিবেচনা করা । **2.** To scorn ; "Goliath *disdains* David ;" অবজ্ঞা করা । **–ful,** *adj.* Full of, or expressing, contempt ; অবজ্ঞাপূর্ণ, অবজ্ঞাসূচক । **–ful-ly,** *adv.* **–ful-ness,** *n.*

dis-ease' (-ēz), *n.* **1.** Uneasiness ; trouble ; অস্থিরতা, অসোয়াস্তি ; কষ্ট । **2.** Any morbid state of the body generally or any particular organ or part of it ; sickness ; malady ; অসুস্থতা ; রোগ ; ব্যাধি । **3.** Deranged or depraved state of the mind or moral character ; মানসিক-বিকৃতি, চরিত্র-ভ্রষ্টতা । **4.** (*Bot.*) A morbid condition of plants etc. ; (উদ্ভিদ্-বিদ্যা) বৃক্ষাদির রুগ্নাবস্থা । **–eased',** *adj.* Affected with disease ; morbid ; depraved ; রোগাক্রান্ত ; রোগ-দুষ্ট, বিকৃত ; ভ্রষ্ট ।

dis-edge' (-ĕj), *v. t.* To deprive of edge ; to blunt ; ধার নষ্ট করা ; ভোঁতা করা, কুণ্ঠিত করা ।

dis-ĕm-bark', *v. t.* & *i.* To remove from on board a vessel ; to put on shore ; জাহাজ বা নৌকা হইতে নামান ; তীরে রাখা । ***Verb i.*** To go ashore out of a ship or boat ; to debark ; জাহাজ বা নৌকা হইতে তীরে অবতরণ করা ; উত্তরণ করা । **–bar-ka'-tion,** *n.*

dis ĕm-băr'-răss, *v. t.* To free from embarrassment ; to disentangle, (with *from*) ; ঝঞ্ঝাট হইতে মুক্ত করা ; সঙ্কট বা দায় হইতে উদ্ধার করা । **–ment,** *n.*

dis-ĕm-bĕl'-lish, *v. t.* To deprive of embellishment ; নিরাভরণ করা, অলঙ্কার বিরহিত করা, ভূষণহীন করা ।

dis-ĕm-bŏd'-y̆, *v. t.* **1.** To divest (a soul) of the corporeal existence ; to free or separate (an idea) ; দৈহিক সত্তা বিরহিত করা, অশরীরী করা, দেহবিযুক্ত করা, অমূর্ত্ত করা, দেহাবচ্ছিন্ন করা ; অবচ্ছিন্ন করা । **2.** (*Fig.*) To disarm or disband a body of soldiers ; (লক্ষণায়) সৈন্যদল নিরস্ত্র করা, সৈন্যদলভঙ্গ করা । **–ied,** *adj.* Incorporeal ; অশরীরী, দেহসম্বন্ধশূন্য, বিদেহী, বীতশরীর (আঃ বঃ), দেহাবচ্ছিন্ন, বায়ুভূত । **–i-ment,** *n.* **1.** The act of disembodying or the state of being disembodied; অশরীরীকরণ,অমূর্ত্তাবস্থা, দেহাবচ্ছিন্নাবস্থা ।

dis-ĕm-bogue' (-bōg), *v. t.* & *i.* **1.** To pour out or discharge at the mouth ; as, a river *disembogues* itself or waters into a sea ; মুখ বা মোহনা দিয়া নিঃস্রাবিত করা । **2.** (*Fig.*) To discharge ; to pour fourth ; as, to *disembogue* a speech ; (লক্ষণায়) নিঃস্রাবিত করা ; নিঃসৃত করা । ***Verb i.*** **1.** To flow (into) ; to pour out contents ; as, a river *disembogues* into a sea ; প্রবাহিত হওয়া ; ঢালা । **2.** (*Fig.*) To come forth ; to emerge ; (লক্ষণায়) নিঃসৃত হওয়া, বহির্গত হওয়া । **–ment,** *n.* Discharge ; নিঃস্রাব ।

dis-ĕm-bos'-om (-bōōz-ŭm), *v. t.* & *i.* To disclose ; to reveal ; প্রকাশ করা ; ব্যক্ত করা । ***Verb i.*** To disclose what is in one's bosom ; প্রাণের কথা প্রকাশ করা ।

dis-ĕm-bōw'-ĕl, *v. t.* To take out the bowels ; to eviscerate ; নিরন্ত্রীকৃত করা ; অন্ত্রবহিষ্কার করা নাড়ীভুঁড়ি বাহির করা, অন্ত্রাপসারিত করা । **–ment,** *n.* The act of disembowelling ; নিরন্ত্রীকরণ ।

dis-ĕm-broil', (-broil), *v. t.* To free from perplexity ; জটিলতা দূর করা ।

dis-ĕm-pōw'-ĕr, *v. t.* To deprive of power, (*rare*) ; ক্ষমতাহীন করা (কচিৎ ব্যবহৃত) ।

dis-ĕn-chănt', *v. t.* To free from enchantment or illusion ; মায়ামুক্ত করা, কুহক-মুক্ত করা, কুহকপাশ ছেদন করা, মোহ দূর করা ।

dis-ĕn-cŭm'-bĕr, *v. t.* To free from encumbrance ; to disburden ; as, to *disencumber* troops of their baggage ; ঝঞ্ঝাট, বোঝা বা দায় হইতে মুক্ত করা ; ভার-মুক্ত করা ।

dis-ĕn-dōw', *v. t.* To strip of endowment, as a church etc. ; বৃত্তিরহিত করা । **–ment,** *n.*

dis-ĕn-frăn'-chīse, *v. t.* To deprive of the rights of a citizen ; নাগরিক অধিকার বিরহিত করা, পৌর-জনাধিকার চ্যুত করা ।

dis-ĕn-gāge', *v. t., i.* & *n.* **1.** To free ; to loosen ; to detach ; to liberate ; as, to *disengage* a metal from extraneous substances ; পৃথক্ করা, স্বতন্ত্র করা ; বিশ্লিষ্ট করা ; বিযুক্ত করা, বিচ্ছিন্ন করা ; মুক্ত করা, ছাড়াইয়া দেওয়া । **2.** (*Fencing*) To shift the sword from one side of an adversary's sword to the other ; (অসি-ক্রীড়া) প্রতিপক্ষের তরবারির এক পার্শ্ব হইতে অপর পার্শ্বে স্বীয় তরবারি ঘুরাইয়া নেওয়া । ***Verb i.*** To withdraw one's self ; as, he *disengaged* from the world ; নিবর্ত্তিত হওয়া, বিষয়বিবিক্ত হওয়া । ***Noun.*** (*Fencing*) Act of disengaging ; (অসিক্রীড়া) প্রতিপক্ষের তরবারির অপর পার্শ্বে স্বীয় অসি সঞ্চারণ। **—gaged'**, *adj.* Not engaged ; at leisure ; free ; vacant ; অব্যাপৃত, কার্য্যবিরত ; অবসর ; মুক্ত ; চিন্তাশূন্য। **—ment,** *n.* **1.** The act of setting free ; state of being disengaged ; বিমোচন ; বিমুক্তাবস্থা, বিশ্লিষ্টাবস্থা। **2.** Leisure ; অবকাশ, অবসর। **3.** Liberation, as of a chemical component ; রাসায়নিক উপাদান পৃথকীকরণ। **4.** Freedom from constraint ; easy natural manner ; সঙ্কোচ-শূন্যতা ; স্বচ্ছন্দভাব, সহজভাব। **5.** The dissolution of an engagement of marriage ; বিবাহ-ভঙ্গ। **6.** (*Fencing*) Disengage ; (অসিক্রীড়া) স্বীয় অসি প্রতিপক্ষের অসির অপর পার্শ্বে সঞ্চারণ। **When disengaged**—অবকাশ মত।

dis-ĕn-nŏ'-ble, *v. t.* To degrade ; to render ignoble ; মর্য্যাদাহীন করা ; অবনমিত করা।

dis-ĕn-tail' (-tāl), *v. t.* & *n.* (*Law*) To break the entail of (an estate) ; (আইন) কোন সম্পত্তি পুত্র পৌত্রাদি ক্রমে ভোগের অধিকারচ্যুত করা। ***Noun.*** The act of breaking the entail of an estate ; পুত্রপৌত্রাদি ক্রমে ভোগের অধিকার লোপ।

dis-ĕn-tan'-gle (-tăng-), *v. t.* & *i.* **1.** To free from entanglement ; to unravel ; to untwist ; গ্রন্থি-মোচন করা ; গাঁইট খোলা, জট খোলা ; পাক খোলা। **2.** (*Fig.*) To extricate from complication ; as, to *disentangle* truth from errors : (লক্ষণায়) ঝঞ্ঝাট বা গোলযোগ হইতে মুক্ত করা ; ***Verb i.*** To become disentangled ; ঝঞ্ঝাট-মুক্ত হওয়া। **—ment,** *n.*

dis-ĕn-thrall', *v. t.* To release from thraldom or slavery, (written also DISENTHRAL) ; দাসত্ব হইতে মুক্ত করা। **—ment,** *n.*

dis-ĕn-tomb' (-tōōm), *v. t.* **1.** To take out from a tomb ; গোর হইতে উঠাইয়া লওয়া, সমাধি হইতে উত্তোলিত করা। **2.** To unearth ; to find by research ; উদ্ভেদ করা ; গবেষণার ফলে আবিষ্কার করা।

dis-ĕn-trănce' (-trăns), *v. t.* To awaken from a trance or enchantment ; যোগনিদ্রা হইতে জাগ্রত করা, সম্মোহিত অবস্থা হইতে জাগ্রত করা, ভাব-সমাধি ভঙ্গ করা।

dis-ĕn-twine' (-twīn), *v. t.* To free from being twisted ; পাক খোলা।

dis-ĕs-tăb'-lish, *v. t.* **1.** To annul the establishment of ; বিপ্রতিষ্ঠিত করা। **2.** To deprive, as a church, of its connection with the state ; খৃষ্টীয় ধর্ম্ম-সংঘের সহিত সরকারী সম্বন্ধ রহিত করা। **—ment,** *n.*

dis-fā'-vour (-vêr), *n.* & *v. t.* **1.** Dislike ; disregard ; disapproval ; অনাদর, অপ্রীতি, বিরাগ, বামতা, অপ্রসাদ ; অশ্রদ্ধা ; অননুমোদন, অস্বীকার। **2.** State of being disliked ; as, to be in *disfavour* at court ; অনাদৃত অবস্থা, সম্মানহীনতা। **3.** An unkindness ; অসদয় ব্যবহার। ***Verb t.*** To regard with disfavour ; to treat with disapprobation ; অপ্রীতির চক্ষে দেখা ; অনাদর করা।

dis-fea'-tūre (-fē-), *v. t.* To mar features of ; to disfigure ; বিরূপ করা ; শ্রীভ্রষ্ট করা।

dis-fĭg'-ūre, *v. t.* To deform ; to deface ; to mar the beauty of ; বিকৃত করা, বিরূপ করা, কদাকার করা ; শ্রীভ্রষ্ট করা ; সৌন্দর্য্য নাশ করা। **—ment,** *n.* **1.** Act of deisfiguring ; defacement ; বিরূপীকরণ ; বৈরূপ্য। **2.** That which disfigures ; শ্রীনাশক, সৌন্দর্য্য-বিঘাতক। **—u-ra'-tion,** *n.* Deformity ; বিকৃতি।

dis-fŏr'-ĕst, *v. t.* **1.** To disafforest ; বনহীন করা। **2.** To clear of forests ; জঙ্গল কাটিয়া পরিষ্কার করা।

dis-frăn'-chise (-chīz or -chĭz), *v. t.* **1.** To dispossess of the rights of a citizen or of a particular privilege as of voting, holding office, etc. ; to deprive (a place) of the right of sending parliamentary representatives ; নাগরিক অধিকার লোপ করা, পৌরজনাধিকার বিরহিত করা, পৌরত্ব লোপ করা ; নির্ব্বাচন ক্ষমতা প্রভৃতি লোপ করা। **2.** To deprive of any right or privilege ; অধিকার চ্যুত করা, অধিকার নাশ করা। **—ment,** *n.* The act disenfranchising ; পৌরত্ব-হরণ, পৌরত্বলোপ।

dis-frock' (-frŏk), *v. t.* To deprive of a clerical garb or office ; যাজকীয় পদ বা পরিচ্ছদ বিরহিত করা।

dis-fur'-nish (-fêr-), *v. t.* To deprive of furniture, equipments, etc. ; গৃহ-সজ্জাহীন করা, সজ্জাহীন করা। **—ment,** *n.*

dis-gâr'nĭsh, *v. t.* To divest of garniture ; ভূষণরিক্ত করা, সজ্জাশূন্য করা, মণ্ডনশূন্য করা।

dis-gorge' (-gŏrj), *v. t.* & *i.* **1.** To eject or discharge by the throat and mouth ; উদ্গিরণ করা, উদ্বমিত করা। **2.** To discharge violently ; as, volcanoes *disgorge* streams of burning lava, ashes and stones ; উদ্গিরণ করা, নিঃস্রাবিত করা। **3.** (*Fig.*) To yield what has been taken wrongfully ; as, he was compelled to *disgorge* his ill-gotten gains ; (লক্ষণায়) অন্যায় পূর্ব্বক গৃহীত দ্রব্য প্রত্যর্পণ করা। ***Verb i.*** **1.** To discharge ; নিঃসৃত করা। **2.** To make restitution ; পুনঃপ্রদান করা, প্রত্যর্পণ করা। **—ment,** *n.*

dis-grāce', *n.* & *v. t.* **1.** Loss of favour, regard or respect ; downfall from one's position ; অযশ, অপযশ, অখ্যাতি, অপমান, অবমাননা, লাঞ্ছনা ; কলঙ্ক, অধঃপতন। **2.** Dishonour ; ignominy ; shame ; অসম্মান ; পরিভব, অসম্ভ্রম, অমর্য্যাদা, অপ্রতিষ্ঠা (মঃ ইঃ) ; লজ্জা। **3.** That which brings dishonour ; cause of shame ; as, every vice is a *disgrace* to a rational being ;

অপমানজনক বিষয়; লজ্জার কারণ। *Verb t.* **1.** To dismiss with dishonour; as, Pitt had been *disgraced* and the old Duke of Newcastle dismissed; লাঞ্ছিত করিয়া পদচ্যুত করা। **2.** To bring shame or discredit upon; to be a disgrace to; to lower in estimation; অপমানিত করা, লাঞ্ছিত করা; সম্ভ্রম নাশ করা; মর্য্যাদাহীন করা। **–ful,** *adj.* Bringing disgrace; dishonorable; shameful; অপমানজনক, অমর্য্যাদাজনক; অকীর্ত্তিকর, (মঃ ইঃ), গর্হিত, অপমানকর, অসম্মানজনক; লজ্জাকর, লজ্জার্হ, লজ্জাবহ। **–ful-ly,** *adv.* **–ful-ness,** *n.* **To disgrace one's self**—ঢলান (*colloq.*)।

dis-grē-gā'-tion, *n.* (*Phys.*) The process of separation or the condition of being separated; (পদার্থ-বিজ্ঞান) বিয়োজন, বিযুক্তাবস্থা।

dis-grŭn'-tle, *v. t.* To render discontented; to disgust, (chiefly used in *p. p.*); অসন্তুষ্ট করা; বিরক্ত করা। **–tled,** *p. p.*

dis-guise' (-gīz), *n.* & *v. t.* **1.** A dress put on for concealment or deception; কপটবেশ, ছদ্মবেশ, কৃত্রিমবেশ (মঃ ইঃ)। **2.** (*Fig.*) A false pretence or show; an assumed appearance intended to deceive; artificial manner; deception; a disguised condition; as, a blessing in *disguise*; (লক্ষণায়) ছল, ভাণ; কপটভাব; কপট আচরণ; বঞ্চনা; ছদ্মভাব। *Verb t.* **1.** To change the guise or appearance of by assuming an unusual or strange dress; ছদ্মবেশ পরিধান করা। **2.** (*Fig.*) To conceal or obscure by any covering or mask; to cloak; as, to *disguise* one's intentions or feelings; (লক্ষণায়) লুকান; প্রচ্ছন্ন করা, গোপন করা। **–ment,** *n.* **Disguised in** or **with drink** or **liquor**—Drunk; মাতাল।

dis-gŭst', *n.* A strong aversion; loathing; repugnance; (generally followed by *at, for, towards, against*); বিরক্তি, বিতৃষ্ণা; অরুচি, বিরাগ; ঘৃণা, জুগুপ্সা।

dis-gŭst', *v. t.* **1.** To provoke loathing, aversion or indignation in; বিরক্তি উৎপাদন করা, অরুচি জন্মান, বিতৃষ্ণা জন্মান। **2.** (*Fig.*) To offend the reason or sensibility of; (with *at* or *with*); (লক্ষণায়) ক্ষুণ্ণ করা। **3.** To dissuade from a proposed or intended purpose, (with *from, of* or *against*); "Which thoroughly *disgusted* him *of* attacking us;" নিবৃত্ত করা। **–ed-ly, –ing-ly,** *advs.*

dis-gŭst'-fŭl, *adj.* Exciting disgust; repulsive; disgusting; বিতৃষ্ণাজনক, অরুচিজনক, বিরাগজনক, উদ্বেগকর; ঘৃণোৎপাদক (মঃ ইঃ), বীভৎস; বিরক্তিকর।

dish, *n., v. t.* & *i.* **1.** A shallow flat-bottomed vessel to serve up food at the table; স্থাল, স্থালী, থালা, রেকাব, শরাব। **2.** A dish-shaped receptacle used for any purpose; থালার আকার পাত্র, বারকোষ। **3.** The food served in a dish; hence any particular kind of food; as, a cold *dish*; থালায় পরিবেষিত খাদ্য; ব্যঞ্জনাদি খাদ্যদ্রব্য। **4.** (*Min.*) A trough in which ore is measured—about 20 inches long; (খনিজ-বিদ্যা) আকরোত্তলিত বিমিশ্র ধাতু মাপিবার জন্য বৃহৎ পাত্র বিশেষ। **5.** (*Agri.*) A hollow place in the field where water lies; ক্ষেত্রমধ্যস্থ জলপূর্ণ গর্ত্ত। **6.** The contents or capacity of a dish; a dishful; থালার জিনিষ, থালার ধারণ-শক্তি; একথালা। **7.** The state of being concave or like a dish; as, the *dish* of a wheel; নতোদরতা, অন্তর্বর্ত্তুলতা, স্থালীসন্নিভতা। *Verb t.* **1.** To put in a dish ready for the table; ভোজনোপবিষ্ট ব্যক্তিগণকে প্রদান করার জন্য স্থালীতে রাখা। **2.** To make concave or depress in the middle, like a dish; স্থালীর মত নতোদর করা। **3.** To make (a hole) like a dish; স্থালীর আকার (ছিদ্র) করা। **4.** To frustrate; to circumvent; to defeat; as, to *dish* the Whigs; পণ্ড করা, বিফল করা; ফাঁকি দেওয়া; পরাভূত করা। *Verb i.* **1.** To have a form resembling that of a dish (said of wheels); as, this wheel *dishes* very much; (চক্র-সম্বন্ধে) স্থালীর ন্যায় আকার প্রাপ্ত হওয়া। **2.** (*Fig.*) To present attractively; as, to *dish* up facts, arguments, etc.; (লক্ষণায়) চিত্তাকর্ষকভাবে উপস্থাপিত করা। **3.** (Of a horse) To swing the fore feet sidewise in trotting; (অশ্ব-সম্বন্ধে) কদমে চলিবার সময় সম্মুখের দুই পা একপার্শ্বে দোলান। **Dish-cloth,** (*archaic*) **Dish-clout**—থালা বাসন মুছিবার নেকড়া, সম্মার্জ্জন-পট (আঃ বঃ)। **Dish-cover**—স্থালীস্থিত খাদ্য উষ্ণ রাখার জন্য ধাতুনির্ম্মিত ঢাকনি। **Dish-wash, –water**—যে জলে স্থালী প্রভৃতি ধৌত করা হয়। **Earthen dish**—খর্পর। **Made-dish**—নানাপ্রকার উপাদানে প্রস্তুত বিচিত্র ব্যঞ্জন। **Standing dish**—যে ব্যঞ্জন প্রত্যহ বা প্রতিবার পরিবেষিত করা হয়। **To dish out**—To serve out of a dish; to distribute in portions at table; স্থালী হইতে পরিবেষণ করা; ভোজনোপবিষ্ট ব্যক্তিগণের প্রত্যেককে কিয়দংশ করিয়া পরিবেষণ করা। **To dish up**—To serve (a meal); পরিবেষণ করা।

dis-ha-bille' (-ă-bĭl), *n.* See DESHABILLE.

dis-hă-bĭt'-ū-āte, *v. t.* To make unaccustomed; অনভ্যস্ত করা।

dis-hăl'-low (-lō), *v. t.* To profane; to make unholy; অমেধ্য করা; অপবিত্র করা।

dis-hăl-lū-cĭ-nā'-tion, *n.* Disillusion; মায়ামুক্তি, মোহমোচন।

dis-hâr'mŏ-ny̆, *n.* Discord ; dissonance ; বিরোধ, অনৈক্য ; ভিন্ন-স্বরতা (হিঃ কোঃ)। **—mo'-ni-ous,** *adj.* **—nize,** *v. t.* & *i.* To put, or be, out of harmony ; সঙ্গতিশূন্য করা, অনৈক্য হওয়া, সঙ্গতিশূন্য হওয়া।

dis-heart'-en (-hârt-n), *v. t.* To discourage ; to deject ; নিরুৎসাহিত করা, দমাইয়া দেওয়া, উৎসাহহীন করা, হতাশ করা, মনোভঙ্গ করা, ভগ্নোদ্যম করা; বিষণ্ণ করা, বিমনাঃ করা। **—ment,** *n.*

dis-hĕr'-i-son (-zn), *n.* Disinheriting ; উত্তরাধিকার স্বত্ব হইতে বঞ্চিত করণ।

di-shĕv'-ĕl, *v. t.* **1.** To suffer the hair to hang loosely, (used chiefly in *p. p.*) ; as, with garments rent and hair *dishevelled* ; কেশরাশি অবেণী-বদ্ধ করিয়া দোলায়িত করা, কেশকলাপ আলুলায়িত করা, আলুথালু করা। **2.** (*Fig.*) To scatter ; to ruffle ; as, like the fair flower *dishevelled* in the wind ; (লক্ষণায়) প্রস্থত করা, ছড়ান, বিছান, মেলান, বিকীর্য্যমাণ করা ; কুঞ্চিত করা, আলোড়িত করা। **—elled,** *adj.* **1.** With disordered hair ; loose ; unconfined as hair ; আলুথালু-কেশপাশ, বিকীর্ণমূর্দ্ধজ, প্রকীর্ণকেশ, অসংযতাকুলালক; বিস্রস্ত (কুঃ) আলুলায়িত (বেহুলা), প্রস্থত (কুঃ), বিলুলিত (ঐ); আলুথালু, বিকীর্য্যমাণ (বাৎস্যঃ)। **2.** Untidy; ruffled; unkempt; as, a *dishevelled* person ; অপরিচ্ছন্ন ; এলোমেলো ; উস্কা-খুস্কা। **—ment,** *n.*

dis-hon'-ĕst (-ŏn), *adj.* Fraudulent ; void of probity ; as, *dishonest* gain ; শঠতাপূর্ণ, কুটিল, খল, প্রবঞ্চক ; অসাধু, অসৎ, অধার্ম্মিক। **—ly,** *adv.* In a dishonest manner ; অসদুপায়ে, শঠতাপূর্ব্বক।

dis-hon'-ĕs-ty̆ (-ŏn-), *n.* **1.** Want of honesty or integrity ; deceitfulness; অসাধুতা ; বঞ্চনাশীলতা, প্রতারণ-পরায়ণতা। **2.** A dishonest act ; theft ; fraud ; অন্যায় কার্য্য ; চৌর্য্য ; প্রতারণা।

dis-hon'-our (dîs-ŏn-êr or dîz-ŏn-êr), *n.* & *v. t.* **1.** Disgrace ; ignominy ; insult ; অমর্য্যাদা, অগৌরব, অনাদর, (মঃ ইঃ) ; অসম্ভ্রম ; অপমান। **2.** (*Law*) The non-payment or non-acceptance of commercial paper by the party on whom it is drawn ; (আইন) হুণ্ডী প্রভৃতি অগ্রাহ্য করণ। ***Verb t.*** **1.** To deprive of honour ; to disgrace ; to treat with indignity ; মানহানি করা, সম্ভ্রম নষ্ট করা, মর্য্যাদা হানি করা ; কলঙ্কিত করা, অখ্যাতি করা, অপযশ করা ; অমর্য্যাদা করা, অসম্মান করা। **2.** To violate the chastity of ; to debauch ; সতীত্ব লঙ্ঘন করা, বে-ইজ্জত করা, ভ্রষ্টকরা ; ব্যভিচারদোষে দুষ্টকরা। **3.** To refuse to accept or pay ; as, to *dishonour* a cheque or bill of exchange ; হুণ্ডী প্রভৃতি অগ্রাহ্য করা, টাকা না দিয়া হুণ্ডী প্রভৃতি ফেরৎ দেওয়া। **—a-ble,** *adj.* **1.** Involving or deserving disgrace ; ignominious ; base ; অপমানজনক, অপযশস্কর ; কলঙ্কজনক ; হেয়, নীচ। **2.** Unprincipled ; সম্মান জ্ঞানহীন, নীতিজ্ঞানহীন। **—a-ble-ness,** *n.* **—a-bly,** *adv.* **—oured,** *adj.* Deprived of honour অমানিত (রবিঃ), অপমানিত, অসম্মানিত।

dis-hŏrn', *v. t.* To deprive of horns ; শৃঙ্গ বিহীন করা।

dis-house' (-howz), *v. t.* To deprive of house or home as a person or persons or a place ; গৃহশূন্য করা, গৃহহীন করা।

dis-il-lū'-sion, *n.* & *v. t.* Disenchantment ; freedom from illusion ; মোহনাশ, মায়াপাশচ্ছেদন, ভ্রান্তি-নিরাশ, ভ্রমোপনোদন ; মায়ামুক্তি, মোহ-বিমুক্তি, মায়া-মোচন। ***Verb t.*** To free from an illusion ; মোহ নাশ করা, মায়ামুক্ত করা, ভ্রান্তি দূর করা। **—ize,** *v. t.* **—ment,** *n.*

dis-in-clīne', *v. t.* & *i.* To excite dislike or aversion ; to make indisposed or unwilling ; as, his timidity *disinclined* him to such an arduous enterprise ; অনাসক্ত করা, বিতৃষ্ণা জন্মান, বিরাগ জন্মান, বিরক্তি উৎপাদন করা, অপ্রীতি সঞ্চার করা, বীতরাগ করা, অপ্রবৃত্তি জন্মান, বিমুখ করা, বীতশ্রদ্ধ করা, পরাঙ্মুখ করা ; অনিচ্ছা জন্মান, নিবৃত্ত করা। ***Verb i.*** To be unwilling or indisposed ; অনিচ্ছুক হওয়া, বিমুখ হওয়া। **—cli-na'-tion,** *n.* Want of liking or willingness ; বিতৃষ্ণা, বীতশ্রদ্ধা, অপ্রবৃত্তি, অনাসক্তি, বিরাগ, অপ্রীতি, অনিচ্ছা, বিরক্তি, বৈমুখ্য।

dis-in-cŏr'-pŏ-rāte, *v. t.* **1.** To deprive of the rights, powers and privileges of a corporate body ; to dissolve (a corporation); সংঘবদ্ধ জনগণের ক্ষমতা বা অধিকার চ্যুত করা ; সংঘবদ্ধ সমাজ ভঙ্গ করা। **2.** To separate from a corporation ; সংঘবদ্ধ সমাজ হইতে বিচ্ছিন্ন করা।

dis-in-fĕct', *v. t.* To cleanse of infection ; to make innocuous ; as, to *disinfect* a room, clothes, etc. ; রোগ-সংক্রমণবিনাশী ঔষধদ্বারা বিশোধিত করা ; সংক্রমণ দোষ দূর করা। **—fec'-tion,** *n.* Act of disinfecting ; purification from infection; সংক্রমণদোষ নিরাকরণ; সংক্রমণদোষ বিশোধন।

dis-in-fĕct'-ănt, *adj.* & *n.* Rendering free from infection ; নিঃসংক্রামক (হিঃ কোঃ), সংক্রামকারি (প্রবাসী ১৩১৯ বাং)। ***Noun.*** An agent used for destroying the germs of infectious diseases ; রোগসংক্রমণ বিনাশক দ্রব্যাদি।

dis-in-gĕn'-ū-ous (-ŭs), *adj.* Not ingenuous ; insincere ; having secret motive ; as, so *disingenuous* as not to confess them (faults) ; অসরল ; খল, কপট, অনৃজু (আঃ বঃ), অদক্ষিণ (মঃ ইঃ) ; গুপ্ত-অভিসন্ধিপূর্ণ। **—ly,** *adv.* **—ness,** *n.*

dis-in-hĕr'-it, *v. t.* To cut off hereditary rights ; to deprive of inheritance ; অনধিকারী করা, নিরংশী

করা ; উত্তরাধিকার হইতে বঞ্চিত করা। **—ance,** *n.* Act of disinheriting ; state of being disinherited ; উত্তরাধিকার হইতে বঞ্চিতকরণ ; উত্তরাধিকার হইতে বঞ্চিতাবস্থা।

dis-in′-tĕ-grāte, *v. t.* & *i.* To separate into component parts ; to reduce to fragments or to powder ; বিশ্লিষ্ট করা, সংহতি ভেদ করা ; খণ্ডবিখণ্ড করা, বিচূর্ণিত করা। ***Verb i.*** To be disintegrated ; to loose cohesion ; বিঘটিত হওয়া (হিঃ কোঃ) ; বিশ্লিষ্ট হওয়া। **—gra-ble,** *adj.* **—gra′-tion,** *n.* Act of disintegrating ; চূর্ণ-ক্রিয়া (হিঃ কোঃ), ভ্রংশ, (ঐ), বিচূর্ণন, সংহতিভেদ (আঃ বঃ), বিশ্লেষণ।

dis-in-têr′, *v. t.* **1.** To unbury ; to exhume ; কবর খুঁড়িয়া লাশ বাহির করা ; সমাধি হইতে মৃতদেহ উত্তোলিত করা। **2.** To bring out of concealment ; to unearth ; লুক্কায়িত স্থান হইতে বাহির করা ; উদ্ভেদ করা, আবিষ্কার করা। **—ment,** *n.*

dis-in′-têr-ĕst-ĕd, *adj.* Not biassed by personal interest or advantage ; impartial ; অহেতুক ; অহৈতুক, অসম্পর্কীয়, নিঃসংশ্রবী। **—ly,** *adv.* **—ness,** *n.* **Disinterested action**—নিঃস্বার্থকর্ম্ম।

disjecta membra, *n. pl.* (*L.*) Fragments ; scattered remains ; বিক্ষিপ্ত দেহাবশেষ।

dis-jĕc′-tion, *n.* Destruction ; disperson ; ধ্বংস ; ছত্রভঙ্গ।

dis-join′ (-jo͝yn), *v. t.* & *i.* To separate ; to disunite ; বিচ্ছিন্ন করা ; বিযুক্ত করা, সংযোগ-ভ্রষ্ট করা। ***Verb i.*** To be parted ; to part ; বিযুক্ত হওয়া ; বিচ্ছিন্ন হওয়া।

dis-joint′ (-jo͝ynt), *v. t.* & *i.* **1.** To put out of joint ; to dislocate as bones ; গ্রন্থিচ্যুত করা ; অস্থি প্রভৃতি সন্ধিচ্যুত করা। **2.** To separate at joints ; গাঁইট ছাড়ান। **3.** To make incoherent, (chiefly used in *p. p.*) ; as, a *disjointed* talk ; অসংলগ্ন করা, অসম্বদ্ধ করা। ***Verb i.*** To fall in pieces ; খণ্ড খণ্ড হইয়া পড়া। **—ed,** *adj.* Separated at joints ; disconnected ; desultory or incoherent as a speech etc. ; গ্রন্থি-বিচ্যুত, সন্ধিচ্যুত ; অসম্বদ্ধ ; অসংলগ্ন। **—ed-ly,** *adv.* **—ed-ness,** *n.*

dis-jŭnc′-tion, *n.* Act of disjoining ; state of being disjoined ; separation ; বিভাগ (সাঃ পঃ), বিশ্লেষ ; পৃথকত্ব, বিপ্রয়োগ, সম্ভেদ, বিয়োগ। **—tive,** *adj.* & *n.* **1.** Tending to disjoin ; involving separation ; disjoining ; বিভাজক ; পৃথকত্বসূচক ; বিয়োজনকারী। **2.** (*Log.*) Alternative ; (তর্ক-বিজ্ঞান) বৈকল্পিক। **3.** (*Gram.*) Involving choice between two words etc. as, a *disjunctive* conjunction ; বৈকল্পিক। (*Noun.*) (*Log.* & *Gram.*) The disjunctive premise or conjunction ; (তর্ক-বিজ্ঞান ও ব্যাকরণ) বৈকল্পিক পূর্ব্বাবয়ব, বৈকল্পিক অব্যয় (either, or, neither, nor, but, etc.) **—tive-ly,** *adv.*

disk, disc, *n.* **1.** A discus ; a quoit ; (*poetic*) ; চক্রাস্ত্র ; লৌহময় ক্রীড়াচক্র (কবিতায়)। **2.** A flat, circular plate ; as, a *disk* of paper ; চাক্‌তি। **3.** (*Astron.*) The round (apparently) flat surface of a celestial body ; as, the sun's *disk* ; (রবিবিম্ব) (জ্যোতির্বিজ্ঞান) জ্যোতিষ্কের বিম্ব। **4.** (*Biol.*) A circular structure either in plants or animals ; as, a blood *disk* ; (জীব-বিজ্ঞান) জীব বা উদ্ভিদের গোলাকার দেহাংশ। **5.** A disk harrow ; এক প্রকার বিদা। **Disk harrow**—See DISK 5.

dis-like′, *n.* & *v. t.* Disapprobation ; aversion ; জুগুপ্সা, দ্বেষ, অপ্রীতি ; বিরাগ। ***Verb t.*** To disapprove of ; to disrelish ; বিরাগ প্রকাশ করা, অপ্রীতি প্রকাশ করা ; অপ্রবৃত্তি বোধ করা, বিরক্তিকর লাগা, ভাল না লাগা, অপসন্দ করা। **—lik′-ing,** *adj.*

dis′-lō-cāte, *v. t.* **1.** To displace ; to put out of joint ; as, to *dislocate* a bone, limb, etc. ; সরান, স্থানচ্যুত করা ; সন্ধিচ্যুত করা। **2.** (*Geol.*) To make (strata etc.) discontinuous ; (ভূবিদ্যা) (স্তরাদি) বিচ্ছিন্ন করা। **3.** To disarrange ; as, to *dislocate* a machinery, plan, affairs, etc. ; বিশৃঙ্খল করা, শৃঙ্খলাভ্রষ্ট করা। **—ca′-tion,** *n.* The act of displacing or the state of being displaced ; অস্থিবিতান, অস্থিচ্যুতি, গ্রন্থিবিশ্লেষ (সাঃ পঃ), সন্ধিভঙ্গ (মঃ উঃ), স্থানচ্যুতি।

dis-lodge′ (-lŏj), *v. t.* To drive from a lodge or fortified position ; as, to *dislodge* an enemy ; to drive from a place of defence or hiding ; as, to *dislodge* a deer ; স্থানচ্যুত করা, বাসস্থান হইতে চ্যুত করা ; আশ্রয়স্থান চ্যুত করা, লুক্কায়িত স্থান হইতে বাহির করা। **—lodg(e)′-ment,** *n.*

dis-loy′-ăl, *adj.* **1.** Not true to allegiance ; as, a *disloyal* subject ; রাজভক্তিহীন। **2.** False ; treacherous ; as, a *disloyal* friend ; অবিশ্বাসী ; বিশ্বাসঘাতক। **—ist,** *n.* **—ly,** *adv.* **—ty,** *n.*

dis′-măl, *adj.* **1.** Disastrous ; calamitous ; (rare) ; দুর্দ্দৈবপূর্ণ ; বিপৎপূর্ণ। **2.** Depressing ; sombre ; gloomy ; cheerless ; dreary ; "It looked very *dismal* and threatening all the time ;" অবসাদকর ; অপ্রফুল্লকর ; বিষাদপূর্ণ ; নিরানন্দ ; ঘোর। **—ly,** *adv.* **—ness,** *n.* **The dismals**—Low spirits ; dumps ; স্ফূর্ত্তিহীনতা ; বিষণ্ণতা।

dis-măn′-tle *v. t.* **1.** To deprive of dress or covering ; to uncloak ; পরিচ্ছদশূন্য করা ; অনাবৃত করা। **2.** (*Fig.*) To deprive of defences, equipments, etc. ; as, to *dismantle* a fortress or a ship ; to break down and render useless ; (লক্ষণায়) আসবাবশূন্য করা ;

সজ্জাহীন করা, ভাঙ্গিয়া ফেলা। **—ment,** *n.*

dis-mâst′, *v. t.* To break off or carry down the mast from; মাস্তুল ভাঙ্গিয়া ফেলা, মাস্তুলহীন করা।

dis-may′ (-mā), *n.* & *v. t.* Consternation; loss of strength and courage through fear; সন্ত্রাস, ভয়ত্রস্ততা; ভয়বিহ্বলতা, ভয়বিকলতা। ***Verb t.*** To terrify; to disable with alarm or fear; to discourage; ভয়-সন্ত্রস্ত করা; ভয়স্তম্ভিত করা, ভীতি-বিহ্বল করা, ভয়াভিভূত করা; নিরুৎসাহিত করা।

dis-mĕm′-bĕr, *v. t.* **1.** To tear limb from limb; to mutilate; অঙ্গচ্ছেদ করা, খণ্ডবিখণ্ড করা; অঙ্গহীন করা। **2.** (*Fig.*) To partition; as, to *dismember* a kingdom; (লক্ষণায়) বিভাগ করা। **—ment,** *n.* The act of dismembering; অঙ্গচ্ছেদ, অঙ্গচ্ছেদন।

dis-miss′, *v. t.* **1.** To send away; to disperse; to disband as an army; (also used as a word of command closing drill); বিদায় করা, বিদায় দেওয়া; ভঙ্গ করা; সৈন্যদল ভঙ্গ করা। **2.** To discard; to remove from office; ফেলিয়া রাখা; বরতরফ করা, পদচ্যুত করা, পদভ্রষ্ট করা, জবাব দেওয়া, বরখাস্ত করা। **3.** To put out of mind or consideration; as, to *dismiss* idle fears; মন হইতে দূর করা, মনে না আনা। **4.** (*Law*) To refuse hearing to; as, to *dismiss* a petition or case; (আইন) ডিস্মিস করা, খারিজ করা। **—al, —mis′-sion,** *ns.* Act of dismissing or the state of being dismissed; পদচ্যুতি, অধিকার-চ্যুতি, জবাব, বরতরফ, ডিসমিস, খারিজ। **—i-ble, —mis′-sive,** *adjs.*

dis-mount′ (-mownt), *n., v. i.* & *t.* Alighting; অবরোহণ, অবতরণ। ***Verb i.*** **1.** To alight from a horse; অশ্ব হইতে অবরোহণ করা। **2.** To come or go down (*poet*); নামা, অবতরণ করা (কবিতায়)। ***Verb t.*** **1.** To throw or remove from a horse; to unhorse; as, the soldier *dismounted* his adversary; to alight from, as horse etc.; অশ্বপৃষ্ঠ হইতে ফেলিয়া দেওয়া, অশ্বপৃষ্ঠ-চ্যুত করা; অশ্বপৃষ্ঠ হইতে পাতিত করা; অশ্বাদির পৃষ্ঠ হইতে অবতরণ করা। **2.** To remove as cannon or other artillery from their carriage; শকট হইতে কামানাদি স্থানান্তরিত করান। **3.** (*Mech.*) To take down, as a machine; (যন্ত্র-বিজ্ঞান) যন্ত্রাদি নামান।

dis-ō-bē′-di-ence (-ĕns), *n.* Act of disobeying; refusal to obey; আজ্ঞা-ভঙ্গ, আদেশ লঙ্ঘন; অবাধ্যতা। **—ent,** *adj.* **1.** Refractory; rebellious; (used of persons, acts); as, the *disobedient* spirit in the colonies; অবাধ্য, আজ্ঞালঙ্ঘনকারী; বিদ্রোহী। **2.** Unyielding; intractable; মগ্‌রা; অদম্য। **—ent-ly,** *adv.*

dis-ō-bey′ (-bā), *v. t.* & *i.* To disregard, as rule; not to obey; as, refractory children *disobey* their parents; অমান্য করা; আজ্ঞা-পালন না করা, কথা না শোনা। ***Verb i.*** To violate commands; to be disobedient; আজ্ঞা না মানা, আজ্ঞা লঙ্ঘন করা, আদেশ লঙ্ঘন করা; অবাধ্য হওয়া।

dis-ō-blīge′, *v. t.* To do something against the wishes of; to be unaccommodating to; কোন ব্যক্তির ইচ্ছার বিরুদ্ধে কার্য্য করা; কোন ব্যক্তির অপ্রীতির কারণ হওয়া, অনুপকার দ্বারা ক্ষুণ্ণ করা। **—blig′-ing,** *adj.* Unaccommodating; অনুগ্রহবিমুখ, অবশম্বদ। **—blig′-ing-ly,** *adv.* **—blig′-ing-ness,** *n.*

dis-ŏrb′, *v. t.* To throw out of the proper orbit; কক্ষচ্যুত করা।

dis-ŏr′-dêr, *n.* & *v. t.* **1.** Confusion; disarray; as, the troops are in *disorder*; গোলমাল; বিশৃঙ্খলা, অব্যবস্থা। **2.** Irregularity neglect of order; ব্যতিক্রম (হিঃ কোঃ); ক্রমভঙ্গ (মঃ ইঃ), দুর্ব্যবস্থা (হিঃ কোঃ)। **3.** Breach of public order; tumult; riot; as, the city is sometimes troubled with the *disorder* of its citizens; শান্তিভঙ্গ; হুলস্থুল ব্যাপার; হাঙ্গামা। **4.** Sickness; derangement; as, *disorder* of bowels; অসুস্থতা; গোলমাল। ***Verb t.*** **1.** To disturb the order of; to throw into confusion; বিশৃঙ্খল করা, বেসিজিল করা; অবিন্যস্ত করা, লণ্ডভণ্ড করা, উলট্‌পালট্ করা। **2.** To produce sickness or indisposition in; পীড়া বা অসুস্থতা জন্মান। **—li-ness,** *n.* **—ly,** *adj.* **1.** Confused; untidy; unruly; বিশৃঙ্খল, অস্তব্যস্ত (মঃ ইঃ); অপরিপাটী; অদম্য। **2.** (*Law*) Violating public order or morality; constituting a nuisance; as, a *disorderly* conduct, house, etc.; (আইন) শান্তিভঙ্গ-কারী, উচ্ছৃঙ্খল, নীতিভ্রষ্ট; ব্যভিচার পূর্ণ। **Disorderly house**—বেশ্যালয়, জুয়ার আড্ডা। **Disorderly person**—দাঙ্গাবাজ, জুয়ারী, শান্তিভঙ্গকারী।

dis-ŏr-găn-īze, *v. t.* To destroy the organic structure of; to throw into utter disorder; ব্যবস্থাচ্যুত করা, ব্যবস্থাভঙ্গ করা; লণ্ডভণ্ড করা, উলট্‌পালট্ করা। **—i-za′-tion,** *n.* The act of disorganizing; উচ্ছেদ, ব্যবস্থাচ্যুতি, ব্যবস্থাভঙ্গ।

dis-ō′-ri-ĕn-tāte, *v. t.* **1.** To turn from the east; পূর্ব্বদিক্ হইতে প্রবাহিত করা। **2.** To confuse (a person) as to his bearings (*lit.* & *fig.*); দিগ্‌ভ্রান্ত করা, দিগ্‌ভ্রম জন্মান।

dis-own′ (-ōn), *v. t.* **1.** To disavow; to disclaim; অস্বীকার করা; প্রত্যাখ্যান করা। **2.** To repudiate; to renounce allegiance to; ত্যাগ করা; বশ্যতা অস্বীকার করা। **—ment,** *n.*

dis-păr′-āge, *v. t.* To bring discredit on; to lower in esteem; to speak slightingly of; to depreciate; খ্যাতি নষ্ট করা; মর্য্যাদা হানি করা; কোন ব্যক্তি সম্পর্কে অবজ্ঞা সহকারে বলা, তাচ্ছিল্যের সহিত কাহারো

বিষয় উল্লেখ করা ; মূল্যাপকর্ষ করা, দর কমান। **—ag-ing-ly,** *adv.* **—ment,** *n.*

dis'-pă-rāte, *adj.* & *n.* Unlike; dissimilar; incommensurable; without relation; বিসদৃশ; বিপরীত; বিষম; সম্বন্ধশূন্য। ***Noun.*** (Usu. *pl.*) Things so unequal or unlike that they cannot be compared with each other; বিসদৃশ বস্তু সমূহ।

dis-păr'-i-tȳ, *n.* Inequality; incongruity; difference; অসাম্য, বৈষম্য, অসমানতা; বৈসাদৃশ্য, অসাদৃশ্য, বৈলক্ষণ্য; প্রভেদ, অন্তর।

dis-pârk', *v. t.* **1.** To convert (a park-land) to other uses; নগরোদ্যানের ভূমি অন্য কার্য্যে নিয়োগ করা। **2.** To release from inclosure; as, he *disparks* his seraglio; অনাবৃত করা, অপরিবেষ্টিত করা, বৃতিবিহীন করা।

dis-pârt', *n.* **1.** (*Gunnery*) Difference between the semi-diameters of a gun at the base-ring and at the muzzle, to be allowed for in aiming; (কামানাদিতে) কামানের নিম্নপ্রান্তস্থ ও অগ্রভাগস্থ ব্যাসার্দ্ধদ্বয়ের বিভেদ, যাহা লক্ষ্য করার সময় বাদসাদ দিয়া লইতে হয়। **2.** A piece of metal placed on the muzzle or on the top of a piece of ordnance to make the line of sight parallel to the axis of the bore, (also *dispart-sight, muzzle-sight*); কামানের উপরিভাগে স্থাপিত ধাতুখণ্ড, যৎসাহায্যে দৃষ্টিরেখা রন্ধ্রের অক্ষের সহিত সমান্তরাল করা হয়।

dis-pârt', *v. t.* & *i.* **1.** To part asunder; to separate; বিযুক্ত করা; পৃথক্ করা, বিচ্ছিন্ন করা। **2.** To distribute; বিতরণ করা। ***Verb i.*** **1.** To separate; to open; বিচ্ছিন্ন হওয়া; বিদারিত হওয়া। **2.** To go in different directions; বিভিন্ন দিকে ধাবিত হওয়া।

dis-pas'-sion (-păsh-ŭn), *n.* Apathy; বিরাগ, উদাসীনতা। **—ate,** *adj.* **1.** Free from passion; অনাসক্ত, বীতরাগ, বীতস্পৃহ। **2.** Impartial; as, *dispassionate* proceedings; পক্ষপাতশূন্য, অপক্ষপাত। **—ate-ly,** *adv.* **—ate-ness,** *n.*

dis-patch', dĕs- (-păch), *n.*, *v. t.* & *i.* **1.** Sending off a message or messenger; সংবাদপ্রেরণ, সংবাদবাহক প্রেরণ। **2.** Putting to death; "We made a keen *despatch* of them all; যমালয়ে প্রেরণ, শমনসদনে প্রেরণ। **3.** Prompt execution; efficiency; rapidity; ক্ষিপ্র-সম্পাদন; কর্ম্মদক্ষতা; ক্ষিপ্রতা। **4.** A written message sent off promptly and speedily; especially an official communication on state affairs; as, naval *dispatches*, ; দ্রুতপ্রেরিত বার্ত্তা; বিশেষতঃ কোন সরকারী পত্র। **5.** An agency for conveying goods etc.; মাল সরবরাহের জন্য যৌথ কারবারের প্রতিনিধির কার্য্যালয়। **6.** A message transmitted by telegram; তারযোগে প্রেরিত বার্ত্তা, তাড়িতবার্ত্তা। ***Verb t.*** **1.** To send off to a destination or for a purpose, (particularly applied to messengers or letters on special business and often implying haste); উদ্দিষ্ট স্থানে প্রেরণ করা, কোন বিশেষ উদ্দেশ্যে প্রেরণ করা। **2.** To execute quickly; to finish off; দ্রুতসম্পাদন করা; শেষ করা। **3.** To send out of the world; যমালয়ে প্রেরণ করা। **4.** To eat promptly or quickly; as, to *dispatch* food, meal, etc.; তাড়াতাড়ি আহার করা। ***Verb i.*** To make haste; to conclude an affair, (*archaic*); তাড়াতাড়ি করা; কোন বিষয় শেষ করিয়া ফেলা (অপ্রচলিত)। **Dispatch-boat**—সরকারী বার্ত্তাবাহী দ্রুতগামী পোত। **Dispatch-box**—সরকারী পত্রাদি-বহনার্থ পেটক বিশেষ, ভ্রমণকালে কাগজ পত্রাদি রাখার জন্য এক প্রকার পেটক। **Happy dispatch**—জাপানীদিগের মধ্যে প্রচলিত আত্মহত্যা।

dis-pau'-pêr (-pä-), *v. t.* To deprive of the claim of a pauper to public support; নিঃস্ব ব্যক্তিকে সাধারণের সাহায্য প্রাপ্তির অধিকার হইতে বঞ্চিত করা।

dis-pĕl', *v. t.* To dissipate; as, to *dispel* fears, darkness, etc.; ভঞ্জন করা, ঘুচিয়ে দেওয়া, অপনোদন করা, নিরসন করা, দূর করা।

dis-pĕn-sā'-tion, *n.* **1.** Distribution; act of managing or ordering; as, to respect the *dispensation* of Providence; বিতরণ, বণ্টন; নির্ব্বাহ, পরিচালন। **2.** An arrangement by Providence or nature; বিধির বিধান, প্রকৃতির বিধান। **3.** Special dealing of Providence with a community or person; দেব-নিয়োগ (হিঃ কোঃ), দেবাজ্ঞা (ঐ)। **4.** Exemption from penalty or duty laid down, esp. in ecclesiastical law, (followed by *with, from*); নিষ্কৃতি, রেহাই, অব্যাহতি। **5.** The religious system prevalent at a period; as, the new *dispensation* (নববিধান); ধর্ম্মব্যবস্থা (হিঃ কোঃ), বিধান। **6.** A dispensing or doing without, (followed by *with*); কোন কিছু ছাড়া চালান বা ব্যবস্থাকরণ।

dis-pĕnse', *v. t.* & *i.* **1.** To deal out in portions; to distribute; as, nature *dispenses* her bounties; অংশ অংশ করিয়া দেওয়া; বিতরণ করা, ভাগ করা, বাঁটিয়া দেওয়া, বণ্টন করা। **2.** To administer; to manage; প্রয়োগ করা; নির্ব্বাহ করা, পরিচালনা করা। **3.** To exempt; to excuse; (used with *from*); অব্যাহতি দেওয়া, নিষ্কৃতি দেওয়া; মাফ করা। **4.** To prepare according to the prescription of a physician; চিকিৎসকের ব্যবস্থাপত্র অনুযায়ী প্রস্তুত করা। **5.** To relax; to give exemption from; as, to *dispense* a rule in a special case; শিথিল করা; নিয়ম পালন হইতে নিষ্কৃতি দেওয়া,

রেহাই দেওয়া। 6. To annul the binding force of ; as, to *dispense* an oath ; প্রতিজ্ঞাবন্ধন হইতে মুক্ত করা। 7. To render needless ; (usually to *dispense* the need of etc.) ; অনাবশ্যক করা। 8. To forego ; to do without ; ত্যাগ করা ; কোন কিছু ছাড়া চালান। ***Verb i.*** To give dispensations ; নিস্কৃতি দেওয়া, ক্ষমা করা। **—pen′-sa-ble,** *adj.* 1. (*Eccles.*) Condonable ; (যাজকীয় শাস্ত্র) ক্ষমার্হ। 2. Capable of being dispensed with ; পরিহার্য্য। 3. Capable of being relaxed, as a canon, law, oath, etc. ; শিথিল করণীয়। **—pen′-sa-ry,** *n.* 1. A place, esp. a charitable institution, where medicines are dispensed ; দাতব্য ঔষধালয়, ডাক্তারখানা। 2. An apothecary's shop ; ঔষধের দোকান, ঔষধালয়। **To dispense with**—To do without ; কোন কিছু ছাড়া চালান, পরিহার করা, ত্যাগ করা।

dis-peo′-ple (-pē), *v. t.* To depopulate ; জনশূন্য করা, উজাড় করা, লোকশূন্য করা।

di-spêr′-mous (-mŭs), *adj.* (*Bot.*) Containing only two seeds ; (উদ্ভিদ্-বিদ্যা) দ্বি-বীজ।

dis-perse′ (-pêrs), *v. t.* & *i.* 1. To scatter ; to send or drive in different directions ; বিক্ষিপ্ত করা, আস্তৃত করা, ছড়ান ; চতুর্দ্দিকে বিশৃঙ্খল ভাবে বিতাড়িত করা, ছিন্নভিন্ন করা। 2. To dissipate ; as, to *disperse* vapours ; বিলীন করা, অন্তর্হিত করা। 3. To distribute ; ভাগ করিয়া দেওয়া। 4. To disseminate ; to put in circulation ; as, to *disperse* news ; বিস্তার করা, পরিব্যাপ্ত করা, বিকীর্ণ করা ; প্রচার করা। 5. (*Opt.*) To divide as white light into its coloured rays ; (দৃষ্টি-বিজ্ঞান) শ্বেত আলোক-রশ্মি বিশ্লিষ্ট করত সপ্তবর্ণের রশ্মিতে বিভক্ত করা। ***Verb i.*** To separate ; to go in different directions ; to dissipate ; to vanish ; as, a cloud *disperses* ; বিচ্ছিন্ন হওয়া, ছিন্ন ভিন্ন হওয়া ; বিভিন্ন দিকে গমন করা, বিকীর্ণ হওয়া ; উড়িয়া যাওয়া, মিলাইয়া যাওয়া ; বিলীন হওয়া, অন্তর্হিত হওয়া, অন্তর্ধান হওয়া। **—pers′-al,** *n.* Act of dispersing ; dispersion ; বিকিরণ (হিঃ কোঃ) ; ছিন্নভিন্নতা, অন্তর্ধান। **—pers′-ed-ly,** *adv.* **—per′-sive,** *adj.* Tending to disperse ; ছিন্নভিন্নকারী। **—per′-sive-ly,** *adv.* **—per′-sive-ness,** *n.*

dis-pêr′-sion, *n.* 1. Scattering or state of being scattered ; ছিন্নভিন্নকরণ, বিসর্পণ, বিশ্লেষণ, বিদ্রাবণ, বিক্ষেপ, বিকিরণ। 2. (*Med.*) The removal of an inflammation ; (ভৈষজ্য-শাস্ত্র) প্রদাহ-শান্তি। 3. (*Opt.*) The separation of light into its different rays ; (দৃষ্টি-বিজ্ঞান) আলোক-বিশ্লেষণ। **Dispersion of light**—আলোক-বিকিরণ, প্রকাশ-বিকিরণ।

dis-pir′-it, *v. t.* To depress ; to dishearten ; নিরুৎসাহিত করা দমাইয়া দেওয়া ; ভগ্নহৃদয় করা, মন ভাঙ্গিয়া দেওয়া, নিস্তেজ করা, নিরাশ করা। **—ed,** *adj.* Disheartened ; নিরুৎসাহিত, স্ফূর্ত্তিহীন, ভগ্ন-হৃদয়। **—ed-ly,** *adv.*

dis-pit′-ē-ous (-ŭs), *adj.* Pitiless ; নিষ্করুণ, নির্ম্মম, নির্দ্দয়।

dis-plăce, *v. t.* 1. To remove from the usual or proper place ; স্থানচ্যুত করা, স্থানভ্রষ্ট করা, বিপর্য্যস্ত করা, স্থানান্তরিত করা, সরান। 2. To oust ; to take the place of ; উচ্ছেদ করা ; স্থানাধিকার করা। 3. To remove from any state, condition, office, or dignity ; পদচ্যুত করা, অবসৃত করা। **—a-ble,** *adj.* **—ment,** *n.* 1. Displacing ; state of being displaced ; স্থানচ্যুতকরণ, স্থানান্তর ; স্থানচ্যুতি, অপসরণ। 2. The amount of a fluid displaced by a body floating or immersed in it ; প্রবমান বা নিমজ্জমান বস্তুদ্বারা স্থানচ্যুত তরল পদার্থের পরিমাণ। 3. Replacement ; স্থানাবরোধকতা।

dis-plănt′, *v. t.* To uproot as plants ; উন্মূলিত করা, উৎপাটিত করা।

dis-play′ (-plā), *n.* & *v. t.* 1. An opening or unfolding ; exhibition ; প্রকাশ, বিকাশ, বিস্তার, জাহির, উদ্ঘাটন ; প্রকটন, প্রদর্শন। 2. Ostentatious show ; "Without *display*, without parade ;" সমারোহ, বাহার, ঠাট, ধূমধড়ক্কা, আড়ম্বর। 3. (*Print.*) Arrangement of types with a view to calling attention ; (মুদ্রণ) মনোযোগ আকর্ষণার্থ (বৃহৎ বা সুপ্রকট) অক্ষর-সন্নিবেশ। ***Verb t.*** 1. To exhibit ; to expose to view ; প্রদর্শন করা, প্রথিত করা, প্রকটন করা ; বিস্তার করা, উদ্ঘাটিত করা। 2. To show ostentatiously ; আড়ম্বর সহকারে প্রদর্শন করা। 3. To reveal ; to betray ; প্রকাশ করা ; জাহির করা, ব্যক্ত করা। 4. (*Print.*) To make conspicuous by large or prominent type ; (মুদ্রণ) বৃহৎ বা সুপ্রকট অক্ষর দ্বারা দৃষ্টি আকর্ষণ করা।

dis-please′ (-plēz), *v. t.* & *i.* To offend ; to annoy ; to be disagreeable to ; অসন্তুষ্ট করা, রুষ্ট করা ; বেজার করা, বিরক্ত করা, উত্ত্যক্ত করা ; অপ্রীতিকর হওয়া। ***Verb i.*** To give displeasure or offence ; অসন্তোষ জন্মান, অসন্তুষ্ট করা, অপ্রীতি জন্মান। **—pleased′,** *adj.* Offended ; annoyed ; (often followed by *at*, or *with*) ; অসন্তুষ্ট, রুষ্ট ; বিরক্ত। **—pleas′-ing** Causing displeasure ; অসন্তুষ্টিকর, বিরক্তিকর, অপ্রীতিকর। **—pleas′-ing-ly,** *adv.* **—pleas′-ure,** *n.* & *v. t.* 1. Dissatisfaction ; disapprobation ; anger ; অসন্তোষ, অপ্রীতি ; অননুমোদন ; রোষ। 2. That which displeases ; causes of annoyance ; অসন্তোষের বিষয় ; বিরক্তির কারণ। (*Verb t.*) To cause displeasure to ; to annoy ; অসন্তোষ জন্মান ; বিরক্ত করা।

dis-plĕn′-ish, *v. t.* To deprive of furniture, implements, etc. ;

আসবাবহীন করা, যন্ত্রাদিশূন্য করা, সাজসজ্জাহীন করা।

dis-plūme′, *v. t.* (*Poet.*) To strip of feathers ; (*fig.*) to strip of decoration, honour ; (কবিতায়) পালকশূন্য করা ; (লক্ষণায়) গৌরবসূচক ভূষাহীন করা, গৌরবহীন করা, হৃত-গৌরব করা।

dis-pŏn′-dee (-dē), *n.* (*Gr. & Lat. prosody*) A double spondee ; a foot consisting of four long syllables ; (গ্রীক ও ল্যাটিন ছন্দঃশাস্ত্র) দ্বিগুণিত কর্ণ ; দীর্ঘ-শব্দাংশ চতুষ্টয় বিশিষ্ট কবিতাপাদ পংক্তি।

dis-pōne′, *v. t.* (*Scot. Law*) To make over to another ; (স্কটলণ্ডদেশের আইন) হস্তান্তরিত করা। **—po-nee′**, *n.* The person to whom anything is disponed ; যে ব্যক্তির নিকট কোন সম্পত্তি হস্তান্তরিত করা হয়।

dis-pōrt′, *n., v. t. & i.* Frolic ; relaxation ; pastime ; আমোদ-প্রমোদ ; লীলা, ক্রীড়া-কৌতুক ; কেলি। ***Verb t.*** (Usually reflexive) To frolic ; to make merry ; রঙ্গ তামাসা করা, ক্রীড়া কৌতুক করা, আমোদপ্রমোদ করা; কেলি করা। ***Verb i.*** To play; ক্রীড়া করা, কেলি করা, বিহার করা।

dis-pōse′, *v. t. & i.* **1.** To place suitably ; to arrange ; যথাস্থানে সন্নিবেশ করা ; সুবিন্যস্ত করা, সজ্জিত করা, সাজান, বিলিব্যবস্থা করা। **2.** To settle ; মীমাংসা করা, নির্দ্দিষ্ট করা, চুকান, নিষ্পত্তি করা, ঠিক করা। **3.** To incline ; উন্মুখ করা, প্রবৃত্ত করা, প্রবণ করা, আসক্ত করা। **4.** To bring (a person, mind, etc.) into a certain state ; (esp. in *p. p.* as ill-or well-*disposed*) ; কোন বিশেষ অবস্থায় আনা। **5.** To bestow ; অর্পণ করা, প্রদান করা। ***Verb i.*** To determine course of events ; as, man proposes, God *disposes* ; ব্যবস্থা করা, বিধান করা। **—pos′-a-ble**, *adj.* **—pos′-al**, *n.* **1.** Arrangement ; as, the *disposal* of troops in two lines ; সন্নিবেশ, বিন্যাস, বিরচনা। **2.** Regulation ; management ; control ; as, to be at one's *disposal* ; ব্যবস্থাপন ; পরিচালন, নির্ব্বাহ ; কর্তৃত্ব, আয়ত্তত্ব (মঃ উঃ), আয়ত্তি, আয়ত্ততা। **3.** Alienation ; parting with ; as, a *disposal* of property ; হস্তান্তর; পরিত্যাগ। **4.** Getting rid of ; settling ; নিষ্কৃতি-লাভ ; মীমাংসা। **5.** Assignment ; bestowal : "The *disposal* of an employment ; নির্দ্দেশ ; অর্পণ, সম্প্রদান। **To dispose of**—To determine the fate of ; to regulate or manage ; ভাগ্য নির্ণয় করা ; নিয়ন্ত্রিত করা, পরিচালন করা। To put away ; to get rid of ; to kill ; to demolish, as an argument etc. ; to consume, as food ; ফেলিয়া রাখা ; নিষ্কৃতি পাওয়া ; নিকাশ করা, বধ করা ; (যুক্তি) খণ্ডন করা ; (অন্নাদি) ধ্বংস করা। To settle as cases, claims, etc. ; নিষ্পত্তি করা। To sell ; to alienate ; বিক্রয় করা ; হস্তান্তর করা।

dis-pō-si′-tion, *n.* **1.** The act of arranging, regulating or transferring ; as, the *disposition* of a property by will ; বিন্যাস, সন্নিবেশ, নিয়ন্ত্রণ, পরিচালন, বিলিব্যবস্থা, হস্তান্তর। **2.** Manner of being disposed or arranged ; as, the *disposition* of the trees in the orchard ; সন্নিবেশ-প্রণালী, সংবিধান (ভাগঃ), সংবিধি (মঃ ভাঃ)। **3.** Natural tendency ; aptitude ; স্বাভাবিক আসক্তি ; প্রবণতা। **4.** Temper of mind ; as, a man of turbulent *disposition* ; স্বভাব, প্রকৃতি, সর্গ, শীল, প্রবৃত্তি, মনোবৃত্তি, মেজাজ, তবীয়ত। **5.** Ordinance ; dispensation ; বিধি, ব্যবস্থা ; বিধান। **6.** (Usu. *pl.*) Plan, preparation and stationing of troops ready for attack, defence, etc. ; (সাধারণতঃ বহুবচন) সৈন্যসন্নিবেশ, সৈন্য-সংস্থান, ব্যূহবদ্ধকরণ। **7.** Control ; কর্তৃত্বাধীনতা, আয়ত্তি। **8.** Inclination ; প্রবৃত্তি, ঝোঁক। **At the disposal of**—কাহারো কর্তৃত্বাধীনে।

dis-pŏs-sĕss′, *v. t.* **1.** To put out of possession ; to oust ; to deprive (of) ; (usu. foll. by *of*) ; as, to *dispossess* a king *of* his crown ; অধিকারচ্যুত করা ; বে-দখল করা ; বঞ্চিত করা, স্বত্ব হরণ করা। **2.** To rid as a possessed person of an evil spirit ; ভূত ছাড়ান। **—ses′-sion**, *n.* **—or**, *n.*

dis-pōst′, *v. t.* To displace ; স্থানভ্রষ্ট করা, স্থানচ্যুত করা, স্থানান্তরিত করা।

dis-praise′ (-prāz), *n. & v. t.* Blame ; reproach ; দোষ, অখ্যাতি, নিন্দা ; তিরস্কার, ভৎর্সনা। ***Verb t.*** To disparage ; to censure ; দোষ দেওয়া, নিন্দা করা ; তিরস্কার করা।

dis-pread′ (-prĕd), *v. t.* To spread in different ways ; চতুর্দ্দিকে আস্তৃত করা, পরিব্যাপ্ত করা, বিকীর্ণ করা।

dis-prĭs′-ŏn, *v. t.* To let loose from prison ; কারামুক্ত করা।

dis-proof′, *n.* **1.** Refutation ; খণ্ডন, নিরাকরণ। **2.** That which disproves, as a piece of evidence ; খণ্ডনকারী বিষয়।

dis-prō-pōr′-tion, *n. & v. t.* Want of proportion ; lack of symmetry ; state of being out of proportion ; অসামঞ্জস্য ; বৈষম্য ; অসৌষ্ঠবসম্পন্নতা। ***Verb t.*** To violate symmetry in; অসৌষ্ঠবসম্পন্ন করা, বেডৌল করা। **—a-ble, —al, —tioned**, *adjs.* **—ate**, *adj.* Unsymmetrical ; relatively too large or small; অসৌষ্ঠবসম্পন্ন, অসুষ্ঠু, অসমঞ্জস ; বে-মানান, বে-মিল। **—a-ble-ness, —ate-ness**, *ns.* **—ate-ly**, *adv.*

dis-prōve′, *v. t.* To prove to be false or erroneous ; to refute ; মিথ্যা বা ভ্রমপূর্ণ বলিয়া প্রমাণ করা ; খণ্ডন করা, নিরাকরণ করা, নিরসন করা। **—prov′-a-ble**, *adj.*

dis′-pū-ta-ble, *adj.* Open to question ; uncertain ; বিচার্য্য, বিবদনীয়, বিতর্কণীয় ; অনিশ্চিত, সন্দেহযোগ্য।

dis-pūte′, *n., v. t. & i.* **1.** Verbal controversy ; debate ; বাক্‌কলহ ;

বিপ্রলাপ, বিচার। 2. Contest ; quarrel ; তর্কবিতর্ক, বিতণ্ডা, বাদপ্রতিবাদ ; বিবাদ। *Verb t.* 1. To make a subject of disputation ; to discuss ; তর্কের বিষয়ীভূত করা, তর্কবিতর্ক করা, বাদবিতণ্ডা করা, বাদানুবাদ করা, তর্ক দ্বারা প্রতিবাদ করা ; বাদপ্রতিবাদ করা, আলোচনা করা। 2. To attempt to overthrow ; to controvert ; as, to *dispute* an assertion, fact or statement ; বিপক্ষের যুক্তি খণ্ডন করিতে চেষ্টা করা ; বাদানুবাদ করা, তর্ক-যুদ্ধ করা। 3. To strive or contend for ; to contest ; as, to *dispute* victory, every inch of ground ; প্রয়াস পাওয়া, সংগ্রাম করা ; প্রতিদ্বন্দ্বিতা করা। 4. To resist ; as, to *dispute* landing, advance, etc. ; প্রতিরোধ করা, বাধা দেওয়া। *Verb i.* To debate, (*with* or *against* a person *on* or *about* a subject) ; to altercate ; to wrangle ; তর্কবিতর্ক ; করা ; বচসা করা ; বাদানুবাদ করা।

Dis′-pu-tant, *n.* & *adj.* One who disputes ; তর্ককারী, বিবাদকারী, বাদবিতণ্ডাকারী। (*Adj.*) Engaged in disputes ; তর্ক-রত, বিবদমান। **—pu-ta′-tion,** *n.* The act of disputing ; argument ; controversy ; বাদপ্রতিবাদ, তর্কযুদ্ধ ; বাদানুবাদ, তর্কবিতর্ক, বাদবিতণ্ডা। **—pu-ta′-tious,** *adj.* Fond of disputing ; তর্কপ্রিয়। **—pu-ta′-tious-ly,** *adv.* **—pu-ta′-tious-ness,** *n.* **—put′-a-tive,** *adj.* 1. Inclined to dispute ; তর্ক-প্রবণ, তর্কপ্রিয়। 2. Of, or pertaining to, disputation ; তর্কঘটিত, বাদানুবাদ-সংক্রান্ত। **Beyond, past** or **without dispute**—Indisputably ; certainly ; অখণ্ডনীয়রূপে ; নিশ্চয়ই। **In dispute**—In controversy ; বিরোধীয়।

dĭs-quăl′-i-fȳ, *v. t.* 1. To make unfit ; to disable ; অনুপযুক্ত করা, অযোগ্য করা ; অকর্মণ্য করা, অক্ষম করা। 2. To debar legally ; to pronounce unqualified ; (আইনতঃ) বর্জ্জিত করা ; অনুপযুক্ত বলিয়া ব্যক্ত করা। **—fi-ca′-tion,** *n.* 1. Act of disqualifying ; state of being disqualified ; incompetency ; অনুপযোগীকরণ, অকর্ম্মণ্যকরণ ; অনুপযোগিতা ; অক্ষমতা, অযোগ্যতা। 2. That which disqualifies ; as, sickness is a *disqualification* for labour ; অযোগ্যকর বিষয়, অক্ষমতাজনক বিষয়।

dĭs-quī′-ĕt, *adj., n.* & *v. t.* Impatient ; restless ; disturbed ; অধীর ; অস্থির, চঞ্চল ; বিক্ষুব্ধ, উদ্বিগ্ন। *Noun.* Want of tranquillity in body or mind ; uneasiness ; anxiety ; উদ্বেগ, অশান্তি, আঁকুবাঁকু ; অস্থিরতা, অধীরতা, ব্যাকুলতা ; উৎকণ্ঠা। *Verb t.* To render unquiet ; to deprive of peace, rest or tranquillity ; অস্থির করা, আকুল করা, উদ্বিগ্ন করা, অশান্ত করা, অধীর করা ; শান্তিশূন্য করা, বিরামহীন করা। **—e-tude,** *n.* Uneasiness ; anxiety ; অস্থিরতা, অধৈর্য্য, অশান্তি ; উদ্বেগ, উৎকণ্ঠা। **—ness,** *n.*

dĭs-qui-sĭ′-tion, *n.* 1. (*Archaic*) Investigation ; inquiry ; (অপ্রচলিত) অনুসন্ধান ; গবেষণা, অনুশীলন। 2. (*Mod.*) A long and elaborate treatise or discourse on a subject ; (আধুনিক) কোন বিষয়ে বিস্তৃত আলোচনা, বিস্তৃত প্রবন্ধ বা সুদীর্ঘ গ্রন্থ। **—al, —a-ry, —quis′-i-tive** *adjs.* Pertaining to, or of the nature of, a disquisition ; অনুসন্ধান বিষয়ক, অনুসন্ধানাত্মক।

dĭs-rāte′, *v. t.* (*Naut.*) To reduce to a lower rating or rank ; (নৌ-বিদ্যা) নিম্নপদে অবনীত করা, অপদস্থ করা।

dĭs-rē-gärd′, *n.* & *v. t.* Neglect ; indifference ; (gen. foll. by *of* or *for*) ; অসম্মান, অনাদর, অবজ্ঞা, তাচ্ছিল্য, অবহেলা, উপেক্ষা ; উদাসীনতা। *Verb t.* To ignore ; to treat as of no importance ; অবহেলা করা, উপেক্ষা করা ; তুচ্ছ বলিয়া গণ্য করা, নগণ্য বলিয়া মনে করা। **—ful,** *adj.* Neglectful ; negligent ; অবহেলাকারী ; অনবহিত, অমনোযোগী, যত্নবিহীন, বেপরোয়া, উপেক্ষাপরায়ণ।

dĭs-rĕl′-ĭsh, *n.* & *v. t.* 1. Distaste ; as, a *disrelish* for some kinds of food ; অরুচি, বিস্বাদ। 2. (*Fig.*) Aversion ; antipathy ; (লক্ষণায়) অপ্রবৃত্তি ; অপ্রীতি, অপছন্দ, বিরাগ, বিতৃষ্ণা। *Verb t.* To dislike the taste of ; বিস্বাদ লাগা।

dĭs-rē-pair′ (-pār), *n.* Bad condition for want of repairs ; as, to be in *disrepair* ; বেমেরামত অবস্থা, ভগ্নাবস্থা, অসংস্কৃতাবস্থা।

dĭs-rĕp-ū-tȧ-ble, *adj.* Of bad repute ; discreditable ; অখ্যাতিভাজন ; অখ্যাতিজনক, অপযশস্কর, অপমানজনক, অকীর্ত্তিকর। **—bly,** *adv.* **—ness,** *n.*

dĭs-rē-pūte′, *n.* Want or loss of reputation ; ill-repute ; অখ্যাতি, অপযশ ; বদনাম, নিন্দা।

dĭs-rē-spĕct′, *n.* & *v. t.* Want of respect ; incivility ; rudeness ; অশ্রদ্ধা, অসম্মান, অবজ্ঞা, অপমান, অবমাননা, অমর্য্যাদা, অসৌজন্য, অভদ্রতা ; অশিষ্টতা ; বেআদবি, রূঢ়তা। *Verb t.* To show disrespect to ; অসম্মান প্রদর্শন করা, অপমান করা, অবজ্ঞা করা, উপেক্ষা করা, অভদ্রতা করা। **—ful,** *adj.* **—ful-ly,** *adv.* **—ful-ness,** *n.*

dĭs-rōbe′, *v. t.* & *i.* 1. To divest of a robe ; to undress ; পরিচ্ছদ হীন করা ; বিবস্ত্র করা, বিবসন করা। 2. (*Fig.*) To divest of that which covers or decorates ; as, autumn *disrobes* the fields of verdure ; (লক্ষণায়) আবরণহীন করা, আবরণ উন্মোচন করা, বিভূষণহীন করা, নিরাভরণ করা, ভূষা রিক্ত করা।

dĭs′-rōōt′, *v. t.* To tear up by the roots ; hence, to tear from a foundation ; নির্ম্মূল করা, উন্মূলিত করা ; উৎখাতিত করা।

dĭs-rŭpt′, *v. t.* To separate forcibly ; to break asunder ; to shatter ; ছিন্ন করা, বিদীর্ণ করা ; ভাঙ্গিয়া ফেলা ;

চূর্ণ বিচূর্ণ করা, চুরমার করা। **—rup′-tion,** *n.* Bursting asunder; violent dissolution; ভঙ্গ; বিদারণ, বিভেদন। **—rup′-tive,** *adj.* Causing or tending to cause disruption; বিদারণশীল।

dis-săt′-is-fȳ, *v. t.* To make discontented; অসন্তুষ্ট করা, বেজার করা, রুষ্ট করা। **—fac′-tion,** *n.* Discontent; অসন্তোষ, বিরক্তি। **—fac′-to-ry,** *adj.* Causing dissatisfaction; displeasing; অসন্তোষজনক; অসন্তোষকর, অপ্রীতিকর।

dis-seat′ (-sēt), *v. t.* To unseat; আসন-চ্যুত করা।

dis-sĕct′, *v. t.* **1.** (*Anat.*) To divide as animals, plants, etc. into separate parts, to show structure etc.; (শারীর-সংস্থান বিদ্যা) (শব) ব্যবচ্ছেদ করা। **2.** To analyse for the purpose of science or criticism; to examine part by part; বিশ্লেষণ করা; প্রত্যেক অংশ পৃথগ্ রূপে পরীক্ষা করা। **—ed,** *adj.* **1.** Divided into sections; as, a *dissected* map; বিভিন্ন বিভাগে বিভক্ত। **2.** (*Bot.*) Cut deeply into many lobes or divisions; as, a *dissected* leaf; (উদ্ভিদ্-বিদ্যা) ব্যবচ্ছিন্ন (সাঃ পঃ)। **—i-ble,** *adj.* **—sec′-tion,** *n.* **1.** Act of dissecting; ব্যবচ্ছেদ, ছেদন (সাঃপঃ)। **2.** That which is dissected or is in a dissected condition; ব্যবচ্ছিন্ন বস্তু। **3.** (*Com.*) The separation of accounts according to departments; (বাণিজ্য) বিভাগ অনুসারে হিসাব পৃথকীকরণ। **—sec′-tor,** *n.* **Dissected map** or **picture**—যে চিত্র বা মানচিত্র ভিন্ন ভিন্ন খণ্ডে বিভক্ত থাকে এবং এই সমস্ত খণ্ড যথাস্থানে সন্নিবেশ করিয়া সম্পূর্ণ চিত্র বা মানচিত্রটী গঠন করিতে হয়। **Dissection wound**—স্পর্শ সংক্রামক রোগাদিতে মৃত ব্যক্তির শব ব্যবচ্ছেদকালে ঘটনাক্রমে ব্যবচ্ছেদকারীর রক্তে মৃত ব্যক্তির রোগ বীজাণু প্রবেশ হেতু যে বিষাক্ত ক্ষত উপজাত হয়।

dis-seise′, —seize′, (-sēz), *v. t.* (*Law*) To deprive of possession; to oust wrongfully; (followed by *of*); as, to *disseize* a tenant *of* his free-hold; অধিকার-চ্যুত করা; অন্যায় রূপে উচ্ছেদ করা, অন্যায় মতে বেদখল করা। **—sei-zee′, —see′,** *n.* A person disseized; অধিকারচ্যুত ব্যক্তি। **—sei′-zin —sin,** *n.* The act of disseizing; অধিকারচ্যুত করণ, বেদখল করণ, স্বত্ব বা অধিকার ভ্রষ্টকরণ, অন্যায়রূপে উচ্ছেদকরণ।

dis-sĕm′-ble, *v. t.* & *i.* **1.** To hide under a false appearance; to conceal; আত্মগোপন করা, ছদ্মবেশ ধারণ করা; কপটতা করা, গোপন করা, লুকান। **2.** To feign; (*obs.*) as, he soon *dissembled* a sleep; ভাণ করা, ছল করা। **3.** To ignore; to pretend not to see; as, to *dissemble* an insult; উপেক্ষা করা; দেখিয়াও না দেখা। **4.** To fail to mention; as, to *dissemble* a fact; উল্লেখ করিতে অবহেলা করা। ***Verb i.*** To play the hypocrite; কপটতা করা। **—bler,** *n.*

dis-sĕm′-i-nāte, *v. t.* **1.** To scatter or sow, as seed; ছড়ান, বপন করা, বোনা। **2.** (*Fig.*) To propagate; to diffuse (doctrines, sedition, etc.); (লক্ষণায়) বিস্তার করা; বিকীর্ণ করা, জাহির করা, প্রচারিত করা, পরিব্যাপ্ত করা। **—na′-tion,** *n.* The act of disseminating; বিস্তার, প্রচার। **—na-tor,** *n.*

dis-sĕn′-sion, *n.* Disagreement in opinion; strife; মতানৈক্য, মতবিরোধ, মতভেদ, ভেদ; বিবাদ, কলহ, দ্বন্দ্ব।

dis-sĕnt′ *n.* & *v. t.* **1.** Non-agreement; difference of opinion; expression of disagreement; অনৈক্য; মতভেদ, মতবিরোধ, বিমত; মতভেদজ্ঞাপন। **2.** (*Eccles.*) Separation from an established church, esp. that of England; non-conformity; (collectively) the dissenters; রাজ-বিধি দ্বারা প্রতিষ্ঠিত খৃষ্টীয় ধর্ম্ম-সজ্ঞ হইতে বিচ্যুতি; প্রচলিত ধর্ম্মের প্রতিপন্থিতা; (সমষ্টিবাচক ভাবে) রাজবিধি দ্বারা প্রতিষ্ঠিত খৃষ্টীয় ধর্ম্মসজ্ঞ হইতে বিচ্ছিন্ন ব্যক্তিগণ। ***Verb t.*** **1.** To refuse to assent; to disagree; সম্মতিদানে অস্বীকার করা; অসম্মত হওয়া, ভিন্নমত হওয়া। **2.** To differ from the doctrine of an established church; রাজবিধি দ্বারা প্রতিষ্ঠিত ধর্ম্মসজ্ঞের অনুমোদিত মতের বিরোধী হওয়া। **—er,** *n.* One who dissents, esp. from a national church; member of a sect that has separated itself from the church of England or Scotland; ভিন্ন মতাবলম্বী, মতান্তরাবলম্বী, মতান্তরধারী, মতান্তরগ্রাহী, বিশেষতঃ রাজবিধি দ্বারা প্রতিষ্ঠিত ধর্ম্মসজ্ঞ হইতে বিচ্ছিন্ন ব্যক্তি; ইংলণ্ড অথবা স্কট্‌লণ্ডের জাতীয় ধর্ম্মসংঘ হইতে বিচ্ছিন্ন সম্প্রদায় বিশেষভুক্ত ব্যক্তি, ভিন্নবাদী। **—ing-ly,** *adv.* **Dissenting ministers**—ভিন্নবাদীদিগের যাজক-সজ্ঞ।

dis-sĕn′-tient (-shĕnt), *adj.* & *n.* Disagreeing, esp. with a majority; ভিন্নমতাবলম্বী, বিশেষতঃ অধিকাংশ লোক হইতে ভিন্নমতালম্বী। ***Noun.*** One who dissents, esp. from the opinion of the majority; ভিন্নমতাবলম্বী ব্যক্তি, বিশেষতঃ অধিকাংশ লোক হইতে ভিন্নমতাবলম্বী ব্যক্তি। **—tious,** *adj.* Quarrelsome, (now rare); ঝগড়াটে। **Dissentient Liberals** — Liberal Unionists; আয়র্লণ্ড দেশে স্বায়ত্তশাসন প্রচলনের বিরোধী উদার নৈতিক সম্প্রদায়ভুক্ত ব্যক্তি।

dis-sĕp′-i-mĕnt, *n.* **1.** A partition; বিভাগ। **2.** (*Bot.* & *Zool.*) A partition in some part of organ; a septum; (উদ্ভিদ্-বিদ্যা এবং জন্তু-বিদ্যা) দৈহিক অংশ বা যন্ত্র; কোঠ বা গহ্বর ব্যবধায়ক অস্থিখণ্ড।

dis-sêrt′, dis′-sêr-tāte, *v. i.* To discourse; to give an exposition; আলোচনা করা; ব্যাখ্যা করা। **—ser-ta′-tion,** *n.* A formal or elaborate argumentative discourse; a disquisition;

an essay ; বিস্তৃত প্রবন্ধ ; নিবন্ধ ; রচনা ।

dis-sĕrve′, *v. t.* To do an ill turn to ; to harm ; অনুপকার করা, অহিত করা, অপকার করা ; অনিষ্ট করা, লোকসান করা । **—serv′-ice**, *n.* Injury ; harm ; অহিত, অনুপকার, অপকার ; অনিষ্ট, লোকসান ।

dis-sĕv′-êr, *v. t.* & *i.* To sever ; to divide ; বিচ্ছিন্ন করা, ছেদন করা ; বিভাগ করা ।

dis′-si-dĕnce, *n.* Disagreement ; dissent ; অনৈক্য ; মতবিরোধ, মতভেদ, মতানৈক্য ।

dis′-si-dĕnt, *adj.* & *n.* **1.** Dissenting ; at variance ; ভিন্নমতাবলম্বী; বিরুদ্ধভাবাপন্ন । **2.** Dissentient ; ভিন্ন মতপ্রকাশী । ***Noun.*** (*Eccl.*) A dissenter ; (যাজকীয় শাস্ত্র) রাজবিধিদ্বারা প্রতিষ্ঠিত খৃষ্টীয় ধর্ম্মসংঘ হইতে বিচ্ছিন্ন ব্যক্তি।

dis-sight′ (-sīt), *n.* An unsightly thing ; an eyesore ; অপ্রিয়দর্শন, কদাকার বস্তু ; চক্ষুশূল ।

dis-sil′-i-ĕnt, *adj.* Bursting open with elastic force, as a ripe capsule, (esp. in *Bot.*) ; স্থিতি-স্থাপকতা বলে বিদারণশীল (যথা, পক্ব বীজকোষ) ।

dis-sim′-i-lâr, *adj.* Not similar ; unlike ; (gen. foll. by *to* and rarely by *from*, *with*) ; ভিন্ন, অসম ; অসদৃশ, বিসদৃশ । **—lar′-i-ty**, *n.* Unlikeness ; heterogeny ; অসাম্য ; বৈসাদৃশ্য, বৈভিন্ন্য, বৈষম্য ।

dis-sim′-i-lē, *n.* (*Rhet.*) A comparison or illustration by contraries ; (অলঙ্কার-শাস্ত্র) বিরুদ্ধ বস্তুদ্বারা উপমা বা উদাহরণ প্রদান ।

dis-si-mil′-i-tūde, *n.* Want of resemblance ; অসাদৃশ্য, বৈসাদৃশ্য, অনৈক্য, অসাম্য, প্রভেদ ।

dis-sim′-ū-lāte, *v. t.* & *i.* To dissemble ; to feign ; to pretend not to have or feel ; কপটাচরণ করা ; ভাণ করা ; ছলনা করা । ***Verb i.*** To be hypocritical ; to dissemble ; কপট হওয়া ; ভাণ করা । **—la′-tion**, *n.* Act of dissembling ; false hypocrisy ; কপটাচরণ, আকার-গোপন, কপট ব্যবহার ; ভাণ, কপটতা, অবহিত্থা (দশরূঃ) ।

dis′-si-pāte, *v. t.* & *i.* **1.** To disperse ; to drive away ; to destroy completely ; দূরীভূত করা ; বিতাড়িত করা ; চূর্ণবিচূর্ণ করা, বিধ্বংস করা । **2.** To spend lavishly ; to squander ; উড়াইয়া দেওয়া ; অপব্যয় করা । **3.** To distract or fritter away (energy, attention); বিক্ষিপ্ত করা ; ক্রমশঃ ক্ষয় করা । ***Verb i.*** **1.** To separate into parts and disappear ; মিলাইয়া যাওয়া । **2.** To become disintegrated ; বিচূর্ণিত হওয়া । **3.** (*Colloq.*) To engage in frivolous or dissolute pleasures ; লম্পটাচারে রত হওয়া, বিলাসব্যসনে নিরত হওয়া । **—pat′-ed**, *p. p.* **1.** Dispersed ; wasted, as money etc. ; distracted or frittered away, as attention etc. ; বিক্ষিপ্ত ; অপব্যয়িত (যথা ধন) ; বিভ্রান্ত, ক্রমশঃ ক্ষয়প্রাপ্ত । **2.** Dissolute ; লম্পট, ব্যসনী ।

dis-si-pā′-tion, *n.* **1.** Dispersion ; disintegration ; ছিন্নভিন্নকরণ, তিরোধান, বিলয় ; বিচ্ছিন্নতা, বিচূর্ণন । **2.** Wasteful expenditure, as of wealth or resources ; অপচয়, অপব্যয় । **3.** Dissoluteness ; vicious practices ; লাম্পট্য, পাপাচার, অমিতাচার, ভ্রষ্টাচার, দুর্বৃত্তি । **4.** Distraction, as of attention etc. ; a trifle which wastes time or distracts attention ; বিক্ষেপ ; যে তুচ্ছবিষয় দ্বারা মন বিক্ষিপ্ত হয় বা সময় নষ্ট হয় ।

dis-sō′-cial-īze (-shăl-), *v. t.* To render unsocial ; অসামাজিক করা । **—cia-ble**, *adj.* **1.** Incongruous ; অসংলগ্ন। **2.** Unsociable; অসামাজিক । **—cial**, *adj.* Unfriendly to society ; selfish ; সমাজবিরোধী ; স্বার্থপর । **—cia′-tion**, *n.* **1.** Disunion ; পৃথগ্ভাব, বিচ্ছেদ, বিশ্লেষ । **2.** (*Chem.*) The process by which a compound body breaks up into simple constituents ; (রসায়ন-শাস্ত্র) বিশ্লেষণ ।

dis′-sō′-ci-āte (shī-), *v. t.* **1.** To separate from fellowship or union ; পৃথক্ করা, স্বতন্ত্র করা, বিযুক্ত করা, বিচ্ছিন্ন করা । **2.** (*Chem.*) To decompose as by heat ; উত্তাপাদি দ্বারা বিশ্লেষণ করা ।

dis′-sō-lū-ble, *adj.* **1.** Capable of being disintigrated or disconnected ; দ্রাবণীয়, দ্রবীকরণযোগ্য, গলনীয়, দ্রাব্য, দ্রাবণার্হ । **2.** Capable of being disunited, as knot etc. ; (গ্রন্থি প্রভৃতি সম্বন্ধে) উন্মোচনীয়, বিযোজ্য । **—bil′-i-ty**, *n.*

dis′-sō-lūte, *adj.* Loose in conduct and morals ; licentious ; লম্পট, অসংযত-চরিত্র, ব্যসনী ; কামাসক্ত, কামুক, ইন্দ্রিয়পরায়ণ, স্খলিতচরিত্র, ইন্দ্রিয়পরতন্ত্র । **—ly**, *adv.* **—ness** *n.*

dis-sō-lū′-tion, *n.* **1.** The act of dissolving, or separating into component parts ; decay ; বিশ্লেষণ ; ক্ষয়, লয়, বিলয় । **2.** Change from a solid to a fluid body ; liquefaction ; বিদ্রাবণ, বিগলন, নির্গলন, দ্রবীকরণ ; তরলীভবন । **3.** Decomposition ; পৃথগ্ভবন, বিচ্ছেদন । **4.** Dismissal of an assembly, esp. ending of parliament with a view to fresh election ; সভাভঙ্গ, বিশেষতঃ পুনর্নির্ব্বাচনের জন্য পার্লেমেণ্ট মহাসভা ভঙ্গ । **5.** Death ; as, we expected immediate *dissolution* ; মৃত্যু, মরণ । **6.** Ruin ; নাশ, প্রলয়, বিনাশ, ধ্বংস । **7.** Undoing of bond, partnership, marriage, alliance, etc. ; সম্বন্ধ, অংশিত্ব, বিবাহ, সন্ধি, প্রভৃতি ভঙ্গ ।

dis-sŏlve′, *v. t.* & *i.* **1.** To disintegrate ; to break up ; to destroy ; বিচূর্ণিত হওয়া ; ভাঙ্গিয়া দেওয়া, ভঙ্গ করা ; ধ্বংস করা, নাশ করা । **2.** To disconnect ; to disunite ; পৃথক্ করা ; বিযুক্ত করা, বিচ্ছিন্ন করা । **3.** To melt ; to liquefy ; as, to *dissolve* salt in water ; (*lit.* & *fig.*) ; দ্রব করা, গলান ; তরলিত করা, দ্রবীভূত করা । **4.** (*Archaic*)

To solve ; to clear up ; (অপ্রচলিত) সমাধান করা ; উদ্ঘাটন করা। 5. To disperse or terminate ; as, to *dissolve* the parliament ; ভঙ্গ করা। 6. To release ; to enervate ; শিথিল করা ; ক্ষীণ করা। 7. (*Law*) To annul ; as, to *dissolve* an injunction ; to put an end to, as partnership etc. ; (আইন) বাতিল করা, রদ করা, অসিদ্ধ করা ; (অংশিত্ব প্রভৃতি) শেষ করিয়া ফেলা। ***Verb i.*** 1. To waste away ; to decompose ; ক্ষয় হইয়া যাওয়া ; বিশ্লিষ্ট হওয়া। 2. To become fluid ; to be melted ; দ্রব হওয়া, তরলিত হওয়া ; নির্গলিত হওয়া। 3. To vanish ; মিলান, মিলাইয়া যাওয়া, বিলীন হওয়া। 4. To break up ; as, an assembly *dissolves* ; ভঙ্গ হওয়া। **—solv′-a-ble,** *adj.* Capable of being dissolved ; দ্রাব্য, দ্রবণীয়, গলনশীল। **A dissolving view** (as of a magic lantern) — যাদু-প্রদীপে যে দৃশ্য ক্রমশঃ অস্পষ্টতর হইয়া অন্য দৃশ্যে ক্রমশঃ মিলাইয়া যায় এবং দ্বিতীয় দৃশ্যটী প্রথম দৃশ্যের স্থানে সমুজ্জল হইয়া উঠে। **To be dissolved in tears**—To weep copiously ; অশ্রু-পরিপ্লুত হওয়া, অশ্রুপ্লাবিত হওয়া। **To dissolve**—To declare dissolution of Parliament ; (পার্লেমেণ্ট) ভঙ্গ হইবে বলিয়া ঘোষণা করা।

dis-sŏlv′-ĕnt, *adj.* & *n.* Having power to dissolve something ; বিদ্রাবক। ***Noun.*** 1. A menstruum ; দ্রাবক পদার্থ। 2. (*Med.*) A remedy supposed capable of dissolving concretions in the body ; (ভৈষজ্য-শাস্ত্র) শরীরস্থ নিরেট পদার্থের পিণ্ড সমূহ দ্রাবণোপযোগী ঔষধ বিশেষ।

dis′-sŏ-nănt, *adj.* 1. Discordant ; not harmonious ; বেসুর, বিস্বর ; কর্কশ। 2. Disagreeing ; incongruous ; অনৈক্যবিশিষ্ট ; অসঙ্গত, অসমঞ্জস। **—ly,** *adv.* **—nance,** *n.* 1. A discordant combination of sounds ; ভিন্ন-স্বর-সম্মিলন। 2. Incongruity ; অসামঞ্জস্য।

dis-suade′ (-swād), *v. t.* 1. To advise against ; to deprecate, as an action ; প্রতিকূলে পরামর্শ দেওয়া ; দোষারোপ করা। 2. To divert by persuasion, (foll. by *from*) ; নিবৃত্ত করা, অপাবৃত্ত করা, মন ফিরান, নিরস্ত করা, নিবর্ত্তিত করা। **—sua′-sion,** *n.* 1. The act of dissuading ; নিবর্ত্তন, অপ্রবৃত্তি-জনন। 2. A motive or consideration tending to dissuade ; অপ্রবৃত্তি-জনক কারণ বা উদ্দেশ্য। **—sua′-sive,** *adj.* & *n.* Tending to dissuade ; অপ্রবৃত্তিজনক, নিবর্ত্তক, নিবৃত্তিকর। (*Noun*) A dissuasive argument or speech ; অপ্রবৃত্তিজনক যুক্তি বা বক্তৃতা।

dis-sȳl′-lă-ble, *n.* A word of two syllables ; দ্বিশব্দাংশবিশিষ্ট শব্দ। **—lab′-ic,** *adj.*

dis-sȳm′-mĕ-trȳ, *n.* Absence or defect of symmetry ; অসৌষ্ঠব। **—met′-ri-cal,** *adj.* Symmetrical in opposed directions, as the two hands ; বিপরীতদিকে সমঞ্জস।

dis′-tăff, *n.* 1. A cleft stick about 3 ft. long which holds the bunch of flax, tow or wool in spinning work ; চরকী, সূত্রতকুটী (মঃ ইঃ)। 2. Woman's work ; women collectively ; "The *distaff* was too busy ;" স্ত্রীলোকের কাজ ; স্ত্রীগণ। **Descent by distaff**—মাতৃপুরুষ পরম্পরায় জন্ম। **Distaff day** or **St. Distaff's day**—প্রাচ্যদেশীয় পণ্ডিতগণের নিকট খৃষ্টের আবির্ভাবের স্মরণার্থ ৬ই জানুয়ারী যে উৎসব হয় তৎপরবর্ত্তী দিবস (অর্থাৎ ৭ই জানুয়ারী) [খৃষ্টমাস উৎসবের পর ঐ দিবসে পুনরায় সূতা কাটার কাজ আরম্ভ করা হইত।] **Distaff side**—কোন পরিবারের স্ত্রী-শাখা।

Distaff.

dis′-tăl, *adj.* (*Anat.* & *Bot.*) Terminal ; (শারীর-সংস্থানবিদ্যা ও উদ্ভিদ্-বিদ্যা) অন্তদেশবর্ত্তী, অন্ত্য, অন্তিম।

dis′-tance (-tăns), *n.* & *v. t.* 1. The space between two objects ; দূরত্ব, ব্যবধান, অন্তর, তফাৎ। 2. A remote place or point ; দূরবর্ত্তী স্থান। 3. Remoteness ; দূরবর্ত্তিতা, দূরত্ব। 4. (*Racing*) A length of 244 yards from the winning post ; জয়-সূচক স্তম্ভ হইতে ২৪৪ গজপরিমিত স্থান, ঐ স্থানের সীমায় একটী স্তম্ভ প্রোথিত থাকে, ইহার নাম দূরত্ব স্তম্ভ। দৌড়ের সময় প্রথম ঘোড়া জয়-স্তম্ভে পৌছিলেও যদি পশ্চাদ্বর্ত্তী কোন অশ্ব দূরত্বস্তম্ভে পৌছিতে না পারে তবে আর সেই অশ্ব পুনরায় দৌড়ে প্রতিযোগিতা করার অধিকার পায় না। 5. Avoidance of familiarity ; reserve ; as, to keep one's *distance* ; ঘনিষ্ঠতা-পরিহার ; দূর দূর ভাব, পৃথক্ পৃথক্ ভাব। ***Verb t.*** 1. To place or keep at a distance ; দূরে স্থাপিত করা, দূরে রাখা। 2. To cause to seem remote ; দূরবর্ত্তী বলিয়া প্রতিভাত করান। 3. To leave far behind in race or competition ; প্রতিযোগিতায় বা দৌড়ে বহু পশ্চাতে ফেলা। **Angular distance** — কৌণিক দূরত্ব। **Middle distance** — (*Painting*) (চিত্রবিদ্যা) চিত্রের যে ভাগ দ্রষ্টার চক্ষুর সর্ব্বাপেক্ষা নিকটবর্ত্তী সেই অংশ, ভাগ এবং চিত্রের দূরবর্ত্তী স্থলের মধ্যস্থিত স্থান। **To be within striking distance**—To be near enough to deliver a blow ; যতটা নিকটে থাকিলে আঘাত করা যাইতে পারে, ততটা নিকটে থাকা। **To keep one's distance**—To stand aloof ; to refrain from familiarity ; দূরে দূরে থাকা, তফাৎ থাকা ; ঘনিষ্ঠতা পরিহার করা।

dis′-tănt, *adj.* 1. At a distance ; away ; দূরস্থ ; দূরবর্ত্তী। 2. Remote ; সুদূর। 3. Not intimate ; reserved ; cool ; as, he passed me with a *distant* look ; অঘনিষ্ঠ ; চাপা, অনালাপী ; অনুরাগবিহীন, আন্তরিকতা শূন্য। 4. Indistinct ; faint, as, some *distant* knowledge ; অস্পষ্ট ; অস্ফুট। **5.** Discrepant ; repugnant ; as, a practice so widely *distant* from Christianity ; বিভিন্ন ; বিরোধী। **—ly,** *adv.* **Distant signal**—লৌহবর্ত্মের সর্ব্বাপেক্ষা দূরবর্ত্তী সঙ্কেত-স্তম্ভ।

dis-tāste′, *n.* & *v. t.* **1.** A dislike of food or drink, (*rare*) ; (ক্বচিৎ ব্যবহৃত) বিস্বাদ, অরুচি। **2.** Aversion ; dislike ; repugnance ; (with *for*); বিতৃষ্ণা, অরতি ; অপ্রীতি ; বিরাগ, অভক্তি, দ্বেষ, ঘৃণা। ***Verb t.*** **1.** To disrelish ; to loathe ; to dislike ; বিস্বাদ লাগা ; ঘৃণা করা ; অপছন্দ করা। **2.** To excite the dislike of ; to offend ; অপ্রীতি উৎপাদন করা ; মনঃক্ষুণ্ণ করা, রুষ্ট করা। **—ful,** *adj.* **1.** Disagreeable to the taste ; বিস্বাদপূর্ণ। **2.** Offensive ; অপ্রীতিকর, বিরাগজনক, বিরক্তিকর।

dis-tĕm′-pêr, *n.* & *v. t.* **1.** Bad temper ; বদমেজাজ। **2.** A disease of young dogs with catarrh, cough and weakness ; কুক্কুর শাবকের সর্দ্দি-রোগ বিশেষ। **3.** Political disorder ; রাজনীতিক বিক্ষোভ। **4.** Mental or bodily derangement ; a malady ; শারীরিক বা মানসিক অসুস্থতা ; রোগ, ব্যাধি। ***Verb t.*** To derange in brain or mind ; চিত্তবিক্ষিপ্ত করা, মতিভ্রান্ত করা, মাথা বিগড়াইয়া দেওয়া, মস্তিষ্ক বিকৃত করা।

dis-tĕm′-pêr, *n.* & *v. t.* (*Painting.*) A method of painting on plates or chalk with yolk of eggs, size, instead of oil in scene-painting and internal walls ; the pigment or the prepared ground used in this process ; (চিত্রবিদ্যা) শিরিস্, ডিম্বের পীতাংশ প্রভৃতি মিশ্রিত রঙ্গ দ্বারা চূণ, বালি বা খড়িমাটির উপর চিত্র করার প্রণালী বিশেষ ; উক্তরূপে চিত্রে ব্যবহৃত রঙ্গ বা উক্তরূপ রঙ্গ লাগাইবার জন্য প্রস্তুত আলেখ্য ভূমি। ***Verb t.*** **1.** To paint (wall etc.) in distemper ; (প্রাচীর প্রভৃতি) উক্ত প্রণালীতে চিত্রিত করা। **2.** To mix as colours etc. in the way of distemper ; উক্ত পদার্থ সমূহের সহিত রঙ্গ মিশ্রিত করা।

dis-tĕnd′, *v. t.* & *i.* **1.** To swell by pressure from within ; to dilate ; স্ফীত করা, ফুলান ; বিস্ফারিত করা। **2.** To stretch out in length (*obs.*) ; বিছাইয়া দেওয়া, সম্প্রসারিত করা, বিস্তৃত করা (অপ্রচলিত)। ***Verb i.*** To become inflated ; as, now his heart *distends* with pride ; স্ফীত হওয়া, ফুলিয়া উঠা। **—ten′-si-ble, —ten′-sive,** *adjs.* **—ten-si-bil′-i-ty,** *n.* **—ten-sion, —ten-tion,** *ns.* Act of distending or state of being distended ; স্ফীত করণ, বিস্ফারণ, প্রসার, বিস্তার, প্রসারণ, স্ফীতি।

dis′-tich, *n.* A couple of lines or verses making a complete sense ; a couplet ; দ্বিপংক্তিবিশিষ্ট কবিতার কলি, দোঁহা ; পরস্পর মিলবিশিষ্ট কবিতা-পংক্তিদ্বয়।

dis′-tich-ous (-ŭs), *adj.* (*Bot.*) Arranged in two rows ; দ্বিপংক্তিতে সজ্জিত, দ্বি-শ্রেণীক (সাঃ পঃ)।

dis-til′, —till, *v. i.* & *t.* **1.** To fall in drops ; to trickle down ; ফোঁটা ফোঁটা হইয়া পড়া, বিন্দু বিন্দু করিয়া ক্ষরিত হওয়া ; চুয়াইয়া পড়া। **2.** To flow gently, (*lit.* & *fig.*) ; "The wisdom...will *distil* in honeyed sweetness ;" মৃদুমন্দ গতিতে প্রবাহিত হওয়া, মন্দ মন্দ প্রবাহিত হওয়া। **3.** To perform or undergo distillation ; পরিস্রুত করা, পরিস্রুত হওয়া। ***Verb t.*** **1.** To let fall or send down in drops ; to subject to the process of distillation, as of liquid ; ফোঁটা ফোঁটা করিয়া ফেলা, চুয়ান ; পরিস্রুত করা। **2.** To obtain by distillation ; to extract as whisky, essence, etc. by distillation ; to purify ; "Wine hath *distilled* our bloods ;" পরিস্রুত করিয়া প্রাপ্ত হওয়া ; পরিস্রুত করিয়া (চোয়াইয়া) হুইস্কি, পুষ্পসার প্রভৃতি বাহির করা ; বিশুদ্ধ করা। **3.** To extract the essence of, as plants etc., (also *fig.*) ; as, to *distil* a doctrine ; সার নিষ্কষিত করা, সারভাগ বাহির করা। **4.** To drive off or out by heat etc. ; as, to *distil* a volatile constituent ; উত্তাপদ্বারা বহিষ্কৃত করা। **—a-ble,** *adj.* **—ate,** *n.* (*Chem.*) Product from distillation ; (রসায়ন শাস্ত্র) পরিস্রুত পদার্থ। **Distilled water**—পরিস্রুত জল।

dis-til-lā′-tion, *n.* **1.** The act or process of distilling ; that which is formed by distillation ; সংস্রাবণ, নিঃসরণ, ক্ষরণ ; ক্ষরিত পদার্থ। **2.** The act of converting a substance into vapour by means of heat and of again condensing this into liquid form ; পরিস্রবণ। **3.** The abstract or essence of anything ; সার ভাগ, আরক।

dis-till′-êr, *n.* One who distils esp. alcoholic spirit ; পরিস্রবণকারী, সুরাকার, সুরাজীবী, শুঁড়ী। **—y,** *n.* The building and works where distilling, esp. of alcoholic liquors, is carried on ; পরিস্রবণাগার, মদের ভাটি, মদ্যসন্ধানাগার।

dis-tinct′, *adj.* **1.** Separate ; individual ; as, a herd of *distinct* animals ; different in quality or kind ; distinctive ; পৃথক, আলাহিদা ; ব্যক্তিগত ; ভিন্ন ; স্বতন্ত্র, বিশিষ্ট। **2.** Plain ; definite ; পরিস্ফুট, স্ফুট ; সুস্পষ্ট, অবধারিত। **3.** Unmistakable ; positive ; "His volume is a *distinct* enrichment of our literature ;" অভ্রান্ত ; প্রত্যক্ষ। **—ly,** *adv.* **—ness,** *n.*

dis-tinc′-tion, *n.* **1.** Act of distinguishing ; discrimination ; as, without *distinction* of caste or creed ; স্বতন্ত্রীকরণ ; ভেদ, বিভিন্নতা, প্রভেদ, ইতরবিশেষ, তারতম্য। **2.** State of being different ; as, the *distinction* of the persons of the Trinity ; স্বাতন্ত্র্য, স্বতন্ত্রতা। **3.** A note or mark of difference ;

as, the only *distinction* between the two is the colour ; name ; title ; পার্থক্য-সূচক চিহ্ন ; নাম ; উপাধি । **4.** Distinguishing quality ; as, a *distinction* between the animal and vegetable kingdoms ; বিভেদক গুণ, পার্থক্যসূচক গুণ । **5.** Estimation of difference ; প্রভেদনির্ণয়, ভেদদর্শন । **6.** A mark of honour ; eminence ; superiority ; as, a man of *distinction* ; সম্মানচিহ্ন ; প্রতিষ্ঠা, সমুন্নতি ; বরেণ্যতা, প্রাধান্য । **7.** Individuality, as of a literary style ; স্বাতন্ত্র্য, ব্যক্তিগত বিশেষত্ব । **–tive,** *adj.* Marking distinction or difference ; characteristic ; পার্থক্যসূচক, ভেদক, বিশেষক, বিশেষত্বদ্যোতক ; ইতরব্যবচ্ছেদক । **–tive-ly,** *adv.* **–tive-ness,** *n.* **Distinction without a difference** — নামমাত্র প্রভেদ, কৃত্রিম প্রভেদ । **Without distinction**— নির্বিশেষে ।

distingue, *adj.* (*F.*) Distinguished ; of superior manner or bearing ; strong ; বিখ্যাত, প্রসিদ্ধ ; সমুন্নত ভাবসম্পন্ন ; শক্তিশালী ।

dis-tin′-guish (-tĭng-gwĭsh), *v. t.* & *i.* **1.** To mark off by some characteristic ; as, the farmer *distinguishes* his sheep by marking their ears ; পার্থক্যসূচক চিহ্ন দ্বারা পৃথক্ করা, প্রভেদ করা । **2.** To divide into classes or categories ; as, to *distinguish* sounds *into* high and low ; শ্রেণীবদ্ধ করা, শ্রেণী বিভাগ করা । **3.** To recognise or make out the differences of by seeing, hearing or feeling etc. ; বুঝা, নির্ণয় করা, চিনা, ঠাহর করা । **4.** To perceive or point out the difference of by marks, signs, etc. ; as, to *distinguish* gold from iron ; পার্থক্য অবধারণ করা, ভেদ দর্শন করা, পার্থক্য নির্দ্দেশ করা । **5.** To make eminent ; as, to *distinguish* oneself by gallantry etc. ; খ্যাতিসম্পন্ন করা, প্রখ্যাত করা, প্রতিষ্ঠাবান করা, সম্মানিত করা । ***Verb i.*** **1.** To perceive the difference ; to draw distinctions ; (foll. by *between*) ; প্রভেদ অবধারণ করা ; পার্থক্য বা স্বাতন্ত্র্য অবধারণ করা । **2.** To characterize ; to be distinctive mark of ; চিহ্নিত করা ; পার্থক্যসূচক চিহ্ন হওয়া । **–a-ble,** *adj.* Capable of being distinguished ; প্রভেদ্য । **–a-bly,** *adv.* **–guished,** *adj.* Marked ; notable ; remarkable ; প্রসিদ্ধ ; খ্যাতিসম্পন্ন ; খ্যাতনামা, লব্ধপ্রতিষ্ঠ ; বিখ্যাত, প্রখ্যাত । **–guish-ing,** *adj.* That which distinguishes ; প্রভেদক, বিশেষক, ভেদসূচক, ভেদপ্রদর্শক ।

dis-tŏrt′, *v. t.* **1.** To put out of shape ; to twist aside physically ; as, to *distort* the face or a limb ; বিকৃতাঙ্গ করা, বিরূপ করা ; আকুঞ্চিত করিয়া বা বাঁকাইয়া বিরূপ করা, মোচড়ান । **2.** To give a twist or erroneous turn to, as thoughts, views, etc. ; to misrepresent, as statements, facts, etc. ; মিথ্যা বা অযথা বর্ণনা করা ; ভ্রান্তপথে পরিচালন করা । **3.** To wrest from the true meaning ; প্রকৃত অর্থ বিকৃত করা । **–ed-ly,** *adv.* **–tor′-tion,** *n.* **1.** Act of distorting ; state of being distorted ; a twisting ; আকুঞ্চন ; আকার-বিকৃতি ; রজ্জুবৎ বিজড়িতাবস্থা । **2.** Perversion, as of a meaning ; misrepresentation, as of facts, statements, etc. ; বিকৃতি, অর্থ-বিকৃতি ; অযথা-বর্ণন, অসত্যবর্ণন । **–tor′-tion-ist,** *n.* **1.** A caricaturist ; হাস্যোদ্দীপক বা বিদ্রূপাত্মক অভিনয়কারী । **2.** An acrobat who distorts his body ; যে বাজীকর অঙ্গ প্রত্যঙ্গাদি বিকৃত করিয়া বাজি দেখায় । **–tor′-tive,** *adj.* Causing distortion ; বিকৃতিকারক ।

dis-tract′, *v. t.* **1.** To divert ; to draw away ; (usually with *from*) ; as, to *distract* the mind or attention *from* a subject ; বিষয়ান্তরে প্রেরণ করা ; নিবর্ত্তিত করা, অন্যদিকে ফিরাইয়া লওয়া । **2.** To confuse the attention of ; (usually used as *p.p.* with *between*) ; to perplex ; to confound ; to harass ; বিভ্রান্ত করা ; আকুলিত করা, ব্যস্ত করা, উতালা করা ; উদ্বেজিত করা, হতবুদ্ধি করা ; উত্ত্যক্ত করা । **3.** To drive mad, (chiefly *p. p.*) ; মতিভ্রান্ত করা, বুদ্ধিভ্রষ্ট করা, উন্মাদ করা । **–ed,** *adj.* In a state of distraction ; উদ্ভ্রান্ত, ব্যস্তচিত্ত, ব্যাকুলিত, বিমনাঃ, উতালা, বিমনস্ক । **–ed-ly,** *adv.* **–ed-ness,** *n.* **–ing-ly,** *adv.*

dis-trăc′-tion, *n.* **1.** Diversion of the mind or attention ; চিত্তবিক্ষেপ, অন্যমনস্কতা । **2.** That which diverts attention ; diversion ; "Domestic *distractions* ;" চিত্তবিক্ষেপকর বিষয় ; বিষয়ান্তরে আকর্ষণ । **3.** Amusement ; relief from over-absorption ; আমোদ প্রমোদ ; চিত্তবিনোদন । **4.** Perplexity ; embarrassment ; চিত্তবৈকল্য, ব্যাকুলতা, বিভ্রান্তি, মোহ ; হতবুদ্ধিতা । **5.** Tumult ; disorder ; as, political *distraction* ; হুলস্থূল ; বিশৃঙ্খলা, বিক্ষোভ । **6.** Perturbation of mind ; madness ; insanity ; চিত্তবিভ্রম, চিত্তবিভ্রংশ, চিত্তবিক্ষেপ, মতিভ্রংশ ; উন্মাদ ; ক্ষিপ্ততা । **To distraction**—To a mad degree ; উন্মত্তবৎ ।

dis-train′ (-trān), *v. i.* & *t.* (*Law*) To levy a distress by sale of the chattels ; (আইন) ক্রোক করা, আটক করা । ***Verb t.*** To seize as chattels etc. for the realisation of a debt etc. ; ক্রোক করা । **–ment, –traint,** *ns.* Act or proceeding of distraining ; ক্রোক করণ, ক্রোক । **–ee, –er, –or,** *ns.*

dis-trait (-trā), *adj.* Absent-minded ; distracted in attention ; অন্যমনস্ক ; আনমনা, উন্মনা ; বিক্ষিপ্ত-চিত্ত ।

dis-traught′ (-trăt), *adj.* **1.** (*Archaic*) Violently agitated ; (অপ্রচলিত) অতিশয় বিক্ষোভিত । **2.** Crazy ; বিকৃত-মস্তিষ্ক, ক্ষিপ্ত, মাথা-পাগল ।

dis-tress' (-trĕs), *n.* & *v. t.* **1.** Anguish ; মর্ম্মান্তিক যন্ত্রণা, সন্তাপ। **2.** Misfortune ; poverty ; misery ; দুর্ভাগ্য, বিপাক ; দারিদ্র্য ; দুঃখ, ক্লেশ, যাতনা, বিড়ম্বনা, দুর্গতি, দুর্দ্দশা। **3.** Dangerous position ; as, a ship is in *distress* from leaking ; বিপৎ-সঙ্কুলাবস্থা, বিপদাপন্নাবস্থা, সঙ্কটাবস্থা। **4.** Exhaustion ; breathlessness ; অবসন্নতা ; নিরতিশয় ক্লান্তি। **5.** (*Law*) Distraint ; (আইন) ক্রোক। ***Verb t.*** **1.** To cause pain to ; to afflict ; to exhaust ; যন্ত্রণা দেওয়া ; কষ্ট দেওয়া ; অবসন্ন করা। **2.** To cause anxiety to ; to make unhappy ; to vex ; উৎকণ্ঠাকুল করা ; অসুখী করা ; উত্যক্ত করা। **3.** (*Law*) To levy a distress upon ; ক্রোকের টাকা আদায় করা। **–ful,** *adj.* **–ing-ly,** *adv.* **–tressed',** *adj.* In a state of distress ; ক্লিষ্ট, বিপন্ন, কাতর, দুঃপাতুর, বিধুর, আর্ত্ত, বিহ্বল, সন্তপ্ত, দুর্দ্দশাপন্ন। **Distress-gun, –rock-et**—বিপদাপন্ন জাহাজ হইতে তোপধ্বনি দ্বারা বা হাউই-বাজি উড়াইয়া যে সঙ্কেত প্রদান করা হয়। **Distress warrant**—ক্রোকের পরওয়ানা।

dis-trib'-üte, *v. t.* **1.** To divide among many ; to deal out ; বিতরণ করা ; বিভাগ করা, বণ্টন করা, অংশ করা, বিলি করা, বাঁটিয়া দেওয়া। **2.** To dispense ; বিধান করা। **3.** To scatter ; as, to *distribute* manure ; ছড়ান। **4.** To arrange ; to classify ; as, to *distribute* propositions into true and false ; শ্রেণীবদ্ধ করা ; শ্রেণী বিভাগ করা। **5.** To apply a term to all the individuals of a class ; শ্রেণীর প্রত্যেকটীর সম্পর্কে কোন পদ প্রয়োগ করা। **6.** (*Print.*) To separate as a used type and return it to its compartment ; (মুদ্রণ) মুদ্রণকার্য্য সমাপ্তির পর বিন্যস্ত অক্ষর সমূহ পৃথক করিয়া বিভিন্ন বিভিন্ন কোটরে রাখা, অক্ষর বণ্টন করা, অক্ষর ঠিক ঘরে ফেলা। **–u-tor,** *n.*

dis-tri-bü'-tion, *n.* **1.** Act of distributing ; state of being distributed ; apportionment ; বিতরণ ; সংবিভাগ ; অংশবিভাগ। **2.** Classification ; division into parts ; শ্রেণীবিভাগ ; বিভাগ। **3.** (*Log.*) Application of a term to all the individuals of the class ; (তর্কবিজ্ঞান) শ্রেণীর প্রত্যেকটীর সম্পর্কে কোন পদপ্রয়োগ। **4.** (*Pol economy*) The dispersal among consumers, of commodities produced ; (অর্থনীতি) ব্যবহারকারী-দিগের মধ্যে উৎপন্ন জিনিষের পরিব্যাপ্তি। **5.** The state or manner of being spread or dispersed ; as, the *distribution* of population or stars ; বিস্তৃতি, বিস্তার-প্রণালী। **6.** That which is distributed ; as, charitable *distributions* ; বিতরিত বস্তু। **7.** (*Print.*) Distributiug types ; (মুদ্রণ) অক্ষরবণ্টন। **Distribution of land water**—সন্নিবেশ (সাঃ পঃ), অবস্থান (ঐ)। **Geographical distribution**—বিশেষ বিশেষ অঞ্চল বা বিভাগে জন্তু ও উদ্ভিদের স্বাভাবিক সংস্থান, নিবসন (সাঃ পঃ)।

dis-trib'-ü-tive, *adj.* & *n.* **1.** Of or relating to distribution ; tending or serving to distribute ; বিভাগসম্বন্ধীয় ; বিভাগাত্মক, বিতরণাত্মক, বিতরণোপযোগী। **2.** (*Log.*) Referring to each individual of a class and not to the class collectively ; (তর্ক-বিজ্ঞান) শ্রেণীর প্রত্যেকটির সম্পর্কে প্রযোজ্য। **3.** (*Gram.*) Expressing distribution, separation or division ; বিভাগাত্মক, পৃথগ্-ভাবসূচক। ***Noun.*** (*Gram.*) A distributive word, as, *each, either, neither, every, etc.* ; (ব্যাকরণ) বিভাগাত্মক শব্দ। **–ly,** *adv.*

dis'-trict, *n.* & *v. t.* **1.** (*India*) An administrative territory, four or five of which generally make a division ; জেলা। **2.** A territory marked off for special administrative purpose ; a defined portion of city or town ; শাসন সম্পর্কীয় বিভাগ ; (সহরের) মহল্লা। **3.** (*Feudal law*) The territory within which the lord has the power of coercing and punishing, (*obs.*) ; (সামন্ত-তন্ত্র সম্বন্ধীয় আইন) সামন্ত তন্ত্রাধীন ভূস্বামীর অধিকারভুক্ত স্থান। **4.** A division of a parish with its own church or chapel and clergymen ; যাজকপল্লীর বিভাগ-বিশেষ,—যাহাতে স্বতন্ত্র যাজক, ধর্ম্মমন্দির কিংবা উপাসনা-মণ্ডপ আছে। **5.** (*England*) A rural division of a county with a district-council ; (ইংলণ্ডে) প্রদেশের পল্লী-বিভাগ। **6.** Sphere of operation ; কার্য্যক্ষেত্র। ***Verb t.*** To divide into districts ; as, legislatures *district* states for the choice of representatives ; শাসন-সম্পর্কীয় বিভাগ সমূহে বিভক্ত করা। **District Board**—জেলা সমিতি। **District Council** — ইংলণ্ড দেশের পল্লীবিভাগের স্থানীয় সমিতি। **District Railway**—লণ্ডন নগরীর কোন কোন অংশ ও নগরোপকণ্ঠস্থ স্থান সমূহ সংযোগকারী লৌহবর্ত্ম। **District visitor** — যাজকের অধীনস্থ পল্লী পুরোহিত,—যিনি যাজক পল্লীর কোন অংশে যাজকের নির্দেশানুসারে কাজ করেন।

dis-trŭst', *n.* & *v. t.* Want of trust ; suspicion ; অবিশ্বাস, অপ্রত্যয় ; আশঙ্কা, সন্দেহ, সংশয়। ***Verb t.*** To have no confidence in ; to doubt ; ভরসা না করা, অবিশ্বাস থাকা ; সন্দেহ করা, সংশয় করা। **–ful,** *adj.* Full of distrust ; apt to distrust ; অবিশ্বাসপূর্ণ ; শঙ্কাশীল, শঙ্কিত, সংশয়াকুল, অপ্রত্যয়ী, সন্দিগ্ধ-চিত্ত, সন্দিহান।

dis-tûrb', *v. t.* **1.** To interrupt the settled state of ; to agitate ; to trouble ; গোলমাল করা, অস্থির করা, বিক্ষোভিত করা ; আলোড়িত করা, বিশৃঙ্খল করা, লণ্ডভণ্ড করা ; ব্যতিব্যস্ত করা, উদ্বেজিত করা। **2.** To rend r uneasy ; to disquiet ; to perplex ; as, a person is *disturbed* by an insult ; বিক্ষুব্ধ করা ; উদ্বিগ্ন করা ; ব্যাকুল করা। 3. (*Law*) To deprive of the peaceful enjoyment or possession (of) ; (আইন) নির্ব্বিবাদে ভোগ বা অধিকার হইতে বঞ্চিত করা। **—ance,** *n.* 1. Interruption of tranquillity ; perplexity ; uneasiness ; অশান্তি ; বিলোড়ন, বিক্ষোভ, সংক্ষোভ ; উদ্বেগ, ব্যাকুলতা। 2. Tumult ; a public agitation ; অশান্তির ভাব, হাঙ্গামা, গোলযোগ ; জন-বিক্ষোভ। 3. (*Law*) Molestation ; interference with rights or property ; (আইন) পীড়ন ; অন্যের স্বত্ব বা সম্পত্তিতে হস্তক্ষেপ।

dis'-tȳle, *adj.* (*Arch.*) Having two columns in front, (said of temple, portico or the like) ; (স্থপতি-বিদ্যা) সম্মুখভাগে দ্বিস্তম্ভ-বিশিষ্ট।

dis-ūn'-iŏn, *n.* 1. Separation ; ভেদন, দ্বৈধীকরণ, বিচ্ছেদ, অসংযোগ। 2. A breach of concord ; dissension ; মতান্তর, অমিল ; মতভেদ, পার্থক্য, অনৈক্য। **—ist,** *n.*

dis-ū-nīte', *v. t.* & *i.* To break the concord of ; to divide ; বিযুক্ত করা, সংযোগ-বন্ধন ছিন্ন করা ; বিচ্ছিন্ন করা, বিভক্ত করা, পৃথক্ করা। ***Verb i.*** To become separated ; বিযুক্ত হওয়া, বিভক্ত হওয়া, সংযোগ-বন্ধন ছিন্ন হওয়া।

dis-ū'-ni-tȳ, *n.* Want of unity ; একতাভাব, অনৈক্য, সংযোগাভাব।

dis-use' (-ūs or ūz), *n.* & *v. t.* Cessation of use, practice, or exercise discontinuance ; অপ্রচলন, অব্যবহার, অনাচরণ ; বিরতি, ক্ষান্তি, নিবৃত্তি। ***Verb t.*** To cease to use ; to discontinue the practice of ; ব্যবহারে বিরত হওয়া ; ব্যবহার বন্ধ করা।

dī-sȳl'-lā-ble, *n.* A word or metrical foot of two syllables ; দ্বি-শব্দাংশ বিশিষ্ট শব্দ বা কবিতা-পংক্তি-পদ। **—lab'-ic,** *adj.* **—lab'-i-cal-ly,** *adv.*

dī'-tā, *n.* A forest tree of Eastern Africa and India ; ছাতিয়ান (খোরীঃ)। ***Dita bark***—ছাতিয়ানের ছাল।

ditch (dĭch), *n.*, *v. i.* & *t.* 1. A long narrow excavation, esp. to hold or conduct water or serve as a boundary ; উপকুল্যা, গড়, নর্দ্দামা, খাত, খানা, পরিখা, পগাড়। 2. A channel or watercourse ; জলপ্রণালী, নালা। 3. An embankment ; a dyke ; বাঁধ ; বন্যাপ্রবাহ রোধার্থ বাঁধ। ***Verb i.*** To make or repair ditches ; খাত প্রস্তুত করা ; খাতের জীর্ণ সংস্কার করা। ***Verb t.*** 1. To surround with a ditch or ditches ; to dig ditches in ; to drain ; as, to *ditch* a moist land ; খাত বা খাত সমূহ দ্বারা পরিবৃত করা ; খাত খনন করা; জল নিকাশের ব্যবস্থা করা। 2. To repair, as a ditch etc. ; খাত প্রভৃতির জীর্ণ-সংস্কার করা। **Ditch'-er,** *n.* 1. One who makes or repairs ditches ; খাত খননকারী, খাতের জীর্ণ-সংস্কারকারী। 2. A machine for digging ditches ; খাতখননার্থ যন্ত্র বিশেষ। **Ditch-dog** — খাত-মধ্যস্থ গলিত কুক্কুর-দেহ। **Ditch-water**—খাতের বদ্ধজল। **Dull as ditch water**—মোটেই চিত্তাকর্ষক নয়, অত্যন্ত নীরস। **To die in the last ditch**—To resist to the uttermost ; to hold out to the very last or to the bitter end ; শেষ পর্য্যন্ত বাধা দেওয়া ; চরম মুহূর্ত্ত পর্য্যন্ত দৃঢ় থাকা।

dī'-thē-ĭsm, *n.* The doctrine of those who maintain the existence of two gods, one good and one evil ; দ্বি-ঈশ্বর-বাদ। **—ist,** *n.* A holder of this doctrine ; দ্বি-ঈশ্বর-বাদী। **—is'-tic, —is'-ti-cal,** *adjs.* Pertaining to ditheism ; দ্বি-ঈশ্বর-বাদ-সম্বন্ধীয়।

dĭth'-ȳ-rămb, *n.* 1. A hymn in honour of Bacchus or some of the other Greek divinities, sung to the music of the flute ; সুরা দেবতা ব্যাকাস বা অন্য কোন গ্রীক দেবদেবীর স্তোত্র, সুরাদেবীর অর্চ্চনা। 2. A vehement or inflated poem, speech or writing ; তেজোপূর্ণ বা অতিরঞ্জিত কবিতা, বক্তৃতা বা রচনা। **—ram'-bic,** *adj.* & *n.* Pertaining to dithyramb ; wild and boisterous ; উক্তরূপ কবিতা সম্পর্কীয় ; প্রচণ্ড। (*Noun*) A dithyramb ; (see above).

dit'-ō-kous (-kŭs), *adj.* (*Zool.*) Producing two at a birth ; (জন্তু-বিদ্যা) যুগপৎ সন্তানযুগল প্রসবকারিণী।

dit'-tā-nȳ, *n.* A herb formerly of medical repute ; এক প্রকার শাক, পূর্ব্বে ঔষধে ব্যবহার হইত।

dit'-tō, *adj.* & *n.* (abbr. d^o ; or *do*) The aforesaid ; the same ; পূর্ব্বোক্ত ; ঐ, তাহাই, তথা, পূর্ব্ববৎ। ***Noun.*** 1. The aforesaid thing ; পূর্ব্বোক্ত বিষয়। 2. A duplicate ; একই প্রকারের দ্বিতীয় বস্তু, অনুরূপ বস্তু। **A ditto suit, a suit of ditto**—একই প্রকার বস্ত্রের ও রঙের এক প্রস্থ পোষাক। **To say ditto to**—To agree with ; কাহারও কথায় সায় দেওয়া।

dit-tŏg'-rā-phȳ, *n.* Unintentional repetition of a letter, word or phrase by a copyist ; অনুলিপি-লেখক কর্ত্তৃক একই অক্ষর, শব্দ বা বাক্যাংশ পুনর্লিখন। **—to-graph'-ic,** *adj.*

dit-tŏl'-ō-ġȳ, *n.* A double reading or twofold interpretation of a text ; পাঠ-ভেদ, ব্যাখ্যা-ভেদ বা ব্যাখ্যা-দ্বৈধ।

dit'-tȳ, *n.* A short simple song ; ক্ষুদ্রগীতি, গাথা, ঠুংরি, টপ্পা। **Ditty-bag** or **—box**—নাবিক বা ধীবরের সূচ, সুতা প্রভৃতি রাখার আধার।

dī-ū-rĕt'-ic, *adj.* & *n.* (*Med.*) Tending to increase the secretion and discharge of urine ; মূত্রল (সাঃ পঃ), মূত্র-বিরেচক (ঠাকুর), মূত্রবর্দ্ধক (ঐ), ইন্দ্রিয় জুলাব (কেম্ভিঃ), ইন্দ্রিয়রেচক (ঐ), মূত্ররেচক, মূত্রোৎপাদক। ***Noun.*** A medicine with diuretic properties ; মূত্রবর্দ্ধক ঔষধ।

dī-ŭr'-năl, *adj.* & *n.* 1. (*Astron.*) Occupying one day ; (জ্যোতির্বিজ্ঞান) আহ্নিক, দৈনিক, দৈনন্দিন, দিবাতন। 2. Relating to day-time ; daily ; as, a *diurnal* heat ; দিবাভাগ-সম্বন্ধীয়,

দিবাভাগের ; প্রাত্যাহিক। 3. (*Zool.*) Active during the day, as some animals ; (জন্তুবিদ্যা) দিবাভাগে কার্য্যপর। ***Noun.*** (*R. C. C.*) A service book containing the daily service for the "little hours ;" রোমান ক্যাথলিকদিগের নিত্য কর্ম্ম পদ্ধতি। **—ly,** *adv.*

div, *n.* An evil spirit in Persian mythology ; দেউ, জিন।

dï'-vâ, *n.* (*Ital.*) A great woman singer ; a prima donna ; সুপ্রসিদ্ধা গায়িকা ; গীতি-নাট্যের প্রধানা গায়িকা।

dï'-vă-gāte, *v. i.* To stray ; to digress ; বিপথে চলা ; মূল বিষয় ছাড়িয়া অবান্তর বিষয় ধরা। **—ga'-tion,** *n.* Digression ; deviation ; বিপথগমন ; ব্যত্যয়।

dĭv'-ă-lĕnt, *adj.* Having two units of combining power ; দ্বি-একক সংযোগ-শক্তি সম্পন্ন, দ্বৈধা (হিঃ কোঃ)।

dĭ-văn', *n.* 1. An oriental council of state, esp. Turkish privy council ; মন্ত্রি-সভা, বিশেষতঃ তুরস্কদেশের মন্ত্রিসভা। 2. (*India*) A chief officer of state ; (ভারতবর্ষ) দেওয়ান। 3. (In oriental countries) A saloon or hall where a council is held ; as, *divan-i-am* (=a court of justice) ; (ভারতবর্ষ প্রভৃতি দেশে) সভা-গৃহ ; ধর্ম্মাধিকরণ। 4. A long seat against a room-wall ; কক্ষ-প্রাচীরে ঠেস-দেওয়া পালঙ্ক বিশেষ। 5. A coffee or smoking saloon ; a cigar-shop ; কাফিপানশালা, ধূমপানশালা ; চুরুটের দোকান। 6. A book, esp., a collection of poems by one author ; as, the *divan* of Hafiz ; গ্রন্থ, বিশেষতঃ কবিতা-সংগ্রহ।

dĭ-văr'-ĭ-cāte, *adj.* & *v. i.* Widely diverging, (*Bot.* & *Zool.*) ; (উদ্ভিদ্‌বিদ্যা ও জন্তুবিদ্যা) পার্শ্ব-বিস্তৃত। ***Verb i.*** To part into two branches ; দ্বিশাখায় বিভক্ত হওয়া। **—ca'-tion,** *n.*

dīve, *n.* & *v. i.* 1. A plunge headforemost into water or other liquids ; a swim under water ; ডুবা, নিমজ্জন ; জলতলে সন্তরণ। 2. A sudden dart out of sight ; "He made a *dive* into the nearest shop ;" সহসা তীর বেগে দৃষ্টিপথ হইতে অন্তর্ধান। 3. A drinking den, (chiefly U. S.) ; মাতালের আড্ডা। ***Verb i.*** 1. To plunge headforemost into water or other liquids ; ডুব দেওয়া, নিমজ্জিত হওয়া। 2. To thrust the hand into water, a vessel or pocket ; জলে, পাত্রে বা জেবে হাত ঢুকান। 3. To go down or disappear suddenly ; সহসা নামা বা অন্তর্ধান হওয়া। 4. To plunge or to go deeply into a subject ; "To *dive* into the mysteries of God ; কোন বিষয়ে গভীর অনুসন্ধানে নিরত হওয়া, প্রবেশ করা। **Diving-bell**—কোন

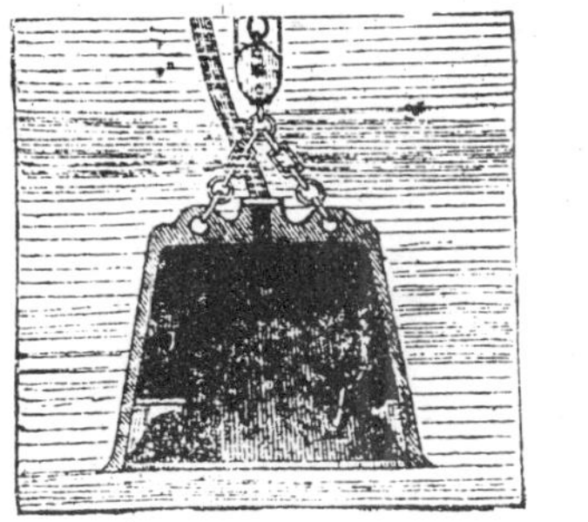

Diving-bell.

ব্যক্তিকে গভীর জলের ভিতর নামাইবার জন্য অনাচ্ছাদিততল আধারবিশেষ।

dīv'-ēr, *n.* 1. Person who dives for pearls or to examine sunk ships etc. ; ডুবুরী, ডুবারী, নিমজ্জক। 2. One of a kind of diving birds ; ডুবুরী পক্ষী, পানকৌড়ি। 3. (*Slang*) A pick-pocket ; (ইতর ভাষায়) পকেট-মারা, গাঁইট-কাটা।

dĭ-verge' (-vêrj), *v. i.* & *t.* 1. To extend from a common point in different directions ; as, the rays of light *diverge* as they proceed from the sun ; একবিন্দু হইতে প্রসৃত হওয়া, একস্থান হইতে চতুর্দ্দিকে বিকীর্ণ হওয়া, কেন্দ্রাপসরণ করা। 2. To go aside from a track or course ; মূল পথ ছাড়িয়া অবান্তর পথ ধরা। 3. (*Fig.*) To differ from a typical form or state ; to differ in opinion ; (লক্ষণায়) কোনরূপ আদর্শীভূত আকার বা অবস্থা হইতে ব্যতিক্রম হওয়া ; মতভেদ হওয়া। ***Verb t.*** To make divergent ; পরস্পর হইতে দূরে অপসৃত করা। **—ment, —ver'-gence, —ver'-gen-cy,** *ns.* 1. Act of diverging ; state of being divergent ; একবিন্দু হইতে নানাদিকে প্রসৃত হওন, বিকিরণ, প্রসারণ ; অপসৃতাবস্থা। 2. Difference ; deviation from a standard ; বৈভিন্ন্য, ব্যভিচার, বৈলক্ষণ্য ; আদর্শ হইতে ব্যতিক্রম **—ver'-gent,** *adj.* 1. Receding farther and farther from each other ; diverging ; (opp. to *convergent*) ; পরস্পর হইতে ক্রমশঃ দূরাপসরণশীল ; বিসর্পী, কেন্দ্রপরাঙ্মুখ, বহির্ম্মুখ। 2. Characterised by divergence or difference ; পরস্পরবিরোধী। 3. (*Opt.*) Causing divergences of rays as lens ; (দৃষ্টি-বিজ্ঞান) কিরণাপসরণকর। **—ver'-gent-ly,** *adv.* **—verg'-ing-ly,** *adv.*

dī'-vērs, *adj.* Several ; sundry ; various ; বিভিন্ন, নানা ; বিবিধ। [Divers is now limited to the plural ; as, *divers* ways (not, *divers* way)]

dī'-verse (-vêrs), *adj.* 1. Unlike in nature or qualities ; ভিন্ন, পৃথক্। 2. Multiform ; varied : as, a *diverse* colour ; বিবিধ, নানাবিধ ; নানা, বিভিন্ন, বিচিত্র। **—ly,** *adv.*

dĭ-vêr'-sĭ-fôrm, *adj.* Of varied forms ; নানারূপ, বহুরূপী।

dĭ-vêr'-sĭ-fȳ, *v. t.* To make diverse ; to modify ; to variegate ; বিভিন্ন করা, বৈচিত্র্যপূর্ণ করা ; রূপান্তর করা, প্রকারান্তর করা, রূপভেদ করা, পরিবর্ত্তন করা ; নানাবর্ণে চিত্রিত করা। **—fi-a-ble,** *adj.* **—fi-ca'-tion,** *n.*

dĭ-vêr'-sion, *n.* 1. The act of turning aside from any course, occupation or object ; বিক্ষেপ, অপসরণ, অন্যদিকে আকর্ষণ, ফিরান। 2. Recreation ; play ; pastime ; as, the *diversions* of youth ; চিত্তবিনোদন, অনুরঞ্জন ; কেলি ; ক্রীড়া-কৌতুক, আমোদপ্রমোদ। 3. (*Mil.*) The act of drawing the attention and force of an enemy from the point where the principal attack is to be made ; (সামরিক-শাস্ত্র) ছলপূর্ব্বক উদ্দিষ্টস্থান হইতে অন্যত্র আক্রমণের ভাণ প্রদর্শন করিয়া শত্রু সৈন্যের মনোযোগ তদ্দিকে আকর্ষণ।

di-vĕr′-si-tȳ, *n.* 1. Difference ; unlikeness ; as, there may be *diversity* without contrariety ; বৈভিন্ন্য, ভিন্নতা, ভেদ, তফাৎ ; অসাদৃশ্য, অনৈক্য। 2. Multiplicity with difference ; variety ; a different kind ; "People have *diversities* of tastes ;" বৈচিত্র্য ; নানাত্ব (বেদান্ত) ; বিভিন্ন প্রকার। 3. Variegation ; "In bright *diversities* of day ;" বর্ণবৈচিত্র্য, চিত্রবিচিত্রতা।

di-vĕrt′, *v. t.* 1. To turn aside ; to deflect ; মূল পথ হইতে সরান ; অপহৃত করা, বিক্ষেপ করা। 2. To turn from business or study ; hence, to please ; to amuse ; ব্যবসায়ের কাজ বা অধ্যয়ন হইতে বিষয়ান্তরে ফিরান; চিত্ত বিনোদন করা, আমোদিত করা, অনুরঞ্জন করা। 3. To distract, as a person, attention or mind (from one thing to another) ; বিক্ষিপ্ত করা, উদ্ভ্রান্ত করা, অন্যমনস্ক করা। 4. To interrupt the progress of ; to ward off ; উন্নতি রোধ করা ; নিবারণ করা, রোধ করা। **–ing,** *adj.* 1. Entertaining ; distracting ; আমোদজনক, চিত্তরঞ্জক, মনোরঞ্জক ; চিত্তবিক্ষেপকর। **–ingly,** *adv.* **–ive,** *adj.*

Dī′-vēs, *n.* A rich man ; ধনবান ব্যক্তি। (See Luke XVI. 19.) **Dives cost**—(আইন) উচ্চহারের খরচ।

di-vĕst′, *v. t.* 1. To unclothe ; to strip of garments etc., (with *of*) ; বিবস্ত্র করা, নগ্ন করা ; পরিচ্ছদ বিরহিত করা। 2. (*Fig.*) To strip ; to deprive ; (with *of*) ; as, to *divest* one *of* his rights ; (লক্ষণায়) বিচ্যুত করা, রিক্ত করা ; বঞ্চিত করা, কাড়িয়া লওয়া, অধিকারচ্যুত করা, অধিকারভ্রষ্ট করা। 3. (*Law*) To take away, as a vested right ; (আইন) সম্পত্তি বা অধিকার হইতে বঞ্চিত করা। **–ment, –i-ture,** *ns.*

dī-vīde′, *v. t., i.* & *n.* 1. To sunder ; to separate into parts ; পৃথক করা, বিভিন্ন করা, বিচ্ছিন্ন করা ; বিযুক্ত করা, বিভাগ করা। 2. To keep apart by a partition ; as, a wall *divides* two houses ; to part ; প্রাচীর বা পর্দ্দা দ্বারা স্বতন্ত্র রাখা ; বিচ্ছিন্ন করা। 3. To distribute ; as, *divide* these fruits among the boys ; বিতরণ করা, বাঁটিয়া দেওয়া, বিলি করা। 4. To cause to disagree ; "Men are *divided* in their opinion ;" অনৈক্য ঘটান, মতভেদ সংঘটন করা। 5. To make way through ; ভেদ করিয়া যাওয়া। 6. To classify ; শ্রেণীবদ্ধ করা, শ্রেণী বিভাগ করা। 7. To separate into two parts in order to ascertain the votes for and against a measure ; as, to *divide* a legislative house or a meeting upon a question ; কোন বিধির অনুকূল ও প্রতিকূল মত সংখ্যা নির্দ্ধারণার্থ দুই ভাগে বিভক্ত করা। 8. (*Math.*) To subject to mathematical division ; ভাগ করা। 9. (*Log.*) To separate into species ; (তর্ক-বিজ্ঞান) বিভিন্ন জাতিতে বিভক্ত করা। 10. (*Mech.*) To graduate ; as, to *divide* a sextant ; (যন্ত্র-বিজ্ঞান) ক্রমাঙ্কিত করা। ***Verb i.*** 1. To part ; বিভক্ত হওয়া, বিচ্ছিন্ন হওয়া। 2. To disunite ; বিযুক্ত হওয়া। 3. To fall out ; as, brothers *divide* ; মনান্তর হওয়া। 4. To part into two sets in voting, as a house of parliament or a meeting ; কোন বিধির অনুকূল ও প্রতিকূল মত সংখ্যা নির্দ্ধারণার্থ দুই শ্রেণীতে বিভক্ত হওয়া। ***Noun.*** A watershed ; জলবাঁধ। **–vid′-er,** *n.* 1. One who or that which divides ; বিভাজক, ভাজক, ভেদক, ছেদক, বিচ্ছেদক। 2. A distributor ; বিতরণকারী। 3. (*Pl.*) Measuring compasses ; রেখা-বিভাজক যন্ত্র।

dĭv′-i-dĕnd, *n.* 1. (*Math.*) A number to be divided by a divisor ; (গণিত-শাস্ত্র) ভাজ্য। 2. A sum payable as interest on loan or as profit of joint stock company ; a sum payable to creditors of an insolvent's estate ; লভ্যাংশ, ঋণের সুদ স্বরূপ প্রদত্ত অর্থ ; দাউলিয়া ব্যক্তির মহাজনগণকে প্রদেয় অর্থ। **–ly,** *adv.*

di-vĭd′-ū-ăl, *adj.* Separate ; separable ; স্বতন্ত্র ; বিয়োজ্য।

dī-vīne′, *adj.* & *n.* 1. Of or belonging to God ; as, the *divine* will ; ঐশ্বরিক, ঐশী, ঈশ্বরীয়, দৈব, ভাগবতী। 2. Like God ; সুরোপম, দেবোপম। 3. Religious ; pious ; as, *divine* songs ; ধর্ম্ম বিষয়ক ; ধর্ম্মনিষ্ঠ, ভক্তি-পরায়ণ। 4. Partaking of the nature of a god or gods ; দেবাত্মা, দেব-স্বভাব। 5. Heavenly ; excellent in the highest degree ; "The *divinest* mind ;" দিব্য, স্বর্গীয় ; পরমোৎকর্ষ-সম্পন্ন। 6. Relating to divinity or theology ; as, *divine* learning ; দেবদেবী-সম্বন্ধীয়, ধর্ম্মশাস্ত্র সম্বন্ধীয়। ***Noun.*** 1. A theologian ; ধর্ম্ম-শাস্ত্রবেত্তা। 2. (*Formerly*) A clergyman ; (পূর্ব্বে) যাজক্য পাদ্‌রি। **–ly,** *adv.* **Divine favour**—ভগবৎ কৃপা। **Divine grace**—ঈশ্বর প্রসাদ। **Divine right of kings**—নৃপতিগণের দেবদত্ত অধিকার (অর্থাৎ প্রজার ইচ্ছা অনিচ্ছার দিকে দৃক্‌পাত না করিয়া স্বাধীনভাবে রাজ্য শাসনের অধিকার)। **Divine service**—সম্মিলিত প্রার্থনা বা উপাসনা। **Divine strength**—দৈবশক্তি। **Divine will**—ঈশ্বরেচ্ছা।

di-vine′, *v. t.* & *i.* **1.** To detect by inspiration, magic or guessing ; to conjecture ; অলৌকিক উপায়ে বাহির করা; অনুমান করা, আন্দাজ করা। **2.** To foresee ; to predict ; পূর্ব্বেই দেখিতে পাওয়া ; ভবিষ্যৎ কহা। ***Verb i.*** **1.** To practise divination ; as, the prophets thereof *divine* for money ; অলৌকিক উপায়ে ভবিষ্যৎ কহা। **2.** To conjecture ; to guess ; as, to *divine* rightly ; আন্দাজ করা ; অনুমান করা, ঠাহর করা। **—vi-na′-tion,** *n.* **1.** Act of divining ; insight into or discovery of the unknown or future by supernatural means ; অলৌকিক উপায়ে ভবিষ্যৎ কথন ; শকুন বিচার (হিঃ কোঃ), নিমিত্ত-বিচার (ঐ), দৈব-বিচার (ঐ)। **2.** A good guess ; সঠিক অনুমান। **—vin′-er,** *n.* **1.** One who divines ; a soothsayer ; অনুমানকারী ; ভবিষ্যৎকথক। **2.** One who guesses correctly ; যে ব্যক্তি ঠিক অনুমান করে।

di-vin′-i-ty, *n.* **1.** The state of being divine ; Godhood ; দেবত্ব ; ঈশ্বরত্ব, ঈশত্ব, ঈশতা। **2.** God ; the supreme Being ; ঈশ্বর ; পরম পুরুষ। **3.** A celestial being ; one of the deities belonging to a polytheistic religion inferior to the supreme Being ; দেবযোনি ; দেবদেবী। **4.** Supernatural power or virtue ; as, they say there is *divinity* in odd numbers ; অলৌকিক শক্তি বা ধর্ম্ম। **5.** Science of divine things ; theology ; the theological faculty in universities ; দেবতত্ত্ব ; ধর্ম্মশাস্ত্র, দেবজ্ঞান, পরমার্থজ্ঞান, ব্রহ্মজ্ঞান, অধ্যাত্মজ্ঞান, অধ্যাত্মশাস্ত্র ; বিশ্ববিদ্যালয়ের ধর্ম্মশাস্ত্র পরিষৎ। (*Scot.*) **Divinity Hall**—(স্কটল্যাণ্ড) ধর্ম্মশাস্ত্র-শিক্ষাদানার্থ উচ্চ বিদ্যালয় ; বিশ্ববিদ্যালয়ের ধর্ম্মশাস্ত্র সম্বন্ধীয় বিভাগ। **The divinity** — ঈশ্বর। (*Book-binding*) **Divinity calf**—(পুস্তক বাঁধাইবার কাজ) খৃষ্টীয় ধর্ম্ম গ্রন্থ বাঁধাইর কাজে ব্যবহৃত গাঢ় বাদামী বর্ণে রঞ্জিত শোধিত গোবৎস-চর্ম্ম।

div′-i-nize, *v. t.* To deify ; দেবত্ব আরোপ করা।

di-vis′-i-ble, *adj.* Capable of being divided ; বিভাজ্য, অংশনীয়, অংশয়িতব্য। **—bil′-i-ty,** *n.*

di-vi′-sion, *n.* **1.** The act of dividing anything into parts ; বিভাজন, ভাগ। **2.** That which divides ; a partition ; বিভাজক বস্তু ; পর্দ্দা, যবনিকা, বৃতি, বেড়া, প্রাচীর। **3.** A distinct segment or section ; খণ্ড, বিভাগ, কাণ্ড। **4.** A territorial or administrative section of a province etc. ; বিভাগ। **5.** Disunion ; alienation ; discord ; as, *division* among the brothers ; অমিল, পার্থক্য, অনৈক্য ; স্নেহচ্যুতি ; মতান্তর। **6.** Distribution ; sharing ; as, *division* of labour ; হিস্যা, বণ্টন, বিতরণ ; অংশবিভাগ। **7.** Contrast ; distinction ; ভেদ, সম্ভেদ, প্রভেদ, বৈপরীত্য ; বিরোধ, স্বাতন্ত্র্য। **8.** (*Log.*) Classification of a genus into its constituent species ; (তর্ক-বিজ্ঞান) বিভাগ (সাঃ পঃ)। **9.** Separation of the members of the house of Parliament to ascertain vote ; কোন বিধি বা প্রস্তাবের অনুকূল এবং প্রতিকূল মত সংখ্যা-নির্দ্ধারণের জন্য পার্লেমেণ্ট মহাসভার সভ্যগণকে দুইভাগে বিভক্ত করণ। **10.** (*Mil.*) A body of men usually two brigades, under the command of a major general ; মেজর জেনারেলের অধীন সুবৃহৎ সৈন্য-দল, সৈন্যবিভাগ। **11.** (*Naut.*) A portion of a fleet or a number of vessels under one command ; (নৌ-বিদ্যা) একজন অধিনায়কের অধীন কতিপয় সংখ্যক রণপোত বা রণপোত বহরের অংশ। **12.** (*Biol.*) A group forming part of a larger group of genera or families ; (জীব-বিজ্ঞান) বর্গ। **13.** (*Math.*) The process of finding how many times one number is contained in another ; (গণিত-শাস্ত্র) হরণ, ভাগহার, ভাগ অঙ্ক। **—al,** *adj.* Pertaining to or making a division ; বিভাগীয়, বিভাগাত্মক। **—al-ly,** *adv.* **—sive,** *adj.* **1.** Forming division ; বিভাগাত্মক। **2.** Creating discord ; বিরোধজনক। **—sive-ness,** *n.* **—sor,** *n.* (*Math.*) The number which divides the dividend ; ভাজক, ছেদক (সাঃ পঃ), ভাগ (ঐ), হর (ঐ), হারক (ঐ), হার (ঐ)। **Division of labour** — শ্রম-বিভাগ (হিঃ কোঃ), কার্য্য-বিভাগ (ঐ), ক্রিয়া-বিভাগ (ঐ)।

di-vōrce′, *n.* & *v. t.* **1.** Legal dissolution of marriage ; বিবাহ-ভঙ্গ, বিবাহ-বিচ্ছেদ, পরিণয়চ্ছেদ, দাম্পত্য-বিচ্ছেদ। **2.** (*Fig.*) Severance ; sundering ; as, to make *divorce* of their incorporate league ; (লক্ষণায়) ছেদন, বিচ্ছেদ, খণ্ডন। ***Verb t.*** **1.** To dissolve the marriage contract between ; to separate by divorce ; বিবাহ-বিচ্ছেদ করা, দাম্পত্য-সম্বন্ধ ছেদন করা ; স্ত্রী-ত্যাগ করা, তালাক দেওয়া। **2.** (*Fig.*) To sunder ; to disunite ; as, the word was *divorced* from its original sense ; বিচ্ছিন্ন করা ; বিযুক্ত করা। **3.** To make away ; to put away ; to repudiate ; অপসারিত করা ; তফাৎ করা, দূরীভূত করা ; অস্বীকার করা। **—ment,** *n.* **—vorce′-a-ble,** *adj.* **—vor-cee′,** *n.* A divorced person ; পরিত্যক্তা স্ত্রী বা পরিত্যক্ত স্বামী। **—vor′-cive,** *adj.*

div′-ŏt, *n.* (*Scot.*) A thin turf or sod for thatching ; ঘর ছাওয়ার উপযোগী তৃণ বিশেষ।

di-vŭlge′, *v. t.* To disclose ; to make public ; as, to *divulge* a secret ; প্রকাশ করা, ফাস করা, উদ্ঘাটন করা ; সাধারণ্যে প্রচার করা, গুপ্ত কথা ব্যক্ত করা। **—vul-ga′-tion,** *n.*

di-vŭl′-sion, *n.* The act of pulling or plucking away ; a rendering asunder ; বিপাটন, উৎপাটন ; বিচ্ছেদন, বিদারণ। **—sive,** *adj.*

diz′-en (-n) *v. t.* To dress gaudily ; সুসজ্জিত করা, জমকালো পোষাক পরান।

diz′-zȳ, *adj.* & *v. t.* **1.** Giddy ; having in the head a whirling sensation with a tendency to fall ; mentally confused or unsteady ; ঘূর্ণ্যমান ; ঘূর্ণিতশির ; বিভ্রান্ত, হতবুদ্ধি। **2.** Causing giddiness ; শিরোঘূর্ণনজনক, ভ্রমিজনক। **3.** Very high as a mountain, tower, etc. ; অত্যুচ্চ। **4.** Whirling rapidly ; as, a *dizzy* stream, wheel, etc. ; সবেগে ঘূর্ণ্যমান। **5.** (*Fig.*) Unreflecting ; "*Dizzy* multitude ;" (লক্ষণায়) বিচারণাশূন্য, চিন্তাশক্তিহীন। ***Verb t.*** To make dizzy ; to confuse or bewilder ; মাথা ঘুরাইয়া দেওয়া, শিরোঘূর্ণিত করা ; বিভ্রান্ত করা, হতবুদ্ধি করা। **–zi-ly,** *adv.* **–zi-ness,** *n.* Giddiness ; ভ্রমি, শিরোঘূর্ণন।

dō, *n.* (*Slang*) A cheat ; an imposture ; a swindle ; (ইতর ভাষায়) প্রতারণা ; ঠকামি ; জুয়াচুরি।

dō, *n.* (*Mus.*) The first of the seven syllables used for the solfeggio of the scale ; (সঙ্গীত-শাস্ত্র) স্বরগ্রামের প্রথমস্বর 'সা'।

dŏ, *v. t., i.* or *aux.* **1.** To perform ; to execute ; to discharge, as right, penance etc. ; করা ; সম্পাদন করা, সংসাধন করা, সাঙ্গ করা ; পালন করা। **2.** To bestow ; to impart ; to render or give ; as, to *do* one credit : to *do* one harm etc. ; অর্পণ করা ; সঞ্চার করা ; প্রদান করা। **3.** To finish ; to bring to an end ; "I have *done* weeping ;" শেষ করা ; সমাপ্ত করা, অবসান করা। **4.** To treat or deal with in any way ; to get in order ; as, to *do* one's hair ; to repair ; to clean or put in order ; as, a paper hanger *does* a house : a housemaid *does* a room ; কোনরূপ ব্যবহার করা ; বিন্যাস করা, সংস্কার করা ; মেরামত করা ; পরিস্কার করা, গোছান। **5.** To solve, as a problem or sum ; সমাধান করা, কষা। **6.** To play the part of ; as, to *do* Hamlet ; (অভিনেয় অংশ) অভিনয় করা। **7.** To translate as a book, (with *into*) ; অনুবাদ করা, অনূদিত করা। **8.** To work at, or learn as, a lesson ; পড়া শিখা, পাঠ শিক্ষা করা। **9.** To traverse as a distance ; ভ্রমণ করা। **10.** To exhaust ; to overcome ; অবসন্ন করা ; অভিভূত করা। **11.** (*Slang*) To provide food etc. for ; as, they *do* you very well ; (ইতর ভাষায়) আহার জোগান। **12.** (*Slang*) To undergo as a term of punishment ; (ইতর ভাষায়) জেল খাটা। **13.** To bring about ; to pronounce ; as, neglecting the duty will *do* much danger ; সংঘটন করা, উৎপাদন করা ; ব্যক্ত করা। **14.** To exert ; as, to *do* one's best ; (শক্তি, ক্ষমতা প্রভৃতি) প্রয়োগ করা। **15.** To transact ; as, to *do* business with another ; নির্ব্বাহ করা। **16.** To have recourse to ; as, in this crisis we know not what to *do* ; কোন উপায় অবলম্বন করা। **17.** (*Slang*) To cheat ; to hoax ; as, he *did* me out of five shillings ; (ইতরভাষায়) প্রতারণা করা ; ফাঁকি দেওয়া। **18.** To outdo, as in fighting ; to beat ; as, I have *done* the few and am in good health ; অতিক্রম করা ; পরাজিত করা। **19.** (*Colloq.*) To inspect the sights of ; to visit as a tourist ; as, I have *done* France and Italy ; (চলিতভাষায়) কোন স্থানের প্রাকৃতিক দৃশ্যাবলী দর্শন করা ; পরিব্রাজকরূপে পরিভ্রমণ করা। **20.** To prepare ; to cook ; as, be sure to *do* the meat thoroughly ; প্রস্তুত করা ; পাক করা, রান্না করা। ***Verb i.*** **1.** To act ; করা। **2.** To conduct ones' self ; to behave ; "The maxim of *doing* as we would be *done* by ;" চলা ; আচরণ করা। **3.** To fare ; to be, as regards health ; as, I asked him how he *did* ; থাকা, চলা ; (স্বাস্থ্যসম্পর্কে) থাকা। **4.** To succeed ; to serve a purpose ; to suffice ; as, will this plan *do* ; কৃতকার্য্য হওয়া ; উদ্দেশ্য সিদ্ধি করা ; প্রচুর হওয়া। **5.** To perform deeds ; as, *do* or die ; কার্য্য সম্পাদন করা। **6.** To conclude ; to make an end ; as one word more and I have *done* ; শেষ করা ; সমাপ্ত করা। **7.** To contrive ; to shift ; as, how shall we *do* for money for these wars ; কৌশল করা ; ফন্দি করা। [As an elliptical auxiliary ; as in "did you sell it ? yes I *did*]"

Do′-ing, *n.* (Usually *pl.*) A deed ; conduct ; কার্য্য ; আচরণ, চালচলন। **Do′-a-ble,** *adj.* **Do′-er,** *n.* **To do away with**—To abolish ; to destroy ; বিলোপ করা, রহিত করা ; ধ্বংস করা। **To do brown**—To cook or roast to brownness ; ভাজিয়া বাদামী রঙ্গ করা। (*Slang*) To make a fool of ; (ইতর ভাষায়) বোকা সাজান। **To do by**—To deal with ; to behave towards ; ব্যবহার করা ; কাহারও প্রতি আচরণ করা। **To do for**—To serve the purpose ; আবশ্যকোপযোগী হওয়া, কাজ চলা। To ruin ; to kill ; as, he is *done for* ; ধ্বংস করা ; সর্ব্বনাশ করা। **To do into**—To translate ; অনুবাদ করা। **To do Macbeth etc.**—To represent that part in a play ; ম্যাক্‌বেথের ভূমিকা অভিনয় করা। **To do one in the eye**—To cheat one ; চোখে ধূলি দেওয়া। **To do over**—To do again ; পুনরায় করা। To cover over ; উপরদিকে আচ্ছাদিত করা। **To do to death**—To murder ; বিনাশ করা, বধ করা। **To do to** or **unto**—To act or behave to ; ব্যবহার করা। **To do up**—To restore ; to repair ; to wrap up as a parcel ; প্রত্যর্পণ করা ; জীর্ণ-সংস্কার করা ; মোড়া। To tire out ; ক্লান্তকরা, পরিশ্রান্ত করা। To ruin ; as, the debtor was *done up* (made bankrupt) by a creditor ; ধ্বংস করা, সর্ব্বনাশ করা। **To do with**—To make use of ; ব্যবহার করা। To get on with ; to tolerate ; to find sufficient ; চলা ; সহা ; প্রচুর মনে করা। To deal with ; (কাহারও প্রতি) ভাল বা মন্দ ব্যবহার করা। **To do without**—To dispense with ; ছাড়া চলা। **To have to do with**—To have a connection or concern with ; সম্পর্ক থাকা, সংস্রব থাকা। **Well-to-do**—Rich ; wealthy ; সঙ্গতিসম্পন্ন, সঙ্গতিশালী ; ধনবান। [*A to-do*—Bustle ; fuss ; গোলমাল ; হৈ-চৈ। *Do-nothing*, *adj.* & *n.* Idle ; নিষ্কর্ম্মা। (*Noun*) Idler ; নিষ্কর্ম্মা লোক, অলস-ব্যক্তি। *Do tell*—Very strange ; you astonish me ; (American phrase) ; ভারী আশ্চর্য্য ; তুমি আমাকে অবাক্ কল্লে। *To do or die*—মন্ত্রের সাধন কিংবা শরীর পাতন।]

dō'-ăb (dō- or dô-), *n.* A tract of land between two rivers ; দুই নদীর মধ্যবর্ত্তী প্রদেশ, অন্তর্বেদী (মঃ উঃ)।

doat (dōt), *v. i.* See DOTE.

dŏb'-bin, *n.* A farm-horse ; কৃষি-ক্ষেত্রে ব্যবহৃত অশ্ব।

Dō-cēt'-ic, *adj.* Pertaining to heresy that Christ's body was not human but phantasmal or of celestial substance ; খ্রীষ্টের চিন্ময়-দেহবাদ সম্বন্ধীয়। **—ce'-tism,** *n.* The Docetic doctrine ; খৃষ্টের দেহ সাধারণ মানবের মত রক্তমাংসময় ছিল না—পরন্ত চিন্ময় পদার্থে গঠিত ছিল, এইরূপ মতবাদ, চিন্ময়দেহবাদ। **—ce'-tist,** *n.* A holder of this doctrine ; চিন্ময়দেহবাদী।

dŏch'-mi-ŭs, *n.* A foot of five syllables (⏑ - - ⏑ -) (usually *pl.* DOCHMII) ; কবিতা পংক্তির পঞ্চ শব্দাংশ বিশিষ্ট পাদ। **—mi-ac,** *adj.* & *n.*

doc'-ile (dŏs-ïle, or dŏs-îl), *adj.* Teachable ; submissive ; শিক্ষাপ্রবণ, শিক্ষণীয় ; সুশাস্ত, বিনেয়, বশ্য। **—cil'-i-ty,** *n.* The state of being docile ; সুশিক্ষ্যতা, সুশান্ততা।

dŏck, *n.* Kinds of coarse weedy herb, a popular antidote for nettle stings ; একপ্রকার ওষধি, লোলিকা (আঃ বঃ), রক্ত সৌগন্ধিক (ঐ)।

dŏck, *n.* **1.** A solid fleshy part of an animal's tail ; জন্তুর লাঙ্গুলের কঠিন এবং মাংসল অংশবিশেষ। **2.** A case of leather to cover the dipped or cut tail of a horse ; অশ্বের ছিন্নলাঙ্গুল ঢাকিবার জন্য চর্ম্মনির্ম্মিত আবরণবিশেষ।

dŏck, *v. t.* **1.** To cut short, (animal in tail, person in hair) ; "His horses are not *docked* :" to *dock* a tail ; আগা কাটিয়া ছোট করা, ছাঁটা, কেশ, লাঙ্গুলাগ্র প্রভৃতি কর্ত্তন করা। **2.** To lessen ; to deduct from ; as, to *dock* wages ; to deprive of ; as, to *dock* a man of supplies ; কমান ; বাদ দেওয়া ; বঞ্চিত করা। **3.** (*Law*) To cut off ; (আইন) ছিন্ন করা। **Dock-tailed**—ছিন্নপুচ্ছাগ্র, হ্রস্বপুচ্ছ (মঃ উঃ)।

dock, *n.* The place in a criminal court where the prisoner stands ; আসামীর কাঠগড়া।

dŏck, *n., v. t.* & *i.* **1.** A basin with flood-gates in which ships may be loaded, unloaded or repaired ; স্রোতোদ্বারবিশিষ্ট জলাশয় বিশেষ, যেখানে জাহাজ মেরামত করা হয় অথবা জাহাজের মাল উঠান বা নামান হইয়া থাকে, পোতাশয় (আঃ বঃ)। **2.** (*Pl.*) A dockyard ; পোত-নির্ম্মাণ স্থলী, নৌ-নির্ম্মাণস্থলী, নৌ-নির্ম্মাণ-কারখানা। **3.** *(In railway)* A platform-enclosure in which a line terminates ; লৌহবর্ত্মের বিরামস্থানের প্রাঙ্গণস্থ বৃতিবেষ্টিত স্থল—যথায় লৌহ-বর্ত্ম শেষ হইয়া থাকে। ***Verb t.*** To bring (a ship) in a dock for repairing or clearing the bottom etc. ; জীর্ণসংস্কারাদির জন্য পোতসংস্কার স্থানে (জাহাজ) আনয়ন করা। ***Verb i.*** (*Of a ship*) To come into dock ; (পোত-সম্পর্কে) পোতাশ্রয়ে আগত হওয়া। **Dock'-age,** *n.* **1.** A charge for the use of a dock ; নৌ-নির্ম্মাণস্থলী ব্যবহারের জন্য দেয় অর্থ। **2.** The docking of vessels ; পোত-নির্ম্মাণ-স্থলীতে পোত আনয়ন। **Dock'-ize,** *v.t.* To transform as a river into a harbour for docking ; নদীকে পোতাশয়ে পরিবর্ত্তিত করা। **Dock-i-za'-tion,** *n.* **Dock dues**—পোতাশয় ব্যবহারের জন্য প্রদেয় অর্থ। **Dock master**—পোতাশয় পরিদর্শক। **Dock-yard**—A yard or storage place for all sorts of naval stores and timber for ship-building ; নৌ-নির্ম্মাণস্থলী, নৌ-নির্ম্মাণ কারখানা, নৌকা নির্ম্মাণ স্থান (হিঃ কোঃ)। **Dry** or **graving dock**—শুষ্কীকৃত পোতাশয়, পোত-নির্ম্মাণস্থলী। **Floating dock**—প্লবমান পোতাশয়। **Wet dock**—জলপূর্ণ পোতাশয় বা পোত সংস্কারস্থলী।

dŏck'-ĕr, *n.* A labourer in a dock ; পোতাশয়ের মজুর।

dŏck'-ĕt, *n.* & *v. t.* **1.** (*Law*) A register of legal judgments ; (আইন) রায় বা ফয়সলার বহি। **2.** Endorsement on a letter or document indicating its contents or subject ; a summary or digest of a long paper or papers ; কোন চিঠি বা দলিলের সারকথা—যাহা তৎপৃষ্ঠে লিখিত হয় ; সুদীর্ঘ পত্রাদির চুম্বক বা সারমর্ম্ম, সার-লিপি। **3.** A custom-house warrant certifying payment of duty ; প্রদত্ত শুল্কের রসিদ। **4.** A certificate of cotton-clearing house entitling the presenter to delivery ; যে নিদর্শন পত্রের বলে তুলার গুদাম হইতে তুলা খালাস করা যায়। ***Verb t.*** **1.** (*Law*) To make a brief abstract of, and inscribe in a book ; (আইন) (পত্রাদির)

সারমর্ম্ম বা চুম্বক কোন বহিতে লিখিয়া রাখা, সারমর্ম্ম লিপিবদ্ধ করা। **2.** To indorse with an abstract as a letter or bill ; কোনও চিঠি বা হুণ্ডীর পৃষ্ঠে সারমর্ম্ম লিখা। **3.** To mark with tickets ; as, to *docket* goods ; ক্ষুদ্র ক্ষুদ্র স্থূল কাগজ খণ্ড সমূহ দ্বারা চিহ্নিত করা।

dŏc′-tor (-têr), *n., v. t.* & *i.* **1.** A holder of the highest university degree in any faculty ; a learned man ; কোন বিষয়ে বিশ্ববিদ্যালয়ের সর্ব্বোচ্চ উপাধিধারী [যথা—D. L., L. L. D., M. D., PH. D.] ; পণ্ডিত ; জ্ঞানী, শাস্ত্রী। **2.** A person only licensed to practise medicine ; a physician ; চিকিৎসক, ভিষক্, বৈদ্য ; ডাক্তার। **3.** An honorary mark of literary or other distinction conferred by a university ; সাহিত্য বা অন্য কোন বিভাগে অনন্য সাধারণ প্রসিদ্ধি লাভের জন্য বিশ্ব-বিদ্যালয় কর্ত্তৃক কোন ব্যক্তিকে যে সম্মানসূচক উপাধি প্রদত্ত হয়। **4.** A part in a machine for regulating quantity, adjusting or feeding ; as, the *doctor* of a calico-printing machine ; যন্ত্রের গতি প্রভৃতি নিয়মিত করণার্থ যন্ত্রাংশ বিশেষ। **5.** A kind of fish ; (also called a *doctor* or *surgeon-fish*) ; একপ্রকার মৎস্য। **6.** (*Angling*) An artificial fly ; (বড়শীর জন্য) কৃত্রিম মক্ষিকা। **7.** (*Archaic*) A teacher ; a learned man ; (অপ্রচলিত) আচার্য্য, উপদেশক ; পণ্ডিত ব্যক্তি। ***Vreb t.*** **1.** To confer the degree of doctor on; বিশ্ববিদ্যালয়ের সর্ব্বোচ্চ উপাধি প্রদান করা, ডাক্তার উপাধি প্রদান করা। **2.** To treat as a physician ; as, to *doctor* a patient ; চিকিৎসা করা। **3.** To patch up (machinery etc.) ; (যন্ত্রাদিতে) পটি লাগান। **4.** (*Slang*) To adulterate ; as, to *doctor* wines etc. ; (ইতর ভাষায়) ভেজাল দেওয়া। ***Verb i.*** To practise as a physician ; চিকিৎসা ব্যবসায় করা, চিকিৎসকের কার্য্য করা। **—al,** *adj.* **—ate,** *n.* The degree, title or rank of a doctor ; বিশ্ব-বিদ্যালয়ের সর্ব্বোচ্চ উপাধি বা গৌরব, বিশারদোপাধি (আঃ বঃ)। **—hood, —ship,** *ns.* **—less,** *adj.* **Doctors' commons**—ইংলণ্ড দেশের প্রাচীন বিচারালয় বিশেষ। **Doctors of the Church**—কতিপয় আদিম যুগের খৃষ্টীয়াচার্য্য। **Doctor's stuff**—Medicine ; ঔষধ।

dŏc-tri-naire′ (-nār), *n.* & *adj.* A pedantic theorist ; a person who applies principles without allowance for circumstances ; পাণ্ডিত্য-প্রদর্শন সহকারে আত্মমত প্রকাশক ; যে ব্যক্তি ঘটনার বিশেষ অবস্থার দিকে দৃষ্টিপাত না করিয়া মূলনীতি প্রয়োগ করিয়া থাকে। ***Adj.*** Theoretical and impractical ; as, *doctrinaire* notions ; কল্পনাত্মক, অকার্য্যকর। **—ism,** *n.*

dŏc-tri-nā′-ri-ăn, *adj.* & *n.* Same as DOCTRINAIRE. **—ism,** *n.*

dŏc′-tri-năl, *adj.* & *n.* Pertaining to doctrines ; inculcating doctrines ; মত-সম্বন্ধীয়, তত্ত্ব-সম্পর্কীয় ; মত-প্রতিপাদক, তত্ত্বোপদেশক। ***Noun.*** (*Pl.*) Matters of doctrine or instruction ; মত বা উপদেশের বিষয়। **—ly,** *adv.*

dŏc′-trine, *n.* **1.** That which is taught ; a body of instructions ; মত, শিক্ষা ; উপদেশাবলী। **2.** A religious, political or scientific belief, dogma or tenet ; as, the *doctrine* of gravitation ; মত, বাদ, তত্ত্ব, সিদ্ধান্ত। **—trin-ism,** *n.* Devotion to, or enunciation of, a doctrine ; মত বা সিদ্ধান্তের প্রতি নিষ্ঠা, মত বা সিদ্ধান্ত নির্দ্দেশন। **—trin-ist,** *n.* **—trin-ize,** *v. i.* To theorize ; মত প্রকটন করা, সিদ্ধান্ত করা। **The Monroe doctrine** — আমেরিকার শাসন সংক্রান্ত ব্যাপারে ইয়ুরোপের হস্তক্ষেপের অধিকার নাই—এই বিষয়ক মত। [রাষ্ট্রপতি Monroe এই মতের পূর্ব্বাভাস প্রদান করেন।]

dŏc′-ü-mĕnt, *n.* & *v. t.* A deed writing or inscription furnishing evidence, information, etc. ; দলীল, লেখ্য, পত্র। ***Verb t.*** To prove by, or provide with, documents or evidence ; as, to *document* a claim ; দলীল পত্র দ্বারা প্রমাণ করা, দলীল পত্র দেওয়া। **—men′-tal,** *adj.* Pertaining to written evidence ; লিখিত প্রমাণ সম্বন্ধীয়, দলীলঘটিত। **—men′-ta-ry,** *adj.* **1.** Of the nature of documents ; contained or certified in writing ; দলীল-ঘটিত ; লেখ্য। **2.** Pertaining to documentation in literature or art ; সাহিত্য বা কলাশাস্ত্রের দলীল ঘটিত প্রমাণ সংগ্রহ বা ব্যবহার সম্বন্ধীয়। **—men-ta′-tion,** *n.* **1.** Preparation, or use of, documentary evidence and authorities ; দলীল-ঘটিত প্রমাণ এবং প্রামাণিক পত্রাদি সংগ্রহ বা প্রয়োগ। **2.** Act of furnishing as a ship with documents ; জাহাজের অধ্যক্ষকে কাগজ পত্র প্রদান। **Human document**—মানব-প্রকৃতি নির্দ্দেশক বর্ণনা, ঘটনা প্রভৃতি।

dŏd, *v. t.* To clip ; to lop ; (*obs.*) ছাঁটা ; ছাড়ান।

dŏd′-dĕd, *adj.* Homeless ; as, *dodded* cattle ; গৃহহীন, গৃহহারা।

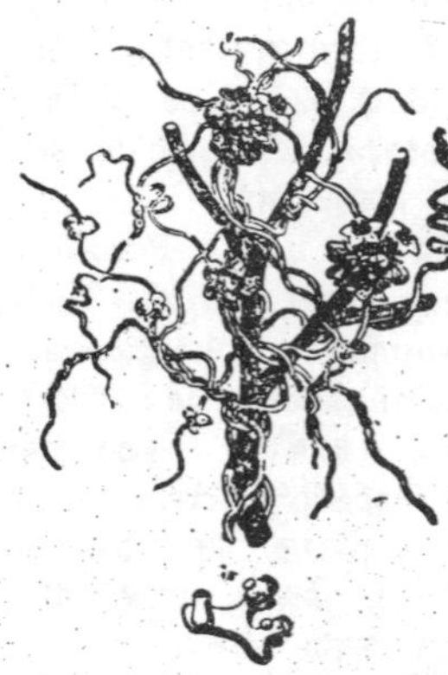

Dodder plant.

dŏd′-dêr, *n.* Kinds of slender leafless, threadlike, parasitic plant ; অমরবল্লী (খোরী), আকাশবল্লী (ঐ), অমরশ্রী (ঐ), আলকলতা (ঐ)।

Dodder grass—একপ্রকার ঘাস।

dŏd′-dêr, *v. t.* & *i.* To tremble ; to nod ; to totter ; to be feeble ; কাঁপা ; কাঁপান ; টলমল করা ; দুর্ব্বল হওয়া।

dŏd′-dered (-dêrd), *adj.* Having lost thetop or branches (of oaks andother trees) ; মুণ্ডিত-শির, মুণ্ডিত-শাখ ; মুড়ো মাগ ; স্থাণু।

dö-dĕc′-ă-gŏn, *n.* A plane figure of twelve sides ; দ্বাদশভুজ (হিঃ কোঃ), দ্বাদশাস্র (মঃ উঃ)।

dö-dĕc-ă-hē′-drŏn, *n.* A solid figure of twelve faces ; দ্বাদশফলক, দ্বাদশফলক বিশিষ্ট ঘনক্ষেত্র (হিঃ কোঃ)।

dö-dĕc-ă-pĕt′-ăl-ous (-ŭs), *adj.* Having twelve petals ; দ্বাদশদল, দ্বাদশপত্রী (সাঃ পঃ)।

dö-dĕc-ă-sȳl′-lă-ble, *n.* A verse of twelve syllables ; দ্বাদশ শব্দাংশ বিশিষ্ট কবিতা পংক্তি-পাদ।

dö-dĕc-ă-tĕm′-ŏ-rȳ, *n.* One of the twelve signs of the zodiac ; রাশি।

dodge (dŏj), *n.*, *v. t.* & *i.* **1.** A quick side movement ; কোন কিছু এড়াইবার জন্য হঠাৎ একপাশে সরিয়া পড়ন। **2.** The act of evading by some skilful movement ; হঠাৎ একপাশে সরিয়া কোন কিছু এড়ান। **3.** (*Colloq.*) A clever expedient ; a contrivance ; চাতুরী, শাঠ্য, ফাঁকি ; ফন্দী, কলকৌশল। ***Verb t.*** **1.** To trifle with ; to play fast and loose with ; তুচ্ছ তাচ্ছিল্য করা ; (চাতুরীপূর্ব্বক) নিতান্ত অব্যবস্থিত ব্যক্তির মত কার্য্য করা। **2.** To evade by sideward movement ; as, to *dodge* a blow, pursuers etc. ; এক পার্শ্বে সরিয়া এড়ান। **3.** To evade by craft ; as, to *dodge* responsibility (*Colloq.*) ; চাতুরীপূর্ব্বক এড়ান (চলিতভাষায়)। **4.** To move (a thing) to and fro ; to shuffle ; ইতস্ততঃ সঞ্চালিত করা ; এদিক ওদিক ফিরান বা চালাচালি করা। **5.** To ask a question unexpectedly ; হঠাৎ কোন প্রশ্ন জিজ্ঞাসা করা। ***Verb i.*** **1.** To move to and fro ; ইতস্ততঃ সঞ্চালিত হওয়া। **2.** To shift place by a sudden start or movement in order to evade a blow, pursuer, etc. ; হঠাৎ চমকিয়া এক পাশে সরা। **3.** To play fast and loose ; to quibble ; (চাতুরীপূর্ব্বক) অব্যবস্থিতের মত কার্য্য করা ; বাক্ চাতুরীদ্বারা আসল কথা এড়ান। **Dodg′-y,** *adj.* Evasive ; tricky ; এড়ানিয়া ; ফন্দিবাজ।

dodg′-êr (dŏj-), *n.* One who or that which dodges ; an artful or elusive person ; ফন্দিবাজ ; কৌশলী, চক্রী।

dŏd′-i-pāte, –pöll, *n.* A fool ; a blockhead ; গোবর গণেশ ; জড়বুদ্ধি।

Dodo

dö′-dö, *n.* A large extinct bird of the island of Mauritius; মরিসাস্ দ্বীপবাসী অধুনালুপ্ত বৃহৎকায় পক্ষিবিশেষ।

doe (dö), *n.* A female of the fallow deer, rabbit or hare ; মৃগী, হরিণী, কুরঙ্গিণী, স্ত্রী-শশক। **Doe-skin**—The skin of the doe ; a leather made of it ; মৃগীচর্ম্ম, অজিন ; শোধিত মৃগীচর্ম্ম। A fine woollen cloth resembling it ; মৃগচর্ম্মের অনুকরণে প্রস্তুত একপ্রকার কোমল পশমী বস্ত্র।

dŏff, *v. t.* **1.** To take off (dress, hat, etc.) ; উন্মোচন করা, খুলিয়া ফেলা। **2.** (*Rarely*) To abandon ; (ক্বচিৎ ব্যবহৃত) ত্যাগ করা।

dŏg, *n.* **1.** A quadruped of many breeds wild and domesticated ; কুক্কুর, কুকুর, শ্বান, সারমেয় কৌলেয়ক, মৃগদংশক, শুনক, ভষক। **2.** A mean worthless fellow ; a wretch ; হীনচেতাঃ অকর্ম্মণ্য লোক ; নরাধম। **3.** A fellow (used humourously or contemptuously) ; as, a sly *dog* ; লোক। **4.** (*Pl.*) A pair of metal supports for burning wood ; অগ্নিকুণ্ডে দহ্যমান কাষ্ঠ ধারণার্থ যন্ত্রবিশেষ, দহ্যমান কাষ্ঠধারণার্থ ধাতুনির্ম্মিত ধারক যুগল। **5.** (*Astron.*) One of the two constellations, *Canis Major* and *Canis Minor* or the Greater Dog and the Lesser Dog ; (জ্যোতিবিজ্ঞান) দিব্য-শ্বান, মৃগব্যাধ, শ্ব-তারা, (হিঃ কোঃ)। **6.** (*Mech.*) Kinds

Eskimo dog.

of mechanical device for gripping etc. ; (যন্ত্র-বিজ্ঞান) কোন কিছু আঁকড়াইয়া ধরিবার জন্য কৌশল বিশেষ। **7.** A light near the horizon portending a storm, (also called *sea-dog*) ; দিক্‌চক্রবালের নিকটবর্ত্তী ঝঞ্ঝাসূচক আলোকচ্ছটা। **Dog′-gish,** *adj.* Currish ; cynical ; spiteful ; কুক্কুরবৎ ; শ্ব-স্বভাব, মানববিদ্বেষী ; দ্বেষপূর্ণ। **Dog′-gy, –gie,** *ns.* A small dog ; a pet name for any dog ; বাচ্চা কুকুর ; কুকুরের আদুরে নাম। **Dog′-hood,** *n.* **Dog′-less, Dog′-like,** *adjs.* **Dog-berry**—একপ্রকার ফল। **Dog-biscuit**—কুকুরের আহারের জন্য একপ্রকার বিস্কুট। **Dog-box**—রেলওয়ের যে শকটে কুকুর বহন করা হয়। **Dog-cart**—একপ্রকার দুই ঘোড়ার গাড়ী। **Dog-cheap**—Very cheap ; অতিশয় সস্তা, মাটীর দর। **Dog-collar** — কুকুরের গলাসি বা হাঁসুলি। A straight high collar worn by persons ; একপ্রকার খাড়া এবং উচ্চ গলবন্ধ। **Dog days**—জুলাই ও আগষ্ট মাসের গরম দিন। **Dog's ear,** *n.* & *v. t.* The corner of the leaf of a book turned down like a dog's ear; কুকুরের কাণের মত মোড়া পুস্তকের পাতা। (*Verb t.*) To turn down the corners of the page of a book so as to make them look like dog's ears; অসাবধান ব্যবহারে পুস্তকের পাতার কোণ মোড়া বা কোণ ভাঙ্গা। **Dog-fall**—একপ্রকার পতন, যাহাতে মল্লদ্বয় এক সঙ্গে ভূমি স্পর্শ করে। **Dog-fennel**—Stinking Camomile; পচা বাবুনা ফুল। **Dog-fish**—একজাতীয় ক্ষুদ্র হাঙ্গর বা অন্য প্রকার মৎস্য। **Dog** or **dog's grass**—দুর্ব্বা। **Dog-hole**—কদর্য্য বাসস্থান। **Dog Latin** — Ungrammatical Latin; ব্যাকরণ-দুষ্ট লাটিন ভাষা। **Dog lead**—কুকুরের শিকল, রজ্জু প্রভৃতি। **Dog-rose**—জয়ঘণ্টী গোলাপ (প্রবোধ)। **Dog skin**—কুকুরের চর্ম্ম। **Dog-sleep**—জাগ্রৎ নিদ্রা, সামান্য ঘুম, তন্দ্রা। **Dog's letter**—The letter or sound of r; R এই অক্ষর বা ইহার ধ্বনি। **Dog's meat**—Horse-flesh; offal; ঘোড়ার মাংস; নিহত জন্তুর দেহের নাড়ী ভুড়ি প্রভৃতি অখাদ্য অংশ, বিমাংস (মঃ উঃ)। **Dogs of war**—Famine, sword or fire; অসি, অগ্নি বা দুর্ভিক্ষ। **Dog-star**—Sirius; সীরিয়াস, লুব্ধক (হিঃ কোঃ)। **Dog's tongue**—এক প্রকার গাছ। **Dog** or **Dog's tail**—A kind of grass—এক প্রকার ঘাস। **Dog-tired, —weary** — নিরতিশয় ক্লান্ত। **Dog tooth**—প্রাচীন গথিক স্থাপত্য রীত্যনুযায়ী স্থাপত্য ভূষাবিশেষ। **Dog violet** — একপ্রকার নির্গন্ধ ভায়োলেট পুষ্প। **Dog watch**—(4-6 & 6-8 P. M.); (নৌ-বিদ্যা) জাহাজের উপরে দুই ঘণ্টার জন্য প্রহরা (অপরাহ্ণ ৪-৬ এবং ৬-৮)। **Dog-whip** — কুকুরের চাবুক। **Sea-dog**—See DOG. (7) **Sun-dog**—Parhelion; সূর্য্যাভাস। **A dog in a blanket**—A kind of pudding; একপ্রকার পিষ্টক। **A dog in the manger** — A churlish fellow who will neither enjoy a thing himself nor let others enjoy; যে অশিষ্ট ব্যক্তি নিজে কোন বিষয় ভোগ করিবে না কিম্বা অপরকেও ছাড়িয়া দিবে না। **Barking dogs seldom bite**—যে গর্জ্জায় সে বর্ষায় না, অসারের তর্জ্জনগর্জ্জন সার। **Every dog has his day**—সুখের দিন ক্ষণস্থায়ী। **Fire-dogs**—See DOG (4). **It rains cats and dogs**—It rains heavily; মুষলধারে বৃষ্টি পড়িতেছে। **Love me, love my dog**—Accept my friends as yours; আমার বন্ধুগণকে তোমার নিজের বন্ধু বলিয়া গ্রহণ করিও। **To die a dog's death** or **like a dog**—To die shamefully or miserably; হেয় ভাবে মরা, দুঃখ দুর্দ্দশায় পড়িয়া মরা। **To give a dog ill name and hang him**—To spoil the reputation of a man and thus spoil his life; কোন ব্যক্তির সুনাম নষ্ট করিয়া তাহার জীবন মাটি করা। **To go to the dogs**—To be ruined; চুলোয় যাওয়া, নিপাত যাওয়া, গোল্লায় যাওয়া, অধঃপাতে যাওয়া, মাটি হওয়া, উচ্ছন্ন যাওয়া, জাহান্নমে যাওয়া। **To help a lame dog over stile**—To be a friend in need; অসময়ে বন্ধু হওয়া। **To lead a dog's life**—To be worried; দুঃখময় জীবন যাপন করা। **To lead one a dog's life**—To worry another; জ্বালাতন করা। **To let sleeping dogs die**—To let alone (as some people, when there is chance of their creating a disturbance if aroused); নিরুপদ্রবে থাকিতে দেওয়া। **To take hair of a dog that bit you**—To drink more in order to cure effects of drink; মাতলামি দূর করার জন্য আরও বেশী মদ খাওয়া। **To throw to the dogs**—To throw away; দূর করিয়া ফেলিয়া দেওয়া।

dŏg, *v. t.*, **1.** To follow closely; কাহারও পায়ে পায়ে বেড়ান। **2.** To grip; to secure; আকড়াইয়া ধরা; দৃঢ়-মুষ্টিতে ধরা।

doge (dōj), *n.* Chief magistrate of Venice or Genoa; ভেনিস অথবা জেনোয়া নগরীর সর্ব্বোচ্চ শাসনকর্তা। **Dog'-ate,** *n.*

dŏg'-gĕd, *adj.* Obstinate; persistent; unyielding; একগুঁয়ে, একরোখা; অটল, নির্ব্বন্ধাতিশয়পূর্ণ, নাছোড়বান্দা; দৃঢ়ব্রত। **—ly,** *adv.* **—ness,** *n.*

dŏg'-gêr, *n.* A two-masted Dutch fishing boat; হলণ্ডদেশীয় দ্বিমাস্তুলবিশিষ্ট পোতবিশেষ।

dŏg'-gêr-ĕl, *adj.* & *n.* Low in style and irregular in measure; trivial; as, *doggerel* rhymer; ছড়ার মত; তুচ্ছ। ***Noun.*** A loose or irregular verse; হাল্‌কা কবিতা, কুকবিতা, ছড়া।

dŏg'-gȳ, *adj.* **1.** Fond of dogs; কুকুর-প্রিয়, কুকুর-ভক্ত। **2.** Of or relating to dogs; কুকুর-সংক্রান্ত। **—gi-ness,** *n.*

dŏg'-mă, *n.* **1.** A tenet; a doctrine; মূলসূত্র; নির্দ্দিষ্ট মত (হিঃ কোঃ), সিদ্ধান্ত। **2.** An arbitrary dictum; an arrogant declaration of opinion; মনগড়া উক্তি; হঠোক্তি। **—mat'-ic, —mal,** *adjs.* **1.** Doctrinal; relating to dogmas; মতগ্রাহী, হঠবাদী, মতাভিমানী, মতবাদী, মতনির্দ্দেশানুযায়ী; সিদ্ধান্ত সম্বন্ধীয়। **2.** Based on *apriori* principles, not on induction; প্রাগ্‌জ্ঞানতত্ত্ব-মূলক। **3.** Authoritative; laying down the law; arrogant; as, a *dogmatic* man or book; প্রামাণিক; ব্যবস্থানির্দ্ধারক, নিয়মনির্দ্ধারক; উদ্ধত, প্রগল্‌ভ। **—mat'-ics,** *n.* The science which treats of Christian doctrines; খৃষ্টীয় মতবাদ সম্বন্ধীয় বিজ্ঞান। **—mat'-i-cal-ly,** *adv.* **—tism,** *n.* Arrogance; positiveness in assertion; হঠোক্তি; যুক্তি-নিরপেক্ষ বাদ। **—tist,** *n.* **—tize,** *v. i.* & *t.* To speak or write authoritatively or arrogantly; প্রামাণিক ভাবে লিখা, উদ্ধতভাবে লিখা। (*Verb t.*) To express (principles) etc. as a dogma; (মত বা সিদ্ধান্ত) ব্যক্ত করা।

doi′-lȳ (dȯy-), *n.* A small napkin used at dessert to place glasses on ; ভোজের শেষে আচার বা ফলাদি পরিবেষণ কালে যে তোয়ালের উপর গ্লাস সকল রাখা হয়।

doit (dȯyt), *n.* **1.** A very small sum or coin ; অতিক্ষুদ্র পরিমাণ অর্থ বা

Doit from British Museum.

অতিক্ষুদ্র মুদ্রা। **2.** (*Fig.*) Merest trifle ; as, I do not care a *doit* ; (লক্ষণায়) অতি সামান্য বস্তু।

doit′-ĕd (dȯyt-) *adj.* Crazed, esp. with age ; বার্দ্ধক্য হেতু বিকৃত-বুদ্ধি।

dolce-far-niente, (*Ital.*) Delightful idleness ; সুখপূর্ণ আলস্য।

dŏl′-drŭms, *n.* **1.** Dullness ; depression ; নীরসতা, জড়তা ; অবসাদ, চিত্তগ্লানি, অবসন্নতা, বিষণ্ণতা। **2.** A becalmed state, as of a ship ; (পোতাদির) অচঞ্চলাবস্থা। **3.** Those parts of the ocean about the equator where calms and baffling winds prevail ; নিরক্ষ বৃত্তের নিকটবর্ত্তী নির্ব্বাতমণ্ডল। **To be in the doldrums**—To be in a state of depression or ennui ; বিষণ্ণ অবস্থায় থাকা, অবসাদ পীড়িত থাকা, চিত্তগ্লানি ভোগ করা।

dōle, *n.* & *v. t.* **1.** Charitable distribution ; দান। **2.** A gift or charity ; ভিক্ষা। **3.** (*Archaic*) Lot ; destiny ; (অপ্রচলিত) ভাগ্য ; নিয়তি। ***Verb t.*** To distribute sparingly as alms etc. ; ভিক্ষা দেওয়া। **Doles-man** or **woman**—A recipient of a dole ; ভিক্ষুক, ভিখারিণী। **Happy man be his dole**—May he be happy ; সে সুখী হউক।

dōle, *n.* (*Poet.*) Grief ; woe ; lamentation ; (কবিতায়) বিষাদ ; দুঃখ ; বিলাপ। **Dole′-ful** *adj.* **1.** Full of woe ; করুণ, বিষাদপূর্ণ। **2.** Sorrowful ; sad ; বিষণ্ণ ; ম্লান। **3.** Causing grief ; শোকাবহ, শোকপ্রদ। **Dole′-ful-ly,** *adv.* **Dole′-ful-ness,** *n.*

dŏl-i-chō-cē-phăl′-ic, *adj.* Long-headed, (of a skull with breadth less than $\frac{4}{5}$ of length, of a person or race with such skull) ; দীর্ঘ-কপাল (হিঃ কোঃ), দীর্ঘ-করোটী (সাঃ পঃ)।

dŏll, *n.* **1.** A puppet ; পুতুল, পুত্তলিকা, পুত্তলী। **2.** A pretty silly woman ; "No worker cares to espouse a *doll* ;" বুদ্ধিহীনা সুন্দরী। **Doll′-ish** *adj.* **Doll′-ish-ly** *adv.* **Doll′-ish-ness,** *n.*

dŏl′-lar (-lêr), *n.* **1.** A coin of United States, Canada, Singapore, etc. ; মার্কিণ যুক্তরাজ্য, ক্যানেডা এবং সিঙ্গাপুরের মুদ্রাবিশেষ। [মার্কিণ যুক্ত-রাজ্যের ডলারের মূল্য প্রায় ৩/০] **2.** (*Slang*) A five shilling piece ; (ইতর ভাষায়) ৫ শিলিং মুদ্রা। **The Almighty dollar**—See ALMIGHTY.

dŏl′-tŏp, *n.* A lump as of food etc. ; দলা, ডেলা, পিণ্ড।

dŏl′-lȳ, *n.* **1.** A pet name for a doll : পুতুল। **2.** Any of the various appliances in clothes-washing, pile-driving, ore-washing etc. ; ভূগর্ভে স্তম্ভ-নিবেশন এবং বস্ত্র ও আকরিক ধাতু ধৌত করণে ব্যবহৃত বিভিন্ন প্রকার যন্ত্র। **Dolly-shop**—নিম্নশ্রেণীর বন্ধকী মালের দোকান, পুরাতন জাহাজি মাল (রেশি, লোহা, ক্যামবিস্) প্রভৃতির ভাণ্ডার।

Dŏll′-ȳ Vâr-dĕn, *n.* **1.** A female character in Dickens' 'Barnaby Rudge' ; ডিকেন্স্‌কৃত "Barnaby Rudge" নামক উপন্যাসের স্ত্রী চরিত্র বিশেষ। **2.** A kind of woman's hat ; একপ্রকার স্ত্রীলোকের টুপি। **3.** A style of dress ; এক ধরণের পোষাক।

dŏl′-măn, *n.* **1.** A long Turkish robe open in front ; সম্মুখভাগে খোলা তুর্কীদেশীয় দীর্ঘ পোষাক বিশেষ **2.** A cloak of a peculiar fashion worn by ladies ; স্ত্রীলোকদিগের বিশেষ ধরণের শ্লথ পরিচ্ছদ বিশেষ। **3.** A hussar's jacket worn with sleeves hanging loose ; হুসার সৈন্যের কুর্ত্তা বিশেষ।

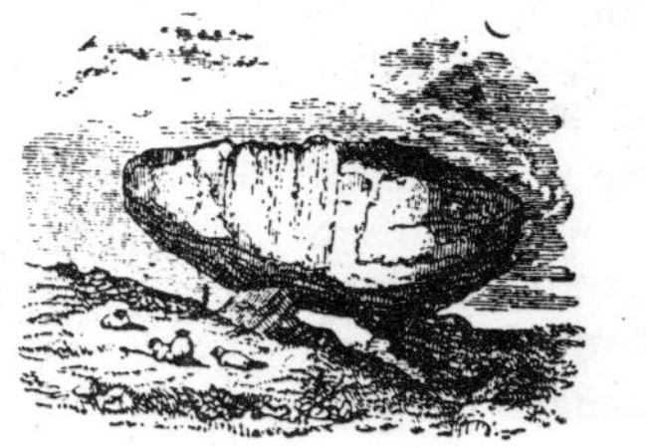

Dolmen.

dŏl′-mĕn, *n.* Same as CROMLECH (which see).

dŏl′-ō-mīte, *n.* A magnesian limestone, so called after French geologist Dolomieu ; এক প্রকার চুণা পাথর। **—mit′-ic,** *adj.*

dŏl′-or-ous (-êr-ŭs), *adj.* **1.** Sorrowful ; dismal ; as, a *dolorous* region ; বিষাদপূর্ণ, শোকপরিপ্লুত, শোকাবহ ; নিরানন্দজনক, অপ্রফুল্লকর। **2.** Distressing ; painful ; "A very *dolorous* thirst ;" দুঃখজনক ; বেদনাপূর্ণ, কষ্টকর, যন্ত্রণাদায়ক। **3.** Distressed ; "A *dolorous* heart ;" আর্ত্ত, ক্লিষ্ট। **—ly,** *adv.*

dō-lōse′, *adj.* **1.** (*Law*) Having a criminal intent ; (আইন) অপরাধজনক অভিপ্রায় বিশিষ্ট। **2.** Intentionally deceitful ; ইচ্ছাপূর্ব্বক প্রবঞ্চনাকারী।

dō′-lour (-lêr), *n.* (*Poet.*) Sorrow ; distress ; দুঃখ, কষ্ট, সন্তাপ, ক্লেশ, যন্ত্রণা ; দুর্দ্দশা, আধি।

dŏl′-phin *n.* **1.** A small species of whale remarkable for gambolling in the water ; একপ্রকার ক্ষুদ্রজাতীয় তিমি মৎস্য। **2.** A fish about 5 ft. in length noted for changing to many colours in dying ; একপ্রকার মৎস্য ইহারা দৈর্ঘ্যে প্রায় ৫ ফিট হইয়া থাকে, এবং মৃত্যুকালে

ইহাদের দেহ নানা উজ্জ্বল বর্ণে রঞ্জিত হয়। 3. (*Naut.*) Any of various contrivances ; (নৌ-বিদ্যা) নানা-প্রকার কল।

dŏlt, *n.* A blockhead ; a dunce ; হাব, জড়ভরত, স্থূলবুদ্ধি ; মূর্খ। **Dolt′-ish,** *adj.* **Dolt′-ish-ness,** *n.*

Dŏm, *n.* A title prefixed to names of Roman Catholic dignitaries, esp. Benedictine and Carthusian monks ; উচ্চশ্রেণীর রোমান্ ক্যাথলিক যাজকগণের নামের পূর্ব্বে সংযোজিত উপাধি বিশেষ।

dō-main′ (-mān), *n.* **1.** Dominion ; estate ; রাজ্য, অধিকার ; ভূসম্পত্তি। **2.** Scope of thought or action ; as, the *domain* of authentic history ; কার্য্যক্ষেত্র, চিন্তারাজ্য, রাজ্য, ক্ষেত্র। **–ma′-ni-al,** *adj.* **Eminent domain**—একাধিপত্য, বিশেষতঃ দেশের সমস্ত সম্পত্তির উপর রাজার একাধিপত্য। **Public domain**—সরকারী ভূসম্পত্তি।

dōme, *n.* & *v. t.* **1.** (*Arch.*) A rounded vault forming a roof with a circular elliptical or polygonal base ; গুম্বজ, গম্বুজ, গোল ছাত, হর্ম্ম্যশিখর (মঃ উঃ)। **2.** An edifice ; a mansion (*poet*) ; (কবিতায়) প্রাসাদ ; হর্ম্ম্য। **3.** A canopy ; as, the *dome* of a tree ; চন্দ্রাতপ। **4.** A rounded summit of a mountain, wave, etc. ; পর্ব্বত, তরঙ্গ, প্রভৃতির গোলাকৃতি চূড়া, শীর্ষভাগ। ***Verb t.*** To cover with a dome ; to shape like a dome ; গুম্বজ মণ্ডিত করা ; গুম্বজাকৃতি করা। **Domed,** *adj.* **Dom′-ic, Dom′-i-cal, Dome′-like, Dom′-y,** *adjs.*

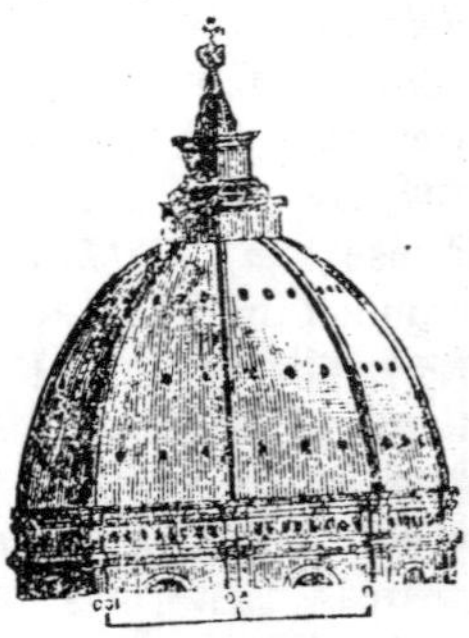

Dome of Florence.

Domes′-day (dōmz-dā), *n.* **1.** ইংলণ্ডেশ্বর প্রথম উইলিয়েম্ কর্তৃক সংগৃহীত সমগ্র ইংলণ্ডের ভূমির পরিমাণ, ভূম্যধিকারিগণের নাম ও বিভিন্ন ব্যক্তির অধিকৃত ভূমির মূল্য প্রভৃতির বিবরণী। **2.** A day of judgment ; খৃষ্টীয় ও মহম্মদীয় ধর্ম্মানুসারে অন্তিম বিচার দিবস।

dō-mĕs′-tic, *adj.* & *n.* **1.** Household ; pertaining to house ; গার্হস্থ্য, পারিবারিক ; গৃহসম্বন্ধীয়, গৃহ্য (আঃ বঃ)। **2.** Intestine ; not foreign ; as, foreign wars, and *domestic* dissensions ; অভ্যন্তরীণ ; ঘরাও। **3.** Home-made ; as, *domestic* manufactures ; গৃহজাত, গৃহনির্ম্মিত, স্বদেশোৎপন্ন, স্বদেশজাত। **4.** Domesticated ; tame, (as distinguished from *wild*) ; as, *domestic* animals ; গৃহপালিত, গ্রাম্য ; পোষা। **5.** Fond of home ; keeping at home ; গৃহ-প্রিয় ; ঘরমুখো। ***Noun.*** A household servant ; গৃহভৃত্য, গৃহকিঙ্কর, ভৃত্য, চাকর। **Domestic affairs**—গৃহ-কার্য্য। **Domestic dissension**—গৃহবিবাদ, কুটুম্বকলহ, গৃহকলহ, অভ্যন্তরীণ বিবাদ। **Domestic economy**—গার্হস্থ্য-ব্যবস্থা, গৃহস্থালী।

dō-mĕs′-ti-cāte, *v. t.* **1.** To naturalize ; as, to *domesticate* a colonist or an animal ; স্বদেশীয় রূপে গ্রহণ বা গণ্য করা। **2.** To make fond of home ; গৃহপ্রিয় করা। **3.** To tame ; as, to *domesticate* an animal ; পোষ মানান। **4.** To civilize ; as, to *domesticate* savages ; সভ্য করা। **–ca-ble,** *adj.* **–ca′-tion,** *n.* The act of domesticating ; গ্রাম্যতাপাদন।

dō-mĕs-tĭć′-i-tȳ, *n.* **1.** Domestic character ; domestic life ; homeliness ; state of being domesticated ; গার্হস্থ্য ভাব ; গার্হস্থ্য জীবন ; ঘরোভাব ; গৃহপালিতাবস্থা। **2.** (*pl.*) Domestic affairs ; গৃহকার্য্য।

dŏm′-ĕtt, *n.* A kind of plain cloth in which the warp is cotton and the weft woollen ; একপ্রকার বস্ত্র যাহার টানা সূতা তুলার ও পড়েনের সূতা পশমের হইয়া থাকে।

dŏm′-i-cīle, *n., v.t.* & *i.* **1.** Home ; a dwelling place ; গৃহ ; বাসস্থান, আবাস, নিবাস। **2.** (*Law*) A place of permanent residence ; a fact of residing ; (আইন) স্থায়ী বাসস্থান। বসতবাটী ; সমাবাস। **3.** A place at which a bill of exchange is made payable ; যে স্থানে হুণ্ডীর টাকা প্রদেয় করা হয়। ***Verb t.*** **1.** To settle in a place ; স্থায়ী আবাস স্থাপন করা। **2.** To make as a bill of exchange etc., payable at a certain place ; কোন নির্দ্দিষ্ট স্থানে হুণ্ডীর টাকা প্রদেয় করা। ***Verb i.*** To settle ; to dwell permanently ; বসবাস স্থাপন করা ; স্থায়িরূপে বাস করা। **–cil′-i-a-ry,** *adj.* Pertaining to a dwelling place ; আবাস-সম্পর্কীয়। **–cil′-i-ate,** *v. t.* & *i.* To establish or settle in a place ; কোনস্থানে স্থায়িরূপে আবাস স্থাপন করা। **–cil-i-a′-tion,** *n.* **Domiciliary visit**—(আইন) খানাতল্লাস বা পরিদর্শনের জন্য রাজকর্ম্মচারিগণের কোন ব্যক্তির বাটিতে গমন, আবাস-পরিদর্শন।

dŏm′-i-nănt, *adj.* & *n.* **1.** Prevailing ; governing ; most influential ; "The *dominant* party persecuted both ;" প্রবল, প্রতাপশালী ; শক্তিশালী, শক্তিমান, প্রভুত্বকারী ; ক্ষমতাশালী, প্রভাবশালী। **2.** Overlooking others ; as, *dominant* height ; অপেক্ষাকৃত উন্নত স্থানে অবস্থান হেতু আধিপত্যকারী। ***Noun.*** The fifth note of the scale of any key ; (সঙ্গীতশাস্ত্র) পঞ্চম স্বর। **–ly,** *adv.* **–nance, –nan-cy,** *ns.* The state or quality of being dominant ; predominance ; শক্তিমত্তা, ক্ষমতা-সম্পন্নতা ; প্রাধান্য।

dŏm′-i-nāte, *v. t.* & *i.* **1.** To govern ; to predominate or prevail over ; শাসনকরা ; প্রাধান্য স্থাপন করা, প্রবল হওয়া ; প্রভুত্ব করা। **2.** To hold a commanding position over ; as, a height *dominates* a plain ; অপেক্ষাকৃত উন্নতস্থানে অবস্থান হেতু আধিপত্য করা। ***Verb i.*** To be the most influential ; to predominate ; অতিশয় ক্ষমতা সম্পন্ন হওয়া ; প্রবল হওয়া, প্রাধান্যশালী হওয়া। **2.** To occupy a commanding position, (with *over*) ; প্রভুত্বকারী হওয়া।

dŏm-ĭ-nā′-tion, *n.* **1.** Ascendency ; sway ; প্রাধান্য ; কর্তৃত্ব, শাসন, প্রভুত্ব, আধিপত্য। **2.** (*Pl.*) A high order of angels in the celestial hierarchy ; উচ্চশ্রেণীর দেবদূত বিশেষ।

dŏm-i-neer (-nēr), *v. t.* & *i.* **1.** To rule arbitrarily ; to tyrannize ; যথারুচি শাসন করা ; অত্যাচার করা। **2.** To tower over ; অত্যুচ্চ হইয়া উঠা। ***Verb i.*** To act imperiously ; to tyrannize ; to be over-bearing ; উদ্ধত ভাবে ব্যবহার করা ; অত্যাচার করা ; উদ্ধত হওয়া, প্রভুত্বকারী হওয়া। **–ing,** *adj.* Tyrannical ; imperious ; অত্যাচারী, পীড়নকারী ; উদ্ধত, প্রভুত্বকারী। **–ing-ly,** *adv.*

dŏ-mĭn′-ĭ-căl, *adj.* **1.** Of the Lord (Christ) ; as, the *dominical* prayer ; ঐশ, প্রভু (যীশুখৃষ্ট) সম্বন্ধীয়। **2.** Pertaining to the Lord's day or Sunday ; প্রভুর দিবসসম্বন্ধীয়, রবিবাসরীয়। **Dominical letter**—ইংরাজী বর্ণমালার প্রথম সপ্ত অক্ষরের অন্যতম, যাহা ইংলণ্ডীয় পঞ্জিকায় কোন কোন বৎসরের প্রতি রবিবারের চিহ্নস্বরূপ ব্যবহৃত হইয়া থাকে। **Dominical year**—খৃষ্টাব্দ।

Dŏ-mĭn′-ĭ-căn, *adj.* & *n.* Of or pertaining to St. Dominic or his order of preaching friars ; খৃষ্টীয় সিদ্ধপুরুষ ডমিনিক বা তৎপ্রতিষ্ঠিত প্রচারক সন্ন্যাসি-সম্প্রদায় সম্বন্ধীয়। ***Noun.*** A friar or monk of the order of St. Dominic; ডমিনিক সম্প্রদায়ভুক্ত সন্ন্যাসী।

dŏm′-ĭ-nie (-nĭ), *n.* A schoolmaster ; a pedagogue ; শিক্ষক ; গুরুমহাশয়।

dŏ-mĭn′-ĭŏn, *n.* **1.** Lordship ; sovereignty ; sway ; "Foreign *dominion* in any shape...becomes hateful ;" চক্রবর্ত্তিতা ; রাজত্ব; আধিপত্য, কর্ত্তৃত্ব। **2.** Domain of a feudal lord ; territory of a sovereign or government ; সামন্ততন্ত্রাধীন জমিদারের জমিদারী ; রাজ্য। **3.** (*Law*) Right of possession ; ownership ; "Held their lands...in absolute *dominion* ;" (আইন) স্বত্ব, অধিকার ; স্বামিত্ব।

dŏm′-ĭ-nō, *n.* **1.** A loose cloak with half mask worn to conceal identity esp. at masquerades ; একপ্রকার শ্লথ ছদ্মবেশ,—যদ্দ্বারা, মুখের অৰ্দ্ধভাগ পর্য্যন্ত আবৃত হয়, মুখসধারণপূর্ব্বক নৃত্য কালে পরিধেয় শ্লথ প্রাবরণ বিশেষ। **2.** A person wearing such a cloak ; উক্তরূপ পরিচ্ছদ পরিহিত ব্যক্তি। **3.** One of the 28 pieces with which the game of dominoes is played ; ডমিনো ক্রীড়ার গুটিকা। **4.** (*Pl.*) The game itself ; (বহুবচন) ডমিনো ক্রীড়া, চতুরস্র ক্রীড়া (আঃ বঃ)।

dŏn, *n.* & *v. t.* **1.** A Spanish title prefixed to Christian name corresponding to English "Sir" ; স্পেনদেশীয় ভদ্রলোকগণের নামের পূর্ব্বে সংযোজিত উপাধি বিশেষ [ইংরাজী 'Sir' উপাধির অনুরূপ]। **2.** A Spanish gentleman ; স্পেনদেশীয় ভদ্রলোক। **3.** A person of high position ; adept at something ; as, a *don* at cricket ; উচ্চ পদস্থ ব্যক্তি ; পারদর্শী, ওস্তাদ। **4.** A head, fellow or tutor of a college ; কলেজের অধ্যক্ষ, সভ্য বা শিক্ষক। ***Verb t.*** To put on (garments), — opposite of *doff* ; পোষাক পরা, পরিচ্ছদ পরিধান করা। **Don′-nish** *adj.* Of or pertaining to a don ; learned ; কলেজের সভ্য, অধ্যক্ষ বা অধ্যাপক সম্বন্ধীয় ; পণ্ডিত। **Don Juan**—A rake ; a libertine ; (বাইরন কৃত ডনজুয়ান নামক কাব্যের নায়কের নাম), দুশ্চরিত্র ব্যক্তি, স্খলিত চরিত্র ব্যক্তি ; লম্পট। **Don Quixote** — সার্ভেন্টিস্ নামক স্পেনদেশীয় সুপ্রসিদ্ধ গ্রন্থকারকৃত বিশ্ববিখ্যাত Don Quixote নামক উপন্যাসের নায়ক।

dŏ′-nă(t), *n.* **1.** (*Slang*) A woman ; (ইতর ভাষায়) মেয়ে লোক। **2.** A sweet-heart ; প্রণয়িনী।

dŏ-nā′-tion, *n.* **1.** Act of bestowing ; a grant ; দানকরণ ; দান। **2.** A gift of money or goods, (esp. of money given to an institution) ; এক কালীন চাঁদা দান (অর্থ বা সম্পত্তি)। **3.** (*Law*) The act by which a person freely transfers his title to anything to another; (আইন) দানপত্র-সম্পাদন।

dŏn′-ă-tive (-tĭv), *adj.* & *n.* Vested or vesting by donation ; দানপত্র দ্বারা অর্পিত বা অর্পণকারী। ***Noun.*** **1.** Gift ; present ; esp. largess ; দান ; উপহার ; বক্শিশ। **2.** (*Eccles.*) A benefice presented by the founder or patron without reference to the bishop ; (যাজকীয় শাস্ত্র) খৃষ্টীয় ধৰ্ম্মাধ্যক্ষের নিকট উল্লেখ না করিয়া প্রতিষ্ঠাতা বা পৃষ্ঠপোষক কর্ত্তৃক প্রদত্ত যাজকীয় বৃত্তি।

dŏn′-ă-tŏ-rȳ *n.* The recipient of a gift or donation ; দানগ্রহীতা।

done (dŭn), *p. p.* of DO. **Done brown** — Duped ; swindled ; প্রতারিত ; প্রবঞ্চিত। **Done up**—worn out ; exhausted ; শীর্ণ ; অবসন্ন। **Over-done**—অতিরিক্ত পাচিত। **Under-done**—অসম্যক্ পাচিত। **Well done**—রীতিমত পাচিত।

dŏ-nee′ (ē), *n.* Recipient of gift ; দানগ্রহীতা, দানগ্রাহক, দানগ্রহণকারী, গৃহীতা।

don′-gă (dŏng-), *n.* A gully ; a ravine ; গলি ; গভীর ও সংকীর্ণ পাৰ্ব্বত্য পথ।

dŏn′-jŏn, *n.* The principal tower of a castle forming the strongest part of the fortification, (also called the KEEP) ; পরিখা-বেষ্টিত প্রাসাদের প্রধান বুরুজ।

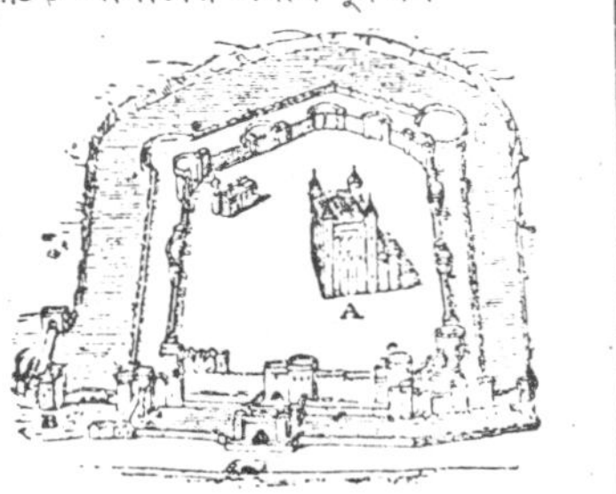

A donjon or keep of castle,

don′-key (dŏng-kē), *n.* **1.** An ass ; গাধা, গর্দ্দভ, খর, রাসভ, লম্বকর্ণ। **2.** A stupid person ; নির্ব্বোধ ব্যক্তি, গাধা, গর্দ্দভ। **Donkey engine**—ক্ষুদ্র বাষ্পীয় যন্ত্রবিশেষ,—জাহাজের সামান্য সামান্য কার্য্যে ব্যবহৃত হয়।

dō′-nor (-nêr), *n.* A giver ; দাতা, দানকর্ত্তা।

doo′-dle (-dl), *n.* A lazy idle trifler ; ভোলানাথ, গোবরগণেশ।

doo′-lie, —ly (-lĭ), *n.* An Indian litter used as army ambulance ; a palanquin ; ডুলি, দোলা ; পাল্কী।

doom *n.* & *v. t.* **1.** (*Hist.*) A statute ; law ; decree ; (ইতিহাস) রাজবিধি ; আইন ; বিধান। **2.** (*Archaic*) Sentence ; judgment ; condemnation ; trial ; (অপ্রচলিত) দণ্ডাজ্ঞা ; বিচার ফল ; দণ্ড ; বিচার। **3.** Unhappy destiny ; fate ; বিপাক (হিঃ কোঃ) ; নিয়তি। **4.** Ruin ; death ; ধ্বংস, নাশ ; মৃত্যু। **5.** The Last Judgment ; as, day of *doom* ; (খৃষ্টীয় ও মহম্মদীয় ধর্ম্মশাস্ত্রানুসারে) অন্তিম বিচার দিবস। ***Verb t.*** **1.** To pronounce sentence against ; to condemn ; as, a criminal *doomed* to chains ; দণ্ডাজ্ঞা প্রচার করা ; দণ্ডাদেশ দেওয়া, দণ্ডিত করা। **2.** To consign to misfortune or destruction ; to destine ; বিপাকে ফেলা, ধ্বংস মুখে প্রেরণ করা; ভাগ্যে নির্দ্দিষ্ট রাখা। **3.** (*Archaic*) To decree ; to ordain as a sentence ; বিধান করা ; শাস্তি বিধান করা।

door (dōr), *n.* **1.** A hinged or sliding barrier usually of wood or metal for closing entrance to a building, room, safe, etc. ; দ্বার, দরজা, দুয়ার, কপাট, প্রতিহার। **2.** House ; room ; as, he lives next *door* to me ; বাটী ; কক্ষ। **3.** Passage ; means of access ; প্রবেশ পথ ; প্রবেশোপায়। **4.** Front door ; chief door from a house to the street ; সম্মুখের দ্বার ; সদর দরজা। **Doored,** *adj.* **Door′-less** *adj.* **Door-bell**—গৃহাভ্যন্তরস্থ ঘণ্টা বিশেষ, দ্বারের বাহিরে সংলগ্ন হাতল দ্বারা এই ঘণ্টা বাজাইতে হয়। **Door case** or **frame**—চৌকাঠ। **Door-keeper** — প্রতিহারী, দৌবারিক, দ্বারবান, দ্বারপাল, দ্বারী, দ্বাররক্ষক। **Door-mat**—পাপোস। **Door money**—নাটক, সার্কাস প্রভৃতির দ্বারদেশে সংগৃহীত অর্থ। **Door-plate**—দ্বারদেশে সংলগ্ন গৃহস্বামীর নামাঙ্কিত (সাধারণতঃ পিত্তল নির্ম্মিত) ফলক। **Door-post** — দ্বার-স্তম্ভ। **Door-sill**—চৌকাঠের নীচের কাঠ, গোবরাট, দ্বার পিণ্ডী (আঃ বঃ)। **Door-step**—দ্বারের নীচের ধাপ। **Door-way**—দেউড়ী। **At death's door**—At the point of death ; মরণের পথে, শিয়রে শমন। **In doors** or **within doors**—Within the house ; বাটীতে, বাটীর ভিতর। **Next door to**—(*Fig.*) Approaching closely to ; very near to ; almost ; (লক্ষণায়) সন্নিহিত ; অতি নিকট ; প্রায়। **Out of doors** — Abroad ; in the open air ; বাহিরে ; মুক্ত বাতাসে। **To close the door upon** — To make impossible ; অসম্ভব করা। **To darken a door**—To cross the threshold of a house ; কাহারও গৃহে পদার্পণ করা। **To lay** or **lie at the door of**—To impute or be imputable to ; আরোপ করা, আরোপনীয় হওয়া। **To live next door** — To live in the next house or room ; পার্শ্বের বাটীতে বা পার্শ্বের কক্ষে বাস করা। **To open a door to**—To make possible ; সম্ভবপর করা। **To show one the door** — To expel one ; বাটী হইতে বাহির করিয়া দেওয়া।

dōpe, *n.* & *v. t.* **1.** Thick liquid used as food or lubricant ; খাদ্য স্বরূপ বা মর্দ্দনাদি কার্য্যে ব্যবহৃত ঘন তরল পদার্থ বিশেষ। **2.** (*Slang*) A narcotic drink ; (ইতর ভাষায়) নিদ্রাজনক পানীয় বিশেষ। ***Verb t.*** (*Slang*) To administer dope to ; (ইতর ভাষায়) উক্তরূপ ঘন তরল পদার্থ লাগান বা ব্যবহার করা।

dŏp′-pĕl-găng-ĕr, *n.* A spiritual double or counterpart ; a co-walker ; আত্মিক প্রতিরূপ ; সহযাত্রী।

dŏr *n.* **1.** An insect flying with a buzzing noise; একপ্রকার কীট। **2.** A black dung-beetle ; গোবরে পোকা।

dō-rā′-dō *n.* **1.** A splendid coloured sea-fish ; সমুজ্জ্বলবর্ণ-রঞ্জিত সামুদ্রিক মৎস্য বিশেষ। **2.** (*Astron.*) A small Southern constellation, (also called the *Sword-fish*) ; দক্ষিণ নভোমণ্ডলীয় ক্ষুদ্র তারা-প্রকোষ্ঠ বিশেষ, খড়্গ-মৎস্য তারা (হিঃ কোঃ)।

Dŏr′-căs *n.* A meeting of ladies to make clothes for the poor ; দরিদ্রদিগের ব্যবহারার্থ পোষাক প্রস্তুতের জন্য মহিলা-সম্মিলন।

Dō′-rĭ-ăn *adj.* & *n.* Pertaining to the ancient Greeks of Doris (a district of Ancient Greece) ; প্রাচীন গ্রীসদেশের অন্তঃপাতী ডরিস্ নামক জেলার অধিবাসী সম্বন্ধীয়। ***Noun.*** **1.** A native of Doris ; ডরিস্ নামক জেলার অধিবাসী। **2.** A member of one of the three divisions of the Ancient Greeks, (the two others being Aeolian and Ionian) ; প্রাচীন গ্রীসজাতির প্রধান বিভাগত্রয়ের অন্যতমের অন্তর্ভুক্ত ব্যক্তি। **Dorian mode**—(সঙ্গীতশাস্ত্র) গাম্ভীর্য্য ও সারল্য-ব্যঞ্জক রাগ বিশেষ।

Dŏr′-ĭc, *adj.* & *n.* **1.** Belonging or pertaining to Doris or Dorians ; গ্রীস দেশের ডরিস্ জেলা বা ঐ জেলার

অধিবাসিসম্বন্ধীয়। **2.** (*Arch.*) Relating to or designating the oldest or simplest of the Greek orders; (স্থপতি-বিজ্ঞান) গ্রীস দেশের প্রাচীন স্থাপত্য রীতি বিশেষ সম্বন্ধীয়। **3.** Broad; rustic; "The *doric* dialect of the Lake District;" স্থূল; কদর্য্য, গ্রাম্য। ***Noun.*** **1.** A dialect of Ancient Greece; প্রাচীন গ্রীস-দেশের উপভাষাবিশেষ। **2.** A rustic dialect of English; ইংলণ্ড দেশীয় গ্রাম্য উপভাষা বিশেষ। **3.** The Doric order of architecture; গ্রীসদেশীয় স্থাপত্য রীতি বিশেষ। **Doric order**—(স্থপতি-বিজ্ঞান) গ্রীসদেশের প্রাচীনতম ও সরলতম স্থাপত্য-রীতিবিশেষ।

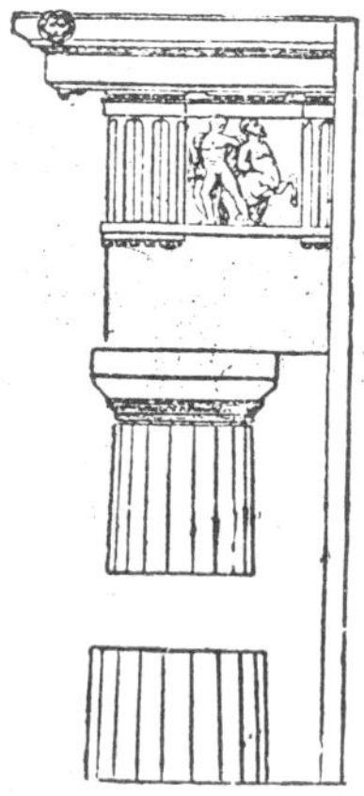

Grecian Doric order.

dŏr'-mănt, *adj.* **1.** Asleep; inactive; at rest; (*fig.*) in abeyance; as, *dormant* person, talent or claim; সুপ্ত, নিদ্রিত; নিষ্ক্রিয়; বিশ্রান্ত; অনুদ্ভূত, গুপ্ত, অপ্রকট, প্রচ্ছন্ন। **2.** (*Herald.*) With head on paws; in a sleeping posture; as, a lion *dormant*; (কুল-বিদ্যা) থাবার উপর ন্যস্তমস্তক; নিদ্রিতাবস্থ। **3.** (*Bot.*) With development suspended; as, a *dormant* bud; (উদ্ভিদ-বিদ্যা) রুদ্ধবিকাশ। **—măn-cy,** *n.* **Dormant partner**—যে অংশীদার কোন ব্যবসায়ে মূলধনাদি দেয়, কিন্তু কোন কাজ করে না। **Dormant warrant**—একপ্রকার পরওয়ানা, যাহাতে নামধামাদির স্থান খালি থাকে, এবং আবশ্যক মত পূরণ করা হয়।

dŏr'-mêr, *n.* (Also DORMER WINDOW) A window standing vertically on a sloping roof; ঢালু ছাদের উপরের খাড়া জানালা।

Dormer window.

dŏr'-meuse (-mŭz), *n.* **1.** A travelling carriage for sleeping; শয়নোপযোগী গাড়ী। **2.** A kind of coach or reclining seat; একপ্রকার গাড়ী বা আরাম কেদারা।

dŏr'-mi-tive (-tĭv), *adj.* & *n.* Soporific; নিদ্রাকর, নিদ্রাজনক। ***Noun.*** A soporific medicine; নিদ্রাজনক ঔষধ।

dŏr'-mi-tō-rȳ, *n.* A large sleeping chamber with many beds; বহু শয্যাসমন্বিত সুবৃহৎ শয়নপ্রকোষ্ঠ, শয়নালয়, শয়নাগার, শেজঘর, শয়নমন্দির।

dŏr'-mouse (-mows), *n.* A small rodent which passes the winter in a lethargic state; মূষিক জাতীয় জন্তুবিশেষ—ইহারা সারা শীতকাল নিদ্রায় কাটায়, বৃক্ষ মূষিক (আঃ বঃ)।

dŏr'-săl *adj.* **1.** (*Anat.* & *Zool.*) Pertaining to, or belonging to, the back; situated on or near the back; পৃষ্ঠসম্বন্ধীয়, পৃষ্ঠ্য; পৃষ্ঠের, পিঠের। **2.** (*Bot.*) Relating to the back of a leaf etc.; (উদ্ভিদ্-বিদ্যা) পত্র প্রভৃতির পৃষ্ঠভাগ সম্বন্ধীয়। **3.** Ridge-shaped; জাঙ্গালাকৃতি। **—ly,** *adv.* **Dorsal suture**—পার্শ্বিক-সন্ধি (জোড়া)।

dŏ'-rȳ, *n.* **1.** A sea-fish used as food, (also called *John dory*); খাদ্যস্বরূপ ব্যবহৃত সামুদ্রিক মৎস্য বিশেষ। **2.** A flat-bottomed boat, esp. one used by fishing vessels in U. S.; একপ্রকার জেলে ডিঙ্গি।

dōs'-āge, *n.* **1.** (*Med.*) Administration of medicine in doses; (ভৈষজ্য-শাস্ত্র) মাত্রা হিসাবে ঔষধ প্রয়োগ। **2.** Size of a dose; ঔষধের এক মাত্রার আকার।

dōse, *n.* & *v. t.* **1.** The quantity of medicine to be taken at one time; মাত্রা, একবার সেবনীয় ঔষধের পরিমাণ। **2.** (*Fig.*) Anything nauseous or unpleasant which has to be taken "To repeat and daily increase the *dose* of flattery;" (লক্ষণায়) অরুচিজনক বস্তু, বিতৃষ্ণাজনক বস্তু। ***Verb t.*** **1.** To give doses to; to administer medicine to; ঔষধের মাত্রা প্রদান করা; ঔষধ প্রদান করা। **2.** To administer as medicine etc. in doses; মাত্রা হিসাবে ঔষধ প্রভৃতি প্রয়োগ করা। **3.** To give anything esp. unpleasant to; কোনরূপ জিনিষ দেওয়া, কোন অপ্রীতিকর জিনিষ দেওয়া। **4.** To adulterate, esp. wine with spirit; ভেজাল দেওয়া, বিশেষতঃ মদ্যে সুরাসার মিশ্রিত করা।

dŏss, *n.* & *v. i.* (*Slang*) A bed n a common lodging house: (ইতর ভাষায়) সাধারণ বাসবাটীতে বিছানা। ***Verb i.*** To sleep in a doss; উক্তরূপ বিছানায় শয়ন করা। **Dos'-ser,** *n.* **Doss-house**—সাধারণ বাসবাটী।

dŏs'-săl, *n.* A cloth hanging at the back of an altar or round a chancel; বেদীর পশ্চাদ্‌ভাগে বা চতুর্দ্দিকে টাঙ্গানো কাপড়।

dŏs-siêr', *n.* A set of documents; esp. a record of a person's antecedents; এক তাড়া দলিল; বিশেষতঃ কোন ব্যক্তির পূর্ব্বচরিত্রের বিবরণ।

dŏs'-sil, *n.* **1.** (*Print.*) A cloth roll for wiping ink from an engraved plate; (মুদ্রণ) খোদিত ফলক হইতে কালি মুছিয়া লইবার জন্য জড়ানো কাপড়। **2.** (*Surg.*) A portion of lint made into a cylindric form for keeping a sore etc. open; (অস্ত্রোপচার বিদ্যা) ঘা প্রভৃতির মুখ খোলা রাখার জন্য ক্ষত স্থানে প্রয়োগের কোমল বস্ত্রের যে অংশ চোঙ্গের আকার করা হয়, স্থূল-পটিকা (সাঃ পঃ)।

dŏt, *n., v. t.* & *i.* **1.** A roundish pen-mark; a small speck usually round বিন্দু; ফুটকি। **2.** A point over i or j; ইংরাজি i অথবা j অক্ষরের উপরের ফুট্‌কি। 3. A small child; a tiny object; "Troops of children from the little *dots* of four or five......to big girls;" ক্ষুদ্র শিশু; অতি ক্ষুদ্র পদার্থ। *Verb t.* 1. To mark with dots; ফুট্‌কি চিহ্নে চিহ্নিত করা। 2. To put dots upon i and j; as, *dot* the i's and cross the t's; ইংরেজী j অথবা i অক্ষরের উপর ফুট্‌কি চিহ্ন দেওয়া। 3. To diversify with small detached objects; as, a sea *dotted* with ships; ফুট্‌ ফুট্‌ চিহ্ন বিশিষ্ট করা, ক্ষুদ্র ক্ষুদ্র বিক্ষিপ্ত বস্তু-দ্বারা বৈচিত্র্য সম্পাদন করা। 4. To scatter or distribute like dots; "All about were *dotted* leafy trees;" বিন্দুবৎ আস্তৃত করা, ফোঁটা ফোঁটা করিয়া ছড়ান। *Verb i.* To make dots or spots; বিন্দুসৃষ্টি করা। **Dot-wheel**—বিন্দু-রেখা অঙ্কনার্থ চক্রবিশেষ। **Dot and carry (one)**—(A school boys' formula for remembering); যোগ অঙ্ক করার সময় এককের অঙ্কগুলি নামান এবং দশকের অঙ্কগুলি পরবর্ত্তী স্তম্ভে লইয়া যাওয়া। **Dot and carry one**—Irregularly; বিশৃঙ্খলভাবে, এলোমেলোভাবে। **Dot and go one**—(*n., adj. & adv.*) The limp of a person; পঙ্গুতা। (*Adj.*) Limping; খঞ্জচরণ, পঙ্গুচিত (মঃ উঃ)। (*Adv.*) Limpingly; খোঁড়াইয়া। **To dot down**—To jot down; টুকিয়া লওয়া। **To dot the i's and cross the t's**—To put in minute details; to make the meaning quite clear; পুঙ্খানুপুঙ্খ-ভাবে বিবৃত করা; অর্থ সুবিশদ করা।

dŏ'-tāge, *n.* 1. Childishness of old age; senility; জরা, জরাজীর্ণতা; বুদ্ধিবৈকল্য, ভীমরথী, বাহাত্তুরে। 2. The object of doting; "Being his father's *dotage*;" অতিরিক্ত স্নেহ বা অনুরাগের পাত্র, সোহাগের পাত্র, সোহাগিনী (*Fem.*)। 3. Excessive fondness; অতিরিক্ত স্নেহ বা অনুরাগ, সোহাগ।

dŏ'-tăl, *adj.* Pertaining to a woman's marriage portion; স্ত্রীধন সম্বন্ধীয়, যৌতুক-সম্বন্ধীয়, যৌতুক-বিষয়ক।

dŏ'-tard (-têrd), *n.* One showing the weakness of old age or excessive fondness; জরাজীর্ণেন্দ্রিয় ব্যক্তি, থুরথুরে বুড়ো, অতিমাত্রায় আদর ও সোহাগপ্রদর্শনকারী।

dōte, doat (dōt), *v. i.* 1. To be delirious; to have the intellect impaired by age; to be silly or infatuated; মতিভ্রান্ত হওয়া; বার্দ্ধক্য হেতু বুদ্ধি বিকল হওয়া; বালিশবুদ্ধি হওয়া, বুদ্ধিশূন্য হওয়া। 2. To be excessively fond; to be foolishly in love; (with *on* or *upon*): as, to *dote on* a person; অত্যাসক্ত হওয়া; অত্যধিক অনুরাগ প্রদর্শন করা, অতিমাত্রায় সোহাগ করা। **Dot'-ing-ly,** *adv.*

dŏt'-tĕd, *adj.* Marked with dots; diversified with dot-like spots; distributed like dots; বিন্দুচিহ্নাঙ্কিত; ফুট্‌কির মত চিহ্নদ্বারা চিত্রিত; ফুট্‌কির মত বিক্ষিপ্ত। **Dotted line**—বিন্দু-রেখা।

dŏt'-têr-ĕl, *n.* A kind of plover; একপ্রকার তিত্তির পক্ষী।

dŏt'-tle (-tl), *n.* The plug of tobacco left or unsmoked or half-smoked in a pipe; ধূমপানের পর অর্দ্ধদগ্ধ বা অদগ্ধ তাম্রকূটখণ্ড।

dŏt'-tȳ, *adj.* 1. Marked with dots; ফুট্‌কি চিহ্নাঙ্কিত। 2. (*Colloq.*) Unsteady in gait; silly; (চলিত ভাষায়) টলমলিয়া; বোকারাম।

douane, *n.* A foreign custom-house; বৈদেশিক শুল্কাগার।

dou'-ble (dŭ-bl), *adj. & adv.* Two-fold; multiplied by two; দ্বিগুণিত, দ্বিক; দোহারা, ডুনা (*Colloq.*)। 2. Folded; as, *doubled* fist; বদ্ধ। 3. Stooping much; with some parts twofold; as a *double* axe; অত্যধিক নত; দ্বি-মুখ। 4. Twice as much or many; দ্বিগুণ। 5. Ambiguous; দ্ব্যাত্মক, দ্ব্যর্থক। 6. Of two-fold or extra size, value, strength, etc.; as, *double* ale, pice, etc.; দ্বিগুণায়তন, দ্বিগুণমূল্যের, দ্বিগুণ শক্তিশালী। 7. (*Fig.*) Deceitful; hypocritical; "They were not of *double* heart;" (লক্ষণায়) দ্বিজিহ্ব, প্রতারণাপর; কপট, খল। *Adv.* 1. To twice the amount etc.; as, "Eyes were *double* bright;" দ্বিগুণসংখ্যা পর্য্যন্ত, দ্বিগুণিত ভাবে, দ্বিগুণ তেজে। 2. Two together; as, to ride *double*; দুইজন এক সঙ্গে, একত্রে দুই জনায়। **—bly,** *adv.* **—ness,** *n.* **Double-acting**—উভয়-দিকে কার্য্যকারী বা শক্তিপরিচালক। **Double barrel**—(*adj. & n.*) Double-barrelled; দোচুঙ্গী, দ্বিনাল। (*Noun*) A double barrelled gun; দ্বিনাল বন্দুক। **Double-barrelled**—With two barrels, as a gun; দ্বিনাল। (*Fig.*) Having a double purpose or effect; as, a *double-barrelled* compliment; (লক্ষণায়) দ্বি-উদ্দেশ্য বিশিষ্ট, দ্বিবিধফলদায়ক। **Double-bass**—বেহালার ন্যায় বাদ্য-যন্ত্র বিশেষ। [ইহা তন্ত্রীযুক্ত বাদ্য-যন্ত্র সমূহের মধ্যে সর্ব্বাপেক্ষা বৃহত্তম।] **Double-biting**—উভয়দিকে ধারাল। **Double-breasted** — কুর্ত্তার বুকের এক পার্শ্ব অপর পার্শ্বের উপর অপর এক শ্রেণী বোতাম দ্বারা সংবদ্ধ। **Double-dealer**—A trickish person; a deceitful fellow; as, I am no *double-dealer*:—(আমার মুখে এক-খানা পেটে একখানা নাই); দ্বি-হৃদয়, শঠ, কপট, খল; দ্বিজিহ্ব, মনে এক মুখে আর। **Double-dealing** — (*adj. & n.*) Deceitful; practising duplicity; দ্বিহৃদয়, কপট; কপটাচরণ-কারী। (*Noun*) A deceitful action; duplicity; কপটাচরণ; কপটতা। **Double decomposition**—দ্বি-বিঘটন। **Double-dyed**—(Usually *fig.*) Deeply stained with guilt; (প্রায়শঃ লক্ষণায়) মহাপাপ-লিপ্ত, পাপকলুষিত। **Double-edged**—দুইদিকে ধারবিশিষ্ট, দ্বি-ধার। **Double entendre**—*n.* (*Fr.*) A phrase with two meanings one being usually indecent ; দ্ব্যর্থবাচক বাক্য, ইহার মধ্যে, একটী সাধারণতঃ অশ্লীলতাদুষ্ট হইয়া থাকে, বক্রোক্তি, শ্লেষ, দ্ব্যর্থ। Use of such phrases ; উক্তরূপ বাক্য ব্যবহার। **Double-entry**—(See ENTRY.) **Double-faced**—কপট, ছলনাপর, অসরল্য, —খল। **Double-first**—দুই বিষয়ে প্রথম শ্রেণীর সম্মান লাভকারী। **Double-ganger**—অপচ্ছায়া, ভুত। **Double mind**—দ্বিমনস্ক, দ্বিমনাঃ। **Double quick**—(*n.* & *adv.*) See DOUBLE TIME. (*Adv.*) Very quickly ; অতি দ্রুতবেগে। **Double salt** — দ্বিধাতুক লবণ। **Double star**—A star which in the telescope is resolved in two stars ; যে নক্ষত্র দূরবীক্ষণ যোগে দেখিলে দুইটী দেখায়, যুগ্ম তারা (হিঃ কোঃ)। **Double-time**—(সৈন্যদলের যাত্রা কালে) প্রতি মিনিটে ৩৩ ইঞ্চি পরিমাণ ১৬৫ বার পদক্ষেপ। **Double-tongued**—একই বিষয়ে একই সময়ে ভিন্ন ভিন্ন মত প্রকাশকারী ; ছলনাপর, কপট।

dou'-ble (dŭ-bl), *n.* **1.** Twice the number, amount or quality ; দ্বিগুণ পরিমাণ, দ্বিগুণ সংখ্যা, দ্বিগুণ। **2.** A counterpart ; a wraith ; "I have met a *double* of myself ;" প্রতিরূপ, আত্মিক প্রতিরূপ, সূক্ষ্মদেহ, লিঙ্গ-দেহ ; অপচ্ছায়া, ছায়ামূর্ত্তি। **3.** (*Obs.*) A fold or plait ; (অপ্রচলিত) ভাঁজ। **4.** A copper coin current in Guernsey ($=\frac{1}{8}d$) ; গার্ণেসি দ্বীপের তাম্রমুদ্রা বিশেষ। **5.** (*Lawn tennis etc.*) A game between two pairs ; (আণ্ডা খেলা প্রভৃতিতে) যে খেলায় প্রত্যেক পক্ষে দুই জন ক্রীড়ক থাকে। **6.** (*Mil.*) A double pace ; as, at the *double* (running) ; দ্বিগুণ গতি। **7.** (*Whist*) A game in which one side scores 5 before the other has scored 3 (at short whist) ; (at long whist) one in which one side scores 10 while the other none ; একপ্রকার তাস খেলা,—যাহাতে এক পক্ষ তিন ক্রীড়াঙ্ক পাইবার পূর্ব্বে-অন্যপক্ষ ৫ ক্রীড়াঙ্ক লাভ করে, ক্রীড়ার প্রকার ভেদ) যাহাতে এক পক্ষ কোন ক্রীড়াঙ্ক পাইবার পূর্ব্বে অন্য পক্ষ ১০ ক্রীড়াঙ্ক লাভ করে। **8.** (*Astron.*) A double star ; যুক্ত-তারা (সাঃ পঃ), দ্বিতারা, নক্ষত্র-যুগ্ম।

dou'-ble (dŭ-bl), *v. t.* & *i.* **1.** To multiply by two ; to increase two-fold ; দুইদ্বারা গুণ করা ; দ্বিগুণ করা, দুনা করা। **2.** To bend or turn as cloth, paper, etc., over upon itself ; to fold, (often with *up*) ; as, to *double up* the leaf (of a book) ; to clench as a fist ; to cause to bend by a blow etc. ; দুভাঁজ করা ; ভাঁজ করা, মোড়া, দুমড়ান ; (মুষ্টি) বদ্ধ করা ; আঘাত প্রভৃতি দ্বারা নোয়ান। **3.** (*Mil.*) To unite as ranks or files ; (সামরিক-শাস্ত্র) সৈন্য শ্রেণী বা পংক্তি সংযোগ করা। **4.** To exceed by two-fold ; to contain twice as much as ; "The adverse flee still *doubling* ours ;" দ্বিগুণ সংখ্যক হওয়া ; দ্বিগুণ থাকা। **5.** (*Naut.*) To get round ; as, to *double* a headland ; (নৌবিদ্যা) ঘুরিয়া আসা। **6.** To avoid or escape by doubling ; to elude ; as, to *double* a pursuer ; সহসা মোড় ফিরিয়া এড়ান বা পলান ; চতুরতা সহকারে পলায়ন করা। **7.** (*Bil'iards*) To make to rebound ; (বিলিয়ার্ড ক্রীড়ায়) ঠিকরান। **8.** To line as a garment or ship with additional material ; বস্ত্র বা জাহাজে আস্তরণ দেওয়া। **9.** To put a passenger (in the same quarters) with another, (some times with *up*) ; একজন যাত্রীকে অপর ব্যক্তির সহিত এক বাটীতে বাস করিবার জন্য স্থান দেওয়া। ***Verb i.*** **1.** To increase to twice the quantity ; দ্বিগুণ পরিমাণ হওয়া, দুনা হওয়া। **2.** To turn sharply and go back over the same ground ; to pursue a tortuous course হঠাৎ ঘুরিয়া পুনরায় পূর্ব্ব পথে দৌড়া আঁকা বাঁকা পথে চলা। **3.** (*Mil.*) To move in double time ; (সামরিক শাস্ত্র) দ্বিগুণ গতিতে চলা। **4.** To bend ; "His knees *doubled* up under him ;" to become folded as a piece of cloth or paper etc. (with *up*) ; নত হওয়া ; ভাঁজ হওয়া **5.** (*Billiards*) To rebound ; (বিলিয়ার্ড) ঠিকরাইয়া আসা। **To double lock**—To turn the key of (some locks) twice ; দুইবার চাবি ঘুরান। **To double reef**—(*Naut.*) To contract the spread of (a sail) by two reefs ; (নৌ-বিদ্যা) প্রান্ত সংবদ্ধ অবান্তর অংশদ্বয় মুড়িয়া পাইল সংকীর্ণ করা। **To double up,** *v. t.* & *i.* To fold up ; to make to bend or stoop as by blow etc. ; ভাঁজ করা, দ্বিপাটিত করা, মোড়া ; প্রহারাদি দ্বারা নোওয়াইয়া দেওয়া। (*Verb i.*) To share with another accommodation designed for one ; একজনের বিছানায় দুইজন শয়ন করা। To bend over as in pain or violent laughter ; বেদনায় বা উৎকট হাস্যে নুইয়া পড়া। **To double upon**—(সামরিক শাস্ত্র) উভয়দিকে গোলাগুলি বর্ষণ করা যায় এরূপ অবস্থায় আবদ্ধ করা। **To double a part** or **parts**—(Of actors) To play two parts in the same piece ; একই নাটকে দুই ব্যক্তির অভিনেয় অংশ অভিনয় করা।

doub'-lĕt (dŭb-), *n.* **1.** (*Hist.*) A close-fitting body-garment worn by men with or without sleeves and short skirts, [worn in 15th to 17th century] ; (ঐতিহাসিক) একপ্রকার আঁটা অঙ্গরাখা, ভিতরের জামা। **2.** One of a pair ; যুগলের একটী, জোড়ার একটী। **3.** (*Phil.*) One of two words of the same derivation but of different sense ; (as, fashion and faction) ; (ভাষাবিজ্ঞান) একই ধাতু হইতে উৎপন্ন বিভিন্নঅর্থবোধক শব্দদ্বয়ের অন্যতর

4. (*Pl.*) The same number turning up on both the dice at a throw ; (বহুবচন) পাশক ক্ষেপে দুইটী পাশকে একরূপ অঙ্ক প্রদর্শন। 5. A factitious gem ; কৃত্রিম মণি। 6. Two birds killed with double-barrelled gun ; দ্বিনল বন্দুকদ্বারা নিহত পক্ষি-দ্বয়। 7. (*Microscope*) Combination of two simple lenses ; (অণুবীক্ষণ যন্ত্র) দুইটী সাধারণ কাচতালের সংযোগ। 8. (*Print.*) A word or words unintentionally set up a second time ; (মুদ্রণ) কোন শব্দ বা শব্দসমূহের অজ্ঞাতসারে দ্বিতীয়বার সন্নিবেশ। **Doublet and hose**—পুরুষের পরিচ্ছদ, বিশেষতঃ যে পুরুষ-পরিচ্ছদ পরিধান করিয়া অভিনেত্রীগণ রঙ্গমঞ্চে অবতীর্ণ হয়।

doub-loon' (dŭb-), *n.* A Spanish gold coin, (formerly varying from 33 to 36 shillings, now worth a little more than a pound) ; স্পেনদেশীয় স্বর্ণমুদ্রা বিশেষ (বর্ত্তমানে এক পাউণ্ড অপেক্ষা কিঞ্চিদধিক মূল্যের)।

doublure, (*F.*) *n.* An ornamental lining usually of leather on the inside of a book-cover ; পুস্তকের মলাটের ভিতরের দিকের শোভাজনক আস্তরণ।

doubt (dowt), *n.* 1. Hesitation ; uncertainty of judgment or mind ; as, to have *doubts* regarding the theory o tides ; সন্দেহ, আশঙ্কা, শঙ্কা, সংশয় ; বিতর্ক। 2. Uncertain state of things ; want of full proof ; as, to give one the benefit of *doubt* ; অনিশ্চয়তা ; প্রমাণাভাব। **No doubt**—সন্দেহ নাই, নিশ্চিতই। **To give one the benefit of the doubt**—আসামীর অপরাধ সম্বন্ধে বিচারকের সন্দেহ হইলে তাহাকে অব্যাহতি দেওয়া **To make no doubt**—To feel sure ; নিশ্চিত বোধ কর। **Without doubt**—নিঃসন্দেহে।

doubt (dowt), *v. t.* & *i.* 1. To hold questionable ; to hesitate ; to distrust ; সন্দেহ করা ; শঙ্কা করা, আশঙ্কা করা ; দ্বিধা করা, অবিশ্বাস করা। 2. (*Archaic* & *dial.*) To be afraid, (with an objective clause) ; as, I *doubt* we are late ; (অপ্রচলিত বা উপভাষায়) আশঙ্কা হওয়া। ***Verb i.*** To waver in opinion or belief ; to feel uncertain ; ইতস্ততঃ করা ; অনিশ্চিত বোধ করা।

doubt'-fŭl (dowt-), *adj.* 1. Uncertain ; indistinct ; ambiguous ; as, a word of *doubtful* origin and meaning ; সন্দিগ্ধমনাঃ; সংশয়াত্মক, সন্দেহসঙ্কুল, দ্বিমনাঃ, সংশয়পর, সাংশয়িক, শঙ্কনীয়, সন্দেহাত্মক, সংশয়াপন্ন, সংশয়গ্রস্ত, সংশয়ালু, সন্দিগ্ধমতি ; অস্পষ্ট ; দ্ব্যর্থক। 2. Of questionable character ; সন্দিগ্ধচরিত্র। 3. Of uncertain issue ; "The *doubtful* fray ;" অনিশ্চিত-পরিণাম। **–ly,** *adv.* **–ness,** *n.* The state of being doubtful ; সংশয়পরতা, সংশয়ত্ব।

doubt'-lĕss (dowt-), *adj.* & *adv.* Undoubted ; free from doubt; নিঃসন্দেহ ; সন্দেহমুক্ত। ***Adv.*** Undoubtedly ; নিঃসন্দেহে, নিঃসংশয়িতরূপে।

douce (dōōs), *adj.* Sober ; gentle ; স্থিরমতি ; শান্ত।

douceur, *n.* Gratuity, bribe ; পারিতোষিক ; বক্‌শিশ, উৎকোচ।

douche (dōōsh), *n.*, *v. t.* & *i.* A jet of water applied to body externally or internally as a form of bathing or medical purpose ; স্নানার্থ বা চিকিৎসার্থ শরীরের বহির্ভাগে বা অভ্যন্তরে জলধারা প্রক্ষেপ, জলযন্ত্রিকা। ***Verb t.*** To administer a douche to ; জলযন্ত্রিকা প্রয়োগ করা। ***Verb i.*** To take a douche ; জলযন্ত্রিকা হইতে প্রক্ষিপ্ত জলধারা গ্রহণ করা।

dough (dō), *n.* Paste of bread ; kneaded flour ; ময়দার তাল ; খমির। **Dough'-y,** *adj.* **Dough'-i-ness,** *n.*

dough'-tŷ (dow-), *adj.* (*Archaic*) Valiant ; formidable ; সাহসী, প্রতাপশালী ; বাহাদুর, প্রবলপ্রতাপাক্রান্ত, মহাশক্তিশালী। **–ti-ly,** *adv.* **–ti-ness,** *n.*

Dou-khŏ-bŏrs (dōw-), *n. pl.* A religious sect, with some likeness in doctrines to Quakers, of which large numbers migrated from Russia to Canada after persecution for refusing military service ; রুশিয়াদেশের ধর্ম্ম সম্প্রদায় বিশেষ—এই সম্প্রদায় ভুক্ত ব্যক্তিগণ সেনা-বিভাগের কার্য্য করিতে অস্বীকৃত হওয়ায় নিদারুণ নির্য্যাতন সহ্য করে এবং পরে ইহাদের অনেক লোক ক্যানাডাদেশে আশ্রয়লাভ করে।

doum (dōōm), *n.* An Egyptian palm-tree, (also called *doum-palm*) ; মিশরদেশীয় তালবৃক্ষ।

dour (dōōr), *adj.* (*Scot.*) Severe ; obstinate ; (স্কট্‌লণ্ড্) কঠোর ; ঠেঁটা। **Dour'-li-ness,** *n.* **Dour'-ly,** *adv.*

douse, dowse (dows), *v. t.* 1. To throw water over ; to drench ; জলধারা প্রক্ষেপ করা ; জলসিক্ত করা। 2. (*Naut.*) To strike or lower in haste ; as, to *douse* the top-sail ; (নৌ-বিদ্যা) তাড়াতাড়ি নামান। 4. To put out ; নির্ব্বাপিত করা, নিভান। 5. To put off ; খোলা। **To douse the glim**—(ইতরভাষায়) বাতি নিভান।

dove (dŭv), *n.* 1. A pigeon ; ঘুঘু, কপোত, পায়রা, পারাবত। 2. Darling ; "Oh, my *dove,* let me hear thy voice ;" যাদু, ময়না, ধন। 3. (*Bible*) The Holy Spirit ; (বাইবেল) পবিত্রাত্মা। 4. An emblem of innocence and gentleness ; নম্রতা ও শুভ্র-স্বভাবের নিদর্শন। **Dove'-like,** *adj.* Like a dove ; pure and gentle ; loveable ; কপোত-তুল্য ; নম্রচরিত্র এবং শুভ্রস্বভাব ; প্রেমাস্পদ। **Dove-colour** — ঈষদ্ গোলাবিবর্ণাভ উজ্জ্বল ধূসর বর্ণ। **Dove-cot(e)**—পায়রার টং, বিটঙ্ক, কপোতপালঙ্ক, কপোতপালিকা, কপোতাবাস, কবুতরের খোপ। **Dove-eyed**—কপোত-নয়ন ; নম্র-নয়ন। **Dove-hawk** — একপ্রকার পক্ষী।

To flutter the dove cot(e)s—To alarm quiet people ; শান্তিপ্রিয় ব্যক্তিগণকে সন্ত্রস্ত করা।

dove′-tail (dŭv-tāl), *n., v. t. & i.* A flaring tenon shaped like a dove's spread tail or a reversed wedge fitting into corresponding mortise and forming a joint ; খাঁজ কাটিয়া তক্তায় জোড়, কপোত পুচ্ছ বন্ধ (আঃ বঃ)। ***Verb t.*** **1.** To put together with dovetails ; খাঁজ কাটিয়া তক্তা জোড়া দেওয়া। **2.** (*Fig.*) To unite compactly ; (লক্ষণায়) আঁটসাঁট করিয়া লাগান। ***Verb i.*** (*Fig.*) To fit together compactly ; (লক্ষণায়) আঁটসাঁট হইয়া জোড়া লাগা।

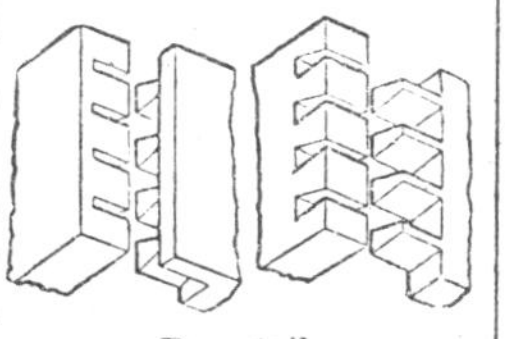

Dove-tail.

dow′-ā-gēr, *n.* A woman with a title or property derived from her husband ; as, a queen *dowager* ;' পরলোকগত স্বামীর উপাধি ও সম্পত্তি প্রাপিকা নারী।

dow′-dȳ, *adj. & n.* **1.** Unfashionably or shabbily dressed as woman ; কুবেশী, জীর্ণ-বেশধারিণী, মলিনবেশ পরিহিতা, ছিন্নবেশা। **2.** Unattractive ; unfashionable as a dress ; অচিত্তাকর্ষক ; রীতিবহির্ভূত। ***Noun.*** A vulgarly dressed indecent woman ; হীনবেশা নারী, অভব্যা স্ত্রীলোক, মলিনবেশধারিণী। **—di-ly,** *adv.* **—di-ness,** *n.* **—ism,** *n.* **—ish,** *adj.*

dow′-ĕl, *n. & v. t.* A headless pin used to connect adjacent pieces, penetrating a part of its length into each piece at right angles to the plane of junction ; পাশাপাশি লাগ দুই তক্তা জোড়া দিবার জন্য একপ্রকার মাথাহীন পেরেক, আধারিয়া, যোগসূচী। ***Verb t.*** To fasten with dowels ; আঁধারিয়া দ্বারা জোড়া দেওয়া।

dow′-ēr, *n. & v. t.* **1.** The portion of a deceased husband's estate which the law allows to his widow for life ; স্ত্রীধন, স্ত্রী বৃত্তি, স্ত্রীভরণধন। **2.** Property or money which a wife brings to her husband on marriage ; a dowry ; শুল্ক ; যৌতুক। **3.** Endowment gift of nature ; talent ; দান ; নিসর্গপ্রদ ক্ষমতা, নৈসর্গিক ক্ষমতা ; ধীশক্তি। ***Verb t.*** **1.** To give dowry to ; স্ত্রীধন প্রদান করা, যৌতুক দেওয়া। **2.** To endow with talent ; ধীশক্তি-সম্পন্ন করা। **—less,** *adj.*

dow′-lăs, *n.* A kind of strong calico ; একপ্রকার স্থূল শ্বেত কার্পাস বস্ত্র।

down, *n.* **1.** An open highland ; esp. (*pl.*) treeless undulating chalk uplands of South England used for pasture ; অধিত্যকা ; বিশেষতঃ ইংলণ্ডদেশের দক্ষিণদিগ্‌বর্ত্তী তরুশূন্য তরঙ্গায়িত খটিক-ভূমি। **2.** A sand-hill ; a dune ; বালুকাগিরি, বালুকা-শৈল ; বালিয়াড়ী।

down, *n.* **1.** A covering o soft leathers possessed by young birds ; birds' under-plumage used in cushions ; etc. ; রোঁয়া, তুলা, (পাখীর) পর। **2.** The hairy covering of seeds of certain plants ; কোন কোন বৃক্ষের বীজের লোমময় আবরণ। **3.** Fluffy substance ; তুলার মত জিনিষ। **4.** Fine short hair, esp. first hair on the face ; সূক্ষ্ম এবং খর্ব্বকেশ ; কোমল রোম, বিশেষতঃ নবজাত শ্মশ্রু ও গুম্ফ। **Down′-y,** *adj.* (see page 623).

down, *n.* **1.** A downward fluctuation ; as, ups and *downs* (উত্থান পতন) of life ; পতন। **2.** (*Colloq.*) A dislike ; grudge ; as, to have a *down* on a person ; (চলিত ভাষায়) অপ্রীতি ; আক্রোশ। **3.** (*Dominoes*) Pose ; (নৃত্যবিশেষে) ভঙ্গী, ঢঙ্গ।

down, *adv.* **1.** From higher to a lower position, degree or place ; as, he is going *down* in life : to come *down* (from a bedroom) ; নীচে, নিম্নদিকে, নিম্নস্থানাভিমুখে, অধোদেশে। **2.** On the ground ; at the bottom ; as, the blinds are *down* : the tide was *down* ; ভূমিতে ; নীচে। **3.** (*Fig.*) In humiliation ; "He that is *down* can fall no more ;" (লক্ষণায়) পতিত অবস্থায়। **4.** Below the horizon ; as, the sun is *down* ; চক্রবালের নিম্নে, দিঙ্মণ্ডলের নীচে। **5.** Into disrepute or disgrace ; as, he may write *down* himself ; কলঙ্কিত অবস্থায়, অপমানিত অবস্থায়। **6.** Away from the capital or university ; "His health compelled him to stay *down* for the whole of our first year ;" রাজধানী অথবা বিশ্ববিদ্যালয় হইতে অন্যত্র। **7.** From a larger to a less bulk ; as, to boil *down* in decoctions and culinary process ; ঘনীভূত করিয়া। **8.** From an earlier to a later time ; "Throughout all ages *down* to our own ;" প্রাচীনকাল হইতে পরবর্ত্তী সময় পর্যান্ত। **9.** Extended or prostrate on the ground ; as, to lie *down* ভূমিতে লুটাইয়া। **10.** Down the throat ; as, food got *down* (*i.e.* is swallowed) ; গলার ভিতর দিয়া নীচে। **11.** On paper or other writing materials ; as, to write, take or note *down* ; কাগজ, শ্লেট, প্রভৃতিতে। **12.** In cash ; on the spot ; as, to pay *down* ; নগদ ; তদ্দণ্ডেই, তৎক্ষণাৎ। [Down শব্দ কখন কখন ন্যূনপদ সহকারে (elliptically) ব্যবহৃত হয় ; as, go *down,* come *down* ; আতিশয্য দ্যোতনার্থও ব্যবহৃত হয়—যথা :—To be waded *down,* to hang *down,* to pay *down,* etc.] **Down-hearted**—ভগ্নহৃদয়, হতোৎসাহ। **Down helm**—Put down the helm ; দাঁড় রাখিয়া দেও। **Bread is down**—It is cheaper ;

রুটি পূর্ব্বাপেক্ষা সস্তা হইয়াছে। **Down in the mouth** — Dispirited; হতোৎসাহ। **Down on one's luck**—In ill luck; very unfortunate; দুর্ভাগ্যগ্রস্ত; অতিশয় দুর্ভাগ্য। In low spirits; স্ফূর্ত্তিহীন মনে। **Down to Scotland** or **the country**—From London; লণ্ডন হইতে স্কটলণ্ড্ বা ইংলণ্ডের অন্যত্র। **Down to the ground** — Completely; thoroughly; সম্পূর্ণরূপে; সম্যক্রূপে। **Down with**—Put down; take down (used in energetic command); "*Down with* the palace, fire it;" ভূপাতিত কর, পাতয়; উচ্ছন্ন দাও। **He is not down yet**—He has not yet come out of his bed-room; সে এখন পর্য্যন্তও শয়ন-কক্ষ হইতে বাহিরে আসে নাই। **Many down with fever**—Prostrate or laid with fever; অনেকেই জ্বরে শয্যাগত। **The book goes down** — It finds acceptance; পুস্তক জনসাধারণের সমাদর লাভ করিয়াছে। **To be down upon a person**—To treat harshly; to bear a grudge against; কাহারও প্রতি কর্কশ ব্যবহার করা; কাহারও উপর আক্রোশ থাকা। **To get down** — To swallow; গলাধঃকরণ করা। To alight; নামা, অবতরণ করা। **To hiss** or **shout down**—To silence as a speaker or actor; টিটকারী দিয়া বক্তা বা অভিনেতাকে চুপ করাইয়া দেওয়া। **To hunt, ride** or **run down**—To bring to bay; এরূপ অবস্থায় ফেলা যাহাতে পলায়ন অসম্ভব হয়, কোণঠাসা করা। **Up and down**—To and fro; এদিক ওদিক, একবার সম্মুখের দিকে একবার পশ্চাতের দিকে।

dŏwn, *prep.* **1.** In a descending direction; along; as, *down* a hill; নিম্নাভিমুখে; অনুলম্বভাবে। **2.** Towards the mouth of a river; as, to swim *down* the stream; নদীর মোহানার দিকে, ভাটারদিকে। **Down town** — Into the town from a higher part; উচ্চতর স্থান হইতে সহরে। **Down the wind**—In the direction in which the wind is blowing; বায়ুর অনুকূলে, অনুকূল বায়ুতে। **To let go down the wind**—To discard; to abandon; অগ্রাহ্য করা; ত্যাগ করা। **Up and down a room**—To and fro along a room; কক্ষের এদিকে ওদিকে।

dŏwn, *adj.* [Having no degree of comparison.] Directed downward; as, *down*-leap; নিম্নাভিমুখীন, নিম্নগামী। **A down grade**—A descending slope in a rail-road; লৌহবর্ত্মের প্রবণতা। (*Fig.*) Deterioration; (লক্ষণায়) অবনতি। **Down look** — A down-cast look; অধোদৃষ্টি। **Down platform** — লৌহবর্ত্মের যে প্রাঙ্গণ হইতে ভাটিয়াল গাড়ী যাত্রা করে। **Down train**—ভাটিয়াল গাড়ী।

dŏwn, *v. t.* (*Colloq.*) To throw or put down; to knock down; (চলিত ভাষায়) ভূপাতিত করা; আঘাত করিয়া ভূপাতিত করা।

dŏwn'-căst, *n.* & *adj.* **1.** (*Geol.*) Downthrow; (ভূ-বিদ্যা) চতুষ্পার্শ্ববর্ত্তী স্তরসমূহ হইতে কোন স্তরের অধোগমন। **2.** A melancholy look; বিষাদপূর্ণ দৃষ্টি, মলিন মুখ। **3.** A shaft for introducing fresh air into a mine; খনির ভিতর নির্ম্মল বাতাস প্রবিষ্ট করণার্থ সুড়ঙ্গ বিশেষ। ***Adj.*** **1.** Directed downwards (of looks); অধোক্ষিপ্ত, মৃত্তিকাপ্রমুখ। **2.** Dejected; "A few looked *downcast*" অধোবদন, অধোমুখ, বিরস, অপ্রসন্ন, বিষন্ন।

dŏwn'-fall, *n.* **1.** A heavy fall of rain, snow, etc.; প্রচুর বৃষ্টি, বরফ প্রভৃতি পতন। **2.** Fall from prosperity; ruin; as, the *downfall* of the kingdom; পতন, অধঃপতন, বিনিপাত; বিনাশ, ধ্বংস, ক্ষয়।

dŏwn'-hill, *n., adj.* & *adv.* Downward slope; decline; as, the *down-hill* of life (=later half of life); প্রবণতা; পতন। ***Adj.*** Sloping down; declining; গড়ানিয়া, ক্রমনিম্ন; পতনশীল। ***Adv.*** Down the slope of a hill; downwards; as, a stream runs *downhill*; পর্ব্বতের ঢালু পার্শ্ব দিয়া নিম্নে; নিম্নাভিমুখে।

Dŏwn'-ing Street (strēt), *n.* A street in London containing some government offices; British Government; as, *Downing-Street* disapprover; লণ্ডননগরীর রাজপথ বিশেষ, এই পথের উপর কতিপয় সরকারী কার্য্যালয় অবস্থিত আছে; ব্রিটিশশাসনতন্ত্র।

dŏwn'-pour (-pōr), *n.* A heavy fall of rain etc.; ধারাসম্পাত, মূষলধারে বৃষ্টিবর্ষণ, অববর্ষণ, ভূরি-বর্ষণ।

dŏwn'-right (-rīt), *adj.* & *adv.* **1.** Positive; thorough; as, a *downright* falsehood or atheist; স্পষ্ট, ডাহা; নিরবচ্ছিন্ন, পুরা। **2.** Unceremonious; straightforward; blunt; as, he spoke in his *downright* way: *downright* character; অভব্য; সোজাসুজি, অকুটিল; রুখা। ***Adv.*** **1.** Thoroughly; positively; quite; পুরা; স্পষ্টরূপে, ডাহা; সম্যক্, সম্পূর্ণরূপে। **2.** Downward; নীচের দিকে, নিম্নাভিমুখে। **—ness,** *n.*

dŏwn'-stairs (-stārz), *adj., adv.* & *n.* Below stairs; as, *downstairs* room; of a lower floor; সিঁড়ির নীচের, সোপান নিম্নে; নীচের তলার। ***Adv.*** Down the stairs; below; as, he is *downstairs*; নীচের তলায়; নীচে। ***Noun.*** The lower part of a house below the stairs; নীচের তলা।

dŏwn'-throw (-thrō), *n.* (*Geol.*) A sinking of strata below the level of the surrounding beds; (ভূ-বিদ্যা) চতুষ্পার্শ্ববর্ত্তী স্তরসমূহ হইতে কোন স্তরের অধোগমন।

dŏwn'-trŏd-den (-dn), *adj.* Oppressed; পদদলিত, চরণদলিত, মর্দ্দিত।

dōwn′-ward (-wêrd), *adj.* & *adv.* Descending ; নিম্নাভিমুখ, অধোগামী, প্রবণ। ***Adv.*** **1.** In a descending course or line ; নিম্নাভিমুখে। **2.** From higher to a lower or inferior condition ; অপেক্ষাকৃত হীনাবস্থায়। **3.** From earlier to later time ; অপেক্ষাকৃত পরবর্ত্তী কালে। **—wards,** *adv.*

dōwn′-ȳ, *adj.* **1.** Covered with downs ; রোঁয়াদ্বারা আবৃত, পরদ্বারা ঢাকা। **2.** Made of, or resembling, down ; (*fig.*) soft ; soothing ; কোমল রোমময়, রোঁয়ার তৈয়ারী, রোঁয়ার মত ; (লক্ষণায়) সুকোমল ; আরামদায়ক। **3.** (*Slang*) Wide awake ; knowing ; cunning ; (ইতর ভাষায়) সজাগ ; জ্ঞাতসার ; চালাক। **—i-ly,** *adv.* **—i-ness,** *n.* **To do the downy**—To sleep ; নিদ্রা যাওয়া।

dōw′-rȳ, *n.* **1.** A portion which a bride brings to her husband on marriage ; যৌতুক, শুল্ক। **2.** Natural gift ; talent ; নৈসর্গিক ক্ষমতা ; ধীশক্তি।

dowse (dōws), *v. i.* To use divining rods in search of water or mineral veins ; জল কিম্বা খনিজ পদার্থের অবস্থিতি নির্ণয়ার্থ অনুসন্ধান-দণ্ড ব্যবহার করা।

dŏx-ŏl′-ŏ-ġȳ, *n.* Liturgical formula of praise to God ; স্তুতি-বাদ, স্তুতিপাঠ, স্তোত্র।

dŏx′-ȳ, *n.* **1.** A beggar's wench ; নেড়ী। **2.** (*Slang*) A paramour ; ব্যভিচারিণী, উপপত্নী।

dŏx′-ȳ, *n.* An opinion, esp. on theology ; মত বিশেষ, বিশেষতঃ খৃষ্টীয় শাস্ত্রসম্বন্ধীয় মত।

doy′-ĕn, *n.* A senior member of a body or group, esp. a senior ambassador at a court ; কোন সম্মিলনীর সর্ব্বাপেক্ষা কর্ম্মপ্রবীণ সভ্য, কোন বৈদেশিক রাজসভায় প্রেরিত কর্ম্মচারিগণের মধ্যে সর্ব্বাপেক্ষা কর্ম্ম-প্রবীণ ব্যক্তি।

doy′-ley (-li), *n.* See DOILY.

dōze, *n., v. i.* & *t.* A light sleep ; তন্দ্রা, কাক-নিদ্রা। ***Verb i.*** To sleep drowsily ; to be half asleep ; ঝিমান, ঢুলা, কাকনিদ্রা যাওয়া ; অর্দ্ধ-নিদ্রিত থাকা। ***Verb t.*** To spend or pass as time in dozing ; ঝিমাইয়া কাল কাটান।

doz′-en (dŭz′n), *n.* A collection of twelve objects ; ডজন, দ্বাদশক। **Baker's dozen**— See BAKER. **Dozens of times**—Many times ; বহুবার। **Some dozen people**—About a dozen of people ; দশ বার জন লোক। **To talk nineteen to the dozen**—To talk incessantly or very fast ; পেচাল পাড়া।

drăb, *n.* & *v. i.* A strumpet ; বারাঙ্গনা, গণিকা, বেশ্যা, খান্‌কী, রাঁড়। ***Verb i.*** To whore ; to associate with strumpets ; রাঁড় বাজি করা ; খান্‌কীদিগের সহিত মিশা।

drăb, *adj.* & *n.* **1.** Of a dull light brown colour ; পিঙ্গলবর্ণ। **2.** Monotonous ; dull ; "The lives of the people were dull and *drab* ;" একটানা, একঘেঁয়ে ; নীরস। ***Noun.*** **1.** Monotony ; একঘেঁয়ে ভাব। **2.** A dull light brown colour ; পিঙ্গলবর্ণ, পাটকিলে রঙ্গ। **3.** A cloth of dull brownish yellow colour ; এক-প্রকার পাটকিলে রঙ্গের কাপড়।

drăb′-bĕt, *n.* A coarse drab linen fabric ; একপ্রকার পাটকিলে রংয়ের স্থূল পশমী বস্ত্র।

drăb-ble (-bl), *v. i.* & *t.* **1.** To go splashing through water and mud ; to become wet and dirty ; জল ও কাদার ভিতর দিয়া ছপাঙ্ ছপাঙ্ করিয়া যাওয়া ; জল কাদা মাখা। **2.** To fish as for barbels etc. with a rod and a long line passed through a piece of lead ; নড়কাইয়া ছিপদ্বারা মাছ ধরা। ***Verb t.*** To besmear with mud and water ; জল কাদা মাখান।

drachm (drăm), *n.* **1.** An ancient Greek silver coin ; প্রাচীন গ্রীসের রৌপ্য মুদ্রাবিশেষ। **2.** An apothecary's weight of 60 grains = $\frac{1}{8}$ oz. (Avord. $27\frac{1}{3}$ grains) ; এক আউন্সের অষ্টমাংশ, ৬০ গ্রেণ। **3.** A small quantity ; কিঞ্চিৎ পরিমাণ, কণা।

drăch′-mă, *n.* **1.** An ancient Greek coin = drachm ; প্রাচীন গ্রীসের মুদ্রাবিশেষ। **2.** A modern Greek franc ; আধুনিক গ্রীসের ফ্রাঙ্ক মুদ্রা।

Dră′-cō, *n.* (*Astron.*) The Dragon ; (জ্যোতি-বিজ্ঞান) অজগর তারা (হিঃ কোঃ)।

Dră-cō′-ni-ăn, Dră-cŏn′-ic, *adjs.* (Of *laws*) Rigorous ; harsh ; (আইন সম্বন্ধে) কঠোর ; কঠিন। [প্রাচীন এথেন্স নগরীর ব্যবস্থাকর্ত্তা DRACO এর নাম হইতে গৃহীত।]

drăff, *n.* **1.** Dregs ; lees ; hog-wash ; ময়লা, ফেনা, কাইট, তলানি ; গাদ ; আঁস্তাকুরের ময়লা। **2.** Refuse of malt brewing or distilling ; জলে পর্য্যুষিত যব হইতে মদ্য প্রস্তুত করিবার কালে পরিত্যক্ত জঞ্জাল, যবসুরার মেয়া।

drăft, draught (drăft), *n.* **1.** (*Mil.*) A number of men selected for some special purpose ; a selection of men for special duty ; as, these important posts were weakened by heavy *drafts* ; (সামরিক শাস্ত্র) কোন বিশেষ উদ্দেশ্যে নির্ব্বাচিত ব্যক্তিবর্গ ; কোন বিশেষ কার্য্য সাধনের জন্য ব্যক্তি-নির্ব্বাচন। **2.** Drawing of money by written order ; a bill or cheque drawn, esp. by one branch of a bank on another ; লিখিত আদেশ দ্বারা টাকা তোলন ; হুণ্ডী। **3.** A demand ; as, a *draft* on national resources or on one's patience, confidence, etc. ; দাবি। **4.** A sketch of work to be executed ; an outline ; as, a *draft* of a poem or painting ; পাণ্ডু, মুসাবিদা ; পাণ্ডুলিপি। **5.** A rough copy of a document ; খসড়া। **6.** (*Masonry*) A chisel-dressing along the margin of a stone's surface ; (গাঁথুনির কাজ) স্থাপত্য ভূষাবিশেষ। 7. (*Naut.*) The depth of water necessary to float or the depth a ship sinks in water ; (নৌ-বিদ্যা) জাহাজ ভাসিতে হইলে জল যতটা গভীর হওয়া আবশ্যক হয়, গহেরা।

drăft, draught (drăft), *v. t.* **1.** To draw as a party esp. of troops by selection for a special duty from a larger body ; কোন, বিশেষ কার্য্যের জন্য একদল লোক বিশেষতঃ সেনাবাহিনী হইতে একদল সেনা নির্ব্বাচিত করা। **2.** To prepare a rough copy of a document, esp. a Parliamentary Bill ; to draw up ; খসড়া খাড়া বা প্রস্তুত করা ; মুসাবিদা করা, পাণ্ডুলিপি প্রস্তুত করা। **Draft'-, Draught'-er,** *ns.*

drăfts'-măn, draughts'-măn (drăfts-), *ns.* **1.** One who makes drawings or designs ; নকসানবীস। **2.** One who drafts or draws up documents or Parliamentary Bills ; পাণ্ডুলিপি প্রস্তুতকারী, যে ব্যক্তি দলীল প্রভৃতি মুসাবিদা করে, যে ব্যক্তি পার্লেমেন্টের আইনের পাণ্ডুলিপি প্রস্তুত করে।

drăg, *v. t.* & *i.* **1.** To pull along with force ; to haul ; as, to *drag* a net in fishing ; to allow to trail ; as, the ship *drags* her anchor ; টানিয়া নেওয়া, ছেঁচড়ান ; জোরে টানা (জাল) ; ঘষড়াইতে দেওয়া। **2.** To continue tediously; "I *drag* a wretched life without him ;" অতিকষ্টে অতিবাহিত করা। **3.** To harrow as lands ; (ক্ষেতে) বিদা দেওয়া। **4.** To sweep with a drag as a river, pond, etc., in search of anything ; (also *fig.*) "I *dragged* my brains for such a song ;" জালদিয়া পুকুর ছাকা (অপিচ লক্ষণায়)। **5.** To catch with a drag-net ; as, to *drag* pearls ; বেড় জাল বা টানা জাল দ্বারা ধরা। ***Verb i.*** **1.** To be moved onward along the ground ; to trail behind or move with friction ; as, an anchor *drags* (fails to hold) ; ছেঁচড়াইয়া যাওয়া ; মাটীতে ঘষড়াইয়া যাওয়া। **2.** To go on lingeringly ; to be tediously protracted ; আস্তে আস্তে যাওয়া ; মন্দ মন্দ গতিতে অগ্রসর হওয়া। **To drag an anchor** — (*Naut.*) To trail the anchor along the bottom when it will not hold the ship ; (নৌবিদ্যা) নোঙ্গর জলতলের মৃত্তিকাতে ঘষড়াইয়া নেওয়া। **To drag in**—To introduce as a subject needlessly ; অনর্থক কোন কথা পাড়া। **To drag in by the head and shoulders**— সজোরে টানিয়া লওয়া। **To drag on**—(*v. t.* & *i.*) To continue or protract tediously ; অতিশয় কষ্টে অতিবাহিত করা, অবসাদক ভাবে দীর্ঘ করিয়া তোলা। **To drag out**— To protract to a tedious end ; অবসাদকর ভাবে দীর্ঘ করা। To draw out by main force ; সবলে টানিয়া বাহির করা। **To drag up**— (*Colloq.*) To rear roughly as a child ; (চলিত ভাষায়) রুক্ষভাবে লালন পালন করা।

drăg, *n.* **1.** A heavy harrow ; একপ্রকার ভারি বিদা বা মৈ। **2.** A kind of sledge for conveying heavy goods ; গুরুভার পদার্থ বহনের জন্য একপ্রকার (বরফের উপর টানার উপযোগী) ক্ষুদ্র চক্র বিশিষ্ট বা চক্রহীন গাড়ী। **3.** A four-horsed private vehicle like a stage-coach ; একপ্রকার চারি ঘোড়ার গাড়ী। **4.** A device for dredging or recovering a drowned person etc. ; জলমগ্ন ব্যক্তিকে উত্তোলনার্থ কৌশলবিশেষ। **5.** An iron-shoe for retarding a vehicle down-hill ; পর্ব্বত হইতে অবতরণ কালে শকটের গতি মন্দীভূত করার জন্য লৌহময়-পাদুকা বিশেষ। **6.** An obstacle to progress or enjoyment ; "She was a *drag* on his carrier ;" উন্নতির বাধা, আনন্দের বিঘ্ন। **7.** A drag net ; টানা জাল। **8.** (*Hunting*) A strong smelling thing (drawn along the ground to leave a scent) for animals, esp. hounds to follow instead of a fox ; a club or association for pursuing this sport ; (মৃগয়া) একপ্রকার উগ্রগন্ধ দ্রব্য (ইহাদ্বারা ভূমিতে একটী রেখা টানায় শিকারী জন্তুগণ বিশেষতঃ কুক্কুরসকল শৃগালের পশ্চাদ্ধাবন পরিত্যাগ করিয়া ঐ রেখার অনুসরণ করে) ; উক্তপ্রকার ক্রীড়ার জন্য সম্মিলনী। **9.** Slow and heavy motion ; "A *drag* in his walk ;" ধীর-মন্থর গতি, গজেন্দ্র গমন। **Drag-anchor**—রজ্জুদ্বারা সংবদ্ধপ্রবমান আধার বিশেষ — ইহাদ্বারা বাতাহত জাহাজের পার্শ্ববিচলন নিবারিত হয়। **Drag-chain**—শৃঙ্খলবিশেষ — যদ্দারা চক্রসকল নিবদ্ধ হইয়া শকটের গতি হ্রাসপ্রাপ্ত হয়। (*Fig.*) An impediment ; (লক্ষণায়) বিঘ্ন, বাধা, প্রতিবন্ধক। **Drag-net**— বেড় জাল, টানা জাল।

drăg'-gle, *v. t.* & *i.* To make wet and dirty by dragging along the ground ; মাটীর উপর ছেঁচড়াইয়া ভিজান বা কাদা লাগান, কর্দ্দম-লুণ্ঠিত করা। ***Verb i.*** **1.** To trail on the ground ; ছেঁচড়ান। **2.** To straggle in the rear ; পশ্চাদ্দিকে পথ হারাইয়া বিপথে ঘূরা। **Draggle-trail(ed) woman**—যে স্ত্রীলোকের কাপড়ের আঁচল বা গাউনের প্রান্তভাগ মাটীতে ঘষড়াইয়া যায়।

drăg'-ō-măn, *n.* An interpreter esp. in Arabic, Turkish, Persian ; দোভাষী, বিশেষতঃ আরব, তুরস্ক, পারস্য ভাষায়।

drăg'-ŏn, *n.* **1.** A mythical winged monster (like a crocodile or a snake with wings and claws and breathing fire) ; গ্রীক পুরাণোক্ত সপক্ষ, সনখর এবং অগ্নিশ্বাসী সর্পবিশেষ। **2.** The guardian of treasure or of female chastity ; a fierce violent or a strict person specif. such a woman ; a duenna ; ধনরক্ষক, যক্ষ, সতীত্বধর্ম্ম রক্ষাকারী ; অতিশয় উগ্রস্বভাব

ব্যক্তি, অতিশয় কড়া লোক; যুবতীর অভিভাবিকা বর্ষীয়সী স্ত্রীলোক; উগ্রচণ্ডা-নারী। 3. (*Astron.*) Draco; (জ্যোতির্বিজ্ঞান) অজগর তারা (হিঃ কোঃ)। 4. (*Bible*) A serpent; a crocodile; a jackal; a whale or a shark; (বাইবেল) সর্প; কুম্ভীর; শৃগাল; তিমি বা হাঙ্গর। 5. A kind of pigeon; এক প্রকার কপোত। 6. A kind of lizard; এক প্রকার টিকটিকি। **Dragon fly**—ঝিল্লী ফড়িং। **Dragon's blood**—A wing-leaved, slender-stemmed palm, similar to that which furnishes the chair-canes; অপ্রং (বেত্র সদৃশ বৃক্ষ বিশেষ) (যোঃ)। Bright red gum exuding from a kind of palm fruit; রক্তভরত (ওয়াট্), লালবণ (ঐ), আমতল (ঐ)। **Dragon's head**—রাহু। **Dragon's tail**—কেতু। **Dragon's teeth**—Seeds of future ruin or destruction; ভবিষ্যৎ ধ্বংসের বীজ, বিষবৃক্ষের বীজ। [Jason এবং Cadmus স্বপক্ষ সর্পের দন্ত বপন করিয়াছিলেন, এবং তাহা হইতে সশস্ত্র সৈন্যগণ উত্থিত হইয়া পরস্পরকে যুদ্ধে নিহত করে। এই শব্দটী গ্রীক্ পুরাণের উল্লিখিত বর্ণনা হইতে গৃহীত হইয়াছে।] **The old Dragon**—Satan; শয়তান।

Dragon fly.

drăg-ŏn-nāde′, *n.* & *v. t.* 1. (*Pl.*) Persecutions of Protestants under Louis XIV by quartering dragoons on them; ফরাসীরাজ চতুর্দ্দশ লুই কর্ত্তৃক প্রটেষ্টাণ্ট খৃষ্টানগণের নির্য্যাতন। 2. Persecution by troops; সৈন্যদ্বারা নির্য্যাতন, উৎপীড়ন। ***Verb t.*** To persecute by means of troops; সৈন্যদ্বারা উৎপীড়ন বা নির্য্যাতন করা।

dră-goon, *n.* & *v. t.* 1. (*Mil.*) Formerly a soldier who was taught and armed to serve either on horse-back or on foot; now, a mounted soldier; a heavy cavalry man; (সামরিক-শাস্ত্র) (পূর্ব্বে) যে সৈন্য পদাতিক ও অশ্বারোহিরূপে কার্য্য করার জন্য শিক্ষাপ্রাপ্ত হইত; (বর্ত্তমানে) অশ্বারোহী সৈন্য; গুরুভার অস্ত্রশস্ত্রে সজ্জিত অশ্বারোহী সৈন্য, সাদী (মঃ উঃ)। 2. A rough fierce fellow; দুর্দ্দান্ত ব্যক্তি। 3. A kind of pigeon, (also called *dragon*); একপ্রকার কপোত। ***Verb t.*** 1. To persecute by abandoning to the mercies of soldiers; সৈন্যদল ছাড়িয়া দিয়া নির্য্যাতন করা। 2. To force into a course by persecution; নির্য্যাতন দ্বারা ইচ্ছার বিরুদ্ধে কোন কাজ করান।

drail (drāl), *n.* A fish-hook and a line weighed with lead for dragging at depth through water; সীসার টুকরা-বাঁধা সূতা ও ছিপ।

drain (drān), *n.*, *v. t.* & *i.* 1. A channel through which water or other liquid flows; a sewer; জলনির্গম, প্রণালী, অববাহিকা, নর্দ্দমা, মুহুরী; পয়োনালা। 2. (*Surg.*) A tube for drawing off discharge from abscess etc.; (অস্ত্রোপচারবিদ্যা) ক্ষতাদি হইতে পুয নিঃসরণার্থ নল বিশেষ। 3. A constant outlet, demand or expenditure; as, a great *drain* on my resources; অবিরত নির্গম, দাবি, খরচ কিম্বা ব্যয়। 4. (*Slang*) A small draught; drink; এক চুমুক; পানীয়। ***Verb t.*** 1. To draw (liquid) by a conduit; নলদ্বারা জল টানিয়া লওয়া, চোয়ান। 2. To empty to the dregs; as, to *drain* a cup; to drink as a liquid; নিঃশেষে পান করা; পান করা। 3. To remove the superfluous water from; as, a river *drains* a district; জল নিকাশ করা। 4. To deprive of moisture; as, to *drain* a land; শুষ্ক করা। 5. To exhaust; শূন্য করা, নিঃশেষ করা। ***Verb i.*** 1. To flow off gradually; ক্রমশঃ জল নিকাশ হইয়া যাওয়া। 2. To get rid of moisture or liquor; as, set the wet cloth there to *drain*; শুষ্ক হওয়া। **Drain-traps**—পয়োনালী হইতে দূষিত বায়ুর নির্গম নিবারণের জন্য কৌশল বিশেষ।

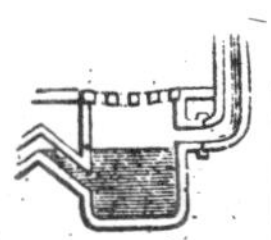

Drain traps shown in section.

drain′-āge (drān-), *n.* 1. Draining; জল নিকাশ করণ। 2. An artificial or natural system of drains: as, the *drainage* is skilfully extended; জলনিকাশের ব্যবস্থা, জলনির্গম প্রণালী (আঃ বঃ), পরিবাহ (হিঃ কোঃ)। 3. Area or district drained; as, the *drainage* of the Thames; জলনিকাশক্ষেত্র, পরিবাহক্ষেত্র। 4. (*Surg.*) The removal by a tube pus etc. from a wound; সচ্ছিদ্র রবারের সূক্ষ্ম নল প্রবিষ্ট করিয়া গভীর-মূল ক্ষতাদি হইতে পূযনিঃসরণ।

drain′-êr (drān-), *n.* 1. One who or that which drains; জল নিকাশকারী, নিঃশেষকারী। 2. A vessel in which things are put to drain; যে সচ্ছিদ্র পাত্রে জল ঝরাণের জন্য তরকারী প্রভৃতি রাখা হয়, ঝাঁঝরি।

drāke, *n.* A kind of ephemeral fly used in angling; একপ্রকার দিবসজীবী কীট, ইহা বড়শীর টোপস্বরূপ ব্যবহৃত হয়। **Green drake**—দিনজীবী কীটবিশেষ।

drāke, *n.* A male duck; হংস, মরাল, পাতিহাস।

drăm, *n.* 1. A weight of sixty grains; ৬০ গ্রেইণ। 2. A small draught of spirit etc.; এক চুমুক বা এক ঢোক সুরাসার প্রভৃতি। 3. A small or minute quantity; "Having not one *dram* of learning;" ঈষৎ পরিমাণ, কণা, বিন্দুমাত্র। **Dram-drinker**—যে ব্যক্তি অনুক্ষণ একটু একটু করিয়া মদ্যপান করে, মদখোর, সরাপখোর। **Dram-shop** — A public house; মদের দোকান, শুঁড়িখানা, শৌণ্ডিকালয়।

drâ′-mă, *n.* 1. A stage-play; দৃশ্যকাব্য, নাটক। 2. The dramatic art, literature, affairs (collectively);

as, one skilled in *drama* ; নাট্যকলা, নাট্যসাহিত্য, নাটকীয় বিষয়।

drā-măt′-ic, –i-căl, *adjs.* **1.** Pertaining to drama ; নাটক-সম্বন্ধীয়। **2.** Theatrical ; নাটকীয়। **3.** Fit for theatrical representation ; impressive ; as, a *dramatic* picture ; অভিনয়োপযোগী ; হৃদয়গ্রাহী। **4.** Representing another person's thoughts ; as, a *dramatic* utterance ; অন্যব্যক্তির চিন্তা প্রদর্শনকারী। **–i-cal-ly,** *adv.*

dramatis personæ, *n. pl.* List of characters in a play ; নাটকের পাত্রপাত্রীগণ, কুশীলবগণ।

drăm′-ăt-ist, *n.* A play-wright ; নাট্যকার, নাটকলেখক, নাটকপ্রণেতা।

drăm′-ă-tīze, *v. t.* & *i.* **1.** To convert into a play ; as, to *dramatize* a novel ; নাট্যাকারে পরিণত করা। **2.** To represent dramatically ; নাট্যবৎ প্রদর্শন করা। ***Verb i.*** To admit of being dramatized ; নাট্যাকারে পরিবর্ত্তন সহ হওয়া। **–ti-za′-tion,** *n.*

drăm′-ă-turge (-tŭrj), *n.* A play-wright ; নাট্যকার, নাট্যলেখক। **–tur′-gic, –tur′-gi-cal,** *adjs.*

drăm′-ă-tŭr-ġy̆, *n.* The art of dramatic composition and representation ; নাট্যকলা। **–gist,** *n.*

drāpe, *v. t.* **1.** To cover or adorn with cloth ; as, *to drape* a building ; বস্ত্রাবৃত করা, বস্ত্রমণ্ডিত করা। **2.** To arrange in graceful folds ; as, to *drape* clothes, hangings, etc. ; সুন্দর সুন্দর ভাঁজে সাজান।

drā′-pêr′, *n.* A dealer in cloth, linen, etc. ; বস্ত্র বিক্রেতা, সুতা ও পশমের কাপড়ের ব্যবসায়ী।

drā′-pêr-y̆, *n.* **1.** Cloth and woollen stuffs in general ; সুতা ও পশমের বস্ত্র, বস্ত্র-পণ্য। **2.** The trade of making and selling cloth ; a draper's trade ; বস্ত্র প্রভৃতির ব্যবসায়, বস্ত্র-ব্যবসায়। **3.** The representation of the clothing or dress of human figures in sculpture, painting, etc. ; মূর্ত্তিশিল্পে মনুষ্য-মূর্ত্তির পরিচ্ছদ প্রদর্শন, প্রচ্ছদপট (মঃ উঃ)। **4.** Clothing or hangings disposed in folds ; পাটকরা কাপড় বা ঝালর। **–ied,** *adj.*

drăs′-tic, *adj.* & *n.* **1.** Acting strongly ; extreme or radical in effect ; উগ্র ; চূড়ান্ত, আমূল-সংস্কারাত্মক। **2.** (*Med.*) Strongly purgative ; (ভৈষজ্যশাস্ত্র) অতিবিরেচক। ***Noun.*** (*Med.*) A strong purgative ; (ভৈষজ্যশাস্ত্র) অতিবিরেচক ঔষধ, স্রংসন (ঠাকুর)। **–ti-cal-ly,** *adv.*

drăt, *v. t.* (*Vulgar*) To curse ; to bother ; (ইতরভাষায়) শাপ দেওয়া ; উত্যক্ত করা, জ্বালাতন করা। **Drat′-ted,** *adj.*

draught (drăft), *n.* **1.** Drawing ; traction ; as, a beast of *draught* (বাহন) ; আকর্ষণ ; টান। **2.** Act of drawing a net ; the number of fishes taken in one sweep of a net ; জাল টানন ; একবার জাল টানিয়া যে পরিমাণ মৎস্য ধরা হয়। **3.** A single act of drinking ; ঢোক, চুমুক। **4.** The quantity of liquor taken at once, (also fig.) ; as, a *draught* of love, joy, etc. ; এক চুমুক, এক ঢোক। **5.** A dose of medicine ; a purgative ; একমাত্রা ঔষধ ; বিরেচক ঔষধ, জোলাপ। **6.** (*Naut.*) The depth of water necessary to float a ship ; জাহাজ ভাসাইতে হইলে জলের যতটা গভীরতা আবশ্যক হয়। **7.** (*Pl.*) A current of air in a room, chimney, etc. ; কক্ষ, ধূমনির্গম-নালী প্রভৃতিতে বায়ু-প্রবাহ। **8.** An outline ; a preliminary drawing for work or art ; নক্সা ; আদড়া। **9.** (*Pl.*) A game with 24 similar pieces on a board like that used in chess ; শতরঞ্চ ক্রীড়ার অনুরূপ ক্রীড়া বিশেষ, অষ্টাপদ ক্রীড়া (আঃ বঃ)। **10.** A rough copy of a document, (usu. *draft*) ; পাণ্ডুলিপি, খসড়া, মুশাবিদা। **11.** (*Mil.*) The force drawn, (usu. *draft*) ; (সামরিক শাস্ত্র) কোন বিশেষ কার্য্যের জন্য নির্ব্বাচিত সৈন্যদল। **12.** (*Comm.*) A written order for the payment of money ; withdrawing of money from a fund in a bank ; (usu. *draft*) ; হুণ্ডী ; কোন ধনাগার হইতে টাকা তোলন। **Draught′-i-ness,** *n.* **Draught′-y,** *adj.* **Beast of draught**—বাহন। **Black-draught** — বিরেচক ঔষধ, জোলাপ। **Draught-horse**—ভারবাহী অশ্ব। [Draught as verb see DRAFT.]

draughts′-măn(drăfts-), *n.* **1.** One who makes drawings, plans or sketches, (see *drafts-man*) ; নক্সা-নবীস, চিত্রকর, পটুয়া। **2.** One who drafts documents ; পাণ্ডুলিপি প্রস্তুতকারী। **3.** A man or piece used in the game of draught ; শতরঞ্চের অনুরূপ ক্রীড়াবিশেষে ব্যবহৃত গুটিকা, শারি (আঃ বঃ)। **–ship,** *n.*

draw (drä), *v. t.* & *i.* & *n.* **1.** To pull along ; to haul ; টানা ; বলপূর্ব্বক আকর্ষণ করা, টানিয়া আনা। **2.** To pull out ; to unsheathe ; as, to *draw* a dagger ; টানিয়া ব্যবহার করা ; নিষ্কাসিত করা। **3.** To drag a criminal to the place of execution ; অপরাধীকে বধ্যভূমিতে লইয়া যাওয়া। **4.** To bring out from a receptacle ; as, to *draw* water from a well ; টানিয়া তোলা। **5.** To attract ; as, a popular speaker *draws* the eyes of an assembly ; আকর্ষণ করা। **6.** To contract ; to distort ; as, to speak with a *drawn* face ; সঙ্কুচিত করা ; বিরূপ করা। **7.** To inhale ; as, to *draw* sultry air ; নাসিকা দ্বারা টানিয়া লওয়া, শ্বাস দ্বারা গ্রহণ করা। **8.** To take from an oven ; as, to *draw* bread ; চুল্লী হইতে তুলিয়া লওয়া। **9.** To extract ; as, to *draw* spirit from grain ; to extract the essence of ; as, to *draw* tea ; নিষ্কর্ষিত করা ;

নির্যাস বাহির করা। **10.** To deduce as a conclusion from premise; to derive; "We do not *draw* the moral lessons from history;" উপপাদন করা; প্রাপ্ত হওয়া। **11.** To move gradually; as, they *drew* themselves more westerly; ক্রমশঃ অগ্রসর হওয়া। **12.** To extract the bowels of; as, to *draw* a fowl; অন্ত্র বহিষ্কার করা, নাড়ীভুঁড়ি বাহির করা। **13.** To cause to slide; to pull open or shut; as, to *draw* a curtain or veil; খোলা; উন্মোচন করা, বন্ধ করা, টানিয়া দেওয়া, টানিয়া সরান। **14.** To lengthen; "How long her face is *drawn*;" লম্বা করা, দীর্ঘ করা। **15.** To give vent to; as, to *draw* a deep sigh; বহির্গত করা। **16.** To make (one) reveal information, talent, etc.; কাহারো নিকট হইতে কোন খবর বাহির করা, ধীশক্তি প্রভৃতি ব্যক্ত করান। **17.** (*Cards*) To cause to be played; as, to *draw* all the trumps; (তাসক্রীড়া) খেলান। **18.** To take from a place of deposit; as, to *draw* money from a bank; (গচ্ছিত টাকা) তুলিয়া লওয়া, তোলা। **19.** To drain by emptying; to suck dry; as, a calf *draws* a cow; নিঃশেষে পান করা; চুষিয়া শুষ্ক করা। **20.** (*Hunting*) To search as a cover etc. for game; শিকারের উদ্দেশ্যে বন অনুসন্ধান করা। **21.** To drag a net through for fish; জাল টানা। **22.** To set forth in due form; as, to *draw* comparison or distinction; যথারীতি প্রদর্শন করা। **23.** To require a depth for floating; as, the ship *draws* 20 ft. of water; ভাসিবার পক্ষে (গভীরতা) আবশ্যক হওয়া, গহেরা হওয়া। **23.** To represent by lines drawn on a plain surface; as, to *draw* the figure of a man; রেখাঙ্কন করা, অঙ্কিত করা। **24.** To entice; to allure; প্রলুব্ধ করা; প্রলোভন দ্বারা আকৃষ্ট করা। **25.** To gain; to earn; as, the shop-keeper *draws* a hundred pounds; to get; as, to *draw* one's salary; লাভ করা; অর্জ্জন করা; পাওয়া। **26.** To describe in words; as, to *draw* men as they ought to be, not as they are; বর্ণনা করা। **27.** To bend; as, to *draw* a bow; নত করা, বক্র করা, বাঁকান। **28.** (*Cricket*) To divert a ball with the bat; (ক্রীকেট ক্রীড়ায়) ব্যাটদ্বারা আঘাত করিয়া বল একপার্শ্বে চালিত করা। **29.** (*Golf*) To drive a ball too much to the left; (গল্‌ফ্ ক্রীড়া) কোন বল অনেকটা বেশী বাম দিকে চালিত করা। **30.** To leave undecided; as, a *drawn* game or contest; অনিশ্চিত রাখা। **31.** To bring about or entail; as, he *drew* ruin upon himself; সংঘটিত করা, ঘটান, ডাকিয়া আনা। **32.** To drag out of a hole, as a fox, etc.; গর্ত্ত হইতে টানিয়া বাহির করা। **33.** To get from a source; as, to *draw* information from etc.; মূলস্থান হইতে প্রাপ্ত হওয়া। ***Verb i.*** **1.** To pull; to exert strength in pulling anything; as, the horse *draws* well; টানা; কোন কিছু টানার জন্ত জোর করা। **2.** To attract; as, play *draws* well; আকর্ষণ করা। **3.** To unsheathe a sword; as, he *drew* upon me; অসি নিষ্কাসিত করা। **4.** To delineate; as, he *draws* with exactness; অঙ্কিত করা। **5.** (*Med.*) To cause to suppurate; (ভৈষজ্য-শাস্ত্র) পুযোৎপাদন করা। **6.** (*Naut.*) To swell with wind; as, sails *draw*; (নৌ-বিদ্যা) বাতাসে ফুলিয়া উঠা। **7.** To assemble round some centre; as, we *drew* round the table; কোন কিছুর চতুঃপার্শ্বে জড় হওয়া। **8.** To move; সরা। **9.** To shrink; "To *draw* into less room;" সঙ্কুচিত হওয়া। **10.** To produce a draft or current; বায়ু-প্রবাহ উৎপাদন করা। **11.** To advance; as, the day *draws* on; অগ্রসর হওয়া। **12.** To make a draft or demand; (also *fig.*); as, to *draw* on one's imagination; দাবি করা; (অপিচ লক্ষণায়) কল্পনাবলে রচনা করা। **13.** To sink in water; জলে ডুবা, নিমজ্জিত হওয়া। ***Noun.*** **1.** Act of drawing; pull; আকর্ষণ; টান। **2.** Attraction; a thing that draws custom or attention; আকর্ষণ; চিত্তাকর্ষক দ্রব্য। **3.** Act of drawing lots; সুরতি খেলায় ভাগ্য-পরীক্ষা করণ। **4.** A drawn game; যে ক্রীড়ায় ফলাফল অনিশ্চিত থাকে, চটা-বাজি। **5.** A thing or person employed to elicit from a person what he knows or intends to do; যে ব্যক্তি বা বস্তুর সাহায্যে কোন ব্যক্তির নিকট হইতে কোন খবর বা তাহার উদ্দেশ্য বাহির করা হয়। **Drawn,** *p. p.* of DRAW. **A drawn game**—যে ক্রীড়ার ফলাফল অনিশ্চিত থাকে। **Long drawn agony**—Protracted agony; দীর্ঘ কালস্থায়ী যন্ত্রণা। **To draw a blank** — To be unsuccessful in the drawing of lottery; স্ফূর্তিখেলায় বাজি হারা। **To draw a cover**—To clear a cover of the game it contains; বন হইতে শিকার বাহির করা। **To draw a curtain**—To shut out of sight or expose to view; পর্দ্দা টানিয়া দেওয়া, পর্দ্দা সরান। **To draw a prize** — To be successful in the drawing of a lottery; স্ফূর্তি খেলায় বাজি জিতা। **To draw aside**—টানিয়া সরাইয়া নেওয়া। **To draw a veil over**—To conceal from public view; অবগুণ্ঠন টানিয়া দেওয়া, লোক-চক্ষুর অন্তরাল করা। **To draw back**—To withdraw from an undertaking;

কোন কার্য্য হইতে নিবৃত্ত হওয়া বা সরিয়া পড়া। **To draw blank**—(মৃগয়া) শিকারের অনুসন্ধানে বনে যাইয়া সফলকাম না হওয়া। **To draw breath**—To hold life; বাঁচিয়া থাকা, জীবন ধারণ করিয়া থাকা। **To draw briddle, bit or rein**—To stop riding or driving by checking horses etc.; লাগাম টানা, বল্গা সংযত করা। (*Fig.*) To check or control oneself; (লক্ষণায়) আত্ম-সংযত করা, নিজকে দমন করা। **To draw by**—To draw aside; টানিয়া সরান। **To draw cloth**—To clear table after meal; ভোজনান্তে মেজ পরিষ্কার করা। **To draw down**—To cause to fall upon a person etc.; to bring down; কাহারও উপর আপতিত করান; অবনত করা। (*Cookery*) To stew or boil down; (রন্ধন-বিদ্যা) মৃদু-সন্তাপে সিদ্ধ করা। **To draw in**—To entice; to induce to take part; প্রলুব্ধ করা; কোন কার্য্যে যোগ দেওয়ার জন্য প্রলুব্ধ করা। To close in as a day; to become shorter (of successive days); শেষ হইয়া আসা; দিবস (পরম্পর সম্পর্কে) ক্রমশঃ ছোট হওয়া। **To draw it mild**—To refrain from exaggeration; অতিরঞ্জিত বর্ণনা না করা। **To draw level**—To overtake; নিকটে আসিয়া পড়া, লাগাইল ধরা। **To draw nigh** or **near**—To approach; ঘনিয়ে আসা। **To draw off,** *v. t.* & *i.* To withdraw as troops from a position; কোন স্থান হইতে সৈন্যদল উঠাইয়া লওয়া। (*Verb i.*) (Of troops) To withdraw; to retire; (সৈন্য-সম্পর্কে) চলিয়া আসা; সরিয়া পড়া। **To draw on,** *v. t.* & *i.* To bring about; to lead to; ঘটান; উৎপাদন করা, আনয়ন করা। To entice; to allure; প্রলুব্ধ করা; ভুলান, ফুসলান। (*Verb i.*) To approach; "Evening *drew on*;" সমীপবর্ত্তী হওয়া। **To draw one against**—To attack; আক্রমণ করা। **To draw out,** *v. t.* & *i.* To array or detach as troops; ব্যূহবদ্ধ করা কিম্বা বিশেষ কার্য্যের জন্য মূল সৈন্য দল হইতে বিচ্ছিন্ন করা। To prolong; as, to *draw out* one's prayers; দীর্ঘ করা। To induce to talk; to elicit; কথা বলিতে প্রলুব্ধ করা; বাহির করা। (*Verb i.*) To become longer as days; দীর্ঘ হওয়া (দিবস সম্বন্ধে)। To draw up, as a bill; to delineate; পাণ্ডুলিপি প্রস্তুত করা; নক্সা করা। **To draw over**—To obtain by distillation; পরিস্রুত করিয়া পাওয়া। To convert to one's party or interest; কাহারও পক্ষভুক্ত করা। **To draw the long bow**—See BOW. **To draw the line at**—To refuse to go as far as or beyond; কোন নির্দ্দিষ্ট রেখা পর্য্যন্ত কিংবা তাহার বাহিরে যাইতে অস্বীকার করা। **To draw the sword**—যুদ্ধ আরম্ভ করা। **To draw the wool over**—To deceive; চোখে ধূলি দেওয়া। **To draw to a head**—To begin to suppurate; পাকিয়া উঠা। **To draw together**—To collect or come together or closer; নিকটে আসা, কাছে আসা। **To draw up,** *v. i.* & *t.* To stop; to come to a halt; to come, (with *to* or *with*, meaning *to overtake*); থামা; চলিতে চলিতে হঠাৎ থামা; লাগাইল ধরা। To come into regular order as troops; ব্যূহবদ্ধ হওয়া, সজ্জিত হওয়া। (*Verb t.*) To arrange in order—as a body of troops; ব্যূহবদ্ধ করা, শৃঙ্খলা পূর্ব্বক স্থাপন করা। To compose as a document etc.; দলিলাদি মুসাবিদা করা। (Reflexive) To assume a stiff attitude; রুক্ষভাব ধারণ করা। **To draw upon**—To allure; প্রলুব্ধ করা। **To draw up with**—To enter into a state of intimacy; ঘনিষ্ঠতা স্থাপন করা। To be in a state of courtship; বিবাহের উদ্দেশ্যে পরস্পরের হৃদয়-পরিচয়ের জন্য মিলিত হওয়া।

draw'-băck (drä-) *n.* **1.** An amount of excise or import duty paid back or remitted on goods exported; ফেরৎ হাসিল, রেয়াইত নগদ। **2.** A deduction (*from*); "A *drawback from* his strength;" a hindrance; a disadvantage; "A serious *drawback* to our enjoyment;" কমি, অভাব, ন্যূনতা, ত্রুটি; বিঘ্ন, প্রতিবন্ধক; অসুবিধা। **A drawback lock**—যে দরজার তালা ভিতরের দিক হইতে হাতল ঘুরাইয়া ও বাহিরের দিক হইতে চাবিদ্বারা খোলা যায়।

draw'-bridge (drä-brĭj), *n.* A bridge that can be pressed up or let down at pleasure; একপ্রকার সেতু যাহা আবশ্যক মত উঠান ও নামান যায়।

Draw-bridge.

Draw'-căn-sir (drä-) *n* & *adj.* **1.** A person formidable both to friend and foe; শত্রু মিত্র উভয়ের পক্ষে করাল ব্যক্তি। (Villiersকৃত *Rehearsal* নামক গ্রন্থের চরিত্র বিশেষ।) **2.** A fierce swashbuckler; ষণ্ডা, গুণ্ডা। ***Adj.*** Formidable to both friend and foe; শত্রু মিত্র উভয়ের পক্ষে করাল।

draw-ee' (drä-ē), *n.* A person on whom a draft or a bill of exchange is drawn; যে ব্যক্তির নিকট হইতে হুণ্ডীর টাকা আদায় করা হয়, আদিষ্টনিষ্কর্ষ (অঃ বঃ)।

draw'-êr (drä-), *n.* **1.** One who, or that which, draws; আকর্ষক। **2.** One who issues a draft or bill of exchange; যে ব্যক্তি হুণ্ডী কাটে,

হুণ্ডীদাতা, হুণ্ডীর মহাজন, নিষ্কর্ষক (আঃ বঃ)। 3. A sliding box or case in a table, desk, etc., which can be drawn out or pushed in at pleasure ; টানা দেরাজ। 4. A draftsman ; নক্সা-নবীস। 5. (*Pl.*) An undergarment worn on the lower body and the legs ; পোষাকের নীচে পরার জন্য একপ্রকার আঁট-সাঁট ইজের, জজ্বাবার (আঃ বঃ)। **—ful,** *adj.* **Chest of drawers**—টানা দেরাজ।

draw'-ing (drä-), *n.* 1. The act of pulling, hauling or attracting, etc. ; আকর্ষণ, টানন। 2. Act of taking lots etc. ; the act of distributing prizes in a lottery ; স্ফূর্তিখেলায় বাজি রাখন ; স্ফূর্তিখেলায় প্রাপ্ত পুরস্কার বিতরণ। 3. The art or act of representing by lines ; delineation without colour ; রেখাঙ্কন ; অঙ্কন। 4. A representation drawn by pen, pencil, etc. ; a picture ; a sketch ; রেখা-চিত্র ; চিত্র, আলেখ্য ; নক্সা। **Drawing-board**—যে ফলকোপরি চিত্রাঙ্কণের কাগজ প্রসারিত করা হয়। **Drawing-compass(es)**—একপ্রকার বৃত্তাঙ্কন-যন্ত্র, যাহার একটী বাহুতে কলম কিংবা পেন্সিল সংযুক্ত থাকে। **Drawing-pin**—যে আলপিন দ্বারা চিত্রাঙ্কণের কাগজ ফলকোপরি সংবদ্ধ করা হয়। **Drawing-room**—A room for reception of a company ; the room to which ladies retire after dinner ; বৈঠকখানা, রঙমহল ; ভোজনান্তে মহিলাগণ যে কক্ষে বিশ্রাম করেন। A levee ; a formal reception esp. at court ; প্রাভাতিক দরবার ; দরবার।

drawl (dräl), *v. t., i.* & *n.* To utter in a slow and sleepy manner ; তন্দ্রাজড়িত স্বরে ধীরে ধীরে উচ্চারণ করা, গেঙ্গাইয়া গেঙ্গাইয়া কথা বলা। ***Verb i.*** To speak with slow and lingering utterance from laziness, lack of spirit, or affection, etc. ; চিবাইয়া চিবাইয়া কথা বলা, মন্দ মন্দ উচ্চারণ করা। ***Noun.*** Slow utterance ; চিবাইয়া চিবাইয়া কথা। **Drawl'-ing-ly** *adv.*

drawn (drän), *p. adj.* 1. Undecided ; অনিশ্চিতজয়-পরাজয়। 2. Unsheathed ; নিষ্কাষিত। **At daggers drawn**—পরস্পরের প্রতি খড়্গহস্ত।

draw'-wĕll (drä-), *n.* A deep well with a rope and a bucket ; পাতকূয়া, কূপ।

dray (drā), *n.* A low (esp. a brewer's) cart without sides for carrying heavy loads ; গুরুভার-দ্রব্য বহনোপযোগী পার্শ্ববিহীন অনুচ্চ শকট বিশেষ অপার্শ্ব শকট। **Dray-horse**—অপার্শ্ব শকটের অশ্ব। **Dray-man**—অপার্শ্ব শকট চালক।

dread (drĕd), *adj., n.* & *v. t.* 1. Causing terror ; frightful ; ভয়াবহ, ভীষণ, ভয়ানক, ভয়ঙ্কর, লোমহর্ষণ, ঘোর ; করাল। 2. Awe-inspiring ; ভীতি সঞ্চারক। ***Noun.*** 1. Great fear ; মহাভয়, ত্রাস। 2. Reverential fear ; ভক্তিজড়িত ভীতি। 3. An object of fear or awe ; ভয়ের পাত্র। ***Verb t.*** To fear greatly ; মহাভয়াকুল হওয়া।

dread'-fûl (drĕd-), *adj.* 1. Terrible ; awe-inspiring ; করাল, রৌদ্র ; ঘোর, বিকট, ভৈরব, ভয়ানক, ভয়াবহ, ভীষণ, ভয়ঙ্কর। 2. Troublesome ; disagreeable ; extremely bad, great or long ; "We awaited a *dreadful* time ;" কষ্টদায়ক ; অপ্রীতিকর ; নিতান্ত মন্দ, অত্যন্ত অধিক, অতি দীর্ঘ। **—ly,** *adv.* **A penny dreadful**—নরহত্যা, স্ত্রীলোকের উপর পাশব অত্যাচার, প্রভৃতি ভয়াবহ ঘটনার বিবরণপূর্ণ পেনি মূল্যের পত্রিকা।

dread'-nought (drĕd-nŏt), *n.* 1. A thick cloth used for garments for stormy weather ; such a garment ; একপ্রকার স্থূল বস্ত্র ; উক্তরূপ বস্ত্রনির্ম্মিত পরিচ্ছদ। 2. A superior type of warship ; একপ্রকার উচ্চশ্রেণীর রণপোত, অভয়পোত।

dream (drēm), *n., v. t.* & *i.* 1. A series of pictures or events passing through the mind during sleep ; স্বপ্ন। 2. (*Fig.*) A matter which has only an imaginary reality ; "The *dream* of youth ;" reverie ; as, to live in a *dream* ; a vision ; (লক্ষণায়) অলীক কল্পনা, খেয়াল, ভ্রান্তি ; ধ্যান, বিচিন্তা ; অলৌকিক দৃশ্য। 3. Something of dreamlike beauty or charm ; স্বপ্নবৎ সুন্দর ও মুগ্ধকর বিষয়। ***Verb t.*** To see or hear in a dream ; স্বপ্নে দর্শন বা শ্রবণ করা। ***Verb i.*** 1. To have visions in sleep ; স্বপ্নে দর্শন করা। 2. To think ; to imagine ; as, he little *dreamed* of his approaching fate ; to consider even the possibility (of) ; as, you can *dream* of your success ; ভাবা ; কল্পনা করা ; সম্ভবপর বলিয়াও মনে করা। 3. To be inactive or unpractical ; নিশ্চেষ্ট হওয়া, অসাংসারিক হওয়া। **Dream'-er,** *n.* **Dream'-less,** *adj.* **Dream'-like,** *adj.* **Day-dream, waking dream**—দিবাস্বপ্ন, জাগ্রৎ স্বপ্ন, অলীক কল্পনা, আকাশকুসুম, গগননগর। **Dream-hole**—বুরুজ প্রভৃতির প্রাচীরে আলোক প্রবেশের ছিদ্র। **Dream-reader** — স্বপ্নফলবিচারক, স্বপ্ন-বিচারী (মঃ উঃ), স্বপ্নবিৎ (ঐ)। **Dream-world, —land**—স্বপ্নজগৎ, স্বপ্নলোক, স্বপ্নরাজ্য, মায়ারাজ্য, কল্পনারাজ্য। **To dream away** or **out etc.**—নিশ্চেষ্টতায় কিম্বা অলীক কল্পনায় সময় কাটাইয়া দেওয়া।

dream'-ŷ (drēm-), *adj.* 1. (*Poet.*) Full of dreams ; (কবিতায়) স্বপ্নময়। 2. Fanciful ; given to reverie ; কাল্পনিক ; ধ্যানশীল। 3. Visionary ; misty ; স্বাপ্নিক ; অস্পষ্ট। **—i-ly,** *adv.* **—i-ness,** *n.*

drear (drēr), *adj.* (*Poet*) Same as DREARY. **Drear'-ly,** *adv.* **Drear'-ness,** *n.*

drear'-ŷ (drēr-), *adj.* Comfortless ; gloomy ; dull ; আরামহীন ; নিরানন্দ, অপ্রসন্ন ; মলিন। **—i-ly,** *adv.* **—i-ness,** *n.*

dredge (drĕj), *n., v. t. & i.* **1.** A kind of drag-net for bringing oysters, shell-fish, etc. from the bottom ; একপ্রকার টানা জাল—যদ্দারা সমুদ্রতলস্থ শুক্তি, কড়ি প্রভৃতি ধরা হয়। **2.** A machine for clearing beds of rivers etc. ; নদী প্রভৃতির গর্ভ হইতে কর্দ্দমাদি উত্তোলনার্থ যন্ত্রবিশেষ, তলকর্ষিণী। ***Verb t.*** **1.** To bring up or clear away with a dredge ; টানাজালদ্বারা শুক্তি, কড়ি প্রভৃতি ধরা, তলকর্ষিণী দ্বারা নদ্যাদির গর্ভ হইতে কর্দ্দমোত্তোলন করা। **2.** To excavate with a dredge ; তলকর্ষিণী দ্বারা খনন করা। ***Verb i.*** To use a dredge ; তলকর্ষিণী ব্যবহার করা। **Dredg′-er,** *n.* Same as DREDGE 2 above.

dredge (drĕj), *v. t.* **1.** To sprinkle with flour or other powder ; as, to *dredge* a roast ; ময়দা কিম্বা অন্য কোনরূপ চূর্ণ ছিটাইয়া দেওয়া। **2.** To sprinkle (flour etc.) over roast-meat etc. ; ভর্জ্জিত মাংসাদির উপর (ময়দা প্রভৃতি) ছড়ান। **Dredg′-er,** *n.* A box with perforated lid for sprinkling, (also called a *dredge-box*) ; ময়দা প্রভৃতি ছড়াইবার জন্য সচ্ছিদ্র ঢাকনিযুক্ত পাত্রবিশেষ।

dree (drē), *v. t.* (*Archaic*) To endure ; (অপ্রচলিত) সহ্য করা, বরদাস্ত করা। **To dree one's weird**—To submit to one's lot ; নিয়তির হস্তে আত্মসমর্পণ করা।

drĕg, *n.* (*Usu. pl.*) **1.** Sediment ; lees ; তলানি, গাদ, তলছাট, মল ; শিটা, কাইট, কিট্ট। **2.** Worthless part ; refuse ; অসার অংশ ; জঞ্জাল, আবর্জ্জনা। **3.** (*Sing.*) A remnant ; a residue ; (একবচন) উচ্ছিষ্ট ; অবশেষ। **Dreg′-gy,** *adj.* **Dregs of society**—সমাজের আবর্জ্জনা। **To drink or drain to the dregs**—To drink completely, leaving nothing ; নিঃশেষে পান করা।

drĕnch, *n. & v. t.* **1.** A dose of medicine for a beast ; গবাদি পশুর জন্য একমাত্রা ঔষধ। **2.** A soaking or downpour ; ধারাবর্ষণ, মুষলধারে বারিবর্ষণ। ***Verb t.*** **1.** To cause or make to drink ; পান করান। **2.** To force (an animal) to take a draught of medicine ; বলপূর্ব্বক (পশুকে) ঔষধসেবন করান। **3.** To soak ; to steep ; ভিজান ; ডুবান। **4.** To wet all over with liquid falling or thrown upon the object ; সর্ব্বাঙ্গ ভিজাইয়া দেওয়া, আপাদমস্তক আর্দ্র করা, সম্পূর্ণরূপে ভিজাইয়া দেওয়া।

drĕnch′-êr, *n.* **1.** One who or that which wets ; আর্দ্রকারী। **2.** A drenching shower of rain ; ধারাবর্ষণ, মুষলধারে বারিবর্ষণ। **3.** An apparatus for giving drench to a beast ; পশুদিগকে ঔষধ সেবন করাইবার জন্য যন্ত্রবিশেষ।

drĕss, *n., v. t. & i.* **1.** Clothes ; esp. ceremonial or distinctive apparel ; বেশ, বেষ, পরিচ্ছদ ; পোষাক। **2.** A lady's gown ; স্ত্রীলোকের ঘাগরা। **3.** Attention to apparel or skill in adjusting it ; as, men of pleasure, *dress* and gallantry ; বেষানুরাগ, পরিচ্ছদানুরাগ বেষরচনা-কুশলতা। **4.** External covering ; as, birds in their winter *dress* ; বহিরাবরণ, গাত্রাবরণ। **5.** Outward form ; as, a French book appearing in English *dress* ; বাহ্যাকার। ***Verb t.*** **1.** To provide (one self) with dress etc. ; বেষসমন্বিত করা। **2.** (*Mil.*) To arrange in exact continuity of line as soldiers ; as, *dress* your ranks ; (সামরিক শাস্ত্র) সৈন্য প্রভৃতি এক অবিচ্ছিন্ন রেখায় সজ্জিত করা। **3.** To clothe ; সজ্জিত করা। **4.** (*Med.*) To treat medically with remedies, bandages, etc. ; as, the surgeon *dressed* the wound ; (ভৈষজ্য-শাস্ত্র) ক্ষতস্থান ধৌত করত তাহাতে ঔষধ লাগাইয়া বস্ত্র দ্বারা বন্ধন করা। **5.** To fit for any use ; to get ready ; to prepare for cooking ; as, to *dress* a fowl ; কোন কার্য্যের জন্য ঠিকঠাক করা ; প্রস্তুত করা ; রন্ধনের জন্য প্রস্তুত করা। **6.** To train and smoothe as a stone ; পাথর কাটিয়া পালিশ করা। **7.** To smooth or finish off, as leather, a fabric, etc. ; চর্ম্ম প্রভৃতি মসৃণ করা, পরিকর্ম্মীকৃত করা। **8.** To cleanse from impurities ; as, to *dress* grain etc. ; পরিষ্কার করা, ঝাড়া। **9.** To provide or equip with costumes ; as, to *dress* a play ; পোষাক জোগান। **10.** To comb ; as, to *dress* one's hair ; আঁচড়ান, সংস্কার করা, রচনা করা। **11.** To curry ; as, to *dress* a horse ; খড়রা দ্বারা ঘোড়ার শরীর পরিষ্কার করা, খড়রা মারা। **12.** To deck ; to adorn ; as, to *dress* a ship with flags ; সজ্জিত করা ; ভূষিত করা, মণ্ডিত করা। **13.** To prune ; as, to *dress* a plant ; ছাঁটা। **14.** To till or weed as lands ; কর্ষণ করা, নিড়ান। **15.** To manure ; as, to *dress* the beds of a garden ; সার দেওয়া। ***Verb i.*** (*Mil.*) **1.** To come into correct place in a line, (a word of command to form alignment in ranks) ; (সামরিক শাস্ত্র) সৈন্যশ্রেণীতে যথাস্থানে আসা। **2.** To put on one's garments ; as, to *dress* for a ball ; পোষাক পরা। **Dress circle**—See under CIRCLE. **Dress-coat**—সন্ধ্যাকালে সম্ভ্রান্ত ব্যক্তিগণের পরিধেয় পশ্চাদ্দিকে তালচঞ্চু পক্ষীর পুচ্ছাকারে কর্ত্তিত অঙ্গাবরণ (কোর্ত্তা), কোর্ত্তা বিশেষ। **Dress-guard**—দ্বিচক্রযানের চক্রোপরিস্থ ধূলি-বারক, পরিচ্ছদ রক্ষক। **Dress-improver**—ইয়ুরোপীয় স্ত্রীগণের জঘন-বসন স্ফীত করিবার জন্য তল্প (গদি) বিশে **Dress-maker**—মহিলাগণের পে প্রস্তুতকারিণী। **Dress-parade**—পরিচ্ছদে শোভিত হইয়া সামরিক

প্রদর্শন। **Evening dress** (or simply *dress*) — অপরাহ্ন ভোজন বা সান্ধ্যসম্মিলনীতে পরিহিত পরিচ্ছদ বিশেষ, সান্ধ্য-পরিচ্ছদ। **Full dress**—উৎসবাদি উপলক্ষে পরিহিত পূর্ণ পরিচ্ছদ। **Morning dress**—প্রাভাতিক পরিচ্ছদ, সাধারণ পোষাক। **To dress down**—To thrash ; to scold ; উত্তম মধ্যম দেওয়া ; তিরস্কার করা। **To dress out** — To attire conspicuously ; জমকালো পোষাকে সজ্জিত করা। **To dress up**—To dress oneself (or another) elaborately ; জমকালো পোষাকে সজ্জিত হওয়া বা করা।

drĕss'-ĕr, *n.* A kitchen sideboard with shelves for dishes etc.; রান্নাঘরের বাসনপত্র রাখিবার তাক।

drĕss'-ĕr, *n.* **1.** One who dresses ; বেষকার, প্রসাধক। **2.** A surgeon's assistant in hospital operations ; ক্ষতাদি পরিষ্কারক ও বন্ধনকারক। **—ship,** *n.*

drĕss'-ing, *n.* **1.** Scolding ; thrashing ; তিরস্কার, গঞ্জনা ; প্রহার। **2.** Sauce ; stuffing of fowl etc. ; আচার, চাটনি ; মুরগী প্রভৃতির ভিতরে মসলাদির পুর দেওন। **3.** Manure ; সার। **4.** Bandages, ointments, etc. for a wound or sore ; ক্ষতাদির জন্য মলম, বস্ত্র-বন্ধনী, প্রভৃতি। **Dressing-case** — বেষভূষা রাখিবার আধার। **Dressing gown**—বেষভূষা করিবার সময় পরিহিত ঢিলা জামা। **Dressing-room**—শয়নকক্ষের সংলগ্ন কক্ষ বিশেষ, সাজঘর, প্রসাধন-কক্ষ বেষ-কক্ষ, নেপথ্য। **Dressing table**—যে মেজে বেষভূষা করিবার জন্য দর্পণ প্রভৃতি থাকে।

drĕss'-ȳ, *adj.* **1.** Fond of, or given to, showy dress ; পরিচ্ছদপ্রিয়, বেষানুরাগী, খুশ-পোষাকী। **2.** Stylish ; as, *dressy* clothes ; পোষাকী।

drib'-ble, *n., v. t.* & *i.* A small trickling stream or flow ; ক্ষুদ্র-জলপ্রবাহ। **2.** (*Foot-ball*) Act of dribbling a ball ; (পাদকন্দুক ক্রীড়ায়) আস্তে আস্তে কন্দুক তাড়ন। *Verb t.* **1.** To let fall in drops ; বিন্দু বিন্দু পাতিত করা, ক্ষরিত করা। **2.** (In foot-ball) To keep the ball moving forward little by little ; (পাদকন্দুক ক্রীড়ায়) আস্তে আস্তে কন্দুক সম্মুখের দিকে চালিত করা। *Verb i.* **1.** To fall in drops ; to trickle ; টপ্ টপ্ করিয়া পড়া, টুব্ টাব্ করিয়া পড়া, বিন্দু বিন্দু পতিত হওয়া, ফোঁটা ফোঁটা করিয়া পড়া ; ক্ষরিত হওয়া, ঝরা। **2.** (Of a child, idiot, etc.) To slaver ; (শিশু, জড়-বুদ্ধি ব্যক্তি প্রভৃতি সম্পর্কে) লালাস্রাব হওয়া, লালা বাহিয়া পড়া। **—bler,** *n.*

drib' –(b)lĕt, *n.* A small quantity or sum ; কিঞ্চিন্মাত্র জিনিষ, নামমাত্র জিনিষ, ঈষৎ পরিমাণ দ্রব্য, সামান্য টাকা, অকিঞ্চিৎকর অর্থ, অত্যল্প মুদ্রা। **By drib(b)lets**—By small quantities ; অল্প পরিমাণে।

drift, *n., v. t.* & *i.* **1.** State of being driven by current ; slow course or current ; প্রবাহতাড়িতাবস্থা ; ধীরপ্রবাহ, মৃদুবেগ, ধীরগতি। **2.** A heap of any matter driven together ; as, a *drift* of snow ; স্তূপাকারে সঞ্চিত বিতাড়িত পদার্থ সমূহ। **3.** Shower ; as, a *drift* of bullets ; বর্ষণ। **4.** Tendency ; meaning ; aim or scope ; "Now thou knowest my *drift* ;" উদ্দেশ্য, অভিপ্রায়, ঝোঁক ; মর্ম্ম, তাৎপর্য্য ; ভাব, আশয়। **5.** The deviation of a projectile owing to its rotatory movement ; ঘূর্ণনহেতু গোলার সরল রেখা হইতে বিচলন। **6.** A ship's deviation from its set course due to current ; স্রোতোবেগ হেতু পোতের পার্শ্ব-বিচলন। **7.** (*Forest law*) Gathering of cattle etc. at one place on a fixed day for determination of ownership etc. ; (আরণ্য আইন) স্বত্ব সাব্যস্ত করিবার জন্য কোন নির্দ্দিষ্ট দিবসে একস্থানে গোমহিষাদি জড়করণ। **8.** (*Geol.*) Earth, rock, etc. conveyed by glaciers and deposited over a country while submerged ; (ভূ-বিদ্যা) তুষার-নদীর দ্বারা স্থানান্তরিত স্তূপীকৃত মৃত্তিকা, কঙ্কর প্রভৃতি, হিমনীত (হিঃ কোঃ)। **9.** (*Mining*) A passage within the earth following a mineral vein ; (খনিজ-বিদ্যা) খনিজ পদার্থের শিরার অনুগামী পথবিশেষ। **10.** (*S. Africa*) A ford in a river ; (দক্ষিণ আফ্রিকা) নদীর (পদব্রজে) উত্তরণ-স্থান। **11.** A tool for enlarging or shaping a hole in metal ; ধাতু-ফলকের ছিদ্র গঠন বা বৃদ্ধি করণার্থ যন্ত্রবিশেষ। **12.** A large net arranged to drift with the tide, (also called a DRIFT-NET) ; একপ্রকার বৃহৎ জাল, যাহা স্রোতোবেগে ধীরে ধীরে ভাসিয়া চলে। *Verb t.* **1.** To drive or carry ; as, a current (of air or water) *drifts* a feather ; তাড়িত করা, বহিয়া নেওয়া, ভাসাইয়া নেওয়া। **2.** To drive into heaps ; as, wind *drifts* sand ; স্তূপীকৃত করা। **3.** To cover with drifts ; as, to *drift* roads, fields, etc. ; তুষারপ্রবাহসমানীত মৃত্তিকা, কঙ্কর প্রভৃতি দ্বারা আচ্ছাদিত করা। *Verb i.* **1.** To float ; to be driven along by a current of water or air ; as, the ship *drifted* astern ; to go passively or aimlessly ; as, the lazy *drift* through life ; ভাসা ; জলস্রোত বা বায়ুপ্রবাহদ্বারা চালিত হওয়া ; উদাসভাবে বা উদ্দেশ্য-হারার মত চলা। **2.** To be piled into heaps by wind etc. ; as, sand *drifts* ; বায়ু প্রভৃতি দ্বারা স্তূপাকার হওয়া। **3.** (*Mining*) To make a drift ; (খনিজ-বিদ্যা) খনিজ ধাতুর শিরার অনুগামী পথ প্রস্তুত করা। **4.** To become covered with drifts, as road etc. ; বালি, কঙ্কর, প্রভৃতিদ্বারা সমাচ্ছাদিত হওয়া। **Drift'-age,** *n.* **Drift'-less,** *adj.* Having no direction ; aimless ; লক্ষ্যহীন ; উদ্দেশ্যহীন। **Drift-current**—বায়ব্য স্রোত। **Drift-ice, —wood**—Ice, wood, driven by, water etc. ; জলে যে বরফ বা কাঠ ভাসিয়া আসে। **To drift in the streets**—To be left in the streets a-begging without any means to get on in the world ; পথে বসা, পথে দাঁড়ান।

drill *v., v. t.* & *i.* **1.** A pointed instrument for boring holes ; বেধন-যন্ত্র বিশেষ, বর্ম্মা। **2.** A kind of boring shell-fish ; একজাতীয় ছিদ্রকারী শঙ্খ। **3.** The act of training soldiers to their duty ; military exercise ; সামরিক-শিক্ষা প্রদান ; সৈন্য-ব্যায়াম, কসরৎ। **4.** (*Fig.*) A strict training or discipline ; কঠোর শিক্ষা, সুশিক্ষা। ***Verb t.*** **1.** To pierce with a drill ; to perforate ; as, to *drill* a piece of metal ; বর্ম্মাদ্বারা ছিদ্র করা ; ছিদ্র করা। **2.** To train in the military art ; সামরিক শাস্ত্রে সুশিক্ষিত করা। **3.** (*Fig.*) To discipline ; (লক্ষণায়) সুশিক্ষিত করা। ***Verb i.*** **1.** To pierce, (with *through* etc.) ; ভেদ করা। **2.** To undergo military exercise etc. ; to train oneself ; কসরৎ শিক্ষা

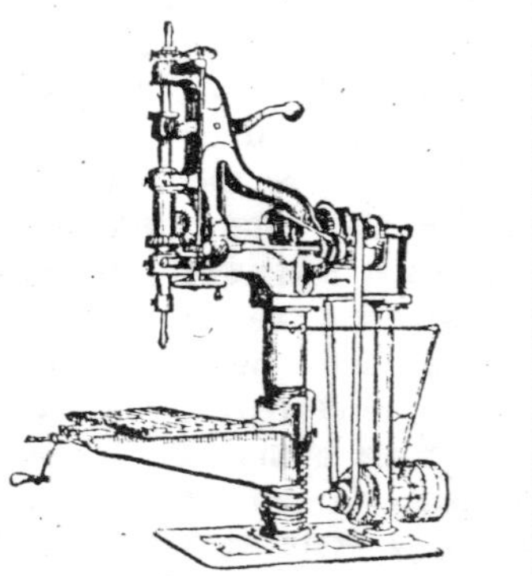

Drill-press.

করা ; শিক্ষিত হওয়া। **Drill-press**—বেধক যন্ত্র, বর্ম্মা। **Drill-sergent**—কসরৎ-শিক্ষক।

drill, *n.* & *v. t.* **1.** A small furrow for sowing seeds in ; বীজ-বপনের জন্য লাঙ্গল-পদ্ধতি, সীতা, নালা। **2.** A machine for making furrows for sowing seeds ; বীজ-বপনের নালা খনন করণার্থ যন্ত্রবিশেষ। **3.** A row of plants sown in a furrow ; লাঙ্গল-পদ্ধতিতে রোপিত তরু-পংক্তি। ***Verb t.*** To sow (seeds) in rows ; সারি সারি নালাতে বীজ-বপন করা।

drill, *n.* A kind of baboon ; এক প্রকার বানর।

drill, *n.* A coarse twilled linen or cotton fabric ; একপ্রকার টের্চ্চা-বুনা স্থূল কার্পাসবস্ত্র।

drī'-lȳ, *adv.* In a dry manner, শুষ্কভাবে।

drink *v. t.* & *i.* **1.** To swallow as liquid ; পান করা। **2.** To suck in ; to absorb ; "And let the purple violets *drink* the stream ;" চুষিয়া নেওয়া ; শুষিয়া নেওয়া, শোষণ করা। **3.** To take medicinally ; ঔষধরূপে সেবন করা। **4.** To spend on drink etc. ; "He *drinks* his whole earnings" মদ্যাদি পানে ব্যয় করা। **5.** To drink a toast to ; to wish good to, in drinking ; as, to *drink* one's health ; কাহারও মঙ্গল কামনা করিয়া পান করা ; মদ্য পানকালে কাহারো মঙ্গল কামনা করা। ***Verb i.*** **1.** To swallow liquor for quenching thirst or other purpose ; as, to *drink* of the brook ; পান করা। **2.** To take spirituous liquor, esp. to excess ; as, he *drinks* hard ; মদ্য পান করা, বিশেষতঃ অতিরিক্ত মদ্য পান করা। **3.** To have a certain taste ; "Burgundy *drinks* as flat as Port ;" স্বাদ লাগা। **Drink'-er,** *n.* **A drinking bout**—মদ্য-পানোৎসব, মদের বৈঠক। **To drink deep**—To drink to excess ; অতি-মাত্রায় পান করা। **To drink hard, heavily or like a fish**—To drink spirituous liquors to excess ; অতি মাত্রায় মদ্য পান করা, মদ্য পানে বিভোর হওয়া। **To drink in**—(*Lit.*) To absorb readily ; (শব্দানুযায়ী) তৎক্ষণাৎ শুষিয়া নেওয়া। (*Fig.*) To receive or take in greedily as with the senses ; to listen to or contemplate with delight ; "I stopped to *drink in* the beauty of the scene ; (লক্ষণায়) সাগ্রহে ইন্দ্রিয়দ্বারা গ্রহণ করা ; সানন্দে শ্রবণ বা অনুধ্যান করা। **To drink off or up**—To drink the whole at a draught ; এক চুমুকে সব টুকু পান করিয়া ফেলা। **To drink one's health**—To drink while expressing good-wishes for the health and welfare of one ; কোন ব্যক্তির স্বাস্থ্য বা মঙ্গল কামনা করিয়া মদ্য পান করা। **To drink one's self drunk**—To continue drinking until one is quite drunk ; মদ খাইতে খাইতে মাতাল হইয়া পড়া। **To drink (others) down or under the table**—To outlast in retaining control of one's self while drinking ; মদ্য পান করিয়া অপর সকলে মাতাল হইয়া পড়িলেও নিজে স্থির থাকা। **To drink till all's blue**—To continue drinking until everything around one looks blue ; চতুর্দ্দিকস্থ পদার্থনিচয় নীলবর্ণ না দেখা পর্য্যন্ত মদ্য পান করিতে থাকা। **To drink to**—To pledge ; to toast ; as, to *drink to* one's health ; মদ্য পান দ্বারা কোন বিষয়ে সম্মতি প্রদান করা ; কোন ব্যক্তির স্বাস্থ্যাদি কামনা করিয়া মদ্য পান করা। **To drink up or in**—To absorb (moisture) as plants ; রস শোষণ করা।

drink, *n.* **1.** Liquid to be swallowed or absorbed for quenching thirst etc. ; beverage ; পেয়, পানীয় ; সরবৎ, পানীয় দ্রব্য। **2.** Intoxicating liquor ; মদ্য, মদিরা, সুরা। **3.** A glass etc. or portion of liquor ; a draft ; এক গ্লাস মদ ; একঢোক মদ। **4.** Excessive drinking ; intemperance ;

as, to take to *drink ;* পানদোষ ; অমিতাচার। **Drink-offering** — Libations ; তর্পণ, দেবোদ্দেশ্যে পেয়-নিষেক। **In drink**—Drunk ; মত্ত, মাতাল। **On the drink** — Given way to this ; মদ্যপানানুরক্ত।

drink'-ǎ-ble, *adj.* & *n.* Good to drink ; পানযোগ্য, সুপেয়। *Noun.* (Esp. in *pl.*) A thing or things to drink ; a beverage ; পানীয় দ্রব্য, পেয় ; সরবৎ প্রভৃতি পানীয় দ্রব্য।

drip, *n., v. t.* & *i.* **1.** A falling, or letting fall, in drops ; that which falls in drops ; বিন্দু বিন্দু পতন, ক্ষরণ, স্রংসন, বিন্দুপাত ; যাহা ফোঁটা ফোঁটা হইয়া পড়ে। **2.** (*Arch.*) A projection keeping rain-water from the parts below ; (স্থপতি-বিজ্ঞান) ঘরের ছাঁইচ। *Verb t.* To let fall in drops ; বিন্দু বিন্দু করিয়া ফেলা, ফোঁটা ফোঁটা করিয়া ফেলা, টস্ টস্ করিয়া ফেলা। *Verb i.* **1.** To fall in drops ; as, water *drips* from cave ; টস্ টস্ করিয়া পড়া, টুব্‌টাব্ করিয়া পড়া, ফোঁটা ফোঁটা করিয়া পড়া। **2.** To let fall drops of moisture or liquid ; as, a wet garment *drips*; ফোঁটা ফোঁটা জল পড়া। **Drip'-py,** *adj.* **Drip-drop**—Persistent dripping ; অবিরল বারি-বিন্দু-পাত।

Drip or Dripstone.

drip'-ping, *n.* **1.** Falling in drops a sound produced in so doing ; বিন্দু বিন্দু পতন ; টস্ টস্ শব্দ, টুব্‌টাব্ শব্দ। **2.** Fat melting from roasting meat and used in frying or as food ; ভর্জ্জনশীল মাংস হইতে গলিত মেদ। **Drippings**—Water, grease, etc. dripping from anything ; কোন বস্তু হইতে নির্গত জল, রস বা চর্ব্বির বিন্দু।

drive, *n., v. t.* & *i.* **1.** An excursion in a carriage etc. ; গাড়ীতে ভ্রমণ। **2.** A stroke at cricket, golf, etc. ; (ক্রীকেট, গল্‌ফ প্রভৃতি ক্রীড়ায়) কন্দুক-তাড়ন। **3.** Energy ; উদ্যম। **4.** (*Rare*) Tendency ; (অপ্রচলিত) আসক্তি, প্রবণতা, ঝোঁক। **5.** A road for driving on ; গাড়ীর রাস্তা। **6.** Urging onward of game or enemy etc. ; the mass of animals so driven together ; as, a *drive* of cattle ; শিকার, শত্রুদল প্রভৃতি সম্মুখের দিকে বিতাড়ন ; বিতাড়িত গো মহিষাদির দল, গবাদি পশুর পাল। **7.** (*Mining*) A tunnel ; সুড়ঙ্গ। *Verb t.* **1.** To impel or urge onward by force ; as, we *drive* a nail into wood with a hammer ; বসান। **2.** To cause to move forward ; as, to *drive* cattle to market ; সম্মুখের দিকে চালিত করা। **3.** To chase ; to hunt ; "To *drive* deer with hound and horn ;" মৃগয়ার্থ পশ্চাদ্ধাবন করা ; শিকার করা। **4.** To force or urge to a point or state ; as, to *drive* one mad or out of one's senses ; বলপূর্ব্বক কোন বিশেষ অবস্থায় আনা। **5.** To guide or regulate (a machine) ; (যন্ত্র) চালান। **6.** To search as a district etc. for game ; শিকারের জন্য বনপ্রদেশ অন্বেষণ করা। **7.** To overwork ; as, to be very hard *driven* ; অতিশয় পরিশ্রম করান। **8.** To convey (a person) in a carriage ; as, to *drive* a person to his door ; কোন ব্যক্তিকে গাড়ীতে নেওয়া। **9.** To defer ; as, *drive* it to the last moment ; স্থগিত রাখা। **10.** To urge ; to press ; as, to *drive* an argument ; নির্ব্বন্ধাতিশয় সহকারে উপস্থিত করা ; চাপিয়া ধরা। **11.** To negotiate as a bargain ; to carry on ; as, he *drove* a roaring trade ; কোন চুক্তি ঠিক করা ; চালান। **12.** (*Mining*) To dig horizontally ; (খনিজ-বিদ্যা) দিক্ চক্রবালের সহিত সমান্তরালভাবে খনন করা। *Verb i.* **1.** To rush and press with violence ; as, time *driveth* onward fast ; প্রচণ্ডবেগে ধাবিত বা অগ্রসর হওয়া। **3.** To be forced along ; to be impelled ; as, a ship *drives* before the wind ; সম্মুখের দিকে চালিত হওয়া ; সজোরে চালিত হওয়া। **4.** To go in a carriage ; as, he *drove* to London ; গাড়ীতে যাওয়া। **5.** To aim or tend, (with *at*) ; as, we know the end the author is *driving at* ; লক্ষ্য করা, অভিপ্রায় করা। **6.** To work hard (*at*) ; অতিশয় পরিশ্রম করা। **7.** To aim a blow ; প্রহার সন্ধান করা। **To drive a hard bargain**—To be hard or harsh in making a bargain ; কঠোরভাবে দর কশাকশি করা। **To drive a nail in one's coffin**—See COFFIN. **To drive a quill or pen**—To write ; লিখা। **To drive at** — To aim at ; to mean ; as, what are you *driving at* ; লক্ষ্য করা ; অভিপ্রায় করা। **To drive into a corner**—See CORNER. **To drive one's pigs to market**—To snore ; নাক ডাকা। **To drive tandem**—একটী ঘোড়ার আগে আর একটী যুড়িয়া গাড়ী চালান। **To drive to one's wits' end**—To perplex utterly ; বিভ্রান্ত করা। **To let drive**—To aim a blow, (with *at*) ; সন্ধান করা।

driv'-el (-'l), *n., v. t.* & *i.* A silly talk ; a twaddle ; আবল তাবল কথা ; বড়বড়ানি। *Verb t.* **1.** To waste or fritter away ; ক্ষয় করিয়া দেওয়া, ক্রমশঃ ক্ষয় করা। **2.** To utter in a childish or idiotic way ; আবল তাবল বকা। *Verb i.* **1.** To run at the mouth or nose like a child ; লালাস্রাব হওয়া, নাসিকা হইতে জল পড়া। **2.** To talk childishly or idiotically ; আবল তাবল বকা। **—ler,** *n.*

driv'-ėr, *n.* One who drives ; a coachman ; one who controls locomotives, motor-cars, etc. ; তাড়নকারী ; শকটচালক, গাড়োয়ান ; বাষ্পীয় শকটচালক। **2.** An over-seer of a slave-gang ; ক্রীতদাসদলের তত্ত্বাবধায়ক। **3.** (*Golf*) A supple wooden-headed club for driving long distance ; গল্‌ফ ক্রীড়ার তাড়ন-দণ্ডবিশেষ। **4.** (*Mech.*) The wheel of a locomotive to which power is directly communicated ; (যন্ত্র বিজ্ঞান) বাষ্পীয় শকটের যে চক্রে সাক্ষাৎ-সম্বন্ধে বল সঞ্চারিত করা হয়। **—less,** *adj.*

driv'-ing-wheel (-whēl), *n.* **1.** A wheel communicating motion to other parts of machine ; যে চক্রের সাহায্যে যন্ত্রের অন্যান্য অংশে গতি সঞ্চারিত হয়। **2.** A large wheel of a locomotive ; বাষ্পীয়-শকটের বৃহচ্চক্র। **3.** A cycle wheel that is directly worked ; দ্বি-চক্রযানের যে চক্রে সাক্ষাৎ-সম্পর্কে শক্তি প্রয়োগ করা হয়।

driz'-zle, *n.* & *v. i.* Fine dense drops of rain ; টিপ্ টিপ্ বৃষ্টি, গুঁড়ি গুঁড়ি বৃষ্টি, ফিন ফিনা বৃষ্টি, শীকর। ***Verb i.*** **1.** To rain in small fine drops ; ফিন্ ফিন্ বৃষ্টি পড়া, টিপির টিপির বৃষ্টি পড়া, গুঁড়ি গুঁড়ি বৃষ্টি পড়া। **2.** To be wet with minute drops ; টিপ্ টিপ্ বৃষ্টি পড়িয়া ভিজা। **—zly,** *adj.*

drō'-gher (-gêr), *n.* **1.** West Indian coasting vessel ; পশ্চিম ভারতীয় দ্বীপপুঞ্জের উপকূলগামী জাহাজ। **2.** A slow heavy craft ; একপ্রকার ভারী ও মন্দগামী ক্ষুদ্র জাহাজ।

drogue (drōg), *n*, A buoy at the end of a harpoon line ; তিমি মাছ মারিবার টেঁটার সুতার প্রান্তে সংলগ্ন বয়া।

droit (droyt), *n.* Right ; due ; legal perquisite ; স্বত্ব ; প্রাপ্য ; দস্তুরী। **Droits of admiralty**—শত্রুপক্ষীয় জাহাজের মালামাল, যাহা নৌ-বিভাগের প্রাপ্য হইয়া থাকে।

drōll, *adj., n.* & *v.i.* **1.** Facetious ; amusing ; কৌতুকপূর্ণ ; রঙ্গরসপূর্ণ, নর্ম্ম-সংযুক্ত, মজার। **2.** Queer ; surprising ; অদ্ভুত ; আজব। ***Noun.*** (Now *rare*) A jester ; a buffoon ; a wag ; হাস্যরসিক ; ভাঁড়, বিদূষক ; মস্করা। ***Verb i.*** To play the buffoon ; to jest ; (followed by *with*, *at* or *on*) ; ভাঁড়ামি করা, মস্করামি করা, ফষ্টি নষ্টি করা ; রঙ্গ রস করা।

Drol'-ly, *adv.* **Droll'-ness,** *n.*

drōll-êr-ȳ, *n.* **1.** Idle sportive jokes ; comical gestures ; buffoonery ; নর্ম্ম, পরিহাস, রঙ্গ রস ; ফষ্টিনষ্টি, হাস্যোদ্দীপক অঙ্গভঙ্গী ; ভাঁড়ামি, মস্কারি। **2.** A facetious composition ; রঙ্গরসপূর্ণ রচনা।

drom'-ĕ-dă-rȳ (drŭm-), *n.* The Arabian or one-humped camel

Dromedary.

bred for riding ; আরব দেশীয় উষ্ট্র ; [ইহাদের একটী মাত্র ককুদ থাকে।]

drŏm'-ond (-ŭnd), *n.* (*Hist.*) A large mediæval ship for war or commerce ; (ইতিহাস) মধ্যযুগের প্রকাণ্ড বাণিজ্য বা সমরপোত।

drōne, *n., v. i.* & *t.* **1.** The male of honey bee which does not work ; পুং মধুকর, পুং মৌমাছি। **2.** (*Fig.*) One who lives on the labour of others ; an idle fellow ; (লক্ষণায়) পরভাগ্যোপজীবী, নিষ্কর্ম্মালোক ; অলস লোক। **3.** A deep humming sound ; গুঞ্জন, ভন্ ভন্ শব্দ। **4.** A monotonous speech or speaker ; ভনভনানি, যে ব্যক্তি ভন্‌ভন্ করে। **5.** The largest tube of the bag-pipe, which emits a continued deep-note ; স্কট্‌লণ্ড্ দেশীয় শুষির যন্ত্র বিশেষের সর্ব্বাপেক্ষা বৃহৎ নল। ***Verb i.*** **1.** To live in idleness ; আলস্যে কাল কাটান। **2.** To hum ; to snore ; গুঞ্জন করা ; নাসিকা গর্জ্জন করা, নাক ডাকা। **3.** To make use of a dull monotonous tone ; as, he *drones* while reading ; to talk monotonously ; নীরস এক ঘেয়ে সুর তোলা ; ভন্ ভন্ করা। ***Verb t.*** **1.** To read or utter in a dull monotonous manner ; একঘেয়ে সুরে পড়া, ভন্ ভন্ করা। **2.** To pass or spend as life etc., in idleness ; আলস্যে (জীবন বা সময়) কাটান। **Dron'-ing-ly,** *adv.*

drŏn'-gō, *n.* A bird of the family Dicruridæ ; ফিঙ্গা। (black—যোঃ)। **Large racket-tailed Drongo**—ভৃঙ্গরাজ (যোঃ)।

droop, *n., v. t.* & *i.* Bending attitude ; loss of spirit ; অবনত ভাব ; স্ফূর্ত্তিহীনতা, নিরুৎসাহ, অবসন্নতা। ***Verb t.*** To let sink or hang down ; as, to *droop* the head, face, or eyes ; অবনত করা, হেঁট করা, নোয়ান, অধোবদন করা। ***Verb i.*** **1.** To bend or hang down as from weakness or exhaustion ; অবনত হওয়া, নুইয়া পড়া, হেঁট হওয়া, অধোবদন হওয়া, নতশির হওয়া। **2.** To languish ; to be depressed ; as, to animate the soldier's *drooping* courage ; মদালস হওয়া, মন্থরাঙ্গ হওয়া, ম্লান হওয়া ; হতোৎসাহ হওয়া, দমিয়া যাওয়া। **3.** To sink as the sun ; to decline ; অস্তমিত হওয়া, ডুবা ; পতন হওয়া। **4.** To look downwards as the eyes ; নীচের দিকে চাওয়া, অধোদৃষ্টি করা। **Droop'-ing-ly,** *adv.*

drŏp', *n.* **1.** The quantity of liquid that falls in one spherical mass ; বিন্দু, ফোঁটা, কণা, শীকর। **2.** (*Pl.*) Any medicine the dose of which is measured by drops ; যে ঔষধ ফোঁটা ফোঁটা হিসাবে মাপা হয়। **3.** A minute quantity ; as, a *drop* in a bucket or ocean ; কণা। **4.** A glass etc. of intoxicating liquor ; as, to take a *drop* ; এক গ্লাস বা এক পাত্র মদ্য বা অন্যবিধ তরল মাদক দ্রব্য। **5.** That which resembles or hangs in the form of a drop, as a hanging diamond ornament, a glass pendant of a chandelier, etc. ; ফোঁটার মত জিনিষ, যাহা ফোঁটার মত ঝুলিয়া থাকে, দোলক, দুল, ঝাড়ের কলম। **6.** Sugarplum ; as, chocolate *drops* ; চিনির লাড়ু, কদমা। **7.** That part of gallows which sustains the criminal before he is executed and which is suddenly dropped ; the distance he is allowed to fall ; as, a *drop* of 3 ft. ; ফাঁসি-মঞ্চের যে অংশে ফাঁসীর পূর্ব্বে অপরাধীকে দণ্ডায়মান করান হয়—এবং যাহা হঠাৎ নীচে টানিয়া লওয়া হয় ; ফাঁসি-মঞ্চ হইতে যতটা নিম্নে অপরাধীর দেহ ঝুলিতে থাকে। **8.** Act of dropping ; sudden fall ; descent in prices, temperature, etc. ; পতন ; আকস্মিক পতন ; মূল্যের পড়তি (বায়ুমণ্ডলাদির) তাপ-হ্রাস, ইত্যাদি। **9.** A contrivance for lowering heavy weights to a ship's deck ; জাহাজের পাটাতনে গুরুভার দ্রব তুলিবার যন্ত্র বিশেষ। **10.** The curtain which conceals the stage of a theatre from the audience, (also called a *drop-curtain*) ; সর্ব্বাগ্রবর্ত্তী দৃশ্যপট, যবনিকা। **11.** An abrupt fall or descent in the level of a surface ; amount of this ; কোন কিছুর সমতল পৃষ্ঠে আকস্মিক প্রবণতা ; ঐরূপ প্রবণতার পরিমাণ। **12.** A kick of foot-ball made by dropping the ball and kicking it as it rises, (also called a *drop-kick*) ; ভূতলে পাদগোলক নিক্ষেপ করিয়া উত্থানকালে পদদ্বারা তাড়ন। **Drop'-let,** *n.* **Drop-kick**—See DROP (12). **Drop-off, out** — পাদগোলক তাড়ন। **Drop-scene**—যবনিকা, জবনিকা (আ: বঃ)। **Drop-shutter**—আলোক-চিত্রের ফলক তৎক্ষণাৎ আলোকে অনাবৃত করিবা জন্য যন্ত্র বিশেষ। **Drop-sulphur, —tin**—দানাদার টিন বা গন্ধক। [গলিত টিন বা গন্ধক বিন্দু বিন্দু করিয়া জলে ফেলিয়া এইরূপ দানা প্রস্তুত করা হয়।] **Dropwort** — একপ্রকার বৃক্ষ। **A drop in a bucket** or **ocean**—A very small contribution ; সমুদ্রে শিশির বিন্দু, কণা মাত্র। **Drop by drop**—In small successive quantities ; little by little ; ফোঁটা ফোঁটা করিয়া ; অল্পে অল্পে। **To have a drop in one's eye**—To show signs of having drunk ; মাতলামির চিহ্ন দেখান। **To take a drop too much**—To become intoxicated ; মাতাল হওয়া।

drŏp, *v. i.* & *t.* **1.** To fall in drops ; ফোঁটা ফোঁটা হইয়া পড়া ; টুপ্ টুপিয়ে পড়া, টুবটাব্ করিয়া পড়া। **2.** To give off moisture in drops ; ফোঁটা ফোঁটা করিয়া জল পড়া। **3.** To fall by force of gravity ; as, ripe fruits *drop* from the tree ; ভূতলে পতিত হওয়া। **4.** (*Fig.*) To be uttered casually ; as, the remark *dropped* from him ; (লক্ষণায়) হঠাৎ উচ্চারণ করা। **5.** To disappear ; as, the meaning has *dropped* out of memory ; লোপ পাওয়া, তিরোহিত হওয়া। **6.** To sink to ground exhausted or wounded ; আহত বা অবসন্ন দেহে ভূশায়ী হওয়া। **7.** To die ; as, we see one friend after another *dropping* round us ; মরা। **8.** To cease ; to lapse ; as, the affair was allowed to *drop* ; স্থগিত হওয়া ; বাতিল হওয়া। **9.** To fall lower ; as, prices *drop* ; পড়া। **10.** To come unexpectedly, (with *in*) ; as, he *dropped in* at time ; হঠাৎ আসিয়া পড়া। **11.** To go down a stream, (usually with *down*) ; as, barges *drop down* a river ; ভাটার দিকে যাওয়া। **12.** To fall behind, to the rear, etc. ; as, the artillery has *dropped* to the rear ; পাছে পড়া। **13.** (Of animals) To let fall youngs etc. in giving birth ; (জন্তু-সম্পর্কে) বাচ্চা প্রসব করা। **14.** To come down (*upon*) ; to reprimand (with *on* or *upon*) ; "Do the police ever *drop upon* the parties and frustrate their plans ;" আক্রমণ করা ; তীব্র ভর্ৎসনা করা। ***Verb t.*** **1.** To pour or let fall in small portions ; ফোঁটা ফোঁটা করিয়া ফেলা, বিন্দু বিন্দু মোচন করা। **2.** To let fall as any substance ; as, to *drop* the anchor (*i. e.* to anchor a ship) ; ফেলা। **3.** To give birth to ; as, to *drop* a lamb ; বাচ্চা দেওয়া। **4.** To utter casually, as if unconciously ; as, to *drop* a hint ; হঠাৎ বলিয়া ফেলা। **5.** To leave ; to permit to subside ; as, to *drop* an affair ; ত্যাগ করা, ছাড়া ; মিটাইয়া ফেলিতে দেওয়া। **6.** To lose (money esp. in gaming) ; (টাকা) খোয়ান (বিশেষতঃ জুয়া খেলায়)। **7.** To fell with axe, blow of fist or bullet ; কুঠারাঘাতে ভূপাতিত করা, গুলি করিয়া বা মুষ্ট্যাঘাতে ধরাশায়ী করা। **8.** To set down (passenger, parcel) ; লিখিয়া লওয়া। **9.** To leave out in speech etc. ; as, to *drop* a letter ; বক্তৃতা প্রভৃতিতে ছাড় দেওয়া। **10.** To lower or depress ; as, to *drop* the curtain or voice ; to droop, as eyes etc. ; নামান ; অবনত করা। **12.** To send as a letter etc. by dropping it in the letter-box ; "I will *drop* a line as often as I can ;" চিঠির বাক্সে ফেলিয়া চিঠি প্রভৃতি পাঠান। **11.** (*Naut.*) To leave behind ; as, a ship *drops* all other vessels astern ; (নৌ-বিদ্যা) পশ্চাতে ফেলা। **Let the matter drop**—একথা ছেড়ে দাও। **To drop a curtsey**—To make a curtsey by lowering the body ; প্রণাম করা। **To drop astern**—To leave in the rear ; (জাহাজ সম্বন্ধে) পশ্চাতে ফেলা। **To drop away**—To depart one by one ; একে একে যাওয়া। **To drop down**—To sail, row or move down a river or towards a sea ; as, the sailors *dropped down* at full speed ; নদীর ভাটার দিকে যাওয়া, পাইল তুলিয়া বা দাঁড় টানিয়া নদীর ভাটার দিকে অগ্রসর হওয়া, সমুদ্রাভিমুখে যাওয়া। **To drop down on a person**—To find fault with him ; to reprove him ; কোন ব্যক্তির দোষ উদ্ঘাটন করা ; তিরস্কার করা। **To drop in**—To pay an informal visit ; অনিয়মিতভাবে সাক্ষাৎ করা। **o drop off**—To fall asleep ; ঘুমাইয়া পড়া। To depart one by one ; একে একে প্রস্থান করা। **To drop on** or **across**—To reprimand or punish ; ধমকাইয়া দেওয়া, শাস্তি দেওয়া। **To drop on one's knee**—To kneel ; প্রণতজানু হওয়া। **To drop out**—To withdraw ; প্রত্যাহার করা। **To drop short**—To fall short ; কোন কিছু অপেক্ষা ন্যূন হওয়া। **To drop the curtain**—To end the tale ; to close the performance ; গল্প শেষ করা ; অভিনয় শেষ করা। **To drop through**—To fail of success ; নিষ্ফল হওয়া।

drŏp′-ping, *n.* (*Pl.*) **1.** What falls in drops, *e. g.* wax from candles ; যাহা ফোঁটা ফোঁটা হইয়া পতিত হয়, যথা মোমবাতি হইতে গলিত মোম। **2.** Dung of beasts or birds ; পশু বা পক্ষীর বিষ্ঠা, নাদ।

drŏp′-scene (-sēn), *n.* The drop-curtain with a scene painted on it ; যবনিকা। **2.** The final scene of a drama in real life ; জীবন-নাট্যের অন্তিম দৃশ্য।

drŏp′-sy̆, *n.* **1.** A disease in which watery fluid collects in cavities or tissues of the body ; শোথ রোগ, উদরী রোগ, উদকোদর, জলোদর (সাঃ পঃ)। **2.** (*Fig.*) An over-swollen state or condition ; (লক্ষণায়) অতিশয় স্ফীতি। **–si-cal,** *adj.* **–si-cal-ly,** *adv.*

drŏs(h)′-kȳ, *n.* Russian or Prussian low four-wheeled carriage ; রুশিয়া বা প্রুশিয়া দেশের চারিচাকার গাড়ি।

drŏss, *n.* **1.** Scum thrown off from metals in melting ; মল, ধাতুমল, খাইদ। **2.** Refuse ; rubbish ; অসার ভাগ ; জঞ্জাল। **Dross′-y,** *adj.*

drought, (drouth, *poet*), (drowt. drowth), *n.* **1.** Continuous dry weather ; want of rain ; অনাবৃষ্টি, অবৃষ্টি, অবর্ষণ, জলশোষ, অগ্রহ (বঃ)। **2.** Thirst ; want of drink ; তৃষ্ণা ; পানাভাব। **Drought′-y,** *adj.* Dried ; thirsty ; শুষ্ক, নীরস, নিরুদক, বৃষ্টিশূন্য ; তৃষিত।

drōve, *n.* **1.** A flock or herd driven or collected for driving ; তাড়িত পশুর পাল, যূথ। **2.** A crowd of people in motion ; a shoal ; সচল লোকসংঘ ; ঝাঁক। **3.** A mason's broad chisel ; রাজমিস্ত্রির প্রশস্ত বাটালী।

drōve, *v. t.* **1.** To drive as cattle, sheep, etc. on long journey ; গবাদি পশুর পাল তাড়াইয়া নেওয়া। **2.** To finish as a stone with a drove chisel ; প্রশস্ত বাটালী দ্বারা প্রস্তর প্রভৃতি কর্তন করা।

drō′-vêr, *n.* A driver of droves to market ; a dealer in cattle ; যে ব্যক্তি বিক্রয়ের জন্য পশুপাল বাজারে লইয়া যায় ; গবাদি পশু ব্যবসায়ী।

drown, *v. t.* & *i.* **1.** To suffocate by submersion ; ডুবাইয়া মারা, জলমগ্ন করিয়া নিহত করা। **2.** To overflow ; to inundate ; as, to *drown* land ; (also *fig.*), as, *drowned* in tears, sleep or wine ; প্লাবিত করা ; ভাসাইয়া দেওয়া। **3.** To overcome ; as, a louder voice *drowns* a milder one ; পরাস্ত করা, অভিভূত করা, ঢাকা, ডুবাইয়া দেওয়া। ***Verb i.*** To suffer death by suffocation in liquid, (now usually to be *drowned*, but *drowning* men etc.) ; ডুবিয়া মরা, জলমগ্ন হইয়া মরা। **A drowning men catches at a straw**—মজ্জমান ব্যক্তি তৃণ পাইলেও আকড়াইয়া ধরে, জলমগ্ন ব্যক্তি তৃণের ভরসা করে। **Like a drowned rat**—In a soaked condition ; ভিজা অবস্থায়। **To drown out** — To drive out by flood ; জলপ্লাবন দ্বারা বিতাড়িত করা। **To drown the miller**—To combine water and wine so disproportionally as to make the mixture unpalatable (from too much water) ; অতিরিক্ত জল মিশাইয়া মদ পানিসা করা।

drowse (drowz), *n.*, *v. t.* & *i.* Half asleep condition ; a doze ; তন্দ্রা ; ঝিমানি। ***Verb t.*** **1.** To make drowsy ; to make heavy with sleepiness ; তন্দ্রাজড়িত করা ; তন্দ্রাবিষ্ট করা। **2.** To pass (time) in drowsing ; ঝিমাইয়া কাল কাটান। ***Verb i.*** **1.** To be half asleep ; to doze ; তন্দ্রাতুর হওয়া, তন্দ্রাবিষ্ট হওয়া ; ঝিমান, ঢুলা, ঢুলু ঢুলু করা। **2.** To be sluggish ; অলস হওয়া, ঢিলা হওয়া।

drows′-ȳ, *adj.* **1.** Sleepy ; half asleep ; dozing ; নিদ্রাপ্রবণ, ঢুলু ঢুলু ; তন্দ্রাবিষ্ট ; তন্দ্রাতুর। **2.** Lulling ; soporific ; ঘুমপাড়ানো ; নিদ্রাজনক। **3.** Sluggish ; stupid ; ঢিলা, অলস ; জড়-বুদ্ধি। **–i-ly,** *adv.* **–i-ness,** *n.* **Drowsy head**—A sleepy person ; তন্দ্রাবিষ্ট ব্যক্তি।

drŭb, *v. t.* **1.** To cudgel ; to beat with a stick ; লাটিপেটা করা, ঠেঙ্গান ; যষ্টিদ্বারা আঘাত করা, বেত্রাঘাত করা। **2.** To beat in fight ; যুদ্ধে প্রহার করা। **3.** To beat (a notion) into or out of a person ; কোন ব্যক্তির মাথায় (কোন ধারণা) ঢুকান, কাহারও কোন ধারণা ছাড়ান। **Drub′-bing,** *n.*

drudge (drŭj), *n.* & *v. i.* A menial worker ; a slave ; হীনকার্য্যে নিযুক্ত দাসদাসী, নিকৃষ্টকর্ম্মকর (আঃ বঃ) ; ক্রীতদাস, দাসী, বাঁদী। ***Verb i.*** To work slavishly at distasteful work ; দাস্যবৃত্তি করা।

drudg'-êr-ỳ (drŭj-), *n.* Act of drudging; disagreeable and wearisome work; ignoble toil; দাস্যবৃত্তিকরণ; নীরস এবং অবসাদ-জনক কর্ম্ম; হীনবৃত্তি, দাস্যবৃত্তি, হীন-কর্ম্ম। **—ing-ly,** *adv.*

drŭg, *n.* & *v. t.* **1.** Original simple medicinal substance, organic or inorganic, used alone or as an ingredient; ঔষধ দ্রব্য, ঔষধি, ভেষজ। **2.** Unsalable commodity; an article no longer in demand; as, a *drug* in the market; অবিক্রেয় জিনিষ; যে জিনিষের আর চাহিদা নাই। ***Verb t.*** **1.** To season or mix with drugs, esp. with narcotic or poison; ভেষজ মিশ্রণদ্বারা কোমল করা, ভেষজ মিশ্রিত করা, বিশেষতঃ বিষ বা নিদ্রাজনক ঔষধ মিশান। **2.** To stupefy by a narcotic drug; "Whom he has *drugged* to sure repose;" নিদ্রাজনক ঔষধ প্রয়োগ করিয়া অজ্ঞান বা অচেতন করা। **3.** To nauseate; ন্যক্কার জন্মান। **4.** To dose to excess with drugs; অতিরিক্ত মাত্রায় ঔষধ সেবন করান। **Drug'-gy,** *adj.* Pertaining to drugs; ভেষজ-সম্বন্ধীয়।

drŭg'-gĕt, *n.* Coarse woollen stuff used for floor or table covering; একপ্রকার স্থূল পশমী বস্ত্র, স্থূল প্রাবার (আঃ বঃ)।

drŭg'-gist, *n.* A dealer in drugs; ঔষধ ব্যবসায়ী, ঔষধবিক্রেতা।

Drû'-id, *n.* **1.** A priest, magician or soothsayer among the ancient Celts; প্রাচীন কেল্ট জাতির পুরোহিত, দৈবজ্ঞ বা ঐন্দ্রজালিক। **2.** An officer of the Welsh Gorsedd or national assembly; ওয়েলস্ দেশের জাতীয় সমিতির কর্ম্মচারি-বিশেষ। **—ess,** *n.* (fem.) **—id'-ic, —i-cal,** *adjs.* **—ism,** *n.*

drŭm, *n.* **1.** A hollow cylindrical instrument of music beaten with sticks; ঢোল, দুন্দুভি, আনক, পটহ, ঢক্কা, ঢাক, জয়ঢাক, দামামা। **2.** The sound of a drum; any similar sound, esp. bittern's cry; ঢক্কা-নিনাদ, দুন্দুভিনাদ, দুন্দুভিধ্বনি; দুন্দুভিবৎ নিনাদ, বিশেষতঃ ক্রৌঞ্চ পক্ষীর ডাক। **3.** Any thing resembling a drum; ঢক্কাকার বস্তু। **4.** (*Anat.*) The tympanum of the ear; (শারীরসংস্থান বিদ্যা) কর্ণ-পটহ, ঢক্কাদ্বক্ (হিঃ কোঃ)। **5.** A cylinder or barrel in machinery on which something is wound or for other purposes; যন্ত্রের চোঙ্গা বা ঢক্কাকার অংশ—যাহাতে কোন বস্তু জড়ানো যায় এবং অন্য উদ্দেশ্যও সাধিত হয়। **6.** A cylindrical box etc. for packing dried fruits, holding oil, etc.; শুষ্কফল প্যাক্ করার জন্য বা তৈল রাখার জন্য চোঙ্গার আকার পেটক বিশেষ। **7.** (*Arch.*) The solid part of the Corinthian and composite capitals; (স্থপতি-বিজ্ঞান) কোরিন্থিয়ান ও বিমিশ্র আইওনিক ও কোরিন্থিয়ান স্থাপত্য-রীত্যনুযায়ী নির্ম্মিত স্তম্ভের নিরেট অংশ। **8.** (*Zool.*) A natural organ producing a loud or bass sound; (জন্তুবিদ্যা) যে দৈহিক যন্ত্র হইতে উচ্চস্বর উত্থিত হয়, ঢক্কা-যন্ত্র। **9.** (*Mil.*) A drummer; (সামরিকশাস্ত্র) দুন্দুভি-বাদক। **10.** An evening or afternoon tea-party; সান্ধ্য চা-পান-সম্মিলনী, বৈকালিক চা-পানসম্মিলনী। **11.** The drum-fish; আমেরিকা দেশীয় কয়েকপ্রকার মৎস্যের সাধারণ নাম। **Drum-fish**—See above. **Drum-head** — The skin of a drum; ঢক্কার অগ্রভাগের চর্ম্ম, ঢক্কাশীর্ষ। The membrane across the drum of an ear; কর্ণপটহের অনুপ্রস্থগামী ঝিল্লী বিশেষ। The heads of the capstan; জাহাজের অগ্রভাগস্থ কাছি জড়াইবার যন্ত্রের শীর্ষভাগ। **Drum-head court-martial**—See COURT-MARTIAL. **Drum-major** — সৈন্য-দলের ঢক্কাবাদকদিগের নায়ক। **Drum-stick**—ঢাকের কাঠি। The lower joint of a cooked fowl's leg; পক্ব মুর্গীর নিম্নতর পদগ্রন্থি। **The drum of ear** — কর্ণের মধ্যভাগের ফাঁকা জায়গা।

drŭm, *v. t.* & *i.* **1.** To perform on a drum as a tune; ঢাক বাজান, ঢক্কাবাদন করা, দুন্দুভি নিনাদ করা। **2.** To strike as hands etc. continuously *on* or *upon* something; to beat or thump (anything) as in beating a drum; হস্তাদি দ্বারা অনবরত কোন কিছুর উপর আঘাত করা; তাল ঠুকা। **3.** To summon or assemble as by beat of drums, (usually with *up*); as, to *drum up* recruits; to obtain by canvassing; as, to *drum up* customers; ঢোল পিটাইয়া আহ্বান করা, ঢেঁটরা পিটাইয়া আহ্বান বা একত্র করা; যোগাড়যন্ত্র করার ফলে পাওয়া। **4.** To expel ignominiously by beat of drums, (with *out down*, etc.); ঢাক বাজাইয়া অপমান-জনকভাবে তাড়াইয়া দেওয়া। **5.** (*Fig.*) To din or beat into a person etc.; as, to *drum* lesson etc. into a dull mind; (লক্ষণায়) বার বার আবৃত্তি করিয়া মনের মধ্যে ঢুকান। ***Verb i.*** **1.** To play the drum; ঢাক বাজান, ঢক্কা বাদন করা। **2.** To make loud hollow noise with quivering wings, (of birds, insects, etc.); (পক্ষী, পতঙ্গাদির পক্ষে) কম্পনশীল পক্ষ দ্বারা ঢক্কাবৎ নিনাদ করা। **3.** To go about as a drummer to gather recruits, customers, etc., (with *for*); ঢাক বাজাইয়া খরিদদার প্রভৃতি সংগ্রহ করিতে যাওয়া। **4.** To beat, tap or thump continuously with fingers on something; আঙ্গুল প্রভৃতি দ্বারা তালঠুকা। **Drum'-mer,** *n.* **To drum into**—To instil into by repetition; as, to *drum* a matter *into* one's mind; বারবার বলিয়া মনের মধ্যে ঢুকান। **To drum out**—To drive out with shame; as, a soldier is *drummed out* of a regiment; অপমানিত করিয়া তাড়াইয়া দেওয়া।

To drum up—To gather by going round with a drum ; ঢক্কা বাজাইয়া চতুর্দ্দিকে ঘুরিতে ঘুরিতে জড় করা। To collect by the exercise of influence and exertion ; শক্তি বা প্রভাব বিস্তার দ্বারা সংগ্রহ করা।

drŭm, drŭm'-lin, *ns.* (*Geol.*) A long narrow hill of drift or dilluvial formation ; (ভূ-বিদ্যা) জলপ্রবাহ সমানীত মৃত্তিকা, কঙ্করাদি দ্বারা রচিত দীর্ঘ এবং সংকীর্ণ পর্ব্বত।

drŭm'-mŏnd-light (-līt), *n.* Same as LIME LIGHT, which see.

drunk (drŭngk), *p.p.* & *n.* Intoxicated ; (also *fig.*) ; as, *drunk* with joy, success or rage ; মত্ত, প্রমত্ত ; (অপিচ লক্ষণায়) মত্ত (as in আনন্দ-মত্ত), মাতোয়ারা। ***Noun.*** 1. A drunken man ; মাতাল। 2. A drinking bout ; a drunken fit ; মদ্যপানোৎসব ; মাতলামি।

drunk'-ard (drŭngk-ẽrd), 1. *n.* One who habitually drinks strong liquor immoderately ; a sot ; মদ্যপ, মদ্যপায়ী ; নেশাখোর, বদ্ধ মাতাল। 2. (*Pl.*) The marsh marigold ; (বহুবচন) জলাভূমিতে জাত একপ্রকার গাঁদাফুল।

drunk'-ĕn (drŭngk-), *adj.* 1. Intoxicated, (rarely predicative) ; মত্ত, মদ্যপানে উন্মত্ত। 2. Given to drunkenness ; as, my *drunken* butler ; মদ্যাসক্ত, নেশাখোর। 3. Caused by or exhibting drunkenness ; as, a *drunken* quarrel, brawl or frolic ; মদ্যপানজনিত, মদ্যপানসূচক। 4. Unsteady as if reeling from being drunk; নেশায় টলটলায়মান। **—ness,** *n.* 1. The state of being drunk ; পানমত্ততা, মদমত্ততা। 2. The habit of indulging in intoxication ; অতিরিক্ত মদ্যপানাভ্যাস, পানদোষ। **—ly,** *adv.*

drupe (drôp), *n.* A fleshy or pulpy fruit enclosing stone or nut with kernel, as olive, plum, or cherry ; আঁঠি ফল (সাঃ পঃ)। **Dru-pa'-ceous,** *adj.* Pertaining to, or of the nature of, drupes ; bearing drupes ; ওপাষ্ঠিক (সাঃ পঃ) ; আষ্ঠিফল-প্রসূ।

drup'-ĕl, drupe'-lĕt (drôp-), *n.* A small drupe as one of the pulpy grains of the black-berry ; ক্ষুদ্রাষ্ঠিক (সাঃ পঃ)।

druse (drôs), *n.* 1. A crust of crystals lining the sides of a cavity in a rock ; পাষাণ-শৈলের গহ্বর-পার্শ্বের স্ফটিকময় কঠিন আবরণ। 2. A cavity in a rock having the sides studded with crystals ; স্ফটিক-খচিত-পার্শ্ব গহ্বর।

druse (drôs), *n.* A member of a political and religious sect of Muhammadan origin inhabiting the regions round Mt. Lebanon in Syria ; সিরিয়ার অন্তঃপাতী লেবানন-শৈলাঞ্চলবাসী রাজনীতিক এবং ধর্ম্মসংক্রান্ত মহম্মদীয় সম্প্রদায় বিশেষের সভ্য।

drȳ, *adj., v. t.* & *i.* 1. Without moisture ; শুষ্ক, শুক্‌না, নীর্জল, নীরস। 2. Not rainy ; with deficient rainfall ; as, a *dry* season ; বৃষ্টিশূন্য ; অপ্রচুর বৃষ্টিপাতযুক্ত। 3. Not shedding tears ; "Not a *dry* eye was to be seen in the assembly ;" অশ্রুপাতহীন, অশ্রুশূন্য। 4. Thirsty ; "Give the *dry* fool drink ;" শুষ্ককণ্ঠ, তৃষিত, তৃষ্ণার্ত্ত। 5. Without butter ; as, *dry* bread or toast ; মাখন-ছাড়া। 6. Free from sweetness and fruity flavour ; as, *dry* wine ; স্বাদহীন, অবিশুদ্ধ। 7. Unconnected with blood or water ; as, a *dry* death ; রক্তলেশহীন, জললেশহীন। 8. Not giving milk ; as, the cow is now *dry* ; দুধাল নয়। 9. Not submerged ; as, tide leaves it *dry* ; অনিমগ্ন। 10. Solid ; not liquid ; as, *dry* goods ; নিরেট ; অতরল। 11. Barren ; unembellished ; as, a *dry* style ; রসহীন ; অনলঙ্কৃত। 12. Sarcastic ; sneering ; as, a *dry* remark ; বিদ্রূপাত্মক ; অবজ্ঞাসূচক। 13. Severe ; hard ; as, a *dry* blow (causing no bloodshed) ; গুরুতর ; কঠিন। 14. Plain ; as, *dry* facts ; সাদাসিধা। 15. Uninteresting ; dull ; unprofitable ; নীরস ; একঘেয়ে ; অলাভজনক। 16. Untinged by prejudice or interest ; অপক্ষপাতদুষ্ট। ***Verb t.*** 1. To free from water or moisture of any kind and by any means, as by wiping, evaporation, or exhalation ; to exsiccate ; as, to *dry* the eyes ; শুষ্ক করান, শুকান ; সম্পূর্ণ শুষ্ক বা নীরস করা। 2. To cause to cease giving milk ; as, to *dry* a cow ; দুগ্ধ বন্ধ করান, দুধ ছাড়ান। ***Verb i.*** 1. To become free from wetness, (sometimes with *up*) ; শুষ্ক হওয়া, শুকাইয়া যাওয়া। 2. (*Colloq.*) To cease talking or doing something ; (চলিত ভাষায়) কথা বলিতে বিরত হওয়া, কোন কার্য্য হইতে বিরত হওয়া। **Dry'-ish,** *adj.* **Dry-, dri'-ly,** *advs.* In a dry manner ; coldly ; sarcastically ; শুষ্কভাবে ; অনুরাগশূন্য ভাবে ; বিদ্রূপাত্মকভাবে। **Dry'-ness,** *n.* **Dri'-, dry'-er,** *ns.* **Dry-blow**—যে আঘাতে কোনরূপ ক্ষত কিম্বা রক্তপাত হয় না। **Dry-bone**—অস্থিচর্ম্মসার। **Dry-cooper**—শুষ্কদ্রব্য রাখার উপযোগী পিপা প্রস্তুতকারী। **Dry-cough**—শুক্‌না কাসি। **Dry-cure**—(*v. t.*) মৎস্য প্রভৃতি লবণাক্ত করিয়া শুষ্ক করা। **Dry-fly**—(*noun.*) মক্ষিকার আকার বড়শীর টোপ,—জলে কীটের ন্যায় ভাসিয়া থাকে। (*Adj.*) With a fly dangled just over water ; জলোপরি দোলায়মান কীটবৎ টোপ বিশিষ্ট। (*Verb t.*) To fish with a dry-fly ; উক্তরূপ টোপ দ্বারা মৎস্য ধরা। **Dry-goods**—Non-liquid goods, as corn etc. ; শুষ্ক মাল, যথা শস্য প্রভৃতি। (*U. S.*) Textile fabrics or wares as distinguished from groceries, etc. ; (মার্কিণ যুক্তরাজ্যে) বস্ত্রাদি। **Dry-light**—A clear unobstructed light ; (hence) an unprejudiced view ; অবারিত স্বচ্ছালোক ; (অতএব) পক্ষপাতশূন্য দৃষ্টি। **Dry lodging**—যে বাসাতে কেবল বাসের স্থান থাকে, কিন্তু আহারের কোন প্রকার বন্দোবস্ত থাকে না। **Dry measure**—শুষ্ক দ্রব্যের পরিমাণ। **Dry-nurse**—(*n.*) যে ধাত্রী শিশুকে পালন করে, কিন্তু স্তন দান করে না, অস্তন্যপায়িনী ধাত্রী (আঃ বঃ)। (*Verb t.*) To bring up by hands ; স্তন্য না দিয়া পালন করা। **Dry pile**—যে বিদ্যুদ্‌ঘটমালা বা বিদ্যুৎ-প্রবাহ-উৎপাদক ধাতুখণ্ডস্তূপে জল ব্যবহৃত হয় না। **Dry-plate**—(*Phot.*) শুষ্ক প্রলেপাবৃত কাচফলক, এই প্রলেপের উপর আলোকের ক্রিয়া হইয়া থাকে এবং তদ্দারা অনার্দ্র অবস্থায় ফলকোপরি বিপরীত চিত্র উঠাইতে পারা যায়। **Dry point**—(*Fine arts*) (ললিত কলা) খোদাই-কারের বাটালীর পরিবর্ত্তে সূচীদ্বারা খোদাইর কাজ,—যাহাতে দ্রাবক ব্যবহার করিতে হয় না ; যে সূচীদ্বারা-উৎকৃরূপ খোদাইর কাজ হয় ; উক্তরূপে খোদিত ফলক হইতে মুদ্রিত চিত্র। (*Verb t.*) উক্তরূপে খোদাই করা। **Dry rot**—ছেতো পড়িয়া কাঠের পচা বা ধসা অবস্থা ; ছেতো ; (লক্ষণায়) নৈতিক বা সামাজিক অবনতি। **Dry-salt**—(*v. t.*) লবণ মিশাইয়া মৎস্যাদি শুষ্ক করা। **Dry-salter**—রং, ভেষজ দ্রব্য, গদ, তৈল, আচার প্রভৃতির ব্যবসায়ী। **Dry saltery**—রং, গদ, ভেষজ দ্রব্য প্রভৃতির দোকান বা ব্যবসায়। **Dry-shod**—(*adj.* & *adv.*) অসিক্তপদ, অনার্দ্রপদ ; অনার্দ্রপদে। **A stirring of the dry bones**—A revival of life where all seems dead ; মৃতদেহে জীবনসঞ্চার। **To die a dry death**—জলে না ডুবিয়া বা রক্ত পাত না হইয়া মরা।

drȳ'-ăd, *n.* (*Class. mythol.*) A wood nymph ; nymph inhabiting a tree ; (গ্রীক ও রোমীয় পুরাণে) বনদেবী ; তরুবাসিনী পরী।

drȳ'-ăs-dŭst, *adj.* & *n.* Very dry ; hopelessly uninteresting ; অতি শুষ্ক ; নিরতিশয় নীরস। ***Noun.*** (With the capital initial letter) An uninspired pedantic writer of antiquities, history, etc. ; ইতিহাস-বা প্রত্নতত্ত্ব লেখক। **Dr. Dry-as-dust**—যে কল্পিত ব্যক্তির নামে Sir Walter Scott তাঁহার কতিপয় উপন্যাস উৎসর্গীকৃত করেন।

dū'-ăd, *n.* Incorrectly used for DYAD.

dū'-ăl, *adj.* & *n.* **1.** Expressing the number two ; pertaining to two ; দ্বিবাচক ; দ্বৈত। **2.** Divided in two ; twofold ; দ্বিধা বিভক্ত ; দ্বিগুণিত। ***Noun.*** (*Gram.*) That number which is used when two things or persons are spoken of ; (ব্যাকরণ) দ্বিবচন। **—al'-i-ty,** *n.* The quality or state of being dual ; দ্বিত্ব, দ্বৈত, দ্বৈধ, দ্বন্দ্বরূপতা। **—ize,** *v. t.* To make dual to ; to regard as two ; দ্বৈত করা ; দুইটী বলিয়া গণ্য করা। **—ly,** *adv.*

dū'-ă-lin, *n.* A powerful explosive of nitre, nitroglycerine and saw-dust ; সোরা, করাতের গুঁড়া এবং নাইট্রো গ্লিসারিণের মিশ্রণে প্রস্তুত শক্তিশালী বিস্ফোরক দ্রব্য বিশেষ।

dū'-ăl-ĭsm, *n.* **1.** Duality ; a two-fold division ; দ্বিত্ব ; দ্বিধা-বিভাগ। **2.** Use of dual number ; দ্বিবচন প্রয়োগ। **3.** (*Phil.*) The doctrine that mind and matter exist as distinct entities ; (দর্শন-শাস্ত্র) মন এবং বাহ্য জগৎ এই দুইয়ের স্বতন্ত্র সত্তা রহিয়াছে—এইরূপ দার্শনিকবাদ, দ্বৈতবাদ (হিঃ কোঃ)। **4.** Duality ; দ্বৈধীভাব। **5.** (*Theol.*) A system which accepts two original principles, one good and the other evil ; (খৃষ্টীয় ধর্ম্মশাস্ত্র) ধর্ম্ম সম্বন্ধীয় মতবাদ বিশেষ, — এই বাদানুসারে সু ও কু এই দুইটী মৌলিক তত্ত্ব গৃহীত হইয়া থাকে। **6.** (*Chem.*) The dualistic theory or system ; (রসায়ন-শাস্ত্র) দ্বৈতসিদ্ধান্ত (হিঃ কোঃ)। [Lavoisier কর্ত্তৃক উদ্ভাবিত এবং তৎপরবর্ত্তী Berzelius কর্ত্তৃক সম্প্রসারিত মত বিশেষ। এই মতানুসারে প্রত্যেক যৌগিক পদার্থ দুই বস্তুর মিশ্রণে উৎপন্ন বলিয়া কল্পিত হইয়া থাকে এবং এই দুই বস্তুর তাড়িদ্‌ধর্ম্ম পরস্পরের বিপরীত হইয়া থাকে।] **—ist,** *n.* **—is'-tic,** *adj.* **—is'-ti-cal-ly,** *adv.*

dŭb, *v. t.* **1.** To strike with a sword and make a knight ; তরবারি দ্বারা স্কন্ধদেশে মৃদু আঘাত করত নাইট্ সম্প্রদায়ভুক্ত করা। **2.** To confer any dignity on ; as, a man of wealth is *dubbed* a man of worth ; to style or name ; গৌরবজনক পদবী প্রদান করা, নূতন আখ্যা প্রদান করা ; নামকরণ করা, নাম প্রদান করা। **3.** To smear (leather) with grease ; (চর্ম্মে) চর্ব্বি মাখান। **4.** To dress with an edge ; as, to *dub* a stick smooth ; বাইশ দ্বারা চাঁছা, ছোলা। **5.** To cut off the comb and wattles of ; as, to *dub* a cock ; মোরগাদির শিখা বা কণ্ঠনিম্নস্থ মাংসপিণ্ড কাটিয়া ফেলা। **6.** To trim as trees, hedges, etc. ; গাছ, গাছের বেড়া প্রভৃতির আগা ছাটিয়া দেওয়া। **To dub a fly**—To dress or make up an artificial fly ; কৃত্রিম মক্ষিকা তৈয়ার করা।

dŭb'-bing, *n.* **1.** Conferring of knighthood ; investment with a dignity or title ; নাইট উপাধি অর্পণ ; গৌরব-সূচক উপাধি প্রদান। **2.** A preparation of grease for leather, (also called *dubbin*) ; চর্ম্মে মাখিবার জন্য চর্ব্বিযুক্ত জিনিষ।

dū-bĭ'-ŏ-tȳ, *n.* **1.** Doubtfulness, সংশয়পরতা। **2.** A doubtful matter ; সন্দিগ্ধ বিষয়।

dū'-bĭ-ous (-ŭs), *adj.* Doubtful ; wavering ; unsettled ; as, the mind is in a *dubious* condition ; সন্দেহপূর্ণ, সাংশয়িক (বাঃ) ; সন্দিগ্ধ, সংশয়ী, সন্দিহান, সংশয়পূর্ণ, দ্বিধাকারী ; অস্থির। **2.** Indistinct ; as, *dubious* light ; ঝাপ্‌সা, অস্পষ্ট। **3.** Unreliable ; as, a *dubious* friend ; অবিশ্বসনীয়। **4.** Of questionable value or truth ; as, a *dubious* compliment ; সন্দেহজনক। **5.** Of doubtful issue ; as, a *dubious* undertaking ; অনিশ্চিত-পরিণাম। **6.** Of suspected character ; as, a *dubious* company or gains ; সন্দিগ্ধ-চরিত্র। **—ly,** *adv.* **—ness,** *n.* Doubtfulness ; সংশয়াচ্ছন্নতা, অনিশ্চয়তা, অস্পষ্টতা।

dū-bĭ-tā'-tion, *n.* Doubt ; hesitation ; সন্দেহ, সংশয় ; শঙ্কা, দ্বিধা, সন্দিগ্ধতা।

dū'-bĭ-tā-tive (-tĭv), *adj.* Of or expressing hesitation ; inclined or given to doubt ; সংশয়সূচক ; সাংশয়িক, সন্দেহরত। **—ly,** *adv.*

dū'-căl, *adj.* Of or pertaining to a duke ; ডিউক্ সম্বন্ধীয়, ডিউকীন (আঃ বঃ)।

dŭ'-căt, *n.* **1.** A gold coin, about 9s., formerly current in most European countries ; প্রায় ৯ শিলিং মূল্যের স্বর্ণমুদ্রাবিশেষ। [এই মুদ্রা পূর্ব্বকালে ইয়ুরোপের অনেক দেশে প্রচলিত ছিল।] **2.** Coin ; মুদ্রা। **3.** (*Pl.*) Money ; "Holmes was...out of *ducats* ;" (বহুবচন) টাকা কড়ি।

dŭch'-ĕss, *n.* **1.** The wife or widow of a duke ; ডিউক্‌পত্নী। **2.** An imposing woman ; প্রভাবশালিনী নারী। **3.** (*Slang*) A costermonger's wife, (abbr. *duch*) ; (ইতরভাষায়) ফলবিক্রেতার স্ত্রী।

dŭch'-ȳ, *n.* **1.** The territory of a duke or duchess ; ডিউক্ বা ডিউক্‌পত্নীর অধিকারভুক্ত ভূসম্পত্তি। **2.** Royal dukedom of Cornwall or Lancaster, each with certain courts of its own ; কর্ণওয়াল ও ল্যান্‌কেষ্টারের রাজবংশীয় ডিউকদ্বয়ের অধিকারভুক্ত সম্পত্তি,—যাহাতে ডিউকগণের নিজস্ব ধর্ম্মাধিকরণ প্রতিষ্ঠিত আছে।

dŭck, *n.* **1.** A kind of swimming bird, esp. the domesticated form of the mallard ; হংস, মরাল, পাঁতিহাস। **2.** A female duck as distinguished from a drake ; হংসী। **3.** (*Pl.*) Troops of the Bombay Presidency ; (বহুবচন) বোম্বাইপ্রদেশের সৈন্যগণ। **4.** (*Cricket*) A batsman's score of zero, (specially *duck's egg*) ; (ক্রীকেট ক্রীড়ায়) ব্যাটধারীর o ক্রীড়াঙ্ক-প্রাপ্তি। **5.** (*Colloq.*) Darling ; a word of endearment ; যাদু ; ময়না, বাছা। **Duck'-ling,** *n.* A young duck ; হাঁসের ছানা, হংসশাবক। **Duck'-y,** *n.* A term of endearment ; যাদু, ময়না, সোণা। **Duck-bill** — একপ্রকার গোধূম ; স্তন্যপায়ী ক্ষুদ্র জলচর জন্তুবিশেষ। **Duck-hawk**—একপ্রকার বাজ পক্ষী। **Duck's egg**—(*Cricket*) A score of o ; nothing ; as, to get a *duck's egg* at an examination ; (ক্রীকেট ক্রীড়ায়) ব্যাটম্যানকর্ত্তৃক o ক্রীড়াঙ্ক প্রাপ্তি ; অশ্বডিম্ব, শূন্য, ডিম। **Duck-shot**—হংস-শিকারের উপযোগী গুলি। **Duck-weed** — গুঁড়িপানা। **Duck and drake**—ছিনিমিনি খেলা। **Fine day for young ducks** — Rainy weather ; বৃষ্টির দিন, বাদ্‌লা দিন। **In two shakes of duck's tail**—In an instant ; মুহূর্ত্তমধ্যে। **Lame duck** — A disabled person ; অকর্ম্মণ্যাবস্থাপ্রাপ্ত ব্যক্তি। A defaulter on stock-exchange ; কোম্পানীর কাগজ ক্রয়-বিক্রয়স্থলীর ঋণ পরিশোধে অসমর্থ ব্যক্তি। **Like duck in thunderstorm**—With upturned eyes ; quite chap-fallen ; উর্দ্ধ-নেত্র ; নিরতিশয় ক্লান্তি বা দুর্ব্বলতা প্রযুক্ত লোলচিবুক। **Like water off duck's back** — Producing no effect ; হংসপৃষ্ঠে বারিবিন্দুবৎ, অকার্য্যকর। **To make ducks and drakes of,** or **to play ducks and drakes with**—To squander ; টাকা লইয়া ছিনিমিনি খেলা, ছকর নকর করা, অপব্যয় করা। **To take to anything like duck to water**—To be immersed in anything ; কোন বিষয়ে নিমগ্ন হওয়া।

dŭck, *n., v. t. & i.* A quick dip below water in bathing ; চুবনি, নিমজ্জন। ***Verb t.*** **1.** To dip or plunge in water and suddenly withdraw ; as, to *duck* a seaman ; চুবনি দেওয়া। **2.** To bow or nod ; হেঁট করা, নত করা। **3.** To avoid as blow etc. by ducking ; সহসা নত হইয়া প্রহার প্রভৃতি হইতে অব্যাহতি পাওয়া। ***Verb i.*** **1.** To dip ; to plunge the head in water or other liquid ; চুবনি দেওয়া। **2.** To stoop quickly to avoid a blow, etc. ; to bow ; আঘাত প্রভৃতি হইতে রক্ষা পাইবার জন্য মস্তক নত করা ; নত হওয়া। **Duck'-ing,** *n.* **Ducking stool**—যে আসনে বসাইয়া উদ্দামস্বভাবা এবং কটুভাষিণী স্ত্রীলোকদিগকে জলে ডুবান হইত।

dŭck, *n.* **1.** Strong untwilled linen or cotton fabric lighter and finer than canvas ; ক্যাম্বিস অপেক্ষা সূক্ষ্ম এবং লঘু শক্ত ক্ষৌম বা কার্পাস বস্ত্র। **2.** (*Pl.*) Trousers of this material ; (বহুবচন) উক্ত বস্ত্রের পাজামা।

dŭck'-ĕr, *n.* **1.** A diving bird, esp. dabchick and water-ouzel ; ডুবুরী পক্ষী, পানকৌড়ী। **2.** A diver ; a bather ; ডুবুরী, প্লব (মঃ উঃ) ; স্নানকারী।

dŭck'-ĕr, *n.* A breeder of ducks ; হংসশাবক উৎপাদন ও পালনকারী।

dŭct, *n.* **1.** A tube for conveying liquid ; নালী, প্রবাহিকা। **2.** (*Anat.*) A tube or canal in an animal body by which blood, chyle, lymp, etc., are conveyed ; (শারীরসংস্থান-বিদ্যা) শরীরাভ্যন্তরস্থ তরল পদার্থবাহী নাড়ী, শিরা, ধমনী। **3.** (*Bot.*) A vessel of plants' vascular tissue holding air, water, etc. ; (উদ্ভিদ্-বিদ্যা) উদ্ভিদদেহস্থ বায়ু, জল, প্রভৃতি পূর্ণ নালী।

dŭc'-tile (-tĭl), *adj.* **1.** (Of metals) Malleable ; flexible ; (technically) capable of being drawn out into wire or thread ; ঘাতসহ ; আনম্য, নমনীয় ; তার বা সূত্র রূপে পরিণত হওয়ার যোগ্য, তান্তব। **2.** (Of clay etc.) Plastic ; (মৃত্তিকা ইত্যাদি সম্বন্ধে) আকারপ্রদ, কোমল। **3.** Tractable ; yielding to motives, persuasion or instruction ; as, a *ductile* people ; সুবিনেয়, বশ্য ; সাধ্য ।

dŭc-til′-i-tȳ, *n.* **1.** The state or quality of being ductile ; তান্তবতা, পরিকর্ষ । 2. Tractableness ; বশ্যতা, বিনেয়তা, শাসনীয়তা ।

dūde, *n.* (*U. S. Slang*) A dandy ; a fop ; (মার্কিণযুক্তরাজ্যের ইতরভাষায়) ফুল বাবু ; খুশপোষাকী বাবু । **Dud′-ish,** *adj.*

dudg′-eon (dŭj-ŏn), *n.* Resentment ; feeling of offence ; রোষ, আক্রোশ, দ্বেষভাব ; বিরক্তির ভাব ।

dŭ-d(h)een′ (-d(h)ēn), *n.* A short clay pipe ; একপ্রকার খর্ব্ব মৃন্ময় ধূমপানের নল ।

dūds, *n. pl.* (*Slang*) Clothes ; (বহুবচন, ইতরভাষায়) কাপড়চোপড় ।

due (dū), *n., adj.* & *adv.* **1.** That to which one has a right legal or moral ; as, to give the devil his *due* ; প্রাপ্য । **2.** What one owes ; debt ; as, to pay one's *dues* ; দেনা ; ঋণ । **3.** (*Usu. pl.*) Toll legally demandable ; as, harbour *dues* ; মাশুল, শুল্ক । ***Adj.*** **1.** Owing ; payable as a debt or obligation ; দেয় ; প্রাপ্য । **2.** That ought to be given to a person ; as, the first place is *due* to Milton ; প্রদেয় । **3.** Appropriate ; suitable ; যথাযোগ্য ; সমুচিত । **4.** Rightful ; proper ; calculated or foreseen ; as, in *due* time ; যথার্থ ; উপযুক্ত ; পূর্ব্ববিবেচিত, পূর্ব্ব হইতে দৃষ্ট । **5.** Ascribable (to a cause, agent, etc.) ; as, the difficulty is *due* to our ignorance ; আরোপণীয় । **6.** Under an engagement to do something ; as, he is *due* to speak this evening ; appointed to arrive (at a certain time) ; as, the train is *due* at 10-30 ; কোন কার্য্য করার জন্য প্রতিশ্রুতি-বদ্ধ ; পৌছার জন্য নিদ্দিষ্ট । ***Adv.*** Exactly ; directly ; as, *due* north wind ; ঠিক ; সোজা । **Due to**—Owing to ; জন্য, কারণ, হেতু, বশতঃ । Occasioned by ; as, his prosperity is *due to* his own diligence ; কোন কিছু দ্বারা জনিত হওয়া । **For a full due**—(*Naut.*) For good ; thoroughly ; completely ; (নৌ-বিদ্যা) চিরকালের জন্য ; পূরাপূরি ; সম্পূর্ণভাবে । **To be already due**—(Of a train etc.) Ought, according to the time tables, to be already here ; ইতঃপূর্ব্বেই পৌছা উচিত হওয়া । **To be overdue**—(Of a train) (ট্রেণ প্রভৃতি সম্পর্কে) পৌছিবার সময় উত্তীর্ণ হওয়া । **To fall** or **become overdue**—(Of a bill) To reach maturity ; হুণ্ডীর টাকা পরিশোধের নিরূপিত সময় উত্তীর্ণ হওয়া । **To give the devil his due**—See DEVIL.

dū′-ĕl, *n.* & *v. i.* **1.** A single combat ; a fight with deadly weapons between two persons in presence of two seconds to settle a quarrel ; দ্বৈরথ যুদ্ধ (কৃঞ্চঃ) ; দ্বন্দ্বযুদ্ধ, মলযুদ্ধ (মঃ উঃ) । **2.** Any quarrel between two persons, animals, parties, etc. ; দুই ব্যক্তি, জন্তু বা পক্ষের মধ্যে বিবাদ । ***Verb i.*** To fight in a single combat ; দ্বন্দ্ব যুদ্ধ করা । **The duel**—Duelling and its code of rules etc. ; দ্বন্দ্বযুদ্ধ এবং তৎসম্পর্কীয় নিয়মাবলী প্রভৃতি ।

dū-ĕn′-nă, *n.* **1.** An elderly woman acting as governess and companion in charge of girls ; প্রকাশ্যস্থলে গমনকালে অবিবাহিতা যুবতীগণের সহিত শোভনতার জন্য যে বর্ষীয়সী মহিলা গমন করেন । **2.** The chief lady in waiting on the queen of Spain ; স্পেনদেশীয় রাণীর প্রধানা সহচরী ।

dū-ĕt(t)′, *n.* **1.** A musical composition for two performers ; দুই ব্যক্তির দ্বারা সম্পাদ্য সঙ্গীত বা বাদ্য । **2.** (*Fig.*) A dialogue ; a scolding match ; (লক্ষণায়) কথোপকথন, কথাবার্ত্তা ; তরজার লড়াই । **3.** A pair ; a couple ; যুগল ; জোড়া । **—et′-tist,** *n.*

dŭff, *n.* **1.** (*Naut.*) A stiff flour pudding boiled in a bag ; (নৌবিদ্যা) ময়দার পিষ্টক—ইহা থলিয়াতে পুরিয়া সিদ্ধ করা হয় । **2.** (*Eng. Dial.*) Dough ; (প্রাদেশিক ইংরেজী) মাখা ময়দা বা গুজি ।

dŭff, *v. t.* **1.** (*Slang*) To take up (goods) ; to cheat ; (ইতর-ভাষায়) পুরাতন জিনিষ রঙ্গ পালিশ করিয়া নূতন বলিয়া ভ্রম জন্মান ; ঠকান । **2.** (*Australia*) To alter the brands on (cattle etc.) ; to steal (cattle etc.) by changing brands ; (অষ্ট্রেলিয়া) (গবাদি পশুর) দাগ বদলাইয়া দেওয়া ; দাগ বদলাইয়া (গবাদি পশু) হরণ করা । **Duf′-fing,** *adj.* Counterfeit ; মেকি, জাল ।

dŭf′-fĕl, —fle, *n.* **1.** A kind of coarse woollen cloth having a thick nap or frieze ; একপ্রকার স্থূল পশমী বস্ত্র । **2.** Sportman's change of clothes ; খেলোয়ারের পোষাক ।

dŭff′-ĕr, *n.* **1.** One who sells trash as valuable, pretending it to be smuggled, stolen, etc. ; যে ব্যক্তি চোরাই মাল বা বিজোড়া মাল বলিয়া সস্তায় দিতেছে এই রূপ ফাঁকি দিয়া অকিঞ্চিৎকর জিনিষ মূল্যবান বলিয়া বিক্রয় করে । **2.** A hawker ; ফেরিওয়ালা । **3.** A faker of sham articles ; যে ব্যক্তি ঝুঁটা বা পুরাণ মাল রঙ্গ পালিশ করিয়া নূতন বা আসল বলিয়া চালায় । **4.** (*Slang*) A counterfeit or worthless thing, as coin, picture, etc. ; (ইতর ভাষায়) মেকি টাকা, জাল ছবি, অসার বস্তু । **5.** An unproductive mine ; অনুৎপাদক খনি । **6.** An unefficient, awkward or stupid person ; নিষ্কর্ম্মা লোক, নির্ব্বোধ লোক ।

dŭg, *p. p.* of DIG, which see.

dŭg, *n.* The udder of female mammals, (also) a teat or nipple (no longer used of women except in contempt) ; পশুর স্তন বা বাঁট, চুচুক, স্তনাগ্র । (বর্ত্তমানে অবজ্ঞার্থে ভিন্ন স্ত্রীলোক সম্পর্কে ব্যবহৃত হয় না ।)

dū-gŏng′, *n.* A large herbivorous mammal of the Indian seas ;

ভারতসাগরবাসী অতিকায়, তৃণভোজী, স্তন্যপায়ী পশুবিশেষ।

dŭg′-out (-owt), *n.* **1.** A canoe made by hollowing the trunk of a tree ; ডোঙ্গা, শালতি, কুঁদা নৌকা (নোয়াখালী)। **2.** A kind of dwelling excavated in the ground and roofed with turf, canvas, etc. ; ভূগর্ভে খোদিত বাস-গুহা, ইহার উপরিভাগ তৃণ বা ক্যাম্বিস কাপড় দ্বারা আচ্ছাদিত করা হয়।

dūke, *n.* **1.** (In Great Britain) The highest rank in the peerage ; ডিউক্। [গ্রেট ব্রিটেনে সম্ভ্রান্ত সমাজের মধ্যে সর্ব্বোচ্চ পদবী।] **2.** (In some countries of the continent) A sovereign prince ; the ruler of a small state or duchy ; (ইয়ুরোপের কোন কোন দেশে) উপরাজ ; ক্ষুদ্র রাজ্যের রাজা। **3.** (*Hist.*) The provincial military commanders under the Roman emperors ; (ইতিহাস) রোমীয় সম্রাটগণের অধীন প্রাদেশিক সামরিক শাসনকর্ত্তা। **4.** (*Bible*) The chief of a tribe ; (বাইবেল) কোন বংশের নায়ক। **5.** A kind of cherry ; এক প্রকার চেরি ফল। **6.** (*Slang*) A hand or fist ; (ইতর ভাষায়) হাত বা মুঠা। **Duke′-dom,** *n.* A duchy ; the dignity of a duke ; ডিউকের অধিকারভুক্ত সম্পত্তি ; ডিউকের গৌরব বা পদবী। **To dine with Duke Humphrey**—See DINE.

Dū-kêr-ies (-iz), *n. pl.* A district in Nottinghamshire containing several ducal estates ; নটীংহাম্‌শায়ারের অন্তর্ভুক্ত ভূভাগ বিশেষ, যাহাতে কতিপয় ডিউকীয় ভূসম্পত্তি রহিয়াছে।

dŭl′-cĕt, *adj.* Sweet ; soothing ; (esp. of sounds) ; সুমিষ্ট, সুললিত ; শ্রুতিহর (বাৎস্যঃ), শ্রুতিসুভগ, শ্রবণ-সুভগ, কর্ণাপহারী (উজ্জ্বলঃ), সুমধুর, শ্রুতিমধুর, শ্রুতিসুখদ।

dŭl′-cĭ-fy̆, *v. t.* To render gentle ; to mollify ; মৃদু করা ; কোমল করা। **—fi-ca′-tion,** *n.*

dŭl′-cĭ-mêr, *n.* A stringed instrument of music, played on by two sticks ; একপ্রকার তন্ত্রিযুক্ত বাদ্য-যন্ত্র।

Italian Dulcimer.

Dŭl-cĭn′-ē-ă, *n.* An idolized and idealized mistress ; দেবীপ্রতিমাসমা স্বপ্নসুন্দরীরূপিণী প্রণয়িনী। [Don-quixoteএর প্রণয়িনীর নাম।]

dŭll, *adj., v. t.* & *i.* **1.** Blockish ; stupid ; slow of understanding ; as, a lad of *dull* genius ; স্থূলবুদ্ধি ; জড়বুদ্ধি, মূঢ় ; হীনবুদ্ধি, মন্দবুদ্ধি। **2.** Without keen perception or sensibility ; as, *dull* eyes ; অপ্রখর, অতীক্ষ্ণ। **3.** Sluggish ; stagnant ; as, a *dull* stream, trade or person ; অলস, খেতো, ঢিলা, ঢিমা ; নরম, মন্দা। **4.** Indistinctly felt ; as, *dull* pain ; অস্পষ্টভাবে অনুভূত। **5.** Insensible; gross ; inert; "Look on the *dull* earth with disturbed mind ;" অচেতন ; স্থূল ; জড়, নির্জ্জীব। **6.** Depressed ; cheerless ; হতোৎসাহ ; বিরস, অপ্রফুল্ল, অপ্রসন্ন, বিষণ্ন। **7.** Tedious ; monotonous ; as, a *dull* story ; অবসাদজনক ; একঘেয়ে। **8.** Blunt ; as, the murderous knife was *dull* and blunt ; ভোঁতা। **9.** Not bright or vivid ; not keen, as a colour, light, sound or taste ; অনুজ্জ্বল, স্বল্পকান্তি ; স্তিমিত, নিস্তেজ, বিবর্ণ, মন্দদ্যুতি। **10.** Cloudy ; overcast ; মেঘাচ্ছন্ন ; ঘোরাল। **11.** (Of goods, stocks) Not easily salable ; not in demand ; কাটতিহীন ; চাহিদাশূন্য। *Verb t.* **1.** To render less acute ; to stupefy ; "Those dungs will *dull* the sense awhile ;" অপ্রখর করা ; স্তব্ধ করা, স্তম্ভিত করা। **2.** To deprive of sharpness of edge or point ; as, this *dulled* their swords ; অধারাল করা, ভোঁতা করা। **3.** To make slow to perceive ; as, to *dull* the ears ; অনুভূতি-শক্তি মন্দীভূত করা। **4.** To render dim ; to sully ; as, breath *dulls* a mirror ; নিষ্প্রভ করা ; ঝাপ্‌সা করা ; মলিন করা। *Verb i.* To become stupid, blunt, dim, etc. ; to lose force, intensity, keenness, etc.; স্থূলবুদ্ধি হওয়া, ভোঁতা হওয়া, নিষ্প্রভ হওয়া, অপ্রখর হওয়া ; শক্তি হ্রাস হওয়া, ধারালতা বা প্রখরতা নষ্ট হওয়া। **Dull′-ish,** *adj.* **Dul(l)′-ness,** *n.* The state of being dull ; মান্দ্য। **Dul′-ly,** *adv.* **Dull as ditch water**—নিরতিশয় নীরস। **To dull the edge of**—To blunt as a sword etc. ; তরবারি প্রভৃতি ভোঁতা করা। To make less sensitive, interesting or effective ; সংবেদন-শক্তি মন্দীভূত করা, কৌতুহল হ্রাস করা, কার্য্যকারিতাশক্তি ক্ষুণ্ন করা। **To feel dull**—গা মাটী মাটী করা।

dŭll′-ard (-ērd), *n.* A stupid person ; স্থূলবুদ্ধি ব্যক্তি, মূঢ়।

dulse (dŭls), *n.* An edible species of sea-weed ; আহারোপযোগী সামুদ্রিক তৃণবিশেষ।

dū′-ly̆, *adv.* **1.** Rightly ; properly ; যথাযোগ্যরূপে ; সমুচিতরূপে। **2.** Sufficiently ; fully ; প্রচুরভাবে ; পুরা, পূর্ণভাবে। **3.** Punctually ; orderly ; যথাসময়ে ; সুষ্ঠুরূপে।

dū′-mā, *n.* Russian parliament ; রুশিয়া দেশের প্রাকৃত সভা। [এই পার্লেমেণ্ট ১৯০৬ খৃষ্টাব্দে প্রতিষ্ঠিত হয়।]

dumb (dŭm), *adj.* **1.** Unable to utter articulate sound ; as, *dumb* brutes ; বোবা, মূক, হাবা। **2.** Mute ; not accompanied by words ; as, a *dumb* show ; নীরব, মৌন ; নির্ব্বাক, অবাক, বাক্‌রহিত। **3.** Inarticulate ; having no voice in government etc. ; as, the *dumb* millions ; অস্ফুটবাক ; শাসন সম্পর্কীয় ব্যাপারাদিতে মতামত প্রকাশের ক্ষমতা-বিহীন। **4.** Deprived of the power of speech, by surprise, shyness, etc. ; as, to be struck *dumb* with astonishment ; বাক্‌শক্তিহীন, রুদ্ধবাক্, জড়, রুদ্ধ-কণ্ঠ। 5. Taciturn ; reticent ; as, the English are a *dumb* people ; সংযতবাক্, স্বল্পভাষী; তুষ্ণীশীল, মৌনী। 6. Emitting no sound ; unheard ; "All the while his whip is *dumb* ;" নীরব ; অশ্রুত। **Dumb'-ly,** *adv.* **Dumb'-ness,** *n.* The state of being dumb ; মূকত্ব, মূকতা। **Dumb-barge**—দাঁড় বা পাল বিহীন বজরা। **Dumb-dog**—যে ব্যক্তি যখন কথা বলা কিম্বা প্রতিবাদ করা উচিত তখন নিৰ্বাক্ থাকে। **Dumb-show**—নাটকের যে অংশ কেবলমাত্র অঙ্গভঙ্গী দ্বারা অভিনীত হয়, মূক-অভিনয়। Significant gesture without speech ; বিশেষ ভাব প্রকাশক অঙ্গভঙ্গী, মূকচেষ্টা। **Dumb-waiter**—এক প্রকার কাঠাম—যাহার উপর থালা, খাদ্য প্রভৃতি রাখিয়া যান্ত্রিক ব্যবস্থার সাহায্যে এক তল হইতে অপর তলে কিম্বা কক্ষ হইতে কক্ষান্তরে নীত হয়। A portable serving table or stand with revolving shelves enabling the waiter to be dispensed with in a dining room ; পরিবেষকের সাহায্য বিনা ভোজনকালে পরিবেষণ কার্য্য নির্ব্বাহের জন্য ঘূর্ণনশীল তাকবিশিষ্ট কাঠাসন বা পরিবেষণমঞ্চ। **Dumb ox of Cologne**—Thomas Aquinas (১২২৬—১২৭৪) নামক মধ্যযুগের সুপ্রসিদ্ধ পণ্ডিত ; ইনি স্বল্পভাষী ও কল্পনাপ্রিয় ছিলেন বলিয়া এই আখ্যাপ্রাপ্ত হইয়াছেন।

dumb (dŭm), *v. t.* To make dumb ; মূক করা, বোবা করা।

dumb'-bĕll (dŭm-), *n.* & *v. i.* Short bar with weight at each end used in pairs for exercising muscles ; দৈহিক পেশীসমূহের অনুশীলনের জন্য উভয়প্রান্তে ভারী খর্ব্ব লৌহদণ্ড, অয়োদণ্ড (আঃ বঃ)। *Verb i.* To use these ; অয়োদণ্ড ব্যবহার করা।

Dumb-bell.

dumb'-found (dŭm-fownd), *v. t.* To strike dumb ; to confound ; মূক করা, বাক্‌শক্তি লোপ করা ; স্তম্ভিত করা, হতবুদ্ধি করা, জড়ীভূত করা, অবাক্ করা।

dŭm'-dŭm (bullet), *n.* A kind of soft-nosed bullet that expands and inflicts laceration ; একপ্রকার গুলি — যাহা দেহে প্রবেশের পর ফাটিয়া মাংস ছিন্নভিন্ন করিয়া ফেলে। ইহা কলিকাতার নিকটবর্ত্তী দমদম্ নামক স্থানে প্রথম প্রস্তুত হয়। এইরূপ গুলির ব্যবহার Hague নগরের আন্তর্জাতিক শান্তিসমিতি কর্ত্তৃক নিষিদ্ধ হইয়াছিল।

dŭm'-mÿ, *adj.* & *n.* Sham, as a watch etc. ; নকল, কৃত্রিম, অপ্রকৃত। ***Noun.*** 1. One who is dumb (*Colloq*) ; মূক, বোবা লোক, (চলিত ভাষায়)। 2. A mere tool of another ; a man of straw ; ক্রীড়া-পুত্তলিকা ; খড়ের পুতুল, সাক্ষীগোপাল, সামান্য লোক। 3. A dolt ; a blockhead ; হাবা, জড়ভরত ; জড়বুদ্ধি ব্যক্তি। 4. A counterfeit object ; a sham drawer or package etc. in shops ; a man's figure for rifle practice etc. ; কৃত্রিম জিনিষ ; মাল প্রভৃতি আছে বলিয়া লোকের ভ্রম জন্মাইবার জন্য দোকানে যে কৃত্রিম দেরাজ, বস্তা প্রভৃতি রাখা হয়, ভড়ঙ্গে বস্তা ; বন্দুকাদি দ্বারা লক্ষ্যভেদ শিক্ষার্থ কৃত্রিম মনুষ্যমূর্ত্তি। 5. The fourth or exposed hand when three persons play at whist ; a game of whist with a dummy ; (৪ জনের তাস খেলায়) তিন জনে খেলিতে হইলে যাহাকে চতুর্থ ব্যক্তির স্থানীয় বলিয়া ধরা হয় ; উক্ত প্রকারে তাসখেলা। 6. A person who appears in the stage but has no word to speak ; যে অভিনেতাকে রঙ্গমঞ্চে অবতীর্ণ হইতে হয় কিন্তু কোন কথা বলিতে হয় না। 7. A set of sheets or leaves made up, as by binding, to represent a book to be printed etc. ; মুদ্রিতব্য পুস্তকাদির সাদা কাগজে বাঁধাই করা প্রতিরূপ।

dŭmp, *n.* 1. A clumsy medal of metal cast in moist sands ; a leaden counter used by boys in games ; একপ্রকার স্থূল পদক ; ছেলেদিগের খেলার জন্য সীসার ঘুঁটি। 2. An obsolete Australian coin ; অষ্ট্রেলিয়া দেশীয় অপ্রচলিত মুদ্রা বিশেষ। 3. A kind of nail or bolt used in ship-building ; পোতনির্ম্মাণে ব্যবহৃত পেরেক বিশেষ। 4. A small coin or sum ; as, not worth a *dump* ; সামান্য মূল্যের মুদ্রা বা অর্থ। 5. A rope-quoit for game on board ship ; জাহাজের উপরে ক্রীড়ার জন্য একপ্রকার রজ্জুনির্ম্মিত চাক্তি। 6. A kind of sweet-meat ; একপ্রকার মিঠাই। 7. A stout person of short stature ; খর্ব্বকায় অথচ হৃষ্টপুষ্ট ব্যক্তি, বজ্রবাটুল।

dŭmp, *v. t., i.* & *n.* 1. To throw into a heap ; গাদা করা। 2. To let fall with a bump ; ধপাৎ করিয়া ফেলা, ধপ্ করিয়া ফেলা। 3. (*Comm.*) To sell (goods etc.) abroad at less than the market price at home (in order to avoid lowering home-price and capture new market) ; (বাণিজ্য) স্বদেশের বাজার দর অপেক্ষা অল্প মূল্যে বিদেশে (জিনিষ) বিক্রয় করা। 4. To land in foreign countries ; as, to *dump* superfluous immigrants ; বিদেশে নামাইয়া দেওয়া। ***Verb i.*** 1. To fall with a thud ; ধপাৎ করিয়া পড়া, ধুপ্‌ধাপ্ করিয়া পড়া। 2. To land in foreign countries ; বিদেশে নামা। 3. (*Comm.*) To dump goods ; (বাণিজ্য) স্বদেশের বাজারদর অপেক্ষা কম মূল্যে বিদেশে জিনিষ বিক্রয় করা। ***Noun.*** 1. A thud or bump as from falling ; ধপাৎ শব্দ, ধুপ্‌ধাপ্ শব্দ। 2. (*U. S.*) A heap of refuse ; a place for tilting refuse ; (যুক্তরাজ্য) জঞ্জালস্তূপ, আবর্জ্জনাস্তূপ ; যে স্থানে জঞ্জাল আবর্জ্জনাদি ফেলা হয়। **Dump'-er,** *n.*

dŭmp'-ling, *n.* A mass of dough boiled or baked either with or without fruit in it ; মালপোয়ার মত মিঠাই বিশেষ, কুলরী।

dŭmps, *n. pl.* Depression ; melancholy ; চিত্তগ্লানি, অবসাদ ; বিষাদ, বিষণ্ণতা। **In the dumps**—Sulky ; in low spirits ; মুখভারী ; দুর্মনায়মান, স্ফূর্তিহীন-চিত্ত।

dŭmp'-ÿ, *adj.* & *n.* Short and stout ; বেঁটে ও মোটসোটা, হ্রস্বস্থূল। ***Noun.*** 1. One of the breed of short-legged fowls ; এক জাতীয় মোরগ। 2. (*Pl.*) 19th Hussars ; ১৯ গণিত হুসার সৈন্য। **—i-ness,** *n.* **Dumpy level**—জরীপে ব্যবহৃত সমতল-নির্ণায়ক যন্ত্রবিশেষ।

dŭn, *adj.* & *n.* 1. Of a dark brown colour ; as, a *dun* cow ; ধূসর, কপিশ, পিঙ্গল। 2. (*Poet.*) Dark ; gloomy ; কৃষ্ণ ; ঘোর। ***Noun.*** 1. Greyish brown colour ; কপিশ বর্ণ। 2. A dun horse ; কপিশবর্ণ অশ্ব। 3. A kind of artificial fly for fishing ; বড়শীর জন্য একপ্রকার কৃত্রিম মক্ষিকা। **Dun bird**—একপ্রকার পক্ষী।

dŭn, *n.* & *v. t.* 1. An importunate creditor who urges for payment ; অত্যন্ত তাগিদদার মহাজন। 2. One who collects debts ; ঋণের টাকা সংগ্রহ-কারী। 3. An urgent demand for payment ; as, to send a *dun* to a debtor ; খতের টাকা পরিশোধের জন্য কড়া তাগিদ। ***Verb t.*** To ask or importune as a debtor etc. ; খতের টাকা পরিশোধের জন্য কড়া তাগিদ দেওয়া। 2. To pester constantly ; অনবরত জ্বালাতন করা, সর্ব্বদা ঝালা-পালা করা।

dunce (dŭns), *n.* One slow in learning ; a dullard ; a dolt ; হীন-বুদ্ধি লোক, স্থূলবুদ্ধি-লোক ; গণ্ডমূর্খ, হাবা। **Dunce's cap**—(মূর্খছেলের) মাথার টুপি।

dŭn'-dêr-head (-hĕd), *n.* A blockhead ; জড়বুদ্ধি ব্যক্তি, আহাম্মক, মাথা-মোটা। **—ed,** *adj.* Stupid ; নির্ব্বোধ, বোকা।

dūne, *n.* A hill ; specifically a ridge of sand piled up on the seacoast ; পাহাড় ; বালিয়াড়ী (সাঃ পঃ), সৈকত-শৈল।

dŭng, *n.* & *v. t.* Excrement or fæces of an animal ; manure ; গোময়, পশুর বিষ্ঠা, পশুমল, গু, নাদ, গোবর, গোপুরীষ ; পশুবিষ্ঠার সার। ***Verb t.*** To manure with dung ; পশুবিষ্ঠার সার দেওয়া। **Dung-beetle** — গোবরে পোকা। **Dung cake**—ঘুঁটে। **Dung-fly**—একপ্রকার মাছি, যাহারা গোবর আহার করিয়া প্রাণধারণ করে। **Dung-worm**—গোময়ে প্রাপ্ত কীট বিশেষ,—ইহা বড়শীর টোপে ব্যবহৃত হয়।

dŭn'-geon (-jŏn), *n.* & *v. t.* (Now usually *donjon*) 1. The innermost and strongest tower of a castle ; গড়বন্দী প্রাসাদের সর্ব্বমধ্যবর্ত্তী এবং সুদৃঢ়তম বুরুজবিশেষ, গূঢ়াগার। 2. A strong underground cell used as a prison ; ভূগর্ভস্থ সুদৃঢ় কারাকক্ষ, আন্তর্ভৌম কারাকক্ষ, অন্ধকূপ। ***Verb t.*** To confine in a dungeon ; গূঢ়াগারে বদ্ধ করা, ভূগর্ভস্থ সুদৃঢ় কারাকক্ষে রুদ্ধ করা।

dŭng'-hill, *n.* 1. A heap of dung or refuse ; পশুপুরীষ, গোময়-স্তূপ, আবর্জ্জনা-স্তূপ, সারকুড়। 2. A vile abode ; a mean situation ; জঘন্য বাসস্থান ; হীনকর্ম্ম। **Dung-hill cock** — গৃহকুক্কুট। **Every cock crows on its own dung-hill**—আপনার কোটে বসিয়া সকলেই নিজ কার্য্যের বড়াই করিতে পারে।

dŭn'-i-wăs-săl, *n.* A gentleman of the secondary rank, (Scot. Highlands) ; (স্কটলণ্ডের পার্ব্বত্য প্রদেশে) দ্বিতীয় শ্রেণীর ভদ্রলোক।

dŭn'-lin, *n.* A species of sandpiper ; একপ্রকার পক্ষী।

dŭn'-năge, *n.* Branches, brushwood, etc. used as a support for cargo ; fagots, bough or loose materials of any kind, laid on the bottom of a ship to prevent injury to goods by water in the hold ; loose articles of merchandise wedged between parts of the cargo to prevent rubbing and to hold them steady ; জাহাজের সকল মাল কাত হইয়া পড়িয়া না যায়, তজ্জন্য যে ডালপালা দ্বারা মালগুলি স্থির রাখা হয় ; জল উঠিয়া মাল ভিজিতে না পারে তজ্জন্য জাহাজের খোলে যে ডালপালা দেওয়া হয় ; জাহাজের মাল পরস্পরের সহিত ঘৃষ্ট হইয়া নষ্ট না হয় তজ্জন্য মাল সকলের মধ্যের ফাঁকা জায়গায় যে আল্লামাল ঢুকাইয়া দেওয়া হয়।

dŭn'-nock(-nŭk), *n.* The common hedgesparrow ; একপ্রকার চটক পক্ষী।

dū-ō-dĕc'-i-măl, *adj.* & *n.* Proceeding by twelves ; pertaining to twelve or twelfths ; দ্বাদশমিক ; দ্বাদশ-সম্পর্কীয়, দ্বাদশতম সংখ্যার বস্তু-সম্পর্কীয়। ***Noun.*** (*Pl.*) 1. A rule in Arithmetic in which the denominations rise by twelves, chiefly applied to the calculation of square feet and inches, (also called *cross-multiplication*) ; দ্বাদশমিক অঙ্ক, দ্বাদশলব (হিঃ কোঃ)। 2. A twelfth part ; দ্বাদশতম অংশ।

dū-ō-dĕc'-i-mō, *adj.* & *n.* Having twelve leaves to a sheet ; as, a *duodecimo* form ; দ্বাদশাংশিত, দ্বাদশপৃষ্ঠাত্মক। ***Noun.*** 1. A size of a book resulting from folding each sheet into twelve leaves ; প্রতি মুদ্রিত কাগজ ভাঁজ করিয়া ১২ পৃষ্ঠা করিলে পুস্তকের যে আকার হয়। 2. A book in which a sheet is folded into twelve leaves ; প্রতি মুদ্রিত কাগজ দ্বাদশ অংশে (২৪ পৃষ্ঠায়) ভাঁজ করিয়া যে পুস্তক হয়। [সাধারণতঃ 12 mo. অথবা ১২° লিখিত হয়।] 3. A thing or person of diminutive form ; খর্ব্বকায় ব্যক্তি, বামন, ক্ষুদ্রবস্তু।

dū-ō-dĕn'-ă-rÿ, *adj.* Proceeding by twelves ; relating to twelve ; containing twelve ; দ্বাদশমিক ; দ্বাদশসম্পর্কীয় ; দ্বাদশাত্মক।

dū-ō-dē'-nŭm, *n.* (*Anat.*) The first portion of the small intestines ; (শারীর-সংস্থান বিদ্যা) দ্বাদশাঙ্গুলান্ত্র

(হঃ চঃ), ক্ষুদ্র অন্ত্রের প্রথমাংশ, গ্রহণী (সুশ্রুঃ), পিত্তাশয় (বিনয়ঃ)। **—nal,** *adj.* **—ni′-tis,** *n.* (*Med.*) Inflammation of the duodenum; দ্বাদশাঙ্গুলান্ত্র-প্রদাহ।

dü-ŏ-logue (-lŏg), *n.* A dialogue between two persons ; a dramatic piece with two actors ; দুই ব্যক্তির মধ্যে কথোপকথন ; যে নাটকে দুই জন মাত্র অভিনেতা থাকে।

duo′-mö (dwö-), *n.* An Italian cathedral ; ইতালীদেশীয় মহামন্দির।

düpe, *n.* & *v. t.* One who is easily deceived ; যে ব্যক্তি সহজে প্রতারিত হয়, বেকুব, সাদাসিধা লোক। ***Verb t.*** To deceive ; to make a fool of ; as, to *dupe* one by flattery ; প্রতারণা করা, বঞ্চনা করা, বোকা বানান ; উপহাসাস্পদ করা। **Dup-a-bil′-i-ty,** *n.* **Dup′-a-ble,** *adj.* **Duped,** *adj.* **Dup′-er,** *n.* **Dup′-er-y,** *n.* Deception ; trickery ; প্রতারণা ; চাতুরী।

dü′-plĕx, *adj.* **1.** Double ; twofold ; দ্বিগুণ ; দ্বিগুণিত, দুভাঁজ। **2.** (*Mech.*) Composed of two parts or elements operating at the same time or in the same way ; একসময়ে ও একভাবে কার্য্যকারী অংশদ্বয়-সমন্বিত। **Duplex escapement**—See ESCAPEMENT. **Duplex gas-burner**—যে বাষ্প-নিঃসারী বর্ত্তিমুখের অংশদ্বয় হইতে অগ্নিচ্ছটা নির্গত হইয়া একমাত্র শিখায় সম্মিলিত হয়। **Duplex lamp**—দুই শলিতার প্রদীপ.

cä′-pē-line (-lin), *n.* **1.** ... worn by ladies going out to an evening party ; মহিলাগণ সান্ধ্য সম্মিলনে যাইবার কালে যে শিরোবস্ত্র পরিধান করিয়া থাকেন। **2.** A surgical bandage for the head ; মস্তকের ক্ষত বন্ধনী বিশেষ।

că-pĕl′-lă, *n.* A brilliant star in the constellation Auriga ; ব্রহ্মহৃদয় (সাঃ পঃ)।

căp′-ĕl-lĕt, *n.* A tumour-like swelling on a horse's elbow or on the back part of his hock ; with him ; বন্ধকী মালের রসিদ। **3.** One of several species of a thing exactly similar ; কতিপয় অনুরূপ বস্তুর অন্যতম। **4.** A synonym ; সমার্থ শব্দ, প্রতিশব্দ। **5.** Exact correspondence between two things ; দুই বস্তুর অনুরূপতা। ***Verb t.*** **1.** To double ; দ্বিগুণিত করা, দ্বিরাবৃত্ত করা। **2.** To make a copy or transcript of ; to make in duplicate ; নকল করা, প্রতিলিপি প্রস্তুত করা ; অনুরূপ অন্য একটী প্রস্তুত করা। **—ca′-tion,** *n.* **—ca-tor,** *n.* A copying-machine ; পত্রাদির অনুলিপি তোলার জন্য যন্ত্রবিশেষ।

dü-plĭc′-i-tў, *n.* **1.** Double-dealing ; dissimulation ; কপটতা, কাপট্য ; ভণ্ডতা, অবহিত্থ, ধোকা। **2.** Doubleness ; দ্বৈধভাব।

dü′-ră-ble (-bl), *adj.* Lasting ; as, *durable* clothes ; permanent ; not wearing out or decaying soon ; স্থায়ী ; স্থিতিমান ; মজবুত, শক্ত, পাকা, টেকসই। **—bil′-i-ty, —ness,** *ns.* **1.** The state of being durable ; স্থায়িত্ব, স্থিরতা, অক্ষয়তা, দৃঢ়তা। **2.** Duration of life ; আয়ু। **—bly,** *adv.* **—ra′-tion,** *n.* Continuance in time ; power of continuance ; permanency ; স্থিতিকাল, স্থিতি, মিয়াদ, মুদ্দৎ, সত্তাকাল ; স্থিতিশক্তি ; স্থায়িত্ব।

dü′-ră mă′-têr, *n.* (*Anat.*) The outer membrane of the brain and spinal cord ; (শারীর সংস্থান বিদ্যা) মস্তিষ্ক এবং মেরুদণ্ডের বাহিরের দিকের প্রথম পরদা, দৃঢ়মাতৃকা (হঃ চঃ), শবকাষ্ঠ (সাঃ পঃ), মস্তিষ্কের বহির্ঝিল্লী।

dür′-ance (-ăns), *n.* Imprisonment, (now usually in the phrase *in durance vile*) ; হাজতে রাখন, কারাবন্ধন।

dur′-bâr (dêr-), *n.* **1.** The court of an Indian ruler ; রাজদরবার, মজলিস। **2.** An official levee held by an Indian prince or the viceroy ; as, *durbar-dress* ; দরবার।

dü-ress(e)′ (-rĕs), *n.* **1.** Imprisonment ; restraint of liberty ; কয়েদ ; আটক, হাজত। **2.** Compulsion illegally used to force persons to do something ; কোন ব্যক্তিকে তাহার ইচ্ছার বিরুদ্ধে কোন কার্য্য করিতে বাধ্য করণ। **A plea of duress**—ইচ্ছার বিরুদ্ধে বলপূর্ব্বক কোন কার্য্য করিতে বাধ্য হইয়াছে এই কারণে চুক্তি নাকচ করার জন্য হেতুবাদ। **Under duress**—Under compulsion ; বাধ্য হইয়া।

dür′-ing, *prep.* Throughout the course of ; in the time of ; as, *during* the space of one year ; ধরে, ধরিয়া, ব্যাপিয়া, যাবৎ ; কোন সময়ের মধ্যে।

Durian.

dü′-ri-ăn, *n.* A kind of tree ; its fruit ; একজাতীয় বৃক্ষ ; উক্ত বৃক্ষের ফল।

dur′-măst (dêr-), *n.* A kind of oak ; একপ্রকার ওক বৃক্ষ।

durn (dêrn), *v. t.* To darn ; রিফু করা।

dŭr′-ră, dhŭr-, *n.* A kind of millet ; একপ্রকার চিনা।

dŭsk, *adj., n., v. t.* & *i.* Shadowy ; ঝাপসা। ***Noun.*** **1.** Middle degree between light and darkness ; gloom ; সন্ধ্যাকাল, গোধূলি ; আঁধার। **2.** The darker stage of twilight ; as, the *dusk* of the evening, প্রদোষ। ***Verb t.*** To make shadowy or dusky ; অস্পষ্ট করা, ঝাপসা করা, ধূম্রবর্ণ দেখান। ***Verb i.*** (*Poet.*) To become shadowy ; to look dusky ; অস্পষ্ট হওয়া ; ঝাপসা হওয়া। **Dusk′-i-ness,** *n.* **Dusk′-i-ly,** *adv.* **Dusk′-ish,** *adj.* **Dusk′-y,** *adj.* **1.** Partially dark ; ঈষদন্ধকার। **2.** Of a dark colour ; ধূম্রবর্ণ, সধূম্র। **3.** Not bright ; dim ; অনুজ্জ্বল ; অস্পষ্ট। **4.** Gloomy ; melancholy ; বিষাদাচ্ছন্ন ; বিষণ্ণ।

dŭst, *n.*, *v. t.* & *i.* **1.** Fine dry particles of earth or other matter; powder; বালু, বালুকা, ধূলি, সিকতা, রজঃ, রেণু, পাংশু; চূর্ণ, গুড়া। **2.** Earth; "For *dust* thou art, shalt to *dust* return;" মৃত্তিকা, মাটী। **3.** Household refuse; as, a *dust*-man (a scavenger who empties dust-bin or -hole); গৃহের আবর্জ্জনা। **4.** (*Bot.*) Pollen of the anther; (উদ্ভিদ-বিদ্যা) ফুলের কেশরের দানা, পরাগ, পুষ্পরেণু। **5.** A cloud of dust; as, to make or raise a *dust* by sweeping etc.; ধূলি-পটল। **6.** The remains of a dead body; as, honoured *dust*; মৃত ব্যক্তির দেহাবশেষ। **7.** The body; "The soul...dwells within your *dust*;" দেহ। **8.** A low or mean condition; humiliation; "My soul lies humbled in the *dust*;" হীনাবস্থা, পাতিত্য; হীনতা। **9.** Something worthless; অসার বস্তু। **10.** Confusion; a disturbance or row; "Raise a *dust* about nothing;" গোলমাল; হাঙ্গামা। **11.** (*Slang*) Cash; (ইতর ভাষায়) টাকা কড়ি। **12.** (*Obs.*) The grave; (অপ্রচলিত) কবর। ***Verb t.*** **1.** To free from dust; to brush or sweep away dust from; as, to *dust* a table; ধূলিমুক্ত করা, ধূলা ঝাড়া; ধূলা ঝাটাইয়া ফেলা। **2.** To sprinkle with dust or powder; to strew; as dust etc; ধূলি বা চূর্ণ ছড়ান; ছড়ান, প্রক্ষেপ করা। **3.** To make dusty; ধূলিময় করা। ***Verb i.*** (Of birds) To take a dust-bath; (পক্ষিগণের) ধূলি-স্নাত হওয়া। **Dust'-less,** *adj.* **Dust-bin** or **-hole**—আবর্জ্জনা-কুণ্ড। **Dust-brand**—শস্য-রোগ বিশেষ। **Dust-cloak, -coat, -gown, -wrap, -cloth**—ধূলিবারক আবরণ, ধূলিবারক প্রাবরণ। **Dust-colour**—ধূসর বর্ণ। **Dust-guard**—ধূলি হইতে পরিচ্ছদ রক্ষার জন্য দ্বি-চক্রযান প্রভৃতি-সংলগ্ন চক্র বিশেষ। **Dust-man**—যে ব্যক্তি আবর্জ্জনা-কুণ্ড পরিষ্কার করে। **Dust-pan**—মেজের ধূলা ঝাঁটাইয়া যে পাত্রে রাখা হয়। **Dust-shot**—অতি ক্ষুদ্র আকারের গুলি। **Dust and heat**—The burden of a struggle; সংগ্রামের চাপ। **In the dust**—Dead; মৃত। **To bite the dust**—See BITE. **To dust a dam**—To fill up the interstices between the planks with earth or gravel; তক্তার মধ্যের ফাঁক ধূলি ও কঙ্কর দ্বারা পূর্ণ করা। **To dust one's jacket**—To give one a sound thrashing; বেদম প্রহার করা, উত্তম মধ্যম দেওয়া। **To dust the eyes of**—To deceive; চোখে ধূলি দেওয়া। **To raise** or **keep up dust**—(*Fig.*) To make a commotion; (লক্ষণায়) গোলমাল বাঁধান, হাঙ্গামা সৃষ্টি করা। **To shake off the dust of one's feet**—To depart indignantly; রোষাবিষ্ট হইয়া প্রস্থান করা। **To throw dust in one's eyes**—To try to lead a man astray; to deceive; কাহারও চক্ষুতে ধূলি দেওয়া; ঠকান। **To turn to dust and ashes**—To become utterly worthless; একেবারে অসার হইয়া যাওয়া।

dŭst'-ėr, *n.* **1.** A piece of cloth for brushing furniture etc.; ঘরের আসবাবপত্র ঝাড়ার জন্য কাপড়ের টুকরা, ধূলি-মার্জ্জনী। **2.** One who does this; ধূলিমার্জ্জক।

dŭst'-ing, *n.* **1.** Act of freeing from dust; ধূলি-মার্জ্জন। **2.** (*Slang*) Thrashing; (ইতরভাষায়) উত্তম মধ্যম, বেদম প্রহার।

dŭst'-ȳ, *adj.* **1.** Filled or sprinkled with dust; like dust; as, *dusty* white; ধূলিময়, ধূলি-ধূসরিত, পাংশুল; ধূলিবৎ। **2.** Powdery; সরজঃ। **3.** Dry as dust; uninteresting; ধূলিবৎ শুষ্ক; নীরস। **—i-ly,** *adv.* **—i-ness,** *n.* **Dusty miller**—The plant auricula; একপ্রকার গাছ। An artificial fly for fishing; বড়শীর টোপস্বরূপ ব্যবহৃত কৃত্রিম মক্ষিকা বিশেষ। **Not so dusty**—(*Slang*) Fairly good; (ইতর ভাষায়) ততটা মন্দ নয়, একরকম ভাল, মন্দ নয়।

Dutch (dŭch), *adj.* & *n.* **1.** Pertaining to Holland or to its inhabitants or to its language; হলন্দ দেশ সম্বন্ধীয়, ওলন্দাজ জাতি-সম্বন্ধীয়, ওলন্দাজদিগের ভাষা সম্বন্ধীয়। **2.** (*Hist.*) Pertaining to Germany including Netherlands; (ইতিহাস) হলণ্ড সমেত জার্ম্মেণী সম্বন্ধীয়। **3.** Made by the Dutch; হলন্দদেশে প্রস্তুত। ***Noun.*** **1.** The people of Holland; ওলন্দাজ। **2.** Language spoken in Holland; ওলন্দাজদিগের ভাষা। **3.** (*Hist.*) The German language in any of its forms; (ইতিহাস) জর্ম্মণ ভাষা। **Double Dutch**—অর্থশূন্য ভাষা। **Dutch-auction**—See AUCTION. **Dutch-concert**—একপ্রকার ঐক্যতান বাদ্য—যাহাতে প্রত্যেক ব্যক্তি স্বতন্ত্রভাবে স্বীয় সঙ্গীত গান বা যন্ত্র বাদন করে। **Dutch courage**—See COURAGE. **Dutch drops**—তার্পিণ তৈল এবং অন্যান্য কতিপয় ভেষজের সহযোগে প্রস্তুত ঔষধ। **Dutch-gold, metal** or **mineral**—অত্যধিক তাম্রমিশ্রিত পিত্তল। **Dutch-man**—A Hollander; ওলন্দাজ। (*Naut.*) A Dutch vessel; (নৌ-বিদ্যা) হলন্দ দেশীয় জাহাজ। **Dutch-nightingales**—ভেক, মণ্ডূক। **Dutch-pink**—বৃক্ষ বিশেষ হইতে প্রাপ্ত লোহিতবর্ণ রঞ্জক পদার্থ। **Dutch school**—ওলন্দাজ চিত্রকর সম্প্রদায়;—এই সম্প্রদায়ের চিত্রকরগণ মনুষ্যজীবনের দৈনন্দিন ঘটনা সমূহের চিত্রাঙ্কণে কলা-নৈপুণ্য প্রদর্শন করিয়া থাকেন। **Dutch uncle**—অশিষ্ট, অমার্জ্জিত ব্যক্তি। **Dutch wife**—গ্রীষ্মপ্রধান দেশে আরামের জন্য বেত্রনির্ম্মিত উপাধানবিশেষ, একপ্রকার কাগজ-ভরা কোল বালিশ। **Flying Dutch man**—ভৌতিক জাহাজ (উক্ত জাহাজ উত্তমাশা অন্তরীপের নিকটবর্ত্তী সমুদ্রে দৃষ্ট হইয়া থাকে—ইহার অধ্যক্ষ অনন্তকাল সমুদ্রে পোতচালনের দণ্ডে দণ্ডিত বলিয়া কল্পিত হইয়া থাকে); গ্রেট

ওয়েষ্টারণ রেলওয়ের (লণ্ডন হইতে ব্রিষ্টলগামী) দ্রুতগামী বাষ্পীয় শকট বিশেষ। **High Dutch**—জর্ম্মণ ভাষা। **Low Dutch**—হলণ্ড প্রভৃতি দেশের ভাষা। **I am a Dutchman, I am a Dutchman, if I do**—A strong refusal; দৃঢ়ভাবে অস্বীকার। **I will talk to you like a Dutch uncle**—I will reprove you smartly; আমি তোমাকে তীব্র তিরস্কার করিব।

dū'-tē-ous (-ŭs), *adj.* Pertaining to duty; dutiful; obedient; as, a *duteous* boy or conduct; কর্ত্তব্য-সম্পর্কীয়; কর্ত্তব্যপরায়ণ; বাধ্য, আজ্ঞাকারী, আজ্ঞাবহ, অনুগত, বশ্য **—ly,** *adv.* **—ness,** *n.*

dū'-ti-ă-ble, *adj.* Subject to customs or other duties as imported goods; শুল্ক-যোগ্য।

dū-ti'-fûl, *adj.* Submissive to natural or legal superiors; as a *dutiful* son; আজ্ঞাকারী, কর্ত্তব্যনিষ্ঠ, কর্ত্তব্যপরায়ণ। **—ly,** *adv.* **—ness.** *n.*

dū'-tȳ, *n.* **1.** Obligation; that which one is bound to do; কর্ত্তব্য, ধর্ম্ম, স্বধর্ম্মপালন (কৃষ্ণঃ); অনুষ্ঠেয় কর্ম্ম। **2.** Any assigned service or business; as, the *duties* of a policeman; কর্ত্তব্যকর্ম্ম, নিয়োগ, নির্দ্দিষ্ট কর্ম্ম। **3.** Obedience or submission due to superiors; an act of respect; deference; as, they both did their *duty* to their lady; বাধ্যতা, আনুগত্য; শ্রদ্ধা; ভক্তি। **4.** Tax; impost or customs; কর, টেক্স; শুল্ক, মাশুল। **5.** The amount of weight which is lifted by a steam-engine as measured by the consumption of a certain quantity of fuel; বাষ্পীয় যন্ত্রদ্বারা উত্তোলিত ভারের পরিমাণ—যাহা নির্দ্দিষ্ট ওজনের জ্বালানি কাঠ, কয়লা প্রভৃতির ব্যয় দ্বারা পরিমিত হয়। **6.** (*Eccl.*) Performance of the offices of the church; ধর্ম্ম-সংক্রান্ত কার্য্যাদির অনুষ্ঠান। **Duty-call**—কর্ত্তব্যের অনুরোধে কাহারো সহিত সাক্ষাৎ। **Duty-free**—মুক্ত-শুল্ক, কর-রহিত, বে-মাশুল। **Duty-paid**—(মাল-সম্পর্কে) শুল্ক-প্রদত্ত। **Off duty**—কর্ত্তব্যকার্য্য সমাপনান্তে প্রাপ্তাবসর। **On duty**—কর্ত্তব্য কার্য্যে নিযুক্ত। **Sense of duty**—কর্ত্তব্য-বুদ্ধি। **To do duty for**—To serve; to pass for (something else); কোন কাজ করা; (কোন কিছু বলিয়া) গণ্য হওয়া।

dū-ŭm'-vir (-vêr), *n.* (*Pl.* -VIRI) One of two Roman officers or magistrates united in the same public functions; one of two officials united in the same office; একই কার্য্যসাধনে নিযুক্ত প্রাচীন রোমের রাজকর্ম্মচারী অথবা শাসন-কর্ত্তৃদ্বয়ের অন্যতর; একই কর্ত্তব্য সম্পাদনে নিযুক্ত রাজকর্ম্মচারিদ্বয়ের অন্যতর, দ্বিপুরুষ (আঃ বঃ)। **—vi-rate,** *n.*

dŭx, *n.* The head of a class in a school, (chiefly Scottish); কোন শ্রেণীর প্রধান ছাত্র, কোন শ্রেণীর ছাত্রগণের নেতা, পটুশিষ্য, শির-পড়ো।

dwarf, *adj., n.* & *v. t.* **1.** Below the common size (in many plant names); খর্ব্বকায়, খর্ব্বাকৃতি, হ্রস্বমূর্ত্তি, হ্রস্বাঙ্গ, বেঁটে। **2.** Relating to a dwarf; stunted; খর্ব্বসম্বন্ধীয়; খাটো। *Noun.* **1.** A person or plant much below the ordinary size; খর্ব্বকায় ব্যক্তি, বামন, খর্ব্বাকৃতি বৃক্ষ। **2.** A small supernatural being in Scandanavian mythology skilled in metal working; নরওয়ে ও সুইডেনের পুরাণে বর্ণিত ধাতব-শিল্প-কার্য্যে নিপুণ খর্ব্বকায় দেবতা। *Verb t.* **1.** To stunt in physical or mental growth; to make or keep small; খর্ব্ব করা, খাটো করা, হ্রস্ব করা; ক্ষুদ্রকায় করা বা ক্ষুদ্রকায় করিয়া রাখা। **2.** To make look small by contrast or distance; দূরত্ব বা বৈপরীত্যদ্বারা ক্ষুদ্র দেখান।

dwarf'-ish, *adj.* Like a dwarf; very small; বামনতুল্য, খর্ব্বাকৃতি, বেঁটে; অতি ক্ষুদ্র। **—ly,** *adv.* **—ness,** *n.*

dwĕll, *n.* & *v. i.* (*Mech.*) A short intermission for some purpose in the motion of a machine; (যন্ত্র-বিজ্ঞান) কোন যন্ত্রের গতিতে ক্ষণিক অবকাশ। *Verb i.* **1.** To live in a place; to reside; বাস করা; অবস্থান করা। **2.** To continue fixed in attention; to write or speak at length, (with *on* or *upon*); কোন বিষয়ে ক্রমাগত নিবিষ্ট থাকা; কোন বিষয় অবলম্বনে সবিস্তারে লিখা বা বলা। **3.** (Of horse) To pause before or after taking fence etc.; (অশ্ব-সম্পর্কে) বৃতি উল্লঙ্ঘনের পূর্ব্বে বা পরে থামা। **To dwell on** or **upon**—To spend time or words upon; to treat at length or with insistence in speech or writing; to stick to; as, to *dwell on* a subject; কোন বিষয়ে সময় বা বাক্য ব্যয় করা; কোন বিষয়ে সবিস্তারে বর্ণনা করা বা লিখা; (কোন বিষয়ে) লাগিয়া থাকা। **To dwell upon a note, syllable, etc**—To prolong it; সুর, শব্দাংশ প্রভৃতি দীর্ঘ করা।

dwĕll'-êr, *n.* **1.** A resident; নিবাসী, অধিবাসী, বাসিন্দা। **2.** A horse that pauses before taking a fence; যে অশ্ব বেড়া ডিঙ্গাইবার পূর্ব্বে ক্ষণকাল থামিয়া থাকে।

dwĕll'-ing, *n.* Habitation; a place of residence or house; abode; গৃহ, ধাম; নিবসন, আলয়; বাসস্থান। **Dwelling house**—বসত বাটী, বাস-গৃহ।

dwin'-dle (-dl), *v. i.* **1.** To become less; to shrink; to waste away; as, the body *dwindles* by pining; খর্ব্ব হওয়া, খাটো হওয়া, হ্রাস হওয়া; সঙ্কুচিত হওয়া; ক্ষয় পাওয়া। **2.** To lose importance; to decline; গুরুত্ব হীন হওয়া; পতন হওয়া।

dȳ'-ăd, *n.* **1.** The number two; দ্বি, দুই। **2.** A pair; a couple; জোড়া; যুগল, মিথুন। **3.** (*Chem.*) An element, atom or radical, with combining power of two atoms of hydrozen; (রসায়ন-শাস্ত্র) যে পরমাণু, মূলক বা মৌলিক পদার্থের

উদজন বাষ্পের দ্বি-পরমাণু সংযোজনী শক্তি আছে, দ্বি-বন্ধন (হিঃ কোঃ)। **—ad'-ic,** *adj.*

dye (dī), *n., v. t. & i.* **1.** A colouring liquor ; tinge ; রঞ্জন, রং ; রাগ, বর্ণ। **2.** A dye-stuff ; রঞ্জক পদার্থ, রংয়ের মালমসলা, রক্তবর্গ (রঃ প্রঃ)। ***Verb t.*** To colour ; রঞ্জিত করা। ***Verb i.*** To take a colour or hue in dyeing ; as, the material *dyes* well or badly ; রং ধরা। **Dye-house, —works**—রঞ্জনশালা, রঞ্জন-গৃহ, রঞ্জন-কার্য্যালয়। **Dye-oak**—মাজুফল। **Dye-stuff**—রঞ্জক পদার্থপ্রদ বস্তু, রংয়ের মালমসলা। **Fast dye** — পাকা রঙ্, অক্ষয় রাগ (ধাঃ প্রঃ)। **Of the blackest** or **deepest dye**—(as a crime, criminal, scoundrel, etc.)—অতি ঘোর বর্ণের, ঘোর। **To dye in the wool, in grain** — To dye while the material is in a raw state giving a more permanent result ; অপেক্ষাকৃত দীর্ঘকালস্থায়ী করার উদ্দেশ্যে কাঁচা অবস্থায় রং করা।

dy'-ėr, *n.* One whose occupation is to dye cloth and the like ; রঞ্জক, রংরেজ, রঙ্গাজীব (আঃ বঃ)। **Dyer's oak, broom, etc.**—বিবিধ রঞ্জক পদার্থপ্রদ বৃক্ষ।

dy'-ing, *adj.* Connected with death ; at the point of death ; at the time of death ; as, a *dying* bed ; মৃত্যু-সংক্রান্ত ; মরণোন্মুখ, মুমূর্ষু ; মরণকালীন। **Dying declaration**—মৃত্যুকালীন উক্তি, আসন্নমৃত্যু ব্যক্তির এজাহার।

dyke, *n.* Same as DIKE, which see.

dy̆-năm'-ic, *adj. & n.* **1.** Pertaining to physical force or energy ; ভৌতিক বল বা শক্তি সম্বন্ধীয়। **2.** Relating to forces producing motion, (opposed to *static*) ; গত্যাত্মক। **3.** Active ; potent ; সক্রিয় ; শক্তিশালী, বীর্য্যবান। **4.** Relating to dynamics ; গতিবিজ্ঞান-সম্বন্ধীয়। **5.** (*Med.*) Functional, as a disease ; (ভৈষজ্যশাস্ত্র) শারীরিক যন্ত্রাদির ক্রিয়া-বিকাশজনিত। **6.** (*Philos.*) Accounting for matter or mind as the action of forces ; জড় ও চৈতন্য বল সমূহের ক্রিয়ার ফলে সঞ্জাত বলিয়া নির্দ্দেশকারী, গত্যাত্মক (হিঃ কোঃ)। ***Noun.*** Motive force ; গতিজননী শক্তি। **—i-cal,** *adj.* **1.** Relating to dynamics ; গতিবিদ্যা সম্বন্ধীয়। **2.** Pertaining to mechanical power ; যান্ত্রিক শক্তি সম্বন্ধীয়। **—i-cal-ly,** *adv.* **—ics,** *n.* **1.** The science which investigates the action of force ; গতিবিদ্যা (হিঃ কোঃ)। **2.** Moving forces physical or moral in any sphere ; ভৌতিক বা নৈতিক রাজ্যে গতিপ্রদায়ক বল। **Dynamic economy** — গত্যাত্মক অর্থশাস্ত্র (হিঃ কোঃ)। **Dynamic theory**—(ক) (দর্শন-শাস্ত্র) ক্যান্ট্ প্রবর্ত্তিত দার্শনিক বাদ বিশেষ ; ক্যান্টের মতে সমস্ত পদার্থ (তন্মাত্র) আকর্ষণ ও বিকর্ষণ এই দুই পরস্পরবিরোধী শক্তির ক্রিয়ার ফলে উদ্ভূত হইয়াছে। (খ) (তাপ-সম্বন্ধে) পদার্থ বিজ্ঞানের সিদ্ধান্ত বিশেষ ; এই সিদ্ধান্তানুসারে যে সকল বস্তুর কণা সমূহ কম্পমান অবস্থায় আছে, কোন মাত্র তৎসমস্ত বস্তুই উত্তপ্ত বস্তু বলিয়া পরিগণিত হয় ; বস্তু যতই অধিক উত্তপ্ত হ[illegible] কণা সমূহের কম্পনও ততই বৃদ্ধি পাইতে থাকে।

dy̆'-nă-mišm, *n.* **1.** (*Philos.*) A theory holding the universe as essentially constituted by forces ; (দর্শন-শাস্ত্র) বিশ্ব মূলতঃ বল-সমবায়ে সংঘটিত এইরূপ মতবাদ, বলবাদ। **2.** The mode of the energizing operation of force or energy ; বল বা শক্তির শক্তিপ্রকাশ-প্রণালী। **—mist,** *n.*

dy̆'-nă-mite, *n. & v. t.* An explosive substance constituting of some powdery matter impregnated with nitro-glycerine ; মহাশক্তিশালী বিস্ফোরক দ্রব্যবিশেষ, ডিনামাইট। ***Verb t.*** To shatter or blow up with dynamite ; ডিনামাইট্ দ্বারা চূর্ণবিচূর্ণ করা বা উড়াইয়া দেওয়া। **—mi-tard, —ter,** *ns.* One who uses explosives for revolutionary purposes ; যে ব্যক্তি বিপ্লব সংক্রান্ত উদ্দেশ্য সাধনের জন্য বিস্ফোরক দ্রব্য ব্যবহার করে। **—mit'-ic,** *adj.* **—mit-ism,** *n.* **—mit-ist,** *n.*

dy̆-nă-mi-zā'-tion, *n.* (*Med.*) A[illegible] of making drugs effective b[illegible] dilution etc. ; (ভৈষজ্য-শাস্ত্র) তর[illegible]করণ প্রভৃতি ক্রিয়াদ্বারা ঔষধের কা[illegible]কারিতা শক্তি বৃদ্ধিকরণ।

dy̆'-nă-mö, *n.* (*Pl.* -MOS) [illegible] machine for producing an electric current by mechanical power যান্ত্রিক-শক্তি দ্বারা তাড়িত প্রবাহ উৎপাদনের জন্য যন্ত্রবিশেষ, তাড়িতোৎপাদক **Dynamo-electric machine** - তাড়িতোৎপাদক যন্ত্র।

dy̆-nă-mö-ė-lĕc'-tric, *adj.* Pertaining to the conversion o[illegible] mechanical energy into electrica[illegible] energy or vice versa ; যান্ত্রি[illegible] শক্তি তাড়িত শক্তিতে অথবা তাড়িত শ[illegible] যান্ত্রিক-শক্তিতে পরিবর্ত্তন-সম্বন্ধীয়।

dy̆-nă-mö-gĕn'-ė-sis, *n.* The pr[illegible]duction of increased nervo[illegible] force ; বিবর্দ্ধিত স্নায়বিক শক্তি উৎপা[illegible] গতিজনি (হিঃ কোঃ)। **—gen'-ic,** *ad[illegible]*

dy̆-nă-mŏm'-ė-tėr, *n.* **1.** A[illegible] instrument for measuring for[illegible] or power, esp. of men, anima[illegible] machines, etc. ; শক্তিমাপক য[illegible] বিশেষতঃ মনুষ্য, পশু, যন্ত্র প্রভৃতির শা[illegible] মাপক যন্ত্র, শক্তিমাপক। **2.** A gaug[illegible] for the magnifying power o[illegible] a telescope ; দূরদর্শন যন্ত্রের আকার বর্দ্ধিনী শক্তি-মাপক।

dy̆'-năst, *n.* **1.** A ruler ; a chief শাসক ; নেতা। **2.** A dynasty রাজবংশ।

dy̆'-năs-ty̆, *n.* A line or succession of kings of the same family ; also the period during which a certain family reigns ; রাজবংশ, একবংশীয় রাজপরম্পরা ; কোন নির্দ্দিষ্ট রাজবংশের রাজত্বকাল। **—nas'-tic,** *adj.* **—nas'-ti-cal-ly,** *adv.*

dȳne, *n.* (*Phys.*) A unit of force which acting on a gramme for one second generates a velocity of a centimetre per second ; (পদার্থ-বিজ্ঞান) বল পরিমাণ বিশেষ,—যাহা এক সেকেণ্ড সময় এক গ্রামের উপর ক্রিয়া করিয়া প্রতি সেকেণ্ডে ১০০ শত মিটার গতিবেগ উদ্ভূত করে, বল-পরিমাণ (হিঃ কোঃ)।

dȳ-ŏth'-ē-lete (-lēt), *n.* One of those who maintain the doctrine of two wills in Christ,—the human and the divine ; যে ব্যক্তি খৃষ্টের দৈবী ও মানুষী দুইটী ইচ্ছা আছে এই মত-সমর্থন করিয়া থাকে, প্রকৃত-দ্বিত্ববাদী। **—le-tism,** *n.*

dȳs-crā'-si-ă, *n.* An ill habit of the body ; রক্তদুষ্টিতা, ধাতুদোষ, রক্তে তন্ত্বিকার (হঃ চঃ)।

dȳs'-ĕn-tĕr-ȳ, *n.* A flux in which the stools consist chiefly of blood and mucus ; আমাশয়, গ্রহণী, অতিসার, আমাতিসার, আমরক্ত, পক্কাতিসার,উদাবর্ত্ত (সাঃ পঃ), প্রবাহিকা (ঐ)। **—ter'-ic,***adj.*

dȳs-lō-ḡis'-tic, *adj.* Opprobrious; expressing disapproval ; কুৎসাত্মক ; অননুমোদনসূচক। **—ti-cal-ly,** *adv.*

dȳs-mĕn-ŏr-rhe'-ă, —rhoe'-ă (-rē-), *n.* (*Med.*) Difficult and painful menstruation ; (ভৈষজ্যশাস্ত্র) রজঃকৃচ্ছ্র, বাধক রোগ।

dȳs-ŏp'-sȳ, *n.* Dimness of sight ; দৃষ্টিকৃচ্ছ্র, ঝাপ্‌সা দৃষ্টি।

dȳs-ŏr-ĕx'-i-ă, *n.* (*Med.*) A bad or depraved appetite ; ক্ষুধামান্দ্য।

dȳs-pĕp'-si-ă, —sȳ, *n.* Indigestion ; মন্দাগ্নি, অগ্নিমান্দ্য, অজীর্ণতা, পরিণামশূল (সাঃ পঃ), অপাক।

dȳs-pĕp'-tic, *adj.* & *n.* **1.** Afflicted with dyspepsia ; অজীর্ণ রোগাক্রান্ত। **2.** Pertaining to dyspepsia ; অজীর্ণ রোগ সম্বন্ধীয়। **3.** (*Fig.*) Depressed or gloomy, with or as with dyspepsia ; (লক্ষণায়) অজীর্ণ রোগহেতু বিষণ্ণ বা অবসাদ-গ্রস্ত, অজীর্ণ রোগাক্রান্ত ব্যক্তির মত অবসাদ-গ্রস্ত। *Noun.* A person having dyspepsia ; অজীর্ণ রোগগ্রস্ত ব্যক্তি।

dȳs-phā'-ḡi-ă, *n.* Difficulty in swallowing ; নিগীরণ-কৃচ্ছ্র।

dȳs-phō'-ni-ă, *n.* (*Med.*) Difficulty in producing sounds ; বাক্ কৃচ্ছ্র।

dȳsp-nœ'-ă, —nē'-ă (-nē-), *n.* Difficult and painful breathing ; শ্বাসকৃচ্ছ্র, শ্বাসাবরোধ।

dȳs-ū'-ri-ă, *n.* Difficult or painful discharge of urine ; মূত্রকৃচ্ছ্র।

E

E **1.** The fifth letter of the English alphabet ; ইংরাজী বর্ণমালার পঞ্চম অক্ষর। **2.** (*Mus.*) The third note of the diatonic scale of C major ; (সঙ্গীত শাস্ত্র) সপ্তকের তৃতীয় স্বর গা (গান্ধার)। **3.** A second class ship in Lloyd's register; লয়েডের জাহাজের তালিকার দ্বিতীয় শ্রেণীর জাহাজ। **E. and O. E.**—Errors and omissions excepted, (often added to an account when presented) ; ভুল চুক বাদ দিয়া।

each (ēch), *adj.* & *pron.* Every one of two or more persons or things taken separately ; every ; প্রত্যেক জন, প্রত্যেকটী ; প্রতি, প্রত্যেক, ফি (*colloq.*)। **Each other**—পরস্পর, অন্যোন্য। **Are equal each to each**—(জ্যামিতি) কোণ ক্ষেত্রের নিদ্দিষ্ট অংশ অপর ক্ষেত্রের অনুরূপ অংশের সমান।

ea'-gêr (ē-), *adj.* **1.** Ardent ; earnest ; intense ; impatient as passions etc. ; ব্যগ্র ; নির্ব্বন্ধাতিশয়-পূর্ণ, আগ্রহান্বিত ; তীব্র, প্রবল ; অধীর, উৎসুক, উৎকণ্ঠাকুল, উৎকণ্ঠিত। **2.** (*Archaic*) Cold ; biting ; sour ; as, *eager* air (cold) ; শীতল; কন্‌কনে ; টক। **—ly,** *adv.* In an eager manner ; সাগ্রহে, উৎকণ্ঠিত ভাবে, ব্যগ্রভাবে, সৌৎসুক্যে। **—ness,** *n.* The state of being eager ; ব্যগ্রতা, অধীরতা, আগ্রহাতিশয্য, ঔৎসুক্য।

ea'-gle (ē-gl), *n.* **1.** A bird remarkable for its keenness of vision ; ঈগল, উৎক্রোশ পক্ষী, গরুড় (যোঃ)। **2.** Standard of the ancient Roman or of the French army bearing the figure of an eagle ; "Where her *eagles* never flew ;" প্রাচীন রোম এবং ফরাসীদেশের গরুড়াঙ্কিত পতাকা। **3.** A golden coin worth 20 dollars current in the U. S. ; মার্কিণ যুক্তরাজ্যে প্রচলিত ২০ ডলার মূল্যের স্বর্ণমুদ্রাবিশেষ। **Double eagle** — See *eagle* (3.) **Eagle-eyed** — শ্যেন-চক্ষু, তীক্ষ্ণদৃষ্টি, খরনজর। **Eagle owl**—ইয়ুরোপদেশীয় বৃহত্তম পেচক পক্ষী। **Eagle-stone**—লৌহগর্ভ প্রস্তর বিশেষ। **Eagle-wood**—অগুরু কাষ্ঠ। **Fishing eagle**—কুরল। **Ring-tailed sea-eagle**—মাছরাঙ্গা (বেলঃ)। **White-tailed sea-eagle** — মাছ মোড়ল (বেলঃ)।

Eagle.

eag'-lĕt (ēg-), *n.* A young eagle ; ঈগল শাবক, উৎক্রোশ শাবক।

ea'-gre (ē-gĕr), *n.* A tidal wave of great height and force (bore) ; বান, কটালের বান।

ean'-ling (ēn-), *n.* A lamb just brought forth ; সদ্যোজাত মেষ শাবক।

ear (ēr), *n.* **1.** The organ of hearing ; কান, কর্ণ, শ্রবণ, শ্রোত্র, শ্রুতি, শ্রবণেন্দ্রিয়। **2.** The sense of hearing ; the power of making nice discrimination between different sounds ; as, he has an *ear* for music : শ্রবণশক্তি, শ্রুতিশক্তি; বিভিন্ন প্রকার স্বরের মধ্যে সূক্ষ্ম প্রভেদ নির্ণয়ের শক্তি। **3.** Favourable hearing ; heed ; regard ; as, he gave an *ear* to my prayer ; সদয়ভাবে কর্ণপাত ; মনোযোগ ; লক্ষ্য। **4.** A handle ; any projection from anything ; as, the *ear* of a tub ; হাতল, কর্ণ (কাঃ শ্রোঃ) ; কোনও বস্তুর উদ্গত অংশ। **5.** One of a pair of tufts of feathers on the head of a bird ; পক্ষীর মস্তকের পালকগুচ্ছদ্বয়ের অন্যতর। **Ear′-less,** *adj.* Devoid of hearing ; deaf ; শ্রবণশক্তিহীন ; বধির। **Ear-ache**—কর্ণশূল, কর্ণবেদনা। **Ear-bored** — কানফোড়া, বিদ্ধকর্ণ। **Ear-drop** — কর্ণিকা, কুন্তল, কানের দুল, উত্তংশ, অবতংশ। **Ear-drum**—কর্ণশষ্কুলী (বিনয়), কর্ণপটহ। **Ear-lap**—কর্ণের নিম্নভাগস্থ মাংসল অংশ, কর্ণলতিকা, কর্ণপাটা। **Ear-lock**—জুলপি, কর্ণান্তিকস্থ কেশগুচ্ছ, পক্ষ (মঃ উঃ)। **Ear-mark**—(*n.* & *v. t.*) A distinguishing mark on the ear of sheep as a sign of ownership ; (*fig.*) a distinctive mark of ownership ; মেষের কর্ণে প্রদত্ত চিহ্ন বিশেষ,—যদ্দ্বারা মালিক তাহাদিগকে পরিচয় করিতে পারে ; (লক্ষণায়) স্বাতন্ত্র্য-সূচক চিহ্ন। (*Verb t.*) To mark as sheep etc. with this sign ; (*fig*) to assign to a definite purpose as a fund etc. ; স্বাতন্ত্র্যসূচক চিহ্ন দ্বারা মেষকে চিহ্নিত করা ; (লক্ষণায়) কোন বিশেষ উদ্দেশ্যের জন্য নির্দ্দেশ করা। **Ear-pick** — কানখুসকি। **Ear-shot** — শ্রবণযোগ্য দূরত্ব, শ্রুতিসীমা, কর্ণপথ। [Beyond *ear-shot* (শ্রবণাতিক্রম)।] **Ear-stealing**—কর্ণাপহারী (উজ্জ্বলঃ)। **Ear-ring**—কুণ্ডল, মাকড়ী, কর্ণালঙ্কার, কর্ণভূষণ, অবতংশ, দুল, কর্ণশোভন। **Ear-trumpet**—শ্রুতিসহায়ক যন্ত্রবিশেষ, কর্ণশৃঙ্গ। **Ear-wax** — কর্ণ গূথিকা, কাণের খইল, কর্ণমল, কানের মল বা খলি। **Ear-wig** — কানের পোকা, কন্নাই, কানকোটারী। (*Verb t.*) To influence (persons) by secret communications ; গুপ্ত-সংবাদ প্রদানে প্রভাবিত করা। **Ear-witness**—শোনা-সাক্ষী, যে ব্যক্তি শ্রুত বিষয়ে সাক্ষ্য প্রদান করিতে পারে। **About one's ears**—All around one, as something falling ; কাহারো চতুর্দ্দিকে বিক্ষিপ্ত ভাবে, চতুর্দ্দিক জুড়িয়া। **A deaf ear**—One that refuses to listen ; যে ব্যক্তি কোন কথায় কর্ণপাত করিতে অস্বীকার করে। **Bow down thine ear** — Condescend to hear or listen ; হীনতা স্বীকার করিয়া শ্রবণ করুন। **I would give my ears**—I would make any sacrifice ; আমি প্রাণপণ চেষ্টা করিব। **Little pitchers have long ears**—See under PITCHERS. **To be all ears**—To hear with great attention ; তন্ময় হইয়া শোনা। **To be at one's ear**—To keep near to whisper a secret into one's ear ; গোপনীয় কথা বলার উদ্দেশ্যে কাহারও কাছে থাকা। **To be by the ears**—To quarrel ; কলহ করা। **To be over head and ears**—To be completely immersed, as in debt ; নিমজ্জিত হওয়া, জড়িত হওয়া। **To din into one's ears**—To repeat continually into one's ear ; বারংবার বলা। **To give ear to**—To attend to ; মনোযোগ পূর্ব্বক শোনা, কান দেওয়া। **To go at one ear and out at the other**—To leave no impression ; এক কান দিয়া যাইয়া অন্য কান দিয়া বাহির হইয়া আসা। **To have an ear for**—To have a liking for ; রুচি থাকা, অনুরাগ থাকা। **To have a person's ear**—To gain one's favourable attention ; সানুগ্রহ কর্ণপাতের অনুমতি প্রাপ্ত হওয়া। **To have itching ears**—To love to hear news or current gossip ; সাময়িক সংবাদাদি শ্রবণের জন্য কর্ণ কণ্ডূয়ন করা। **To poison one's ear**—To prejudice one against another ; কান ভাঙ্গাইয়া দেওয়া, কান ভারি করা, কুমন্ত্রণা দেওয়া, কানে মন্ত্র দেওয়া। **To prick (up) one's ears**—To assume an attitude of expectant attention ; উৎকর্ণ হওয়া, কান খাড়া করা। **To pull or drag by the ear**—To pull or drag violently or roughly ; কান ধরা, কান মলিয়া দেওয়া। **To set (persons) by the ears** — To occasion a quarrel between them ; কলহ বাঁধাইয়া দেওয়া, ঝগড়া বাঁধান। **To tickle one's ear** — To flatter ; তোষামোদ করা। **To turn a deaf ear to**—To refuse to hear ; কর্ণপাত করিতে অসম্মত হওয়া। **Up to the ears**—Almost overwhelmed ; অভিভূত, জড়িত। **Walls have ears**—দেয়ালেরও কান আছে (অর্থাৎ কেহ লুকাইয়া থাকিয়া তোমার কথা শুনিতে পারে, বিশেষ সতর্ক হও)। **Were your ears burning last night**—We were talking about you last night ; আমরা কাল রাত্রে তোমার বিষয়ে কথা বলিতেছিলাম।

ear (ër), *n.* & *v. i.* A spike as of corn ; ধান্য প্রভৃতি শস্যের শীস, মঞ্জরী। ***Verb i.*** To form ears ; শীস বাহির হওয়া। **Ear-cock**—কীট জনিত গোধূমরোগ বিশেষ।

ear (ër), *v. t.* To plough or till ; কর্ষণ বা চাষ করা।

ear′-ing (ër-), *n.* Tilling ; কর্ষণ।

ear′-ing (ër-), *n.* (*Naut.*) A rope attached to the cringle of a sail by which it is bent or reefed ; a rope at the upper corner of a sail ; (নৌ-বিদ্যা) পাইলের রজ্জুর আংটাতে বাঁধা যে রজ্জুর সাহায্যে পাইল নোয়ান যায় বা ইহার কিয়দংশ গুটান যায় ; পাইলের কোণে সংবদ্ধ রজ্জু।

earl (êrl), *n.* An English nobleman next in rank to a marquis ; ইংলণ্ডের সম্ভ্রান্ত সম্প্রদায় বিশেষ ভুক্ত ব্যক্তি। **Earl′-dom,** *n.* The territorial possessions or dignity of an earl ; উক্ত সম্ভ্রান্ত সম্প্রদায়ভুক্ত ব্যক্তির ভূ-সম্পত্তি বা আভিজাত্য-গৌরব। **Earl-marshal**—যে কর্ম্মচারী কুলবিদ্যা-বিশারদগণের সভা প্রভৃতিতে অধ্যক্ষতা করেন।

ear'-ly̆ (êr-), *adj.* & *adv.* **1.** In good season ; soon ; সময়োচিত ; শীঘ্র। **2.** Towards morning ; appearing earlier in the season ; at the beginning of period or sessions ; as, *early* fruit : *early* flowers ; ঊষাকালীন ; ঋতুর প্রথমভাগে আগত ; কোন সময়ের প্রারম্ভে। ***Adv.*** In good time or season ; betimes ; soon ; সুসময়ে ; সকাল সকাল ; শীঘ্র। **—li-ness,** *n.* Promptitude ; সত্বরতা। **Early-bird** — প্রাতরুত্থানশীল ব্যক্তি। **At your earliest convenience**—As soon as you conveniently can ; যত শীঘ্র আপনার সুবিধা হয়। **The early part of**—The beginning of ; প্রারম্ভ। **To keep early hours**—To rise and sleep early or at the proper hour ; যথা সময়ে শয্যাত্যাগ করা বা নিদ্রা যাওয়া, অল্পরাত্রে নিদ্রিত হইয়া প্রত্যুষে শয্যাত্যাগ করা।

earn (êrn), *v. t.* **1.** To acquire ; অর্জ্জন করা, উপার্জ্জন করা, রোজগার করা। **2.** To deserve ; "The effort of men to *earn* rather to receive their salvation ;" যোগ্য হওয়া, উপযুক্ত হওয়া। **Earn'-ings,** *n.* What is earned ; wages; রোজগার, উপার্জ্জন, কামাই (*Colloq.*) ; মাহিয়ানা

ear'-nĕst (êr-), *adj.* & *n.* Zealous ; sincere ; serious ; ardent ; উৎসাহী, তৎপর, ব্যগ্র ; অকপট, আন্তরিক ; প্রকৃত প্রস্তাবে কার্য্যে প্রবৃত্ত ; ঐকান্তিক। ***Noun.*** Zeal ; seriousness ; eagerness ; উৎসাহ, নির্ব্বন্ধাতিশয় ; তৎপরতা ; ব্যগ্রতা, ঐকান্তিকতা। **—ly,** *adv.* **—ness,** *n.* **In earnest**—Serious or seriously ; সত্য সত্যই, প্রকৃত প্রস্তাবে।

ear'-nĕst (êr-), *n.* **1.** Money paid as an instalment esp. to confirm contract etc. ; অগ্রিম, দাদন বায়না, আগাম। **2.** (*Fig.*) A pledge of anything to come ; (লক্ষণায়) কোন অনাগত বিষয়ের জন্য প্রতিভূ। **Earnest money** — বায়নার টাকা আগাম টাকা, সত্যঙ্কার (জাতক)।

earth (êrth), *n.* **1.** The globe or planet in which we live ; পৃথিবী, পৃথ্বী, ধরণী, অচলা, মহী, মেদিনী, বসুন্ধরা, ক্ষিতি, বসুমতী, বসুধা, উর্ব্বী, অবনী, ভূমণ্ডল, ধরিত্রী, ধরা, ভূ, দুনিয়া, (*colloq.*) মুল্লুক, (*colloq.*) জ্যা, ইলাতন (সাঃ পঃ), ক্ষিতি-মণ্ডল। **2.** The ground ; as, to fall to the *earth* ; ভূমি, ভূতল, ধরাতল। **3.** The world of land and sea in distinction from heaven and hell ; মর্ত্ত্য। **4.** (*Pl.*) The hole or lair of a burrowing animal ; (বহুবচন) বিবর, গর্ত্ত। **5.** The inhabitants of this globe ; পৃথিবীবাসী লোকবৃন্দ। **6.** Soil ; "Alternate strata of *earth* and limestone ;" মৃত্তিকা, মাটি। **Earth'-en,** *adj.* মৃন্ময়, মৃত্তিকাময়, মৃদাত্মক। **Earth-born** — পৃথিবীজাত, মানবীয়। **Earth bound**—সংসারাবদ্ধ। **Earth closet**—একপ্রকার পায়খানা—এইরূপ পায়খানায় মলমূত্রাদি শুষ্ক মৃত্তিকা দ্বারা আবৃত করা হয়। **Earth-hunger**—ভূ-সম্পত্তি বৃদ্ধির লালসা, রাজ্য বিস্তার লালসা। **Earth-light, —shine**—চন্দ্রের অন্ধকারাবৃত অংশে পৃথিবী হইতে যে জ্যোতিঃ প্রতিফলিত হয়। **Earth-nut** — ইংলণ্ডদেশজাত বন্য ফলবিশেষ। **Earth-plate** — তাড়িত বার্ত্তাবহের তারের ভূসংযোগ স্থাপনের জন্য ভূগর্ভে প্রোথিত ধাতুফলক। **Earth-quake**—ভূদোল (হিন্দিঃ), ভূমিকম্প, ভূকম্প। **Earth's circumference**—ভূ-পরিধি, ভূবেষ্টন। **Earth's surface** — ভূপৃষ্ঠ (জিঃ)। **Earth work**—মৃদুত্তোলন, মাটীর কাজ, মেটেগড় ; দুর্গাদির জন্য মৃত্তিকাস্তূপ। **Earth-worm**—মহীলতা, কেঁচো, কেঁচুয়া কিঞ্চলুক, কিঞ্চুলুক, কিঞ্চিলিকা ; (লক্ষণায়) নরাধম।

earth (êrth), *v. t.* & *i.* **1.** To conceal in the earth ; to bury ; মাটীর ভিতর লুকান ; ভূগর্ভে সমাহিত করা। **2.** To drive as fox etc. to earth ; বিজ্জুর গর্ত্তে তাড়িত করা। ***Verb i.*** To burrow ; বিবরে লুক্কায়িত হওয়া।

earth'-ĕn-wâre (êrth-), *n.* Vessels etc. made of baked clay ; মৃন্ময় পাত্রাদি, মৃদ্ভাণ্ড, মাটীর বাসন।

earth'-ly̆ (êrth-), *adj.* **1.** Belonging to the earth ; worldly ; পার্থিব ; সাংসারিক, ঐহিক। **—li-ness,** *n.* **Earthly-minded**—সংসারাসক্ত। **No earthly use** — No use at all (*collq.*) ; কোন কাজের নয়।

earth'-ward(s) (êrth-wêrd), *adv.* Towards the earth ; ভূতলাভিমুখে।

earth'-y̆ (êrth-), *adj.* Relating to, or resembling, earth or soil ; (*fig.*) grossly material ; পার্থিব, মৃত্তিকা সম্বন্ধীয়, মৃত্তিকাবৎ ; (লক্ষণায়) স্থূল।

ease (ēz), *n.* **1.** Freedom from pain or trouble ; rest ; comfort ; repose ; নিরুদ্বেগ ; স্বস্তি, সোয়াস্তি ; সুখ, স্বাচ্ছন্দ্য ; আয়েস, অনায়াস, আসান (*colloq*)। **2.** Tranquility ; as, *ease* of mind ; শান্তি। **3.** Facility ; naturalness ; as, *ease* in writing ; freedom from stiffness ; সৌকর্য্য, সুকরতা ; স্বাভাবিকতা ; স্বচ্ছন্দতা, সলীলভাব, অনাড়ষ্টতা। **Ease'-ful,** *adj.* Full of ease ; soothing ; আরামদায়ক ; প্রশামক। **Ease'-less,** *adj.* **At ease**—Free from pain, trouble or anxiety ; আরামে, নিরুদ্বেগে। (*Mil.*) In an informal or unconstrained attitude ; as, to stand *at ease* ; (সামরিক-শাস্ত্র) অনিয়মিত ভাবে। **Ill at ease**—In trouble ; in anxiety ; ঝঞ্ঝাটে ; উদ্বেগে। **With ease**—Without stiffness ; স্বচ্ছন্দ ভাবে, অবলীলাক্রমে।

ease (ēz), *v.t.* & *i.* **1.** To free from pain or trouble ; to give mental ease to ; নিরুদ্বেগ করা, আশ্বাস দেওয়া ; শান্তি প্রদান করা। **2.** To mitigate ; প্রশমিত করা, উপশম করা। **3.** (*Slang*) To rob ; as, to *ease* a man of his purse ; (ইতর ভাষায়) কাড়িয়া লওয়া,

লুঠ করিয়া নেওয়া। **4.** To relax, as that which is too tight ; শ্লথ করা, শিথিল করা। **5.** To facilitate ; to make easier ; সুকর করা ; অধিকতর সহজ করা। ***Verb i.*** To become less burdensome ; (with *off*) ; অপেক্ষাকৃত অল্প পীড়াদায়ক হওয়া। **Ease'-ment,** *n.* **1.** (*Archaic*) Relief ; gratification ; convenience ; বিরাম, উপশম ; আয়াস, তৃপ্তি ; সুবিধা। **2.** (*Law*) Right of passage of light, air, etc. in another man's possesion ; ব্যবহার-স্বত্ব, সাধারণ-সুখাধিকার (হিঃ কোঃ)। **3.** A supplementary building, shed, room, etc. ; অতিরিক্ত ইমারত, চালা, কোঠা, প্রভৃতি। **Ease her**—Reduce the speed of the engine ; জাহাজের যন্ত্রের গতি কমাও। **To ease oneself**—To feel relieved after having satisfied calls of nature ; মলমূত্রাদি ত্যাগের পর সচ্ছন্দতা বোধ করা।

ea'-šĕl (ē-), *n.* The frame on which pictures are placed while being painted ; যে কাঠের কাঠামে রাখিয়া চিত্রকর চিত্র অঙ্কন করে, চিত্রফলক, চিত্রাধার, চিত্রকরের পাটা।

Easel.

east, (ēst), *n., adj.* & *adv.* **1.** The point of the horizon where the sun is seen to rise ; the corresponding point of the earth ; পূর্ব্ব, প্রাচী ; উদয়দিক, পূর্ব্বদিক, উদয়াচল। **2.** The east wind ; পূর্ব্বদিগের বাতাস। **3.** Countries lying to the east of Europe ; as, the wisdom of the *east* ; প্রাচ্যদেশ, ইয়ুরোপের পূর্ব্বদিগ্‌বর্ত্তী দেশসমূহ। ***Adj.*** Toward or at the east ; as, the *east* side ; পূর্ব্বাভিমুখীন, পূর্ব্বাস্থ। ***Adv.*** Eastward ; পূর্ব্বদিকে। **East-end** — লণ্ডন নগরীর পূর্ব্বাঞ্চল (এই অঞ্চলে সাধারণতঃ সঙ্গতিহীন ব্যক্তিগণ বাস করিয়া থাকে)। **East-Indian**—ভারতবাসী। **Far east**—চীন, জাপান প্রভৃতিদেশ। **Near-east**—তুরস্ক ও তন্নিকটবর্ত্তী দেশ সমূহ।

Eas'-tēr (ēs-), *n.* A Christian festival observed in commemoration of Jesus Christ's resurrection, occurring on Sunday after Good-Friday ; যীশুখৃষ্টের পুনরুত্থানের স্মৃতি-সূচক পর্ব্ব বিশেষ — এই পর্ব্ব গুড্ ফ্রাইডের পরবর্ত্তী রবিবারে অনুষ্ঠিত হয়। **Easter-day, -Sunday**—যে রবিবার দিবস ঈষ্টার পর্ব্ব অনুষ্ঠিত হয়। **Easter-eggs**—ঈষ্টার পর্ব্বোপলক্ষে ব্যবহৃত ডিম্ব। **Easter-eve**—ঈষ্টার পর্ব্বের পূর্ব্ব দিবস। **Easter-week**—ঈষ্টার পর্ব্বের দিবস হইতে যে সপ্তাহের আরম্ভ হয়।

east'-ēr-lȳ (ēst-), *adj.* & *adv.* In an eastern position or direction ; (blowing) from the east ; as, *easterly* wind ; পূর্ব্বদিকে, পূর্ব্বাভিমুখে ; পূর্ব্বদিক্ হইতে প্রবহমান।

east'-ērn (ēst-), *adj.* & *n.* Dwelling in the east ; towards the east ; being in the east ; পূর্ব্বদেশীয়, প্রাচ্য ; পূর্ব্বাভিমুখীন ; পূর্ব্বদিকস্থ। ***Noun.*** An inhabitant of the east ; a member of the *eastern* church ; পূর্ব্বদেশবাসী, প্রাচ্যদেশবাসী ; গ্রীস, রুষ প্রভৃতি দেশীয় খৃষ্টীয় ধর্ম্মসঙ্ঘের সভ্য। **—most,** *adj.* **Eastern Church**—গ্রীস, রুষ প্রভৃতি দেশের খৃষ্টীয় ধর্ম্ম। **Eastern question** — ইয়ুরোপের পূর্ব্বদিগ্‌বর্ত্তী, বিশেষতঃ তুরস্ক দেশ সংক্রান্ত রাজনীতিক প্রশ্ন।

east'-ing (ēst-), *n.* Departure in an easterly direction ; easterly direction ; পূর্ব্বদিকে যাত্রা ; পূর্ব্বদিক্।

east'-ward (ēst-wērd), *adj., n.* & *adv.* Moving or looking towards the east ; পূর্ব্বদিগ্‌গামী ; পূর্ব্বাভিমুখীন। ***Noun.*** The eastern direction ; "Sailing to the *eastward* ;" পূর্ব্বদিক্। ***Adv.*** (also EAST-WARDS) Toward the east ; পূর্ব্বাভিমুখে।

eas'-ȳ (ēz-), *adj.* **1.** Free from trouble, pain ; as, *easy* circumstances (স্বচ্ছল অবস্থা) ; উদ্বেগশূন্য আরামযুক্ত। **2.** Peaceful, as the mind ; উদ্বেগশূন্য, শান্ত, আরামময়। **3.** Free from stiffness or constraint ; as, *easy* manners ; সলীল, স্বচ্ছন্দ, অবাধ, নিঃসঙ্কোচ। **4.** (*Comm.*) Not in much demand ; (of market) not showing much demand ; অধিক চাহিদাশূন্য, নরম ; মন্দা। **5.** Not difficult ; সহজ, অকঠিন, সহজসাধ্য, অনায়াসসাধ্য, সুগম, সুসাধ্য, সুকর। **6.** Compliant or tractable ; as, an *easy* victim ; বশ্য, বচনগ্রাহী, অনুকূল, বিনেয়, প্রণেয়। **7.** Comfortable ; as, an *easy* chair ; আরামপ্রদ, আরামদায়ক। **8.** Given to ease or idleness ; "The *easy* colonist ;" আরামপ্রিয়, শ্রমকুণ্ঠ, আলস্যপরবশ। **9.** Gentle ; moderate ; as, to be proved by *easy* stages ; মৃদু, ধীর ; পরিমিত। **10.** Affluent ; as, *easy* circumstances ; সুখস্বাচ্ছন্দ্য-পূর্ণ, স্বচ্ছল। **—i-ly,** *adv.* In an easy manner ; without difficulty ; with ease ; স্বচ্ছন্দভাবে, সহজে, অবলীলাক্রমে ; অক্লেশে, অনায়াসে ; নিরুপদ্রবে। **—i-ness,** *n.* **Easy-chair**—আরামকেদারা। **Easy-going**—(অশ্বসম্বন্ধে) লীলাগতি, ঢিলা, আরামপ্রিয়, শ্রমবিমুখ। **A woman of easy virtue**—স্খলিত-চরিত্রা স্ত্রীলোক, যে স্ত্রীলোক সহজেই সতীধর্ম্ম বিসর্জ্জন করে। **Easy-come easy-go**—যাহা অক্লেশে লাভ করা যায়, তাহা সহজেই ব্যয় করা যায়।

eas'-ȳ (ēz-), *adv.* & *n.* In an easy manner ; as, to take it *easy* ; নিরুদ্বিগ্নচিত্তে। ***Noun.*** A short rest ; স্বল্পবিশ্রাম।

eas'-ȳ (ēz-), *Int.* (A command) Move gently ; ধীরে চালাও। **Easy all**—Stop, esp. rowing ; থাম, বিশেষতঃ দাড়টানা বন্ধ কর।

eat (ēt), *v. t.* & *i., n.* **1.** To masticate and swallow one's solid food ; আহার করা, খাওয়া,

ভোজন করা। 2. To devour or destroy; to ravage; as, the locusts *ate* the country clean; গ্রাস করা, কুক্ষিগত করা; ধ্বংস করা। 3. To corrode; to wear away gradually; খাইয়া দেওয়া; ক্রমশঃ ক্ষয় করা। 4. To take in, as a soup; উদরস্থ করা। ***Verb i.*** 1. To take a meal; আহার করা। 2. To have a certain flavour when eaten; as, the cakes *eat* crisp; খাইতে (স্বাদ) লাগা। 3. To wear or waste away; ক্ষয় হইয়া যাওয়া, খাইয়া যাওয়া। **Eat'-a-ble,** *adj.* & *n.* Worth to be eaten; ভক্ষণীয়, ভক্ষণার্হ, খাদ্য, খাদনীয়, ভোজ্য, খাওয়ার যোগ্য, ভক্ষিতব্য, ভক্ষ্য। (*Noun.*) (*pl.*) Something fit to be eaten; আহার্য্য, ভোজ্যদ্রব্য, ভক্ষ্যদ্রব্য। **Eat'-er,** *n.* One who eats; খাদক, ভোজনকারী। **Eat'-ing,** *n.* The act of eating; আহারক্রিয়া, ভোজন, দক্ষিণ হস্তের ব্যাপার। **Eating-house**—An inn; হোটেল বা সরাই, ভোজন শালা, ভোজনাগার। **A horse etc. eats its head off**—It costs more to feed than it is worth; (ঘোড়ার) যতটা মূল্য তার চেয়ে খোরাকী খরচ অধিক লাগা। **To eat a humble pie**—To be submissive esp. when compelled to retract something; to yield under humiliating circumstances; অন্যায় স্বীকার করা, ঘাট মানা; হীনতা স্বীকার করা। **To eat crow** — See CROW. **To eat dirt**—To apologise or yield under humiliating circumstances; ঘাট মানা, হীনতা স্বীকার করা। **To eat for the bar**—ব্যারিষ্টারীর জন্য প্রস্তুত হওয়া। **To eat one's term**—To study law in some of the inns; ব্যারিষ্টারীর জন্য আইন অধ্যয়ন করা। **To eat one's words**—To retract one's statement in a humiliating manner; ঘাট মানা, প্রত্যাহার করা, কথা ফিরাইয়া নেওয়া। **To eat (a person) out of house and home**—To ruin him by eating all he has, (*lit.* & *fig.*); খাইয়া কোন ব্যক্তিকে সর্ব্বস্বান্ত করা। **To eat the air**—To have vain hopes; বৃথা আশা পোষণ করা। **To eat (out) one's heart**—To mourn bitterly and silently; তীব্র সন্তাপে প্রাণ বিদগ্ধ করা, নীরবে শোক করা। **To eat the mad cow** — দুরবস্থার শেষ সীমায় আসা (অর্থাৎ যে অবস্থায় আসিলে মানুষ যাহা তাহা আহার করিতে থাকে)। **To eat up** — To consume completely; to waste; বিধ্বংস করা; নষ্ট করা। To absorb; as, he is *eaten up* with pride; অভিভূত করা।

eau (ō), *n.* French word for water; (ফরাসী ভাষায়) জল। ***Eau-de-Cologne*** — জর্ম্মণীদেশের কলোন নগরীতে প্রস্তুত সুগন্ধি দ্রব্য বিশেষ। ***Eau-de-Luce***—সর্প বিষঘ্ন ঔষধ বিশেষ। ***Eau-de-vie***—ব্রাণ্ডি।

eaves (ēvz), *n. pl.* The part of the roof of a thatched house or building that overhangs the walls; ঘরের ছাঁইচ, ছাঁচি।

eaves'-drŏp (ēvz-), *v. i.* & *n.* To stand under the eaves of a house with a view to overhear conversation within the house; ছাঁইচের নীচে দাঁড়াইয়া কান পাতিয়া কথা শোনা, আড়ি পাতা, কানাচি পাতা। ***Noun.*** The space on the ground within which water falls from the eaves; the water that falls in drops from the eaves of a house; ছাঁচিতলা, কাণাচি; যে জল ফোঁটা ফোঁটা করিয়া ছাঁচি তলায় পড়ে। **—per,** *n,* যে ব্যক্তি আড়ি পাতিয়া কথা শুনে, কানাচে, কানাচিয়া, শ্রবণ-কামুক (আঃ বঃ), গূঢ় শ্রোতা।

ebb (ĕb), *n.* & *v. i.* 1. The flowing back of the tide; ভাটা। 2. Decline; downfall; "Painting was at its lowest *ebb*; অবনতি; অধঃপতন, পতন। ***Verb i.*** 1. To flow back; ভাটা পড়া। 2. To decline; to fall back from a better to a worse state; অবনতি প্রাপ্ত হওয়া; দুরবস্থায় পতিত হওয়া। **Ebb-tide**—ভাটার টান। **Ebb and flow**—জোয়ার ভাটা; উত্থান ও পতন; উন্নতি অবনতি। **At a (low) ebb**—In a state of decline; ভাটা-পড়া অবস্থায়; পতনাবস্থায়।

Eb'-lĭs (ĕb-), *n.* The Satan in Mahomedan mythology; ইবলিস্, শয়তান।

ēb'-ŏn, *adj.* (*Poet.*) Made of ebony; dark as ebony; আবলুস কাঠের তৈয়ারী; আবলুস-কৃষ্ণ।

ĕb'-ŏn-īte, *n.* & *adj.* Vulcanite; চিরুণী প্রভৃতি প্রস্তুতের জন্য কঠিনীকৃত রবর, গন্ধকময় রবর (হিঃ কোঃ)। ***Adj.*** Looking like ebony; আবলুসবৎ।

ĕb'-ŏn-ȳ, *n.* & *adj.* 1. A hard durable black-coloured wood; আবলুস কাঠ। 2. A kind of tree yielding wood resembling ebony; কুন্দাল (বিনয়), কাকতিন্দুক। ***Adj.*** Made of ebony; black as ebony; আবলুস কাষ্ঠ নির্ম্মিত; আবলুস-কৃষ্ণ। **—on-ist,** *n.* One who works in ebony; আবলুস কাঠের আসবাব নির্ম্মাতা। **—on-ize,** *v. t.* To colour black so as to resemble ebony; আবলুসের মত কৃষ্ণবর্ণ করা। **Ebony-black**—আবলুস-কৃষ্ণ, নিবিড় কৃষ্ণ।

ē-brī'-ĕ-tȳ, *n.* Drunkenness; মদের নেশা, মদ্যপান জনিত মত্ততা।

ē'-brĭ-ous (-ŭs), *adj.* Inclined to drinking excess; drunk; অতিরিক্ত মদ্যপানশীল; নেশায় মত্ত, মাতাল।

ē-bŭl'-lĭ-ĕnt, *adj.* Boiling; enthusiastic; স্ফোটনশীল; উদ্দীপনাপূর্ণ। **—lience, —lien-cy,** *ns.*

ē-bŭl'-lĭ-ō-scōpe, *n.* An instrument for observing the boiling point of liquids; কথন-মাপক (হিঃ কোঃ), স্ফোটনমাপক (ঐ), কথন-দর্শক (ঐ)।

ĕb-ŭl-lĭ'-tion, *n.* 1. Boiling; স্ফোটন, কথন। 2. Effervescence; বুদ্বুদোদ্গম। 3. An outburst (as of feeling, war, etc.); উচ্ছ্বাস।

e-car-te′ (ā-câr-tā), *n.* A game at cards for two persons ; দুই জনের তাস খেলা।

Ec′-cē Hō-mō (ĕk-), *n.* A portrait of Jesus Christ wearing a crown of thorns ; যীশুখৃষ্টের কণ্টক-মুকুট পরিহিত প্রতিকৃতি। [বিচারক পাইলেট কর্তৃক যীশুকে ক্রুশে বিদ্ধ করার জন্য জনসাধারণের হস্তে সমর্পণ করার ঘটনা অবলম্বনে।]

ĕc-cĕn′-tric, *adj.* & *n.* **1.** Not having common centre with another ; অনৈককেন্দ্রিক, অসমকেন্দ্রিক। **2.** Not having its axis in the centre ; not circular as an orbit ; কেন্দ্রত্যাগী, কেন্দ্রাপসারী, কেন্দ্রভ্রষ্ট, উৎকেন্দ্রিক, কেন্দ্রাপসারিতাক্ষ ; অবৃত্তাকার। **3.** Passing along an eccentric orbit as a heavenly body ; অবৃত্তাকার কক্ষানুগামী। **4.** Anomalous ; odd ; whimsical ; উৎকট ; সৃষ্টিছাড়া ; বাতিকগ্রস্ত, খামখেয়ালীভাবের, মাথা-পাগলা, ছিটগ্রস্ত। ***Noun.*** **1.** A circle not having the same centre as another ; অনৈককেন্দ্রিক বৃত্ত, অসমকেন্দ্রিক বৃত্ত, উৎকেন্দ্রিক বৃত্ত। **2.** (*Mech.*) A mechanical contrivance for converting circular into backward and forward motion ; (যন্ত্র-বিজ্ঞান) চক্রবৎ গতি অগ্রপশ্চাৎ গতিতে পরিণত করার জন্য যন্ত্রব্যবস্থা-বিশেষ, গতি-পরিবর্ত্তক। **3.** A wheel with axis not in its centre ; যে চক্রের অক্ষ কেন্দ্র হইতে অপসারিত থাকে। **4.** A person whose conduct is irregular or odd ; ছিটগ্রস্ত লোক। **—tri-cal-ly,** *adv.* In an eccentric manner ; whimsically ; সৃষ্টিছাড়া ভাবে ; খামখেয়ালী ভাবে। **—tric′-i-ty,** *n.* **1.** The state or quality of having a different centre from that of another circle ; অসমকেন্দ্রতা, উৎকেন্দ্রতা, কেন্দ্রভ্রষ্টতা। **2.** The distance between the centre of a heavenly body and the centre of the sun ; সূর্য্যের কেন্দ্র হইতে গ্রহাদির কেন্দ্রের দূরত্ব, মন্দ-পরিধির ব্যাসার্দ্ধ (সাঃ পঃ), অন্ত্যফলজ্যা (ঐ)। **3.** Oddness ; whim ; সৃষ্টিছাড়া ভাব, ছিট, মাথাপাগলামি ; খামখেয়ালী। **Eccentric rod** or **strap**—(Mech.) Parts of the eccentric ; (যন্ত্র-বিজ্ঞান) গতি-পরিবর্ত্তক যন্ত্রের অংশসমূহ।

ĕc-chȳ-mō′-sis, *n.* (*Med.*) Appearance of livid spots on the skin occasioned by effusion of extravasated blood ; (ভৈষজ্য-শাস্ত্র) কালশিরা (ডাঃ), কালিসা (হঃ চঃ)।

ĕc-clē′-sī-ă, *n.* A regular assembly, esp. of Athenian citizens ; নিয়মিত সভা, বিশেষতঃ প্রাচীন এথেন্স নগরবাসীদিগের সভা।

ĕc-clē′-sī-ăst, *n.* A member of the Athenian ecclesia ; প্রাচীন এথেন্স নগরবাসীদিগের সভার সভ্য।

ĕc-clē-sī-ăs′-tic, —ti-căl, *adjs.* Pertaining to the church or the clerk ; খৃষ্টধর্ম্ম-সংঘ সম্বন্ধীয়, খৃষ্টীয় যাজক সম্পর্কীয়। **—tic,** *n.* A clergyman ; যাজক, পুরোহিত। **—ti-cal-ly,** *adv.* **—ti-cism,** *n.*

ĕc-clē-sī-ŏl′-ō-ġy, *n.* The science of church institutions, esp. of church building and decoration ; খৃষ্টীয় ধর্ম্ম-সংঘের প্রতিষ্ঠানসমূহ সংক্রান্ত বিজ্ঞান, খৃষ্টীয় ধর্ম্মসংঘের অট্টালিকা ও সৌধ-ভূষা সম্বন্ধীয় বিজ্ঞান। **—gist,** *n.* **—o-log′-ic, —o-log′-i-cal,** *adjs.*

ĕc′-dȳ-sis, *n.* Casting off slough or outer covering, as in the case of serpents etc. ; নির্ম্মোক (চামড়া) মোক্ষণ (সর্পাদির মত), ত্বক-পরিবর্ত্তন।

ech′-ē-lŏn (ĕsh-), *n.* & *v. t.* The position of troops in parallel lines, each line being a little to the right or left of the preceding one ; ব্যূহরচনার প্রকার বিশেষ। [ইহাতে সৈন্যশ্রেণীকে সমান্তরাল পংক্তিতে সমাবেশ করা হয়, এবং প্রত্যেক পংক্তি পূর্ব্ববর্ত্তী পংক্তির অল্প বাম বা দক্ষিণ-দিকে সংস্থিত থাকে।] ***Verb t.*** To draw up in this way as troops ; উক্ত প্রকারে সৈন্যদল ব্যূহবদ্ধ করা।

ē-chid′-nă, *n.* A burrowing animal of Australia like hedgehog ; অষ্ট্রেলিয়া দেশীয় বিবরবাসী জন্তু বিশেষ,—এই জন্তুটি দেখিতে কতকটা ক্ষুদ্র শজারুর মত।

ē-ch′-i-nīte, *n.* A fossil sea-urchin শিলীভূত সমুদ্র-শজারু।

ē-chin′-ō-dêrm, *n.* A class of animals including sea-urchins ; কণ্টকদেহী, কণ্টকচর্ম্মী।

ē-chī′-nŭs, *n.* **1.** A hedge-hog ; ক্ষুদ্র শজারু। **2.** A sea-urchin সামুদ্রিক জন্তু বিশেষ।

ē-chī′-tēs, *n.* A large genus of twining herbs ; মালত্যাদি।

ĕch′-ō, *n., v. t.* & *i.* **1.** Repetition of a sound ; প্রতিধ্বনি, প্রতিশব্দ, প্রতিনাদ, অনুনাদ, অনুধ্বনি, অনুশব্দ, আকাশ-দুহিতা, অনুরণন। **2.** The personified cause of this phenomenon ; প্রতিধ্বনি দেবী। [গ্রীক পুরাণে বর্ণিত আছে Echo পবনদেবতা ও পৃথিবীর কন্যা ছিলেন। তিনি Narcissus নামক যুবকের প্রণয়ে মুগ্ধা হন ; কিন্তু সেই প্রণয়ের প্রতিদান না পাইয়া ব্যর্থ প্রেমের ব্যথায় দিনে দিনে ক্ষীণা হইতে হইতে কেবল শব্দ মাত্রে বর্ত্তমানা রহিলেন।] **3.** A sylvan or mountain nymph ; বনদেবী বা গিরিদেবী। **4.** A favourable response ; অনুকূল উত্তর। **5.** A servile imitator ; close imitation ; দাসবৎ অনুকরণকারী ; অবিকল অনুকরণ। ***Verb t. & i.*** **1.** To send back or repeat as a sound ; প্রতিধ্বনি করা। **2.** To imitate ; to flatter in a slavish manner ; অনুকরণ করা ; হীনভাবে তোষামোদ করা। **3.** (Of a piece of writing) To resemble ; (রচনা সম্বন্ধে) সদৃশ হওয়া। ***Verb i.*** To resound with an echo as a place ; প্রতিধ্বনিত হওয়া। **—ism,** *n.* **—less,** *adj.* **To the echo**—Enthusiastically—সোৎসাহে।

ĕch-ō-lā′-li-a, *n.* (*Med.*) Automatic and purposeless repetition of words ; শব্দানুকরণ রোগ (হিঃ কোঃ), প্রতিজল্প রোগ (ঐ)।

eclaircissement, (*F.*), *n*. **1.** Unravelling of a mystery, plot, etc. ; রহস্যোদ্ঘাটন। **2.** An explanation, esp. of conduct, (as in phrase *to come to an eclaircissement*) ; কৈফিয়ৎ।

e-clat′ (ā-clâ), *n*. **1.** Pomp and magnificence ; acclamation ; glory ; জাঁক, জাঁকজমক, ধুমধাম, সমারোহ, আড়ম্বর, ঘটা ; জয়ধ্বনি ; গৌরব। **2.** Social distinction ; "A diplomatist of great *eclat* ;" সামাজিক গৌরব, সামাজিক মর্য্যাদা। **With great eclat**—With great pomp and splendour ; মহাসমারোহে, মহাড়ম্বরে, ধুমধামের সহিত।

ĕc-lĕc′-tic, *adj.* & *n*. **1.** Selecting such doctrines as seem best from the writings of other philosophers ; সর্ব্বদর্শনসারসংগ্রাহক। **2.** Borrowing freely from diverse sources ; নানা গ্রন্থ-সার-সংগ্রহকারী। **3.** Containing selections from works of others ; নানা গ্রন্থ-সার-সংগ্রহ-পূর্ণ। ***Noun.*** A person who follows an eclectic method in philosophy etc. ; সর্ব্বদর্শনসারসঙ্কলনকারী। **—ti-cal-ly,** *adv.* **—ti-cism,** *n*. The doctrine or practice of an eclectic ; সর্ব্বদর্শন সারসংগ্রহবাদ, সর্ব্বদর্শন সার সংগ্রহ, সর্ব্বমতগুণগ্রাহকতা (হিঃ কোঃ), সর্ব্বতন্ত্রগুণৈকদর্শন (ঐ), সর্ব্বশাস্ত্র সারসংগ্রহণ (ঐ), সার-সংগ্রহ, সার-সংগ্রহ বাদ।

ē-clipse′ (-clîps), *n.* & *v. t.* **1.** (*Astron.*) The obscuring of the light of one heavenly body by

Solar eclipse.

Lunar eclipse.

another ; গ্রহণ, উপরাগ, গ্রাস, রাহুগ্রাস (সাঃ পঃ)। **2.** Interception of light, esp. of the light-house ; আলোকাবরোধ (বিশেষতঃ আলোক-মন্দিরের)। **3.** Darkening of splendour ; obscuration ; তেজোহানি ; নিষ্প্রভীকরণ। ***Verb t.*** **1.** To cause an eclipse ; to darken ; গ্রহণ উৎপাদন করা ; অন্ধকারাচ্ছন্ন করা। **2.** To intercept as light, esp. of a light-house ; (আলোক) অবরোধ করা, বিশেষতঃ আলোক-মন্দিরের আলোকাবরোধ করা। **3.** (*Fig.*) To outshine ; to surpass ; to obscure ; অধিকতর দীপ্তি প্রকাশ করা ; অতিক্রম করা ; নিষ্প্রভ করা, দীপ্তিহীন করা, তিমিরাচ্ছন্ন করা। **To suffer an eclipse**—To be thrown into the shade ; নিষ্প্রভ হওয়া, পরিম্লান হওয়া, মলিন হওয়া।

ē-clip′-tic, *adj.* & *n*. Pertaining to an eclipse or to the ecliptic ; গ্রহণ- বা অয়নমণ্ডল-সম্পর্কীয়, গ্রাহণিক। ***Noun.*** Apparent path of the sun ; রাশিচক্র, সৌরঅয়নমণ্ডল, অয়নমণ্ডল, ক্রান্তিমণ্ডল (সুঃ সিঃ), গ্রহণ-রেখা, ক্রান্তিবৃত্ত, ক্রান্তিবলয়, অপথমণ্ডল (ঐ)। **Line of ecliptic**—ক্রান্তিজ্যা। **Nodes of the ecliptic**—ক্রান্তিপাত। **Obliquity of the ecliptic**—পরমক্রান্তি, পরক্রান্তি, পরমাপম (কেঃভিঃ), পরাপম (ঐ)।

ĕc′-logue (-lŏg), *n*. A pastoral poem ; গোষ্ঠগীতি, চারণিক গাথা, পল্লীগাথা, গ্রাম্যগীতি, গোষ্ঠগাথা, গ্রাম্য কবিতা।

ē-cō-nŏm′-ic, *adj.* & *n*. **1.** Pertaining to economy ; frugal ; গৃহস্থালী-সম্পর্কীয় ; হিসাবী, মিতব্যয়ী। **2.** Maintained for the sake of profits ; connected with industrial art ; as, *economic* applications of electricity ; লাভের জন্য রক্ষিত ; শ্রমশিল্পসংক্রান্ত, শ্রমশিল্পসম্পর্কীয়। ***Noun.*** (*Pl.*) **1.** The science of domestic manangement ; political economy ; গার্হস্থ্য-বিজ্ঞান ; অর্থনীতিশাস্ত্র, অর্থশাস্ত্র। **2.** The condition of a country with regard to material property ; সমৃদ্ধিসম্বন্ধে কোন দেশের অবস্থা। **—i-cal,** *adj.* **1.** Pertaining to economics or political economy ; অর্থনীতিশাস্ত্রসম্বন্ধীয়। **2.** Thrifty ; মিতব্যয়ী। **—i-cal-ly,** *adv.* Frugally ; from an economic point of view ; মিতব্যয়িতার সহিত ; অর্থনীতির দিক্ হইতে দেখিলে।

ē-cŏn′-ō-mȳ, *n*. **1.** Domestic management ; গার্হস্থ্য ব্যবস্থা বা গৃহস্থালী। **2.** Administration of the affairs of a state, community, etc. ; নির্ব্বাহ, সুব্যবস্থা। **3.** Frugality ; a saving, (esp. in *pl.*) ; মিতব্যয় ; মিতব্যয়িতা। **4.** The structure or proportion of any work ; "*Economy* observed in the minutest parts of epic poem ;" organisation ; কোন গ্রন্থের অনুপাত বা বিষয়বিন্যাস-পদ্ধতি ; ব্যবস্থা। **5.** An organized body, society, etc. ; ব্যবস্থাবদ্ধ সমাজ প্রভৃতি। **6.** The operations of nature in the generation, nutrition and preservation of animals and plants ; জীব ও উদ্ভিদের সৃষ্টি, স্থিতি, ও পরিপুষ্টি বিধানের জন্য প্রকৃতির নিয়মিত ক্রিয়া। **—mist,** *n*. **1.** One who observes frugality ; one well-versed in political economy ; মিতব্যয়ী, পরিমিতব্যয়ী ; অর্থশাস্ত্রজ্ঞ, অর্থশাস্ত্রবেত্তা, অর্থবিজ্ঞানবৎ, অর্থনীতিশাস্ত্রবিৎ। **—mize,** *v. t.* & *i*. To spend or use frugally ; মিতব্যয় করা, পরিমিত ব্যয় করা। **To turn to the best account** ; যতদূর সম্ভব ভাল কাজে লাগান। (*Verb i.*) To practise economy ; মিতব্যয়ী হওয়া। **—mi-za′-tion,** *n*. **Economy of nature** — See ECONOMY (6). **Political economy**—অর্থনীতিশাস্ত্র, ধনবিজ্ঞান, অর্থশাস্ত্র।

e′-crû (â-), *n*. The colour of unbleached linen ; অধৌত ক্ষৌমবস্ত্রের বর্ণ।

ĕc′-stă-sȳ, *n*. **1.** Rapture ; excessive delight ; পরমানন্দ ; উল্লাস, হর্ষ, আনন্দাভিবেশ, হর্ষাবেশ। **2.** An exalted state of mind when no longer being susceptible to sense impressions it can contemplate divine mysteries; trance; ভাবসমাধি, ভাবোন্মাদ; রসোন্মত্ততা (রবীঃ), সংরাধ (বেদান্ত), আনন্দময় দশা (বিশ্বঃ)। **3.** (*Med.*) A morbid condition of nervous system marked by mental exaltation, suspension of voluntary motion, etc.; (ভৈষজ্য-শাস্ত্র) হর্ষোন্মাদ (হঃ চঃ), রসোন্মাদ (ঐ)। **—size,** *v. t.* & *i.* To throw or go into ecstasies; হর্ষাবিষ্ট করা, রসোন্মত্ত হওয়া। **—stat'-ic,** *adj.* Pertaining to ecstasy; causing ecstasy; in a state of ecstasy; হর্ষাবেশ-সম্বন্ধীয়; উল্লাসকর, রসোন্মাদজনক; রসোন্মত্ত, হর্ষাবিষ্ট। **—stat'-i-cal-ly,** *adv.*

ĕc'-tŏ, in combination as **Ecto-blast**—কোষের বহিস্তর। **Ecto-derm**—জন্তু বা উদ্ভিদের বহিশ্চর্ম্ম বা বহিস্তর। **Ecto-parasite** — জন্তুর শরীরের বহির্ভাগবাসী পরজীবী (চাটুয়া) কীটবিশেষ। **Ecto-plasm**—স্ত্রীজীবের অণ্ডাশয়স্থ বৃদ্ধিশীল অণ্ড বা উদ্ভিদ কোষের বহির্ভাগ-আবরক, জৈবনিক স্তর।

ĕc-ū-mĕn'-i-căl, *adj.* General; universal; সর্ব্বজনীন; সার্ব্বভৌমিক।

ĕc'-zē-mă, *n.* An inflammation or eruption of the skin; ঝামা, কাউর, ত্বগ্‌ব্রণ।

ē-dā'-cious (-shŭs), *adj.* Pertaining to eating; greedy; ভোজন-সম্বন্ধীয়; উদরসর্ব্বস্ব, ঔদরিক, পেটুক, উদরম্ভরী। **—dac'-i-ty,** *n.* Greediness; voracity; পেটুকত্ব, ভুরিভোজন-প্রিয়তা; ঔদরিকতা, উদরম্ভরিতা। **—ly,** *adv.*

Ed'-dă (ĕd-), *n.* A collection of old poems of Iceland, (also called *order* or *poetic edda*); আইস্‌লণ্ড্ দেশীয় প্রাচীন কবিতা-সংগ্রহ।

ĕd'-dy̆, *n., v. i.* & *t.* A whirlpool; a current of air; জলাবর্ত্ত, বাতাবর্ত্ত, ঘূর্ণি, অবঘূর্ণ, আবর্ত্ত, ঘূর্ণজল, পাকচক্র; উন্টাবাও (হিন্দি)। ***Verb i. & t.*** To move or cause to move in an eddy; পাক দেওয়া, ঘূরা, ঘূর্ণিত হওয়া; আবর্ত্তিত করা, ঘূর্ণিত করা। **Eddy current** — (*Elect.*) An induced electric current circulating wholly within a mass of metal; আবর্ত্তন-প্রবাহ (সাঃ পঃ)।

e-del-weiss (ā-dl-vīs), *n.* An Alpine plant with white flowers growing in rocky places; শ্বেতপুষ্পপ্রসূ বৃক্ষ বিশেষ।

E'-dĕn (ē-), *n.* The garden where Adam and Eve lived before their fall; paradise; a place of pleasure; a state of bliss; যে সুরম্য উদ্যানে আদি মানব আদম ও তদীয় পত্নী ইভ বাস করিতেন, স্বর্গোদ্যান, নন্দন কানন; স্বর্গ; প্রমোদ নিকেতন, আনন্দ নিকেতন; আনন্দময় দশা।

ē-dĕn'-tāte, *n.* & *adj.* A toothless animal; দন্তহীন প্রাণী, অদন্তক প্রাণী। ***Adj.*** Not possessing teeth or incisor; দন্তহীন, অদন্তক, কৃন্তন দন্তহীন।

edge (ĕj), *n., v. t.* & *i.* **1.** Sharp side of a sword or other cutting instrument; অস্ত্রের ধারালো পার্শ্ব। **2.** Keenness; sharpness; effectiveness; as, the *edge* of sarcasm; তীব্রতা; তীক্ষ্ণতা; কার্য্যকারিতা। **3.** Border; margin; কিনারা; প্রান্ত। **4.** A critical position or time; সঙ্কটপূর্ণ অবস্থা, সঙ্কট কাল। ***Verb t.*** **1.** To sharpen; ধার দেওয়া, শাণিত করা, ধারাল করা। **2.** To furnish with a border; পাইড় লাগান, কিনারা লাগান, হাঁসিয়া লাগান। **3.** To push (a thing, oneself, etc.) little by little; as, to *edge* one's chair forward; অল্পে অল্পে ঠেলিয়া দেওয়া। ***Verb i.*** **1.** To advance slantwise; তির্য্যগ্‌ভাবে অগ্রসর হওয়া। **2.** To proceed or recede little by little; অল্পে অল্পে অগ্রসর হওয়া বা পশ্চাদ্দিকে যাওয়া। **3.** To enthuse: উৎসাহিত করা। **Edg'-ing,** *n.* **1.** A row of plants round a bed of flowers; ফুলের কেয়ারীর চতুর্দ্দিকে বৃত্তাকারে রোপিত ক্ষুদ্র ক্ষুদ্র বৃক্ষশ্রেণী, খরঞ্জা (প্রবোধ)। **2.** A border or fringe; কিনারা, পাইড়, মগজি, ঝালর, হাসিয়া। **Edge'-less,** *adj.* Not sharp; blunt; obtuse; অধারাল; ভোঁতা; স্থূল। **Edge'-ways** or **—wise.** *adv.* Sidewise; with the edge foremost; পাশাপাশি; কিনারার দিকে। **Edge** or **edged tool**—ধারাল অস্ত্র। **Edging shears**—তৃণভূমির প্রান্ত ছাঁটিবার জন্য কাঁচি। **To be on edge**—To be anxious; উদ্‌গ্রীব হওয়া। **To get a word in edgeways**—To get one in a talkative person's silent interval; বাচাল ব্যক্তির কথার অবকাশের মধ্যে অতি কষ্টে একটী কথা পাড়া। **To play with edge-tools**—To play with what is dangerous; শাণিত অস্ত্র লইয়া ক্রীড়া করা, সাপ লইয়া ক্রীড়া করা। **To set the teeth on edge**—To cause unpleasant sensation in the teeth, (also *fig*); দাঁত সিড়সিড় করান। **To take the edge off one's argument** — To take the effectiveness off one's argument; কোন যুক্তির কার্য্যকারিতাশক্তি নষ্ট করা।

edg'-y̆ (ĕj-), *adj.* **1.** Sharp; keen; তীক্ষ্ণ; ধারাল, খরধার, খরশাণ। **2.** Irritative; as, *edgy* temper; চটা। **3.** Having the outlines too sharp; অতি সুপ্রকট বাহ্যরেখা বিশিষ্ট।

ĕd'-i-ble, *adj.* & *n.* Eatable; খাদ্য, ভক্ষ্য। ***Noun.*** A thing fit to be eaten; ভোজনোপযোগী দ্রব্য। **—bil'-i-ty, —ness,** *ns.*

ē'-dict, *n.* Proclamation; a command of a sovereign issued to his subjects; অনুশাসন, শাসন, ঘোষণাপত্র; রাজাজ্ঞা, আজ্ঞাপত্র, শাসনবাণী (আঃ বঃ), ফরমাণ (হিন্দিঃ)। **Edict of Nantes**—ফরাসী রাজ চতুর্থ হেনরী কর্ত্তৃক ১৫৯৮ খৃঃ অব্দে প্রচারিত শাসনবাণী বিশেষ। এই শাসনবাণীদ্বারা প্রোটেষ্টেণ্ট খৃষ্টানগণকে আশ্রয় প্রদান করা হয়।

ĕd-i-fi-cā'-tion, *n.* Instruction ; intellectual, moral and spiritual advance ; শিক্ষা, উপদেশ ; নৈতিক, মানসিক এবং আধ্যাত্মিক উন্নতি।

ĕd'-i-fice (-fĭs), *n.* A buildiug ; a colossal structure, (*lit* & *fig*) ; অট্টালিকা, হর্ম্ম্য ; সৌধ, প্রাসাদ (শব্দানুযায়ী এবং লক্ষণায়)।

ĕd'-i-fȳ, *v. t.* 1. (*Arch.*) To build ; (অপ্রঃ) ইমারতাদি নির্ম্মাণ করা। 2. To instruct or improve, esp. in moral or religious knowledge ; উপদেশ প্রদানে উন্নত করা, বিশেষতঃ নৈতিক বা ধর্ম্মোপদেশ প্রদানে উন্নতি বিধান করা। **-ing,** *adj.* Serving to improve or instruct ; শিক্ষাপ্রদ, উপদেশপ্রদ, নৈতিক উন্নতিবিধায়ক।

ĕd'-it, *v. t.* To act as editor of (a news-paper) ; to superintend the publication of ; to prepare for publication ; সম্পাদকতা কার্য্য করা, পত্রিকাসম্পাদন করা; পুস্তক বা পত্রিকা প্রকাশের কার্য্যের তত্ত্বাবধান করা, প্রকাশ করা ; প্রকাশের জন্য প্রস্তুত করা।

ĕ-dĭ'-tion, *n.* 1. The whole number of the copies published at one time ; একবারে যতসংখ্যক পুস্তক প্রকাশিত হয়, সংস্করণ। 2. The form in which a literary work is published ; as, Macmillan's *edition* ; সংস্করণ।

edition de luxe, (*F.*), *n.* Handsome edition ; রাজসংস্করণ।

editio princeps, (*L.*) *n.* The first edition of a book ; কোন পুস্তকের প্রথম সংস্করণ।

ĕd'-i-tor (-têr), *n.* 1. One who prepares the work of another for publication ; সম্পাদক। 2. One who conducts a news-paper ; পত্রিকা-সম্পাদক, পত্রিকাধ্যক্ষ। **-ship,** *n.* The work of an editor; সম্পাদকতা। **-tress,** *n.* (*Fem.*)

ĕd-i-tō'-ri-ăl, *adj.* & *n.* Of or written by an editor ; সম্পাদকীয়, সম্পাদক-লিখিত। ***Noun.*** The heading article in a news-paper written by the editor ; সম্পাদকীয় প্রবন্ধ বা মন্তব্য। **-ly,** *adv.*

ĕd'-ū-cāte, *v.t.* To train ; to teach ; to develop some faculty or sense ; as, to *educate* the eye ; শিক্ষা দেওয়া ; জ্ঞানোপদেশ দান করা ; কোন ইন্দ্রিয় বা বৃত্তির বিশেষ উৎকর্ষ সাধন করা। **-cat-ed,** *adj.* Trained ; learned ; শিক্ষিত, কৃতবিদ্য ; বিদ্বান, পণ্ডিত।

ĕd-ū-cā'-tion, *n.* 1. Instruction ; discipline ; শিক্ষা, উপদেশ ; শাসন, সংস্কার। 2. Development of character or mental powers ; as, intellectual or moral *education* ; চরিত্র বা মানসিক শক্তির উন্নতি। **-al,** *adj.* Pertaining to education ; শিক্ষা-সংক্রান্ত। **-al-ist, -ist,** *ns.* One who is well-versed in the science of education ; শিক্ষানীতিবিৎ। **-al-ly,** *adv.* **-ca-bil'-i-ty,** *n.* **-ca-ble,** *adj.* **-ca-tive,** *adj.* Giving or facilitating education ; শিক্ষাদায়ক, শিক্ষোৎকর্ষ-বিধায়ক। **-ca-tor,** *n.* One who imparts education ; শিক্ষাদাতা। **Educated community** — শিক্ষিত সম্প্রদায়, কৃতবিদ্য সম্প্রদায়। **To educate public opinion**—To enlighten the public, in order to make them fit to give proper opinion ; শিক্ষা ও উপদেশ প্রদান দ্বারা লোকমত গঠন করা।

ē-dūce' *v. t.* 1. To bring out ; to elicit or evolve ; বাহির করা ; তর্কের দ্বারা উদ্ধার করা, উদ্‌ঘাটন করা। 2. (*Chem.*) To separate a substance from a compound ; to infer as a principle etc. from a data ; (রসায়ন-শাস্ত্র) যৌগিক পদার্থ পৃথক করা, নিষ্কর্ষণ করা ; অনুমান করা। **-du'-ci-ble,** *adj.* Capable of being educed ; নিষ্কর্ষণীয়, নিঃসরণীয়, অনুমন্তব্য।

ē'-dūct, *n.* 1. That which is educed ; inference ; নিষ্কর্ষিত বস্তু ; অনুমান। 2. (*Chem.*) A body separated from another in which it already existed ; (রসায়ন-শাস্ত্র) যৌগিক পদার্থ হইতে পৃথকীকৃত পদার্থ।

ē-dŭc'-tion, *n.* 1. The act of bringing into view or drawing out ; inference ; বহিষ্করণ, নিষ্কর্ষণ, নিঃসারণ ; অনুমান। 2. (*Steam-engine*) Exhaustion of steam, (chiefly in combination as *eduction-pipe* = exhaustion-pipe) ; (বাষ্পীয় যন্ত্র) বাষ্পক্ষয়।

ē-dŭl'-cō-rāte, *v.t.* 1. To sweeten, (*obs.*) ; মিষ্ট করা, স্বাদু করা, মধুর করা, (অপ্রঃ)। 2. To free from acrid properties or soluble particles ; to purify ; অম্লগুণ হইতে বিমুক্ত করা বা দ্রবণশীল কণা বিরহিত করা, নির্ম্মল করা ; বিশুদ্ধ করা। **-ra'-tion,** *n.*

eel (ēl), *n.* 1. A fish looking like a serpent ; (*fig.*) any slippery creature ; বাইন মাছ, কুঞ্চিকা, কুঁচে ; (লক্ষণায়) পিচ্ছিল-দেহ প্রাণী। 2. A kind of worm found in vinegar ; সির্কায় প্রাপ্ত কীট বিশেষ। **Eel-grass**—উত্তর আটলান্টিক উপকূলে প্রাপ্ত উদ্ভিদ বিশেষ। **Eel-pont**—এক জাতীয় ক্ষুদ্র বাইন মৎস্য। **Eel-spear**—বাইন মৎস্য বিদ্ধ করার জন্য বর্শা।

e'er (âr), *adv.* See EVER.

ee'-rie (ē-rĭ), **-rȳ,** *adj.* 1. Timid ; ভীত। 2. Weird ; exciting superstitious fear; অপ্রাকৃত; (ডাকিনী, ভূত, পিশাচ বা অপদেবতার ভয়ে) শরীরে ছম্ ছম্ ভাব সঞ্চারক, ভয়োদ্দীপক। **-ri-ness,** *n.* Excitement of fear from hearing ghost stories or by supernatural things ; ভূত প্রেতাদির গল্প শ্রবণে শরীর ছম্‌ছমানি, ছমছম ভাব। **-ri-ly,** *adv.*

ĕf-fā-ble, *adj.* Expressible ; utterable, (*obs.*) ; নির্ব্বচনীয় ; কথ্য, কথনীয়, (অপ্রঃ)।

ĕf-fāce', *v. t.* 1. To rub out ; to wipe out ; to destroy ; (*lit.*&*fig.*) ; ঘসিয়া উঠান ; মুছিয়া ফেলা, অপহার করা; নষ্ট করা। 2. To regard oneself as insignificant ; আত্মবিলোপ করা। 3. To utterly surpass ; "Her beauty *effaced* every thing I have seen ; সম্পূর্ণরূপে অতিক্রম করা,

বিলুপ্ত করা। **—a-ble,** *adj.* Capable of being effaced ; অপনেয়, বিলোপনীয়। **—ment,** *n.* The act of effacing or the state or condition of being effaced ; অপনয়ন, বিলোপ, ক্ষয়, বিলয়। **Self-effacement**—আত্মবিলোপ।

ĕf-fĕct′, *n.* & *v. t.* **1.** Result ; consequence ; efficacy ; as, of no *effect* ; পরিণাম ; ফলাফল, ফল ; গুণ। **2.** Purport ; as, to that *effect* ; মর্ম্ম। **3.** Execution ; performance ; as, to give *effect* to ; সম্পাদন, সাধন ; কার্য্য-পরিণতি। **4.** Event ; purpose ; ঘটনা ; উদ্দেশ্য, অভিপ্রায়। **5.** The power to produce result ; as, cause and *effect* ; ফলোৎপাদিকা শক্তি, কার্য্য। **6.** Impression produced by a work of art etc. ; "Conversation......calculated, for *effect* ;" combination of colour or form in picture etc. ; চিত্রাদির কলা-নৈপুণ্য সঞ্জাত ভাব ; চিত্রাদিতে বর্ণ অথবা রূপের সুসমাবেশ। **7.** (*Pl.*) Goods ; personal estate ; মালপত্র ; জায়দাদ, অস্থাবর সম্পত্তি। ***Verb t.*** To produce ; to execute ; to accomplish ; উৎপাদন করা ; সাধন করা, সম্পাদন করা ; নিষ্পন্ন করা। **—less,** *adj.* **In effect**—Indeed ; বাস্তবিক, বস্তুগত্যা। **For effect**—To give an exaggerated notion ; আড়ম্বর প্রদর্শনের জন্য, চটক লাগাইবার জন্য, লোক দেখাইবার অভিপ্রায়ে। **No effects**—কাহারো নামে ব্যাঙ্কে টাকা জমা না থাকিলে তাহার চেকের উপর এই কথাগুলি লিখা হয়। **To carry into effect**—To accomplish ; সম্পাদন করা, কার্য্যে পরিণত করা। **To effect a policy**—To take out a policy of insurance ; বীমা করা। **To give effect to**—To carry out in practice ; কার্য্যে পরিণত করা। **To no effect**—To be unproductive of any result ; নিষ্ফল হওয়া। **To the effect** — Purporting ; মর্ম্মে। **To take effect** — To come into operation ; আমলে আসা। **With effect**—With result or efficacy ; অবর্থ্য, অমোঘরূপে।

ĕf-fĕc′-tive (-tîv), *adj.* & *n.* **1.** Serviceable as a soldier etc. ; producing effect ; (সৈন্য সম্পর্কে) কার্য্যক্ষম, কার্য্যকারী, কার্য্য-সাধক, সিদ্ধিকারক ; ফলদায়ী, ফলপ্রদ। **2.** Actual ; "*Effective* losers ;" প্রকৃত। **3.** Producing a striking impression ; as, an *effective* narrative ; মর্ম্মস্পর্শী, হৃদয়গ্রাহী। **4.** Powerful in effect ; শক্তিশালী। ***Noun.*** An effective soldier ; as, twenty thousand *effectives* ; কার্য্যক্ষম সৈন্য। **—ly,** *adv.* In an effective manner ; কার্য্যকারিভাবে, ফলদায়কভাবে। **—ness,** *n.* The quality of being effective ; কার্য্যকারিতা, কার্য্যশক্তি, হৃদয়-গ্রাহিতা। **Effective range**—(of weapons) (অস্ত্র-সম্পর্কে) যে পাল্লার ভিতর বন্দুকের গুলি প্রভৃতি কার্য্যকরী হয়।

ĕf-fĕc′-tū-ăl, *adj.* Having power to produce desired result ; operative ; অভীষ্ট ফলদায়ক, সফল, ফলোৎপাদক, ফলানুবন্ধী ; কার্য্যকরী, ফলবতী, সফল। **—ly,** *adv.* In an effectual manner ; ফলপ্রদায়ক ভাবে, কার্য্যকারিভাবে। **—ness,** *n.* **Effectual calling**—দিব্যাহ্বান (হিঃ কোঃ), দৈবী প্রেরণা (ঐ)।

ĕf-fĕc′-tū-āte, *v. t.* To bring to pass ; to accomplish ; সংঘটন করা ; সম্পাদন করা, সংসাধন করা। **—a′-tion,** *n.*

ĕf-fĕm′-i-nā-cy̆, *n.* Woman-like softness or weakness ; voluptuousness ; cowardice ; স্ত্রীজনসুলভ কোমলতা বা দুর্ব্বলতা, মেয়েলি স্বভাব ; ভোগাসক্তি, বিলাসপরায়ণতা ; নির্ব্বীর্য্যতা, কাপুরুষতা।

ĕf-fĕm′-i-nāte, *adj.*, *v. t.* & *i.* Womanish ; voluptuous ; cowardly ; unmanly ; স্ত্রীজনসুলভ, স্ত্রীময় ; বিলাসরত ; ভীরু, কাপুরুষ ; স্ত্রৈণ, নির্বীর্য্য, হীনবীর্য্য। ***Verb t.*** To make womanish ; স্ত্রীভাবাপন্ন করা। ***Verb i.*** To become effeminate ; স্ত্রীবৎ হওয়া, হীনবীর্য্য হওয়া, দুর্ব্বল হওয়া। **—ness,** *n.*

ĕf-fĕn′-dĭ, *n.* Turkish title of high Government officials and erudite persons ; তুরস্কদেশীয় উচ্চ রাজকর্ম্মচারী এবং পণ্ডিত ব্যক্তিদের সম্ভ্রমসূচক উপাধিবিশেষ।

ĕf′-fĕr-ĕnt, *adj.* (*Physiol.*) Conveying outward ; বহিঃসঞ্চালক, আজ্ঞাবহ (স্রজঃ), বহির্বাহিনী (হিঃ কোঃ), ক্রিয়াবাহিনী (ঐ)।

ĕf-fĕr-vesce′ (-vĕs), *v. i.* **1.** To froth up ; to bubble with a hissing sound ; ফেনাইয়া উঠা ; ফেনিল হওয়া, ফেনময় হওয়া, স্ফুরিত হওয়া, ফুটিয়া উঠা, ফুস্ ফুস্ শব্দে ফেনাইয়া উঠা, বুদ্বুদান্বিত হওয়া। **2.** To exhibit signs of excitement ; উত্তেজনার চিহ্ন-প্রদর্শন করা। **—ves′-cence, —ves′-cen-cy,** *ns.* **1.** A kind of natural ebullition ; বুদ্বুদোদ্গম, স্ফোটন, ফেনিলতা। **2.** Exhibition of excitement ; উত্তেজনা-প্রদর্শন, উচ্ছ্বাস। **—ves′-cent, —ves′-cing,** *adjs.* Bubbling ; স্ফোটনশীল, ফুটন্ত, বুদ্বুদান্বিত।

ĕf-fete′ (-fēt), *adj.* Exhausted ; feeble ; barren ; অবসন্ন ; জরা-জর্জ্জরিত, জরাগ্রস্ত ; অনুর্ব্বর, জননশক্তিরহিত, বন্ধ্যা, পুনঃ পুনঃ প্রসবের পর উৎপাদনে অক্ষম। **—ness,** *n.*

ĕf-fi-că′-cious (-shŭs), *adj.* Productive of desired effect ; অভীষ্ট ফলপ্রদ, অব্যর্থ, অমোঘ। **—ly,** *adv.* **—ness,** *n.*

ĕf′-fi-că-cy̆, *n.* **1.** Power to produce effect ; উপকারিতা, গুণ, ফলপ্রদান শক্তি, সাফল্য। **2.** Virtue ; energy ; ধর্ম্ম, সাধকতা (হিঃ কোঃ) ; সামর্থ্য, প্রভাব, ক্ষমতা, শক্তি।

ĕf-fĭ′-cien-cy̆ (-shĕn-), *n.* **1.** Power of producing desired effect ; ঈপ্সিতফল-প্রদানশক্তি। **2.** Competency ; fitness ; কার্য্যক্ষমতা, কর্ম্মশক্তি, দক্ষতা ; যোগ্যতা। **3.** (*Mech.*) Amount of the really effective force ; (যন্ত্রবিজ্ঞান) যন্ত্রবল। **—cient,** *adj.* Competent ; capable ; effective ; কর্ম্মদক্ষ, কার্য্যদক্ষ ; কর্ম্মক্ষম,

কার্য্যক্ষম ; ফলপ্রদ । **—cient-ly,** *adv.* **Efficient cause**—নিমিত্ত কারণ।

ĕf′-fĭ-ġy̆, *n.* **1.** An image ; প্রতিমা, মূর্ত্তি । **2.** The likeness of a person ; প্রতিকৃতি, প্রতিমূর্ত্তি, প্রতিকায়, কুশ-পুত্তলিকা । **To burn, or hang in effigy**—To burn or hang the likeness of (a person) in expression of hate or abhorrence ; কোন ব্যক্তির কুশপুত্তলিকা দাহ করা, কোন ব্যক্তির কুশপুত্তলিকা ফাঁসি-কাষ্ঠে ঝুলান।

ĕf-flŏ-resce′ (-rĕs), *v. t.* **1.** To blossom into flower, (*lit.* & *fig.*) ; পুষ্পিত হওয়া, কুসুমিত হওয়া, বিকসিত হওয়া, (শব্দানুযায়ী এবং লক্ষণায়)। **2.** (*Chem.*) To form into tiny crystals ; (রসায়ন-শাস্ত্র) অতিক্ষুদ্র দানা বাঁধা । **3.** To be covered with a whitish powder ; শ্বেতাভচূর্ণ দ্বারা আচ্ছাদিত হওয়া । **—res′-cence,** *n.* **1.** Blossoming into flowers ; the time of bursting into flowers ; পুষ্পোৎপাদন, পুষ্পোৎপত্তি, প্রপুষ্পণ, প্রস্ফোটন, পুষ্পোদ্গম ; পুষ্পোদ্গমকাল। **2.** An eruption ; redness of skin ; উদ্ভেদ (হঃ চঃ), স্ফোট (ঐ) উদর্দ্দ ; চর্ম্মলৌহিত্য। **3.** A whitish powder or minute crystals forming on the surface (as of salt) ; লবণক পদার্থাদির উপরিভাগে যে শ্বেতবর্ণ ক্ষুদ্র ক্ষুদ্র দানা বা চূর্ণ গঠিত হয়। **—res′-cent,** *adj.*

ĕf′-flû-ence (-ĕns), *n.* (Of light etc.) The act of flowing out ; (*lit* & *fig.*) that which flows out ; নির্গম, বহির্নিঃসরণ, বহিঃপ্রবহন ; প্রবাহ, নিঃস্রব, (শব্দানুযায়ী এবং লক্ষণায়)। **—ent,** *adj.* & *n.* Flowing out ; বহিঃ-প্রবহমান, বহির্নিঃসরণশীল, নির্ব্বাহী। (*Noun*) A stream that flows out of another stream or lake ; শাখানদী, উপনদী।

ĕf-flŭ′-vi-ŭm, (*pl.* EFFLUVIA), *n.* **1.** Noxious vapour ; a disagreeable smell ; দূষিত বাষ্প ; দুর্গন্ধ, পূতিগন্ধ। **2.** (*Phys.*) A (supposed) stream of minute particles emitted by magnet etc. ; (পদার্থবিজ্ঞান) চুম্বকাদি হইতে নিঃসৃত (কল্পিত) সূক্ষ্ম-কণিকা-প্রবাহ। **—vi-al,** *adj.*

ĕf′-flŭx, *n.* **1.** The act of flowing out ; emanation ; নির্গম ; নিঃসরণ। **2.** That which flows out ; স্রাব। **3.** Expiry as of time etc. ; অবসান, শেষ। **—flux′-ion,** *n.*

ĕf′-fort (-fĕrt), *n.* **1.** Attempt ; struggle ; exertion ; উদ্যম ; প্রয়াস, প্রযত্ন, চেষ্টা, বিচেষ্টিত, আয়াস ; পুরুষকার। **2.** A display of oratorial power etc. ; বাগ্মিতা প্রভৃতি প্রদর্শন। **—less,** *adj.* Taking no effort ; inert ; উদ্যমহীন, নির্যত্ন; জড়, শিথিল-প্রযত্ন, নির্জীব।

ĕf-front′-ĕr-y̆ (-frŭnt-), *n.* Impudence ; shamelessness ; shameless audacity ; ঔদ্ধত্য ; নির্লজ্জতা ; ধৃষ্টতা।

ĕf-fŭl′-gence (-jĕns), *n.* Great radiance ; splendour ; flood of light ; মহাজ্যোতিঃ, মহাদ্যুতি, পরমৌজ্জ্বল্য ; দীপ্তি ; প্রভা-সংহতি, আলোক-স্রোতঃ। **—gent,** *adj.* Extremely radiant ; মহাদ্যুতিপূর্ণ, মহা-জ্যোতির্ম্ময়, দেদীপ্যমান, মহাজ্যোতিষ্মান, পরমোজ্জ্বল, অতি দীপ্তিমান। **—gent-ly,** *adv.*

ĕf-fūse′, *v. t.* **1.** To pour forth or out, as liquid, light, air, smell, etc. ; to shed ; ঢালা ; বর্ষণ করা, নিঃসৃত করা। **2.** To pour out words (in composition) ; (রচনায়) শব্দের ছড়াছড়ি করা। **—fu′-sion,** *n.* **1.** The act of pouring out ; shedding ; বর্ষণ, নিঃস্রাবণ ; স্রাব, নিষেক, নির্গম, পাত, ক্ষরণ। **2.** Overflowing kindness ; উচ্ছ্বসিত করুণা। **3.** Overflow of words (in composition) ; শব্দের ছড়াছড়ি (রচনায়)। **4.** That which is poured out ; স্রাব, নিঃস্রব। **—fu′-sive,** *adj.* Emotional ; demonstrative ; আবেগপূর্ণ ; আবেগ-প্রদর্শনাত্মক। **—fu′-sive-ly,** *adv.* **—fu′-sive-ness,** *n.*

ĕft, *n.* A European lizard; ইয়ুরোপীয় গোধা বিশেষ, তৃণগোধা (আঃ বঃ)।

ĕft-sōōn(s)′, *adv.* (*Archaic*) Soon afterwards ; (অপ্রচলিত) অনতিকাল পরে।

ē-găd′, *inter.* By God ; হরি ! হরি !! মাইরি !

ĕgg, *n.* **1.** An oval roundish body laid by birds and tortoise etc. ; ডিম্ব, ডিম, অণ্ড। **2.** Something resembling an egg ; ডিম্বাকৃতি বস্তু। **Egg-apple** — বার্ত্তাকু, বেগুণ, বঙ্গন, হিঙ্গীর, হিঙ্গুলী, বৃহতী, ব্যাকুড়। **Egg-bag** — যাদুকরের ডিম বাহির করার থলিয়া। **Egg-cup**—সিদ্ধ ডিম্ব রাখার পাত্র। **Egg-dance**—চোখ বাঁধা অবস্থায় ডিম্ব সকলের মধ্যে নাচ। (*Fig.*) An intricate task ; (লক্ষণায়) জটিল কার্য্য। **Egg-flip, —nag**—তপ্ত মদ্য,—যাহাতে ডিম্ব ভাঙ্গিয়া নাড়িয়া লওয়া হয়। **Egg-ler, Eg-ger,** *ns.* ডিম্ব-সংগ্রাহক। **Egg-slice** — কড়া হইতে ডিমের তরলাংশ-ভাজা তুলিবার জন্য পাত্র বিশেষ। **Egg-spoon**—সিদ্ধ ডিম তুলিয়া খাওয়ার জন্য চামচে, অণ্ডখাদনচমস (আঃ বঃ)। **Egg-whisk**—ডিম্ব ফোটানের জন্য পাত্র বিশেষ। **A bad egg**—A worthless man ; অকর্ম্মণ্য ব্যক্তি, অপদার্থ ব্যক্তি। **As sure as eggs is eggs** — Undoubtedly ; (perhaps a corruption of *as sure as x is x*); নিশ্চিতই। **Egg and spoon race** — এক প্রকার দৌড়, যাহাতে ধাবনকারী চামচার মধ্যে ডিম্ব রাখিয়া ধাবিত হয়। **From the egg to the apples**—From first to last ; আগাগোড়া। **I have eggs on the spit**—I am very busily occupied and cannot attend to anything else ; আমি কার্য্যে অতিশয় ব্যাপৃত আছি, অন্য কোন বিষয়ে মনোযোগ দেওয়ার আমার অবকাশ নাই। **In the egg**—In an early stage ; অঙ্কুরা-বস্থায়। **To put or have all one's eggs in one basket**—কোন ঝুঁকিদার ব্যবসায়ে যথাসর্ব্বস্ব ফেলা। **To take eggs for money**—To delay payment of money by vain promises ; টাল বাহানা করিয়া পাওনার টাকা দিতে বিলম্ব

করা। **To teach one's grand mother to suck eggs** — To offer advice to an older and wiser person ; বয়োবৃদ্ধ বা জ্ঞানবৃদ্ধ ব্যক্তিকে উপদেশ দিতে যাওয়া, জেঠামি করা। **To tread upon eggs**—To walk continuously ; to move warily in a delicate situation ; সতর্কতার সহিত পদক্ষেপ করা ; গুরুতর অবস্থায় বিশেষ সতর্কতার সহিত অগ্রসর হওয়া। **Will you take eggs for your money**—Will you suffer yourself to be imposed upon ; তুমি কি ঠকিতে চাও ?

ĕgg *v. t.* To instigate ; to urge on ; উত্তেজিত করা ; উৎসাহিত করা। **To egg on**—To incite ; উত্তেজিত করা, প্রোৎসহিত করা।

ĕg'-lăn-tīne, *n.* The sweet briar ; কণ্টকাকীর্ণ গোলাপবিশেষ, বন্যসেবতী।

ē'-gō, *n.* (*Metaph.*) The thinking subject, as opposed to the *non-ego* (object) ; অহং, আত্মা, বিষয়ী, ক্ষেত্রজ্ঞ। **–ism,** *n.* **1.** (*Philos.*) A doctrine of philosophy which admits of nothing but existence of self ; (দর্শন-শাস্ত্র) অহংবাদ (হিঃ কোঃ), মায়াবাদ। **2.** (*Ethics*) The theory that finds in self-interest the foundation of all moral acts ; (নীতি-বিজ্ঞান) প্রত্যেক সৎকার্য্য স্বার্থমূলক এইরূপ দার্শনিকবাদ, স্বার্থবাদ (হিঃ কোঃ)। **3.** Selfishness ; স্বার্থপরতা, আত্মপরতা, অহংকার। **4.** Self-opinionatedness ; আত্মম্ভরিতা। **–ist,** *n.* **1.** One who holds the doctrine of egoism ; আত্মবাদী, স্বার্থবাদী, অহংবাদী (হিঃ কোঃ)। **2.** One who thinks too much of himself ; আত্মাভিমানী, আত্মরত, আত্মশ্লাঘী, অহংশীল। **–is'-tic, –is'-ti-cal,** *adjs.* **–is'-ti-cal-ly,** *adv.*

ē'-gō-tĭsm, *n.* **1.** Constant use of *I* and *me* ; অহংসর্ব্বস্বতা, অহমহমিকা, অহংকৃতি, মমতা, অহংকার। **2.** Selfishness ; self-exaltation ; self-conceit ; self-praise ; স্বার্থপরতা, অহংবুদ্ধি ; আত্ম-গৌরব, আত্মম্ভরিতা ; আত্ম-শ্লাঘা ; আত্ম-গর্ব্ব ; আত্মাভিমান ; আত্মগুণ-কীর্ত্তন। **–the'-ism,** *n.* The deification of self ; সোঽহংভাব, অহং-ব্রহ্মাস্মি। **–tist,** *n.* **–tis'-tic, –tis'-ti-cal,** *adjs.* **–tis'-ti-cal-ly,** *adv.* **–tize,** *v. t.*

ē-grē'-gious (-jĭ-ŭs), *adj.* **1.** Distinguished ; excellent ; প্রসিদ্ধ, বিখ্যাত ; শ্রেষ্ঠ, উৎকৃষ্ট। **2.** Flagrant ; gross ; extraordinary ; as, *egregious* folly ; জলন্ত, উৎকট, বিষম, ডাহা ; ভয়ঙ্কর, ভয়ানক, ঘোর ; অসাধারণ। **–ly,** *adv.* **–ness,** *n.*

ē'-grĕss, *n.* **1.** The act of going out ; নির্গম, প্রস্থান, প্রয়াণ, নির্যাণ, নিষ্ক্রমণ, বহির্গমন। **2.** Right of going out ; বহির্গমনের অধিকার। **3.** A means or place of exit, (*lit.* & *fig.*) ; নির্গমের উপায় বা স্থান। **4.** (*Astron.*) The emergence of heavenly body from eclipse etc. ; the end of an eclipse or transit ; (জ্যোতিবিজ্ঞান) গ্রহণাদি হইতে জ্যোতিষ্কের নির্গম ; গ্রহণাবসান, যাম্যোত্তরগমনাবসান, পরমাস্তান্তর কাল (হিঃ কোঃ)। **–gres'-sion,** *n.* **Egress and ingress**—আগমনির্গম, গমনাগমন।

ē'-grĕt, *n.* **1.** The lesser white heron ; বকজাতীয় পক্ষিবিশেষ। **2.** The down on the seeds of dandelion ; ডেণ্ডিলিয়ন (ভুধাল) পুষ্পের বীজ-সংলগ্ন রোঁয়ার মত শূক।

E-gyp'-tian (ē-jĭp-shăn), *adj* & *n.* Pertaining to Egypt ; মিশরদেশ সম্পর্কীয়, মিশ্রদেশীয়। *Noun.* **1.** A native of Egypt ; মিশর বা মিশ্র দেশবাসী। **2.** A kind of printing type ; একপ্রকার মুদ্রণের হরফ। **3.** A gipsy ; যাযাবর, বেদিয়া, হাঘড়িয়া।

E-gȳp-tŏl'-ŏ-gist (ē-), *n.* One well-versed in the science of Egyptian antiquities ; প্রাচীন মিশর দেশের পুরাতত্ত্ববিৎ, মিশরতত্ত্ববিৎ। **–gy,** *n.* The science or study of Egyptian antiquities ; প্রাচীন মিশর দেশের প্রত্নবিদ্যা, প্রাচীন মিশ্রদেশের পুরাতত্ত্ব বিজ্ঞান।

eh (ā), *inter.* An interjection expressing surprise or inquiry ; এঁ, কি !

ei'-dêr (ī-), *n.* A species of duck found in Arctic region ; the downy feathers of the eider ; উত্তরমেরুর সন্নিহিত দেশের একজাতীয় হংস, সুমেরু-মরাল ; সুমেরু-মরালের তুলাবৎ পালক।

Eider ducks.

ei'-dō-grăph (ī-), *n.* An instrument for copying drawings on the same or a different scale ; সমান বা বর্দ্ধিত আকারে নক্সার প্রতিলিপি অঙ্কনের জন্য যন্ত্রবিশেষ।

ei dŏ'-lŏn (ī-), *n.* A visible representation or apparition ; a visible spirit ; প্রতিমূর্ত্তি (হিঃ কোঃ), অনুবিম্ব (ঐ) ; আভাসিকা, ছায়ামূর্ত্তি।

Eif-fĕl tow-êr (īf-), *n.* A lofty structure ; সুবিশাল অত্যুচ্চ হর্ম্ম্য। [প্যারী নগরীর সুবিখ্যাত বুরুজের নাম হইতে গৃহীত। উক্ত বুরুজের উচ্চতা ৯৮৫ ফুট্ এবং ইহা ১৮৮৯ খৃষ্টাব্দে Gustave Eiffel কর্ত্তৃক নির্ম্মিত হয়।]

eight' (āt), *adj.* & *n.* One more than seven ; অষ্ট, আট, অষ্ট সংখ্যক। *Noun.* **1.** The figure representing this number ; আট। **2.** (*Pl.*) The crew of a boat, esp. a racing boat, manned by oarsmen (at Oxford and Cambridge) ; নৌকার মাঝিমাল্লা, বিশেষতঃ অক্সফোর্ড ও কেম্ব্রিজে যে দৌড়ের নৌকায় আট জন চালক থাকে। **An eight days**—এক সপ্তাহ। **An eight oar**—আটমাল্লার নৌকা। **Eight-day**—একবার চাবি দিলে আট দিন চলে এইরূপ। **The eights** — অক্সফোর্ড এবং কেম্ব্রিজ বিশ্ববিদ্যালয়ের নৌকাদৌড়।

eight'-een (ā-tēn), *adj.* & *n.* One more than seventeen ; অষ্টাদশ। *Noun.* The figure representing this number ; আঠার (১৮)। **–eenth,** *adj.* & *n.*

eighth (ātth), *adj.* & *n.* Next after the seventh ; অষ্টম। *Noun.*

An eighth part ; the unit next in order after the seventh ; অষ্টমাংশ ; অষ্টম সংখ্যা । **—ly,** *adv.*

eight'-ў (āt-), *adj.* & *n.* Eight times ten ; অশীতি । ***Noun.*** The number representing eighty ; আশী (৮০) । **—i-eth,** *adj.* & *n.* Next in order after the seventy-ninth ; অশীতিতম । (*Noun*) **1.** One of eighty equal parts ; অশীতি সংখ্যক সমান অংশের এক অংশ । **2.** The unit or object next after the seventy-ninth ; অশীতিতম সংখ্যা বা বস্তু ।

ei-rĕn'-ĭ-cŏn (ĭ-), *n.* A proposal tending to promote peace ; শান্তি-সংস্থাপন-সহায়ক প্রস্তাব, শান্তিবর্দ্ধক প্রস্তাব ।

eiș-tedd'-fod (ĭ-stĕth-vŏd), *n.* A congress of the bards of Wales ; ওয়েল্‌স্ দেশীয় কবি-সম্মিলনী ।

ei'-ther (ē- or ĭ-), *adj., pron., adv.* & *conj.* One of two ; both ; one or the other ; দুইয়ের মধ্যে একটী, অন্যতর ; উভয় ; একতর । ***Adv. conj.*** (Followed by *or*) **1.** On one or other supposition ; as, he is *either* killed *or* missing ; হয় না হয়, হয় নতুবা, হয় কিম্বা । **2.** Any more than the other ; as, if you do not do it, I shall not *either* ; ও ।

ē-jăc'-ū-lāte, *v. t.* **1.** To utter suddenly or briefly ; to exclaim ; সহসা উচ্চারণ করা, সহসা সংক্ষেপে উচ্চারণ করা ; আবেগভরে উচ্চারণ করা । **2.** To cast forth or eject as fluids etc. from the body ; নির্গত করা, উদ্গিরণ করা । **—la'-tion,** *n.* A sudden exclamation ; an utterance of a sudden prayer ; a short prayer ; মনের আবেগে সহসা উচ্চারণ ; সংক্ষিপ্ত প্রার্থনা উচ্চারণ; সংক্ষিপ্ত প্রার্থনা। **—la-to-ry,** *adj.*

ē-jĕct', *v. t.* **1.** To throw out ; to emit ; to expel ; as, to *eject* one from a room ; নিক্ষেপ করা ; উদ্গিরণ করা, নির্গত করা ; নিঃসারিত করা । **2.** (*Law*) To dispossess ; as, to *eject* a tenant ; (আইন) বেদখল করা, উচ্ছেদ করা । **—jec'-tion,** *n.* Discharge ; expulsion ; নিঃসারণ, বহিষ্করণ ; বে-দখল, বাসোচ্ছেদ । **—jec-tor,** *n.* **—ment,** *n.* Expulsion ; dispossession ; বহিষ্করণ ; উচ্ছেদ ।

ē'-jĕct, *n.* (*Psychol.*) A mental state of (another person etc.) as directly inferred from physical actions ; শারীরিক ক্রিয়া হইতে অনুমিত (অপর ব্যক্তি প্রভৃতির) মানসিক অবস্থা, প্রতিকল্পিত (হিঃ কোঃ), প্রতিকল্প (ঐ) ।

ē-jĕc'-tive, *adj.* **1.** Tending to eject ; উদ্গিরণশীল । **2.** (*Psychol.*) Relating to an eject ; প্রতিকল্পাত্মক (হিঃ কোঃ) । **—ly,** *adv.*

eke (ēk), *v. t.* To increase ; to lengthen, (with *out*) ; বৃদ্ধি করা ; দীর্ঘ করা । **To eke out**—To make up the deficiencies of anything ; কোন কিছুর অভাব পূরণ করা ।

eke (ēk), *adv.* (*Archaic*) Also ; (অপ্রচলিত) অপিচ, আরও ।

eke (ēk), *n.* An addition ; something added ; সংযোগ ; সংযোজিত বস্তু।

ē-lăb'-ō-rāte, *v. t.* & *adj.* **1.** To produce with labour ; বহুশ্রমে উৎপন্ন করা । **2.** To perfect or refine by successive operations ; to work out in detail ; as, to *elaborate* a literary or artistic work ; প্রক্রিয়া-পরম্পরা দ্বারা উৎকর্ষ-সম্পাদন করা ; পরিশ্রম করিয়া বিস্তারিত ভাবে সম্পাদন করা । ***Adj.*** Wrought with much labour ; refined with great effort ; বহুশ্রম-সম্পাদিত, বহুশ্রমসিদ্ধ (আঃ বঃ) ; বহু যত্নে উৎকর্ষ সাধিত । **—ly,** *adv.* **—ra'-tion,** *n.* Act of elaborating ; improvement or refinement by successive operations ; বহুযত্নে সম্পাদন ; প্রক্রিয়া পরম্পরার ফলে উৎকর্ষসাধন, সংস্কার (আঃ বঃ) । **—ra-tive,** *adj.* **1.** Constructing with labour and minute attention to details ; বহু পরিশ্রমে সবিস্তারে গঠনকারী । **2.** (Animal and vegetable *physiol.*) Process by which substances as tissue or sap, are produced by the organs of plants or animals ; (জন্তু ও উদ্ভিদের শারীর বিজ্ঞান) যে প্রক্রিয়া দ্বারা জন্তু ও উদ্ভিদের দৈহিক যন্ত্র সমূহ উদ্ভিদ-রস বা জান্তবতন্তু উৎপাদন করে । **Elaborate faculty** — (*Metaph.*) (তত্ত্ব-বিদ্যা) সম্বন্ধ-নির্ণয়শক্তি এবং সম্বন্ধদ্বারা কিম্বা সম্বন্ধের ভিতর দিয়া বস্তুসমূহ দর্শনের শক্তি, বিস্তারশক্তি (হিঃ কোঃ), উপবৃংহণ শক্তি (ঐ) ।

Elæocarpus ganitrus—রুদ্রাক্ষ (বেলঃ) ।

e-lan' (ā-lâng), *n.* (*F.*) Sprightly animation ; vivacity ; স্ফূর্ত্তি, উৎফুল্লতা ; সজীবতা ।

ē'-lănd, *n.* A species of large African antelope ; আফ্রিকাদেশীয় বৃহৎকায় কৃষ্ণসার বিশেষ ।

ē-lapse' (-lăps), *v. i.* To glide ; to pass away (as time) ; অতিবাহিত হওয়া, অতীত হওয়া, গত হওয়া ; চলিয়া যাওয়া ।

ē-lăs'-tic, *adj.* & *n.* **1.** Having the power of resuming the original form from which it is bent or distorted ; স্থিতিস্থাপক, স্থিতিস্থাপকগুণোপেত (হিঃ কোঃ), সঙ্কোচ-প্রসারশীল । **2.** Springy ; সঙ্কোচ-প্রসারধর্ম্মা, প্রকৃতি-প্রাপক । **3.** Buoyant ; স্ফূর্ত্তিযুক্ত । **4.** Adaptable ; as, *elastic* conscience ; প্রয়োজন মত পরিবর্ত্তন-শীল । ***Noun.*** An elastic cord or string usually woven with India-rubber ; রবার রজ্জু বিশেষ । **—ti-cal-ly,** *adv.* **—tic'-i-ty,** *n.* **1.** Stage of being elastic ; springiness ; স্থিতিস্থাপকতা ; প্রত্যবস্থায়িতা । **2.** (*Mech.*) Flexibility ; (যন্ত্র-বিজ্ঞান) নমনীয়তা । **3.** Buoyancy ; স্ফূর্ত্তি-যুক্ততা । **Elastic conscience**—যে ধর্ম্মবুদ্ধি ভাল মন্দ যে কোনরূপ কার্য্যের অনুমোদন করিয়া থাকে ।

ē-lāte′, *adj.* & *v.t.* Puffed up with success; exultant; exalted; জয়োল্লাস-স্ফীত; উল্লসিত, উৎফুল্ল; স্পর্দ্ধিত। ***Verb t.*** To make exultant; to make proud; to exalt; উল্লসিত করা; স্পর্দ্ধিত করা; বাড়ান, গৌরবান্বিত করা। **—la′-tion,** *n.* Buoyancy; pride arising from success; উল্লাস, উৎফুল্লতা, চিত্তসমুন্নতি, প্রহর্ষ, প্রমোদ, উৎসেক (আঃ বঃ); সফলতাজনিত গর্ব্ব।

ĕl′-ā-tĕr, *n.* (*Bot.*) An elastic spiral filament attached to spores; (উদ্ভিদ্-বিদ্যা) রেণু-ক্ষেপক (সাঃ পঃ)।

ĕl′-bow (-bō), *n., v. t.* & *i.* **1.** The outer angle formed by the fore and the upper arm; কনুই, কফোণি, কূর্পর, অরত্নি (আঃ বঃ)। **2.** Any bend or turn in the course of a river, path, etc.; a corner; বাঁক, মোড়; কোণ। ***Verb t.*** To push with elbow; to force as one's way etc. through crowd; কনুই দ্বারা ঠেলিয়া যাওয়া; ভিড় ঠেলিয়া অগ্রসর হওয়া। ***Verb i.*** **2.** To bend in the manner of an elbow; কনুইএর আকারে বাঁকান। **2.** To push rudely along; হুড় হুড় করিয়া অগ্রসর হওয়া। **Elbow-chair**—বাজুদার কেদারা, কুর্শি। **Elbow-grease**—শ্রমজল, শ্রমজনিত ঘর্ম্ম; কঠোর পরিশ্রম। **Elbow-room**—হাত ছড়াইবার জায়গা, যথেষ্ট স্থান, পর্য্যাপ্ত স্থান, প্রসর, অবকাশ (আঃ বঃ)। **At one's elbow**—Close at hand; হাতের কাছে, সন্নিকটে। **Out at the elbows**—Torn as a coat; poor; ছিন্ন, জীর্ণ; জীর্ণবাস পরিহিত, দরিদ্র। **To be elbowed out**—To be superseded; অন্য ব্যক্তির দ্বারা স্থানভ্রষ্ট হওয়া। **To elbow one's way in**—To get a position by hook or crook; যে কোন প্রকারে বা উপায়েই হউক কোন পদ লাভ করা। To push one's way through in a crowd; ভিড় ঠেলিয়া অগ্রসর হওয়া, ঠেলেঠুলে আসা। **Up to the elbows**—Deeply engrossed in; অভিনিবিষ্ট, তন্ময়।

el′-chee (ĕl-shī), (*F.*), *n.* An ambassador; রাজদূত।

ĕld, *n.* (*Archaic, poet.* or *dial.*) **1.** Old age; (অপ্রচলিত, কবিতায় বা উপভাষায়) বার্দ্ধক্য। **2.** Former days; পুরাকাল।

ĕld′-ĕr, *adj.* & *n.* Older; পূর্ব্বজ, জ্যেষ্ঠ, বয়োজ্যেষ্ঠ, বয়োবৃদ্ধ। ***Noun.*** **1.** A man older in age; the senior of two relations; an aged person; বয়োজ্যেষ্ঠ ব্যক্তি; অগ্রজ; প্রাচীন ব্যক্তি। **2.** A member of a senate etc.; সিনেট সভার সভ্য। **3.** An officer in the early Christian church; প্রাচীন যুগের খৃষ্টীয় ধর্ম্মসংঘের কর্ম্মচারি বিশেষ। **—ly,** *adj.* Advanced beyond middle age; প্রৌঢ়, বৃদ্ধপ্রায়, বুড়-হেন ((*colloq.*), স্থবিরপ্রায়। **—ship,** *n.* **Elder hand**—তাসখেলাতে যে ব্যক্তিকে সর্ব্বাগ্রে খেলিতে হয়।

ĕld′-ĕr, *n.* A species of shrub; গুল্ম বিশেষ। **Elder-wine** — উক্ত গুল্মজ ফল হইতে প্রস্তুত সুরা।

ĕld′-ĕst, *adj.* Oldest; সর্ব্বজ্যেষ্ঠ, সর্ব্বাগ্রজ।

El Dō-râ′-dō (ĕl-), *n.* (*Sp.*) **1.** A legendary land in South America imagined to abound in gold and precious gems; দক্ষিণ আমেরিকার কল্পিত দেশ বিশেষ, এই স্থানে প্রচুর স্বর্ণ ও মণিরত্ন পাওয়া যাইত বলিয়া বর্ণিত হইয়াছে, স্বর্ণরাজ্য, স্বর্ণভূমি, সোণার লঙ্কা। **2.** Any place where fortune may be made easily; যে স্থানে অনায়াসে প্রচুর ধনার্জ্জন করা যাইতে পারে।

ĕl′-dritch (-drĭch), *adj.* (*Scot.*) Weird; hideous; অমানুষিক, ভৌতিক; বিকট।

E-lē-ăt′-ic (ē-), *adj.* & *n.* Pertaining to a school of Greek philosophers who held that true knowledge is attainable only by the reason, they did not believe in the testimony of senses; গ্রীস দেশীয় দার্শনিক সম্প্রদায় বিশেষ সম্পর্কীয়। [এই মতাবলম্বী দার্শনিকগণের মতে বিশুদ্ধ জ্ঞান বা প্রমা কেবল মাত্র প্রজ্ঞা দ্বারা লাভ করা যাইতে পারে, তাহারা ইন্দ্রিয় জনিত জ্ঞানকে অলীক বলিয়া গণ্য করিতেন। Parmenides, Zeno প্রভৃতি দার্শনিকগণ এই সম্প্রদায়ভুক্ত ছিলেন।] ***Noun.*** A philosopher of the Eleatic school; প্রজ্ঞাবাদী। **—i-cism,** *n.*

ĕl-ē-căm-pāne′, *n.* **1.** A plant having aromatic leaves etc.; সুগন্ধি পত্র বিশিষ্ট বৃক্ষবিশেষ, রাস্না (বেলঃ), পিলঘুস (পারসী—খোরী), ফটমেল (হিন্দী—ঐ)। **2.** A sweet-meat made from the root of this plant; রাস্নার মূল হইতে প্রস্তুত মিষ্ট দ্রব্য।

ē-lĕct′, *adj.* & *v. t.* **1.** Select; chosen; মনোনীত, নির্ব্বাচিত; বৃত। **2.** (*Theol.*) Chosen by God for salvation or eternal life; ঈশ্বর কর্ত্তৃক মুক্তি বা অনন্ত জীবন লাভের জন্য মনোনীত। ***Verb t.*** **1.** To choose; to select; পছন্দ করা, বাছনি করা, নির্ব্বাচন করা; মনোনীত করা। **2.** To select by votes for an office etc.; as, to *elect* a magistrate; কোনরূপ পদ প্রভৃতির জন্য নির্ব্বাচিত করা। **3.** (*Theol.*) To choose for eternal life etc. in preference to others; (খৃষ্টীয়ধর্ম্মশাস্ত্র) মুক্তি প্রভৃতির জন্য মনোনীত করা।

ē-lĕc′-tion, *n.* **1.** The act of electing, esp. by votes; নির্ব্বাচন, মনোনয়ন, বাছনী, ইচ্ছা (আঃ বঃ)। **2.** (*Theol.*) Divine choice; (খৃষ্টীয় ধর্ম্মশাস্ত্র) ঈশ্বর কর্ত্তৃক মুক্তির জন্য নির্ব্বাচন। **By′-election** — পার্লেমেন্টের কোন সভ্যের শূন্যপদ পূরণের জন্য নির্ব্বাচন, উপনির্ব্বাচন। **General election**—সমগ্র দেশ ব্যাপিয়া প্রতিনিধি-নির্ব্বাচন, সাধারণ নির্ব্বাচন।

ē-lĕc-tion-eer′ (-ēr), *v. t.* To labour to secure votes for a candidate; নির্ব্বাচনপ্রার্থীর জন্য নির্ব্বাচন-মত সংগ্রহার্থ পরিশ্রম করা। **—er,** *n.* **—ing,** *n.* & *adj.*

ē-lĕc′-tive (-tĭv), *adj.* **1.** Pertaining to or exerting the power of choice;

selecting ; নির্ব্বাচন-সংক্রান্ত, নির্ব্বাচন-ক্ষমতা-পরিচালনকারী ; নির্ব্বাচনশীল। **2.** Dependent on choice ; appointed by election, as an officer ; নির্ব্বাচন-সাপেক্ষ ; নির্ব্বাচনদ্বারা নিযুক্ত। **—ly,** *adv.* **Elective affinty**—কতিপয় বিশেষ বিশেষ রাসায়নিক দ্রব্যের সহিত সম্মিলনের আসক্তি, সংযোগ-প্রীতি (হিঃ কোঃ)। **Elective franchise**—নির্ব্বাচনাধিকার।

ĕ-lĕc′-tor (-tĕr), *n.* **1.** One who elects, esp. an M. P. ; নির্ব্বাচক, নির্ব্বাচনাধিকারী (আঃ বঃ), বিশেষতঃ পার্লেমেণ্ট মহাসভার সভ্য-নির্ব্বাচক। **2.** The title of the German noblemen and archbishops who had formerly the right of electing the emperor ; জর্ম্মণ দেশীয় যে সকল সম্ভ্রান্ত পুরুষ এবং প্রধান ধর্ম্মাধ্যক্ষ পূর্ব্বে সম্রাট মনোনয়ন করিতেন তাঁহাদের উপাধি। **—ship,** *n.* **—to-ral,** *adj.* Pertaining to election ; নির্ব্বাচন-সংক্রান্ত। **—to′-ri-al,** *adj.* **—to-rate,** *n.* **1.** The territory or dignity of a German elector ; জর্ম্মণ দেশের যে সমস্ত সম্ভ্রান্ত পুরুষ এবং প্রধান ধর্ম্মাধ্যক্ষ পূর্ব্বে সম্রাট নির্ব্বাচন করিতে পারিতেন তাহাদের অধিকারভুক্ত স্থান বা পদমর্য্যাদা। **2.** A body of electors ; নির্ব্বাচক-সম্প্রদায়, নির্ব্বাচক-সমিতি, নির্ব্বাচক-সমাজ। **Electoral college** — নির্ব্বাচক-সমিতি।

ĕ-lĕc′-tric, *adj.* & *n.* Pertaining to, or capable of producing, electricity ; containing electricity ; বৈদ্যুতিক, তাড়িত-সম্বন্ধীয়, তাড়িতোৎপাদনক্ষম, বৈদ্যুত (আঃ বঃ) ; বিদ্যুদ্গর্ভ। ***Noun.*** A non-conductor of electricity as amber, glass etc. ; তাড়িত অপরিচালক পদার্থ,—কাচ, তৈল-স্ফটিক প্রভৃতি। **—tri-cal,** *adj.* Same as ELECTRIC. **—tri-cal-ly,** *adv.* **Electrical accumulator**—বিদ্যুৎসঞ্চায়ক (হিঃ কোঃ)। **Electric alarm**—বৈদ্যুতিক ঘণ্টা, বিজুলী ঘণ্টা (হিঃ কোঃ)। **Electric at atmosphere**—বৈদ্যুমণ্ডল (হিঃ কোঃ)। **Electrical cable** — তার, বিজলীর তার। **Electrical conductor**—বিদ্যুচ্চালক (হিঃ কোঃ)। **Electric arc**—বিদ্যুল্লাট। **Electric attraction**—তাড়িত আকর্ষণ। **Electric battery**—তাড়িত-কোষ, বিদ্যুদ্ঘটমালা (হিঃ কোঃ)। **Electric blue**—ইস্পাতের মত নীলবর্ণ। **Electric charge**—See CHARGE. **Electric chime**—বিদ্যুন্নাদ (হিঃ কোঃ)। **Electric condenser** — বিদ্যুদ্ঘনকারী। **Electric oscillation** — তাড়িত-কম্প, বিদ্যুৎ-কম্পন। **Electric current** — তাড়িত-প্রবাহ, তাড়িত-স্রোতঃ, বিজুলী-প্রবাহ। **Electric eel**—বাইন জাতীয় তড়িন্ময় মৎস্যবিশেষ,—ইহার স্পর্শে শরীরে বিদ্যুৎস্পর্শের মত ধাক্কা লাগে। **Electric field**—তাড়িত-ক্ষেত্র। **Electric fluid**—বিদ্যুৎ-তরল। **Electric light**—বিদ্যুৎ-প্রকাশ, তাড়িতালোক, বিজলীবাতি, বৈদ্যুতিক আলোক। **Electric machine**—বিজলীর কল, তাড়িত-যন্ত্র, তাড়িতোৎপাদক-যন্ত্র ; তাড়িচ্ছক্তি-চালিত বাষ্পীয় শকট। **Electric railway**—যে লৌহবর্ত্মের উপর তাড়িচ্ছক্তি-চালিত বাষ্পীয় শকট চলিয়া থাকে। **Electric spark** — বিদ্যুৎ-স্ফুলিঙ্গ, তাড়িন্মোচন, বিদ্যুৎস্ফুরণ। **Electric storm** — বৈদ্যুতিক অবস্থার ঘোরতর বিপর্য্যয়। **Electric telegraph**—তাড়িত বার্ত্তাবহ। **Electric wave**—তাড়িতোর্ম্মি, তাড়িত-তরঙ্গ। **Electric wave apparatus**—তাড়িতোর্ম্মি যন্ত্র।

ĕ-lĕc-tri′-cian (-shăn), *n.* One who studies, or is well-versed in, the science of electricity ; বিদ্যুদ্বিদ্ ; তাড়িদ্বিদ্।

ĕ-lĕc-tric′-i-tў, *n.* The matter or force that causes eletric phenomena ; the science that deals with the laws and phenomena of electricity ; তাড়িত, বিদ্যুৎ, ইরম্মদ, তড়িচ্ছক্তি ; তাড়িতবিজ্ঞান। **Atmospheric electricity** — বায়ববিদ্যুৎ (আঃ বঃ)। **Dynamical electricity** — চলবিদ্যুৎ (হিঃ কোঃ)। **Frictional electricity**—ঘর্ষণ বিদ্যুৎ (হিঃ কোঃ), ঘর্ষণ তাড়িত। **Magnetic electricity** — চুম্বকীয় বিজলী (হিঃ কোঃ)। **Negative electricity**—ঋণাত্মক বিজলী (হিঃ কোঃ), ঋণতাড়িত (সাঃ পঃ)। **Positive electricity**—ধনাত্মক বিজলী (হিঃ কোঃ), ধনতাড়িত (সাঃ পঃ), ধনাত্মক তাড়িত (ঐ)। **Resinous electricity**—লাক্ষ বিজলী (হিঃ কোঃ)। **Statical electricity**—স্থিত বিজলী (হিঃ কোঃ), অচল তাড়িত, স্থির তাড়িত। **Vitreous electricity**—কাচ বিজলী (হিঃ কোঃ)।

ĕ-lĕc′-tri-fў, *v. t.* **1.** To charge with electricity ; তাড়িতবিশিষ্ট করা, বিদ্যুন্ময় করা, বিদ্যুৎ সঞ্চার করা, তড়িদ্বিদ্ধ করা (আঃ বঃ)। **2.** To give an electric shock to ; বৈদ্যুতিক ধাক্কা দেওয়া। **3.** (*Fig.*) To startle ; to rouse ; to surprise ; (লক্ষণায়) চমকিত করা, চমকান ; উদ্বোধিত করা ; অত্যন্ত বিস্ময় জন্মান। **—fi-a-ble,** *adj.* **—fi-ca′-tion,** *n.*

ĕ-lĕc′-trīze, *v. t.* To electrify ; বিদ্যুদ্‌যুক্ত করা। **—tri-za′-tion,** *n.* The act of electrizing ; বিদ্যুৎসঞ্চারণ (হিঃ কোঃ)।

ĕ-lĕc′-trŏ—Combining form of *electric, electrical.* **Electro-biology**—জীববিজ্ঞানের যে শাখায় জীবসমূহের বৈদ্যুতিক অবস্থা সম্পর্কে আলোচিত হইয়া থাকে, তাড়িৎ-জীববিজ্ঞান। **—capillarity** — বিদ্যুৎ-কৈশিকতা। **—chemistry**—রসায়নের যে শাখায় রাসায়নিক পরিবর্ত্তন সংঘটনে বিদ্যুতের ক্রিয়া সম্বন্ধে আলোচিত হইয়া থাকে, তাড়িত-রসায়ন, বিদ্যুদ্রসায়ন। **—chronograph** — বিদ্যুৎসূক্ষ্মকালদর্শক। **—dynameter** — বিদ্যুদ্গতি-মাপক। **—engraving** — বিদ্যুন্মুদ্রণ (হিঃকোঃ)। **—magnet**—তাড়িত চুম্বক (সাঃ পঃ), বিদ্যুচ্চুম্বক ; তাড়িত প্রবাহ দ্বারা চৌম্বক ধর্ম্মাক্রান্ত লৌহদণ্ড। **—magnetism**—বিদ্যুচ্চুম্বকত্ব (হিঃ কোঃ)। **—metallurgy**—বিদ্যুদ্ ধাতু শোধন (হিঃ কোঃ)। **—motive force**—বিদ্যুৎ-প্রবাহক বল (হিঃ কোঃ),

তাড়িত-প্রবাহোৎপাদিকা শক্তি। **–polar**—বিদ্যুদ্-ধ্রুব (হিঃ কোঃ)। **–therapeutics**—বিদ্যুচ্চিকিৎসা (হিঃ কোঃ)। **–thermancy** — বিদ্যুৎতাপবিজ্ঞান (হিঃ কোঃ)।

ē-lĕc-trō-cū′-tion, *n.* Punishment of death by means of electricity, as practised in the U.S. of America; তাড়িতের সাহায্যে প্রাণদণ্ডে দণ্ডিত ব্যক্তির বধ-সাধন, তড়িন্নিহনন। [আমেরিকার যুক্তরাজ্যে প্রচলিত আছে।] **–cute,** *v. t.*

ē-lĕc′-trōde, *n.* The poles of electric wires or conductors; বৈদ্যুতিক তারের উভয় প্রান্ত, তাড়িদ্দ্বার (সাঃ পঃ), তাড়িদ্ধাম (ঐ), বিদ্যুন্মার্গ (হিঃ কোঃ)।

ē-lĕc-trō-dȳ-năm′-ics, *n.* The branch of physical science that treats of the mechanical actions of electricity; তাড়িদ্বলবিজ্ঞান। **–ic,** *adj.*

ē-lĕc′-trō-grăph, *n.* An instrument for registering electric conditions; বৈদ্যুতিক অবস্থা লিখনার্থ যন্ত্র বিশেষ, বিদ্যুল্লেখ (হিঃ কোঃ)।

ē-lĕc-trō-ki-nĕt′-ics, *n.* The branch of electric science which treats of electricity in motion; তড়িদ্গতি বিজ্ঞান, বিদ্যুদ্গতি শাস্ত্র।

ē-lĕc-trō-lier′ (-lēr), *n.* A cluster of electric lamps; বৈদ্যুতিক আলোকশ্রেণী।

ē-lĕc-trō′-lȳse, *v. t.* To decompose by means of electricity; তাড়িতপ্রবাহের সাহায্যে রাসায়নিক বিশ্লেষণ করা। **–lyt′-ic,** *adj.* Liable to be decomposed by electricity; তাড়িত-প্রবাহের সাহায্যে বিশ্লেষণশীল, বৈদ্যুৎ-বিঘটনশীল (হিঃ কোঃ)। **–trol′-y-sis,** *n.* The decomposition of compounds into their component elements by means of electricity; তাড়িত প্রবাহের সাহায্যে রাসায়নিক-বিশ্লেষণ, তাড়িত-বিশ্লেষণ, বৈদ্যুদ-বিশ্লেষণ।

ē-lĕc-trŏm′-ē-têr, *n.* An apparatus for measuring electricity; তড়িন্মান যন্ত্র, তড়িন্মাপক (সাঃ পঃ)।

ē-lĕc-trō-mō′-tor (-têr), *n.* An engine moved by the power of electricity; an apparatus for producing electric current; তাড়িত-বলে চালিত যন্ত্র, তাড়িদ্বাহক (হিঃ কোঃ); তড়িতপ্রবাহোৎপাদক যন্ত্র, তড়িতবর্দ্ধক (হিঃ কোঃ), বৈদ্যুদ্-বর্দ্ধক (ঐ)।

ē-lĕc′-trŏn, *n.* Same as ELECTRUM below. Also atom of negative electricity; electric charge of an atom; ঋণ-তাড়িত পরমাণু; এক পরমাণু তড়িন্ময় করিতে হইলে যে পরিমাণ তাড়িতের আবশ্যক হয়।

ē-lĕc-trō-nĕg′-ă-tive, –pŏs′-i-tive, *adjs* & *ns.* Relating to negative or positive electricity; ঋণাত্মক বা ধনাত্মক তাড়িত সম্বন্ধীয়। ***Nouns.*** A body or substance that passes to the anode or to the cathode in electrolysis; ঋণ-বিদ্যুৎপদার্থ (-negative), ঘনবিদ্যুৎ পদার্থ (-positive), ঋণাত্মক বিদ্যুৎ (হিঃ কোঃ), ধনাত্মক বিদ্যুৎ (ঐ), ঋণাত্মক বিজলী, ধনাত্মক বিজলী।

ē-lĕc-trŏp′-ă-thȳ, *n.* (*Med.*) Treatment of disease by electricity; তাড়িতের সাহায্যে চিকিৎসা, তড়িচ্চিকিৎসা।

ē-lĕc-troph′-ō-rŭs, *n.* An apparatus for getting statical electricity by means of induction; তাড়িদ্দহ যন্ত্র, বিদ্যুৎস্ফুরক (হিঃ কোঃ), তাড়িত প্রবর্ত্তন ক্রিয়া দ্বারা স্থির তাড়িত উৎপাদনের জন্য যন্ত্রবিশেষ।

ē-lĕc′-trō-plāte, To give a coating at silver or other metals by means of electricity; তাড়িত-প্রবাহের সাহায্যে গিল্টি করা বা রূপার হল করা। ***Noun.*** An electro-plated wire; তাড়িত প্রবাহ দ্বারা গিল্টি-করা তার। **–plat-ing,** *n.* তাড়িত-রঞ্জন।

ē-lĕc′-trō-scōpe, *n.* An instrument for detecting the presence of free electricity; তাড়িত-নির্দ্দেশক যন্ত্র, তাড়িদ্দর্শক (সাঃ পঃ), বিদ্যুদ্দর্শক (হিঃ কোঃ)।

ē-lĕc-trō-stăt′-ics, *n.* The branch of science that deals with electricity at rest; তাড়িত-স্থিতি-বিজ্ঞান, স্থির বিদ্যুচ্ছাস্ত্র (হিঃ কোঃ)।

ē-lĕc′-trō-tȳpe, *n.* & *v. t.* **1.** The art or process of producing copies of types, wood-cuts, etc., by depositing copper with the help of electric current on mould taken from the original; ছাঁচের উপর বিদ্যুৎপ্রবাহের সাহায্যে তাম্র সঞ্চিত করত মুদ্রণাক্ষর, কাষ্ঠফলকে ক্ষোদিত চিত্রাদির প্রতিলিপি প্রস্তুতের প্রণালী বা কৌশল, তাড়িতাঙ্কন। **2.** A model or copy of a thing found by the deposition of copper on a mould by galvanic action; উক্ত প্রক্রিয়ায় প্রস্তুত প্রতিলিপি বা আদর্শ। ***Verb t.*** To copy (by the electrotype process); উক্ত প্রক্রিয়ায় অক্ষর, ছবি প্রভৃতির প্রতিলিপি প্রস্তুত করা।

ē-lĕc′-trŭm, *n.* **1.** Amber; তৈল-স্ফটিক। **2.** An alloy of gold and silver; স্বর্ণ ও রৌপ্যের মিশ্রণে উৎপন্ন ধাতু, চন্দ্রহেম (রঃ প্রঃ)।

ē-lĕc′-tū-ă-rȳ, *n.* Medicinal powder mixed with honey or syrup; আলেহ্য, অবলেহ।

ĕl-ee-mŏs′-ȳ-nă-rȳ (-ē-), *adj.* **1.** Given in charity or alms; relating to charitable donations; দান-স্বরূপ প্রদত্ত, ভিক্ষাস্বরূপ প্রদত্ত; ভিক্ষাদান-সম্বন্ধীয়। **2.** Supported by alms or charity as the poor; দান অথবা ভিক্ষাদ্বারা পালিত বা রক্ষিত, খয়রাতি।

ĕl′-ĕ-gance (-găns), *n.* Refinement; grace; rich ornamentation; beauty resulting from perfect propriety; as, *elegance* of manners; style of composition, etc.; মার্জ্জিতত্ব; মাধুর্য্য, সুষ্ঠুতা, সুষমা; শোভা, কান্তি, লালিত্য, কমনীয়তা; চারুতা, সমুজ্জ্বল ভূষা বা মণ্ডন; সৌকুমার্য্য। **–gant,** *adj.* **1.** Graceful; refined; tasteful; richly ornamental; symmetrical; সুকুমার, চারু, মধুর, ললিত, সুচারু, মাধুর্য্যপূর্ণ, সুললিত; মার্জ্জিত;

সুরুচিসম্পন্ন, সুরুচিপূর্ণ ; সমুজ্জ্বল শোভা-সম্পন্ন ; সৌষ্ঠবসম্পন্ন। 2. Characterised by refined luxury as a mode of life etc. ; মাৰ্জ্জিত বিলাসিতাপূর্ণ। 3. (*Vulgar*) Fine or excellent ; (ইতর ভাষায়) তোফা, চমৎকার। **—gant·ly,** *adv.*

ĕ-lē'-gĭ-ăc, *adj.* & *n.* Mournful ; belonging or suited to an elegy as a metre ; বিষাদজনক, শোকজনক ; শোকগীতি সম্বন্ধীয়, শোকগাথার উপযোগী, করুণার্থ-গ্রথিত (আঃ বঃ)। ***Noun.*** An elegiac verse ; শোকগাথা, বিষাদ-গীতি।

ĕl'-ĕ-ġy̆, *n.* A funeral song ; a mournful poem ; শ্মশান-সঙ্গীত ; শোক-গীতি, বিষাদজনক কবিতা, করুণার্থগ্রথিত কাব্য বা গীত (আঃ বঃ)। **—gise,** *v. t.* & *i.* To lament in an elegy ; to mourn as in an elegy ; শোকগাথায় বিলাপ করা ; বিলাপ করা।

ĕl'-ĕ-mĕnt, *n.* 1. A fundamental part or principle ; মৌলিক অংশ, মূল তত্ত্ব। 2. (*Chem.*) A substance that cannot be analysed ; (রসায়ন-শাস্ত্র) সূক্ষ্ম-পদার্থ, মূলপদার্থ, বীজভূত (হিঃ কোঃ), মূলভূত (ঐ), অসঙ্করিতভূত (ঐ), আদিভূত (ঐ), রূঢ়পদার্থ। 3. An ingredient ; মূল উপাদান। 4. (*Pl.*) First principles of an art or science ; rudiments ; শিল্প বা বিজ্ঞানের মূলতত্ত্ব, বীজতত্ত্ব (হিঃ কোঃ) ; প্রাথমিক শিক্ষা বা শিক্ষাগ্রন্থ। 5. Atmospheric agencies ; as, the war of *elements* ; বায়ুমণ্ডলস্থ জল, বিদ্যুৎ, বায়ু প্রভৃতি। 6. Proper sphere or state of anything ; স্বাভাবিক বা প্রকৃতির উপযোগী স্থান। 7. (*Pl.*) The bread and wine used in holy Eucharist ; খৃষ্টের শেষ ভোজন উৎসবের সুরা ও রুটিকা। 8. A data used in a calculation ; গণনায় প্রদত্ত বিষয়। **—men'-tal,** *adj.* & *n.* 1. Fundamental ; of the four elements ; মূলতত্ত্ব বা মূলসূত্র সম্বন্ধীয় ; আধিভৌতিক, পাঞ্চভৌতিক। 2. Pertaining to the agencies of nature ; as, *elemental* worship ; ভৌতিক। 3. Comparable to the powers of nature ; as, *elemental* grandeur or tumult ; প্রাকৃতিক শক্তির তুল্য। 4. Essential as ingredients ; মৌলিক। (*Noun*) (*Theos.*) A spirit of earth, air, water or fire ; (ব্রহ্মবিদ্যা) ক্ষিতি, বায়ু, জল ও অগ্নিবাসী অপদেবতা। **—men'-tal-ism,** *n.* Worship of the elements or elemental spirits ; পিশাচ-পূজা, ভূত-পূজা। **—men'-tal-ly,** *adv.* **—men'-ta-ri-ly,** *adv.* **—men'-ta-ri-ness,** *n.* **—men'-ta-ry,** *adj.* 1. Pertaining to first principles ; introductory ; teaching rudiments ; তাত্ত্বিক, মৌলিক ; প্রারম্ভিক, মুখবন্ধ-স্বরূপ ; প্রাথমিক শিক্ষাপ্রদায়ী। 2. (*Chem.*) Undecomposable ; অবিশ্লেষণীয়, রূঢ়। **Euclid's elements**—প্রাথমিক জ্যামিতি। **Five elements** — ক্ষিত্যপ্‌তেজোমরুদ্ব্যোম, পঞ্চভূত। **Four elements**—Earth, air, water and fire ; ক্ষিত্যপ্‌তেজোমরুৎ, পৃথিবী, বায়ু, জল এবং অগ্নি। **To be in or out of one's elements**—To be in or out of one's proper sphere ; কাহারও স্বাভাবিক বা প্রকৃতির উপযোগী স্থানে থাকা বা তাহা হইতে ভ্রষ্ট হওয়া (জল হইতে উত্তোলিত মৎস্যের মত)।

ĕl'-ĕ-mi, *n.* A resinous substance used in the preparation of stimulant ointments etc. ; মলম, বলকারক ঔষধ প্রভৃতি প্রস্তুতে ব্যবহৃত ধুনার মত দ্রব্য বিশেষ।

ĕ-len'-chŭs (-lĕng-), *n.* (*Pl.* *-chi.*) Logical refutation ; খণ্ডন। **—chic,** *adj.* **Socratic elenchus**—সংক্ষিপ্ত প্রশ্নোত্তরদ্বারা সত্য নির্ণয় করণ।

ĕ-lĕn'-tic, *adj.* Relating to, or given to, refutation ; খণ্ডন-সম্বন্ধীয়, খণ্ডনাত্মক, প্রত্যাখ্যানাত্মক।

ĕl'-ĕ-phănt, *n.* 1. A species of large quadrupeds ; হস্তী, হাতী, গজ, বারণ, কুঞ্জর, মাতঙ্গ, করী, পিল (হিন্দিঃ), নাগ, দন্তী, দ্বীপ, দ্বিরদ। 2. A size of paper (28×23 in.) ; কাগজের আয়তন বিশেষ। **—phan'-tine,** *adj.* 1. Pertaining to an elephant ; large as an elephant ; হস্তিসম্বন্ধীয় ; হাস্তেয়ক, গজবৎ প্রকাণ্ড, গজাকার। 2. Clumsy ; unwieldy ; কদর্য্য ; গুরুভার, গোব্দা। **—phan'-toid,** *adj.* **Elephant apple**—কৎবেল, কপিথ। **White elephant**—অতিশয় ব্যয়সাপেক্ষ অথচ অলাভকর বিষয়। [শ্যামদেশের রাজা কোন সভাসদের সর্ব্বনাশ সাধনে অভিলাষী হইলে ঐ সভাসদকে একটী শ্বেত হস্তী উপহার প্রদান করিতেন। এই হস্তীর ভরণ-

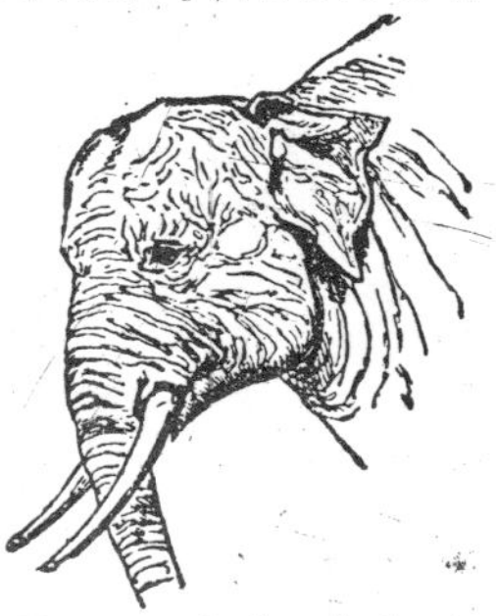

Head of an Indian elephant.

পোষণ অসম্ভব ব্যয়সাপেক্ষ হওয়ায় সভাসদ অচিরেই সর্ব্বস্বান্ত হইত।] **Elephantine epoch**—যে যুগে বৃহৎ স্থূলচর্ম্মী জন্তুগণ বহুসংখ্যায় বর্ত্তমান ছিল। **To have seen the elephant**—To have the knowledge of all latest movements ; সমস্ত সাময়িক আন্দোলনাদির বিষয় অবগত থাকা।

ĕl-ĕ-phăn-tī'-ă-sis, *n.* A skin disease consisting of the overgrowth of the skin and its connecting tissues causing it to resemble an elephant's hide ; শ্লীপদ, শিলীপদ।

El-eu-sin'-i-ăn (ĕl-ū-), *adj.* Pertaining to Eleusis, in Greece ; pertaining to secret rites in honour of Ceres celebrated at Eleusis ; গ্রীসদেশের অন্তঃপাতী Eleusis নামক স্থান-সম্বন্ধীয় ; সীরীস দেবীর সম্মানার্থ তান্ত্রিক ক্রিয়াকলাপ ও রহস্য-পূজা সম্বন্ধীয়। **Eleusinian mysteries** — সীরীস-দেবীর সম্মানার্থ অনুষ্ঠিত তান্ত্রিক ক্রিয়া-কলাপ বা রহস্য-পূজা।

ĕl'-ĕ-vāte, *v. t.* 1. To lift up ; to raise to a more exalted position ; উত্তোলিত করা ; উন্নত করা। 2. To animate ; to intoxicate slightly to cheer; উত্তোলিত করা; গোলাবী নেশা জন্মান; উৎফুল্ল করা। **3.** To raise morally or intellectually; নৈতিক বা মানসিক উন্নতি সাধন করা। **—vat-ed,** *adj.* Uplifted; সমুচ্ছ্রিত,উচ্ছ্রিত,সমুন্নত। **—va-**

Elevated railway.

to-ry, *adj.* **Elevated railway**—স্তম্ভপংক্তির উপরি উত্তোলিত লৌহবর্ত্ম। সাধারণতঃ বড় বড় সহরে এইরূপ লৌহবর্ত্ম নির্ম্মিত হইয়া থাকে এবং ইহার নীচে মালপত্র ও লোকজনের চলাচলের রাস্তা থাকে।

ĕl-ĕ-vā′-tion, *n.* **1.** The act of elevating or the state of being elevated; exaltation; dignity; grandeur; উন্নমন, উন্নয়ন, ঔন্নত্য; অভ্যুদয়, সমুন্নতি; পদগৌরব; জাঁকজমক। **2.** An elevated place; a hill; উচ্চস্থান; পাহাড়। **3.** The angle of elevation as of a gun with the horizon; দিক্ চক্রবালের সহিত কামানাদির কোণ। **4.** A height or altitude above a given level, esp. of the sea; উচ্চতা, উচ্ছ্রায়, বিশেষতঃ সাগর পৃষ্ঠ হইতে উচ্চতা। **Elevation of a mountain**—নাগোচ্ছ্রায়।

ĕl′-ĕ-va-tor (-têr), *n.* **1.** One who, or that which, elevates; উত্তোলক, উত্তোলনকারী। **2.** A muscle that raises or moves a limb; হস্তপদাদি সঞ্চালক বা উত্তোলক পেশী। **3.** A machine for raising grain into a grain-store; শস্যাগারে শস্য উত্তোলিত করার জন্য যন্ত্রবিশেষ, শস্যোত্তোলক। **4.** (*Surg.*) An instrument for raising any depressed bone; পিচ্ছিত অস্থি উত্তোলনে ব্যবহৃত যন্ত্রবিশেষ।

ĕ-lĕv′-ĕn, *adj.* & *n.* One more than ten; একাদশ, এগার। ***Noun.*** **1.** The sum of 10+1; এগার (১১)। **2.** Players of a side of foot-ball, cricket, etc.; ফুটবল বা ক্রীকেট খেলার প্রত্যেক দলের লোক সংখ্যা। **—enth,** *adj.* & *n.* Next in order after the tenth; একাদশতম। (*Noun*) An eleventh part; an object next in order after the tenth; একাদশভাগের এক ভাগ; একাদশতম বস্তু। **At the eleventh hour**—At the very last moment; শেষ মুহূর্ত্তে, অন্তিম মুহূর্ত্তে। **The Eleven**—জুদাস্ ব্যতীত যীশুখৃষ্টের একাদশ শিষ্য।

ĕlf, *n.* **1.** A supernatural being of short size; খর্ব্বকায় ভূত বা অপদেবতা, বেঁটে ভূত। **2.** A mischievous fellow; অনিষ্টকারী ব্যক্তি। **3.** A pet name of a mischievous child; দুরন্ত ছেলের আদুরে নাম। **4.** A dwarf; বামন। **Elf′-in,** *adj.* & *n.* Pertaining to elves or dwarfs; বামন বা অপদেবতা সম্পর্কীয়। (*Noun*) An elf; a dwarf; a child; বেঁটে ভূত; বামন; শিশু। **Elf′-ish, Elv′-an,** *adjs.* **Elf-bolt**—অগ্নিপ্রস্তরনির্ম্মিত বাণাগ্র। **Elf-child**—পরী সুন্দর শিশু চুরি করিয়া নিয়া তৎপরিবর্ত্তে যে কদাকার শিশু রাখিয়া যায়। **Elf-fire**—আলেয়া। **Elf-land**—ভূত বা পরীর দেশ, পরীরাজ্য। **Elf-lock**—জটা। **Elf-struck**—ভূতাবিষ্ট।

El′-gin mâr′-bles (bls-), *n.* Celebrated Greek sculptures kept in the British Museum—they were found in Athens in 1811 by Lord Elgin; লর্ড এলগিন কর্ত্তৃক ১৮১১ খৃঃ অব্দে এথেন্স নগরীতে প্রাপ্ত প্রাচীন গ্রীসের ভাস্কর্য্য-শিল্পের নিদর্শন-স্বরূপ মূর্ত্তি প্রভৃতি, যাহা বর্ত্তমানে ব্রিটিশ মিউজিয়মে রক্ষিত আছে।

ĕ-lĭc′-it, *v. t.* To draw forth; to deduce; to bring to light; to evoke; টানিয়া বাহির করা, নিষ্কর্ষণ করা; উপপাদন করা, সিদ্ধান্ত করা; প্রকাশ করা; বাহির করা। **—i-ta′-tion,** *n.*

ē-līde′, *v. t.* To suppress (a vowel or a syllable) in pronunciation; উচ্চারণ কালে (স্বরবর্ণ অথবা শব্দাংশ) উহ্য করা। **—li′-sion,** *n.* The suppession of a vowel or syllable; স্বরবর্ণ লোপ, শব্দাংশ-লোপ।

ĕl′-i-ġi-ble, *adj.* **1.** Suitable; fit to be selected; যোগ্য, যথোচিত গুণসম্পন্ন, গ্রহণীয়; বরণীয়, নির্ব্বাচন-যোগ্য। **2.** Desirable; বাঞ্ছনীয়, উপাদেয়। **—bil′-i-ty, —ness,** *ns.* Desirableness; the state of being eligible; স্পৃহনীয়তা; নির্ব্বাচন-যোগ্যতা, বরণীয়তা, যোগ্যতা, উপযোগিতা, গ্রহণীয়তা, গ্রাহ্যতা। **—bly,** *adv.*

ē-lim′-i-nāte, *v. t.* **1.** To exclude; to remove; বাহির করা, বিতাড়িত করা; দূর করা, অপসারিত করা। **2.** (*Chem.* & *physiol.*) To expel; (রসায়নশাস্ত্র ও শারীরবিজ্ঞান) বাহির করা, নিঃসারিত করা। **3.** (*Alg.*) To get rid of; (বীজগণিত) নিষ্কাশিত করা। **4.** To cancel; বাতিল করা। **—i-na-ble,** *adj.* **—na′-tion,** *n.* Act of eliminating; পাশ, নিষ্কাশন, অপনয়ন, বহিষ্করণ, বিতাড়ন, লোপ, নাশ।

e-lite′ (ā-lēt), *n.* The best part of anything; a choice or select company; as, the *elite* of society; সর্ব্বোৎকৃষ্ট অংশ; গণ্যমান্য ব্যক্তিগণ, শ্রেষ্ঠজনগণ।

ē-lix′-ir (-êr), *n.* **1.** A liquor sought after by the alchemists to transmute baser metals into gold or to prolong life; প্রাচীন রাসায়নিক বা তান্ত্রিকগণ দীর্ঘজীবন লাভের জন্য কিম্বা অপকৃষ্ট ধাতু স্বর্ণে পরিণত করার উদ্দেশ্যে যে একপ্রকার তরল দ্রব্য প্রস্তুতের চেষ্টা করিয়াছিলেন, তাহা। **2.** Panacea; সর্ব্বরোগনাশক ঔষধ, মহৌষধি। **3.** Quintessence; ঔষধের বীর্য্য, সারাংশ। **4.** A cordial which invigorates; উত্তেজক ঔষধ। ***Elixir vitæ***—জীবন-সুধা, অমরত্ব-প্রদায়ক ঔষধ, রসায়ন।

E-liz-ā-bē′-thăn (ĕ-), *adj.* & *n.* Pertaining to Queen Elizabeth or her times ; রাজ্ঞী এলিজাবেথ সম্বন্ধীয় বা তাঁহার সামসময়িক। *Noun.* A person or writer of the Elizbethan period ; রাণী এলিজাবেথের যুগের লেখক বা ব্যক্তি।

ĕlk, *n.* The largest species of deer found in Europe and North

Head of an elk.

America ; ইয়ুরোপ এবং উত্তর আমেরিকায় প্রাপ্ত বৃহত্তম জাতীয় হরিণ।

ĕll, *n.* A measure of length of 45 inches, (now *obs.*) ; ২।৹ হাত পরিমিত দৈর্ঘ্যের মাপ বিশেষ। **Give him an inch and he will take an ell**—Give him a little and he will claim for much ; একটুকু দিলে দশটুকু চা'বে।

ĕl-lipse' (-lĭps), *n.* A geometrical figure produced by cutting a cone by a plane making a smaller angle with the base than the side of the cone makes ; an oval figure or object ; বৃত্তাভাস ক্ষেত্র, অবক্ষেত্র, দীর্ঘক্ষেত্র (সাঃ পঃ) অণ্ডবৃত্ত, অপবৃত্ত (আঃ বঃ) ; ডিম্বাকার ক্ষেত্র বা বস্তু। **—lip-tic, —lip-ti-cal,** *adjs.* **—lip-ti-cal-ly,** *adv.* **—lip-tic'-i-ty,** *n.*

ĕl-lip'-sis, —lipse (-lĭps), *n.* (*Pl.* **—lipses**) **1.** Omission from sentence of words necessary for making a complete sense or construction ; পদশূন্যতা, পদাপেক্ষা, পদাকাঙ্ক্ষা, লোপ, লোপালঙ্কার। **2.** (*Print.*) A mark or marks as ...... or * * * * to indicate omission of letters etc. ; (মুদ্রণ) অক্ষর প্রভৃতির লোপসূচক চিহ্ন। **—lip'-tic, —lip'-ti-cal,** *adjs.* Relating to ellipsis; having a part omitted, as a phrase ; লোপালঙ্কারবাচক ; সংবৃতাংশ শূন্য, ন্যূনপদ (আঃ বঃ), উহ্যশব্দাদিসূচক। **—lip'-ti-cal-ly,** *adv.* **Supplying of an ellipsis**—অধ্যাহার (পাণিঃ), আকাঙ্ক্ষাপূরণ।

ĕl-lip'-soid (-sȳd), *n.* A solid figure, as the earth, of which all the plane sections are ellipses or circles ; যে ঘনক্ষেত্রের প্রত্যেকটী খণ্ড বৃত্ত বা বৃত্তাভাস হইয়া থাকে, দীর্ঘগোলাভ (হিঃ কোঃ)।

ĕlm, *n.* A tree found in Europe and America, valued for its timber ; দেবদারুজাতীয় ছায়াবহুল বৃক্ষ বিশেষ। **Elm'-y,** *adj.*

El-mö's fire (ĕl-), *n.* A popular name of an electric appearance seen on the masts of ship, (from Saint Elmo, the patron saint of sailors) ; জাহাজের মাস্তুলাগ্রে দৃষ্ট তড়িচ্ছটার সাধারণ নাম।

ĕl-ō-cü'-tion, *n.* The style or art of delivering an impressive speech ; eloquence ; বাক্‌কৌশল, বাক্‌চাতুর্য্য, বাক্‌পাটব, বক্তৃতাকুশলতা, বাগ্‌ধারা, বক্তৃতাপটুতা, বাগ্‌বিদগ্ধতা ; বাগ্মিতা। **—a-ry,** *adj.* Pertaining to elocution ; বাক্‌কৌশল-সম্বন্ধীয়। **—ist,** *n.* One versed in, or teaching, elocution ; গীষ্পতি, বাচস্পতি, সদ্বক্তা, বক্তৃতাকুশল ব্যক্তি।

e-loge' (ă-lōzh), (*F.*), *n.* A discourse in honour of a deceased person ; a speech made by a member of French Academy in honour of his deceased predecessor ; মৃত ব্যক্তির প্রতি সম্মান প্রদর্শনার্থ বক্তৃতা, শ্মশান-বক্তৃতা, মৃত ব্যক্তির গুণানুবাদ ; ফরাসীদেশের বিদ্বজ্জনসভার কোন সভ্য তাহার পূর্ব্ববর্ত্তী মৃত সভ্যের প্রতি সম্মান-প্রদর্শনার্থ যে বক্তৃতা দান করেন।

ē-lon'-gate (-lŏng-), *v. t., i.* & *adj.* To lengthen ; to prolong ; প্রবর্দ্ধিত করা ; দীর্ঘ করা। *Verb i.* (*Bot.*) To have a slender or tapering form ; (উদ্ভিদ্-বিদ্যা) সরু বা ক্রমসূক্ষ্মাগ্র আকৃতি বিশিষ্ট হওয়া। *Adj.* (*Bot.* & *Zool.*) Slender ; tapering ; long ; সরু ; ক্রমসূক্ষ্মাগ্র ; লম্বা। **—ga'-tion,** *n.* **1.** Lengthening ; the part of a line produced ; দীর্ঘীকরণ ; রেখার বর্দ্ধিতাংশ। **2.** (*Astrol.*) The distance of a planet from the sun as it appears to a terrestrial observer ; (জ্যোতির্বিজ্ঞান) পৃথিবীস্থ দ্রষ্টার নিকট প্রতিভাত সূর্য্য হইতে গ্রহের দূরত্ব, গ্রহের প্রতান (সূর্য্যঃ বিঃ) ; (of an inferior planet) শীঘ্রফল (সাঃ পঃ), (of moon) তিথি।

ē-lōpe', *v. t.* To run away with a lover or paramour ; প্রণয়ীর সহিত পলায়ন করা, পতিকুলত্যাগ করা। **2.** To run away privately ; to abscond ; গোপনে পলায়ন করা ; ফেরার হওয়া। **—ment,** *n.* Running away with a paramour or mistress ; পরপুরুষ বা পররমণীর সহিত পলায়ন, সংগৃহণ্‌ (অর্থঃ)।

ĕl'-ō-quence (-kwĕns), *n.* **1.** The art of fine speaking ; persuasive speech ; বাগ্মিতা ; প্ররোচনাজনক বক্তৃতা। **2.** Rhetoric ; as, a professor of *eloquence* ; অলঙ্কারশাস্ত্র। **—quent,** *adj.* **1.** Endowed with eloquence; বাগ্মী, বাক্যকোবিদ (আঃ বঃ)। **2.** Characterised by eloquence ; বাগ্মিতা-পূর্ণ। **3.** Exciting emotion ; as, *eloquent* looks ; আবেগপূর্ণ, ভাবোদ্দীপক। **—quent-ly,** *adv.*

else (ĕls), *adv.* & *pron.* Otherwise ; had it not been so ; besides ; other ; নতু, নতুবা ; তাহা না হইলে, অন্যথা ; এতদ্ব্যতীত, ছাড়া ; অপর। **Elsewhere**—In or to some other place ; অন্যত্র, স্থানান্তরে।

ē-lū'-ci-dāte, *v. t.* To make clear ; to explain ; to throw light upon ; সহজবোধ্য করা ; সরল করা, স্পষ্ট করা, বিশদ করা, অর্থপ্রকাশ করা ; স্পষ্টতঃ বোধগম্য করা। **—da'-tion,** *n.* **1.** The act of elucidating or making clear ; স্পষ্টীকরণ, বিশদীকরণ, উদ্ভাসন। 2. Explanation ; exposition ; ব্যাখ্যান ; টীকা। **–da-tive, –da-to-ry,** *adjs.* **–da-tor,** *n.*

ē-lūde′, *v. t.* To evade ; to escape ; to avoid by stratagem ; to baffle as the understanding etc. ; এড়ান, দৃষ্টি এড়ান ; ধরা না দেওয়া, পলায়ন করা ; কৌশল বা চাতুরীপূর্ব্বক ধরা না দেওয়া, কৌশলপূর্ব্বক পরিহার করা ; বুদ্ধি প্রভৃতি পরাভূত করা। **–lu′-sion,** *n.* Evasion ; the act of eluding ; পলায়ন, এড়ানো ; কৌশলপূর্ব্বক পরিহার। **–lu′-sive,** *adj.* Delusive ; using stratagem to escape ; ভ্রান্তিজনক, মোহজনক, ভ্রমাত্মক, মোহাত্মক ; পলায়নের জন্য কৌশল অবলম্বনকারী। **–lu′-sive-ly,** *adv.* **–lu′-sive-ness,** *n.* **–lu′-so-ry,** *adj.* Fraudulent ; fallacious ; evasive ; প্রতারণাপূর্ণ ; ভ্রান্ত ; চাতুরীপূর্ব্বক পরিহারকারী, এড়ানিয়া।

ē-lū′-tri-āte, *v. t.* To purify by washing and straining ; to separate fine particles of metal from an ore by washing and straining ; ছাঁকিয়া পরিষ্কার করা, ধুইয়া পরিষ্কার করা ; ধৌত করিয়া খনিজ বিমিশ্র পদার্থ হইতে ধাতুরেণু পৃথক করা। **–a′-tion,** *n.*

ĕl′-văn, *n.* A hard rock of igneous origin ; a vein of this rock ; কঠিন আগ্নেয় প্রস্তর বিশেষ ; উক্তরূপ প্রস্তরপূর্ণ পাহাড়ের ফাটোল।

ĕl′-ish, *adj.* See under ELF.

E-ly′-si-an (ē-lĭ-zĭ-ăn or ē-lĭzh-ĭ-ăn), *adj.* Pertaining to Elysium or the region of delight ; extremely delightful ; আনন্দধাম-সম্পর্কীয়, স্বর্গীয় (আঃ বঃ) ; পরমানন্দদায়ক।

E-lў′-si-ŭm (ē-), *n.* 1. (*Gr. Myth.*) The abode of happy souls after death ; (গ্রীকপুরাণোক্ত) স্বর্গধাম, পরদেশ, অমরলোক। 2. A place or condition of ideal happiness ; আনন্দধাম, পরমানন্দময় দশা।

ĕl′-ў-trŏn, –trŭm, *n.* 1. The wing sheath which covers the true wing in beetles ; গোবরে-পোকার প্রকৃত পক্ষ আবরক বহির্পক্ষ। 2. The vagina ; যোনি-দ্বার।

El′-ze-vir (ĕl-zē-vêr), *adj.* 1. Printed by the Elzevir family of Amsterdam as a book ; আমষ্টার্ডম-নগরীর Elzevir পরিবারকর্ত্তৃক মুদ্রিত। (ইঁহারা মধ্যযুগে প্রাচীন গ্রীস ও রোমের শ্রেষ্ঠ গ্রন্থ সমূহ মুদ্রিত করিতেন।) 2. Relating to a sort of printing types ; এক জাতীয় মুদ্রণাক্ষর সম্বন্ধীয়।

ĕm, *n.* 1. (*Print.*) The unit of measure for printed matter in a line ; প্রতি মুদ্রিত পংক্তির পরিমাণের একক। [এই অভিধানের প্রত্যেকটী পংক্তি ১১ em পরিমাণ।] 2. The letter M ; ইংরেজী M অক্ষর।

ē-mā′-ci-āte (-shĭ-), *v. t.* To make lean ; to cause to lose flesh ; to waste ; কৃশ করা, কাহিল করা, বিশীর্ণ করা ; ক্ষীণ করা, অস্থিচর্ম্মসার করা ; ক্ষয় করা। **–at-ed,** *adj.* Deprived of flesh ; lean ; অস্থিচর্ম্মসার ; কৃশ, শীর্ণকায়, শীর্ণদেহ, প্রক্ষীণ, কাহিল, ক্ষীণাঙ্গ। **–a′-tion,** *n.* Act of emaciating ; leanness ; কার্শ্যপ্রাপন ; কৃশতা, শীর্ণতা।

ĕm′-ă-nănt, *adj.* Issuing or flowing out from something else ; নিঃসরণশীল, প্রবহমান, বহির্গামী।

ĕm′-ă-nāte, *v. t.* To issue from something else ; to originate ; বহির্গত বা নিঃসৃত হওয়া, উদ্গত হওয়া (আঃ বঃ) ; উদ্ভূত হওয়া। **–na′-tion,** *n.* 1. Flowing out from a source ; as, the *emanation* of the universe from God; নির্গম, প্রভব, নির্যাণ, উদ্গাম (আঃ বঃ)। 2. Effluvium ; দূষিত বাষ্প। 3. That which emanates, (*lit.* & *fig.*) ; নিঃসৃত বস্তু, নিঃস্রব, ব্যূহ (ব্রজঃ বৈষ্ণঃ), কায়ব্যূহ (ঐ)। 3. An ancient system of philosophy according to which all existences have successively flowed or emanated from the divine essence of God ; that which has come into being by this process ; (দর্শন-শাস্ত্র) প্রাচীন দার্শনিক মত বিশেষ, যদনুসারে প্রত্যেক বস্তু পরম্পরা-ক্রমে ঈশ্বর হইতে উদ্ভূত হইয়াছে ; সৃষ্টি, সর্গ, বিশ্ব-বিকাশ, বিবর্ত্ত। **–na′-tion-al, –na-tive, –na-to-ry,** *adjs.*

ē-măn′-ci-pāte, *v. t.* 1. To set free from slavery ; to liberate ; to liberate from subjection ; দাসত্ব-মুক্ত করা, বন্ধন-মুক্ত করা ; স্বাধীনতা-প্রদান করা ; অধীনতা হইতে মুক্ত করা। 2. (*Rom. Law*) To free as a child etc. from the paternal power ; (রোমক আইন) পিতার প্রভাব হইতে সন্তানাদিকে মুক্ত করা। **–pa′-tion,** *n.* Act of making free ; liberation, esp. from slavery ; deliverance ; স্বাধীনতা-প্রদান ; দাসত্ব বিমোচন ; উদ্ধার, খালাস, বন্ধন-মুক্তি, মুক্তত্ব, মোক্ষ (আঃ বঃ), ত্রাণ, পরিত্রাণ, কৈবল্য (ব্রজঃ বৈষ্ণঃ)। **–pa′-tion-ist,** *n.* An advocate for the liberation of slaves ; দাসত্ব-প্রথার উচ্ছেদ-কামী। **–pa-tor,** *n.* One who emancipates ; স্বাধীনতা-প্রদাতা, মুক্তিদাতা, উদ্ধারকর্ত্তা। **–pa′-to-ry,** *adj.*

ē-măn′-ci-pist, *n.* An ex-convict who has served his term of punishment ; কারা-মুক্ত বন্দী।

ē-mâr′-gi-nāte, *adj.* Notched at the apex as leaf etc. ; পরিনিম্ন (সাঃ পঃ), তীক্ষ্ণাগ্র (সাঃ পঃ)।

ē-măs′-cū-lāte, *v.t.* 1. To castrate ; to deprive of virility ; to render effeminate ; মুষ্কচ্ছেদন করা, খোজা করা, খাসী করা ; জননশক্তি নষ্ট করা, পুরুষত্ব লোপ করা ; স্ত্রীস্বভাবাপন্ন করা, নিস্তেজ করা, হীনবীর্য্য করা। 2. To impoverish (language) ; (ভাষা) শক্তিহীন করা। **la′-tion,** *n.* The act of emasculating ; মুষ্কচ্ছেদন, বৃষণোৎপাটন, পুরুষত্ব-লোপকরণ, নির্বীর্য্যকরণ, খাসী-করণ। **–la-tive,** *adj.* **–la-tor,** *n.*

ĕm-balm′ (-bâm), *v. t.* 1. To perfume ; সুরভি করা, সুগন্ধিময় করা, সুবাসিত করা। 2. To preserve (as a dead body) from being rotten by aromatic spices ; সুগন্ধি মসলাদি দ্বারা মৃতদেহ তাজা রাখা, রক্ষা করা (আঃ বঃ)। **3.** To cherish in memory with love and affection ; সপ্রেমে ও সস্নেহে স্মৃতিপথে জাগরূক রাখা। **—ment,** *n.*

ĕm-bank′ (-băngh), *v.t.* To shut in by banks or raised stone structure etc. (as a river) ; বাঁধ দেওয়া। **—ment,** *n.* A bank or dike constructed to enclose water within a fixed limit ; বাঁধ, রোধ, জাঙ্গাল, ভেড়ি, বপ্র, বন্ধ।

ĕm-bâr′-gō, *n.* & *v. t.* **1.** A royal edict forbidding a commercial ship to leave any ports of the country or any foreign ships to enter any ports ; বাণিজ্য জাহাজের বন্দর ত্যাগ ও বৈদেশিক জাহাজের বন্দর-প্রবেশ-নিষেধক রাজাজ্ঞা, প্রস্থান-নিষেধ (আঃ বঃ)। **2.** Temporary suspension of commerce by royal order ; রাজাজ্ঞায় সাময়িকভাবে বাণিজ্য স্থগিত রাখন, রোক (হিঃ কোঃ)। **3.** Restraint or hindrance ; প্রতিরোধ, বাধা। *Verb t.* **1.** To put an embargo on ships, trade, etc. ; রাজাজ্ঞায় জাহাজাদির গমনাগমন নিষেধ করা। **2.** To seize for state services (as a ship, goods, etc.) ; রাজকার্য্যের জন্য আটক করা (জাহাজ, মাল প্রভৃতি)। **To lay an embargo on.**—To seize ships or goods for the service of the state ; to seize ; রাজকার্য্যের জন্য জাহাজ কিম্বা জাহাজের মালপত্র আটক করা ; আটক করা।

ĕm-bârk′, *v. i.* & *t.* **1.** To go on board a ship ; জাহাজ বা নৌকায় চড়া কিম্বা উঠা। **2.** To engage in any affair ; as, to *embark* in a business speculation ; কোনও কার্য্যে প্রবৃত্ত হওয়া। *Verb t.* **1.** To put on board a ship or boat ; জাহাজ কিম্বা নৌকায় চড়ান। **2** To engage in any affair ; to invest ; কোন ব্যাপারে লাগান ; (মূলধন) খাটান। **—bar-ka′-tion,** *n.*

embarras de richesse, (*F.*), *n.* Too much material ; confusion arising from the difficulty of choosing among a very large number of things ; অত্যধিক পরিমাণ উপাদান বা সামগ্রী ; অত্যধিক পরিমাণ বস্তু বর্ত্তমান থাকাতে কোনটী নির্ব্বাচন করা উচিত তদ্বিষয়ে দুঃসাধ্যতা-নিবন্ধন হতবুদ্ধিতা।

ĕm-băr′-răss, *v. t.* **1.** To involve in difficulty (esp. in financial matters) ; ঝঞ্ঝাটে বা অর্থাভাবে ফেলা, অস্বচ্ছলতায় ফেলা। **2.** To encumber ; to confuse ; to impede ; ভারগ্রস্ত করা ; গোলমালে ফেলা ; বাধা দেওয়া, ব্যাহত করা। **3.** To complicate as a question etc. ; জটিল করা। **—ing,** *adj.* **—ment,** *n.* Entanglement ; difficulty arising from pecuniary wants ; confusion of mind ; জড়িতাবস্থা, প্রতিহতাবস্থা, বিভ্রাট, জটিলতা ; অর্থকৃচ্ছ্রতা, অর্থকষ্ট, টানাটানি (*colloq.*) ; হতবুদ্ধিতা, ব্যামোহ, কিংকর্ত্তব্যবিমূঢ়তা ; অপ্রতিভতা।

ĕm′-băs-sy̆, *n.* **1.** The office or function of an ambassador ; the residence of an ambassador ; দৌত্য ; দূতাবাস, দূতনিবাস, রাজদূত-ভবন। **2.** An important message to a foreign court ; সন্দেশ, দূতদ্বারা প্রেরিত বার্ত্তা। **3.** The person or persons sent as ambassadors ; রাজদূত, রাজদূতবৃন্দ।

ĕm-băt′-tle, *v. t.* To set an army in battle array ; ব্যূহ বিন্যাস করা, ব্যূহ-রচনা করা, যুদ্ধার্থ সজ্জিত করা।

ĕm-băt′-tle, *v. t.* To furnish as a wall etc. with battlements ; সচ্ছিদ্র প্রাকার সমন্বিত করা। **—ment,** *n.* Same as BATTLEMENTS (which see.)

ĕm-bay′ (-bā), *v. t.* To enclose in a bay ; (of wind etc.) to force as vessels into a bay ; to landlock ; খাড়ীর মধ্যে আটক রাখা ; (বাতাস প্রভৃতি সম্পর্কে) খাড়ির মধ্যে (জাহাজাদি) ঢুকান ; চতুর্দ্দিক অথবা প্রায় চতুর্দ্দিক ভূমিদ্বারা বেষ্টিত এইরূপ খাড়ির মধ্যে বদ্ধ করা। **—ment,** *n.* A portion of the sea closed by capes or promontories ; খাড়ি, উপসাগর।

ĕm-bĕd′, ĭm—, *v. t.* **1.** To lay in a bed ; শয্যায় শায়িত করা। **2.** To fix in a surrounding mass ; বসান, প্রোথিত করা।

ĕm-bĕl′-lish, *v. t.* **1.** To adorn ; to illustrate with a profusion of beautiful pictures ; to beautify ; বিভূষিত করা, অলঙ্কৃত করা, মণ্ডিত করা ; চিত্রসম্পদে সুশোভিত করা ; শোভাসম্পাদন করা। **2.** To heighten as a narrative with fictitious additions; নানারূপ কাল্পনিক বিবরণ সংযোগ দ্বারা কোন বর্ণনা রসাল করা। **—ment,** *n.* Adornment ; act of adorning ; decoration ; বিভূষণ, অলঙ্কার ; শোভাসম্পাদন ; প্রসাধন, সৌন্দর্য্য-বিধান।

ĕm′-bêr, *n.* Live coal or wood in a smouldering fire ; red-hot ashes ; (*lit.* & *fig.*) ; জ্বলদঙ্গার ; জ্বলন্ত ভস্ম (শব্দানুযায়ী এবং লক্ষণায়)।

ĕm′-bêr, *n.* An Orkney sea-fowl ; (also called -GOOSE, -DIVER) ; একপ্রকার সামুদ্রিক পক্ষী।

ĕm′-bêr days (dāz), *n. pl.* Three days (Wednesday, Friday and Saturday) set apart for fasting and prayer in each of the four seasons of the year ; রোমান ক্যাথলিক খৃষ্টানদিগের উপবাস দিবসত্রয় (বুধ, শুক্র, শনি), প্রতি তিনমাসের দিবসত্রয় (বুধ, শুক্র, শনি)।

ĕm′-bêr-goose (-gōōs), *n.* Same as EMBER 2. (which see).

ĕm-bĕz′-zle, *v. t.* To appropriate fraudulently money, property, etc. intrusted to a person's care ; গচ্ছিত ধন আত্মসাৎ করা, তহবিল তছরুপ করা, তহবিল ভাঙ্গা। **—ment,** *n.* Misappropriation ; গচ্ছিত ধন আত্মসাৎকরণ, তহবিল তছরুপাত। **—zler,** *n.*

ĕm-bĭt′-têr, *v. t.* **1.** To make bitter or sad ; তিক্ত বা দুঃখজনক

করা। 2. To exasperate ; উত্ত্যক্ত করা। **–ing,** *adj.* **–ment,** *n.*

ĕm-blāze′, *v. t.* To illuminate ; to kindle ; উজ্জ্বলিত করা ; প্রদীপ্ত করা, প্রজ্বালিত করা।

ĕm-blā′-zon (-zn), *v. t.* **1.** To depict or inscribe conspicuously as on a heraldic shield ; চর্ম্মাদির উপর কোন বংশ, প্রতিষ্ঠান বা পরিবারের বিশেষ চিহ্ন অঙ্কিত করা। **2.** To deck in bright colours ; to extol ; সমুজ্জ্বল বর্ণে চিত্রিত করা; উচ্চ প্রশংসা করা, গুণকীর্ত্তন করা। **–ment, –ry,** *ns.*

ĕm′-blĕm, *n.* & *v. t.* **1.** A symbol ; a visible sign of an immaterial thing ; a type ; চিহ্ন, নিদর্শন, লিঙ্গ, লক্ষণ, লাঞ্ছন ; প্রতীক (ছান্দোগ্য), মূর্ত্তি, বিগ্রহ ; প্রতিরূপ। **2.** A picture appearing to the understanding something different from that it appears to the eye ; রূপক। **3.** A heraldic device ; কুল-চিহ্ন। ***Verb t.*** To represent by an emblem ; to symbolize ; প্রতিরূপদ্বারা প্রদর্শন করা; চিহ্ন বা সঙ্কেত দ্বারা প্রদর্শন করা। **–at′-ic, –at′-i-cal,** *adj.* Symbolical ; pertaining to or comprising a symbol ; নিদর্শনীকৃত, নিদর্শনাত্মক ; প্রতিরূপস্বরূপ। **–at′-i-cal-ly,** *adv.* **–blem′-a-tist,** *n.*

ĕm′-blĕ-mĕnt, *n.* (Usu. *pl.*) The profits of sown land ; natural product of land as grass etc. ; কৃষিক্ষেত্রজাত লাভ ; ভূমির স্বাভাবিক উৎপন্ন দ্রব্য, যথা ঘাস প্রভৃতি।

ĕm-bŏd′-ȳ, ĭm–, *v. t.* & *i.* **1.** To invest with a body ; শরীরবিশিষ্ট করা, শরীরী করা। **2.** To incorporate ; to collect into a whole ; অঙ্গীভূত করা ; একত্র সমাবিষ্ট করা। **3.** To give concrete forms to (ideas) ; (of things) to be an expression of (idea or principles) ; to include ; সবিগ্রহ করা, বিগ্রহবান করা, মূর্ত্ত করা ; (বস্তু-সম্পর্কে ভাব বা তত্ত্বের) প্রকাশ-রূপ হওয়া; অন্তর্ভুক্ত করা। ***Verb i.*** To coalesce ; to unite in a body or mass ; সংশ্লিষ্ট হওয়া, সংলগ্ন হওয়া ; একত্র সংবদ্ধ হওয়া, পিণ্ডাকারে পরিণত হওয়া। **–i-ment,** *n.* **1.** Incarnation ; as, he is the very *embodiment* of piety ; অবতার, প্রতিমূর্ত্তি। **2.** The act of embodying or the state of being embodied ; শরীর-পরিগ্রহ, কলেবর-ধারণ, দেহধারণ।

ĕm-bŏg′, *v. t.* To sink into a bog ; to hamper in a bog, (*lit.* & *fig.*) ; বিলে ডুবান ; জলাভূমিতে আবদ্ধ করা।

ĕm-bōld′-en (-n), *v. t.* To encourage ; to make bold or courageous ; উৎসাহিত করা ; সাহসান্বিত করা, সাহস সঞ্চার করা, সাহসী করা।

ĕm′-bō-lĭsm, *n.* **1.** (*Astron.*) The insertion of days in an account of time to produce regularity ; (জ্যোতির্বিজ্ঞান) সৌর ও চান্দ্রবৎসর সমীকরণের জন্য মলমাস গ্রহণ। **2.** (*Med.*) The presence of obstructing clots in the blood-vessels ; (ভৈষজ্য-শাস্ত্র) দেহের তন্তুময় উপাদানদ্বারা রক্তবহা নাড়ীর অবরোধ, অনুসমবরোধন (হিঃ কোঃ)।

embonpoint, (*F.*), *n.* & *adj.* Plumpness ; স্থূলতা, হৃষ্টপুষ্টতা। ***Adj.*** Plump ; গোলগাল, মোটাসোটা, হৃষ্টপুষ্ট, স্থূলাঙ্গ।

ĕm-bos′-om (-bōōz-ŭm), *v.t.* **1.** To clasp or embrace ; আলিঙ্গন করা, আশ্লেষ করা, সাদরে বক্ষে ধারণ করা। **2.** To enclose or surround ; পরিবেষ্টন করা, পরিবৃত করা।

ĕm-bŏss′, *v. t.* **1.** To carve figure etc. out on (surface) ; চাপপ্রয়োগে ধাতুর চাদর প্রভৃতির উপর উদ্গত চিত্রাদি তোলা। **2.** To carve in relief ; উদ্গত কারুকার্য্যখচিত করা। **3.** To form or raise bosses or protuberances ; বুটা তোলা, টোপ তোলা। **4.** To decorate with raised work ; উদ্গত কারুকার্য্যদ্বারা বিভূষিত করা। **–ment,** *n.* **–er,** *n.* **Embossed envelope**—যে খামে উদ্গত টিকিট মুদ্রিত থাকে।

embouchure, (*F.*), *n.* **1.** The mouth of a river ; নদী-মুখ, মোহানা। **2.** The mouth-hole of a musical instrument ; বাঁশী প্রভৃতির মুখ।

ĕm-bow′ (-bō), *v. t.* & *i.* To bow or arch ; ধনুকাকারে বক্র করা বা হওয়া।

ĕm-bow̄′-ĕl, *v. t.* **1.** To remove the bowels or entrails of (a body) ; অন্ত্র বা নাড়ীভুঁড়ি বাহির করা, অন্ত্রশূন্য করা, নিরন্ত্রীকৃত করা। **2.** To imbed or bury ; মাটীতে বসান, ভূগর্ভে সমাহিত করা, প্রোথিত করা। **–er, –ment,** *ns.*

ĕm-bow̄′-ĕr, ĭm–, *v. t.* To cover or inclose with a bower ; to place in a bower ; কুঞ্জ দ্বারা আবৃত বা পরিবেষ্টিত করা, কুঞ্জ-কুটীরে বা লতা-মণ্ডপে স্থাপন করা।

ĕm-brāce′ *v. t., i.* & *n.* **1.** To hug ; to clasp within arms ; to press to the bosom with affection ; আলিঙ্গন করা, কোলাকুলি করা ; বাহুযুগলে বেষ্টন করা ; কণ্ঠাশ্লেষ করা ; সাদরে বক্ষে ধারণ করে। **2.** To adopt eagerly ; as, to *embrace* a cause ; পরিগ্রহ করা। **3.** To inclose ; "The woods *embracing* lawns ;" বেষ্টন করা। **4.** To comprise ; অন্তর্নিবিষ্ট করা, সামিল করা, অন্তর্ভুক্ত করা। ***Verb i.*** To join in an embrace ; আলিঙ্গন-বদ্ধ হওয়া। ***Noun.*** Fond pressure in the arms ; sexual intercourse ; আলিঙ্গন, কোলাকুলি, প্রেমাশ্লেষ, কণ্ঠাশ্লেষ, উপগূহন (আঃ বঃ), পরিরম্ভ ; রতিক্রিয়া। **–a-ble,** *adj.* **–ment,** *n.*

ĕm-brāc′-ĕr, *n.* (Also *embraceor, embrasor*). (*Law*) One who influences a juror by bribes or other corruptness ; যে ব্যক্তি উৎকোচ কিম্বা অন্য কোনরূপ গর্হিত উপায়ে জুরিদিগকে বশীভূত করে। **–y,** *n.*

ĕm-brănch′-mĕnt, *n.* A branching forth or out ; শাখা-বিস্তার।

ĕm-bran′-gle (-brăng-l), **ĭm–,** *v. t.* To confuse ; to entangle ; হতবুদ্ধি করা ; জড়িত করা। **–ment,** *n.*

ĕm-brā′-sure (-zhūre), *n.* Opening in parapet for firing cannons ; আবক্ষঃ উচ্চ দুর্গপ্রাচীরোপরি কামানাদি

দাগিবার রন্ধ্র বা খাঁজ, আকাশ-জননী (মঃ ভাঃ)।

Embrasures.

ĕm′-brō-cāte, *v. t.* To wash and rub as a diseased part of the body ; ধৌত, মর্দ্দন বা মালিস করা। **—ca′-tion,** *n.* The act of embrocating ; the lotion used in embrocation ; ধৌত বা মালিস করণ ; শরীরে মর্দ্দনার্থ তরল ঔষধ।

ĕm-bro′-gliō (-brōl-yō), *n.* See IMBROGLIO.

ĕm-broid′-ēr (-broyd-), *v. t.* **1.** To ornament with needle-work ; সূচীকর্ম্ম করা, চিকন তোলা। **2.** To embellish ; to exaggerate, as a narrative ; "He *embroidered* his own story with...some legends ;" অলঙ্কৃত করা ; অতিরঞ্জিত করা। **—y,** *n.* Ornamental needle-work ; চিকণ কাজ, কসিদার কাজ, সূচীকার্য্য, সূচি-শিল্প। **Embroidered cloth**—কার্ম্মিক বস্ত্র।

ĕm-broil′ (-broyl), *v. t.* **1.** To entangle in a quarrel ; কলহ বা হাঙ্গামায় জড়িত করা। **2.** To throw into confusion ; গোলমালে ফেলা, আকুলিত করা, গণ্ডগোলে ফেলা। **—ment,** *n.*

ĕm-brown′, *v. t.* To make brown ; পিঙ্গলবর্ণ করা, বাদামি রঙ্ করা।

ĕm′-bry̆-ō, —ŏn, *n.* & *adj.* **1.** The rudiments of an animal ; ভ্রূণ, জরায়ুস্থ জীব, আমগর্ভ (ভাবঃ প্রঃ), অপরিণত গর্ভ, কলল (হিঃ কোঃ)। **2.** (*Bot.*) The germ of the future plant enclosed in the seed ; (উদ্ভিদ্-বিদ্যা) বীজাভ্যন্তরস্থ বৃক্ষ-বীজাণু। **3.** The beginning of anything ; অঙ্কুর, উদ্গম, প্রারম্ভ, আদ্যাবস্থা। *Adj.* In the first stages of development ; ভ্রূণাবস্থ। **—oc′-to-my,** *n.* The destruction of fetus in a womb ; ভ্রূণহত্যা। **—og′-e-ny,** *n.* The generation of an embryo ; ভ্রূণোৎপত্তি। **—o-log′-ic, —o-log′-i-cal,** *adjs.* **—ol′-o-gist,** *n.* One who is well-versed in embryology ; ভ্রূণতত্ত্বজ্ঞ। **—ol′-o-gy,** *n.* The science of the embryo ; ভ্রূণতত্ত্ব, ভ্রূণ-বিদ্যা, গর্ভশাস্ত্র (হিঃ কোঃ)। **—on′-ic,** *adj.* Pertaining to an embryo ; ভ্রূণঘটিত, ভ্রৌণিক। **—ot′-o-my,** *n.* The cutting of fetus in the uterus to effect delivery ; প্রসবার্থ জরায়ুস্থ ভ্রূণব্যবচ্ছেদ, ভ্রূণব্যবচ্ছেদ। **Embryo-sack**—ভ্রূণস্থলী (সাঃ পঃ)। **In embryo**—In a rudimentary state ; অব্যক্ত অবস্থায়, অপ্রকট অবস্থায়, ভ্রূণাবস্থায়।

ē-mĕnd′, *v. t.* To correct ; to amend as a literary work ; পরিশোধিত করা ; সংশোধন করা। **—a-tor,** *n.* **—a-to-ry,** *adj.* **—men-da′-tion,** *n.* Correction ; সংশোধন, পরিশোধন, ভ্রমনিরসন।

ĕm′-ēr-ăld, *n.* & *adj.* **1.** A gem of a brilliant velvety green colour ; হরিন্মণি, মরকত, পান্না, গরলারি, গরুড়মণি, গারুড়, গরুড়োদ্গার, রাজনীল (মঃ উঃ)। **2.** (*Print.*) A sort of printing type ; (মুদ্রণ) একপ্রকার ক্ষুদ্র মুদ্রণের হরফ। *Adj.* Of a rich green colour like that of emerald ; মরকত বর্ণ, মারকত, মারকতী। **—ine,** *adj.* & *n.* **1.** Of a bright green colour like emerald ; মারকত-হরিৎ, মরকত-শ্যামল। **2.** Pertaining to emerald types ; উক্ত ক্ষুদ্র মুদ্রণাক্ষর সম্বন্ধীয়। (*Noun*) A green dyeing stuff ; হরিদ্বর্ণ রঞ্জক পদার্থ। **Emerald Isle**—আয়র্লণ্ড।

ē-merge (-mērj), *v. i.* **1.** To rise out of a fluid or substance, "The ocean out of which (Great Britain) emerges ;" উত্থিত হওয়া। **2.** To issue ; to reappear ; to come to view ; নির্গত হওয়া ; পুনরাবির্ভূত হওয়া ; দৃষ্টিপথে আবির্ভূত হওয়া। **3.** To arise ; to become manifest ; উঠা ; প্রকট হওয়া, প্রকাশমান হওয়া। **—mer′-gence,** *n.* **1.** Act of emerging ; arising out from water ; নির্গমন ; জল হইতে উত্থান, উন্মজ্জন। **2.** (*Astron.*) Same as EMERSION 2. **—mer′-gen-cy,** *n.* An unforeseen event ; অভাবনীয় ঘটনা, দৈব ঘটনা। **3.** Sudden crisis ; আকস্মিক সঙ্কট, বিভ্রাট। **—mer′-gent,** *adj.* **1.** Rising out of a fluid or other covering or surrounding substance ; তরল বস্তু হইতে উত্থানশীল, প্রকাশমান। **—mer′-gent-ly,** *adv.*

ē-mĕr′-ĭ-tŭs, *adj.* & *n.* Discharged from public service with honour on account of old age or infirmity ; অবসরপ্রাপ্ত, ভূতপূর্ব্ব। *Noun.* A retired professor ; অবসরপ্রাপ্ত অধ্যাপক।

ĕm′-ēr-ŏds, *n. pl.* (*Bible*) Hemorrhoids ; (বাইবেল) রক্তস্রাবী অর্শ।

ē-mēr′-sion, *n.* **1.** Act of emerging ; নিষ্ক্রমণ, নিমজ্জন, বহির্গমন, নিঃসরণ, উন্মজ্জন। **2.** (*Astron.*) Reappearance of the sun, moon, etc. after eclipse or occultation ; গ্রহণ বা অদর্শনান্তে চন্দ্র সূর্য্যাদির পুনরাবির্ভাব, উন্মজ্জন (হিঃ কোঃ), উন্মীলন (ঐ)।

ĕm′-ĕr-y̆, *n.* A variety of corundum the powder of which is used in polishing metals, gems or other hard substances ; শিরীষ, কুরুন্দ-চূর্ণ, কুরঙ্গ (হিঃ কোঃ)। **Emery-nut**—মদনফল (প্লোরী)। **Emery-paper**—শিরীষ কাগজ। **Emery-stone**—কুরুন্দ্ (ওয়াট্)।

ē-mĕt′-ic, *adj.* & *n.* Causing vomiting ; (also *fig.*) ; বমনজনক, বমনকারক, উদ্বামক, ছর্দ্দন (চঃ), বমনীয় (সুশ্রুঃ), বামক (সাঃ পঃ), সংশোধক (ঠাকুর)। *Noun.* A medicine that promotes vomiting ; বমন জনক ঔষধ।

ĕm′-ĕ-sis, *n.* A vomiting ; বমন।

emeute, (*F.*), *n.* A popular rising ; জনবিপ্লব, প্রজাবিদ্রোহ।

ē-mic'-tion, *n.* The discharge of urine ; urine ; মূত্রত্যাগ ; মূত্র।

ĕm'-i-grănt, *n.* One who leaves his own country to settle into another ; যে ব্যক্তি পরদেশে বসবাস করার উদ্দেশ্যে স্বদেশ ত্যাগ করে, স্বদেশ-ত্যাগী ব্যক্তি।

ĕm'-i-grāte, *v. i.* & *t.* To leave one's own country to settle in another ; (*colloq.*) to change the place of residence ; বিদেশে বসবাসের উদ্দেশ্যে স্বদেশ ত্যাগ করা ; (চলিত ভাষায়) বাসস্থান পরিবর্ত্তন করা। ***Verb t.*** To send out to settle in a foreign country ; বিদেশে বসবাস করার জন্য প্রেরণ করা। **—gra'-tion,** *n.* **1.** The act of emigrating ; বাসার্থে পরদেশ-গমন, স্বদেশ-ত্যাগ, দেশান্তর-বাস, প্রবাসন, বিদেশগমন। **2.** A body of emigrants ; স্বদেশত্যাগী ব্যক্তিবৃন্দ। **—gra'-tion-ist,** *n.* An advocate or promoter of emigration ; পরদেশ-গমনে উৎসাহদাতা বা সাহায্যদাতা, পরদেশ-গমনপক্ষপাতী।

emigre, (*F.*), *n.* A Frenchman leaving his country for another, esp. a royalist who fled at the French revolution ; দেশত্যাগী ফরাসী, বিশেষতঃ যে রাজপক্ষভুক্ত ব্যক্তি ফরাসী রাষ্ট্রবিপ্লবকালে পলায়ন করেন।

ĕm'-i-nence (-nĕns), **—nĕn-çy̆,** *ns.* **1.** A high ground ; a height ; উচ্চভূমি; উচ্চ স্থান, শীর্ষস্থান। **2.** Social, moral or intellectual elevation ; distinction ; high rank ; celebrity ; সামাজিক, নৈতিক বা মানসিক উন্নতি, সমুন্নতি ; গৌরব, খ্যাতি ; উচ্চপদবী ; প্রতিষ্ঠা। **3.** A title of high honour given to cardinals etc. in R. C. Church ; রোমান ক্যাথলিক কার্ডিন্যালগণের সম্মানসূচক উপাধিবিশেষ। **—nent,** *adj.* High : exalted ; famous ; prominent ; exalted in rank or position ; উন্নত ; সমুন্নত ; প্রখ্যাত, লব্ধপ্রতিষ্ঠ, শ্রুতকীর্ত্তি ; মুখ্য ; উচ্চপদস্থ, উচ্চমর্য্যাদান্বিত। **—nent-ly,** *adv.* **Eminent domain** — See under DOMAIN.

ē'-mir, —meer (-mēr), *n.* A Mahommedan governor or prince ; a descendent of Mohammed ; আমীর ; মহম্মদের বংশধর।

ĕm'-is-să-ry̆, *n.* **1.** A person sent on a secret mission ; a secret agent ; a spy ; চর ; গুপ্তচর ; গোয়েন্দা। **2.** A subterranean channel by which the water of a lake passes out ; হ্রদের জল নির্গমের জন্য আন্তর্ভৌমিক প্রণালী।

ē-mit', *v. t.* To give out ; to throw out ; to discharge ; নির্গত করা ; ক্ষেপণ করা ; নিঃসৃত করা, মোচন করা। **—mis'-sion,** *n.* **1.** Act of emitting ; নিঃস্রাবণ, নির্গমন, নিঃসরণ, ক্ষরণ, পাত, প্রসেক, সঙ্কলন, বিকিরণ, মোচন, ক্ষেপণ। **2.** That which is emitted at one time ; একবারে নিঃসৃত পদার্থ, স্রাব, পাত। **—mis'-sive,** *adj.* **Emission theory**—আলোক জ্যোতিষ্মান পদার্থ হইতে নিঃসৃত অতি লঘু কণিকা-প্রবাহ ভিন্ন আর কিছুই নহে—এইরূপ মতবাদ, নির্গম-মীমাংসা (হিঃ কোঃ)।

Em-măn'-ū-ĕl (ĕm-), *n.* See IMMANUEL.

ĕm-mĕn'-ă-gogue (-gŏg), *n.* A medicine taken to promote the menstrual discharge ; রজোনিঃসারক ঔষধ, ঋতুজনক ঔষধ, ঋতুপ্রবাহক ঔষধ।

ē-mŏl'-li-āte, *v. t.* To soften ; to make effeminate ; কোমল করা, মৃদু করা, স্নিগ্ধ করা, নরম করা ; স্ত্রীজনবৎ করা, হীনবীর্য্য করা।

ē-mŏl'-li-ĕnt, *adj.* & *n.* Softening ; স্নিগ্ধতাকারী, প্রদাহ-উপশামক, মৃদুকারী। ***Noun.*** A medicinal application used to soften hard texture (also *fig.*); প্রদাহনিবারক প্রলেপ, স্নেহোপযোগ, স্নিগ্ধতাকারক ঔষধ, স্নেহন, অভ্যঞ্জন।

ē-mŏl'-ū-mĕnt, *n.* Profit arising from a post or office ; salary ; পারিশ্রমিক ; বেতন, ভৃতি।

ē-mō'-tion, *n.* Mental agitation ; excitment of the feelings ; feeling ; মানসিক আবেগ ; হৃদয়োচ্ছ্বাস, মর্ম্মোচ্ছ্বাস, হৃদয়াবেগ, ভাবতরঙ্গ ; চিত্তবৃত্তি, রস। **—al,** *adj.* **—al-ism,** *n.* **—al-ist,** *n.* **—al-i-ty,** *n.* **—al-ly,** *adv.* **—less,** *adj.* **—tive,** *adj.*

ĕm-pāle', *v.t.* See IMPALE. **—ment,** *n.* Same as IMPALEMENT. (which see).

ĕm-păn'-ĕl, im—, *v. t.* & *i.* To form or enroll (jurors) ; বিচারালয়ে জুরীদল গঠন করা বা জুরীদলভুক্ত করা। **—ment,** *n.*

ĕm-pĕr'-il, *v. t.* See IMPERIL.

ĕm'-pêr-or (-ĕr), *n.* A title of dignity superior to that of a king ; সম্রাট্, রাজরাজেশ্বর, রাজচক্রবর্ত্তী, সার্ব্বভৌম, রাজাধিরাজ, মণ্ডলেশ্বর। **—ship,** *n.* **Purple emperor**—এক-প্রকার প্রজাপতি।

ĕm'-phă-sis, *n.* **1.** A stress laid on particular word(s) or syllables ; উচ্চারণে শব্দ বা শব্দাংশবিশেষের উপর জোর। **2.** Importance assigned to a thing ; গুরুত্ব-প্রদান। **3.** Intensity ; impressiveness ; vividness ; আতিশয্য ; হৃদয়গ্রাহিতা ; সজীবতা। **4.** Sharpeness of contour ; "By a gradual *emphasis* of the brick wall ;" আকার-রেখার সুপ্রকটতা। **—phat'-ic, —phat'-i-cal,** *adjs.* **1.** Uttered with an emphasis ; impressive ; জোরের সহিত উচ্চারিত ; হৃদয়গ্রাহী। **2.** Forcible ; significant ; বলবৎ ; গুরুত্বপূর্ণ। **—phat'-i-cal-ly,** *adv.* **—size, —sise,** *v. t.* To lay stress on ; to make emphatic ; উচ্চারণে শব্দ বা শব্দাংশ-বিশেষের উপর জোর দেওয়া ; জোর দেওয়া।

ĕm'-pire(-pīr), *n.* **1.** A government with an emperor at the head ; সাম্রাজ্য। **2.** Supreme control over anything ; একাধিপত্য। **Empire-city**—নিউ ইয়র্ক। **The empire**—৮০০ খৃষ্টাব্দে চার্লস দি গ্রেট কর্ত্তৃক

প্রতিষ্ঠিত সাম্রাজ্য,—এই সাম্রাজ্য প্রতীচ্য রোমীয় সাম্রাজ্যের পুনরুজ্জীবন বলিয়া গণ্য হইয়া থাকে।

ĕm-pĭr'-ic, *adj.* & *n.* Based on observation and experiment; relying on experience without due regard to theory; পর্য্যবেক্ষণ বা অভিজ্ঞতার উপর প্রতিষ্ঠিত, ভূয়োদর্শন-লব্ধ, বহুদর্শনসিদ্ধ; পরীক্ষাসিদ্ধ কিন্তু বিজ্ঞানানুমোদনসাপেক্ষ নহে। ***Noun.*** 1. A quack; হাতুড়িয়া বৈদ্য, গোবৈদ্য, কুবৈদ্য। 2. One relying solely on observation or experiments; যে ব্যক্তি কেবল পর্য্যবেক্ষণ ও পরীক্ষার উপর নির্ভর করে। **–i-cal**, *adj.* **–i-cal-ly**, *adv.* **–i-cism**, *n.* 1. Pursuit of knowledge by observation and experiment; পর্য্যবেক্ষণ ও পরীক্ষা দ্বারা জ্ঞানানুসরণ। 2. Quackery; হাতুড়িয়া চিকিৎসা, অশাস্ত্র-চিকিৎসা। 3. (*Philos.*) The doctrine that knowledge comes solely from experience; কেবলমাত্র ভূয়োদর্শন হইতে জ্ঞানলাভ হয়—এইরূপ মতবাদ, অনুভবৈকবাদ (হিঃ কোঃ), অনুভাবালম্বন (ঐ), প্রত্যক্ষৈকবাদ (ঐ)। **–i-cist**, *n.*

ĕm-plăce'-mĕnt, *n.* 1. Putting in a definite place; নিরূপিত স্থানে স্থাপন। 2. Situation as of a building etc.; (অট্টালিকাদির) অবস্থান। 3. (*Mil.*) A platform for guns etc.; (সামরিক শাস্ত্র) কামানাদির মঞ্চ।

ĕm-plăs'-trŭm, *n.* A plaster; একপ্রকার কঠিন মিশ্র-পদার্থ,—এতই আঠালো যে শরীরের স্বাভাবিক উত্তাপেই গাত্রে লাগিয়া থাকে, পলস্ত্রা।

ĕm-ploy', *v. t.* & *n.* 1. To use; ব্যবহার করা, খাটান। 2. To give work to; to keep at service; কাজ দেওয়া, কাজে রাখা। 3. To occupy or devote as time; ব্যাপৃত করা, নিয়োগ করা। ***Noun.*** Service; as, I am in the *employ* of Ram babu; কার্য্য, কর্ম্ম, চাকুরী। **–a-ble**, *adj.* **–e', –ee'**, *ns.* One employed by another; ভৃত্য, চাকর। **–er**, *n.* One who gives employment; স্বামী, প্রভু, নিয়োগকর্ত্তা, নিযোক্তা, মনীব। **–ment**, *n.* 1. Act of employing; state of being employed; নিয়োজন; নিযুক্তি। 2. Occupation; post; ব্যবসায়; কাজ, কর্ম্ম, নিয়োগ, চাকুরী।

ĕm-plȳ-sē'-mă, *n.* (*Med.*) An unnatural distension of a part with air; বায়ুকর্ত্তৃক শারীরিক যন্ত্রের অস্বাভাবিক স্ফীতি-উৎপাদন।

ĕm-poi'-son (-poy-zn), *v. t.* To poison as food, drink, etc.; to corrupt; to taint; খাদ্য, পানীয় প্রভৃতি বিষাক্ত করা; দূষিত করা; কলঙ্কিত করা।

ĕm-pō'-rĭ-ŭm, *n.* 1. A great mart; a commercial centre; আড়ত, আড়ঙ্গ, গঞ্জ; বাণিজ্যকেন্দ্র। 2. (*Vulgar*) A shop; (ইতর ভাষায়) দোকান।

ĕm-pow'-ĕr, *v. t.* 1. To authorise; ক্ষমতা প্রদান করা, ক্ষমতার্পণ করা, অধিকার দেওয়া, ক্ষমতাবান করা। 2. To enable; সমর্থ করা।

ĕm'-prĕss, *n.* 1. The consort of an emperor; a female sovereign; মহারাণী, সম্রাজী, সম্রাজ্ঞী, সম্রাট-মহিষী; রাজরাজেশ্বরী, অধিরাণী, পট্টমহিষী। 2. (*Fig.*) A sovereign mistress; "*Empress* of my soul;" অধীশ্বরী।

empressement, (*F.*)*n.* Display of cordiality; হৃদ্যতা-প্রদর্শন, আন্তরিকতা-প্রদর্শন।

ĕm-prīse', *n.* (*Archaic*) Enterprise, esp. one of a chivalrious nature; অসমসাহসিক কার্য্য, বিশেষতঃ আর্ত্তত্রাণার্থ অসমসাহসিক কার্য্য।

ĕm-prŏs-thŏt'-ō-nŏs, *n.* A spasmodic contraction of muscle by which the body is drawn forward; সম্মুখ-বক্রটঙ্কার।

emp'-tȳ (ĕm-), *adj.* & *n.* 1. Vacant; void; hollow; খালি; শূন্য, রিক্ত; ফাঁপা, শূন্যগর্ভ। 2. Unreal; unsubstantial; unburdened; ঝুটা, অপ্রকৃত, মায়িক; অসার; ঝঞ্ঝাটশূন্য, উদ্বেগশূন্য। 3. (*Colloq.*) Hungry; (চলিত ভাষায়) ক্ষুধিত। 4. Destitute of sense, as a person etc.; বুদ্ধি-শূন্য, কাণ্ডজ্ঞানহীন। 5. Meaningless, as words etc.; অর্থশূন্য। 6. Without any burden or load, as a ship etc.; খালি। 7. Devoid, (with *of*); as, a man *empty of* virtues; হীন, বিহীন, শূন্য। ***Noun.*** An empty car, box, etc.; খালি গাড়ী, বাক্স্ প্রভৃতি। **–ti-ness**, *n.* The state of being empty; vanity; want of substance; শূন্যতা, রিক্ততা, অসারতা, বুদ্ধিহীনতা; গর্ব্ব; শূন্যগর্ভতা। **Empty-bluster**—ফাঁপা আওয়াজ। **Empty-handed**—শূন্যহস্ত, রিক্তহস্ত। **Empty-headed** — Ignorant; senseless; ক্ষীণমস্তিষ্ক, লঘুমতি, অজ্ঞ, নির্ব্বোধ; বিবেচনাশূন্য। **Empty vessels sound much**—ফাঁপা ঢাকের শব্দ বড়।

emp'-tȳ (ĕm-), *v.t.* & *i.* 1. To discharge the contents of; to make empty or void; to transfer the contents of (into another receptacle); to deprive of contents, inhabitants, or the like; as, the town was *emptied*; ঢালা; শূন্য করা, রিক্ত করা, খালি করা; এক পাত্র হইতে অপর পাত্রে ঢালা; খালি করা, উজাড় করা। 2. (Of a river) To discharge (itself) into another river or a sea; (নদী-সম্বন্ধে) অন্য নদী বা সমুদ্রে পতিত হওয়া। 3. To deprive (of); "He *emptied* himself of his glory;" বিহীন করা, বঞ্চিত করা, বিচ্যুত করা। ***Verb i.*** To become empty; to pour out contents; খালি হওয়া; শূন্য হওয়া।

ĕmp'-tȳ-sis, *n.* Hemorrhage from the lungs; ফুসফুস্ হইতে রক্তস্রাব।

ĕm-pŭr'-ple (-pl), *v. t.* To tinge with a purple colour; আনীল লোহিত বর্ণে রঞ্জিত করা।

ĕm-pȳ-ē'-mă, *n.* A collection of pus in the pleura; ফুসফুস-বেষ্টন-গহ্বরে পূয-সঞ্চার।

ĕm-pȳr'-ē-ăl, *adj.* Pertaining to the highest and purest regions of heaven; formed of pure fire or light; সত্যলোক-সম্বন্ধীয়; পবিত্র জ্যোতিঃ বা অগ্নি-রচিত।

ĕm'-pȳ-rē'-ăn, *n.* & *adj.* **1.** The highest heaven; সত্যলোক, বৈকুণ্ঠ, গোলোকধাম। **2.** The visible heavens or firmament; দৃশ্যমান আকাশ-মণ্ডল। ***Adj.*** Same as EMPYREAL.

Emu, with young.

ē'-mū, ē'-meue (-mü), *n.* A large Australian bird; অষ্ট্রেলিয়া দেশীয় বৃহৎ পক্ষি-বিশেষ।

ĕm'-ū-lāte, *v. t.* To imitate with a view to equal or excel; to rival; to vie with; সমতা কিম্বা উৎকর্ষ সাধনের ইচ্ছায় অনুকরণ করা, বিজিগীষা করা; প্রতিযোগিতা করা; প্রতিদ্বন্দ্বিতা করা। **–la'-tion,** *n.* Rivalry; competition; প্রতিযোগিতা, বিজিগীষা; প্রতিদ্বন্দ্বিতা, প্রতিস্পর্দ্ধা। **–la-tive,** *adj.* Inclined to imitation, rivalry or competition; প্রতিযোগী, বিজিগীষু। **–la-tor,** *n.* One who emulates; প্রতিপক্ষ, প্রতিযোগী, প্রতিদ্বন্দ্বী, প্রতিস্পর্দ্ধী। (*fem. -la-tress*) **–la to-ry,** *adj.* **–lous,** *adj.* Vying with; প্রতিস্পর্দ্ধী, প্রতিযোগী। **–lous-ly,** *adv.*

ē-mŭl'-gĕnt, *adj.* & *n.* Milking or drawing out, (used generally in reference to kidneys); নিঃসারক, নিঃস্রাবক, পিত্ত-নিঃসারক। ***Noun.*** Emulgent vessels; নিঃস্রাবক নাড়ী সমূহ।

ē-mŭl'-sion, *n.* A medical preparation consisting of oil, water and another substance that combine with them; as, codliver *emulsion*; তৈল, জল এবং অপর কোন পদার্থের মিশ্রণে প্রস্তুত ঔষধ, দুগ্ধবৎ ঔষধ। **–ize,** *v. t.* To emulsify; দুগ্ধবৎ বিমিশ্র পদার্থে পরিণত করা। **–si-fy,** *v. t.* **–sive,** *adj.*

ē-munc'-tō-rȳ (-mŭngk-), *n.* & *adj.* An excretory duct; মলমূত্রাদি নিঃসারক নাড়ী প্রভৃতি। ***Adj.*** Relating to the flowing of the nose; conveying waste matters from the body, as duct etc.; শ্লেষ্মা-নিঃসারণ-সম্পর্কীয়; শরীরস্থ গ্লানিকর পদার্থবাহী।

ĕn-ā'-ble, *v. t.* **1.** To make able; to authorise; to give strength; to empower; পারগ করা; অধিকার দেওয়া; সমর্থ করা; ক্ষমতা দেওয়া, শক্তিমান করা। **2.** To supply with means to do any act; কোন কার্য্য সাধনের উপযোগী উপায় সমন্বিত করা।

ĕn-ăct', *v. t.* **1.** To ordain; to establish by law; to perform; to decree; ব্যবস্থা করা; বিধিবদ্ধ করা, ব্যবস্থাপন করা; সম্পাদন করা, নির্ব্বাহ করা; বিধান করা। **2.** To act the part of; অভিনয় করা। **–ac'-tion,** *n.* **–ment,** *n.* A law; the passing of a bill into law; a decree; an act; আইন, বিধি; বিধিবদ্ধ করণ, ব্যবস্থাপন; বিধান; কার্য্য। **–ac'-tive,** *adj.* **–ac'-to-ry,** *adj.* **–or,** *n.*

ĕn-ăl'-lă-gē, *n.* (*Rhet.*) A figure of speech in which one mood, tense or case is exchanged for another; as, *it is him* for *it is he*; পদান্তর-ন্যাস অলঙ্কার।

ĕn-ăm'-ĕl, *n.* **1.** A semi-transparent coating on the surface of metal pots etc.; এনামেল, মীনা। **2.** The coating of teeth; দন্তবেষ্টের বহিরাবরণ। **3.** Any smooth hard coating; স্বচ্ছ এবং কঠিন বহিরাবরণ। **4.** An enamel painting; মীনাকরা বাসনের উপর চিত্রাঙ্কণ। **5.** (*Poet.*) A smooth and bright colour on the surface of anything; verdure; কোন পদার্থের উপরিভাগের মসৃণ এবং উজ্জ্বল বর্ণ; শ্যামলতা, শ্যামশ্রী। **6.** A kind of cosmetic or paint for the face; মুখরাগ বিশেষ। ***Verb t.*** **1.** To coat or inlay with enamel; এনামেল করা, মীনা করা, এনামেলদ্বারা খচিত করা। **2.** To decorate with a variety of colours; নানা বর্ণে চিত্রিত করা। **3.** To form a glossy enamel surface upon; as, to *enamel* paper; উপরিভাগ মীনার মত মসৃণ করা। **–eled,** *p. adj.* **–er, –ist,** *ns.*

ĕn-ăm'-our, –or (-êr), *v. t.* To charm; to inspire or inflame with love; to delight; মুগ্ধ করা, বিমোহিত করা; প্রণয়বিহ্বল করা; পরমানন্দিত করা। **–oured,** *adj.* **To be enamoured of** (books)—To be extremely fond of; অতিশয় মুগ্ধ বা আসক্ত হওয়া। **To be enamoured with**—To be captivated by; কাহারও দ্বারা বিমোহিত হওয়া।

ē-năn-ti-ō'-sis, *n.* (*Rhet.*) A figure of speech in which a statement is affirmed by the negation of its contrary; as, I am no coward; (অলঙ্কারশাস্ত্র) এক প্রকার অলঙ্কার,—যাহাতে কোন উক্তি, তৎবিপরীত উক্তির প্রতিষেধদ্বারা দৃঢ়ীভূত করা হয়, বিপর্য্যয়ালঙ্কার, বিপরীত কথন-অলঙ্কার।

ĕn-âr-thrō'-sis, *n.* (*Anat.*) A ball-and-socket joint; (শারীরসংস্থান-বিদ্যা) কন্দুক-কোটর-সন্ধি।

en bloc, (*F.*), *adv.* Wholesale; in a lump; পাইকারী; একলাটে, থাউকো।

ĕn-cæ'-ni-ă, ĕn-ce'-ni-ă (-sē-), *ns.* **1.** Annual festival in the university of Oxford, held in commemoration of the founders and benefactors of the university; অক্সফোর্ড বিশ্ববিদ্যালয়ের প্রতিষ্ঠাতৃ ও সাহায্যদাতৃগণের স্মরণার্থ সাম্বৎসরিক উৎসব। **2.** A dedicatory festival; প্রতিষ্ঠা-উৎসব।

ĕn-cāge', –in-, *v. t.* To confine in a cage; পিঞ্জরাবদ্ধ করা।

ĕn-cămp′, *v. i.* & *t.* To pitch tents ; to halt on a march ; to lodge in a tent ; শিবির সন্নিবেশ করা, তাঁবু ফেলা ; ছাউনি করা ; শিবিরে বাস করা। ***Verb t.*** To form into a camp ; to lodge in a tent ; বস্ত্রাবাস বা শিবির শ্রেণীতে সজ্জিত হওয়া ; শিবিরে বাস করিতে দেওয়া। **—ment,** *n.* **1.** Act of encamping ; শিবির-সন্নিবেশ। **2.** The place where an army or a party is encamped ; a halting place ; a camp ; শিবির সন্নিবেশস্থলী, নিবেশ (স্ত্রঃ) ; ছাউনীর স্থান ; শিবির, স্কন্ধাবার, ছাউনী।

ĕn-căse′, in—, *v. t.* **1.** To put in a case ; কোনরূপ দৃঢ় আবরণের ভিতর রাখা। **2.** (*Humorous*) To cover ; (কৌতুকচ্ছলে) ঢাকা। **3.** To surround as with case ; বাক্সবন্দী করা। **—ment,** *n.* That which encases ; a covering ; a sheath ; দৃঢ় আবরণ ; আবরণ ; কোষ, খাপ।

ĕn-căsh′, *v. t.* **1.** To cash (a bill or note) ; নোট, হুণ্ডী প্রভৃতি ভাঙ্গান। **2.** To realize ; "The revenue *encashed* ;" আদায় করা। **—ment,** *n.*

ĕn-caus′-tic (-cäs-) *adj.* & *n.* Prepared by means of heat ; relating to the art of enamelling and of painting in burnt wax ; উত্তাপদ্বারা প্রস্তুতীকৃত ; দগ্ধীভূত মোম দ্বারা মীনা বা চিত্রকরণের শিল্প সম্বন্ধীয়। ***Noun.*** The method of painting in heated or burnt wax ; উত্তপ্ত অথবা দগ্ধীভূত মধূথ দ্বারা চিত্রণ-প্রণালী। **Encaustic brick, —tile—** রঙ্গীন মৃত্তিকা দ্বারা খচিত ইষ্টক বা টালি।

enceinte, (*F.*), *adj.* & *n.* Pregnant ; গর্ভবতী, গুর্ব্বিণী, অন্তঃসত্ত্বা, অন্তর্ব্বত্নী। ***Noun.*** An enclosure (chiefly in fortification) ; (দুর্গাদির) আবেষ্টক প্রাচীর।

ĕn-cĕph-ă-lī′-tis, *n.* Inflammation of the brain ; মস্তিষ্ক-প্রদাহ।

ĕn-cĕph′-ăl-ŏn, *n.* Brain ; মস্তিষ্ক। **—ce-phal′-ic,** *adj.*

ĕn-chain′ (-chān), *v. t.* **1.** To chain up ; to fetter ; শৃঙ্খলিত করা, শৃঙ্খলাবদ্ধ করা ; নিগড়বদ্ধ করা, নিগড়িত করা ; **2.** To hold fast as attention etc. ; দৃঢ়রূপে সংযোগ করা। **—ment,** *n.*

ĕn-chănt′, *v. t.* **1.** To bewitch ; to act on by charms or spells ; মন্ত্রমুগ্ধ করা, মায়ামুগ্ধ করা ; যাদুমন্ত্র-দ্বারা প্রভাবিত করা, সম্মোহিত করা। **2.** To delight in a high degree ; to captivate ; পরমপুলকিত করা ; বিমুগ্ধ করা। **—ed,** *adj.* **1.** Bewitched ; সম্মোহিত, মন্ত্রমুগ্ধ। **2.** Delighted ; possessed by witches or spirits ; পুলকিত ; ভূতগ্রস্ত। **—er,** *n.* One who enchants or charms ; যাদুকর, সম্মোহক, কুহক-বিদ্যাবিশারদ, চিত্তবিমোহক, মায়াবী, ঐন্দ্রজালিক। [**—ress,** (fem.) *n.* কুহকিনী, মায়াবিনী, ডাকিনী, মোহিনী।] **—ing,** *adj.* Charming ; fascinating ; মোহন, মোহময়, মুগ্ধকর। **—ing-ly,** *adv.* **—ment** *n.* **1.** The act of enchanting ; state of being enchanted ; যাদুকরণ, অভিচার, বিমুগ্ধকরণ, সম্মোহন, বশীকরণ ; বিমোহিতাবস্থা। **2.** Incantation ; the use of magic arts, spells or charms ; witchcraft ; যাদুমন্ত্র, মোহ, কুহক, যাদু ; তন্ত্রমন্ত্র ও ঐন্দ্রজালিক ক্রিয়ার প্রয়োগ ; ডাইনী বিদ্যা, কুহকবিদ্যা, আসুরী মায়া। **3.** Rapturous delight ; পরমানন্দ। **Enchanted city**—মায়াপুরী।

ĕn-chăse′, *v. t.* **1.** To set with jewels ; to surround with an ornamental casing as a gem etc. with gold ; মণিখচিত করা, রত্নখচিত করা, জড়াও করা ; কারুকার্য্য শোভিত স্বর্ণময় আবেষ্টন দ্বারা পরিবেষ্টন করা, সোণা দ্বারা বাঁধা। **2.** To decorate by embossed work ; উদ্গাত কারুকার্য্যদ্বারা বিভূষিত করা।

ĕn-cir′-cle (-sêr-cl), *v. t.* **1.** To enclose within a circle ; to surround ; বলয়িত করা ; পরিবেষ্টিত করা, পরিবৃত করা, ঘেরা। **2.** To pass round ; চক্রাকারে ভ্রমণ করা, চক্কর দেওয়া, ঘুরিয়া আসা। **3.** To embrace ; ভুজ-পাশে বেষ্টন করা, আলিঙ্গন বদ্ধ করা।

ĕn-clăsp′, *v. t.* To clasp ; to embrace ; আলিঙ্গন করা ; ভুজপাশে বেষ্টন করা।

ĕn-clāve′, *n.* & *v. t.* A territory inclosed within the dominion of an alien power ; পররাজ্য পরিবৃত রাজ্য। ***Verb t.*** To inclose within the territory of an alien power ; পররাজ্য দ্বারা বেষ্টিত করা।

ĕn-clōsĕ′, in—, *v. t.* **1.** To surround ; to fence in ; পরিবেষ্টিত করা, ঘিরিয়া ফেলা, ঘেরা ; পরিবৃত করা। **2.** To shut up in a case or envelope, esp. a letter etc. into the cover of another ; "I beg to *enclose* my price list ;" খাম বা মোড়কে বদ্ধ করা, বিশেষতঃ পত্র প্রভৃতি অন্যপত্রের খামে পুরা। **3.** To hem in on all sides ; পরিবেষ্টিত করা, অবরুদ্ধ করা। **4.** To contain ; ধারণ করা। **—clo′-sure,** *n.* **1.** Act of enclosing ; an encompassing ; a fence ; a covering or envelope ; আবেষ্টন ; ঘের ; বেড়া, বৃতি ; আবরণ, মোড়ক। **2.** An enclosed place ; আবৃত স্থল, ঘেরা জায়গা। **3.** Paper etc. enclosed with a letter in the envelope ; খামের ভিতরে চিঠির সহিত যে কাগজাদি থাকে।

ĕn-clōthe′, *v. t.* To clothe ; কাপড় পরান, বস্ত্রাচ্ছাদিত করা।

ĕn-cloud′ (-clowd), *v. t.* To cover with clouds ; মেঘাবৃত করা, মেঘাচ্ছন্ন করা, জলদাবৃত করা।

ĕn-cō′-mi-ŭm, *n.* High praise ; panegyric ; eulogy ; উচ্চ প্রশংসাবাদ বা গুণকীর্ত্তন, গুণশ্লাঘা, গুণস্তুতি, গুণবচন (উচ্ছ্বলঃ) ; মহিমাকীর্ত্তন ; স্তুতিবাদ। (*Pl.* **—ums**) **—ast,** *n.* One who writes panegyrics or utters them ; a praiser ; a flatterer ; স্তুতিবাদ-লেখক, স্তুতিপাঠক, স্তাবক, গুণানুবাদক, গুণকীর্ত্তনকারী ; প্রশংসাকারী ; তোষামোদকারী। **—as′-tic, —as′-ti-cal,** *adjs.*

ĕn-com′-păss (-cŭm-), *v. t.* **1.** To surround or enclose ; বেষ্টন বা পরিবৃত করা, ঘেরা। **2.** To contain ; ধারণ করা। **—ment,** *n.*

en-core′ (âng-kör), *n., interj.* & *v. t.* A call for a repetition of a song ; পুনরায় গাহিবার জন্য আহ্বান। ***Interj.*** Again ; once more ; পুনর্ব্বার, পুনরায় ; আবার। ***Verb t.*** To call for the repetition of a song or a particular part in a theatre or concert ; নাটক কিম্বা ঐক্যতান বাদ্যাদিতে পুনর্ব্বার গাহিবার, অভিনয় করিবার বা বাজাইবার জন্য বলা।

ĕn-coun′-têr (-cown-), *v. t.* & *i.* & *n.* **1.** To meet in opposition or contest ; to oppose ; সম্মুখীন হওয়া ; বাধা দেওয়া, প্রতিরোধ করা। **2.** To meet, as a friend or a difficulty ; সাক্ষাৎকার করা। ***Verb i.*** To meet face to face ; to meet unexpectedly ; to be engaged in battle ; সামনা সামনি হওয়া ; হঠাৎ সাক্ষাৎ হওয়া ; যুদ্ধে প্রবৃত্ত হওয়া। ***Noun.*** **1.** A fight ; a battle ; সম্মুখসমর ; রণ। **2.** A meeting accidentally with a person or thing ; হঠাৎ সাক্ষাৎকার।

ĕn-cour′-āge (-cŭr-), *v. t.* **1.** To inspire with courage ; to incite ; to animate ; উৎসাহপূর্ণ করা, আশ্বাসিত করা, প্রোৎসাহিত করা ; উত্তেজিত করা ; জীবনীশক্তি সঞ্চার করা। **2.** To promote ; to cherish ; to patronize ; উন্নতিসাধন করা, শ্রীবৃদ্ধি করা ; সযত্নে রক্ষা করা, সযত্নে পোষণ করা ; পৃষ্ঠপোষকতা করা। **—ag-er,** *n.* One who encourages ; উৎসাহদাতা, পৃষ্ঠপোষক। **—ag-ing,** *p. adj.* Exciting courage ; furnishing grounds to hope for success ; উৎসাহবর্দ্ধক, উৎসাহজনক ; আশাজনক, আশ্বাসপ্রদায়ক। **—ag-ing-ly,** *adv.* **—ment,** *n.* **1.** Act of encouraging ; state of being encouraged ; সাহসদান, উৎসাহদান, সমাশ্বাসন ; উৎসাহিতাবস্থা। **2.** That which encourages ; উৎসাহবর্দ্ধক বিষয় (যথা পুরস্কার, অনুগ্রহ প্রভৃতি)।

ĕn-crim′-son (-zn), *v.t.* To make crimson ; সুলোহিত করা।

ĕn-croach″ (-crōch), *v. i.* To intrude ; to trespass, (with *on* or *upon*) ; অনাহূতভাবে প্রবেশ করা ; চড়াও করা, সীমালঙ্ঘন করা, বলপূর্ব্বক প্রবেশ করা, অনধিকার প্রবেশ করা। **—ment,** *n.* **1.** Act of encroaching ; unlawful intrusion ; invasion ; পরসম্পত্তিতে বলপূর্ব্বক বা অনভিমতে প্রবেশ, অনধিকার প্রবেশ ; শনৈঃ শনৈঃ পরের অধিকৃত ভূমিদখল বা পরাধিকারে প্রবেশ ; আক্রমণ। **2.** That which is taken by encroaching on another ; অন্যায়রূপে, অনভিমতে বা অবৈধরূপে অধিকৃত বস্তু বা সম্পত্তি, অবৈধরূপে দখল-করা সম্পত্তি। **Encroachment of a river**—গাঙ্গসিকস্তি, তীরভাঙ্গন।

ĕn-crŭst′, *v. t.* See INCRUST.

ĕn-cŭm′-bêr, *v. t.* **1.** To load ; to retard the motion of something with a burden ; to obstruct or embarrass ; ভারগ্রস্ত করা, ভারাক্রান্ত করা ; ভার চাপাইয়া গতিরোধ করা ; প্রতিরোধ করা, প্রতিবন্ধক দেওয়া। **2.** To load with debts or other legal claim ; ঋণভারাক্রান্ত করা, দায়গ্রস্ত করা। **—brance,** *n.* **1.** Burden ; impediment ; embarrassment ; a trouble ; ভার, বোঝা, দায় ; বাধা, বিঘ্ন, প্রতিবন্ধক ; জঞ্জাল, ঝঞ্ঝাট, উৎপাত ; কষ্ট। **2.** A dependent person, esp. a child ; as, the lady is without any *encumbrances, i. e.* unencumbered with children ; পরিবারস্থ পোষ্য, ঘাড়ে-পড়া ছেলেপিলে। **—bran-cer,** *n.* (*Law*) One who has a legal claim on an estate ; যে ব্যক্তির কোন সম্পত্তিতে বৈধ অধিকার আছে। **—ment,** *n.* **Without encumbrance**—শিশুসন্তানশূন্য।

ĕn-cўc′-lic, —li-căl, *adj.* & *n.* Sent to many persons or places ; বহুজনসমীপে বা বহুস্থানে প্রেরিত। ***Noun.*** (Only **—lic**) An encyclical letter, esp. a circular letter addressed by the pope to all the bishops ; বহু ব্যক্তির নিকট বা বহুস্থানে প্রেরিত পত্র, সমস্ত ধর্ম্মাধ্যক্ষগণের নামে প্রেরিত রোমীয় ধর্ম্মসম্রাটের পত্র।

ĕn-cў-clō-pæ′-di-ă (-pē-), **—pē′-di-ă,** *ns.* **1.** A comprehensive summary of all branches of knowledge or of a particular branch of knowledge arranged in alphabetical order ; মহাকোষ, বিদ্যাকল্পদ্রুম, বিশ্বকোষ। **2.** The French works of French philosophers Diderot, D'Alembert and others who lived in the third quarter of the 18th century ; খৃষ্টীয় অষ্টাদশ শতাব্দীর শেষার্দ্ধভাগের দিদারো, দা এলেম্বার প্রভৃতি ফরাসী দার্শনিকগণের গ্রন্থসমূহ। **—ped′-ic, —ped′-i-cal,** *adjs.* Pertaining to encyclopædia ; full of or possessing universal knowledge and information ; বিশ্বকোষসম্বন্ধীয় ; সার্ব্বভৌমিক জ্ঞানসম্পন্ন, নিখিল শাস্ত্রকুশল। **—pæ′- or —pe′-dism,** *n.* **—pe′-dist,** *n.* The compiler or writer of an encyclopædia ; one whose knowledge embraces all the branches of science and arts ; বিশ্বকোষরচক বা সংগ্রাহক, বিশ্বকোষকার ; সর্ব্বশাস্ত্রবেত্তা, বিদ্যাসাগর। **The encyclopædists**—The writers of the great French Encyclopædia ; বিরাট ফরাসী বিশ্বকোষের লেখকগণ। [Diderot এবং D'Alembert উক্ত বিশ্বকোষের সম্পাদক ছিলেন এবং Voltaire এবং Rousseau প্রভৃতি প্রবন্ধলেখক ছিলেন।]

ĕn-cўst′, *v. t.* & *i.* To enclose, or to be enclosed, in a cyst or bag ; থালী বা থলিয়ার মধ্যে রাখা বা থাকা। **—cys-ta′-tion,** *n.* **—ed,** *adj.* **—ment,** *n.*

ĕnd, *n., v. t.* & *i.* **1.** Limit ; extremity ; surface bounding a thing at either extremity ; সীমা, অবধি, প্রান্ত ; শেষ সীমা, চরমসীমা ; উভয় প্রান্তস্থিত আবরণ বা ঢাকনি। **2.** Consequence ; result ; ultimate state or condition ; ফল ; পরিণাম ; অন্তিম দশা বা অবস্থা। 3. Conclusion ; close ; as, the *end* of a month or speech ; উপসংহার ; অন্ত, অবসান, শেষ, অত্যয়, সমাপ্তি। 4. Purpose ; aim ; অভিপ্রায় ; উদ্দেশ্য, লক্ষ্য। 5. The final cause ; পরম কারণ। 6. Cessation ; death ; destruction ; নিবৃত্তি ; মৃত্যু ; বিনাশ। 7. A fragment ; remnant ; as, the *ends* of a candle ; খণ্ড ; অবশিষ্টাংশ। ***Verb t.*** 1. To bring to an end or conclusion ; শেষ করা, সমাপ্ত করা, উপসংহার করা, অবসান করা। 2. To destroy or put an end to ; বিনাশ করা, ধ্বংস করা। ***Verb i.*** To come to an end ; to cease ; to terminate ; to result (in) ; সমাপ্ত হওয়া, পর্য্যবসিত হওয়া ; বিরামপ্রাপ্ত হওয়া ; অবসান হওয়া ; পরিণত হওয়া। **End′-ing,** *n.* 1. Termination ; conclusion ; সমাপ্তি, অবসান ; উপসংহার। 2. (*Gram.*) The terminating syllable of a word ; as, case-*endings* ; প্রত্যয়, বিভক্তি, অন্ত্যবর্ণ। **End′-less,** *adj.* 1. Without an end ; infinite ; eternal ; incessant ; অশেষ ; অসীম, সীমাহীন ; অনন্ত ; অবিরাম, নিরবচ্ছিন্ন। 2. Fruitless ; objectless ; নিষ্ফল, নিরর্থক ; উদ্দেশ্য-বিহীন। **End′-less-ly,** *adv.* **End′-less-ness,** *n.* The state of being endless ; সীমাশূন্যতা, সমাপ্তিহীনতা (রবিঃ)। **End′-long,** *adv.* Lengthwise ; লম্বার দিকে। **End′-most,** *adj.* Farthest ; নিতান্ত দূরবর্ত্তী। **End′-ways, End′-wise,** *advs.* Lengthwise ; লম্বালম্বি। **End-all**—The ending ; the conclusion ; অবসান ; উপসংহার। **End-iron**—See ANDIRON. **End-less band, cable** or **chain**—অন্তহীন শৃঙ্খল। **A rope's end**—রজ্জু নির্ম্মিত কষা বিশেষ। **A shoe-maker's end**—প্রান্তভাগে লৌহকণ্টকযুক্ত চর্ব্বিমার্জ্জিত সূত্র। **At a loose end**—In disorder ; unoccupied ; বিশৃঙ্খল অবস্থায় ; অব্যাপৃত। **Cannot make both ends meet**—কাছা দিতে কোঁচা আঁটে না। **End for end**—One end for another ; এক প্রান্তের পরিবর্ত্তে অন্য প্রান্ত, বিপর্যস্ত ভাবে। **End on**—With the end fronting one ; প্রান্তভাগ সম্মুখে থাকা (যেমন জাহাজাদির অগ্রভাগ দ্রষ্টার সম্মুখে লক্ষিত হওয়া)। **End to end**—Lengthwise ; with ends in contact ; লম্বার দিকে ; প্রান্ত সকল পরস্পরের সহিত সংলগ্নভাবে। **In the end**—Ultimately ; শেষে, পরিণামে। **My later end**—The close of life ; জীবনের দিনান্ত, শেষ বয়স। **No end**—(*Colloq.*) A great deal ; অনেক। **No end of a fellow**—A very good fellow ; অতি ভাল মানুষ। **Odds and ends**—Scraps ; গুঁড়া গাড়া, টুকরা টাকরা। **On end**—Erect ; upright ; খাড়া ; দণ্ডায়মান। In succession ; "For years *on end* ;" ক্রমাগত। **The end does not justify the means**—শুভ উদ্দেশ্য সাধনের জন্য নিন্দনীয় উপায় অবলম্বন করা নিন্দনীয়। **To be at one's wit's ends**—To be quite unable to decide what further step is to be taken ; কিংকর্ত্তব্যবিমূঢ় হওয়া, হতবুদ্ধি হওয়া। **To begin at the wrong end**—To attempt to do something unmethodically ; to manage badly ; বিশৃঙ্খল ভাবে নির্ব্বাহ বা সম্পাদন করা ; কদর্য্যভাবে সম্পাদন করা। **To be the end of**—To occasion the death of ; মৃত্যু সংঘটন করা। **To come to or be at the end of one's tether**—To go to the utmost limit of one's power ; যতদূর সাধ্য ততদূর অগ্রসর হওয়া। **To end in smoke**—ধূম্রমাত্রে পর্য্যবসিত হওয়া, ফাঁসিয়া যাওয়া। **To get the better end of**—To get the advantage of ; সুবিধালাভ করা। **To go end for end**—(Of a boat) To be upset ; উল্টাইয়া যাওয়া। **To have something at one's finger's ends**—To be perfectly acquainted with ; করামলকবৎ করা, নখদর্পণের মত করা। **To make an end of**—To put a stop to ; বন্ধ করিয়া দেওয়া, শেষ করিয়া দেওয়া। **To make both ends meet**—To live within one's income ; আয়ব্যয়ের সামঞ্জস্য করা, কষ্টে সৃষ্টে খরচপত্র চালান। **To turn end**—(*Naut.*) To reverse, as a rope ; to upset, as a boat ; পাল্টান (যথা রজ্জু) ; উল্টাইয়া ফেলা (যথা নৌকা)। **World without end**—For ever ; চিরকালের জন্য।

ĕn-dăn′-gĕr, *v. t.* To imperil ; to put in hazard ; বিপদগ্রস্ত করা, বিপদাপন্ন করা, সংশয়াপন্ন করা ; আপদে ফেলা। **—ment,** *n.*

ĕn-dear′ (-dēr), *v. t.* 1. To make dear or dearer ; প্রিয় করা, প্রিয়পাত্র করা, প্রিয়তর করা। 2. To raise the price of, (*obs.*) ; মূল্য বৃদ্ধি করা, মহার্ঘ করা (অপ্রঃ)। **—deared′,** *adj.* Beloved ; প্রেমাস্পদ। **—ing,** *adj.* **—ment,** *n.* The act of endearing ; tender affection ; caress (in this sense generally *pl.*) ; প্রীতিজনন ; প্রেমানুরাগ, প্রীতিমাধুর্য্য ; আদর, সোহাগ, হাব, বিলাস।

ĕn-deav′-our (-dĕv′-ēr), *v. t.* & *i.* & *n.* To try to use effort ; to effect ; চেষ্টা করা, উদ্যম করা, প্রযত্ন করা ; সম্পাদন করা। ***Verb i.*** To exert oneself mentally or physically to attain an object ; to attempt ; ইষ্ট বস্তু লাভের জন্য শারীরিক বা মানসিক প্রয়াস পাওয়া ; চেষ্টা পাওয়া। ***Noun.*** Attempt ; effort ; exertion ; চেষ্টা ; উদ্যম ; প্রযত্ন। **—ment,** *n.* **To do one's endeavour**—To try one's utmost ; যথাসাধ্য চেষ্টা করা।

ĕn-dĕm′-ic, *adj.* & *n.* Peculiar to a people, or a land ; কোন বিশেষ দেশ বা জাতিতে সীমাবদ্ধ, স্থানীয়, (রোগাদি সম্বন্ধে) কোন বিশেষ স্থান, ঋতু বা জাতিতে সীমাবদ্ধ। ***Noun.*** A disease of endemic nature ; স্থানিক রোগ। **—i-cal,** *adj.* **—i-cal-ly,** *adv.* **—ic′-i-ty,** *n.*

ĕn-dêr'-mic, *adj.* (*Med.*) Acting on the skin ; (ভৈষজ্য-শাস্ত্র) চর্ম্মের উপর ক্রিয়াজনক ।

ĕn'-dive (-dīv), *n.* An annual or biennial plant of the same genus as *chicory*, used as salad ; কাশনি (খোরী) ।

ĕn-dŏ-câr'-di-ŭm, *n.* A colourless transparent membrane which lines the interior of the heart ; হৃৎপিণ্ডের আবরণ-ঝিল্লী, হৃদন্তবেষ্ট । **—tis,** *n.* Inflammation of the endocardium ; হৃদন্তবেষ্ট-প্রদাহ ।

ĕn'-dŏ-cârp, *n.* The inner covering of a fruit ; ফলের আভ্যন্তরীণ আবরণ, অন্তঃপেশী (সাঃ পঃ) ।

ĕn'-dŏ-chrōme, *n.* (*Bot.*) The colouring matter in the cell of plants; (উদ্ভিদ্-বিদ্যা) রঞ্জকরস (সাঃ পঃ) ।

ĕn-dŏ-dêr'-mis, *n.* (*Bot.*) The innermost layer of the cortex ; (উদ্ভিদ্-বিদ্যা) অন্তস্তক্ (সাঃ পঃ) ।

ĕn-dŏg'-ă-mȳ, *n.* **1.** Marriage within the tribe ; স্বগোত্রে বা স্ববংশে বিবাহ, স্ববর্ণ-পরিণয়, অন্তর্ব্বিবাহ । **2.** The custom which forbids a man to marry outside his tribe ; স্বগোত্র বিবাহ বিধি, অন্তর্ব্বিবাহ রীতি । **—mous,** *adj.*

ĕn'-dŏ-gĕn, *n.* A plant that grows from within; অন্তর্জনি উদ্ভিদ, তাল, কদলী প্রভৃতি যে সমস্ত বৃক্ষ ভিতরের দিক্ হইতে বর্দ্ধিত হয় । **—dog'-e-nous,** *adj.*

ĕn-dŏ-mē-trī-tis, *n.* (*Med.*) Inflammation of mucous membrane lining the uterus ; জরায়ুর অভ্যন্তরের প্রদাহ ।

ĕn-dŏ-phlœ'-ŭm (-flē-), *n.* (*Bot.*) The inner bark ; (উদ্ভিদ্-বিদ্যা) অন্তর্বল্কল (সাঃ পঃ) ।

ĕn'-dŏ-plăsm, *n.* The inner or central portion of the cytoplasm in a cell ; অন্তঃরস (সাঃ পঃ) ।

ĕn'-dŏ-pleu'-ră (-plü-), *n.* (*Bot.*) The innermost skin of a seed-coat ; (উদ্ভিদ্-বিদ্যা) অন্তর্বীজাবরণ (সাঃ পঃ) ।

ĕn-dōrse', *v. t.* **1.** To write something on the back of ; to sign one's name etc. on the back of ; to write (comments) on the back of a letter or document ; হুণ্ডীর পৃষ্ঠে লিখা কিম্বা চেকের পৃষ্ঠে নাম সহি করা ; পৃষ্ঠে নাম সহি করিয়া বরাত দেওয়া ; কোন পত্র বা দলিলের পৃষ্ঠে মন্তব্য লিপিবদ্ধ করা । **2.** To confirm ; to approve ; দৃঢ় করা, বলবৎ করা ; অনুমোদন করা । **—dor'-sa-ble,** *adj.* **—dor-see',** *n.* **—ment,** *n.* **1.** The act of endorsing ; the comment or signature written on a letter or document ; পৃষ্ঠে লিখন ; কোন পত্র বা দলিলের পৃষ্ঠে লিখিত মন্তব্য বা স্বাক্ষর । **2.** Sanction ; ratification ; approval ; মঞ্জুর ; দৃঢ়ীকরণ ; অনুমোদন, সম্মতি ।

ĕn'-dŏ-scōpe, *n.* An instrument for examining the interior of the body; অভ্যন্তরবীক্ষণ যন্ত্র, অন্তর্বীক্ষণ যন্ত্র ।

ĕn-dŏs-mō'-sis, *n.* The passage of a fluid inwards through an organic membrane, to mix with another fluid inside, (also called *endosmose*) ; তরল-নিবেশ (সাঃ পঃ), অন্তর্ব্বাহ (হঃ চঃ), অন্তর্গমন (সাঃ পঃ), জীবদেহাভ্যন্তরস্থ ঝিল্লীভেদপূর্ব্বক রসাদির অভ্যন্তরে সঞ্চার ।

en'-dŏ-spêrm, *n.* (*Bot.*) The albumen of a seed ; (উদ্ভিদ্-বিদ্যা) বীজাভ্যন্তরস্থ অণ্ডলালা, অন্তর্বীজ ।

ĕn-dow', *v. t.* **1.** To furnish with the means of permanent support ; চিরদিনের জন্য ব্যয় নির্ব্বাহের উপযোগী অর্থ প্রদান করা, স্থায়ী বৃত্তি প্রদান করা । **2.** To furnish with any gift, quality or faculty ; (মানসিক কিম্বা আধ্যাত্মিক) প্রকৃতি-দত্ত বা স্বভাবজাত গুণবিশিষ্ট করা । **3.** To invest as a person with something ; সম্পন্ন করা, সমন্বিত করা । **—er,** *n.* **—ment,** *n.* **1.** Act of endowing ; যৌতুক প্রদান, বৃত্তিদান, স্থায়ীবৃত্তি নির্দ্ধারণ । **2.** Property or money endowed for the permanent maintenance of a person or an institution ; স্থায়ী-বৃত্তি, ধর্ম্মোত্তর (হিঃ কোঃ) । **3.** Natural gifts ; প্রকৃতিদত্ত গুণাবলী, নৈসর্গিক গুণ সমূহ । **Endowment insurance**—এক প্রকার জীবনবীমা,—যাহাতে নিরূপিত সময়ের (কিংবা তৎপূর্ব্বে মৃত্যু হইলে, মৃত্যুর) অন্তে নির্দ্দিষ্ট পরিমাণ টাকা পাওয়া যায় ।

ĕn-due' (-dü), *v. t.* **1.** To invest to endow, as with qualities etc. ; প্রদান করা ; অন্বিত করা, সমন্বিত করা, বিশিষ্ট করা । **2.** To clothe বসন পরিধান করান ।

ĕn-dūre', *v. i.* & *t.* To last টিকিয়া থাকা, টেঁকসই হওয়া, স্থায়ী হওয়া *Verb t.* **1.** To bear ; সহ্য করা সহা । **2.** To tolerate ; অবাধে চলিতে দেওয়া, প্রশ্রয় দেওয়া । **—dur'-a-ble** *adj.* That can be endured or borne ; সহনীয় । **—dur'-ance,** *n.* **1.** Lastingness ; স্থায়িত্ব । **2.** Sufferance ; patience ; সহন ; সহিষ্ণুতা ধৈর্য্যশীলতা, স্থৈর্য্য, তিতিক্ষা, সহনশীলতা । **—dur'-ing,** *adj.* **1.** Lasting টেঁকসই, স্থায়ী । **2.** Patient ; ধীর সহিষ্ণু, ধৈর্য্যশালী ।

ĕn'-ĕ-mă, *n.* A liquid medicine thrown into the rectum ; an injection ; গুহ্য মধ্যে পিচকারী দ্বারা প্রক্ষিপ্ত তরল ঔষধ ; বস্তিক্রিয়া, গুহ্য দ্বারে পিচকারী প্রয়োগ ।

ĕn'-ĕ-mȳ, *n.* **1.** A foe ; an adversary ; an antagonist ; শত্রু, রিপু, অরি, বিরোধী, বিপক্ষ, প্রতিদ্বন্দ্বী ; বৈরী ; প্রতিপক্ষ । **2.** A hostile army or naval force ; শত্রু, শত্রু-পক্ষীয় সৈন্য বা নৌবল । **Last enemy**—মৃত্যু । **Rear enemy**—পার্ষ্ণি-গ্রাহ । **The enemy or the old enemy**—শয়তান । **How goes the enemy**—(*Vulgar*) What is the time ; কয়টা বাজিয়াছে (ইতর-ভাষায়) ।

ĕn-êr-gü'-mĕn, *n.* **1.** One under the influence of evil spirit ; ভূতগ্রস্ত ব্যক্তি, ভূতাবিষ্ট ব্যক্তি । **2.** A fanatic ধর্ম্মোন্মত্ত ব্যক্তি ।

ĕn'-ĕr-ġȳ, *n.* **1.** Internal power inherent power ; অন্তর্বল, অন্তর্নিহিত শক্তি ; স্বাভাবিক বা সহজাত শক্তি

2. (*Pl.*) Individual power in exercise ; শক্তিবিকাশ, কার্য্যকরী শক্তি। 3. Strength ; spirit ; force ; vigour ; শক্তি, প্রৈতি, বলশালিতা ; তেজঃ ; বল, পরাক্রম, বীর্য্য ; তেজস্বিতা, ওজস্বিতা, জীবনী-শক্তি। 4. Power efficiently exerted ; as, the *energy* of a magistrate ; বিচক্ষণতা সহকারে প্রযুক্ত ক্ষমতা। 5. Capacity performing work ; কার্য্য-শক্তি। **–get′-ic,** *adj.* & *n.* 1. Possessing or full of energy ; active ; তেজস্বী, বলবৎ, তেজোপূর্ণ, বীর্য্যবান, শক্তিসম্পন্ন ; অতন্দ্রিত, কর্ম্মিষ্ঠ। 2. Relating to energy ; শক্তি-সম্বন্ধীয়। (*Noun*) (*Pl.*) The science of energy ; প্রৈতিবিজ্ঞান। **–get′-i-cal,** *adj.* **–get′-i-cal-ly,** *adv.* Vigorously ; তেজস্বিতা সহকারে। **–er′-gic, –er′-gi-cal,** *adjs.* (*Rare*) 1. In a state of action ; ক্রিয়মাণ, সক্রিয়। 2. Energetic ; তেজস্বী। **–gism,** *n.* (*Ethics*) The doctrine that the supreme good consists in the efficient exercise of normal human activities, rather than in happiness ; (নীতিবিজ্ঞান) কর্ত্তব্যকর্ম্মসম্পাদনই পরম মঙ্গলের হেতু, সুখভোগ নয়,—এইরূপ মতবাদ, কর্ম্মপক্ষ (হিঃ কোঃ), কর্ম্মমার্গ (ঐ)। **–gize, –gise,** *v. t.* & *i.* To give strength to ; to give vigour to ; বলবৎ করা, শক্তিসঞ্চার করা ; সঞ্জীবিত করা। (*Verb i.*) To act with strength ; to act with force or vigour ; শক্তিসহকারে ক্রিয়া করা ; সবলে ও সতেজে ক্রিয়া করা। **Actual, kinetic** or **motive energy** — গতিশক্তি, গতিজশক্তি, প্রৈতিশক্তি, ব্যক্তশক্তি, উদ্ভূতশক্তি, সঞ্জাতশক্তি। **Conservation of energy**—See CONSERVATION. **Dissipation of energy**—শক্তির অপব্যয়। **Potential, static** or **latent energy**—অব্যক্ত, প্রচ্ছন্ন, বা গূঢ়শক্তি, স্থিতিশক্তি। **Waste of energy**—পণ্ডশ্রম।

ē-nêr′-vāte, *v. t.* & *adj.* 1. To make feeble ; to make effeminate ; to deprive of courage ; to impair the moral power of ; দুর্ব্বল করা, অশক্ত করা, নির্ব্বীর্য্য করা ; স্ত্রীজনবৎ করা ; সাহস লোপ করা ; নৈতিক শক্তি হীন করা। ***Adj.*** weakened ; debilitated ; without vigour ; ক্ষীণ ; শক্তিহীন, দুর্ব্বল ; নির্ব্বীর্য্য, নিস্তেজ। **–va′-tion,** *n.* The act of enervating ; the state of being enervated ; ক্ষীণীকরণ ; দুর্ব্বলতা, ক্ষীণতা, শক্তিহীনতা, নির্ব্বীর্য্যতা, ক্লৈব্য।

enfant terrible, (*F.*), *n.* A child who by its remark puts its elders into awkward positions ; জ্যেঠা ছেলে।

ĕn-fee′-ble (-fē-bl), *v. t.* To make feeble ; to weaken ; দুর্ব্বল করা, হীনবল করা ; অশক্ত করা, ক্ষীণ করা। **–ment,** *n.*

ĕn-feoff′ (-fĕf), *v. t.* 1. To invest with a fief ; জায়গীর দেওয়া, মৌরশী দেওয়া। 2. (*Fig.*) To deliver ; to surrender entirely ; (লক্ষণায়) প্রদান করা ; সমর্পণ করা। **–ment,** *n.*

ĕn-fĕt′-têr, *v. t.* To bind in fetters ; to enchain ; to enslave ; শৃঙ্খলিত করা ; নিগড়িত করা ; দাসত্ব শৃঙ্খলে শৃঙ্খলিত করা।

ĕn-fi-lāde′, *n.* & *v. t.* 1. The fire from artillery sweeping a whole line of works or troops from end to end ; শত্রুসৈন্য বা দুর্গপ্রাকারাদির উপর লম্বালম্বিভাবে কামানের গোলাবর্ষণ। 2. A number of rooms with the doors opening into a common passage ; সাধারণ নির্গম পথসমন্বিত সারিবন্দী প্রকোষ্ঠ সমূহ। ***Verb t.*** To rake with shot through the entire length of works of troops from end to end ; লম্বালম্বিভাবে শত্রুসৈন্য বা সামরিক প্রাকারাদি ভেদ করিয়া গোলাবর্ষণ করা।

ĕn-fōld′, in–, *v. t.* 1. To wrap up ; to clasp ; to embrace ; আবৃত করা ; আলিঙ্গন করা ; আশ্লেষ করা। 2. To shape into folds ; ভাঁজ করা। **–ment,** *n.*

ĕn-fōrce′, *v. t.* 1. To compel ; বাধ্য করা। 2. To put in force ; to give effect to ; as, to *enforce* a law ; কার্য্যে পরিণত করা, প্রবর্ত্তন করা ; বাহাল করা, আমলে আনা। 3. To urge, as a demand etc. ; to impress on the mind, as an argument etc. ; নির্ব্বিন্ধাতিশয় সহকারে উপস্থাপিত করা ; মনোমধ্যে মুদ্রিত করা। **–a-ble, –for′-ci-ble,** *adjs.* **–forced′,** *adj.* Compulsory ; বলদ্বারা প্রবর্ত্তিত, অনিচ্ছাকৃত। **–for′-ced-ly,** *adv.* **–ment,** *n.* Act of enforcing ; compulsion ; a giving effect to ; urging ; বলবৎকরণ, দৃঢ়ীকরণ ; বাধ্যতা ; প্রবর্ত্তন ; নির্ব্বন্ধাতিশয়।

ĕn-frāme′, *v. t.* To set in a frame as a picture ; to serve as a frame ; ফ্রেমে আঁটা ; ফ্রেমের কাজ করা।

ĕn-frăn′-chīse, *v. t.* 1. To set free ; স্বাধীন করা, মুক্ত করা। 2. To endow as, a town etc., with the right of voting for a member of parliament ; to invest with the rights and privileges of a citizen ; পার্লেমেণ্টের সভ্যনির্ব্বাচনের জন্য ভোট প্রদানের ক্ষমতা দেওয়া ; নাগরিকের অধিকার প্রদান করা। **–ment,** *n.* 1. Liberation ; দাসত্ব-বিমোচন, দাস্য-মোচন, মুক্তিদান, স্বাধীনতা-প্রদান। 2. Admission to the rights and privileges of a citizen ; পৌরজনাধিকার দান, নির্ব্বাচন-ক্ষমতা প্রদান।

ĕn-gāge′, *v. t.* & *i.* 1. To bind by a pledge or contract ; চুক্তি বা অঙ্গীকারে আবদ্ধ করা। 2. To bind by a promise of marriage ; as, an *engaged* couple ; বিবাহের অঙ্গীকারে আবদ্ধ করা, বাগ্‌দান করা। 3. To allure ; to attract ; to win over ; "Good nature *engages* everybody ;" প্রলুব্ধ করা ; আকর্ষণ করা, আকৃষ্ট করা ; বশীভূত করা। 4. To hire or employ ; ভাড়া করা, নিযুক্ত করা। 5. To occupy ; to engross ; as, to *engage* one in a conversation ;

ব্যাপৃত করা ; অভিনিবিষ্ট করা। 6. To attack in a contest ; to bring into conflict as troops etc. ; (যুদ্ধে) আক্রমণ করা ; যুদ্ধে নিরত করা। 7. (*Mach.*) To join or interlock with ; as, the teeth of a wheel *engage* those of another ; (যন্ত্র-বিজ্ঞান) সংযোগ করা, পরস্পর সংলগ্ন করা। 8. To persuade ; to induce ; "He *engaged* them to declare in his favour ;" প্ররোচিত করা, প্রবর্ত্তিত করা ; প্রবৃত্তি-জন্মান। *Verb i.* 1. To pledge oneself ; বাক্যদান করা, বাগ্দান করা। 2. To embark in a commercial enterprise; বাণিজ্যাদিতে ব্যাপৃত হওয়া। 3. To join in battle ; যুদ্ধে প্রবৃত্ত হওয়া। **—gaged′**, *p. adj.* 1. Employed ; occupied ; busy ; নিযুক্ত ; ব্যাপৃত, রত ; ব্যস্ত, নিষ্ঠ। 2. Promised ; betrothed ; প্রতিজ্ঞাবদ্ধ ; বাগ্দত্ত। 3. Involved, esp. in an encounter ; জড়িত। **—ment,** *n.* 1. Act of engaging ; state of being engaged ; অঙ্গীকারবদ্ধকরণ ; প্রতিজ্ঞাবদ্ধতা। 2. A promise ; a pledge to take some one as husband or wife ; প্রতিজ্ঞা, অঙ্গীকার, চুক্তি, করার ; বাগ্দান, প্রতিশ্রুত-সম্বন্ধ। 3. Employment ; occupation ; কার্য্য ; ব্যবসায়, ব্যাপার। 4. A battle ; contest ; যুদ্ধ ; সংগ্রাম। 5. An appointment ; as, I have an *engagement* elsewhere ; প্রতিশ্রুতি। **—gag′-ing,** *adj.* Attractive ; winning ; মনোহারী, হৃদয়হারী ; চিত্তবিনোদক, চিত্তাকর্ষক। **—gag′-ing-ly,** *adv.* **To engage to**—To become responsible for ; দায়ী হওয়া।

ĕn-gâr′-lănd, *v. t.* To wreathe or encircle with a garland ; মাল্য-শোভিত করা।

ĕn-gĕn′-dêr, *v. t.* & *i.* 1. To beget, (now only figurative) ; উৎপাদন করা, জন্মদান করা, (বর্ত্তমানে কেবল লক্ষণায় ব্যবহৃত হয়)। 2. To bring about ; সংঘটন করা।

ĕn′-gine (-jĭn), *n.* & *v. t.* 1. A machine to drive machinery, to prepare railway trains etc. ; বাষ্পীয় শকটাদির কল, বাষ্পীয়-যন্ত্র। 2. An instrument used in war ; as, an *engine* of death ; যুদ্ধে ব্যবহৃত যন্ত্র বিশেষ, যন্ত্রপাষাণ। 3. A machine for raising and pouring water on burning houses ; জলন্তগৃহে জল উত্তোলন বা প্রক্ষেপের জন্য যন্ত্রবিশেষ, জল-প্রক্ষেপক। 4. A means ; an instrument ; "The state has two *engines*—punishment and reward ;" উপায়, সাধন ; যন্ত্র। *Verb t.* To furnish with an engine or engineer ; যন্ত্র-সমন্বিত করা বা যন্ত্রচালক নিযুক্ত করা। **Engine-driver**—বাষ্পীয় শকট-চালক, যন্ত্রচালক। **Engine-lathe** — যন্ত্র-চালিত ভ্রমি-যন্ত্র বা কুন্দন যন্ত্র। **Engine-sized**—যন্ত্রদ্বারা নির্দ্দিষ্ট আয়তনে কর্ত্তিত। **Engine-turning**— যন্ত্রদ্বারা ধাতু-ফলকোপরি সমায়তন আদর্শ উল্লেখন। **Fire-engine**—দমকল। **Steam-engine**—বাষ্পীয়-যন্ত্র।

ĕn-gĭ-neer′ (-nër), *n., v. i.* & *t.* 1. An engine-maker ; one well-versed in the science of engineering ; যন্ত্র-নির্ম্মাতা ; পূর্ত্তবিদ্যাবিশারদ। 2. (*Mil.*) One who plans and constructs works of offence or defence ; (সামরিক শাস্ত্র) সামরিক পূর্ত্তকার্য্যবিশারদ। 3. One who constructs roads, railways, etc. ; রাস্তা, লৌহবর্ত্ম প্রভৃতি নির্ম্মাতা। 4. One having charge of a steam-engine ; বাষ্পীয় যন্ত্রাধ্যক্ষ। (ইংলণ্ডে কেবল মাত্র পোতাদির বাষ্পীয়-যন্ত্র সম্পর্কে ব্যবহৃত হয়।) 5. An efficient manager (*colloq.*) ; সুদক্ষ কর্ম্মকর্ত্তা (চলিতভাষায়)। *Verb i.* To act as an engineer ; পূর্ত্তকার্য্যে নিযুক্ত হওয়া। *Verb t.* 1. To construct or manage in the capacity of an engineer ; পূর্ত্তাদি কার্য্য পরিদর্শন করা বা লৌহ-সেতু, বর্ত্ম, প্রভৃতি নির্ম্মাণ করা। 2. (*Colloq.*) To arrange ; to contrive ; (চলিত-ভাষায়) বন্দোবস্ত করা ; সুকৌশলে উদ্ভাবন করা। **—ing,** *n.* The art or profession of an engineer ; যন্ত্র-বিদ্যা, পূর্ত্তবিদ্যা। **—ship,** *n.* **Civil engineering** —সেতু, বর্ত্ম, প্রণালী, প্রভৃতি নির্ম্মাণরূপ সাধারণ পূর্ত্তকার্য্য। **Military engineering**—দুর্গপরিখাদি নির্মাণ ও খননরূপ সামরিক পূর্ত্তকার্য্য। **The engineer hoisted with his own petard**—গুটি পোকা গুটি করে নিজের ফাঁদে নিজে মরে।

ĕn′-gine-rȳ (-jĭn-), *n.* 1. Engines or machines in general ; যন্ত্রাদি। 2. Machinery, (often *fig.*) ; যন্ত্র।

ĕn-gir′-dle (-gêr-dl), *v. t.* To encircle ; to surround, as with a girdle ; বেষ্টিত করা ; চন্দ্রহারাকারে বেষ্টিত করা।

Eng′-lănd-êr (ĭng-), *n.* An Englishman ; ইংরেজ, ইংলণ্ডবাসী। **A little Englander** — সাম্রাজ্যবাদীদের বিরুদ্ধ মতাবলম্বী।

Eng′-lish (ĭng-), *adj., n.* & *v. t.* 1. Pertaining, or belonging, to England or its people ; ইংলণ্ডীয়, ইংলণ্ডজাত, ইংরাজ-জাতীয়, ইংরাজী, বিলাতী, ইঙ্গ। 2. Belonging to the English language ; ইংরাজী ভাষা সম্বন্ধীয়। *Noun.* 1. The language of the people of England ; ইংরাজী ভাষা। 2. A size of type ; একপ্রকার মুদ্রণের হরফ। *Verb t.* To translate into English ; to make English ; ইংরাজীতে অনুবাদ করা ; ইংরাজিভাবাপন্ন করা। **—er, —man,** *n.* A native of England ; ইংরাজ, ইংলণ্ডবাসী। **English type**—একপ্রকার ছাপার হরফ। **Old English**—৪৫০ হইতে ১১৫০ খৃষ্টাব্দ পর্য্যন্ত সময়ের ইংরাজী ভাষা। **Middle English** — ১১৫০ হইতে ১৫০০ খৃষ্টাব্দ পর্য্যন্ত সময়ের ইংরাজী ভাষা। **In plain English**—সোজা ভাষায়। **The English** — ইংরাজ জাতি। **The king's** or **queen's English**—ইংরাজী ভাষা।

ĕn-gorge′ (-gŏrj), *v.t.* 1. To devour greedily ; to swallow ; অতিভোজন

করা, গুরুভোজন করা ; গ্রাস করা, গেলা। **2.** (*Passive*) To be crammed or filled to excess ; to be congested with blood (of an animal tissue etc.) ; ঠাসাঠাসিভাবে পূর্ণ হওয়া ; রক্তাধিক্য বশতঃ রুদ্ধ হওয়া। **—gorg-ed′,** *p. adj.* **—ment,** *n.* **1.** The act of engorging ; গুরুভোজন, অতিভোজন, আকণ্ঠ-ভোজন। **2.** (*Med.*) Congestion ; (ভৈষজ্য-শাস্ত্র) রক্তাধিক্যজনিত শিরা, ধমনী, প্রভৃতির রোধ।

ĕn-grăft′, *v. t.* **1.** To insert (scion of one tree) into or upon another ; কলম বসান, কলম করা। **2.** To fix or implant deeply ; as, to *engraft* a principle in the mind ; গভীরভাবে নিবদ্ধ করা। **3.** To incorporate ; অঙ্গীভূত করা। **4.** To add ; সংযোগ করা।

ĕn-grail′ (-grāl), *v. t.* To notch or indent ; খাঁজ কাটা।

ĕn-grain′ (-grān), *v. t.* **1.** To dye with a fast colour ; পাকা রঙ্গ করা। **2.** To cause to sink deeply ; as, to *engrain* a dye into a fabric ; (also *fig.*) ; অনুপ্রবিষ্ট করা। **—grained′** *p. adj.* Inveterate ; as, an *engrained* rascal (হাড়ে হাড়ে দুষ্ট); পাকা।

ĕn-grāve′, *v. t.* **1.** To carve ; মূর্ত্তি প্রভৃতি ক্ষোদিত করা। **2.** To inscribe ; ক্ষোদিত করা, উৎকীর্ণ করা। **3.** To imprint ; to impress deeply ; "To *engrave* them on his memory ;" মুদ্রিত করা, গভীরভাবে মুদ্রিত বা অঙ্কিত করা। **—grav′-er,** *n.* One who engraves ; ভাস্কর, ত্বষ্টা, খোদক, তক্ষক, খোদাইকার। **—grav′-ing,** *n.* **1.** The art of cutting out figures or other devices on wood, stone or metal ; খোদাই-কার্য্য, তক্ষণ-শিল্প। **2.** An impression taken from an engraved plate ; ক্ষোদিত-ফলক হইতে গৃহীত প্রতিরূপ। **3.** An engraved plate ; খোদিত ফলক, উৎকীর্ণ ফলক।

ĕn-grŏss′, *v. t.* **1.** To occupy wholly : to absorb ; ব্যাপৃত করা ; নিবিষ্ট করা। **2.** To write or copy in a large clear hand ; বড় বড় অক্ষরে স্পষ্ট করিয়া লিখা বা নকল করা। **3.** To buy up whole or a large quantity with a view to sell again at a higher price ; to monopolize ; অধিক মূল্যে বিক্রয় করিবার উদ্দেশ্যে কোন জিনিষ অধিক পরিমাণে ক্রয় করা, রাখি করা ; একচেটিয়া করা। **4.** To write out or express in a legal form ; যথারীতি লিখা বা প্রকাশ করা। **—er,** *n.* **1.** One who engrosses ; নকলনবীস, অভিনিবিষ্টকারী। **2.** One who buys up whole or large quantity in order to sell at an enhanced rate ; যে ব্যক্তি অধিক লাভের আশায় সমস্ত কিম্বা প্রচুর পরিমাণে মাল ক্রয় করিয়া মজুত রাখে, পরিক্রয়ী (আঃ বঃ)। **3.** A monopolist ; একচেটিয়াকারী। **4.** One who writes in large characters ; যে ব্যক্তি বড় বড় অক্ষরে স্পষ্ট করিয়া লিখে। **—ment,** *n.* **1.** A copy of document written in a large legible hand ; স্পষ্ট বৃহৎ অক্ষরে লিখিত দলিলাদির প্রতিলিপি। **2.** Act of engrossing ; একচেটিয়াকরণ। **Engrossing deed** — স্পষ্ট অক্ষরে লিখিত দলিল। **Engrossing hand**— বড় বড় অক্ষরে স্পষ্ট করিয়া দলিলাদি লিখিবার ছাঁদ।

ĕn-gŭlf, in—, *v. t.* To plunge into a gulf ; to swallow up, as in a gulf ; উপসাগরে নিক্ষেপ করা ; কুক্ষিগত করা, গ্রাস করা। **—ment,** *n.*

ĕn-hance′ (-hăns), *v. t.* **1.** To increase ; বৃদ্ধি করা, বাড়ান। **2.** To exaggerate ; as, to *enhance* the infirmity ; অতিরঞ্জিত করা, অত্যুক্তি করা। **3.** To raise ; to heighten ; as, to *enhance* price ; বাড়ান ; চড়ান, চেতান। **4.** To intensify ; to aggravate ; গাঢ়তর করা, প্রগাঢ় করা ; গুরুতর করা। **—ment,** *n.* Increase ; aggravation ; বৃদ্ধি ; বর্দ্ধন, উপচয়।

ē-nig′-mă, *n.* **1.** A riddle ; a conundrum ; ধাঁধা, হেঁয়ালি, প্রহেলিকা, সমস্যা। **2.** A puzzling person or thing ; any obscure thing ; প্রহেলিকাময় মানব বা বস্তু ; প্রহেলিকাবৎ দুর্ব্বোধ বিষয়। **—mat′-ic, —mat′-i-cal,** *adjs.* Relating to or resembling an enigma ; puzzling ; obscure ; প্রহেলিকাবৎ, প্রহেলিকাপূর্ণ ; দুর্ব্বোধ, দুজ্ঞেয়, হতবুদ্ধিতাজনক ; অস্পষ্ট। **—mat′-i-cal-ly,** *adv.* **—tise, —tize,** *v. t.* To make or deal in enigmas or riddles ; ধাঁধা রচনা করা, হেঁয়ালির ছন্দে কথা বলা, সমস্যা প্রয়োগ করা। **—tist,** *n.*

ĕn-isle′ (-īl), *v. t.* **1.** To make an island of ; দ্বীপে পরিণত করা। **2.** To place on an island ; দ্বীপে স্থাপন করা। **3.** To isolate ; বিচ্ছিন্ন বা স্বতন্ত্র অবস্থায় রাখা।

ĕn-jamb′-mĕnt (-jăm-), *n.* (*Pros.*) Continuation of the sense in a phrase beyond the end of a verse or couplet ; (ছন্দঃশাস্ত্র) কোন বাক্যাংশের অর্থ শ্লোক বা কলির বাহিরে প্রসারণ।

ĕn-join′ (-joyn), *v. t.* **1.** To prescribe ; to command ; to order or direct with authority ; to admonish ; (with *on* or *upon* before the person enjoined) ; ব্যবস্থা করা, বিহিত করা, নির্দ্দেশ করা ; অনুজ্ঞা করা ; আদেশ করা, হুকুম করা ; অনুযোগ দেওয়া। **2.** (*Law*) To prohibit by an injunction ; (আইন) আদেশ প্রচার দ্বারা নিষেধ করা। **—ment,** *n.*

ĕn-joy′, *v. t.* **1.** To feel gladness or joy in ; to take delight in ; আনন্দ উপভোগ করা ; আনন্দ লাভ করা। **2.** To have the use or enjoyment of ; ভোগ বা ব্যবহারের জন্য প্রাপ্ত হওয়া। **3.** To have sexual intercourse with, (*obs.*) ; সম্ভোগ করা (অপ্রঃ)। **4.** To experience ; as, to *enjoy* poor health ; ভোগ করা। **—a-ble,** *adj.* Capable of being enjoyed ; yielding joy ; ভোগ্য, উপভোগ্য ; আনন্দদায়ক, সুখকর। **—a-ble-ness,** *n.* **—a-bly,** *adv.* **—er,** *n.* One who enjoys ; ভোক্তা । **—ment,** *n.* The condition of enjoying any thing ; satisfaction ; pleasures ; gratification ; সুখভোগ, ভোগ, উপভোগ, সম্ভোগ ; তৃপ্তি, তুষ্টি ; বিলাস ; চরিতার্থতা ।

ĕn-kin′-dle, *v. t.* **1.** To set on fire ; to kindle ; প্রজ্বলিত করা, অগ্নিসংযোগ করা ; জ্বালান । **2.** To rouse ; to inflame with passion ; উত্তেজিত করা, উদ্দীপ্ত করা, উদ্দীপিত করা, সন্ধুক্ষিত করা ।

ĕn-lāce′, *v. t.* **1.** To lace ; to encircle ; to enfold ; রজ্জু বা ফিতাদ্বারা বাঁধা ; বেষ্টিত করা, জড়ান । **2.** To interlace or entwine ; পরস্পরের সঙ্গে জড়ান, একত্র পাকান বা জড়ান । **—ment,** *n.*

ĕn-large′ (-lârj), *v. t.* & *i.* **1.** To make large or larger ; to expand ; to dilate ; বৃদ্ধি করা ; বিকাশ করা, প্রসারিত করা ; বিস্তারিত করা ; স্ফীত করা । **2.** To amplify (a discourse) ; সবিস্তারে বর্ণনা করা বা পল্লবিত করা । **3.** (*Archaic*) To set free ; (অপ্রচলিত) মুক্ত করা, স্বাধীনতা প্রদান করা । ***Verb i.*** **1.** To grow large or larger ; to magnify ; বাড়া, বৃদ্ধিপ্রাপ্ত হওয়া ; আয়তন বৃদ্ধি হওয়া । **2.** To expatiate ; to write or speak in detail, (with *upon*) ; সবিস্তারে রচনা করা ; প্রসঙ্গ বিস্তৃতি করা, প্রপঞ্চিত করা । **—larg′-er,** *n.* **—ment,** *n.* **1.** Act of enlarging ; state of being enlarged ; বিবর্দ্ধন, প্রসারণ ; বিপুলতা, বিবৃদ্ধি । **2.** Diffuseness ; amplification ; প্রসঙ্গ-বাহুল্য; অতিবিস্তৃতি, প্রসঙ্গ-বিস্তৃতি । **3.** Release from confinement, servitude ; liberty ; মুক্তিদান, স্বাধীনতাদান ; মুক্তি । **4.** Expansion, as of mental power etc. ; মানসিক শক্তি প্রভৃতির বিকাশ । **5.** Something added so as to enlarge ; বর্দ্ধিত করার জন্য যাহা সংযোগ করা হয় । **6.** (*Photog.*) An enlarged picture (আলোক-চিত্র) বিবর্দ্ধিত চিত্র । **To enlarge an order**—(*Law*) আদেশ প্রতিপালনের সময় বাড়াইয়া দেওয়া বা আরও সময় দেওয়া । **To enlarge one's self**—To amplify a discourse ; প্রসঙ্গ বিস্তার করা । **To enlarge the heart** — To expand or swell the heart with gratitude or affection ; আনন্দে বা কৃতজ্ঞতায় হৃদয় স্ফীত করা ।

ĕn-light′-ĕn (-līt-), *v. t.* **1.** (*Archaic*) To illuminate ; to shed light on ; আলোকিত করা ; উদ্ভাসিত করা । **2.** To free a person's mind from prejudice or superstition ; to elevate intellectually or morally ; to instruct ; to inform ; as, to *enlighten* one on a subject ; পূর্ব্ব-সংস্কার বা কুসংস্কার দূর করা ; জ্ঞান বা নীতিবিষয়ে উন্নত করা, মানসিক বা আধ্যাত্মিক উন্নতি সাধন করা ; উপদেশ দান করা, শিক্ষাদান করা ; জ্ঞাত করা । **—ened,** *adj.* Illuminated ; civilized ; unprejudiced ; আলোকিত, আলোকপ্রাপ্ত, জ্ঞানদীপ্ত ; সভ্য ; পূর্ব্ব-সংস্কারবর্জ্জিত । **—er,** *n.* **—ment,** *n.* **1.** The act of enlightening ; the state of being enlightened or instructed ; the imparting or receiving mental or spiritual light ; আলোক-বিকিরণ, আলোকদান ; জ্ঞানালোক, বুদ্ধি প্রকাশ (হিং কোঃ), প্রকাশ (ঐ), জ্ঞানোদয় (ঐ), বুদ্ধ্যুদয় (ঐ) । **2.** The spirit of the French philosophers of the 18th century ; অষ্টাদশ শতাব্দীর ফরাসী দার্শনিকদিগের তত্ত্ব ।

ĕn-link′, *v. t.* To chain together ; to connect closely ; একত্র শৃঙ্খলিত করা ; সংযোগ করা ।

ĕn-list′, *v. t.* & *i.* **1.** To enrol ; তালিকাভুক্ত করা । **2.** To engage for military service ; সৈন্যশ্রেণীভুক্ত করা । **3.** To engage in public service ; to secure the co-operation or support of ; to employ in promoting some cause, as one's sympathy ; সরকারী কর্ম্মে নিযুক্ত করা ; সাহায্য বা সাহচর্য্য লাভ করা ; কোন উদ্দেশ্য সাধনের মানসে নিযুক্ত করা । ***Verb i.*** **1.** To enrol oneself voluntarily in military service ; স্বেচ্ছাপূর্ব্বক সৈন্যশ্রেণীভুক্ত হওয়া । **2.** To enter heartily into a cause ; আন্তরিক আগ্রহ সহকারে কোন কার্য্য সাধনে প্রবৃত্ত হওয়া । **—ment,** *n.*

ĕn-lĭv′-ĕn, *v. t.* To give life or vivacity to ; to animate ; to make merry and cheerful ; to inspire ; to heighten as a picture, screen, etc. ; জীবনদান করা, সজীব করা, জীবদান করা, উজ্জীবিত করা, নবজীবন সঞ্চার করা ; জীবন্ত করা ; উল্লসিত করা, হর্ষোৎফুল্ল করা ; অনুপ্রাণিত করা, তেজঃসঞ্চার করা ; চিত্র, যবনিকা প্রভৃতি বর্ণোজ্জ্বলিত করা । **—ment,** *n.*

en masse, (*F.*) *adv.* In a mass ; all together ; একলাটে, একত্রে ; সর্ব্বশুদ্ধ ।

ĕn-mĕsh′, ĕm–, ĭm–, *v. t.* To entangle in or as in meshes ; জালে জড়িত করা, জালবদ্ধ করা । **—ment,** *n.*

ĕn′-mi-tȳ, *n.* Animosity ; hostility ; antipathy ; শত্রুতা, অরিত্ব, অমিত্রতা, বৈর ; বিরোধ, দ্বেষ, জিগীষা ; বিতৃষ্ণা, বিরাগ ।

ĕn-nō′-ble (-bl), *v. t.* **1.** To make noble; to dignify ; সম্ভ্রান্ত করা, সম্ভ্রান্ত-সমাজভুক্ত করা ; উন্নত করা, উন্নীত করা । **2.** To raise to the rank of nobility ; as, Mr. Calvin was *ennobled* for his scientific discoveries ; অভিজাত শ্রেণীতে উন্নীত করা, কৌলিন্য প্রদান করা । **—ment,** *n.*

en-nui′ (âng-nwē), (*F.*), *n.* Mental weariness or disgust from want of occupation or lack of interest ; অরুচি, অরতি, বিতৃষ্ণা, বিরতি, ক্লান্তি, খেদ, শ্রান্তি, উদাসভাব । **—nuied,** *adj.*

ē-nŏr′-mi-tȳ, *n.* **1.** The state of being immoderate or excessive ; ঔৎকট্য, বিকটতা, আত্যন্তিকতা, ঘোরতা । **2.** Outrageous wickedness ; monstrous crime ; atrocity ; দুষ্কর্ম্ম ; পৈশাচিক অপরাধ, উৎকট পাপাচার,

ঘোরপাতক ; নৃশংসতা। **—mous,** *adj.* **1.** Huge; prodigious; colossal; অতিবৃহৎ ; প্রকাণ্ড, বিপুল; সুবিশাল। **2.** Outrageous, (*rare*); উৎকট। **—mous-ly,** *adv.* **—mous-ness,** *n.*

ē-nough' (-nŭf), *adj., n., adv. & interj.* Sufficient; satisfying desire; satisfying want; প্রচুর, ঢের; যথেষ্ট, পর্য্যাপ্ত; বহুল। ***Noun.*** **1.** A sufficiency; adequate quantity; প্রাচুর্য্য; পর্য্যাপ্ত পরিমাণ। **2.** That which is equal to the powers or abilities: শক্তি বা ক্ষমতার অনুরূপ চেষ্টা প্রভৃতি, যথাসাধ্য চেষ্টা প্রভৃতি। ***Adv.*** **1.** Sufficiently; fully; quite; as, you know well *enough* (quite well) what I have in my mind; যথেষ্টভাবে, প্রচুর রূপে, পর্য্যাপ্ত পরিমাণে; সম্যগ্‌রূপে; বেশ, ভালরূপে। **2.** Tolerably; as, she sings well *enough*; এক রকম, একপ্রকার। ***Interj.*** An exclamation denoting sufficiency: বস্‌! যথেষ্ট হইয়াছে। **Enough!** Speak no more; থাম থাম। **Enough and enough**—More than sufficient; ছড়াছড়ি। **Enough is as good as a feast**—অভাব মিটিলেই ভরপুর হইল। **Enough of this folly**—Stop; ঢের হইয়াছে থাম। **I had enough to do to catch the train**—I had to exert all my powers to catch the train: গাড়ী ধরিতে আমার যথাসাধ্য চেষ্টা করিতে হইয়াছে। **I have enough and to spare**—I have in sufficient quantity, even to the extent of sparing; আমার যথেষ্ট পরিমাণে আছে, এমন কি ইচ্ছা করিলে কিছু দানও করিতে পারি। **To cry enough**—To admit defeat; পরাজয় স্বীকার করা। **To have enough of a person or thing**—To be tired of him or it; কোন লোক বা বস্তুর প্রতি সম্পূর্ণ বিতৃষ্ণ হওয়া।

ē-nounce' (-nowns), *v. t.* **1.** To enunciate; স্পষ্টরূপে নির্দ্দেশ করা। **2.** To declare; to pronounce; প্রকাশ করা, প্রচার করা; ব্যক্ত করা, ঘোষণা করা। **—ment,** *n.* Act of enouncing; proclamation; declaration; statement: প্রচার করণ; ঘোষণা; প্রচার; প্রতিজ্ঞাদির নির্দ্দেশ বা কথন।

en passant, (*F.*), *adv.* By the bye; প্রসঙ্গক্রমে, কথাপ্রসঙ্গে, প্রসঙ্গতঃ।

ĕn-quīre', *v. t. & i.* See INQUIRE.

ĕn-rāge', *v. t.* To make angry or furious; ক্রুদ্ধ করা, কুপিত করা, রোষাবিষ্ট করা। **—raged,** *p. adj.* Furious; frenzied with rage; রোষাবিষ্ট; ক্রোধোন্মত্ত।

ĕn-răp'-tūre, *v. t.* To delight beyond measure; to fill with transcendent joy: পরমানন্দিত করা, আহ্লাদানন্দাভিভূত করা, হর্ষাবিষ্ট করা; অলৌকিক আনন্দে বিহ্বল করা, আনন্দ-প্লাবিত করা। **—tured,** *p. adj.* Delighted beyond measure; পরমানন্দিত, ভাবে গদগদ, আনন্দ-বিহ্বল, হর্ষোন্মত্ত, মাতোয়ারা।

ĕn-răv'-ish, *v. t.* To enrapture; to fill with unbounded delight; to fascinate; অত্যুল্লসিত করা; পরমানন্দিত করা; বিমোহিত করা, সম্মোহিত করা, বিমুগ্ধ করা। **—ment,** *n.*

ĕn-rĕg'-i-mĕnt, *v. t.* To form into a regiment; to bring under discipline; সৈন্য পল্টন গঠন করা; শাসনাধীনে আনা।

en regle, (*F.*) *adv.* In due form; যথারীতি, যথাবিধানে।

ĕn-rich', *v. t.* **1.** To make rich; ধনশালী করা, ধনাঢ্য করা। **2.** To fertilize; উর্ব্বরতা সম্পাদন করা। **3.** To add to the existing stock; as, to *enrich* a library with a book; পরিপুষ্টি সাধন করা, নব নব বস্তু সংযোগ করা, সমৃদ্ধ করা। **4.** To embellish; to adorn; to set off with carving; বিভূষিত করা; মণ্ডিত করা, অলঙ্কৃত করা; সুশোভিত করা। **5.** To supply with knowledge; as, to *enrich* the mind; জ্ঞানসম্পন্ন করা। **6.** To heighten taste or flavour; as, to *enrich* a soup with spices; স্বাদুতা বৃদ্ধি করা। **—ment,** *n.* Act of enriching; state of being enriched; ধনসম্পন্ন-করণ, উর্ব্বরতা সম্পাদন, স্বাদগন্ধবর্দ্ধন, অলঙ্করণ; ধনসম্পন্নতা, উর্ব্বরতা-বৃদ্ধি, স্বাদগন্ধবৃদ্ধি।

ĕn-rōbe', *v. t.* To invest with robe or dress; পরিচ্ছদ শোভিত করা।

ĕn-rōl', —rōll', *v. t.* **1.** To enlist; তালিকাভুক্ত করা। **2.** To enter on the rolls of a court; to leave in writing; as, to *enroll* a petition or a law; ফর্দ্দেতে নাম লিখা, ফিরিস্তিতে নাম লিখা; লিপিবদ্ধ করা, লিখিয়া রাখা। **3.** To incorporate as an acknowledged member in a society, etc.; কোন সভাসমিতি বা পরিষদের সভ্য তালিকাভুক্ত করা। **4.** To record with honour or celebrate; "To *enroll* your triumphs;" গৌরবের সহিত লিপিবদ্ধ বা কীর্ত্তন করা। **—er,** *n.* **—ment,** *n.* Act of enrolling; state of being enrolled; তালিকাভুক্তকরণ; তালিকাভুক্তি। **2.** A register; a record; খাতা, দলীল, দস্তাবেজ; নথী।

en route [*F.*], *adv.* On the way; পথিমধ্যে।

ĕns, *n.* (*Pl.* ENTIA) An entity; সৎবস্তু, নিত্যপদার্থ, সত্তা, সৎ।

ĕn-săm'-ple *n.* (*Archaic*) Example; দৃষ্টান্ত (অপ্রঃ)।

ĕn-san'-guine (-săng-gwĭn), *v. t.* To stain with blood; to make of a blood-red colour; রক্তরঞ্জিত করা রুধির-সংলিপ্ত করা, শোণিতদিগ্ধ করা; রুধিরারুণবর্ণে রঞ্জিত করা। **—guined,** *adj.*

ĕn-sconce' (-skŏns), *v. t.* **1.** To cover with a sconce or fort; to hide safely; ক্ষুদ্র দুর্গাদিদ্বারা রক্ষিত করা; নিরাপদে লুক্কায়িত রাখা। **2.** To establish (one's self) in a safe secret or snug place; সুখোপবিষ্ট করা, সুপ্রতিষ্ঠিত করা।

ensemble (or *tout ensemble*) [*F.*], *n.* The whole; all the parts viewed in relation to the whole ; the general effect (of a person, appearance, a whole work of art etc.); সমগ্র, সমুদায়, সমুচ্চয় ; ব্যাপকভাবে গৃহীত অংশসমূহ ; আলেখ্য, সঙ্গীত বা অন্যবিধ সুকুমার কলা-জাত বস্তুকে ব্যাপকভাবে দর্শন করিয়া যে ধারণা জন্মে, ব্যাপক-ধারণা, সামগ্রিক-দৃশ্য, মোট-দৃশ্য।

ĕn-shrīne′, *v. t.* **1.** To inclose in a shrine or chest ; to cherish or preserve as something sacred ; মন্দির-মধ্যে রক্ষা করা ; সযত্নে রক্ষা করা, ভক্তি-সহকারে পোষণ করা, স্মৃতি-মন্দিরে প্রতিষ্ঠিত করা। **2.** To serve as a shrine for (a precious thing), (*lit.* & *fig.*) ; মূল্যবান বস্তু রক্ষার উপযোগী মন্দিরের কার্য্য করা। **—ment,** *n.*

ĕn-shroud′ (-shrōwd), *v. t.* To cover with a shroud ; to cover completely ; to hide ; শবাচ্ছাদন বস্ত্রে আবৃত করা ; সমাচ্ছন্ন করা, আচ্ছাদিত করা; লুক্কায়িত করা।

ĕn′-si-fōrm, *adj.* Having the form of a sword ; খড়্গাকৃতি (সাঃ পঃ), অসি-পত্রাকৃতি, যথা বক্ষঃস্থলের উপাস্থি।

ĕn′-sign (-sīn), *n.* **1.** A sign or mark ; a badge of office or rank ; চিহ্ন, নিদর্শন, নিশানা ; পদসূচক-চিহ্ন। **2.** A banner ; a flag ; a standard ; a national flag ; পতাকা, ধ্বজা, নিশান ; কেতু, কেতন ; বৈজয়ন্ত ; জাতীয় পতাকা। **3.** A flag-bearer ; পতাকাবাহী, পতাকী, বৈজয়ন্তিক। **4.** A signal to give notice ; বিপৎ-সূচক চিহ্ন। **5.** (*Formerly*) A commissioned officer of the lowest rank in the British infantry ; (পূর্ব্বকালে) ব্রিটিশ পদাতি সেনাদলের সর্ব্বনিম্নপদস্থ সৈনিক কর্ম্মচারী। **—cy, —ship,** *ns.* **Ensign bearer**—ধ্বজাবাহক, ধ্বজাধর। **Blue ensign**—ভবিষ্যতের ব্যবহারের জন্য সংরক্ষিত নৌ-সৈন্যদল প্রভৃতির নীলবর্ণ পতাকা। **Red ensign**—সওদাগরী জাহাজের রক্তপতাকা। **White ensign**—রাজকীয় নৌসৈন্যের শ্বেতপতাকা।

ĕn′-si-lāge, *n.* & *v. t.* Preserving of green fodder etc. in pits ; the fodder thus preserved ; গবাদির খাদ্য কাঁচা ঘাস প্রভৃতি গর্ত্ত মধ্যে রক্ষাকরণ ; উক্ত প্রকারে রক্ষিত হরিৎ তৃণাদি। ***Verb t.*** To subject as fodder to the process of ensilage ; হরিৎ তৃণাদি গর্ত্তমধ্যে রক্ষা করা।

ĕn-slāve′, *v. t.* To make a slave of ; to reduce to slavery ; to master or bring under complete subjection, (*lit.* & *fig.*) ; ক্রীতদাস করা ; গোলাম করা ; দাসত্বনিগড়ে বদ্ধ করা, প্রাধান্য-সংস্থাপন করা, পরাভূত করা, সম্পূর্ণরূপে বশীভূত করা। **—ment,** *n.* **—slav′-er,** *n.* দাসকারী ; যে রমণী সদ্‌গুণ ও লাবণ্য দ্বারা পুরুষকে দাসবৎ করিয়া রাখে।

ĕn-snāre′, —in, *v. t.* To entrap ; to entangle ; ফাঁদে ফেলা, পাশবদ্ধ করা, জালবদ্ধ করা ; কল বা কূটযন্ত্রে আটক করা, বিজড়িত করা।

ĕn-soul′ (-sōl), **in-,** *v. i.* **1.** To receive or put into the soul ; প্রাণে গ্রহণ করা, প্রাণে প্রবেশ করাইয়া দেওয়া। **2.** To infuse a soul into ; to animate ; প্রাণ-সঞ্চার করা ; উজ্জীবিত করা।

ĕn-sphere′ (-sfēr), *v. t.* **1.** To encircle ; to enclose ; বেষ্টিত করা ; ঘেরা। **2.** To give spherical form to, (*lit.* & *fig.*) ; মণ্ডলাকার করা।

ĕn-sue′ (-sû), *v. t.* **1.** To succeed or to happen afterwards ; to result ; পরে আসা বা ঘটা, অনুবর্ত্তী হওয়া, অনুসরণ করা, পরম্পরাক্রমে আগত হওয়া ; পরিণত হওয়া, ফলস্বরূপ সংঘটিত হওয়া। **2.** (*Bible*) To seek after ; (বাইবেল) অন্বেষণ করা। **—su′-ing,** *adj.* Coming ; আগামী।

ĕn-sure′ (-shōōr), *v. t.* **1.** To make certain ; to make secure ; নিশ্চিত করা ; নিরাপদ করা। **2.** See INSURE.

ĕn-swāthe′, *v. t.* To bind or cover in a bandage ; বস্ত্র-বন্ধনী দ্বারা বন্ধন বা আবৃত করা। **—ment,** *n.*

ĕn-tăb′-lă-tūre, *n.* (*Arch.*) In classical architecture the part of a structure above the column, comprehending the architrave, frieze and cornice ; (প্রাচীন গ্রীস ও রোমান স্থাপত্য-শিল্পে) কার্ণিশ ও সর্দ্দালাদি সম্বলিত স্তম্ভ-শীর্ষ, প্রস্তার (রাঃ রাঃ), উত্তীরা (উরিষ্যা), স্তম্ভ-শিরঃশাখা (আঃ বঃ)।

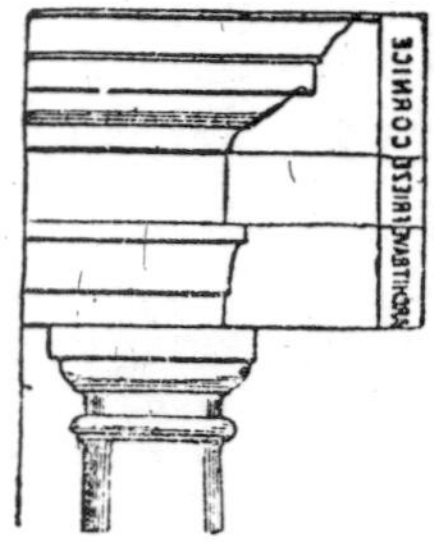

Entablature.

ĕn-tail′ (-tāl), *v. t.* & *n.* **1.** (*Law*) To settle inalienably (an estate) on some one or a series of heirs ; পুত্রপৌত্রাদিক্রমে ভোগদখল করণার্থ সম্পত্তি প্রভৃতি দান করা, দান বিক্রয়ের স্বত্ব রহিত করিয়া কেবল ভোগ দখলের জন্য ব্যক্তিবিশেষ বা তাঁহার উত্তরাধিকারি-পরম্পরাকে স্থাবর সম্পত্তি দান করা। **2.** To necessitate ; to bring on as an unavoidable consequence ; "The scheme was found to *entail* greater evil ;" আবশ্যক করা ; অবশ্যম্ভাবী ফলস্বরূপ সংঘটন করা। **3.** To impose ; চাপান। ***Noun.*** **1.** An estate which has been entailed ; the act of entailing ; পুত্রপৌত্রাদিক্রমে ভোগ দখলের জন্য প্রদত্ত সম্পত্তি, অনুচ্ছেদ্য সম্পত্তি, অবিভাজ্য সম্পত্তি ; উক্তরূপে সম্পত্তি দান করণ। **2.** (*Fig.*) Inalienable inheritance ; as, of quality, belief, etc. ; অপরিত্যাজ্য সহজাত গুণ বা প্রবৃত্তিসমূহ। **—ment,** *n.* **—er,** *n.*

ĕn-tan′-gle (-tăng-gl), *v. t.* **1.** To twist into tangles ; to make disordered or intricate ; জড়িত করা, পেঁচান, জড়ান ; বিশৃঙ্খল করা, জটিল করা। **2.** To ensnare ; to embarrass ; ফাঁদে ফেলা, পেঁচে ফেলা ; ঝঞ্ঝাটে ফেলা। **—gled,** *p. adj.* Involved ;

জড়িত। **—gler,** *n.* **—ment,** *n.* Act of entangling ; state of being entangled ; perplexity ; বিজড়ন ; জড়িতাবস্থা ; ঝঞ্ঝাট, প্রমুগ্ধতা।

Ented a pursaetha—গিলা (বেলঃ)।

ĕn-tĕl′-ĕ-chȳ, *n.* (*Metaph.*) Realisation of form-giving cause or energy ; actual existence ; আকার-প্রদায়ক কারণ বা শক্তির বাস্তবতা-প্রাপ্তি, প্রকৃত্যাপুর, পরিণতি ; বাস্তবতা (হিঃ কোঃ)।

entente cordiale, [*F.*], *n.* Cordial or friendly understanding between two governments ; রাজাদ্বয়ের মধ্যে মৈত্রীভাব।

ĕn′-tĕr, *v. i.* & *t.* **1.** To come or go in ; ঢুকা, প্রবেশ করা, পশা (কাব্যতায়)। **2.** To come upon a stage (as a stage direction,—usually 3rd person imperative, as, *enters* Bheem) ; রঙ্গমঞ্চে প্রবেশ করা, রঙ্গমঞ্চে অবতীর্ণ হওয়া। **3.** To penetrate ; ভেদ করিয়া প্রবেশ করা। **4.** To get admitted, (with *into*) ; to engage ; as, to *enter into* a business ; ভর্ত্তি হওয়া ; নিযুক্ত হওয়া, প্রবৃত্ত হওয়া, আবদ্ধ হওয়া, ব্যাপৃত হওয়া। **5.** To form a part of ; to be an ingredient in ; (with *into*) ; as, hydrogen *entered into* the composition of water ; অংশীভূত হওয়া ; উপাদানীভূত হওয়া। **6.** To sympathise with, (with *into*) ; as, I can *enter into* your feelings ; সমবেদনা প্রকাশ করা। **7.** To be a party, (with *into*) ; as, to *enter into* a contract ; পক্ষ হওয়া। **8.** To begin, (with *on* or *upon*) ; আরম্ভ করা। **9.** To assume possession of, (with *on* or *upon*) ; as, he *entered on* his paternal property ; অধিকার গ্রহণ করা। **10.** To deal with, (with *on* or *upon*) ; as, now I must *enter on* the most abstruse part of metaphysics ; আলোচনা করা। ***Verb t.*** **1.** To go or come into ; to penetrate ; প্রবেশ করা, প্রবিষ্ট করা, ঢুকান ; ভেদ করিয়া প্রবেশ করা। **2.** To set down in writing ; to enroll ; to record the name of ; as, *enter* him for the race (*i. e.* as a competitor) ; লিপিবদ্ধ করা ; তালিকাভুক্ত করা ; সরকারী খাতায় লিখিয়া রাখা। **3.** To become a member of ; to join ; সভ্যশ্রেণীভুক্ত হওয়া ; যোগ দেওয়া। **4.** To admit (some one) ; ভর্ত্তি করা। **5.** To engage ; to begin ; প্রবৃত্ত করা, ব্যাপৃত করা ; আরম্ভ করা। **6.** (*Law*) To go in or upon and take possession of ; সম্পত্তির অধিকারে প্রবৃত্ত হওয়া বা অধিকার গ্রহণ করা। **7.** To place in proper form before the court, আদালতের সমক্ষে যথাবিধি উপস্থাপিত করা। **8.** To report the arrival of a ship at the custom house ; জাহাজাদির বন্দরে আগমন বার্ত্তা শুল্কাগারে বিজ্ঞাপিত করা। **9.** To train ; to break in as a horse etc. ; "Hounds ready to be *entered* ;" শিক্ষিত করা ; (অশ্ব প্রভৃতি সম্পর্কে) শিক্ষিত করা বা বশে আনা। **—a-ble,** *adj.* **—er,** *n.* **Enter-close**—কক্ষদ্বয়ের মধ্যবর্ত্তী পথ। **To enter a bill short**—ধনাগারে গচ্ছিত হুণ্ডীর সংক্ষিপ্ত বিবরণ লিখিয়া রাখা। **To enter an appearance**—To cause one's presence to be noted down ; হাজিরা লিখান। **To enter appearance**—উপস্থিত হওয়া, হাজির হওয়া। **To enter a protest** — To record one's protest in a minute or journal ; to protest ; কোনও মন্তব্য-পুস্তক বা খাতায় প্রতিবাদ লিপিবদ্ধ করা, লিখিত আপত্তি দাখিল করা ; প্রতিবাদ করা। **To enter goods at the custom house**—শুল্কাগারে মালের তালিকা দেখাইয়া জাহাজ হইতে মাল খালাস করার অনুমতি পাওয়া। **To enter into**—To pass into the interior of ; অভ্যন্তরে প্রবেশ করা। To engage in ; as, to *enter into* business ; প্রবৃত্ত হওয়া, ব্যাপৃত হওয়া। To deal with ; to examine ; আলোচনা করা ; পরীক্ষা করা। To be an ingredient or element in ; উপাদানীভূত হওয়া। **To enter into a bond**—খত বা তমঃসুক লিখিয়া দেওয়া। **To enter into a case**—অনুসন্ধান করা, তদন্ত করা। **To enter into a recognisance** — To be bound down ; মুচলেকা বদ্ধ হওয়া। **To enter into a security**—জামিন দেওয়া। **To enter on or upon**—To begin ; আরম্ভ করা। To treat of ; to examine ; আলোচনা করা ; অনুসন্ধান করা। **To enter one's head**—To occur to some one ; মনে উদিত হওয়া। **To enter satisfaction on a decree** — ডিক্রীর টাকা শোধ হইয়াছে এমত লিখা বা কহা। **To enter the list**—To engage in a quarrel ; to accept a challenge ; বিবাদে প্রবৃত্ত হওয়া ; দ্বন্দ্ব-যুদ্ধে সম্মত হওয়া। **To enter up**—To complete the series of entries in (an account book) to a certain date ; নির্দ্দিষ্ট তারিখ পর্য্যন্ত খাতায় লিখা উঠান। (*Law*) To cause to be written down in the records of a court ; বিচারালয়ের নথিতে লিপিবদ্ধ করান।

ĕn-tĕr′-ic, *adj.* Belonging or relating to the intestines ; আন্ত্রিক, অন্ত্র-সম্পর্কীয়। **Enteric fever**—আন্ত্রিক জ্বর, বাত-শ্লেষ্মাজ্বর, টাইফয়েড্ জ্বর।

ĕn-tĕ-rī′-tis, *n.* Inflammation of the intestines ; অন্ত্র-প্রদাহ।

ĕn-tĕr′-ö-cele (-sēl), *n.* A hernial tumour containing part of the intestines ; অন্ত্রবৃদ্ধি (হঃ চঃ)।

ĕn′-tĕr-prīse, *n.* **1.** An adeventure ; a bold or hazardous undertaking ; উদ্যম, উদ্যমজনক ব্যাপার ; অসমসাহসিক কার্য্য, বিপৎসঙ্কুল বা দুঃসাহসিক কর্ম্ম। **2.** An adventurous spirit ; courage ; as, a man of *enterprise* ; অসমসাহসিকতা ; সাহস ; **—pris′-er,** *n.* Adventurer ; অসমসাহসিক কর্ম্মে প্রবৃত্ত ব্যক্তি।

–pris-ing, *adj.* Ready to undertake enterprises; resolute; adventurous; দুঃসাহসিক কার্য্য সাধনে প্রস্তুত; স্থিরসঙ্কল্প, দৃঢ়প্রতিজ্ঞ; উদ্যমশীল, উদ্যোগী, দুঃসাহসিক। **–pris-ing-ly,** *adv.*

ĕn-têr-tain' (-tān), *v. t.* **1.** To divert; to amuse; as, to *entertain* friends with music or conversation; আমোদিত করা; চিত্তবিনোদন করা। **2.** To receive as guest; to treat hospitably; অতিথির সম্বর্দ্ধনা বা অভ্যর্থনা করা, পান-ভোজনে আপ্যায়িত করা, অতিথি সৎকার করা। **3.** To harbour; to cherish; as, to *entertain* an idea; মনে স্থান দেওয়া; পোষণ করা। **4.** To receive or take into consideration; বিবেচনা করা, গ্রাহ্য করা। **5.** To keep up; as, to *entertain* correspondence etc.; চালান। **–er,** *n.* One who entertains; অতিথিসেবক, চিত্তবিনোদক। **–ing,** *adj.* Amusing; pleasing; আমোদজনক, চিত্ত-বিনোদক, আনন্দকর, তুষ্টিকর, মনোমদ। **–ing-ly,** *adv.* **–ment,** *n.* **1.** Act of entertaining; hospitable treatment; চিত্তবিনোদন, ভোজন-পানীয় দ্বারা আপ্যায়ন; অতিথি-সৎকার। **2.** Feast; repast; festival; নিমন্ত্রণ; ভোজ, আহার; উৎসব, পর্ব্ব। **3.** Amusement; diversion; আমোদ-প্রমোদ; ক্রীড়া-কৌতুক, রঙ্-তামাসা। **4.** Public performance or show; নাচগান, ক্রীড়া-প্রদর্শনী প্রভৃতি। **5.** Reception of something into mind or consideration; গ্রহণ, গ্রাহ্যকরণ, বিবেচনাকরণ।

en-thrall', **–thral,** *v. t.* **1.** To enslave, (*lit.* & *fig.*); ক্রীতদাস করা (শব্দানুযায়ী এবং লক্ষণায়)। **2.** To captivate; to charm; বিমোহিত করা; বিমুগ্ধ করা। **–dom,** *n.* Slavery; দাসত্ব। **–ment,** *n.*

ĕn-thrōne', *v. t.* **1.** To place on a throne; to invest with royalty; to raise on an elevated situation; সিংহাসনস্থ করা, সিংহাসনে অধিষ্ঠিত করা, রাজপাটে স্থাপিত করা; রাজপদে অভিষিক্ত করা, রাজ্যাভিষিক্ত করা; উচ্চপদে অভিষিক্ত করা। **2.** To instal, as a bishop, into a vacant see; বিশপের পদে অধিষ্ঠিত করা। **–ment,** *n.*

ĕn-thrŏn'-ize, *v. t.* To place on throne; to induct (a bishop) into office; রাজতক্তে বসান সিংহাসনাধিরূঢ় করা; বিশপের পদে প্রতিষ্ঠিত করা। **–i-za'-tion,** *n.*

ĕn-thūse', *v. i.* (*Colloq.*) To display enthusiasm; উৎসাহ প্রদর্শন করা।

ĕn-thū'-sĭ-ăsm, *n.* **1.** An ecstasy of mind caused as if by divine possession, (*rare*); আবেশ, শক্ত্যাবেশ। **2.** Ardent zeal; উৎসাহ, আগ্রহ, ব্যগ্রতা। **–ast,** *n.* **1.** One actuated by enthusiasm; a person of ardent zeal; অত্যুৎসাহী; উৎসাহদীপ্ত ব্যক্তি। **2.** A highly imaginative person; উৎকট কল্পনাপ্রিয় ব্যক্তি। **3.** A zealot; ধর্ম্মোন্মত্ত ব্যক্তি, গোঁড়া। **–as'-tic, –as'-ti-cal,** *adjs.* **1.** Ardent; zealously excited in any cause or pursuit; visionary; উৎসাহশীল, আগ্রহান্বিত; উৎসাহোন্মত্ত; উৎকট কল্পনাপ্রিয়। **2.** Devoted; অনুরক্ত, ভক্ত, অনুরাগী। **–as'-ti-cal-ly,** *adv.* In an enthusiastic manner; সোৎসাহে।

ĕn'-thȳ-meme (-mēm), *n.* A syllogism with one premise suppressed; যে ন্যায় বাক্যে একটা অবয়ব অনুক্ত থাকে, যথা—"পর্ব্বত অগ্নিময়" "ধূম হইতে" (অনুমিত হইল) অতএব যাহা যাহা ধূমায়মান তাহা তাহাই বহ্নিমান, এই তৃতীয় অবয়বটী এস্থলে অনুক্ত রহিয়াছে, অব্যক্ত ন্যায় (সাঃ পঃ), অবয়বহীন বাক্য (হিঃ কোঃ), লুপ্তাবয়বতর্ক (ঐ), উপলক্ষিত তর্ক (ঐ)।

ĕn-tīce', *v. t.* **1.** To allure; to tempt to evil; প্রলুব্ধ করা, আকর্ষণ করা, প্রলোভিত করা; ভুলান, ফুসলান। **2.** To lead astray; বিপথে পরিচালিত করা, ফুসলাইয়া পাপকর্ম্মে প্রবৃত্ত করা। **–a-ble,** *adj.* **–ment,** *n.* **1.** Act of enticing; state of being enticed; প্রলোভন, লোভন, বিমোহন; বিমোহিতাবস্থা। **2.** That which entices; allurement; blandishment; প্রলোভক; লোভ; প্রিয়বাক্য, সোহাগ। **–tic'-er,** *n.* One who entices; প্রলোভক।

ĕn-tīre', *adj.* & *n.* **1.** Whole; complete; perfect; as, *entire* confidence; সমগ্র, নিখিল, ষোল আনা, আস্ত; সমস্ত; পূর্ণ। **2.** Unmixed; pure as a quality or feeling; as, *entire* affection; অবিমিশ্র, খাঁটি; বিশুদ্ধ। **3.** Unbroken; not mutilated or decayed; অভগ্ন, অটুট, অখণ্ড; অখণ্ডিত, অক্ষয়িত। **4.** Sincere; cordial; faithful (*obs.*); সরল; আন্তরিক; বিশ্বস্ত (অপ্রঃ)। **5.** Not castrated as an animal; অচ্ছিন্ন-মুষ্ক। **6.** Continuous throughout, (now only in scientific use); অবিচ্ছিন্ন, নিরবচ্ছিন্ন। **7.** Mere; as, an *entire* delusion; কেবল, শুদ্ধ। **8.** (*Bot.*) Not in the least toothed, as leaves; (উদ্ভিদ্-বিদ্যা) অদন্তুর (পত্র-সম্পর্কে)। **9.** (*Archaic*) In full strength; as, he is *entire*; (অপ্রচলিত) পূর্ণ শক্তিসম্পন্ন। ***Noun.*** Entirety; সম্পূর্ণতা, সামগ্র্য। **2.** A kind of wine; একপ্রকার মদিরা। **3.** An entire (not castrated) horse; অচ্ছিন্নমুষ্ক অশ্ব। **–ly,** *adv.* Wholly; completely; সম্পূর্ণরূপে, অখণ্ডভাবে; সমগ্ররূপে। **–ness,** *n.* The whole; completeness; সমস্তটা, আস্তটা; সমগ্রতা, সম্পূর্ণতা, সামগ্র্য, সাকল্য, অখণ্ডতা। **–ty,** *n.* Completeness; that which is entire; sum total; অখণ্ডতা, সমগ্রতা; অখণ্ড বস্তু; সর্ব্বসাকল্য, মোট। **Possession by entireties**—(*Law*) অবিভক্ত অধিকার। **Tenancy by entireties**—(*Law*) একপ্রকার স্বত্ব—যাহাতে দুই ব্যক্তি (স্বামী স্ত্রী) এক যোগে কোন সম্পত্তির অধিকারী হইয়া থাকে।

ĕn-tī'-tle (-tl), *v. t.* **1.** To style; to give a title to; আখ্যা দেওয়া, নামকরণ করা, নাম দেওয়া, অভিহিত করা; উপাধিদান করা। **2.** To qualify for; to give a claim to; as his talents *entitle* him to respect ; যোগ্য করা ; অধিকারী করা । **3.** (*Law*) To settle a legal title to ; (আইন) স্বত্ববান করা ।

ĕn′-ti-tȳ, *n.* A thing that has real existence ; being ; সৎবস্তু ; অস্তিত্ব, সত্ত্ব, সত্তা, পরম সত্তা । **—ta-tive,** *adj.*

ĕn-tomb′ (-tōōm), *v. t.* To bury ; to inter ; to deposit in a tomb ; (*lit.* & *fig.*) ; ভূগর্ভে প্রোথিত করা, গোর দেওয়া ; সমাহিত করা ; কবরস্থ করা । **—ment,** *n.* Burial ; সমাধি-কার্য্য ।

ĕn-tŏm′-ic, *adj.* Relating to insects ; কীট-সম্বন্ধীয় ।

ĕn-tŏ-mŏl′-ŏ-ġȳ, *n.* The science that treats of insects ; কীটবিদ্যা, পতঙ্গবিদ্যা, কীটতত্ত্ব । **—gise,** *v. i.* To collect specimens to study or practise entomology ; কীটবিদ্যা-শিক্ষার উদ্দেশ্যে বা আলোচনার্থ বিভিন্ন প্রকারের কীটাদি সংগ্রহ করা । **—gist,** *n.* One well-versed in the science of entomology ; কীটতত্ত্বজ্ঞ, পতঙ্গ-বিদ্যা-বিশারদ । **—mo-log′-i-cal,** *adj.*

ĕn-tŏ-mŏph′-i-lous (-lŭs), *adj.* (*Bot.*) Pollinated by the agency of the insects ; (উদ্ভিদ্-বিদ্যা) পতঙ্গমেলক (সাঃ পঃ) ।

ĕnt-ŏp′-tic, *adj.* (*Physiol.*) Relating to objects situated within the eye ; আন্তশ্চাক্ষুষ (হিঃ কোঃ) । **Entoptic phenomenon**—আন্তশ্চাক্ষুষ দৃশ্য ।

entourage, (*F.*), *n.* Surroundings ; followers ; attendants ; পারিপার্শ্বিক ; অনুচর ; অনুযায়ী ।

en-tout-cas, (*F.*), *n.* Umbrella ; sunshade ; ছত্র ; আতপত্র ।

Entozoa.

ĕn-tŏ-zŏ′-ă, *n.* Animals that live inside other animals ; শরীরের অভ্যন্তরস্থ ক্রিমি, অন্তর্জীব ।

entra'cte, (*F.*), *n.* **1.** Interval between two acts of play ; অভিনয়ের অঙ্ক-দ্বয়ের মধ্যবর্ত্তী সময় । **2.** A music performed between two acts of a drama ; নাটকের অঙ্কদ্বয়ের মধ্যবর্ত্তী সময়ের বাদ্য ।

ĕn′-trails (-trāls), *n.* (*Pl.*) **1.** Bowels ; intestines ; অন্ত্র ; আঁতড়ী, নাড়িভুঁড়ী । **2.** (*Fig.*) The internal parts, as of the earth etc. : (লক্ষণায়) পৃথিব্যাদির অভ্যন্তর ভাগ ।

ĕn-train′ (-trān), *v. t.* & *i.* To put or go into a railway train as troops ; ট্রেনে চাপান, ট্রেনে যাওয়া, বাষ্পীয় শকটে স্থাপন করা, বাষ্পীয় শকটে গমন করা ।

ĕn-trăm′-mĕl, *v. t.* To trammel ; to entangle ; to hamper ; আটক করা ; জড়িত করা ; আবদ্ধ করা ।

ĕn′-trance (-trăns), *n.* **1.** Coming or going in ; আগম, প্রবেশ, প্রবেশন । **2.** A door or passage for entering ; প্রবেশ-পথ, প্রবেশদ্বার, প্রবেশিকা । **3.** Power or right to enter ; প্রবেশাধিকার । **4.** The commencement, (*obs.*) ; প্রারম্ভ (অপ্রঃ) । **5.** Appearance of an actor on a stage ; রঙ্গমঞ্চে প্রবেশ । **6.** Entrance-money or fee ; প্রবেশিকা, ভর্ত্তিফিস ।

ĕn-trance′ (-trăns), *v. t.* To put into a trance ; যোগ-নিদ্রাভিভূত করা, সম্মোহিত করা, মোহাবিষ্ট করা, সম্মোহন ক্রিয়াদ্বারা অচৈতন্য করা । **2.** To enrapture ; to overpower with any strong feeling, as delight etc. ; হর্ষাবিষ্ট করা, পরমানন্দিত করা ; চিত্ত অভিভূত করা । **—ment,** *n.*

ĕn-trăp′, *v. t.* **1.** To catch as in a trap ; to beguile ; to inveigle ; ফাঁদে ধরা, পাশবদ্ধ করা, জালবদ্ধ করা, কলে আটকান ; ভুলান ; প্রতারণা করা । **2.** To involve in difficulties or contradictions ; ঝঞ্ঝাটে ফেলা, বিজড়িত করা ।

ĕn-treat′ (-trēt), *v. t.* To solicit ; to ask earnestly ; to beseech ; to supplicate ; যাচ্ঞা করা, প্রার্থনা করা ; সনির্ব্বন্ধ অনুরোধ করা ; অনুনয় করা ; বিনীত প্রার্থনা করা । ***Verb i.*** To pray ; প্রার্থনা করা । **—ing,** *adj.* **—ing-ly,** *adv.* In an entreating manner ; সবিনয়ে, কাতরভাবে । **—y,** *n.* An earnest request ; সনির্ব্বন্ধ অনুরোধ, কাতর-প্রার্থনা, অনুনয়, বিনয় মিনতি, যাচ্ঞা, বিনতি ।

en-tree′ (äng-trā), *n.* **1.** Right or freedom of admission ; প্রবেশাধিকার বা অবাধপ্রবেশ । **2.** A made dish served in the interval of chief courses ; (in the French usage) a dish served at the beginning of dinner to increase appetite ; প্রধান প্রধান ব্যঞ্জনাদি বিতরণের মধ্যসময়ে প্রদত্ত উপচারাদি ; (ফরাসী রীত্যনুযায়ী) ভোজনের প্রারম্ভে প্রদত্ত রুচিকর উপচার (আচার) । **The right of private entree**—সম্ভ্রান্ত পুরুষের গৃহ-প্রবেশের বিশেষ অধিকার ।

entremets, (*F.*), *n.* Side-dishes ; মুখ-রোচক উপচার ।

ĕn-trĕnch′, in-, *v. t.* & *i.* To surround (army, position, etc.) with trenches, (*lit.* & *fig.*) ; পরিখাবেষ্টিত করা । ***Verb i.*** To encroach ; পরসম্পত্তিতে অধিকার বিস্তার করা । **—ment,** *n.* **To entrench upon**—To encroach upon ; অনধিকারে চাপিয়া পড়া ।

entre nous, (*F.*), *adv.* Between you and me ; তোমাতে আমাতে ।

entrepot, (*F.*), *n.* A store-house for depositing goods temporarily ; a commercial centre ; গুদাম, আমানতি গুদাম (হিঃ কোঃ) ; বাণিজ্য-কেন্দ্র, আড়ত, গঞ্জ ।

entre preneur, (*F.*), *n.* An organiser of amusements, esp. musical performances ; আমোদ-প্রমোদের ব্যবস্থাপক বা অনুষ্ঠাতা ।

entresol, (*F.*), *n.* A low story between the first and the ground floor ; একতল ও দ্বিতলের মধ্যবর্ত্তী অনুচ্চ তল ।

ĕn-trŏ-pi′-ŏn, *n.* (*Med.*) The turning inward against the eye-ball of the border of the eye-lids ; (ভৈষজ্য-শাস্ত্র) বীপর্য্যস্ত অক্ষিপুট (হঃ চঃ) ।

ĕn-trŭst′, in-, *v. t.* To trust ; to confide to the care of ; to confide (duty, person, thing or it safety) to a person; as, to *entrust* one with an object of care etc.: to *entrust* thing to a person; অর্পণ করা; ভারার্পণ করা, সঁপা; বিশ্বাসপূর্ব্বক কোন কিছুর ভার ন্যস্ত করা।

ĕn'-trў, *n.* 1. Act of entering; প্রবেশ, আগম, অন্তর্নিবেশ। 2. A passage leading into a courtyard; প্রাঙ্গণ-প্রবেশ-পথ, প্রবেশ-পথ, প্রবেশ-দ্বার, তোরণ। 3. A ceremonial entrance as of a king etc.; "Their solemn *entry* into the imperial city;" সমারোহের সহিত প্রবেশ। 4. Act of committing to writing; act of recording in a book; the thing written; an item; লিখন; খাতায় লিপিবদ্ধকরণ; লিখিত বস্তু; জায়; দফা। 5. (*Law*) Act of entering or taking possession of a property; সম্পত্তির অধিকার গ্রহণ, সম্পত্তিদখল। 6. A list of competitors for a race etc.: ঘোড় দৌড়ের প্রতিযোগিগণের তালিকা। 7. (*Comm.*) The exhibition or depositing of a ship's papers at the custom-house to procure license to land goods; (বাণিজ্য) মাল নামাইবার অনুমতির জন্য শুল্কাগারে জাহাজের কাগজপত্র প্রদর্শন বা গচ্ছিতকরণ। **Entry-money** — প্রবেশ-দক্ষিণা, ভর্ত্তিফিস। **Book-keeping by double entry** or **single entry**—সওদাগরী কার্য্যালয়ের জমাখরচের বহিতে কোন দফা বা বিষয় একবার (*single*) বা দুইবার (*double*) লিখনের পদ্ধতি।

ĕn-twīne', ĭn—, *v. t.* & *i.* 1. To interweave; to interlace; to wreathe; জড়িত করা বা হওয়া, পাকান বা প্যাকাইয়া যাওয়া, সংগ্রথিত করা বা হওয়া, মাল্যাকারে বেষ্টন করা, বলয়িত করা। 2. To embrace; বুকে জড়াইয়া ধরা। **—ment,** *n.*

ĕn-twist' —ĭn—, *v. t.* To twist or wreathe round; জড়িত করা, পাকান, মাল্যাকারে বেষ্টন করা, বলয়িত করা।

ē-nū'-clē-āte, *v. t.* To make clear; বিশদ করা, পরিষ্কার করা, স্পষ্ট করা।

ē-nū'-mĕr-āte, *v. t.* To count; to specify number; গণনা করা, সংখ্যা নির্দ্দেশ করা। **—a'-tion,** *n.* 1. Act of enumerating; সংখ্যান, পরিগণন, গণনা, হিসাব, গণতি, সংখ্যা-নির্দ্দেশ। 2. A detailed account in which each particular thing is mentioned; এক একটী করিয়া সমস্ত-বিষয়ের বিবৃতি। 3. (*Rhet.*) A recapitulation in the preroration; পুনরাবৃত্তি, সংক্ষেপে পুনরুক্তি। **—a-tive,** *adj.* **—a-tor,** *n.*

ē-nŭn'-ci-āte (-shĭ-), *v. t.* 1. To state definitely as a theory, proposition, etc.; to proclaim; to declare; স্পষ্ট বাক্যে নির্দ্দেশ করা; রটনা করা, রাষ্ট্র করা, ঘোষণা করা। 2. To utter; to pronounce; বলা; উচ্চারণ করা। **—a'-tion,** *n.* 1. Mode of pronunciation; উচ্চারণ-ভঙ্গী। 2. Statement; declaration; উক্তি, স্পষ্ট কথন; ঘোষণা। 3. The form of words in which a proposition is stated; প্রতিজ্ঞা-বাক্য। **—a-tive,** *adj.* **—a-tor,** *n.*

ĕn-ūre', *v. t.* See INURE.

ĕn-vĕl'-op (-ŭp), *v. t.* 1. To wrap up; to surround on all sides; আবৃত করা, আচ্ছাদিত করা, মোড়া, ঢাকিয়া ফেলা; অবগুণ্ঠিত করা, চতুর্দ্দিকে বেষ্টিত করা। 2. To cover so as to conceal; সংগোপন করা, লুক্কায়িত করা। **—ment,** *n.*

ĕn'-vĕl-ōpe, *n.* 1. Covering; a wrapper; (*lit.* & *fig.*); আচ্ছাদন, আবরণ; মোড়ক, আবেষ্টন। 2. The cover of a letter; খাম, পত্র-পুটক। 3. (*Astron.*) The nebulous covering of the head of a comet etc.; (জ্যোতির্বিজ্ঞান) ধূমকেতু-শীর্ষের নীহারিকা-ময় আবরণ। 4. (*Bot.*) The calyx or the corolla; (উদ্ভিদ্-বিদ্যা) পুষ্পের বহিরাবরণ বা অন্তরাবরণ।

ĕn-vĕn'-om (-ŭm), *v. t.* 1. To poison; to put poison into; as, to *envenom* a weapon etc.; বিষাক্ত করা, বিষদিগ্ধ করা, বিষলিপ্ত করা, বিষান্বিত করা; হলাহল সঞ্চার করা। 2. To taint with bitterness or malice; as, to *envenom* feelings, words, etc.; বিদ্বেষ কলুষিত করা। 3. To vitiate or corrupt as the mind; কলুষিত করা।

ĕn'-vĭ-ă-ble, *adj.* Calculated to excite envy; capable of awakening desire to possess; ঈর্ষণীয়, স্পৃহণীয়, বাঞ্ছনীয়, আকাঙ্ক্ষণীয়। **—bly,** *adv.*

ĕn'-vĭ-ous (-ŭs), *adj.* 1. Feeling or exhibiting envy, (with *of*); "My soul is *envious of* mine eye;" দ্বেষ-প্রদর্শক। 2. Full of envy; সমৎসর, দ্বেষী, ঈর্ষালু, ঈর্ষাপর। **—ly,** *adv.* **—ness,** *n.* The quality of being envious; পরশ্রীকাতরতা, ঈর্ষালুতা (বাৎস্যঃ)।

ĕn-vī'-rŏn, *v. t.* 1. To surround; to encircle; to be round about; to envelop; পরিবেষ্টিত করা; বলয়িত করা, চক্রাকারে পরিবেষ্টিত করা; ঘেরা; পরিবৃত করা। 2. To besiege; অবরোধ করা। 3. To be placed round as guards etc.; চতুর্দ্দিকে স্থাপিত হওয়া। **—rons,** *n. pl.* Neighbourhood; suburbs; চতুষ্পার্শ্ববর্ত্তী স্থানসমূহ, প্রান্তদেশ; নগরোপকণ্ঠ, সহরতলী। **—ment,** *n.* 1. Act of environing or state of being environed; বেষ্টন, বেষ্টিতাবস্থা। 2. A surrounding; surrounding conditions or circumstances; বেষ্টনী পারিপার্শ্বিক অবস্থা, প্রতিবেশ, পরিপার্শ্ব (অভিঃ), জন্মনিকেতন (প্রবাসী ১৩১৯ অবচার (ঐ), আবরণিক অবস্থা।

ĕn-vĭs'-āge, *v. t.* 1. To look in the face of; to confront; as, to *envisage* danger etc.; সাহসের সহিত কোন কিছুর সম্মুখীন হওয়া; সম্মুখীন হওয়া। 2. To apprehend directly or by intuition; to contemplate; অবধারণ করা, সহজ বুদ্ধিদ্বারা অবধারণ করা; ভাবা, অনুধ্যান করা। **—ment,** *n.*

ĕn'-vŏy, *n.* A messenger; a king's messenger; a representative; a royal plenipotentiary rankin[g]

সূক্ষ্ম নাড়ী বা নালী বিশেষ, কৈশিক নালী (সাঃ পঃ)। **2.** One of the smallest vessels connecting the arteries and veins ; ধমনী এবং শিরাসংযোজক অতি ক্ষুদ্রতম নাড়ী বিশেষ, শরীরের অভ্যন্তরস্থ কেশের ন্যায় সূক্ষ্ম সূক্ষ্ম নাড়ী, কৈশিকা (হঃ চঃ)। **—lar′-i-ty,** *n.* **Capillary attraction, Capillary repulsion**—কৈশিক নালীতে তরল পদার্থের উত্থান পতন, কৈশিকাকর্ষণ (সাঃ পঃ), কেশাকর্ষণ (হিঃ কোঃ), কেশনিরাকরণ (হিঃ কোঃ), কৈশিক বিপ্রকর্ষণ।

căp′-i-tăl, *n.* (*Arch.*) The head or upper portion of a column ; স্তম্ভের শীর্ষ বা উর্দ্ধ ভাগ, বোধিকা (রাঃ রাঃ)।

căp′-i-tăl, *adj.* & *n.* **1.** Relating to the head ; মস্তক-সম্বন্ধীয়। **2.** Involving loss of life ; punishable by death ; as, *capital* sentence ; প্রাণহানিঘটিত ; বধদণ্ডার্হ, বধদণ্ডযোগ্য, প্রাণদণ্ডার্হ। **3.** Vitally injurious ; fatal ; as, *capital* error ; সাংঘাতিক ; মারাত্মক। **3.** First in importance ; chief ; as, a *capital* article in religion ; metropolitan ; as, a *capital* town or city ; মুখ্য ; প্রধান ; রাজধানীস্বরূপ। **5.** (*Colloq.*) Excellent ; first class ; as, *capital* singer or player ; (কথিতভাষায়) চমৎকার ; সবার সেরা। **6.** Original ; principal ; as, *capital* stock or fund ; মূলস্বরূপ, পুঁজিস্বরূপ ; আসল। ***Noun.*** **1.** The seat of governmet ; the head city of any country ; রাজধানী ; কোন দেশের সর্ব্বশ্রেষ্ঠ নগর। **2.** Money or wealth employed in trade, manufactures, etc. ; মূলধন, পুঁজি, ধনমূল (অঃ), ধন (যাজ্ঞঃ), আসল, পরিপণ, নীবী (অমরঃ)। **3.** (*Fig.*) Means of influence or of increasing one's power ; as, to make a *capital* out of something ; প্রভাব বা ক্ষমতা বৃদ্ধির উপায়। **4.** Capital letters

সৌর ও চান্দ্র মাস বা বৎসরের প্রভেদ। সৌরচান্দ্রান্তর (annual), সৌরচান্দ্রমাসান্তর (monthly)।

ĕp-ă-gö′-gē, *n.* (*Log.*) Argument in which universal propositions are proved by particulars ; এক প্রকার ন্যায়,—যাহাতে ব্যাপ্তিপ্রতিজ্ঞা ব্যাপ্যপ্রতিজ্ঞা দ্বারা প্রমাণিত করা হয়, আগমনামূলক ন্যায় (হিঃ কোঃ)।

ĕp-ăn′-ă-phör-ă, *n.* (ফলিতজ্যোতিষ) পণফর (সাঃ পঃ)।

ĕp′-ârch, *n.* The ruler or bishop of an eparchy in modern Greece ; বর্ত্তমান গ্রীস্‌দেশের বিভাগীয় শাসনকর্ত্তা বা ধর্ম্মাধ্যক্ষ। **—y,** *n.* **1.** A subdivision of the modern Greece ; বর্ত্তমান গ্রীসরাজ্যের বিভাগ বিশেষ। **2.** A diocese of the Greek Church in Russia ; রুষদেশে খৃষ্টীয় ধর্ম্মসংঘের গ্রীকশাখার অধীন ধর্ম্মাধ্যক্ষের অধিকারভুক্ত স্থান।

ĕp′-au-lĕt (-ä-), **—lette** (-lĕt), *n.* **1.** (*Mil.*) An ornamental shoulder-piece on the uniforms of military officers ; সৈনিকপুরুষদের পরিচ্ছদের স্কন্ধ-ভূষা। **2.** An ornament on the shoulder of woman's dress ; মহিলাদের পরিচ্ছদের স্কন্ধাভরণ। **To win one's epaulets**—(Of a private soldier) To be promoted to the rank of an officer ; (সাধারণ সৈন্যদের পক্ষে) সৈনিক-কর্ম্মচারীর পদে উন্নীত হওয়া।

ē-pergne′ (-pārn), *n.* An ornamental stand for a large dish etc. (usually in a branched form) placed on the centre of the dinner table; ভোজনাগারের মেজে বৃহৎ পাত্রাদি রাখার জন্য কারুকার্যশোভিত বৈঠক।

ĕp-ĕx-ĕ-gē′-sis, *n.* A word or words added to make the meaning clear ; addition of words to make the meaning clear ; অর্থ বিশদীকরণার্থ সংযোজিত শব্দ বা শব্দসমূহ ; অর্থ বিশদীকরণার্থ শব্দ-সংযোজন। **—get′-ic, —get′-i-cal,** *adjs.* **—get′-i-cal-ly,** *adv.*

ē-phebe′ (-fēb), *n.* A citizen aged from 18 to 20 ; (গ্রীসদেশীয় পুরাতত্ত্ব) ১৮ হইতে ২০ বৎসর বয়সের নাগরিক।

ē-phĕm′-ĕ-ră, *n.* **1.** A fly that lives for one day only ; দিবসজীবী পতঙ্গ, দিনায়ুঃ পতঙ্গ। **2.** A short-lived creature ; ক্ষণস্থায়ী জীব, অল্পায়ুঃ জীব। **—er-al,** *adj.* & *n.* **1.** Existing for a day ; lasting for a day or a few days, as a kind of insects, flowers, etc. ; দিনমাত্রস্থায়ী ; একাহজীবী, দিনায়ুঃ। **2.** Short-lived ; fleeting ; ক্ষণজীবী ; ক্ষণিক, অস্থায়ী, ক্ষণস্থায়ী, উৎপন্নবিনাশী, অল্পায়ুঃ, ক্ষণভঙ্গুর, ক্ষণবিধ্বংসী। (*Noun*) Anything lasting but a day, esp. an ephemeral animal or plant ; একদীবসজীবী প্রাণী বা উদ্ভিদ্‌। **—er-al′-i-ty,** *n.* Transitoriness ; ক্ষণস্থায়িত্ব, ক্ষণভঙ্গুরতা। **—ron,** *n.* Singular of EPHEMERA.

ē-phĕm′-ĕ-ris, *n.* (*pl.* -RIDES) **1.** (*Obs.*) A diary ; (অপ্রচলিত) রোজনামচা। **2.** Astronomical almanac ; (*astron.*) a table showing the daily positions of a planet etc. during a given period; পঞ্জিকা ; গ্রহস্থিতি-পত্র। **3.** An account of daily transactions ; দৈনিক-হিসাব। **4.** Periodical literature ; মাসিক ও সাপ্তাহিক পত্রিকাদি, ক্ষণিক সাহিত্য।

ĕph′-ŏd, *n.* A linen surplice worn by the Jewish priests ; ইয়ুদী পুরোহিতগণের আলখাল্লা বিশেষ।

ĕph′-ŏr, *n.* One of the magistrates of ancient Sparta ; প্রাচীন স্পার্টাদেশীয় শাসনকর্তৃগণের অন্যতম।

ĕp′-ic, *adj.* & *n.* **1.** Pertaining to a great poem composed in a lofty style ; heroic ; narrated in a grand style ; মহাকাব্যসম্বন্ধীয় ; বীররসাত্মক ; গুরুগম্ভীর ভাষায় বর্ণিত। **2.** Lofty ; grand ; উন্নত ; গুরুগম্ভীর। ***Noun.*** A narrative poem written in elevated style deserving the glorious achievements of heroes ; মহাকাব্য। **—i-cal,** *adj.* **—i-cal-ly,** *adv.* **Epic dialect**—যে প্রকার গ্রীক

ভাষায় ইলিয়দ, ওডেসী, প্রভৃতি মহাকাব্য লিখিত হইয়াছিল। **National epic**—জাতীয় মহাকাব্য (যথা রামায়ণ)।

ĕp'-i-căl-ȳx, *n.* (*Bot.*) An external or accessory calyx outside of the true calyx ; উপচ্ছদ (সাঃ পঃ), উপকুণ্ড (ঐ)।

ĕp-i-cē'-di-ŭm, *n.* A funeral song or ode ; শোকগীতি, শ্মশান-সঙ্গীত।

Epicarpus orientalis—সেওরা (বেলঃ)।

ĕp'-i-cene (-sēn), *adj.* & *n.* 1. (*Latin* & *Greek Gram.*) Of either gender; উভলিঙ্গক। 2. Worn or used by both sexes ; as, *epicene* linen ; স্ত্রীপুরুষ উভয়ের পরিধেয়। 3. Having characteristics of both sexes ; effeminate ; পুংস্ত্রীলক্ষণাত্মক, হিজড়া ; স্ত্রীজনসুলভ। ***Noun.*** A person having characteristics of both sexes ; পুংস্ত্রীলক্ষণ-বিশিষ্ট ব্যক্তি।

ĕp'-i-cĕn-trŭm, -tre (-tĕr), *n.* The point at which earthquake breaks out ; ভূমিকম্পের কেন্দ্রের অব্যবহিত উপরিস্থ পৃথিবী-পৃষ্ঠ।

ĕp-i-chī-rē'-mī, *n.* (*Log.* & *Rhet.*) A syllogism in which the proof of a major or minor premise, or both, is introduced with the premises themselves and the conclusion is drawn in the usual way ; সহেতুকাবয়বানুমান।

Ep'-i-cūre (-ĕp), *n.* 1. (*Obs.*) A disciple of Epicurus, a Greek philosopher, according to whom sensual pleasures are the *summum bonum* of human life ; গ্রীক দার্শনিক এপিকিউরিসের শিষ্য। [তাঁহার মত অনেকটা আমাদের দেশের চার্ব্বাকের মতের অনুরূপ ; Eat, drink and be merry : Do not care for tomorrow ; খাও দাও আমোদ কর, কল্যকার ভাবনা করিও না ; চার্ব্বাকের মতে "যাবজ্জীবেৎ সুখং জীবেৎ, ঋণং কৃত্বা ঘৃতং পিবেৎ"।] 2. (*Rare*) Voluptuary ; sensualist ; ভোগ-বিলাসী ব্যক্তি ; ইন্দ্রিয়পরতন্ত্র ব্যক্তি। 3. (*L. C.*) One who indulges in the luxuries of the table ; ঔদরিক, ভোজনবিলাসী। **-cu-rise,** *v. i.* (*Obs.*) 1. To profess the doctrine of Epicurus ; এপিকিউরাসের মতাবলম্বী হওয়া। 2. To play the part of an epicure ; ইন্দ্রিয়জ সুখ বা ভোগ-বিলাসে প্রমত্ত হওয়া। **-cu-rism,** *n.* 1. (*Obs.*) The doctrine of Epicurus ; এপিকিউরাসের মত, লোকায়তবাদ। 2. Luxury in the table ; the habit and taste of an epicure ; ভোজন-বিলাস ; ভোগ-বিলাস।

ĕp-i-cū-rē'-ăn, *adj.* & *n.* 1. Pertaining to Epicurus or following Epicurus ; এপিকিউরাস-সম্বন্ধীয়, এপিকিউরাসের মতাবলম্বী। 2. Given to pleasure, esp. refined sensual enjoyment ; ভোগপরায়ণ, ইন্দ্রিয়পরতন্ত্র। ***Noun.*** 1. A follower or disciple of Epicurus ; গ্রীকদার্শনিক এপিকিউরাসের শিষ্য। 2. One who makes pleasure ; ভোগবিলাসপরায়ণ ব্যক্তি। **-ism,** *n.* The doctrines of Epicurus ; attachment to his doctrine : এপিকিউরাসের মতবাদ, লোকায়তবাদ ; তন্মতানুবর্ত্তিতা।

ĕp'-i-cȳ-cle (-cl), *n.* (*Geom.* & *Astron.*) A small circle whose centre revolves round the circumference of a greater circle ; (জ্যামিতি ও জ্যোতির্বিজ্ঞান) যে ঘূর্ণায়মান ক্ষুদ্র বৃত্তের কেন্দ্র বৃহত্তর বৃত্তের চতুর্দ্দিকে আবর্ত্তিত হয়, অপচক্র (হিঃ কোঃ), নীচোচ্চবৃত্ত (সুঃ সিঃ), পরিবৃত্ত (ঐ)। **-cyc'-lic,** *adj.* **-cy'-cloid,** *n.* (*Geom.*) A curve traced by a point of a circle that rolls on the outside of a fixed circle ; (জ্যামিতি) স্থিরবৃত্তের বহির্ভাগে ঘূর্ণায়মান বৃত্ত-বিন্দু দ্বারা অঙ্কিত বক্ররেখা, উপজনি, পশ্চাজ্জনি, উপচক্রালদ (হিঃ কোঃ) নীচোচ্চ বৃত্ত, উপনীচোচ্চ বৃত্ত (ঐ)। **-cy'-cloi-dal,** *adj.*

ĕp-i-deic'-tic (-dīk-), *adj.* Meant for display ; প্রদর্শনীয়।

ep-i-dĕm'-ic, -i-cal, *adj.* & *n.* (*Med.*) Prevalent among the whole country at a particular time ; as, an *epidemic* disease ; ব্যাপক, দেশব্যাপী। ***Noun.*** **(-ic),** A disease which prevails among a community, at the same period ; মারী, মহামারী, মড়ক, ব্যাপক রোগ। **-i-cal-ly,** *adv.* **-de-mi-ol'-o-gy,** *n.* The science treating epidemics ; মহামারী চিকিৎসা-বিজ্ঞান।

ĕp-i-dêr'-mis, *n.* 1. The outer layer of the skin of animals ; উপত্বক্, বহিস্তক্, বাহ্যত্বক্, বহিশ্চর্ম্ম, দেহের উপরের সূক্ষ্মত্বক, যে পর্দ্দা ত্বকের উপরিভাগ আবৃত করিয়া রাখে। 2. (*Bot.*) The outermost coating of the leaves or stem of a plant, পত্রাদির সর্ব্বোপরিস্থ আবরণ (পর্দ্দা), অধিত্বক (সাঃ পঃ)। **-mal, -mic. -moid, -moi-dal,** *adjs.*

ĕp'-i-dōte, *n.* A silicate of aluminium, iron and calcium ; ভল্লাতক।

ĕp-i-găs'-tric, *adj.* Pertaining to the upper regions of the abdomen ; উদরের ঊর্দ্ধভাগ সম্বন্ধীয়। **-gas'-tri-um,** *n.* The upper region of the abdomen ; উদরের সম্মুখ ও ঊর্দ্ধভাগ, উদরোর্দ্ধ প্রদেশ। **Epigastric plexus**—মণিপুর (বামনদাস বসু)।

ĕp'-i-gene (-jēn), *adj.* 1. (*Geol.*) Formed on the surface of the earth ; (ভূ-বিদ্যা) ভূ-পৃষ্ঠে গঠিত। 2. Not natural to a substance ; কোন পদার্থের পক্ষে অস্বাভাবিক।

ĕp-i-gĕn'-ĕ-sis, *n.* Formation of organic germ as a new product ; the doctrine of generation holding that the germ is created entirely new, not merely expanded and unfolded by the procreative power, (also called *theory of epigenesis*) ; জীবাণুসমূহের নূতন পদার্থরূপে উৎপত্তি ; প্রজনন-সম্বন্ধীয় মতবাদবিশেষ, — এই বাদানুসারে জীবাণু নূতনভাবে উৎপাদি

হয়, প্রজনন-শক্তিদ্বারা কেবলমাত্র বিস্তার ও বিকাশ প্রাপ্ত হইয়া থাকে না।

ĕp-i-glŏt'-tis, *n.* The cartilage plate at the root of the tongue; উপজিহ্বা, অলিজিহ্বা, আলজিভ্।

ĕp'-i-grăm, *n.* **1.** A short keenly satirical poem; তীব্র শ্লেষাত্মক ক্ষুদ্র কবিতা। **2.** A pointed or antithetical saying; a witty thought sharply expressed; অল্পাক্ষর গ্রথিত সরস বাক্য বা কবিতা; বিদগ্ধমুখমণ্ডন। **—mat'-ic, —mat'-i-cal,** *adjs.* **1.** Pertaining to an epigram; তাদৃশ কবিতা সম্পর্কীয়। **2.** Pointed; piquant; concise and pointed; তীক্ষ্ণ; তেজাল, উগ্র; তীক্ষ্ণ অথচ সংক্ষিপ্ত, মর্ম্মভেদী। **—mat-i-cal-ly,** *adv.* **—ma-tise,** *v. t.* & *i.* To represent or express by epigrams; তীব্র সংক্ষিপ্ত কবিতাদ্বারা ব্যক্ত করা। (*Verb i.*) To write epigrams; তীব্র সংক্ষিপ্ত কবিতা লিখা। **—ma-tist,** *n.* One who writes epigrams or deals in them; সরস ক্ষুদ্র কবিতা-লেখক।

ĕp'-i-grȧph, *n.* **1.** An inscription on coin, stone, statue or metal plate; শিলা, মুদ্রা, মূর্ত্তি অথবা ধাতুফলকাদিতে উৎকীর্ণ লিপি, উৎকীর্ণ লিপি। **2.** A motto or quotation placed at the beginning of a book or one of its chapter; গ্রন্থারম্ভে অথবা পরিচ্ছদের উপরে উদ্ধৃত কবিতা বা প্রবচন। **—graph'-ic, —graph'-i-cal,** *adjs.*

ē-pig'-ră-phist, *n.* A student of, or one well versed in, epigraphy; উৎকীর্ণ লিপিচর্চ্চানিরত বা উৎকীর্ণলিপিপাঠকুশল ব্যক্তি। **—phy,** *n.* The science of inscriptions; inscriptions collectively; উৎকীর্ণলিপিবিদ্যা; উৎকীর্ণ-লিপিমালা। ***Epigraphica Indica***—ভারতীয় উৎকীর্ণ লিপিমালা।

ĕp'-i-lĕp-sȳ, *n.* A disease of the brain which causes the sufferer to fall to the ground unconscious; মৃগীরোগ, সন্ন্যাস রোগ, অপস্মার। **—lep'-tic,** *adj.* & *n.* Pertaining to epilepsy; affected with epilepsy; মৃগীরোগ সংক্রান্ত; মৃগীরোগগ্রস্ত, অপস্মার রোগগ্রস্ত। (*Noun*) **1.** One affected with epilepsy; অপস্মার রোগগ্রস্ত ব্যক্তি। **2.** A medicine for epilepsy; মৃগীরোগের ঔষধ।

ĕp-il'-ŏ-gist, *n.* The writer or speaker of an epilogue; কাব্যাদির উপসংহার-শ্লোক লেখক।

ĕp'-i-logue (-lŏg), *n.* **1.** A speech or short poem at the end of a play; নাটকের উপসংহার কবিতা বা বক্তৃতা, ভরতবাক্য, উপসংহার শ্লোক, শেষবন্ধ, অন্ত্যমঙ্গল (কেণ্ডিঃ)। **2.** The conclusion of a book; উপসংহার। **—log'-ic, —log'-i-cal,** *adjs.*

ē-piph'-ȧ-nȳ, *n.* **1.** Appearance or manifestation of Christ to the Magi; (পূর্ব্বদেশীয় জ্ঞানিগণের নিকট) খৃষ্টের আবির্ভাব, অবতার, প্রকাশ। **2.** A church festival celebrated on the 6th of January to commemorate the manifestation of the new-born Christ to the wise men of the East; খৃষ্টীয় পর্ব্ব বিশেষ (৬ই জানুয়ারী), অবতরণোৎসব। **3.** Manifestation of a superhuman being; দেব, গন্ধর্ব্ব বা দেবদূতাদির আবির্ভাব।

ĕp'-i-phȳte, *n.* **1.** A plant growing on another but not fed by the latter; পরবৃক্ষাশ্রয়ী বৃক্ষ, পরবৃক্ষী (সাঃ পঃ)। **2.** (*Med.*) A vegetable parasite on the body; (ভৈষজ্য শাস্ত্র) দেহের উপরে জাত পরগাছা বিশেষ। **—phy'-tal,** *adj.*

ē-pis'-cŏ-pă-cȳ, *n.* **1.** The government of the church by the bishops; খৃষ্টীয় ধর্ম্মাধ্যক্ষ দ্বারা ধর্ম্মসংঘ-শাসন, ধর্ম্মাধ্যক্ষ-শাসন-তন্ত্র। **2.** The collective body of bishops; ধর্ম্মাধ্যক্ষ-সংঘ। **—pal,** *adj.* **1.** Pertaining to bishops; governed by bishops; vested in bishops; ধর্ম্মাধ্যক্ষ সম্পর্কীয়; ধর্ম্মাধ্যক্ষ শাসিত; ধর্ম্মাধ্যক্ষের হস্তেন্যস্ত। **2.** Relating to Protestant episcopal church; ধর্ম্মাধ্যক্ষশাসিত ধর্ম্মসংঘ সম্বন্ধীয়। **—pa'-li-an,** *adj.* & *n.* Relating to episcopacy; ধর্ম্মাধ্যক্ষ-শাসিত, ধর্ম্মসংঘ সংক্রান্ত। (*Noun*) One who belongs to an episcopal church; ধর্ম্মাধ্যক্ষ-শাসিত ধর্ম্ম-সংঘ-ভুক্ত ব্যক্তি। **2.** One who adheres to episcopacy; ধর্ম্মাধ্যক্ষশাসিত ধর্ম্মসংঘানুরাগী। **—pa'-li-an-ism, —pal-ism,** *ns.* **—pate,** *n.* **1.** The dignity or office of a bishop; ধর্ম্মাধ্যক্ষের পদ। **2.** The whole body of bishops; ধর্ম্মাধ্যক্ষ-সমাজ। **3.** The term of office of a bishop; ধর্ম্মাধ্যক্ষের পদের স্থিতিকাল।

ĕp'-i-sōde, *n.* **1.** (*Gr. drama.*) The part of a tragedy between two choric songs; (গ্রীকনাট্য শাস্ত্র) বৃন্দ-সংগীতদ্বয়ের মধ্যবর্ত্তী বিয়োগান্ত নাটকের অংশ, পতাকা (দশরূঃ), প্রকরী (ঐ), প্রকরিকা (ঐ)। **2.** An incidental narrative; মূলবিষয়ের অন্তর্গত প্রাসঙ্গিক বর্ণনা, উপাখ্যান, অবান্তর কথা, প্রাসঙ্গিক কাহিনী। **3.** An interesting incident in a series of events; কৌতুকাবহ ঘটনা, আমোদপ্রদ ঘটনা, ঘটনাপরম্পরার অন্তর্গত কোন বিশেষ ঘটনা। **—so'-dal, —so'-di-al, —sod'-ic, —sod'-i-cal,** *adjs.* Pertaining to, or contained in, an episode; প্রাসঙ্গিক, উপাখ্যানঘটিত বা তদন্তর্ভুক্ত। **—sod'-i-cal-ly,** *adv.* By way of episode; প্রসঙ্গক্রমে, বর্ণনাপ্রসঙ্গে।

ĕp-i-spăs'-tic, *adj.* & *n.* (*Med.*) Causing a blister; ফোস্কাকারক, শোফকর (ঠাকুর)। ***Noun.*** A blister; a blistering agent; ফোস্কা; ফোস্কা উৎপাদক ঔষধ।

ĕp'-i-spêrm, *n.* (*Bot.*) The outer integument of a seed; বহির্বীজাবরণ (সাঃ পঃ)।

ĕp'-i-stă-sis, *n.* Suppression of secretion or excretion; মূত্রাবরোধ, আনাহ, কুষ্ঠবদ্ধরোগ।

ĕp-i-stăx′-is, *n.* Bleeding from the nose ; নাসারন্ধ্র হইতে রক্তস্রাব।

ē-pis-tē-mŏl′-ō-gў, *n.* The theory or science of the method or grounds of knowledge ; জ্ঞানবিদ্যা (হিঃ কোঃ), জ্ঞানশাস্ত্র (ঐ)।

ē-pis′-tle (-l), *n.* **1.** A letter ; লেখ্য, পত্র, লিপি। **2.** A letter of an apostle in the New Testament ; as, the *epistles* of St. Paul ; নিউ টেষ্টামেণ্ট গ্রন্থান্তর্গত যীশুখৃষ্টের শিষ্যগণের লিপি। **3.** A selection from the epistles of the apostles read in the communion service ; উপাসনাকালে পঠিত খৃষ্ট শিষ্যগণের পত্রাবলীর অংশবিশেষ। **4.** A literary or poetical work composed in the form of a letter ; পত্রাকারে রচিত পদ্য বা পদ্য গ্রন্থ। **—tler,** *n.* **1.** One who reads from the epistles in church service ; গির্জ্জায় উপাসনাকালে যিনি খৃষ্ট শিষ্যগণের পত্রাবলী হইতে স্থান বিশেষ পাঠ করেন। **2.** A writer of epistles ; পত্রলেখক। **—to-la-ry,** *adj.* Pertaining to, or carried on, by a letter ; suitable to correspondences ; as, *epistolary* style ; পত্রীয়, পত্রসম্বন্ধীয়, পত্রবিষয়ক, পত্রবাহিত; পত্রোপযোগী।

ē-pis′-trŏ-phē, *n.* (*Rhet.*) A figure of speech in which each sentence or clause ends with the same word ; (অলঙ্কারশাস্ত্র) একপ্রকার শব্দালঙ্কার—যাহাতে প্রত্যেক বাক্য বা বাক্যাংশের শেষে একই শব্দ থাকে, (যথা—Are they Hebrew—so am I, are they Israelites—so am I.)

ĕp-i-stўle, *n.* (*Arch.*) Architrave ; (স্থপতি-বিজ্ঞান) অধঃপ্রস্তার।

ĕp′-i-tăph, *n.* An inscription on a tomb etc. in honour of the dead ; মৃত ব্যক্তির সমাধি বা স্মৃতিস্তম্ভের গাত্রে খোদিত লিপি, চৈত্য-লিপি, স্তম্ভ লিপি, সমাধি-লিপি। **—ist,** *n.* **—taph′-ic,** *adj.*

ĕp-i-thă-lā′-mi-ŭm, *n.* (*Pl. -miums, -mi-a*) A nuptial poem or song ; বিবাহ সঙ্গীত, উদ্বাহ-গীতি, বিবাহের প্রীতি-উপহার কবিতা। **—mi-al, —lam′-ic,** *adjs.*

ĕp-i-thē′-li-ŭm, *n.* **1.** The tissue forming the outer layer of the mucous membrane etc. ; স্তনাগ্র, ওষ্ঠ এবং শ্লৈষ্মিক ও স্নৈহিক ঝিল্লীর উপরিস্থ পাতলা ত্বক বা আচ্ছাদন, উপচর্ম্ম (হঃ চঃ)। **—al,** *adj.*

ĕp′-i-thĕt, *n.* **1.** An adjective expressing some quality of a person or a thing, কোন ব্যক্তি বা বস্তুর গুণ, ধর্ম্ম বা লক্ষণ জ্ঞাপক বিশেষণ, গুণবাচক শব্দ, গুণনাম। **2.** A significant name or title ; অর্থযুক্ত (অন্বর্থ) নাম, আখ্যা বা উপাধি। **—thet′-ic, —thet′-i-cal,** *adjs.* **—thet′-i-cal-ly,** *adv.*

ē-pit′-ō-me (-mi), *n.* **1.** A short summary ; সারমর্ম্ম, সারসংগ্রহ, সংক্ষিপ্তসার, সার, চুম্বক। **2.** A condensed representation of anything ; as, the man is the world's *epitome* ; সংক্ষিপ্ত প্রতিরূপ। **—mize,** *v. t.* To make an epitome of ; to summarize ; সংক্ষেপ করা, সারসংগ্রহ করা ; মর্ম্মসংগ্রহ করা, সারোদ্ধার করা। **—mist,** *n.* One who makes an epitome ; সারসংগ্রহকার।

ep′-ŏ<u>ch</u> (ĕp- or ēp-), *n.* **1.** The beginning of a new era or distinctive period in history, life, science, etc. ; as, an *epoch*-making event ; যুগারম্ভ, যুগ, কল্প। **2.** A period of time marked by important events ; বিশেষ বিশেষ ঘটনাদ্বারা প্রসিদ্ধ ঐতিহাসিক কাল, অব্দপ্রবর্ত্তক কাল। **3.** A fixed time ; a date ; "The precise *epoch* on which they were to be executed ;" নির্দ্দিষ্টকাল ; তারিখ। **4.** (*Astron.*) The longitude of a planet at any given time ; (জ্যোতিবিজ্ঞান) অবধি (বাপুদেব শাস্ত্রী), দ্যুগণ (সাঃ পঃ), অহর্গণ (ঐ)। **—o-chal,** *adj.* **Epoch-making** — নবযুগপ্রবর্ত্তক, অব্দারম্ভক, নবযুগারম্ভসূচক, যুগান্তকর। **To make or mark an epoch**—To begin a new era ; নবযুগ প্রবর্ত্তিত করা বা হওয়া।

ĕp′-ōde, *n.* **1.** A kind of lyric poem ; একপ্রকার গীতি-কবিতা। **2.** The third part of a lyric ode ; গাথা-কবিতার তৃতীয় বা শেষ অংশ।

ĕp′-ō-nŷm(e), *n.* **1.** A name of a place or people derived from that of a person ; কোন ব্যক্তির নাম হইতে গৃহীত স্থান বা জাতির নাম। **2.** A real or mythical person giving his name to a country, people, &c. ; যে প্রকৃত বা পৌরাণিক ব্যক্তি জাতি বা দেশবিশেষের নামের আদি কারণ বলিয়া কল্পিত হইয়া থাকে। (যথা—Europa হইতে Europe, Romulus হইতে Rome, চন্দ্র is the eponym, of চন্দ্রবংশ।) **—nym′-ic, E pon′-y-mous,** *adjs.*

ĕp′-ō-pœ (-pē), *n.* An epic poem ; the subject of an epic poem ; মহাকাব্য ; মহাকাব্যের বর্ণনীয় বিষয়।

ĕp′-ŏs, *n.* An epic poem ; মহাকাব্য।

Ep′-som-īte, Ep′-som-sălt (ĕp-sŭm-), *ns.* Magnesium sulphate (from Epsom, a town in Surrey) ; বিরেচক ঔষধ বিশেষ।

ĕp′-ŭ-lăt-ing, *adj.* Cicatrizing ; পর্পটীকর।

ē-quā′-ble (-bl), *adj.* **1.** Uniform ; সমান, সমভাবাপন্ন, সদা একই রূপ, সমতাবিশিষ্ট। **2.** Free from extremes of heat and cold, as a climate ; tranquil ; as, an *equable* temper ; নাতিশীতোষ্ণ ; প্রশান্ত, ধীর, গম্ভীর, নির্ব্বিকার, সমবৃত্তি। **—bil-i-ty, —ness,** *ns.* The quality or state of being equable ; সমতা, সাম্য, সমরূপতা, শান্তভাব। **—bly,** *adv.* In an equable manner ; প্রশান্তভাবে, সমভাবে।

ē′-quăl, *adj., n. & v. t.* **1.** Identical in weight, extent, degree, number, rank, magnitude, measure, value, etc. ; তুল্য, সদৃশ,

সমতুল, সমান, সমসংখ্যক, সমকক্ষ, সমযোগ্য, অনুরূপ, সমায়তন, সমমূল্য। 2. Adequate; "Commendations *equal* to your merit;" having competent power or abilities; as, to be *equal* to the task; ঠিক, যথোচিত, যথানুরূপ, সমভাবাপন্ন, অপরিবর্ত্তনীয়, সমুচিত; কার্য্যানুরূপ শক্তিসম্পন্ন। 3. Uniform; "The English govern India with *equal* laws (uniform in operation); একরূপ, সমতাসম্পন্ন, সমঞ্জস। 4. Just; impartial; equitable; as, I do not regard him an *equal* (unbiassed) judge; ন্যায়পর; নিরপেক্ষ, সমদর্শী; ন্যায়পরায়ণ। 5. Evenly balanced or proportioned; as this is an *equal* fight; সমতুলিত, সমকক্ষ, সমানুপাতসম্পন্ন। ***Noun.*** 1. A person equal to another in rank, power, position, etc.; as, mix with your *equals*; সমযোগ্য ব্যক্তি, সমকক্ষ ব্যক্তি। 2. (*Pl.*) Equal things; as, if *equals* be added to *equals*; সমান বস্তুসকল। ***Verb t.*** 1. To make equal, (*archaic*); সমান করা (অপ্রঃ)। 2. To be or become equal to; সমান হওয়া, সমতুল্য হওয়া, সদৃশ হওয়া, সমকক্ষ হওয়া, সমযোগ্য হওয়া, সমুচিত হওয়া। **–i-za'-tion,** *n.* The act of making equal or the state of being equalized; সমীকরণ, সদৃশীকরণ, সমতাপ্রাপ্তি, সমতাসম্পন্নতা। **–ize,** *v. t.* To make equal; (with *to* or *with*); সমান করা। **–ly,** *adv.* In an equal manner; justly; in equal shares; uniformly; তুল্যরূপে, সমভাবে; ন্যায়সঙ্গতরূপে; সমাংশে; সমরূপে। **–qual'-i-ty,** *n.* The state or quality of being equal; sameness; সাম্য, সমভাব সাম্যাবস্থা, সমতা, সমানতা, তুল্যতা; অভিন্নতা। **Equal to the occasion**—Having strength, courage and fitness for an emergency; কার্য্যোচিত ক্ষমতা বা যোগ্যতাসম্পন্ন, সমুচিত-শক্তিসম্পন্ন। **To be on an equality with**—To be on equal terms with; সমাবস্থ হওয়া।

ē-quă-nim'-i-tȳ, *n.* Calmness of mind; steadiness of temper; মানসিক স্থৈর্য্য, ধৃতি, প্রশান্তচিত্ততা, নির্ব্বিকার ভাব, শান্তভাব; সমবৃত্তিতা, সমভাব, সমচিত্ততা, ধীরতা।

ē-quāte', *v. t.* 1. To make equal; to represent as equivalent; সমান করা; তুল্য বলিয়া প্রদর্শন করা। 2. To reduce to mean time or motion; as, *equated* distances; মধ্যবর্ত্তী সময় বা গতিতে পরিণত করা।

ē-quā'-tion, *n.* 1. The act of making equal; as, the *equation* of demand and supply; সমীকরণ, তুলীকরণ। 2. (*Alg.*) A statement or expression affirming the equality of two algebraic or other quantities; (বীজগণিত) সমীকরণ। 3. (*Astron.*) The quantity to be added to or subtracted from the mean position of a heavenly body to obtain the true position; (জ্যোতির্বিজ্ঞান) কোন জ্যোতিষ্কের প্রকৃত অবস্থান নির্দ্ধারণের জন্য ইহার মধ্য অবস্থানে যে সংখ্যা যোগ বা উক্ত স্থান হইতে যে সংখ্যা বিয়োগ করিতে হয়, গ্রহসমীকরণ (হিঃ কোঃ)। **–al,** *adj.* **–al-ly,** *adv.* **Binomial equation**—দ্বিপদসমীকরণ (হিঃ কোঃ)। **Biquadratic equation** — চতুর্ঘাত সমীকরণ (হিঃ কোঃ)। **Cubic equation**—ঘনসমীকরণ (হিঃ কোঃ)। **Differential equation** — চলন সমীকরণ (হিঃ কোঃ)। **Elliptic equation**—দৈর্ঘ্যসমীকরণ (হিঃ কোঃ)। **Equation of the equinoxes**—সমপাত সমীকরণ (হিঃ কোঃ)। **Equation of payments**—(পাটীগণিত) বিভিন্ন সময়ে দেয় বিভিন্ন সংখ্যক মুদ্রার পরিশোধের মধ্য কাল। **Equation of time**—মধ্য ও স্ফুট (আপাতঃ বোধ্য) সময়ের মধ্যে প্রভেদ, অর্থাৎ সূর্য্যঘড়ী ও উৎকৃষ্ট সময় পরিচালক ঘটিকাযন্ত্রদ্বারা প্রদর্শিত সময়ের মধ্যে প্রভেদ, কালসমীকরণ। **Personal equation**—(জ্যোতির্বিজ্ঞান) ব্যক্তিবিশেষের পরিবীক্ষণের বিলম্বহেতু গ্রহাদি পর্য্যবেক্ষণে ভ্রান্তি হইলে গণনায় যে বাদসাদ দেওয়া হয়, নিজসমীকরণ (হিঃ কোঃ); (লক্ষণায়) মানবের ব্যক্তিগত, প্রকৃতিগত, অথবা পূর্ব্বসংস্কারাদি হইতে সঞ্জাত অপসিদ্ধান্ত-প্রবণতা। **Quadratic equation**—বর্গীয় সমীকরণ (হিঃ কোঃ), বর্গসমীকরণ (লীলাবতী)। **Reciprocal equation** — ব্যতিহার সমীকরণ (হিঃ কোঃ)। **Simultaneous equation**—সমকালিক সমীকরণ (হিঃ কোঃ)।

ē-quā'-tor (-tēr), *n.* 1. An imaginary circle equidistant from the poles, dividing the earth's surface into two hemispheres; ভূমধ্যরেখা, বিষুবরেখা, নিরক্ষবৃত্ত, ভূপরিধি (আঃ বঃ), ভূকক্ষ (ঐ)। 2. (*Astron.*) A celestial circle coinciding with the plane of the earth's equator; (জ্যোতির্বিজ্ঞান) নাড়ীমণ্ডল, আকাশ, ব্যোমকক্ষ, পরিধি (আঃ বঃ)। **–to'-ri-al,** *adj.* Pertaining to, or adjoining to, the equator; নৈরক্ষিক। **–to'-ri-al-ly,** *adv.* In a direction parallel to the equator; নিরক্ষবৃত্তের সমান্তরালদিকে। **Celestial equator** — খ-নিরক্ষবৃত্ত, খগোলীয় নাড়ীমণ্ডল। **Equatorial telescope**—নাড়ীমণ্ডল দর্শক।

eq'-uer-rȳ (ĕk-wĕr- or ē-kwĕr-), *n.* 1. An officer of princes or nobles who has the care of horses; রাজা বা সম্ভ্রান্ত ব্যক্তির অশ্বাধ্যক্ষ, বাজিশালার ভারপ্রাপ্ত রাজকর্ম্মচারী, মন্দুরাপাল (কুমার)। 2. In England, an officer of the Royal house-hold; (ইংলণ্ডে) রাজপ্রাসাদের কর্ম্মচারি-বিশেষ।

ē-quĕs'-tri-ăn, *adj.* & *n.* 1. Pertaining to a horse, or horse-riding; skilled in horse-manship; অশ্ববিষয়ক, অশ্বসম্বন্ধীয়, আশ্বিক, অশ্বীয়, আশ্ব, অশ্বারোহণ বিষয়ক; অশ্বারোহণ-পটু, অশ্বারোহণকুশল। 2. Mounted on horse-back; as, an *equestrian* statue; অশ্বারূঢ়, অশ্বপৃষ্ঠারূঢ়। ***Noun.*** A rider on horse-back;

one performing feats of horsemanship in a circus etc. ; অশ্বারোহী, ঘোড়ার সোয়ার, সাদী ; অশ্বারোহণ কৌশল প্রদর্শনকারী। (Fem. *equestrienne.*) **—ism,** *n.* Horsemanship ; অশ্বারোহণ বিদ্যা, অশ্বারোহণকুশলতা।

ē-qui-an′-gu-lar (-ăng-gū-lĕr), *adj.* Having equal angles ; তুল্য কৌণিক, সমকৌণিক, সমকোণী, সমকোণ, সমাস্র।

ē-qui-dis′-tănt, *adj.* Equally distant ; সমদূরবর্ত্তী, সমান্তর।

ē-qui-lăt′-ĕr-ăl, *adj.* Having all the sides equal ; সমভুজ, সমবাহু।

ē-qui-li′-brāte, *v. t.* & *i.* **1.** To keep in equipoise ; to balance ; ভারসাম্য করা ; তুল্য পরিমাণ করা। **2.** To counterpoise ; (তুলা-দণ্ডের দুই দিগে) সমভার দ্বারা ভারসাম্য করা, সমতুলিত করা। ***Verb i.*** To equipoise ; to balance ; সমতুলিত হওয়া ; সমভার হওয়া। **—bra′-tion, —lib′-ri-ty,** *ns.*

ē-quil′-i-brist, *n.* A rope-dancer ; রজ্জুনর্ত্তক।

ē-qui-lib′-ri-ŭm *n.* **1.** Equipoise ; balance, (*lit.* & *fig.*) ; ভারসাম্য, তুলাসাম্য ; ভার-সংস্থান। **2.** Mental neutrality ; suspense ; as, infidels live in a state of *equilibrium* ; উদাসীনতা ; দোদুল্যমানাবস্থা, অনিশ্চয়তা। **3.** (*Phys.*) The state of balance between opposing forces ; (পদার্থ বিজ্ঞান) পরস্পর-বিরোধী বলদ্বয়ের মধ্যে সামঞ্জস্য, বল-সামঞ্জস্য। **In equilibrium**—ভারসাম্যাবস্থায়। **Stable equilibrium**—সদৃশ পরিণাম (সাঃ পঃ)। **Unstable equilibrium**—অসদৃশ পরিণাম (সাঃ পঃ)।

ē-qui-mŭl′-ti-ple (-pl), *n.* (Chiefly *Pl.*) A number having a common factor with another ; সমগুণিতক।

e-quine, *adj.* Pertaining to or like a horse ; অশ্বসম্বন্ধীয়, আশ্বিক।

ē-quin-i-ă *n.* Horse-pox ; অশ্ব-বসন্ত।

ē′-qui-nŏx, *n.* **1.** The time when the day and night are of equal length, (21st March, 23rd September) ; বৎসরের যে সময়ে সর্ব্বত্র রাত্রি ও দিনমান সমান হয়, ক্রান্তিপাত, সায়ন। **2.** One of the two points at which the sun's path crosses the equator ; অয়ন, ক্রান্তিপাত। **—noc′-tial,** *adj.* & *n.* **1.** Pertaining to the time of equal day and night ; occurring at or about the time of the equinox ; as, the *equinoctial* gales ; সমদিবারাত্র-সম্পর্কীয়, বিষুব ; হরিপদ বা বিষুপদ সময়ে সংঘটিত। **2.** Pertaining to or near the terrestrial equator ; as, *equinoctial* heat ; নিরক্ষবৃত্তস্থিত বা তৎসমীপস্থ স্থানসমূহে সংঘটিত; বৈষুব, বিষুবীয়, নিরক্ষমণ্ডলীয়। (*Noun*) **1.** The celestial equator ; খ নিরক্ষবৃত্ত। **2.** An equinoctial gale ; নিরক্ষদেশে প্রবাহিত ঝঞ্ঝা। **Autumnal equinox**—September 22 or 23 ; হরিপদ, শারদীয় ক্রান্তিপাত, তুলা-সংক্রান্তি, জলবিষুব (সাঃ পঃ), সায়ন তুলা (হিঃ কোঃ)। **Equinoctial circle** — সায়ন বৃত্ত (হিঃ কোঃ)। **Equinoctial point**—ক্রান্তিপাত (হিঃ কোঃ), অয়ন (ঐ)। **Equinoctial flowers**—যে সমস্ত পুষ্প নিয়মিত ভাবে নির্দ্দিষ্ট সময়ে প্রস্ফুটিত হয়। **Equinoctial line** — (জ্যোতির্বিজ্ঞান) নাড়ীমণ্ডল। **Procession of the equinoxes**—অয়নচলন, ক্রান্তিপাতগতি, অয়নাংশ। **Vernal equinox**—(২০শে কি ২১শে মার্চ্চ) বিষুপদ, বাসন্তী ক্রান্তিপাত, মেষ সংক্রান্তি, মহাবিষুব (সাঃ পঃ), সায়ন মেষ (হিঃ কোঃ)।

ē-quip′, *v. t.* **1.** To furnish or fit out (a ship, army, person, etc.) with what is necessary for service ; আবশ্যক সাজসরঞ্জাম বা আসবাবপত্রে সজ্জিত করা, সুসজ্জিত করা। **2.** To dress ; as, he *equipped* himself for a journey ; পোষাক পরিচ্ছদদ্বারা সজ্জিত করা। **—ment,** *n.* **1.** Act of equipping ; the state of being equipped ; সজ্জীকরণ ; সজ্জা। **2.** Outfit ; equipage as of a soldier, army, etc. ; সাজসজ্জা ; সৈনিকদিগের সাজসজ্জা।

eq′-ui-pāge (-ĕk-wi-), *n.* **1.** Furniture or outfit required for an army, men-of-war or a soldier etc. ; outfit for a journey, expedition, etc. ; সৈন্যদল, রণপোত অথবা কোন সৈনিকের আবশ্যক সাজসজ্জা, সরঞ্জাম ও অস্ত্রশস্ত্রাদি সাজসজ্জা ; ভ্রমণ বা যুদ্ধযাত্রার উপযোগী সাজসজ্জা, সন্নাহ। **2.** A carriage and horses with attendants; অনুচরবর্গ সমেত অশ্ব শকট। **3.** (*Obs.*) Accoutrements ; habiliments ; রণসজ্জা, সমর-সরঞ্জাম ; পোষাক পরিচ্ছদ। **4.** A set of articles for table-service ; ভোজনকালে ব্যবহৃত এক প্রস্থ চা, চামচা, প্রভৃতি।

ē′-qui-poise (-pōyz), *n.* & *v. t.* **1.** Equality of weight or force ; balance ; সমগুরুত্ব, বলসাম্য ; ভারসাম্য, সাম্যাবস্থা, সমতুলত্ব, সমবৃত্তি (আঃ বঃ) (প্রায়ই লক্ষণায়)। **2.** A counterpoise ; তুল্যভার। ***Verb t.*** **1.** To counterbalance ; ভারসামঞ্জস্য করা। **2.** To hold in suspense ; as, to *equipoise* the mind ; সংশয়দোলায় দোদুল্যমান করা।

ē-qui-pŏl′-lĕnt, *adj.* & *n.* Having equal power or force ; equivalent ; তুল্য শক্তিমান, সমবল ; সমতুল্য। ***Noun.*** An equivalent ; সমতুল্য বস্তু। **—lence, —len cy,** *ns.* **1.** Equality of power or force ; an equivalent ; শক্তিসাম্য, বলসাম্য, সমতুল্যতা, সমকক্ষতা ; সমতুল্য বস্তু।

ē-qui-pŏn′-dĕr-āte, *v. t.* To counterbalance ; সমভার করা। **—ance,** *n.* **—ant,** *adj.* & *n.* Of equal weight, importance, force, etc., (with *to* or *with*) ; সমভার, সমগুরুত্ববিশিষ্ট, সমবলসম্পন্ন। (*Noun*) Things of equal weights ; সমভার বস্তুসমূহ।

ē-qui-pō-tĕn'-tial (-shăl), *adj.* (*Phys.*) Having the same potential; (পদার্থবিজ্ঞান) সমশক্তিভাগিক।

ē-qui-tā'-tion *n.* The art of riding on horseback; অশ্বারোহণ-বিদ্যা।

ĕq'-ui-tȳ (ĕk-wĭ-), *n.* **1.** Natural justice or right giving to each man his due; শাশ্বত ন্যায় বা অধিকার। **2.** Fairness; impartiality; ন্যায্যতা, সুবিচার; অপক্ষপাত, সমদৃষ্টি। **3.** (*Law*) A system of law based on eternal principles of justice, supplementary or superseding the common law; (আইন) শাশ্বত ন্যায় বিচারের মূলতত্ত্বের উপর প্রতিষ্ঠিত ব্যবহারশাস্ত্রের শাখা বিশেষ,—ইহা দেশ প্রচলিত সাধারণ আইনের পরিশিষ্ট স্বরূপ,—সাধারণ আইনের বিধানের সহিত ইহার অনৈক্য হইলে, ইহার বিধানই বলবৎ থাকে। **4.** An equitable claim or right; ন্যায্য দাবী বা অধিকার। **—ta-ble,** *adj.* **1.** Just; impartial; ন্যায়সম্মত, ন্যায্য, ন্যায়ানুগত, ন্যায়নিষ্ঠ, নীতিমান্, ন্যায়সঙ্গত, ন্যায়পরায়ণ; নিরপেক্ষ, সমদর্শী। **2.** (*Law*) Valid in equity as opposed to law; as, an *equitable* claim; শাশ্বতন্যায়সিদ্ধ। **—ta-ble-ness,** *n.* The state or quality of being just or impartial; ন্যায়পরায়ণতা, অপক্ষপাতিত্ব, সমদর্শিতা। **—ta-bly,** *adv.* In an equitable manner; fairly; ন্যায়ানুমোদিতরূপে।

Equity of redemption—বন্ধকী জমি মুক্ত করার জন্য সময় দেওন [অর্থাৎ কোন লোক কিছু টাকা কর্জ্জ করিয়া অধিক মূল্যের জমি বন্ধক রাখিলে, যদি নিরূপিত মিয়াদের মধ্যে ঐ কর্জ্জ শোধ করিতে না পারে, তবে আদালতে দরখাস্ত করিলে আদালত কর্ত্তৃক ঋণগ্রহীতাকে সময় প্রদান।]

ē-quiv'-ă-lence (-lĕns), **—lĕn-cȳ,** *ns.* **1.** Equality of value; state of being equivalent; তুল্যমূল্যতা; সমপরিবৃত্তি, সমানার্থতা। **2.** (*Chem.*) Equality of valence; (রসায়ন-শাস্ত্র) সংযোগ্য শক্তিসাম্য(হিঃ কোঃ)। **—lent,** *adj.* & *n.* **1.** Equal in value (to); equal in meaning; তুল্যমূল্য; তুল্যার্থক, অভিন্ন। **2.** Identical in effect; একরূপ কার্য্যকারী। **3.** Corresponding; "The *equivalent* strata of different countries;" অনুরূপ। **4.** (*Chem.*) Equal in combining value to a quantity of another substance; (রসায়নশাস্ত্র) তুল্যশক্তিক (হিঃ কোঃ)। (*Noun*) **1.** Anything equal in value, import, weight, etc. to something else; তুল্যমূল্য, তুল্যার্থক বা তুল্যপরিমাণ বস্তু। **2.** Compensation; ক্ষতিপূরণ। **3.** (*Chem.*) A combining weight of a radical or compound; সংযোগ-ভারাঙ্ক (হিঃ কোঃ)। **The equivalents of the signs in right ascension** — লঙ্কোদয় (সূঃ সিঃ), লগ্নাসব (সাঃ পঃ), লঙ্কোদয়াসব (ঐ)।

ē-quiv'-ō-căl, *adj.* **1.** Capable of two interpretations; ambiguous; দ্ব্যর্থবোধক; সন্দিগ্ধার্থক, অস্পষ্টার্থক। **2.** Uncertain; undecided; as, an *equivocal* attitude; সন্দিগ্ধ; অনিশ্চিত, দ্বিকল্প। **3.** Questionable; সংশয়যোগ্য। **—cal'-i-ty, —ness,** *ns.* **—ly,** *adv.*

ē-quiv'-ō-cāte, *v. t.* To use ambiguous words with a view to mislead; to prevaricate; ভ্রান্তি জন্মাইবার উদ্দেশ্যে অস্পষ্টার্থ বাক্য প্রয়োগ করা; সত্যের অপলাপ করা, কথার মারপেঁচ করা, বাক্চাতুরীদ্বারা মূল বিষয় পরিহার করিয়া বিষয়ান্তরে লইয়া যাওয়া। **—ca'-tion,** *n.* Act of equivocating; prevarication; quibble; দ্ব্যর্থবোধক বাক্য-প্রয়োগ, সত্যের অপলাপ; সত্যাভাস, কথার মারপেঁচ, বক্রোক্তি, বাক্ছল, কূটোক্তি; দ্ব্যর্থবোধক বাক্য-প্রয়োগ। **—ca'-tor,** *n.* **—ca-to-ry,** *adj.*

eq'-ui-voke (ĕk-wĭ), **—voque**(-vōk), *n.* **1.** Equivocation; ambiguity; দ্ব্যর্থক ভাষণ; বাক্ছল, বক্রোক্তি, কূটোক্তি। **2.** An ambiguous term; a pun; দ্ব্যর্থবাক্য; শব্দশ্লেষ।

Equula edentula — টেকা চাঁদা (গুপ্তঃ)।

ē'-ră, *n.* **1.** A system or order of chronology beginning from a certain given date; as, the Christian *era*; সম্বৎ, শক, সন, অব্দ। **2.** An epoch; a historical period; যুগ; ইতিহাসপ্রসিদ্ধ কাল।

ē-rā'-di-āte, *v. i.* To shoot forth, as rays of light; রশ্মিবিকীর্ণ হওয়া, আলোক-চ্ছটা বিসারিত হওয়া। **—a'-tion,** *n.* Emission of rays; কিরণ বিকিরণ।

ē-răd'-i-cāte, *v. t.* **1.** To root up or out; মূলোৎপাটিত করা, উপড়াইয়া ফেলা, উৎপাতিত করা। **2.** To destory; বিধ্বংস করা, বিনষ্ট করা, উন্মূলিত করা, মূলোচ্ছেদ করা, নির্ম্মূল করা। **—ca-ble,** *adj.* **—ca'-tion,** *n.* Act of plucking up by the roots; state of being eradicated; extirpation; সমূলোৎপাটন, নির্ম্মূলন, উন্মূলন; উন্মূলিতাবস্থা; মূলোচ্ছেদ। **—ca-tive,** *adj.*

ē-rāse', *v. t.* **1.** To scrape or rub out; to efface; অপহ্নব করা, বিলুপ্ত করা; মুছিয়া ফেলা। **2.** (*Fig.*) To obliterate (from the mind or memory); (লক্ষণায়) ঘসিয়া তোলা, চাঁচিয়া তোলা। **—ment, —ra'-sion, —ra'-sure,** *ns.* **1.** Obliteration; a rubbing or scraping out; বিলোপ; ঘসিয়া বা চাঁচিয়া তোলন। **2.** (Only **—ra'-sure**) The place where something written has been rubbed out; an instance of erasing; যে স্থান হইতে কোন লেখা ঘষিয়া তোলা হইয়াছে; ঘসিয়া তোলার চিহ্ন। **—ras'-a-ble,** *adj.* **—ras'-er,** *n.* One who, or that which, erases; an instrument or piece of rubber used to erase marks of inks etc.; যে ব্যক্তি চাঁচিয়া বা ঘসিয়া তুলিয়া ফেলে; চাঁচন যন্ত্র, চাঁচনী, রবরের টুকরা।

E-răs'-tiăn (ē-), *n.* & *adj.* A follower of Erastus, a theologian of the 16th century; খৃষ্টীয় ষোড়শ শতাব্দীতে প্রাদুর্ভূত ইরেষ্টাস্ নামক

জনৈক ধর্ম্মশাস্ত্রবেত্তার মতাবলম্বী। [যাজকসম্প্রদায় রাজ্যের সাধারণ শাসনব্যবস্থা ও আইনকানুনের অধীন হইবে—ইহা তাঁহার মত ছিল।] *Adj.* Of or relating to Erastus or his doctrines ; ইরেষ্টাস্ বা তৎপ্রবর্ত্তিত মতসম্পর্কীয়। **—ism,** *n.* **—ize,** *v. t.* & *i.*

ere (âr), *prep.* & *conj.* (*Poet.* & *archaic*) Before (of time) ; (কবিতায় বা অপ্রচলিত) পূর্ব্বে, অগ্রে, প্রাক্‌কালে। **2.** Sooner than ; অবিলম্বে, অচিরে, শীঘ্র। **Ere-long** — শীঘ্র, অবিলম্বে। **Ere-now**—ইতঃপূর্ব্বে ; পূর্ব্বে। **Ere while** — পূর্ব্বে ; অনতিকাল পূর্ব্বে, কিঞ্চিৎপূর্ব্বে।

Er'-ë-bŭs (ĕr-), *n.* (*Gr. Mythol.*) A gloomy region between the earth and Hades ; (গ্রীক্‌পুরাণে বর্ণিত) যমালয় ও পৃথিবীর মধ্যস্থিত অন্ধকারময় স্থান।

ë-rĕct', *adj.* & *v. t.* **1.** Upright ; not bending ; vertical ; দণ্ডায়মান ; সোজা ; খাড়া। **2.** Elevated ; uplifted ; উন্নত ; উত্তোলিত। **3.** Bristling, as hair etc. ; কণ্টকিত, পুলকিত। **4.** Bold ; unshaken ; সাহসী ; অকম্পিত, অটল, অবিচলিত। **5.** (*Optics*) Not inverted as an image ; (দৃষ্টিবিজ্ঞান) অবিপর্য্যস্ত। *Verb t.* **1.** To raise ; to build ; as, to *erect* a house ; গাঁথিয়া তোলা ; নির্ম্মাণ করা। **2.** To set upright ; as, to *erect* a post ; to form ; খাড়া করা ; গঠন করা। **3.** To set up ; "To *erect* conclusion ;" প্রতিষ্ঠা করা, স্থাপন করা, দাঁড় করা। **4.** To establish, (obs. except in law) ; "The statute *erected* a summary jurisdiction ;" (কেবলমাত্র আইনে ব্যবহার আছে) প্রতিষ্ঠিত করা। **5.** (*Optics*) To change as an image from an inverted to a normal position ; (দৃষ্টি-বিজ্ঞান) কোন প্রতিবিম্বকে বিপর্য্যস্ত অবস্থা হইতে স্বাভাবিক অবস্থায় পরিবর্ত্তন করা। **—er, —or,** *ns.* One who or that which erects ; a muscle that erects a limb etc. ; উত্থাপক, উত্থাপনকারী, হর্ম্ম্যাদি নির্ম্মাতা ; যে পেশীর সাহায্যে কোন অঙ্গ প্রত্যঙ্গ সোজা করা হয়। **—ly,** *adv.* In an upright manner ; খাড়াভাবে। **—ness,** *n.* Uprightness of posture ; লম্বভাবে অবস্থিতি। **—rec'-tion,** *n.* **1.** The act of erecting ; the state of being erected ; establishment ; গাঁথিয়া তোলন, খাড়াকরণ, নির্ম্মাণ, উন্নয়ন ; উত্থান, উচ্ছ্বাস, সমুচ্ছ্রয় ; সংস্থাপন, প্রতিষ্ঠাপন। **2.** A building, (*lit* & *fig.*) ; সৌধ, ইমারত, মন্দির, প্রভৃতি। **—rec'-tive,** *adj.*

ë-rĕct'-ïle, *adj.* Capable of being erected ; উন্নয়নযোগ্য। **Erectile tissue**—জীবদেহস্থ বিধানতন্তুবিশেষ—যাহা উত্তেজনার সময় প্রসারিত ও দৃঢ়ীভূত হয়।

ĕr'-ë-mīte, *n.* A hermit ; a christian solitary ; তপস্বী, তাপস ; বনচারী, যতি, আরণ্যক। **—mit'-ic, —mit'-i-cal,** *adjs.*

ĕr'-ë-thism, *n.* **1.** (*Med.*) Excessive irritability (of organ, tissue, etc.) ; অতিক্ষোভ্যতা। **2.** (*Fig.*) Excitement, as of the mind ; (লক্ষণায়) উত্তেজনা, বিক্ষোভ।

êr'-gö, *con.* & *adv.* Therefore ; অতএব।

êr'-gŏt, *n.* **1.** Disease of rye and other grasses, caused by fungus ; গোধূমাদির ছত্রাক-জনিত রোগবিশেষ। **2.** Diseased rye-seeds used in medicine ; ঔষধরূপে ব্যবহৃত ছত্রাক রোগাক্রান্ত গোধূম প্রভৃতির বীজ। **—got'-ic,** *adj.* **—ism,** *n.* **1.** A disease caused by eating grain affected with ergot ; ছত্রাক-রোগাক্রান্ত ময়দার প্রস্তুত রুটি-ভক্ষণজনিত রোগবিশেষ।

1. Heads of ergot (a a a) produced on a grass ; 2, fungus (b b b) springing from the ergot.

E'-rin (ĕ-), *n.* Ancient name of Ireland ; আয়র্লণ্ডদেশের প্রাচীন নাম, (অধুনা কবিতায় ব্যবহৃত হয়)।

Eriobotrya Japonica — লকেট ফল (বেলঃ)।

Eriodendron anfractuosum—শ্বেতশিমুল (বেলঃ)।

ĕ-ri-ŏm'-ĕ-têr, *n.* সূক্ষ্ম ব্যাসমাপক (হিঃ কোঃ)।

ĕ-ris'-tic, *adj.* & *n.* Pertaining to disputation ; বাদবিতণ্ডাঘটিত। *Noun.* **1.** The art of disputation ; তর্কবিদ্যা। **2.** A controversialist ; তার্কিক।

Erl'-king (êrl-), *n.* A spirit supposed to create mischief, esp. among children ; জুজু।

êr'-mine (-mĭn), *n.* **1.** An animal of the weasel tribe valued for its

Ermine.

white fur ; নকুল জাতীয় জন্তু বিশেষ,—ইহার বহু মূল্যবান শ্বেতলোম ধনীর পোষাকে ব্যবহৃত হইয়া থাকে। **2.** The fur of the ermine ; উক্ত জন্তুর লোম। **3.** The office or dignity of the judges, peers, etc. from their state robe being ornamented with ermine in emblem of purity of administration ; "The purity of the critical *ermine* like that of the judicial is often soiled by contact with politics ;" বিচারক, সম্ভ্রান্ত বংশীয় পুরুষ ও শাসনকর্ত্তৃগণের পদ বা পদগৌরব। (উচ্চ বিচারপতিগণ পবিত্রতার নিদর্শনস্বরূপ আরমিনের অকলঙ্ক শুভ্র লোমসুশোভিত পরিচ্ছদ ধারণ করিয়া থাকেন।) **—mined,** *adj.*

erne (êrn), *n.* A sea-eagle ; মাছ-মোড়ল।

ë-röde', *v. t.* To eat away ; to corrode ; to wear away ; ক্ষয় করা ; ক্রমশঃ ক্ষয় করা ; খাইয়া দেওয়া। **—ro'-sion,** *n.* The act of wearing away ; corrosion ; ক্ষয়করণ, ক্ষয়।

—ro'-sive, *adj.* Tending to erode; ক্ষয়োন্মুখ; ক্ষয়কারক।

ĕr-ō-tē'-sis, *n.* (*Rhet.*) A figure of speech containing an earnest interrogation; as in "Shall I act against my principle, if all the pleasures of this world tempt me?" অর্থালঙ্কার বিশেষ।

ē-rŏt'-ic, *adj.* & *n.* Pertaining to sexual love; dealing with such love; শৃঙ্গার রসাত্মক, আদিরসাত্মক; শৃঙ্গারবিষয়ক। ***Noun.*** An amorous composition or poem; আদিরসাত্মক রচনা বা কবিতা।

ĕ-rō-tō-mā'-nĭ-ă, *n.* (*Path.*) Madness arising from sexual love; শৃঙ্গার-বিক্ষিপ্ততা (হিঃ কোঃ), শৃঙ্গারোন্মাদ (ঐ), কামোন্মাদ।

ĕrr, *v. i.* **1.** (Now *archaic*) To wander away; to deviate from the true path; বিপথে যাওয়া; পথভ্রষ্ট হওয়া, উন্মার্গগামী হওয়া, বিপথগামী হওয়া। **2.** To be mistaken; to blunder; (of statements &c.) to be incorrect; ভ্রান্ত হওয়া; ভ্রম করা; ভ্রমপূর্ণ হওয়া। **3.** To sin; to do wrong; পাপ করা; অপরাধ করা। **To err is human**—ভ্রম মানুষের পক্ষে স্বাভাবিক, মুনীনাঞ্চ মতিভ্রমঃ।

ĕr'-rănd, *n.* **1.** A journey for a purpose intrusted or undertaken; as, to be sent on an *errand*; কোন ভারার্পিত বা ভারগৃহীত কার্য্য সাধনের জন্য যাত্রা। **2.** The business on which one is sent; ভারার্পিত কার্য্য, ন্যস্ত কর্ম্ম। **3.** Purpose; উদ্দেশ্য। **An errand boy** — সংবাদ-বাহক বালক। **Fool's errand**—অনর্থক কাজ, পণ্ডশ্রম। **To go or run (on) an errand**—To go or run to some place carrying a message; সংবাদ লইয়া গমন করা। **To make an errand**—To invent an excuse for going; যাইবার অজুহাত বাহির করা। To make a journey; যাত্রা করা।

ĕr'-rănt, *adj.* & *n.* **1.** Wandering in quest of adventures; as, a knight *errant*; দুঃসাহসিক কার্য্যের অন্বেষণে ভ্রমণকারী। **2.** Travelling; itinerant; ভ্রমণশীল; ভ্রমণকারী। **3.** Having no fixed course; "With an *errant* motion of his hand;" অনির্দ্দিষ্ট-গতি, অব্যবস্থিত। **4.** Deviating from a proper course or standard; নির্দ্দিষ্ট কার্য্যপ্রণালী, বা আদর্শ হইতে বিচলনশীল, ব্যভিচারী। ***Noun.*** **1.** A knight-errant; আর্ত্ত ও দুর্ব্বলের পরিত্রাণের জন্য গৃহীতব্রত ব্যক্তি। **2.** One who is astray; বিপথগামী ব্যক্তি। **—ran-cy, —ry,** *ns.*

ĕr-răt'-ĭc, —ĭ-căl, *adj.* **1.** Wandering; having no certain course; wild; ইতস্ততঃ পর্য্যটনশীল; অনির্দ্দিষ্ট-গতি; উচ্ছৃঙ্খল, উন্মার্গগামী, উৎপথাশ্রয়ী, ব্যভিচারী। **2.** Eccentric; queer; অদ্ভুত চরিত্র; অপরূপ, কিম্ভুত। **3.** (Of a disease) Changing places; irregular; as, *erratic* fever; এক-স্থান হইতে অপর স্থানে সঞ্চরণশীল; অনিয়মিত। **4.** (*Geol.*) Detached and carried at a distance from its native rock; (ভূবিদ্যা) মূলস্থান হইতে বিশ্লিষ্ট করত দূরবর্ত্তী স্থানে সমানীত **—ĭ-cal-ly,** *adv.* **Erratic blocks** or **erratics**—(ভূবিদ্যা) তুষার স্রোতোদ্বারা বহুদূরবর্ত্তী স্থানে সমানীত প্রস্তর খণ্ড সমূহ।

ĕr-rā'-tŭm, *n.* (*pl.* -TA) **1.** An error or mistake in writing or printing; লিখা বা ছাপার ভুল। **2.** (*Pl.*) Errors noted in a list attached to a book; শুদ্ধিপত্র।

ĕr'-rhine (-rīn), *adj.* & *n.* Causing discharge from the nose; শ্লেষ্ম-বর্দ্ধক, ছিক্কাকর। ***Noun.*** A medicine to be snuffed up the nose to produce discharge of mucus; নস্য।

ĕr-rō'-nē-ous (-ŭs), *adj.* Full of errors; mistaken; incorrect; ভ্রমপূর্ণ; ভ্রান্ত, ভ্রমমূলক; অশুদ্ধ। **—ly,** *adv.* By mistake; ভ্রমতঃ, ভ্রান্তি হেতু; **—ness,** *n.*

ĕr'-ror (-rêr), *n.* **1.** Mistake; oversight; ভ্রম, ভুল, ভ্রান্তি, চুক, অধ্যাস; অনবধানতা। **2.** A mistaken judgment or opinion; ভ্রান্ত মত বা নিষ্পত্তি। **3.** A moral offence; a transgression; ত্রুটি; অপরাধ, দোষ, উন্মার্গগমন, ব্যভিচার। **Clerical error**—কেরাণীর ভুল, লিপিকর প্রমাদ। **Error of a planet**—কোন গ্রহের দৃষ্ট ও প্রকৃত অবস্থানের মধ্যে পার্থক্য। **The writ of error**—(আইন) ভ্রান্তির হেতুতে রায় উল্টাইবার জন্য যে পরওয়ানা বাহির করা হয়।

Erse (ĕrs), *n.* **1.** Celtic language of the Highlands of Scotland; স্কটলেণ্ড দেশের উত্তরাঞ্চলে প্রচলিত ভাষা বিশেষ। **2.** (*Vulgar*) Irish language; (ইতর ভাষায়) আয়র্লণ্ডের ভাষা।

êrst, *adv.* (*Archaic* or *poetic*) Formerly; at first; পূর্ব্বে; প্রথমে। **Erst-while,** *adv.* **1.** (*Rare*) Till then or now; তদবধি বা এযাবৎ। **2.** Formerly; পূর্ব্বে।

ĕr-ū-bĕs'-cĕnt, *adj.* Reddish; blushing; রক্তাভ, আলোহিত; লজ্জারক্তিম। **—cence,** *n.*

ē-rŭc'-tāte, *v. t.* To belch out; উদ্গীর্ণ করা, উদ্বমিত করা।

ē-rŭc-tā'-tion, *n.* **1.** Act of belching; a belch; উদ্গিরণ; বায়ূদ্গার, ঢেকুর, উদ্বমন। **2.** An eruption, esp. of a volcano etc.; অগ্ন্যুৎপাত, ধূমোদ্গার। **3.** That which is belched out; উদ্গীর্ণ-বস্তু।

ĕr'-ū-dīte, *adj.* Learned; as, an *erudite* person or essay; পণ্ডিত, সুশিক্ষিত, সুবিদ্বান, পাণ্ডিত্যপূর্ণ। **—dĭ'-tion,** *n.* Learning in literature etc.; scholarship; পাণ্ডিত্য; বিদ্যাবত্তা। **—ly,** *adv.* **—ness,** *n.*

ē-rŭpt', *v. i.* & *t.* **1.** To break out in eruption as a volcano; উদ্গীর্ণ হওয়া, অগ্ন্যুৎপাত হওয়া। **2.** To break out through the gums, as teeth; দন্তবেষ্টের ভিতর দিয়া উদ্গত হওয়া। ***Verb t.*** To cause to break out, as lava from a volcano etc. or teeth through the gums; উদ্গীর্ণ করা।

ē-rŭp'-tion, *n.* **1.** Act of bursting forth; outbreak; উদ্ভেদ; উদ্গম

2. Violent emission of flames, lava, etc. from a volcano ; অগ্ন্যুৎপাত, ধূমোদ্গিরণ, উৎক্ষেপ (হিঃ কোঃ)। 3. An outburst as of feeling, passion, etc. ; a sally of wit etc. : উচ্ছ্বাস, উদ্গার (cf. রসোদ্গার), লহরী। 4. A breaking out of pimples etc. upon the body ; সর্ব্বাঙ্গে দুষ্ট ব্রণ ও স্ফোটকাদির নির্গম, পীড়কা (on the body), যুবগণ্ড (on the face), প্রস্ফুটন। 5. (Of tooth) Act of breaking out through the gums ; দন্তোদ্গম। **—al,** *adj.* **—tive,** *adj.* 1. Bursting forth ; উদ্ভেদী। 2. (*Med.*) Attended with or producing eruption ; স্ফোটক সহকৃত, স্ফোটকোৎপাদক, স্ফোটনোৎপাদী। 3. Relating to, or produced by, volcanic eruption ; অগ্ন্যুৎপাত-সম্বন্ধীয় বা তজ্জাত। **—tive-ly,** *adv.* **—tive-ness,** *n.* **—tiv'-i-ty,** *n.*

Ervum lens, *n.* মসূর দাল (বেলঃ)।

Er-ȳ-sĭp'-ĕ-lăs, *n.* A disease (also called *St. Anthony's fire* or *the rose*) marked by a deep red colour on the skin ; বিসর্প-রোগ, 'ইরি বেল্লিকা', সপ্রদাহ জ্বররোগ বিশেষ, চর্ম্ম-প্রদাহ, উদর্দ (ভাব-প্রঃ)। **—si-pel'-a-tous,** *adj.*

ĕr-ȳ-thē'-mă, *n.* A kind of skin disease ; একপ্রকার চর্ম্মরোগ, অরুণিমা (হঃ চঃ)।

Erythina Indica—মন্দার।

Er-ȳ-thrī'-nă (ĕr-), *n.* The coral tree ; মন্দার, পারিজাত।

ĕs-că-lāde', *n.* & *v. t.* Scaling of walls, esp. of a fortified place with ladders ; মইয়ের সাহায্যে দুর্গাদির প্রাচীর উল্লঙ্ঘন। ***Verb t.*** To mount or enter by means of ladders ; মইয়ের সাহায্যে আরোহণ বা প্রবেশ করা।

ĕs-căl-lō'-ni-ă, *n.* A South-American shrub or tree ; দক্ষিণ আমেরিকা দেশীয় বৃক্ষ বা গুল্মবিশেষ।

ĕs-căl'-lŏp, *n.* A bivalve shell ; দ্বিখোল শঙ্খ, শুক্তি, প্রভৃতি।

ĕs-că-pādĕ', *n.* 1. Act of escaping from confinement or restraint ; পলায়ন। 2. A breaking loose from rules of propriety ; a freak ; "Churchill's latest *escapade* is the theme of general remark ;" শিষ্টাচারের নিয়ম ভঙ্গ, সদাচার-লঙ্ঘন ; স্খলিত, খেয়াল, মর্জ্জি।

ĕs-cāpe', *v. i., t.* & *n.* 1. To flee and become secure ; to be free, (with *from, out of,* etc.) ; পলায়ন করা ; মুক্ত হওয়া। 2. To avoid an evil ; to go unpunished ; to get off safely ; to free oneself from restraint or custody ; as, he has *escaped* from prison ; দুর্দ্দৈব পরিহার করা, এড়ান, পার পাওয়া ; শাস্তি হইতে পরিত্রাণ পাওয়া ; নিষ্কৃতি পাওয়া, নিস্তার পাওয়া ; কারামুক্ত হওয়া। 3. (Of steam, fluids, etc.) To issue from a confining enclosoure ; (বাষ্পাদির পক্ষে) রন্ধ্রপথে নির্গত হওয়া। ***Verb t.*** 1. To shun ; to flee from ; পরিহার করা, পলায়ন করা ; এড়ান। 2. To elude notice or memory of ; as, the name of that boy has *escaped* me ; মন হইতে অপসৃত হওয়া। 3. To issue unawares from ; "No word of courtesy *escaped* his lips ;" অতর্কিতভাবে নির্গত হওয়া। ***Noun.*** 1. Act of fleeing from danger, evil, etc. ; পলায়ন। 2. Flight from or evasion of legal restraint or custody ; অব্যাহতি, পরিত্রাণ, নিষ্কৃতি, নিস্তার। 3. Leakage or outflow, as of gas, steam, etc. ; ছিদ্রপথে বাষ্প, প্রভৃতির নির্গম, বা নিঃসরণ। **—ment,** *n.* 1. An outlet ; নির্গমপথ। 2. A mechanism in watch or clock regulating the movement of the regulator ; ঘটিকাযন্ত্রের নিয়ামকের (দোলন প্রভৃতির) গতি নিয়ামক যান্ত্রিক ব্যবস্থাবিশেষ। **Escape-pipe**—রন্ধ্র হইতে যে নল-সহযোগে বাষ্প বাহির হইয়া যায়। **Escape-wheel**—(Also called *escapement wheel*) ঘটিকা যন্ত্রের নিয়ামকের (দোলকাদির) গতি-নিয়ামক যান্ত্রিক ব্যবস্থার অঙ্গীভূত চক্রবিশেষ, ঘড়ীর দাঁতাল চাকা। **Escape-valve**—বাষ্পীয় যন্ত্রের বাষ্প-স্থলীর অতিরিক্ত বাষ্পনিঃসারণ রন্ধ্র। **To have a narrow escape**—সামান্যের জন্য বাঁচিয়া যাওয়া।

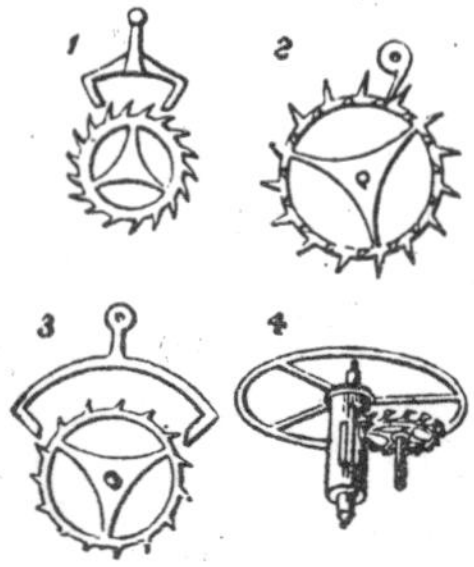

Watch and Clock escapements. 1, anchor escapement of a common clock ; 2, duplex escapement ; 3, lever escapement ; 4, horizontal or cylinder escapement.

ĕs-cârp', *v. t.* & *n.* To form into a sudden slope ; ঢালু করিয়া নির্ম্মাণ করা, ক্রমনিম্নাকার করা। ***Noun.*** A steep slope immediately in front of and below the rampart ; উচ্চ ঢালু। **—ment,** *n.* 1. A steep slope ; a ground cut away nearly vertically for fortification ; ঢালু স্থান ; শত্রু সৈন্য প্রতিরোধার্থ দুর্গাদির চতুর্দ্দিগস্থ প্রবণভূমি।

esch-ă-lŏt' (ĕsh-), *n.* Shallot ; গন্ধপিঁয়াজ, গদিনা।

ĕsch'-âr, *n.* (*Surg.*) A hard crust or scar made by hot applications ; দগ্ধাবরণ, দাগ।

ĕs-chă-tŏl'-ŏ-ḡȳ, *n.* The doctrine of the last things, as death, judgment, heaven and hell ; মৃত্যু, অন্তিম বিচার, স্বর্গ, নরক প্রভৃতি বিষয়ক শাস্ত্র, পরলোকশাস্ত্র (হিঃ কোঃ), প্রলয়শাস্ত্র (ঐ)। **—to-log'-i-cal,** *adj.*

ĕs-cheat' (-chēt), *n., v. i.* & *t.* 1. The reversion or lapsing of property to tne original proprietor or to the state on the owner's dying intestate without heirs ; উত্তরাধিকারীর অভাবে সম্পত্তি রাজা বা জমিদারের সরকারে বাজেয়াপ্ত হওন, উত্তরাধিকারীর অভাবে ভূসম্পত্তির স্বত্ব প্রত্যাবর্ত্তন। 2. The land so reverted ; the right of appropriating property subject to escheat ; উক্ত প্রকারে বাজেয়াপ্ত সম্পত্তি, বেওয়ারীশ সম্পত্তি, বেওয়ারীশী মাল ; উত্তরাধিকারী অভাবে সম্পত্তি বাজেয়াপ্ত করার অধিকার। *Verb i.* To revert as land etc. to the state or original proprietor for want of heirs ; উত্তরাধিকারীর অভাবে স্বত্ব প্রত্যাবৃত্ত হওয়া, বেওয়ারীশ সম্পত্তি রাজ সরকারে বর্ত্তা বা বাজেয়াপ্ত হওয়া। *Verb t.* To confiscate ; to hand over as an escheat to a person ; বাজেয়াপ্ত করা ; বেওয়ারীশ সম্পত্তি কোন ব্যক্তির নিকট হস্তান্তরিত করা।

ĕs-chew′ (-chō), *v. t.* To shun or avoid ; to abstain from ; পরিত্যাগ করা, বিসর্জ্জন করা, পরিহার করা, বর্জ্জন করা ; নিবৃত্ত থাকা, বিরত থাকা।

esclandre, (*F.*), *n.* A scandal ; notoriety ; a disturbance ; অপবাদ, কুৎসা, কুকার্য্যে প্রসিদ্ধি ; গণ্ডগোল, হাঙ্গামা।

ĕs′-cŏrt, *n.* **1.** A body of armed men attending great personages, baggages, treasures, etc. ; রক্ষিবর্গ, শরীর রক্ষী সৈন্যদল, প্রহরী সৈন্যদল, তৈনাতী সৈন্যদল। **2.** A person or persons attending another on journey or for the sake of courtesy ; শিষ্টাচারের অনুরোধে বা শরীর রক্ষার জন্য যে লোক বা লোক-সকল কোন ব্যক্তির অনুগমন করে। **3.** Protection ; care or guidance ; as, to go under the *escort* of a friend ; রক্ষণাবেক্ষণ ; তত্বাবধান।

ĕs-cŏrt′, *v. t.* To act as escort to ; as, to *escort* a lady ; শরীর রক্ষার্থ বা ভদ্রতার অনুরোধে অনুগমন করা, অনুগমন করা।

ē-scrībe′, *v. t.* (*Math*) To draw (a circle) touching one side of a triangle externally and the other two (produced) internally ; (গণিত-শাস্ত্র) কোন ত্রিভুজের বহির্দ্দেশে এক বাহু এবং ভিতরের দিকে অপর দুই (বর্দ্ধিত) বাহু স্পর্শ করিয়া (বৃত্ত) অঙ্কিত করা।

ĕs-crī-toire′ (-twär), *n.* A writing desk constructed to contain stationery or documents ; দেরাজযুক্ত লিখিবার ডেস্ক বিশেষ। **—to′-ri-al,** *adj.*

ĕs′-cū-lĕnt, *adj.* & *n.* Fit for food ; edible ; আহারোপযোগী ; ভক্ষ্য, ভোজনীয়, খাদ্য, ভোজ্য। ***Noun.*** An edible thing ; আহার্য্য-বস্তু।

ĕs-cutch′-eon (-kŭch-ŏn) *n.* **1.** (*Herald.*) A shield with armorial bearings ; কুলমর্য্যাদ সূচক চিহ্নাঙ্কিত চর্ম্ম। **2.** The portion of a ship's stern where her name is written ; অর্ণবপোতের পশ্চাদ্ভাগের যে অংশে উহার নাম লিখিত হইয়া থাকে।

Escutcheon.

Escutcheon of pretense—কোন ব্যক্তির পত্নী উত্তরাধিকারিণী হইলে তদীয় কুলচিহ্নাঙ্কিত যে ক্ষুদ্র ঢাল পতির ঢালের মধ্যস্থলে নিবদ্ধ করা হয়। **This is a blot on his escutcheon**—This is a stain on his reputation ; ইহা তাহার শুভ যশের উপর কলঙ্করেখা।

Es′-ki-mo, Es′-qui-mau, (ĕs-kĭ-mō), *n.* (*pls.* -MOS. or -MAUX) A member of a race in North America ; উত্তর আমেরিকাবাসী জাতি-বিশেষ, এস্কুইমো জাতি। **Eskimo dog**—একজাতীয় দীর্ঘলোম কুক্কুর।

ē-sŏph′-ă-gŭs, *n.* (*Anat.* & *Zool.*) The gullet ; গলনালী, কণ্ঠনালী, অন্ননালী।

ĕs-ō-tĕr′-ic, *adj.* & *n* **1.** Intelligible to or designed for, the initiated only ; কেবল বিশেষরূপে দীক্ষিত ব্যক্তি-গণের বোধগম্য, বিশেষ ভাবে দীক্ষাপ্রাপ্ত ব্যক্তিগণের জন্য অভিপ্রেত বা কেবল মাত্র উক্ত প্রকার ব্যক্তির নিকট ব্যক্ত। **2.** Secret ; confidential ; as, an *esoteric* purpose ; গুপ্ত, গুহ্য, নিগূঢ়, বিনিগূহিত, রহস্যপূর্ণ ; আভ্যন্তরীণ, অন্তরঙ্গ, একান্তোপদিষ্ট, রহঃ-কথিত। **3.** Initiated ; as, an *esoteric* disciple ; দীক্ষাপ্রাপ্ত। ***Noun.*** **1.** (*Pl.*) Esoteric doctrines or treatises ; গুপ্তশাস্ত্র, গুহ্যশাস্ত্র, নিগূঢ় খৃষ্টধর্ম্মতত্ব। **2.** One initiated in esoteric doctrines ; নিগূঢ় শাস্ত্রজ্ঞ।

ĕs-pă-gno-lette′ (-nyō-lĕt), *n.* The fastening of a French window ; ফরাসী দেশীয় বাতায়নের অর্গল।

ĕs-păl′-ier (-yĕr), *n.* **1.** A lattice-work on which fruit trees and ornamental shrubs are trained ; ফলতরু বা শোভাসম্পাদক গুল্মসমূহের আশ্রয়স্বরূপ কাষ্ঠনির্ম্মিত জাফ্রি। **2.** Trees or shrubs so trained ; জাফ্রির উপর আশ্রিত তরু-গুল্মসমূহ।

ĕs-pâr′-tō, *n.* A species of Spanish grass, used for making paper, (also called *esparto-grass*) ; স্পেনদেশীয় তৃণবিশেষ,—কাগজ প্রস্তুত করণে ব্যবহৃত হয়।

ĕs-pĕ′-cial (-shăl), *adj.* **1.** Particular, pre-eminent ; as, a thing of *especial* importance ; বিশেষ ; প্রধান, বিশিষ্ট, অগ্রগণ্য। **2.** Belonging chiefly to a particular case ; "Every vice had its *especial* demon ;" নির্দ্দিষ্ট। **—ly,** *adv.* Particularly ; chiefly ; বিশেষ ভাবে ; প্রধানতঃ, মুখ্যতঃ, বিশেষতঃ। (See SPECIAL).

Es-pĕr-ăn′-tō (ĕs-), *n.* An artificial language intended to serve as a medium of communication for all nations ; as, *Esperanto* society ; বিভিন্ন জাতি সমূহের মধ্যে মনোভাব প্রকাশ জন্য আবিষ্কৃত ভাষা বিশেষ, বিশ্বভাষা, আন্তর্জাতিক ভাষা। [Warsaw নগরবাসী Dr. L. L. Zamenhof নামক নেত্রবৈদ্য কর্ত্তৃক ১৮৮৭ খৃঃ অব্দে Esperanto আবিষ্কৃত হয়।]

ĕs-pī′-ăl, *n.* Act of espying ; watching ; acting as a spy ; অবলোকন, দর্শন, পর্য্যবেক্ষণ ; গোয়েন্দা-গিরিকরণ।

espieglerie (*F.*), *n.* Roguishness ; frolicsomeness ; ধড়িবাজি ; ক্রীড়া-কৌতুক।

ĕs′-pi-ō-năge, *n.* Practice of spying or employing spies ; practice of watching others without being suspected ; গুপ্তচর-নিয়োগ, বা গোয়েন্দা-গিরি, চারপ্রয়োগ, চারদ্বারাবলোকন ;

কোন ব্যক্তির গতিবিধি সম্বন্ধে জ্ঞাত হওয়ার জন্য অলক্ষিতে তাহার অনুসরণ।

ĕs-plă-nāde′, *n.* **1.** A level space of ground between the citadel and the first row of houses in a

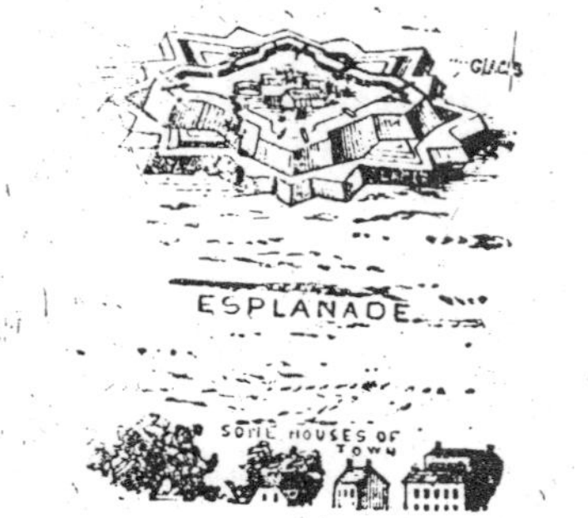

town ; দুর্গ এবং নগরপ্রান্তস্থ সর্ব্বপ্রথম গৃহশ্রেণীর মধ্যবর্ত্তী সমতল প্রান্তর। **2.** Any level space near a town for walks or drives ; ভ্রমণ ও শকটাদি চালনার জন্য নগরোপকণ্ঠস্থিত উন্মুক্ত সমতল প্রান্তর (যথা, গড়ের মাঠ)।

ĕs-pouse′ (-powz), *v. t.* To marry ; বিবাহ দেওয়া বা করা। **2.** To promise in marriage, (*rare*) ; বিবাহের চুক্তি বা অঙ্গীকারে আবদ্ধ হওয়া (কচিৎ ব্যবহৃত)। **3.** To become a supporter of ; to embrace ; as, to *espouse* a cause ; to champion ; পক্ষাবলম্বন করা ; পরিগ্রহণ করা ; পক্ষসমর্থন করা। **–pous′-al** *n.* **1.** (In the *pl.*) Nuptials ; betrothal ; বিবাহ, পরিণয় ; বাগ্দান। **2.** The adopting or taking up of a cause ; ব্রতগ্রহণ বা পক্ষাবলম্বন, পরিগ্রহ। **–pous′-er,** *n.* One who espouses ; বর। **2.** One who takes up the cause of a person, party, etc. ; an upholder ; ব্রতগ্রহণকারী, পক্ষাবলম্বনকারী ; সমর্থক।

espressivo (*It.*), (*Mus.*) *adv.* With expression ; (সঙ্গীত-শাস্ত্র) ভাবের সহিত।

esprit (ĕs-prē) (*F.*), *n.* Sprightliness ; vivacious wit ; সজীবতা, প্রফুল্লতা ; স্ফূর্ত্তি। ***Esprit de corps***—Regard for the honour of a body or association to which one belongs ; কোন সঙ্ঘের পক্ষে স্বকীয় সমিতি বা সম্মিলনীর গৌরব এবং মর্য্যাদা রক্ষার দিকে বিশেষ আগ্রহ, সমাজানুরক্তি, স্বগণাভিমান (হিঃ কোঃ)। ***Esprit-fort***—A strong-minded man ; a free-thinker ; দৃঢ়চিত্ত ব্যক্তি ; ধর্ম্ম সম্বন্ধে স্বাধীন চিন্তাকারী।

ĕs-pȳ′, *v. t.* **1.** To see at a distance ; to catch sight of ; দূরে দর্শন করা ; দেখিতে পাওয়া। **2.** To find out or detect as a fault etc. ; দোষ প্রভৃতি বাহির করা। **–pi-al,** *n.* See above.

Es′-qui-mau, *n.* See ESKIMO.

ĕs-quire′, *n.* **1.** A title appended to the name of a gentleman in addressing letters etc., (*abbr.* ESQ.) ; (পত্রাদির শিরোনামায়) ভদ্রলোকের নামের শেষে সংযোজিত উপাধি বিশেষ। **2.** One who as a candidate for knight-hood attends on a knight, (*archaic*) ; (অপ্রঃ) নাইট উপাধি লাভের উদ্দেশ্যে যে ব্যক্তি কোন নাইটের পার্শ্বচরের কার্য্য করিয়া থাকে। **3.** A landed proprietor, (*archaic*) ; ভূস্বামী (অপ্রঃ)। **4.** A title next in rank to that of a knight ; নাইট উপাধির অব্যবহিত নিম্নতর সম্মানসূচক উপাধি বিশেষ।

ĕs′-say (-sā), *n.* **1.** An attempt ; an experiment ; (with *at*) ; "My second *essay at* authorship ;" উদ্যম, চেষ্টা, যত্ন, প্রযত্ন ; পরীক্ষা। **2.** A literary composition ; রচনা, প্রবন্ধ, নিবন্ধ। **–ist,** *n.* A writer of essays ; প্রবন্ধলেখক, রচনালেখক।

ĕs-say′ (-sā), *v. t.* & *i.* **1.** To attempt ; to try ; চেষ্টা করা ; উদ্যম করা। **2.** To test ; to put to the proof, as a person or thing ; যাচাই করা ; পরখ করা। ***Verb i.*** To make an attempt ; চেষ্টা করা। **–er,** *n.*

ĕs′-sence (-sĕns), *n.* & *v. t.* **1.** Entity ; সদ্বস্তু। **2.** The qualities or properties that make anything be what it is ; বস্তুর প্রকৃতিগত ধর্ম্ম, মৌলিক ধর্ম্ম। **3.** Absolute being ; পরম সত্তা। **4.** Intrinsic nature ; prime character ; "The *essence* of mind being...unknown to that of external bodies ;" প্রকৃতি ; মূল প্রকৃতি। **5.** Indispensable quality or constituent element of anything ; "*Essence* of friendship is entireness ;" সারাংশ। **6.** Extract, as obtained by distillation from a plant, drug, etc. ; (*lit.* & *fig.*) ; আরক, নির্য্যাস, শিকা, সার, সত্ত্ব। **7.** Perfume ; scent ; সুগন্ধি দ্রব্য ; পুষ্পসার। ***Verb t.*** To perfume with essence ; to perfume ; পুষ্পসার দ্বারা সুবাসিত করা ; সুরভিত করা। **–senced,** *p.p.* **–sen′-tial,** *adj.* & *n.* **1.** Pertainting to, or constituting, essence ; সারবিষয়ক, সারভূত, সারগর্ভ, মূলীভূত, স্বাভাবিক, প্রকৃতিসিদ্ধ, নিসর্গসিদ্ধ। **2.** Important in the highest degree ; indispensable ; একান্ত আবশ্যক, অত্যাবশ্যক ; অপরিহার্য্য। **3.** Highly rectified ; diffusible ; as, an *essential* oil ; বিশোধিত ; প্রসরণশীল। **4.** Of the nature of an essence ; as, *essential* odour ; পুষ্পসার-প্রকৃতিক। (*Noun*) Something that is necessary ; the constituent principle ; "The *essentials* of religion ;" আবশ্যকীয় বস্তু ; মূল উপাদান, প্রধান অঙ্গ। **–sen-tial′-i-ty,** *n.* **–sen-tial-ly,** *adv.* In an essential manner ; fundamentally ; indispensably ; বস্তুতঃ ; মূলতঃ ; অপরিহার্য্যরূপে। **Essential character**—(Of a species, genus, etc.)—(জাতি, পরজাতি প্রভৃতির) পার্থক্যসূচক গুণ, ব্যবর্ত্তক গুণ। **Essential definition**—প্রধান লক্ষণ (হিঃ কোঃ), সার লক্ষণ (ঐ)। **Essential oil**—সুগন্ধি উদ্ভিজ্জ হইতে প্রাপ্ত তৈল।

ĕs′-sene (-sēn), *n.* One of a monastic order among the ancient Jews ; প্রাচীন ইহুদি জাতীয় সন্ন্যাসি-সম্প্রদায়ের সভ্যবিশেষ।

ĕs-tăb-lish, *v. t.* **1.** To settle on a firm or permanent basis ;

as, to *establish* a house of business; প্রতিষ্ঠা করা, সুদৃঢ় ভিত্তির উপর প্রতিষ্ঠিত করা, স্থাপন করা, সংস্থাপন করা, (গৃহাদির) পত্তন করা। **2.** To settle as a person, oneself, etc. in office ; to ordain ; স্থাপন করা ; ব্যবস্থাপন করা, বিধান করা। **3.** To confirm ; বলবৎ করা, দৃঢ়তর করা। **4.** (Reflexively) To set up in business ; to settle in any position ; as, they *established* themselves in the citadel; ব্যবসায়ে প্রতিষ্ঠিত করা; কোন স্থানে স্থাপন করা। **5.** To prove and cause to be accepted as true ; to set up permanently ; as, to *establish* a fact, claim, custom, etc. ; প্রতিপন্ন করা ; প্রতিষ্ঠাপিত করা। **6.** To create and regulate as a colony etc. ; উপনিবেশ প্রভৃতি স্থাপন করা। **—er,** *n.* One who establishes; সংস্থাপয়িতা, প্রতিষ্ঠাতা, স্থাপক, প্রতিপাদক। **—lished,** *adj.* Ratified ; set up and supported by the state ; as, the *established* church ; প্রতিষ্ঠিত, দৃঢ়ীভূত ; শাসনতন্ত্রকর্ত্তৃক প্রতিষ্ঠিত ও পৃষ্ঠপোষিত। **—ment,** *n.* **1.** Act of establishing or settling on a firm basis ; state of being established ; settlement, প্রতিষ্ঠা, সংস্থাপন, পত্তন ; ব্যবস্থা ; নিষ্পত্তি, নির্দ্ধারণ। **2.** Confirmation ; দৃঢ়ীকরণ। **3.** That which is established ; সুপ্রতিষ্ঠিত বিষয়। **4.** A place of residence or of business ; as, to keep up a separate *establishment*, (esp. for a paramour) ; a public institution ; বাসভবন বা ব্যবসায়ের স্থান ; নিবেশন, অধিষ্ঠান, সংসার, গৃহস্থালী, প্রতিষ্ঠান। **5.** The staff of servants etc. ; ভৃত্যবর্গ, কর্ম্মচারিবর্গ। **6.** Permanent civil or military force or organisation ; as, civil *establishment* ; সামরিক বা অসামরিক বিভাগীয় স্থায়ী কর্ম্মচারিসম্প্রদায়। **—men-ta'-ri-an,** *n.* One who maintains the doctrine that the church be governed by the laws of the state ; খৃষ্টীয় ধর্ম্মসংঘ রাজবিধি দ্বারা শাসিত ও নিয়ন্ত্রিত হইবে, যিনি এইরূপ মত পোষণ করেন। **Church establishment, The establishment** — রাজবিধি দ্বারা প্রতিষ্ঠিত ধর্ম্মসংঘের শাসনপদ্ধতি। **Peace establishment** — শান্তির সময়ের সৈন্যসংখ্যা। **Separate establishment**—অতিরিক্ত গৃহ-ভৃত্য, আসবাব, প্রভৃতি, (বিশেষতঃ উপপত্নীর জন্য রক্ষিত)। **War establishment** — যুদ্ধসময়ের বর্দ্ধিত সৈন্য-সংখ্যা।

estaminet, (*F.*), *n.* A cafe where smoking is allowed ; যে কাফিগৃহে ধূমপান করিতে দেওয়া হয়।

ĕs-tāte', *n.* **1.** (*Archaic*) Condition; দশা, পদ, গতি, অবস্থা, হাল। **2.** Landed property ; possessions ; collective assets and liabilities of a person ; ভূসম্পত্তি, বিষয় সম্পত্তি, মহাল ; অধিকৃত বা অধিগত বস্তু ; কোনও ব্যক্তির সম্পত্তি ও দেনার সমষ্টি। **3.** An order or class of men in the body politic ; রাষ্ট্রের ভিন্ন ভিন্ন অঙ্গ বা শ্রেণী, বর্গ (আঃ বঃ)। **4.** One's interest in landed property ; as, widow's *estate* in her husband's property ; ভূসম্পত্তিতে ব্যক্তি বিশেষের স্বত্ব। **—tat'-ed,** *adj.* Furnished with, or possessed, esp. of, landed property ; সম্পত্তিশালী, ভূসম্পত্তিশালী। **Personal estate**—অস্থাবর সম্পত্তি। **Real estate** — ভূ-সম্পত্তি, স্থাবর-সম্পত্তি। **The fourth estate**—The press ; মুদ্রাযন্ত্র, সংবাদ-পত্র। **The three estates** — আর্কবিশপ, বিশপ প্রভৃতি উচ্চ পদস্থ ধর্ম্মযাজকগণ, সম্ভ্রান্ত এবং কুলীন-সম্প্রদায় (ডিউক, মারকুইস্ প্রভৃতি) এবং জনসাধারণের প্রতিনিধিগণ। **To reach man's estate**—To attain majority ; সাবালকত্ব প্রাপ্ত হওয়া।

ĕs-teem' (-tēm'), *v. t.* & *n.* **1.** To prize ; to regard with reverence ; বহুমূল্য জ্ঞান করা ; সমাদর করা, শ্রদ্ধা করা, মান্য করা। **2.** To deem ; as, he will *esteem* it as a favour ; গণ্য করা, পরিগণনা করা, বিবেচনা করা, জ্ঞান করা। ***Noun.*** High regard ; respect ; appreciation ; high value ; সমাদর, শ্রদ্ধা, সম্ভ্রম ; সম্মান, বহুমান ; গুণগ্রহণ, গুণগ্রাহিতা ; বহুমূল্য। **—teemed',** *adj.* Respected ; regarded ; সম্মানিত ; সমাদৃত।

ĕs'-tim-ă-ble, *adj.* **1.** Worthy of esteem ; মাননীয়, আদরণীয়, শ্রদ্ধেয়, মান্য, শ্লাঘ্য। **2.** Capable of being estimated ; পরিমেয়, নিরূপ্য, মূল্যাবধারণ-যোগ্য।

ĕs'-ti-māte, *v. t.* & *n.* **1.** To determine the value or worth of (a thing); মূল্যাবধারণ করা। **2.** To make a rough calculation of ; মোটামুটি নির্দ্ধারণ করা, আনুমানিক মূল্য নির্দ্ধারণ করা, বরাদ্দ করা। **3.** To form an opinion regarding ; "To *estimate* the intention and sincerity of a movement ;" কোন ব্যক্তির গুণ বা যোগ্যতা নির্দ্ধারণ বা অনুমান করা। **4.** To fix by estimate, (with *at*) ; আন্দাজ করিয়া নির্দ্ধারণ করা। ***Noun.*** **1.** An approximate calculation (of the value, size, extent, quantity or quality of a thing); valuation ; the quantity estimated ; কোন বস্তুর মূল্য, আয়তন, বিস্তার বা গুণ নির্ণয় ; মূল্যাবধারণ ; অবধারিত সংখ্যা বা পরিমাণ। **2.** A statement of probable expenses of any undertaking ; আনুমানিক ব্যয়াবধারণ, বরাদ্দ, আনুমানিক ব্যয়নির্ণয়। **3.** Judgment of the character or qualities of a person etc. ; "A just *estimate* of us ;" যোগ্যতাবধারণ, কোন ব্যক্তির চরিত্র বা গুণ সম্বন্ধে মতামত। **—ma'-tion,** *n.* **1.** Opinion ; judgment ; as, in any *estimation* ; মতামত; বিচার, বিবেচনা। **2.** Regard ; esteem ; as, to hold in high *estimation* ; সম্মান, শ্রদ্ধা ; সম্ভ্রম, সমাদর। **3.** Act of estimating or reckoning the value, worth, extent or size etc. of a thing etc. ; (কোন ব্যক্তির) যোগ্যতা-নিরূপণ। **4** Manner of estimating ; মূল্যাবধারণ

প্রণালী। —ma-tive, *adj.* —ma-tor, *n.* One who estimates ; a valuer ; আনুমানিক ব্যয় নির্দ্ধারক ; মূল্যনিরূপক। **To be in estimation**—To be in esteem or regard ; সমাদৃত হওয়া। **To hold in estimation** — To regard or respect ; সম্ভ্রম করা, সম্মান করা, সমাদর করা।

ĕs'-tĭv-ăl, *adj.* See ÆSTIVAL.

ĕs-tŏp', *v. t.* **1.** To bar ; to stop ; বাধা দেওয়া; স্থগিত করা। **2.** (*Law*) To impede or bar by one's own act ; (আইন) স্বকার্য্যদ্বারা বাধা দেওয়া, প্রতিবন্ধ করা। **—page,** *n.* **—pel,** *n.* (*Law*) An impediment or bar to a right of action arising from a man's own act or where he is forbidden by law to speak against his own deed ; (আইন) পূর্ব্ববর্ত্তীকালে কোন উক্তি বা কার্য্য করা হেতু পরবর্ত্তী সময়ে তদ্বিপরীত উক্তি বা কার্য্য করিতে গেলে যে প্রতিবন্ধক উপস্থাপিত হয়।

ĕs-tō'-vērs, *n. pl.* (*Law*) The tenant's right of taking necessary wood from an estate for fuel, repairs, etc. ; রন্ধন, গৃহাদি মেরামত প্রভৃতির জন্য কোন জমিদারী হইতে আবশ্যক কাষ্ঠাদি আহরণের অধিকার।

ĕs-trade' (-trād), *n.* A platform ; মঞ্চ।

ĕs-trānge', *v. t.* **1.** To alienate in affection or feeling ; as, to *estrange* a man from his friends ; স্নেহপাশ ছিন্ন করা, স্নেহচ্যুত করা। **2.** (*Archaic*) To withdraw or keep away from ; বিশ্লিষ্ট করা, দূরে রাখা (অপ্রঃ)। **—ment,** *n.* Alienation or withdrawal of the heart or affections from ; স্নেহচ্যুতি, বিচ্ছেদ।

ĕs-tray' (-trā), *n.* (*Law*) Stray animal ; (আইন) যূথভ্রষ্ট পশু।

ĕs-treat' (-trēt), *n.* & *v. t.* A true copy or extract of writing under which fines etc. are to be levied ; কাগজের যথার্থ প্রতিলিপি বা সারমর্ম্ম,—যাহার বলে জরিমানা প্রভৃতি আদায় করা যায়। ***Verb t.*** To levy, as fines etc. under an extract ; উক্ত প্রকার কাগজপত্রের নকল বা সারমর্ম্ম আদালতে দাখিল করিয়া জরিমানা প্রভৃতি আদায় করা।

ĕs'-tū-ā-rȳ, *n.* **1.** The mouth of a river where the tide meets the river current ; a frith ; নদীর মোহানা, সাগর-সঙ্গম ; খাড়ী। **—rine,** *adj.*

ē-sū'-ri-ĕnt, *adj.* & *n.* Hungry ; greedy ; ক্ষুধিত ; লোভী। ***Noun.*** A greedy person ; লোভী ব্যক্তি। **—ence, —en-cy,** *ns.*

etat-major, (*F.*), *n.* (*Mil.*) Staff of an army ; staff-office ; সামরিক দপ্তর খানার কর্ম্মচারিবর্গ ; সামরিক দপ্তর খানা।

ĕt-cĕt'-ēr-ă, —cæt'—, (-sĕt-), (Abbreviation—etc. or &c.) (*pl.* -AS) *phrase.* & *n.* And so on ; and so forth ; and the rest ; আদি, ইত্যাদি ; প্রভৃতি; প্রমুখ। ***Noun.*** (*Pl.*) Extras ; sundries ; "fifty guineas a year without the *etceteras* ;" অতিরিক্ত প্রাপ্য ; এ ও তা পাঁচ রকম জিনিষ।

etch (ĕch), *v. t.* & *i.* **1.** To engrave (metals, glass, etc.) eating out the lines by means of some acids or corrosives ; দ্রাবক অথবা অন্য কোন প্রকার রাসায়নিক ক্ষয়কর দ্রব্য সহযোগে ধাতুফলকে রেখাদি উৎকীর্ণ করা। **2.** To produce as figures etc. on metal, glass, etc. by etching ; to produce (pictures etc.) or to portray (subjects etc.) by this method ; দ্রাবকের সাহায্যে কাচ, ধাতুফলক প্রভৃতির উপর চিত্রাদি উৎপাদন করা ; উক্ত উপায়ে (কোন বিষয়ের) চিত্রাদি অঙ্কন করা। ***Verb i.*** To practise the art of etching ; দ্রাবকের সাহায্যে কাচ, ধাতুফলক, প্রভৃতির উপর অঙ্কনের কার্য্য করা। **Etch'-ing,** *n.* **1.** A picture printed from an etched plate ; দ্রাবকোৎকীর্ণ ফলক হইতে মুদ্রিত চিত্র। **2.** The act or art of etching ; ধাতুফলকের উপর দ্রাবকের সাহায্যে (চিত্রাদি) উৎকীর্ণ করণ, উক্ত প্রকারে চিত্র উৎকীর্ণ করার শিল্প। **Etching-needle**—ধাতুফলকোপরি (চিত্রাদি) উৎকীর্ণ করার কাজে ব্যবহৃত সূচী বিশেষ।

ē-tēr'-năl, *adj.* **1.** Without beginning or end of existence ; everlasting ; without an end ; immortal ; আদ্যন্তহীন, অনাদ্যন্ত, আদ্যন্তরহিত, অনাদিসিদ্ধ, অনাদি, অনন্ত ; নিত্য, অনন্তকাল স্থায়ী, সনাতন, শাশ্বত, চিরন্তন, ধ্রুব ; অশেষ ; অনশ্বর, অবিনাশী, অমর, অক্ষয়। **2.** (*Colloq.*) Incessant ; ceaseless ; as, the *eternal* bickerings ; অবিরাম ; অবিশ্রান্ত। **3.** Unchangeable ; immutable ; as, an *eternal* truth ; অপরিবর্ত্তনীয় ; নিত্য। **4.** (Now *vul.* or *dial.*) Abhorrent ; "An *eternal* rogue" ; (বর্ত্তমানে ইতর ভাষায় বা উপভাষায়) জঘন্য। **—ize, —nize,** *v. t.* **1.** To make eternal or endless ; অনন্ত করা, চিরস্থায়ী করা, অক্ষয় করা। **2.** To immortalize ; as, to *eternalize* one's name ; অমর করা, চিরস্মরণীয় করা। **—ly,** *adv.* **—ter'-ni-ty,** *n.* **1.** Endless time ; অনন্তকাল। **2.** State or quality of being eternal ; duration without beginning or end ; immortality ; শাশ্বততা ; অনন্তকাল-স্থায়িত্ব, অনন্ততা, নিত্যতা ; অমৃতত্ব, অমরত্ব। **3.** State or time after death ; future life ; "They were going to be launched into *eternity* ; মৃত্যুর পরবর্ত্তী কাল বা অবস্থা ; পারলৌকিক জীবন। **4.** Immortal fame ; অমরকীর্ত্তি। **5.** (*Phil.*) That which transcends time ; অনাদ্যন্ততা, আদ্যন্তশূন্যতা। **6.** (*Pl.*) Eternal truth ; শাশ্বত সত্য, ধ্রুব সত্য, নিত্য সত্য। **The eternal city**—রোমনগরী। **The eternal life**—অনন্ত জীবন।

ē-tē'-sĭ-ăn, *adj.* Periodical ; annual ; সাময়িক ; সাম্বৎসরিক। **Etesian wind** — প্রতিবৎসর ভূমধ্যসাগরে প্রায় চল্লিশ দিবস ব্যাপিয়া উত্তর-পশ্চিম কোণ হইতে যে নিদাঘ-পবন প্রবাহিত হয়।

ē'-thēr, *n.* **1.** A thin subtle matter much finer than air supposed to pervade the upper regions of the sky; upper regions beyond clouds; the clear sky; ব্যোম, পঞ্চমভূত, আকাশতত্ত্ব (হিঃ কোঃ); অন্তরীক্ষ, নভঃ, শূন্য; নির্মেঘ আকাশ। 2. (*Chem.*) A light, volatile and inflammable liquid; এক প্রকার লঘু, দাহ্য ও উদ্বায়ী তৈল, উদ্বায়ী তৈল (সাঃ পঃ), ঈথার। 3. (*Phys.*) A subtle fluid of great elasticity permeating space and filling the interstices between molecules of air and other matters; the medium through which light waves, heat etc. are transmitted; এক প্রকার অতিসূক্ষ্ম বায়বীয় পদার্থ,—ইহা আকাশ ও যাবতীয় পদার্থের অণুসকলের মধ্যবর্ত্তী অতি সঙ্কীর্ণ ফাঁকা স্থান ব্যাপিয়া অবস্থান করিতেছে, আকাশতত্ত্ব, তেজোবহ। **–ther′-i-al, –the′-re-al,** *adjs.* **1.** Pertaining to the upper regions of the sky; celestial; আন্তরীক্ষ; স্বর্গীয়। 2. Formed of ether; intangible; ব্যোম-পদার্থ রচিত, আকাশময়; অস্পর্শবেদ্য। 2. Characterised by extreme delicacy; as, an *etherial* form, manner, thought, etc.; সূক্ষ্ম, পরমসুকুমার, পরমকমনীয়। **4.** (*Chem.*) Relating to, or filled with, ether; containing, or like, ether; (রসায়ন-শাস্ত্র) ঈথারীয়; ঈথারপূর্ণ, ঈথারময়, ঈথারবৎ। **5.** (*Phys.*) Of or pertaining to ether; ব্যোম পদার্থ সম্বন্ধীয় বা বিষয়ক। **–the′-re-al-ism, –the-re-al′-i-ty,** *ns.* **–the-re-al-i-za′-tion,** *n.* **–the′-re-al-ize,** *v. t.* **1.** To make ethereal; to convert into ether; ঈথার বা ব্যোম পদার্থে পরিণত করা; উক্ত পদার্থদ্বারা অভিভূত বা অচেতন করা। **2.** To make spiritual; দেবযোনির মত সূক্ষ্মশরীর বিশিষ্ট করা। **–the-re-al-ly,** *adv.* **Ethereal double**—লিঙ্গশরীর (হিঃ কোঃ), লিঙ্গদেহ (ঐ), প্রাণময় কোষ (ঐ), ছায়াদেহ (ঐ)। **Ethereal oil**—উদ্বায়ী তৈল।

ē-thêr′-ĭc, *adj.* (*Phys.*) Ethereal; ব্যোমপদার্থ সম্বন্ধীয়। **Etheric telegraphy** — Wireless telegraphy; তারবিহীন তাড়িতবার্ত্তাবহ।

ē-thē′-rĭ-fȳ, *v. t.* (*Chem.*) To convert as alcohol into ether; (রসায়ন-শাস্ত্র) সুরাবীর্য্য প্রভৃতিকে ঈথরে পরিণত করা। **–fi-ca′-tion,** *n.* The act or process of converting alcohol into ether; ঈথর প্রস্তুত প্রণালী।

ē′-thêr-īze, *v. t.* **1.** To convert (alcohol) into ether; (সুরাবীর্য্য) ঈথরে পরিণত করা। **2.** To stupefy with ether; to put (a patient) under the influence of ether; ঈথর প্রয়োগদ্বারা সংজ্ঞাশূন্য করা; রোগীকে ঈথর প্রয়োগ করা। **–i-za′-tion,** *n.*

ĕth′-ĭc, (now usually) **–i-căl,** *adj.* **1.** Relating to morals; treating of morality and of ethics as a science; নীতিসম্পর্কীয়; নৈতিক, নীতিবিষয়ক, আচার সম্বন্ধীয়। **2.** Pertaining to ethos or character; চরিত্রসম্বন্ধীয়। **–al ly,** *adv.* **–ise,** *v.t.*

ĕth′-ĭc, *n.* **1.** (*Pl.*) The science of morals; নীতিবিজ্ঞান, নীতিশাস্ত্র, শীলবিদ্যা, আচারশাস্ত্র (হিঃ কোঃ)। **2.** (*pl.*) A treatise on moral philosophy; নীতি-শাস্ত্র বিষয়ক পুস্তক। **3.** (*Pl.*) Moral principles; the rules of conduct; নৈতিক বুদ্ধি, নীতি; আচার-নীতি। **–i-cist,** *n.* One who is versed in ethics; নীতিশাস্ত্রবেত্তা। **–i-cize,** *v. t.* To make ethical; শীল সম্পন্ন করা।

E-thi-ŏp′-i-ăn, E′-thi-ŏp, (-ē-), *adjs.* & *ns.* Of or pertaining to Ethiopia or its people; ইথিওপীয়, হাব্সী জাতি সম্বন্ধীয়। ***Noun.*** **1.** A native of Ethiopia, a country lying south of Egypt; মিশরের দক্ষিণে অবস্থিত দেশবিশেষের লোক। **2.** A negro or black man; কাফ্রী অথবা কৃষ্ণকায় পুরুষ, হাব্সী। **–op′-ic,** *n.* The language of the ancient Abyssinian empire; প্রাচীন এবিসিনিয়া সাম্রাজ্যের ভাষা। **The Ethiopian will not change his skin**—অঙ্গারঃ শতধৌতোঽপি মলিনত্বং ন মুঞ্চতি। **To wash an or the Ethiop (white)**—To attempt the impossible; অসম্ভব সাধনে চেষ্টা করা।

ĕth′-nic, –ni-cal, *adjs.* & *ns.* **1.** Pertaining to race; ethnological; জাতিসম্পর্কীয়; জাতিতত্ত্ব বিষয়ক। **2.** (Only *ethnic*) Heathen; pagan; পৌত্তলিক; অখ্রীষ্টান। ***Noun.*** (Only *ethnic*) A heathen; পৌত্তলিক। **–ni-cal-ly,** *adv.* As regards race; জাতি সম্পর্কে। **–ni-cism,** *n.*

ĕth-nŏg′-ră-phȳ, *n.* The science which deals with the origin, distribution, manners, customs an religions, etc. of the different race of men; যে শাস্ত্রে ভূমণ্ডলস্থ বিভিন্ন জাতির রীতি, নীতি, ধর্ম্ম, আচার, উৎপত্তি ও বিস্তার বিষয়ে আলোচিত হইয়া থাকে, নৃকুল বর্ণন (হিঃ কোঃ), নৃকুলবিদ্যা (ঐ) জাতিতত্ত্ব। **–no-graph′-ic, –no-graph′-i-cal,** *adjs.* Pertaining to ethnography; জাতি-বিজ্ঞান বিষয়ক। **–pher,** *n.* A student of ethnography; জাতি-তত্ত্বানুশীলনকারী।

ĕth-nŏl′-ŏ-ğy, *n.* The science that deals with the physical features, manners, religion and other characteristics of the different races of men; যে শাস্ত্র পাঠে বিভিন্ন মানব পরিবারের ভাষা, ধর্ম্ম, রীতিনীতি ও শারীরিক গঠনাদি সম্বন্ধে জ্ঞানলাভ করা যায়, জাতিবিজ্ঞান, নৃজাতিবিজ্ঞান, জাতি-তত্ব, জাতিবিদ্যা। **–no-log′-ic, –no-log′-i-cal,** *adjs.* **–no-log′-i cal-ly,** *adv.* **–gist,** *n.*

ē-thŏl-′ŏ-ğy, *n.* The science of character; the science of the formation of character; চরিত্র-বিজ্ঞান; জাতি, ব্যক্তি বা সম্প্রদায়-গত চরিত্র গঠন বিষয়ক-শাস্ত্র, নরপ্রকৃতি শাস্ত্র। **–gist,** *n.* **–tho-log′-i-cal,** *adj.*

ē′-thŏs′ *n.* **1.** The characteristic spirit, disposition or sentiment of a people or community ; the spirit actuating manners and customs ; কোন জাতি বা সমাজের ভাব বা প্রকৃতির বিশেষত্ব ; আচার এবং রীতির অন্তর্নিহিত প্রণোদক ভাব।

ē′-thȳl, *n.* (*Chem.*) The base of ordinary alcohol, ether and acetic acid ; (রসায়ন-শাস্ত্র) একপ্রকার দাহ্য অবর্ণ রাসায়নিক পদার্থ।

ē′-ti-ö-lāte, *v.t.* & *i.* **1.** To cause as a plant, to become pale or white by depriving the sun's rays ; সূর্য্যালোকপাত বন্ধ করিয়া (বৃক্ষাদি) পরিম্লান বা পাণ্ডুর বর্ণ করা। **2.** To give a pale hue to, as a person or his skin ; বিবর্ণ করা। ***Verb i.*** To become pale or white from want of sunlight ; সূর্য্যালোকের অভাবে বিবর্ণ বা শুক্লবর্ণ হওয়া। **—la′-tion,** *n.* Condition produced by etiolating ; বৈবর্ণ্য।

ē-ti-ŏl-ō-ġȳ, *n.* See ÆTOLOGY.

ĕt-i-quette′ (-kĕt), *n.* **1.** Conventional forms of personal behaviour in polite society ; শিষ্টাচার, আদবকায়দা, সংসমাজানুমোদিত আচার-ব্যবহার, শিষ্টাচার-রীতি। **2.** The prescribed ceremonial of a court ; রাজদরবারের আদবকায়দা। **3.** The rules prohibiting the members of some professions from doing things deemed likely to injure the interests of their breathren or to lower their dignity ; as, medical or legal *etiquette* ; (ডাক্তারি, ওকালাতি প্রভৃতি) ব্যবসায়ে নিযুক্ত ব্যক্তিগণ স্ব স্ব সম্প্রদায়ের স্বার্থ ও গৌরব রক্ষার্থ যে নিয়মাবলীর অনুসরণ করিয়া থাকেন, ব্যবসায় সম্পর্কীয় শিষ্টাচার।

ĕt′-nă, *n.* An utensil for heating small quantity of liquid by a spirit lamp ; সুরাদীপের সাহায্যে তরল পদার্থ উত্তপ্তকরণার্থ ক্ষুদ্র পাত্রবিশেষ।

E′-tŏn (ē-), *n.* Eton jacket or coat ; ইটন বিদ্যালয়ের ছাত্রদের পরিধেয় কুর্ত্তা বিশেষ।

Et-ŏn′-i-ăn (ĕt-), *n.* A student of the famous Eton college in England ; ইংলণ্ডের সুপ্রসিদ্ধ ইটন্ কলেজের ছাত্র। (এই বিদ্যালয়ে ইংলণ্ডের ধনি-সন্তানগণ পাঠ করে।)

E-trŭs′-căn (ē-), *adj.* & *n.* Of or pertaining to ancient Etruria,

Etruscan vases.

in Italy ; ইতালী দেশস্থ প্রাচীন এট্রুরিয়া দেশীয় বা উক্ত দেশ-সংক্রান্ত। ***Noun.*** A native of ancient Etruria ; প্রাচীন এট্রুরিয়া প্রদেশের অধিবাসী।

et se-quen′-tes, -tia, [*L.*]— And the words, pages, etc. that follow ; এবং পরবর্ত্তী বাক্য, পৃষ্ঠা, প্রভৃতি (পুস্তকের সম্পর্কে ব্যবহৃত হয়)। (Abbr. *et seq.* or *et seqq.*)

ĕt-ui′ (-wē), **ĕt-wee′** (-wē), *n.* A small case for holding needles, scissors and other small articles ; সূচী, কাঁচি প্রভৃতি রাখিবার কৌটা।

ĕ-tȳ-mŏl′-ō-ġȳ, *n.* **1.** That department of philology which treats of the origin, primary significations and changes of forms of words and their meanings ; শব্দসাধনবিদ্যা, শব্দের ব্যুৎপত্তি তত্ত্ব ; শব্দ-ব্যুৎপত্তি শাস্ত্র (হিঃ কোঃ), নিরুক্ত। **2.** The part of grammar which deals with inflection and derivations of words ; ব্যাকরণের শব্দরূপ ও ধাতুপ্রকরণ বিষয়ক অংশ। **—mol′-o-ger,** *n.* **—mo-log′-ic, —mo-log′-i-cal,** *adjs.* Pertaining to etymology ; শব্দব্যুৎপত্তি সংক্রান্ত, ব্যুৎপত্তি বিষয়ক। **—mo-log′-i-cal-ly,** *adv.* **—mol′-o-gise,** *v. t.* & *i.* To trace the root of ; to give the etymology or derivation of, as a word ; ব্যুৎপত্তি নির্ণয় করা, শব্দ সাধন করা ; ধাতু নির্ণয় করা। (*Verb i.*) To study etymology ; to form etymologies for words ; শব্দব্যুৎপত্তি বিষয়ক শাস্ত্র আলোচনা করা ; শব্দের ব্যুৎপত্তি নিষ্পাদন করা। **—mol′-o-gist-** *n.* One who investigates the origin of words ; one versed in etymology ; শব্দের ব্যুৎপত্তি অনুসন্ধায়ী ; শব্দ-ব্যুৎপত্তিতত্ত্বজ্ঞ।

ĕt′-ȳ-mŏn, *n.* An original or primary word giving rise to a derivative ; ধাতু প্রাতিপাদিক।

eu-că-lȳp′-tŭs (ū-) *n.* A genus of plants of the myrtle order ; কয়েক প্রকার সুরভি নির্যাসস্রাবী বৃক্ষের সাধারণ নাম,—অষ্ট্রেলিয়া ও তৎসন্নিহিত দ্বীপপুঞ্জের

Eucalyptus.

নির্যাসপ্রদ বৃক্ষসকল এই জাতীয় বৃক্ষ-শ্রেণীর অন্তর্ভুক্ত বলিয়া গণ্য হয়। **Eucalyptus oil** — ইউকেলিপ্টাস পত্র হইতে প্রাপ্ত তৈল বিশেষ। [এই তৈল ঔষধস্বরূপ ব্যবহৃত হয়।]

eu′c͟hă-ris (ū-), *n.* A bulbous plant of South America bearing white bell-shaped flowers ; দক্ষিণ আমেরিকা দেশীয় কন্দজ বৃক্ষ বিশেষ।

eu′-c͟hă-rist (ū-), *n.* **1.** Lord's supper ; প্রভুর নৈশ-ভোজ। [যীশুখৃষ্ট মৃত্যুর পূর্ব্ব রাত্রে শিষ্যগণের সহিত ভোজন করিয়াছিলেন ; তৎস্মরণে খৃষ্টীয় সমাজে একটী ধর্ম্মক্রিয়া অনুষ্ঠিত হইয়া থাকে। ইহাকে Eucharist বলে। উক্ত অনুষ্ঠানে প্রদত্ত রুটি ও সুরা যীশুখৃষ্টের মাংস ও রক্তস্বরূপ আহার করা হয়।] **2.** Consecrated elements, esp. the bread ;

(ধর্ম্মক্রিয়া বিশেষ দ্বারা) শোধিত রুটি। **3.** The communion ; খৃষ্টের শেষ নৈশ-ভোজন-স্মারক অনুষ্ঠান। **4.** Thanksgiving ; "To pay their *eucharist* to the Holy Ghost;" ধন্যবাদ-প্রদান। **—ris′-tial,** *n.* (*Eccles.*) A vessel to hold the consecrated bread for use at the Eucharist ; (যাজকীয় শাস্ত্র) খৃষ্টের শেষ নৈশ ভোজন-স্মারক অনুষ্ঠানের শোধিত রুটি রক্ষার জন্য পাত্র বিশেষ। **—ris′tic, —ris-ti′-cal,** *adjs.* **To give** or **receive the Eucharist**—To give or receive the sacred bread ; পবিত্র রুটি প্রদান বা গ্রহণ করা।

eu′-chre (ū-kêr), *n.* & *v. t.* **1.** A game of cards played by two, three or four players ; একপ্রকার তাস খেলা—দুই, তিন বা চারিজন ব্যক্তি মিলিয়া খেলিয়া থাকে। **2.** Failure to take three tricks in a hand at euchre by a player who has made the trump ; উক্ত রূপ খেলায় ৩ পিঠ গ্রহণে অসমর্থতা। ***Verb t.*** **1.** To gain the advantage over (an adversary) by his failure to take three tricks; উক্তরূপ ক্রীড়ায় প্রতিপক্ষীয় ব্যক্তি ৩ পিঠ গ্রহণে অসমর্থ হইলে, তাহার উপর সুবিধা লাভ করা। **2.** To defeat in any scheme ; to outwit ; as, to *euchre* a person out of a project ; কোন উপায় ব্যর্থ করা ; কৌশল বা বুদ্ধিমত্তায় অতিক্রম করা।

eu-chrō-ic (ū-) *adj.* Pertaining to, or designating, a colourless crystal in organic acids ; স্বচ্ছ (হিঃ কোঃ), বিমল (ঐ)।

eu-dē′-mŏn-ism (-ū), **eu-dæ′-** (ū-dē-), *n.* The system of ethics which makes happiness the test of moral virtue ; নীতি-বিজ্ঞানের শাখা বিশেষ [এই মতানুসারে নৈতিক গুণের অধিকারী না হইলে, প্রাণে প্রকৃত আনন্দ বিরাজ করিতে পারেনা।]. সুখৈকোদ্দেশ্যবাদ (হিঃ কোঃ), সুখৈকপুরুষার্থবাদ (ঐ)। **—ist,** *n.*

eu-di-ŏm′-ĕ-tĕr (ū-), *n.* (*Chem.*) An instrument for determining the quantity of oxygen in air ; বায়ুতে অম্লজান বাষ্পের পরিমাণ নিরূপণার্থ যন্ত্র বিশেষ, বাতলক্ষণমাপক যন্ত্র (হিঃ কোঃ)। **—o-met′-ric, —o-met′-ri-cal,** *adjs.* **—o-met′-ri-cal-ly,** *adv.* **—om′-e-try,** *n.*

eu′-gē (ū-), *inter.* [*L.*] Bravo ! well-done ! সাবাস ! বেশ ! বাহবা !

eugenia caryophyllifolia—ছোট জাম (বেলঃ)।

eugenia jambolana — কাল জাম (বেলঃ)।

eu-gĕn′-ic, (ū-), *adj.* & *n.* Pertaining to the production of fine (human) offspring ; সুস্থ ও সুন্দর সন্তানোৎপাদন-সম্বন্ধীয়। ***Noun.*** (*Pl.*) The science of race culture ; যে বিজ্ঞানে জাতির উৎকর্ষের জন্য সুস্থ ও সুন্দর শিশু-উৎপাদনের বিষয় আলোচিত হইয়া থাকে, সুপ্রজনন-বিদ্যা।

eu-hē′-mêr-ism (ū-), *n.* Interpretation of myths as traditional accounts of historical events and personages ; ঐতিহাসিক ঘটনা ও ব্যক্তি সমূহের কিম্বদন্তীমূলক বিবরণ বলিয়া পৌরাণিক গল্প-সমূহের ব্যাখ্যান। **—ist,** *n.* **—is′-tic,** *adj.* **—ize,** *v. t.* & *i.*

eu′-lŏ-ġy̆ (ū-), *n.* The praise of any one either written or spoken ; praise ; encomium ; প্রশংসাবাদ, গুণকীর্ত্তন, গুণানুবাদ, স্তুতিগীত ; প্রশংসা, সুখ্যাতি; যশোকীর্ত্তন, স্তুতিবাদ, স্তব, স্তোত্র, স্তুতিপাঠ। **—log′-ic,** *adj.* Containing eulogy or praise; স্তুতিপূর্ণ, প্রশংসাপূর্ণ, সুখ্যাতিপূর্ণ। **—log′-i-cal-ly,** *adv.* **—gist,** *n.* One who praises in writing or speech ; encomiast ; প্রশংসাকারী ; স্তুতিপাঠক, স্তুতিব্রত। **—gis′-tic, —gis′-ti-cal,** *adjs.* Pertaining to eulogy ; containing praise ; commendatory ; প্রশংসাত্মক; স্তুতিবাদপূর্ণ ; স্তুতিগর্ভ। **—gis′-ti-cal-ly,** *adv.* **—lo′-gi-um,** *n.* An eulogy ; স্তুতিবাদ, স্তব, স্তুতি, গুণগ্রহণ, গুণস্তবন। **—gize,** *v. t.* To praise in words or writing ; to praise ; প্রশংসাবাদ করা, গুণানুবাদ করা ; গুণকীর্ত্তন করা, গুণবর্ণন করা।

eulophia vireus — সালেপমিশ্রি (বেলঃ)।

eu-nŭch (ū-), *n.* A castrated man, esp. such a man who has the charge of a harem ; a chamberlain ; ছিন্নমুষ্ক পুরুষ, ষণ্ড, অপুংস, বর্ষবর, ছিন্নমুষ্ক, ছিন্নাণ্ড, ক্লীব; খোজা ; কঞ্চুক।

eu-ŏn′-y-mous (ū-ŏn-ĭ-mŭs), *n.* A genus of shrubs ; একজাতীয় গুল্ম।

eu-pĕp′-si-ă (ū-), **—pĕp′-sy̆,** *n.* (Opposed to *dyspepsia*) (*med.*) Good digestion ; (ভৈষজ্য-শাস্ত্র) সুপরিপাক শক্তি। **—pep′-tic,** *adj.* Of or pertaining to good digestion ; having good digestion ; easy of digestion ; পরিপাক-শক্তি সম্পর্কীয় ; উত্তম পরিপাক শক্তিবিশিষ্ট; সুপরিপাচ্য, লঘুপাক।

eu′-phē-mism (ū-), *n.* The substitution of a mild and delicate expression for something harsh, blunt or offensive to good manners ; a word or expression thus substituted ; as, '*queer*' is an euphemism for '*mad*' ; কর্কশ, কঠোর বা শিষ্টাচার বিরোধী বাক্যের স্থলে সাধু, কোমল ও কমনীয় বাক্য প্রয়োগ, মোলায়েম কথা প্রয়োগ ; মোলায়েম শব্দ বা বাক্য, মঙ্গলভাষিত। **—mis′-tic, —mis′-ti-cal,** *adjs.* Softened or sweetened in expression ; ললিত, কোমল, কান্ত, মোলায়েম। **—mis′-ti-cal-ly,** *adv.* By way of euphemism ; মোলায়েম করিয়া। **—mize,** *v. t.* & *i.* To express in a delicate language ; মোলায়েম করিয়া বলা, মিষ্টকথায় বলা।

euphorbia thymifolia — শ্বেত কেওড়া।

euphobia tirraculli—লঙ্কাসীজ (বেলঃ)।

eu′-phŏ-ny̆ (ū-), *n.* **1.** A pleasing or sweet sound ; an agreeable combination of sounds ; the quality of having a pleasant sound ; মনোরম ধ্বনি, মধুর স্বর ; শ্রবণ-সুখদ স্বর-সম্মিলন, মধুর-কোমল-কান্ত স্বর-সম্মিলন ; মনোরম ধ্বনিবিশিষ্টতা। 2. (*Phon.*) A tendency to greater ease of pronunciation ; সুখোচ্চারণ-প্রবণতা। **—nize,** *v. t.* **—phon'-ic,** *adj.* Pertaining to euphony ; having euphony ; মধুর-কোমল কান্ত, সুস্বর, কর্ণ-মধুর, শ্রবণ-মঙ্গল। **—phon'-i-cal,** *adj.* **—phon'-i-cal-ly,** *adv.* **—pho'-ni-ous,** *adj.* Smooth-sounding ; ললিত, সুস্বর। **—pho'-ni-ous-ly,** *adv.*

eu'-phră-sy̆ (ü-), *n.* The eye-bright (a plant) ; একপ্রকার গুল্ম,—পূর্ব্বে অক্ষিরোগে ব্যবহৃত হইত।

eu'-phü-ism (ü-), *n.* High-flown style ; excessive eloquence of language ; অনুপ্রাস ও দীর্ঘ সমাসবহুল রচনাপদ্ধতি ; শব্দাড়ম্বরপূর্ণ রচনা-পদ্ধতি। [Lyly কৃত Euphues নামক আড়ম্বরপূর্ণ-শব্দবহুল গ্রন্থ হইতে এই শব্দটী উৎপন্ন হইয়াছে]। **—ist,** *n.* **—is'-tic, —is'-ti-cal,** *adjs.*

Eur-a'-sian (ür-ā-shĭ-ăn), *adj.* & *n.* [Eur (opean) and Asian] Of, or pertaining to, Europe and Asia ; as, the great *Eurasian* plain ; relating to Eurasians ; ইয়ুরোপ ও এসিয়া সম্পর্কীয় বা বিষয়ক, ইউরোপীয়-এসীয় ; ফিরিঙ্গি সম্পর্কীয়। ***Noun.*** A person of mixed European and Asian parentage ; ইউরোপ ও এসিয়া-দেশীয় পিতা মাতার সংসর্গ-জাত সন্তান, ফিরিঙ্গি।

eu-rē'-kă (ü-), *inter.* & *n.* The exclamation "I have found (it) ;" প্রাপ্তোস্মি ! পেয়েছি রে পেয়েছি ! ***Noun.*** An exulting exclamation ; a discovery achieved, (often used as a trade name in advertising) ; বিজয়োল্লাস-সূচক ধ্বনি ; সমুজ্জ্বল আবিষ্কার, সুবিখ্যাত আবিষ্ক্রিয়া। [গ্রীস-দেশের রাজা হীরো একটী স্বর্ণ-মুকুট নির্ম্মাণ করাইয়াছিলেন ; উক্ত মুকুটে খাইজ আছে কিনা তাহা নিরূপণার্থ মহাপণ্ডিত আর্কিমিডাস্ এর উপর ভারার্পণ করেন ; আর্কিমিডাস্ বহু চিন্তা ও চেষ্টার পরও কিছু নির্ণয় করিতে পারেন নাই। এক দিবস স্নানচিত্তে স্নানার্থ গমন করিয়া স্নানকুণ্ডে নামিলে পর তিনি লক্ষ্য করিলেন যে কতকটা জল উপচিয়া পড়িয়া গেল। এই ঘটনা হইতে বস্তুর আপেক্ষিক গুরুত্ব নিরূপণ বিষয়ের সন্ধান পাইয়া তিনি আনন্দে উন্মত্তবৎ হইয়া "পেয়েছি পেয়েছি" শব্দে উলঙ্গ দেহে দৌড়িতে দৌড়িতে রাজ-সদনে উপস্থিত হইয়াছিলেন। গ্রীক ভাষায় eureka শব্দে 'পেয়েছি' বুঝায়।]

Eu-rö-pē'-ăn (ü-), *adj.* & *n.* Relating to Europe or its inhabitants ; extending over Europe ; as, *European* reputation ; ইয়ুরোপ বা ইয়ুরোপবাসী সম্বন্ধীয়, ইয়ুরোপীয় ; সমগ্র ইয়ুরোপ-ব্যাপী, ইয়ুরোপ জুড়িয়া। ***Noun.*** An inhabitant of Europe ; ইয়ুরোপের অধিবাসী। **—ism,** *n.* Tendency to adop what is European ; ইউরোপীয় রীতিনীতি, জীবনযাত্রা নির্ব্বাহের পদ্ধতি, চিন্তা-প্রণালী প্রভৃতি গ্রহণের প্রবৃত্তি। **—i-za'-tion,** *n.* **—ize,** *v. t.* To make European in manners etc. ; to accustom to European usages ; রীতিনীতি আচার ব্যবহারে ইয়ুরোপীয়দিগের সমকক্ষ করা ; ইয়ুরোপীয় ব্যবহারে অভ্যস্ত করা।

euryale ferox—মাখনা (বেলঃ)।

Eu-stā'-chi-ăn (ü-), *adj.* Relating to Eustachius ; Eustachius নামক রোমনগরবাসী ভিষক-সম্বন্ধীয়। **Eustachian tube**—(*Anat.*) বায়ু চলাচলের জন্য মুখের পশ্চাদ্ভাগ হইতে কর্ণের মধ্য ভাগ পর্য্যন্ত প্রসারিত সূক্ষ্ম নল।

Eu-têr'-pē (ü-), *n.* 1. (*Class. myth.*) The Muse ; রাগরাগিণীর অধিষ্ঠাত্রী বাগ্ দেবী। 2. (*Bot.*) A genus of palms ; তাল-জাতীয় বৃক্ষশ্রেণী বিশেষ। **—an,** *adj.*

eu-thă-nā'-si-ă (ü-), *n.* 1. An easy death ; সুখমৃত্যু। 2 Act or process of causing an easy death, esp. in case of incurable disease ; সুখমৃত্যুজনন (বিশেষতঃ অসাধ্য রোগে।)

Eutropii chythys vacha—বাচা মাছ (গুপ্তঃ)।

ē-văc'-ü-āte, *v. t.* 1. To make empty ; (*fig.*) to deprive, (with *of*) ; শূন্য করা, খালি করা ; রিক্ত করা। 2. To withdraw from or quit ; as, the troops *evacuated* the position ; ছাড়া, ত্যাগ করা। 3. To discharge ; as, to *evacuate* excrements ; (মলমূত্রাদি) ত্যাগ করা, মোচন করা। **—ant,** *adj.* & *n.* **—a'-tion,** *n.* 1. Emptying ; শূন্যীকরণ, রেচন। 2. Withdrawing from ; as, *evacuation* of a fort ; পরিত্যাগকরণ। 3. (*Med.*) The act of causing a discharge by any of the excretory passages ; (ভৈষজ্য শাস্ত্র) মলমূত্রাদি ত্যাগ, রেচন। 4. That which is discharged ; ত্যক্ত মল-মূত্রাদি।

ē-vāde', *v. t.* & *i.* 1. To avoid artfully ; to escape from cleverly ; কৌশলপূর্ব্বক পরিহার করা ; ভাঁড়ান। 2. To elude ; to baffle ; এড়ান ; ফাঁকি দেওয়া, এড়িয়া যাওয়া, কাটাইয়া উঠা, টালবাহানা করা ; ব্যর্থ করা। **—vad'-a-ble,** *adj.* **—va'-sion,** *n.* See BELOW.

ē-văg'-i-nate, *v. t.* (*Physiol.*) To turn inside out, as a tubular organ ; ভিতরের দিক উল্টাইয়া বাহিরে আনা,—যথা নলাকৃতি দৈহিক যন্ত্র। **—na'-tion,** *n.*

ē-văl'-ü-āte, *v. t.* 1. To determine the value or amount of ; মূল্য নিরূপণ করা, সংখ্যা নিরূপণ করা 2. (*Math.*) To express numerically ; (গণিত শাস্ত্র) সংখ্যাদ্বারা প্রকাশ করা। **—a'-tion,** *n.* The process or result of evaluating ; মূল্য-নির্দ্ধারণ।

ĕv-ă-nesce (-nĕs), *v. t.* To fade away ; to vanish ; ক্রমশঃ লোপ বা অদৃশ্য হওয়া ; বিলীন হওয়া, অন্তর্হিত হওয়া। **—es'-cence,** *n.* 1. Vanishing away ; অন্তর্দ্ধান, অদর্শন, ক্রমশঃ দৃষ্টিবহির্ভূত হওন, বিলোপ। 2. Liability to dissipation or vanishing ;

অদৃশ্যমানতা। **—es′-cent,** *adj.* **1.** Vanishing quickly; as, an *evanescent* impression; fleeting; ক্রমশঃ বিলীয়মান, অন্তর্হিয়মান, দ্রুতাপগামী; ক্ষণস্থায়ী। **2.** Infinitesimal, esp. in mathematics; as, an *evanescent* quantity; ক্ষুদ্রতম।

ē-văn′-gĕl *n.* (*Archaic*) The gospel; one of the four gospels; (অপ্রচলিত) সুসমাচার; মার্ক, মথি, জন বা লুক লিখিত সুসমাচারের অন্যতম। **2.** A doctrine or principle (of politics, reform, etc.); "I do not announce a new *evangel* to be ushered in by flourish of trumpets;" রাজনীতি, সংস্কার, প্রভৃতি সম্পর্কীয় মতবাদ বা মূলতত্ত্ব। **3.** An evangelist; খৃষ্টধর্ম্ম-প্রচারক। **—gel-ism,** *n.*

ē-văn-gĕl′-i-căl, *adj.* & *n.* Pertaining or according to the gospel or the Christian religion; সুসমাচার-সম্পর্কীয়, খৃষ্টীয় সুসমাচার নামক গ্রন্থ চতুষ্টয়ের অন্তর্ভুক্ত, সুসমাচারানুযায়ী (also **—ic**)। **2.** Grounding salvation on faith in the atoning sacrifice of Christ for sin; খৃষ্টের দেহত্যাগ মানবের পরিত্রাণের মূলকারণ—এইরূপ মতাবলম্বী। ***Noun.*** One holding evangelical principles; উক্ত মতাবলম্বী ব্যক্তি। **—ism,** *n.* **—ly,** *adv.*

ē-văn′-gĕl-ist, *n.* **1.** Writer of one of the four gospels; সুসমাচার গ্রন্থ-চতুষ্টয়ের অন্যতমের রচয়িতা। **2.** One who preaches the gospel; সুসমাচার প্রচারক, খৃষ্টধর্ম্ম-প্রচারক। **3.** A layman engaged in home missionary work; স্বদেশে প্রচারকার্য্যে নিরত গৃহী ব্যক্তি। **—is′-tic,** *adj.*

ē-văn′-gĕl-ize, *v. t.* & *i.* **1.** To convert (persons) to Christianity; to preach the gospel to; as, to *evangelize* the nation; খৃষ্টধর্ম্মে দীক্ষিত করা; খৃষ্টীয় সুসমাচার প্রচার করা। ***Verb i.*** To preach the gospel; খৃষ্টীয় সুসমাচার প্রচার করা। **—i-za′-tion,** *n.*

ē-văn′-ish, *v. i.* To vanish away; বিলীন হওয়া, অন্তর্হিত হওয়া। **—ment,** *n.*

ē-văp′-or-āte (-ĕr-), *v. t.* & *i.* **1.** To convert into vapour as a solid or liquid substance; বাষ্পে পরিণত করা। **2.** To subject to evaporation; বাষ্পীভূত করা। ***Verb i.*** **1.** To turn into vapour; বাষ্পে পরিণত হওয়া, বাষ্পীভূত হওয়া। **2.** (*Fig.*) To give forth vapour; বাষ্প নির্গত করা। **3.** To be wasted; to disappear; to die (*colloq.*); নষ্ট হওয়া; অন্তর্হিত হওয়া, বিলীন হওয়া; মরা (চলিত ভাষায়)। **—a′-tion,** *n.* **1.** Act of evaporating; conversion into vapour; উৎশোষণ, বাষ্পীকরণ; বাষ্পীভবন। **2.** Vapour formed by evaporating; সঞ্জাত বাষ্প। **—o-ra-ble, —o-ra-tive,** *adjs.* **—o-ra-tor,** *n.* **1.** One who or that which evaporates; বাষ্পকারক, বাষ্পজনক। **2.** An apparatus for evaporating solutions, drying fruits etc.; দ্রববস্তু বাষ্পে পরিণত করার জন্য অথবা ফল প্রভৃতি শুষ্ক করণার্থ যন্ত্রবিশেষ, শোষক-যন্ত্র।

ē-văp-o-rŏm′-ē-têr (-ĕ-), *n.* An instrument for ascertaining the evaporation of liquids; বাষ্পীভবন-মাপক (হিঃ কোঃ)।

ē-vā-sion, *n.* The act of evading; পরিহার, এড়ান; an artifice to elude; an excuse; ফাঁকি, ফন্দি, চাতুরী, কৌশল; ছল, ওজর, বাহানা, অছিলা। **—sive,** *adj.* Elusive; avoiding by artifice; equivocating; as, an *evasive* reply; ছলনাময়; এড়ানিয়া; ফাঁকা, কুটিল। **—sive-ly,** *adv.* **—sive-ness,** *n.*

eve (ēv), *n.* **1.** (*Poet.*) Evening; (কবিতায়) সন্ধ্যাবেলা, সাঁঝের বেলা, দিনান্ত, সায়াহ্ন। **2.** The evening or day before a holiday or date of event; as, the Christmas *eve*; কোনও পর্ব্বাহ বা প্রসিদ্ধ ঘটনার পূর্ব্বদিবস বা পূর্ব্ব-সায়াহ্ন। **3.** Time just before any event; as, on the *eve* of my departure; কোন ঘটনার অব্যবহিত পূর্ব্ববর্ত্তী কাল।

Eve (ēv), *n.* Wife of Adam; the first woman; আদমের স্ত্রী; আদি মানবী। **Daughter of Eve**—(Esp. referring to feminine curiosity); নারী।

ē-vĕc′-tion, *n.* (*Astron.*) An inequality in the longitude of the moon; (জ্যোতির্বিজ্ঞান) চন্দ্রের দেশান্তরে বৈষম্য।

ē′-ven (-vn), *n.* (*Poet.*) Evening; (কবিতায়) সন্ধ্যাকাল। **Even-song**—ইংলণ্ডীয় রাজবিধিদ্বারা প্রতিষ্ঠিত ধর্ম্ম-সংঘের সান্ধ্যউপাসনা বিশেষ। **Even-tide**—সন্ধ্যাকাল, সন্ধ্যাবেলা।

ē′-ven (-vn), *adj.* & *n.* **1.** Level; smooth; সমতল, সম, অবন্ধুর; মসৃণ। **2.** Uniform; equal or regular; as, *even* rhythm; equable; as, an *even* temper; একরূপ; নিয়ত; স্থৈর্য্যসম্পন্ন, প্রশান্ত, অবিক্ষুব্ধ। **3.** In the same plane or line (with); as, a row of houses *even* with each other; এক পংক্তিতে অবস্থিত, সমতলে অবস্থিত। **4.** Not odd; as, an *even* number; যুগ্ম, জোড়। **5.** Equally balanced; impartial; "*Even* reckoning makes lasting friends; সমতুলিত; সমদর্শী, পক্ষপাতশূন্য। **6.** Equal in number, quality, etc.; as, *even* shares; সমসংখ্যক, সমগুণসম্পন্ন। **—ly,** *adv.* **1.** Equally; impartially; সমভাবে; সমদৃষ্টির সহিত, নিরপেক্ষভাবে। **2.** Equably; স্থিরচিত্তে, প্রশান্ত মনে। **3.** Uniformly; সমরূপে। **—ness,** *n.* **Even-handed** — Impartial; as, *even-handed* justice; পক্ষপাতশূন্য। **Even-minded**—Equable; প্রশান্তচিত্ত, স্থিরচিত্ত, ধীরমতি, স্থৈর্য্য সম্পন্ন। **Odd and even**—See under 'ODD.' **Of even date**—(*Law*) Of the same date; (আইন) এক তারিখের। **To be even with some one**—To have one's revenge on a person; প্রতিশোধ লওয়া।

ē′-ven (-vn), *adv.* **1.** Exactly ; quite ; বাস্তবিক ; সম্পূর্ণরূপে। **2.** Just ; as, *even* now you said so ; ঠিক। **3.** Serving to indicate an extreme case or instance ; as, I can *even* prove it ; অধিকন্তু, এমন কি। **Even if** — Although ; যদিও। **Even then**—তখনও, তবু।
ē′-ven (-vn), *v.t.* **1.** To make even or level ; সমান করা, মসৃণ করা, তুল্য করা। **2.** To treat as equal, (with *to*) ; "Idea of *evening* two poets ;" সমান বা তুল্য বলিয়া গণ্য করা।
ē′-ven-ing (-vn-), *n.* **1.** The close of the day ; সায়াহ্ন, সায়ংকাল, সন্ধ্যা-বেলা, দিনান্ত, প্রদোষ, রজনীমুখ, সাঁঝ। **2.** Decline of life ; the declining period of anything ; as, the *evening* of glory ; জীবনের দীনান্ত, শেষকাল ; পতনকাল। **3.** An entertainment in the evening ; as, musical *evenings* ; সান্ধ্য-সম্মিলনী। **Evening-dress**—সান্ধ্য পরিচ্ছদ, সান্ধ্য-বেশ। **Evening-party**—সান্ধ্য-সম্মিলনী, সান্ধ্য-মিলন সভা, সন্ধ্যাসম্মিলনী। **Evening-star**—শুকতারা (শুক্রগ্রহ)।
ē-vĕnt′, *n.* **1.** Occurrence ; as, in the *event* of his coming (if he comes) ; ঘটনা। **2.** An incident, esp. an important one ; as, the *events* of the last month ; ঘটনা, ব্যাপার, বিশেষতঃ গুরুতর ঘটনা। **3.** Result ; "The *event* of his enterprise was doubtful ;" ফল, পরিণাম, ফলাফল। **—ful,** *adj.* Full of important incidents ; as, an *eventful* day ; ঘটনাবহুল, ঘটনাসঙ্কুল, বিচিত্রঘটনাপূর্ণ। **—less,** *adj.* Unmarked by noteworthy events ; প্রসিদ্ধ ঘটনাবিহীন। **—ven′-tu-al,** *adj.* **1.** Consequential ; final ; ফলস্বরূপ আগত ; শেষ, অন্তিম, চরম। **2.** Dependent on certain circumstances ; কতিপয় নির্দ্দিষ্ট অবস্থার অধীন। **—ven-tu-al′-i-ty,** *n.* **1.** A possible event ; a contingency ; অনিশ্চিত ঘটনা ; আকস্মিক ঘটনা। **ven′-tu-al-ly,** *adv.* Ultimately ; অন্তিমে, চরমে, অবশেষে। **—ven′-tu-ate,** *v. i.* To happen ; to result (in) ; "The crisis has *eventuated* favourably ;" ঘটা ; পরিণত হওয়া, পরিণামে সঙ্ঘটিত হওয়া। **At all events**—In any case ; যাহাই ঘটুক না কেন। **Double event**—এক সময়ে দুইটী ঘটনা সংঘটন।
ĕv′-ĕr, *adv.* **1.** (*Archaic*) Always ; perpetually ; সর্ব্বক্ষণ, অনুক্ষণ ; সর্ব্বদা, অনুদিন। **2.** At any time ; as, no man *ever* saw it ; কখনও, কদাচ, কদাচিৎ, কদাপি কোনও কালে। **3.** In any degree ; যে পরিমাণেই হউক, অন্ততঃ। **Ever-after,—since**—All along after or since that ; তদবধি সর্ব্বদা। **Ever and anon**—(*Arch.*) Now and then ; frequently ; সময় সময় ; প্রায়শঃ। **Ever and again**—বারেবারে, পুনঃপুনঃ। **Ever more**—Always ; সর্ব্বদা। **Ever so**—To any extent ; as, *ever so* much money ; যতই, যতই হউক না কেন। **For ever, for ever and ever, for ever and a day**—For all future time ; constantly ; incessantly ; চিরদিনের জন্য ; সর্ব্বদা ; অনবরত।
ĕv′-ĕr-glāde, *n.* (*U. S.*) A swamp ; esp. (*pl.*) one in S. Florida ; (মার্কিণ যুক্ত রাজ্য) অনুপদেশ ; বিশেষতঃ (বহুবচন) দক্ষিণ ফ্লোরিডার অন্তঃপাতী অনুপদেশ।
ĕv′-ĕr-green (-grēn), *adj.* & *n.* (*Bot.*) Always green ; চিরহরিৎ, চিরশ্যামল। ***Noun.*** (*Lit.* & *fig.*) A plant retaining its verdure through all the seasons ; চিরহরিৎ উদ্ভিদ।
ĕv-ĕr-lăst′-ing, *adj.* & *n.* **1.** Eternal ; সনাতন, শাশ্বত, নিত্যস্থায়ী, অনন্ত-কালস্থায়ী। **2.** Lasting long ; repeated too often ; as, *everlasting* nonsense ; বহুকালস্থায়ী ; পুনঃ পুনঃ উচ্চারিত। **3.** Durable ; "Its *everlasting* wear ;" টেঁকসই। ***Noun.*** **1.** Eternity ; অনন্তকাল, অমৃতত্ব। **2.** (With *the*) God ; অনন্তদেব, ঈশ্বর। **3.** (*Bot.*) The everlasting flower ; একপ্রকার গাছ—এই গাছের ফুল চয়নের পর অনেক মাস তাজা থাকে। **4.** A strong twilled woollen stuff, also called *lasting* ; একপ্রকার সুদৃঢ় টেঁচ্চা-বুনা পশমী কাপড়। **—ly,** *adv.* Constantly ; for ever ; সর্ব্বদা ; চিরকাল। **—ness,** *n.* **Everlasting flower** — See EVERLASTING 3.
ē-vĕrt′, *v. t.* (*Physiol.*) To turn inside out as intestine etc. ; (শারীর-বিজ্ঞান) অন্ত্র বা অন্য দৈহিক যন্ত্রের ভিতর দিক উল্টাইয়া বাহিরে আনা।
ĕv′-ĕr-y̆, *adj.* Each ; প্রত্যেক। **Every bit** — Quite ; as, it is *every bit* as good as that ; সম্পূর্ণ। **Every body (else)**—(অন্য) প্রত্যেক লোক, সর্ব্বজন। **Every day**—*adv.* & *adj.* Daily ; প্রাত্যহিক, দৈনিক, দৈনন্দিন ; (*Adj.*) Occurring every day ; common ; usual ; as, *every-day* affairs ; নিত্য-সঙ্ঘটিত ; সাধারণ ; সচরাচর। **Every here and there**—At various points or places ; বিভিন্ন স্থানে বা দিকে। **Every now and then, Every now and again**—From time to time ; at intervals ; মধ্যেমধ্যে ; থাকিয়া থাকিয়া। **Every one**—Each ; (everyone = everybody) ; প্রত্যেক ব্যক্তি, প্রত্যেক, সকলেই। **Every thing** — All things ; সব, সকল জিনিষ। Most important thing ; as, peace is *everything* ; সর্ব্বাপেক্ষা গুরুতর বিষয়। **Every other day** — প্রতি একদিন অন্তর একদিন, প্রতি দ্বিতীয় দিন। **Every three hours**—প্রতি তিন ঘণ্টা অন্তর। **Every-way** — সর্ব্বপ্রকারে। **Every-where**—সর্ব্বত্র। **What is everybody's business is nobody's business**—ভাগের মা গঙ্গা পায় না, সবার কাজ কেউ করে না।
ē-vict′, *v. t.* **1.** To eject ; বাসোচ্ছেদ করা, বেদখল করা। **2.** To recover

by legal process; as, to *evict* property (or title to it) *from* or *of* a person · মোকদ্দমা করিয়া উদ্ধার করা। **—vic′-tion,** *n.* Act of evicting or state of being evicted; বেদখলকরণ, উচ্ছেদ, উচ্ছেদকরণ। **—vic′-tor,** *n.*

ĕv′-i-dence (-dĕns), *n.* & *v. t.* **1.** Clearness; as, in *evidence* (=conspicuous); সুস্পষ্টতা। **2.** (Often *pl.*) Testimony; fact leading to a conclusion, (with *of* or *for*); as, *evidences* of Christianity; সাক্ষ্য; প্রমাণ। **3.** (*Law*) Means of making proof; statements, proofs admissible as testimony in a court; (আইন) প্রমাণের উপায়; বিচারালয়ে সাক্ষ্যস্বরূপ গ্রাহ্য উক্তি, প্রমাণ প্রভৃতি। ***Verb t.*** **1.** To indicate; to prove; to attest; "Occurrences *evidencing* the divinity of Christ; নির্দ্দেশ করা; প্রমাণ করা; সত্য বলিয়া নির্দ্দেশ করা। **-den′-tial,** *adj.* Relating to or affording evidence; resting on evidence; প্রমাণ-ঘটিত, প্রামাণিক; প্রমাণপ্রদ। **—den′-tial-ly,** *adv.* **Circumstantial evidence** — See under CIRCUMSTANCE. **Documentary evidence** — দলীল-ঘটিত প্রমাণ, লিপিবদ্ধ প্রমাণ। **In evidence**—Conspicuous; প্রকাশমান, সুপ্রকট, সুস্পষ্ট। **Internal** or **external evidence**—See under INTERNAL and EXTERNAL. **Presumptive** or **verbal evidence**—See under PRESUMPTIVE and VERBAL. **To bear** or **give in evidence**—To give evidence; প্রমাণ প্রয়োগ করা, প্রমাণ প্রদান করা। **To be,** or **produce in evidence**—To be a part, or to produce as a part, of the evidence before the court; as, the document is not in *evidence*; প্রমাণস্থলীয় হওয়া, প্রমাণস্বরূপ উপস্থাপিত করা। **To call in evidence**—To call as witness; সাক্ষীস্বরূপ আহ্বান করা। **To turn king's, queen's** or **state's evidence**—রাজসাক্ষী হওয়া, মহারাণীর সাক্ষী হওয়া, আত্মদোষ স্বীকার করিয়া সহচরগণের বিরুদ্ধে সাক্ষ্য প্রদান করা।

ĕv′-i-dĕnt, *adj.* Obvious; manifest; প্রত্যক্ষ-গোচর, বিশদ, স্পষ্ট, ব্যক্ত; পরিস্ফুট, প্রতীয়মান। **—dent-ly,** *adv.* Obviously; স্ফুটরূপে, প্রত্যক্ষতঃ, সুস্পষ্টরূপে, স্পষ্টতঃ।

ē′-vil, *adj., n.* & *adv.* **1.** Bad; harmful; বদ্, কু, মন্দ; অনিষ্টকর। **2.** Corrupt; as, an *evil* thought; দূষিত, দুষ্ট; কলুষিত। **3.** Unpropitious; calamitous; as, an *evil* sign; অশুভ; বিপৎ-সূচক। ***Noun.*** **1.** That which is not good; harm; calamity; অসৎ বস্তু বা বিষয়; অপকার, অনিষ্ট, ক্ষতি; দুরদৃষ্ট, দুর্ভাগ্য, বিপদ্, হানি, অশুভ, অহিত। **2.** Sin; depravity; পাপাচার; চরিত্রভ্রংশ, দুশ্চরিত্রতা, দুষ্টতা। **3.** King's evil; গণ্ডমালা। ***Adv.*** **1.** In an evil manner; slanderously; as, to speak *evil* of; (*Bible*) injuriously; মন্দরূপে; দূষণীয়রূপে; অনিষ্টকররূপে। **—ly,** *adv.* In an evil manner; দুষ্টভাবে। **Alleppo evil**—একপ্রকার ব্রণ রোগ। **An evil tongue** — A slanderous tongue; পরনিন্দাদ্বারা কলুষিত রসনা। **Evil company** — কুসংসর্গ। **Evil-doer**—কুকর্ম্মান্বিত ব্যক্তি, দুষ্কৃত, দুরাচার। **Evil-eye** — কুনজর, দৃষ্টিদোষ, কুদৃষ্টি; কুপ্রভাব। **Evil-minded** — দুষ্টমতি, দুষ্টপ্রকৃতি, পাপমতি, দুষ্টচেতাঃ, দুষ্টাত্মা, কুমতি, দুষ্প্রকৃতি, দুরাচার। **Evil worker**—অনিষ্টকারী। **King's evil**—Scrofula; স্ফোটকরোগ; গণ্ডমালা। **Evil to him who evil thinks**—পরের মন্দ চিন্তিলে নিজের মন্দ আগে হয়, পরের জন্য কুয়ো খোঁড়ে নিজে কুয়োয় পড়ে। **Of evil repute**—Of bad reputation; দুর্নাম গ্রস্ত। **Origin of evil**—জরামরণের উৎপত্তি। **The evil one** — The devil; শয়তান। **To speak evil of**—To slander; কুৎসা রটনা করা, অপবাদ করা।

ē-vince′ (-vîns), *v. t.* **1.** To show clearly; স্পষ্টরূপে প্রদর্শন করা; স্পষ্টরূপে প্রতীয়মান করা। **2.** To display; "His answers *evinced* wisdom;" প্রদর্শন করা। **—vin′-ci-ble,** *adj.* **—vin′-cive,** *adj.* Tending to prove; indicative; প্রমাণানুকূল; নির্দ্দেশক।

ē′-vir-āte (-vêr-), *v. t.* **1.** To castrate; মুষ্কচ্ছেদন করা। **2.** (*fig.*) To deprive of manly qualities or attributes; পুরুষত্ব নষ্ট করা, নির্ব্বীর্য্য করা, হীনবীর্য্য করা। **—tion,** *n.*

ē-vĭs′-cĕr-āte, *v. t.* To disembowel; (*fig.*) to deprive of forcefulness of vital contents, as an argumemt, clause, etc.; অন্ত্র নিষ্কাশিত করা, নিরন্ত্রীকৃত করা; (লক্ষণায়) শক্তি নষ্ট করা, অসার করা। **—a′-tion,** *n.* **1.** The act of eviscerating: নিরন্ত্রীকরণ।

ĕv-ō-cā′-tion, *n.* **1.** The act of calling out or forth; আহ্বান, কার্য্যার্থ আহ্বান, সযত্ন স্মরণ, স্মৃত্যুদ্বোধ। **2.** (*Law*) Removal from an inferior to a superior court; (আইন) নিম্ন আদালত হইতে উচ্চতর আদালতে স্থানান্তর।

ē-vōke′, *v. t.* **1.** To call up or forth, as a spirit, memory, etc.; আহ্বান করা, উদ্বুদ্ধ করা, টানিয়া বাহির করা, বহিরাকর্ষণ করা। **2.** To summon as a cause to a higher court; উচ্চতর আদালতে নেওয়া। **—voc′-a-tive,** *adj.*

ĕv′-ō-lūte, *adj.* & *n* Applied to a curve as stated below; নিম্ন-বর্ণিত বক্ররেখা সম্বন্ধে প্রযোজ্য। ***Noun.*** A curve which is the locus of the centres of curvature of another curve called its *involute*; (গণিত শাস্ত্র) যে বক্ররেখা অন্য বক্ররেখার বক্রতার কেন্দ্রস্থলের বিন্দুপথরূপে অবস্থিত থাকে, অনুবক্র-কৈন্দ্রিক (হিঃ কোঃ)।

ĕv-ō-lū′-tion, *n.* **1.** The act of unfolding; development; as, the *evolution* of a plot or organism;

appearance (of events etc.) in due succession ; প্রকটন, উদ্ঘাটন, প্রস্ফুটন, উদ্ভেদ, বিকাশ ; ক্রমবিকাশ, ক্রমস্ফূর্তি, ক্রমোন্নতি, অভিব্যক্তি ; বিবর্ত্তন। 2. A thing or series of things unfolded ; as, the tree is the *evolution* of the seed ; ক্রমবিকাশশীল বস্তু বা বস্তুপরম্পরা। 3. (*Math.*) The extraction of roots in arithmetic and algebra, (the reverse of *involution*) ; (গণিত) বর্গ-ঘনাদির মূলাকর্ষণ, মূলক্রিয়া (হিঃ কোঃ)। 4. The orderly movement of troops or ships in changing their position ; সেনাদল বা রণতরী শ্রেণীর সুশৃঙ্খল ভাবে সঞ্চালন। 5. The process of evolving or giving off ; as, the *evolution* of gas etc. ; উদ্ভবন। 6. (*Geom.*) The opening or unfolding of a curve ; (জ্যামিতি) বক্ররেখার বিকাশ, বিকাশ (হিঃ কোঃ)। **–al, –a-ry,** *adjs.* Relating to or produced by, evolution ; বিবর্ত্তন সংক্রান্ত। **–ism,** *n.* The theory of evolution ; অভিব্যক্তিবাদ। **–ist,** *n.* One who holds the doctrine of evlution ; অভিব্যক্তিবাদী। **–is'-tic,** *adj.* **–lu'-tive,** *adj.* **Evolution of matter**—তান্মাত্রিক সৃষ্টি। **Theory of evolution** — যে দার্শনিক মতবাদানুসারে যাবতীয় জীব ও জড় পদার্থ সরল আদিম অবস্থা হইতে ক্রমশঃ জটিলতর ও উন্নততর অবস্থায় বিকাশ প্রাপ্ত হয় (যথা, কোন কোন বৈজ্ঞানিকের মতে, বানর ক্রমশঃ উন্নতি লাভ করিয়া মনুষ্যে পরিণত হইয়াছে ; বালুকা বহুযুগের ক্রমবিকাশের ফলে প্রস্তরে পরিণত হইয়াছে), অভিব্যক্তিবাদ, বিবর্ত্তনবাদ, ক্রমবিকাশবাদ, ক্রমোন্নতিবাদ, পরিণামবাদ।

ē-volve' (-vŏlv), 1. *v.t.* & *i.* To unfold; to develop; to deduce ; উদ্ঘাটন করা; বিকাশ করা, অভিব্যক্ত করা; উপপাদন করা। 2. To emit ; as, to *evolve* odour or heat ; বিকীর্ণ করা, নির্গত করা, নিঃসৃত করা। ***Verb i.*** 1. To become open or disclosed ; অভিব্যক্ত হওয়া। 2. To develop naturally ; স্বাভাবতঃ বিকাশ প্রাপ্ত হওয়া। **–ment,** *n.*

ē-vŭl'-sion, *n.* Act of plucking out forcibly ; উৎপাটন, উৎকর্ষণ, উন্মূলন।

ewe (ū), *n.* A female sheep ; ভেড়ী, মেষী। **Ewe-cheese** — মেষীর দুগ্ধ হইতে প্রস্তুত পনীর। **Ewe-lamb**—A female lamb ; (স্ত্রী) মেষশাবক ; a poor man's only possession ; দরিদ্র ব্যক্তির একমাত্র ধন, সবে ধন নীলমণি।

ew'-ĕr (ū-), *n.* 1. A jug or pitcher ; গাড়ু, ভৃঙ্গার, বড় বদ্‌না, ঘটি। 2. (*Com.*) A bed-room water-jug ; শয়নকক্ষের জলের ঘড়া।

ĕx, *prep.* (*Com.*) Out of ; sold from ; as, *ex* ship ; (বাণিজ্য) (মজুত মাল) হইতে ; হইতে বিক্রীত। **Ex divident** (Abbr. *ex div.* or *x. d.*)—পরবর্ত্তী লভ্যাংশ অন্তর্ভুক্ত না করিয়া।

ĕx-, *prefix.* Late ; as, *ex*-king ; ভূতপূর্ব্ব। **Ex-officio**—By virtue of one's office ; কোন কার্য্যে নিযুক্ত থাকা হেতু। **Ex-parte**—Partial ; biassed ; পক্ষপাতী ; পক্ষপাতদুষ্ট। (*Law*) One-sided ; একতরফা। **Ex-parte evidence**—পক্ষপাতদুষ্ট প্রমাণ। **Ex-parte decree**—একতরফা ডিক্রী। **Ex-post facto**—After the act is done ; কার্য্য সমাপনান্তে।

ĕx-ă'-cĕr-bāte, *v. t.* To make more violent or bitter; to irritate ; as a person ; অধিকতর প্রবল ও কষ্টপ্রদ করা ; কুপিত করা, রোষাবিষ্ট করা। **–ba'-tion,** *n.* ক্রোধোদ্দীপন।

ĕx-ăct' (ĕgz-), *adj., v. t.* & *i.* 1. Precise ; strict ; as, *exact* rules or command ; যথার্থ, প্রকৃত, ঠিক, নিশ্চিত, অবিকল, হুবহু (*colloq*) ; কড়া, কঠোর। 2. Accurate; correct; as, an *exact* report ; বিশুদ্ধ, নির্ভুল ; প্রকৃত, সত্য। ***Verb t.*** 1. To enforce the payment of ; to extort ; as, to *exact* money *of* or *from* a person ; অর্থপ্রদান করিতে বাধ্য করা ; বলপূর্ব্বক আদায় করা। 2. To demand or claim as of right ; as, to *exact* obedience from the inferiors ; অধিকার স্বরূপ দাবী করা। 3. To require urgently ; নির্ব্বন্ধাতিশয় সহকারে দাবী করা। ***Verb i.*** (*Obs.*) To practise extortion ; বলপূর্ব্বক অর্থ আদায়ে রত হওয়া। **–ac'-tion,** *n.* 1. Act of exacting ; extortion ; বলপূর্ব্বক আদায় ; পীড়ন। 2. That which is extorted ; বলপূর্ব্বক গৃহীত অর্থ প্রভৃতি। **–er, –or,** *n.* One who exacts, esp. by authority ; বলপূর্ব্বক আদায়কারী। **–ing,** *adj.* Disposed to claim too much ; অত্যধিক দাবীকারী। **–i-tude,** *n.* State or quality of being exact ; nicety ; accuracy ; সূক্ষ্মতা ; বিশুদ্ধতা, নির্ভুলতা ; যথার্থতা। **–ly,** *adv.* 1. In an exact manner ; nicely ; correctly ; যথাযথ রূপে, সঠিকরূপে ; সূক্ষ্মরূপে ; বিশুদ্ধরূপে। 2. Quite so ; তাইতো। **–ness,** *n.* Accuracy ; nicety ; বিশুদ্ধতা ; সূক্ষ্মতা। **Exact copy** — অবিকল প্রতিলিপি, হুবহু নকল। **Exactly so**—তাইতো, বটে।

ex-ăg'-gĕr-āte (ĕgz-), *v t.* 1. To depict extravagantly ; অতিরঞ্জিত করা, বাহুল্য বর্ণনা করা। 2. To aggravate ; "The distress *exaggerated* by social change ;" গুরুতর করা, প্রগাঢ়তর করা। 3. To make abnormal in size ; "A nose *exaggerated* by intemperance ; অস্বাভাবিকরূপে আয়তন বৃদ্ধি করা। **–a-ted,** *adj.* 1. Magnified beyond due limits ; অতিরঞ্জিত। 2. Abnormally enlarged ; অস্বাভাবিকরূপে বর্দ্ধিত। **-a-ted-ly,** *adv.* **–a'-tion,** *n.* The act of exaggerating ; hyperbolical representation ; অতিরঞ্জন ; অত্যুক্তি, অতিশয়োক্তি, অতিবাদ, অতিরিক্তকথন। **–a-tive,** *adj.* Tending or given to exaggeration ; hyperbolical ; অত্যুক্তি প্রবণ, অতিশয়োক্তিপূর্ণ। **–a-tive-ly,** *adv.* **–a'-tor,** *n.*

ex-ălt′ (ĕgz-), *v. t.* **1.** To lift up; as, to walk with an *exalted* head; উন্নত করা। **2.** To raise in rank, power, etc.; to dignify; "Righteousness *exalteth* a nation;" উন্নীত করা; উচ্চপদে প্রতিষ্ঠিত করা, গৌরব বা মর্য্যাদাজনক স্থানে স্থাপিত করা। **3.** To intensify; to heighten; as, to *exalt* colour or imigration; প্রগাঢ়তর করা; রঙ্গ চড়ান। **4.** To extol; প্রশংসা দ্বারা উচ্চে তোলা, গৌরবান্বিত করা। **–al-ta′-tion,** *n.* **1.** The act of exalting; elevation to power, office, etc.; উন্নয়ন, সমুন্নতি, সমুচ্ছ্রয় (মঃ ভাঃ), মানবৃদ্ধি, প্রতিষ্ঠাবৃদ্ধি; উচ্চপদে উন্নয়ন। **2.** Elation; সফলতাজনিত গর্ব্ব, উল্লাস। **3.** Augmentation in intensity; বিবৃদ্ধি, তেজোবৃদ্ধি। **4.** (*Astrol.*) The place of a planet in the zodiac where it exerts its strongest influence; (জ্যোতিষ-শাস্ত্র) তুঙ্গস্থান, উচ্চসংশ্রয় (রঃ)। **–ed,** *adj.* Elevated; dignified; উন্নীত, উচ্চপদাভিষিক্ত; উচ্চ, সম্ভ্রান্ত, মর্য্যাদান্বিত। **–ed-ness,** *n.* **–er,** *n.*

ex-am′-ine (ĕgz-ăm-ĭn), *v. t.* & *i.* **1.** To enquire into; to inspect carefully; to test; অনুসন্ধান করা, তদন্ত করা, তদারক করা; পর্য্যবেক্ষণ করা; পরখ করা, যাচাই করা। **2.** To test by question; as, to *examine* a witness or an accused person; প্রশ্ন জিজ্ঞাসা করা। **3.** To test the capacity or knowledge of by questioning; as, to *examine* a pupil, candidate, etc.; পরীক্ষা করা। ***Verb i.*** To inquire, (with *into*); "To *examine into* the nature of royal good;" অনুসন্ধান করা। **–i-nant,** *n.* An examiner; পরীক্ষক। **–i-na′-tion,** *n.* **1.** Act of examining; investigation; পরীক্ষাগ্রহণ, পরীক্ষণ; অনুসন্ধান, আবিষ্কারার্থ পুঙ্খানুপুঙ্খ অনুসন্ধান। **2.** A process for testing qualification etc. of a student, candidate, (colloq. abbr. *exam.*); পরীক্ষা। **–i-na′-tion-al, –i-na-to′-ri-al,** *adjs.* **1.** Of, or relating to, examination; পরীক্ষাসম্বন্ধীয়। **2.** (Only **–i-na-to′-ri-al**) Relating to an examiner; পরীক্ষক-সম্বন্ধীয়। **–i-nee′,** *n.* A person examined; পরিক্ষার্থী। **–in-er,** *n.* One who examines; পরীক্ষক, অনুসন্ধানকারক। **Cross-examination** — প্রতি-প্রশ্ন, জেরা। **Examination-in-chief** — যে পক্ষ হইতে সাক্ষী মানা হয়, সেই পক্ষের উকিল, ব্যারিষ্টার প্রভৃতি দ্বারা সাক্ষীর জবানবন্দী। **Examination paper** — প্রশ্নপত্র। **Post mortem examination** — See POST MORTEM. **Re-examination** — জেরার পর স্বপক্ষের উকীল প্রভৃতি দ্বারা সাক্ষীর পুনঃ পরীক্ষা, পুনঃ পরীক্ষা।

ex-am′-ple (ĕgz-ăm-pl), *n.* & *v. t.* **1.** A sample; model; নমুনা; আদর্শ, প্রতিরূপ। **2.** A person or thing proposed to be imitated; আদর্শ স্থানীয় ব্যক্তি বা বস্তু। **3.** A problem etc. designed to illustrate a general rule; উদাহরণ, দৃষ্টান্ত। **4.** A precedent; as, such an instance is without *example*; নজীর, পূর্ব্বদৃষ্টান্ত। **5.** Warning to others; as, I shall make an *example* of (punish) you (অর্থাৎ তোমাকে এমন শাস্তি প্রদান করিব যাহা দেখিয়া সকলের কাণ খাঁড়া হয়); অন্য সকলের সাবধান হইবার বিষয়। ***Verb t.*** To exemplify, (usu. in *p. p.*); দৃষ্টান্ত প্রদর্শন করা। **Beyond** or **without example**— অভূত-পূর্ব্ব। **Following the example**—দেখাদেখি। **For example**— For instance; দৃষ্টান্ত-স্বরূপ। **To set an example** — To show an example intending others to follow; অন্যে অনুসরণ করিবে এই অভিপ্রায়ে দৃষ্টান্ত প্রদর্শন করা, পথ দেখান। To be a model of imitation; আদর্শ-স্থলীয় হওয়া। **To take example by**—To copy; নকল করা।

ex-ăm′-plă-rȳ (ĕgz-), *adj.* (*Rare.*) Serving for an example or pattern, (cf. *exemplary*); দৃষ্টান্ত-স্থলীয়, নমুনা-স্বরূপ।

ex-ăn′-i-māte (ĕgz-), *adj.* & *v. t.* Dead; lifeless; spiritless; মৃত; গতজীবিত; নির্জীব, নিস্তেজ।

ĕx-ăn-thē′-mȧ (*pl.* -MA-TA), *n.* A febrile disease such as small-pox, measles, etc., marked by an eruption on the skin; স্ফোট জ্বর (হঃ চঃ)। **–mat′-ic, –them′-a-tous,** *adjs.*

ĕx′-ârch, *n.* **1.** The title of the viceroys of the Byzantine emperors; (East. Church) a bishop or patriarch's deputy; বাইজেন্টাইন সম্রাটগণের প্রতিনিধির উপাধি; (প্রাচ্য-দেশীয় খৃষ্টীয় ধর্ম্মসংঘ) ধর্ম্মাধ্যক্ষ বা মহাধর্ম্মাধ্যক্ষের প্রতিনিধি।

ex-ăs′-pêr-āte (ĕgz-), *v. t.* **1.** To irritate; to enrage; উত্যক্ত করা; ক্রোধাবিষ্ট করা, রোষাবিষ্ট করা। **2.** To aggravate; to make worse; as, to *exasperate* enmity; গুরুতর করা; মন্দতর করা। **–at-ing,** *adj.* **–at-ing-ly,** *adv.* **–a′-tion,** *n.* Irritating; provocation; embittering; প্রকোপন, সংক্ষোভন; তীব্র-ক্রোধোদ্দীপন, উৎকোপন; উত্যক্তকরণ।

ex-ca-the′-dra, [*L.*] *adj.* & *adv.* Authoritative; প্রামাণিক। ***Adv.*** Authoritatively; প্রামাণিকরূপে।

ĕx′-că-vāte, *v. t.* **1.** To form a hole in; as, to *excavate* a hill etc.; খনন করা, খোঁড়া। **2.** To form by digging as a tank, hole etc.; খনন করা। **3.** To dig out and remove as soil, mineral matter; খনন করিয়া স্থানান্তরিত করা। **4.** To expose to view by digging, as a buried city etc.; মৃত্তিকা খনন করিয়া বাহির করা। **–va′-tion,** *n.* **1.** Act of excavating; খনন। **2.** A cavity formed by digging, scooping, etc.; গর্ত্ত, গহ্বর, খাত। **–va-tor,** *n.* One who excavates; a machine for digging out earth etc.; খনক ; খন্তা, খনিত্র।

ex-ceed′ (ĕk-sēd), *v. t. & i.* **1.** To go beyond the limit of; as, to *exceed* one's power or authority; সীমা-লঙ্ঘন করা, মাত্রার বাহিরে যাওয়া। **2.** To be greater than; to surpass; অধিকতর হওয়া; অতিক্রম করা, ডিঙ্গাইয়া যাওয়া। ***Verb i.*** **1.** To go too far; নির্দ্দিষ্ট বা সঙ্গত সীমার বাহিরে যাওয়া। **2.** To preponderate; গুরুতর হওয়া। **3.** (Chiefly in Cambridge use) To have more than usual at a meal; (প্রধানতঃ কেম্ব্রিজে ব্যবহৃত হয়) অতিরিক্ত আহার করা। **—ing,** *adj. & adv.* More than usual; excessive; অতিরিক্ত; অতিশয়, অধিক। (*Adv.*) (*Archaic*) To a very great extent; অত্যধিক পরিমাণে। **—ing-ly,** *adv.* Extremely; immoderately; সমধিক, নিরতিশয়, অত্যন্ত, নিতান্ত; অমিতরূপে, অপরিমিতরূপে।

ĕx-cĕl′, *v. t. & i.* To surpass (in good qualities etc.); সদ্‌গুণে অতিক্রম করা। ***Verb i.*** To outdo others in good qualities; সদ্‌গুণাদিতে অন্যসকলকে অতিক্রম করা।

ĕx′-cĕl-lence (-ĕns), *n.* **1.** The quality of being excellent; pre-eminence; গুণোৎকর্ষ, পরমোৎকর্ষ, প্রকর্ষ, উত্তমতা, মহত্ত্ব; শ্রেষ্ঠতা, প্রকৃষ্টতা। **2.** A valuable quality; সদ্‌গুণ। **—len-cy,** *n.* **1.** Same as EXCELLENCE. **2.** A title of honour; as, His *Excellency* the Viceroy; সম্ভ্রমসূচক উপাধি বিশেষ,—ভারতবর্ষে এই উপাধি রাজপ্রতিনিধি (বড় লাট), প্রধান সেনাপতি (জঙ্গী লাট), এবং বঙ্গ, বোম্বাই ও মান্দ্রাজ প্রেসিডেন্সির শাসনকর্ত্তার (Governors) নামের পূর্ব্বে ব্যবহৃত হয়। **—lent,** *adj.* Of great value; very good; pre-eminent; উৎকৃষ্ট, প্রকৃষ্ট; চমৎকার, তোফা (*colloq.*), সুশোভন; শ্রেষ্ঠ, বরেণ্য। **—lent-ly,** *adv.*

ĕx-cĕl′-si-ŏr, *adj. & n.* Higher; উন্নততর, উচ্চতর। [এই শব্দটী ব্যবসায়চিহ্ন (trade mark), ব্যবসায়ের নাম প্রভৃতিতে ব্যবহৃত হয়] ***Noun.*** (*U. S.*) Curled shreds of wood for stuffing; (মার্কিন যুক্তরাজ্য) কাঠের কোমল চাঁচনি, যাহা কোন কিছুর ভিতরে ঠাসিয়া পূরা হয়। **Excelsior State**—New-York; নিউইয়র্ক।

ĕx-cĕpt′, *v. t. & i.* To omit from enumeration etc.; to exclude; গণনায় বাদ দেওয়া, অনুল্লেখ করা; বর্জ্জন করা, ছাড়িয়া দেওয়া। ***Verb i.*** to object, (foll. by *against*); আপত্তি উত্থাপন করা, আপত্তি করা। **—cep′-tive,** *adj.* **1.** Containing or making an exception; as, an *exceptive* clause; বর্জ্জনকারী। **2.** Captious; ত্রুটি গ্রহণশীল।

ĕx-cĕpt′, *prep & conj.* Exclusively of; but; as, we all succeeded *except* Ram; ব্যতিরেকে, ছাড়া, ভিন্ন, বাদে, বাদ দিয়া, ছাড়িয়া, ব্যতীত। ***Conj.*** (*Archaic*) Unless; as, *except* he be born again; যদি না।

ĕx-cĕpt′-ing, *prep. & conj.* Same as EXCEPT (*prep. & conj.*); it is used only after *not, without*; as, all failed to answer not *excepting* the first boy.

ĕx-cĕp′-tion, *n.* **1.** Act of excepting; exclusion; গণনায় বাদ দেওন; বর্জ্জন। **2.** That which is excepted; as, every rule has its *exceptions*; বর্জ্জিত বিষয়, ব্যতিরেক, ব্যভিচার, ব্যতিক্রম। **3.** Objection; offence; as, to take *exception* to a person's remarks; আপত্তি; দোষ, ত্রুটী। **—a-ble,** *adj.* আপত্তিযোগ্য, আপত্তিসহ। **—al,** *adj.* Not ordinary; unusual; as, of *exceptional* value; অসাধারণ, অতুলনীয়; অলোকসামান্য, অনন্যসাধারণ। **—al′-i-ty,** *n.* Exceptional quality or character; অনন্যসাধারণ গুণ বা স্বভাব। **—al-ly,** *adv.* **1.** Unprecedently; unusually; especially; অভূতপূর্ব্বরূপে, অপূর্ব্বরূপে; অনন্যসাধারণ ভাবে; বিশেষরূপে। **An exception to a rule**—A person or thing not included in a general rule; সাধারণ নিয়মের বহির্ভূত ব্যক্তি বা বস্তু। **Exception proves the rule**—The excepting of some cases proves the existence of the rule; ব্যভিচারই নিয়মের অস্তিত্বের প্রমাণ [অর্থাৎ 'ব্যভিচার' এই শব্দ দ্বারা নিয়মেরই ব্যভিচার বুঝায়, নিয়ম না থাকিলে ব্যভিচারও থাকে না।] **Open to exception**—Subject, or liable to objection; আপত্তিসহ। **To take exception (to)**—To object; to find fault with, (with *to*); আপত্তি করা; ত্রুটি বাহির করা, দোষ ধরা। To take offence, (with *at*); as, to *take exception* at a remark; অপরাধ গ্রহণ করা।

ĕx-cêrpt′, *v. t. & n.* To select or cite as a literary passage; নির্ব্বাচন করা, উদ্ধৃত করা। ***Noun.*** A passage picked out from an author; an extract; গ্রন্থাদি হইতে উদ্ধৃত বাক্য; উদ্ধৃত অংশ। **—cerp′-tion,** *n.* **—i-ble,** *adj.*

ĕx-cĕss′, *n.* **1.** Going beyond due limits; superfluity; extreme degree; as, *excess* of provision or cruelty; সঙ্গতসীমালঙ্ঘন; আধিক্য, বাহুল্য, প্রাচুর্য্য; চরমমাত্রা। **2.** Intemperance esp. in eating and drinking; অমিতাচার, অপচার। **3.** The degree or amount by which one thing exceeds another; অতিরেক। **5.** (Usually *pl.*) Outrage; "The *excesses* of the Star Chamber;" অত্যাচার। **—ces′-sive,** *adj.* **1.** Exceeding due limits; immoderate; extreme; সঙ্গত সীমাতিক্রামী; অমিত, অপরিমিত, অতিরিক্ত; অতীব, সমধিক, অত্যন্ত, নিরতিশয়, নিতান্ত। **2.** Intemperate; as, *excessive* drinkers; অমিতাচারী। **—ces′-sive-ly,** *adv.* In an excessive degree or manner; immoderately; অতিশয়িতরূপে; অপরিমিতরূপে, বাহুল্যরূপে। **—ces′-sive-ness,** *n.* **Excess fare**—যে স্থানের জন্য টিকিট ক্রয় করা হয়, তদতিরিক্ত স্থান ভ্রমণের জন্য

যে অতিরিক্ত ভাড়া দিতে হয়, অতিরিক্ত ভাড়া। **Excess luggage** — যতটা মাল বিনা ভাড়ায় নেওয়া যাইতে পারে, কিংবা যতটা মালের ভাড়া দেওয়া হইয়াছে, তদতিরিক্ত মাল। **In excess of**—More than ; অধিকতর। **To carry to excess**—To do too much ; অতিরিক্ত করা ; বাড়াবাড়ি করা। **To, or in, excess**—Immoderately ; as, to drink, eat or run *to excess* ; অতিরিক্ত পরিমাণে ; অমিতরূপে।

ĕx-chānġe′, *n.*, *v. t.* & *i.* **1.** Act of exchanging ; interchange ; as, *exchange* of civilities or of prisoners in war ; পরিবর্তন ; বিনিময়, আদানপ্রদান, অদলবদল। **2.** Barter ; বিনিময়, অদলবদল, পরাবর্ত্ত, পরিদান। **3.** Exchanging of coin for its equivalent in coin of the same or a foreign country ; the money-changer's trade ; মুদ্রাবিনিময় ; মুদ্রা-বিনিময়ের ব্যবসায়। **4.** The things interchanged, esp. a newspaper ; বিনিময়ে প্রাপ্ত বা প্রদত্ত বস্তু, বিশেষতঃ সংবাদপত্রের বিনিময়ে প্রাপ্ত সংবাদপত্র। **5.** The place where the merchants etc., of a city meet to transact business ; বাণিজ্য-সংক্রান্ত কার্য্যনির্ব্বাহার্থ যে হর্ম্ম্যে নগরের বণিক, ব্যাঙ্কওয়ালা (মহাজন) ও দালালগণ সমবেত হইয়া থাকে (এই অর্থে সাধারণতঃ *change* ব্যবহৃত হয়), বিনিময় বিপণি, শ্রেষ্ঠি-চত্বর। **6.** The difference between the value of money in different lands ; বাটা। ***Verb t.*** **1.** To give or take (one thing) in return for another, (with *for*) ; as, to *exchange* a house *for* a garden ; বিনিময় করা, প্রতিদান করা। **2.** To interchange ; as, to *exchange* blows or glances ; পরস্পর আদানপ্রদান করা ; অদলবদল করা। ***Verb i.*** To be exchanged *(for)* ; as, a rupee *exchanges for* 64 pice ; পরিবর্ত্তিত হওয়া। **–a-bil′-i-ty,** *n.* The quality or state of being exchangeable ; পরিবর্ত্তনীয়তা। **–a-ble,** *adj.* **1.** Capable of being exchanged ; fit for exchange ; পরিবর্ত্তনীয়, বিনিময় যোগ্য ; পরিবর্ত্তনসহ। **2.** Available for making exchanges ; as, an *exchangeable* value ; বিনিময়ের জন্য প্রাপ্য। **–chang′-er,** *n.* **Bill of exchange**—See BILL. **In exchange for**—In return for ; বিনিময়ে। **Par of exchange**—বিভিন্ন দেশের মুদ্রার তুলনা মূলক নির্দ্ধারিত মূল্য [যথা £1 sterling at par = 25. 22½ francs French money.] **Rate or course of exchange**—বিভিন্নদেশের মুদ্রা বিনিময়ের হার।

ĕx-cheq′-uer (-chĕk-ĕr), *n.* **1.** (England) An ancient court of law dealing only with the king's revenue ; a division of the High Court of Justice, now merged in the Queen's Bench division, (also called a *court of exchequer*) ; (প্রাচীন ইংলণ্ডের) রাজস্ব-সংক্রান্ত বিচারালয় ; ইংলণ্ডের প্রধান বিচারালয়ের বিভাগ বিশেষ। **2.** The department of a state charged with receipt and custody of the national revenue ; রাজস্ববিভাগ। **3.** A royal or national treasury ; রাজকোষ, জাতীয় ধনাগার, সরকারী তহবিল। **4.** A person's funds ; কোন ব্যক্তির ধনসম্পত্তি। **Chancellor of the exchequer** — See CHANCELLOR. **Court of exchequer**—See EXCHEQUER. **Exchequer bill**—পার্লেমেণ্টের বিধানানুসারে গভর্ণমেণ্ট জনসাধারণ হইতে ঋণ-স্বরূপ প্রাপ্ত অর্থের জন্য যে প্রতিশ্রুতি-পত্র (promissory bill) প্রদান করেন।

ĕx-cīse′, *n.* & *v. t.* **1.** A tax on articles as beer, opium, produced or consumed in a country ; দেশজ বা দেশে ব্যবহৃত সুধা, গঞ্জিকা, অহিফেন প্রভৃতি কতিপয় মাদক দ্রব্যের উপর শুল্ক, আবকারী শুল্ক। **2.** Government office collecting excise ; আবকারী আফিস। ***Verb t.*** **1.** To impose an excise upon, *(obs.)* ; দেশজ বা দেশে ব্যবহৃত মাদক দ্রব্যাদির উপর মাশুল নির্দ্ধারণ বা স্থাপন করা। **2.** To force as a person to pay excise ; to overcharge, (also *fig.*) ; আবকারী মাশুল প্রদানের জন্য বাধ্য করা ; অতিরিক্ত দাবী করা। **–cis′-a-ble,** *adj.* Liable to excise duty ; আবকারী শুল্ক স্থাপন-যোগ্য। **Excise man** — আবকারী বিভাগের কর্ম্মচারী।

ĕx-cīse′, *v. t.* **1.** To cut out or off, as a passage of a book or limb etc. ; কাটিয়া ফেলা, ছাঁটিয়া ফেলা। **2.** (*Bot.* & *Zool.*) To notch ; খাঁজ কাটা। **–ci′-sion,** *n.* **1.** The act of excising or cutting off ; extirpation ; উৎকর্ত্তন, ছেদন, উচ্ছেদ, ছাঁটন, অঙ্গচ্ছেদ ; উৎপাটন, উন্মূলন, মূলচ্ছেদ, উচ্ছেদ।

ĕx-cīte′, *v. t.* **1.** To provoke ; to rouse ; to move a strong emotion ; উদ্দীপ্ত করা, প্রকোপিত করা, উস্কাইয়া দেওয়া, উত্তেজিত করা, সঙ্ক্ষিত করা, উদ্রেক করা ; বলসঞ্চার করা ; গভীর আবেগ উদ্রিক্ত করা। **2.** To stimulate ; as, to *excite* a bodily organ ; উত্তেজিত করা। **4.** (*Electr.*) To induce magnetic activity in ; to set in motion ; তড়িন্ময় করা, চুম্বক ধর্ম্মাক্রান্ত করা ; চালাইয়া দেওয়া। **5.** (*Photog.*) To sensitize as a plate ; রাসায়নিক বস্তুদ্বারা লিপ্ত করিয়া আলোক চিত্রের ফলক প্রতিবিম্ব-গ্রহণক্ষম করা। **–cit-a-bil′-i-ty,** *n.* State of being excitable ; irritability ; উত্তেজনীয়তা ; উত্তেজন-প্রবণতা, ক্ষোভশীলতা, ক্ষোভ্যতা। **–cit′-a-ble,** *adj.* Susceptible of excitement ; easily excited ; উত্তেজনীয়, ক্ষোভ্য ; সহজে উত্তেজিত, শীঘ্রকোপী। **–ci-ta′-tion,** *n.* Exciting ; electric energising ; উত্তেজন, উদ্দীপক ; বিদ্যুন্ময়করণ। **–cit′-ant,** *adj.* & *n.* Stimulating ; উত্তেজক, সন্দীপক। (*Noun*) **1.** A stimulent ; উত্তেজক ঔষধাদি, রুচক, দীপক, তেজক। **2.** (*Electr.*) An agent for inducing electric action ; বৈদ্যুতিক ক্রিয়া উৎপাদনার্থ যন্ত্র বিশেষ। **–cit′-a-tive,** *adj.* **–cīt′-a-to-ry,** *adj.*

—cit′-ed, *adj.* **—cit′-ed-ly,** *adv.* **—cit′-ing,** *adj.* Producing excitement ; thrilling ; উত্তেজনাজনক ; রোমাঞ্চকর। **—ment,** *n.* **1.** Act of exciting ; stimulation ; agitation ; উদ্দীপন, উত্তেজন ; উত্তেজনা ; আন্দোলন, চাঞ্চল্য, ব্যাকুলতা, বিক্ষোভ, সংক্ষোভ। **2.** That which excites ; উত্তেজনাকর বিষয়।

ĕx-claim′ (-clām), *v. i.* & *t.* **1.** To shout, esp. from pain, anger, etc. ; উচ্চরব করা, উচ্চৈঃস্বরে চীৎকার করা। **2.** To accuse loudly, (with *against*) ; as, to *exclaim against* oppression or an offender ; উচ্চকণ্ঠে বা তীব্রভাবে প্রতিবাদ বা দোষারোপ করা। ***Verb t.*** To speak loudly ; উচ্চকণ্ঠে বলা। **—cla-ma′-tion,** *n.* **1.** Act of exclaiming ; a loud cry or utterance ; চীৎকার করণ, উদ্ঘোষণ, নির্ঘোষ, চীৎকার, সোরগোল ; কোলাহল। **4.** (*Gram.*) An interjection ; (ব্যাকরণ) হর্ষ বিস্ময়াদিসূচক অব্যয়। **—clam′-a-to-ry,** *adj.* Containing, or expressing, exclamation ; উদ্ঘোষক, চীৎকারব্যঞ্জক। **—er,** *n.* **To exclaim aginst** — See EXCLAIM *v. i.* **2. The note of exclamation**—The sign !

ĕx-clūde′, *v. t.* **1.** To hinder from entering ; to shut out ; to refuse participation ; to omit ; পথরোধ করা, বহিষ্কার করা, বাহির করিয়া দেওয়া ; বর্জ্জন করা ; যোগদান করিতে না দেওয়া, বাদ দেওয়া। **2.** To eject ; to expel ; উচ্ছেদ করা ; বলপূর্ব্বক বহিষ্কৃত করা। **3.** To prevent the occurrence of ; as, to *exclude* a doubt ; সংঘটনে বাধা দেওয়া। **—clu′-sion,** *n.* The act of excluding ; state of being excluded ; rejection ; বহিষ্কার, বহিষ্করণ, নিঃসারণ, নিরাকরণ, নিষ্কাশন ; বর্জ্জিতাবস্থা, বর্জ্জন ; প্রত্যাখ্যান। **—clu′-sion-ist,** *n.* One who would preclude others from some privilege ; যে ব্যক্তি অন্যকে কোনরূপ সুবিধাভোগ হইতে বঞ্চিত করিতে চায়। **—clu′-sive,** *adj.* **1.** Shutting out ; possessed, or enjoyed, to the exclusion of others, as a privilege etc. ; বর্জ্জনকারী, পরিবর্জ্জনশীল ; একাধিকৃত, অনন্যসাধারণ। **2.** Desirous of excluding others ; illiberal ; as, an *exclusive* member ; বর্জ্জনেচ্ছু ; অনুদার। **3.** Not taking into account, (opposed to *inclusive*, foll. by *of*) ; as, 200 men *exclusive of* our own ; ব্যতিরিক্ত। **4.** Excluding all except what is specified ; as, an *exclusive* term or proposition ; নির্দ্দিষ্ট বিষয় ব্যতীত অপর সমস্ত বর্জ্জনকারী। **—clu′-sive-ly,** *adv.* In an exclusive manner ; একান্ত ভাবে। **—clu′-sive-ness,** *n.* The quality or state of being exclusive ; বর্জ্জনশীলতা, অনন্যসাধারণতা, কেবলত্ব। **—clu′-sive-ism,** *n.* **Law of excluded middle**—মধ্যমনিরাসন্যায় (হিঃ কোঃ)।

ĕx-cŏg′-i-tāte, *v. t.* To think out ; to devise ; ভাবিয়া বাহির করা ; কৌশলক্রমে উদ্ভাবন করা, পরিকল্পনা করা। **—ta′-tion,** *n.* Act of excogitating ; contrivance ; invention ; কৌশলক্রমে উদ্ভাবন ; কৌশল ; উদ্ভাবন, পরিকল্পন। **—ta-tive,** *adj.*

ĕx-cŏm-mū′-ni-cāte, *v. t.* & *n.* To cut off from communion or from all connection with the Church ; to expel from any fellowship ; ধর্ম্মসমাজ-চ্যুত করা, সমাজচ্যুত করা, একঘরে করা ; অপাংক্তেয় করা। **—ca′-tion,** *n.* The act of excommunicating ; expulsion from the communion of the Church ; সমাজচ্যুতি, জাতিবহিষ্করণ, জাতিভ্রংশন ; ধর্ম্মসমাজ হইতে বহিষ্কার। **—ca-tive,** *adj.* **—ca-to-ry,** *adj.* **—mun′-i-ca-ble,** *adj.*

ĕx-cō′-ri-āte, *v. t.* To strip a part of the skin of by abrasion etc. ; to peel, as the skin ; ঘর্ষণদ্বারা চর্ম্ম তুলিয়া লওয়া, লু... তোলা ; চর্ম্ম উত্তোলন করা। **—tion,** *n.*

ĕx′-crē-mĕnt, *n.* Waste matt... discharged from the bowels ; dung ; বিষ্ঠা, গু, বাহ্যি, অমেধ্য ; পুরীষ শকৃৎ। **—men′-tal, —man-ti′-tious,** *adjs.* Pertaining to, o... consisting of, excrements ; lik... excrement ; বৈষ্ঠিক, পুরীষপূ... পুরীষবৎ।

ĕx crĕs′-cence (-sĕns), *n.* **1.** An... thing growing unnaturally an... uselessly on something elses, as wart etc., (*lit.* & *fig.*) ; যাহা ... কোন পদার্থের দেহ হইতে অস্বাভা... রূপে উদ্ভূত হয়, আঁচিল, উপমা... অর্ব্বুদ, কড়া, আচ, গ্যাঁজ। **2.** (*Ra...* Exuberance as of joy etc. ; (ক্ব... ব্যবহৃত) আতিশয্য।

ĕx-crĕs′cĕnt, *adj.* **1.** Growing ab... normally ; superfluous ; অস্বাভাবি... রূপে বর্দ্ধমান ; অতিরিক্ত। **2.** (*Philo...* Not properly or originally b... longing ; as, 'p' is *excrescent* i... empty ; (ভাষা-বিজ্ঞান) সঙ্গতরূপে ... মূলতঃ অঙ্গীভূত নয়। **—crĕs-ce...tial,** *adj.* **Excrescent cons...nant**—Another term for 'EPEN... THESIS', (which see.)

ĕx-crē′-tă, *n. pl.* (*Sing.* -TES... Matter, esp. urine and pus, discharged from the animal body ; জীবদেহ নিস্থত পদার্থ, বিশেষতঃ মূত্র এবং পূয।

ĕx-crete′ (-crēt), *v. t.* (Of animals or plants) To separate and discharge as waste matter etc from the system ; নিঃসৃত কর... ক্ষরণ করা, ত্যাগ করা। **—cre′-tio...** *n.* **1.** The act of excreting, es... waste matter from the body ; বহির্নিক্ষেপ, বহির্নিসারণ, নিষ্ক্রমণ (হি... কোঃ), ত্যাগ, উৎসর্জ্জন। **2.** Tha... which is excreted ; মলমূত্রাদি। **—cre′-tive,** *adj.* Having the power of excreting or promoting cretion ; ভেদনীয় (সাঃ পঃ)। **—cre′-o-ry,** *adj.* & *n.* Pertaining to, or concerned with, excretion ; মল-নিঃসারী। (*Noun*) An excretory organ ; মল-নিঃসারিকা নাড়ী, মল-বাহিকা নাড়ী।

ĕx-crû′-ci-āte (-shĭ-), *v. t.* To torture ; to torment mentally ; পীড়ন করা, অসহ্য যন্ত্রণা দেওয়া, অসহনীয় যাতনা প্রদান করা ; দুঃসহ মানসিক ক্লেশ প্রদান করা। **—at-ing,** *adj.* Extremely painful ; agonising ; নিরতিশয় যন্ত্রণাপ্রদ ; মর্ম্মান্তিক যন্ত্রণাদায়ক, অসহ্য পীড়াদায়ক, তীব্র যন্ত্রণাপ্রদ, অতিবেদনাজনক, অরুন্তুদ। **—at′-ing-ly,** *adv.* **—a′-tion,** *n.*

ĕx-cŭl′-pāte, *v. t.* To relieve of blame ; to clear (a person) from a charge ; দোষ বিমোচন করা, দোষ-নির্ম্মুক্ত করা ; (কোন ব্যক্তির) নির্দ্দোষতা প্রতিপন্ন করা, অপবাদ বা দোষ খণ্ডন করা, দোষমোচন করা। **—pa′-tion,** *n.* Act of exculpating ; দোষ-বিমোচন, দোষ-খণ্ডন, অপরাধ-ভঞ্জন, দোষ-ক্ষালন, শুদ্ধি, দোষ-মোচন, দোষ-নিরসন। **—pa′-to-ry,** *adj.* Tending to exculpate ; clearing from blame ; দোষাপবাদ-বিমোচক, দোষ-খণ্ডনশীল ; দোষক্ষালক।

ĕx-cŭr′-rĕnt, *adj.* **1.** Running or flowing out ; (of arterial blood etc.) flowing from the heart ; প্রবহমান, ধাবমান ; (ধমনীর রক্ত সম্পর্কে) হৃৎপিণ্ড হইতে প্রবহমান। **2.** (*Bot.*) Projecting beyond the apex ; (উদ্ভিদ্-বিদ্যা) শীর্ষ হইতে উদ্গত।

ĕx-cur′-sion (-kêr-) *n.* **1.** A journey for pleasure or health ; a tour ; as, an *excursion* into the country ; প্রমোদ বা স্বাস্থ্যোন্নতিকল্পে পর্য্যটন, প্রমোদভ্রমণ, বিহার ; পরিভ্রমণ। **2.** Deviation from a definite path ; নির্দ্দিষ্ট পথ হইতে চ্যুতি ; অপচার, ব্যভিচার, উৎক্রম। **—al,** *adj.* **—sive,** *adj.* Rambling ; digressive ; desultory ; "*Excursive* reading ;" পরিভ্রমণকারী ; মূল-বিষয় পরিত্যাগ করিয়া অবান্তর বিষয়গামী, অপচারী, ব্যভিচারী ; শৃঙ্খলাশূন্য। **—sive-ly,** *adv.* **—sive-ness,** *n.* **—ist,** *n.* One of a party making a pleasure trip ; প্রমোদ-ভ্রমণকারী। **Excursion train**—যে বাষ্পীয় শকটে অল্প ভাড়াতে প্রমোদ-ভ্রমণকারী আরোহিগণ ভ্রমণ করিতে পারে।

ĕx-cur′-sŭs (-kêr-), *n.* (*Pl.* -SUSES.) **1.** A dissertation appended to a book ; পুস্তকের পরিশিষ্টভাগে সংযোজিত নিবন্ধ। **2.** An incidental discussion ; বিস্তৃত অপ্রাসঙ্গিক আলোচনা।

ĕx-cūse′, *v. t.* **1.** To attempt to remove blame from (a person) or the blame of (a fault) ; as, to *excuse* oneself or a fault ; দোষ মোচন করিতে চেষ্টা করা, অপরাধ-ভার লঘু করিতে চেষ্টা করা। **2.** To serve as an excuse for ; "The wife's presence will not *excuse* the husband ;" অজুহাতস্বরূপ হওয়া। **3.** To pardon or forgive ; ক্ষমা করা, মার্জ্জনা করা। **4.** To overlook ; as, to *excuse* an impropriety ; উপেক্ষা করা, দৃক্‌পাত না করা, গায়ে না মাখা, প্রশ্রয় সহকারে দৃষ্টি করা। **5.** To seek or obtain release for or from ; as, to *excuse* oneself from attendance ; মুক্ত করা, রেহাই পাওয়া। **6.** To remit by a favour ; as to *excuse* a student his fine ; to free from an obligation or duty ; অনুগ্রহ পুরঃসর মাপ করা ; কর্ত্তব্যপালন বা বাধ্যবাধকতা হইতে মুক্তি দেওয়া, রেহাই দেওয়া, নিষ্কৃতি দেওয়া। **—cus′-a-ble,** *adj.* Admitting of excuse or justification ; pardonable ; অজুহাত গ্রহণের-যোগ্য, ন্যায্যতা প্রতিপাদনযোগ্য ; ক্ষমার্হ, ক্ষন্তব্য, মার্জ্জনীয়। **—cus′-a-bly,** *adv.* **—cus′-a-to-ry,** *adv.* **Excuse me**—আমার ত্রুটি গ্রহণ করিবেন না। (কোনও পূজনীয় ব্যক্তির সহিত মতভেদ হইলে, সময় সময় এই কথা দ্বারা স্বীয় মত ব্যক্ত করা হয়।) **He who excuses himself accuses himself**—ঠাকুর ঘরে কে রে? আমি কলা খাই না। **To excuse one's self**—See EXCUSE 5.

ĕx-cūse′, *n.* **1.** Pardoning ; exculpation ; as, in *excuse* of ; মাপ, ক্ষমা, মার্জ্জনা ; দোষ-খণ্ডন। **2.** A plea in extenuation of a fault ; an apology ; as, an *excuse* for neglect of duty ; ওজর, হেতুবাদ, অজুহাত, ছুতা ; ত্রুটিস্বীকার। **3.** A ground or reason for excuse ; ক্ষমার কারণ বা হেতু।

ĕx′-ē-ăt, *n.* (England) Permission for temporary absence from a college or a religious house ; (ইংলণ্ডে) কলেজ বা ধর্ম্মমন্দির হইতে সাময়িক অনুপস্থিতির জন্য অনুমতি।

ĕx′-ē-cră-ble (-bl), *adj.* **1.** Detestable ; ঘৃণ্য, ঘৃণার্হ, গর্হ্য, জঘন্য। **2.** Extremely bad ; as, *execrable* weather ;" নিতান্ত মন্দ, অতি খারাপ। **—bly,** *adv.*

ex′-ē-crāte, *v. t.* & *i.* To curse ; to detest utterly ; অভিসম্পাত করা, অভিশাপ দেওয়া ; বিজাতীয় ঘৃণা করা। *Verb i.* To utter curses ; অভিশাপ-বাক্য উচ্চারণ করা। **—cra′-tion,** *n.* **1.** Act of execrating ; a curse ; imprecation ; অভিশাপ প্রদান ; অভিসম্পাত ; অভিশাপ। **2.** An object of execration ; বিজাতীয় ঘৃণার পাত্র। **—cra-tive, —cra-to-ry,** *adjs.*

ex-ĕc′-ū-tănt (ĕgz-), *n.* One who executes or performs, (with *of*) ; as, an *executant of* music ; সম্পাদক নির্ব্বাহক।

ĕx′-ē-cūte, *v. t.* **1.** To carry out ; to perform ; as, to *execute* a plan, order ; পালন করা ; সম্পাদন করা, সমাপ্ত করা, নির্ব্বাহ করা। **2.** To complete or give validity to, as legal instrument or deed etc. by signing, sealing, etc. ; স্বাক্ষর ও শীলমোহর প্রভৃতি দ্বারা দলিলাদি যথাবিধিরূপে সম্পাদন করা, সম্পাদন করা। **3.** To give effect to :

as, to *execute* a decree or will; কার্য্যে পরিণত করা, জারি করা। 4. (*Mus.*) To perform as a piece of music; বাদ্য প্রভৃতি সম্পাদন করা। 5. To inflict capital punishment on; as, to *execute* a traitor; মৃত্যুদণ্ডপ্রাপ্ত ব্যক্তিকে নিধন করা। 6. To fulfil or discharge; as, to *execute* an office or function; সম্পন্ন করা, নির্ব্বাহ করা। **–cut-a-ble,** *adj.* Capable of being executed; সম্পাদনীয়, কার্য্যকরী।

ĕx-ē-cū′-tion, *n.* 1. Carrying into effect; performance; সম্পাদন; নিষ্পাদন, পালন, নির্ব্বাহ। 2. The infliction of capital punishment; প্রাণদণ্ডে দণ্ডিত ব্যক্তির বধ সাধন। 3. Completion of legal instruments by signing, sealing, etc.; দলিলাদি সম্পাদন। 4. Facility of voice or finger in music; গীতবাদ্য-সম্পাদনে স্বরনৈপুণ্য বা অঙ্গুলিচালন-চাতুর্য্য। 5. Carrying into effect the decree of a court; জারীকরণ। 6. Seizure of goods of a debtor in default of payment; (আইনে) ক্রোক। 6. The act or mode of performing a work of art; শিল্পকার্য্য সম্পাদন বা উৎপাদনের ধারা কিম্বা প্রণালী। 7. Destructive effect; slaughter; as, these weapons did great *execution*; ধ্বংসজনকতা; হত্যা। **–er,** *n.* One who executes criminals condemned by law; জল্লাদ, ঘাতক। **To do execution**—See EXECUTION 7. above.

ex-ec′-u-tive (ĕgz-ĕk-ū-tĭv), *adj.* & *n.* Relating to execution; having the function of, or fitted to, execution; as, an *executive*; officer or authority; carrying laws etc. into effect or superintending their enforcement, (opp. to *judicial* and *legislative*); as, the *executive* government; কার্য্যকারী, কার্য্যনির্ব্বাহক; কার্য্যনির্ব্বাহক্ষম, কার্য্যকুশল, কার্য্যনির্ব্বাহোপযোগী, কার্য্য-সম্পাদনার্থ অভিপ্রেত; শাসনবিভাগীয়, শাসনসম্পর্কীয়। ***Noun.*** 1. The branch of government concerned with the execution of laws, decrees, etc.; শাসনবিভাগ। 2. A person or body of persons charged with executive work; শাসনবিভাগীয় কর্ম্মচারী, শাসকসম্প্রদায়। **–ly,** *adv.*

ex′-ec-u-tor (ĕk-sĭ-kūt-ēr or ĕgs-ĕk′-ūt-ėr), *n.* 1. One who executes or performs; সম্পাদনকারী। 2. (*Law*) One appointed by a testator to execute his will or to see it carried into effect; (আইন) মৃত ব্যক্তির সম্পত্তির তত্ত্বাবধায়ক বা অছি, চরমপত্রের কার্য্যনির্ব্বাহক। (*fem.* -TRESS, TRIX, মৃতব্যক্তির সম্পত্তির তত্ত্বাবধায়িকা)। **–ship,** *n.* **–to′-ri-al,** *adj.* **–to-ry,** *adj.* Pertaining to administration; performing official duties; executive; শাসন-সংক্রান্ত; সরকারী কার্য্য-নির্ব্বাহক; শাসনবিভাগীয়। **Literary executor** — লেখকের অপ্রকাশিত পুস্তকাবলী যাহার তত্ত্বাবধানে রাখা হয়।

ĕx-ē-ġē′-sĭs, *n.* Exposition; critical expianation of the scripture; ব্যাখ্যা, বিবৃতি, অর্থবিবরণ (হিঃ কোঃ); খৃষ্টীয় ধর্ম্মগ্রন্থের ভাষ্য। **–get′-ic, –get′-i-cal,** *adjs.* Expository; ব্যাখ্যাসূচক। **–get′-i-cal-ly,** *adv.*

ex-em′-plar (ĕgz-ĕm-plêr), *n.* 1. A pattern; an ideal model; নমুনা; আদর্শ, প্রতিরূপ। 2. A parallel or typical instance; a type as of a class; অনুরূপ দৃষ্টান্ত, আদর্শস্বরূপ দৃষ্টান্ত; কোন শ্রেণী বা জাতির আদর্শস্বরূপ বস্তু।

ex′-ĕm-plă-rȳ (ĕgz-), *adj.* 1. Serving as model for imitation; fit to be imitated; "Popular tales with *exemplary* morals;" আদর্শ-স্থানীয়; অনুকরণযোগ্য। 2. Serving as a warning; as, an *exemplary* punishment; অপরের পক্ষে সতর্কতা-জনক। 3. Illustrative; as, an *exemplary* passage or drawing; উদাহরণস্বরূপ। **–ri-ly,** *adv.* **–ri-ness,** *n.*

ex-ĕm′-plĭ-fȳ (ĕgz-), *v. t.* 1. To illustrate by example; to serve as an example of; উদাহৃত করা, দৃষ্টান্ত প্রদর্শন করা, উদাহরণদ্বারা স্পষ্ট করা; দৃষ্টান্ত স্বরূপ হওয়া। 2. To make an attested copy or transcript of (a document) under official seal; সহিমোহরের নকল প্রস্তুত করা। **–fi-ca′-tion,** *n.* 1. The act of exemplifying; দৃষ্টান্ত-প্রদর্শন। 2. An example, উদাহরণ। 3. An attested copy of a document; সহিমোহরের নকল।

ex-empt′ (ĕgz-ĕmt), *v. t.* To free or grant immunity (from); as, to *exempt* a person from taxation; মুক্তি দেওয়া, কোনও দায় হইতে নিস্কৃতি বা অব্যাহতি দেওয়া, রেহাই দেওয়া। **–emp′-tion,** *n.* Act of exempting; immunity; মোচন মুক্তি; অব্যাহতি, দায়-মুক্তি।

ex-empt′ (ĕgz-ĕmt), *n.* & *adj.* 1. A person exempted, esp. from taxation; অব্যাহতিপ্রাপ্ত ব্যক্তি। 2. An exon, (see EXON). ***Adj.*** Free or released from some liability; not liable, (with *from*); মুক্ত, অনধীন; দায়-মুক্ত, বিমুক্তিপ্রাপ্ত।

ĕx-ĕn′-têr-āte (ĕgz-), *v. t.* To disembowel, (only *fig.*); অন্ত্রহীন করা। **–a′-tion,** *n.*

ĕx-ē-quā′-tur (-têr), *n.* [*L.*] A written official recognition of a country's consul or commercial agent by a foreign government; বিদেশীয় গভর্ণমেণ্টকর্ত্তৃক কোন দেশের রাজদূত বা বাণিজ্য-সংক্রান্ত প্রতিনিধিকে পত্রদ্বারা স্বীকার।

ĕx′-ē-quies (-kwĭs), *n.* (*pl.*) Funeral rites; অন্ত্যেষ্টিক্রিয়া, ঔর্দ্ধদেহিক-ক্রিয়া, প্রেতকর্ম্ম।

ĕx′-êr-cīse, *n.* 1. A setting in action; practice; use; application; as, the *exercise* of the eyes or of power, authority, etc.; সঞ্চালন, চালনা, পরিচালনা, কার্য্যে নিয়োগ;

ব্যবহার, চর্য্য (মঃ ইঃ), পালন, অভ্যাস, অনুষ্ঠান; প্রয়োগ; বিনিয়োগ। **2.** Exertion of the body for health or amusement ; as, dumb-bell *exercise* ; অঙ্গচালনা, অঙ্গচেষ্টা, কসরৎ (ব্যায়ামাদি)। **3.** Mental, physical or spiritual training ; শারীরিক, মানসিক বা আধ্যাত্মিক উন্নতির উদ্দেশ্যে চর্চ্চা বা অনুশীলন। **4.** A lesson for practice ; a school task ; as, give him an *exercise* ; কর্ত্তব্যকার্য্য, নির্দ্দিষ্টকার্য্য ; পাঠ, অনুশীলনী। **5.** (*Pl. Mil.*) Drill ; athletics ; সামরিক কসরৎ ; মল্লক্রীড়া। **6.** Performance ; as, the *exercise* of an office function ; সম্পাদন। **7.** An academical declamation etc. required from candidates for degree ; বিলাতে বিশ্ববিদ্যালয়ের উপাধি-প্রার্থীকে যে সালঙ্কার বক্তৃতা প্রদান করিতে হয়। **8.** The act of divine worship ; দেবার্চ্চনা।

ĕx′-ê̤r-cīse, *v. t.* & *i.* To employ ; to set in action ; as, to *exercise* a right or faculty ; বিনিয়োগ করা ; চালান, সঞ্চালন করা। **2.** To train by use or practice ; as, to *exercise* oneself in an art ; to practise for training ; অভ্যাস বা অনুশীলনদ্বারা শিক্ষিত করা ; শিক্ষার জন্য অভ্যাস বা অনুশীলন করা। **3.** To vex ; to worry ; as, do not *exercise* your mind about that ; ব্যাকুল করা, উত্ত্যক্ত করা ; ব্যথিত করা, ক্লিষ্ট করা। **4.** To perform ; to use ; as, to *exercise* a function or authority ; সম্পাদন করা, কার্য্য সম্পাদন করা ; পরিচালন করা। ***Verb i.*** To take exercise ; ব্যায়াম করা। **—cis-a-ble,** *adj.* Capable of being exercised, employed or enforced ; as, an *exerciseable* right ; পরিচালনীয়, প্রযোজ্য, আমলে আনিবার যোগ্য। **—cis-er,** *n.*

ĕx-ê̤r-cĭ-tā′-tion, *n.* **1.** Exercise ; training ; literary or oratorial exercise ; পরিচালনা ; অভ্যাস, ব্যবহার ; প্রবন্ধ বা বক্তৃতার অনুশীলন।

ex-ergue′ (ĕgz-ĕrg), *n.* The small space beneath the main device, on the reverse of a coin or model ; also the inscription engraved there on ; মুদ্রা বা পদকের বিপরীত পৃষ্ঠের প্রতিমূর্ত্তির নিম্নস্থিত স্বল্পায়তন স্থান (ইহাতে তারিখ প্রভৃতি মুদ্রিত হইয়া থাকে) ; উক্ত স্থানে উৎকীর্ণ তারিখ প্রভৃতি।

ex-êrt′ (ĕgz-), *v.t.* **1.** To put forth ; to put in action ; as, to *exert* one's strength, ability, etc. ; যত্ন করা, চেষ্টা করা, উদ্যোগ করা, উদ্যম করা ; পরিচালনা করা, কার্য্য সাধনে নিয়োগ করা। **2.** To bring to bear ; "The influence was *exerted* on the side of order and peace ;" প্রয়োগ করা। **—er′-tion,** *n.* Act of exerting ; effort ; পরিচালনা ; চেষ্টা, প্রচেষ্টা, প্রযত্ন, উদ্যম, উদ্যোগ। **—er′-tive,** *adj.* **To exert oneself**—To strive ; চেষ্টা করা।

exeunt *v. i.* [*L.*] (A stage direction) They *i. e.* the actors leave the stage (তাহারা রঙ্গমঞ্চ হইতে প্রস্থান করিতেছে) ; (নাটক) প্রস্থান (করিতেছে)। ***Exeunt omness***—All leave the stage ; (সকলে প্রস্থান করিতেছে) সকলের প্রস্থান।

ĕx-fō′-lĭ-āte, *v.i.* & *t.* To separate and come off in scales ; to throw off scales or layers etc. ; as, some minerals *exfoliate* when heated ; ছিল্কা উঠা ; শল্ক উঠিয়া যাওয়া। ***Verb t.*** To scale off ; শল্ক মুক্ত করা। **—a′-tion,** *n.* The process of exfoliating ; শল্ক স্খলন, ছিল্কা উঠন।

ex-hāle′ (ĕgz-), *v. t.* & *i.* **1.** To emit as vapour ; to give off ; "They (plants) *exhales* oxygen : the rose *exhales* fragrance ; নিঃসৃত করা ; নির্গত করা। **2.** To evaporate ; as, the sun *exhales* vapour from the sea ; বাষ্পীভূত করা। **3.** To get rid of as if by blowing ; as, he has *exhaled* his anger ; যেন শ্বাস ছাড়িয়া অব্যাহতি পাওয়া। ***Verb i.*** **1.** To rise or be emitted as vapour ; বাষ্পাকারে উত্থিত বা নির্গত হওয়া। **2.** To emit breath or vapour ; নিশ্বাস বায়ু মোচন করা ; বাষ্প নির্গত করা। **—hal′-a-ble, —hal′-ant,** *adjs.* **—ha-la′-tion,** *n* **1.** The act of exhaling ; evaporation ; expiration ; মোচন, নির্গম ; বাষ্পনির্গম ; নিশ্বাসমোচন। **2.** Steam ; effluvium ; mist ; as, the *exhalations* from a corpse ; বাষ্প ; দূষিত বাষ্প ; কুহেলিকা। **3.** A short burst (of anger etc.) ; উদ্গম (ক্রোধাদির)। **—hale′ment,** *n.*

ex-haust′ (ĕgz-häst), *v. t.* **1.** To drain off completely ; as, to *exhaust* air from a glass tube ; সম্পূর্ণরূপে নিঃশেষিত করা। **2.** To use the whole of ; as, to *exhaust* strength, resources, etc. to deprive (a nation etc.) of strength, resources, etc. ; to tire out ; সমস্তটা প্রয়োগ করা ; শক্তিহীন করা, সঙ্গতি হীন করা, উপায় হীন করা, সম্বল শূন্য করা ; পরিক্লান্ত করা। **3.** To empty of contents ; as, to *exhaust* a well ; খালি করা, শূন্যগর্ভ করা, ফুরান, পর্য্যবসিত করা, নিঃশেষিত করা, রিক্ত করা। **4.** To treat or discuss completely ; (কোন বিষয়ে) সম্যগ্‌রূপে আলোচনা করা। **—ed,** *adj.* **1.** Emptied ; নিঃশেষিত, শূন্যীকৃত। **2.** Quite fatigued ; অতিশ্রান্ত, খিন্ন, অবসন্ন। **3.** Used up ; ব্যয়িত। **—er,** *n.* **—i-bil′-i-ty,** *n.* **—i-ble,** *adj.* **—ing,** *adj.* Producing exhaustion ; অবসাদকর। **—ing-ly,** *adv.*

ex-haust′ (ĕgz-häst), *n.* **1.** (*Steam-Engine*) The escape of steam from a cylinder after its work is done ; কার্য্য সমাপনান্তে নল হইতে বাষ্প-নির্গম। **2.** The process of emptying a vessel of air ; বায়ুশূন্য করণ। **3.** Generation of air-currents by creating a partial vacuum ; an apparatus for this purpose ; আংশিক শূন্যতা উৎপাদন

করত বায়ুপ্রবাহজনন; উক্ত উদ্দেশ্য সাধনোপযোগী যন্ত্রবিশেষ। **Exhaust-pipe**—বাষ্পীয় যন্ত্রের যে নল দ্বারা অব্যবহার্য্য বাষ্প যন্ত্রের বৃহত্তম নল হইতে বায়ুমণ্ডলে বা বাষ্পসংকোচক যন্ত্রাংশে নীত হয়। **Exhaust-steam**—বাষ্পীয় যন্ত্রের নলদণ্ড (piston) চালনার পর যে অব্যবহার্য্য বাষ্প বৃহত্তম নল হইতে উড়িয়া যায়। **Exhaust-valve**—বাষ্পীয় যন্ত্রের যে বাষ্প-নিঃসরণ পথে বৃহত্তম চোঙ্গার অব্যবহার্য্য বাষ্প নির্গত হইয়া থাকে।

ex-haus′-tion (ĕgz-hăst-yŏn) *n.* **1.** The act of exhausting; state of being exhausted; শূন্যীকরণ, রিক্তীকরণ নিঃশেষকরণ; নিঃশেষতা, শূন্যতা, বলক্ষয়, পরম ক্লান্তি, অবসাদ, খেদ, গ্লানি, নিস্তেজতা, পরিশ্রান্তি। **2.** (*Math.*) A method of proving the equality of two magnitudes by a *reductio ad absurdum i. e.* by showing that if either is greater or less than the other a contradiction will follow; as, proof by *exhaustion*; (গণিতশাস্ত্র) অসঙ্গতি প্রদর্শন দ্বারা দুইটী আয়তনের সমতা-প্রমাণের উপায় বিশেষ, অর্থাৎ আয়তনদ্বয় পরস্পরাপেক্ষা বৃহত্তর বা অল্পতর হইলে অসঙ্গতি হইয়া থাকে।

ex-haus′-tive (ĕgz-hăs-tĭv), *adj.* Tending to exhaust; thorough; as, an *exhaustive* treatment of a subject; নিঃশেষকর; চূড়ান্ত। **—ly,** *adv.* **—ness,** *n.*

ex-hib′-it (ĕgz), *v. t.* & *n.* **1.** To present to view, as goods in a shop; to manifest, as a quality; to show publicly as a magic lantern; প্রদর্শন করা; ব্যক্ত করা, প্রকটিত করা, প্রকাশ করা; সর্ব্বসাধারণ্যে প্রদর্শন করা। **2.** (*Med.*) To administer as a medicine; (ভৈষজ্য-শাস্ত্র) ঔষধাদি প্রয়োগ করা। **3.** To submit as a document etc. to a court for consideration; আদালতের বিবেচনার্থ দলিল দস্তাবেজ দাখিল করা। ***Noun.*** **1.** Something as a document etc., produced in court to be used as evidence; মোকদ্দমার প্রমাণস্বরূপ আদালতে উপস্থাপিত দলিলাদি, নিদর্শন পত্র, দস্তাবেজ। **2.** A thing or collection of things exhibited; প্রদর্শিত বস্তু বা বস্তুসমূহ। **3.** Act of showing; প্রদর্শন। **—i-tor,** *n.* One who exhibits; প্রদর্শক। **—i-to-ry, —ive,** *adjs.* **To exhibit an essay**—To present an essay in public; কোন রচনা বা নিবন্ধ জনসাধারণের সমক্ষে উপস্থাপিত করা।

ĕx-hi-bi′-tion, *n.* **1.** The act of exhibiting; প্রদর্শন, প্রকটীকরণ, ব্যক্তীকরণ। **2.** Any public show, esp. of works of art, manufacture, etc.; as, agricultural *exhibition*; প্রদর্শনী, মেলা। **3.** (*In Eng.*) A sum given to a student for a term of years from the funds of an institution; (ইংলণ্ডীয় বিশ্ববিদ্যালয় সমূহে) বৃত্তি। **4.** The act of administering a remedy; ঔষধপ্রদান। **—er,** *n.* A student who has been granted an allowance for support; (ইংলণ্ডীয় বিশ্ববিদ্যালয়ে) বৃত্তিধারী ছাত্র। **The Great Exhibition**—১৮৫১ খৃঃ অব্দের লণ্ডন নগরীর বিরাট প্রদর্শনী। **To make an exhibition of oneself**—(*colloq.*) (চলিত ভাষায়) এমন নির্ব্বোধের মত ব্যবহার করা যাহাতে লোকের নিকট উপহাসাস্পদ হইতে হয়।

ex-hil′-ă-rāte (ĕgz-), *v. t.* To cheer; to enliven; as, to *exhilarate* a man, mind or spirits; সমুল্লসিত করা, উৎফুল্ল করা, স্ফূর্ত্তিযুক্ত করা, প্রহৃষ্ট করা; উজ্জীবিত করা। **—rant,** *adj.* & *n.* Exciting joy; হর্ষোদ্দীপক, হর্ষকর, উল্লাসকর। (*Noun*) That which exhilarates; উল্লাসজনক বস্তু। **—rat-ing,** *adj.* Cheering; আনন্দোদ্দীপক, উল্লাসকর, আনন্দদায়ক, স্ফূর্ত্তিজনক। **—rat-ing-ly,** *adv.* **—ra′-tion,** *n.* The act of enlivening or cheering; lively cheerfulness; সমুল্লসন, স্ফূর্ত্তিজনন; সমুল্লাস, প্রফুল্লতা। **—ra-tive,** *adj.*

ex-hŏrt′ (ĕgz-), *v. t.* **1.** To urge strongly, as to do a good thing; to admonish; to insist upon; as, to *exhort* reform; সনির্ব্বন্ধ অনুরোধ করা, পীড়াপীড়ি করা; উপদেশ প্রদান করা; জেদ করা। **—hor-ta′-tion,** *n.* **1.** Exhorting; সনির্ব্বন্ধ অনুরোধ। **2.** Advice; a homily; পরামর্শ, উপদেশ; ধর্ম্মোপদেশ, ধর্ম্মবিষয়ক বক্তৃতা। **—hor′-ta-tive, —hor′-ta-to-ry,** *adjs.*

ĕx-hūme′, *v. t.* To dig out; to disinter, (*lit.* & *fig.*); খনন করিয়া ভূগর্ভ হইতে উত্তোলিত করা, উৎখনিত করা; সমাধি হইতে উত্তোলিত করা। **—hu-ma′-tion,** *n.* Act of exhuming; disinterment; ভূগর্ভ হইতে উত্তোলন; সমাধি হইতে উত্তোলন, শবোৎখাতন, উৎখনন।

ĕx′-i-gence (-jĕns), **—gĕn-cy̆,** *n.* **1.** Pressing necessity; emergency; "The extreme *exigency* of the moment;" নিতান্ত আবশ্যক, অত্যন্ত প্রয়োজন, গরজ, জরুরীয়ৎ (*colloq.*); গুরুতর প্রয়োজন। **—gent,** *adj.* **1.** Pressing; critical; নির্ব্বন্ধাতিশয়পূর্ণ, জরুরী, অত্যাবশ্যক; গুরুতর। **2.** Exacting; as, an *exigent* man etc.; পীড়নপূর্ব্বক আদায়কারী। **—gi-ble,** *adj.* **Exigent of**—Demanding; দাবীকারী।

ĕx-ig′-ū-ous (-ŭs), *adj.* Scanty; small; অপ্রচুর; অল্প, কণামাত্র। **—i-gu′-i-ty,** *n.* Smallness or scantiness; অল্পতা, অপ্রাচুর্য্য। **—ness,** *n.*

ex′-īle (ĕgz-), *n.* & *v. t.* **1.** Banishment; long absence from one's native land; নির্ব্বাসন, বিবাসন; সুদীর্ঘপ্রবাস। **2.** A banished person, (*lit.* & *fig.*); নির্ব্বাসিত ব্যক্তি। ***Verb t.*** To banish; নির্ব্বাসিত করা, বিবাসিত করা। **—ment,** *n.* Banishment; নির্ব্বাসন, বিবাসন। **—il′-ic,** *adj.* Pertaning to exile or banishment, esp. to that of Jews in Babylon; নির্ব্বাসন-সংক্রান্ত, (বিশেষত বাইবেলে বর্ণিত) ইয়ুদীজাতির বেবিলনরাজ্যে নির্ব্বাসন-বিষয়ক।

ex-il'-i-an, *adj.* Same as EXILIC above.
ex-il'-i-tŷ (ĕgz-), *n.* Thinness ; subtlety ; তনুতা ; সূক্ষ্মতা।
ex-ist' (ĕgz-), *v. t.* **1.** To be ; অস্তিত্ব থাকা, বর্ত্তমান থাকা, রহা, বিদ্যমান থাকা, অবস্থান করা। **2.** To occur ; as, salt *exists* in sea-water ; বর্ত্তমান থাকা, দৃষ্ট হওয়া। **3.** To live ; as, man cannot *exist* in water ; বাঁচিয়া থাকা, জীবিত থাকা। **4.** To continue to be ; as, what is untrue can not *exist* ; থাকা। **—ence,** *n.* **1.** The state of existing or being ; continuance ; অস্তিত্ব, সত্তা, ভাব, বিদ্যমানতা, সদ্ভাব, বর্ত্তমানতা ; অবস্থিতি, অবস্থান, স্থিতি। **2.** Life ; as, a wretched *existence* ; জীবন। **3.** An existing thing ; an entity ; সৎপদার্থ ; অস্তিত্ববান পদার্থ। **4.** A mode of existing ; "New *existence* led by men and women ;" জীবন-প্রণালী। **5.** Occurrence ; সংঘটন। **—ent,** *adj.* Existing ; actual ; current ; বিদ্যমান ; প্রকৃত ; প্রচলিত। **—is-ten'-tial,** *adj.* Involving, or pertaining to existence ; সত্তাসম্পর্কীয়, সত্তাসংসৃষ্ট। **—ing,** *adj.* Present ; current ; বর্ত্তমান, উপস্থিত, বিদ্যমান ; প্রচলিত **Struggle for existence**—জীবন-সংগ্রাম (জিঃ), জীবন-দ্বন্দ্ব (ঐ)।
ĕx'-it, *v. i.* (A stage direction) Goes off the stage, (*lit,* & *fig.*) ; (নাটকে) রঙ্গমঞ্চ পরিত্যাগ করিতেছে (প্রস্থান)।
ĕx'-it, *n.* **1.** Departure from the stage, as of a player, (*lit.* & *fig.*) : রঙ্গমঞ্চ হইতে অভিনেতা বা অভিনেত্রীর প্রস্থান। **2.** Death ; as, he made his *exit* *i. e.* died ; জীবনের রঙ্গমঞ্চ পরিত্যাগ, তিরোভাব, মৃত্যু। **3.** Going out or forth ; "The *exit* of the steam ;" liberty to go out ; a departure ; বহির্গমন, নিঃসরণ, নিক্রমণ, নির্যাণ ; বহির্গমনের স্বাধীনতা ; নির্গম-পথ, প্রয়াণ-পথ।
ĕx-lī'-bris, *n.* A label or inscription in a book indicating its ownership ; পুস্তকের মলাটের ভিতরের দিকে আঁটা কাগজ খণ্ড,—ইহাতে মালিকের নামধামাদি লিখা থাকে, নাম-পট্ট।
ĕx'-ōde, *n.* (*Greek antiq.*) The concluding part of a Greek drama ; a farce ; গ্রীসদেশীয় নাটকের উপসংহার ভাগ ; প্রহসন, ব্যঙ্গনাট্য।
ĕx'-ō-dŭs, *n.* **1.** Going forth as of a body of emigrants ; the departure of the Israelites from Egypt ; প্রস্থান, গমন, নির্যাণ ; মিসর দেশ হইতে ইজরেলাইটগণের প্রস্থান। **2.** The second book of the Old Testament ; প্রাচীন বাইবেলের অন্তর্ভুক্ত দ্বিতীয় পুস্তক। (ইজরেলাইটগণ মিসরদেশ হইতে বিতাড়িত হইয়া মুশার (Moses) নেতৃত্বে ঈশ্বরের প্রতিশ্রুত দেশের অন্বেষণে বহির্গত হয় ; তাহাদের মিশর হইতে প্রস্থানের কাহিনী প্রাচীন বাইবেলের (Old Testament) 'Exodus' নামে একটী অধ্যায়ে লিখিত হইয়াছে।)
ex officio, *adj.* & *adv.* [*L.*] By virtue of one's office ; as, an *ex-officio* member ; পদহেতুক।
ĕx-ŏg'-ă-mŷ, *n.* A custom compelling men to marry outside of the tribe ; অসবর্ণ বিবাহ, গোত্রান্তর বিবাহ, ভিন্ন গোত্রে বিবাহ, বহির্ব্বিবাহ। **—mous,** *adj.*
ĕx'-ō-gĕn, *n.* (*Bot.*) A plant whose stem grows by additions to the outside of the wood ; যে সমস্ত উদ্ভিদ বাহিরের দিক হইতে পুষ্ট হইয়া বৃদ্ধি পায়, বহির্জনি উদ্ভিদ্ [এই জাতীয় উদ্ভিদের কাণ্ড, বল্কল, কাষ্ঠ ও মজ্জা এই তিনভাগে বিভক্ত ; যথা, আম্র, কাঁঠাল, তিন্তিড়ী প্রভৃতি ; ইহা endogen অর্থাৎ অন্তর্জনি (যথা — কলাগাছ) উদ্ভিদের বিপরীত]। **—og'-e-nous,** *adj.* (*Bot.*) Growing by additions on the frontside ; অন্তঃসার, বহির্জনিষ্ণু।
ĕx'-ōn, *n.* (In England) One of four officers of the Yeomen of the Royal body-guard ; ইংলণ্ডাধিপতির শরীর-রক্ষক ইয়োম্যান সৈন্যদলের কর্ম্মচারি চতুষ্টয়ের অন্যতম।
ex-ŏn'-ĕr-āte (ĕgz-), *v. t.* **1.** To relieve from a charge or obligation etc. ; to justify ; অভিযোগ হইতে মুক্তি দেওয়া, বাধ্যবাধকতা হইতে রেহাই দেওয়া ; ন্যায্যতা প্রতিপাদন করা। **2.** To exculpate ; দোষ মুক্ত করা। **—a'-tion,** *n.* Act of exonerating ; acquittal ; দোষবিমোচন, দোষক্ষালন, দোষনিরসন ; অব্যাহতি। **—a-tive,** *adj.*
ĕx-ō-păth'-ic, *adj.* (*Med.*) Having an external source, as a disease ; (ভৈষজ্য-শাস্ত্র) বাহ্য কারণমূলক (রোগাদি সম্বন্ধে)।
ĕx-ŏph'-ă-gŷ, *n.* Cannibalism in which only persons of a different tribe are eaten ; ভিন্নজাতীয় লোকের মাংসাহার। **—gous,** *adj.*
ĕx-ŏph-thăl'-mŭs, —mŏs, —mi-ă, *ns.* (*Med.*) The protrusion of the eye-ball so that the eye-lid cannot cover it ; বহিরাগত অক্ষিগোলক রোগ (হঃ চঃ)।
ĕx'-ō-ră-ble (-bl), *adj.* Capable of being persuaded by entreaty ; অনুনয়দ্বারা প্রসাদনীয়, তোষণীয়।
ex-ŏr'-bi-tănt (ĕgz-), *adj.* Grossly excessive ; অতিরিক্ত, অত্যধিক, বেজায়, অপরিমিত, নিয়মাতীত। **—tance,** *n.* State or quality of being exorbitant ; extravagance ; আতিশয্য, বাহুল্য ; অতিরেক। **—ly,** *adv.* Excessively ; অতিশয়িতরূপে, বাহুল্যভাবে, অত্যন্ত।
ĕx'-ŏr-çīse, —çīze, *v. t.* To expel as evil spirits by some holy name from a person or a place ; to relieve as a person or place of malignant spirits ; ভূত ঝাড়া, ভূত ছাড়ান ; ভূত, পিশাচাদি দুষ্ট যোনির প্রভাব হইতে মুক্ত করা। **—cism,** *n.* The act of exorcising ; a formula for exorcism ; ভূত-বিতাড়ন, ভূতাপসরণ ; ভূত-বিদ্যা, ওঝাগিরি, ভূত ছাড়ানের মন্ত্র। **—cist,** *n.* **1.** One who exorcises ভূতের ওঝা, রোজা।

ex-ŏr'-dĭ-ŭm (ĕgz-), *n.* (*pl.* -ums, -a) The introductory part of a discourse or treatise ; বাক্যারম্ভ, ভূমিকা, মুখবন্ধ, উপক্রমণিকা, অবতরণিকা। **—di-al,** *adj.*

ĕx'-ŏs-mōse, —mō'-sĭs, *n.* Passage of a fluid outwards through a porus membrane ; সচ্ছিদ্র আবরণ ভেদ পূর্ব্বক তরল পদার্থের বহির্নিঃসরণ, বহির্গমন (সাঃ পঃ)।

ĕx-ŏs-tō'-sĭs, *n.* (*Med.*) Morbid enlargement of a bone ; অস্থির অস্বাভাবিক বিবর্দ্ধন, অস্থি-অর্ব্বুদ।

ĕx-ō-tĕr'-ĭc, *adj.* & *n.* **1.** Suitable to be imparted to the public ; readily intelligible, (opp. to *esoteric* or *secret*) ; সাধারণ্যে প্রচার-যোগ্য ; সহজ বোধগম্য। **2.** Not admitted to esoteric teaching ; নিগূঢ় উপদেশ লাভে অনধিকারী, বহিরঙ্গ, বাহ্য। **3.** Popular ; ordinary ; লোকপ্রিয়, লৌকিক ; সাধারণ। ***Noun.*** (*Pl.*) Exoteric doctrines or treatises ; বহিরঙ্গ লোকের নিকট প্রকাশ যোগ্য উপদেশ বা পুস্তক, অপরা বিদ্যা (ডিউসেন)। **—i-cal,** *adj.* **—i-cal-ly,** *adv.*

ĕx-ŏt'-ĭc (ĕgz-), *adj.* Introduced from a foreign country ; foreign ; as, an *exotic* plant, word or fashion ; বিদেশ হইতে প্রবর্ত্তিত ; বৈদেশিক, পরদেশী, বিদেশী, অন্তদেশজ, বিদেশজ, দেশান্তরজ, বিদেশীয়। ***Noun.*** An exotic plant, word, etc. ; বিদেশ হইতে প্রবর্ত্তিত উদ্ভিদ, পরদেশীয় উদ্ভিদ, পরদেশ হইতে প্রবর্ত্তিত দ্রব্য বা শব্দ। **—i-cism,** *n.*

ĕx-pănd', *v. t.* **1.** To spread out ; "The rose *expands* her paradise of leaves ;" বিস্তার করা, বিস্ফারিত করা, প্রস্ফুটিত করা, বিকচ করা, উৎফুল্ল করা। **2.** To dilate ; to distend, (opp. to *contract*) ; as, heat *expands* bodies ; প্রসারিত করা ; বিতানিত করা, বিতত করা, বিস্ফারিত করা, বিসারিত করা ; আয়তন বৃদ্ধি করা, বিস্ত্যার্ষিত করা। **3.** To write out or express in full ; to develop ; as, to *expand* a stanza or line ; সবিস্তারে লিখা বা প্রকাশ করা ; উন্নত করা। ***Verb i.*** To dilate ; to spread wide ; to swell ; বিসারিত হওয়া ; প্রসারিত হওয়া, বিস্ফারিত হওয়া ; স্ফীত হওয়া। **—panse',** *n.* **1.** Wide extent or surface ; (with *the*) the firmament ; "The *expanse* of the sea ;" প্রসার, বিস্তার ; নভোমণ্ডল। **2.** Expansion ; বিস্তার। **—pan-si-bil'-i-ty,** *n.* The capacity of being expanded ; প্রসার্যতা। **—pan'-si-ble,** *adj.* Capable of being expanded ; বিস্তরণীয়, বিস্তার-ক্ষম। **—pan'-sile,** *adj.* **1.** Expansible ; বিস্তরণীয়। **2.** Pertaining to expansion ; বিসারণ সম্বন্ধীয়।

ĕx-păn'-sion, *n.* **1.** The act of expanding ; state of being expanded ; extension ; as, *expansion* of territory or business ; বিসারণ, প্রসারণ, প্রসর্পণ, প্রস্ফুটন ; বিস্তৃতি, বিবৃতি, ব্যাপ্তি, প্রসার, প্রসর, প্রস্থতি ; স্ফীতি ; বিস্তার। **2.** Extended surface ; (কোন বস্তুর) প্রসারিত অংশ। **3.** An expanded part or termination ; বিস্তারিত অংশ বা শেষ অংশ। **—sive,** *adj.* **1.** Tending to expand ; wide-extending ; comprehensive ; effusive, as a speech, feeling etc. ; প্রসরণ-প্রবণ, প্রসরণ-ক্ষম, প্রসরণধর্ম্মী, বিস্তারশীল ; প্রসারী, প্রসর্পী, বহুদূরব্যাপ্ত, সুবিস্তৃত, দিগন্ত-বিসারী ; ব্যাপক, বহুব্যাপ্তিবিশিষ্ট ; আবেগপূর্ণ। **2.** Working, by or capable of, expansion ; বিস্তারদ্বারা ক্রিয়া-শীল, বিস্তার-যোগ্য। **—ist,** *n.* An advocate of the expansion of the paper currency ; ব্যাঙ্ক নোটের বিস্তৃত প্রচারের পক্ষপাতী। **—sive-ly,** *adv.* **—sive-ness,** *n.* **—siv'-i-ty,** *n.*

ĕx-pā'-ti-āte (-shĭ-), *v. i.* & *t.* (with *on* or *upon*) **1.** To move at large, (usu. *fig.*) ; যথেচ্ছ বিচরণ করা, স্বচ্ছন্দে বিচরণ করা। **2.** To be copious in discourse or writing, (with *on* or *upon*) ; প্রসঙ্গ-বিস্তার করা, বাগ্‌বাহুল্য করা, বাগ্‌জাল বিস্তার করা, নিরঙ্কুশভাবে লিখিয়া যাওয়া, লিপিবিস্তার করা। **—a'-tion,** *n.* Act of expatiating ; স্বচ্ছন্দ-গমন, প্রসঙ্গ-বিস্তার, বাগ্‌বিস্তার, বাক্ প্রপঞ্চ। **—a-tor,** *n.* **—a-to-ry,** *adj.* Expansive ; diffusive ; প্রসারণশীল ; বিস্তারশীল।

ĕx-pā'-tri-āte, *v. t.* **1.** To exile or banish ; নির্ব্বাসিত করা, জন্মভূমি হইতে বিতাড়িত করা। **2.** (*Reflexively*) To emigrate ; (*law of nations*) to renounce citizenship ; বসবাসের জন্য দেশান্তরে গমন করা ; নাগরিক অধিকার ত্যাগ করা। **—a'-tion,** *n.* The act of banshing ; state of being expatriated ; নির্ব্বাসন ; স্বেচ্ছাকৃত-নির্ব্বাসন।

ĕx-pĕct', *v. t.* **1.** To look for ; to regard as likely ; as, I *expect* a bad weather ; প্রত্যাশা করা ; সম্ভবপর বলিয়া মনে করা। **2.** (*Colloq.*) To suppose ; (চলিত ভাষায়) বোধ করা, মনে করা। **—ance, —an-cy,** *ns* Act or state of expecting ; hope as of future possession ; উন্মুখতা, আশংসা, আশঙ্কা ; প্রত্যাশা। **—ant** *adj.* & *n.* **1.** Expecting ; prospective ; as, *expectant* heirs ; প্রত্যাশী, আশান্বিত ; সম্ভাবনীয়। **2.** (*Law*) Reversionary ; (আইন) কোন নির্দ্দিষ্ট ঘটনার পর সম্পত্তি পুনঃ প্রাপ্তি বিষয়ক। (*Noun*) One who expects ; a candidate for office ; প্রত্যাশাকারী ; কোন কার্য্যের প্রার্থী। **—ant-ly,** *adv.* **Expectant method of treatment** — (ভৈষজ্য-শাস্ত্র) যে চিকিৎসা প্রণালীতে রোগের আরোগ্য বিষয় প্রায় সম্পূর্ণরূপে প্রকৃতির উপর নির্ভর করা হইয়া থাকে—এবং মূলরোগের কোন বিশেষ ঔষধ প্রয়োগ না করিয়া উপসর্গাদি উপশমনের জন্য কেবল পথ্যাদি প্রদান করা হয়।

ĕx-pĕc-tā'-tion, *n.* **1.** The act or state of expecting ; awaiting ; আশাপোষণ, আশান্বিত অবস্থা ; প্রতীক্ষা। **2.** Prospect of future good, as of wealth, possessions, etc. ; (usu. in *pl.*) ground for expectation ;

প্রত্যাশা ; প্রত্যাশার কারণ। 3. That which is expected ; প্রত্যাশিত বস্তু। 4. The probability of the occurrence of an event ; কোন ঘটনা সংঘটনের সম্ভাব্যতা। **—pect'-a-tive,** *adj.* Pertaining to expectation ; reversionary ; প্রত্যাশা সম্বন্ধীয় ; ভাবি-স্বত্ব-বিশিষ্ট। **—pect'-ing-ly,** *adv.* In a state of expectation ; আশান্বিত ভাবে। **In expectation of** — In anticipation or hope of ; প্রতীক্ষায়, প্রত্যাশায়। **Beyond expectation**— আশাতীত।

ĕx-pĕc'-tŏ-rāte, *v. t.* & *i.* To eject (phlegm etc.) from the lungs by coughing ; to spit forth ; কফ নিঃসরণ করা, কাসিয়া কফ প্রভৃতি নির্গত করা ; থু থু ফেলা, নিষ্ঠীবন নিক্ষেপ করা। ***Verb i.*** To spit ; থু থু ফেলা। **—rant,** *adj.* & *n.* Tending to promote expectoration ; শ্লেষ্মাবর্জ্জক, কফ-নিঃসারক, কফতরলকর, শ্লেষ্মাহর, কণ্ঠ্য (ঠাকুরঃ)। (*Noun*) A medicine which facilitates expectoration ; কফ নিঃসারক ঔষধ। **—ra'-tion,** *n.* The act of expectorating ; that which is expectorated ; কফ নিঃসারণ ; কফ, শ্লেষ্মা। **—ra-tive,** *adj.* & *n.*

ĕx-pē'-di-ence (-ĕns), **—ĕn-cy̆,** *n.* 1. State or quality of being expedient ; propriety ; advisability ; উপযোগিতা, স্বার্থানুকূলতা ; উপযুক্ততা, সুবিধা, ঔচিত্য, যুক্ততা, যৌক্তিকতা, যুক্তিযুক্ততা, সমীচীনতা, সুসাধকতা ; স্বার্থানুকূলতা ; পরামর্শ-সিদ্ধতা। 2. Seeking self-interest by the sacrifice of principles ; time-servingness ; ধর্ম্মবুদ্ধি বিসর্জ্জন করত স্বার্থান্বেষণ ; যখন যেমন তখন তেমন ব্যবহার করার প্রবৃত্তি।

ĕx-pē'-di-ĕnt, *adj.* & *n.* 1. Suitable ; advisable ; advantageous ; as, do what-ever is *expedient* ; উপযোগী ; যুক্তিযুক্ত, পরামর্শসিদ্ধ, উচিত, বিহিত ; সুবিধাজনক। 2. Politic rather than just ; কূটবুদ্ধিপ্রসূত। ***Noun.*** An end, (*rare*) ; উদ্দেশ্য-সাধনোপযোগী উপায়। 2. Shift ; device ; as, every *expedient* exhausted ; ফিকির ; কৌশল, ফন্দী, উদ্ভাবনা, হেকমত ; মতলব, কল্পনা, উপায়। **—en'-tial,** *adj.* **—en'-tial-ly,** *adv.* **—ly,** *adv.* In an expedient manner ; suitably ; যুক্তিযুক্তরূপে ; যথাযোগ্যভাবে।

ĕx'-pē-dite, *v. t.* 1. To accelerate ; to facilitate ; "Nature *expedites* the progress of flowering ;" ত্বরান্বিত করা, সত্বর করা, দ্রুত করা, সুকর করা। 2. To perform quickly ; as, to *expedite* business ; সত্বর সম্পাদন করা।

ĕx-pē-di'-tion, *n.* 1. Promptness ; despatch ; speed ; "With all *expedition* ;" সত্বরতা, ক্ষিপ্রতা ; তৎপরতা ; দ্রুততা, ত্বরা, শীঘ্রতা। 2. A journey or voyage for a specific purpose ; warlike enterprise ; the collective body on an expedition ; অভিযান, সংযান, যাত্রা ; সামরিক অভিযান যুদ্ধযাত্রা; সামরিক অভিযানের জন্য প্রস্তুত সৈন্যদল। **—a-ry,** *adj.* Pertaining to an expedition ; forming an expedition ; as, an *expeditionary* force ; অভিযান-সম্বন্ধীয় ; অভিযানরচক। **—ist,** *n.* One going on an expedition ; অভিযানকারী, অভিযায়ী। **—tious,** *adj.* Speedy ; prompt ; done speedily ; ক্ষিপ্র, দ্রুত, ত্বরান্বিত, অবিলম্বিত, সত্বর ; তৎপর ; শীঘ্র সম্পাদিত। **—tious-ly,** *adv.* **—tious-ness,** *n.*

ĕx-pĕl', *v. t.* 1. To eject ; বাহির করিয়া দেওয়া, বহিষ্কৃত করা। 2. To exile ; নির্ব্বাসিত করা। 3. To drive out, as from any society or constitution ; বর্জ্জন করা, বিতাড়িত করা, নাম কাটিয়া বাহির করিয়া দেওয়া, বহিষ্কৃত করা। **—la-ble, —lant,** *adjs.* **—ler,** *n.* **To expel from society**— সমাজচ্যুত করা ; অপাংক্তেয় করা।

ĕx-pĕnd, *v. t.* To consume by use ; ব্যয় করা, খরচ করা।

ĕx-pĕnd'-i-tūre, *n.* 1. Expending ; laying out of money ; ব্যয়করণ ; (অর্থাদির) বিনিয়োগ। 2. Money expended ; expense ; ব্যয়িত অর্থ ; অর্থ-ব্যয়, খরচ। 3. Consumption ; as, *expenditure* of ammunition ; ব্যয়।

ĕx-pĕnse' (-pĕns), *n.* 1. Disbursement ; expenditure ; ব্যয় ; খরচ, খরচপত্র। 2. Outlay ; (ব্যবসায় প্রভৃতিতে) যে ধন খাটানো হয়। 3. A source of expenditure ; as, his sons have become a great *expense* to him ; ব্যয়ের কারণ। **A laugh at one's expense**— A laugh at him ; কাহাকেও উপলক্ষ করিয়া বিদ্রূপের হাসি। **At a great expense**—At a great cost ; বহু-ব্যয়ে। **At an expense of**—At a cost or loss amounting to ; নির্দ্দিষ্ট পরিমাণ ব্যয়ে। **At the expense of**—At the sacrifice of ; বিসর্জ্জন দিয়া। By bringing discredit on ; ক্ষুণ্ণ করিয়া। **To be at (the) expense of**—To pay the cost of ; ব্যয় বহন করা।

ĕx-pĕn'-sive (-sĭv), *adj.* Costly ; বহুব্যয়-সাধ্য, মূল্যবান, দুর্ম্মূল্য, মহার্ঘ, মহার্হ। **—ly,** *adv.* **—sive-ness,** *n.*

ĕx-pē'-ri-ence (-ĕns), *n.* & *v. t.* 1. Actual observation of facts and events ; অনুভব (হিঃ কোঃ), অনুভূতি (ঐ)। 2. Practical knowledge derived by personal trial, proof or observation ; ভূয়োদর্শন-লব্ধজ্ঞান, অভিজ্ঞতা। 3. (Usu. *pl.*) The state of religious emotion ; ধর্ম্মসম্বন্ধীয় অনুভূতি, আধ্যাত্মিক অভিজ্ঞতা। ***Verb t.*** 1. To have experience of ; to undergo ; to feel ; as, to *experience* good and evil ; ভূয়োদর্শনদ্বারা জ্ঞাত হওয়া ; ভোগ করা ; অনুভব করা। 2. To learn ; to find ; শিক্ষা করা ; পরীক্ষা দ্বারা জানিতে পারা। **—enced',** *adj.* Taught by experience ; skilful by use or observation ; অভিজ্ঞ ; বহুদর্শী, পরিপক্ক-বুদ্ধি, পাকা, বিচক্ষণ, বিজ্ঞ। **—en'-tial,** *adj.* **—en'-tial-ly,** *adv.* **—en'-tial-ism,** *n.* A doctrine of philosophy, treating all knowledge as derived from experience ; দার্শনিক মত বিশেষ—এই মতানুসারে জ্ঞান মাত্রই অভিজ্ঞতা প্রসূত বলিয়া পরিগণিত হয়, অভিজ্ঞতাবাদ। **—en'-tial-ist,** *n.* **Experience meeting**—যে ধর্ম্মসভায় সভ্যগণ স্ব স্ব আধ্যাত্মিক অভিজ্ঞতা ব্যক্ত করেন।

ĕx-pĕr'-i-mĕnt, *n.* & *v. t.* A trial ; an operation designed to discover something unknown or to establish it when discovered ; পরীক্ষা, পরীক্ষণ, পরখ, কষ্টি ; কোন সন্দিগ্ধ বিষয়ের প্রমাণ বা খণ্ডনের জন্য পরীক্ষা। ***Verb t.*** To make experiment, (with *on* and *with*) ; পরীক্ষা করা, পরখ করা, পরীক্ষাদ্বারা তত্ত্বানুসন্ধান করা। **—men-ta'-tion,** *n.* **—men'-ta-tive,** *adj.*

ĕx-pĕr-i-mĕn'-tăl, *adj.* **1.** Based on personal experience ; empirical ; ব্যক্তিগত অনুভবমূলক ; অনুভবমূলক, পরীক্ষামূলক। **2.** Relating to, or based on, experiment ; as, *experimental* science ; tentative ; পরীক্ষা-সম্বন্ধীয় ; পরীক্ষাত্মক। **—ism,** *n.* Empiricism ; অনুভবৈকবাদ (হিঃ কোঃ), প্রত্যক্ষৈকবাদ, অনুভবমূলক বিজ্ঞানবাদ (হিঃ কোঃ)। **—ist,** *n.* **—ize,** *v. t.* To make experiments ; পরীক্ষা করা। **—ly,** *adv.* By, or by way of, experiment ; পরীক্ষণপূর্ব্বক, পরীক্ষাদ্বারা, পরীক্ষাচ্ছলে।

ĕx-pērt', *adj.* & *n.* Trained by skilful practice, (with *at* or *in*) ; বিজ্ঞ, বিশারদ, প্রবীণ, বিচক্ষণ, দক্ষ, নিপুণ, কুশল, কর্ম্মজ্ঞ, সিদ্ধহস্ত, ধুরন্ধর, পটু, কৃতী। ***Noun.*** One having special skill or knowledge, (foll. by *at, in*) ; as, a mining *expert* ; (শিল্প বিজ্ঞানাদিতে) সুদক্ষ ব্যক্তি, বিশেষজ্ঞ। **—ly,** *adv.* Adroitly ; skilfully ; সুনিপুণভাবে; দক্ষতাসহকারে। **—ness,** *n.*

ĕx'-pi-āte, *v. t.* To pay the penalty of ; to atone for ; as, to *expiate* a crime, guilt or sin ; পাপের প্রায়শ্চিত্ত ভোগ করা ; প্রায়শ্চিত্ত করা। **—a-ble,** *adj.* Capable of being expiated ; প্রায়শ্চিত্তার্হ, প্রায়শ্চিত্তসাধ্য, ক্ষমার্হ, শোধনীয়। **—a'-tion,** *n.* **1.** Act of expiating ; atonement ; প্রায়শ্চিত্তকরণ ; প্রায়শ্চিত্ত। **2.** The means by which atonement is made ; প্রায়শ্চিত্তের ক্রিয়াকলাপ। **—a-tor,** *n.* One who makes expiation ; প্রায়শ্চিত্তকারী। **—a-to-ry,** *adj.* Atoning ; "*Expiatory* sacrifice ;" প্রায়শ্চিত্ত-সম্বন্ধীয়, শান্তিক, পাপশোধক, পাপঘ্ন, পাপনিষ্কৃতিকর, পাপক্ষয়-বিধায়ক।

ĕx-pīre', *v. t.* & *i.* To breathe out ; as, to *expire* air etc. ; শ্বাসমোচন করা। ***Verb i.*** **1.** To emit the breath ; শ্বাস ফেলা। **2.** To die ; প্রাণবায়ু বহির্গত হওয়া। **3.** To end ; to become extinct ; as, period, lease or fire *expires* ; অবসান হওয়া, শেষ হওয়া ; নির্ব্বাপিত হওয়া, নির্ব্বাণ-প্রাপ্ত হওয়া, নিভিয়া যাওয়া। **4.** To become void as a law, patent, etc. ; বাতিল হওয়া, রদ হওয়া। **—pir'-a-ble,** *adj.* **—pi-ra'-tion,** *n.* **1.** The act of breathing out ; নিশ্বসিত বায়ু পরিত্যাগ, প্রশ্বাস-ক্রিয়া। **2.** Termination ; end ; অবসান, পর্য্যবসান ; বিরতি, শেষ, অন্ত, পরিসমাপ্তি, নির্ব্বাণ। **—pir'-a-to-ry,** *adj.*

ĕx'-pi-rȳ, *n.* End ; termination ; শেষ ; অবসান, অন্ত, পর্য্যবসান।

ĕx-pis'-cāte, *v. t.* To search out by scrutiny, (*Scottish* or *humorously*) ; তন্ন তন্ন করিয়া খুঁজিয়া বাহির করা। **—ca'-tion,** *n.*

ĕx-plain' (-plān), *v. t.* & *i.* **1.** To elucidate ; to make intelligible ; সরল করা, বিবৃতি করা ; অর্থ বুঝাইয়া দেওয়া, অর্থ স্পষ্ট করা, সুবোধ্য করা, সুগম করা। **2.** To account for ; as, to *explain* a conduct ; কৈফিয়ৎ দেওয়া। ***Verb i.*** To give explanations ; কৈফিয়ৎ দেওয়া। **—a-ble,** *adj.* Capable of being explained ; ব্যাখ্যেয়। **—er,** *n.* **To explain a way**—(used in a bad sense) To get rid of by explanation ; যেন তেন প্রকারেণ বুঝাইয়া দেওয়া, একরকম করিয়া গোঁজামিল দিয়া বুঝাইয়া দেওয়া। **To explain one's self**—To make clear the meaning of one's statements or the reasons for one's conduct ; স্বীয় উক্তির অর্থ স্পষ্ট করা, অথবা কোন রূপ আচরণের কারণ প্রদর্শন করা, কৈফিয়ৎ দেওয়া।

ĕx-plă-na'-tion, *n.* **1.** The act of expounding ; অর্থপ্রকাশন, স্পষ্টীকরণ, ব্যাখ্যাকরণ, ব্যাখ্যা, বিবৃতি, বার্ত্তিক, অর্থ-বিস্তার। **2.** A mutual clearing up of matters between parties at variance ; কোনও বিবাদীয় বিষয় সম্পর্কে পরস্পরের মনের গ্লানি বা অস্পষ্টতার নিরসন, মনখোলাসা। **3.** That which explains or makes clear ; as, a satisfactory *explanation* ; কৈফিয়ৎ, জবাবদিহী। **4.** Sense ; meaning ; "Different *explanations* of the doctrine of the Trinity ;" অভিপ্রায় ; অর্থ। **To come to an explanation** — সরলভাবে পরস্পরের মনোভাব ব্যক্ত করিয়া মনোমালিন্য বা বিবাদের নিবৃত্তি করা।

ĕx-plăn'-ă-tŏ-rȳ, *adj.* Serving to explain ; containing explanation ; বাচক, বোধক, অর্থপ্রকাশক, কৈফিয়ত-সূচক ; ব্যাখ্যাসম্বলিত। **—ri-ly,** *adv.*

ĕx'-plĕ-tive (-tĭv), *adj.* & *n.* Serving to fill out ; superfluous ; as, *expletive* epithets ; পাদপূরক, অনুপূরক ; অতিরিক্ত। ***Noun.*** A word, syllable inserted to fill a vacancy etc. ; an oath or exclamation ; বাক্যপূরণার্থ সংযোজিত পদ বা পদাংশ, পাদপূরক শব্দ, বাক্যালঙ্কার উপাক্ষর ; পাদপূরক (বা, তু, হি প্রভৃতি)। **—ly,** *adv.*

ĕx'-plĕ-tŏ-rȳ, *adj.* Same as EXPLETIVE.

ĕx'-pli-cāte, *v. t.* **1.** (*Archaic*) To explain ; (অপ্রচলিত) অর্থ-প্রকটন করা, ব্যাখ্যা করা, বিবৃতি করা। **2.** To bring out what is implied in as, to *explicate* a notion or principle ; ভাব প্রভৃতির অন্তর্নিহিত তত্ত্ব প্রকটন করা, বিস্তার করা। **—ca-ble,** *adj.* Capable of being explicated ; ব্যাখ্যেয়, হেতু-প্রদর্শন-যোগ্য। **—ca′-tion,** *n.* **1.** Developing what is involved or implied in a notion etc. ; ভাব প্রভৃতির অন্তর্নিহিত তত্ত্ব-প্রকটন। **2.** Explanation ; interpretation ; অর্থপ্রকটন ; বিবৃতি, ব্যাখ্যান। **—ca-tive,** *adj.* Analytical ; বাচক, ব্যাখ্যাত্মক, বোধগম্যকর। **—ca-to-ry,** *adj.*

ĕx-plĭc′-it, *adj.* (Opp. to *implicit*) **1.** Express ; not merely implied ; plain in language ; as, *explicit* consent ; definite ; সুব্যক্ত ; স্ফুট, স্পষ্ট ; স্পষ্টভাবে উক্ত ; স্পষ্টভাষিত। **2.** Outspoken ; as, he was *explicit* in his terms ; অবাক্‌সংযত, মুক্তভাষ, অকপট, স্পষ্টবাদী। **—ly,** *adv.* Plainly ; clearly ; সোজাসোজি ভাবে, খোলাখোলি ভাবে ; স্পষ্টভাবে। **—ness,** *n.*

ĕx-plĭc′-it, *v. t.* Here ends (a word formerly used at the end of a book to indicate conclusion of) ; সম্পূর্ণ হইল।

ĕx-plōde′, *v. t.* & *i.* **1.** To bring into disrepute and reject ; as, to *explode* a theory etc. ; (কোন বাদ, মত, প্রভৃতি) খণ্ডন বা অবজ্ঞেয় করা, উড়াইয়া দেওয়া। **2.** To cause to burst out ; as, to *explode* a shell ; সশব্দে বিদীর্ণ করা। ***Verb i.*** **1.** To burst violently with noise, as gun powder, gas, etc. ; সশব্দে বিদীর্ণ হওয়া, ভীমরবে ফাটিয়া বাহির হওয়া। **2.** To burst into activity or into passion ; as, his wrath *exploded* instantly ; উচ্ছ্বসিত হওয়া। **—plod′-ed,** *n.* Rejected ; discarded ; as, an *exploded* theory ; খণ্ডিত ; অবজ্ঞাত। **—plod′-er,** *n.*

ĕx-ploit′ (-ploÿt), *n.*, *v. t.* & *i.* A brilliant achievement ; মহাকর্ম্ম, মহৎকার্য্য, কৃতকৃত্য, অদ্ভুতকার্য্য, অবদান। ***Verb t.*** **1.** To utilise ; to turn to account ; as, to *exploit* a mine ; ব্যবহারে আনা, প্রয়োজনীয় করা, স্বার্থসাধনের বিষয়ীভূত করা ; কাজে লাগান। **2.** To make use of for one's own profit ; as, capitalists *exploit* labourers ; অর্থ লাভের জন্য কাজে লাগান। **—a-ble,** *adj.* **—age,** *n.* **—ploi-ta′-tion,** *n.* The act of exploiting ; utilisation ; কার্য্যে প্রয়োগ ; ভূমি, খনি প্রভৃতির উপর লাভজনক শ্রমশিল্পের প্রয়োগ। **2.** Selfish utilisation ; স্বার্থ-পরতার সহিত ব্যবহার।

ĕx-plōre′, *v.t.* **1.** To travel and examine for discovery ; as, to *explore* a new country ; to inquire into ; আবিষ্কারের উদ্দেশ্যে পর্য্যটন ও পর্য্যবেক্ষণ করা ; অনুসন্ধান করা। **2.** (*Med.*) To examine by touch ; as, to *explore* a wound ; স্পর্শদ্বারা পরীক্ষা করা। **—plor′-a-ble,** *adj.* **—plo-ra′-tion,** *n.* **1.** The act of exploring, as for geographical discovery etc. ; strict examination ; আবিষ্কারার্থ পর্য্যটন ও পরীক্ষণ, ভূমি-আবিষ্কার (সাঃ পঃ) ; পুঙ্খানুপুঙ্খরূপে পরীক্ষণ। **2.** (*Med.*) Examination as of a wound etc. by means of a probe or finger ; অঙ্গুলি বা শলাকার সাহায্যে ক্ষতাদি পরীক্ষণ। **—plor′-a-tive,** *adj.* **—plor′-a-to-ry,** *adj.* **—plor′-er,** *n.* One who explores ; a traveller in unknown regions ; আবিষ্কারার্থ পর্য্যটন ও পরীক্ষাকারী ; অপরিচিত দেশে ভ্রমণকারী।

ĕx-plō′-sion, *n.* **1.** The act of exploding or bursting with noise ; as, the *explosion* of a bomb ; সশব্দ-স্ফোটন, সশব্দ-বিদারণ। **2.** Such noise ; স্ফোটন-শব্দ, আওয়াজ। **3.** A violent outburst (of anger etc.) ; প্রবল উচ্ছ্বাস।

ĕx-plō′-sive (-sĭv), *adj.* & *n.* **1.** Causing explosion ; readily exploding, (*lit.* & *fig.*) ; as, *explosive* temper ; বিস্ফোরক ; বিস্ফোরণশীল, স্ফোটন-ধর্ম্মী। **2.** Tending to drive forth something with loud noise ; ভীমশব্দে বিদারণকারী। ***Noun.*** **1.** Explosive agent or material, as gun powder etc. ; বিস্ফোরক পদার্থ। **—ly,** *adv.* **—ness,** *n.*

ĕx-pō′-nĕnt, *adj.* & *n.* Interpreting or explaining ; ব্যাখ্যাকারী, অর্থপ্রকটনকারী। ***Noun.*** **1.** A person or a thing that explains ; an interpreter ; ব্যাখ্যাতা ; অর্থ-প্রকটনকারী। **2.** A representative ; কোন সমিতি বা সম্প্রদায়ের মূলতত্ত্ব, শিক্ষা বা মতাদির ব্যাখ্যাকারী। **3.** The index of a power in Algebra ; (বীজগণিতে) কোন রাশির ঘাত-চিহ্ন বা বৈজিকশক্তি, ঘাত (হিঃ কোঃ)। **—nen′-tial,** *adj.* Pertaining to, or involving, exponents ; বীজগণিতের ঘাত সম্বন্ধীয়, বৈজিকশক্তি-সংক্রান্ত। **An exponential equation**—ঘাতরাশিক সমীকরণ।

ĕx-pōrt′, *v. t.* To carry or send (goods etc.) to foreign countries ; (opp. to *import*) ; রপ্তানি করা, বিদেশে মালপত্র চালান দেওয়া। **—a-ble,** *adj.* Suitable for exportation ; রপ্তানি-যোগ্য। **—por-ta′-tion,** *n.* The act of exporting ; রপ্তানিকার্য্য। **—er,** *n.* One who oxports, (opp. to *importer*) ; রপ্তানিকারী।

ĕx′-pōrt, *n.* **1.** The act of exporting ; exportation ; পণ্যদ্রব্যাদি স্থানান্তরে প্রেরণ ; রপ্তানি। **2.** A commodity exported ; (usu. *pl.*) quantity of goods exported ; দেশান্তরে প্রেরিত দ্রব্য, রপ্তানিমাল ; রপ্তানিমালের পরিমাণ। **Export-duty**—রপ্তানি শুল্ক।

ĕx-pōse′, *v. t.* **1.** To lay bare or open ; to make liable ; as, to *expose* one to a risk ; অনাবৃত করা, উদ্‌ঘাটিত করা, রৌদ্র, বৃষ্টি বা বায়ুতে অনাবৃত রাখা ; অধীন করা। **2.** To exhibit ; to put up for sale ; to make public, as a plan, secret, etc.; প্রদর্শন করা; বিক্রয়ার্থ সজ্জিত বা প্রসারিত করা; সর্ব্বজনগোচর করা, সাধারণ্যে প্রকাশ করা। 3. To unmask or disclose; as, *expose* a liar or the faults of a man; মুখস খুলিয়া দেওয়া, কোন ব্যক্তির প্রকৃত চরিত্র বা কদাচার লোকসমাজে প্রকাশ করিয়া তাহাকে ঘৃণ্য বা উপহাসাস্পদ করা, গুপ্ত কথা ব্যক্ত করা। 4. To cast out unprotected or uncared for; as, to *expose* children (this practice prevailed among the ancient Greeks); অরক্ষিতভাবে ও অযত্নে বাহিরে ফেলিয়া দেওয়া। 5. (*Phot.*) To subject (a plate) to light; আলোকচিত্রের ফলক আলোকে স্থাপিত করা। **—pos'-er,** *n.*

ĕx-pō'-se (-zā), *n.* Exposure as of something discreditable; উদ্ঘাটন, দোষ-প্রকাশন।

ĕx-pō-sĭ'-tion, *n.* 1. Act of exposing; exposure; abandonment to chance, as of a child; উদ্ঘাটন; দোষপ্রকটন; শিশু প্রভৃতিকে অরক্ষিত স্থানে পরিত্যাগ। 2. The act of setting forth; বিন্যাস। 3. Interpretation; commentary; ব্যাখ্যা, বিবৃতি; টীকা, ভাষ্য, চূর্ণক। 4. A public exhibition or show; মেলা বা প্রদর্শনী।

ĕx-pŏs'-i-tive (-tîv), *adj.* Descriptive; explanatory; বিবৃতিপূর্ণ; ব্যাখ্যাত্মক।

ĕx pŏs'-i-tor (-têr), *n.* A commentator; বিবৃতিকার, টীকাকার, ভাষ্যকার। **—to-ry,** *adj.* Pertaining to exposition; explanatory; ব্যাখ্যাবিষয়ক; ব্যাখ্যাত্মক।

ex post facto, *adj.* [*L.*] Acting retrospectively; after the deed is done; অতীতকাল হইতে কার্য্যকরী; কৃত্যুত্তর। **Expost facto law**—কৃত্যুত্তর ব্যবস্থাপিত বিধি,—বিধিবদ্ধ হইবার পূর্ব্বসাময়িক ঘটনাদি সম্বন্ধেও যে আইন কার্য্যকরী হয়; যথা—পুষ্করিণী প্রভৃতি জলাশয় অপরিষ্কার রাখা বর্ত্তমান আইনানুসারে দণ্ডনীয় নয়; এখন যদি এইরূপ একটা আইন বিধিবদ্ধ হয় যে, যাহারা পুষ্করিণী প্রভৃতি উপযুক্তমত পরিষ্কার না রাখিবে, তাহাদিগকে দণ্ডিত হইতে হইবে, এবং এইরূপ বিধানও থাকে—যাহারা এই আইন বিধিবদ্ধ হইবার পূর্ব্ববর্ত্তী সময়েও পুষ্করিণী প্রভৃতি অপরিষ্কার রাখিয়াছে, তাহারাও এই আইনের আমলে আসিবে, তাহা হইলে এইরূপ আইনকে ex post facto বা কৃত্যুত্তর ব্যবস্থাপিত বিধি বলা যায়।

ĕx-pŏs'-tū-lāte, *v. i.* To remonstrate; to reason with a person on impropriety, (foll. by *with*): অনুযোগ করা; কোন ব্যক্তি অসঙ্গত আচরণ করিলে তৎসম্বন্ধে তাহার সহিত বাদানুবাদ করা। **—la'-tion,** *n.* Expostulating; remonstrance; অনুযোগ; আপত্তি। **—la-tor,** *n.* **—la-to-ry,** *adj.* Containing expostulation; অনুযোগপূর্ণ।

ĕx-pō'-sure (-zhür), *n.* 1. Act of exposing or laying open; abandonment (of a child); উদ্ঘাটন; অনাবৃত স্থানে শিশু পরিত্যাগ। 2. State of being exposed as to view or inconvenience etc.; as, *exposure* to cold etc.; অনাবৃতত্ব। 3. Showing up or unmasking; as, the *exposure* of a fraud or importor; দোষোদ্ঘাটন, দোষপ্রকাশন। 4. Situation with respect to sun and wind; aspect; "Under southern *exposure*:" সূর্য্য অথবা বায়ু সম্পর্কে অবস্থিতি; অভিমুখতা, মুখ, রোক। 4. (*Photo.*) Exposing a sensitized surface to light; (আলোকচিত্রণ) প্রতিবিম্ব-গ্রহণক্ষম ফলকাদি আলোকে অনাবৃতকরণ।

ĕx-pound' (-pownd), *v. t.* 1. To set forth in detail; as, to *expound* a theory; বিবৃত করা, বিন্যাস করা। 2. To interprete; as, to *expound* the scripture; to construe as a law; অর্থপ্রকটন করা; অর্থ করা, ব্যাখ্যা করা। **—er,** *n.* An explainer or interpreter; প্রবক্তা, ব্যাখ্যাতা, অর্থপ্রকাশক। **To expound the *samasa*** — কোনও সমাসযুক্ত বাক্যের ব্যাসবাক্য লিখা বা বলা।

ĕx-prĕss', *v. t.* 1. To press or squeeze out; to extort; as, to *express* the juice; নিষ্পীড়ন করিয়া, পিষিয়া বা চিপিয়া বাহির করা, নিঙ্ড়াইয়া বাহির করা, নিষ্কর্ষণ করা। 2. To set forth in words; as, to *express* a thought; to betoken; to exhibit; as, to *express* feeling or quality; to signify; as, these words *express* my intention; বিবৃত করা, বাক্যদ্বারা প্রকাশ করা; (আকার ইঙ্গিত প্রভৃতি লক্ষণদ্বারা) সূচনা করা; প্রদর্শন করা; অভিপ্রায় ব্যক্ত করা। 3. (Reflexive) To declare what is in the mind of; as, to *express oneself*; মনোভাব ব্যক্ত করা। **—i-ble,** *adj.* Capable of being expressed; নির্ব্বচনীয়, কথনীয়। **To express oneself**—See EXPRESS 5.

ĕx-prĕss', *n., adj.* & *adv.* 1. A messenger or vehicle sent on a particular occassion; a message specially sent; কোনও বিশেষ ঘটনা উপলক্ষে প্রেরিত যান বা সংবাদবাহক; বিশেষভাবে প্রেরিত বার্ত্তা বা সংবাদ। 2. Express train or rifle; (see below). ***Adj.*** 1. Exact; as, *express* resemblance; অবিকল। 2. Distinctly stated; not implied; explicit; as, an *express* statement; সুব্যক্ত; স্পষ্টরূপে ব্যক্ত; স্পষ্টার্থ, অসন্দিগ্ধার্থ, সুস্পষ্ট। 3. Sent or travelling, with special speed; done, made or sent for special purpose; as, an *express* messenger or train; বিশেষ দ্রুততা সহকারে প্রেরিত, বিশেষ দ্রুতগামী; বিশেষ উদ্দেশ্য সাধনের জন্য কৃত, সম্পাদিত বা প্রেরিত। ***Adv.*** With special haste; by an express train or messenger; বিশেষ দ্রুতগতিতে; বিশেষ দূতদ্বারা বা দ্রুতগামী বাষ্পীয় শকটে। **—ly,** *adv.* In an express, clear or distinct manner ; particularly ; স্পষ্টরূপে, স্পষ্টাক্ষরে ; বিশেষতঃ, বিশেষ ভাবে। **Express delivery**—বিশেষ পত্রবাহকদ্বারা পত্রবণ্টন। **Express messenger**—বিশেষ কার্য্যে বা সংবাদ প্রদানে প্রেরিত বার্ত্তাবহ। **Express rifle**—দ্রুতবেগে গুলিবর্ষী বন্দুক। **Express-train**—অতি দ্রুতগামী বাষ্পীয় শকট,—এই গাড়ী অল্পসংখ্যক ষ্টেশনে থামিয়া থাকে।

ĕx-pres'-sion (-prŏ-), *n.* **1.** The act of pressing out ; product of this process ; নিষ্পীড়ন, নিষ্পেষণ, নিষ্কর্ষণ ; নিষ্পীড়ন পূর্ব্বক প্রাপ্ত বস্তু। **2.** The act of expressing in words ; utterance ; শব্দে প্রকাশকরণ ; উক্তি। **3.** A significant word or phrase ; as, an odd *expression* ; বিশেষভাব দ্যোতক শব্দ বা বাক্য, বাক্য (কাব্যঃ)। **4.** Mode of representation in language ; diction ; "*Expression* is the dress of thought ;" শব্দদ্বারা প্রকাশের প্রণালী ; শব্দবিন্যাস-প্রণালী। **5.** (*Art.*) The mode of representation in art ; a vivid indication of mood and sentiment ; as, a picture characterized by *expression* ; (কলাশাস্ত্র) শিল্পে ভাবাদি দ্যোতনার প্রণালী ; চিত্রাদিতে ভাবের প্রকাশ, ভাব-দ্যোতনা, ভাব-ব্যঞ্জনা। **6.** Aspect (of face) ; intonation (of voice) ; as, she sings with *expression* ; মুখের বাহ্য দৃশ্য, মুখাকৃতি, আকার ; নাদপদ্ধতি। **7.** (*Algeb.*) A collection of symbols expressing a quantity ; (বীজগণিত) রাশি। **8.** (*Music*) The mode of performance that expresses the feeling of a passage ; ভাবের সহিত সঙ্গীতাদি গাহিবার রীতি। **—al,** *adj.* **—ist,** *n.* An artist whose work aims at expression ; যে শিল্পী তৎ-সম্পাদিত শিল্প-কার্য্যে ভাব দ্যোতনার দিকে বিশেষ লক্ষ্য রাখে। **—less,** *adj.* Destitute of expression ; অভিব্যঞ্জনাশূন্য।

ĕx-prĕs'-sive (-sĭv), *adj.* **1.** Serving to express, (with *of*) ; as, words *expressive of* sorrow ; সূচক, নির্দ্দেশক, ব্যঞ্জক, দ্যোতক, বাচক, প্রতিরূপপ্রদর্শক। **2.** Full of expression ; significant ; as, an *expressive* look or word ; ভাবব্যঞ্জক, দ্যোতনাপূর্ণ ; গূঢ়ার্থ প্রকাশক, গভীরার্থ জ্ঞাপক। **—ly,** *adv.* **—ness,** *n.*

ĕx-prō-brā'-tion, *n.* Reproachful language ; দুর্ব্বাক্য, দুরুক্তি।

ĕx-prō'-pri-āte, *v.t.* **1.** To deprive of possession ; as, to *expropriate* one from an estate ; অধিকারচ্যুত করা, বেদখল করা। **2.** To take away (property) ; সম্পত্তিহরণ করা। **—a'-tion,** *n.* The act of expropriating ; state of being expropriated ; অধিকারচ্যুতকরণ ; সম্পত্তিহরণ, অধিকারচ্যুতি।

ĕx-pŭl'-sion, *n.* Act of expelling ; বহিষ্করণ, বহিষ্কার, দূরীকরণ, অপসারণ, নিঃসারণ, নির্ব্বাসন, নিষ্কাশন। **—sive,** *adj.* & *n.* (Med.) Able, or serving, to expel ; (ভৈষজ্য-শাস্ত্র) নিঃসারণক্ষম, নিঃসারক, অপসারক, নিষ্কাশনশক্তি বিশিষ্ট, নিষ্কাশন-সমর্থ। (*Noun.*) An expulsive drug ; নিঃসারক ঔষধ।

ĕx-punge' (-pŭng), *v. t.* To erase ; to strike out ; as, to *expunge* a line from a book ; মুছিয়া ফেলা ; কাটিয়া দেওয়া, লোপ করা, বিলুপ্ত করা, তুলিয়া দেওয়া। **—punc'-tion,** *n.*

ĕx'-pur-gāte (-pêr-), *v. t.* To purify ; as, to *expurgate* a book ; to remove as noxious or erroneous matter from a book etc. ; বিশোধিত করা, নির্ম্মল করা, শোধন করা ; অশ্লীল বা অন্যবিধ আপত্তিকর অংশ পরিবর্জ্জন করত গ্রন্থাদি পরিশোধিত করা। **—ga'-tion,** *n.* The act of exprugating ; purification ; গ্রন্থশোধন ; বিশোধন, নির্ম্মলীকরণ, পাবন, পবিত্রীকরণ, পরিষ্করণ। **—ga-tor,** *n.* One who expurgates, esp. a book ; গ্রন্থশোধক। **—ga-to'-ri-al,** *adj.* **—ga-to-ry,** *adj.* Purifying ; শোধক, পাবক, বিশোধক।

ĕx'-qui-site (-zĭt), *adj.* & *n.* **1.** Very excellent or beautiful ; as, jewels of *exquisite* form ; পরমোৎকর্ষ-সম্পন্ন, অত্যুত্তম, চমৎকার, অতি ললিত, অতিরম্য, পরমশোভাসম্পন্ন। **2.** Acute ; intense, as pain or pleasure ; তীক্ষ্ণ, সান্দ্র, তীব্র। **3.** Delicate ; nice ; as, *exquisite* sensibility, taste, etc. ; সূক্ষ্ম ; সূক্ষ্মবিশ্লেষণ-ক্ষম। ***Noun.*** A dandy or fop ; ফুলবাবু। **—ly,** *adv.* In an exquisite manner ; nicely ; as, *exquisitely* done or written ; পরমরুচিররূপে, চমৎকার রূপে ; নিখুঁত ভাবে।

ĕx-san'-guine (-săng-gwĭn), *adj.* Bloodless ; রক্তশূন্য, রক্তহীন। **—guin-ate,** *v. t.* (*Med.*) To drain of blood ; (ভৈষজ্য-শাস্ত্র) রক্তহীন করা, শোণিতশূন্য করা।

ĕx-scĭnd', *v. t.* To cut off or out ; to excise, (*lit.* & *fig.*) ; (শব্দানুযায়ী এবং লক্ষণায়) ; কাটিয়া ফেলা, বাদ দেওয়া, কাটিয়া বাহির করা, ছাঁটিয়া ফেলা ; কর্ত্তন করা, ছেদন করা।

ĕx-sĕc'-tion, *n.* A cutting off or out ; ছেদন, কর্ত্তন, বিচ্ছিন্নকরণ।

ĕx-sêrt', *v. t.* (*Biol.*) To thrust out or protrude ; (জীব-বিজ্ঞান) নিষ্ক্রান্ত করা, প্রলম্বিত করা।

ĕx'-sic-cāte, *v. t.* To dry up ; to exhaust of moisture ; শুষ্ক করা ; নীরস করা, আর্দ্রতাশূন্য করা। **—cant,** *adj.* & *n.* Drying ; শোষক। (*Noun*) (*Med.*) A drug having drying properties ; (ভৈষজ্য-শাস্ত্র) শোষণ-ধর্ম্মা ভেষজ।

ĕx'-tănt, *adj.* Still existing, as a document etc. ; অদ্যাপি বর্ত্তমান বা বিদ্যমান, উপলভ্য, প্রচলিত (বিশেষভাবে দলিলাদি সম্বন্ধে ব্যবহৃত হয়।)

ĕx'-tă-sȳ, *n.* See ECTASY.

ĕx-tĕm'-pō-rē, *adj.* & *adv.* Unpremeditated ; off-hand ; without preparation ; as, he speaks *extempore* ; পূর্ব্ববিচার-রহিত ; তৎক্ষণ কল্পিত, তৎকালবিহিত, অচিন্তিত-পূর্ব্ব, অযত্নসম্ভূত, অযত্নসাধিত ; উপস্থিত-মত,

অপূর্ব্বকল্পিত, সময়স্ফূর্ত্ত। **—ra′-ne-ous,** *adj.* **1.** Extemporary, as a speech etc.; অচিন্তিত-পূর্ব্ব, উপস্থিত। **2.** Made for the occasion, as a shelter; তৎসময়ের জন্য নির্ম্মিত। **—ra′-ne-ous-ly,** *adv.* On the spur of the moment; তৎক্ষণাৎ, উপস্থিত ক্ষেত্রে। **—ra′-ne-ous-ness,** *n.* **—ra-ri-ly,** *adv.* **—ra-ry,** *adj.* **1.** Extemporaneous; unpremeditated; উপস্থিত; অচিন্তিত-পূর্ব্ব। **2.** Made or done, for the occasion; কালোপযোগী, সময়োপযোগী।

ĕx-tĕm′-pŏ-rīze, *v.t.* & *i.* To utter or compose without forethought; to make extempore; উপস্থিত ক্ষেত্রে বলা বা লিখা; উপস্থিত মত প্রস্তুত করা। ***Verb i.*** To speak extempore; উপস্থিতক্ষেত্রে বলা। **—ri-za′-tion,** *n.* **—ri-zer,** *n.*

ĕx-tĕnd′, *v. t.* & *i.* **1.** To stretch out; to lengthen or prolong as a line or period; বিস্তৃত করা, বিতত করা; বর্দ্ধিত করা (যেমন রেখাদি), প্রসারিত করা। **2.** To lay out at full length; as, to *extend* one's legs or body; ছড়াইয়া দেওয়া। **3.** To expand in size, as a metal by hammering; বিস্তারিত করা, বাড়ান। **4.** To make more comprehensive; as, to *extend* commerce; to enlarge; ব্যাপকতর করা; অর্থ বিস্তার করা, প্রসঙ্গ-বাহুল্য করা। **5.** To write out at full length, (esp. shorthand notes into long hand); সবিস্তারে লিখা। **6.** To reach forth; as, I *extend* my hand to him; প্রসারিত করা, বাড়াইয়া দেওয়া, নাগাল পাইবার জন্য হাত বাড়াইয়া দেওয়া। **7.** To bestow; as, to *extend* mercy to a person; প্রদান করা। **8.** (*Law*) To value as lands etc.; to seize (a land) for a debt; মূল্যাবধারণ করা; ঋণের জন্য ভূসম্পত্তি প্রভৃতি ক্রোক করা। ***Verb i.*** **1.** To spread; to reach; "Whose goodness *extendeth* to all men;" to be comprehensive; বিস্তারিত হওয়া, বিতানিত হওয়া, ক্রমশঃ বিস্তার লাভ করা; প্রসারিত হওয়া; ব্যাপক হওয়া। **2.** To move at full stride (of a horse); (অশ্ব-সম্পর্কে) দীর্ঘ পদক্ষেপ সহকারে চলা। **—er,** *n.* **—i-ble,** *adj.* Capable of being extended; প্রসার্য্য, প্রসারণক্ষম। **—ten-si-bil′-i-ty,** *n.* **—ten′-si-ble, —ten′-sile,** *adjs.* Capable of being extended; প্রসার্য্য, বিস্তরণীয়, বিস্তারক্ষম। **To extend over**—To stretch or spread over; বিস্তারিত বা প্রচলিত হওয়া, প্রসারিত বা প্রচলিত করা।

ĕx-tĕn′-sion, *n.* The act of extending; the state of being extended; enlargement; prolongation; extent; প্রসারণ, প্রসার; প্রসর, বিস্তরণ, বিসার; বর্দ্ধন; সম্প্রসারণ, প্রসৃতি, বিততি, ব্যাপ্তি, ব্যাপকতা, বিস্তার্য্যতা, বিস্তৃতি, বৃদ্ধি, প্রবর্দ্ধন; বিস্তার। **2.** (*Phys.*) The property of a body in virtue of which it occupies a space; (পদার্থ-বিজ্ঞান) স্থানাবরোধকতা। **3.** A line in a railway extended beyond the original terminus; পূর্ব্বতন সীমা হইতে রেলপথের বিস্তার। **4.** (*Log.*) Denotation, (correlative of *intension*); (তর্ক-বিজ্ঞান) ব্যাপ্তি।

ĕx-tĕn′-sive (-sĭv), *adj.* **1.** Pertaining to, or characterised by, extension; বিস্তার-সম্পর্কীয়, সুদূর-বিস্তৃত, সুদূর-প্রসারিত। **2.** Having great extent; large; wide; comprehensive; as, an *extensive* field; বিশাল; বিপুল, প্রকাণ্ড; বিস্তীর্ণ; ব্যাপক। **—ly,** *adv.* **—ness,** *n.*

ĕx-tĕn′-sor (-sêr), *n.* One of the muscles that serves to straighten a part of the body, (opp. to *flexor*); প্রসারক-পেশী, প্রসারক।

ĕx-tĕnt′, *n.* **1.** The space or degree to which anything is extended; compass; size; আয়তন; প্রসর, পরিধি, পরিসর, বিস্তার মাত্রা; পরিমাণ। **2.** Large space; বিস্তীর্ণ স্থান। **3.** (*Log.*) Extension; ব্যাপ্তি, দৈর্ঘ্য। **4.** Valuatian of a property; সম্পত্তির মূল্যাবধারণ। **5.** (*Law*) A writ to seize the property of a debtor; পাওনা আদায়ের জন্য যে পরওয়ানা দ্বারা অধমর্ণ ব্যক্তির সম্পত্তি ক্রোক করা হয়। **6.** Seizure of lands etc. in execution of a writ; ভূমি ক্রোককরণ।

ĕx-tĕn′-ū-āte, *v.t.* **1.** To palliate; as, to *extenuate* a crime or guilt; (of circumstances) to serve as an excuse for; হ্রাস করা, ন্যূন করা, পাতলা করা, লঘু করা, গুরুত্ব-হ্রাস করা; কারণ প্রদর্শন পূর্ব্বক অপরাধ হ্রাস করিতে চেষ্টা করা। **2.** To lessen the apparent guilt of, as oneself, conduct, etc.; দোষ প্রশমন করা। **3.** (*Archaic*) To weaken; to render thin; (অপ্রচলিত) দুর্ব্বল করা; কৃশ করা। **—at-ing,** *adj.* Palliating; দোষপ্রশমক, দোষনিরাসক। **—a′-tion,** *n.* **1.** Palliation; excuse; mitigation; as, in *extenuation* of; লঘূকরণ; অপরাধ-ভঞ্জন, পাপাপনোদন; উপশম, প্রশমন, লাঘব। **—a-to-ry,** *adj.* Serving to extenuate or palliate; দোষ-প্রশামক, অপরাধ-ভঞ্জক, দোষ-লাঘবকর।

ĕx-tēr′-ĭ-or (-êr), *adj.* & *n.* **1.** External; outer; as, the *exterior* part of a thing; বাহ্য, বহিঃ; বহিরঙ্গ। **2.** Situated without; as, a point *exterior* to a circle; বহিরস্থ বহিরাগত, বহির্ব্বর্ত্তী। **3.** Foreign; as, the *exterior* relations of a state; বৈদেশিক, বিদেশবাসী জাতি সমূহ সম্পর্কীয়। ***Noun.*** **1.** The outer surface or part; বহিস্তর, বহির্ভাগ, বাহ্যাকার, উপরিভাগ। **2.** Outward deportment, form or ceremony; as, the *exteriors* of religion; বহিরঙ্গ ভাব, আবরণ বা ক্রিয়াকলাপ। **—ly,** *adv.* On the outside or surface; superficially; বহিঃপৃষ্ঠে; উপর উপর, ভাসা ভাসা। **—or′-i-ty,** *n.* **Exterior angle** — (*Geom.*) An angle made by producing any side of a figure ; বাহ্যকোণ, বহিঃস্থকোণ।

ĕx-tē'-ri-or-īze (-êr-), *v. t.* To make external ; to give external form to, as a conception etc.; to attribute external existence to ; বহির্ব্বর্ত্তী করা ; মূর্ত্ত করা ; বহির্জ্জগতের পদার্থে পরিণত করা।

ĕx-têr'-mi-nāte, *v. t.* To destroy utterly ; to root out ; as, to *exterminate* a race, a species or opinions, etc. ; বিনষ্ট করা, উচ্ছেদ করা, ধ্বংস করা ; উন্মূলন করা, মূলোচ্ছেদ করা, উৎপাটিত করা। **—na'-tion,** *n.* Complete destruction ; eradication ; উচ্ছেদ ; নাশ, লয়, বিনাশ, উৎপাটন, ধ্বংস, উন্মূলন, সমূলনাশ। **—na-tor,** *n.* **—na-to-ry,** *adj.* Exterminating ; destroying utterly ; উচ্ছেদকারী, উচ্ছেদক, বিনাশকর ; সর্ব্বনাশী, সর্ব্বনাশক।

ĕx-têrn', *n.* A pupil in a seminary who lives and boards outside its walls; যে ছাত্র বিদ্যালয়-সংলগ্ন ছাত্রাবাসে বাস করে না।

ĕx-têr'-năl, *adj.* & *n.* **1.** Exterior ; outside ; বাহ্য, বহিঃস্থ ; বহির্ব্বিষয়ক। **2.** Physical, as opposed to mental or moral ; "His virtues graced with *external* gifts ;" দৈহিক, শারীরিক। **3.** Foreign ; as, an *external* loan ; বৈদেশিক, বিজাতীয়। **4.** Accidental ; not essential or intrinsic ; আকস্মিক ; আনুষঙ্গিক, অপ্রধান। **5.** (Of remedies etc.) Applied to the outside of the body ; বহির্জ্জাত, বহির্ভব, অনাভ্যন্তর, বহিঃস্থ। **6.** Belonging to the external world ; "The knowledge of *external* nature ;" বহির্জ্জাগতিক। **7.** (*Theol.*) Consisting in outward acts ; (খৃষ্টীয় শাস্ত্র) বাহ্য ক্রিয়াকলাপাত্মক। ***Noun.*** (*Pl.*) External parts, forms, features or characteristics ; non-essential rites etc. ; বহির্ভাগ, বাহ্যাকার, বহিরবয়ব, বহির্লক্ষণ ; বাহ্য-ক্রিয়া পার্ব্বণাদি, বাহ্যানুষ্ঠান, ক্রিয়াকলাপ। **—ism,** *n.* **1.** Phenomenalism ; যে দার্শনিক বাদানুসারে কেবল মাত্র বাহ্যবস্তুর সত্তা স্বীকৃত হইয়া থাকে, বাহ্যবস্তুবিজ্ঞানবাদ (হিঃ কোঃ), প্রত্যক্ষবাদ (ঐ)। **2.** Attention to externals, as rites etc. বাহ্যবিষয় মগ্নতা, অনুষ্ঠান-পার্ব্বণাদি বাহ্যবিষয়ে মনোনিবেশ। **—i-za'-tion,** *n.* **—ize,** *v. t.* To make external ; to exteriorize ; বহিঃস্থ করা, বহির্ব্বর্ত্তী করা ; বহির্জ্জগতের বিষয়ে পরিণত করা। **—ly,** *adv.* Outwardly ; apparently ; superficially ; বহির্দ্দিকে, বাহ্যতঃ ; স্পষ্টতঃ, আপাতঃ ; বহির্ভাগে। **—nal'-i-ty,** *n.* The quality or state of being external ; বাহ্যতা, বহিরঙ্গতা, বহির্ব্বিষয়তা। **External evidence**—আলোচ্য প্রশ্নের বহির্ভূত বিষয় হইতে প্রাপ্ত প্রমাণ, বাহ্যপ্রমাণ।

ĕx-tĕr-ri-tō'-ri-ăl, *adj.* Beyond the jurisdiction of the laws of the country in which one resides, as an ambassador ; কোন ব্যক্তি (রাজদূত প্রভৃতি) যে দেশে অস্থায়িভাবে বাস করে তদ্দেশীয় আইন-কানুনের অধিকারের বহির্ভূত। **—ly,** *n.*

ĕx-tinct' (-tĭngkt), *adj.* **1.** Extinguished ; quenched ; as, an *extinct* fire, volcano or life ; নির্ব্বাপিত ; সমাপ্ত, অবসানপ্রাপ্ত, গতায়ু। **2.** Obsolete ; out of force ; as, an *extinct* law or office ; having died out ; without an inheritor ; as, an *extinct* race or title ; অনাচরিত, অপ্রচলিত ; লুপ্ত ; মৃত ; নির্ব্বংশ। **—tinc'-tion,** *n.* **1.** The act of extinguishing ; the state of being extinguished, as of a fire or light etc. ; নির্ব্বাণ, নির্ব্বাপণ ; বিলুপ্তি। **2.** Making, or becoming, extinct ; destruction ; suppression ; as, the *extinction* of a family, claim or debt ; বিনাশ, বিলোপ ; ধ্বংস ; দমন। **—tinc'-tive,** *adj.* **The great extinction of Buddha**—বুদ্ধদেবের মহাপরিনির্ব্বাণ।

ĕx'-tīne, *n.* (*Bot.*) The outer coat of the pollen grain or a spire ; পরাগত্বক (সাঃ পঃ)।

ĕx-tin-guish (-tĭng-), *v. t.* **1.** To put out, as a fire, light, etc. ; to destroy ; to annihilate ; to suppress ; as, to *extinguish* a life, race, family, right or debt ; নিভাইয়া দেওয়া, নির্ব্বাপিত করা ; বিনষ্ট করা, ধ্বংস করা ; নাশ করা ; দমন করা। **2.** To obscure by superior splendour ; পরিম্লান করা, মলিনপ্রভ করা, নিস্প্রভ করা। **3.** To reduce to silence ; as, to *extinguish* an adversary ; চুপ করান। **—a-ble,** *adj.* Capable of, or liable to, extinction ; নির্ব্বাপ্য, নির্ব্বাণশীল, বিনশ্য। **—er,** *n.* One who, or that which extinguishes ; a hollow conical utensil to extinguish a candle ; নির্ব্বাপক, নির্ব্বাণকারী ; দীপনির্ব্বাপণের টোপর, দীপনির্ব্বাপক। **—ment,** *n.*

ĕx'-tir-pāte (-têr-), *v. t.* To eradicate ; to root out ; as, to *extirpate* weed, species, nation, heresy, etc. ; মূলোচ্ছেদ করা, মূলোৎপাটিত করা ; সমূলে ধ্বংস করা। **—pa'-tion,** *n.* The act of extirpating ; total destruction ; মূলোচ্ছেদন, মূলোৎপাটন, উন্মূলন, উৎসাদন ; বিনাশ, বিধ্বংস। **—pa'-tor,** *n.* One who extirpates ; উন্মূলক, উচ্ছেদক, ধ্বংসকারী, সংহারক, বিনাশক।

ĕx-tŏl', *v. t.* To praise highly ; to laud ; প্রশংসা করা ; প্রশংসাদ্বারা উচ্চে তোলা, উৎকীর্ত্তন করা, বাড়াইয়া তোলা, অতি সুখ্যাতি করা, গুণকীর্ত্তন করা। **—ler,** *n.* One who extols ; অতিপ্রশংসাকারী। **—ment,** *n.* **To extol one to the skies** (to laud to the skies)—To overpraise one প্রশংসা দ্বারা আকাশে তোলা।

ĕx-tŏrt, *v. t.* **1.** To wrest (*from* a person, by force, threats, or torture etc.) ; to exact ; as, to *extort* money, promise, etc. from a person ; বলপ্রয়োগ, ভয়প্রদর্শন বা পীড়নপূর্ব্বক আদায় করা, নিঙ্গড়াইয়া বা শাসাইয়া বাহির করা ; নিষ্কর্ষণ করা। **2.** To extract forcibly ; as, to *extort* a meaning, inference, etc. ; জোর করিয়া বাহির করা। **—er,** *n.* **—tor'-tive,** *adj.*

ĕx-tŏr'-tion, **1.** The act of extorting ; oppressive or illegal exaction ; নিষ্কর্ষণ ; বলপূর্ব্বক অর্থ-নিষ্কর্ষণ বা পরস্বগ্রহণ। **2.** That which is unduly extorted ; বলপূর্ব্বক গৃহীত বস্তু। **—a-ry, —ate,** *adjs.* **1.** Characterised by extortion ; oppressive ; hard ; পীড়নাত্মক ; ক্লেশ-দায়ক, পীড়াদায়ক ; কঠোর। **2.** (Only **—ate**) Exhorbitant, as a price etc. ; অত্যধিক, বেজায়। **—er, —ist,** *ns.* One who practises extortion ; উৎপীড়ক, পীড়নকারী।

ĕx'-tră-, *pref.* Beyond ; অতি।

ĕx'-tră, *adj. adv.* & *n.* **1.** Supplementary ; as, *extra* charge etc. ; অতিরিক্ত, অতিনির্দ্দিষ্ট, অধিক। **2.** Of superior quality ; as, an *extra* binding ; উৎকৃষ্ট। **3.** Larger than the usual size ; as, an *extra* card : *extra* foolscap ; সাধারণ আকার অপেক্ষা বৃহত্তর। ***Adv.*** Unusually ; as, *extra* strong ; additionally ; অসাধারণরূপে ; অতি-রিক্তভাবে। ***Noun.*** **1.** Something in addition ; as, music is charged as an *extra* ; অতিরিক্ত বস্তু। **2.** Additional issue of a newspaper ; as, the war *extra* ; সংবাদ-পত্রের অতিরিক্ত সংখ্যা। **Extra-judicial** — Beyond jurisdiction ; as, *extra-judicial* oath ; অধিকার-বহির্ভূত, বৈধ ক্ষমতার বহির্ভূত, ব্যবহার-বহির্ভূত, ব্যবহারবাহ্য। **Extra-mundane**—অলৌকিক, অপার্থিব। **Extra-mural**—(নগর বা সহরের) প্রাচীর-বহির্ভূত। **Extra-official** — নিয়মিত কার্য্যের অতিরিক্ত। **Extra-physical**—ভৌতিক নিয়মের বহির্ভূত, আধিভৌতিক। **Extra-territorial**—Outside the earth or its atmospher ; পৃথিবী বা পার্থিব বায়ু-মণ্ডলের বহির্ভূত।

ĕx-trăct', *v. t.* **1.** To draw or pull out ; as, to *extract* a tooth etc. ; to derive ; as, to *extract* good from something evil ; টানিয়া বাহির করা বা তুলিয়া ফেলা ; উৎপন্ন করা। **2.** To draw out by pressure, distillation, etc. ; as, to *extract* an essence ; নিষ্কর্ষণ করা, পরিস্রুত করা। **3.** To choose out ; to copy out ; as, to *extract* a passage from a book ; to make extracts from ; as, to *extract* a book ; অংশবিশেষ নির্ব্বাচন করা ; কোন পুস্তক বা রচনা হইতে স্থানবিশেষ নির্ব্বাচিত বা উদ্ধৃত করা ; সারোদ্ধার করা। **4.** To draw forth, as money, admission, etc. against one's will ; পীড়ন পূর্ব্বক আদায় করা, উৎপীড়নপূর্ব্বক বাহির করা। **5.** (*Math.*) To find as the root of a number ; বর্গমূল প্রভৃতি নিষ্কর্ষণ করা। **—a-ble,** *adj.* **—or,** *n.*

ĕx'-trăct, *n.* **1.** That which is extracted ; essence ; নিষ্কর্ষিত বস্তু ; সার। **2.** (*Pharm.*) A solid preparation got by evaporating a solution of a drug, or the fresh juice of a plant ; উদ্ভিদ বা জান্তব পদার্থ হইতে বাষ্প নির্গত করণান্তর প্রস্তুত গাঢ় ঔষধ দ্রব্য, সত্ত্ব (ঠাকুর), কষায় (হিঃ কোঃ)। **3.** An excerpt or quotation ; গ্রন্থাদি হইতে উদ্ধৃত অংশ বা বাক্য, সারোদ্ধার।

ĕx-trăc'-tion, *n.* **1.** The act of extracting ; operation of drawing essences, tinctures, etc. ; উন্মূলন, উৎপাটন ; নিষ্কর্ষণ, উদ্ধারণ। **2.** Birth ; lineage ; জন্ম, বংশ, উদ্ভব, সম্ভব ; কুল, বংশ। **Extraction of square roots**—বর্গমূল বাহির করণ।

ĕx-trăc'-tive (-tĭv), *adj.* & *n.* Capable of being extracted ; নিষ্কর্ষণীয়। **2.** Serving to extract ; নিষ্কর্ষণকারী। ***Noun.*** **1.** An extract ; a thing like an extract ; সত্ত্বসার, ঘনরস ; ঘনরসবৎ পদার্থ। **Extractive industries**—যে শ্রমশিল্প-দ্বারা নৈসর্গিক পদার্থ প্রাপ্ত হওয়া যায়, যথা কৃষি, খনির কার্য্য প্রভৃতি।

ĕx'-tră-dīte, *v. t.* To deliver up to proper authorities, as a fugitive criminal ; to procure extradition ; পরদেশ হইতে পলায়িত অপরাধীকে তদীয় দেশের শাসনকর্ত্তৃপক্ষ-গণের হস্তে সমর্পণ করা ; বিদেশে পলাতক অপরাধীকে ধৃত করার বন্দোবস্ত করা। **—di'-ta-ble,** *adj.*

ĕx-tră-dĭ'-tion, *n.* **1.** The delivery by one nation to another of fugitives from justice ; পরদেশ হইতে পলায়িত অপরাধীকে তদ্দেশের শাসন-কর্ত্তৃকপক্ষগণের হস্তে সমর্পণ। **2.** (*Psychol.*) Act of localising a sensation at a distance from the centre of sensation ; (মনো-বিজ্ঞান) অনুভূতি-কেন্দ্র হইতে দূরে কোন সংবেদনের স্থান-নির্দ্দেশ।

ĕx-tră'-dŏs, *n.* (*Arch.*) The exterior curve of an arch ; (স্থপতি-বিজ্ঞান) তোরণের বহির্দ্দিকের বক্রতা।

ĕx-tra'-nĕ ous (-ŭs), *n.* Not belonging to a thing ; foreign ; external ; not essential ; বাহ্য ; স্বতন্ত্র, ভিন্ন, বিজাতীয়, অপর, বহির্ভূত ; বহিরঙ্গ ; অপ্রধান। **—ly,** *adv.* **—ness,** *n.*

ĕx-tră-ŏr'-dĭn-ă-rȳ, *adj.* & *n.* **1.** Beyond or out of ordinary course ; unusual ; অসাধারণ, অসামান্য, লোকোত্তর, অপ্রাকৃত, অলোকসামান্য, অপূর্ব্ব ; অদৃষ্টচরদৃষ্ট। **2.** Remarkable ; rare as a faculty or influence etc. ; অদ্ভুত, আশ্চর্য্য ; বিরল, দুর্লভ। **3.** Sent or appointed for a special purpose ; as, an ambassador *extraordinary* ; বিশেষ উদ্দেশ্যে নিযুক্ত বা প্রেরিত। ***Noun.*** (*pl.*) Extra allowance to troops ; সৈন্যদিগের অতিরিক্ত ভাতা। **—ri-ly,** *adv.* **—ri-ness,** *n.*

ĕx-trăv'-ă-gance (-găns), **—găn-çȳ,** *n.* **1.** Quality of being extravagant ; excess ; excessive expenditure ; prodigality ; উচ্ছৃঙ্খলতা ; আতিশয্য ; অমিতব্যয় ; অপব্যয়। 2. An absurd statement or action etc.; অসাধারণ উক্তি বা কার্য্য। **—gant,** *adj.* 1. Excessive ; exceeding due bounds ; immoderate ; অতিরিক্ত ; সীমাতিক্রান্ত ; অমিত। 2. Wasteful ; prodigal ; অপব্যয়ী, অপচয়ী ; অমিতব্যয়ী। 3. Exhorbitant, as a price etc. ; অত্যধিক। **—gant-ly,** *adv.* Unreasonably ; excessively ; wastefully ; অযৌক্তিকরূপে ; অতিরিক্ত ভাবে ; অপব্যয়ের সহিত।

ĕx-trăv-ă-găn'-ză, *n.* 1. A wild literary or musical composition ; উৎকট সাহিত্যিক প্রবন্ধ বা সঙ্গীত, উদ্ভ্রান্তগীত বা প্রবন্ধ। 2. A fantastic language or behaviour ; উৎকট ভাষা বা ব্যবহার।

ĕx-trăv'-ă-sate, *v. t.* & *i.* To force or let out of proper vessel, as blood etc. ; (শোণিতাদি) স্বস্থান হইতে নিঃসারিত করা। *Verb i.* (Of blood etc.) To flow out ; (রক্তাদি সম্বন্ধে) প্রবাহিত করা। **—sa'-tion,** *n.* Effusion ; রসরক্তাদির আধার নালী হইতে নির্গমন ও নিকটস্থ বিধানাদিতে সঞ্চরণ, পর্য্যুৎপ্লাবন (হিঃ কোঃ)।

ĕx-treme' (-trēm), *adj.* & *n.* 1. Farthest ; at the utmost edge or border ; as, *extreme* point of a thing ; নিতান্ত দূরবর্ত্তী ; অতিবহিঃস্থ। 2. Last in point of time ; as, the *extreme* hour of life ; অন্তিম, চরম। 3. The best or worst ; greatest ; as, *extreme* pain, suffering or pleasure ; উৎকৃষ্ট, অপকৃষ্ট ; পরম, মহত্তম, উচ্চতম। 4. Reaching a great dregree ; very great ; as *extreme* old age ; immoderate ; stringent, as measure ; নিতান্ত, অত্যন্ত, একান্ত ; যৎপরোনাস্তি, নিরতিশয় ; অমিত, অপরিমিত ; কঠোর, কড়া। 5. Radical, (opp. *moderate*) ; as, *extreme* opinions ; উৎকট উদারনৈতিক। *Noun.* 1. An extremity; অন্ত্যসীমা, শেষসীমা। 2. (*Pl.*) Things as remote or as different as possible ; as, *extremes* of heat and cold : *extremes* always meet ; পরস্পর হইতে নিতান্ত দূরে অবস্থিত বস্তুসমূহ। 3. An excessive degree ; as, to go to *extreme* ; চরম মাত্রা। 4. (*Math.*) The first or last term of a ratio or series ; (গণিত শাস্ত্র) অনুপাত বা শ্রেঢ়ীর প্রথম বা শেষ সংখ্যা। **—ly,** *adv.* In an extreme manner or state ; নিতান্ত, একান্ত, নিরতিশয়, পরম। **—ness,** *n.* **—trem'-ism,** *n.* Radicalism ; চরম উদার-নীতিক মত, চরম-পন্থা। **—trem'-ist,** *n.* A supporter of extreme doctrines ; চরমপন্থী। **Extreme unction**—মুমূর্ষু ব্যক্তিদের চক্ষু, কর্ণ, মুখ, হস্ত, পদ এবং নাসারন্ধ্রে খৃষ্টীয় পুরোহিত কর্ত্তৃক তৈল-ম্রক্ষণ, অন্তিমম্রক্ষণ। **An extreme case** — যে ঘটনায় কতকগুলি বিশেষত্ব চরম মাত্রায় বর্ত্তমান থাকে। **Extremes meet**—সুখ দুঃখ প্রভৃতি চরম সীমায় অভিন্ন হইয়া যায়, চরম সুখ ও দুঃখের অনুভূতি একরূপ। **In the extreme**—Extremely ; in the highest degree ; নিতান্ত, নিরতিশয় ; অতিমাত্রায়। **To go to extremes, To run to an extreme**—To take an extreme course ; চরম উপায় অবলম্বন করা।

ĕx-trĕm'-i-tў, *n.* 1. The extreme part or point ; utmost limit ; অন্তিমপ্রান্ত ; চরমসীমা, অন্তাবধি, পরমাবধি (হিঃ কোঃ)। 2. The utmost point or highest degree ; as, the *extremity* of physical suffering ; পরাকাষ্ঠা, আত্যন্তিকতা, চরম মাত্রা। 3. (Usu. in *pl.*) Limbs, esp. hands and feet ; অঙ্গপ্রত্যঙ্গ, বিশেষতঃ হস্তপদ। 4. Utmost distress ; utmost difficulty ; "Driven to *exiremity* ;" চরম দুর্দ্দশা ; নিদারুণ সঙ্কট। 5. (Usu. *pl.*) An extreme measure or measures ; চরম উপায়, অন্তিমপন্থা। **Driven to extremity**—See EXTREMITY 4. **Man's extremity is God's opportunity** — মনুষ্যের চরম সঙ্কটই ঈশ্বরের সুবিধাজনক সময় ; অর্থাৎ মনুষ্য চরম দুর্দ্দশায় পতিত হইলেই শ্রীভগবানকে ভাবিয়া থাকে। **To go to extremities**—চরম উপায় অবলম্বন করা।

ĕx'-tri-cāte, *v. t.* 1. To free ; to disentangle ; as, to *extricate* a man from difficulty, debt, etc. ; মুক্ত করা, ত্রাণ করা ; ঝঞ্চাট হইতে উদ্ধার করা, নিস্তার করা। 2. (*Chem.*) To liberate (gas etc.) from combined state ; (রসায়ন-শাস্ত্র) যৌগিক অবস্থা হইতে (বাষ্প প্রভৃতি) মোচন করা। **—cable,** *adj.* Capable of being extricated ; মোচ্য, উদ্ধরণীয়। **—ca'-tion,** *n.*

ĕx-trin'-sic, *adj.* 1. Not belonging to a body ; not essential ; as, *extrinsic* differences ; acting from without ; as, an *extrinsic* influence ; আরোপিত, বাহ্য, বহিরঙ্গ ; অপ্রধান ; বহির্দ্দিক হইতে ক্রিয়াশীল। **—si-cal,** *adj.* **—si-cal-ly,** *adv.*

ĕx-trorse' (-trŏrs), *adj.* (*Bot.*) (Of anthers) Turned outwards ; (উদ্ভিদ-বিদ্যা—পরাগকোষ সম্পর্কে) বহির্মুখ (সাঃ পঃ)।

ĕx-trŏ-vêr'-sion, *n.* (*Med.*) The state of being turned inside out as, the *extroversion* of the bladder ; (ভৈষজ্য-শাস্ত্র) অভ্যন্তরের দিক বহির্দ্দিকে অবস্থান, বাহ্যাবর্ত্তন (হঃ চঃ)।

ĕx-trude' (-trûd), *v. t.* To force or thrust out ; as, to *extrude* a fetus ; ধাকাদিয়া বাহির করা, সবলে বাহির করা, ঠেলিয়া বাহির করা, নিঃসারিত করা। **—tru'-sion,** *n.* Thrusting out ; expulsion ; বহিষ্কার, অপসারণ ; নিঃসারণ। **—tru'-sive,** *adj.*

ĕx-ū'-bêr-ance (-ăns), *n.* Superabundance ; excessive luxuriance or richness ; অতিপ্রাচুর্য্য, অতিসমৃদ্ধি ; আতিশয্য, বাহুল্য, ছড়াছড়ি (*colloq.*)।

ĕx-ū'-bêr-ănt, *adj.* 1. Plenteous ; rich ; as, *exuberant* growth ; luxuriant as a plant etc. ; বহুল, অজস্র ; সমৃদ্ধ, সম্পন্ন ; অতিপ্রচুর ; অতিশয় বর্দ্ধনশীল। 2. Luxuriantly productive, as soil or fancy ; অতিশয়-উৎপাদিকা

শক্তিবিশিষ্ট। **3.** Overflowing; effusive; উদ্বেল; ভূয়িষ্ঠ। **4.** Copious, as a language; (ভাষাসম্বন্ধে) অতিবিস্তৃতিপূর্ণ, পুষ্কল। **–ly,** *adv.*

ĕx-ū′-bêr-āte, *v. i.* **1.** To be in abundance; to indulge freely (in); প্রচুর পরিমাণে থাকা; গা ঢালিয়া দেওয়া।

ĕx-ūde′, *v. i.* & *t.* To flow through pores like sweat; "Honey *exuding* from flowers;" স্বেদবৎ নির্গত হওয়া, চুয়াইয়া পড়া, নিষ্ঠ্যূত হওয়া। ***Verb t.*** To discharge through pores or incisions; স্বেদবৎ রসাদি নির্গত করা, নিঃসৃত করা। **–u-da′-tion,** *n.* The act of exuding; the substance exuded; স্রাব, স্বেদস্রাব, নিঃস্রাব, নির্গম; রস, নির্যাস, স্রাব, নিঃসৃত বস্তু। **–u′-da-tive,** *adj.* **Exudation of elephants**—গজমদ।

ex-ŭlt′ (ĕgz-), *v. i.* To leap for joy; to rejoice exceedingly; to triumph, (with *at, in* or *over*); উল্লাসে নৃত্য করা; পরমানন্দিত হওয়া; বিজয়োল্লাসে মত্ত হওয়া। **–ance, –an-cy,** *ns.* See EXULTATION. **–ant,** *adj.* Exulting; হর্ষোৎফুল্ল প্রমোদিত, বিজয়োল্লাসমত্ত। **–ant-ly,** *adv.* Rejoicingly; triumphantly; উল্লসিতভাবে; জয়োল্লাসের সহিত। **–ing-ly,** *adv.* **–ul-ta′-tion,** *n.* Lively joy; rapturous delight; triumph; উল্লাস; ভূমানন্দ, পরমানন্দ; বিজয়োল্লাস।

ex-u′-vi-æ (ĕgz-ū-vĭ-ē), *n.* (*Pl.*) Cast skins, shells or other coverings of animals whether recent or fossil; জন্তুর পরিত্যক্ত খোলস (নির্মোক), খোলা বা অন্যবিধ আবরণ, ভূস্তরে পরিত্যক্ত শিলীভূত জন্তুসমূহের দেহাবরণ প্রভৃতি। **–al,** *adj.*

ex-ū′-vi-āte (ĕgz-), *v. t.* & *i.* To cast or throw off (exuviæ); খোলস ছাড়া। ***Verb i.*** To slough; নির্মোক মোচন করা, খোলসা ছাড়া।

ĕx-vō′-tō, *adv.* & *n.* According to a vow; যেরূপ মানত করা হইয়াছে, তদনুযায়ী। ***Noun.*** An offering fulfilling a vow; দেবতার নিকট মানত (বা মানসিক) বলি বা উপহার প্রদান।

ey′-ăs (ī-), *n.* A young hawk taken from nest for training; শিক্ষাদানের উদ্দেশ্যে কুলায় হইতে আনীত বাজপক্ষীর শাবক।

eye (ī), *n.* **1.** Organ of vision; চক্ষু, নয়ন, আঁখি, লোচন, নেত্র, বিলোচন, অক্ষি। **2.** The iris of the eye; as, a brown *eye*; the region of eyes; as, a black *eye*; চক্ষুর তারার চতুর্দ্দিকস্থ রঞ্জিত মণ্ডল,—যাহার অভ্যন্তরে চক্ষুর তারা অবস্থিত আছে, নেত্র তারকামণ্ডল; চক্ষুর নিকটবর্ত্তী প্রদেশ। **3.** Sight; as, to look with a malicious *eye*; দৃষ্টি। **4.** The power of seeing; keenness of perception; as, to have an *eye* for colour; দৃষ্টিশক্তি; সূক্ষ্ম অনুভবশক্তি, সূক্ষ্মদৃষ্টি। **5.** Observation; attention; "To keep *eyes* on a person;" পর্য্যবেক্ষণ; অবহিত দৃষ্টি। **6.** Mental perception; opinion; point of view; as, it is a crime in the *eye* of law; মানসিক প্রত্যক্ষ; অভিমত; যেভাবে কোন বিষয় বিবেচনা করা যায়। **7.** That which resembles an eye; যাহার আকার, অবস্থান বা রূপ চক্ষুসদৃশ; যথা, (a) a spot on peacock's tail, চন্দ্রক (গীতঃ); (b) the bud or sprout of a plant; as, the *eye* of a potato; আলু প্রভৃতি কন্দের চোক; (c) a bull's eye; চাঁদমারির মধ্যস্থল বা লক্ষ্য; (d) a small loop to receive a hook; as, hooks and *eyes* on a dress; ফাঁস, পুঁটে-ঘরা; (e) a small opening; the thread-hole of a needle; ক্ষুদ্র ফাঁক বা রন্ধ্র; সূচের সূত্রপ্রবেশের রন্ধ্র। **Eyed,** *adj.* Having eyes or eye-like spots; নেত্রবিশিষ্ট, অক্ষিবৎ-বিন্দুবিশিষ্ট। **Eye′-less,** *adj.* Wanting eyes; blind; চক্ষুহীন, দৃষ্টিশক্তিহীন; অন্ধ। **Eye-ball**—অক্ষিগোলক। **Eye-bolt**—যে পেরেক, দণ্ড প্রভৃতির একদিকে ছিদ্র থাকে। **Eye-bright**—একপ্রকার গুল্ম,—ইহা পূর্ব্বে চক্ষ রোগের ঔষধ প্রস্তুত করিতে ব্যবহৃত হইত। **Eye-brow**—ভ্রূ, ভ্রূলতা। **Eye-doctor**—নেত্র বৈদ্য। **Eye-drop**—(*Poet.*) A tear; (কবিতায়) অশ্রু-বিন্দু। **Eye-glass**—উপনেত্র, উপলোচন, চসমা। **Eye-hole**—গোলাকার ক্ষুদ্র ছিদ্র, পুঁটে-ঘরা। **Eye-lash**—অক্ষিপক্ষ্ম, অক্ষিলোম, চক্ষুর পাতার লোম। **Eye-let,** *n.* & *v. t.* (a) ক্ষুদ্র ছিদ্র; ধাতুনির্ম্মিত অতি ক্ষুদ্র চক্র বা নল,—ইহা পাদুকা, পরদা প্রভৃতি চর্ম্ম বা বস্ত্র নির্ম্মিত বস্তুর ছিদ্র মধ্যে সংলগ্ন করিয়া দুই দিকের উদ্গত অংশ আটিয়া দেওয়া হয়—তাহাতে চর্ম্মাদি ছিড়িতে পারে না; (b) a small eye; ক্ষুদ্র চক্ষু। (c) a loop-hole; পুঁটেঘরা, ফাঁস। (*Verb t.*) To make eyelets in; পুঁটে-ঘরা তৈয়ার করা। **Eye-let punch**—যন্ত্র-বিশেষ,—এই যন্ত্রের সাহায্যে (পাদুকা, টেলিগ্রামের খাম প্রভৃতি) ছিদ্র করত ঐ ছিদ্রে ধাতুনির্ম্মিত ক্ষুদ্র নল প্রবেশ করাইয়া ফিতা লাগাইবার রন্ধ্র করা যায় বা দুই বা ততোধিক খণ্ড কাগজ সংলগ্ন করা হয়। **Eye-lid**—নেত্রচ্ছদ, অক্ষিপুট, চক্ষুর পাতা, নয়নপুট, চক্ষু-পল্লব, অক্ষি-পল্লব। **Eye-opener**—যে অবস্থায় লোকের চক্ষু খুলিয়া যায় বা বিস্ময় উৎপাদন করে; চক্ষুরুন্মীলক। **Eye-piece**—দূরবীক্ষণাদি যন্ত্রের যে কাচখণ্ড বা কাচখণ্ডসকল চক্ষুর নিকটে থাকে, নেত্রতাল, উপনেত্র খণ্ড। **Eye-salve**—অঞ্জন, নেত্রাঞ্জন। **Eye-servant**—যে চাকর যতক্ষণ প্রভুর চোখের উপর থাকে ততক্ষণ ঠিকরূপে কাজ করে। **Eye-service**—যতক্ষণ নজর ততক্ষণ কাজ, মনিবের চক্ষের আড়াল হইলেই যে কাজে ফাঁকি দেওয়া হয়, প্রত্যক্ষসেবা, প্রত্যক্ষশুশ্রূষা। **Eye-shot**—চক্ষুর্বিষয় দৃষ্টির সীমা (*Beyond eye-shot*—দৃষ্টি-বহির্ভূত।) **Eye-sight**—দৃষ্টিশক্তি। **Eye-sore**—চক্ষুঃশূল, দুই চক্ষের বিষ, চোখের বালি; কলঙ্ক। **Eye-strings**—যে পেশী বা শিরার সাহায্যে চক্ষু সঞ্চালিত, হয়। **Eye-tooth**—উপরের চোয়ালের শৌবন দন্ত বিশেষ। **Eye-water**—অক্ষি-জল, অশ্রুজল; নেত্রশোধনজল। **Eye-witness**—প্রত্যক্ষদর্শী সাক্ষী,

প্রত্যক্ষ দ্রষ্টা। **Bull's-eye** — See under BULL. **Glass-eye** — কাচ নির্ম্মিত কৃত্রিম চক্ষু। **Evil-eye**—See under EVIL. **An eye for an eye**—Retaliation ; প্রতিহিংসা। **Apple of the eye**—See under APPLE. **All my eyes, All my eye and Betty Martin**—Humbug ; nonsense ; চালাকি, ফাঁকি ; বাজেকথা, প্রলাপ। **Eye of day** or **heaven** — Sun ; সূর্য্য, দিনমণি, নভশ্চক্ষু (অঃ)। **Eyes right, left** or **front**—(*Mil.*) To turn eyes in those directions ; (সামরিক-শাস্ত্র) সম্মুখে, দক্ষিণে বা বামে চক্ষু ফিরান। **Eyes of ship**—Part in the bows of a ship, where, formerly, eyes were painted ; জাহাজের অগ্রভাগের যে অংশে পূর্ব্বে চক্ষু অঙ্কিত করা হইত। **Hook and eye**—পোষাক আটিবার কৌশল বিশেষ (যাহাতে কুর্ত্তার একদিকে একটী আঁকড়া এবং অপর দিকে ঐটী আটকাইবার জন্য একটী ক্ষুদ্র ছিদ্র থাকে)। **If you had half an eye**—If you were not completely blind or dull ; তুমি যদি চোখের মাথা না খাইতে। **In the twinkling of an eye**—চক্ষুর নিমিষে। **In his eyes**—In his estimation or opinion ; তাহার চক্ষুতে, তাহার মতে। **In the eyes of**—In the judgment of ; বিচারে, বিবেচনায়। **In the eye of the law**—See EYE 6. **In the mind's eye**—In imagination or anticipation ; মানসচক্ষুতে, কল্পনার নেত্রে। **In the wind's eye**—যে দিক হইতে বাতাস বহিতেছে। **Mind your eye**—সাবধান হও (অবজ্ঞা সূচক)। **My eye** or **eyes**—(An interjection expressing astonishment) ; বিস্ময়সূচক অব্যয়। **The eye of Greece** — এথেন্সনগরী। **The eye of the Baltic**—Gothland ; বাল্টিকসাগরস্থ গথল্যাণ্ড দ্বীপ। **To be all eyes** — To watch intently ; অত্যন্ত অভিনিবেশ সহকারে পর্য্যবেক্ষণ করা। **To cast sheep's eye at**—To graze at in a modest diffident but longing way like a bashful lover ; সলজ্জ প্রণয়ীর মত সরমজড়িত, সঙ্কোচপূর্ণ অথচ লালসাময় দৃষ্টিতে চাওয়া। **To catch one's eyes** — To attract one's notice ; কোন ব্যক্তির মনোযোগ আকৃষ্ট করা। **To find favour in one's eyes**—To be graciously received and treated ; কাহারও সুদৃষ্টিলাভ করা বা সুনজরে পড়া। **To hang on by the eyelids**—To be in a dangerous position ; সঙ্কটাপন্ন অবস্থায় থাকা। **To have a good eye to anything**—To look well after anything ; কোন বিষয়ে বিশেষ দৃষ্টি রাখা। **To have (all) one's eyes about one**—To be at all times on guard ; চতুর্দ্দিকে নজর রাখা, সর্ব্বদা সতর্ক থাকা। **To have an eye for**—To have a due sense of ; সবিশেষ জ্ঞান থাকা। **To have an eye to**—To have as one's object ; উদ্দেশ্যের বিষয়ীভূত হওয়া। **To keep an eye on**—To watch ; দৃষ্টি রাখা, নজর রাখা। **To lose an eye**—To lose its sight ; দৃষ্টিশক্তি লোপ পাওয়া। **To make eyes at**—To look at amorously ; তেরছ নয়নে দৃষ্টিপাত করা, কটাক্ষ শর নিক্ষেপ করা, সপ্রেম দৃষ্টিপাত করা। **To make one open his eyes**—To make one stare with astonishment ; বিস্মিত নেত্রে চাহিয় থাকে এরূপ অবস্থায় আনা। **To pass eye over**—চোখ বুলান। **To put one's finger in one's eye, To pipe one's eye**—To weep ; অশ্রুপাত করা। **To run one's eyes over**—To glance hastily at ; তাড়াতাড়ি চোখ বুলাইয়া যাওয়া। **To see eye to eye**—To agree entirely as with a person ; কোনও বিষয়ে সম্পূর্ণ একমত হওয়া। **To set** or **clap eyes on**—To behold ; দর্শন করা। **To shut one's eyes to**—Not to see wilfully ; ইচ্ছা করিয়া চোখ বুজিয়া থাকা। **To throw dust in the eyes of**—To deceive ; চোখে ধূলি দেওয়া। **To view with a friendly** or **jealous eye**—To view with such feelings ; বন্ধুতার চক্ষুতে দেখা, বিদ্বেষের চক্ষুতে দেখা। **Up to the eyes**—Completely or deeply (engaged) ; as, *up to the eyes* in work ; গভীর ভাবে, সর্ব্বপ্রযত্নে। **With an eye to**—With a view to ; উদ্দেশ্যে।

eye (ī), *v. t.* To view ; to watch with fixed attention ; দৃষ্টিপাত করা, দৃষ্টি করা, দেখা ; স্থিরনেত্রে দৃষ্টিপাত করা।

ey'-ŏt (ī-), *n.* A little island in a river ; নদীগর্ভস্থ ক্ষুদ্র দ্বীপ।

eyre (âr), *n.* Circuit ; circuit court ; as, Justices in *eyre* ; পরিভ্রমণ ; পর্য্যটনশীল বিচারালয়।

eye'-rie (ī rî), *n.* See AERIE.

F

F, (*Pl.* FS., F'S.), **1.** The sixth letter of the English Alphabet ; ইংরাজী বর্ণমালার ষষ্ঠ অক্ষর। **2.** (*Mus.*) The fourth note in the diatonic scale of *C* major ; (also, called *fa*) ; (সঙ্গীত-শাস্ত্র) স্বরগ্রামের অন্তর্গত চতুর্থ স্বর 'মা' ; the sixth in a series ; অনুক্রমিক ষষ্ঠ-সংখ্যক পদার্থ।

fa (fâh), *n.* (*Mus.*) Same as F 2. (which see).

fā-bā'-ceous (-shŭs), *adj.* Of the nature of, or resembling, a bean ; শিম্বি-প্রকৃতিক, শিম্বি-সদৃশ।

fā'-bi-ăn, *adj.* Delaying ; dilatory ; cautious ; বিলম্বকারী ; দীর্ঘ-সূত্র

চিরক্রিয়; সতর্ক। [প্রাচীন রোম-নগরীর সৈন্যাধ্যক্ষ Q. Fabiusএর নাম হইতে গৃহীত। ইনি নিশ্চায়ক-যুদ্ধ পরিহার করত, Punic যুদ্ধে মহাবীর Hannibalকে পরাস্ত করেন]। **Fabian policy**—Fabiusএর আদর্শানুযায়ী রণনীতি,—ইহাতে নিশ্চায়ক-যুদ্ধে বিলম্ব করিয়া শত্রুকে নিগৃহীত করা হয়।

fa'-ble (-bl), *n.* **1.** A fictitious narrative to instruct or amuse, often to enforce a precept; an apologue; উপকথা, আখ্যায়িকা; নীতিকথা, নৈতিক গল্প। **2.** A false statement; an untruth; a fabrication; as, the story is all a *fable*; মিথ্যা উক্তি; অসত্য, মিথ্যা; মিথ্যা রচনা। **3.** A story of supernatural or highly marvellous happenings; myths; legendary tales; রূপকথা; পৌরাণিক গল্প; উপকথা, উপাখ্যান। **4.** An idle story; "Old wives' *fables*;" গালগল্প, গল্পগাছা। **5.** The plot of a poem or drama; কাব্য বা নাটকের আখ্যান বস্তু। **—bu-lous**, *adj.* See below.

fa'-ble (-bl), *v. i.* & *t.* (*Archaic* & *poet.*) To tell or write fables; to tell falsehood or untruths; (অপ্রচলিত এবং কবিতায়) রূপকথা বলা বা লিখা; অলীক কথা বলা। ***Verb t.*** To tell of falsely; to invent; "The hell thou *fablest*;" কোন বিষয় সম্পর্কে মিথ্যা বর্ণনা করা; অপ্রকৃত ভাবে কল্পনায় গড়া। **—bled**, *p. adj.* **1.** Celebrated in fables; legendary; উপকথায় প্রসিদ্ধ; পৌরাণিক। **2.** Ficticious; কাল্পনিক। **—bler**, *n.*

fă-bli-au' (-blë-ö), *n.* (*pl.* -AUX) A kind of metrical tale common in early French literature; ফরাসী সাহিত্যের আদি যুগের ছন্দোবদ্ধ গল্প।

făb'-ri-c, *n.* **1.** A building; an edifice; অট্টালিকা, ইমারৎ; সৌধ। **2.** Frame or structure of anything; workmanship; texture; as, a cloth of nice *fabric*; গঠন; রচনা-কৌশল; বুনট, জমিন। **3.** Woven material; বস্ত্র।

făb'-ri-cāte, *v. t.* **1.** To frame; to construct; to manufacture; as, to *fabricate* a bridge or woollens, (*rare*); রচনা করা; নির্ম্মাণ করা; প্রস্তুত করা। **2.** To invent; to forge; to devise falsely; as, to *fabricate* a lie or story: to *fabricate* a document; উদ্ভাবন করা; জাল করা; মিথ্যা সাজান। **—ca'-tion**, *n.* **1.** (*Rare*) Act of fabricating; manufacture; (অপ্রঃ) গঠন; নির্ম্মাণ। **2.** Act of inventing; forging; উদ্ভাবন, মিথ্যারচন; জালকরণ। **3.** A falsehood; an invention; মিথ্যা কথা; মন-গড়া কথা, মনঃকল্পিত বিষয়। **—ca-tor**, *n.* **1.** One who makes or fashions; গঠনকারী, নির্ম্মাতা, রচয়িতা। **2.** One who invents a false statement; a forger; মিথ্যারচনাকারী; জালিয়াৎ।

făb'-ū-list, *n.* **1.** A writer or inventor of fables; আখ্যায়িকাকার, রূপকথা রচক। **2.** A liar; মিথ্যাবাদী।

făb'-ū-lous (-lŭs), *adj.* **1.** Feigned as a story etc.; related in fables; not real; fictitious; invented; mythical; as, a *fabulous* hero; given to legends; as, a *fabulous* historian; কল্পিত; উপকথায় বর্ণিত, আখ্যানকীর্ত্তিত; অবাস্তব, অবাস্তবিক; কাল্পনিক; মিথ্যারচিত; পৌরাণিক; উপকথানুরাগী। **2.** Exceedingly great; exaggerated; incredible; as, to sell at a *fabulous* price; অত্যধিক, নিরতিশয়; অতিরঞ্জিত; অবিশ্বাস্য। **—los'-i-ty**, *n.* **—ly**, *adv.* **—ness**, *n.*

fă-çāde', *n.* The face or front of a building towards a street or other open place; রাজপথ বা মুক্ত প্রান্তরের অভিমুখীন অট্টালিকার পার্শ্ব, অট্টালিকার সম্মুখভাগ, হর্ম্ম্যমুখ।

fāce, *n.*, *v.t.* & *i.* **1.** The front part of the head; the visage; countenance; মুখ, আনন, বক্ত্র, বদন, তুণ্ড; আস্য; মুখমণ্ডল। **2.** Expression of countenance; look; cast of features; মুখের ভাব; মুখাকৃতি; চেহারা। **3.** Boldness; effrontery; "He has the *face* to charge others with false citations;" প্রগল্‌ভতা; ঔদ্ধত্য। **4.** Presence; sight; as, in the very *face* of the court; উপস্থিতি, সমক্ষ, সম্মুখ; দৃষ্টি। **5.** The surface; the front; as, the *face* of the earth or of a house; উপরিভাগ; সম্মুখভাগ। **6.** A plane surface of a solid; as, a cube or die has six *faces*; the marked side of a playing card etc.; the dial of a watch etc.; পার্শ্ব; তাসের চিত্রিত পার্শ্ব; টেক ঘড়ী প্রভৃতির মুখপট্ট। **7.** Outward appearance; surface show; disguise; "We set the best *face* on it we could;" বাহ্যাকার; বাহ্যদৃশ্য; ছদ্মভাব। **8.** A distortion of the features; as, he made a wry *face*; মুখভঙ্গী। ***Verb t.*** **1.** To meet; to encounter; as, to *face* an enemy in the field of battle; to oppose; সাক্ষাৎ হওয়া; সম্মুখীন হওয়া, অভিমুখীন হওয়া; প্রতিরোধ করা। **2.** To stand opposite to; to stand with the face or front toward; as, the building *faces* the park; সম্মুখে অবস্থান করা; বিপরীত দিকে অবস্থান করা। **3.** To cover in front; as, a fortification *faced* with marble; সম্মুখদেশ আবৃত করা। **4.** To confront impudently or defiantly; উদ্ধতভাবে সম্মুখীন হওয়া, স্পর্দ্ধিতভাবে সম্মুখীন হওয়া। **5.** To smooth the face of; as, to *face* a stone; সম্মুখভাগ মসৃণ করা। **6.** To cause to turn a face or front in a certain direction; কোন দিকে অভিমুখীন করা। **7.** To furnish as a dress with facings; পোষাকে জরি, ফিতা প্রভৃতি লাগান। **8.** To put an appearance on; as, to *face* tea with colouring matter; কৃত্রিম করা। ***Verb i.*** **1.** To turn the face;

as, to *face* to the right or left ; মুখ ফিরান। **2.** To stand with the face in a certain direction ; as, the house *faces* toward the south ; অভিমুখ হওয়া। **Face-ache**—মুখের স্নায়ুতে বেদনা। **Face-card**—মুখবিশিষ্ট তাস, সাহেব, বিবি, গোলাম। **Face-cloth** — মৃতদেহের মুখাচ্ছাদন বস্ত্র। **Face-guard**—রৌদ্র-তাপ হইতে শ্রমজীবিদিগের মুখ রক্ষার্থ মুখস বিশেষ। **Face-value**—উপরিভাগে লিখিত মূল্য ; ষ্ট্যাম্প, নোট, মুদ্রা প্রভৃতির উপরিভাগে মুদ্রিত মূল্য। **Face-wall**—বাটীর সদর দেওয়াল। **A brazen face**—A bold defiant look ; উদ্ধত দৃষ্টি। **A wry face** — মুখ-বিকৃতি। **Face to face**—In the presence of each other; confronted; মুখোমুখী; সামনা সামনি। **Face to face with**—Confronting ; সম্মুখীন। **In the face of**—Opposite to ; in front of ; বিরুদ্ধে ; সম্মুখে। Notwithstanding ; স্বত্ত্বেও। **In the face of day**—Openly ; স্পষ্ট দিবালোকে ; প্রকাশ্যে। **In the face of the world**—Before the public at large ; সর্ব্বজনসমক্ষে। **On the face of it** — Manifestly ; to judge by appearance ; স্পষ্টতঃ ; দৃষ্টতঃ। **To draw a long face**—To look dissatisfied or sorrowful ; অসন্তুষ্ট বা বিষাদ-মলিন হওয়া। **To face about** — To look all around ; চতুর্দ্দিকে দৃষ্টিপাত করা। **To face down** — To browbeat as an opponent etc. ; চোখ রাঙাইয়া বা ধমক দিয়া দমাইয়া দেওয়া। **To face out** — To maintain impudently ; to carry through by effrontery ; as, to *face* a matter *out* ; প্রগল্‌ভভাবে সমর্থন করা, ঔদ্ধত্য সহকারে সাধন করা। **To face the music**—To meet an unpleasant situation or a danger resolutely ; not to quail at the time of trial ; দৃঢ়তার সহিত কোনরূপ অপ্রীতিকর অবস্থা বা বিপদের সম্মুখীন হওয়া ; সঙ্কট সময়ে ধৈর্য্য পরিত্যাগ না করা। **To fly in the face of** — To defy ; to set at nought ; to oppose ; তুচ্ছ করা ; অকিঞ্চিৎকর জ্ঞান করা ; বিরুদ্ধাচরণ করা। **To keep two faces under one head**—To be double-faced ; বিষকুম্ভ পয়োমুখ হওয়া, কপটাচারী হওয়া। **To look one in the face**—To confront or meet one with a steady gaze implying courage, confidence, etc. ; নির্ভয়ে সম্মুখীন হওয়া, সাহসের সহিত মুখের দিকে তাকান। **To make a wry face**—মুখ বাঁকান। **To make** or **pull a face** or **faces**—To distort the countenance ; মুখভঙ্গী করা, ভেঙ্গচান। **To one's face**—Openly in his sight or hearing ; মুখের উপর। **To pull grave faces**—To be solemn ; গম্ভীর ভাব ধারণ করা। **To put a bold face upon**—To act boldly as if there was nothing to be ashamed of ; বেহায়ার মত আচরণ করা। **To put a good face on a matter**—To make it look well ; to bear up under something disagreeable ; কোন বিষয় অনুকূলভাবে প্রদর্শন করা ; অপ্রীতিকর কোন কিছু ঘটিলে প্রসন্নতা অক্ষুণ্ণ রাখা। **To put a new face on**—To change the aspect of ; নূতন আকার প্রদান করা। **To save one's face**—To forbear from, or evade, shaming him or oneself openly ; মুখ রক্ষা করা। **To set one's face against**—To oppose ; বাধা দেওয়া, প্রতিরোধ করা। **To show one's face**—To appear; মুখ দেখান, উপস্থিত হওয়া। **To stare one in the face**—To be before one's eyes ; চক্ষুর সম্মুখে উপস্থিত হওয়া। **With black faces**—With dejected look ; বিষণ্ণদৃষ্টিতে, ম্লান-বদনে। **With good faces**—Without being ashamed ; লজ্জিত না হইয়া, সপ্রতিভ ভাবে। **With long faces**—Chapfallen ; ম্লান, বিষণ্ণ। **With wind** or **sun in one's face**—বাতাস, সূর্য্যালোক প্রভৃতি মুখের উপর প্রবাহিত বা পতিত অবস্থায়।

faced (fāst), *adj.* **1.** Having a face ; marked with a face as court-card ; মুখবিশিষ্ট ; (তাসের পক্ষে) সাহেব, বিবি, গোলামের) চিত্রসমন্বিত। **2.** With the upper or outer surface dressed or smoothed ; as, a *faced* stone ; (প্রস্তর পক্ষে) উপরিভাগ মসৃণীকৃত।

fā'-cĕr, *n.* **1.** One who puts on a false show, (*obs.*) ; কৃত্রিম ভাবভঙ্গী প্রদর্শনকারী (অপ্রচলিত)। **2.** A blow on the face (in boxing) ; a sudden hindrance or difficulty ; (মুষ্টিযুদ্ধে) মুখে মুষ্ট্যাঘাত ; আকস্মিক বাধা বা বিপদ্।

făc'-ĕt, fă-cette' (-sĕt), *n.* **1.** One of the small smooth surfaces on a cut gem ; as, the *facet* of a diamond ; হীরকাদির পল। **2.** (*Anat.*) A small circumscribed portion of the surface of a bone ; (শারীর-সংস্থানবিদ্যা) অস্থির উপরিভাগের ক্ষুদ্র সীমাবদ্ধ অংশ।

făc'-ĕt, *v. t.* To cut facets or small faces upon ; as, to *facet* a diamond ; পল কাটা। **—ed,** *adj.* Having facets ; পল-কাটা।

fă-cē'-ti-æ (-shĭ-ē), *n.* (*Pl.*) Witty or humorous sayings or writings ; books of humourous or obscene character ; হাস্যরসপূর্ণ উক্তি বা রচনা সমূহ ; অশ্লীল বা হাস্যরসপূর্ণ পুস্তক সমূহ।

fă-cē'-tious (-shŭs), *adj.* **1.** Addicted to pleasantry ; jocular ; as, a *facetious* companion ; পরিহাসরসিক ; রঙ্গপ্রিয়, নর্ম্মসংযুক্ত। **2.** Characterised by pleasantry ; exciting laughter ; as, a *facetious* expression ; রঙ্গ-রসাত্মক ; হাস্যোদ্দীপক। **—ly,** *adv.* Merrily ; humorously ; with pleasantry ; আমোদ করিয়া ; সকৌতুকে, পরিহাসপূর্ব্বক ; রঙ্গরসের সহিত। **—ness,** *n.*

fā'-ci-ă (-shĭ-), *n.* A plate over the front of a shop bearing the name of the merchant etc. ; বিপণীর সম্মুখে মালিকের নামপট্ট।

fā′-ci-ăl (-shî-), *adj.* **1.** Pertaining to the face; as, the *facial* artery; মুখ-সম্বন্ধীয়। **2.** Relating

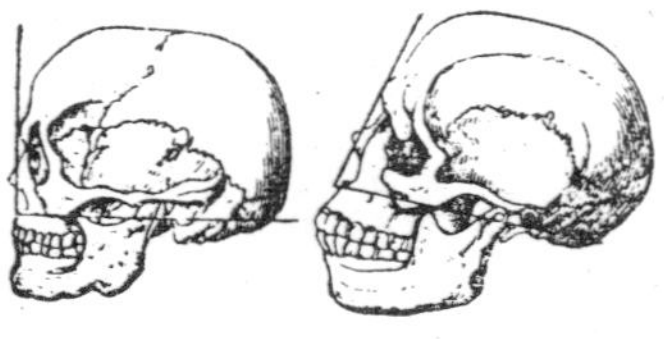

Facial angle.

to the face or surface of anything; কোন পদার্থের উপরিভাগ সম্বন্ধীয়। **—ly,** *adv.* **Facial angle**—নাসারন্ধ্র হইতে কর্ণ এবং ললাট পর্য্যন্ত গামী রেখাদ্বয়ের সংযোগে উৎপন্ন কোণ, আস্য-কোণ।

fă′-cile (-sîl), *adj.* **1.** Easily done or performed; not difficult; সুসাধ্য, সুকর, অনায়াস-সাধ্য, অযত্ন-সাধ্য, অনায়াস-নিষ্পাদ্য, সুখসাধ্য; সহজ। **2.** Easy to be surmounted or removed; easily conquerable; "The *facile* gates of hell too slightly barred;" সহজে অতিক্রমণীয়; সহজে পরাজেয়। **3.** Flexible; gentle; yielding; নমনীয়, কোমল; নম্র; বশ্য। **4.** Ready; expert; fluent; working easily; তৎপর; দক্ষ, নিপুণ; অনর্গল; অনায়াসে কার্য্যকারী। **5.** Courteous; affable; শিষ্ট, ভদ্র; মিষ্টভাষী। **—ly,** *adv.* ***Facile princeps***—*pred. adj.* (*L.*) Easily first; অনায়াসে সর্ব্বাগ্রগণ্য।

fā-cĭl′-i-tāte, *v. t.* **1.** To make easy; to further; সহজ করা, সুগম করা; অগ্রসর করা। **—ta′-tion,** *n.* Act of faciliating or making easy; সৌকর্য্য-সাধন, অনায়াস-সাধ্যকরণ।

fā-cĭl′-i-tŷ, *n.* **1.** Quality of being easy; easiness to be performed; absence of difficulty; সুকরতা; সৌকার্য্য; অনায়াসসাধ্যতা, অযত্নসাধ্যতা। **2.** Readiness proceeding from skill or practice; dexterity; aptitude; "He performed it with *facility*;" fluency; তৎপরতা; দক্ষতা; লীলা, অনায়াস; অনর্গলতা। **3.** (*Now* in *pl.*) Opportunity; as, to give *facilities* for doing something; সুবিধা।

făc′-ing, *n.* **1.** A covering in front for ornament or other purpose; সম্মুখভাগের আবরণ, মুখচ্ছদ। **2.** A lining placed at the edge of a garment; হাঁসিয়া, জরি, মুড়ি। **3.** (*Mil. pl.*) Trimmings on regimental garments; সামরিক পরিচ্ছদের জরি, গোটা, প্রভৃতি। **4.** (*Mil.* chiefly *Pl.*) The movements of soldiers to the right, left or about; বামে, দক্ষিণে বা চতুর্দ্দিকে সৈন্যদিগের গতি। **5.** A mode of adulterating tea by mixing it with colouring matter; রঞ্জকপদার্থ মিশ্রণ দ্বারা চা বিকৃত করণ। **To put one through one's facings**—To examine; to inspect; পরীক্ষা করা; পরিদর্শন করা।

făc-sĭm′-i-lē, *n.* & *v. t.* An exact copy, esp. of handwriting, printing, picture, etc.; as, the *facsimile* of the handwriting of a famous man; প্রতিলিপি, হস্তলিপি, আলেখ্য প্রভৃতির অবিকল অনুলিপি, প্রতিরূপ। ***Verb t.*** To reproduce or to make a facsimile of; to copy exactly; অবিকল প্রতিলিপি প্রস্তুত করা; অবিকল নকল করা। **Reproduced in facsimile**—Reproduced exactly; অবিকলভাবে পুনরুৎপাদিত।

făct, *n.* **1.** An event; a deed; ঘটনা; কার্য্য। **2.** Reality; truth; (without *a*) a datum of experience; "*Facts* are more powerful than arguments;" তথ্য; সত্য; দৃষ্টসিদ্ধি, উপপত্তি। **3.** Occurrence of an event; perpetration of an act; (now only in the phrases,—*after* or *before the fact, to confess the fact*); কোন ঘটনা সংঘটন; দুষ্কর্ম্ম-সাধন। **4.** The assertion of a thing done or existing; a thing supposed to be done or to exist; as, his *facts* are disputable: with false *facts*; কৃতকর্ম্ম বা বর্ত্তমান বিষয় সম্বন্ধে নিঃসন্দিগ্ধ ভাবে কথিত বাক্য; কৃত বা বর্ত্তমান বলিয়া কল্পিত বিষয়। **Matter-of-fact,** *n.* & *adj.* Something which has really happened; সত্য ঘটনা, প্রকৃত ঘটনা বা ব্যাপার। (*Adj.*) (Words conn. with hyphen) Prosaic; not imaginative; গদ্যময়, নীরস, ভাবাবেগবিহীন; অকাল্পনিক। **As a matter of fact**—In reality; যথার্থতঃ, বাস্তবিক পক্ষে। **In fact, in point of fact**—In reality; বাস্তবিক পক্ষে, বস্তুতঃ, প্রত্যুত। **The fact of the matter**—কোন বিষয়ের তথ্য বা প্রকৃত কথা, উপপত্তি, দৃষ্টসিদ্ধি। **To confess the fact**—To confess the perpetration of a thing; প্রকৃত কথা প্রকাশ করা।

făc′-tion, *n.* **1.** A party in politics combined or acting together in opposition to the ruling power; an unscrupulous party seeking self-interest only; রাজশক্তির বিরুদ্ধাচারী রাজনীতিকদল; কুচক্রিদল। **2.** Discord; tumult; dissention; "In great *faction* among themselves;" বিরোধ; গোলযোগ; দলাদলি, ভেদ, বিবাদ, বিসংবাদ। **—al,** *adj.* **—a-ry,** *n.* A member of a faction; কুচক্রিদলভুক্ত ব্যক্তি। **—ist,** *n.* **—tious,** *adj.* Given to faction; seditious; হাঙ্গামাকারী; রাজদ্রোহী। **—tious-ly,** *adv.* **-tious-ness,** *n.*

făc-ti-tious (-shŭs), *adj.* Artificial; "*Factitious* wants created by luxury;" কৃত্রিম, কপট। **—ly,** *adv.* In a factitious manner; কৃত্রিম ভাবে। **—ness,** *n.*

făc′-ti-tive (-tĭv), *adj.* (*Gram.*) Causative; (applied to verbs) expressing an action that produces a new condition in the object; as, in "He made him king;" *made* is a factitive verb; (ব্যাকরণ) ণিজন্ত।

făc′-tor (-têr), *n.* **1.** A transactor of business for another; a deputy;

a mercantile agent ; a commission merchant ; গোমস্তা ; প্রতিনিধি ; কুঠিয়াল ; পাইকার, আড়তদার। **2.** (*Math.*) One of the quantities or numbers which multiplied together, produce a product—*e. g.* 3 and 8 are *factors* of 24 ; গুণনীয়ক, উৎপাদক, গুণ্যগুণাবয়ব (হিঃ কোঃ), গুণবাচক (ঐ), গুণ্যপদ। **3.** An element in the composition of anything ; a circumstance, fact or influence tending to produce a result ; কারণ ; অবয়ব। **—age,** *n.* The fees or commission given to a factor by his employer ; প্রতিনিধির বেতন বা কুঠিয়ালের পারিশ্রমিক, দস্তুরি। **—ship,** *n.*

făc-tō′-ri-ăl, *adj.* & *n.* **1.** Pertaining to a factor or factory ; কুঠিয়াল বা কুঠি-সম্বন্ধীয়। **2.** (*Math.*) Relating to factors ; (গণিত শাস্ত্র) গুণনীয়ক সম্বন্ধীয়। ***Noun.*** (*Math.*) The product of the consecutive integers from 1 up to any given number ; as, *factorial n* (written *n*7) is the product of all numbers from 1 to *n* ; (গণিত-শাস্ত্র) এক হইতে আরম্ভ করিয়া কোনও অখণ্ড রাশি পর্য্যন্ত সংখ্যা সমূহের পূরণ ফলকে ঐ রাশির factorial কহে।

făc′-tor-īze (-têr-), *v. t.* **1.** (*Math.*) To resolve into factors ; (গণিত-শাস্ত্র) গুণনীয়কে বিশ্লিষ্ট করা। **2.** (*U. S. law*) To attach goods (belonging to a debtor) in the hands of a third person ; (মার্কিণ যুক্তরাজ্যের আইন) (অধমর্ণ ব্যক্তির মাল পত্র) ক্রোক করিয়া তৃতীয় ব্যক্তির হস্তে সমর্পণ করা।

făc′-tō-rȳ, *n.* **1.** A trading house or station in a distant country where factors transact business for their employers ; কুঠী। **2.** A building or buildings appropriated to the manufacture of goods ; as, a cotton *factory* ; a manufactory ; কারখানা ; শিল্পশালা। **3.** The body of factors in any place, (*obs.*) ; কুঠীওয়ালাগণ (অপ্রঃ)। **Factory Acts**—কারখানার শ্রমজীবিগণের স্বার্থরক্ষার্থ রাজবিধি।

făc-tō′-tŭm, *n.* **1.** A servant employed to do all kinds of business of his master ; সর্ব্বকর্ম্মসম্পাদনার্থ নিযুক্ত ভৃত্য। **2.** A man of all work ; সর্ব্বকর্ম্মসাধনে সুনিপুণ ব্যক্তি।

făc′-tū-ăl, *adj.* Relating to facts ; of the nature of a fact ; actual ; তথ্যসম্বন্ধীয় ; তথ্যাত্মক ; বাস্তবিক, যথার্থ। **—ly,** *adv.*

făc′-tŭm, *n.* (*pl.* -TA) **1.** A statement of facts ; সত্য বিবরণ। **2.** (*Law*) A thing done ; an act or deed ; কৃতকার্য্য ; কার্য্য।

făc′-tūre, *n.* **1.** (*Comm.*) An invoice or bill of parcels ; (বাণিজ্য) পুলিন্দাসমূহের চালান-তালিকা। **2.** Act or result of making a thing, (now used esp. of literary and musical porductions) ; বিরচন বা বিরচিত পুস্তকাদি।

făc′-ū-lă, *n.* (*pl.* -LÆ) (*Astron.*) A spot seen on the sun's disk ; সূর্য্যমণ্ডলস্থ উজ্জ্বল বিন্দু। **—lar, —lous,** *adjs.*

făc′-ŭl-tă-tive (-tĭv), *adj.* **1.** Permissive ; optional ; as, *facultative* celibacy ; অনুমোদক, অনুমতিদায়ক ; ইচ্ছাধীন। **2.** (*Psychol.*) Relating to a faculty ; (মনোবিজ্ঞান) মনোবৃত্তিসম্বন্ধীয়।

făc′-ŭl-tȳ, *n.* **1.** Capacity for any function ; as, the *faculty* of speech ; কার্য্যশক্তি, বৃত্তি। **2.** Mental gift ; knack ; as, *faculty* for mimicry ; প্রতিভা, কার্য্যকৌশল; নৈপুণ্য। **3.** Powers of the mind, *e. g.* the will, reason, etc. ; ঈশ্বরদত্ত বুদ্ধি বা গুণ, মনোবৃত্তি। **4.** The power inherent in the body or in any of its organs ; as, the *faculty* of hearing ; শক্তি (যথা, ঘ্রাণশক্তি)। **5.** A department of a university ; the branch of university teaching it ; as, the *faculty* of medicine ; বিশ্ববিদ্যালয়ে যে সকল বিষয় শিক্ষাদান করা হয় তাহার অঙ্গ বিশেষ ; বিশ্ববিদ্যালয়ের যে শাখায় কোন শাস্ত্রের কোন বিশেষ অঙ্গ শিক্ষাদান করা হয়। **6.** The members of a profession ; as, the medical or legal *faculty* ; কোন ব্যবসায়ি সমাজের অন্তর্ভূত ব্যক্তিবর্গ। **7.** (*Chiefly in U. S.*) Executive ability ; (প্রধানতঃ মার্কিণ যুক্তরাজ্যে) শাসন-ক্ষমতা। **8.** Licence, (esp. ecclesiastical) ; বিশেষ অধিকার, বিশেষ সনন্দ। **9.** The tutors and professors in a university etc. ; বিশ্ববিদ্যালয়ের শিক্ষক ও অধ্যাপক-মণ্ডলী। **The four faculties** — (University) Theolgoy, Law, Medicine, and Arts ; (বিশ্ববিদ্যালয়) ধর্ম্মশাস্ত্র, আইন, ভৈষজ্য-শাস্ত্র ও সুকুমার সাহিত্য। **The Faculty**—চিকিৎসা-ব্যবসায়ি-সমাজ।

făd, *n.* A hobby ; whim ; সখ ; খেয়াল, মর্জ্জি। **Fad′-dish, fad′-dy,** *adjs.* **Fad′-dish-ness, fad′-di-ness, fad′-dism,** *ns.* **Fad′-dist,** *n.* One who indulges in fads or whims ; খেয়াল-পরবশ ব্যক্তি।

făd′-dle (-dl), *v. i.* To trifle ; to play ; তুচ্ছ করা ; খেলা করা।

fāde, *v. i.* & *t.* **1.** To lose freshness or vigour gradually ; to wither ; as, the plant has *faded* ; ক্ষীণ হওয়া, তেজোহীন হওয়া, পরিম্লান হওয়া, নিস্তেজ হওয়া ; বিশুষ্ক হওয়া। **2.** To grow dim ; as, a colour *fades* ; ক্রমশঃ মন্দপ্রভ হওয়া, ঝাপ্‌সা হওয়া। **3.** To disappear gradually ; ক্রমশঃ অদৃশ্য হওয়া, ক্রমশঃ বিলীন হওয়া। ***Verb t.*** To cause to wither ; শুষ্ক করা, নিস্তেজ করা, মলিন করা। **Fad′-ed,** *adj.* Withered ; grown dim ; as, a *faded* cheek ; পরিম্লান, শুষ্ক ; বিবর্ণ। **Fad′-ed-ly,** *adj.* **Fade′-less,** *adj.* Unfading ; অম্লান। **Fade′-less-ly,** *adv.*

fadge (făj), *v. i.* (*Obs.*) To agree ; to suit ; (অপ্রঃ) ঐক্য হওয়া ; যোগ্য হওয়া, মানান।

fæ′-cēs (fē-), **fē′-cēs,** *n.* (*pl.*) **1.** Sediments ; গাদ, সিটা, তলানি। **2.** Excrements ; বিষ্ঠা, মল, পুরীষ, গুথ, অবস্কর। **–cal,** *adj.* Pertaining to fæces ; containing or consisting of fæces ; মল-সম্বন্ধীয় ; মলপূর্ণ, পুরীষপূর্ণ।

fā′-êr-ȳ, –êr-ie (-ĭ), *n.* & *adj.* The world of fairies ; the fairies (as described in Spencer's Faery Queen) ; পরীরাজ্য; পরীসমাজ। ***Adj.*** Relating to, or like, faery or fairy land ; visionary ; পরী-সম্বন্ধীয়, পরীবৎ, পরীরাজ্য-সম্বন্ধীয়, পরীরাজ্যবৎ ; কল্পিত, স্বাপ্নিক, কাল্পনিক।

făg, *v. i., t.* & *n.* **1.** To labour assiduously ; to work hard ; অবিশ্রান্ত পরিশ্রম করা ; কঠোর পরিশ্রম করা। **2.** (In some English schools of junior boys) To do services for seniors ; বয়োজ্যেষ্ঠ ব্যক্তির জন্য কোনরূপ হীনকর্ম্ম করা। ***Verb t.*** **1.** To compel to drudge ; as, senior boys *fag* juniors at school ; হীনকর্ম্ম করিতে বাধ্য করা। **2.** To tire ; to exhaust ; খাটাইয়া হয়রান করা ; অবসন্ন করা। ***Noun.*** **1.** A school boy who has to fag ; বিদ্যালয়ের যে অল্পবয়স্ক ছাত্রকে বয়োধিক এবং উচ্চশ্রেণীর ছাত্রের জন্য হীনকর্ম্ম করিতে হয়। **2.** Drudgery ; a tiresome work ; as, what a *fag* ; exhaustion ; as, brain *fag* ; হীনকর্ম্ম ; ক্লান্তি বা অবসাদ-জনক কার্য্য ; অবসাদ। **Fag′-ging,** *n.* **Fag-end**—কাপড়ের দশী বা ছিলা ; রজ্জুর পাক-খোলা প্রান্ত ; কোন বস্তুর অসার নিকৃষ্ট অংশ ; অসার অবশিষ্ট ভাগ। **Brain-fag** — Brain exhaustion ; মস্তিষ্কের অবসাদ। **To fag out**—To become untwisted, as the end of a rope ; রজ্জু প্রভৃতির প্রান্তের পাক খুলিয়া যাওয়া।

făg′-gŏt, fă′-gŏt, *n.* & *v. t.* **1.** A bundle of sticks used for fuel etc. ; জ্বালানী কাঠের আঁটি। **2.** A bundle of pieces of iron or steel for remanufacture ; পুনর্ব্বার দ্রব্যাদি প্রস্তুতের জন্য লৌহ বা ইস্পাত খণ্ড সমূহের পুঁটলি। **3.** An old shrivelled woman ; অস্থিচর্ম্মসার বৃদ্ধা স্ত্রীলোক, থুড়থুড়ে বুড়ী। ***Verb t.*** To tie together as in a bundle ; আঁটি বাঁধা। **2.** To collect promiscuously ; এলোমেলোভাবে জমান। **–ing,** *n.* A kind of embroidery ; একপ্রকার চিকণের কাজ। **Faggot vote**—কতিপয় ব্যক্তির অধিকৃত সম্পত্তি ক্রয় করিয়া যে নির্ব্বাচন-মত প্রাপ্ত হওয়া যায়] এইরূপ সম্পত্তি ক্রয়কারীর স্বপক্ষে অবিভক্ত-সম্পত্তির প্রত্যেক মালিক নামমাত্র নির্ব্বাচন মত প্রদানে অধিকারী হয়।]

fă-gŏt′-tō, *n.* (*Mus.*) The bassoon ; (সঙ্গীত-শাস্ত্র) সানাই।

Fah′-ren-heit (fâ-rĕn-hĭt), *adj.* (abbr. F.) The name of a thermometer invented by a German of that name, with 32° & 212° for freezing and boiling points ; তাপমান যন্ত্রবিশেষ [ইহাতে সংহনন-বিন্দু ৩২° ডিগ্রী এবং স্ফুটন-বিন্দু ২১২° ডিগ্রী চিহ্নিত থাকে]।

fă-ience′ (-îns), *n.* [F.] A kind of pottery glazed and painted in various designs ; একপ্রকার চিত্রিত এবং কাচের সূক্ষ্ম-স্তরাচ্ছাদিত মৃৎপাত্র।

fail (fāl), *v. i., t.* & *n.* **1.** To fall short ; to be wanting (in) ; "The dialogue *fails* in unity ;" ন্যূন হওয়া ; অভাব হওয়া। **2.** To decline ; to become extinct ; "The eldest line *failing*;" to die out as an odour or sound ; পতন হওয়া, ক্ষয় হওয়া ; নির্ব্বাণ-প্রাপ্ত হওয়া ; ক্রমশঃ অন্তর্হিত হওয়া, লোপ পাওয়া, বিলীন হওয়া। **3.** To become weaker ; as, a sick man *fails* everyday ; ক্রমশঃ ক্ষীণ বা দুর্ব্বল হওয়া। **4.** To come short (*of*) ; as, to *fail of* beauty ; ত্রুটি হওয়া, অপূর্ণ হওয়া। **5.** To be unsuccessful ; as, the attack *failed* ; ব্যর্থকাম হওয়া, বিফল মনোরথ হওয়া, অকৃতকার্য্য হওয়া। **6.** To be guilty of omission or neglect ; as, to *fail* in duty or respect ; ত্রুটি করা। **7.** To become insolvent ; দেউলিয়া হওয়া। **8.** To get plucked as in an examination ; পরীক্ষায় অনুত্তীর্ণ বা অকৃতকার্য্য হওয়া। ***Verb t.*** Not to be sufficient for ; "Time would *fail* me to tell ;" to desert ; to disappoint ; as, wind *failed* us ; অপ্রতুল হওয়া, অপ্রচুর হওয়া ; পরিত্যাগ করা ; নিরাশ করা। ***Noun.*** Failure ; deficiency ; বিফলতা ; অন্যথাচরণ, দোষ, ত্রুটি। **Failed,** *p. adj.* Decayed ; worn out ; ক্ষয়প্রাপ্ত ; বিশীর্ণ। **Fail′-ing,** *n.* & *prep.* A fault ; a shortcoming ; failure ; weakness ; as, the mental *failing* ; দোষ ; ত্রুটি ; কসুর; দুর্ব্বলতা। (*Prep.*) In default of ; as, *failing* this (*i. e.* if this does not happen) ; অন্যথায়। **To fail of**—To come short of ; to lose ; ত্রুটি হওয়া ; হারান। **Without fail**—Without failure ; certainly ; অন্যথা না করিয়া ; নিশ্চয়ই।

fail′-ūre (fāl-), *n.* **1.** failing ; deficiency ; as, *failure* of rain o crops ; অভাব; ন্যূনতা, কমি। **2.** Non-performance ; omission ; অসম্পাদন ত্রুটি, কসুর। **3.** Decay or defect from decay ; as, *failure* of memory ; ক্ষয়, লোপ। **4.** Illsuccess ; অকৃতকার্য্যতা। **5.** Bankruptcy ; দেউলিয়া অবস্থা। **6.** An unsuccessful person, thing or attempt ; অকৃত কার্য্য ব্যক্তি, নিষ্ফল বিষয়, নিষ্ফল চেষ্টা।

fain (fān), *adj.* & *adv.* (predicative) **1.** Glad ; সন্তুষ্ট। **2.** Inclined ; as, *fain* to be wise ; রত, ইচ্ছুক। **3.** Content for want of something better ; অগত্যা-সন্তুষ্ট। ***Adv.*** Gladly (with *would*) ; "I would very *fain* speak with you ;" সানন্দে। **Fain′-ness,** *n*, Eagerness; আগ্রহ।

faineant (fā-nā-ân), [*F.*] *adj.* & *n.* Doing nothing ; idle ; নিষ্কর্ম্মা,

অলস ; নিশ্চেষ্ট, জড়। *Noun.* An idle fellow ; অলস ব্যক্তি, নিষ্কর্ম্মা লোক, কুড়ে।

faint (fānt), *adj., v. i., t. & n.* **1.** Languid ; feeble ; inclined to swoon ; as, *faint* with thirst ; অলসাঙ্গ, অবশাঙ্গ, অবসন্ন ; দুর্ব্বল, ক্ষীণ; ম্লানাঙ্গ (মঃ ভঃ); মূর্চ্ছাপ্রবণ। **2.** Timid ; dejected ; as, a *faint* heart ; ভীরু ; বিরস, দীন। **3.** Sluggish ; ঢিলা। **4.** Not vigorous ; half-hearted ; as, a *faint* attempt or resistance ; নিস্তেজ, নির্ব্বীর্য্য ; নিরুৎসাহ। **5.** Not bright or vivid ; indistinct ; pale ; as, a *faint* colour or voice ; ম্লান, ফিকা, মন্দ ; অস্পষ্ট ; বিবর্ণ। **6.** Oppressive ; sickly ; as, a *faint* smell, air, etc. ; পীড়াদায়ক ; রোগপ্রবণ। ***Verb i.*** **1.** To become feeble, (*poet.*) ; দুর্ব্বল হওয়া, ক্ষীণ হওয়া (পদ্যে)। **2.** (*Archaic*) To loose courage or spirit ; to give way ; (অপ্রঃ) হতাশ্বাস হওয়া, নিরুৎসাহ হওয়া ; ভাঙ্গিয়া পড়া। **3.** To swoon, (sometimes with *away*) ; মূর্চ্ছা যাওয়া। ***Verb t.*** (*Rare*) To cause to faint ; (অপ্রঃ) মূর্চ্ছিত করা। ***Noun.*** A swoon ; মূর্চ্ছা। **Faint'-ing,** *n.* **1.** Depression ; অবসন্নতা। **2.** Syncope ; মূর্চ্ছা। **Faint'-ish,** *adj.* Slightly faint ; ঈষৎ দুর্ব্বল। **Faint'-ly,** *adv.* **Faint'-ness,** *n.* **1.** Loss of consciousness ; exhaustion ; feebleness ; সংজ্ঞালোপ, চৈতন্যলোপ ; অবসন্নতা, অবসাদ ; দৌর্ব্বল্য, শক্তিহীনতা, দুর্ব্বলতা। **2.** Feebleness of colour, light, etc. ; বর্ণ, আলোক প্রভৃতির মান্দ্য বা ম্লানিমা। **3.** Dejection ; timorousness ; (now only in the phrase *faintness of heart*) ; বিষাদ ; হৃদয়দৌর্ব্বল্য। **Faint-heart**—A coward ; দুর্ব্বলচিত্ত, ভীরু। **Faint-hearted**—Cowardly ; timorous ; দুর্ব্বলহৃদয়, ভীরু ; কাপুরুষ। (*Faint-heartedness, n.*) **Faint** or **feint lines**—সোজা রেখায় লিখিবার জন্য কাগজের উপর অঙ্কিত ফিকা নীলবর্ণের রেখা সমূহ। **A faint idea**—সামান্য আভাস। **In a dead faint**—সম্পূর্ণ সংজ্ঞাহীন অবস্থায়।

faints (fānts), *n. (Pl.)* The impure spirit coming over first and last in the distillation of whisky ; (বহুবচন) হুইস্কী মদ্য চোলাই করার সময় প্রথম ও শেষ অবস্থায় যে অপরিষ্কার সুরাসার বাহির হয়।

fair (fār), *adj. & n.* **1.** Handsome ; সুন্দর, সুরূপ, সুশ্রী। **2.** Unblemished ; clear ; as, *fair* fame etc. ; অনবদ্য ; নিষ্কলঙ্ক। **3.** Not dark ; blond ; as, a *fair* complexion ; পরিষ্কার, ফর্সা ; গৌর। **4.** Just ; impartial ; as, *fair* field and no favour ; ন্যায্য ; পক্ষপাতশূন্য। **5.** Distinct ; legible ; স্পষ্ট ; সুখপাঠ্য। **6.** Specious ; plausible ; আপাতরম্য, আপাতসুন্দর ; আপাতমনোজ্ঞ। **7.** Favourable ; fine ; cloudless ; as, a *fair* wind, day, sky, weather, etc. ; অনুকূল ; নির্ম্মল, বিমল ; মেঘনির্ম্মুক্ত, নির্মেঘ। **8.** Uninterrupted ; direct ; as, a *fair view* ; অবাধিত, অবারিত ; প্রত্যক্ষ। **9.** Moderately good ; as, a *fair* income ; মাঝারি রকমের, মধ্যবিত্ত। **10.** Satisfactory ; abundant ; as, a *fair* heritage ; সন্তোষজনক ; পর্য্যাপ্ত। **11.** Promising ; আশাপ্রদ। ***Noun.* 1.** (*Archaic*) A fair woman ; (অপ্রঃ) সুন্দরী স্ত্রী। **Fair'-ness,** *n.* The quality of being free from stains or blemishes ; honesty ; impartiality ; candour ; fineness or clearness, as of weather etc. ; distinctness ; নিষ্কলঙ্কতা, অনবদ্যতা ; সাধুতা ; সমতা, সমদর্শিতা, নিরপেক্ষতা ; সরলতা, অকপটতা, অকৃত্রিমভাব ; নির্ম্মলতা, মেঘমুক্ততা ; সুস্পষ্টতা। **Fair chance**—সুবর্ণ-সুযোগ। **Fair-copy** — বিশুদ্ধ প্রতিলিপি, পরিষ্কার নকল। **Fair-faced**—সুবদন ; গৌর, গৌরবর্ণ ; আপাত-সুন্দর, আপাতরমণীয়। **Fair game**—ঠাট্টা, উপহাসের পাত্র ; যে ব্যক্তি নিজেকে উপহাসাস্পদ করে। **Fair-haired**—স্বর্ণাভ পিঙ্গলবর্ণ কেশযুক্ত। **Fair-minded**—ন্যায়পর ; সংস্কার-বিমুক্ত ; সাধু। **Fair-name**—সুনাম, সুখ্যাতি, সুযশ। **Fair-natured**—সুশীল। **Fair one**—রূপবতী স্ত্রী, সুন্দরী, রূপসী। **Fair play**—Impartial and just behaviour ; justice ; নিরপেক্ষ ও ন্যায্য ব্যবহার ; ন্যায়বিচার। **Fair-spoken**—মিষ্টভাষী, সদালাপী, প্রিয়ম্বদ। **Fair-trade**—অবাধ বাণিজ্য, নিষ্পক্ষব্যাপার (চিঃ কোঃ)। Smuggling, (*slang*) ; (ইতরভাষায়) ঘাটমারণ, মাশুল চুরি করণ। **Fair-way**—নৌ তার্য্য-প্রণালী। **Fair-weather**—ঝঞ্ঝাবৃষ্টিশূন্য কালের উপযোগী, সুসময়ের, সুদিনের। **A fair field and no favour**—Opportunity and impartiality ; সুযোগ এবং সমদর্শিতা। **All's fair in love and war**—যুদ্ধে এবং প্রণয় ব্যাপারে কৃত পাতক অপাতক মধ্যে গণ্য। **By fair means**—সদুপায়ে। **By fair means or foul**—By hook or by crook ; যেন তেন প্রকারেন। **Fair and square**—*Adj. & Adv.* Above board ; সাধু, নিষ্কপট। (*Adv.*) Honestly ; justly ; সততার সহিত ; ন্যায্যভাবে। **Fair fall you**—Good befall you ; তোমার মঙ্গল হউক, স্বস্তি **Fairer the paper fouler the blot**—কাগজ যত সাদা হয়, দাগ তত বিশ্রী দেখায়। **Fair-weather-friends**—সুসময়ের বন্ধু। [cf. লক্ষ্মীর বরযাত্রী, সুখের পায়রা, ভালর ভাগী, মন্দের কেহ নয়।] **Fair** (or **fine**) **words butter no parsnips**—See BUTTER. **February Fair-maids** — তুষারবিন্দু। **The fairest rose is at last withered**—মা কুরু ধনজন যৌবন গর্ব্বং, হরতি নিমেষাৎ কালঃ সর্ব্বম্। **The fair sex**—স্ত্রীজাতি। **To be in a** (or **the**) **fair way** or **road to**—To be likely to attain or reach ; as, he is *on the fair way to* fortune ; সিদ্ধির পথে অগ্রসর হওয়া।

fair (fār), *v. t. & i.* To make fair, (*obs.*) ; সুন্দর করা (অপ্রঃ)। ***Verb t.*** To clear up, as the weather from rain etc.; মেঘনির্মুক্ত হওয়া, পরিষ্কার হওয়া।

fair (fār), *adv.* 1. Gracefully; brightly; as, the moon shone *fair*; সুন্দররূপে, মনোহররূপে; উজ্জ্বলভাবে। 2. Frankly; courteously; সরলভাবে, অকপটভাবে; শিষ্টভাবে। 3. Honestly; equitably; according to rule; as, to play *fair*; সততার সহিত; সমতার সহিত; যথানিয়মে। 4. Favourably; promisingly; as, the weather promises or bids *fair*; অনুকূলভাবে; আশাজনকভাবে। 5. Clearly; legibly; as, he writes *fair*; স্পষ্টভাবে; সুপাঠ্যভাবে। 6. Straight; clear; as, he was struck *fair* between the eyes; সোজাভাবে; সাফ। **Fair and softly**—Honestly and courteously; সাধুভাবে ও ভদ্রভাবে। **Fair and softly goes far in a day**—(চলিত ভাষায়) সাধুতা ও ভদ্রব্যবহার দ্বারা অল্প সময়েই উদ্দেশ্য সিদ্ধ হয়। **To bid fair** — To promise well; আশা প্রদান করা, আশাপ্রদ হওয়া। **To keep fair with** — (অপ্রঃ) সদ্ভাব রাখা। **To lead fair**—(*Naut.*) To suffer little friction in a pulley, (said of ropes etc.); (নৌ বিদ্যা) (রজ্জু প্রভৃতি সম্পর্কে) কপিকলের সহিত অল্পমাত্র সংঘৃষ্ট হওয়া। **To speak one fair**—To address him courteously; মিষ্টবাক্যে বলা। **To stand fair with**—(অপ্রঃ) কাহারও অনুগ্রহভাজন হইয়া থাকা।

fair (fār), *n.* A gathering of buyers and sellers at a place at a fixed season; মেলা। **Fancy fair**—সখের মেলা, মোহন-মেলা, আনন্দ-বাজার, রুচির মেলা (আঃ বঃ)। **Fair'-ing,** *n.* A present bought at a fair; মেলায় ক্রীত উপহার দ্রব্য। **After the fair, A day after the fair**—Too late; মেলা ভাঙ্গিলে, অর্থাৎ সময় অতীত হইলে।

fair'-ly̆ (fār-), *adv.* 1. Honestly; justly; legitimately; সাধুতার সহিত; ন্যায্যভাবে; বৈধভাবে। 2. Properly; suitably; "His time *fairly*......employed"; উপযুক্তরূপে; সমীচীনরূপে, সমুচিতরূপে, যথোচিতরূপে; যথার্থ। 3. Clearly; plainly; স্পষ্টরূপে; সরলভাবে। 4. Completely; "We were *fairly* in the trap"; সম্পূর্ণরূপে। 5. Moderately, মধ্যমরকম, মাঝারি গোছের, একরূপ। **Fairly beside himself**—একেবারে আত্মহারা।

fair'-y̆ (fār-), *n.* & *adj.* 1. A small supernatural being with magical power; পরী। ***Adj.*** 1. Pertaining to fairies; like fairies; পরী-সম্বন্ধীয়; পরীতুল্য। 2. Given by fairies; as, *fairy* money; পরীদত্ত। 3. Imaginary; "*fairy* isles"; কাল্পনিক। **—dom, —hood,** *ns.* **—i-ly,** *adv.* **—ism,** *n.* Belief in fairies; পরীতে বিশ্বাস। **Fairy-land** —পরীরাজ্য, পরীস্থান, মায়ারাজ্য। **Fairy-money**—পরীপ্রদত্ত অর্থ, —যাহা অচিরেই শুষ্কপত্রে পরিণত হয়। **Fairy-rings or circles**—চতুষ্পার্শ্ববর্তী তৃণ হইতে বিভিন্নবর্ণের তৃণবলয়, বৃদ্ধিবলয় (সাঃ পঃ)। **Fairy's hair** — হংসরাজ (খোরী), হংসপদী (ঐ)। **Fairy tale**—রূপকথা। **Fairy-sparks** — গলিত কাষ্ঠ, মৎস্য বা অন্য পদার্থ হইতে নির্গত ফুস্ফুরক জ্যোতিঃ। **Fairy-stone** — শিলীভূত মৎস্য বিশেষ; অগ্নিপ্রস্তর নির্মিত বাণাগ্র।

fait accompli, (*F.*), *n.* An accomplished fact; a thing already done; নির্দ্ধারিত বিষয়; নিষ্পন্ন বিষয়।

faith (fāth), *n.* 1. Confidence; trust, (with *in*); বিশ্বাস; প্রত্যয়। 2. A system of religious truths; as, the Christian *faith*; ধর্ম্ম। 3. (*Theol.*) Belief in the truths of religion; ধর্ম্মবিশ্বাস। 4. Trust in Christ; খৃষ্টে বিশ্বাস। 5. Belief founded on testimony or authority; প্রমাণ বা প্রামাণ্যের উপর প্রতিষ্ঠিত বিশ্বাস। 6. Fidelity; বিশ্বস্ততা, নিষ্ঠা, আনুরক্তি। 7. Promise; as, to violate one's *faith*; প্রতিজ্ঞা, সত্য। **Faith'-ful,** *adj.* 1. Loyal; as, a *faithful* wife; conscientious; অনুরক্ত, নিষ্ঠ, পতিব্রতা; ধর্ম্ম-বুদ্ধিসঙ্গত। 2. Trustworthy; true to fact or original; accurate; বিশ্বাসযোগ্য, বিশ্বসনীয়; যথার্থ; ঠিক, অবিকল। **Faith'-ful-ly,** *adv.* 1. In a faithful manner; exactly; যথাযথরূপে; অবিকলভাবে। 2. Sincerely; loyally; বিশ্বস্তভাবে, সরলভাবে, অকপটভাবে; নিষ্ঠার সহিত। **Faith'-ful-ness,** *n.* **Faith'-less,** *adj.* 1. Without faith; বিশ্বাসবিহীন, অবিশ্বাসী। 2. Not believing in God or religion, esp. in Christianity; নাস্তিক, ধর্ম্মবিশ্বাসহীন, খৃষ্টধর্ম্মে অবিশ্বাসী। 3. False; perfidious; সত্যভঙ্গকারী, অবিশ্বাসী; বিশ্বাসঘাতক। 4. Deceptive; unreliable; প্রতারণাশীল; অবিশ্বাসযোগ্য। **Faith'-less-ly,** *adv.* **Faith'-less-ness,** *n.* Bad faith intent to deceive; বিশ্বাসঘাতকতা; প্রতারণার অভিপ্রায়। **Faith-cure**—Faith-healing; প্রার্থনা দ্বারা রোগ-চিকিৎসার প্রণালীবিশেষ, শ্রদ্ধা-চিকিৎসা (হিঃ কোঃ); উক্তপ্রকার চিকিৎসাদ্বারা রোগের প্রতিকার। **Faith Philosophy** — ঈশ্বরাপরোক্ষবাদ (হিঃ কোঃ)। **Faith-worthy** — Trust-worthy; বিশ্বাসযোগ্য। **By my faith**—Verily; ধর্ম্মতঃ, সত্যসত্য। **In good faith**—With sincerity; honestly; সরলভাবে; সাধুভাবে। **Defender of the Faith**—See under DEFENDER. **Father of the faithful**—মুসলমানদিগের খলিফা; এব্রাহম। **Good-faith**—Honesty of intention; সদভিপ্রায়। **On the faith of**—In reliance on the security of; কাহারও জামিনের উপর নির্ভর করিয়া। **Punic faith**—Treachery; বিশ্বাসঘাতকতা। [Punic অথবা কার্থেজবাসিগণ রোমানদিগের সহিত বিশ্বাসঘাতকতা করিয়াছিল বলিয়া *Punic faith* বলিতে

বিশ্বাস-ঘাতকতা বুঝায়।] **The faith**—The true religion, esp. Christianity ; সত্যধর্ম্ম, বিশেষভাবে খৃষ্টধর্ম্ম। **The faithfuls**—Believers, esp. Mahammadans ; বিশ্বাসিগণ, বিশেষতঃ মুসলমানগণ। **To break faith**—প্রতিজ্ঞা ভঙ্গ করা, সত্যভঙ্গ করা। **To deal faithfully with**—To speak home-truths to or of ; কাহাকে বা কাহারো সম্বন্ধে আঁতে ঘা দিয়া কথা বলা। **To give, pledge, keep** or **violate one's faith**—To give, pledge, keep or violate one's promise ; সত্য বাক্য প্রদান করা, সত্যরক্ষা করা, সত্য লঙ্ঘন করা। **To pin one's faith to** or **upon**—To believe implicitly ; অটল বিশ্বাস করা। **To promise faithfully** — To promise emphatically ; দৃঢ়ভাবে প্রতিজ্ঞা করা।

fāke, *v. t.* & *n.* (*Naut.*) To coil or fold as a rope etc. ; (নৌ বিদ্যা) কাছি গুটাইয়া বা কুণ্ডলী পাকাইয়া রাখা। ***Noun.*** A single coil of a rope etc. ; কাছির এক একটী পাক বা কুণ্ডলী।

fāke, *v. t.* & *n.* **1.** (*Slang*) To steal ; (ইতরভাষায়) চুরি করা, ছিঁচকে চুরি করা। **2.** (*Slang*) To make so as to hide (its) defects, (with *up*) ; as, a horse *faked up* for sale ; (ইতরভাষায়) চালাকি করিয়া খুঁত প্রভৃতি ঢাকা। ***Noun.*** A faking ; something faked up ; a cooked report ; প্রতারণার উদ্দেশ্যে কৃত্রিমকরণ, প্রতারণাপূর্ব্বক খুঁত প্রভৃতি ঢাকন ; যাহার বা যে বস্তুর খুঁত প্রভৃতি ঢাকিয়া দেওয়া হইয়াছে ; সাজানো বা রং চড়ানো খবর।

fâ-kir' (-kēr), *n.* A dervish ; a yogi ; ফকির, দরবেশ ; যোগী। **–ism,** *n.* ফকিরী।

făl'-bâ-lâ, *n.* A trimming or flounce ; পোষাকের ঝালর।

făl'-cāte, *adj.* (*Anat., bot.* & *zool.*) Bent or hooked like a sickle ; (শারীর-সংস্থান বিদ্যা, উদ্ভিদ-বিদ্যা এবং প্রাণি-বিদ্যা) কাস্তের মতন বাঁকা। **–cat-ed,** *adj.* (*Astron.* said of the moon etc.) Hooked ; (জ্যোতির্বিজ্ঞান, চন্দ্র অথবা অন্যান্য গ্রহসম্বন্ধে) বক্র।

făl'-chion (-shŭn), *n.* A short crooked sword ; a scimitar ; ক্ষুদ্র খড়্গ বিশেষ ; খড়্গা দা।

făl'-ci-fórm, *adj.* Sickle-shaped ; কাস্তের ন্যায় বক্র।

fal'-con (fä-kn), *n.* **1.** A small bird of prey ; শিকারী শ্যেন পক্ষী। **2.** A hawk of any kind trained to sport, (applied only to the

Falcon.

female birds) ; বাজ পক্ষী। **–er,** *n.* One who breeds and trains, or sports with, falcons ; one who hunts with hawks ; শ্যেনজীবী (মঃ সং), শ্যেনপালক ; শ্যেনদ্বারা মৃগয়াকারী। **–ry,** *n.* The art of training falcons ; the sport of hunting with falcons ; শ্যেনপক্ষীকে শিক্ষিতকরণ ; শ্যেনপক্ষী দ্বারা মৃগয়া, শ্যেন পক্ষী দ্বারা অপর পক্ষিশিকার। **Falcon-eyed**—শ্যেন-চক্ষু, তীক্ষ্ণদৃষ্ট।

făl'-cō-nĕt, *n.* A small cannon ; ষোড়শ শতাব্দীর একপ্রকার ছোট কামান।

făl'-dē-răl, *n.* A gew-gaw ; a trifle ; খেলনা, ফটকীনাটকী ; অকিঞ্চিৎকর জিনিষ।

făld-stool, *n.* **1.** A bishop's armless chair ; খৃষ্টীয় ধর্ম্মাধ্যক্ষের আসন। **2.** A desk at which the litany is read ; যে গড়ানিয়া মেজের উপর পুস্তক রাখিয়া প্রার্থনা-বিশেষ পাঠ করা হয়।

Fă-lêr'-ni-ăn, *adj.* & *n.* Pertaining to Falernus in Italy ; ইতালীর অন্তর্গত জেলাবিশেষ সম্বন্ধীয়। ***Noun.*** A wine of ancient Campania ; প্রাচীন ক্যাম্পেনিয়া প্রদেশের মদ্যবিশেষ।

făll, *v. i.* **1.** To drop down ; as, a fruit *falls* from a tree ; to hang or depend freely ; as, a coat or hair *falls* gracefully ; অধঃপতিত হওয়া, পতন হওয়া, পতিত হওয়া, পড়া ; ঝুলিয়া পড়া। **2.** To drop from an erect posture ; as, a worshipper *falls* on his knees ; প্রণত হওয়া। **3.** To flow, (with *into*) ; as, a river *falls into* a lake ; প্রবাহিত হইয়া পড়া। **4.** To lose high position, good name, etc. ; as, statesmen *fall* ; (of women) to lose chastity ; উচ্চপদ ভ্রষ্ট হওয়া ; (স্ত্রীলোকের পক্ষে) ভ্রষ্টা হওয়া, সতীত্ব হারান। **5.** To be uttered ; to drop ; as, words *fall* from his lips ; উচ্চারিত হওয়া ; নির্গত হওয়া। **6.** To die by violence (as in a battle) ; (রণ-ক্ষেত্রে) পতিত হওয়া (মরা)। **7.** To be born, as the young of certain animals ; প্রসূত হওয়া। **8.** To droop, as the eyes etc. ; আনত হওয়া। **9.** To sound less loud ; as, a voice *falls* ; অপেক্ষাকৃত অনুচ্চ হওয়া, মন্দীভূত হওয়া। **10.** To be overthrown or captured ; as, a fortress *falls* ; বিপর্য্যস্ত হওয়া, বন্দী হওয়া, ধ্বংসপ্রাপ্ত হওয়া, বিধ্বংস হওয়া। **11.** To subside ; to ebb ; as, a storm or tide *falls* ; শান্ত হওয়া, থামা ; ভাটা পড়া। **12.** To become feeble or faint ; as, hope rises and *falls* ; দুর্ব্বল হওয়া, ক্ষীণ হওয়া। **13.** To be entangled ; to stumble ; as, to *fall* into a difficulty or error ; জড়িত হওয়া ; পদস্খলিত হইয়া পড়া, হোঁচট খাইয়া পড়া। **14.** To slope ; "The ground of the plateau *falls* towards this strait" ; ঢালু হওয়া, প্রবণ হওয়া। **15.** To come ; to occur ; "Easter *fell* early that year" ;

পড়া, হওয়া, আসা ; ঘটা। 16. To decrease, as price etc. ; to suffer a decline in price etc. ; as, the market is *falling* ; বাজার পড়া ; পড়্তি হওয়া। 17. To assume an appearance of dejection, shame or disappointment, etc. ; as, his face *fell* ; নৈরাশ্যপূর্ণ হওয়া, বিরস ভাব ধারণ করা, লজ্জিত ভাব ধারণ করা। 18. To begin ; as, to *fall* a-laughing ; আরম্ভ করা। 19. To belong or appertain (*to*) ; to be suitable ; অন্তর্ভূত হওয়া, সংসৃষ্ট হওয়া ; উপযোগী হওয়া। 20. To come down in fragments ; as, a house *falls* ; ভাঙ্গিয়া পড়া। 21. To pass or be transferred by inheritance, distribution, etc. ; as, the estate *fell* to his widow ; উত্তরাধিকার সূত্র বা দানপত্রাদি দ্বারা আগত বা হস্তান্তরিত হওয়া। 22. To come in a fitting manner or order ; as, this event *falls* into the third chapter ; উপযুক্তরূপে বা যথাক্রমে আসা। 23. To have its place ; as, the accent *falls* on the second syllable ; পড়া। 24. To be divisible, (with *into*) ; as, this subject *falls into* three parts ; বিভাজ্য হওয়া। 25. To swoop ; as, vengeance *fell* ; ছোঁ মারা, আপতিত হওয়া। 26. To revert ; to lapse ; as, revenues *fall* to the Crown ; প্রত্যাবৃত্ত হওয়া ; খাস হইয়া যাওয়া। 27. To take such a direction ; as, his eyes *fell* upon me ; অভিমুখীন হওয়া। 28. To come by chance ; as, the cost *falls* to you ; ঘটনাক্রমে পড়া, আগত হওয়া। **Fall'en,** *adj.* Dropped ; degraded ; lost to virtue ; ruined ; decreased ; অবনত ; পতিত ; ভ্রষ্ট ; ধ্বংসপ্রাপ্ত ; হ্রাসপ্রাপ্ত। **A lion fell to his rifle**—তাহার বন্দুকের গুলিতে একটী সিংহ হত হইয়াছিল। **Fall back, Fall edge**—No matter what may happn ; যা' হবার তা' হউক, যৎভবেৎ তদ্‌ভবিষ্যতি। **To fall aboard of**—(*Naut.*) To collide with another vessel ; (নৌ-বিদ্যা) অন্য পোতের সহিত সংঘর্ষ লাগা। **To fall across**—To meet by chance ; দৈবক্রমে সাক্ষাৎ হওয়া, ঘটনাক্রমে দেখা হওয়া। **To fall among**—To come into the midst of ; মধ্যে আসিয়া পড়া। **To fall a prey, sacrifice** or **victim to**—To be destroyed by ; কাহারও দ্বারা বিনষ্ট হওয়া। **To fall a-rowing, a-laughing, etc.**—To begin rowing, laughing, etc. ; দাঁড় টানিতে আরম্ভ করা, হাসিতে আরম্ভ করা, ইত্যাদি। **To fall astern**—(*Naut.*) To lessen a ship's way so as to allow another to go ahead of her ; to be driven backward or to remain behind as a ship ; (নৌ-বিদ্যা) অন্য জাহাজকে আগে যাইতে দেওয়ার জন্য কোন জাহাজের গতি হ্রাস করা ; পশ্চাদ্দিকে চালিত হওয়া, পশ্চাতে পড়া। **To fall at**—To be engaged ; নিযুক্ত হওয়া। **To fall away**—To decline gradually ; to fade ; to languish ; "Colour *falls away* by such slow degrees" ; অপকর্ষ প্রাপ্ত হওয়া ; ক্ষীণ হওয়া ; অবসন্ন হওয়া, অলসাঙ্গ হওয়া। To grow lean ; কৃশ হওয়া, কাহিল হওয়া। To revolt ; বিদ্রোহী হওয়া। To perish ; "How can the soul *fall away* into nothing" ; বিনষ্ট হওয়া। To apostatize ; স্বধর্ম্মত্যাগী হওয়া। **To fall away from**—To abandon ; as, *to fall away from* a person ; পরিত্যাগ করা। **To fall back**—To retreat ; to give way ; to go from good to bad ; পশ্চাৎপদ হওয়া ; হটিয়া আসা ; ক্রমশঃ অধঃপতন হওয়া। To fail of performing a promise etc. ; প্রতিজ্ঞাদি পালন করিতে না পারা। **To fall back upon**—To have recourse to (some expedient or resource in reserve) ; সর্ব্বশেষ অবলম্বনস্বরূপ কোন উপায়ের আশ্রয় গ্রহণ করা। (*Mil.*) To retreat for safety to, as a stronger position etc. ; (সামরিক শাস্ত্র) নিরাপদ্ হওয়ার জন্য (অধিকতর সুরক্ষিত স্থানে) হটিয়া আসা। **To fall behind**—To be passed by ; to be in arrears ; পিছে পড়া, পশ্চাদ্‌বর্ত্তী হওয়া ; বাকী থাকা। **To fall by**—To be lost ; হারাইয়া যাওয়া। To be afflicted, esp. in childbirth ; যন্ত্রণাক্লিষ্ট হওয়া (বিশেষতঃ সন্তান প্রসবকালে)। **To fall by one's rest**—Not to sleep ; নিদ্রা না যাওয়া। **To fall calm**—To become calm ; as, the wind or sea *falls calm* ; শান্ত হওয়া। **To fall dead**—To strike the ground as a golf-ball so as to roll slightly or not at all ; (ক্রীড়াকন্দুক সম্পর্কে) ভূমিতে আহত হইয়া স্থির থাকা বা অল্পদূর মাত্র গড়াইয়া যাওয়া। **To fall dead from the press**—Books are said *to fall dead from the press,* when they are not sold after being published ; (পুস্তকের পক্ষে) প্রকাশিত হওয়ার পর বিক্রীত না হওয়া। **To fall down**—To prostrate one's self in worship or supplication ; "I *fell down* before the Lord" ; সাষ্টাঙ্গে প্রণিপাত করা। To come to the ground ; ভূপতিত হওয়া, সটান হইয়া পড়া। **To fall dumb**—To become dumb ; মূক হওয়া। **To fall flat**—To fail of the intended effect ; to produce no result or interest ; as, his speech *fell flat* ; ফলপ্রদানে অসমর্থ হওয়া ; নিষ্ফল হওয়া, নীরস বোধ হওয়া, চিত্তাকর্ষক না হওয়া, অনুরাগের উদ্রেগ না করা। **To fall foul of**—(*Naut.*) To collide with, (of ships) ; সংঘর্ষ লাগা। To attack ; আক্রমণ করা। To quarrel with ; কলহ করা, ঝগড়া করা। **To fall from**—To recede from (an engagement or agreement etc.) ; not to adhere to ; কোন কিছু হইতে পশ্চাৎপদ হওয়া ;

অনুরক্ত না থাকা। To give up or renounce; to cease from; to revolt; পরিত্যাগ করা, বর্জ্জন করা; বিরত হওয়া; বিদ্রোহী হওয়া। **To fall from grace to sin**—পাপপথে পদার্পণ করা। **To fall home**—(*Naut.*) To curve inwards; (নৌবিদ্যা) ভিতরের দিকে বাঁকিয়া যাওয়া (জাহাজের তক্তা বা পার্শ্বের উপরিভাগের অংশ সমূহ সম্বন্ধে)। **To fall in**—To agree; to concur; as, he *fell in* with my views; সম্মত হওয়া; একমত হওয়া। To sink or fall inwards; as, the roof *fell in*; বসিয়া যাওয়া। (*Mil.*) To take one's assigned place in a line; (also) to cause to take place in a line; as, *to fall in* on the right; নির্দ্দিষ্ট স্থান পরিগ্রহ করা; নির্দ্দিষ্ট স্থান পরিগ্রহ করান। To come to an end; to lapse; as, the lease has recently *fallen in*; শেষ হওয়া, অবসান হওয়া; মিয়াদ ফুরান। To become due; as, a debt or rent *falls in* on the 10th; দেয় হওয়া। To become available, as land etc.; প্রাপ্য হওয়া। To droop; as, his eyes *fell in*; আনত হওয়া। To subside, as a river after rain; নামিয়া যাওয়া। To come into the possession of the owner after a lease; পাট্টার মিয়াদ শেষ হওয়ার পর মালিকের অধিকারে আসা। **To fall in love**—To become enamoured of; প্রেমে পড়া, প্রেমাসক্ত হওয়া। **To fall into**—(*Lit.* & *fig.*) To take as one's place; to take one's place in, as the ranks etc.; (শব্দানুযায়ী ও লক্ষণায়) স্বস্থান পরিগ্রহ করা; পদমর্য্যাদানুসারে স্বীয় স্থান পরিগ্রহ করা। To engage in, as a talk etc.; to begin the discussion of, as a subject etc.; কোন কার্য্য-সাধনে প্রবৃত্ত হওয়া; কোন বিষয়ের মীমাংসায় প্রবৃত্ত হওয়া। To comply with; to agree to; অনুরোধ রক্ষা করা; সম্মত হওয়া, রাজি হওয়া। To get into, as a habit etc.; অভ্যাসাদির অধীন হওয়া। **To fall into oblivion**—To come to be forgotten; বিস্মৃতিগর্ভে নিমজ্জিত হওয়া। **To fall into one's hand**—To pass suddenly into one's control or ownership; কাহারও হাতে পড়া, কাহারও অধিকারে আসা। **To fall in two** — To separate; পৃথক হওয়া, বিচ্ছিন্ন হওয়া। To bear a child, (*rare*); প্রসব করা (অপ্রঃ)। **To fall in upon** — To come upon unexpectedly; to meet or visit unexpectedly; হঠাৎ আপতিত হওয়া; অপ্রত্যাশিতভাবে সাক্ষাৎ হওয়া, ঘটনাক্রমে দেখা হওয়া। **To fall in with** — To meet with accidentally; as, to *fall in with* a friend or ship; হঠাৎ সাক্ষাৎ হওয়া। To agree with; একমত হওয়া। To come near, or discover, as a land; (স্থল প্রভৃতির) নিকটে আসা বা আবিষ্কার করা। To comply; to accede to; as, to *fall in with* one's project or views; সম্মত হওয়া; স্বীকার করা। To coincide with; সম্পূর্ণরূপে মিলা। **To fall off**—To drop; as, fruits *fall off* when ripe; খসিয়া পড়া, স্খলিত হওয়া, বৃন্তচ্যুত হওয়া। To withdraw; to separate; as, friends *fall off* in adversity; to apostatize; to revolt; সরিয়া পড়া; পৃথক্ হওয়া; স্বধর্ম্মচ্যুত হওয়া; বিদ্রোহী হওয়া। To perish; to become obsolete; as, words *fall off* by disuse; মৃত হওয়া; অপ্রচলিত হওয়া। To decrease; to degenerate; to become less interesting; as, a magazine or its circulation *falls off*; হ্রাস পাওয়া; অপকর্ষ প্রাপ্ত হওয়া; অপেক্ষাকৃত নীরস হওয়া। To decline in health or strength; স্বাস্থ্য বা বলহানি হওয়া। **To fall on**—To begin eagerly and suddenly; to meet with; to light upon; as, to *fall on* evil days; হঠাৎ আগ্রহের সহিত আরম্ভ করা; সাক্ষাৎ করা; পড়া, পতিত হওয়া। To attack; to join battle; আক্রমণ করা; যুদ্ধে যোগদান করা। **To fall on (or upon) one's feet or legs**—To come well out of a difficulty; কোনও হাঙ্গামা হইতে সৌভাগ্যক্রমে নিষ্কৃতি পাওয়া। To have marked good luck; বিশেষ সৌভাগ্যের অধিকারী হওয়া। **To fall on one's sword**—To come down on one's sword in suicide; নিজের তরবারীর উপর পতিত হইয়া আত্মহত্যা করা। **To fall out**—To quarrel; বিবাদ করা, কলহ করা। To come to pass; ঘটা। (*Mil.*) To leave the ranks; (সামরিক-শাস্ত্র) সৈন্যদল ত্যাগ করা। To turn out; to prove to be; as, it will *fall out* for the best; ফলে দাঁড়ান; প্রমাণিত হওয়া। **To fall out of**—To give up, as a habit etc.; অভ্যাসাদি ত্যাগ করা। **To fall over**—To revolt; to desert from one side to another; বিদ্রোহী হওয়া; একপক্ষ ত্যাগ করিয়া অপরপক্ষে যোগদান করা। **To fall short**—To be deficient or insufficient; as, the corn *falls short*; ন্যুন হওয়া, অপ্রচুর হওয়া, অকুলান হওয়া। Not to go far enough, as a shot or missile; গুলি বা প্রহরণ যতটা দুরে যাওয়া আবশ্যক ততটা দুরে না যাওয়া। **To fall short of**—To fail to obtain; to fail in performing; as, to *fall short of* one's duty; লাভ করিতে অক্ষম হওয়া; সম্পাদনে অসমর্থ হওয়া। To fail of attaining to (a certain amount, degree, etc.); "They *fell short of* the number they told us of"; বিশেষ সংখ্যা বা মাত্রা অপেক্ষা ন্যূন হওয়া। **To fall through**—To come to nothing; to fail; as, the project *has fallen through*; পণ্ড হওয়া; নিষ্ফল হওয়া, বিফল হওয়া। **To fall to**—To begin hastily and eagerly ; to set to ; as, *to fall to* work or working ; to begin eating ; তাড়াতাড়ি আগ্রহের সহিত আরম্ভ করা ; প্রবৃত্ত হওয়া ; আহার করিতে আরম্ভ করা, খাইতে সুরু করা। To come to blows ; হাতাহাতি হওয়া, মারামারি লাগা। **To fall to one's lot**—To happen to one without his planning; ভাগ্যে ঘটা, অদৃষ্টে পতিত হওয়া। **To fall to the ground**—To come to nothing ; to be abandoned, as a plan, project, etc. ; পণ্ড হওয়া, নিষ্ফল হওয়া ; পরিত্যক্ত হওয়া। **To fall under**—To come under or within the limit of ; অন্তর্ভুক্ত হওয়া। To become the subject of ; as, it does not *fall under* human observation ; বিষয়ীভূত হওয়া। To be ranged ; as, it does not *fall under* this class ; শ্রেণীভুক্ত হওয়া। **To fall under one's notice**—To be noticed by one ; কাহারো চোখে পড়া, কাহারো লক্ষ্যের বিষয়ীভূত হওয়া। **To fall upon** (or **on**)—See TO FALL ON. To attack ; আক্রমণ করা, আপতিত হওয়া। To have recourse to ; আশ্রয় গ্রহণ করা, শরণ লওয়া। **To fall within**—To be included in ; অন্তর্ভুক্ত হওয়া। **Wicket falls**—The batsman is out ; (ক্রীকেট ক্রীড়ায়) ব্যাটধারী "আউট" হইয়াছে।

fall, *n.* 1. The act of falling ; a descent ; as, a *fall* from a tree : a *fall* of rain etc. ; পতন ; পাত। 2. Downfall ; loss of greatness ; degradation ; as, the *fall* of the Mogul Empire ; অধঃপতন ; মহিমাহানি ; অবনতি, পতন। 3. Ruin ; overthrow ; as, they conspire thy *fall* ; death ; ধ্বংস ; উচ্ছেদ ; মৃত্যু। 4. That which falls ; the quantity that falls or has fallen ; as, 1 inch-*fall* of rain :- a *fall* of fruits ; পতিত বস্তু ; পতিত বস্তুর পরিমাণ। 5. A slope or declivity ; ঢালু, প্রবণতা। 6. Diminution or decrease in price etc ; মূল্যের হ্রাস। 7. (*Pl.*) A cataract ; a cascade ; as, the *falls* of Niagra ; জলপ্রপাত ; নির্ঝর, প্রস্রবণ (সাঃ পঃ), ঝরণা (ঐ)। 8. The act of felling, as trees etc. ; কর্ত্তন, ছেদন। 9. The surrender of a beseiged fortress or town ; as, the *fall* of Sebastopol ; অবরুদ্ধ দুর্গ বা নগরীর পতন। 10. Cadence ; subsidence ; as, the rise and *fall* of the waves or voice etc. ; a sinking ; as, a *fall* of mercury in thermometer ; কণ্ঠস্বরের বিরাম বা স্বরপতন ; বিরাম ; পতন। 11. A lapse into sin ; a moral ruin ; "The moral *fall* of a fellow creature" ; the apostasy of rebellious angels ; the act of Adam and Eve in eating fruits of the forbidden tree ; ধর্ম্মচ্যুতি ; নৈতিক সর্ব্বনাশ ; ঈশ্বরদ্রোহী দেবদূতগণের ভ্রষ্টতা ; আদম ও ইভা কর্ত্তৃক নিষিদ্ধ তরুর ফল ভক্ষণ। 12. Falling off (of leaves etc.) ; স্খলন। 13. Autumn ; শরদৃতু, শরৎকাল। 14. Discharge of a river etc. into a sea, lake, etc. ; as, the *fall* of the Ganges into the Bay of Bengal ; নদীর সমুদ্রাদিতে পতন। 15. Tumbling or dropping from an erect posture ; "By a *fall* in his flight" ; পতন। 16. Birth, as of lambs etc. ; the number of lambs etc. born ; মেষশাবক প্রভৃতির জন্ম ; প্রসূত মেষশাবকাদির সংখ্যা। 17. Extent of descent ; the distance through which anything falls ; as, the water of a stream has a *fall* of 5 ft. ; পতনের পরিমাণ ; যে স্থান অতিক্রম করিয়া কোন কিছু পতিত হয় তাহার দূরত্ব। 18. (*Wrestling*) A bout at wrestling ; (মল্লযুদ্ধ) কুস্তিলড়ন ; পাছাড়লড়ন। 19. A woman's veil ; স্ত্রীলোকের অবগুণ্ঠন, ঘোমটা। **Fall-trap** — একপ্রকার ফাঁদ—যাহা পশ্বাদির উপর পতিত হয়। **The fall, The fall of man**—আদিমানব আদমের ঈশ্বরাদেশ লঙ্ঘন হেতু মানব জাতির মধ্যে প্রথম পাপের প্রবেশ। **The fall of the leaf** or **year**—যে ঋতুতে বৃক্ষ হইতে পত্র চ্যুত হয়, শরদৃতু। **To try a fall**—To try a bout at wrestling ; কুস্তি লড়া।

făll'-ing, *p. adj.* & *n.* ধ্বংসমান, ভ্রশ্যমান, পতিষ্যমাণ। ***Noun.*** (*Med.*) Displacement of a part ; as, the *falling* of the uterus ; (ভৈষজ্য-শাস্ত্র) স্থানচ্যুতি। **Falling-off**—Degeneration ; deterioration ; decrease ; অধঃপতন ; অপকর্ষ ; হ্রাস। **Falling-sickness**—মৃগী রোগ। **Falling-star**—উল্কাপিণ্ড, উল্কা (হিঃ কোঃ)। **Falling-stone**—A portion of an exploded meteor ; বিদীর্ণ উল্কার খণ্ড। **Falling-tide**—ভাটা।

făl'-lă-çy̆, *n.* 1. (*Log.*) An unsound argument or mode of arguing ; sophism ; a flaw that vitiates a syllogism ; any of the types to which such flaws are reducible ; (তর্ক-বিজ্ঞান) ভ্রান্তযুক্তি, অপসিদ্ধান্ত ; কুতর্ক ; আভাস ; হেত্বাভাস (হিঃ কোঃ), নিগ্রহস্থান (ঐ) 2. Deceptiveness ; deceitfulness that which misleads the e or mind ; deception ; as, t *fallacy* of our senses ; ভ্রান্তিজনকতা; প্রতারণাপূর্ণতা; ভ্রান্তিজনক বিষয়; ছলনা। 3. An erroneous idea or notion ; delusion ; error ; "We being...... obnoxious to *fallacy* in our...... judgments" ; ভ্রমপূর্ণ ভাব বা ধারণা, ভ্রান্ত ধারণা ; ভ্রান্তি, মোহ ; ভ্রম। 4. Unsoundness ; delusiveness ; disappointing character ; as, the *fallacy* of argument, beliefs, etc. ; ভ্রমসঙ্কুলতা ; মোহজনকতা ; নৈরাশ্যজনক ভাব। **—la'-cious,** *adj.* 1. Pertaining to or embodying a fallacy ; হেত্বাভাস সম্পর্কীয়, হেত্বাভাসাত্মক। 2. Deceptive ; প্রতারণাশীল। 3. Causing disappointment ;

delusive ; as, a *fallacious* hope ; নৈরাশ্যজনক ; ভ্রান্তিজনক, মোহজনক। **–la'-cious-ly,** *adv.* **–la'-cious-ness,** *n.* **Fallacy of many questions**—অনেকপ্রশ্নাত্মক-হেত্বাভাস। **Logical fallacy** — শব্দহেত্বাভাস (হিঃ কোঃ), তর্কাভাস (ঐ)। **Material fallacy**—বাস্তবহেত্বাভাস (হিঃ কোঃ), উদাহরণশুদ্ধি (ঐ), ব্যাপ্যাভাস (ঐ)। **Pathetic fallacy** — See under PATHETIC.

fal'-li-ble (-bl), *adj.* Liable to error or be deceived ; ভ্রমযোগ্য। **–bil'-i-ty,** *n.* Liability to mistake or deception ; ভ্রান্তি, ভ্রমশীলতা। **–bly,** *adv.*

fal'-low (-lō), *adj., n.* & *v. t.* Left untilled or unsowed for a time ; uncultivated ; as, *fallow* land ; পতিত (কিছুকাল যাবৎ) ; অকৃষ্ট। ***Noun.*** **1.** A land that has been lain a year or more untilled or unsown after having been ploughed ; একবৎসরের কিম্বা তদধিকের অকৃষ্ট এবং পতিত ০ জমি, অনুপ্ত জমি। **2.** State of being fallow ; পতিত অবস্থা। ***Verb t.*** To break up (land) for sowing or destroy weeds ; আবাদ করা।

fȧl'-low (-lō), *adj.* Of a brownish yellow colour ; pale yellow, (now only in *fallow deer*) ; পিঙ্গলাভ পীত-বর্ণ, মৃদু পীত-বর্ণ ; আপীত। **Fallow deer**—একপ্রকার আপীতবর্ণের হরিণ। **Fallow flinch**—ইয়ুরোপ দেশীয় ক্ষুদ্র পক্ষিবিশেষ।

false (fāls), *adj.* & *adv.* **1.** Lying ; given to deceit ; dishonest ; অসত্যভাষী, মিথ্যাবাদী, অনৃতভাষী ; প্রতারণাপর ; অসাধু। **2.** Not true ; not conformable to fact ; as, a *false* deposition ; অসত্য, অলীক ; মিথ্যা। **3.** Unfaithful ; treacherous ; as, a *false* friend : *false* to promises and vows ; অবিশ্বাসী ; বিশ্বাসঘাতক। **4.** Counterfeit ; hypocritical ; not genuine ; as, *false* tears or coin : a *false* prophet ; artificial, as teeth etc. ; কৃত্রিম, জাল ; কপট ; নকল,মেকি ; ঝুঁটা। **4.** Not well-founded ; erroneous ; incorrect ; wrong ; as, a *false* claim : a *false* conclusion ; অমূলক ; অশুদ্ধ ; ভ্রান্ত ; ভ্রমাত্মক। **5.** Pseudo ; as, *false* acacia ; তথাকথিত। **6.** Deceptive ; as, a *false* miror ; ভ্রান্তিজনক। ***Adv.*** **1.** Wrongly ; incorrectly ; ভুলে ; অশুদ্ধভাবে। **2.** Faithlessly ; treacherously ; as, to play one *false* ; অবিশ্বস্ততার সহিত ; বিশ্বাসঘাতকের মত। **3.** Not truly or honestly ; মিছামিছি ; অসাধুভাবে। **False'-ly,** *adv.* In a false manner ; not truly ; erroneously ; treacherously ; মিথ্যাভাবে ; অসত্যভাবে ; ভ্রান্তভাবে ; বিশ্বাসঘাতকতার সহিত। **False'-ness,** *n.* State of being false ; false-hood ; want of integrity ; double dealing ; deceitfulness ; treachery ; অলীকতা ; মিথ্যাবাদ, অনৃত ; অসাধুতা ; কপটতা ; প্রতারণশীলতা ; বিশ্বাসঘাতকতা। **False analogy** — সাদৃশ্যাভাস (হিঃ কোঃ)। **False-bottom**—(জাহাজে) শায়িত বিভাজক ফলক। **False cause**—কারণাভাস (হিঃ কোঃ)। **False-colours** — (শত্রুকে প্রতারিত করার উদ্দেশ্যে) যে বিদেশীয় পতাকা উঠান হয়। **False concord** — ব্যাকরণের সূত্রের নিয়ম-ব্যতিক্রম। **False face** — মুখস। **False-faced**—কপট। **False-hearted**—Treacherous ; বিশ্বাসঘাতক। **False imprisonment** — অবৈধভাবে কারাগারে প্রেরণ। **False personation**—প্রতারণার উদ্দেশ্যে অন্য ব্যক্তির নাম গ্রহণ। **False pretence**—ছল, ব্যপদেশ, ওজর। **False pride, shame**—মিথ্যা অহঙ্কার, কৃত্রিম লজ্জা। **False step**—Stumble ; transgression ; পদস্খলন, হোঁচট ; অপরাধ। **False start** — (ঘোড়দৌড়ে) মিথ্যা যাত্রা। **To play one false**—To cheat one ; কাহারও সহিত কপট ব্যবহার করা, কাহাকেও প্রতারণা করা। **To put one in a false position**—মুস্কিলে ফেলা, গোলে ফেলা, এমন অবস্থায় ফেলা যাহাতে কোন ব্যক্তিকে অপ্রস্তুত, অপ্রতিভ বা উপহাসাস্পদ হইতে হয়।

false'-hood (fāls-), *n.* **1.** Want of conformity to fact or truth ; an untrue assertion ; অসত্য, মিথ্যা ; মিথ্যোক্তি। **2.** That which is contrary to fact or truth ; a lie or lies ; lying ; মিথ্যা ; অসত্য ; মিথ্যাকথন, অনৃতভাষণ।

fal'-si-fȳ, *v. t.* **1.** To make false ; মিথ্যা করা। **2.** To misrepresent ; "coldly *falsifying* facts and dates" ; মিথ্যা বর্ণনা করা। **3.** To alter fraudulently ; to tamper with ; as, to *falsify* a record or account etc. ; প্রতারণাপূর্ব্বক পরিবর্ত্তন করা ; অপ্রকৃত করা। **4.** To prove to be false ; "No man can *falsify* any fact stated here" ; মিথ্যা বলিয়া সপ্রমাণ করা। **5.** To babble ; as, to *falsify* a blow etc. ; to disappoint, as hope, fear, etc. ; ব্যর্থ করা ; নিরাশ করা। **6.** To make untrue ; "to *falsify* our standards" ; মিথ্যা করা। **7.** To violate, *(rare)* ; as, to *falsify* one's word or faith ; লঙ্ঘন করা (কচিৎ ব্যবহৃত)। **8.** To counterfeit, *(obs.)* ; জাল করা (অপ্রঃ)। **–fi-ca'-tion,** *n.* **1.** The act of falsifying ; অসত্য বা কৃত্রিমকরণ, মিথ্যাকরণ। **2.** Wilful misrepresentation ; ইচ্ছাপূর্ব্বক মিথ্যাবর্ণন। **3.** A showing anything to be false or erroneous ; মিথ্যাপ্রদর্শন। **–fi-er,** *n.*

fal-sĕt'-tō, *n.* A false voice ; a forced voice above the natural compass ; কৃত্রিম স্বর ; কৃত্রিম উচ্চ স্বর জিল সুর।

fal'-sid'-i-cȧl, *adj.* (Of false images, premonitions, etc.) Illusory ; ভ্রান্তিজনক, মোহজনক।

fals'-ism, *n.* *(Rare)* Self-evident falsity ; স্বতঃসিদ্ধ মিথ্যাবাক্য।

fal'-si-ty, *n.* **1.** The quality of being false; inconformity to truth; falsehood; deceitfulness; অলীকতা; অসত্যতা; মিথ্যা-কথা; প্রতারণশীলতা। **2.** That which is false or untrue; a false assertion; অনৃত, মিথ্যাবিষয়; মিথ্যা উক্তি।

Fal-staff'-i-an, *adj.* Like Shakespeare's fool Falstaff; hence, jovial; humorous; সেক্ষপীয়রের নাটকের (Merry Wives of Windsor and Henry IV) বিদূষক ফলষ্টাফের মত; কৌতুকপ্রিয়, রঙ্গপ্রিয়; পরিহাস-রসিক।

fal'-ter, *v. i., t.* & *n.* **1.** To tremble; to walk with an unsteady gait; টলা; টলিতে টলিতে চলা। **2.** To stammer; to hesitate in speech; তোত্‌লান; কথা বলিতে ইতস্ততঃ করা। **3.** To waver; to lose courage; to give way; দ্বিধা করা; সাহস হারান; ভাঙ্গিয়া পড়া। ***Verb t.*** To utter with hesitation or in a broken manner; ইতস্ততঃ করিয়া বলা, ভাঙ্গা ভাঙ্গা স্বরে কথা বলা, জড়িত স্বরে কথা বলা। ***Noun.*** A faltering; quivering; unsteadiness; তোত্‌লামি; কম্পন; অস্থিরতা। **–ing,** *p. adj.* Hesitating; stammering; দ্বিধাকারী; তোত্‌লা। **–ing-ly,** *adv.* In a faltering or hesitating manner; তোত্‌লাইয়া, ইতস্ততঃ করিয়া, গদ্‌গদ স্বরে।

fame, *n.* **1.** Public report or rumour; জনরব, জনশ্রুতি। **2.** Reputation favourable or unfavourable; যশঃ, খ্যাতি, নাম। **3.** Celebrity; renown; প্রসিদ্ধি; কীর্ত্তি। **Fame'-less,** *adj.* Without renown; অবিখ্যাত, যশোহীন, অপ্রসিদ্ধ। **A house of ill-fame**—বেশ্যালয়।

fame, *v. t.* (*Usu. passive*) **1.** To report correctly; সঠিক ভাবে বিবৃত করা, যথাযথ বর্ণনা করা। **2.** To make famous; বিখ্যাত করা, প্রসিদ্ধ করা।

famed (fāmd), *p. adj.* Renowned; much spoken of; বিখ্যাত; প্রথিত, খ্যাতনামা, প্রসিদ্ধ, প্রথিতনামা।

fa-mil'-iar (-yer), *adj.* & *n.* **1.** Well-acquainted or well-versed in, (foll. by *with*); as, I am *familiar with* the subject; intimate; সুপরিচিত, চিরপরিচিত; ঘনিষ্ঠ, অন্তরঙ্গ। **2.** Well-known; as, it is *familiar* to him; common: current; usual; as, a *familiar* illustration; সুবিদিত, সুবিজ্ঞাত; সাধারণ; প্রচলিত; প্রায়িক, সচরাচর ব্যবহৃত। **3.** (Of animals) Domesticated; tame; (জন্তুসম্পর্কে) গৃহপালিত; পোষা। **4.** Free as among friends; "In his house as *familiar* was he"; too free; "With *familiar* access to his person"; খোলা, সহজ, অবাধ, স্বচ্ছন্দ; অতিশয় খোলা। ***Noun.*** **1.** One long or well acquainted; an intimate; সুপরিচিত ব্যক্তি; অন্তরঙ্গ বন্ধু। **2.** A spirit or demon supposed to attend at a call; অনুগত দানব, বেতাল। **3.** (*R. C. Church*) A person rendering certain services in the Pope's or Bishop's household; রোমান ক্যাথলিক ধর্ম্মসম্রাট্ বা ধর্ম্মাধ্যক্ষের পারিবারিক পরিচারক। **–i-ar'-i-ty,** *n.* **1.** Close intercourse or intimacy (with a person etc.); freedom from ceremony; as, *familiarity* breeds contempt (ঘনিষ্ঠতা হইতে অবজ্ঞা প্রসূত হয়—দ্বিজেন্দ্রনাথ ঠাকুর); ঘনিষ্ঠতা, সৌহার্দ্দ, অন্তরঙ্গতা; স্বচ্ছন্দভাব, মাখামাখি ভাব। **2.** Close acquaintance with, or knowledge of, anything; as, *familiarity* with a subject; সুবিজ্ঞতা, পারদর্শিতা। **–i-za'-tion,** *n.* **–ize,** *v. t.* **1.** To make thoroughly acquainted; as, to *familiarize* one with a book etc.; to make to feel at ease; as, to *familiarize* a friend in one's home; সুপরিচিত করা; নিজ বাটীতে থাকার মত স্বচ্ছন্দ বোধ করান। **2.** To make well known; as, to *familiarize* the idea of liberty; সুপ্রসিদ্ধ করা, প্রখ্যাত করা। **–ly,** *adv.* Intimately; unceremoniously; commonly; সুপরিচিতভাবে, ঘনিষ্ঠভাবে, অন্তরঙ্গভাবে; লৌকিকতার ধার না ধারিয়া; সাধারণভাবে।

fam'-i-ly, *n.* **1.** Members of a household — parents, children, servants, etc.; পরিবার, পরিজন—পিতামাতা, সন্তান, দাসদাসী, ইত্যাদি। **2.** The descendents of one common progenitor; a race; a tribe; as, the *family* of Abraham; lineage; কুল; জাতি; গোষ্ঠী; বংশ। **3.** Honourable or noble descent; as, a man of *family*; সম্ভ্রান্ত বংশ বা সদ্বংশ। **4.** The parents and children alone or a group of relations; পিতামাতা ও সন্তানবর্গ, কুটুম্ববর্গ। **5.** A person's children regarded collectively; as, he has a large *family*; পুত্রকন্যাগণ। **6.** A group of animals or plants, more comprehensive than a genus; জন্তু বা উদ্ভিদের শ্রেণী, বংশ (সাঃ পঃ)। **7.** A group of objects distinguished by common features; as, a *family* of languages; সাধারণ লক্ষণবিশিষ্ট বস্তু সমূহ। **–lism,** *n.* (*Cap.*) Tenets of Familists; প্রেমই একমাত্র ধর্ম্ম—প্রেমের দ্বারাই মানব ঈশ্বরের সহিত সম্মিলিত হয়—এইরূপ মতবাদ। [হলণ্ডবাসী David Toris (1501-56) এই মত প্রবর্ত্তন করেন।] **–list,** *n.* (*Cap.*) A member of the sect called the Family of Love; প্রেমবাদী। **Family Bible**—বৃহৎ পারিবারিক বাইবেল—যাহাতে পরিবারস্থ ব্যক্তিদের জন্ম, মৃত্যু প্রভৃতি ঘটনার বিবরণ লিখিবার জন্য সাদা পাতা থাকে। **Family butcher etc.** — কসাই প্রভৃতি,—যাহারা গৃহস্থদিগকে মাংসাদি বিক্রয় করে (সৈন্য কিংবা ক্লাব প্রভৃতির নিকট নয়)। **Family coach** — পারিবারিক যান [যাহাতে পরিবারের সমস্ত লোক ধরে বা বসা যায়]। **Family Compact**—ফ্রান্স, স্পেন এবং সিসিলীর বুরবোনদিগের

সম্মিলন—ইংলণ্ডের প্রভাব বিস্তারে বাধা প্রদানের উদ্দেশ্যে এই সম্মিলনের প্রতিষ্ঠা হয়। **Family connection**—জন্ম বা বিবাহসূত্রে সম্পর্ক। **Family hotel**—যে ভোজনাগারে পরিবারের জন্য বিশেষ হার নির্দ্দিষ্ট থাকে। **Family living**—কোন পরিবারের প্রধান ব্যক্তির হস্তে যে যাজকীয় বৃত্তি প্রদানের ভার থাকে। **Family man**—স্ত্রীপুত্রবান ব্যক্তি; সংসারী লোক। **Family likeness**—পারিবারিক সাদৃশ্য। **Family tie**—পারিবারিক ঐক্য-বন্ধন, পারিবারিক প্রীতি। **Family tree**—বংশাবলী। **Family name** — বংশনাম (যথা ঘোষ, বসু, চক্রবর্ত্তী প্রভৃতি)। **Family priest**—কুল-পুরোহিত। **Happy family**—বিভিন্ন জাতীয় জন্তুবর্গ,—যাহাদিগকে পোষ মানাইয়া এক পিঞ্জরে আবদ্ধ রাখা হয়। **Holy Family**—চিত্রপটে একত্র অঙ্কিত কুমারী মেরী, যীশু, সেণ্ট যোশেফ এবং সচরাচর সেণ্ট এলিজেবেথ এবং সেণ্ট জন দি ব্যাপটিষ্ট। **Joint family**—একান্নবর্ত্তী পরিবার, অবিভক্ত কুটুম্ব (হিং কো:)। **Family of Love**—Same as FAMILISM (which see.) **Family of nations**—(আন্তর্জাতিক আইন) নীতি, রাজনীতি বা সভ্যতা সম্পর্কে সমোন্নত রাষ্ট্রপুঞ্জের সম্মিলন, রাষ্ট্রপরিবার। [বর্ত্তমানে ইয়ুরোপের সমস্ত জাতি, তুরুস্ক, জাপান ও আমেরিকার শ্বেতাঙ্গ জাতিসমূহ উক্ত শ্রেণীভুক্ত বলিয়া গণ্য হইয়া থাকে।] **In a family way**—In a domestic manner; পারিবারিক ভাবে। **In the** (or a) **family way**—Pregnant; অন্তঃসত্ত্বা, গর্ভবতী, সসত্ত্বা।

făm'-ine (-ĭn), *n.* 1. General scarcity of food in a district etc.; dearth; দুর্ভিক্ষ; অন্নকষ্ট, আকাল। 2. Scarcity of anything; as, water *famine*; অভাব, দুষ্প্রাপ্যতা। 3. Want of food; starvation; খাদ্যাভাব; অনাহার, উপবাস, অনশন। **Famine fever**—সান্নিপাতিক জ্বর। **Famine price**—দুর্ভিক্ষহেতু বৃদ্ধিপ্রাপ্ত মূল্য।

făm'-ish *v. t.* & *i.* 1. To starve; to kill or destroy with hunger; দুর্ভিক্ষপীড়িত করা; আহার না দিয়া বিনাশ করা, উপবাস করাইয়া মারা। 2. To exhaust the strength of by means of hunger; to distress with hunger; উপবাস-কৃশ করা; অনাহারক্লিষ্ট করা, ক্ষুৎপীড়িত করা। ***Verb i.*** 1. To die of hunger; to starve; অনশনে মৃত্যুমুখে পতিত হওয়া; দুর্ভিক্ষ-পীড়িত হওয়া। 2. To suffer extreme hunger or thirst; ক্ষুৎ-পিপাসায় অবসন্ন হওয়া। **—ment,** *n.* **To be famishing** — (*Colloq.*) To feel hungry; (চলিতভাষায়) ক্ষুধিত হওয়া।

fa'-mous (-mŭs), *adj.* 1. Renowned; known to fame; স্বনাম-খ্যাত, স্বনামধন্য, প্রসিদ্ধ, বিখ্যাত, রূঢ়, লব্ধকীর্ত্তি, লব্ধপ্রতিষ্ঠ, খ্যাতনামা, কীর্ত্তিমান্, বিশ্রুতনামা, সুবিদিত; যশস্বী। 2. (*Colloq.*) Excellent; first-rate, as a dinner etc.; (চলিতভাষায়) অত্যুৎকৃষ্ট, চমৎকার, উম্দা; প্রথম শ্রেণীর। **—ly,** *adv.* 1. In a famous manner; প্রখ্যাতভাবে। 2. (*Colloq.*) Excellently; (চলিত-ভাষায়) উৎকৃষ্টরূপে, চমৎকাররূপে। **—ness,** *n.*

făm'-ū-lŭs, *n.* (*pl.* -LI) An attendant as upon a scholar or magician; ঐন্দ্রজালিক বা পণ্ডিত ব্যক্তির সহচর।

făn, *n.* 1. An instrument for

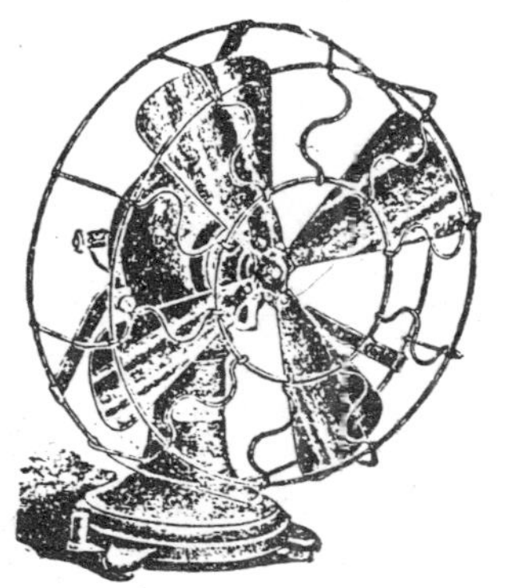

Electric fan.

agitating air; পাখা, বীজন, ব্যজনী। 2. A winnowing machine; কুলা, শূর্প। 3. Something in the shape of a spread fan, as a bird's tail; ছড়ানো পাখার আকার বস্তু। **Electric fan**—বৈদ্যুতিক পাখা, বিজলী-বীজন। **Fan-light** — দ্বারোপরিস্থ ব্যজনাকৃতি বাতায়ন। **Fan-palm**—তাল বৃক্ষ। **Fan-tail**—লক্কা পায়রা; কয়লা উত্তোলনকারীর টুপি। **Fan-tail**

Fan-tracery.

warbler— একপ্রকার পাখী। **Fan-tracery**—খিলানের উপরিভাগের পাখার আকার কাজ।

făn, *v. t.* & *i.* 1. To winnow; শস্য ঝাড়া। 2. To cool and refresh with a fan, as one's face etc.; to drive away; as, to *fan* away flies; to kindle; as, to *fan* fuel into blaze; to excite or stir up to activity; as, to *fan* one's rage etc.; পাখাদ্বারা বাতাস করা, বীজন করা; বাতাস দিয়া তাড়াইয়া দেওয়া; পাখার বাতাস দিয়া আগুন জ্বালান; সন্ধুক্ষিত করা, উত্তেজিত করা, উদ্দীপ্ত করা। 3. To move with a fan; as, to *fan* air; পাখাদ্বারা চালিত করা। 4. To blow gently upon; to cool; as, the breeze *fans* me; (বায়ু) মৃদুমন্দ প্রবাহিত হওয়া; শীতল করা। 5. To spread out like a fan; পাখার আকারে ছড়াইয়া দেওয়া। ***Verb i.*** 1. To spread out like a fan, (often with *out*); পাখার মত মেলিয়া যাওয়া।

Fan'-ner, *n.* 1. One who fans; ব্যজনকারী। 2. A ventilator; বিশুদ্ধ বায়ু সঞ্চালন কিম্বা দূষিত বায়ু নিঃসরণের জন্য যন্ত্র-বিশেষ। 3. A machine used for winnowing grains; শস্য ঝাড়িবার যন্ত্র।

To fan into blaze or **flame**—To kindle by fanning ; বাতাস দিয়া জ্বালান, অগ্নিশিখা উদ্দীপ্ত করা। **To fan the flame**—To increase excitement etc. ; উত্তেজনা বৃদ্ধি করা।

fá-năt′-ĭc, *adj.* & *n.* Filled with excessive and mistaken enthusiasm, esp in religion ; ধর্ম্মোন্মত্ত, উৎকট ধার্ম্মিক। ***Noun.*** A person excessively enthusiastic, esp. in religion ; a visionary zealot ; ধর্ম্মোন্মত্ত ব্যক্তি ; স্বপ্নাবিষ্ট ব্যক্তি, গোঁড়া। **—i-cal**, *adj.* Unreasonably zealous ; উৎকট আগ্রহবান। **—i-cal-ly**, *adv.* **—i-cism**, *n.* Wild and excessive enthusiasm, esp. in religion ; ধর্ম্মোন্মাদ। **—i-cize**, *v. t.* & *i.* To make fanatical ; ধর্ম্মোন্মত্ত করা। (*Verb i.*) To act as a fanatic ; ধর্ম্মোন্মত্তের মত কার্য্য করা।

făn′-cĭ-ēr, *n.* **1.** One who is governed by fancy ; খেয়াল-পরবশ ব্যক্তি। **2.** One who has special liking for, or interest in, certain objects, as birds, dogs, etc. ; যে ব্যক্তির কোন বিশেষ জন্তু প্রভৃতির জন্য সখ বা প্রীতি আছে।

făn′-cȳ, *n.* & *adj.* **1.** That faculty of the mind by which it forms an image or representation of anything not present ; imagination ; কল্পনাবৃত্তি, কল্পনাশক্তি ; কল্পনা। **2.** An image or representation thus formed in the mind ; a conception ; a thought ; কল্পনা ; ধারণা ; চিন্তা। **3.** An arbitrary notion or supposition ; caprice ; as, that's a mere *fancy* ; খেয়াল ; বাহানা, মর্জ্জি। **4.** Inclination ; liking ; as, to take a *fancy* for a thing ; আসক্তি ; রুচি। **5.** (*Collectively*, with *the*) Those who have a certain hobby ; (সংঘবাচকভাবে) কোন বিষয়ের জন্য একান্ত সখ আছে এরূপ লোকের সমবায়। ***Adj.*** **1.** Pleasing to the fancy or caprice ; as, *fancy* goods or articles ; মনোহারী, পসন্দসই, বিচিত্র। **2.** Above real value ; extravagant ; as, a *fancy* price ; প্রকৃত মূল্যের অতিরিক্ত ; অসম্ভব, কাল্পনিক। **3.** Whimsical ; irregular ; "A display of *fancy* shooting" ; খেয়াল-পরবশ ; অব্যবস্থিত। **4.** Based on imagination ; as, a *fancy* picture ; কল্পনামূলক, কাল্পনিক। **5.** Bred for particular points of beauty etc. ; as, *fancy* pigeons ; বিশেষ গুণ, সৌন্দর্য্য প্রভৃতির জন্য পালিত, সখের। **6.** Particoloured ; as, a *fancy* flower ; বিচিত্র-বর্ণ। **—ci-ful**, *adj.* **1.** Guided by fancy ; full of fancy ; খেয়ালপরবশ ; কাল্পনিক। **2.** Imaginary ; unreal ; "Spake at shadows *fanciful* and vain" ; কাল্পনিক ; অবাস্তব। **2.** Fantastically designed ; peculiarly shaped ; as, a *fanciful* head-dress ; অপরূপভাবে কল্পিত ; সৃষ্টিছাড়া রকমের। **—ci-less**, *adj.* **Fancy-ball**—যে নৃত্যোৎসবের নর্ত্তক-নর্ত্তকীগণ কোন বিশেষ যুগ, জাতি বা ঐতিহাসিক ব্যক্তির অনুকরণে বিচিত্র পরিচ্ছদ পরিধান করে। **Fancy dress** — উক্তরূপ নৃত্যোৎসবে পরিহিত পরিচ্ছদ। **Fancy dog etc.** — See FANCY, *adj.* 5. **Fancy-fair**—See FAIR. **Fancy franchise** — জটিল অথবা খামখেয়ালভাবে যোগ্যতার উপর প্রতিষ্ঠিত নির্ব্বাচনক্ষমতা। **Fancy-free**—অপ্রণয়বদ্ধ। **Fancy goods**—সখের জিনিষ, মনোহারী জিনিষ। **Fancy man** — A sweet heart ; প্রণয়ী ; যে ব্যক্তি বেশ্যার অর্থে জীবনধারণ করে, পিরীতের লাং (ইতর ভাষায়)। **Fancy picture**—See FANCY, *adj.* 4. **Fancy-sick**—বিকৃতমতি ; প্রণয়পীড়িত। **Fancy work** — শোভাসাধক সূচীকর্ম্ম। **The fancy**—মল্লক্রীড়কগণ, বিশেষতঃ মুষ্টি-যুদ্ধকারিগণ। **To catch the fancy of**—To please ; খুসী করা, সুখ দেওয়া। **To take** or **have a fancy to, for** — To have a liking or fondness for ; সখ থাকা।

făn′-cȳ, *v. t.* & *i.* **1.** To form a conception of ; to imagine ; ধারণা করা ; কল্পনা করা। **2.** To like ; to be pleased with ; "Which (face) I could *fancy* more than any other" ; পসন্দ করা ; ভাল লাগা। **3.** To be inclined to think ; to suppose ; ভাবা ; অনুমান করা, বোধ করা, মনে করা। **4.** To believe without sufficient evidence ; "He *fancies* he was welcome" ; উপযুক্ত প্রমাণাভাবে বিশ্বাস করা। ***Verb i.*** To imagine ; to suppose without proof ; কল্পনা করা ; ভাবা। **—ci-er**, *n.* Which see.

făn-dan′-gle (-dăng-gl), *n.* Fantastic ornament ; nonsense ; কিম্ভুত কিমাকার অলঙ্কার ; আজগুবি কথা।

făn′-dan′-gō (-dăng-), *n.* **1.** A lively Spanish dance ; স্পেনদেশীয় নৃত্যবিশেষ। **2.** The time for this ; উক্ত নৃত্যের সময়।

fāne, *n.* A temple, (*poetic*) ; (কবিতায়) মন্দির, দেবালয়, দেবমন্দির।

făn′-fare (-fâr), *n.* A flourish of trumpets or bugles ; তূরী বা শিঙ্গার ধ্বনি।

făn′-fă-rŏn, *n.* One who uses bravado ; a braggart ; আস্ফালনকারী ; দম্ভকারী।

făn-fă-rŏn-āde′, *n.* **1.** Vain boasting ; ostentation ; গর্ব্ব, বড়াই ; আস্ফালন, জাঁক, ধুমধাম। **2.** Same as FANFARE (which see).

făng, *n.* **1.** The canine tooth of some beasts, as dogs, wolves, etc. ; the venom tooth of a serpent ; কুকুর, নেকড়ে বাঘ, প্রভৃতির শোবন দন্ত ; সর্পের বিষ-দাঁত। **2.** The root of a tooth ; দন্তমূল। **3.** The tang

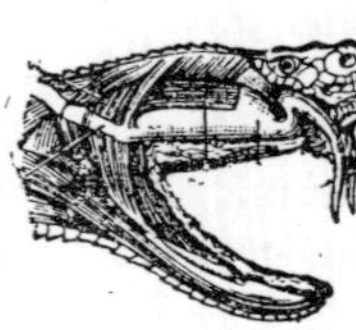

Fangs of Rattle snake.

of a tool ; যন্ত্রাদির সূক্ষ্মাগ্র নিম্নাংশ,—যাহা হাতলে প্রবিষ্ট করা হয়। 4. A claw or talon, (*rare*) ; নখর (অপ্রঃ)। **Fang′-ed,** *adj.* **Fang′-less,** *adj.* Having no fangs ; দংষ্ট্রাহীন। **In a fang**—Fast entangled ; দৃঢ়রূপে জড়িত। **To lose the fang**—Said of a pump, when the water has gone out ; জলশূন্য হওয়া। To miss one's aim ; to fail ; উদ্দেশ্য ব্যর্থ হওয়া, বিফলমনোরথ হওয়া, ব্যর্থকাম হওয়া ; অকৃতকার্য্য হওয়া।

făng, *v. t.* To supply as a pump with water so as to make it work ; দমকল চালাইবার জন্য উহাতে জল সরবরাহ করা।

fan′-gle (făng-gl), *n.* A new fashion or crotchet ; a novelty, (*rare*) ; নূতন ধারা, উৎকট খেয়াল ; নূতন রকমের বিষয় বা ঘটনা (অপ্রঃ)।

făn′-iŏn, *n.* A small flag for marking the stations in surveying ; জরীপের কার্য্যে ব্যবহৃত ক্ষুদ্র ধ্বজা-বিশেষ।

făn-tâ′-sia (-zēâ), *n.* A fantastic musical composition in which form is subservient to fancy ; আজগুবি গান।

făn′-tăst, phăn′–, *ns.* **1.** A visionary ; কল্পনাপ্রিয় ব্যক্তি। **2.** One who is eccentric in thought or style ; উৎকটরুচি ব্যক্তি।

făn-tăs′-tic, phăn–, *adjs.* **1.** Of or pertaining to fantasy or fancy ; fancied, (*rare*) ; কাল্পনিক ; কল্পিত (অপ্রঃ)। **2.** Fanciful ; whimsical ; eccentric ; as, a *fantastic* mind or person ; কল্পনাপ্রিয় ; খেয়ালপরবশ ; ছিটগ্রস্ত। **3.** Grotesque ; quaint ; odd ; as, *fantastic* gestures or style ; অদ্ভুত, অপরূপ, আজগুবি ; সৃষ্টিছাড়া ; কিম্ভূতকিমাকার। **4.** Unreal; irrational ; as, *fantastic* fears ; অপ্রকৃত, মিথ্যা, অসত্য ; অযৌক্তিক। **–ti-cal,** *adj.* **–ti-cal′-i-ty,** *n.* **–ti-cal-ly,** *adv.* **–ti-cal-ness,** *n.* **–ti-cism,** *n.*

făn′-tă-sȳ, phăn′–, *n.* & *v. t.* **1.** Fancy ; কল্পনা। **2.** A mental image or phantom ; hallucination ; মানসিক প্রতিমা, অপচ্ছায়া, ভ্রান্তি, মায়া। **3.** A fantastic design or invention ; উৎকটকল্পনা বা আবিষ্কার। **4.** (*Music*) Same as FANTASIA. ***Verb t.*** To fancy ; to conceive mentally ; কল্পনা করা ; ধারণা করা। **–sied,** *adj.* **–tasque′,** *adj.*

făn′-toc-ci-ni (tŏ-chē-nē), *n. Pl.* Puppets which are made to go through revolutions by concealed wires or strings ; dramatic performances by puppets ; নাচের পুতুল ; পুতুল নাচ।

fâ-quir′ (-kēr), *n.* Same as FAKIR.

fâr, *adj., adv.* & *n.* (*comp.* & *sup.* — *farther, farthest,* also *further, furthest*) **1.** Remote ; as, the *far* east ; দূরবর্ত্তী। **2.** Distant ; long ; as, a *far* journey ; সুদূর ; দীর্ঘ। **3.** The more distant of two ; as, the *far* side (also *offside*) of a house ; দুইএর মধ্যে অধিকতর দূরবর্ত্তী। ***Adv.*** **1.** At, or to, a great distance of space ; বহু দূরে, অতি দূরে। **2.** Distantly in time ; as, he pushed his researches very *far* into antiquity ; দূরবর্ত্তীকালে, দূরে। **3.** In great part ; "The night is *far* spent" ; to a great extent ; অধিকাংশে ; অধিক পরিমাণে। **4.** Greatly ; exceedingly ; "Which *far* exceeds his skill" ; অতিশয় ; নিরতিশয়। ***Noun.*** **1.** A distance ; as, I come from *far* ; দূরবর্ত্তী স্থান। **2.** A great extent or amount ; as, by *far* ; বহু পরিমাণ, বহু সংখ্যা। **Far-away**—Distant ; long past ; অতি দূরবর্ত্তী ; বহুকালগত। Abstracted ; dreamy ; as, a *far-away* look or eye ; তন্ময় ; স্বপ্নাবিষ্ট। **Far-between**—Infrequent ; বহুদিন অন্তর। **Far-famed** — বিশ্রুতকীর্ত্তি, দেশবিশ্রুত, প্রখ্যাতনামা, প্রথিতযশ। **Far-fetched**—(*Lit.*) Brought from a far or distant place ; (শব্দানুযায়ী) দূরবর্ত্তী স্থান হইতে আনীত। Strained ; as, the idea was *far-fetched* ; কষ্টকল্পিত। **Farmost**—নিতান্ত দূরবর্ত্তী। **Far-reaching** — Exerting influence to a great distance and for a long time ; বহুদূর প্রভাববিস্তারী। **Far-seeing**—দূরদৃষ্টিসম্পন্ন, দূরদর্শী। **Far-sighted**—দূরদৃষ্টিসম্পন্ন, দূরদর্শী ; নিকটস্থ বস্তু স্পষ্ট দেখিতে অসমর্থ। **Far-sightedness**—দূরদর্শিতা। **Far-spent**—Far advanced ; বহু দূরে অগ্রসর; অধিকাংশগত। **A far cry**—A long distance ; বহু দূরবর্ত্তী স্থান। **As far as**—Not short of (place) ; যতদূর। **As or so far as, In so far as**—To whatever extent ; যে পরিমাণে। **At (the) farthest**—Making the largest possible allowance of time ; বড় জোর। **By far**—In a great degree ; greatly ; exceedingly ; বহু পরিমাণে ; অনেকাংশে ; অত্যধিকরূপে। **Far and near**—At a distance and close by ; দূরে ও নিকটে। **Far and away**—By much ; decidedly ; as, it is *far and away* the best course ; অধিক পরিমাণে ; নিশ্চিতরূপে, সুনিশ্চিত। **Far and wide** — Distantly and broadly ; comprehensively ; "*Far and wide* his eye commands" ; বহুদূর-ব্যাপিয়া ; ব্যাপকভাবে। **Far be it from me**—I would on no account etc. ; আমাদ্বারা কোন ক্রমেই নয়। **Far from it** — Not at all ; by no means ; একবারেই নয় ; কোন ক্রমেই নয়। **Far better, different, etc.**—Much better, different, etc. ; অনেকটা ভাল, অনেকটা বিভিন্ন। **Far gone** — Advanced in some progress ; as, he is *far gone* in love ; বহুদূর অগ্রসর। **Far off**—At a great distance ; অতিদূরে। **Far other**—Very different ; অত্যন্ত

বিভিন্ন। **From far**—From a great distance ; বহু দূর হইতে। **He will go far**—He will do much ; সে অনেক দূর করিবে। **How far**—To what extent ; কতদূর। **So far**—To such a distance ; up to now ; ততদূর ; এপর্য্যন্ত।

făr'-ăd, *n.* (*Electr.*) The unit of quantity in the measurement of electricity ; (তাড়িতবিদ্যা) তাড়িতের একক।

făr-ă-dā'-ic, *adj.* (*Electr.*) Inductive ; induced ; as, *faradaic* current ; (তাড়িত বিদ্যা) উৎপাদনীয় (হিঃ কোঃ) ; উৎপাদিত (ঐ)।

farce (fârs), *n.* & *v. t.* **1.** A dramatic work of comic character, full of extravagant drollery ; প্রহসন। **2.** Ridiculous or empty show ; mockery ; as, it is a mere *farce* ; হাস্যজনক বা অসার দৃশ্য ; বিদ্রূপ। ***Verb t.*** (*Archaic*) To fill with spice, (in *cookery and fig.*) ; (অপ্রঃ) মসলা পুরা।

fâr'-cĭ-căl, *adj.* Relating to a farce ; absurdly futile ; ludicrous ; প্রহসনসম্বন্ধীয় ; হাস্যজনক ; বিদ্রূপাত্মক। **—cal'-i-ty**, *n.* **—ly**, *adv.*

farceur, *n.* (*F.*) **1.** A writer or player of farces ; প্রহসন-লেখক বা অভিনেতা। **2.** A joker ; ব্যঙ্গকারী, বিদূষক, বৈহাসিক।

fâr'-cy̆, *n.* A disease of horses like glanders ; অশ্বের গ্রন্থি-রোগ। **Farcy bud** or **button**—উক্ত রোগ-জনিত ক্ষুদ্র স্ফোটক।

fâr'-dāge, *n.* (*Naut.*) Same as DUNNAGE (which see).

fâr'-dĕl, *n.* (*Archaic*) **1.** A bundle ; a burden ; (অপ্রঃ) আঁটি ; বোঝা। **2.** A collection ; সংগ্রহ।

fâr'-dĕl-bound (-bownd), *adj.* Marked by costiveness, (esp., of cattle, sheep etc.) ; কোষ্ঠ-কাঠিন্য রোগাক্রান্ত (সাধারণতঃ গো মেষাদির কোষ্ঠবদ্ধ রোগসম্বন্ধে)।

fāre, *v. i.* **1.** To go ; to pass ; to travel ; to journey ; গমন করা ; চলা ; ভ্রমণ করা ; পর্য্যটন করা। **2.** To be in any rate good or bad ; "Ill *fares* the land" ; to have good or bad fortune or experience ; ভাল অথবা মন্দ অবস্থায় থাকা ; সৌভাগ্য বা দুর্ভাগ্যের অধীন হওয়া। **3.** To happen well or ill ; to turn out, (with *it* impersonally) ; as, let us see how *it fares* with him ; শুভ বা অশুভ সংঘটন হওয়া ; ফলে দাঁড়ান। **4.** To be entertained or provided with food ; খাদ্য প্রদান করা ; খাদ্যদ্বারা আপ্যায়িত করা। **To fare as though** or **if**—To act as if ; to pretend ; এরূপ কার্য্য করা যেন ; ভাণ করা। **To fare ill** or **well**—See FARE 2 above. **To fare with**—To deal with ; ব্যবহার করা, আচরণ করা। **To fare with oneself**—To behave ; আচরণ করা।

fāre, *n.* **1.** The sum paid for conveying a person by land or water ; ভাড়া, বাহিক। **2.** The person or persons conveyed in a vehicle ; as, a full *fare* of passengers ; আরোহী, চড়ন্দার, যাত্রী। **3.** Food ; as, good, bad or rich *fare* ; খাদ্য। **4.** State of things ; fortune, (*archaic*) ; ব্যাপার ; ভাগ্য (অপ্রঃ)। **5.** The catch of fish on a fishing vessel ; জেলে জাহাজে একবারে ধৃত মৎস্যের পরিমাণ। **Bill of fare**—See under BILL.

fāre-wĕll', *interj.* & *n.* May you farewell ; good-bye ; adieu ; স্বস্তি, তোমার মঙ্গল হউক, শিবমস্তু ; বিদায় হই ; তবে আসি। ***Noun.*** **1.** A wish of happiness or welfare at parting ; a good-bye ; বিদায়কালীন মঙ্গলকামনা ; নমস্কার, বিদায় হই ইত্যাকার অভিবাদন-বাক্য। **2.** Act of departure or leave-taking ; a last look, reference or attention ; as, *farewell* happiness ; প্রস্থান, বিদায়, বিদায়গ্রহণ ; বিদায় সম্ভাষণ। **Farewell to**—No more of ; আর নয়।

fāre'-wĕll, *adj.* **1.** Parting ; as, *farewell* speech ; বিদায়কালীন। **2.** Valedictory ; বিদায়-সূচক। **3.** Final ; অন্তিম।

fă-rī'-nă, *n.* **1.** Fine flour or meal of corn, nuts or starchy roots ; সূক্ষ্ম শস্যচূর্ণ, আটা। **2.** (*Chem.*) Starch ; (রসায়ন-শাস্ত্র) শ্বেতসার-চূর্ণ। **3.** (*Bot.*) Pollen ; (উদ্ভিদ্‌বিদ্যা) পরাগ, পুষ্পরেণু। **4.** A powdery or flour-like substance ; সূক্ষ্মচূর্ণ। **—na'-ceous**, *adj.* **1.** Consisting of or made of meal or flour ; শস্যচূর্ণঘটিত, ময়দা বা আটার তৈয়ারী। **2.** Yielding farina or flour ; ময়দা উৎপাদক। **3.** Pertaining to meal ; like meal ; শস্যচূর্ণ সম্বন্ধীয় ; শস্যচূর্ণবৎ।

făr'-i-nōse, *adj.* **1.** Yielding farina ; সূক্ষ্মশস্যচূর্ণপ্রদ। **2.** Covered with mealy powder ; mealy ; সূক্ষ্ম শস্যচূর্ণদ্বারা আবৃত ; সূক্ষ্ম শস্যচূর্ণময়।

fârm, *n.*, *v. t.* & *i.* **1.** A piece of land devoted to agricultural or other purposes under the management of a tenant or the owner ; landed estate ; কৃষিক্ষেত্র ; ভূসম্পত্তি, খাস জমি। **2.** (*Originally*) A tract of land held on lease for cultivation ; (পূর্ব্বে) ইজারা জমি। **3.** A place where children etc. are farmed ; শিশুদিগের রক্ষণাবেক্ষণের স্থান। **4.** A farm house ; কৃষিক্ষেত্র-বাটিকা, গোলাবাড়ী। ***Verb t.*** **1.** To let out for an equivalent, as land for a rent, (*rare*) ; ইজারা দেওয়া, জমা করিয়া দেওয়া। **2.** To take proceeds of on payment of a fixed sum ; as, to *farm* an office, tax, etc. ; ইজারা নেওয়া। **3.** To devote to cultivation ; to till, as a farm ; কৃষিকার্য্যে নিয়োগ করা ; চাষ করা। **4.** To give up to another, as an estate, a business, the revenue, etc. on condition of receiving in return of a fixed sum, (sometimes with *out*); as, to *farm* the taxes; ইজারা দেওয়া। **5.** To let the labour of (persons) for hire; মজুরি করা। **6.** To contract for the maintenance and care of (persons, esp. children) at a fixed price; (কোন ব্যক্তি বা শিশুদিগকে) নির্দ্দিষ্ট পরিমাণ অর্থ গ্রহণে রক্ষণাবেক্ষণের চুক্তি করা। ***Verb i.*** To cultivate the soil; ভূমি কর্ষণ করা। **Farm'-er,** *n.* **1.** One who cultivates lands; one who manages a farm; কৃষক, কৃষাণ; কৃষিক্ষেত্রের অধ্যক্ষ, কৃষিক্ষেত্রের পতি। **2.** One who undertakes to collect taxes etc. for a certain payment per cent.; as, a *farmer* of the revenues; কর-সংগ্রাহক, ইজারাদার। **Farm'-er-y,** *n.* The buildings and yards of a farm; গোলাবাড়ীর গৃহাদি এবং প্রাঙ্গণসমূহ। **Farm'-ing,** *n.* & *adj.* **1.** The act or business of cultivating; management of a farm; কৃষিকর্ম্ম, চাষ-আবাদ; কৃষিক্ষেত্রের কার্য্য-নির্ব্বাহ। **2.** The practice of letting or leasing taxes for collection; কর-সংগ্রহের জন্য ভারার্পণ, ইজারা দেওন। (*Adj.*) Relating to agriculture; কৃষি বিষয়ক। **Farm-house**—কৃষিক্ষেত্র সংশ্লিষ্ট কৃষক-ভবন, গোলাবাড়ী। **Farm-stead**—জোত সংক্রান্ত গৃহাদি। **Farm-yard**—গোলাবাড়ীর প্রাঙ্গণ, খামার। **Home farm**—খামার। **Farmer-general**—প্রাচীনকালে ফরাসীদেশে যে ব্যক্তি নির্দ্দিষ্ট অর্থ প্রদানপূর্ব্বক কোন নির্দ্দিষ্ট বিভাগ কিংবা জেলার কর-সংগ্রহের ক্ষমতা প্রাপ্ত হইতেন। **To farm, let** or **let to farm**—To lease on rent; জমা লইয়া পত্তন করা।

far niente—Idleness; আলস্য।

far'-ō, *n.* A game of hazard played with cards; একপ্রকার তাসের জুয়াখেলা। **Faro-bank**—উক্তরূপ তাস খেলায় গচ্ছিত অর্থ, উক্তরূপ তাসখেলার পণ; উক্তপ্রকার জুয়া খেলার গৃহ বা কক্ষ।

fa-rouche, *adj.* (*F.*) Sullen; shy; কোপন-স্বভাব; লাজুক, লজ্জাশীল।

far-ra'-gō, *n.* Hotch-potch; মিশ্র বস্তু; জগা খিচড়ী। **—rag'-i-nous,** *adj.* Miscellaneous; mixed; বিবিধ; মিশ্রিত।

far'-ri-êr, *n.* **1.** A shoeing smith; a horse-shoer; যে ব্যক্তি ঘোড়ার পায়ে নাল লাগায়; নালবন্দ। **2.** One who treats the diseases of horses; horse-doctor; অশ্ব-চিকিৎসক; অশ্ববৈদ্য। **3.** An official who has care of horses in a cavalry regiment; অশ্বারোহী পল্টনের অশ্বাধ্যক্ষ কর্ম্মচারী। **—y,** *n.* **1.** The art of shoeing horses; নালবাঁধাই। **2.** The veterinary surgery; পশুর অস্ত্র-চিকিৎসাবিদ্যা। **3.** The place where a smith shoes horses; অশ্বাদির নাল বাঁধনের স্থান।

far'-row (-rō), *n., v. t.* & *i.* **1.** A pig; a litter of pigs; শূকর; শূকর-ছানা সমূহ। **2.** Act of farrowing; শূকর-শাবক প্রসব করণ। ***Verb t. & i.*** To give birth to (pigs), (said only of swine); শূকর-শাবক প্রসব করা।

far'-row (-rō), *adj.* Not producing young in a given season or year, (said only of cows); নির্দ্দিষ্ট ঋতুতে বা বৎসরে বৎস অপ্রসবকারিণী, কালনী (কেবল গাভী-সম্পর্কে)।

fart, *n.* & *v. i.* A noisy emission of wind from the anus; বাতকর্ম্ম, অধোবায়ু মোচন। ***Verb i.*** To emit wind from the anus; অপান বায়ু ত্যাগ করা, অধোবায়ু নিঃসরণ করা।

fär'-thêr, *adj., adv.* & *v. t.* (*Compar.* of FAR) **1.** More remote; অধিকতর দূরবর্ত্তী। **2.** Additional; further; অতিরিক্ত; আরো। ***Adv.*** **1.** At or to a greater distance; more remotely; as, to look *farther*; আরও দূরে; অধিকতর দূরে। **2.** Moreover; also; (now usually *further*); আরও; অধিকন্তু, অপরন্তু। **3.** To a greater extent or degree; as, he can suffer no *farther*; অতিশয়, অতিমাত্রায়। ***Verb t.*** (*Rare*) To help onward; (now *further*); (অপ্রঃ) অগ্রসর করা।

fär'-thêr-most, *adj.* At the greatest distance; সর্ব্বাপেক্ষা অধিক দূরবর্ত্তী।

fär'-thest, *adj.* & *adv.* Most distant or remote; দূরতম। ***Adv.*** To or at the greatest distance; সর্ব্বাপেক্ষা দূরবর্ত্তী। **At the** or **at farthest**—At the greatest distance; নিতান্ত পক্ষে। At most; বড় জোর।

fär'-thing, *n.* **1.** A British coin, being the quarter of a penny; ইংলণ্ডীয় ক্ষুদ্র তাম্রমুদ্রা বিশেষ (এক পেনির চতুর্থাংশ)। **2.** The least possible amount; ক্ষুদ্র বা সামান্য কোন কিছু, লেশ ক্রান্তি। **Not to care** or **matter a farthing**—Not to care or matter a bit or little; অণুমাত্রও গ্রাহ্য না করা; কিছুই ক্ষতি না হওয়া।

fär'-thin-gale (-thing-), *n.* (*Hist.*) A hooped petticoat formed of whale-bone; (ঐতিহাসিক) তিমি মৎস্যের অস্থিনির্ম্মিত ঘাগরার অন্তর্বেষ্টন-পঞ্জর।

fas'-cēs, *n. pl.* (*Rom. Antiq.*) A bundle of rods with axe in the middle carried before high magistrates as a badge of authority; (রোমীয় প্রত্নতত্ত্ব) দণ্ডবাহক (Lictor) গণ কর্ত্তৃক প্রাচীন রোমের উচ্চপদস্থ কর্ম্মচারিগণের সম্মুখে বাহিত মধ্যদেশে কুঠারনিবিষ্ট ক্ষমতার নিদর্শন-স্বরূপ দণ্ডসমুচ্চয়, দণ্ডপরশু (আঃ বঃ)। **2.** (*Fig.*) Emblems of authority; (লক্ষণায়) ক্ষমতার চিহ্ন।

fas'-ci-a (fă-shĭ-ă), *n. Pl.* (*Arch.*) A long flat surface of wood or stone; (স্থপতি-বিজ্ঞান) কাষ্ঠ বা প্রস্তর নির্ম্মিত সুদীর্ঘ সমতল উপরিভাগ।

fas'-ci-āte (fă-shĭ-), **fas'-ci-āt-ĕd** (fă-shĭ-), *adjs.* **1.** Marked with bands or stripes; বন্ধনী চিহ্নিত, ডোরা-কাটা। **2.** (*Bot.*) Growing in bundles or bunches from the same point ; গুচ্ছিত। **–a′-tion,** *n.*

făs′-ĭ-cle (-cl), *n.* **1.** A small bundle ; a cluster ; as, a *fascicle* of flowers or roots ; স্তবক ; গুচ্ছ। **2.** A part of a book published by instalments ; খণ্ডশঃ প্রকাশিত পুস্তকের অংশ। **–cled,** *adj.* Growing in fascicles ; as, *fascicled* tuft of hair ; গুচ্ছাকারে উৎপন্ন। **–cic′-u-lar, –cic′-u-late, –cic′-u-lat-ed,** *adjs.* গুচ্ছিত, পুঞ্জিত। **–cic′-u-late-ly,** *adv.* **–cic-u-la′-tion,** *n.*

făs′-ĭ-nāte, *v. t.* **1.** To deprive (victim) of power of escape or resistance by one's look or presence, (esp. of serpents) ; দৃষ্টিশক্তি দ্বারা বিমোহিত করা, চলচ্ছক্তি রহিত করা, (বিশেষতঃ সর্পাদির পক্ষে)। **2.** To allure irresistibly ; to charm ; to captivate ; to enchant ; অপ্রতিহতভাবে প্রলুব্ধ করা ; মন্ত্রমুগ্ধ করা, যাদু করা ; বশীভূত করা ; বিমোহিত করা, বিমুগ্ধ করা। **–nat-ing,** *adj.* Charming ; enchanting ; delightful ; মনোমুগ্ধকর ; মোহকর, মনোহারী, মোহন, চিত্তগ্রাহক (বাৎস্যঃ) ; আনন্দজনক। **–nat-ing-ly,** *adv.* **–na′-tion,** *n.* **1.** The act of fascinating, bewitching or enchanting ; enchantment ; charm ; বশীকরণ, যাদুকরণ, বিমোহন, সম্মোহন ; কুহক ; যাদু। **2.** The state of being fascinated ; মোহ। **3.** Fascinating quality or influence ; as, a lady of *fascination* ; মোহকর গুণ বা প্রভাব। **–na-tor,** *n.* One who fascinates ; বিমোহনকারী, মোহিনী।

făs-cine′ (-sēn), *n.* A bundle of rods or sticks used in raising batteries, in filling ditches, etc. ; কামান উত্তোলন, পরিখাদি পূর্ণকরণ প্রভৃতির জন্য যষ্টিগুচ্ছ। **Fascine dwelling**—অনৈতিহাসিক যুগের কুটীর।

făsh, *v. t.* & *n.* (*Scot.*) To bother ; to trouble ; to tease ; বিরক্ত করা ; কষ্ট দেওয়া, যন্ত্রণা দেওয়া ; ক্ষ্যাপান। ***Noun.*** Vexation ; trouble ; as, without further *fash* on my part ; বিরক্তি ; কষ্ট।

făsh′-ion (-ŏn), *n.* & *v. t.* **1.** The make or form of anything ; style ; আকৃতি, গঠন, কল্পন ; পদ্ধতি বা ধরণ। **2.** Manner ; mode ; sort (*rare*) ; workmanship ; execution ; রীতি, প্রকার ; ধারা ; রকম (অপ্রঃ) ; শিল্পনৈপুণ্য ; সম্পাদন। **3.** Prevailing mode, esp. of dress, ornaments, etc. ; as, to import *fashions* from France ; prevailing custom ; as, it is the *fashion* of the age ; বেশভূষা প্রভৃতির চলিত ধারা ; চলিত রীতি বা প্রথা। **4.** Pattern ; model ; নমুনা ; আদর্শ। **5.** Gentle society or life ; as, a man of *fashion* ; fashionable people collectively ; "When heart met heart in *fashion's* hall" ; সুসভ্য সমাজ বা ভদ্র সমাজ ; বিলাসিসম্প্রদায়। **6.** Something in accord with conventional usages for the time being ; প্রচলিত রীত্যনুযায়ী বস্তু। ***Verb t.*** **1.** To give shape or figure to ; গঠন করা, নির্ম্মাণ করা, গড়া। **2.** To adapt, (with *to*) ; যোগ্য বা উপযোগী করা। **–a-ble,** *adj.* & *n.* **1.** Following, or suited to, the fashion prevailing at a particular time ; as, *fashionable* dress ; (প্রচলিত) প্রথানুরূপ, রীতিসম্মত। **2.** Patronised by, or characteristic of, persons of fashion ; বিলাসিসমাজ কর্ত্তৃক আদৃত। **3.** Observant of the fashion ; stylish ; as, a *fashionable* man ; প্রচলিত প্রথানুগামী ; বস্ত্রবিলাসী। (*Noun*) A person of fashion ; প্রথানুযায়ী, বিলাসী, বস্ত্রবিলাসী। **–a-ble-ness,** *n.* **–a-bly,** *adv.* **–ist,** *adj.* **–ioned,** *p. adj.* **Fashion-monger** — বস্ত্রবিলাসী ব্যক্তি, ফুলবাবু। **Fashion-plate**—পরিচ্ছদ-রীতি প্রদর্শক চিত্র। **After or in a fashion** — To a certain extent ; কোন প্রকারে। **After the fashion of**—Like ; মত, অনুরূপ। **In (the) fashion**—Agreeing with current usage ; প্রচলিত রীত্যনুযায়ী। **Out of (the) fashion**—Not agreeing with current usage ; not in vogue ; প্রচলিত রীতির বহির্ভূত ; অপ্রচলিত। Old* fashioned ; সেকেলে, পুরাতন। **Men of fashion**—ভদ্রসমাজ। **To walk crab etc. fashion**—To walk in the manner of a crab etc. ; কাঁকড়া প্রভৃতির মত চলা। **To set or lead the fashion**—To be an example in dress etc. for others to follow ; পোষাক-পরিচ্ছদাদি সম্বন্ধে অন্যের অনুকরণস্থলীয় হওয়া। **The fashion**—Whatever is in accord with conventional usages of upper society for the time being ; সাময়িকভাবে উচ্চশ্রেণীর লোকদিগের রীতিনীতির অনুযায়ী বিষয়। A person or thing that is fashionable to admire or discuss ; যে ব্যক্তি বা বস্তুর প্রশংসা বা আলোচনা সাময়িক প্রথা হইয়া দাঁড়াইয়াছে।

fāst, *v. i.* **1.** To abstain from food partly or wholly ; to go without food ; উপবাসে থাকা ; নিরাহার থাকা। **2.** To abstain from food on religious grounds or in mourning ; ধর্ম্মার্থ বা শোক-প্রদর্শনার্থ উপবাস করা। **Fasting day**—উপবাস-দিবস।

fāst, *n.* **1.** Abstinence from food ; অনশন, অনাহার, উপবাস, অভুক্তি, হরিবাসর, হরিমটর (*colloq.*)। **2.** Season or day appointed for fasting ; উপবাসবাসর, হরিবাসর, উপবাস-দিবস। **3.** Abstinence from food on religious grounds ; উপবাস। **Fast day or fasting day** — উপবাস-দিবস। **To break one's fast**—To put an end to a period of abstinence by taking food ; especially to take one's morning meal ; উপবাসান্তে আহার করা, পারণ।

করা ; (বিশেষতঃ) প্রাতর্ভোজন করা, প্রাতরাশ করা। **To fast to death**—To die of starvation ; অনশনে প্রাণত্যাগ করা।

făst, *adj.* & *adv.* **1.** Firmly adhering ; closely fixed ; not loose ; tight ; as, to make *fast* the door ; দৃঢ়লগ্ন; দৃঢ়বদ্ধ ; আঁটা; শক্ত। **2.** Rapid ; quickly moving ; swift ; as, a *fast* horse ; done or accomplished quickly ; as, *fast* race ; ক্ষিপ্র দ্রুতগামী, শীঘ্রগামী ; সত্বর, শীঘ্র ; দ্রুত-সম্পন্ন। **3.** Durable ; lasting ; as, *fast* colours ; চিরস্থায়ী ; পাকা। **4.** Steadfast ; faithful ; as, a *fast* friend (=ঘনিষ্ঠ মিত্র, অন্তরঙ্গ বন্ধু) ; অটল ; বিশ্বস্ত। **5.** Deep ; sound ; as, *fast* sleep ; গভীর ; প্রগাঢ়। **6.** Given to pleasure-seeking ; dissipated ; ইন্দ্রিয়সুখপরতন্ত্র, ইন্দ্রিয়সুখলালসা পরায়ণ ; অসচ্চরিত্র, লম্পট। **7.** Indicating more advanced time than it really is ; as, a *fast* watch or clock ; দ্রুতগামী। ***Adv.*** **1.** Securely ; soundly ; দৃঢ়রূপে, অচলভাবে ; গাঢ়ভাবে। **2.** Swiftly ; quickly ; in quick succession ; দ্রুতবেগে ; সত্বর ; দ্রুত। **3.** Extravagantly ; in a dissipated manner ; as, to live *fast* ; অমিতব্যয়ীর মত ; ব্যভিচারীর মত, লম্পটের মত **Fast'-ness,** *n.* **1.** State or quality of being fast ; দৃঢ়তা, অটলতা। **2.** A stronghold ; a fortress ; সুরক্ষিত স্থান ; দুর্গ। **A ship fast aground**—A ship aground ; চড়ায় লাগা জাহাজ। **Fast and loose**—Now cohering, now disjoined ; inconstant ; অব্যবস্থিতচিত্ত ; চঞ্চলপ্রকৃতি, অস্থিরমতি। **Fast bind fast find**—Lock up what you would not lose ; যাহা হারাইতে না চাও, তাহা তালাদ্বারা বন্ধ করিয়া রাখ। **Fast cricket-ground, racqet-court, billiard-table**—যে সকল মাঠের উপর কন্দুক সতেজে চলে। **Fast girl**—A young girl aping the manners of young men ; পুরুষস্বভাবা বালিকা, প্রগল্ভা বালিকা। **Fast man**—A man of dissolute habits ; লম্পট, বিলাসব্যসনরত ব্যক্তি। **Fast on** or **upon**—Near upon (a specified quantity etc.) ; নির্দিষ্ট সংখ্যা প্রভৃতির কাছাকাছি। **Fast ways**—Dissipated ways of living ; লাম্পট্য, ব্যভিচারপরায়ণতা। **Fast with gout**—Confined with gout ; গেঁটেবাতে শয্যাগত। **Hard and fast** — Strict ; বাঁধাধরা, বাঁধাবাঁধি। **The door is fast**—It is locked ; তালা দ্বারা বন্ধ। **To make fast** — To fasten ; দৃঢ়বদ্ধ করা। **To play (at) fast and loose**—To act with reckless inconstancy ; to say one thing and do another ; to be unreliable ; অব্যবস্থিতচিত্তের ন্যায় কায করা ; একরূপ কথা বলিয়া অন্যরূপ কায করা ; অবিশ্বাসী হওয়া। **To stand fast**—To stand still ; স্থিরভাবে দণ্ডায়মান থাকা। To show constancy or courage ; not to yield ; স্থিরানুরাগ বা সাহস প্রদর্শন করা ; অটল থাকা। **To take fast hold of**—To grasp tightly ; দৃঢ়ভাবে ধরা, দৃঢ়মুষ্টিতে ধরা।

făst, *n.* (*Naut.*) A rope etc. which fastens a ship, boat, etc. ; (নৌবিদ্যা) জাহাজ বা নৌকা বাঁধিবার রজ্জু।

fás'-ten (-n), *v. t.* & *i.* **1.** To fix firmly or closely ; to make fast ; as, to *fasten* a thing to a post ; to *fasten* a door ; to secure, as by a tie, lock, bolt, etc. ; দৃঢ়সংলগ্ন করা ; বদ্ধ করা ; তালা, হুড়কা, প্রভৃতি দ্বারা দৃঢ়রূপে বন্ধ করা। **2.** To join in close union ; as, to *fasten* boards together ; to cause to cleave together ; as, to *fasten* a nick-name on or upon a person ; দৃঢ়রূপে বদ্ধ করা ; পরস্পরের সহিত জোড়া দেওয়া। **3.** To direct steadily or keenly, (with *on* or *upon*) ; as, to *fasten* the eyes, thoughts or hopes etc. *on* or *upon* something ; নিবদ্ধ করা। ***Verb i.*** **1.** To take firm hold ; to seize ; to cling, (with *on*) ; "He *fastened on* my neck" ; দৃঢ়মুষ্টিতে ধরা ; ধরা ; সংলগ্ন হওয়া, সংসক্ত হওয়া। **2.** To become fast ; নিবদ্ধ হওয়া। **–er,** *n.* **–ing,** *n.* That which fastens, as a lock, bolt, bar, etc. ; যদ্দ্বারা আটক বা বদ্ধ করা যায়, যথা, তালা, অর্গল প্রভৃতি। **To fasten a quarrel upon**—To drag into a quarrel against one's inclination ; ইচ্ছার বিরুদ্ধে কাহাকে কলহে জড়িত করা। **To fasten off thread etc.**—To secure with a knot or otherwise ; সূতা প্রভৃতিতে গেরো দেওয়া। **To fasten on** or **upon**—See FASTEN *v. t.* 3. (Also *Verb i.*) To single out for attack or censure ; আক্রমণ বা তিরস্কারের জন্য বাছিয়া ঠিক করা। To seize upon eagerly ; as, to *fasten on* a pretext ; সাগ্রহে আঁকড়াইয়া ধরা।

fás'-tï, *n. Pl.* **1.** Chronological register of events ; কালানুক্রমিক ঘটনা-বিবরণী। **2.** (*Rom. antiq.*) A calendar indicating days for festivals, courts, etc. ; (রোমীয় পুরাতত্ত্ব) পঞ্জিকা-বিশেষ।

făs-tid'-i-ous (-ŭs), *adj.* Easily disgusted ; difficult to please ; squeamish ; সহজে বিরক্ত ; দুস্তোষণীয়, দুষ্প্রসাদ, কষ্টপ্রীত ; খুঁতখুঁতে, উৎকট-রুচি। **–ness,** *n.* **–ly,** *adv.*

făt, *n., v. t., i.* & *adj.* **1.** A solid oily substance found in parts of animal bodies ; চর্ব্বি, মেদ, বসা, স্নেহ। **2.** The best part of anything ; কোন জিনিষের উৎকৃষ্টাংশ বা সারভাগ। **3.** (*Print.*) A work with many blank places and paying well ; (মুদ্রণ) যে কাজে অনেক ফাঁকা জায়গা থাকে বলিয়া লাভ বেশী হয়। **4.** (*Theatre*) The part of a robe that enables a player to show off ; (রঙ্গালয়) পরিচ্ছদের আড়ম্বর প্রদর্শক অংশ

5. (*Chem.*) An organic compound of glycerine with acid ; (রসায়ন-শাস্ত্র) গ্লিসেরিণ ও দ্রাবকের সহযোগে উৎপন্ন একরূপ জৈব মিশ্র পদার্থ। ***Verb t.*** To make plump or fat ; to make fleshy with abundant food, as for slaughter etc. ; as, to *fat* fowls or sheep ; হৃষ্টপুষ্ট করা, মোটা করা ; মেদস্বী করা, স্থূলাঙ্গ করা। ***Verb i.*** To grow fat ; মোটা হওয়া, স্থূলাঙ্গ হওয়া, মেদস্বী হওয়া। ***Adj.*** **1.** Fleshy ; plump ; corpulent ; মাংসল ; পীন, পীবর, পুষ্ট, মোটাসোটা ; স্থূলকায়, স্থূলাঙ্গ, পুষ্টাঙ্গ। **2.** Oily ; greasy, said of food ; তৈলাক্ত, স্নেহময় ; চর্ব্বিময়, চর্ব্বিযুক্ত, মেদযুক্ত। **3.** Coarse ; gross ; dull ; stupid ; মোটা ; স্থূল ; স্থূলবুদ্ধি ; বোকা। **4.** Fertile ; productive ; as, *fat* land ; উর্ব্বর ; শস্যপ্রদ। **5.** Producing a large income ; as, a *fat* job or benefice ; অতি লাভকর, মোটা। **6.** Thick ; extended (esp. of printing types) ; স্থূল ; প্রসারিত, (বিশেষতঃ মুদ্রাক্ষর সম্পর্কে)। **7.** Bituminous, as coal ; sticky, as clay etc. ; শিলাজতুময় ; আঠাল। **Fat'-ish,** *adj.* Somewhat fat ; কতকটা স্থূল। **Fat'-less,** *adj.* **Fat'-ness,** *n.* Quality or state of being fat ; corpulence ; পুষ্টি, স্থূলতা ; স্থৌল্য, বিপুলাঙ্গতা, তুন্দিলত্ব। **Fat-brained**—Dull of apprehension ; স্থূল-মস্তিষ্ক, স্থূলধী। **Fat-guts**—A corpulent person ; স্থূলাঙ্গ ব্যক্তি। **Fat-head**—A dolt ; হাবা। **Fat-headed, —witted** — Dull ; stupid ; বোকা ; স্থূলবুদ্ধি। **Fat-hen**—নানা প্রকার গুল্মের সাধারণ নাম। **The fat is on the fire**—There is going on a great splutter and confusion, (in allusion to the process of frying) ; মহা হুলস্থূল কাণ্ড বাঁধিয়া গিয়াছে। **To cut it fat**—To make a display ; আড়ম্বর প্রদর্শন করা। **To cut up fat**—To leave much money ; অনেক টাকা রাখিয়া মরা।

To kill the fatted calf for—To receive as a returned prodigal with joy ; দেশত্যাগী অমিতব্যয়ী পুত্র প্রভৃতি অনুতপ্ত চিত্তে গৃহে ফিরিয়া আসিলে তাহাকে সাদরে সম্বর্দ্ধনা করা। **To live on the fat of the land**—To have the best of every thing ; প্রত্যেক জিনিসের সারভাগের অধিকারী হওয়া।

fa'-tal, *adj.* **1.** Proceeding from, or appointed by, fate ; inevitable ; necessary ; ভাগ্যসম্ভূত, ভাগ্যনির্দ্দিষ্ট ; অনিবার্য্য, অপরিহার্য্য ; আবশ্যক। **2.** Pertaining to, or concerned with, fate or destiny ; fateful ; decisive ; important ; as, *fatal* hour ; অদৃষ্ট-সম্বন্ধীয়, অদৃষ্ট-সংক্রান্ত ; নিয়তিনির্দ্দিষ্ট ; নিশ্চায়ক ; গুরুতর। **3.** Deadly ; as, a *fatal* weapon ; mortal ; destructive ; calamitous ; as, a *fatal* wound or day ; মারাত্মক ; প্রাণঘাতী ; বিনাশক, বিধ্বংসী ; অশুভকর, বিপজ্জনক। **4.** Causing mischief ; ill-advised ; "You no longer are *fatal,* but ugly and hateful" ; অনিষ্টজনক ; কুপরামর্শ দ্বারা প্রণোদিত। **-ism,** *n.* **1.** The doctrine that all events or things are predetermind by fate ; অদৃষ্টবাদ, নিয়তিবাদ, ভবিতব্যতাবাদ (হিঃ কোঃ)। **2.** Submission to whatever happens as inevitable ; অদৃষ্টের হস্তে আত্মসমর্পণ। **-ist,** *n.* & *adj.* One who maintains that all things are subject to fate ; ভবিতব্যতাবাদী (হিঃ কোঃ), অদৃষ্টবাদী। (*Adj.*) Fatalistic ; কপালঠুকা। **-is'-tic,** *adj.* Pertaining to fatalism ; অদৃষ্টবাদ-সম্বন্ধীয়। **-is'-ti-cal-ly,** *adv.* **-ize,** *v. i.* & *t.* To incline to fatalism ; অদৃষ্টবাদানুরাগী হওয়া। (*Verb t.*) To bring under the control of fate ; নিয়তির অধীন করা। **-ly,** *adv.* **1.** Mortally ; ruinously ; সাংঘাতিকরূপে ; অনিষ্টজনকভাবে। **2.** As decreed by fate ; নিয়তিনির্দ্দিষ্টভাবে। **-tal'-i-ty,** *n.* **1.** Subjection to fate ; invincible necessity ; ভবিতব্যতা ; বিধিনির্ব্বন্ধ, দৈবনির্ব্বন্ধ। **2.** Tendency to danger or destruction ; fatal influence ; বিপদাধীনতা, ধ্বংসশীলতা ; মারাত্মক প্রভাব। **3.** Destiny ; state of being liable to disaster ; নিয়তি ; বিপদাধীনতা। **4.** A disaster resulting in death ; a calamity ; death by accident, in war etc. ; অপমৃত্যুজনক দুর্ঘটনা ; দুর্ঘটনা ; অপঘাত মৃত্যু, অপমৃত্যু। **Fatal shears** — Death ; মৃত্যু। **Fatal sisters** —The three Fates (see FATE 4.) ; গ্রীক-পুরাণোক্ত নিয়তি দেবীত্রয়।

fata morgana, *n.* **1.** A fairy celebrated in the tales of chivalry etc. ; প্রাচীন বীরগণের কাহিনীতে উক্ত পরীবিশেষ। **2.** A mirage frequently seen in the strait of Messina ; মেসিনা প্রণালীতে দৃষ্ট মরীচিকা বিশেষ, গগননগর, খপুর।

fate, *n.* & *v. t.* **1.** The destiny that foredooms everything ; inevitable and unalterable necessity ; অদৃষ্ট, নিয়তি ; ভবিতব্যতা, বিধি। **2.** Appointed lot ; what is destined to happen ; doom ; death ill fortune ; ভাগ্য ; ভবিতব্য ; ধ্বংস, বিনাশ ; মৃত্যু ; দুর্দ্দৈব, দুর্ভাগ্য **3.** Ultimate condition ; "Plumer's *fate* is sealed" ; অন্তিম অবস্থা। **4.** (*Myth.*) The goddess of destiny (esp. *plu.*) [The three Greek goddesses, Clotho, Lachesis and Atropos, sometimes called the Destinies or Parcæ, who were supposed to determine the course of human life. They are represented,—one as holding the distaff, second as spinning and the third as cutting off the thread (of life.)] গ্রীক পুরাণোক্ত ক্লথো, ল্যাকিসিস এবং এট্রোপাস্ নাম্নী নিয়া দেবীত্রয়। ***Verb t.*** (Usually *pass* To pre-ordain ; to destine পূর্ব্বনির্দ্দিষ্ট করা ; নির্দ্দিষ্ট করা, নিরূপিত

করা। **Fat'-ed,** *adj.* Decreed by fate; doomed to ruin or destruction; controlled by fate; নিয়তিনির্দ্দিষ্ট, দৈববিহিত, বিধিকৃত; নিয়তিকর্ত্তৃক মৃত্যুর জন্য নিরূপিত; নিয়তিনিয়ন্ত্রিত। **Fate'-ful,** *adj.* **1.** Fraught with destiny; involving important consequences; important; as, *fateful* hour or decision; নিয়তিপূর্ণ; গুরুতরপরিণামজনক; গুরুতর। **2.** Significant of fate; ominous; as, the *fateful* cawings of the crow; দুর্ভাগ্যসূচক; অমঙ্গলসূচক। **3.** Showing the power of fate; controlled by fate; "As *fateful* as a Greek tragedy"; অদৃষ্টের ক্ষমতাপ্রদর্শী; নিয়তি-নিয়ন্ত্রিত। **Fate'-ful-ly,** *adv.* **Fate'-ful-ness,** *n.* **An irony of fate**—A providence which brings about events most curiously; অদৃষ্টের ফের, অদৃষ্ট-চক্র, অদৃষ্টের নিষ্ঠুর পরিহাস (রমেশ চন্দ্র দত্ত)। **To seal, decide or fix one's fate**—To seal, decide or fix one's ultimate condition; ভাগ্য নিরূপিত করা। **To share the fate of**—To share the same fate; to meet with the same kind of misfortue; কাহারও অদৃষ্টের সমভাগী হওয়া, সমসুখদুঃখভাগী হওয়া; একইরূপ দুর্দ্দৈবে পতিত হওয়া, একদশা প্রাপ্ত হওয়া।

fâ'-thêr, *n.* & *v. t.* **1.** A male parent; a generator; পিতা; জনক। **2.** A forefather; a founder of a race, family, etc.; (*pl.*) ancestors; পিতার ঊর্দ্ধতন পুরুষ, পূর্ব্বপুরুষ, পিতৃপুরুষ; কোন বংশের প্রতিষ্ঠাতা বা আদিম পুরুষ; (বহুবচন) পূর্ব্বপুরুষগণ, পিতৃপিতামহগণ। **3.** Inventor of anything; the author or contriver; as, the *father* of English poetry; উদ্ভাবক, আবিষ্কর্ত্তা; গ্রন্থকর্ত্তা, রচক। 4. One who performs the offices of a parent by maintenance, affectionate care, etc.; as, he was a *father* to the poor; পিতৃস্বরূপ ব্যক্তি, পিতৃস্থানীয় ব্যক্তি, প্রজাবৎসল রাজা (cf. স পিতা পিতরস্তাসাং কেবলং জন্মহেতবঃ — রঃ)। **5.** One who assumes the relationship of a parent by marriage, adoption, etc; as, *father*-in-law; শ্বশুর প্রভৃতি। **6.** God; the First Person of the Trinity; পরমেশ্বর; জগৎপিতা। [খৃষ্টীয় ধর্ম্মানুসারে ভগবানের ত্রিমূর্ত্তি, — পিতা, পুত্র ও পবিত্রাত্মা।] **7.** Christian writers of first five centuries; প্রথম পঞ্চশতাব্দীর খৃষ্টীয় শাস্ত্রকারগণ। **8.** A senator of ancient Rome; প্রাচীন রোমনগরীর ব্যবস্থাপক সভার সভ্য। **9.** A religioust eacher; ধর্ম্মোপদেষ্টা। **10.** A title given to dignitaries of the Church, superiors of convents and to Roman Catholic confessors; খৃষ্টীয় ধর্ম্মাধ্যক্ষ, মঠাধ্যক্ষ প্রভৃতির উপাধি। **11.** A priest; পুরোহিত। **12.** (*Pl.*) The leading men or elders of a city or council; কোন নগরীর বা সভার নেতৃস্থানীয় ব্যক্তিবৃন্দ। **13.** The eldest or senior member of a profession or body; কোন ব্যবসায় বা সম্মিলনীর সর্ব্বাপেক্ষা বয়োজ্যেষ্ঠ সভ্য। ***Verb t.*** **1.** To make oneself the father of; to beget; পিতা হওয়া; জন্ম দেওয়া। **2.** To originate, as a statement etc.; উদ্ভূত করা। **3.** To adopt, (*rare*); পোষ্যপুত্রগ্রহণ করা (অপ্রঃ)। **4.** To appear, or acknowledge oneself, as the author of (a book, statement, etc.); কোন পুস্তকের গ্রন্থকার বা কোন উক্তির কর্ত্তা বলিয়া স্বীকার করা। **5.** To confess as one's own child; to pass as the father of; নিজপুত্র বলিয়া স্বীকার করা; পিতা বলিয়া গৃহীত হওয়া। **6.** To fix the paternity, (with *on* or *upon*); as, to *father* a child or book *on* ~~or~~ *upon* a person; পিতৃত্ব নির্দ্দিষ্ট করা, জনকত্ব বা গ্রন্থকর্ত্তৃত্ব আরোপ করা। **7.** To act as a father to; to look after; পিতৃবৎ আচরণ করা; তত্ত্বাবধান করা। **—hood,** *n.* State of being a father; fatherly character or authority; পিতৃত্ব; পিতৃক্ষমতা, পিতৃপ্রকৃতি। **—less,** *adj.* **1.** Destitute of a living father; পিতৃহীন। **2.** Without a known author, as a book etc,; অজ্ঞাত-লেখক। **—less-ness,** *n.* **—ly,** *adj.* & *adv.* Like a father in affection and care; tender; paternal; পিতৃস্বরূপ, পিতৃবৎ; কোমল; পৈত্রিক। (*Adv.*) In a fatherly manner; with fatherly affection and care; পিতার ন্যায়, পিতৃবৎ; অপত্যনির্ব্বিশেষে। **—ship,** *n.* Position, state or relation of a father; পিতৃভাব, পিতৃত্ব। **Adoptive father**—পোষ্যপুত্রগ্রাহী, দত্তকগ্রহীতা। **Conscript Fathers**—Senators of ancient Rome; প্রাচীন রোমের ব্যবস্থাপক সভার সভ্যগণ। **Father-in-law**—শ্বশুর। **Father-land**—জন্মভূমি। **Father of the bar**—The oldest member of the bar; ব্যবহার-জীবি সমাজের সর্ব্বাপেক্ষা বয়োজ্যেষ্ঠ সভ্য। **Father of English poetry**—See FATHER *n.* 3. **Father of lies**—The Devil; শয়তান। **Father of the faithful**—(ক) এব্রাহেম; (খ) মহম্মদ বা তদীয় উত্তরাধিকারী সুলতানগণ, বর্ত্তমানে তুরুস্কের সুলতান। **Father of the House of Commons**—যে ব্যক্তি নিরবচ্ছিন্নভাবে সর্ব্বাপেক্ষা দীর্ঘকাল পার্লেমেন্টের প্রতিনিধি হইয়া আসিতেছেন। **Fathers of the Church** or **Fathers**—See FATHER *n.* 7. **Fathers of the City**—See FATHER *n.* 12. **Right** or **Most Reverened Father in God**—The title of a bishop or archbishop; খৃষ্টীয় ধর্ম্মাধ্যক্ষ বা প্রধান ধর্ম্মাধ্যক্ষের উপাধি। **The Father-land** — Germany; জর্ম্মণদেশ। **The father of water** — মিসরের নীলনদ। **The Holy Father**—রোমান ক্যাথলিক ধর্ম্মসম্রাট্, পোপ। **To be gathered to one's father**—To die and be buried; মরার পর কবরস্থ হওয়া। **To father on a person**—See FATHER *v. t.* 6.

făth'-om (-ŭm), *n.* & *v. t.* A measure of six feet, chiefly used in sounding ; ছয় ফুট অর্থাৎ ৪ হাত পরিমাণ, সাধারণতঃ সমুদ্রের গভীরতা পরিমাপে ব্যবহৃত হয়। ***Verb t.*** **1.** To measure by a sounding line ; গভীরতা মাপক সূত্র দ্বারা পরিমাপ করা। **2.** To sound the depth of water etc.; (*fig.*) to get to the bottom of; to understand ; জল প্রভৃতির গভীরতা নিরূপণ করা ; (লক্ষণায়) তলাইয়া দেখা; গভীরভাবে প্রবেশ করা। **a-ble,** *adj.* Capable fo being fathomed ; পরিমেয়। **–less,** *adj.* **1.** Bottomless ; অতলস্পর্শ। **2.** Incapable of being measured ; incomprehensible ; অপরিমেয়, অপ্রমেয়, অগাধ; দুর্ব্বোধ, দুর্জ্ঞেয়। **Fathom-line** — জলের গভীরতা মাপিবার রজ্জু।

fă-tid'-i-căl, *adj.* Having the power to foretell future events ; ভবিষ্যৎকথনক্ষম।

fă-tigue' (-tēg), *n.* & *v. t.* **1.** Weariness from labour or mental exertion ; exhaustion ; labour ; a task that fatigues one ; কায়িক বা মানসিক ক্লান্তি, আয়াস, খেদ ; গ্লানি, অবসন্নতা ; শ্রম, শ্রান্তি ; শ্রমজনক কর্ম্ম। **2.** (*Mil.*) Labours of soldiers distinct from the use of arms ; সৈন্যদিগের যুদ্ধ ব্যতিরিক্ত শ্রমজনক কার্য্য। **3.** (*Mech.*) Weakness in metals after repeated blows or long strain ; (যন্ত্রবিজ্ঞান) বহুক্ষণব্যাপী ব্যবহারের পর যন্ত্রাদির অবসন্নতা। ***Verb t.*** **1.** To weary or harass with toil; to exhaust ; পরিশ্রান্ত করা ; অবসন্ন করা। **2.** (*Mech.*) To induce a condition of fatigue in ; as, to *fatigue* a metal ; (যন্ত্রাদি) অবসাদগ্রস্ত করা। **–tigued,** *adj.* Tired ; ক্লান্ত, পরিশ্রান্ত, পরিক্লান্ত, খিন্ন। **–less,** *adj.* Tireless ; অক্লান্ত, অশ্রান্ত। **–ti'-guing,** *adj.* Exhausting ; ক্লান্তিজনক, অবসাদজনক। **Fatigue-dress**—যুদ্ধ ব্যতিরিক্ত কার্য্যে নিযুক্ত থাকার কালে সৈন্যগণ যে পোষাক পরিয়া থাকে। **Fatigue duty**—সৈন্যদিগের যুদ্ধ ভিন্ন অপর শ্রমজনক কার্য্য। **Fatigue-party** or **fatigue**—যুদ্ধ ভিন্ন অপর শ্রমজনক কার্য্যে নিযুক্ত সৈন্যদল।

făt'-ting, *n.* A young animal fattened for slaughter ; a fat animal ; বধার্থ যে পশু-শাবককে হৃষ্টপুষ্ট করা হয় ; মেদস্বী পশু।

făt'-ten (-n), *v. t.* & *i.* **1.** To make fat ; to feed, as animal etc. for slaughter ; স্থূল করা, মেদস্বী করা ; বধের জন্য পশুকে স্থূল বা পুষ্ট করা। **2.** To fertilize ; as, to *fatten* soil ; উর্ব্বরতা সম্পাদন করা। ***Verb i.*** To grow fat ; স্থূল হওয়া, মোটা হওয়া, হৃষ্টপুষ্ট হওয়া।

făt'-tȳ *adj.* **1.** Containing or resembling fat ; greasy ; বসাময়, চর্ব্বিবৎ, বসাসিক (সাঃ পঃ) ; তৈলাক্ত। **2.** Fertile ; উর্ব্বর। **3.** Having a morbid deposit of fat ; as, *fatty* kidney ; বিকৃত বসাপূর্ণ। **Fatty clay**—চিকণ মাটী (হিঃ কোঃ)।

făt'-tȳ, *n.* (*Usu. voc.*) A fat child etc ; নাদুসনুদুস শিশু প্রভৃতি।

fă-tū'-i-tous (-tŭs), *adj.* Stupid ; বুদ্ধিহীন, বোকা।

fă-tū'-i-tȳ, *n.* **1.** Stupidity ; বুদ্ধিহীনতা, বুদ্ধিভ্রংশ, মূঢ়তা। **2.** Imbecility of the mind ; বুদ্ধিদৌর্ব্বল্য।

făt'-ū-ous (-ŭs), *adj.* **1.** Foolish ; vacantly silly ; idiotic ; নির্ব্বোধ ; জড়বুদ্ধি ; হাবা। **2.** Illusory ; unreal like the ignis fatuus ; as, *fatuous* fire or light ; ভ্রান্তিজনক ; আলেয়ার মত অবাস্তব। **–ly,** *adv.* **–ness,** *n.*

faubourg, *n.* (*F.*) A suburb of a city, esp. of Paris ; নগরোপকণ্ঠ, সহরতলী (বিশেষতঃ প্যারী নগরীর)।

fau'-cĭl (fä-), *adj.* Pertaining to fauces or throat ; (*phonol.*) deeply guttural, as a sound ; কণ্ঠসম্বন্ধীয় ; (শব্দ-বিজ্ঞান) গভীরভাবে কণ্ঠ্য।

fau'-cēs (fä-), *n.* (*Pl.*) The back part of the mouth terminated by the pharynx and the larynx মুখ-মধ্য ও গলমধ্যের অভ্যন্তরস্থ গহ্বর,—জিহ্বা, উপজিহ্বা, তালুপার্শ্বগ্রন্থি ও গলনলী দ্বারা এই গহ্বর সীমাবদ্ধ।

fau'-cĕt (fä-), *n.* (*Dial.* & *U. S.*), A pipe inserted in a barrel to draw liquid ; (উপভাষায়) মদ্যাদি বাহির করার জন্য পিপায় প্রবিষ্ট নল।

faugh (fä), *interj.* An exclamation of contempt or disgust ; ছি! ছি!! রাম! রাম!! তোবা! তোবা!! মহাভারত !

fault (fält), *n.* & *v. t.* **1.** A defect ; a blemish ; অঙ্গহীনতা, অসম্পূর্ণতা ; অভাব, খুঁত, ছিদ্র। **2.** An offence less serious than a crime ; a neglect of duty ; a transgression ; a wrongful act ; দোষ ; কর্ত্তব্যের ত্রুটী ; কসুর, ঘাট (*colloq.*) ; অন্যায় কার্য্য। **3.** Responsibility ; blame ; as, the *fault* is not mine ; দায়িত্ব ; দোষ। **4.** (*Hunting*) Loss of scent ; a check caused by failure of scent ; (মৃগয়া) পশ্চাদ্ধাবিত জন্তুর গন্ধ অপ্রাপ্তি ; পশ্চাদ্ধাবিত জন্তুর গন্ধ অপ্রাপ্তিজনিত প্রতিবন্ধক। **5.** (*Tennis*) Failure to serve the ball to proper court ; (টেনিস্ ক্রীড়া) নির্দ্দিষ্ট অঙ্গনে কন্দুকতাড়নে অকৃতকার্য্যতা। **6.** (*Geol.*) A break or dislocation of strata ; (ভূ-বিদ্যা) স্তর-ভ্রংশ (হিঃ কোঃ), স্তরচ্যুতি (ঐ)। **7.** (*Telegr.*) Imperfect insulation ; a leakage ; (তাড়িত বার্ত্তাবহ) অসম্যক বিদ্যুদরোধন ; ছিদ্রপথে প্রবেশ বা নিঃসরণ। ***Verb t.*** **1.** To find fault with, (*rare*) ; দোষ ধরা (অপ্রঃ)। **2.** (*Geol* & *mining*) To cause a fault or displacement in strata or veins ; (ভূ- ও খনিজ বিদ্যা) স্তর-ভ্রংস করা।

Fault'-i-ly, *adv.* In a faulty manner ; অসম্পূর্ণভাবে, দোষের সহিত। **Fault'-i-ness,** *n.* **Fault'-less,** *adj.* Without any fault ; নির্দ্দোষ, নিখুঁত, সর্ব্বাঙ্গ-সম্পন্ন, অনবদ্য, অনিন্দ্য, নিরবদ্য। **Fault'-less-ly,** *adv.*

নির্দ্দোষভাবে, নিখুঁতভাবে। **Fault'-less-ness,** *n.* **Fault'-y,** *adj.* Marked by faults ; imperfect ; defective ; blamable ; দোষী, অপরাধী ; অসম্পূর্ণ ; দোষযুক্ত ; নিন্দার্হ। **Fault-finder**—One who makes a practice of discovering others' faults, esp. unreasonably ; পরদোষান্বেষণে রত ব্যক্তি, ত্রুটিগ্রাহক, দোষগ্রাহী, দোষদর্শী। **Fault-finding**—*adj.* & *n.* Censorious ; দোষদর্শী, দোষগ্রাহী, ত্রুটিগ্রাহী। (*Noun*) The act or practice of finding fault ; ত্রুটিগ্রহণ, দোষদৃষ্টি। **At fault**—Unable to find the scent and continue chase ; ঘ্রাণ হারাইয়া শিকারানুসরণে অসমর্থ। Puzzled ; at a loss ; embarrassed ; হতভম্ব, ভ্যাবাচ্যাকা ; কিংকর্ত্তব্যবিমূঢ় ; বিভ্রাটে পতিত। **For fault of**—In default of ; কোন কিছুর অভাবে বা অন্যথায়। **In fault**—To blame ; দোষী। **To a fault**—Excessively ; as, he is gentle *to a fault* ; অতিরিক্ত মাত্রায়। **To find fault**—To complain ; অভিযোগ করা। **To find fault with**—To attribute blame to ; to censure ; as, to *find fault with* a man or his conduct ; দোষ ধরা, ছিদ্র বাহির করা ; ভর্ৎসনা করা। **With all faults**—At the buyer's risk ক্রেতার দায়িত্বে। **Without fault**—Certainly ; without fail ; নিশ্চিতভাবে; অন্যথা না করিয়া।

Faun (făn), *n.* A rural deity with horns and tail among the Romans ; রোমকদিগের সশৃঙ্গ ও সক্ষুর বনদেবতা বিশেষ।

fau'-nă (fă-), *n.* (*Pl.* -NAE, -NAS) **1.** The animals of any given area or epoch ; কোন দেশ বা কাল বিশেষের জন্তুনিচয়, প্রাণিবর্গ, প্রাণিনামমালা (সাঃ পাঃ), প্রাণিমালা (ঐ)। **2.** A treatise on the animals of a region or period ; কোন বিশেষ দেশ বা যুগের প্রাণিবিষয়ক গ্রন্থ। **—nal,** *adj.* Relating to fauna ; কোন দেশ বা কাল বিশেষের জন্তু সম্বন্ধীয়। **—nic, —ni-cal,** *adjs.* **—nist,** *n.* One who studies a fauna ; দেশ বা কাল বিশেষের প্রাণিতত্ত্বানুশীলনকারী।

fauteuil, *n.* (*F.*) **1.** An arm-chair ; বাজুদার কুশি, কেদারা। **2.** A theatre stall ; (রঙ্গালয়ের নিম্নতলস্থ) সম্মুখবর্ত্তী আসন।

faux pas, *n.* (*F.*) A false step ; a breach of manners or moral conduct ; a lapse from chastity ; পদস্খলন ; সদাচারস্খলন ; ব্যভিচার।

fă-vē'-ō-lāte, *adj.* Honey-combed ; having cavities or cells ; মৌচাকের মত ছিদ্রাবিশিষ্ট, শরঘাবৎ ; ছিদ্রাবিশিষ্ট, কোষবিশিষ্ট।

fă-vō'-ni-ăn, *adj.* Pertaining to the west wind ; favourable ; পাশ্চমানিলসম্বন্ধীয় ; অনুকূল।

fă-vōse', *adj.* Like a honey-comb ; মধুচক্রবৎ।

fā'-vour (-vêr), *n.* **1.** Kind or friendly regard ; good will ; kindness ; as, to find *favour* in the eyes of a man ; approval ; "Who looked with *favour* on his enterprise" ; অনুগ্রহ, সৌহার্দ্দ ; প্রীতি ; দয়া, সদাশয়তা ; অনুকূল দৃষ্টি। **2.** Support ; as, under the *favour* of night ; সাহায্য, পোষকতা, সহায়তা। **3.** An act of grace or good will done as a kindness and not as an act of justice or right ; an exceptional kindness ; as, I should esteem it a *favour* ; অনুগ্রহ বা দয়ার কার্য্য ; প্রীতি। **4.** A gift or present ; a token of love or affection ; a knot of ribbons worn at a ceremony ; a badge ; উপহার ; প্রীতি বা ভালবাসার চিহ্ন ; উৎসবকালে পরিহিত ফিতার গুচ্ছ ; নিদর্শন-চিহ্ন। **5.** Partiality ; পক্ষপাত। **6.** Letter ; as, I have received your *favour* of yesterday ; পত্র। **7.** (*Archaic*) Countenance ; looks ; (অপ্রঃ) চেহারা ; আকৃতি। **In favour**—Favoured ; অনুগ্রহলব্ধ। **In favour of**—On behalf of ; favourable to ; on the side of ; in support of ; as, I am *in favour of* women's suffrage ; to the advantage or account of ; as, a cheque to be drawn *in his favour* ; স্বপক্ষে ; অনুকূলে ; পক্ষে ; সহায়তায়, পোষকতায়। **In favour with**—Favoured by or encouraged by ; কাহারও দ্বারা অনুগৃহীত বা উৎসাহিত। **Out of favour**—Disliked ; কুদৃষ্টিতে পতিত, কাহারও অনুগ্রহ হইতে বঞ্চিত। **To be or stand high in one's favour**—To be in one's good graces ; কাহারও অনুগ্রহপাত্র হওয়া, কাহারও সুনজরে পড়া, কাহারও অনুগ্রহ-দৃষ্টি লাভ করা **To curry favour**—To seek to gain favour by flattery ; তোষামোদ দ্বারা অনুগ্রহলাভের চেষ্টা করা, প্রসাদ প্রার্থনা করা। **Under favour**—With your permission ; subject to correction ; আপনার অনুমতি লইয়া ; সংশোধনাধীনে। **With or by one's favour**—With one's leave or kind permission ; কাহারও অনুমতিক্রমে।

fā-vour (-vêr), *v. t.* **1.** To look with favour upon ; to approve ; to aid ; to treat with kindness ; to show partiality towards ; প্রীতির চক্ষুতে দেখা, করুণাকটাক্ষপাত করা ; অনুমোদন করা ; সাহায্য করা ; সদয়ভাবে ব্যবহার করা ; পক্ষপাত প্রদর্শন করা। **2.** To be advantageous to (a person) ; to facilitate ; as, he *favoured* the entrance of the enemy ; সুবিধাজনক হওয়া ; সুকর করা, সুবিধাজনক করা। **3.** To resemble in appearance or features ; as, the child *favours* his father ; চেহারা বা আকৃতিতে সদৃশ হওয়া। **4.** To lend confirmation to ; দৃঢ়তা সম্পাদন করা। **5.** To oblige ; as, to *favour* a person with a copy of a book ; বাধিত

করা। **—a-ble,** *adj.* **1.** Kind; propitious; friendly; approving; সদয়; প্রীতিপূর্ণ, প্রসন্ন; বন্ধুভাবাপন্ন; অনুমোদনকারী। **2.** Advantageous; partial; সুবিধাজনক; পক্ষপাতী। **3.** Suitable (to); উপযুক্ত, উপযোগী। **4.** Promising; auspicious; as, he has a *favourable* aspect; আশাপ্রদ; শুভ। **—a-bly,** *adv.* In a favourable manner; অনুকূলভাবে, সদয়ভাবে, প্রীতির সহিত। **—ing,** *adj.* Showing favour or good will; facilitating; অনুগ্রহপ্রদর্শক, প্রীতিপ্রদর্শক; সৌকর্য্যসাধক। **—voured,** *p. adj.* **1.** Regarded with favour; অনুগ্রহপ্রাপ্ত। **2.** Having a certain appearance or looks; as, ill or well *favoured*; বিশেষ আকৃতি বা চেহারা বিশিষ্ট। **3.** Having unusual advantages or blessings; as, a *favoured* nation; বিশেষ অনুগ্রহপ্রাপ্ত।

fā'-vour-ite (-vẽr-ĭt), *n.* & *adj.* **1.** A person or thing regarded with special favour; one unduly favoured by a man of high rank or authority; প্রিয়পাত্র, প্রিয়বস্তু, বল্লভ; বড়লোকের প্রিয়পাত্র। **2.** (*Sporting*) A competitor generally expected to win; ঘোড়দৌড়ে যে প্রতিদ্বন্দ্বী জয়ী হইবে বলিয়া আশা করা যায়। ***Adj.*** Regarded with special favour or fondness; as, a *favourite* child or walk; প্রিয়, আদৃত, বিশেষভাবে অনুগৃহীত। **—it-ism,** *n.* **1.** A disposition to favour a person or a class to the exclusion of others having equal claims; partiality; কোন বিশেষ ব্যক্তি বা সম্প্রদায়ের প্রতি সবিশেষ অনুগ্রহশীলতা; পক্ষাপাতিত্ব। **2** The condition of being a favourite; অনুগ্রহভাজনতা, প্রিয়পাত্রত্ব। **A favourite of fortune**—লক্ষ্মীর বরপুত্র।

fawn (fän), *n.*, *adj.* & *v. t.* **1.** A young deer; a buck or doe of the first year; মৃগশিশু, হরিণশাবক, বালকুরঙ্গম; একবর্ষবয়স্ক মৃগশাবক। **2.** A fawn colour; light brown; মৃগশাবকবর্ণ; মৃদু পিঙ্গলবর্ণ। ***Adj.*** Of the colour of a fawn; কুরঙ্গশাবকবর্ণ। ***Verb t.*** To bring forth (a fawn); (মৃগশাবক) প্রসব করা। **Fawn-coloured**—Of light brown colour; মৃদুপিঙ্গলবর্ণ। **Fawn-eyed** — বালকুরঙ্গমনেত্রা, মৃগশিশুলোচনা, মৃগশাবকাক্ষী, (পুরুষপক্ষে) বালমৃগাক্ষ। **In fawn**—Pregnant; (হরিণী-পক্ষে) সসত্ত্বা।

fawn (fän), *v. i.* **1.** To show affection by wagging the tail, crouching, etc.; as, a dog *fawns* upon his master; লাঙ্গুল নাড়িয়া গুড়িশুড়ি মারিয়া ভালবাসা দেখান। **2.** To cringe in order to gain favour, (with *on* or *upon*); জঘন্যভাবে তোষামোদ করা, হীনতোষামোদ করা। **Fawn'-ing,** *adj.* & *n.* Courting servilely; হীনভাবে তোষামোদকারী; পদলেহনকারী (*Noun*). Gross flattery; হীনতোষামোদ। **Fawn'-ing-ly,** *adv.* **To fawn on** or **upon**—To flatter servilely; হীনভাবে তোষামোদ করা, পদলেহন করা। To practise blandishment; আদর বা সোহাগ করা।

fay (fā), *n.* & *v. t.* **1.** A fairy; an elf; পরী; দেবযোনি বিশেষ, উপদেবতা। **2.** (*Shakes.*) Faith; বিশ্বাস (অপ্রঃ)। ***Verb t.*** To fit (pieces of timber) together; (কাষ্ঠফলক সকল) সংলগ্ন করা, জোড় দেওয়া।

fē'-āl-tȳ, *n.* **1.** The vassal's oath of fidelity to his feudal lord; সামন্ততন্ত্রের নিয়মাধীন ভূমিগ্রহণকারী ব্যক্তির ঊর্দ্ধতন ভূস্বামির প্রতি নিষ্ঠা। **2.** Faithfulness; constancy, as of a friend to a friend, or of a wife to her husband; বিশ্বস্ততা; নিষ্ঠা।

fear (fēr), *n.*, *v. t.* & *i.* **1.** A painful emotion caused by apprehension of impending danger or evil; dread; আতঙ্ক; ভীতি, ভয়, ডর। **2.** Reverence and awe; as, the *fear* of God; ভয়মিশ্রিত ভক্তি। **3.** The cause or object of dread; "I was a *fear* to mine acquaintance"; ভয়-হেতু, ভীতিজনক বস্তু, ভয়ের কারণ। **4.** Anxiety for the safety, (with *of*); as, I am in *fear of* his life; উদ্বেগ, উৎকণ্ঠা। ***Verb t.*** **1.** To regard with fear; to be afraid of; ভয় করা; ভীত হওয়া। **2.** To revere or venerate (God); ভক্তি করা, শ্রদ্ধা করা। ***Verb i.*** **1.** To be afraid; to be in apprehension of evil; ভীত হওয়া; শঙ্কিত হওয়া। **2.** To feel painful uncertainty; as, you shall get it, never *fear*; উৎকণ্ঠাকুলিত হওয়া, উদ্বেগপূর্ণ হওয়া। **Fear'-ful,** *adj.* **1** Afraid; frightened; ভীত, সভয়, শঙ্কিত; ভয়ার্ত্ত। **2.** Exciting fear; dreadful; ভয়াবহ, ভীতিজনক, আতঙ্কজনক; ভীষণ, বিভীষণ, ভয়ানক, ভয়ঙ্কর, লোমহর্ষণ। **3.** Timid; apprehensive; wanting resolution (to); শঙ্কিত; ভীত; সংশয়াকুলিত। **4.** Reverential; ভক্তি-পূর্ণ। **5.** Extremely bad or annoying; "A *fearful* outcry"; ভয়ঙ্কর, ভয়ানক, ভীষণ। **Fear'-ful-ly,** *adv.* In a fearful manner; ভীতভাবে, সত্রাসে, সভয়ে। **Fear'-less,** *adj.* Free from fear; bold; daring; অকুতোভয়, নির্ভীক, নিঃশঙ্ক, ভয়হীন; সাহসী; দুঃসাহসী। **Fear'-less-ly,** *adv.* In a fearless manner; নির্ভীকভাবে, অকুতোভয়ে, নির্ভয়ে। **Fear'-less-ness,** *n.* The state of being fearless; নির্ভীকতা, সাহসিকতা। **For fear of** — In apprehension of; ভয়ে, পাছে। **For fear that** or **lest**—Lest; ভয়ে, পাছে। **In a fearful mess** — See FEARFUL 5. **No fear**—It is not likely; শঙ্কার কারণ নাই।

fear'-nought (fẽr-nät), *n.* A thick shaggy woollen staff used for lining portholes in ships and for other purposes ; একপ্রকার স্থূল পশমের কাপড়,—যদ্দ্বারা জাহাজের পার্শ্বদেশস্থ ছিদ্রে আস্তর দেওয়া হয়।

fear'-some (fēr-sŭm), *adj.* Causing fear ; frightful in apprehension etc. ; ভীতিজনক ; ভীষণদর্শন। **—ly,** *adv.* **—ness,** *n.*

fea'-si-ble (fē-zĭ-bl), *adj.* **1.** Practicable ; possible to be done ; সাধ্য, শক্য ; সুকর। **2.** Serviceable ; manageable ; suitable ; কার্য্যকরী, কার্য্যকর ; পরিচালনীয় ; উপযোগী। **3.** Probable ; সম্ভবপর। **—bil'-i-ty,** *n.* Practicability ; সুকরতা, সৌকর্য্য, সাধ্যতা, শক্যতা। **—bly,** *adj.* **—ness,** *n.*

feast (fēst), *n., v. i.* & *t.* **1.** A festival, esp. religious ; a holiday ; a joyous anniversary ; পর্ব্ব, ধর্ম্মোৎসব ; ছুটীর দিন ; সাম্বৎসরিক আনন্দোৎসব। **2.** An annual village festival ; সাম্বৎসরিক পল্লী-উৎসব। **3.** A sumptuous repast of which many guests partake ; a banquet ; (*fig.*) an exquisite gratification to the senses or mind ; as, a *feast* of reason ; মহোৎসব, ভোজোৎসব ; ভোজ ; (লক্ষণায়) ঐন্দ্রিয় বা মানসিক পরিতৃপ্তি বা পরিতুষ্টি। ***Verb i.*** To partake of a feast ; to eat sumptuously ; to be highly gratified or pleased ; "Let her eyes *feast* incessantly on a laughing sea" ; ভোজে যোগদান করা ; সমৃদ্ধভাবে ভোজন করা ; পরিতৃপ্ত হওয়া, পরিতুষ্ট হওয়া। ***Verb t.*** **1.** To entertain sumptuously ; as, he was *feasted* by the king ; to gratify ; as, to *feast* one's eyes on a picture ; সমৃদ্ধভাবে ভোজন করান ; পরিতৃপ্ত করা, পরিতুষ্ট করা। **2.** To pass in feasting, (with *away*); as, he *feasted away* the night ; ভোজোৎসবে অতিবাহিত করা। **Feast'-er,** *n.* **1.** One who fares sumptuously ; ভোজাহারী। **2.** One who entertains others sumptuously ; ভোজদাতা। **Feast-day**—স্মরণার্থ পর্ব্ব-দিবস। **Movable** or **immovable feast**—যে পর্ব্ব নির্দ্দিষ্ট বা বিভিন্ন দিবসে প্রত্যাবৃত্ত হয়। **Feast of reason and flow of soul**—উচ্চাঙ্গের মানসিক বা আধ্যাত্মিক বিষয়ক কথা-বার্ত্তার প্রবাহ।

feat (fēt), *n.* **1.** A deed of valour ; a noteworthy act ; "Your *feats* of arms" ; বীরোচিত কর্ম্ম, সাহসিক কর্ম্ম ; অবদান। **2.** An extraordinary act showing dexterity or strength or cunning ; a surprising trick ; as, *feast* of horsemanship ; শক্তি, দক্ষতা বা চাতুর্য্যসূচক অসাধারণ কর্ম্ম, অদ্ভুত কর্ম্ম ; বিস্ময়জনক কৌশল।

feat (fēt), *adj.* (*Archaic*) Smart ; dexterous ; nice ; neat ; (অপ্রঃ) চালাক ; সুদক্ষ ; সুন্দর, সুশ্রী ; ফিট্‌ফাট্। **Feat'-ly,** *adv.*

feath'-êr (fĕth-), *n.* **1.** One of the growths which form the covering of a bird's skin ; পক্ষীর (গাত্রাচ্ছাদক) পাখা, পালক। **2.** Plumage ; a tire ; as, fine *feathers* make fine birds, (a proverb) ; পাখীর পালকসমূহ ; টোপর। **3.** A plume worn in a hat ; টুপির কোমল পালক। **4.** A piece or pieces of feather attached to an arrow ; বাণের পক্ষ। **5.** Kind ; species ; (from the proverbial phrase — *birds of a feather*) ; প্রকার, রকম; জাতি। **6.** Anything very light ; as, he could have knocked me down with a *feather* ; অতি লঘু বস্তু, অসার পদার্থ। **7.** A feathery tuft of hair ; পালকবৎ কেশগুচ্ছ। **8.** (*Mech.*) A projection on a board to fit into another board ; (যন্ত্রবিজ্ঞান) অন্য ফলকের সহিত জোড়া দিবার জন্য কোন ফলকের উদ্গাত অংশ। **9.** A feather-like flaw in the eye or in a gem ; চক্ষু বা মণিতে পালকাকার খুঁত। **10.** (*Rowing*) The horizontal adjustment of an oar as it rises from the water ; (দাঁড়টানায়) জল হইতে তুলিবার সময় পাখীর ডানার মত দাঁড়ের অবস্থান। **—ered,** *adj.* **1.** Clothed or covered with feathers ; পালকাচ্ছাদিত, পালক-শোভিত। **2.** Covered with anything like feather or ornamented ; কারুকার্য্যশোভিত। **—i-ness,** *n.* **—y,** *adj.* Pertaining to, resembling, or covered with, feathers ; পালক-সম্বন্ধীয়, পালকসদৃশ, সপক্ষ, পালক-শোভিত **—less,** *adj.* Having no feathers ; পালক-বিহীন। **Feather-bed** — পালক-পূরিত গদি। **Feather-edge** — কাষ্ঠফলকের কপোত-পুচ্ছাকার উদ্গাত অংশের প্রান্ত। **Feather-flower**—রমণীদিগের শিরোভূষণের জন্য পালকনির্ম্মিত কৃত্রিম পুষ্প। **Feather-grass**—এক প্রকার ঘাস। **Feather-head, —brain, —pate** — ক্ষীণ-মস্তিষ্ক ব্যক্তি, নির্ব্বোধ ব্যক্তি। **Feather-headed, —brained, —pated** — ক্ষীণমস্তিষ্ক, নির্ব্বোধ। **Feather-let**—A small feather ; ক্ষুদ্র পালক। **Feather-stitch** — একপ্রকার কারুকার্য্যশোভি আঁকাবাঁকা সেলাইর কাজ। **Feather-weight**—দৌড়ের অশ্বদ্বারা বাহ্য অতি লঘু ভার ; অতি লঘু বস্তু বা ব্যক্তি ; গুরুত্বহীন ব্যক্তি, নগণ্য ব্যক্তি, তুচ্ছ ব্যক্তি। **A feather in one's cap**—An honour, trophy or mark of distinction ; মান, গৌরব, বিজয়চিহ্ন, সম্মানচিহ্ন। **Birds of a feather**—See BIRD. **Fur and feather**—Game beasts and birds ; শিকারের উপযোগী পশু বা পক্ষী। **To be in full feather**—To be in one's best clothes ; সর্ব্বোত্তম ভূষণে বা পরিচ্ছদে সজ্জিত হওয়া। **To be in high feather**—To be in high spirits ; to be greatly elated ; উৎফুল্ল হওয়া, হর্ষোৎফুল্ল হওয়া ; উল্লসিত হওয়া। **To cut a feather**—(*Naut.*) To make the water foam in moving,—in allusion to the ripple which a ship throws off from her bows ; (নৌবিদ্যা) জল ফেনিল করিয়া চলা। To make one's self conspicuous ; নিজকে সবিশেষ লক্ষ্য বা দৃষ্টির বিষয়ীভূত করা। **To show** or **fly the white feather**—To betray cowardice,—(white feather in a game-bird's tail being the mark of bad breeding) ; ভীরুতা বা কাপুরুষতার চিহ্ন প্রদর্শন করা।

feath'-ēr (fĕth-), *v. t.* & *i.* **1.** To furnish with feather or feathers ; as, to *feather* an arrow ; পক্ষযুক্ত করা, সপক্ষ করা, পক্ষদ্বারা বিভূষিত করা, পালক শোভিত করা। **2.** To adorn, as with feathers ; to form featherlike covering or adornment for ; as, to *feather* a hat : a hill *feathered* with birch ; পালকবৎ ভূষিত করা ; পালকবৎ আবরণ বা আভরণ রচনা করা। **3.** To cover or line with feathers ; as, to *feather* a nest ; পালকাচ্ছাদিত করা, পালকাবৃত করা। **4.** To turn, as an oar horizontally over water : জল হইতে দাঁড় তুলিয়া ভূপৃষ্ঠের সহিত সমান্তরাল করা। **5.** To knock a few feathers from (a bird) without killing ; (গুলি করিয়া) পক্ষীর শরীর হইতে কয়েকটী পালক ছিন্ন করা। **6.** (*Mech.*) To join by a groove and tongue ; (যন্ত্র-বিজ্ঞান) খাজ বা উদ্গাত অংশদ্বারা জোড়া লাগান। *Verb i.* **1.** To become feathered ; পালকযুক্ত হওয়া। **2.** To turn to a horizontal plane, as an oar ; (দাঁড়ের পক্ষে) পক্ষীর ডানার মত ভূপৃষ্ঠের সহিত সমান্তরাল হওয়া। **3.** To float, move or wave like feathers ; "Cedars *feathering* in evergreen beauty" ; পালকের মত ভাসিয়া চলা, সঞ্চালিত হওয়া, আন্দোলিত হওয়া। **To feather an oar**—See FEATHER *v. t.* 4. **To feather one's nest** — To collect wealth for one's self while serving others in the position of a trust, (an expression taken from the practice of birds which collect feathers for the lining of their nests) ; অন্যের সম্পত্তি হইতে নিজের বাসা পুরু করা, অন্যের কার্য্যে নিযুক্ত থাকার সময় বেশ দু'পয়সা সংস্থান করিয়া লওয়া, অন্যের অধীনে বিশ্বাসের কার্য্যে নিযুক্ত থাকার সময় নিজের স্বার্থ উদ্ধার করা। **To tar and feather a person**—To smear him with tar and cover him with feathers as a punishment or indignity ; সর্ব্বাঙ্গে আলকাত্‌রা মাখাইয়া পালকদ্বারা আচ্ছাদিত করা, হোঁদল কুতকুতে সাজান।

feath-ēr-ing (fĕth-), *n.* **1.** Plumage ; পক্ষীর পালকসমূহ। **2.** The fitting of feathers to arrows ; the feathers of an arrow ; বাণে পক্ষ সংযোজন ; বাণের পক্ষ। **3.** A fringe of hair, as on the legs of a dog ; কুকুরাদির পায়ের রোমরেখা। **4.** (*Arch.*) Foliation ; (স্থপতি-বিজ্ঞান) পত্রাকার ভূষা। **5.** A feather-like marking in a flower ; পুষ্পের উপর পালকাকৃতি চিহ্ন।

fea'-tūre (fē-), *n.* & *v. t.* **1.** The make or cast of the face or any part of it ; (*pl.*) the countenance ; মুখের গঠন ; (বহুবচনে) চেহারা, মুখাবয়ব। **2.** A peculiar mark or characteristic ; a prominent part ; as, the chief *feature* of a work or thing ; বিশেষ নিদর্শন ; বিশেষত্ব। *Verb t.* **1.** To delineate or sketch the prominences ; প্রধান প্রধান লক্ষণসমূহ উল্লেখ করা, স্থূল স্থূল বিষয়সমূহ প্রদর্শন করা। **2.** To stand, as a feature or distinctive mark upon ; কোন কিছুর বিশেষত্বসূচক লক্ষণ স্বরূপে অবস্থান করা। **—less,** *adj.* Having no distinct features ; ugly, (*rare*) ; বিশিষ্ট আকৃতিবিহীন, নিরবয়ব ; কদাকার (বিরল)। **—ly** *adj.* Handsome, (*rare*) ; সুন্দর (বিরল)। **—tured,** *p. adj.* Having features of a certain cast ; বিশিষ্ট মুখাবয়বসম্পন্ন।

fē-bric'-ū-lă, *n.* A slight fever ; অল্পজ্বর, মৃদুজ্বর।

fē-brif'-ic, *adj.* Producing fever ; জ্বরোৎপাদক, জ্বরজনক, জ্বরকর।

fĕb'-ri-fūge, *n.* A medicine that removes or mitigates fever ; a cooling drink ; জ্বরহর ঔষধ, জ্বরঘ্ন ঔষধ, জ্বরাঙ্কুশ ; শৈত্যজনক পানীয়।

Fe-brif'-u-gal, *adj.* Having the quality of mitigating or removing fever ; জ্বরঘ্ন, জ্বরহর, জ্বরোপশামক।

fē'-brīle, *adj.* Of or relating to fever ; feverish ; জ্বরঘটিত, জ্বরসংক্রান্ত ; সজ্বর।

Fĕb'-rū-ă-rȳ, *n.* The second month in the year, said to have been introduced into the Roman calendar by Numa (a Roman emperor), in common years it contains twenty-eight days, but in a leap year, twenty-nine days ; ইংরেজী বৎসরের দ্বিতীয় মাস, ফেব্রুয়ারী। **February fill-dike**—বৃষ্টি এবং তুষারপাতের বাহুল্যহেতু ফেব্রুয়ারী মাসের নাম।

fē-cēs, *n. Pl.* See FACES.

fecit, fecerunt, (*abbr. fec.*) They made it (esp. this picture etc.)—used with an artist's signature ; তাহাদের দ্বারা রচিত বা প্রস্তুত (বিশেষতঃ এই চিত্র প্রভৃতি)।

fĕck'-lĕss, *adj.* Spiritless ; feeble ; inefficient ; নিস্তেজ ; দুর্ব্বল, অশক্ত, অকর্ম্মণ্য। **—ly,** *adv.* **—ness** *n.*

fĕc'-ū-lă, *n.* Starch obtained as a sediment by breaking down certain plants and seeds in water ; starch ; কোন কোন গাছগাছড়া বা বীজ ছেঁচিয়া জলে ভিজাইলে তলানি স্বরূপ যে শ্বেতসার পাওয়া যায় ; শ্বেতসার।

fĕc'-ū-lĕnt, *adj.* Containing feces or sediment ; muddy ; গাদযুক্ত, তলানি বা মলপূর্ণ ; আবিল, পঙ্কিল, সমল। **—lence,** *n.* **1.** Muddiness ; foulness ; আবিলতা ; মলিনতা। **2.** Lees ; dregs ; গাদ ; তলানি।

fĕc′-ŭnd, *adj.* **1.** Fruitful in progeny ; fertile ; ফলপ্রসূ, ফলবতী, বহুপ্রজ ; উর্ব্বর। **2.** Fertilizing ; উর্ব্বরতা-সম্পাদক। **Fe-cun′-di-ty,** *n.* Fruitfulness ; power of producing or bringing forth ; উৎপাদিকা শক্তি ; উর্ব্বরাশক্তি। **3.** (*Bot.*) The power of germinating, as some seeds possess ; (উদ্ভিদ-বিদ্যা) অঙ্কুরোদ্গমকারিণী শক্তি। **4.** Fertility ; richness of invention ; উর্ব্বরতা, বহুপ্রজতা ; উদ্ভাবনী শক্তির প্রাচুর্য্য।

fĕc′-ŭn-dāte, *v. t.* **1.** To make fruitful or prolific ; ফলবান করা, ফলপ্রসূ করা, ফলপ্রদ করা, বহুপ্রজ করা। **2.** To impregnate ; গর্ভসঞ্চার করা, গর্ভাধান করা। **—da′-tion,** *n.* Act of fecundating ; impregnation ; ফলোৎপাদন ; গর্ভোৎপাদন, গর্ভসঞ্চার, গর্ভাধান।

fĕd, *v.* See FEED.

fĕd′-ĕr-ă-çy̆, *n.* A confederacy ; পরস্পরের সাহায্যার্থ মিত্রতাসূত্রে আবদ্ধ রাষ্ট্র বা জাতিসমূহ।

fĕd′-ĕr-ăl, *adj.* **1.** Pertaining to a league or treaty ; derived from an agreement or covenant between parties, esp. between states or nations confederated ; সন্ধিসম্বন্ধীয়, সন্ধিঘটিত ; পরস্পরের সাহায্যের জন্য সন্ধি বা মিত্রতা সূত্রে আবদ্ধ জাতি বা রাজ্যদ্বয়ের মধ্যে চুক্তি হইতে জাত। **2.** Founded on alliance between states which unite for national purpose ; জাতীয় স্বার্থসাধনের জন্য মিলিত রাষ্ট্রসমূহের মধ্যে সন্ধি বা মিলনের উপর প্রতিষ্ঠিত। **3.** Friendly or devoted to such a government ; মৈত্রীবদ্ধ শাসনের পক্ষপাতী বা সংহততন্ত্রের অনুরাগী। **—ism,** *n.* The principles of federalists ; মৈত্রীবদ্ধশাসন, মৈত্রীতন্ত্র, সংহত-তন্ত্র। **—ist,** *n.* **—ly,** *adv.* **Federal states**—যে সমস্ত রাজ্য আভ্যন্তর কার্য্য পরিচালনে সর্ব্বতোভাবে স্বাধীন থাকিয়া স্বজাতির স্বার্থসিদ্ধির উদ্দেশ্যে পরস্পরের সাহচর্য্যের জন্য ভিন্ন রাজ্যের সহিত সন্ধি বা মিলনসূত্রে বদ্ধ হয়, মৈত্রীবন্ধনে আবদ্ধ রাষ্ট্রসমূহ।

fĕd′-ĕr-ăl-īze, *v. t.* To unite or bring under a federal government ; মৈত্রীবন্ধনে বদ্ধ রাষ্ট্রসমূহের সহিত মিলিত বা উক্ত রাষ্ট্রসমূহের অন্তর্ভূত করা। **—i-za′-tion,** *n.*

fĕd′-ĕr-āte, *adj., v. t. & i.* United by league ; confederate ; সন্ধিসূত্রে মিলিত ; মৈত্রীবন্ধনে আবদ্ধ। ***Verb t. & i.*** To unite in a league or federation ; to organize on a federal basis ; সন্ধি বা মিত্রতাবন্ধনে আবদ্ধ করা ; মৈত্রীমূলক ব্যবস্থার অধীন করা। **—a′-tion,** *n.* **1.** The act of uniting in a league or confederacy ; সন্ধিসূত্রে মিলন, মৈত্রীবন্ধন। **2.** A league ; a confederacy ; a federal government ; a federal empire ; দুই বা ততোধিক জাতির সন্ধিসূত্রে মিলন ; সন্ধি বা মিত্রতাসূত্রে মিলিত রাজ্যসমূহ ; মৈত্রীতন্ত্র ; মৈত্রীবন্ধনে আবদ্ধ রাজ্যসমূহের সমবায়ে গঠিত সাম্রাজ্য, মৈত্রী সাম্রাজ্য। **—a-tive,** *adj.* **Imperial federation** — See under IMPERIAL.

fee (fē), *n. & v. t.* **1.** An inherited estate being either a *fee-simple* or *fee-tail* ; উত্তরাধিকার-সূত্রে প্রাপ্ত ভূসম্পত্তি। **2.** The sum payable to a public officer for performing his function or for the use of a privilege etc. ; as, license *fees* ; পারিশ্রমিক, ফিস। **3.** A recompense for service rendered or to be rendered by any professional man ; ডাক্তারের দর্শনী, উকিলের দক্ষিণা বা বায়না, রসুম। **4.** Charge ; ব্যয়, খরচ। **5.** A payment for admission to a place of amusement or instruction, an association, etc. ; as, school-*fees* ; ভর্ত্তিফিস, বিদ্যালয়ের বেতন, পরীক্ষার ফিস। **6.** A fief ; any federal benefice ; আয়মা ; জায়গীর। **7.** Gratuity ; পারিতোষিক। ***Verb t.*** **1.** To give a fee or reward to ; দর্শনী দেওয়া, উকিলাদির দক্ষিণা দেওয়া, পারিতোষিক দেওয়া। **2.** To engage for a fee ; দর্শনী কিম্বা বায়না প্রদানে নিযুক্ত করা। **Fee-simple**—যে সম্পত্তি বিশেষ উত্তরাধিকারিগণের মধ্যে সীমাবদ্ধ নয় এবং যাহা ইচ্ছামত হস্তান্তরিত করা যাইতে পারে। **Fee-tail**—যে উত্তরাধিকারসূত্রে প্রাপ্ত সম্পত্তি নির্দ্দিষ্ট উত্তরাধিকারিগণের মধ্যে সীমাবদ্ধ থাকে।

fee′-ble (fē-bl), *adj. & n.* **1.** Deficient in physical strength ; দুর্ব্বল, শক্তিহীন, হীনবল। **2.** Wanting in energy, force, intelligence or efficiency in character ; as, a *feeble* mind ; উৎসাহহীন, নিস্তেজ, হীনবীর্য্য। **3.** Indistinct ; faint ; dull ; as, a *feeble* colour ; অস্পষ্ট ; ক্ষীণ ; নিষ্প্রভ। ***Noun.*** **1.** A foible of character ; চরিত্রের দুর্ব্বলতা। **2.** (*Fencing*) The foible of a sword-blade ; (অসি-ক্রীড়া) অসিফলকের মধ্যভাগ হইতে অগ্রভাগ পর্য্যন্ত অংশ। **—blish,** *adj.* **—bly,** *adv.* In a feeble manner ; indistinctly ; দুর্ব্বলভাবে, ক্ষীণভাবে ; অস্পষ্টভাবে। **—ness,** *n.* Debility ; infirmity ; দৌর্ব্বল্য, দুর্ব্বলতা ; জরাজীর্ণতা। **Feeble-minded** — Weak-minded ; irresolute ; দুর্ব্বলমনাঃ ; অস্থির-চিত্ত।

feed (fēd), *v. t. & i.* **1.** To give food to ; to supply with food or nourishment ; as, to *feed* an infant ; to put food into mouth of ; as, he cannot *feed* himself ; খাওয়ান ; খাদ্য প্রদান করা, পোষণ করা, ক্ষুন্নিবৃত্তি করা ; মুখে খাদ্য প্রদান করা। **2.** To satisfy ; to gratify ; as, to *feed* desire of vengeance ; to comfort with hopes etc. ; পরিতৃপ্ত করা ; পরিতুষ্ট করা ; আশ্বাসাদি প্রদানে সান্ত্বনা দেওয়া। **3.** To fill the wants of ; to furnish with what is used or consumed ; as, to *feed* a furnace with coal ; অভাব পূরণ করা ; ইন্ধনাদি প্রদান করা। **4.** To graze (cattle) ; to use (land) for pasture ; চরান ; পশুচারণের জন্য

(ভূমি) ব্যবহার করা। 5. To nourish; to foster; "The trees had been *fed* by other roots", "Poetry *feeds* the passion"; পোষণ করা; পুষ্ট করা। 6. To supply to a machine as some materials; যন্ত্রে (ইন্ধনাদি) সরবরাহ করা। 7. To serve as a food for; as, this quantity is sufficient to *feed* all: ভোজনের জন্য পর্য্যাপ্ত হওয়া। *Verb i.* 1. To take food: to eat; খাওয়া; আহার করা। 2. To subsist by eating; to prey; (with *on* or *upon*); as, some birds *feed on* seeds etc., others on flesh; আহার দ্বারা জীবনধারণ করা; শিকার করা। 3. To pasture; to graze; পশুচারণ করা; ঘাস খাওয়ান। 4. To grow fat, (*dial*); (উপ-ভাষায়) হৃষ্টপুষ্ট হওয়া। 5. To be nourished or gratified as if by food; as, to *feed* on hope; পুষ্ট হওয়া, পরিতৃপ্ত হওয়া। **To feed to market**—To feed for sale; বিক্রয়ের জন্য হৃষ্টপুষ্ট করা। **To feed up**—To fatten; to satiate; হৃষ্টপুষ্ট করা; পরিতৃপ্ত করা।

feed (fēd), *n.* 1. Act of feeding; as, three biscuits at one *feed*; ভোজন, আহার। 2. That which is eaten; fodder; as, the best *feed* for sheep; খাদ্য; ঘাস, শস্যাদি। 3. A grazing or pasture ground; পশুচারণ-ভূমি। 4. An allowance of oats etc. for horse, cows, etc.; as, a *feed* of corn or oats; অশ্বাদির (একবারের) খোরাক। 5. (*Colloq.*) Meal; feast; (চলিত ভাষায়) আহার; ভোজ। 6. Act or process of feeding a machine; যন্ত্রাদিতে ইন্ধনাদি প্রদান। 7. Material supplied, as water, to an engine; the charge of a gun; যন্ত্রাদিতে যে জল সরবরাহ করা হয়; কামানাদিতে যে বারুদ, গুলি ভরা হয়। **Feed-bag** — অশ্বাদির দানা খাওয়ার তোবড়া। **Feed-door**—চুল্লীতে কয়লা দিবার দ্বার। **Feed-head**—যে জলকুণ্ড হইতে বাষ্পীয় যন্ত্রের বাষ্পাধারে জল সরবরাহ করা হয়। **Feed-heater** — বাষ্পাধারের জল উত্তপ্ত করিবার যন্ত্র। **Feed-pipe**—বাষ্পীয় যন্ত্রের বাষ্পাধারে জল সরবরাহের নল। **Feed-pump**—বাষ্পীয় যন্ত্রের বাষ্পাধারে জল সরবরাহের জন্য দমকল। **Feed-tank, —trough**—বাষ্পীয় যন্ত্রের জলাধার। **Off one's feed**—Without appetite; ক্ষুধাশূন্য। **On the feed**—(Of fish) Feeding or looking out for food; (মৎস্য-সম্পর্কে) আহারে রত, খাদ্যান্বেষণে রত। **Out at feed**—Turned out to graze; চরিবার জন্য ছাড়িয়া দেওয়া।

feed (fĕd), *v.* Past tense of FEE.

feed'-ēr (fēd-), *n.* 1. One who feeds; one who gives food or supplies nourishment; ভোজনদাতা, অন্নদাতা, খাদ্যদাতা; পোষণকর্ত্তা। 2. One who fattens cattle; a shepherd; যে ব্যক্তি বিক্রয়ের মেষাদি পুষ্ট করে; মেষপালক। 3. A device, as a feeding bottle etc., for nourishment; ভোজন করাইবার জন্য যন্ত্রবিশেষ। 4 An encourager; উৎসাহদাতা। 5. One who eats or feeds; ভোক্তা, যে ব্যক্তি আহার করাইয়া দেয়। 6. A stream that flows into another body of water; a tributary, (*lit.* & *fig.*); উপস্রোত; শাখানদী। 7. A branch railway; শাখা লৌহবর্ত্ম। 8. A feeding apparatus in a machine; যন্ত্রে সংলগ্ন কৌশল বিশেষ,—যদ্দ্বারা কোন উপকরণ (মুদ্রিতব্য কাগজ প্রভৃতি) যন্ত্রে নীত হয়। **A gross feeder**—One who eats much; মহাশন, ভূরিভোজনকারী।

feed'-ing (fed-), *n.* 1. Act of giving food; act of eating; খাদ্যপ্রদান; ভক্ষণ, ভোজন। 2. That which is eaten; provender; খাদ্য, ভোজদ্রব্য; গবাদির খাদ্য,—তৃণ বিচালি। **Feeding bottle**—শিশুদিগকে দুধ পান করাইবার জন্য রবরের নলযুক্ত বোতল। **Feeding storm**—ক্রমশঃ বর্দ্ধমান ঝঞ্ঝা।

fee-faw-fŭm (fē-fā-), *interj.* & *n.* An exclamation attributed to ogres etc.; (রাক্ষসীর) হাউ মাউ খাউ! *Noun.* A nonsense fit only to terrify a child etc.; শিশুদিগের ভীতি উৎপাদনের উপযোগী বিষয়।

feel (fēl), *v. t., i* & *n.* 1. To perceive by the touch; স্পর্শদ্বারা অনুভব করা। 2. To handle; to examine by touch; as, to *feel* the pulse; to test; (*mil.*) to reconnoitre; as, the cavalry *felt* the ground of the enemy; স্পর্শ করা; স্পর্শপূর্ব্বক পরীক্ষা করা; পরীক্ষা করা; যুদ্ধ বা পূর্ত্তকার্য্যের জন্য পরিদর্শন করা। 3. To experience; to be conscious of; as, to *feel* pleasure, pain, pity, hunger, etc.; অনুভব করা; বোধ করা। 4. To know or to have a real and just view of; as, he *felt* its truth; অবগত হওয়া, উপলব্ধি করা। *Verb i.* 1. To have perception by the touch; স্পর্শ দ্বারা অনুভূত হওয়া। 2. To have the emotions excited or moved; as, to *feel* for the poor; প্রাণ আকুল হওয়া, প্রাণ বিচলিত হওয়া। 3 To have perception mentally; to perceive oneself to be, (followed by an adjective descriptive of the state); as, to *feel* sick, weak or grieved; উপলব্ধি হওয়া; বোধ করা। 4. To search for something with the hand; to grope, (with *about*, *after* and *for*); as, to *feel for* something in the pocket; কোন কিছুর জন্য অনুসন্ধান করা; হাতড়ান। 5. To seem; to appear; as, air *feels* chilly; বোধ হওয়া; লাগা। *Noun.* 1. The sense of touch; as, it is soft to the *feel*; স্পর্শ, স্পর্শ-বোধ। 2. A sensation or impression produced by touch; স্পর্শজনিত অনুভূতি। 3. Examining by touch; স্পর্শদ্বারা পরীক্ষা। **To feel after**—To search for; to seek as a person groping in the dark ; অনুসন্ধান করা ; অন্ধকারে হাতড়ান। **To feel for**—To sympathize ; to pity ; সমবেদনা বোধ করা, ব্যথার ব্যথী হওয়া ; করুণা করা। To seek with uncertainty ; খুঁজা, হাতড়ান। **To feel one's legs**—To begin to support oneself upright ; to gain confidence ; পায়ে ভর দিয়া দাঁড়াইবার উপক্রম করা ; বিশ্বাস লাভ করা। **To feel like doing**—To have an inclination or willingness for doing ; কোন কাজ করার আসক্তি বা ইচ্ছা বোধ করা। **To feel quite oneself**—To be fit, self-possessed, etc. ; স্থৈর্য সম্পন্ন হওয়া, আত্মস্থ হওয়া, ধীরচেতা হওয়া। **To feel one's oats**—(Of a horse etc.) To be spirited or frisky ; (অশ্বসম্পর্কে) তেজস্বিতা দেখান, উল্লম্ফন করা। (Of a person) To be conceited or self-important ; (কোন ব্যক্তির পক্ষে) গর্ব্বিত হওয়া, আত্মাভিমানী হওয়া, অহম্মন্য হওয়া। **To feel one's pulse**—To ascertain by feeling the condition of the pulse ; কাহারও শিরা ধরিয়া নির্ণয় করা। To sound one's opinion ; কোন ব্যক্তির মত জানিবার চেষ্টা করা। **To feel one's way**—To grope it out ; to proceed carefully ; অন্ধকারে হাতড়াইতে হাতড়াইতে চলা ; সাবধানে অগ্রসর হওয়া। **To feel out**—To explore ; to try ; পরীক্ষা করা ; চেষ্টা করা।

feel'-ẽr (fēl-), *n.* **1.** One who or that which feels ; স্পর্শকারী, ভাবুক। **2.** An organ in certain animals for testing things by touch or for searching food ; জন্তুদিগের মস্তকস্থ অনুভূতিশক্তিসম্পন্ন শুণ্ড বা শূঁয়া। **3.** An observation or remark etc. put forth to ascertain the views of others ; অন্য ব্যক্তির মনোগত ভাব অবধারণের জন্য যে মন্তব্য বা মত ব্যক্ত করা হয়। **4.** (*Mil.*) A scout ; (সামরিকশাস্ত্র) যুদ্ধকালে বিপক্ষের গতিবিধি অনুসন্ধানার্থ প্রেরিত চর।

feel'-ing (fēl-), *n.* & *adj.* **1.** Act or condition of one that feels ; বোধকরণ, অনুভূতি। **2.** Sense of touch ; স্পর্শেন্দ্রিয়, স্পর্শানুভূতি বা জ্ঞান। **3.** A sensation of touch ; স্পর্শবোধ। **4.** Sensation or perception by any of the senses ; as, the *feeling* of warmth or of cold ; অনুভব, বোধ, সংবেদন। **5.** Emotion or mental sensation ; as, a *feeling* of pride or anger ; (*pl.*) susceptibilities ; (*pl.*) the affections or passions ; হৃদয়ের আবেগ, মনোভাব ; হৃদয়বৃত্তি, মনোবৃত্তি ; রাগদ্বেষাদি। **6.** Fine sensibility ; sympathetic emotion or sentiment ; as, a man of *feeling* ; সূক্ষ্মসংবেদন-শক্তি সহানুভূতি, সমবেদনা। **7.** Sentiment ; as, the general *feeling* was against it ; ভাব। **8.** Consciousness ; conviction ; "A *feeling* of safety" ; জ্ঞান ; দৃঢ়প্রতীতি। **9.** (*Psychol.*) (a) Brown, Mill and others—A fact or state of consciousness ; (b) other writers—sensation, emotion or desire (excluding thought or perception) ; (c) after Kant—an element of pleasure or pain in any mental state ; (d) an intuitive belief ; (মনোবিজ্ঞান) (ব্রাউন, মিল প্রভৃতি) জাগ্রত চৈতন্যের ভাব বা অবস্থা ; (অন্যান্য দার্শনিকগণ) সংবেদন, আবেগ, হৃদয়বৃত্তি, বাসনা ; (ক্যাণ্টের অনুযায়ী) যে কোনরূপ মানসিক অবস্থায় সুখ বা দুঃখ ; আত্ম-প্রত্যয়লব্ধ বিশ্বাস। **10.** (*Art*) The quality of a work of art embodying the emotion of the artist and similarly affecting the spectator ; (কলাশাস্ত্র) চিত্রার্পিত মূর্তি প্রভৃতিতে শিল্পীর ভাব ও হৃদয়াবেগের প্রস্ফুটন দ্বারা চিত্রাদিতে যে গুণ সঞ্জাত হয়, চিত্রাদিদর্শনে দর্শকের চিত্তে যে ভাবাবেগ সঞ্জাত হয়। ***Adj.*** **1.** Perceiving by touch ; sensitive ; স্পর্শানুভূত ; সংবেদনশীল। **2.** Possessing great sensibility ; easily moved ; as, a *feeling* heart ; showing or evincing emotion ; তীক্ষ্ণ অনুভূতিসম্পন্ন ; সকরুণ, দরার্দ্র, মরমী ; আবেগপূর্ণ, আবেগদ্যোতক। **3.** Heartfelt ; as, a *feeling* pleasure ; আন্তরিক। **—ly,** *adv.* Pathetically ; tenderly ; সকরুণভাবে, সুকোমলভাবে। **Feeling eloquence**—আবেগপূর্ণ বক্তৃতা। **Fellow feeling**—Sympathy ; সহানুভূতি, সমবেদনা।

feet (fēt), *n.* Plural of FOOT.

feign (fān), *v. t.* & *i.* **1.** To invent ; as, to *feign* an excuse, accusation, etc. ; to forge, as a document ; (*archaic*) to imagine ; রচনা করা, উদ্ভাবন করা ; জাল করা ; মনে মনে কল্পনা করা (অপ্রঃ)। **2.** To make a shew of ; to simulate ; as, to *feign* sickness or madness ; ভাণ করা ; কপটভাব ধারণ করা। ***Verb i.*** To practise simulation ; to pretend ; ভাণ করা ; কপটতা করা, ছলনা করা। **Feign'-ing-ly,** *adv.* In a deceitful manner ; ছলনাপূর্ব্বক।

feigned (fānd), *adj.* Not genuine ; pretended ; insincere ; as, a *feigned* friend ; অপ্রকৃত, কৃত্রিম ; কপট, ছদ্ম, কুতক ; অসরল। **Feign'-ed-ly,** *adv.* Not really ; অপ্রকৃতভাবে। **Feign'-ed-ness,** *n.*

feint (fānt), *n.* & *v. i.* **1.** A Pretence ; a false appearance ; ছল, ভাণ ; কপটাচার, কপটভাব, কৈতব। **2.** A mock blow or attack at one part while another is the real object of attack ; উদ্দিষ্ট স্থান হইতে অন্যত্র কপট আক্রমণ, কৃত্রিম আক্রমণ। ***Verb i.*** To make a feint or mock attack, (with *at*, *upon* and *against*) ; ভাণ করা, কপট আক্রমণ করা।

fĕld'-spâr, *n.* Same as FELSPAR.

fē'-li-cīde, *n.* Killing of a cat ; মার্জ্জার-হত্যা, বিড়াল-বধ।

fē-lĭ-cĭf′-ĭc, *adj.* Causing happiness ; সুখাবহ, সুখজনক।

fē-lĭc′-i-tāte, *v. t.* **1.** To make happy, (*rare*) ; সুখী করা (অপ্রঃ)। **2.** To wish joy or pleasure to ; to congratulate, (usually with *on*) ; আনন্দ বা সুখ কামনা করা ; অভিনন্দন করা। **–ta′-tion,** *n.* Wishing of joy or happiness ; congratulation ; (usually *pl.*) ; আনন্দ-কামনা, সুখ-কামনা ; অভিনন্দন।

fē-lĭc′-i-tȳ, *n.* **1.** The state of being happy ; intense happiness ; সৌখ্য ; পরমসুখ, পরমানন্দ। **2.** Blessing or source of happiness ; a fortunate trait (in an individual) ; "It was the *felicity* of Cromwell to detect this gift of Government"; শ্রেয়, সৌভাগ্য ; অভ্যুদয় (বেদান্তঃ)। **3.** A pleasing faculty in expression ; appropriateness ; as, the *felicity* of an expression ; মনোভাবাদি দ্যোতনার সুষ্ঠুতা ; সমীচীনতা, যথাযোগ্যতা। **4.** An apt expression or phrase ; যথাযোগ্য বাক্য। **–tous,** *adj.* **1.** Happy, (*rare*) ; সুখী (অপ্রঃ)। **2.** Delightfully ingenuous ; extremely appropriate ; as, a *felicitous* expression or quotation ; সুষ্ঠু ; অতিশয় সুপ্রযুক্ত। **–tous-ly,** *adv.* In a felicitous manner ; সুখজনকভাবে, সুষ্ঠুরূপে, স্বচ্ছন্দে।

fē′-lĭd, *n.* One of the Felidæ or the cat tribe ; মার্জ্জার-জাতীয় জন্তু।

Fē′-lĭ-dæ (-dē), *n.* The family or tribe of the cat ; মার্জ্জারবর্গ, মার্জ্জার পরিবার।

fē′-līne, *adj.* & *n.* **1.** Of or relating to cats ; like a cat ; বিড়াল-সম্বন্ধীয় ; বিড়ালসদৃশ, মার্জ্জারবৎ। **2.** Characteristic of cat ; মার্জ্জারসুলভ। **3.** Sly ; treacherous ; as, *feline* nature ; ধূর্ত্ত ; বিশ্বাসঘাতক। ***Noun.*** An animal of the cat tribe ; মার্জ্জার জাতীয় জন্তু। **–lin′-i-ty,** *n.* The quality of being feline ; catlike disposition ; মার্জ্জারত্ব ; মার্জ্জারপ্রকৃতি। **Feline amenities**—Veiled spite ; a woman's seemingly innocent thrusts ; প্রচ্ছন্ন দ্বেষ ; স্ত্রীলোকের আপাতসরল মর্ম্মভেদী বাক্য।

Felis catus—বিড়াল, মার্জ্জার (বেলঃ)।

Felis chaus—বনবিড়াল (বেলঃ)।

Felis leo—সিংহ (বেলঃ)।

Felis pardus—চিতাবাঘ (বেলঃ)।

Felis tigris — ব্যাঘ্র (বেলঃ)।

Felis viverrina—বাঘ ডাঁস (বেলঃ)।

fĕll, *n.* **1.** A barren hill, (*obsolete,* except in proper names) ; উদ্ভিজ্জহীন পাহাড়। **2.** A stretch of moorland, as in North England ; জলাভূমি।

fĕll, *n.* A hide or skin of animals, esp. with the hair ; a fleece ; a covering of hair or wool ; পশুচর্ম্ম, সলোম পশুচর্ম্ম ; লোম ; কেশ বা পশমের আবরণ। **Fell of hair**—মাথার উস্‌কো-খুস্‌কো চুল।

fĕll, *v. t.* & *n.* **1.** To cause to fall ; to bring to the ground by a blow or cut ; as, to *fell* an animal, person or tree ; পাতিত করা ; ভূশায়িত করা, ছেদন করা। **2.** To sew or hem down in a certain fashion ; as, to *fell* a seam ; এক প্রকার সেলাই করা, এক রকমের মুড়ি সেলাই করা। ***Noun.*** **1.** A quantity of timber felled ; কর্ত্তিত কাষ্ঠফলক সমূহ। **2.** A seam formed by felling ; সেলাইয়ের জোড়মুখ। **Fell′-a-ble,** *adj.* **Fell′-er,** *n.* **1.** A cutter of wood ; কাষ্ঠচ্ছেদক, কাঠুরিয়া। **2.** A sewing machine attachment for felling seams ; সেলাইয়ের কলে সংযুক্ত মুড়ি সেলাইয়ের জন্য অংশ বিশেষ।

fĕll, *adj.* (*Poet.*) Cruel ; fierce ; terrible ; ruinous ; (কবিতায়) নিষ্ঠুর, ক্রূর, নির্ম্মম ; হিংস্র ; রুদ্র, ভীষণ ; ধ্বংসকারী।

fĕll, *p. t.* of FALL.

fĕl′-lah (-lâ), *n.* (*Pl.* -LAHEN, -LAHS) An Egyptian peasant or agricultural labourer ; মিসরদেশীয় কৃষক বা কৃষিক্ষেত্রের শ্রমজীবী।

fĕl′-loe (-lö), *n.* The outer circle (or a segment of it) of a wheel supported by spokes ; পরিধি, চক্রনেমি। (See also FELLY).

fĕl′-low (-lö), *n.* **1.** A companion ; a comrade ; সঙ্গী ; সহচর, সাথী। **2.** A contemporary ; one of a company ; সমসাময়িক ব্যক্তি ; কোন দলভুক্ত ব্যক্তি। **3.** An equal ; one of the same class ; a mate ; সমকক্ষ ব্যক্তি ; এক শ্রেণীর লোক ; প্রতিযোগী, প্রতিদ্বন্দ্বী। **4.** One of a pair , or of two things used together and suited to each other ; a counterpart ; জোড়ার একটী ; অনুরূপ অংশ। **5.** A person ; an individual : as, he is a good *fellow* ; মানুষ, লোক, ব্যক্তি। **6.** A man without good breeding ; a worthless person ; "Worth makes the man, the want of it the *fellow*" ; অসভ্য বা ইতর লোক, বর্ব্বর, চাষ ; নীচাশয় ব্যক্তি। **7.** (In an American College or University) One of the trustees of a college ; (আমেরিকার বিশ্ববিদ্যালয়ে) অন্যতম ন্যাসরক্ষক। **8.** A member of an incorporated learned society ; as, a *fellow* of the Royal Society ; বিদ্বজ্জন পরিষদের সভ্য। **–ship,** *n.* **1.** State of being a fellow ; সহচরত্ব। **2.** Familiar intercourse ; friendliness ; পরস্পর সখ্যভাব, সংসর্গ, সঙ্গ, সাহচর্য্য ; বন্ধুত্ব। **3.** Association ; community of interest ; সাহচর্য্য ; স্বার্থের ঐক্য। **4.** A corporation ; a body of associates ; a company ; বিধিবদ্ধ সমাজ ; সভ্যগণ, সহযোগিগণ ; সমাজ, দল। **5.** Brotherhood ; সৌভ্রাত্র, ভ্রাতৃপ্রেম, মৈত্রী। **6.** (In English and American Universities) An establishment for the maintenance of fellows ; dignity or income of college fellows ; ইংলণ্ড ও আমেরিকার বিশ্ববিদ্যালয়ের বৃত্তিবিশেষ ; বিশ্ববিদ্যালয়ের শাসন-পরিষদের সভ্যগণের

পদমর্য্যাদা বা আয়। 7. (*Arith.*) The rule for dividing profit and loss among partners; (গণিতশাস্ত্র) সম্ভূয় সমুত্থান। [*Good fellowship*—Love of society; the temper and disposition of a good fellow; সমাজপ্রিয়তা; সুজনের স্বভাব বা প্রকৃতি।] **Fellow-citizen** — সহনাগরিক, এক নগরবাসী, পুরসখা। [*Fellow-citizenship*—পৌরসখ্য (মনুঃ)।] **Fellow-commoner**—যে সমস্ত অপ্রাপ্ত-উপাধি ছাত্রের বিশ্ববিদ্যালয়ের শাসন-পরিষদের সভ্যগণের সহিত একত্র অপরাহ্ণ ভোজনের অধিকার আছে। **Fellow-creature**—স্বজাতীয় ব্যক্তি বা প্রাণী। **Fellow-countryman**—স্বদেশবাসী। **Fellow-feeling** — সহানুভূতি, সমবেদনা। **Fellow-heir** — A joint heir; সহ-উত্তরাধিকারী, সহদায়াদ। **Fellow-servant**—এক প্রভুর অধীনে নিযুক্ত ভৃত্য, সহভৃত্য। **Fellow-soldier** — একযোগে যুদ্ধে নিরত সৈনিক, সহযোদ্ধা। **Fellow-student**—সহাধ্যায়ী, সতীর্থ। **Fellow-traveller**—সহযাত্রী। **Good fellow**—সুসঙ্গী। **Hail-fellow-well-met**—See under HAIL. **Stone dead hath no fellow**—There is no keeper of secrets like a deadman; গোপনীয় কথা অপ্রকাশ রাখিতে মৃত ব্যক্তির দোসর কেহ নাই।

fĕl'-lȳ, *n.* See FELLOE.

fē'-lō-dē-sē', *n.* (*Pl.* FELONES, FELOS.) 1. Self-murderer; আত্মঘাতী, আত্মহন্তা। 2. (*Sing.*) Self-murder; আত্মহত্যা।

fĕl'-ŏn, *n.* & *adj.* One who has committed heinous crimes; গুরুতর অপরাধী। ***Adj.*** (*Poet.*) Cruel; wicked; murderous; (কবিতায়) নির্দ্দয়, নিষ্ঠুর, ক্রূর; দুষ্ট; হত্যাকারী। **–lo'-ni-ous**, *adj.* 1. Wicked; villainous; criminal; perfidious; দুশ্চরিত্র, পাপিষ্ঠ; অপরাধী; বিশ্বাসঘাতক। 2. (*Law*) Relating to, or of the nature of, a felony; done with the deliberate intention to commit crime; ঘোর অপরাধ সম্পর্কীয়, মহাপরাধাত্মক; অপরাধ করার অভিপ্রায়ে কৃত। **lo'-ni-ous-ly**, *adv.* **–lo'-ni-ous-ness**, *n.* **–ry**, *n.* The felon or convict class; দুর্বৃত্তের দল। **–y**, *n.* 1. A crime incurring the forfeiture of lands, goods, etc.; যে অপরাধের দরুণ স্থাবর অস্থাবর সম্পত্তি প্রভৃতি বাজেয়াপ্ত হইতে পারে। 2. A crime graver than a misdemeanour; মহাপরাধ, ঘোর অপরাধ, মহাপাতক।

fĕl'-ŏn, *n.* (*Med.*) A whitlow; আঙ্গুলহাড়া।

fĕl'-spâr, *n.* A crystalline mineral; স্ফটিকবৎ খনিজপদার্থ, ফেনোপল (হিঃ কোঃ)। (Also FELD-SPAR).

fĕl'-stōne, *n.* A rock of quartz and felspar; স্ফটিকপ্রস্তর ব ফেনোপলরচিত শৈল।

fĕlt, *P. t.* and *p. p.* of FEEL.

fĕlt, *n.*, *v. t.* & *i.* 1. A kind of cloth made of wool etc. by rolling, heating and pressure; পশমী বস্ত্রবিশেষ, নেমদা। 2. A hat made of felt; নেমদার টুপী। ***Verb t.*** 1. To make into felt; to mat together; নেমদা তৈয়ার করা; জট পাকান। 2. To cover with, or as with, felt; নেমদাদ্বারা আচ্ছাদিত করা, নেমদার মত আচ্ছাদিত করা। ***Verb i.*** To become matted; জটা বাঁধা। **Felt'-y** *adj.* **Felt-hat** — One made of felt; নেমদার টুপী।

fĕlt'-ĕr-ĭc, *n.* A disease of a horse; অশ্বরোগ-বিশেষ।

Felucca.

fē-lŭc'-că, *n.* A small coasting vessel with oars and sails used in the Mediterranean; ভূমধ্যসাগরের উপকূলগামী পূর্ব্বকালীন পালের জাহাজ

fē'-māle, *n.* & *adj.* 1. One of that sex which conceives and brings forth youngs; a female animal; স্ত্রীলোক, অঙ্গনা, নারী, অবলা, যোষিৎ, সিমন্তিনী, বামা, বণিতা, মহিলা, বধূ, কামিনী, রমণী, বামলোচনা, ললনা, নিতম্বিনী, কান্তা, রমা, বরারোহা (excellent woman), ভীরু, প্রমদা, ভামিনী (angry woman), কোপনা (ঐ); স্ত্রী-জন্তু, মাদী। 2. (*Bot.*) A pistillate plant or one bearing fruit; স্ত্রী-বৃক্ষ, ফলপ্রসূবৃক্ষ। ***Adj.*** 1. Belonging to the sex which produces young; pertaining to women; as, *female* sex, education, etc.; স্ত্রীজাতীয়; স্ত্রীসংক্রান্ত, স্ত্রীসুলভ। 2. Characteristic of women; delicate; as, *female* tenderness; স্ত্রীসুলভ; কোমল, পেলব, সুকুমার। 3. (*Bot.*) Fruit-bearing; having pistils and no stamens; (উদ্ভিদ-বিদ্যা) ফলপ্রসূ; স্ত্রীকেশরবান। 4. Weakly; paler in colour; as, a *female* sapphire; দুর্ব্বল; অপেক্ষাকৃত মলিন-বর্ণ। 5. (*Mech.*) Suited to receive a corresponding male part; (যন্ত্র-বিদ্যা) অনুরূপ যন্ত্রাংশ গ্রহণের উপযোগী। **Female suffrage**—স্ত্রীলোকের নির্ব্বাচনাধিকার।

fē-măl'-ĭ-tȳ, *n.* The female nature and characteristics; effeminacy; স্ত্রী-চরিত্র, স্ত্রীস্বভাব; স্ত্রৈণতা, নারীত্ব।

feme-cov'-ĕrt (fĕm-kŭv-), *n.* A married woman; a woman under the covert of her husbad; বিবাহিতা স্ত্রীলোক; স্বামীর আশ্রয়াধীনা স্ত্রীলোক।

feme'-sōle (fĕm-), *n.* An unmarried woman or a widow; a married woman independent of her husband as regards property; অবিবাহিতা মহিলা, বিধবা; স্বামীর সম্পত্তি হইতে স্বতন্ত্র সম্পত্তির অধিকারিণী স্ত্রী।

fĕm-ĭ-năl'-ĭ-tȳ, *n.* 1. Female nature; a female peculiarity;

স্ত্রীপ্রকৃতি ; স্ত্রীজনের বিশেষত্ব। **2.** Something that women delight in ; a knick-knack ; স্ত্রীলোকের প্রিয়বস্তু ; ফটকীনাট্কী।

fĕm-i-nē'-i-tȳ, *n.* The quality of being female ; womanishness ; নারীত্ব ; স্ত্রীপ্রকৃতি।

fĕm'-i-nine (-nĭn), *adj.* **1.** Relating to female sex, (*rare*) ; স্ত্রীজাতি-সম্বন্ধীয় (অপ্রঃ)। **2.** Pertaining to women ; womanly ; স্ত্রীসংক্রান্ত ; স্ত্রী-সুলভ। **3.** (*Gram.*) Denoting the gender proper to women's name ; স্ত্রীলিঙ্গবাচক। **4.** (*Rare*) Effeminate ; (অপ্রঃ) স্ত্রীজনসুলভ, মেয়েলী। **5.** (In *prosody*—of a rhyme etc.) Of two syllables one accented and one unaccented ; (ছন্দঃশাস্ত্রে—মিত্রাক্ষরাদি সম্পর্কে) যে ছন্দে একটী স্বর-চিহ্নিত অপরটী অস্বরচিহ্নিত তৎসম্বন্ধে প্রযোজ্য। **—ly,** *adv.* **—ness, —nin'-i-ty,** *ns.* The qualities or manners becoming a woman ; womankind ; স্ত্রীত্ব, নারীত্ব, স্ত্রীজনসুলভত্ব ; স্ত্রীজাতি, নারীজাতি, মহিলাসমাজ।

fĕ-mĭn'-i-tȳ, *n.* Same as FEMININITY.

fĕm'-i-nīze, *v. t.* & *i.* To make feminine ; স্ত্রীবৎ করা, নারীসদৃশ করা, স্ত্রীজনসুলভ করা। ***Verb i.*** To become feminine ; স্ত্রীবৎ হওয়া, স্ত্রীত্ব প্রাপ্ত হওয়া। **—ni-za'-tion,** *n.*

femme-de-chambre, (*F.*) A lady's maid ; a chambermaid ; ভদ্রমহিলার সহচরী ; শয্যাগৃহের পরিচারিকা।

fē'-mur (-mêr), *n.* (*pl.* -MORA) **1.** The thigh bone; ঊর্বস্থি। **2.** The third segment of an insect's leg ; পতঙ্গের পায়ের তৃতীয় পর্ব্ব। **Fem'-o-ral,** *adj.*

fĕn, *n.* A marsh or moor ; বিল, জলাভূমি, অনূপভূমি, বিলান জমী, বাদা, কচ্ছভূমি। **Fen-berry**—বিলাভূমিতে জাত গুল্ম-বিশেষ। **Fen-fire**—আলেয়া। **Fen-man**—অনূপদেশবাসী ব্যক্তি। **Fen-pole**—লম্ফপ্রদানে পরিখাদি উল্লঙ্ঘনের জন্য দণ্ডবিশেষ। **Fen-reeve**—অনূপ-দেশের ভারপ্রাপ্ত কর্ম্মচারিবিশেষ। **The fens**—The low lying districts in Lincolnshire and other counties of England ; ইংলণ্ডের অন্তঃপাতী লিঙ্কলন সায়ার এবং অন্যান্য জেলার বিলাভূমি।

fen(s), *n.* See FAIN.

fence (fĕns), *n., v. t.* & *i.* **1.** (*Archaic*) A defence ; (অপ্রঃ) দুর্গপ্রাকারাদি। **2.** The art and practice of fencing and sword play ; skill in debate etc. ; অসি-ক্রীড়া, অসিচালনা-কৌশল ; তর্কপটুতা। **3.** A wall, railing or hedge etc. forming a boundary or inclosure ; বেড়া, বৃতি। **4.** Guard, gauge, etc. in various machines ; বিভিন্ন প্রকার যন্ত্রের চতুঃপার্শ্বস্থ বৃতি। **5.** A receiver of stolen goods ; the place of receiving such goods ; অপহৃত দ্রব্য গ্রহণকারী ; চোরাই মাল গ্রহণের স্থান। ***Verb t.*** **1.** To give security to ; to protect, (with *from, against*) ; as, to *fence* oneself *from* a danger ; নিরাপদ্ করা ; রক্ষা করা। **2.** To inclose or secure by a fence, as hedge, wall, etc. ; to fortify ; বৃতি প্রভৃতি দ্বারা পরিবেষ্টিত করা ; সুরক্ষিত করা। **3.** To keep out ; to repel ; নিবারণ করা, প্রতিরোধ করা ; প্রতিহত করা। **4.** (*Slang*) To purchase or sell, as stolen goods ; (ইতর ভাষায়) চোরাই মাল প্রভৃতি কেনা বা বেচা। **5.** To ward or parry by argument ; as, to *fence* a question ; যুক্তিদ্বারা প্রতিহত করা। ***Verb i.*** **1.** To practise the use of the sword or foil in order to learn the art of attack and defence ; অসি-ক্রীড়া অভ্যাস করা, অসিচালন-কৌশল শিক্ষা করা। **2.** To parry arguments ; to prevaricate ; যুক্তি ব্যর্থ করা ; কথার মারপেঁচ করা। **3.** To deal in stolen goods ; চোরাই মাল কেনাবেচা করা। **Fenced,** *adj.* Enclosed with a fence ; বৃতি-বেষ্টিত, বেড়ায় ঘেরা। **Fence'-less,** *adj.* Without a fence ; uninclosed ; open ; (*poet.*) unfortified ; বৃতিহীন, অবেষ্টিত ; অনাবৃত, মুক্ত, খোলা ; (কবিতায়) অরক্ষিত। **Fence-time, —season, —month**—মৃগয়া বা মৎস্য শিকারের অবসানপ্রাপ্ত কাল। **A sunk fence**—One placed along the bottom of a ditch ; পগাড়ের নীচের বেড়া। **Master of fence**—A good swordsman ; অসিচালনায় সুনিপুণ ব্যক্তি, পাকা তলোয়ার খেলোয়াড়। (*Fig.*) A good debator ; (লক্ষণায়) সুতার্কিক, উচ্চদরের তার্কিক। **To be on one's side of the fence** — To take one's side ; কাহারো পক্ষাবলম্বন করা। **To come down on the right side of the fence**—To take the side of the winner ; বিজয়ী ব্যক্তির পক্ষাবলম্বন করা। **To put one's horse at a fence**—To spur him on to leap it ; পাদুকা সংবদ্ধ লৌহকণ্টক দ্বারা তাড়না করত অশ্বকে বৃতি উল্লম্ফনের জন্য অগ্রসর করা। **To sit or stand on the fence**—To be undecided in opinion ; to remain neutral in a contest ; not to take sides ; মত প্রদানে ইতঃস্তত করা ; উদাসীন থাকা, নির্লিপ্ত থাকা ; কোনও পক্ষ অবলম্বন না করা।

fĕnc'-ĕr *n.* **1.** One who practises or teaches the art of fencing with sword ; যে ব্যক্তি অসিচালনা-কৌশল শিক্ষা করে বা শিক্ষা দান করে, অসিযোধ। **2.** A horse good at leaping fences ; বৃতিলঙ্ঘনপটু অশ্ব।

fĕn'-ci-ble (-bl), *n.* (*Mil. usu. pl.*) A soldier liable only for a defensive service at home ; (সামরিক-শাস্ত্র) যে সৈনিক কেবলমাত্র স্বদেশ রক্ষার জন্য দায়ী থাকে, স্বদেশরক্ষী সৈনিক।

fĕnc'-ing, *n.* **1.** The act of constructing a fence ; the materials used in making fences ; বৃতিনির্ম্মাণ-কৌশল ; বৃতিনির্ম্মাণোপযোগী সামগ্রী। **2.** The art of using skilfully a sword or foil in attack or defence ; অসিচালন-বিদ্যা, অসিচর্য্যা। **3.** The aggregate of the fences put up for inclosure or protection; railing; as, the *fencing* of a farm or machine; বৃতিসমষ্টি; গড়া। **Fencing-cully, —ken**—The storer or the store of stolen goods; অপহৃত দ্রব্যের ভাণ্ডারী, অপহৃত দ্রব্য সংগ্রহ।

fĕnd, *v. t.* & *i.* To keep or ward off; to shut out; as, to *fend* off blows; আটকান, নিবারণ করা; প্রবেশ করিতে না দেওয়া। ***Verb i.*** **1.** To parry; আটকান। **2.** To provide (for); জীবিকার সংস্থান করা।

fĕnd'-ĕr, *n.* **1.** Something used to keep off anything harmful, to prevent collision, etc.; অনিষ্টজনক কোন কিছুর প্রতিরোধক বস্তু, সংঘর্ষাদি নিবারক ব্যবস্থা, রক্ষক। **2.** A utensil used to prevent coals of fire from rolling into the room; গৃহমধ্যস্থ অগ্নিকুণ্ডের সম্মুখস্থ ধাতুনির্ম্মিত বৃতি-বিশেষ—যদ্দ্বারা বাধা প্রাপ্ত হইয়া কয়লা গৃহতলে গড়াইয়া আসিতে পারে না, পাষাণাঙ্গার-রোধক। **3.** (*Naut.*) Anything serving as a cushion to lessen the shock when a vessel comes in contact with another vessel or a wharf; (নৌ-বিদ্যা) কোন কিছুর সহিত সংঘৃষ্ট হইয়া জাহাজের অনিষ্ট না হয় তজ্জন্য তৎপার্শ্বে বিলম্বিত কাষ্ঠখণ্ড, পুরাতন রজ্জু-রাশি প্রভৃতি, সংঘর্ষবাধক। **—less** *adj.*

fĕn-ĕs-tĕl'-lă, *n.* (*Arch.*) Any small window-like opening or recess, esp. one to show the relics within an altar, or the like; (স্থপতি-বিজ্ঞান) পরলোকগত সাধু মহাপুরুষদিগের দেহাবশেষ বা স্মৃতি-সামগ্রী প্রদর্শনের জন্য বেদী কিম্বা তদ্বৎ কোন কিছুর মধ্যস্থ গবাক্ষসদৃশ ছিদ্র বা কুলঙ্গি বিশেষ।

fĕ-nĕs'-tră, *n.* A window; an aperture; গবাক্ষ, বাতায়ন; রন্ধ্র।

fē-nĕs'-trăl, *adj.* (*Arch.*) Relating to a window or windows; (স্থপতি-বিজ্ঞান) গবাক্ষ-সম্বন্ধীয়, বাতায়ন-সম্পর্কীয়।

fē-nĕs'-trāte, *adj.* (*Bot.* & *zool.*) Having window-like perforations; (উদ্ভিদ্-বিদ্যা ও প্রাণি-বিদ্যা) গবাক্ষবৎ ছিদ্রবিশিষ্ট।

fē-nĕs-tră'-tion, *n.* **1.** (*Arch.*) The series or arrangement of windows in a building; স্থপতি-বিজ্ঞান) গবাক্ষ-শ্রেণী, বাতায়ন-শ্রেণী। **2.** (*Bot.* & *zool.*) The state of being fenestrate; (উদ্ভিদ্-বিদ্যা ও প্রাণি-বিদ্যা); গবাক্ষবৎ ছিদ্রবিশিষ্টতা।

fĕn'-gīte, *n.* A kind of transparent marble used for window; বাতায়নের জন্য ব্যবহৃত একপ্রকার স্বচ্ছ মর্ম্মরপ্রস্তর।

Fē'-ni-ăn, *n.* & *adj.* A member of a secret society having for its principal object the overthrow of English rule in Ireland; নিউইয়র্ক নগরীতে (১৮৫৭ খৃঃ অব্দে) প্রতিষ্ঠিত আইরিসদিগের গুপ্ত সমিতি বিশেষ—আয়র্লণ্ডে ইংরাজ রাজত্বের উচ্ছেদ সাধন এই সম্প্রদায়ের মূল উদ্দেশ্য ছিল, ফিনিয়ান-সম্প্রদায়। ***Adj.*** Of, or relating to, the Fenians; ফিনিয়ান সম্প্রদায়সংক্রান্ত বা তৎসম্পর্কীয়। **—ism** *n.* The principle of the Fenians; ফিনিয়ান সম্প্রদায়ের মূল নীতি।

fenks (fĕngks), *n.* (*Pl.*) The fibrous parts of a whale's blubber; the refuse of a whale-blubber; তিমি-মৎস্যের মেদের তন্তুময় অংশ; তিমি-মৎস্যের মেদের অসার ভাগ।

fĕn'-nĕc *n.* A small African fox-like animal; আফ্রিকাদেশীয় শৃগালবৎ ক্ষুদ্র প্রাণিবিশেষ।

fĕn'-nĕl, *n.* A plant cultvaied for the aromatic flavour of its seeds and for its leaves; মৌরী, পানমৌরি।

fĕn'-ū-greek (-grēk), *n.* A leguminous plant with seeds used in farriery; মেথী (বেলঃ), মেথিকা (ঐ)।

feoff (fĕf), *n.* & *v. t.* A fief or fee; যৌবভূমি, জায়গীর। ***Verb t.*** To grant possession of a fief or property in land; জায়গীর প্রদান করা। **Feoff-ee',** *n.* A person to whom a freehold estate in land is conveyed by a feoffment; জায়গীরপ্রাপ্ত ব্যক্তি। **Feof-fer, —for,** *ns.* He who grants the feoff; জায়গীরপ্রদাতা। **Feoff'-ment** *n.* The legal gift or transference to a person of a fee or freehold or estate; the deed or instrument by which such property is conveyed; জায়গীর প্রদান; জায়গীর দান-পত্র।

fē-ra'-cious (-shŭs), *adj.* Fruitful; producing abundantly; ফলপ্রদ, শস্যপ্রদ; প্রচুর উৎপাদনশীল।

fē'-ræ (-rē), *n.* (*Pl.*) Wild animals; বন্য জন্তু, আরণ্য জন্তু।

fē'-ræ-na-tu'-ræ (-rē-nā-tū-rē), *adj.* (*Used predicatively or after the noun*) Living in a wild state; not domesticated; as, animals *feræ-naturæ*; বন্য; বন্যভাবাপন্ন।

fē'-răl, (*adj.*) Uncultivated or wild; untamed; brutal; বন্য, বন্যপশুবৎ; অপোষা; পাশবিক।

fĕr-dĕ-lance' (-lângs), *n.* A very venomous serpent of Brazil and the West Indies; ব্রাজীল দেশ ও পশ্চিম ভারতীয় দ্বীপপুঞ্জের বিষধর সর্প-বিশেষ।

fĕr'-ē-tŏ-rȳ, *n.* **1.** A shrine used for containing saints' relics; a tomb; সাধু মহাপুরুষগণের পবিত্র দেহাবশেষ বা স্মৃতিসামগ্রী রক্ষার স্থান; সমাধিস্তম্ভ। **2.** A bier; শবযান; মড়ার খাটুলী। **3.** A chapel in which shrines were deposited; যে ক্ষুদ্র ধর্ম্মমন্দিরে সাধু মহাপুরুষগণের পবিত্র দেহাবশেষ প্রভৃতি রক্ষিত হইত।

fē'-ri-ăl *adj.* Relating to a holiday; (of a day) not appointed for festival or feast; বন্ধ-দিবস সম্পর্কীয়; (দিন-সম্পর্কে) পর্ব্ব বা উপবাসের জন্য নির্দ্দিষ্ট নয়। **Ferial service**—উপবাস দিবসের উপাসনা।

fē'-rīne, *adj.* Wild; untamed; feral; বন্য; অসভ্য; হিংস্র।

Fē-rin'-ghee (-rĭng-gē), *n.* An Indian name for a Eurasian, esp. of

Portugese Indian—a derogatory native term ; ফিরিঙ্গী।

fêr′-mĕnt, *n.* **1.** That which causes fermentation, as yeast, leaven, etc. ; কিণ্ব, খমীর। **2.** Tumult ; agitation ; গোলমাল ; আন্দোলন, আলোড়ন, উত্তেজনা, বিক্ষোভ। **3.** A gentle internal motion of constituent parts of a fluid ; fermentation ; তরল পদার্থের উপাদান সমূহের অন্তরুৎসেচন ; স্ফোটন।

fêr-mĕnt′, *v. t.* & *i.* **1.** To cause or excite fermentation in ; to set in motion ; গাঁজাইয়া বা মাতাইয়া তোলা ; অন্তরুৎসিক্ত করা। **2.** To foment ; to agitate ; উত্তেজিত করা ; উচ্ছলিত করা, আলোড়িত করা। ***Verb i.*** **1.** To undergo fermentation ; to effervesce ; মাতিয়া উঠা ; গাঁজিয়া উঠা। **2.** To be excited by violent emotion ; উত্তেজিত হওয়া, বিক্ষুব্ধ হওয়া, উচ্ছলিত হওয়া। **–a-ble,** *adj.* **–a-tive,** *adj.* Causing, or consisting in fermentation ; অনরুৎসেচক, সন্ধানাত্মক (অভিঃ)। **–a-tively,** *adv.*

fêr-mĕn-tā′-tion, *n.* **1.** The act or process of fermenting ; the decomposition or conversion of an organic substance into new compounds through the agency of a ferment, generally indicated by the development of heat, bubbles, etc. ; কিণ্বন ; অন্তরুৎসেক (হঃ চঃ), সন্ধান (সাঃ পঃ), গাঁজন। **2.** Restless state of the mind or feelings ; উত্তেজনা, অস্থিরতা, চাঞ্চল্য, বিক্ষোভ, আন্দোলন, আলোড়ন।

fêrn, *n.* A cryptogamous plant producing leaves called fronds ; পর্ণাঙ্গ (সাঃ পঃ), (রসবহানালী এবং শাখার স্থলে) কাণ্ড-সংলগ্ন সবৃন্তক পত্র বিশিষ্ট গুল্মশ্রেণীর অন্যতম। **Fern′-er-y,** *n.* A place for rearing ferns ; গুল্মবাড়ী (প্রবোধ), গুল্মবাটিকা, পর্ণাঙ্গবাটিকা। **Fern′-less,** *adj.* **Fern′-y,** *adj.* Overgrown with ferns ; পর্ণাঙ্গবহুল।

Fern-owl — একপ্রকার পোকা।

Fern-shaw—পর্ণাঙ্গ-কুঞ্জ।

Fern.

fē-rō′-cious (-shŭs), *adj.* Fierce ; savage ; wild ; cruel ; হিংস্র ; অসভ্য, বর্ব্বর ; বন্য ; নিষ্ঠুর, ক্রুর, নির্ম্মম। **–ly,** *adv.* In a ferocious manner ; হিংস্রভাবে, ক্রুরভাবে। **–ness,** *n.*

fē-rŏc′-i-tȳ, *n.* Fierceness ; a ferocious act ; হিংস্রত্ব, হিংস্র স্বভাব, ভীষণত্ব, ভয়ানকত্ব, নিষ্ঠুরতা, ক্রুরতা ; ক্রুরতার কার্য্য।

Feronia Elephantum, *n.* কৎবেল (বেলঃ)।

fĕr′-răn-dīne, *n.* A stuff made of silk and wool ; রেশম ও পশমে প্রস্তুত একপ্রকার কাপড়, উর্ণা ও পট্টসূত্রে প্রস্তুত বস্ত্রবিশেষ।

Fêr-râ′-râ, *n.* A sword of excellent quality ; অতি উৎকৃষ্ট তরবারী [ইতালীদেশীয় সুবিখ্যাত অসি-নির্ম্মাতা Andrea Ferrarar নাম হইতে গৃহীত]।

fĕr′-rē-ous (-ŭs), *adj.* Pertaining to iron ; made of, or containing, iron ; আয়স ; লৌহময়, লৌহনির্ম্মিত।

fĕr′-rĕt, *n., v. i.* & *t.* **1.** An animal of the weasel family employed in unearthing rabbits ; একপ্রকার অর্দ্ধ-বন্য গন্ধগোকুলা—ইহারা শশকদিগকে গর্ত্ত হইতে বাহির এবং ইন্দুরাদি বিনাশ করিয়া থাকে। **2.** A kind of narrow tape made of cotton, wool or silk ; একপ্রকার সূতী, রেশমী বা পশমী ফিতা। **3.** A detective ; গোয়েন্দা, টিকটিকি। ***Verb i.*** To hunt with ferrets ; to search, (with *about, for*) ; উক্তরূপ জন্তুদ্বারা শিকার করা ; পাঁতি পাঁতি করিয়া খুঁজা, তন্নতন্ন করিয়া তল্লাস করা। ***Verb t.*** **1.** To drive out of a lurking place ; to catch with a ferret ; as, to *ferret* a rabbit ; to search (often with *out*) ; as, to *ferret out* a secret ; গুপ্ত স্থান হইতে বাহির করা ; গন্ধ গোকুলাদ্বারা ধৃত করা ; অন্বেষণ করা, খোঁজা। **2.** To hunt over (a ground, place, etc.) with a ferret ; কোন স্থানে অর্দ্ধবন্য গন্ধগোকুলা দ্বারা শিকার করা। **–y,** *adj.*

fĕr′-ri-āge, *n.* The fare to be paid at a ferry ; conveyance by a ferry ; পারের কড়ি, খেয়ার মাশুল, তরপণ্য, দান (প্রাচীন সাহিত্য); পারাণি।

fĕr′-ric, *adj.* Of, or relating to, iron ; (*chem.*) containing iron in its highest combining power ; as, *ferric* acid ; লৌহ-সম্বন্ধীয়, আয়স ; (রসায়ন-শাস্ত্র) লৌহময়। **Ferric-Oxide**—পূতিত লৌহ (ভারতী ১৩২২)। **Ferric sulphide** — সোণামুখী, সুবর্ণমক্ষিকা।

fĕr-rō-măg-nĕt′-ic, *adj.* Magnetic as opposed to diamagnetic ; চৌম্বক।

fĕr′-rō-tȳpe, *n.* A photographic process with salts of iron ; a photograph taken on a thin iron plate ; আয়সলবণক দ্বারা আলোকচিত্র পরিস্ফুরণ ; লোহার পাতের উপর গৃহীত আলোকচিত্র।

fĕr′-rous (-rŭs), *adj.* (*Chem.*) Having a considerable quantity of iron in its composition ; (রসায়ন-শাস্ত্র) লৌহময়, লৌহজাত, লৌহসঙ্কুল।

fĕr-rû′-gi-nous (-nŭs), *adj.* **1.** Containing, or relating to, iron or iron rust ; লৌহকণাময়, লৌহগর্ভ, লৌহ-সঙ্কুল, আয়সকণীয় (সাঃ পঃ), লৌহময় (ঐ)। **2.** Like iron rust in colour ; brownish red ; মরিচার মত লালবর্ণ ; পিঙ্গলবর্ণ।

fĕr-rû'-gō, *n.* A disease of plants commonly called rust ; বৃক্ষরোগ বিশেষ।

fĕr'-rule (-rûl), **—rĕl**, *ns.* **1.** A metallic ring or cap on the end of a stick etc. ; লাঠির মাথার গুলো, সামি। **2.** A band strengthening or forming a joint ; গ্রন্থির দৃঢ়তা-সংসাধক বেষ্টনী, গাঁইট। **—rul-ed**, *adj.*

fĕr'-rÿ, *v. t., i.* & *n.* To convey or carry over a river etc. in a boat ; খেয়া নৌকায় পার করা। ***Verb i.*** To pass over water in a boat or by a ferry ; (of a boat) to pass to and fro over a river etc. ; খেয়া নৌকায় পার হওয়া ; খেয়া দেওয়া। ***Noun.*** **1.** A place where persons or things are carried across a river in a ferry boat; খেয়া ঘাট, পার ঘাট। **2.** (*Law*) A right to maintain a vessel for carrying passengers and freight across a river etc. by charging tolls ; (আইন) খেয়া পার করিবার অধিকার। **3.** (*Archaic*) A ferry boat ; (অপ্রঃ) খেয়া নৌকা। **Ferry boat**—খেয়া-নৌকা, তরণ নৌকা। **Ferry bridge**—এক প্রকার বৃহৎ তরণ নৌকা,—যাহার উপর দিয়া বাষ্পীয় শকট নদী বা উপসাগর পার হয়। **Ferry man**—One who keeps a ferry ; পাটনী, খেয়া মাঝি, দানী (প্রাচীন সাহিত্য)।

fêr'-tile, *adj.* **1.** Productive; fruitful; inventive (often with *of, in*) ; as, he is *fertile* in resources ; *fertile* land ; *fertile* mind ; উর্ব্বর ; শস্যপ্রদ; উদ্ভাবনক্ষম, উদ্ভাবনী। **2.** (*Bot.*) Fruit-bearing ; (উদ্ভিদ বিদ্যা) ফলপ্রসূ। **3.** Causing or tending to promote fertility ; উর্ব্বরতাজনক, উর্ব্বরতা সম্পাদক। **—ly**, *adv.*

fêr-til'-i-tÿ, *n.* The state or quality of being fertile ; fruitfulness ; productiveness ; fertile invention ; উর্ব্বরতা ; ফলশালিতা ; উৎপাদিকাশক্তি ; প্রচুর উদ্ভাবন।

fêr-ti-li-zā'-tion *n.* The act or process of rendering fertile ; act of fecundating ; উর্ব্বরতা সাধন ; গর্ভাধান (হিঃ কোঃ), আধান (ঐ), ডিম্বনিষেক।

fêr'-ti-lïze, *v. t.* **1.** To make fertile or enrich ; as, to *fertilize* soil ; উর্ব্বরতাসাধন করা, উর্ব্বর করা। **2.** To fecundate ; as, to *fertilize* an individual or organ ; গর্ভাধান করা, ডিম্বনিষেক করা। **—liz-a-ble**, *adj.* **—zer**, *n.* One who or that which fertilizes ; উর্ব্বরতাসাধক ব্যক্তি বা বস্তু।

fêr'-ü-lă, *n.* **1.** A ferule ; বেত। **2.** (*Bot.*) The giant fennel, (*obs.*) ; একপ্রকার গুল্ম (অপ্রঃ)।

fĕr'-üle, *n.* & *v. t.* A rod for punishing boys in schools ; বিদ্যালয়ের ছাত্রদিগকে শাস্তি দেওয়ার জন্য দণ্ডবিশেষ, গুরুমহাশয়ের বেত্র। ***Verb t.*** To punish with a ferule ; বেত্রাঘাত করা।

fĕr'-vĕnt, *adj.* **1.** Hot ; glowing ; burning ; as, a *fervent* summer ; উষ্ণ ; উদ্দীপ্ত ; জ্বলন্ত। **2.** Ardent ; zealous ; as, a *fervent* lover ; a *fervent* hatred ; প্রচণ্ড, তীব্র ; আগ্রহবান, আগ্রহপূর্ণ ; **—ven-cy**, *n.* Ardour; zeal ; প্রচণ্ডতা, তীব্রতা ; জ্বলন্ত উৎসাহ। **—ly**, *adv.* In a fervent manner ; তীব্রভাবে, প্রচণ্ডভাবে।

fêr-vĕs'-cĕnt, *adj.* Growing hot ; উচ্চণ্ড।

fêr'-vid, *n.* **1.** (*Poet.*) Very hot ; (কবিতায়) অত্যন্ত উত্তপ্ত। **2.** Ardent; zealous ; সোৎসাহ ; আগ্রহান্বিত। **—ly**, *adv.* **—vid'-i-ty**, **—ness**, *ns.* প্রচণ্ডতা।

fêr'-vour (-vêr), *n.* **1.** Heat or warmth ; উষ্ণতা, উত্তাপ। **2.** Ardour ; intensity of feeling ; vehemence ; আগ্রহ ; হৃদয়োচ্ছ্বাস ; প্রচণ্ডতা।

fĕs'-cĕn-nine, *adj.* Scurrilous ; obscene ; as, *fescennine* verse ; কুরুচিপূর্ণ ; অশ্লীল। [প্রাচীন রোম রাজ্যের অন্তঃপাতী Fescenninm নামক নগরীতে প্রথম প্রচলিত হয়।]

fĕs'-cue (-kü), *n.* **1.** A small stick, pin, etc. used for pointing out letters to children ; শিক্ষকদিগের অক্ষর প্রদর্শক কাষ্ঠিকা, শিশুদিগের বর্ণপরিচয় করাইবার জন্য যষ্টি বা শলকা বিশেষ। **2.** A kind of grass ; একপ্রকার ঘাস।

fĕss, fesse (fĕs), *ns.* (*Herald.*) A broad band crossing the shield horizontally and possessing one-third of it ; (কুলবিদ্যা) চর্ম্ম ফলকের বেষ্টনী-বিশেষ।

fĕs'-tăl, *adj.* Pertaining to a feast ; keeping holiday ; joyous ; gay ; পর্ব্ব সম্বন্ধীয় ; উৎসবানন্দ সম্ভোগকারী ; আনন্দময়, আনন্দপূর্ণ ; উৎফুল্ল। **—ly**, *adv.* In a festal manner ; উৎফুল্লভাবে।

fĕs'-têr, *v. t., i.* & *n.* To cause to fester or rankle ; পচান, সপূয করা। ***Verb i.*** **1.** To generate matter or pus ; to suppurate ; সপূয হওয়া ; পূয জন্মা। **2.** To putrefy ; to rot ; গলিত হওয়া ; পচা। ***Noun.*** **1.** A small inflammatory sore ; প্রদাহজনক ক্ষুদ্র ব্রণ। **2.** A festering state or condition ; গলিতাবস্থা।

fĕs'-ti-văl, *n.* & *adj.* A time of feasting ; a festive celebration ; merry-making ; পর্ব্বকাল ; পর্ব্ব, উৎসব ; আমোদপ্রমোদ। ***Adj.*** (Not *predicative*) Festive ; joyous ; পর্ব্ব সম্বন্ধীয় ; উৎফুল্ল।

fĕs'-tive (-tiv), *adj.* Pertaining to a feast ; joyous ; gay ; jovial ; উৎসবসম্বন্ধীয়, পর্ব্বসম্বন্ধীয় ; আনন্দপূর্ণ ; উৎফুল্ল ; আমোদপূর্ণ। **—ly**, *adv.* **—tiv-i-ty**, *n.* **1.** Mirth ; rejoicing ; as, a day of great *festivity* ; আমোদপ্রমোদ ; আনন্দ। **2.** A festive celebration ; (*pl.*) festive proceedings ; উৎসব ; (বহুবচন) উৎসবক্রিয়া।

fĕs'-tōōn', *n.* & *v. t.* **1.** A garland of flowers, foliage, etc. suspended in a curve between two posts ; স্তম্ভযুগলের মধ্যদেশে বিলম্বিত পত্রপুষ্পাদি রচিত মালা, তোরণ-স্রজ (সঃ)।

2. (*Arch.* & *sculp.*) An ornament of curved work in imitation of such a garland ; (ভাস্কর্য্য এবং স্থাপত্য-শিল্প) তোরণস্রজাকারে ক্ষোদিত সৌধ-ভূষা। ***Verb t.*** To adorn with festoons ; তোরণস্রজদ্বারা বিশোভিত করা। **–er-y,** *n.*

fē'-tăl, *adj.* Pertaining to a fetus ; পূর্ণাঙ্গ ভ্রূণসম্বন্ধীয়।

fetch (fĕch), *v. t., i.* & *n.* **1.** To go for and bring back ; to bring ; যাইয়া আনা; আনা, আনয়ন করা। **2.** To bring in ; "His land *fetched* 15*s.* an acre" ; আনয়ন করা। **3.** To cause to come ; to draw forth ; as, to *fetch* blood, tears, etc. আনা ; টানিয়া আনা, আকর্ষণ করা। **4.** To make or perform ; as, to *fetch* a compass ; to heave (sigh); to draw (breath) ; to deal, as a blow; সম্পন্ন করা, সম্পাদন করা; নিঃশ্বাস ফেলা ; শ্বাস টানা ; দেওয়া। **5.** To please ; to attract irresistibly ; as, the costume will *fetch* the audience ; তুষ্ট করা ; প্রবলভাবে চিত্তাকর্ষণ করা। **6.** (*Naut.*) To arrive at ; (নৌ-বিদ্যা) পৌঁছা। ***Verb i.*** **1.** To bring things ; কোন জিনিষ আনা। **2.** To move and turn ; as, to *fetch* about ; ঘূর, ফেরা করা। **3.** (*Naut.*) To arrive ; (নৌ-বিদ্যা) পৌঁছা। ***Noun.*** **1.** A stratagem or trick ; কৌশল, ফিকির, ছল। **2.** (*Archaic*) A far-reaching effort ; (অপ্রঃ) সুদূরব্যাপী চেষ্টা। **Fetch'-ing,** *p. adj.* Attractive ; delighting ; চিত্তাকর্ষক ; আনন্দজনক। **Far-fetched**—See under FAR. **Fetch-candle** — মৃত্যুসূচক নৈশ আলোক। **To fetch about**—To adopt a round-about way or method ; to swing round, as a weapon ; বক্রতা অবলম্বন করা ; ঘুরান। **To fetch a compass**—To take a circuitous route in going to a place ; সোজা পথে না যাইয়া ঘুরিয়া যাওয়া। **To fetch and carry**—To perform humble services for another ; দাস্যবৃত্তি করা, নীচ কার্য্য করা। To run to and fro with news of gossip ; গল্পগুজব করিয়া বেড়ান, সংবাদ প্রচার করিয়া বেড়ান। **To fetch a pump**—To pour water into it so as to make it draw water ; জল টানিয়া তোলার জন্য দম কলের ভিতর জল ঢালা। **To fetch away**—To move or shift from its proper place ; স্বস্থানচ্যুত করা, স্থানভ্রষ্ট করা। **To fetch back**—To bring back ; ফিরাইয়া আনা, প্রত্যানয়ন করা। **To fetch down**—To bring to the ground by a shot or blow ; আঘাত করিয়া বা গুলিদ্বারা বিদ্ধ করিয়া ভূপাতিত করা। To bring down, as price etc. ; দাম প্রভৃতি কমান। **To fetch forth**—To bring out ; টানিয়া বাহির করা। **To fetch in**—To seize ; ধরা, গ্রেপ্তার করা। **To fetch off**—To carry off ; জিতিয়া লওয়া। **To fetch out**—To bring out ; to draw forth ; টানিয়া বাহির করা ; আকর্ষণ করা। **To fetch to**—To revive, as from a swoon ; সংজ্ঞা সম্পাদন করা, চৈতন্যসম্পাদন করা। **To fetch up**—To vomit ; বমন করা। To come to a standstill ; হঠাৎ থামা। To overtake ; লাগাইল ধরা।

fetch (fĕch), *n.* The apparition of a living person ; a wraith ; ভূত ; অপচ্ছায়া।

fête (fāt), *n.* & *v. t.* (*F.*) **1.** A feast or festival ; উৎসব, পর্ব্ব। ***Verb t.*** **1.** To feast ; to honour with a festival ; পানভোজন করান, ভোজ প্রদান করা ; পানভোজনাদি দ্বারা আপ্যায়িত করা। **2.** The day of the saint after whom one is named,—observed like a birthday in Roman Catholic countries, (also called a FETE-DAY, as below) ; যে সিদ্ধপুরুষের নামে কাহারো নামাকরণ হয় তদীয় দিবস — যে দিবসে রোমান ক্যাথলিকগণ জন্ম দিনের মত উৎসব করিয়া থাকে। **Fete-day** —A day appointed for fete ; পর্ব্বদিবস, উৎসবদিন, পর্ব্বাহ।

fete champetre (*F.*) An out door feast or entertainment মুক্ত স্থানে ভোজ বা উৎসব।

fē'-tich(e) (-tĭsh), **–tĭsh,** *n.* **1.** An inanimate object worshipped by some savage races for its magical power or as being inhabited by a spirit ; অসভ্য জাতিসমূহদ্বারা পূজিত পিশাচাশ্রিত বৃক্ষ, পাষাণ প্রভৃতি, কাষ্ঠলোষ্ট্রদেবাঃ (ব্রজ—বৈষ্ণবঃ)। **2.** An object or principle irrationally regarded with reverence অতিরিক্ত নিষ্ঠা বা আসক্তির বিষয়। **–er –eer,** *ns.* A sorcerer ; পিশাচসিদ্ধ ব্যক্তি, মায়াবী। **–ism,** *n.* Belief in fetishes ; practice of fetish worship ; জড়চেতনা (সাঃ পঃ), জড়চৈতন্যবাদ (ঐ) ; পিশাচাশ্রিত বোধে কাষ্ঠলোষ্ট্রাদির পূজা, জড়-পূজা, জড়োপাসনা। **–ist,** *n.* A believer in fetishes কাষ্ঠলোষ্ট্রদেবাদিতে বিশ্বাসী ব্যক্তি। **–is'-tic,** *adj.* Pertaining to fetichism; জড়পূজা-সম্বন্ধীয়, জড়োপাসনা সম্পর্কীয়।

fē'-ti-cīde, *n.* The destruction of the fetus in the womb ; ভ্রূণ-হত্যা।

fĕt'-id, fœt'-id (fĕt-), *ns.* Having a strong offensive odour ; পূতিগন্ধময়, দুর্গন্ধময়। **–ly,** *adv.* **–ness,** *n.*

fĕt'-lŏck *n.* A tuft of hair growing behind the pastern joint of horses ; that part of a horse's leg where it grows ; অশ্বপদের পশ্চাদ্‌ভাগস্থ লোমগুচ্ছ ; অশ্বপদের যে গ্রন্থিতে তাদৃশ লোমগুচ্ছ জাত হইয়া থাকে। **–locked,** *adj.* Having fetlocks ; ঐরূপ লোমসমন্বিত গ্রন্থিযুক্ত।

fĕt'-têr, *n.* & *v. t.* **1.** A chain for the feet ; a bond ; (generally used in the *plural*) ; শৃঙ্খল, বেড়ী, নিগড় ; বন্ধন। **2.** (*Pl.*) Captivity ; আটক। **3.** A restraint ; আটক।

Verb t. To put fetters upon; to shackle; to confine; to check; শৃঙ্খলবদ্ধ করা; নিগড়িত করা; রুদ্ধ করা; নিরোধ করা, সংযত করা। **—tered,** *p.p.* **1.** Bound by fetters; শৃঙ্খলাবদ্ধ, নিগড়বদ্ধ, নিগড়িত। **2.** (*Zool.*) Of feet bent backward and apparently unfit for walking; (প্রাণিবিদ্যা) চলচ্ছক্তিরহিত বলিয়া প্রতীয়মান (যথা কচ্ছপাদির পক্ষে পদ সঙ্কুচিত করিয়া ভিতরের দিকে টানিয়া নেওয়া হেতু।) **—less,** *adj.* Free from fetters; শৃঙ্খলমুক্ত, নিগড়নির্ম্মুক্ত।

fét'-têr-lŏck, *n.* See FETLOCK 2.

fĕt'-tle (-tl), *v. t.* & *n.* To put in right order; ঠিক করা, মেরামত করা, ঠিকঠাক করা, সারা। *Noun.* Good condition; trim; ভাল অবস্থা; ঠিকঠাক, পরিপাটী। **In fine fettle**—In good spirits; খোস মেজাজে।

fē'-tŭs, *n.* (*Pl.* -TUSES) The young or embryo in the womb or in the egg; ভ্রূণ (see also FŒTUS).

fĕt'-wâ, *n.* A decision given by a Moslem authority; ফতোয়া।

fēu (fü), *n.* **1.** (In Scotland) Perpetual lease for a fixed rent; নির্দ্দিষ্ট জমায় চিরস্থায়ী বন্দোবস্ত, কায়েমী-জোত। **2.** A piece of land held in feu; মকররী ভূমি।

feud (füd), *n.* A lasting mutual hostility; a deadly quarrel between families or parties to avenge wrong; চিরশত্রুতা; কুলবৈরিতা, পারিবারিক শত্রুতা। **To be at a feud with**—To have lasting mutual hostility with any one; কাহারও সহিত চিরশত্রুতা থাকা।

feud (füd), *n.* A fief; a fee or feudal benefice; চাকরাণ জমী; সামরিক জায়গীর।

feu'-dăl (fü-), *adj.* **1.** Of, or relating to, a feud or fief; চাকরাণ জমী বা জায়গীর সম্বন্ধীয়। **2.** Pertaining, or according, to the feudal system; সামন্ততন্ত্র-সম্পর্কীয়। **—ism,** *n.* Same as FEUDAL SYSTEM. **Feudal system**—মধ্যযুগে ইংলণ্ডের ভূম্যধিকার বিশেষ,—যাহাতে সামরিক বা অন্য প্রকার কার্য্য করার চুক্তিতে রাজা ভূম্যধিকারিগণকে এবং তাঁহারা ক্ষুদ্র ক্ষুদ্র জমীদারদিগকে এবং তাঁহারা প্রজাদিগকে ভূমিদান করিতেন, ভৌমিকতা (সাহিত্য), সামন্ত-তন্ত্র (প্রবাসী ১৩১৯)।

feu'-dăl-ĭst (fü-), *n.* An upholder of feudalism; সামন্ততন্ত্রসমর্থক। **—is'-tic,** *adj.* Inclined to feudalism; সামন্ততন্ত্রানুরাগী।

feu-dăl'-ĭ-tȳ (fü-), *n.* The state of being feudal; the feudal system or principles; ভৌমিকতা; সামন্ত-তন্ত্র, সামন্ত-তন্ত্রের মূলনীতি।

Feu'-dal-ize, *v. t.* **—za'-tion,** *n.*

feu'-dă-tō-rȳ (fü-), *adj.* & *n.* Holding lands or power by a feudal tenure; (of a kingdom) under the overlordship of a foreign state; জায়গীর ভোগী; (রাজ্য সম্বন্ধে) অধীন, করদ। *Noun.* The tenant of a feud or fief; অধীন ভূম্যধিকারী, সামন্ত।

feu de joie, (*F.*), *n.* Gun-firing on the occasion of a public procession; a bonfire; সাধারণের শোভাযাত্রাকালীন তোপধ্বনি; উৎসবাগ্নি, বহ্ন্যুৎসব।

feuilleton, (*F.*), *n.* The part at the end of a French newspaper devoted to fiction, criticism, light literature, etc.; ফরাসী সংবাদপত্রের যে অংশে চুট্‌কী, উপন্যাস, সমালোচনা, প্রভৃতি থাকে।

fē'-vêr, *n., v. t.* & *i.* **1.** A morbid condition of the system or a disease characterised by accelerated pulse, high temperature, thirst, etc.; জ্বর। **2.** Excitement; agitation; "The quarrel has set my blood in a *fever*;" ক্রোধাদির উত্তেজনা; বিক্ষোভ। *Verb t.* To put in a fever; জ্বরাক্রান্ত করা। *Verb i.* To contract fever; জ্বরাক্রান্ত হওয়া। **—vered,** *p. p.* Affected with fever; excited; জ্বরাক্রান্ত; উত্তেজিত। **Fever-heat**—জ্বরাবস্থায় দৈহিক উষ্ণতা। **Fever-nut** — করঞ্জা। **Fever-trap** — জ্বররোগাণু সঞ্চয়ের স্থান।

fē'-vêr-few (-fü), *n.* A herb formerly used in medicine; পূর্ব্বকালে ঔষধে ব্যবহৃত গুল্মবিশেষ।

fē'-vêr-ĭsh, *adj.* **1.** Having a slight fever; as, he feels *feverish*; অল্প জ্বরাক্রান্ত, ঈষৎ জ্বরগ্রস্ত, জ্বরজ্বর, সজ্বর। **2.** Indicating, or pertaining to, fever; as, *feverish* symptoms; জ্বরসূচক, জ্বরসম্পর্কীয়। **3.** Excited; restless; inconstant; উত্তেজিত; অস্থির; চঞ্চল। **4.** Infected by fever, as a locality; জ্বরসমাকুল। **—ly,** *adv.* **—ness,** *n.* The state of being feverish; জ্বরজ্বর ভাব।

fē'-vêr-ous (-ŭs), *adj.* **1.** Having the nature of a fever; pertaining to fever; জ্বরাত্মক; জ্বরসম্পর্কীয়। **2.** Excited; restless; উত্তেজিত; চঞ্চল, বিক্ষুব্ধ, অস্থির। **3.** Apt to cause fever; as, a *feverous* climate or locality; জ্বরজননপ্রবণ।

few (fü), *adj.* Small in number; not many; as, a man of *few* words; অল্পসংখ্যক, অনধিক; কতিপয়, গোটাকয়েক। **Few'-ness,** *n.* Smallness of number; অল্পতা, অল্পসংখ্যা। **A few**—Not many; a small number; as, *a few* know the truth; গোটাকয়েক; অল্পসংখ্যা। (*Slang*) Very much beyond a doubt; (ইতর-ভাষায়) একেবারে নিঃসন্দেহে। [*Few* is opposed to *many* and *a few* to *none*.] **Every few days**—Once in every group of a few days; মাঝে মাঝে, সময় সময়। **Good few**—A considerable number (of); অনেকগুলি, বড় কম নয়। **Few and far between** — See BETWEEN. **In few**—Briefly; সংক্ষেপে। **Not a few**—Many; অনেক। **Some few**—No great number; অল্পসংখ্যক, গোটাকয়েক। **The few** — The minority; opposed to the majority or the many ; অধিক নয়, অল্প।

fey (fā), *adj*. **1.** (*Scot.*) Doomed to die ; at the point of death ; নিশ্চিত-মৃত্যু ; মুমূর্ষু। **2.** Disordered in mind like a person about to die ; মুমূর্ষু ব্যক্তির মত বিকৃত মতি।

féz, *n*. A close-fitting red cap with a tassel, much worn in Turkey, Egypt, etc.; তুরস্ক, মিসর এবং উত্তর-আফ্রিকার মুসলমানদিগের একপ্রকার লাল টুপী, লাল তুর্কি টুপী।

1, Egytian fez.
2, Turkish fez.

fiacre (*F.*), *n*. A kind of French hackney coach ; ফরাসীদেশীয় একপ্রকার ভাড়াটিয়া গাড়ী।

fiance' (*Mas.*), ***-cee*** (*Fem.*), (*F.*) *ns*. A betrothed man or woman ; বিবাহের জন্য স্থিরীকৃত পাত্র কিম্বা স্থিরীকৃতা পাত্রী, বাগ্‌দত্তা কন্যা।

fi-ăs'-cō (fē-) *n*. A ridiculous failure, (originally in dramatic and musical performances); ignominious result ; হাস্যজনক অকৃতকার্যতা, হাস্যকর বিফলতা ; অখ্যাতিজনক পরিণাম।

fī'-ăt, *n*. & *v. t.* A decree ; a command to do something ; an authorization ; আদেশ, আজ্ঞা ; হুকুম ; ক্ষমতার্পণ। ***Verb t.*** To sanction ; মঞ্জুর করা।

fib, *n*. & *v. i.* A falsehood ; (a word used as a softer expression than *lie*) ; অনৃত, সত্যের অপলাপ। ***Verb i.*** To tell a fib or lie ; সত্যের অপলাপ করা।

fib, *n*. & *v. t.* A blow ; আঘাত। ***Verb t.*** To strike, as in pugilism ; আঘাত করা।

fib'-bêr, –stêr, *ns*. One who tells fibs ; অসত্যভাষী, অনৃতভাষী, সত্যের অপলাপকরী।

fī'-bre (-bêr), **–bêr,** *ns*. **1.** A thread or thread-like filament or structure ; তন্তু, অংশু, আঁশ, রেশা। **2.** (*Collectively*) A substance consisting of fibres whether of animal, vegetable or mineral origin ; a thing capable of being spun woven etc. ; (সমষ্টিবাচক ভাবে) আঁশওয়ালা জিনিষ, অংশুময় পদার্থ ; যে জিনিষ বুনা যাইতে পারে বা যাহা হইতে সূতা কাটা হয়। **3.** (*Bot.*) A small root or twig ; (উদ্ভিদ্-বিদ্যা) ক্ষুদ্র শিকড় বা ডগা। **4.** Sinew ; strength ; character ; as, a man of coarse *fibre* ; মাংসপেশী ; শক্তি, বল ; স্বভাব, প্রকৃতি। **–bred,** *adj*. Having fibres or made up of fibres ; আঁশাল, অংশুরচিত। **–bri-form,** *adj*. Having the form of a fibre ; resembling a fibre ; অংশুর ন্যায় আকৃতিবিশিষ্ট ; অংশুসদৃশ। **–brous,** *adj*. Composed of fibres ; containing or resembling fibres ; অংশুনির্মিত ; অংশুময়, তন্তুময়, আঁশাল, সৌত্রিক, তন্তুনিভ, তান্তব। **–brous-ly,** *adv*. **–brous-ness,** *n*. **–less,** *adj*. Having no fibres ; অংশুবিহীন।

fī'-bril, *n*. **1.** A small fibre ; a very slender thread ; ক্ষুদ্রতন্তু ; অতি সূক্ষ্ম তন্তু বা সূত্র। **2.** (*Bot.*) A root-hair ; (উদ্ভিদ্-বিদ্যা) তন্তু। **–lar, –la-ry,** *adjs*. Pertaining to or like fibres ; (জীব বা উদ্ভিদ দেহের) তন্তুবৎ উপাদান-সম্বন্ধীয় বা তদ্বৎ। **–late, –lat-ed,** *adjs*. Having a fibrillous structure ; তন্তুবৎ গঠিত। **–bril'-li-form,** *adj*. Having the form of a fibril or fibrils ; (জীব বা উদ্ভিদ্‌দেহের) তন্তুময় উপাদানকারী। **–lose,** *adj*. (*Bot.*) Furnished with hair-like appendages ; (উদ্ভিদ্-বিদ্যা) তন্তুবিশিষ্ট, অংশুল। **–lous,** *adj*. Pertaining to, or composed of fibrils ; সূক্ষ্মতন্তু নির্মিত অথবা তৎসম্পর্কীয়।

fī-bril-lā'-tion, *n*. The process of becoming fibrillated ; তন্তুবৎ গঠন।

fī'-brin, *n*. An organic compound found in animals and vegetables distinguished by its disposition to form into filaments ; প্রাণী ও উদ্ভিদ্ দেহের তন্তুময় উপাদান,—রক্তে এই পদার্থ বিশিষ্টরূপে পাওয়া যায়।

fī-bri-nā'-tion, *n*. State of acquiring or having an excess of fibrin ; তন্তুময়পদার্থবত্তা, (ভৈষজ্য শাস্ত্র) তন্তুময়পদার্থের প্রাচুর্য্য।

fī'-brin-ous (-ŭs), *adj*. Of or like fibrin ; আঁশযুক্ত, তন্তুময়োপাদানবিশিষ্ট, তন্তুময় উপাদানবৎ।

fī'-broid (-broyd), *adj*. & *n*. Resembling fibre or fibrous tissue ; অংশুসদৃশ। ***Noun.*** A fibroid uterine tumour ; জরায়ুর তন্তুময় অর্ব্বুদ।

fī'-brō-in, *n*. The chief ingredient of silk, cobwebs, etc. ; রেশম, লূতাতন্তু অথবা তদ্বৎ পদার্থের প্রধান রাসায়নিক উপাদান।

fī-brō'-mâ, *n*. (*pl*. -MATA). A fibrous tumour ; তন্তুময় অর্ব্বুদ (হঃ চঃ)।

fĭb'-ū-lā, *n*. (*pl*. -AE, -AS) **1.** A brooch ; পোষাকে লাগাইবার আঁকড়া। **2.** The outer and lesser bone of the lower leg ; জঙ্ঘার দীর্ঘাস্থির সম্মুখস্থ ক্ষুদ্র অস্থি, নলকাস্থি (হঃ চঃ), জানুর নিম্নস্থ একমাত্র অস্থি, অপ্রজঙ্ঘাস্থি (সাঃ পঃ)। **3.** (*Surg.*) A needle for sewing up wound ; (অস্ত্রোপচার বিদ্যা) ক্ষতের মুখ সেলাই করিবার সূচী।

Fibula.

fĭb'-ū-lar (-lêr), *adj*. Pertaining to or situated near fibula ; নলকাস্থি সম্বন্ধীয়, নলকাস্থির অস্তিকস্থ।

fich'-u (fi-shō), *n*. An article of laces worn by ladies over the neck, throat and shoulders ; একপ্রকার লেসের শাল,—যাহাতে স্ত্রীলোকদিগের গ্রীবা, স্কন্ধ ও কণ্ঠ আবৃত হয়।

fick'-le (-l), *adj*. Changeable ; inconstant ; as, fortune's *fickle* wheels (*shak.*) ; চঞ্চল, পরিবর্ত্তনশীল; চপল-প্রকৃতি, তরল-মতি, চঞ্চল-বুদ্ধি, চলবুদ্ধি, অস্থির-মতি, তরল-প্রকৃতি, অব্যবস্থিত-চিত্ত। **—ness,** *n.* Instability ; inconstancy; অস্থিরতা, চাঞ্চল্য ; অব্যবস্থিত-চিত্ততা, চাপল্য, চপলতা, চলচিত্ততা।

fi'-cō (fē-), *n.* (*Obs.*) A fig, (as used in expression of scorn or contempt) ; (অপ্রঃ) কলা (অবজ্ঞাসূচক বাক্যে ব্যবহৃত হয়)।

fic'-tīle, *adj.* Moulded into form by art ; made of clay by the potter ; relating to the pottery ; শিল্পকলাদ্বারা বিশেষ আকারে গঠিত; কুম্ভকাররচিত, কুলালরচিত ; মৃৎশিল্প-সম্পর্কীয়। **—ness, —til'-i-ty,** *ns.*

fic'-tion, *n.* **1.** Feigning ; inventing or imagining ; কল্পনা ; উদ্ভাবন। **2.** Thing feigned or imagined ; an invented statement or story ; কল্পিত বর্ণনা বা গল্প, ছল (বাৎস্য) ; কাল্পনিক বৃত্তান্ত। **3.** Fictitious literature esp. novels and romances ; গল্প, উপন্যাস, নবন্যাস, গুপ্তকথা প্রভৃতি। **4.** (*Law*) An assumption of a possible thing as a fact whether true or not ; as, a legal *fiction* ; (আইন) সত্যাসত্য বিচার না করিয়া কোন সম্ভাবিত বিষয় সত্য বলিয়া ধরিয়া লওন। **—al,** *adj.* **—ist,** *n.* A writer of fiction ; উপন্যাসলেখক, ঔপন্যাসিক।

fic-ti'-tious (-shŭs), *adj.* **1.** Counterfeit ; not genuine ; imaginary ; assumed as a character or name ; কৃত্রিম, নকল, জাল ; অপ্রকৃত ; কাল্পনিক ; ছদ্ম। **2.** Relating to, or like, fiction ; ঔপন্যাসিক, উপন্যাসবৎ। **3.** Regarded as such by a legal or conventional fiction; as, a *fictitious* son ; কৃত্রিম, কৃতক। **—ly,** *adv.* **—ness,** *n.*

fic'-tive (-tĭv), *adj.* **1.** Created by imagination ; কাল্পনিক, কল্পনা-রচিত। **2.** Imaginary ; sham ; as, *fictitious* tears ; কাল্পনিক ; কপট।

Ficus carica—ডুমুর (বেলঃ)।

Ficus elastica—রবর গাছ (বেলঃ)।

Ficus glomerata — যজ্ঞ ডুমুর (বেলঃ)।

Ficus Indica—বট (বেলঃ)।

Ficus religiosa—অশ্বত্থ (বেলঃ)।

fid, *n.* (*Naut.*) **1.** A tapering pin of wood used in splicing ; (নৌ-বিদ্যা) রজ্জু প্রান্তের পাক খুলিয়া গেলে যে সূক্ষ্মাগ্র কাষ্ঠকীলক দ্বারা সেই খোলা অংশ পুনরায় পাকান হয়। **2.** (*Naut.*) A square bar of wood or iron to support the top mast ; (নৌবিদ্যা) মাস্তুলের অবলম্বন স্বরূপ চতুষ্কোণ লৌহময় দণ্ড। **3.** A wooden or iron bar to support or steady anything ; কোন জিনিষ অবলম্বিত বা স্থির রাখিবার জন্য কাষ্ঠ অথবা লৌহদণ্ড। **4.** (*Dial.*) A small thick piece of anything ; (উপভাষায়) কোন জিনিষের ক্ষুদ্র স্থূল খণ্ড।

fid'-dle (-dl), *n., interj., v. i. & t.* **1.** A stringed instrument of music ; a violin ; (now only in familiar or contemptuous use) ; সারঙ্গী, সারঙ্গ ; বেহালা। **2.** (*Naut.*) A rack or the like to keep things from rolling off the cabin-table in bad weather ; (নৌ-বিদ্যা) এক প্রকার তাক বা তদ্বৎ কোন কিছু,—যাহা থাকাতে কোন জিনিষ ঝটিকাদির সময়ে জাহাজের কামরার মেজে হইতে গড়াইয়া পড়িতে পারে না। ***Interj.*** Nonsense; বাতুলের প্রলাপ। ***Verb i.*** To play on a fiddle ; বেহালা বাজান। ***Verb t.*** **1.** To play (a tune) on the fiddle ; বেহালায় সুর বাজান। **2.** To trifle ; to make aimless movements ; to be idle or frivolous ; তুচ্ছ বিষয় লইয়া মত্ত হওয়া ; লক্ষ্যহীন ভাবে চলা, উদ্দেশ্যহারা ভাবে চলা ; অলস ও চপল হওয়া। **Fiddle-bow**—বেহালার ছড়। **Fiddle-case**—বেহালার বাক্স। **Fiddle-head** — An ornament on a ship's head curved like the volute ; পোতাগ্রস্থ বেহালা-প্রকৃতি ভূষা-বিশেষ। **Fiddle's news**—বিলম্বে আগত সংবাদ। **Fiddle-stick** — বেহালার ছড় ; বাজে কথা (also called a *fiddle stick end*)। **Fiddle-string**—বেহালার তার। **Fiddle-wood**—মার্কিণ দেশীয় বৃক্ষবিশেষ।

fid-dle-dee-dee' (-dl-dē-dē) *Interj.* & *n.* Nonsense ! পাগল আর কি ! বাজে কথা ! ***Noun.*** Nonsense ; বাজে কথা।

fid'-dle-fad-dle (-l-făd-l), *v. i., n., adj.* & *interj.* To trifle ; to fuss ; তুচ্ছ বিষয় লইয়া মত্ত হওয়া ; বাজে কথা বকা। ***Noun.*** Trivial matters ; trifling talk ; তুচ্ছ ব্যাপার, সামান্য বিষয়, বাজে বিষয় ; নিরর্থক কথা, প্রলাপ। ***Adj.*** Petty ; fussy ; তুচ্ছ, অকিঞ্চিৎকর ; বৃথা গোলযোগকারী। ***Interj.*** Nonsense ; বাজে প্রলাপ।

fid'-dler (-lėr), *n.* **1.** One who fiddles (esp. for hire) ; বেহালাদার, বেহালাবাদক। **2.** A small crab ; ক্ষুদ্রজাতীয় কর্কট-বিশেষ।

fid'-dling (-lĭng). *adj.* Trifling ; petty ; তুচ্ছ ; নগণ্য, ক্ষুদ্র।

fi-dĕl'-i-tȳ, *n.* **1.** Faithfulness ; loyalty, (with *to*) ; বিশ্বস্ততা ; নিষ্ঠা। **2.** Adherence to the marriage contract ; পতিনিষ্ঠা, পাতিব্রত্য, পরদার-বিমুখতা। **3.** Accuracy ; as, the *fidelity* of a copy ; বিশুদ্ধতা, যাথার্থ্য।

fidg'-ĕt (fĭj-), *n.* **1.** (Often *the fidgets*) An uneasy restless motion ; উস্‌খুস্। **2.** Restlessness ; অস্থিরতা, চাঞ্চল্য, আইঢাই। **3.** One who fidgets or causes others to fidget ; অস্থির ব্যক্তি, যে ব্যক্তি অপরকে অস্থির করিয়া তোলে। **4.** Rustle of dress etc. ; পোষাকের খস্‌খসানি। **—i-ness,** *n.* **—y,** *adj.* Uneasy ; restless ; চঞ্চল ; অস্থির।

fidg'-ĕt (fĭj-), *v. i. & t.* **1.** To move nervously and uneasily, (often with *about*) ; অস্থির ও চঞ্চল ভাবে চলা। **2.** To worry ; জ্বালাতন করা, ত্যক্ত করা। ***Verb t.*** To put in a fidget ; to worry ; অস্থির করা, জ্বালাতন করা ; উত্যক্ত করা।

fid'-i-bŭs, *n.* A spill of paper to light candles etc. ; চর্ব্বির বাতি প্রভৃতি জ্বালাইবার জন্য কাগজের নল।

fī-dū'-cial (-shăl), *adj.* **1.** Confident ; বিশ্বাসী। **2.** Of the nature of a trust ; বিশ্বাসাত্মক। **3.** (*Phys.*) Taken as a standard of reference ; (পদার্থ-বিজ্ঞান) কোন বিষয় নিষ্পত্তির জন্য প্রামাণিক মানস্বরূপ গৃহীত। **Fiducial-line,–point**—See FIDUCIAL 3.

fī-dū'-ci-ă-rȳ (-shī-), *adj.* & *n.* **1.** Held in trust ; বিশ্বাসপূর্ব্বক রক্ষিত। **2.** Of the nature of a trust ; confidential ; বিশ্বাসাত্মক ; বিশ্বস্ত। **3.** Depending on public confidence for value, as notes etc. ; (নোট প্রভৃতি সম্পর্কে) মূল্য সম্বন্ধে লোকসাধারণের বিশ্বাসের উপর নির্ভরশীল। ***Noun.*** A trustee ; ন্যাসপত্ররক্ষক, অন্যের বিষয় রক্ষাকারী, জিম্মাদার।

fidus Achates, (*L.*), *n.* A trusty companion ; বিশ্বস্ত সহচর।

fie (fī), *interj.* An exclamation denoting impatience, contempt or dislike ; ছি ছি ! ধিক্ ধিক্ ! দূর দূর !

fief (fēf), *n.* An estate held of a superior on condition of military service ; a fee ; যোধ-ভূমি, সামরিক জায়গীর ; আয়মা।

fie'-fie (-fī-fī), *adj.* Improper ; scandalous ; অনুচিত ; কলঙ্কজনক।

field (fēld), *n., v. i.* & *t.* **1.** Ground ; a piece of grouud ; a piece of land suitable for tillage or pasture; ভূমি; ময়দান, প্রান্তর; ক্ষেত্র, জমি। **2.** A tract of land containing some natural product ; as, a gold *field* ; যে ভূমিখণ্ডে কোন প্রকার খনিজ পদার্থ পাওয়া যায়, খনিজ ক্ষেত্র। **3.** The ground on which a battle is fought ; as, to take the *field* ; রণভূমি, যুদ্ধক্ষেত্র, সমরক্ষেত্র, রণাঙ্গন, সমরভূমি। **4.** The battle itself ; রণ, যুদ্ধ, আহব। **5.** The ground for playing cricket, foot-ball, etc. ; ক্রীড়া-ক্ষেত্র, খেলার মাঠ, ক্রীড়াঙ্গন। **6.** The body of fielders in cricket ; ক্রীকেট ক্রীড়ায় যে সকল ক্রীড়ক মাঠে থাকিয়া বল লুফে বা আটকাইয়া থাকে। **7.** All competitors in any athletic or sporting contest ; মল্লক্রীড়া প্রভৃতির প্রতিযোগিগণ। **8.** A wide expanse ; as, a *field* of snow ; (also *fig.*) as, whole *field* of history ; বিস্তীর্ণ স্থান, বিস্তার। **9.** The ground-work of a picture, flag, coin, etc. ; চিত্র, পতাকা, মুদ্রা প্রভৃতির জমি। **10.** (*Her.*) The whole surface of a shield or escutcheon ; (কুল-বিদ্যা) কুল-মর্য্যাদা-চিহ্নাঙ্কিত চর্ম্মের উপরিভাগ। **11.** The sphere or range of activity, observation etc. ; as, each supreme in his own *field* : the *field* of a telescope or vision ; কার্য্যক্ষেত্র, দৃষ্টির প্রসর। ***Verb i.*** To act as a fielder in cricket etc. ; ক্রীকেট ক্রীড়ায় বল লুফা বা থামান। ***Verb t.*** To catch or stop (the ball) in cricket ; ক্রীকেট ক্রীড়ায় বল লুফা বা থামান। **Field'-er,** *n.* (*Cricket*) A ball player who stands out in the field to catch or stop the ball ; (ক্রীকেট ক্রীড়ায়) যে ব্যক্তি ক্রীড়াক্ষেত্রে বল থামাইবার বা লুফিবার জন্য দণ্ডায়মান থাকে। **Field'-ward(s),** *adv.* **Field-allowance**—যুদ্ধেনিযুক্ত সৈনিক কর্ম্মচারীকে যে অতিরিক্ত ভাতা দেওয়া হয়। **Field-artillery**—যুদ্ধক্ষেত্রে ব্যবহারের উপযোগী কামান। **Field-battery**—অশ্বারোহী বা পদাতিক সৈন্যদলের সঙ্গীয় কামানশ্রেণী। **Field-book**—যে পুস্তকে জরীপের আমিন জরীপসম্পর্কীয় বিবরণ লিপিবদ্ধ করিয়া থাকেন। **Field-cornet**—কেপকলোনিতে ক্ষুদ্র নগরীর শাসনকর্ত্তা। **Field-day**—যে দিবস সৈন্যগণকে যুদ্ধকার্য্য শিক্ষাদানার্থ ময়দানে সজ্জিত করা হয় ; সর্ব্বজনীন উৎসবের দিন ; (লক্ষণায়) গুরুতর বিষয়ে বাদানুবাদ। **Field-dressing**—যুদ্ধক্ষেত্রে আহত সৈন্যগণের পটী, মলম প্রভৃতি। **Field-fare**—পক্ষিবিশেষ। **Field-glass**—দৃষ্টিক্ষেত্রনির্দ্ধারক তাল (হিঃ কোঃ) ; একপ্রকার শক্তিশালী দুনলা দূরবীণ। **Field-gun**—যুদ্ধক্ষেত্রে ব্যবহারোপযোগী ক্ষুদ্র কামান, ময়দানী কামান (প্রবাসী)। **Field-hospital**—রণক্ষেত্রের সন্নিকটস্থ অস্থায়ী আরোগ্যশালা। **Field-map**—থাকবস্ত নক্সা। **Field-marshal** — ইংলণ্ডের সেনাবিভাগের সর্ব্বোচ্চ কর্ম্মচারী। **Field-mouse**—প্রান্তরবাসী ক্ষুদ্র মূষিক মেঠো ইন্দুর। **Field-night** — কোন বিশেষ ঘটনা বা সভাধিবেশনের রজনী। **Field-officer** — কাপ্তানের উর্দ্ধতন এবং সেনাপতির অধস্তন কর্ম্মচারী (যথা—Major, Colonel, Lieutenant colonel)। **Field-piece** — রণক্ষেত্রে ব্যবহৃত কামান। **Field-preacher**—যে ধর্ম্মপ্রচারক মুক্ত মাঠে উপদেশ প্রদান করেন। **Fieldsman**—ক্রীকেট ক্রীড়ায় যে ক্রীড়ক বল লুফে বা থামায়। **Field-sports**—মৃগয়াদি। **Field-telegraph** — যুদ্ধক্ষেত্রে ব্যবহারোপযোগী বহনযোগ্য তাড়িত-বার্ত্তাবহ। **Field-traiu** — যুদ্ধক্ষেত্রে যুদ্ধোপকরণ সরবরাহের ভারপ্রাপ্ত রাজকীয় গোলন্দাজ সৈন্যের বিভাগ-বিশেষ। **Field-work**—(*Pl.*) অস্থায়ী পরিখাদি ; (*sing.*) জরিপ-আমিন, ভূতত্ত্ববিদ, এবং পুরাতত্ত্ববিদ্যাবিশারদ প্রভৃতির ময়দানী কাজ। **A fair field and no favour**—See under FAIR. **A good field**—Many and good competitors ; অনেক ভাল ভাল প্রতিযোগী। **Field of consciousness** — সংবিৎক্ষেত্র (হিঃ কোঃ), সংবিদ্গোচর (ঐ)। **Field of ice**—প্রবমান বিপুল হিমানী রাশি। **Field of touch**—স্পর্শক্ষেত্র (হিঃ কোঃ)। **Field of view** — [See FIELD *n.* (11)] অণুবীক্ষণের দৃষ্টি-ক্ষেত্র। **Field of vision**—দৃগ্গোচর (হিঃ কোঃ)। **In the field**—Campaigning; যুদ্ধক্ষেত্রে। **To be in the field**—To be a competitor for any prize ; কোন পুরস্কারের জন্য প্রতিযোগী হওয়া। **To hold the field**—Not to be superseded ; স্বস্থান রক্ষা করা। **To keep the field**—To continue the campaign ; to maintain one's grouud;

যুদ্ধ চালান ; নিজের কোট বজায় রাখা। **To take the field**—To enter upon a campaign ; যুদ্ধে প্রবৃত্ত হওয়া, রণাঙ্গনে অবতীর্ণ হওয়া।

fiend (fēnd), *n.* The devil ; a demon ; A person diabolically wicked or cruel ; শয়তান ; পিশাচ, দানব ; নরপিশাচ। **Fiend-like**—পিশাচবৎ, পৈশাচিক।

fiend'-ish (fēnd-), *adj.* Like a fiend ; diabolically wicked or cruel ; পিশাচবৎ, শয়তানী, পৈশাচিক ; নৃশংস, উগ্রকর্ম্মা, রৌদ্র, ক্রূর, বিদ্বেষপরায়ণ।

fierce (fērs), *adj.* **1.** Furious ; violent ; as, a *fierce* storm ; ভীষণ, করাল, রৌদ্র, ভয়ঙ্কর ; প্রচণ্ড, দারুণ। **2.** Vehement in rage ; ferocious ; প্রচণ্ডক্রোধোদ্দীপ্ত ; হিংস্র। **3.** Very eager or zealous ; অতিশয় আগ্রহান্বিত, অত্যুৎসাহী। **Fierce'-ly,** *adv.* **Fierce'-ness,** *n.*

fī'-ē-rī-fā'-ci-ŭs (-shī-), *n.* (*Law—abbr. fi. fa.*) A visit to a sheriff for executing judgment ; (আইন) রায়ের আদেশ কার্য্যে পরিণত করার জন্য আদালতের নাজিরকে যে পরওয়ানা দেওয়া হয়।

fī'-ēr-ȳ, *adj.* **1.** Consisting of, or attended with, fire ; like fire ; containing fire ; অগ্নিময়, জ্বলন্ত ; অগ্নিতুল্য, অগ্নিকল্প, কৃশানুপ্রতিম (রঃ) ; অগ্নিগর্ভ। **2.** Vehement ; ardent ; as, *fiery* spirit ; flashing ; as, *fiery* eyes ; mettlesome, as a horse ; প্রচণ্ড, উচ্চণ্ড ; অগ্নিবর্ষী ; তেজস্বী। **3.** Passionate ; irritable ; ক্রোধজ্বলিত ; কোপনস্বভাব। **4.** Heated by fire ; acting like fire ; অগ্নিতপ্ত ; অগ্নিতুল্য ক্রিয়াকারী। **5.** Inflammable, as gases etc. ; liable to explosion, as a mine etc. ; দাহ্য ; সশব্দে স্ফোটনশীল। **—i-ly,** *adv.* **—i-ness,** *n.* State or quality of being fiery ; অগ্নিময়তা, অগ্নিকল্পতা, উচ্চণ্ডতা, প্রচণ্ডতা। **Fiery-cross**—(স্কটলণ্ডদেশে) ক্রুশাকার চিহ্ন বিশেষ—প্রাচীনকালে যুদ্ধে আহ্বানের জন্য উহা স্থান হইতে স্থানান্তরে নীত হইত। [ঐরূপ ক্রুশের প্রান্তদেশে অগ্নি সংযোগ পূর্ব্বক তৎপর ঐ অগ্নি অচিরনিহত মেষরক্তে নির্ব্বাপিত করা হইত।]

fīfe *n., v. i.* & *t.* **1.** A small shrill flute used chiefly in military music ; শিঙ্গাবিশেষ, বাঁশী। **2.** A fifer ; বংশিবাদক। ***Verb i.*** To play on a fife ; বাঁশী বাজান। ***Verb t.*** To play as an air on the fife ; বংশিধ্বনি করা। **Fif'-er,** *n.* One who plays on a fife ; বংশিবাদক। **Fife-rail**—(নৌ-বিদ্যা) জাহাজের মাস্তুলের চারিদিকের গরাদ।

fif'-teen (-tēn), *adj.* & *n.* Five and ten ; পঞ্চদশ। ***Noun.*** **1.** The sum of 5 and 10 ; পনর, পঞ্চদশ। **2.** The symbol representing this number ; পনর সংখ্যা (১৫)। **3.** (*Rugby-football*) A side of fifteen players ; (রাগ্‌বী পাদগোলক ক্রীড়ায়) যে পক্ষে পনের জন ক্রীড়ক থাকে। **The fifteen**—The Jacobite rising of 1715 in Scotland ; স্কট্‌লণ্ডদেশে ১৭১৫ খৃঃ অব্দের জেকোবিট বিদ্রোহ।

fif'-teenth (-tēnth), *adj.* & *n.* **1.** The fifth after the tenth ; পঞ্চদশতম। **2.** Forming one of fifteen equal parts ; পঞ্চদশাংশস্বরূপ। ***Noun.*** A fifteenth part ; পঞ্চদশাংশ।

fifth, *adj.* & *n.* **1.** The next to the fourth ; পঞ্চম। **2.** Constituting one part in five ; পঞ্চমাংশস্বরূপ। **3.** (*Pl.*) Fifth-rate material ; (বহুবচন) পঞ্চম শ্রেণীর জিনিষ। ***Noun.*** A fifth part ; পঞ্চমাংশ। **Fifth'-ly,** *adv.* **A fifth part**—One of a five equal parts of a whole ; পঞ্চমাংশ। **Fifth-monarchy**—যীশুখ্রীষ্টের পৃথিবীতে সহস্রবর্ষব্যাপী রাজত্ব। **Fifth-monarchy men** — ইংলণ্ডে (Cromwellএর সময়ের) রাষ্ট্রবিপ্লবের সমকালীন সম্প্রদায় বিশেষ—এই সম্প্রদায়ভুক্ত ব্যক্তিগণ যীশুখৃষ্টের পার্থিব রাজত্বকাল অতি সন্নিকট বলিয়া মনে করিতেন **Fifth wheel of a coach etc.**—Something superfluous ; অতিরিক্ত জিনিষ। **To smite under the fifth rib**—বধ করা, বিনাশ করা।

fif'-tȳ, *adj.* & *n.* **1.** Five times ten ; পঞ্চাশৎ। **2.** Large or indefinite number ; as, I have *fifty* things to tell you ; অনেক। **1. *Noun.*** The sum of five tens ; a set of fifty persons or things ; পঞ্চাশৎ ; পঞ্চাশৎসংখ্যক ব্যক্তি বা বস্তু। **2.** The figure indicating this number ; পঞ্চাশ (৫০) এই সংখ্যা। **The fifties**—The years between 50 and 60 in life or a century ; কোন শতাব্দীর বা ব্যক্তি-বিশেষের জীবনের ৫০ হইতে ৬০ বর্ষ পর্য্যন্ত কাল।

fif'-ti-ēth, *adj.* & *n.* **1.** Next after fortyninth ; পঞ্চাশত্তম। **2.** Forming one of fifty equal parts ; পঞ্চাশত্তমাংশ ($\frac{১}{৫০}$)। ***Noun.*** A fiftieth part ; পঞ্চাশত্তম অংশ।

fig, *n.* **1.** A broad-leaved tree bearing fruits ; আঞ্জীর বৃক্ষ, ডুমুর বৃক্ষ। **2.** The fruit of a fig tree ; আঞ্জীর ফল, ডুমুর ফল [Fig বলিতে সচরাচর কাবুলের ডুমুর বা আঞ্জীর বুঝায়, এই ফল অতি উপাদেয় ও রসনারোচক।]

Fig.

3. Something of little value ; a trifle ; (as, *I don't care a fig for it*—তৃণবৎ জ্ঞান করি) ; অকিঞ্চিৎকর বস্তু, নগণ্য বস্তু ; তুচ্ছ জিনিষ। **Fig-leaf**—ডুম্বর-পত্র ; প্রতিকৃতি বা পাষাণ-মূর্ত্তির গোপনীয় অঙ্গ আবরণের জন্য ডুম্বরপত্রাকার ভূষা [আদি মানব ও মানবী আদম ও ইভের গোপনীয় অঙ্গ আঞ্জীর পত্রদ্বারা আবৃত ছিল—বাইবেলের (See Genesis iii. 7) এই উক্তি হইতে গৃহীত] ; কৃত্রিম লজ্জার চিহ্ন। **Fig-wort**—একপ্রকার গুল্ম। **A fig for**—An exclamation of contempt ; as, *a fig for* Peter ; অবজ্ঞাসূচক

চীৎকার। **Under one's vine and fig tree**—স্বগৃহে নিরাপদে।

fig, *n.* **1.** Dress ; equipment ; as, in full *fig* ; পোষাক ; সাজসজ্জা, পূর্ণ-পরিচ্ছদ। **2.** Condition ; form ; as, in good *fig* ; অবস্থা ; রূপ, আকার।

fig, *v. t.* To dress or furnish up ; as, to *fig* out a person ; to make lively or spirited, as a horse ; (with *out*) ; সজ্জিত করা ; তেজস্বী করা, সতেজ করা।

Fi-gä-rō′, *n.* An adroit or unscrupulous intriguer ; শঠশিরোমণি [*Beaumarchais* কৃত নাটকদ্বয়ের নায়কের নাম হইতে গৃহীত]।

fight (fīt), *v. i.* & *t.* **1.** To strive or contend in battle or single combat, (with *against, with,* or *for*) ; যুদ্ধ বা লড়াই করা, বিরোধ করা। **2.** To struggle ; to contend ; to act in opposition ; সংগ্রাম করা ; বিরোধ করা ; বাধা দেওয়া, প্রতিরোধ করা। ***Verb t.*** **1.** To carry on or wage, as a battle etc. ; to win or gain by struggle, as one's way ; to sustain by fighting, as a cause ; যুদ্ধ আরম্ভ করা ; যুদ্ধ দ্বারা লাভ করা ; যুদ্ধ করিয়া বজায় রাখা। **2.** To contend with in battle or duel, or with the fists ; কাহারও সহিত যুদ্ধ করা, দ্বৈরথ যুদ্ধ করা বা মুষ্টিযুদ্ধ করা। **3.** To cause to fight, as cocks etc. ; to manœuvre, as troops or ship in battle ; লড়াই বাঁধাইয়া দেওয়া, যুদ্ধে প্রবৃত্ত করা ; যুদ্ধে সৈন্য, রণপোত প্রভৃতি কৌশলে চালিত করা। **Fight′-er,** *n.* A warrior ; যোদ্ধা। **Fight′-ing,** *p. p.* **To fight for**—To fight on behalf of (a person) or to secure any right ; কাহারও পক্ষে যুদ্ধ করা, কোনও অধিকার প্রাপ্তির জন্য যুদ্ধ করা। **To fight for one's own hand**—To struggle for one's own interest ; স্বীয় স্বার্থসিদ্ধির উদ্দেশ্যে চেষ্টা করা। **To fight (it) out** — To settle (it) by fighting ; যুদ্ধদ্বারা মীমাংসা করা। **To fight off**—To repel with effort ; আয়াস সহকারে প্রতিহত করা। **To fight shy of**—To avoid or keep aloof from ; as, to *fight shy of* an undertaking ; ভয় বা অবিশ্বাস হেতু পরিহার করা বা দূরে দূরে থাকা। **To fight windmills**—To combat imaginary evils ; কাল্পনিক অশুভের সহিত সংগ্রাম করা।

fight (fīt), *n.* **1.** A battle ; a combat between two or more persons, animals or parties ; যুদ্ধ, রণ, সংগ্রাম, আহব, সমর, আয়োধন ; লড়াই। **2.** Strength or disposition for fighting ; as, he has a great deal of *fight* in him ; যুদ্ধপ্রবণতা, যুদ্ধসামর্থ্য। **3.** (*Fig.*) A contest of any kind ; যে কোনরূপ প্রতিযোগিতা। **A running fight**—A fight in which one party is continually chased ; শত্রু-কর্তৃক পশ্চাদ্ধাবিত হইয়া যুদ্ধ। **A stand-up fight** — One in which the combatants stand up manfully to each other ; an open and formal fight ; যে যুদ্ধে যোদ্ধৃগণ পরস্পরের সম্মুখে বীরের মত দণ্ডায়মান হয় ; সম্মুখযুদ্ধ। **Sham fight**—Fight between troops for practice or display ; কৃত্রিম যুদ্ধ, লীলা রণ, ছদ্মযুদ্ধ। **To show fight**—Not to yield tamely ; ঘাড় বাঁকাইয়া দাঁড়ান।

fig′-mĕnt, *n.* An invented statement or story ; a thing existing only in imagination ; স্বকপোলকল্পিত উক্তি, উপকথা ; কাল্পনিক বিষয়। **–men′-tal,** *adj.* Fictitious ; feigned ; কাল্পনিক, স্বকপোলকল্পিত ; ছদ্ম।

fig-ū-rant, *n.* (*Fem.* -RANTE.) **1.** A ballet dancer ; যে নর্তক রঙ্গমঞ্চে অপর সকলের সহিত নৃত্য করে। **2.** An accessory character on the stage who figures in its scenes, but has nothing to say ; যে অভিনেতা রঙ্গমঞ্চে আসিয়া মৌন থাকে।

fig-ū-rā′-tion, *n.* **1.** The act of giving determinate form ; নির্দ্দিষ্ট আকার প্রদান। **2.** Shape ; form ; গঠন, অবয়ব, আকার, রূপ ; আকৃতি। **3.** Figurative or typical representation ; লাক্ষণিক বাক্য, আলঙ্কারিক বাক্য। **4.** Adornment by designs ; লতাপাতাপুষ্পাদি রচিত ভূষাদ্বারা (বস্ত্রাদি) অলঙ্করণ।

fig′-ūr-ā-tive (-tĭv), *adj.* **1.** Emblematical ; typical ; সাঙ্কেতিক ; আদর্শস্বরূপ, প্রতিরূপস্বরূপ। **2.** Metaphorical ; as, a *figurative* expression ; রূপকস্বরূপ, আলঙ্কারিক, লাক্ষণিক। **3.** Abounding in figures of speech ; অলঙ্কার-বহুল। **–ly,** *adv.* **–ness,** *n.*

fig′-ūre, *n.* **1.** Form ; shape ; বাহ্যাবয়ব, বাহ্যাকৃতি ; গঠন, অবয়ব, রূপ। **2.** A representation of the human body, as by drawing, sculpture, etc. ; a likeness ; a statue ; চিত্র, চিত্রপট ; প্রতিকৃতি ; প্রতিমূর্ত্তি **3.** A numerical symbol ; সংখ্যা। **4.** A design or pattern, esp. decoration ; as, the muslin of a pretty *figure* ; কাগজ, কাপড় প্রভৃতির উপর পুষ্প, লতাপাতা প্রভৃতির নক্সা। **5.** A person or thing as observed ; as, I saw a *figure* leaning against the door ; মূর্ত্তি, প্রতিমূর্ত্তি। **6.** A character ; as, great *figures* of history ; চরিত্র। **7.** Price ; as, at a low or high *figure* ; মূল্য, দাম। **8.** A type ; representative ; আদর্শ ; প্রতিরূপ, অনুরূপ। **9.** (*Geom.*) A diagram ; (জ্যামিতি) ক্ষেত্র। **10.** A mode of expression in which words are turned from their ordinary signification ; উপমাদি অলঙ্কার, লক্ষণা। **11.** (*Astrol*) A horoscope ; (জ্যোতিষ-শাস্ত্র) কোষ্ঠী, ঠিকুজি। **12.** (*Log.*) A particular form of syllogism according to the relative position of the middle term ; (তর্কবিজ্ঞান) অনুমান বাক্যের প্রকার বিশেষ।

13. Steps or movements made by a dancer in accordance with the music ; নৃত্যে পদবিক্ষেপ, নর্তকের অঙ্গসঞ্চালন। **14.** An illustrative diagram, (*abbr. fig.*) উদাহরণ প্রদর্শক চিত্র, চক্র, যন্ত্র। **–ured,** *adj.* Marked or adorned with figures ; লতা পাতা পুষ্পাদিদ্বারা ভূষিত। **Figure-dance**—বিভিন্ন বিভাগাত্মক নৃত্যবিশেষ। **Figure-dancer**—উক্ত প্রকার নৃত্যের নর্তক। **Figure-head** — পোতাগ্র-সংবদ্ধ কাষ্ঠরচিত মনুষ্যমস্তক। A nominal leader ; নামে মাত্র অধ্যক্ষ। (*Jocular*) The face of a preson ; (রহস্যচ্ছলে) আস্য, আনন, তুণ্ড। **A person of figure**—A distinguished man ; সুবিখ্যাত ব্যক্তি, প্রথিতনামা ব্যক্তি। **Double figures**—৯ হইতে ১০০ পর্য্যন্ত সংখ্যা। **Figure of fun**—A grotesque ; সৃষ্টি ছাড়া বস্তু। **Income of five figures**—১০,০০০ পাউণ্ডের উপর ও ১০০,০০০ পাউণ্ডের নীচে আয়। **To figure up**—যোগ দেওয়া, ঠিক দেওয়া। **To make or cut a figure**—To persent a (good or bad) appearance ; to occupy a conspicuous or distinguished position ; নিজকে ভাল বা মন্দ ভাবে জাহির করা ; উচ্চ পদবী অধিকার করা, লোকসাধারণের দৃষ্টি আকর্ষণ করা, বড়মানুষি ফলান। **To reach three figures**—(*Cricket*) To get century ; (ক্রীকেট) একশত জয়াঙ্ক লাভ করা।

fig'-üre, *v. t.* & *i.* **1.** To represent in a diagram or picture ; to shape ; to form a mental image of ; চিত্রাদি দ্বারা প্রদর্শন করা ; গঠন করা, আকার প্রদান করা ; মানস-চিত্র অঙ্কিত করা। **2.** To adorn with figures or designs ; as, a *figured* satin ; নানা প্রকার পুষ্পলতাদির চিত্রদ্বারা বস্ত্রাদি বিভূষিত করা। **3.** To mark with numbers or prices ; to indicate by numerals ; মূল্য চিহ্নিত করা ; সংখ্যাদ্বারা নির্দেশ করা। **4.** To symbolize ; লক্ষণায় প্রকাশ করা, সঙ্কেতে প্রকাশ করা। ***Verb i.*** **1.** To make a figure ; to be distinguished or conspicuous ; to appear ; জাঁকজমক দেখান, জাহির করা ; বিখ্যাত বা সুপ্রকট হওয়া ; বোধ হওয়া, প্রতিভাত হওয়া। **2.** To use figures in Arithmetic ; পাটীগণিতে—সংখ্যা ব্যবহার করা। **–ur-a-ble,** *adj.* **To figure out**—To give result in figures ; as, it *figures out* at £20 ; সংখ্যাদ্বারা ফল প্রকাশ করা। **To figure up**—To reckon the amount of ; to add ; সমষ্টি নির্ণয় করা, যোগফল গণনা করা ; যোগ করা, ঠিক দেওয়া।

fig-ü-rine' (-rīn), *n.* A statuette ; ক্ষুদ্র মূর্ত্তি।

fil'-ă-mĕnt, *n.* **1.** A thread or thread-like body ; a fibre esp. in animal or vegetable structure ; সূত্র বা সূত্রবৎ পদার্থ ; অংশু বা তন্তু। **2.** (*Bot.*) A long thread-like part that supports the anther ; (উদ্ভিদ্-বিদ্যা) কিঞ্জল্ক, কেশর (সাঃ পঃ)। **3.** A non-fusible conductor in incandescent electric lamp raised to incandescence by current ; বিজলী বাতির ফিতা বা সূত্রাকার বস্তু—তাড়িত প্রবাহদ্বারা উদ্দীপ্ত হইয়া যাহা হইতে আলোক বিকীর্ণ হয়। **–men'-ta-ry,** *adj.* Of the nature of, or formed by, filament ; সূত্রাত্মক, অংশুরচিত। **–ment-ed, –men'-tous,** *adjs.*

fi'-lar (-lêr), *adj.* Relating to a thread ; সূত্র-সম্বন্ধীয়, তান্তব।

fil'-ă-türe, *n.* **1.** The reeling of silk from cocoons ; গুটী হইতে নাটাইয়া রেশম জড়ান। **2.** An establishment for reeling silk ; গুটী হইতে নাটাইয়া রেশম জড়ানের জন্য কারখানা।

fil'-bêrt, *n.* The nut or fruit of the cultivated hazel ; the tree itself ; জঙ্গলী আখরোট ; ঐ গাছ।

filch, *v. t.* To steal ; to pilfer ; চুরি করা ; ছিঁচকে চুরি করা, পাতিচুরি করা। **Filch'-er,** *n.* One who filches ; ছিঁচকে চোর, পাতি চোর।

fīle, *n., v. t.* & *i.* **1.** A line or wire on which papers are strung for preservation ; কাগজপত্র গাঁথিয়া রাখিবার শিক বা তার। **2.** A collection of papers so strung or otherwise arranged in order for reference ; as, *files* of letters or of newspapers ; নথী। **3.** A row of soldiers arranged one behind another from front to rear ; অগ্রপশ্চাৎক্রমে সজ্জিত সৈন্য-শ্রেণী। **4.** A row of persons, animals or things arranged one behind another ; অগ্রপশ্চাৎক্রমে সজ্জিত জনগণ বা বস্তুশ্রেণী। ***Verb t.*** **1.** To place papers etc., on a file ; কাগজপত্র শিকে গাঁথিয়া রাখা। **2.** To arrange in order ; শৃঙ্খলাপূর্ব্বক রাখা, সাজাইয়া রাখা। **3.** To bring before a court by presenting the proper papers ; as, to *file* a petition ; আদালতে দাখিল করা, পেশ করা। **4.** To put upon the files or among the records of a court ; আদালতের নথীতে ভুক্ত করা। **5.** To order, as soldiers, to move off by filing ; সৈন্যদিগকে অগ্রপশ্চাৎক্রমে সারি বাঁধিয়া যাত্রা করিতে আদেশ করা। ***Verb i.*** To march in a file ; অগ্রপশ্চাৎ-ক্রমে সারবন্দী হইয়া যাত্রা করা। **A file of men**—Two men told off for some purpose ; কোন উদ্দেশ্য-সাধনে নিযুক্ত ব্যক্তিদ্বয়। **In file**—one behind the other ; in succession ; অগ্রপশ্চাৎক্রমে, পরস্পরের পশ্চাতে ; ক্রমান্বয়ে। **Rank and file**—See under RANK. **Single file, Indian file** — অগ্রপশ্চাৎক্রমে সজ্জিত সৈন্যপংক্তি। **To file off or away**—To go off by files ; অগ্র-পশ্চাৎক্রমে শ্রেণীবদ্ধ হইয়া চলা। **To file with**—To follow closely ; to keep pace ; পশ্চাৎ পশ্চাৎ চলা, সমানে চলা, পিছাইয়া না পড়া।

fīle, *n.* & *v. t.* **1.** A steel instrument for cutting and smoothing iron, wood, etc.; উখা, ঘর্ষণ-যন্ত্র, খরগাত্র ইস্পাত, রেতি। **2.** (*Slang*) A shrewd or artful person; (ইতর-ভাষায়) ধূর্ত্ত লোক, ধড়ীবাজ-লোক। ***Verb t.*** **1.** To rub, cut or polish with a file; উখাদ্বারা কাটা, ঘষা বা পালিস করা। **2.** To polish; to elaborate to perfection, as a literary work; ঘষিয়া মাজিয়া পালিস করা; শ্রমসহকারে উৎকর্ষতা সম্পাদন করা। **3.** To remove, as roughness, with a file, (with *off* and *away*); উখাদ্বারা ঘষিয়া উচ্চাবচতা দূর করা। **An old** or **deep file**—See FILE. *n.* 2. **To bite** or **gnaw a file**—To attempt a vain task; অসাধ্য সাধনে চেষ্টা করা।

fĭl'-ĕ-mŏt, *adj.* & *n.* Of the colour of a dead leaf; মৃতপত্রবর্ণ, পুরাণ-পত্র সমবর্ণ। ***Noun.*** The colour of a faded leaf; a yellowish brown colour; মৃত পত্রের বর্ণ; পীতাভ পিঙ্গল-বর্ণ।

fĭl'-ĭ-ăl, *adj.* Pertaining to a son or daughter; becoming a child in relation to his parents; পুত্রকন্যা-সম্বন্ধীয়, অপত্যসম্বন্ধীয়; সন্তানোচিত। **—ly,** *adv.* In a filial manner; অপত্যনির্ব্বিশেষে (সীতা), অপত্যবৎ, সন্তানোচিত ভাবে। **Filial piety**—Regard for parents; জনকজননীর প্রতি শ্রদ্ধা, পিতৃমাতৃভক্তি।

fĭl'-ĭ-āte, *v. t.* To adopt as son or daughter; পুত্র বা কন্যারূপে গ্রহণ করা। **To filiate itself**—To declare its author; ইহার রচক বা গ্রন্থকার বলিয়া প্রকাশ করা।

fĭl-ĭ-ā'-tion, *n.* **1.** The state of being a child to some one; অপত্যত্ব, সন্তানত্ব। **2.** Descent (from); as, to ascertain the *filiation* of a language; relationship like that of a son; উদ্ভব; পুত্রবৎ সম্পর্ক। **3.** An offshoot; প্ররোহ। **4.** The formation of branches or offshoots; শাখা বা প্ররোহ উৎপাদন।

fĭl'-ĭ-bĕg, *n.* (*Scot.*) Kilt; (স্কটলণ্ডে) এক প্রকার জাঙ্গিয়া।

fĭl'-ĭ-bŭs-têr, *n.* & *v. i.* **1.** One who engages in unauthorized warfare against a foreign country; যে ব্যক্তি ক্ষমতাপ্রাপ্ত না হইয়া বৈদেশিক রাজ্যের সহিত যুদ্ধে প্রবৃত্ত হয়। **2.** A lawless pirate; বোম্বেটিয়া, জলদস্যু। ***Verb i.*** To act as a filibuster; ক্ষমতাপ্রাপ্ত না হইয়া বৈদেশিক রাজ্যের সহিত যুদ্ধে প্রবৃত্ত হওয়া, বোম্বেটিয়াগিরি করা। **—bus'-ter-ism,** *n.*

fĭl'-ĭ-fŏrm, *adj.* Having the shape of a thread or filament; সূত্রাকার, তন্তুনিভ।

fĭl'-ĭ-gree (-grē), *n.* **1.** Ornamental open-work in fine gold or silver or copper wire; সূক্ষ্ম স্বর্ণ, রৌপ্য ও তাম্রের তারের শোভাজনক কাজ। **2.** Anything delicate and showy; অতি সূক্ষ্ম চটকদার জিনিষ। **—greed,** *p. p.*

fīl-ĭng, *n.* (Usu. *pl.*) A particle or particles rubbed off by the act of filing; উখাদ্বারা লৌহ প্রভৃতি ঘর্ষণ করিলে যে চূর্ণ পতিত হয়, উখার গুঁড়া।

fĭll, *v. t., i.* & *n.* **1.** To make full; পূর্ণ করা। **2.** To supply abundantly; to occupy completely; to pervade; প্রচুর পরিমাণে প্রদান করা; পূর্ণভাবে ব্যাপিয়া থাকা; ব্যাপ্ত হওয়া। **3.** To satisfy; to surfeit; পরিতৃপ্ত করা; আকণ্ঠ ভোজন করান। **4.** To press and dilate; as, the wind *fills* the sail; ঠেলিয়া স্ফীত করা, বিস্তার করা। **5.** To hold and discharge duties of (office etc.); to officiate in, as an incumbent; to occupy; as, to *fill* an office, position, etc.; অধিকার পূর্ব্বক কর্ত্তব্য-কার্য্য সম্পাদন করা; কাহারো স্থলবর্ত্তী হইয়া কার্য্য করা; অধিকার করা। **6.** To appoint the holder of; as, to *fill* a vacant post; শূন্যপদ পূরণ করা, লোক নিযুক্ত করা। **7.** To block up with gold etc.; as, to *fill* a hollow tooth; স্বর্ণাদিদ্বারা বন্ধ করা বা বুজাইয়া দেওয়া। **8.** To adulterate; as, *filled* cottons; ভেজাল দেওয়া। ***Verb i.*** **1.** To become or grow full; পূর্ণ হওয়া, পরিতৃপ্ত হওয়া। **2.** To pour out, as tea, wine, etc.; ঢালা। ***Noun.*** As much as fills or satisfies; a full supply; as, to eat one's *fill*; enough to fill something; যে পরিমাণ বস্তু দ্বারা পরিপূর্ণতা বা পরিতৃপ্তি সাধিত হয়; পূর্ণ পরিমাণ সরবরাহ; কোন কিছু পূর্ণ করার পক্ষে যথেষ্ট বস্তু। **To fill in**—To pour or put in for the purpose of filling something; কোন কিছু পূর্ণ করিবার উদ্দেশ্যে ঢালা ন্যস্ত করা। To complete by supplying omissions; as, to *fill in* an outline, document, etc.; লিখিয়া পূরণ করা, শূন্যস্থান পূর্ণ করা। **To fill out**—*v. t.* & *i.* To enlarge or extend to the desired limit; যথেচ্ছ বিস্তারিত বা প্রসারিত করা। (*Verb i.*) To become enlarged to the proper limit; প্রকাম প্রসারিত হওয়া। **To fill the bill**—To be the only conspicuous item; একমাত্র দৃষ্টি-আকর্ষক বিষয় হওয়া। (*U. S. colloq.*) To do all that is required; (মার্কিণ যুক্তরাজ্যের চলিত ভাষায়) যাহা কিছু আবশ্যক করা। **To fill up**—*v. t.* & *i.* To make quite full; পরিপূর্ণ করা, পরিপূরিত করা। To fill, as a deficiency, vacancy, post etc.; (শূন্য পদ ইত্যাদি) পূরণ করা। To insert what is necessary in; as, to *fill up* a design or form; (লিখিয়া) পূরণ করা। To do away with by filling; as, to *fill up* a hole, pond, etc.; বুজিয়া দেওয়া। (*Verb i.*) To grow full; as, the river *fills up* with sand; পূর্ণ হওয়া।

fĭll'-ĕr, *n.* One who, or that which, fills; a tube for filling bottles, etc; পরিপূরক; বোতল প্রভৃতি পূর্ণ করার জন্য নল-বিশেষ।

fill'-ing, *n.* That which fills or is used to fill a cavity etc.; যদ্দারা কোন রন্ধ্রাদি বুঁজিয়া দেওয়া হয়, বা যাহা রন্ধ্রাদি বুঁজিয়া দিবার জন্য ব্যবহৃত হয়।

fille, (*F.*), *n.* A daughter; a girl; কন্যা; বালা, বালিকা, কিশোরী। ***Fille de chambre***—A chambermaid; শয়নমন্দিরের পরিচারিকা। ***Fille de joie*** — A prostitute; বারাঙ্গনা, বেশ্যা, বারযোষিৎ।

fil'-lĕt, *n.* & *v. t.* **1.** A little band to tie about the hair; চুল বাঁধিবার ফিতা, শিরোবন্ধ, কেশবন্ধনী। **2.** A thin narrow strip of anything; ফালি, ছিল্‌কা। **3.** A piece of meat rolled together and tied round; a slice from the fleshy part of the thigh in veal; a thick slice cut from a fish; একত্র গুটাইয়া বাঁধা মাংসখণ্ড; বাছুরের দাবনার মাংসের ফালি; মৎস্য হইতে কর্ত্তিত স্থুল অস্থি-শূন্য অংশ। **4.** An animal's loins; জন্তুর দাবনা, রাং। **5.** (*Arch.*) A narrow flat band separating two mouldings; a small band between the flutes of a column; (স্থপতি-বিদ্যা) যে স্বল্পায়ত এবং চ্যাপ্টা বন্ধনীদ্বারা কার্ণিসাদির স্থাপত্য-ভূষা পৃথগ্‌কৃত হয়; থামের পিঠের ডুঙ্গি বা ঝিঙ্গের খোলের মধ্যের বন্ধনী। **6.** (*Book-binding*) A line impressed on the cover of a book; (পুস্তক বাঁধাইর কাজ) পুস্তকের মলাটের উপর ছাপ দিয়া অঙ্কিত রেখা। **7.** Any raised rim; উদ্গত ধার বা প্রান্ত। ***Verb t.*** **1.** To bind or adorn with a fillet; ফিতা দ্বারা (চুল) বাঁধা বা ভূষিত করা। **2.** To cut into fillets or slices, as fishes; ফালি ফালি করিয়া কাটা।

fil'-li-bĕg, *n.* See FILIBEG.

fil'-lip, *v. t., i.* & *n.* **1.** To strike with the nail of the finger forced from the thumb with a sudden spring; বৃদ্ধাঙ্গুলিতে চাপিয়া তর্জ্জনী বা মধ্যমাঙ্গুলীর নখ হঠাৎ ছাড়িয়া দিয়া আঘাত করা, নখ দ্বারা টোকা মারা। **2.** To strike quickly; to stimulate; as, to *fillip* one's memory; চট্ করিয়া মারা; উত্তেজিত করা, চেতান, জাগাইয়া দেওয়া। ***Verb i.*** To make a fillip; টোকা মারা। ***Noun.*** **1.** A jerk of the finger from the thumb; টোকা, তুড়ি। **2.** A stimulus; উত্তেজনা। **3.** A trifle; as, it is not worth a *fillip*; অতি তুচ্ছ বিষয়, নগণ্য বিষয়।

fil'-lis-têr, *n.* A plane for grooving; একপ্রকার খাঁজ কাটিবার রেঁদা।

fil'-lȳ, *n.* **1.** A female foal; বাচ্চা ঘোড়ী, বাচ্চা ঘোটকী। **2.** A young lively girl; চপলা তরুণী, চটুলা বালা।

film, *n., v. t.* & *i.* **1.** A thin skin; a thin coating or layer; a haze; dimness over the eyes; পাতলা পরদা; পটল (হিঃ কোঃ), ঝিল্লী (ঐ), পাতলা আবরণ বা প্রলেপ; ঘোর; চক্ষুর ছানি। **2.** A very slender thread; as that of a cobweb; লুতাতন্তুবৎ অতি সুক্ষ্ম সুত্র। **3.** The layer of gelatin or collodion used on photographic paper or plates; আলোকচিত্রের কাগজ বা ফলকের উপর শিরিষ প্রভৃতির লেপ। ***Verb t.*** To cover with, or as with, a film; পাতলা পরদা বা তদ্বৎ কোন কিছু দ্বারা আচ্ছাদিত করা। ***Verb i.*** To become covered with, or as with, a film; পাতলা পরদা বা তদ্বৎ কোন কিছু দ্বারা আচ্ছাদিত হওয়া।

fi'-lose (-lös), *adj.* Terminating in a thread-like process; অন্ত্যভাগে সুত্রবৎ উপাঙ্গবিশিষ্ট।

fil-o-selle' (fĕl-ö-zāl), *n.* A ferret or floss silk; একপ্রকার রেশম।

fils, (*F.*), *n.* A son (often used with a proper name to distinguish between father and son of same names); পুত্র।

fil'-têr, *n., v. t.* & *i.* A contrivance for purifying liquids by passing them through sand, charcoal, etc.; a strainer; তরল পদার্থশোধক যন্ত্র, জলশোধক যন্ত্র; ছাঁকনি। ***Verb t.*** **1.** To pass through a filter for purification; (of a filter) to purify as a liquid; জলশোধক যন্ত্রদ্বারা তরল পদার্থ পরিষ্কার বা নির্ম্মল করা; ছাঁকিয়া পরিষ্কার করা। **2.** To obtain by filtering; ছাঁকিয়া পাওয়া। ***Verb i.*** To pass through a filter; to percolate; ছাঁকনির ভিতর দিয়া পড়া; চুয়াইয়া পড়া। **Filter-bed**—বহু পরিমাণ জল পরিষ্কার করার জন্য বালি, কঙ্কর প্রভৃতির স্তর। **Filter-paper**—জলাদি ছাঁকিবার জন্য সচ্ছিদ্র কাগজ।

filth, *n.* **1.** Foul matter; loathsome dirt; nastiness; দূষিত পদার্থ; মল, ময়লা; মলিনতা, মালিন্য। **2.** Anything that defiles the moral character; কলুষতা, কল্মষ। **3.** Foul language; অপভাষা, কলুষিত ভাষা, কুবচন, কদর্য্য ভাষা, জঘন্য ভাষা। **Filth'-i-ly,** *adv.* In a filthy manner; foully; দূষিত বা কলুষিতভাবে; অপরিষ্কাররূপে। **Filth'-i-ness,** *n.* The state of being filthy; অপরিচ্ছন্নতা, জঘন্যতা, অশ্লীলতা, কদর্য্যতা। **Filth'-y,** *adj.* Foul; dirty; licentious; impure; obscene; কলুষিত, দূষিত, জঘন্য; অপরিষ্কার; ময়লা, মলিন, সমল; লম্পট; অপবিত্র; অশ্লীল। **Filthy lucre**—Dishonourable gain; (*facet.*) money; নিন্দনীয় উপায়ে অর্জ্জিত অর্থ; (কৌতুকচ্ছলে) টাকা কড়ি।

fil'-trate *v. t.* & *n.* To filter; ছাঁকনি দিয়া ছাঁকা। ***Noun.*** Filtered liquor; ছাঁকা তরল পদার্থ। **–tra'-tion,** *n.* Act or process of filtering; ছাঁকন, গালন (সাঃ পঃ)।

fim'-bri-āte, –ā-tĕd, *adjs.* (*Zool.* & *Bot.*) Having a fringe or border; (প্রাণি-বিদ্যা ও উদ্ভিদ্‌ বিদ্যা) প্রান্তবিশিষ্ট।

fim'-bri-ate *v. t.* To fringe; কিনারা লাগান।

fin, *n.* **1.** One of the organs by which a fish balances itself and swims; মৎস্যের ডানা, পাখ্‌না, পর

2. (*Slang*) The hand ; (ইতরভাষায়) হাত। 3. Anything like a fin ; পাখ্‌নার আকার কোন কিছু। **Fin'-less,** *adj.* **Finned, Fin'-ny** *adjs.* Havig fins ; furnished with fins ; পাখ্‌নাওয়ালা ; ডানাযুক্ত। **Fin-footed** — লিপ্তপাদ। **Fin-toed**— লিপ্তাঙ্গুলি। **Tip us your fin**—Shake hands ; আমাদের সহিত করকম্পন কর।

fi'-năl, *adj.* & *n.* **1.** Pertaining to an end ; last ; ultimate ; অন্ত্য; অন্তিম; চূড়ান্ত, শেষ, চরম, পরম। **2.** Conclusive ; decisive ; as, a *final* victory ; নিশ্চায়ক; নির্ণায়ক। **3.** Regarding the purpose or end in view ; উদ্দেশ্যঘটিত। ***Noun.*** **1.** (*Athlet.*) A deciding game, hit or trial ; (মল্লক্রীড়া) নির্ণায়ক ক্রীড়া, আঘাত বা চেষ্টা। **2.** (*Sing. or pl.*) The last of a series of examinations ; সর্ব্বশেষ পরীক্ষা। **—ly,** *adv.* Eventually ; lastly ; conclusively ; অন্তিমে, অবশেষে, পরিশেষে ; সর্ব্বশেষে ; নির্ণায়করূপে। **Final cause** — নিমিত্ত কারণ, প্রয়োজন (হিঃ কোঃ), উদ্দেশ্য (ঐ)। **Final utility** — অন্তিম তোষ (হিঃ কোঃ), অন্তিম উপযোগ (ঐ)।

fi-na'-le (fē-nâ-lā), *n.* **1.** (*Mus.*) The last movement of the instrumental composition ; the last piece in any act of an opera ; সঙ্গীতের শেষ অংশ ; নাটক প্রভৃতির চরম ঘটনা। **2.** The close of any performance, as drama etc. ; নাটক প্রভৃতির উপসংহার। **3.** Close ; termination ; উপসংহার; সমাপ্তি, অন্ত।

fi-năl'-i-ty, *n.* **1.** State of being final ; the belief that something is final ; চরমতা ; কোন কিছুর চরমতায় বিশ্বাস। **2.** A final act, state or utterance ; সর্ব্বশেষ কার্য্য, অন্তিম অবস্থা, অন্তিম উক্তি, শেষ কথা। **3.** The doctrine that nothing exists except for a determined end ; প্রতি বস্তুর সত্তারই একটা বিশেষ উদ্দেশ্য আছে—এইরূপ মতবাদ।

fi-nance' (-năns), *n., v. t.* & *i.* **1.** (*Pl.*) The pecuniary resources of a ruler, state, company or individual ; রাজা, রাজ্য, ব্যবসায়ী সম্মিলন বা ব্যক্তি-বিশেষের আর্থিক সম্পদ, রাজধন (হিঃ কোঃ), অর্থ (ঐ)। **2.** The science of public revenue ; management of money matter, esp. of public money ; রাজস্বসংক্রান্ত বিজ্ঞান, রাজস্ববিজ্ঞান ; রাজস্ব-সংক্রান্ত বিষয়ের পরিচালন, রাজস্ব-পরিচালন। ***Verb t.*** To furnish with finances : to provide capital for ; as, to *finance* a business ; অর্থ দিয়া চালান ; মূলধন যোগান। ***Verb i.*** To conduct or engage in financial operations ; আয়ব্যয় সম্বন্ধে তত্ত্বাবধান করা।

fi-năn'-cial (-shăl), *adj.* Pertaining to finance or money matter ; রাজস্ববিষয়ক, ধনসম্বন্ধীয় (হিঃ কোঃ)। **—ist,** *n.* (*Colloq.*) A financier ; (চলিত ভাষায়) অর্থপ্রয়োগকুশল ব্যক্তি। **—ly,** *adv.* In relation to finances ; রাজস্বসংক্রান্ত বিষয়ে, আয়ব্যয় সম্বন্ধীয় ব্যাপারে, অর্থ ঘটিত ব্যাপারে।

fin-ăn-cier' (-sēr), *n., v. i.* & *t.* **1.** One who manages the public revenue ; রাজস্বসচিব। **2.** A capitalist concerned with financial operations ; যে ব্যক্তি জনসাধারণের নিকট হইতে টাকা তুলিয়া তাহা লাভজনক ব্যবসায়ে নিয়োগে দক্ষতা লাভ করিয়াছে, অর্থ-বিদ্যা-বিশারদ। ***Verb i.*** To conduct financial operations, (chiefly *contemptuously*) ; রাজস্ব-ঘটিত কাজ পরিচালন করা, জনসাধারণ হইতে টাকা তুলিয়া তাহা লাভজনক ব্যবসায়ে প্রয়োগ করা (প্রধানতঃ অবজ্ঞাচ্ছলে)। **3.** (*U. S.*) To swindle ; (মার্কিণ যুক্তরাজ্যে) জুয়াচুরি করা, প্রবঞ্চনা করা। ***Verb t.*** To finance ; মূলধন যোগান, অর্থদ্বারা চালান। **To financier money away**—To swindle money ; টাকা কাড়ু ঠকাইয়া নেওয়া। **To financier one out of**—To dupe one out of ; কাহাকে কোন কিছু হইতে বঞ্চিত করা।

finch (finsh), *n.* A kind of small singing bird ; কয়েক প্রকার ক্ষুদ্র কলকণ্ঠ পক্ষীর সাধারণ নাম। **Finch-backed** — same as FINCHED below. **Finch-lark** — ধূলিচটক (যোঃ)। **Rose-finch**—তুতীপাখী (ঐ)।

finched (finsht), *adj.* Spotted on the back ; পিঠে ফুট্ ফুট্ দাগ-বিশিষ্ট।

find, *v. t.* & *n.* **1.** To meet with ; to come across ; সাক্ষাৎ হওয়া ; হঠাৎ দেখিতে পাওয়া। **2.** To gain ; to procure ; as, to *find* favour, time, leisure, etc. ; লাভ করা ; সংগ্রহ করা, প্রাপ্ত হওয়া, পাওয়া। **3.** To discover by search ; to discover by study or experience ; খুঁজিয়া পাওয়া ; পাঠ বা অভিজ্ঞতার ফলে আবিষ্কার করা। **4.** To discover by sounding ; as, to *find* bottom ; মানরজ্জু দ্বারা মাপিয়া নির্ণয় করা। **5.** To perceive ; as, he *found* himself puzzled ; to detect ; as, to *find* an argument absurd ; বোধ করা, অনুভব করা ; বাহির করা, ধরা। **6.** To come home to ; as the books *found* me and taught me ; হৃদয়ঙ্গম হওয়া। **7.** To reach ; as, the bullet *found* its mark ; উপনীত হওয়া, পৌঁছা। **8.** To furnish ; as, they *found* him in clothes ; to supply ; as, a hotel does not *find* tea ; যোগান ; সরবরাহ করা। **9.** To determine and declare ; as, to *find* a verdict or to *find* a man guilty ; কোন সিদ্ধান্তে উপনীত হইয়া তাহা প্রকাশ করা। **10.** To gain or regain the use or highest power of ; as, to *find* one's tongue ; কোন কিছু ব্যবহারের শক্তি বা কোন কিছুর পূর্ণ শক্তি প্রাপ্ত বা পুনঃ প্রাপ্ত হওয়া। ***Noun.*** **1.** Finding of a fox ; শৃগাল বাহির করণ। **2.** Anything found ; a discovery of anything valuable ; প্রাপ্ত বা আবিষ্কৃত বস্তু ; কোনরূপ মূল্যবান

বস্তু আবিষ্কার, গুপ্ত ধন, খনিজ পদার্থ, প্রভৃতি আবিষ্কার। **Find'-a-ble,** *adj.* Capable of being found ; প্রাপ্য। **All found**—With all necessaries provided ; যাবতীয় আবশ্যক সাজ-সরঞ্জাম দ্বারা সজ্জিত। **Find-fault** (*Shakes.*)—One who finds fault with another ; দোষদর্শী ব্যক্তি। **Sure find**—A place where something *e. g.*, a fox is sure to be found ; যে স্থানে কোন কিছু, যথা শৃগালাদি প্রাপ্তির সম্ভাবনা নিশ্চিত। **To find a clue to**—To discover that which will lead to the desired object ; সন্ধান পাওয়া, খেই পাওয়া, অনুসন্ধানের সূত্র পাওয়া। **To find a market** — To meet with a purchaser ; ক্রেতা জুটা। **To find a true bill**—To determine and declare the grounds of accusation ; অভিযোগের হেতু নির্দ্ধারণ পূর্ব্বক প্রকাশ করা। **To find fault with**—To blame ; to censure ; নিন্দা করা ; দোষ দেওয়া। **To find favour**—To be graciously received and treated ; সাদরে গৃহীত হওয়া, সাদর ব্যবহার পাওয়া। **To find (it) in one's heart**—To be willing or disposed ; as, I *found it in my heart* to ask your pardon ; ইচ্ছুক হওয়া, প্রবণ হওয়া। **To find one in**—To supply one with (something) ; কাহাকেও কোন কিছু যোগান। **To find one's account in (anything)**—To find satisfactory profit or advantage in it ; কোন কাজে সন্তোষ-জনক লাভ হওয়া, কোন বিষয়ে বিশেষ সুবিধা হওয়া। **To find one's legs**—To rise or to recover the use of one's legs, as after being drunk etc. ; দাঁড়ান, নেশা কাটিলে দাঁড়াইতে পারা। **To find one's self**—To provide for one's own needs ; আবশ্যক দ্রব্যাদি সংগ্রহ করা। To fare, chiefly as regards health ; as how do you *find yourself* this evening ; থাকা (সাধারণতঃ স্বাস্থ্য-সম্বন্ধে)। **To find one's way to**—To contrive to reach ; to arrive at ; পথ করিয়া লওয়া ; পৌঁছা, উপনীত হওয়া। **To find out**—To discover, as a secret ; to solve, as an enigma ; to detect, as a thief ; to understand ; বাহির করা ; সমাধান করা ; ধরা ; বুঝা।

Find'-ĕr, *n.* **1.** (*Astron.*) A small telescope attached to a larger one to find objects ; (জ্যোতির্বিজ্ঞান) পদার্থ সমূহ অনুসন্ধান করিয়া বাহির করার জন্য বৃহত্তর দূরদর্শন যন্ত্রে সংবদ্ধ ক্ষুদ্র দূরদর্শন যন্ত্র, উপদূরদর্শক (হিঃ কোঃ)। **2.** A contrivance for a similar purpose in a photographic camera or in microscope ; অনুবীক্ষণ বা আলোকচিত্র গ্রহণের যন্ত্রে সংবদ্ধ ক্ষুদ্র দূরদর্শন যন্ত্র।

finde siecle, (*F.*) *adj.* Characteristic of the end of the nineteenth century ; advanced ; modern ; ঊনবিংশ শতাব্দীর শেষ ভাগের বিশেষত্ব প্রকাশক ; অগ্রসর ; আধুনিক।

fīne, *adj., n., adv., v.t. & i.* **1.** Refined ; pure ; (of metal) having a specified proportion of pure metal ; as, silver 11 oz. *fine* ; পরিমার্জ্জিত, পরিষ্কৃত, বিশোধিত ; বিশুদ্ধ ; (ধাতু-সম্পর্কে) নির্দ্দিষ্ট পরিমাণ বিশুদ্ধ ধাতুবিশিষ্ট। **2.** Nice ; delicate ; light ; as, *fine* linen ; খাসা ; সুকুমার, মোলায়েম ; মিহি, ফিনফিনে। **3.** Not coarse ; in small particles ; as, *fine* sand ; সূক্ষ্ম ; মিহি। **4.** Subtle ; sensitive ; elevated ; as, a *fine* sense ; "A movement of *finer* joy" ; সূক্ষ্ম ; সংবেদনশীল ; উন্নত। **5.** Sharp ; as, *fine* edge ; তীক্ষ্ণ, ধারাল। **6.** (*Athlet.*) Reduced to perfect condition ; (মল্লক্রীড়া) পরমোৎকর্ষ সম্পাদিত। **7.** Slender ; as, a *fine* thread ; সূক্ষ্ম, সরু, মিহি। **8.** Capable of delicate perception ; as, a *fine* distinction ; সূক্ষ্ম অনুভব-গম্য। **9.** Bright ; cloudless ; as, a *fine* weather ; beautiful ; as a *fine* face ; উজ্জ্বল ; মেঘমুক্ত, নির্ম্মেঘ ; সুন্দর, সুচারু, মনোহর, শোভন, মঞ্জু, মঞ্জুল, মনোরম, রুচির। **10.** Excellent ; of great merit ; good ; as, a *fine* man or thing ; skilful ; as, a musician etc. ; চমৎকার, উৎকৃষ্ট ; অতি গুণবান, শ্রেষ্ঠগুণ-সম্পন্ন ; উত্তম ; নিপুণ, বিচক্ষণ, দক্ষ। **11.** Euphemistic ; মোলায়েম। **12.** Ornate ; showy ; fastidious ; as, a *fine* dress, writing or speech ; সালঙ্কার ; জমকালো, জাঁকালো ; উৎকট-রুচি। **13.** Flattering ; complimentary as, to say *fine* things about a person ; তুষ্টিজনক, প্রীতিপ্রদ ; প্রশংসাত্মক, গুণানুবাদপূর্ণ। ***Noun.*** Fine weather ; as, in rain or *fine* ; সুদিন (বৃষ্টিঝটিকাদি শূন্য)। ***Adv.*** Finely ; as, to talk *fine* : সুন্দরভাবে, চমৎকাররূপে, রুচিররূপে। ***Verb t.*** To make pure or clear, as beer ; স্বচ্ছ বা বিশুদ্ধ করা। ***Verb i.*** To become clear, as a liquid ; স্বচ্ছ হওয়া, পরিষ্কার হওয়া। **Fin'-er-y,** *n.* Gaudy, decorated, showy clothes ; জমকালো পোষাক বা বেশভূষা। **Fine'-ly,** *adv.* সূক্ষ্মভাবে, সুন্দররূপে। **Fine'-ness,** *n.* The quality of being fine ; সূক্ষ্মতা, রুচিরতা, নির্ম্মলতা। **Fine arts**—Arts which appeal to the senses, as, poetry, music, etc. ; সুকুমার কলা, সুকুমার বিদ্যা, ললিতকলা, সুকুমার শিল্প, (চিত্র, ভাস্কর্য্য, নৃত্যগীতাদি)। **Fine-draw**—*v. t.* To sew up with so much nicety that the rent or joint is not perceived ; সেলাই করা হইয়াছে বলিয়া মালুম হয় না এরূপভাবে রিফু করা। To draw out to extreme subtlety ; as, to *finedraw* an argument ; টানিয়া টানিয়া নিতান্ত সূক্ষ্ম করা। **Fine drawn**—*p. p.* Subtle ; very thin ; (of athletes etc.) reduced in weight by exercise or training ; সূক্ষ্ম ; অতিশয় সরু বা পাতল ; ব্যায়ামাদিদ্বারা দেহের গুরুত্ব হ্রাস-প্রাপ্ত। **Fine-spoken**—মিষ্টভাষী, প্রিয়ম্বদ। **Fine-spun**—Delicate ; flimsy ; excessively subtle ; unpractical ; as, a *finespun* theory ; সুকুমার ; পাতল ; অতিশয় সূক্ষ্ম ; অকার্য্যকর। **A fine gentleman** or **lady**—A person of fashion ; বেশবিলাসপ্রিয় ব্যক্তি বা বেশ-বিলাসানুরাগিণী মহিলা। **A fine pen**—A narrow pointed pen ; সরু লিখার জন্য কলম। **A fine pencil**—One with hard lead for making fine lines ; সূক্ষ্ম রেখাঙ্কনের জন্য পেন্সিল। **A man of fine presence**—*i. e.* of dignified presence ; গৌরবমণ্ডিত ব্যক্তি। **Fine feathers do not make fine birds**—Fine clothing does not make a person better than he is ; ভাল কাপড়চোপড় পরিলেই ভাল লোক হয় না। **Fine potatoes**—বড় গোল আলু। **Fine words butter no parsnips**—Same as FAIR WORDS etc. which see under BUTTER. **One fine day**—Once upon a time ; একদা, একদিন। **One of these fine days**—(In prophecies) Some day ; (ভবিষ্যদ্বাণী সম্পর্কে) কোন একদিন। **To fine away, down** or **off**—*v. t. & i.* To make finer, less coarse ; সূক্ষ্ম করা, মিহি করা। To whittle away or down ; চাঁচিয়া বা মুছিয়া ফেলান। (*Verb i.*) To become finer, thinner, etc. ; to dwindle ; সুন্দরতর হওয়া, মঞ্জুতর হওয়া, কৃশতর হওয়া ; হ্রাস হওয়া।

fīne, *n., v. t. & i.* **1.** A sum of money paid by an incoming tenant in order to make his rent small or nominal ; কোন প্রজা অল্প বা নামমাত্র রাজস্বে ভূমি বন্দোবস্ত গ্রহণের জন্য জমিদারকে যে নজরানা প্রদান করিয়া থাকে। **2.** Sum of money fixed as penalty for offence ; অর্থদণ্ড, জরিমানা, ধনদণ্ড। **3.** Conclusion, (only in the phrase *in fine*) ; শেষ, অবশেষ, পরিশেষ। ***Verb t.*** To punish by a fine ; অর্থদণ্ড করা, জরিমানা করা। ***Verb i.*** To pay a consideration for a privilege or for appointment to an office ; কোনপ্রকার সুবিধা লাভের জন্য অথবা কোন কর্ম্মে নিযুক্ত হওয়ার দরুণ কিছু অর্থ প্রদান করা। **Fine'-a-ble,** *adj.* Liable to fine ; অর্থদণ্ডার্হ, জরিমানার যোগ্য।

fĭn'-ĕr-ў, *n.* A hearth where cast iron is made malleable or sheet is made from pig iron ; যে চুল্লীতে লৌহাদি পোড়ান হয়, লৌহ-শোধন-শালা, লোহার কারখানা।

fi-nesse' (-nĕs'), *n., v. i. & t.* **1.** Skill ; subtle discrimination ; নিপুণতা, দক্ষতা; সূক্ষ্মবিশ্লেষণ। **2.** Artifice ; stratagem ; চাতুর্য্য, কলাকৌশল; চাতুরী, ফন্দি। ***Verb i.*** To use finesse or artifice ; কলাকৌশল প্রয়োগ করা। ***Verb t.*** To bring by finesse or artifice (into a certain state), (with *into, away*) ; কলাকৌশল প্রয়োগদ্বারা কোন বিশেষ অবস্থায় আনা।

fin'-gêr (fĭng-), *n., v. t. & i.* **1.** One of the five terminating members of the hand ; করাঙ্গুলী, অঙ্গুলী, আঙ্গুল, করশাখা, কররুহ। **2.** The pointer of a clock etc. ; ঘড়ী প্রভৃতির কাঁটা। **3.** The breadth of a finger ; as, three *fingers* thick ; অঙ্গুলীর প্রস্থ। **4.** Skill in playing on a keyed instrument ; চাবি বিশিষ্ট বাদ্য-যন্ত্র বাদনে নিপুণতা। ***Verb t.*** **1.** To touch with the fingers ; to handle ; অঙ্গুলীদ্বারা স্পর্শ করা ; হস্তদ্বারা ব্যবহার করা। **2.** To touch lightly ; মৃদু স্পর্শ করা। **3.** (*Music*) To play upon (an instrument) with the fingers ; (সঙ্গীত-শাস্ত্র) হস্ত সঞ্চালন দ্বারা বাদ্যযন্ত্র বাজান। **4.** To pilfer ; to steal ; ছিঁচকে চুরি করা ; চুরি করা। **5.** To perform, as a delicate work with the fingers ; অঙ্গুলীদ্বারা সূক্ষ্ম কার্য্য সম্পাদন করা। ***Verb i.*** To use the fingers in playing on a musical instrument ; বাদ্যযন্ত্র বাদনে অঙ্গুলী সঞ্চালন করা। **—gered,** *adj.* Having fingers ; অঙ্গুলীযুক্ত। **—less,** *adj.* **Finger-alphabet, —language** — বধির ব্যক্তিগণের সহিত আলাপ করার জন্য সাঙ্কেতিক চিহ্ন, অঙ্গুলী-ভাষা। **Finger-board** — বাদ্যযন্ত্রের ঘাট বা চাবি। **Finger-bowl, —glass**—আহারান্তে অঙ্গুলী প্রক্ষালনের জন্য পাত্র-বিশেষ। **Finger-breadth**—The breadth of a finger ; the fourth part of a palm ; অঙ্গুলীর প্রস্থ ; এক ইঞ্চির ত্রিচতুর্থাংশ। **Finger-fern**—একপ্রকার গুল্ম। **Finger-fish**—একপ্রকার মৎস্য, তারা মাছ। **Finger-mark**—অঙ্গুলীর ময়লা দাগ বা ছাপ। **Finger-plate**—অঙ্গুলীর ময়লা দাগ বা ছাপ না লাগিতে পারে তজ্জন্য দ্বারোপরি যে ধাতু বা চীনা মাটীর ফলক লাগান হয়। **Finger-post**—যে স্তম্ভের উপরে পথ নির্দ্দেশনার্থ হস্ত চিত্রিত থাকে। **Finger-print**—অঙ্গুলীর ছাপ [দুই ব্যক্তির অঙ্গুলীর ছাপ একরূপ হয় না বলিয়া ঐরূপ ছাপ দ্বারা অপরাধীকে সহজে চিনিতে পারা যায়]। **Finger-stall**—চর্ম্মনির্ম্মিত অঙ্গুলিত্রাণ (শবব্যবচ্ছেদ কালে ব্যবহৃত হয়)। **Done by the finger of God**—Done by the agency of God ; ঈশ্বরকৃত। **His fingers are all thumbs**—He is clumsy ; সে বড় আনাড়ী বা অপটু। **My fingers itch**—I am impatient (to do etc.) ; আমি অস্থির হইয়া উঠিয়াছি। **The fore-finger** — তর্জ্জনী। **The little finger**—কনিষ্ঠাঙ্গুলী। **The middle finger**—মধ্যমা। **The ring-finger**—অনামিকা। **To arrive at one's fingers' end**—To be reduced to poverty ; দুরবস্থায় পতিত হওয়া। **To burn one's fingers**—See under BURN. **To have a finger in**—To be concerned in ; লিপ্ত থাকা, জড়িত থাকা। **To have a finger in every pie**—To take part in all matters ; সকল নৈবেদ্যে ঠোকর মারা। **To have at one's finger ends** — To be perfect master of the subject ; to be quite familiar with ; কোনও বিষয় কাহারো নখদর্পণের মত থাকা, করামলকবৎ করা ; সুবিদিত থাকা। **To lay** or **put a**

finger upon—To touch however slightly ; অঙ্গুলীস্পর্শ করা। **To lay or put one's fingers on**—To point with precision to ; সঠিক ভাবে প্রদর্শন করা। **To let slip through one's fingers**—To lose hold of ; ছাড়িয়া দেওয়া। **To look through one's fingers at**—To pretend not to see ; দেখে নাই বলিয়া ভাণ করা, দেখিয়াও না দেখা। **To snap one's finger**—তুড়ি দেওয়া। **To stir a finger**—To make the least effort ; অণুমাত্রও চেষ্টা করা। **To turn or twist a person round one's (little) finger**—To cajole him ; মিঠা কথায় ভুলান। **With a wet finger**—With ease ; অনায়াসে, অক্লেশে।

fin'-gêr-ing (fing-), *n.* **1.** The act of touching with the fingers ; অঙ্গুলীস্পর্শ। **2.** The movement of the fingers in playing on a musical instrument ; বাদ্যযন্ত্র বাদনে অঙ্গুলীসঞ্চালন। **3.** Delicate work made with the fingers ; অঙ্গুলীদ্বারা সম্পাদিত সূক্ষ্ম শিল্পকার্য্য।

fin'-gêr-ing (fing-), *n.* A worsted yarn for stockings ; মোজার জন্য পশমী সূতা।

fin'-i-ăl, *n.* (*Arch.*) The ornamental termination of a pinnacle, gable, etc. ; the pinnacle itself ; (ভাস্কর্য্য) গৃহের পাশকপালী (gable) প্রভৃতির শোভাজনক শীর্ষ দেশ, কলস (রাঃ রাঃ) ; চূড়া।

fin'-i-căl, *adj.* Over-nice ; fastidious ; অতিরিক্ত সূক্ষ্মবিচারী ; উৎকট-রুচি। **—cal'-i-ty,** *n.* **—ick-ing,** *adj.* **—ly,** *adv.* **—ness,** *n.* বাবুগিরি।

fin'-i-kin, *adj.* A sort of pigeon ; এক প্রকার কপোত (ইহার ঝুঁটি কতকটা অশ্বের কেশরের ন্যায়)।

fi'-nis, *n.* The end (generally put at the end of a book); the end of anything, esp. the life ; সম্পূর্ণ, সমাপ্তি ; শেষ, উপসংহার।

fin'-ish, *v. t., i.* & *n.* **1.** To bring to an end ; সম্পন্ন করা। **2.** To complete ; to perfect ; to complete the education of ; সমাপ্ত করা, শেষ করা, সম্পূর্ণ করা ; সুসম্পন্ন করা ; বিদ্যা সাঙ্গ করা। **3.** To consume ; to get through the whole or remainder of ; as, to *finish* food or a book ; নিঃশেষ করা ; পড়িয়া শেষ করা। **4.** To kill ; to overthrow ; as, to *finish* an enemy ; বধ করা, বিনাশ করা, নিকাশ করা ; বিপর্য্যস্ত করা। ***Verb i.*** To come to an end ; to terminate ; শেষ হওয়া, সমাপ্ত হওয়া ; অবসান হওয়া। ***Noun.*** **1.** That which serves to give completeness ; যদ্দ্বারা পরিসমাপ্ত হয়। **2.** Last stage ; end ; অন্তিম অবস্থা ; শেষ, পরিসমাপ্তি, উপসংহার। **3.** State of being perfected ; manner or style of finishing ; সম্পূর্ণতা, সর্ব্বাঙ্গসম্পন্নতা ; সম্পাদন-প্রণালী। **—er.** *n.* **1.** One who or that which finishes ; সমাপক। **2.** A workman or machine that gives the finishing touch in manufacture ; যে শ্রমজীবী বা যন্ত্রদ্বারা কোন নির্ম্মিত দ্রব্যের শেষ চানকান হয়। **—ing,** *adj.* **—ished** *adj.* Polished to the highest degree ; complete ; perfect ; terminated ; অতি মাত্রায় পরিকর্ম্মীকৃত ; সমাপ্ত ; সর্ব্বাঙ্গসম্পন্ন ; অবসানপ্রাপ্ত। **A finisher of the law**—A hangman ; যে ব্যক্তি ফাঁসি দেয়, জল্লাদ। **Finishing stroke or touch**—The final act or work ; শেষ পোঁচ, শেষ চানকান। A discomfiting thing ; a crushing blow ; পরাভবজনক বিষয় ; সাংঘাতিক আঘাত, খতম ঘা। **To be in at the finish**—To be at the last stage ; অন্তিম অবস্থা প্রাপ্ত হওয়া। **To fight to a finish**—To fight till one party is completely worsted ; এক পক্ষ সম্পূর্ণরূপে বিধ্বস্ত না হওয়া পর্য্যন্ত যুদ্ধ করা। **To finish off**—To provide with an ending ; শেষ করিয়া ফেলা।

fi'-nite, *adj.* **1.** Bounded or limited ; not infinite ; সীমাবদ্ধ, নির্দ্দিষ্টসীম, সসীম, সান্ত, পরিচ্ছিন্ন ; আদ্যন্তবান, সাবধি। **2.** (*Gram.*) Limited by number and person ; as, a *finite* verb ; (ব্যাকরণ) সমাপিকা। **—ly,** *adv.* In a finite manner ; সান্তভাবে। **—ness** *n.* The state of being finite ; সীমাবদ্ধতা, সান্ততা।

Fin(n), *n.* **1.** A native of Finland ; ফিন্‌ল্যাণ্ডের অধিবাসী। **2.** One of a race of people of North-Eastern Europe ; উত্তর-পূর্ব্ব ইয়ুরোপের জাতি-বিশেষ।

fin'-i-tüde, *n.* Finite state ; সীমাবচ্ছিন্নতা, সীমাবদ্ধতা, সসীমতা।

fin'-nêr, *n.* A fin-backed whale ; একপ্রকার তিমি মৎস্য।

Finn'-ic, *adj.* Pertaining to the Finns ; ফিন্‌ল্যাণ্ডের অধিবাসি-সম্বন্ধীয়।

Finn'-ish, *adj.* & *n.* Finnic ; ফিন্‌ল্যাণ্ডবাসিগণ সম্পর্কীয়। ***Noun.*** The language of the Finns ; ফিন্‌ল্যাণ্ডবাসিগণের ভাষা।

fin'-ny, *adj.* With, or like, fins ; relating to, or abounding in, fishes ; পাখনা-বিশিষ্ট, পাখনার মত ; মৎস্যসম্বন্ধীয়, মৎস্যবহুল।

fiord, fjord (fyŏrd), *ns.* A rock-bound narrow inlet from the sea, as in Norway ; নরওয়ে প্রভৃতি দেশের পাষাণশৈলবেষ্টিত সাগরশাখা।

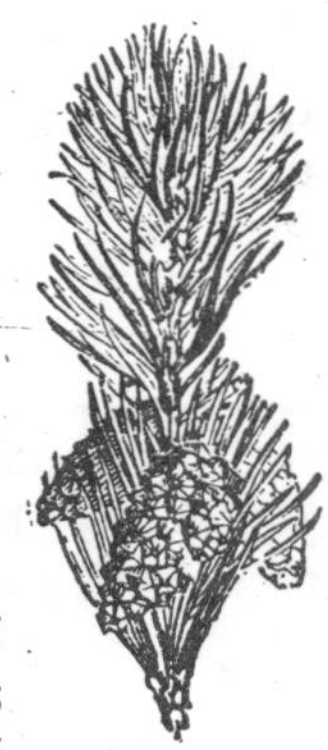

Scotch fir.

fi'-ō-rin, *n.* A kind of grass ; একপ্রকার ঘাস।

fir (fêr), *n.* **1.** A name for various coniferous trees ; দেবদারু প্রভৃতি বৃক্ষ। **2.** The wood of these trees ; দেবদারু প্রভৃতির কাঠ। **Fir'-ry,** *adj.* Abounding in firs ; দেবদারু বৃক্ষবহুল। **Fir-apple, —ball, —cone**—The fruit of the fir ; দেবদারুফল। **Fir-needle**—দেবদারু পত্র। **Silver-Fir**—তালীশপত্র।

fire, *n., v. t.* & *i.* **1.** Heat and light emanating from burning a body ; combustion ; state of ignition ; অগ্নি, আগুন, পাবন, অনল, হুতাশন, বহ্নি, কৃশানু, বৈশ্বানর, জাতবেদাঃ, বর্হিঃ, কৃষ্ণবর্ত্ম, বায়ুসখ, দহন, চিত্রভানু, বিভাবসু, শুচি, রোহিতাশ্ব, হিরণ্যরেতা, হব্যবাহন, সপ্তার্চ্চিঃ; দাহন; প্রজ্বলিতাবস্থা। **2.** Burning fuel in a grate, furnace, etc. ; চুল্লি প্রভৃতির ইন্ধন জ্বলন। **3.** Burning, as of a town or house etc. ; a conflagration ; অগ্নিকাণ্ড, গৃহদাহ ; দাবানল, দাবাগ্নি, বনানল। **4.** Ardour or violence of passion ; spirit ; কামানল, প্রেমানল, ক্রোধাগ্নি, রোষবহ্নি ; তেজ। **5.** Fervour ; জ্বলন্ত আগ্রহ, জ্বলন্ত উৎসাহ, মনের আবেগ। **6.** Liveliness of imagination ; vivacity ; poetic inspiration ; সজীব বা সতেজ কল্পনা ; সজীবতা ; কবির প্রেরণা। **7.** Glow ; lustre ; দীপ্তি ; চাক্‌চিক্য, দ্যুতি। **8.** Torture by burning ; severe affliction ; severe trial ; অঙ্গদাহপূর্ব্বক যন্ত্রণা প্রদান ; মর্ম্মান্তিক যন্ত্রণা ; অগ্নিপরীক্ষা। **9.** The discharge of fire-arms ; (বন্দুকাদি) আওয়াজ করণ,(তোপ) দাগন। **10.** Fever ; জ্বর। ***Verb t.*** **1.** To set on fire with the intention of destroying ; as, to *fiire* a house ; to kindle ; অগ্নি সংযোগ করা, আগুন লাগান বা দেওয়া, জ্বালাইয়া দেওয়া ; প্রজ্বালিত করা। **2.** To cauterize ; তপ্ত লৌহ দ্বারা কোন স্থান দগ্ধ করা। **3.** To bake ; to turn in a kiln ; as, to *fire* pottery ; সেঁকা ; পোয়ানে উল্টাইয়া দেওয়া। **4.** To supply with fuel ; as, to *fire* a furance or engine ; জ্বালানি কাঠ যোগান। **5.** To animate ; to give life to ; সজীব করা ; সঞ্জীবিত করা। **6.** To irritate, as the passions ; উত্তেজিত করা। **7.** To illuminate ; আলোকিত করা। **8.** To cause to explode ; as, to *fire* a mine ; to discharge, as a gun etc. ; (বারুদ দ্বারা) উড়াইয়া দেওয়া ; আওয়াজ করা। **9.** To hurl, as a missile from a gun etc. ; (also *fig.*) as, to *fire* a remark ; বন্দুকাদি আওয়াজ করা, গুলি করা ; (লক্ষণায়) ক্ষেপণ করা। **10.** (*U. S.*) To expel or dismiss (a person), (sometimes with *out*) ; (মার্কিণ যুক্তরাজ্যে) বিতাড়িত করা, পদচ্যুত করা। ***Verb i.*** **1.** To take fire ; to be kindled ; to glow or redden ; আগুন ধরা, আগুন লাগা ; প্রজ্বলিত হওয়া ; দীপ্তি পাওয়া, লাল হইয়া উঠা। **2.** To become irritated with passion ; ক্রোধানলে উদ্দীপ্ত হওয়া। **3.** To discharge cannon, firearms, etc. ; বন্দুকাদি আওয়াজ করা, (তোপ) দাগা। **4.** To go off, as a gun etc. ; বন্দুকাদি আওয়াজ হওয়া। **Fire′-less,** *adj.* **Fire alarm** — অগ্নিকাণ্ডের সংবাদ বিজ্ঞাপনের জন্য যন্ত্র-বিশেষ, অগ্নিজ্ঞাপক **Fire-arm**—(Usu. *Pl.*) Rifle, gun, pistol, etc. ; আগ্নেয়াস্ত্র,—বন্দুক, কামান প্রভৃতি। **Fire-arrow**—জাহাজাদিতে অগ্নিসংযোগের জন্য দাহ্য পদার্থ সমন্বিত লৌহ সায়ক-বিশেষ, অগ্নিবাণ। **Fire-back**—সুমাত্রা দ্বীপবাসী উজ্জ্বল বর্ণ রঞ্জিত পক্ষাবিশিষ্ট বিহঙ্গ বিশেষ। **Fire-ball**—অগ্নিগর্ভ গোলা, অগ্নিগোলক (কেণ্ডি), বম্ ; উজ্জ্বল উল্কাপিণ্ড। **Fire-balloon**—ফানুস বাজী। **Fire-bell**—অগ্নিদাহজ্ঞাপক ঘণ্টা। **Fire-bird**—পক্ষিবিশেষ। **Fire-blast** — ডাণ্ডজ্জ রোগ-বিশেষ। **Fire-blight**—A disease of hops ; হপ লতার রোগবিশেষ। **Fire-box**—A fuel chamber of the steam-boiler ; বাষ্পীয় পোত, বাষ্পীয়-শকট প্রভৃতির বাষ্পজনকের (boiler) যে প্রকোষ্ঠে কয়লা প্রভৃতি রক্ষিত হয়। **Fire-brand**—জ্বলন্ত কাঠ-খণ্ড, অগ্নিকাঠ (কেণ্ডি), অঙ্গার (ঐ) ; দুরন্ত ব্যক্তি, অনিষ্টকারী ব্যক্তি। **Fire-brick**—যে ইষ্টক প্রবল অগ্নিতাপেও নষ্ট বা বিকৃত হয় না, অগ্নীষ্টক। **Fire-brigade** — অগ্নিনির্ব্বাপণার্থ সম্প্রদায়-বিশেষ, অগ্নিবাহিনী। **Fire-bucket**—আগুন নিবাইবার জল বহনের জন্য বাল্‌তি, অগ্নি-জলদ্রোণি। **Fire-clay**—একপ্রকার মাটী,—যাহা হইতে প্রস্তুত ইষ্টক প্রবল অগ্নিতাপেও নষ্ট বা বিকৃত হয় না, অগ্নিমৃত্তিকা। **Fire-cock**—অগ্নি নির্ব্বাপণার্থ জলনিঃস্রাবী নল, অগ্নি নির্ব্বাপক নল। **Fire-cross** — Same as FIERY-CROSS which see. **Fire damp** — খনিজ দাহ্য বাষ্প-বিশেষ। **Fire-dog** — Same as ANDIRON which see. **Fire-drake**—অগ্নিময় উল্কাপিণ্ড ; একপ্রকার আতস বাজী ; আগ্নেয় সর্প। **Fire-dress**—A dress which resists fire ; অগ্নিরোধক পরিচ্ছদ, অগ্নিবেশ। **Fire-eater**—যে ঐন্দ্রজালিক অগ্নিভক্ষণ করে বলিয়া ভ্রম জন্মায়, অগ্নিখাদক ; ঝগড়াটে লোক, কোন্দলিয়া লোক ; মহাযোদ্ধা, দ্বন্দ্বযুদ্ধকারী। **Fire-engine** — অগ্নিনির্ব্বাপণার্থ যন্ত্রবিশেষ, অনল যন্ত্র, আগ্নেয় যন্ত্র। **Fire-escape** — দহ্যমান অট্টালিকাদির উপর হইতে রক্ষা পাওয়ার জন্য মই-বিশেষ, অগ্নিত্রাতা। **Fire-flair**—একপ্রকার মৎস্য। **Fire-fly** — খদ্যোত, খদ্যোতিকা, জোনাকী পোকা, দীপমক্ষিকা, প্রভাকীট, জ্যোতিরিঙ্গণ। **Fire-guard** — শিশু প্রভৃতিকে অগ্নিপতন হইতে রক্ষার্থ অগ্নিস্থলীর সম্মুখস্থ তাররচিত বৃতি, অগ্নিরক্ষক। **Fire-hose** — অগ্নিনির্ব্বাপক নল। **Fire-insurance**—যে বীমাতে অগ্নিদাহ হইয়া বীমাকারীর সম্পত্তি নষ্ট হইলে তাহার জন্য ক্ষতিপূরণ পাওয়া যায়, অগ্নিবীমা। **Fire-irons**—Tongs, poker and shovel ; চিম্‌টা, আগুন উস্কাইবার জন্য ধাতুময় শলাকা এবং শাবল। **Fire light** — অগ্নিসেবনস্থলী হইতে আগত আলোক। **Fire-lock**—একপ্রকার প্রাচীন ধরণের বন্দুক—যাহাতে লৌহ ও চক্‌মকি পাথরের সংঘর্ষণে অগ্নি প্রজ্বালিত হয়। **Fire-man**—যে ব্যক্তি চুল্লী বা বাষ্পীয়যন্ত্রের অগ্নিরক্ষা করিয়া থাকে। **Fire-new** — (*Archaic*) Brand new ; (অপ্রঃ) আনকোরা নূতন। **Fire-office** — অগ্নিবীমা কার্য্যালয়। **Fire-pan**—অগ্নিপাত্র, অঙ্গারধানিকা।

Fire-place — A hearth for room-fire ; শীতপ্রধানদেশে গৃহাভ্যন্তরস্থ

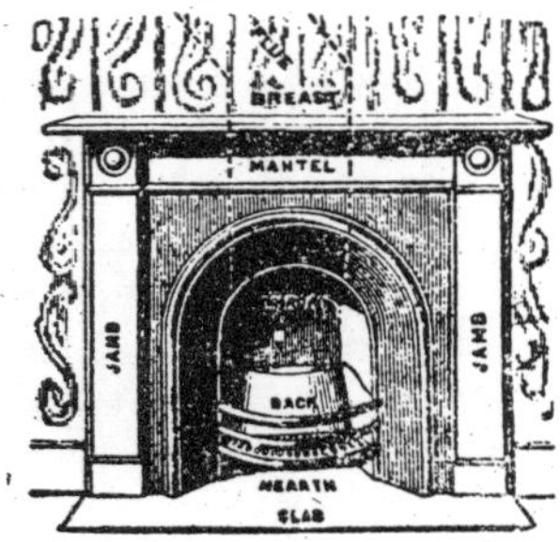

Fire-place.

অগ্নি-সেবনস্থলী। **Fire-plug** — অগ্নি-কাণ্ডের সময় যে নলের সাহায্যে জলপ্রক্ষেপ করা হয়। **Fire-policy**—অগ্নিদাহের ক্ষতিপূরণার্থ অগ্নিবীমা কোম্পানীর অঙ্গীকারপত্র। **Fire-pot**—অগ্নিপাত্র ; (সামরিক-শাস্ত্র) পূর্ব্বকালে যুদ্ধাস্ত্রস্বরূপ ব্যবহৃত বিস্ফোরক পদার্থপূর্ণ ক্ষুদ্র মৃন্ময় পাত্র। **Fire-proof** — অগ্নিপরীক্ষিত, অদাহ্য। **Fire-raising**—The crime of arson ; অগ্নিদাহাপরাধ। **Fire-robed**—(*Shakes.*) Robed in fire ; অনল-বসন। **Fire-ship** — শত্রুপোত দহনার্থ দাহ্যদ্রব্য পূর্ণ ক্ষুদ্র অর্ণবযান-বিশেষ, অগ্নিপোত। **Fire-screen**—অগ্নিতাপ বারণের জন্য পরদা, অগ্নিযবনিকা। **Fire-side** — গৃহাভ্যন্তরস্থ অগ্নিসেবন-স্থলী ; গার্হস্থ্যজীবন, গৃহ। **Fire-stone** — চকমকি পাথর, অগ্নিপ্রস্তর (কেণ্ডি)। **Fire-teazer** — Same as STOKER which see. **Fire-trap** — অগ্নিকাণ্ডের সময় বহির্গমনের উপযুক্ত দ্বারাদিবিহীন গৃহ, অনলকূটযন্ত্র, আগুনের ফাঁদ। **Fire-water**—তীব্র সুরা, উগ্রবীর্য্য সুরা। **Fire wood**—জ্বালানি কাঠ, ইন্ধন। **Fire-works**—আতসবাজি। **Fire-worship**—অগ্নিপূজা, অনলোপাসনা, অগ্ন্যুপাসনা, অগ্নিহোত্র (হিঃ কোঃ) [অগ্নিপূজা প্রাচীন পারস্য প্রভৃতি দেশে প্রচলিত ছিল]। **Fire-worshipper** — অগ্নিপূজক ; পার্শী। **Greek-fire** — শত্রুপোত দাহের জন্য প্রস্তুত দাহ্য দ্রব্যবিশেষ। **Kentish-fire**—করতালি। **A burnt child dreads the fire** — See under BURN. **A line of fire**—The path of a bullet about to be shot ; গোলাগুলির পথ। **Between two fires**—Shot at from two directions ; উভয়দিক হইতে গোলাগুলি লাগিতে পারে এরূপ স্থানে অবস্থিত; উভয় সঙ্কটে পতিত। **Cross-fire** — যুগপৎ বিভিন্ন দিক্ হইতে গোলাগুলি বর্ষণ। **Fat is in the fire**—See under FAT. **Fire**—A call for aid at a fire ; আগুন ! আগুন ! **Fire away**—Begin ; go ahead ; say on ; আরম্ভ কর ; অগ্রসর হও ; বলিয়া যাও। **No smoke without fire**—There is always some ground for rumour ; ধূম ভিন্ন অগ্নি ঘটিতে পারে না, কারণ ভিন্ন কার্য্য হয় না, জনরবের প্রায়ই কোন না কোনরূপ একটা মূল থাকে। **On fire**—Burning ; excited ; as, the house or the man is *on fire* ; জ্বলন্ত ; উত্তেজিত, উদ্দীপ্ত। **Out of the frying pan into the fire**—See FRY. **Running fire** — The rapid discharge of fire-arms in succession by a line of troops ; শ্রেণীবদ্ধ সৈনিকগণের ক্রমান্বয়ে দ্রুত গোলাগুলিবর্ষণ। **St. Anthony's fire**—বিসর্প রোগ। **St. Elmo's fire**—আলেয়া। **To fire away**—To begin ; to go ahead ; আরম্ভ করা ; এগিয়ে যাওয়া। **To fire broadside** — To discharge all the guns on one side of a ship ; রণপোতের একপার্শ্বস্থ কামানশ্রেণী হইতে যুগপৎ গোলাবর্ষণ করা। **To fire off**—To discharge a shot ; গোলা বর্ষণ করা। To stop the burning as of a kiln ; পোয়ান প্রভৃতির অগ্নি নির্ব্বাপণ করা। **To fire out**—See FIRE *v. t.* to. **To fire salute**—To discharge a number of guns as salute ; সম্মানসূচক তোপধ্বনি করা। **To fire up**—To light a fire, as in a furnace ; অগ্নি প্রজ্বলিত করা। To become irritated or angry ; to show anger ; রাগান্বিত হওয়া, অগ্নিশর্ম্মা হওয়া, রাগিয়া উঠা ; ক্রোধ প্রদর্শন করা। **To fire upon**—To discharge fire-arms aiming at ; গুলিবর্ষণ করা। **To go through fire and water**—To face all perils ; সর্ব্বপ্রকার বিপদের সম্মুখীন হওয়া। **To heap coals of fire on the head**—To return good for evil ; মন্দ ব্যবহারের পরিবর্ত্তে সদ্ব্যবহার করা। **To pour oil on fire**—To add to excitement while deprecating it ; অগ্নিতে ঘৃতাহুতি প্রদান করা। **To set fire**—To kindle ; to inflame ; আগুন লাগাইয়া দেওয়া, অগ্নি সংযোগ করা, প্রজ্বলিত করা ; উদ্দীপ্ত করা। **To set on fire** — To ignite ; to excite ; অগ্নিসংযোগ করা, প্রজ্বলিত করা ; উত্তেজিত করা, উদ্দীপ্ত করা। **To set the Thames on fire**—To do something remarkable ; অসাধ্য সাধন করা। **To strike fire**—To elicit sparks by friction or blow ; ঘর্ষণ বা আঘাত দ্বারা অগ্নি প্রজ্বলিত করা। **To take** or **catch fire**—To be inflamed ; আগুন লাগা, প্রজ্বলিত হওয়া, আগুন ধরা।

fīr'-ēr *n.* One that fires ; গুলি-গোলা বর্ষক। **Single-firer**—যে কামান পুনরায় গোলা-বারুদ না পুরিয়া কেবলমাত্র একবার দাগিতে পারা যায়, সকৃদগ্নিবর্ষী।

fīr'-ing *n.* 1. A putting fire to ; অগ্নি সংযোগ। 2. Discharge of guns ; বন্দুকাদির আওয়াজ। **Firing point**—তাপের যে মাত্রায় তৈল স্বতঃ জ্বলিয়া উঠে, অগ্নিতাপাঙ্ক।

fir'-kin (fêr-), *n.* 1. A measure, being equal to the fourth part of a barrel ; 9 gallons ; এক ব্যারেলের চতুর্থাংশ ; নয় গ্যালন। 2. A small cask for liquids, butter, etc. ; মাখন প্রভৃতির জন্য ক্ষুদ্র পিপা।

firm (fêrm), *adj. adv., v. t. & i.* 1. Of compact structure ; as, *firm* flesh ; দৃঢ়, সংহত, ঘন-সন্নিবিষ্ট, সান্দ্র, নিরেট। 2. Staple ;

not easily excited or disturbed ; established ; constant ; resolute ; স্থির, অচল, অটল, অকম্পিত ; স্থিরধী, অবিচলিত ; দৃঢ়প্রতিষ্ঠিত, অচলপ্রতিষ্ঠ ; নিত্য ; দৃঢ়প্রতিজ্ঞ, স্থিরপ্রতিজ্ঞ। 3. Indicating firmness ; as, a *firm* tread ; দৃঢ়তাব্যঞ্জক। 4. (*Comm*) Not fluctuating ; as, a *firm* price ; (বাণিজ্য) স্থির। ***Adv.*** Firmly; as, to stand *firm* ; দৃঢ়ভাবে। ***Verb t.*** To fix securely ; to make solid or compact ; দৃঢ়বদ্ধ করা ; নিরেট করা, সংহত করা। ***Verb i.*** To solidify ; to become firm ; ঘনীভূত হওয়া, জমাট বাঁধা ; দৃঢ় হওয়া। **Firm′-ly,** *adv.* In a firm manner ; দৃঢ়ভাবে, অটলভাবে, অবিচলিতচিত্তে, স্থিরভাবে। **Firm′-ness,** *n.* The state or quality of being firm ; দৃঢ়তা, অটলভাব, অবিচলিতভাব, দার্ঢ্য, কাঠিন্য, স্থৈর্য্য।

firm (fêrm), *n.* The name or title under which a company of partners transacts business ; partners carrying on business ; a commercial house ; partnership in business ; যৌথব্যবসায়ের নাম ; ব্যবসায়ি-সম্প্রদায়, ব্যবসায়ি-গোষ্ঠী ; বাণিজ্যশালা, বাণিজ্যাগার ; যৌথ কারবার, ব্যবসায়ে অংশভাগিতা। **Long firm**—যে জুয়াচোরের দল ক্রীত জিনিষের মূল্য প্রদান করে না।

fir′-mă-mĕnt (fêr-), *n.* The vault of the sky with its clouds and stars ; নভোমণ্ডল, অন্তরীক্ষ, নক্ষত্রলোক, ভবলয় (স্থঃ সিঃ), ব্যোম (হিঃ কোঃ), ঘনাশ্রয় (কেশিঃ)। **—men′-tal,** *adj.*

fir′-măn (fêr-), *n.* A license, grant or edict of an oriental sovereign, as of Turkey ; সম্রাট বা বাদশাহের হুকুম, ফর্ম্মান।

first (fêrst), *adj., n.* & *adv.* 1. Earliest in time or succession ; প্রথম, সর্ব্বপ্রথম, আদ্য। 2. Foremost in rank, position, importance or worth ; as, the *first* man in the country ; সর্ব্বপ্রধান, অগ্রগণ্য, বরেণ্য, মুখ্য, অগ্রণী, শীর্ষস্থানীয়। 3. Coming next after a specified time ; as, he shall take the *first* train ; নির্দ্দিষ্ট সময়ান্তে যেটা প্রথম আসে সেই। ***Noun.*** 1. A person or thing that is mentioned first ; the beginning ; প্রথমোক্ত ব্যক্তি বা বস্তু, প্রথম ব্যক্তি বা বস্তু ; প্রারম্ভ। 2. A place in the first class in an examination list ; one who takes this place ; পরীক্ষোত্তীর্ণ ব্যক্তিগণের তালিকায় প্রথম বিভাগের সর্ব্বপ্রথম স্থান ; পরীক্ষায় সর্ব্বপ্রথম স্থানাধিকারী ব্যক্তি। 3. The first day of a month ; মাসের ১লা তারিখ। 4. (*Pl.*) The best quality of an article, as butter etc. ; কোন জিনিষের সর্ব্বোৎকৃষ্ট প্রকার। ***Adv.*** 1. Before all other time, place, etc. ; সর্ব্বাগ্রে, সর্ব্বপ্রথমে। 2. For the first time ; সর্ব্বপ্রথম। 3. Rather ; বরং। **First′-ly,** *adv.* In the first place ; প্রথমতঃ, আদৌ। **First aid**—হঠাৎ আঘাতপ্রাপ্ত বা ব্যাধিগ্রস্ত ব্যক্তিকে চিকিৎসকের আগমনের পূর্ব্বে যে সাহায্য প্রদান করা হয়। **First-born**—First brought forth ; eldest ; সর্ব্বপ্রথম সন্তান, সর্ব্বাগ্রজ ; জ্যেষ্ঠ। **First-cause**—See under CAUSE. **First-chap**—First rate ; প্রথমশ্রেণীর। **First-class**—*n., adj.* & *adv.* প্রথম শ্রেণীর গাড়ী ; প্রথম বিভাগ ; প্রথম স্থানপ্রাপ্ত ব্যক্তি। 2. A set of persons or things grouped together as better than others ; প্রথম শ্রেণীর বস্তু বা ব্যক্তি সমূহ। (*Adj.*) উৎকৃষ্ট ; প্রথম শ্রেণীর ; প্রথম শ্রেণী সম্পর্কীয়। (*Adv.*) প্রথম শ্রেণীতে। **First-coat**—First layer of a paint ; রঙ্গের প্রথম পোঁচ। **First-day**—রবিবার। **First-floor**—দ্বিতল, দোতলা। **First-form**—বিদ্যালয়ের সর্ব্বনিম্ন শ্রেণী। **First-fruit**—(Usu. *pl.*) বৎসরের প্রথম উৎপন্ন শস্য বা ফল ; নবান্ন (মঃ সং) ; প্রথম লাভ ; যাজকীয় বৃত্তি প্রভৃতির প্রথম বর্ষের আয় ; (ইতিহাস) কোন পদে নবনিযুক্ত ব্যক্তি কর্তৃক ঊর্দ্ধতন কর্ম্মচারীকে প্রদত্ত অর্থ। **First-hand**—মূল স্থান হইতে প্রাপ্ত নির্ম্মাণকারী বা উৎপাদনকারীর নিকট হইতে প্রাপ্ত। (*At first hand*—মূল স্থান হইতে, সাক্ষাৎসম্বন্ধে)। **First intention** — প্রথম অভিপ্রায়। **First-night**—প্রথম অভিনয়রজনী। **First-nighter**—যে ব্যক্তি প্রতি অভিনয়ের প্রথম রজনীতে রঙ্গালয়ে গমন করিয়া থাকে, প্রথমরজনীগামী। **First-rate**—সর্ব্বশ্রেষ্ঠ, প্রথম শ্রেণীর, অত্যুত্তম। **First-water** — (হীরকাদি সম্বন্ধে) প্রথম শ্রেণীর, অতিশয় উজ্জ্বল, সর্ব্বশ্রেষ্ঠ। **At first** or **at the first**—প্রথমতঃ, আদৌ। **At (the) first sight, view** or **blush**—At the first appearance, view or consideration ; প্রথমদৃষ্টিতে, আপাতদৃষ্টিতে। **First and last**—Altogether ; সর্ব্বথা, সর্ব্বতোভাবে। **First come first served** — যে প্রথম আসে তাহার কাজ প্রথম করা হয়। **First Gentleman of Europe**—ইংলণ্ডেশ্বর চতুর্থ জর্জ্জের উপনাম। **First of all, First and foremost**—Before all others ; সর্ব্বাগ্রে, সর্ব্বপ্রথম, সর্ব্বোপরি। **First or last**—At one time or another ; এক সময়ে না এক সময়ে। **First stroke is half the battle** — Well begun is half done ; কোন কাজ ভালরূপে আরম্ভ করা হইলে উহা অতি সহজেই সম্পন্ন হয়। **Head etc. first**—With head in front ; মস্তক সম্মুখে। **In the first place**—To begin with ; প্রথমতঃ, আদৌ। **I shall do it first thing** — (*Colloq.*) I shall do it before anything else ; (চলিত ভাষায়) সকলের আগে এই কাজ সমাধা করিব। **To come in first**—To win a race ; ঘোড়দৌড়ে জিতা।

first′-ling (fêrst-), *n.* The first produce or result of anything ; first offspring, esp. of animals ; প্রথম উৎপন্ন বস্তু, কোন কার্য্যের প্রথম ফল ; প্রথমজাত শাবক, পহিলা বাচ্চা।

th (fêrth), **frith**, *ns.* An arm f the sea ; খাড়ী, সমুদ্রের বাহু, াগের শাখা।

sc, fisk, *ns.* **1.** The treasury of state ; the exchequer (*rare*) ; ধন-ভাণ্ডার ; রাজকোষ (অপ্রঃ)। **2.** The treasury of ancient Rome ; প্রাচীন রোমের ধনাগার।

fis'-căl, *adj.* & *n.* Pertaining to the public treasury or revenue ; রাজস্ববিষয়ক, রাজস্বসম্বন্ধীয়, রাজস্ব-সংক্রান্ত। ***Noun.*** A legal official, as a public prosecutor in some foreign country ; সরকারী উকিল। **—ly,** *adv.* **Fiscal-system**—রাজকর প্রণালী (হিঃ কোঃ), রাজস্ব-প্রণালী।

fish, *n., v. t.* & *i.* (*Pl.* FISH, -ES), **1.** An animal that lives in water ; (more strictly) a vertebrate aquatic animal with gills, fins, etc. ; জলচর জন্তু ; মৎস্য, মাছ, মীন, ঝষ, পৃথুরোমা, বিসার, শকলী, অণ্ডজ। **2.** The flesh of fish used as food ; কাটা মাছ। **3.** (*Colloq.*) A man of certain kind ; (চলিত ভাষায়) এক রকমের লোক। **4.** [*Astron.* (*cap.*)] The twelfth sign of the zodiac ; (জ্যোতির্বিজ্ঞান) মীনরাশি। ***Verb t.*** **1.** To catch or try to catch fish in ; as, to *fish* a pool ; মৎস্য ধরা, মৎস্য ধরার চেষ্টা করা। **2.** To draw *out* or *up* from water or a deep place ; as, to *fish out* a thing from water or a pocket ; to get (*out*) ; as, to *fish out* a fact, opinion or secret ; জল বা গভীর স্থান হইতে টানিয়া তোলা ; পাওয়া। **3.** To search, as by raking, sweeping, etc. ; আঁচড়াইয়া বা ঝাঁটাইয়া খুঁজা। ***Verb i.*** **1.** To attempt to catch fish ; মাছ ধরার চেষ্টা করা। **2.** To search *for* anything in or under water ; as, to *fish for* pearls ; জলের মধ্যে অনুসন্ধান করা। **3.** To seek indirectly (with *for*) ; as, to *fish for* a compliment ; পরোক্ষভাবে চেষ্টা করা। **Fish'-a-ble** *adj.* মৎস্যধরণযোগ্য। **Fish'-er**, *n.* **1.** A fishing animal ; মৎস্যশিকারী জন্তু। **2.** (*Rare*) A fishing man ; (অপ্রঃ) মৎস্যজীবী, ধীবর, জেলে। **Fish'-er-y**, *n.* **1.** The business or industry of catching fish ; মৎস্য ধরার কার্য্য বা ব্যবসায়। **2.** A place for catching fish ; মৎস্যধরার স্থান, মৎস্যস্থলী। **3.** (*Law*) The right to catch fish in certain water ; (আইন) কোন কোন জলাশয়ে মৎস্যধরার অধিকার। **Fish'-i-ly,** *adv.* **Fish'-i-ness**, *n.* **Fish'-ing** *adj.* Used in fishery ; engaged in fishing ; মৎস্য ব্যবসায়ে ব্যবহৃত, মৎস্য ধরায় ব্যবহৃত ; মৎস্য শিকারে নিযুক্ত। **Fish'-y**, *adj.* **1.** Consisting of fish ; fish-like ; abounding in fish ; মৎস্যপূর্ণ ; মৎস্যবৎ ; মৎস্যসমাকুল, মৎস্যবহুল। **2.** Tasting or smelling like a fish ; মৎস্যগন্ধী, মৎস্যাস্বাদ, আঁশটিয়া। **3.** (*Slang*) Of dubious character ; questionable ; (ইতরভাষায়) সন্দিগ্ধ ; সন্দেহযোগ্য। **4.** Dull ; vacant ; as, *fishy* eyes ; মন্দপ্রভ ; শূন্য। **Fish-bellied** — মৎস্যোদরের মত নিম্নদিকে স্ফীত। **Fish-carver**—মৎস্য কাটার জন্য বৃহৎ ছুরী, মৎস্য-কর্ত্তরিকা। **Fish-creel**—মাছের খালুই, মৎস্যাধানী (অমরঃ)। **Fish-day**—যে দিবস মাংসের পরিবর্ত্তে মৎস্য খাওয়া হয়, মৎস্যদিবস। **Fisherman** — জেলে, ধীবর। **Fish-fag**—মেছুনী, জেলেনী, ধীবরপত্নী। **Fish-garth**—মৎস্য রক্ষা বা ধরার জন্য সাগর বা নদীমধ্যস্থ বেষ্টিত স্থান। **Fish-gig**—টেঁটা। **Fish-globe**—যে কাচগোলকে জীবিত মৎস্য রক্ষিত হয়, মৎস্য গোলক। **Fish-glue**—Same as ISINGLASS which see. মাছের পটকা হইতে প্রস্তুত শিরীষ। **Fish hook**—বড়শী, মৎস্যবেধন, বড়িশ ; (নৌ-বিদ্যা) নোঙ্গরের যে অংশদ্বারা রজ্জু তোলা হয়। **Fishing boat**—জেলে ডিঙ্গী, জেলে নৌকা। **Fishing-line**—বড়শীর সূতা। **Fishing-net**—মৎস্য ধরার জাল। **Fishing-rod**—বড়শীর ছিপ। **Fishing-tackle**—মৎস্য ধরার জন্য জাল, ছিপ, সূতা, বড়শী ইত্যাদি সরঞ্জাম। **Fish-kettle**—মৎস্য পাক করার জন্য ডিম্বাকার পাত্র। **Fishknife**—মাছ কাটার ছুরী। **Fish-louse**—একপ্রকার মৎস্যবিনাশক পোকা। **Fish meal**—মৎস্য ভোজন। **Fishmonger** — মৎস্যবিক্রয়ী, ধীবর, মৎস্যব্যবসায়ী, মৎস্যজীবী। **Fish-pond**—মাছের পুকুর। **Fish-pot**—বাইন প্রভৃতি মাছ ধরার জন্য ঘুণি বা আটল। **Fish-slice**—ভোজনের সময় মাছ কাটার জন্য ছুরি ; মাছ উল্টাইবার জন্য যন্ত্রবিশেষ। **Fish-sound**—মাছের পটকা। **Fish-spear**—টেঁটা। **Fish-tail** — মৎস্য পুচ্ছাকৃতি ধারা (গ্যাস প্রভৃতি-সম্পর্কে)। **Fish-tail wind**—বন্দুক ছোঁড়ার মাঠে চাঁদমারির দিকে প্রবহমাণ পরিবর্তনশীল বায়ু। **Fish-torpedo**—মৎস্যাকৃতি স্বয়ংবহ জলবজ্রবিশেষ (See TORPEDO.) **Fish-trap** — ঘুণি, হোঁচা, আটল। **Fish-wife, —woman** — ধীবরপত্নী, মেছুনী, জেলেনী। **A fish out of water** — A person out of his element ; জলছাড়া মীন (কোনরূপ অপ্রীতিকর ও অস্বচ্ছন্দ অবস্থায় পতিত ব্যক্তি সম্বন্ধে উক্ত হয়)। **All's fish that comes to his net** — He takes all he can get ; সে যাহা পায় তাহাই গ্রহণ করে। **A loose-fish**—A man of loose character ; ব্যভিচারাসক্ত লোক, লম্পট ব্যক্তি। **A loose or queer fish**—A person of odd habits ; সৃষ্টিছাড়া লোক, মাথা পাগলা লোক। **A pretty kettle of fish**—Confusion ; muddle ; গোলমাল ; বিশৃঙ্খলা। **A ripe fish**—A fish with eggs ; ডিমওয়ালা মাছ, ডিমভরা মাছ। **Give your own fish-guts to your own sea-maws**—Give what you can spare to those who belong to you and not to others ; যাহা বাঁচাইতে পার তাহা তোমার নিজের আত্মীয় স্বজনকে দিও,—পরকে দিও না। **Neither fish, flesh, nor good red herring**—Having no definite character or qualities ; এও নয় তাও নয়, নির্দিষ্ট

গুণ বা প্রকৃতি বিহীন। **Neither fish nor fowl**—Difficult to classify ; odd ; শ্রেণী বিভাগ দুঃসাধ্য ; সৃষ্টিছাড়া। **Other fish to fry**—More important business to attend to ; অন্য কোন গুরুতর কাজ করিতে হইবে। **There is a good fish in the sea as ever came out of it**—There is no fear of scarcity ; অভাব কিম্বা আকালের ভয় নাই। **To drink like a fish**—To drink excessively ; অতিমাত্রায় মদ্যপান করা। **To feed the fishes**—To be drowned ; to be sea-sick ; জলমগ্ন হওয়া ; সমুদ্র-পীড়ায় আক্রান্ত হওয়া। **To fish for**—To seek ; অনুসন্ধান করা, অন্বেষণ করা, খুঁজা, তল্লাস করা। To search out ; খুঁজিয়া বাহির করা। **To fish out**—To exhaust the supply of fish by fishing ; মৎস্যশূন্য করা। **To fish for compliments**—To induce others indirectly to praise one ; কাহাকেও প্রশংসা করার জন্য অন্যকে পরোক্ষভাবে প্ররোচিত করা। **To fish in troubled waters**—To make one's profit out of disturbances ; কোনরূপ গোলযোগ ও দেশবাসীর বিপদের সময় ব্যক্তিগত সুবিধা লাভের জন্য চেষ্টা করা। **To fish the anchor**—(*Naut.*) To draw flukes up to gunwale ; (নৌ-বিদ্যা) নোঙ্গরের হুল-ফলা জাহাজের পার্শ্বদেশের উপরিভাগে রাখা। **To make fish of one and flesh of another**—To make invidious distinction ; to show undue partiality ; ঈর্ষামূলক পক্ষপাত করা ; অনুচিত পক্ষপাত প্রদর্শন করা।

fish, *n.* & *v. t.* **1.** (*Naut.*) A piece of timber used to strengthen a mast etc. ; (নৌ-বিদ্যা) মাস্তুলদণ্ড প্রভৃতি দৃঢ়ীকরণার্থ কাষ্ঠখণ্ড। **2.** A piece of wood etc. fastened to another for strengthening it ; কাষ্ঠখণ্ড দৃঢ়ীকরণার্থ উহাতে সম্বদ্ধ অপর কাষ্ঠখণ্ড। ***Verb t.*** To strengthen or mend, as a spar etc. with a fish ; to join (rails etc.) with a fish ; কাঠের বাতা লাগাইয়া দৃঢ় করা ; (পাতা রেল প্রভৃতি) চ্যাপ্টা লৌহ ফলক আঁটিয়া জোড়া দেওয়া। **Fish-plate**—বর্গা লৌহবন্ধের পাতা রেল প্রভৃতির জোড়ার উপর দিকে পেরেকদ্বারা আঁটা চ্যাপ্টা লৌহফলক।

fish, *n.* A counter used in various games ; বিভিন্ন প্রকার ক্রীড়ায় গণনার জন্য ব্যবহৃত ধাতু বা গজদন্ত খণ্ড।

fisk, *n.* See FISC.

fis'-sile, *adj.* Capable of being split or cleft, as wood etc. ; বিদার্য্য। **—sil'-i-ty,** *n.* cleavableness ; বিদারণশীলতা, বিদার্য্যতা।

fis'-sion (fi-), *n.* **1.** A cleaving or breaking up in two parts ; খণ্ডশঃ বিদারণ। **2.** (*Biol.*) The division of a cell into new cells as a mode of reproduction ; (জীব-বিজ্ঞান) পুনরুৎপাদনের জন্য জীবদেহের অনুকোষের নূতন অনুকোষসমূহে বিভাজন। **—sive,** *adj.*

fis-sip'-a-rous (-rŭs) *adj.* Reproducing by fission ; অনুকোষ সমূহ বিভাজন দ্বারা পুনরুৎপাদনকারী।

fis'-si-pĕd, *adj.* (*Zool.*) Cloven-footed ; (প্রাণিবিজ্ঞান) খণ্ডিত-ক্ষুর, দ্বিশফ।

fis'-sure (fi-shür), *n., v. t.* & *i.* **1.** A cleft ; a longitudinal opening ; as, the *fissure* of a rock ; ফাটা, ফাইট, ফাটোল ; ফাঁক, চির। **2.** Cleavage ; বিদারণ। ***Verb t. & i.*** To cleave ; to divide ; বিদারণ করা, বিদীর্ণ হওয়া ; বিভক্ত করা বা হওয়া।

fist, *n.* & *v. t.* **1.** A clenched hand esp. as used in boxing ; মুষ্টি, মুঠা। **2.** Handwriting ; as, he writes a good *fist* ; হস্তলিপি। **3.** (*Colloq.*) The hand ; (চলিত-ভাষায়) হাত। ***Verb t.*** **1.** To strike with the fist ; মুষ্ট্যাঘাত করা, ঘুষি মারা। **2.** (*Naut.*) To handle ; as to *fist* an oar ; (নৌ-বিদ্যা) হস্ত দ্বারা ব্যবহার করা। **Fist'-ing,** *adj.* Pertaining to boxing (*humourous*) ; (কৌতুকচ্ছলে) মুষ্টি-যুদ্ধ সম্পর্কীয়। **Fist-law**—The right of the strongest ; জোর যার মুলুক তার—এই নীতি। **I know his fist**—See FIST, *n.* 2. **Give us your fist**—Shake hands with us ; আমাদের সহিত করকম্পন কর।

fis-ti-a'-na, *n.* Anecdotes about boxing and boxer ; মুষ্টা-মুষ্টির কাহিনী, মুষ্টিযোদ্ধার গল্প।

fist'-i-cŭff, *n.* A blow with the fist ; মুষ্ট্যাঘাত, ঘুষি। (*Pl.*) Boxing ; ঘুষাঘুষি।

fis'-tü-la, *n.* **1.** A pipe or spout ; নল, মুখনল। **2.** (*Surg.*) A deep narrow sinuous pipe-like ulcer ; নালী ঘা, নাড়ীব্রণ (হঃ চঃ)। **—lar, —lous,** *adjs.* Hollow like a pipe or reed ; নল বা বাঁশীর মত শূন্যগর্ভ। Having the form of a fistula ; নালীক্ষত সদৃশ। **Fistula-in-ano**—মলদ্বারে নালীক্ষত, ভগন্দর।

fit, *adj.* **1.** Well adapted ; suitable ; competent ; worthy ; উপযোগী ; উপযুক্ত ; যোগ্য ; গুণসম্পন্ন। **2.** Proper ; becoming ; সমুচিত, যথাযোগ্য, যথোচিত, সঙ্গত, বিহিত ; সমীচীন, শোভন। **3.** Ready ; prepared ; প্রস্তুত ; সজ্জিত। **4.** In good condition ; in good health ; ভাল অবস্থায় ; সুস্থ। **5.** Angry ; troubled or exhausted enough (*to* do something) ; as, he was *fit* to strike you or drop you to the ground ; ক্রুদ্ধ ; বিরক্ত বা অবসন্ন। **Fit'-ly,** *adv.* In a fit manner ; suitably ; যথাযোগ্যভাবে, যথানুরূপ, সমুচিতরূপে ; সমীচীনরূপে, বিহিতরূপে। **Fit as a fiddle**—ভাল অবস্থায়, খোস্ মোজাজে। **Is not fit to hold a candle to**—See under CANDLE.

fit, *v. t., i.* & *n.* **1.** To be suitable to ; to befit ; to suit ; "Such boldness does not *fit* a stranger" ; the coat *fits* you ; উপযোগী হওয়া ; মানান, সাজা ; ঠিক লাগা। **2.** To make fit or suitable ; to qualify ; অনুরূপ

করা, যোগ্য করা; উপযুক্ত করা, যথাযোগ্য করা, যোগ্যতাসম্পন্ন করা। **3.** To adapt *(to)*; as, to *fit* conduct to circumstances; উপযোগী করা। **4.** To shape; to adjust; as, the tailor *fits* the belt best; গঠন করা; ঠিকঠাক করা। **5.** To supply, as a ship or, rarely, a person *with* something fit or suitable; উপযুক্ত দ্রব্যাদি যোগান, উপযুক্ত দ্রব্যাদি সরবরাহ করা। ***Verb i.*** **1.** To be proper or becoming; সঙ্গত হওয়া, সমীচীন হওয়া, শোভন হওয়া। **2.** To suit; to be adapted; as the coat *fits* well; উপযোগী হওয়া; মানানসই হওয়া, মানান। ***Noun.*** Adjustment; adaptation; the style in which a dress fits; "Ashamed of his rustic *fit*"; ঠিকঠাক করণ; উপযোগীকরণ; পোষাক লাগার ধরণ। **Fit'-ter,** *n.* One who fits on articles of dress or adjusts the parts of a machine; যে ব্যক্তি পোষাক ঠিক গায়ে লাগে কিনা দেখে, যে ব্যক্তি যন্ত্রের বিভিন্ন অংশ ঠিক করিয়া লাগায়। **Fit-out**—Equipment; সাজসজ্জা। **To be fit**—To be in good health; to be worthy; শারীরিক সুস্থ থাকা; উপযুক্ত হওয়া, যোগ্য হওয়া। **To fit in with**—To agree exactly with; ঠিক মিলা। **To fit on**—To try on (a garment) in order to see whether it fits the person; পোষাক ঠিক লাগে কিনা গায়ে দিয়া দেখা। **To fit out**—To equip; সজ্জিত করা। **To fit up**—To supply with necessary fittings, furniture, or stores; as to *fit up* a room; আবশ্যকীয় সাজসরঞ্জাম, আসবাবপত্র দ্বারা সজ্জিত করা।

fit, *n.* **1.** A sudden temporary attack of disease; a paroxysm; a stroke of hysteria, epilepsy, etc. attended with unconsciousness or convulsions; রোগের হঠাৎ আক্রমণ; প্রকোপ; মূর্চ্ছা, তড়কা। **2.** A passing humour or caprice; as, when the *fit* was on him; an outburst; as, a *fit* of laughter; খেয়াল, হিড়িক; উচ্ছ্বাস। **Fit'-ful,** *adj.* Full of fits; spasmodic; variable; অস্থির, চপল, চঞ্চল; সবিরাম; খামখেয়ালী, পরিবর্ত্তনশীল। **A fit of the face** — Grimace; মুখভঙ্গী। **By fits and starts** — Spasmodically; অনিয়মিতরূপে, থাকিয়া থাকিয়া। **Survival of the fittest**—যোগ্যতমাবশেষ (হিঃ কোঃ), যোগ্যতমাতিজীবন (ঐ), যোগ্যতমের উদ্বর্ত্তন।

fitch (fĭch), *n.* **1.** The polecat; its fur; গন্ধগোকুলা, গন্ধমার্জ্জার, খট্টাশ; ঐ জন্তুর লোম। **2.** A small brush made of the hair of the fitch; উক্ত জন্তুর লোমদ্বারা প্রস্তুত ক্ষুদ্র বুরুষ।

fitch'-ew (fĭch-ü), *n.* A polecat; গন্ধগোকুলা।

fil'-mĕnt, 1. *n.* A piece of furniture; মেজ, কেদারা প্রভৃতি সাজসজ্জা; **2.** *(Pl.)* fittings; সাজসজ্জা।

fit'-nĕss, *n.* **1.** State of being fit; উপযোগিতা, সমীচীনতা, শোভনতা। **2.** Appropriateness; propriety; ঔচিত্য; শোভনতা। **3.** *(Ethics)* Moral worthiness; (নীতি-শাস্ত্র) নৈতিক গুণবত্তা। **Consciousness** or **sense of fitness** — যোগ্যতাবুদ্ধি (হিঃ কোঃ), ঔচিত্যবুদ্ধি (ঐ)।

fit'-ting, *adj.* & *n.* Fit; becoming; proper; উপযুক্ত; যোগ্য, শোভন; সঙ্গত, সমুচিত। ***Noun.*** Anything used in fitting up; *(esp. in pl.)* fixtures or apparatus; furniture; সাজসজ্জার জন্য ব্যবহৃত দ্রব্য; সরঞ্জাম; আসবাব। **—ly,** *adv.* In a fitting manner; যথোপযুক্তরূপে। **Fitting-place**—*(Engineering)* A place where parts are put together; (পূর্ত্ত-বিদ্যা) যে স্থানে যন্ত্রের বিভিন্ন অংশ লাগান হয়।

five, *adj.* & *n.* One more than four; পঞ্চ, পাঁচ। ***Noun.*** **1.** The number next to four; পঞ্চম। **2.** The symbol representing five; ৫ এই সংখ্যা। **3.** A set of five things; পঞ্চদ্রব্য। **4.** A card with five pips; তাসের পাঞ্জা। **5.** *(Cricket)* A hit for which five runs are scored (also called FIVER); (ক্রীকেট ক্রীড়ায়) যে আঘাতে ৫টা জয়াঙ্ক লব্ধ হয়। **6.** *(Pl.)* Gloves or shoes of the fifth size; (also) five per cent.; ৫ নম্বরের দস্তানা বা জুতা; শতকরা পাঁচ। **7.** A five-pound note (also called FIVER); পাঁচ পাউণ্ড মূল্যের নোট। **Fiv'-er,** *n.* See FIVE, *n.* 5 and 7. **Five-finger**—A kind of plant; একপ্রকার গুল্ম। A star-fish; তারা-মাছ। **Five penny**—Costing or worth 5*d.*; ৫ পেন্স মূল্যের। **Five-per cents**—Stock or shares paying 5%; শতকরা পাঁচ পাউণ্ড মূল্যের কোম্পানীর কাগজ। **A bunch of fives**—Hand; হস্ত। **Five-and-twenty** — Twenty-five; পঁচিশ। **Five-fold** — Consisting of five in one; পঞ্চগুণিত। **Five-o'clock tea**—A light afternoon meal; অপরাহ্ণ বেলার জলযোগ। **Five-finger exercise**—An exercise on a piano for practising all fingers; পিয়ানোতে সকল অঙ্গুলি চালনার অভ্যাস।

fives (fīvz), *n.* A game at ball in which the ball is struck against a wall; একপ্রকার কন্দুক ক্রীড়া—যাহাতে কন্দুক প্রাচীরে অভিহত করা হয়।

fix, *v. t., i.* & *n.* **1.** To make firm or fast; to fasten; as, to *fix* a post in the ground; to direct or hold steadily; as, to *fix* one's eye or attention on an object; দৃঢ় করা, স্থায়ী করা; আবদ্ধ করা, সংবদ্ধ করা লাগান, আঁটা; নিবদ্ধ করা। **2.** To place definitely or permanently; as, to *fix* one's residence in a place; to settle; as, to *fix* a date, price or place, etc.; প্রতিষ্ঠিত করা, সংস্থাপন করা; ধার্য্য করা, নির্দ্ধারিত করা। **3.** To determine the form of; as, a *fixed* idiom;

রূপ নির্দ্ধারণ করা। **4.** (*Chem.*) To render solid ; as, to *fix* nitrogen ; (রসায়ন-শাস্ত্র) কঠিন করা, ঘন করা, জমাট করা, সংহত করা। **5.** To make permanent or fast ; as, to *fix* a colour or photographic image ; স্থায়ী করা, পাকা করা। **6.** To place or settle (with *on* or *upon*) ; as, to *fix* a crime on a person ; স্থাপন করা। **7.** (*U. S.* often with *up*) To arrange ; to adjust ; (*colloq.*) to set right ; as, to *fix* the furniture of a room ; (মার্কিণ যুক্তরাজ্য) সুবিন্যস্ত করা ; ঠিকঠাক করা ; (চলিত ভাষায়) দুরস্ত করা। ***Verb i.*** **1.** To become firm ; to settle permanently ; দৃঢ়প্রতিষ্ঠিত হওয়া ; চিরস্থায়ী হওয়া। **2.** To decide ; as, he *fixes* to do that ; নির্দ্ধারণ করা, স্থির করা। **3.** To congeal ; শক্ত হওয়া, জমিয়া যাওয়া। ***Noun.*** A dilemma ; a difficulty ; as, to be in a *fix* ; সমস্যা ; ফাঁপর, মুস্কিল, সঙ্কট। **Fix'-a-ble,** *adj.* **Fix'-er,** *n.* **Fix'-i-ty,** *n.* **1.** Fixedness ; stability ; দৃঢ়বত্তা ; দৃঢ়বদ্ধতা। **2.** The property of enduring heat without volatilization or loss of weight ; উদ্বায়িতা-শূন্যতা। **To be in a fix**—See FIX, *n.* **To fix on** or **upon**—To fix one's choice on or upon ; কোন জিনিষ পসন্দ করা।

fix-ā'-tion, *n.* **1.** The state of being fixed ; the act of fixing ; as, *fixation* of attention etc. ; স্থির ভাব ; স্থিরীকরণ। **2.** Solidification ; as, the *fixation* of mercury ; ঘনীভূত করণ। **Fixation point**—দৃষ্টিযোগ স্থান (হিঃ কোঃ)। **Fixation of memories**—স্মৃতি-স্থৈর্য্য (হিঃ কোঃ)।

fix'-ā-tive (-tĭv), *adj.* & *n.* Tending to fix ; সংবদ্ধকারক। ***Noun.*** A substance used for fixing colours etc. ; রং প্রভৃতি পাকা করার মসলা।

fix'-ā-türe, *n.* A preparation for stiffening the hair etc. ; কেশ শক্ত করিবার সামগ্রী-বিশেষ।

fixed (fĭkst), *adj.* **1.** Firmly placed or fastened ; settled ; unalterable ; দৃঢ়-প্রতিষ্ঠিত, দৃঢ়-বদ্ধ, অচল-প্রতিষ্ঠ ; নির্দ্ধারিত, ধার্য্য ; অটল, ধ্রুব, অপরিবর্ত্তনীয়, নিশ্চল। **2.** (*Chem.*) Deprived of volatility ; (রসায়ন-শাস্ত্র) উদ্বায়িতাশূন্য। **Fix'-ed-ly,** *adv.* In a fixed manner ; firmly ; intently ; as, to look *fixedly* at a person ; বদ্ধভাবে ; দৃঢ়ভাবে ; একাগ্রচিত্তে, অনন্যমনে। **Fix'-ed-ness,** *n.* The state of being fixed ; permanence ; steadfastness ; স্থিরতা, অটলতা ; চিরস্থায়িতা ; দৃঢ়তা। **Fixed air**—Carbonic acid or carbon-dioxide, so called by Dr. Black ; অঙ্গারাম্ল, অঙ্গারাম্ল বায়ু। **Fixed idea**—One tending to become a monomania ; যে ভাব কতকটা এক বিষয়াত্মক বাতুলতায় পরিণত হইয়া উঠে, স্থিরভ্রান্তপ্রত্যয় (হিঃ কোঃ)। **Fixed oil** or **acid**—যে তৈল বাষ্পাকারে উড়িয়া যায় না, অনুদ্বায়ী তৈল। **Fixed point**—One where a police-man is permanently stationed ; যে স্থানে পুলিস প্রহরী স্থায়ীভাবে স্থাপিত হয়। **Fixed stars**—অচল নক্ষত্রপুঞ্জ, স্থির নক্ষত্র (হিঃ কোঃ), অচল নক্ষত্র (সূর্য্যসিদ্ধান্ত) [অর্থাৎ যে সকল নক্ষত্রের পরস্পরের সহিত আপেক্ষিক দূরত্ব নিয়ত একরূপ থাকে]।

fix'-ing, *n.* **1.** Act or process of making fixed ; দৃঢ়ীকরণ। **2.** (*Pl.*) (*U. S.*) Trimmings ; accompaniments ; equipment ; apparatus ; ফিতা, জরি প্রভৃতি ; আনুষঙ্গিক পদার্থ ; সাজসজ্জা ; যন্ত্র।

fix'-ture (-tür), *n.* **1.** That which is fixed or attached to something permanently ; দৃঢ়নিবদ্ধ বস্তু। **2.** (*Law pl.*) (আইন—বহুবচনে) ঘর কিম্বা ভূমিতে সংবদ্ধ অথবা সংগ্রথিত দ্রব্য। **3.** The state of being fixed ; দৃঢ়তা। **4.** A thing or person firmly established in a place ; স্থাবর বস্তু, এক পদে সুদীর্ঘকাল যাবৎ প্রতিষ্ঠিত ব্যক্তি। **4.** A settled date or time for anything to take place ; কোন কার্য্যের জন্য নির্দ্ধারিত দিবস।

fiz'-gig, *n.* **1.** A flirty girl ; চপলা বালিকা। **2.** A fire-work of damp powder ; একপ্রকার আতসবাজী।

fizz, *v. i.* & *n.* To make a hissing or sputtering sound ; ফোঁস্ ফোঁস্ শব্দ করা, সোঁ সোঁ করা। ***Noun.*** **1.** A hissing sound ; liveliness ; fuss ; ফোঁস্ ফোঁস্ শব্দ ; সজীবতা ; জটলা। **2.** Any frothy drink esp. champagne ; ফেনিল পানীয়, বিশেষতঃ স্যাম্পেন মদ্য। **Fizz'-y,** *adj.*

fiz'-zle (-zl), *v. i.* & *n.* To hiss or sputter ; ফোঁস্ ফোঁস্ করা, সোঁ সোঁ শব্দ করা। ***Noun.*** A hissing sound ; সোঁ সোঁ শব্দ, ফোঁস্ ফোঁস্ শব্দ। **To fizzle out**—To fail disgracefully ; লজ্জাজনকরূপে অকৃতকার্য্য হওয়া।

flăb'-bĕr-găst, *v. t.* To astonish utterly ; to confound ; অবাক করা ; বিস্ময়স্তম্ভিত করা, কিংকর্ত্তব্য-বিমূঢ় করা।

flăb'-bȳ, *adj.* Flaccid ; as, *flabby* flesh ; feeble ; as, *flabby* language or character ; ভস্‌কা, থলথলিয়া, শিথিল, লোল ; ক্ষীণ, দুর্ব্বল। **—bi-ly,** *adv.* **—bi-ness,** *n.*

flā-bĕl'-lāte, flā-bĕl'-li-fôrm, *adjs.* (*Bot.* & *Zool.*) Fan-shaped ; (উদ্ভিদ্‌ ও প্রাণিবিদ্যা) ব্যজনাকার।

flăc'-cĭd, *adj.* Hanging loose ; flabby ; soft ; drooping ; as, *flaccid* muscle or flesh ; wanting vigour ; weak ; শিথিল ; ভস্‌কা, থলথলিয়া, লোল ; কোমল ; শ্লথ ; নিস্তেজ ; দুর্ব্বল। **—cid'-i-ty,** *n.* Want of stiffness ; limpness ; want of vigour ; শিথিলতা ; লোলতা ; নির্জ্জীবতা।

flăg, *n., v. t.* & *i.* **1.** A wide strip of decorated fabric intended to float in the wind ; পতাকা, নিশান, বৈজয়ন্তী, ধ্বজা, কেতু, কেতন। 2. The ensign carried by a flag-ship : রণপোত বহরের অধিনায়কের জাহাজের পতাকা। *Verb t.* 1. To inform or communicate by means of flag signals ; as, to *flag* an order ; পতাকা-সঙ্কেতদ্বারা জ্ঞাপন করা। 2. To place a flag on or over ; as, to *flag* a house, a race-course, etc. : কোন কিছুর উপর পতাকা স্থাপন করা। 3. To signal to, with a flag ; as, to *flag* a train ; নিশান দ্বারা সঙ্কেত করা, পতাকা দ্বারা সঙ্কেত প্রদর্শন করা। *Verb i.* 1. To hang down; to flap loosely : as, *flagging* sail ; ঝুলিয়া পড়া, অবনত হওয়া, লোল হওয়া ; নড়বড় করা। 2. To lose vigour ; to droop ; to languish ; to fall off in interest, as an author or his work ; তেজোহীন হওয়া ; ম্লান হওয়া ; অলসাঙ্গ হওয়া ; কৌতূহল হ্রাস হওয়া। **Black Flag** — জলদস্যুদিগের কৃষ্ণপতাকা ; মৃত্যুদণ্ডে দণ্ডিত ব্যক্তির ফাঁসীর সময় কারাগৃহের বহির্দ্দেশে উড্ডীন পতাকা। **Black Flags**—Irregular Chinese soldiers ; চীনদেশের অব্যবস্থিত সৈন্য। **Flag-captain**—রণপোতবহরের অধিনায়কের জাহাজের অধ্যক্ষ। **Flag-lieutenant**—রণপোতবহরের সর্ব্বপ্রধান অধ্যক্ষের আজ্ঞাবহ কর্ম্মচারী। **Flag-man**—ঘোড়দৌড় প্রভৃতিতে পতাকাধারী ব্যক্তি। **Flag-officer**—সমরপোতশ্রেণীর অধিনায়ক যথা, Admiral, Vice-admiral or Rear-admiral। **Flag ship** — রণপোতসমূহের অধিনায়কের নিজস্ব পোত। **Flagstaff**—পতাকাদণ্ড, ধ্বজাদণ্ড, ধ্বজযষ্টি। **Flag-station**—যে স্থানে পতাকা প্রদর্শন করিলে গাড়ী থামিয়া থাকে। **Flag-waver** — পতাকা আন্দোলনকারী। **Red flag**—বিপৎসূচক রক্তপতাকা ; যুদ্ধাহ্বানসূচক রক্তধ্বজা ; রাষ্ট্রবিপ্লবসূচক লোহিত পতাকা। **White flag**—যুদ্ধবিশ্রান্তিসূচক শ্বেতপতাকা। **Yellow flag**—স্পর্শ সংক্রামক রোগের সময় পোতোপরি উড্ডীন পীতপতাকা। **Flag of distress**—বিপৎকালে উড্ডীন পতাকা। **Flag-wagging**—Signalling ; সঙ্কেতপ্রদান। **To dip the flag**—To lower the flag and quickly restore it to its place as a token of respect ; সম্মান-প্রদর্শনার্থ পতাকা উন্নমিত ও পরে উত্থিত করা। **To hang out the red flag**—To give a challenge to battle ; to intimate danger ; যুদ্ধার্থ আহ্বান করা ; বিপৎসঙ্কেত প্রদান করা। **To hang out the white flag**—To ask truce or manifest friendly design by exhibiting or fixing a white flag ; শ্বেতপতাকা প্রদর্শন পূর্ব্বক আত্মসমর্পণ করা অথবা যুদ্ধবিশ্রান্তি প্রার্থনা করা। **To hang the flag half-mast-high or half-staff**—To raise it only half-way to the top of the mast or staff as a token or sign of mourning ; শোক চিহ্নস্বরূপ ধ্বজাবস্ত্র পতাকাদণ্ডের অথবা মাস্তুলের মধ্য ভাগে বদ্ধ করা। **To hoist or strike one's flag**—To assume or relinquish command ; অধিনায়কতা গ্রহণ বা পরিত্যাগ করা। **To strike or lower the flag**—To take it down as a salute or sign of surrender ; সম্মান-প্রদর্শন বা আত্মসমর্পণের জন্য পতাকা অবনত করা।

flăg, *n.* 1. An aquatic plant with sword-shaped leaves, particularly a species of Iris ; জলজ অসি-পত্র উদ্ভিদবিশেষ, বিশেষতঃ এক জাতীয় দশবাই চণ্ডী। 2. A long slender blade of a plant ; অসিফলকাকৃতি বৃক্ষপত্র [cf. অসিপত্র = *Sugarcane*]। **Fla'-gy,** *adj.*

flăg, *n.* The quill-feather of a bird's wing ; (also called *flag feather*) ; পাখীর বড় পালক—যাহা হইতে কলম তৈয়ার হয়।

flăg, *n.* & *v. t.* 1. A flat slab of stone for paving (also called *flag-stone*) ; টালি পাথর। 2. (*Pl.*) A pavement made of flag-stone ; টালি পাথরে বাঁধানো মেঝে। *Verb t.* To pave with flag-stone ; টালি পাথরদ্বারা বাঁধান। **flag'-ging,** *n.* Flag-stone ; টালি পাথর।

flăg'-ĕl-lănt, *adj.* & *n.* Scourging oneself ; given to scourging ; (নিজ অঙ্গে) বেত্রাঘাতকারী ; বেত্রাঘাততৎপর। *Noun.* One who scourges himself ; (পাপের প্রায়শ্চিত্তস্বরূপ যে ব্যক্তি নিজ অঙ্গে বেত্রাঘাত করে।

flăg'-ĕl-lāte, *v. t.* To whip ; to scourge : কষাঘাত করা ; বেত্রাঘাত করা। **—la'-tion,** *n.* Whipping ; scourging ; বেত্রাঘাত ; কষাঘাত। **—la-tor,** *n.* One who practices flagellation ; বেত্রাঘাতকারী, কষাঘাতকারী। **—la-to-ry,** *adj.*

flā-gĕl'-lŭm, *n.* 1. (*Bot.*) A long thread-like shoot ; (উদ্ভিদ বিদ্যা) সুদীর্ঘ সূত্রবৎ প্ররোহ। **Flag'-el-late, —li-form,** *adjs.*

flăg-eo-lĕt' (-ŏ-), *n.* A small

Flageolet.

wind instrument of music with a mouthpiece ; একপ্রকার বাঁশী।

flăg'-eo-lĕt' (-ŏ-), *n.* A kidney-bean ; মুগ।

flā-gĭ'-tious (-shŭs), *adj.* 1. Deeply criminal ; atrocious ; grossly wicked, as an act or desire ; ঘোরতর অপরাধী ; অতি নিষ্ঠুর, অতি দুর্ব্বৃত্ত ; অতিশয় দুষ্ট, মহাদুর্জ্জন, মহাপাপী, পাপিষ্ঠ। 2. Corrupt ; profligate villainous, as a person; দুশ্চরিত্র ভ্রষ্ট ; লম্পট ; দুরাচার, মহাপাতকী। **—ly,** *adv.* **—ness,** *n.*

flăg'-ŏn, *n.* A vessel for liquors with a handle, a spout and a lid ; a bulging bottle ; (*as a measure*) two quarts; কুঁজো, সোরাই ; এক প্রকার ন্যুব্জাকৃতি বোতল ; দুই কোয়ার্ট।

flā'-grănt, *adj.* Glaring ; enormous ; scandalous ; as, *flagrant* blunder, offence or offender ; জলন্ত

ঘোর, মহা ; কলঙ্কজনক। **–gran-cy,** *n.* Atrocity ; heinousness ; enormity ; অমানুষিক অত্যাচার ; ক্রূরতা ; বিকটতা। **–ly,** *adv.* In a flagrant manner ; অমানুষিক ভাবে।

flail (flāl), *n.* A wooden instrument for thrashing or beating grain from the ear by hand ; শীষ হইতে শস্য ঝাড়িয়া বাহির করার জন্য যন্ত্র বিশেষ।

flair (flâr), *n.* Instinctive discernment ; হৃৎস্থিত সহজজ্ঞানজাত সূক্ষ্মদর্শিতা।

flāke, *n., v. t.* & *i.* **1.** A layer of anything ; a scale ; a thin broad piece peeled off ; a light fleecy particle esp. of snow ; as, a *flake* of a fish, tallow or snow ; পর্দা ; আঁইশ, শল্ক ; চিল্‌তা ; বরফের ছিল্‌কা। **2.** A particle of burning matter thrown off ; অগ্নিকণা, স্ফুলিঙ্গ। **3.** (*Horti.*) A kind of carnation having white petals ; (উদ্যানবিদ্যা) একপ্রকার পুষ্প। ***Verb t.*** **1.** To form into flakes ; to take off in flakes or layers ; শল্কাকারে গঠিত হওয়া ; ছিল্‌কা উঠান। **2.** To cover with or as with flakes (of snow etc.) ; ছিল্‌কা দ্বারা আবৃত করা, শল্কবৎ আবৃত করা। ***Verb i.*** To fall like flakes ; to scale off ; ছিল্‌কার মত খসিয়া পড়া ; আঁইশের ন্যায় উঠিয়া যাওয়া। **Flak′-y,** *adj.* **Flake-white—** সফেদা হইতে প্রাপ্ত শল্কাকার রঞ্জক পদার্থ।

flāke, *n.* A rack for storing provisions etc ; a platform for drying fish etc. ; খাদ্য দ্রব্যাদি রাখার জন্য তাক ; মৎস্য প্রভৃতি শুষ্ক করার জন্য মঞ্চ।

Flambeau.

flăm, *n.* A false story ; a deception ; a trick ; মিথ্যা গল্প ; প্রতারণা, ছলনা।

flăm′-beau (-bō), *n.* A flaming torch ; জ্বলন্ত মশাল।

flăm-boy′-ănt, *adj.* & *n.* **1.** (*Of a style of Gothic architecture*) Marked by wavy flame-like lines ; (স্থপতি-বিদ্যা) তরঙ্গায়িত অগ্নিশিখাবৎ রেখাশ্রেণী বিশিষ্ট **2.** Gorgeously decorated or coloured ; সমুজ্জ্বল ভূষায় বিমণ্ডিত, সমুজ্জ্বল বর্ণে রঞ্জিত।

flāme, *n., v. i.* & *t.* **1.** A blaze ; fire ; অর্চ্চি, অগ্নিশিখা, দীপশিখা, জ্বালা, (হিঃ কোঃ), লব (হিঃ কোঃ) ; অগ্নি। **2.** A ray of light ; brilliance ; আলোকরশ্মি ; কিরণ, দ্যুতি, জ্যোতিঃ, প্রভা। **3.** Burning passion ; excitement ; ardour ; "In a *flame* of zeal" ; জ্বলন্ত ক্রোধ ; প্রবলোত্তেজনা ; উদ্দীপনা। **4.** The passion of love ; প্রেমানল, অনুরাগ, প্রেম, প্রণয়। **5.** (*Joc.*) A sweet-heart ; as, an old *flame* of mine ; (রহস্যচ্ছলে) প্রেমিকা, প্রণয়ী, প্রেমিক। **6.** A kind of moth ; এক প্রকার তসরে কীট। ***Verb i.*** **1.** To blaze ; to burn with a flame ; শিখা বিস্তার করা ; জ্বলিয়া উঠা। **2.** To be kindled with rage or ardour ; as, he *flamed* with indignation ; to burst out as a passion ; "Their malice *flames* out" ; ক্রোধজ্বলিত হওয়া, উৎসাহদীপ্ত ; হওয়া রোষানল প্রদীপ্ত হওয়া, ক্রোধবহ্নি উদ্দীপ্ত হওয়া। **3.** To appear or move like a flame ; to shine brightly : শিখাবৎ প্রতীয়মান হওয়া ; উজ্জ্বল প্রভা বিস্তার করা। ***Verb t.*** **1.** To convey as a signal by flaming ; শিখাসঞ্চালন দ্বারা সঙ্কেত প্রদান করা। **2.** To subject to the action of flame ; অগ্নিতে সমর্পণ করা। **Flame′-less,** *adj.* Destitute of flame ; শিখাবিহীন। **Flam′-ing,** *adj.* **1.** Emitting flame ; very hot ; as, a *flaming* sun ; জ্বলন্ত, শিখাবিস্তারী ; অত্যুষ্ণ। **2.** Bright coloured, সমুজ্জ্বলবর্ণ, দীপ্তবর্ণ। **3.** Ardent ; passionate ; as, a *flaming* harangue ; exaggerated, as a description ; আগ্রহবান ; অত্যন্তানুরক্ত ; অত্যুক্তিপূর্ণ। **Flam′-ing-ly,** *adv.* **Flam′-ma-ble,** *adj.* **Flam′-y,** *adj.* Blazing ; flame-coloured ; অর্চিষ্মান, জ্বালাময়, জ্বলন্ত ; অগ্নিবর্ণ। **The flames**—Fire, esp. as consuming ; অগ্নি, বিশেষতঃ ধ্বংসজনক অগ্নি। **In flames**— On fire ; (*fig.*) inflamed with anger, passion or zeal ; জ্বলন্ত ; ক্রোধজ্বলিত, কামানল দগ্ধ, উৎসাহোদ্দীপ্ত। **To burst into flame** or **flames**—জ্বলিয়া উঠা। **To fan the flame**—To excite passion, emotion etc. ; জ্বলন্ত অনলে ঘৃতাহুতি প্রদান করা, ক্রোধানল বৃদ্ধি করা প্রেমাগ্নি সন্দীপিত করা। **To flame up**—To blush violently ; লজ্জারুণ হওয়া, লজ্জায় লাল হইয়া উঠা। **To flame out** or **up**—To break out into anger ; ক্রোধে জ্বলিয়া উঠা, রাগে তেলে বেগুনে জ্বলিয়া উঠা।

flāme′-lĕt, *n.* A small flame ; ক্ষুদ্র শিখা।

flā′-mĕn, *n.* (*Rom. Antiq.*) A priest devoted to some special god ; প্রাচীন রোমকদিগের বিশেষ দেবতার পুরোহিত।

Flamingo.

flă-min′-gō, *n.* A large long-legged and web-footed bird ; দীর্ঘ এবং লিপ্ত-পাদ পক্ষিবিশেষ।

flâ-neur′ (-nêr), **fla-ne-rie′** (flân-rī) *ns.* (*U. S.*) One who strolls about aimlessly ; (মার্কিণ যুক্তরাজ্যে ব্যবহৃত) যে ব্যক্তি নিষ্কর্ম্মার মত ঘুরিয়া বেড়ায়, ভবঘুরে।

flange (flănj), *n.* & *v. t.* A projecting edge or rim as of a wheel etc. ; চক্রাদির উদ্গত বা বহিঃপ্রসৃত প্রান্ত। ***Verb t.*** To furnish with a flange ; চক্রাদিতে উদ্গত প্রান্ত সংযোজিত করা। **Flanged,** *adj.*

flank (flăngk), *n.*, *v. i.* & *t.* 1. The fleshy part of the side of an animal between the ribs and the hip ; জন্তুদেহের পার্শ্বভাগস্থ মাংসল অংশ। 2. The side or wing, of a building, hill, etc. ; প্রাসাদ, পর্ব্বত প্রভৃতির পার্শ্বদেশ। 3. (*Mil.*) The right or left of an army, fleet etc. ; সৈন্যদল, রণতরী প্রভৃতির পার্শ্বদেশ। ***Verb i.*** 1. To be situated at the side of (with *on*) ; পার্শ্বদেশে অবস্থিত হওয়া, পার্শ্ববর্তী হওয়া। ***Verb t.*** 1. (*Mil.*) To attack or threaten the side of ; (সৈন্যের) পার্শ্বদেশে আক্রমণ করা। 2. (*Mil.*) To guard or strengthen the flank ; সৈন্যের পার্শ্বদেশ রক্ষা করা বা সুদৃঢ় করা। 3. (*Mil.*) To pass round the flank of ; (সৈন্যের) পার্শ্বদেশ বেষ্টন করিয়া চলা। **Flank'-er,** *n.* A fortification projecting so as to command the side of an assailing army ; a body of troops employed on the flank of an army to reconnoitre or guard a line of march ; যে বহিঃপ্রসৃত দুর্গ পরিখাদি হইতে আক্রমণকারী সৈন্যের পার্শ্বদেশ আক্রমণ করা যাইতে পারে; সৈন্যযাত্রাপথ রক্ষার্থ বা শত্রুসৈন্যের গতিবিধি পরিদর্শনার্থ সৈন্যদলের পার্শ্বভাগে নিযুক্ত লোকবর্গ। **Flank-movement**—শত্রুসৈন্যের পার্শ্বদেশ বেষ্টন বা আক্রমণের উদ্দেশ্যে সৈন্যচালনা। **In flank**—At the side ; পার্শ্বভাগে, পার্শ্বদেশে।

flăn'-nĕl, *n.* & *v. t.* 1. A soft woollen cloth of loose texture ; একপ্রকার গরম পশমী কাপড়, ফ্লানেল কাপড়। 2. (*Pl.*) Flannel underclothes ; ফ্লানেল কাপড়ের ভিতরের জামা, প্রভৃতি। 3. (*Pl.*) Garments of flannel ; esp. for games ; ফ্লানেল কাপড়ের পোষাক, বিশেষতঃ খেলোয়াড়দিগের। ***Verb t.*** To clothe or rub with flannel ; ফ্লানেলের পোষাক পরান, ফ্লানেল দ্বারা ঘষা। **—nelled,** *adj.* Covered or wrapped up in flannel ; made of flannel ; ফ্লানেল কাপড়ে আবৃত ; ফ্লানেল কাপড়ে তৈয়ারী। (*Flannelled fool*—ক্রীকেট খেলোয়াড় প্রভৃতি।) **—ly,** *adj.* Flannel-like; ফ্লানেলের মত। **Flan'-nel-ette,** *n.* A soft narrow flannel ; এক প্রকার কোমল ফ্লানেল।

flăp, *n.*, *v. t.* & *i.* 1. Something broad and flexible or a thing that hangs loose ; প্রশস্ত এবং নমনীয় বস্তু, শিথিলভাবে বিলম্বমান বস্তু 2. The motion or sound of anything broad and loose or a stroke with it ; পাখ্‌সাট্, ঝাপ্‌টা। 3. (*Pl.*) A disease in the lips of horses ; অশ্বের ওষ্ঠাধরের রোগবিশেষ। ***Verb t.*** To beat or strike with a flap ; as, to *flap* the wings ; পাখ্‌সাট্ মারা, পৎ পৎ করিয়া উড়ান। 3. To drive (*away*, *off*), as flies : তাড়ান। ***Verb i.*** To fly with wings beating the air ; to flutter ; to oscillate ; পৎ পৎ শব্দ করিয়া উড়িয়া যাওয়া ; পৎ পৎ শব্দ করা ; আন্দোলিত করা। 2. To fall and hang like a flap ; শিথিলভাবে ঝুলা।

flăp'-dōō-dle (-dl), *n.* Food for fools ; nonsense ; নির্ব্বোধের খাদ্য ; বাজে কথা।

flăp'-drăg-ŏn, *n.* & *v.t.* 1. A game in which raisins etc., are snatched from the burning brandy and swallowed ; একপ্রকার ক্রীড়া যাহাতে জ্বলন্ত ব্রাণ্ডী হইতে কিস্‌মিস্ প্রভৃতি তুলিয়া গলাধঃকরণ করা হয়। 2. The thing thus caught and eaten ; উক্ত প্রকার ক্রীড়ায় ভক্ষিত কিস্‌মিস্ প্রভৃতি। ***Verb t.*** To gulp ; গ্রাস করা, গলাধঃকরণ করা।

flăp'-pêr, *n.* 1. One that flaps ; (referring to *Laputans*) a person or thing rousing another's memory etc. by flapping ; যে অথবা যাহা ঝাপ্‌টা মারে ; যে বা যাহা ঝাপটা মারিয়া কোন ব্যক্তির স্মৃতি জাগরূক করে [Gulliver's Travels নামক পুস্তকে বর্ণিত ল্যাপুটা দ্বীপের স্বপ্নাবিষ্ট দার্শনিকগণকে দার্শনিক বিষয় হইতে বৈষয়িক ব্যাপারে প্রবর্ত্তিত করার জন্য যে সকল লোক বায়ুপূর্ণ ভস্ত্রাদ্বারা তাহাদের মুখ ও নাসিকায় আঘাত করার জন্য নিযুক্ত ছিল তাহাদের সম্পর্কে উক্ত]। 2. A flat fly-killing instrument ; একপ্রকার চ্যাপ্টা মাছি-মারা কল। 3. A hinged or hanging piece ; কব্জার উপর ঘুরে এরূপ বস্তু, শিথিলভাবে লম্বমান বস্তু। 4. A broad fin ; প্রশস্ত পাখ্‌না। 5. A young wild duck ; তরুণ বন্য হংস। 6. (*Slang*) The hand ; (ইতর ভাষায়) হাত। **Flap-eared**—(*Shakes.*) Having broad, loose ears ; আলম্বিত কর্ণ।

flāre, *v. i.*, *t.* & *n.* 1. To burn or blaze with unsteady flame ; দপ্ দপ্ করিয়া জ্বলা। 2. To gleam with dazzling lustre ; প্রভা বিকিরণ করা, চোখ ঝল্‌সাইয়া দেওয়া। 3. To open or spread outwards ; বহির্দ্দেশে উন্মুখ বা প্রসৃত হওয়া। ***Verb t.*** To cause to bulge upwards gradually as the sides of a ship etc. ; জাহাজের পার্শ্ব প্রভৃতি উপরের দিকে ক্রমশঃ স্ফীত করা। ***Noun.*** 1. A dazzling unsteady light ; লোল তীব্রোজ্জ্বল শিখা। 2. A sudden outburst of flame ; হঠাৎ প্রজ্বলন। 3. Ostentation ; জাঁকজমক। 4. A spreading outward, as in the sides of a ship ; বহিরুদ্গম। **Flar'-ing,** *adj.* 1. Flaming or blazing unsteadily ; dazzling ; gaudy ; অস্থির ভাবে জ্বলনশীল ; চোখ ঝল্‌সানো, তীব্রোজ্জ্বল ; জমকালো। **Flar'-ing-ly,** *adv.* উজ্জ্বলভাবে। **To flare up**—To burst into sudden blaze or anger ; দপ্ করিয়া জ্বলিয়া উঠা, তেলে বেগুণে জ্বলিয়া উঠা।

flāre'-ŭp, *n.* 1. A sudden breaking into flame ; হঠাৎ প্রজ্বলন। 2. A sudden outburst of anger ; হঠাৎ রাগের প্রকাশ। 3. Uproarious merry-making ; তুমুল আনন্দ-কোলাহল।

4. Short, brilliant popularity ; অল্পকালস্থায়ী অনন্য-সাধারণ লোকপ্রীতি।

flăsh, *v. t., i.* & *n.* 1. To send out in flashes ; to cause to gleam ; as, he *flashed* his sword ; বিদ্যুতের মত চমকান ; আলোকচ্ছুরিত করা। 2. To convey by telegraph ; as, to *flash* a message ; তারযোগে প্রেরণ করা। 3. (*Glass-making*) To spread out into a sheet ; to coat (plain glasses) with a coloured film ; (কাচ নির্ম্মাণ) চাদরের আকারে বিস্তার করা ; (সাদা কাচ) সূক্ষ্ম রঞ্জিত স্তরদ্বারা আবৃত করা। 4. To fill, as a stream with water ; জল প্রভৃতি দ্বারা পরিপূর্ণ করা। ***Verb i.*** 1. To break forth into flame ; to burst with a flash ; to give out flame or sparks ; to gleam ; দপ্ করিয়া জ্বলিয়া উঠা ; আলোকস্ফুরণ হওয়া ; কিরণ বিকিরণ করা, স্ফুলিঙ্গ বিক্ষেপ করা ; দীপ্তি পাওয়া, উদ্যোতিত হওয়া। 2. To burst suddenly into view or perception ; হঠাৎ দৃষ্টিপথে আবির্ভূত হওয়া বা মনোমধ্যে উদিত হওয়া। 3. To gleam with animation or passion ; as, *flashing* eyes ; আবেগদীপ্ত হওয়া, কোপজ্বলিত হওয়া। 4. (Of water) To dash ; (জল সম্বন্ধে) প্রচণ্ড বেগে ধাবিত হওয়া। ***Noun.*** 1. A sudden momentary outburst of light or flame ; চমক, আলোকস্ফুরণ, স্ফুরিত (মঃ ভাঃ)। 2. A sudden burst, as of wit or feeling ; বুদ্ধির চমক, প্রতিভাস্ফুরণ। 3. An instant ; নিমেষকাল, মুহূর্ত্ত কাল। 4. Ostentation ; জাঁকজমক, সমারোহ, ধূমধাম্। 5. A preparation for colouring spirits ; সুরাসার রঞ্জনার্থ প্রস্তুত দ্রব্য বিশেষ। 6. A rush of water at a shoal etc. for letting a boat descend ; নৌকা নামাইবার জন্য চড়ার দিকে জল প্রবাহ প্রেরণ। **Flash'-i-ly,** *adv.* Gaudily ; showily ; জমকালো ভাবে ; জাঁকালোভাবে। **Flash'-i-ness,** *n.* **Flash'-y,** *adj.* 1. Temporarily or superficially bright ; ক্ষণ-প্রভ, ক্ষণ-রুচি, অচির-দ্যুতি চটকদার, বহিরুজ্জ্বল। 2. Fiery ; vehement ; অগ্নিময় ; প্রচণ্ড। 3. Showy ; gaudy ; বাহ্যসুন্দর, চাক্‌চিক্যময় ; আড়ম্বরপূর্ণ, জমকালো। **Flash-board**—বাঁধের জল হইতে অধিকতর পরিমাণে জল চক্রঘূর্ণনকারী জলস্রোতে প্রেরণের জন্য ফলক-বিশেষ। **Flah-light**—সঙ্কেত-প্রদানে, আলোক-মন্দিরে এবং রজনীতে আলোক-চিত্র গ্রহণে ব্যবহৃত নানা প্রকার আলোক। **Flash-point**—More usually *Flashing point* which see. **A flash in the pan**—An abortive effort ; বৃথা উদ্যম, নিষ্ফল প্রয়াস। **A flash of hope**—A sudden short access of hope ; আশার আলোক। **A flash of lightning**—চপলা-চমক, বিদ্যুৎস্ফুরণ, দামিনী চমক। **In a flash**—In an instant ; নিমেষে, চক্ষুর পলকে। **His eyes flash fire**—His eyes throw angry or passionate glances or burn with emotion ; তাহার চক্ষু হইতে অগ্নি শিখা ছুটিতেছে, তাহার চক্ষু হইতে বিদ্যুৎ শিখার মত আবেগতরঙ্গ স্ফুরিত হইতেছে। **The news was flashed all over the country**—It was sent to by telegraph all over the country ; ঐ সংবাদ দেশের সর্ব্বত্র তারযোগে প্রেরিত হইয়াছিল। **To flash in the pan** — To fail after a showy start ; জাঁকজমকের সহিত আরম্ভ করিয়া পরিণামে বিফলমনোরথ হওয়া। **To flash on the mind**—To occur suddenly in the mind ; হঠাৎ মনে উদয় হওয়া, হঠাৎ মনে পড়া, মনোগগনে বিদ্যুতের মত চমকিয়া উঠা, টনক্ নড়া। **To flash up** or **out**—To show sudden passion ; হঠাৎ ক্রোধ প্রকাশ করা, সহসা রাগিয়া উঠা।

flăsh, *adj.* 1. Showy ; counterfeit ; as, *flash* notes or money ; জমকাল ; কৃত্রিম, জাল। 2. Showily dressed ; as, *flash* man or woman ; জমকালো পোষাক পরিহিত। 3. Relating to thieves, tramps etc. ; as, *flash* language ; চোর, ভবঘুরে প্রভৃতি সম্পর্কীয়। **Flash-house** — A house frequented by thieves ; a brothel ; চোরের আড্ডা ; বেশ্যালয়, গণিকাভবন। **Flash-jewellery**—Counterfeit jewellery ; কৃত্রিম অলঙ্কার। **The flash gentry**—তস্কর সম্প্রদায়।

flăsh'-ing, *n.* The act of blazing ; a flash ; a sudden burst, as of water ; উদ্দ্যোতন ; চমক, স্ফুরণ ; বেগে প্রধাবন। **Flashing point**—উত্তাপের যে মাত্রায় তৈলাদির বাষ্প জ্বলিয়া উঠে, প্রজ্বলনবিন্দু, (হিঃ কোঃ) জ্বলনতাপাঙ্ক।

flăsk, *n.* 1. A narrow-necked bottle for carrying fluids ; তরল পদার্থ রাখিবার সরুগলাওয়ালা বোতল। 2. A leather or metal case for carrying gunpowder ; বারুদদান। **Florence flask**—বকভাণ্ড (সাঃ পঃ)।

flăs'-kĕt, *n.* 1. (*Archaic*) A long shallow basket ; (অপ্রঃ) লম্বা এবং অপ্রশস্ত ঝুড়ি। 2. A small flask ; মদ্যাদি রাখিবার সরুগলাওয়ালা ক্ষুদ্র ভাণ্ড।

flăt, *adj., adv., n.* & *v. t.* 1. Horizontal ; level ; smooth ; চক্রবালের সহিত সমান্তরাল ; সমতল ; মসৃণ। 2. Spread out ; prostrate ; as, to lie *flat* on the ground ; ছড়ানো ; সটান। 3. Tasteless ; as, a drink *flat* to the taste ; স্বাদহীন, স্বাদশূন্য, নীরস। 4. Dull ; monotonous ; as, a *flat* speech ; নীরস ; একঘেয়ে, একটানা। 5. Clear ; plain ; downright ; as, *flat* denial ; পরিষ্কার, সাফ্ ; সুস্পষ্ট ; ডাহা, অভ্রান্ত, নিশ্চিত, ধ্রুব 6. Dejected ; without energy ; slow-witted ; বিষণ্ণ, বিরস ; নিস্তেজ, নিরুদ্যম ; মন্দ-বুদ্ধি। 7. Depressed, as, a market or price ; মন্দা। 8. (*Fine arts*) Uniform in hue and shade ; wanting relief ; (ললিত কলা) একরঙ্গা ; উদ্গাতকারুকার্য্য বিহীন। 9. (*Mus.*) Below the true pitch ; (সঙ্গীত-শাস্ত্র) অনুচ্চ, কোমল। 10. (*Phonetics*) Soft-voiced (of certain consonants) ; (কতিপয়

ব্যঞ্জনবর্ণ সম্বন্ধে) কোমল। *Adv.* In a flat manner ; directly ; সটান, সাফ ; প্রত্যক্ষভাবে। *Noun.* **1.** A flat surface ; a plain ; সমতল পৃষ্ঠ ; সমতলভূমি। **2.** A shoal ; a strand ; a swamp ; চড়া ; হ্রদ বা নদীর ধার ; জলাভূমি, বাদা। **3.** Something broad and flat in form ; চ্যাপ্টা বস্তু। **4.** A flat-bottomed boat ; চ্যাপ্টা তলার নৌকা। **5.** A straw hat with a broad brim and low crown ; কিনারা চওড়া এবং মাথা নীচু খড়ের টুপী। **6.** A roofless car ; ছাদ-বিহীন শকট। **7.** A flat basket ; চ্যাপ্টা ঝুড়ী। **8.** (*Theatre*) A flat piece of scenery pushed on from the wings or lowered from over-head or raised from below ; (রঙ্গমণ্ডপ) যে সমতল দৃশ্যপট রঙ্গমঞ্চের পার্শ্বদেশ হইতে ঠেলিয়া দেওয়া হয় অথবা ঊর্দ্ধ হইতে অবনমিত কিম্বা নিম্ন হইতে উত্থিত করা হয়। **9.** The flat surface of anything ; as, the *flat* of the hand or sword ; কোন কিছুর (যথা, হাতের বা অসি ফলকের) সমতল পৃষ্ঠ, (হাতের), চেটো। **10.** A simpleton ; নির্ব্বোধ, বোকা। **11.** (*Mus.*) A note lowered a semitone below natural pitch ; a sign indicating this lowering ; (সঙ্গীত-শাস্ত্র) কোমল ; কোমল চিহ্ন। **Flat'-ly,** *adv.* In a flat manner ; evenly ; horizontally ; without spirit ; positively ; চ্যাপ্টা ভাবে ; সমতল ভাবে ; সটান হইয়া, সটাং করিয়া ; নিস্তেজ ভাবে ; নিশ্চিতভাবে, অসঙ্কুচিত চিত্তে, সোজাসুজি, স্পষ্টাক্ষরে, স্পষ্টভাষায়, সাফ্। **Flat'-ness,** *n.* **Flat'-tish,** *adj.* Somewhat flat ; ঈষৎ চ্যাপ্টা। **Flat-boat**—অগভীর জলে চলার উপযোগী চ্যাপ্টাতলওয়ালা নৌকা। **Flat-denial**—See FLAT *adj.* 5. **Flat-fish**—একজাতীয় মৎস্য। **Flat-foot(ed)**—(Having) flat feet ; (*U. S.*) resolute ; চ্যাপ্টাপদযুক্ত ; (মার্কিণ যুক্তরাজ্যে) দৃঢ়প্রতিজ্ঞ। **Flat-head**—Characterised by flatness of head ; চ্যাপ্টা মাথাওয়ালা। **Flat-iron**—ইস্ত্রী। **Flat-nosed**—Having a depressed nose ; খাঁদা। **Flat-race**—(Opposed to *hurdle race*) ; সমতল ভুমিতে দৌড়। **Flat-tint**—Uniform tint ; সর্ব্বত্র একরূপ রঙ্গ। **Flat-wise,** **-ways**—With the flat side downward ; চ্যাপ্টাদিক নিম্নে রাখিয়া। **Flat worm**—একপ্রকার কীট। **Sharps and flats**—কড়ি ও কোমল। **That's flat**—Let there be no doubt about it ; এই বিষয়ে কোন সন্দেহ করিও না। **To fall flat**—To fall prostrate ; সটান হইয়া পড়া। To fail to cause interest or amusement ; নীরস হওয়া। **To sing flat**—To sing with a flat voice ; কোমল স্বরে গান করা।

flăt, *n.* A floor in a building ; set of rooms on one floor as residence ; (অট্টালিকার) তল ; প্রাসাদের কোন তলস্থ বাসোপযোগী কক্ষশ্রেণী।

flăt'-ten (-tn), *v. t.* & *i.* **1.** To level ; to make flat ; সমতল করা ; চ্যাপ্টা করা। **2.** To bring to the ground ; to prostrate ; to dispirit ; ধরাশায়ী করা ; সটান করিয়া ফেলা ; ভগ্নোৎসাহ করা। **3.** To make insipid ; নীরস করা, স্বাদহীন করা। **4.** (*Mus.*) To render less acute or sharp ; (সঙ্গীত-শাস্ত্র) অনুচ্চ করা, কোমল করা। *Verb i.* **1.** To grow flat or even ; চ্যাপ্টা হওয়া, সমতল হওয়া। **2.** To become depressed, dull or insipid ; বিষণ্ণ হওয়া, বিরস হওয়া। **3.** To grow less sharp, as a sound ; কোমল হওয়া।

flăt'-tĕr, *v. t.* & *i.* **1.** To compliment unduly ; তোষামোদ করা, চাটুবাদ করা। **2.** To raise hopes in (usually false) ; to please oneself with false hopes etc. ; বৃথা আশা দেওয়া, মিথ্যা আশায় আশান্বিত করা ; মিথ্যা আশাদ্বারা মনোরঞ্জন করা। **3.** To caress ; to fawn on ; আদর করা ; সোহাগ করা। **4.** To exaggerate good looks of ; as, his portrait *flatters* him ; কাহারও সৌন্দর্য্য অতিরঞ্জিত করা। **5.** To gratify, as an eye or ear ; চক্ষু বা কর্ণ পরিতৃপ্ত করা। *Verb i.* To make use of flattery ; চাটুবাক্য প্রয়োগ করা। **-er,** *n.* One who flatters ; চাটুকার, খোসামুদে, তোষামোদকারী। **-ing,** *adj.* Coaxing ; gratifying ; agreeable to one's self-love or vanity ; raising false hopes ; তোষামোদপূর্ণ ; প্রীতিকর ; আত্মতুষ্টিকর ; বৃথা আশাপ্রদ, মিথ্যা আশাপ্রদ। **-ingly,** *adv.* **-y,** *n.* The act of flattery ; adulation ; false praise ; তোষামোদ ; অনুচিত প্রশংসা বা স্তুতি ; চাটুবাদ, চাটূক্তি (উজ্জ্বলঃ), চাটুবচন, মিথ্যা প্রশংসা। **To flatter oneself**—আত্মপ্রসাদ অনুভব করা।

flăt'-ting, *n.* **1.** The process of making flat ; চ্যাপ্টা করণ। **2.** A mode of house-painting in which the paint is left without gloss ; এক প্রণালীর গৃহচিত্রণ যাহাতে রঙ্গের উপর জিল্লা দেওয়া হয় না। **3.** The process of making metal into sheets ; ধাতুর চাদর প্রস্তুত প্রণালী।

flăt'-ū-lĕnt, *adj.* **1.** Generating wind in the stomach ; উদর-বায়ু জনক, উদরাধ্মান জনক। **2.** Attended or affected with accumulation of wind in the stomach and intestines ; উদরস্ফীতি সহকৃত, উদরাধ্মান রোগাক্রান্ত। **3.** Inflated ; pretentious ; as, a *flatulent* writer ; স্ফীত, শূন্যগর্ভ, অসার ; মিথ্যাদাবীপূর্ণ। **-lence, -len-cy,** *ns.* The state of being flatulent ; উদরাধ্মান, পেটফাঁপা, আধ্মান (হঃ চঃ), উদাবর্ত্ত, (সাঃ পঃ) বায়ুদ্গার (ঐ)। **-ly,** *adv.*

flā'-tŭs, *n.* Wind generated in the stomach or intestines ; অগ্নি-মান্দ্যাদি হেতু আমাশয়ে যে বায়ু উৎপন্ন হয়।

flaunt (flänt), *v. i., t.* & *n.* **1.** To wave showily, as a flag etc. ; আড়ম্বরসহকারে আন্দোলিত করা। **2.** To display oneself or other things ostentatiously ; জাঁক দেখান, ভড়ং দেখান, বেশভূষার বাহার দেখান।

Verb t. To show, as oneself, finery etc. ostentatiously ; আড়ম্বর সহকারে প্রদর্শন করা, জাঁকজমকের সহিত প্রদর্শন করা। ***Noun.*** Ostentatious display or motion ; আড়ম্বর সহকারে প্রদর্শন বা আন্দোলন। **Flaunt'-er,** *n.* **Flaunt'-ing, Flaunt'-y,** *adjs.* Boastfully showy ; ostentatious; ভড়ংপূর্ণ; আড়ম্বরপূর্ণ। **Flaunt'-ing-ly,** *adv.*

flau'-tist (flä-), *n.* A flute player ; বংশিবাদক, বেণুবাদক, মুরলীধর, বংশি-ধারি।

flā-vês'-cĕnt, *adj.* Growing yellow ; yellowish ; পীতায়মান ; ঈষৎ-পীত, পীতাভ।

flā'-vour (-vêr), *n.* & *v. t.* **1.** Fragrance ; as, the *flavour* of a flower ; গন্ধ, পরিমল, বাস, ঘ্রাণ। **2.** That quality of a substance which affects the taste ; relish ; zest ; as, the *flavour* of food ; স্বাদ ; রুচি ; তার, রস। **3.** Characteristic quality ; বিশেষত্ব। ***Verb t.*** To give flavour to ; to season ; সুগন্ধি বা সুস্বাদু করা, সুরস করা ; মসলাদি মিশ্রিত করিয়া স্বাদু করা, রসাল করা। **–ing,** *n.* Anything, as an essence etc., used to give a particular flavour ; পুষ্পসার প্রভৃতি, যদ্দারা কোন কিছু সুবাসিত বা সুরস করা হয়। **–less,** *adj.* Having no flavour ; স্বাদগন্ধ হীন। **–ous, –some,** *adjs.* Pleasant to the taste or smell ; সুগন্ধি বা সুস্বাদু।

flaw (flä), *n., v. t.* & *i.* **1.** A crack ; a breach ; ফাটা ; চিড়, (মণি সম্বন্ধে) দোষ, ছিদ্র, চিড়, ত্রাস (অঃ) মণিদোষ, শঙ্খলিখিত (মঃ ভাঃ)। **2.** A defect ; দোষ, ত্রুটী, খুঁত। **3.** (*Law*) An invalidating fault ; (আইন) দোষ, ত্রুটী। ***Verb t.*** **1.** To crack ; বিদীর্ণ করা, ভাঙ্গা, ফাটান। **2.** To make a defect in ; to mar ; দোষযুক্ত করা ; নষ্ট করা। ***Verb i.*** To crack ; ফাটা। **Flaw'-less,** *adj.* Without any flaw or defect ; as, a *flawless* character ; নিঁখুত, নিষ্কলঙ্ক, নির্দ্দোষ, অনবদ্য। **Flaw'-less-ly,** *adv.* **Flaw'-less-ness,** *n.* **Flaw'-y,** *adj.*

flaw (flä), *n.* A sudden gust of wind ; a short storm ; ঝাপ্‌টা বাতাস, দম্‌কা বাতাস; ক্ষণস্থায়ী ঝটিকা।

The Flax plant (*Linum usitatissimum*) with section of seed vessel.

flăx, *n.* **1.** A plant cultivated for its textile fabric and its seeds, called linseed ; তিসি বা মসিনার গাছ, অতসীর গাছ,—ইহার সুতা হইতে বস্ত্র ও বীজ হইতে তৈল উৎপন্ন হয়। **2.** The fibres of this plant ; তিসি গাছের সূক্ষ্ম তন্তু বা আঁশ। **3.** Cloth made of flax ; মসিনা গাছের সুতায় তৈয়ারী কাপড়। **Flax'-en,** *adj.* **1.** Of the colour of flax ; flowing and fair ; as, *flaxen* hair ; তিসির বর্ণ, পীতাভ কপিশ বর্ণ ; নিম্নে প্রসৃত এবং মনোহর। **2.** Relating to flax ; তিসিসম্বন্ধীয়। **Flax'-y,** *adj.* Like flax ; তিসির ন্যায়। **Flax-comb**—তিসির আঁশ পরিষ্কারক যন্ত্রাবশেষ। **Flax-dresser** — তিসিতন্তুনির্ম্মাতা। **Flax-seed**—মসিনা, তিসি।

flay (flā), *v. t.* **1.** To strip off the skin of ; as, to *flay* a cow ; চাম উঠান, খাল ছাড়ান, চর্ম্ম উন্মোচন করা। **2.** To plunder, as a person ; to criticise severely ; লুটিয়া নেওয়া ; কঠোর সমালোচনা করা। **3.** To take off, as skin, bark etc. ; চামড়া বা বাকল তুলিয়া ফেলা। **Flay'-er,** *n.* One who strips off the skin ; যে চর্ম্ম উন্মোচন করে, মুচি। **Flay-flint**—An extortioner ; a miser ; পীড়ন পূর্ব্বক অর্থ আদায়কারী ; কৃপণ, কঞ্জুষ। **To flay one alive**—To strip off one's skin when he is living ; কাহারও জীবদ্দশায় দেহ-চর্ম্ম উন্মোচন করা। **To flay the fox**—(*Obs.*) To vomit ; (অপ্রঃ) বমি করা।

flea (flē), *n.* **1.** An insect that leaps with agility and whose bite is troublesome ; পিশু (নৃত্যঃ), চিমড়া-মাছি (যোঃ)। **2.** A small or hateful creature ; ক্ষুদ্র অথবা ঘৃণ্য জন্তু। **Flea-bane, –wort,** , এক জাতীয় উগ্র-গন্ধ গুল্ম। **Flea-bite**—পিসুর কামড় ; পিসুর দংশনজনিত লোহিত-বর্ণ চিহ্ন। **Flea-bitten**—চিমড়া পোকা দ্বারা দষ্ট ; অপেক্ষাকৃত পাতলা রঙ্গের উপর লাল ফুট্‌ ফুট্‌ দাগবিশিষ্ট। **Flea-louse** — একপ্রকার উৎকুণ। **With a flea in his ear**—Discomfited by a reproof, repulse or unexpected reply ; তিরস্কার, প্রত্যাখ্যান বা অপ্রাত্যাশিত উত্তরদ্বারা পরাভবপ্রাপ্ত।

fleam (flēm), *n.* A lancet for bleeding horses ; অশ্বের রক্তমোক্ষণার্থ ছুরিকা বিশেষ।

fleche, *n.* (*Arch.*) A slender spire at the intersection of the nave and transepts ; (স্থপতি-বিজ্ঞান) গির্জ্জার মধ্যভাগ এবং ঢেড়ার আকার গির্জ্জার অন্তর বাহুর সংযোগ-স্থলের ক্রমসূক্ষ্মাগ্র চূড়া।

flĕck *n.* & *v. t.* **1.** A spot ; a freckle ; a speckle ; দাগ ; তিল, মেচেতা ; ফুট্‌ ফুট্‌ দাগ। **2.** A small particle ; কণিকা। ***Verb t.*** To spot ; to dapple ; to variegte ; দাগবিশিষ্ট করা ; ফুট্‌ ফুট্‌ দাগবিশিষ্ট করা ; চিত্রবিচিত্র করা। **Flecked,** *adj.* Dappled ; ফুট্‌ ফুট্‌ বিন্দুবিশিষ্ট, ফুট্‌ ফুট্‌ দাগবিশিষ্ট। **Fleck'-less,** *adj.* Without spot ; দাগশূন্য।

flĕck'-êr, *v. t.* To fleck ; ফুট্‌ ফুট্‌ দাগ দেওয়া।

flĕc'-tion, *n.* Same as FLEXION which see.

flĕd, *p. t.* and *pp.* of FLEE.

fledge (flĕj), *v. t.* & *i.* To furnish with feathers or wings for flight ; to cover or adorn with feathers or down ; পালকবিশিষ্ট করা,

পক্ষবিশিষ্ট করা; পালকশোভিত করা, পালকাবৃত করা, পালকদ্বারা ভূষিত করা। ***Verb i.*** To acquire feathers for flying; উদ্গাতপক্ষ হওয়া। **Fledge′-less,** *adj.* Unfledged; অজাতপক্ষ। **Fledg′-y,** *adj.* (*Keats*) Feathered; পক্ষযুক্ত, সপক্ষ।

Fledg(e)′-ling (flĕj-), *n.* **1.** A little bird just fledged; নবোদ্গাত-পক্ষ পক্ষিশাবক। **2.** An inexperienced person; অনভিজ্ঞ লোক।

flee (flē), *v. i.* & *t.* **1.** To run away, as from dangers etc.; পলায়ন করা। **2.** To disappear; to pass away; as, life has *fled*; তিরোহিত হওয়া, চলিয়া যাওয়া; অন্তর্হিত হওয়া। ***Verb t.*** **1.** To run away from; to shun; পলাইয়া যাওয়া, সরিয়া পড়া; পরিহার করা। **2.** To quit abruptly, as a place or person; সহসা ত্যাগ করা।

fleece (flēs), *n.* & *v. t.* **1.** The woolly covering of sheep or other similar animals; the quantity of wool shorn from a sheep at one time; মেষ লোম; এককালে কর্ত্তিত মেষ লোমরাশি। **2.** Any soft woolly covering like fleece; a white cloud; falling snow; পশমবৎ কোমল আবরণ; শুভ্রমেঘ; পতিষ্যমাণ তুষার। **3.** A head or mass of hair; কেশরাশি। ***Verb t.*** **1.** To deprive of fleece; লোমশূন্য করা বা লোমহীন করা। **2.** To strip of money or property; টাকা পয়সা কাড়িয়া নেওয়া, বিত্তহীন করা। **3.** To spread, as fleece; লোমাবৃত করা। **Fleece′-a-ble,** *adj.* **Fleeced,** *adj.* **Fleec′-ing,** (*Dial.*) Curd separated from whey; (উপভাষায়) দধি, দৈ। **Fleece′-less,** *adj.* Without fleece; লোমশূন্য। **Fleec′-y,** *adj.* Covered with, made of, or resembling a fleece; লোমাচ্ছাদিত; লোমনির্ম্মিত, পশমী, লোমসদৃশ। **Fleece-wool**—জীবজন্তু হইতে কর্ত্তিত লোমরাশি। **The Golden Fleece**—The Austrian and the Spanish order of Knighthood; অষ্ট্রিয়া ও স্পেনদেশীয় সম্ভ্রান্তসম্প্রদায় বিশেষ।

fleer (flēr), *v. i.* & *n.* To laugh or grin mockingly: to make wry faces in contempt; to jeer; বিদ্রূপের হাসি হাসা; মুখ বাঁকান, মুখ সিটকান, নাসিকা কুঞ্চিত করা; বিদ্রূপ করা, পরিহাস করা। ***Noun.*** A speech or look of mockery; বিদ্রূপব্যঞ্জক দৃষ্টি, বিদ্রূপবাক্য। **Fleer′-er,** *n.* উপহাসকারী। **Fleer′-ing-ly,** *adv.* In a fleering manner; মুখবাঁকাইয়া।

fleet (flēt), *n.* **1.** The number of warships under one commander-in-chief; navy; রণপোত বহর, সমরপোতশ্রেণী; নৌবল। **2.** A group of vessels sailing in company; বহর (কপালঃ), নৌ-সাধন। **Fleet of the desert** — A caravan; একত্র ভ্রমণকারী বণিকসমূহ, বণিক কটক।

Fleet (flēt), *n.* A creek or bay; খাড়ী, উপসাগর। **Fleet-parson**—ফ্লীট ষ্ট্রীটের নিকটাঞ্চলবাসী যে সকল কলঙ্কিত ধর্ম্মযাজকগণ অবৈধ বিবাহকার্য্য সম্পাদন করিত। **The Fleet**—A stream (now a coverd sewer) near Fleet Street in London; former prison near this stream; লণ্ডন নগরীস্থ ফ্লীটষ্ট্রীটের নিকটবর্ত্তী স্রোতস্বতী (বর্ত্তমানে আবৃত নর্দ্দমায় পরিণত); উক্ত স্রোতস্বতীর নিকটবর্ত্তী প্রাচীন কারাগার।

fleet (flēt), *v. i.* To pass or fly swiftly; to flit; to slip away; to glide, as day; to vanish; to be transient; দ্রুতবেগে অতিক্রম করা বা উড়িয়া যাওয়া; উধাও হইয়া ছুটা; অলক্ষ্যে চলিয়া যাওয়া; বহিয়া যাওয়া; অন্তর্হিত হওয়া, বিলীন হওয়া; ক্ষণস্থায়ী হওয়া। **Fleet′-ing,** *adj.* Passing swiftly; transitory; দ্রুতগামী; ক্ষণস্থায়ী। **Feet′-ing-ly,** *adv.*

fleet (flēt), *adj.* (*Poet.*) Swift of pace; nimble; (পদ্যে) দ্রুতগামী, ক্ষিপ্র-গতি; চটুল, চপল। **Fleet′-ly,** *adv.* **Fleet′-ness,** *n.*

fleet (flēt), *adj.* & *adv.* (of water) Shallow; (জল-সম্পর্কে) অগভীর। ***Adv.*** To no great depth; as, to plough or sow *fleet*; অগভীরভাবে।

Flĕm′-ing, *n.* A native of Flanders; ফ্লাণ্ডার্স দেশের অধিবাসী।

Flĕm′-ish, *adj.* & *n.* Of, or pertaining to, Flanders; ফ্লাণ্ডার্স দেশসম্বন্ধীয় [বর্ত্তমানে বেলজিয়ম, নেদারলেণ্ডের দক্ষিণ ভাগ এবং ফরাসী দেশের কতক স্থান এই দেশের অন্তর্ভুক্ত]। ***Noun.*** The language of Flanders; ফ্লাণ্ডার্স দেশের ভাষা।

flĕm′-ish, *v. i.* (*Hunting*) To feather, as a hound; (মৃগয়া—শিকারী কুকুর সম্পর্কে) শিকারের গন্ধ অনুসরণকালে লাঙ্গুল ও দেহ কম্পিত করা।

flench (flĕnsh), **flense** (flĕns), **flinch** (flĭnsh), *v. t.* To cut up and obtain the blubber of a whale; to flay, as a seal; তিমি মৎস্য কাটিয়া চর্ব্বি সংগ্রহ করা; সীল প্রভৃতি মৎস্যের চর্ম্ম উন্মোচন করা।

flĕsh, *n.* & *v. t.* **1.** The soft muscular part of the animal body; মাংস (বিশেষতঃ মাংসপেশী), আমিষ, পলল, ক্রব্য, পিশিত। **2.** Animal food in distinction from vegetable, fish, etc.; আমিষাহার, আমিষখাদ্য। **3.** The human body as distinguished from the soul; মানবদেহ। **4.** Kindred; near relations; as, one's own *flesh* and blood; জ্ঞাতি; ঘনিষ্ঠ আত্মীয়। **5.** The human race; mankind; মনুষ্যবংশ; মানবজাতি, মনুষ্যজাতি। **6.** Human nature with its emotions and infirmities; মানবপ্রকৃতি, মানবস্বভাব। **7.** The sensual appetites; ইন্দ্রিয় লালসা, কামাদি বৃত্তিসমূহ, ইন্দ্রিয় সেবার ইচ্ছা। **8.** The pulpy substance of a fruit or plant; ফলের শাঁস। **9.** Plumpiness; as to lose *flesh* (=to grow thin; ক্ষীণ-দেহ হওয়া) হৃষ্টপুষ্টতা, মাংসলতা। **10.** The surface of the human body (referring to colour); as, a man of fair *flesh*; শরীরের রঙ্গ, দেহের বর্ণ। *Verb t.* **1.** To feed, as dogs etc. with flesh so as to incite to further exertion; শিকারী কুকুর প্রভৃতিকে মাংসাহার দ্বারা উত্তেজিত করা। **2.** To initiate in bloodshed; to thrust (swords etc.) into flesh; to incite by foretaste of success; রক্তপাতে দীক্ষিত করা; মাংসের ভিতর অসি প্রবিষ্ট করা; সফলতার পূর্ব্বাস্বাদ প্রদানে প্রোৎসাহিত করা। **3.** To gratify; পরিতৃপ্ত করা, চরিতার্থ করা। **Flesh'-er,** *n.* A butcher; কসাই, শৌনিক। **Flesh'-i-ness,** *n.* Plumpness; হৃষ্টপুষ্টতা। **Flesh'-less,** *adj.* Having no flesh; lean; মাংসবিহীন; ক্ষীণ, কাহিল। **Flesh'-li-ness,** *n.* Carnal passions and appetites; ইন্দ্রিয়সুখলালসা বিষয়বুদ্ধি (কেওি), বিষয়াসক্তি, (ঐ) বিষয়পরতা (ঐ)। **Flesh'-ly,** *adj.* **1.** Corporeal; carnal; lascivious, as appetites or desires; worldly; দৈহিক; ঐন্দ্রিয়; লম্পট, ভোগাসক্ত, কামোদ্দীপক; বৈষয়িক। **2.** Mortal; material; not spiritual; নশ্বর, অনিত্য, বিনাশী; জড়, স্থূল; অনাত্ম। **Flesh'-y,** *adj.* **1.** Relating to, or like, flesh; plump; corpulent; without bone; মাংস-সম্বন্ধীয়, মাংসসদৃশ; মাংসল, হৃষ্টপুষ্ট; স্থূলকায়; অস্থিশূন্য। **2.** (*Bot.*) Pulpy; (উদ্ভিদ-বিদ্যা) শাঁসাল। **Flesh-broth**—মাংসের যূষ। **Flesh-brush, –glove**—যে বুরুশ বা দস্তানা দ্বারা ঘর্ষণ পূর্ব্বক রক্ত সঞ্চালন ক্রিয়া উত্তেজিত করা হয়। **Flesh-colour(ed)**—মাংসবর্ণ। **Flesh-fly** — মাংসভুক্ কীট, যে কীট মাংসের উপর ডিম পাড়িয়া থাকে। **Flesh-hood**—The state of being in the flesh; bodily existence; দেহবদ্ধতা; জীবভাব। **Flesh-hook** — পাত্রাদি হইতে মাংসাদি উত্তোলনের জন্য কাঁটা। **Flesh-tights** — Same as FLESHINGS which see. **Flesh-meat**—মাংস, আমিষ। **Flesh-pot** — মাংস রন্ধনের পাত্র। (*Pl.*) ভোগ-বিলাসপূর্ণ জীবন; বড়মানুষী চাল। **Flesh-side** (or **Flesh**)—চর্ম্মের যে দিকে মাংস সংলগ্ন থাকে। **Flesh-tint** — মানব দেহের অনুরূপ বর্ণ। **Flesh-worm** — একপ্রকার মাংস-ভুক্ কীট, চর্মপোকা। **Flesh-wound**—সামান্য আঘাত, যে আঘাতে মাংসমাত্র বিদ্ধ হয়। **After the flesh** — After the manner of man; in a gross or earthly manner; মনুষ্যানুরূপভাবে; লৌকিকভাবে, সাংসারিকভাবে। **An arm of flesh**—Human strength or aid; মানবীয় শক্তি, মানবীয় সাহায্য। **Flesh and blood**—The body or its material; রক্তমাংসের শরীর। Human nature with its emotions and infirmities; মানব প্রকৃতি। Blood relations; descendants; as, he is my own *flesh and blood*; রক্তগত সম্পর্ক; বংশধর। **Flesh and fell**—*n.* & *adv.* The whole body; সমগ্র দেহ। (*Adv.*) Entirely; সম্পূর্ণরূপে। **Fleshly-minded** — Given to sensual pleasures; ইন্দ্রিয়সুখপরতন্ত্র, ইন্দ্রিয়সুখপরায়ণ। **Ill that flesh is heir to**—Disease which human body is subject—মানবদেহ স্বভাবতঃ যে সকল রোগের অধীন। **Sins of the flesh**—Unchastity; অসতীত্ব। **To be one flesh** — To become closely united as in marraige etc.; এক দেহ এক প্রাণ হওয়া। **To make his flesh creep**—To terrify him especially with dread of the supernatural; গা ছম্ ছম্ করিয়া উঠান। **To flesh one's valour** — To show one's prowess by killing an enemy for the first time; প্রথমবার শত্রু নিধন করত বিক্রম দর্শন করা।

flĕsh'-ings, *n.* (*pl.*) Tight fitting flesh coloured garments worn by dancers, actors, etc.; নর্ত্তক, নর্ত্তকী, কিম্বা অভিনেতা ও অভিনেত্রীগণের ঈষৎ রক্তবর্ণ আঁটসাঁট পোষাক।

fletch (flĕch), *v. t.* To feather, as an arrow; বাণে পালক লাগান। **Fletch'-er,** *n.* One who makes arrows; সায়ক নির্ম্মাতা।

Fleur de lis, *n.* (*Pl.* FLEURS-), ***Flower de luce,*** **1.** (*Archaic*), *n.* **1.** Iris flower; lily; দশবাই চণ্ডী (প্রবোধ); কুমুদ। **2.** The royal insignia of France; the royal family of France; France; ফরাসীদেশের রাজচিহ্ন; ফরাসীদেশের রাজপরিবার; ফরাসীদেশ।

Flower de luce.

fleu-rĕt' (floo-), An ornament like a small flower; ক্ষুদ্র পুষ্পবৎ ভূষা।

Fleuron, (*F.*), *n.* A flower-shaped ornament in architecture on coins etc.; (স্থপতি-বিজ্ঞান) মুদ্রা, প্রভৃতির উপর ক্ষুদ্র পুষ্পাকৃতি ভূষা।

fleur'-ȳ (flôr-), *adj.* (*Her.*) Decorated at the end with fleur-de-lis; (কুলবিদ্যা) দশবাই চণ্ডীর চিত্র দ্বারা প্রান্তদেশ শোভিত।

flew (flü), *p. t.* of FLY.

flews (flüz), *n.* (*Pl.*) The hanging part of the upper lip of hounds; শিকারী কুকুরের ওষ্ঠের ঝুলানো অংশ।

flĕx, *v. t.* To bend; নত করা, নোয়ান।

flĕx'-i-ble (-bl), *adj.* **1.** Capable of being bent without breaking; pliable; নমনীয়, নমনশীল; কোমল। **2.** Tractable; manageable; বশ্য; শাসনীয়। **3.** Plastic; as, a *flexible* language; কোমল। **4.** Supple; "*Flexible* politics"; নমনীয়, কোমল। **–bil'-i-ty, –ness,** *ns.* Quality of being flexible; pliancy; readiness to comply; নমনীয়তা; কোমলতা; বশ্যতা। **–bly,** *adv.*

flĕx'-ile, *adj.* Flexible; supple; tractable; নমনীয়; কোমল; বশ্য **–il'-i-ty,** *n.*

flex'-ion (flĕk-shŭn), *n.* 1. The act of bending; state of being bent, as of a limb etc.; curvature; অবনমন; নমনীয়তা; বক্রতা। 2. A part bent; a bending; নত অংশ; বাঁক। 3. (*Gram.*) Inflexion; (ব্যাকরণ) বিভক্তিযোগ, বিভক্তি রূপান্তর, ধাতু রূপান্তর। **–al, –less,** *adjs.*

Flĕx'-or (-êr), *n.* A muscle that bends a limb or part etc.; (opposed to *extensor*); যে পেশী দ্বারা দেহের কোন অংশ নোয়ান যায়।

flex'-ū-ous (-ŭs), **–ose** (-ōs), *adjs.* 1. Bending; winding; আঁকাবাঁকা; বক্র। 2. (*Only* -OSE) (*Bot.*) Serpentine; waving; (উদ্ভিদ-বিদ্যা) সর্পাকৃতি তরঙ্গায়িত, ঢেউ-খেলানিয়া। **–ly,** *adv.* **–os'-i-ty,** *n.*

flĕx'-ūre, *n.* 1. Act of bending bent state; অবনমন; বক্রভাব। 2. A bend; a turn; বাঁক; মোড়; 3. (*Math.*) The curving of a line or surface; (গণিত) রেখা বা ধরাতলের বক্রতা। **Flexure of a curve**—সরল রেখা হইতে কোন বক্রের অবনতি।

fl·b'-bêr-ti-ğib-bĕt, *n.* Gossiping frivolous person; ছ্যাবলা গল্পিয়া লোক, চপল-চিত্ত এবং গল্পগুজবপ্রিয় ব্যক্তি।

flick (flĭk), *v. t.* & *n.* To strike with a flick; as, to *flick* a horse; to jerk off or away, as dust etc.; সপাং করিয়া চাবুক মারা; ধূলি প্রভৃতি ঝাড়িয়া ফেলা। ***Noun.*** A smart sudden blow, as with a whip etc.; a jerk; a sound made by such a blow; সপাং শব্দে আঘাত; ঝাঁকুনি; সপাং শব্দ।

flick'-êr (flĭk-), *v. i.* & *n.* 1. To quiver; to flutter; কম্পিত করা; পাখসাট মারা। 2. To wave to and fro, as a flag etc.; আন্দোলিত করা, দোলান। 3. To blow lightly and unsteadily as wind; ধীর চঞ্চল ভাবে বহা। 4. To burn fitfully, as a dying fire; (*fig.*) to waver unsteadily; as, a *flickering* hope; মিট্ মিট্ করিয়া জ্বলা, টিম্ টিম্ করিয়া জ্বলা; টিপ্‌টিপ্ করিয়া জ্বলা, নিবুনিবু করিয়া জ্বলা; (লক্ষনায়) মিট্ মিট্ করা। ***Noun.*** A flickering movement of light; as, the last *flicker* of the dying lamp; স্ফুরণ, স্ফুরিত। **–ing,** *n.* **–ingly,** *adv.*

flī'-êr, *n.* See FLYER.

flight (flīt), *n.* & *v. t.* 1. Act or mode of flying, as of a bird, balloon, arrow etc.; swift passage as, of time; the distance covered at a flight; flying of a hawk in pursuit of a game; উড্ডয়ন, শূন্য পথে গমন, গগনমার্গে বিচরণ; দ্রুত অতিক্রান্ত হওন; একবার উড্ডয়নে যে পরিমাণ স্থান অতিক্রম করা যায়; শিকার অন্বেষণে বাজপক্ষীর উড্ডয়ন। 2. Soaring; sally; as, a *flight* of wit, fancy etc.; ঊর্দ্ধগমন; উচ্ছ্বাস। 3. A body of migrating or flying birds; a flock of birds or insects; a migration; a volley (of arrows); একত্র উড্ডীয়মান পাক্ষিশ্রেণী; প্রব্রজন; বর্ষ, বর্ষণ। 4. A reach of steps from one landing to another; এক অবতরণস্থল হইতে অপর অবতরণস্থল পর্যন্ত প্রসারিত সোপানশ্রেণী। 5. The husk of oats; যই এর খোসা। ***Verb t.*** To shoot while flying; উড্ডীন অবস্থায় গুলি করা। **Flight'-i-ly,** *adv.* **Flight'-i-ness,** *n.* **Flight'-y,** *adj.* 1. Whimsical; fickle; খেয়ালপরবশ; চপলমতি, অস্থিরচিত্ত। 2. Crazy; মাথা-পাগলা। **Flight feather or muscle**—যে পক্ষ অথবা পেশী উড্ডয়নে ব্যবহৃত হয়। **Flight of fancy** — The exercise of the power of imagination; কল্পনাশক্তির পরিচালনা। **In the first flight** — Taking a leading place; নেতৃত্ব গ্রহণ করিয়া। **To put to flight, To turn to flight**—To compel to run away; পলায়নে বাধ্য করা। **To take (to) flight** — To betake oneself to flight; to run away; পলায়ন করা; ভাগিয়া যাওয়া। **To wing one's flight**—To fly; উড্ডীন হওয়া, উড়া।

Flight(flīt), *n.* Act of fleeing or running away; hasty retreat; উড্ডয়ন, পলায়ন; দ্রুত হটিয়া যাওন।

flim'-flăm, *n.* 1. A trifle; trick; তুচ্ছ বিষয়; চাতুরী, ফন্দী। 2. Nonsense; humbug; deception; বাজে কথা; ধোঁকা, ছলনা; প্রতারণা।

flĭm'-sy *adj.* & *n.* Weak; frail; trivial; superficial; দুর্ব্বল; ভঙ্গুর; অকিঞ্চিৎকর, নগণ্য, তুচ্ছ, অসার; ভাসাভাসা, অগভীর। ***Noun.*** (*Slang*) 1. A banknote; (ইতরভাষায়) ব্যাঙ্কের নোট। 2. A thin paper; the copy of a reporter; পাতলা কাগজ; সংবাদদাতৃ পাতলা কাগজে যে প্রতিলিপি লিখিয়া থাকে। **–si-ly** *adv.* **–si-ness,** *n.*

flinch (flĭnsh), *v. i.* To withdraw *from* any course, duty etc.; to shrink; পরাঙ্মুখ হওয়া, পশ্চাৎপদ হওয়া; সঙ্কুচিত হওয়া। **Flinch'-er,** *n.* **Flinch'-ly,** *adv.*

flin-dêrs, *n.* (*Pl.*) Small pieces; fragments; অংশ; টুকরা।

fling, *v. t.* *i.* & *n.* 1. To hurl; to throw; নিক্ষেপ করা, ত্যাগ করা; ছোড়া মোচন করা। 2. To scatter; to emit; as, to *fling* rays of light; বিকীর্ণ করা, বিকিরণ করা; ছড়ান। 3. To throw to the ground; as, a horse *flings* the rider; ভূপাতিত করা, মাটীতে ফেলা, ধরাশায়ী করা। 4. To extend or spread suddenly; to toss; as, to *fling* out arms: the horse *flung* up his heels; ছোড়া, বিক্ষেপ করা; চাইট দেওয়া। 5. To cast off; পরিত্যাগ করা। ***Verb i.*** 1. To rush or go with violence or anger; সরোষে বা প্রচণ্ড বেগে ধাবমান হওয়া, বেগে নিষ্ক্রান্ত হওয়া। 2. To flounce; to plunge; as, a horse began to kick and *fling*; হাত পা ছোড়া; হস্তপদবিক্ষেপ করা, চাইট দেওয়া। 3. To utter abusive language; গালি দেওয়া, কটূক্তি করা

4. To put a person suddenly or violently *into* prison ; কারাগারে নিক্ষেপ করা। *Noun*. 1. A throw or cast ; a flounce ; a kick ; as, the *fling* of a horse ; নিক্ষেপ ; চাইট ; লাথি। 2. A sneer ; a gibe ; ব্যঙ্গোক্তি ; বিদ্রূপ, ঠাট্টা, ব্যঙ্গ। 3. A kind of dance esp. Highland *fling* ; এক প্রকার নৃত্য। 4. A time of free and full indulgence, pleasure and dissipation ; as, to have one's *fling* ; আলস্য, যথেচ্ছ আমোদ বা বিলাসভোগের কাল। **To fling about**—To throw on all sides ; চতুর্দ্দিকে ছড়ান। **To fling as a fact etc. in one's teeth**—To reproach one with it ; কোন বিষয় নিয়া কাহাকে তিরস্কার করা। **To fling away**—To reject ; to discard ; ত্যাগ করা ; অগ্রাহ্য করা। **To fling down**—To demolish ; ধ্বংস করা। To throw to the ground ; ভূপাতিত করা, ধরাশায়ী করা। **To fling from**—To quit in ill temper ; সরোষে পরিত্যাগ করা। **To fling in**—To throw in ; নিক্ষেপ করা। To add as an extra or bonus ; অতিরিক্ত পুরস্কারস্বরূপ দেওয়া। **To fling off**—To baffle in the chase ; অনুসরণ ব্যর্থ করা। **To fling open**—To open suddenly or with violence ; as, to *fling open* a door ; সজোরে খোলা, সবলে উদ্ঘাটিত করা। **To fling out**—*v. t.* & *i.* To utter harshly ; রূঢ়ভাবে বলা। (*Verb i.*) To utter sneers etc. ; বিদ্রূপোক্তি বা ব্যঙ্গোক্তি করা, বিদ্রূপ-বাণ বর্ষণ করা। **To fling up**—To abandon, as a design etc. ; ত্যাগ করা। **To have a fling at**—To make an attempt at ; চেষ্টা করা। To jeer at ; উপহাস করা, বিদ্রূপ করা। **To have one's fling**—To indulge in a fun or dissipation ; কৌতুক উপভোগ করা ; আমোদ প্রমোদে গা ঢালিয়া দেওয়া, বিলাসিতার স্রোতে ভাসিয়া চলা। **To indulge in a fling at**—To jeer at ; বিদ্রূপ করা, উপহাস করা।

flint, *n.* 1. A very hard silicious stone which strikes fire with steel ; আগ্নেয় প্রস্তরবিশেষ, অগ্নিপ্রস্তর (অভিঃ), চকমকি পাথর (কৃষ্ণঃ)। 2. Anything hard and unyielding like flint ; অগ্নিপ্রস্তরবৎ কঠিন বস্তু। 3. A quartz of any kind ; যে কোন প্রকার স্ফটিকপ্রস্তর। **Fint'-i-fy**, *v. t.* To turn to flint ; অগ্নিপ্রস্তরে পরিণত করা। **Flint'-i-ness**, *n.* **Flint'-y**, *adj.* Consisting of, composed of, abounding in, or like, flint ; আগ্নেয় প্রস্তরময়, অগ্নিপ্রস্তর রচিত, অগ্নিপ্রস্তর বহুল, আগ্নেয় প্রস্তর সদৃশ। **Flint glass**—একপ্রকার সুদৃশ্য কাচ (পূর্ব্বে চকমকি পাথরের চূর্ণ হইতে প্রস্তুত হইত), চকমকি কাচ। **Flint-hearted**—Having hard heart ; পাষাণ-হৃদয়। **Flint-implement** — আদিম নিবাসিদিগের আগ্ন প্রস্তরাদি রচিত অস্ত্র সমূহ। **To set another's flint for him**—To punish him ; শাস্তি দেওয়া। **To set one's face like a flint**—To be determined ; স্থির-সংকল্প হওয়া, দৃঢ়-প্রতিজ্ঞ হওয়া। **To skin a flint**—To be miserly ; মাছি টিপিয়া গুড় বাহির করা, কৃপণ হওয়া, কঞ্জুষ হওয়া। **To wring water from a flint**—To work miracles ; পাষাণ নিংড়াইয়া পানি বাহির করা, অসম্ভব সম্ভব করা।

flip, *n.* A mixture of beer and spirit sweetened with sugar and heated with hot iron ; চিনিদ্বারা স্বাদুকৃত ও তপ্ত লৌহদ্বারা উষ্ণীকৃত বীয়র মদ্য এবং সুরাসারের মিশ্র।

flip, *n.*, *v. t.* & *i.* A slight smart blow ; টোকা। *Verb t.* 1. To fillip or strike lightly, as one's cheek etc. ; to move with a sudden jerk, as a whip, fan, etc. ; টোকা মারা ; সপাং করিয়া ঘুরান, হঠাৎ ঝিঁকা মারিয়া নাড়া। 2. To fillip or toss, as a coin etc. ; টোকা দিয়া উপরে তোলা। *Verb i.* 1. To make a fillip তুড়ি দেওয়া। 2. To strike light' (at) with a whip etc. ; to mov with jerk ; টোকা মারা ; ঝাঁকি দি, সরান।

flip'-flăp, *adv.* & *n.* With lapping sound ; পৎপৎ শব্দে *Noun*. 1. A form of somersault এক প্রকার ডিগবাজী। 2. A fire-cracker ; পট্‌কা।

flip'-pănt, *adj.* Treating serious subjects or respectful persons lightly ; lacking in gravity ; inconsiderate ; গুরুতর বিষয় বা সম্মানিত ব্যক্তি সম্বন্ধে তাচ্ছিল্যভাবে আলোচনাকারী ; তরল-চিত্ত, চপল-স্বভাব, গাম্ভীর্য্যহীন ; অবিবেচক। **—ly**, *adv.* **—ness**, *n.* **—pan-cy**, *n.* The quality of being flippant ; তরলচিত্ততা, চপল স্বভাব, তরলতা, চাপল গাম্ভীর্য্যহীনতা, ফাজলিমি, বাকচাপল্য।

flip'-pêr, *n.* 1. (*Slang*) A hand ; (ইতরভাষায়) হাত। 2. A broad limb for swimming, as of a turtle, seal, etc. ; শীল মৎস্য, কচ্ছপ প্রভৃতির সাঁতার দেওয়ার জন্য প্রশস্ত প্রত্যঙ্গবিশেষ। **A tip of the flipper**—(*Slang*) A shake of the hand ; (ইতরভাষায়) করকম্পন।

flip'-pêr-tў, flŏp'-pêr-tў, *adj.* Dangling ; loose ; ঝুলানো ; শিথিল

flirt (flērt), *v. t.*, *i.* & *n.* 1. To throw with a jerk ; to fillip ; সজোরে বা সবলে নিক্ষেপ করা, হঠাৎ নিক্ষেপ করা ; টোকা মারা। 2. To toss about jerkily ; to open or close briskly, as a fan, tail of a bird etc. ; ঝিঁকা মারিয়া ঘুরান ; চট্‌পট্ খোল বা বন্ধ করা। *Verb i.* 1. To run and dart about ; to trifle ; ইতস্তত ঘুরিয়া বেড়ান, ছুটাছুটী করা ; তুচ্ছতাচ্ছিল করা। 2. To play at courtship (*with*) ; to coquet ; to [illegible] to make love ; প্রণয়রঙ্গ করা ; [illegible] ভাব প্রদর্শন করা, ছিনালি [illegible] মেকানি করা ; প্রেমপ্রদর্শনের ভাব [illegible]

Noun. 1. A sudden jerk; a darting motion; ঝিকা; ঝাঁকুনি। 2. A man or woman playing at courtship or amusement; a coquette; প্রণয়রঙ্গী পুরুষ, হাবভাবময়ী নারী; ছেনাল, প্রণয়রঙ্গিণী, রসবতী। **Flir-ta'-tion** *n.* Flirting; playing at courtship; coquetry; হাবভাব প্রদর্শন; ছিনালি, প্রণয়রঙ্গ, মেকানি। **Flir-ta'-tious, Flrit'-y,** *adjs.* **Flirt'-ing,** *n.* **Flirt-ing-ly.** *adv.* **Flirt'-ish,** *adj.* হাবভাবপূর্ণ, হাবভাবময়।

flit, *v. i.* & *n.* 1. To dart along; to pass rapidly, softly or lightly; as a *flitting* cloud, a bird; ছুটিয়া চলা; ভাসিয়া চলা। 2. To migrate; to depart; বসবাসের জন্য স্থানান্তরে গমন করা; প্রস্থান করা। 3. To flutter; to change abode; পৎপৎ শব্দে উড়া; বাসস্থান পরিবর্তন করা। *Noun.* 1. A flutter; পৎপৎ শব্দ। 2. Change of abode; বাসস্থান পরিবর্তন।

flitch (flich), *n.* & *v. t.* 1. The side of a hog salted and cured; লবণাক্ত এবং ধূমপ্রয়োগে শুষ্কীকৃত শূকরের পার্শ্বদেশের মাংস। 2. An outside slice of wood cut from a tree-trunk; বৃক্ষকাণ্ডের বহির্ভাগ হইতে কর্ত্তিত কাষ্ঠের পাতলা খণ্ড, চেলা। 3. A square piece of blubber; তিমি বা তৎসদৃশ সামুদ্রিকজন্তুর চর্ব্বির চতুষ্কাকার খণ্ড। 4. A steak of halibut; সামুদ্রিকমৎস্য বিশেষের খণ্ড বা ফালি। *Verb t.* To cut into flitches, as logs, halibuts etc.; ফালি ফালি করিয়া কাটা।

flit'-têr, *v. i.* To flutter; to move quickly; ইতস্ততঃ ছুটাছুটি করা; দ্রুত সঞ্চালিত হওয়া। **Flitter-mouse**—A bat; বাদুড়।

flix, *n.* Fur; the down of a beaver; জন্তুর কোমল লোম; বীবরের কোমল লোম।

float (flöt), *v. i., t.* & *n.* 1. To rest on the surface of liquid; ভাসা, প্রবমান হওয়া। 2. To drift along; as, to *float* on water or air; ভাসিয়া, যাওয়া, ভাসিয়া চলা। 3. (*Com.*) To be current; to get public support, as a company etc.; (বাণিজ্য) প্রচলিত হওয়া, প্রচারিত হওয়া; লোক সাধারণের সাহায্য প্রাপ্ত হওয়া। *Verb t.* 1. To cause to float; (of water) to support as a buoyant object; ভাসাইয়া দেওয়া, ভাসান; প্রবমান করা। 2. To flood; জলপ্লাবিত করা। 3. To circulate, as a rumour etc; প্রচার করা, রটনা করা। 4. (*Plastering*) To smooth with a float; (চূণকাম) কর্ণিকবিশেষ দ্বারা প্রাচীরাদির চূণবালি মসৃণ করা। 5. (*Com.*) To get afloat or fully started, as a company, scheme etc.; (বাণিজ্য) যৌথকারবার প্রভৃতি স্থাপন করা, সমবায় প্রতিষ্ঠা করা। *Noun.* 1. Anything that floats on water; প্রবমান বস্তু। 2. A floating mass of weeds, ice, etc.; a raft; প্রবমান শৈবাল, হিমানী, প্রভৃতি; ভেলা, উড়ুপ, প্রব। 3. Cork or quill used on a fishing line; বড়শীর ফাত্‌না। 4. An inflated bag or pillow used by persons learning to swim; সন্তরণশিক্ষার্থিগণ কর্ত্তৃক ব্যবহৃত বায়ুপূরিত থলিয়া বা উপাধান বিশেষ। 5. A tool for smoothing plaster; চূণবালির আস্তর মসৃণ করার জন্য কর্ণিক বিশেষ। 6. (Often *pl.*) The foot-lights on a theatre stage; (সচরাচর বহুবচনে) রঙ্গমঞ্চের সম্মুখস্থ দীপাবলী, দীপশ্রেণী। 7. A kind of file; একপ্রকার উখা। 8. A hollow ball regulating cistern tap; জলকুণ্ডের নল হইতে জলস্রাবনিয়ামক শূন্য-গর্ভ কন্দুক। 9. A kind of cart for carrying heavy goods; গুরুভার দ্রব্য বহনার্থ শকট বিশেষ। 10. A platform on wheels in procession; শোভাযাত্রায় ব্যবহৃত চক্রবিশিষ্ট মঞ্চ। **Float'-y,** *adj.* Buoyant; light; প্রবনশীল; লঘু। **Float-bridge** — প্রবমান সেতু। **Float grass**—একপ্রকার শৈবাল। **Float stone** — A kind of light stone that floats; এক প্রকার প্রবনশীল লঘু প্রস্তর। A stone for smoothing curved bricks; বক্রীভূত ইষ্টক মসৃণ করার জন্য প্রস্তরবিশেষ। **On the float**—Afloat; প্রবমান।

float'-a-ble (flöt-ă-bl), *adj.* Capable of floating; (of a stream) enabling rafts etc. to float; প্রবনযোগ্য; (নদী-সম্পর্কে) নাব্য (রঃ)।

float'-ăge (flöt-), **flöt–,** *ns.* 1. Floating; the floating capacity of a thing; প্রবন; প্রবন-শক্তি। 2. Anything that floats; প্রবমান বস্তু, প্রবমান পদার্থ। 3. The part of a ship above the water-line; জল রেখার উপরিস্থ জাহাজের অংশ।

float-ā'-tion (flöt-) **flöt–,** *ns.* 1. Act of floating; ভাসন, প্রবন। 2. (*Com.*) Act of starting a company or enterprise; (বাণিজ্য) যৌথকারবার প্রভৃতি স্থাপন। **Centre of floatation** — প্রবমান বস্তুর ভারকেন্দ্র।

float'-êr (flöt-), *n.* 1. One who or that which floats; প্রবক, প্রবনকারী। 2. (*Fin.*) A bond etc. recognised as a security; (রাজস্ব) কোম্পানীর কাগজ প্রভৃতি।

float'-ing (flöt-), *adj.* & *n.* 1. Buoyed up or in a fluid; ভাসমান, প্রবমান। 2. Unattached; as the *floating* ribs in some fishes; অসংলগ্ন। 3. Not fixed or invested; as *floating* capital or debt; অনিশ্চিত, অপ্রযুক্ত। 4. Fluctuating, as a population; হ্রাসবৃদ্ধিশীল। 5. (*Com.*) (of cargo) At sea; (বাণিজ্য—মাল প্রভৃতি সম্পর্কে) সমুদ্রোপরি। **–ly,** *adv.* **Floating anchor**—একপ্রকার নঙ্গর। **Floating-battery**—গোলাবর্ষণ দ্বারা কোন স্থান বিধ্বংস করার জন্য উপকূলাদি রক্ষার মানসে ভেলা অথবা রণপোতের খোলের

উপর স্থাপিত কামানশ্রেণী। **Floating-bridge**—ভাসমান সেতু, প্রবমান সেতু।

Floating-dock.

Floating-dock—প্রবমান নৌ-নির্ম্মাণ স্থলী। **Floating-light** — আলোক মন্দিররূপে ব্যবহৃত নঙ্গরবদ্ধ পোত। **Floating trade or price**—Relating to, or concerned with, cargoes at sea ; সমুদ্রোপরিস্থ জাহাজের মালের ব্যবসায় বা মূল্য সম্পর্কীয়।

flŏc-cĭ-nau-cĭ-nĭ-hi-li-pĭ-li-fi-ca′-tion (-nā-), *n.* Estimating as worthless ; তুচ্ছ বলিয়া পরিগণন।

flŏc′-cōse, *adj.* (*Bot.*) Having tufts ; (উদ্ভিদ্-বিদ্যা) লোমশ, গুচ্ছিত।

flŏc′-cūle, *n.* A small portion of matter resembling a tuft of wool ; পশমগুচ্ছবৎ বস্তু।

flŏc′-cü-lĕnt, —lose (-lōs), **—lous** (-lŭs), *adjs.* **1.** Resembling tufts of wool ; পশমগুচ্ছবৎ। **2.** Covered with, or showing, tufts ; গুচ্ছাবৃত, গুচ্ছপ্রদর্শী। **—lence,** *n.*

flŏc′-cü-lŭs, *n.* (*pl.* -LI). **1.** Same as FLOCCULE. **2.** (*Anat.*) A small lobe in the under surface of the cerebellum : মস্তিষ্কের পশ্চাতে ও নিম্নে প্রবর্দ্ধিত দীর্ঘ ও সূক্ষ্ম খণ্ড।

flŏc′-cŭs, *n.* (*Pl.* -CI) **1.** (*Bot.*) Tuft of woolly hairs or filaments ; (উদ্ভিদ্-বিদ্যা) পশমগুচ্ছ, কেশরগুচ্ছ। **2.** (*Zool.*) The down of unfledged birds ; (প্রাণি-বিদ্যা) অজাত-পক্ষ পক্ষিশাবকের নরম লোম।

flŏck, *n.* & *v. i.* **1.** A large number or company, as of sheep, birds etc ; পশুপক্ষীর দল বা ঝাঁক, ব্রজ, যূথ, পাল। **2.** A company of people, as in the phrase, *to come in flocks* ; একদল লোক। **3.** The body of all Christian people under a pastor ; a company in relation to one in a charge ; as, a *flock* of children in a family ; খৃষ্ট ধর্ম্মাবলম্বী জনসম্প্রদায়, খৃষ্টীয়ান পল্লীযাজকের অধীন খৃষ্টীয় উপাসকমণ্ডলী ; কোন ব্যক্তির রক্ষণাবেক্ষণের অধীন ব্যক্তিগণ। ***Verb i.*** To gather or move in companies or crowds ; জড় হওয়া, একত্র হওয়া, দলে দলে মিলিত হওয়া, দল বাঁধা, দল বাঁধিয়া চলা, দলবদ্ধ হইয়া চলা। **Flock-master**—মেষজীবী, মেষপালক। **Flocks and herds**—Sheep and cattle ; মেষ ও গোমহিষাদি গৃহপালিত পশু।

Flŏck, *n.* & *v. t.* **1.** A lock of wool, hair etc. ; পশমগুচ্ছ, কেশগুচ্ছ। **2.** (*Pl.*) Material for quilting and stuffing made of wool-refuse or torn up cloth ; গদি, লেপ, প্রভৃতির ভিতর ঠাসিবার জন্য পশুলোম, আবর্জ্জনা বা পুরাতন কাপড়ের টুকরা। **3.** Powdered wool or cloth for making flock-paper ; প্রাচীরাদি আবরণের কাগজ প্রস্তুত করার জন্য পশম বা কাপড়ের গুঁড়া। **4.** A tuft-like mass, as of a chemical precipitate ; রাসায়নিক তলছাটের গুচ্ছিত রাশি। **5.** A flock-bed ; (see below). ***Verb t.*** To coat with flock, as wallpaper ; বস্ত্র বা পশমের গুঁড়াদ্বারা আবৃত করা।

flock′-y, *adj.* Abounding with flocks or little tufts like wool ; গুচ্ছিত পশমবহুল। **Flock-bed**—পশম বা ছিন্ন বস্ত্রের টুকরা দ্বারা ভরা লেপ, তোষক প্রভৃতি। **Flock-paper**—এক প্রকার প্রাচীরগাত্র মণ্ডনের কাগজ, যাহার উপরি পৃষ্ঠ পশম ও ছিন্ন বস্ত্রের গুঁড়া দ্বারা আবৃত করা হয়।

floe (flō), *n.* A mass or sheet of floating ice ; সমুদ্রে প্রবমান তুষার রাশি।

flŏg, *v. t.* **1.** To beat with a whip or rod ; to chastise with repeated blows ; to drive, as learning laziness *into* or *out* of a person ; কষাঘাত করা, পুনঃ পুনঃ প্রহার করা ; পিটিয়া ঢুকান বা বাহির করা। **2.** To cast fishing line repeatedly over (a stream etc.) ; পুনঃ পুনঃ বড়শী ফেলা। **3.** (*Slang*) To excel ; (ইতর ভাষায়) ছাড়াইয়া যাওয়া, অতিক্রম করা। **4.** To urge forward, as a horse by whipping ; চাবুক মারিয়া অগ্রসর করা। **Flog′-ger,** *n.* One that flogs ; বেত্র প্রহারকারী। **Flog′-ing,** *n.* A whipping for punishment ; বেত্রাঘাত, বেত্রদণ্ড। **To flog a dead horse**—To waste energy ; শক্তির অপচয় করা। **To flog the dead horse**—To try to revive an interest in a subject out of date ; পুরাতন বিষয়ে লোকের উৎসাহ ও অনুরাগ উৎপাদনের চেষ্টা করা।

flood (flŭd), *n., v.t.* & *i.* **1.** A great flow of water over land ; an inundation : প্রবল জলপ্রবাহ, জলোচ্ছ্বাস (কপালঃ),ধারা, ওঘ ; জলপ্লাবন, বন্যা, জলপ্রলয় (কেন্ডি)। **2.** The flowing or rising of the tide (opposed to *ebb*) ; জোয়ার। **3.** Torrent ; downpour, as of rain, tears etc. ; আধিক্য, বাহুল্য, প্রাচুর্য্য, অতিশয্য ; বর্ষণ। **4.** (*Poet.*) The sea ; (কবিতায়) সাগর। **5.** The menstrul discharge ; ঋতু, রজঃ। ***Verb t.*** **1.** To inundate ; to deluge ; to fill to overflowing ; জলপ্লাবিত করা ; বন্যাপ্লাবিত করা ; ডুবাইয়া দেওয়া। **2.** To cover with water, as for irrigation etc. ; to fill to excess, as a country etc. with currency papers ; জলপূর্ণ করা, জলপ্লাবিত করা ; পরিপ্লাবিত করা। ***Verb i.*** **1.** To come in great quantity (*usu.* with *in*) "Thoughts *flooded in* upon us" ; প্রচুর পরিমাণে আসা। **2.** To suffer from uterine hemorrhage ; জরায়ু হইতে প্রচুর রক্তস্রাব হওয়ার দরুণ কষ্ট ভোগ করা। **Flood′-ing,** *n.* **1.** The act of overflowing or inundation ; inundation ; জলপ্লাবিত করণ ; বন্য

2. An excessive discharge of blood from the uterus ; জরায়ু হইতে অতিমাত্রায় রক্তস্রাব। **Flood-gate**—জলনির্গম পথ, স্রোতোদ্বার। **Flood-mark**—The mark or line to which the tide or flood rises ; জলপ্লাবন বা জোয়ারের সর্ব্বোচ্চ সীমা-চিহ্ন, সর্ব্বোচ্চ জলোচ্ছ্বাস-চিহ্ন। **Flood-tide** — জোয়ার, জলোচ্ছ্বাস। **The Flood, Noah's Flood**—The deluge in the days of Noah as stated in Genesis ; বাইবেলের Genesis গ্রন্থে বর্ণিত নোয়ার সময়ের জলপ্রলয়। **Flood and field**—(*Poet.*) Sea and land ; (কবিতায়) ভূমি ও সাগর।

floor (flŏr), *n.* & *v. t.* **1.** The lower surface of a room ; মেঝে, গৃহতল, কুট্টিম (paved floor)। **2.** A storey of buildings ; a set of rooms on a level ; as, the first or second *floor* ; অট্টালিকার তল ; অট্টালিকার কোন তলস্থ কক্ষশ্রেণী। **3.** The platform of a structure ; as, the *floor* of the bridge ; সেতু প্রভৃতির মঞ্চ। **4.** A part of the House of Parliament where members sit and speak ; ইংলণ্ডের মহাসভার যে অংশে সদস্যগণ উপবেশন ও বক্তৃতা করেন। **5.** The bottom of the sea, lake etc. ; হ্রদ, সাগর প্রভৃতির তলদেশ। **6.** A level area ; সমতল ক্ষেত্র। ***Verb t.*** **1.** To furnish with a floor ; to pave ; মেঝেযুক্ত করা ; পাকা করা, শাণদ্বারা বাঁধা। **2.** To knock down on the ground ; ধাক্কা দিয়া মাটিতে ফেলা, ধরাশায়ী করা, ভূপাতিত করা। **3.** To finish ; to get through successfully, as an examination ; to overcome ; শেষ করা, স[illegible]ন্ন করা ; উত্তীর্ণ হওয়া ; পরাজিত করা, পরাস্ত করা। **4.** To confound or silence by a conclusive answer or retort ; নিরুত্তর করা, ভ্যাবাচ্যাকা লাগান, তর্কে পরাস্ত করা। **Floor'-ing,** *n.* **1.** Material for the construction of a floor ; গৃহতল নির্ম্মাণের উপকরণ। **2.** A floor ; গৃহতল। **Floor'-less,** *adj.* Without a floor ; মেঝেহীন, কুট্টিমহীন। **First-floor** — দ্বিতল। **Floor-cloth**—গৃহতলাচ্ছাদন বস্ত্র। **Ground-floor**—নিম্নতল, নীচের তলা। **To floor the question paper** — To answer every question in it ; প্রশ্নপত্রের সমস্ত প্রশ্নের উত্তর করা। **To have the floor**—To have the right of speaking in a meeting before other speakers ; কোন সভায় অপর সকল বক্তার পূর্ব্বে বক্তৃতা প্রদানের ক্ষমতা থাকা। **To take the floor**—(*Esp. U. S.*) To rise to address a public meeting ; (সাধারণতঃ মার্কিণ যুক্তরাজ্যে) প্রকাশ্য সভায় বক্তৃতা করিবার জন্য দণ্ডায়মান হওয়া।

floor'-ẽr (flŏr-), *n.* **1.** A blow that floors one ; যে আঘাতে লোক ভূতলশায়ী হয়। **2.** A disconcerting news or argument ; হতবুদ্ধিতাজনক যুক্তি বা সংবাদ। **3.** A too difficult paper or question ; অতি কঠিন প্রশ্নপত্র বা প্রশ্ন।

flŏp, *v. i., t., n.* & *adv.* **1.** To swing or sway about heavily ; "The sail *flops* against the mast" ; to make a noise ; as, the *flopping* of wings ; ঝাপ্‌টা মারা ; (পাখ্‌সাটের মত) শব্দ করা। **2.** To sit or lie down heavily or clumsily ; to move clumsily ; ধপ্ করিয়া বসিয়া পড়া বা শয়ন করা ; ধুব্‌ধাব্ করিয়া চলা। ***Verb t.*** **1.** To clap or strike frequently ; as to *flop* the wings ; ঝাঁকড়ান, বার বার ঝাপ্‌টা মারা। **2.** To drop down suddenly or noisily ; as, to *flop* oneself down ; ধপাৎ করিয়া ফেলিয়া দেওয়া। ***Noun.*** Act or sound of flopping ; ধপাৎ শব্দ, ধুব্‌ধাব্ শব্দ। ***Adv.*** With a flop ; ধুব্‌ধাব্ করিয়া, ধপাস্ করিয়া।

flō'-rȧ, *n.* **1.** (*Myth.*) (cap.) The goddess of flowers and gardens ; রোমানদিগের বাসন্তীদেবী বা পুষ্পের অধিরাণী, পুষ্পদেবী। [এই দেবীর মস্তকে কুসুমকিরীট, কণ্ঠে পুষ্পমালিকা এবং অঙ্গের স্থানে স্থানে অন্যান্য কুসুমাভরণ শোভা পাইত]। **2.** The plants of a particular district or period ; বিশেষ অঞ্চল বা যুগের উদ্ভিদ্‌বর্গ। **3.** A list of plants of a particular region or period ; দেশ বা কাল-বিশেষের সমগ্র উদ্ভিদের তালিকা বা বিবরণ, উদ্ভিদ-নামমালা (সাঃ পঃ), উদ্ভিদবর্গ (ঐ), উদ্ভিদমালা (ঐ)। **—ral,** *adj.* **1.** Relating to Flora ; রোমানদিগের পুষ্পদেবী সম্বন্ধীয়। **2.** Relating to, or like, flowers ; made of flowers ; as a *floral* wreath ; পুষ্প-সম্পর্কীয়, পৌষ্পিক, কুসুমোপম, পুষ্পবৎ ; পুষ্পময়, পুষ্পরচিত। **Floral-zone**—বিশেষ উদ্ভিজ্জ প্রভৃতি সম্পন্ন ভূ-ভাগ।

Flora.

Flŏr'-ĕn-tīne, *adj.* & *n.* Of, or pertaining to, Florence in Italy ; ইতালীর অন্তঃপাতী ফ্লোরেন্স নগর-সম্বন্ধীয়। ***Noun.*** **1.** An inhabitant of Florence ; ফ্লোরেন্স্ নগরের অধিবাসী। **2.** A kind of twilled silk stuff ; একপ্রকার টের্চ্চাবুনা রেশমী কাপড়।

flō-rĕs'-cence (-sĕns), *n.* A blossoming state or season ; তরুলতাদির পুষ্পোদ্গমকাল বা কুসুমিতাবস্থা, পুষ্পবিকাশকাল, পুষ্পোদ্গমকাল, কুসুমপ্রসূতি সময়। **—cent,** *adj.* In a blooming state ; উদ্ভিন্ন-কুসুম।

flō'-rĕt, *n.* **1.** A small flower ; (*Bot.*) one of the little flowers making up a composite flower ; ক্ষুদ্র পুষ্প, পুষ্পিকা ; (উদ্ভিদ্-বিদ্যা) কুসুমস্তবকান্তর্গত এক একটী পুষ্পিকা। **2.** A silk yarn or floss ; রেশমের সূতা বা গুটীর বাহিরের নিকৃষ্ট রেশম। **The floret of the disk**—কুসুমস্তবকের মধ্যস্থলবর্ত্তী পুষ্পিকা। **The floret of the ray** — কুসুমস্তবকের প্রান্তবর্ত্তী পুষ্পিকা।

flo′-ri-cŭl-tūre, *n.* The cultivation of flowering plants ; পুষ্পের চাষ। **–cul′-tur-al,** *adj.* **–cul′-tur-ist,** *n.*

flŏr′-id, *adj.* **1.** Excessively ornate, as a literary, musical or artistic style ; অলঙ্কারবহুল। **2.** Bright in colour ; flushed with red ; উজ্জ্বলবর্ণ, দীপ্তবর্ণ ; অরুণিত। **3.** Ostentatious ; জাঁকাল, জমকালো, আড়ম্বরপূর্ণ। **–ly,** *adv.* **Flo-rid′-i-ty, Flor′-id-ness,** *ns.*

Flŏr′-i-dă, *n.* One of the United States ; মার্কিণ যুক্তরাজ্যের অন্তর্গত রাজ্যবিশেষ। **Florida water**—এক প্রকার সুবাসিত জল। **Forida wood** — খচিত করার কার্য্যে ব্যবহৃত কাষ্ঠবিশেষ।

flŏr′-in, *n.* **1.** Foreign gold or silver coin current at different times ; বিভিন্ন সময়ে প্রচলিত বৈদেশিক (ইংলণ্ডের পক্ষে) স্বর্ণ বা রৌপ্য মুদ্রা। **2.** (*Hist.*) An English gold coin of Edward III. ; (ইতিহাস) তৃতীয় এড্‌ওয়ার্ডের সময়ের ইংলণ্ড দেশীয় স্বর্ণমুদ্রা-বিশেষ। **3.** A British silver coin worth 2*s.* ; ২ শিলিং মূল্যের ইংলণ্ডীয় রৌপ্যমুদ্রা বিশেষ।

flŏ′-rū-it, *n.* The period during which a person flourishes ; মানবের উন্নতি ও সমৃদ্ধির কাল।

flō′-rȳ, *n.* & *v. i.* See FLURRY.

flŏs′-cūle, *n.* A floret of an aggregate flower ; পুষ্পিকা। **–cu-lar, –cu-lous,** *adjs.* Composed of many floscules or florets ; বহু পুষ্পিকা রচিত।

flŏss, *n.* **1.** Silky substance in certain plants ; কোন কোন বীজের খোসায় প্রাপ্ত রোম বা তুলার মত পদার্থ। **2.** Untwisted filaments of silk, used in embroidery ; চিকণের কাজে ব্যবহৃত অপাকান রেসমী সূতা। **Floss′-y,** *adj.* **Floss-silk**—গুটীর বাহিরের নিকৃষ্ট রেসম।

flō′-tă, *n.* (*Span.*) A commercial fleet ; (স্পেন) বাণিজ্য পোত শ্রেণী।

flō′-tănt, *adj.* (*Her.*) Represented as floating in the air ; (কুলবিদ্যা) বায়ুতে উড্ডীন বা প্রবমান ভাবে চিত্রিত।

flō-tā′-tion, *n.* Same of FLOATATION.

flō-til′-lă, *n.* A little fleet ; a fleet of small vessels ; ক্ষুদ্র পোতবহর ; ক্ষুদ্র জাহাজের বহর।

flŏt′-săm, *n.* **1.** (*Law*) Goods lost by shipwreck and found floating on the sea—in distinction from JETSAM ; জলমগ্ন এবং বিধ্বস্ত পোতের যে সকল অংশ বা মাল জলে ভাসিয়া থাকে, অস্বামিক তরিত-দ্রব্য (কেণ্ডি)। **2.** Oyster-spawn ; ঝিনুকের ডিম, শুক্তিডিম্ব।

flounce (flowns) *v. i.* & *n.* To throw about the body or limbs ; to go with agitated or violent motion ; হাবুডুবু খাওয়া, আছাড়ি পিছাড়ি খাওয়া ; আছাড়ি পিছাড়ি খাইতে খাইতে চলা। ***Noun.*** A sudden jerk of the body or limb ; আছাড়ি পিছাড়ি, হাবুডুবু।

flounce (flowns), *n.* & *v. t.* A strip of cloth sewed round a frock gown, with the lower border loose and spreading ; পোষাকের ঝালর। ***Verb t.*** To adorn with a flounce ; পোষাকে ঝালর লাগান।

floun′-dêr (flown-), *v. i.* & *n.* **1.** To fling the limbs and body, as in making efforts to move, struggle, as a horse in mire ; to toss and tumble ; হাত পা ছোঁড়া ; আছাড়ি পিছাড়ি করা। **2.** To make mistakes ; to manage business badly or with difficulty ; ভুল করা ; কদর্য্যভাবে কার্য্য নির্ব্বাহ করা, আনাড়ীর মত কাজ করা, কষ্টে নির্ব্বাহ করা। ***Noun.*** A floundering ; staggering attempts to go on ; হাবু ডুবু ; আছাড়ি পিছাড়ি।

floun′-dêr (flown-), *n.* A small flat fish ; একপ্রকার ক্ষুদ্র চ্যাপ্টা মৎস্য।

flour (flowr), *n.* & *v. t.* Finely ground meal of wheat or other grain ; the fine powder of any substance ; ময়দা, আটা ; সূক্ষ্মচূর্ণ। ***Verb t.*** **1.** (*U. S.*) To grind and bolt, as wheat ; পিষিয়া চূর্ণ করা, পেষা। **2.** To sprinkle with flour ; কোন কিছুর উপর ময়দা ছিটাইয়া দেওয়া। **Flour′-y,** *adj.* ময়দার মত। **Flour-box**—ময়দা ছড়ানের জন্য টীনের বাক্স।

flour′-ish (flŭr-), *v. i., t.* & *n.* **1.** To grow luxuriantly ; to thrive, as a plant ; সতেজে বর্দ্ধিত হওয়া ; প্রচুর পরিমাণে জন্মা। **2.** To prosper ; to be in one's prime ; (of authors, painters, etc.) to be active *in* or *about* a certain time ; উন্নতি করা, শ্রীমান্ হওয়া, সমৃদ্ধ হওয়া, সমৃদ্ধিমান হওয়া, শ্রীসম্পন্ন হওয়া ; উন্নতির পরাকাষ্ঠা প্রাপ্ত হওয়া ; কোন বিশেষ সময়ে কার্য্যতৎপরতা প্রদর্শন করা। **3.** To use florid language in writing or speech ; বক্তৃতা বা লিখায় সালঙ্কার ভাষা প্রয়োগ করা, অলঙ্কারবহুল ভাষা প্রয়োগ করা। **4.** To play with bold and irregular notes ; তালমানের দিকে দৃষ্টি না রাখিয়া জমকালো ভাবে বাজান। **5.** To use flourishes in handwriting ; টানটোন দিয়া সাজাইয়া লিখা। **6.** To boast ; to brag ; গর্ব্ব করা ; আস্ফালন করা, বড়াই করা। ***Verb t.*** **1.** To embellish with flowers or figures ; to embellish ; পুষ্পাদিদ্বারা বিভূষিত করা ; মণ্ডিত করা, ভূষিত করা। **2.** To brandish, as a sword etc. ; to throw about as limbs ; to display ostentatiously ; তরবারি প্রভৃতি ঘুরান, অস্ত্রাদি ভাঁজা ; (হাত পা) ছোড়া, সঞ্চালন করা ; আড়ম্বর সহকারে প্রদর্শন করা। ***Noun.*** **1.** (*Rare*) Prosperity ; vigour ; (অপ্রঃ) সমৃদ্ধি ; তেজ। **2.** Ostentatious decoration ; a parade of words and figures ; a florid expression ; show ; as, a *flourish* of wit or rhetoric ; জমকালো ভূষা ; শব্দালঙ্কারের আড়ম্বর প্রদর্শন,

শব্দাড়ম্বর ; অলঙ্কারবহুল উক্তি ; বাহার। **3.** A fanciful stroke of the pen in handwriting ; লেখার টানটোন। **4.** A florid musical passage ; a fanfare, as of trumpets ; জমকালো বাদ্য ; বাদ্যভাণ্ড। **5.** Ostentatious waving, as of weapon, hand, etc. ; আড়ম্বর সহকারে (অস্ত্রাদি) ঘূর্ণন। **—er,** *n.* **—ing,** *adj.* Thriving ; prosperous ; showy ; উন্নতিশীল, বর্দ্ধমান, বর্দ্ধিষ্ণু ; সমৃদ্ধিশালী, শ্রীমান্, শ্রীসম্পন্ন ; আড়ম্বরপূর্ণ।

flout (flowt), *v. t., i.* & *n.* To mock ; to insult ; to treat with contempt ; ব্যঙ্গ করা, বিদ্রূপ করা ; অবমাননা করা ; অবজ্ঞার সহিত ব্যবহার করা, হেয় জ্ঞান করা। ***Verb i.*** To scoff or sneer (at) বিদ্রূপ করা। ***Noun.*** A mock ; an insult ; ব্যঙ্গ ; অবমাননা, অপমান। **Flout'-ing-ly,** *adv.* Insultingly ; অবজ্ঞার সহিত। **Flouting-stock** — (*Shaks.*) An object of flouting ; অবজ্ঞার পাত্র, বিদ্রূপের পাত্র।

flow (flō), *v. i., t.* & *n.* **1.** To slide along, as a stream ; to circulate, as a liquid ; to run ; as, tears *flow* from eyes ; প্রবাহিত হওয়া ; সঞ্চালিত হওয়া ; বহিয়া যাওয়া, বহা। **2.** To proceed ; to issue ; নির্গত হওয়া ; নিঃসৃত হওয়া। **3.** To pass smoothly, as a period etc. ; to move easily, as a talk, style etc. ; to be uttered easily ; to sound smoothly to the ear ; অতিবাহিত হওয়া ; অনায়াসে বহিয়া যাওয়া ; সুখোচ্চার্য্য হওয়া ; সুশ্রাব্য হওয়া, শ্রবণসুখদ হওয়া। **4.** (*Archaic*) To be plentifully supplied *with* ; (অপ্র:) প্রচুর পরিমাণে প্রাপ্ত হওয়া। **5.** To hang loose and waving, as a lock of hair etc. ; শিথিল ভাবে লম্বমান হওয়া, দোদুল্যমান হওয়া, বিলম্বিত হওয়া। **6.** To rise, as the tide, (opposite to *ebb*) ; স্ফীত হওয়া, জোয়ার হওয়া। **7.** (*Math.*) To vary uniformly ; (গণিতশাস্ত্র) নিয়ত এক রূপ পরিবর্ত্তিত হওয়া। **8.** To discharge blood excessively from the uterus ; জরায়ু হইতে অতিরিক্ত রক্তস্রাব হওয়া। **9.** (Of blood) To be split ; পাত হওয়া, ক্ষরিত হওয়া। ***Verb t.*** To cover with water ; to flood ; জলপ্লাবিত করা ; বন্যাপ্লাবিত করা। ***Noun.*** **1.** Flowing or streaming, as of a river etc. ; প্রবহণ। **2.** A stream of any liquid ; current ; স্রোতঃ, প্রবাহ ; প্রবাহিনী, স্রোতস্বতী। **3.** A continuous gentle movement like that of a river ; copious outpouring ; as, a *flow* of thought or words ; প্রবাহ ; প্রচুর নিঃস্রব। **4.** The rise of tide ; জোয়ার। **5.** The quantity that flows ; যে পরিমাণ প্রবাহিত হয়। **6.** Undulating as of a dress etc. ; পোষাক প্রভৃতির তরঙ্গায়িত ভাব। **7.** Overflowing of the Nile etc. ; নীল নদ প্রভৃতির কূলপ্লাবন। **Flow'-age,** *n.* Act of flowing ; state of being flooded ; প্রবহণ, ক্ষরণ, গলন, বিস্রব ; প্লাবিতাবস্থা। **Flow'-ing,** *adj.* Moving, as a fluid ; fluent, as a style ; hanging loose and waving as hair ; সঞ্চরণশীল, সঞ্চরমান ; প্রবহমাণ ; বিলম্বমান। **Flow'-ing-ly,** *adv.* **Flowing tide**—Progressive tendency ; প্রবহমাণ স্রোতঃ। **Flow of spirits**—স্বভাবসিদ্ধ হাবভাব। **To flow with milk and honey**—ধনধান্যে পূর্ণ হওয়া।

flow'-ĕr, *n., v. t.* & *i.* **1.** The blossom of a plant ; ফুল, প্রসূন, পুষ্প, কুসুম, সুমনস। **2.** A flowering plant ; ফুলগাছ, পুষ্পবৃক্ষ, কুসুমতরু। **3.** The best and choicest part or example of anything ; the state or time of bloom or of vigour ; as, in the *flower* of one's age ; উৎকৃষ্টাংশ, সারভাগ ; পুষ্পিতাবস্থা, পুষ্পপ্রসব কাল, সতেজভাব, নবীনতার কাল। **4.** The prime, as of life etc. ; জীবনের প্রথমভাগ, যৌবনকাল, নবযৌবন, প্রথমযৌবন, নবতারুণ্য। **5.** (*Usu. pl.*) Figures of speech ; ornamental phrases ; শব্দালঙ্কার ; সালঙ্কারবাক্য, অলঙ্কারঘটিত বাক্য। **6.** (*Old Chem.*) *pl.* A powdery substance left after sublimation ; (প্রাচীন রসায়ন-শাস্ত্র) ঊর্দ্ধপাতন ক্রিয়ার পর স্থিত সূক্ষ্ম চূর্ণাকার পদার্থ। **7.** Scum formed by fermentation, as of tan ; গাঁজন দ্বারা উৎপন্ন গাদ। **8.** (*Pl.*) Menstrual discharges ; স্ত্রীরজঃ, পুষ্প, আর্ত্তব। ***Verb t.*** (*Gardening*) **1.** To cause, as some plants to bear flowers ; (উদ্যানকর্ম্ম) পুষ্পোৎপাদনক্ষম করা। **2.** To adorn with figures of flowers or floral designs ; কৃত্রিম পুষ্পে ভূষিত করা, পুষ্পচিত্রিত করা। ***Verb i.*** To blossom ; to bloom ; as, the plant *flowers* in April ; প্রস্ফুটিত হওয়া ; বিকশিত হওয়া, উৎফুল্ল হওয়া। **—er,** *n.* Plant that flowers at a particular time ; যে বৃক্ষ কোন বিশেষকালে পুষ্পপ্রসব করে। **—et,** *n.* A small flower ; ক্ষুদ্র পুষ্প, পুষ্পিকা। **—i-ness,** *n.* **—ing,** *adj.* Producing flowers ; blossoming ; পুষ্পপ্রসূ ; কুসুমিত। **—less,** *adj.*

Parts of a flower.

having no flowers ; অপুষ্পক। **—y,** *adj.* **1.** Full of flowers ; abounding in flowers ; সপুষ্প, পুষ্পময় ; পুষ্পবহুল, কুসুমবহুল। **2.** Highly embellished with figurative language ; florid ; অলঙ্কারবহুল, অলঙ্কারঘটিত ; সালঙ্কার। **Flower-age**—Flowering state ;

flowers in general ; floral ornament ; কুসুমিতাবস্থা ; পুষ্পসমূহ ; পুষ্পসংহতি, পুষ্পাভরণ। **Flower-bed**—A bed made of flowers; কুসুমশয্যা, কুসুমাস্তরণ, পুষ্পশয্যা। **Flower-bell**—ঘণ্টাকৃতি পুষ্প। **Flower-bud**—An unopened flower ; কুসুমকলিকা, ফুলকলি কুসুমকোরক। **Flower-clock**—পুষ্পঘড়ী [ইহাতে এরূপভাবে পুষ্পবৃক্ষ সমূহ সাজান হয় যাহাতে পুষ্পের প্রস্ফোটন ও সঙ্কোচদ্বারা সময় নিরূপণ করা যায়]। **Flower-girl**—One who sells flowers ; পুষ্পবিক্রেত্রী বালিকা, পুষ্পবালা, ফুলওয়ালী। **Flower-head**—পুষ্পস্তবক। **Flower-piece**—পুষ্পালেখ্য, পুষ্পচিত্র। **Flowerpot**—A pot in which plants are grown ; পুষ্পপাত্র, ফুলের টব বা গামলা। **Flower-show** — পুষ্প প্রদর্শনী। **Flower-stalk**—পুষ্পবৃন্ত, কুসুম বৃন্ত। **Flower-vase**—পুষ্পাধান, সাজি। **In flower**—In a state of blooming : ফুটন্ত, প্রস্ফুট। **The Flowery Kingdom**—চীনদেশ।

flower-de-luce — See FLEUR DE LIS.

flown (flōn), *p. p.* Of FLY.

flown (flōn), *adj.* (*Archaic*) Swollen ; puffed up ; (অপ্রঃ) স্ফীত ; গর্ব্বস্ফীত।

flŭc'-tū-āte, *v. i.* 1. (*Rare*) To move as waves; (অপ্রঃ) তরঙ্গবৎ উর্দ্ধাধঃ চালিত হওয়া। 2. To be wavering or unsteady ; to vary irregularly ; to oscillate ; এদিক ওদিক করা; অনিশ্চিত হওয়া ; উঠা নামা, উঠ্‌তি পড়তি হওয়া ; ইতস্ততঃ করা। **—ant,** *adj.* Moving like wave; তরঙ্গবৎ সঞ্চারী। **—a-ting,** *adj.* Unsteady ; waving ; changeable ; অস্থির ; তরঙ্গায়িত; হ্রাসবৃদ্ধিশীল। **—a'-tion,** *n.* A Wavering ; unsteadiness, as of opinion, price etc. ; vicissitude ; হ্রাসবৃদ্ধি ; ঘাট্‌তি বাড়্‌তি, উঠ্‌তি, পড়্‌তি; অবস্থা বিপর্য্যয়।

flue (flū), *n.* 1. A passage for smoke or heated air etc. ; ধূম অথবা উষ্ণবাষ্প নির্গম পথ, ধূমনির্গমনালী, ধূমমার্গ (আঃ বঃ)। 2. A pipe for conveying heat ; উত্তাপসঞ্চালক নলবিশেষ। 3. A tube for heating water in some kind of boiler ; কোন কোন প্রকার বাষ্পজনকে জল উষ্ণ করার জন্য চুঙ্গী-বিশেষ। 4. An opening in organ mouthpipes ; বাদ্যযন্ত্রের মুখ-নলের ছিদ্র-বিশেষ।

flue (flū), *n.* A kind of fishing net ; এক প্রকার মাছ ধরার জাল।

flue (flū), *n.* A light downy matter ; এক প্রকার হাল্কা তুলার মত জিনিষ। **Flue'-y,** *adj.*

flu(e) (flū), *n.* (*Colloq.*) Short for INFLUENZA which see.

flue (flū), *v. i.* & *t.* To expand ; বিস্তার করা। ***Verb t.*** To make (an opening) to expand inwards and outwards ; বাহিরের দিকে ও ভিতরের দিকে (ছিদ্র) বিস্তার করা।

flū'-ĕnt, *adj.* & *n.* 1. (*Rare*) Easily moving ; flowing ; (অপ্রঃ) লীলাগামী, অনায়াসগামী ; প্রবহমাণ। 2. (*Rare*) Liable to change ; (অপ্রঃ) পরিবর্ত্তনশীল, পরিবর্ত্তনসহ। 3. Graceful ; easy, as a curve, motion etc. ; মাধুর্য্যময় ; স্বচ্ছন্দ, সলাল। 4. Copious ; coming easily ; as, a *fluent* speech, style etc. ; অনর্গলবাক্, বচস্বী (আঃ বঃ), চপলজিহ্ব (কেঙি), চপলবাক্ (ঐ), বাক্‌চপল (ঐ) ; অনর্গল। 5. (*Math.*) Fluential ; পরিবর্ত্তনশীল সংখ্যা সম্পর্কীয়। ***Noun.*** (*Math.*) A variable quantity considered as increasing or diminishing ; পরিবর্ত্তনশীল সংখ্যা। **—en-cy,** *n.* The quality of being fluent ; ready utterance ; easy flow ; অনর্গলভাষিতা ; বাক্‌পাটব ; অনর্গল প্রবাহ। **—ly,** *adv.* In a fluent manner ; অনর্গল ভাবে।

flū-ĕn'-tial (-shăl), *adj.* (*Math.*) (গণিত) পরিবর্ত্তনশীল সংখ্যা-সম্পর্কীয়।

flŭff, *n., v. t.* & *i.* 1. Light down or nap such as rises from blankets etc. ; soft fur ; কম্বলাদির আঁশ বা শুঁয়া, নরম পাতলা তুলা, পেঁজা তুলা ; শশকাদি জন্তুর কোমল লোম। 2. Soft short hair on the lip or cheek ; কোমল গুম্ফ বা শ্মশ্রু। 3. (*Slang—theatre*) A part imperfectly learned ; অসম্পূর্ণভাবে শিক্ষিত অভিনেয় অংশ, যে ভূমিকা বা অভিনেয় অংশ সুচারুরূপে শিক্ষা করা হয় নাই। ***Verb t.*** 1. To put soft surface on (the flesh-side of leather) ; চর্ম্মের মাংসসংলগ্ন দিক মসৃণ করা। 2. To make into fluff ; পেঁজা তুলার মত করা। 3. To shake *out* or *up* as one's feathers etc. into a mass like fluff ; ঝাঁকিয়া কোমল পশমের মত করা। ***Verb i.*** (*Slang*) To blunder in a theatrical part ; নাটকের অভিনেয় অংশ বলিতে ভুল করা।

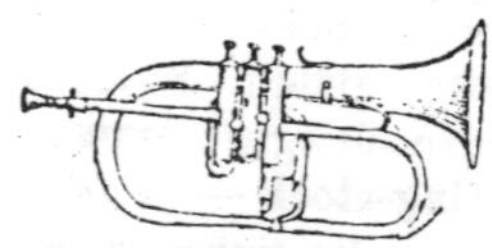

Flugelhorn.

flū'-gĕl-hŏrn, *n.* A hunting horn ; মৃগয়ার জন্য শিঙ্গা।

flū'-id, *adj.* & *n.* 1. Liquid or gaseous ; capable of flowing, জলীয়, বাষ্পীয় ; প্রবহণক্ষম। 2. (*Fig.*) Not solid, rigid or stable; (লক্ষণায়) দ্রব, সরিল (রাঃ সুঃ ত্রিঃ)। ***Noun.*** 1. A substance whose particles move easily among themselves ; তরল দ্রব্য, দ্রবদ্রব্য। 2. A liquid constituent or secretion ; তরল উপাদান বা স্রাব। **—al,** *adj.* **—id'-i-fy,** *v. t.* To render fluid ; তরল করা, দ্রব করা। **—id'-i-ty,** *n.* A liquid or gaseous state ; তরলতা, দ্রবত্ব, আর্দ্রত্ব।

flūke, *n.* 1. A flat fish (now rare); চেপ্টা মৎস্য-বিশেষ (অধুনা লুপ্ত)। 2. A parasitic worm found in sheep's liver ; মেষের যকৃতে প্রাপ্ত তদঙ্গপুষ্ট ক্রিমিকীট বিশেষ। 3. A kind of kidney potato ; এক প্রকার ডিম্বাকার বিলাতী আলু।

flüke, *n.* **1.** That part of an anchor which fastens in the ground ; নঙ্গরের যে অংশ মৃত্তিকাতে প্রোথিত থাকে, নঙ্গরের হুল-ফলা। **2.** (*Pl.*) The tail of a whale ; (বহু বচন) তিমিমৎস্তের পুচ্ছ। **3.** The barbed head of an arrow, lance, etc. ; তীর বা বড়শার হুলযুক্ত অগ্রভাগ। **4.** An accidentally successful stroke in billiards ; as, he won by a *fluke* ; (*fig.*) an accidental or unexpected advantage ; আংটাল খেলায় — দৈবজনিত সুবিধাজনক আঘাত ; দৈবপ্রেরিত সুযোগ, সৌভাগ্য। **Fluk'-i-ly,** *adv.* **Fluk'-i-ness,** *n.* **Fluk'-y,** *adj.*

flüme, *n., v. i.* & *t.* (*Chiefly U. S.*) **1.** An artificial channel conveying water for industrial use ; (প্রধানতঃ মার্কিণ যুক্তরাজ্যে) কলকারখানাদির কাজের জল সরবরাহের জন্য কৃত্রিম খাত, যন্ত্রজলবাহিকা। **2.** (*U. S.*) A ravine or gorge with a stream ; (মার্কিণ যুক্তরাজ্যে) নদী-সমন্বিত সঙ্কীর্ণ গিরিবর্ত্ম। ***Verb i.*** To construct a flume ; যন্ত্রজলবাহিকা খনন করা। ***Verb t.*** To convey down a flume ; যন্ত্রজলবাহিকা দ্বারা প্রবাহিত করা। **To be, or go, up the flame**—বিপদ্ বা দুর্ঘটনায় পড়া, সর্ব্বনাশ হওয়া।

flüm'-mêr-ȳ, *n.* **1.** (*Dial.*) Jelly-like food made of flour or meal ; (উপভাষায়) ময়দা বা আটা হইতে প্রস্তুত খাদ্যবিশেষ। **2.** A sweet dish made with milk, flour, eggs, etc. ; দুগ্ধ, ডিম্ব, ময়দা প্রভৃতিদ্বারা প্রস্তুত পিষ্টকবিশেষ। **3.** Empty compliments ; trash ; nonsense ; অসার স্তুতি, শূন্য, গর্ভ প্রশংসা ; তুচ্ছ বিষয় ; বাজে কথা।

flüm'-mŏx, *v. t.* (*Slang*) To confound ; to disconcert ; (ইতর ভাষায়) হতবুদ্ধি করা, ভ্যাবা চ্যাকা লাগান ; ব্যর্থ করা, বিফল করা।

flŭmp, *v. i., t.* & *n.* To fall or move suddenly and heavily ; ধপাস্ করিয়া পড়া, ধুব্ ধাব্ করিয়া যাওয়া, ঢিব্ করিয়া পড়া। ***Verb t.*** To set or throw *down* with a dump ; ধপাস্ করিয়া ফেলা বা রাখা। ***Noun.*** The act of flumping ; the dull sound caused by the act ; ঢিব্ করিয়া পড়ন ; ঢিব্ শব্দ।

flŭng, *p. t.* & *p. p.* of FLING.

flun'-key, flunk'-y (flŭng-kĭ), *ns.* **1.** A liveried servant ; a foot-man ; পরিচ্ছদধারী ভৃত্য, তক্‌মাপরাভৃত্য ; চাপরাসী। **2.** (*Slang*) A toady ; চাটুকার, পা চাটা, ধামাধরা। **—dom,** *n.* The flunkey world ; পরিচ্ছদধারী সম্প্রদায়, চাটুকারসম্প্রদায়, ধামাধরার দল। **—ism,** *n.* The characteristic of a flunkey ; toadyism ; হীনানুগত্য ; চাটুকারিতা।

flü'-ŏr, *n.* (*Min.*) A beautiful transparent mineral, usually coloured and sometimes crystalline, (also called FLUOR SPAR) ; একপ্রকার স্বচ্ছ সুন্দর খনিজ পদার্থ—ইহা সচরাচর রঞ্জিত এবং কখনও কখনও স্ফটিকবৎ হইয়া থাকে।

flü-ŏ-rĕs'-cence (-sĕns), *n.* **1.** A peculiar blue appearance exhibited by certain substances exposed to sunlight ; সূর্য্যালোকে রক্ষিত কুইনাইন প্রভৃতি দ্বারা প্রদর্শিত নীলিমা, ঝলক (হিঃ কোঃ), স্বদীপক, তরলজ্যোতি (প্রবাসী)। [জলমিশ্রিত কুইনাইন সালফেটের উপর সূর্য্যরশ্মি কেন্দ্রীভূত করা হইলে উহাতে বেগুনে বা বেগুনে বর্ণের অতীত রশ্মিদ্বারা সূচীক্ষেত্রের আকার নীলবর্ণ যে আলোক রচিত হইয়া থাকে। কাচ, হরিদ্রার আরক, ইউরেনিয়ম্ প্রভৃতি পদার্থেও উক্ত ধর্ম্ম দৃষ্ট হয়। ১৮৩৩ খৃঃ অব্দে Sir D. Brewster উক্ত পদার্থ সমূহের এই বিশেষ ধর্ম্ম আবিষ্কার করেন। Sir G. G. Stokesএর ঝলক বিষয়ক মৌলিক গবেষণাও অতি মূল্যবান বলিয়া বৈজ্ঞানিক সমাজে গৃহীত হইয়াছে।] **2.** The property of rendering ultra-violet rays visible ; অতি-নীলারুণকিরণ দর্শনযোগ্য করার ধর্ম্ম, অতিনীলারুণরশ্মি-প্রদর্শনধর্ম্মিতা। **—cent,** *adj.* Having the property of fluorescence ; স্বদীপকধর্ম্মা। **—resce',** *v. i.* To produce or exhibit fluorescence ; স্বদীপক উৎপাদন বা প্রদর্শন করা।

flü'-ŏr-īde, *n.* (*Chem.*) Compound of fluorine with another element ; (রসায়ন-শাস্ত্র) অপর কোন মূল পদার্থের সহিত প্লবের সংমিশ্রণ।

flü-ŏr-ine (-ĭn), *n.* (*Chem.*) A non-metallic element grouped with bromine, chlorine and iodine : (রসায়নশাস্ত্র) প্লব (হিঃ কোঃ), একপ্রকার অধাতব মূল পদার্থ।

flü'-ŏr-spâr, *n.* See FLUOR.

flŭr'-rȳ, *n.* & *v. i.* **1.** A sudden gust of wind ; a light temporary breeze ; দম্‌কা বাতাস ; মৃদু বাতাস। **2.** Commotion ; excitement ; nervous hurry ; বিক্ষোভ ; অস্থিরতা, ব্যস্ততা, উত্তেজনা, চাঞ্চল্য ; তাড়াহুড়া, সংরম্ভ, ত্বরা, হুড়মুড়। **3.** The violent spasm of a dying whale ; তিমি মৎস্যের মৃত্যুকালীন প্রবল আক্ষেপ বা খেঁচুনি। ***Verb i.*** To excite or agitate ; to confuse by haste or noise ; চঞ্চল করা, অস্থির করা, ব্যতিব্যস্ত করা, উদ্বেজিত করা, ব্যস্তসমস্ত করা ; তাড়াহুড়া বা গণ্ডগোল করিয়া ভ্যাবাচ্যাকা লাগান।

flŭsh, *v. i.* & *t.* **1.** To rush ; to flow suddenly ; "blood *flushes* into the face" ; প্রধাবিত হওয়া ; সহসা বেগে প্রবাহিত হওয়া। **2.** To glow ; দীপ্তি পাওয়া। **3.** To turn red ; to blush ; রক্তবর্ণ হওয়া, লাল হইয়া উঠা, অরুণবর্ণ ধারণ করা ; লাজে লাল হওয়া, সরমরক্তিম হওয়া, লজ্জায় গণ্ডস্থল আরক্তিম হওয়া, লজ্জারুণিত হওয়া। **4.** To throw out fresh shoots, as a plant ; নূতন প্ররোহ জন্মা, নবপল্লবোদ্গম হওয়া। ***Verb t.*** **1.** To flood, as a meadow etc ; to cleanse, as a drain etc. by a rush of water ; জলপ্লাবিত করা ; জলস্রোত প্রবাহিত করিয়া নর্দ্দমা প্রভৃতি পরিষ্কার করা। **2.** To cause to glow or blush ; to suffuse with worm colour ; দীপ্ত করা, লজ্জারুণিত করা ; লোহিত বর্ণোচ্ছ্বাস দ্বারা আপ্লুত

করা। 3. To excite; to encourage; to elate; উত্তেজিত করা, উদ্দীপ্ত করা; প্রোৎসাহিত করা; উল্লসিত করা, উৎফুল্ল করা, প্রফুল্ল করা।

flŭsh, *n.* 1. A sudden flow or rush of water, as for cleansing purpose; নর্দমাদি পরিষ্করণের জন্য জলপ্রবাহ বা জলস্রোতঃ। 2. A rush of blood to face; a redness thus produced; as, a *flush* on a cheek or cloud; vigour, as of youth etc.; freshness; মুখমণ্ডলে সবেগে রক্ত সঞ্চলন; (তজ্জনিত) রক্তিমা, লালিমা, আরক্তিম আভা, মুখমণ্ডলের গোলাবি বিভা, লজ্জারুণিমা, মুখমণ্ডলের আরক্তিম শোভা, কপোলরাগ; তেজ; নবীনতা। 3. A sudden abundance of anything; as, a *flush* of passengers in the street; প্রাচুর্য্য, বাহুল্য, ছড়াছড়ি। 4. A rush of emotion; elation caused by it or by victory etc.; as, a *flush* of joy; আবেগোল্লাস; প্রফুল্লতা, উৎফুল্লতা, উল্লাস। 5. A fresh growth, as of grass etc.; নবপল্লবোদ্গম। 6. A hot fit in fever; হঠাৎ জ্বরের প্রকোপ বৃদ্ধি।

flŭsh, *n., v. i. & t.* A flock of birds suddenly started up or flushed; অকস্মাৎ চমকিত হইয়া উড্ডীয়মান পক্ষিশ্রেণী। ***Verb i.*** To start up and fly away, as birds; চমকিয়া উড়া। ***Verb t.*** To cause (birds) to take wing and fly away; পক্ষীদিগকে উড়াইয়া দেওয়া।

flŭsh, *n.* A set of cards all of one suit; এক রঙ্গের এক প্রস্থ তাস।

flŭsh, *adj. & v. t.* (*Used predicatively*) 1. Having a plentiful supply of; as, one *flush with,* or *of,* money; abundant, as money; prosperous, as time; বহুল, প্রচুর; সমৃদ্ধিপূর্ণ, সঙ্গতিপন্ন। 2. Well filled; in flood; as, a stream is *flush* in the rainy season; পরিপূর্ণ; বন্যাপ্লাবিত। 3. Even or level in surface; on a level with adjacent surface; সমতল; সমোচ্চ। ***Verb t.*** To level; to make, as a joint etc. level in masonry; সমান করা; সমোচ্চ করা।

flŭs'-têr, *v. t., i. & n.* To make hot and excited with drinking; to confuse; to flurry; সুরাপানদ্বারা উষ্ণ ও উত্তেজিত করা; ভ্যাবাচ্যাকা লাগান; উদ্বেজিত করা, চঞ্চল করা, অস্থির করা। ***Verb i.*** To be agitated and confused; ব্যস্ত হওয়া, ব্যাকুল হওয়া, উত্তেজিত হওয়া। ***Noun.*** Agitation mingled with confusion; flurry; ব্যাকুলতা, চাঞ্চল্য, অস্থিরতা; তাড়াহুড়া, ব্যস্ততা।

flūte, *n., v. t. & i.* 1. A small wind-instrument with fingerholes

Flute.

and keys; বংশী, বেণু, বাঁশী, মুরলী, বাঁশরী। 2. (*Arch.*) A furrow or channel cut along the shaft of a column or pilaster; (স্থপতিবিজ্ঞান) থামের পিঠে ঝিঙ্গার খোলের আকার ডুঙ্গী বা নালী। 3. A similar groove or channel elsewhere, as in frills and a lady's ruffle; পোষাক প্রভৃতির ঝালরে ঝিঙ্গার খোলের মত নালী। 4. A flute-player; বেণুবাদক, মুরলীবাদক, বংশীবাদক। ***Verb t.*** 1. To play, as an air etc., on a flute; বংশীবাদন করা, বাঁশী বাজান, মুরলী বাজান। 2. To form flutes or grooves in; ঝিঙ্গার খোলের মত নালী বা ডুঙ্গী গঠন করা। ***Verb i.*** To play on a flute; to sing, whistle or speak in flute-like tones; বাঁশী বাজান; বাঁশীর সুরে শিটী দেওয়া বা কথা বলা। **Flut'-ed,** *adj.* 1. Ornamented with channels or grooves; ডুঙ্গী বা নালিবিশিষ্ট। 2. Flute-like, as notes; বংশীধ্বনিবৎ। **Flut'-er,** *n.* One who makes grooves etc.; যে ব্যক্তি থাম প্রভৃতির নালী বা ডুঙ্গী গঠন করে। **Flut'-ing,** *n.* 1. The act of playing the flute; বংশীবাদন, বেণুবাদন। 2. Decoration by means of flutes or grooves; fluted work; থামের পিঠে ঝিঙ্গার খোলের মত নালী গঠন; উক্তরূপ নালী বা ডুঙ্গী। **Flut'-ist,** *n.* One who plays on a flute; বংশীবাদক, বেণুবাদক। **Flut'-y,** *adj.* Sounding like a flute; soft; clear; বংশীবৎধ্বনিকারী; কোমল; স্পষ্ট। **Fluting machine**—লোহার চাদরে ঢেউ তোলার জন্য যন্ত্রবিশেষ।

flŭt'-têr, *v. i., t. & n.* 1. To flap wings rapidly without flying or with short flights; পক্ষসঞ্চালন করা, পাখসাট মারা, পাখা নাড়া। 2. To move with quick vibrations, as a sail, pulse etc.; দ্রুত সঞ্চালিত হওয়া, দ্রুতস্পন্দিত হওয়া। 3. To move about in a bustling way; to flit; "Mr. Thrale *flutters* about the rooms"; ব্যস্তভাবে ছুটাছুটি বা হুট্‌হাট্ করিয়া চলা; ছুটিয়া চলা। 3. To quiver with excitement; to be agitated; আবেগকম্পিত হওয়া, থরথর করিয়া কাঁপা; বিক্ষুব্ধ হওয়া, ব্যাকুল হওয়া। ***Verb t.*** 1. To flap, as wings rapidly; to move quickly or irregularly, as a flag etc.; পক্ষবিধুনিত করা, পাখঝাড়া দেওয়া; পত্‌পত্ করিয়া উড়া। 2. To throw into confusion or agitation; ব্যাকুল করা, বিক্ষুব্ধ করা, বিভ্রান্ত করা। ***Noun.*** 1. Fluttering, quick and irregular motion, as of a flag, fan, etc.; পক্ষবিধুনন; পত্‌পত্ শব্দে সঞ্চালন। 2. Agitation of the mind; confusion; as, to be in a *flutter*; মানসিক চাঞ্চল্য, বিক্ষোভ, চিত্তচাঞ্চল্য, উদ্বেগ; গোলমাল, বিশৃঙ্খলা। 3. (*Slang*) A venture at gambling; (ইতর ভাষায়) জুয়া খেলা। 4. Stir; sensation; as, to make a *flutter*; চাঞ্চল্য; উত্তেজনা, হুলস্থুল ব্যাপার, হৈ চৈ। **To be or put in a flutter**—See FLUTTER, *n.* 2.

flū'-vĭ-ăl, *adj.* Of, or relating to, a river or rivers; found in a river ; নদী বা স্রোতস্বিনীসংক্রান্ত, নাদেয় ; নদীজাত, নদীবাসী।

flü'-vi-a-tile, *adj.* Of, or existing in, rivers ; produced by river-action ; নদী-সংক্রান্ত, নদীতে বর্ত্তমান ; নদীকৃত।

flŭx, *n., adj., v. i.* & *t.* **1.** A flowing ; প্রবহণ। **2.** (*Phys.*) The rate of flow of any fluid across a given area ; (also) the amount crossing an area in a given time ; (পাদার্থ-বিদ্যা) বিশেষ স্থানে কোন তরল পদার্থের প্রবাহের হার ; নির্দ্দিষ্ট সময়ে কোন স্থানে যে পরিমাণ তরল পদার্থ প্রবাহিত হয়। **3.** The moving and passing of anything in continued succession ; নিরবচ্ছিন্ন প্রবাহ। **4.** The flow of the tide, (opposite to *reflux*) ; জোয়ার। **5.** A liquid state from the action of heat ; fusion ; দ্রবীভবন ; বিগলন। **6.** (*Chem. and Metallurgy*) Any substance used to promote fusion ; (রসায়ন-শাস্ত্র এবং ধাতুবিদ্যা) খনিজ পদার্থ প্রভৃতি গলাইতে যে পদার্থ ব্যবহৃত হয়, বিদ্রাবক। **7.** Issue, as of humours etc.; স্রাব। **8.** (*Fig.*) A stream, as of people ; a copious flow, as of talk etc. ; (লক্ষণায়) স্রোতঃ ; প্রবাহ, স্রাব, বিস্রব। **9.** An excessive or morbid discharge of blood, excrement, etc. ; (formerly) dysentery ; অত্যধিক দূষিত রক্ত, মল প্রভৃতির স্রাব ; (পূর্ব্বে) আমাশয়। **10.** (*Math.*) A continued motion ; as, line is the *flux* of a point ; (গণিত-শাস্ত্র) নিরবচ্ছিন্ন গতি। ***Adj.*** Flowing ; inconstant ; variable ; প্রবহমাণ ; অনিত্য ; পরিবর্ত্তনশীল। ***Verb i.*** To flow copiously ; to issue in a flux ; বহুল পরিমাণে নির্গত হওয়া ; স্রাব হওয়া। ***Verb t.*** **1.** To melt ; to fuse ; দ্রবীভূত করা, বিদ্রাবিত করা ; তরল করা।

lux'-ion (flŭk-shŭn), *n.* **1.** An excessive discharge of blood etc. to any organ ; কোন শারীরিক-যন্ত্রের অভিমুখে অত্যধিক রক্ত-প্রবহণ। **2.** (*Math.*) The rate or proportion at which a flowing or varying quantity increases its magnitude ; (গণিত-শাস্ত্র) নিত্য পরিবর্ত্তনশীল সংখ্যার বৃদ্ধির হার, সূক্ষ্ম-বৃদ্ধি (হিঃ কোঃ)। **3.** (*Math.—pl.*) Newtonian Calculus ; as, the method of *fluxions* ; (গণিতশাস্ত্র) নিউটন কর্ত্তৃক উদ্ভাবিত ব্যাস-গণিত। **—al, —a-ry,** *adjs.* **—ist,** *n.*

flȳ, *v. i.* & *t.* **1.** To move through the air with wings ; as, the crow *flies* ; উড়া, উড্ডীন হওয়া। **2.** To pass quickly through the air by any impulse, as bullets etc. ; আকাশপথে ছুটিয়া চলা। **3.** To wave or rise in the air, as a flag, hair, kite etc. ; আকাশে উড়া, আকাশে উঠা। **4.** To take to flight ; পলায়ন করা। **5.** To move swiftly, as a racer, rumour etc. ; দ্রুতবেগে চলা। **6.** To pass rapidly, as time etc. ; দ্রুত গতিতে চলিয়া যাওয়া। **7.** To rush or spring ; as, to *fly* to arms ; ধাবিত হওয়া, লাফাইয়া পড়া। To burst ; as, the door *flew* open ; উদ্ভিন্ন হওয়া, সহসা উদ্ঘাটিত হওয়া। ***Verb t.*** **1.** To cause to fly or float in the air ; উড্ডীন করা, উড়াইয়া দেওয়া। **2.** To flee from ; to shun ; as, I must *fly* from the country ; কোন স্থান হইতে পলায়ন করা ; পরিত্যাগ করিয়া যাওয়া। **Fly-away**—streaming loose, as garments ; flighty, as a person ; absurd ; ঝল্ ঝল্ ; চঞ্চলমতি ; অসম্ভব, আজগুবি। **Fly-by-night** (or **at night**)—One who decamps at night ; যে ব্যক্তি রাত্রিতে চম্পট দেয়। **Fly-the-garter**—A kind of leap-frog ; বালকদিগের ক্রীড়াবিশেষ (See LEAP-FROG.) **Glass flies**—Glass breaks in pieces ; কাচ ভাঙ্গিয়া চুরমার হয়, কাচ ভাঙ্গিয়া খণ্ড বিখণ্ড হয়। **The bird is flown**—The person wanted has escaped ; যে লোককে খুঁজা হইয়াছিল সে পলাইয়া গিয়াছে। **To fly about**—To change frequently, (said of the wind) ; (বাতাসের পক্ষে) পুনঃ পুনঃ পরিবর্ত্তন হওয়া। **To fly around**—To move about in haste ; ব্যস্তভাবে ছুটাছুটি করা। **To fly at, on** or **upon**—To attack violently ; to rush on ; প্রচণ্ড তেজে আক্রমণ করা ; ধাবিত হওয়া। **To fly at a higher game**—To have noble ambitions ; উচ্চাকাঙ্ক্ষা থাকা। **To fly away**—To depart ; to escape ; প্রস্থান করা ; পলায়ন করা। **To fly away with**—To carry off ; জিতিয়া লওয়া। **To fly high**—To be ambitious ; উচ্চাভিলাষী হওয়া। **To fly in the face of**—To act in direct opposition to ; to resist ; to set at defiance ; বিরুদ্ধাচরণ করা ; প্রতিরোধ করা ; তুচ্ছ করা, উড়াইয়া দেওয়া। **To fly in the face of providence**—To do deliberately an imprudent thing ; to court death or danger ; ভাবিয়া চিন্তিয়া অবিবেচনার কার্য্য করা ; বিপদ্ বা মৃত্যুকে আলিঙ্গন করা। **To fly into passion**—To become suddenly furious or angry ; তেলে বেগুনে জ্বলিয়া উঠা, রাগিয়া উঠা। **To fly off**—To separate and depart suddenly ; সহসা প্রস্থান করা। To revolt ; to break away, as from an engagement ; বিদ্রোহী হওয়া ; চুক্তিভঙ্গ করা। **To fly off at a tangent**—See TANGENT. **To fly off at the handle**—To be excited ; to do anything in a fit of excitemet ; উত্তেজিত হওয়া ; উত্তেজনাবশে কার্য্য করা। **To fly on**—To attack ; আক্রমণ করা। **To fly open**—To open suddenly ; সহসা উদ্ঘাটিত হওয়া, সহসা খুলিয়া যাওয়া, হঠাৎ উন্মুক্ত হওয়া। **To fly out**—To rush out ; সবেগে ধাবিত হওয়া, ছুটা। To burst into passion, violent language or action (with *at, against*); হঠাৎ রাগিয়া উঠা, রাগের মাথায় বলা বা করা। **To fly the kite**—To raise money by accommodation bill; also to try how the wind blows; সিকামী হুণ্ডী দ্বারা টাকা তুলিতে চেষ্টা করা; লোক সাধারণের কিরূপ অভিমত তাহা জানিতে চেষ্টা করা। **To fly to arms**—To take up arms eagerly; ব্যগ্রভাবে অস্ত্র ধারণ করা। **To let fly**—To discharge, as missiles; to shoot, hit or use strong language *at*; ক্ষেপণ করা; সবলে বা সজোরে নিক্ষেপ করা। **To make the money fly**—To spend quickly; টাকা পয়সা উড়ান।

flÿ, *n.* **1.** A two-winged insect; মক্ষিকা, মাছি। **2.** A fishing-hook

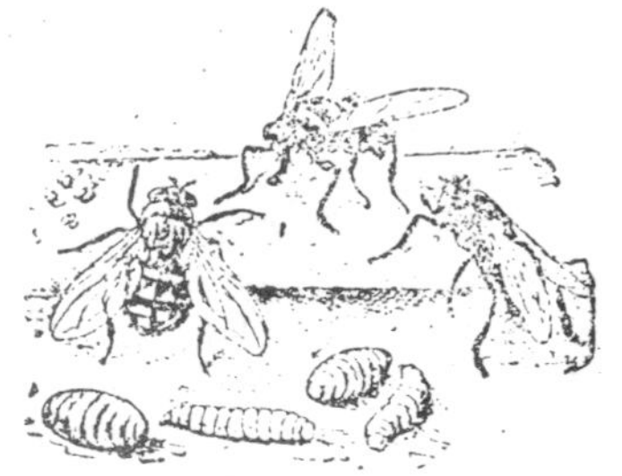

Bluebottle fly; 1, fly; 2, eggs; 3, larvæ; 4, chrysalis.

dressed like a fly; natural or artificial fly used as a bait; মক্ষিকার আকারে সজ্জিত বড়শী; বড়শীর টোপস্বরূপ ব্যবহৃত কৃত্রিম মক্ষিকা। **3.** A kind of plant-disease caused by various flies; মক্ষিকা-রচিত বৃক্ষরোগ-বিশেষ। **4.** A fly shaped ornament for woman's hair etc.; স্ত্রীলোকের মক্ষিকাকৃতি কেশ-ভূষা। **Blue bottle fly** or **Blow fly** — কাচ মাছি। **Fly-bane**—একপ্রকার গুল্ম। **Fly-bitten**—Marked by the bite of flies; মক্ষিকাদষ্ট, মক্ষিকা-দংশন চিহ্নিত। **Fly-blow**—*n.* & *v. t.* মাংসাদির উপর পাড়া মাছির ডিম। (*Verb t.*) To deposit eggs in; to taint; মাংসাদির উপর ডিম পাড়া; দূষিত করা। **Fly-blown**—(*lit.* & *fig.*) ডিম্বদ্বারা দূষিত। **Fly-boat**—দ্রুতগামী লঘু নৌকা। **Fly-book**—বড়শীর টোপ রাখার জন্য পুস্তকাকার আধার। **Fly-catcher**—মাছি ধরার ফাঁদ; কটকটিয়া পাখী, চোক দয়াল। **Fly-fish**—To fish with flies; মাছির টোপ দ্বারা মাছ ধরা। **Fly-flap** — মক্ষিকা তাড়াইবার জন্য আঘাত। **Fly-flapper**—যে ব্যক্তি মাছি তাড়ায়। **Fly-net**—ঘোড়ার শরীরে মাছি বসিতে না পারে তজ্জন্য যে জাল ব্যবহৃত হয়। **Fly-paper**—মাছি মারার জন্য বিষাক্ত কাগজ। **Fly-trap**—One for catching flies; মাছি ধরার ফাঁদ। A plant; গুল্ম-বিশেষ। **Fly-whisk**—Whisk for driving away flies; মক্ষিকা তাড়াইবার জন্য চামর-বিশেষ। **A fly in amber** — A curious relic; বিচিত্র প্রাচীন স্মৃতিচিহ্ন। **A fly in the ointment**—Some slight flaw which corrupts a thing of value; মূল্যবান দ্রব্যে সামান্য দোষ, এক কলস দুধে এক বিন্দু গোমূত্র। **The fly on the wheel**—A person who overestimates his own influence; আত্মম্মন্য ব্যক্তি, হামবড়া লোক। **To break a fly on wheel** — To expend disproportionate energy; মশা মারিতে কামান দাগা। **Venus' fly trap**—এক প্রকার গুল্ম, রতির ফাঁদ (প্রবাসী ১৩২২)।

flÿ, *n.* **1.** Flying; the course or distance flown; উড্ডয়ন; উড্ডয়নের দিক, উড্ডয়ন দ্বারা অতিক্রান্ত স্থান। **2.** A carriage drawn by one horse; একাশ্ববাহিত শকট, এক ঘোড়ার গাড়ী। **3.** The length of an extended flag from its staff; the loose end of a flag; বিস্তারিত পতাকার দণ্ড হইতে উহার অপর প্রান্তের দূরত্ব; পতাকার মুক্ত প্রান্ত। **4.** A revolving mechanism to regulate the motion of machinery; যন্ত্রের গতিনিয়ামক আবর্ত্তনশীল যন্ত্রাংশ-পরম্পরা। **5.** A lap on a garment to contain or cover button-holes; বোতাম লাগাইবার বা ঢাকিবার জন্য পোষাক প্রভৃতির পার্শ্বে সংলগ্ন ঝুল (?) ঝুল অংশ। **6.** (*Weaving*) A shuttle driven by a blow or jerk; মাকু। **7.** (*Theatre—pl.*) A large space over the proscenium from which the scenes are controlled; (রঙ্গমঞ্চ) যবনিকা ও বাদ্যমঞ্চের মধ্যবর্ত্তী স্থানের উপরিস্থ মঞ্চ বিশেষ—যথা হইতে দৃশ্যপট সমূহ নিয়ন্ত্রিত হয়। **8.** The flap at the entrance forming the door of a tent; তাঁবুর প্রবেশপথের দ্বারের পরদা। **9.** (*Print.*) One who takes the sheets from the press; (মুদ্রণ) যে ব্যক্তি মুদ্রাযন্ত্র হইতে কাগজ উঠায়। **Fly-leaf**—পুস্তকের প্রারম্ভ বা শেষের অমুদ্রিত পৃষ্ঠা। **Fly-man**—যে ব্যক্তি রঙ্গমঞ্চের উপরিস্থ স্থানবিশেষে থাকিয়া দৃশ্যপট সমূহ সঞ্চালিত করিয়া থাকে; এক ঘোড়ার গাড়ী চালক। **Fly-wheel**—যন্ত্র প্রভৃতি নিয়ামক গুরুভার চক্র। **Fly-shuttle-loom**—ঠক্‌ঠকি তাঁত। **On the fly**—On the wing, as a bird; in motion, as a ball etc.; উড্ডীয়মান, উড্ডীন; চলন্ত।

flÿ, *adj.* (*Slang*) Knowing; wide awake; (ইতর ভাষায়) জ্ঞাতসার; সজাগ।

flÿ'-êr, -flï'-êr, *ns.* **1.** One that flies, as a bird etc.; উড্ডয়নকারী। **2.** One that goes with exceptional speed, as a vehicle, animal etc.; অতিদ্রুতগামী জন্তু, শকট প্রভৃতি।

flÿ'-ing, *adj.* **1.** Moving in the air; waving; fleeting; temporary, as a bridge; hasty; as, a *flying* visit; উড্ডীন; দোলয়মান দ্রুতগামী; অস্থায়ী; ত্বরিত। **2.** Designed for rapid movement; as, a *flying* squadron; দ্রুত গমনের জন্য অভিপ্রেত। **Flying-bridge** — A temporary bridge suspended or floating; ভাসমান বা দোদুল্যমান অস্থায়ী সেতু। **Flying-dog**—একপ্রকার শোণিতশোষক বাদুড়। **Flying dragon**—কাগজের ঘুড়ি; উল্কা। **Flying Dutchman**--See under

DUTCH. **Flying-fish**—উড়ুক্কু মৎস্য, উড্ডয়নশীল মৎস্য। **Flying-fox**—এক

Flying-fish.

জাতীয় বৃহৎ ফলভুক্ বাদুড়। **Flying handicap, mile** or **start**—(ঘোড়-দৌড়) যাহাতে যাত্রার স্থান পূর্ণবেগে অতিক্রম করা হয়। **Flying-man**—ব্যোমপোতচালক, আকাশপোতচালক। **Flying-party** — দ্রুতগমনের জন্য সজ্জিত সৈন্যসমূহ। **Flying shot**—চলদ্বস্তুর উপর নিক্ষিপ্ত গুলি। **Flying-squid** — একপ্রকার মৎস্য। **Flying-squirrel**—একপ্রকার কাঠ-বিড়ালী—ইহা লাফাইয়া অল্প উপরে উঠিতে পারে। **Flying-visit** — A hasty visit ; অল্প সময়ের জন্য সাক্ষাৎ। **With flying colour** — Honourably ; triumphantly ; সসম্মানে ; জয়োল্লাসের সহিত।

foal (fōl), *n.*, *v. t.* & *i.* The young of a mare, she-ass etc. ; অশ্বশাবক, ঘোড়ার বাচ্চা, গাধার বাচ্চা, বাল-ঘোটকী। ***Verb t. & i.*** To give birth to (a foal) ; (অশ্বের পক্ষে) শাবক প্রসব করা, বাচ্চা দেওয়া। **Foal-foot**—টগর। **In or with foal**—(অশ্বাদির পক্ষে) গর্ভিন্, গর্ভিণী।

foam (fōm), *n.*, *v. i.* & *t.* **1.** Froth ; foaming saliva ; froth of perspiration, as on the body of the horse etc. ; ফেন, ফেনা ; মুখের ফেনা ; অশ্বাদির গায়ে ঘামের ফেনা। **2.** (*Poet.*) The sea ; (কবিতায়) সাগর। ***Verb i.* 1.** To form or gather foam ; to froth at the mouth ; to rush or run foaming ; ফেনিল হওয়া, সফেন হওয়া, ফেনায়িত হওয়া ; মুখে ফেনা উঠা ; ফেনায়িত অঙ্গে ধাবিত হওয়া। **2.** To be filled with foam ; as, a *foaming* in cup ; ফেনপূর্ণ হওয়া। **3.** To be in a rage ; রাগান্বিত হওয়া, ক্রুদ্ধ হওয়া। ***Verb t.*** To throw out with violence or rage ; সবলে নিক্ষেপ করা, রাগের সহিত ছুড়িয়া ফেলা। **Foam′-ing-ly,** *adv.* **Foam′-less,** *adj.* Having no foam ; ফেনশূন্য। **Foam′-y,** *adj.* Frothy ; সফেন, ফেনিল, ফেনায়িত, ফেনময়।

fŏb, *n.* & *v. t.* A small pocket for a watch ; কোমরবন্ধে ঘড়ির ছোট পকেট বা জেব। ***Verb t.*** To put in one's fob ; জেবে রাখা।

fŏb, *v. t.* **1.** To palm or pass *off upon* ; as, to *fob off* a thing of inferior quality *upon* a person ; ফাঁকি দিয়া চালাইয়া দেওয়া। **To fob off**—To shift off by an artifice ; কৌশলে সরাইয়া রাখা। To put off (a person) *with* a thing of inferior quality ; ধোঁকা দিয়া খারাপ জিনিষ ভাল বলিয়া চালান।

fō′-cŭs, *n.* & *v. t.* (*Pl.* -CI, -ES) **1.** (*Phys.*) A point in which the rays of light, heat or sound meet after being reflected or refracted ; (পদার্থবিজ্ঞান) রশ্মি সমূহের সম্মিলনবিন্দু, কিরণকেন্দ্র (হিঃ কোঃ) অধিশ্রয়ণ (ঐ), নাভি (সূর্য্য-সিদ্ধান্ত), তেজঃসংকর্ষ দেশ (কেণ্ডি)। **2.** (*Plane Geom.*) One of the points from which distances to any point of a given curve are connected by linear relation ; (জ্যামিতি-শাস্ত্র) যে বিন্দুদ্বয় হইতে নির্দ্দিষ্ট বক্ররেখাস্থ কোন বিন্দুর দূরত্ব রৈখিক সম্বন্ধদ্বারা অন্বিত তাহাদের অন্যতর, কেন্দ্র (কেণ্ডি), নাভি (ঐ)। **3.** Focal length ; মুকুর বা পরকলার মধ্যস্থল হইতে অধিশ্রয়ণবিন্দুর দূরত্ব। **4.** Adjustment of an eye or eye-glasses, necessary to produce a clear image ; স্পষ্ট প্রতিবিম্ব উৎপাদনের জন্য চক্ষু বা চক্ষুসহায়ক কাচের সংযোজনা। **5.** Any central point ; the centre of activity etc. ; সম্মিলনবিন্দু, মধ্যবিন্দু ; কর্ম্মকেন্দ্র, কেন্দ্রস্থল। ***Verb t.* 1.** To bring to a focus ; to concentrate ; অধিশ্রয়ণবিন্দুগত করা ; কেন্দ্রীভূত করা। **2.** To adjust the focus of, as eyes, lens etc. ; চক্ষু, পরকলা (lens) প্রভৃতির অধিশ্রয়ণবিন্দু ঠিক করা। **3.** To bring into a focus, as an image ; অধিশ্রয়ণবিন্দুগত করা। **—cal,** *adj.* Of, or relating to, a focus ; অধিশ্রয়ণবিন্দুসম্বন্ধীয়, অধিশ্রয়াণিক। **—cal-i-za′-tion, —cal-ize,** *v. t.* Same as FOCUS *v. t.* **Aplanatic focus**—প্রসাধকনাভি (হিঃ কোঃ)। **Conjugate focus**—সম্বদ্ধ নাভি (হিঃ কোঃ)। **Focal-chord**—নাভিগত পূর্ণজ্যা (হিঃ কোঃ) **Focal length, —distance**—(*Optics*) মুকুর বা পরকলার মধ্যস্থল হইতে অধিশ্রয়ণবিন্দুর দূরত্ব, নাভিগতান্তর (হিঃ কোঃ)। **Focal point**—অগ্রকর (কেণ্ডি), অগ্রাংশু (ঐ)। **Principal focus, Solar focus**—মুখ্য নাভি (হিঃ কোঃ)। **Virtual focus**—ভ্রামক কেন্দ্র (হিঃ কোঃ)। **In focus**—অধিশ্রয়ণবিন্দুর মধ্যগত। **Out of focus**—Not in focus ; অধিশ্রয়ণ-বিন্দুর বহির্ভূত।

fō-cĭm′-ē-têr, *n.* (*Phot.*) An assisting instrument for focussing an object in or before a camera ; (আলোক-চিত্র) আলোক-চিত্রগ্রাহক যন্ত্রের মধ্যে বা সম্মুখে কোন বস্তুর প্রতিরূপ কেন্দ্রীকরণে সহায়ক যন্ত্র।

fŏd′-dĕr, *n.* & *v. t.* Dried food, as, hay, straw etc. for cattle ; অশ্বগবাদির জন্য খড় প্রভৃতি শুষ্ক খাদ্য, গবাদন। ***Verb t.*** To feed (cattle) with fodder ; গবাদির খাদ্য যোগান। **—less,** *adj.*

foe (fō) *n.* **1.** An enemy ; an adversary ; শত্রু, বৈরী, রিপু অরি, অরাতি ; বিপক্ষ, দ্বিষদ্, অমিত্র, অভিঘাতী, পরিপন্থী, প্রতিপক্ষ। **2.** An enemy in war ; a hostile force ; যুদ্ধকালে শত্রু ; বিপক্ষ সৈন্য, অরাতি সৈন্য। **3.** An ill wisher ; অহিতকামী, অহিতাকাঙ্ক্ষী। **Foe-man**—(*Archaic*) An enemy in war ; (অপ্রঃ) যুদ্ধকালে শত্রু।

Foeniculum Panmori — মৌরি (বেলঃ), গুয়ামৌরি (বেলঃ)।

foe′-tŭs (fē-), **fē′-tŭs**, *ns*. A fully developed embryo in the womb or egg ; জ্রূণ। **–tal**, *adj*. Pertaining to a fetus ; জ্রূণসম্বন্ধীয়, জ্রৌণিক। **Dead fœtus** — মূঢ়গর্ভ (কেণ্ডি), নষ্টগর্ভ (ঐ)।

foet′-i-cīde (fĕt-), **fĕt-i-cīde**, *ns*. Destruction of the fetus ; জ্রূণ-হত্যা।

fŏg, *n*. & *v*. *t*. **1.** Second growth of grass ; প্রথম কাটার পর দ্বিতীয়বার উৎপন্ন ঘাস। **2.** Long grass left standing on land during winter ; শীতকালে জমিতে যে মরা ও শুষ্ক ঘাস থাকে। ***Verb t.*** **1.** To graze (cattle) on the fog ; দ্বিতীয়বার উৎপন্ন ঘাস খাওয়ান। **2.** To leave land under fog ; কুজ্ঝটিকাচ্ছন্ন ভূমি ত্যাগ করা।

fŏg, *n*., *v*. *t*. & *i*. **1.** A dense vapour near the earth's surface ; an obscurity caused by this ; কুয়াসা, কুজ্ঝটিকা (সাঃ পঃ), খ-বাষ্প, ধূমিকা, কুহা, কুহেলিকা ; কুয়াসার অন্ধকার। **2.** A thick or darkened state of the atmosphere ; কুয়াসাচ্ছন্ন ভাব। **3.** (*Phot.*) Cloudiness on a developed plate ; (আলোক-চিত্র) যে ফলকের উপর চিত্র পরিস্ফুট করা হইয়াছে তদুপরিস্থ অস্পষ্টতা। **4.** A state of mental confusion ; as, he was in a *fog* ; মনের ঘোর। ***Verb t.*** **1.** To envelop with fog ; to confuse; to perplex ; কুয়াসাচ্ছন্ন করা ; হতবুদ্ধি করা ; বিহ্বল করা। **2.** (*Phot.*) To make negative, obscure or clumsy ; (বিপর্য্যস্ত আলোক-চিত্র) অস্পষ্ট বা ঘোরালো করা। ***Verb i.*** **1.** To be covered with fog ; কুয়াসায় ঢাকা, কুজ্ঝটিকাচ্ছন্ন হওয়া। **2.** (*Gardening*) To perish from damp, (with *off*) ; (উদ্যান-কর্ম্ম) আর্দ্রতাহেতু নষ্ট হওয়া। **3.** (*Railway*) To put fog-signals on the line ; (রেলওয়ে) লৌহবর্ত্মের উপর কুয়াসা-সঙ্কেত রাখা। **Fog′-ger**, *n*. One who puts fog-signals on a railway line ; যে ব্যক্তি লৌহবর্ত্মে কুয়াসা-সঙ্কেত স্থাপন করে। **Fog′-gi-ly**, *adv*. **fog′-gi-ness**, *n*. **Fog′-gy**, *adj*. **1.** Filled with fog ; misty ; কুয়াসাপূর্ণ, কুয়াসাচ্ছন্ন ; কুজ্ঝটিকাচ্ছন্ন। **2.** Clouded ; dull ; obscure ; confused ; মেঘাচ্ছন্ন ; হীনপ্রভ ; অস্পষ্ট ; ঘোরাল। **Fog′-less**, *adj*. Without fog ; clear ; কুয়াসাশূন্য, কুজ্ঝটিকাহীন ; নির্ম্মল, স্বচ্ছ। **Fog-bank**—সাগরোপরি লম্বমান স্থলবৎ প্রতিভাত কুজ্ঝটিকাপুঞ্জ। **Fog-bell**—কুয়াসার সময় পাষাণ শৈল প্রভৃতিতে সংস্পৃষ্ট হইয়া জাহাজ নষ্ট হইতে না পারে তজ্জন্য ঢেউ কিম্বা বায়ুর সাহায্যে যে ঘণ্টা বাদন পূর্ব্বক নাবিকদিগকে সতর্ক করা হয়। **Fog-horn**—কুয়াসার সময় জাহাজাদি সতর্কতা অবলম্বন করিতে পারে তন্নিমিত্ত এক প্রকার শিঙ্গা। **Fog-signal** — বাষ্পীয়শকট চালকের পথ নির্দ্দেশনার্থ কুয়াসার সময় লৌহবর্ত্মের উপর যে বিস্ফোরক দ্রব্যপূর্ণ ভাণ্ড রাখা হয়, কুয়াসা-সঙ্কেত।

fō′-gle (-gl), *n*. (*Thieves' slang*) A silk handkerchief ; (চোরদিগের ভাষায়) রেসমী রুমাল।

fō′-gў, fō′-gey (-gî), *ns*. A dull old fellow ; an old fashioned fellow ; সেকেলে বুড়ো ; সেকেলে লোক, প্রাচীন লোক। **–dom**, *n*. The fogey as a class ; বুড়োর দল, বৃদ্ধসমাজ। **–ish**, *adj*. Antiquated ; সেকেলে, প্রাচীন। **–ism**, *n*. The principles and conduct of a fogey ; সেকেলে মত, সেকেলে ভাব।

foh (fō), *interj*. An exclamation of abhorrence or contempt ; ছি ছি! ধিক্ ধিক্ !

Fohn (fŏn), *n*. Hot southerly wind in the Alps ; আল্পস্ পর্ব্বতে প্রবহমাণ উষ্ণ দক্ষিণ পবন।

foi′-ble (foy-bl), *n*. **1.** A moral weakness ; a weak point in character ; a failing ; নৈতিক দুর্ব্বলতা ; চরিত্রের ক্রটী ; ক্রটী। **2.** A part of a sword-blade from middle to point ; অসিফলকের মধ্য হইতে অগ্রভাগ পর্য্যন্ত অংশ।

foil (foyl), *v*. *t*., *i*. & *n*. **1.** (*Hunting*) To trample ; hence, to spoil by crossing or retracing a trail or scent ; (মৃগয়া) পদদলিত করা ; অতএব প্রত্যাবর্ত্তন বা অতিক্রম করিয়া পলায়িত জন্তুর ঘ্রাণ, পদচিহ্ন প্রভৃতি বিলুপ্ত করা। **2.** To frustrate ; to baffle ; to defeat ; to disappoint ; বিফল করা ; ব্যর্থ করা ; পরাজিত করা, পরাভব করা ; বিমুখ করা, নিরাশ করা। ***Verb i.*** (Of a deer etc.) To spoil the scent by crossing or running over it ; (মৃগাদির পক্ষে) পলায়িত জন্তুর গমনপথের উপর দিয়া অতিক্রম করিয়া বা দৌড়িয়া উহার ঘ্রাণ নষ্ট করা। ***Noun.*** **1.** (*Archaic*) Frustration ; defeat ; বিফলতা, অসিদ্ধি, অকৃতকার্য্যতা, নিষ্ফলতা ; পরাজয়, পরাভব। **2.** The track or trail of a hunted animal ; অনুসৃত জন্তুর গমন পথ, গন্ধ, পদচিহ্ন প্রভৃতি। **To run (upon) the foil**—To run over the same track a second time ; পুনরায় পূর্ব্ব পথে দৌড়ান।

foil (foyl), *n*. & *v*. *t*. **1.** A leaf or thin sheet of metal ; as, a gold *foil* ; ধাতুর পাতলা পাত, তবক। **2.** A thin leaf of metal placed under precious stones etc. to heighten their brilliancy, to give them a particular colour ; প্রভা-বৃদ্ধি ও বর্ণ পরিবর্ত্তনার্থ মূল্যবান প্রস্তরের পশ্চাদ্দেশে সংলগ্ন ধাতুর পাত। **3.** A thin coat of tin with quicksilver placed behind the mirror-glass ; দর্পণের পশ্চাদ্দেশে বিলেপিত পারদ ও রঙ্গের মিশ্র। **4.** Anything setting off something by contrast ; যে বিরুদ্ধ রূপ বা গুণসম্পন্ন বস্তু দ্বারা অপর বস্তুর সৌন্দর্য্য ও উজ্জ্বল্য বৃদ্ধি প্রাপ্ত হয়। ***Verb t.*** **1.** To back or cover with foil ; ধাতুর পাতলা পাত দ্বারা মোড়া বা ঢাকা, দর্পণাদির পশ্চাদ্দেশে পারদ ও রঙ্গের মিশ্র লাগান। **2.** To set off by contrast ; বিরুদ্ধ রূপ বা গুণ-বিশিষ্ট বস্তু দ্বারা সৌন্দর্য্য কিংবা ঔজ্জ্বল্য বৃদ্ধি করা। **To be the foil to**

one—To serve the purpose of setting off one's power to advantage ; কোন লোকের ক্ষমতা সুবিধাজনক রূপে প্রদর্শনে সাহায্য করা।

foil (foyl), *n.* A blunt sword-like weapon used in fencing ; অসিক্রীড়া শিক্ষায় ব্যবহৃত ভোতা তলোয়ারের মত একপ্রকার অস্ত্র।

foi'-son (fŏy-zn), *n.* (*Archaic*) Plenty ; (অপ্রঃ) প্রাচুর্য্য।

foist (foyst) *v. t.* **1.** To introduce or insert surreptitiously or without warrant, (with *in* or *into*) ; প্রক্ষিপ্ত করা। **2.** To pass off (with *on* or *upon*) ; to father *upon* ; as, to *foist* a composition *upon* a person ; নকল মাল আসল বলিয়া চালান ; পিতৃত্ব আরোপ করা, অর্থাৎ কোন ব্যক্তিকে কোন কিছুর মূল বলিয়া নির্দ্দেশ করা। **Foist'-er,** *n.*

fōld, *v. t., i.* & *n.* **1.** To lay in folds ; to double ; ভাঁজ করা ; দুপাট করা। **2.** To bend a portion (of a thing), (with *back, down*) ; কোন বস্তুর একাংশ বক্র করা। **3.** To double or lay together ; to entwine ; as, he *folds* his arms in despair ; to clasp ; অঞ্জলিবদ্ধ করা, (হাত) যোড় করা ; বেষ্টন করা ; আলিঙ্গন করা, বাহুপাশে বদ্ধ করা, পরিরম্ভ করা। **4.** To envelop ; to cover ; as, he *folded* it in paper ; hills *folded* in mist ; আবৃত করা, জড়ান ; ঢাকা। ***Verb i.*** To become folded ; to be capable of being folded ; as, a *folding* door ; to close together ; অঞ্জলিবদ্ধ হওয়া, যুক্ত হওয়া ; দ্বিপাটিত হওয়া ; মুদ্রিত হওয়া। ***Noun.*** **1.** A doubling or folding ; a plait ; as, a thing in the *fold* of her dress ; ভাঁজ, দুপাট, তহ ; চুনট, উর্ম্মি। **2.** Hollow or nook in mountain ; গিরিগহ্বর, কন্দর। **3.** A coil of serpent, string etc. ; সর্প বা রজ্জুর কুণ্ডলী, ভোগ [hence ভোগী = সর্প]। **4.** The line or mark made by folding ; ভাঁজের দাগ। **Fold'-er,** *n.* **1.** One who, or that which, folds ; যে বা যাহা ভাঁজ করে। **2.** An instrument for folding paper ; কাগজ ভাঁজ করার জন্য যন্ত্রবিশেষ। **3.** (*Pl.*) Folding eye-glasses ; দোমুড়ান চশমা। **Fold'-ing,** *adj.* **Folding door** or **doors**—দ্বিপাটি কপাট, দ্বিপাট-বিশিষ্ট কপাট, দ্বিপক্ষদ্বার (মঃ ভাঃ)। **To fold one's hands** — To be idle ; হাত পা গুটাইয়া থাকা। **To fold up** — To make more compact by folding ; ভাঁজ করা, পাট করা। **With folded hands** — যোড়হস্তে, যুক্তপাণি হইয়া, কৃতাঞ্জলিপুটে, করযোড়ে, বদ্ধাঞ্জলি হইয়া, যুক্তকরে।

fōld, *v. t.* & *n.* **1.** To enclose in a fold, as sheep ; খোঁয়াড়ে আবদ্ধ করা। **2.** To confine sheep in a fold upon (land) to manure it ; জমিতে সার দেওয়ার উদ্দেশ্যে উহার উপর খোঁয়াড় প্রস্তুত করিয়া মেষ রাখা। ***Noun.*** **1.** An inclosure for sheep ; মেষশালা, খোঁয়াড়। **2.** (*Fig.*) The church ; a body of believers ; (লক্ষণায়) খৃষ্টীয় উপাসনা মন্দির, ভজনালয় ; খৃষ্টীয় ধর্ম্ম-সংঘ, খৃষ্টধর্ম্মে আস্থাবান্ জনমণ্ডলী, খৃষ্টীয় উপাসকমণ্ডলী।

fō-li-ā'-ceous (-shŭs), *adj.* **1.** (*Bot.*) Relating to a leaf ; like a leaf ; leafy in form or nature ; with leafy organs ; (উদ্ভিদ্-বিদ্যা) পত্র সম্বন্ধীয় ; পত্রবৎ ; পর্ণাকার, পত্রাকৃতি, পত্র-ধর্ম্মা ; পত্রবৎ উপাঙ্গবিশিষ্ট। **2.** (*Min.*) Consisting of leaves or thin laminæ ; (খনিজ) পত্রযুক্ত, পত্রাত্মক।

fō'-li-āge, *n. n.* **1.** Leaves collectively ; leafage ; পত্ররাজি, পল্লবগুচ্ছ ; পত্রগুচ্ছ, পত্রপুঞ্জ। **2.** Ornamental representation of leaves, as, in architecture etc. ; সৌধশিল্পে পত্রাকার ভূষা। **—aged,** *adj.* Furnished or decorated with foliage ; পত্রযুক্ত, পত্ররাজি-বিভূষিত। **—ar,** *adj.* Consisting of, or pertaining to, leaves ; পত্রযুক্ত, পত্রময়, পত্র-সম্বন্ধীয়। **Foliage plant**—(*Bot.*) (উদ্ভিদ্-বিদ্যা) পাতাবাহার গাছ।

fō'-li-āte, *v. t.* & *i.* **1.** To foil, as a looking-glass ; দর্পণাদির পশ্চাদ্দেশে রঙ্গ ও পারদের মিশ্র লাগান। **2.** To mark the leaves of (a book) with consecutive numbers ; পুস্তকে পত্রাঙ্ক দেওয়া। **3.** (*Archaic*) To decorate with foliage ; (অপ্রঃ) পত্রাকার ভূষাদ্বারা অলঙ্কৃত করা। ***Verb i.*** To put forth leaves ; পত্রোদ্গম হওয়া।

fō'-li-āt-ĕd, *p. adj.* **1.** Having leaf or leaf-like projections ; পত্রযুক্ত অথবা পত্রবৎ উদ্গত অংশবিশিষ্ট। **2.** Covered with a thin plate or foil ; পাত বা তবকদ্বারা মোড়ানো। **3.** Having leaf-shaped ornaments পত্রাকার ভূষাবিশিষ্ট।

fō-li-ā'-tion, *n.* **1.** The leafing of plants পত্রোদ্গম। **2.** The act of applying foil to glass ; দর্পণের পশ্চাদ্ভাগে রঙ্গ এবং পারদের মিশ্র সংযোজন। **3.** (*Arch.*) The decoration with foils ; (স্থপতি-বিজ্ঞান) পত্রাকার ভূষা দ্বারা মণ্ডন। **4.** Numbering the leaves of a book ; পুস্তকের পত্রাঙ্ক প্রদান।

fō'-li-ō, *n., v. t.* & *adj.* (*Pl.* -os) **1.** A leaf of a book or a manuscript ; পুস্তকাদির পত্র, পাতা, পৃষ্ঠা। **2.** A sheet of paper folded once ; কাগজের আধা তা। **3.** A book made of such sheets ; a volume of the largest size ; উক্ত আকারের কাগজে বাঁধাই পুস্তক ; বৃহত্তম আকারের পুস্তক। **4.** The page number of a printed book ; মুদ্রিত পুস্তকের পত্রাঙ্ক। **5.** (*Book-binding*) A page ; the two opposite pages of an account book having the same serial number ; পত্র ; হিসাবের খাতার বাম ও ডানদিকের একই প্রকার ক্রমিক পত্রাঙ্ক-চিহ্নিত পত্র **6.** (*Law*) A number of words (72 or 90) taken as unit in reckoning the length of a document; (আইন) দলিলে লিখিত শব্দ সমূহের নির্দ্দিষ্ট সংখ্যা (১২ বা ৯০)। ***Verb t.*** To put a serial number in each folio or page of a book; to page; পত্রাঙ্ক দেওয়া; পত্রাঙ্কিত করা। ***Adj.*** Formed of sheets each folded once (making two leaves or four pages); as, in ten volumes *folio*: a *folio* book; একবার ভাঁজ-করা কাগজের তায় প্রস্তুত। **In folio**—(Of a book) In sheets folded once; (পুস্তক সম্পর্কে) এক বার ভাঁজ করা কাগজের তায়।

fō'-lĭ-ōle, *n.* (*Bot.*) **1.** Leaflet; (উদ্ভিদ্ বিদ্যা) ক্ষুদ্র পত্র। **2.** (*Zool.*) A leaf-shaped organ or part; (জন্তু-বিদ্যা) পত্রাকার অঙ্গ বা অংশ।

folk (fōk), *n.* (*Pl.* the *sing.* being *Archaic* or *Dial.*) **1.** People in general; people of a particular class; as, the old *folks*, the poor *folks*; লোকসাধারণ; কোন নির্দ্দিষ্ট শ্রেণীর লোক। **2.** (*Archaic*) A nation or race; (অপ্র:) জাতি, বংশ। **3.** (*Pl.*) Relative; আত্মীয়স্বজন, স্বজনবর্গ, আত্মীয় কুটুম্ব। **Folk-land**—(এংলো স্যাকসনদিগের সময়ে) সাধারণ ভূমি। **Folk-lore** — কোন দেশের প্রাচীন জনশ্রুত, রীতিনীতি, আচার পদ্ধতি ও উপাখ্যানাবলী, জনশ্রুতি (হিঃ কোঃ), পুরাবৃত্ত, পুরাকাহিনী। **Folk-song**—লোক গাথা, লোকগীতি। **Folk-speech** — সাধারণ লোকদিগের অথবা অশিক্ষিত লোকদিগের (চলিত) ভাষা, ইতর ভাষা। **Folk-tales**—উপকথাসমূহ, উপকথামালা।

fŏl'-lĭ-cle (-kl), *n.* **1.** (*Bot.*) A seed vessel; (উদ্ভিদ্-বিদ্যা) বীজকোষ। **2.** (*Anat.*) A small sac or gland; (শারীর-সংস্থান বিদ্যা) গ্রন্থি বা ক্ষুদ্র কোষ। **3.** (*Zool.*) A cocoon; (প্রাণি-বিদ্যা) গুটীপোকার গুটী। **–lic'-u-lar, –lic'-u-lat-ed,** *adjs.*

fŏl'-low (-lō), *v. t., i. & n.* **1.** To go or come after; to accompany; to attend upon; অনুবর্ত্তী হওয়া; অনুগমন করা, অনুগামী হওয়া, পরিচর্য্যার্থ কাছে থাকা বা সঙ্গে সঙ্গে গমন করা। **2.** To pursue; to seek to gain; to chase; অনুসরণ করা; পাইতে চেষ্টা করা; পশ্চাদ্ধাবিত হওয়া, পাছু পাছু ছুটা, পশ্চাদনুসরণ করা। **3.** To take as a leader or master; to adopt the opinions or cause of; to obey; as, to *follow* a rule of action; to *follow* a good advice; কাহাকেও প্রভু বলিয়া গণ্য করা; কাহারো মত বা পক্ষ গ্রহণ করা; আজ্ঞাপালন করা, আজ্ঞানুবর্ত্তী হওয়া, আদেশানুবর্ত্তী হওয়া। **4.** To succeed in order of time; সময় হিসাবে পরবর্ত্তী হওয়া। **5.** To walk in, as a road or course; to practise, as a profession or calling; পথ ধরিয়া চলা; অনুসরণ করা। **6.** To result from; "Peace *follows* virtue"; পশ্চাৎ আসা, পরে আসা, পরবর্ত্তী হওয়া, পশ্চাদ্‌বর্ত্তী হওয়া, ফলস্বরূপ আগত হওয়া। **7.** To imitate; অনুকরণ করা, অনুসরণ করা। **8.** To pursue with the eye or mind; to understand; as, to *follow* a speker or argument; অনুধাবন করা; হৃদয়ঙ্গম করা, বোঝা। ***Verb i.*** **1.** To come after another; to ensue; to attend; পরবর্ত্তী হওয়া, অনুবর্ত্তী হওয়া, পশ্চাৎ আসা; পশ্চাৎ ঘটা; অনুগমন করা। **2.** To result; ফলস্বরূপ হওয়া, ফলে দাঁড়ান। ***Noun.*** Act or process of following; অনুসরণ, অনুগমন, অনুবৃত্তি **–er,** *n.* **1.** One who follows; an adherent; a disciple; অনুগামী, অনুযায়ী, অনুসরণকারী, অনুবর্ত্তী, মতাবলম্বী; সহচর, অনুগ, অনুচর; শিষ্য, অন্তেবাসী। **2.** A man who courts a maid-servant; পরিচারিকার প্রেম যাচ্‌ঞাকারী ব্যক্তি। **–ing,** *n. & adj.* One's follower or adherents collectively; সহচরবর্গ, অনুযায়িবর্গ, দলবল। (*Adj.*) **1.** Succeeding; as, the *following* day; পরবর্ত্তী, পশ্চাদ্‌বর্ত্তী, অনুযায়ী। **2.** That is to be immediately mentioned; as, the *following* are noteworthy; নিম্নলিখিত, নিম্নোক্ত, পশ্চাদুক্ত। **Follow-my-leader** — একপ্রকার ক্রীড়া যাহাতে প্রতি ক্রীড়ক নেতার অনুসরণ করে। **To follow from** — To become deducible from; as, it *follows* from his argument; প্রতিপন্ন হওয়া। **To follow home**—To follow up to a conclusion; শেষ পর্য্যন্ত অনুসরণ করা। **To follow in one's tracks**—To follow exactly behind; hence, to follow one's example; পশ্চাদনুসরণ করা; দৃষ্টান্ত অনুসরণ করা। **To follow in the footsteps of**—কাহারও পদাঙ্কানুসরণ করা। **To follow on**—To continue following; চলিতে থাকা। **To follow one's nose**—To go straight on; to leave one's route to chance; সোজাসুজি চলা; দৈবের উপর নির্ভর করিয়া পথ চলা। To pursue to the end; শেষ পর্য্যন্ত অনুসরণ করা। **To follow suit**—(*Card playing*) To play a card of the same suit as the first played; to do as a person has done before; রঙ্গে রঙ্গ দেওয়া; অপরের দেখাদেখি কোন কাজ করা, অপরের দৃষ্টান্ত অনুসরণ করা। **To follow the plough**—To be a ploughman; কৃষিকার্য্য করা। **To follow the sea**—To be a sailor; নাবিক হওয়া। **To follow up**—To pursue indefatigably or closely; to prosecute to a conclusion, as victory; অক্লান্তভাবে বা অবিশ্রান্তভাবে অনুসরণ করা; শেষ পর্য্যন্ত অনুসরণ করা। **To follow the hounds**—To hunt with dogs; কুকুর লইয়া শীকার করা।

fŏl'-low (-lō), *n.* (*Billiard*) A stroke which causes the ball to follow the one which it has struck; (আণ্টাল খেলায়) যে আঘাতে কোন কন্দুক অপর কন্দুকের সহিত টক্কর লাগার পর উহার পশ্চাদনুসরণ করে।

fŏl'-lȳ, *n.* **1.** Foolishness; imbecility of mind; নির্ব্বুদ্ধিতা, বুদ্ধিহীনতা, মূঢ়তা, মূর্খতা; মানসিক দুর্ব্বলতা। **2.** A foolish act, idea or practice;

unbecoming or unwise conduct ; বোকামি, মূঢ়তার কার্য্য ; অনুচিত আচরণ, অবিবেচনার কাজ। 3. A structure left unfinished by the builder on its proving too great for his resources ; নির্ম্মাতার অর্থবলের অতিরিক্ত হইয়া পড়ায় যে অট্টালিকা প্রভৃতি অসম্পন্ন রাখা হইয়াছে।

fō-mĕnt', *v. t.* 1. To apply a warm lotion to ; সেক দেওয়া, উষ্ণ স্বেদ দেওয়া। 2. To foster ; to instigate ; to rouse ; as, to *foment* sedition ; উৎকর্ষ সাধন করা ; প্রোৎসাহিত করা, প্ররোচিত করা ; উদ্দীপ্ত করা, উত্তেজিত করা। **—er,** *n.* One, or that which foments ; যে ব্যক্তি সেক দেয় ; উৎসাহদাতা, প্ররোচক, প্ররোচনাকারী। **—men-ta'-tion,** *n.* 1. The act of fomenting ; the application of warm medicinal substances for fomenting purposes ; the lotion used ; উষ্ণস্বেদ, দ্রবস্বেদ, তাপ সেক, সেকপ্রদান, উত্তাপন; বেদনা নিবারণ অথবা রোগাক্রান্ত স্থানের উত্তেজনার্থ উষ্ণ ঔষধ মিশ্রিত জল প্রয়োগ ; সেক প্রদানার্থ ঔষধ মিশ্রিত জল। 2. Instigation ; উৎসাহ প্রদান, প্রোৎসাহন, উৎসাহ, প্ররোচনা।

fō'-mĕnt, *n.* 1. Fomentation ; উষ্ণস্বেদ। 2. State of excitement উত্তেজনার ভাব।

fŏnd, *adj.* 1. Foolishly tender and loving ; অনুরক্ত, আসক্ত। 2. Affectionate ; tender ; as, a *fond* mother or wife ; স্নেহপ্রবণ, স্নেহশীল, মমতামাখা ; সকরুণ। 3. Foolishly credulous ; as, he was *fond* enough to believe it ; আশুবিশ্বাসী, অতি বিশ্বাসী। 4. Having a strong affection or liking for (with *of*) ; অনুরক্ত বা আসক্ত, অনুরাগী, অনুরাগবান, বৎসল, প্রিয়। **Fond'-ler, Fond'-ling,** *ns.* The act of caressing ; a caress ; a person or thing caressed or fondled ; আদর ; সোহাগ; আদরের বস্তু, সোহাগের বস্তু, দুলাল। **Fond'-ly,** *adv.* **Fond'-ness,** *n.*

fŏn'-dănt, *n.* A kind of sweetmeat ; একপ্রকার মিঠাই, মিষ্টদ্রব্যবিশেষ।

fŏn'-dle (-dl), *v. t.* & *i.* 1. To treat with fondness ; to caress ; আদর করা ; সোহাগ করা। ***Verb i.*** To toy amorously (followed by *with, together*) ; কান্দর্পিক লীলা করা, কামক্রীড়া করা।

fŏnt, *n.* 1. A basin to contain water for baptising ; খৃষ্টীয়ধর্ম্মে দীক্ষা দানকালে ব্যবহৃত পবিত্র জলপাত্র। 2. An oil reservoir of a lamp ; প্রদীপের তৈলাধার। 3. A receptacle for holy water ; (খৃষ্টীয় জল দীক্ষায় ব্যবহৃত) পবিত্র জল রাখার জন্য আধার বা ভাণ্ড, পবিত্র জলভাণ্ড। 4. A fountain ; a source ; উৎস ; উৎপত্তিস্থল। **Font'-al,** *adj.* Original ; baptismal ; মৌলিক ; খৃষ্টধর্ম্মে দীক্ষানম্পকীয়। **Font-stone**—A baptismal font of stone ; পবিত্র জল রাখার জন্য পাষাণ কুণ্ড।

fŏnt, *n.* An assortment of type of one size and style ; মুদ্রাক্ষরের সাট।

fŏn-tă-nĕl', —nelle' (-nĕl), *ns.* (*Anat.*) A vacancy in the infant cranium ; (শারীর-সংস্থান-বিদ্যা) শিশুর মস্তকের অস্থি-শূন্য স্থান, ব্রহ্মরন্ধ্র।

fōōd, *n.* 1. What is eaten by animals etc. for nourishment ; victuals ; আহার সামগ্রী ; খাদ্যদ্রব্য, আহার, খোরাক। 2. Nutriment ; as, *food* and drink ; পুষ্টিকর দ্রব্য। 3. That which nourishes or develops ; as, mental or intellectual *food* ; পুষ্টিকর বস্তু। **Food'-less,** *adj.* Without food ; নিরন্ন, উপবাসী। **Food-stuff** — খাদ্যদ্রব্য। **Food and raiment**—গ্রাসাচ্ছাদন। **Food for powder** — Soldier ; সৈনিক পুরুষ। **To be food for fishes**—To be drowned ; জলমগ্ন হইয়া মৃত্যুমুখে পতিত হওয়া, জলে ডুবিয়া মরা। **To be food for worms**—To be dead ; মরা, মৃত্যুমুখে পতিত হওয়া।

fōōl, *n., v. i.* & *t.* 1. A simpleton ; a silly person ; নির্ব্বোধ ব্যক্তি, আহাম্মক ; বেকুব লোক, বোকা। 2. A professional jester or buffoon ; as, to play *fool* ; বিদূষক, ভাঁড়, বৈহাসিক। 3. A dupe ; আশু-প্রবঞ্চিত ব্যক্তি। ***Verb i.*** To play the fool ; to trifle ; বোকামি করা ; তুচ্ছ করা। ***Verb t.*** 1. To make a fool of ; to deceive ; to cheat ; as, to *fool* a man out of money etc. ; (=to get, as money etc. by dupery out of a person) ; বোকা বানান ; প্রতারণা করা ; ঠকান। 2. To spend foolishly, as times etc. (with *away*); নির্ব্বোধের মত সময় কাটান। **Fool'-er-y,** *n.* 1. Habitual folly ; absurdity ; মূর্খতা, নির্ব্বুদ্ধিতা ; অযৌক্তিকতা, অসঙ্গতি। 2. An act of folly ; নির্ব্বুদ্ধিতা, বোকামি। **Fool-hardiness**—Courage without sense or judgment ; recklessness ; দুঃসাহস, অসমসাহস ; গোঁয়ারতামি, হঠকারিতা, অসমসাহসিকতা। **Fool-hardy**—Daring without judgment ; foolishly bold ; গোঁয়ারগোবিন্দ, অসম সাহসী, দুঃসাহসী, প্রমত্ত। **Foolscap, Fool's cap**—A dunce's cap of conical shape ; বিদূষকের মোচাকার টুপি। A size of paper (about 13*in.*×8*in.* when folded) ; ফুলস্কেপ কাগজ—এই কাগজ ভাঁজ করিলে প্রায় ১৩"×৮" ইঞ্চি আয়তনের হয় [সপ্তদশ শতাব্দীতে এই কাগজে বিদূষকের মস্তকের জলীয় ছাপ অঙ্কিত থাকিত বলিয়া এই নাম]। **Fool's-errand**—An absurd or fruitless search or enterprise ; বৃথা অন্বেষণ, নিষ্ফল প্রয়াস। **Fool's mate**—See under MATE. **Fool's paradise**—Illusory happiness ; মায়িক সুখ, অলীক সুখ, সুখ-স্বপ্ন। **A fool's bolt is soon shot**—His stock of argument is soon exhausted ; মূর্খের যুক্তিভাণ্ডার শীঘ্রই নিঃশেষিত হয়। **All Fool's day**—1st April ; ১লা এপ্রিল। **April fool**—See APRIL. **Every man hath a fool in his sleeve**—No one is always wise; মুনীনাঞ্চ মতিভ্রমঃ [cf. জিহ্বা টলতি ধীরস্য পাদস্খলতি হস্তিনঃ। ভীমস্যাপি রণে ভঙ্গো মুনীনাঞ্চ মতিভ্রমঃ ॥] **Fools build homes and wise men buy them, Fools give feast and wise men eat them**—Wise men reap the benefit of the extravagance of the foolish; নির্ব্বোধেরা অপব্যয় করে এবং বুদ্ধিমানগণ তাহা হইতে নিজের সুবিধা করিয়া লয়। **Man is fool or physician at thirty**—Sensible man needs no doctor; সুবিবেচক লোকের চিকিৎসকের প্রয়োজন হয় না। **Fools rush in where angels fear to tread**—দেবতারা যেখানে পা বাড়াইতে ভয় করেন কাণ্ডাকাণ্ড জ্ঞানহীন মূর্খেরা তথায় হুড়মুড় করিয়া প্রবেশ করে—দ্বিজেন্দ্রনাথ ঠাকুর। **To be a fool for one's pains**—To take unnecessary and thankless troubles; অকারণ কষ্ট স্বীকার করা। **To be a fool to**—To be nothing in comparison with; তুলনায় কিছু না হওয়া। **To fool away**—To spend foolishly; নির্ব্বোধের মত ব্যয় করা। **To fool one to the top of one's bent**—To fool in the superlative degree—যৎপরোনাস্তি নির্ব্বুদ্ধিতা প্রকাশ করা। **To fool with**—To be meddlesome; গায়ে পড়িয়া পরের ব্যাপারে হস্তক্ষেপ করা। **To make a fool of**—To bring a person to ridicule; to disappoint; to dupe; হাস্যাস্পদ করা; নিরাশ করা; বোকা সাজান। **To play the fool**—To conduct oneself foolishly or recklessly; নির্ব্বোধের মত আচরণ করা, কাণ্ডজ্ঞানহীনের ন্যায় কাজ করা। To indulge in buffoonery; ভাঁড়ামি করা। To blunder; to trifle; ভুল করা; তুচ্ছতাচ্ছিল্য করা।

fōōl, *n.* A viand made of gooseberries and cream; সর ও গুজবেরী ফলদ্বারা প্রস্তুত খাদ্য দ্রব্য।

fōōl'-ish, *adj.* 1. Silly; without judgment or discretion; নির্ব্বোধ, বুদ্ধিহীন, মূর্খ, মূঢ়; মন্দবুদ্ধি, হীনবুদ্ধি, কাণ্ডজ্ঞানহীন। 2. Proceeding from, or exhibiting, silliness, as an act; নির্ব্বুদ্ধিতাপ্রসূত, নির্ব্বুদ্ধিতাব্যঞ্জক। 3. Absurd; অযৌক্তিক, অসঙ্গত। **—ly**, *adv.* **—ness**, *n.*

fōōl-ŏc'-ra-cy̆, *n.* A government by fools; নির্ব্বোধ ব্যক্তিগণ দ্বারা পরিচালিত শাসন ব্যাপার, মূঢ়তন্ত্র।

fōōt, *n., v. i.* & *t.* (*Pl.* FEET) 1. The lower extremity of the leg; পাদ, পদ, পা, চরণ, অঙ্ঘ্রি। 2. Tread; pace; as, he is swift of *foot*; পদক্ষেপ; পদবিক্ষেপ। 3. The part as of a stocking that covers the feet; the lower end of a bed, grave etc.; মোজা প্রভৃতির পা; পায়ের দিক, শয্যা, সমাধিমন্দির প্রভৃতির পায়ের দিক। 4. The lowest part or base; the bottom, as of a hill, wall, etc,; the last of a row or series; নিম্নভাগ, পাদদেশ; নিম্নদেশ; কোন শ্রেণী বা পংক্তির সর্ব্বশেষটী। 5. A measure of length equivalent to 12 inches; এক ফুট, ১২ ইঞ্চি। 6. The infantry; পদাতিক সৈন্য। 7. (*Prosody*) A division of a line of poetry; পদ্যের চরণ বা পাদ। ***Verb i.*** 1. To dance; নৃত্য করা। 2. (*Rare*) To walk; (অপ্রঃ) ভ্রমণ করা। ***Verb t.*** 1. (*Rare*) To walk or dance on or over; as, to *foot* the grass; (অপ্রঃ) কোন কিছুর উপর হাঁটিয়া যাওয়া বা নাচা। 2. To sum up, as an account; যোগ করা, ঠিক্ দেওয়া। 3. To pay, as bill; শোধ করা। 4. To attach a new foot to, as a stocking; নূতন পা লাগান। **Foot'-ed**, *p. p.* 1. Provided with a foot or feet; পাদবিশিষ্ট, পাদযুক্ত, সপাদ। 2. (*Shaks.*) Having gained a footing; established; অধিকার-প্রাপ্ত; সুপ্রতিষ্ঠিত, সংস্থিত। **Foot'-less**, *adj.* Having no feet; পাদবিহীন, নিষ্পদ, চরণহীন। **Foot-artillery**—পদাতিক গোলন্দাজ সৈন্য। **Foot-ball**—চর্ম্মনির্ম্মিত বায়ুপূর্ণ কন্দুক, পাদগোলক, পাদকন্দুক; পাদগোলক ক্রীড়া। **Foot-bath** — জানু অবধি পা পর্য্যন্ত ভিজান, পাদমজ্জন; উক্ত উদ্দেশ্য সাধনের জন্য পাত্রবিশেষ। **Foot-board**—শকটাদিতে আরোহণার্থ পা-দান, পাদফলক (আঃ বঃ); শকটের পশ্চাতে ভৃত্য বা খানসামার দাঁড়াইবার স্থান। **Foot-boy**—তকমাপরা ভৃত্য; ছোকরা চাকর। **Foot-breadth**—চরণের প্রস্থ বা পরিসর। **Foot-bridge, —path, —road, —way, etc.**—পাদচারী যাত্রীদিগের নিমিত্ত সঙ্কীর্ণ সেতু ইত্যাদি। **Foot-drill, —pump etc.**—পদ দ্বারা চালিত বর্ম্মা, দমকল, প্রভৃতি। **Foot-fall**—পদবিক্ষেপ শব্দ; পদন্যাস, চরণপাত। **Foot gear** — পাদাবরণ, জুতা মোজা ইত্যাদি, পদত্রান। **Foot-guards**—পদাতিক রক্ষি সৈন্য। **Foot-hill**—সানুদেশস্থ ক্ষুদ্র শৈল, পাদশৈল। **Foot-hold** — পাদাবলম্বন, পাদাশ্রয়; পাদধারণ স্থান। **Foot-licker**—তোষামোদকারী, চরণসেবী, পাদলেহী, পদলেহনকারী, পা-চাটা। **Foot-lights** — রঙ্গমঞ্চের সম্মুখস্থ দীপপংক্তি। **Footman**—পদাতিক সৈন্য; (প্রভুর) নির্দ্দিষ্ট পরিচ্ছদধারী ভৃত্য, তকমাপরা ভৃত্য, যে ভৃত্য প্রভুর গাড়ী ঘোড়া প্রভৃতির সহিত দৌড়িয়া যায়। **Foot-mark**—পদচিহ্ন, পদাঙ্ক। **Foot-muff** — পা গরম রাখার জন্য আবরণ। **Foot-note** — গ্রন্থপৃষ্ঠার নিম্নে সন্নিবিষ্ট টীকা, পাদটীকা। **Foot-pace**—Walking pace; dais; পাদচারণ গতি; মঞ্চ। **Foot-pad**—রাহাজান বা দস্যু। **Foot-page** — বালকভৃত্য, ছোকরা চাকর। **Foot-pan**—পদপ্রক্ষালন পাত্র। **Foot-passenger**—পদব্রজে ভ্রমণকারী ব্যক্তি, পথিক। **Foot-path**—পাদচারণ পথ (অর্থাৎ পথের যে অংশে গাড়ী, ট্রাম প্রভৃতি চলে না), পাদমার্গ। **Foot-plate**—বাষ্পীয় শকটের ইঞ্জিন চালক কিংবা অগ্নিরক্ষকের দাঁড়াইবার মঞ্চ। **Foot-pound**—এক পাউণ্ড ওজনের জিনিষ এক ফুট উর্দ্ধে তুলিতে যে পরিমাণ শক্তির প্রয়োজন হয়। **Foot-print** — পদচিহ্ন; পদবী

(কুমাঃ), পদ্ধতি (মঃ সং); দৃষ্টান্ত। **Foot-race** — পাদধাবন। **Foot-rule** — এক ফুট লম্বা মাপের কাঠি। **Foot-soldier**—পদাতিক সৈন্য, পদাতি, পত্তি। **Foot-sore** —পদক্ষত। **Foot-stalk** — (*Bot.* & *Zool.*) পত্রবৃন্ত। **Foot-stall**—স্ত্রীলোকের ঘোড়ায় চড়িবার জন্য রেকাব। **Foot-step**—পাদন্যাস, পাদপংক্তি, পদবিক্ষেপ, চরণপাত; পদাঙ্ক। (*Pl.*) Example; as, to follow in a person's *footsteps* (=to do as he did); দৃষ্টান্ত। **Foot-stone**—Foundation stone; ভিত্তিপ্রস্তর, মংলেষ্টক। A stone at the foot of a grave; সমাধিস্তম্ভের পাদদেশস্থ (জাতক) পাষাণ ফলক। **Foot stool** — পাদপীঠ (কুমাঃ), পদাসন (কেণ্ডি)। **Foot-warmer**— পদ উষ্ণ করিবার যন্ত্র। **At one's feet**—As his disciple; subject or suppliant; শিষ্যস্বরূপ; অধীন, পদ-প্রণত, চরণপ্রণত। **Foot-and-mouth (disease)** — A kind of fever especially in horned cattle; গো মহিষাদির মুখরোগ বিশেষ। **On foot**—By walking; হাঁটিয়া, পদব্রজে। Active; busy; proceeding; projected; কর্ম্মঠ; কর্ম্মব্যস্ত; প্রবর্ত্তিত; কল্পিত। In motion; চলন্ত। **On one's feet**—Standing; দণ্ডায়মান। In health; with a livelihood; as, to put one *on foot*; সুস্থ; জীবিকার সংস্থান-বিশিষ্ট। **The cloven foot**— See CLOVEN. **The first foot**—যে ব্যক্তি নববর্ষের প্রথম দিবসে সর্ব্বপ্রথম দ্বার অতিক্রম করে। **To carry one off his feet**—To make him enthusiastic; to excite greatly; উৎসাহসম্পন্ন করা; অতিশয় উত্তেজিত করা। **To fall on one's feet**—See under FALL. **To find, know, length of one's foot**—To learn his weakness; to be able to manage him; কোন লোকের দুর্ব্বলতার বিষয় অবগত হওয়া; কাহাকেও শাসন সংরক্ষণ করিতে পারা। **To have the ball at one's feet**—(See BALL.) To see one's way to success; কোন বিষয়ে কৃতকার্য্য হওয়া। **To keep one's feet**—Not to fall; দাঁড়াইয়া থাক, দণ্ডায়মান থাকা, না নড়া। **To keep the foot**— (*Script.*) To preserve decorum; শোভনতা, শীলতা বা ভব্যতা রক্ষা করা। **To measure another's foot by one's own last**—To judge other by oneself; নিজের সহিত তুলনায় অপরের বিচার করা। **To put one's feet down**—(*Fig.*) To take up a firm position; (লক্ষণায়) দৃঢ়প্রতিজ্ঞ হওয়া, অচলপ্রতিষ্ঠ হওয়া। **To put one's foot on anothers neck**—To trample upon him; পদদলিত করা। **To put one's foot in it**—To blunder; ভুল করা। **To put the best foot foremost onward**—To make as good an appearance as possible; যতদূর সম্ভব ভাল ভাব দেখান। To walk most rapidly; to do one's best; অতি দ্রুত চলা; যথাসাধ্য বা যথাশক্তি চেষ্টা করা, প্রাণপণে চেষ্টা করা। **To set on foot**— To put in motion; আরম্ভ করা; প্রবর্ত্তন করা। To assist to start; প্রতিষ্ঠায় সাহায্য করা। **To tread under foot**—To oppress; পদদলিত করা, পদমর্দ্দিত করা। **With foal at foot**—(ঘোটকী সম্পর্কে) সবৎসা। **With one foot in the grave**— Near death; having but short time to live; মৃতকল্প; আসন্ন-মৃত্যু। **With one's foot foremost**— Being carried to burial; সমাধিক্ষেত্রে নীত, শ্মশানে বাহিত।

foot'-ĕr, *n.* (*Slang*) The game of foot-ball; (ইতর ভাষায়) পাদগালক ক্রীড়া।

foot'-ing, *n.* **1.** Placing of feet; পদন্যাস, পদক্ষেপ। **2.** Place or surface to stand upon; foothold; secure position; basis; দাঁড়াইবার স্থান; পাদাবলম্বন; বদ্ধমূল অবস্থা; ভিত্তি। **3.** Firm foundation; stability; দৃঢ়ভিত্তি; স্থায়িত্ব। **4.** Relative condition; status; rank; as, he lived on a *footing* of equality with nobles; আপেক্ষিক অবস্থা; পদবী; পদমর্য্যাদা। **5.** The act of adding up a column of figures; the sum total of such a column; এক স্তম্ভ সারি যোগ করণ; এক স্তম্ভ রাশির যোগফল বা সংখ্যা। **6.** Act of entering on a new position; admittance to any trade, society, etc.; as, to pay for (one's) *footing* (=to pay a customary fee for it); নূতন পদে প্রবেশ; কোন ব্যবসায় বা সমিতি প্রভৃতিতে প্রবেশ। **7.** A narrow cotton lace; অতি সূক্ষ্ম সূতার ফিতা। **To gain footing**— To obtain possession of something which is to form the basis of future operation; এমন কোন বস্তু অধিকার করা যাহাতে ভবিষ্যতে কাজের সুবিধা হয়। **To live on the same footing with another**— সমাবস্থাপন্ন হওয়া। **To make good one's footing** — To establish firmly one's position; অচলপ্রতিষ্ঠ হওয়া, দৃঢ়প্রতিষ্ঠ হওয়া, সুপ্রতিষ্ঠিত হওয়া।

foo'-tle (-tl), *v. i.* & *n.* (*Slang*) To talk or act foolishly; to trifle; (ইতরভাষায়) নির্ব্বোধের মত কথা বলা বা কাজ করা; তুচ্ছ বিষয়ে রত থাকা। ***Noun.*** Twaddle; বাজে কথা, বাজে গল্প।

foots, *n.* (*Pl.*) Dregs; residue; গাদ; অবশিষ্টাংশ।

foo'-zle (-zl), *v. t.* & *n.* (*Slang*) To bungle; to manage clumsily; as, to *foozle* a stroke in golf; (ইতর ভাষায়) ভুল করা; আনাড়ীর মত কাজ করা। ***Noun.*** A clumsy failure; আনাড়ীর মত নিষ্ফলতা বা অকৃতকার্য্যতা।

fŏp, *n.* A dandy; a coxcomb; ফুলবাবু, নবকার্ত্তিক; খোস পোষাকী বাবু, ফটিক চাঁদ, (*colloq.*); **Fop'-ling**, *n.* **Fop'-per-y**, *n.* Vanity in dress or manners; showy affectation or folly; বাবুগিরি, বাবুয়ানি, সৌখীনতা, বস্ত্রবিলাস; ভড়ং, বোকামি।

Fop′-pish, *adj.* Vain and showy in dress ; বাবুয়ানা। **Fop′-pish-ly,** *adv.* **Fop′-pish-ness,** *n.*

fŏr, *prep.* & *conj.* **1.** In the place of ; instead of ; in exchange of : স্থানে ; পরিবর্ত্তে ; বিনিময়ে। **2.** In behalf of ; in favour of ; on the side of ; স্থলে ; অনুকূলে ; পক্ষে। **3.** Because of ; on account of ; জন্য ; নিমিত্ত, কারণ, বিধায়, বশতঃ, দরুণ, হেতু। **4.** In spite of ; notwithstanding ; as, *for* all his learning he has no sense ; সত্ত্বেও ; হইলেও। **5.** In the character of ; স্বরূপে। **6.** Towards ; as, we sailed *for* China ; দিকে, অভিমুখে। **7.** During ; as, he was imprisoned *for* life ; ব্যাপিয়া, পর্য্যন্ত। **8.** Considering ; in proportion to ; as, he is tall *for* his age: বিবেচনায়, হিসাবে ; অনুপাতে। **9.** To the amount or extent of ; as, a bill *for* Rs. 100 : সংখ্যায় বা পরিমাণে। **10.** With a view to ; in order to be ; conducive to ; as, to do a thing *for* the good of mankind ; to go *for* a soldier ; it is *for* his good ; উদ্দেশ্যে ; হওয়ার উদ্দেশ্যে ; জন্য। **11.** To get, win or save ; as, to go *for* a cab ; আনিতে, লাভ করিতে বা রক্ষা করিতে। **12.** In respect to ; concerning ; as far as concerns ; as, *for* my part ; সম্পর্কে ; সম্বন্ধে ; বিষয়ে। **13.** In quest of ; অনুসন্ধানে, অন্বেষণে। ***Conj.*** Because ; since ; seeing that ; কারণ ; যেহেতু ; কেননা। **Bulk for bulk**—Taking equal bulk of each ; উভয় বস্তু সমপরিমাণে লইয়া। **For all that** — In spite of that ; সত্ত্বেও। **For all the world**—Wholly ; exactly ; সম্পূর্ণরূপে ; ঠিক-ভাবে। **For as much as**—(*Conj.*) Since ; because ; যেহেতু, কেননা ; কারণ। **For aught one knows**—So far as one knows ; যতদূর অবগত আছে। **For sale** — To be sold ; বিক্রেয়। **For the better**—Resulting in a better condition of affairs ; ভালর জন্য। **For the life of me**—If my life depended on it ; যদি আমার জীবন ইহার উপর নির্ভর করিত। **For the present**—আপাততঃ। **For the worse**—Resulting in a worse condition ; মন্দের জন্য। **He is not long for this world**—He will soon die ; সে শীঘ্রই মরিবে, সে আর বেশী দিন বাঁচিবে না, তাহার দিন ফুরাইয়া আসিয়াছে। **It is usual for hats to be worn**—It is usual that hats should be worn ; সচরাচর টুপী পরা উচিত। **Nothing for it but to submit**—Submission being the only course open ; বশ্যতা স্বীকার ছাড়া উপায়ান্তর নাই। **Oh for wings** — Would that I had wings ; আমার যদি পাখা থাকিত। **Once for all**—Finally ; আখেরের মত, চিরদিনের জন্য। **To go for**—(*Slang*) To attack ; (ইতর ভাষায়) আক্রমণ করা। **Were it not but for**—Leaving out of account ; তাহা না হইলে, তাহা না ধরিলে, যদি তাহা না হইত। **Word for word**—Literally ; কথার কথায়, শব্দানুযায়ী।

fŏr′-āge, *n.*, *v. t.* & *i.* **1.** Food for horses and cattle ; অশ্বগবাদির খাদ্য। **2.** The act of foraging ; অশ্ব গবাদির খাদ্য অন্বেষণ, খাদ্যান্বেষণ। ***Verb t.*** **1.** To gather forage from ; to ravage ; অশ্বগবাদির খাদ্য-সংগ্রহ করা ; লুণ্ঠন করা। **2.** To supply with forage ; অশ্ব গবাদির খাদ্য সরবরাহ করা। ***Verb i.*** To rove in search of forage or any other thing (*lit.* & *fig.*) ; (লক্ষণায় ও শব্দানুযায়ী) খাদ্যাদির অনুসন্ধানে বিচরণ করা। **—ag-er,** *n.*

fō-rā′-mĕn *n.* (*Pl.* -MINA) A small opening, orifice or hole (esp. in *Bot., Anat.* & *Zool.*) ; (উদ্ভিদ্, শরীর-ব্যবচ্ছেদ ও প্রাণিবিদ্যা) রন্ধ্র, ছিদ্র। **—ram′-i-nate, —ram′-i-nat-ed,** *adjs.* সচ্ছিদ্র, রন্ধ্রবিশিষ্ট।

fō-răm′-i-nĭf-ĕr-ă, *n.* (*pl.*) An order of Rhizopoda, furnished with a shell or test ; রন্ধ্রী (সাঃ পঃ)।

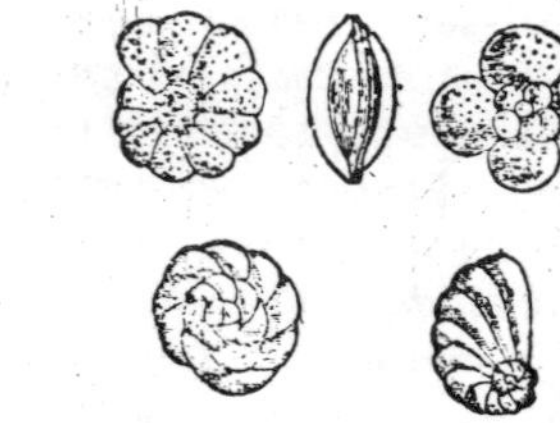

Foraminifera.

fŏr′-ay (-ā), *n.* & *v. i.* A sudden incursion ; লুণ্ঠনার্থ হঠাৎ আক্রমণ। ***Verb i.*** To make a raid ; to ravage ; লুণ্ঠনার্থ হঠাৎ আক্রমণ করা ; লুটপাট করা। **—er,** *n.*

fŏr-bade′ (-băd), *Pt.* of FORBID.

fŏr-bear′ (-bār), *v. t.* & *i.* To keep away from ; not to use or mention ; বিরত থাকা, নিবৃত্ত থাকা ; উল্লেখ বা ব্যবহার না করা। ***Verb i.*** **1.** To refrain or abstain (with *from*) ; ক্ষান্ত হওয়া, বিরত হওয়া। **2.** To be patient ; ধৈর্য্যশীল হওয়া, সহিষ্ণু হওয়া। **—ance,** *n.* **1.** Act of forbearing ; the exercise of patience ; ধৈর্য্য অবলম্বন, সহিষ্ণুতা অবলম্বন ; সহিষ্ণুতা, তিতিক্ষা। **2.** Indulgence ; mildness ; long-suffering ; অপরাধীর প্রতি অনুগ্রহ-শীলতা ; নম্রতা, মৃদুতা ; দীর্ঘকালব্যাপী কষ্টভোগ। **—er,** *n.* **—ing,** *adj.* Patient ; long suffering ; ধৈর্য্যশীল, সহিষ্ণু, তিতিক্ষু ; দীর্ঘকালব্যাপী কষ্ট-ভোগকারী। **—ing-ly,** *adv.*

fŏr-bear′ (-bār), *n.* (*Usu. pl.*) An ancestor or ancestors ; পূর্ব্ব-পুরুষ, পূর্ব্বপুরুষগণ।

fŏr-bid′, *v. t.* **1.** To prohibit ; as, to *forbid* bull-fights ; নিষেধ করা, বারণ করা, মানা করা, প্রতিষেধ করা। **2.** To oppose ; as, his death *forbids* its completion ; বাধা দেওয়া, প্রতিরোধ করা। **—den,** *adj.* Prohibited ; as, *forbidden* degress, *forbidden* fruit ; নিষিদ্ধ, বারিত (কেণ্ডি), নিবারিত (ঐ), নিষেধিত (ঐ), প্রতিষিদ্ধ (ঐ), বর্জ্জিত (ঐ), পরিবর্জ্জিত (ঐ), প্রত্যাখ্যাত। **–ding,** *adj.* Repelling ; repulsive ; disagreeble ; ঘৃণাজনক ; অভক্তিজনক, অপ্রীতিকর। **–ding-ly,** *adv.* **–ding-ness,** *n.* **Forbidden or prohibited degrees**—সম্পর্কের যে গণ্ডীর মধ্যে বিবাহ চলিতে পারে না। **Forbidden fruit**—আদম ও ঈভ ইডেন উদ্যানের যে ফল ভক্ষণ করিতে ঈশ্বর কর্তৃক নিষিদ্ধ হইয়াছিলেন; [See Genesis, ii. 9, iii. 3-6, 11, 17]। একপ্রকার কমলা লেবু। অধিক বা অনুচিত সুখ-সম্ভোগ। **May God forbid**—May it not happen ; ঈশ্বর না করুন।

fŏr-bōre′, *p.t.* of FORBEAR.

fōrce, *n.* & *v. t.* **1.** Strength; power ; vigour ; বল, শক্তি ; ক্ষমতা; তেজ। **2.** Power to convince ; efficiency ; binding effect ; validity, as of an argument, appeal etc. ; vividness of effect ; as, described with much *force*; প্রতীতি-জনন-শক্তি; কার্য্যকারিতা; অবশ্যকরণীয়তা; বৈধতা, সিদ্ধতা ; সজীবতা, জীবন্তভাব। **3.** Military strength ; a body of soldiers ; (*pl.*) troops ; সামরিক শক্তি; সৈন্য; (বহুবচন) সৈন্যদল, বল (তদপরিমিতং বলং — কুমাঃ)। **4.** Violence ; compulsion ; coercion ; as, by *force* ; জুলুম, জবরদস্তি ; বাধ্যতা ; বলপ্রয়োগ। **5.** Mental or moral strength ; মানসিক বল, নৈতিক বল। **6.** Real import or meaning ; ভাব, অভিপ্রায়, যথার্থ অর্থ, প্রকৃত অর্থ, তাৎপর্য্য। **7.** (*Phys.*) A measurable and determinable influence inclining a body to motion ; intensity of this (পদার্থ-বিজ্ঞান) বল ; বলের প্রাবল্য। ***Verb t.*** **1.** To constrain ; to coerce ; to compel ; বলপ্রয়োগে রুদ্ধ করা ; বলপ্রয়োগ করা ; বলপ্রয়োগে বাধ্য করা। **2.** To do violence to ; to ravish : বলপ্রয়োগ করা, অত্যাচার করা ; বলাৎকার করা। **3.** To urge ; to strain ; as, to *force* one's voice ; to produce by unnatural effort, as a smile etc. ; বলপূর্ব্বক উত্তেজিত করা ; অতিরিক্ত মাত্রায় খাটান ; কৃত্রিম বা অস্বাভাবিক চেষ্টা দ্বারা উৎপাদন করা। **4.** To capture by force ; to storm, as a fort etc. ; বলপূর্ব্বক অধিকার করা ; প্রচণ্ডভাবে আক্রমণ পূর্ব্বক অধিকার করা। **5.** To break open, as a gate etc. ; ভাঙ্গিয়া ফেলা। **6.** To make way through, as a hostile country, by force; পথ করিয়া যাওয়া, জোর করিয়া যাওয়া। **7.** To drive or impel by force ; to extort or take by force ; বলপূর্ব্বক প্রবিষ্ট বা চালিত করা ; বলপূর্ব্বক গ্রহণ করা, জোর করিয়া লওয়া, পীড়নপূর্ব্বক আদায় করা। **8.** (*Whist*) To cause (a player) to trump or reveal his strength ; to compel a player to play (a certain card) ; (তাস খেলায়) তুরুপ করিতে বা রং খেলিতে বাধ্য করা ; কাহারও শক্তি (হাতের তাস) বুঝিবার নিমিত্ত রং খেলিতে বাধ্য করা। **9.** To impose, as something (*upon* a person) ; স্কন্ধে চাপান, ভারার্পণ করা, জোর করিয়া চাপাইয়া দেওয়া। **10.** To hasten artificially the maturity ; কৃত্রিম উত্তাপে (ফল প্রভৃতি) পাকান, জাক দেওয়া। **Force′-less,** *adj.* Having little or no force ; ক্ষীণ-শক্তি, হীন-শক্তি। **Force′-ful,** *adj.* Forcible ; সজীব, ওজস্বী, তেজোপূর্ণ, শক্তিশালী। **Force′-ful-ly,** *adv.* **Force′-ful-ness,** *n.* **Animal force**—জীব-বল (হিঃ কোঃ)। **Biological force**—জীবনবল (হিঃ কোঃ)। **Bionomic force**—বীজনিয়ামক বল (হিঃ কোঃ), জীববৃদ্ধি নিয়ামক বল (ঐ)। **Centrifugal force** — See CENTRIFUGAL. **Centripetal force**—See CENTRIPETAL. **Equilibrium force**—বলসাম্য (হিঃ কোঃ)। **Co-planer force**—একধরাতল বল (হিঃ কোঃ)। **Force diagram** — বল পরিলেখ (হিঃ কোঃ)। **Force majeure**—Irresistible force ; অপ্রতিরোধনীয় বল-প্রয়োগ। **Force meat**—মসলাদার মাংসের পুর। **Force-pump**—একপ্রকার দমকল—যাহা হইতে জলধারা সবেগে উর্দ্ধে উৎসারিত হয়, জলোৎক্ষেপক নলিকা (হিঃ কোঃ)। **Opposite force**—সম্মুখ-বল (হিঃ কোঃ)। **Parallel-force**—সমানান্তরবল (হিঃ কোঃ)। **Psychological force**—মানসবল (হিঃ কোঃ), অন্তঃকরণবল (ঐ)। **Psychonomic force** — অন্তঃকরণ-বিকাশ-নিয়ামক বল (হিঃ কোঃ)। **Social force**—সামাজিক বল (হিঃ কোঃ)। **Socionomic force** — সমাজপ্ররোহ-নিয়ামক বল (হিঃ কোঃ)। **Resultant-force**—লব্ধবল (হিঃ কোঃ)। **Vital force**—আত্মবল (হিঃ কোঃ)। **By force**—By means of force ; বলদ্বারা, সবলে, বলপূর্ব্বক। **In force**—In vogue ; current ; চলিত ; প্রচলিত। (*Mil.*) In great number ; (সামরিক শাস্ত্র) বহু সংখ্যায়। **In great force**—Vigorous ; fit ; lively ; তেজস্বী ; উপযুক্ত ; সতেজ। **Parallelogram of force** — বলসমানান্তরচতুর্ভুজ (হিঃ কোঃ)। **The force** — The Police ; পুলিসগণ। **To come into force** — To attain validity or binding effect ; আমলে আসা, চলিত হওয়া। **To force a card**—(*In conjuring*) To make one choose a particular card unconsciously ; (ভোজবাজীতে) কাহাকেও অজ্ঞাতসারে কোন নির্দ্দিষ্ট তাস নির্ব্বাচিত করান। **To force a scholar, plant**—To hasten artificially the maturity of a scholar, plant ; কৃত্রিম উপায়ে অকালপক্ব করা। **To force the pace or running**—To adopt high speed in a race ; to tire out an adversary quickly ; (so at auction, *to force the bidding*) ; প্রতিযোগীকে শীঘ্র ক্লান্ত করার উদ্দেশ্যে ঘোড়দৌড় প্রভৃতিতে অতি দ্রুত ধাবিত হওয়া ; প্রতিযোগীকে শীঘ্র ক্লান্ত করা। **To force one's hand**—To compel him to act prematurely or adopt a policy unwillingly ; নিরূপিত

কালের পূর্ব্বে কার্য্য করিতে বাধ্য করা, অনিচ্ছা সত্ত্বেও কোন নীতি অবলম্বনে বাধ্য করা। **To force one's way**—To make one's way etc. by force; বলপূর্ব্বক পথ করিয়া চলা। **To force the game**—To run risk to score quickly ; দ্রুত জয়াঙ্ক লাভের জন্য ঝুঁকি লওয়া। **To force words etc.** — To put strained sense upon words etc. ; শব্দাদির কষ্ট-কল্পিত অর্থ করা। **To put in force**—To enforce ; আমলে আনা, চলিত করা, প্রবর্ত্তন করা। **Triangle of force**—বলত্রিভুজ (হিঃ কোঃ)।

förce, *n.* A water-fall ; জল-প্রপাত।

forced (först), *adj.* **1.** Compelled by force ; কৃচ্ছ্রসাধিত, আয়াসসাধিত। **2.** Strained ; affected, as a smile, style, etc. ; কষ্টকল্পিত ; কৃত্রিম, অস্বাভাবিক। **Forc'-ed-ly,** *adv.* **Forc'-ed-ness,** *n.* **Forced-labour**—বেগার। **Forced march**—বিশেষ আয়াসকর রণযাত্রা। **Forced meaning**—কষ্টকল্পিত অর্থ। **Forced smile**—কাষ্ঠ হাসি।

för'-cĕps, *n.* (*Sing.* & *pl.*) **1.** Pincers used in surgery ; সন্দংশ, দন্তাদি উৎপাটনের জন্য সাঁড়াশী যন্ত্র, কঙ্ক-মুখ (সুশ্রুঃ), খণ্ডধারা, স্বস্তিক (ঠাকুরঃ)। **2.** (*Zool.*, *Anat.*, etc.) An organ or part like forceps ; (প্রাণি-বিদ্যা, শারীরসংস্থান-বিদ্যা ইত্যাদি) সাঁড়াশীর আকার অঙ্গ। **—ci-pate,** *adj.* Forceps-like ; কঙ্কমুখাকৃতি।

för'-ci-ble (-bl), *adj.* **1.** Effected by or involving force ; as, a *forcible* entry ; বলসম্পাদিত, বল-সাধিত, বলসাধ্য, শক্তিসাধ্য। **2.** Impressive ; convincing ; vivid ; as, a *forcible* style ; হৃদয়গ্রাহী ; প্রতীতিজনক, প্রত্যয়কর ; ওজস্বী। **—bly,** *adv.* **—ness,** *n.* **Forcible-feeble** — Seemingly strong while really weak ; আপাতদৃষ্টিতে বলবান বলিয়া প্রতীয়মান কিন্তু প্রকৃত পক্ষে দুর্ব্বল।

förc'-ing, *n.* (*Hort.*) The art of hastening the growth of plants etc. ; (উদ্যান-রচনা) বৃক্ষের দ্রুতবর্দ্ধন-কৌশল। **Forcing engine**—প্রেরক ইঞ্জিন (হিঃ কোঃ)। **Forcing machine** — প্রেরক কল (হিঃ কোঃ)। **Forcing-house** — A hot house ; যে গৃহে দ্রুতবর্দ্ধনার্থ বৃক্ষাদি রক্ষিত হয়।

förc'-īte, *n.* An explosive ; এক প্রকার বিস্ফোরক।

förd, *n.*, *v. t.* & *i.* A shallow place in a river etc. where it may be passed by wading ; নদী প্রভৃতির পদব্রজে উত্তরণযোগ্য স্থান, সুপ্রতর স্থল, গাধ (রঃ)। ***Verb t.*** To cross by walking, as a river etc. ; নদী প্রভৃতি পদব্রজে পার হওয়া। ***Verb i.*** To cross a river etc. on foot ; হাঁটিয়া নদী পার হওয়া। **Ford'-less,** *adj.*

förd'-ā-ble (-bl), *adj.* Capable of being forded ; পদব্রজে উত্তরণ-যোগ্য, সুপ্রতর (রঃ), সুতর। **—ness,** *n.*

för-dô', *v. t.* **1.** (*Archaic*) To destroy ; to kill ; (অপ্রঃ) ধ্বংস করা ; বিনাশ করা। **2.** To tire out, (only *p. p.*) ; ক্লান্ত করা, পরিশ্রান্ত করা, খিন্ন করা।

fōre, *adj.*, *n.*, *adv.* & *prep.* Advanced in position ; coming first ; (opposed to *back, behind* etc. ; as, the *fore*-leg = অগ্রপাদ) ; সম্মুখবর্ত্তী, পুরোবর্ত্তী ; অগ্রবর্ত্তী। ***Noun.*** The front ; the front part ; the bow of a ship ; সম্মুখ ; সম্মুখভাগ, অগ্রভাগ ; পোতাগ্র। ***Adv.*** In front ; (*naut.*) in, or towards, the bows of a ship ; সম্মুখস্থ ; (নৌ-বিদ্যা) পোতাগ্রস্থ, পোতাগ্র প্রদেশস্থ। ***Prep.*** Before ; পূর্ব্বে, অগ্রে। **Fore and aft**—(*Naut.*) Lengthwise of a ship ; from stem to stern ; জাহাজের লম্বালম্বি ; জাহাজের আগা হইতে পাছা পর্য্যন্ত। **Fore George**—By George ! জর্জ্জের নামে ! **To bring to the fore**—To bring to the front ; সম্মুখে আনয়ন করা, অগ্রবর্ত্তী করা, পুরোবর্ত্তী করা। **To come to the fore**—To be conspicuous ; পুরোবর্ত্তী হওয়া। **To the fore**—On the spot ; ready to hand ; available ; alive ; স্থানে ; হাতের নিকট ; প্রাপ্য ; জীবিত।

fōre, *interj.* (*Golf*) A word warning people in front of a stroke ; গল্ফ ক্রীড়ায় আঘাতের সময় সম্মুখবর্ত্তী লোকদিগকে সাবধান করার শব্দ।

fōre'-ärm, *v. t.* & *n.* To arm before the time of need ; পূর্ব্ব হইতেই অস্ত্রশস্ত্রে সজ্জিত করা। ***Noun.*** (*Anat.*) The part of the arm from elbow to wrist or to finger tops ; the corresponding part in a fore-leg or wing ; (শারীর-সংস্থান বিদ্যা) কনুই হইতে হাতের কব্জী পর্য্যন্ত অংশ, প্রকোষ্ঠ, অগ্রবাহু ; অগ্রপাদ, আগালীপা, ডানার অগ্রভাগ।

fōre-bōde', *v. t.* **1.** (*Rare*) To foretell ; (অপ্রঃ) পূর্ব্বে বলা। **2.** To portend ; অমঙ্গল সূচনা করা, ভাবী অশুভ সূচনা করা। **3.** To be prescient of, as a calamity etc. ; পূর্ব্ব হইতেই ভাবী অমঙ্গলাদি অনুভব করা। **—bod'-er,** *n.* One who forebodes ; ভাবী অমঙ্গল সূচনাকারী। **—bod'-ing,** *n.* Presage ; omen, esp. of coming evil ; পূর্ব্ব সূচনা ; ভাবী অমঙ্গল সূচনা, অনিষ্টসূচনা, ভাবী অমঙ্গল অনুভব। **—bod'-ing-ly,** *adv.*

fōre'-cā-bin, *n.* A cabin in forepart of a ship, usually for second class passengers ; জাহাজের সম্মুখ ভাগের কামরা (সাধারণতঃ দ্বিতীয় শ্রেণীর যাত্রীদিগের জন্য)।

fōre-cāst', *v. t.*, *i.* & *n.* **1.** To plan beforehand ; পূর্ব্বে কল্পনা করা। **2.** To calculate or conjecture beforehand ; পূর্ব্বেই গণনা করা বা আন্দাজ করা, পূর্ব্বানুমান করা। ***Verb i.*** To form schemes beforehand ; অগ্রে মতলব আঁটা। ***Noun.*** **1.** An estimate or conjecture of a future happening, esp. of coming weather ; পূর্ব্বানুমান, পূর্ব্বযোজনা (কেঙি), পূর্ব্বসংসাধন (ঐ), বৃষ্টিবাত্যাদি সম্বন্ধে পূর্ব্বসূচনা। **2.** (*Rare*) Foresight ; (ক্বচিদ্ ব্যবহৃত) দূরদৃষ্টি,

পরিণামদর্শিতা। **–er,** *n.* One who forecasts : পূর্ব্বাভাস প্রদানকারী।

fōre'-căs-tle (-l), **fo'c'sle** (fōksl), *ns.* **1.** The part of the upper deck of a war-ship forward of the foremast; রণপোতের অগ্রভাগস্থ ক্ষুদ্র পাটাতন। **2.** The fore-part of a merchant-vessel under the deck where sailors live; জাহাজের পাটাতনের নিম্নস্থ পুরোবর্ত্তী অংশ,—যথায় মাল্লাগণ বাস করে।

fōre-clōse', *v. t.* & *i.* **1.** To preclude; to prevent; to debar from enjoyment of; বারণ করা, প্রতিবন্ধকতা করা; নিষেধ করা; ভোগাধিকার হইতে বঞ্চিত করা। **2.** (*Law of mortgage*) To bar (a person entitled to redemption) on non-payment of debts; to bar as the right of redemption; (বন্ধকী-আইন) অধমর্ণকে (ঋণ অপরিশোধ হেতু) বন্ধকী মাল খালাস করণের অবকাশ না দেওয়া; বন্ধকী মাল খালাস করার অধিকারচ্যুত করা। **3.** To complete or settle beforehand; পূর্ব্বে মীমাংসা বা সম্পাদন করা। **–clo'-sure,** *n.* A proceeding which bars or extinguishes a mortgager's right redeeming a mortgaged estate; যে কার্য্যদ্বারা বন্ধকদাতার বন্ধকী সম্পত্তি পুনরুদ্ধারের অধিকার লোপ করা যায়, বয়বাৎ (রঃ অঃ)।

fōre'-court (-kōrt), *n.* The front or outcourt of a building; দালানের সম্মুখ অথবা বহির্ভাগস্থ চত্বর।

fōre'-dĕck, *n.* (*Naut.*) The forepart of a deck; (নৌ-বিদ্যা) জাহাজের পাটাতনের অগ্রভাগ।

fōre'-dōom, *v. t.* & *n.* To doom beforehand; পূর্ব্ব হইতে নির্দ্দিষ্ট বা নিরূপিত করা। ***Noun.*** Previous doom or sentence; অগ্রেই বিহিত দণ্ড বা দণ্ডাজ্ঞা।

fōre'-fä-thêr, *n.* An ancestor; পূর্ব্বপুরুষ, পিতৃপুরুষ, পিতৃপিতামহগণ। **Our forefathers**—Earlier generations; আমাদের পূর্ব্বপুরুষগণ।

fōre-fĕnd', *v. t.* To ward off; to avert; প্রতিরোধ করা, নিবারণ করা, আটকান; প্রতিনিবৃত্ত করা, ফিরাইয়া দেওয়া।

fōre'-fin-gêr (-fing-), *n.* The finger next to the thumb; তর্জ্জনী, প্রদেশিনী (কেভি)।

fōre'-fōot, *n.* **1.** One of the anterior feet of a beast; জন্তু প্রভৃতির অগ্রপাদ, আগালী পা।

fōre'-front (-frŭnt), *n.* The foremost part or place; as, in the *forefront* of the battle; পুরোভাগ, সম্মুখদেশ।

fōre-găth'-êr, *v.* See FORGATHER.

fōre'-gift, *n.* A premium paid for a lease; ইজারাভূমির জন্য ইজারাদার কর্ত্তৃক যে টাকা প্রদত্ত হয়।

fōre-gō', *v. t.* & *i.* To go before in time or place; অগ্রে গমন করা, পূর্ব্বে গমন করা। **–er,** *n.* A predecessor; পূর্ব্বগামী ব্যক্তি, অগ্রগামী ব্যক্তি। **–ing,** *adj.* Preceding; previously mentioned; পূর্ব্ববর্ত্তী, পূর্ব্বগামী; পূর্ব্বোক্ত, প্রাগুক্ত। **–gone',** *p. p.* পূর্ব্বসংকল্পিত (কেভি)। **Foregone conclusion**—A decison or opinion come to before argument or examination; পূর্ব্বকল্পিত সিদ্ধান্ত, পূর্ব্ব স্থিরীকৃত সিদ্ধান্ত। A result that was inevitable; নিশ্চিত পরিণাম।

fōre-gō' *v. t.* To abstain from; to neglect; to renounce; বিরত হওয়া, ক্ষান্ত হওয়া, নিবৃত্ত হওয়া; উপেক্ষা করা; ছাড়া, ত্যাগ করা, পরিত্যাগ করা।

fōre'-ground (-grownd), *n.* **1.** The part of a scene or picture which is nearest to the spectator; দৃশ্য বা চিত্রের যে অংশ দ্রষ্টার সর্ব্বাপেক্ষা নিকটে থাকে, চিত্রের সম্মুখভূমি (মন্মথ), অগ্রভূমি (কিঃ রাঃ)। **2.** The most conspicuous position; অতিশয় সুস্পষ্ট স্থান।

fōre'-hănd, *n.* & *adj.* The part of a horse before the rider; অশ্ব-দেহের যে অংশ আরোহীর সম্মুখে থাকে। ***Adj.*** **1.** (*Dial.*) Done beforehand; (উপভাষায়) অগ্র-সাধিত, পূর্ব্বকৃত। **2.** (*Tennis*) Not back-handed, as a stroke; (টেনিস ক্রীড়া) পশ্চাদভিমুখীন। **–ed,** *adj.* **1.** Timely; সময়োচিত, কালোচিত। **2.** (*U. S.*) Prosperous; (মার্কিণ যুক্ত রাজ্যে) সমৃদ্ধ, সমৃদ্ধিশালী।

fore'-head (fōre-hĕd, fŏr-ĕd), *n.* **1.** The part of the face above the eyes; কপাল, ললাট, ভাল। **2.** Countenance; মুখাবয়ব, চেহারা। **3.** Assurance; audacity; "My refuter's *forehead* is stronger with a weaker wit"; প্রত্যয়, নিশ্চয়; ধৃষ্টতা।

fŏr'-eign (-in), *adj.* **1.** Belonging to, or derived from, another country or nation; not native; as, a *foreign* language; বৈদেশিক, বিদেশীয়, পরদেশীয়, দেশান্তরীয়, পারদেশ্য, অন্যদেশীয়, ভিন্ন-দেশীয়; বিজাতীয়। **2.** Proceeding from, or belonging to, other persons or things; introduced from outside; as, a *foreign* substance; ভিন্ন ব্যক্তি বা বস্তু হইতে প্রসূত; বহির্দ্দিক্ হইতে আগত, বাহ্য, বহিরঙ্গ, আগন্তুক। **3.** Alien (with *to* or *from*); Not appropriate; irrelevant, (with *to*); as, *foreign to* the purpose; বিদেশীয়; অনুপযোগী; অপ্রাসঙ্গিক। **4.** Related to, or dealing with, other countries; as, *foreign* trade; coming from another district, society, etc.; বৈদেশিক; অপর জেলা, সম্প্রদায়, প্রভৃতি হইতে আগত। **–er,** *n.* **1.** A person born in a foreign country or speaking a foreign language; an alien; বিদেশী লোক; পরদেশী, বিদেশী, বৈদেশিক, দেশাতিথি (মঃ ভাঃ)। **2.** A foreign vessel; বৈদেশিক জাহাজ। **3.** An animal or article imported from abroad; বিদেশ হইতে সমানীত জন্তু বা দ্রব্য। **–ism,** *n.* Imitation of what is foreign; a foreign idiom or custom; বৈদেশিক ভাবের অনুকরণ; বৈদেশিক বাক্‌পদ্ধতি বা রীতিনীতি।

—ize, *v. t.* & *i.* To make, or become, foreign ; বৈদেশিক ভাবাপন্ন করা বা হওয়া। **Foreign-commerce**—বৈদেশিক বাণিজ্য। **Foreign exchange** — বহির্বিনিময়। **Foreign goods**—পরদেশী মাল, বিলাতী মাল। **Foreign labour**—বিদেশী মজুরী। **Foreign minister**—পররাষ্ট্র-সচিব। **Foreign parts**—Foreign countries ; বিদেশ। **Foreign office**—পররাষ্ট্র বিভাগ ; পররাষ্ট্র বিভাগের কার্য্যালয়।

före-judge′ (-jŭj), *v. t.* To judge beforehand or before hearing the facts and proof ; প্রমাণাদি গ্রহণের পূর্ব্বে সিদ্ধান্ত বা নিষ্পত্তি করা, পূর্ব্বসিদ্ধান্ত করা।

före-know′ (-nō), *v. t.* To know beforehand ; পূর্ব্বে অবগত হওয়া, পূর্ব্বে জানা বা বিদিত হওয়া। **—a-ble,** *adj.* **—er,** *n.* ভবিষ্যজ্ঞ (কেণ্ডি), ভবিষ্যদর্শী (ঐ), দৈবজ্ঞ (ঐ)। **—knowl′-edge,** *n.* Knowledge of a thing before it happens ; ভাবী বিষয়ের পূর্ব্বজ্ঞান, ভবিষ্যদ্‌জ্ঞান, ভবিষ্যজ্ঞান (হিঃ কোঃ)।

fŏr′-ĕl, —rĕl, *ns.* A kind of parchment for the covers of books ; পুস্তকের প্রচ্ছদপটের একপ্রকার চর্ম্মপট্ট।

före′-lănd, *n.* **1.** A promontory or cape ; অন্তরীপ, শৈলান্তরীপ, ভূশলাকা (কেণ্ডি), ভূশির (ঐ)। **2.** A strip of land before something ; অগ্রভূমি।

före′-lĕg, *n.* One of the front legs of animals, chairs etc. ; অগ্রপদ (অভিঃ), অগ্রচরণ, আগালী পা।

före′-lŏck (-lŏk), *n.* The lock of hair growing just above forehead ; মস্তকের সম্মুখভাগজাত কেশগুচ্ছ, অগ্রশিখ, ভ্রমরক (কেণ্ডি), ভ্রমরালক (ঐ), অগ্রকেশ, অগ্রশিখা (আঃ বঃ)। **To take time** or **occasion by the forelock**—To seize an opportunity ; not to let a chance slip ; সুযোগ গ্রহণ করা ; সুযোগ না ছাড়া।

före′-lŏck, *n.* & *v. t.* A wedge driven through the end of a bolt to prevent its drawing ; খিল। ***Verb t.*** To fasten with a forelock ; খিল দিয়া বন্ধ করা।

före′-măn, *n.* **1.** The president and spokesman of a jury ; জুরীদলের অগ্রণী বা মুখপাত্র, সভ্যপ্রধান (আঃ বঃ)। **2.** The chief workman superintending others ; শ্রমজীবিগণের প্রধান তত্ত্বাবধায়ক, পরিদর্শক, মজুরদলের সর্দ্দার, কার্য্যপরিদর্শক। **Working foreman** — যে শ্রমজীবিগণের কার্য্যপরিদর্শক নিজে কার্য্য করে এবং অপরের কার্য্যও পরিদর্শন করিয়া থাকে।

före′-măst, *n.* The mast nearest the bow ; জাহাজের সম্মুখভাগস্থ সর্ব্বাগ্রবর্ত্তী গুণবৃক্ষ। **Foremast-band, —man, —seaman**—সাধারণ নাবিক।

före-mĕn′-tioned (-shŏnd), *adj.* Mentioned before ; পূর্ব্বোল্লিখিত, প্রাগুক্ত, প্রোক্ত, উল্লিখিত।

före′-mōst, *adj.* & *adv.* First in time, place or rank ; most advanced ; most notable ; best ; সর্ব্বপ্রধান, মুখ্যতম, অগ্রগণ্য, সর্ব্বাগ্রগণ্য, অগ্রস্থিত, অগ্রবর্ত্তী ; পরমোন্নত ; প্রসিদ্ধতম, অতিশয় প্রসিদ্ধ, সেরা, প্রধানতম ; অত্যুত্তম। ***Adv.*** First ; in the first place ; সর্ব্বপ্রথম ; প্রথমস্থানবর্ত্তী। **Head etc. foremost** — With head etc. in front ; মস্তক প্রভৃতি সম্মুখে রাখিয়া।

före′-nāme, *n.* A person's first name ; কোন ব্যক্তির পূর্ব্বনাম।

före′-noon, *n.* The portion of the day before noon ; পূর্ব্বাহ্ণ, প্রাহ্ণ।

fō-rĕn′-sic, *adj.* Belonging to, or used in, courts of judicature ; ধর্ম্মাধিকরণ বা আদালত সংক্রান্ত, ধর্ম্মাধিকরণে ব্যবহৃত, ন্যায়সভাসম্বন্ধীয় (কেণ্ডি)। **Forensic medicine** — Medical jurisprudence ; ভৈষজ্যশাস্ত্র সম্পৃক্ত ব্যবস্থাবিজ্ঞান। **—si-cal,** *adj.* **—si-cal-ly,** *adv.*

före-ŏr-dain′ (-dān), *v. t.* To predestinate ; to ordain or appoint beforehand ; পূর্ব্বনির্দ্ধারিত করা, অগ্রে নির্দ্ধারিত করা, পূর্ব্ব হইতে নির্দ্দিষ্ট করা। **—di-na′-tion,** *n.* নিয়তি (হিঃ কোঃ)।

före′-pârt, *n.* The part most advanced or first in time or place ; the front ; সর্ব্বোৎকৃষ্ট অংশ, প্রথম অংশ ; সম্মুখভাগ, অগ্রভাগ, পূর্ব্বভাগ।

före′-peak (-pēk), *n.* (*Naut.*) The part of a vessel close to the bow ; (নৌ-বিদ্যা) পোতাগ্রভাগের সন্নিহিত জাহাজের অংশ।

före′-plāne, *n.* (*Carpentry*) The first plane used after saw and plane ; (তক্ষণ কার্য্য) কুঠার দ্বারা কাটা ও করাত দ্বারা চিরার পর প্রথম যে রেঁদা ব্যবহৃত হয়।

före′-rank (-răngk), *n.* The first rank ; the front ; প্রথম পংক্তি ; সম্মুখভাগ, পুরোভাগ।

före-reach′ (-rēch), *v. i.* & *t.* To go ahead ; পূর্ব্বে যাওয়া, অগ্রে যাওয়া। ***Verb t.*** To gain upon ; as, a vessel *forereaches* another, পশ্চাতে ফেলিয়া যাওয়া।

före-rŭn′, *v. t.* To foreshadow, as a future event ; পূর্ব্বাভাস দেওয়া, পূর্ব্বসূচনা করা। **—ner,** *n.* **1.** A harbinger ; a precursor ; a prognostic ; অগ্রপ্রেরিত ব্যক্তি, অগ্রদূত, অগ্রবর্ত্তী সংবাদবাহক ; অগ্রগ, পুরোগামী, অগ্রগামী ব্যক্তি ; ভাবী সূচনা। **2.** A predecessor ; পূর্ব্ববর্ত্তী। **3.** (*Pl.*) An advance guard ; অগ্রগামী সৈন্য-অগ্রানীক।

före′-said (-săd), *adj.* Said or spoken before ; পূর্ব্বকথিত, পূর্ব্বোক্ত, প্রাগুক্ত, প্রোক্ত।

före′-sail′ (-sāl), *n.* The principal sail of the foremast ; জাহাজের সর্ব্বাগ্রবর্ত্তী মাস্তুলের প্রধান পাইল।

före-see′ (-ē), *v.t.* To see beforehand ; to foreknow ; পূর্ব্বে দর্শন করা ; পূর্ব্বে বুঝিতে পারা। **—ing,** *adj.* Characterised by foresight ; পূর্ব্বদৃষ্টিসম্পন্ন, ভবিষ্যদ্দর্শী, ভবিষ্যৎপ্রেক্ষী। **—ing-ly,** *adv.*

före-shăd′-ow (-ō), *v. t.* To shadow beforehand ; to serve as a type or presage of ; অগ্রে ছায়া প্রদান করা ; পূর্ব্বাভাস দেওয়া, আদর্শ বা পূর্ব্বাভাস স্বরূপ হওয়া।

före′-sheets (-shēts), *n.* (*Pl.*) The inner part of the bow of a boat ; নৌকার অগ্রাংশের অন্তর্ভাগ।

före′-shöre, *n.* The sloping part of a shore between the high and low water-marks ; the beach ; নদী বা সমুদ্রতীরের যে ঢালু অংশে জোয়ারের সময় জল আসে এবং ভাঁটার সময় সরিয়া যায় ; সৈকত।

före-shŏrt′-en (-n), *v. t.* (*Painting*) To depict a figure which is viewed either from below, or directly in front of it, and which has, in consequence, to be portrayed in a smaller space, so that the idea of its projecting forward may be accurately conveyed ; ঠিক নিম্ন হইতে দৃষ্ট বস্তুর চিত্র অঙ্কিত করা, হ্রস্ব চিত্রাঙ্কণ করা। [ঐরূপ চিত্রে অঙ্কিত মূর্ত্তির সম্মুখ-দিকে উদ্গমের সঠিক ধারণা উৎপাদনের উদ্দেশ্যে উহা অপেক্ষাকৃত স্বল্পায়ত স্থানে অঙ্কিত করিতে হয়। Melezzo da Forli এবং Correggio ঐরূপ চিত্রাঙ্কণে বিশেষ কৃতকার্য্যতা লাভ করেন]। **–ing,** *n.* (*Fine arts*) Representing in a foreshortened mode or way ; (চিত্র-বিদ্যা) হ্রস্বচিত্রাঙ্কণ, অগ্রসংহার (আঃ বঃ), বক্রচিত্রিত (ঐ)।

Foreshortened figure.

före-show′ (-shō), *v. t.* To show beforehand ; to foretell ; to portend ; to prefigure ; অগ্রে প্রদর্শন করা ; পূর্ব্বে বলা ; অগ্রসূচনা করা, ভাবিসূচনা করা, পূর্ব্বসূচনা করা ; পূর্ব্বে কল্পনা করা।

före′-sīde, *n.* The front side ; সম্মুখবর্ত্তী পার্শ্ব।

före′-sight (-sīt), *n.* **1.** The act or power of foreseeing ; ভবিষ্যদর্শন, ভবিষ্যদৃষ্টি (কেণ্ডি), দূরদর্শন (ঐ), দূরদৃষ্টি (ঐ), দূরদর্শিতা, দীর্ঘদর্শিতা, দীর্ঘদর্শন (কেণ্ডি), দীর্ঘদৃষ্টি (ঐ), ভবিষ্যদর্শন-শক্তি। **2.** Prudence, prudent care, দূরদৃষ্টি ; পরিণামদর্শিতা। **–ed,** *adj.* Sagacious ; prudent ; দূরদর্শী ; পরিণামদর্শী।

före′-skin, *n.* The prepuce ; লিঙ্গমুণ্ডের আবরণ-ত্বক্, মেঢ্র-ত্বক।

fŏr′-ĕst, *n., adj.* & *v.t.* **1.** A large tract of land covered with trees etc. ; the trees of a forest ; অরণ্যানী, অরণ্য, কান্তার, বন, জঙ্গল, অটবী, বিপিন, কানন; আরণ্য তরুরাজি। **2.** (*Law.*) A hunting ground usually owned by a sovereign ; মৃগয়াভূমি, রাজগণের মৃগয়ার্থ রক্ষিত আরণ্য ভূমি। **3.** (With a proper name prefixed) A district once a wood but now cultivated ; as, Sherwood *Forest* ; যে জেলা একসময়ে অরণ্য ছিল বর্ত্তমানে আবাদ হইয়াছে। ***Adj.*** Pertaining to a forest ; sylvan ; বন সম্বন্ধীয় ; বন্য, আরণ্য। ***Verb t.*** To cover with trees ; to convert into a forest ; বৃক্ষাচ্ছাদিত করা ; অরণ্যে পরিণত করা। **–al,** *adj.* **–er,** *n.* **1.** An officer appointed to watch a forest or growing timber; অরণ্য-রক্ষক কর্ম্মচারী। **2.** An inhabitant of a forest ; বনবাসী। **3.** A kind of moth ; একপ্রকার ধেপসো বা তসরে পোকা। **4.** A bird or beast of a forest ; বন্য পাখী, বন্য জন্তু। **–ry,** *n.* **1.** The service or art of cultivating or managing forests ; অরণ্য-রচনা বিদ্যা, অরণ্য-সংরক্ষণ বিদ্যা। **2.** A forest land ; forest ; আরণ্য-ভূমি ; অরণ্য।

före-stall′, *v. t.* **1.** To anticipate and so to baffle ; as, to *forestall* one's thoughts ; পূর্ব্ব হইতে কোন কাজ করিয়া কাহারো উদ্দেশ্য ব্যর্থ করা। **2.** To act or think of beforehand ; to anticipate ; অগ্রে কার্য্য করা, অগ্রে ভাবা ; অগ্রে অনুমান করা। **3.** (*Hist.*) To buy up (goods) to profit by enhanced price ; (ইতিহাস) ফড়েমি করা। **- er,** *n.* **To forestall the market**—অধিক মূল্যে বিক্রয়ার্থ বাজারে আসার পূর্ব্বে রাস্তায় জিনিষ কিনিয়া রাখা।

före′-stay (-stā), *n.* A rope reaching from the foremast head, to the bowsprit end ; a sail hoisted on this ; সর্ব্বাগ্রবর্ত্তী মাস্তুল এবং জাহাজের অগ্রদেশ হইতে প্রলম্বিত দণ্ডের প্রান্তভাগ পর্য্যন্ত প্রসারিত রজ্জু ; উক্ত রজ্জুতে যে পাইল খাটানো হয়।

före′-tāste, *v. t.* & *n.* To taste before possession ; to anticipate ; পূর্ব্বাস্বাদ করা, পূর্ব্বে অনুভব করা, পূর্ব্বাববোধ করা; প্রত্যাশা করা। ***Noun.*** A taste beforehand ; anticipation ; পূর্ব্বাস্বাদ, পূর্ব্বাববোধ, পূর্ব্বভোগ (কেণ্ডি), আদিভোগ (ঐ), পূর্ব্বানুভব (ঐ), কালাপকর্ষভোগ (ঐ); প্রত্যাশা।

före-tĕll′, *v. t.* To predict ; to presage ; ভবিষ্যসূচনা করা, অনাগত বলা ; ভবিষ্যদ্বাণী উচ্চারণ করা। **–er,** *n.* ভবিষ্যকথক (কেণ্ডি), ভবিষ্যদ্বক্তা (ঐ), দৈবজ্ঞ (ঐ)।

före′-thought (-thät), *n.* Thinking or planning beforehand ; deliberate intention ; provident care ; ভবিষ্যৎচিন্তা, ভবিষ্যৎ কল্পনা, পূর্ব্ববিচার (কেণ্ডি); সুচিন্তিত ইচ্ছা ; পরিণামদর্শিতা, প্রসমীক্ষ্যা।

före′-tīme, *n.* The past ; old days ; অতীতকাল ; প্রাচীনকাল।

före-tö′-ker (-kn), *n.* A previous sign ; prognostic ; পূর্ব্বলক্ষণ ; ভাবী শকুন, নিমিত্ত।

före-tö′-ken (-kn), *v. t.* To betoken beforehand ; to portend ; পূর্ব্বসূচনা করা, পূর্ব্বলক্ষণ প্রকাশ করা ; ভবিষ্যসূচনা করা।

före′-tŏp, *n.* **1.** A platform at the head of the fore-mast

জাহাজের সর্ব্বাগ্রবর্ত্তী মাস্তলের উপরিস্থ ক্ষুদ্র মাস্তল। **Foretop-mast**—জাহাজের সর্ব্বাগ্রবর্ত্তী মাস্তলের উপরিস্থ মাস্তল।

fōre′-tȳpe, *n.* The type of a coming thing ; অনাগত বস্তুর প্রতিরূপ।

fōre-wârn′, *v. t.* To warn beforehand ; পূর্ব্বে সমাধান করা, অগ্রে সতর্ক করা। **Forewarned is forearmed**—সাবধানের মার নাই।

fōre′-wom-ăn (-wŭm-), *n.* The chief of jury, of matrons or of a workshop, of women ; তত্ত্বাবধায়িকা।

fōre′-word (-wêrd), *n.* A preface ; ভূমিকা, মুখবন্ধ, অবতরণিকা।

fōre′-yărd, *n.* (*Naut.*) The lowest yard on the foremast ; (নৌ-বিদ্যা) জাহাজের সম্মুখস্থ সর্ব্বাগ্রবর্ত্তী গুণ-বৃক্ষের সর্ব্বনিম্ন মঞ্চ।

fōre′-yârd, *n.* A yard in front ; সম্মুখবর্ত্তী মঞ্চ, অগ্রাঙ্গণ।

fŏr′-fârs, *n.* A coarse heavy linen cloth ; একপ্রকার স্থূল ক্ষৌম বস্ত্র।

fŏr′-feit (-fĭt), *n., v. t.* & *adj.* **1.** A thing forfeited ; a fine ; a penalty ; অপরাধের জন্য যাহা বাজেয়াপ্ত করা হয় ; জরিমানা, অর্থদণ্ড, ধনদণ্ড, শাস্তি। **2.** A deposit that is redeemable by a fine ; যে গচ্ছিত দ্রব্য অর্থদণ্ড প্রদান দ্বারা উদ্ধার করা যাইতে পারে। **3.** Forfeiture; বাজেয়াপ্তি। ***Verb t.*** To lose the right to by some fault or crime ; as, to *forfeit* an estate by treason ; to pay, as a penalty ; ত্রুটি কিম্বা অপরাধাদির নিমিত্ত (কোন বস্তু) অধিকারচ্যুত হওয়া, বাজেয়াপ্ত হওয়া, জব্দ হওয়া; দণ্ডস্বরূপ প্রদান করা। ***Adj.*** Lost for a crime or fault ; দোষ বা অপরাধহেতু বিচ্যুত, জব্দ, বাজেয়াপ্ত। **–a-ble,** *adj.* Liable to be forfeited ; বাজেয়াপ্ত করার যোগ্য, জব্দ হওয়ার যোগ্য। **–fei-ture,** *n.* **1.** The act of forfeiting ; the loss of right, estate etc. for a crime or fault ; বাজেয়াপ্তকরণ; দোষ বা অপরাধ হেতু স্বত্ববিচ্যুতি, বাজেয়াপ্তি, স্বত্বলোপ। **2.** (*Obs.*) A penalty ; (অপ্রঃ) দণ্ড, শাস্তি।

fŏr-fĕnd′, *v. t.* To avert ; to prevent ; আট্‌কান ; প্রতিরোধ করা।

fŏr′-fĭ-cāte, *adj.* (*Zool.*) Shaped like scissors ; (প্রাণি-বিদ্যা) কাঁচির আকার, পট্ট-সন্দাংশ আকৃতি।

fŏr-găth′-ĕr, *v. i.* To meet together ; to associate to gossip ; একত্র হওয়া, সম্মিলিত হওয়া, জড় হওয়া ; গল্প গুজব করার জন্য একত্র হওয়া।

fŏr-gāve′, *p. t.* Of FORGIVE.

forge (fōrj), *n.* **1.** A furnace for melting or refining metal ; a smithy ; কামারের হাপর, উদধ্মান (আঃ বঃ), কুটালিকা (ঐ) ; কামারশালা।

forge (fōrj), *v. t.* & *i.* **1.** To form by heating and hammering ; আগুনে পোড়াইয়া হাতুড়ী দ্বারা পিটিয়া প্রস্তুত করা। **2.** To fabricate, as a tale etc. ; to write in fraudulent imitation, as a document, signature etc. ; মিথ্যা রচনা করা ; জাল করা। ***Verb i.*** **1.** To work at the forge ; হাপরে কাজ করা। **2.** To commit forgery ; জালিয়াতি করা। **Forged,** *adj.* Counterfeited ; as, a *forged* document ; কৃত্রিম, জাল। **forg′-er,** *n.* **1.** One who forges metal ; যে ব্যক্তি হাপরে কাজ করে। **2.** A fabricator ; one guilty of forgery ; উদ্ভাবক, কৃত্রিম রচক ; জালিয়াৎ, কূটকারক।

forge (fōrj), *v. i.* To move forward or advance gradually or slowly ; ধীরে ধীরে বা শনৈঃ শনৈঃ অগ্রসর হওয়া। **To forge ahead**—To take lead in a race ; দৌড় প্রভৃতিতে অগ্রগামী হওয়া।

fōr′-gĕr′-y, *n.* **1.** The act or art of forging or counterfeiting documents etc. ; জালকরণ, জালিয়াতি, জাল। **2.** That which is forged or counterfeited ; কৃত্রিম বা জাল-করা জিনিষ।

fŏr-gĕt′, *v. t.* **1.** To lose the remembrance of ; বিস্মৃত হওয়া, ভুলা, পাসরা (কবিতায়)। **2.** To neglect ; অবহেলা করা। **3.** To treat with disregard ; to slight ; তাচ্ছিল্য করা ; অবহেলা করা। **4.** To become unmindful of one's own interest ; নিজের স্বার্থের দিকে দৃষ্টি না করা। **5.** To be lost in thought ; চিন্তামগ্ন হওয়া। **6.** To act unbecomingly or unworthily ; অন্যায় কিংবা অযুক্ত ব্যবহার করা। **7.** To be unconscious, as in sleep ; অচেতন হওয়া, সংজ্ঞাশূন্য হওয়া। **–a-ble,** *adj.* **–ful,** *adj.* **1.** Apt to forget ; বিস্মরণশীল, স্বল্পস্মৃতি (মুচ্ছঃ)। **2.** Heedless ; neglectful ; (with *of* or infinitively) ; অসাবধান ; অনবধান। **3.** Causing oblivion ; বিস্মৃতিজনক। **–ful-ly,** *adv.* **–ful-ness,** *n.* **Forget-me-not**—A small bright blue flower ; the herb bearing this flower ; as, *forget-me-not* blue eyes ; উজ্জ্বল নীলবর্ণ ক্ষুদ্র পুষ্পবিশেষ ; উক্ত ফুলের গাছ। **Forgive and forget**—Pardon me and put out of mind everything ; আমাকে ক্ষমা কর এবং সব ভুলে যাও। **To forget one's self**—আত্মবিস্মৃত হওয়া।

fŏr-give′ (-gĭv), *v. t.* **1.** To remit ; as, to *forgive* a debt ; (ঋণাদি) মাপ করা। **2.** To pardon, as an offence, offender, etc. ; ক্ষমা করা, মার্জ্জনা করা, মাপ করা। **–giv′-a-ble,** *adj.* Capable of being forgiven ; ক্ষমার্হ, ক্ষমার যোগ্য, মার্জ্জনীয়, ক্ষন্তব্য। **–giv′-ing,** *adj.* Disposed to forgive ; merciful ; compassionate ; ক্ষমাশীল, ক্ষান্ত, ক্ষমান্বিত, ক্ষমাপর ; দয়ালু, কারুণিক, কৃপালু ; সকরুণ। **–giv′-ing-ly,** *adv.* **–giv′-ing-ness, –ness,** *ns.* Pardon ; remission ; disposition to pardon ; ক্ষমা, ক্ষান্তি (উজ্জ্বলঃ), মার্জ্জনা ; মাপ ; ক্ষমাশীলতা।

fŏr-gō′, *v. t.* See FOREGO.

fŏr-gŏt′, *pt.* & *pp.* of FORGET.

fŏrk, *n., v. i.* & *t.* **1.** An instrument with two or more prongs at the end used in agriculture etc. ; such a small instrument used at table etc. ; কৃষিকার্য্যে ব্যবহৃত দুই বা ততোধিক ফেঁকড়াওয়ালা কাঁটা ; ইয়ুরোপীয়গণ যে কাঁটাদ্বারা খাদ্যদ্রব্য মুখে তুলিয়া থাকেন, ত্রিমুখকণ্টক (আঃ বঃ)। **2.** A prong ; a branch, as of a road etc. ; ফেঁকড়া ; রাস্তা প্রভৃতির শাখা। **3.** Forking or bifurcation ; the place where a division or union occurs ; বিভাগ ; মিলনস্থল, সংযোগস্থল। **4.** A flash of forked lightning ; শাখায়িত বিদ্যুতের চমক। ***Verb i.*** To shoot into two or three branches ; to divide into branches, as a road etc. ; দ্বিশাখায়িত হওয়া, ত্রিশাখায়িত হওয়া ; শাখায়িত হওয়া। ***Verb t.*** To raise, pitch or carry with a fork, as hay ; to dig or turn over with a fork, as the soil ; (*slang*) to hand or pay over, as money ; কাঁটাদ্বারা তোলা, নাড়া বা বিদ্ধ করা ; কাঁটাদ্বারা খুঁড়া বা উল্টান ; (ইতর ভাষায়) দেওয়া। **Forked,** *adj.* Shaped like a fork ; branching ; divergent ; bifurcated ; দ্বিমুখ কণ্টকাকৃতি ; শাখায়িত ; ক্রমশঃ বিপ্রকৃষ্ট বা দূর প্রস্থিত ; দ্বিশাখ, দ্বিকণ্টক (কেণ্ডি), দুফেঁকড়া, দ্বিধাবিভক্ত। **Fork'-y,** *adj.* (*Poet.*) Shaped like a fork ; (কবিতায়) দ্বি বা ত্রিমুখ কণ্টকাকৃতি।

fór-lórn', *adj.* **1.** Deserted ; পরিত্যক্ত। **2.** In pitiful condition ; hopeless ; desperate ; দুর্দ্দশাগ্রস্ত, দুঃস্থ ; হতাশ, আশাহীন ; মরিয়া। **A forlorn hope**—A body of soldiers selected for some service of uncommon danger ; অসমসাহসিক কার্য্য সম্পাদনার্থ নির্ব্বাচিত সৈন্যদল। An almost hopeless enterprise ; যে অসম সাহসিক কার্য্যে সিদ্ধি লাভের আশা সম্পূর্ণ অসম্ভব।

fŏrm, *n., v. t.* & *i.* **1.** The shape of anything ; arrangement of parts ; visible appearance (excluding colour) ; আকার, আকৃতি, অবয়ব, ডৌল, গঠন ; আকার সংস্থান ; বাহ্যাবয়ব। **2.** An animal or person as visible ; as, I saw a *form* before me ; মূর্ত্তি। **3.** Customary method ; a formula ; as, a *form* of prayer ; প্রচলিত প্রথা ; নির্দ্দিষ্ট পদ্ধতি, নিয়ম বা অবস্থা। **4.** A document with blanks ; as, to fill up a *form* ; পরে লিখিয়া পূরণ করার জন্য সাদা স্থান বিশিষ্ট দলিল, ফারম। **5.** Manner or mode ; রীতি ; প্রকার, পদ্ধতি, ধারা। **6.** A mode of existence or manifestation of a thing ; a species ; রূপ, রকম ; জাতি। **7.** A mere ceremony ; a formality ; বাহ্যরীতি ; লৌকিকতা। **8.** A prescribed manner of behaving ; as, a good or bad *form* ; আচরণের নির্দ্দিষ্ট রীতি। **9.** Arrangement of parts and style in a literary or musical composition ; mould ; model ; সাহিত্যিক রচনা বা সঙ্গীতে বিভিন্ন অংশের সন্নিবেশ, অঙ্গ-সংস্থান ; ছাঁচ ; আদর্শ। **10.** (*Gram.*) The particular shape or structure of a word or part of a speech ; as participial *forms* ; (ব্যাকরণে) শব্দাদির বিশেষ আকার, সুপ্তিঙন্ত পদ। **11.** (*Philos.*) The qualities which make an object or body be what it is ; conditions of a thing's existence by knowing which we can produce it ; that which the mind itself contributes as the condition of knowing (*Baconian*) ; a formative principle of perception and recognition regarded as a subjective factor moulding reality as given in sensation into systematic experience (*Kantian.*) ; (দর্শন-শাস্ত্র) যে গুণ সমূহের সমবায়ে কোন বস্তুর বিশিষ্ট বস্তুত্ব উৎপন্ন হয় ; কোন বস্তুর সত্তার যে সমস্ত অবস্থা অবগত হইলে আমরা উহাকে উৎপাদন করিতে পারি ; প্রত্যক্ষীকরণ (perception) এবং অববোধের আকারপ্রদ বীজ বিশেষ—যাহা সংবেদনে প্রদত্ত বাস্তবতাকে প্রণালীবদ্ধ অনুভবে (recognition) পরিণত করার শক্তিসম্পন্ন বিষয়ীস্বরূপ (অবয়ব) বলিয়া পরিগণিত হইয়া থাকে। **12.** (*Print.*) A body of type composed and made ready for printing ; (মুদ্রাঙ্কণ) মুদ্রাঙ্কণার্থ সজ্জিত অক্ষর-পংক্তি, ছাপিবার ফর্‌মা। **13.** A long seat ; a bench ; সুদীর্ঘ আসন ; বেঞ্চ। **14.** A class of a boy in a school ; বিদ্যালয়ের শ্রেণী। **15.** Condition or fitness for competing or performing ; as, a horse in or out of *form* ; প্রতিযোগিতার জন্য বা কোন কার্য্য সম্পাদনের উপযোগী অবস্থা বা যোগ্যতা। **16.** The seat or bed of a hare ; খরগোসের আসন বা নিলয়। ***Verb t.*** **1.** To shape or mould ; to fashion *into* a certain shape ; to make or frame ; to produce ; নির্ম্মাণ করা, গঠন করা ; আকার প্রদান করা, গড়িয়া তোলা ; রচনা করা ; উৎপাদন করা। **2.** To mould by instruction and discipline ; to train ; শিক্ষা ও শাসনদ্বারা গঠন করা ; শিক্ষিত করা। **3.** To act as a constituent of ; উপাদানীভূত হওয়া। **4.** (*Gram.*) To make as a new word etc. by derivation or by suffixes or affixes ; উপসর্গ ও প্রত্যয়যোগে নূতন শব্দাদি গঠন করা। **5.** (*Mil. etc.*) To arrange as troops etc. ; সৈন্য সংস্থান করা, ব্যূহ রচনা করা। **6.** To conceive, as an idea ; ধারণা করা। **7.** To organize ; ব্যবস্থাবদ্ধ করা। **8.** To contract, as an alliance or habit ; to articulate ; অর্জ্জন বা গ্রহণ করা ; স্পষ্টরূপে উচ্চারণ করা। ***Verb i.*** **1.** To take a form or shape ; আকার ধারণ করা, আকার পরিগ্রহ করা। **2.** (*Mil.*) To assume a specified formation ; (সামরিক-শাস্ত্র) ব্যূহবদ্ধ হওয়া। **Form'-er,** *n.* One who forms ; নির্ম্মাণকারী, নির্ম্মাতা। **Form'-less,** *adj.* Shapeless ; without determinate form ; আকারহীন,

নিরাকার ; নির্দ্দিষ্ট আকৃতি বিহীন। **Form'-less-ly,** *adv.* **Form'-less-ness,** *n.* **Form quality**—প্রাকারিক গুণ (হিঃ কোঃ)। **In bad form**—Contrary to current ideals; প্রচলিত আদর্শের বিপরীত। **In due form**—In customary method; যথারীতি, যথাবিধি। **In good form**—প্রচলিত আদর্শানুযায়ী। **To be in great form**—To be in good spirits; স্ফূর্ত্তিতে থাকা বা উৎফুল্লচিত্ত হওয়া। **To form a counsel**—পরামর্শ আঁটা। **To form a line**—সারি বাঁধা। **To lose one's form**—To be in bad spirits; স্ফূর্ত্তিহীন হওয়া।

fŏr'-măl, *adj.* **1.** Of, or relating to, form; conventional; আকার-সম্বন্ধীয়, গঠনসম্বন্ধীয়; লৌকিক। **2.** (*Metap.*) Relating to the essence of a thing; (দর্শন-শাস্ত্র) মৌলিক, সারভূত, বৈজিক। **3.** According to regular method; ceremonial; express; প্রচলিত প্রথানুযায়ী, আচারানুগত (আঃ বঃ); আনুষ্ঠানিক, লৌকিক, বৈধী, ব্যক্ত, স্ফুট। **4.** Ceremonious; punctilious; methodical; prim; বাহ্যাচারনিষ্ঠ, বাহ্যানুষ্ঠাননিষ্ঠ, বাহ্যাচার রত; সূক্ষ্মবিষয়ে মনোযোগী, সূক্ষ্মাচারনিষ্ঠ; নিয়মানুগত, প্রণালীসঙ্গত; ফিট্‌ফাট, কেতাদুরস্ত, লেফাফাদুরস্ত। **5.** Having, or relating to, the outward form or appearance only; external; as, *formal* worship; বাহ্যাচার সম্পর্কীয়; বাহ্যিক, বহিরঙ্গ, বাহ্য। **—ism,** *n.* The doctrine or practice of strict adherence to external forms, esp. in religion; বাহ্যাচারানুষ্ঠান, বৈধীমার্গ, নৈষ্ঠিকতা, কলা-আকারবাদ (হিঃ কোঃ), প্রকার-প্রাধান্যবাদ (ঐ), আকার-প্রাধান্যবাদ (ঐ)। **—ist,** *n.* One who observes forms; বাহ্যাচারনিষ্ঠ ব্যক্তি, বাহ্যোপচারী (কেণ্ডি), বাহ্যধর্ম্মনিষ্ঠ (ঐ), বাহ্যধর্ম্ম প্রবৃত্তি (ঐ), নৈষ্ঠিক, বাহ্যধর্ম্ম-সেবী। **—is'-tic** *adj.* **—mal'-i-ty** *n.* **1.** Quality of being formal; ceremoniousness; strict regularity; বাহ্যানুষ্ঠান প্রিয়তা; বাহ্যাচারনিষ্ঠা, নৈষ্ঠিকতা; নিয়মনিষ্ঠা। **2.** Compliance with, or comformity to, rule; নিয়মানুগামিতা, নিয়মনিষ্ঠা। **3.** Conventional rule of procedure; a ceremony; সামাজিক রীতি, আচার; লৌকিকতা। **4.** A formal or ceremonial act; social or customary requirement; আনুষ্ঠানিক কার্য্য; সামাজিক আচার বা নিয়ম। **—ize,** *v. t.* **1.** To give a definite form to; নির্দ্দিষ্ট আকার প্রদান করা। **2.** To make precise or ceremonious; to imbue with formalism; অনুষ্ঠানাত্মক করা; লৌকিকাচারান্বিত করা। **3.** To render legally formal, as a document etc.; বিধিসঙ্গত করা, আইনানুযায়ী করা। **—i-za'-tion,** *n.* **—ly,** *adv.* In a formal manner; precisely; লৌকিকভাবে, বিধিসঙ্গত ভাবে, যথারীতি; ঠিকরূপে। **Formal cause**—স্থূলকারণ (হিঃ কোঃ), কারণাত্মক আকার (ঐ)। **Formal culture**—প্রাকারক শিক্ষা (হিঃ কোঃ), শক্ত্যুৎপাদক শিক্ষা (ঐ)। **Formal Logic**—তর্কশাস্ত্রের যে শাখায় যুক্তির মূল বিষয় সম্বন্ধে আলোচিত হয় না, কেবল বহিরবয়ব সম্বন্ধে আলোচিত হইয়া থাকে, প্রাকারক ন্যায় (হিঃ কোঃ)। **Formal rightness**—প্রাকারক ঋততা (হিঃ কোঃ)। **Formal steps**—প্রকারক্রমিক অঙ্গ (হিঃ কোঃ)। **Formal studies**—প্রাকারক-শাস্ত্র (হিঃ কোঃ)।

format, *n.* The shape and size of a book; পুস্তকের আকার বা আয়তন, ফর্ম্মা।

fŏr'-māte, *n.* A salt of formic acid; পিপীলিকাম্লের লবণক।

fŏr-mā'-tion, *n.* **1.** The act of forming; state of being formed; নির্ম্মাণ, রচনা, গঠন; নির্ম্মিতি। **2.** That which is formed; গঠিত বস্তু। **3.** (*Geol.*) A group of strata of one period; (ভূ-বিদ্যা) কোন বিশেষ যুগের স্তর-সংহতি। **4.** (*Mil.*) The arrangement of troops; সেনা-সন্নিবেশ, সেনাসংস্থান, ব্যূহরচনা। **Form'-a-tive,** *adj.* & *n.* **1.** Serving to form; relating to formation; গঠনক্ষম, আকারপ্রদ, রচনাকারী, সৃষ্টিক্ষম; গঠনসম্পর্কীয়। **2.** (*Gram.*) Serving to form words; (ব্যাকরণ) উৎপাদী, ব্যুৎপত্তিলব্ধ। (*Noun*) (*Gram.*) A formative element; (ব্যাকরণ) প্রত্যয়, বিভক্তি।

forme (fŏrm), *n.* (*Print.*) See FORM *n.* II.

fŏr'-mêr, *adj.* **1.** Relating to the past; previous; ancient; পূর্ব্বতন, পূর্ব্বকালীন, প্রাক্‌কালীন; পূর্ব্ববর্ত্তী; প্রাচীন। **2.** Near the beginning; as, the *former* part of a discourse; first-mentioned; প্রারম্ভাংশের নিকট বর্ত্তী; প্রথমোক্ত। **—ly,** *adv.* In times past; পূর্ব্বে, পূর্ব্বকালে। **The former**—The first or first mentioned of two,—opposed to *the latter*; প্রথম, প্রথমোক্ত।

fŏr'-mic, *adj.* Pertaining to or derived from, ants; পিপীলিকা সম্বন্ধীয়, পিপীলিকাজাত। **Formic acid**—(*Chem.*) An acid contained in a fluid emitted by ants; (রসায়ন-শাস্ত্র) পিপীলিকার শরীর নিঃসৃত রস হইতে প্রাপ্ত দ্রাবক-বিশেষ, পিপীলিকাম্ল।

fŏr'-mi-că-rȳ, *n.* An ant-hill; বল্মীক, উই-ঢিবি।

fŏr'-mi-dă-ble (-bl), *adj.* **1.** Causing fear; difficult to deal with or overcome; ভয়াবহ, করাল, রৌদ্র, দারুণ, উচ্চণ্ড, ভৈরব; দুর্দ্ধর্ষ, দুর্ব্বার, দুর্ম্মদ, উগ্র। **—bly,** *adv.*

fŏr'-mü-lă, *n.* (*Pl.* -LÆ, -LAS), **1.** A prescribed form; an established rule; a set form of words; নির্দ্দিষ্ট পদ্ধতি; অচলপ্রতিষ্ঠ নিয়ম; সূত্র। **2.** A conventional usage or belief; প্রচলিত প্রথা বা বিশ্বাস। **3.** A recipe; ব্যঞ্জনাদির প্রস্তুত প্রণালী-বিষয়ক ব্যবস্থা। **4.** (*Alg.*) A rule or principle expressed in algebraic symbols; বীজগণিতের অঙ্ক-সমাধানের সঙ্কেত। **5.** (*Chem.*) The symbolic expression of the constituents of a substance; রাসায়নিক পদার্থের উপাদানসূচক সাঙ্কেতিক চিহ্ন, নির্দ্দেশ (প্রবাসী ১৩১৯), সঙ্কেত (হিঃ কোঃ), সিদ্ধান্ত (ঐ)। 6. (*Eccl.*) A formal statement of doctrines; (যাজকীয় শাস্ত্র) প্রণালীবদ্ধভাবে মতাদি বিবৃতি। **—late,** *v. t.* To reduce to, or express into, a formula; to set forth in systematic statement; সূত্রাকারে নিবদ্ধ করা, সূত্রাকারে ব্যক্ত করা; প্রণালীবদ্ধ ভাবে বর্ণনা করা। **—lar-i-za'-tion, —li-za'-tion,** *ns.* **—la-ry,** *adj.* & *n.* Relating to formulas; prescribed; সূত্র সম্বন্ধীয়; নির্দ্ধারিত। (*Noun*) A book or document containing prescribed forms; a collection of formulas; ক্রিয়াকাণ্ডের বিধিব্যবস্থা সমন্বিত পুস্তক, ক্রিয়াকাণ্ডবারিধি, বিধানমালা (কেণ্ডি), বিধানসংগ্রহ (ঐ); সূত্রসংগ্রহ, সূত্রগ্রন্থ। **—la'-tion, —lar-ize, —lize,** *v. t.* To state in formula; to formulate; সূত্রদ্বারা ব্যক্ত করা; সূত্রাকারে নিবদ্ধ করা।

fŏr'-ni-cāte, *v. i.* To commit fornication; অনূঢ়া স্ত্রীলোকের সহিত ব্যভিচার করা। **—ca'-tion,** *n.* Unlawful sexual intercourse between unmarried persons; অবিবাহিত স্ত্রী পুরুষের সঙ্গম, অনূঢ়া স্ত্রীলোকের সহিত সঙ্গম, অনূঢ়াগমন (কেণ্ডি), কন্যাগমন (ঐ)। **—ca-tor,** *n.* অনূঢ়াগামী (কেণ্ডি)।

fŏr'-pained (-pānd), *adj.* (*Archaic*) Wasted by torture, hunger etc.; (অপ্রঃ) যন্ত্রণাশীর্ণ, অনশনকৃশ ইত্যাদি।

fŏr'-ra-dêr, see under FORWARD.

fŏr'-rĕl, *n.* See FOREL.

fŏr-sāke', *v. t.* 1. To desert; to abandon; পরিত্যাগ করা; পরিবর্জ্জন করা। 2. To renounce; to give up; পরিহার করা; ছাড়িয়া দেওয়া। **—sak'-er,** *n.*

fŏr-sōōth', *adv.* In truth; certainly; সত্যসত্যই; নিশ্চয়ই।

fŏr-spĕnt', *p. adj.* Tired out; পরিক্লান্ত।

fŏr-swear' (-swār), *v. t.* & *i.* To renounce or reject upon oath; শপথপূর্ব্বক অস্বীকার করা বা পরিবর্জ্জন করা। ***Verb i.*** To swear falsely; মিথ্যা শপথ করা। **—sworn',** *p. p.* **To forswear one's self**—To swear falsely; to perjure oneself; মিথ্যা শপথ করা; হলফ লইয়া মিথ্যা সাক্ষ্য প্রদান করা।

fōrt, *n.* 1. A strong fortified place; দুর্গ, গড়, কেল্লা, কোট। 2. A trading station in North America; উত্তর আমেরিকার বাণিজ্যস্থান, আড়ত, গঞ্জ।

fŏr'-tă-lice (-lĭs), *n.* Formerly a fortress, now a small fort; an outwork of fortification; (পূর্ব্বে) দুর্গ, (বর্ত্তমানে) ক্ষুদ্র দুর্গ; দুর্গপারখার বহিস্থ উপদুর্গাদি।

forte (fōrt), *n.* 1. The strong point; chief excellence; প্রধান বল; প্রধান উৎকর্ষ, প্রধান গুণ। 2. The strongest part of the blade of a sword; অসিফলকের কঠিনতম অংশ।

fŏr'-te (-tā), *adv.* (*Direction to sing or play*) With force; সতেজে।

fŏr'-te (-tā), *interj.* Loud; উচ্চৈঃস্বরে। **Forte-forte**—(*Abbr. ff.*) Very loud; অতিশয় উচ্চৈঃস্বরে। **Forte-piano**—*adj.* (*Abbr. fp.*) Loud and then immediately soft; পূর্ব্বে উচ্চ অব্যবহিত পরে মৃদু।

fōrth, *adv.* 1. Forward; onward in time or place; পুরঃসর; অগ্রে। 2. Out; into view; as, to come or bring *forth*; বাহিরে; দৃষ্টিগোচর। 3. Out of doors; as, to cast *forth*; বাটীর বাহিরে। 4. Away from home; as, to sail *forth*; বিদেশে। **And so forth**—And so on; ইত্যাদি, এই। **Back and forth**—To and fro; ইতস্ততঃ। **So far forth**—To that extent; সেই পরিমাণে, সেই মাত্রায়। **So far forth as**—To whatever extent; যতদূর হউক, যে পরিমাণেই হউক।

fōrth'-com-ing (-kŭm-), *adj.* About, or likely, to come forth; approaching; ready to appear; আগামী; আসন্ন; আগতপ্রায়।

fōrth'-right (-rīt), *adv.* Straightway; সোজাসুজি।

fōrth-with', *adv.* Immediately; without delay; তৎক্ষণাৎ, ঝটিতি তন্মুহূর্ত্তে; অবিলম্বে।

fŏr'-ti-ĕth, *adj.* See FORTY.

fŏr'-ti-fȳ, *v. t.* 1. To strengthen the structure of; দৃঢ় করা। 2. To strengthen and secure by forts or batteries; to encourage; দুর্গাদি নির্ম্মাণ এবং কামানাদি স্থাপন দ্বারা সুদৃঢ় অথবা সুরক্ষিত করা, গড়বন্দি করা; উৎসাহিত করা, প্রোৎসাহিত করা। 3. To strengthen (liquor) with alcohol; সুরাবীর্য্য দ্বারা মদিরা তেজাল করা। 4. To invigorate; to give physical strength to; সতেজ করা; দৈহিক শক্তি প্রদান করা। **—fi-ca'-tion,** *n.* 1. Act of fortifying; দুর্গাদিসন্নিবেশ। 2. Strengthening of wines with alcohol; সুরাবীর্য্য সংযোগে মদিরা তেজাল করণ। 3. (*Mil.*) The act, art or science of fortifying a place in order to defend it against an enemy; (সামরিকশাস্ত্র) দুর্গাদি দ্বারা দৃঢ়ীকরণ, দুর্গনির্ম্মাণ শাস্ত্র, দুর্গনির্ম্মাণকৌশল, দুর্গপ্রাকারাদি রচনবিদ্যা (কেণ্ডি)। 4. That which fortifies; a defensive work or works; যদ্দ্বারা কোনও স্থান দৃঢ়ীকৃত হয়; দুর্গপ্রাকারাদি।

fortissimo, *adv.* (*Abbr. ff., ffor., fortiss.*) (*Mus. Direction*) Very loud; (গীতবাদ্যে নির্দেশ) অতি উচ্চৈঃস্বরে।

fŏr'-ti-tūde, *n.* The strength of mind or courage in adversity or pain; বিপৎ বা দুঃখের কালে ধীরতা বা মনের বল, মানসিক স্থৈর্য্য, ধৃতি, ধৈর্য্য, দৃঢ়তা।

fōrt'-night (-nīt-), *n.* The space of two weeks; দ্বিসপ্তাহ কাল, পক্ষ, মাসার্দ্ধ। **—ly,** *adj.* & *adv.* Occurring or appearing once in a fortnight; পাক্ষিক। (*Adv.*) Once in a fortnight ; পক্ষে একবার। **To-day, this day** or **Monday fortnight**—A fortnight from to day etc. ; অদ্য হইতে এক পক্ষ, সোমবার হইতে এক পক্ষ।

fŏr′-trĕss, *n.* & *v. t.* A strongly fortified place ; a stronghold ; সুরক্ষিত স্থান ; দুর্গ, গড়, কেল্লা। ***Verb t.*** To furnish with a fortress ; to protect ; দুর্গাদি সমন্বিত করা ; রক্ষা করা।

fŏr-tü′-i-tism, *n.* The belief that evolutionary adaptations in nature are produced by the operation of natural laws operating fortuitously ; প্রাকৃতিক বস্তু সমূহের ক্রমবিকাশমূলক নব নব রূপ নৈসর্গিক নিয়মনিচয়ের আকস্মিক বা নৈমিত্তিক ক্রিয়াদ্বারা উৎপন্ন হয়— এইরূপ বিশ্বাস। **–tist,** *n.* One who believes in fortuitism ; ঐরূপ মতবাদী।

ŏr-tü′-i-tous (-tŭs), *adj.* Happening by chance ; casual ; accidental ; as, *fortuitous* concourse of atoms ; দৈবিক ; নৈমিত্তিক ; আকস্মিক, আগন্তুক। **–ly,** *adv.* In a fortuitous manner ; নৈমিত্তিকভাবে, আকস্মিকভাবে, দৈবযোগে। **–ness,** *n.*

ŏr-tü′-i-tȳ, *n.* Fortuitousness ; chance ; accident ; দৈব ; দৈবঘটনা ; দৈবযোগ।

ŏr′-tü-nāte, *adj.* **1.** Having good fortune ; lucky ; prosperous ; সৌভাগ্যশালী ; ভাগ্যবান ; সমৃদ্ধ, সুভগ, পয়মন্ত। **2.** Auspicious ; favourable ; শুভকর, মঙ্গল্য, শুভ ; সুপ্রসন্ন। **–ly,** *adv.* By good fortune ; happily ; সৌভাগ্যবলে, সৌভাগ্যক্রমে, কপালক্রমে ; ভাগ্যবশতঃ।

ŏr′-tüne, *n.* & *v. i.* **1.** Luck ; chance ; hap ; the personified power regarded as determining the lots of life ; ভাগ্য ; দৈব ; অদৃষ্ট, কপাল ; ভাগ্যদেবী, নিয়তিদেবী, কমলা, লক্ষ্মীদেবী, শ্রী। **2.** Good or bad luck falling to a person or to a.. enterprise ; success ; good luck ; prosperity ; কোন ব্যক্তির অদৃষ্টে বা কোন অসমসাহসিক কার্য্যের পরিণামে যে সৌভাগ্য, দুর্ভাগ্য ঘটিয়া থাকে ; কৃতকার্য্যতা, সিদ্ধি ; সৌভাগ্য ; সমৃদ্ধি, ঋদ্ধি, ঐশ্বর্য্য। **3.** Fate ; coming lot ; as, to tell one's *fortune* ; ভাগ্য ; কপাল, ললাটলিপি। **4.** Prosperous condition ; riches ; সমৃদ্ধাবস্থা ; ধনদৌলত। ***Verb i.*** (*Archaic* & *Poet.*) To happen ; (অপ্রঃ বা কবিতায়) ঘটা। **–less,** *adj.* Luckless ; দুরদৃষ্ট, ভাগ্যহীন। **Fortune-book** — যে পুস্তকের সাহায্যে শুভাশুভ নির্ণয় করিয়া বলা যায়, ভাগ্যগণনা পুস্তক। **Fortune-hunter**— ধনশালিনী রমণীর পাণিগ্রহণে সচেষ্ট ব্যক্তি। **Fortune-teller** — দৈবজ্ঞ, গণক। **A soldier of fortune**— ভাগ্যান্বেষী সৈন্য। **Fortune favours the brave** — The brave alone are favoured by good fortune ; কেবল সাহসী পুরুষেরাই কমলার কৃপা লাভ করিয়া থাকে, বীরেরাই কেবল ভাগ্য দেবীর অনুগ্রহ লাভ করিয়া থাকে। **The wheel of fortune**—অদৃষ্টচক্র, নিয়তিচক্র, ভাগ্যচক্র, দৈবচক্র (কোং), সংসারচক্র (ঐ)। **To make one's fortune**—To be rich ; ধনশালী হওয়া। **To marry a fortune**— To marry an heiress ; ধনসম্পত্তির উত্তরাধিকারিণী কুমারীর পাণিগ্রহণ করা। **To spend a small fortune on a thing**—To spend a large sum on it ; কোন ব্যাপারে বহু অর্থ ব্যয় করা। **To tell one's fortune** — To presage one's coming lot ; কাহারও ভবিষ্যৎ শুভাশুভ বলা। **To try one's fortune** — To take some risky step ; অদৃষ্ট পরীক্ষা করা, ভাগ্য পরীক্ষা করা।

fŏr′-tȳ, *adj.* & *n.* Four times ten ; চত্বারিংশৎ, চল্লিশ। ***Noun.*** **1.** The sum of four tens ; 40 units or objects, as years etc. ; চত্বারিংশৎ ; চাল্লশটী বস্তু। **2.** A symbol expressing forty units ; as, 40 ; 80 এই সংখ্যা। **–ti-eth,** *adj.* & *n.* Following the thirty-ninth ; চত্বারিংশ, চত্বারিংশত্তম। (*Noun*) One of the forty equal parts of a thing ; চত্বারিংশত্তমাংশ। **Forties**— Years of life between 39 to 50 ; ৩৯ হইতে ৫০ বর্ষ পর্য্যন্ত জীবনের কাল। **Forty-winks** — A short nap, specially after dinner ; অপরাহ্ণ ভোজনান্তে স্বল্প নিদ্রা। **Roaring-forties** — ৩৯° হইতে ৫০° উত্তর অক্ষাংশের মধ্যবর্ত্তী অতলান্তিক মহাসাগরের ঝটিকাবিক্ষুব্ধ অংশ। **After** or **over forty**—After or over the age of forty years, চল্লিশোর্দ্ধ। **The forty-five** — The Jacobite rebellion of 1745 ; ১৭৪৫ খৃঃ অব্দের জেকোবিট বিদ্রোহ।

fō′-rŭm, *n.* (*Rom. Ant.*) **1.** A market-place ; a public place where causes were judicially tried and orations delivered to the people ; (রোমীয় প্রত্নতত্ত্ব) হট্ট ; যে জনসাধারণের সমাগম স্থলে মোকদ্দমার বিচার ও বক্তৃতা প্রদান করা হইত, ন্যায়স্থান (হিঃ কোঃ), ন্যায়াঙ্গন (ঐ), শাসনপ্রদেশ (ঐ)। **2.** A tribunal ; a court ; বিচারালয় ; ধর্ম্মাধিকরণ।

fŏr′-ward (-wērd), *adj.*, *adv.*, *v. t.* & *n.* **1.** (*Naut.*) Near or at the fore-part of a ship ; (নৌবিদ্যা) পোতাগ্রভাগস্থ, পোতাগ্রভাগসন্নিহিত। **2.** Toward a position in front ; onward ; সম্মুখবর্ত্তী, পুরোবর্ত্তী ; অগ্রগামী। **3.** Advanced ; early ; precocious ; as, a *forward* spring or child ; অগ্রসর ; অকালাগত ; আকালিক, অকালজাত ; অকালপক্ক। **4.** Prompt ; ready ; সত্বর ; তৎপর। **5.** Eager ; pert ; bold ; as, the boy is too *forward* for his years ; ব্যগ্র ; প্রগল্ভ, মুখর, সপ্রতিভ ; সাহসী। **6.** Extreme ; radical ; চরম ; আমুল। **7.** (*Com.*) Relating to future produce, as a contract etc. ; (বাণিজ্য) ভাবী-উৎপাদন সম্বন্ধীয়, আগাম। ***Adv.*** Towards what is before or in front ; towards the future; in advance; progressively; সম্মুখদিকে; ভবিষ্যতের দিকে; অগ্রে; উন্নতির দিকে। ***Verb t.*** **1.** To help onward; to promote; to hasten; অগ্রসর করা, অগ্রবর্তী করা; উন্নীত করা; ত্বরান্বিত করা। **2.** To send to the place of destination, as a letter etc.; প্রেরণ করা। **3.** To despatch, as goods etc.; মাল প্রভৃতি প্রেরণ করা। ***Noun.*** One of players at foot-ball stationed at the front line; পাদগোলক ক্রীড়ায় পুরোবর্ত্তী রেখায় অবস্থিত ক্রীড়কগণের অন্যতম। **–ly,** *adv.* **–ness,** *n.* **1.** Eagerness; promptness; ব্যগ্রতা; সত্বরতা। **2.** Earliness; precocity; অগ্রবর্ত্তিতা; অকালপক্কতা। **3.** Pertness; প্রগল্‌ভতা, ধৃষ্টতা। **Forward**—(*A military command*) Go forward in advance; (সামরিক আদেশ) অগ্রসর হও! আগে চল! **Forward movement**—Special effort at political movement etc.; progress; রাজনীতিক আন্দোলন প্রভৃতিতে বিশেষ প্রচেষ্টা; অগ্রপ্রয়াণ, উন্নতি। **Forward party, –opinions**—See FORWARD *adj.* 6. **Backward(s) and forward**—To and fro; অগ্র পশ্চাতে। **I can't get any forwarder** or **forrader** (*Colloq.*)—I make no progress; অগ্রসর হইতে পারি না। **To bring forward**—To draw attention to; মনোযোগ আকর্ষণ করা। **To come forward**—To offer oneself for a task, post, etc.; কোন কার্য্যের জন্য প্রার্থী হওয়া। **To go forward**—To advance; to progress; অগ্রসর হওয়া; উন্নতি করা। **To look forward** — To look ahead; অগ্রে দৃষ্টি করা। **To put** or **set forward**—To allege; to make oneself too conspicuous; আরোপ করা; নিজকে অতিশয় জাহির করা।

fór'-wards (-wêrdz), *adv.* Same as FORWARD, *adv.*

fŏr-wea'-ried (-wĕ-rĭd), **–wōrn',** *adjs.* (*Archaic*) Exhausted; (অপ্রঃ) অবসন্ন।

fŏss, fosse (fŏs), *ns.* **1.** A ditch; a canal; a trench esp. in fortification; খাত; খাল; পগাড়, যুদ্ধ খাড়ি, গড়খাই। **2.** (*Anat.*) A cavity or depression in a bone; (শারীর-সংস্থান-বিদ্যা) অস্থিমধ্যস্থ ছিদ্র বা টোল।

fŏs-sette' (-sĕt), *n.* **1.** A dimple; টোল। **2.** (*Med.*) A small ulcer of the transparent cornea; (ভৈষজ্য-শাস্ত্র) চক্ষুর সম্মুখভাগস্থ স্বচ্ছাবরণের ক্ষুদ্র ব্রণ।

fŏs'-sick (-sĭk), *v. i.* (*Slang*) To search about; (ইতর ভাষায়) খুঁজিয়া বেড়ান।

fŏs'-sil, *adj* & *n.* **1.** (*Obs.*) Dug out of the earth; (অপ্রঃ) ভূগর্ভ হইতে উৎখাতিত। **2.** Petrified and preserved in rocks, as a bone etc.; শিলীভূতাবস্থায় এবং শিলাভ্যন্তরে রক্ষিত। **3.** Antiquated; প্রাচীন। ***Noun.*** **1.** The petrified remains of a plant or animal found in stratified rocks; ভূগর্ভস্থ ভিন্ন ভিন্ন স্তরে প্রাপ্ত প্রাণী ও উদ্ভিদের শিলীভূত দেহাবশেষ, শিলীভূত কঙ্কাল, জীবশেষ (সাঃ পঃ), জীবাবশেষ (ঐ), শিলীভূতাবয়ব (ঐ), জৈবাশ্ম (ঐ), প্রশীল (অভিঃ)। **2.** A person of antiquated notions or habits; সেকেলে লোক, দাদা আদমের কালের লোক। **–ate,** *v. t.* To make fossil; শিলীভূত কঙ্কালে পরিণত করা। **–a'-tion,** *n.* **–if'-fer-ous,** *adj.* **–i-za'-tion,** *n.* **–ize,** *v. t.* & *i.* To convert into a fossil state, (*lit.* & *fig.*); শিলীভূত কঙ্কালে পরিণত করা। (*Verb i.*), **1.** To become a fossil; শিলীভূত কঙ্কালে পরিণত হওয়া। **2.** To become antiquated or fixed; প্রাচীন বা বদ্ধমূল হওয়া।

fŏs-sō'-rĭ-ál, *adj.* (*Zool.*) Digging or burrowing; used in burrowing; (প্রাণি-বিদ্যা) খনক, গর্ত্তকারী; খননকার্য্যে ব্যবহৃত।

fŏs'-têr, *v. t.* **1.** (*Archaic*) To tend with affection; (অপ্রঃ) লালন পালন করা। **2.** To promote the growth of; to cherish; to nurse; to encourage; to be favourable, as a circumstance etc.; বর্দ্ধন করা; পোষণ করা; লালনপালন করা; প্রোৎসাহিত করা; অনুকূল হওয়া। **–age,** *n.* **1.** Act of fostering; লালন পালন। **2.** The custom of engaging foster-mother; ধাত্রীনিয়োগ-পদ্ধতি। **–er,** *n.* **–tress,** *n.* (*Fem.*) A woman who fosters; পালয়িত্রী। **Foster-brother** — পালিত ভ্রাতা। **Foster-child** — পালিত সন্তান। **Foster-daughter** — পালিত-কন্যা। **Foster-father** — পালক পিতা। **Foster-mother** — উপমাতা, ধাত্রী। **Foster-parent** — পালক পিতা বা ধাত্রী। **Foster-sister** — পালিতা ভগিনী, ধাত্রেয়িকা, ধাত্রেয়ী। **Foster-son**—পালিত পুত্র।

fŏs'-têr, *n.* (*Obs.*) Food; (অপ্রঃ) খাদ্য।

fŏs'-têr-ling, *n.* A foster-child; পালিত সন্তান।

fought (fät) *p. t.* and *p. p.* of FIGHT.

foul (fowl), *adj., n., adv., v. i.* & *t.* **1.** Loathsome; disgusting; filthy; as, a *foul* disease, air or odour; জঘন্য, ঘৃণ্য, গর্হিত, জুগুপ্সিত, বীভৎস; বিরক্তিকর; অপরিষ্কার। **2.** Not clear; soiled; clogged; as, *foul* linen or chimney; অপরিষ্কার; মলিন, মলপূর্ণ, অশুচি, অমেধ্য, ময়লা, সমল; মলাবরুদ্ধ। **3.** Obscene or profane; abusive; as, a *foul* word; অশ্লীল, কলুষিত, কুৎসিৎ; কুৎসাপূর্ণ। **4.** Unfavourable, as wind; not advantageous; wet; stormy, as weather; প্রতিকূল; অসুবিধাজনক; ভিজা, সিক্ত; ঝটিকাচ্ছন্ন, ঝটিকাময়, ঝটিকাসঙ্কুল। **5.** Unfair; dishonest; against rules of game etc.; as, *foul* play; অসঙ্গত; অন্যায়, অসাধু; ক্রীড়াদির নিয়ম বিরুদ্ধ।

6. Entangled; as, a rope may get *foul* while paying it out; বিজড়িত। 7. Defaced, as by changes or markings; as, a *foul* copy; বিকৃত, কদর্য্য। 8. Ugly; as, fair or *foul*; কুরূপ, কুৎসিত, বিশ্রী, কদাকার। 9. In bad condition, as a fish at or after spawning; হীনাবস্থ। ***Noun.*** 1. That which is foul; বিরক্তিকর বিষয়, জঘন্য বিষয়, কুৎসিত বিষয়। 2. Entanglement; collision, as in riding, rowing etc.; বিজড়ন; সংঘর্ষ। 3. A foul stroke, hit or play; নিয়মবিরুদ্ধ আঘাত বা ক্রীড়া। ***Adv.*** In a foul or irregular way; নিয়মবিরুদ্ধভাবে। ***Verb i.*** 1. To become foul or clogged, as a gun etc.; মলিন হওয়া, মলরুদ্ধ হওয়া। 2. To get entangled, as a rope etc.; to collide; জড়িত হওয়া; সংঘৃষ্ট হওয়া। 3. To make a foul play or stroke; অন্যায় ক্রীড়া বা আঘাত করা। ***Verb t.*** 1. To make foul or dirty; to pollute; to defile; মলিন করা, অপরিষ্কার করা, নোংরা করা; কলুষিত করা; দূষিত করা। 2. To disgrace; to dishonour; কলঙ্কিত করা; অসম্মানিত করা। 3. To entangle, as a cable etc.; to collide with; জড়িত করা; সংঘর্ষ লাগা। **Foul′-ly,** *adv.* In a foul manner; cruelly; wickedly; as, he was *foully* murdered; দূষিতভাবে; নির্ম্মমভাবে; গর্হিতভাবে। **Foul′-ness,** *n.* Foul state; foul matter; wickedness; মালিন্য; দূষিত পদার্থ; গর্হিত আচরণ। **Foul-anchor** — জাহাজের রজ্জুর সহিত বিজড়িত হইয়াছে এইরূপ নোঙ্গর। **Foul-copy**—খস্‌ড়া। **Foul-mouthed, —spoken**—অশ্লীলভাষী, দুর্ম্মুখ। **Foul-play**—অন্যায় ক্রীড়া; বিশ্বাসঘাতকতা। **The foul fiend**—The devil; শয়তান। **The rope is foul** — The rope is entangled; রজ্জুটী জড়াইয়া গিয়াছে। **Through foul and fair**—Through everything; সুদিনে দুর্দ্দিনে। **To claim a foul**—To assert that the recognised rules have been broken and that a victory is therefore invalid; ক্রীড়ার নির্দ্ধারিত নিয়মভঙ্গ হইয়াছে এই অজুহাতে জয়লাভ অবৈধ বলিয়া দাবী করা। **To fall foul**—To quarrel; ঝগড়া করা। **To fall foul of**—See under FALL. **To make foul water**—(Of a ship) To come into such shoal that the keel comes near the bottom so that the water under it, being greatly agitated, gets muddy; অগভীর জলে আসা হেতু তলদেশের ঘর্ষণে কর্দ্দম তোলা। **To fall or run foul of**—To come in collision with; সংঘর্ষ হওয়া। **To play one foul**—To deal with one treacherously; কাহারো সহিত বিশ্বাসঘাতকতা করা। **To run foul of**—To collide with; সংঘৃষ্ট হওয়া।

fou-lard′ (fô-lâr), *n.* 1. A kind of silk material; একপ্রকার রেসমী কাপড়। 2. A handkerchief of foulard; ঐরূপ রেসমী কাপড়ের রুমাল।

fou′-mârt (fô-), *n.* The European polecat; ইয়ুরোপদেশীয় নকুল জাতীয় জন্তু বিশেষ।

found (fownd), *p. t.* of FIND which see.

found (fownd), *v. t.* 1. To form by melting and moulding a metal; to cast; ছাঁচে ঢালাই করিয়া নির্ম্মাণ করা; ঢালাই করা। 2. To fuse, as materials for glass; to make (glass) in this way; দ্রব করা, কাচ প্রস্তুতের জন্য নানাদ্রব্য ঢালাই করা; নানাদ্রব্য ঢালাই করিয়া কাচ প্রস্তুত করা। **Found′-er,** *n.* **Found′-er-y, Found′-ry,** *ns.* 1. Art or business of casting metals etc.; ঢালাই কাজ। 2. An establishment for casting metals; ঢালাইখানা, কুপ্যশালা (কেণ্ডি), সন্ধানী (আঃ বঃ)।

found (fownd) *v. t.* & *i.* 1. To lay the basis of; to base; to establish, (*lit.* & *fig.*); as, to *found* one's fortunes *on* a support; ভিত্তিপত্তন করা; প্রতিষ্ঠিত করা; প্রতিষ্ঠাপিত করা, সংস্থাপিত করা। 2. To be the original builder of; to begin to raise, as an edifice; to set up; to originate; as, to *found* a college; প্রথম প্রতিষ্ঠাতা হওয়া; গড়িয়া তুলিতে আরম্ভ করা; প্রতিষ্ঠিত করা; সৃষ্টি করা। ***Verb i.*** To be based; to rely or depend; প্রতিষ্ঠিত হওয়া, দাঁড় হওয়া; নির্ভর করা।

foun-dā′-tion (-fown-), *n.* 1. The act of founding; state of being founded; সংস্থাপন, প্রতিষ্ঠাপন; প্রতিষ্ঠা। 2. Solid ground or base on which a building etc. stands; the lowest part of a structure; basis; as, the report has no *foundation*; ভিত্তি; বুনিয়াদ; মূল, পত্তন। 3. Fund invested for a benevolent purpose; an endowment; জনহিতকর প্রতিষ্ঠানের সাহায্যার্থ স্থায়ীবৃত্তি বা ধনভাণ্ডার, বৃত্তি, ধর্ম্মদায় (কেণ্ডি)। 4. An endowed institution, *e. g.* a college, hospital etc.; স্থায়ীবৃত্তি প্রদত্ত প্রতিষ্ঠান। **—er,** *n.* One who derives support from the funds or foundation of a college or school; বিদ্যালয়ের দত্তসম্পত্তির আয় হইতে বৃত্তিভোগী ছাত্র। **Foundation-muslin, —net** — Gummed fabrics for stiffening dresses and bonnets; পোষাক টুপি প্রভৃতি শক্ত করার জন্য গঁদ মাখানো জাল বা মসলিন কাপড়। **Foundation school**—Endowed school; বৃত্তিপ্রাপ্ত বিদ্যালয়। **Foundation stone**—One of the stones forming the foundation of a building, esp. a stone laid with public ceremony; ভিত্তি-প্রস্তর, বিশেষভাবে, যে প্রস্তর ধূমধামের সহিত মৃত্তিকাতলে প্রোথিত হয়, মঙ্গলেষ্টক। **Laying the**

foundation stone—মঙ্গলেষ্টকস্থাপন (বৌদ্ধ জাতক)। **On the foundation**—স্থায়ীবৃত্তি প্রাপ্তির অধিকারী। **To lay the foundation of**—To lay the basis of; ভিত্তি স্থাপন করা, মঙ্গলেষ্টক স্থাপন করা। **To shake to its foundation**—মূল প্রদেশ পর্য্যন্ত কম্পিত করা।

found'-ėr (fownd-), *n.* One who founds or establishes; one who founds an institution; সংস্থাপক, উদ্ভাবক; প্রতিষ্ঠাতা। **–ėss**, *n.* (*Fem.*) **–ship**, *n.* **Founders' shares**—কোন কোম্পানীর প্রতিষ্ঠাতৃবর্গের ধুরন্ধর (organisers) গণকে যে নির্দ্দিষ্ট সংখ্যক অংশ প্রদান করা হয়। **Founders' skin**—Relatives of a founder entitled to election or preference; স্থায়িবৃত্তিদাতার আত্মীয় কুটুম্বগণ,—যাহাদের নির্ব্বাচিত হওয়ার অধিকার থাকে।

found'-ėr (fownd), *v. i., t.* & *n.* **1.** To fall down or in; to slide down; as, earth *founders*; পতিত হওয়া; পিছলাইয়া পড়া। **2.** To become filled with water and sink, as a ship; জলপূর্ণ হইয়া নিমগ্ন হওয়া। **3.** To stumble; to stumble and so lame, as a horse; হোঁচট্ খাওয়া; হোঁচট খাইয়া খোঁড়া হওয়া। ***Verb t.*** **1.** To cause to sink, as a ship; নিমগ্ন করা, ডুবান। **2.** To cause, as a horse, to be disabled and lame; অকর্ম্মণ্য করা, অক্ষম করা। ***Noun.*** Inflammation of a horse's foot from overwork; শ্রমাধিক্য হেতু অশ্বের পদস্ফীতি। **Chest or body founder**—অশ্বের বক্ষ ও পেশীর বাত।

found'-ling (fownd-), *n.* A child found without any one to care for it; পরিত্যক্ত শিশু, কুড়ানো ছেলে, অজ্ঞাতপিতৃক (কেণ্ডি), অপবিদ্ধ বাল (আঃ বঃ)।

fount (fownt), *n.* Same as FONT which see.

fount (fownt), *n.* (*Poet.* or *rhet.*) A fountain; a source; (কবিতায়) উৎস, ফোয়ারা; উৎপত্তিস্থল।

foun'-tain (fown-tăn), *n.* **1.** A spring of water; the source of a river; প্রস্রবণ, নির্ঝর; নদীর উৎপত্তিস্থল। **2.** An artificial spring of water; কৃত্রিম উৎস। **3.** A reservoir in a pen, lamp, etc. for ink, oil, etc.; লেখনীর মস্যাধার, প্রদীপের তৈলাধার প্রভৃতি। **4.** Origin; source; উৎপত্তিস্থান; মূল। **Fountain-head**—মূল, উৎপত্তিস্থল, আদি কারণ, মুখ্যস্থান (কেণ্ডি)। **Fountain-pen**—যে লেখনীতে অনর্গল মসী নিঃসরণের ব্যবস্থা থাকে, উৎস-লেখনী।

four (fōr), *adj.* & *n.* One more than three; চারি। ***Noun.*** **1.** The sum of four units; a set of four persons or objects; চতুর; চারিজন ব্যক্তি, চতুষ্টয় বস্তু, চতুষ্টয়। **2.** A symbol representing four; ৪ এই সংখ্যা। **3.** A card or domino with four pips; তাসের চৌকা। **4.** Four-oared boat and crew; (*pl.*) races for fouroared boats; চারি দাঁড়ের নৌকা এবং উহার মাল্লা; চারি দাঁড়ের নৌকার দৌড়। **5.** Short for four o'clock; চারিটা। **6.** (*Mil.*) (*Pl.*) A formation four deep; as, form *fours*; (সামরিক-শাস্ত্র) চারি গভীর পংক্তি। **7.** (*Pl.*) Four per cent. stock; শতকরা চারি টাকা সুদের কোম্পানীর কাগজ। **8.** Four penny worth (*of* spirits); ৪ পেনি দামের (সুরাসার)। **Carriage and four**—See under CARRIAGE. **Four-ale**—Ale sold at 4*d*. a quart; এল মদ্য প্রতি কোয়ার্ট ৪ পেনি হিসাবে। **Four and twenty**—Twenty-four; চতুর্বিংশতি। **Four-course**—(*Of crops*) With four-fold rotations; বৎসরে চারিবার জন্মে এরূপ। **Four figures**—Some number between 1000 and 9999; ১০০০ এবং ৯৯৯৯এর মধ্যবর্ত্তী কোন সংখ্যা। **Four-fold**—*adj.* Fourtimes; quadruple; চারিগুণ; চতুর্গুণ, চতুর্গুণিত। **Four footed**—Quadruped; চতুষ্পদ। **Four-foot way**—Space (4 ft. $8\frac{1}{2}$ inch) between a pair of rails; লৌহবর্ত্মের দুইটী পাতা রেলের মধ্যবর্ত্তী (৪ ফিট ৮½ ইঃ) স্থান। **Four-handed**—Quadra-manus, as a monkey; চতুর্হস্ত। (*Of games*) For four persons; চারি জনের; (*Of a piece of music*) For two players; দুইজন ক্রীড়কের জন্য। **Four-horse(d)**—Drawn by four horses; অশ্বচতুষ্টয় চালিত। **Four-in-hand**—*n.* & *adv.* A vehicle drawn by four horses; চারি ঘোড়ার গাড়ী। (*Adv.*) In such a vehicle; as, to drive etc. *four-in-hand*; ঐরূপ যানে। **Four-oar**—*adj.* & *n.* With four oars; চারি দাঁড় বিশিষ্ট। (*Noun*) A boat with four oars; চারি দাঁড়ের নৌকা। **Four o'clock**—The plant Marvel-of-Peru; কৃষ্ণকেলি। **Four-pence**—A sum or coin equal to 4*d*.; ৪ পেন্স্। **Four-penny**—Costing or worth 4*d*.; ৪ পেনি মূল্যের। **Four-post**—(*Of a bed*) With four posts to support curtain; (শয্যা-সম্পর্কে) চারি খুঁটাওয়ালা। **Four-poster**—মশারী ঝুলানের জন্য চারিটী খুঁটীযুক্ত প্রশস্ত খট্টা। **Four-pounder**—A gun throwing 4lb shot; ৪ পাউণ্ড ওজনের গোলাবর্ষী কামান। **Four-score**—80; age of 80 years; অশীতি; অশীতি বর্ষ। **Four-square**—Having four equal sides and angles; solidly based or steady; সমচতুরস্র এবং সমচতুর্ভুজ; দৃঢ়প্রতিষ্ঠিত, অটল। **Four wheel**—Four wheeled carriage; চারিচাকার গাড়ী; **Four wheeler**—Four wheeled hackney carriage; চারিচাকার ভাড়াটীয়া গাড়ী। **Four corners of a document**—Its scope; কোন দলিলের আশয় বা অভিপ্রায়। **Four corners of earth**—Remotest parts; পৃথিবীর সুদূর প্রান্ত। **Within the four seas**—In Great Britain; গ্রেট্ ব্রিটেনে।

fourgon, *n.* (*F.*) Luggage-van; মালের শকট।

Fou'-ri-êr-ism (fô-), *n.* ফরাসী সাম্যবাদ। [ফরাসীদেশবাসী Charles Fourier এই মত প্রবর্ত্তন করেন। তাঁহার মতে দেশের প্রতি ১৮০০ ব্যক্তি এক পরিবারের মত এক বাটীতে বাস করিবে এবং প্রত্যেকের পরিশ্রমের ফল সকলে ভোগ করিবে। প্রতিভাবান ও পরিশ্রমী ব্যক্তিদিগের জন্য বিশেষ পুরস্কারের ব্যবস্থা থাকিলেও প্রত্যেক ব্যক্তিরই নির্দ্দিষ্ট পরিমাণ সুখ সম্ভোগের ব্যবস্থা ছিল। এতদ্ভিন্ন সাধারণ ভাষা এবং সাধারণ শাসনতন্ত্রের প্রচলন ও প্রতিষ্ঠার কল্পনাও ছিল।

four'-some (fōr-sŭm), *n.* A game of golf between two pairs; এক প্রকার গল্‌ফ্ ক্রীড়া।

four'-teen (fōr-tēn), *adj.* & *n.* Four and ten; চতুর্দ্দশ। ***Noun.*** The number 14; the symbol representing this number; চৌদ্দ; ১৪।

four'-teenth (fōr-tēnth), *adj.* & *n.* **1.** The ordinal of 14; চতুর্দ্দশতম। **2.** Being one of 14 equal parts; সমচতুর্দ্দশাংশ বিশিষ্ট। ***Noun.*** One of 14 equal parts of a thing; চতুর্দ্দশাংশ।

fourth (fōrth), *adj.* & *n.* Next after the third; চতুর্থ। ***Noun.*** **1.** Fourth part; চতুর্থাংশ। **2.** (*Pl.*) Articles of the fourth quality; চতুর্থ-শ্রেণীর জিনিষ। **Fourth'-ly,** *adv.* In the fourth place; চতুর্থতঃ। **Fourth estate**—মুদ্রাযন্ত্র, সংবাদপত্র। [এডমাণ্ড বার্ক এই শব্দটী প্রথম ব্যবহার করেন।] **Fourth part**—A quarter; এক চতুর্থাংশ। **The fourth** — The fourth day of the month; মাসের ৪ঠা তারিখ। **The fourth of July** — মার্কিণ যুক্তরাজ্যের জাতীয় উৎসবের দিন।

fowl, *n.* & *v. i.* **1.** Any bird (*rare*); bird (*obs.* except in *wild fowl*); যে কোন পাখী (ক্বচিৎ ব্যবহৃত); পাখী (অপ্রঃ)। **2.** A domestic cock or hen মোরগ, কুক্কুট, কুক্কুটী। **3.** The flesh of fowls used as food; কুক্কুটের মাংস, মোরগের মাংস। ***Verb i.*** To catch, kill or snare wild fowl for game or food; পাখী ধরা, পাখী মারা। **Fowl'er,** *n.* A sportsman who pursues or kills wild fowl; যে ব্যক্তি বন্য পক্ষী শিকার করে, শাকুনিক। **Fowl'-ing,** *n.* The art or practice of hunting, shooting or snaring; বন্য পাখী শিকার। **Fowling-piece** — A light gun used in fowling; পাখী মারিবার ক্ষুদ্রবন্দুক। **Fowl run**—A place where fowls may run; a breeding establishment for fowls; কুক্কুটগণের দৌড়ের উপযোগী স্থান; কুক্কুট উৎপাদনের স্থান।

fŏx, *n.*, *v. t.* & *i.* **1.** A carnivorous animal closely allied to the dog, remarkable for cunning; খেঁকশেয়ালী, ভাক্ষের (জিঃ)। **2.** A sly, cunning fellow; ধূর্ত্তলোক, চালাক লোক, সেয়ানা লোক। ***Verb t.*** To discolour as the leaves of a book etc. with brownish spots; পুস্তকের পত্র প্রভৃতি পিঙ্গলবর্ণের ফুট ফুট দাগদ্বারা নষ্ট করা। ***Verb i.*** **1.** To turn sour (of beer etc.); (বীয়র মদ্য প্রভৃতি সম্পর্কে) টকিয়া যাওয়া। **2.** To become discoloured, as the leaves of a book etc.; পুস্তকের পত্র প্রভৃতিতে দাগ ধরা। **3.** To act cunningly; চালাকি করা। **Fox'-i-ness,** *n.* **Fox'-y,** *adj.* **1.** Like, or pertaining to, the fox; wily; খেঁকশিয়ালবৎ, খেঁকশিয়াল সম্পর্কীয়; ধূর্ত্ত, চালাক, সেয়ানা। **2.** Of reddish brown or fox colour, as painting; কপিশবর্ণ, পিঙ্গলবর্ণ। **3.** Damaged with mildew etc.; ছাতা-ধরা। **4.** Sour, as beer etc.; টক। **Fox-brush**—খেঁকশিয়ালের পুচ্ছ। **Fox-earth**—খেঁকশিয়ালীর গর্ত্ত। **Fox-evil**—একপ্রকার টাক রোগ। **Fox-glove**—শ্বেত বা ধূমলবর্ণ পুষ্পপ্রসূ দীর্ঘ তরুবিশেষ। **Fox-hound** — খেঁকশিয়াল-শিকারী কুকুর। **Fox-hunt**—*n.* & *v. t.* The chase of a fox; খেঁকশিয়ালের অনুসরণ। (*Verb t.*) To chase (fox) with hounds; কুকুরদ্বারা খেঁকশিয়াল শিকার করা। **Fox-hunter** — One who hunts foxes; খেঁকশিয়াল শিকারী। **Fox-hunting**—*adj.* & *n.* Devoted to hunting of foxes; খেঁকশিয়াল শিকারে রত। (*Noun*) The sport of hunting foxes; খেঁকশিয়াল শিকার। **Fox-sleep**—Pretended sleep; কপট নিদ্রা। **Fox-tail**—The tail of a fox; a kind of grass; খেঁকশিয়ালের লেজ; একপ্রকার ঘাস। **Fox terrier**—A kind of terrier to unearth foxes; খেঁকশিয়ালীকে গর্ত্ত হইতে বাহির করার জন্য শিক্ষাপ্রাপ্ত একপ্রকার ক্ষুদ্র কুকুর। **Fox and geese**—একপ্রকার বড়ে খেলা।

foyer, *n.* (*F.*) A lobby in a theatre; রঙ্গমঞ্চের উপপ্রকোষ্ঠ।

frā'-căs, *n.* An uproar; a noisy quarrel; গোলমাল; হাঙ্গামা।

frăc'-tion, *n.* **1.** A fragment; a scrap; অংশ, টুকরা, খণ্ড, শকল; একাংশ, একদেশ। **2.** (*Arth.*) One or more aliquot parts of a unit or whole number; (পাটীগণিত) ভগ্নাংশ, অপূর্ণাঙ্ক (কেঃণ্ডি)। **–al,** *adj.* **1.** Pertaining to fractions; consisting of a fraction; ভগ্নাংশ-সম্পর্কীয়, ভগ্নাংশাত্মক, ভিন্নাত্মক (হিঃ কোঃ)। **2.** Insignificant; as, a *fractional* part; সামান্য, তুচ্ছ, অকিঞ্চিৎকর। **–ate,** *v. t.* To separate, as a mixture, into different portion, as in the distillation of liquids; ভিন্ন ভিন্ন অংশে বিভক্ত করা। **–ize,** *v. t.* To separate into fractions; ভগ্নাংশে বিশ্লিষ্ট করা। **Complex fraction**—মিশ্রিত ভিন্ন (হিঃ কোঃ), জটিল ভগ্নাংশ। **Compound fraction**—যুক্ত ভিন্ন (হিঃ কোঃ), প্রভাগজাতি (কেঃণ্ডি), প্রভাগজাতি অপূর্ণাঙ্ক (ঐ)। **Decimal fraction**—দশমিক ভগ্নাংশ, দশাংশ, অপূর্ণাঙ্ক (কেঃণ্ডি)। **Fractional distillations** — রাশিভাগ নিষ্কর্ষণ (হিঃ কোঃ)। **Improper fraction**—যে ভগ্নাংশের হর লব অপেক্ষা বৃহত্তম, বিষম ভিন্ন (হিঃ কোঃ), বিষম অপূর্ণাঙ্ক (কেঃণ্ডি)। **Mixed fraction** — মিশ্র ভগ্নাংশ,

Proper fraction—যে ভগ্নাংশের হর লব অপেক্ষা ক্ষুদ্রতর, সম অপূর্ণাঙ্ক (কেভি)। Simple fraction — সরল ভগ্নাংশ, সামান্য ভগ্নাংশ। Vulgar fraction—ব্যবহারী অপূর্ণাঙ্ক (কেভি), শুদ্ধ অপূর্ণাঙ্ক (ঐ)।

frac'-tious (-shŭs), *adj.* Snappish ; peevish ; unruly ; cross ; রুক্ষস্বভাব ; খিট্‌খিটে ; অদম্য, দুর্দ্দমনীয় ; চটা, রাগী। **—ly,** *adv.* **—ness,** *n.*

frac'-türe, *n. v. t.* & *i.* **1.** The act of breaking ; state of being broken ; breach ; ভাঙ্গন ; ভঙ্গপ্রবণতা ; ভঙ্গ, বিভঙ্গ। **2.** The breaking of a bone or of a cartilage ; তরুণাস্থিভঙ্গ। ***Verb t.*** To break continuous parts of ; to crack ; ভাঙ্গিয়া ফেলা, ভগ্ন করা ; ফাটান। ***Verb i.*** To undergo fracture; ভাঙ্গিয়া যাওয়া, ভগ্ন হওয়া। **Comminuted fracture**—অস্থির একাধিক স্থানে ভঙ্গ, বহুভঙ্গ। **Compound fracture**—(See COMPOUND.) অস্থিভঙ্গের সহিত বিদারিত-মুখক্ষত, মিশ্রভঙ্গ। **Simple fracture**—কেবলমাত্র অস্থিভঙ্গ, সামান্যভঙ্গ।

fræ'-nŭm (frē-), **frē—,** *ns.* (*Pl.* -NA). A small ligament restraining the motion of an organ ; কোন দৈহিকযন্ত্র স্বস্থানে রক্ষার জন্য ঝিল্লীময় ক্ষুদ্র বল্গাকার পদার্থ, বল্গাঝিল্লী।

frăg'-ile (-ĭl), *adj.* Easily broken ; brittle ; frail ; weak ; perishable ; ভঙ্গুর, ভঙ্গপ্রবণ ; ঠুন্‌কো ; ক্ষণভঙ্গুর, ক্ষণস্থায়ী ; ক্ষীণ ; ধ্বংসশীল। **Fra-gil'-i-ty,** *n.* The quality of being fragile ; frailness ; weakness ; ভঙ্গপ্রবণতা ; ক্ষণভঙ্গুরতা ; ক্ষীণতা। **—ly,** *adv.*

frăg'-mĕnt, *n.* **1.** A small portion broken off or detached ; ক্ষুদ্র অংশ, টুকরা, খণ্ড। **2.** An imperfect or incomplete part, as of a writing or work of art ; অসমাপ্ত অংশ, অপূর্ণ অংশ। **—men-ta-ry,** *adj.* Composed of fragments ; disconnected ; অংশাত্মক ; অসম্বদ্ধ।

frā'-grănt, *adj.* Sweet-scented ; সুবাসিত, সুগন্ধি, সুরভি, সুবাসময়। **—grance,** *n.* Sweetness of smell ; a pleasing odour ; সুবাস, পরিমল, সৌগন্ধ, সৌরভ, আমোদ ; সুগন্ধ। **—ly,** *adv.*

frail (frāl), *n.* A basket of rushes for figs, raisins, etc. ; আঞ্জীর, কিসমিস প্রভৃতি রাখার জন্য ঝুড়ি।

frail (frāl), *adj.* **1.** Weak ; transient, as life, bliss, etc. ; easily broken or destroyed ; in weak health ; ক্ষীণ, দুর্ব্বল, নির্জ্জীব ; ক্ষণভঙ্গুর, ক্ষণবিধ্বংসী, নশ্বর, ক্ষণস্থায়ী ; ভঙ্গুর, ভঙ্গপ্রবণ ; স্বাস্থ্যহীন। **2.** Morally weak ; unchaste as, a woman ; দুর্ব্বলচিত্ত ; ভ্রষ্টা। **Frail'-ty,** *n.* **1.** Physical, mental or moral weakness ; liability to err or yield to temptation ; শারীরিক, মানসিক বা নৈতিক দুর্ব্বলতা, দুর্ব্বলচিত্ততা ; সহজে প্রলোভনে পড়িবার বা পাপপথে পদার্পণ করিবার প্রবণতা। **2.** A failing ; a fault ; a foible ; দোষ ; অপরাধ, কসুর (*colloq.*) ; চরিত্রের ক্রটী বা দুর্ব্বলতা।

fraise (frāz), *n.* (*Fort.*) A palisade of pointed stakes on a rampart ; দুর্গপ্রাচীরের উপরিস্থ সূক্ষ্মাগ্র কীলকরচিত বৃতি।

fraise (frāz), *n.* A tool used in enlarging a hole made by a drill or in cutting teeth in watch-wheels ; বেধন-যন্ত্র দ্বারা কৃত ছিদ্র বৃহৎ করার জন্য যন্ত্র-বিশেষ, ঘড়ীর চাকার দাঁত কাটার যন্ত্রবিশেষ।

fram-bœ'-si-ă (-bē-), *n.* (*Med.*) The yaws ; (ভৈষজ্য-শাস্ত্র) কণ্টক-গুটী (হঃ চঃ)।

frame, *v.t.* & *i.* **1.** To fashion ; to shape ; to adapt or fit, (*to* or *into*) ; to dispose to a purpose ; রচনা করা ; গঠন করা ; উপযোগী করা ; কোন বিশেষ উদ্দেশ্যে নিয়োগ করা। **2.** To construct by uniting several parts ; বিভিন্ন অংশ সংযোজন দ্বারা গঠন করা। **3.** To plan ; to invent ; to express or utter ; to conceive or imagine ; পরিকল্পনা করা ; উদ্ভাবন করা ; ব্যক্ত করা, উচ্চারণ করা ; কল্পনা করা, ধারণা করা। **4.** To set in a frame, as a picture etc. ; to be a frame to ; ছবি প্রভৃতি বাঁধান ; ঠাট বা কাঠাম স্বরূপ হওয়া। ***Verb i.*** To give promise of becoming skilful ; দক্ষ বা কুশল হইবে বলিয়া আশা হওয়া। **Fram'-a-ble,** *adj.* **Fram'-er,** *n.* **Fram'-ing,** *n.* **1.** Act of making a frame ; a frame ; কাঠাম রচনা ; ঠাট, কাঠাম।

frame, *n.* **1.** Construction ; structure ; constitution ; scheme ; system ; as, the *frame* of Government ; রচনা ; গঠন ; সংস্থান ; ব্যবস্থা ; পদ্ধতি। **2.** A structure or frame-work ; কাঠাম, ঠাট। **3.** A temporary state of mind ; mood ; as, happy *frame* of mind ; মনের অস্থায়ী ভাব ; মানসিক ভাব, মনোগতি, চিত্তবৃত্তি (কেভি), মনোবিকার (ঐ) মনোবৃত্তি (ঐ)। **4.** The skeleton of a building ; অট্টালিকাদির কাঠাম বা কঙ্কাল। **5.** Support or substructure of anything, a pane of glass etc. ; a case enclosing a picture ; কাঠাম, ঠাট ; ছবির চারি কিনারের কাঠ, ফ্রেম। **6.** The bodily structure ; as, a man of gigantic *frame* ; শারীরিক গঠন, অঙ্গরচনা (কেভি), অঙ্গযষ্টি (ঐ)। **7.** (*Mining*) A plain table ; (খনির কাজ) সমতল মেজ। **8.** (*Gardening*) A glazed structure to protect plants from frost ; (উদ্যান-কার্য্য) তুষার হইতে বৃক্ষাদি রক্ষার জন্য সূক্ষ্ম কাচস্তরাচ্ছাদিত আবরণ বিশেষ। **Frame'-less,** *adj.* **Framehouse**—কাঠের ঘর। **Frame-saw**—ফ্রেম বা কাঠামে আঁটা করাত। **Frame-work**—A structure or fabric for supporting anything, (*lit.* & *fig.*) ; কাঠাম, ঠাট।

franc (frăngk), *n.* A French silver coin of about $9\frac{1}{2}$*d.* ; ফরাসী দেশীয়

রৌপ্যমুদ্রা বিশেষ—ইহার মূল্য প্রায় ৯½ পেন্স।

Franc.

frăn'-chīse, *n.* **1.** (*Hist.*) A privilege or exceptional right, granted to person, corporation, etc. রাজদত্ত বিশেষাধিকার। **2.** The right of voting especially for a member of parliament; নির্ব্বাচনাধিকার, বিশেষতঃ পার্লেমেণ্ট মহাসভার সভ্য নির্ব্বাচনাধিকার। **3.** Full membership of a corporate body or state; citizenship; কোন সমবায়ের পূর্ণ সভ্যপদ; নাগরিকত্ব।

Frăn-cĭs'-căn, *adj.* & *n.* Relating to the order of St. Francis, or the Franciscans; সেণ্ট ফ্রান্সিস্ নামক খৃষ্টীয় সিদ্ধপুরুষ কর্ত্তৃক ১২০৯ খৃঃ অব্দে প্রবর্ত্তিত সন্ন্যাসিসম্প্রদায়সম্বন্ধীয়। ***Noun.*** A monk of the order of St. Francis in the Roman Catholic Church; উক্ত সম্প্রদায়ভুক্ত সন্ন্যাসী।

fran'-cŏ-lin (frăng-), *n.* A kind of partridge; কালতিত্তির পক্ষী।

franc-tireur, (*F*) *n.* (*Pl.* -CS, -RS), A soldier of irregular light infantry corps; লঘু অস্ত্রধারী অনিয়মিত সৈন্য-দলভুক্ত যোদ্ধা।

frăn'-gĭ-ble (-bl), *adj.* Brittle; ভঙ্গুর, ভঙ্গপ্রবণ, ঠুন্‌কা (*colloq.*)। **—bil'-i-ty, —ness,** *ns.*

frăn'-gĭ-pāne, *n.* **1.** A perfume of red jasmine; আমেরিকাদেশীয় রক্তবর্ণ পুষ্পবিশেষ হইতে প্রস্তুত সুগন্ধি দ্রব্য। **2.** A species of pastry; মাংসপূরিত পিষ্টক, একজাতীয় মিষ্ট দ্রব্য।

frank (frăngk), *adj.* **1.** Open; sincere; candid; outspoken; সরল; অকপট; অমায়িক; স্পষ্টবাদী। **2.** Avowed; স্বীকৃত। **Frank'-ly,** *adv.* In a frank manner; openly; unreservedly; সরলভাবে; অকপটভাবে; খোলাখুলিভাবে। **Frank'-ness,** *n.*

frank (frăngk), *v. t.* & *n.* **1.** To convey, as a person gratuitously; বিনা ব্যয়ে স্থানান্তরে নেওয়া। **2.** (*Hist.*) To exempt from charge for postage, as a letter; (ইতিহাস) বিনা মাশুলে পত্রাদি পাঠান। **3.** To facilitate the passage of, as a person; to give social passport to; কাহারো পথ সুগম করা; সমাজে প্রবেশের অধিকার দেওয়া। ***Noun.*** **1.** (*Hist.*) The privilege of sending letters etc. free of postage etc; (ইতিহাস) বিনা মাশুলে পত্রাদি প্রেরণের অধিকার। **2.** (*Hist.*) The signature ensuring free transmission of a letter; a franked cover; বিনা ব্যয়ে পত্রাদি প্রেরণে ক্ষমতাপন্ন ব্যক্তির স্বাক্ষর; ঐরূপ স্বাক্ষরযুক্ত লেফাফা।

Frank (frăngk), *n.* **1.** One of the ancient German races; যে সকল জর্ম্মাণ জাতীয় লোক ষষ্ঠ শতাব্দীতে ফরাসী দেশ বিজয় করে তাহাদের অন্যতম। **2.** A native of Western Europe; ইয়ুরোপের পশ্চিমভাগের অধিবাসী। **Frank'-ish,** *adj.* Like or pertaining to the Franks; ফ্রাঙ্কজাতীয় লোকের মত, ফ্রাঙ্কজাতীয় লোক-সম্পর্কীয়।

Frank'-en-stein (frăngk-ĕn-stīn), *n.* Any creation bringing trouble or disaster to its author [from Mrs. Shelly's (1797—1851). Tale Frankenstein]; যে সৃষ্টি সৃষ্টিকর্ত্তার বিপদ্, উৎকণ্ঠা ও দুর্ভাগ্যের কারণস্বরূপ হইয়া থাকে।

Frank'-fōrt —blăck (-frăngk), *n.* A pigment used in copper plate engraving; তাম্র ফলকে খোদাইর কাজে ব্যবহৃত একপ্রকার রঞ্জক পদার্থ।

frank'-in-cense (frăngk-ĭn-sĕns), *n.* An aromatic gum resin used for burning as incense; আরব দেশীয় ধূনা বিশেষ, শ্বেত-কুন্দুরু।

frank'-lin (frăngk-), *n.* (*Hist.*) An English free-holder; (ইতিহাস) ইংলণ্ডদেশীয় আয়মাদার প্রজা।

frank'-pledge (frăngk-plĕj) *n.* (*Hist.*) The system under which every member of a tithing is responsible for the conduct of the rest; (ইতিহাস) যে ব্যবস্থানুসারে ইংলণ্ডের প্রতি ক্ষুদ্র পল্লীবাসী দশজন গৃহস্থ প্রত্যেকে অপর সকলের আচরণের জন্য দায়ী থাকিত।

frăn'-tic, *adj.* Wildly moved or excited; furious; transported with rage, grief etc; frenzied; raving; উন্মত্ত, বুদ্ধিভ্রষ্ট; উচ্চণ্ড; ক্রোধোন্মত্ত শোকোন্মত্ত; ক্ষিপ্ত; প্রলাপভাষী। **—ly, —ti-cal-ly,** *advs.* In a frantic manner; উন্মত্তবৎ, ক্রোধোন্মত্ত হইয়া।

frăp, *v. t.* (*Naut.*) To bind tightly; (নৌ-বিদ্যা) শক্ত করিয়া বাঁধা।

frăss, *n.* The refuse or excrement left by insect larvæ; ক্রিমির শরীর হইতে নিঃসৃত ক্লেদ।

frā'-te (-tā), *n.* (*Pl.* -TI.) A friar; খৃষ্টীয় সন্ন্যাসী।

fră-têr'-năl, *adj.* Becoming, or or relating to, a brother or brothers; brotherly; ভ্রাতৃ-সম্বন্ধীয়, ভ্রাত্রীয়; ভ্রাতৃতুল্য।

fră-têr'-nĭ-tў, *n.* **1.** State of being fraternal; brotherliness; ভ্রাতৃভাব; সৌভ্রাত্র, মৈত্রী। **2.** A religious brotherhood or society; ধর্ম্মসম্প্রদায়, ভ্রাতৃমণ্ডলী। **3.** Men of the same class, profession, occupation, etc.; এক শ্রেণী বা ব্যবসায়ের লোক সমূহ।

frat'-ĕr-nīze, *v. t.* To associate as brothers or intimates; to have friendly feeling; ভ্রাতৃভাবে মিলিত হওয়া, অন্তরঙ্গভাবে মিলিত হওয়া, ভ্রাতৃত্ব বন্ধনে বদ্ধ হওয়া; বন্ধুভাব থাকা। **—ni-za'-tion,** *n.*

frăt'-rĭ-cīde, *n.* **1.** The act of murdering one's own brother or sister; ভ্রাতৃহত্যা, ভ্রাতৃবধ, ভগ্নীহত্যা, ভগ্নীবধ। **2.** One who kills his own brother or sister ; ভ্রাতৃহন্তা, ভগ্নীহন্তা। **—cid-al,** *adj.* Pertaining to fratricide ; ভ্রাতৃহত্যা-সম্বন্ধীয়, ভ্রাতৃঘাতী, ভগ্নীঘাতী।

frau, (*F.*), *n.* (*In Germany*) A woman ; (also) the title Mrs. (applied to a married woman or widow) ; (জর্ম্মণ দেশে) স্ত্রীলোক ; (বিবাহিতা বা বিধবা স্ত্রীলোকের) উপাধি, শ্রীযুক্তা।

fraud (fräd), *n.* **1.** Deception by which the right or interest of another is injured ; also deceptive representations ; জুয়াচুরী, প্রতারণা, প্রবঞ্চনা ; প্রবঞ্চনাপূর্ণ বিবরণ। **2.** A deceptive device or trick ; ছল, চাতুরী, ফিকিরফন্দী, ফেরেব (*colloq.*)। **3.** A person or thing that does not fulfil an expectation or description ; যে ব্যক্তি বা বস্তু আশানুরূপ বা বর্ণনানুরূপ হয় নাই। **Fraud'-ful,** *adj.* Full of fraud ; প্রতারণাপূর্ণ। **Fraud'-ful-ly,** *adv.* **Fraud'-ful-ness,** *n.* **A pious fraud**—সদুদ্দেশ্যে প্রতারণা। **In frand of, To the fraud of**—So as to defraud ; প্রতারণার উদ্দেশ্যে।

fraud'-ü-lĕnt (fräd-), *adj.* **1.** Using fraud ; guilty of fraud ; প্রতারণাপূর্ণ, প্রবঞ্চনামূলক, বঞ্চনামূলক ; প্রতারণা দোষে দোষী। **2.** Characterised by, or of the nature of, fraud ; effected by fraud ; প্রতারণাত্মক, বঞ্চনা-ঘটিত ; প্রতারণাদ্বারা সাধিত। **—lence, —len-cy,** *ns.* প্রতারণা-শীলতা, প্রবঞ্চনাশীলতা, ঠকবাজী (কেণ্ডি)। **—ly,** *adv.* In a fraudulent manner ; প্রতারণাপূর্ব্বক।

fraught (frät), *adj.* **1.** (*Poet.*) Filled ; stored (*with*) ; (কবিতায়) পূর্ণ ; পুরিত। **2.** (*Fig.*) Attended or teeming with ; as, it is *fraught* with dangers, meaning etc. ; সংসৃষ্ট, পূর্ণ, ভারাক্রান্ত।

frau-lein, *n.* (*In Germany*) An unmarried woman ; a governess ; (also) the title Miss, applied to unmarried ladies ; (জর্ম্মণ দেশে) অবিবাহিতা স্ত্রীলোক ; পারিবারিক শিক্ষয়িত্রী ; কুমারী (উপাধি)।

fray (frā), *n.* A tumult ; brawl ; a contest ; a fight (*lit.* & *fig.*) ; দাঙ্গা ; হাঙ্গামা ; প্রতিযোগিতা ; লড়াই।

fray (frā), *v. t.* & *i.* To rub ; to wear off by rubbing ; to fret, as a cloth etc. ; ঘষা ; ঘষিয়া ক্ষয় করা ; (কাপড় ইত্যাদি) ঘষিয়া খাইয়া দেওয়া। ***Verb i.*** **1.** To rub ; ঘর্ষণ করা। **2.** To wear out ; ক্ষয় হওয়া। **To fray** or **fray head**—(Of a deer) To rub velvet off new horns ; (হরিণ সম্পর্কে) নবোদ্গত শৃঙ্গ হইতে সলোম কোমল ত্বক্ ঘষিয়া উঠান।

frăx-i-nĕl'-lă, *n.* A kind of dittany ; একপ্রকার সুগন্ধি গুল্ম।

freak (frēk), *n.* **1.** A whim or caprice ; খেয়াল, মর্জ্জি, সখ। **2.** Capriciousness ; অব্যবস্থিতচিত্ততা। **3.** The product of freakish thought or action ; a monstrosity ; a specimen abnormally developed ; মনের খেয়াল ; বিকট জীব, অদ্ভুত জীব ; অস্বাভাবিক ভাবে বর্দ্ধিত জীব প্রভৃতি। **Freak'-ish,** *adj.* Whimsical ; capricious ; খামখেয়ালী ; স্বেচ্ছাচারী, কামাচারী। **Freak'-ish-ly,** *adv.* **Freak'-ish-ness,** *n.* **A freak of nature**—প্রকৃতির খেয়াল।

frĕck'-le (-l), *n., v. t.* & *i.* **1.** A yellowish spot on the skin ; মেছেতা, জড়ুল, আঁচিল। **2.** A small spot or discolouration ; ক্ষুদ্র দাগ, বর্ণ-বিকৃতি। ***Verb t.*** To spot or mark with freckles ; তিল, মেছেতা প্রভৃতি দ্বারা চিহ্নিত করা। ***Verb i.*** To become marked with freckles ; তিল, মেছেতা প্রভৃতি দ্বারা চিহ্নিত হওয়া।

free (frē), *adj.* & *v. t.* **1.** Not in bondage to another ; মুক্ত, অনন্যাধীন, (কেণ্ডি)। **2.** Possessed of personal rights and social and political liberty ; as, a *free* Negro ; ব্যক্তিগত অধিকার এবং সামাজিক ও রাজনৈতিক স্বাধীনতা বিশিষ্ট। **3.** Independent, as a state or nation ; স্বাধীন, স্বতন্ত্র। **4.** Unrestricted ; loose ; অবাধ, স্বতন্ত্র, অপ্রতিবদ্ধ, উদ্দাম, অবারিত, অব্যাহত ; আল্গা। **5.** Not confined or imprisoned ; as, a *free* person or animal ; মুক্ত, খালাস। **6.** Frank ; unreserved ; familiar ; forward ; সরল ; সঙ্কোচ-শূন্য, স্বচ্ছন্দ ; অন্তরঙ্গ ; প্রগল্‌ভ, সপ্রতিভ। **7.** Lavish ; liberal ; as, a *free* gift ; অতিব্যয়ী ; মুক্তহস্ত, বদান্য। **8.** Exempt (*from*) ; মুক্ত, রহিত, হীন, বিহীন, শূন্য। **9.** Without trade restrictions ; not liable to tax, duty or fees ; as, a *free* port or ship etc. ; ব্যবসায়সম্বন্ধে প্রতিবন্ধকতা শূন্য ; কর, শুল্ক প্রভৃতি হইতে মুক্ত, নিষ্কর, শুল্কশূন্য। **10.** Furnished without cost etc. ; gratuitous ; as, a *free* pass or admission ; বিনামূল্যে প্রদত্ত ; মূল্য-রহিত, অবৈতনিক, দাতব্য। **11.** Spontaneous ; as, *free* choice or will ; স্বতঃস্ফুট, স্বতঃস্ফূর্ত্ত, স্বপ্রণোদিত। **12.** (*Of literary style etc.*) Irregular ; (*of translation*) not literal ; (রচনা-রীতি-সম্পর্কে) অনিয়মিত ; (অনু-বাদ সম্পর্কে) অনাক্ষরিক। **13.** Allowable ; as, it is *free* for him to do so ; বৈধ। **14.** Profuse ; copious ; as, *free* use of liquor ; প্রচুর ; প্রভূত। **15.** (*Chem.*) Uncombined ; (রসায়ন-শাস্ত্র) অমিশ্র। **16.** Favourable, as a wind ; অনুকূল। **17.** Not quite decent as, a *free* talk ; শ্লীলতাবর্জ্জিত। **18.** Ready ; "I am *free* to confess" প্রস্তুত। **19.** Immoderate ; licentious ; as, a *free* life ; মাত্রাছাড়া, লম্পট, ভ্রষ্ট। **20.** Devoid, (with *of* or *from*) ; as, *free of* a burden ; রহিত, বিহীন, শূন্য। **21.** Not fixed ; unattached ; আল্‌গা ; অসম্বদ্ধ, অসংলগ্ন। ***Verb t.*** To set at liberty ; to relieve (*from*) ; to release ; to disengage ; to clear ; to rid (*of*) ; মুক্ত করা ; উদ্ধার করা ; বিযুক্ত করা ;

মুক্তি দেওয়া; পরিষ্কার করা; বিমুক্ত করা। **Free'-ly**, *adv.* In a free manner; liberally; readily; স্বাধীনভাবে; উদারভাবে; তৎপরতার সহিত। **Free-agency** — অব্যাহত কার্য্যক্ষমতা, স্বাধীনভাবে কার্য্য করিবার ক্ষমতা, স্বতন্ত্রতা (কেঙি), স্বাতন্ত্র্য (ঐ)। **Free-and-easy** — স্বচ্ছন্দ। **Free board**—জলপৃষ্ঠ এবং পাটাতনের সমতল রেখার মধ্যবর্ত্তী জাহাজের অংশ। **Free-boot** — *v. i.* To plunder; লুণ্ঠন করা। **Free-booter**—A plunderer; a pirate; লুণ্ঠনকারী; জলদস্যু, বোম্বেটিয়া। **Free-booting**—*n.* & *adj.* Robbery; দস্যুবৃত্তি। *(Adj.)* Robbing; দস্যুবৃত্তিপরায়ণ। **Free-bootery**—The act of a free-booter; লুণ্ঠনকার্য্য। **Free-born**—স্বাধীন (অর্থাৎ ক্রীতদাস বা ক্রীতদাসী নয়) পিতামাতা হইতে জাত। **Free boy**—অবৈতনিক ছাত্র। **Free-breakfast-table** — যে সকল দ্রব্য সচরাচর খাদ্যস্বরূপ ব্যবহৃত হয় তাহা সর্ব্বপ্রকার শুল্ক হইতে বিমুক্ত হইবে—এইরূপ মত। **Free-Church**—যে ধর্ম্ম-মন্দিরে সর্ব্বসাধারণ অবাধে বিনা ব্যয়ে প্রবেশ করিতে পারে। One unconnected with the state; শাসনতন্ত্রের সহিত অসংসৃষ্ট খৃষ্টীয় ধর্ম্মসংঘ। *(Pl.* with *the)* Nonconformists, which see. **Free-city**—A city independent in its government and franchise; শাসন ও নির্ব্বাচনাদি বিষয় সম্বন্ধে স্বাধীন নগরী। **Free-fight**—One in which any one present joins; যে দাঙ্গায় উপস্থিত যে কোন ব্যক্তি যোগ দান করে; হাঙ্গামা। **Free-fooder**—যে ব্যক্তির মতে সর্ব্বপ্রকার সাধারণ খাদ্যদ্রব্য বিনা শুল্কে আমদানী করিতে দেওয়া উচিত। **Free gift**—দান। **Free-hand**—Done by the hand, without support, or the guidance of instrument; as, *freehand* drawing; যন্ত্রাদির সাহায্য ব্যতীত কেবল মাত্র হস্তদ্বারা অঙ্কিত। **Free-handed**—Open-handed; liberal; মুক্ত-হস্ত; বদান্য। **Free-hearted**—অমায়িক। **Free-hold** — অল্প মালগুজারির আয়মা। **Free-labour**—Labour of workmen not belonging to the trade unions; স্বেচ্ছাকৃত শ্রম। **Free-lance**—A mercenary soldier of the middle ages; মধ্যযুগের যে সকল সৈনিক বীর বেতন গ্রহণপূর্ব্বক যুদ্ধ করিত। A politician or controversialist unattached to any party; যে তার্কিক বা রাজনীতিক কোন পক্ষে যোগ দান করেন না। **Free-liver**—One who freely indulges in the pleasures, especially of the table; ভোগবিলাসী ব্যক্তি, ভোগবিলাসপরায়ণ ব্যক্তি, ভোগবিলাসী। **Free-living**—Unrestrained indulgence in pleasures, especially of the table; ভোগবিলাস। **Free-love**—Sexual relations without marriage; বিবাহবন্ধন ব্যতীত স্ত্রীপুরুষের যৌন সম্বন্ধ, অবাধপ্রেম। **Free-man**—One who enjoys liberty, (not a slave or serf etc.) স্বাধীন ব্যক্তি। A citizen of a free state; one having the freedom of a city or company; স্বাধীন রাজ্যের নাগরিক; কোন নগরী বা ব্যবসায়নিকেতনের বিশেষ অধিকার প্রাপ্ত ব্যক্তি। **Free martin**—এঁড়ে বাছুরের সহিত যমজ ভাবে জাত বকনা বাছুর,—যাহা সাধারণতঃ বন্ধ্যা হইয়া থাকে। **Free mason**—A member of the society called *Free and Accepted Masons*; (পূর্ব্বে) প্রস্তর শিল্পীদিগের গুপ্ত সমিতি বিশেষের সভ্য, (বর্ত্তমানে) সামাজিক সুখভোগ ও পারস্পরিক সাহায্যের জন্য প্রতিষ্ঠিত সম্প্রদায় বিশেষের সভ্য। **Free-masonry**—উক্ত সম্প্রদায়ের মত, প্রতিষ্ঠান, প্রভৃতি। Secret understanding between like characters; instinctive sympathy; সমপ্রকৃতিক ব্যক্তি সমূহের মধ্যে গোপনীয় যোগ; প্রকৃতিসিদ্ধ সহানুভূতি। **Free pass**—বাষ্পীয়-পোত ও শকটাদিতে গমনাগমনের জন্য বিনামূল্যের টিকিট। **Free port**—যে বন্দরে পণ্যদ্রব্যের উপর কোনরূপ শুল্ক, মাশুল, প্রভৃতি আদায় হয় না। **Free school**—অবৈতনিক বিদ্যালয়। **Free spoken**—Not concealing one's opinions; blunt; স্পষ্টবাদী, স্পষ্টভাষী; রুক্ষ। **Free stone**—বেলে পাথর; একপ্রকার পিচ ফল,—যাহা পাকিলে পর আঁটি সকল শিথিল হইয়া যায়। **Free-thinking**—*n.* & *adj.* Independent thinking, esp. when carried into scepticism; স্বাধীন চিন্তা। *(Adj.)* Sceptical; unbelieving; সংশয়বাদী; অবিশ্বাসী। **Free thinker**—Sceptic; a rationalist; অজ্ঞেয়বাদী; স্বাধীনচেতা, শাস্ত্রদ্বেষী (কেঙি), যুক্তিবাদী **Free thought**—স্বাধীন চিন্তা; স্বাধীন চিন্তার মূলতত্ত্ব। **Free trade**—যেরূপ বাণিজ্যে বৈদেশিক দ্রব্যের উপর শুল্ক প্রদান করিতে হয় না, অবাধবাণিজ্য। **Free trader** — অবাধবাণিজ্যানুরাগী। **Free wheel**—দ্বিচক্রযানের যে চক্র পাদান স্থির থাকিলেও ঘুরিতে পারে, মুক্তচক্র। **Free-will**—*n.* & *adj.* স্বাধীন ইচ্ছা [যাহা দৈব কর্ত্তৃক নিয়ন্ত্রিত হয় না], স্বেচ্ছাকর্ত্তৃত্ব (কেঙি)। *(Adj.)* Spontaneous; voluntary; স্বতঃপ্রবৃত্ত; স্বেচ্ছাপ্রবৃত্ত। [*Doctrine of free will* — পৌরুষবাদ (কেঙি), প্রযত্নবাদ (ঐ)]। **Free church of Scotland**—১৮৪৩ খৃঃ অব্দে স্কটলণ্ড দেশে প্রতিষ্ঠিত ধর্ম্মসংঘ-বিশেষ। **Free on board** (f. o. b.)—ইহার অর্থ এই যে জাহাজ প্রভৃতিতে মাল বিনা ব্যয়ে তুলিয়া দিতে হইবে। **Free of the house**—Having the entrance and use of the house; গৃহে অব্যাহত প্রবেশ ও গৃহ ব্যবহারের অধিকার বিশিষ্ট। **I am free to confess**—I am not unwilling to confess; আমি স্বীকার করিতে নারাজ নই। **To be free of one's money**—To be open-handed; মুক্তহস্ত হওয়া। **To make free**—সাহসী হওয়া। **To make or be free with**—To take undue liberties with; অনুচিত ব্যবহার করা। **free'-dom** (frē-dŭm), *n.* 1. Personal or civil liberty; independence;

ht (to do etc.) ; স্বাধীনতা ; রতন্ত্রতা ; (কার্য্যাদি করার) অধিকার। Exer tion from necessity, fate . in choice and action ; as, freedom of the will ; মুক্তি, ধীনতা। 3. Participation in ivileges of membership of a mpany or citizenship of a y ; নাগরিকের বা ব্যবসায়িনিকেতনের ভ্যর অধিকারের সহভাগিতা। 4. Franise ; privilege, as possessed y a city, corporation, etc. ; াজদত্ত অধিকার ; নগরী, বিধিবদ্ধ .জ, প্রভৃতি দ্বারা প্রদত্ত অধিকার। Ease ; facility ; as, he speaks acts with freedom ; স্বচ্ছন্দতা, নায়াস, স্বাচ্ছন্দ্য ; সুকরতা, অনায়াস-য্যতা। 6. Outspokenness ; frank-ss ; স্পষ্টবাদিতা, স্পষ্টভাষিতা ; সরলতা, কপটতা। 7. Improper familiarity ; নুচিত ঘনিষ্ঠতা বা অন্তরঙ্গতা। (Phys.) Capability of moving ; পদার্থ-বিজ্ঞান) চলচ্ছক্তি। 9. Boldess of conception ; কল্পনার তেজ।

e'-höld (frē-), *n.* & *adj.* A roperty held free of duty except o the king ; tenure by which uch an estate is held ; নিষ্কর ভূমি, আয়মা ; মিরাস (কেণ্ডি)। *Adj.* Held by freehold ; আয়মাস্বরূপ অধিকৃত। **-er**, *n.* One who possesses a reehold estate ; নিষ্কর ভূম্যধিকারী, আয়মাদার, মিরাসদার (কেণ্ডি)।

eeze (frēz), *v. i.*, *t.* & *n.* 1. To e hardened into ice or a like olid body ; জমিয়া যাওয়া, জমাট াধা। 2. To become rigid, as esult of cold ; to be chilled th fear ; শীতে আড়ষ্ট হওয়া, ার্ত্ত হওয়া, শীতে জড়সড় হওয়া ; য় আড়ষ্ট হওয়া। *Verb t.* 1. To ngeal ; to harden into ice ; মাট বাধান ; বরফে পরিণত করা। To chill, as feelings ; to tery greatly ; আড়ষ্ট করা ; ভয়ে আড়ষ্ট , ভয়ে জড়সড় করা। 3. To rden, damage or kill by chilling, as to death ; শৈত্য প্রয়োগে কঠিন করা, শীতদ্বারা নষ্ট বা নিহত করা। 4. To preserve by refrigeration ; as, to *freeze* meat ; শৈত্য-সঞ্চারদ্বারা তাজা রাখা। *Noun.* State of being frozen ; coming or period of frost ; জমাট অবস্থা ; তুষারাগম, তুষারস্থিতিকাল। **Freez'-er**, *n.* **Freez'-ing**, *adj.* Extremely cold ; (*colloq.*) cold or distant as manners ; নিতান্ত শীতল ; (চলিত ভাষায়) অনুরাগশূন্য। **Freez'-ing-ly**, *adv.* **Freezing mixture**—লবণ এবং বরফ বা অন্য পদার্থের মিশ্রণ,—যদ্দ্বারা তরল পদার্থ জমান হয়, শীতজনকমিশ্রণ। **Freezing point**—তাপমানযন্ত্রের যে তাপাঙ্কে জল জমিয়া বরফ হইয়া যায় বা অন্যবিধ তরলপদার্থ জমিয়া যায়। **To freeze one's blood**—To terrify him ; ভয়ে রক্ত জমাট বাঁধান। **To freeze on to**—(*Slang*) To take or keep tight hold of ; (ইতর ভাষায়) দৃঢ় মুষ্টিতে ধরা। **To freeze out**—(*Slang*) To exclude from business, society, etc. by competition, boycotting, etc. ; (ইতর ভাষায়) সমাজচ্যুত করা। **To freeze to death**—To die by frost ; শীতে রক্ত জমাট হইয়া মরা।

freight (frāt), *n.* & *v. t.* 1. The hire of a ship for transport of goods ; charge for this ; মাল চালানের জাহাজ ভাড়া করণ ; মাল জাহাজের ভাড়া। 2. Cargo ; any burden or load ; জাহাজ প্রভৃতিতে বোঝাই মাল ; বোঝা। 3. Transportation of goods by water ; জলপথে মাল প্রেরণ। *Verb t.* 1. To load, as a ship with goods ; জাহাজে মাল বোঝাই করা। 2. To hire or let, as a ship for conveyance of goods or passengers ; মাল বা যাত্রী বহনের জন্য জাহাজ ভাড়া করা বা ভাড়া দেওয়া। **Freight'-age**, *n.* 1. Expense of the carriage of goods ; মালের ভাড়া। 2. Hiring or letting of a ship for freight ; মাল বহনের জন্য জাহাজ ভাড়া করণ, বা ভাড়া প্রদান। 3. Freight ; cargo ; জাহাজ বা মালের ভাড়া ; জাহাজাদিতে বোঝাই মাল। **Freight'-er**, *n.* 1. One who charters and loads a ship ; যে ব্যক্তি জাহাজ ভাড়া করিয়া মালদ্বারা বোঝাই করে। 2. One employed in receiving and forwarding freight ; যে কর্ম্মচারী মালের ভাড়া আদায় এবং প্রেরণ করে। 3. One who consigns goods for carriage inland ; স্বদেশের সীমার ভিতর মালপ্রেরক। 4. A cargo-vessel ; মালজাহাজ।

Frĕnch *adj* & *n.* Belonging to France or its people ; like French people ; ফরাসীদেশীয়, ফরাসী ; ফরাসীগণের মত। *Noun.* 1. The people of France ; ফারাসীজাতি। 2. The language of France ; ফরাসী ভাষা। **French'-ness**, *n.* **French'-y**, *adj.* & *n.* Like or characteristic of French people ; ফরাসী জাতির মত ; ফরাসী জাতি মূলক। (*Noun*) A Frenchman ; ফরাসীস্। **French bean**—মুগ। **French bread** — একপ্রকার বিচিত্র রুটী। **French chalk**—কাপড়ের উপর রেখা টানার জন্য শঙ্কময় অভ্র। **French-grey** — একপ্রকার ধূসর বর্ণ। **French horn**—একপ্রকার সানাই। **French-man**—ফরাসীদেশীয় লোক। **French-roof**—একপ্রকার ছাদ, যাহার পার্শ্বদ্বয় বক্র বা আনত এবং উপরিভাগ সমতল বা প্রায় সমতল থাকে। **French window**—সূক্ষ্মকাচস্তরাচ্ছাদিত দ্বার,—যদ্দ্বারা দ্বার ও বাতায়ন উভয়ের কার্য্য সাধিত হয়। **French-polish**—*n.* & *v. t.* কাঠের আসবাবে লাগাইবার একপ্রকার বার্ণিস। (*Verb t.*) উক্ত প্রকার বার্ণিস দ্বারা বার্ণিস করা। **French-polisher**—যে ব্যক্তি উক্তরূপ

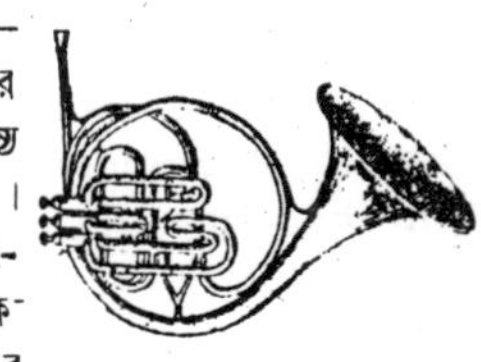

French horn.

বার্ণিস লাগায়। **To take French leave**—To depart without notice or permission; to use anything without permission; না বলিয়া গোপনে প্রস্থান করা; বিনা অনুমতিতে কোন দ্রব্য ব্যবহার করা।

Frĕnch, Frĕnch'-i-fȳ, *v. t.* To make French in character or manners; চালচলন ও স্বভাবে ফরাসীর অনুরূপ করা। **–i-fi-ca'-tion,** *n.*

frē'-nŭm, *n.* Same as FRAENUM which see.

frĕn'-zȳ, *n.* & *v. t.* Mental derangement; delirious rage or fury; temporary insanity; wild folly; মানসিক বিকৃতি; প্রচণ্ড ক্রোধ, উন্মদ; ক্ষণিক উন্মাদ; ভয়ানক নির্ব্বুদ্ধিতা। ***Verb t.*** (Usu. in *p. p.*) To drive to frenzy or madness; উন্মত্ত করা। **Frenzied rage**—উন্মদরোষ।

frē'-quen-cȳ (-kwĕn-), *n.* **1.** Occurrence often repeated; state of being frequent; rapidity, as of pulse etc.; পুনঃ পুনঃ সংঘটিত ঘটনা; পৌনঃপুন্য; দ্রুততা। **2.** (*Phys.*) The number of vibrations etc. in a unit of time; (পদার্থ-বিদ্যা) নির্দ্দিষ্ট সময়ের কম্পন-সংখ্যা।

fre'-quent (-kwĕnt), *adj.* **1.** Numerous; abundant; বহুসংখ্যক; প্রচুর। **2.** Happening or repeated at short intervals; common; rapid, as a pulse etc.; পুনঃ পুনঃ সংঘটনশীল, সচরাচর সংঘটিত, বারংবার আগত; সচরাচর দৃষ্ট, সাধারণ; দ্রুত। **3.** Habitual; constant; as, a *frequent* caller; নিত্য; সতত। **–ly,** *adv.* Often; repeatedly; প্রায়শঃ, সচরাচর; বারংবার, পুনঃপুন।

frē-quent' (-kwĕnt), *v. t.* To visit or attend often or habitually, as a house, meeting, etc.; সর্ব্বদা গতিবিধি কর, নিয়ত গতিবিধি করা, সর্ব্বদা আসা যাওয়া করা। **–er,** *n.* **–quen-ta'-tion,** *n.*

frē-quen'-tă-tive (-kwĕn-), *adj.* & *n.* (*Gram.*) Serving to express the frequent repetition of an action; as, a *frequentative* verb; (ব্যাকরণ) পৌনঃপুন্য জনক, যঙন্ত, বীপ্সাব্যঞ্জক, সমভিহারার্থক (আঃ বঃ)। ***Noun.*** A frequentative verb; পৌনঃপুন্যবাচক ক্রিয়া, যঙন্ত ক্রিয়া।

frĕs'-cō, *n.* & *v. t.* A method of painting on walls the plaster of which is not yet dry; দেওয়ালের চূণবালির আস্তরের উপর চিত্রাঙ্কণ-প্রণালী। ***Verb t.*** To paint in fresco, as a wall, picture or subject; ঐরূপ চিত্রাঙ্কণ করা। **Fresco-painting**—প্রাচীরাদির আস্তরের উপর চিত্রাঙ্কণ, প্রাচীর গাত্রাঙ্কিত চিত্র, আঁট চিত্র।

frĕsh, *adj., adv.* & *n.* **1.** Newly produced, gathered, made; not preserved by salting, pickling etc.; as, *fresh* fruit, meat, etc.; নবজাত, নবনির্ম্মিত, নবরচিত; টাট্‌কা, তাজা। **2.** Not stale or vapid; as, *fresh* fish, fruit etc.; টাট্‌কা, তাজা। **3.** Vigorous; active; as, one is *fresh* in the morning; refreshed; সতেজ; কর্ম্মঠ; স্ফূর্ত্তিযুক্ত। **4.** Not salt; as, *fresh* water (in distinction from sea water); not bitter; drinkable; as, *fresh* water; অলবণাক্ত; মিঠা; পানযোগ্য। **5.** Healthy; youthful; "*Fresh* country ladies"; of a bright colour; not faded; as, a *fresh* complexion, flower or memory; সুস্থ; তরুণ; উজ্জ্বলবর্ণ; অম্লান। **6.** Inexperienced; raw; as, to be *fresh* in society; অনভিজ্ঞ; কাঁচা। **7.** Recent; novel; additional; another; as, to begin a *fresh* chapter: *fresh* news; নব, নূতন; অভিনব; অতিরিক্ত; অপর। **8.** Cool; refreshing; pure; as, *fresh* air or wind; শীতল; স্নিগ্ধ, সরস; নির্ম্মল, বিশুদ্ধ। ***Adv.*** Newly; freshly; as, *fresh* caught: *fresh* coined; নূতনভাবে; নবভাবে।

Fresh'-en, *v. t.* & *i.* **1.** To make fresh; to make less salt, as water; নবীন করা, সতেজ করা অলবণাক্ত করা। **2.** To refresh to revive; পুনরায় সতেজ করা পুনরুজ্জীবিত করা। (*Verb i.*) grow fresh; সতেজ হওয়া, ন হওয়া। **Fresh'-ly,** *adv.* **1.** I cently (only with participial adjs as, *freshly* published or torn; দিন হইল, সম্প্রতি, ইদানীং। **2.** W unabated energy or vigour; অ মিত তেজে বা শক্তিতে, অপ্রতিহততেজে **Fresh'-ness,** *n.* **Fresh-butter**-টাট্‌কা মাখন (অর্থাৎ যাহাতে লবণ মিশ্রি হয় নাই)। **Freshman**—A novice a first-year student in a University; নবপ্রবিষ্ট ব্যক্তি; বিশেষভাবে বিশ্ববিদ্যালয়ের প্রথম বার্ষিক শ্রেণীর ছাত্র। **Fresh news**—নূতন খবর, টাট্‌কা খবর। **Fresh-run**—(Of a salmon) Lately come up from the sea; (স্যামন মৎস্য সম্পর্কে) সাগর হইতে অচিরাগত। **Fresh-water**—*adj.* & *n.* Pertaining to, o living in, water not salt; as, *fresh water* fish, fishing etc.; অলবণাক্ত জলীয় বা জলসম্বন্ধীয়। Accustomed to sail on fresh water only; as, a *freshwater* sailor; কেবলমাত্র নদী, প্রভৃতির অলবণাক্ত জলে জাহাজাদি চালনায় অভিজ্ঞ। **A fresh wind**—A wind of some strength; কতকটা সতেজ বাতাস। **As fresh as paint**—Quite brisk; অতিশয় সতেজ। **To break fresh ground**—To try something u. hackneyed; নূতন কোন বিষয়ে চেষ্টা করা। **To freshen the way**—To increase the speed of a ship; জাহাজের গতিবৃদ্ধি করা।

frĕsh, *n.* **1.** The fresh part of a day, year or life time; as, in the *fresh* of the morning; দিবস, বৎসর বা জীবনের প্রথমভাগ। **2.** A flow or rush of water in a river; a flood; জলপ্রবাহ; নদীর বান।

frĕsh'-ĕr, *n.* (*Slang*) Same as FRESHMAN, under FRESH.

frĕt, *v. t., i.* & *n.* **1.** To wear away by friction; to gnaw; to eat away; to chafe; ঘষিয়া ক্ষয় করা; ক্রমশঃ ক্ষয় করা; খাইয়া ফেলা; ঘষিয়া লুণছাল তোলা। **2.** (*Fig.*) To wear away; to consume; to torment, as the heart etc.: ক্ষয় করা; ধ্বংস করা; জ্বালাতন করা, অসুখী করা, যন্ত্রণা দেওয়া। **3.** To agitate or disturb, as water; বিক্ষোভিত করা। **4.** To make, as a passage etc., by wearing away a substance; কোন কিছু ক্ষয় করিয়া পথ করা। ***Verb i.*** **1.** To distress oneself with regret or discontent অনুশোচনা বা অসন্তুষ্টি দ্বারা পীড়িত করা **2.** (Of a stream etc.) To be agitated; as, a river *frets* over a rock: বিক্ষোভিত হওয়া। ***Noun.*** **1.** Disturbance of mind or temper: vexation: বিক্ষোভ; বিরক্তি। **2.** The agitation of the surface of a fluid by fermentation; তরল পদার্থাদির স্ফোটন বা আন্দোলন। **Fret′-ful,** *adj.* Peevish; irritable; angry; খিট্‌খিটে; কোপন; চটা। **Fret′-ful-ly,** *adv.* **Fret′-ful-ness,** *n.* **Fret′-ty,** *adj.* Fretful; খিট্‌খিটে। **On the fret**—In a state of agitation, irritation or impatience; বিরক্ত, খিট্‌খিটে, অধীর, বিক্ষুব্ধ।

frĕt, *n.* & *v. t.* **1.** (*Arch.*) An ornament consisting of small fillets intersecting each other at

Grecian fret.

right angles; (also Greek or Grecian fret); নকাশী কাজ বিশেষ, যাহাতে ক্ষুদ্র সরল রেখাসমূহ সমকোণ উৎপাদনপূর্ব্বক পরস্পরকে কর্ত্তিত করিয়া থাকে। **2.** One of the cross-bars on the finger-board of a stringed instrument; সেতার, এস্রাজ প্রভৃতি বাদ্যযন্ত্রের ঘাট। ***Verb t.*** **1.** To enrich with carved or embossed patterns; as, to *fret* ceiling; (ছাদের ভিতরের দিক) উদ্গত বা উৎকীর্ণ কারুকার্য্যদ্বারা শোভিত করা। **Fre-ted,** *adj.* **Fret-saw**—ক্রেমে আঁটা অতি সরু করাত,—যদ্দ্বারা কাঠের উপর নানা প্রকার নমুনা কাটা হয়। **Fret-work**—এক প্রকার উদ্গত বা খোদিত কারুকার্য্য।

frī′-ȧ-ble(-bl), *adj.* Apt to crumble; easily reduced to powder; ক্ষয়প্রবণ; সুচূর্ণনীয়, চূর্ণযোগ্য, আশু চূর্ণনীয় (কেণ্ডি), চূর্ণবশ্যক (ঐ)। **—bil′-i-ty, —ble-ness,** *ns.* চূর্ণধর্ম্ম (কেণ্ডি), চূর্ণযোগ্যতা (ঐ)।

frī′-ar (-êr), *n.* A member of certain religious orders, especially the four mendicant orders of Franciscans, Augustines, Dominicans and Carmelites; খৃষ্টীয় সন্ন্যাসী। **—ly,** *adj.* Relating to, or like, friar; খৃষ্টীয় সন্ন্যাসি-সম্পর্কীয় অথবা তদ্বৎ। **—y,** *n.* A convent of friars; খৃষ্টীয় সন্ন্যাসিগণের মঠ। **Austin Friars** or **Augustines**—সেণ্ট অগাষ্টিন্ কর্ত্তৃক প্রবর্ত্তিত খৃষ্টীয় সন্ন্যাসি সম্প্রদায়। **Black Friars**—Same as DOMINICANS which see. **Grey Friars**—Same as FRANCISCANS which see. **White Friars**—Same as CARMELITES which see. **Friar's balsam**—ক্ষত, নালী ঘা, প্রভৃতিতে প্রয়োগের জন্য লোবানের আরক।

frib′-ble (-bl), *v. i.* & *n.* To act frivolously; to trifle; চাপল্য প্রকাশ করা; ছেব্‌লামি করা। ***Noun.*** A trifler; ছেব্‌লা।

fric-an-deau′ (frĕk-ân-dö), *n.* & *v. t.* (*Pl.* -DEAUX, -DEAUZ) A slice of veal larded and stewed; মৃদু সন্তাপে সিদ্ধ চর্ব্বিমাখানো বাছুরের মাংসের কালিয়া। ***Verb t.*** To make into fricandeau; চর্ব্বি মাখানো বাছুরের মাংস মৃদু সন্তাপে সিদ্ধ করত কালিয়া প্রস্তুত করা।

fric-ȧs-see′(-së), *n.* & *v. t.* A dish made of fowls etc. cut into pieces and cooked with sauce; প্রচুর মসলাদি যোগে প্রস্তুত কুক্কুটশশকাদির মাংসের কালিয়া। ***Verb t.*** To make a fricassee of; কুক্কুটশশকাদির মাংসের কালিয়া প্রস্তুত করা।

fric′-tion, *n.* **1.** Rubbing of two bodies; ঘর্ষণ, সংঘর্ষণ, সংঘর্ষ। **2.** (*Mech.*) The resistance which a body meets with from a surface on which it moves; (যন্ত্র-বিজ্ঞান) কোন বস্তু সঞ্চালন কালে ভূমি প্রভৃতির সহিত ঘর্ষণ হেতু যে বাধাপ্রাপ্ত হইয়া থাকে, সংঘটন, সংঘট্ট। **3.** (*Fig.*) A clashing between unlike opinions or temperaments; (লক্ষণায়) সংঘর্ষ, অপ্রীতি, মনকষাকষি। **—al,** *adj.* Relating to, or produced by, friction। সংঘর্ষোৎপন্ন, ঘর্ষণজাত, ঘর্ষণসম্পর্কীয়; **—less,** *adj.* Having no friction; সংঘর্ষণবিহীন। **Frictional electricity**—ঘৃষ্টতাড়িত। **Friction-ball**—ঘর্ষণ হ্রাসার্থ ক্ষুদ্র লৌহ গোলক। **Friction clutch**—ঘর্ষণদ্বারা গতি সঞ্চারের জন্য কৌশল বিশেষ।

Frī′-day (-dā), *n.* The sixth day of the week; শুক্রবার, শুক্রবাসর, ভৃগুবাসর। **Black-Friday**—শুক্রবারে যে সমস্ত দুর্ঘটনা সংঘটিত হইয়াছে তাহাদের সাধারণ নাম। **Good-Friday**—See GOOD.

friend (frĕnd), *n.* & *v. t.* **1.** One attached to another by mutual goodwill and affection; বন্ধু, মিত্র, সখা, বয়স্য। **2.** One not inimical or hostile; an acquaintance or stranger; নিরপেক্ষজন; পরিচিত বা অপরিচিত ব্যক্তি। **3.** A favourer; a patron; as, a *friend* to commerce; অনুগ্রাহক; পৃষ্ঠপোষক, মুরুব্বি; **4.** A Quaker; খৃষ্টীয় সম্প্রদায় বিশেষের সভ্য। **5.** (*Pl.*) Near relations; ঘনিষ্ঠ আত্মীয়, বান্ধব। **6.** A useful thing; as, my shyness was here my best *friend*; আবশ্যক

বস্তু। ***Verb t.*** (*Poet.*) To befriend ; (কবিতায়) বন্ধুতা করা, বন্ধুত্ব স্থাপন করা। **Friend′-less,** *adj.* Destitute of friends ; বন্ধুহীন, অসহায়, অনাশ্রয়, নিরাশ্রয়, অনাথ, নিরালম্ব, অগতিক, অসহায়। **Friend′-less-ness,** *n.* **Friend′-ly,** *adj.* & *n.* **1.** Having disposition of a friend ; acting as a friend ; kind ; মিত্রভাবাপন্ন ; মিত্রবৎ ; সদয়। **2.** Befitting or characteristic of friends ; বন্ধুজনোচিত। **3.** Not hostile ; as, a *friendly* power or state ; মিত্রতাসূত্রে বদ্ধ, মিত্রপক্ষীয়। **4.** Favourable ; propitious ; ready to help ; serviceable ; অনুকূল, সদয় ; প্রসন্ন; সাহায্যদানে প্রস্তুত; কার্য্যকর। **Friend′-ship,** *n.* The state of being friends ; friendly relation or disposition ; favour ; বন্ধুতা, বন্ধুত্ব, বন্ধুভাব, মিত্রতা, সখ্য ; সৌহৃদ্য, সৌহার্দ্দ্য; আনুকূল্য। **Bosom friend**—অন্তরঙ্গ বন্ধু, পরাণবন্ধু (cf. পরাণ বঁধুয়া—চণ্ডীদাস), প্রাণবন্ধু। **Fair weather friend**—Friend in prosperity only; সুসময়ের বন্ধু, সুদিনের বন্ধু। **Friendly action**—(*At law*) An action brought merely to get a point decided ; (আইন) কেবল মাত্র কোন আইনের তর্ক মীমাংসার জন্য যে মোকদ্দমা করা হয়। **Friendly lead**—Among the poorer classes in London, an entertainment to raise funds for a distressed person ; লণ্ডন-নগরীতে দরিদ্রশ্রেণীর মধ্যে আর্ত্ত ব্যক্তির সাহায্যার্থ চাঁদা তোলার জন্য ভোজ। **Friendly-match**—সদ্ভাবসূচক ক্রীড়া, অর্থাৎ যেরূপ ক্রীড়ায় বিজয়ীদিগকে কারুকার্য্যখচিত পাত্রাদি উপহার দেওয়া হয় না। **Friendly Society**—যে সমিতিতে নির্দ্দিষ্ট হারে অর্থ প্রদান করিয়া রোগ, বৈধব্য, বার্দ্ধক্য ইত্যাদিতে সাহায্য পাওয়া যায়, পরস্পরহিতকারিণী সভা। **A friend at or in court**—যে ব্যক্তি রাজদ্বার প্রভৃতিতে প্রভাব থাকা হেতু বিপদ্ বা অভাবের সময় কোন বন্ধুকে সাহায্য করিতে পারে। **A friend in need**—One who befriends in time of adversity ; বিপদের বন্ধু, অসময়ের বন্ধু। **My honourable friend**—মাননীয় বন্ধু [পার্লেমেণ্ট বা ব্যবস্থাপক সভার সভ্যগণ পরস্পরকে এই বাক্যে সম্বর্দ্ধনা করিয়া থাকেন]। **My learned friend**—The address of one lawyer to another ; আমার শিক্ষিত বন্ধু [এই বাক্যে ব্যবহারজীবিগণ পরস্পরকে সম্বোধন করিয়া থাকেন]। **The Society of Friends**—খৃষ্টীয় ধর্ম্মসম্প্রদায় বিশেষ, বান্ধব-সমিতি। **To make friends with**—To be or get on good terms with ; কাহারও সহিত সখ্যভাব স্থাপন করা, কাহারও সহিত বন্ধুত্ব স্থাপন করা।

frieze (frēz), *n.* A coarse woollen cloth with a nap on one side ; একপ্রকার স্থূল পশমী বস্ত্র।

frieze (frēz), *n.* **1.** A member of the entablature between the architrave and the cornice ; কার্ণিসের অব্যবহিত নিম্নবর্ত্তী অট্টালিকার মাথাড়ীর কারুকার্য্যসমন্বিত উর্দ্ধভাগ, কপোত (মঃ উঃ)। **2.** A band of sculptured decoration in a building etc. ; অট্টালিকাদিতে ভাস্কর্য্য-ভূষার বেষ্টনী।

frig′-ate, *n.* (*Hist.*) A ship of war next in size to a ship of the line ; (now loosely) a cruiser; (ঐতিহাসিক) প্রাচীনকালের যুদ্ধ জাহাজ—যাহা পাইলে চলিত ; বর্ত্তমানে *cruiser* জাহাজ ইহার স্থান অধিকার করিয়াছে। **Frigate-bird**—একপ্রকার সামুদ্রিক শিকারী পক্ষিবিশেষ।

fright (frīt), *n.* & *v. t.* **1.** A sudden and violent fear ; terror ; alarm ; ত্রাস, বিত্রাস ; আতঙ্ক ; ঘোর ভয়। **2.** An ugly grotesque looking person ; বিকটাকৃতি ব্যক্তি। ***Verb t.*** (*Poet.*) To terrify ; (কবিতায়) ত্রস্ত করা, আতঙ্কিত করা। **Fright′-en,** *v. t.* **1.** To terrify ; to alarm ; ত্রস্ত করা ; আতঙ্কিত করা। **2.** To drive *away, out of* a place or *into* submission by fr[illegible] ভয়প্রদর্শন করিয়া তাড়াইয়া [illegible] ভয়প্রদর্শনে বশীভূত করা। **Fr[illegible]ful,** *adj.* **1.** Exciting a[illegible]rn dreadful ; shocking ; as, *frightful* chasm ; hed[illegible] ত্রাসজনক, আতঙ্কজনক ; ভীষণ, [illegible]াব ভয়ঙ্কর, ভৈরব, ভীম ; লোমহর্ষণ ; বীভৎ[illegible] বিকট, ঘোর। **2.** (*Slang*) Awful very great ; (ইতরভাষায়) ভয়ানক অতিপ্রকাণ্ড। **Fright′-ful-ly,** *ad[illegible]* **Fright′-ful-ness,** *n.*

frig′-id, *adj.* **1.** Very cold ; a[illegible] a *frigid* climate ; অতি শীতল **2.** Dull and unanimated ; as, *frigid* look ; stiff and formal, a[illegible] a style ; depressing ; প্রীতিশূন্য, উদা[illegible] অনুরাগশূন্য ; কঠোর, নীরস, কাঠখোট্টা অবসাদজনক। **Fri-gid′-i-ty,** *n.* **1.** Coldness ; শৈত্য। **2.** Want [illegible] ardour or animation ; dull[illegible]ess coldness of affection; want of vi[illegible]our ; as, the *frigidity* of old ag[illegible] formality; আগ্রহহীনতা, তেজোহীনতা জড়তা ; অনুরাগশূন্যতা ; উৎসাহহীনতা আচারানুগতত্ব। **–ly,** *adv.* **–ness,** *n.* **Frigid zone**—তুষারমণ্ডল, হিম[illegible] হিমবলয় (সাঃ পঃ)।

frill *v. i., t.* & *n.* (*Photo[illegible].*) T[illegible] wrinkle, as a film ; (আলোকচিত্র কুঞ্চিত হওয়া। ***Verb t.*** To provi[illegible] or decorate with frills ; as, t[illegible] *frill* a cap ; কুঁচি দেওয়া। ***Noun*** **1.** A plaited edging on any artic[illegible] of dress ; a ruffle ; বস্ত্রাদির চুনট[illegible] বেল। **2.** (*Zool.*) A fringe of hair feathers on a bird, animal plant ; পক্ষী, জন্তু বা উদ্ভিদের [illegible] বা পালকরেখা। **3.** (*Pl.*) Affec[illegible]tion ; as, to put on *frill* ; কৃ[illegible] ভাব। **4.** The mesentery an animal ; জন্তুর অন্ত্রবেষ্টের দ্বিভাজ দ্বারা ক্ষুদ্রান্ত্র যথাস্থানে [illegible] থাকে। **5.** (*Photog.*) The wri[illegible]ling of a gelatine film at [illegible] edge of a plate ; (আলোকচি[illegible] আলোকচিত্রের ফলকপ্রান্তে শিরি[illegible]

ছাদনের কুঞ্চন। **Frilled,** *adj.* nished with frills ; বেলদার। **il'-er-y,** *n.* Frills ; বেল, কুঁচি, জ্বলিতদশা (আঃ বঃ) ; বেলদার কিনারা। **Frill'-ing,** *n.* Frilled edging ; f s ; বেলদার কিনারা ; বেল।

ringe (frînj), *n.* & *v. t.* **1.** An ornamental bordering consisting of loose threads ; ঝালর, ফুঁপি, দশি, ছিলা। **2.** A border ; edging ; margin ; প্রান্ত ; হাঁসিয়া, পাড় ; কিনারা। **3.** Front hair cut short and allowed to hang over forehead ; ললাটোপরি লম্বমান কেশগুচ্ছ। **4.** A fringe-like growth of hair or bristles in animals or plants ; জন্তু বা উদ্ভিদের গাত্রের রোম-রেখা, লোমলতাবলী। ***Verb t.*** To adorn the edge of with a fringe ; to serve, as a fringe to ; ঝালরদ্বারা প্রান্তভাগ শোভিত করা ; ঝালরস্বরূপ হওয়া। **Fringed,** *adj.* Furnished with a fringe ; ঝালরযুক্ত। **Fringe'-less,** *adj.* Having no fringe ; ঝালরহীন। **Fring'-ing,** *n.* **Fring'-y,** *adj.* Adorned with, or like, fringes ; ঝালরশোভিত, ঝালরসদৃশ।

frip'-pĕr-ȳ, *n.* & *adj.* **1.** Cheap and tawdry decoration especially in dress ; empty display, as in literary style ; চটকদার সাজ ; বৃথা ভাষার আড়ম্বর। **2.** Trifles ; অকিঞ্চিৎকর বিষয়। ***Adj.*** Trifling ; contemptible ; তুচ্ছ ; ঘৃণার্হ, হেয়।

'-sette (-zĕt), *n.* A cluster (usually artificial) of curls worn on the forehead ; a pad made of combings of natural hair, horse-hair or silk over which women arrange their hair to puff out ; অলক, চূর্ণকুন্তল, ললাটোপরি স্থিত কৃত্রিম কেশগুচ্ছ ; মনুষ্য বা ...র রোম বা রেসমে প্রস্তুত গদি-বিশেষ—...বা স্ত্রীলোকের চুল ফুলান হয়।

'-siăn, *adj.* & *n.* Of, or relating to, Friesland ; ফ্রিজ্‌লেণ্ড দেশসম্পর্কীয়। ***Noun.*** A native of Friesland ; the language of Friesland ; ফ্রিজ্‌ল্যাণ্ডের অধিবাসী ; ফ্রিজ্‌ল্যাণ্ডের ভাষা।

frisk, *v. i.* & *n.* To leap or dance in frolic or gaiety ; লাফালাফি ছুটাছুটি করা, নর্ত্তনকুর্দ্দন করা। ***Noun.*** A frolic ; a little playful leap ; নর্ত্তনকুর্দ্দন ; ক্রীড়াচ্ছলে লম্ফঝম্প। **Frisk'-er,** *n.* **Frisk'-i-ly,** *adv.* **Frisk'-i-ness,** *n.* **Frisk'-y,** *adj.* Inclined to frisk ; Frolicsome ; নৃত্যপর ; ক্রীড়াশীল।

fris'-kĕt, *n.* (*Print.*) An iron frame to keep paper in position while printing ; মুদ্রণ সময় মুদ্রাযন্ত্রের কাগজ ঠিকভাবে রাখার জন্য লৌহময় বেষ্টনী বিশেষ।

frit, *n.* & *v. t.* **1.** The material of which glass is made after it is calcined ; কাচ নির্ম্মাণের উপাদান। **2.** The composition from which soft porcelain is made ; যে মিশ্রিত পদার্থ হইতে কোমল চিনামাটি প্রস্তুত হয়। ***Verb t.*** To make into frit ; to fuse partially ; উক্তরূপ মিশ্র উপাদান প্রস্তুত করা ; আংশিকভাবে দ্রব করা। **Frit-fly**—একপ্রকার গোধূমনাশক কীট।

frith, *n.* Same as FIRTH which see.

frit'-ĭl-lă-rȳ, *n.* **1.** A kind of butterfly ; একপ্রকার প্রজাপতি। **2.** A kind of plant, esp. snakeshead ; একপ্রকার গুল্ম।

frit'-têr, *n.* **1.** A piece of fried batter containing slices of fruit, meat, etc. ; মাংস এবং ফলের টুকরা মিশ্রিত ডিম, দুধ ও আটার লেইয়ের বড়া। **2.** (*Pl.*) Fenks ; তিমি প্রভৃতি মৎস্যের অংশময় অংশ।

frit'-têr, *n.* & *v. t.* A minute subdivision ; (*pl. now rare*) Fragments ; ক্ষুদ্র বিভাগ ; (বহুবচন—বর্তমানে অপ্রচলিত) খণ্ড, টুকরা। ***Verb t.*** To cut or divide into small pieces ; to scatter ; to waste ; as, to *fritter* away time or energy ; কুচি কুচি করিয়া কাটা, ক্ষুদ্র ক্ষুদ্র অংশে বিভাগ করা ; ছড়ান ; অপব্যয় করা।

friv'-ŏl, *v. i.* & *t.* To act frivolously ; to trifle ; ছেব্‌লামি করা, ছেলেমি করা ; তুচ্ছতাচ্ছিল্য করা। ***Verb t.*** To spend foolishly, as money, time etc. ; নির্ব্বোধের মত ব্যয় করা।

friv'-ŏ-lous (-lŭs), *adj.* **1.** Of little importance ; futile ; slight ; তুচ্ছ, অকিঞ্চিৎকর ; অসার ; নগণ্য। **2.** Given to trifling ; silly ; not serious ; ছেবলা, ক্ষুদ্রচিত্ত, লঘুচিত্ত ; বেকুব ; চপল। **Fri-vol'-i-ty,** *n.* Act or habit of trifling ; levity ; ছেবলামি ; চাপল্য, লঘুতা। **–ly,** *adv.* **–ness,** *n.*

friz(z), *v. t.* & *n.* **1.** To crisp ; to curl, as hair etc. ; কোঁকড়ান ; (কেশ) কুঞ্চিত করা। **2.** To form into little knobs etc. like the nap of cloth ; কাপড় প্রভৃতির উপরে ফুঁপি বা এঁশোর মত করা। **3.** To dress with pumice or blunt knife etc. ; as, to *friz* leather etc. ; প্রস্তর কিম্বা ভোঁতা ছুরী দ্বারা মসৃণ করা। ***Noun.*** A frizzed hair ; curled state ; a row of crisp curls ; কোঁকড়ান চুল ; কুঞ্চিতাবস্থা ; কুঞ্চিত কেশ রেখা।

frizz, *v. i.* To produce a spluttering noise in frying ; চড় চড় শব্দে ভাজা হওয়া।

friz'-zle (-zl), *v. t., i.* & *n.* To curl or crisp, as hair, (often with *up*) ; কেশ কুঞ্চিত করা, কোঁকড়ান, কুঞ্চিত হওয়া। ***Noun.*** A curl ; a lock of hair crisped ; অলক ; কুঞ্চিত কেশদাম, চূর্ণ কুন্তল। **–zly,** *adj.* Curled or crisped ; কুঞ্চিত, কোঁকড়ান।

friz'-zle (-zl), *v. i.* & *t.* To fry, toast or boil with a sputtering noise ; চড় চড় শব্দে ভাজা, সিদ্ধ করা বা হওয়া।

frŏ, *adv.* Away ; from ; back or backwards ; দূরে ; হইতে ; পশ্চাৎদিকে। **To and fro**—(*i. e.*) *To and from*, backwards and forwards এদিকওদিক, ইতস্ততঃ, এখানে সেখানে।

frock (frŏk), *n.* & *v. t.* **1.** A loose outer garment for men; পুরুষাদিগের ঢিলা জামা। **2.** A gown worn by females and children; স্ত্রীলোকদিগের এবং শিশুদিগের ঢিলা জামা। **3.** A monk's gown with loose sleeves; (*fig.*) a priestly character; সন্ন্যাসিদিগের আলখেল্লা; (লক্ষণায়) যাজকীয় ভাব। **4.** A sailor's woollen jersey; নাবিকদিগের পশমী কামিজ। **5.** A military coat like frockcoat; একপ্রকার সামরিক কোর্ত্তা। ***Verb t.*** To invest with priestly office; যাজকীয় পদে প্রতিষ্ঠিত করা। **Frock coat**—এক প্রকার কোর্ত্তা—যাহার সম্মুখ ও পশ্চাদ্‌ভাগ সমান লম্বা।

frŏg, *n.* **1.** A tailless amphibious animal remarkable for its rapid swimming and leaping;

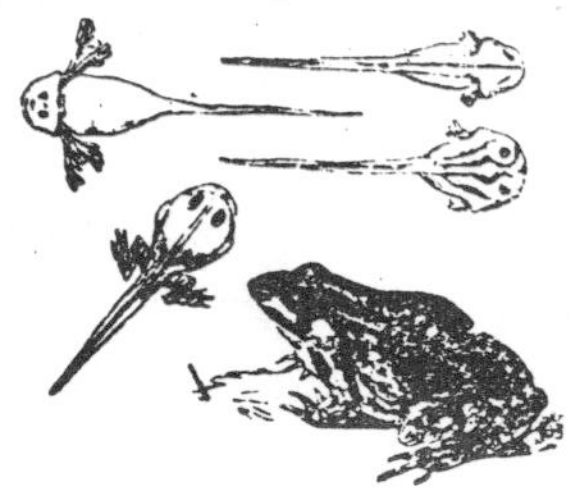

Frog and its metamorphosis.

ভেক, ব্যাঙ্গ, মণ্ডুক, দর্দ্দুর, বর্ষাভু, প্লব, বৃষ্টিভূ। **2.** An elastic horny substance in the middle of the sole of a horse's foot; অশ্বের পদতলের মধ্যভাগের স্থিতিস্থাপক শৃঙ্গময় পদার্থ। **3.** An ornamental fastening or tasselled button for frock or vestment; সামরিক কোর্ত্তার জন্য ঝাপ্পাওয়ালা বোতাম এবং উহা আটকাইবার জন্য ঘুণ্টিঘরা। **4.** The loop attached to a belt for supporting a sword, bayonet, etc.; সঙ্গীন, তরবারী প্রভৃতি আবদ্ধ করার জন্য পেটির মধ্যে পুঁটে-ঘরা-বিশেষ। **5.** (*Railways*) A grooved piece of iron placed at the junction of rails where one track crosses another; (রেলওয়ে) লৌহবর্ত্ম দ্বয়ের সংযোগস্থলে স্থাপিত খাঁজ কাটা লৌহ খণ্ড। **6.** (*Contempt.*) A Frenchman; (অবজ্ঞাচ্ছলে) ফরাসী [ফরাসীগণ ভেক আহার করে বলিয়া এই নাম।] **Frogged,** *adj.* **Frog'gy,** *n.* & *adj.* (*Slang—contempt.*) A Frenchman; (ইতরভাষায়) ব্যাঙ্গু (ফরাসীদিগের অবজ্ঞাসূচক নাম)। (*Adj.*) Abounding in frogs or froglike; মণ্ডূকবহুল, মণ্ডূকবৎ। **Frog-eater**—মণ্ডূকভুক্; (অবজ্ঞাচ্ছলে) ফরাসী। **Frog-hopper**—ফড়িঙ্-বিশেষ।

Frog-hopper.

Frog's-march or **frog-march**—চারিজনে উপুড় করিয়া হাত পা ধরিয়া বন্দীকে লইয়া চলন।

frŏl'-ic, *adj., v. i.* & *n.* (*adj. Archaic*) Merry; dancing; frisky; উৎফুল্ল; নর্ত্তনপর; লম্ফঝম্পকারী। ***Verb i.*** To play merry pranks; to gambol; ফষ্টিনষ্টি করা, রঙ্গরস করা; ক্রীড়াকৌতুক করা। ***Noun.*** **1.** A prank; ক্রীড়াকৌতুক, ফষ্টিনষ্টি, রঙ্গরস। **2.** Merry-making; a gay party; আমোদপ্রমোদ; আমোদপ্রমোদকারী ব্যক্তির দল। **—some,** *adj.* Full of gaiety and mirth; given to prank; কৌতুকপ্রিয়; রঙ্গপ্রিয়। **—some-ly,** *adv.* **—some-ness,** *n.*

frŏm, *prep.* **1.** It generally denotes source, distance, absence, departure, etc.; সাধারণতঃ ইহাতে উৎপত্তি, দূরত্ব, অনুপস্থিতি, প্রস্থান, ইত্যাদি বুঝায়। **2.** Out of; as, *from* a source; হইতে। **3.** Since; as, *from* last mouth; অবধি। **4.** By reason of; বশতঃ, কারণ, হেতু, নিমিত্ত, জন্য, দরুণ। **5.** By the aid of; দ্বারা, সাহায্যে। [*From* sometimes governs an adverb, preposition or adverbial or prepositional phrases; as, *from* above: *from* of old: *from* under the spectacles: *from* out the bed (meaning *out from the bed*)]. **From a child From a boy**—From childhood; বাল্যাবধি, আশৈশব। **From age to age**—যুগে যুগে। **From among**—Out of; হইতে **From birth**—আজন্ম, জন্মাবধি। **From day to day**—Daily; প্রতিদিন, প্রত্যহ। **From head to foot**—আপাদমস্তক, সর্ব্বাঙ্গ। **From his point of view**—As he sees things; তিনি যে ভাবে দেখেন। **From home**—Away; out; দূরে; বাহিরে। **From pillar to post**—From one refuge to another; harassed; এক আশ্রয়স্থান হইতে অন্যত্র তাড়িত; উৎপীড়িত। **From saving comes having**—Wealth comes from economy: মিতব্যয়িতা হইতে অর্থ সঞ্চয় হয়। **From the bottom of one's heart**—Sincerely; হৃদয়ের অন্তঃস্থল হইতে, অন্তরের অন্তরতম প্রদেশ হইতে। **From time immerorial**—From a very ancient time which cannot be remembered; স্মরণাতীত কাল হইতে। **From time to time**—Occasionally; মধ্যে মধ্যে, সময় সময়, কখন কখন। **From title to colophon**—Throughout the book; পুস্তকের আদ্যন্ত, বহির আগাগোড়া। **Repeated from mouth to mouth**—মুখে মুখে প্রচারিত।

frŏnd, *n.* **1.** (*Bot.*) A combined leaf and stem; (উদ্ভিদ্-বিদ্যা) সবৃন্ত পত্র, জন্ম-পত্র, জনন-পত্র (সাঃ পঃ) (যেমন তাল প্রভৃতি বৃক্ষের)। **2.** (*Zool.*) A leaf-like expansion in some animal organisms; (প্রাণি-বিদ্যা) কোন কোন জন্তুর দেহযন্ত্রের পত্রাকার বিস্তার। **Frond'-age,** *n.* Fronds collectively; পত্ররাজি। **Frondose',** *adj.* Bearing fronds; like a frond; সবৃন্তপত্রধারী; সবৃন্ত পত্রবৎ।

Fronde (frŏnd), *n.* **1.** A political party in France opposed to the Court, in the minority of Louis XIV; চতুর্দ্দশ লুই নাবালক থাকার

কালে ফরাসীদেশের রাজনীতিক দল-বিশেষ। 2. A malcontent party; stern political opposition; অসন্তুষ্ট রাজনীতিক দল; কঠোর রাজনীতিক প্রতিরোধ।

front (frŭnt), *n., adj., v. i. & t.* **1.** The forehead (now *usu. in poetry*); the whole face; (সাধারণতঃ কবিতায়) কপাল, ললাট, ভাল; মুখমণ্ডল। **2.** Boldness; impudence; as, a bold *front*; সাহসিকতা; নির্লজ্জতা, ধৃষ্টতা। **3.** Any face of the building, especially that of the main entrance; as, the *front* of a house; গৃহাদির সম্মুখভাগ, বিশেষ ভাবে মুখ্য দ্বার বা প্রধান প্রবেশদ্বারের সম্মুখভাগ। **4.** The foremost line of an army; সৈন্যদলের সর্ব্বাগ্রবর্ত্তী শ্রেণী। **5.** The most advanced portion of the field of active operation; the scene of active fighting; যুদ্ধক্ষেত্রের সর্ব্বাগ্রবর্ত্তী অংশ; যুদ্ধক্ষেত্র, রণক্ষেত্র। **6.** The direction in which a formed line of troops faces; সৈন্যশ্রেণীর সম্মুখদিক। **7.** The foremost part of a thing, (opposed to back, rear etc.); সর্ব্বাগ্রবর্ত্তী অংশ। **8.** A band of false hair worn over women's forehead; স্ত্রীলোকের ললাটের উপর পরিহিত কৃত্রিম কেশ। **9.** Forward position; as, in *front* of; সম্মুখ। **10.** The breast of a shirt; কামিজের আল্‌গা বুক। ***Adj.*** Of, or relating to, the front or forward part; foremost; as, a *front* view; সম্মুখভাগ-সম্বন্ধীয়; সর্ব্বাগ্রগণ্য। ***Verb i.*** **1.** To face, (with *to, towards, upon, on*); তাকান বা মুখ ফিরান। **2.** *(Mil.)* To turn to the front, (usu. as a word of command); (সামরিক-শাস্ত্র) সম্মুখদিকে ফিরা। ***Verb t.*** **1.** To oppose directly; to confront; সাক্ষাৎভাবে প্রতিরোধ করা; সম্মুখীন হওয়া। **2.** To face towards; as, the house *fronts* the street; অভিমুখীন হওয়া। **3.** To stand opposite to; as, his house *fronts* the church; বিপরীতদিকে অবস্থান করা। **4.** To adorn in front; to furnish with a front; as, to *front* a house with marble; সম্মুখভাগ মণ্ডিত করা; সম্মুখভাগসমন্বিত করা। **5.** *(Mil)* To turn to the front; (সামরিক-শাস্ত্র) সম্মুখদিকে ফিরা। **Front-age,** *n.* **1.** The front of a building; extent of front land abutting on a road, river etc.; অট্টালিকার সম্মুখভাগ; পথ, নদী প্রভৃতি উপর অবলম্বিত সম্মুখভূমির পরিসর বা বিস্তার। **2.** Fronting or facing a certain way; exposure; অভিমুখীনতা; অনাবৃতত্ব। **3.** Ground occupied by troops in camp or on parade; শিবিরস্থিত বা কুচকাওয়াজে নিযুক্ত সৈন্যগণের অধিকৃত ভূমি। **Fron'-tal,** *adj. & n.* Relating to, or on, the front part; as, a *frontal* attack; of, or relating to, the forehead; as, a *frontal* bone; সম্মুখভাগসম্পর্কীয়, সম্মুখভাগস্থ; ললাটস্থ, ললাটসম্পর্কীয়। *(Noun)* **1.** The facade of a building; অট্টালিকার সম্মুখভাগ, হর্ম্ম্য-মুখ। **2.** A covering for the front of an altar; বেদীর সম্মুখভাগের আচ্ছাদন। **Front'-less,** *adj.* **1.** Void of shame or modesty *(rare)*; নির্লজ্জ, বেহায়া (ক্বচিদ্ ব্যবহৃত)। **2.** Without front; সম্মুখভাগহীন। **Front bench**—পার্লেমেণ্ট মহাসভার গৃহে মন্ত্রী এবং ভূতপূর্ব্ব মন্ত্রীদিগের উপবেশনের জন্য সম্মুখবর্ত্তী দীর্ঘ আসন। **Front door**—বাটীর প্রধান দরজা, প্রদ্বার (মঃ ভাঃ), সদর দরজা। **Fronts-man**—দোকানের সম্মুখের তলপত্তনে স্থিত পণ্যবিক্রেতা। **Frontward(s)** — *adj. & adv.* সম্মুখের দিক বা দিকে। *(Adv.)* সম্মুখভাগে। **Front to front**—Face to face; সাম্‌নাসাম্‌নি। **Head and front**—Chief part or item; প্রধান অংশ, প্রধান দফা। **In front of**—Before; confronting; in advance of; অগ্রে, সম্মুখে; সামনাসামনি; অগ্রভাগে। **To come to the front**—To become conspicuous; to become prominent; to rise to a chief place; সুপ্রসিদ্ধ হওয়া; অগ্রগণ্য হওয়া; পুরোবর্ত্তী হওয়া। **To go to the front**—To join troops on a campaign; রণক্ষেত্রে সৈন্যগণের সহিত যুদ্ধার্থ যোগদান করা। **To have the front**—To be impudent enough (to do etc.); ততটা ধৃষ্ট হওয়া; **To present** or **show a bold front**—To show impudence; ধৃষ্টতা প্রদর্শন করা। **Two pair front**—A second floor room in front; দ্বিতলের সম্মুখভাগে স্থিত কক্ষ।

frŏn'-tier (-tër), *n. & adj.* That part of a country which fronts another country; the border of a country; সীমান্ত প্রদেশ; দেশের সীমা। ***Adj.*** **1.** On the frontier; as, a *frontier* town; সীমান্তস্থিত; **2.** Of, or relating to, a frontier; সীমান্ত সম্বন্ধীয়।

frŏn-ti-gnac' (-tin-yăk), *n.* A muscat wine; মুস্কট নগরীতে প্রস্তুত মদ্য-বিশেষ।

frŏn'-tis-piece (-pēs), *n. & v. t.* **1.** The principal part of a building; a decorated entrance; a pediment over the door; অট্টালিকার সম্মুখদেশ; কারুকার্য্য মণ্ডিত প্রবেশদ্বার; দ্বারোপরিস্থ ত্রিকোণাকার ভূষা। **2.** An illustration facing the title-page of a book or of its divisions; পুস্তকের প্রথম পৃষ্ঠার চিত্র, মুখপাতের ছবি, পুরশ্চিত্র (প্রবাসী ১৩২১), গ্রন্থাগ্রবর্ত্তিচিত্র (কেভি), মুখপত্র। **3.** *(Slang*—esp. in boxing) Face; (ইতর ভাষায়) মুখ। ***Verb t.*** To supply with a frontispiece; পুরশ্চিত্র-সমন্বিত করা।

front'-lĕt (frŭnt-), *n.* **1.** A band worn on the forehead; ললাট-বন্ধনী। **2.** An altar frontal; বেদী; অট্টালিকার সম্মুখভাগ। **3.** The forehead of animal জন্তুর

ললাটদেশ। 4. A phylactory; তাবিজ, মাদুলী।

frŏn-tŏn′, *n.* A pediment; দ্বার, বাতায়ন, প্রভৃতির উপরিভাগস্থ ত্রিকোণাকৃতি সৌধভূষাবিশেষ।

frōre, *adj.* (*Poet.*) Frozen; frosty; (কবিতায়) শীতে জমাট-বাঁধা; তুষারময়।

frŏst, *n.* & *v. t.* **1.** The act of freezing; জমাট বাঁধন। **2.** Temperature below freezing point; frozen state; সংহনন বিন্দুর নিম্নবর্ত্তী তাপাঙ্ক; জমাট অবস্থা। **3.** Frozen dew or vapour; কঠিনীভূত নীহার বা বাষ্প, তুষার, তুহিন। **4.** Influence that chills or makes grey etc.; শৈত্যজনক প্রভাব, শুভ্রতাজনক প্রভাব। **5.** (*Slang*) Failure; (ইতর ভাষায়) বিফলতা। ***Verb t.*** **1.** To injure by frost, as plants etc.; তুষারদ্বারা নষ্ট করা। **2.** To cover with rime or as with rime; to produce a surface like frost on, as glass, metal etc.; ঘনীভূত নীহার বা তদ্বৎ কোন কিছু দ্বারা, আচ্ছাদিত করা; কাচ, ধাতু প্রভৃতির উপরিভাগ তুষারবৎ করা। **3.** To sharpen the points of a horse's shoe that it may not slip on ice; বরফের উপর পদস্খলন নিবারণার্থ অশ্বের নালের কাঁটাসমূহ সুতীক্ষ্ণ করা। **4.** To turn white, as hair; শ্বেতবর্ণ ধারণ করা। **Frost′-i-ly**, *adv.* **Frost′-i-ness**, *n.* **Frost′-less**, *adj.* Free from frost; তুষারবিহীন। **Frost′-y**, *adj.* **1.** Cold; freezing; শীতল; জমাটকারী। **2.** Covered with frost; তুষারাচ্ছাদিত। **3.** Chill in affection; অনুরাগবিহীন, অনুরাগশূন্য, প্রীতিবিহীন। **4.** Hoary; তুষারধবল। **Frost-bite** — The freezing of some part of a body by exposure to cold; তুষারজনিত অবসাদ। **Frost bitten**—Affected with frost bite; তুষার-ক্ষত, তুষার-ক্লিষ্ট, হিমগ্রস্ত (কেভি), হিমদগ্ধ (ঐ)। **Frost bound**—Confined by frost; হিমবদ্ধ, তুষারবদ্ধ। **Frost work**—Tracery made by frost on glass etc.; তুষার দ্বারা কাচপ্রভৃতির উপর রচিত বিচিত্র কারুকার্য্য।

frŏst′-ing, *n.* A composition of sugar with beaten egg, used to cover cake etc; পিষ্টকাদি আচ্ছাদনের জন্য ফেটান ডিম ও চিনি দ্বারা প্রস্তুত তুষারকণাবৎ দ্রব্য।

frŏth, *n.*, *v. i.* & *t.* **1.** A collection of bubbles caused by agitation etc.; ফেন, ফেনা, গাজলা, মণ্ড। **2.** Scum; গাদ। **3.** Any empty show in speech; worthless matter; বৃথা বাগাড়ম্বর, ফেনিল ভাষা প্রয়োগ; অসার জিনিষ। ***Verb i.*** To foam; to emit or gather froth; ফেনায়িত হওয়া, ফেনিল হওয়া, ফেনাইয়া উঠা; ফেন নির্গত করা, ফেন নিঃসৃত হওয়া, ফেন সঞ্চিত হওয়া। ***Verb t.*** **1.** To cause to foam; ফেনা উঠান, ফেনিল করা, সফেন করা, ফেনায়িত করা। **2.** To cover with froth; ফেনাবৃত করা। **Froth′-i-ly**, *adv.* **Froth′-i-ness**, *n.* **Froth′-less**, *adj.* ফেনবিহীন। **Froth′-y**, *adj.* **1.** Full of foam; foamy; ফেনময়; ফেনিল, সফেন। **2.** Light; empty; unsubstantial; as, a *frothy* speaker; লঘু; শূন্য; অসার।

frou′-frou (frōō-frōō), *n.* A rustling, as of dresses; পোষাক প্রভৃতির খস্‌খস্ শব্দ।

frounce (frowns), *v. t.* (*Archaic*) To form wrinkles in or upon; to plait; to curl, as the hair; (অপ্রঃ) কোঁচকান; চুনট করা; কুঞ্চিত করা।

frow, *n.* A Dutch or German woman; ওলন্দাজ বা জর্ম্মণ নারী।

frow (frō), *n.* A cleaving tool with handle at right angles to the blade; পরশু, কুঠার।

frō′-ward (-wẽrd), *adj.* (*Archaic*) Perverse; refractory; (অপ্রঃ) একগুঁয়ে, ঠেঁটা; বে-আড়া। **—ly**, *adv.* **—ness**, *n.*

frown, *v. i.*, *t.* & *n.* **1.** To knit the brows in displeasure, sternness etc; to put on a grim or surly look; ভ্রূকুটি করা, ভ্রূকুঞ্চিত করা, ভ্রূভঙ্গী করা, রোষকটাক্ষপাত করা; চোক পাকান, চোক রাঙান, ভ্রূকুটি কুটিল-দৃষ্টি সম্পন্ন হওয়া। **2.** To manifest disapprobation; বিরাগ প্রদর্শন করা। ***Verb t.*** To put down or repel with a frown; as, to *frown down* an interrupter; to manifest as defiance with a frown; চোক পাকাইয়া দাবাইয়া দেওয়া; ভ্রূকুটি প্রদর্শন দ্বারা অগ্রাহ্য করা। ***Noun.*** **1.** A wrinkling of the face in displeasure; a scowl; ভ্রূকুটী, ভ্রূভঙ্গী, ভ্রূকুটীভঙ্গ, (কেভি), ভ্রূভঙ্গ; চোকপাকানি, চোকরাঙ্গানি। **2.** A look expressing anger, severity, disapproval or deep thought; রোষদৃষ্টি, বিরাগব্যঞ্জক-দৃষ্টি, গভীর চিন্তাব্যঞ্জক দৃষ্টি। **Frown′-ing-ly**, *adv.* **To frown at** or **on a person**—To look sternly at a person; ভ্রূকুটিকুটিল দৃষ্টিক্ষেপ করা, রোষকটাক্ষপাত করা।

frowst, *n.* & *v. i.* Fusty heat in a room; কোন কোঠার ভাপ্‌সা তাপ ***Verb i.*** To enjoy it; ঐরূপ তাপ উপভোগ করা। **Frowst′-y**, *adj.*

frow′-zȳ, *adj.* Offensive to the smell; nasty; slovenly; unkempt; দুর্গন্ধময়; ছেঁতলা-ধরা; নোঙ্‌রা উস্কাখুস্কা।

frōze, *p. t.* Of FREEZE. **Fro′-zen**, *p. p.* Congealed with cold শীতে জমাট-বাঁধা, হিমস্তব্ধ (কেভি), হিমস্তম্ভিত (ঐ), হিমগ্রস্ত (ঐ)।

frŭc-tif′-ẽr-ous (-ŭs), *adj.* Bearing fruit; ফলপ্রসূ, ফলোৎপাদক, ফলবান্ (কেভি), ফলদ (ঐ)।

frŭc′-ti-fȳ, *v. t.* & *i.* To make fruitful; to fertilize; ফলবন্ত করা; উর্ব্বর করা। ***Verb i.*** To bear fruit; ফলপ্রসূ হওয়া, ফলবান হওয়া। **—fi-ca′-tion**, *n.* **1.** (*Bot.*) Act of fructifying; (উদ্ভিদ্ বিদ্যা) ফলোৎপাদন, ফলপ্রসব। **2.** The reproductive organs of a plant esp. of ferns and mosses; পর্ণাঙ্গ, শৈবাল প্রভৃতির পুনরুৎপত্তিজনক অংশ।

frŭc-tōse′, *n.* Fruit-sugar ; ফলের চিনি।

frŭc′-tŭ-ous (-ŭs), *adj.* Fruitful ; producing fruits ; profitable ; ফলপূর্ণ ; ফলপ্রসূ ; ফলদায়ক।

fru′-găl (frô-), *adj.* **1.** Economical in the use of resources ; thrifty ; sparing ; হিসাবী ; স্বল্পব্যয়ী, মিতব্যয়ী ; পরিমিতব্যয়ী। **2.** Sparingly supplied or used ; of small cost ; পরিমিত ভাবে প্রদত্ত ও ব্যবহৃত ; অল্প-মূল্য। **–gal′-i-ty,** *n.* The quality of being frugal ; thrift ; মিতব্যয়িতা, পরিমিতব্যয়িতা ; মিতব্যয়। **–ly,** *adv.*

fru-gif′-er-ous (frô-jĭf-ĕr-ŭs), *adj.* Producing fruit or corn ; ফলপ্রসূ, শস্যপ্রসূ।

fru-giv′-o-rous (frô-jĭv-ŏr-ŭs), *adj.* Feeding on fruits, corn, etc. ; ফলমূলভোজী, শস্যাহারী।

fruit (frôt), *n., v. i.* & *t.* **1.** (*Usu. pl.*) Vegetables fit for food ; as, *fruits* of the earth ; ফলমূল। **2.** The produce of a plant or tree ; ফল। **3.** (*Bible*) Offspring ; as, *fruits* of the body, loins, womb etc. ; (বাইবেল) সন্তানসন্ততি। **4.** A vegetable seed as a means of reproduction ; বীজ। **5.** Product ; consequence ; as, the *fruits* of labour ; profit or advantage ; ফল ; পরিণাম ; লাভ, সুবিধা। ***Verb i.*** To bear fruit ; ফলপ্রসূ হওয়া, ফল ধরা। ***Verb t.*** To cause to bear fruit ; ফলপ্রসূ করা, ফল ধরান। **Fruit′-age,** *n.* **1.** Fruits collectively ; ফলসমূহ। **2.** The state or process of bearing fruit ; ফলশালিতা, ফলবত্তা। **3.** Result of any action ; কর্ম্মফল। **Fruit′-er,** *n.* **1.** A ship for carrying fruit ; ফলবাহী অর্ণবপোত। **2.** A tree that bears fruits ; as, a sure *fruiter* ; ফলতরু। **3.** A fruit grower ; ফলোৎপাদক। **Fruit′-er-er,** *n.* One who deals in fruits ; ফলব্যবসায়ী, ফলবিক্রয়ী। **Fruit′-er-y,** *n.* Repository for fruits ; ফলালয়, ফলাগার। **Fruit′-ful,** *adj.* Full of fruits ; bearing fruits or results ; causing fertility ; fertile ; prolific, as marriage etc. ; beneficial ; ফলপূর্ণ ; ফলপ্রসূ, ফলবান (কেঙি), সফল (ঐ), ফলিত (ঐ), ফলপ্রদ (ঐ), বহুফল (ঐ), ফলদায়ক, অমোঘ (ঐ) ; উর্ব্বরতাজনক ; উর্ব্বর ; প্রসবশীল (কেঙি), বহুপ্রসব (ঐ), গর্ভধারণশীল (ঐ) ; হিতকর। **Fruit′-ful-ly,** *adv.* **Fruit′-ful-ness,** *n.* **Fruit′-less,** *adj.* **1.** Not bearing fruit ; barren ; ফলহীন, নিষ্ফল, অফলদায়ক ; বন্ধ্যা। **2.** Not profitable or beneficial ; useless ; vain ; অলাভজনক, অহিতকর ; অপ্রয়োজনীয় ; নিরর্থক, নিষ্ফল। **Fruit′-less-ly,** *adv.* **Fruit′-less-ness,** *n.* **Fruit′-y,** *adj.* Of, or relating to, fruits ; having the taste of the grape, as a wine ; ফলসম্পর্কীয় ; আঙ্গুরের আস্বাদবিশিষ্ট, দ্রাক্ষাস্বাদ। **Fruit cake**—কিস্‌মিস্ জাতীয় ফলবিশেষ দ্বারা পরিপূরিত পিষ্টক। **Fruit-clipper**—দ্রুতগামী ফলবাহী অর্ণবপোত। **Fruit knife**—রৌপ্যাদি ধাতুর ফলকবিশিষ্ট ফল-কর্ত্তরিকা। **Fruit piece**—ফলচিত্র। **Fruit show**—ফলপ্রদর্শনী। **Fruit sugar** — ফলজশর্করা, ফলের চিনি। **Fruit tree** — ফলতরু। **Small fruits**—কিস্‌মিস্ প্রভৃতি ক্ষুদ্র ফল। **To bear fruits**—See BEAR. **To reap fruit**—(স্বকার্য্যের) ফলভোগ করা। **To reap the fruits of**—To take consequences of one's action ; স্বকার্য্যের ফল ভোগ করা।

fru-i′-tion (frô-), *n.* Enjoyment, use or possession of things desired ; realization of hopes etc. ; ভোগ, সম্ভোগ ; চরিতার্থতা, সফলতা, সিদ্ধি।

fru′-mĕn-tȳ (frô-), **fŭr′-mē-tȳ,** *ns.* Food made of wheat boiled in milk and seasoned with cinnamon, sugar etc. ; শর্করাদি মিশ্রিত এবং দারুচিনি দ্বারা বাসিত দুগ্ধে পক্ব গোধূম।

frŭmp, *n.* A cross-tempered old-fashioned female ; রুক্ষ-স্বভাবা সেকেলে বুড়ী। **Frump′-ish, Frump′-y,** *adjs.*

frŭsh, *n.* The frog of a hore's foot ; অশ্বের পদতলের স্থিতিস্থাপক শৃঙ্গময় পদার্থ।

frŭs′-trāte, *v. t.* & *adj.* **1.** To balk ; ব্যর্থ করা, বিফল করা, পণ্ড করা। **2.** To baffle ; to make vain ; পরাহত করা, পণ্ড করা ; ব্যর্থ করা। ***Adj.*** (*Archaic*) Baffled ; defeated ; (অপ্রঃ) বিফলীকৃত ; পরাহত। **–tra′-tion,** *n.* The act of frustrating ; disappointment ; defeat ; বিফলীকরণ ; নৈরাশ্য ; পরাজয়।

frŭs′-tŭm, *n.* (*pl.* -TA, -TUMS) (*Geom.*) The part of a cone which remains when the top is cut off by a plane parallel to the base ; (জ্যামিতি) ছিন্নাগ্র-মোচাকার ঘনক্ষেত্র।

fru-tĕs′-cĕnt (frô-), *adj.* Growing or becoming like a shrub ; shrubby ; গুল্মায়মান ; গুল্মময়।

fru′-tĕx (frô-), *n.* (*Bot.*) Shrub ; (উদ্ভিদ্-বিদ্যা) গুল্ম।

fru′-ti-cōse (frô-), *adj.* (*Bot.*) **1.** Shrublike ; গুল্মাকার। **2.** (Of minerals etc.) Looking like a shrub ; (খনিজ-পদার্থ-সম্পর্কে) গুল্মবৎ।

frȳ, *v. t., i.* & *n.* To cook with oil or fat in a pan over the fire ; as, to *fry* fish ; ভর্জ্জিত করা, ভাজা। ***Verb i.*** To cook food with oi in a pan ; ভাজা। ***Noun.*** **1.** Anything fried ; ভাজাপোড়া। **Fried-meat**—ভাজা মাংস। Internal parts of an animal usually eaten fried ; জন্তুদেহের অভ্যন্তরের যে অংশসমূহ সাধারণতঃ ভাজিয়া খাওয়া হয়। **Frying-pan**—ভাজিবার পাত্র, তাওয়া, চাটু, তপ্তক। **Other fish to fry**—See under FISH. **Out of the frying pan into the fire**—From bad to worse ; কটাহ হইতে জ্বলন্ত অনলে, এক বিপদ্ হইতে অধিকতর বিপদে, মন্দ হইতে মন্দ অবস্থায়, ধোঁয়ার হাত এড়াইতে গিয়া আগুনে পুড়িয়া মরা।

frȳ, *n.* **1.** A swarm of fishes just spawned ; the young of other creatures, *e. g.* bees, frogs, etc. ; মাছের পোনা ; মৌমাছি, ভেক, প্রভৃতির ঝাঁক বা পাল। **2.** The young of salmon in the second year ; দুই বৎসরের স্যামন মৎস্য। **Small fry**—Young or insignificant beings ; children etc. ; নগণ্য লোক, চুণোপুঁটি; কচিশিশু।

frȳ'-er, frī-ĕr, *ns.* A vessel for frying ; তপ্তক, তাওয়া, চাটু।

fŭb'-sy (-zĭ), *adj.* Plump ; fat ; মোটাসোটা, গোলগাল ; মোটা, হৃষ্টপুষ্ট।

fuch'-si-a (fū-shĭ-ă, fôk-sĭ-ă), *n.* A kind of drooping flowering shrub : একপ্রকার নমনশীল পুষ্পগুল্ম।

fuch'-sīne (fôk-), *n.* A dye-stuff consisting of salts of rosaniline etc. ; একপ্রকার রঞ্জক-পদার্থ।

fū'-cŭs, *n.* (*Pl.* -CI) A genus of sea-weed ; একপ্রকার সমুদ্রজ শৈবাল। **Fu'-coid**, *adj.*

fŭd'-dle (-dl), *v. i., t.* & *n.* To tipple ; to booze ; বার বার একটু একটু মদ্য পান করা; অপরিমিত মদ্য পান করা। ***Verb t.*** To intoxicate ; to muddle ; to confuse ; মাতাল করা ; গোলমাল করা ; হতবুদ্ধি করা। ***Noun.*** A drinking bout ; intoxication ; confusion ; মদের বৈঠক ; মত্ততা ; গোলযোগ।

fudge (fŭj), *n.* & *interj.* Nonsense ; humbug; বাজে কথা ; ধোকা। ***Interj.*** An exclamation of contempt ; nonsense ; ফুস্ ; পাগল আর কি।

fudge (fŭj), *v. t., i.* & *n.* To make up or to devise in a dishonest way ; to patch together or fake *up* ; উপস্থিত কাজ চালাইবার মত বা অসাধু উদ্দেশ্যে কোন জিনিষ জোড়াতাড়া দেওয়া ; পুরাতন খুঁতবিশিষ্ট জিনিষ রঙ্গ পালিস করিয়া আসল বলিয়া চালান। ***Verb i.*** To practise such methods ; অসাধুতা করিয়া কোন জিনিষ জোড়াতোড়া দিয়া চালান। ***Noun.*** A piece of fudging ; পুরাতন বা খুঁত বিশিষ্ট জিনিষ আসল বলিয়া চালানের কাজ।

fū'-ĕl, *n., v. t.* & *i.* **1.** Materials used to produce heat by burning, *e. g.* coal, wood, etc. ; ইন্ধন, জ্বালানি কাঠ, সমিৎ কাঠ। **2.** Anything that serves to increase passion or excitement ; ক্রোধানলে ইন্ধন বা ঘৃতাহুতি। ***Verb t.*** To furnish, as fire with fuel ; আগুনে জ্বালানি কাঠ দেওয়া। ***Verb i.*** To procure fuel ; জ্বালানি কাঠ সংগ্রহ করা। **To add fuel to fire**—To say or do something to increase the anger of a person already angry ; জ্বলন্ত অগ্নিতে ঘৃতাহুতি দেওয়া, ক্রোধানলে ইন্ধন প্রদান করা।

fŭg, *n.* Fustiness of air in a room ; fluff and dust collected in a corner ; কক্ষের বাতাসের দুর্গন্ধময়ত্ব ; গৃহকোণ প্রভৃতিতে সঞ্চিত ধূলি, তুলার আঁশ প্রভৃতি। **Fug'-gy**, *adj.*

fū-ga'-cious (-shŭs), *adj.* Lasting but a short time ; evanescent ; volatile ; ক্ষণস্থায়ী ; অন্তর্হিয়মাণ, দ্রুত-সঞ্চরণশীল ; উদ্বায়ী। **–gac'-i-ty**, *n.*

fū-găl, *adj.* Of the nature of a fugue ; (see FUGE.)

fū'-ğĭ-tive, *adj.* & *n.* **1.** Running away ; fleeing, as from pursuit or danger ; as, a *fugitive* soldier; পলাতক; পলায়নকারী। **2.** Not durable ; evanescent ; quickly fading ; অস্থায়ী, অচিরস্থায়ী, চঞ্চল ; ক্রমবিলীয়মান ; দ্রুতবিলীয়মান। **3.** Of temporary interest ; occasional, as an essay, verse etc ; ক্ষণিক কৌতূহলোদ্দীপক, অচিরকৌতূহলপ্রদ ; নৈমিত্তিক। ***Noun.*** **1.** One who flees from duty, pursuit, danger, etc. as, a *fugitive* from justice ; পলাতক। **2.** An exile or refugee ; নির্ব্বাসিত ব্যক্তি, আশ্রিতজন, শরণাগত ব্যক্তি। **A fugitive from justice**—(আইনে) এক এলাকায় অপরাধ করিয়া অপর এলাকায় পলাতক ব্যক্তি।

fū'-gle (-gl), *v. i.* To act as a fugleman, guide or model ; কুচকাওয়াজের সময় সেনা শ্রেণীর অগ্রনায়কের কাজ করা, পথপ্রদর্শক বা আদর্শস্বরূপ হওয়া।

fū-'gle-măn (-gl-), *n.* (*Pl.* -MEN) **1.** A soldier who stands in front of a line of soldiers under drill and whose movements others are to follow ; যে ব্যক্তি কুচকাওয়াজের সময় সৈন্যদিগের সম্মুখে দাঁড়াইয়া তাহাদিগকে অঙ্গচালনা কৌশল শিক্ষা দান করে, অগ্রনায়ক। **2.** A leader ; a spokesman ; নেতা, নায়ক ; মুখপাত্র।

fugue (fŭg), *n., v. i.* & *t.* (*Mus.*) A composition in which the parts follow or pursue one another at certain distances ; (সঙ্গীত-শাস্ত্র) এক প্রকার সঙ্গীত,—যাহাতে বিভিন্ন অংশ নির্দ্দিষ্ট সময়ান্তে পরস্পরের অনুসরণ করে। ***Verb i. & t.*** To compose or perform a fugue ; উক্তরূপ সংগীত গান বা রচনা করা। **Fu'-guist**, *n* One who composes or performs fugues ; উক্তরূপ সঙ্গীত গায়ক, উক্তরূপ সঙ্গীত রচক।

fŭl'-crŭm, *n.* (*Pl.* -CRA) **1.** A prop or support ; অবলম্বন। **2.** (*Mech.*) That by which a lever is sustained or on which it moves ; (*fig.*) means by which an influence is brought to bear ; (যন্ত্র-বিজ্ঞান) দণ্ডযন্ত্রের অবলম্বন স্থল, আলম্ব ; (লক্ষণায়) যে উপায় অবলম্বনে কোনরূপ প্রভাব বিস্তার করা হয়। **3.** (*Bot.*—Usu. *pl.*) Accessory organs, as tendrils etc. ; (উদ্ভিদ্-বিদ্যা — সাধারণতঃ বহুবচন) উপাঙ্গ, যথা প্রতান।

fûl-fil, *v. t.* **1.** To carry into effect, as a promise etc ; to satisfy, as a desire etc. ; to perform or execute, as a command, law etc ; to comply with, as a condition ; to answer, as a purpose ; কার্য্যে পরিণত করা, রক্ষা করা, প্রতিপালন করা ; পূরণ করা ; সম্পাদন করা, সম্পন্ন করা, সম্পূর্ণ করা, সাধন করা ; পালন করা ; কার্য্যোপযোগী হওয়া। 2. To bring to an end, as a period ; to complete, as a work ; শেষ করা ; সমাপন করা। **—ment,** *n.* Completion ; performance ; পরিপূর্ণতা, সমাপ্তি, সমাপন, সম্পাদন ; সাধন, সংসাধন।

fŭl′-gĕnt, *adj.* (*Poet.* and *rhet.*) Exquisitely bright ; shining ; dazzling ; মহাদ্যুতিমান ; দীপ্তিমান ; তীব্রোজ্জ্বল।

fŭl′-gū-rīte, *n.* **1.** (*Geol.*) Rocky substance vitrified by lightning ; a tube made by passage of lightning through loose sand ; (ভূ-বিদ্যা) বিদ্যুৎদ্বারা কাচতুল্য পদার্থে পরিণত পাষাণ ; শিথিল বালুকারাশির ভিতর দিয়া বিদ্যুৎশিখা অতিক্রম করা হেতু যে পথ রচিত হয়। **2.** A kind of explosive ; একপ্রকার বিস্ফোরক দ্রব্য।

fū-lĭg′-ĭ-nous (-nŭs), *adj.* Sooty ; dark ; dusky ; দীপকাটুময় ; অন্ধকার ; ধূসর।

fûll, *adj., adv., n., v. t.* & *i.* **1.** Filled ; having all it can contain ; as, a basket *full* of corn ; *full* to the brim ; পূর্ণ ; ভরা। **2.** Entirely occupied ; as, a *full* house ; পরিপূর্ণ। **3.** Adequate ; complete ; perfect ; as, a *full* narrative ; of *full* age : *full* stop ; যথানুরূপ, যথোচিত ; সম্পূর্ণ ; সর্ব্বাঙ্গসুন্দর। **4.** Engrossed with the thought of : চিন্তানিমগ্ন, ধ্যাননিবিষ্ট, ধ্যানমগ্ন। **5.** Overcharged with emotion ; as, a *full* heart : to the *full* of one's project ; ভাবাবেগপূর্ণ। **6.** Swelling ; plump ; স্ফীত ; মোটা। **7.** (*Archaic*) Filled with food ; (*Bible*) sated ; (অপ্রঃ) পূর্ণোদর ; (বাইবেল) সন্তৃপ্ত। **8.** (Of animals) Pregnant ; (জন্তু-সম্পর্কে) গর্ভবতী। **9.** (Of light) Intense ; (of colour) deep ; (of motion) vigorous ; (আলোক সম্বন্ধে) তীব্র ; (বর্ণ-সম্বন্ধে) গাঢ়, ঘন ; (গতি-সম্পর্কে) সতেজ। **10.** Abundant ; copious ; ample ; as, *full* notes : a *full* purse ; প্রচুর ; প্রভূত ; পর্য্যাপ্ত। **11.** (Of sound) Deep ; as, *full* voice ; (শব্দ সম্পর্কে) গভীর। **12.** (Of dress) Containing superfluous material arranged in fold ; (পরিচ্ছদ-সম্পর্কে) বিভিন্ন ভাঁজে সজ্জিত অতিরিক্ত বস্ত্রসমন্বিত। **13.** Having reached the height of its development ; as, the *full* moon ; পূর্ণতাপ্রাপ্ত, পূর্ণ। ***Adv.*** **1.** Very (*chiefly poet.*) : as, *full* many a gem etc. (বহু বহু মণি) ; অত্যন্ত (প্রধানতঃ কবিতায়)। **2.** Quite full ; as, *full* ten miles ; পুরা, ঝাড়া, পাকা। **3.** To the full, (*chiefly in combination*) ; as, *full*-blown : *full*-grown ; পূর্ণ-পরিমাণে, পূর্ণমাত্রায়। **4.** Exactly ; as, hit him *full* on the nose ; ঠিক, সঠিকরূপে। ***Noun.*** **1.** Utmost extent ; fulness ; as, to the *full* ; height ; acme ; as, the season is past the *full* ; শেষসীমা ; পরিপূর্ণতা ; উচ্চসীমা ; পরাকাষ্ঠা। **2.** Whole ; as, he can tell you the *full* of it ; সমস্তটা। ***Verb t.*** To make full, as a garment etc. ; বহুভাঁজে সজ্জিত অতিরিক্ত বস্ত্রদ্বারা শোভিত করা। ***Verb i.*** To pucker ; as, a sleeve *full* too much ; কুঞ্চিত হওয়া। **Full′-er,** *n.* One whose occupation is to full cloth ; যে ব্যক্তি চাপ দিয়া এবং আর্দ্র ও উত্তপ্ত করিয়া বস্ত্র পরিষ্কার করে। **Full′-ly,** *adj.* & *adv.* Somewhat full ; কিয়দংশপূর্ণ। (*Adv.*) **1.** Completely ; entirely ; without defect ; সম্পূর্ণভাবে; পূর্ণভাবে ; সম্যক্‌রূপে, সম্যক্‌ভাবে, সর্ব্বতোভাবে, নিখুঁতরূপে। **Ful(l)′-ness,** *n.* **1.** The state of being full ; পরিপূর্ণতা। **2.** Abundance ; প্রাচুর্য্য, ভূয়িষ্ঠতা। **3.** Richness ; volume, as of sound, colour etc. ; প্রাচুর্য্য ; বর্ণ, শব্দ প্রভৃতির পরিমাণ বা পূর্ণতা। **Full age**—পূর্ণবয়স, সাবালক অবস্থা। **Full-aged**—পূর্ণবয়স্ক, প্রাপ্তবয়স্ক। **Full-back**—A foot-ball player stationed behind ; পশ্চাদ্দিকে অবস্থিত ক্রীড়ক। **Full-blooded**—Of pure blood ; সদ্বংশজ ; তেজস্বী ; ইন্দ্রিয়পরায়ণ। **Full-bloomed** — পূর্ণবিকশিত ; পূর্ণপ্রস্ফুটিত পুষ্প-নিভ। **Full-blown**—পূর্ণবিকশিত ; বায়ুদ্বারা সম্যক্ স্ফীত। **Full bottomed**—পূর্ণ অথবা বৃহৎ তলবিশিষ্ট। **Full brother** or **sister**—সহোদর ভাই বা সহোদরা ভগ্নী। **Full dress**—See under DRESS. **Full-bodied**—(Of wine) With much body ; অতিশয় ঘন। **Fuller's earth**—সাজিমাটী। **Full-eyed** — আয়তাক্ষ, আকর্ণবিশ্রান্তনেত্র। **Full face**—দর্শকাদির দিকে আবর্ত্তিত মুখ। **Full-faced**—আয়তাস্য। **Full-grown**—Grown to maturity ; প্রবৃদ্ধ, প্রৌঢ়, বয়ঃস্থ। **Full-hearted** — Full of courage or confidence (*shaks.*) ; অতি সাহসী, অতিবিশ্বাসী। Filled with eomtion ; আবেগপূর্ণ। **Full-mouthed**—(Of dogs) Braying loudly ; (of cattle) with full complement of teeth ; (of style, oratory, etc.) sonorous ; vigorous ; (কুকুর-সম্পর্কে) উচ্চৈঃস্বরে চীৎকারকারী ; (মহিষাদি সম্পর্কে) পূর্ণদন্তপংক্তিসমন্বিত ; স্নিগ্ধগম্ভীর-নাদী ; তেজস্বী, সতেজ। **Full-pay**—পূর্ণ বেতন পুরামাহিনা। **Full-point**—A period in punctuation ; পূর্ণচ্ছেদ, দাঁড়ি। **Full-timer**—(opposed to *halftimer*) A child who attends during all school hours ; যে ছাত্র বিদ্যালয়ে প্রতিদিন পূর্ণসময় অধ্যয়ন করে। **Full-winged** — পূর্ণবিস্তারিত পক্ষ. **A full house**—A house with a good proportion of members present ; পূর্ণ সভা। **At full length**—Lying stretched out ; সটান। **At the full**—At the height ; চরম অবস্থায়। **Full dress**

debate—(পার্লেমেণ্ট মহাসভায়) যে বাদানুবাদের বিষয় পূর্ব্বেই স্থিরীকৃত থাকে এবং যাহাতে উভয়পক্ষ হইতে গুরুত্বপূর্ণ বক্তৃতা প্রদত্ত হয়। **Full length portrait**—A portrait of full figure; পূর্ণায়তন চিত্র, সমগ্র দেহের চিত্র। **Full of the news**—Unable to keep from talking of it; সংবাদ না বলিয়া থাকিতে অসমর্থ। **In full**—Without abridgment; পূর্ণভাবে, সংক্ষেপ না করিয়া। **In full cry**—Pursuing; পশ্চাদ্ধাবমান। **In full swing**—With free course; as, the work is in *full swing*; পুরাদমে, অপ্রতিহতগতিতে। **In fulness of time**—কালপূর্ণ হইলে। **The fulness of heart** — হৃদয়োচ্ছ্বাস, হৃদয়াবেগ। **Of the full blood**—Of pure descent; সদ্বংশজ, কুলীন, উচ্চবংশজাত। **The full moon**—পূর্ণচন্দ্র, পূর্ণেন্দু, রাকেন্দু (কৃষ্ণঃ কঃ), পূর্ণশশধর; পৌর্ণমাসী। **The fulness of time**—The destined time; নিরূপিত কাল, যথাকাল। **The fulness of the world**—All that fills it; যাবতীয় পার্থিব বস্তু। **To the full**—To the utmost extent; পূর্ণমাত্রায়।

fûll'-êr, *n.* & *v. t.* A kind of hammer for forming grooves; a groove made by this, esp. in horse shoes; খাঁজ কাটার জন্য হাতুড়ী বিশেষ; উক্ত প্রকার হাতুড়ীদ্বারা ঘোড়ার নাল প্রভৃতিতে যে খাঁজ কাটা হয়।

fûl'-mâr, *n.* A sea-fowl of the petrel kind; একপ্রকার সামুদ্রিক পক্ষী।

fŭl'-mi-nāte, *v. i.* & *t.* **1.** To thunder or make a loud noise; to detonate; বজ্রধ্বনি হওয়া অশনিবৎ গর্জ্জিত হওয়া; সশব্দে বিদীর্ণ হওয়া, ভীম শব্দে বিদীর্ণ হওয়া। **2.** To issue forth decrees or censures with the assumption of supreme authority; প্রভুত্বসহকারে তিরস্কার করা বা আদেশ প্রচার করা। ***Verb t.*** To utter or publish; to thunder forth; as, to *fulminate* censures; উচ্চারণ করা, প্রকাশ করা; বজ্রনাদে ব্যক্ত করা। **—na'-tion,** *n.* **1.** The act of fulminating or thundering; explosion; অশনিবৎ গর্জ্জন; বিদারণ, সশব্দস্ফোটন। **2.** Vehement censure; denunciation; তীব্র গঞ্জনা; নিন্দাবাদ। **—na-tor-y,** *adj.* Thundering; striking terror; ভীমনাদী, গর্জ্জনকারী; ভীতি-সঞ্চারক।

fŭl'-mi-nāte, *n.* A compound of fulminic acid with mercury etc.; একপ্রকার মিশ্র পদার্থ,—যাহা ঘর্ষণ বা উত্তাপ প্রয়োগে সশব্দে বিদীর্ণ হয়।

fŭl'-mi-nănt, *adj.* **1.** Fulminating; বজ্রনাদী। **2.** (Of a disease) Developing suddenly; (রোগ-সম্পর্কে) সহসা বর্দ্ধমান।

fŭl'-mine (-mĭn), *v. t.* & *i.* **1.** (*Poet.*) To fulminate; (কবিতায়) বজ্রগর্জ্জনে উচ্চারণ করা বা উচ্চারিত হওয়া।

fŭl'-some (-sŭm), *adj.* Cloying; disgusting; as, *fulsome* praise, flattery, etc.; অবসাদজনক, বিতৃষ্ণাজনক; বিরক্তিকর। **—ly,** *adv.* **—ness,** *n.*

fŭl'-vous (-vŭs), *adj.* Tawny; dull yellow; জরদ; কমলাবর্ণ। **—ves'-cent,** *adj.*

fū-māde' *n.* A smoked pilchard; শুষ্ক মৎস্যবিশেষ।

fū'-mă-rōle, *n.* A hole in a volcano from which fumes issue; আগ্নেয়গিরির ধূমোদ্গম রন্ধ্র।

fŭm'-ble (-bl), *v. i., t.* & *n.* To grope about clumsily (*for* or *after* a thing sought); to use the hand awkwardly; হাতড়ান; আনাড়ীর মত কোন কাজ করার চেষ্টা করা। ***Verb t.*** To handle or manage awkwardly; as, to *fumble* a ball; হাতড়ান বা আনাড়ীর মত কাজ করা। ***Noun.*** A bungling attempt; আনাড়ীর মত চেষ্টা। **—bler,** *n.* **To fumble the ball**—To fail to stop it cleanly; নিপুণ হস্তে কন্দুক থামাইতে অসমর্থ হওয়া।

fūme, *n., v. t.* & *i.* **1.** Odorous smoke as of an incense, tobacco etc.; ধোঁয়া, ধূম। **2.** Vapour or exhalation; a noxious exhalation from the stomach, as of liquor etc.; as, the *fumes* of wine; বাষ্প, বাষ্পোদ্গম; পাকস্থলী হইতে মদ্য প্রভৃতির দূষিত বাষ্পোদ্গম। **3.** Water vapour, as rising from the earth, sea etc.; জলীয় বাষ্প। **4.** Anything unsubstantial; idle conceit; অসার বস্তু; বৃথা গর্ব্ব। **5.** A fit of anger or vexation; as, to be in a *fume*; একচোট রাগ, ক্রোধোচ্ছ্বাস, অসন্তোষ, বিরক্তি। **6.** Inordinate flattery; অতিরিক্ত তোষামোদ, বেজায় খোসামুদি। ***Verb t.*** **1.** To expose to chemical fumes; রাসায়নিক ধূম লাগান। **2.** To perfume, as with an incense; ধূপাদি দ্বারা সুবাসিত করা। **3.** To disperse in vapours; বাষ্পাকারে ছড়ান। ***Verb i.*** **1.** To smoke; to give off fumes; to rise up, as vapour; ধূমায়িত হওয়া; ধোঁয়া উঠা; (বাষ্প) উদ্গম হওয়া। **2.** To be in a rage; ক্রোধান্বিত হওয়া, ক্রোধাবিষ্ট হওয়া। **Fume'-less,** *adj.* Free from fumes; নির্ধূম। **Fum'-y,** *adj.* Producing smoke; full of fumes or vapours; ধূমোদ্গারী; ধূমময়, বাষ্পময়, সধূম।

fū'-mi-gāte, *v. t.* **1.** To apply fumes to; to purify or free from infection by the use of smoke; ধোঁয়া লাগান, উপধূমিত করা; ধূমপ্রয়োগ দ্বারা বিশুদ্ধ করা অথবা সংক্রামকতা দোষ নষ্ট করা। **2.** To perfume; সুবাসিত করা, সুরভিত করা। **—ga'-tion,** *n.* Applying smoke or vapour, as for disinfection; ধূমপ্রয়োগ, ধূপন (সাঃ পঃ) উদ্ধূপন (ঐ)। **—ga-tor,** *n.* One who or that which fumigates; ধূমপ্রদায়ক, সংক্রামক রোগের বীজ নাশক দ্রব্যাদি প্রজ্বালনের জন্য পাত্রবিশেষ, ধূপ যন্ত্র (সাঃ পঃ)।

...mi-tŏ-rў, *n.* A herb formerly used in medicine ; ক্ষেত্রপর্পটী (খোরা), ক্ষেতপাপড়া (ঐ)।

fŭn, *n.* & *v. i.* Sport ; merriment ; drollery ; ক্রীড়াকৌতুক ; আমোদ ; রঙ্গ, মজা। ***Verb i.*** (*Rare*) to joke ; to make fun of ; (অপ্রঃ) ঠাট্টা করা, তামাসা করা ; হাস্যাস্পদ করা। **For fun**—As a joke ; তামাসাচ্ছলে, কৌতুকচ্ছলে, রঙ্গচ্ছলে। **Like fun**—Vigourously ; quickly ; much ; সতেজে ; দ্রুত ; অতিশয়। **To be good** or **great fun**—To be very amusing ; অতীব কৌতুকজনক হওয়া, ভারি মজার বিষয় হওয়া। **To poke fun at**—To ridicule ; বিদ্রূপ করা। **What fun**—How amusing ; কি মজা !

fū-năm′-bū-lāte, *v. i.* To walk or to dance on a rope ; রজ্জুর উপর হাঁটা বা নৃত্য করা। **–list,** *n.* রজ্জু-নর্ত্তক, দড়াবাজীকর।

func′-tion (fŭngk-), *n.* & *v. i.* **1.** The appropriate action of any special organ or part of an animal or vegetable organism ; as, the *function* of the heart ; ব্যাপার, বৃত্তি, কার্য, ধর্ম্ম [যথা, নিঃশ্বাস প্রশ্বাস, ফুস্‌ফুসের ক্রিয়া]। **2.** The activity appropriate to any business or profession ; official duty ; কর্ত্তব্য ; সরকারী কার্য্য। **3.** Profession ; employment ; calling ; ব্যবসায় ; বৃত্তি ; পেশা। **4.** A religious ceremony ; a public or social ceremony or gathering ; পর্ব্ব, উৎসব ; সামাজিক সম্মিলনী। **5.** (*Math.*) A variable quantity so connected with another that any change in the one causes corresponding changes in the other ; (গণিত) অন্যোন্য সম্বন্ধ বিশিষ্ট রাশিদ্বয়,—যাহার একটীর পরিবর্তন হইলে অপরটীর অনুরূপ পরিবর্ত্তন হয়, ফল (হিঃ কোঃ)। ***Verb i.*** To execute or perform an action ; to act ; কোন কার্য্য সম্পন্ন করা ; কাজ করা। **–al,** *adj.* **1.** Pertaining to, or connected with, a function or office ; formal (*rare*) ; কার্য্যসম্বন্ধীয়, কর্ত্তব্য-কার্য্য বিষয়ক ; আনুষ্ঠানিক (অপ্রঃ)। **2.** Pertaining to the function of an organ ; having or performing a function ; as, a *functional* organ ; দৈহিক যন্ত্রের কার্য্যসম্বন্ধীয় ; কার্য্য সমন্বিত বা কার্য্য সম্পাদনকারী। **–al-ly,** *adv.* **–a-ry,** *n.* & *adj.* One charged with the performance of a function or office ; as, a public *functionary* ; কর্ম্মচারী, রাজকর্ম্মচারী। (*Adj.*) Same as FUNCTIONAL which see. **–ate,** *v. i.* **–less,** *adj.*

fŭnd, *n.* & *v. t.* **1.** A permanent stock or supply of anything ; as, a *fund* of knowledge ; ভাণ্ডার। **2.** A stock of money set apart for a purpose ; capital ; as, the *fund* of a bank ; (*pl.*) pecuniary resources ; ধনভাণ্ডার, তহবিল, কোষ (হিঃ কোঃ) ; পুঁজি, মূলধন ; আর্থিক অবস্থা। **3.** (*Pl.* with *the*) The stock of a national debt, as a mode of investment ; as, he had £2000 in *funds* ; কোম্পানীর কাগজ। ***Verb t.*** **1.** To convert into a more or less permanent debt at a fixed interest ; স্থায়ী ঋণে পরিণত করা। **2.** (*Rare*) To place in a fund, as money ; to store up ; (অপ্রঃ) ধনভাণ্ডারে জমা দেওয়া ; ভাণ্ডার-জাত করা। **3.** To invest, as money in the funds ; টাকা খাটান, ধনপ্রয়োগ করা। **Funded debt**—স্থায়ী সরকারী ঋণের যে অংশের সুদ প্রদত্ত হয়। **In funds**—Having money ; ধনশালী। **Sinking fund**—সরকারী ঋণ ক্রমশঃ পরিশোধ করার জন্য যে টাকা পৃথক করিয়া রাখা হয়। **The funds** or **public funds**—কোম্পানীর কাগজ।

fŭn′-dă-mĕnt, *n.* The buttocks ; নিতম্ব, গুহ্য প্রদেশ (কেণ্ডি)।

fŭn-dă-mĕn′-tăl, *adj.* & *n.* (Usu. *Pl.*) Pertaining to the foundation or basis ; serving as the base ; essential ; original ; primary ; as, a *fundamental* change, trait, etc. ; মৌলিক ; মূলীভূত ; মূলতত্ত্বসম্বন্ধীয় ; আদিম ; প্রাথমিক। ***Noun.*** **1.** A leading or primary principle ; essential part ; as, the *fundamentals* of the Christian faith ; মূলতত্ত্ব, মূলসূত্র ; মূল অংশ। **–ly,** *adv.* **–tal′-i-ty,** *n.* **Fundamental colours**—Red, green, violet, blue ; লোহিত, সবুজ, নীল এবং বেগুনে রং।

fū-nē′-bri-ăl, *adj.* (*Rare*) Funeral ; (অপ্রঃ) ঊর্দ্ধদেহিক।

fū′-nêr-ăl, *n.* & *adj.* **1.** A burial with attendant observances ; obsequies ; অন্ত্যেষ্টি ক্রিয়া, সমাধি কার্য্য ; মৃতসৎকার, ঊর্দ্ধদেহিক কার্য্য, প্রেত-কার্য্য, শবসংস্কার (কেণ্ডি), প্রেতসংস্কার (ঐ)। **2.** A burial procession ; প্রেতযাত্রা (কেণ্ডি), শবযাত্রা (ঐ), শ্মশান যাত্রা (ঐ)। ***Adj.*** Pertaining to, or used at, funeral ; as, *funeral* rites ; অন্ত্যেষ্টিক্রিয়া সম্বন্ধীয়, ঊর্দ্ধদেহিক। **–a-ry,** *adj.* Of, or relating to funeral ; অন্ত্যেষ্টিক্রিয়াসম্পর্কীয়। **Funeral pile** or **pyre**—চিতা। **Funeral rites and ceremonies**—প্রেতকর্ম্ম (কেণ্ডি), প্রেতকার্য্য (ঐ) ; উত্তরক্রিয়া (ঐ)।

fū-nē′-rē-ăl, *adj.* Pertaining to a burial ; suiting a funeral ; dismal ; gloomy ; mournful ; অন্ত্যেষ্টি ক্রিয়া-সম্বন্ধীয় ; সমাধি কার্য্য সমুচিত ; বিষাদাচ্ছন্ন ; বিষাদমলিন ; শোকাবহ। **–ly,** *adv.* **Funereal urn**—শ্মশানভস্ম পাত্র।

fŭn′-gī, *n.* (*Pl.*) See FUNGUS.

fŭn′-gi-ble (-bl), *adj.* & *n.* (*Law.*) That can serve or be replaced by another answering to the same definition ; (of goods etc.) contracted for ; (আইন) অপর বস্তুর পরিবর্ত্তে দেয় বস্তু ; (মাল প্রভৃতি সম্পর্কে) যাহার জন্য চুক্তি করা হইয়াছে—এইরূপ

Noun. A fungible thing; অপর বস্তুর পরিবর্তে দেয় বস্তু।

fŭn'-gĭ-cīde, *n.* Any substance that destroys fungus; ছত্রাকনাশী, শিলীন্ধ্র বিনাশক।

fŭn'-gĭn, *n.* A substance forming cell walls of fungus; ছত্রাকের কোষ প্রাচীরে প্রাপ্ত পদার্থবিশেষ।

fun-goid (fŭng-goyd), *adj.* Resembling a mushroom; ছত্রাকবৎ শিলীন্ধ্রতুল্য।

fun'-gous (fŭng-gŭs), *adj.* **1.** Relating to, or of the nature of, fungi; ছত্রাক-সম্বন্ধীয়, শিলীন্ধ্র-সম্বন্ধীয়, ছত্রাক ধর্ম্মা। **2.** Growing suddenly, but not durable; transitory; দ্রুতবর্দ্ধনশীল কিন্তু অস্থায়ী; ক্ষণিক, ক্ষণভঙ্গুর, ক্ষণস্থায়ী।

fun'-gŭs (fŭng-), *n.* (*Pl.* -GI, -GUSSES.) **1.** Mushroom; (*Bot.*) a cryptogamous plant feeding on organic matter; ব্যাঙের ছাতা, ছত্রক, ছত্রাক, শিলীন্ধ্র; (উদ্ভিদ্-বিদ্যা) জৈব পদার্থ-ভোজী অপুষ্পক-উদ্ভিদ্। **2.** (*Med.*) A spongy excrescence, as proud-flesh formed in a wound; স্পঞ্জের ন্যায় সচ্ছিদ্র ক্যানসার প্রভৃতির উন্নত মাংস বা অর্ব্বুদ। **3.** A thing that forms suddenly; সহসা জাত বস্তু। **4.** A skin disease of fish; মৎস্যের চর্ম্মরোগ বিশেষ। **–gal,** *adj.* **–gi-form,** *adj.* Shaped like a mushroom; শিলীন্ধ্রাকার। **–y,** *adj.*

fŭn-gĭv'-o-rous, *adj.* (-êr-ŭs), *adj.* Eating fungi; শিলিন্ধ্র-ভোজী।

fū'-nĭ-cle (-cl), *n.* A small cord or fibre; অতিসূক্ষ্ম সূত্র, ক্ষুদ্র রজ্জু। **–nic'-u-lar,** *adj.* **1.** Relating to, or consisting of, a rope; রজ্জু-সম্বন্ধীয়, রজ্জু-সম্পর্কীয়। **2.** Pertaining to, or dependant on, the tension of a rope; রজ্জু সম্পর্কীয়, রজ্জুর প্রসার্য্যতার উপর নির্ভরশীল। **Funicular railway** — একপ্রকার লৌহবর্ত্ম,—যাহাতে বাষ্পীয়শকট সমূহ ধাতব রজ্জু দ্বারা টানিয়া পর্ব্বতাগ্রিতে তোলা হয়—উক্ত রজ্জু অচল বাষ্পীয় যন্ত্রের সাহায্যে ঘূর্ণ্যমান চোঙ্গার চতুর্দ্দিকে আবর্ত্তিত করা হয়—তাহাতে উপরে উঠে।

funk (fŭngk), *n., v. i.* & *t.* **1.** (*Slang*) Panic; (ইতর ভাষায়) ত্রাস, আতঙ্ক, বিভীষিকা। **2.** A coward; ভীরু, কাপুরুষ। ***Verb i.*** To shrink back; to flinch; to show cowardice; সঙ্কুচিত হওয়া; পরাঙ্মুখ হওয়া; ভীরুতা প্রদর্শন করা। ***Verb t.*** **1.** To shrink from; to be afraid of; সঙ্কুচিত হইয়া আসা; ভীত হওয়া। **2.** To frighten; ভীত করা, সন্ত্রস্ত করা। **3.** To evade or try to evade, as an undertaking etc.; to shrink; এড়ান, এড়ানের চেষ্টা করা; সঙ্কুচিত হওয়া, পরাঙ্মুখ হওয়া।

fŭn'-nĕl, *n.* **1.** A passage for air, light, smoke, etc.; the metal chimney of an engine, ship, etc.; ধূমনির্গমনালী; জাহাজ, প্রভৃতির চুঙ্গী। **2.** An instrument for pouring fluids into bottles etc; তৈল প্রভৃতি বোতলে ভরিবার জন্য ফাঁদল, ফণ্ডিল।

fŭn'-nĭ-mĕnt, *n.* Joke; drollery; তামাসা, কৌতুক; রঙ্গ।

fŭn'-nȳ, *adj.* **1.** Droll; comical; মজাদার; কৌতুকজনক, কৌতুকাবহ, হাস্যকর। **2.** Queer; perplexing; strange; সৃষ্টিছাড়া; হতবুদ্ধিতাজনক; অদ্ভুত, আজগবী। **–ni-ly,** *adv.* **Funny-bone**—কনুইয়ের যে অংশের উপর দিয়া প্রকোষ্ঠাস্থির শিরা অতিক্রম করে। **Funny-man**—A professional jester; ভাঁড়, বিদূষক, বৈহাসিক।

Fun'-ny, *n.* A small clinker-built boat for one sculler; একপ্রকার নৌকা।

fŭr, *n., v. t.* & *i.* **1.** The short, soft hair of certain animals, as distinguished from the longer hair; কোমল লোম। **2.** (*Pl.*) The skins of certain animals with the fur worn as a trimming or lining to a garment; পোষাকের ভূষা-স্বরূপ পরিহিত সলোম পশুচর্ম্ম খণ্ড। **3.** (Usu. *pl.*) Articles of clothing made of, or having, fur; লোমরচিত বা লোম-সমন্বিত পোষাকের অংশ। **4.** Furred animals collectively; লোমশ জন্তুবর্গ। **5.** A coat of morbid matter collected on the tongue in persons affected with fever etc.; জ্বরকালে জিহ্বাদির উপরিভাগে সরের ন্যায় দূষিত পদার্থের যে স্তর সঞ্চিত হয়, জিহ্বামল। **6.** A fur-like coating on the interior of a tea kettle; চার কেটলীর ভিতরে সঞ্চিত মলাবরণ। ***Verb t.*** **1.** To line or cover with fur; লোমদ্বারা আচ্ছাদিত করা বা আস্তর দেওয়া। **2.** To coat, as the tongue or the inside of a kettle etc. with fur; জিহ্বা, কেটলীর অভ্যন্তর মলাচ্ছাদিত করা। **3.** To remove fur from (a boiler etc.) বাষ্পজনকের মলাচ্ছাদন দুর করা। **4.** (*Carpentry*) To level, as floor timbers by inserting strips of wood; কাঠের লম্বা সরু ফালি প্রবিষ্ট করিয়া মেঝের তক্তা সকল সমতল করা। ***Verb i.*** To become coated with fur; লোমাচ্ছাদিত হওয়া; মলাচ্ছাদিত হওয়া। **Fur'-ry,** *adj.* **1.** Coated or dressed with fur; লোমাবৃত, লোমশ। **2.** Consisting of, or like, fur; লোমান্বিত, লোমবৎ, রোমবৎ। **Fur and feather** — See under FEATHER. **To hunt fur**—To hunt hares; শশক শিকার করা।

fur'-be-low (fêr-bē-lö), *n.* & *v. t.* **1.** A plaited flounce on a woman's garment; স্ত্রীলোকের পোষাকের কুঁচিওয়ালা ঝালর। **2.** (*Pl.*) Showy ornaments; জমকালো অলঙ্কার। **3.** A kind of sea weed; একপ্রকার সামুদ্রিক শৈবাল। ***Verb t.*** To adorn with furbelow; কুঁচিওয়ালা ঝালর দ্বারা শোভিত করা।

fŭr'-bĭsh, *v. t.* To rub or scour to brightness; to clean; to burnish; to renovate; to revive, (sometimes with *up*); ঘষিয়া মাজিয়া চক্চকে করা; পরিষ্কার করা; পালিস করা; নবীভূত করা; পুনরুজ্জীবিত করা।

fŭr′-cāte, *adj.* & *v. i.* Forked ; দু-ফেঁকড়া । ***Verb i.*** To branch or divide like a fork ; দু-ফেঁকড়া করা । **—ca′-tion,** *n.*

fur-fu-ra′-ceous (fêr-fêr-ā-shŭs), *adj.* Like bran ; scurfy ; তুষবৎ ; খুস্কিযুক্ত ।

fū′-ri-ous (-ŭs), *adj.* **1.** Raging ; violent ; fierce ; ক্রোধোদ্দীপ্ত, মত্ত ; প্রচণ্ড, উচ্চণ্ড, উন্মদ ; রৌদ্র, করাল । **2.** Moving into violence : as, a *furious* storm ; প্রবলবেগে প্রবহমাণ । **—ly,** *adv.* **Fast and furious**—(Of mirth etc.) Eager ; uproarious ; আগ্রহপূর্ণ ; কোলাহলপূর্ণ ।

furl (fêrl), *v. t.* & *i.* **1.** To roll up, as a sail close to the yard etc. ; পাইল প্রভৃতি গুটান, জড়ান । **2.** To close or fold up, as an umbrella, wings, etc ; to relinquish, as hopes etc ; জড়াইয়া গুটান, বন্ধ করা ; পরিত্যাগ করা । ***Verb i.*** To become curled or folded ; to roll away like clouds ; গুটান, জড়ান ; আবর্ত্তিত হওয়া ।

fur-lŏng (fêr-), *n.* $\frac{1}{8}$ th of a mile ; এক মাইলের অষ্টমাংশ ।

fur′-lough (fêr-lō), *n.* & *v. t.* Leave of absence especially given to a soldier ; বিদায়, ছুটী, অবকাশ, কর্ম্মাবসর । ***Verb t.*** To grant a furlough to ; বিদায় দেওয়া ।

fur′-mĕ-tў (fêr-), *n.* Same as FURMENTY, which see.

fur′-nace (fêr-nās), *n.* & *v. t.* **1.** An inclosed place in which heat is produced by the combustion of fuel etc., for melting ores, warming houses etc. ; a place or time of severe affliction or trial ; a severe test ; চুল্লী, উনন, হাপর, অগ্নিশালা, অগ্নিকুণ্ড ; মহা যন্ত্রণার স্থল, অগ্নিপরীক্ষার কাল বা স্থান ; অগ্নিপরীক্ষা । **2.** A hot place ; উষ্ণ স্থান । ***Verb t.*** To heat in a furnace ; চুল্লীতে উত্তপ্ত করা ।

fur′-nish (fêr-), *v. t.* **1.** To equip ; to fit up or out ; as, to *furnish* a man for a journey ; to *furnish* a table ; সজ্জিত করা, সাজান ; ঠিকঠাক করা । **2.** To supply with furniture and fittings, as a house, room etc. ; আসবাবপত্র, সরঞ্জাম প্রভৃতি দ্বারা সজ্জিত করা । **3.** To supply, as a man or thing (*with* something) ; কোন জিনিষ সরবরাহ করা । **4.** To afford ; to give ; to yield ; প্রদান করা ; দেওয়া ; অর্পণ করা ।

fur′-ni-tūre (fêr-), *n.* **1.** Outfit ; contents of a receptacle ; as, the *furniture* of one's pocket (*i. e.* money) ; সাজসজ্জা ; কোন আধারের অভ্যন্তরস্থ জিনিষ । **2.** Movables either for use or ornament, such as tables, chairs, etc. ; খাট, চেয়ার, টেবিল, আয়না প্রভৃতি আসবাব সামগ্রী, গৃহসজ্জা, গৃহালঙ্কার । **3.** (*Archaic*) The trappings of a horse ; (অপ্র:) অশ্ব সজ্জা । **Furniture of one's mind**—Knowledge and intelligence ; বিদ্যাবুদ্ধি ।

fū′-rŏr, *n.* Rage ; fury ; রাগ ; প্রচণ্ডতা ।

fu′-ro-re (fô-rō-rā), *n.* Enthusiastic admiration ; mania ; rage ; উৎসাহপূর্ণ প্রশংসা ; বাতিক ; প্রবল অভিলাষের বিষয় ।

fur′-ri-êr (fêr-), *n.* A dealer in furs ; লোমব্যবসায়ী, লোমনির্ম্মিত বস্তুর ব্যবসায়ী । **—y,** *n.* **1.** Furs in general ; লোমসমূহ । **2.** Trade in furs ; লোম-ব্যবসায় ।

fur′-ring (fêr-), *n.* **1.** Act of putting on fur ; লোম রচিত ভূষা পরিধান । **2.** (*Ship-building*) Doubling of planks on a ship's side ; জাহাজের পার্শ্বভাগের কাষ্ঠফলক সকল দ্বিগুণিত করণ ।

fŭr′-row (-rō), *n.* & *v.t.* **1.** A trench in the earth made by a plough ; হলপদ্ধতি, লাঙ্গলমার্গ, লাঙ্গলপদ্ধতি, নালা (প্রবোধ) । **2.** A groove ; a long indentation ; a wrinkle on the face ; খাঁজ ; নালা ; মুখমণ্ডলের কুঞ্চিত রেখা, বলি । ***Verb t.*** To plough ; to make furrows or grooves in ; to mark with wrinkles ; হলদ্বারা কর্ষণ করা ; নালী, বা খাঁজ কাটা ; কুঞ্চিত করা । **—less, —y,** *adjs.*

fur′-thêr (fêr-), *adj., adv.* & *v. t.* **1.** More remote ; as, the *further* side ; অধিকতর দুরবর্ত্তী । **2.** Additional ; as, without *further* delay ; আর, অতিরিক্ত । ***Adv.*** **1.** To, or at, a greater distance ; to a greater extent or degree ; আরো দূরে, অধিকতর দূরে ; অধিকতর মাত্রায় বা পরিমাণে । **2.** In addition ; besides ; আরো ; ছাড়া, ব্যতীত বিনা । ***Verb t.*** To help forward ; to promote ; to favour ; সাহায্য করা, অগ্রসর করা, আগুয়ান করা ; উন্নতিবিধান করা ; অনুগ্রহ করা । **—ance,** *n.* A helping forward ; promotion ; অগ্রসর করাণ, উন্নয়ন; উন্নতিবিধান, উন্নতিসাধন । **Furthermore**—*adv.* Moreover ; besides ; আরো ; এতদ্ব্যতীত । **Furthermost**—Most remote ; সর্ব্বাপেক্ষা দুরবর্ত্তী, নিতান্ত দূরবর্ত্তী, দূরতম । **Furthersome**—*adj.* Helping forward ; উন্নতিবিধায়ক ।

fur′-thĕst, (fêr-), **fâr′—,** *adjs.* & *advs.* দূরতম ।

fur′-tive (fêr-tĭv), *adj.* **1.** Done or got by stealth ; clandestine ; sly ; stealthy ; গোপনে সাধিত, গোপনে প্রাপ্ত ; গোপন, গুপ্ত ; ধূর্ত্ত ; চোরা (as, *furtive looks*=চোরা চাহনি) । **2.** Stolen ; thievish ; অপহৃত ; চৌর্য্যপর । **—ly,** *adv.* **—ness,** *n.*

fū′-run-cle (-rŭng-kl), *n.* A boil or tumour ; স্ফোটক, ব্রণ । **—cu-lar —cu-lous,** *adjs.* Of, or pertaining to, a furuncle ; স্ফোটকসম্বন্ধীয় ।

fū′-rў *n.* **1.** Violent anger ; rage ; passion ; প্রচণ্ডরোষ ; ক্রোধাবেশ ; ক্রোধাগ্নি । **2.** Frenzy ; ক্রোধোন্মাদ । **3.** Violence, as of storm, disease, etc. ; প্রচণ্ডতা, প্রবলতা প্রাবল্য । **4.** (Cap. *usu. pl., Greek Myth.*)

snakehaired goddess or goddesses; গ্রীক পুরাণোক্ত সর্পকেশী প্রতিহিংসাদেবীত্রয়ের অন্যতম [ইঁহাদের নাম Alecto, Megaera, Tisiphone]। **5.** A violent woman; a virago; উগ্রচণ্ডা নারী; রায়বাঘিনী। **In a fury**—In a fit of rage; রাগের মাথায়,ক্রোধাবেশে। **Like fury**—Furiously; প্রচণ্ডভাবে। **The Spanish Fury**—The massacre by the Spaniards at Antwerp in 1576; এণ্টওয়ার্প নগরীতে ১৫৭৬ খৃষ্টাব্দে স্পেনিয়ার্ডগণকর্ত্তৃক অনুষ্ঠিত হত্যাকাণ্ড।

… (fêrz), *n.* A thorny evergreen shrub with beautiful yellow flowers; ইয়ুরোপদেশীয় পীতপুষ্পপ্রদ চিরশ্যামল গুল্মবিশেষ। **Fur'-zen, Fur'-zy,** *adjs.*

fu'-să-rŏb, *n.* (*Arch.*) A kind of moulding; (স্থপতি-বিজ্ঞান) একপ্রকার সৌধভূষা।

fus'-cous(-kŭs), *adj.* Dark; dusky; ধূমসাচ্ছন্ন; অনুজ্জ্বল, ঈষদন্ধকারাচ্ছন্ন।

fuse (füz), *v. t.* & *i.* **1.** To liquify by heat; to melt; দ্রবীভূত করা; গালান। **2.** To unite or blend, as by melting together; গালাইয়া মিশান বা একত্র করা। ***Verb i.*** **1.** To be reduced to a liquid; to be melted; তরলপদার্থে পরিণত হওয়া; দ্রবীভূত হওয়া। **2.** To be blended, as if melted together; মিশা। **Fused,** *adj.* গলিত, দ্রবীভূত, ধ্মাপিত (রঃ রঃ সঃ—প্রঃ)। **Fu'-si-ble,** *adj.* Capable of being melted; দ্রাব্য, গলনীয়। **Fu-si-bil'-i-ty,** *n.* গলনীয়তা, দ্রাব্যতা, দ্রবণীয়তা। **Fusing point**—যে তাপমাত্রায় কোন পদার্থ দ্রবীভূত হয়, গলনাঙ্ক।

fuse (füz), *n.* & *v. t.* A tube filled with combustible matter for firing mines, discharging shells etc.; বিস্ফোরক দ্রব্যপূর্ণ চুঙ্গী। ***Verb t.*** To fit a fuse to; বিস্ফোরক দ্রব্যপূর্ণ চুঙ্গী লাগান।

fu-see' (-zē), *n.* **1.** A conical pulley or wheel, esp. in a watch or clock; ঘড়ী বা টেঁকঘড়ী প্রভৃতির মোচাকার কপিকল। **2.** A large headed match for lighting cigar etc. in wind; বাতাসে চুরুট প্রভৃতি ধরাইবার জন্য একপ্রকার দেয়াশলাই।

fū-sĕl-oil (-ŏyl), *n.* A colourless oily spirit separated in the rectification of ordinary distilled spirits; একপ্রকার অবর্ণ তৈলময় সুরাসার।

fū'-sĭl, *n.* A light musket formerly in use; সাবেক কালে ব্যবহৃত একপ্রকার হাল্কা বন্দুক, চকমকির বন্দুক। **–er, –eer,** *ns.* Formerly a soldier armed with a fusil, (now usu. *pl.*); a soldier of some British regiments; certain British regiments; as, the Royal *fusilers*; সাবেক কালের চকমকি বন্দুকধারী সৈনিক; (বর্ত্তমানে) কতিপয় বৃটীশ পল্টনের সৈন্য; কতিপয় ব্রিটীশ সৈন্য পল্টনের নাম।

fū'-sĭl-lāde (-ād), *v. t.* & *n.* To attack (a place) or shoot down persons by a simultaneous discharge of firearms; যুগপৎ গোলাগুলি বর্ষণ দ্বারা আক্রমণ বা ভূপাতিত করা। ***Noun.*** A simultaneous discharge of firearms; wholesale execution by it; যুগপৎ বা অবিশ্রান্ত অগ্নিবর্ষণ; যুগপৎ অগ্নি বর্ষণ দ্বারা বহু লোক নিধন।

fū'-sion (-zhŏn), *n.* **1.** The act of melting together; as, the *fusion* of metals; উত্তাপ দ্বারা দ্রবীকরণ, গলন, বিদ্রাবণ। **2.** The state of fluidity from heat; as, metals in *fusion*; দ্রবত্ব। **3.** Blending or union of different things into one; মিশ্রণ। **4.** (*Politics*) Coalition; (রাজনীতি) সম্মিলন, সংযোগ, সমবায়। **–ist,** *n.* (*Politics*) An upholder of the policy of fusion; (রাজনীতি) সংযোগবাদী, সম্মিলনবাদী। **–si-form,** *adj.* Shaped like a spindle; tapering at each end; as, a *fusiform* root; টেকুয়াবৎ (সাঃ পঃ), তকুবৎ (ঐ); উভয় প্রান্তে ক্রমসূক্ষ্মাগ্র।

fuss ([illegible]) … & *n.* To make a bustle or ado; to busy oneself restlessly with trifles; হল্লা করা, গোলমাল করা; সামান্য বিষয় লইয়া হৈ চৈ করা। ***Verb t.*** To disturb with trifles; to worry; সামান্য বিষয় নিয়া বিরক্ত করা; জ্বালাতন করা। ***Noun.*** A bustle or tumult; treatment of trifles as important; হল্লা, গোলমাল, জটলা; তুচ্ছ বিষয় গুরুতর বলিয়া গণন। **Fus'-si-ly,** *adv.* In a fussy manner; গোলমেলে ভাবে। **Fus'-si-ness,** *n.* **Fus'-sy,** *adj.* **1.** Making a fuss; nice; হৈ চৈ কারী; অতিসূক্ষ্মবিচারী। **2.** Bustling; হল্লাকারী।

fŭst, *n.* (*Arch.*) The shaft of a column; (স্থপতি-বিদ্যা) স্তম্ভ-দণ্ড স্তম্ভবপু।

fŭs-tā-nĕl'-lā, *n.* A man's white petticoat in modern Greece; আধুনিক গ্রীসের পুরুষদিগের শ্বেতবর্ণ ঘাগ্‌রা বিশেষ।

fŭs'-ti-ăn, *n.* & *adj.* **1.** A kind of thick twilled cotton cloth; একপ্রকার টের্চ্চা-বুনা স্থূলবস্ত্র। **2.** An inflated style of writing or speaking; bombast; বাগাড়ম্বরপূর্ণ লিখন বা কথনের রীতি; শব্দাড়ম্বর বাগাড়ম্বর। ***Adj.*** **1.** Made of fustian; টের্চ্চাবুনা স্থূল বস্ত্রবিশেষ দ্বারা, নির্ম্মিত। **2.** Bombastic; শব্দাড়ম্বরপূর্ণ, বাগাড়ম্বরপূর্ণ। **3.** Worthless; pretentious; অসার; আড়ম্বরপূর্ণ, জাঁকাল।

fŭs'-tic, *n.* A kind of wood yielding a yellow dye; the dye got from it; একপ্রকার কাষ্ঠ—ইহা হইতে একপ্রকার পীতবর্ণ রঞ্জক পদার্থ প্রাপ্ত হওয়া যায়: ঐরূপ কাষ্ঠ হইতে প্রাপ্ত হরিদ্রাবর্ণ রঞ্জক পদার্থ।

fŭs'-ti-gāte, *v. t.* To cudgel; লগুড়াঘাত করা, যষ্টিদ্বারা প্রহার করা। **–ga'-tion,** *n.* A punishment by beating with a stick; যষ্টি দ্বারা প্রহার।

fŭs'-tў, *adj.* **1.** Musty; ill smelling; ভাপ্‌সা, ছাঁতা-পড়া, ভাকন্দো-পড়া;

দুর্গন্ধ। 2. Without freshness ; old-fashioned ; নবীনতাহীন ; সেকেলে, সাবেক ধরণের। 3. Stuffy ; ঠাসাঠাসি। **–ti-ness,** *n.*

futch′-ĕl(l) (fŭch-), *n.* A piece of timber supporting the axle-bar, pole or shafts of a carriage ; শকটের অক্ষদণ্ড, যুগন্ধর।

fu′-thŏrc (fōō-) *n.* The Runic alphabet : প্রাচীন টিউটনদিগের বর্ণমালা।

fū′-tīle, *adj.* 1. Useless ; ineffectual ; vain ; অকারণ ; নিষ্ফল, বিফল ; বৃথা, পণ্ড। 2. Trifling ; frivolous ; তুচ্ছ, অকিঞ্চিৎকর ; ছেবলা। **–ly,** *adv.* **–til′-i-ty,** *n.* 1. নিষ্ফলতা, বিফলতা, অসিদ্ধি, নিরর্থকতা। 2. Worthlessness ; অসারতা, অকিঞ্চিৎকরতা, অগণ্যতা।

fŭt′-tŏck, *n.* One of the separate pieces of timber composing the frame of a ship ; জাহাজের খোলের তক্তা।

fū′-tūre, *n.* & *adj.* 1. Time to come ; (*collectively*) events that are to happen in time to come ; as, lay the *future* open ; ভবিষ্যৎ কাল, ভবিষ্য, অনাগত কাল, ভাবী কাল, আইন্দা (*colloq*) ; ভাবী ঘটনাবলী। make a mislead at cards—কাটে as of a person, country, etc. ; as, he had a great *future* before him ; ভবিষ্যৎ। 3. (*Gram.*) The future tense ; (ব্যাকরণ) ভবিষ্যৎকাল। 4. (*Pl.—Comm.*) Goods and stocks for future delivery ; contracts for these ; (বহুবচন—বাণিজ্য) ভবিষ্যৎকালে প্রদেয় মাল ; ঐরূপ মালের জন্য চুক্তি। 5. One's affianced wife or husband ; বিবাহের জন্য স্থিরীকৃত পাত্র বা পাত্রী। *Adj.* 1. That is to be or come hereafter ; about to happen ; ভবিষ্যৎ, ভাবী, ভবিষ্য, অনাগত ; আসন্ন। 2. Relating to, or expressing, futurity ; ভবিষ্যৎকাল সম্বন্ধীয়, ভাবীকালবোধক। **–less,** *adj.* Without prospect of betterment in the future ; ভবিষ্যৎ উন্নতির আশাশূন্য। **–tur-ist,** *n.* & *adj.* (*Theol.*) One believing that the prophecies of the Bible are still to be fulfilled ; (খ্রীষ্টীয় ধর্মশাস্ত্র) বাইবেল গ্রন্থে উক্ত ভবিষ্যদ্‌বাণী অদ্যাপি পূর্ণ হয় নাই বলিয়া যাহারা বিশ্বাস করে, ভবিষ্যবাদী ব্যক্তি। (*Adj.*) Believing that the prophecies of the Bible are still to be fulfilled ; ঐরূপমতবাদী। **–tur′-i-ty,** *n.* 1. Future state ; existence after death ; ভবিষ্য অবস্থা ; পরকাল। 2. Future time ; ভাবীকাল। 3. An event or events to happen in future ; ভাবীঘটনা, ভবিষ্যঘটনা।

fŭzz, *v. i.* & *n.* To fly in minute particles ; সূক্ষ্মকণাকারে উড়িয়া যাওয়া। *Noun.* Fine light particles ; volatile matter ; সূক্ষ্ম লঘু কণিকাসমূহ ; উদ্বায়ী পদার্থ। **Fuz′-zi-ly,** *adv.* **Fuz′-zi-ness,** *n.* **Fuz′-zy,** *adj.* Blurred ; indistinct ; ঝাপ্‌সা ; অস্পষ্ট। **Fuzz-ball**—A fungus ; ছত্রাক। **Fuzzy-wuzzy**—A Soudanese warrior ; সুদানবাসী যোদ্ধা।

fȳ, fye (fī), Same as FIE which see.

fȳke, *n.* A bag-net for catching fish ; মাছ ধরার জন্য একপ্রকার জাল।

fȳl′-fŏt, *n.* A rectangular cross with arms of equal length and each bent at right angles at the end ; একপ্রকার আয়ত ক্ষেত্রাকার সমবাহু বিশিষ্ট ক্রুশ—ইহার প্রত্যেক বাহু প্রান্তদেশে সমকোণ অবস্থায় আনত থাকে।

fyrd (fĕrd), *n.* (*Hist.*) The military array of a whole country ; all males capable of bearing arms ; (ইতিহাস) সমগ্রদেশের সামরিক সজ্জা ; দেশের অস্ত্রধারণে সমর্থ পুরুষগণ।

ললাটদেশ। 4. A phylactory ; কবিচ, মাদুলী।

frŏn-tŏn′, *n.* A pediment ; দ্বার, বাতায়ন, প্রভৃতির উপরিভাগস্থ ত্রিকোণাকৃতি সৌধভূষাবিশেষ।

frōre, *adj.* (*Poet.*) Frozen ; frosty ; (কবিতায়) শীতে জমাট-বাঁধা ; তুষারময়।

frŏst, *n.* & *v. t.* **1.** The act of freezing ; জমাট বাঁধন। **2.** Temperature below freezing point ; frozen state ; সংহনন বিন্দুর নিম্নবর্তী তাপাঙ্ক ; জমাট অবস্থা। **3.** Frozen dew or vapour ; কঠিনীভূত নীহার বা বাষ্প, তুষার, তুহিন। **4.** Influence that chills or makes grey etc. ; শৈত্যজনক প্রভাব, শুভ্রতাজনক প্রভাব। **5.** (*Slang*) Failure ; (ইতর ভাষায়) বিফলতা। ***Verb t.*** **1.** To injure by frost, as plants etc. ; তুষারদ্বারা নষ্ট করা। **2.** To cover with rime or as with rime ; to produce a surface like frost on, as glass, metal etc. ; ঘনীভূত নীহার বা তদ্বৎ কোন কিছু দ্বারা আচ্ছাদিত করা ; কাচ, ধাতু প্রভৃতির উপরিভাগ তুষারবৎ করা। **3.** To sharpen the points of a horse's shoe that it may not slip on ice ; বরফের উপর পদস্খলন নিবারণার্থ অশ্বের নালের কাঁটাসমূহ সুতীক্ষ্ণ করা। **4.** To turn white, as hair ; শ্বেতবর্ণ ধারণ করা। **Frost′-i-ly,** *adv.* **Frost′-i-ness,** *n.* **Frost′-less,** *adj.* Free from frost ; তুষারবিহীন। **Frost′-y,** *adj.* **1.** Cold ; freezing ; শীতল ; জমাটকারী। **2.** Covered with frost; তুষারাচ্ছাদিত। **3.** Chill in affection ; অনুরাগবিহীন, অনুরাগশূন্য, প্রীতিবিহীন। **4.** Hoary ; তুষারধবল। **Frost-bite** — The freezing of some part of a body by exposure to cold ; তুষারজনিত অবসাদ। **Frost bitten**— Affected with frost bite ; তুষার-ক্ষত, তুষার-ক্লিষ্ট, হিমগ্রস্ত (কেভি), হিমদগ্ধ (ঐ)। **Frost bound**—Confined by frost ; হিমবদ্ধ, তুষারবদ্ধ। **Frost work**— Tracery made by frost on glass etc. ; তুষার দ্বারা কাচপ্রভৃতির উপর রচিত বিচিত্র কারুকার্য্য।

frŏst′-ing, *n.* A composition of sugar with beaten egg, used to cover cake etc ; পিষ্টকাদি আচ্ছাদনের জন্য ফেটান ডিম ও চিনি দ্বারা প্রস্তুত তুষারকণাবৎ দ্রব্য।

frŏth, *n.*, *v. i.* & *t.* **1.** A collection of bubbles caused by agitation etc. ; ফেন, ফেনা, গাজলা, মণ্ড। **2.** Scum ; গাদ। **3.** Any empty show in speech ; worthless matter ; বৃথা বাগাড়ম্বর, ফেনিল ভাষা প্রয়োগ ; অসার জিনিষ। ***Verb i.*** To foam ; to emit or gather froth ; ফেনায়িত হওয়া, ফেনিল হওয়া, ফেনাইয়া উঠা ; ফেন নির্গত করা, ফেন নিঃসৃত হওয়া, ফেন সঞ্চিত হওয়া। ***Verb t.*** **1.** To cause to foam ; ফেনা উঠান, ফেনিল করা, সফেন করা, ফেনায়িত করা। **2.** To cover with froth ; ফেনাবৃত করা। **Froth′-i-ly,** *adv.* **Froth′-i-ness,** *n.* **Froth′-less,** *adj.* ফেনবিহীন। **Froth′-y,** *adj.* **1.** Full of foam ; foamy ; ফেনময় ; ফেনিল, সফেন। **2.** Light ; empty ; unsubstantial ; as, a *frothy* speaker ; লঘু ; শূন্য ; অসার।

frou′-frou (frōō-frōō), *n.* A rustling, as of dresses ; পোষাক প্রভৃতির খস্‌খস্ শব্দ।

frounce (frowns), *v. t.* (*Archaic*) To form wrinkles in or upon ; to plait ; to curl, as the hair ; (অপ্রঃ) কোঁচকান ; চুনট করা ; কুঞ্চিত করা।

frōw, *n.* A Dutch or German woman ; ওলন্দাজ বা জর্ম্মণ নারী।

frow (frō), *n.* A cleaving tool with handle at right angles to the blade ; পরশু, কুঠার।

frō′-ward (-wẽrd), *adj.* (*Archaic*) Perverse ; refractory ; (অপ্রঃ) একগুঁয়ে, ঠেঁটা ; বে-আড়া। **—ly,** *adv.* **—ness,** *n.*

frōwn, *v. i.*, *t.* & *n.* **1.** To knit the brows in displeasure, sternness etc ; to put on a grim or surly look ; ভ্রূকুটি করা, ভ্রূকুঞ্চিত করা, ভ্রূভঙ্গী করা, রোষকটাক্ষপাত করা ; চোক পাকান, চোক রাঙান, ভ্রূকুটি কুটিল-দৃষ্টি সম্পন্ন হওয়া। **2.** To manifest disapprobation ; বিরাগ প্রদর্শন করা। ***Verb t.*** To put down or repel with a frown ; as, to *frown down* an interrupter ; to manifest as defiance with a frown ; চোক পাকাইয়া দাবাইয়া দেওয়া ; ভ্রূকুটি প্রদর্শন দ্বারা অগ্রাহ্য করা। ***Noun.*** **1.** A wrinkling of the face in displeasure ; a scowl ; ভ্রূকুটী, ভ্রূভঙ্গী, ভ্রূকটীভঙ্গ, (কেভি), ভ্রূভঙ্গ ; চোকপাকানি, চোকরাঙ্গানি। **2.** A look expressing anger, severity, disapproval or deep thought ; রোষদৃষ্টি, বিরাগব্যঞ্জক-দৃষ্টি, গভীর চিন্তাব্যঞ্জক দৃষ্টি। **Frown′-ing-ly,** *adv.* **To frown at** or **on a person**—To look sternly at a person ; ভ্রূকুটিকটিল দৃষ্টিক্ষেপ করা, রোষকটাক্ষপাত করা।

frowst, *n.* & *v. i.* Fusty heat in a room ; কোন কোঠার ভাপ্‌সা তাপ ***Verb i.*** To enjoy it ; ঐরূপ তাপ উপভোগ করা। **Frowst′-y,** *adj.*

frōw′-zȳ, *adj.* Offensive to the smell ; nasty ; slovenly ; unkempt ; দুর্গন্ধময় ; তেঁতলা-ধরা ; নোংরা ; উস্কোখুস্কো।

frōze, *p. t.* Of FREEZE. **Fro′-zen,** *p. p.* Congealed with cold ; শীতে জমাট-বাঁধা, হিমস্তব্ধ (কেভি), হিমস্তম্ভিত (ঐ), হিমগ্রস্ত (ঐ)।

frŭc-tif′-ẽr-ous (-ŭs), *adj.* Bearing fruit ; ফলপ্রসূ, ফলোৎপাদক, ফলবান্ (কেভি), ফলদ (ঐ)।

frŭc′-ti-fȳ, *v. t.* & *i.* To make fruitful ; to fertilize ; ফলবন্ত করা ; উর্ব্বর করা। ***Verb i.*** To bear fruit ; ফলপ্রসূ হওয়া, ফলবান হওয়া। **—fi-ca′-tion,** *n.* **1.** (*Bot.*) Act of fructifying ; (উদ্ভিদ্‌ বিদ্যা) ফলোৎপাদন, ফলপ্রসব। **2.** The reproductive organs of a plant esp. of ferns and mosses ; পর্ণাঙ্গ, শৈবাল প্রভৃতির পুনরুৎপত্তিজনক অংশ।

urrency — To be current ; প্রচলিত হওয়া, চল্তি হওয়া। **To gain ground**—To advance; to acquire strength : অগ্রসর হওয়া ; শক্তি অর্জ্জন করা, বল লাভ করা। **To gain ground on or upon**—To encroach on or upon ; to get closer to (a person or thing pursued) ; কোন কিছুর উপর চড়াও হওয়া ; অধিকতর সন্নিহিত হওয়া, কাছে আসা, ক্রমশঃ নিকটবর্ত্তী হওয়া। **To gain head**—To gain or collect strength ; শক্তিলাভ করা, প্রবল হইয়া উঠা। **To gain into**—To persuade to join in ; কোন ব্যাপারে যোগদানে প্ররোচিত করা। **To gain on or upon**—To come closer to ; to encroach on or upon, as a sea on land ; to win the favour of ; to have an advantage over ; ক্রমশঃ নিকটবর্ত্তী হওয়া ; চাপিয়া পড়া ; অনুগ্রহ লাভ করা ; কাহারও উপর সুবিধা থাকা। **To gain one's point**—To accomplish one's aim ; উদ্দেশ্য সিদ্ধ করা, অভীষ্ট পূরণ করা। **To gain over**—To win over ; to draw to another party or interest ; উৎকোচাদি দানে বশীভূত করা ; পক্ষভুক্ত করা, দলভুক্ত করা। **To gain the day**—To win the victory ; জয়লাভ করা। **To gain the ear of**—To get favourable hearing from ; কোন ব্যক্তি সদয়ভাবে কর্ণপাত করিবেন এরূপ সৌভাগ্য লাভ করা। **To gain the honours of the day**—To win the victory honourably ; সসম্মানে জয় লাভ করা। **To gain the upperhand** — To become victorious ; জয়ী হওয়া। **To gain the wind**—(*Naut.*) To reach the windward side of another ship ; অপর জাহাজের বাতাহত দিকে পৌঁছা। **To gain time**--To take time by pretexts or slow methods ; নানা অছিলায় ও অজুহাতে সময় লওয়া।

gain-say' (gān-sā), *v. t.* To contradict or deny ; to dispute ; প্রতিবাদ করা, অস্বীকার করা ; বাদানুবাদ করা। **—er,** *n.* **—ing,** *n.* বিপরীত কথন, বিরুদ্ধ কথন।

gainst, 'gainst (gĕnst), *preps.* Poetic form of AGAINST which see.

gait (gāt), *n.* 1. Walk ; way ; "Go your *gait* and let poor folks pass" ; ভ্রমণ, গতি, চলন ; পথ। 2. Manner of walking or stepping ; "My limping *gait*" ; গতি-ভঙ্গী, গতিবিলাস (উজ্জ্বলঃ), চলনভঙ্গী। **Gait'-ed,** *adj.* **To gang one's gait**—To go on one's way ; আপন পথে চলা। **To gang to the gait**—To go to the wreck ; ধ্বংস প্রাপ্ত হওয়া। **To hold the gait**—To advance ; to prosper ; অগ্রসর হওয়া ; উন্নতি করা, শ্রীবৃদ্ধি প্রাপ্ত হওয়া। **To take the gait**—To start ; to depart ; যাত্রা করা ; প্রস্থান করা।

gai'-têr (gā-), *n.* 1. A covering of cloth or leather for the leg ; বস্ত্র বা চর্ম্মরচিত পাদচ্ছদ, গুল্‌ফত্রাণ। 2. A kind of half boot with a cloth top ; একপ্রকার বুট জুতা—উহার উপরিভাগ চর্ম্মরচিত

ga'-la (gā-lă, gä-lă), *n.* A festive occasion ; festivity ; উৎসবকাল ; উৎসব। **A gala day**—Festivity ; a holiday ; উৎসবদিন, উৎসব দিবস ; পর্ব্বদিন। **A gala dress**—উৎসববেশ, উৎসব-পরিচ্ছদ।

gă-lăc'-tă-gogue (-gŏg), *n.* A medicine which promotes the secretion of milk ; স্তন্যজনক ঔষধ, স্তন্যজনন (ঠাকুরঃ)।

gá-lăc'-tic, *adj.* 1. Relating to milk ; দুগ্ধ-সম্বন্ধীয়। 2. Pertaining to the Galaxy ; ছায়াপথ-সম্পর্কীয়। **Galactic circle** — মন্দাকিনী বৃত্ত (হিঃ কোঃ)। **Galactic poles**—মন্দাকিনী ধ্রুব (হিঃ কোঃ)।

găl-ăc-tŏm'-ĕ-tĕr, *n.* A lactometer ; দুগ্ধমান যন্ত্র।

găl'-ă-lith, *n.* A horn-like preparation made from caesin of milk and other substances as a substitute for horn, ivory etc. ; সরতোলা দুধের ছানা প্রভৃতি হইতে প্রস্তুত শৃঙ্গবৎ পদার্থ।

găl'-ăn-tine (-tēn), A dish of veal etc. boned and served cold ; গোবৎসের মাংস হইতে হাড় ছাড়াইয়া মসলা মিশ্রণপূর্ব্বক সিদ্ধকরত রক্ষিত ব্যঞ্জন-বিশেষ।

gă-lăn'-tȳ-show (-shō), *n.* Pantomime on a screen made by shadows of puppets ; একপ্রকার মূক অভিনয়,—যাহা পর্দ্দার উপর পুতুলের ছায়া ফেলিয়া অভিনীত হয়।

Găl'-ă-tē-ă, *n.* A sea-nymph beloved by the Cyclops Polyphemus who in jealous rage killed her lover Acis with a rock torn from the mountain side ; গ্যালেটিয়া গ্রীকপুরাণোক্ত সাগর-পরী বিশেষ। এই পরী Polyphemus নামক একচক্ষু দৈত্যের প্রণয়পাত্রী ছিলেন। ঐ পরী Acis নামক কোন ব্যক্তির প্রেমে পতিত হইলে Polyphemus পর্ব্বত গাত্র হইতে একখণ্ড পাষাণ চ্যুত করিয়া Acis কে শমনাগারে প্রেরণ করেন।

găl'-ăx-ȳ, *n.* 1. (*Astron.*) The Milky Way ; (জ্যোতি-বিজ্ঞান) ছায়াপথ, সুরনদী (সাঃ পঃ), নাগবীথী, (ঐ), সুরনদী (ঐ), আকাশগঙ্গা, স্বর্গগঙ্গা, স্বর্নদী, স্বর্গঙ্গা। 2. (*Fig.*) Brilliant persons or things; as, a *galaxy* of beauties ; প্রতিভাসমুজ্জ্বল ব্যক্তিগণের সমাগম, শ্রেষ্ঠ বস্তুসমূহের সংহতি। **A galaxy of beauties**—A coterie of handsome women ; লাবণ্যোজ্জ্বলা ললনাসমাজ।

găl'-bă-nŭm, *n.* A gum resin from certain Asiatic plants ; গন্ধবিরজা।

gāle, *n.* 1. A strong wind ; (*naut.*) storm ; প্রবল বায়ু ; ঝড়, তুফান, প্রভঞ্জন, ঝঞ্ঝা, চণ্ডবাত। 2. (*Poet.*) A gentle breeze ; (কবিতায়) মন্দ পবন, ধীর সমীর (গীতঃ), মৃদুপবন, মন্দানল, মৃদুমন্দ পবন। 3. A state of excitement ; উত্তেজিত অবস্থা, গোলযোগ, হাঙ্গামা, হুলস্থুল।

gāle, *n.* A periodical payment of rent ; খাজানার কিস্তি। **The gale day**—The day on which rent or interest is due ; খাজানা প্রদানের দিন, সুদ প্রদানের দিন। **The hanging gale**—Arrears of rent; বাকী খাজানা, বকেয়া বাকী (Arrears of rent of a previous year)।

gāle, *n.* A small shrub found in bogs ; বিলাভূমিতে জাত ক্ষুদ্র গুল্ম-বিশেষ।

gă′-lē-ă, *n.* (*Zool.*) **1.** A helmet-like structure in shape, position, etc. ; (জন্তু-বিদ্যা) জন্তুগণের মস্তকস্থ শিরস্ত্রাকার উপাঙ্গ। **2.** (*Bot.*) Any helmet-shaped part of a calyx or corolla ; (উদ্ভিদ্-বিদ্যা) হরিদ্বর্ণ পুষ্পাচ্ছাদন পত্র অথবা পুষ্পের গর্ভদলের শিরস্ত্রাকার অংশ। **3.** (*Pathol.*) Headache extending all over the head ; (নিদান-শাস্ত্র) সর্ব্ব মস্তকব্যাপী শিরোবেদনা। **–ate, –at-ed,** *adjs.* **1.** Shaped like a helmet ; শিরস্ত্রাকার (সাঃ পঃ)। **2.** Wearing a helmet ; covered with a helmet ; শিরস্ত্রাণ শোভিত, শিরস্ত্রাবৃত।

gă-lee′-nȳ (-lē-), *n.* Guinea fowl ; গিনি প্রদেশ হইতে সমানীত ধূসরবর্ণ পক্ষিবিশেষ।

Gă′-lĕn, *n.* A famous ancient Greek physician ; hence humourously a physician ; প্রাচীন গ্রীসের জনৈক সুবিখ্যাত চিকিৎসক; (কৌতুকচ্ছলে) চিকিৎসক, ধন্বন্তরি।

gă-lē′-nă, (*Min.*) *n.* The principal ore of lead ; অঞ্জন (সাঃ পঃ), সৌবীরাঞ্জন (ঐ), কৃষ্ণসুর্ম্মা (ঐ), স্রোতোঽঞ্জন (আয়ুরসঃ)।

gă-lĕn′-ic, *adj.* Of, or relating to, Galen : প্রাচীন গ্রীসবাসী সুবিখ্যাত বৈদ্য গেলেন সম্বন্ধীয়।

gă-lĕn′-i-căl, *adj.* & *n.* Same as GALENIC. ***Noun.*** A vegetable medicine ; উদ্ভিজ্জ ঔষধ, বনৌষধ।

găl′-i-lee (-lē), *n.* (*Arch.*) A porch or chapel at the entrance of a church ; (স্থপতি-বিদ্যা) খৃষ্টীয় ধর্ম্মমন্দিরের দ্বারমণ্ডপ, খৃষ্টীয় ধর্ম্মমন্দিরের দ্বারদেশস্থ ক্ষুদ্র ভজনালয়।

galimatias, (*F.*), *n.* Confused meaningless talk ; gibberish ; প্রলাপ ; বিড়বিড়, বড়বড়ানি।

găl′-in-gale, *n.* **1.** Aromatic root of certain East Indian plants ; চীনা কালাঞ্জন (খোরী), সুগন্ধ বচ, সর্ব্বজয়া। **2.** (Also *English galingale*) A kind of sedge, জলাভূমিতে জাত একপ্রকার শৈবাল।

găl′-i-pŏt, *n.* A kind of hardened turpentine ; একপ্রকার কঠিনীকৃত তার্পিণ।

găll, *n.* **1.** The bitter fluid secreted in the liver of animals ; bile ; পিত্তরস ; পিত্ত। **2.** The gall bladder ; পিত্তাশয়, পিত্তকোষ, পিত্ত, ক্লোম (ব্রজঃ হিন্দু)। **3.** Any extremely bitter substance ; নিতান্ত তিক্ত বস্তু। **4.** (*Fig.*) Rancour ; asperity ; "Lips ···· imbued with *gall*" ; bitterness ; বিদ্বেষ, দ্রোহভাব ; রুক্ষতা, উগ্রতা, কর্কশতা ; তিক্ততা। **Gall-stone**—পিত্তকোষে যে পাথরের ন্যায় পদার্থ সঞ্চিত হয়, পিত্তশিলা, পিত্তাশ্মরী। **Gall and wormwood**—Extremely disagreeable and annoying ; নিরতিশয় তিক্ত বা অপ্রীতিকর। **The gall of bitterness** — Extreme affliction or grief ; অসীম কষ্ট বা দুঃখ। **To add gall to bitterness** — কাটা ঘায়ে নুনের ছিটা দেওয়া, জ্বালার উপর জ্বালা দেওয়া।

găll, *n.* An excrescence produced by certain insects on trees, esp. the oak, (also called *oak-gall*) ; ওক প্রভৃতি বৃক্ষগাত্রে জাত কীটজনিত অর্ব্বুদ, মাজুফল। **Gall-fly**—An insect producing galls ; বৃক্ষগাত্রে অর্ব্বুদ উৎপাদক কীট-বিশেষ। **G. moth**—সরু গোঁফুয়া (যোঃ)। **G. nut**—Same as GALL ; মাজুফ কর্কটশৃঙ্গী।

Oak galls and gall-fly.

găll, *n.* **1.** A painful blister, in horse ; a sore in the made by rubbing ; ফুস্কুড়ী, (বিশেষতঃ ঘোটকের) ; ঘর্ষণদ্বারা উপর উৎপন্ন ক্ষত। **2.** (*Fi* state of mental soreness irritation ; (লক্ষণায়) মর্ম্ম মর্ম্মক্ষত। **3.** Flaw ; "Take that your hair be ····free fi *gall*" ; খুঁত, ত্রুটি।

găll, *v. t.* & *i.* **1.** To chafe ; hurt the skin of by rubbi রগড়াইয়া গরম করা ; রগড়াইয়া নুণ তোলা। **2.** To vex ; to humilia to harass ; "The multit *galled* them with a clou arrows" ; বিরক্ত করা, দিক (*colloq.*) ; অবমানিত করা, মর্য্য করা ; উত্ত্যক্ত করা, জ্বালাতন ***Verb i.*** To become worn rubbing ; ঘর্ষণ হেতু ক্ষয়প্রাপ্ত হও **Gall′-ing,** *adj.* Irritati বিরক্তিজনক, জ্বালাকর।

găl′-lănt, *adj.* & *n* **1.** (*Arch* Showy ; well-dressed ; (অ জমকালো, চটকদার, শোভন ; স্ব সম্পন্ন। **2.** Grand ; stately ship, horse, etc.) ; জাঁকাল ; (ঘোটক প্রভৃতি সম্পর্কে) বি **3.** Brave ; শূর, শৌর্য্যসম্পন্ন। **4.** (Usu. **–lant′**) Polite and courteous to women ; স্ত্রীলোকের প্রতি শিষ্টাচার পরায়ণ, রমণীরঞ্জক, স্ত্রীসম্মানী (কেভি), স্ত্রীজনতোষী (ঐ), স্ত্রীজনানুবর্ত্তী (ঐ), স্ত্রীপ্রেমী (ঐ), স্ত্রীসম্মানপর (ঐ)। **5.** Amatory ; amorous ; শৃঙ্গারভাবোদ্দীপক ; শৃঙ্গাররসিক। ***Noun.*** **1.** A gay or fashionable man ; আমোদী লোক আমোদতরল ব্যক্তি, সৌখীন লোক **2.** (Usu. **–lant**) A man attentiv to ladies ; a paramour ; a suitor স্ত্রীলোকের প্রতি সৌজন্য প্রদর্শনকারী জার, উপপতি, নাগর,

নটবর ; বিবাহার্থ প্রণয়প্রার্থী ব্যক্তি। **—lant'-ly, —ly,** *advs.*

găl-lănt', *v. t. & i.* To wait on or attend to ; to escort ; as, to *gallant* a lady ; পরিচর্য্যা করা ; শরীর রক্ষার্থ অনুগমন করা। ***Verb i.*** To make love, (followed by *with*) ; প্রেম করা, প্রণয় করা।

găl'-lănt-rÿ, *n.* **1.** Bravery ; as, the *gallantry* of the soldiers ; শৌর্য্য, বীরত্ব। **2.** Behaviour of a gallant ; নাগরালি। **3.** Polite attention to ladies ; স্ত্রীলোকের পরিচর্য্যা, রমণীরঞ্জন। **4.** Amorous intrigue ; sexual immorality ; প্রণয়চক্রান্ত, গুপ্তপ্রণয় ; লাম্পট্য, অবৈধ কামোপভোগ। **5.** A gallant act or speech ; "To exchange a few *gallantries* with a lady" ; রমণী রঞ্জনার্থ অনুষ্ঠিত কার্য্য, রমণীজনমনোরঞ্জক বাক্য।

găl-lē-ŏn, *n.* A large ship formerly used by the Spaniards ; পূর্ব্বে স্পেনদেশীয়গণ কর্ত্তৃক ব্যবহৃত একপ্রকার বৃহৎ জাহাজ।

găl'-lêr-ÿ, *n. & v. t.* **1.** A corridor ; a portico ; a colonnade ; বারদালান ; দ্বারমণ্ডপ, গাড়ী-বারান্দা ; স্তম্ভপংক্তি। **2.** A balcony surrounded by rails ; (*naut.*) a frame like a balcony ; গরাদবেষ্টিত অলিন্দ ; অলিন্দাকৃতি প্রলম্বিত মঞ্চ। **3.** A room for exhibition of works of art ; a collection of paintings etc. ; শিল্পদ্রব্য প্রদর্শনের জন্য কক্ষ বা গৃহ, চিত্রশালা, চিত্রশালিকা ; চিত্রাদির সংগ্রহ। **4.** A platform projecting from the inner wall of a church hall etc. providing extra room for audience etc. ; (গির্জ্জা বা নাট্যশালার) উপাসকমণ্ডলী বা শ্রোতৃবৃন্দের উপবেশনের জন্য প্রাচীরের মধ্যভাগ হইতে প্রলম্বিত মঞ্চ। **5.** The upper floor of seats in a church or theatre ; ভজনালয় বা রঙ্গালয়ের প্রাচীর হইতে প্রলম্বিত আসনরাজি সমন্বিত সর্ব্বোর্দ্ধ মঞ্চ। **6.** The assemblage of persons occupying the gallery of a theatre ; (*fig.*) the less refined portion of the audience ; নাট্যশালার উক্ত প্রলম্বিত মঞ্চে উপবিষ্ট দর্শকবৃন্দ ; ইতর শ্রেণীর দর্শক। **7.** (*Mil.*) An underground passage ; (সামরিক শাস্ত্র) অন্তর্ভৌম বর্ত্ম, সুড়ঙ্গ পথ। *Verb t.* To furnish with a gallery ; প্রলম্বিত মঞ্চবিশিষ্ট করা। **—ful,** *adj.* **—y-ite,** *n.* One who occupies a seat in a gallery ; যে ব্যক্তি রঙ্গালয়ের প্রলম্বিত মঞ্চে উপবেশন করিয়া থাকে। **To play the gallery**—To appeal to the lower taste ; নিম্নশ্রেণীর দর্শকবৃন্দের মনোরঞ্জনার্থ অভিনয় করা, ইতর লোকদিগের বাহবা লাভের চেষ্টা করা। **To play with one eye on the gallery** — To work for popularity ; লোকপ্রিয় হওয়ার উদ্দেশ্যে কাজ করা।

găl'-ley (-lĭ), *n.* **1.** (*Chiefly Hist.*) A single-decked ship using oars and sails ; (প্রধানতঃ ইতিহাসে) একতলবিশিষ্ট প্রাচীন পোতবিশেষ—যাহা দাঁড় এবং পাইলে চলিত। **2.** The boat of a warship used by the captain ; পোতাধ্যক্ষের ব্যবহারার্থ রণপোত-সংলগ্ন নৌকা। **3.** An ancient Greek or Roman warship propelled by oars ; প্রাচীন গ্রীস বা রোমের দাঁড় দ্বারা চালিত পোত। **4.** The cook room of a ship ; জাহাজের রন্ধনাগার। **5.** (*Print.*) An oblong frame used is printing ; বিন্যস্ত অক্ষরপংক্তি সমূহ রাখিবার জন্য দস্তা বা কাঠের লম্বা ফলক। **Galley-proof**—ঐরূপ ফলক হইতে চাপ দিয়া যে মুদ্রনী পত্র তোলা হয়। **Galley-slave**—A person condemned to row in a galley ; (*fig.*) a drudge ; পূর্ব্বে যে অপরাধীকে জাহাজে বাঁধিয়া রাখিয়া অবিশ্রান্ত দাঁড় টানান হইত, নৌ-দাস, পোতদাস ; (লক্ষণায়) কঠিন পরিশ্রমজনক কার্য্যে নিযুক্ত ব্যক্তি। **Galley-worm**—একপ্রকার বহুপদী কীট।

Găl'-lī, *n.* (*Pl.—Rom. antiq.*) The priests of Cybele at Rome ; রোম নগরীর শিবীলী দেবীর (Cybele) পুরোহিত বৃন্দ।

găl'-liard (-yȧrd), *n.* A brisk, gay dance ; উল্লাসপূর্ণ নৃত্যবিশেষ।

Găl'-lic, *adj.* Pertaining to Gaul or the Gauls ; French ; গল্ বা ফ্রান্সদেশ সম্পর্কীয় ; ফরাসীদেশীয়, ফরাসীজাতীয়। **—li-cism,** *n.* A French idiom ; a French custom ; ফরাসী ভাষার রীতিসিদ্ধ প্রয়োগ, ফরাসী ভাষা-রীতি ; ফরাসীয় রীতি। **—li-cize,** *v. t. & i.* To conform to the French idiom or language ; ফরাসীভাষার রীতিসিদ্ধ প্রয়োগের অনুযায়ী হওয়া, ফরাসীভাষার অনুযায়ী হওয়া। (*Verb i.*) To use Gallicism ; ফরাসীভাষার রীতি-অনুযায়ী প্রয়োগ করা।

găl'-lic, *adj.* Of, or derived from, galls of oak, apples, etc. : মাজুফল-সম্পর্কীয়, মাজুফল হইতে উৎপন্ন। **Gallic acid**—মাজুফল হইতে প্রাপ্ত অম্লবিশেষ—উহা কালি প্রস্তুতে ব্যবহৃত হয়।

Găl'-li-căn, *adj. & n.* **1.** Of the ancient church of Gaul or France ; গল বা ফরাসীদেশের প্রাচীন ধর্ম্মসংঘসম্বন্ধীয়। **2.** (*Palæograph.*) Relating to Gaul or France ; (পুরালিপি-বিদ্যা) ফরাসীদেশীয়। ***Noun.*** One holding Gallican doctrine ; ফরাসীদেশে পোপের আধিপত্যে প্রতিরোধী ব্যক্তি। **—ism,** *n.* Resistance to Papal domination in France ; ফরাসীদেশে পোপের আধিপত্য প্রতিরোধ। **—ist,** *n.*

Găl'-li-cē, *adv.* In French ; ফরাসী ভাষায়।

găl'-li-găs-kin, *n.* (*Pl.*) Trousers ; loose breeches ; পাজামা ; ঢিলা ইজের।

găl-li-mau'-frÿ (-mä-), *n.* **1.** A ragout ; গরমমসলা সহযোগে রান্ধিত মাংস। **2.** A medley ; মিশ্র।

găl-li-nā'-ceous (-shŭs), *adj.* Of, or pertaining to, the order of birds including domestic fowl, pheasants etc. ; কুক্কুটাদি জাতীয়। **—cean,** *adj. & n.*

găl′-lĭ-nūle, *n.* A genus of aquatic birds closely allied to the coots ; একজাতীয় জলচর পক্ষী, কাকমদ্গু, জলকুক্কুট, কালকণ্ঠ।

găl′-lĭ-ō, *n.* A man refusing to meddle outside his province ; a careless easy going man ; নিজের নির্দ্দিষ্ট প্রভাবমণ্ডল বা কার্য্যক্ষেত্রের বাহিরে হস্তক্ষেপ করিতে নারাজ—এইরূপ ব্যক্তি ; আরামপ্রিয় ব্যক্তি [Junius Annaeus Gallilo নামক Achaia প্রদেশের রোমীয় শাসনকর্ত্তা,—যিনি ইহুদীগণের আন্দোলন স্বত্ত্বেও St. Paulএর বিরুদ্ধে হস্তক্ষেপ করেন নাই—তদীয় নাম হইতে গৃহীত, See Acts xviii, 12—17] ।

găl′-lĭ-ŏt, –ĭ-ŏt, *ns.* A two masted Dutch cargo vessel ; হলেণ্ড দেশীয় দ্বি-মাস্তুল মালের জাহাজ।

găl′-lĭ-pŏt, *n.* A small glazed earthen pot for holding medicines ; মলমাদি রাখার জন্য চিনামাটীর কৌটা।

găl′-lĭ-ŭm, *n.* A soft bluish-white metal ; একপ্রকার নীলাভ-শ্বেত কোমল ধাতু।

găl-lĭ-vănt′, *v. i.* To go about esp. with one of the other sex ; নাগরালি করিয়া বেড়ান, (পুরুষের পক্ষে) স্ত্রীলোকের পাছু পাছু ছুটিয়া বেড়ান, (স্ত্রীলোকের পক্ষে) পুরুষের সঙ্গে সঙ্গে ঘুরিয়া বেড়ান।

găl′-lĭ-văt, *n.* (*Obs.*) A vessel used on the Malabar coast ; (অপ্রঃ) মালাবার উপকূলে ব্যবহৃত দ্বি-মাস্তুল নৌকা।

găl′-lon (-lŭn), *n.* A liquid measure of 4 quarts ; তরলপদার্থের পরিমাণ বিশেষ, দ্রবমান বিশেষ।

Găl′-lō–, A combining form for Gallic.

găl-lo͞on′, *n.* A narrow lace or ribbon made of gold, silver, silk or cotton ; রেসম, সূতা বা জরীর সরু ফিতা, জরি, গোটা।

găl′-lop (-lŭp), *n., v. i. & t.* The quickest springing gait of various quadrupeds, esp. the horse ; a ride at a gallop ; অশ্বের প্লুত বা রেচিত গতি ; প্লুতগতিতে অশ্বচালন। ***Verb i.*** **1.** To runwith leaps, as a horse ; to run rapidly ; (অশ্ব পক্ষে) লাফাইয়া ছুটা ; পূর্ণবেগে ধাবিত হওয়া, দ্রুতবেগে ধাবিত হওয়া। **2.** To ride a horse at a gallop ; "He *galloped* up to join them" ; পূর্ণবেগে অশ্ব ছুটাইয়া দেওয়া। **3.** (*Fig.*) To hurry (in reading or reciting) ; to talk fast, (with *over, through*) ; as, I will *gallop* through the discourse as fast as I can ; (লক্ষণায়) অতি দ্রুত পাঠ বা আবৃত্তি করা, অতি তাড়াতাড়ি কথা বলা। ***Verb t.*** To cause to gallop ; দ্রুতবেগে অশ্ব ছুটান। **–ing,** *p. adj.* Going at a gallop ; (*fig.*) advancing rapidly ; প্লুত গতিতে ধাবমান ; (লক্ষণায়) দ্রুতগামী। **Canterbury gallop**—A moderate gallop of a horse ; ঘোটকের অনতিদ্রুত দৌড় বা ধাবন। **Full gallop**—*n. & adv.* The quickest pace of a horse ; অশ্বের পূর্ণগতি, রেচিত (বিনয়)। (*Adv.*) At a full gallop ; পূর্ণবেগে। **Galloping consumption**—রাজযক্ষ্মা। **Hand gallop**—A slow or gentle gallop ; মৃদু ধাবন, মৃদু রেচিত গতি। **Snail's gallop**—(*Jocularly*) An extremely slow pace ; (কৌতুকচ্ছলে) শম্বুকগতি, অতি মৃদুগতি। **At a full gallop**—পূর্ণ বেগে। **To gallop away**—To talk fast ; তাড়াতাড়ি কথা বলা। **To gallop over, through**—See GAPLLOP *v. i.* 3.

găl-lo-pāde′ (-lŭ-), *n.* **1.** A lively dance ; উল্লাসপূর্ণ নৃত্য-বিশেষ। **2.** (In horsemanship) A side-long gallop ; অশ্বের পার্শ্ব প্লুতগতি।

gal′-lop-êr (-lŭp-), *n.* **1.** A man or horse that gallops ; পূর্ণবেগে ধাবনশীল অশ্ব বা ঐরূপ অশ্বের আরোহী। **2.** (*Mil.*) Aide-de-camp ; a light field gun ; (সামরিক শাস্ত্র) সেনাপতির আজ্ঞাবহ সৈনিক কর্ম্মচারী ; একপ্রকার হাল্কা ময়দানী কামান।

găl′-lō-way (-wā), *n.* A small strong horse from Gallow-way in Scotland ; a small horse ; স্কটল্যাণ্ডের অন্তর্গত গেলওয়ে প্রদেশের ক্ষুদ্রকায় বলবান অশ্ব ; ক্ষুদ্রকায় ঘোটক।

găl′-lows (-lōz), *n.* (*Pl. treated as sing.*) **1.** A wooden frame for hanging criminals ; similar frame for suspending anything ; ফাঁসীকাঠ, বধ্যকাষ্ঠ ; কোন কিছু ঝুলাইয়া রাখিবার জন্য ফাঁসী কাঠের আকার কাঠাম। **2.** A gymnastic apparatus ; ব্যায়ামের যন্ত্র-বিশেষ। **3.** Punishment by hanging ; ফাঁসী। **4.** (*Print.*) The rest for the tympan when raised ; (মুদ্রণে) ছাপিবার সাদা কাগজ যে চর্ম্মাবৃত ঢাকনির উপর লাগান হয় তাহা উত্তোলিত অবস্থায় যে কাঠামের উপর রক্ষিত হয়। **Gallows-bird**—ফাঁসী কাঠে ঝুলিবার উপযুক্ত লোক, নরাধম। **Gallows-ripe** — ফাঁসীর উপযুক্ত। **Gallows-tree**—ফাঁসীকাষ্ঠ। **A gallows look** — A sinister appearance ; অশুভ দর্শন। **To have the gallows in one's face**—To have the look of one deserving the gallows ; ফাঁসীকাঠে ঝুলিবার উপযুক্ত লোকের মত দেখান, হত্যাকারীর মতন দেখান।

Gallus Ferrugineus — বনমোরগ (বেলঃ), জঙ্গলী মোরগ (ঐ)।

găl′-op (-ŭp), *n. & v. i.* A lively dance ; একপ্রকার উল্লাস-পূর্ণ নৃত্য। ***Verb i.*** To dance a gallop ; ঐরূপ নৃত্য করা।

gă-lore′ (-lōr), *adv. n.* Plentifully ; প্রচুর ভাবে, প্রচুররূপে, প্রচুর পরিমাণে, পর্য্যাপ্ত পরিমাণ। ***Noun.*** Plenty ; প্রাচুর্য্য, ছড়াছড়ি।

gă-lŏsh′, gă-loshe′ (-lŏsh), **gŏ-lŏsh′,** *ns.* **1.** An over-shoe ; বর্ষাকালে চর্ম্ম পাদুকার উপর পরিহিত পাদুকা বিশেষ। **2.** A gaiter covering the upper part of the shoe and part of the leg ; জুতার উপরিভাগ এবং পদের অংশ আচ্ছাদক পাদচ্ছদ। **–loshed,** *p. adj.*

gă-lŭmph′, *v. i.* To go prancing in triumph ; জয়োল্লাসে নৃত্য করিতে করিতে যাওয়া ।

găl-văn′-ic, *adj.* **1.** Relating to galvanism ; exhibiting or containing it ; রাসায়নিক ক্রিয়া দ্বারা উৎপন্ন তাড়িত সম্পর্কীয় ; উক্তরূপ তাড়িত প্রদর্শক, রাসায়নিক বিদ্যুদ্গর্ভ । **2.** (*Fig.*) (Of smile etc.) Sudden and forced ; (হাস্যাদি সম্পর্কে) কৃত্রিম এবং আকস্মিক ।

Galvanic battery ; *c*, copper plates ; *z*, zinc plates.

—i-cal-ly, *adv.* **Galvanic-battery**—বিজলীপ্রবাহ উৎপাদক যন্ত্র-বিশেষ [এতদ্দ্বারা রুগ্ন ব্যক্তির দেহে তাড়িত-প্রবাহ সঞ্চারিত হয়] । **Galvanic-belt**—দেহে রাসায়নিক বিদ্যুৎ প্রয়োগের জন্য কটিবন্ধনী বিশেষ । **Galvanic electricity** — রাসায়নিক বিদ্যুৎ । **Galvanic pile**—রাসায়নিক তাড়িত উৎপাদনের জন্য ধাতব চক্রের স্তূপ বিশেষ ।

găl′-vă-nĭsm, *n.* **1.** Electricity generated by chemical action ; দস্তা, তাম্র প্রভৃতি ধাতু হইতে ভিন্ন ভিন্ন প্রকার দ্রাবকাদির সংযোগে রাসায়নিক ক্রিয়া বশতঃ সমুৎপন্ন তাড়িত [আবিষ্কারক Lugi Galvani র নাম হইতে গৃহীত], রাসায়নিক ক্রিয়া দ্বারা সঞ্জাত বিদ্যুৎ, রাসায়নিক বিদ্যুৎ । **2.** Application of this for medical purposes ; চিকিৎসার উদ্দেশ্যে উক্তরূপ বিদ্যুৎপ্রবাহ প্রয়োগ । **3.** The branch of electrical science treating dynamical electricity ; চলবিদ্যুৎ শাস্ত্র-সম্বন্ধীয় তাড়িত-বিজ্ঞান । **—nist**, *n.* One versed in galvanism ; রাসায়নিক তাড়িত-তত্ত্বজ্ঞ ।

găl′-vă-nīze, *v. t.* **1.** To affect with galvanism ; রাসায়নিক তাড়িত দ্বারা প্রভাবিত করা । **2.** To electroplate ; to coat, as iron with zinc etc. ; তাড়িত প্রবাহ দ্বারা গিল্টি করা ; তাড়িত প্রবাহ দ্বারা কালাই করা । **3.** To restore to consciousness by galvanic action ; to stimulate thus ; as, her approach *galvanized* him to new life ; রাসায়নিক তাড়িতশক্তির ক্রিয়া দ্বারা চৈতন্য সম্পাদন করা ; রাসায়নিক তাড়িতপ্রবাহ সঞ্চারদ্বারা সঞ্জীবিত করা । **—ni-za′-tion**, *n.* **—niz-er**, *n.* **Galvanized iron**—দস্তামণ্ডিত লোহার পাত ।

găl-vă-nŏm′-ĕ-têr, *n.* An instrument for measuring the strength of galvanic current ; রাসায়নিক

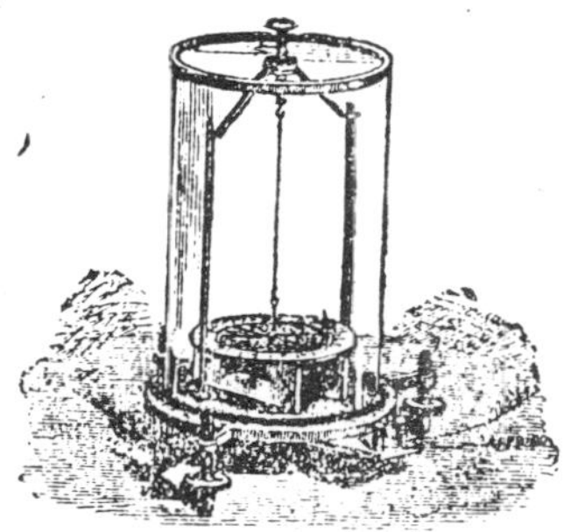

Galvanometer.

তাড়িত প্রবাহের স্থিতি, শক্তি এবং দিঙ্‌নির্ণয়ার্থ যন্ত্র-বিশেষ, বিদ্যুৎশক্তিমাপক (হিঃ কোঃ), প্রবাহ মাপক (সাঃ পঃ) ।

găl-vă-nŏm′-ĕ-trȳ, *n.* The measurement of galvanic current ; তড়িৎপ্রবাহশক্তি পরিমাপ ।

găl′-vă-nō-scōpe, *n.* An instrument for detecting the existence and direction of an electric current ; তাড়িতের স্থিতি ও গতি নিরূপক যন্ত্র, বিদ্যুত্তরঙ্গ দর্শক (হিঃ কোঃ), বিদ্যুৎপ্রবাহদর্শক, প্রবাহ দর্শক (সাঃ পঃ) ।

găm′-bă, *n.* A stringed instrument, (also called *Viola da gamba*) ; একপ্রকার বেহালা ।

găm-bāde′, —bā′-dō, *ns.* (*Pl.* -DOES) **1.** A leap of a horse ; অশ্বের লম্ফ, ঘোড়ার লাফ । **2.** A prank ; a freak ; ফষ্টিনষ্টি ; খেয়াল, মর্জ্জি ।

găm-bā′-dō, *n.* (*Pl.* -DOES), Leather leggings ; চর্ম্মনির্ম্মিত জঙ্ঘাত্রাণ ।

găm′-bier (-bër), **—beer** (-bër), **—bir**, *ns.* A vegetable extract used in tanning etc. ; খয়ের, কৎ, খদির, হরিদ্রুম (ঠাকুরঃ), গায়ত্রী (অমরঃ), বালতনয় (ঐ), দন্তধাবন, অরিমেদ (বিট্‌ খদির), কদর (white), সোমবল্ক (*ibid.*) ।

găm′-bĭt, *n.* (In chess) A mode of opening the game incurring the sacrifice of a pawn ; (দাবাখেলা) খেলার প্রথম অবস্থায় আক্রমণের পক্ষে সুবিধাজনক স্থান লাভের উদ্দেশ্যে অগ্রেই একটী বড়ে ত্যাগ ।

găm′-ble (-bl), *v. i., t.* & *n.* **1.** To play for money, esp. for high stakes ; দ্যূত-ক্রীড়া করা, জুয়াখেলা, স্ফূর্ত্তি খেলা । **2.** To take great risks to secure great results in war, finance, etc. ; যুদ্ধ, অর্থ-ঘটিত ব্যাপার প্রভৃতিতে সুমহান্ ফল লাভের উদ্দেশ্যে বড় ঝুঁকি লওয়া । ***Verb t.*** To squander (*away*) by gambling ; জুয়া খেলিয়া উড়াইয়া দেওয়া । ***Noun.*** Act of gambling ; risky undertaking or attempt ; জুয়াখেলা, স্ফূর্ত্তি-খেলা ; ঝুঁকিদার কার্য্য বা চেষ্টা । **—bler**, *n.* One who gambles ; জুয়াড়ী, দ্যূতকার (মৃচ্ছঃ) । **—bling**, *n.* The act of one who gambles ; দ্যূত-ক্রীড়া, জুয়াখেলা, দেবন, দ্যূত । **—some**, *adj.* Frolicsome ; ক্রীড়াপ্রিয়, রঙ্গপ্রিয়, লীলাপ্রিয় । **Gambling board**—দ্যূতফলক । **Gambling house**—দ্যূতশালা, দ্যূতগৃহ দ্যূতসদন, জুয়ার আড্ডা, দ্যূতমণ্ডল (মঃ ভাঃ) । **On the gamble**—Engaged in a spell of gambling ; জুয়াখেলায় নিযুক্ত ।

găm-boge′ (-bŏj, -bōj), *n.* Gum resin obtained from various trees used as a pigment ; গটীফেরী-জাতীয় বৃক্ষবিশেষের অতিবিরেচক নির্য্যাস,—ইহা ঔষধাদি প্রস্তুতে ও রঞ্জন কার্য্যে ব্যবহৃত হয় ।

găm′-bŏl, *v. i.* & *n.* To leap in frolick ; to frisk ; লাফালাফি করা, নর্ত্তনকুর্দ্দন করা, নাচাকুঁদা করা,

ধেই ধেই করিয়া নাচা; ক্রীড়াচ্ছলে লম্ফঝম্প দেওয়া। ***Noun.*** A skip; a sportive prank; ক্রীড়াচ্ছলে লম্ফঝম্প, নর্ত্তনকুর্দ্দন; ফষ্টিনষ্টি।

game, *n.* **1.** Sport of any kind; fun; as, pleasant *game*; jest; "To make *game* of his scruples"; ক্রীড়া, খেলা; কৌতুক; ঠাট্টা, তামাসা। **2.** A pleasant incident; "Oh, what a game!" প্রীতিপ্রদ ঘটনা। **3.** An exercise or play for amusement testing skill etc.; as, the *games* of cricket; প্রতিযোগিতামূলক মল্লক্রীড়া। **4.** A single match at play; as, a *game* at cards; খেলার বাজি, এক বাজি। **5.** The winning score in a game; "... and ten constitute *game*"; কোন ক্রীড়ায় জয়াঙ্ক। **6.** A scheme pursued; a plan; "Your murderous *game* is nearly up"; ব্যবস্থা; কল্পনা। **7.** A hunted animal; an object of pursuit; "I fly at a higer game"; মৃগয়ালব্ধ জন্তু, শিকার; অনুসৃত বস্তু, ইষ্ট পদার্থ। **8.** A diversion or pastime; আমোদ প্রমোদ, চিত্তবিনোদন, ক্রীড়া কৌতুক। **9.** (*Collectively*) Wild beasts, birds, etc. hunted for sport or food; their flesh; (সংঘবাচক ভাবে) বন্য জন্তু, পক্ষী প্রভৃতি যাহাদিগকে আমোদ বা আহারের জন্য শিকার করা হয়, শিকার, জাঙ্গল (জাঙ্গলাঃ প্রায়শঃ সর্ব্বে লঘবো বলবর্দ্ধনাঃ—ভাবপ্রকাশ।); শিকারের মাংস। **10.** (*Commer.*) Apparatus for a game; (বাণিজ্য) ক্রীড়া-যন্ত্র। **11.** Tricks; "... are up to such *games*"; চাতুরী। **Gam'-y,** *adj.* **1.** Abounding in games; মৃগয়ার উপযোগী জন্তুদ্বারাপূর্ণ। **2.** Courageous (*rare*); সাহসী (ক্বচিদ্ ব্যবহৃত)। **Big game**—The large animals hunted; সিংহ, ব্যাঘ্র প্রভৃতি মৃগয়ালব্ধ বৃহৎ জন্তুসমূহ। **Fair game**—A legitimate object of pursuit; অনুসরণযোগ্য বিষয়। **Game-bag**—শিকার রাখার জন্য থলিয়া। **Game-ball**—আণ্টাল প্রভৃতি ক্রীড়ায় যে অবস্থায় এক পক্ষ এক জয়াঙ্ক লাভ করিতে পারে। **Game-cock, -fowl**—লড়াইর জন্য শিক্ষিত কুক্কুট, যোধকুক্কুট। **Game-keeper** — শিকার-রক্ষক। **Game-laws**—মৃগয়ার উপযোগী জন্তু রক্ষার্থ বিধি। **Game-license** — শিকারের জন্য কিম্বা শিকারে নিহত পশুর ব্যবসায় করার জন্য অনুমতি। **Game-preserver**—যে ভূম্যধিকারী মৃগয়ার্থ পশু পালন করেন এবং মৃগরক্ষা-সম্বন্ধীয় আইন কঠোরভাবে প্রয়োগ করিয়া থাকেন। **Game-tenant**—পশু বা মৎস্য শিকারের জন্য ভূমি বা জলার ইজারাদার। **A game at which two can play**—A course of action equally open to another person; যে কার্য্যপ্রণালী উভয়েই সমভাবে অনুসরণ করিতে পারে। **A game of chance**—ভাগ্য পরীক্ষার খেলা, যে খেলায় জয় পরাজয় অদৃষ্টের উপর নির্ভর করে। **Are you game for a spree**—Are you inclined to join in a bit of fun (in allusion to game-cocks); তুমি কি একটু মজা করিতে চাও? **A round game**—A game, as at cards, in which the number of players is not fixed; যে তাস খেলায় ক্রীড়কগণের সংখ্যা নির্দ্দিষ্ট থাকে না। **Game and game**—One game scored to each side; প্রত্যেক দিকে এক জয়াঙ্ক লাভ হইয়াছে। **He is game for anything** — He is ready to venture upon anything; full of life; সে যে কোনরূপ কার্য্যে সাহসের সহিত প্রবৃত্ত হইতে প্রস্তুত; প্রাণপূর্ণ। **That's your little game**—That is your policy or plan of action; তাহাই হইতেছে তোমার কার্য্যপ্রণালী। **The game's afoot**—The enterprise has begun; সেই কার্য্য আরম্ভ হইয়াছে। **The game is not worth the candle**—The thing is not worth the labour; এই ব্যাপারে পরিশ্রমের অনুরূপ ফললাভ হইবে না। **The game is up**—The scheme has failed; the hope of success is gone; ঐ ব্যবস্থা নিষ্ফল হইয়াছে; সিদ্ধিলাভের আশা নাই, ভুর ভাঙ্গিয়াছে, বাজিমাৎ। **To die game**—To die fighting; যুদ্ধ করিতে করিতে রণক্ষেত্রে দেহ ত্যাগ করা। **To have the game in one's hand**—To be sure to win; ক্রীড়ায় জয়লাভে কৃতনিশ্চয় থাকা। **To have the game out**—To play it to the end; শেষ পর্য্যন্ত খেলা। **To make game of**—To make fun of; to ridicule; কাহাকেও লইয়া পরিহাস করা; ঠাট্টা করা, উপহাস করা। **To play a good** or **poor game**—To be skilful or not; নিপুণ বা অনিপুণ হওয়া। **To play one's game**—To advance one's scheme unintentionally; অজ্ঞাতসারে নিজের সংকল্প বা কল্পনা উপস্থাপিত করা। **To play the game**—To observe the rules; to behave honourably; নিয়ম পালন করা; সম্ভ্রান্তজনোচিত আচরণ করা। **To play the game of**—To act so as to secure the advantage or interests of; এরূপ ভাবে কাজ করা যাহাতে স্বার্থ বা সুবিধা অক্ষুণ্ণ থাকে।

game, *adj.* **1.** Of, or belonging to, such animals as are hunted; মৃগয়ালব্ধ জন্তু-সম্বন্ধীয়। **2.** Spirited like a game cock; plucky; willing; "I am *game* to try"; লড়াইয়ের জন্য শিক্ষিত কুক্কুটের মত তেজস্বী, যোধকুক্কুটতুল্য সাহসী; সাহসী, নির্ভীক; ইচ্ছুক। **Game'-ly,** *adv.* **Game'-ness,** *n.*

game, *v. i.* & *t.* **1.** To gamble; জুয়া খেলা, স্ফূর্ত্তি খেলা। **2.** To play at any sport; to amuse oneself; খেলা করা, ক্রীড়া করা; আমোদিত করা। ***Verb t.*** To gamble away; as, let us *game away* these dismal hours; আমোদপ্রমোদে কাটান।

gāme′-some (-sŭm), *adj.* Sportive ; gay ; ক্রীড়াপ্রিয়, কেলিপর, খেলাপর ; আমুদে, রঙ্গী, রঙ্গপ্রিয়। **—ly,** *adv.* **—ness,** *n.*

gāme′-stêr, *n.* A competitor in a game of contest ; an athlete ; প্রতিযোগিতামূলক ক্রীড়ায় প্রতিদ্বন্দ্বী ; মল্লক্রীড়ক।

găm′-ete (-ēt), *n.* (*Biol.*) A sexual protoplasmic body, which unites with another for reproduction ; (জীব-বিজ্ঞান) যৌনধর্ম্ম বিশিষ্ট জীবপঙ্কাত্মক বস্তু—যাহা অপর বস্তুর সহিত সংযুক্ত হইয়া থাকে, জম্পতী (সাঃ পঃ)।

gamin, (*F.*), *n.* A neglected street-boy ; a street Arab ; যে গৃহহীন বালক সহরের রাস্তায় রাস্তায় ঘুরিয়া বেড়ায়, সহরের পরিত্যক্ত বালক ; সহরের গৃহহীন বালক।

găm′-ing, *n.* Gambling ; জুয়া খেলা। **Gaming house**—দ্যূতশালা, জুয়াখেলার আড্ডা ; নরক। **Gaming table**—জুয়া খেলিবার মেজ, দ্যূতফলক (মঃ উঃ)।

găm′-mă, *n.* **1.** The third letter of the Greek alphabet ; গ্রীক বর্ণমালার তৃতীয় অক্ষর। **2.** A kind of moth ; একপ্রকার তসরে পোকা।

găm-mă′-dī-ŏn, *n.* A cruciform ornament ; একপ্রকার ক্রুশাকৃতি ভূষা।

găm′-mêr, *n.* An old woman (*cf.* GAFFER) ; বৃদ্ধা নারী, ঠানদিদি, বুড়ী।

găm′-mon (-mŭn), *n.* & *v. t.* The thigh of a hog pickled and dried ; the lower end of a flitch ; শূকরের শুষ্ক ও লবণাক্ত জঙ্ঘা ; শূকর-জঙ্ঘা। ***Verb t.*** To salt and dry in smoke ; লবণাক্ত করিয়া ধোঁয়ায় শুষ্ক করা।

găm′-mon (-mŭn), *n.*, *v. i.*, & *interj.* Deception ; a hoax ; প্রবঞ্চনা, ফাঁকি, ছল ; ধোঁকা, ধাপ্পা। ***Verb i.*** To talk plausibly ; to pretend ; "*Gammoning* to read it (the document)" ; আপাতযুক্তিপূর্ণভাবে কথা বলা ; ভাণ করা। ***Verb t.*** To hoax ; to impose upon ; ধোঁকা দেওয়া, ঠকান ; চোখে ধূলি দেওয়া। ***Interj.*** Nonsense ; বাজে কথা ! পাগলের প্রলাপ !

găm′-mon (-mŭn), *v. t.* & *n.* (*Naut.*) To fasten as a bowsprit to the stem of a ship by several turns of a rope ; (নৌ-বিদ্যা) পোতাগ্র হইতে প্রলম্বিত দণ্ড কয়েক পাক রজ্জুদ্বারা পোতাগ্রের সহিত বন্ধন করা। ***Noun.*** The lashing of the bowsprit (also called *gammoning*) ; কয়েক পাক রজ্জু দ্বারা পোতাগ্রের সহিত পোতাগ্র হইতে প্রলম্বিত দণ্ড বন্ধন।

găm′-mon (-mŭn) *n.* & *v. t.* **1.** Backgammon (*rare*) ; ক্রীড়া-বিশেষ (কচিদ্ ব্যবহৃত)। **2.** Victory scoring two games at backgammon ; উক্ত ক্রীড়ায় পূর্ণ জায়ঙ্ক লাভ। ***Verb t.*** To beat in the game of backgammon ; উক্ত ক্রীড়ায় প্রতিপক্ষকে পরাভূত করা।

găm-ŏ-gĕn′-ĕ-sis, *n.* Sexual generation ; যোনিজনি (হিঃ কোঃ)।

găm-ŏ-gĕ-nĕt′-ic, *adj.* Of, or relating to, gamogenesis ; উদ্বাহিক (সাঃ পঃ)।

găm-ŏ-phȳl′-lous (-ŭs), *adj.* Having the perianth leaves united ; যুক্তপত্রী (সাঃ পঃ)।

găm-ŏ-sĕp′-ăl-ous (-ŭs), (*Bot.*) Having the calyx composed of united sepals ; যুক্তচ্ছদ (সাঃ পঃ)।

gamp, (*F.*), *n.* (*Facet.*) A large umbrella ; (কৌতুকচ্ছলে) প্রকাণ্ড ছত্র।

găm′-ŭt, *n.* **1.** The whole musical scale ; (সঙ্গীতে) স্বরগ্রাম, সপ্তস্বর, স্বরসপ্তক (হিঃ কোঃ)। **2.** The whole range of a thing ; "In the whole *gamut* of crime" ; পূর্ণ প্রসার। **Flat gamut**—উত্তর স্বর (হিঃ কোঃ)। **Semi-tones gamut**—কোমলস্বর (হিঃ কোঃ)।

Gamut.

găn′-dêr, *n.* **1.** The male of the goose ; রাজহংস, রাজহাঁস। **2.** A fool or simpleton ; মূর্খ, মূঢ়, নির্ব্বোধ ব্যক্তি। **A gander party**—(*U. S.*) A gathering of males only ; (মার্কিণ যুক্তরাজ্যে) পুরুষসম্মিলনী। **What is sauce for the goose is sauce for the gander**—Two of the same class must be treated alike ; সমশ্রেণীর লোকের মধ্যে এক জনের প্রতি যেরূপ ব্যবহার করিবে অপরের প্রতি ঠিক সেইরূপ ব্যবহার করা উচিত।

găng, *n.* **1.** A band of workmen under a foreman ; a company of slaves or prisoners ; a squad ; সরদারের অধীন মজুরগণ ; ক্রীতদাসের দল, বন্দীর দল ; কসরৎ শিক্ষার্থ সৈন্যদল। **2.** A band of persons associted for a criminal purpose ; কুকর্ম্মিদল, কুলোকদিগের দল, দল। **3.** A set of tools etc. arranged so as to act together ; এককালে কাজ করার জন্য সজ্জিত একপ্রস্থ যন্ত্র। **4.** A vein in mining ; পাষাণাদির মধ্যস্থ ধাতু প্রভৃতির শিরা। **Gang′-er,** *n.* Foreman of a gang of workmen ; মজুরদলের সর্দ্দার। **Gang board**—জাহাজ বা নৌকা হইতে উঠা নামার জন্য বাতা দ্বারা আঁটা তক্তা। **Gang's man**—A labourer in a gang, (also a *ganger*) ; মজুর দলের লোক।

gange (gănj), *v. t.* To protect (fish hook etc.) with fine wire ; সূক্ষ্ম তার দ্বারা (বড়শী প্রভৃতি) রক্ষা করা। **—gang′-ing,** *n.*

Găn-gĕt′-ic, *adj.* Of the Ganges ; গাঙ্গেয়, গাঙ্গ, (মঃ ভাঃ), গাঙ্গ্য।

gan′-glī-ŏn (găng-) *n.* (*Pl.* -GLIA) **1.** A knot or enlargement in the course of a nerve ; স্নায়ুগ্রন্থি, বাতগ্রন্থি (সাঃ পঃ), স্নায়ুগণ্ড (ঐ), স্নায়ুবন্ধুল (ঐ), বাতগণ্ড (ঐ), বাতগ্রন্থি (ঐ)। **2.** A mass of nervous matter giving origin to nerve fibres ; শিরার উপাদান বস্তু, গুচ্ছক (হিঃ কোঃ), নাড়ীগুচ্ছক (ঐ)। **3.** (*Fig.*) A centre of force, activity or interests ; (লক্ষণায়) শক্তিকেন্দ্র, কর্ম্মকেন্দ্র। **–ate, –ated, –o-form, –on'-ic,** *adjs.* **Ganglionic cell**—স্নায়ুকোষ। **Ganglionic centres**—চক্র (ব্রজঃ হিন্দু)।

gan'-grene (găng-grēn), *n.*, *v. t.* & *i.* **1.** An eating away of the flesh ; the mortification of some part of the body (*lit.* & *fig.*) ; শরীরের যে কোন স্থানের মাংস পচন, বিগলন, কোথ, নালী ; অজীব (সাঃ পঃ)। ***Verb t.*** To mortify ; জীবিত প্রাণিদেহের কোন অংশের জীবনী-শক্তি নষ্ট করা। ***Verb i.*** To become putrid ; পচা, পচিয়া যাওয়া। **–grenous,** *adj.*

gangue (găng), *n.* (*Mining*) The mineral matters in which metallic ores are imbedded ; (খনিজ-বিদ্যা) যে সকল খনিজ পদার্থে খনিজ বিমিশ্র ধাতু প্রোথিত থাকে।

găng-way (-wā), *n.* **1.** A way, esp. between rows of seats ; (in the House of Commons) a passage across the house, (it separates the ministers, ex-ministers and others from the neutral members) ; পথ, আসন শ্রেণীসমূহের মধ্যবর্ত্তী পথ ; পার্লেমেন্টের প্রাকৃত সভার অনুপ্রস্থগামী পথ-বিশেষ। [এই পথের এক পার্শ্বস্থ আসন শ্রেণীতে (অর্থাৎ যে পার্শ্বে মুখপাত্র speaker উপবেশন করেন) মন্ত্রিগণ, ভূতপূর্ব্ব মন্ত্রিগণ এবং তাহাদের সমর্থকগণ উপবিষ্ট হন এবং অপর পার্শ্বের আসন শ্রেণীতে নিরপেক্ষ সভ্যগণ (যাহারা উদার-নৈতিক বা রক্ষণশীল—কোন দলভুক্ত নহেন) উপবিষ্ট থাকেন।] **2.** (*Naut.*) An opening in the bulwarks of a ship by which one enters or leaves a vessel ; a bridge laid across from this to the shore etc. ; (নৌ-বিদ্যা) পাটাতনের উপরিস্থ পোত-পার্শ্বভাগস্থ প্রবেশ ও নির্গমের রন্ধ্র ; জাহাজে উঠা নামার জন্য উক্ত রন্ধ্র হইতে আরম্ভ করিয়া কাষ্ঠফলকাদিদ্বারা রচিত পথ, জাহাজের এক অংশ হইতে অপর অংশে উঠা নামা বা যাওয়ার জন্য মঞ্চ-বিশেষ। **To bring to the gangway**—To whip a sailor ; জাহাজের মাল্লাকে বেত্রাঘাত করা।

Common gannet.

găn'-nĕt, *n.* A web-footed sea-bird ; জালপাদ সামুদ্রিক পক্ষি-বিশেষ।

găn'-oid (-ȯyd) *adj.* & *n.* **1.** (Of fish scale) Having a smooth shining surface ; (মৎস্যের শল্ক-সম্বন্ধে) স্নিগ্ধোজ্জ্বল ; **2.** (Of fish etc.) Having ganoid scales ; (মৎস্যাদি-সম্পর্কে) স্নিগ্ধোজ্জ্বল শল্ক-বিশিষ্ট। ***Noun.*** An order of fish having smooth and bright scales ; স্নিগ্ধোজ্জ্বল শল্ক-বিশিষ্ট মৎস্য-বিশেষ, চিক্কণ-শল্কী।

gănt'-lĕt, *n.* Same as GAUNTLET which see.

găn'-trȳ, gaun'–(gän-), *n.* A four footed wooden stand for barrels ; পিপা রাখার জন্য কাঠের চৌপায়া।

Găn'-ȳ-mede (-mēd), *n.* **1.** (*Facet.*) Pot-boy ; a cup-bearer ; hence a catamite ; (কৌতুকচ্ছলে) মদ্য-বিক্রেতার সাহায্যকারী বালক ; (মদ্য পাত্র হইতে) মদিরা পরিবেষক। [Hebe-র পরে যে সুন্দর বালক Zeus দেবের সুরাপরিবেষক নিযুক্ত হন এবং যিনি তদীয় উৎক্রোশ পক্ষীকর্ত্তৃক দেবাধ্যুষিত অলিম্পাস্ পর্ব্বতে নীত হইয়াছিলেন] ; অতএব, অবৈধ সঙ্গমের জন্য রক্ষিত বালক, লৌণ্ডা। **2.** (*Astron.*) The largest satellite of the planet Jupiter ; বৃহস্পতি গ্রহের বৃহত্তম উপগ্রহ।

gaol (jāl), *n.* Same as JAIL which see.

găp, *n.* & *v. t.* **1.** An opening or breach, as in a hedge etc. ; ফাঁক, ছিদ্র। **2.** A vacant space or interval ; a blank ; অবচ্ছেদ, অবকাশ, ফাঁকা জায়গা ; শূন্যস্থান, সাদা জায়গা। **3.** A mountain pass ; a gorge ; গিরিবর্ত্ম ; গিরি-সঙ্কট, গিরিদ্বার। **4.** A wide divergence in character or sympathies ; "......a *gap* between him and clergy" ; (চরিত্র বা সহানুভূতিতে) মহা বৈলক্ষণ্য, আকাশ পাতাল তফাত। ***Verb t.*** (*Rare*) To notch ; খাঁজ কাটা। **Gap'-ped,** *adj.* **Gap'-py,** *adj.* Full of gaps ; শূন্যস্থান বহুল। **Gap-toothed**—ফাঁক ফাঁক দন্তবিশিষ্ট ; কতিপয় দন্তবিহীন। **To stand in the gap**—(*Rare*) To act as a defender ; (ক্কচিদ্ ব্যবহৃত) রক্ষা করা। **To stop, to fill (in or up), to supply, a gap**—To supply a want ; to fill a vacant place ; অভাব পূরণ করা ; শূন্য স্থান পূরণ করা।

gāpe, *v. i.* & *n.* **1.** To open the mouth wide ; to yawn ; হাঁ করা, মুখ ব্যাদান করা, বদন ব্যাদান করা ; হাঁই তোলা, জৃম্ভণ করা। **2.** To open or part widely ; to split ; as, a *gaping* wound, chasm, etc. ; ব্যাদিত হওয়া ; বিদীর্ণ হওয়া। **3.** To stare ; to gaze curiously (usu. followed by *at*) ; "To gape at new sights" ; বিস্ময়ে হাঁ করিয়া এক দৃষ্টিতে চাহিয়া থাকা ; কৌতুহলাক্রান্ত দৃষ্টিতে চাহিয়া থাকা। ***Noun.*** The act of gaping ; a yawn ; মুখ ব্যাদান, মুখ বিস্তার ; হাঁই, জৃম্ভণ। **2.** An open-mouthed stare ; বিস্ময়বিদারিত- সহকৃত দৃষ্টি। **3.** An opening ; rent ; ফাঁক, ছিদ্র, ফাটল। **4.** (*Zool.*) The expanse of a an open mouth or beak ; (জন্তু-বিজ্ঞান) ব্যাদিত বা মুখের বিস্তার, হাঁ। **Gap'-ing,** *adj.* **The gapes**—Poultry disease with gaping as symptom ; কুক্কুটাদির চঞ্চু বিস্তার রোগবিশেষ। (*Facet.*) A fit of yawning ; (কৌতুকচ্ছলে) হাঁই, জৃম্ভণ। **To gape at**—See GAPE *v.* 3. **To gape away**—To pass, as time in yawning ; হাঁই তুলিয়া সময় কাটান। **To gape for** or **after**—To wait for ; to crave ; to desire or covet eagerly ; প্রতীক্ষা করা; আকাঙ্ক্ষা করা; আকুলভাবে আকাঙ্ক্ষা করা।

gāp'-ėr, *n.* One that gapes, esp. a kind of bird ; a kind of mollusc ; মুখব্যাদানকারী, বিশেষতঃ একপ্রকার পক্ষী ; একপ্রকার শম্বূক।

gâr, gâr'-fish, *ns.* A long slender sea-fish ; a sword-fish ; দীর্ঘ সামুদ্রিক মৎস্যবিশেষ ; অসি-মৎস্য, খড়্গ-মৎস্য।

gă-rage' (-rîj), (*Has not acquired a settled pronunciation.*) *n.* A place for housing automobiles, esp. motor-cars ; হাওয়া গাড়ী প্রভৃতি রাখার স্থান।

gârb, *n.* & *v. t.* **1.** Dress, esp. one indicating rank or office ; fashion of dress ; পোষাক, পরিচ্ছদ, বেশ ; পরিচ্ছদ-রীতি। **2.** External appearance ; "His customary *garb* of indifference" ; বাহ্যদর্শন, বহিঃদৃশ্য, বাহিরের ভাব। ***Verb t.*** To dress ; to clothe ; পোষাক পরাণ ; সজ্জিত করা, সাজান।

gâr'-bāge, *n.* **1.** Offal ; waste matter ; নিহত জন্তুর নাঁড়ীভুঁড়ি; অসার পদার্থ, আবর্জ্জনা, জঞ্জাল, উচ্ছিষ্ট। **2.** Foul or worthless reading ; অশ্লীল বা অসার পাঠ্য অংশ।

[gâ]r'-ble (-bl), *v. t.* **1.** (*Rare*) To [t]ake the pick of ; (অপ্রঃ) শ্রেষ্ঠ [অ]ংশ গ্রহণ করা। **2.** To make election for a bad purpose ; [অ]সদুদ্দেশ্যে পুস্তকাদি হইতে অংশবিশেষ নির্ব্বাচন করা। **3.** To mutilate, [so] as to cause a false impression ; ভ্রান্ত ধারণা জন্মাইবার উদ্দেশ্যে অঙ্গহানি করা। **—bler,** *n.* **Garbled account** — বিকৃত বিবরণ। **Garbled quotation**—বিকৃতি সাধন পূর্ব্বক উদ্ধৃত অংশ।

gâr'-board (-börd), **—strāke,** *ns.* (*Naut.*) The first range of planks [a]ttached to the keel of a ship ; (নৌ-বিদ্যা) জাহাজের পাণি তরাসের সংলগ্ন প্রথম তক্তার শ্রেণী।

Garcinia Cambogia — রক্তস্রবা (বেলঃ)।

garcon, (*F.*), *n.* A waiter in a French hotel ; ফরাসী দেশীয় সাধারণ ভোজনাগারের পরিচারক।

gâr'-den (-dn), *n.* & *v. i.* **1.** A piece of ground appropriated to cultivating flowers, fruits or plants ; উদ্যান, বাগান, বাগিচা, পুষ্পোদ্যান, পুষ্পবাটিকা, আরাম (*pleasure garden*)। **2.** (*Pl.*) Ornamental ground for public resort ; সাধারণের ভ্রমণের জন্য পুষ্পালোক বৃক্ষাদি শোভিত সুরম্য স্থান। **3.** Fertile, well cultivated tract ; as, the garden of England (Kent, Worcestershire etc.) ; সুকর্ষিত শস্যপ্রদ স্থান। [*Attrib. adj.* Pertaining to, produced, or living in, a garden ; উদ্যান সম্বন্ধীয়, উদ্যানজাত।] ***Verb i.*** To cultivate a garden ; উদ্যান-কর্ম্ম করা। **—dened,** *adj.* **—er,** *n.* One who cultivates, or has charge of, a garden ; উদ্যান-পালক, উদ্যানরক্ষক, বাগানের মালী, উদ্যানপাল। **—esque,** *adj.* Somewhat like a garden ; উদ্যান-কল্প। **—ing,** *n.* উদ্যানকর্ম্ম, উদ্যানরক্ষণ। **Garden-engine**—A portable force-pump for watering ; একপ্রকার দমকল। **Garden-glass** — Bell-glass for covering plant ; বৃক্ষাদি আচ্ছাদনের জন্য ঘণ্টাকৃতি কাচ। **Garden house**—উদ্যানবাটিকা, পুষ্পবাটিকা, বাগানবাড়ী। **Garden-party** — উদ্যান সম্মিলনী, উদ্যানমিলন, উদ্যান-ভোজ। **Garden-pea**—বড় মটর। **Garden-seat**—Bench etc. for use in a garden ; a similar seat on the lop of an omnibus ; বাগানে বসিবার বেঞ্চি ; বিশ্বযানের (*omnibus*) উপরিস্থ উক্তরূপ আসন। **Garden-white**—প্রজাপতি-বিশেষ। **Hanging gardens** — বেবিলোনের শূন্যোদ্যান (পৃথিবীর সপ্তাশ্চর্য্যের অন্যতম)। [সম্ভবতঃ শূন্যোদ্যান প্রথমতঃ Nebuchadnezzar (খৃঃ পূঃ ৬০৪—৫৬১) এর আদেশে নির্ম্মিত হইয়াছিল। এই উদ্যানের উপরি উপরি রচিত চাতালসমূহ বুরুজাকারে শোভা পাইত। ঐ সকল চাতাল খিলানের উপর ৭৫ হইতে ৩০০ ফিট দীর্ঘ শূন্য স্তম্ভরাজি দ্বারা বিধৃত এবং তরু, গুল্ম, উৎস, কুঞ্জবন এবং ভোজমণ্ডপ দ্বারা পরিশোভিত ছিল। *See* Ward, *The Master of the Magicians* ; Rawlinson, *Ancient Monarchies,* ii and iii.]। **Kitchen garden**—পারিবারিক ব্যবহারের জন্য শাকসব্জীর বাগান, তরিতরকারীর বাগান, শাকোদ্যান। **Market-garden** — বাজারে বিক্রয়ার্থ শাকসব্জী উৎপাদনের জন্য বাগান। **Market gardener**—যে ব্যক্তি বাজারে বিক্রয়ার্থ ফল তরিতরকারী উৎপাদন করে। **The garden** — Epicurus এর দর্শন [ইনি উদ্যানে শিষ্যমণ্ডলীকে শিক্ষা দান করিতেন]। **Garden of Eden**—আদম ও ঈভের বাসোদ্যান। **Garden of Europe**—ইটালী। **Garden of India**—অযোধ্যা। **Garden of Italy**—সিসিলী দ্বীপ। **Garden of the sun**—ভারতবর্ষীয় দ্বীপপুঞ্জ, মালয়দ্বীপপুঞ্জ। **Garden of the world**—The region of the Missisipi ; মিসিসিপি নদীর সন্নিহিত প্রদেশ। **The garden of England**—কেণ্ট। **Get on, gardener**—Get on, you slow and clumsy coachman ; চালাও, ঢিলা আনাড়ী গাড়োয়ান।

gâr-dē'-nĭ-ă, *n.* A genus of plants ; একজাতীয় পুষ্পবৃক্ষ।

Gardenia florida—গন্ধরাজ (বেলঃ)।

gâr'-fish, *n.* See GAR.

gāre'-fowl, *n.* The great auk ; উত্তর সাগরচর বৃহৎ জালপাদ পক্ষিবিশেষ।

Gâr-găn'-tū-ăn, *adj.* (From Rabelais's Gargantua, a gigantic king having an extraordinary appetite.) Enormous ; prodigious ; gigantic ; প্রকাণ্ড ; বিরাট ; অতিকায়, রাক্ষুসে।

gâr'-gĕt, *n.* **1.** Swelling in the throat or head of cattle etc. ;

গোমেষাদি পশুর কণ্ঠ বা মস্তকে স্ফীতি। **2.** A disease in a cow's or ew's udder; গাভীর বা ভেড়ীর পালানের রোগবিশেষ।

gâr'-gle (-gl), *v. t., i.* & *n.* **1.** To wash, as the throat or mouth with a liquid; কুলি করা, কুলকুচি করা, কুলকুচি করিয়া ধোওয়া। *Verb i.* To wash throat or mouth; কুলি করা। *Noun.* A liquid for washing the throat or the mouth; কণ্ঠ বা মুখ ধাবনার্থ তরল পদার্থ বিশেষ।

gâr'-goyle (-goyl), **gŭr'–**, *ns.* The projecting water spout on a

Gargoyle.

building, frequently in the form of a human or other figure; মনুষ্য বা পশুমুখাকৃতি প্রলম্বিত জলনির্গম নল।

gâr-i-bâl'-di, *n.* A kind of blouse worn by women and children; স্ত্রীলোকদিগের একপ্রকার ঢিলা জামা [ইতালীর স্বাধীনতা প্রদাতা প্রেমিক Garibaldiর লোহিতবর্ণ জামার অনুকরণে তৈয়ারী বলিয়া এই নাম]।

gâr'-ish, gair'- (gār-), *adjs.* **1.** Showy; gaudy; dazzling; too highly decorated; as, *garish* signboards; বাহ্যচাকচিক্যময়; জাঁকালো, জমকালো; তীব্রোজ্জ্বল; অতিমাত্রায় ভূষিত, অত্যলঙ্কৃত। **—ly,** *adv.* **—ness,** *n.*

gâr'-lănd, *n.* & *v. t.* **1.** A wreath or chaplet of flowers, leaves etc.; হার, মালা, মাল্য, মালিকা, স্রক্, দাম, পুষ্পহার, পুষ্পমাল্য, শিরোমাল্য, মৌলি, মাল্য (উজ্জ্বলঃ), পত্র-পুষ্পাদিরচিত মুকুট। **2.** A prize or distinction for victory; বিজয়মাল্য, জয়মালা, বিজয়-গৌরব। **3.** (*Archaic*) Collection of extracts; an anthology; (অপ্রঃ) প্রবন্ধমালা; কবিতা-সংগ্রহ। *Verb t.* To deck with a garland; to act as a garland to; পুষ্পমাল্যে শোভিত করা, পুষ্পমুকুট ভূষিত করা; মাল্যাকারে শোভা পাওয়া। **Civic garland**—যুদ্ধক্ষেত্রে সহনাগরিকের জীবনরক্ষার্থ কোন সৈনিককে যে ওকপত্র নির্ম্মিত মুকুট প্রদত্ত হয়। **Wild garland**—বনমালা।

gâr'-lic, *n.* A bulbous rooted plant having a pungent taste; রশুন, লশুন, গৃঞ্জন, মহাকন্দ (ব্রজঃ হিন্দু)। **—lick-y,** *adj.*

gârm, *n.* Hell's watchdog; (স্ক্যান্ডিনেভিয়ার পুরাণ) নরকরক্ষক কুকুর।

gâr'-mĕnt, *n.* & *v. t.* **1.** An article of dress, as gown, coat, etc.; a vestment; পোষাক; পরিচ্ছদ, অংশুক, বাস। **2.** (*Pl.*) Clothes; কাপড় চোপড়, পরিচ্ছদ। **3.** (*Fig.*) The external covering in which any thing is manifested; "The mysterious *garment* of the unseen"; (লক্ষণায়) বহিরাবরণ। *Verb t.* (*Poet.*) To attire (*usu. in past. part.*) (কবিতায়) সজ্জিত করা। **Bridal garment** — আনন্দপট (মঃ ভাঃ), বৈবাহিক-পরিচ্ছদ।

gâr'-nêr, *n.* & *v. t.* A granary; ধান্যাগার, শস্যাগার। *Verb t.* To store in a granary; to store up; to collect; শস্যাগারে সঞ্চিত করা; গোলাজাত করা; সংগ্রহ করা।

gâr'-nĕt, *n.* A precious stone of a red colour; রক্তবর্ণ মণি-বিশেষ, বৈক্রান্তমণি।

gâr'-nish, *v. t.* & *n.* **1.** To adorn; to decorate; সজ্জিত করা, সাজান, ভূষিত করা; মণ্ডিত করা, শোভিত করা, অলঙ্কৃত করা, খচিত করা, অলঙ্কারাদি দ্বারা ভূষিত বা শোভিত করা। **2.** (*Cook.*) To embellish, as a dish for the table; (রন্ধন-কার্য্য) চতুর্দ্দিকে নানা উপকরণ বিন্যস্ত করত পাত্রস্থিত ব্যঞ্জনাদি সজ্জিত করা। **3.** (*Obs.*) To furnish; to equip; (অপ্রঃ) সরবরাহ করা, যোগান; সাজান। **4.** (*Law*) To give notice to; to summon (a person) as party to a litigation; (আইন) জ্ঞাপন করা; কোন মোকদ্দমার পক্ষভুক্ত কোন ব্যক্তিকে আদালতে উপস্থিত হওয়ার জন্য আহ্বান করা। *Noun.* Things round a dish as an embellishment; (also *fig.*) literary embellishment; "Such a *garnish* o misrepresentation"; ভোজন পাত্রে ভোজ্যদ্রব্যের চতুর্দ্দিকে স্থাপিত উপকরণ (লক্ষণায়) রচনার অলঙ্কার। **—ee',** *n* A person warned not to pa money which he owes to third party indebted to th warner; যে ব্যক্তিকে তৃতীয় ব্যক্তি নিকট সে যে টাকা ধারে তা না দেওয়ার জন্য ঐ তৃতীয় ব্যক্তি পাওনাদার সতর্ক করিয়া থাকে।

gâr'-ni-türe, *n.* **1.** Furniture outfit; গৃহসজ্জা, আসবাব; সাজ সজ্জা **2.** Embellishment; dressing of dish; অলঙ্কার, মণ্ডন, ভূষা; ভো পাত্রস্থ ভোজ্য দ্রব্যের চতুর্দ্দিকে বি উপকরণ। **3.** Dress; পোষাক, বেশ

gâr'-rĕt, *n.* & *v. t.* **1.** A apartment in the highest sto of a house; an attic; শিরোগৃ সর্ব্বোচ্চ প্রকোষ্ঠ; চিলঘর, চিলে কো চন্দ্রশালা (বৃঃ নং), উত্তরাগার (হরিঃ **2.** (*Slang*) Head; as, to ha one's *garret* unfurnished; (ইত ভাষায়) মুণ্ড। *Verb t.* To ins small pieces of stone etc. in t joints of (coarse masonry (মোটা গাঁথনির) জোড়াতে ক্ষুদ্র প পাথরের টুকরা ভরা। **—eer',** **1.** One who lives in a garre esp. an impecunious autho চন্দ্রশালাবাসী; বিশেষতঃ নিঃস্ব গ্রন্থকা **To be wrong in the garre** To be wrong in the hea মাথার গোল হওয়া।

gâr'-ri-son (-sn), *n.* **1.** A bo of soldiers stationed in a f or town to defend them; রক্ষী সৈন্য, দুর্গস্থিত সৈন্য। *Vert* **1.** To place a garrison in; to *garrison* a fort; দুর্গে

সমাবেশ করা। **2.** To occupy, as a garrison ; সৈন্যসমাবেশ পূর্ব্বক র্গাদি অধিকার করা। **3.** To put ·n garrison duty ; দুর্গ রক্ষার র্য্যে নিযুক্ত করা। **Garrison town**—দুর্গরক্ষিসৈন্যদল-সন্নিবিষ্ট নগরী। **In garrison**—Doing duty of a garrison ; দুর্গ রক্ষায় নিযুক্ত।

·ăr-rotte′ (-rŏt), **găr-rote′** (-ŏt), · & *v. t.* **1.** A Spanish mode of pital punishment by strang-ng ; apparatus used in such xecution ; লৌহময় গলবন্ধনী দ্বারা রোধ পূর্ব্বক মৃত্যুদণ্ড বিধান (স্পেনদেশে লিত) ; উক্তরূপ মৃত্যুদণ্ড বিধানার্থ হময় গলবন্ধনী। **2.** Throttling, as h a garrote esp. for robbery ; রূপ যন্ত্রদ্বারা শ্বাসরোধ পূর্ব্বক রাহাজানি রণ। ***Verb t.*** **1.** To strangle th the garrotte ; লৌহগলবন্ধ দ্বারা রোধ করিয়া মারা। **2.** To throttle order to rob; রাহাজানি করার দশ্যে পশ্চাৎ হইতে কোন ব্যক্তির গলা পিয়া ধরা। **–rot′-er, –rot′-ter,** *ns.*

·′-rû-lous (-lŭs), *adj.* **1.** Talka-ive ; loquacious ; as, the most *irrulous* people ; wordy ; as, a *irrulous* story ; বাচাল, বাবদুক, বর ; বহুভাষী, অতিভাষী, জল্পাক, টট ; শব্দবহুল। **2.** Chatter-· ; babbling ; as, a *garrulous* 1 or river ; কিচ্‌মিচ্ শব্দকারী ; খর, কুলুকুলুনাদী। **ly,** *adv.* **–ness, ru′-li-ty,** *ns.* he quality of ing garru-; বাচালতা, াদুকতা, মুখরতা, ভাষিতা।

Star and jewel of the Order of the Garter.

·′-têr, *n.* & *t.* **1.** A band hold up a ·king on the মোজাবন্ধ, ার, পাদাবরণ-·নী। **2.** (*Cap.* — With *the* prefixed) The badge of the highest order of knighthood in Great Britain ; the order itself ; ইংলণ্ডের সর্ব্বোচ্চ অভিজাত সম্প্রদায়ের চিহ্ন ; উক্ত সম্প্রদায়। ***Verb t.*** **1.** To bind with a garter ; মোজাবন্ধন দ্বারা বাঁধা। **2.** To invest with the Order of the Garter ; উক্ত অভিজাত সম্প্রদায়-ভুক্ত করা। **Garter King of Arms**—উক্ত অভিজাত সম্প্রদায়ের প্রধান কুলাচার্য্য।

gärth, *n.* **1.** (*Archaic or Dial.*) A close ; a yard ; a garden ; the open area within cloisters ; (অপ্রঃ কিম্বা উপভাষায়) সীমাবদ্ধ স্থান, ঘেরা জায়গা ; প্রাঙ্গণ, আঙ্গিনা ; উদ্যান, বাগান ; খৃষ্টীয় মঠ বা ধর্ম্মমন্দিরের চতুর্দ্দিকস্থ আচ্ছাদিত পথের মধ্যবর্ত্তী উন্মুক্ত স্থান। **2.** A dam etc. in a river for catching fish ; মৎস্য ধরিবার জন্য নদীতে বাঁধ।

găs, *n., v. t.* & *i.* **1.** An elastic fluid in the form of air ; বাষ্প, অনিল (রাঃ সুঃ ত্রিঃ), গ্যাস (সাঃ পঃ), মরুৎ (জঃ রাঃ), বায়ু (ঐ), ধূম (ঐ)। **2.** The coal-gas commonly used for lighting or heating purposes ; কয়লার বাষ্প। **3.** (*Mining*) Explosive mixture of fire-damp with air ; বিস্ফোরক দ্রব্য-বিশেষ। **4.** Laughing gas ; হাস্যজনক বাষ্প। **5.** Hydrogen etc. for filling a balloon ; ব্যোমযান প্রভৃতি পূর্ণ করার জন্য উদজন বাষ্প, প্রভৃতি। **6.** A jet of gas for lighting purposes ; গ্যাসের বাতি জ্বালাইবার জন্য বাষ্পধারা। **7.** Empty or boastful talk ; humbug ; অসার বাগাড়ম্বর ; ধোঁকা। ***Verb t.*** **1.** To supply with gas, as a room etc. ; গৃহ প্রভৃতিতে গ্যাস সরবরাহ করা। **2.** To clear (thread etc.) of loose fibres etc. by passing through gas flame ; গ্যাসের শিখার ভিতর দিয়া নিয়া (সূতা-প্রভৃতির) আল্গা আঁশ প্রভৃতি পরিষ্কার করা। ***Verb i.*** To make use of empty talk ; বৃথা বাগাড়ম্বর করা। **Gas-e′-i-ty,** *n.* **Gas′-e-ous,** *adj.* In the form of a gas ; aeriform ; light as gas ; বাষ্পময়, বাষ্পীভূত, বাষ্পাকার ; বাত্যাকার ; বাষ্পতুল্য লঘু, গ্যাসের মত হাল্কা। **Gas′-e-ous-ness,** *n.* **Gas′-i-fi-a-ble,** *adj.* **Gas′-i-form,** *adj.* Gaseous ; বাষ্পীয়। **Gas′-i-fy,** *v. t.* To convert into gas ; বাষ্পে পরিণত করা। **Gas′-sy,** *adj.* Full of gas ; gaseous ; বাষ্পপূর্ণ, সবাষ্প, বাষ্পময় ; বাষ্পীয়। **–i-fi-ca′-tion,** *n.* **Gas-bag**—বাষ্পাধার। A boastful or empty talker ; বাগাড়ম্বরকারী। **Gas-bracket**—প্রাচীর হইতে উদ্গত দীপমুখসমন্বিত নল। **Gas-burner**—বাষ্পীয় দীপের মুখ। **Gas-coal**—একপ্রকার কয়লা—যাহা হইতে বাতি প্রভৃতির গ্যাস প্রস্তুত করা হয়। **Gas-coke** — গ্যাস প্রস্তুত করার পর কয়লার

Gas-engine.

যে অংশ অবশিষ্ট থাকে। **Gas-engine, -motor** — কয়লার বাষ্পের শক্তিতে চালিত কল বা গতিশক্তিসঞ্চারক যন্ত্র। **Gas-fitter**—যে ব্যক্তি গ্যাসের নলাদি বসাইয়া দেয়। **Gas-fittings**—গ্যাসের দ্বারা উত্তাপ সঞ্চার বা আলোক প্রদানের জন্য যন্ত্র। **Gas-holder** — বাষ্পাধার, বাষ্পধারক। **Gas-jet**—বাষ্পীয় দীপের মুখ, গ্যাসদীপক (হিঃ কোঃ)। **Gas-lamp** — বাষ্পীয় দীপ, গ্যাসের বাতি। **Gas-light**—গ্যাসের আলো। **Gas-main**—গ্যাস সরবরাহের প্রধান নল। **Gas-man**—গ্যাস প্রস্তুতকারী ; গ্যাস সরবরাহের জন্য পাওনা টাকা উশুলকারী। **Gas-meter**—কোন নির্দ্দিষ্ট স্থানে নির্দ্দিষ্ট সময়ে যে পরিমাণ গ্যাস খরচ হয় তাহা পরিমাপের জন্য যন্ত্রবিশেষ, বাষ্পমান। **Gas-ring**—রন্ধনাদি কার্য্যে ব্যবহৃত

সচ্ছিদ্র চক্র। **Gas-tar, Coal-tar**—গ্যাস প্রস্তুত কালে উৎপন্ন আলকাত্‌রা। **Gas-works**—গ্যাসের কারখানা।

Găs'-cŏn, *n.* **1.** An inhabitant of Gascony in France ; ফরাসীদেশের অন্তর্গত গ্যাস্‌কনি নামক প্রদেশের অধিবাসী। **2.** A braggart ; দম্ভকারী, গর্ব্বকারী।

găs-cŏn-āde', *n.* & *v. i.* A boast or boasting ; a bravado ; দম্ভোক্তি, দর্প ; বড়াই। ***Verb i.*** To boast : to brag ; গর্ব্ব করা, আত্মশ্লাঘা করা ; বড়াই করা।

găs-ĕ-lier' (-lēr), **—ă-lier** (-lēr), *ns.* A hanging gas lamp with several branches for burning gas ; বাষ্পালোকের ঝাড়।

găsh, *v. t.* & *n.* To make a deep incision in ; to cut (applied chiefly to a cut in flesh) ; to slash ; অস্ত্র বসাইয়া গভীর ক্ষত করা ; লম্বালম্বি চিরা বা ফালি ফালি করিয়া কাটা ; হাঁসান। ***Noun.*** **1.** A long deep cut ; a wound ; a cleft such as might be made by a slashing cut ; দীর্ঘ গভীর ক্ষত ; ক্ষত ; অস্ত্রঘাতজনিত গভীর ক্ষত, দীর্ঘ গভীর ছেদ। **2.** Act of making gash ; অস্ত্রদ্বারা গভীর ক্ষতকরণ।

găs'-kĕt, *n.* **1.** A small cord for tying the sail to the yard ; মাস্তুল-সংলগ্ন পাইল-দণ্ডে পাইল বাঁধিবার জন্য ক্ষুদ্র রজ্জু। **2.** A strip of tow etc. to pack a piston joint or caulking ; নলদণ্ড আঁটসাট করা অথবা জোড়ার ফাঁক রুদ্ধ করার জন্য ফেঁসো।

găs'-ŏ-gene (-jēn), **găz'—,** *ns.* An apparatus for manufacturing ærated water ; লেমনেড, সোডা-ওয়াটার প্রভৃতি প্রস্তুতের জন্য যন্ত্রবিশেষ।

găs'-ŏ-lene (-lēn), **—line** (-lēn), *ns.* A volatile liquid obtained from petroleum ; কেরোসিন তৈল হইতে প্রাপ্ত উদ্বায়ী তরল পদার্থবিশেষ।

găs-ŏm'-ĕ-têr, *n.* A large reservoir in which gas is stored for distribution by pipes ; বৃহৎ বাষ্পাধার—যাহা হইতে নলদ্বারা বিভিন্ন স্থানে গ্যাস বিতরিত হইয়া থাকে, বাষ্পাধার।

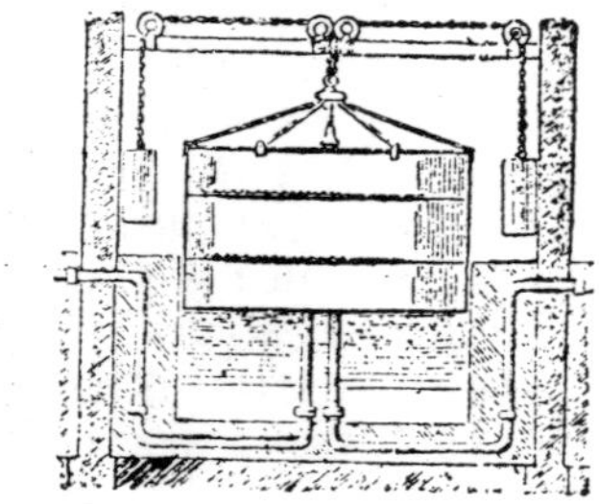

Gasometer.

găsp, *v. i., t.* & *n.* **1.** To open the mouth wide to catch breath ; to labour for breath ; নিশ্বাস গ্রহণার্থ মুখ ব্যাদান করা ; কষ্টে শ্বাস গ্রহণ করা, হাঁপান, খাবি খাওয়া। **2.** To pant eagerly ; to long ; "Doors and windows *gasping* for air" ; হাঁপান, হাঁস ফাঁস করা, আকুলি বিকুলি করা ; লালসা করা। ***Verb t.*** To emit with gasps, (with *forth, out, away*) ; to utter gaspingly, (with *out*) ; as, he *gasped out* a plea for mercy ; হাঁপাইতে হাঁপাইতে বাহির করা ; হাঁপাইতে হাঁপাইতে উচ্চারণ করা। ***Noun.*** Convulsive catching of breath ; হাঁপানি, খাবি। **Gasp'-ing,** *adj.* **Last gasp**—নাভিশ্বাস। **At one's last gasp**—At the point of one's death ; মুমূর্ষু অবস্থাপন্ন। **To gasp for or after**—To desire eagerly for ; কোন কিছুর জন্য আকুলি বিকুলি করা। **To gasp life out or away** — To expire ; প্রাণবায়ু ত্যাগ করা। **To gasp out**—See GASP *v. t.*

găs-têr-ō-mȳ-cē'-tēs, *n.* One of the six great divisions of fungi ; দাশস্যছত্রিকা (সাঃ পঃ)।

găs'-têr-ŏ-pŏd, —trŏ—, *ns.* A mollusc, such as snails having a muscular foot attached to the ventral surface ; শম্বুকাদি, উদরপদী (সাঃ পঃ), উদরগ (ঐ)।

găs-trăl'-gĭ-ă, *n.* (*Path.*) Pain in the stomach ; পাকস্থলীতে বেদনা, আমাশয়ের বেদনা, আমাশয় শূল (হঃ চঃ)।

găs'-trĭc, *adj.* Of, or pertaining to, the stomach ; পাকস্থলী-সম্বন্ধীয়, আমাশয়িক। **Gastric fever**—পিত্তশ্লৈষ্মিক অবিরাম জ্বর। **Gastric juice**—পাকস্থলী হইতে উৎপন্ন এক প্রকার অম্লরস—এই রসে ভুক্তদ্রব্য জীর্ণ হয়, পাচক রস, আমাশয়িক রস, জারক রস, জাঠর দ্রব (আঃ বঃ)। **Gastric tympanis**—আধ্মান (সাঃ পঃ)।

găs-trī'-tĭs, *n.* Inflammation of the stomach ; আমাশয় অর্থাৎ পাকস্থলীর প্রদাহ।

găs-trŏl'-ŏ-ġy, *n.* The science of cookery ; রন্ধন-বিজ্ঞান, পাক-বিদ্যা, রন্ধন বিদ্যা। **—ger, —gist,** *ns.*

găs'-trŏ-nōme, *n.* One versed in gastronomy ; a judge of cookery ; an epicure ; সুভোজনশিল্পজ্ঞ ; রন্ধনের দোষ গুণ বিচারক ; ভোগবিলাস পরায়ণ ব্যক্তি।

găs-trŏn'-ŏ-mȳ, *n.* The art or science of good eating ; epicurism ; সুভোজনশিল্প, সুভোজন বিদ্যা, ভোজনবিলাস কলা ; ভোগবিলাস। **—mer, mist,** *ns.* **—tro-nom'-i-cal,** *adj.* **—tro-nom'-i-cal-ly,** *adv.*

găs'-trŏ-pŏd, *n.* Same as GASTEROPOD which see.

găs-trŏs'-tŏ-mȳ, *n.* An operation of opening the stomach for the introduction of food ; খাদ্যদ্রব্য উদরাভ্যন্তরে প্রবেশ করাইবার জন্য পাকস্থলীর প্রাচীর-কর্ত্তন।

găs-trŏt'-ŏ-mȳ, *n.* A cutting or opening of the stomach ; পাকস্থলী ছেদন, পাকস্থলী উন্মোচন।

gāte, *n.* & *v. t.* **1.** A large door or passage in the wall of a city etc. or large building etc. ; তোরণ, ফটক, সিংহদ্বার। **2.** A passage with an enclosure, fence etc. ; (*fig.*) means of entrance or exit ; দুর্গ প্রভৃতি দ্বারা বেষ্টিত পথ ; (লক্ষণায়) প্রবেশোপায়, নির্গমোপায়, প্রবেশ পথ

নির্গম পথ। 3. (*Bible*) The place of a judicial assembly in a city; (বাইবেল) নগরীর বিচারাধিবেশনের স্থান। 4. A mountain pass; গিরিসঙ্কট, গিরিবর্ত্ম। 5. A frame regulating the passage of water through a dam etc.; স্রোতোদ্বার। 6. The number of persons entering by payment at the gates to see an athletic contest etc.; the sum of money thus received; দ্বারদেশে অর্থ প্রদান পূর্ব্বক মল্লক্রীড়া দর্শনার্থ রঙ্গক্ষেত্রে প্রবেশকারী ব্যক্তিবর্গ; মল্লক্রীড়া দর্শনার্থিগণ হইতে দ্বারদেশে গৃহীত অর্থ। ***Verb t.*** 1. (In Oxford and Cambridge) To punish (an undergraduate) by confining him within the college gates by a certain hour; (অক্সফোর্ড ও কেম্ব্রিজে) অনুপাধিপ্রাপ্ত যুবককে নির্দ্দিষ্ট সময় পর্য্যন্ত কলেজের ভিতর আটক রাখিয়া শাস্তি প্রদান করা। **Gate'-less,** *adj.* **Gate-keeper, Gate-man,** দ্বারবান, দ্বাররক্ষক, দৌবারিক, প্রতিহারী, দ্বারপাল, দ্বারী, দ্বারপ (ছান্দোগ্য)। **Gate-money**—কোন পরিবেষ্টিত স্থানে প্রবেশের জন্য গৃহীত অর্থ। **Gate-way** — The way through a gate; a frame in which a door is hung; means of entrance or exit; দ্বারতোরণ, দ্বারবর্ত্ম (মঃ ভাঃ); চৌকাঠ; আগম বা নির্গমের পথ, প্রবেশ পথ, নির্গম পথ। **Gate(s) or jaws of death**—The near approach of death; আসন্ন মৃত্যু। **Gate of horn** — শৃঙ্গ-নির্ম্মিত দ্বার [যাহার ভিতর দিয়া সফল স্বপ্ন সমাগত হয়; দ্বিরদরদ রচিত দ্বার (*Gates of ivory*) হইতে নিষ্ফল স্বপ্ন আগত হয়]। **Gate of tears**—Babelmandeb; বাবলমণ্ডপ [ঐ স্থানে বহুসংখ্যক পোত ধ্বংস হইয়াছিল বলিয়া আরবগণ এই নাম প্রদান করিয়াছে]। **To break gates**—(In English Universities) To enter the college inclosure after the prescribed hour; নির্দ্দিষ্ট সময়ের পর কলেজের বেষ্টিত অঙ্গনে প্রবেশ করা। **To open a gate for or to**—To provide facility or opportunity for; সুবিধা বা সুযোগ প্রদান করা। **To stand in the gate(s)**—To occupy a position of defence; আত্মরক্ষার উপযোগী স্থান অধিকার করা।

gāte, *n.* A street (with a prefixed name); as, in North *Gate* etc.; রাজপথ।

găth, *n.* (In Dryden's *Absalom and Achitophal*) Brussels where Charles II. lived long while in exile; ব্রাসেল্‌স্ নগরী (যথায় দ্বিতীয় চার্লস্ নির্ব্বাসিত অবস্থায় বহুদিন বাস করিয়াছিলেন)। **Tell it not in gath**—Don't let your enemies hear of it; তোমার শত্রুরা যেন এই কথা না শোনে।

găth'-ẽr, *v. t. & i.* 1. To collect or bring together; to cause to assemble; একত্র করা, সমবেত করা; জড় করা। 2. To get in or collect as harvest; to pluck or cull; "A rose just *gathered* from the stalk"; সংগ্রহ করা, সমাহরণ করা; কুড়ান, চয়ন করা। 3. To amass; to accumulate; "We *gather* the honey of world by wisdom not from flowers but from thorns"; সঞ্চয় করা; রাশীকৃত করা। 5. To receive addition of; as, a rolling stone *gathers* no moss; অতিরিক্ত দ্রব্য গ্রহণ করা। 6. To contract; to plait; to pucker; as, to *gather* the brow, a garment or ruffle; কুঞ্চিত করা; চুনট করা; কোঁচান। 7. To infer; to conclude; "*Gather* the sequel by that went before"; অনুমান করা, অবধারণ করা; সিদ্ধান্ত করা। ***Verb i.*** 1. To come together; to assemble; to congregate; একত্র হওয়া; সম্মিলিত হওয়া; সমবেত হওয়া, জড় হওয়া। 2. To grow larger by accretion; as, the tale *gathered* like a snowball; ক্রমশঃ বর্দ্ধিত হওয়া। 3. To come to a head; to generate

চুম্বক করা। To summon up for an effort ; (মানসিক বল প্রভৃতি) সংগ্রহ করা। **To gather way**—(*Naut.*) To begin to move ; to move with increasing speed ; (নৌ-বিদ্যা) চলিতে আরম্ভ করা ; উত্তরোত্তর বেগে চলা।

gă'-thêrs, *n.* (*Pl.*) The plaits of a cloth etc. gathered by a thread etc. ; কাপড়ের চুনট। **Out of gathers**—Out of order; in distress ; বিশৃঙ্খল ; দুর্দ্দশায়।

Găt'-lĭng, *n.* (Also *Gatling gun*) An American machine-gun, so named from the inventor ; আমেরিকা দেশীয় যান্ত্রিক কামান-বিশেষ [আবিষ্কারক Gatlingএর নাম হইতে গৃহীত]।

gauche, (*F.*), *adj.* Tactless ; clumsy ; awkward ; অকৌশলী ; আনাড়ী ; অপটু।

gauche'-rie (gŏsh-rē), (*F.*), *n.* Awkward action or manner ; অভব্যতা, অপটুতা।

gau'-chō (gâô-), *n.* A native of the South American Pampas, of Spanish descent ; দক্ষিণ আমেরিকার তরুহীন প্রান্তরের স্পেনিয়ার্ডদিগের বংশোৎপন্ন অধিবাসী।

gaud (găd), *n.* 1. A showy ornament or finery ; চটকদার অলঙ্কার। 2. (*Pl.*) Showy ceremonies ; gaieties ; "With *gauds* of this world" ; ধূমধাম, সমারোহপূর্ণ উৎসব ; আমোদ-প্রমোদ, উল্লাস, উৎসব। **Gaud'-i-ly**, *adv.* **Gaud'-i-ness**, *n.* **Gaud'-y**, *n.* & *adj.* A grand feast esp. an annual college dinner to old members etc. ; মহাভোজ, বিশেষতঃ কলেজের পুরাতন ছাত্র প্রভৃতিকে যে বাৎসরিক-ভোজ দেওয়া হয়। (*Adj.*) Excessively showy ; tastelessly fine ; as, *gaudy* dress or style of writing ; জমকালো, বাহ্য চাকচিক্যময় ; উজ্জ্বল, শোভন, চটকদার, রংদার, রংচঙ্গে। **Gaudy day**—যে দিবস কলেজের পুরাতন ছাত্র প্রভৃতিকে ভোজ দেওয়া হয়।

gauf'-fêr (gă-), See GOFFER.

gauge (gāj) **gāge**, *v. t.* 1. To measure accurately ; মাপ কাঠি দিয়া ঠিকরূপে পরিমাপ করা। 2. To ascertain the contents or capacity of, as a barrel etc. ; পিপা প্রভৃতির ধারণাশক্তি বা অভ্যন্তরস্থ তরল পদার্থ পরিমাপ করা। 3. To estimate ; to judge of ; as, I *gauged* his character very accurately ; অনুমান করা, ধারণা করা ; দোষগুণ বিচার করা। 4. To bring to uniform standard, size or shape ; "The stones are *gauged* and dressed by the hammer" ; একরূপ আদর্শ, আয়তন বা আকৃতি-বিশিষ্ট করা। **Gauge'-a-ble, Gage'-a-ble**, *adjs.* **Gaug'-er, Gag'-er**, *ns.* One who gauges ; an excise officer ; পরিমাপক ; আবকারী বিভাগের কর্ম্মচারী। **Gauging rod**—মদ্যাদি পরিমাপের জন্য আবকারী কর্ম্মচারিগণ কর্ত্তৃক ব্যবহৃত দণ্ড-বিশেষ।

gauge (gāj) **gāge**, *n.* 1. A standard measure of dimensions, distance or capacity ; নির্দ্দিষ্টমান। 2. Capacity ; extent ; estimate ; ধারণাশক্তি ; প্রসার, বিস্তার ; অনুমান। 3. The distance between the rails of a railway (nearly *4ft.* $8\frac{1}{2}$*in.*) ; দুইটী পাতা রেলের মধ্যবর্ত্তী দূরত্ব (প্রায় ৪ ফিট ৮॥০ ইঞ্চি)। 4. An instrument for measuring force or quantity of rainfall, stream, tide, wind, etc. ; বৃষ্টিপাত, প্রবাহ, জোয়ার ভাঁটা, বায়ু প্রভৃতির বল ও পরিমাণ নির্ণায়ক যন্ত্র। 5. A device for indicating the height of contents in a boiler etc. ; বাষ্পজনক প্রভৃতির অভ্যন্তরস্থ পদার্থের উচ্চতা প্রদর্শন যন্ত্র। 6. The relative position of two or more vessels with reference to the wind ; বায়ু সম্পর্কে দুই বা ততোধিক পোতের আপেক্ষিক অবস্থান। 7. The depth to which a vessel sinks in water ; পোতের যে অংশ জলের নীচে থাকে। 8. (*Print.*) A strip of reglet with a notch cut in it to indicate the length of a page ; (মুদ্রণ) পৃষ্ঠার দৈর্ঘ্য নির্দ্দেশের খাঁজ বিশিষ্ট কাষ্ঠখণ্ড। 10. A criterion ; a test ; "The *gauge* of a pensioner's disability is his unfitness to do etc." ; গুণাগুণ নির্ণয়ের আদর্শ ; পরখ, পরীক্ষা। **Broad gauge** or **narrow gauge**—(In railway construction) A distance between the rails greater or less than 4 ft. 8 in. called *standard gauge* ; লৌহ বর্ত্মের পাতা রেল দুইটীর মধ্যে ব্যবধান। [এই ব্যবধান ৪ ফিট ৮½ ইঞ্চির কম হইলে উহাকে *Narrow gauge* বলে ও তদপেক্ষা অধিক হইলে *Broad gauge* বলে]। **Carpenter's gauge**—The joiner's gauge ; ছুতারের সমান্তরাল রেখাপাত করিবার যন্ত্র, কুর্ুৎ। **Rain gauge**—বৃষ্টিমান যন্ত্র, বর্ষমান যন্ত্র (কৌটিল্যঃ), বৃষ্টিপরিমাপক (হিঃ কোঃ)। **Salt gauge**—ক্ষারপরিমাপক (হিঃ কোঃ)। **Siphon gauge**—বক্রনলিকা পরিমাপক (হিঃ কোঃ)। **Water gauge**—জলপরিমাপকযন্ত্র। **To have** or **keep the weather gauge of**—(*Naut.*) To be to windward of ; (*fig.*) to have the advantage of ; (নৌ-বিদ্যা) বাতাহতদিকে থাকা ; (লক্ষণায়) সুবিধা থাকা। **To take the gauge of**—অনুমান করা।

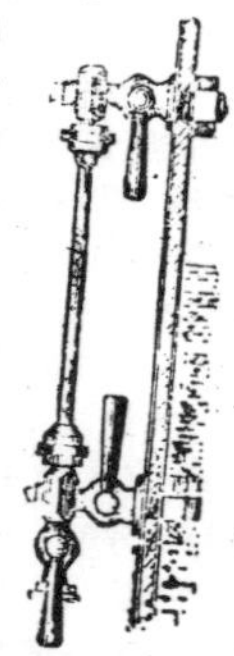

Water gauge.

Gaul (găl), *n.* A native of Gaul or ancient France ; (*facet.*) a Frenchman ; গল বা প্রাচীন ফ্রান্সের অধিবাসী ; (কৌতুকচ্ছলে) ফরাসী। **Gaul'-ish**, *adj.* & *n.* Of, or relating to, the Gauls ; French ; প্রাচীন ফরাসী জাতি-সম্বন্ধীয় ; ফরাসী। (*Noun*) The language of the Gauls ; ফরাসীজাতির ভাষা।

gaunt (gänt), *adj.* **1.** Lean ; emaciated ; কৃশ, ক্ষীণ, কাহিল, ক্ষীণকায় ; অস্থিচর্ম্মসার, কঙ্কালসার। **2.** Grim or desolate ; "The naked trees of the *gaunt* wood" ; ঘোর-দর্শন, বিজন, জনমানবহীন। **Gaunt′-ly,** *adv.* **Gaunt′-ness,** *n.*

gaunt′-lĕt (gänt-), *n.* **1.** An iron glove used as armour ; লৌহ বা ইস্পাত নির্ম্মিত করত্রাণ, ধাতু নির্ম্মিত দস্তানা। **2.** A long glove covering the wrist ; একপ্রকার লম্বা দস্তানা,—যদ্দ্বারা হাতের কব্জা ও প্রকোষ্ঠের কতকাংশ আবৃত হয়। **—ed,** *adj.* Wearing a gauntlet ; দস্তানাপরিহিত। **To fling** or **throw down the gauntlet**—To offer a challenge ; যুদ্ধার্থ আহ্বান করা, যুদ্ধং দেহি বলিয়া সগর্ব্বে অহ্বান করা। **To run the gauntlet** — (শাস্তিভোগের জন্য) ক্রমাগত যষ্টি, চাবুক, প্রভৃতি দ্বারা প্রহৃত হইতে হইতে দুইসারি লোকের মধ্য দিয়া চলিয়া যাওয়া ; (লক্ষণায়) অপ্রীতিজনক ব্যবহার বা সমালোচনা করা। **To take** or **pick up the gauntlet**—যুদ্ধের আহ্বান পরিগ্রহণ করা, যুদ্ধ করিতে সম্মত হওয়া।

gaun′-trȳ (gän-), **gaun′-tree** (gän-trē), *ns.* See GANTRY.

gauze (gäz), *n.* **1.** A very thin transparent fabric of silk, cotton etc. ; এক প্রকার অতি সূক্ষ্মবস্ত্র, সূক্ষ্মাংশুক, হাওয়ার কাপড়। **2.** Anything resembling a gauze ; as, wire *gauze* ; সূক্ষ্মাংশুকবৎ বস্তু। **3.** A thin haze ; "A *gauze* of smoke over the chimney" ; অতি লঘু ধূম বা কুজ্ঝটিকা। **Gauz′-y,** *adj.* **Wire-gauze**—তারের জালি।

găv′-ĕl-kĭnd, *n.* (*Law*) An old English land tenure by which, when the owner died without will, the land descended to all the sons in equal shares ; (আইন) ইংলণ্ডের অন্তঃপাতী কেণ্ট্ দেশের প্রাচীন দায়াধিকারবিশেষ—যাহাতে পৈত্রিক সম্পত্তি পুত্রগণের মধ্যে সমাংশে বিভক্ত হইত। *Gavæus Gaurus*—বনগাই (বেলঃ)।

gā′-vĭ-ăl, *n.* A large piscivorous crocodile (*Gavialis Gangeticus*) of India inhabiting chiefly the basins of the Ganges, Brahmaputra and Indus rivers ; ঘড়িয়াল।

gă-votte′ (-vŏt), *n.* **1.** A lively kind of dance ; একপ্রকার উল্লাসপূর্ণ নৃত্য। **2.** The music for such a dance ; উক্ত প্রকার নৃত্যোপযোগী বাদ্য।

gawk (gäk), *n.* An awkward person ; a simpleton ; আহাম্মক লোক ; বোকা, বেকুব, হাবা, গোবর-গণেশ। **Gawk′-i-ness,** *n.* **Gawk′-y,** *adj.* & *n.* Awkward ; stupid ; ungainly ; আনাড়ী ; মূর্খ, নির্ব্বোধ ; কদাকার। (*Noun.*) A fool ; বোকা লোক।

gay (gā), *adj.* **1.** Lively ; merry ; sportive ; উৎফুল্ল, প্রফুল্ল, উল্লসিত ; স্ফূর্ত্তিময়, আমুদে, প্রমোদপূর্ণ, প্রমোদতরল, রঙ্গপ্রিয় ; সলীল, লীলাপ্রিয়, ক্রীড়াপ্রিয়। **2.** Fine ; brilliant in colour ; as, a *gay* costume ; richly dressed ; সুন্দর, রুচির, শোভন ; উজ্জ্বল-বর্ণ ; জমকালো পোষাক পরিহিত, সমুজ্জ্বলবেশধারী। **3.** (*Euphem.*) Loose ; dissipated ; immoral ; as, to lead a *gay* life ; (মোলায়েম ভাষায়) ভ্রষ্ট ; লম্পট ; দুর্নীতিপূর্ণ। **4.** Airy ; "*Gay* indifference" ; হালকা। **Gay′-ly, Gai′-ly,** *advs.* **Gay′-ness,** *n.*

gāze, *v. i.* & *n.* To look steadfastly (*at, on, upon*) ; "Long, long they *gaze* with meeting eyes" ; স্থিরভাবে চাহিয়া থাকা, অনিমেষ নেত্রে দৃষ্টিপাত করা, স্থির দৃষ্টিতে নিরীক্ষণ করা, একদৃষ্টিতে তাকাইয়া থাকা। ***Noun.*** **1.** A fixed or intent look ; স্থিরদৃষ্টি, বদ্ধদৃষ্টি। **Gaz′-er,** *n.* **Gaz′-ing,** *v. n.* The act of looking intently ; অনিমেষনয়নে দর্শন। **Gaze-hound** — যে শিকারী কুকুর সাধারণতঃ ঘ্রাণ দ্বারা শিকার না করিয়া দৃষ্টি দ্বারাই শিকার অন্বেষণ করে। **Gazing stock**—লোক সাধারণে ঘৃণা বা অবজ্ঞার দৃষ্টিতে পতিত ব্যক্তি, দৃষ্টিপাত্র (কেউঃ), উপহাসদর্শনাস্পদ (ঐ)। **To give (one) the gaze**—To be a spectator of (one) ; দ্রষ্টা হওয়া। **To have in gaze**—To have in prospect ; আশা থাকা। **To set oneself at gaze**—To display oneself ; আড়ম্বর সহকারে প্রদর্শন করা। **To stand at gaze**—To stand in the attitude of gazing esp. in wonder, bewilderment, etc. ; বিস্ময়-স্তম্ভিতভাবে দণ্ডায়মান হওয়া।

gă-zē′-bō, *n.* Summer-house commanding an extensive prospect ; উচ্চস্থানে নির্ম্মিত নিদাঘ-বাটিকা।

gă-zelle′ (-zĕl), *n.* A small species of graceful antilope ; একপ্রকার

Gazelles.

ক্ষুদ্রকায় কোমলনেত্র কৃষ্ণসার মৃগ, এণ। **Gazelle-eyed**— হরিণনয়নী, মৃগাক্ষী, মৃগনয়না, মৃগলোচন, এণক্ষি, এণাক্ষী।

gă-zette′ (-zĕt), *n.* & *v. t.* **1.** A newspaper ; a printed sheet published periodically ; সংবাদ-পত্র, বার্ত্তাবহ ; সাময়িক সংবাদপত্র। **2.** (*Cap.*) One of the three official journals (London, Edinburgh and Dublin Gazettes) published twice a week ; the official journal of any government ; লণ্ডন গেজেট, এডিন্‌বার্গ গেজেট ও ডাব্‌লিন গেজেট নামক সরকারী সংবাদপত্রত্রয়ের অন্যতম ; সরকারী সংবাদপত্র—যাহাতে কর্ম্মচারিগণের নিয়োগ, বদলী, বৃষ্টিপাত, প্রভৃতির বিবরণ নিয়মিতরূপে প্রকাশিত হয়, গেজেট। ***Verb t.*** To publish or announce officially in a gazette ; গেজেটে প্রকাশিত বা বিজ্ঞাপিত করা। **A gazetted officer**—যে কর্ম্মচারীর নিয়োগ বা বদলীর বিষয় সরকারী গেজেটে প্রকাশিত

হয়। **To apper** or **have one's name in the gazette**—To be mentioned in an official newspaper as a bankrupt ; গেজেটে নাম উঠান—বিশেষভাবে দাউলিয়াদিগের। **To be gazetted**—To be the subject of an announcement in the official gazette ; গেজেটে প্রকাশিত হওয়া। **To be gazetted out**—(Of an officer) To be announced as having resigned his post ; (রাজকর্ম্মচারি-সম্পর্কে) পদত্যাগ করিয়াছেন বলিয়া ঘোষিত করা।

găz-ĕt-teer′ (-tēr), *n.* **1.** (*Hist.*) A writer in a gazette ; (ইতিহাস) গেজেটের লেখক, বার্ত্তাবহ-লেখক। **2.** A geographical dictionary ; কোন দেশের নানাস্থানের ভৌগোলিক বিবরণ সম্বলিত অভিধান, ভৌগোলিক অভিধান, দেশ, নগর ইত্যাদির বর্ণানুক্রমিক বর্ণনা-সম্বলিত গ্রন্থ, স্থানকোষ (আঃ বঃ)।

găz′-ō-gene (-gēn), **găs—**, *ns.* A portable apparatus for making aerated waters on a small scale ; অল্প পরিমাণ সোডা, লেমনেড্ প্রভৃতি প্রস্তুতের জন্য কল।

Ge (jē), *n.* The Greek goddess of Earth ; গ্রীক পুরাণোক্ত পৃথিবী দেবী [ইনি সর্ব্বপ্রথম সৃষ্টির প্রাক্কালীন বিশৃঙ্খলা (Chaos) হইতে উদ্ভূতা হন। Uranus এবং Pontus ইঁহার পুত্র। ইঁহার প্রথম পুত্রের ঔরসে Titans নামক দৈত্যগণ এবং দ্বিতীয় পুত্রের ঔরসে Nereus, Ceto, Eurybia, Thaumus এবং Phorcysএর জন্ম হয়।

gear (gēr), *n., v.t.* & *i.* **1.** (*Archaic*) Clothing ; garments ; (অপ্রঃ) কাপড়চোপড় ; পরিচ্ছদ, বেষ। **2.** Goods ; household utensils ; জিনিষপত্র, মালপত্র ; তৈজসপত্র। **3.** Tools ; implements ; appliances ; যন্ত্রপাতি, হাতিয়ার ; অস্ত্র-শস্ত্র ; যন্ত্র, উপকরণ, সাধন, উপায়। **4.** The harness of horses or cattle ; অশ্বা দর সজ্জা **5.** (*Naut.*) Rigging in general ; জাহাজের রশারশি, দড়ি **6.** (*Mech.*) Toothed wheels working one on another ; (যন্ত্র-বিজ্ঞান) পরস্পরের উপর কার্য্যকারী দন্তুর চক্র-সমূহ। **7.** (*Mech.*) Working relation or adjustment of parts ; (যন্ত্র-বিজ্ঞান) যন্ত্রের বিভিন্ন অংশের কার্য্যগত সম্বন্ধ বা সুসমাবেশ। ***Verb t.*** **1.** (*Obs.*) To dress ; (অপ্রঃ) সজ্জিত করা। **2.** To harness, (often with *up*) ; ঘোড়ার সাজ পরান। **3.** (*Mech.*) To connect by, or provide with, gearing ; (যন্ত্র-বিজ্ঞান) পরস্পরের উপর কার্য্যকারী দন্তুর চক্র-সমন্বিত করা, পরস্পরের উপর কার্য্যকারী দন্তুর চক্রসমূহদ্বারা সংযোগ করা। ***Verb i.*** (*Mach.*) (Of a wheel) To get exactly *into* or be in gear *with* ; (চক্র-সম্পর্কে) অপর চক্র ঠিক লাগা, অপর চাকার দাঁতের ফাঁকে ফাঁকে দাঁত ঠিক লাগা। **Gear′-ing,** *n.* Harness ; a train of toothed wheels with logs for transmitting motion ; অশ্বসজ্জা ; পরস্পর সংলগ্ন দন্তুর চক্রশ্রেণী। **Gear′-less,** *adj.* **Driving gear**—যে যন্ত্রাংশসমূহের সাহায্যে যন্ত্র চালিত হয়। **Gear-box**—দ্বিচক্রযানের দন্তুর চক্র আবরক। **Gear cutter**—A maker of toothed wheels for transmitting motion in machines ; a machine for cutting such wheels ; যন্ত্রে গতি সঞ্চারের দন্তুর চক্র নির্ম্মাতা ; দন্তুর চক্র রচন-যন্ত্র। **Gear-wheel**—যে দন্তুর চক্র অন্য দন্তুর চক্রের উপর ক্রিয়া করিয়া গতি সঞ্চার করে। **High gear**—দ্বিচক্রযানের ব্যবস্থা বিশেষ—যদ্দ্বারা যন্ত্র দ্রুতবেগে চালিত হয়। **Low gear**—দ্বিচক্রযান মন্দবেগে চালাইবার জন্য উহার গতিসঞ্চারক অংশের ব্যবস্থা-বিশেষ। **In (good) gear** — In (good) working order ; বেশ (ভাল) চলে—এরূপ। **Out of gear**—(*Mech.*) Out of working order ; in disorder ; বিকল, নষ্ট ; বিশৃঙ্খল। **To throw in** or **out of gear**—(*Mech.*) To connect or disconnect (wheel-work, couplings etc.) ; সংযোগ সংলগ্ন করা ; বিশ্লিষ্ট করা, বিলগ্ন করা।

gĕck′-ō, *n.* A lizard ; টিক্‌টিকি (ষোঃ)।

Gecko.

gee (jē), **gee′-gee** (jē-jē), *n* (*Colloq.*) A horse ; (চলিত ভাষায়) ঘোড়া।

gee (jē), **gee′-hō** (jē-), **gee′-(h)ŭp** (jē-), **gee′-wō** (jē-), *interjs.* (Expression commanding a horse etc.) Go on ; move faster ; or (sometimes) turn to the right ; আগে চল ; জল্‌দি চল ; অথবা (কখন কখন) ডাইনে চল।

geese (gēz), *n. pl.* of GOOSE which see.

Gē-hĕn′-nă, *n.* **1.** (New Testament) Hell ; নরক, জাহান্নম। **2.** A place of torture or misery ; যন্ত্রণাগার।

gei′-shâ (gā-), *n.* A dancing girl of Japan ; জাপানী নর্ত্তকী বালিকা, জাপানী নাচওয়ালী।

gĕl′-ă-tin, —tine (-tĭn), *ns.* An animal substance which dissolves in hot water and forms a jelly when cold ; শিরীষ। **Ge-lat′-i-nate, Ge-lat′-i-nize,** *v. t.* & *i.* To convert or to be converted into gelatin ; শিরিষে পরিবর্ত্তন করা অথবা শিরিষে পরিবর্তিত হওয়া। **Ge-lat′-i-nous,** *adj.* **Ge-lat′-i-noid,** *adj.* & *n.* Relating to gelatine ; of the nature or consistency of jelly ; শিরীষ সম্পর্কীয় ; শিরিষের মত আঠালো বা চট্‌চটে। (*Noun*) A gelatinous substance ; শিরীষ-বৎ পদার্থ। **—tin′-i-form,** *adj.* Resembling gelatine ; শিরীষবৎ। **Blasting** or **Explosive gelatine**—একপ্রকার শক্তিশালী বিস্ফোরক

দ্রব্য। **Gelatine paper**—আলোকের রাসায়নিক ক্রিয়া-দ্বারা বিকারশীল শিরীষ-লিপ্ত কাগজ।

gĕ-lā′-tion, *n.* Solidification by cooling or freezing ; শৈত্যপ্রয়োগে সংহনন বা ঘনীকরণ।

gĕld, *v. t.* **1.** To castrate ; to emasculate ; to extirpate the ovaries of a female ; খাসী করা, হিজড়া করা ; মুষ্কচ্ছেদ করা, বৃষণোৎপাটন করা ; স্ত্রীলোকের ডিম্বাশয় নষ্ট করা। **Geld′-er,** *n.* One who gelds ; মুষ্কচ্ছেদক। **Geld′-ing,** *n.* **1.** The act of castrating ; মুষ্কচ্ছেদন। **2.** A castrated horse etc. ; ছিন্নমুষ্ক অশ্ব বা অপর জন্তু, আখ্তা ঘোড়া, খাসী, দামড়া।

gĕl′-id, *adj.* Icy ; very cold ; cool ; হিমানীশীতল, তুষারশীতল ; অতি-শীতল ; শীতল।

gĕm, *n.* & *v. t.* **1.** A precious stone, esp. when cut and polished for ornaments ; বহুমূল্য প্রস্তর, বিশেষতঃ পরিকর্ম্মীকৃত মণি, রত্ন, মণি। **2.** Anything extremely valuable or attractive ; a prized thing ; বহুমূল্য বা চিত্তাকর্ষক কোন পদার্থ ; অতি সমাদৃত বস্তু। **3.** A precious or semi-precious stone with engraved designs ; as, antique *gems* ; নানাপ্রকার নক্সা-খোদিত মণি। ***Verb t.*** **1.** To adorn with gems ; রত্নভূষিত করা, মণিমণ্ডিত করা, রত্নখচিত করা, মণিমাণিক্যাদি দ্বারা ভূষিত করা। **2.** To embellish, as with gems ; as, foliage *gemmed* with dew drops ; ভূষিত করা, মণ্ডিত করা। **Gem′-my,** *adj.*

gĕm′-i-nāte, *adj.* & *v. t.* (*Bot.*) In pairs ; twin ; as, *geminate* leaves ; (উদ্ভিদ্-বিদ্যা) যুগ্ম (সাঃ পঃ) ; যুগল। ***Verb t.*** To double ; দ্বিগুণিত করা। **–na′-tion,** *n.*

Gem′-i-ni (jĕm-), *n.* & *interj.* The third Zodiacal constellation pictorially represented as the twins—Castor and Pollux ; মিথুন, জিতুম (সাঃ পঃ), মিথুন রাশি ; ***Interj.*** A mild form of oath or exclamation ; আঃ কপাল, আহা মরি !

gĕm′-mă, *n.* (*Pl.* -MÆ) **1.** (*Bot.*), A leaf-bud ; (উদ্ভিদ্-বিদ্যা) পত্র-মুকুল, কুট্যাল (সাঃ পঃ)। **2.** (*Zool.*) An outgrowth which develops into a new organism ; (প্রাণি-বিদ্যা) যে উপাঙ্গ নূতন নূতন জীবে পরিণত হয়।

gĕm′-māte, *adj.* & *v. t.* Reproducing by buds ; having buds ; মুকুল দ্বারা পুনরুৎপাদনশীল ; মুকুলবিশিষ্ট, কুট্যালী। ***Verb t.*** To produce or propagate by buds ; মুকুল দ্বারা উৎপাদন বা বংশ বিস্তার করা।

gĕm-mā′-tion, *n.* **1.** Act or manner of budding ; the time when buds are put forth ; কুট্যালোদ্গম (সাঃ পঃ), কুট্যালোদ্গম-রীতি ; কুট্যালোদ্গম কাল। **2.** (*Zool.*) The formation of a new individual by the process of budding ; method of reproduction by buds ; (প্রাণি-বিদ্যা) কোন জন্তুর বর্দ্ধিত উপাঙ্গ হইতে অপর জন্তু প্রজনন ; উক্তরূপ প্রজনন-প্রণালী। **3.** The arrangement of buds on the stalk ; বৃন্তোপরি কুট্যাল-সন্নিবেশ। **Gem′-ma-tive,** *adj.*

gĕm-mĭf′-ĕr-ous (-ŭs), *adj.* Producing gems or buds ; মুকুলোৎপাদী, রত্নপ্রসূ।

gĕm-mĭp′-ă-rous (-rŭs), *adj.* Producing buds ; reproducing by buds ; মুকুলোৎপাদী ; মুকুল বা বর্দ্ধিত উপাঙ্গ দ্বারা পুনরুৎপাদী। **–ly,** *adv.*

gĕm′-mūle, *n.* **1.** (*Bot.*) The plumule of the embryo in a seed ; (উদ্ভিদ-বিদ্যা) বীজাঙ্কুর। **2.** (*Bot.*) One of the reproductive cells of cryptogamous plants ; (উদ্ভিদ-বিদ্যা) অপুষ্পক উদ্ভিদের পুনরুৎপাদক কোষ। **3.** (*Zool.*) A small gemma ; (প্রাণি-বিদ্যা) জীবদেহের ক্ষুদ্র বর্দ্ধিত উপাঙ্গ—যাহা নূতন জীবে পরিণত হয়।

gĕ-nappe′ (-năp), *n.* A worsted yarn used with silk in fringes etc. ; একপ্রকার পশমী সূতা।

gendarme, (*F.*), *n.* **1.** An armed policeman esp. in France ; ফরাসী-দেশের সশস্ত্র পুলিস প্রহরী। **2.** A projecting piece of rock on a ridge ; উদ্গত পাষাণস্তূপ।

gendarmerie, (*F*), *n.* The body of a gendarmes ; ফরাসী দেশের সশস্ত্র পুলিস প্রহরী দল।

gendarussa vulgaris — নীল-নির্গুন্ড (বেঙ্গঃ)।

gĕn′-dĕr, *n.* & *v. t.* **1.** (*Jocular*) A sex ; (কৌতুকচ্ছলে) স্ত্রী বা পুং চিহ্ন। **2.** (*Gram.*) The classification of nouns according to sex ; one of three classes of objects corresponding to two sexes and sexlessness ; (ব্যাকরণ) বিশেষ্যের লিঙ্গভেদ ; লিঙ্গ। ***Verb t.*** (*Poet.*) To engender ; (কবিতায়) উৎপাদন করা, জন্মদান করা। **–less,** *adj.* Without gender ; লিঙ্গশূন্য, অলিঙ্গ, লিঙ্গহীন।

gĕn-ē-ăl′-ō-ġy̆, *n.* **1.** An account of the descent of a person or family ; a pedigree ; কোন ব্যক্তি বা পরিবারের বংশবিবরণ, বংশ-তালিকা, বংশবৃত্তান্ত, কুলক্রমচরিত্র (কেঙ্গিঃ), কুলক্রম, (ঐ), বংশচরিত্র (ঐ) ; বংশানুক্রম, বংশাবলী, কুলজী, বংশ-পরম্পরা (কেঙ্গিঃ)। **2.** Investigation of pedigrees ; বংশবৃত্তান্তানুসন্ধান। **3.** (*Obs.*) Lineage ; (অপ্রচলিত) বংশ। **4.** (*Biol.*) The line of development of an animal or plant from older forms ; (জীব-বিজ্ঞান) জীব বা উদ্ভিদের বংশানুক্রম। **–gise,** *v. t.* & *i.* To draw up a genealogy of ; বংশাবলী প্রস্তুত করা। (*Verb i.*) To trace genealogies ; কোন রূপ সূত্র ধরিয়া বংশবৃত্তান্ত অনুসন্ধান করা। **–gist,** *n.* One who traces genealogies or descents ; কুলাচার্য্য, বংশবিবরণজ্ঞ পণ্ডিত, কুলক্রমজ্ঞ (কেঙ্গিঃ), কুলক্রমদর্শক (ঐ), বংশক্রমদর্শক (ঐ), অন্বয়জ্ঞ। **–a-log′-ic, –a-log′-i-cal,** *adjs.* Pertaining to, or exhibiting, the descent of a person or families ; ব্যক্তি বা

বংশসমূহের উৎপত্তি বিষয়ক বা উৎপত্তি প্রদর্শক, বংশানুক্রমিক, কুলসংক্রান্ত, বংশানুক্রমবিষয়ক (কেঙিঃ)। **Genealogical tables** — বংশাবলীপত্র, গোত্রপট। **Genealogical tree**—কুলক্রম।

gĕn'-ĕ-ră, *n. Pl.* of GENUS which see.

gĕn'-ĕr-ăl, *adj.* & *n.* **1.** Relating to a whole class or order; not particular; সাধারণ; সামান্য (সাঃ পঃ)। **2.** Public; common; as, the *general* interest of a nation; সাধারণ, সামান্য; সর্ব্বজনীন, সার্ব্বজনিক, সার্ব্বভৌমিক, সর্ব্বসম্বন্ধী (কেঙিঃ), সর্ব্বসাধারণ (ঐ)। **3.** Prevalent; usual; extensive, though not universal; as, a *general* custom; প্রবল; প্রায়িক, ব্যবহারিক, সচরাচরিক; ব্যাপক। **4.** Not specialized; not restricted to one department; as, a *general* reader (one who reads miscellaneous literature); বিশেষ বিষয়ে একনিষ্ঠ নয়; কোন বিশেষ বিভাগে সীমাবদ্ধ নয়। **5.** All collectively; whole; as, the *general* body of citizens; সমুদায়; সমগ্র। **6.** Indefinite; vague; as, some *general* remarks on fishing; অনিশ্চিত, অনির্দ্দিষ্ট; অস্পষ্ট। **7.** Taken as a whole; "His *general* behaviour"; মোটের উপর। ***Noun.*** **1.** (*Archaic*) The public; (অপ্রঃ) জনসাধারণ, লোকসাধারণ। **2.** The whole; the total; the aggregate; আস্ত জিনিষ, গোটা জিনিষ; সমষ্টি; সমূহ, সমুদায়। **3.** The chief of a religious order, as of Jesuits, Dominicans, etc.; সন্ন্যাসি-সম্প্রদায়ের নেতা। **4.** (*Mil.*) The chief commander of an army or of a division or brigade; সেনানী, সেনানায়ক, সেনাপতি, সৈন্যাধ্যক্ষ, সৈন্যাধিপতি, সেনাকর্ত্তা (কেঙিঃ), বলাধ্যক্ষ, চমূপতি। **5.** (*Mil.*) A strategist; রণনীতিজ্ঞ ব্যক্তি, রণপণ্ডিত ব্যক্তি। **6.** A general servant; সাধারণ ভৃত্য, সর্ব্বকর্ম্ম সম্পাদনার্থ ভৃত্য। **7.** (*Pl. rare.*) General notions, principles or rules; (অপ্রঃ) সাধারণ ধারণা, মতসমূহ বা নিয়মাবলী। **—ly,** *adv.* On the whole; in general sense or way; মোটের উপর; সাধারণভাবে, সাধারণ উপায়ে। **General agent**—এজেন্ট, আমমোক্তার। **General concept**—সামান্য প্রত্যয় (হিঃ কোঃ)। **General confession** — A confession to be made by whole congregation; সমস্ত উপাসকমণ্ডলী দ্বারা করণীয় পাপ স্বীকারোক্তি। **General consciousness**—সামাজিক সংবিৎ (হিঃ কোঃ)। **General council**—খৃষ্টীয় ধর্ম্মসংঘের সভ্যগণের সাধারণ সভা। **General dealer**—যে ব্যবসায়ী সচরাচর ব্যবহার্য্য সর্ব্বপ্রকার জিনিষ বিক্রয় করে। **General election**—See under ELECTION. **General good**—সর্ব্বহিত (হিঃ কোঃ), সাধারণের উপকার, লোকহিত। **General idea, notion** — সামান্য প্রত্যয় (হিঃ কোঃ)। **General issue**—বাদীর অভিযোগ সাধারণভাবে অগ্রাহ্য করা হেতু মোকদ্দমার যে নিষ্পত্তি হয়। **General officer** — কর্ণেলের উর্দ্ধতন সামরিক কর্ম্মচারী। **General Post**—First morning delivery; প্রাতঃকালের প্রথম পত্রবন্টন। A kind of indoor game; একপ্রকার ক্রীড়া—যাহা বাটীতে খেলা যায়। **General practitioner** — যে চিকিৎসক সর্ব্বপ্রকার রোগের চিকিৎসা করেন, সর্ব্বরোগচিকিৎসক, ভিষক। **General property**—সামান্য ধর্ম্ম। **General servant**—See GENERAL *n.* 6. **General term**—সাধারণপদ (হিঃ কোঃ), সামান্যব্যাপক পদ (ঐ); **General will**—সামাজিক ইচ্ছা (হিঃ কোঃ)। **Lover-general** — (*Jocularly*); (কৌতুকচ্ছলে) যে ব্যক্তি নির্ব্বিচারে সকল রমণীর সহিতই প্রেম করিয়া থাকে, সাধারণ প্রেমিক। **A general word, term** or **notion**—One including points common to individuals of a class and neglecting differences; সামান্য শব্দ, সামান্য প্রত্যয়, সামান্যবাচক পদ। **As a general rule**—In most cases; সাধারণতঃ। **Generally speaking**—In general; স্থূলতঃ, বলিতে গেলে, স্থূল কথায়। **In a general way** — Ordinarily; সাধারণতঃ। **In general** — Commonly; extensively; সাধারণতঃ, সামান্যতঃ; ব্যাপকভাবে। As a general rule; usually; সাধারণ নিয়মস্বরূপ; প্রায়শঃ। **The General Assembly**—See ASSEMBLY.

gĕn-ĕr-ăl-is'-si-mō, *n.* A commander of a combined military and naval force or of several armies; সম্মিলিত নৌ এবং স্থল-সৈন্যের অধিনায়ক, একাধিক সৈন্যদলের অধিনায়ক, প্রধান সেনাপতি।

gĕn-ĕr-ăl'-i-tȳ, *n.* **1.** State or quality of being general. সাধারণতা। **2.** Vagueness; "Let us descend from *generalities* to particulars"; অস্পষ্টতা, অনিশ্চয়তা। **3.** The main body; majority; as, the *generality* of a nation; প্রধান অংশ, প্রধান ভাগ; অধিকাংশ। **4.** A general principle, point or law; সাধারণ তত্ত্ব, বিষয় বা বিধি।

gĕn'-ĕr-ăl-īze, *v. t.* & *i.* **1.** To reduce to general laws; to include under a general term; to call by a general name; সাধারণ নিয়মের অন্তর্ভুক্ত করা, সাধারণ নিয়মাধীন করা; সামান্যবাচক পদের অন্তর্ভুক্ত করা, সমশ্রেণীভুক্ত করা, একজাতীয় করা; সাধারণ সংজ্ঞা দান করা। **2.** To make general in use or application; to make common or familiar; বিশ্বজনীন বা সর্ব্বজনীন ভাবে প্রয়োগ করা; সুপরিচিত করা, সর্ব্বসাধারণ করা। **3.** To infer; to deduce (a law etc.) from particulars; as, to *generalize* fact; সিদ্ধান্ত করা; বিশেষ বিশেষ ঘটনা হইতে সাধারণ নিয়ম বা তত্ত্ব উপপাদনকরা। ***Verb i.*** **1.** To form general notions from particular instances; to classify under general heads; বিশেষ বিশেষ দৃষ্টান্ত

হইতে সাধারণ ধারণা করা, সামান্য কয়েকটী দৃষ্টান্ত হইতে সাধারণ নিয়ম স্থির করা ; পদার্থ সকলের শ্রেণী বিভাগ করা, সাধারণ অনুমান করা। 2. (*Math.* & *Philos.*) To throw (a proposition etc.) into a general form of which the original becomes a particular case ; (গণিত বা দর্শন-শাস্ত্র) কোন প্রতিজ্ঞা বা উপপাদ্যকে সাধারণ নিয়মের আকার দান করা (যাহার ফলে মৌলিক প্রতিজ্ঞা বা উপপাদ্য একটী বিশেষ দৃষ্টান্ত হইয়া দাঁড়ায়)। 3. (*Painting*) To render only the typical characteristics of ; কোন বস্তুর প্রধান প্রধান বিশেষত্ব চিত্রিত করা। 4. To render indefinite ; to speak vaguely ; অস্পষ্ট করা ; অস্পষ্ট ভাবে বলা। **—iz-a-ble,** *adj.* **—i-za′-tion,** *n.* 1. The act or process of generalizing ; শ্রেণীবিভাগ, সাধারণ নিয়মের অন্তর্ভুক্ত করণ, শ্রেণীভেদ-পদ্ধতি, শ্রেণীভাগের নিয়ম। 2. A general inference ; সাধারণ সিদ্ধান্ত, সাধারণ অনুমান, অনুগম (হিঃ কোঃ)। **—iz-er,** *n.* **Hasty generalization** — সামান্য কয়েকটী দৃষ্টান্তের উপর সাধারণ অনুমান বা সিদ্ধান্ত দাঁড়করণ।

gĕn′-êr-ăl-ship, *n.* 1. The office or dignity of a general ; সেনাপতিত্ব, সৈনাপত্য, সৈনান্য। 2. Military skill ; strategy ; সমর-কৌশল, রণকৌশল ; রণনীতি, রণপাণ্ডিত্য, যুদ্ধকৌশল, রণ-চাতুর্য্য, রণনৈপুণ্য। 3. Judicious management ; skilful tact ; সুপরিচালন ; কার্য্যকৌশল।

gĕn′-êr-āte, *v. t.* 1. To beget ; জন্ম দেওয়া, জন্মদান করা। 2. To bring into life or existence ; to produce ; পুনর্জীবিত করা, সত্তা প্রদান করা ; উৎপাদন করা। 3. (*Math.*) To make ; as, a point *generates* a line or figure ; সৃষ্টি করা। **—at-ing,** *v. n.* **—a-tive,** *adj.* 1. Relating to generation ; জনন-সংক্রান্ত। 2. Productive ; as, *generative* principles of social peace ; জননক্ষম, উৎপাদক, উৎপাদনক্ষম, প্রজননক্ষম, প্রজননী। **—a-tor,** *n.* 1. One who begets or produces ; জনক, উৎপাদক, উৎপাদনকারী ব্যক্তি বা বস্তু। 2. An apparatus for the production of gas, steam, electricity, etc. : বাষ্প, তাড়িত, প্রভৃতি উৎপাদক যন্ত্র। **Generating line**—উৎপাদক-রেখা (হিঃ কোঃ)।

gĕn-êr-ā′-tion, *n.* 1. Act of procreation ; propagation of species ; state of being generated ; জনন, প্রজনন ; বংশবিস্তার ; উৎপত্তি। 2. Production ; formation ; উৎপাদন ; গঠন। 3. (*Obs.*) Progeny ; offspring ; (অপ্রঃ) প্রসূতি ; সন্তান-সন্ততি। 4. A single step in descent or pedigree ; পুরুষ। 5. The people living at the same time ; (also) the average in which children are ready to replace the parents (reckoned at $\frac{1}{3}$ of a century or at 30 years as a time-measure) ; সমকালীন তাবৎ লোক ; গড়পড়তা মানুষের জীবনকাল, যুগ, আমল। **Alternate generation**—(প্রাণি-বিদ্যা) উৎপাদনের প্রকারান্তর—যাহাতে সন্তানগণ পিতামাতার সদৃশ না হইয়া পিতামহী বা তদূর্দ্ধতন পূর্ব্ব-পুরুষের সদৃশ হইয়া থাকে, একান্তরিত জনন। **Spontaneous or equivocal generation** — অজৈব পদার্থ হইতে জীবের উৎপত্তি, স্বতঃজনন, স্বয়ংজন্ম (হিঃ কোঃ), অজীবজনি (ঐ)। **From generation to generation** — পুরুষানুক্রমে, পুরুষপরম্পরায়। **The present generation**—The living men of the present time ; বর্তমান কালের জীবিত লোকসমূহ।

gē-nĕr′-ic, —i-căl, *adjs.* 1. Pertaining to, or characteristic of, a genus or kind ; applied to a large class ; as, a *generic* name ; জাতীয়, জাতি-বিষয়ক, জাতিগত, শ্রেণীগত, গণসম্বন্ধীয় ; জাতিবাচক। 2. Very comprehensive ; not specific or special ; অতিবিস্তৃতার্থ, বহুব্যাপকার্থ, ব্যাপকার্থযুক্ত ; সামান্য, সাধারণ। **—i-cal-ly,** *adv.* **Generic distinctions**—যে বিশেষত্ব দ্যোতক লক্ষণ সমূহ দ্বারা এক জাতি হইতে অপর জাতির পার্থক্য নিরূপিত হয়। **Generic properties**—সামান্য ধর্ম্ম (সাঃ পঃ), জাতিধর্ম্ম (হিঃ কোঃ)।

gĕn-êr-ŏs′-i-tȳ, *n.* 1. Noble-mindedness ; মহানুভবতা, ঔদার্য্য, মহত্ত্ব, মহাপ্রাণতা, সদাশয়তা। 2. Liberality ; munificence ; বদান্যতা, দানশীলতা ; মুক্তহস্তত্ব, দানশৌণ্ডত্ব।

gĕn′-êr-ous (-ŭs), *adj.* 1. Noble ; high-minded ; not mean ; magnanimous ; মহৎ ; উন্নতমনা ; মহানুভব, মহাপ্রাণ ; সদাশয়, উদার, মহাত্মা। 2. Open-handed ; munificent ; মুক্তহস্ত ; দানশৌণ্ড, দানশীল, ত্যাগশীল, বদান্য, বহুপ্রদ। 3. Abundant ; copious ; প্রচুর ; অপর্য্যাপ্ত, বহুল। 4. Fertile ; as, *generous* fields ; উর্ব্বর, শস্য-প্রদ। 5. Rich, as a diet, colour, etc. ; strong ; stimulating ; as, *generous* wine etc. ; গুরুপাক, মসলাদার ; উগ্র, তেজাল ; উত্তেজক। **—ly,** *adv.*

gĕn′-ĕ-sis, *n.* (*Pl.* -SES) 1. (*Cap.*) The first book of the Old Testament cotaining an account of the creation ; বাইবেলের পুরাতন নিয়মের অন্তর্গত প্রথম পুস্তক—যাহাতে জগৎসৃষ্টি বর্ণিত হইয়াছে। 2. Origin ; production ; mode of formation or generation ; মূল, আদিকারণ ; উৎপাদন, জনন, সৃষ্টি, উৎপত্তি, গঠন ; উৎপাদন বা গঠন-প্রণালী। **Ge-nes′-ic, —sit′-ic,** *adjs.* **Genesis of species**—বিভিন্ন জাতির উৎপত্তি।

Genet.

gĕn′-ĕt, *n.* 1. An animal allied to the civet ; গন্ধগোকুলা জাতীয়

জন্তু-বিশেষ। **2.** The fur of the genet ; উক্ত জন্তুর লোম বা পশম।

gĕ-nĕt′-ic, –i-căl, *adjs.* Relating to, or concerning, origin or mode of production ; উৎপাদন-সম্বন্ধীয়, প্রজননরীতি-সম্পর্কীয়, জননসম্বন্ধী (হিঃ কোঃ)। **–i-cal-ly,** *adv.* **Genetic method**—জন্মপ্রদর্শক রীতি (হিঃ কোঃ)। **Genetic selection**—বহুপ্রজবরণ (হিঃ কোঃ)। **Genetic spiral**—পত্রমূলাবর্ত্ত (সাঃ পঃ)।

gĕ-nē′-vă, *n.* A liquor flavoured with juniper berries (also called) Hollands) ; একপ্রকার মদিরা।

Ge-nē′-vă (jē-), *n.* & *adj.* The chief city of Switzerland ; সুইজারল্যাণ্ডের প্রধান নগরী। ***Adj.*** Made at, or belonging to, Geneva ; জেনেভা নগরীতে নির্ম্মিত, জেনেভা নগরী সম্পর্কীয়।

Gen-e-vese′, –van, *adjs.* & *ns.* Pertaining to Geneva ; Calvanistic ; জেনেভা নগরী সম্পর্কীয় ; জেনেভা নগরবাসী ধর্ম্মপ্রবর্ত্তক ক্যালভিনের ধর্ম্মমত সম্বন্ধীয়। (*Noun*) **1.** A native of Geneva ; জেনেভা নগরবাসী। **2.** An adherent of Calvanism ; ক্যাল্‌ভিনের মতাবলম্বী। **Geneva Convention**—১৮৬৪ খৃঃ অব্দে ইংলণ্ড ব্যতীত ইয়ুরোপের প্রধান শক্তিসমূহ কর্ত্তৃক স্বাক্ষরিত সম্মতি-পত্র—ইহাতে যুদ্ধক্ষেত্রে আহত ও পীড়িত ব্যক্তিগণের প্রতি সকরুণ ব্যবহার করা হইবে স্থিরীকৃত হয়। গ্রেটব্রিটেন ১৮৬৫ খৃঃ অব্দে এই সম্মতি-পত্র স্বাক্ষর করেন। **Geneva-cross**—যুদ্ধকালে আহত সৈনিকদিগের যান প্রভৃতিতে প্রদর্শিত লোহিতবর্ণ ক্রুশ-চিহ্ন। **Geneva-gown**—ক্যালভিন্ সম্প্রদায়ের পুরোহিতগণ কর্ত্তৃক ধর্ম্মপ্রচারকালে পরিহিত কৃষ্ণবর্ণ বহিঃপরিচ্ছদ। **Geneva theology** — Calvinism ; জেনেভাবাসী ধর্ম্মপ্রবর্ত্তক ক্যালভিন প্রবর্ত্তিত ধর্ম্মমতসমূহ।

gē′-ni-ăl, *adj.* **1.** *(Rare.)* Pertaining to marriage ; generative ; "The *genial* bed" ; (অপ্রঃ) ঔদ্বাহিক ; জন্মদ, উৎপাদক। **2.** Cheering ; sociable ; kindly ; cordial ; as, *genial* disposition ; healthful ; স্ফূর্ত্তিজনক, সুখদ, চিত্তপ্রফুল্লকর ; সদালাপী, মিশুক, সঙ্গপ্রিয় ; সদয়, দয়ার্দ্র ; আন্তরিক ; স্বাস্থ্যকর, স্বাস্থ্যজনক। **3.** Favourable to growth or comfort ; warm ; as, a *genial* climate ; বৃদ্ধির পক্ষে অনুকূল, আরামদায়ক, আরামপ্রদ ; উষ্ণ। **–al′-i-ty,** *n.* The quality of being genial ; cheerfulness or cordiality ; আরামজনকতা ; আন্তরিকতা, প্রসন্নতা, প্রফুল্লতা। **–ize,** *v. t.* To render pleasant or agreeable ; প্রীতিপ্রদ করা, মনোজ্ঞ করা, রুচির করা। **–ly,** *adv.*

gē-nī′-ăl, *adj.* (*Anat.*) Pertaining to the chin ; চিবুক-সম্বন্ধীয়।

gē-nĭc′-ū-lāte, –lāt-ĕd, *adjs.* Having joints or bent like a knee ; as, a *geniculate* stem ; জানুর মত সন্ধিবিশিষ্ট বা নত, জানুমান (সাঃ পঃ)।

gē′-nie (-nē), *n.* A jinnee ; ভূত, অপদেবতা, জিন।

gē′-ni-ī, *n. pl.* (*Sing.* GENIUS) Spirit ; জিনসমূহ।

gĕn′-i-tăl, *adj.* & *n.* Pertaining to animal generation ; প্রজনন-সম্বন্ধীয়, প্রজোৎপাদন সম্বন্ধীয়। ***Noun.*** (*Pl.*) The generative or sexual organs ; জননেন্দ্রিয়, সঙ্গমেন্দ্রিয়, জননাঙ্গ (কেন্ডিঃ), গোপনীয় অঙ্গ, উপস্থ।

gĕn′-i-tive (-tĭv), *adj.* & *n.* (*Gram.*) Pertaining to that case which denotes source or possession ; (ব্যাকরণ) সম্বন্ধবাচক কারক-সম্পর্কীয়। ***Noun.*** The genitive case ; possessive case ; সম্বন্ধকারক, সম্বন্ধ পদ ; সম্বন্ধসূচক বিভক্তি, ষষ্ঠী। **–ti′-val,** *adj.* **–ti′-val-ly,** *adv.* **Objective genetive** — কর্ম্মণি ষষ্ঠী। **Subjective genetive**—কর্ত্তরি ষষ্ঠী।

gĕn′-i-ŭs, *n.* (*Pl.* -USES, GENII) **1.** An attendant spirit of a person or place ; a tutelary deity ; a supernatural being ; অধিদেবতা, স্থলদেবতা (কেন্ডিঃ), বাস্তুদেবতা (ঐ), বাস্তুপুরুষ (ঐ) ; অধিষ্ঠাতা ; অপদেবতা, পিশাচ, জিন, দৈত **2.** Natural aptitude ; disposition as, a *genius* for history ; স্বাভাবিব প্রবৃত্তি ; প্রকৃতি, মেজাজ। **3.** Peculiar character, sentiment, opinion taste or spirit ; drift ; as, the *genius* of a nation, language, period, etc. ; বিশেষ প্রকৃতি, ভাব, মত, রুচি ; মর্ম্ম, তাৎপর্য্য। **4.** (*No pl.*) Uncommon intellectual power ; superior power of invention or creation ; as, Homer was a man of *genius* ; অসাধারণ ধীশক্তি, প্রতিভা ; নবনবোন্মেষশালিনী প্রজ্ঞা, নবনবোন্মেষশালিনী প্রতিভা, প্রাকৃতশক্তি (প্রঃ চিঃ)। **5.** (*Pl.* -USES) A man having uncommon intellectual power ; as, Shakespeare was a rare *genius* ; অসাধারণ ধীশক্তি-সম্পন্ন ব্যক্তি, প্রতিভাসম্পন্ন ব্যক্তি, প্রতিভাবান ব্যক্তি। **6.** The associations, traditions, etc. (of a place) ; as, his character moulded by the *genius* of Edinburgh ; (কোন স্থানের) সহচার, জনশ্রুতি, প্রভৃতি। **Genius loci**—The presiding divinity, associations, etc. of a place ; কোন স্থানের অধিদেবতা, অধিষ্ঠাত্রী দেবী, কোন স্থানের সহচার, জনশ্রুতি, প্রভৃতি। **A person's good** or **bad genius**—Two opposed spirits or angels working for a person's salvation or damnation ; (*fig.*) a person who powerfully influences others for good or evil ; যে দেবদূত কোন ব্যক্তির মুক্তিলাভে সাহায্য করে, যে দেবদূত কাহারও নরকের পথ প্রশস্ত করে ; (লক্ষণায়) যে ব্যক্তি অন্য ব্যক্তির মনের উপর দুর্জ্জয় প্রভাব বিস্তার করিয়া তাহাকে সুপথে বা কুপথে চালিত করে।

Gen′-ō-ă (jĕn-), *n.* A city of Italy ; ইটালীদেশের নগরীবিশেষ। **–ese′, –vese′,** *adjs.* & *ns.* **Genoa cakes**—উপরে বাদাম-দেওয়া পিষ্টক-বিশেষ।

genre, (*F.*), *n.* **1.** A kind, sort or style ; রকম, প্রকার, রীতি, ধারা।

(Also GENRE PAINTING) A inting etc. depicting scenes of dinary life ; দৈনন্দিন জীবনের নামূলক চিত্র প্রভৃতি। **Genre-inting**—See GENRE 2.

ns, *n.* (*Pl.* GENTES) (*Rom. ntiq.*) A clan among Romans or Greeks ; প্রাচীন রোমের গোত্র বা বংশ।

ent, *adj.* **1.** (*Vulg.*) A gentleman ; (ইতর ভাষায়) ভদ্র ব্যক্তি। **2.** (*Jocular*) One who apes the gentleman ; (কৌতুকচ্ছলে) যে হীনশ্রেণীর লোক ভদ্রলোকের আচার আচরণ অনুকরণের হাস্যোদ্দীপক চেষ্টা করে।

gĕn-teel′ (-tēl), *adj.* **1.** Polite ; having the manners of the upper classes ; ভদ্র ; ভদ্রজনোচিত শিষ্টাচারপরায়ণ। **2.** Elegant in dress etc. ; fashionable ; সুবেশ ; কেতাদুরস্ত। **3.** Suited to the position of gentleman or lady ; as, a *genteel* occupation ; ভদ্রোচিত, ভদ্রমহিলার উপযোগী। **—ly,** *adv.*

gĕn′-ti-ăn (-shĭ-), *n.* A kind of blue-flowered plant ; একপ্রকার তিক্ত ওষধি, কিরাততিক্ত (আঃ বঃ), ভূনিম্ব (ঐ), চিরতিক্ত (ঐ), পাষাণভেদ (খোরী)। **Gentian bitter**—উক্ত গুল্মের মূল হইতে নিষ্কর্ষিত বলপ্রদ ঔষধ।

gĕn -tīle, *adj.* & *n.* **1.** Belonging to the non-Jewish nations ; অ-ইহুদী জাতি সম্পর্কীয়। **2.** Relating to a nation or tribe ; জাতিসম্বন্ধীয়, বংশ-সম্পর্কীয়। **3.** (*Gram.*) Denoting a race or country ; as, a *gentile* noun ; (ব্যাকরণ) জাতি অথবা দেশ সম্পর্কীয়। ***Noun.*** **1.** Any one not Jew ; a heathen ইহুদী ভিন্ন অন্য জাতীয় লোক, যে ব্যক্তি ইহুদী নয় ; বিধর্ম্মী, পৌত্তলিক। **2.** A non-Mormon ; মর্ম্মন সম্প্রদায়ের বাহিরের লোক। **3.** (*Gram.*) A word denoting nationality ; (ব্যাকরণ) জাতিবাচক শব্দ। **—dom,** *n.*

gĕn-til′-i-tȳ, *n.* **1.** Good birth (*rare*) ; আভিজাত্য, কুলীনতা (অপ্রঃ)। **2.** Politeness ; good breeding ; social superiority ; শিষ্টাচার ; সৌজন্য; সামাজিক শ্রেষ্ঠতা। **To shabby gentility**—To try to keep up genteel appearances ; বাহিরে ভদ্রলোকের ঠাট বজায় রাখিতে চেষ্টা করা।

gĕn′-tle (-tl), *adj.* & *n.* **1.** Of good birth ; (*herald.*) having a right to bear arms ; সদ্বংশজাত, সম্ভ্রান্তবংশীয়, কুলীন, ভদ্রবংশীয়, ভদ্রবংশ, কুলবন্ত (কেডিঃ), জাতিবন্ত (ঐ), অভিজাত (ঐ), সদ্বংশ (ঐ), বংশবিশুদ্ধ (ঐ) ; (কুলবিদ্যা) কুলচিহ্নধারণে অধিকারী। **2.** Honourable ; suited to high birth or position ; as, a *gentle* occupation ; সম্মানজনক ; সম্ভ্রান্তজনোচিত। **3.** Quiet ; mild ; amicable ; tender ; as, a *gentle* nature ; শান্ত, সৌম্য, ধীর, নম্র, বিনীত ; কমনীয় ; কোমল, মৃদু। **4.** (*Archaic*) Noble ; courteous ; (অপ্রঃ) উন্নতমনাঃ ; ভদ্র, শিষ্ট। **5.** Tame ; quiet and docile ; as, a *gentle* horse ; পোষা ; শান্ত, ঠাণ্ডা, সুশান্ত, বশ্য। **6.** Not violent or rough ; soothing ; as, a *gentle* breeze or music ; not severe, as a rule etc. ; moderate ; as, a *gentle* heat ; অপ্রচণ্ড, অনুগ্র, অবিক্ষুব্ধ ; স্তিমিত, স্নিগ্ধ, আরামপ্রদ, আরামদায়ক, মৃদু, মন্দ, ধীর ; অকঠোর ; পরিমিত। **7.** Not steep ; as, a *gentle* slope ; অসরলোন্নত, খাড়া নয়। ***Noun.*** **1.** (*Pl. vulg.*) Gentle folks ; (বহুবচন—ইতরভাষায়) ভদ্রসমাজ। **2.** Maggot ; a dipterous larva used as a fish bait ; কীট, পোকা ; মাছ ধরার জন্য টোপ স্বরূপ ব্যবহৃত পোকা বিশেষ। **—hood,** *n.* Position or character attaching to gentle birth ; ভদ্র স্বভাব, ভদ্রত্ব। **—ness,** *n.* Quality of being gentle ; softness of manners or disposition ; mildness ; freedom from violence, severity, etc. ভদ্রতা ; কোমলতা, শান্ত স্বভাব ; মৃদুতা, নম্রতা, ধীরতা ; অনুগ্রতা, অকঠোরতা। **—tly,** *adv.* **1.** Softly ; mildly ; slowly ; meekly ; with tenderness ; kindly ; কোমলভাবে ; নম্রভাবে ; মন্দ মন্দ, শনৈঃ শনৈঃ, ধীরে ধীরে, আস্তে আস্তে, মৃদু মৃদু, মৃদুমন্দভাবে ; শান্তভাবে ; সকরুণ ভাবে ; সদয়ভাবে। **Gentle folk(s)**—People of high position and family ; ভদ্র সমাজ, সম্ভ্রান্ত সমাজ। **Gently born**—Of gentle birth ; সদ্বংশজাত, উচ্চ বংশ জাত। **Gentle and simple**—High born and low born ; ভদ্রেতর, আপামরসাধারণ। **The gentle craft**—Shoe-making ; চর্ম্মপাদুকা নির্ম্মাণ, জুতা তৈয়ারী। Angling ; বড়শী দ্বারা মৎস্য শিকার। **The gentle (gentler) sex**—The female sex ; অবলা জাতি।

gĕn′-tle-măn (-tl-), *n.* **1.** (*Chiefly Hist.*) A man entitled to bear arms but not included in the nobility ; (প্রধানতঃ ইতিহাসে) সম্ভ্রান্ত সমাজভুক্ত নয় অথচ কুলচিহ্নধারণে অধিকারী ব্যক্তি। **2.** A man of refined manners ; a well-bred man ; a man of high social position ; ভদ্রলোক ; সুশিক্ষিত লোক ; সম্ভ্রান্ত লোক। **3.** The servant or attendant of a man of rank ; "A *gentleman*-in-waiting" ; ভদ্রলোকের অনুচর। **4.** (*Law*) A respectable man having no specific profession ; (আইন) যে সম্ভ্রান্ত ব্যক্তির কোন বিশেষ কাজ নাই। **5.** (A polite term for) man ; (in plural) used generally in addressing assemblies of men ; শিষ্ট সম্বোধন সূচক পদ ; (বহুবচনে) ভদ্রমহোদয়গণ। **—hood, —ship,** *ns.* **—like, —ly,** *adjs.* **1.** Relating to, or resembling, a gentleman ; befitting a gentleman ; ভদ্র ব্যক্তি সম্বন্ধীয়, ভদ্রবৎ ; ভদ্রোচিত। **—li-ness,** *n.* **Gentleman-at-arms**—রাজকীয় উৎসবাদিতে যে চল্লিশজন ভদ্রলোক রাজার শরীররক্ষকের কার্য্য করে তাহাদের অন্যতম। **Gentleman commoner**—অক্সফোর্ড বিশ্ববিদ্যালয়ের

যে ছাত্র নিজের সর্ব্বপ্রকার ব্যয় নির্ব্বাহ করে এবং বিশ্ববিদ্যালয়ের ধনভাণ্ডার হইতে কোন প্রকার সাহায্য প্রাপ্ত হয় না। **Gentleman farmer**—কৃষিক্ষেত্রের অধিকারী, ভূস্বামী। **Gentleman usher** — যে কর্ম্মচারী দর্শনার্থী ব্যক্তিগণকে রাজা বা সম্ভ্রান্ত ব্যক্তিগণের নিকট লইয়া গিয়া পরিচিত করাইয়া দেয়। **My gentleman**—The fellow of whom I was speaking ; যে ব্যক্তির কথা আমি বলিতেছিলাম। **A gentlemam at large**—কাজ কর্ম্মশূন্য লোক, নিষ্কর্ম্মা লোক। **A gentleman in brown**—(*Humourous* or *slang*) A bed bug ; (কৌতুকচ্ছলে বা ইতরভাষায়) ছারপোকা। **A gentleman in red** — A soldier ; সৈনিক পুরুষ। **A gentleman of fortune**—A pirate ; জলদস্যু। **A gentleman of the four outs**—A vulgar upstart, with*out* manners, with*out* wit, with*out* money and with*out* credit ; ইতর ভুঁইফোড় লোক — যে শিষ্টাচারের ধার ধারে না, যাহার বুদ্ধি, অর্থ বা সম্ভ্রম নাই। **A gentleman of the long robe**—A gentleman belonging to the legal profession ; ব্যবহারজীবী। **A gentleman of the short staff**—A constable ; পুলিশ কনেষ্টবল। **A gentleman's gentleman**—A valet ; খানসামা, খাসকামরার চাকর, খিদমদ্গার। **The gentleman in black velvet**—A male ; পুরুষ। **The gentleman in black** or **the old gentleman**—The devil ; শয়তান। **To be a gentleman**—(*Jocularly*) To have no work to do ; (কৌতুকচ্ছলে) নিষ্কর্ম্মা হওয়া।

gĕn'-tle-wo-man (-tl-wûˈ-măn), *n.* **1.** A woman of good family or a lady of good breeding ; উচ্চবংশীয়া মহিলা, ভদ্রমহিলা। **2.** (*Hist.*) A woman who attends a lady of high rank ; সম্ভ্রান্ত মহিলার সহচরী, সখী। **—hood,** *n.* **—like, —ly,** *adjs.* **—li-ness,** *n.*

gĕn-too', *n.* (*Archaic*) A Hindoo ; (অপ্রঃ) হিন্দু।

gĕn'-trȳ, *n.* **1.** People of good birth and breeding ; the class of people below the rank of nobility ; ভদ্রমণ্ডলী ; মধ্যবিত্তশ্রেণীর লোক, মধ্যবিত্ত জনগণ। **2.** (*Contempt.*) People ; (অবজ্ঞাচ্ছলে) সাধারণ লোক।

gĕn'-ü-ăl, *adj.* Pertaining to the knee ; জানু-সম্বন্ধীয়।

gĕn-ü-flĕct', *v. i.* To bend the knee, as in worship ; (উপাসনা বা সম্মান প্রদর্শনার্থ) জানু নত করা, হাঁটু গাড়িয়া বসা। **—flec'-tion, —flex'-ion, —flec'-tor,** *ns.* **—flec'-to-ry,** *adj.*

gĕn'-ü-ine (-în), *adj.* **1.** Belonging to the original stock ; not counterfeit or false or spurious ; real ; true ; pure ; মৌলিক, আদিম ; অকৃত্রিম, সাঁচ্চা, (মণি সম্বন্ধে) জাত্য (মঃ ভাঃ), সমঙ্গল, খাঁটি, অকৃত্রিম ; প্রকৃত, আসল, সত্য, যথার্থ ; বিশুদ্ধ (কথাঃ লঃ)। **2.** (*Colloq.*) Trustworthy, as a man ; (চলিতভাষায়) বিশ্বাসভাজন। **—ly,** *adv.* **—ness,** *n.*

gē'-nŭs, *n.* (*pl.* -NERA, -NUSES) **1.** (*Log.*) A class of objects divided into several subordinate species ; (তর্কবিজ্ঞান) পরজাতি, সামান্য, (সাঃ পঃ), পরসামান্য (হিঃ কোঃ), জাতি (ঐ)। **2.** (*Zool. & Bot.*) Assemblage of species having distinctive characteristics ; গণ [অর্থাৎ অনেকগুলি জাতি যাহার অন্তর্ভুক্ত থাকে,—যথা, সিংহ, ব্যাঘ্র, চিতা, বিড়াল প্রভৃতি "বিড়াল" এই গণের অন্তর্ভুক্ত।] **3.** A class ; a kind ; a tribe ; শ্রেণী ; জাতি ; কুল। **Subaltern genus**—A genus which is also a species of a higher genus ; যে 'গণ' উচ্চতর গণের জাতি স্বরূপ। **The genus homo**—Mankind ; মনুষ্যজাতি। **The summum genus**—উচ্চতম জাতি।

gē-ō-cĕn'-tric, —tri-căl, *adjs.* **1.** Relating to, or having, the earth as centre ; ভূকেন্দ্রিক, ভূকেন্দ্রসম্পর্কীয়, ভূকেন্দ্রক (হিঃ কোঃ) ভূসহকেন্দ্রিক (ঐ)। **2.** Relating to, or reckoned from, the centre of the earth ; ভূকেন্দ্র সম্পর্কীয়, ভূকেন্দ্র হইতে পরিমিত, পৃথিবীকে কেন্দ্র করিয়া স্থিত, পৃথ্বীকেন্দ্রক (সাঃ পঃ)। **—ly,** *adv.* **Geocentric place of a heavenly body**—পৃষ্টস্থান (সাঃ পঃ)।

gē-ō-cȳc'-lic, *adj.* Relating to, or illustrating, the revolutions of the earth ; as, a *geocyclic* machine ; পৃথিবীর আবর্ত্তন সম্বন্ধীয়, পৃথিবীর আবর্ত্তন প্রদর্শী।

gē'-ōde, *n.* A roundish lump of stone with a cavity ; রন্ধ্র বিশিষ্ট গোলাকৃতি শিলাখণ্ড। **—od'-ic,** *adj.*

gē-ŏd'-ĕ-sȳ, *n.* The geometry of the earth or large portions of it ; গণিত শাস্ত্রের যে শাখায় পৃথিবী কিম্বা বৃহৎ ভূভাগের আকার ও পরিমাণ সম্বন্ধে আলোচিত হইয়া থাকে, ভূপরিমাণ বিদ্যা। **—o-des'-ic, —o-det'-ic, —o-det'-i-cal,** *adjs.* **—sist,** *n.* One versed in geodesy ; ভূমানবিৎ। **—o-des'-i-cal-ly,** *adv.* **Geodesic line**—বিন্দুদ্বয়ের মধ্যবর্ত্তী ক্ষুদ্রতম রেখা।

gē-ŏg'-nō-sȳ, *n.* **1.** Geology ; the science of the structure of the earth ; ভূবিদ্যা, ভূতত্ত্ব ; যে শাস্ত্রে পৃথিবীর পৃষ্ঠদেশ ও তন্মধ্যস্থ বিভিন্ন স্তর সমূহের সম্বন্ধ এবং পরিবর্ত্তন সম্বন্ধে আলোচিত হইয়া থাকে। **2.** Local geology ; স্থানীয় ভূতত্ত্ব। **—nos'-tic, nos'-ti-cal,** *adjs.* **—nos'-ti-cal-ly,** *adv.*

gē-ŏg'-ră-phȳ, *n.* **1.** The science of the external features of the earth ; ভূগোল শাস্ত্র, ভূগোলবিদ্যা, ভূগোলবর্ণন (কেঃডিঃ), ভূগোল। **2.** The subject matter of this science ; ভূগোল বিদ্যার আলোচ্য বিষয়। **3.** A treaties on geography ; ভৌগোলিক পাঠ, ভৌগোলিক বিবরণ সম্বলিত পুস্তক, ভূগোল গ্রন্থ। **4.** The geographical features (of a place etc.) ; কোন স্থানের ভৌগোলিক অবস্থা। **—o-graph'-ic, —o-graph'-i-cal,** *adjs.*

Relating to geography ; ভূগোল বিদ্যা বিষয়ক। **—pher,** *n.* One who is skilled in, or compiles a treaties on, geography ; ভূগোলবেত্তা, ভূগোল বিদ্যাবেত্তা, ভূগোল গ্রন্থ লেখক। **Astronomical geography** — জ্যোতি-ভূগোল (সাঃ পঃ)। **General geography** — ভূগোল (সাঃ পঃ)। **Geographical mile**—৬০৮০ ফিট। [আমেরিকায় ৬০৮০·২৭ ফিট, ফরাসীদেশে ১৮৫১·৯ মিটার।] **Historical geography** — ঐতিহাসিক ভূগোল। **Physical geography**—পৃথিবীর পর্ব্বতশ্রেণী, সাগরীয়স্রোতঃ,প্রাণীও ...দের সংস্থান, জল বায়ুর অবস্থাদি সম্বন্ধীয় প্রাকৃতিক ভূগোল। **Political geography**—শাসন সম্পর্কীয় ভূগোল বিদ্যা, রাজতন্ত্রীয় ভূগোল (সাঃ পঃ), রাষ্ট্রিক ভূগোল (ঐ)।

-ŏl′-ă-trȳ, *n.* Earth worship ; পৃথিবী দেবীর পূজা, পৃথ্বীপূজা।

-ŏl′-ŏ-ġȳ, *n.* **1.** The science relating to the earth's crust, its strata and their relations and changes ; ভূতত্ত্ব-বিজ্ঞান, ভূতত্ত্ব-বিদ্যা, ভূপঞ্জর-বিদ্যা (সাঃ পঃ), ভূরচনা-শাস্ত্র (কেণ্ডিঃ), ক্ষিতিরচনা-শাস্ত্র (ঐ), ভূগর্ভ-শাস্ত্র (ঐ), ভূগর্ভবিদ্যা (হিঃ কোঃ)। **2.** Geological features, as of a place etc. ; (কোন স্থানের) ভূতত্ত্ব-বিষয়ক অবস্থা। **—gist,** *n.* One versed in geology ; ভূতত্ত্ববিৎ পণ্ডিত, ভূতত্ত্ববিদ্যা-বিশারদ। **—gize,** *v. i.* & *t.* To make geological investigations ; ভূ-বিদ্যার অনুশীলন করা, ভূ-বিদ্যা বিষয়ক তত্ত্বানুসন্ধান করা। (*Verb t.*) To examine geologically ; ভূতত্ত্ব সম্বন্ধে অনুসন্ধান করা। **—o-log′-ic, —o-log′-i-cal,** *adjs.* **—o-log′-i-cal-ly,** *adv.*

ġe′-ŏ-măn-cȳ, *n.* Divination by means of figures or lines drawn on the earth ; ভূতলে রেখাদি পাত দ্বারা ভবিষ্যৎ কথন, রমল (কেণ্ডিঃ)। **-cer,** *n.* **—man′-tic,** *adj.*

-ŏm′-ĕ-trȳ, *n.* **1.** The science of properties and relations of magnitudes, such as lines, surfaces and solids ; ক্ষেত্র-তত্ত্ব, জ্যামিতি, জ্যামিতি শাস্ত্র, ক্ষেত্রতত্ত্ববিদ্যা, রেখাগণিত, ভূমিতি (ঠাকুর), ক্ষেত্রব্যবহার (কেণ্ডিঃ)। **2.** Treaties on geometry ; জ্যামিতি পুস্তক। **—o-met′-ric, —o-met′-ri-cal,** *adjs.* Pertaining to geometry ; according to the rules and principles of geometry ; জ্যামিতিবিষয়ক ; জ্যামিতির নিয়মানুযায়ী, জ্যামিতির মূলতত্ত্বের অনুসারী। **—ter,** *n.* **1.** One skilled in geometry ; জ্যামিতি শাস্ত্রবিৎ, জ্যামিতিজ্ঞ, রেখাগণিত পণ্ডিত। **2.** Kinds of caterpillar (so called from its mode of walking) ; বিভিন্ন জাতীয় কীরা। **—tri′-cian,** *n.* One skilled in geometry ; ক্ষেত্রতত্ত্ববিৎ, ক্ষেত্রতত্ত্ববেত্তা, জ্যামিতিবিৎ, জ্যামিতিবেত্তা, রেখাগণিত-পণ্ডিত। **—trize,** *v. i.* & *t.* To work or form by geometrical methods ; জ্যামিতি শাস্ত্রানুসারে গঠন বা সমাধান করা। **Abstract geometry**—সূক্ষ্মজ্যামিতি। **Analytic or co-ordinate geometry**—জ্যামিতি-সম্পর্কীয় আয়তন সমূহের ধর্ম্ম ও সম্বন্ধ বিষয়ে বৈশ্লেষণিক অনুসন্ধানের জন্য জ্যামিতি-বিশেষ, বৈশ্লেষিক জ্যামিতি। **Geometrical progresssion** — গুণোত্তর বৃদ্ধি (অভিঃ), সমগুণ শ্রেঢ়ী। **Geometrical spider** — এক প্রকার মাকড়সা—যাহা নানা প্রকার জ্যামিতিক নক্সায় জাল প্রস্তুত করে। **Geometrical tracery**—পাষাণের উপর জ্যামিতিক নমুনায় ক্ষোদিত কারুকার্য্য। **Plane geometry**—সমতল জ্যামিতি। **Projective geometry**—প্রলম্বীয় ভূমিতি (হিঃ কোঃ)। **Solid geometry**—ঘন জ্যামিতি। **Synthetic Geometry**—সংশ্লেষক জ্যামিতি।

ġĕ-oph′-ă-ġȳ (-ŏf-), **—ġism,** *ns.* Earth-eating ; মৃত্তিকা-ভক্ষণ। **—gist,** *n.* An earth-eater ; মৃত্তিকা ভোজী।

ġĕ-ŏ-pŏn′-ic, —i-căl, *adjs.* Pertaining to agriculture ; ভূমিকর্ষণ-বিদ্যা-সম্বন্ধীয়।

George (jŏrj), *n.* **1.** A figure of St. Geogre on horse-back, worn by Knights of the Garter ; বিলাতের সর্ব্বোচ্চ নাইট শ্রেণীর গ্রীবা-বন্ধনীলম্বিত সেণ্ট জর্জ্জের অশ্বারূঢ় প্রতিমূর্ত্তি। **St Geogre** — ইংলণ্ডের রক্ষাকারী সিদ্ধ পুরুষ। **St. George's day**—২৩-শে এপ্রিল। **By George**—শপথ-বাক্য বিশেষ।

Geor′-ġi-ăn (jŏr-), *adj.* **1.** Pertaining to the reigns of the four Georges, kings of Great Britain ; গ্রেট ব্রিটেনের জর্জ্জ নামক নৃপতি চতুষ্টয়ের রাজত্বকাল ঘটিত।

Geor′-ġi-ăn (jŏr-), *adj.* & *n.* Belonging to Georgia in the Caucasus or in the United States ; ককেশাস্ পর্ব্বতের অন্তঃপাতী অথবা মার্কিণ যুক্ত রাজ্যের জর্জ্জিয়া দেশ সম্বন্ধীয়। *Noun.* A native or inhabitant of Georgia ; জর্জ্জিয়া দেশের আদিম নিবাসী বা অধিবাসী।

geor′-ġic (jŏr-), *n.* A rural or pastoral poem ; as, the *Georgics* of Virgil ; গ্রাম্য কবিতা, গোষ্ঠগীতি, পল্লীগীতি, পল্লীগীতিকা, কৃষি-কবিতা, কৃষিকাব্য (আঃ বঃ)।

ġĕ-ŏt′-rŏ-pism, *n.* Disposition or tendency to turn or incline towards the earth ; ভূকেন্দ্রাভিমুখীনতা। **—o-trop′-ic,** *adj.* **Negative geotropism**—বৃক্ষাদির কাণ্ডের ভূমিকেন্দ্রের প্রতিমুখে বৃদ্ধির উন্মুখতা। **Positive geotropism**—বৃক্ষাদির কাণ্ডের ভূমিকেন্দ্রের অভিমুখে বৃদ্ধির উন্মুখতা।

ġĕ-ra′-ni-ŭm, *n.* **1.** A genus of plants with seed-vessels like a crane's bill ; একজাতীয় গুল্ম—ইহার বীজকোষের আকার বকচঞ্চুর মত। **2.** A cultivated pelargonium ; এক প্রকার গুল্ম। **3.** The colour of the scarlet geranium ; লোহিতবর্ণ জেরেনিয়াম কুসুমের রক্তিমা।

ġĕr′-fal-con (-fă-kn), *n.* A species of falcon ; একপ্রকার বাজপক্ষী।

ġĕrm, *n.* & *v. i.* **1.** A rudimentary form of a living thing whether a plant or animal ; জীবাঙ্কুর, উদ্ভিজ্জাঙ্কুর। 2. A microbe esp. one believed to cause disease ; জীবাণু, সূক্ষ্মজীব, রোগবীজাণু। 3. Origin ; a first principle ; "The *germ* of dissensions" ; আদি বীজ, মূল ; আদিম অবস্থা, মূলতত্ত্ব। ***Verb i.*** To germinate (*fig.* only) ; (কেবল লক্ষণায়) অঙ্কুরিত হওয়া। **Germ theory**—কেবল জীবাঙ্কুর হইতে জীবের উৎপত্তি হইতে পারে—এইরূপ মতবাদ, জীবাণুবাদ, জীবাণু যাবতীয় রোগের মূল কারণ — এইরূপ মতবাদ। **Germ-plasm**—কলল (ব্রজঃ হিন্দু)। **Germ vescicle**—কললনাভি (সাঃ পঃ)। **In germ**—Not yet developed ; অঙ্কুরাবস্থায়। **Germ and sperm**—শোণিত-শুক্র (হিঃ কোঃ)।

gêr'-măn, *adj.* **1.** Related in the first degree, (only in *cousin-german*, *brother-german* and *sister-german*); ঘনিষ্ঠ সম্পর্কীয়, অতি নিকট সম্পর্কীয়। 2. Appropriate ; relevant ; "*German* to the subject" ; সমুচিত ; প্রাসঙ্গিক। **Cousin-german**—See under COUSIN.

Ger'-măn (jêr-), *n.* & *adj.* **1.** A native or inhabitant of Germany ; জর্ম্মণ দেশের আদিম নিবাসী বা অধিবাসী, জর্ম্মণ দেশীয় লোক। 2. The German language ; জর্ম্মণ ভাষা। ***Adj.*** Pertaining to Germany, its people or language ; জর্ম্মণ দেশ, তদ্দেশের অধিবাসী বা ভাষা-সম্পর্কীয়। **—ism,** *n.* **1.** An idiom or phrase peculiar to the German language ; জর্ম্মণ ভাষার নিজস্ব বাক্যাংশ বা রীতিসিদ্ধ প্রয়োগ। **2.** Characteristics of the German ; জর্ম্মণ-সুলভতা। **—ish,** *adj.* **—i-za'-tion, —i-zer,** *ns.* **—ize,** *v. t. & i.* To make German in character, appearance, etc. ; জর্ম্মণস্বভাব করা, জর্ম্মণ ভাবাপন্ন করা। (*Verb i.*) To become German, as in style, taste, etc. ; রীতিনীতি এবং বেশভূষায় জর্ম্মণ সদৃশ হওয়া, জর্ম্মণ ভাবাপন্ন হওয়া। **—man'-ic,** *adj.* & *n.* **1.** Of, or relating to, Germany or the Germans ; জর্ম্মণি বা তদ্দেশের অধিবাসিগণ সম্পর্কীয়। 2. Teutonic ; টিউটন জাতীয়। (*Noun*) The language of the German people ; জর্ম্মণ ভাষা। **—man'-i-ty,** *n.* German characteristics or nature ; জর্ম্মণত্ব, জর্ম্মণ প্রকৃতি। **—ma-no-ma-nia,** *n.* Extreme leaning towards things German in one not a German ; জর্ম্মণীর রীতি, নীতি, আচার ব্যবহার, জিনিস প্রভৃতির প্রতি আত্যন্তিক অনুরাগ, জর্ম্মণোন্মাদ। **—ma-noph'-i-list,** *n.* An admirer of German people and their institutions and customs ; জর্ম্মণ জাতি এবং উহাদের রীতি নীতির প্রশংসাকারী ব্যক্তি, জর্ম্মণ-প্রেমিক। **—ma-no-pho'-bi-a,** *n.* A morbid fear or dislike of Germany ; জর্ম্মণাতঙ্ক। **German sausage**—একপ্রকার অর্দ্ধসিদ্ধ মাংসের কাবাব। **German silver**—নিকেল, দস্তা ও তামা মিশ্রিত শুভ্রধাতু, রূপদস্তা। **German-text**—প্রাচীন ইংরাজী বা বর্ত্তমান জর্ম্মণ ভাষার অক্ষর ; **High German**—পূর্ব্ব-জর্ম্মণীর দক্ষিণাঞ্চলের ভাষা (বর্ত্তমানে সমগ্র জর্ম্মণ দেশে প্রচলিত সাধুভাষা)। **Low German** — জর্ম্মণীর উপভাষা সমূহ (High German ব্যতীত), জর্ম্মণীর পশ্চিমাঞ্চলের ভাষা এবং তন্মূলক ইংরাজী, ওলন্দাজ প্রভৃতি ভাষা। **The East Germanic** — গথিক বা অধুনালুপ্তপ্রায় বারগণ্ডিয়ান বা ভ্যাণ্ডাল ভাষা। **The North Germanic**—Scandinavian ; স্ক্যাণ্ডিনেভিয়ান। **The West Germanic**—High and Low German, English Dutch, etc. ; হাইজর্ম্মণ, লোজর্ম্মণ, ইংরেজী, ওলন্দাজ প্রভৃতি ভাষা।

gêr-măn'-dêr, *n.* **1.** A genus of plants ; একজাতীয় গুল্ম।

gêr-māne', *adj.* Closely connected ; relevent ; appropriate, (with *to*) ; "Evidences *germane to* the subject" ; ঘনিষ্ঠ ; প্রাসঙ্গিক ; যথাযোগ্য।

gêr'-mĕn, *n.* (*Bot.*) An ovary ; (উদ্ভিদ্-বিদ্যা) ডিম্বাশয়।

gêr'-mi-cīde, *n.* & *adj.* A substance or agent destroyi germs esp. of diseases ; বীজ বা জীবাণুনাশক পদার্থ, রোগজীবাণুনা দ্রব্য। ***Adj.*** Destructive of ge esp. diseases ; জীবাণুনাশক, রো জীবাণুনাশক। **—cid-al,** *adj.*

gêr'-mi-năl, *adj.* **1.** Of, or rela ting to, a germ ; of the natu of a germ ; বীজাণু-সম্পর্কীয়, জীব সম্পর্কীয় ; বীজাণুপ্রকৃতিক। **2.** the earliest state of developmen "*Germinal* ideas" ; অঙ্কুরাবস্থায় স্থি **—ly,** *adv.*

gêr'-mi-nate, *v. i.* & *t.* **1.** spring from a germ ; to bud ; to shoot, (*lit.* & *fig.*) ; অঙ্কুর হইতে উৎপন্ন হওয়া ; মুকুলিত হওয়া, অঙ্কুরিত হওয়া; উদ্গত হওয়া, অঙ্কুরোদ্গত হওয়া। ***Verb t.*** To cause to

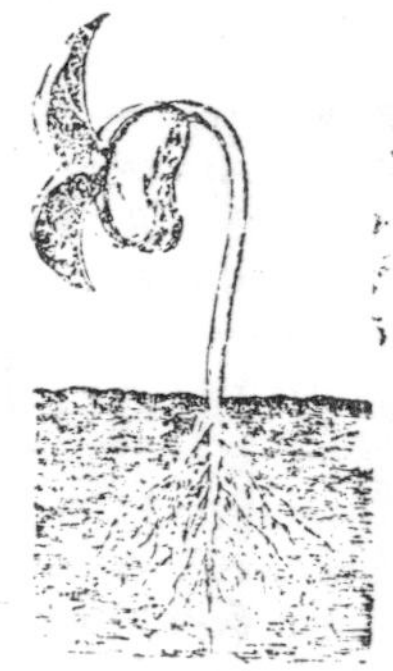

Germination of bean.

sprout or develop ; to prod ; অঙ্কুরিত করা, বিকাশ করা ; উৎপাদ করা। **—nant, —na-tive,** *adjs.* Pertaining to germination ; অঙ্কুরোদ্গম সম্পর্কীয়। **—na'-tion,** *n.* The act or process of germinating ; অঙ্কুরোদ্গম, অঙ্কুরোদ্ভেদ, অঙ্কুরোৎপত্তি (সাঃ পঃ), প্ররোহণ (ঐ)।

germon, (*F.*), *n.* A kind of fish ; একজাতীয় মৎস্য।

gĕr-ŏn-tŏc'-ră-cy̆, *n.* Government by, or a governing body of, old men ; বৃদ্ধব্যক্তিগণ দ্বারা গঠিত শাসনতন্ত্র, বৃদ্ধগণ দ্বারা শাসন, স্থবির-তন্ত্র।

gĕr-ry̆-măn'-dêr, *v. t.* & To re-arrange unfairly the voting districts in the interests of a particular party ndidate ; কোন বিশেষ দল বা সভ্য-দপ্রার্থীর অনুকূলে নির্ব্বাচনমত প্রদানে বিকারী জেলা সমূহ অসাধু ভাবে নবিভাগ করা। *Noun.* Such an rangement, ঐ প্রকার বন্দোবস্ত। -er, *n.*

r'-ŭnd, *n.* 1. A kind of verbal oun in Latin ল্যাটিন ভাষায় ক্রিয়ার প বিশেষ—যাহা বিশেষ্য রূপে প্রয়োগ [illegible] বাহকক্রিয়া [illegible] 2. An English erbal noun in *-ing* when used listinctly as a part of the verb, uch as *teaching* in "fit for *eaching* boys" ; বর্ত্তমান ইংরাজীতে য সকল *-ing* যুক্ত ক্রিয়ামূলক বিশেষ্য পষ্টরূপে ক্রিয়ার অংশ স্বরূপ ব্যবহৃত য়। **Ge-run'-di-al,** *adj.* Pertaining to, or like, a gerund ; nce denoting purpose ; ক্রিয়া-ক বিশেষ্য-সম্বন্ধীয়, বা তৎসদৃশ ; ভপ্রায় বা নিমিত্তার্থ বাচক। **Gerund-rinder**—A teacher of Latin ; টিন ভাষার শিক্ষক। **Gerundial nfinitive**—নিমিত্তার্থক ক্রিয়া।

ē-rŭn'-dive (-dĭv), *n.* & *adj.* The future passive participle of Latin verb ; ল্যাটিন ভাষায় ভবিষ্যৎ-ালের কর্ম্মবাচ্যের অসমাপিকা ক্রিয়া। *dj.* Of, or like, the gerund ; বাহক ক্রিয়াবৎ, বাহকক্রিয়া সম্বন্ধীয়।

ĕs'-sō, *n.* Plaster of Paris or gypsum prepared for use in painting and in sculpture ; প্যারী নগরীর সন্নিকটে সমুৎপন্ন শ্বেতবর্ণ সঙ্কোচক চূর্ণ বিশেষ।

ĕs-tā'-tion, *n.* Carrying, or being carried, in the womb from conception to delivery ; the period of pregnancy ; গর্ভধারণ, অন্তঃসত্ত্বাবস্থা ; গর্ভধারণ-কাল।

ĕs-ta-tō'-ri-ăl, *adj.* Designating the chair in which the Pope is carried on ceremonial occasions ; পর্ব্বোপলক্ষে রোমান ক্যাথলিক ধর্ম্মসম্রাট্ পোপকে যে আসনে বহন করা হয় তৎসম্পর্কীয়।

gĕs-tic'-ū-lāte, *v. i.* & *t.* To make expressive gestures or motions with or instead of speech ; (বাক্য কথন কালে) অঙ্গভঙ্গী করা, অঙ্গভঙ্গী পূর্ব্বক কথা বলা। ***Verb t.*** To indicate by gestures ; অঙ্গভঙ্গী দ্বারা সূচনা করা। **—la'-tion,** *n.* Gesticulatings ; gestures ; অঙ্গ-বিক্ষেপ (কেঁচিঃ) ; অঙ্গভঙ্গী। **—la-to-ry, —la-tive,** *adjs.*

gĕs'-tūre, *n.*, *v. i.* & *t.* A significant movement of the body or limb ; an action expressive of sentiment or passion ; হাবভাব, আকার-ইঙ্গিত, অঙ্গভঙ্গী, মুদ্রা (এভেলন)। ***Verb i. & t.*** To gesticulate ; অঙ্গভঙ্গী করা। **—less,** *adj.* Without a gesture ; অঙ্গভঙ্গী হীন। **Gesture language**—ইঙ্গিত ভাষা (হিঃ কোঃ)।

gĕt, *v. t.* & *i.* **1.** To obtain ; to procure ; to earn ; as, I cannot *get* a living ; to win ; to gain ; as, to *get* the upperhand : we *get* wealth by industry and economy ; to attain ; to realize ; প্রাপ্ত হওয়া, পাওয়া ; সংগ্রহ করা, হস্তগত করা ; অর্জ্জন করা, উপার্জ্জন করা, রোজগার করা ; (প্রতিযোগিতায়) জয় করিয়া লওয়া ; লাভ করা ; পাওয়া ; সম্যক্ ধারণা করা, অনুভব করা। **2.** To have ; as, thou has *got* the face of man ; থাকা। **3.** (Of animals) To beget ; জন্মদান করা, (জন্তু সম্পর্কে) প্রসব করা। **4.** To learn ; to memorize ; as, to *get* a lesson by heart ; (পাঠাদি) শিক্ষা করা, অভ্যাস করা ; (পাঠ) কণ্ঠস্থ করা, স্মরণ রাখা, মুখস্থ করা। **5.** To determine ; to obtain as result of calculation ; as, we *get* 9.5 as the average ; স্থির করা ; গণনা করিয়া পাওয়া। **6.** To prevail on ; to persuade ; as, *get* him to do this ; প্রবর্ত্তিত করা, প্রবৃত্তি লওয়ান ; (যুক্তি বা অনুরোধে) সম্মত করা, মত লওয়ান, প্ররোচিত করা। **7.** To extract by prayer, demand, enquiring, etc. ; as, I could not *get* leave ; পাওয়া, প্রাপ্ত হওয়া। **8.** To cause to be in any state or condition ; "*Get* them done soon" ; কোন অবস্থায় আনা, হওয়ান, ঘটান। **9.** To betake ; to remove ; "*Get* thee out from this land"—Genesis xxxi. 13 ; গমন করা ; স্থানান্তরিত করা। **10.** To suffer or receive as one's lot or penalty ; as, to *get* a fall ; ভোগ করা। **11.** To capture ; to puzzle ; "That's where you've *got* me" ; বন্দী করা ; হতবুদ্ধি করা, কিংকর্ত্তব্যবিমূঢ় করা। **12.** To catch, as fish etc. ; মৎস্য ধরা। **13.** To gather or bring in, as a crop ; শস্যাদি সংগ্রহ করা। ***Verb i.*** **1.** To arrive (*at*) ; to become ; as, to *get* to be friends ; to *get* tired ; to come to be (doing something) ; "They *got* talking together" ; পৌঁছা ; হওয়া ; (কোন কিছু) করিতে আরম্ভ করা। **2.** To succeed in coming or going, (with *to*, *out of*, *from*, *into* etc.) ; আসিতে বা যাইতে কৃতকার্য্য হওয়া। **3.** To make acquisition ; to gain ; "We lose, they daily *get*" ; অর্জ্জন করা ; লাভ করা। **4.** To acquire habit, (with *infinitive*) ; as, one soon *gets* to like it ; অভ্যস্ত হওয়া। **Get'-a-ble, Get'-ta-ble,** *adjs.* **Get'-ter, Get'-ting,** *ns.* **Get along with you**—(*Colloq.*) Be off ; nonsense ; (চলিত ভাষায়) দূর হও, তফাৎ যাও ; বাজে কথা ! বাতুলের প্রলাপ ! **Get away with you**—Go away ; be off ; দূর হও ; ভাগো। **Get there**—(*Slang*) Succeed ; (ইতর ভাষায়). তোমার কার্য্য-সিদ্ধি হউক। **It has got to be done**—It must be done ; এই কাজ অবশ্যই করিতে হইবে। **To be getting on for**—To approach, as an age etc. ; কাছাকাছি হওয়া, নিকটবর্ত্তী হওয়া। **To get**

about—To go about ; to begin to walk after illness etc. ; ইতস্ততঃ বিচরণ করা ; পীড়াদি হইতে আরোগ্য লাভের পর হাঁটিতে আরম্ভ করা। (Of rumours etc.) To be circulated ; প্রচারিত হওয়া। **To get above**—To rise higher than ; কোন কিছু অপেক্ষা অধিকতর উপরে উঠা। **To get abroad**—(Of rumours) To be circulated ; প্রচারিত হওয়া। **To get a change for the better**—To get a change into a better or more favourable state ; (স্বাস্থ্য প্রভৃতি সম্বন্ধে) ক্রমশঃ উন্নতি লাভ করা। **To get ahead**—To advance ; to prosper ; অগ্রসর হওয়া ; উন্নতি লাভ করা, শ্রীবৃদ্ধি হওয়া। **To get a living** — To earn livelihood ; জীবিকার্জ্জন করা। **To get along**—To proceed ; to prosper ; অগ্রসর হওয়া ; উন্নতি লাভ করা। **To get a mile**—To pass over it ; এক মাইল পথ অতিক্রম করিয়া যাওয়া। **To get a person on one's nerves**—To be irritably affected by him ; কাহারও দ্বারা জ্বালাতন হওয়া। **To get a person** or **thing on the brain**—To think of a person or thing exclusively : কোন বস্তু বা ব্যক্তি সম্বন্ধে একান্তভাবে চিন্তা করা। **To get asleep**—To fall asleep ; ঘুমাইয়া পড়া, নিদ্রিত হওয়া। **To get astray**—To wander out of the right way ; বিপথে যাওয়া, পথভ্রষ্ট হওয়া। **To get at** — To reach ; to attain ; "*Getting at* the thoughts of men" ; পৌঁছা ; পাওয়া, প্রাপ্ত হওয়া। (*Slang*) To tamper with ; to bribe ; to attack ; to banter ; বিনা অনুমতিতে পরিবর্ত্তন করা ; ঘুষ দেওয়া ; আক্রমণ করা ; ব্যঙ্গ করা, বিদ্রূপ করা। **To get away**—To escape ; to start ; (*Imperative*) to be off ; পলায়ন করা ; যাত্রা করা ; দূর হও, তফাৎ হও, ভাগো। **To get back**—To come home ; to recover (a lost thing) ; (গৃহে) প্রত্যাবর্ত্তন করা ; ফিরিয়া পাওয়া, পুনঃপ্রাপ্ত হওয়া। **To get before**—To arrive in front of ; অগ্রে যাওয়া, অগ্রবর্ত্তী হওয়া। **To get behind**—To fall into the rear ; পিছে পড়া। **To get by heart**—To commit to memory ; পাঠাদি মুখস্থ বা কণ্ঠস্থ করা। **To get by oneself**—To escape from company ; একেলা থাকা। **To get clear of** — To disengage oneself from ; to become free from (some difficulty) ; (কোন কাজ হইতে) নিজকে তফাৎ করা ; বিপদ হইতে উদ্ধার হওয়া। **To get credit for**—To get honour or merit for ; সম্মান বা গৌরব লাভ করা। **To get done with**—To bring to an end ; শেষ করা, সমাপ্ত করা, সাঙ্গ করা। **To get down**—To dismount ; অবতরণ করা। **To get drunk**—To become intoxicated ; মাতাল হইয়া পড়া। **To get forward**—To advance ; to prosper ; অগ্রসর হওয়া ; উন্নতি করা। **To get free**—To be released ; মুক্তি পাওয়া, খালাস হওয়া। **To get hold of**—To obtain or catch hold of ; ধরা। **To get home**—To arrive at one's own house ; বাড়ীতে পৌঁছা। **To get in**—*v. t.* & *i.* To bring in, or gather, as crop etc. ; to collect ; সংগ্রহ করা ; সঞ্চয় করা। To enter, as a carriage etc. ; গাড়ী প্রভৃতিতে প্রবেশ করা। (*Print.*) To set close ; (মুদ্রণ) ঘনসন্নিবিষ্ট করা। (*Verb i.*) To arrive at or make way within any place or body ; to be elected as an M. P. ; as, he *got in* for the country ; পৌঁছা, ঢুকা ; পার্লেমেন্টের সভ্যরূপে নির্ব্বাচিত, মনোনীত বা বৃত হওয়া। **To get in a word edgeways**—To succeed in saying something in a pause of another talk ; অন্যের কথার মাঝে কথা পাড়া। **To get into** — To enter into ; প্রবেশ করা, ঢুকা। **To get into a mess, To get into a muddle**—হাঙ্গামায় পড়া, গোলে পড়া। **To get into a scrape**—To come into trouble and difficulty ; বিপদে পড়া, হাঙ্গামায় পড়া, গোলমালে পড়া, ঝঞ্চাটে পড়া। **To get into bad odour**—To become unpopular ; লোকসাধারণের অপ্রীতিভাজন হওয়া। **To get into debt**—To be involved in debt ; ঋণগ্রস্ত হওয়া। **To get into hot water (with)** — To get into a state of trouble (with) ; কাহারও সহিত বাদ বিসম্বাদ হওয়া। **To get into one's head**—(Of liquor etc.) To affect ; to confuse ; (মদ্যাদি সম্পর্কে) ক্রিয়া করা ; বিভ্রান্ত করা। **To get it**—To be punished, scolded, etc. ; শাস্তি পাওয়া, তিরস্কৃত হওয়া। **To get it into one's head**—To be convinced ; হৃদ্বোধ হওয়া। **To get more kicks than half-pence**—(*Colloq.*) To get more rebuffs than money ; (ইতর ভাষায়) টাকা পয়সা যতটা না পাওয়া যায় তাহার চেয়ে বেশী ধাক্কা ধমক খাওয়া। **To get near**--To approach ; কাছে আসা। **To get off**—*v. t.* & *i.* To take off ; to remove ; to sell ; to get rid of ; to escape ; to procure acquittal or slight penalty (for a person) ; ছাড়া, উন্মোচন করা ; সরান, স্থানান্তর করা ; বিক্রয় করা ; নিষ্কৃতি পাওয়া, পরিত্রাণ পাওয়া ; পলায়ন করা ; নিষ্কৃতি পাওয়ান, সারাইয়া দেওয়া। To succeed in uttering, as a joke ; কৌতুক করা। To learn ; অবগত হওয়া। (*Verb i.*) To alight ; as, to *get off* a horse ; অবতরণ করা। To escape ; to start ; পলায়ন করা ; রওয়ানা হওয়া। To be acquitted, as in a criminal trial etc. ; অব্যাহতি লাভ করা, বেকসুর খালাস পাওয়া। **To get off goods**—To dispose of the goods by sale or onward despatch ; মাল চালাইয়া ফেলা। **To get on (upon)**—*v. i.* & *t.* To advance or proceed; to succeed; to prosper; অগ্রসর হওয়া, উন্নতি লাভ করা; কৃতকার্য্যতা লাভ করা; শ্রীবৃদ্ধি প্রাপ্ত হওয়া। (*Verb t.*) To mount, as a horse etc.; আরোহণ করা। To put on; পরিধান করা। **To get one into trouble**—To bring one into trouble; কাহাকেও বিপদে ফেলা। **To get one's back up**—To be angry; ক্রুদ্ধ হওয়া, কাহাকেও ক্রুদ্ধ বা জ্বালাতন করা। **To get oneself up**—To appear in a striking costume; জমকালো পোষাক পরিয়া উপস্থিত হওয়া। **To get one's fingers burned**—To get oneself into unexpected trouble; অপ্রত্যাশিত বিপদে পড়া। **To get one's hand in**—To become at home with some operation; কোন বিষয়ে সিদ্ধহস্ত হওয়া। **To get one's head above water**—To tide over difficulties; অতি কষ্টে বিপদ্ সাগর হইতে উদ্ধার হওয়া। **To get on like a house on fire**—To fare in an easy gliding manner; আরামে দিন কাটান, সুখে স্বচ্ছন্দে কাল যাপন করা। **To get on one's legs** or **feet**—To stand up, esp. for speaking in public; দণ্ডায়মান হওয়া, বিশেষতঃ বক্তৃতা প্রদানের জন্য দণ্ডায়মান হওয়া। **To get on the high horse**—To be overbearing; উদ্ধত হওয়া। **To get on with one**—To find oneself in congenial company; বনিবনাও হওয়া, মিলিয়া মিশিয়া থাকা। **To get out**—*v. t.* & *i.* To draw out or extract; to get rid of; as, to *get out* a tooth; to elicit; to succeed in uttering publishing, etc.; উৎপাটিত করা; নিষ্কৃতি পাওয়া; বাহির করা; উচ্চারণ কিম্বা প্রচার করিতে কৃতকার্য্য হওয়া। (*Verb i.*) To escape from any place or state of confinement; অবরুদ্ধ স্থান হইতে পলায়ন করা। To be off; চলিয়া যাওয়া। To become known; "The fact did not *get out* till etc."; পরিচিত হওয়া। To transpire; বাহির হইয়া পড়া। **To get out a secret**—*v. i.* To draw forth concealed fact; গুপ্ত বিষয় বাহির করা। **To get out of**—To issue or escape from; বহির্গত হওয়া, উদ্ধার পাওয়া। **To get out of bed on wrong side**—To be in bad temper; মেজাজ খারাপ থাকা। **To get out of hand**—To go out of reach; হাতছাড়া হওয়া। To break control; হাত হইতে ছুটিয়া পালান। **To get out of one's depth**—To be in too deep water to stand; সাঁতার জলে পড়া। **To get out of sight**—To disappear; অদৃশ্য হওয়া, দৃষ্টির অগোচর হওয়া। **To get over**—To pass over; অতিক্রম করা। (*Fig.*) To surmount; to recover from; (লক্ষণায়) লঙ্ঘন করা; আরোগ্য লাভ করা। (*Slang*) To circumvent; (ইতর ভাষায়) ফাঁদে ফেলা। To bring to an end, as a troublesome task; শেষ করা। **To get over a person**—To ingratiate oneself with him; অনুগ্রহভাজন হওয়া। **To get religion**—To be religious or pious; ধার্ম্মিক হওয়া, সাধু হওয়া। **To get rid** or **quit of**—To free one's self from; অব্যাহতি লাভ করা, নিষ্কৃতি পাওয়া। **To get round (a person)**—*v. t.* & *i.* To gain an advantage over; to circumvent; সুবিধা লাভ করা; ফাঁদে ফেলা, বুদ্ধি বলে পরাজয় করা। (*Verb i.*) To recover from illness; আরাম হওয়া। **To get the best of**—To be victorious; জয়ী হওয়া। **To get the better of a person**—To subdue; পরাভূত করা, পরাস্ত করা। **To get the boot**—To be dismissed from employment; চাকুরী হইতে বরখাস্ত হওয়া। **To get the credit of**—To receive praise for; (কোন কিছুর জন্য) প্রশংসা লাভ করা। **To get the day**—To gain the victory; যুদ্ধে জয়লাভ করা। **To get the hang of**—(*Colloq.*) To understand the arrangement or construction of; (চলিত ভাষায়) রচনা, বিন্যাস বা গঠন বুঝা। **To get the mitten**—To be rejected as a suitor; প্রণয়প্রার্থী হইয়া প্রত্যাখ্যাত হওয়া। **To get the right scent**—To get a clue to some mystery; কোন রহস্যের সন্ধান পাওয়া। **To get the sack**—Same as TO GET THE BOOT. **To get the start of a person**—To be in advance of a person; আগে থাকা। **To get the upperhand of**—To gain mastery over; প্রাধান্য লাভ করা, প্রভুত্ব লাভ করা। **To get the worst of it**—To be defeated in a contest; পরাস্ত হওয়া। **To get through**—To pass through; কাটান। To finish; to accomplish; শেষ করা; সমাপ্ত করা। To pass away, as time etc.; কাটান, অতিবাহিত করা, যাপন করা। To be passed by (the Lords, Commons etc.); অনুমোদিত হওয়া, মঞ্জুর হওয়া। **To get through with**—To succeed in doing; করিতে কৃতকার্য্য হওয়া। **To get to**—To arrive at; to reach; to begin; পৌঁছা; লাগাইল ধরা; আরম্ভ করা। **To get to blows**—To come to blows; to begin to fight; হাতাহাতি আরম্ভ করা; যুদ্ধারম্ভ করা। **To get together**—*v. t.* & *i.* To collect; to convene; সংগ্রহ করা, জড় করা; সম্মিলিত করা। (*Verb i.*) To assemble; to meet together; জড় হওয়া; মিলিত হওয়া। **To get to the bottom of**—To penetrate into mysteries of; রহস্য ভেদ করা, রহস্যোদ্ভেদ করা। **To get under**—To subdue, as fire etc.; বশে আনা। **To get under way**—To begin to sail; জলযাত্রা আরম্ভ করা। **To get up**—*v. i.* & *t.* To rise as from bed etc.; to climb up; to mount, esp. on horse back;

শয্যা হইতে গাত্রোত্থান করা, শয্যা ত্যাগ করা ; আরোহণ করা ; চড়া। To begin to be violent, as fire, wind or sea ; প্রবল হইয়া উঠিতে আরম্ভ করা। To rise from cover, as a game ; আশ্রয় স্থান হইতে উঠিয়া দাঁড়ান। (*Verb t.*) To prepare ; to organize ; to set on foot ; "The revolt had been *got up*" ; উদ্যোগ করা ; বন্দোবস্ত করা, ব্যবস্থা করা ; সূচনা করা। To learn ; as, *to get up* a lesson; শিক্ষা করা। To dress ; to fit out ; as, *to get up* linen, hair, etc. ; সজ্জিত করা ; সাজান। To produce ; as, *to get up* steam ; উৎপাদন করা। **To get up steam**—To produce steam enough to work an engine ; যন্ত্র চালাইবার পক্ষে আবশ্যকানুরূপ বাষ্প উৎপাদন করা। (*Fig.*) To work oneself into anger or energy ; (লক্ষণায়) ক্রোধে ফুলিয়া উঠা, উৎসাহ সম্পন্ন হওয়া। **To get wind**—To be divulged ; প্রকাশ হইয়া পড়া। To recover breath ; হাঁপ ছাড়া। **To get wind or knowledge of**—To learn ; to get intimation of ; অবগত হওয়া ; সন্ধান পাওয়া। **To get with child**—To make pregnant ; সসত্ত্বা করা। **To get word**—To receive intimation ; খবর পাওয়া, সংবাদ পাওয়া। **What has got him**—What has become of him ; তার কি হলো ? **Where has it got to**—What has become of it ; ইহার কি হইয়াছে ?

gĕt, *n.* Act of begetting ; offspring ; "The *get* of a stallion" ; সন্তান-উৎপাদন, প্রজনন ; সন্তানসন্ততি, বাচ্চা।

gĕt'-ŭp, *n.* The style of dress, equipment, etc ; style of production or finish, as of a book etc ; পোষাকের ধরণ, পরিচ্ছদ-রীতি, সাজ-সজ্জা ; পুস্তকের ছাপা, বাঁধাই প্রভৃতি।

gē'-ŭm, *n.* (*Bot.*) A genus of perennial rosaceous herbs ; একপ্রকার বহুবর্ষজীবী গোলাপজাতীয় গুল্ম।

gew'-gaw (gü-gä), *n.* A toy ; a splendid plaything ; a bauble ; a showy trifle ; খেলনা ; অল্প মূল্যের চটকদার জিনিষ ; তুচ্ছ জিনিষ ; ফট্‌কীনাট্‌কী।

gey (gī), *adv.* (*Scot.*) Considerably ; very ; (স্কটল্যাণ্ড) অতিশয়, অত্যন্ত ; ভারি।

gey'-sêr (gī-), *n.* **1.** A hot-spring which intermittently spouts water into the air ; উষ্ণপ্রস্রবণ। **2.** An apparatus for heating water ; জল উত্তপ্ত করার জন্য যন্ত্রবিশেষ।

Ghan'-nâ (gä-) *n.* A Babylonian goddess ; প্রাচীন কেলডিয়া সাম্রাজ্যের রাজধানী বেবিলন নগরবাসিগণ কর্তৃক সম্পূজিত দেবী বিশেষ।

ghast'-lȳ (găst-), *adj.* & *adv.* **1.** Death-like ; pale ; dismal ; as, a *ghastly* face ; মরণমলিন, শববৎ, মৃতবৎ, প্রেতবৎ ; পাংশুবর্ণ, ম্লান, বিবর্ণ, ফেকাসিয়া, পাঙ্গাশবর্ণ ; নিরানন্দ। **2.** Horrible ; shocking ; hideous ; as, *ghastly* wounds ; ভয়ঙ্কর, ভীষণ, করাল, বিকট, ভয়াবহ, ভীতি-জনক ; লোম-হর্ষণ ; বিকটাকার, বীভৎস। **3.** Objectionable ; আপত্তিজনক। **4.** (Of smile etc.) Painfully forced ; কাষ্ঠ (হাসি)। ***Adv.*** In a ghastly manner ; hideously ; as, *ghastly* pale ; ভয়ঙ্করভাবে ; বিকটরূপে। **—i-ly,** *adv.* **Ghastly smile**—See GHASTLY *adj.* 4.

ghaz'-ăl (găz-), *n.* **1.** In Persian poetry an ode ; পার্সী গীতি কবিতা, গজল। [এইরূপ কবিতায় পাঁচটীর অধিক এবং আঠারটীর অনধিক মিল বিশিষ্ট যুগ্ম পংক্তি থাকে। ইহাতে প্রথম দুই চরণ মিলযুক্ত থাকে, এবং প্রতি পরবর্তী যুগ্ম-পংক্তির দ্বিতীয় পংক্তির শেষ অক্ষর উক্ত চরণ-দ্বয়ের শেষ অক্ষরের সহিত মিল রাখিতে হয়।] **2.** A piece of music in which a simple thing is constanly reviving ; গজল।

Gha'-zi (gâ-), *n.* A Mahomedan soldier fighting for his faith ; a religious warrior ; one who has slain an infidel ; ধর্ম্মার্থ যুদ্ধকারী মুসলমান সৈনিক ; ধর্ম্ম-যোদ্ধা ; যে ব্যক্তি বিধর্ম্মী বা কাফেরকে হত করিয়াছে।

gher'kin (gêr-), *n.* A small cucumber used for pickling ; এক প্রকার ক্ষুদ্র শশা, ক্ষীরা।

ghet'-tō (gĕt-), *n.* A quarter the Jews in a city ; নগরীর অংশে ইহুদীগণ বাস করে, ইহুদী-পল্লী।

Ghib'-ĕl-līne (gĭb-), *n.* & (*Hist.*) A member of a great political faction in mediæval Italy ; (ইতিহাস) মধ্যযুগে ই দেশে বর্ত্তমান বৃহৎ রাজনৈতিক দল-বি ভুক্ত ব্যক্তি। [মহাকবি দান্তে (Dante উক্ত সম্প্রদায়ভুক্ত ছিলেন]। ***Adj.*** Of, or pertaining to, this faction ; উক্ত দলসম্পর্কীয়। **—lin-ism,** *n.*

ghost (gōst), *n.* **1.** Principle of life ; জীবাত্মা। **2.** Soul or spirit appearing after death ; as, to raise a *ghost* ; a spectre ; প্রেতাত্মা; ভূত, প্রেত, পিশাচ, বেতাল, অপদেবতা, ছায়ামূর্ত্তি। **3.** A shadow or semblance ; a slight trace ; as, he had not the *ghost* of a chance ছায়া, আভাস ; ছায়ামাত্র, লেশমাত্র **4** An emaciated person ; অস্থি চর্ম্মসার ব্যক্তি, কঙ্কালসার ব্যক্তি তালপাতার সিপাই। **5.** One who does artistic or literary work for another who takes the credit ; যে ব্যক্তি অন্যের অধীনে নিযুক্ত থাকিয়া তাহার জন্য শিল্পকার্য্য সম্পাদন ব পুস্তকাদি রচনা করে এবং যাহার জন্য শেষোক্ত ব্যক্তি প্রতিষ্ঠা লাভ করিয়া থাকে **6.** (*Opt.*) A bright spot or secondary image in the field of a telescope due to the defect of lens ; পরকলার (lens) ত্রুটী হেতু দূরবীক্ষণ যন্ত্রের দৃষ্টিক্ষেত্রে যে বে উজ্জ্বল বিন্দু বা গৌণ প্রতিমূর্ত্তি দৃষ্ট হয়। **Ghost'-hood,** *n.* **Ghost'-like,** *adj.* **Holy Ghost**—The Spirit of God ; পবিত্রাত্মা। **Not the ghost of a chance**—No chance at all.

লেশমাত্রও সম্ভাবনা নাই। **To give up or yield up the ghost**—To die; মৃত্যু প্রাপ্ত হওয়া, অক্কা পাওয়া (*slang*), টল তোলা (*slang*), শিঙ্গে ফুঁকা (*slang*)। **To raise or lay a ghost** — To cause a ghost to appear or cease appearing; ভূত নামান, ভূত তাড়ান।

ghost'-lȳ (gōst-), *adj.* 1. (*Archaic*) Spiritual; (অপ্রঃ) অনাত্ম, পারমার্থিক (কেণ্ডিঃ), পরমার্থ বিষয়ক (ঐ)। 2. Concerned with sacred or ecclesiastical matters; পবিত্র বিষয় সংক্রান্ত, ধর্মীয় বিষয় সংক্রান্ত। 3. Of, or relating to, apparitions; spectral; অপদেবতা সম্বন্ধীয়; ভৌতিক, ভূতুড়ে। **—li-ness,** *n.* **Ghostly comfort, counsel**—Comfort, counsel, etc. administered by a priest; যাজক কর্ত্তৃক প্রদত্ত উপদেশ বা সান্ত্বনা। **Ghostly father, adviser, director etc.**—A confessor; যে ধর্ম্মযাজক পাপ স্বীকারোক্তি শ্রবণ করেন। **Ghostly weapons**—Religious arguments; ecclesiastical penalties; ধর্ম্ম সম্বন্ধীয় বাদানুবাদ; যাজকীয় দণ্ড। **Our ghostly enemy**—The Devil; শয়তান।

ghoul (gôl), *n.* A spirit fabled to prey on the dead (as stated in Eastern tales); ডাকিনী, যোগিনী [আরব্য দেশীয় উপকথায় বর্ণিত যে শ্মশানচারিণী ডাকিনী নিশাকালে মৃতদেহ ভক্ষণ করে]। **Ghoul'-ish,** *adj.* **Ghoul'-ish-ly,** *adv.*

gi-ăl'-ō—ăn-tĭ'-cō, *n.* A rich yellow marble found among Italian ruins; ইতালী দেশের প্রাচীন ধ্বংসাবশেষ সমূহে প্রাপ্ত উজ্জ্বল পীতবর্ণ মর্ম্মর-প্রস্তর-বিশেষ।

gī'-ănt, *n.* & *adj.* 1. (*Orig.—Gr. Myth.*) One of the sons of Gaea (Earth) and Uranus (Heaven) or Tartarus (Hell) who warred against the gods; (গ্রীক পুরাণ) দৈত্য, দানব, অসুর। 2. A very powerful agency; "Electricity our docile giant"; দানবীয় শক্তি, মহাশক্তি। 3. A person of extraordinary strength or powers, bodily or intellectual; as, the judge is a *giant* in his profession; অসাধারণ-শক্তিশালী ব্যক্তি, অসাধারণ প্রতিভাসম্পন্ন ব্যক্তি, অমানুষিক মনীষাসম্পন্ন ব্যক্তি। 4. A man of extraordinary size or bulk; an animal, plant or thing of extraordinary size or power; অতিকায় মনুষ্য, মহাকায়, দিগ্‌গজ পুরুষ (কেণ্ডিঃ); বিশালাকৃতি বা অমিতশক্তিসম্পন্ন বৃক্ষ, বস্তু বা জন্তু। ***Adj.*** Extraordinary in size, strength or power; monstrous; gigantic; মহাকায়, অতিকায়, অতিমানুষশক্তিসম্পন্ন; বিকট; বিরাট। **—ess,** *n.* (*Fem.*) A she giant; a woman of extraordinary size; দানবী; বিপুলাঙ্গী নারী। **Giant cement**—অত্যন্ত সংলাগশীল একপ্রকার বিলাতী মাটী। **Giant powder**—এক প্রকার ডিনামাইট। **Giant('s) stride**—একপ্রকার ব্যায়াম-দণ্ড—ইহার অগ্রভাগ ঘূর্ণনশীল এবং উহা হইতে রজ্জু সমূহ ঝুলানো থাকে। ঐ রজ্জুতে ধরিয়া ব্যায়ামকারী উক্ত কাষ্ঠ দণ্ডের চতুর্দ্দিকে দীর্ঘ পাদবিক্ষেপ করিতে পারে, দানবপাদক্ষেপ যন্ত্র। **There were giants in those days**—Our fathers were superior to us; আমাদের পিতৃ-পিতামহগণ আমাদের চেয়ে শ্রেষ্ঠ ছিলেন।

giaour (jowr), *n.* An infidel; অবিশ্বাসী, নাস্তিক, কাফের। [তুর্কিগণ অ-মুসলমানদিগকে এই নামে আখ্যাত করিয়া থাকে।]

gĭb'-bĕr, *v. i.* & *n.* To speak rapidly and inarticulately; to chatter like an ape; হড়্‌বড় করিয়া কথা বলা; বানরের মত কিচির মিচির করা। ***Noun.*** Rapid inarticulate sound or speech; অর্থহীন ধ্বনি, বড়বড়ানি, প্রলাপ, বর্ব্বর ভাষা। **—ish,** *n.* Unintelligible language; jargon; unmeaning words; ungrammatical talk; দুর্ব্বোধ ভাষা, পিশাচভাষা (কেণ্ডি), বর্ব্বর ভাষা; অপভাষা; অর্থহীন বাক্য, প্রলাপ; ব্যাকরণ-বিরুদ্ধ বাক্য।

gĭb'-bĕt, *n.* & *v. t.* 1. (*Orig.*) A gallows; (*later*) an upright post with an arm from which the bodies of criminals were hung in chains or irons after execution; (পূর্ব্বে) ফাঁসীকাষ্ঠ, বধ্য কাষ্ঠ, উদ্বন্ধন কাষ্ঠ; (পরবর্ত্তীকালে) দণ্ড-বিশেষ—যাহার বাহু হইতে নিহত অপরাধিগণের মৃতদেহ শৃঙ্খল দ্বারা ঝুলান হইত। 2. Death by hanging; ফাঁসি কাষ্ঠে মৃত্যু। ***Verb t.*** 1. To hang on a gibbet; to expose on a gibbet; ফাঁসীকাষ্ঠে ঝুলান; বাহুসমন্বিত প্রোথিত কাষ্ঠ দণ্ডে নিহত অপরাধী ব্যক্তির শব প্রদর্শন করা। 2. To expose to infamy or contempt; লোকসাধারণের অবজ্ঞা বা কলঙ্কভাজন করা।

gĭb'-bŏn, *n.* A long armed ape of the Indian Archipelago; উল্লুক।

gĭb'-bous (-ŭs), *adj.* 1. Hunch-backed; কুব্জ, কুব্জপৃষ্ঠ, কূর্ম্মপৃষ্ঠবৎ, বহির্ব্বর্ত্তুল, ন্যুব্জাকার। 2. (Of moon or planet) Having the bright part greater than a semicircle but less than a circle; "Mars likewise appears *gibbous*"; (চন্দ্র বা অন্য গ্রহ সম্পর্কে) উজ্জ্বল অংশ অর্দ্ধবৃত্ত অপেক্ষা বৃহত্তর কিন্তু বৃত্ত অপেক্ষা ন্যূনতর, অণ্ডমণ্ডল (সাঃ পঃ), কুবৃত্ত (ঐ), ন্যূনবৃত্ত (ঐ), অর্দ্ধাধিক (হিঃ কোঃ)। 3. Convex; protuberant; as, the *gibbous* substance on their head; বহির্ব্বর্ত্তুল; ন্যুব্জ। **—bos'-i-ty,** *n.* **—ly,** *adv.* **Gibbous moon**—অষ্টমী ও পূর্ণিমার মধ্যবর্ত্তী চন্দ্র, খণ্ডমণ্ডল।

gībe, jībe, *v. t., i.* & *n.* To mock; to taunt; to jeer; বিদ্রূপ করা; ঠাট্টা করা; ব্যঙ্গ করা। ***Noun.*** A taunt; a sneer; ঠাট্টা, বিদ্রূপ, ব্যঙ্গ; নাকসিট্‌কানি। **Gib'-er, Jib'—,** *n.* **Gib'-ing-ly,** *adv.*

gĭb'-lĕts, *n.* (*Pl.*) The internal eatable parts of a goose taken out before cooking; রাজহংসীর যকৃৎ, হৃৎপিণ্ড, পাকস্থলী প্রভৃতি আহার্য্য অংশ — যাহা স্বতন্ত্র ভাবে রান্ধা হয়।

Giblet-soup—রাজহংসীর মেটে, কলিজা প্রভৃতি র ঝোল।

gī′-bŭs, *n.* A crush hat so named from the original maker in Paris; একপ্রকার টুপি—যাহা সঙ্কাপিত হওয়ার পর পুনরায় পূর্ব্বাকার ধারণ করে।

gid′-dy̆, *adj., v. t. & i.* **1.** Affected with vertigo; ঘূর্ণিগ্রস্ত, ঘূর্ণিরোগগ্রস্ত, বায়ুরোগগ্রস্ত। **2.** Causing or inducing giddiness; as, a *giddy* height; ভ্রমিজনক, শিরোঘূর্ণনকর। **3.** Circling or whirling with bewildering speed; "The *giddy* mill"; মহাবেগে ঘূর্ণায়মান। **3.** Unstable; frivolous; fickle; flighty; inconstant; "*Giddy* girls of gay fifteen"; অস্থির, চপল; ছেবলা; অস্থির-মতি, চঞ্চল-মতি, চপল চিত্ত, অস্থির-চিত্ত, তরল-মতি; খামখেয়ালী; অব্যবস্থিতচিত্ত, চলচিত্ত। ***Verb t. & i.*** To make or become dizzy; শিরোঘূর্ণি জন্মান, ঘূর্ণিজনক হওয়া, ভ্রমি দেওয়া। **—di-ly,** *adv.* **—di-ness,** *n.* তরলতা। **Giddy-brained**—Giddy headed; চঞ্চল; তরলমস্তিষ্ক; thoughtless তরল-মতি; বিবেচনাহীন; চপল, চলচিত্ত। **Giddy-go-round**—যে বস্তু অতি দ্রুতবেগে ঘূর্ণিত হয়। **Giddy-headed**—Thoughtless; foolish; চিন্তাহীন, বিবেচনাহীন, বিচারমূঢ় (রঃ), ভাবনাহীন, বিচারশূন্য; নির্ব্বোধ, বোকা। **To play the giddy goat**—To play the fool; বোকামি করা।

gift, *n. & v. t.* **1.** The act, right or power of giving; as, the office is not in his *gift*; প্রদান, দান, প্রদানের ক্ষমতা। **2.** Anything given; a present; a donation; দান; উপহার, উপঢৌকন, ইনাম, সওগাত, খয়রাত; এককালীন দান। **3.** (*Law*) Voluntary transference of property without consideration; (আইন) সম্পত্তিদান। **4.** A natural quality or a faculty regarded as conferred by God; as, *gift* of tongues; স্বভাবদত্ত গুণ বা বুদ্ধি, প্রতিভা, স্বাভাবিক বুদ্ধি, স্বাভাবিক বৃত্তি। **5.** A white speck on finger nails; করনখের উপরিস্থ শ্বেতবর্ণ চিহ্ন, নখের ফুল। ***Verb t.*** **1.** To confer, as a gift; to present with, as a gift; উপহার প্রদান করা; উপঢৌকন দেওয়া, উপহার দেওয়া। **2.** To endow with any power or faculty; as, I am better *gifted* than another; ক্ষমতাদি প্রদান করা। **Gift′-ed,** *adj.* Talented; endowed with natural gifts; প্রতিভাবান, প্রতিভাশালী; স্বাভাবিক বুদ্ধিসম্পন্ন। **Gift-book**—উপহার পুস্তক। **Do not look a gift horse in the mouth**—দানে পাওয়া জিনিষের খুঁত ধরিও না, ভিক্ষার চাল কাঁড়া আর আকাঁড়া। **Resumption of a gift**—দত্তাপহার (কেঃডিঃ)। **The gift of the gab**—বাক্‌পটুতা, মুখের জোর। **To be in the gift of**—To belong to one; to have right or power to bestow; কাহারো অধিকারে থাকা, কাহার হাতে থাকা, দানের অধিকার থাকা। **Would not have it at a gift**—এমন কি বিনামূল্যে পাইলেও ইহা লইবে না।

gig, *n.* **1.** A light two-wheeled carriage drawn by one horse; একপ্রকার দুই চাকার হাল্‌কা গাড়ী, বগী (কেঃডিঃ)। **2.** A rowing boat usually for racing; একপ্রকার বাইচের নৌকা। **3.** A light ship's boat designed for rapid motion; জাহাজের একপ্রকার হালকা ডিঙ্গী। **Gig-lamps**—(ইতর ভাষায়) চস্‌মা। **Gig-man**—বগী গাড়ী-চালক।

Gig.

gig, *n.* A kind of fish-spear; একপ্রকার টেঁটা।

Gi-găn′-tēs (jī-), *n.* Giants who dwelt in the island of Trinacria in the Western Ocean, and whom the gods warred upon; পশ্চিম-সাগরস্থ ট্রিনেক্রিয়া দ্বীপবাসী দানবগণ—যাহাদের সহিত দেবতাগণ যুদ্ধ করিয়াছিলেন।

gī-găn′-tic, *adj.* **1.** Giant-like in size and stature; অতিমানুষ, বৃহৎকায়, মহাকায়, রাক্ষুসে ভীমবিগ্রহ (কেঃডিঃ)। **2.** Enormous; huge "This *gigantic* telescope"; অতি বৃহৎ, প্রকাণ্ড; বিরাট, বিশাল **—tesque′,** *adj.* Be-fitting a giant অসুরোচিত। **—ti-cal-ly,** *adv.*

gig′-gle (-l). *v. i. & n.* To laugh in an affected or silly manner to titter; খিল্ খিল্ করিয়া হাসা; হি করিয়া হাসা। ***Noun.*** A light silly laugh; a laugh with short catches of the voice or breath খিল্ খিল্ হাস্য; হিহি করিয়া হাস্য **—gler,** *n.*

gig′-lĕt, —lŏt, *ns.* A giggling girl; খিল্ খিল্ করিয়া হাসে এরূপ বালিকা।

gig-măn′-i-ty̆, *n.* The respectable unimaginative middle classes; Philistines; সম্ভ্রান্ত এবং কল্পনাশক্তি-শূন্য মধ্যবিত্তশ্রেণী সমূহ; বিষয়-সুখ-সর্ব্বস্ব ব্যক্তি সমূহ। [এই শব্দটী *Gig-man* (অর্থাৎ যে ব্যক্তির হালকা গাড়ী আছে, অতএব যে ব্যক্তি সাংসারিক সুখই জীবনের একমাত্র পুরুষত্ব মনে করে) শব্দ হইতে উদ্ভূত হইয়াছে। Carlyle এই শব্দটী সৃষ্টি করিয়াছেন।]

gig-mill, *n.* A machine in which woollen cloth is napped or teaseled; a building in which these machines are used; যে যন্ত্র দ্বারা পশমী কাপড়ের ফুঁপি বা এঁশো তুলা হয়; যে গৃহে ঐরূপ যন্ত্র চালান হয়।

Gi′-hil, *n.* The Babylonian god of fire; বেবিলোন নগরবাসিগণের অগ্নিদেব।

gild, *v.t.* **1.** To overlay with gold; সুবর্ণমণ্ডিত করা, সোণার পাতলা পাত দিয়া মোড়ান, সোণার জল লাগান, গিল্টি করা, সোণার হল করা, সোণার গিল্টি করা, কলস্বা করা, সোণালি করা। **2.** (*Fig.*) To tinge or adorn with golden colour or light; "The crests of...the headland were *gilded* by...sunshine"; (লক্ষণায়) সুবর্ণাভ করা, স্বর্ণাভ করা, স্বর্ণবর্ণে রঞ্জিত করা।

স্বর্ণজ্যোতির্বিমণ্ডিত করা। 3. (*Fig.*) To supply with gold or money; esp. to make reputable or tolerable; "I'll *gild* that poverty...."; (লক্ষণায়) স্বর্ণ বা মুদ্রা প্রদান করা; বিশেষতঃ গণ্যমান্য বা একরকম চলনসই করার জন্য স্বর্ণ বা অর্থ প্রদান করা। 4. (*Fig.*) To give a specious appearance to; as, to *gild* a lie; আপাতমনোরম করা, আপাতরম্য করা। **Gild'-ed, Gilt,** *adjs.* Overlaid with a covering of gold; tinged with a golden colour; গিল্টি-করা, হল-করা, স্বর্ণমণ্ডিত, সুবর্ণীকৃত; স্বর্ণ-বর্ণ-রঞ্জিত। **Gild'-er,** *n.* **Gild'-ing,** *n.* 1. The act or practice of overlaying things with gold; গিল্টি করণ। 2. A thin coating of gold; সূক্ষ্ম স্বর্ণ-স্তরাচ্ছাদন। 3. Fair, superficial show; বাহিরের চটক, জেল্লা। **Gilded Chamber**—The House of Lords; পার্লেমেন্টের লর্ড সভা। **Gilded** (or **gilt) spurs** — An emblem of knighthood; নাইট উপাধিধারিগণের চিহ্ন। **Gilded youth**—ধনী ও বিলাসী যুবক সম্প্রদায়। **Giltcup**—Buttercup; পীত পুষ্পবান গুল্ম বিশেষ। **To gild refined gold**—To do what is not essential in the hope of making it better; পাকা সোণার উপর গিল্টি করা। **To gild the pill**—To soften down a disagreeable necessity; কোন অপ্রীতিকর বিষয়কে কতকটা মোলায়েম করা।

gild, *v. t.* See GUILD.

Gilgames or ***Ghisdubar***—The Babylonian name of Nimrod; নিমরোড্ (বেবিলোন নগরীতে প্রচলিত নাম)।

g̃ill, *n.* & *v. t.* (*Usu. pl.*) 1. The organ of respiration in fishes and some other aquatic animals; (মৎস্যাদি জলচর প্রাণীর) কান্‌কো, ফুল্‌কো, মৎস্যাদির শ্বাসেন্দ্রিয়। 2. Dew-lap of a fowl; কুক্কুটাদির চঞ্চুর অধোদেশে লম্বমান চর্ম্ম। 3. The radiating plates on the underside of a mushroom; ছত্রাকের অন্তর্ভাগস্থ বিকীর্য্যমান ফলক সমূহ, মুণ্ডতবক (সাঃ পঃ)। ***Verb t.*** 1. To gut (fish); মাছের নাড়ীভুঁড়ি বাহির করা। 2. To cut gills from (a mushroom); ছত্রাকের অন্তর্ভাগ হইতে বিকীর্য্যমান ফলক সমূহ ছিন্ন করা। 3. To catch (fish) by the gills in a gill-net; মাছের কান্‌কো আট্‌কাইয়া কই-জালে মাছ ধরা। **Gilled,** *adj.* **Gill-net**—একপ্রকার মাছ ধরিবার জাল—যাহাতে মাছের কান্‌কো আটকাইয়া যায়, কই-জাল। **Rosy** or **red about the gills**—Flushed with drink: সুরাপানে আরক্তবদন। **White about the gills** — Showing signs of fear or sickness; ভয় বা পীড়া-বশতঃ পাণ্ডুর বা বিবর্ণ, পাঙ্গাশ-বর্ণ।

g̃ill, *n.* A measure equal to $\frac{1}{4}$ of a pint; (তরলপদার্থের পরিমাণ) এক পাইন্টের এক চতুর্থাংশ (৴১০ ছটাক)।

gill, *n.* A sportive name for a lass; a sweetheart; বালা; প্রণয়িনী। **Gill-flirt**—চপলা বালিকা, রসিকা বালিকা, তরুণী। **Jack and Gill**—বালকবালিকা।

gill, *n.* A wooded ravine; a mountain torrent; তরুসমাচ্ছাদিত গিরিবর্ত্ম; গিরি-প্রবাহিনী।

gil'-lie (-lĭ-) **—lȳ,** *n.* 1. (*Hist.*) A Highland chief's attendant; (ইতিহাস) লেংটা গোরার নায়কের সহচর। 2. A male attendant of a sportsman in Scotland; (স্কটলণ্ডে) শিকারীর অনুচর।

Gilly-flower, *n.* Clove-scented pink; একপ্রকার লবঙ্গগন্ধী পুষ্প।

gilt, *n.* Gilding; গিল্টিকরণ। **Gilt-edged paper, securities, stocks etc.**—যে কোম্পানীর কাগজ ক্রয় করিলে টাকা মারা যাইবার সম্ভাবনা থাকে না। **To take the gilt off the ginger bread**—To deprive a thing of adventitious attraction; to destroy the illusion; কোন জিনিষের ক্ষণিক চটক নষ্ট করা; মোহ দূর করা।

gĭm'-băl, *n.* A contrivance for suspending the mariner's compass etc., so as to keep it always horizontal; (জাহাজে) দিগ্দর্শন যন্ত্রাদি নিয়ত শয়ানভাবে বিলম্বিত রাখার জন্য যন্ত্র-বিশেষ।

g̃ĭm'-crăck, *n.* & *adj.* A trivial mechanism; a knick-knack; a toy; অকিঞ্চিৎকর ক্রীড়াযন্ত্র; অসার তুচ্ছ পদার্থ; খেলনা, ক্রীড়নক। ***Adj.*** Showy but of little worth; trumpery; as, the cheap church is generally a *grimcrack* affair; চটকদার অকিঞ্চিৎকর দ্রব্য; ফট্‌কীনাট্‌কী, খেলনা। **—er-y,** *n.* Gimcracks collectively; ফট্‌কীনাট্‌কী জিনিষ। **—y,** *adj.*

gĭm'-lĕt, *n.* A small boring tool; বেধনিকা, আস্ফোটন-যন্ত্র, তুরপুণ, ভ্রমর, যন্ত্র, স্ফোটনী, আবিধ, বরমা।

g̃ĭmp, g̃ȳmp, *ns.* 1. A silk or cotton twist with a cord or wire running through it; দড়ি বা তারের উপর জড়ান রেশমী বা কার্পাসের সূতা। 2. A silk fishing line strengthened with wire; তারদ্বারা পেঁচানো বড়শীর রেশমী সূতা। 3. (Lace-making) The coarser thread forming the outline of a design; কোনরূপ নমুনার নক্সাস্বরূপ মোটা সূত্রসমূহ।

g̃ĭn, *n.* A distilled spirit flavoured with juniper berries; শস্য বা পর্য্যুসিত যব হইতে পরিস্রুত মদ্য, উগ্র মদ্য-বিশেষ, সরাপ, শীধু। **Gin palace**—A gaudily decorated public house, সুসজ্জিত মদির-বিপণি। **Ginshop—**A dram-shop esp. for gin; মদের দোকান, শুঁড়িখানা। **Gin-sling** Gin flavoured and sweetened (used in America); আমেরিকায় প্রচলিত সুবাসিত এবং সুমিষ্ট জিন মদ্য।

g̃ĭn, *n.* & *v. t.* 1. A snare; a trap; পাশ, জাল; ফাঁদ। 2. (*Fig.*) An apparatus for lifting weights etc.; ভারোত্তলন যন্ত্র। 3. A machine for separating seeds from cotton; তুলার বীচি ছাড়াইবার কল।

Verb t. **1.** To clear of seeds by a cotton-gin ; (যন্ত্র সাহায্যে) তুলার বীচি ছাড়ান। **2.** To catch in a trap ; ফাঁদে ধরা।

Gin for raising heavy weights.

gĭn′-gall, jin-, *ns.* A light swivel gun (used in China and India) ; একপ্রকার হাল্‌কা বন্দুক।

gĭn′-gĕl-lȳ, *n.* Sesamum ; তিল। **Gingelly oil**—The sesamum oil ; তিলের তৈল।

gĭn′-gĕr, *n., adj.* & *v. t.* **1.** A plant with a hot spicy root ; the root of this plant ; আদা গাছ ; আদা, আর্দ্রক, শৃঙ্গবের। **2.** A light sandy colour like that of ginger ; আদার মত রং। **3.** (*Slang*) Mettle ; spirit ; "I'll take the *ginger* out of him" ; (ইতর ভাষায়) শক্তি ; তেজ। ***Adj.*** Of light sandy colour, as hair etc. ; আর্দ্রক-বর্ণ। ***Verb t.*** **1.** To flavour with ginger ; আর্দ্রক-রসদ্বারা সুবাসিত করা। **2.** To treat (a horse) with ginger ; (ঘোড়াকে আদা দ্বারা চিকিৎসা করা। **3.** To inspire, as a person ; অনুপ্রাণিত করা। **—y,** *adj.* **Gingerade, Gingerette**—আর্দ্রক-রস-সুবাসিত উত্তেজক পানীয়। **Ginger ale, —beer, —pop**—আর্দ্রকবাসিত সুরা, আর্দ্রকাসব। **Ginger-brandy** — আর্দ্রকরসদ্বারা সুবাসিত ব্রাণ্ডি। **Ginger-bread**—*n.* & *adj.* A cake flavoured with ginger juice ; আর্দ্রকরসবাসিত পিষ্টক বিশেষ। (*Adj.*) Gaudy ; tawdry ; showy ; as, *ginger-bread* work ; জমকালো ; চটকদার ; বাহ্যসুন্দর। **Ginger-bread nut, Ginger-nut**—আর্দ্রকবাসিত পিষ্টক-বিশেষ। **Ginger-bread work**—ইমারত প্রভৃতির চটকদার কাজ। **Ginger-race**—A root of ginger ; আদা। **Ginger-wine**—জল, চিনি এবং ছেঁচা আদা গাঁজাইয়া যে একপ্রকার মদ্য প্রস্তুত করা হয়, আর্দ্রক-সুরা। **To take the gilt off the ginger-bread**—See GILT.

Ginger.

gĭn′-gĕr-lȳ, *adv.* & *adj.* Cautiously ; timidly ; gently ; with soft steps ; সতর্কভাবে, সন্তর্পণে ; ভয়ে ভয়ে, সভয়ে ; শান্তভাবে, মৃদুভাবে, ধীরে ধীরে ; মৃদুপদসঞ্চারে, ধীরপাদ-বিক্ষেপে। ***Adj.*** Extremely cautious ; নিতান্ত সাবধান।

gĭng′-ham (-ăm), *n.* **1.** A kind of striped cotton or linen cloth of dyed yarn ; একপ্রকার ডোরা-কাটা সুদৃঢ় ক্ষৌম বা কার্পাস বস্ত্র। **2.** (*Colloq.*) An umbrella ; (চলিত ভাষায়) ছাতা।

gĭn′-gĭ-li, *n.* An East Indian plant ; a sweet oil obtained from it ; তিল গাছ ; তিলের তৈল।

gĭn′-gĭ-văl, *adj.* Of, or relating to, the gums ; দন্তবেষ্টনী সম্পর্কীয়।

gĭng′-kō, *n.* A tree of fan-shaped leaves in Japan ; ব্যজনাকৃতি পত্র-বিশিষ্ট জাপানদেশীয় বৃক্ষবিশেষ।

gin′-glȳ-mŭs (gĭng-), *n.* (*Anat.*) A hinge-joint admitting only of flexion and extension (*e. g.*, the elbow, knee-joints) ; (শারীর-সংস্থান-বিদ্যা) কেবল অবনমন এবং প্রসারণ গতি-বিশিষ্ট সন্ধি, কব্জা-সন্ধি—যথা কনুই, হাঁটু।

Ginnungagap, *n.* The chaotic condition in Norse mythology before creation ; নরওয়ে ও সুইডেনের পুরাণে উক্ত সৃষ্টির প্রাক্কালীন মহা বিশৃঙ্খলার অবস্থা।

gĭn′-sĕng, *n.* **1.** A medicinal plant of the genus Aralia found in China, Nepal, etc. ; চীন, নেপাল প্রভৃতি দেশের বনৌষধি বিশেষ। **2.** A root of this plant ; ঐ গুল্মের মূল।

gĭp′-sȳ, *n.* See GYPSY.

gĭ-raffe′ (-răf), *n.* A ruminant quadruped found in Africa with spotted skin and a long neck and leg ; the camel-opard ; আফ্রিকা-দেশীয় দীর্ঘগ্রীব রোমন্থনকারী চতুষ্পদ জন্তুবিশেষ, জিরাফ ; চিত্রোষ্ট্র, দীর্ঘগ্রীব।

Giraffe.

gĭr′-ăn-dōle, *n.* **1.** A rotating fire work ; একপ্রকার চরকী বাজী। **2.** An ornamental branched candlestick ; একপ্রকার বাতির ঝাড়। **3.** A revolving fountain jet ; ফোয়ারার ঘূর্ণ্যমান ধারা। **4.** An ear-ring or pendant with a large central stone surrounded by small ones ; ক্ষুদ্র ক্ষুদ্র মণিবেষ্টিত বৃহৎ মধ্যমণি-সমন্বিত কর্ণভূষা।

gĭr′-ă-sōl, —sōle, *ns.* An opal reflecting a reddish glow in a bright light ; একপ্রকার উপল মণি।

gird (gĕrd), *v. t.* **1.** To encircle or bind (waist etc.) with any flexible band, as a belt etc. ; বেড়িয়া বাঁধা। **2.** To make fast as clothes on the body with a girdle ; কটিবন্ধনীদ্বারা বস্ত্র প্রভৃতি দেহে বদ্ধ করা। **3.** To provide or equip (*with* a sword in belt) ; সজ্জিত করা। **4.** To invest (with strength, powers, etc.) ; to make ready ; as, to *gird* oneself for a contest ; সমন্বিত করা ; প্রস্তুত করা। **5.** To surround ; to encircle ; as, to *gird* a town with besiegers : a belt *girds* his waist; বেষ্টিত করা ; বলয়িত করা। 6. To put as a cord etc. (round) ; ফিতা প্রভৃতি দ্বারা ঘুরাইয়া বাঁধা, পেঁচাইয়া বাঁধা। **Gird′-er,** *n.* The main beam supporting a superstructure : প্রধান কড়ি কাঠ, আধার দারু (আঃ বঃ), সাথির : **To gird on, upon** or **to**—To fasten, as a sword etc. to one's person with a belt etc. ; তরবারি প্রভৃতি কোমর-বন্ধ দ্বারা কটিতে বদ্ধ করা। **To gird (up) one's self, To gird (up) one's loins**—To prepare for an action or contest ; বদ্ধপরিকর হওয়া, কোমর বাঁধিয়া প্রস্তুত হওয়া।

gird (gêrd), *v. i.* & *n.* To sneer ; to jibe, (with *at*) ; নাক সিঁট্‌কান ; মুখভঙ্গী করা, মুখ বাঁকান। ***Noun.*** A sarcastic remark ; a jibe ; ব্যঙ্গোক্তি ; মুখ বাঁকানি। **To gird at**—See GIRD *v. i.*

gir′-dle (gêr-dl), *n.* & *v.t.* **1.** That which girds ; a band, cord or belt to gird waist ; বন্ধনী, বেষ্টনী ; মেখলা, রশনা, কাঞ্চী, পরিকর, সারসন, কক্ষ্যা, শৃঙ্খলী, কোমরবন্ধ, কটিবন্ধ, পেটি। **2.** (*Anat.*) Bony supports for upper and lower limbs ; (শারীর-সংস্থান-বিদ্যা) হস্তপদাদি অঙ্গপ্রত্যঙ্গের অবলম্বনস্বরূপ অস্থি-সমূহ। **3.** A ring round a tree trunk made by removing the bark ; বল্কল উন্মোচন দ্বারা বৃক্ষকাণ্ডের চতুর্দ্দিকে রচিত বেষ্টনী। ***Verb t.*** **1.** To surround or bind with a girdle, (often with *about, in, round*) ; বন্ধনীদ্বারা পরিবেষ্টন বা বন্ধন করা। **2.** To kill a (tree) or make it more fruitful by girdling ; কাণ্ডের ত্বক্ চক্রাকারে ছেদন করিয়া বৃক্ষকে মারিয়া ফেলা বা ফলশালী করা। **A good name is better than a golden girdle**—A good name is better than money ; ধনের চেয়ে সুনাম বড়, বিত্ত হইতে সুখ্যাতি বড় জিনিষ। **Children under the girdle**—Children not yet born ; গর্ভস্থ শিশু। **He has large mouth but small girdle**—He has great expenses but small means ; তাহার আয়ের চেয়ে ব্যয় বেশী। **He has undone her girdle**—He has taken her for his wedded wife ; সে তাহার সহিত পরিণয়পাশে বদ্ধ হইয়াছে। **Like a hen on a het (hot) girdle**—Indicating a state of great uneasiness or discomfort ; অতিশয় ছট্‌ফটে, আন্‌ছান্। **To hold** or **have under one's girdle**—To keep under control and submission ; নিজের অধীন রাখা, হাতের মুঠোয় রাখা। **To put a girdle round the earth**—To travel or go round the earth ; পৃথিবী পর্য্যটন করা, ভূপ্রদক্ষিণ করা।

gir′-dle (gêr-dl), *n.* (*Scot.* & *prov. Eng.*) A griddle, (which see).

girl (gêrl), *n.* **1.** A female child ; a young maiden ; কন্যা, কন্যকা ; বালিকা, কুমারী, বালা। **2.** A maid servant ; ঝি, চাকরাণী, দাসী। **3.** A sweetheart, (also *best girl*) ; প্রণয়িনী, প্রেমিকা, প্রেয়সী। **Girl′-hood,** *n.* The state of being girl ; কন্যাকাল, কৌমার্য্য, বালিকাবস্থা, বালভাব (কুমারঃ)। **Girl′-ish,** *adj.* Like or befitting a girl ; artless ; immature ; বালিকাবৎ, বালিকাসুলভ ; সরল ; কাঁচা। **Girl′-ish-ness,** *n.* **Girl′-ishly,** *adv.* **The girls**—Daughters of a family married or not ; কন্যাবর্গ, দুহিতৃগণ।

girl′-ie (gêr-lĭ), *n.* A little girl ; ছোট মেয়ে।

Gi-rŏn′-dist (zhĭ-), *n.* & *adj.* One of the moderate republican party during the French Revolution ; প্রথম ফরাসী বিপ্লবের কালে (১৭৮৯—৯৬) প্রতিষ্ঠিত মধ্যপন্থী বিপ্লববাদিগণের সম্প্রদায় বিশেষের সভ্য। [ফরাসী দেশের দক্ষিণ-পশ্চিম ভাগের Gironde জেলা হইতে উক্ত সম্প্রদায়ের নেতৃস্থানীয় কতিপয় ব্যক্তি আসিয়াছিলেন বলিয়া এই নাম। Vergniaud, Gaudet, Isnard প্রভৃতি এই সম্প্রদায়ের মুখপাত্র ছিলেন।] ***Adj.*** Relating to the views of the Girondists ; উক্ত রাজনীতিক সম্প্রদায়ের মত-সম্পর্কীয়।

girt (gêrt), *n.* & *v. t.* The measurement round a person's body or any other thing of a more or less cylindrical shape ; বেড়ের মাপ। ***Verb t.*** **1.** To gird ; to encircle ; to invest with a girdle ; to measure the girth of ; as, to *girt* a tree ; বেষ্টিত করা ; বলয়িত করা ; চন্দ্রহার দ্বারা ভূষিত করা ; বেড় মাপা। **2.** To measure in girth ; as, the tree *girts* $18\frac{1}{2}$ ft. ; বেড়ের মাপ হওয়া, কাণ্ডের মাপ হওয়া।

girth (gêrth), *n.* & *v. t.* **1.** A strap for a saddle ; ঘোড়ার পেটি, বরত্রা (আঃ বঃ)। **2.** The measure round a (almost) cylindrical thing ; বেড়ের মাপ। ***Verb t.*** **1.** To surround ; to secure (the saddle) with a girth ; to fit or bind, as a horse with a girth ; বেষ্টিত করা ; পেটি দ্বারা জিন আঁটিয়া বাঁধা ; পেটিদ্বারা ঘোড়া বাঁধা। **2.** To measure in girth ; "He *girthed* 8 ft." ; বেড়ে হওয়া।

g̈ist, *n.* The main point ; the substance or pith of a matter ; মুখ্য বিষয় ; সারাংশ, সারকথা, সারভাগ, মর্ম্ম, সার সত্য, আসল কথা, ফলার্থ, ফলিতার্থ, তাৎপর্য্য, চুম্বক।

git′-têrn, *n.* A guitar-like instrument ; একপ্রকার সেতার।

give (gĭv), *v.t.* & *i.* **1.** To bestow ; to confer gratuitously ; অর্পণ করা, প্রদান করা ; দান করা। **2.** To deliver or hand over without reference to ownership ; "The letter you *gave* me to deliver at Breme" ; to put before one as food etc. ; দেওয়া ; খাদ্যাদি সম্মুখে রাখা। **3.** To commit ;

to entrust ; "He was *given* into custody" ; অর্পণ করা ; বিশ্বাসপূর্ব্বক ন্যস্ত করা। **4.** To administer medicine ; (ঔষধ) প্রদান করা। **5.** To pledge ; as, to *give* one's word ; (কথা) দেওয়া। **6.** To yield ownership of ; to sell for price ; to pay ; স্বত্ব ত্যাগ করা ; বিক্রয় করা ; টাকা দেওয়া। **7.** To communicate ; as, to *give* a message, compliments or love ; to pronounce (a judgment) ; to utter (a shout) ; জ্ঞাপন করা ; রায় দেওয়া ; উচ্চারণ করা। **8.** To put forth (some action or effort) to affect another or simply ; as, *give* him a kick : to *give* a jump ; দেওয়া। **9.** To provide, as a host ; as, to *give* a dinner, ball, etc. ; প্রদান করা, দেওয়া। **10.** To yield, as a product or result ; as, the analysis *gives* the following figures ; to present ; to offer ; to expose ; "*Give* to the wanton winds their flowing hair ;" to show ; as, it *gives* no sign of life ; উৎপাদন করা ; উপস্থিত করা ; অর্পণ করা ; দৃষ্টি পথে স্থাপন করা ; প্রদর্শন করা। **11.** To devote ; to apply ; to addict ; as, he *gives* his life to it : the soldiers *gave* themselves to plunder : *given* to luxury, study, etc. ; নিয়োগ করা, উৎসর্গ করা ; প্রয়োগ করা ; রত করা, আসক্ত করা। **12.** To attribute ; to assign ; as, he was *given* the name of John ; to assume ; *given* health, the thing can be done ; নির্দ্দেশ করা ; আরোপ করা ; ধরিয়া লওয়া, অনুমান করা। **13.** To excite, as pleasure or pain ; to cause or allow to have ; as, this *gives* him a right to complain ; সুখ বা দুঃখ প্রদান করা ; দেওয়ান। **14.** To emit ; as, flint and stone *give* sparks ; নির্গত করা। **15.** To cause (*infinitive*এর সঙ্গে ব্যবহৃত হয়) ; as, he *gave* me to understand ; (বুঝিতে বা জানিতে) দেওয়া। ***Verb i.*** **1.** To yield as to pressure ; as, the earth *gives* under the feet ; to relax ; to shrink ; বসিয়া যাওয়া ; শিথিল হওয়া, ঢিলা হওয়া ; সঙ্কুচিত হওয়া। **2.** To fade, as a colour ; to become soft or mild ; ম্লান হওয়া, বিবর্ণ হওয়া ; কোমল হওয়া, মৃদু হওয়া। **3.** To open ; to lead ; to afford a view or passage, (with *upon, on, to, into,* etc.) "No window *giving on* to the street" ; উন্মুক্ত করা ; চালিত করা ; দর্শনীয় করা, পথ দেওয়া। **4.** To give gifts ; as, he *gave* liberally to charitable institutions ; দান করা। **5.** To recede ; "Now back he *gives*, then rushes on amain" ; হটিয়া যাওয়া, পশ্চাদাবর্ত্তন করা। **Giv'-er, Giv'-ing,** *ns.* **Giv'-en,** *p. p.* Assumed ; supposed to be known ; stated ; fixed ; addicted ; কল্পিত, অনুমিত ; বিদিত বলিয়া অনুমিত ; নির্দ্দিষ্ট ; স্থিরীকৃত, অবধারিত ; আসক্ত, রত। **Give and take**—*adj.* & *n.* Characterised by fair measures on both sides ; উভয় পক্ষ কর্ত্তৃক ন্যায্য পন্থা অনুসৃত। (*Noun*) An exchange, as of talk etc. ; compromise ; mutual concession ; বিনিময়, আদান-প্রদান ; আপোষ ; উভয় পক্ষের ত্যাগ-স্বীকার। **Give and take policy**—A policy of mutual accommodation and forbearance ; একে অন্যের সুবিধা দেখিবে—একজনের দোষে অপরে সহিয়া লইবে—এইরূপ নীতি **Given over**—Abandoned (to evil course etc.) ; পরিত্যক্ত। **Give you joy**—I wish you joy ; তুমি আনন্দে থাক। **It is not given to one**—It is not in his lot ; তাহার ভাগ্যে ইহা নির্দ্দিষ্ট নহে, তাহার কপালে নাই। **To be given to**—To be devoted or addicted to ; আসক্ত হওয়া, অনুরক্ত হওয়া, রত হওয়া। **To give a back** — To stand to be leap-frogged over ; এরূপ ভাবে দাঁড়ান যাহাতে ক্রীড়া বিশেষে অপর ব্যক্তি লাফ দিয়া পার হইয়া যাইতে পারে। **To give a broadside**—(*Naut.*) To discharge at once all the guns along one side of a ship ; রণপোতের কোন পার্শ্বের কামানশ্রেণী হইতে যুগপৎ গোলা বর্ষণ করা। **To give a helping hand**—To help ; সাহায্য করা। **To give a loose rein to**—To give license to ; লাগাম ছাড়িয়া দেওয়া, যথেচ্ছভাবে চলিতে দেওয়া। **To give and take**—To give and get fairly ; সাধুভাবে আদান প্রদান করা। To exchange freely, as blows, sarcasms etc. ; (ঠাট্টা, মুষ্ট্যাঘাতাদি) বিনিময় করা। **To give a person the cold shoulder**—To treat or to receive him coldly ; কাহারও প্রতি অপ্রীতি বা ঔদাসীন্য প্রদর্শন করা। **To give a person to understand, know**—To give him reason to believe ; to assure ; to inform ; বিশ্বাসের হেতু প্রদান করা ; সুনিশ্চিত ভাবে বলা ; বিদিত করা, জানান। **To give a person up**—To despair of seeing him ; to abandon or renounce him ; কাহাকে দেখার আশা ত্যাগ করা ; কাহাকে বর্জ্জন করা। **To give a piece of one's mind** — To chide or reproach ; বেশ দুকথা শুনাইয়া দেওয়া। **To give a Roland for an Oliver** — To retort effectively ; কড়া জবাব দেওয়া। **To give as good as one gets**—To retort sufficiently in words or blows ; পাল্টা শোধ দেওয়া। **To give away**—To alienate by gift ; to hand over, as a bride in marriage ; to expose to ridicule, deception etc. ; to betray ; to distribute, as prize ; হস্তান্তর করা ; সম্প্রদান করা ; উপহাসাস্পদ করা, বিদ্রূপের পাত্র করা ; প্রতারিত করা, ব্যক্ত করা, প্রকাশ করা ; (পুরস্কারাদি) বিতরণ করা। **To give away the show**—To betray its inadequacy or pretentiousness; কোন প্রদর্শনীর অসম্পূর্ণতা বা কৃত্রিমতা দেখাইয়া দেওয়া। **To give a wide berth to**—To keep at a distance; দূরে দূরে থাকা, দূর হইতে প্রণাম করা। **To give back** — To return or restore; প্রত্যর্পণ করা, ফেরত দেওয়া। **To give birth to**—To bring forth, as a child; প্রসব করা, জন্ম দেওয়া। To originate; উৎপাদন করা। **To give chase**—To pursue; পশ্চাদ্ধাবিত হওয়া। **To give countenance to a project** — To favour it; প্রস্তাবিত বিষয় সমর্থন করা। **To give credit**—To sell goods on credit; ধারে জিনিষ বিক্রয় করা, ধারে বেচা। **To give ear to**—See under EAR. **To give forth**—To tell; to report; to publish; to emit; বলা; সংবাদ জ্ঞাপন করা; প্রকাশ করা; নির্গত করা, নিঃসৃত করা। **To give ground**—To retrace; পশ্চাদ্‌বর্ত্তন করা, হটিয়া যাওয়া। **To give heed to**—See under HEED. **To give in**—To yield; to cease opposition; to deliver as documents etc. to a proper official; to announce; বশ্যতা স্বীকার করা; বাধা প্রদানে বিরত হওয়া; উপযুক্ত কর্ম্মচারীর হস্তে দলীলাদি প্রদান করা; ঘোষণা করা। **To give it (him)**—To attack him with words or blows; বাক্যবাণ বর্ষণ করা, প্রহার করা। **To give line**—To allow a person apparent freedom, so as to gain him at last; সূত ছাড়া, শত্রুকে জব্দ করার উপায় হাতে রাখিয়া তাহাকে স্বাধীনভাবে চলিতে দেওয়া। **To give off**—To emit; বিকীর্ণ করা। **To give one a bit of another's mind, To give one a trimming**—(*Colloq.*) To scold or to find fault with him; (চলিত-ভাষায়) বেশ দু'কথা শুনাইয়া দেওয়া। **To give one credit for,** (or) **the credit of**—To praise one for; কোন বিষয়ে কাহারো প্রশংসা করা। **To give one his due**—To admit any merits he may have; কাহারো কোন গুণ থাকিলে তাহা স্বীকার করা। **To give oneself airs**—To be pretentious; জাঁক দেখান, ভড়ং দেখান, চাল দেখান। **To give oneself trouble about a thing**—To take pains about the doing of it; কোন কার্য্য সম্পাদনে যত্ন নেওয়া। **To give oneself out as** or **for**—To declare oneself to be; নিজকে কোন কিছু বলিয়া ঘোষণা করা। **To give one's self away**—To betray one's secret by a slip of the tongue etc.; হঠাৎ অসাবধানে পেটের কথা বাহির হইয়া পড়া, অসাবধানে গুপ্ত কথা ফাঁস করিয়া ফেলা। **To give one's self up** — To abandon hope; to surrender one's self to the police; to devote or addict to: আশা ত্যাগ করা; পুলিসের নিকট আত্মসমর্পণ করা; নিয়োগ করা, আসক্ত করা, রত করা। **To give one the head**—To free from restraint; অসংযত হওয়া, বাধামুক্ত করা। **To give one the right scent**—To afford one an inkling of a thing; কাহাকেও কোন বিষয়ে ইঙ্গিত বা আভাস দেওয়া, অনুসন্ধানের সূত্র দেওয়া। **To give one the slip**—To escape from one secret by trick or fraud; কৌশলে কাহারো হাত এড়ান। **To give on, upon, to** or **into**—To open on or upon; to lead into; দৃষ্টি পথবর্ত্তী করা; অতিক্রম করিয়া যাইতে পারা। **To give out**—*v. t.* & *i.* To announce or declare; to emit; to distribute; "The king *gave out* arms to them"; প্রকাশ করা, প্রচার করা; নিঃসৃত করা, নির্গত করা; ছড়ান, বিকিরণ করা; বিতরণ করা। **To give over**—To abandon, as a habit etc.; to cease from; as, to *give over* play; to hand over (*intr.*); ছাড়িয়া দেওয়া, পরিবর্জ্জন করা; বিরত হওয়া, নিবৃত্ত হওয়া; হস্তান্তর করা। (*Verb i.*) To cease or break down from exhaustion; to fall short; অবসন্ন হইয়া ভাঙ্গিয়া পড়া; ত্রুটী হওয়া, কম্‌তি পড়া। To cease; বিরত হওয়া, নিবৃত্ত হওয়া। **To give place (to)**—To make room (for); to be superseded or succeeded (by); (কাহাকেও) সরিয়া স্থান দেওয়া; কোন ব্যক্তি স্বপদে নিযুক্ত হওয়া হেতু স্থানচ্যুত হওয়া, কাহারো দ্বারা স্বস্থান অধিকৃত হওয়া। **To give quarter**—To show mercy to the conquered; পরাজিত শত্রুর প্রতি করুণা প্রদর্শন করা। **To give rise to**—To originate; to occasion; উৎপাদন করা; সংঘটন করা। **To give the boot**—See under BOOT. **To give the case (or it) for or against a person**—To deliver judgment in a case for or against a person; কোন ব্যক্তির স্বপক্ষে বা বিরুদ্ধে রায় দেওয়া। **To give the devil his due**—See under DEVIL. **To give the hand**—To pledge friendship; বন্ধুত্ব স্থাপন করা। **To give the hand of** — To espouse; বিবাহ করা, পাণিগ্রহণ করা, পাণিপীড়ন করা। **To give the lie to a person**—To accuse him of falsehood; কাহাকে মিথ্যাবাদী বলা। **To give the mitten** — To dismiss (a lover); to dismiss from office; (প্রণয়ীকে) প্রত্যাখ্যান করা; পদচ্যুত করা, বরখাস্ত করা। **To give the sack**—To dismiss from service etc.; বরখাস্ত করা, বরতরফ করা। **To give the time of day**—To say good morning, good evening etc., appropriate to the hour; যথাকালে 'সুপ্রভাত' ইত্যাদি বাক্যোচ্চারণপূর্ব্বক অভিবাদন করা। **To give tone to**—To invigorate; সতেজ করা, তেজাল করা। **To give tongue** — To bark, (of dogs); ঘেউ ঘেউ করা। To speak out in a loud voice; উচ্চৈঃস্বরে কথা বলা। **To give up**—To relinquish or abandon; ত্যাগ করা। To sacrifice; as, to *give up* one's life; উৎসর্গ করা। To resign; to surrender; to hand over, as a fugitive into the hands of pursuers etc.; ত্যাগ করা, ছাড়িয়া দেওয়া; আত্মসমর্পণ করা; পলাতক ব্যক্তি প্রভৃতিকে অনুসরণকারীর হস্তে প্রদান করা। To cease to have to do with (a person); কাহারো সহিত সংশ্রব ত্যাগ করা। To stop (*intr.*); থামা। To abandon (oneself) to a feeling etc.; ভাবস্রোতে গা ঢালিয়া দেওয়া। (*Reflex.* & *p. p.*) To devote or addict to; অনুরক্ত করা, আসক্ত করা, রত করা। To reveal, as the names of accomplices etc.; সহাপরাধী প্রভৃতির নাম প্রকাশ করা। To pronounce incurable or insoluble; অসাধ্য বলিয়া প্রকাশ করা। To renounce the hope of; "He had *given himself up* for lost"; আশা ত্যাগ করা। **To give up a riddle**—To cease attempting to answer it—ধাঁধার উত্তর প্রদানের চেষ্টায় বিরত হওয়া। **To give up for lost**—To give up all hopes of; সমস্ত আশা ত্যাগ করা। **To give up the ghost**—See under GHOST. **To give way**—To yield; to succumb; to retire, as fighting men; to be superseded by, (with *to*); to make concessions; to abandon oneself (to anger, grief etc.); to fall in price, as stocks etc.); (*naut.*) to begin to row; হার মানা; ভাঙ্গিয়া পড়া; হটিয়া যাওয়া; পৃষ্ঠভঙ্গ দেওয়া; উল্লঙ্ঘিত হওয়া; ত্যাগ স্বীকার করা; গা ঢালিয়া দেওয়া; দর কমা, মূল্য হ্রাস হওয়া; (নৌ-বিদ্যা) দাঁড় টানিতে আরম্ভ করা। **To give way together**—(*Naut.*) To row in time; to keep stroke; এক সময়ে দাঁড় টানিয়া নৌকা চালান; তালে তালে দাঁড় ফেলা। **To give vent to**—To give expression to; প্রকাশ করা।

giz'-zard (-ĕrd), *n.* **1.** The second muscular stomach of a bird; পক্ষীর দ্বিতীয় পৈশিক পাকস্থলী। **2.** The muscular stomach of some fish, insects, etc.; কোন কোন কীট বা মৎস্যের পেশীময় পাকস্থলী, আমাশয় (সাঃ পঃ)। **To fret one's gizzard**—To harass; to worry; উত্ত্যক্ত করা; জ্বালাতন করা। **To stick in one's gizzard**—(*Fig.*) To be disagreeable or unpalatable; (লক্ষণায়) অরুচিকর বা অতৃপ্তিকর হওয়া।

glā'-brous (-brŭs), *adj.* Without hair or down; smooth; smooth-skinned; নির্লোম, পালকহীন; মসৃণ; মসৃণ-চর্ম্ম।

glace, (*F.*) *adj.* **1.** Smooth or polished, as leather etc.; মসৃণ বা মসৃণীকৃত। **2.** Iced or sugared, as fruits etc.; (ফলাদি সম্পর্কে) বরফ-মিশ্রিত, শর্করাবৃত।

glā'-cial (-shĭăl), *adj.* **1.** Pertaining to, or consisting of, ice; frozen; icy; হিমানী-সম্বন্ধীয়, তুষারাত্মক; জমাট-বাঁধা; তুষারময়, হৈম (হিঃ কোঃ), হিমবৎ (ঐ) **2.** (*Chem.*) Crystallized; (রসায়ন শাস্ত্র) স্ফটিকীভূত। **3.** (*Geol.*) Characterised by the presence of ice; as, *glacial* epoch, era, period, (the period when the northern hemisphere was mostly covered with ice-sheet): তুষারাত্মক। **—ci-at-ed,** *adj.* **1.** Rubbed or polished by the action of ice; তুষারাঙ্কিত, তুষারঘৃষ্ট, তুষারের ক্রিয়াদ্বারা মসৃণীকৃত। **2.** Covered with ice; হিমানীসমাবৃত, তুষারাবৃত। **—cia'-tion,** *n.* The act of freezing; হিমসংহনন (সাঃ পঃ), হিমানীঘর্ষণ (হিঃ কোঃ)। **—ly,** *adv.* **Glacial period**—যে যুগে পৃথিবীর উত্তর গোলার্দ্ধের অধিকাংশ স্থান তুষারাচ্ছন্ন ছিল, তুষারযুগ, হিমানীযুগ।

glă'-cier (-shĭêr-), *n.* A slowly moving field or stream of ice;

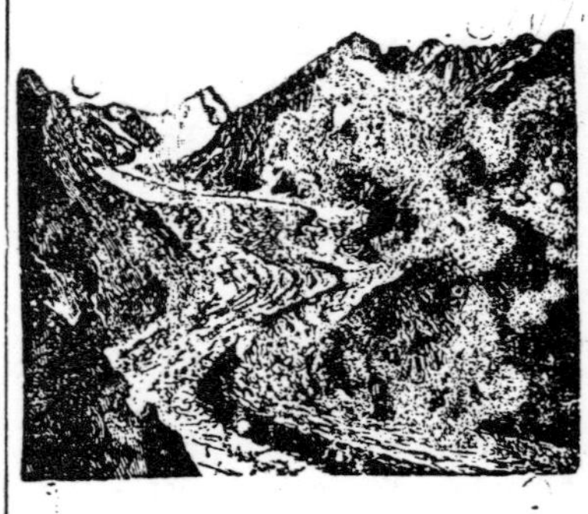

Glacier.

তুষারনদী, হিমানী নদী (সাঃ পঃ), হিমসরিৎ (ঐ), হিমসংহতি (ঐ), চিরনীহার বাহু, হিমানীক্ষেত্র, সংহত হিমক্ষেত্র, শিলীভূত হিমভূমি।

glă'-cis, *n.* A gentle slope; the outer slope of a fortification; প্রবণ ভূমি, ঢালু স্থান; দুর্গের বহির্ভাগস্থ প্রবণ ভূমি, দুর্গান্তিকস্থ ক্রমনিম্নভূমি, বহিঃপ্রবণ-ভূমি।

glăd, *adj.* & *v. t.* (*Predicative*) **1.** Pleased; happy; as, I am *glad* to hear etc.; সন্তুষ্ট, আনন্দিত, সানন্দ, উৎফুল্ল, হৃষ্টমানস, প্রীত, আহ্লাদিত; সুখী। **2.** Expressive of, or marked by, joy; as, a *glad* countenance; (of nature etc.) beautiful; bright; exhilarating; "*Glad* summer"; আনন্দব্যঞ্জক, আনন্দময়, হর্ষোৎফুল্ল; (প্রকৃতি-সম্বন্ধে) সুন্দর; উজ্জ্বল; উল্লাসকর। **3.** (Of news or events) Imparting pleasure; joyous; (সংবাদ বা ঘটনা সম্বন্ধে) প্রীতিপ্রদ; হর্ষজনক। ***Verb t.*** (*Archaic*) To make glad; to cheer; (অপ্রঃ) হর্ষোৎফুল্ল করা; আহ্লাদিত করা। **Glad'-den,** *v. t.* To make glad; to cheer; to please; to animate; to exhilarate; আনন্দিত করা, নন্দিত করা, আহ্লাদিত করা; হর্ষোৎফুল্ল করা; সন্তুষ্ট করা; অনুপ্রাণিত করা; প্রহৃষ্ট করা। **Glad'-ly,** *adv.* With pleasure;

joyfully ; সানন্দে ; সহর্ষে। **Glad'-ness,** *n.* The state of being glad ; হৃষ্টতা, প্রফুল্লতা। **Glad'-some,** *adj.* (*Poet.*) Pleased ; joyful ; cheerful ; pleasing ; gay ; (কবিতায়) আনন্দিত, সন্তুষ্ট ; আনন্দপূর্ণ, আনন্দদায়ক ; প্রফুল্ল, আনন্দময় ; আনন্দোদ্দীপক ; উৎসবদায়ী (উজ্জ্বলঃ)। **Glad'-some-ly,** *adv.* **Glad'-some-ness,** *n.*

glāde, *n.* An open passage through a wood ; a grassy open space in a forest ; অরণ্যপথ, বনপথ, বনবীথিকা, বনমার্গ ; বনমধ্যস্থ মুক্ত শ্যামল প্রান্তর।

glăd'-i-ā-tor (-tėr), *n.* **1.** (*Rom. antiq.*) A man who fought with men or beasts in the arena ; প্রাচীন রোমে যে ব্যক্তি দর্শকগণের চিত্ত-বিনোদনের জন্য বৃতিবেষ্টিত রঙ্গভূমিতে (সাধারণতঃ) অসিধারণপূর্ব্বক মনুষ্য বা পশুর সহিত যুদ্ধ করিত, অসিযোধ (আঃ বঃ), অসিমল্ল (ঐ)। **2.** A disputant ; a controversialist ; "Intellectual *gladiator*" ; বাদবিতণ্ডাকারী ; বাদানুবাদকারী। **–to'-ri-al,** *adj.* Relating to a gladiator ; অসিমল্ল-সম্বন্ধীয়।

glă-dī'-ŏ-lŭs, *n.* (*Pl.* -LUSES, -LI) The sword-lily plant ; এক-জাতীয় গুল্ম।

Gladsheimir, *n.* The world of gladness, where Odin dwelt with his two wolves and ravens, and where the hall of heroes, Valhalla, was situated ; নোর্সজাতির পুরাণোক্ত আনন্দলোক। এই স্থানে দেবরাজ Odin তদীয় বৃকদ্বয় ও দাঁড়কাকগণকে লইয়া বাস করিতেন। বীরগণের Valhalla নামক প্রমোদ-সৌধও এই স্থানেই অবস্থিত ছিল।

Glăd'-stōne, *n.* A kind of four-wheeled carriage ; একপ্রকার চারি চাকার গাড়ী। **Gladstone-bag**—ভ্রমণকারীদিগের একপ্রকার হাল্কা চামড়ার ব্যাগ। **Gladstone-claret** — এক প্রকার সুলভ ক্লারেট মদ্য [১৮৬৯ খৃঃ অব্দে প্রধান মন্ত্রী Gladstone এই মদ্যের শুল্ক হ্রাস করিয়া দেওয়াতে উহা বহুল পরিমাণে ব্যবহৃত হয়।]

glair (glār), *n.* & *v. t.* **1.** The white of an egg ; an adhesive preparation made from it used in book-binding etc. ; ডিম্বের শ্বেতাংশ ; ডিম্বের শ্বেতাংশ হইতে প্রস্তুত একপ্রকার আঠালো দ্রব্য,—যাহা পুস্তক বাঁধাই প্রভৃতি কাজে লাগে। **2.** Any viscous transparent substance ; স্বচ্ছ আঠালো জিনিষ। ***Verb t.*** To smear with white of eggs ; ডিম্বের শ্বেতাংশ দ্বারা মাখান। **Glair'-e-ous, Glair'-y,** *adjs.* Covered with glair ; viscid ; ডিম্বের শ্বেতাংশ দ্বারা ম্রক্ষিত ; আঠালো, চট্‌চটে।

glaive (glāv), *n.* (*Archaic* or *poet.*) Broadsword ; a sword ; (অপ্রচলিত বা কবিতায়) খড়্গ ; অসি, তরবারি।

glăm'-our (-ėr), *n.* & *v. t.* **1.** Magic ; a spell ; মায়া, ভেল্কি ; মন্ত্র, যাদু, গুণ। **2.** Delusive beauty or charm ; মোহজনক সৌন্দর্য্য, মুগ্ধকরী শোভা। **3.** A kind of haze in the air, causing things to appear different from what they are ; একপ্রকার লঘু কুজ্‌ঝটিকা,—যাহার ভিতর দিয়া কোন বস্তু ভিন্ন রূপ দেখায়। ***Verb t.*** To affect with glamour ; to charm ; to enchant ; ধাঁধা লাগান, ভেল্কি লাগান ; বিমোহিত করা ; সম্মোহিত করা। **–or-ous,** *adj.* **–or-ous-ly,** *adv.* **To cast a glamour over**—To enchant ; ধাঁধা লাগান, বিমোহিত করা, বিমুগ্ধ করা।

glance (glăns), *n., v. i.* & *t.* **1.** A sudden movement producing a flash etc. ; a flash or gleam ; প্রভা, চমক, ক্ষণিক প্রভা ; ছটা। **2.** A quick or a casual look ; কটাক্ষ, চকিতদৃষ্টি, ঈষৎদৃষ্টি, দৃষ্টি-বিক্ষেপ (কেঙিঃ), নেত্র-বিক্ষেপ (ঐ)। **3.** An incidental or passing thought ; আকস্মিক চিন্তা, প্রাসঙ্গিক চিন্তা। **4.** A swift oblique movement ; দ্রুত বক্রগতি। ***Verb i.*** **1.** To shine ; to flash ; to dart ; "When through the gloom the *glancing* lightnings fly" ; দীপ্তি পাওয়া ; চমকান ; স্ফুরিত হওয়া। **2.** To strike obliquely and turn aside ; "Your arrow hath *glanced*" ; বক্রভাবে আঘাত করিয়া এক পাশে পিছলাইয়া পড়া, ঘষড়াইয়া যাওয়া। **3.** (Of eye etc.) To cast a hasty look ; to snatch a momentary view ; কটাক্ষক্ষেপ করা, চকিতদৃষ্টিক্ষেপ করা ; কটাক্ষপাত করা চমকান। **4.** (Of talk or talker) To pass quickly over ; to glide (*off* or *from* a subject etc.) ; to allude ; to hint ; দ্রুত অতিক্রম করা ; পিছলাইয়া যাওয়া ; আভাস দেওয়া ; ইঙ্গিত করা। ***Verb i.*** **1.** To cast for a moment ; as, to *glance* the eye ; to catch a glimpse of ; দৃষ্টিক্ষেপ করা ; কটাক্ষপাত করা, অপাঙ্গ-বিক্ষেপ করা, ক্ষণেকের তরে দেখা, মুহূর্ত্তের জন্য দর্শন করা। **2.** To express or convey with a glance ; "*Glancing* sublime devotion" ; চকিত দৃষ্টিপাতদ্বারা প্রকাশ করা। **Glanc'-ing,** *p. pr.* **Glanc'-ing-ly,** *adv.* **A sidelong glance**—কটাক্ষ, অপাঙ্গ দর্শন, আড়দৃষ্টি, তেরছ চাহনি (প্রাঃ সাঃ), তির্য্যকপ্রেক্ষণ (মঃ উঃ)। **At a glance**—At a rapid survey ; এক নজরে, কটাক্ষে, দৃষ্টিমাত্রেই। **To glance at**—To make passing and usually sarcastic allusion to ; কটাক্ষপাত করা, কটাক্ষ করা। To give a brief look at ; ক্ষণকালের জন্য দৃষ্টি করা, ক্ষণিক দৃষ্টিপাত করা। **To glance one's eye (at or over)**—To direct it (at or over) ; দৃষ্টি নিক্ষেপ করা। **To glance over**—To read cursorily ; উপর উপর দেখিয়া যাওয়া, চোখ বুলাইয়া যাওয়া, তাড়াতাড়ি পড়িয়া যাওয়া।

glănd, *n.* **1.** (*Physiol.*) An organ of the human body secreting some fluid from the blood ;

(শরীর-বিজ্ঞান) নিঃস্রবনিঃসরণশীল গ্রন্থি, বীচি, পিণ্ড (সাঃ পঃ), মাংসগ্রন্থি (কেণ্ডিঃ), মাংসপিণ্ড (ঐ), গণ্ড (সাঃ পঃ)। **2.** (*Bot.*) Secreting organs in some plants ; বৃক্ষাদির নির্যাসনিঃসারী গ্রন্থি। **Gland′-less**, *adj.* **Glan′-du-lar, Glan′-du-lose, Glan′-du-lous,** *adjs.* Containing, or pertaining to, glands ; মাংসগ্রন্থি বিশিষ্ট (কেণ্ডিঃ), মাংসগ্রন্থিময় (ঐ), মাংসগ্রন্থিযুক্ত বা তদ্বিষয়ক। **Glan′-dule,** *n.* **Glan-du-lif′-er-ous,** *adj.* **Axillary gland** — কক্ষ-গ্রন্থি। **Salivary gland**—লালাগ্রন্থি।

glăn′-dêrs, *n.* **1.** (*Pl.*) A contagious disease of the mucous membrane about the mouth in horses ; অশ্বের মুখরোগ-বিশেষ। [ইহাতে চোয়ালের নিম্নদেশ স্ফীত হয় এবং নাসারন্ধ্র হইতে শ্লেষ্মা স্রাব হইয়া থাকে।] **2.** The same disease communicated to man ; অশ্ব হইতে সংক্রামিত ব্রণবিশিষ্ট একপ্রকার উৎকট রোগ, লাসাদূষিকা (হঃ চঃ)। **—dered,** *adj.* Affected with glanders ; উক্ত রোগাক্রান্ত। **—der-ous,** *adj.*

glănd′-i-fôrm, *adj.* Acorn-shaped ; resembling a gland ; ওকবৃক্ষের ফলের আকার ; গ্রন্থিসদৃশ।

glare (glâr), *v. i., t.* & *n.* **1.** To shine with a bright dazzling light ; ঝলসিয়া উঠা, ঝক্‌মক্ করা, চক্‌মক্ করা, আলো ঝলমল করা। **2.** To look fixedly and fiercely ; "They *glared* like angry lions" ; কটমট্ করিয়া চাওয়া। **3.** To be intensely bright as a colour etc. ; to be over-conspicuous or obtrusive ; তীব্রোজ্জ্বল হওয়া ; অতিশয় সুপ্রকট হওয়া, গায়ে-পড়া হওয়া। ***Verb t.*** To send forth or express by look ; as, to *glare* defiance, hatred, etc. ; দৃষ্টি দ্বারা প্রেরণ বা প্রকাশ করা। ***Noun.*** **1.** A dazzling over-powering light ; oppressive unrelieved sunshine ; চাক ঝল্‌সানো আলোক, তীব্রোজ্জ্বল আলোক, তীব্রজ্যোতিঃ ; প্রচণ্ড সূর্য্য-রশ্মি। **2.** Tawdry brilliance ; showiness ; "Maidens like moths, are ever caught by *glare*" ; চাকচিক্য, জলুষ, ঝলক, ঝক্‌মকি, রং-চঙ্গ, চটক ; বাহ্য চাকচিক্য। **3.** A fierce piercing look ; তীক্ষ্ণ দৃষ্টি, কটমট্ চাহনি। **Glar′-y,** *adj.*

glâr′-ing, *adj.* **1.** Staring fiercely (said of eyes) ; তীব্র, তীক্ষ্ণ। **2.** Excessively bright ; অতি দীপ্ত (কেণ্ডিঃ), অতিদীপ্যমান (ঐ), তীব্রোজ্জ্বল। **3.** Plainly evident as an error ; notorious ; as, a *glaring* crime ; স্পষ্ট, সুস্পষ্ট ; জাজ্বল্যমান (কেণ্ডিঃ)। **—ly,** *adv.*

glăss, *n.* & *v. t.* **1.** A hard, brittle transparent substance composed of silica and an alkali ; কাচ, সাসী। **2.** (*Chem.*) A substance having properties, or composition of, glass ; as, *glass* of antimony ; কাচবৎ পদার্থ। **3.** Anything made of glass ; (*collectively*) (*a*) a looking glass ; (*b*) an hour-glass ; (*c*) a drinking vessel or its contents, esp. liquor ; (*d*) a lens ; a telescope ; opera-glass ; microscope ; (*e*) a carriage-window ; (*f*) a glass-plate or disc covering a picture or watch-face etc. ; (সংঘবাচক ভাবে) (ক) আয়না, দর্পণ, মুকুর, আদর্শ ; (খ) বালির ঘড়ী ; (গ) কাচনির্ম্মিত পাত্র, গ্লাস, ঐরূপ পাত্রস্থিত জল, সুরা প্রভৃতি ; (ঘ) দূরদর্শন যন্ত্র ; ক্ষুদ্র দূরবীণ ; অণুবীক্ষণ যন্ত্র ; (ঙ) গাড়ীর জানালা ; (চ) ছবির উপরের কাচ, টেঁক ঘড়ি প্রভৃতির উপরের কাচ। **4.** (*Pl.*) Spectacles ; চসমা। ***Verb t.*** **1.** To reflect, as in a mirror, (*used reflexively*) ; as, trees *glass* themselves in the lake ; প্রতিফলিত করা, প্রতিবিম্বিত করা। **2.** (*Rare*) To glaze ; (ক্বচিদ্ ব্যবহৃত) সূক্ষ্ম কাচস্তরাচ্ছাদিত করা। **3.** (*Rare*) To case in glass ; (ক্বচিদ্ ব্যবহৃত) কাচাবৃত করা। **4.** (*Rare*) To make glassy, as the eye ; কাচবৎ করা (ক্বচিদ্ ব্যবহৃত)। **Glass′-ful,** *n.* The contents of a glass ; এক গ্লাস। **Glass′-i-ly,** *adv.* **Glass′-i-ness,** *n.* **Glass′-y,** *adj.* **Cut-glass**—বেলোয়ারী কাচ। **Frosted glass** or **ground glass**—অস্বচ্ছীকৃত কাচ। **Glass-blower**—যে ব্যক্তি ফুৎকার দ্বারা ফুঁকা শিশি প্রভৃতি গঠন করে, শিশি বোতল নির্ম্মাতা। **Glass-case**—যে কাচের ডালাবিশিষ্ট আধারে দোকানের জিনিষপত্র প্রদর্শিত হয়, কাচাধার। **Glass-cloth**—কাচের সূক্ষ্ম অংশু রচিত বস্ত্র ; কাচচূর্ণাবৃত বস্ত্র (পালিশের কার্য্যে ব্যবহৃত)। **Glass-culture**—কাচের আবরণের নীচে বৃক্ষগুল্মাদি উৎপাদন। **Glass-cutter**—অগ্রভাগে হীরক সংযুক্ত কাচ কাটিবার যন্ত্র, কাচচ্ছেদক। **Glass-dust**—কাচচূর্ণ (পালিসে ব্যবহৃত হয়)। **Glass-eye**—কাচনির্ম্মিত কৃত্রিম চক্ষু ; অশ্বের ছানিরোগ বিশেষ। **Glass-house**—কাচের কারখানা ; শীতপ্রধান দেশের কাচাচ্ছাদিত উদ্ভিদশালা বা হরিৎগৃহ, কাচভবন, সাসী মন্দির (প্রবোধ)। **Glassing-jack**—চর্ম্মসংস্কার যন্ত্র। **Glass-paper**—কাচ চূর্ণদ্বারা আচ্ছাদিত কাগজ, একপ্রকার শিরিষ কাগজ। **Glass-painting**—রাসায়নিক ক্রিয়ার সাহায্যে কাচ-চিত্রণ। **Glass-shade**—কৃত্রিম-পুষ্পের উপর স্থাপিত কাচের আবরণ। **Glass-ware**—কাচের বাসন। **Glass work**—কাচের জিনিষ। **Glass-wort**—একপ্রকার গুল্ম — ইহা হইতে কাচ নির্ম্মাণোপযোগী সোডা প্রস্তুত হয়। **Glassy surface**—কাচবৎ মসৃণ তল। **Musical glass**—জলতরঙ্গ (কেণ্ডিঃ)। **He has taken a glass too much**—He is intoxicated ; সে মাতাল হইয়া পড়িয়াছে। **Those who live in a glass-house shouldn't throw stones**—যাহার নিজের শত দোষ তাহার পক্ষে পরের ছিদ্রানুসন্ধান করা অনুচিত। **To live in a glass-house**—To be open to attack or retort ; সহজে আক্রমণীয় হওয়া।

Glau'-bêr's-sält(s) (glä-), *n.* Sulphate of sodium ; খাড়ী নুণ।

Glauce (gläs), *n.* (১) গ্রীক পুরাণোক্ত সাগরদেবী। এই দেবী সাগর-নীলিমার বিগ্রহ রূপিণী। (২) জেসনের পত্নীর নাম।

glau-cō'-mă (glä-), *n.* A disease in the eye involving gradual loss of sight etc. ; এক প্রকার চক্ষুরোগ—রূপবহা নাড়ীর শীর্ণতা হেতু এই রোগের উৎপত্তি হইয়া থাকে, ঝাপ্‌সা রোগ (যোঃ), কাচবিন্দু (কেণ্ডিঃ), ধূসর মন্থ (হঃ চঃ)। **—ma-tous,** *adj.*

glau'-cous (glä-kŭs), *adj.* **1.** Of a sea-green colour ; greyish blue ; সাগর-শ্যামল, ধূসরাভ নীল। **2.** (*Bot.*) Covered with bloom, as of grapes ; (উদ্ভিদ্‌-বিদ্যা) সূক্ষ্ম চূর্ণাচ্ছাদিত।

Glau'-cŭs (glä-), *n.* (১) ক্রীটদ্বীপের রাজা Minos এর পুত্র। এই রাজপুত্র এক বৃহৎ মধুপূর্ণ পাত্রে পতিত হইয়া ইহলোক ত্যাগ করেন। ভাববাদী Polyidus রাজপুত্রের জীবন দানে বিফলপ্রযত্ন হওয়াতে তাঁহার সহিত জীবন্ত সমাহিত হন। এক সর্প ফণাবিস্তার করিয়া রাজপুত্রের মৃতদেহের সন্নিহিত হইলে Polyidus উহাকে যষ্টির আঘাতে সংহার করেন। কিয়ৎক্ষণ পরে অপর এক ফণী সেই মৃত সর্পের শরীরে একটী ওষধি স্থাপন করিলে শেষোক্ত সর্প পুনর্জীবিত হয়। Polyidus সেই ওষধি রাজপুত্রের দেহে স্থাপন করিয়া—তাঁহাকে প্রাণদান করেন। (২) বিয়োসিয়াবাসী জনৈক ধীবর—ইনি এপোলোদেবের বরে ভবিষ্যকথনের ক্ষমতা প্রাপ্ত হন। (৩) Lycia র রাজপুত্র। ইনি ট্রয়ের যুদ্ধে ট্রোজানদিগের পক্ষে যুদ্ধ করিয়াছিলেন। এই রাজপুত্র যুদ্ধ ক্ষেত্রে Diomedesকে দর্শন করিয়া পুরাতন বন্ধুত্বের চিহ্ন স্বরূপ তাঁহাকে স্বীয় স্বর্ণময় বর্ম্ম প্রদান পূর্ব্বক তৎপরিবর্ত্তে তদীয় পীতলময় বর্ম্ম গ্রহণ করেন। ইনি Ajax কর্ত্তৃক নিহত হন। (৪) Sisyphusএর পুত্র। স্বীয় ঘোটকী কর্ত্তৃক ইহার দেহ খণ্ড বিখণ্ড হয়। (৫) Bulwar Lytton কৃত Last days of Pompey নামক উপন্যাসের নায়ক। Niydia নাম্নী কাণা ফুলওয়ালী ইহাকে গোপনে ভালবাসিত।

glāze, *v. t., i. & n.* **1.** To furnish a window, picture, etc. with glass or a house etc. with glass windows etc. ; ছবি, জানালা প্রভৃতিতে কাচ লাগান, গৃহাদিতে কাচের জানালা প্রভৃতি লাগান। **2.** To incrust or overlay with a vitreous substance, as, to *glaze* earthenware ; to overlay with a smooth lustrous coating, as a cloth, etc. ; মৃণ্ময় পাত্রাদি সূক্ষ্ম কাচের স্তর দ্বারা আচ্ছাদিত করা, বর্ণক দেওয়া ; বস্ত্রাদি মসৃণোজ্জ্বল প্রলেপ দ্বারা প্রলিপ্ত করা। **3.** To render smooth, glass-like or glossy ; মসৃণ করা, কাচবৎ করা, উজ্জ্বল করা। **4.** (*Paint.*) To apply a thin coat of different transparent colour to (a painted surface) to modify tone ; (চিত্র-বিদ্যা) কোন বর্ণের প্রভা প্রশমিত করার জন্য উহার উপর ভিন্ন প্রকার স্বচ্ছবর্ণের লঘু আবরণ দেওয়া। **5.** To cover as an eye with a film ; ছানি দ্বারা আচ্ছাদিত করা। ***Verb i.*** To become glassy as eyes etc. ; কাচবৎ হওয়া, নিষ্প্রভ হওয়া। ***Noun.*** **1.** The vitreous coating of porcelain etc. ; anything used as a coating or colour in glazing ; কাচবৎ প্রলেপ ; বর্ণক। **2.** A polished or glossy appearance ; চটক, চাকচিক্য, মসৃণতা, জেল্লা। **Glaz'-y,** *adj.* **Full of glaze**—চটকদার, চাকচিক্যশালী।

glāz'-êr, *n.* A workman who glazes pottery, paper, window, house etc. ; যে লোক বাসনাদি ও কাগজ প্রভৃতি চক্‌চকে ও মসৃণ করে।

glā'-zier (-zhêr), *n.* One whose business is to set window glass ; যে ব্যক্তি জানালায় কাচ লাগায়। **Is your father a glazier**—(*Vulg.*) Do you think I can see through you ; (ইতর ভাষায়) তুমি কি স্বচ্ছ পদার্থ ? (কোন ব্যক্তির সম্মুখে অপর ব্যক্তি দাঁড়াইয়া দৃষ্টিরোধ করিলে এই বাক্য ব্যবহৃত হয়।)

glāz'-ing, *n.* **1.** The act or art of setting glass ; the art of covering with a vitreous substance ; কাচসন্নিবেশ, কাচসন্নিবেশ শিল্প ; কাচের সূক্ষ্ম স্তর দ্বারা আচ্ছাদন। **2.** Windows ; বাতায়নশ্রেণী, গবাক্ষ-পংক্তি। **3.** A substance used to produce glaze ; বর্ণক।

gleam (glēm), *v. i., t. & n.* To glow ; to shine rather faintly ; to flash ; উজ্জ্বল হওয়া ; দীপ্তি পাওয়া ; আলোক স্ফুরণ হওয়া, স্ফুরিত হওয়া, চমকান। ***Verb t.*** To shoot out as flashes of light ; স্ফুরিত করা। ***Noun.*** A transient or subdued light ; moderate brightness ; a beam ; a glimpse ; as, a *gleam* of humour or hope ; ক্ষণিক আলোক ; মৃদু আলোক ; দীপ্তি, ভাতি, দ্যুতি ; রশ্মি, কিরণ ; আলোকস্ফুরণ, চমক। **Gleam'-y,** *adj.* Casting beams or rays of light ; flashing ; আলোক রশ্মিবর্ষী, কিরণ বিকিরণকারী ; স্ফুরৎ ;

glean (glēn), *v. i. & t.* **1.** To gather ears of corn left by reapers ; শস্য কাটিয়া গেলে পর ক্ষেত্রে যাহা কিছু অবশিষ্ট থাকে তাহা খুঁটিয়া লওয়া। **2.** To pick up or gather from various sources or with difficulty ; নানা স্থান হইতে বা কষ্টে সংগ্রহ করা। ***Verb t.*** **1.** To collect as ears of corn left by reapers ; উঞ্ছবৃত্তির অনুসরণ করা। **2.** To gather slowly and assiduously ; to scrape together ; as, a few examples have been *gleaned* from mediaeval chronicles ; আস্তে আস্তে শ্রমসহকারে সংগ্রহ করা ; অল্পে অল্পে সংগ্রহ করা। **Glean'-er,** *n.* **Glean'-ing,** *n.* The act of gathering after reaping ; (*usu. pl.*) that which is gleaned ; উঞ্ছবৃত্তির অনুসরণ, উঞ্ছন, উঞ্ছন ; শীলতা ; উঞ্ছবৃত্তি দ্বারা লব্ধ বস্তু, অতি কষ্টে ও পরিশ্রমের ফলে নানা স্থান হইতে সংগৃহীত বস্তু।

glebe (glēb), *n.* **1.** (*Poet.*) Soil ; ground ; (কবিতায়) মৃত্তিকা ; ভূমি । **2.** The land belonging to a parish church or ecclesiastical benefice ; গ্রাম্য গির্জ্জার অধিকৃত ভূসম্পত্তি, যাজকোত্তর ভূমি ।

glee (glē), *n.* **1.** Joy ; mirth ; gaiety ; হর্ষ, উল্লাস ; আমোদ, আহ্লাদ ; হাসি তামাসা, আমোদপ্রমোদ । **2.** (*Mus.*) A musical composition for voices in three or more parts ; (সঙ্গীত-শাস্ত্র) বিভিন্ন অংশে বিভক্ত সঙ্গীত বা বিভিন্ন গায়ক দ্বারা পর্য্যায়ক্রমে গেয় সঙ্গীত, পর্য্যায়-সঙ্গীত । **Glee'-ful, Glee'-some,** *adjs.* **Glee'-ful-ly,** *adv.* **Glee club** — পর্য্যায়-সঙ্গীত সম্প্রদায় । **Glee-man**—A minstrel ; চারণ, বন্দী ।

gleet (glēt), *n.* (*Med.*) A transparent mucous discharge from the urethra—an effect of gonorrhea ; (ভৈষজ্য-শাস্ত্র) প্রমেহের পুরাতন অবস্থায় জ্বালা যন্ত্রণা ব্যতিরেকে অল্প অল্প স্রাব-নিঃসরণ, লালামেহ (হঃ চঃ), শুক্রমেহ । **Gleet'-y,** *adj.*

glĕn, *n.* A secluded narrow valley ; a depression between hills ; সংকীর্ণ নির্জ্জন উপত্যকা ; পর্ব্বতদ্বয়ের মধ্যস্থ নিম্নভূমি ।

Glendoveer, *n.* In Southey's *Kehama,* one of a race of beautiful sprites, (as occurring in Hindu myths) ; দেবযোনি-বিশেষ (Prob. গন্ধর্ব্ব) ।

glē'-noid (-noyd), *adj.* (*Anat.*) Having the form of a smooth and shallow depression ; (শারীর-সংস্থান বিদ্যা) মসৃণ এবং স্বল্পায়ত কোটরাকৃতি । **Glenoid cavity, fossa, surface** — (শারীর সংস্থান-বিদ্যা) যে অস্থি-গহ্বরে অন্য অস্থির মস্তক প্রবিষ্ট থাকে ।

glib, *adj.* & *adv.* **1.** (*Rare*) Smooth ; slippery ; unimpeded, as movement etc. ; (অপ্রঃ) মসৃণ ; পিচ্ছিল ; সহজ, অনায়াস, স্বচ্ছন্দ, অবাধ । **2.** Fluent ; as, a *glib* tongue ; voluble ; বাক্পটু, অনর্গল ; দ্রুতভাষী, তড়্বড়ে, ফর্ফরে, চপলজিহ্ব (কেভিঃ), চপল-বাক্, বাক্চপল । ***Adv.*** (*Rare*) Volubly ; গল্ গল্ করিয়া । **Glib'-ly,** *adv.* In a glib manner ; volubly ; অনায়াসে, অনর্গলভাবে ; গল্ গল্ করিয়া । **Glib'-ness,** *n.*

glīde, *v.i., t.* & *n.* **1.** To move gently and smoothly ; as, a bird *glides* through the air : a skater *glides* over ice ; to pass gently and imperceptibly, as time etc. ; অনায়াসে চলা, সহজে চলা, মসৃণ ভূমির উপর পিছ্লাইয়া যাওয়া ; মৃদুমন্দ গতিতে অগ্রসর হওয়া, বহিয়া যাওয়া, প্রবাহিত হওয়া, চলিয়া যাওয়া । **2.** To go quietly and stealthily ; as, the cat *glides* through the bushes ; চুপি চুপি চোরের মত যাওয়া । **3.** To pass gradually or insensibly (*into*) ; (*Phon.*) To pass with a glide, as voice etc. ; কাটিয়া যাওয়া, বহিয়া যাওয়া ; (ধ্বনিশাস্ত্র) শব্দাদি অনায়াসে চলিয়া যাওয়া । ***Verb t.*** To cause to glide ; as, light airs *glided* her on her course ; অনায়াসে চালিত করা । ***Noun.*** **1.** Act of gliding ; a sliding movement ; অনায়াসে প্রবহণ ; অনায়াসগতি, লীলাপ্রবাহ, লীলাগতি । **2.** (*Phon.*) The joining of two sounds without a break ; (শব্দ-যন্ত্র) নিরবচ্ছিন্নভাবে ধ্বনিদ্বয়ের সংযোগ । **Glid'-ing-ly,** *adv.*

glim, *n.* (*Slang*) A light ; a candle ; (ইতর ভাষায়) আলো ; বাতি । **To douse the glim**—To put out the light ; আলো নিবান ।

glĭm'-mêr, *v. i.* & *n.* To shine faintly ; to flicker ; মন্দ মন্দ দীপ্তি পাওয়া, ক্ষীণালোক বিকীর্ণ করা ; মিট্ মিট্ করা, টিম্‌টিম্ করা । ***Noun.*** **1.** A feeble scattered ray of light ; a gleam, as of hope ; ক্ষীণালোক, মৃদুভাতি, মন্দদীপ্তি, আভা, মন্দপ্রভা, মন্দদ্যুতি, টিম্‌টিম্ আলো ; আশার আলোক । **2.** A glimpse or half view ; ঈষদ্দর্শন (কেভিঃ) । **3.** An inkling ; আভাস, টের, নামগন্ধ । **—ing,** *n.* **—ing-ly,** *adv.* **Glimmer-gowk**—An owl ; পেচক ।

glimpse (glĭmps), *n., v. i.* & *t.* **1.** A sudden flash ; transient lustre ; স্ফুরণ ; চমক । **2.** A short transitory view ; "Last year I caught a *glimpse* of his face" ; ক্ষণিকদৃষ্টি, ঈষদ্দৃষ্টি, ঈষদ্দর্শন ; ক্ষণদৃষ্টি, মুহূর্ত্তদর্শন । ***Verb i.*** (*Poet.*) To appear faintly or by glimpses ; (কবিতায়) স্ফুরিত হওয়া, চমকান । ***Verb t.*** To catch a glimpse of ; to see by glimpses ; হঠাৎ একবার দেখিতে পাওয়া ; কোন কিছুর ক্ষণিক দর্শন লাভ করা । **Glimpses of the moon** — The earth by night ; sublunary affairs ; নৈশ পৃথিবী ; পার্থিব ব্যাপার । **To catch a glimpse of**—To take a hurried view of ; ক্ষণেকের জন্য দর্শন করা ।

glint, *n., v. i.* & *t.* A glance ; a glimpse ; a gleam ; a flash ; কটাক্ষ ; ক্ষণিক দৃষ্টি ; মন্দদ্যুতি ; চমক । ***Verb i.*** To glance ; to shine ; to glitter ; কটাক্ষক্ষেপ করা, দৃষ্টি হানা ; দীপ্তি পাওয়া ; ঝক্‌মক্ করা । ***Verb t.*** To cause to flash ; to reflect as light ; চমকান ; প্রতিফলিত করা ।

glis-sade' (-ād), *n.* & *v. i.* A sliding, as down a snow slope ; পিছলান, সংসর্পণ । ***Verb i.*** To slide, as in mountaineering ; পিছলাইয়া পড়া ।

glist, *v. i.* & *n.* To glisten ; ঝক্‌মক্ করা । ***Noun.*** (*Rare*) A gleam ; আভা, দীপ্তি ।

glis'-ten (-n), *v. i.* & *n.* To shine with a fitful lustre ; to sparkle ; to glitter ; as, the *glistening* stars ; ঝল্‌মল্ করা ; ঝিক-মিক করা, চক্ চক্ করা ; চিক্‌মিক্ করা ।

glis'-têr, *v. i.* & *n.* (*Archaic*) To glisten ; to shine ; to glitter ; (অপ্রঃ) ঝক্‌ঝক্ করা ; দীপ্তি পাওয়া ; চক্‌চক্ করা, ঝিক্‌মিক্ করা । ***Noun.***

(*Archaic*) Glitter ; lustre ; দীপ্তি ; উজ্জ্বলতা।

glit′-tēr, *v. i., t.* & *n.* **1.** To sparkle with light ; to glisten ; to gleam ; as, a *glittering* sword ; চকমক্ করা ; ঝলমল করা ; চকচক করা, ঝক্ঝক্ করা। **2.** To be splendid ; as, the *glittering* scenes of the court ; জমকালো হওয়া। ***Noun.*** A bright sparkling light ; brightness ; brilliancy ; lustre ; ঝলমল আলো ; ঔজ্জ্বল্য ; দীপ্তি ; প্রভা। **—ing**, *adj.* Shining with a sparkling light ; আলোঝলমল (গীতাঞ্জঃ), ঝলঝলায়মান, স্ফুরৎপ্রভাময়। **—ing-ly**, *adv.* **All that glitters is not gold**—চকচক্ করিলেই সোণা হয় না, ঝিনুক মাত্রেই কি মুক্তা থাকে? শৈলে শৈলে ন মাণিক্যং।

gloam′-ing (glōm-), *n.* Twilight of the evening ; dusk ; প্রদোসকাল; গোধূলিবেলা, রজনীমুখ।

gloat (glōt), *v. i.* To look steadfastly ; to gaze with passionate desire, lust, avarice or ill-will, (with *on, upon* or *over*) ; একদৃষ্টিতে চাহিয়া থাকা ; লালসাপূর্ণ নেত্রে দৃষ্টিপাত করা, সতৃষ্ণ নয়নে দৃষ্টিপাত করা। **Gloat′-ing-ly**, *adv.*

glōbe, *n., v. t.* & *i.* **1.** A round or spherical body ; বর্ত্তুল, গোলক, পরিমণ্ডল, গোল। **2.** Anything spherical or globular in shape ; as, the *globe* of the eye ; মণ্ডল (সাঃ পঃ)। **3.** (With *the* prefixed) The Earth ; ধরণীমণ্ডল, ইলা (সাঃ পঃ), গোল (ঐ), ভূগোল (কেণ্ডিঃ), ভূমণ্ডল (ঐ)। **4.** One of the celestial bodies ; খগোল (কেণ্ডিঃ), আকাশমণ্ডল (ঐ)। **5.** A spherical representation of the earth or heavens ; as, a celestial *globe* ; ভূমণ্ডলের গোলাকার আদর্শ। **6.** A golden orb, as an emblem of sovereignty ; রাজচিহ্নস্বরূপ হিরণ্ময় গোলক। ***Verb t. & i.*** To make or become globular ; গোলাকার করা, গোলাকৃতি হওয়া। **Glo′-boid**, *adj.* & *n.* Approximately globular ; গোলপ্রায়। (*Noun*) A globoid figure ; গোলাভাস। **Glo′-bose**, *adj.*

Globe-fish.

Glo-bos′-i-ty, *n.* **Globe-fish**—গোলাকার সামুদ্রিক মৎস্যবিশেষ — এই মৎস্য ইচ্ছানুসারে দেহ গোলাকৃতি করিতে পারে। **Globe-flower** — পীতবর্ণ গোলাকার পুষ্পপ্রসূ ইয়ুরোপীয় বৃক্ষবিশেষ। **Globe-lightning**—Fire-ball ; শত্রু-সৈন্যের উপর নিক্ষেপার্থ দাহ্যপদার্থপূর্ণ গোলক। **Globe-trotter**—ভূ-প্রদক্ষিণকারী, ভূপর্য্যটক, পৃথিবী ভ্রমণকারী। **Globe trotting**—ভূপর্য্যটন, পৃথিবীভ্রমণ, ভূ-প্রদক্ষিণ।

glŏb′-ū-lar (-lēr), *adj.* **1.** Spherical ; round ; বর্ত্তুলাকার, গোলাকার ; মণ্ডলাকার। **2.** Composed of globules ; গুলিকারচিত। **—lar′-i-ty**, *n.* **—ly**, *adv.*

glŏb′-ūle, —ū-lĕt, *ns.* **1.** A little ball or round particle ; বর্ত্তুল, গুলিকা। **2.** A small pill or pillule, such as is used in Homeopathy ; বটিকা, সর্ষপপ্রমাণ ক্ষুদ্র বটিকা। **3.** (*Biol.*) A blood corpuscle etc. ; (জীব-বিজ্ঞান) রক্তকণিকা প্রভৃতি।

glŏb′-ū-lin, *n.* The main ingredient of blood globules and resembling albumen ; রক্তকণিকার অম্লালাবৎ প্রধান উপাদান।

glŏm′-ēr-āte, *adj.* (*Bot.* & *anat.*) Growing in rounded or massive forms ; conglomerate (উদ্ভিদ্ ও শারীরসংস্থান বিদ্যা) বর্ত্তুলাকারে বৃদ্ধিশীল ; পিণ্ডীভূত।

glŏm′-ēr-ūle, *n.* (*Bot.*) **1.** A clustered head of flowers ; (উদ্ভিদ্-বিদ্যা) গুচ্ছিতপুষ্প নিবিড়গুচ্ছ (সাঃ পঃ)। **2.** A cluster of small organisms, animal tissues etc. ; জীবদেহস্থ বিধানতন্ত প্রভৃতির গুচ্ছ।

glōōm, *n.* **1.** Partial or total darkness ; obscurity ; as, the *gloom* of midnight ; (আংশিক বা সম্পূর্ণ) অন্ধকার, তিমির, নিবিড় ছায়া, তমঃ, তমিস্র, ধ্বান্ত, তমস ; অস্পষ্টতা, ম্লানালোক। **2.** Heaviness of mind ; melancholy ; "The uncertainty of morrow casts a *gloom* upon him" ; dullness ; বিমর্ষতা ; বিষাদ, নিরানন্দ ; স্ফূর্ত্তিহীনতা।

glōōm, *v. i.* & *t.* **1.** To look sullen ; to frown ; to scowl ; to look dejected ; as, he was *gloomy* over her daughter's prolonged absence ; মুখ ভার করিয়া থাকা, বিষণ্ণ দেখান ; রোষকটাক্ষপাত করা, চোক পাকান, ভ্রূভঙ্গী করা ; বিমর্ষ দেখান। **2.** (Of sky etc.) To be cloudy, dark etc. ; to be threatening ; মেঘাচ্ছন্ন হওয়া, অন্ধকার হওয়া ; ভীতিপ্রদ হওয়া। **3.** To appear dimly ; অস্পষ্টভাবে দেখান। ***Verb t.*** **1.** To render dark ; to darken ; অন্ধকারময় করা ; অন্ধকারাচ্ছন্ন করা, তমসাবৃত করা। **2.** (*Fig.*) To make sullen or melancholy ; (লক্ষণায়) বিষণ্ণ করা, বিরস করা, নিরানন্দ করা, বিষাদমলিন করা।

glōōm′-ȳ, *adj.* **1.** Dark ; imperfectly lighted ; dusky ; dim ; অন্ধকার ; অনুজ্জ্বল ; ধূসর ; নিষ্প্রভ, মন্দ। **2.** (Of persons and their attributes) Sad ; melancholy ; dejected ; দুঃখিত ; বিষণ্ণ ; ভগ্নোৎসাহ, বিরস। **3.** Dismal ; disheartening ; "In *gloomy* reflections" ; নিরানন্দজনক ; নিরুৎসাহকর, নৈরাশ্যজনক। **—i-ly**, *adv.* **—i-ness**, *n.*

glō′-ri-ă, *n.* A doxology ; স্তোত্র, স্তব। **Gloria in excelsis**—(The greater Doxology) Glory be to God on high ; হে স্বর্গস্থ পরমেশ্বর, তোমার জয় হউক। **Gloria patri**—(The lesser Doxology) Glory be to the Father, the Son and Holy Ghost ; পিতা, পুত্র ও পবিত্রাত্মার জয়।

glō'-ri-fȳ, *v. t.* 1. To make glorious ; to elevate to celestial glory ; "Jesus was not yet *glorified*" ; মহিমান্বিত করা, গৌরবান্বিত করা ; স্বর্গীয় মহিমায় মণ্ডিত করা, দিব্য শোভান্বিত করা। 2. To invest with radiance ; জ্যোতির্বিমণ্ডিত করা। 3. To invest as an inferior or common thing with charm or beauty ; as, to *glorify* everyday life ; সৌন্দর্য্যসমন্বিত করা, লাবণ্যোদ্ভাসিত করা। 4. To adore ; to extol ; to exalt ; আরাধনা করা ; গুণকীর্ত্তন করা ; গৌরবান্বিত করা। **—fi-ca'-tion,** *n.*

glō'-ri-ōle, *n.* An aureole ; কিরণ-কিরীট, ছটামুকুট।

glō'-ri-ous (-ŭs), *adj.* 1. Illustrious ; possessing glory ; noble ; "O *glorious* King" ; গৌরবান্বিত ; মহিমাময়, কীর্ত্তিমান, মহিমামণ্ডিত, মহীয়ান্, মহান্, প্রতাপান্বিত (কেণ্ডিঃ), তেজশালী (ঐ), প্রভান্বিত (ঐ) ; গৌরবোন্নত, গৌরবোজ্জ্বল। 2. Conferring glory ; conspicuously honourable ; গৌরবপ্রদ, গৌরবজনক ; নিরতিশয় সম্মানজনক। 3. (*Colloq.*) Extremely delightful ; magnificient ; as, a *glorious* view ; (চলিত ভাষায়) পরমানন্দপ্রদ ; জমকালো। 4. Resplendent ; bright ; as, the sky was *glorious* with stars ; সমুজ্জ্বল, সুপ্রভ ; উজ্জ্বল, জ্যোতির্ম্ময়। 5. Hilarious ; elated with drink ; হর্ষোৎফুল্ল ; সুরাপানোল্লসিত। **—ly,** *adv.*

glō'-rȳ, *n.* 1. Honourable fame ; renown ; "Paths of *glory* lead but to the grave" ; celebrity ; গৌরব, গরিমা, মহিমা, জয়শ্রী (কেণ্ডিঃ), বীরশ্রী (ঐ) ; কীর্ত্তি, প্রতিষ্ঠা (কেণ্ডিঃ) ; যশ। 2. An object of pride ; a distinguished honour or ornament etc. ; "Babylon, the glory of kingdoms" ; গৌরবের বিষয় ; গরিমা, গৌরব। 3. Adoring praise and thanksgiving ; মহিমাকীর্ত্তন, মহিমা গান। 4. The divine presence or its manifestation ; celestial honour and bliss ; ঈশ্বরের প্রকাশ বা আবির্ভাব ; স্বর্গীয় মহিমা, স্বর্গীয় আনন্দ, মোক্ষ, নির্ব্বাণ, অপবর্গ, পরমপদ। 5. Resplendent majesty, beauty or splendour ; "Jewels lose their *glory* if neglected" ; সমুজ্জ্বল মহিমা, সমুজ্জ্বলশ্রী, সমুজ্জ্বল শোভা। 6. An unearthly beauty attributed by imagination ; (লক্ষণায়) অপার্থিব সৌন্দর্য্য, স্বপ্নলোকের সৌন্দর্য্য। 7. Height of prosperity ; exaltation ; as, Spain was then at its *glory* ; সমৃদ্ধির চরমসীমা ; অভ্যুদয়। 8. A circle of light round the head or figure of a deity or saint ; a halo ; দেবতা বা সিদ্ধপুরুষগণের দেহ বা মস্তকের চতুর্দ্দিগবর্ত্তী প্রভামণ্ডল, অংশুমালা (কেণ্ডিঃ) ; দ্যুতিমণ্ডল (কৃষ্ণ কঃ), ছটামুকুট, কিরণ-কিরীট। **Glory-hole** — (ইতরভাষায়) যে কোঠা বা দেরাজে এলোমেলোভাবে জিনিষ রাখা হয়। **To go to glory**—To go to heaven ; to die ; স্বর্গপ্রাপ্ত হওয়া ; পরলোক গমন করা। **To send to glory**—(*Facet.*) To kill ; (কৌতুকচ্ছলে) বধ করা।

glō'-rȳ, *v. i.* 1. To exult with joy ; to rejoice ; আনন্দমত্ত হওয়া ; হর্ষোৎফুল্ল হওয়া। 2. To be proud ; কোন বিষয়ে গর্ব্বিত হওয়া (প্রায়শঃ ভাল অর্থে ব্যবহৃত)। **—ing-ly,** *adv.*

glŏss, *n.* & *v. t.* 1. Lustre, as from a polished surface ; polish ; (মসৃণ পদার্থাদির) উজ্জ্বলতা ; চাকচিক্য। 2. Fair outside ; "Till the *gloss* of novelty is worn away" ; বাহ্যচাক্‌চিক্য, চটক, জলুষ, জিল্লা, চিক্‌নাই, ঝলক, চমক। ***Verb t.*** 1. To give a superficial lustre to ; to make smooth and shining ; বাহ্যচাকচিক্য সম্পাদন করা ; চকচকে করা, জিল্লা দেওয়া। 2. To give a specious appearance to ; "You have the art to *gloss* the foulest cause" ; আপাতরম্য করা, আপাতশোভন করা। **Gloss'-i-ly,** *adv.* **Gloss'-i-ness,** *n.* **Gloss'-y** *adj.* 1. Smooth and shining ; lustrous ; চক্‌চকে, চিক্কণ (cf. চিক্কণ কালা) ; চিক্কণ, চমকদার, জিল্লাদার। 2. Specious ; plausible ; আপাতরম্য ; আপাতশোভন।

glŏss, *n.*, *v. t.* & *i.* 1. An interlinear or marginal note ; a comment ; an interpretation or commentary ; paraphrase ; টীকা ; টিপ্পনী, ভাষ্য ; বার্ত্তিক ; ব্যাখ্যা। 2. A false or specious explanation ; misrepresentation ; মিথ্যা ব্যাখ্যা, আপাতমনোরম ব্যাখ্যা ; মিথ্যা বর্ণন। 3. A glossary ; নিঘণ্ট। ***Verb i.*** 1. To write glosses ; টীকা রচনা করা, বার্ত্তিক প্রণয়ন করা, ভাষ্য রচনা করা। 2. To make unfavourable comments ; প্রতিকূল মন্তব্য প্রকাশ করা, টিপ্পনী কাটা, টিপ্‌নী কাটা। ***Verb t.*** 1. To insert glosses in (texts etc.) ; to explain ; to illustrate ; টীকা সন্নিবেশ করা ; ব্যাখ্যা করা ; চিত্র, দৃষ্টান্ত প্রভৃতি দ্বারা ব্যাখ্যা করা। 2. To explain away ; "To *gloss* the truth" ; এক রকম করিয়া গোঁজা মিল দিয়া বুঝাইয়া দেওয়া।

glŏs'-săl, *adj.* (*Anat.*) Of, or pertaining to, the tongue ; (শারীরসংস্থান-বিদ্যা) জিহ্বা-সম্বন্ধীয়।

glŏs'-sa-rȳ (-ă-), *n.* A collection of glosses ; a vocabulary explaining antiquated or difficult words or phrases ; টীকা-সংগ্রহ ; অপ্রচলিত, প্রাদেশিক বা বৈজ্ঞানিক শব্দ সমূহের অভিধান, পরিভাষা, নির্ঘণ্ট, অনুক্রমণিকা, অপ্রসিদ্ধ শব্দ-কোষ (কেণ্ডিঃ), কূটার্থশব্দ-কোষ (ঐ), গূঢ় শব্দার্থবোধিনী (ঐ)। **—rist,** *n.* A writer of a gloss or glossary ; টীকাকার, বার্ত্তিককার, ভাষ্যকার। **—sa'-ri-al,** *adj.* **—sa'-tor,** *n.* A commentator, esp. mediaeval one ; টীকাকার।

glŏs-sī′-tis, *n.* Inflammation of the tongue ; রসনাপ্রদাহ, রসনার স্ফীতি, জিহ্বাপ্রদাহ (জাহিঃ), অলাস (সাঃ পঃ)।

glŏs-sŏg′-ră-phêr, *n.* A writer of glosses ; a commentator ; টীকাকার; ভাষ্যকার, বার্তিককার। **–phy,** *n.*

glŏs-sol′-ŏ-ġȳ (-ŏl-), *n.* Terminology ; পরিভাষা।

glŏt′-tis (-ĭs), *n.* The narrow opening at the upper part of the windpipe ; স্বরযন্ত্রের উপরিভাগের অপ্রশস্ত রন্ধ্র, স্বরযন্ত্রমুখ, কণ্ঠনালী, শ্বাসমার্গ (কেণ্ডিঃ)। **–tal, –tic,** *adjs.*

glŏt-tol′-ŏ-ġȳ (-ŏl-), *n.* The science of languages ; comparative philology ; ভাষাবিজ্ঞান ; তুলনামূলক ভাষাতত্ত্ব। **–gist,** *n.* **–to-log′-ic, –to-log′-i-cal,** *adjs.*

Glouces′-têr (glŏs-), *n.* A cheese made in Gloucestershire ; গ্লষ্টারসায়ার নামক স্থানে প্রস্তুত পনীর বিশেষ।

glove (glŭv), *n.* & *v. t.* **1.** A cover for the hand with a separate sheath for each finger ; করত্রাণ, অঙ্গুলীত্র, দস্তানা। **2.** A boxing glove ; মুষ্টিযোদ্ধার দস্তানা। ***Verb t.*** **1.** To cover with, or as with, a glove ; দস্তানা দ্বারা আবৃত করা, দস্তানার স্থায় আবৃত করা। **Gloved,** *adj.* Covered with a glove ; দস্তানা দ্বারা আবৃত। **Glov′-er,** *n.* One who trades in, or sells, gloves ; দস্তানা-ব্যবসায়ী, দস্তানা-বিক্রেতা। **Glove′-less,** *adj.* **Boxing glove**—মুষ্টিযোদ্ধার দস্তানা। **Glove fight**—যে মুষ্টিযুদ্ধে হস্ত দস্তানা দ্বারা আবৃত করা হয়। **Glove-sponge**—দস্তানার আকার স্পঞ্জ-বিশেষ। **Glove-stretcher** দস্তানার অঙ্গুলী বিস্তার করার জন্য যন্ত্র-বিশেষ। **Glove-silver, Glove-money**—বখসিস্। **To be hand and glove with**—To be on intimate terms with ; কাহারও সহিত হরিহর আত্মা হওয়া। **To bite one's gloves**—To be resolved on mortal revenge ; ভীষণ প্রতিহিংসা সাধনে কৃতসংকল্প হওয়া। **To fit like a glove**—To fit exactly ; ঠিক লাগা। **To handle without gloves**—To treat without reserve or tenderness ; to deal roughly with ; কঠোর ব্যবহার করা ; কর্কশ ব্যবহার করা। **To put on** or **wear gloves**—To attack an opponent mildly ; শত্রুকে মৃদুভাবে আক্রমণ করা। **To take up the glove**—To accept a challenge ; যুদ্ধের আহ্বান গ্রহণ করা। **To throw down the glove**—To challenge to combat ; যুদ্ধে আহ্বান করা।

glow (glō), *v. i.* & *n.* **1.** To shine with an intense or white heat ; অত্যুত্তাপে শ্বেতবর্ণ হইয়া জ্বলা, তাপোজ্জ্বল হওয়া। **2.** To exhibit a strong bright colour ; to be flushed with heat or animation ; তীব্রোজ্জ্বল বর্ণ প্রদর্শন করা ; উত্তাপ বা উত্তেজনা হেতু অরুণ বর্ণ ধারণ করা। **3.** To feel great heat or passion ; to be animated ; as, the heart *glows* with love, zeal, or patriotism ; উদ্দীপ্ত হওয়া, উত্তেজিত হওয়া ; অনুপ্রাণিত হওয়া। **4.** To burn with bodily heat ; দৈহিক তাপে দগ্ধ হওয়া। ***Noun.*** **1.** A glowing state ; as, the *glow* of a sunset sky ; জ্বালা, দীপ্তি, বিভা, দ্যুতি, তাপদীপন, তাপোজ্জ্বলতা। **2.** Brightness of colour ; as, the *glow* of health in the cheeks ; ঔজ্জ্বল্য, রক্তিমাভা, গোলাপি বিভা, অরুণিমা, রাগ। **3.** Intense excitement ; animation ; vehemence ; ardour ; passion ; তীব্রোত্তেজনা ; সজীবতা, তেজস্বিতা ; প্রচণ্ডতা ; জ্বলন্ত আগ্রহ ; চিত্তক্ষোভ, চিত্তবেগ, অনুরাগ। **4.** Heat of body ; দৈহিক তাপ, শারীরিক উত্তাপ। **Glow′-ing,** *p. adj.* **1.** Shining with intense light ; প্রদীপ্ত, সমুজ্জ্বল, দীপ্তিমান (কেণ্ডিঃ), দেদীপ্যমান (ঐ), তাপশুভ্র। **2.** Ardent ; fervent ; fiery ; জ্বলন্ত আগ্রহপূর্ণ ; প্রচণ্ড ; জ্বলন্ত, অগ্নিদীপ্ত (কেণ্ডিঃ)। **Glow′-ing-ly,** *adv.* **Glow-lamp**—An incandescent lamp ; বিজলী বাতি, শ্বেততেজদীপ (হিঃ কোঃ), শিখাহীন দীপ (ঐ)। **Glow-worm**—খদ্যোত, খদ্যোতিকা, জ্যোতিরিঙ্গণ, প্রভাকীট, কীটমণি। **In a glow, All of a glow** — Hot or flushed ; উষ্ণ, লজ্জাদিবশতঃ অরুণিত, রোষকষায়িত।

glow′-êr, *v. i.* To stare ; to look angrily, (with *at*) ; একদৃষ্টে চাহিয়া থাকা ; রোষকষায়িত নেত্রে দৃষ্টিপাত করা।

glŏx in′-i-ă, *n.* A genus of tropical American plant with ball-shaped flowers ; আমেরিকার উষ্ণমণ্ডলজাত ঘণ্টাকৃতি পুষ্পপ্রদ গুল্ম-শ্রেণী বিশেষ।

glōze, *v. i.* & *t.* **1.** (*Archaic*) To comment (*upon* or *on*) ; টীকা করা। **2.** To talk smoothly ; to flatter ; to fawn ; প্রিয়বাক্য বলা ; তোষামোদ করা ; হীনতোষামোদ করা, পা চাটা। **3.** To give a specious meaning ; আপাতযুক্তিপূর্ণ অর্থ করা। ***Verb t.*** **1.** To explain away ; to palliate ; (frequently with *over*) ; "To *gloze over* the sin" ; এক রকম করিয়া গোঁজামিল দিয়া বুঝাইয়া দেওয়া ; দোষ প্রশমন করা, দোষ ঢাকা। **2.** To flatter ; তোষামোদ করা। **Gloz′-ing-ly,** *adv.*

glū-cĭ′-nŭm, *n.* A metallic element resembling magnesium ; একপ্রকার ধাতব মূলপদার্থ।

glū′-cose (-kōs), *n.* **1.** (*Chem.*) Grape sugar ; (রসায়ন-শাস্ত্র) দ্রাক্ষাফলজাত শর্করা, দ্রাক্ষশর্করা। **–co′-sic, –co-side,** *adjs.*

glue (glū), *n.* & *v. t.* **1.** A sticky substance obtained by boiling skins, horns, hoofs, etc. with water ; শিরিষ। **2.** A gum-like cement or sticky substance ; শিরিষের মত বিলাতি মাটী বা আঠা। ***Verb t.*** **1.** To join with glue or viscous substance ; আঠা দিয়া জোড়া দেওয়া। **2.** To attach lightly or closely; "Ear *glued* to the key-hole"; আঁটসাট করিয়া লাগান। **Glu'-ey,** *adj.* Like glue; sticky; viscous; শিরীষবৎ; আঠাল; চট্চটে। **Glue-pot**—A vessel for melting glue; শিরিষ গালাইবার জন্য পাত্র বিশেষ।

glŭm, *adj.* Frowning; sullen; gloomy; dejected; ভ্রূকুটিকুটিল; মুখভার, মলিনমুখ (কেণ্ডিঃ), খিন্ন-বদন (ঐ), অপ্রসন্ন; বিষাদকালিমাচ্ছন্ন; বিমর্ষভাবাপন্ন, নিরানন্দ, বিরস। **Glum'-ly,** *adv.* **Glum'-ness,** *n.*

glūme, *n.* (*Bot.*) The husk or chaff of grain; a bract of plants, such as grasses and sedges; তুষ, তুষপত্র (সাঃ পঃ); উপতুষ (ঐ)। **Glu-ma'-ceous, –glu'-mose.** *adjs.* Bearing glumes; তুষপত্রযুক্ত।

glŭt, *v. t.* & *n.* **1.** To feed to repletion; "Is this your fate to *glut* the dogs with gore"; to overload with food, (*lit.* & *fig.*); to satiate; উদরপূর্ণ করিয়া খাওয়ান; আকণ্ঠভোজন করান; সন্তৃপ্ত করা, পরিতৃপ্ত করান। **2.** To fill to excess; অতিরিক্ত মাত্রায় পূর্ণ করা। **3.** To overstock with mercantile goods; as, to *glut* a market; কোন জিনিষ অতিরিক্ত পরিমাণে আমদানী করিয়া বাজার পূর্ণ করিয়া ফেলা। ***Noun.*** **1.** One's fill; surfeit; plenty to satiety or loathing; আকণ্ঠভোজন; পূর্ণ পরিতৃপ্তি; পরিতৃপ্তি বা বিতৃষ্ণাজনক প্রাচুর্য্য। **2.** A full supply; hence, a supply beyond demand; as, a *glut* in the market; পূর্ণ পরিমাণে সরবরাহ; চাহিদার অধিক সরবরাহ। **To glut the market**—To furnish an over-supply of any article of trade, so that there is no sale for it; প্রয়োজনাতিরিক্ত মাল দ্বারা বাজার পূর্ণ করা।

glū'-tĕn, *n.* **1.** An adhesive substance, as gum or glue; আঠা। **2.** A sticky nitrogenous substance found in the flour of wheat etc.; গোধূম প্রভৃতির যবক্ষারজান বিশিষ্ট অংশ—যাহা জলে দ্রব হয় না। **3.** A viscid animal secretion; জন্তুদেহের আঠালো স্রাব। **–ti-nize,** *v. t.* To make viscous or gluey; আঠালো করা, চট্চটে করা। **–ti-nos'-i-ty,** *n.* **–ti-nous,** *adj.* **–ti-nous-ly,** *adv.*

glŭt'-ton (-n), **1.** One who eats to excess; a gormandizer; অতি-ভোজনকারী, অতিভোক্তা; ঔদরিক ব্যক্তি, বহুভোজী ব্যক্তি, মহাশন, বহুভুক্ (বৃঃ সং), উদরপিশাচ (কেণ্ডিঃ), রাক্ষস (ঐ), উদরম্ভরি (ঐ)। **2.** One who is excessively fond of an object or pursuit, esp. a glutton of books; কোন বিষয়ের অনুসরণে অতিরিক্ত অনুরাগী ব্যক্তি। **3.** A carnivorous quadruped, $2\frac{1}{2}$ ft. long, inhabiting N. Europe and America; ইয়ুরোপের উত্তরাংশ ও আমেরিকার মাংসাশী জন্তু-বিশেষ। **–ize,** *v. i.* To eat to excess; আকণ্ঠ ভোজন করা, অতিরিক্ত ভোজন করা। **–ous,** *adj.* Given to gluttony; eating to excess; voracious; উদরপরায়ণ, ঔদরিক; উদরপ্রধান, অমিতভোজী; বহ্বাশী (কেণ্ডিঃ), বহুভোজী, অত্যাশী। **–ous-ly,** *adv.* **–y,** *n.* Excess in eating; voracity; অতিভোজন, অত্যাশন, অত্যাহার; ঔদরিকতা, উদরসেবা, পেট-পূজা।

glȳ-cĕr'-ic, *adj.* (*Chem.*) Pertaining to, or derived from glycerine; (রসায়ন-শাস্ত্র) গ্লিসিরিণ-সম্পর্কীয়, গ্লিসিরিণ হইতে জাত।

glȳc'-ĕr-in, –ine (-ĭn), *n.* An oily colourless viscid liquid with a hot sweetish taste; চর্ব্বি হইতে প্রাপ্ত একপ্রকার মিষ্ট, ঘন এবং অবর্ণ তরল পদার্থ—যাহা সাবানাদি প্রস্তুতে ব্যবহৃত হয়। ইহার বৈজ্ঞানিক নাম glycerol. **–ate, –ide,** *ns.* **–in-ate,** *v. i.* To treat with glycerine; as, *glycerinated* lymph; গ্লিসিরিণের ক্রিয়ার অধীন করা। **–ite,** *n.*

glȳc'-ĕr-ŏl, *n.* (*Chem.*) A scientific name for glycerine; (রসায়ন-শাস্ত্র) গ্লিসিরিণের বৈজ্ঞানিক নাম।

glȳ'-cō-gĕn, *n.* (*Chem.*) A substance producing sugar in animal tissues; (রসায়ন-শাস্ত্র) একপ্রকার পদার্থ,—যদ্দ্বারা জীবদেহস্থ বিধান-তন্তু সমূহে শর্করা উৎপাদিত হয়, শর্করোৎপাদক, শর্করাদ। **–gen'-e-sis,** *n.* **–gen'-ic,** *adj.* Relating to, or caused by, glycogen; শর্করোৎপাদক সম্পর্কীয়, শর্করাজনিত।

glȳ'-cŏl, *n.* A colourless thick fluid being a compound intermediate between glycerine and alcohol; গ্লিসিরিণ এবং সুরাবীর্য্যের মাঝামাঝি একপ্রকার অবর্ণ ঘন পদার্থ। **–col'-ic,** *adj.*

glȳ-cŏn'-ic, *adj.* & *n.* (Applied to a kind of verse in Greek and Latin poetry) Consisting of three feet—a spondee, a choriamb, a pyrrhic; ল্যাটিন ও গ্রীক কবিতার চরণবিশেষ সম্পর্কীয়। ***Noun.*** A glyconic verse; উক্তরূপ চরণ বিশিষ্ট কবিতা।

glȳ-cō-sū'-ri-ă, *n.* (*Pathol.*) A diseased state with sugar in the urine; (নিদানশাস্ত্র) ইক্ষুমেহ (সাঃ পঃ)। **–ric,** *adj.*

glȳph, *n.* (*Arch.*) An ornamental channel usually vertical; শোভাসাধক প্রণালিকা। **Glyph'-ic,** *adj.*

glȳph'-ō-grăph, *n., v. t.* & *i.* A plate or copy formed by the process of glyphography; তড়িন্মুদ্রণ দ্বারা গৃহীত চিত্রফলক বা প্রতিচ্ছবি। ***Verb t. & i.*** To form (plates) by glyphography; তড়িন্মুদ্রণ দ্বারা চিত্রফলক প্রস্তুত করা। **–graph'-ic,** *adj.*

glȳ-phŏg'-ră-phȳ, *n.* A process of taking a raised copy of a drawing by electrotype; তড়িন্মুদ্রণ দ্বারা বস্তুর চিত্রের প্রতিচ্ছায়া গ্রহণের জন্য প্রণালী-বিশেষ, তড়িচ্চিত্রাঙ্কণ বিদ্যা। **–pher,** *n.*

glŷp'-tic, *adj.* Of, or relating to, carving, esp. on precious stones ; তক্ষণশিল্পসম্পর্কীয়, বিশেষ মূল্যবান প্রস্তরের উপর ক্ষোদন সম্পর্কীয়। **—tics,** *n.* The art of engraving on precious stones ; মণিতক্ষণশিল্প।

glŷp'-tŏ-dŏn, *n.* A genus of large extinct mammals related

Glyptodon.

to the armadillos ; বর্ম্মধারীর অনুরূপ অধুনা-লুপ্ত বৃহৎ স্তন্যপায়ী জীব-বিশেষ।

glŷp-tŏg'-ră-phŷ, *n.* Art, or process, of gem-engraving ; মণিক্ষোদন-শিল্প, মণিক্ষোদন-প্রণালী।

gnarled (nârld), **gnarl'-ŷ** (nârl-), *adjs.* (*Lit.* & *fig.*) Full of knots ; knotty ; twisted ; rugged ; as, a *gnarled* tree ; গ্রন্থিল ; পেঁচাল ; মোচড়ান, জড়ানো ; আব্‌ড়োথাব্‌ড়ো।

gnash (năsh), *v. i.* & *t.* To strike or grind the teeth together in rage or pain ; (of teeth) to grind together ; ক্রোধে বা বেদনায় দাঁত কিড়ামড় করা ; দন্তে দন্তে ঘর্ষণ করা। ***Verb t.*** To srike or grind together as teeth ; কিড়মিড় করা, ঘর্ষণ করা, দন্ত কড়মড় করা।

gnat (nât), *n.* **1.** A small fly, the female of which bites ; মশা, মশক।

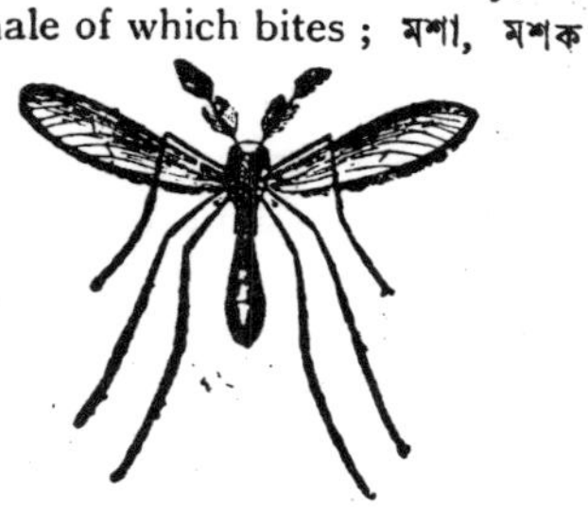

Gnat.

2. A tiny insignificant thing ; ক্ষুদ্র নগণ্য বস্তু। **A gnat strainer—** One who is scrupulous about trifles ; যে ব্যক্তি অতি সামান্য বিষয়ে সূক্ষ্মভাবে প্রণিধান করে। **To strain at**

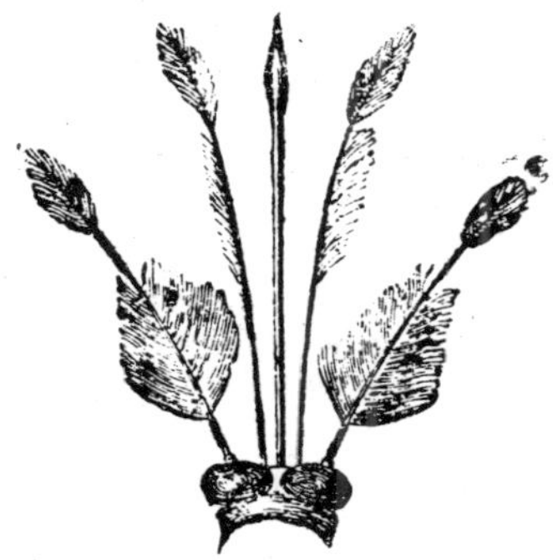

Head of gnat magnified.

a gnat (and swallow a camel)— সহরেতে ছুঁচ চলে না মফঃস্বলে হাতী চলে।

gnath'-ic (năth-), **gna'-thăl** (nă-), *adjs.* Pertaining to the jaws ; চোয়াল সম্বন্ধীয়, হনুসম্পর্কীয়। **Gna'-thism,** *n.* The classification of mankind based on the measurement of the jaw ; চোয়ালের পরিমাপ অনুসারে মানব জাতির শ্রেণীবিভাগ।

gna-thī'-tis (nă-), *n.* Inflammation of the cheek or upper jaw ; গণ্ড বা উপরের চোয়ালের প্রদাহ।

gnaw (nä), *v.t.* & *i.* **1.** To bite off little by little ; to wear or eat away by continued biting ; to wear or eat away ; as, rats *gnaw* a plank ; (*usu.* with *of*, *away*, *out*, *in two* etc.) একটু একটু করিয়া কামড়াইয়া কাটা ; দাঁত দিয়া কটু কটু করিয়া কাটা ; ক্ষয় করিয়া ফেলা। **2.** To bite in agony or rage ; ক্রোধে বা যন্ত্রণায় দংশন করা। **3.** To corrode ; to torture ; ক্রমশঃ ক্ষয় করা ; যন্ত্রণা দেওয়া। ***Verb i.*** To use the teeth in biting ; to cause steady annoying pain ; দাঁত দিয়া কামড়ান ; জ্বালাতন করা। **Gnaw'-ing-ly,** *adv.*

gneiss (nīs), *n.* (*Geol.*) A species of stratified rock composed mainly of quartz, feldspar and mica ; (ভূবিদ্যা) স্তরবিন্যস্ত প্রস্তর বিশেষ। **Gneiss'-oid, Gneiss'-ose, Gneiss'-y,** *adjs.*

gnome (nōm), *n.* A maxim ; an aphorism ; নীতিবাক্য ; সূত্র। **Gno'-mic,** *adj.* **1.** Sententious ; relating to, uttering, or containing, maxims ; সারগর্ভ ; নৈতিক, নীতিগর্ভ, সূত্রাত্মক।

gnome (nōm), *n.* **1.** A sprite guarding the inner parts of the earth and its treasures ; খনি প্রভৃতির অধিষ্ঠাতা, পাতালবাসী বালখিল্য দৈত্য বিশেষ, বামনভূত। **2.** A dwarf ; a goblin ; বামন ; ভূত, পিশাচ, প্রেত। **3.** (*U. S.*) A small owl ; (মার্কিণ যুক্তরাজ্যে) ক্ষুদ্রাকার পেচক। **Gnom'-ish,** *adj.*

gno'-mŏn (nō-), *n.* **1.** The pointer of a sundial casting a shadow which points the hour or the day ; সূর্য্যঘড়ীর শঙ্কু বা কীলক, কীল (সাঃ পঃ), কীলক (ঐ), শঙ্কু (ঐ), নর (সূঃ সিঃ)। **2.** (*Astron.*) A column etc. used in observing the sun's meridian altitude ; (জ্যোতিবিজ্ঞান) সূর্য্যের মাধ্যন্দিন উচ্চতার সীমা পর্য্যবেক্ষণের জন্য স্তম্ভ-বিশেষ। **3.** (*Geom.*) The name given to the sum of any three parts of a rectangle when divided into four parts by cross lines parallel to its sides ; কোন সমান্তরাল ক্ষেত্র হইতে উহার যে কোন কোণস্থ তৎসদৃশ অপর সমান্তরাল ক্ষেত্র বাদ দিলে যাহা অবশিষ্ট থাকে, শঙ্কুক্ষেত্র। **—mon'-ic,** *adj.* **Distance of the sun from the gnomon —** উদয়াস্তসূত্র (সাঃ পঃ)। **Midday shadow of the gnomon on the equinoxes—**বিষুবচ্ছায়া (সাঃ পঃ), পলভা (ঐ), অক্ষভা (ঐ)। **Shadows of the gnomon –** শঙ্কুচ্ছায়া (সাঃ পঃ)।

gno'-sis (nō-), *n.* The knowledge of spiritual mysteries ; mystical knowledge ; Gnosticism ; আধ্যাত্মবিদ্যা, গুপ্তবিদ্যা, রহস্যবিদ্যা ; জ্ঞানপথ (হিঃ কোঃ), জ্ঞানমার্গ (ঐ) ;

প্রাচীন তাত্ত্বিক খৃষ্টিয়ান সম্প্রদায় বিশেষের মত, খৃষ্টীয় তত্ত্ববিদ্যা। **–si-ol′-o-gy,** *n.* জ্ঞান-শাস্ত্র।

gnos′-tic (nŏs-), *n.* & *adj.* One of a sect in the beginning of the Christian era which maintained that knowledge and not faith was the way to salvation and represented individual life as the result of a process of emanation from the original essence; খৃষ্টীয় প্রথম শতাব্দীর ধর্ম্ম-সম্প্রদায় বিশেষ—তাঁহারা জ্ঞানমার্গকেই মুক্তির শ্রেষ্ঠ পন্থা বলিয়া গণ্য করিতেন। তাঁহাদের মতে ব্যক্তিগত মানবজীবন সেই পরম সত্তার বিকাশ প্রক্রিয়ার পরিণাম বলিয়া বিবেচিত হয়, জ্ঞানবাদী (হিঃ কোঃ)। ***Adj.*** **1.** Pertaining to the Gnostics or their belief; mystic; খৃষ্টীয় তাত্ত্বিক বা তত্ত্ববিদ্যা সম্পর্কীয়; রহস্যাত্মক। **2.** Relating to knowledge; cognitive; জ্ঞান-সম্পর্কীয়; জ্ঞানাত্মক। **3.** Possessing esoteric spiritual knowledge; অধ্যাত্মতত্ত্বজ্ঞ, অধ্যাত্মরহস্যজ্ঞ। **–ti-cism,** *n.* The doctrines or system of philosophy taught by the Gnostics; উক্ত সম্প্রদায়ের ধর্ম্ম মত বা দার্শনিক তত্ত্ব। **–ti-cize,** *v. t.* & *i.*

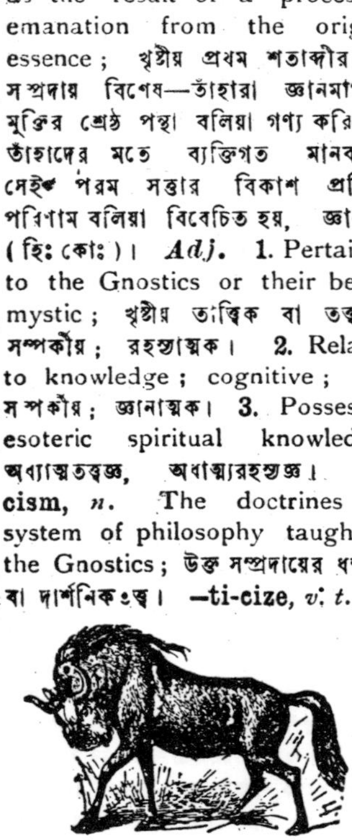

Gnu.

gnu (nü), *n.* An ox-like antelope; বৃষভাকৃতি কৃষ্ণসার বিশেষ।

gō, *v. i.* **1.** To move on; to advance or make progress; as, to *go* slowly; চলা, যাওয়া; অগ্রসর হওয়া। **2.** To depart; to start: (opposed to come); as, the mail *goes* and comes everyday; যাওয়া; যাত্রা করা। **3.** To walk or travel; ভ্রমণ করা। **4.** To be circulated; as, a good story is *going* about; to be current; to be accepted; as, sound money *goes* everywhere; প্রচারিত হওয়া; প্রচলিত হওয়া; গৃহীত হওয়া। **5.** To pass or elapse; "How *goes* the night boys?"; অতিবাহিত হওয়া, কাটা, চলা। **6.** (Of events) To turn out; "Things *go* well"; to succeed; as, the play *went* well; to fare; ফলে দাঁড়ান; সুসম্পন্ন হওয়া; ভাল বা মন্দ অবস্থায় থাকা। **7.** (Of lines etc.) To lie or point in a certain direction; (রেখাদি সম্পর্কে) কোন বিশেষ দিকে অবস্থিত হওয়া বা নির্দ্দেশ করা। **8.** To apply; as, this argument *goes* to this point only; to tend; as, it *goes* to show; to conduce; to contribute; উপযোগী হওয়া; প্রবণ হওয়া; উৎপাদন করা, সহায়তা করা; আংশিক সাহায্য করা। **9.** To take certain course or views; as, Liverpool *went* Tory; কোন মত অবলম্বন করা, কোন পক্ষ গ্রহণ করা। **10.** To be guided by; as, a good rule to *go* by; পরিচালিত হওয়া, মানিয়া চলা। **11.** To be with young; to be pregnant; গাভীন হওয়া; সসত্ত্বা হওয়া, গর্ভবতী হওয়া। **12.** To be sold; as, the thing *goes* cheap; বিক্রীত হওয়া, যাওয়া (as সস্তায় যাওয়া)। **13.** To extend or reach; to lead; প্রসারিত হওয়া, পৌঁছা; পরিচালিত করা। **14.** To run; to read; as, the second clause *goes* thus; লিখিত হওয়া; পঠিত হওয়া। **15.** To pass away; to depart for ever; to be lost or ruined; to perish; to decline; as, our trade is *going*; to die; চলিয়া যাওয়া; চির বিদায় লওয়া; নষ্ট হওয়া, ধ্বংস প্রাপ্ত হওয়া; বিনষ্ট হওয়া; মন্দা পড়া; মরা। **16.** To have recourse; to resort; as, to *go* to blows; আশ্রয় লওয়া; সাহায্য লওয়া। **17.** To give way; as, the sails *went* in the gale; ভাঙ্গিয়া পড়া। **18.** To be about to do; as, I was *going* to say; উদ্যত হওয়া। **19.** To carry action to a certain point; as, he will *go* so far as to say; অগ্রসর হওয়া। **20.** To sink; to penetrate; as, this *goes* to his heart (=grieves him); ডুবা; ভেদ করিয়া প্রবেশ করা। **21.** To admit of passing or being contained in another; as, five will not *go* into four; অতিক্রম করিয়া যাইতে পারা, অন্তর্ভুক্ত হইতে পারা। **22.** To amount together to; as, 12 inches *go* to the foot; মোটে হওয়া, সমষ্টিতে হওয়া। **23.** To attain a given limit or condition; as, to *go* to seed; to be changed or reduced; to become; as, to *go* mad; নির্দ্দিষ্ট সীমা বা অবস্থা প্রাপ্ত হওয়া; হইয়া পড়া, পরিণত হওয়া, পরিবর্ত্তিত হওয়া; হওয়া। **24.** To sound; as, a bell, clock or gun *goes*; নিনাদিত হওয়া, বাজা, আওয়াজ হওয়া। **25.** To escape as, to *go* unpunished; পরিত্রাণ পাওয়া, নিষ্কৃতি পাওয়া। **26.** To be spent (of money); ব্যয়িত হওয়া, খরচ হওয়া, লাগা, চলিয়া যাওয়া। **27.** To pass or be alloted (to a person); as, the prize *goes* to him; ভাগে পড়া, হস্তগত হওয়া। **Far gone**—Very ill; deeply entangled; অতিশয় পীড়িত; অত্যন্ত জড়িত। **Go-ahead**—Enterprising; কষ্ট-সাধ্য কার্য্যসাধনে অগ্রসর। **Go-as-you-please**—Unrestrained by regulations; উচ্ছৃঙ্খল। **Go-between**—An intermediary; মধ্যস্থ, দূত, কুটনী (কোঃ), সঙ্কারিকা, দূতী। **Go-by** — Passing; as, to give the *go-by,* (which see.) **Go-cart**—A wheeled framework for teaching infants to walk; a litter; a palanquine; a hand-cart; একপ্রকার চক্রবিশিষ্ট

কাঠাম—যাহার সাহায্যে শিশুগণ হাঁটিতে শিখিয়া থাকে ; তাঞ্জাম ; পাল্‌কী ; ঠেলা

Go-cart.

গাড়ী। **A going concern** — A prosperous business ; সমৃদ্ধ ব্যবসায়, ভাল কারবার। **As or so far as it goes**—Caution against taking a statement too widely ; যতটা গ্রহণ করা যাইতে পারে। **Going fifteen etc.**—In one's fifteenth year ; পঞ্চদশ বর্ষে। **Going ! gone !**—গেল ! গেল !! যায় ! যায় !! নিলামের ডাক শেষ হইয়া যায় ! [নিলামকারী এই শব্দ উচ্চারণ করিয়া থাকে।] **Going on for**—Approaching a time, age etc. ; কোন বিশেষ সময় বা বৎসরের কাছাকাছি। **Going strong**—Going with vigour ; সতেজে অগ্রসর। **Going to**—About to ; intending to ; উদ্যত, উন্মুখ ; ইচ্ছুক। **Gone** (also *dead and gone*)—Dead ; গতায়ু। **Gone on**—(*Slang*) Infatuated with ; (ইতর ভাষায়) কাহারও জন্য পাগল। **Go it blind**—Don't stop to deliberate অন্ধভাবে করিয়া যাও। **Go off**—Start ; as, at the first *go off* ; যাত্রা। **Go to** — (*Imperative—Archaic*) An interjection of remonstrance, incredulity, impatience, etc. ; থাম ! চুপ থাক ! **Go-to-meeting**—Such as people have on when they go to church ; respectable ; ধর্ম্মমন্দির গমনোচিত, ভজনালয় গমন সমুচিত ; ভদ্রোচিত। **Her tongue goes nineteen to the

(trade mark), ব্যবসায়ের নাম প্রভৃতিতে ব্যবহৃত হয়] *Noun.* (*U. S.*) Curled shreds of wood for stuffing ; (মার্কিন যুক্তরাজ্য) কাঠের কোমল

লাভ করিবে। **I'll go bail**—I assure you ; আমি তোমাকে নিশ্চিত বলিতেছি। **Six months gone with child**—Having spent that time in gestation ; ছয়মাস গর্ভাবস্থায় কাটাইয়াছে। **The case goes by default**—The case takes its course against the absent party ; মোকদ্দমা অনুপস্থিত পক্ষের বিরুদ্ধে যাইবে। **The song goes to a tune**—It is adaptable to a tune ; এই গানে স্বরসংযোগ করা যাইতে পারে। **They have been and gone and done it**—(*Vulg.*) They have been so foolish or unlucky as to have done it ; (ইতর ভাষায়) হায় তাহারা কি নির্ব্বোধ, কি হতভাগ্য যে এই কাজ করিয়া ফেলিল ! **Things go well (or ill) with him**—He is in prospering (or dwindling) condition ; তাহার উন্নতি (বা অবনতি) হইতেছে। **To be gone**—To take oneself off ; চলিয়া যাওয়া। **To give the go-by to**—To pass without notice ; to neglect ; to treat with intentional disregard or avoidance ; অলক্ষিতে চলিয়া যাওয়া ; অবহেলা করা ; পাশ কাটিয়া যাওয়া। **To go a-begging**—See BEGGING. **To go about**—To move from place to place ; to set to work at ; to be circulated as money, report, etc. ; to endeavour to do ; স্থানে স্থানে গমন করা, ঘুরা ফিরা করা, বেড়াইয়া বেড়ান ; কোন কাজে লাগিয়া যাওয়া ; প্রচলিত হওয়া, রেওয়াজ হওয়া ; করিতে চেষ্টা করা, করিতে প্রয়াস পাওয়া। **To go about one's business**—To attend to one's duties ; to be off ; নিজের কাজে মন দেওয়া, নিজের চরকায় তেল দেওয়া ; চলিয়া যাওয়া। **To go abroad**—To go to a foreign country ; to become public ; বিদেশে গমন করা ;

included in a general rule ; সাধারণ নিয়মের বহির্ভূত ব্যক্তি বা বস্তু। **Exception proves the rule**—The excepting of some cases

to visit as a wooer or disciple ; অনুসরণ করা ; প্রয়োগ করা ; বিদ্যার্থী বা প্রণয়প্রার্থী হইয়া অনুগমন করা। **To go against**—To resist ; to go contrary to ; to be disagreeable to ; to result unfavourably to ; বাধা দেওয়া ; বিরুদ্ধে যাওয়া ; অপ্রীতিকর হওয়া ; পরিণাম মন্দ হওয়া। **To go ahead**—To go in advance ; to make rapid progress ; অগ্রসর হওয়া ; দ্রুত উন্নতি করা। **To go all lengths**—To strive to the utmost or fullest extent ; প্রাণপণ চেষ্টা করা। **To go a long way**—To go far ; to have a great little, etc. effect : to be nearly sufficient for ; অধিক দূর অগ্রসর হওয়া ; বিশেষ ফল হওয়া, বিশেষ ফল না হওয়া ; প্রায় যথেষ্ট হওয়া। To take much trouble ; to go beyond the limits of prudence ; বহু কষ্ট স্বীকার করা ; সুবিবেচনার সীমা লঙ্ঘন করা। **To go along with**—To accompany ; সঙ্গে সঙ্গে যাওয়া। **To go aside**—To withdraw ; to deviate from the right path ; প্রস্থান করা ; সৎপথ ভ্রষ্ট হওয়া। **To go at**—To attack ; to take in hand energetically ; আক্রমণ করা ; সোৎসাহে আরম্ভ করা। **To go away** — To depart ; to leave ; প্রস্থান করা ; ত্যাগ করা। **To go back**—To retire ; to recede ; to withdraw ; চলিয়া যাওয়া ; হটিয়া যাওয়া ; সরিয়া পড়া। **To go back from, upon one's words etc.**—To fail to keep it ; সত্য রক্ষা করিতে না পারা, কথা রাখিতে না পারা। **To go back on**—To retrace ; as, to *go back on* one's footsteps ; পশ্চাৎপদ হওয়া। To prove faithless to ; to betray ; অবিশ্বাসী হওয়া ; বিশ্বাসঘাতকতাপূর্ব্বক

another ; অন্য ব্যক্তির সমকক্ষ ব্যক্তি । **—ly,** *adv.* **—qual'-i-ty,** *n.*

cō-erce' (-ērs), *v. t.* **1.** To restrain by force ; বলপূর্ব্বক সংযত করা, নিরোধ করা, প্রতিরোধ করা, শাসন করা, নিগৃহীত করা । **2.** To compel or enforce ; বাধ্য করা, বলপ্রয়োগদ্বারা বাধ্য করা । **—er-ci-bil'-i-ty,** *n.* **—er'-**

পুনরায় অনুসন্ধান করা । **To go better** or **one better** — To outbid or outdo an adversary ; প্রতিপক্ষ অপেক্ষা অধিক ডাকা, প্রতিপক্ষকে অতিক্রম করা । **To go by—** To pass near ; as, to *go by* a village ; নিকট দিয়া যাওয়া । To proceed by way or means of ; as, to *go by* rail ; কোন কিছুতে যাওয়া । To elapse (of time etc.) ; to pass away, as things *gone by* ; গত হওয়া, অতীত হওয়া ; চলা, অতিবাহিত হওয়া । To abide by ; as, to *go by* a principle ; মানিয়া চলা, পালন করা, অনুসরণ করা । **To go by a name—** To be known by that name ; কোন নামে পরিচিত হওয়া । **To go down—**To descend ; to sink ; to go below the horizon ; to be recorded in writing ; to fall (before a conqueror) ; to fail ; অবতরণ করা ; ডুবিয়া যাওয়া ; অস্তমিত হওয়া ; লিপিবদ্ধ হওয়া ; ধ্বংসপ্রাপ্ত হওয়া ; ব্যর্থ হওয়া, নিষ্ফল হওয়া । To be swallowed (followed by *with*) ; to be accepted without opposition by ; গ্রস্ত হওয়া ; এক বাক্যে গৃহীত হওয়া । To get lower in price ; মূল্য হ্রাস হওয়া, দর কমা । **To go down in the world—** To sink in the social scale ; সমাজে পতিত হওয়া । **To go down on one's knees —** To kneel down as to ask for some favour etc. ; জানু পাতিয়া উপবেশন করা, হাঁটু গাড়িয়া বসা । **To go far—**To go to a distance ; to have much weight

cō-ĕx-tĕnd', *v. t. & i.* To extend equally with ; সমায়ত হওয়া । ***Verb i.*** To be co-extensive ; সমস্থান ব্যাপিয়া বিস্তৃত থাকা । **—ten'-sion,** *n.* **—ten'-sive,** *adj.* Equally extensive ; সহব্যাপী (জিঃ), সমব্যাপক । **—ten'-sive-ness,** *n.*

cŏf'-fee (-fē), *n.* **1.** A drink made

পোষকতা করা । To go to fetch ; আনিতে যাওয়া । To be sold for ; নির্দ্দিষ্ট দরে বিক্রীত হওয়া । **To go for nothing—**To be useless ; to be of no value, weight or influence ; ব্যর্থ হওয়া, নিষ্ফল হওয়া ; নিরর্থক হওয়া, নগণ্য হওয়া । **To go forth —** To depart out of a place ; to issue as a decree etc. ; প্রস্থান করা, চলিয়া যাওয়া ; প্রচার করা । **To go (for) to (do something)—**(*Vulg.*) To be so inconsiderate as to (do it) ; (ইতর ভাষায়) এরূপ অবিবেচক হওয়া যে । **To go further and fare worse —** To take extra trouble and find oneself in a worse position than before ; অতিরিক্ত কষ্ট সহ্য করার পর পূর্ব্বাপেক্ষা অধিকতর সঙ্কটে পড়া । **To go halves,** or **shares—**To divide a thing equally between two persons ; to take equal portions ; সমাংশে বিভাগ করা ; সমান দুই ভাগ করিয়া লওয়া, সমান অংশে গ্রহণ করা । **To go hand in hand—**To agree in pursuing the same course ; to be in union ; to agree ; একমত হওয়া, ঐক্য হওয়া ; একসঙ্গে থাক ঘটা ; মিলা । **To go hard with—** To trouble; to pain or endanger ; কষ্ট দেওয়া, যাতনা দেওয়া ; বিপদাপন্ন করা । **To go home to—**To appeal directly to ; সাক্ষাৎভাবে অনুরোধ বা প্রার্থনা করা । **To go hot and cold—**To have access of fever or shame ; জ্বরাধিক্য হওয়া, লজ্জাভিভূত হওয়া । **To go in—**To enter ; to enter as a competitor ; (cricket) to take or begin innings ; (of sun) to be obscured by a cloud ; প্রবেশ করা ; প্রতিদ্বন্দ্বিরূপে নাম তালিকাভুক্ত করা ; (ক্রীকেট ক্রীড়া) খেলা আরম্ভ করা ; (সূর্য্য সম্বন্ধে) মেঘাবৃত হওয়া । **To go in and out—**To come and go freely ; অবাধে গমনাগমন করা । **To go in for—** To take as one's object, pursuit, style, principle, etc. ; কোন ব্যক্তির লক্ষ্য, ধারা, মূলমন্ত্র বা অনুসরণের বিষয় হওয়া । **To go into—**To enter, as a profession, parliament, etc. ; to frequent, as a society etc. ; to investigate ; পার্লেমেণ্টে প্রবেশ করা, ব্যবসায় প্রভৃতিতে প্রবৃত্ত হওয়া ; সর্ব্বদা গতিবিধি করা ; অনুসন্ধান করা । **To go in unto—**To have sexual intercourse with ; অভিগমন করা, রতিক্রিয়া করা । **To go it—**(*Slang*) To act vigorously, furiously, etc. ; to indulge in dissipation ; (ইতর ভাষায়) উৎসাহের সহিত কাজ করা, প্রচণ্ড তেজে কার্য্য করা ; বিলাস ব্যসনে মত্ত হওয়া । To go on with furious vigour or speed ; প্রচণ্ড তেজে বা বেগে অগ্রসর হওয়া । **To go mad, crazy** or **blind—** To become mad, crazy or blind ; পাগল হওয়া, উন্মাদগ্রস্ত হওয়া, বিকৃত-মস্তিষ্ক হওয়া বা অন্ধ হওয়া । **To go off—** To leave ; to depart ; ত্যাগ করা ; প্রস্থান করা । To explode ; to be discharged ; আওয়াজ হওয়া ; সশব্দে বিদীর্ণ হওয়া, ফুটা । To leave the stage, as an actor ; রঙ্গমঞ্চ হইতে প্রস্থান করা । To die ; মরা । To cease to be felt as a sensation ; অসাড় হওয়া । To deteriorate ; "Her...looks...were...*going off*" ; অপকর্ষ প্রাপ্ত হওয়া । To pass into unconsciousness ; as, to *go off* to sleep, or in or into a fit etc. ; চৈতন্য লোপ হওয়া, অচেতন হওয়া, মূর্চ্ছিত হওয়া । To be got rid of by sale ; মাল খালাস করা ।

To succeed; সফল হওয়া। To happen; ঘটা। **To go off at a tangent**—See TANGENT. **To go off one's head**—To be crazy; মাথা নষ্ট হওয়া, মাথার গোল হওয়া। To go off or **go to sleep**—To fall asleep; নিদ্রিত হওয়া, ঘুমাইয়া পড়া। **To go on**—To become chargeable to (a parish, relief fund etc.); কোন কিছুর উপর ব্যয়ভার পড়া। To continue; to persevere; to proceed; to proceed to do something as the next step; as, he *goes on* to quote a passage; বারংবার চেষ্টা করা, চেষ্টা করা; পুনঃ পুনঃ চেষ্টা করা; অগ্রসর হওয়া; করিতে থাকা। To conduct one's self shamefully etc.; লজ্জাজনক আচরণ করা। (*Colloq.*) To rail or storm (*at*); (চলিত-ভাষায়) বিদ্রূপ করা, ব্যঙ্গোক্তি করা, তর্জ্জন গর্জ্জন করা। (*Theatre*) To appear on the stage; (রঙ্গালয়) রঙ্গমঞ্চে প্রবেশ করা। (*Cricket*) To begin to bowl; বল করিতে আরম্ভ করা। (*Colloq. -Imperative*) Go your ways; don't talk nonsense; নিজের কাজ দেখ; বাজে কথা বকিও না। **To go on a fool's errand** — To go on an expedition which leads to a foolish bootless end; নিষ্ফল কাজে প্রবৃত্ত হওয়া, পরিণামে বোকা সাজিতে হয় এরূপ কাজে প্রবৃত্ত হওয়া। **To go on all fours**—To be prefect in all points; সর্ব্বাঙ্গসম্পন্ন হওয়া। **To go one's way**—To depart; to act according to one's will; প্রস্থান করা; নিজের খুসী মত কাজ করা। **To go on foot to a place**—To walk to a place; কোন স্থানে পদব্রজে গমন করা, কোন স্থানে হাঁটিয়া যাওয়া। **To go on sick leave**—To obtain leave of absence when an official becomes unwell; পীড়া বশতঃ বিদায় লওয়া। **To go on strike**—To strike; ধর্ম্মঘট করা। **To go on the stage**—To become an actor; অভিনেতা হওয়া। **To go on the streets**—To become a prostitute; বেশ্যাবৃত্তি অবলম্বন করা। **To go on to the bitter end**—To carry on a contest reckless of the consequences; চরমসীমায় যাওয়া। **To go on with a work**—To keep on doing it; কাজ করিতে থাকা। **To go out**—To go outside; to become public; বাহির হওয়া; সাধারণ্যে প্রচারিত হওয়া, প্রকাশিত হওয়া। To cease to burn; to cease to be fashionable; নিভিয়া যাওয়া; বে-রেওয়াজ হওয়া। To recede; to ebb; পশ্চাদ্দিকে সরা, হটিয়া যাওয়া; ভাটা পড়া। To retire from office (of government); সরকারী চাকুরী হইতে অবসর গ্রহণ করা। (Of girls) To find employment away from home; to mix in society; (বালিকার পক্ষে) বাহিরে চাকরী পাওয়া; সমাজে মেলামেশা করা। (Of work-men) To strike; ধর্ম্মঘট করা। (Of heart etc.) To expand with love etc. (to a person); স্ফীত হওয়া, বিস্তারিত হওয়া। **To go out of**—To go outside of; বাহিরে যাওয়া। **To go out of one's way**—To depart from one's habitual course of conduct; to trouble oneself; to agitate or discompose oneself; চিরাভ্যস্ত আচরণ বা পন্থা পরিত্যাগ করিয়া নূতন পথে চলা; কষ্ট স্বীকার করা; উদ্বেগ বা অশান্তি ভোগ করা। **To go over** — To pass across, as a river, boundary, etc.; to pass (to another owner); to change one's party or religion; to inspect the details of; পার হওয়া, উত্তীর্ণ হওয়া; হস্তান্তরিত হওয়া; মত পরিবর্ত্তন করা, ধর্ম্মান্তর পরিগ্রহ করা; সূক্ষ্মরূপে পরীক্ষা করা। To peruse; to review; to revise; পাঠ করা; আলোচনা করা; দেখিয়া দেওয়া, সংশোধন করা। **To go round**—To pay an informal visit (to); to be long enough to encompass; (of food etc.) to be sufficient for a whole party; অনিয়মিতভাবে সাক্ষাৎ করা; পরিবেষ্টন করার পক্ষে যথেষ্ট দীর্ঘ হওয়া; (খাদ্য সম্পর্কে) দলের সকল লোকের জন্য প্রচুর হওয়া। **To go the pace**—To go at great speed; (*fig.*) to indulge in dissipation; মহাবেগে ধাবিত হওয়া, প্রচণ্ডবেগে ছুটা; (লক্ষণায়) বিলাস-ব্যসনে প্রমত্ত হওয়া। **To go the way of all flesh (or the earth)**—To die; পঞ্চত্বপ্রাপ্ত হওয়া। **To go through** — To pass through to the other side; ভেদ করিয়া অপর পার্শ্বে যাওয়া। To endure to the end; to undergo; to accomplish; to finish; শেষ পর্য্যন্ত টিকিয়া থাকা; ভোগ করা, সহ্য করা; সম্পন্ন করা, শেষ করা; সমাধা করা। To peruse from beginning to end; to discuss in details; to scrutinize; to be sold out; as, the book has *gone through* 3 editions; আদ্যোপান্ত পাঠ করা; সবিস্তারে আলোচনা করা; বিশেষ ভাবে পরীক্ষা করা; বিক্রীত হওয়া। To exhaust or waste, as a fortune; উড়াইয়া দেওয়া, অপব্যয় করা। **To go through fire and water**—To undertake any trouble or risks for one's end; স্বর্গ মর্ত্ত্য তোলপাড় করা। **To go through thick and thin**—To go through difficulties great or small as they arise; সর্ব্বপ্রকার সঙ্কটের ভিতর দিয়া অগ্রসর হওয়া। **To go through with**—To go to the end; to perform completely; শেষ পর্য্যন্ত যাওয়া; সুসম্পন্ন করা। **To go to a ball, church or market**—To attend it; যাওয়া। **To go to a better world**—To die; স্বর্গধামে গমন করা। **To go to destruction**—ধ্বংসপ্রাপ্ত হওয়া। **To go together**—To be concomitant or compatible; সহচারী হওয়া,

সংশ্লিষ্ট হওয়া, আনুষঙ্গিক হওয়া। **To go to great expense**—To expend much ; বহু অর্থ ব্যয় করা। **To go to law**—To litigate ; আদালতের আশ্রয় গ্রহণ করা। **To go to one's account** or **own place**—To die ; পরলোকে গমন করা, চিত্রগুপ্তের খাতায় নাম উঠা। **To go to one's heart**—To grieve him ; মর্মে প্রবেশ করা। **To go to pieces**—To break ; চুরমার হওয়া, খণ্ডবিখণ্ড হওয়া। **To go to rack and ruin**—To fall into utter disrepair ; ভাঙ্গিয়া চুরিয়া যাওয়া। **To go to sea**—To become a sailor ; নাবিক হওয়া। **To go to school**—To get instruction ; বিদ্যালয়ে যাওয়া, শিক্ষালাভ করা। **To go to the bad**—To become a wreck ; ধ্বংসপ্রাপ্ত হওয়া। **To go to the bar**—To become a barrister ; কৌঁসুলী হওয়া। **To go to the country**—To test opinion by general election ; সাধারণ নির্ব্বাচন দ্বারা কোন মত পরীক্ষা করা। **To go to the dogs**—To become of depraved character ; গোল্লায় যাওয়া, চুলোয় যাওয়া, জাহান্নমে যাওয়া। **To go to the wall**—To be discomfited ; to be compelled to retire ; পরাভবপ্রাপ্ত হওয়া ; অবসর গ্রহণ করিতে বাধ্য হওয়া। **To go under**—To be called by some title ; কোন উপাধিতে অভিহিত হওয়া। To fail ; to succumb ; to be overwhelmed or ruined ; to die ; অকৃতকার্য্য হওয়া ; ভাঙ্গিয়া পড়া ; অভিভূত হওয়া, বিনষ্ট হওয়া ; মরা। **To go up**—To rise, as price etc. ; চড়া। **To go upon**—To act upon as a principle, basis or foundation ; কোন কিছুর ভিত্তিস্বরূপ হওয়া। **To go well**—To prosper ; সমৃদ্ধিশালী হওয়া, শ্রীবৃদ্ধি হওয়া, উন্নতি লাভ করা। **To go with**—To accompany ; to be concomitant of ; to agree with ; to follow the drift of ; সঙ্গে যাওয়া ; সহচারী হওয়া ; মিলা ; মর্ম্ম বা তাৎপর্য্যের অনুযায়ী হওয়া। **To go without**—To be, or remain, destitute or unprovided ; কোন কিছু হইতে বঞ্চিত হওয়া, কোন কিছু হইতে বঞ্চিত হইয়া থাকা। **To go without saying**—To be an evident fact or natural conclusion ; স্বতঃসিদ্ধ কথা, বলাই বাহুল্য, স্পষ্টই বুঝা যায়, না বলিলেও চলে। **To go with the stream**—To do as other people do ; লোকে সাধারণতঃ যেরূপ করে সেরূপ করা, দশজনে যেরূপ করে সেরূপ কাজ করা। **To go with tide** or **times**—To do as others do ; আর সকলের মত কাজ করা, গড্ডলিকা প্রবাহের মত চলা, সকলের দেখাদেখি প্রচলিত মতের অনুবর্ত্তী হইয়া চলা। **To go wrong**—To take a wrong direction ; to stray ; to depart from virtue ; ভ্রান্ত পথে চলা ; বিপথগামী হওয়া ; ধর্ম্মভ্রষ্ট হওয়া, সৎপথচ্যুত হওয়া। **To let go**—To release ; ছাড়িয়া দেওয়া। **Who goes there**—A sentry's challenge ; কে যাও? [পরিচয় প্রদানের জন্য সান্ত্রীর আহ্বান-বাক্য।]

gō, *n.* (*Pl.* GOES) **1.** Act of going ; গমন। **2.** (*Colloq.*) The fashion or mode ; প্রচলিত রীতি, ধারা, রেওয়াজ। **3.** (*Colloq.*) Noisy merriment ; (চলিত ভাষায়) কোলাহলপূর্ণ আমোদ প্রমোদ। **4.** Energy ; spirit ; dash ; animation ; as, the piece has plenty of *go* in it ; শক্তি ; তেজ ; প্রচণ্ডতা ; সজীবতা। **5.** (*Cribbage*) That condition of the game when a player cannot play a card which will not carry the count above thirty one ; (একপ্রকার তাস খেলায়) খেলার যে অবস্থায় কোন খেলোয়াড় যদ্দ্বারা মোট ক্রীড়াঙ্ক একত্রিশের অধিক হইয়া না পড়ে এমন কোন তাস খেলিতে পারে না। **6.** A portion of liquor or food served ; পরিবেষিত খাদ্য বা মদ্যের অংশ, উচ্ছিষ্ট। **7.** An embarrassing state of affair ; as a queer *go* ; ঝঞ্ঝাট। **All** or **quite the go**—(*Colloq.*) In fashion ; (চলিত ভাষায়) প্রচলিত, রেওয়াজ। **A pretty go**—A pretty state of affair ; মজার ব্যাপার। **Come and go**—Traffic ; movement to and fro ; জাহাজ বা রেলযোগে মাল-পত্রের গমনাগমন ; গমনাগমন, আসা যাওয়া, যাতায়াত। **It's no go**—(*Colloq.*) Nothing can be done ; (চলিত ভাষায়) কিছুই করা যাইতে পারে না। **Near go**—(*Colloq.*) A near approach ; a close shave ; (চলিত ভাষায়) প্রায় কাছাকাছি ; ঘষড়াইয়া চলন। **To have a go at**—To turn at doing something ; কোন কার্য্য করিতে উন্মুখ হওয়া।

goad (gōd), *n.* & *v. t.* Spiked stick for urging ; hence anything that torments or stimulates ; অঙ্কুশ, প্রতোদ, ডাঙ্গস, আজনি (সাঃ পঃ) ; উত্তেজক বস্তু, যন্ত্রণাদায়ক বস্তু, তাড়না। *Verb t.* To prick ; to urge with a goad ; to stimulate ; অঙ্কুশদ্বারা বিদ্ধ করা ; অঙ্কুশদ্বারা তাড়না করা ; উত্তেজিত করা।

goal (gōl), *n.* **1.** A point or place at which a race or journey is to end ; destination ; দৌড়ের সীমা, ধাবনসীমাস্তম্ভ ; চরম গম্যস্থান, গন্তব্যস্থল। **2.** The final purposes ; the object of effort ; ambition ; চরম লক্ষ্য, চরম উদ্দেশ্য, পুরুষার্থ (ছান্দোগ্য) ; অভীষ্ট ; উচ্চাকাঙ্ক্ষা। **3.** (In foot-ball) The two upright posts between which the ball is kicked in order to score ; a point won in that way ; পাদগোলক ক্রীড়ায় যে স্তম্ভযুগলের মধ্য দিয়া গোলক তাড়িত করা হয় ; পাদগোলক ক্রীড়ায় জয়াঙ্ক। **Goal-keeper**—পাদগোলক ক্রীড়ায় সীমাস্তম্ভ রক্ষক। **Goal-line**—পাদগোলক ক্রীড়ায় সীমাস্তম্ভ যুগলের মধ্যবর্ত্তী রেখা। **To drop a goal**—To make a goal by a drop-kick ; ভূতলে নিক্ষিপ্ত পাদগোলক

ঠিকরাইয়া উঠিলে তাহাতে পদাঘাত করিয়া "গোল" করা।

goat (gōt), *n.* **1.** A well-known ruminant quadruped; (*pl.*) the sub-family to which the goat

Goat.

belongs; অজ, ছাগ; (বহুবচনে) অজজাতি। **2.** (*Cap.—Astron.*) The sign of Capricorn in the Zodiac; (জ্যোতি-বিজ্ঞান) মকর-রাশি। **3.** A licentious man; কামুক ব্যক্তি, লোচ্চা। **Goat′-ish, Goat′-y,** *adjs.* **1.** Resembling a goat, esp. in smell; ছাগসদৃশ, অজগন্ধী। **2.** Lustful; wanton; কামুক; লম্পট, ছাগবৃত্ত। **Goat′-ish-ly,** *adv.* **Goat′-ish-ness,** *n.* **Goat-god**—Same as PAN which see. **Goat-herd** — One who tends goats; ছাগরক্ষক, অজাপাল, অজাপালক, অজপ (মঃ উঃ)। **Goat's beard** — একপ্রকার গুল্ম। **Goat skin**—ছাগ-চর্ম্ম; ছাগচর্ম্ম নির্ম্মিত বস্ত্র, বোতল প্রভৃতি। **Goat-sucker** — একপ্রকার চাতক পক্ষী [এই পাখী ছাগ-দুগ্ধ পান করে বলিয়া ভ্রান্ত বিশ্বাস প্রচলিত আছে।] **Goat's wool** — কাল্পনিক বস্তু, — শিয়ালের সিং, সাপের পা। **He goat** — পাঁঠা, অজ, ছাগ। **She goat**—পাঁঠী, অজা, ছাগী, ছাগল। **Sheep and goats**—The good and the wicked; ভাল এবং মন্দ লোক। **To play the giddy goat**—To frolic foolishly; ক্রীড়া কৌতুক করা।

goat-ee′ (gōt-ē), *n.* A chin tuft like the beard of a goat; থুতনির উপর ছাগলের মত দাড়ী।

goat′-ling (gōt-), *n.* A young goat above 12 months and under 2 years old; ছাগশিশু (এক বৎসরের অধিক এবং দুই বৎসরের অনধিক বয়স্ক)।

gŏb, *n.* & *v. i.* **1.** (*Vulg.*) A lump or mass; (ইতর ভাষায়) খণ্ড, ডেলা, পিণ্ড। **2.** Spittle; থুথু। ***Verb i.*** To spit; থুথু ফেলা।

gō-băng′, *n.* A game played on the chequer-board; একপ্রকার খেলা।

gŏb′-bet (-ĕt), *n.* (*Archaic*) A mouthful; a lump; a small piece, esp. of raw flesh or food; এক গ্রাস; পিণ্ড, ডেলা; ক্ষুদ্র খণ্ড, বিশেষতঃ কাঁচা মাংস বা খাদ্যদ্রব্যের খণ্ড।

gŏb′-ble (-l), *v. t.* & *i.* To swallow or eat hastily and noisily; to gulp; গপ্ গপ্ করিয়া গেলা, আড়ে গেলা, গড়গড় করিয়া গেলা; গিলিয়া ফেলা। **—bler,** *n.* **Gobble-stitch**—ব্যস্ততা বশতঃ সূঁচের লম্বা ফোঁড়।

gŏb′-ble (-l), *v. i.* To make a noise in the throat as a turkey; to make such a sound while speaking from rage etc.; গড় গড় শব্দ করা; রাগে গর গর করা।

gŏb′-ē-lin, *adj.* Pertaining to tapestry produced at the state factory in Paris, called *Gobelins*, after its founders; প্যারী নগরীস্থ গবেলিন নামক সরকারী (রাষ্ট্রীয়) শিল্পশালায় প্রস্তুত চিত্র-যবনিক-সম্বন্ধীয়।

gōbe-mouche′ (-mōsh), *n.* A credulous person or news-monger; আশু-বিশ্বাসী ব্যক্তি বা সংবাদ-প্রচারক।

gŏb′-lĕt, *n.* **1.** (*Archaic*) A large drinking cup without a handle; (*poet.*) a drinking vessel; মদ্য পানের জন্য হাতল শূন্য বড় পেয়ালা; (কবিতায়) পানপাত্র, চষক, সুরাপাত্র। **2.** (*Commr.*) A glass with foot and stem as distinguished from a tumbler; (বাণিজ্য) হুকার বৈঠকের আকার পানপাত্র।

gŏb′-lin, *n.* An evil mischievous ugly spirit; দুষ্ট ভূত, পিশাচ।

gō′-bȳ, *n.* A genus of small fishes; একজাতীয় ক্ষুদ্র মৎস্য।

gŏd, *n.* (*Cap.*) **1.** The Supreme Being, the Creator and Preserver of the world; পরমেশ্বর, ঈশ্বর, পরম-পুরুষ, সৃষ্টিকর্ত্তা, বিশ্বপিতা, ভগবান। **2.** A divinity; a deity; an object of worship; an idol; "This man is now become a *god*"; দেব; দেবতা; পূজ্য বস্তু; দেবমূর্ত্তি, প্রতিমা। **3.** Any person or thing highly adored and honoured; an object of supreme regard; "Whose *god* is their belly"; অতিশয় সম্মানিত বস্তু; পরম ভক্তির পাত্র। **4.** (*Pl.*) The audience in the gallery of a theatre; রঙ্গালয়ের সোপানাকারে সজ্জিত আসন-শ্রেণী সমূহের মধ্যে সর্ব্বোচ্চ আসন-শ্রেণীতে উপবিষ্ট শ্রোতৃবর্গ। **God′-hood, God′-ship,** *ns.* Divinity; ঈশ্বরত্ব। **God′-less,** *adj.* Having or acknowledging no God; impious; wicked; নিরীশ্বর, দেবভক্তিবিমুখ (কোঃ); অসাধু, ধর্ম্মবিমুখ (কেঃ); দুষ্ট, দুর্বৃত্ত। **God′-li-ness,** *n.* ঈশ্বর-পরায়ণত্ব। **God′-ly,** *adj.* Like God in character; according to God's laws; pious; devout; righteous; দেবস্বভাব, দেবপ্রকৃতিক; ঈশ্বরবিধানানু-সারী; সাধু; ধর্ম্মনিষ্ঠ, ঈশ্বরভক্ত, ঈশ্বর-পরায়ণ, পরমার্থিক, ধার্ম্মিক। **God′-ward,** *adv.* & *adj.* **God′-wards,** *adv.* **By God**—A confirmatory oath; ঈশ্বরের নামে শপথ। **God-daughter**—ধর্ম্ম-কন্যা। **God-father**—যে ব্যক্তি দীক্ষাকালে দীক্ষাপ্রাপ্ত শিশুর ধর্ম্মশিক্ষার দায়িত্ব গ্রহণ করে, ধর্ম্মপিতা। **God-fearing** — ঈশ্বরভীরু, ধর্ম্মভীরু। **God-forsaken** — ঈশ্বর পরিত্যক্ত। **Godhead, Godship** — Divinity or divine nature; a deity; দেবত্ব, ঈশ্বরত্ব (হিঃ কোঃ), দেবস্বভাব; দেবতা। (With *the*) The Supreme Being; পরমেশ্বর। **God-like**—Like a god or God; divine; hence, pre-eminently good; ঈশ্বর সদৃশ, দেবতুল্য,

দেবোপম, সুরোপম, দেবরূপ, দেবস্বরূপ ; স্বর্গীয়, দিব্য ; সর্ব্বোত্তম, সর্ব্বশ্রেষ্ঠ। **Godling**—ক্ষুদ্র দেবতা। **God-man**—One both God and man ; Christ ; নরদেব ; যীশুখ্রীষ্ট। **God's acre**—A church-yard ; গির্জ্জার প্রাঙ্গণ। **God's earth** — পৃথিবী। **God's book**—বাইবেল। **Godsend** — অপ্রত্যাশিত সৌভাগ্যলাভ, অপ্রত্যাশিত ঘটনা। **God's image**—Human body ; মানব দেহ। **Godson**—ধর্ম্মপুত্র। **God-speed**—*n.* (A contraction of the phrase *God speed you*) Success ; prosperity ; as, I wish you *god-speed* ; সিদ্ধি, সাফল্য ; উন্নতি, সমৃদ্ধি। A wish for one's success ; শুভকামনা। **God's truth**—An absolute truth ; পরম সত্য। **Household gods**—রোমানদিগের গৃহদেবতাগণ ; পারিবারিক কল্যাণসংশ্লিষ্ট কোন পদার্থ। **Under-god**—A secondary cause or mediate object of gratitude ; "The blessedness of this good work *under god* is to be attributed to the king alone" ; ঈশ্বরের পরে বা নীচে কৃতজ্ঞতা প্রকাশের পাত্র। **A feast** or **sight for the gods**—Something exquisite etc. ; অতি চমৎকার দৃশ্য, দেবদুর্লভ দৃশ্য। **For god's sake**—With urgent petitions ; ঈশ্বরের খাতিরে। **God forbid**—May God forbid such a calamity ; ঈশ্বর না করুন। **God knows**—I do not know ; ঈশ্বর জানেন। **God of day**—The Sun ; দিনেশ, দিননাথ (মঃ উঃ), দিনরাজ (ঐ), দিনপতি (বৃঃ সং), দিনেশ্বর (হরিঃ)। **God of love, Blind God**—Cupid ; কামদেব, বাল-কন্দর্প। **God of this world**—The Devil ; শয়তান। **God of war**—Mars ; সমর-দেবতা, রণদেব, রণস্বামী (Siva as the Lord of battle রাজতরঙ্গিণী), রণেশ, রণেশ্বর (মঃ উঃ), রণেন্দ্র [Cf. our রণচণ্ডী, রণদুর্গা, রণলক্ষ্মী (কথাঃ সঃ)]। **God of wine**—Bacchus ; সুরা দেবতা — ব্যাকাস্। **God the Father, Son, Holy Ghost**—Persons of Trinity ; খৃষ্টীয় বাইবেলোক্ত ত্রিমূর্ত্তি—ঈশ্বর, যীশুখ্রীষ্ট, পবিত্রাত্মা। **God willing**—If circumstances allow ; ঈশ্বরেচ্ছা থাকিলে, যদি ঈশ্বর করেন। **Oh my good etc. God**—Exclamations of pain, grief or anger ; হায় ঈশ্বর ! হরি ! হরি ! **Thank God**—ঈশ্বরকে ধন্যবাদ। **To bid a person God-speed**—To wish him success in an undertaking, journey, etc. ; কোন ব্যক্তির কার্য্যারম্ভকালে বা যাত্রাকালে শুভকামনা করা। **With God**—Dead and in heaven ; স্বর্গধামে ঈশ্বরের নিকট।

gŏd, *v. t.* To deify ; দেবত্ব আরোপ করা, দেবত্বে উন্নীত করা, দেবতুল্য করা। **To god it**—To play the god ; দেবতার অভিনয় করা।

gŏd'-dĕss (-ĕs), *n.* (*Fem.* of GOD). **1.** A female deity ; ঈশ্বরী, দেবী। **2.** A woman of great charms or one adores ; পরম রূপবতী নারী, দেবী।

gō'-dōwn, *n.* (*Anglo Ind.*) A store house for goods ; গুদাম ঘর, মাল ঘর, আড়ত (কেবল ভারতবর্ষে প্রচলিত)।

God-wits.

gŏd'-wit, *n.* A bird having long slender legs and long bills ; এক জাতীয় বক।

gō'-êr, *n.* A person or thing that goes ; গমনকারী, গামী।

Goe'-thi-ăn (gŭ-tî-), *adj.* & *n.* Of, or relating to, Goethe, his writings or views ; like Goethe ; জর্ম্মাণদেশীয় কবি গেটে সম্পর্কীয়, উক্ত কবির মত বা রচনা সম্পর্কীয় ; গেটের তুল্য।

gŏf'-êr, gŏf'-fêr (-êr), **gō'-phêr, gauf'-fêr** (găf-êr), *v. t.* & *n.* To plait ; to make wavy ; to crisp (with a heated iron) ; কুচিযুক্ত করা ; কুঞ্চিত করা ; কোঁচান। ***Noun.*** **1.** The iron used for goffering ; কাপড় কোঁচাইবার জন্য লৌহ-বিশেষ। **2.** Ornamental plaiting ; নকাশী কুঁচি।

gŏg'-gle (-l), *v. i.*, *t.*, *adj.* & *n.* To squint ; to roll the eyes about ; to stare ; (of eyes) to project ; "And wink and *goggle* like an owl" ; আড়চোখে চাওয়া ; চোক ঘুরান ; এক দৃষ্টে হাঁ করিয়া তাকান ; (চক্ষু সম্বন্ধে) উদ্গত হওয়া। ***Verb t.*** To turn as the eyes sideways ; আড়দৃষ্টি করা, অপাঙ্গ দৃষ্টি করা, দৃষ্টি হানা। ***Adj.*** (Of eyes) Rolling ; staring ; protuberant ; (নেত্রাদি সম্বন্ধে) ঘূর্ণিত ; অনিমেষ-দৃষ্টি ; উদ্গত। ***Noun.*** **1.** (*Pl.*) Spectacles for protecting eyes from glare, dust, etc. ; ঠুলি চসমা। **2.** (*Pl.*) Sheep disease ; staggers ; মেষরোগ ; অশ্ব গবাদির মস্তিষ্ক-রোগ বিশেষ। **Goggle-eyed**—Having prominent distorted or rolling eyes ; বিকৃতনেত্র, ঘূর্ণিত-লোচন, লোলনেত্র, বহিরুদ্গতনেত্র।

gŏg'-lĕt, gŭg'-glet (-lĕt), *ns.* (*Anglo-Ind.*) A long-necked earthen jar for cooling water ; কুঁজো, সোরাই (ভারতবর্ষে ব্যবহৃত)।

Goi'-dĕl (goy-), *n.* One of the Celtic races represented by the Irish and the Highlanders of Scotland ; কেল্‌ট জাতির শাখা বিশেষ (বর্ত্তমান আইরিস ও হাইল্যাণ্ডারগণ)। **—del'-ic**, *adj.* & *n.* উক্ত জাতি-সম্পর্কীয়। (*Noun*) The language of the Goidels ; উক্ত জাতির ভাষা।

gō'-ing, *n.* & *adj.* **1.** The act of moving or walking ; travelling ; গমন, চলন ; ভ্রমণ। **2.** Departure ; "Have a safe *going* and return" ; প্রস্থান। **3.** Condition of the ground for walking, racing, etc. ; ভ্রমণ, ঘোড়দৌড় প্রভৃতির জন্য ভূমির অবস্থা। **4.** Pregnancy ; child-bearing ; গর্ভাবস্থা ; গর্ভধারণ। **5.** (*Pl.*)

Course of life ; জীবন-গতি। ***Adj.*1.** Prevalent; "The best style *going*" ; to be had ; "There is cold beef *going*" ; প্রচলিত ; প্রাপ্য। **2.** (With *a* prefixed) In action ; as, set the clock *agoing* ; চলন্ত অবস্থায়। **Goings on**—Behaviour or conduct (usually strange) ; ব্যবহার, আচরণ। **Going strong**—See under GO.

goi′-têr (gŏy-), **-tre** (-têr), *n.* Bronchocele ; a tumour on the forepart of throat ; গলগণ্ড, গড়গল (হঃ চঃ)। **-tered, -tred,** *adjs.* Affected with goitre ; গলগণ্ড-রোগাক্রান্ত। **-trous,** *adj.* Pertaining to the goitre ; affected with the goitre ; of the nature of goitre; গলগণ্ড-সম্বন্ধীয়; গলগণ্ডাক্রান্ত, গড়্কণ্ঠ (কেণ্ডিঃ); গলগণ্ডাত্মক।

Goiter neck.

Gŏl-cŏn′-dă, *n.* The mine of wealth, (*lit.* or *fig.*); ঐশ্বর্য্যের খনি। [হায়দ্রাবাদের প্রাচীন নাম। পূর্ব্বে হীরকের খনির জন্য বিখ্যাত ছিল।]

gōld, *n.* & *adj.* **1.** A precious metal of bright yellow colour and of high specific gravity ; স্বর্ণ, সুবর্ণ, সোণা, হেম, হিরণ্য, কনক, কাঞ্চন, দ্রবিণ, সূর্য্য, (সাঃ পঃ), সুরঙ্গ (ঐ), বহ্নিরোচন (ঐ), দেবধাতু (ঐ), হাটক (ঐ), শিখি (ঐ), রসজ (ঐ), পীত (ঐ), তপনীয়, শাতকুম্ভ, গাঙ্গেয়, ভস্ম, কর্ব্বূর, চামীকর, জাতরূপ মহারজত, রুক্ম, কার্ত্তস্বর, জাম্বূনদ, অষ্টাপদ (cf. কাঠের সেঁউতি মোর হইল অষ্টাপদ—অন্নদামঙ্গল)। **2.** Coins made of this ; money ; riches ; wealth ; স্বর্ণমুদ্রা ; অর্থ ; ঐশ্বর্য্য ; ধন। **3.** A bright yellow colour ; স্বর্ণবর্ণ, পীতবর্ণ, হেমবর্ণ। **4.** (*Fig.*) Something brilliant, precious or pure ; as, a heart of *gold* ; (লক্ষণায়) উজ্জ্বল, বহুমূল্য বা বিশুদ্ধ বস্তু [cf. our সোণার মানুষ।] **5.** The metal used for coating a surface ; gilding ; গিল্টিকরণে ব্যবহৃত ধাতু ; গিল্টি। ***Adj.*** Made of, or coloured like, gold ; স্বর্ণনির্ম্মিত বা স্বর্ণ তুল্য, হেমময়, স্বর্ণবৎ উজ্জ্বল, কনকোজ্জ্বল। **Dead-gold**—See under DEAD. **Gold-amalgam**—পারদ ও স্বর্ণের মিশ্র। **Gold-beater** — One who beats gold into thin leaf ; স্বর্ণপত্রকার। **Gold beater's skin**—বৃষের বৃহদন্ত্রের বহিরাবরণ—যাহা সংস্কৃত হওয়ার পর স্বর্ণপত্রকারগণ কর্তৃক ব্যবহৃত হয়। **Gold cloth**—See CLOTH OF GOLD under CLOTH. **Gold-dust**—স্বর্ণরেণু, কনকপরাগ কাঞ্চনরেণু, চামীকরচূর্ণ (কুমারঃ)। **Gold-fever**—A mania for seeking gold ; স্বর্ণসংগ্রহের জন্য বাতিক, স্বর্ণোন্মাদ, স্বর্ণজ্বর। **Gold-field**—স্বর্ণক্ষেত্র। **Goldfinch**—A bright coloured song-bird ;

Goldfinch.

সমুজ্জ্বল বর্ণ গায়কপক্ষিবিশেষ। (*Slang*) A gold coin ; (ইতর ভাষায়) স্বর্ণমুদ্রা। **Gold-fish**—স্বর্ণবর্ণ ক্ষুদ্র মৎস্য বিশেষ। **Gold-foil**-সোণার পাত। **Gold-leaf**—Gold beaten into extremely thin sheets, (*-foils* being thicker) ; স্বর্ণপত্র, সুবর্ণপত্র (সাঃ পঃ), হেমপত্র (ঐ)। **Gold-lace**—গোট। **Gold mine**—(*Lit.* & *fig.*) Source of wealth ; স্বর্ণখনি (শব্দানুযায়ী ও লক্ষণায়)। **Gold Mohur tree**—কৃষ্ণচূড়া (যোঃ)। **Gold plate** — স্বর্ণপাত্র। **Goldsmith**—সোণার, সেঁকরা, স্বর্ণকার। **Goldsmith beetle**—স্বর্ণবর্ণ পক্ষচ্ছদ বিশিষ্ট কীটবিশেষ, স্বর্ণকীট। **Gold-stick**—The gilt rod borne by the colonel of Life Guards or the captain of Gentlemen-at-arms ; লাইফ গার্ড সেনাদলের কর্ণেল অথবা রাজকীয় উৎসবে চত্বারিংশৎ ভদ্রবংশীয় রাজানুচরগণের অধ্যক্ষকর্তৃক বাহিত স্বর্ণ-মণ্ডিত দণ্ড। **Gold-thread**—সুবর্ণ-সূত্র, স্বর্ণসূত্র, কালাবাত্তু (ফঃ হিঃ), কনকসূত্র, স্বর্ণতন্তু ; **Gold-wire**—শলমা। **Rolled-gold**—সোণার পাত-দ্বারা মোড়া ধাতু-ফলক [ধাতু ফলককে গুরুভার ডলনার ভিতর ডলিয়া স্বর্ণফলক সংশ্লিষ্ট করা হয়।] **All that glisters or glitters is not gold**—See under GLITTER.

gōld′-en (-n), *adj.* **1.** Made of gold ; consisting of, or pertaining to, gold ; স্বর্ণনির্ম্মিত ; হেমময়, স্বর্ণময়, হিরণ্ময়, হৈম, সৌবর্ণ। **2.** Abounding in gold ; স্বর্ণবহুল, স্বর্ণগর্ভ। **3.** Having the colour of gold ; স্বর্ণবর্ণ, কনকবর্ণ। **4.** Precious ; excellent ; important ; "*Golden* opinions" ; বহুমূল্য ; উৎকৃষ্ট, চমৎকার ; গুরুতর। **Golden age**—The most prosperous period of a nation's condition or literature ; as, the Elizabethan has been called the *golden age* of English literature ; কোন জাতির অবস্থা বা সাহিত্যের চরম সমৃদ্ধির যুগ, স্বর্ণযুগ। The fabulous age of simplicity and purity of manners in rural employments followed by the *silver, bronze,* and *iron* ages ; সত্যযুগ। **Golden apple** — See APPLE. **Golden calf**—ধন [ভাববাদী মুশা ঈশ্বরাদেশ শ্রবণের জন্য সিনাই পর্ব্বতে গেলে পর Aaron ইহুদীদিগের পূজার জন্য একটী স্বর্ণময় গোবৎস নির্ম্মাণ করেন।] **Golden-eye** — একপ্রকার সামুদ্রিক হংস। **Golden-fleece** — যে সুবর্ণ মেষলোমের অনুসন্ধানার্থ পুরাকালে জেসন প্রমুখ গ্রীকবীরগণ কলসিস্ দ্বীপে গমন করিয়াছিলেন, সুবর্ণ মেষ-লোম। **Golden house**—Palace ; কনকসৌধ। [রোম

সম্রাট্ নীরোর স্বর্ণ অট্টালিকা। এই অট্টালিকার ছাদ সোনার টালি দ্বারা রচিত হইয়াছিল। এই সৌধের স্বর্ণমণ্ডিত প্রাচীরের ভিতরের পার্শ্ব শুক্তি এবং মণিরাজি এবং ভিতরের ছাদ স্বর্ণ ও গজদন্ত দ্বারা খচিত ছিল]। **Golden jubilee**—See JUBILEE. **Golden-knop**—গোবরে পোকা। **Golden Legend**—মধ্যযুগে Jacobus de Voragine নামক খৃষ্টীয়-সন্ন্যাসিবিরচিত সিদ্ধপুরুষদিগের জীবনী। **Golden mean**—শ্রেয়ঃ মধ্যপথ। **Golden mouthed**—Eloquent—সুবক্তা। **Golden-number**—স্বর্ণাঙ্ক [Easter পর্ব্বের তারিখ নির্ণয়ের জন্য প্রয়োজনীয় সংখ্যা-বিশেষ। প্রাচীন রোম ও এলেকজেণ্ড্রা নগরীর পঞ্জিকায় এই সংখ্যা স্বর্ণাক্ষরে লিখিত হইত বলিয়া এই নাম। কোন বৎসরের সংখ্যার সহিত ১ যোগ করিয়া যোগফলকে ১৯ দ্বারা ভাগ করিলে যে সংখ্যা অবশিষ্ট থাকে তাহাই স্বর্ণাঙ্ক। অবশিষ্ট শূন্য হইলে স্বর্ণাঙ্ক ১৯ ধরা হয়।] **Golden ointment**—অঞ্জন। **Golden opinions**—High respect; গভীর শ্রদ্ধা। **Golden opportunity**—সুবর্ণ সুযোগ। **Golden-rain**—একপ্রকার আতসবাজী, স্বর্ণবৃষ্টি। **Golden-rose**—স্বর্ণময় গোলাপ-গুচ্ছ—যাহা পোপ কর্ত্তৃক প্রতি বৎসর Lent পর্ব্বের চতুর্থ রবিবারে মন্ত্রাদিদ্বারা পূত হইত, এবং উহা কোন ধর্ম্মসংঘ, নগরী, রাজ্য বা ব্যক্তিকে রোমান ক্যাথলিক ধর্ম্মসংঘের উপকারজনক কার্য্য সাধনের পুরস্কারস্বরূপ অথবা রোমান ক্যাথলিক জগতের সর্ব্বপ্রধানা ধর্ম্মপরায়ণা নারীকে উপহারস্বরূপ প্রদত্ত হইত। **Golden shower**—ধন; উৎকোচ। **Golden-wedding**—স্বামী স্ত্রীর জীবিতাবস্থায় বিবাহের পঞ্চাশত্তম সাম্বৎসরিক উৎসব। **The golden bowl is broken**—Death has supervened; দেহপিঞ্জর ভাঙ্গিয়া প্রাণপাখী পালাইয়াছে। **The golden rule**—সুবর্ণনীতি, আচারসার (হিঃ কোঃ), নীতিসার (ঐ), আচারসর্ব্বস্ব (ঐ), নীতিসর্ব্বস্ব (ঐ)। **(1)** "Do unto others as you would have others do unto you" (Matt. vii, 12); অন্যের নিকট হইতে যেরূপ ব্যবহার পাইতে আশা কর তাহার সহিত সেরূপ ব্যবহার কর। (2) (*Arith.*) The Rule-of-three; (পাটীগণিত) ত্রৈরাশিক। **The golden State**—California; ক্যালিফোর্ণিয়া। **To worship the golden calf**—To bow down before a unworthy thing; কোন অযোগ্য পদার্থের সম্মুখে মস্তক নত করা।

gōld'-ĭ-lŏck, *n.* A kind of flower plants; কাঞ্চনবর্ণ পুষ্পপ্রদ বৃক্ষ-বিশেষ।

gŏlf, *n.* & *v. i.* A game played with clubs and balls; এক প্রকার দণ্ডকন্দুক ক্রীড়া। [এই ক্রীড়ায় যে ব্যক্তি দণ্ড দ্বারা সর্ব্বাপেক্ষা অল্পসংখ্যক আঘাতে কন্দুক ক্রমান্বয়ে কতকগুলি নির্দ্দিষ্ট গর্ত্তে নিক্ষেপ করিতে সমর্থ হন তিনিই জয় লাভ করিয়া থাকেন।] ***Verb i.*** To play golf; গল্‌ফ্ ক্রীড়া করা। **Golf'-er,** *n.* **Golf-club**—An implement used in the game; গোল্‌ফ ক্রীড়ার দণ্ড। A society for playing golf; গোল্‌ফ ক্রীড়া সমিতি।

Gŏl'-gö-thă, *n.* **1.** The scene of the crucifixion of Jesus Christ, near Jerusalem; জেরুশালেমের নিকটবর্ত্তী স্থান বিশেষ—যথায় যীশুখ্রীষ্ট ক্রুশে নিহত হন। **2.** (*L. c.*) A charnel house; শবাস্থি সংরক্ষণ-গৃহ, অস্থিগৃহ।

Gö-lī'-ăth, *n.* A giant (*Sam.* xvii); দৈত্য-বিশেষ।

gŏl'-lĭ-wŏg, *n.* A grotesque doll; কিম্ভূতকিমাকার পুত্তলিকা।

gŏl'-lȳ, *interj.* By God (used esp. by the Negroes); ঈশ্বরের নামে।

gö'-lŏsh, *n.* See GALOSH.

gö-lŭp'-tious (-shŭs), **–lŏp–,** *adjs.* Luscious; delightful; রসাল, সুরস; আনন্দময়।

Gö-mŏr'-rah (-ră), *n.* A wicked town; the type of such a town; (*Gen.* xvii, xix); বাইবেলের প্রাচীন নিয়মে উক্ত পাপাচারপূর্ণ নগরী; পাপাচারপূর্ণ নগরী, পাপপুরী।

gŏm-phĭ'-ă-sĭs, *n.* Looseness of the teeth; দন্তের শিথিলতা।

gŏn'-dö-lă, *n.* A long narrow boat used on Venetian canals; ভিনিস নগরীর খাল সমূহে ব্যবহৃত এক প্রকার হাল্‌কা অপ্রশস্ত নৌকা, ভিনীস

Gondola.

নগরীর কেলিনৌকা। **–lier',** *n.* One who rows a gondola; উক্ত নৌকাবাহক।

gŏne (*P. P.* of GO) **1.** Lost; hopeless; ruined; undone; "A *gone* case"; "A *gone* man"; হৃত; নিরাশ; ধ্বংসপ্রাপ্ত; নষ্ট, হত। **2.** Past; "The *gone* ages"; গত, অপগত, অতীত, বিগত। **A gone case**—A hopeless case; a person despaired of; নিরাশাজনক বিষয়; যে ব্যক্তির সম্পর্কে সমস্ত আশা পরিত্যক্ত হইয়াছে। **A gone coon**—A person who is ruined or lost, (*coon* is short for *racoon*); হৃতসর্ব্বস্ব ব্যক্তি, সর্ব্বস্বান্ত ব্যক্তি। **Too far gone**—In a desperate or hopeless condition; অতিশয় সঙ্কটে পতিত।

gŏn'-ĕr, *n.* (*Slang*) One who is dead or undone; (ইতরভাষায়) মৃত, সর্ব্বস্বান্ত।

gŏn'-fă-lŏn, *n.* An ensign or standard with tails or streamer, esp. a standard of some Italian republics; ইটালী দেশীয় পতাকা বিশেষ। **–ier',** *n.* **1.** A standard bearer; ধ্বজাবাহক, পতাকাধারী। **2.** The chief magistrate of any of the republics in mediæval Italy; মধ্যযুগে ইটালী দেশীয় নগরের প্রধান শাসনকর্ত্তা।

gŏng, *n.* **1.** A metal disc with upturned rim producing a resonant note when struck; কাঁসর, ঝাঁঝ। **Gong metal**—An alloy of copper and tin of which gongs are made; টীন ও তামা মিশ্রিত ধাতু—যদ্দ্বারা কাঁসর প্রস্তুত হয়।

gŏ-ni-ŏm′-ĕ-têr, *n.* An instrument for measuring angles ; কোণমাপক যন্ত্র। **–o-met′-ric, –o-met′-ri-cal,** *adjs.* **–try,** *n.* The art of measuring angles ; trigonometry ; কোণমিতি ; ত্রিকোণমিতি।

gŏn-ŏr-rhe′-ă (-ē-), *n.* **–rhœ′-** (-ē-), *ns.* An inflammatory discharge of mucus from the urethra or vagina ; প্রমেহ রোগ। **–al,** *adj.*

good, *adj.* & *n.* **1.** Not bad ; useful ; fit ; proper ; excellent ; satisfactory ; সু, ভাল ; প্রয়োজনীয় ; উপযুক্ত ; উপযোগী ; উত্তম ; সন্তোষজনক। **2.** Having the right qualities ; adequate ; as, *good* fire ; যথোচিতগুণসম্পন্ন ; যথোচিত, সমুচিত। **3.** Possessing moral qualities ; virtuous ; pious ; just ; সৎ, সাত্ত্বিক ; ধাৰ্ম্মিক, ধৰ্ম্মিষ্ঠ ; সাধু ; ন্যায়বান। **4.** Commendable ; as, his wife is far too *good* for him ; প্রশংসনীয়। **5.** Kind ; benevolent ; দয়ালু ; হিতকর, পরোপকারী, উপকারী। **6.** (Of child) Well behaved ; not giving trouble ; (শিশু-সম্পর্কে) সুশীল ; শান্ত, সুধীর। **7.** Suitable ; efficient, (with *for*) ; as, it is *good for* the purpose ; যোগ্য ; কাৰ্য্যকর। **8.** Clever ; as, a *good* workman ; he is *good* at drinking ; নিপুণ, দক্ষ, তৎপর। **9.** Pleasant ; agreeable ; as, a *good* company ; favourable ; beneficial ; wholesome ; মনোরম, মনোমদ ; প্রীতিপ্রদ ; অনুকূল ; হিতকর ; স্বাস্থ্যকর। **10.** Sound ; thorough ; valid ; as, gave her a *good* beating ; a *good* lesson ; নিখুঁৎ ; চূড়ান্ত, পুরা, সম্যক্ ; প্রমাণসিদ্ধ, সিদ্ধ। **11.** Reliable ; solvent ; বিশ্বস্ত ; সাউকার। **12.** Real ; actual ; serious ; as, in *good* earnest ; বাস্তব ; যথার্থ, প্রকৃত ; সত্যসত্য ইচ্ছুক। **13.** Not small or insignificant ; considerable ; as, a *good* deal ; অনল্প ; অসামান্য। **14.** Full ; complete ; as, he played for a *good* hour ; thorough ; পুরা ; পাকা ; ঝাড়া, বিলকুল। **15.** Not blemished ; unsullied ; as, a *good* name ; নিষ্কলঙ্ক, অকলঙ্ক ; নির্ম্মল। **16.** Honourable ; noble ; as, he comes of a *good* family ; মাননীয়, সম্মানিত ; সম্ভ্রান্ত। ***Noun.*** **1.** Virtuous persons ; as, *good* and bad alike respect him ; ধাৰ্ম্মিক ব্যক্তিগণ। **2.** That which is contributed to happiness, benefit or convenience etc. ; a desirable end or object ; সুখজনক বস্তু, হিতজনক বস্তু, সুবিধাজনক বিষয়, কল্যাণজনক বিষয় ; স্পৃহণীয় বস্তু বা আদর্শ, ইষ্টবস্তু। **3.** Welfare ; profit ; benefit ; advantage ; as, do it for the *good* of your country ; মঙ্গল, কল্যাণ, ভদ্র, শিব, শুভ, শ্রেয়ঃ ক্ষেম ; লাভ ; হিত, উপকার ; সুবিধা। **4.** (*Pl.*) Movable property ; অস্থাবর সম্পত্তি। **5.** (*Pl.*) Merchandise ; wares ; chattels ; things for transmission by rail etc. ; বাণিজ্য দ্রব্য ; মালপত্র ; দ্রব্যজাত, জিনিষ-পত্র ; মাল। **Good′-ish,** *adj.* Pretty good ; tolerable ; একপ্রকার ভাল ; মন্দ নয়। **Good′-ness,** *n.* সত্ত্ব (হিঃ কোঃ), সত্ত্বগুণ (ঐ)। **Good-breeding**—শিষ্টাচার, সভ্যতা, সৌজন্য, ভদ্রতা, সুশিক্ষা। **Good by, –bye**—স্বস্তি (কেঙিঃ), বিদায় হই, তবে আসি। **Good conditioned**—ভাল অবস্থায়। **Good day**—*n.* & *interj.* A common salutation at meeting or parting ; শুভদিন। **Good debts**—Debts which are sure to be paid ; যে সমস্ত ঋণ নিশ্চিতই পরিশোধ হইবে। **Good-fellow**—A person of compassionate qualities ; সুজন, মরমী জন। **Good-fellowship**—সামাজিকতা ; সঙ্গিপ্রিয়তা। **Good-folk**—সুজনসমাজ, সৎসমাজ। **Good-for-nothing, –nought**—*adj.* & *n.* worthless ; useless ; অকেজো, নিষ্কৰ্ম্মা, কাজেরবার ; অকৰ্ম্মণ্য, অপদার্থ। (*Noun*) An idle person, অলস ব্যক্তি **Good Friday**—যীশুখ্রীষ্টের ক্রুশারোহণ দিবস, যীশুখ্রীষ্টের ক্রুশারোহণ স্মারক খৃষ্টীয় পৰ্ব্ব দিবস। **Good heavens, Good gracious**—An exclamation of surprise ; হা ভগবন্ ! **Good humour**—A cheerful disposition ; amiability ; খোস্ মেজাজ ; কমনীয়তা। **Good humoured**—সুরসিক, খোসমেজাজী। *Good-humouredly*—*adj.* & *adv.* সুরসিক, খোস মেজাজে। (*Adv.*) খোসমেজাজে। **Good lady**—Wife ; madam ; স্ত্রী ; মহাশয়া। **Good law**—Valid or sound law ; অভ্রান্ত বিধি। **Good-looking**—Having a good appearance esp. referring to the beauty of the countenance ; সুন্দর, সুরূপ, সুশ্রী, সুদৃশ্য, ভদ্রদর্শন (বাৎস্যঃ), রূপান্বিত (বৃঃ সং), সুদর্শন প্রিয়দর্শন। **Good looks**—Personal beauty ; সৌন্দৰ্য্য, রূপ। **Good luck**—Good fortune ; success ; সৌভাগ্য ; সিদ্ধি। **Goodman**—(*Archaic*) The head of a household ; a husband, father etc. ; (অপ্রঃ) গৃহস্বামী, কর্ত্তা ; স্বামী, পিতা, প্রভৃতি। **Good manners**—Polite manners ; শিষ্টাচার। **Good money**—Genuine money ; খাঁটি টাকা। **Good-morning**—A salutation at meeting in the morning ; সুপ্রভাত (অভিবাদন বাক্য)। **Good-morrow**—(*Archaic*) Good morning ; (অপ্রঃ) শুভ প্রভাত, সুপ্রভাত। **Good nature**—Naturally mild and kind disposition ; সৎপ্রকৃতি। **Good-natured**—Kind and benignant ; সদাশয়, সৎস্বভাব, সুধীর। *Good-naturedly, adv.* *Good-natured-ness, n.* Virtue ; kindness ; সদ্গুণ ; দয়ালুতা। **Good-neighbourship**—Friendly conduct ; বন্ধুবৎ ব্যবহার। **Good news**—সুসংবাদ, খোসখবর। **Good night**—A salutation in parting at night ;

নিশাকালীন বিদায় সূচক অভিবাদন। **Goods engine**—মালগাড়ী টানিবার ইঞ্জিন। **Good sense**—Soundness of judgment ; practical wisdom ; সুবুদ্ধি ; কার্য্যকরী বুদ্ধি। **Good soil**—Fertile soil ; উর্ব্বরা ভূমি। **Goods train**—মালগাড়ী। **Good temper**—ভাল মেজাজ। **Good-tempered**—ধীর-প্রকৃতি, সৎপ্রকৃতি, মৃদু-প্রকৃতি। **Good Templar**—A member of a temperate society of the United States and of England ; (মার্কিণ যুক্ত রাজ্য এবং ইংলণ্ডের) মাদকতা নিবারণী সমিতির সভ্য। **Goodwife**—The mistress of a house ; গৃহিণী, গিন্নী। **Good will**—Benevolence ; kindly feeling ; হিত ; প্রীতি। Heartiness ; zeal ; cheerful consent ; আন্তরিকতা ; উৎসাহ ; আনন্দপূর্ণ সম্মতি। The custom of any trade or business ; ব্যবসায়ের পসার, গ্রাহক সম্বন্ধ (হিঃ কোঃ)। **A good fire**—A fire not too small or dull ; জ্বলন্ত অগ্নি। **A good hand at**—Expert or skilful at ; সিদ্ধহস্ত, সুদক্ষ, সুচতুর, সুনিপুণ। **A good leg**—A well-shaped leg ; সুগঠিত চরণ। **A good life**—One that is likely to last long, such as is accepted by an insurance office ; যে জীবন দীর্ঘস্থায়ী হওয়ার সম্ভব। **A good man**—See GOOD *adj.* II. **A good name** — An unsullied name ; সুনাম, অকলঙ্ক নাম। **A good round sum**—A large sum of money ; অনেক টাকা। **A good Samaritan**—A philanthrophist ; পরোপকারী ব্যক্তি। **A good thing**—An advantageous bargain or speculation ; a witty saying ; (*pl.*) dainties ; সুবিধাজনক দরে ক্রয় ; সরস উক্তি ; (বহুবচন) রসনা তৃপ্তিকর খাদ্য। **A good turn, office, etc.**—A good service; অনুগ্রহ, দয়ার কার্য্য, উপকার। **As good as** — The same as ; essentially ; practically ; সেইরূপ ; মূলতঃ ; কার্য্যতঃ। **As good as a play** — Very amusing or interesting ; অতিশয় কৌতূহলজনক, অতীব আমোদজনক। **As good as gold**—Thoroughly good and trustworthy ; অতিশয় সৎ ও বিশ্বাসযোগ্য। **For good**—Altogether; completely ; for ever ; একেবারে ; সম্পূর্ণরূপে ; জন্মের মত, চিরদিনের জন্য। **For good and all**—Finally ; permanently ; আগেরের মত, চিরকালের জন্য, জনমের শোধ ; চিরস্থায়িভাবে। **Good for anything**—Ready for any kind of work ; যে কোন কাজ করিতে প্রস্তুত। **Good Homer sometimes nods**—Great men even sometimes err ; মুনীনাঞ্চ মতিভ্রমঃ। **Good man's croft**—(In Scotland) A corner of a field untilled to avert the malice of the devil from the crop ; স্কটলণ্ডে শয়তানের দৃষ্টি হইতে শস্য রক্ষার জন্য কোণে যে নামমাত্র ভূমি অকর্ষিত রাখা হয়। **Good morning to anything**—Good bye or farewell to it ; কোন ব্যাপারের সহিত সংশ্রব ত্যাগ করা ; **I am as good as my word**—আমার যেই কথা সেই কাজ। **In good faith** — See under FAITH. **In good spirits** — Not depressed ; স্ফূর্ত্তিতে, খোস মেজাজে। **In good time**—In proper time ; যথাসময়ে, যথাকালে। **No good**—Some mischief ; as, to be after *no good* ; নষ্টামি। **Piece of goods**—(*Facet.*) A person ; (রঙ্গচ্ছলে) লোক। **The good**—শ্রেয়স্ (হিঃ কোঃ)। **The good folk** or **people**—Fairies ; পরীগণ। **The greatest good**—নিঃশ্রেয়স্ (হিঃ কোঃ), পরমপুরুষার্থ (ঐ)। **To be any, some, no, much good**—To be of any, some, etc. use ; কোন কাজের হওয়া, কিছুটা কাজের হওয়া। **To be in** or **get into one's good graces**—To be in favour with ; কাহারো অনুগ্রহভাজন হওয়া, কাহারও সুনজরে পড়া, কাহারও প্রিয়পাত্র হওয়া। **To come to good**—To yield good result ; সুফলপ্রদ হওয়া। **To do good**—To show kindness to ; to act philanthrophically ; to benefit ; to be beneficial to ; দয়া প্রকাশ করা ; জনহিতকর কার্য্য করা ; উপকার করা ; হিতকারী হওয়া। **To have a good mind**—To be much inclined (to do etc.) ; খুব ইচ্ছুক হওয়া। **To have a good night**—To sleep well ; সুনিদ্রা যাওয়া। **To have a good time**—To enjoy oneself ; সুখভোগ করা, আমোদপ্রমোদ করা। **To hold good**—To be valid, firm or sure ; to be operative ; to remain in force ; বৈধ হওয়া, দৃঢ় হওয়া, নিশ্চিত হওয়া ; কার্য্যকর হওয়া ; বলবৎ থাকা। **To make good**—To fulfil ; to perform ; to make up or compensate for ; to gain and hold, as a position ; to carry out with success ; to prove or verify as a statement ; to vindicate ; to replace or restore, as a thing lost or damaged ; পূরণ করা ; সম্পাদন করা ; ক্ষতিপূরণ করা ; দখল রাখা ; কৃতকার্য্যতার সহিত সম্পন্ন করা ; প্রমাণিত করা, সত্য বলিয়া সপ্রমাণ করা, সাব্যস্ত করা ; সমর্থন করা, সত্যতা প্রতিপাদন করা ; (নষ্ট বা হারান জিনিষ) পরিবর্ত্তে দেওয়া, পুনঃ স্থাপিত করা। **To say a good word for**—To recommend ; to defend ; কাহারও পক্ষে দুই একটা কথা বলা ; সমর্থন করা। **To stand good**—To be firm or valid; to hold good ; দৃঢ় হওয়া, বৈধ হওয়া ; বলবৎ হওয়া। **To take in good part**—Not to be annoyed at ; ভালভাবে গ্রহণ করা। **To the good**—As a balance on the profit side ; লাভের দিকে। **To think good**—To be pleased or satisfied with ; to consider good, advisable or expedient ; সন্তুষ্ট হওয়া, তৃপ্ত হওয়া ; ভাল মনে করা, উপযুক্ত মনে করা, উচিত মনে করা। **To write a good**

hand — To write clearly and legibly ; হস্তাক্ষর সুন্দর হওয়া।

gŏŏd'-lȳ, *adj.* **1.** Handsome ; fair ; সুদৃশ্য ; সুন্দর, সুশ্রী, ভদ্রদর্শন (বাংস্থঃ), প্রিয়দর্শন। **2.** Large ; বৃহৎ, বড়। **3.** (*Iron.*) Worthless or trifling ; (কৌতুকচ্ছলে) অসার, তুচ্ছ। **—li-ness,** *n.*

gŏŏd'-nĕss, *n.* **1.** The state or quality of being good ; virtue ; উৎকৃষ্টতা, গুণবত্তা ; সদ্গুণ। **2.** Excellence ; শ্রেষ্ঠতা। **3.** Kindness ; benevolence ; generosity ; দয়ালুতা ; পরোপকারিতা ; বদান্যতা। **4.** Strength or essence of a thing ; "Stew till all the *goodness* be got from the meat" ; সত্ব, সার। **5.** A euphemism for God ; as, *goodness* knows ; (মোলায়েম ভাষায়) ঈশ্বর। **Goodness gracious**—An exclamation of surprise or indignation ; হা ঈশ্বর ! **Goodness knows** — I do not know ; ঈশ্বর জানেন। **Have the goodness**—Be kind enough (to) ; দয়া করিয়া।

gŏŏd'-ȳ, *n.* (*Archaic*) An elderly woman of the lower class, (*often prefixed as a title to the surname*) ; নিম্নশ্রেণীর বৃদ্ধা স্ত্রীলোক।

gŏŏd'-ȳ, *n.* A bonbon, cake or the like ; পিঠা, মণ্ডা।

gŏŏd'-ȳ, gŏŏd-ȳ-gŏŏd'-ȳ, *adjs.* Weakly ; sentimentally or pretentiously good or virtuous ; squeamish in morals ; সদিচ্ছাসম্পন্ন অথচ দুর্ব্বলচিত্ত ; ধর্ম্মপ্রাণ অথচ ভাবপ্রবণ ; উৎকট-রুচি, খুঁতখুঁতে। **—i-ness,** *n.* **To talk goody**—To talk in a goody manner ; খুঁতখুঁতেভাবে আলাপ করা।

gōōs-ăn'-dĕr, *n.* A swimming bird, allied to ducks and divers ; হংসজাতীয় জলচর পক্ষিবিশেষ।

gōōse, *n.* **1.** A web-footed bird larger than a duck ; the flesh of this bird ; রাজহংস ; রাজহংসের মাংস। **2.** A tailor's smoothing iron (with handle like goose's neck) ; দরজীর ইস্ত্রী। **3.** A silly stupid person ; a simpleton ; নির্ব্বোধ, নির্ব্বোধলোক ; বোকারাম। **4.** A game played with dice on a card divided into compartments ; একপ্রকার ক্রীড়া। **Goose-club**—দরিদ্র ব্যক্তিকে খৃষ্টমাস পর্ব্বোপলক্ষে হংসমাংস প্রদানের জন্য সমিতি, হংসসমাজ। **Goose-egg**—The egg of a goose ; a zero ; হাঁসের ডিম ; শূন্য। **Goose-flesh**—A peculiar roughness of the human skin produced by cold or fright ; রোমাঞ্চ, পুলক। **Goose-foot**—A kind of plant ; বাস্তুক শাক (বনঃ), বেঁতোশাক (ঐ)। **Goose-herd**—One who tends goose ; হংসপালক। **Goose-quill**—A feather of a goose, used as pen ; হাঁসের পাখ, হাঁসের পাখের কলম। **Goose-step**—(*Mil.*) The marking of time by raising the feet alternately without advancing ; অগ্রসর না হইয়া সৈনিকগণের তালে তালে পা ফেলা। **Ruddy-goose**—চক্রবাক, কোক। **All his geese are swans**—He invariably overestimates ; নিজের ঘোল কেউ টক বলে না। **A sauce for the goose is sauce for the gander**—See under GANDER. **He steals a goose and gives the gibbets in alms**—He amasses wealth by unfair means and salves his conscience by giving small sums in charity ; সে হাঁস চুরি করিয়া তাহার নাড়ি ভুঁড়ি দান করে, অর্থাৎ সে অসদুপায়ে অর্থ উপার্জন করিয়া মনকে প্রবোধ দিবার জন্য সামান্য দুই এক পয়সা দান করে। **It's a gone goose with any one**—There is no more hope for him ; তাহার সম্পর্কে আর আশা নাই। **The goose that lays the golden eggs**—The source of a person's wealth or most cherished possessions ; স্বর্ণডিম্ব প্রসবকারী হংস (cf. our কামধেনু, কল্পতরু), কোন লোকের ধনাগমের মূল বা কাহারও অধিগত অতি মূল্যবান বস্তু। **The older the goose the harder to pluck**—Old men are unwilling to part with their money ; বুড়ো মানুষের কাছ থেকে টাকা বাহির করা অতি শক্ত কাজ। **To cook a person's goose for him**—To bring about his death ; কাহাকেও যমালয়ে প্রেরণ করা। **To get the goose**—To get hissed on the stage ; রঙ্গমঞ্চে টিটকারী পাওয়া। **To kill the goose that laid the golden eggs**—To destroy the source of ones' wealth ; ধনাগমের উপায় নষ্ট করা। **To say bo to the goose**—See under BO. **Wild goose chase**—An attempt to accomplish something impossible or unlikely of attainment ; অসাধ্য সাধনের জন্য বা কোনরূপ অপ্রাপ্য বস্তু অন্বেষণের জন্য পণ্ডশ্রম, নিষ্ফল প্রয়াস, অশ্বডিম্বের অন্বেষণ।

gōōse'-ber-rȳ (-bə-), *n.* **1.** The fruit of a thorny shrub ; the shrub itself ; কণ্টকবহুল গুল্ম বা তাহার ফল ; টেপারি ফল (প্রবোধ), নুরফল (ফার্সিঃ)। **Chinese gooseberry**—কামরাঙ্গা। **Gooseberry picker**—A person who plays gooseberry ; যে ব্যক্তি শোভনতার জন্য প্রকাশ্য স্থানে প্রণয়ী যুগলের সঙ্গে গমন করে। **As green as gooseberry**—Very ignorant of life ; অতিশয় সংসারানভিজ্ঞ। **Like old gooseberry** — Energetically ; সতেজে, সোৎসাহে। **To play gooseberry** — To accompany persons for propriety ; to appear with two lovers in public ; শোভনতার জন্য সঙ্গে যাওয়া ; লোক-নিন্দা বারণের জন্য প্রেমিক-প্রেমিকার সঙ্গে প্রকাশ্য স্থানে গমন করা। **To play up old gooseberry with one**—To take great liberties with his property and abuse it ; বিনানুমতিতে অন্যের জিনিষ ব্যবহার

এবং তাহার অপব্যবহার করা। To defeat or silence promptly: তৎক্ষণাৎ হারাইয়া দেওয়া বা চুপ করিয়া দেওয়া।

goos'-êr-ȳ *n.* **1.** A place for keeping geese; হংসাগার, হংসালয়। **2.** Silliness; মূঢ়তা।

goos'-ey (-i), *n.* A little goose; a blockhead; ক্ষুদ্র রাজহংস; জড়বুদ্ধি ব্যক্তি, নির্বোধ লোক, বোকারাম।

go'-pher *n.* See GOFFER.

Gor'-di-ăn, *adj.* Of Gordius, an ancient king of Phrygia, or of the knot tied by him; intricate; difficult; ফ্রিজিয়ার প্রাচীন রাজা গর্ডিয়াস্ অথবা তদীয় জটিল-গ্রন্থি-সম্পর্কীয়; জটিল; সুকঠিন। **Gordian knot**—ফ্রিজিয়ার রাজা গর্ডিয়াস্ কৃত জটিল গ্রন্থি [গর্ডিয়াস্ নামক জনৈক কৃষক ফ্রিজিয়ার রাজা নির্ব্বাচিত হইলে পর তদীয় শকট জুপিটার দেবকে উৎসর্গ করে। সে সেই শকটের জোয়াল শকটদণ্ডের সহিত এইরূপ সুকৌশলে বাঁধিয়াছিল যে, সেই গ্রন্থি কেহই খুলিতে সমর্থ হয় নাই। দিগ্বিজয়ী আলেকজেণ্ডার (অলীকসুন্দর বা শেকেন্দর শাহ) ফ্রিজিয়ায় উপস্থিত হইলে শ্রবণ করেন যে, যে ব্যক্তি উক্ত গ্রন্থি খুলিতে পারিবে সে সমগ্র প্রাচ্য ভূখণ্ডের উপর আধিপত্য বিস্তার করিবে। এই কথা শ্রবণ মাত্র "আমি এই ভাবে কার্য্য সাধন করি" এই বাক্য বলিতে বলিতে আলেকজেণ্ডার স্বীয় অসি দ্বারা গ্রন্থিটী দ্বিখণ্ডিত করিলেন]। A difficult problem or task; কঠিন কার্য্য; দুষ্কর কার্য্য। **To cut the Gordian knot**—See under CUT.

Gor'-di-ŭs, *n.* ফ্রিজিয়ার জনৈক রাজা। ফ্রিজিয়া রাজ্য অরাজক হইয়া পড়িলে দৈববাণী হয় যে, এক শকটারোহণে রাজা আসিবেন। ইহার কিছু দিন পর গর্ডিয়াস্ স্ত্রীপুত্রসহ শকটারোহণে উপস্থিত হইলে ফ্রিজিয়াবাসিগণ তাহাকে রাজপদে বরণ করে। এই গর্ডিয়াসকৃত জটিল গ্রন্থিই আলেকজেণ্ডার ছেদন করেন।

gōre, *n.* Clotted blood; জমাট রক্ত। **Gor'-y,** *adj.* Covered with gore: bloody; জমাট রক্ত দ্বারা আবৃত; রক্তাক্ত, রুধিরচর্চ্চিত, শোণিত-লিপ্ত। **Gor'-i-ly,** *adv.*

gōre, *n.* & *v. t.* **1.** A triangular piece of cloth inserted into a garment to narrow it; কোন পরিচ্ছদ স্বল্পায়ত করার জন্য তাহাতে যে ত্রিকোণ বস্ত্রখণ্ড সংযুক্ত করা যায়। **2.** A triangular or lune-shaped piece in an umbrella, balloon, dome, etc.; ছত্র, ব্যোমযান, গুম্বজ প্রভৃতিতে সংযুক্ত ত্রিকোণ বা ডিম্বাকার বস্ত্র খণ্ড। ***Verb t.*** To cut in a triangular form; to provide with a gore; ত্রিকোণাকারে কর্ত্তিত করা; ত্রিকোণ খণ্ডসমন্বিত করা।

gōre, *v. t.* **1.** (*Obs.*) To stab or pierce with a pointed instrument; (অপ্রঃ) সূক্ষ্মাগ্র কোন কিছুর দ্বারা বিদ্ধ করা, খোঁচা মারা। **2.** To pierce or wound with horns or tusks: (*fig.* of rocks etc.) to pierce, as a ship; শৃঙ্গ দ্বারা বিদ্ধ করা, শিঙের গুঁতা মারা; (লক্ষণায়—পাষাণ শৈলাদির পক্ষে) বিদীর্ণ করা, ভেদ করা।

gorge (gŏrj), *n.* **1.** The internal throat; the gullet; কণ্ঠমধ্য; গলনালী। **2.** A narrow passage usually with a stream between mountains; গিরিসঙ্কট, গিরিবর্ত্ম, গিরিদ্বার (সাঃ পঃ)। **3.** The entrance into a bastion or other outerwork of a fortress; দুর্গবহিঃস্থ উপদুর্গাদির প্রবেশদ্বার, দুর্গপ্রাকার হইতে বহিরুদ্গত পঞ্চভুজাকৃতি মৃত্তিকা স্তূপের প্রবেশ পথ। **4.** What has been swallowed; contents of the stomach; ভুক্ত দ্রব্য; পাকস্থলীর অভ্যন্তরস্থ বস্তু। **5.** (*U. S.*) Choking of a passage by obstructions; (মার্কিণ-যুক্তরাজ্য) কোনরূপ প্রতিবন্ধক হেতু পথরোধ। **6.** A solid object meant to be swallowed, as bait for a fish; বড়শীর টোপ স্বরূপ ব্যবহৃত কঠিন পদার্থ। **One's gorge rises at**—One is sickend or disgusted by; বিরক্ত হওয়া, অরুচি জন্মা। **To cast the gorge at**—To reject with loathing; ঘৃণার সহিত অগ্রাহ্য করা।

gorge (gŏrj), *v. i., t.* & *n.* To eat greedily; পেটুকের মত আহার করা। ***Verb t.*** **1.** To glut; to satiate; আকণ্ঠ ভোজন করা; পরিতৃপ্ত করা। **2.** To swallow; to devour greedily; as, the fish has *gorged* the hook; গ্রাস করা; লোলুপভাবে গলাধঃ করা। **3.** To choke up; to distend, as a vein with blood; রুদ্ধ করা; সম্প্রসারিত করা। ***Noun.*** Act of gorging; a glut; গলাধঃকরণ; আকণ্ঠ ভোজন।

Gorge (gŏrj), *n.* Calydon এর রাজা Æneus এর দুহিতা। ইঁহার ভগিনীগণ পক্ষিদেহ প্রাপ্ত হন। কেবল ইঁহার ও ইঁহার অপর এক ভগিনীর দেহ রূপান্তর প্রাপ্ত হয় নাই।

gŏr'-gē-ous (-ŭs), *adj.* **1.** Adorned with rich and various colours; splendid; magnificent; নানাবর্ণ-সমুজ্জ্বল, অনেকবর্ণদীপ্ত; উজ্জ্বল; জাঁকালো। **2.** (Of diction) Ornate; অলঙ্কার-বহুল। **—ly,** *adv.* **—ness,** *n.*

gŏr'-gĕt, *n.* **1.** (*Hist.*) A piece of armour to defend the throat or neck; (ইতিহাস) গ্রীবারক্ষণ বর্ম্ম, গলকবচ, গলত্রাণ, কণ্ঠত্রাণ, কণ্ঠকঞ্চুক। **2.** An ornament suspended from the neck, formerly worn by officers on duty; কণ্ঠদেশ হইতে বিলম্বিত ভূষা-বিশেষ, পদক। **3.** (*Hist.*) A wimple of a woman; (ইতিহাস) স্ত্রীলোকের অবগুণ্ঠন বিশেষ। **4.** A necklace; মালা, মালিকা, হার। **5.** (*Zool.*) A coloured patch on the throat of a bird etc.; (প্রাণি-বিদ্যা) পক্ষী প্রভৃতির কণ্ঠ দেশের রঞ্জিত স্থান।

gŏr'-gĕt, *n.* (*Surg.*) A channel-shaped steel instrument used in operation for stone etc.; (অস্ত্রোপচার-বিদ্যা) অশ্মরী প্রভৃতি রোগে অস্ত্র করার জন্য একপ্রকার প্রণালিকাকার যন্ত্র।

Gorgio, (*F.*), *n.* The designation given by gipsies to non-gipsy ; অ-যাযাবর জাতীয় লোক।

gŏr′-gŏn, *n.* (*Gk. myth.*) **1.** One of the snake-haired female monster (Stheno, Euryale and Medusa) whose looks turned the beholder to stone ; (গ্রীকপুরাণোক্ত) ঘোরদর্শনা, সর্প-কেশা দানবীত্রয়ের অন্যতম (Stheno, Euryale এবং Medusa) ইহাদিগের দৃষ্টিমাত্র মানুষ পাষাণে পরিণত হইত। **2.** (*l. c.*) A terrible or ugly person ; a repulsive woman ; ঘোররূপা নারী, উগ্রচণ্ডা, কুরূপা স্ত্রীলোক ; বিকটদর্শনানারী, ঘোরদর্শনা স্ত্রী। **—go′-ni-an,** *adj.* **Gorgon-fruit**—মাখনা (কানাই)।

gŏr-gō′-ni-ă, *n.* (*Pl.* -LE, -IAS), Sea-fan ; একজাতীয় প্রবাল।

gŏr′-gŏn-īze, *v. t.* To petrify ; to stare at with a Gorgon look ; পাষাণে পরিণত করা, শিলীভূত করা ; কটমট করিয়া চাওয়া।

Gŏr-gŏn-zō′-lă, *n.* A good cheese ; একপ্রকার উত্তম পনীর।

Gorilla.

gō-ril′-lă *n.* The largest animal of the ape kind ; আফ্রিকা দেশীয় বৃহৎ বানর, গরিলা।

gŏr′-mănd-īze, *n., v. i. & t.* ***(gourmandize*** *F.*, only *n.*), Gluttony ; বহুভোজন, ঔদরিকতা। ***Verb i. & t.*** To eat greedily ; পেটুকের মত আহার করা, অতিশয় ভোজন করা, অতিরিক্ত ভোজন করা। **-iz-er,** *n.*

gorse (gŏrs), *n.* A prickly shrub ; পীতপুষ্পপ্রসূ কণ্টকাকীর্ণ গুল্ম বিশেষ।

gŏsh, *interj.* By God (also *by gosh*) ; ঈশ্বরের নামে।

gŏs′-hawk (-hăk), *n.* A large hawk with short wings ; এক প্রকার খর্ব্বপুচ্ছ বাজপক্ষী।

Gō′-shĕn, *n.* A place of plenty or light (Genesis xlv. 10 etc.) ; ধনরত্নসম্ভারপূর্ণ স্থান, জ্যোতির্ম্ময় স্থান।

gŏs′-ling, *n.* A young goose ; রাজহংস শাবক।

gŏs′-pĕl, *n.* **1.** Glad tidings preached by Christ ; hence the doctrines of Christ and his apostles ; সুসমাচার, সুবার্ত্তা (কেস্তিঃ), শুভবার্ত্তা (ঐ) ; খৃষ্ট এবং তদীয় শিষ্যবৃন্দের ধর্ম্মমত। **2.** (*Cap.*) One of the four records of Christ's life by his apostles Matthew, Mark, Luke and John ; any of those books ; খৃষ্ট শিষ্য মথি, মার্ক, লুক ও জন কর্তৃক রচিত পুস্তক চতুষ্টয়ে লিখিত খৃষ্টজীবনী ; উক্ত পুস্তক চতুষ্টয়ের অন্যতম। **3.** A selection from one of the Gospels used in church service ; খৃষ্টীয় ধর্ম্মমন্দিরে উপাসনাকালে পঠিত উক্ত কোন পুস্তকের অংশ বিশেষ। **4.** Any general doctrine or principle ; সাধারণ ধর্ম্মমত বা মূলতত্ত্ব। **5.** A thing that may be safely believed ; absolute truth ; as, they took his word for *gospel* ; অনায়াসে বিশ্বাসযোগ্য বিষয় ; বেদবাক্য, আপ্তবাক্য, অকাট্য সত্য, ধ্রুব সত্য। **—ler,** *n.* The reader of gospel in Communion service ; যে ব্যক্তি উপাসনাকালে সুসমাচার গ্রন্থ পাঠ করিয়া থাকে। **Gospel-book**—উপাসনাকালে পঠিত বাইবেলের সুসমাচার পুস্তক। **Gospel oath**—বাইবেল স্পর্শ করিয়া শপথ। **Gospel-shop**— মেথডিষ্টদিগের ধর্ম্মমন্দির। **Gospel-side**—বেদীর উত্তর পার্শ্ব—যথায় বাইবেল গ্রন্থ পঠিত হয়। **Gospel-truth** — বাইবেলের সুসমাচার গ্রন্থোক্ত সত্য সমূহ। Something as true as the Gospel ; বেদবাক্য।

gŏs′-sa-mêr (-ă-), *n.* & *adj.* **1.** A fine filmy substance floating in the air in calm weather ; spider's webs ; বুড়ীর সুতা ; মাকড়সার জাল লূতাতন্তু, ঊর্ণনাভ জাল। **2.** Something flimsy ; অতি সূক্ষ্ম বস্তু। **3.** A very thin fabric ; a delicate gauze ; খুব পাতলা কাপড় ; মিহি জাল। ***Adj.*** Light and flimsy as a gossamer ; মাকড়সার জালের ন্যায় মিহি ও পাতলা, লূতাতন্তু-সূক্ষ্ম। **—mered, —y,** *adjs.* **Gossamer-spider**—একজাতীয় ক্ষুদ্রকায় মাকড়সা।

gŏs′-sip, *n.* & *v. i.* **1.** (*Archaic*) An intimate acquaintance ; friend (esp. of women) ; (অপ্রঃ) সবিশেষ পরিচিত ব্যক্তি ; বন্ধু। **2.** An idle talker ; a newsmonger (mostly a woman) ; যে ব্যক্তি বাজে কথা বলে, গল্পিয়া, গল্পগুজব প্রিয় ব্যক্তি ; যে ব্যক্তি নানা স্থানে প্রচার বা খবর সংগ্রহ করিয়া বেড়ায়। **3.** An idle talk ; an unfounded rumour ; tittle-tattle ; বৃথা গল্প, বাজে কথা ; অমুলক রটনা, জনরব ; গল্পসল্প, গল্পগুজব, গল্পগাছা। **4.** A light talk or writing about a person or social incident ; বৈঠকী আলাপ, চুট্‌কী। ***Verb i.*** **1.** To prate ; to talk idly or lightly ; গল্পসল্প করা, গল্পগুজব করা ; বাজে কথা বকা। **2.** To run about and tattle ; গল্পগুজব করিয়া বেড়ান। **3.** To write in a gossiping style ; চুট্‌কীর ভাষায় লিখা। **—er,** *n.* **—ry,** *n.* **1.** Spiritual relationship or affinity ; আধ্যাত্মিক সম্বন্ধ। **2.** Idle talk ; বাজে গল্প, গালগল্প, বৃথা গল্প। **—y,** *adj.* Full of, or given to, gossip ; গল্পিয়া, গল্পপ্রিয়।

gŏs-sōōn′, *n.* *(Ang. Ind.)* A lad ; ছোকরা, ছেলে।

gŏt, *p. t.* & *p. p.* of GET. **Got-up**—Facetious ; concocted ; কৃত্রিম, কপট ; সাজানো। **Ill got**—অন্যায়োপার্জ্জিত (কেস্তিঃ), অসদুপায়ে অর্জ্জিত। **Well got**—ন্যায়োপার্জ্জিত (কেস্তিঃ)।

Góth, *n.* **1.** One of an ancient Teutonic race who pouring down upon from the North founded kingdoms of Italy, France and Spain; এল্‌ব ও ভিশ্‌চুলা নদীর মধ্যবর্ত্তী প্রদেশবাসী যে প্রাচীন জর্ম্মণজাতি খৃষ্টীয় ৩য় হইতে ৫ম শতাব্দীর মধ্যভাগে ফ্রান্স, স্পেন ও ইতালীদেশে রাজ্যস্থাপন করে। **2.** One who is rude or uncivilized; a barbarian; one destroying works of art or defective in taste; রূঢ় ব্যক্তি, অসভ্য লোক, চোয়াড়; বর্ব্বর; চিত্র প্রভৃতি মূল্যবান কলাদ্রব্য ধ্বংসকারী, সুরুচিহীন ব্যক্তি। **Goth'-ish,** *adj.*

Gŏt'-hăm (-ăm), *n.* A village proverbial for the folly of its inhabitants; গ্রামবিশেষ—যথাকার অধিবাসিগণ অতিশয় নির্ব্বোধ বলিয়া কথিত আছে, হবুচন্দ্রের দেশ; **Go'-tham-ite,** *n.* A simpleton; বেকুব। **A wise man of Gotham**—হবুচন্দ্রের দেশের লোক।

Gŏth'-ic, *adj.* & *n.* **1.** Of, or relating to, the Goths or their language; rude; barbarous; uncivilized; গথজাতি-সম্বন্ধীয়, গথ জাতির ভাষাসম্বন্ধীয়; রূঢ়, অশিক্ষিত; বর্ব্বর; অসভ্য। **2.** Pertaining to the style of architecture with sharp pointed arches; গথিক স্থাপত্য-রীতি সম্পর্কীয় [সূক্ষ্মাগ্র তোরণ মালা গথিক স্থাপত্য রীতির বিশেষত্ব।] **3.** *(Printing etc.)* German etc. as a type; জর্ম্মণ প্রভৃতি (মুদ্রাক্ষর রূপে)। ***Noun.*** **1.** The language of the Goths; গথদিগের ভাষা। **2.** *(Arch.)* The Gothic style of architecture; গথিক স্থাপত্য-রীতি। **3.** *(Print.)* A kind of square-cut type; একপ্রকার হরফ। **—i-cal-ly,** *adv.* **—i-cise,** *v. i.* & *t.* To make Gothic; to bring back to barbarousness; গথ ভাবাপন্ন করা; পুনরায় বর্ব্বরাবস্থা প্রাপ্ত হওয়া। **—i-cism,** *n.* **1.** A Gothic idiom; গথ ভাষার রীতিসিদ্ধ প্রয়োগ। **2.** Rudeness of manners; রূঢ়তা। **3.** Conformity to the Gothic style or architecture; গথিক স্থাপত্য-রীতির অনুযায়ী।

Gothic.

gouache, (*F.*), *n.* A method of painting in opaque colours, ground in water and thickened with gum and honey; গম এবং মধু দ্বারা ঘনীকৃত জলে গুলা অস্বচ্ছ বর্ণ দ্বারা রঞ্জনের প্রণালী-বিশেষ, অনচ্ছরঞ্জন।

gouge (gowj), *n.* & *v. t.* **1.** A chisel with a concave blade, used in carpentry and surgery; সূত্রধর বা অস্ত্রচিকিৎসকের বক্রপৃষ্ঠ বাটালি বিশেষ, কোর-বাটালি। **2.** A book-binder's tool; দপ্তরীর যন্ত্র বিশেষ। ***Verb t.*** **1.** To scoop out or cut (as) with a gouge, (sometimes with *out*); কোর-বাটালি দ্বারা খাঁজ কাটা, খুঁড়িয়া গর্ত্ত করা। **2.** To force out as a person's eye etc. with a gouge or the thumb; to force out the eye of; বৃদ্ধাঙ্গুলি বা অস্ত্রচিকিৎসকের যন্ত্র বিশেষ দ্বারা চাপ দিয়া চক্ষু প্রভৃতি বাহির করিয়া ফেলা; টিপিয়া চক্ষু বাহির করা।

Gou-lârd (gô-), *n.* A lotion of subacetate of lead in solution (from T. Goulard, a French surgeon); একপ্রকার সীসক মিশ্রিত ঔষধ জল।

gourd (görd, gôrd), *n.* **1.** A large fleshy fruit; the gourd plant; লাউ, কুমড়া, তুম্বী, অলাবু; লাউগাছ, অলাবুতরু। **2.** The rind of a gourd emptied and dried for use as a bottle etc.; অলাবু পাত্র, অলাবু (মঃ সং)। **Gourd'-ful,** *n.* As much as a gourd will hold; অলাবুপাত্রপূর্ণ। **Red gourd**—মিষ্ট কুমড়া (ওয়াট্)। **Snake gourd**—চিচিঙ্গা।

gour'-mând (gôr-), *n.* & *adj.* A greedy eater; a glutton; a judge of good eating; পেটুক; ঔদরিক; সুখাদ্যবিচারক্ষম ব্যক্তি। ***Adj.*** Voracious; fond of eating; gluttonous; পেটুক, উদর-পিশাচ (অঃ); ভোজনবিলাসী; উদর-পরায়ণ, ঔদরিক। **—ism,** *n.*

gour-met' (gôr-mā, gôr-mĕt), (*F.*), *n.* A connoisseur in eating and drinking; আহার্য্য ও পানীয়ের দোষ গুণজ্ঞ, খাদ্য ও পানীয়ের উৎকর্ষাপকর্ষ বিচারক।

gout (gowt), *n.* **1.** A painful disease with inflammation of smaller joints and esp. of the great toe; গ্রন্থিপ্রদাহ, গেঁটে বাত, গ্রন্থিবাত, গৃধ্রসী (সাঃ পঃ), বাতরোগ (কেভিঃ), বায়ু (ঐ), সন্ধিবায়ু (ঐ), শূল (ঐ)। **2.** A wheat disease caused by gout-flies; কীটজনিত গোধূমরোগ-বিশেষ। **3.** A drop or splash of blood or other liquids; রক্ত কিম্বা অন্য তরলপদার্থের বিন্দু বা ছিটা। **4.** Spot of colour; বর্ণের দাগ। **Gout'-i-ly,** *adv.* **Gout'-i-ness,** *n.* **Gout'-y,** *adj.* **1.** Relating to gout; গ্রন্থিবাতসম্পর্কীয় **2.** Affected with, or subject to, the gout; গ্রন্থিবাতাক্রান্ত, গ্রন্থিবাত-প্রবণ।

gout (*F.*), *n.* Taste; relish; good taste; স্বাদ; তার, রস; সুস্বাদ।

Govannon, Goibniu — The Celtic god of smithcraft, architecture, etc; কেল্টদিগের বিশ্বকর্ম্মা।

gov'-ĕrn (gŭv-), *v. t.* & *i.* **1.** To direct and control; as, to *govern* and rule multitudes; শাসন করা। **2.** To be in military command of (a fort, town, etc.); দুর্গাধিকারী হওয়া, কোন নগরের সামরিক শাসনকর্ত্তা হওয়া। **3.** To regulate; to influence; to determine; to restrain; to manage; as, to *govern* a house; নিয়মিত করা, নিয়ন্ত্রিত করা; প্রভাবিত করা; স্থির করা, নিরূপিত করা; নিরোধ করা; নির্ব্বাহ করা, পরিচালনা করা। **4.** To curb; to bridle; as, to *govern* oneself or one's passions etc.; সংযত করা, সংযমিত করা; দমন করা। 5. To constitute a law or principle for; to serve in deciding as a case etc.; বিধি বা মূলতত্ত্ব প্রতিষ্ঠিত করা; মোকদ্দমা প্রভৃতির নিষ্পত্তি সাধনে কার্য্যকরী হওয়া। 6. To affect so as to determine the case etc. in Grammar; এরূপ ভাবে ক্রিয়া করা যাহাতে কারক প্রভৃতি নিরূপণ করা যায়। *Verb i.* 1. To exercise authority; to administer the laws; as, king reigns but does not *govern*; ক্ষমতা পরিচালন করা, আধিপত্য খাটান; বিধিপ্রয়োগ করা। 2. To be the predominating influence; প্রভাবশালী হওয়া। **–a-ble,** *adj.* Capable of being governed; controllable; manageable; obedient; শাসনীয়, শাস্য, বশ্য; দমনীয়, দম্য, সংযমনীয়; পরিচালনযোগ্য; বাধ্য। **–a-bil'-i-ty,** *n.* **–ing,** *adj.*

gov'-êrn-ance (gŭv-êrn-ăns) *n.* Act, manner, office or power of governing; control; sway; শাসন, শাসন-রীতি, শাসনকর্ত্তার পদ, শাসনশক্তি; কর্তৃত্ব; প্রভুত্ব, আধিপত্য।

gov'-êrn-ĕss (gŭv-), *n.* 1. A female who governs; শাসনকর্ত্রী, শাসনকারিণী। 2. An instructress or tutoress; উপদেষ্ট্রী, গৃহশিক্ষয়িত্রী, উপদেশিকা। **Governess car(t)**—সামনাসামনি দুইটী আসনওয়ালা একপ্রকার হাল্কা দু' চাকার গাড়ী।

gov'-êrn-mĕnt (gŭv-), *n.* 1. The act of governing; the exercise of authority; administration (of public affairs); control; direction; regulation; শাসন; ক্ষমতা পরিচালন; শাসনকার্য্যপরিচালন; নিয়মন, নিয়ন্ত্রণ, সংযমন; পরিচালন, নির্ব্বাহ; ব্যবস্থাপন। 2. The system of governing; the form of polity; as, a monarchical *government*; (রাজ্য) শাসনপ্রণালী, রাজপ্রবন্ধ (হিঃ কোঃ), শাসনতন্ত্র, রাজ্যতন্ত্র; (সাঃ পঃ), রাষ্ট্রতন্ত্র, রাজ্যব্যবস্থা, রাষ্ট্রব্যবস্থা। 3. A body politic under one authority; a state; a province or territory under a governor; রাষ্ট্র; সরকার, রাজ্য (হিঃ কোঃ), রাজসরকার; শাসনকর্ত্তার অধীন প্রদেশ বা ভূখণ্ড। 4. The person or persons authorized to administer the laws; ruling power; ministry; শাসনকর্ত্তা, শাসকবর্গ; শাসনশক্তি; মন্ত্রিসমাজ, মন্ত্রিবর্গ। 5. The office or function of governing authority; শাসনকর্ত্তার পদ, শাসনকর্ত্তার কার্য্য। 6. (*Gram.*) The influence of one word in determining the form of another; (ব্যাকরণ) কোন অপর শব্দের আকার নিরূপণে প্রভাব, অধিকার (কেঃডিঃ)। **–men'-tal,** *adj.* **–men'-tal-ly,** *adv.* **Government house**—Official residence of a governor; শাসনকর্ত্তার সরকারী আবাসভবন, লাটভবন। **Government paper, securities**—কোম্পানীর কাগজ প্রভৃতি।

gov'-er-nor (gŭv-êr-nêr), *n.* 1. A person who governs, a ruler; শাসক, নিয়ন্তা, নিয়ামক; শাসনকর্ত্তা। 2. A person appointed to govern a province, fort, town etc.; প্রাদেশিক শাসনকর্ত্তা, দুর্গেশ, দুর্গাধিপতি, নগরাধিপতি। 3. (*In India*) The ruler of Bengal, Bombay or Madras presidencies; (ভারতবর্ষে) বঙ্গ, মাদ্রাজ বা বোম্বের শাসনকর্ত্তা। 4. A head of an institution or one of a governing body; as, the *governor* of the Bank of England or of the Pentonville Convict Prison; কোন প্রতিষ্ঠানের অধ্যক্ষ বা কার্য্যনির্ব্বাহক সভ্যগণের অন্যতম। 5. (*Slang*) An employer; a father; (ইতর ভাষায়) মনিব; পিতা। 6. A sort of fishing fly; বড়শীর টোপের জন্য একপ্রকার মাছি। 7. (*Mech.*) A contrivance for maintaining a uniform velocity; (যন্ত্র বিজ্ঞান) নিয়ত একরূপ বেগ অক্ষুন্ন রাখার জন্য যন্ত্র-বিশেষ। **–ship,** *n.* The office of a governor; শাসনকর্ত্তার পদ।

gov'-er-nor–gĕn'-êr-ăl (gŭv-êr-nêr-), The supreme governor having lieutenant or deputy-governor under him; সর্ব্বপ্রধান শাসনকর্ত্তা, রাজপ্রতিনিধি, বড়লাট, উপরাজ। **–ship,** *n.*

gōw'-ăn, *n.* (*Scot.*) The daisy; (স্কটলণ্ডে) আরণ্য পুষ্প-বিশেষ।

gowk, *n.* 1. (*Dial.*) A cuckoo; (প্রাদেশিক) কোকিল। 2. A simpleton; a fool; বোকা, বেকুব, গোকারাম; নির্ব্বোধ।

gown, *n.* & *v. t.* 1. A woman's outer garment; স্ত্রীলোকের ঘাগরা, পেশোয়াজ। 2. The ancient Roman toga; প্রচীন রোমানদিগের উত্তরীয় বা গাত্রবস্ত্র। 3. The official robe of various shapes worn by judges, lawyers, clergymen etc.; বিচারক, ব্যবহারজীবী ও ধর্ম্মযাজক প্রভৃতির বহিঃপরিচ্ছদ, গাউন। *Verb t.* (*Chiefly in p. p.*) To dress in a gown; ঘাঘরা পরান। **Gownsman**—অসামরিক বিভাগের লোক; বিশ্ববিদ্যালয়ের সভ্য। **Town and gown**—অক্সফোর্ড বা কেম্ব্রিজ বিশ্ববিদ্যালয়ের সভ্য বা সভ্যশ্রেণীর বহির্ভূত ব্যক্তিসমূহ।

Graaf'-i-ăn (grăf-), *adj.* Relating to, or discovered by, R. de Graaff, a Dutch physician; ওলন্দাজ ভিষক আর, দা গ্রাফ সম্পর্কীয় বা তদাবিষ্কৃত। **Graafian follicles or vescicles**—ডিম্বকোষের উপরিভাগস্থ ডিম্বাণুধারী ক্ষুদ্র ক্ষুদ্র গোলাকার কোষ (হঃ চঃ)।

grăb, *v. t., i.* & *n.* 1. To seize or clutch suddenly; to grasp; hence to appopriate to oneself rapaciously; as, to *grab* a franchise; খপ্ করিয়া ধরা; মুঠ করিয়া ধরা, আঁকড়াইয়া ধরা; কাড়িয়া আত্মসাৎ করা। 2. To capture; ধরা। *Verb i.* To make a snatch at; কাড়িয়া লইতে চেষ্টা করা।

Noun. **1.** A sudden grasp or clutch ; an attempt to seize ; হঠাৎ মুট করিয়া ধরণ ; আঁকড়াইয়া ধরার চেষ্টা। **2.** The act or practice of grabbing ; rapacious proceedings (esp. in politics or commerce) ; আঁকড়াইয়া ধরণ ; লুণ্ঠন কার্য্য। **3.** An implement or device for clutching objects ; আঁকড়াইয়া ধরার জন্য যন্ত্র বা কৌশল বিশেষ, আঁকড়া। **4.** A children's game at card ; ছেলেদের একপ্রকার তাসখেলা। **Grab'-ber,** *n.*

grăb'-ble (-bl), *v. i.* **1.** To grope about ; to feel with the hands ; হাতড়াইয়া বেড়ান ; হাতড়ান। **2.** To lie prostrate on the belly ; to sprawl on all fours ; to grovel ; উপুড় হইয়া শয়ন করা ; হাত পা ছড়াইয়া উপুড় হইয়া শয়ন করা ; লুটাইয়া পড়া, ভূলুণ্ঠিত হওয়া।

grace (grās), *n.* & *v. t.* **1.** Pleasing or attractive quality ; charm ; "*Grace* was in all her steps" ; ease and refinement of movement ; মাধুর্য্য, বিভ্রম (সাঃ পঃ) ; মনোহারিত্ব, লালিত্য ; গতি-মাধুরী, লীলাগতি, গমন-মাধুর্য্য। **2.** (*Theol.*) The unmerited love and favour of God ; mercy ; divine influence ; enjoyment of divine favour ; প্রসাদ, দেবপ্রসাদ (ব্রজঃ বৈষ্ণঃ) ; ঈশ্বর কৃপা, ভগবদনুগ্রহ, অনুগ্রহ (বেদান্ত) ; ঈশ্বর প্রেরণা (কেঙিঃ), ঈশ্বর-প্রেরিত বুদ্ধি (ঐ) ; ঈশ্বরানুগ্রহ-ভোগ, দেবানুগ্রহ-প্রাপ্তি। **3.** Favour ; good will ; "Came to the court for an act of *grace*" ; a favour conferred ; a kindness ; অনুগ্রহ ; প্রীতি ; উপকার, প্রীতির কার্য্য। **4.** Becomingness ; as, with good *grace* (as if willing) ; শোভনতা, ঔচিত্য, সুষ্ঠুতা। **5.** Beauty ; loveliness ; accomplishment ; embellishment ; রূপ, সৌন্দর্য্য ; লাবণ্য, চারুতা, কান্তি, রমণীয়তা ; অর্জ্জিতগুণাবলী ; বিভূষণ, ভূষা। **6.** (*Pl.—Gr. Myth.*) One of the three ancient sister goddesses (Euphrosyne, Aglaia and Thalia) in whose gift were grace, loveliness and favour ; মাধুর্য্য, লাবণ্য, কান্তি এবং দেবানুগ্রহের অধিষ্ঠাত্রী গ্রীক-পুরাণোক্ত দেবী ভগিনীত্রয়। **7.** A title used in addressing or speaking of a duke or duchess or an archbishop (*preceded by possessive pronoun*) ; as, her *grace* the duchess of Bedford ; ডিউক, ডিউক পত্নী এবং আর্চ বিশপের সম্বোধনে ব্যবহৃত উপাধি বিশেষ। **8.** Favour shown by granting delay ; as, a day's *grace* ; সময় প্রদানে যে অনুগ্রহ প্রদর্শিত হয়। **9.** (*Eng. University*) An act, vote or decree of the senate or governing body ; (ইংলণ্ডীয় বিশ্ববিদ্যালয়) বিশ্ব-বিদ্যালয়ের কার্য্যকরী সভার বিধি, মত বা বিধান। **10.** (*Pl.—Mus.*) Embellishment of an extra note or notes not essential to the harmony or melody, (also *grace note*) ; মাধুর্য্য বর্দ্ধনের জন্য স্বরসঙ্গতি বা সুতানের পক্ষে অনাবশ্যক অতিরিক্ত সুর। **11.** A short prayer before or after a meal ; ভোজনের পূর্ব্বে বা পরে সংক্ষিপ্ত প্রার্থনা বা ঈশ্বরস্তুতি। ***Verb t.*** **1.** To give or add grace to ; to adorn ; to embellish ; মাধুর্য্যসমন্বিত করা, রূপান্বিত করা, মাধুর্য্য বর্দ্ধন করা ; মণ্ডিত করা ; বিভূষিত করা, সুশোভিত করা। **2.** To dignify ; to honour, as with a title etc. ; গৌরবান্বিত করা ; সম্মানিত করা। **3.** To do credit to ; গৌরবের কারণ হওয়া। **Grace'-ful,** *adj.* Elegant ; easy ; marked by prosperity ; agreeable ; মাধুর্য্যপূর্ণ, সুললিত, সুচারু, লাবণ্যময়, কান্ত, সবিভ্রম, রমণীয়, শোভন ; স্বচ্ছন্দ, সহজ, সলীল ; সমৃদ্ধিযুক্ত ; শোভন, প্রীতিপ্রদ। **Grace'-ful-ly,** *adv.* **Grace'-ful-ness,** *n.* **Grace'-less,** *adj.* **1.** (*Archaic* or *facet.*) Depraved ; corrupt ; abandoned ; (অপ্রঃ বা রঙ্গচ্ছলে) ভ্রষ্ট, দুষ্ট ; পাপাসক্ত ; পতিত, দুরাচার। **2.** Wanting sense of decency or propriety ; দুর্বিনীত, অভব্য। **3.** Wanting charm or elegance, (*rare*) ; (কচিদ্ ব্যবহৃত) অসুন্দর, মাধুর্য্যহীন। **Grace'-less-ly,** *adv.* **Grace'-less-ness,** *n.* **Good graces**—Favour ; অনুগ্রহ, সুদৃষ্টি, সুনজর। **Grace-cup, —drink—** ভোজনান্তে পেয় পেয়ালাপূর্ণ সুরা। **Grace stroke** — A finishing stroke or touch ; শেষ চানকান। **Saving grace**—মুক্তিপথের সহায়ক ঈশ্বর-প্রসাদ। **Act of Grace**—A formal or general pardon by an Act of Parliament ; পার্লেমেন্টের আইন দ্বারা সর্ব্বজনীন ক্ষমা। **Airs and graces**—ঠাট, ঠমক। **By the grace of God**—Appended to royal titles ; রাজোপাধির শেষে ব্যবহৃত হয়। **Days of grace**—হুণ্ডীর টাকা দেওয়ার তারিখ অতীত হইলে যে তিন দিবস সময় দেওয়া হয়। **Means of grace**—Means of securing knowledge of God ; opportunities of hearing the Gospel ; ব্রহ্মজ্ঞান লাভের উপায় ; বাইবেলের সুসমাচার শ্রবণের সুযোগ। **The throne of grace** — (*Fig.*) God's seat ; heaven ; (লক্ষণায়) ভগবানের আসন ; স্বর্গ। **To be in the good graces of** — To enjoy the favour or liking of ; কাহারও প্রীতিভাজন হওয়া, অনুগ্রহভাজন হওয়া, কাহারও সুনজরে পড়া। **To fall from grace**—To backslide ; to lapse from the state of grace and salvation ; স্বধর্মভ্রষ্ট হওয়া ; ভগবৎ কৃপা হইতে বঞ্চিত হওয়া, মুক্ত অবস্থা হইতে পতিত হওয়া। **To have the grace to** —To do something that decency requires ; যাহাতে শোভনতা বা সুরুচিসম্পন্নতা রক্ষা হয় তেমন কাজ করা। **To say grace**—To ask the divine blessing before or after a meal ; ভোজনের পূর্ব্বে বা অন্তে ঈশ্বরাশীর্ব্বাদ প্রার্থনা করা। **To take the heart of**

grace—To take courage from favour shown ; অনুগ্রহলাভে উৎসাহিত হওয়া, অনুগ্রহ লাভ করিয়া ভরসা বা সাহস পাওয়া। **With a bad** or **ill grace**—In a reluctant manner ; ungraciously ; অনিচ্ছাপূর্ব্বক, নারাজভাবে ; কদর্য্যভাবে। **With a good grace**—Gracefully ; with a show of willingness ; সুন্দররূপে, মধুরভাবে, সুচারুরূপে ; ইচ্ছার সহিত।

gra'-cious (-shŭs), *adj.* & *interj.* **1.** (*Archaic*) Agreeable ; having pleasing qualities ; excellent ; (অপ্রঃ) প্রীতিপ্রদ, মনোজ্ঞ ; রম্য, সদ্‌গুণসম্পন্ন ; উৎকৃষ্ট। **2.** Merciful ; beneficial ; benignant ; condescending ; as, His most *Gracious* Majesty ; করুণাময়, দয়াময়, কারুণিক, দয়াবন্ত (কেভিঃ), দয়ালু, করুণানিধান ; কল্যাণজনক, হিতকর ; সদয়, অনুগ্রহশীল, প্রসন্ন, সুমনাঃ, সপ্রসাদ ; হীন ব্যক্তির প্রতি অনুগ্রহশীল। **3.** Benevolent ; courteous, (*chiefly poet.*) ; উপকারী; ভদ্র, শিষ্ট (প্রধানতঃ কবিতায়)। ***Interj.*** (*Ellip. for Gracious God*) An exclamation of surprise ; as, good *gracious* ! my *gracious* ! হা ঈশ্বর ! হরি ! হরি ! **—ly,** *adv.* In a gracious manner ; favourably ; kindly ; with kind condescension ; ভদ্রভাবে, প্রীতির সহিত ; অনুগ্রহপূর্ব্বক, কৃপাপূর্ব্বক, কৃপাপুরঃসর; দয়াপূর্ব্বক ; হীনজনের প্রতি দয়া প্রদর্শনে। **—ness,** *n.* The quality of being gracious ; kindness ; অনুগ্রহশীলতা ; কৃপা (কেভিঃ), কৃপাদৃষ্টি (ঐ), কৃপাকটাক্ষ (ঐ), অনুগ্রহ (ঐ), প্রসাদ (ঐ), কৃপালুতা (ঐ)।

gră'-date, *v.i.* & *t.* **1.** (Of colours) To pass gradually from one shade to another ; (বর্ণ সম্বন্ধে) এক বর্ণের আভা অপর বর্ণে ক্রমে মিলাইয়া যাওয়া। **2.** To arrange in grades ; বিভিন্ন স্তরে বা শ্রেণীতে বিন্যস্ত হওয়া। ***Verb t.*** **1.** To cause (colours etc.) to pass gradually from one shade to another ; এক বর্ণের আভা ক্রমশঃ অপর বর্ণের আভায় বিলীন করা।

gră-dā'-tion, *n.* **1.** (*Usu. Pl.*) Progressive movements ; stages of advance ; অগ্রগতি ; উন্নতির ক্রম, অনুক্রম, ক্রমিকগতি। **2.** A series of degrees in rank, merit, intensity, etc. ; arrangement in a series of degrees ; ক্রম, ধাপ, সোপান; ক্রমবিন্যাস, পর্য্যায়, শ্রেণীবিন্যাস। **3.** (*Pl.*) Degrees in any order or series ; "The several *gradations* of the intelligent universe ;" ক্রম, পরম্পরা, শ্রেণীভাব, শ্রেণী। **4.** (*Painting* etc.) The gradual passing from one colour or shade to another ; (চিত্র-বিদ্যা) এক বর্ণের আভা ক্রমশঃ অপর বর্ণের আভায় বিলীন হওন, ক্রমবিলয়ন। **5.** (*Mus.*) A diatonic succession of chords ; (সঙ্গীত-বিদ্যা) সপ্তকানুসারী তন্ত্রীপরম্পরা। **6.** (*Philol.*) Ablaut ; (ভাষা-বিজ্ঞান) প্রণালীসঙ্গতভাবে স্বরবর্ণের পরিবর্ত্তন (as in *sing, song, sung*). **—al-ly,** *adv.* In regular gradation ; যথাক্রমে (কেভিঃ), ক্রমশঃ (ঐ), ক্রমতঃ।

grāde, *n.* & *v. t.* **1.** Step or degree in any series, quality ; the class of persons or things alike in such a grade ; সোপান, শ্রেণী, ধাপ, পরম্পরা ; ক্রমোচ্চ শ্রেণী সমূহের মধ্যে কোন শ্রেণীভুক্ত ব্যক্তি বা বস্তুসমূহ। **2.** (*Cattle breeding*) A class of animals produced by crossing a native stock with a superior breed ; কোনও দেশীয় জন্তুর সহিত তদপেক্ষা উৎকৃষ্ট জাতীয় জন্তুর সংসর্গে জাত জন্তুশ্রেণী, সঙ্কর জন্তুশ্রেণী। **3.** (In a railroad in U. S.) The rate of ascent or descent ; a gradient ; a slope ; (মার্কিণ যুক্তরাজ্যে রেল রাস্তা সম্পর্কে) ক্রমোন্নতি বা ক্রমাবনতির হার; রাস্তার প্রবণতার মাত্রা ; ঢালু স্থান, উতরাই, প্রবণভূমি। **4.** (*Math.*) The hundredth part of a right-angle ; সমকোণের শতাংশের এক অংশ। **5.** (*Philol.*) Relative position in ablaut series ; (ভাষা-বিজ্ঞান) প্রণালী-সঙ্গতভাবে পরিবর্ত্তিত স্বরবর্ণসমূহের আপেক্ষিক অবস্থান। ***Verb t.*** **1.** To arrange in order according to size, quality, rank and the like ; to class ; to sort ; আয়তন, গুণ, মর্য্যাদা প্রভৃতি অনুসারে সজ্জিত করা ; শ্রেণীভাগ করা ; কিসিম করা। **2.** To reduce as a road, canal etc. to a suitable level or slope ; (রাস্তা, খাল প্রভৃতি) উপযুক্ত পরিমাণ ঢালু করা। **3.** To blend with other things so as to affect the quality of ; কোন বস্তুর গুণ বা ধর্ম্মের উপর ক্রিয়া করার জন্য উহার সহিত অন্য বস্তু মিশ্রিত করা। **4.** To colour with shades or tints passing into each other ; পরস্পর ক্রম বিলয়নশীল বর্ণদ্বয়ে রঞ্জিত করা। **5.** (*Cattle breeding*) To cross with some other breeds ; অপেক্ষাকৃত উৎকৃষ্ট শ্রেণীর জন্তুর সংসর্গে সঙ্কর-শাবক উৎপাদন করা। **Grad'-er,** *n.* **Down-grade** or **up-grade**—(লৌহবর্ত্মাদির) ক্রমনিম্ন বা ক্রমোচ্চ অংশ, আরোহাবরোহ। **Graded school** — যে বিদ্যালয়ে বিভিন্ন শ্রেণী আছে। **Graded service** — যে চাকরীতে ক্রমে ক্রমে বেতন বৃদ্ধি হয়। **On the up** or **down grade**—(*Lit.* & *fig.*) Rising or falling ; ক্রমোচ্চ বা ক্রমনিম্ন, উত্থান বা পতনশীল। **To grade up**—To improve by cross-breeding ; উৎকৃষ্ট জাতীয় জন্তুর সংসর্গে উৎকর্ষ সাধন করা।

grā'-dĭ-ĕnt, *adj.* & *n.* Gradually rising or ascending ; ক্রমোচ্চ, ক্রমোত্থানশীল। ***Noun.*** **1.** Amount or degree of slope (of a road, railway, etc.) ; লৌহবর্ত্ম প্রভৃতির প্রবণতার মাত্রা বা পরিমাণ। **2.** The proportional amount of rise or fall of the thermometer or barometer in passing from one place to another ; স্থানান্তরিত হওয়ার কালে তাপমান বা বায়ুমান যন্ত্রের আনুপাতিক উত্থান বা পতন।

grā′-din, gră-dine′ (-dēn), *ns.* **1.** One of a series of steps or seats raised over one another ; সোপান-শ্রেণীর একটী, ক্রমোচ্চ আসন-শ্রেণীর একটী। **2.** A ledge at the back of an altar ; বেদীর পশ্চাদ্‌ভাগস্থ উন্নত অংশ।

grăd′-ū-ăl, *adj.* Proceeding or advancing by degrees ; not rapid, steep or abrupt ; as, a *gradual* increase of light ; ক্রমশঃ অগ্রসর, ক্রমিক, ক্রমোন্নতিশীল ; অসরলোন্নত, ঢালু। **—ly,** *adv.* By degress ; step by step ; ক্রমশঃ ; ক্রমে ক্রমে, ক্রমতঃ, অল্পে অল্পে, শনৈঃ শনৈঃ।

grăd′-ū-ăl, *n.* (*R. C. Church*) The portion of the mass sung between the Epistle and the Gospel ; the book containing such anthems ; (রোমান ক্যাথলিক ধর্ম্মসংঘ) খৃষ্টের শেষ ভোজন-স্মৃতি-অনুষ্ঠান পর্ব্বের অংশ বিশেষ ; উক্ত অংশ সম্বলিত পুস্তক।

grăd′-ū-āte, *v. t.* & *i.* **1.** To divide into regular intervals ; to mark with degrees ; as, to *graduate* a thermometer ; সমান সমান অংশে বিভক্ত করা ; ক্রমাঙ্কিত করা, ক্রমাঙ্ক চিহ্নিত করা। **2.** To confer an academic degree on ; বিশ্ববিদ্যালয়ের উপাধি দান করা। **3.** (*Chem.*) To concentrate as a solution by evaporation ; (রসায়ন-শাস্ত্র) ঘনীভূত করা। **4.** To arrange in grades ; বিভিন্ন শ্রেণীতে বিন্যাস করা, ক্রমবিন্যস্ত করা। ***Verb i.*** **1.** To pass away by degrees ; to change gradually, (with *into*) ; as, carnelian sometimes *graduates* into quartz ; ক্রমশঃ বিলীন হওয়া, বিলীয়মান হওয়া ; ক্রমশঃ পরিবর্ত্তিত হওয়া। **2.** To take a university degree ; "He *graduated* at Oxford" ; বিশ্ববিদ্যালয়ের উপাধি গ্রহণ করা। **3.** To qualify ; "When it *graduated* as a nation" ; উপযুক্ত হওয়া, উপযুক্ত গুণসম্পন্ন হওয়া। **—ā′-tion, —a-tor,** *ns.*

grăd′-ū-āte, *n.* **1.** One who holds a university degree ; বিশ্ববিদ্যালয়ের উপাধিধারী ব্যক্তি। **2.** A graduated measuring glass of a chemist ; রাসায়নিকের ক্রমাঙ্কিত গ্লাস।

grā′-dŭs, *n.* A dictionary of Greek or Latin prosody ; গ্রীক অথবা ল্যাটিন ছন্দঃশাস্ত্রের অভিধান-বিশেষ।

Gr(a)e′-cĭsm (grē-), *n.* **1.** A Greek idiom, esp. as imitated in another language ; গ্রীক ভাষার রীতি-সিদ্ধ প্রয়োগ বিশেষ,—যাহা অন্য ভাষায় অনুকৃত হইয়াছে। **2.** The spirit or style of the Greeks in art etc. ; imitatation of these ; গ্রীক শিল্প প্রভৃতির ধারা বা অন্তঃপ্রকৃতি ; উক্ত ধারা বা অন্তঃপ্রকৃতির অনুকরণ।

Gr(a)e′-cīze (grē-), *v. t.* & *i.* To give a Greek character, cast or form to ; গ্রীকপ্রকৃতিসম্পন্ন করা, গ্রীসীয় ছাঁচে গঠন করা। ***Verb i.*** To imitate the Greeks ; গ্রীকদিগের অনুকরণ করা।

Gr(a)e′-cō-mā-ni-ă (grē-), *n.* A mania for things Greek ; গ্রীসদেশীয় রীতি-নীতি, শিক্ষাদীক্ষা, শিল্প, প্রভৃতির জন্য উৎকট অনুরাগ, গ্রীসোন্মাদ।

graf-fi′-tō (grâ-fē-), *n.* (*Pl.* -ti) **1.** An inscription or drawing found on a wall etc. esp. on an ancient wall as at Pompeii ; প্রাচীর গাত্রে উৎকীর্ণ বা অঙ্কিত লিপি বা রেখা-চিত্র—বিশেষতঃ প্রাচীন পম্পে নগরীর প্রাচীর গাত্রাঙ্কিত লিপি বা রেখাচিত্র। **2.** Decoration by scratches through plaster showing different coloured under-surface ; উল্লেখন দ্বারা চূণ বালির আস্তরের ভিতর দিয়া ভিন্ন বর্ণের নিম্নতল প্রদর্শন পূর্ব্বক রচিত ভূষা।

grăft, *n., v. t.* & *i.* **1.** A scion or shoot of a tree inserted in the stock of another which is to support and nourish it ; জোড় কলম। **2.** (*Surg.*) A portion of living tissue ; জীবিত বিধান তন্তু। **3.** The process of grafting ; জোড়কলম বাঁধার প্রণালী। **4.** The space where a graft is inserted ; যে স্থানে কলম প্রবিষ্ট করান হয়। ***Verb t.*** **1.** To insert (a shoot or scion) *in, into, on,* or *upon* another tree ; কলম করা, শাখা কলম প্রস্তুত করা। **2.** (*Fig.*) To insert or fix *in* or *upon*, so as to produce close union ; সংপ্রবিষ্ট করা, সংশ্লিষ্ট করা। **3.** (*Surg.*) To transplant as a portion of a living tissue, skin, etc. ; (অস্ত্রোপ্রচার বিদ্যা) দেহের এক অংশের সুস্থ চর্ম্ম বা বিধান তন্তু দ্বারা দেহের অন্য অংশের রুগ্ন চর্ম্ম বা বিধান তন্তুর স্থান পূরণ করা। **4.** (*Naut.*) To cover as a ring, bolt, etc. with a weaving of small cord or rope yarns ; (নৌ-বিদ্যা) আংটা, প্রভৃতি ক্ষুদ্র রজ্জু বা রজ্জুর সুতা দ্বারা ঢাকা। ***Verb i.*** **1.** To insert a graft or grafts ; কলম করা। **Graft′-ing,** *n.* **1.** The act, art or process of inserting grafts ; কলম করণ। **2.** The transplanting of a piece of flesh or skin to a denuded surface ; দেহের এক অংশের সুস্থ চর্ম্ম বা বিধান-তন্তু দ্বারা অপর অংশের রুগ্ন চর্ম্ম বা বিধান-তন্তুর স্থান-পূরণ।

grăft, *n.* & *v. i.* (*U. S. colloq.*) Illicit spoils in connection with politics or municipal business ; practices intended to secure these ; (মার্কিণ যুক্তরাজ্যের চলিত-ভাষায়) রাজনীতিক বা মিউনিসিপালিটী সংক্রান্ত ব্যাপারে অবৈধ ভাবে চাকুরী প্রভৃতি প্রাপ্তি ; যে অবৈধ উপায়ে ঐরূপ চাকুরী প্রভৃতি পাওয়া যায়। ***Verb i.*** To seek or make graft ; অবৈধ উপায়ে চাকুরী প্রভৃতি লাভের চেষ্টা করা বা চাকুরী প্রভৃতি পাওয়া। **Graft′-er,** *n.*

grail (grāl), *n.* Gradual ; ক্রমিক।

grail (grāl), *n.* A comb-maker's file ; চিরুণি নির্ম্মাতার উখা বা রেত।

grail (grāl), *n.* (Also *holy or saint grail or sangreal*) The Holy Cup used by Christ at the Last Supper ; খৃষ্টের শেষ ভোজনের পবিত্র পানপাত্র [এই পাত্রে Arimathea

বাসী যোশেফ পবিত্রাত্মা যীশুর ক্রুশনির্গত রক্তধারা সঞ্চিত রাখিয়াছিলেন। উক্ত যোশেফের পরিবারে এই পানপাত্র বহুদিন পর্য্যন্ত রক্ষিত ছিল। কথিত আছে যোশেফ বা তদ্বংশীয় কোন ব্যক্তি ঐ পান-পাত্র ইংলণ্ডে লইয়া যান। এই পাত্র অলৌকিক গুণসম্পন্ন ছিল। ইহাতে রুটি রাখিলে রুটির সংখ্যা বাড়িয়া যাইত। নিষ্পাপ ব্যক্তিগণ ইচ্ছা মাত্র এই পান-পাত্র হইতে নানাবিধ সুখাদ্য প্রাপ্ত হইতেন। পাপীরা ইহার দিকে দৃষ্টিপাত করিলে ইহার তীব্র জ্যোতিতে অন্ধ হইয়া যাইত। মধ্যযুগের গল্পপুস্তক সমূহে এই পান-পাত্র ও ইহার অন্বেষণ সম্পর্কে বহু বিচিত্র ও অলৌকিক ঘটনাবলী লিপিবদ্ধ হইয়াছে। See Malory's *Morted' Arthur*, Tennyson's *Idylls of the King*, Wagner's *Parsifal*, *History of the Holy Grail* (*Dent*, Everyman's Library).]

grain (grān), *n.*, *v. t.* & *i.* **1.** A seed like fruit of any cereal grass; ধান্য যবাদি শস্যের বীজের মত বীজ। **2.** (*Collectively*) Wheat or allied food-grasses or their fruits; corn; ধান্য, যব, ভুট্টা প্রভৃতির বীজ, ধান্য, গোধূম প্রভৃতির গাছ, ধান্য, গোধূম; শস্য। **3.** A small hard particle; hence, the smallest amount; as, a *grain* of sand or wit; দানা; কণা, কণিকা, রেণু, রতি,তিল, লেশ। **4.** The smallest unit of weight equal to $\frac{1}{24}$ of pennyweight Troy; (ইংরেজী ওজন প্রণালীর) তুলামান বিশেষ, ৪ মাষা। **5.** A reddish dye made from some insects; (*poet.*) a fast dye or colour; কোন কোন কীট হইতে জাত রক্তবর্ণ রঞ্জক পদার্থ, অলক্ত, আলতা; (কবিতায়) পাকা রং, অক্ষয় রাগ। **6.** Granular texture; roughness of surface; দানাদার বুনট; কোন কিছুর উপরিভাগের বন্ধুরতা বা অমসৃণতা। **7.** A scarlet dye; অলক্ত বর্ণ, আলতার রং। **8.** The arrangement of fibres or particles in wood, stone, flesh, skin, etc.; texture; কাষ্ঠ, প্রস্তর, মাংস বা চর্ম্মাদিতে অংশু বা কণিকা সমূহের বিন্যাস; বুনট, জমি। **9.** The fibre of wood etc.; the lines of fibre in wood giving a pattern; lamination; কাষ্ঠ প্রভৃতির অংশু; কোনরূপ নমুনায় বিন্যস্ত কাষ্ঠ-তন্তু সমূহ; স্তর-বিন্যাস। **10.** The remains of grain etc. after brewing or distilling; hence, any residuum; মদ্য চোলাই করার পর যব প্রভৃতির যে অংশ অবশিষ্ট থাকে; অবশিষ্টাংশ, অবশেষ। **11.** (*Fig.*) Nature; temper; tendency; as, against the *grain*; (লক্ষণায়) প্রকৃতি; মেজাজ; ঝোঁক, আসক্তি। ***Verb t.*** **1.** To form (powder, sugar etc.) into grains; চিনি, চূর্ণ প্রভৃতিকে দানাদার করা। **2.** To dye in grain; আলতার মত লাল রং করা, অলক্তক বর্ণে রঞ্জিত করা, পশম অবস্থাতে রং করা। **3.** To paint in imitation of the grain of wood or marble; মারবেল পাথর বা কাঠের আঁশের অনুকরণে চিত্রিত করা। **4.** To take hair off hides; চামড়া হইতে লোম তুলিয়া লওয়া। **5.** To impart a granular surface to; উপরিভাগ দানাদার করা। ***Verb i.*** **1.** To form into grains; দানাদার হওয়া, দানা বাঁধা। **2.** To paint in imitation of the grain of wood; কাষ্ঠাদির আঁশের অনুকরণে চিত্রিত করা। **Grain'-er,** *n.* **1.** A painter in imitation of a grain of wood etc.; his brush; যে চিত্রকর কাঠের আঁশের অনুকরণে চিত্র করে; তাহার তুলিকা। **2.** An infusion of pigeon's dung used by tanners; a tanner's knife; চর্ম্মসংস্কারক কর্ত্তৃক ব্যবহৃত পারাবত বিষ্ঠার নির্য্যাস; চর্ম্মসংস্কারকের ছুরিকা। **Grain'-less, Grained,** *adjs.* **Grain'-y,** *-adj.* Resembling grains; granular; শস্যবীজবৎ; দানাদার। **Awned** or **bearded grain**—শূক ধান্য (কেশুঃ)। **Grain allowance** — A small allowance; বেতনের উপর যে সামান্য ভাতা প্রদান করা হয়। **Grain leather**—চর্ম্মের যে দিক হইতে লোম উৎপাটিত হইয়াছে সেই দিক বাহিরে রাখিয়া সংস্কৃত চর্ম্ম। **Grain-sick**—গবাদি পশুর রোগবিশেষ। **Grain-side**—চর্ম্মের যে দিক হইতে লোম তুলিয়া লওয়া হইয়াছে। **Against the grain**—Against the direction of the fibres; against one's wishes; unpleasantly; reluctantly; আঁশের বিপরীত দিকে, বিলোমভাবে, প্রতিলোমভাবে; ইচ্ছার বিরুদ্ধে; অপ্রীতিজনকভাবে; অনিচ্ছার সহিত, নারাজভাবে। **A rogue in grain**—পাকা দাগাবাজ। **In grain**—Of a fast colour; genuine; downright; thorough; by nature; পাকা রঙ্গের; সাঁচ্চা, খাঁটি; ডাহা; পুরা; প্রকৃতিগত, হাড়ে হাড়ে। **The grains of Paradise** or **Guinea grains**—গিনি হইতে আনীত, একপ্রকার ঝাল এবং সুগন্ধি বীজ। **To dye grain**—To dye in scarlet; to dye in fast colour; to dye deeply or thoroughly; আলতার মত লাল রং করা; পাকা রং দেওয়া; গাঢ়ভাবে রঞ্জিত করা। **To go against the grain of (one)**—To be repugnant to; to vex; to trouble; বিরক্তিকর হওয়া; বিরক্ত করা; কষ্ট দেওয়া। **With the grain of salt** — With some reservation; (অবিশ্বাস্য গল্পাদি সম্বন্ধে) কিছু চাপিয়া রাখিয়া, কতকটা সন্দেহের সহিত, বাদসাদ দিয়া। **With the grain**—অনুলোমভাবে।

grains (grānz), *n.* A forked fishing spear or harpoon; একপ্রকার টেঁটা।

Head of a grallatory bird.

grăl-la-tō'-rēs (-ĕ-), *n. pl.* An order of wading and running birds including curlews, cranes, etc.; বকজাতীয় পক্ষী। **-ri-al,** *adj.* উক্ত পক্ষিজাতি-সম্বন্ধীয়।

grăl'-lŏch, *n.* & *v. t.* The viscera of a deer; হরিণের নাড়ীভুঁড়ি

Verb t. To disembowel (deer etc.); (হরিণ প্রভৃতির) নাড়ীভুঁড়ি বাহির করা।

grăm, *n.* The chick-pea; any pulse used as fodder; ছোলা, বুট, চাণা, চণক; গবাদির খাদ্য যে কোন রকম কলাই জাতীয় শস্য। **Black-gram**—মাষ: **Cow-gram**—বরবটী। **Flour of gram**—বেসন। **Green-gram**—মুদ্গ, মুগ। **Horse-gram**—কুর্ত্তিকালাই।

grăm, gramme (grăm), *ns.* The French unit of weight equal to 15·432 grains (Troy); ফরাসীদেশের একক ওজনের পরিমাণ ১৫·৪৩২ গ্রেণ (ট্রয়)। [স্বতন্ত্র শব্দে *gramme* এবং সংযুক্ত শব্দে *gram* ব্যবহৃত হয়।]

grä'-mă, grăm'-mă, *ns.* (Also *grama grass*) A kind of pasture grass in Western U. S.; মার্কিণ যুক্তরাজ্যের পশ্চিমাংশে জাত গবাদির খাদ্যোপযোগী একপ্রকার ঘাস।

grăm'-ă-rye (-rī), *n.* **1.** (*Archaic*) Necromancy; magic; (অপ্রচলিত) পিশাচসিদ্ধি, প্রেতসিদ্ধি; যাদুবিদ্যা। **2.** (*Obs.*) Grammar; (অপ্রচলিত) ব্যাকরণ।

gră-mêr'-çy̆, *interj.* **1.** (*Archaic*) Many thanks; thank you; (অপ্রচলিত) সাধু সাধু, ধন্য ধন্য; আপনাকে ধন্যবাদ।

grăm-i-nā'-ce-ous (-shë-ŭs), **gră-min'-ē-ous** (-ŭs), *adjs.* Of, or relating to, grass; like grass; তৃণজাতীয়, তৃণসম্বন্ধীয়; তৃণসদৃশ, তৃণতুল্য, ঘাসের মত।

grăm-i-niv'-ö-rous (-rŭs), *adj.* Feeding, or subsisting, on grass; তৃণাদ, তৃণভোজী, তৃণভক্ষী, তৃণাহারী।

grăm'-mă-logue (-lŏg), *n.* (*Short hand*) A word represented by a single sign or logogram; a logogram; (সাঙ্কেতিক-লিপি) একমাত্র চিহ্নদ্বারা প্রদর্শিত শব্দ; যে চিহ্নদ্বারা কোন শব্দ প্রদর্শিত বা সূচিত হয়, শব্দ সূচক।

grăm'-măr, *n.* **1.** The science which treats of the principles of a language; ব্যাকরণ-শাস্ত্র। **2.** A treatise or book on the principles of language; ব্যাকরণ পুস্তক। **3.** The elements or rudiments of an art or science; কোন বিজ্ঞান বা শিল্পের প্রাথমিক পুস্তক, উপক্রমণিকা। **—less,** *adj.* **—ma'-ri-an,** *n.* **1.** One versed in grammar; a philologist; ব্যাকরণবিৎ, বৈয়াকরণ; শব্দতত্ত্ববিৎ, শব্দশাস্ত্রজ্ঞ, শাব্দিক। **2.** One who writes on, or teaches, grammar; ব্যাকরণ লেখক বা ব্যাকরণাধ্যাপক, ব্যাকরণকার। **—mat'-ic, —mat'-i-cal,** *adjs.* **1.** Of, or relating to, grammar; ব্যাকরণসম্বন্ধীয়, ব্যাকরণ-বিষয়ক, বৈয়াকরণ। **2.** According to, or conforming to, the rules of grammar; ব্যাকরণের অনুযায়ী, ব্যাকরণশুদ্ধ, ব্যাকরণসিদ্ধ, ব্যাকরণানুসারী, শব্দশাস্ত্র সিদ্ধ, শব্দশাস্ত্রানুসারী। **3.** Relating, or conforming, to the formal principles of an art; কোন শিল্পের বহিস্তত্ত্ব-সম্বন্ধীয় বা তদনুযায়ী। **—mat'-i-cal-ly,** *adv.* According to grammar; ব্যাকরণানুরূপ। **—mat'-i-cize,** *v. t.* To render grammatical; ব্যাকরণানুসারী করা, ব্যাকরণ-সঙ্গত করা। **Comparative grammar**—যে ব্যাকরণে দুই বা ততোধিক ভাষার ব্যাকরণের সম্পর্ক সম্বন্ধে আলোচনা থাকে, তুলনামূলক ব্যাকরণ। **Grammar school**—যে বিদ্যালয়ে প্রধানতঃ ল্যাটিন ও গ্রীক ব্যাকরণ শিক্ষা দেওয়া হয়। **Grammatical accuracy**—ব্যাকরণ-শুদ্ধি, শব্দশুদ্ধি। **Grammatical error**—ব্যাকরণগত ভুল। **Historical grammar**—যে ব্যাকরণে কোন ভাষার বিভক্তি, প্রত্যয় ও পদবিন্যাস প্রকরণের ক্রমবিকাশ সম্বন্ধে আলোচনা থাকে, ঐতিহাসিক ব্যাকরণ।

gramme (grăm), *n.* See GRAM.

grăm'-ō-phōne, *n.* An instrument for recording and reproducing sounds; যে যন্ত্রের সাহায্যে গান, বক্তৃতা প্রভৃতি স্থায়িভাবে রক্ষা ও ইচ্ছানুসারে পুনরুৎপাদন করা যায়, শব্দ-যন্ত্র [১৮৭৭ খৃঃ অব্দে সর্ব্ব প্রথম আমেরিকা দেশীয় প্রখ্যাত নামা বৈজ্ঞানিক Edison কর্ত্তৃক উদ্ভাবিত হয়]।

grăm'-pŭs, *n.* **1.** A large marine fish of the Dolphin family; মকর, শিশুমার। **2.** A person who breathes loud; যে ব্যক্তি নাসিকা-গর্জ্জন করে।

grăn-ă-dil'-lă, grên-, *ns.* A kind of passion flower; এক প্রকার ঝুমকা ফুল।

grăn'-ă-ry̆, *n.* A store-house or repository for thrashed grain; (*fig.*) a region yielding, and esp exporting much corn; শস্যের গোলাঘর, ভাণ্ডার, শস্যাগার, মরাই, ধান্যশালা, ধান্যাগার; (লক্ষণায়) যে প্রদেশে প্রচুর শস্য উৎপন্ন হয়, যে প্রদেশ হইতে প্রচুর শস্য দেশ বিদেশে রপ্তানি হয়।

grănd, *adj.* & *n.* **1.** Of large size or extent; of great consequence; great; as, a *grand* mountain; a *grand* mistake; বৃহদাকার বা বৃহদায়তন, প্রকাণ্ড, বিস্তীর্ণ; গুরুতর; বিরাট, বিশাল, বিপুল, মহা। **2.** Magnificient; splendid; gorgeous; sublime; lofty; as, a *grand* parade; a *grand* view or conception; শোভমান, জমকালো; মহাপ্রভ, দেদীপ্যমান, উজ্জ্বল, সমৃদ্ধ; সমুজ্জ্বল, বিচিত্র; গম্ভীর, গুরু, মহা, উচ্চ, উন্নত। **3.** Chief; of the highest rank; as, a *Grand* Vizier; the *Grand* Duke; মুখ্য, প্রধান, শ্রেষ্ঠ, অগ্রগণ্য; উচ্চপদস্থ। **4.** Imposing in appearance; impressive; dignified; distinguished; ভাবগম্ভীর; মহিমান্বিত; গৌরবান্বিত; প্রখ্যাত। **5.** (*Law*) Great; principal; as, a *grand* assize; (আইন) মহা; প্রধান। **6.** Final; as, a *grand* total; অন্তিম, চূড়ান্ত। **7.** Main; as, the *grand* staircase; প্রধান। **8.** Solemnly or splendidly conducted; "*Grand* wedding festivities"; মহাসমারোহপূর্ণ। **9.** (*Mus.*) Complete in all its parts; of full dimensions or for full orchestra; as, a *grand* chorus ; (সঙ্গীত-শাস্ত্র) সর্ব্বাঙ্গসম্পন্ন ; পূর্ণায়তন, বাদিত্র-স্থলে উপবিষ্ট পূর্ণসংখ্যক বাদ্যকদলের জন্য। 10. (*Colloq.*) Very satisfactory ; as, the ground is in *grand* condition ; (চলিত ভাষায়) বেশ, খুব ভাল। 11. Of the second degree in ascent or descent ; as, *grand*father or *grand*son ; অধঃস্তন বা উর্দ্ধতন দ্বিতীয় পুরুষ সম্পর্কে। *Noun*. 1. A grand piano ; সুবৃহৎ ত্রিভুজ বীণাকৃতি পিয়ানো। 2. (*Sugar making*) The largest evaporating pan of a battery ; (চিনির কল) বাষ্পীকরণের জন্য সুবৃহৎ পাত্র। **Grand'-ly,** *adv.* In a grand manner ; splendidly ; sublimely ; বিরাট ভাবে, জমকালো ভাবে ; দেদীপ্যমান ভাবে ; গম্ভীর ভাবে। **Grand'-ness,** *n.* **Grand air**—Distinguished appearance ; জমকালো চেহারা। **Grand-child**—নাতি বা নাতিনী, নপ্তী, পৌত্রী বা দৌহিত্রী। **Grand committee** — পার্লেমেণ্টের প্রাকৃত সভার স্থায়ী সমিতিদ্বয়ের অন্যতর। **Grand-daughter**—দৌহিত্রী, পৌত্রী। **Grand Duke**—(জর্ম্মণদেশে) কতিপয় নির্দ্দিষ্ট ক্ষুদ্র রাজ্যের অধিপতি, (রুষিয়ার) সম্রাটপুত্রের উপাধি। (*Zool.*) The Great European Horned Owl ; (জন্তু-বিদ্যা) ইয়ুরোপীয় বৃহৎকায় সশৃঙ্গ পেচক। **Grandfather**—পিতামহ বা মাতামহ। **Grand-fatherly**—*adj.* Like a grand-father in age or manner ; kind ; indulgent ; ঠাকুরদাদার বয়সী, ঠাকুরদাদার মত ; দয়ালু ; প্রশ্রয়দায়ক। **Grand jury**—(আইন) যে ২৩ জনের অনধিক সভাসদ্ কোন অভিযোগ বিচারকের কাছে প্রেরণ জন্য যথেষ্ট প্রমাণ আছে কি না তদ্বিষয়ে অনুসন্ধান করেন। **Grandmamma**—ঠাকুরমা। **Grand Master**—সামরিক নাইট সম্প্রদায় বিশেষের অধ্যক্ষ ; ফ্রিমেশন প্রভৃতি সম্প্রদায়ের অধ্যক্ষ। **Grandpapa**—A grandfather; ঠাকুরদাদা। **Grandmother**—পিতামহী বা মাতামহী। **Grand-motherly**—Like a grandmother in age or manner ; kind ; indulgent ; বয়সে বা ব্যবহারে ঠাকুরমার ন্যায় ; দয়াবতী ; প্রশ্রয়দাত্রী। (Of a government, legislation etc.) Excessively paternal ; (শাসন-তন্ত্রব্যবস্থা সম্পর্কে), অতি মাত্রায় পিতৃবৎ পালন ও রক্ষণাবেক্ষণশীল। **Grand piano**—See GRAND. *n.* 1. **Grandsire**—(বিশেষভাবে) কোন জন্তুর জনকের জনক। An ancestor ; পূর্ব্বপুরুষ। An old man ; বৃদ্ধলোক। A method of ringing changes on bells ; সজ্জিত ঘণ্টাশ্রেণী বিভিন্ন ক্রমে বাজাইবার প্রণালীবিশেষ। **Grandson**—A son's or daughter's son ; পৌত্র বা দৌহিত্র, নাতি, নপ্তা। **Grand stand**—ঘোড়দৌড়ের মাঠের দর্শকদিগের উচ্চ মঞ্চ। **Grand Turk**—তুরস্কের সুলতান। **Grand Vizier**—তুরস্কের প্রধান মন্ত্রী। **The Grand Old Man** or **G. O. M.**—Gladstone ; গ্লাডষ্টোন। **Teach your grandmother to suck eggs**—See under EGG. **To do the grand**—To make a great display ; খুব ধুমধড়াক্কা করা।

grăn'-dam(e) (-dăm), *n.* 1. An old woman ; বুড়ী। 2. A grandmother ; ঠাকুরমা। 3. (*-dam* only,—of animals) The dam's dam ; (জন্তু-সম্পর্কে) জনকের জনক।

grăn(d)'-dăd, *n.* Affectionate or childish term for grandfather ; দাদামণি।

grande (*F.*), *n.* (Fem. of GRAND). *Grande toilette* — Ceremonial costume ; উৎসব পরিচ্ছদ। *Grande passion* — An engrossing love affair ; পরম প্রেম।

grăn-dee' (-dē), *n.* In Spain a nobleman of the highest rank ; hence, a nobleman ; a man of elevated rank or eminence ; স্পেনরাজ্যে সর্ব্বোচ্চশ্রেণীর অভিজাত ব্যক্তি ; অভিজাত ব্যক্তি, সম্ভ্রান্ত ব্যক্তি, সম্ভ্রান্ত পুরুষ ; উচ্চপদস্থ ব্যক্তি।

grăn'-deur (-dyėr), *n.* Great power, rank or eminence ; greatness ; splendour ; অসীম ক্ষমতা উচ্চপদ, উচ্চপদবী ; মাহাত্ম্য, গরিমা, মহিমা, মহত্ব ; জাঁক, সমারোহ, শোভা।

grăn-dĭl'-ŏ-quence (-kwĕns), *n.* Lofty speaking ; pompous language ; শব্দাড়ম্বর, বাগাড়ম্বর ; বাগাড়ম্বরপূর্ণ ভাষা। **–quent,** *adj.* Speaking in a lofty style ; expressed in high-sounding words ; bombastic ; গম্ভীর ভাষায় কথিত ; শব্দাড়ম্বরপূর্ণ ভাষায় কথিত ; শব্দাড়ম্বরপূর্ণ, বাগাড়ম্বর পূর্ণ। **–quent-ly,** *adv.*

grăn'-di-ōse, *adj.* 1. Impressive ; imposing ; splendid ; striking (in a good sense) ; গুরুগম্ভীর ; মহান্ ; জাঁকাল ; হৃদয়গ্রাহী। 2. Pompous ; bombastic (in a bad sense) ; as, a *grandiose* style ; সমারোহপূর্ণ, জমকালো ; শব্দাড়ম্বরপূর্ণ, শব্দচ্ছটাযুক্ত। **–ly**, *adv.* **–os'-i-ty,** *adj.*

Grăn-di-sō'-ni-ăn, *adj.* Marked by stately courtesy and chivalric magnanimity (From Sir C. Grandison in Richardson's novel) ; উন্নতশিষ্টাচারসূচক আদর্শ নাইট সমুচিত, মহানুভবত্বসূচক।

grăn-dū'-căl, *adj.* Of, or pertaining to, a Grand Duke ; গ্র্যাণ্ড ডিউক সম্বন্ধীয়।

grānge, *n.* 1. A granary (*archaic*) ; (অপ্রচলিত) শস্যাগার। 2. A farmhouse with buildings, stables, etc. ; অট্টালিকা, আস্তাবল, প্রভৃতি সমন্বিত কৃষিবাটিকা।

grānġ'-ėr-īze, *v. t.* To illustrate (a book) by adding prints etc. often cut from other books ; অন্যান্য পুস্তক হইতে চিত্রাদি কাটিয়া কোন পুস্তকে সন্নিবেশ করা। **–ism, –ite, –i-za'-tion, –iz-er,** *ns.*

grā-nĭf'-ėr-ous (-ŭs), *adj.* Producing grain or seeds like grain ; শস্যোৎপাদী। **Gran'-i-form,** *adj.*

grăn'-īte, *n.* A granular crystalline rock consisting of quartz, feldspar and mica ; একপ্রকার স্ফটিক

প্রস্তর। **Gra-nit′-ic, Gra-nit′-i-form,** *adjs.* **-it-oid,** *adj.* & *n.* Resembling granite; স্ফটিকপ্রস্তরনিভ; (*Noun*) Granitoid rock; স্ফটিক-প্রস্তরশৈল। **Granite ware**—গ্রেনাইটের মত ফুট ফুট বিন্দুবিশিষ্ট এক-প্রকার পাত্র; একপ্রকার কালাই-করা লোহার বাসন।

grā-nĭv′-ō-rous (-rŭs), *adj.* Feeding, or subsisting, on grains; শস্যভোজী, ধান্যভক্ষক (কেণ্ডিঃ), শস্য ভক্ষক (ঐ), অন্নভক্ষক (ঐ), অন্নভোজী (ঐ), অন্নজীবী (ঐ), অন্নসেবী (ঐ)।

Grăn′-nŭs, *n.* কেল্টজাতির দেব বৈদ্য।

grăn′-nȳ, *n.* (Affectionate or contempt. for) a grandmother; an old woman; ঠান্‌দিদি; বুড়ী। **Granny's bend** or **knot**—(*Naut.*) ইংরাজী ৪ অঙ্কের আকার গ্রন্থিবিশেষ।

grăn-ō-lith′-ic, *adj.* Of, or relating to, a kind of concrete; এক প্রকার প্রস্তর সম্বন্ধীয়।

grănt, *v. t.* & *n.* **1.** To give over; to give the possession or title of; to convey; as, the legislative has *granted* all the new land; অর্পণ করা; স্বত্ব বা অধিকার প্রদান করা; প্রদান করা। **2.** To consent to fulfil, of a request, wish etc.; পূরণ করিতে স্বীকার করা। **3.** To permit to have; to bestow; মঞ্জুর করা; অর্পণ করা। **4.** To admit as true; to allow; as, I *grant* in her some sense of shame; to concede; সত্য বলিয়া স্বীকার করা, ধরিয়া নেওয়া; স্বীকার করা মানিয়া লওয়া। ***Noun.*** **1.** Act of granting; a formal conferment; অর্পণ, মঞ্জুর; দান। **2.** The thing or property granted; a gift; a boon; প্রদত্ত বস্তু বা সম্পত্তি; দান; বর। **3.** (*Law*) A transfer of property by written instrument; দানপত্র দ্বারা সম্পত্তি হস্তান্তর। **Grant′-a-ble** *adj.* **Gran-tee′,** *n.* **Grant′-er, Grant′-or,** *ns.* (আইন) দান-কর্ত্তা, দাতা। (*Law*) The person to whom a grant or conveyance is made; গ্রহীতা, প্রতিগৃহীতা (কেণ্ডিঃ)। **Grant-in-aid**—বিদ্যালয় প্রভৃতির সাহায্য। **Deed of grant**—সনদ, দানপত্র। **I grant you**—I admit; আমি মানি, আমি স্বীকার করি। **Resumption of a grant**—দত্তাপহার (কেণ্ডিঃ)। **To take for granted**—To presuppose or assume; সত্য বলিয়া স্বীকার করা, ধরিয়া লওয়া, মানিয়া লওয়া।

grăn′-ū-lar (-lêr), *adj.* Relating to, consisting of, or resembling grains; having granulated surface or structure; দানা সম্বন্ধীয়, দানাময়, দানাসদৃশ; দানাদার। **-la-ry, -lose, -lous,** *adjs.* **-ly,** *adv.*

grăn′-ū-lāte, *v. t.* & *i.* **1.** To form into grains; দানাদার করা। **2.** To make rough on the surface; উপরিভাগ খস্‌খসে (বন্ধুর) করা। ***Verb i.*** **1.** To be formed into grains; দানা বাঁধা, দানা ধরা। **2.** (Of wound etc.) To form prominences as a beginning of healing or junction; to heal or join; (ক্ষতাদি সম্পর্কে) ক্ষতারোগ্য কালে ক্ষতোপরি মাংসাঙ্কুর জাত হওয়া; ঘা শুকাইয়া যাওয়া, জোড়া লাগা। **-late, -lat-ed,** *adjs.* **-la′-tion,** *n.* **1.** The act or process of granulating; দানা বাঁধন, দানা উৎপাদন, দানাবাঁধনের প্রণালী। **2.** The state of being granulated; দানাদার অবস্থা, কণিকাময় ভাব। **3.** The formation of small grain-like prominences on the surface of wounds while healing; (*pl.*) the fleshy grains themselves; ক্ষতারোগ্য কালে ক্ষতোপরি মাংসাঙ্কুর উৎপাদন, ক্ষতারোগ্য কালে তাহাতে যে ক্ষুদ্র ক্ষুদ্র মাংসাঙ্কুর জন্মে; (বহুবচনে) ক্ষতাঙ্কুর (হঃ চঃ), মাংসাঙ্কুর (সাঃ পঃ)। **-tor,** *n.*

grăn′-ūle, *n.* A little grain; a small particle; ক্ষুদ্র দানা; কণা, কণিকা।

grāpe, *n.* **1.** A single berry of the vine; দ্রাক্ষাফল, আঙুর, মৃদ্বীকা (a kind of red grape). **2.** The plant bearing this fruit; দ্রাক্ষালতা। **3.** A mangy tumour on the leg of a horse; অশ্বপদের খোসযুক্ত অর্ব্বুদ। **4.** A grape shot; পেটা লোহার শলাকাতে পর পর সংযুক্ত ৪টী লোহার চাক্‌তির উপর তিন থাকে সাজানো গুলিসকল [সাধারণতঃ প্রতি থাকে তিনটী গুলি থাকে। কাঠের তলাওয়ালা টিনের কানেস্তার ভিতর পুরিয়া ঐরূপ সাজানো গুলিসকল কামান হইতে ছোড়া হইলে উহারা শত্রুসৈন্যের মধ্যে চারিদিকে ছড়াইয়া পড়ে], দ্রাক্ষাগুলিকা। **Grape′-less,** *adj.* **Grap′-er-y,** *n.* A place where grapes are grown; দ্রাক্ষা উৎপাদনের স্থান। **Grap′-y,** *adj.* Composed of, or like, grapes; দ্রাক্ষাময়, দ্রাক্ষাবৎ। **Grape-brandy**—আঙ্গুরের রস হইতে প্রস্তুত ব্রাণ্ডি, দ্রাক্ষাসুরা। **Grape-cure**—রোগীকে প্রচুর পরিমাণ আঙ্গুরের রস পান করাইয়া রোগচিকিৎসার প্রণালী-বিশেষ। **Grape fruit**—The shaddock; বাতাবী লেবু। **Grape-house**—A vinery; দ্রাক্ষা-বাটিকা, দ্রাক্ষারাম (মঃ উঃ), দ্রাক্ষাবলয় ভূমি (রঃ)। **Grape-shot**—See GRAPE 4. **Grape-stone**—আঙ্গুরের বীজ। **Grape-sugar**—দ্রাক্ষাফলজাত শর্করা। **Grape vine**—The vine which bears grapes; দ্রাক্ষালতা, আঙ্গুরলতা। A peculiar skating figure; হিমানী-পাদুকা দ্বারা অঙ্কিত পরস্পরজড়িত লতার মত চিত্র-বিশেষ। **Sour grapes, The grapes are sour**—One disparages what is beyond his reach; কোন ব্যক্তি ঈপ্সিত বস্তু লাভে হতাশ হইয়া সেই বস্তুর নিন্দা করিলে এই বাক্য উক্ত হয়। **The grape, The juice of the grape**—Wine; দ্রাক্ষা ফলের রস হইতে প্রস্তুত মদিরা, দ্রাক্ষাবারুণী, দ্রাক্ষাসব।

grăph, *n.* A symbolic diagram expressing a system of mathematical or chemical connexion; গণিত বা রসায়নশাস্ত্র সম্বন্ধীয় সম্বন্ধ-পরম্পরা প্রদর্শনার্থ রেখাদি।

-grăph, A suffix denoting an agent which writes; as, auto*graph*, tele*graph*, etc.; লেখক-সূচক প্রত্যয়।

grăph, *n.* & *v. t.* An apparatus for copying a writing etc. by pressing it on a gelatinous surface; একপ্রকার আঠালো পদার্থ মাখান ফলকের উপর চাপ দিয়া লিখিত দলীল প্রভৃতির প্রতিলিপি তোলার জন্য যন্ত্র, লেখক-যন্ত্র। ***Verb t.*** To copy or multiply with this; লেখক যন্ত্র দ্বারা এক বা বহু অনুলিপি প্রস্তুত করা।

grăph'-ic, *adj.* **1.** Of, or pertaining to, painting, drawing, engraving, etching, etc.; অঙ্কন, চিত্রণ, ক্ষোদন প্রভৃতি সম্বন্ধীয়। **2.** Pertaining to the art of writing; লিপি-বিদ্যা বিষয়ক। **3.** Of, or relating to, diagrams or symbolic curves; "*Graphic* representations"; ক্ষেত্র বা সাঙ্কেতিক বক্র রেখা সম্পর্কীয়। **4.** Well delineated; vividly descriptive; picturesquely described; vivid; as, a *graphic* description and statement; সুচিত্রিত; জীবন্তভাবে বর্ণিত, সুবর্ণিত; সজীব বর্ণনা পূর্ণ, বিচিত্ররূপে বর্ণিত; সজীব, জীবন্ত। **5.** Having the faculty of describing things graphically; সজীববর্ণনক্ষম। **6.** (Of minerals) Showing marks like writing on surface or in fracture; (খনিজ-পদার্থ সম্পর্কে) লিখনবৎ চিহ্ন-বিশিষ্ট। **—i-cal,** *adj.* (*Rare*) Same as GRAPHIC. **—i-cal-ly,** *adv.* **1.** Picturesquely; vividly; বিচিত্র ভাবে; সজীবভাবে। **2.** By writing; লিখন দ্বারা। **3.** By diagrams or graphs; রেখাচিত্র দ্বারা, সাঙ্কেতিক রেখা দ্বারা। **Graphic algebra**—বীজগণিতের শাখা বিশেষ—ইহাতে সমীকরণের ধর্ম্ম বক্র বা সরল রেখার সাহায্যে আলোচিত হইয়া থাকে। **Graphic arts**—চিত্রণ, অঙ্কন, ক্ষোদন বিদ্যা, প্রভৃতি। **Graphic method**—গণিত-শাস্ত্রে রৈখিকবিশ্লেষপদ্ধতি—ইহাতে কতিপয় শ্রেণীবদ্ধ সংখ্যার সম্পর্ক বা মূলসূত্র বক্র রেখা বা অন্য চিত্র দ্বারা প্রদর্শিত হয়, চিত্র-রীতি (হিঃ কোঃ)।

grăph'-īte *n.* A mineral, commonly called black-lead or plumbago, largely used in making pencils; কৃষ্ণবর্ণ খনিজ পদার্থ বিশেষ—ইহা দ্বারা পেন্সিল তৈয়ার হয়, কৃষ্ণসীসক। **Gra-phit'-ic, –i-toid,** *adjs.*

gră'-phī-ūre *n.* A South-African rodent with tail ending in a pencil of hairs; দক্ষিণ আফ্রিকা দেশীয় দন্তুর জন্তু বিশেষ—এই জন্তুর লাঙ্গুলপ্রান্তে রোমগুচ্ছ বিদ্যমান থাকে।

grăph-ŏl'-ŏ-ġy̆, *n.* **1.** The art or science of estimating character etc. from hand writing; হস্তাক্ষর পরীক্ষা দ্বারা চরিত্রানুমান-বিদ্যা। **2.** The system of graphic formulae; গণিতের সাঙ্কেতিক রেখাবলীর সূত্রপদ্ধতি।

grăph'-ŏ-tȳpe, *n.* A process of obtaining blocks for surface printing; মুদ্রণের জন্য উৎকীর্ণ-ফলক প্রস্তুতের প্রণালী-বিশেষ। [প্রথমতঃ বিশেষ ভাবে প্রস্তুত ফরাসী খড়ী-মাটীর উপর চিত্রের বাহ্যরেখাসমূহ বিশেষ এক প্রকার কালীতে অঙ্কিত হইত, তৎপর ঐ বাহ্যরেখা সমূহের মধ্যবর্ত্তী খড়ী ব্রুশদ্বারা উঠাইয়া ফেলিলে রেখাগুলি উন্নত হইয়া উঠিত। পরে ঐ উন্নতরেখাচিত্র হইতে ক্ষোদিত ফলক প্রভৃতি গৃহীত হইত। ১৮৬০ খৃঃ অব্দে আমেরিকাবাসী Dr. Clinton Hitchcock নামক এক বৈজ্ঞানিক এইরূপ ক্ষোদিত ফলক প্রস্তুতের প্রণালী আবিষ্কার করেন। বর্ত্তমানে এতদপেক্ষা বহুবিধ উন্নততর প্রণালী আবিষ্কার হওয়ায়, ঐ ক্ষোদিত ফলক প্রণালী লুপ্ত হইয়াছে]।

Grapnel.

grăp'-nĕl, *n.* **1.** A small anchor with several arms; ক্ষুদ্র নঙ্গর। **2.** An iron instrument with hooks for grappling anything; আকর্ষী, লোহাকর্ষণী।

grăp'-ple (-l), *v. t., i* & *n.* **1.** To seize as with a grapnel; to lay fast hold of with the hands etc. as, to *grapple* an antagonist: "Which *grapples* the difficulties"; পাকড়ান; শক্ত করিয়া ধরা, সাপটাইয়া ধরা, আঁকড়ান, জাপ্‌টে ধরা, আঁকড়াইয়া ধরা। **2.** To fasten as with a grapple; to attach closely and firmly; "Let us *grapple* this faith to our inmost souls"; লৌহাকর্ষণী দ্বারা বদ্ধ করা; দৃঢ়ভাবে সংশ্লিষ্ট করা। ***Verb i.*** To contend or struggle in close fight as wrestlers; আঁকড়াআঁকড়ি করা, হাতাহাতি করা, হস্তাহস্তি করা (মঃ ভাঃ), ধ্বস্তাধ্বস্তি করা, পাছড়াপাছড়ি করা। ***Noun.*** **1.** A grip or hold as of wrestlers; close hug in contest; close fight; আঁকড়াইয়া ধরণ; বক্ষে বক্ষে পীড়ন; হাতাহাতি যুদ্ধ, লড়াই। **2.** A grappling iron; লৌহনির্ম্মিত আকর্ষণ যন্ত্র, লৌহাকর্ষণী। **—pling,** *n.* **1.** Act of grappling; সাপ্‌টাইয়া ধরণ। **2.** A grappling iron or grapnel; লৌহাকর্ষণী। **A grappling iron**—See GRAPNEL 2. **To grapple with**—To contend with; to try to overcome, accomplish or solve; to deal with; সংগ্রাম করা, ধ্বস্তাধ্বস্তি করা; পরাজয়, সম্পাদন বা সমাধান করার জন্য চেষ্টা করা; আলোচনা করা।

grăsp, *v. t., i.* & *n.* **1.** To seize and hold with the finger or arms; আঁকড়াইয়া ধরা, দৃঢ় মুষ্টিতে ধরা, বাহু পাশে বদ্ধ করা, বাহুদ্বারা জড়াইয়া ধরা, জাপ্‌টে ধরা। **2.** To clutch at; to seize greedily; "He who *grasps* much holds little"; মুঠ করিয়া ধরা; লোলুপভাবে ধরা। **3.** To seize by the intellect; to comprehend; ধারণা করা; বুঝা, মর্ম্ম গ্রহণ করা। ***Verb i.*** To make a clutch at; মুঠ করিয়া ধরা। ***Noun.*** **1.** A gripe of the hand; fast hold; হস্ত দ্বারা ধরণ; দৃঢ় মুষ্টি। **2.** Reach of the arms; hence the power of seizing and holding; as, it is beyond his *grasp*; বাহুর প্রসারসীমা; ধরার ক্ষমতা। **3.** Mastery; control; possession; as, to be in the *grasp* of one; প্রভুত্ব, হাতের মুঠা; শাসন; অধিকার, করতল (as in করতলগত)। **4.** Power of the intellect to seize and comprehend; বুদ্ধির দৌড়, বুঝিবার শক্তি, মর্ম্মগ্রহণের ক্ষমতা। **Grasp'-a-ble,** *adj.* **Grasp'-er,** *n.* **Grasp'-ing,** *n.* & *p. adj.* Seizing; ধরণ। (*p. adj.*) Avaricious; covetous; miserly; গৃধ্নু, গ্রাহী; লোভী, লোলুপ; কঞ্জুষ, হাত-কষা, বদ্ধ-মুষ্টি। **Grasp'-ing-ly,** *adv.* **Grasp'-ing-ness,** *n.* **To grasp at**—To try to seize; to accept with avidity; ধরিতে চেষ্টা করা; লোলুপভাবে ধরা। **To grasp nettle**—To tackle difficulty or danger boldly; নির্ভীকচিত্তে বিপদের সম্মুখীন হওয়া। **Within** or **beyond one's grasp**—Close or not close enough to be grasped; ধরিতে পারা যায় ততটা কাছে, হস্তপ্রাপ্য (মেঘঃ), হস্তাহার্য্য, হাত-দ্বারা নাগাল না পাওয়া যায় ততটা দূরে, হস্তাপ্রাপ্য।

grăss, *n.* & *v. t.* **1.** Herbage forming the food of cattle, sheep etc.; grazing; as, to go or send to *grass*; ঘাস, তৃণ, শষ্প, শাদ, বালতৃণ; গোচারণ, চারণ। **2.** Pasture-land; পশুচারণ ভূমি, পশুচারণ ক্ষেত্র, গোষ্ঠ, বাথান, গোচারণ ভূমি। **3.** A ground covered with grass; "The *grasses* crimsoned with tulips"; তৃণাবৃত ভূমি, শাদ্বল ভূমি, শাদ্বলস্থলী, তৃণশ্যামল ক্ষেত্র। **4.** Spring and early summer; "Two years old next *grass*"; বসন্ত, গ্রীষ্মারম্ভ, নবনিদাঘ। **5.** The surface of a mine; খনির উপরিভাগ। ***Verb t.*** **1.** To cover with grass or with turf; ঘাস দ্বারা আচ্ছাদন করা, শষ্পাবৃত করা, ঘাসের চাপড়া বসান। **2.** To bleach on the grass or ground, as flax; ঘাসের উপর শুকাইয়া সাদা করা। **3.** To bring to the ground; as, to *grass* a bird by a shot; to land; as, to *grass* a fish; ভূপাতিত করা; (মাছ) ডাঙ্গায় তোলা। **4.** To knock down; to fell; as, to *grass* an opponent; ধাক্কা দিয়া মাটীতে ফেলা; ভূপাতিত করা। **Grass'-less,** *adj.* **Grass'-y,** *adj.* **1.** Covered with grass; তৃণাচ্ছাদিত, শষ্পাবৃত, তৃণাকীর্ণ। **2.** Resembling grass; green; তৃণসন্নিভ; শ্যামল হরিৎ। **Grass-cutter**—(ভারতবর্ষে) ঘাসিয়াড়া, ঘেসুড়ে, ঘাসুড়িয়া। **Grass-hopper**—ফড়িঙ্গ, গঙ্গাফড়িঙ্গ (যোঃ), দূর্ব্বাফড়িঙ্গ (অভিঃ)। **Grass-hopper beam**—বাষ্পীয় যন্ত্রের অন্তর্গত যে দণ্ড এক প্রান্তে একটী সূক্ষ্ম কীলকের উপর দোলায়িত হয়। **Grass-hopper beamed**—(Of a golf club) With the face slightly sloped backwards; (গোল্‌ফ্‌ ক্রীড়ার দণ্ড সম্পর্কে) পশ্চাদ্দিকে ঈষৎপ্রবণ মুখবিশিষ্ট। **Grass-snake**—A common ringed snake; ইংলণ্ড দেশীয় এক প্রকার অহিংস্র সর্প। **Grass tree**—অষ্ট্রেলিয়া দেশীয় বৃক্ষ বিশেষ। **Grass widow**—প্রবাসী ব্যক্তির স্ত্রী, প্রোষিতভর্ত্তৃকা, পথিকবধূ (গীতঃ)। **Green grass**—Green with grass; green as grass; তৃণশ্যামল; দূর্ব্বাদলশ্যামল। **At grass**—(*Fig.*) Out of work; making holiday; (লক্ষণায়) বেকার; আমোদ প্রমোদে রত। At pasture; "The colt is *at grass*"; পশুচারণ ক্ষেত্রে। **Not to let the grass grow under one's feet**—Not to waste time in doing something; অবিলম্বে কাজকরা, কালক্ষয় না করা। **To go to grass**—To go to pasture; মাঠে চরিতে যাওয়া। To be knocked down; হঠাৎ ধাক্কা খাইয়া মাটীতে পড়া। **To let the grass grow under one's feet**—To loiter; গৌণ করা, গড়িমসি করা। **To put** or **turn out to grass**—To put or turn out to graze; চরিবার জন্য মাঠে ছাড়িয়া দেওয়া। **To send to grass**—To send to pasture; পশুচারণ ক্ষেত্রে বা মাঠে নেওয়া, মাঠে চরিতে পাঠান। To knock down; ধাক্কা দিয়া মাটীতে ফেলা।

grāte, *n.* The frame of iron bars for holding fuel while burning; a fireplace or furnace; জ্বলন্ত কয়লা রাখার জন্য লৌহশলাকা রচিত আধার, কয়লার উনুনের ঝাঁঝরি; চুল্লী, অগ্নিকুণ্ড।

grāte, *v. t.* & *i.* **1.** To wear away in small praticles by rubbing on a rough surface; as, to *grate* a nutmeg; বস্তুর বস্তর উপর ঘষিয়া সূক্ষ্ম চূর্ণে পরিণত করা। **2.** To rub with a harsh noise; as, to *grate* a thing *on*, *upon* or *against* another; ঘড় ঘড় শব্দে ঘর্ষণ করা। **3.** To grind as teeth; দন্তে দন্তে ঘর্ষণ করা, দাঁত কিড়মিড় করা। **4.** (*Rare*) To irritate; to offend; as, this outrageous merriment *grates* my spirits; (কচিদ্‌ব্যবহৃত) বিরক্ত করা, জ্বালাতন করা; মনোকষ্ট দেওয়া। ***Verb i.*** **1.** To rub with a harsh noise (*on*, or *against* something else); "A dry wheel *grating on* the axle tree"; ঘড় ঘড় শব্দে ঘর্ষণ করা। **2.** To sound harshly; as, a *grating* voice; to crack, as a hinge etc.; কর্কশ শব্দ হওয়া; কট্‌কট্‌ শব্দ হওয়া, কিচির মিচির শব্দ হওয়া। **3.** To have an annoying effect (*on* or *upon*); "What *grates upon* the sense"; বিরক্তিকর হওয়া, বিরক্তিজনক হওয়া, অপ্রীতিকর হওয়া। **Grat'-ed,** *adj.* Having a grate or grating; as, a *grated* window; শলাকাসমন্বিত, ঝাঁঝরি-ওয়ালা। **Grate'-less,** *adj.* **Grat'-er,** *n.* An instrument with a rough surface for grating; ঘর্ষণের জন্য খরগাত্র যন্ত্র বিশেষ। **Grat'-ing,** *adj.* **Grat'-ing-ly,** *adv.*

grāte'-fŭl *adj.* 1. Pleasing ; agreeable ; gratifying ; as, a *grateful* present ; সুখদ, আনন্দপ্রদ ; প্রীতিপ্রদ, সুখপ্রদ, সুখাবহ, মনোরম ; তুষ্টিজনক। 2. Thankful ; feeling or expressing gratitude ; কৃতজ্ঞ ; কৃতজ্ঞতা সূচক। **–ly,** *adv.* **–ness,** *n.*

grăt-ĭ-fĭ-cā'-tion, *n.* 1. Act of gratifying or pleasing ; তর্পণ, বিনোদন, সংরঞ্জন, তোষণ, সন্তোষণ। 2. That which gives satisfaction ; enjoyment ; pleasure ; তৃপ্তিদায়ক-বস্তু ; উপভোগ ; সুখ, পরিতোষ। 3. A reward ; a recompense ; a gratuity ; (in a bad sense) a bribe ; পুরস্কার ; পারিতোষিক ; বখশিশ্ ; ঘুষ। **Illegal gratification**—উৎকোচ, ঘুষ।

grăt'-ĭ-fȳ, *v. t.* 1. To please ; to oblige ; to delight ; to satisfy ; to indulge ; as, beauty *gratifies* the eye ; to *gratify* the taste or vanity ; আনন্দ দান করা ; বাধিত করা ; আনন্দিত করা ; চরিতার্থ করা, মনোরঞ্জন করা ; পরিতৃপ্ত করা, পরিতুষ্ট করা। 2. To remmunerate ; to make present, usually of money, to ; to bribe ; পুরস্কৃত করা, পুরস্কার দেওয়া ; বখ্শিশ্ দেওয়া ; ঘুষ দেওয়া, উৎকোচ প্রদান করা। **–ing,** *adj.* **–ing-ly,** *adv.*

gratin (F.), *n.* A dish cooked with toasted bread crumbs ; the process of preparing it ; ভাজা রুটীর টুকরা সহযোগে রন্ধিত ব্যঞ্জন ; উক্তরূপ ব্যঞ্জন রন্ধনের প্রণালী।

grāt'-ĭng, *n.* 1. A partition of bars or lattice work ; লোহার শিক বা ঝাঁঝরির প্রাচীর। 2. (*Optics*) Set of parallel wires or surface of glass etc. ruled with parallel lines for producing spectra by diffraction ; (দৃষ্টি-বিজ্ঞান) বিকৃতি-ক্রিয়া দ্বারা বর্ণচ্ছত্র উৎপাদনের জন্য সমান্তরাল তারশ্রেণী বা কাচফলকাদির উপর অঙ্কিত সমান্তরাল রেখাসমূহ।

grā'-tis, *adv.* & *adj.* For nothing ; without charge ; কিছু না লইয়া ; বিনা মূল্যে, অমনি, বিনা ব্যয়ে। *Adj.* Given or done for nothing ; gratuitous ; "His *gratis* practice of medicine" ; বিনা মূল্যে প্রদত্ত বা বিনা দক্ষিণায় কৃত ; বিনা মূল্যে প্রাপ্ত বা প্রাপ্য।

grăt'-ĭ-tūde, *n.* The state of being grateful ; কৃতজ্ঞতা।

gră-tū'-ĭ-tous (-tŭs), *adj.* 1. Freely bestowed or obtained ; free ; "The *gratuitous* blessings of Heaven" ; বিনা পারিশ্রমিক বা পুরস্কার ব্যতিরেকে প্রাপ্ত বা প্রদত্ত ; বিনামূল্যে প্রদত্ত, অবৈতনিক। 2. Uncalled for ; unwarranted ; done or acting without any reason ; as, a *gratuitous* lie or liar ; অকারণ, অমূলক ; বিন-সনদী ; অহেতুক, হেতুশূন্য। **–ly,** *adv.* **–ness,** *n.* **Gratuitous utility**—প্রাকৃতিক উপযুক্ততা (হিঃ কোঃ)।

gră-tū'-ĭ-tȳ, *n.* 1. A present (usually of money) in return for favours or services ; (now esp.) such a gift to a servant or inferior official ; পারিতোষিক ; বখ্শিশ্। 2. A free gift ; a donation ; a bounty to soldiers on retirement or other occasions ; দান ; এককালীন দান ; কর্ম্ম হইতে অবসর গ্রহণকালে বা অন্য সময়ে সৈনিকগণকে যে এককালীন অর্থ পুরস্কার দেওয়া হয়।

grăt'-ū-lāte, *v. t.* (*Archaic*) To congratulate ; অভিনন্দন করা। **–la'-tion,** *n.*

grăt'-ū-lă-tō-ry, *adj.* Congratulatory ; complimentary ; অভিনন্দন-সূচক ; প্রশংসাবাচক।

gră-vā'-mĕn, *n.* 1. A grievance ; দুঃখের হেতু, দুঃখের বিষয়। 2. (*Eccl.*) A memorial from the Lower House of Convocation to the Upper relating the disorders or grievances of the church ; (যাজকীয়শাস্ত্র) ধর্ম্মসংঘসম্পর্কীয় অভিযোগ সম্পর্কে নিম্নযাজক সভা হইতে ঊর্দ্ধতন যাজক সভায় আবেদন। 3. The essence or the worst part (of a complaint) ; অভিযোগের স্থূলমর্ম্ম, অভিযোগের সারাংশ, অভিযোগের মন্দতম অংশ।

grāve, *v. t.* 1. (*Archaic*) To sculpture ; to engrave ; (অপ্রঃ) ক্ষোদিত করা ; উৎকীর্ণ করা। 2. To impress deeply or fix indelibly (*on* or *in* the mind etc.) ; গভীর ভাবে মুদ্রিত করা, গভীর ভাবে অঙ্কিত করা। 3. (*Archaic*) To bury ; সমাহিত করা, গোর দেওয়া। **A graven image**—An idol ; শিলামূর্ত্তি, পাষাণ-প্রতিমা।

grāve, *n.* 1. An excavation, as a place of burial ; a tomb ; a mound or monument over a grave ; (*fig.*) death ; Hades ; সমাধিস্থলী, শবখাত, প্রেতকুণ্ড, শবগর্ত্ত ; কবর, গোর ; সমাধি স্তূপ, সমাধি-স্তম্ভ ; (লক্ষণায়) মৃত্যু ; প্রেতাত্মাদিগের বাসভূমি, অধোলোক। 2. A trench for earthing up potatoes etc. ; বিলাতি আলু প্রভৃতি মাটীর ভিতর রাখার জন্য খাত-বিশেষ। **Grave'-ward,** *adv.* & *adj.* **Grave clothes**—সমাহিত ব্যক্তির পরিধেয় বস্ত্র, প্রেতবাস, প্রেতবস্ত্র, শব-বস্ত্র। **Grave digger**—শবখাতখনক ; একপ্রকার কীট। **Grave-stone**—সমাধির উপরে বা নীচে স্থাপিত ক্ষোদিত শিলাফলক, সমাধিপ্রস্তর, সমাধিফলক। **Grave-yard** — সমাধিভূমি, গোরস্থান, সমাধিপ্রাঙ্গণ, সমাধিক্ষেত্র। **Secret as the grave** — Quite secret ; অতি গোপনীয়, গুহ্যাতিগুহ্য। **To make a person turn in the grave** — Of an act etc. which would have pained him while alive ; কোন ব্যক্তি জীবিত থাকিলে যেরূপ কার্য্যে ব্যথা পাইত সেইরূপ কার্য্য করা। **With one foot in the grave**—At the very verge of death—মুমূর্ষু অবস্থাপন্ন, আসন্নমৃত্যু, শিয়রে শমন, গঙ্গামুখো পা, গঙ্গাযাত্রা সন্নিকট।

grāve, *adj.* & *n.* 1. Weighty ; serious ; as, a *grave* and prudent law : a *grave* fault, responsibility or symptom ; গুরু, ভারি ; প্রয়োজনীয়, গুরুতর, সঙ্গীন (*colloq.*) । 2. Not light or gay ; slow moving ; solemn ; as, man of *grave* deportment : "*Grave* steps" : *grave* appearance ; গম্ভীর, গাম্ভীর্যশালী (উচ্ছলঃ) ; মৃদুসঞ্চারী, মন্থরগামী ; প্রশান্তগম্ভীর, গুরুগম্ভীর । 3. (*Mus.*) Low ; deep ; (সঙ্গীত শাস্ত্র) উদাত্ত, অনুচ্চ ; গভীর । 4. (*Obs.*) Heady ; উগ্রপ্রকৃতি । ***Noun.*** A grave accent ; উদাত্ত স্বর ।

grāve, *v. t.* To clean, as a ship's bottom by burning off the weeds etc. and coating it with pitch or tar ; জাহাজের তলার সামুদ্রিক শৈবালাদি পোড়াইয়া দিয়া রং বা আলকাতরা লাগান ।

grăv'-ĕl, *n.* & *v. t.* 1. Very small pebbles intermixed with coarse sand ; কঙ্কর, কাঁকর, উপল (সাঃ পঃ) । 2. (*Geol.* & *Min.*) A stratum of this material esp. one that contains gold ; কঙ্করস্তর, বিশেষতঃ স্বর্ণগর্ভ কঙ্কর স্তর । 3. A disease produced by small concretions in the kidneys and bladder ; অশ্মরী, পাথরী রোগ । ***Verb t.*** 1. To cover or strew with gravel ; as, to *gravel* a street ; কঙ্করাবৃত করা, কাঁকর বিছান, কাঁকর দিয়া বাঁধা । 2. To puzzle ; to embarrass ; to perplex ; "It will *gravel* even a philosopher to comprehend this" ; ধাঁধা লাগান ; ঝঞ্ঝাটে ফেলা ; হতবুদ্ধি করা । **—ly**, *adj.* Abounding with, or consisting of, gravel ; কঙ্করময়, কঙ্করবহুল । **Gravel-blind**—More than SAND-BLIND (which see.) **Gravel-stone**—উপলখণ্ড, কঙ্কর । **Gravel-walk**—কঙ্করদ্বারা বাঁধানো হাঁটিবার পথ, কঙ্করাবৃত পাদপথ । **Pay-gravel**—যে কাঁকরে এমন পরিমাণ সোনা মিশ্রিত থাকে যে তাহা হইতে সোনা বাহির করিয়া ব্যবসায় করিলে, খরচ পোষাইয়া লাভ দাঁড়াইতে পারে ।

grăv'-ĭd, *adj.* Being with young ; pregnant ; গর্ভভারাক্রান্ত, গর্ভবতী, অন্তর্বত্নী ; অন্তঃসত্ত্বা, গুর্ব্বী, গুর্ব্বিণী [cf. উত্তরাং ত্বং অবেক্ষস্ব গুর্ব্বিণীং মা শুচ শুভে !]

grăv'-i-tāte, *v. i.* & *t.* 1. To be acted on by gravitation ; to tend to move under the influence of gravity (towards) ; to tend to the centre ; মাধ্যাকর্ষণের ক্রিয়ার অধীন হওয়া ; মাধ্যাকর্ষণের প্রভাব বশে (কোন কিছুর দিকে) আকৃষ্ট হওয়া ; কেন্দ্রাভিমুখে আকৃষ্ট হওয়া । 2. (*Fig.*) To be strongly attracted (*towards* or *into* some centre of influence) ; (লক্ষণায়) প্রবলভাবে আকৃষ্ট হওয়া । 3. To sink by gravity ; to tend to reach to low level ; to settle down ; (*lit.* & *fig.*) ; গুরুত্ব হেতু নিমজ্জিত হওয়া ; নিম্নবর্ত্তীস্থানে পৌঁছিবার জন্য উন্মুখ হওয়া ; স্থির হওয়া, তলায় বসিয়া যাওয়া, থিতান, স্থায়ীভাবে বসতি স্থাপন করা ; (শব্দানুযায়ী এবং লক্ষণায়) । ***Verb t.*** (*In diamond mining*) To agitate, as gravel so that the weighty parts settle to the bottom ; (হীরকের খনির কাজে) এরূপভাবে কাঁকর নাড়া যাহাতে ভারি অংশ সকল নীচে পড়িয়া যায় । **—ta-tive**, *adj.* Causing to gravitate ; tending to a centre ; মাধ্যাকর্ষণের প্রভাবাধীনকারী ; কেন্দ্রাভিসারী ।

grăv-i-tā'-tion, *n.* 1. Act or process of gravitating ; মাধ্যাকর্ষণ । 2. (*Phys.*) That species of attraction by which all bodies or particles of matter tend toward each other ; (পদার্থবিদ্যা) মাধ্যাকর্ষণ, গুরুত্বাকর্ষণ (হিঃ কোঃ), মধ্যাভিসরণ, মধ্যাভিগমন, গুরুত্বহেতু মধ্যাভিসরণ । **—al**, *adv.* Of, or relating to, gravitation ; মাধ্যাকর্ষণ সম্বন্ধীয় । **Laws of gravitation**—গুরুত্বাকর্ষণ নিয়ম (হিঃ কোঃ), মাধ্যাকর্ষণ নিয়ম ।

grăv'-i-tȳ, *n.* 1. Weight ; as, centre of *gravity* ; গুরুত্ব । 2. State of being grave ; solemnity ; sobriety of demeanour ; as, men of *gravity* and learning ; গাম্ভীর্য ; ধীরতা, প্রশান্তভাব ; স্থিরভাব । 3. Importance ; seriousness ; enormity ; as, the *gravity* of an offence ; গুরুত্ব ; গুরুতা ; আতিশয্য । 4. The attractive force by which all bodies tend to the centre of the earth ; the degree of intensity of this force measured by acceleration ; degree of intensity with which any body is thus attracted by any other ; যে আকর্ষণ শক্তি দ্বারা পদার্থ সমূহ ভূকেন্দ্রের অভিমুখীন হইয়া থাকে, ভূমধ্যাকর্ষণ (সাঃ পঃ), ভূকেন্দ্রাভিমুখীনতা ; ভূমধ্যাকর্ষণের প্রবলতার মাত্রা ; যে শক্তি দ্বারা কোন পদার্থ অপর পদার্থের দিকে আকৃষ্ট হয় তাহার প্রবলতার মাত্রা । 5. Lowness of tone in music ; সঙ্গীতাদিতে স্বরের অনুচ্চতা । **Specific gravity**—সমায়তন জলের সহিত তুলনায় আপেক্ষিক গুরুত্ব । **The centre of gravity**—See under CENTRE.

grā-vūre', *n.* Short for PHOTO-GRAVURE.

grā'-vȳ, *n.* 1. The juices coming from meat while cooking ; a dressing for food made from these with other materials ; রন্ধনকালে মাংস হইতে যে রস বাহির হইয়া থাকে, সিদ্ধ-মাংস রস, পক্ব-মাংস-রস (কেশিঃ) ; পক্বমাংসরসের সহিত অন্যান্য দ্রব্যের সহযোগে ব্যঞ্জনাদির যে ঝোল প্রস্তুত হয় । **Gravy-beef**—গরুর পায়ের যে অংশ রস বাহির করার জন্য সিদ্ধ করা হয় । **Gravy-boat**—পক্বমাংসের রস রাখার জন্য নৌকাকার পাত্র ।

gray, grey (grā), *adj.*, *n.*, *v. t.* & *i.* 1. White mixed with black ; of the colour of hair whitened by age ; ashy coloured ; ধূসর, ধূম্রবর্ণ ; পলিত ; ভস্মবর্ণ । 2. Dull ; cloudy ; "*Gray* twilight" ; dismal ; gloomy ; "*Gray* years" ; স্ফূর্ত্তিহীন ; ম্লান, মলিন ; অপ্রসন্ন ; বিষাদমলিন । 3. Gray-haired, as a man ; turning white with age, as hair etc. ; পলিতকেশ ; শ্বেত, পক্ব। **4.** Mature ; as, a *gray* experience ; পরিপক্ব। **5.** Ancient ; old ; "Of *gray* renown" ; প্রাচীন ; পুরাতন। ***Noun.*** **1.** A gray colour ; a gray pigment ; early morning or evening twilight ; as, in the *grey* of the morning ; ধূসরবর্ণ, ধূম্রবর্ণ ; ধূম্রবর্ণ রঞ্জক পদার্থ ; গোধূলি, ঊষা, কাকজ্যোৎস্না। **2.** A gray animal, as a horse ; ধূসরবর্ণ পশু। **3.** Gray clothes ; ধূসরবর্ণ পরিচ্ছদ। ***Verb t.*** **1.** To make gray ; ধূসরবর্ণ করা, ধূসরিত করা। **2.** (*Photog.*) To give a dull surface to (a glass) ; to give mezzotint effect to (a photograph) by covering a negative with such a glass ; (আলোকচিত্র) (কাচের) উপরিভাগ নিষ্প্রভ করা ; বিপর্য্যস্ত চিত্র উক্ত প্রকার কাচদ্বারা আবৃত করিয়া (আলোকচিত্রে) মেজটিণ্ট ফলকের মত ছায়ালোক প্রদর্শিত করা। ***Verb i.*** To grow or become gray ; ধূসরবর্ণ হওয়া, ধূম্রায়মান হওয়া। **–ish,** *adj.* **–ly,** *adv.* **–ness,** *n.* **Gray beard**—An old man ; পলিতকেশ ব্যক্তি, পক্ব-শ্মশ্রু ব্যক্তি। A large stoneware ; মদ্যাদি রাখিবার জন্য প্রস্তরনির্ম্মিত বৃহৎ পাত্র। **Gray coat**—কাম্বারল্যাণ্ডের মধ্যশ্রেণীর লোক। **Gray crow** or **Gray-back**—একপ্রকার কাক। **Gray drake**—একপ্রকার দিনজীবী কীট। **Gray-eye**—ধূসর নেত্র, কটা চোক। **Gray-eyed**—কটা চোকো। **Gray friar**—ফ্রান্সিস্কান সম্প্রদায়ভুক্ত সন্ন্যাসী। **Gray-haired, –headed**—পক্বকেশ, শুভ্রকেশ, পলিতকেশ। **Gray-hen**—একপ্রকার বন্য কুক্কুটী। **Gray-ling**—রজতাভ ধূসরমৎস্য বিশেষ। A butterfly ; প্রজাপতি। **Gray monk**—সিস্টারসিয়ান্ সম্প্রদায়ভুক্ত সন্ন্যাসী। **Gray-matter**—মস্তিষ্কের ধূসরবর্ণ পদার্থ। **Gray-owl**—The common owl ; পেচক। **The gray mare**—The wife who rules the husband ; যে স্ত্রী স্বামীর উপর কর্তৃত্ব করে। **The gray mare is the better horse**—The wife rules the husband ; স্ত্রী স্বামীর আধিপত্য করে। **The Grays** or **Scots Grays**—গুরুভার অস্ত্রশস্ত্রে সজ্জিত অশ্বারোহী সৈন্য। **The gray of the morning**—ঊষা কাল।

grāze, *v. i.* & *t.* **1.** To eat grass ; to feed on growing herbage ; as, cattle *graze* on the meadows ; ঘাস খাওয়া ; চরা। **2.** To pasture cattle ; "My own friend who *grazed* on the marshes" ; গবাদি চারণ করা, চরান। ***Verb t.*** **1.** To feed with grass ; to furnish pasture for ; as, to *graze* cattle ; ঘাস খাওয়ান ; চরান। **2.** To feed on ; to browze ; "To *graze* the flowery plain" ; খাইয়া প্রাণধারণ করা ; তরুণ শাখা পল্লবাদি ভক্ষণ করা।

Graz'-er, *n.* An animal that grazes ; যে পশু মাঠে চরে, তৃণচারী।

Graz'-ing, *n.* **1.** Pasturing ; পশুচারণ। **2.** Pasture-land ; গোষ্ঠ, পশুচারণ ভূমি।

grāze, *v. t., i.* & *n.* **1.** To rub or touch lightly in passing ; as, the bullet *grazed* the wall ; মৃদু স্পর্শ করিয়া যাওয়া, ঘষড়াইয়া যাওয়া, ঈষৎ স্পর্শ করিয়া যাওয়া, ঠিকরাইয়া যাওয়া। **2.** To abrade slightly ; as, to *graze* the skin or a part of a body ; ঘষিয়া ক্ষত করা, লুণছাল তোলা। ***Verb i.*** To touch or abrade something lightly in passing (with *against, along, through, by, past* etc.) ; ঘষড়াইয়া যাওয়া, ঈষৎ স্পর্শ করিয়া যাওয়া। ***Noun.*** Grazing ; a slight scratch ; ঈষৎ স্পর্শ করিয়া চলন ; সামান্য আঁচড়।

grā'-zier (-zhêr), *n.* One who pastures cattle for the market ; রাখাল, পশুচারণকারী, গোপালক, পশুপ, চারক, পশুপাল। **–y,** The occupation of a grazier ; পশুপালন।

grease (grēz, grēs), *n.* **1.** Animal fat in a soft state ; চর্ব্বি, বসা, মেদ। **2.** Fat of deer or other game ; as, in *grease* (=fit for killing) ; মৃগাদির চর্ব্বি। **3.** An oily matter esp. as lubricant ; তৈলাক্ত পদার্থ, তৈলাক্ত মালিস। **4.** An inflammation in the heels of a horse ; অশ্বের পদস্ফীতি রোগ। **Grease-box**—গাড়ীর চাকায় সংবদ্ধ তৈলাধার বিশেষ। **Grease paint** — অভিনেতৃগণের মুখে মাখিবার জন্য তৈলাক্ত পদার্থ-বিশেষ। **Grease trap**—নর্দ্দমার জলের চর্ব্বি সঞ্চয়ের জন্য যন্ত্র-বিশেষ, চর্ব্বি-ধরা-ফাঁদ। **In grease, In pride** or **prime of grease**—Fit for killing ; fatty ; বধের উপযোগী ; মেদস্বী, চর্ব্বিওয়ালা।

grease (grēz, grēs), *v. t.* **1.** To anoint, soil or lubricate with grease ; as, to *grease* an axle ; চর্ব্বি মাখান, বসা দ্বারা মলিন করা। **2.** To affect (a horse) with the grease disease ; (অশ্বকে) অশ্বপাদ-স্ফীতিরোগাক্রান্ত করা। **3.** (*Rare*) To bribe ; (কচিদ্ ব্যবহৃত) ঘুষ দেওয়া। **To grease the palm of**—To bribe ; ঘুষ দেওয়া। **To grease the wheels** — To make affairs go smoothly ; নির্ব্বিবাদে চালান।

greas'-ėr (grēz-, grēs-), *n.* **1.** One who greases machinery ; যে ব্যক্তি কলে চর্ব্বি মাখায়। **2.** (*Slang, U.S.*) A native Mexican ; (মার্কিণ যুক্তরাজ্যের ইতরভাষায়) মেক্সিকোর প্রাচীন অধিবাসী।

greas'-ȳ (grēz-, grēs-), *adj.* **1.** Composed of grease ; oily ; unctuous ; বসাময় ; তৈলাক্ত ; তেলাল। **2.** Smeared or defiled with grease ; (of wool) uncleansed ; বসালিপ্ত, বসাপ্লুত, বসাদ্বারা মলিনীকৃত ; (পশম) অপরিষ্কৃত। **3.** Like grease or oil ; smooth ; slippery or slimy with mud or moisture as a road etc. ; বসাবৎ, তৈলবৎ ; মসৃণ, চিক্কণ ; পিচ্ছিল। **4.** (Of a horse) Affected with the grease ;

(অশ্ব-সম্বন্ধে) পাদস্ফীতি রোগাক্রান্ত। **5.** Disagreeably unctuous as manners, expressions, etc.; পাঁচাটারকমের। **–i-ly,** *adv.* **–i-ness,** *n.*

great (grāt), *n.* **1.** Large in size; big; extensive; প্রকাণ্ড, বিশাল, বিরাট; বৃহৎ, মহা; বিস্তীর্ণ। **2.** Large in number; numerous; as, a *great* company; বহুসংখ্যক; অসংখ্য। **3.** Long continued; prolonged in time; as, a *great* interval; বহুকালাগত; দীর্ঘকালস্থায়ী। **4.** Endowed with extraordinary powers; powerful; mighty; noble; as, a *great* hero or judge; অসামান্যক্ষমতাসম্পন্ন, অসাধারণ শক্তিসম্পন্ন; শক্তিমান, শক্তিশালী; পরাক্রান্ত, প্রতাপশালী; মহৎ, মহান্। **5.** High in rank or position; illustrious; distinguished; as, a *great* man; সম্ভ্রান্ত, উচ্চপদস্থ; খ্যাতনামা; বিখ্যাত। **6.** Superior; admirable; lofty; grand; as, a *great* thought or idea; শ্রেষ্ঠ; শ্লাঘ্য; উন্নত; মহান্। **7.** Important; weighty; as, *great* occasion; critical; "The *great* movements"; প্রয়োজনীয়; গুরু, গুরুতর; সঙ্কটসঙ্কুল। **8.** Pre-eminent; chief; (with *the* prefixed); as, *the Great* Powers of Europe; মুখ্য; প্রধান। **9.** (*Archaic*) Pregnant; big (with young); গর্ভবতী; অন্তঃসত্ত্বা, গুর্ব্বিণী। **10.** Beyond the ordinary; considerable; as, take *great* care; অসামান্য; অতিশয়, অত্যন্ত। **11.** Distant by one more generation; as, *great* grandfather or *great* grandson; একপুরুষ ঊর্দ্ধতন বা অধস্তন। **12.** Fully deserving the name of; as, a *great* scoundrel or friend; অন্বর্থনামা, সার্থকনামা। **13.** (*Predicatively*) Possessing much skill at, or information on; "Is *great at* cooking etc."; "Very *great on* dogs"; সুদক্ষ, সুনিপুণ, সুবিজ্ঞ, প্রাজ্ঞ। ***Noun.*** (*Pl.* THE GREAT) **1.** Great persons; বড়লোক সকল, মহৎলোক সকল। **2.** That which is great; মহান্ বস্তু। **Great'-ness,** *n.* The state or quality of being great; মহত্ত্ব, মাহাত্ম্য। **Great Assize, Day** or **Inquest**—The Day of Judgment; খৃষ্টীয় ও মুসলমান ধর্ম্মানুসারে অন্তিম বিচার দিবস। **Great Bear** — সপ্তর্ষিমণ্ডল, সপ্তর্ষি (হিঃ কোঃ)। **Great Charter**—Magna Charta নামক ইংলণ্ডের প্রজাধিকার বিষয়ক সনন্দ বিশেষ। **Great coat** — বড় লম্বা কোর্ত্তা। *-ed, -less, adjs.* **Great deal**—অতিশয়। **Greater Britain** — উপনিবেশ ও অধীন দেশসমূহ সমেত গ্রেটব্রিটেন, বৃহত্তর ব্রিটেন। **Great go**—ইংলণ্ডের কেম্ব্রিজ বিশ্ববিদ্যালয়ের বি, এ, উপাধির জন্য শেষ পরীক্ষা। **Great grandfather, grandmother, grandson etc.**—See GREAT *adj.* 11. **Great hearted**—Magnanimous; noble; মহাপ্রাণ, মহাত্মা, মহদন্তঃকরণ; সম্ভ্রান্ত। **Great (or long) hundred**—১২০। **Great Mother** — পৃথিবী। **Great primer** — See under PRIMER. **Greats**—অক্সফোর্ড বিশ্ববিদ্যালয়ের বি, এ, উপাধির জন্য শেষ পরীক্ষা। **Great sea**—ভূমধ্যসাগর। **Great Seal** — কোন রাজ্যের প্রধান শীলমোহর। **Great toe**—(*Now usually*) Big toe; পায়ের বুড়ো আঙ্গুল, পাদাঙ্গুষ্ঠ। **A great hand at**—(*Colloq.*) A person highly skilful in; সিদ্ধহস্ত। **The Great**—The best known (*generally appended to a name*); as, Alexander *the Great*: *the Great* Mogul; জগদ্বিখ্যাত, বিশ্ববিখ্যাত। **The greatest good of the greatest number** — অধিকতম লোকের প্রভূততম সুখ (Bentham প্রবর্ত্তিত নীতি)। **The Great Lakes**—(*Humour.*) The Atlantic; (কৌতুকচ্ছলে) অতলান্তিক মহাসাগর। **The great majority**—অধিকাংশ। **The Great Powers (of Europe)**—ইয়ুরোপের প্রধান শক্তিপুঞ্জ—যথা, ইংলণ্ড, ফ্রান্স, জর্ম্মণি, অষ্ট্রিয়া, রুষ ও ইতালী। **The great spirit**—উত্তর আমেরিকার আদিম নিবাসিগণের প্রধান দেবতা। **The Great Unknown**—স্যর ওয়াল্টার স্কট। ইনি সুপ্রসিদ্ধ Waverly উপন্যাসরাজি স্বীয় নাম গোপন রাখিয়া প্রকাশিত করেন বলিয়া এই উপাধি। **The great unwashed**—Artisan class; শিল্পিশ্রেণী, কারিকর সমাজ। **The great world**—High society; সম্ভ্রান্ত সমাজ। **To be great with one**—(*Dial.*) To be intimate or familiar with him; (উপভাষায়) খুব জানা শোনা থাকা।

great'-en (grāt-n), *v. t.* & *i.* (*Archaic*) To render great or eminent; to aggrandize; (অপ্রঃ) মহান্ করা, সমুন্নত করা; উৎকর্ষসাধন করা। ***Verb i.*** (*Archaic*) To become great or greater; to increase; (অপ্রঃ) মহান্ হওয়া, মহত্তর হওয়া; বৃদ্ধি হওয়া, বৃদ্ধি পাওয়া।

great'-ly (grāt-), *adv.* **1.** In a great degree; much; অতি মাত্রায়; অত্যন্ত। **2.** Nobly; loftily; magnanimously; মহান্ ভাবে; মহানুভবতাসহকারে; সদয়ভাবে।

greave (grēv), *n.* (*Pl.*) The sediment of melted tallow used as fish-bait or food of dogs etc.; গলিত চর্ব্বির তলানি যাহা বড়শীর টোপ স্বরূপ অথবা কুকুর ইত্যাদির খাদ্য রূপে ব্যবহৃত হয়।

greave (grēv), *n.* (*Usu. pl.*) An armour for the leg below the knee; জঙ্ঘাত্রাণ।

grebe (grĕb), *n.* An aquatic web-footed almost tailless bird;

Horned grebe.

the plumage of the grebe; পুচ্ছহীন জালপাদ জলচর পক্ষি-বিশেষ; উক্ত পক্ষীর পালক।

Grē′-cian (-shăn), *adj.* & *n.* (*Rare except of architecture and facial outline*) Of, or pertaining to, Greece ; Greek ; গ্রীস দেশীয় ; গ্রীক জাতীয়। ***Noun.*** **1.** (*Obs.*) A native or inhabitant of Greece ; গ্রীসদেশের অধিবাসী বা প্রবাসী। **2.** A Greek scholar ; গ্রীক ভাষায় সুপণ্ডিত ব্যক্তি। **3.** A first-class student in Christ's Hospital, London ; লণ্ডননগরীস্থ Christ Hospital College এর প্রথম শ্রেণীর ছাত্র। **Grecian-bend**—স্ত্রীলোকদিগের মধ্যে সম্মুখের দিকে দেহ ঈষৎ আনত করিয়া চলিবার ভঙ্গি-বিশেষ। **Grecian knot**—স্ত্রীলোকের কেশবিন্যাসরীতি বিশেষ [এই রীতি অনুসারে কেশপাশ পশ্চাদ্দিকে বাঁধা হয়]। **Grecian slippers**—একপ্রকার চটী জুতা।

Grē′-cīze, *v. t.* & *i.* To make Grecian ; to translate into Greek ; গ্রীসীয়বৎ করা ; গ্রীকভাষায় অনুবাদ করা। ***Verb i.*** To speak Greek ; গ্রীক ভাষায় কথা বলা। **—cism,** *n.* An idiom of the Greek language ; গ্রীক ভাষার রীতিসিদ্ধ প্রয়োগ।

greed (grēd), *n.* An insatiate longing esp. for wealth ; ধন লালসা, লোভ, লুব্ধতা। **Greed′-i-ly,** *adv.* **Greed′-i-ness,** *n.*

greed′-ȳ (grēd-), *adj.* **1.** Having keen appetite for food or drink ; ravenous ; voracious ; gluttonous ; ক্ষুধার্ত্ত বা তৃষ্ণার্ত্ত ; লুব্ধ ; অতিভোজী ; পেটুক, উদরসর্ব্বস্ব, ঔদরিক। **2.** Covetous ; avaricious (with *of*) ; লোভী, লিপ্সু, লোলুপ, লুব্ধ, গৃধ্নু, লালসাপর ; অর্থগৃধ্নু।

Greek (grēk), *adj.* & *n.* **1.** Of, or pertaining to, Greece or the Greeks ; Hellenic ; গ্রীস সম্বন্ধীয়, গ্রীসীয় ; যাবনিক। **2.** Of, according to, written or spoken in, Greek language ; গ্রীকভাষা সম্বন্ধীয়, গ্রীক-ভাষানুযায়ী, গ্রীক ভাষায় লিখিত বা কথিত। ***Noun.*** **1.** A native of Greece ; the language of Greece ; গ্রীস দেশের অধিবাসী, যবন, গ্রীক ; গ্রীস দেশের ভাষা। **2.** A member of the Greek Church ; খৃষ্টীয় ধর্ম্মসংঘ বিশেষের সভ্য। **3.** A cunning person ; a cheat ; "He was an adventurer, a pauper, a blackleg, a regular *Greek*" ; ধূর্ত্তলোক, চালাক লোক ; প্রতারক। **4.** (*Colloq.*) Something unintelligible ; as, it was all *Greek* to me ; দুর্ব্বোধ বিষয়। **Greek calends**—See CALENDS. **Greek Church**—গ্রীস, রুশিয়া ও তুরস্ক সাম্রাজ্যের খৃষ্টীয় ধর্ম্মসংঘ। **Greek cross**—See under CROSS. *n.* **Greek Fathers**—Fathers who wrote in Greek ; প্রাচীন খৃষ্টীয়াচার্য্যগণ—যাঁহারা গ্রীক ভাষায় গ্রন্থ রচনা করিয়াছেন। **Greek fire**—See under FIRE ; অনলবর্ষী পিচকারী (প্রবাসী ১৩২২)। **Greek fret, —key**—Same as FRET, *n.* (*arch.*) **Greek to any one**—See under GREEK, *n.* 4. **When Greek meets Greek then comes the tug of war**—সমানে সমানে লাগিলে ভীষণ লড়াই বাঁধিয়া যায়।

green (grēn), *adj., n., v. t.* & *i.* **1.** Having the colour of growing herbage and plants ; as, *green* fields ; emerald ; verdant ; শ্যামল, হরিৎ, সবুজবর্ণ ; মরকতবর্ণ ; হরিদ্বর্ণ। **2.** (Of complexion) Having a sickly colour ; wan ; pale ; (চেহারা সম্পর্কে) পাংশুবর্ণ ; পাঙ্গাসিয়া, ফেকাসিয়া ; মলিন, বিবর্ণ। **3.** Full of vitality ; vigorous ; as, a *green* old age ; new ; fresh, as wound ; সতেজ ; তেজস্বী ; নব, নূতন ; তাজা। **4.** Unripe ; immature ; young and tender ; as, *green* fruit, vegetables, etc. ; কাঁচা, অপক্ব ; অপরিণত ; কচি ও কোমল। **5.** Inexperienced ; gullible ; "*Green* girl" ; কাঁচা, অনভিজ্ঞ ; সহজে প্রতারিত। **6.** Not dry ; not seasoned ; as, *green* wood or fish etc. ; not tanned, as hide etc. ; কাচা ; অশুষ্কীকৃত ; অশোধিত। ***Noun.*** **1.** The characteristic colour of growing herbage ; anything green ; green part of anything ; শ্যামলবর্ণ ; হরিদ্বর্ণ বস্তু ; কোন বস্তুর কাঁচা অংশ। **2.** A green dye or pigment ; হরিদ্বর্ণ রঞ্জক বস্তু। **3.** Verdure ; vegetation ; শ্যামলতা, শ্যামশ্রী ; তৃণগুল্ম। **4.** Vigour ; youthfulness ; vitality ; তেজ ; তারুণ্য ; ওজস্বিতা। **5.** A grassy plot or plain sometimes used for a special purpose ; as, a bowling *green* ; তৃণশ্যামল ভূমি, শাদ্বলস্থলী। **6.** (*Pl.*) Leaves and stems of young plants before or after cooking ; কচি গাছের পাতা বা ডাঁটা। **Green′-er-y,** *n.* Green plants ; verdure ; সবুজ তরুগুল্ম ; শ্যামলতা, শ্যামশ্রী। **Green′-ish, Green′-y,** *adjs.* Somewhat green ; ঈষৎ সবুজ, হরিদাভ, আহরিৎ। **Green′-ly,** *adv.* **Green′-ness,** *n.* **Green-back**—(মার্কিণ যুক্তরাজ্য) নোট ; ব্যাঙ্কের নোট। **Green-blind**—হরিদ্বর্ণ দর্শনাক্ষম, হরিদ্বর্ণসংবেদনাক্ষম। **Green-book**—সরকারী কার্য্যবিবরণী পুস্তক—বিশেষতঃ ইতালী ও ভারতবর্ষের শাসনতন্ত্রের হরিদ্বর্ণ প্রচ্ছদপটযুক্ত কার্য্যবিবরণী পুস্তক। **Green cheese**—পুঁদিনার মত সুগন্ধি গুল্মবিশেষ দ্বারা হরিতীকৃত পানীয়। **(Board of) Green cloth**—ইংলণ্ডেশ্বরের রাজপ্রাসাদের শান্তিরক্ষার জন্য এবং প্রাসাদের সীমা মধ্যে কোন ব্যক্তি অপরাধ করিলে তাহার বিচারের জন্য সম্মিলনী—পূর্ব্বে যে দ্বারের সম্মুখে ঐ সম্মিলনীর অধিবেশন হইত—তাহা হরিদ্বর্ণ বস্ত্রে আবৃত থাকিত। **Green crop**—যে শস্য কাঁচা অবস্থায় খাওয়া যায়। **Green-eyed**—Having green eyes ; jealous ; শ্যামনয়ন ; ঈর্ষ্যাপরায়ণ। **Green-eyed-monster**—Jealousy ; ঈর্ষ্যা, বিদ্বেষ, পরশ্রীকাতরতা। **Green fat**—চিত্রকচ্ছপের সবুজবর্ণ তৈল বা মেদ (ইহা ভোজনবিলাসিগণ কর্ত্তৃক অতিশয় সমাদৃত হইয়া থাকে। **Green finch** or **green**

linnet—হরিদ্বর্ণ পালকশোভিত ইংলণ্ড-দেশীয় পক্ষি-বিশেষ। **Green gage**—একপ্রকার গোলাকার সবুজবর্ণ কুল ফল। **Green grocer**—তাজা শাকসব্জী বা ফলমূল বিক্রেতা। **Green-grocery**—তাজা শাকসব্জী বা ফলমূলের ব্যবসায়; তাজা শাকসব্জী বা ফলমূল। **Green hand**—A novice; নূতন লোক, কাঁচা লোক। **Greenheart**—পশ্চিম ভারতীয় দ্বীপপুঞ্জের বৃক্ষবিশেষ—এই বৃক্ষের কাষ্ঠে উৎকৃষ্ট আসবাব প্রভৃতি নির্ম্মিত হয়। **Greenhorn** — A raw or inexperienced person; a simpleton; কাঁচা লোক, অনভিজ্ঞ লোক, অপরিপক্বুদ্ধি লোক; বোকা। **Green manure**—সবুজসার, হরিৎসার, কাঁচা সার। **Green parrot** — টিয়া (শিশু)। **Green room** — নাটকের সাজঘর, নেপথ্য (কেণ্ডিঃ), নেপথ্যশালা (ঐ)। **Greensand**—একপ্রকার বেলে পাথর—যাহাতে লৌহের সবুজবর্ণ দাগ দৃষ্ট হয়। **Green sea**—পারস্য উপসাগর। **Green-sick**—হরিৎ পীড়াক্রান্ত। **Green sickness** — Chlorosis; হরিৎপীড়া, মৃৎপাণ্ডু [See CHLOROSIS.] **Greenstick**—একপ্রকার অস্থিভঙ্গ (বিশেষতঃ শিশুদিগের),—যাহাতে অস্থির এক পার্শ্ব ভগ্ন ও অপর পার্শ্ব বক্র হইয়া থাকে, বক্রভঙ্গ (সাঃ পঃ)। **Green stuff**—শাকসব্জী, তৃণগুল্ম। **Greensward**—কাঁচা ঘাসের চাপড়া। **Green table**—সবুজ কাপড়ে ঢাকা মেজ; দ্যূতফলক। **Green-tail**—একপ্রকার গুল্ম। **Green tea**—যে সকল চায়ের পাতা দ্রুত শুষ্ক করত সবুজ রাখা হয়, সবুজ চা। **Green vitriol**—(*Chem.*) Sulphate of iron; হীরাকস। **Green weed**—একপ্রকার গুল্ম—রঞ্জন-কার্য্যে ব্যবহৃত হয়। **Green yard**—An enclosure for stray beasts; a pound; যূথভ্রষ্ট পশুর জন্য বৃতিবেষ্টিত স্থান; খোঁয়াড়। **Green old age**—See under GREEN *adj.* 3. **In the green tree**—In good condition (*In the dry tree*—in bad condition); ভাল অবস্থায়। **The wearing of the green**—The showing of patriotic or rebel sympathies by wearing green (in Ireland); (আয়র্লণ্ডে) সবুজ পরিচ্ছদ পরিধানে দেশ-প্রেম বা রাজদ্রোহীদিগের প্রতি প্রীতি প্রদর্শন [সবুজ আয়র্লণ্ডের জাতীয় বর্ণ]। **To keep the bones green**—To maintain good health—স্বাস্থ্য অক্ষুণ্ণ রাখা। **To look through green glass**—To be jealous of one; চোখ টাটান, ঈর্ষাপরায়ণ হওয়া। **To see green in another's eye**—To see any sign of gullibility in his eye, *i. e.* to consider him to be gullible; কাহারও চোখে ধূলা দেওয়া যাইতে পারে বলিয়া মনে করা।

green (grēn), *v. i.* & *t.* To grow green, esp. with verdure; সবুজ হওয়া, হরিদ্বর্ণ ধারণ করা, শ্যামায়মান হওয়া, শস্যশামল হওয়া। ***Verb t.*** **1.** To dye green; to soil with green; হরিদ্বর্ণে রঞ্জিত করা; সবুজবর্ণ কলঙ্ক দ্বারা বিবর্ণ করা। **2.** (*Slang*) To hoax; 'I have *greened* all the Spaniards"; (ইতর ভাষায়) তামাসা করিয়া ঠকান, ধাপ্পা দেওয়া।

green'-ĕr (grēn-), *n.* (*Slang*) A green hand; esp. a newly arrived foreigner seeking work; (ইতর-ভাষায়) কাঁচা লোক; বিশেষতঃ নবাগত বিদেশী কর্ম্মপ্রার্থী।

green'-ing (grēn-), *n.* A kind of apple green when ripe; একপ্রকার সেও ফল—যাহা পাকিলে সবুজবর্ণ ধারণ করে।

Green'-wich (grĭn-ĭj), *n.* An English town with a state observatory; ইংলণ্ডের নগর-বিশেষ—এই নগরে একটী সরকারী মানমন্দির প্রতিষ্ঠিত আছে। **Greenwich time**—ইংলণ্ড প্রভৃতি দেশের সাধারণ সময়। [গ্রীন-উইচের সময় তারযোগে প্রতিদিন ইংলণ্ড প্রভৃতি দেশের বিভিন্ন স্থানে প্রেরিত হয় এবং তদনুসারে তৎতৎস্থানের ঘড়ী ঠিক হইয়া থাকে।]

greet (grēt), *v. t.* **1.** To salute; to welcome; অভিবাদন বা স্বাগত জিজ্ঞাসা করা, নমস্কার করা, কুশলপ্রশ্ন করা; অভ্যর্থনা করা। **2.** To receive or meeting or arrival with speech or action (friendly or not); as, the candidate was *greeted* with cheers: "To *greet* him with a kiss"; সাক্ষাৎ হইলে বা উপস্থিত হইলে বন্ধু ভাবে বা অন্য ভাবে গ্রহণ করা। **3.** To accost on meeting with expressions of courtesy etc.; সম্বর্দ্ধনা করা, সাদর সম্ভাষণ করা। **4.** To hail (of cheers); to meet; as, a sight or sound *greets* the eye or ear; অভিনন্দন করা; সাক্ষাৎ হওয়া, গোচর হওয়া। **Greet'-ing,** *n.* A salutation at meeting; a compliment from one absent; নমস্কার, অভিবাদন, সম্বর্দ্ধনা, সাদর সম্ভাষণ, কুশল-প্রশ্ন; নমস্কার, অভিনন্দন।

greet (grēt), *v. i.* (*Scot.*) To weep; (স্কটলণ্ডে) ক্রন্দন করা।

grĕf'-fi-ĕr (-ĭ-), *n.* A registrar or recorder; a notary; সরকারী খাতাপত্র রক্ষক, লেখক; সরকারী দলীল নিদর্শক।

grē-gā'-ri-ous (-ŭs), *adj.* **1.** Keeping or living in flocks, herds or communities; দলবদ্ধভাবে বাসকারী, সংঘচারী (মঃ ভাঃ), নৈকচর, সহচারী (চঃ), যূথচারী, বহুচর (সাঃ পঃ), অনেকচর (কেণ্ডিঃ), সঙ্গচর (ঐ)। **2.** Fond of company; সংঘপ্রিয়, দলপ্রিয়। **3.** (*Bot.*) Growing in clusters; (উদ্ভিদ বিদ্যা) গুচ্ছাকারে জাত। **4.** Of, or relating to, a flock, crowd or community; যূথ সম্বন্ধীয়, দল সম্পর্কীয়, সম্প্রদায় সম্পর্কীয়। **—ly,** *adv.* **—ness,** *n.*

Grē-gō'-ri-ăn, *adj.* & *n.* **1.** Of, or relating to, Pope Gregory I.; রোমীয় ধর্ম্মসম্রাট ১ম গ্রেগরী সম্পর্কীয়। **2.** Relating to, or established by, Pope Gregory XIII.; রোমীয় ধর্ম্মসম্রাট ত্রয়োদশ গ্রেগরী সম্পর্কীয় বা তৎপ্রতিষ্ঠিত। ***Noun.*** A Gregorian chant (*see below*). **Gregorian calendar**—বর্ত্তমান সময়ে ইয়ুরোপে প্রচলিত পঞ্জিকা—যাহা পোপ ত্রয়োদশতম গ্রেগরী ১৫৮২ খৃঃ অব্দে সংশোধন

করেন। **Gregorian chant**—পোপ প্রথম গ্রেগরী কর্তৃক প্রবর্তিত খৃষ্টীয় ধর্ম্ম মন্দিরে উপাসনা কালে গেয় সরল সঙ্গীত। **Gregorian style**—New style ; নবপদ্ধতি, নবপ্রণালী। **Gregorian year**—পোপ ত্রয়োদশতম গ্রেগরী কর্তৃক সংশোধিত পঞ্জিকানুসারে গণিত বৎসর, সাধারণ বর্ষ।

Grĕg′-ō-rȳ-pow̄′-dêr, *n.* Compound rhubarb powder ; রেউচিনি প্রভৃতির সংমিশ্র বিরেচক চূর্ণ।

grē′-mi-ăl, *n.* A silk apron placed on a bishop's lap at some ceremonies ; কোন কোন ধর্ম্ম ক্রিয়া উপলক্ষে বিশপের ক্রোড়ে স্থাপিত পট্ট বহির্ব্বাস বিশেষ।

grĕ-nāde′, *n.* **1.** A small explosive ball or shell fired by means of a fuse and thrown by hand ; হস্তদ্বারা ক্ষেপণীয় বিস্ফোরকদ্রব্যপূর্ণ ক্ষুদ্র গোলক, বোমা। **2.** A glass receptacle thrown to disperse its chemical contents for testing drains, fires, etc. ; রাসায়নিক দ্রব্য পূর্ণ কাচাধার—যাহা নিক্ষিপ্ত হইলে ফাটিয়া যাইয়া তদভ্যন্তরস্থ দ্রব্যের সাহায্যে অগ্নি-নির্ব্বাপণ, নর্দ্দামার ছিদ্রাদি আছে কিনা তাহা পরীক্ষা ও অন্যান্য কার্য্য সাধিত করিয়া থাকে। **Drain grenade, Fire grenade**—See GRENADE 2. **Hand grenade**—হস্তদ্বারা শত্রুর পরিখা প্রভৃতিতে যে বিস্ফোরক দ্রব্যপূর্ণ গোলক নিক্ষিপ্ত হয়, হাতবোমা।

grĕn-ă-dier′ (-dēr), *n.* **1.** A soldier who throws hand grenades ; (*pl.* also called *Grenadier Guards*) the first regiment of household infantry ; বিস্ফোরকদ্রব্যপূর্ণ গোলক নিক্ষেপকারী সৈনিক ; (বহুবচন) গার্হস্থ্য পদাতিক সৈন্যের ১ গণিত পল্টন। **2.** A kind of South African weaver-bird ; দক্ষিণ আফ্রিকার একজাতীয় বাবুই পক্ষী।

grĕn′-ă-dīne, *n.* A thin silk or woollen fabric for ladies' dresses etc. ; মহিলাগণের পোষাকের জন্য এক প্রকার পাতলা রেশমী বা পশমী কাপড়।

grĕn′-ă-dīne, *n.* A dish of veal or poultry fillets trimmed, larded and glazed ; মুর্গী বা বাছুরের মাংসের ব্যঞ্জন বিশেষ।

grĕs-sō′-ri-ăl, *adj.* (*Zool.*) Adapted for walking, as the feet of bird etc. ; (প্রাণি-বিদ্যা) পাদচারণোপযোগী।

Gretna Green marriage — A runaway marriage (in allusion to those performed at Gretna Green, a village in Dumfriesshire, Scotland) ; পলায়িত প্রেমিক-প্রেমিকার বিবাহ [ইংলণ্ডের আইন হইতে নিষ্কৃতি লাভের জন্য স্কটলণ্ড দেশের অন্তঃপাতী Gretna Green নামক গ্রামে পলাইয়া গিয়া পূর্ব্বে ইংলণ্ডের বহু প্রেমিক প্রেমিকা এইরূপ বিবাহ বন্ধনে বদ্ধ হইতেন।]

grew (grû), *p. t.* of GROW.

grew′-some (grû-sŭm), *adj.* Same as GRUESOME (which see.)

grey (grā), *adj.* Same as GRAY.

grey′-hound (grā-how̄nd), *n.* A tall, slender and fleet dog kept for the chase; এক প্রকার শিকারী কুকুর। **Ocean greyhound**—দ্রুতগামী জাহাজ।

Greyhound,

grey′-lăg (goose) (grā-), *n.* ইয়ুরোপ দেশীয় বন্য হংস বিশেষ।

grid, *n.* **1.** A grating of thin parallel bar ; ঝাঁঝরি। **2.** A gridrion as for cooking ; কাবাব পাকের জন্য লোহার ঝাঁঝরি।

grid′-dle (-l), *n.* & *v. t.* **1.** A flat iron plate for baking cakes on ; পিঠা ভাজিবার লোহার চাটু বা তাওয়া। **2.** A sieve with a wire bottom used by miners ; খনির মজুরগণ কর্ত্তৃক ব্যবহৃত তারের তলাওয়ালা একপ্রকার চালনি। ***Verb t.*** (*Mining*) To screen with griddle ; (খনির কাজ) তারের চালনি দ্বারা চালা।

grid′-ī-ron (-êrn), *n.* **1.** A grated iron utensil for broiling flesh and fish over the fire ; কাবাব পাকের জন্য লোহার ঝাঁঝরি। **2.** (*Naut.*) A frame upon which a ship rests for inspection or repair ; পরিদর্শন বা জীর্ণসংস্কারের জন্য যে কাঠামের উপর জাহাজ রাখা হয়। **3.** (*Theatre*) A plank structure over a stage supporting mechanism for drop-scenes etc. ; (রঙ্গমঞ্চ) যবনিকা প্রভৃতির উত্থান-পতন-নিয়ামক যন্ত্রের অবলম্বনস্বরূপ কাষ্ঠফলক রচিত মঞ্চ। **4.** Compensation pendulum with parallel rods of different metals (also *gridiron pendulum*) ; বিভিন্ন ধাতু রচিত সমান্তরালশলাকা সমন্বিত শুদ্ধ দোলন-দণ্ড। **5.** A naval evolution ; পোত সমূহের বিন্যাসের পরিবর্ত্তন। **Gridiron pendulum**—See GRIDIRON 4.

grief (grēf), *n.* Deep sorrow ; heavy affliction ; keen regret ; গভীর সন্তাপ, শোক, গভীর দুঃখ ; বিষাদ, চিত্তখেদ, মনস্তাপ, মনোবেদনা, মনোদুঃখ, মনঃপীড়া ; তীব্র অনুশোচনা। **To come to grief** — To come to ruin or disaster ; to fail ; (*sporting*) to fall ; দুঃখে পড়া, দুর্ঘটনা হওয়া ; অকৃতকার্য্য হওয়া ; (ক্রীড়া) পড়া, পতিত হওয়া।

griev′-ance (grēv-ăns), *n.* A cause of complaint whether real or fancied ; অভিযোগের বিষয়, অভিযোগের কারণ।

grieve (grēv), *v. t.* & *i.* **1.** To cause grief to, to give mental pain to ; to afflict ; শোকার্ত্ত করা ; মনোবেদনা দেওয়া, মনঃপীড়া দেওয়া, সন্তপ্ত করা ; ক্লেশ দেওয়া, ক্লিষ্ট করা। **2.** (*Poet.*) To regret deeply ; (কবিতায়) গভীর অনুশোচনা করা। ***Verb i.*** To feel grief, (often with *for*, *over*) ; শোকানুভব করা, সন্তপ্ত হওয়া, শোক করা।

griev′-ous (grēv-ŭs), *adj.* **1.** Causing great trouble ; harmful ; as, a *grievous* folly ; দুঃখজনক, দুঃখপ্রদ, দুঃখকারক, দুঃসহ, ক্লেশদ, ক্লেশকারক ; অনিষ্টকর, অহিতকর। **2.** Severe ; intense ; as, *grievous* pain ; গুরুতর, দুর্ব্বহ ; তীব্র, ভীষণ। **3.** Atrocious ; heinous ; as, *grievous* sin ; ঘোর, নিদারুণ ; বিকট, ভয়ানক। **4.** Causing or exciting grief ; "It was *grievous* to see etc." ; বিষাদজনক, শোকাবহ। **--ly,** *adv.* **—ness,** *n.*

grif'-fin, grif'-fŏn, grȳph'-ŏn, *ns.* **1.** A fabulous monster with a lion's body and an eagle's head and wings ; প্রাচীন রূপকথায় বর্ণিত দৈত্যবিশেষ—ইহার পক্ষ ও মস্তক ঈগল পক্ষী সদৃশ এবং দেহ সিংহাকৃতি ছিল, শ্যেন-সিংহ। **2.** (Only **—fon**) A species of vulture ; এক জাতীয় গৃধ্র।

grif'-fin, griff, *ns.* (*Anglo-Indian*) A newcomer from Europe ; a novice ; a greenhorn ; (ভারতবর্ষে) নবাগত ইয়ুরোপবাসী ; নূতন লোক ; কাঁচা লোক।

grif'-fŏn, *n.* A terrier-like dog ; একপ্রকার ক্ষুদ্র কুকুর।

grig, *n.* **1.** A cricket ; a grasshopper ; ঝিঁঝিঁ পোকা ; গঙ্গা ফড়িঙ্। **2.** A small eel ; এক প্রকার ক্ষুদ্র বাইন মাছ। **Merry** or **lively as a grig**—Exceedingly merry or lively ; বেজায় খুসী।

grill, *v. t., i. & n.* **1.** To boil or roast on a gridiron ; লোহার ঝাঁঝরিতে ভাজা। **2.** To scallop as a shrimp or oyster ; চিংড়িমাছ বা ঝিনুক চাটুতে ভাজা। **3.** To torment with heat ; উত্তাপদ্বারা যন্ত্রণা দেওয়া। ***Verb i.*** **1.** To be cooked on a gridiron ; ঝাঁঝরীতে রন্ধিত হওয়া। **2.** (*Fig.*) To suffer as if from broiling ; (লক্ষণায়) দুঃসহ যন্ত্রণা ভোগ করা। ***Noun.*** **1.** Grilled food ; ভাজা খাদ্য। **2.** A room where chops, steaks, etc. are grilled and served (also *grill room*) ; যে কোঠায় চপ প্রভৃতি ভাজা করা হয়। **Grill'-er,** *n.* One who grills ; a grilling apparatus ; যে ব্যক্তি ভাজা করে ; ভাজা করার জন্য চাটু, ভাজন-খোলা।

grill, *n.* A gridiron ; কাবাব রাঁধিবার জন্য ঝাঁঝরী।

grīl'-lage (-āj), *n.* A frame work of cross-beams etc. as a foundation for building on marshy grounds ; জলাভূমিতে অট্টালিকাদির ভিত্তিস্বরূপ কাষ্ঠফলক রচিত মঞ্চ।

grille (gril), **grill,** *ns.* **1.** A grating ; a latticed screen, esp. in a door for observing callers, in a convent separating nuns from visitors, in front of ladies' gallery in the House of Commons etc. ; ঝাঁঝরি ; জাফরি, জালিদার পর্দ্দা। **2.** (*Tennis*) A square opening in the wall ; (আণ্টাল খেলায়) প্রাচীরে সমচতুষ্কোণ রন্ধ্র। **3.** (*Fish culture*) A frame for spawn-hatching purposes ; (মৎস্যের চাষ) ডিমে তা দেওয়ার জন্য কাঠাম বিশেষ। **Grilled,** *adj.*

Grille of door.

grilse (grils), *n.* A young salmon on its first return from the sea ; সমুদ্র হইতে প্রথম প্রত্যাগত নবজাত স্যামন মৎস্য।

grim, *adj.* **1.** Fierce ; as, *grim* wolves ; stern ; merciless ; unrelenting ; as, *grim* murder ; ভীষণ, ভয়ঙ্কর ; কঠোর ; নিষ্করুণ, নির্দ্দয় ; নির্ম্মম। **2.** Of stern or forbidding aspect ; ugly ; hedious ; as, *grim* figure : *grim* death ; ঘোরদর্শন ; কুৎসিৎ, কদাকার ; বিকটাকার। **3.** Sinister ; ghastly ; unmirthful ; as, a *grim* smile : a *grim* truth ; অশুভ ; পৈশাচিক, বিকট, করাল, ঘোর ; অপ্রফুল্ল। **Grim'-ly,** *adv.* In a grim manner ; fiercely ; ঘোররূপে ; ভীষণভাবে। **Grim'-ness,** *n.* State of being grim ; sternness ; fierceness ; কঠোরতা ; কঠোরভাব ; ভীষণতা।

gri-māce', *n. & v. t.* **1.** A distortion of the countenance ; a wry face ; মুখভঙ্গী, মুখবিকৃতি ; বিকৃতাস্য। **2.** Affectation ; pretence ; "To consider all piety as *grimaces*" ; কপটাচরণ ; ছলনা। ***Verb t.*** To make grimaces ; to distort one's face ; মুখ খিঁচান, ভেঙ্গান, ভেঙ্গচান ; মুখভঙ্গী করা, মুখ বাঁকান। **—mac'-er, —ma'-ci-er,** *ns.* One who grimaces ; যে মুখভঙ্গী করে।

gri-măl'-kin, *n. & v. t.* **1.** An old she cat ; বৃদ্ধবিড়ালী। **2.** A spiteful old woman ; দ্বেষপরায়ণা বৃদ্ধা, বিদ্বেষকারিণী স্ত্রীলোক।

grīme, *n. & v.t.* Foul matter ; soot ; dirt ingrained in the skin etc. ; ময়লা ; ঝুল ; শরীরের ময়লা। ***Verb t.*** To blacken ; to soil deeply ; কজ্জলিত করা ; মলিন করা। **Grim'-i-ly,** *adv.* **Grim'-i-ness,** *n.* **Grim'-y,** *adj.* Foul ; dirty ; দূষিত ; মলিন, মলদূষিত।

Grimm's law—See LAW.

Grim'-nir (-nêr), *n.* নোর্স পুরাণোক্ত দেবরাজ Odin এর উপনাম।

grin, *v. i., t. & n.* To show the teeth as in laughter, scorn or anguish, (often with *at*) ; দন্তরাজি বিকাশ পূর্ব্বক হাস্য করা, দন্ত প্রদর্শন পূর্ব্বক বিদ্রূপ করা, যন্ত্রণায় দাঁত চাপিয়া ঠোঁট খোলা। ***Verb t.*** To express by grinning ; as, to *grin* contempt or satisfaction ; দন্তবিকাশ পূর্ব্বক প্রকাশ করা। ***Noun.*** Showing the teeth ; a forced smile ; দন্ত-প্রদর্শন ; কাষ্ঠহাসি। **To grin and bear it**—To suffer pain with fortitude ; সহিষ্ণুতার সহিত যন্ত্রণা সহ্য করা। **To grin like a Cheshire cat**—See CAT.

grīnd, *v. t., i. & n.* **1.** To reduce to powder as between a millstone, teeth, etc. ; to crush into small fragments ; চূর্ণ করা ; ভাঙ্গিয়া গুঁড়া করা। **2.** To smooth, polish or sharpen by friction ; to whet, as a knife ; to rub against one another, as teeth ; to rub gratingly *on, into,* or *against* ; ঘষিয়া পালিশ করা, ধারাল করা ; শাণ দেওয়া ; পরস্পরের সহিত ঘর্ষণ করা, কড়মড় করা ; ঘস্‌ঘস্ করিয়া ঘষা । **3.** To oppress by severe exaction ; to harass ; as, to *grind* the faces of the poor ; উৎপীড়ন পূর্ব্বক টাকা পয়সা আদায় করা ; নিষ্পেষণ করা । **4.** To produce (flour) by grinding ; যাঁতা দ্বারা পিষিয়া ময়দা প্রস্তুত করা, গম পিষা । **5.** To work (a hand-mill) so as to grind meal etc. ; যাঁতা ঘুরান । **6.** To produce (music) on a hurdy-gurdy or barrel-organ ; "Do, my good girls, *grind* me a pennyworth more of your music" ; বাদ্যযন্ত্র বিশেষ বাজান । **7.** To instruct *in* ; to teach ; as, to *grind* one *in* a subject : to *grind* Latin ; উপদেশ দেওয়া ; শিক্ষা দেওয়া । ***Verb i.*** **1.** To turn a mill or millstones ; জাঁতা ঘুরান । **2.** To be ground or pulverized by friction ; as, the corn *grinds* well ; চূর্ণ হওয়া, পিষ্ট হওয়া । **3.** To be polished or sharpened by friction ; ঘর্ষণ হেতু পালিস হওয়া, শাণিত হওয়া । **4.** To rub gratingly *on* or *against* something ; অন্য কোন কিছুর উপর ঘস্‌ঘস্ শব্দে ঘৃষ্ট হওয়া । **5.** To drudge ; to study hard ; কঠোরশ্রমজনক হীন কার্য্য করা ; কঠোর অধ্যয়ন করা । ***Noun.*** **1.** The act of reducing to powder, or of sharpening, by friction ; পেষণ, বিচূর্ণন, শাণ দেওন । **2.** A hard monotonous work or task ; কঠোর-শ্রমজনক একঘেয়ে কাজ, একঘেয়ে হাড়ভাঙ্গা খাটুনি । **3.** A walk for exercise ; অঙ্গচালনার জন্য ভ্রমণ । **Grindstone**—যাঁতা, পেষণযন্ত্র, চাকী, শিলাপেষ (মার্কণ্ডঃ), পেষণী, পেষণ-প্রস্তর, শিলাপট্ট (for sharpening), শাণ পাথর, শাণযন্ত্র, শিল, যন্ত্রোপল, শাণোপল, শাণাশ্ম, ভ্রম (মঃ উঃ) । **Hard grinder**—কঠোর পরিশ্রমী ছাত্র, উকীল, ডাক্তার, প্রভৃতি । **To grind one down**—To reduce the price asked ; দর কষাকষি করিয়া দাম কমান । **To grind one's teeth**—To have feelings of rage, disappointment or disgust ; দাঁত কিড়মিড় করা, দন্তে দন্তে ঘর্ষণ করা । **To grind out an oath**—To utter an oath while grinding the teeth ; দন্তে দন্তে ঘর্ষণ করিয়া শপথ বাক্য উচ্চারণ করা । **To grind the face**—To oppress ; নিষ্পেষণ করা, নির্যাতন করা, দলন করা । **To hold or keep one's nose to the grindstone**—To make one work incessantly ; to oppress one ; রাত্রি দিন খাটান, অনবরত খাটান ; নিষ্পেষণ করা । **To take a grind**—To take a walk ; বেড়ান ।

grip, *n.* A small open ditch ; a drain ; ক্ষুদ্র খোলা নালা ; নর্দ্দমা ।

grip, *n.* **1.** A fast hold ; firm grasp ; tight clasp ; দৃঢ়গ্রাহ ; দৃঢ়মুষ্টি ; নিবিড় আলিঙ্গন । **2.** A mode of grasping hands peculiar to a secret society ; as, the masonic *grip* ; আত্মপরিচয় প্রদানের জন্য গুপ্তসমিতির সভ্যগণ কর্তৃক বিশেষভাবে হস্ত ধারণ । **3.** A hilt or handle ; as, the *grip* of a sword ; খড়্গাদির মুষ্টি, হাতল, বাঁট, মুঠ, ৎসরু । **4.** A device for grasping or holding fast to something ; আঁকড়া । **5.** Control ; mastery ; "The *grip* of poverty"; intellectual hold ; "Have a *grip* of the facts of the case" ; মুঠা, করতল (as, *within one's grip*= মুঠার ভিতর, করতলগত) ; প্রভুত্ব ; ভাল ধারণা, মানসগ্রাহ । **6.** Power of arresting attention ; "If (a play) lack........*grip*" ; মনোযোগ আকর্ষণের ক্ষমতা, চিত্তাকর্ষিণী শক্তি । **Grip-brake** — হস্তচালিত চক্রগতি-রোধক । **At grips with**—In close combat with ; হাতাহাতি । **In grips**—In custody ; জিম্মায়, হাতে । **To come to grips**—To come to close quarters ; হাতের কাছে যাওয়া ।

grip, *v. t.* & *i.* **1.** To grasp firmly ; to seize or hold tightly ; দৃঢ় মুষ্টিতে ধারণ করা ; আঁকড়াইয়া ধরা । **2.** To compel the attention of ; মনোযোগ আকর্ষণ করা । ***Verb i.*** To take firm hold ; as, the anchor *grips* ; আঁকড়াইয়া ধরা । **Grip'-per,** *n.* **Grip-sack**—(U. S.) A hand bag ; (মার্কিণ যুক্তরাজ্যে) হাতব্যাগ ।

gripe, *v. t., i.* & *n.* **1.** To grasp ; to clutch ; দৃঢ় মুষ্টিতে ধরা ; মুঠা করিয়া ধরা । **2.** To oppress ; to pinch ; to distress ; "How inly sorrow *gripes* his soul" ; নির্যাতন করা ; পীড়ন করা ; ক্লিষ্ট করা । **3.** To give pain in the bowels to ; পেট কামড়ানি জন্মান । **4.** (*Naut.*) To secure gith gripes ; (নৌ-বিদ্যা) আঁকড়া দ্বারা আটকাইয়া রাখা । ***Verb i.*** **1.** To take fast hold ; to clutch ; দৃঢ়মুষ্টিতে ধারণ করা ; মুঠা করিয়া ধরা । **2.** (*Naut.*) To lie too closely to the wind, as a ship ; (নৌ-বিদ্যা) যে দিক হইতে বায়ু প্রবাহিত হইতেছে যতদূর সম্ভব সেই দিকের অভিমুখে থাকা । **3.** To cause gripes ; to suffer griping pains ; অন্ত্রশূল উৎপাদন করা ; পেট কামড়ান, পেট কন্ কন্ করা । ***Noun.*** **1.** Act of grasping ; seizure ; clutch ; দৃঢ়মুষ্টিতে ধরণ, দৃঢ়-গ্রাহ ; ধরণ ; মুষ্টিগ্রাহ । **2.** A handle ; হাতল, বাঁট । **3.** Hold ; as, to be in the *gripe* of ; মুঠা । **4.** (*Pl.*) The pinching pain in the bowels ; অন্ত্রশূল, পেটকামড়ানি, উদরশূল, পেট খোঁচানি । **5.** (*Naut., Pl.*) Lashings securing a boat in its place ; (নৌ-বিদ্যা) যে দড়ী সকল দ্বারা জাহাজ এক জায়গায় বাঁধিয়া রাখা হয় ।

grip'-ing, *p. p.* **1.** Grasping ; গ্রাহী । **2.** Avaricious ; greedy ; গৃধ্নু ; লোলুপ । **3.** Painful ; distressing ; যন্ত্রণাদায়ক ; ক্লেশজনক ।

4. Pinching the bowels; অম্ল-শূলজনক। **—ly,** *adv.*

grippe, (*F.*) *n.* Influenza (which see).

gri-saille' (grë-säl), *n.* A style of decorative painting in gray monochrome representing objects in relief; a stained glass window executed according to this method; এক প্রণালীর শোভাসাধক চিত্রণ—যাহাতে বস্তু সকলের উচ্চাবচতা প্রদর্শিত হয়; উক্ত প্রণালীতে চিত্রিত কাচের জানালা।

Gri-sĕl-'dă, *n.* A woman who was the model of enduring patience and conjugal obedience; প্রাচীন উপন্যাসে বর্ণিতা জনৈকা নারী—যিনি সহিষ্ণুতা ও পাতিব্রত্যধর্ম্মের আদর্শস্থানীয়া ছিলেন। ইনি Janicola নামক জনৈক কয়লাওয়ালার কন্যা ছিলেন। Marquis of Saluzzoর সহিত তাঁহার বিবাহ হয়। স্বামী কর্ত্তৃক তিনবার ভীষণ পরীক্ষানলে নিক্ষিপ্ত হইয়াও Griseldaর সহিষ্ণুতা ও পাতিব্রত্যধর্ম্ম বিশুদ্ধ স্বর্ণসম অধিকতর সমুজ্জ্বল হইয়া উঠিয়াছিল। তিনটী পরীক্ষা এই:—(১) গ্রীসেল্‌ডার শিশু কন্যাকে Paviaর রাণীর বাটীতে প্রেরণ করিয়া তাঁহার স্বামী তাঁহাকে জানাইলেন যে কন্যাটীকে হত্যা করা হইয়াছে। (২) চারি বৎসর পর গ্রীসেল্‌ডা একটী পুত্র সন্তান প্রসব করিলে সেই পুত্রকে মাতৃবক্ষ হইতে ছিনাইয়া লইয়া স্বামী তাঁহার ভগ্নীর নিকট প্রেরণ করিলেন। এ দিকে কন্যাটী দ্বাদশবর্ষে পদার্পণ করিলে মার্কুইস্ গ্রীসেল্‌ডাকে বলিলেন, "আমি তোমাকে পরিত্যাগ করিয়া অপর একটী বিবাহ করিব স্থির করিয়াছি।" এই বলিয়া স্বামী গ্রীসেল্‌ডার অঙ্গ হইতে সমস্ত আভরণ উন্মোচন করিয়া এবং তাঁহার সুন্দর সুন্দর পরিচ্ছদ রাখিয়া দিয়া তাঁহাকে পিতৃগৃহে প্রেরণ করিলেন। বিবাহের দিবস গ্রীসেল্‌ডাকে পুনরায় বাটীতে আনিয়া স্বামী তাঁহাকে নববধূর সম্বর্দ্ধনার জন্য প্রস্তুত হইতে বলিলেন। ইহাতেও গ্রীসেল্‌ডার মুখে ঈষন্মাত্রও ঈর্ষ্যার মলিন ছায়া পড়ে নাই দেখিয়া স্বামী তাহাকে বজ্রকণ্ঠে বলিলেন "তুমি জান আমি কাহাকে বিবাহ করিতেছি? তোমার কন্যাই এই গৃহে তোমার সপত্নীরূপে আসিতেছে।" এই কথায়ও গ্রীসেল্‌ডার ধৈর্য্যচ্যুতি হইল না। See *Boccacio's Decameron*—last tale.]

gris'-ē-ous(-ŭs), *adj.* (*Bot.* & *Zool.*) Bluish or pearly grey; (উদ্ভিদ্-বিদ্যা ও জন্তু-বিদ্যা) নীলাভ, আনীল, মুক্তাধূসর।

grisette, (*F.*), *n.* A young woman of the working class in France given to gaiety and gallantry; ফরাসী দেশের শ্রমজীবি-শ্রেণীর রসবতী যুবতী বা বালিকা।

gris'-kin, *n.* A pork loin, esp. the lean part; শূকরের পৃষ্ঠদেশের নিম্নভাগ সমেত কটিদেশ।

gris̈'-lȳ, *adj.* Dreadful; fearful; ghastly; causing superstitious horror; ভীষণ, ভয়ানক; ভয়ঙ্কর; ভীমদর্শন, উগ্রদর্শন, ঘোরদর্শন, করাল; ত্রাসজনক।

grist, *n.* **1.** Corn for grinding; ground corn; পেষণার্থ শস্য; শস্যচূর্ণ, শক্তু, সাতু, পিষ্ট (আঃ বঃ)। **2.** Malt ground for brewing; চোয়াইয়া মদ প্রস্তুত করার জন্য কলা বেরুনো যবের চূর্ণ। **3.** Profit; লাভ। **All is grist that comes to his mill**—He utilizes everything; সে সব জিনিষই কাজে লাগায়।

grist, *n.* Size or thickness of yarn or rope; সূতা বা দড়ীর আকার বা বেধ।

gris'-tle (-l) *n.* Cartilage; a cartilaginous part; তরুণাস্থি, কোমলাস্থি, মৃদ্বস্থি; তরুণাস্থিময় অংশ। **In the gristle**—Immature (referring to the nature of bones in infancy); কাঁচা, অপরিণত, অপরিপক্ব, তরুণ। **—tly,** *adv.*

grit, *n.* **1.** Small particles of stone or sand, esp. as causing discomfort or clogging machinery etc.; শর্কর, শিলাকণা, বালুকাকণা। **2.** *(Formerly)* Sand or gravel; (পূর্ব্বে) বালি, কাঁকর। **3.** (*Geol.*) A hard coarse-grained sand-stone (also *gritstone*); (ভূ-বিদ্যা) মোটা দানাদার বেলে পাথর। **4.** Texture of stone; পাথরের বুনট। **5.** (*Colloq.*) Strength of mind or character; pluck; endurance; (চলিতভাষায়) মনের বল, চরিত্রবল; বুকের পাটা; সাহস, সহিষ্ণুতা। **Grit'-ti-ness,** *n.* **Grit'-ty,** *adj.*

grit, *v. i.* & *t.* To give forth a grating sound; to move gratingly; কড় মড় করা, কড় কড় করা; কড় মড় শব্দে চলা। ***Verb t.*** **1.** To cover with grit; শিলাকণা দ্বারা আবৃত করা। **2.** To grind; to grate; as, to *grit* teeth; কড় মড় করা; কড় কড় করা।

grit, *n.* (*Pl.*) Husked but unground or coarsely ground oats; খোসা ছাড়ানো যই, যইয়ের ছাতু।

griz'-zled (-ld), *adj.* Gray; having gray-hair; as, *grizzled* hair or man; ধূসর; পলিতকেশ।

griz'-zly (-lĭ), *adj.* & *n.* Somewhat grey; grey-haired; ঈষৎ ধূম্র; পলিতকেশ। ***Noun.*** A Grizzly bear; উত্তর আমেরিকা দেশীয় বৃহৎকায় হিংস্র ভল্লুক। **Grizzly king** or **qneen**—বড়শীর টোপস্বরূপ ব্যবহৃত মক্ষিকা বিশেষ।

groan (grōn), *v. i., t.* & *n.* **1.** To utter a deep moaning sound expressing pain or sorrow or disapprobation; কোঁকান, গোঁগান, গোঁগড়ান। **2.** (*Fig.*) To be afflicted; to be oppressed or loaded (*under, beneath, with*); as, a nation *groans under* the weight of taxes: the shelf *groans with* books; (লক্ষণায়) আর্ত্ত হওয়া, বেদনা পাওয়া; প্রপীড়িত হওয়া। ***Verb t.*** **1.** To utter or give forth with groans, (often with *out*); কোঁকাইয়া, বলা, গোঁগাইয়া বলা। **2.** To show disapprobation by groans; as, the speaker was *groaned* down (silenced); গোঁ গোঁ শব্দে বিরাগ প্রকাশ করা। **3.** To long (*for*); কামনা

করা, আকাঙ্ক্ষা করা। ***Noun.*** A deep moaning sound uttered in pain, disapprobation, etc; কোঁকানি, গোঁগানি, আর্ত্তনাদ। **Groan'-ing,** *adj.* **Groan'-ing-ly,** *adv.* **A groaning board**—ভারাক্রান্ত মেজ। **To groan down** — To silence (a speaker) by groans; গোঁ গোঁ শব্দ করিয়া বক্তাকে চুপ করিয়া দেওয়া। **To groan inwardly**—To be distressed; সন্তপ্ত হওয়া, মনস্তাপ ভোগ করা।

groat (grōt), *n.* 1. (*Hist.*) An English silver-coin worth 4 pence; ৪ পেন্স মূল্যের ইংলণ্ডীয় প্রাচীন রজত মুদ্রা বিশেষ। 2. A very small sum; as, I don't care a *groat*; কাণাকড়ি।

groats (grōts), *n.* (*Pl.*) Grain, esp. oats hulled and sometimes also crushed; খোসা ছাড়ানো যই, আধা ভাঙ্গা যই, শক্তু।

Grō'-bi-ăn, *n.* A rude clownish person; পাড়া গেঁয়ে লোক।

grō'-cĕr, *n.* A dealer in tea, sugar, spices etc.; চা, চিনি ইত্যাদির ব্যবসায়ী, পশারী। **Grocer's itch**—Eczema caused by handling sugar; সর্ব্বদা চিনিতে হাত দেওয়ার দরুণ মুদিদের যে চর্ম্মরোগ জন্মে।

grō'-cĕr-ȳ, *n.* 1. A grocer's shop; পশারীর দোকান, মুদীর দোকান। 2. (*Pl.*) Commodities sold by grocers; পশারীর জিনিষ, চা, মসল্লা প্রভৃতি মুদির দোকানের জিনিষ।

grŏg, *n., v. i.* & *t.* 1. A mixture of spirit and water without sugar; a spirituous liquor; জলমিশ্রিত সুরা; মদিরা। 2. A social meeting with grog; যে প্রীতি-সম্মিলনীতে জলমিশ্রিত সুরা পান করা হয়। ***Verb i.*** To drink grog; জলমিশ্রিত সুরা পান করা। ***Verb t.*** To soak (an empty liquor cask) with hot water so as to draw out the spirits from the wood; কাঠ হইতে সুরাসার বাহির করার জন্য (খালি মদের পিপা) গরম জলদ্বারা সিক্ত করা।

grŏg'-gy (-ĭ), *adj.* 1. Overcome with grog; tipsy; মদ্যপানে অভিভূত; আধ মাতাল। 2. Bibulous; পানাসক্ত। 3. (Of a horse) Moving in a hobbling manner as with weak forelegs; tottering; (অশ্বপক্ষে) সম্মুখের পদদ্বয় দুর্ব্বল হেতু স্খলিত পদে গমনশীল; টলটলায়মান। 4. Unsteady; shaky; "I am *groggy* on my pins"; অস্থির; টলমল। **—gi-ness,** *n.* **Grog-blossom**—অমিত সুরাপান জনিত মুখের আরক্তিম ভাব বা বদনমণ্ডলে জাত লোহিত বর্ণ ব্রণ সমূহ।

grŏg'-răm, *n.* A kind of coarse cloth and silk and mohair often stiffened with gum; মেষ ও ছাগলোমদ্বারা বা মেষ ও ছাগলোমের মিশ্রণে প্রস্তুত এবং গঁদদ্বারা কঠিনীকৃত বস্ত্র-বিশেষ।

groin (groyn), *n.* & *v. t.* 1. The depressed part between the belly and the thigh; কুঁচকি, উরুসন্ধি, কটিসন্ধি, বংক্ষণ। 2. (*Arch.*) The angular curve formed by the crossing of two arches; খিলানদ্বয়ের পরস্পরের ছেদনে উৎপন্ন কোণাকৃতি বক্র। ***Verb t.*** To form into groins; to build with groins; খিলানদ্বয়ের পরস্পরের ছেদন দ্বারা কোণাকৃতি বক্র উৎপন্ন করা; ঐরূপ কোণাকৃতি বক্র উৎপন্ন করিয়া গঠন করা। **Groin'-ing,** *n.*

Groined roof.

grŏm'-wĕll, *n.* A kind of plant; একপ্রকার গুল্ম।

groōm, *n.* & *v. t.* 1. A servant who has the charges of horses or the stable; অশ্বরক্ষক, সহিস, অশ্বপ, অশ্বপাল, তুরগ পরিচারক। 2. One of a certain officers in the Royal Household of Britain; as, a *groom* in waiting; ইংলণ্ডের রাজপ্রাসাদের কর্ম্মচারিবিশেষ। 3. (*Rare*) A bridegroom; (কচিদ্ ব্যবহৃত) বর। ***Verb t.*** To feed, tend or curry, as a horse; সহিসের কাজ করা, অশ্বের পরিচর্য্যা করা। **Groomsman**—মিতবর। **Groom in waiting, Groom of the chamber, Groom of the stole**—See GROOM *n.* 2. **Well-groomed** — Neatly got up, esp. with well-trimmed hair, beard, etc.; as, a *well groomed* man; ফিটফাট।

groove (groōv), *n.* & *v. t.* 1. A furrow, channel or long hollow; সীতা, নালী, খাঁজ, রেখা। 2. (*Fig.*) A routine of action or life; a rut; (লক্ষণায়) নির্দ্দিষ্ট এবং নিয়মিত কার্য্য প্রণালী বা আচার ব্যবহার, জীবনের গতানুগতিক ধারা; চক্রাঙ্ক, চাকার দাগ। ***Verb t.*** To cut a groove or grooves in; to furrow; খাঁজ কাটা; রেখা কাটা। **Groov'-i-ness,** *n.* **Groov'-y,** *adj.*

grōpe, *v. i.* & *t.* To seek for something by feeling about in the dark; to search blindly (*lit.* & *fig.*, — sometimes with *for*, *after*); আঁধারে হাতড়ান; হাতড়াইয়া বেড়ান। ***Verb t.*** To search out by feeling about; হাতড়াইয়া খুঁজিয়া বাহির করা। **Grop'-ing-ly,** *adv.* In a groping manner; হাতড়াইয়া। **To grope one's way**—To find it by feeling; to proceed tentatively; অন্ধকারে হাতড়াইয়া পথ ঠিক করা; পরীক্ষাস্থলে অগ্রসর হওয়া।

grōs'-beak (bēk), *n.* A finch with a thick and stout bill; একপ্রকার পক্ষী।

gros de Naples (*F.*), *n.* A heavy silk fabric; একপ্রকার ক্ষৌমবস্ত্র।

grōss, *adj.* 1. Bulky; fat; corpulent; as, a *gross* body or man; বৃহৎ, প্রকাণ্ড; মোটা; স্থূলকায়। 2. Thick; dense; not ethereal or transparent ; palpable ; as, *gross* matter ; পুরু ; ঘন ; অসূক্ষ্ম, অস্বচ্ছ ; স্পর্শযোগ্য। **3.** Luxuriant ; rank ; as, *gross* vegetation ; প্রচুর ; অতিবর্দ্ধনশীল। **4.** Coarse ; rough ; uncleanly ; repulsive ; "Their diet is extremely *gross*" ; মোটা ; খস্‌খসে ; অপরিষ্কার ; জঘন্য। **5.** Obscene ; vulgar ; unrefined ; indecent ; impure ; অশ্লীল ; অশিষ্ট, অসভ্য, শিষ্টাচারবিরুদ্ধ ; অমার্জ্জিত, শ্লীলতাবর্জ্জিত ; অবিশুদ্ধ। **6.** Dull ; "Things that *gross* ear can hear" ; জড়, নিস্তেজ। **7.** Serious ; flagrant ; shameful ; as, a *gross* mistake or negligence ; গুরুতর ; উৎকট, ঘোর, জ্বলন্ত, পুরা ; লজ্জাজনক। **8.** Whole ; total ; not net ; as, a *gross* amount : *gross* income ; সমগ্র ; মোট ; নিট নয়। **Gross′-ly,** *adv.* In a gross manner ; coarsely ; greatly ; shamefully ; disgracefully ; অশিষ্টভাবে ; স্থূলভাবে ; অতিশয় ; লজ্জাজনকরূপে ; কলঙ্কজনকরূপে। **Gross′-ness,** *n.* **Gross-body, –frame**—স্থূলশরীর। **Gross-matter**—স্থূলভূত (ব্রজঃ হিন্দু)। **Gross receipts** — মোট আয়—যাহা হইতে খরচা বাদ দেওয়া হয় নাই। **A gross feeder** — কদন্নভোজী। **By the gross**—At wholesale ; পাইকারী হিসাবে। **In (the) gross**—In the general way ; on the whole ; সাধারণভাবে ; সর্ব্বসাকল্যে, মোটের উপর। Wholesale ; পাইকারী।

grŏss, *n.* (*Pl.* GROSS) The number of twelve dozens ; বার ডজন, একগ্রোস।

grŏt, *n.* (*Poet.*) Same as GROTTO which see.

grō-tesque′ (-tĕsk), *n.* & *adj.* **1.** Decorative painting or sculpture with fantastic interweaving of human and animal forms with foliage ; অস্বাভাবিক এবং বিকটাকার জন্তু প্রভৃতির প্রতিকৃতিযুক্ত শোভাসাধক চিত্র প্রভৃতি। **2.** A figure or design whimsically or comically distorted ; বিকৃতমূর্ত্তি, হাস্যোদ্দীপকভাবে চিত্রিত মূর্ত্তি, বিকৃত চিত্র, কিম্ভূতকিমাকার মূর্ত্তি বা দৃশ্য। ***Adj.*** **1.** Designating a work or style of art characterized by fantastic exaggeration or combination, esp. of human or animal figures ; বিকট, অস্বাভাবিক, হাস্যোদ্দীপক মূর্ত্তি প্রভৃতি দ্বারা চিহ্নিত কলাপদ্ধতি বা শিল্পকার্য্য সূচক। **2.** Distorted ; as, a *grotesque* figure ; বিকৃত। **3.** Ludicrous ; absurd ; fantastic ; as, *grotesque* theories ; হাস্যোদ্দীপক ; সৃষ্টিছাড়া ; বিকট, কিম্ভূতকিমাকার, অপরূপ। **–ly,** *adv.* **–ness,** *n.*

grō-tĕs′-quer-ie (-kėr-ĭ), *n.* Grotesque objects collectively ; grotesque quality ; কিম্ভূতকিমাকার বস্তুসমূহ ; অদ্ভুত ভাব, সৃষ্টিছাড়া ভাব।

grŏt′-tō, *n.* (*Pl.* -OES, -OS). **1.** A natural cave or cavern ; কন্দর, গুহা, গহ্বর। **2.** An artificial ornamental cave or cave-like apartment serving as a cool retreat ; উদ্যানমধ্যস্থ কৃত্রিম শিলাগৃহ, শিলাবেশ্ম (মেঘঃ)। **–toed,** *adj.* **Grotto-work** — উদ্যান মধ্যে সমুদ্র সৈকতস্থ শিলাগৃহের অনুকরণে কৃত্রিম শোভাসাধক কারুকার্য্য।

ground (grownd), *n.* **1.** The surface of the earth ; ভূতল, ভূপৃষ্ঠ, ক্ষিতি, মহীতল, ধরাতল। **2.** A portion of the earth's surface ; region ; field ; an area of a special kind or use ; as, a hunting *ground* : play *ground* ; ভূখণ্ড, ভূভাগ ; অঞ্চল, মুলুক, দেশ ; ক্ষেত্র ; মৃগয়াভূমি, ক্রীড়াভূমি। **3.** Soil ; ভূমি, মাটী, মৃত্তিকা। **4.** Land ; a person's property ; জমি ; ভূসম্পত্তি। **5.** (*Pl.*) The gardens, lawns etc. attached to a house ; প্রাসাদসংলগ্ন উদ্যান, তৃণভূমি প্রভৃতি। **6.** The bottom of the sea or a body of water ; as, the ship has taken *ground* (stranded) ; সাগরের তলদেশ, জলতল। **7.** Substratum ; background ; the surface worked upon in embroidery, painting, etc. ; অধস্তর ; অধিষ্ঠান ; চিত্রাঙ্কণ বা সেলাইএর জমি। **8.** (*Etching*) A composition spread on a metal and cut through with needle where acid is to act ; (দ্রাবকদ্বারা চিত্রক্ষোদণে) ধাতু ফলকের উপর আস্তৃত মিশ্র দ্রব্যবিশেষ। **9.** Basis ; foundation ; as, the *ground* of the national existence was laid in sacrifice ; reason ; motive ; ভিত্তি, ভিত্তিভূমি, মূল ; বুনিয়াদ ; হেতু, কারণ ; উদ্দেশ্য। **10.** Point of view ; opinion ; belief ; as, politicians shift their *ground* readily ; যেদিক হইতে কোন বিষয় বিবেচনা করা হয় ; মত ; বিশ্বাস। **11.** Sediment ; dregs ; as, coffee *grounds* ; মদ্যাদির তলানি, তলছাট ; শিটা, গাদ, কাইট। **12.** (*Cricket*) The space within which a player may lawfully stand ; as, the *ground* of a batsman ; the paid staff of players attached to a club ; (ক্রীকেট-ক্রীড়া) যে সীমার ভিতর ক্রীড়ক ক্রীড়ার নিয়ম লঙ্ঘন না করিয়া দণ্ডায়মান থাকিতে পারে ; কোন ক্রীড়ক সম্মিলনীর বেতনভোগী ক্রীড়কগণ। **Ground′-age,** *n.* The tax paid by a ship for the space occupied while in port ; বন্দরে স্থানাধিকারের জন্য জাহাজের দেয় শুল্ক। **Ground′-less,** *adj.* Without foundation ; false ; as *groundless* fear : *groundless* report ; ভিত্তিহীন, অমূলক, অকারণ, নির্নিমিত্ত ; অলীক। **Ground′-less-ly,** *adv.* **Ground′-less-ness,** *n.* **Ground′-y,** *adj.* Containing grounds or sediment ; তলানিযুক্ত। **Forbidden ground**—Subjects that must be avoided ; নিষিদ্ধ বিষয়, যে বিষয়ের আলোচনা সর্ব্বথা পরিহার্য্য। **Ground-angling, –fishing**—বড়শীর কয়েক ইঞ্চ উপরে ভারি জিনিষ বাঁধিয়া ফাতনা ছাড়া

বড়শী দ্বারা মাছ ধরা। **Ground-ash**—আশ বৃক্ষের চারা; উহা হইতে নির্ম্মিত যষ্টি। **Ground-bait**—*n.* & *v. t.* Bait dropped to the bottom of the water to attract fish; মাছকে প্রলুব্ধ করার জন্য জলের তলে নিক্ষিপ্ত টোপ। (*Verb t.*) To prepare as a spot etc. for fishing with ground-bait (*lit.* & *fig.*); জলের তলে টোপ ফেলিয়া কোন স্থান মৎস্য ধরার উপযোগী করা। **Ground-colour**—রং-এর প্রথম পোঁচ। **Ground fish**—Same as GROUNDLING I. (which see). **Ground-floor**—নিম্নতল, নীচের তলা। **Ground game**—শশকাদি ভূচর শিকার। **Ground-hog**—আমেরিকার শশকবৎ গিরি মূষিক। **Ground-ice**—উপরে ভাসিয়া উঠিবার পূর্ব্বে তলদেশের জমাট বরফ। **Ground-landlord**—The owner of a ground leased for building; বাস্তুভূমির অধিকারী। **Ground-nut**—Pea nut; the earth nut; ভুঁইমুগ, ভুচনক; চীনাবাদাম। **Ground-plan**—ইমারতের নীচের তলার নক্সা, ভূমিকা; (লক্ষণায়) রেখাণ্যাস, মোটামুটি নক্সা। **Ground plot**—বাস্তুভূমি; ভিত্তি, বুনিয়াদ। **Ground-rent**—বাটীর ভূমির খাজনা। **Ground-sea**—কারণ বিনা আপাত-প্রতিভাত উত্তালতরঙ্গসঙ্কুলিত সাগর। **Ground-swell** — দূরবর্ত্তী ঝটিকা বা ভূমিকম্প হেতু সাগরের বিস্তৃত এবং গভীর তরঙ্গান্দোলন, সামুদ্র বিবর্ত্ত (সাঃ পঃ)। **Ground-torpedo**—সাগরতলে নিবদ্ধ জলবজ্র বিশেষ। **Ground-work**—The basis; the essential or fundamental part; first principle; বুনিয়াদ; সারভাগ, মৌলিক অংশ; প্রধান উপাদান। **Holy ground**—দেবভূমি, পুণ্যভূমি, পুণ্যক্ষেত্র। **Slippery ground**—পিচ্ছিল স্থান। **Above ground**—Alive; মাটীর উপর, জীবিত। **A classic ground**—A historical place; ঐতিহাসিক স্থান, ইতিহাস-প্রসিদ্ধ স্থান। **Down to the ground**—Completely; in all respects; সম্পূর্ণরূপে, পুরোপুরি; সর্ব্বাংশে, সর্ব্বতোভাবে। **On the ground that** — এই কারণে যে। **On the ground of**—By reason of; on the pretext of; যেহেতু; অছিলায়, ছলে। **To be dashed to the ground**—See TO FALL TO THE GROUND. **To be on delicate ground**—To be in a fix; ফাঁপড়ে পড়া। **To be on one's own ground** — To be dealing with a matter in which one is specially versed; যে বিষয়ে যে বিশেষ ব্যুৎপন্ন তৎসম্বন্ধে আলোচনা করা। **To break ground**—See under BREAK. **To cover much ground** — (Of enquiry, report, etc.) To be far-reaching; বিস্তৃত ভাবে আলোচনা করা। **To cut the ground from under one's feet**—To anticipate and satisfy his arguments or plans; কোন ব্যক্তির যুক্তি বা মন্ত্রণা সম্বন্ধে পূর্ব্বাভাস পাইয়া তাহা খণ্ডন করা। **To fall to the ground**—See under FALL. **To gain or get ground**—To advance; to obtain an advantage; to gain credit; অগ্রসর হওয়া; সুযোগ বা সুবিধা পাওয়া; প্রশংসা লাভ করা। **To get in on the ground-floor**—To be admitted to a company etc. on the same terms as the promoter; প্রথম প্রতিষ্ঠাতৃগণের তুল্য অধিকার লাভ করিয়া কোন যৌথ কারবার প্রভৃতির সভ্যশ্রেণী ভুক্ত হওয়া। **To give or lose ground**—To recede; to retreat; to yield advantage; to decline; হটিয়া যাওয়া; পশ্চাৎপদ হওয়া; সুবিধা প্রদান করা; অবনতি প্রাপ্ত হওয়া। **To have the ground cut from under one's feet**—হঠাৎ আশ্রয়ভূমি বা অবলম্বন হইতে চ্যুত হওয়া। **To hold one's ground**—To maintan one's authority or influence; নিজের প্রভাব বা ক্ষমতা বজায় রাখা। **To shift one's ground**—To change one's argument or intention; পূর্ব্ব উদ্দেশ্য ত্যাগ করিয়া ভিন্ন উদ্দেশ্যের অনুসরণ করা, ভিন্নরূপ যুক্তিপ্রণালী অবলম্বন করা। **To stand one's ground**—To be firm; to maintain one's argument; অটল থাকা; নিজের যুক্তি সুপ্রতিষ্ঠিত রাখা। **To take the ground**—(Of a ship) To become stranded; (জাহাজাদি) চড়ায় লাগিয়া যাওয়া। **To touch ground** — (*Fig.*) To come to something solid after vague talk etc.; (লক্ষণায়) নানা প্রকার ফাঁকা কথার পর কতকটা সারবান বিষয়ের আলোচনায় প্রবৃত্ত হওয়া।

ground (grownd), *v. t.* & *i.* **1.** To set or run on the ground; as, to *ground* a ship; ভূমির উপর রাখা, চড়ায় আটকান। **2.** To found; to establish; as, to *ground* a belief on some fact; প্রতিষ্ঠিত করা; প্রতিষ্ঠাপিত করা। **3.** To instruct in elements or first principles; মৌলিক তত্ত্ব বিষয়ে শিক্ষা দেওয়া। **4.** To connect (an electrical current) with the ground; ভূমির সহিত তাড়িৎপ্রবাহ সংযোগ করা। **5.** To prepare the ground of (embroidery etc.); (সূচীকার্য্য প্রভৃতির) জমি প্রস্তুত করা। **6.** To lay on the ground; as, to *ground* arms; মাটীতে রাখা। ***Verb i.*** **1.** To run aground; চড়ায় লাগিয়া যাওয়া, চড়ায় আটকান। **2.** To alight on the ground; ভূতলে অবতরণ করা। **Ground'-ed,** *p. p.* Well-founded; সুপ্রতিষ্ঠিত। **Ground'-ed-ly,** *adv.* In a firmly established manner; সুপ্রতিষ্ঠিত ভাবে। **Ground'-ing,** *n.* **1.** Act of founding or laying a ground-work; ভিত্তি বা বুনিয়াদ স্থাপন। **2.** Elementary instruction; প্রাথমিক শিক্ষা। **3.** A background of embroidery etc.; সূচীকার্য্য প্রভৃতির জমি। **4.** Basis; foundation; ভিত্তি; বুনিয়াদ।

ground (grownd), *p. p.* of GRIND. **Ground glass**—ঘষা কাচ।

ground′-ling (grownd-), *n.* **1.** A fish which keeps near the bottom of the water ; একপ্রকার মৎস্য—ইহারা জলাশয়ের তলদেশে বাস করে। **2.** A spectator in the pit of a theatre ; a reader of inferior taste ; রঙ্গালয়ের গৃহতলে দণ্ডায়মান দর্শক ; হীনরুচি পাঠক। **3.** A creeping or dwarf plant ; লতা, খর্ব্ব বৃক্ষ।

ground′-sĕl (grownd-), *n.* A common weed used as food for cage birds ; পিঞ্জরবদ্ধ পক্ষীর খাদ্যরূপে ব্যবহৃত একপ্রকার আগাছা।

ground′-sĕl (grownd-), **–sill,** *ns.* **1.** (*Archaic*) The timber of a building lying on the ground; ভূতলে রক্ষিত গৃহ নির্ম্মাণোপযোগী কাষ্ঠফলক সমূহ। **2.** A threshold ; দরজার নীচের কাঠ বা পাষাণ ফলক, গোবরাট।

group (grôp), *n., v. t. & i.* **1.** A cluster, crowd or throng ; an assemblage ; গুচ্ছ, সংগ্রহ, পুঞ্জ, সমূহ, বৃন্দ ; সংঘ, দল। **2.** A number of persons or objects classed together ; a class ; মণ্ডলী, সংহতি ; শ্রেণী। **3.** (*Fine arts*) Two or more figures or objects forming an artistic whole ; (ললিত-কলা) এক চিত্রে দুই বা ততোধিক মনুষ্য, পশু, পক্ষী, প্রভৃতির সন্নিবেশ। ***Verb t.*** **1.** To make a group of ; to place in a group with ; শ্রেণীগঠন করা ; শ্রেণীতে সন্নিবেশ করা। **2.** To classify ; শ্রেণীবদ্ধ করা। **3.** To arrange (colours, figures etc.) in a group so as to produce harmonions effect ; (বর্ণ, মূর্ত্তি প্রভৃতি) এক চিত্রে সুসমাবেশ করা। ***Verb i.*** **1.** To form a group or a part of a group ; দলবদ্ধ হওয়া, দলভুক্ত হওয়া। **2.** To fall into harmonious combination ; সুসমাবিষ্ট হওয়া, সমঞ্জস হওয়া, সঙ্গতিবিশিষ্ট হওয়া। **Group′-age,** *n.* Arrangement in a group or groups ; মণ্ডলীসন্নিবেশ। **Grouping of atoms or molecules**—ব্যূহ (সাঃ পঃ), অবয়বসন্নিবেশ (ঐ)।

group′-ĕr (grôp-), *n.* A kind of fish ; এক জাতীয় মাছ।

grouse (grows), *n.* (*Pl.* GROUSE) The heathcock or moor-fowl ; কুক্কুটজাতীয় পক্ষি-বিশেষ। **Red grouse**—ইংলণ্ড দেশীয় আরক্ত পক্ষি-বিশেষ। **White grouse**—একপ্রকার পক্ষী ; উহার মাংস।

grouse (grows), *v. i.* (*Slang*) To grumble ; (ইতর-ভাষায়) গজ্ গজ্ করা।

grout (growt), *n. & v. t.* **1.** Sediment ; dregs ; তলানি, তলছাট ; কাইট, গাদ, সিটা। **2.** A thin fluid mortar for filling interstices ; ছিদ্র, ফাটাল বন্ধ করিবার জন্য একপ্রকার পাতলা চূণসুরকী। ***Verb t.*** To fill up with grout or mortar ; পাতলা চূণসুরকী দ্বারা পূর্ণ করা।

grout (growt), *v. i. & t.* (Of pigs) To turn up earth ; (শূকর ছানার পক্ষে) মাটী উল্টান।

grōve, *n.* A shady cluster of trees ; a small wood ; কুঞ্জ, কুঞ্জবন, নিকুঞ্জ, আরাম (মূচ্ছঃ), বৃক্ষবাটিকা, কুঞ্জবাটিকা, বৃক্ষজাল নিকুঞ্জমন্দির ; উপবন। **Groved,** *adj.* **Grove′-less, Grov′-y,** *adjs.*

grŏv′-ĕl *v. i.* **1.** To lie prone or move with the body prostrate on the earth ; to humble oneself ; as, to *grovel* in the dirt or dust ; ভূলুণ্ঠিত হওয়া, পায়ে লুটাইয়া পড়া ; নিজকে হীন করা। **2.** To be abject or mean ; to act meanly ; নীচতা বা হীনতা প্রদর্শন করা ; হীনজনোচিত কার্য্য করা। **–ler,** *n.* **–ling,** *adj.* Abject ; low ; mean ; হীন ; অধম, নীচ ; নিকৃষ্ট। **To grovel in the dirt or dust**—See *Grovel* 1.

grow (grō), *v. i. & t.* **1.** To develop by a natural and organic power ; বাড়া, বৃদ্ধিপ্রাপ্ত হওয়া, বর্দ্ধিত হওয়া। **2.** To germinate ; to spring up ; to be produced ; to arise ; "States *grow* out of human character" ; অঙ্কুরিত হওয়া, গজান ; উদ্গত হওয়া ; উৎপন্ন হওয়া ; উদ্ভূত হওয়া। **3.** To increase in any way ; to be augmented ; to advance ; to extend ; বৃদ্ধি প্রাপ্ত হওয়া ; বর্দ্ধিত হওয়া ; অগ্রসর হওয়া ; বিস্তৃত হওয়া, প্রসারিত হওয়া। **4.** To thrive ; as, his reputation is *growing* ; to flourish ; to improve ; বর্দ্ধমান হওয়া ; শ্রীবৃদ্ধি হওয়া ; উন্নতি লাভ করা। **5.** To become gradually ; as, to *grow* rich, pale, etc. ; ক্রমশঃ হওয়া। ***Verb t.*** **1.** To cultivate ; to produce ; as, to *grow* wheat ; চাষ করা ; উৎপাদন করা, জন্মান। **2.** To let grow on the body ; "To *grow* a beard" ; শরীরে বাড়িতে দেওয়া। **3.** (*Passive*) To be covered with some growth, (with *up, over*) ; "...*grown up* with wood" ; তৃণবৃক্ষাদি দ্বারা আবৃত হওয়া। **Grow′-a-ble,** *adj.* **Grow′-ing,** *adj.* Developing ; increasing ; বাড়ন্ত, বর্দ্ধিষ্ণু ; বর্দ্ধমান, বৃদ্ধিশীল। **Grown-up**—*adj. & n.* Adult ; বয়োপ্রাপ্ত, পূর্ণবয়স্ক। (*Noun*) An adult ; বয়োপ্রাপ্ত ব্যক্তি, পূর্ণবয়স্ক ব্যক্তি। **To grow downward**—To diminish ; হ্রাসপ্রাপ্ত হওয়া। **To grow into one or together**—To coalesce ; বাড়িতে বাড়িতে জোড়া লাগা। **To grow on or upon**—To become more influential with or admired by ; অধিকতর প্রভাবশালী হওয়া বা প্রশংসাভাজন হওয়া। **To grow out of**—To issue from ; to result from ; কোন কিছু হইতে নির্গত হওয়া, নিষ্ক্রান্ত হওয়া ; উৎপন্ন হওয়া, পরিণত হওয়া। **To grow up**—To become mature or full-grown ; to emerge from soil ; (of a custom) to arise or become common ; পরিণত হওয়া, বাড়িয়া উঠা, বয়োপ্রাপ্ত হওয়া ; অঙ্কুরিত হওয়া ; উদয় হওয়া, প্রচলিত হওয়া। **To grow upon one**—To gradually gain powers upon any one ; কাহারো উপর ক্রমশঃ প্রভাব বিস্তার করা।

grow′-ĕr (grō-) *n.* **1.** One who grows or produces ; উৎপাদক, উৎপাদনকারী। **2.** A plant growing in a specified way ; as, a fast *grower* ; বিশেষ প্রকারে বৃদ্ধিশীল বৃক্ষ।

grōwl, *v. i., t.* & *n.* **1.** To murmur or snarl as a dog ; to utter an angry grumbling sound ; গোঁ গোঁ শব্দ করা ; গর্জ্জন করা, গর গর করা, গজ্ গজ্ করা। **2.** (Of thunder) To rumble ; "Low *growls* the distant thunder" ; গুরু গুরু গর্জ্জন করা। **3.** To grumble ; গজ্ গজ্ করা। ***Verb t.*** To utter or express by growling, (often with *out*) ; গজ্ গজ্ করিয়া প্রকাশ বা উচ্চারণ করা। ***Noun.*** **1.** Grumbling murmur ; গরগরানি, গজ্গজানি। **2.** A rumble, as of cannon, thunder, etc. ; গুরু গুরু গর্জ্জন, গর্জ্জন। **Growl′-ing,** *adj.* **Growl′-ing-ly,** *adv.*

grōwl′-êr, *n.* **1.** One that growls ; যে গজ্গজ্ করে। **2.** A four wheeled cab ; চারি চাকার গাড়ী। **3.** A kind of fish ; একপ্রকার মাছ।

grōwl′-êr-ȳ, *n.* **1.** Act of growling ; গোঁ গোঁ শব্দে চীৎকার, গজ্গজানি। **2.** A place to growl in ; a private room ; a den ; যে স্থানে থাকিয়া গোঁ গোঁ শব্দে চীৎকার বা গর গর করা হয় ; নির্জ্জনপ্রকোষ্ঠ ; গর্ত্ত, বিবর।

grown (grōn), (*p. p.* of GROW) Mature ; পরিণত, বৃদ্ধি-প্রাপ্ত।

growth (grōth), *n.* **1.** Process of growing ; augmentation ; development ; as, the *growth* of trade ; বৃদ্ধি-প্রণালী ; বর্দ্ধন, বৃদ্ধি ; বিকাশ। **2.** Production by cultivation ; কৃষিকার্য্যদ্বারা উৎপাদন। **3.** That which has grown or is growing ; product ; "Nature multiplies her fertile *growth*" ; জাত বা জায়মান বস্তু, উদ্ভব (জিঃ) ; উৎপন্ন বস্তু। **4.** (*Path.*) A morbid formation ; (নিদান-শাস্ত্র) রোগদুষ্ট মাংস। **Full growth**—Size ultimately obtained ; পরিণত আয়তন, পূর্ণ-বিকাশ। **Of foreign growth** — Grown abroad ; বিদেশজাত।

groyne (groyn), *n.* & *v. t.* A frame-work of timber or low broad wall run out to stop encroachment of the sea ; সাগরের বাঁধ। ***Verb t.*** To furnish as a beach with groynes ; সাগর-সৈকতে বাঁধ দেওয়া।

grŭb, *v. i.* & *t.* **1.** To dig ; to be occupied in digging ; খনন করা ; খনন কার্য্যে নিযুক্ত থাকা। **2.** To drudge ; to be employed meanly, (with *on*, *along*, *away*) ; হাড়ভাঙ্গা পরিশ্রম করা ; হীন কার্য্যে নিযুক্ত থাকা। **3.** To search ; to rummage ; খুঁজা ; তন্ন তন্ন করিয়া খুঁজা, পাঁতি পাঁতি করিয়া খুঁজা। **4.** (*Slang*) To take food ; (ইতর ভাষায়) খাওয়া। ***Verb t.*** **1.** To dig superficially ; উপরি উপরি খুঁড়া। **2.** To root out by digging, (followed by *up*) ; as, to *grub up* trees ; উপড়াইয়া ফেলা, উন্মুলিত করা। **3.** To extract by digging ; (*fig.*) to discover in books, (with *up*, *out*) ; "*Grubbing up* antiquities" ; খুঁড়িয়া বাহির করা ; পুস্তক হইতে বাহির করা। **4.** (*Slang*) To provide with food ; (ইতর ভাষায়) খাবার দেওয়া। **Grub′-ber,** *n.* **Grub axe, Grub hoe, Grub hook**—খুরপা, হাতখুরপা, খন্তা।

grŭb, *n.* **1.** The larva of an insect, esp. of a beetle ; a caterpillar ; maggot ; কৃমি (যোঃ) ; শূঁয়া পোকা ; কীড়া। **2.** A dull worker ; a literary hack ; a slovenly person ; ঢিলা মজুর ; বেতনগ্রাহী লেখক ; নোঙ্গরা লোক। **3.** (*Cricket*) A ball bowled along ground , (ক্রীকেট ক্রীড়া) মাটীতে গড়াইয়া যে বল করা হয়। **4.** (*Slang*) Victuals ; food ; (ইতর ভাষায়) খাদ্য দ্রব্য, রসদ ; খাবার। **Grub′-bi-ness,** *n.* **Grub′-by,** *adj.* **1.** Of, or infested with, grubs, as trees etc. ; শূঁয়াপোকা সম্পর্কীয়, কীড়া বা শূঁয়া পোকা সমাকুল। **2.** Dirty ; slovenly ; মলিন ; নোঙ্গরা। **Grub and bub**—Victuals and drink ; অন্নজল।

Grŭb′-street (-strēt), *n.* & *adj.* A London street (now called Milton Street) formerly inhabited by poor authors ; hence, poor, mean or needy authors collectively ; লণ্ডন নগরীর রাজপথ বিশেষ—ইহার বর্ত্তমান নাম Milton Street [পূর্ব্বে এই স্থানে দরিদ্র গ্রন্থকারগণ বাস করিতেন] ; অতএব, দরিদ্র, অভাবগ্রস্ত বা নিম্নশ্রেণীর গ্রন্থকার সমাজ। ***Adj.*** Of, or relating to, Grub street ; mean ; poor ; of the nature of literary hackwork ; গ্রাব্‌ষ্ট্রীট সম্পর্কীয় ; হীন, নীচ ; দরিদ্র ; নিকৃষ্ট (রচনা)।

grudge (grŭj), *v. t., i.* & *n.* **1.** To permit or grant with reluctance ; to begrudge ; to be unwilling to allow ; অনিচ্ছার সহিত অনুমতি দেওয়া বা মঞ্জুর করা ; আক্রোশ করা, দিতে নারাজ হওয়া। ***Verb i.*** (*Obs.*) To murmur or grumble ; গজ্ গজ্ করা, গর্ গর্ করা। ***Noun.*** Reluctance felt in giving ; feeling of resentment or ill will ; secret enmity ; কোন কিছু প্রদানে অনিচ্ছার ভাব ; আক্রোশ, আখেজ ; গুপ্ত শত্রুতা। **Grudg′-ing,** *adj.* Reluctant ;

cō-ē-têr′-năl, *adj.* Equally eternal ; সমনিত্য, সমচিরস্থায়ী, সমসনাতন। **—ly,** *adv.* **—ni-ty,** *n.*

cō-ē′-văl, *adj.* & *n.* Of the same age ; সমকালীন, সমবয়স্ক। ***Noun.*** A contemporary ; সামসময়িক ব্যক্তি।

co-ex-ec′-u-tor (kō-ĕgz-ĕk-ū-têr), (fem. **—trix**) *n.* A joint executor ; সহযোগী কর্ম্মনির্ব্বাহক।

cō-ex-ist′ (-ĕgz-), *v. i.* To exist at the same time or in the same place, etc., (*with*) ; যুগপৎ অবস্থান করা, এক স্থানে অবস্থান করা। **—ence,** *n.* Existence ; conjunction ; এককালিকত্ব, সমকালবিদ্যমানতা ; সহভাব (হিঃ কোঃ), সহাস্তিত্ব (ঐ)। **—ent,** *adj.* এককালিক ; সহবর্ত্তী।

প্রহার করা, উত্তম মধ্যম দেওয়া, মেরে গন্ধর্ব্ব ছুটান ; মারিয়া ফেলা।

grue′-some (grô-sŭm), *adj.* Grisly ; frightful ; repulsive ; করাল, রুদ্র, ভয়ঙ্কর, রৌদ্র লোমহর্ষণ ; ভীষণ, ভয়ঙ্কর, ভয়াবহ ; বীভৎস, বিকট। **—ly,** *adv.* **—ness,** *n.* বাক্‌কঠোরতা, বচন পারুষ্য।

grŭff, *adj.* Rough in manners, voice etc. ; surly ; laconic ; severe ; harsh ; কর্কশ, উগ্রপ্রকৃতি ; চটা, রুখা, কঠোরবাক্, রুক্ষবাক্, পরুষবাক্ অল্পশব্দক ; কঠোর, কড়া ; পরুষ, কর্কশ। **Gruff′-ly,** *adv.* **Gruff′-ness,** *n.*

grŭm′-ble (-bl), *v. i., t.* & *n.* **1.** To murmur ; to mutter ; to growl faintly ; গড় গড় করা ; বক্ বক করা ; গজ্ গজ্ করা। **2.** To rumble ; as, a *grumbling* storm ; গর্জ্জন করা। **3.** To complain, (with *at, about, over*) ; অভিযোগ করা। ***Verb t.*** To express or utter complainingly, (often with *out*) ; গজ্ গজ্ করিয়া বলা। ***Noun.*** **1.** The act of grumbling ; অনুচ্চস্বরে অসন্তোষ প্রকাশ। **2.** A murmur of discontent ; a complaint ; গড়গড়ানি, গজ্‌গজানি, গগানি, গজর গজর ; অভিযোগ। **3.** A rumble ; গুরু গুরু শব্দ, গুরু গুরু গর্জ্জন। **—bler,** *n.* **—bling-ly,** *adv.*

grume (grüm), *n.* A thick viscid fluid ; a clot of blood ; চট্‌চটে জিনিষ ; জমাট রক্ত। **Gru′-mous,** *adj.*

grŭm′-mĕt, *n.* (*Naut.*) A ring of rope as a fastening, row-lock, wad, etc. ; (নৌ-বিদ্যা) রজ্জুর কুণ্ডলী।

grŭmp′-ȳ, —ish, *adjs.* Surly ; ill-tempered ; angry ; কোপনস্বভাব ; বদমেজাজী ; চটা। **—i-ly,** *adv.* **—i-ness,** *n.*

[illegible]ŭn′-dȳ (Mrs.), *n.* A general [illegible]me for public fault-finders etc. ; [illegible]) the opinion of neighbours [illegible] one's actions etc. (from Grundy, a character, in [illegible]orton's play *Speed the Plough,* 1798) ; পরদোষদর্শীদিগের সাধারণ নাম ; কাহারও কার্য্যাদি সম্বন্ধে প্রতিবেশিগণের মতামত। **—ism,** *n.* Conventional propriety ; prudery ; মামুলী শিষ্টাচার, গতানুগতিক লোকাচার ; অতিরিক্ত ভব্যতা। **What will Mrs. Grundy say** or **think**—What will a neighbour or the people say? লোকে কি বলিবে? দশজনে কি বলিবে?

grŭnt, *v. i., t.* & *n.* **1.** To make a deep short noise as a hog ; to utter a deep guttural sound ; ঘোঁৎ ঘোঁৎ করা ; ঘোঁগড়ান। **2.** To express discontent, dissent, fatigue, etc. by grunting ; ঘোঁগড়াইয়া অসন্তোষ প্রকাশ করা। ***Verb t.*** To utter with a grunt, (with *out*) ; ঘোঁগড়াইয়া বলা। ***Noun.*** A deep guttural sound, as of a hog ; ঘোঁৎ ঘোঁতানি। **Grunt′-er,** *n.* **1.** One that grunts ; a pig ; যে ঘোঁৎ ঘোঁৎ করে ; শূকর। **2.** A kind of fish ; এক প্রকার মাছ। **Grunt′-ing,** *adj.* **Grunt′-ing-ly,** *adv.*

grȳph′-ŏn, *n.* A fabulous animal dwelling near the hyperborean ; (গ্রীক পুরাণ) পৃথিবীর উত্তর প্রান্তনিবাসী জন্তু বিশেষ। [ইহার শরীর সিংহের মত এবং মাথা ও পাখা ঈগল পাখীর তুল্য। এই জন্তু ইহার সোণার নীড়ে ডিমের বদলে রোজ এক একটী সুলেমানি পাথর পাড়িত, শ্যেন-কেশরী।]

grȳs′-bŏk, *n.* A small antelope of South Africa ; দক্ষিণ আফ্রিকার ক্ষুদ্রকায় কৃষ্ণসার বিশেষ।

guai′-ac (gwā-yăk), **—a-cŭm** (-yă-), *ns.* **1.** A genus of trees growing in tropical America ; আমেরিকার গ্রীষ্মমণ্ডলে জাত এক জাতীয় বৃক্ষ। **2.** The resin from these ; a drug prepared from it ; ঐ বৃক্ষ হইতে প্রাপ্ত রজন ; ঐ রজন হইতে প্রস্তুত ঔষধ।

guan (gwân), *n.* A South American gallinaceous bird ; দক্ষিণ আমেরিকার কুক্কুটজাতীয় পক্ষিবিশেষ।

gua′-nâ (gwă-), *n.* Iguana ; গোধা।

gua-nâ′-cö (gwă-), *n.* A llama ; দক্ষিণ আমেরিকার উষ্ট্রজাতীয় রোমন্থক জন্তুবিশেষ।

gua′-nö (gwâ-), *n.* **1.** The accumulated excrement of certain sea-fowl found especially in the islands about Peru, much used for manure ; পেরুর পার্শ্ববর্ত্তী দ্বীপ সমূহে সঞ্চিত সামুদ্রিক পক্ষীর মলরাশি—ইহা জমির সার রূপে বহুল পরিমাণে ব্যবহৃত হয়। **2.** Artificial manure made from fish etc. ; মৎস্যাদি হইতে প্রস্তুত কৃত্রিম সার।

guar-an-tee′ (găr-ăn-tē), *n.* & *v. t.* **1.** One who acts as a surety or gives security ; জামিনদার, প্রত্যয়-প্রতিভূ (মিতঃ)। **2.** The act of giving security ; (same as GUARANTEE I.) ; জামিন দেওন। **3.** Something given or held as a security ; জামিন স্বরূপ প্রদত্ত বা রক্ষিত বস্তু, জামিন, জামানত। **4.** The person to whom a guarantee is made, (correlative to *guarantor*) ; যে লোকের অনুকূলে কোন বিষয়ে চুক্তি বা অঙ্গীকারে আবদ্ধ হওয়া যায়। ***Verb t.*** **1.** To be a gurantee or security for ; to become responsible for the fulfilment or genuineness of ; জামিন হওয়া, প্রতিভূ হওয়া ; কোন চুক্তি সম্পাদনের জন্য বা কোন জিনিষের অকৃত্রিমতার জন্য দায়ী থাকা। **2.** To engage that something has happened or will happen ; to warrant ; "I'll *guarantee* that he will never return" ; কোন ঘটনা ঘটিয়াছে বা ঘটিবে বলিয়া নিশ্চয় করিয়া বলা ; নিশ্চিতরূপে বলা। **3.** To furnish security to ; to secure, (with *against, from, in*) ; as, to *guarantee* a person or thing *against* risk or injury ; জামিন প্রদান করা ; নিরাপদ্ করা। **4.** To secure the possession of to a person ; কোন ব্যক্তির অধিকার বহাল রাখা। **Guar′-an-tor,** *n.* One who gives a guarantee ; জামিনদাতা। **Guarantee fund**—দৈবক্রমে কোনরূপ ক্ষতি ঘটিলে তাহা পূরণের জন্য যে টাকা জামিন রাখা হয়।

guar′-ăn-tȳ (găr-), *n.* & *v. t.* **1.** An undertaking by a third person that a covenant shall be observed by the contracting parties or by one of them ; চুক্তিকারিগণ বা চুক্তিকারিগণের এক পক্ষের লোক চুক্তির সর্ত্ত অনুসারে কার্য্য করিবে তদ্বিষয় তৃতীয় ব্যক্তি কর্ত্তৃক অঙ্গীকার, জামিন, জামানত, প্রত্যয় (মৎপ্রত্যয়েনাস্তু দ্রব্যং দেহি—বীরমিত্রোদয়)। **2.** Something which secures the existence or persistence of a thing ; "The best *guaranty* of a peace is a good force to maintain it" ; কোন বস্তুর স্থিতি ও সুপ্রতিষ্ঠার কারণীভূত বিষয়। ***Verb t.*** To guarantee (now *rare*) ; (অধুনা অপ্রঃ) জামিন দেওয়া।

guard (gârd), *v. t.* & *i.* **1.** To protect from danger ; to defend ; বিপদ্ হইতে রক্ষা করা ; নিরাপদে রাখা, রক্ষা করা, সংরক্ষণ করা। **2.** To secure from misunderstanding or abuse by explanations or stipulations ; as, courts *guard* the laws against misapplication ; ব্যাখ্যাদি দ্বারা অপব্যবহার বা ভ্রমাত্মক অর্থগ্রহণ প্রতিষেধ করা। **3.** To keep watch over ; as, to *guard* a prisoner ; to restrain ; to control ; as, to *guard* one's speech ; পাহারা দেওয়া, চৌকী দেওয়া, রক্ষা করা ; সংযত রাখা ; দমন করা। **4.** (*Med.*) To administer correctives with (a drug) ; as, a dose of mercury well *guarded* with opium ; (ভৈষজ্যশাস্ত্র) ঔষধের সঙ্গে উহার দোষশোধক বস্তু প্রদান করা। ***Verb i.*** **1.** To watch ; to take precautions *against* ; as, to *guard against* mistakes ; রক্ষা করা ; সতর্ক হওয়া, সাবধান হওয়া, হুসিয়ার হওয়া। **2.** To use a fencing guard ; অসিক্রীড়ার সময় হস্তত্রাণ ব্যবহার করা। **Guard′-ed,** *adj.* Circumspect ; framed or uttered with caution ; as, *guarded* language ; চৌকস ; অতি সতর্কতার সহিত রচিত বা উচ্চারিত, সাবহিত, অবহিত, অপ্রমত্ত। **Guard′-ed-ly,** *adv.* **Guard′-ed-ness,** *n.*

guard (gârd), *n.* **1.** Defensive posture or motion in fencing, boxing etc. ; অসিযুদ্ধ, মুষ্টিযুদ্ধ প্রভৃতিতে আত্মরক্ষার ভঙ্গীতে অবস্থান। **2.** Watch ; a state of caution or vigilance ; as, a careful *guard* over the tongue ; পাহারা, চৌকি ; সাবধানতা, দৃষ্টি, নজর। **3.** A protector ; a defender ; a sentinel ; রক্ষক ; রক্ষাকর্ত্তা, সংরক্ষক ; প্রহরী, সান্ত্রী, রক্ষী। **4.** One who has charge of a railway train, mail coach, etc. ; বাষ্পীয়শকট, ডাকগাড়ী প্রভৃতির ভারপ্রাপ্ত কর্ম্মচারী, বাষ্পীয় শকট রক্ষক। **5.** (*Pl.*) The household troops of the English army ; ইংলণ্ড দেশের গার্হস্থ্য সৈন্য। **6.** A body of soldiers etc. engaged to protect a place or person ; an escort ; detached part of an army etc. ; "The *guard* which kept the door" : the rear *guard* ; রক্ষি-সৈন্য ; শরীররক্ষী সৈন্য; সৈন্যদলের বিশ্লিষ্ট অংশ। **7.** A contrivance to prevent injury or accident ; as, fire *guard* ; আঘাত বা আকস্মিক দুর্ঘটনাবারক যান্ত্রিক কৌশল বিশেষ — যথা করত্রাণ, জঙ্ঘাত্রাণ, প্রভৃতি। **Guard′-less,** *adj.* **Advanced guard, Vanguard**—অগ্রবর্ত্তী সৈন্যশ্রেণী বা রণপোতশ্রেণী। **Guard-boat**—পোতাশ্রয়স্থিত রণপোত বহরে রীতিমত পাহারা দেওয়া হইতেছে কিনা তাহা ঘুরিয়া দেখিবার জন্য যে নৌকা ব্যবহৃত হয়, প্রহরী তরী ; পোতাশ্রয়স্থিত সরকারী নৌকা বিশেষ। **Guard-chain**—টেঁক ঘড়ী প্রভৃতির চেইন বা শিকল। **Guard-house, –room, –tent**—রক্ষিসৈন্যগণের গৃহ, রক্ষিগৃহ ; বন্দিগৃহ, গারদঘর। **Guard-rail**—সিঁড়ী প্রভৃতির পার্শ্বের রেলিং। **Guard-ring**—অপর অঙ্গুরীয়ক (বিশেষতঃ বিবাহ উপলক্ষে প্রাপ্ত অঙ্গুরীয়ক) স্বস্থানে রক্ষাকারী অঙ্গুরীয়ক, রক্ষকাঙ্গুরীয়ক। **Guard-ship**—পোতাশ্রয়রক্ষী রণপোত। **Guardsman**—সৈনিক, বিশেষতঃ ইংলণ্ডের গার্হস্থ্য সৈন্যদলের কর্ম্মচারী। **Guard of honour**—উচ্চপদস্থ কর্ম্মচারী প্রভৃতির প্রতি সম্মান প্রদর্শনার্থ রক্ষি সৈন্যদল। **On guard**—Acting as a guard or sentinel ; পাহারায় নিযুক্ত। **To be off the guard**—To be careless or heedless ; অসতর্ক হওয়া, অসাবধান হওয়া। **To be on one's guard**—To be vigilant ; to be cautious ; to be careful ; হুসিয়ার থাকা ; সতর্ক হওয়া ; সাবধান হওয়া। **To guard against**—To be in a state of defence against ; বিপদ্ আপদ্ হইতে রক্ষা করা। **To keep guard, To be on guard**—To act as a sentry ; পাহারা দেওয়া, সান্ত্রীর কাজ করা। **To mount guard**—To go on guard duty ; পাহারা দিতে যাওয়া। **To put on one's guard**—To warn one ; সতর্ক করিয়া দেওয়া, হুসিয়ার করা, সাবধান করা। **To relieve guard** — To take other's place in sentry duty ; পাহারা বদলান। **To run the guard**—To pass the watch or sentinel without detection ; অলক্ষিত ভাবে রক্ষী বা সান্ত্রীকে অতিক্রম করিয়া যাওয়া। **To take guard**—(*Cricket*—of a bat's man) To take the position in which the bat is held to defend the wicket ; উইকেট রক্ষার জন্য ব্যাট ধরিয়া অবস্থান করা। **To throw one off one's guard**—To render one inattentive o unsuspicious of danger ; কাহাকে অনবহিত করা, যাহাতে কোন ব অসাবধান বা অসতর্ক থাকে তাহা কর

guard'-i-ăn (gârd-), *n.* **1.** One who guards ; a defender ; রক্ষক, অভিভাবক ; রক্ষাকর্ত্তা। **2.** (*Law*) One having custody of the person or property or both of an infant, idiot, etc. ; (আইন) অভিভাবক, তত্ত্বাবধায়ক। **3.** A superior of a Franciscan convent ; ফ্রান্সিস্কান সম্প্রদায়ের মঠাধ্যক্ষ। **Guardian angel**—An angel conceived as watching over or protecting a particular person or place ; hence (*fig.*) a protector or defender in general ; রক্ষাকারী দেবদূত ; রক্ষাকারী। **Guardian deity**—অধিদেবতা, অধিষ্ঠাত্রী দেবী। **Guardian of the poor** or **guardian**—কোন জেলা বা পল্লীর দরিদ্রসম্বন্ধীয় বিধি ব্যবস্থা পরিচালনের ভার যে সভার উপর অর্পিত আছে, অনাথপালক।

guard'-i-ăn-ship (gârd-), *n.* **1.** The office of a guardian ; অভিভাবকতা। **2.** Protection ; guard ; as, under the *guardianship* of law ; রক্ষণ ; আশ্রয়, প্রহরা।

gua'-vă (gwâ-), *n.* A tropical tree ; its fruit ; পেয়ারা গাছ ; পেয়ারা, সবরী আম।

gü-bêr-nă-tŏ'-ri-al, *adj.* Of, or pertaining to, a governor ; শাসন সম্বন্ধীয় বা শাসনকর্ত্তা সম্পর্কীয়, শাসকীয়।

Gucumatz—Feathered serpent ; (লাল ইণ্ডিয়ানগণের ভাষায়) সপক্ষ সর্প।

gud'-geon (gŭj-ŏn), *n.* **1.** A small European fresh water fish used as bait ; ইয়ুরোপদেশীয় একপ্রকার ক্ষুদ্র মৎস্য—বড়শীর টোপ স্বরূপ ব্যবহৃত হয়। **2.** A person easily cheated ; বেকুব, বোকারাম।

gud'-geon (gŭj-ŏn), *n.* **1.** A pivot fixed in the end of a wooden shaft or axle ; কাষ্ঠদণ্ড বা অক্ষদণ্ডের প্রান্তদেশে সংবদ্ধ সূক্ষ্মাগ্র কীলক। **2.** (*Naut.*) A socket in which rudder works ; (নৌবিদ্যা) দাঁড়ের [illegible]র। **3.** A pin holding two [illegible]ks of stones etc. together ; যে কীলক দ্বারা দুইটী পাষাণফলক যুক্ত থাকে।

Gue'-bêr (gā-, gē-), **-bre** (-bêr), *n.* A Zoroastrian or fire worshipper ; a Parsee ; অগ্নিপূজক, অনলোপাসক ; পারসীক, পার্শি।

guel'-dêr-rösē (gĕl-), *n.* A plant bearing large bunches of white flowers ; শ্বেতপুষ্পপ্রসূ তরুবিশেষ।

Guelf (gwĕlf), **Guelph** (gwĕlf) *ns.* One of medieval Italian party supporting the Pope against the Emperor (cf. GHIBELLINE) ; মধ্যযুগে ইতালী দেশীয় রাজনীতিক সম্প্রদায় বিশেষ—এই সম্প্রদায়ভুক্ত ব্যক্তিগণ পোপের পক্ষাবলম্বী এবং রাজশক্তির বিরুদ্ধাচারী ছিল। **Guelf'-ic,** *adj.*

guer'-dŏn (gêr-), *n.* & *v. t.* (*Poet.*) A reward ; requital ; recompense ; (কবিতায়) পারিতোষিক ; পুরস্কার ; বখ্‌শিশ্‌। ***Verb t.*** (*Poet.*) To reward ; to requite ; (কবিতায়) পুরস্কৃত করা ; বখ্‌শিশ্‌ দেওয়া। **—less,** *adj.*

Guern'-sy (gêrn-sē), *n.* **1.** One of the Channel Islands ; ব্রিটীশ দ্বীপপুঞ্জের অন্যতম দ্বীপ। **2.** (*l. c.*) A close-fitting woollen shirt or jersey, (also *guernsey coat, —shirt, —frock*) ; গঞ্জিফ্রক, গঞ্জি। **3.** One of a breed of dairy cattle originating on Guernsey ; গারন্‌সী দ্বীপ হইতে আনীত গাভী বিশেষ।

guer-ril'-lă, gue-ril'-la (gĕ-), *n.* & *adj.* **1.** An irregular mode of carrying on war as adopted by the Spaniards against the French in the Peninsular war ; পেনিনসুলার যুদ্ধে স্পেনিয়ার্ডগণ কর্তৃক ফরাসীগণের বিরুদ্ধে অবলম্বিত অনিয়মিত যুদ্ধপ্রণালী, অব্যবস্থিত যুদ্ধ, অব্যবস্থিত সমর। **2.** A person engaged in irregular warfare ; অব্যবস্থিত সমরে প্রবৃত্ত ব্যক্তি। ***Adj.*** Irregularly carried on, as a war ; অনিয়মিত, অব্যবস্থিত।

guess (gĕs), *v. i., t.* & *n.* **1.** To estimate without measurement or detailed calculation ; অনুমান করা। **2.** To judge of at random ; to conjecture ; অনুমান করা ; আন্দাজ করা। **3.** To divine ; to solve by correct conjecture ; as, to *guess* a riddle ; ঠাহর করা, ঠাওরান ; আন্দাজ করিয়া ঠিক উত্তরদেওয়া বা সমাধান করা। **4.** To think ; to suppose ; to believe ; to imagine ; বিবেচনা করা ; বোধ করা ; বিশ্বাস করা ; কল্পনা করা। ***Verb t.*** To make a random judgment ; to conjecture, (with *at, about* etc.) ; আঁচা ; অনুমান করা। ***Noun.*** A conjecture ; a surmise ; a hypothesis ; অনুমান ; আন্দাজ, বিতর্ক, ঠাহর ; কল্পনা। **Guess'-er,** *n.* **Guess-work**—Work done by guess ; conjecture ; আন্দাজি কাজ ; আন্দাজ। **By guess**—At haphazard ; খামখেয়ালি ভাবে। **I guess**—(*Chiefly U. S.*) I feel sure or know well ; (প্রধানতঃ মার্কিণযুক্ত রাজ্যে) আমি নিশ্চয় মনে করি বা বিশেষরূপে জানি।

guest (gĕst), *n.* **1.** A visitor or friend entertained in the house, or at the table of another ; অতিথি, অভ্যাগত ব্যক্তি, আগন্তুক। **2.** A lodger at a hotel etc. ; ভোজনাগার প্রভৃতি বাসী। **3.** An animal or vegetable parasite ; জান্তব বা উদ্ভিজ্জ পরাঙ্গপুষ্ট জীব বা উদ্ভিদ। **Guest-chamber** — অতিথিশালা। **Guest night**—যে রজনীতে অভ্যাগত ব্যক্তিগণকে কোন কলেজ, পরিষদ্‌ প্রভৃতির গৃহে পানভোজনাদি দ্বারা আপ্যায়িত করা হয়। **Guest-rites**—অতিথি সৎকার। **Paying guest**—যে ব্যক্তি নির্দ্দিষ্ট হারে টাকা দিয়া কোন ব্যক্তির বাটীতে বা ভোজনালয়ে বাস করে।

gŭf'-faw (-fă), *v. i., t.* & *n.* To laugh loudly or boisterously ; হো হো করিয়া হাসা। ***Verb t.*** To say with a guffaw ; হো হো করিয়া হাসিতে হাসিতে বলা। ***Noun.*** A loud burst of laughter ; a horse laugh ; উচ্চ হাস্য, হি হি রবে হাস্য, অট্টহাস্য ; হোহো রবে হাস্য।

gŭg′-gle (-l), *v. i.* To gurgle; গড় গড় শব্দ করা, কুলুকুলু করা।

guide (gīd), *v. t.* **1.** To lead or direct in a way; to conduct; পথপ্রদর্শন করা; পরিচালনা করা, পরিচালিত করা। **2.** To regulate and manage; as, he will *guide* his affair with discretion; নির্ব্বাহ করা, চালান। **3.** To be the principle, motive or ground of (action, judgment, etc.); হেতু, উদ্দেশ্য বা মূলতত্ত্ব হওয়া। **4.** To train; শিক্ষিত করা। **Guid′-a-ble,** *adj.* **Guid′-ance,** *n.* Act of guiding; direction; government; পরিচালন; নির্ব্বাহ; শাসন।

guide (gīd), *n.* **1.** One who leads in a way or course; as, he followed the *guides*; a hired conductor of a traveller or tourist; পথপ্রদর্শক, পথোপদেশক; যে ব্যক্তি অর্থ গ্রহণ করিয়া কোন যাত্রী বা দেশপর্য্যটনকারীকে কোন নগর প্রভৃতি দ্রষ্টব্য স্থান ও বস্তুসমূহ প্রদর্শন করিয়া থাকে, ভ্রমণকারীর, দেশপর্য্যটনকারীর বেতনগ্রাহী পথপ্রদর্শক। **2.** A director; an adviser; a regulator; "He will be our *guide* even unto death"; তত্ত্বাবধায়ক, পরিচালক; উপদেশক, উপদেষ্টা; নিয়ামক। **3.** A soldier or other person employed to obtain information for an army; কোন সৈন্যদলের সংবাদ সংগ্রহার্থ নিযুক্ত সৈনিক বা অপর ব্যক্তি। **4.** (*Naut.*) A guide ship; (নৌ বিদ্যা) পরিচালক জাহাজ। **5.** A book of instruction or information for beginners; as, a commercial *guide*; a guide book; প্রথম শিক্ষার্থীর জন্য উপদেশ বা জ্ঞাতব্য বিবরণ পূর্ণ পুস্তক; দিগ্‌দর্শন পুস্তক (প্রবাসী ১৩২২)। **6.** (*Mech.*) A bar, rod, etc. directing the motion of something; something which guides a tool etc.; (যন্ত্রবিজ্ঞান) গতিনির্দ্দেশক দণ্ড, যষ্টি, প্রভৃতি; যাহা যন্ত্রাদিকে পরিচালিত করে। **7.** Something that marks a position or guides the eye; স্থান নির্দ্দেশক, অক্ষি পরিচালক। **Guide′-less,** *adj.* **Guide-book** — কোন নগরের যাদুঘর, অট্টালিকা প্রভৃতির জ্ঞাতব্য বিবরণ পূর্ণ পুস্তক, দিগ্‌দর্শন পুস্তক (প্রবাসী ১৩২২)। **Guide-post**—Same as FINGER POST (which see). **Guide way**—A groove; a track; খাঁজ; রাস্তা। **Right and left guide**—(সামরিক-শাস্ত্র) সামরিক কর্ম্মচারি বিশেষ। **Spiritual guide**—গুরু, দীক্ষাগুরু।

gui′-dŏn (gī-), *n.* **1.** A flag pointed at the free end used as a standard of Dragoons; অশ্বারোহী সৈন্যের ত্রিকোণ পতাকা। **2.** An officer carrying such a flag; ত্রিকোণপতাকাবাহী কর্ম্মচারী।

guild (gild), **gild,** *ns.* A society or corporation for mutual aid and protection; পরস্পরের সাহায্য ও স্বার্থ সংরক্ষণের জন্য সমিতি, গণ (মনুঃ), শ্রেণী (শুক্রঃ বিনয়), সার্থ (সাঃ পঃ)। **Guild-hall**—The hall where a gild or corporation meets; শ্রেষ্ঠি-সঙ্গম, গণভবন, সার্থমন্দির। A town-hall esp. in London; সাধারণ সম্মিলন বা সভাগৃহ, নগরমন্দির, পুরমন্দির—বিশেষতঃ লণ্ডন নগরীস্থ যে ভবনে নগরবাসিগণের সভা সম্মিলনী প্রভৃতির অধিবেশন হয়।

guil′-dêr (gil-), *n.* **1.** A silver coin of Holland = 1 8*d.*; হলাণ্ড দেশীয় রৌপ্যমুদ্রা বিশেষ। **2.** An obsolete gold coin of Netherlands; হলণ্ড দেশের অপ্রচলিত স্বর্ণমুদ্রা বিশেষ।

guile (gīl), *n.* Cunning; duplicity; wile; deceit; treachery; প্রবঞ্চনা, ধূর্ত্ততা, চাতুরী; কপটতা; কৌশল; শঠতা, কাপট্য, ছলনা, কুটিলতা, ছল, মায়া, প্রতারণা, শাঠ্য; বিশ্বাসঘাতকতা। **Guile′-ful,** *adj.* Full of guile; crafty; deceitful; treacherous; শঠ, প্রবঞ্চক; চালাক, ধূর্ত্ত; প্রতারক; বিশ্বাসঘাতক। **Guile′-ful-ly,** *adv.* **Guile′-ful-ness,** *n.* **Guile′-less,** *adj.* Free from guile; artless; অকপট, অমায়িক, নিষ্কপট; সরল, সাদা, অখল। **Guile′-less-ly,** *adv.* **Guile′-less-ness,** *n.*

guil′-lĕ-mŏt (gil-), *n.* A marine swimming bird; একপ্রকার সন্তরণপটু সামুদ্রিক পক্ষী।

guil-loche′ (gil-lŏsh), *n.* An architectural ornament imitating braided ribbons; বিনানো ফিতার আকার এক প্রকার স্থাপত্য-ভূষা।

guil′-lo-tine (gil-lö-tēn), *n.* & *v. t.* **1.** An instrument for beheading persons by means of a sharp blade loaded with a mass of lead and sliding between two upright posts; শিরশ্ছেদনের যন্ত্রবিশেষ, মুণ্ডচ্ছেদক [এই যন্ত্রদ্বারা মৃত্যুদণ্ডে দণ্ডিত ব্যক্তির শিরশ্ছেদ করা হইয়া থাকে। এই যন্ত্রের উপরিভাগ হইতে

Guillotine.

একটী গুরুভার কর্ত্তরিকা পতিত হইয়া অপরাধীর মুণ্ডচ্ছেদ করিয়া থাকে। ফরাসী বিপ্লবের সময়—Dr. J. I. Guillotin নামক জনৈক ব্যক্তি কর্ত্তৃক এই যন্ত্র ফরাসীদেশে প্রবর্ত্তিত হয়]। **2.** A machine much used for cutting paper, straw, etc.; কৃন্তন-যন্ত্র, কাগজ, তৃণ প্রভৃতি কাটিবার কল বিশেষ, দপ্তরীর কাগজ-কাটা কল। ***Verb t.*** **(–tine′)** **1.** To behead by the guillotine; to cut with a guillotine as the edges of a book; মুণ্ডচ্ছেদন করা, মস্তকচ্ছেদন করা; কৃন্তন যন্ত্রদ্বারা পুস্তকের কিনারা প্রভৃতি কাটা। **2.** A surgical instrument for excising uvula etc. ; আলজিভ ছাঁটিবার জন্য যন্ত্র-বিশেষ। 3. (*Parliament*) A method of shortening discussion by fixing a date by which the parts of a Bill must be voted on ; (পার্লেমেন্ট) যে দিবসের মধ্যে কোন আইনের অংশ-বিশেষ সম্বন্ধে মত গ্রহণ করা হইবে তাহা নির্দ্দিষ্ট করিয়া আলোচনা কমাইবার প্রণালী বিশেষ। **–tine′-ment,** *n.*

guilt (gĭlt), *n.* **1.** Punishable conduct ; অপরাধ। **2.** (*Obs.*) Crime ; sin ; (অপ্রঃ) দোষ ; পাপ। **3.** Criminality ; culpability ; অপরাধিতা ; সাপরাধতা। **Guilt′-less,** *adj.* **1.** Free from guilt ; innocent ; দোষহীন, নির্দ্দোষ, দোষরহিত ; নিরপরাধ, নিষ্পাপ। **2.** Having no knowledge or possession (of) ; as, *guiltless* of Greek or moustache ; অজ্ঞ, অনভিজ্ঞ, বিরহিত, শূন্য। **Guilt′-less-ly,** *adv.* **Guilt′-less-ness,** *n.*

guilt′-ȳ (gĭlt-), *adj.* **1.** Justly chargeable with a crime ; criminal ; culpable ; as, a *guilty* man or act ; অপরাধী ; সাপরাধ, কৃতাপরাধ ; অপরাধজনক। **2.** Sensible of, or prompted by, guilt ; as, a *guilty* conscience, look etc. ; দোষানুভবপ্রবণ, অপরাধাহত, পাপবিদ্ধ। **3.** Having committed a particular offence, (often with *of*) ; "*Guilty* of a breach of trust" ; অপরাধী। **Guilt′-i-ly,** *adv.* **Guilt′-i-ness,** *n.* **Guilty, Not guilty**—Verdicts in criminal trials ; অপরাধী, নির্দ্দোষ বা দোষী (ফৌজদারী মোকদ্দমায় অভিযুক্ত ব্যক্তি সম্পর্কে জুরিগণের অভিমত)।

guimp (gĭmp), *n.* Same as GIMP which see.

guin′-ea (gĭn-ĕ), *n.* **1.** A gold coin formerly current in Great Britain, of the value of 21 shillings sterling (so called from being struck out of gold from Guinea) ; (now) a sum of money of the same amount ; পূর্ব্বে গ্রেট ব্রিটেনে প্রচলিত স্বর্ণমুদ্রা বিশেষ,—মূল্য ২১ শিলিং [বর্ত্তমানে অপ্রচলিত ; ১৮১৩ খৃঃ অব্দে সর্ব্বশেষবার মুদ্রিত হয়। আফ্রিকার অন্তঃপাতী গিনি নামক স্থানের স্বর্ণ হইতে প্রথম মুদ্রিত হয় বলিয়া এই নাম] ; (বর্ত্তমানে) এক গিনির পরিমাণ অর্থ। **2.** (*Cap.*) A coast region of West Africa ; পশ্চিম আফ্রিকার সমুদ্রোপকূলবর্ত্তী প্রদেশ বিশেষ। **Guinea fowl, –hen**—গিনি হইতে সমানীত কুক্কুটজাতীয় পক্ষি-বিশেষ, চিত্রকুক্কুট, চীনা হাঁস [ধূসরবর্ণের উপর শ্বেত বর্ণের ফুট্ ফুট্ চিহ্নবিশিষ্ট]। **Guinea grains**—Same as GRAINS OF PARADISE. **Guinea pig**—(ক) দক্ষিণ আমেরিকার ক্ষুদ্র ইন্দুর বিশেষ—ইহা দেখিতে ক্ষুদ্র শূকর-ছানার ন্যায়। (খ) কোন সমবায়ের প্রতিনিধি বা পরিচালক [উহাদিগকে প্রতি অধিবেশনে উপস্থিতির জন্য ১ গিনি দক্ষিণা দেওয়া হয় বলিয়া এই নাম]। (গ) যে সমবায়ের পরিচালক প্রভৃতি কেবলমাত্র দক্ষিণার (fees) জন্য কাজ করে। (ইংলণ্ডে সাধারণতঃ উহাদিগকে এক গিনি দক্ষিণা দেওয়া হয়)। *Guinea pigging, n.* **Guinea worm**—গ্রীষ্মপ্রধান দেশে মানুষের চর্ম্মের ভিতর যে সূক্ষ্ম সূত্রবৎ দীর্ঘ ক্রিমি বিশেষ জন্মে, জলসূত্র (সাঃ পঃ)।

Guinivere, Guinever, Gwenhwyvar—ব্রিটনের প্রাচীন রাজা Arthurএর পত্নী। তিনি পরম রূপবতী ছিলেন। রাজা Arthurএর পারিষদ Sir Lancelotএর সহিত Guinivereএর অবৈধ প্রণয় ছিল।

guipure (*F.*), *n.* **1.** A kind of lace ; এক প্রকার জরি, এক প্রকার লেইস। **2.** A kind of gimp ; এক প্রকার ঝালর।

guise (gīz), **1.** (*Archaic*) Style of attire ; dress ; garb ; (কচিদ্-ব্যবহৃত) পরিচ্ছদরীতি ; পোষাক ; বেষ। **2.** External appearance ; semblance ; as, a fox in the *guise* of a priest preaching to a flock of geese ; shape ; রূপ, প্রতিরূপ ; আকার। **3.** Cover ; cloak ; pretence ; as, he did it under the *guise* of religion ; আবরণ ; বেশ ; ছল, অছিলা। **4.** (*Obs.*) Behaviour ; manner ; (অপ্রঃ) আচরণ ; রীতি। **Under the guise of**—See GUISE 3.

gui-târ′ (gĭ-), *n.* & *v.i.* A musical instrument having six strings played with the fingers ; অঙ্গুলি দ্বারা বাদনীয় ষড়তন্ত্রী-বিশিষ্ট বাদ্য-যন্ত্র বিশেষ, সুরদ (বেলঃ), রুদ্রবীণা। ***Verb i.*** To play guitar ; সুরদ বাজান। **–ist,** *n.*

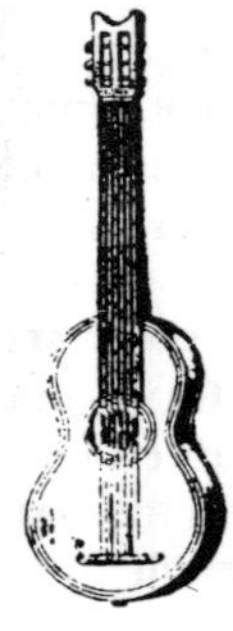

Modern guitar

gŭlch, *n.* (U. S.) A ravine, esp. one with gold deposit ; মার্কিণ যুক্তরাজ্যে সঙ্কীর্ণ গিরিবর্ত্ম,—বিশেষতঃ সঞ্চিত স্বর্ণপূর্ণ সঙ্কীর্ণ গিরিবর্ত্ম।

gul′-dĕn (gōl-), *n.* A silver coin of Holland and Austro-Hungary = 1 8 ; হলণ্ড বা অষ্ট্রিয়া-হাঙ্গেরি রাজ্যের রৌপ্য মুদ্রা বিশেষ।

gules (gūlz), *n.* & *adj.* The term applied to indicate red in heraldry ; (as *adj.* generally used after noun) ; লোহিত (বর্ণ) কুলমর্য্যাদাসূচক চর্ম্ম (ঢাল) প্রভৃতির উপরিস্থ লোহিত বর্ণ সম্বন্ধে ব্যবহৃত।

gŭlf, *n.* & *v. t.* **1.** A hollow place in the earth ; an abyss ; a deep chasm ; hence, an impassable gap ; "Between us and you there is a great *gulf* fixed" ; খাত ; অতলস্পর্শ খাত ; অতলস্পর্শ গহ্বর ; অনতিক্রমনীয় বিরোধ। **2.** A whirlpool ; জলাবর্ত্ত। **3.** (*Geog.*) A portion of an ocean or sea extending into the land ; (ভূ-বিদ্যা) উপসাগর, সাগরশাখা (সাঃ পঃ), খাড়ি (হিঃ কোঃ)। **4.** (*Univ. slang*) ; The degree allowed to an honour candidate who fails but deserves pass ; (বিশ্ববিদ্যালয়ের ইতর ভাষায়) অনর পরীক্ষায় অনুত্তীর্ণ, কিন্তু সাধারণ উপাধি পাইবার যোগ্য ছাত্রকে যে সাধারণ উপাধি প্রদান করা হইয়া থাকে। **5.** (*Poet.*) A profound depth ; the sea ; (কবিতায়) অতলস্পর্শ গভীরতা ; সাগর। ***Verb t.*** **1.** To engulf ; to swallow up ; কুক্ষিগত করা ; গ্রাস করা। **2.** (*Univ.*) To place in the gulf ; (বিশ্ব-বিদ্যালয়) অনর পরীক্ষায় অনুত্তীর্ণ, কিন্তু সাধারণ উপাধি পাওয়ার যোগ্য ছাত্রকে সাধারণ উপাধি প্রদান করা। **Gulf-stream** — মেক্সিকো উপসাগর হইতে নির্গত উষ্ণ সামুদ্রিক স্রোত, উপসাগরীয় স্রোত। **Gulf-weed** — এক-প্রকার সমুদ্রজাত গুল্ম।

Gulf-weed.

To bridge over the gulf — To effect a reconciliation by removing the cause of separation ; পুনর্মিলন সংঘটন করা।

gŭll, *n.* & *v. t.* One easily cheated ; a simpleton ; যে ব্যক্তি সহজে প্রবঞ্চিত হয় ; বোকা, বোকারাম। ***Verb t.*** To beguile ; to deceive ; to cheat ; প্রলুব্ধ করা ; প্রতারিত করা ; প্রবঞ্চিত করা। **Gul-li-bil′-i-ty,** *n.* **Gul′-li-ble,** *adj.* Easily deceived ; আশু প্রতারিত। **Gull′-ish,** *adj.*

gŭll, *n.* A long-winged and web-footed marine bird ; গাঙ্গচিল, গঙ্গাচিল্লী, জলকুক্কুটী, সাগরবলাকা।

gŭll′-ẽr-ȳ, *n.* A haunt or breeding place of gulls ; গঙ্গাচিল্লী নিষেবিত স্থান, গঙ্গাচিল্লীর শাবকোৎপাদনের স্থান।

gŭl′-lĕt, *n.* **1.** The passage for food from mouth to stomach ; throat ; অন্ননালী, অন্নমার্গ, গল (সাঃ পঃ) ; কণ্ঠনালী। **2.** (*Archaic* & *dial.*) A channel for water ; a strait ; (অপ্রচলিত ও উপভাষায়) নালা ; প্রণালী।

gŭl′-lȳ, *n.* & *v. t.* **1.** A channel or ravine worn in the earth by water ; পয়োপ্রণালী। **2.** A deep artificial watercourse a gutter ; a drain ; নালা ; নর্দ্দমা ; প্রণালিকা। ***Verb t.*** To wear into a gully or gullies ; to make (channels) by water action ; ক্ষয় করিয়া নর্দ্দমা বা পয়োপ্রণালী করা ; জলপ্রবাহ দ্বারা নালা করা। **Gully-hole**—রাজপথ হইতে নর্দ্দমা পর্য্যন্ত রন্ধ্র।

gŭl′-lȳ, *n.* A large knife ; বৃহৎ ছুরিকা।

gū-lŏs′-i-tȳ, *n.* (*Rare*) Gluttony ; (কচিৎ ব্যবহৃত) ঔদরিকতা।

gŭlp, *v. t., i.* & *n.* **1.** To swallow eagerly, greedily or in large draughts, (*usu.* with *down*) ; টপাটপ্ গেলা, গল্ গল্ করিয়া গেলা, ঢক্ ঢক্ করিয়া পান করা। **2.** To suppress with difficulty, (with *down*) ; as, to *gulp down* a sob or tears ; কষ্টে সংবরণ করা। ***Verb i.*** To catch the breath, as if in taking a long drink ; to gasp ; to choke ; "She *gulped* when she looked at it" ; অল্পক্ষণের জন্য শ্বাস রোধ করিয়া থাকা ; হাঁস ফাঁস করা, হাঁপান ; শ্বাসরোধ করা। ***Noun.*** **1.** Act of gulping ; as much as is swallowed at once ; a large mouthful ; গপ্ গপ্ করিয়া গেলন ; এক ঢোক ; এক গ্রাস, এক গাল। **3.** Effort to swallow ; গিলিবার প্রয়াস। **Gulp′-ing,** *adj.* গপ্ গপ্। **Gulp′-y,** *adj.*

gŭm, *n.* (*Usu. pl.*) The hard fleshy tissue of the jaw investing the teeth ; দাঁতের গোড়া, দন্তমাড়ি, দন্তমাংস, দন্তবেষ্ট, দন্তমূল। **Gum-boil**—দন্তমাড়ির স্ফোটক, দন্তপুপ্পুট (সুশ্রুঃ), মাড়ির স্ফীতি, দন্তার্ব্বুদ, দ্বিজ-ব্রণ (সাঃ পঃ)।

gŭm, *n., v. t.* & *i.* **1.** A mucilage exuding from trees etc., more or less soluble in water ; গঁদ। **2.** Secretion collecting in the inner corners of the eyes ; চক্ষুর মল, অক্ষি-মল, পিচটি। **3.** A gum tree esp. kinds of eucalyptus ; নির্যাসপ্রদ বৃক্ষ। **4.** A morbid secretion of gum as a disease of fruit-trees ; রুগ্ন ফল-বৃক্ষ হইতে নিঃসৃত দূষিত নির্যাস। ***Verb t.*** To smear or stiffen with gum ; গঁদের আঠা দ্বারা লিপ্ত করা বা কঠিন করা, আঠা দ্বারা জোড়া দেওয়া। ***Verb i.*** To exude or form gum ; গঁদের আঠা নির্গত হওয়া, গঁদের আঠা জমা। **Gum′-mi-ness,** *n.* **Gum′-my,** *adj.* **1.** Viscous or adhesive ; আঠালো, চট্চটে। **2.** Impregnated with gum ; exuding gum ; "The *gummy* bark" ; গঁদপূর্ণ ; নির্যাসস্রাবী। **3.** (Of ankles and legs) Swollen ; (গুল্ফ বা পদ সম্বন্ধে) ফুলা, স্ফীত। **Gum-Arabic**—আরবী গঁদ, কিকর। **Gum-dragon**—Tragacanth ; কয়েক প্রকার গুল্ম হইতে নিঃসৃত শ্বেতাভ বা রক্তাভ নির্যাস বিশেষ [ঔষধ প্রস্তুত প্রভৃতিতে ব্যবহৃত হয়]। **Gum elastic**—India rubber ; রবর। **Gum-tree**—নির্যাস-প্রদ বৃক্ষ বিশেষ, গঁদগাছ। **Up a gum tree**—In a fix ; at the end of one's resources ; মুস্কিলে, ফাঁপরে ; নিরুপায়।

gŭm, *n.* A vulgar euphemism for God ; as, by *gum* (a form of oath) ; (ইতর ভাষায়) ঈশ্বর।

gŭm′-mă, *n.* (*Pl.*-S, -TA) A kind of tumour of syphilitic origin ; এক-প্রকার উপদংশজ অর্ব্বুদ। **—tous,** *adj.*

gump′-tion (gŭm-), *n.* **1.** (*Colloq.*) Ready, practical sense ; go ; understanding ; capacity ; shrewdness ; (চলিত-ভাষায়) প্রত্যুৎপন্নমতিত্ব ; তেজ ; বুদ্ধি ; শক্তি ; বিচক্ষণতা। **2.** (*Painting*) A vehicle for colour ; (চিত্রবিদ্যা) যে তরল পদার্থে রঙ্গ গুলা হয়।

gŭn, *n.* **1.** A fire arm from which balls or other projectiles are discharged ; a musket ; আগ্নেয়াস্ত্র, বৃহন্নালিকাস্ত্র (শুক্র বিনয়ঃ), নালাস্ত্র (ঐ) ; বন্দুক। **2.** A piece of heavy ordnance ; a cannon ; গুরুভার কামান ; কামান। **3.** One who carries a gun ; a member of a shooting party ; বন্দুকবাহক ; মৃগয়াবাহিগণের দলভুক্ত ব্যক্তি। **4.** A discharge of a cannon in a salute; as, a salute of 17 *guns*; সম্মান-সূচক তোপধ্বনি। **Gunned, Gun'-less,** *adjs.* **Barisal guns**—গঙ্গা অথবা ব্রহ্মপুত্রের নিকটবর্ত্তী সাগর হইতে সময় সময় যে বজ্রগর্জ্জনবৎ শব্দ উত্থিত হইয়া থাকে। **Gun-barrel**—বন্দুকের নল বা চুঙ্গী, কামান-নালী। **Gun-boat** — বৃহৎ রন্ধ্রবিশিষ্ট দুই বা ততোধিক কামান দ্বারা সজ্জিত ক্ষুদ্র রণতরী। **Gun-case** — শিকারীর বন্দুকের আধার। **Gun-carriage**—কামানের গাড়ী, কামান শকট। **Gun-cotton**—গন্ধকদ্রাব এবং তাম্রদ্রাবে তূলা ডুবাইয়া ক্রমশঃ শুষ্ক করত প্রস্তুত শক্তিশালী বিস্ফোরক দ্রব্য-বিশেষ। **Gun-fire**—তোপ দাগন; প্রাতে বা সন্ধ্যায় যে সময়ে তোপ পড়ে। **Gun-harpoon**—এক-প্রকার টেঁটা—ইহা বন্দুকের মুখ হইতে নিক্ষিপ্ত হয়। **Gun-house**—যুদ্ধকালে কামান বা গোলন্দাজ সৈনিকের আশ্রয় গৃহ, কামানাগার। **Gun-lock**—বন্দুকাদিতে সংযুক্ত কল বিশেষ—যদ্দ্বারা বারুদ প্রভৃতি প্রজ্বালিত করা হয়, বন্দুকের কল। **Gun-metal**—৯ ভাগ তামা ও ১ ভাগ টীনের সংমিশ্রণে প্রস্তুত কামাননির্ম্মাণোপযোগী ধাতু-বিশেষ। **Gun-pit**—শত্রুর গোলা-বর্ষণ হইতে কামান রক্ষার্থ গর্ত্ত বিশেষ, কামান-বিবর। **Gun-port** — কামান দাগিবার জন্য রণপোতের পার্শ্বস্থ রন্ধ্র বিশেষ। **Gunpowder**—বারুদ, আগ্নেয় চূর্ণ, অগ্নিচূর্ণ (শুক্রঃ বিনয়), আগ্নেয়ৌষধ (নৌলঃ)। **Gunpowder-plot**—১৫০৫ খৃঃ অব্দের ৫ই নভেম্বর দিবসে বারুদ দ্বারা পার্লেমেণ্ট গৃহ উড়াইয়া দিবার জন্য কতিপয় রোমান ক্যাথলিকের ষড়যন্ত্র। **Gun-room**—রণপোতের নিম্নপদস্থ কর্ম্মচারিগণের বাসকক্ষ। **Gun-running**—কোন দেশে গোপনে বন্দুক রপ্তানী। **Gunshot**—কামানের পাল্লা। **Gun-shy** — বন্দুকের আওয়াজে ত্রস্ত (কুক্কুরাদি সম্বন্ধে ব্যবহৃত)। **Gun-smith** — কামান বন্দুকাদি আগ্নেয়াস্ত্র নির্ম্মাতা, বন্দুকাদি মেরামতকারী। **Gun-stock** — বন্দুকের কুঁদা। **Gun-wound**—বন্দুকের গুলি বা কামানের গোলার আঘাত। **A great gun**—An eminent person; বড় মানুষ, হোমরা চোমরা লোক। **As sure as a gun**—Quite sure; certainly; out of question; ঠিক নিশ্চয়; নিশ্চিত-রূপে; নিঃসন্দেহ। **Son of a gun**—A contemptible fellow; নরাধম, ঘৃণাস্পদ ব্যক্তি। **To blow great gun** — প্রচণ্ডবেগে ঝটিকা প্রবাহিত হওয়া। **To stand** or **stick to one's gun**—নিজের কোট বজায় রাখা।

gŭn'-nĕl (-ĕl), *n.* A small eel-shaped marine fish; বাইন মৎস্যের মত একপ্রকার সামুদ্রিক মৎস্য।

gŭn'-nel (-ĕl), *n.* Same as GUNWALE (which see).

gŭn'-ner (-êr), *n.* **1.** One who works a gun or cannon; (*naut.*) a warrant officer who has charge of the ordnance on a vessel; গোলন্দাজ; (নৌবিদ্যা) যে কর্ম্মচারীর উপর রণপোতের কামান গোলাগুলির ভার থাকে। **2.** A game shooter; বন্দুকধারী শিকারী। **Gunner's daughter**—বেত মারিবার জন্য যে কামানের সহিত পূর্ব্বে জাহাজের মাল্লাদিগকে বাঁধা হইত। **To kiss** or **marry the gunner's daughter** — To be flogged; বেত খাওয়া।

gŭn'-ner-ȳ (-êr-), *n.* **1.** Construction and management of large guns; the science of artillery; কামাননির্ম্মাণ ও চালনা; আগ্নেয়াস্ত্র বিদ্যা। **2.** The practical use of guns; কৌশলে কামান চালনা, গোলন্দাজি। **Gunnery lieutenant**—রণপোতের কামান পরিদর্শক কর্ম্মচারী। **Gunnery ship**—কামানচালনাবিদ্যা শিক্ষাদানের জন্য রণপোত।

gŭn'-ning (-ĭng), *n.* Shooting game; as, to go *gunning*; মৃগয়া, শিকার।

gŭn'-nȳ, *n.* A strong coarse sacking made of jute-fibre; also a bag or sack of gunny; চট, গুণ থলে, ছালা। **Gunny bag**—ছালা।

gŭn'-têr, *n.* **1.** A large plain scale invented by Mr. Gunter and used for solving mechanically problems in surveying and navigations (also *Gunter scale*); একপ্রকার শিকল — যাহা দ্বারা যান্ত্রিক কৌশলে জরিপ বা পোতচালনা সম্বন্ধীয় সমস্যার সমাধান হইয়া থাকে। **2.** (*Naut.*) The top mast or its sail sliding up and down the lower mast on rings; জাহাজের মাস্তুলের দ্বিতীয় অংশ বা তৎসংলগ্ন পাইল—যাহা নিম্নতর মাস্তুলে উঠা নামা করিয়া থাকে।

gŭn'-wale, —nel (-ĕl), *ns.* The upper edge of a ship's or boat's side; পোত বা নৌকার পার্শ্বদেশের উপরের প্রান্ত। **Gunwale to** or **under**—Level with or below water; জলের সমতল বা জলের নীচে।

gŭr-gĭ-lā'-tion, *n.* Surging of a liquid; a bubbling motion or sound; কলকল শব্দে প্রবহণ; কলকল বা গরগর শব্দ।

gur'-gle (gêr-gl), *v. i., t. & n.* To flow in an irregular noisy current; to make a bubbling sound; ঝির ঝির শব্দে প্রবাহিত হওয়া; কুলু কুলু ধ্বনি করা। ***Verb t.*** To utter with a gurgling sound; গরগর করিয়া বলা। ***Noun.*** Act or sound of gurgling; কুলু কুলু ধ্বনি, ঝির ঝির শব্দ, গরগর শব্দ।

gur'-jŭn (gêr-), *n.* An East Indian tree yielding oil used medicinally; গর্জ্জন গাছ। **Gurjun balsam** or **oil**—গর্জ্জন।

Gurnard.

gur'-nârd (gêr-), **—nĕt,** *ns.* A kind of certain marine fish with angular bony head ; মদ্‌গুরবৎ সামুদ্রিক মৎস্য বিশেষ।

gŭsh, *v. i., t.* & *n.* **1.** To issue with violence and rapidity ; to flow copiously ; to stream, (*lit.* & *fig.*) ; বেগে ছুটা ; ফিনকি দিয়া ছুটা ; প্রবাহিত হওয়া। **2.** To suffer a free flow of blood, tears, etc. (with *forth, into, out*) ; as, she *gushed into* tears ; অশ্রু ছুটা, রক্ত বহা। **3.** To speak or behave with effusiveness or high sentimentality ; আবেগ বা ভাবোচ্ছ্বাস প্রদর্শন করা। ***Verb t.*** To emit in a copious flow ; "The gaping wound *gushed* out a crimson flow" ; প্রচুর পরিমাণে নিঃসৃত করা, ফিনকি দিয়া ছুটান। ***Noun.*** **1.** A sudden and violent issue of a fluid ; the fluid thus emitted ; a rapid outpouring of anything ; as, a *gush* of light from the East ; তরলপদার্থের নিঃস্রাব ; নিঃসৃত তরল পদার্থ ; ঝলক, ফিন্‌কি। **2.** Effusiveness ; sentimental affectation ; ভাবের ছড়াছড়ি ; ভাবোচ্ছ্বাস, ভাবাবেগ। **Gush'-er,** *n.* **1.** One that gushes : (*U. S.*) an oil-well with a large natural flow ; যে নিঃসৃত করে বা যাহা হইতে নিঃসৃত হয় ; (মার্কিণ যুক্তরাজ্যে) যে কেরোসিন তৈলের কূপ হইতে স্বাভাবিক অবস্থায় অনবরত তৈল নিঃসৃত হয়। **2.** One who is effusively sentimental ; ভাবোচ্ছ্বাস প্রদর্শনকারী, ভাবপ্রবণ ব্যক্তি। **Gush'-ing,** *adj.* **1.** Rushing forth with violence ; flowing copiously ; প্রবলবেগে ধাবমান ; অজস্রবাহী। **2.** Effusive ; exhuberantly and demonstratively affectionate or sentimental ; আবেগপূর্ণ ; অতিরিক্ত স্নেহপ্রবণ, অতিরিক্ত ভাবপ্রবণ। **Gush'-ing-ly,** *adv.* **Gush'-y,** *adj.*

gŭs'-sĕt, *n.* **1.** A small piece of cloth inserted in a garment to strengthen some part ; পরিচ্ছদের কোন অংশ দৃঢ় করার জন্য তদভ্যন্তরে যে ক্ষুদ্র ত্রিকোণাকার বস্ত্রখণ্ড নিবিষ্ট করা হয়। **2.** Iron bracket strengthening the angles of a structure ; গৃহ, সেতু প্রভৃতির কোণ দৃঢ়ীকরণের জন্য লৌহময় কোণ-রক্ষক, লোহার কোণাচী। **—ed,** *adj.*

gŭst, *n.* **1.** A sudden blast or squall of wind ; দমকা বাতাস, চণ্ডবাত। **2.** A burst of passion ; ক্রোধোচ্ছ্বাস। **Gust'-i-ly,** *adv.* **Gust'-y,** *adj.* **1.** Stormy ; ঝটিকাময়, ঝটিকা-বিক্ষুব্ধ, ঝটিকাসঙ্কুল। **2.** Passionate ; উচ্চণ্ড।

gŭst, *n.* (*Archaic or poet.*) **1.** The sense or pleasure of tasting ; স্বাদেন্দ্রিয়, সুস্বাদ, সুরস। **2.** Keen relish ; সুতার, সুস্বাদ, রুচি। **3.** Special flavour or taste ; বিশেষ স্বাদ বা তার। **To have a gust of**—To appreciate ; গুণানুভব করা, গুণগ্রহণ করা।

gŭs-tā'-tion, *n.* Tasting ; স্বাদগ্রহণ।

gŭs'-tā-tō-rȳ, —tive (-tĭv), *adjs.* Pertaining to the sense of taste ; স্বাদেন্দ্রিয়-ঘটিত।

gŭs'-tō, *n.* Special flavour ; relish ; keen relish ; enjoyment ; বিশেষ স্বাদ ; রস ; রুচি ; ভোগ, রসাস্বাদন।

gŭt, *n., v. t.* & *i.* **1.** Bowels or entrails (esp. of animals) ; the contents of anything ; অন্ত্র, নাড়ী, নাড়িভুঁড়ী, আঁতড়ী ; কোন কিছুর ভিতরের জিনিষ। **2.** (*Vulg.*) The belly or stomach as the seat of appetité ; (ইতর ভাষায়) পেট, পাকস্থলী। **3.** Animal intestines prepared for violin strings ; তন্ত্রী, তার। **4.** A material for fishing lines, made from intestines of silk-worm ; বড়শীর সুতা তৈয়ারের জন্য গুটী পোকার অন্ত্র হইতে প্রস্তুত সামগ্রী বিশেষ। **5.** (Oxford and Cambridge) A bend of river in a racing course ; (অক্সফোর্ড ও কেম্ব্রিজ) নদীর বাঁক। **6.** A defile between hills ; a narrow lane ; গিরিসঙ্কট ; গলি। ***Verb t.*** **1.** To take out the entrails of ; to eviscerate ; as, to *gut* a fish ; নাড়িভুঁড়ি বাহির করা ; অন্ত্র বাহির করা। **2.** To plunder of contents ; to destroy the contents of ; as, to *gut* a house ; ভিতরের জিনিষ লুঠ করিয়া লওয়া ; ভিতরের জিনিষ নষ্ট করা। **3.** To extract the essence of ; as, to *gut* a book ; সারোদ্ধার করা, সারসঙ্কলন করা, সার তুলিয়া লওয়া। ***Verb i.*** To eat greedily ; to gormandize ; পেটুকের মত খাওয়া ; আকণ্ঠ ভোজন করা। **Blind gut**—Caecum ; অন্ধান্ত্র (হঃ চঃ)। **It has no guts in it**—It has no real value or force ; ইহার কোন সার নাই, এর মাঝে কোন জিনিষ নাই। **To have guts in the brain** — To be intelligent ; মাথায় জিনিষ থাকা।

gŭt-tă–pĕr'-chă, *n.* The solidified juice of various trees in the Malayan Islands ; মালয়দ্বীপজাত কতিপয় বৃক্ষের ঘনীভূত নির্যাস।

Guttapercha plant.

gŭt'-tāte, *adj.* (*Nat. Hist.*) Speckled ; (জীবজন্তুর বিবরণ) চিত্রবিচিত্র, ফুটফুট দাগ বিশিষ্ট।

gŭt'-tĕr, *n.* & *v. t.* **1.** An eaves channel ; ঘরের ছাঁইচ, ছাদের জলনালী। **2.** An open conduit for outflow of water ; নালা, নর্দ্দমা, প্রণালিকা (সাঃ পঃ), জুলী, স্যন্দনিকা (মিতঃ)। **3.** Any narrow channel or groove ;

নালী, খাঁজ। *Verb i.* 1. To cut or form into small hollows; to channel; to flow in streams; as, tears *gutter* down; ক্ষুদ্র ক্ষুদ্র গর্ত কাটা বা হওয়া; নালি হওয়া; প্রবাহিত হওয়া। 2. To become channelled as a candle when the flame flares in the wind; to sweat; (দীপশিখা বায়ু দ্বারা আন্দোলিত হইলে মোমবাতি) খাঁজ বা নালীবিশিষ্ট হওয়া; চুয়াইয়া পড়া, বিন্দু বিন্দু নির্গত হওয়া। **Gutter-blood**—(*Scot.*) Low born person; ছোট লোক, ইতর লোক, হাড়ী ডোম। **Gutter-child, Gutter-snipe**—উপেক্ষিত বালকবালিকা, গৃহহীন বালক-বালিকা। **Gutter-man** — যে ব্যক্তি অল্পমূল্যের জিনিষ রাস্তায় রাস্তায় ফেরি করিয়া বেড়ায়। **Out of the gutter**—Of low origin; হীন বংশজ। **To take a child out of gutter**—To remove him from poor surroundings; দরিদ্রের ঘর হইতে গ্রহণ করা।

gut'-tle (-l), *v. i.* & *t.* To gourmandize; পেটুকের মত আহার করা। **–tler,** *n.*

gŭt'-tur-ăl (-têr-), *adj.* & *n.* 1. Of, or pertaining to, the throat; কণ্ঠ্য, জিহ্বামূলীয়, কণ্ঠস্থ, কণ্ঠসম্বন্ধীয়। 2. Formed in the throat; produced by the back of the tongue and the palate; as, a *guttural* sound; কণ্ঠজাত; কণ্ঠ্য। *Noun.* A guttural sound or letter, as *g, k,* etc.; কণ্ঠ্যস্বর, কণ্ঠ্যবর্ণ। **–ism,** *n.* **–ize,** *v. t.* **–ly,** *adv.*

gŭt'-tȳ, *n.* (*Golf*) A guttapercha ball; গাটাপারচা নির্ম্মিত গল্‌ফ ক্রীড়ার বল।

guy (gï), *n.* & *v. t.* A rope etc. to steady any suspended weight or hold tent etc. in place; বিলম্বিত ভার স্থির রাখিবার জন্য রজ্জু, তাঁবুর রজ্জু। *Verb t.* To keep steady or in position with a guy or guys; তাদৃশ রজ্জু দ্বারা যথাস্থানে রাখা।

guy (gï), *n., v. t.* & *i.* 1. The effigy of Guy Fawkes paraded and burnt on the anniversary of the Gunpowder plot, Nov. 5; অগ্নিচূর্ণ-ষড়যন্ত্রের নায়ক গাই ফক্‌সের কুশপুত্তলিকা,—যাহা প্রদর্শনের পর ৫ই নভেম্বর দগ্ধ করা হয়। 2. A person dressed grotesquely; a fright; অপরূপ পরিচ্ছদ পরিহিত ব্যক্তি, কোঁদলকুতকুত; বিকট মূর্ত্তি। 3. (*Slang*) Act of decamping; as, to give the *guy* to (=to escape from); (ইতর ভাষায়) চম্পট, সরিয়া পড়ন, পিট্টান। *Verb t.* To exhibit in effigy; to ridicule; কুশপুত্তলিকা প্রদর্শন করা; বিদ্রূপ করা। *Verb i.* (*Slang*) To disappear secretly; সটকান্ দেওয়া। **To do a guy**—To decamp; চম্পট দেওয়া, পিট্টান দেওয়া। **To give the guy to**—See GUY, *n.* 3.

gŭz'-zle (-zl), *v. i.* & *t.* To eat and drink greedily and frequently; গপ্‌গপ্ করিয়া খাওয়া। *Verb t.* To drink or swallow greedily; to use up as money in guzzling, (often with *away*); গপ্‌গপ্ করিয়া খাওয়া, ঢকঢক্ করিয়া পান করা; খাইয়া উড়াইয়া দেওয়া। **–zler,** *n.*

gȳbe, *v. i.* & *t.* (Of fore-&-aft sails etc.) To swing from one side to the other; (পাইল প্রভৃতি) জাহাজের এক পার্শ্ব হইতে অপর পার্শ্বে ঘুরাইয়া নেওয়া। *Verb t.* To cause as a sail to gybe; পাইল জাহাজের একপার্শ্ব হইতে অপর পার্শ্বে ঘুরাইয়া নেওয়া।

gȳle, *n.* 1. Quantity of beer brewed at once; একেবারে যে পরিমাণ বীয়র মদ্য চোলাই করা হয়। 2. A fermenting wort; a fermenting turn; গাঁজাইবার জন্য এক প্রকার গুল্ম; গাঁজানের জন্য পাত্র।

gym-kha'-nă (gĭm-kâ-, jĭm-kâ-), *n.* (*Anglo Ind.*) 1. A public resort or meeting for athletic games etc.; ব্যায়াম, কুস্তি প্রভৃতির জন্য সাধারণ সমাগমস্থল বা সম্মিলন, ক্রীড়াপ্রাঙ্গণ, মল্লক্ষেত্র। 2. Athletic sports display; মল্লক্রীড়া প্রদর্শন।

gȳm-na'-sĭ-ŭm, *n.* (*Pl.* -UMS,-A) 1. A place for athletic exercises; ব্যায়াম-বিদ্যালয়, মল্লভূমি, মল্লাঙ্গন, মল্লযুদ্ধশালা, রঙ্গভূমি, রঙ্গাঙ্গন, আখ্‌ড়া। 2. A continental esp. German school of the highest grade preparing for the universities; জর্ম্মণী প্রভৃতি দেশের উচ্চ বিদ্যালয়। **–al,** *adj.* Of, or relating to, the continental gymnasiums; জর্ম্মণী প্রভৃতি দেশের উচ্চ বিদ্যালয় সম্বন্ধীয়।

gȳm'-năst, *n.* One who teaches or practises gymnastics; ব্যায়াম শিক্ষার্থী, ব্যায়াম-শিক্ষক, কুস্তিগীর, পালোয়ান, ডনগীর।

gȳm-năs'-tic, *adj.* & *n.* 1. Pertaining to athletic exercise of the body; ব্যায়ামসম্পর্কীয়, মল্লযুদ্ধবিষয়ক। 2. Pertaining to disciplinary intellectual exercise; নিয়মানুবর্ত্তিতা বিধায়ক শিক্ষা সম্বন্ধীয়। *Noun.* 1. A course of instruction, regarded as discipline; as, grammar is a good *gymnastic*; নৈতিক ও মানসিক বৈয়ামিকি বিদ্যা (বাৎস্য), নিয়মানু-বর্ত্তিতা বিধায়ক শিক্ষা। 2. (*Pl.*) Athletic exercises to strengthen the muscles and the bones (*lit.* & *fig.*); "Musical *gymnastics*"; মল্লযুদ্ধ, মল্লক্রীড়া, ব্যায়াম, কুস্তি, ডন।

gȳm-nŏs'-ō-phist, *n.* One of a class of Hindu philosophers almost naked and given to contemplation; নাগা সন্ন্যাসী, যোগী। **–phy,** *n.* The doctrine of the gymnosophists; যোগশাস্ত্র।

gȳn-æ cē'-ŭm (-ē-), *n.* 1. (*Gk.* & *Rom. Antiq.*) The part or apartment reserved for females; পূর্ব্বকালে প্রাসাদের যে অংশে কেবল মহিলাগণ বাস করিত, অন্তঃপুর, অন্তঃগৃহ, জেনানামহল, অন্দরমহল, শুদ্ধান্ত, অবরোধ, অন্তর্নিবেশন (মঃ সং), অন্তর্মন্দির (দশঃ)। 2. (*Bot.*) (Sometimes—ŒCIUM) Female organ of flower;

with angular bony head ; মদ্গুরবৎ সামুদ্রিক মৎস্য বিশেষ।

gŭsh, *v. i., t. & n.* **1.** To issue with violence and rapidity; to flow copiously; to stream, (*lit. & fig.*); বেগে ছুটা; ফিন্‌কি দিয়া ছুটা; প্রবাহিত হওয়া। **2.** To suffer a free flow of blood, tears, etc. (with *forth, into, out*); as, she *gushed into* tears; অশ্রু ছুটা, রক্ত বহা। **3.** To speak or behave with effusiveness or high sentimentality; আবেগ বা ভাবোচ্ছ্বাস প্রদর্শন করা। ***Verb t.*** To emit in a copious flow; "The gaping wound *gushed* out a crimson flow"; প্রচুর পরিমাণে নিঃসৃত করা, ফিন্‌কি দিয়া ছুটান। ***Noun.*** **1.** A sudden and violent issue of a fluid; the fluid thus emitted; a rapid outpouring of anything; as, a *gush* of light from the East; তরলপদার্থের নিঃস্রাব; নিঃসৃত তরল পদার্থ; ঝলক, ফিন্‌কি। **2.** Effusiveness; sentimental affectation; ভাবের ছড়াছড়ি; ভাবোচ্ছ্বাস, ভাবাবেগ। **Gush′-er,** *n.* **1.** One that gushes: (*U. S.*) an oil-well with a large natural flow; যে নিঃসৃত করে বা যাহা হইতে নিঃসৃত হয়; (মার্কিণ যুক্তরাজ্যে) যে কেরোসিন তৈলের কূপ হইতে স্বাভাবিক অবস্থায় অনবরত তৈল নিঃসৃত হয়। **2.** One who is effusively sentimental; ভাবোচ্ছ্বাস প্রদর্শনকারী, ভাবপ্রবণ ব্যক্তি। **Gush′-ing,** *adj.* **1.** Rushing forth with violence; flowing copiously; প্রবলবেগে ধাবমান; অজস্রবাহী। **2.** Effusive; exhuberantly and demonstratively affectionate or sentimental; আবেগপূর্ণ; অতিরিক্ত স্নেহপ্রবণ, অতিরিক্ত ভাবপ্রবণ। **Gush′-ing-ly,** *adv.* **Gush′-y,** *adj.*

gŭs′-sĕt, *n.* **1.** A small piece of cloth inserted in a garment to strengthen some part; পরিচ্ছদের কোন অংশ দৃঢ় করার জন্য তদভ্যন্তরে যে ক্ষুদ্র ত্রিকোণাকার বস্ত্রখণ্ড নিবিষ্ট করা হয়। **2.** Iron bracket strengthening the angles of a structure; গৃহ, সেতু প্রভৃতির কোণ দৃঢ়ীকরণের জন্য লৌহময় কোণ-রক্ষক, লোহার কোণাচী। **—ed,** *adj.*

gŭst, *n.* **1.** A sudden blast or squall of wind; দমকা বাতাস, চণ্ডবাত। **2.** A burst of passion; ক্রোধোচ্ছ্বাস। **Gust′-i-ly,** *adv.* **Gust′-y,** *adj.* **1.** Stormy; ঝটিকাময়, ঝটিকা-বিক্ষুব্ধ, ঝটিকাসঙ্কুল। **2.** Passionate; উচ্চণ্ড।

gŭst, *n.* (*Archaic or poet.*) **1.** The sense or pleasure of tasting; স্বাদেন্দ্রিয়, সুস্বাদ, সুরস। **2.** Keen relish; সুতার, সুস্বাদ, রুচি। **3.** Special flavour or taste; বিশেষ স্বাদ বা তার। **To have a gust of—** To appreciate; গুণানুভব করা, গুণগ্রহণ করা।

gŭs-tā′-tion, *n.* Tasting; স্বাদগ্রহণ।

gŭs′-tā-tō-rӯ, —tive (-tĭv), *adjs.* Pertaining to the sense of taste; স্বাদেন্দ্রিয়-ঘটিত।

gŭs′-tō, *n.* Special flavour; relish; keen relish; enjoyment; বিশেষ স্বাদ; রস; রুচি; ভোগ, রসাস্বাদন।

gŭt, *n., v. t. & i.* **1.** Bowels or entrails (esp. of animals); the contents of anything; অন্ত্র, নাড়ী, নাড়িভুঁড়ী, আঁতড়ী; কোন কিছুর ভিতরের জিনিষ। **2.** *(Vulg.)* The belly or stomach as the seat of appetite; (ইতর ভাষায়) পেট, পাকস্থলী। **3.** Animal intestines prepared for violin strings; তন্ত্রী, তার। **4.** A material for fishing lines, made from intestines of silk-worm; বড়শীর সুতা তৈয়ারের জন্য গুটী পোকার অন্ত্র হইতে প্রস্তুত সামগ্রী বিশেষ। **5.** (Oxford and Cambridge) A bend of river in a racing course; (অক্সফোর্ড ও কেম্ব্রিজ) নদীর বাঁক। **6.** A defile between hills; a narrow lane; গিরিসঙ্কট; গলি। ***Verb t.*** **1.** To take out the entrails of; to eviscerate; as, to *gut* a fish; নাড়ীভুঁড়ি বাহির করা; অন্ত্র বাহির করা। **2.** To plunder of contents; to destroy the contents of; as, to *gut* a house; ভিতরের জিনিষ লুঠ করিয়া লওয়া; ভিতরের জিনিষ নষ্ট করা। **3.** To extract the essence of; as, to *gut* a book; সারোদ্ধার করা, সারসঙ্কলন করা, সার তুলিয়া লওয়া। ***Verb i.*** To eat greedily; to gormandize: পেটুকের মত খাওয়া; আকণ্ঠ ভোজন করা। **Blind gut—** Caecum; অন্ধান্ত্র (হঃ চঃ)। **It has no guts in it—**It has no real value or force; ইহার কোন সার নাই, এর মাঝে কোন জিনিষ নাই। **To have guts in the brain —** To be intelligent; মাথায় জিনিষ থাকা।

gŭt-tā-pêr′-chā, *n.* The solidified juice of various trees in the

Guttapercha plant.

Malayan Islands; মালয়দ্বীপজাত কতিপয় বৃক্ষের ঘনীভূত নির্যাস।

gŭt′-tāte, *adj.* (*Nat. Hist.*) Speckled; (জীবজন্তুর বিবরণ) চিত্রবিচিত্র, ফুটফুট দাগ বিশিষ্ট।

gŭt′-tĕr, *n. & v. t.* **1.** An eaves channel; ঘরের ছাঁইচ, ছাদের জলনালী। **2.** An open conduit for outflow of water; নালা, নর্দ্দমা, প্রণালিকা (সাঃ পঃ), জুলী, স্যন্দনিকা (মিতঃ)। **3.** Any narrow channel or groove;

নালী, খাঁজ। *Verb i.* **1.** To cut or form into small hollows; to channel; to flow in streams; as, tears *gutter* down; ক্ষুদ্র ক্ষুদ্র গর্ত্ত কাটা বা হওয়া; নালি হওয়া; প্রবাহিত হওয়া। **2.** To become channelled as a candle when the flame flares in the wind; to sweat; (দীপশিখা বায়ু দ্বারা আন্দোলিত হইলে মোমবাতি) খাঁজ বা নালীবিশিষ্ট হওয়া; চুয়াইয়া পড়া, বিন্দু বিন্দু নির্গত হওয়া। **Gutter-blood**—(*Scot.*) Low born person; ছোট লোক, ইতর লোক, হাড়ী ডোম। **Gutter-child, Gutter-snipe**—উপেক্ষিত বালকবালিকা, গৃহহীন বালক-বালিকা। **Gutter-man**—যে ব্যক্তি অল্পমূল্যের জিনিষ রাস্তায় রাস্তায় ফেরি করিয়া বেড়ায়। **Out of the gutter**—Of low origin; হীন বংশজ। **To take a child out of gutter**—To remove him from poor surroundings; দরিদ্রের ঘর হইতে গ্রহণ করা।

gut'-tle (-l), *v. i.* & *t.* To gourmandize; পেটুকের মত আহার করা। **–tler,** *n.*

gŭt'-tur-ăl (-têr-), *adj.* & *n.* **1.** Of, or pertaining to, the throat; কণ্ঠ্য, জিহ্বামূলীয়, কণ্ঠস্থ, কণ্ঠসম্বন্ধীয়। **2.** Formed in the throat; produced by the back of the tongue and the palate; as, a *guttural* sound; কণ্ঠজাত; কণ্ঠ্য। ***Noun.*** A guttural sound or letter, as *g, k,* etc.; কণ্ঠ্যস্বর, কণ্ঠ্যবর্ণ। **–ism,** *n.* **–ize,** *v. t.* **–ly,** *adv.*

gŭt'-tȳ, *n.* (*Golf*) A guttapercha ball; গাটাপারচা নির্ম্মিত গলফ্ ক্রীড়ার বল।

guy (gĭ), *n.* & *v. t.* A rope etc. to steady any suspended weight or hold tent etc. in place; বিলম্বিত ভার স্থির রাখিবার জন্য রজ্জু, তাঁবুর রজ্জু। *Verb t.* To keep steady or in position with a guy or guys; তাদৃশ রজ্জু দ্বারা যথাস্থানে রাখা।

guy (gĭ), *n., v. t.* & *i.* **1.** The effigy of Guy Fawkes paraded and burnt on the anniversary of the Gunpowder plot, Nov. 5; অগ্নিচূর্ণ-ষড়যন্ত্রের নায়ক গাই ফক্‌সের কুশপুত্তলিকা,—যাহা প্রদর্শনের পর ৫ই নভেম্বর দগ্ধ করা হয়। **2.** A person dressed grotesquely; a fright; অপরূপ পরিচ্ছদ পরিহিত ব্যক্তি, চোদলকুতকুত; বিকট মূর্ত্তি। **3.** (*Slang*) Act of decamping; as, to give the *guy* to (=to escape from); (ইতর ভাষায়) চম্পট, সরিয়া পড়ন, পিট্টান। *Verb t.* To exhibit in effigy; to ridicule; কুশপুত্তলিকা প্রদর্শন করা; বিদ্রূপ করা। *Verb i.* (*Slang*) To disappear secretly; সট্‌কান্ দেওয়া। **To do a guy**—To decamp; চম্পট দেওয়া, পিট্টান দেওয়া। **To give the guy to**—See GUY, *n.* 3.

gŭz'-zle (-zl), *v. i.* & *t.* To eat and drink greedily and frequently; গপ্‌গপ্ করিয়া খাওয়া। *Verb t.* To drink or swallow greedily; to use up as money in guzzling, (often with *away*); গপ্‌গপ্ করিয়া খাওয়া, ঢকঢক্ করিয়া পান করা; খাইয়া উড়াইয়া দেওয়া। **–zler,** *n.*

g̈ȳbe, *v. i.* & *t.* (Of fore-&-aft sails etc.) To swing from one side to the other; (পাইল প্রভৃতি) জাহাজের এক পার্শ্ব হইতে অপর পার্শ্বে ঘুরাইয়া নেওয়া। *Verb t.* To cause as a sail to gybe; পাইল জাহাজের একপার্শ্ব হইতে অপর পার্শ্বে ঘুরাইয়া নেওয়া।

g̈ȳle, *n.* **1.** Quantity of beer brewed at once; একেবারে যে পরিমাণ বীয়র মদ্য চোলাই করা হয়। **2.** A fermenting wort; a fermenting turn; গাঁজাইবার জন্য এক প্রকার গুল্ম; গাঁজানের জন্য পাত্র।

gym-kha'-nă (gĭm-kâ-, jĭm-kâ-), *n.* (*Anglo Ind.*) **1.** A public resort or meeting for athletic games etc.; ব্যায়াম, কুস্তি প্রভৃতির জন্য সাধারণ সমাগমস্থল বা সম্মিলন, ক্রীড়াপ্রাঙ্গণ, মল্লক্ষেত্র। **2.** Athletic sports display; মল্লক্রীড়া প্রদর্শন।

g̈ȳm-nā'-sĭ-ŭm, *n.* (*Pl.* -UMS, -A) **1.** A place for athletic exercises; ব্যায়াম-বিদ্যালয়, মল্লভূমি, মল্লাঙ্গন, মল্লযুদ্ধশালা, রঙ্গভূমি, রঙ্গাঙ্গন, আখ্‌ড়া। **2.** A continental esp. German school of the highest grade preparing for the universities; জর্ম্মণী প্রভৃতি দেশের উচ্চ বিদ্যালয়। **–al,** *adj.* Of, or relating to, the continental gymnasiums; জর্ম্মণী প্রভৃতি দেশের উচ্চ বিদ্যালয় সম্বন্ধীয়।

g̈ȳm'-năst, *n.* One who teaches or practises gymnastics; ব্যায়াম শিক্ষার্থী, ব্যায়াম-শিক্ষক, কুস্তিগীর, পলোয়ান, ডনগীর।

g̈ȳm-năs'-tic, *adj.* & *n.* **1.** Pertaining to athletic exercise of the body; ব্যায়ামসম্পর্কীয়, মল্লযুদ্ধবিষয়ক। **2.** Pertaining to disciplinary intellectual exercise; নিয়মানুবর্ত্তিতা বিধায়ক শিক্ষা সম্বন্ধীয়। ***Noun.*** **1.** A course of instruction, regarded as discipline; as, grammar is a good *gymnastic*; নৈতিক ও মানসিক বৈয়ামিকি বিদ্যা (বাৎস্য), নিয়মানুবর্ত্তিতা বিধায়ক শিক্ষা। **2.** (*Pl.*) Athletic exercises to strengthen the muscles and the bones (*lit.* & *fig.*); "Musical *gymnastics*"; মল্লযুদ্ধ, মল্লক্রীড়া, ব্যায়াম, কুস্তি, ডন।

g̈ȳm-nŏs'-ŏ-phist, *n.* One of a class of Hindu philosophers almost naked and given to contemplation; নাগা সন্ন্যাসী, যোগী। **–phy,** *n.* The doctrine of the gymnosophists; যোগশাস্ত্র।

g̈ȳn-æ cē'-ŭm (-ē-), *n.* **1.** (*Gk.* & *Rom. Antiq.*) The part or apartment reserved for females; পূর্ব্বকালে প্রাসাদের যে অংশে কেবল মহিলাগণ বাস করিত, অন্তঃপুর, অন্তঃগৃহ, জেনানামহল, অন্দরমহল, শুদ্ধান্ত, অবরোধ, অন্তর্নিবেশন (মঃ সং), অন্তর্মন্দির (দশঃ)। **2.** (*Bot.*) (Sometimes—ŒCIUM) Female organ of flower;

(উদ্ভিদ্-বিদ্যা) পুষ্পের স্ত্রী-চিহ্ন, স্ত্রীস্তবক (সাঃ পঃ)।

gȳ-năn′-drous (-drŭs), *adj.* (*Bot.*) Having the stamens and pistils united in one column as in orchids; (উদ্ভিদ্ বিদ্যা) পরাগ-কেশর ও গর্ভ-কেশর একই স্তম্ভে সংযুক্ত, যোষিৎ পুংস্ক (সাঃ পঃ)।

g̃ȳn′-ârch-ȳ, *n.* Government by a female or females; স্ত্রীলোকের রাজত্ব, স্ত্রী-তন্ত্র।

g̃ȳn-e(æ)-cŏc′-ră-c̃ȳ (-ë-), *n.* Government by a woman or women; female rule; petticoat rule; স্ত্রীতন্ত্র; স্ত্রী শাসন, নারীশাসন; স্ত্রীরাজ্য (কেণ্ডিঃ), স্ত্রীপ্রাধান্য (ঐ)।

g̃ȳn-e(æ)-cŏl′-ă-trȳ (-ë-), The extravagant adoration of women; বামার্চ্চনা, নারীপূজা।

g̃ȳn-e(æ)-cŏl′-ŏ-g̃ȳ (-ē-), *n.* The science dealing with the diseases of women; স্ত্রীরোগ বিজ্ঞান।

g̃ȳ-nŏc′-ră-c̃ȳ, *n.* Same as GYNAECOCRACY.

g̃ȳn′-ŏ-phōre, *n.* (*Bot.*) The pedicel or stock supporting the ovary; যোষিদ্বহ (সাঃ পঃ)।

Gynophore of passion-flower.

gȳp, *n.* (Cambridge and Durham) A college servant; (কেম্ব্রিজ ও ডারহামে) কলেজের ভৃত্য। **Gyp-room**—উক্ত ভৃত্যদিগের রুটি এবং অন্যান্য খাদ্যসামগ্রী রাখার কক্ষ।

g̃ȳp′-sŭm, *n.* A mineral from which Plaster of Paris is made; খড়িমাটীর ন্যায় খনিজ দ্রব্য বিশেষ—ইহা দগ্ধ করিয়া চূর্ণ করিলে Plaster of Paris প্রস্তুত হয়। **—se-ous,** *adj.*

g̃ȳp′-sȳ, g̃ĭp′—, *n.* **1.** One of a vagabond race scattered over many countries of Europe and living by basket-making, fortune-telling, etc.; ভ্রমণশীল জাতি বিশেষ, ইহারা চৌর্য্যবৃত্তি, ভাগ্য গণনা প্রভৃতি দ্বারা জীবিকা নির্ব্বাহ করে, যাযাবর, হাবড়িয়া। **2.** (Playfully) A mischievous woman; a dark complexioned woman; (কৌতুকচ্ছলে) দুরন্ত মেয়ে; শ্যামাঙ্গী। **—dom, —hood, —ism,** *ns.* **—fy,** *v. t.* (*Usu. pl*). **—ish,** *adj.* **Gypsy bonnet** or **hat**—স্ত্রীলোক বা শিশুর চওড়া কিনারাওয়ালা টুপি। **Gypsy-rose** — শ্বেত, নীল, গোলাপী প্রভৃতি নানা রংয়ের পুষ্পপ্রসূ গুল্ম বিশেষের সাধারণ নাম। **Gypsy table** — তেপায়ার উপর স্থাপিত গোলাকার হালকা মেজ।

gȳ′-rāte, *adj.* (*Bot.*) Winding in a circle; arranged in rings; কুণ্ডলিত; চক্রাকারে সজ্জিত।

gȳ′-rāte, *v. i.* To turn round; to move spirally; to revolve or whirl; ঘুরা; পাক খাওয়া, ভ্রাম্যমাণ হওয়া; ঘূর্ণিত হওয়া। **—ra′-tion,** *n.* Act of moving round; a spiral motion; revolution; ঘূর্ণন; আবর্ত্ত গতি, ঘূর্ণি; পাক, আবর্ত্তন। **—ra-to-ry,** *adj.* ঘূর্ণনশীল।

gȳre, *v. i.* & *n.* (*Poet.*) To gyrate; (কবিতায়) ঘূর্ণিত হওয়া, ঘুরা, পাক খাওয়া। ***Noun.*** A circular motion; gyration; ঘূর্ণি; ঘূর্ণন, আবর্ত্তন।

gȳ′-rö-grăph, *n.* A device for recording revolution; চক্রঘূর্ণির সংখ্যা লেখনের জন্য যন্ত্র বিশেষ, ঘূর্ণি-লেখক।

gȳ′-rö-măn-c̃ȳ, *n.* Divination practised by walking in a circle till the person falls from dizziness, the prognostic being drawn from the direction of the fall; ভবিষ্যৎ কথনের উপায় বিশেষ—ইহাতে কোন ব্যক্তি ঘুরিতে ঘুরিতে মাথায় ভ্রমি দিয়া পড়িয়া গেলে পতনের দিক্ ও প্রকার হইতে ভবিষ্যৎ বলা হইত।

gȳ′-rö-scōpe, *n.* **1.** An apparatus illustrating dynamics of rotating bodies; ভ্রাম্যমাণ বস্তুর গতি প্রদর্শক যন্ত্র। **2.** A rapidly spinning wheel fixed on something; কোন কিছুর উপর সংবদ্ধ দ্রুত ভ্রাম্যমাণ চক্র।

gȳ′-rōse, *adj.* (*Bot.*) Marked with wavy lines; undulate; (উদ্ভিদ্ বিদ্যা) তরঙ্গায়িত রেখা দ্বারা চিহ্নিত; তরঙ্গায়িত।

gȳve, *n.* & *v. t.* (*Usu. pl.*) A shackle or fetter; শৃঙ্খল, নিগড়। ***Verb. t.*** (*Poet.*) To shackle or fetter; নিগড়িত করা, শৃঙ্খলবদ্ধ করা।

H

H, 1. The eighth letter of the English alphabet; ইংরাজী বর্ণমালার অষ্টম অক্ষর। **2** (*Chem.—Cap.*) A symbol denoting hydrogen; (রসায়ন-শাস্ত্র) উদজন বাষ্পের সাঙ্কেতিক চিহ্ন।

hă, *interj.* & *v. i.* An exclamation of surprise, joy, grief, doubt, triumph, etc.; হাঁ, এঁ, অ্যাঁ, আহা, অহো। ***Verb i.*** To exclaim *ha* in hesitation; এঁ এঁ করা, অ্যাঁ অ্যাঁ করা।

haaf (hâf), *n.* **1.** (In Shetland and Orkney) A deep-sea fishing ground; (সেট্‌ল্যাণ্ড এবং অরকেনিতে) গভীর-সমুদ্র মৎস্য শিকারস্থলী।

hā′-bē-ăs—cŏr′-pŭs, *n.* (*Lat.* = *You must have the body*) A writ to a jailor to produce a prisoner before a court or judge and show the reason of his confinement; (ল্যাটীন-ভাষায় সশরীরে হাজির করিতে হইবে) বন্দীকে বিচারালয়ে উপস্থিত করার জন্য এবং তদীয়

THE MODERN ANGLO-BENGALI DICTIONARY

THE MODERN ANGLO BENGALI DICTIONARY

(In 6 Volumes)

(Volume-3)

CHARUCHANDRA GUHA

Publications

KALPAZ PUBLICATIONS

DELHI - 1100052

THE MODERN ANGLO- BENGALI DICTIONARY

ISBN : 81-7835 - 484 - 5 (Set)
ISBN : 81 - 7835 - 487 - X (Vol.3)

Rs. 4500 (Set)

Published in 2007 in India by
Kalpaz Publications
C - 30, Satyawati Nagar,
Delhi - 110052
E-mail : kalpaz@hotmail.com

Laser Typesetting at : Tact Computer, Delhi
Printed at : Mehra Offset Press, Delhi

H

H, **1.** The eighth letter of the English alphabet; ইংরাজী বর্ণমালার অষ্টম অক্ষর। **2** (*Chem.—Cap.*) A symbol denoting hydrogen; (রসায়ন-শাস্ত্র) উদজন বাষ্পের সাঙ্কেতিক চিহ্ন।

ha, *interj.* & *v. i.* An exclamation of surprise, joy, grief, doubt, triumph, etc.; হাঁ, এঁ, অ্যাঁ, আহা, অহো। ***Verb i.*** To exclaim *ha* in hesitation; এঁ এঁ করা, অ্যাঁ অ্যাঁ করা।

haaf (hâf), *n.* **1.** (In Shetland and Orkney) A deep-sea fishing ground; (সেট্‌ল্যাণ্ড এবং অরকেনিতে) গভীর-সমুদ্র মৎস্য শিকারস্থলী।

hā'-bē-ăs–cŏr'-pŭs, *n.* (*Lat.*= *You must have the body*) A writ to a jailor to produce a prisoner before a court or judge and show the reason of his confinement; (ল্যাটীন-ভাষায় সশরীরে হাজির করিতে হইবে) বন্দীকে বিচারালয়ে উপস্থিত করার জন্য এবং তদীয়

(এই অঞ্চলে সাধারণতঃ সঙ্গতিহীন ব্যক্তিগণ বাস করিয়া থাকে)। **East-Indian**—ভারতবাসী। **Far east**—চীন, জাপান প্রভৃতিদেশ। **Near-east**—তুরস্ক ও তন্নিকটবর্ত্তী দেশ সমূহ।

Eas'-têr (ës-), *n.* A Christian festival observed in commemoration of Jesus Christ's resurrection, occurring on Sunday after Good-Friday; যীশুখৃষ্টের পুনরুত্থানের স্মৃতি-সূচক পর্ব্ব বিশেষ — এই পর্ব্ব গুড্ ফ্রাইডের পরবর্ত্তী রবিবারে অনুষ্ঠিত হয়। **Easter-day, –Sunday**—যে রবিবার দিবস ঈষ্টার পর্ব্ব অনুষ্ঠিত হয়। **Easter-eggs**—ঈষ্টার পর্ব্বোপলক্ষে ব্যবহৃত ডিম্ব। **Easter-eve**—ঈষ্টার পর্ব্বের পূর্ব্ব দিবস। **Easter-week**—ঈষ্টার পর্ব্বের দিবস হইতে যে সপ্তাহের আরম্ভ হয়।

east'-êr-lŷ (ëst-), *adj.* & *adv.* In an eastern position or direction; (blowing) from the east; as, *easterly* wind; পূর্ব্বদিকে, পূর্ব্বাভিমুখে; পূর্ব্বদিক্ হইতে প্রবহমান।

east'-êrn (ëst-), *adj.* & *n.* Dwelling in the east; towards the east; being in the east; পূর্ব্বদেশীয়, প্রাচ্য; পূর্ব্বাভিমুখীন; পূর্ব্বদিকস্থ। ***Noun.*** An inhabitant of the east; a member of the *eastern* church; পূর্ব্বদেশবাসী, প্রাচ্যদেশবাসী; গ্রীস, রুষ প্রভৃতি দেশীয় খৃষ্টীয় ধর্ম্মসঙ্ঘের সভ্য। **–most,** *adj.* **Eastern Church**—গ্রীস, রুষ প্রভৃতি দেশের খৃষ্টীয় ধর্ম্ম। **Eastern question** — ইয়ুরোপের পূর্ব্বদিগ্‌বর্ত্তী, বিশেষতঃ তুরস্ক দেশ সংক্রান্ত রাজনৈতিক প্রশ্ন।

east'-ing (ëst-), *n.* Departure in an easterly direction; easterly direction; পূর্ব্বদিকে যাত্রা; পূর্ব্বদিক্।

east'-ward (ëst-wêrd), *adj., n.* & *adv.* Moving or looking towards the east; পূর্ব্বদিগ্‌গামী; পূর্ব্বাভিমুখীন। ***Noun.*** The eastern direction; "Sailing to the *eastward*;" পূর্ব্বদিক্। ***Adv.*** (also EAST-WARDS) Toward the east; পূর্ব্বাভিমুখে।

eas'-ŷ (ëz-), *adj.* **1.** Free from trouble, pain; as, *easy* circumstances (স্বচ্ছল অবস্থা); উদ্বেগশূন্য আরামযুক্ত। **2.** Peaceful, as the mind; উদ্বেগশূন্য, শান্ত, আরামময়। **3.** Free from stiffness or constraint; as, *easy* manners; সলীল, স্বচ্ছন্দ, অবাধ, নিঃসঙ্কোচ। **4.** (*Comm.*) Not in much demand; (of market) not showing much demand; অধিক চাহিদাশূন্য, নরম; মন্দা। **5.** Not difficult; সহজ, অকঠিন, সহজসাধ্য, অনায়াসসাধ্য, সুগম, সুসাধ্য, সুকর। **6.** Compliant or tractable; as, an *easy* victim; বশ্য, বচনগ্রাহী, অনুকূল, বিনেয়, প্রণেয়। **7.** Comfortable; as, an *easy* chair; আরামপ্রদ, আরামদায়ক। **8.** Given to ease or idleness; "The *easy* colonist;" আরামপ্রিয়, শ্রমকুণ্ঠ, আলস্যপরবশ। **9.** Gentle; moderate; as, to be proved by *easy* stages; মৃদু, ধীর; পরিমিত। **10.** Affluent; as, *easy* circumstances; সুখস্বাচ্ছন্দ্যপূর্ণ, স্বচ্ছল। **–i-ly,** *adv.* In an easy manner; without difficulty; with ease; স্বচ্ছন্দভাবে, সহজে, অবলীলাক্রমে; অক্লেশে, অনায়াসে; নিরুপদ্রবে। **–i-ness,** *n.* **Easy-chair**—আরামকেদারা। **Easy-going**—(অশ্বসম্বন্ধে) লীলাগতি, ঢিলা, আরামপ্রিয়, শ্রমবিমুখ। **A woman of easy virtue**—স্খলিতচরিত্রা স্ত্রীলোক, যে স্ত্রীলোক সহজেই সতীধর্ম্ম বিসর্জ্জন করে। **Easy-come easy-go**—যাহা অক্লেশে লাভ করা যায়, তাহা সহজেই ব্যয় করা যায়।

eas'-ŷ (ëz-), *adv.* & *n.* In an easy manner; as, to take it *easy*; নিরুদ্বিগ্নচিত্তে। ***Noun.*** A short rest; স্বল্পবিশ্রাম।

eas'-ŷ (ëz-), *Int.* (A command) Move gently; ধীরে চালাও। **Easy all**—Stop, esp. rowing; থাম, বিশেষতঃ দাড়টানা বন্ধ কর।

eat (ët), *v. t.* & *i.*, *n.* **1.** To masticate and swallow one's solid food; আহার করা, খাওয়া, চিবাভ্যস্ত। **3.** Constant; usual; "Their *habitual* success": *habitual* topic; নিত্য; প্রাত্যহিক, সাচরাচরিক। **–ly,** *adv.* **–ness,** *n.*

hă-bit'-ū-āte, *v. t.* **1.** To accustom to: "Minds not *habituated* to accurate thinking"; অভ্যস্ত করা, অভ্যাস করা। **2.** (*U. S.*) To frequent; সর্ব্বদা গতিবিধি করা। **–a'-tion,** *n.* The state of being habituated; অভ্যস্ততা (হিঃ কোঃ)।

hăb'-i-tūde, *n.* **1.** Physical or mental constitution; মানস প্রকৃতি, অন্তঃপ্রকৃতি, দেহ-প্রকৃতি, শরীরের ধাত। **2.** Long custom; tendency; habit; চিরপ্রচলিত প্রথা; প্রবণতা, ঝোঁক, আসক্তি; রীতি, অভ্যাস।

habitue, (*F.*) *n.* A habitual frequenter or resident; as, a *habitue* of a theatre; যে ব্যক্তি সর্ব্বদা কোন স্থানে গতিবিধি করে অথবা নিয়ত কোন স্থানে বাস করে, নিত্যযাত্রী, চিরবাসী।

hachures, (*F.*), *n.* (*Pl.*) Lines used in drawing esp. hill-shading to indicate slopes; চিত্রাঙ্কণে প্রবণতা সূচক রেখাবলী।

hacienda, (*F.*), *n.* A large estate or farm with a dwelling house (in Spain or Spanish colonies); (স্পেন অথবা স্পেনাধিকৃত আমেরিকায়) সুবিস্তীর্ণ কৃষিক্ষেত্র বা ভূসম্পত্তি।

hăck, *n.* **1.** (*Falconry*) The board on which a hawk's meat is laid; (বাজপক্ষীদ্বারা শিকার) যে ফলকের উপর বাজপক্ষীর মাংস রক্ষিত হয়। **2.** A frame for drying bricks, fish, etc.; মৎস্য, ইষ্টক, প্রভৃতি শুষ্ক করার জন্য কাঠাম। **To be at hack**—(Of an eyas hawk) Not to be allowed to prey for itself; নিজের জন্য শিকার করিতে না পাওয়া।

hăck, *v. t.* & *i.* **1.** To cut irregularly; to notch; to mangle; কোপাইয়া কাটা; খাঁজ কাটা; কুচি কুচি করা, খোড়া। **2.** To kick the shins of (an opposing player at foot-ball); ফুটবল খেলায় অপর পক্ষের খেলোয়াড়ের জঙ্ঘায় পদাঘাত করা। *Verb i.* **1.** To deal cutting blows (*at*); কোপান। **2.** To cough in a short broken manner; খক্ খক্ করিয়া কাশা। **A hacking cough**—A short dry frequent cough; খক্ খক্ কাশি।

hăck, *n.* & *adj.* **1.** A horse kept for hire; a jade; ভাড়াটীয়া ঘোড়া; অকর্ম্মণ্য অশ্ব। **2.** A hackney carriage (now in *U. S.*); ভাড়াটীয়া গাড়ী (বর্ত্তমানে মার্কিণ যুক্তরাজ্যে)। **3.** A horse for everyday riding; সদা সর্ব্বদা চড়িবার জন্য ঘোড়া। **4.** A drudge, esp. a literary one; কঠোর পরিশ্রমজনক কার্য্যে নিযুক্ত দাস, বেতনভোগী লেখক। **5.** (*Obs.*) A procuress; (অপ্রঃ) দূতী, কুট্টনী। *Adj.* Hired; mercenary; as, a *hack* writer; ভাড়াটীয়া; বৈতনিক; বেতনভোগী। **Hack work**—Work done by a hired drudge; the work of a literary hack; ঠিকালোকের কাজ; বেতনভোগী লেখকের কাজ। **Hack writer**—One who writes for hire; পেশাদার লেখক, যে ব্যক্তি টাকা লইয়া অন্যের জন্য পুস্তকাদি লিখিয়া দেয়, বেতনভোগী লেখক।

hăck, *v. t.* & *i.* **1.** To use frequently; to make common; to hackney; সদা সর্ব্বদা ব্যবহার করা; সাধারণ করা; পুরাতন করা, নূতনত্বহীন করা। **2.** To employ as a literary hack; বেতন দিয়া লেখকের কাজে নিযুক্ত করা। **3.** To ride as a horse, on a road at an ordinary pace; সাধারণ গতিতে ঘোড়া দৌড়ান। *Verb i.* **1.** To be offered to common use for hire; অর্থ গ্রহণে সাধারণের উপভোগ্য হওয়া, গণিকাবৃত্তি অবলম্বন করা। **2.** To live the life of a drudge; to be a literary hack; বেতন লইয়া কঠোর শ্রমজনক কার্য্য করা; পেশাদার লেখকের কাজ করা; বেতনভোগী লেখকের কাজ করা। **3.** To ride a horse at an ordinary pace on a road etc.; সাধারণ গতিতে ঘোড়া চালান।

hăck, *n.* **1.** A pick; a mattock or hoe; খনিত্র; খন্তা, গাঁতি। **2.** A gash or wound as from a kick at football; গভীর ক্ষত, জখম।

hăck, *n.* **At hack (heck) and manger**—Extravagantly; অতিমাত্রায়।

hăck'-êr-ў, *n.* **1.** An Indian bullock cart; (ভারতবর্ষে) গোযান, গরুর গাড়ী।

hăck'-le (-l), *n.* & *v. t.* **1.** A steel comb for dressing flax, raw silk, etc.; পাট, শণ, কাঁচা রেশম প্রভৃতি আঁচড়াইবার জন্য ইস্পাতের কাঁটা। **2.** Long pointed feathers on the neck of a cock and other birds; গৃহপালিত কুক্কুট এবং অন্যান্য পক্ষীর কণ্ঠদেশস্থ দীর্ঘ এবং সূক্ষ্মাগ্র পালকগুচ্ছ। **3.** An artificial fly for angling dressed with such a feather; কুক্কুটাদির গ্রীবাদেশের পালকদ্বারা সজ্জিত বড়শীর টোপস্বরূপ ব্যবহৃত কৃত্রিম মক্ষিকা। *Verb t.* To dress (flax etc.) with hackle; শণ, পাট ইত্যাদি কাঁটাদ্বারা আঁচড়াইয়া পরিষ্কার করা। **With his hackles up** — (Of a cock, dog, man) Angry; ready to fight; ক্রুদ্ধ; যুদ্ধার্থ প্রস্তুত।

hăck'-le (-l), *v. t.* To cut roughly; to mangle; কোপাইয়া কাটা, থোড়া; কুচি কুচি করিয়া কাটা, খণ্ড খণ্ড করিয়া কাটা, ছিন্ন ভিন্ন করা। **—ly,** *adj.* Rough; jagged; খস্‌খসে, আব্‌ড়ো থাব্‌ড়ো; খাঁজ-কাটা।

hăck'-ney (-nē), *n., adj.* & *v. t.* **1.** A horse kept for hire (*obs.*); ভাড়াটীয়া ঘোড়া। **2.** A horse for ordinary riding; সচরাচর আরোহণের জন্য অশ্ব। **3.** A hired drudge; a hireling; হাড়ভাঙ্গা খাটুনির কাজে নিযুক্ত ঠিকা লোক; বেতনগ্রাহী ভৃত্য। **4.** A carriage kept for hire; ভাড়াটীয়া গাড়ী, ঠিকা গাড়ী, ছেকরা গাড়ী। *Adj.* Let out or kept for hire; as, a *hackney* coach; ভাড়াটীয়া। *Verb t.* (esp. *p. p.* **—neyed**) To devote to common use; to make commonplace or trite; সাধারণের উপভোগ্য করা; নীরস করা, নূতনত্বহীন করা, পুরাতন করা। **—neyed,** *p. p.* Much used; commonplace; as, a *hackneyed* joke or phrase; অতিশয়ব্যবহৃত, বহুপ্রযুক্ত; নিত্যব্যবহৃত, সাধারণ, বৈচিত্র্যশূন্য, নূতনত্বহীন, পুরাতন, নীরস। **Hackney coach, -carriage**—See HACKNEY, *adj.* **Hackneyed joke** or **phrase**—See HACKNEYED, *p. p.*

hăd, *p. t.* & *p. p.* of HAVE.

hăd'-dŏck, *n.* A kind of sea-fish allied to cod; একপ্রকার আহারোপযোগী সামুদ্রিক মৎস্য।

hāde, *v. i.* (*Mining* & *Geol.*) To incline from the vertical; প্রবণ হওয়া, ঢালু হওয়া।

Hā'-dēs, *n.* (*Gk. Myth.*) The nether world; the abode of departed spirits; (গ্রীক পুরাণ) অধোভুবন, অধোলোক; যমলোক প্রেতলোক, প্রেতাত্মাদিগের বাসভূমি।

Hadj'-ī (hăj-), **Hăj'-ji** (-ī), *n.* A Mohammedan pilgrim to Mecca; the title of such a Mohammedan; মক্কাযাত্রী মুসলমান; হাজি।

haec-cē'-i-tў (hĕk-), *n.* (*Philos.*) Thisness; individuality; (দর্শনশাস্ত্র) ইদংতা (হিঃ কোঃ), বস্তুতা (ঐ); ব্যক্তিত্ব, পুরুষবিধত্ব।

hae'-măl (hē-), **hē'—,** *adjs.* **1.** (*Anat.*) Of, or pertaining to, the blood; (শারীর-সংস্থান-বিদ্যা) রক্তসম্বন্ধীয়, শোণিত-সম্পর্কীয়। **2.** Situated on the side of the spinal cord where the heart and great blood vessels are placed; হৃৎপিণ্ড এবং বৃহৎ রক্তবহা নাড়ী সকল দেহের যে পার্শ্বে অবস্থিত তৎপার্শ্বস্থ।

hae-măt'-ic (hē-), *adj.* & *n.* Of, relating to, or containing, blood;

রক্তসম্পর্কীয়, রক্তপূর্ণ। ***Noun.*** A medicine acting on the blood; রক্তের উপর ক্রিয়াকারী ঔষধ, রক্ত-বিশোধক ঔষধ।

hae'-mă-tin (hē-), *n.* (*Chem.*) A bluish black amorphous substance existing as a constituent of haemoglobin; (রসায়ন-শাস্ত্র) লোহিত রক্তকণিকার রঞ্জকবস্তুর উপদানীভূত নীলাভকৃষ্ণ নিরবয়ব পদার্থ বিশেষ, লোহিতক।

haem'-ă-tīte (hĕm-), *n.* An iron ore of red, brown or blackish colour; গৈরিক (সাঃ পঃ), গিরিসিন্দুর।

haem-ă-tŏl'-ŏ-ġȳ (hĕm-), **hĕm—,** *ns.* The science of blood; শোণিত-বিজ্ঞান, রক্ততত্ত্ব।

hae-mŏ-glō'-bin (hē-), **hē—,** *ns.* The colouring matter of the red corpuscles of the blood; লোহিত রক্তকণিকার রঞ্জক বস্তু, রাগদ।

Hae'-mŭs (hē-), *n.* Boreuas এবং Orithyaর পুত্র। Haemus ও তৎপত্নী Rhodope প্রগল্‌ভতাপূর্ব্বক দেবরাজ Zeus ও দেবরাণী Heraর নাম গ্রহণ করাতে শাস্তিস্বরূপ পর্ব্বতে পরিণত হয়।

haem'-or-rhoids (hĕm-ŏr-ōydz), **hĕm—,** *ns.* (*Pl.*) Piles; রক্তস্রাবী অর্শ, অন্ত্রপিত্ত (সাঃ পঃ), রক্তপ্রবাহ (ঐ), রক্তপিত্ত (ঐ), লোহিত পিত্ত (ঐ)।

hă'-fiz, *n.* A Mohammedan who knows the Koran by heart; a title of respect; সমগ্র কোরাণ কণ্ঠস্থ আছে এরূপ মুসলমান ধর্ম্মাবলম্বী লোক; সম্মানসূচক উপাধি বিশেষ।

Hăf'-găn, *n.* ব্রিটিশ কেল্ট জাতির পাতালবাসী দেবতা বিশেষ।

hăft, *n.* & *v. t.* A handle or hilt of knife, sword, dagger, etc.; বাঁট। ***Verb t.*** To furnish as a knife etc. with a handle; ছুরি প্রভৃতিতে বাঁট লাগান।

hăg, *n.* **1.** An ugly old woman; কুৎসিতা বৃদ্ধানারী, জরতী (প্রাঃ সদঃ)। **2.** (*Formerly*) A female evil spirit; (পূর্ব্বে) ডাকিনী, যোগিনী, রাক্ষসী। **3.** A witch; ডাইনী, শাকচুন্নী। **Hag'-gish,** *adj.* **Hag-ridden**—Affected with night-mare; স্বপ্নে বুকে চাপ প্রাপ্ত।

hăg, *n.* **1.** A soft bog in a moor etc.; জলাভূমি প্রভৃতির নরম জায়গা। **2.** A firm spot in a bog; জলাভূমির কঠিন জায়গা।

hăg'-gȧrd, *adj.* & *n.* **1.** Lean, weak and hollow-eyed (as a result of fatigue or worry); gaunt; as, a *haggard* look; কৃশ এবং কোটর-প্রবিষ্টচক্ষুঃ; কৃশ, ক্ষীণকায়, অস্থিচর্ম্মসার, কাহিল, শীর্ণ, বিশীর্ণ। **2.** (Of a hawk) Untamed; অপোষা। ***Noun.*** A haggard hawk; অপোষমানানো বাজপাখী। **—ly,** *adv.* **—ness,** *n.*

hăg'-gis, *n.* A dish made of heart, lungs and liver of a sheep or lamb, boiled in a maw with suet, oatmeal, onion, etc.; কুচি কুচি করিয়া কাটা মেষ বা মেষশাবকের কলিজা, ফুস্‌ফুস এবং মেটের সহিত যইএর ময়দা, পেঁয়াজ-বাটা, চর্ব্বি প্রভৃতির সহযোগে প্রস্তুত ব্যঞ্জন বিশেষ।

hăg'-gle (-l), *v. t., i.* & *n.* To cut or mangle; কোপান, কোপাইয়া কাটা। ***Verb i.*** To be difficult in bargaining; to dispute, (with *over, about*); দর কষাকষি করা, দর-দস্তুর করা; বাগ্‌বিতণ্ডা করা, খেঁচাখেঁচি করা, কচাল করা। ***Noun.*** Wrangling about terms; dispute, (with *about, over*); দরদস্তুর, দরকষাকষি; বাগ্‌বিতণ্ডা, বাদানুবাদ।

hăg'-ĭ-âr-chy, *n.* Government, or order, of saints; government by holy persons; সিদ্ধপুরুষতন্ত্র, সিদ্ধপুরুষ সমাজ, মহাপুরুষমণ্ডলী; যাজক-তন্ত্র।

hăg-ĭ-ŏc'-ră-cȳ, *n.* Government by holy persons; যাজকতন্ত্র।

Hăg-ĭ-ŏg'-ră-phă, *n.* The last of the three Jewish divisions of the Old Testament; ইহুদীগণ কৃত প্রাচীন নিয়মের বিভাগত্রয়ের মধ্যে সর্ব্বশেষ বিভাগ। **—o-graph'-ic,** *adj.*

hăg-ĭ-ŏg'-ră-phêr, *n.* A writer of Hagiographa or hagiography; প্রাচীন নিয়মের সর্ব্বশেষ বিভাগ সম্পর্কীয় গ্রন্থ লেখক, সিদ্ধপুরুষগণের জীবনী লেখক।

hăg'-ĭ-ŏg-ră-phȳ, *n.* The biography of the saints; সাধু মহাপুরুষদিগের জীবনী, খৃষ্টীয় সিদ্ধপুরুষগণের জীবনী।

hăg-ĭ-ŏl'-ŏ-ġȳ, *n.* Literature dealing with lives and legends of saints; a catalogue of saints; খৃষ্টীয় সিদ্ধপুরুষ-চরিত, সিদ্ধজীবনী; ভক্তমাল।

Hague (The) (hăg), *n.* হলণ্ডদেশের নগরী বিশেষ। **Hague Tribunal**—অন্তর্জাতিক বিরোধ মীমাংসার জন্য উক্ত নগরীতে প্রতিষ্ঠিত স্থায়ী বিচারালয়। [এই বিচারালয় ১৮৯৯ খৃঃ অব্দে অন্তর্জাতিক শান্তিসমিতির নির্দ্ধারণানুসারে প্রতিষ্ঠিত হয়।]

hah (hâ), *interj.* & *v. i.* See HA.

hâ-hâ', *n.* A sunk fence, wall or ditch; দূর হইতে অদৃশ্য বৃতি, প্রাচীর বা পরিখা।

hâ'-hâ, *interj.* An interjection indicating laughter; হি হি, হো হো।

hai(c)k (hāk), *n.* An outer garment worn by the Arabs; আরব দেশীয়গণ কর্তৃক ব্যবহৃত একপ্রকার পশমী বা সূতি আলোয়ান।

hail (hāl), *n.* Frozen drops of rain etc.; শিলা, করকা, বর্ষোপল। [Some purely Sanskrit synonyms:—পয়োঘন ঘনকফ, মেঘাস্থি, মেঘকফ, তোয়ডিম্ব, পিণ্ডাভ্র, শিলীন্ধ্র।] **Hail'-y,** *adj.* **Hail storm**—A storm accompanied with hail; a shower of hail; শিলাবৃষ্টি সহকৃত ঝঞ্ঝা; শিলাবর্ষণ, করকপাত। **Hail-stone**—শিলা, করকা, বর্ষোপল, ঘনোপল, হিমখণ্ড, পয়োঘন।

hail (hāl), *interj.* An exclamation of salutation or greeting; "*Hail* brave friend"; জয়োঽস্তু, জয়জয়, নমস্কার স্বস্তি। **Hail fellow**—(*Obs.*) An intimate friend; (অপ্রঃ) প্রাণের বন্ধু, পরাণ বন্ধু (রবি)। **Hail fellow, Hail fellow well**

met—Intimate ; as, to be *hail fellow* or *hail fellow well met* with any one ; অন্তরঙ্গ, হরিহরাত্মা।

hail (hāl), *v. i.* & *t.* (*Impersonally*) To fall as hail ; (*fig.*) to come down violently ; শিলাবৃষ্টি হওয়া, শিল পড়া ; (লক্ষণায়) প্রচণ্ডবেগে পতিত হওয়া। ***Verb t.*** To shower down like hail, as words, blows, etc. ; শিলাপাতের মত বর্ষণ করা, বর্ষণ করা।

hail (hāl), *v. t.*, *i.* & *n.* **1.** To salute ; to greet ; to designate in greeting ; as, they *hailed* him king or as king ; অভিবাদন করা, বন্দনা করা ; সম্বর্দ্ধনা করা, অভ্যর্থনা করা ; আখ্যাত করা, অভিহিত করা। **2.** To call to in order to draw attention ; to accost ; as, to *hail* a ship or person ; ডাকা ; সম্ভাষণ করা। ***Verb i.*** To come, (with *from*) ; as, the steamer *hails from* Narayanganj : he *hails from* Dacca ; আসা। ***Noun.*** Act of hailing ; a salutation ; as, to be within *hail* (to be near enough to be hailed) ; সম্ভাষণ ; অভিবাদন, বন্দনা। **To hail from**—See *v. i.*

hair (hār), *n.* **1.** A thread-like filament or filaments collectively growing from the skin of an animal, esp. from the human head ; কেশ, চুল, লোম, রোম, কুন্তল,

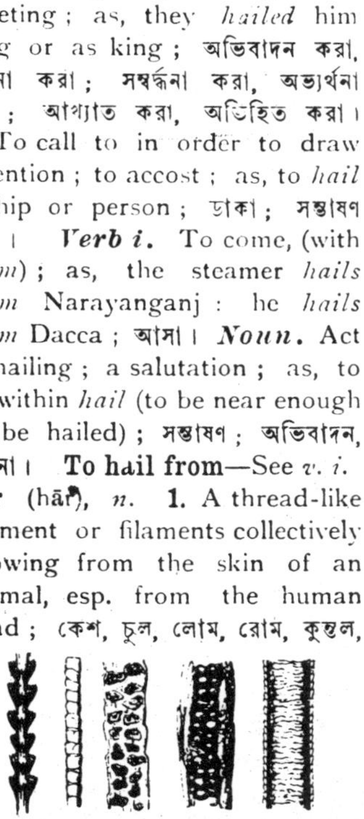

Hairs of various animals magnified.

চিকুর, কচ, বাল, শিরোরুহ, তনূরুহ মূর্দ্ধজ। **2.** (*Bot.*) A minute hair-like filament on the epidermis ; (উদ্ভিদ্-বিদ্যা) রোম। **3.** A hair like thing ; কেশবৎ বস্তু। **4.** A jot ; বিন্দুবিসর্গ, লেশমাত্র। **Haired,** *adj.* **Hair'-i-ness,** *n.* **Hair'-less,** *adj.* **Hair'-y,** *adj.* **Hair breadth, Hair's breadth**—*n.* & *adj.* The breadth of a hair, *i. e.* a very small distance ; কেশপ্রমাণ ব্যবধান। (*Adj.*) Very narrow ; as, a *hairbreadth* escape ; অত্যন্ত সংকীর্ণ, অল্পের জন্য। **Hair-brush** — চুল আঁচড়াইবার বুরুস, কেশমার্জ্জনী। **Hair-cloth** — একপ্রকার লোমনির্ম্মিত বস্ত্র। **Hair dresser**—কেশপ্রসাধক, চুল ছাঁটা নাপিত। **Hair dressing**—কেশবিন্যাস, কেশ রচনা। **Hair-dye**—চুলের কলপ। **Hair line**—চুলের ডোর ; কেশ হইতে প্রস্তুত বড়শীর সূক্ষ্ম সূতা। **Hair-like,** *adj.* **Hair-net**—কেশ আচ্ছাদনের জন্য জাল। **Hair-oil**—কেশ তৈল। **Hair pencil** — চিত্রকরদিগের সূক্ষ্ম তুলিকা। **Hair pin** — চুলের কাঁটা। **Hair powder**—চুলে মাখিবার জন্য সুগন্ধি চূর্ণ, কেশচূর্ণ। **Hair space**—(মুদ্রণে) শব্দদ্বয়ের মধ্যে অতি অল্প ফাঁক রাখার জন্য যে সূক্ষ্ম হরফ ব্যবহৃত হয়। **Hair splitter**—অতিরিক্ত সূক্ষ্মবিচারী ব্যক্তি। **Hair-splitting**—*adj.* & *n.* Over subtle ; চুল-চেরা, সূক্ষ্ম-বিচারী (*Noun*) Making of overnice distinctions ; অতি সূক্ষ্ম প্রভেদ নিরূপণ। **Hair-spring**—টেঁক ঘড়ীর কেশবৎ সূক্ষ্ম তারের দম। **Hair stroke**—লেখার উপরের দিকে অতি সরু টান। **Hair trigger**—বন্দুকাদির দ্বিতীয় টিপকল—যাহা স্পর্শমাত্র প্রধান টিপকল উঠিয়া থাকে। **Against the hair**—Against the nature or grain ; প্রকৃতির বিরুদ্ধে, প্রতিলোমভাবে। **Both of a hair**—Both alike ; উভয়েই তুল্য, এক গোয়ালের গরু। **Hair standing on end** — Hair standing erect through astonishment or fright ; ভয়ে কণ্টকিত, রোমাঞ্চিত, হৃষ্টরোমা (গীতা)। **Not to touch a hair of one's head**—Not to do even the slightest injury to any one; কাহারও কেশাগ্র স্পর্শ না করা। **Not to turn a hair**—No to be discomposed or disturbed ; to show no sign of fatigue ; অবিচলিত থাকা ; ক্লান্তি বা অবসাদের চিহ্ন প্রদর্শন না করা। **Not worth a hair**—অতি অকিঞ্চিৎকর। **To a hair, To the turn of a hair** — Exactly ; চুলমাত্র ব্যতিক্রম না করিয়া, এক চুল তফাৎ না করিয়া। **To comb a person's hair the wrong way** — To irritate a person by running counter to one's prejudices, opinions, etc. ; কোন ব্যক্তির মত বা সংস্কারের বিরুদ্ধে চলিয়া তাহাকে চটান। **To have a hairbreadth escape**—অল্পের জন্য বাঁচিয়া যাওয়া, চুলে চুলে রক্ষা পাওয়া। **To keep ones' hair on**—(*Slang*) To keep cool ; ঠাণ্ডা থাকা। **To let down the hair**—(In toilet) To keep the hair hanging ; চুল ছাড়িয়া দেওয়া, চিকুরদাম বিলম্বিত করা। **To put** or **turn up the hairs (of** or **at)**—To dress the hair up on the head instead of keeping it hanging ; কেশবিন্যাস করা, বেণী বন্ধন করা, চুল বাঁধা। **To split hairs**—To be unduly and uselessly nice in making distinctions ; অতিরিক্ত সূক্ষ্ম বিচার করা, অনর্থক খুঁটিনাটি করা, চুল চিরে বিচার করা। **To take a hair of the dog that bit you**—(From the ancient idea that it was cure for hydrophobia) To drink a little more to cure the effects of previous heavy drinking ; অতিরিক্ত মদ্যপান জনিত অবসাদ দূর করার জন্য অল্প মাত্রায় ব্রাণ্ডি পান করা, খোঁয়ারি ভাঙ্গা। [কুকুর-দংশন জনিত জলাতঙ্করোগে দংশনকারী কুকুরের রোম ক্ষতস্থানে লাগাইলে কুকুর-দষ্ট ব্যক্তি আরোগ্য লাভ করে স্কটলণ্ড দেশবাসিগণের মধ্যে প্রচলিত এই বিশ্বাস হইতে এই বাক্যটী উদ্ভূত হইয়াছে]।

Hake.

hāke, *n.* A kind of sea-fish ; একপ্রকার সামুদ্রিক মৎস্য।

hāke, haik (hāk), *ns.* A wooden framework for drying bricks and other purposes ; কাঁচা ইট প্রভৃতি শুকাইবার জন্য কাঠের কাঠাম।

hâ kim′ (-kēm), *n.* A Mohammedan physician ; হাকিম।

ha′-kim (-kēm), *n.* (India and Mohammedan countries); Judge; ruler ; হাকিম, বিচারক ; শাসনকারী।

hăl′-bêrd, –bêrt, *ns.* A weapon in which spear and battle axe

Halberd.

are combined ; সম্মিলিত বর্শা ও পরশু, টাঙ্গী। **–ier,** *n.* One armed with a halberd ; টাঙ্গীধারী ব্যক্তি।

hăl′-cȳ-ŏn, *n.* & *adj.* A kind of bird fabled by the ancients to lay eggs in nests on the sea at the winter solstice to produce calm weather for the purpose ; গড়িয়াল (যোঃ), খয়রামাথা, মাছরাঙ্গা পক্ষিবিশেষ। [এই পক্ষী উত্তরায়ণের পূর্ব্বে সমুদ্রে প্লবমান নীড়ে ডিম্ব পাড়িয়া ১৪ দিন ব্যাপিয়া তা দিত। এই কালে সমুদ্র শান্তমূর্ত্তি ধারণ করিত বলিয়া প্রাচীন গ্রীকগণের বিশ্বাস ছিল।] ***Adj.*** Calm ; শান্ত। **Halcyon days**—সুখসমৃদ্ধির কাল।

Halcyon fulviventer—মাছরাঙ্গা (বেলঃ)।

Halcyon fuscus—সাদা বক (বেলঃ)।

Halcyon leucocephalus—গড়িয়াল (বেলঃ)।

hāle, *adj.* Healthy ; robust (esp. of the old) ; সুস্থ ; সবল। **Hale′-ness,** *n.*

hāle, *v. t.* (*Archaic*) To pull, draw or drag forcibly (*lit.* & *fig.*) ; (অপ্রঃ) সবলে টানা বা আকর্ষণ করা।

half (hâf), *n., adj.* & *adv.* (*Pl.* HALVES.) One of two equal parts into which a thing is divided or considered as divided ; as, the *half* of 4 is 2 ; অর্দ্ধাংশ, অর্দ্ধভাগ। ***Adj.*** **1.** Consisting of one of two equal parts ; as, a *half* share ; আধা, অর্দ্ধ। **2.** Partial ; imperfect ; as, *half* knowledge ; আংশিক, আধখেচরা (*colloq.*) ; অসম্পূর্ণ। **3.** (Sometimes it is viewed as noun with *of* omitted) ; as, *half* the men : *half* a pound ; অর্দ্ধেক। ***Adv.*** **1.** To the extent of a half ; to some extent or degree ; as, *half* cooked : *half* done ; partially ; অর্দ্ধপরিমাণে, সমপরিমাণে, সমাংশে ; কিয়ৎপরিমাণে ; অল্পমাত্রায়, আংশিকভাবে, অংশতঃ। **2.** (With a negative) Not by great deal ; very little or not at all ; as, not *half* bad : he does not *half* like it ; ততটা নয় ; অত্যল্প বা মোটেই নয়। **Better half**—Wife ; অর্দ্ধাঙ্গিনী, স্ত্রী, অর্দ্ধাঙ্গ। **Half-back**—পাদগোলক ক্রীড়ায় সম্মুখবর্ত্তী ক্রীড়কদলের অব্যবহিত পশ্চাদ্দেশে স্থিত ক্রীড়কদ্বয়ের অন্যতর ; ঐ ক্রীড়কের অবস্থানস্থল। **Half-baked**—(*Fig.*) Incomplete ; not thorough ; not earnest ; অসম্পূর্ণ ; অসম্যক্ ; নিমরাজি। **Half-binding**—একপ্রকার বাঁধাই,—যাহাতে পুস্তকের পৃষ্ঠ ও কোণ চামড়া দ্বারা এবং উভয় পার্শ্ব কাপড় দ্বারা বাঁধানো হয়। (*Half-bound, adj.*) **Half-blood**—A person having one parent in common with another ; this relationship ; (also) a person of mixed nationality ; একই পিতা বা মাতার সন্তান, অন্যপিতৃজ, অন্যমাতৃজ ; ঐরূপ সম্পর্ক ; বিভিন্ন জাতীয় স্ত্রীপুরুষের সংসর্গজাত সন্তান। **Half-blooded**—Born of different races ; বিভিন্নজাতীয় স্ত্রীপুরুষের সংসর্গজাত। **Half-boot**—যে বুট জুতা দ্বারা পায়ের গুল্‌ফদেশমাত্র আবৃত হয়, আগুল্‌ফপাদুকা। **Half-bred**—অর্দ্ধশিক্ষিত ; সংকীর্ণযোনি (মঃ সং), জাতিসঙ্কর। **Half-breed**—সঙ্কর জাতীয় লোক। **Half-brother, –sister**—বৈমাত্রেয় বা বৈপিত্রেয় ভ্রাতা অথবা ভগ্নী, অন্যপিতৃজ বা অন্যমাতৃজ ভ্রাতা বা ভগিনী। **Half-burnt**—আধ-পোড়া, অর্দ্ধদগ্ধ। **Half-caste**—*n.* & *adj.* A half-breed, esp. a child ; জাতিসঙ্কর ব্যক্তি, বিশেষতঃ শিশু। (*Adj.*) Born of European and Indian parents ; ভারতবাসী ও ইয়ুরোপীয়ের সংসর্গজাত, ফিরিঙ্গী। **Half-cock**—বন্দুকের ঘোড়া অর্দ্ধেকটা উঠিয়া যে ঘাটে আট্‌কায়। **Half crown** — ইংলণ্ডে প্রচলিত রৌপ্যমুদ্রা বিশেষ,—মূল্য ২ শিলিং ৬ পেন্স। **Half dead** — অর্দ্ধমৃত, আধমরা, মৃতকল্প। **Half-dollar**—মার্কিণ যুক্তরাজ্যের রৌপ্যমুদ্রা (প্রায় ১৸৹ টাকা)। **Half-done**—অর্দ্ধপক্ব, অর্দ্ধসিদ্ধ। **Half-eaten**—অর্দ্ধোপভুক্ত। **Half-educated**—অর্দ্ধশিক্ষিত। **Half-hearted**—উৎসাহশূন্য, অনুরাগশূন্য, উদাসীন। (*Half-heartedly, adv. Half-heartedness, n.*) **Half-holiday**—যে দিন অর্দ্ধেক ছুটি পাওয়া যায়, অর্দ্ধানধ্যায়। **Half-length**—শরীরের উপরার্দ্ধের চিত্র। **Half-mast**—মৃত ব্যক্তির প্রতি সম্মানপ্রদর্শনার্থ বা বিপৎ সূচনার্থ মাস্তুলের অগ্রভাগ হইতে ঈষৎ নিম্নে যে স্থানে পতাকা বাঁধা হয়। **Half-mast high**—*Adj.* (Of a flag) Lowered to half-mast ; (পতাকা সম্পর্কে) মাস্তুলাগ্র হইতে ঈষৎ নিম্নে অবনমিত। **Half measure**—উদ্দেশ্য সাধনের পক্ষে অপ্রচুর নয়। **Half-moon**—অর্দ্ধচন্দ্র, অষ্টমীর চন্দ্র, চন্দ্রখণ্ড ; অর্দ্ধচন্দ্রাকার বস্তু। **Half-mourning**—A costume in which black is relieved by grey etc. ; যে পরিচ্ছদের কৃষ্ণবর্ণের গাঢ়তা ধূসর প্রভৃতি বর্ণ দ্বারা কতকটা প্রশমিত করা হয়, অর্দ্ধশোকপ্রকাশক পরিচ্ছদ। **Half-naked** — অর্দ্ধনগ্ন, অর্দ্ধ উলঙ্গ। **Half-pay**—নৌ বা সামরিক বিভাগের কর্ম্মচারিগণকে অবসরগ্রহণের পর বা যুদ্ধাদি

ব্যতিরিক্তকালে যে অর্দ্ধেক বা তন্ন্যূন বেতন প্রদান করা হয়। **Half-seas-over**—Half drunk ; আধমাতাল, নেশায় চুরচুর, মদ্যপানে অর্দ্ধমত্ত (cf. মধ্যেন মদেন মত্তঃ—নিদান)। **Half-starved**—অনশনক্লিষ্ট, আধ-পেটা। **Half-timer** — যে ছাত্র দিবসের অর্দ্ধভাগ বিদ্যালয়ে পাঠ করে এবং অপরার্দ্ধভাগে অর্থোপার্জ্জন করে। **Half-tint**—মাঝামাঝি রঙ্গ (অর্থাৎ খুব ঘন কিম্বা খুব ফিকা নয়)। **Half-tone block**—চিত্রফলক বিশেষ—এই ফলকে আলো ও ছায়ার নিবিড়তার তারতম্য আলোকচিত্রণের সাহায্যে উৎপাদিত ক্ষুদ্র ক্ষুদ্র বিন্দু সমূহ দ্বারা প্রদর্শিত হইয়া থাকে। **Half-truth**—আংশিক সত্য উক্তি, সত্যাভাস। **Half-way**—*adv.* & *adj.* In the middle ; midway ; মধ্যপথে ; অর্দ্ধ পথে। (*Adj.*) Situated at an intermediate point ; মধ্যপথে অবস্থিত। **Half-way-house**—নগরদ্বয়ের মধ্যপথে অবস্থিত পান্থশালা। **Half-willing**—নিমরাজি। **Half-witted**—Weak in intellect ; foolish ; হীনবুদ্ধি ; নির্ব্বোধ। **Half-yearly**—*adj.* & *adv.* Happening every half year ; ষাণ্মাষিক, অর্দ্ধবার্ষিক। (*Adv.*) Every half year ; বৎসরে দুইবার। **By halves**—Equally ; imperfectly ; partially ; as, to do a thing *by halves* ; সমাংশে, সমপরিমাণে, আধাআধি, অর্দ্ধাঅর্দ্ধি ; অসম্পূর্ণরূপে ; আধখেচরা করিয়া, আংশিক ভাবে। **Half a loaf is better than no bread**—নেই মামার চেয়ে কাণা মামাও ভাল। **Half and half**—*n.* & *adj.* What is half of one thing and half of another ; esp. a mixture of beer and ale ; যাহাতে এক জিনিষের অর্দ্ধেক ও অপর জিনিষের অর্দ্ধেক আছে ; অর্দ্ধেক বীয়র ও অর্দ্ধেক এল মদ্যের মিশ্রণে প্রস্তুত পানীয় বিশেষ। (*Adj.*) Languid ; spiritless ; as, *half and half* enthusiasm ; ঢিলা, ঢিমা ; নিস্তেজ। **Half is more than the whole**—It is better to be satisfied with half when the whole is at stake ; সর্ব্বনাশে সমুৎপন্নে অর্দ্ধং ত্যজতি পণ্ডিতঃ। **Half the battle**—অর্দ্ধেক সিদ্ধি, অর্দ্ধেক সাফল্য। **In half** or **into halves**—In two parts (equal or otherwise) ; as, to cut a thing *in half* ; দুই সমান অংশে, দ্বিধা, দ্বিভাগে। **Not half**—See HALF. *Adv.* 2. মোটেই না। **Not half-bad**—See HALF *Adv.* 2. **To cry halves**—To claim equal share ; অর্দ্ধাংশ দাবী করা, সমান অংশ দাবী করা। **To go halves** (*with* a person, *in* a thing) To share equally ; তুল্যাংশে ভাগ করিয়া লওয়া, সমাংশে ভাগ করিয়া লওয়া, আধাআধি করিয়া লওয়া।

half-pĕn-nŷ (hā-), *n.* অর্দ্ধ পেনি, আধ পেনি। **Halfpenny worth** (usu. Pronounced *hapeth*), **h'p'orth**—অর্দ্ধ পেনি মূল্যের, আধ পেনির। **A bad half-penny**—That which is supposed to return to the owner however often he tries to get rid of it ; যে অর্দ্ধ পেনি পরকে দিয়া উদ্ধার পাওয়ার জন্য শত চেষ্টা সত্ত্বেও তাহা ঘুরিয়া বার বার তাহার হাতে ফিরিয়া আসে বলিয়া কল্পিত হয়।

hăl'-i-bŭt, hŏl- *ns.* A kind of flat marine fish used for food ;

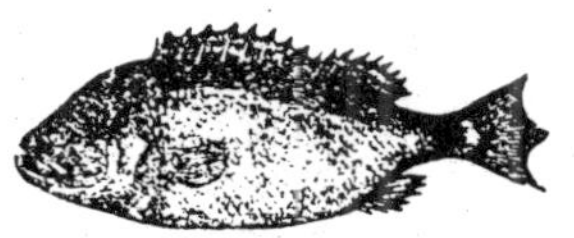

Halibut.

একপ্রকার চ্যাপ্টা, বৃহৎ এবং সুখাদ্য সামুদ্রিক মৎস্য।

hăl'-i-dŏm, *n.* (*Archaic*) Holiness ; a sacred thing, (*used chiefly in oath*) ; "By my *halidom*" ; পবিত্রতা ; পবিত্র বস্তু।

hăl-i-eu'-tic (-ü-), *adj.* & *n.* Of, or relating to, fishing ; মৎস্যশীকার সম্পর্কীয়। ***Noun.*** (*Pl.*) The art or practice of fishing ; ichthyology ; মৎস্যশিকার ; মৎস্যবিজ্ঞান।

hall, *n.* **1.** A large room at the entrance of a house ; a passage or corridor in a building ; কোন গৃহের প্রবেশদ্বারস্থ সুবৃহৎ কক্ষ, শালা ; মণ্ডপ (শুক্রঃ)। **2.** A big spacious public room in a palace ; লোকসাধারণের সম্মিলনের জন্য রাজপ্রাসাদস্থ বৃহৎ কক্ষ। **3.** A large building or room for public purposes as for meetings etc. ; a building of a guild ; সুবৃহৎ সভামণ্ডপ পণভবন। **4.** The residence of a landed proprietor ; a court house ; ভূস্বামীর বাটী, জমিদার বাড়ী ; বিচারালয়। **5.** The name of certain colleges at Oxford and Cambridge ; অক্সফোর্ড ও কেম্ব্রিজের কোন কোন কলেজের নাম। **6.** (*Eng. Univ.*) The great room in which the students dine together ; hence also, the dinner itself ; (বিশ্ববিদ্যালয়ে) ছাত্রগণের সুবৃহৎ অপরাহ্নভোজন-কক্ষ ; অপরাহ্নভোজন। **7.** An apartment in which the servants dine ; ভৃত্যদিগের অপরাহ্নভোজনশালা। **Hall-mark**—*n.* & *v. t.* স্বর্ণরৌপ্যাদির বিশুদ্ধতা সূচক চিহ্ন, ছাপ ; অকৃত্রিমতার চিহ্ন। (*Verb t.*) To stamp with a hall-mark ; সোণার উপর ছাপ দেওয়া। **Liberty Hall**—যে স্থানে কেহ স্বাধীনভাবে যাহা ইচ্ছা তাহা করিতে পারে, স্বাধীনতামন্দির, কামাচারভবন। **Hall of audience**—দেওয়ানী আম, দেওয়ান খানা, দরবার।

Haliastur Indus — শঙ্করচিল (বেলঃ)।

hăl-lĕ-lu'-jah (-lô-yȧ), *n.* See ALLELUIA.

hăl'-liard (-yârd), *n.* See HALYARD.

hăl-lō', -loa (-lö), *interj.*, *n.* & *v. i.* An interjection drawing attention or expressing surprise ; ওহে ! হাহা ! অহো ! ***Noun.*** The cry *hallo* ; হ্যালো শব্দে চীৎকার, হলহলা। ***Verb i.*** To cry *hallo* ; হ্যালো হ্যালো রবে ডাকা বা চীৎকার করা।

hăl-lōō′, *interj.* & *n.* An interjection inciting dogs to the chase, calling attention or expressing surprise ; লে লে ; ওহো ! হাহা ! অহো ! ***Noun.*** The shout halloo ; হ্যালো শব্দে চীৎকার।

hăl′-lōō, *v. i.* & *t.* To cry out to draw attention or to incite dogs or other animals ; as, to *halloo* to a man or dog ; হ্যালো শব্দে চীৎকার করা, লে লে করা। ***Verb t.*** **1.** To encourage or urge on with shouts ; as, he *halloed* his hounds again ; লেলে শব্দে লেলান। **2.** To call or shout to, to draw attention ; হ্যালো শব্দে চীৎকার করিয়া ডাকা। **3.** To shout (something) aloud ; চীৎকার করা। **Do not halloo until you are out of the wood**—Do not rejoice before you are quite out of danger ; সম্পূর্ণরূপে বিপন্মুক্ত হওয়ার পূর্ব্বে আনন্দে অধীর হইও না।

hăl′-low (-lō), *v. t.* **1.** To make holy ; পবিত্র করা, পূত করা। **2.** To regard as holy ; পবিত্র বলিয়া শ্রদ্ধা করা, পবিত্র বলিয়া মান্য করা। **3.** (*Archaic*) To set apart for religious purposes ; (অপ্রঃ) পবিত্র কার্য্যের জন্য পৃথক করিয়া রাখা, ধর্ম্মোদ্দেশ্যে স্বতন্ত্র করিয়া রাখা।

hăl′-low (-lō), *n.* A holy person ; a saint (now only in *all hallows, hallowmas*) ; সাধু ; মহাপুরুষ, সিদ্ধপুরুষ। **Hallowmas**—খৃষ্টীয় মহাপুরুষদিগের সম্মানার্থ উৎসববিশেষ।

hal′-low (-lō), *v. t.* & *i.* **1.** To pursue with shouts ; চীৎকার করিয়া অনুসরণ করা। **2.** To incite with shouts ; লে লে করিয়া লেলান। ***Verb i.*** To cry or shout to incite dogs etc. ; কুকুর প্রভৃতিকে লেলাইবার জন্য লে লে করিয়া চীৎকার করা।

hăl-lū′-cĭ-nāte, *v. t.* To produce a false idea or impression in the mind of (a person) ; ভ্রান্ত ধারণা জন্মান, ভ্রান্ত সংস্কার উপজাত করা।

hăl-lū-cĭ-nā′-tion, *n.* **1.** Delusion ; ভ্রান্তি, মোহ, চিত্তবিভ্রম, ধীবিভ্রম, মায়ামরীচিকা, মতিবিভ্রম, চিত্তভ্রান্তি, ভ্রম। **2.** Perception of external objects with no reality ; অবাস্তব বস্তু দর্শন বা অতীন্দ্রিয় বিষয়ের কল্পনা, প্রত্যক্ষভ্রম (হিঃ কোঃ), ভ্রান্তপ্রত্যক্ষ (ঐ)। **—lu′-ci-na-to-ry,** *adj.*

halm (häm), *n.* See HAULM.

hăl′-mă, *n.* A kind of game played on a chequer board of 256 squares ; এক প্রকার ক্রীড়া।

hā′-lō, *n.* & *v. t.* **1.** A luminous circle round the sun, moon, etc. ; চন্দ্র বা সূর্য্যের চতুর্দ্দিকস্থ জ্যোতির্বলয়, পরিবেষ (যোঃ), অংশুমালা, পরিধি (কেণ্ডিঃ), প্রকাশমণ্ডল (হিঃ কোঃ), প্রভামণ্ডল (ঐ)। **2.** The disc of light round the head of a god or saint in painting ; (দেবতা বা সিদ্ধ পুরুষদিগের) ছটামুকুট, দ্যুতিমণ্ডল (কৃষ্ণ কঃ), প্রভামণ্ডল (রঃ), কিরণকিরীট, প্রভা (হিঃ কোঃ), তেজোমণ্ডল (ঐ)। **3.** An ideal glory investing a person or an object ; "Encircled by a *halo* of literary glory" ; গৌরবমুকুট, মহিমাকিরীট। **4.** A coloured circle round a nipple, a vescicle etc. ; চুচুক, ফোস্কা প্রভৃতির চতুর্দ্দিকস্থ রঞ্জিতমণ্ডল, স্তনাগ্রবর্ণমণ্ডল, আনীলস্তনাগ্রমণ্ডল। ***Verb t.*** To surround or encircle with a halo ; প্রভামণ্ডলদ্বারা পরিবেষ্টন করা, জ্যোতির্বলয় দ্বারা পরিবৃত করা।

hăl′-oid (-ōyd), *adj.* & *n.* (*Chem.*) In composition like that of common salt ; (রসায়ন-শাস্ত্র) লবণবৎ। ***Noun.*** Haloid salt ; লবণবৎ বস্তু।

hält, *v. i., t.* & *n.* To stop temporarily on a march or journey ; পথিমধ্যে বিশ্রাম করা। ***Verb t.*** (*Mil.*) To cause to cease marching ; (সামরিক শাস্ত্র) কুচ করিয়া যাওয়ার কালে থামা। ***Noun.*** A stop in a march or journey ; an arrest of progress ; পথিমধ্যে বিশ্রাম, বিশ্রাম; গতিভঙ্গ, গতিরোধ। **Halting place** — অভিযানকালে বিশ্রামস্থান বিশ্রামস্থলী।

hält, *v. i.* & *n.* **1.** To walk unsteadily or hesitatingly ; শঙ্কিত ভাবে চলা, টলিতে টলিতে চলা, অস্থির পদে চলা, কম্পিত পদে চলা। **2.** To hesitate ; to vacillate ; as, to *halt* between two opinions ; ইতঃস্তত করা ; দ্বিধা করা। **3.** To be defective ; as, *halting* argument or verse ; খুঁত থাকা, অসম্পূর্ণতা থাকা, ত্রুটী থাকা। **4.** (*Archaic*) To walk lamely ; (অপ্রঃ) খোঁড়াইয়া খোঁড়াইয়া চলা। ***Noun.*** (*Archaic*) A halting or limping ; (অপ্রঃ) থামন, খোঁড়াইয়া চলন, নেংচান। **Halt′-ing,** *adj.* **Halt′-ing-ly,** *adv.* **The halting foot of justice**—The slow but sure punishment which follows wrongdoers ; অন্যায়কারিগণের বিলম্বিত অথচ স্থিরনিশ্চিত দণ্ড। **To halt between two opinions** — To be in a dilemma ; দুই নৌকায় পা দেওয়া, দোটানায় পড়া।

hält, *adj.* (*Archaic*) Lame ; limping in walking ; (অপ্রঃ) খঞ্জ ; খোঁড়াইয়া খোঁড়াইয়া চলে—এরূপ।

hält′-ẽr, *n.* & *v. t.* **1.** A rope with noose or headstall for a horse or other animal ; অশ্বাদির গলায় বাঁধিবার দড়ী, কণ্ঠপাশ, অশ্বাভিধানী (সাঃ পঃ)। **2.** A rope for hanging criminals ; hence, death by hanging ; ফাঁসির দড়ী ; ফাঁসি দ্বারা মৃত্যু। ***Verb t.*** **1.** To fasten with a halter ; অশ্বাদির গলদেশে রজ্জু বন্ধন করা। **2.** To hang with halter ; ফাঁসি দেওয়া।

halve (hâv), *v. t.* **1.** To divide into two equal parts ; to share equally ; as, to *halve* a fruit ; আধাআধি ভাগ করা, সমান দুই অংশে বিভক্ত করা ; সমাংশে গ্রহণ করা। **2.** To reduce to half ; অর্দ্ধাংশে পরিণত করা ; অর্দ্ধেক করা। **3.** To fit together (two pieces of wood) by cutting away half the thickness of each ; প্রত্যেকের বেধের অর্দ্ধেক কাটিয়া দুই খণ্ড কাঠ জোড়া দেওয়া, পাতাম তোলা (Dacca)।

hăl′-yărd, hăl′-liard (-yărd), **haul′-yărd** (hăl-), *ns.* The rope for hoisting or lowering sails, yards, etc.; জাহাজের পাইল, পাইল দণ্ড প্রভৃতি তুলিবার বা নামাইবার রজ্জু।

hăm, *n.* **1.** (*Formerly*) The hind part of the knee ; (পূর্ব্বে) জানুর পশ্চাদ্ভাগ। **2.** The back of the thigh ; the thigh and buttock, (*usually pl.*) ; উরুর পশ্চাদ্ভাগ ; নিতম্ব। **3.** The thigh of an animal, especially of a hog salted and dried in smoke for food ; খাদ্যার্থ লবণাক্ত ও শুষ্ক (শূকরের) জঙ্ঘা, রাং, দাব্না।

hăm, *n.* (*Hist.*) A town ; a village ; (ইতিহাস ; সহর ; গ্রাম।

hăm′-ă-dry̆-ăd, *n.* **1.** A wood-nymph who lived and died with the tree in which she dwelt ; গ্রীক ও রোমীয় পুরাণোক্ত তরুবাসিনী বনদেবী — আশ্রয়বৃক্ষের জীবনে ইঁহার জীবন এবং মৃত্যুতে মরণ। **2.** A venomous Indian serpent ; এক প্রকার বিষধর সর্প। **3.** A baboon of Abyssinia ; আবিসিনিয়া দেশীয় বানর বিশেষ।

Hăm′-burg (-bêrg), *n.* **1.** A city in Germany near the mouth of the Elbe ; জর্ম্মাণির নগর বিশেষ। **2.** A black species of grape (also *Hamburg grape*) ; একপ্রকার কালো রঙ্গের আঙ্গুর ফল। **3.** A small variety of domestic fowl ; এক জাতীয় ক্ষুদ্র গৃহপালিত মোরগ।

hāme, *n.* One of the two curved pieces of wood or metal forming the collar of a draught horse ; ভারবাহী ঘোটকের গলবন্ধনীস্বরূপ বক্র কাষ্ঠ বা ধাতুখণ্ডদ্বয়ের অন্যতর।

Hăm′-hit, *n.* A goddess of Egypt ; প্রাচীন মিশর দেশীয়গণের দেবী বিশেষ—এই দেবীর মস্তকে একটী মৎস্য শোভা পাইত।

Hăm′-īte, *n.* **1.** A descendant of Ham, the second son of Noah (*Gen.* x. 6.-20.) ; নোয়ার পুত্র হ্যামের বংশধরগণ। **2.** A member of the Egyptian or other African race ; মিসর দেশীয় লোক বা আফ্রিকা দেশের অন্যান্য জাতীয় লোক। **–it-ic,** *adj.*

hăm′-lĕt, *n.* A small village, esp. one without a church ; ক্ষুদ্র গ্রাম, পল্লীগ্রাম, পাড়া গাঁ [বিশেষতঃ যে গ্রামে খৃষ্টীয় ভজনালয় নাই]।

hăm′-mêr, *n.* **1.** An instrument for driving nails and beating metals etc. ; a machine with a metal block serving the same purpose ; হাতুড়ি, মুদ্গর ; কলের হাতুড়ি। **2.** Something resembling a hammer in form and function, *e. g.* the contrivance for striking to indicate the hour of a clock, for exploding charge in gun, for striking the string of a piano ; বন্দুকের ঘোড়া, পিয়ানোর তারে ঘা দিবার যন্ত্র। **3.** An auctioneer's mallet to strike the article with when it is sold ; নীলামকারীর ক্ষুদ্র হাতুড়ী। **–less,** *adj.* **Hammer-beam**—প্রাচীর হইতে উদ্গত ক্ষুদ্র কড়ি কাঠ,—যাহা বর্গার পাদদেশে আবদ্ধ থাকে। **Hammer cloth**—শকটচালকের আসনাচ্ছাদন বস্ত্র, গাড়ীর কোচ বাক্স ঢাকিবার কাপড়। **Hammer head**—The head of a hammer ; হাতুড়ির মাথা। A kind of shark ; এক প্রকার হাঙ্গর। A species of African bird ; আফ্রিকাদেশীয় পক্ষি-বিশেষ। **Hammer-man**—কর্ম্মকার। **Gone to the hammer**—Sent to a sale by auction ; নিলামে বিক্রয়ের জন্য প্রেরিত। **Hammer and tongs**—With might and main; violently ; মহাবলে ; খুব জোরে। **Knight of the hammer**—কর্ম্মকার। **They live at hammer and tongs**—They are always quarrelling ; তাহাদের আদা কাঁচকলা সম্বন্ধ। **To come under the hammer**—To be sold by auction ; নিলামে বিক্রয় হওয়া। **To go it hammer and tongs**—To act violently and recklessly ; to throw all one's energies into anything ; মরিয়া হইয়া লাগা ; উঠিয়া পড়িয়া লাগা। **To sell under the hammer, To bring to the hammer**—নিলামে বিক্রয় করা। **Up to the hammer**—First rate ; সর্ব্বশ্রেষ্ঠ, প্রথম শ্রেণীর।

hăm′-mêr, *v. t.* & *i.* **1.** To strike, beat or drive or shape with a hammer ; হাতুড়ি দ্বারা আঘাত করা পিটা বা পিটিয়া বসান, হাতুড়িদ্বারা পিটিয়া গড়া। **2.** To attack or work at assiduously ; বারংবার আক্রমণ করা, অভিনিবেশ পূর্ব্বক পাঠ করা। **3.** To device or contrive by intellectual labour, (with *out*) ; মাথা ঘামাইয়া বাহির করা। **4.** To force as an idea etc. (into a person's head) ; মাথায় ঢুকান। **5.** (*Colloq.*) To belabour ; উত্তম মধ্যম দেওয়া, পিটুনি দেওয়া, ঠেঙ্গান। ***Verb i.*** **1.** To strike repeated blows with or as with a hammer ; হাতুড়ী দ্বারা বা হাতুড়ীর মত পুনঃ পুনঃ আঘাত করা। **2.** To belabour hard ; to toil, (with *at*) ; উত্তম মধ্যম দেওয়া ; কঠোর পরিশ্রম করা। **To hammer an idea into a person's head**—See HAMMER *v. t.* 4. **To hammer at**—To work hard at ; হাড়ভাঙ্গা পরিশ্রম করা। **To hammer out**—To devise ; মাথা ঘামাইয়া বাহির করা।

hăm′-mŏck, *n.* A swinging bed

Sailor's hammock.

esp. for sailors ; জাহাজের নাবিকদিগের ঝোলা খাট, দোলন-শয্যা, হিন্দোল খট্টা, দোলনশয়ন (আঃ বঃ), ঝোলা,

Hammock chair — ক্যাম্বিসের দোলায়মান আসন।

hăm′-pêr, *n.* A large basket for packing things ; প্যাক করার জন্য বড় ঝুড়ি।

hăm′-pêr, *v. t.* & *n.* To obstruct the movement (of a person) by material obstacles ; hence, to hinder ; to embarrass ; গতিরোধ করা ; বাধা দেওয়া, প্রতিরোধ করা, ব্যাঘাত করা, প্রতিবন্ধকতা জন্মান ; ঝঞ্ঝাটে ফেলা। ***Noun.*** **1.** (*Obs.*) A shackle ; an obstacle ; নিগড় ; বাধা। **2.** A cumbrous but necessary part of the equipment of a vessel ; (নৌ-বিদ্যা) জাহাজের সাজ-সজ্জার অপরিহার্য্য অথচ প্রতিবন্ধকতা-জনক অংশ।

hăm′-shăck-le (-l), *v. t.* To shackle (an animal) with a rope binding the head with a foreleg ; রজ্জুদ্বারা ঘোড়ার মাথার সহিত একটী আগালি পা বাঁধা।

hăm′-stêr, *n.* A species of rat with two cheek-pouches for holding grain ; এক-প্রকার মুষিক—ইহাদের গালে ধান্যাদি রাখার জন্য দুইটী থলি আছে।

Hamster.

hăm′-strĭng, *n.* & *v. t.* A tendon of the ham ; জঙ্ঘাশিরা, মন্দিরশিরা। ***Verb t.*** To lame or cripple by cutting the hamstring ; জঙ্ঘা-শিরা কাটিয়া পঙ্গু করা।

hăm′-ū-lŭs, *n.* (*Anat. Zool.* & *Bot. Pl.* -LI.) A hook or hook-like process ; (শারীর-সংস্থান বিদ্যা, প্রাণিবিদ্যা, উদ্ভিদবিদ্যা) বড়িশ বা বঁড়িশের মত অস্থি প্রভৃতির বিবর্দ্ধিত অংশ।

hănd, *n.* **1.** The terminal part of the human arm beyond the wrist ; হস্ত, হাত, কর, পাণি [Some purely Sanskrit synoyms :—শয়, শম, পঞ্চশাখ, হরণ, ভুজাদন] ; **2.** The terminal part of all four limbs of an ape ; the fore-foot of a quadruped ; বানরের হস্ত ও পদের অন্ত্যভাগ ; চতুষ্পদ জন্তুর অগ্রপদ, আগালি পা। **3.** Something resembling a human hand ; the pointer of a clock or watch ; হাতের মত কোন কিছু ; ঘড়ীর কাঁটা। **4.** A linear measure of about 4 inches used chiefly in measuring the height of horses ; প্রায় চার ইঞ্চি রৈখিক মাপ (সাধারণতঃ অশ্বের উচ্চতা মাপে ব্যবহৃত হয়)। **5.** Pledge of marriage ; বিবাহের অঙ্গীকার, বাগ্‌দান। **6.** Side ; direction ; পার্শ্ব ; দিক্। **7.** Authority ; disposal ; as, it is in the *hands* of ; কর্ত্তৃত্ব ; হাত। **8.** One doing something with one's own hand ; a workman or labourer ; যে ব্যক্তি গায়ে খাটিয়া খায় ; শ্রমজীবী, শ্রমিক, মজুর। **9.** A person with some special faculty ; বিশেষ বৃত্তি বা ক্ষমতাসম্পন্ন ব্যক্তি। **10.** Agency ; as, by the *hand* of ; part in any action ; as, he has *hand* in it ; কর্ত্তৃত্ব ; কোন কার্য্যে সহযোগিতা। **11.** Handwriting ; as, he writes a good *hand* ; signature ; হস্তাক্ষর, হস্তলিপি ; স্বাক্ষর। **12.** Possession ; control ; management ; as, he could not keep the government in his own *hand* ; অধিকার ; শাসন ; নির্ব্বাহ, পরিচালনা। **13.** Source ; as, knowledge at first *hand* ; মূল, উৎপত্তিস্থল। **14.** Skill ; dexterity ; as, he has a *hand* for pastry ; চাতুর্য্য, পটুতা, নৈপুণ্য ; দক্ষতা। **15.** Style of execution ; as, to judge the *hand* of an artist ; touch ; সম্পাদনরীতি ; সংশোধন বা উৎকর্ষসাধনার্থ কলমের আঁক, তুলির স্পর্শ। **16.** (*Cards*) One of the players ; the cards dealt to a player ; (তাসখেলা) ক্রীড়কগণের অন্য-তম ; এক হাতের তাস। **17.** (*Cricket, billiard, etc.*) An inning or turn of play ; (ক্রীকেট প্রভৃতি খেলায়) খেলিবার পালা, বাজি। **18.** A fixed quantity of various commodities, *e. g.* a bundle of tobacco leaves ; নানা প্রকার জিনিষের নির্দ্দিষ্ট পরিমাণ। **Hand′-less,** *adj.* **1.** Without hands ; হস্তহীন, করহীন, নুলো, ঠুঁটা। **2.** Inefficient with the hands ; আনাড়ী। **Clean hands**—(*Fig.*) Innocence ; (লক্ষণায়) নির্দ্দোষতা। **Hand-bag**—হাত ব্যাগ, হস্তপেটিকা। **Hand-ball**—বল লুফালুফি খেলা ; ঐরূপ খেলার বল। **Hand-bell**—কাঁসর ; মেজের উপর রক্ষিত ঘণ্টা। **Hand-bill** — বিজ্ঞাপন। **Hand-book**—হাতে করিয়া নেওয়া যাইতে পারে এইরূপ পুস্তক, করণ (প্রবাসী ১৩২২)। **Hand-canter**—A gentle canter ; একপ্রকার কদম। **Hand-cart**—হাত গাড়ী, ঠেলা গাড়ী। **Hand-cuff**—*n.* & *v. t.* হাতকড়ি। (*Verb t.*) To confine or secure with manacles ; হাতকড়ি লাগান। **Hand-gallop**—An easy gallop ; তুরকী ছুটন। **Hand-glass**—Magnifying glass held in the hand ; হাতে ধরিয়া ব্যবহারের উপযোগী বিপুল-দর্শক কাচ ; হাতলওয়ালা ক্ষুদ্র আয়না। **Hand grenade** — হস্তদ্বারা নিক্ষিপ্ত বিস্ফোরক দ্রব্যপূর্ণ গোলা, হাত বোমা। **Hand-grip**—A grasping with the hand (either friendly or hostile) ; করমর্দ্দন। **Hand-hold** — বৃক্ষাদি আরোহণকালে যাহা হাতদ্বারা মুঠাইয়া ধরা হয়। **Hand-line**—যে বড়শীর সুতা হাতে ধরিয়া মাছ ধরা হয়। **Hand-loom**—তাঁত। **Hand-made**—Made by hand (opp. to *machine made*) ; হস্ত নির্ম্মিত, হাতে তৈয়ারী। **Hand-maid(en)**—A maidservant ; দাসী, পরিচারিকা (লক্ষণায় ভিন্ন কচিদ্ ব্যবহৃত হয়।) **Hand-mill**—হস্ত-চালিত যন্ত্র।

Hand-mill.

Hand-organ — একপ্রকার বাদ্যযন্ত্র

Hand-press — One operated by hand ; হস্তচালিত মুদ্রা-যন্ত্র। **Hand-rail**—সিঁড়ি প্রভৃতির কিনারার গরাদ। **Hand-shake**—করমর্দ্দন, করকম্পন। **Hand-writing**—হস্তলিপি হস্তাক্ষর, হাতের লেখা। **Hand wrought** — হস্তনির্ম্মিত। **Second hand**—See under SECOND. **A great hand at anything**—Very skilful or expert in it ; কোন কার্য্যে অতি নিপুণ বা সুদক্ষ, সিদ্ধহস্ত। **All hands**—The whole crew ; জাহাজের সকল মাল্লা। **An old hand**—An experienced person ; পাকা লোক, অভিজ্ঞ লোক। **At first hand**—Directly from the producer etc. ; as, to buy an article *at first hand* ; সাক্ষাৎসম্বন্ধে উৎপাদনকারীর নিকট হইতে। **At hand**—Near or close by ; about to happen ; soon ; হাতের কাছে, সন্নিকটে ; আসন্ন ; শীঘ্র। **At second hand**—Not from the producer ; through the intermediary ; উৎপাদনকারীর নিকট হইতে নয় ; কোন মধ্যবর্ত্তী ব্যক্তি হইতে। **At the hand (or hands) of**—From ; হইতে, হাতে। **By hand**—By manual labour ; হস্তদ্বারা (অর্থাৎ কলে নয়, হাতে)। **Cap in hand**—Humbly ; সসম্ভ্রমে, বিনীত ভাবে। **Empty hand is no lure for a hawk**—You must not expect anything without giving a return ; কোন জিনিষ অমনি পাইবে বলিয়া আশা করিও না। **For one's own hand**—For one's own advantage or interest ; for one's own account ; নিজের সুবিধা বা স্বার্থের জন্য ; নিজের জন্য। **From good hands**—From a reliable source ; বিশ্বস্ত সূত্রে। **From hand to hands**—From one person to another ; এক হাত হইতে অপর হাতে, হাতে হাতে, এক ব্যক্তির নিকট হইতে অপর ব্যক্তির নিকট। **From hand to mouth** — Without provision for the morrow ; as, to live *from hand to mouth* ; কষ্টে সৃষ্টে, ডাইনে আনতে বাঁয়ে কুলায় না এরূপ ভাবে, কায়ক্লেশে, আজ খাইলে কাল নাই এমন ভাবে। **Hand in (and) glove with**—Intimate with ; মাখামাখি, হরিহর আত্মা, গলাগলি, মাণিকজোড়। **Hand in hand**—With hands mutually clasped; conjointly ; হাতে হাতে ধরিয়া ; একযোগে। **Hand over hand**—With each hand successively passing over the other as in climbing a rope ; (*fig.*) rapidly or with steady advance ; ক্রমান্বয়ে হাতের উপর হাত রাখিয়া ; (লক্ষণায়) দ্রুতবেগে, ক্রমশঃ অগ্রসর হইয়া। **Hand over head**—Negligently; rashly; leisurely; তাচ্ছিল্যের সহিত, অবহেলার সহিত; বেপরওয়াভাবে; ধীরে সুস্থে। **Hands down**—Easily ; as, to win *hands down* ; অনায়াসে, অক্লেশে। **Hands off**—Keep off ; do not touch ; তফাৎ ; ছুঁইও না। **Hands up**—A direction to persons to raise their hands as a sign of assent etc. or to preclude resistance ; সম্মতি প্রভৃতি প্রকাশের জন্য হস্তোত্তলনের আদেশ, অস্ত্রশস্ত্র পরিত্যাগ পূর্ব্বক হাত উঠাইবার জন্য পুলিশ কর্ম্মচারীর আদেশ। **Hand to hand**—In close proximity ; as, a *hand to hand* contest ; হাতাহাতি। **He is my right hand**—He is my best man ; সে আমার দক্ষিণহস্তস্বরূপ। **His hand is out**—He is out of practice ; তিনি আর ব্যবসায় করেন না। **In hand**—Held in the hand ; under control ; at one's disposal ; under discussion ; করধৃত, হস্তধৃত ; শাসনাধীন ; কর্ত্তৃত্বাধীন ; আলোচ্য। **Note of hand**—হাত চিঠা। **Off hand**—Without previous preparation ; then and there ; না ভাবিয়া চিন্তিয়া ; উপস্থিত মত। **Off one's hands**—No longer under one's responsibilities ; হাতছাড়া। **On all hands, On every hand**—From or to all sides or quarters ; সকল দিক্ হইতে। **On hand**—In one's possession ; কাহারো হাতে, কাহারো অধিকারে। **On one's hands**—Under one's care or management ; resting on one as a responsibility ; কাহারো তত্ত্বাবধানে কাহারো দায়িত্বের উপর। **Out of hand**—At once ; promptly ; অগৌণে, তৎক্ষণাৎ ; অমনি। Completed ; done ; সম্পন্ন ; সমাপ্ত। Beyond control ; শাসনের বাহিরে। **On the one hand**—এ দিকে, এক পক্ষে। **On the other hand**—পক্ষান্তরে। **The handwriting on the wall**—The omen of an approaching catastrophe (Bible, Daniel v. 5-31) ; আসন্ন বিপদের পূর্ব্বাভাস। **To bear a hand** — (*Naut.*) To give assistance quickly ; ত্বরায় সাহায্য করা। To take part (*in*) ; যোগদান করা। **To be on the mending hand**—To be improving ; ক্রমশঃ উন্নতির পথে অগ্রসর হওয়া, ক্রমশঃ ভালর দিকে যাওয়া। **To bring up by hand**—To rear (an infant) without suckling ; স্তন্যপ্রদান না করিয়া শিশু পালন করা। **To change hands**—To pass from one person to another, as a property ; হস্তান্তরিত হওয়া। **To clap hands**—To express joy or approval by striking hands together ; হর্ষ বা অনুমোদন সূচক করতালি দেওয়া, করধ্বনি করা। **To come to hand**—To be received ; to turn up ; হস্তগত হওয়া ; আসিয়া পড়া। **To fight for one's own hand**—To look after one's own interest ; নিজের স্বার্থের দিকে দৃষ্টি রাখা। **To get or gain the upperhand**—To get the mastery ; প্রবল হওয়া। **To give one's hand upon anything**—To promise to fulfil an undertaking ; কোন কার্য্য সম্পাদনে প্রতিশ্রুত হওয়া। **To go hand in hand with**—To keep step with (*lit.* & *fig.*) ; অনুসরণ

করা, সঙ্গে সঙ্গে থাকা; অনুবর্ত্তী হওয়া। **To hand**—Within reach; into possession; as, the letter is *to hand*; হাতের কাছে; হস্তগত। **To have a hand**—To be concerned (*in*); হাত থাকা, সংশ্রব থাকা। **To have or keep one's hand in**—To be in practice; হাত ঠিক রাখা, অর্থাৎ কোন কাজে অভ্যাস ঠিক রাখা। **To have in hand**—To be engaged in; কোনও কাজ হাতে নেওয়া। **To have one's hands full**—To be pressed with work; হাতে অনেক কাজ থাকা। **To have upon one's hands**—To be responsible for; to have charge of; দায়ী থাকা; কোন কাজের ভার থাকা। **To hold in hand**—(*Obs.*) To keep in expectations; (অপ্রঃ) আশান্বিত রাখা। **To hold one's hands**—To do nothing or refrain from interfering; কোন কাজ না করা; হাত না দেওয়া, হস্তক্ষেপ না করা। **To keep in hand**--To direct or manage; পরিচালন করা, নির্ব্বাহ করা। **To lay hands on**—To seize; to touch; ধরা; হস্তার্পণ করা। **To lend a hand**—To assist; সাহায্য করা। **To live from hand to mouth**--See FROM HAND TO MOUTH. **To make a hand**—To gain advantage; to profit; সুবিধা করিয়া নেওয়া; লাভ করা। **To make a poor hand at**—To make little impression upon; to make very little progress with; মনে সামান্য মাত্র লাগা; সামান্য মাত্র অগ্রসর হওয়া। **To make no hand of**—To be unable to explain; বুঝাইতে না পারা। **To one's hands**—Ready for one; prepared; "Here's a subject made *to your hands*"; কাহারো জন্য প্রস্তুত; প্রস্তুত। **To put forth hand against**—To attack; আক্রমণ করা। **To put the last (or finishing) hand**—To give the last touch or polish to as a work of art etc.; শেষ চানকানদেওয়া। **To serve one hand and foot**—To serve assiduously; প্রাণপণে সেবা করা, কায়মনোবাক্যে সেবা করা। **To set the hand to**—To undertake; কোন কাজে হাত দেওয়া। **To shake hands**—To clasp the right hand mutually in token of friendship, greeting, etc.; করমর্দ্দন করা, করকম্পন করা। **To take in hand**—To undertake; to take charge of; to pay attention to; হাতে নেওয়া; ভার লওয়া; মন দেওয়া। **To take off one's hands**—To free from a burden; ভারমুক্ত করা। **To try one's hand at**—To try one's power to accomplish (a work); কোন কার্য্য সাধনে নিজের শক্তি পরীক্ষা করা। **To wait upon hand and foot**—To wait upon assiduously; অতি যত্নের সহিত পরিচর্য্যা করা। **To wash one's hands of (a business)**—To renounce all concern in; সংশ্রব ত্যাগ করা, হাত ধুইয়া ফেলা। **Under one's hand**—Under one's action, care, charge or treatment; কাহারও হাতে (কাহারও তত্ত্বাবধানে বা চিকিৎসাধীনে)। **Under the hand of**—With one's signature; কাহারো স্বাক্ষরযুক্ত। **With a heavy hand**—Severely; কঠোর হস্তে। **With a high hand**—Boldly; arrogantly; উদ্ধতভাবে; সগর্ব্বে। **With clean hands**—Innocently; নির্দ্দোষভাবে।

hănd, *v. t.* **1.** To give or transmit with the hand; as, to *hand* over a letter to a person; হস্তদ্বারা অর্পণ করা, হাতে করিয়া দেওয়া। **2.** To lead or guide with the hand; as, he *handed* a lady into or out of the carriage; হাত ধরিয়া গাড়ী প্রভৃতিতে তুলিয়া দেওয়া। **3.** (*Naut.*) To furl (as a sail); (পাইল) জড়ান, (পাইল) গুটান। **To hand down**—To transmit in succession, as traditions; as, *handed down* from generation to generation; পুরুষানুক্রমে সংক্রমণ করা, পুত্রপৌত্রাদিক্রমে অর্পণ করা। **To hand in**—To give in; to tender; as, to *hand in* an application; প্রদান করা; পেশ করা, দাখিল করা। **To hand on**—To transmit; হস্তান্তরিত করা। **To hand over** — To deliver over; অর্পণ করা, সমর্পণ করা, সম্প্রদান করা।

hănd'-fûl, *n.* (*Pl.* -s) **1.** As much as a hand can contain; এক মুঠা। **2.** A small number as of persons etc.; অল্প পরিমাণ, অল্প সংখ্যা, গোটা কয়েক। **3.** (*Colloq.*) A troublesome person or task; (চলিত-ভাষায়) উৎপাত।

hănd'-i-căp, *n.* & *v. t.* **1.** Special disadvantage imposed upon superior competitors in order to equalize chance of success in a race or contest of agility, strength or skill; প্রতিদ্বন্দ্বিগণের মধ্যে সমতাসাধনের জন্য শ্রেষ্ঠতর প্রতিযোগীর উপর যে অতিরিক্ত ভার বা অসুবিধা চাপান হয়। **2.** A race or contest so arranged; যে ঘোড়দৌড় প্রভৃতি প্রতিযোগিতার ক্রীড়ায় শ্রেষ্ঠতর প্রতিদ্বন্দ্বীর উপর অতিরিক্ত ভার চাপাইয়া কিম্বা দৌড় আরম্ভের পূর্ব্বে তাহাকে কতকটা পশ্চাতে রাখিয়া অথবা অন্য কোন প্রকারে প্রতিদ্বন্দ্বিগণের মধ্যে সমতা সাধিত হয়। ***Verb t.*** **1.** To put a handicap on; ঘোড়দৌড় প্রভৃতি প্রতিযোগিতার ক্রীড়ায় শ্রেষ্ঠতর প্রতিদ্বন্দ্বীর উপর অতিরিক্ত ভার বা অন্য কোনরূপ অসুবিধা চাপান। **2.** (*Fig.*) To place at a disadvantage; (লক্ষণায়) অসুবিধায় ফেলা। **-per,** *n.*

hănd'-i-crăft, *n.* **1.** Manual skill; হস্তকৌশল। **2.** Manual art; হস্তশিল্প। **Handicrafts man**—হস্তশিল্পী, কারিগর, শিল্পী, শিল্পকার।

hănd'-i-work (-wêrk), *n.* Work of the hand; a thing made by the hand; a work done personally;

হস্তশিল্প, হস্তক্রিয়া (কেডিঃ), হস্তকৃতি (ঐ); হস্তনির্ম্মিত বস্তু, হাতের তৈয়ারী জিনিষ; স্বয়ংকৃত কার্য্য।

hănd'-kêr-chief (-chĕf), *n.* **1.** A piece of cloth for wiping face etc.; রুমাল। **2.** A neckcloth; (also *neck-handkerchief, neck-kerchief*): গলায় বাঁধিবার রুমাল। **To throw the handkerchief to** — (কোন কোন ক্রীড়ায়) রুমাল নিক্ষেপ করিয়া পশ্চাদ্ধাবন করিতে ইঙ্গিত করা; অতঃপর কাহাকে বক্তৃতা প্রদান করিতে আহ্বান করা; কাহাকে অনুগ্রহ প্রকাশে অন্যাপেক্ষা অধিকতর সমাদর করা।

hăn'-dle (-dl), *v. t.* **1.** To touch, hold or feel with hand; হস্তদ্বারা স্পর্শ বা অনুভব করা, হস্তদ্বারা ধারণ করা। **2.** To manage in doing, (as a bow or gun etc.); হস্তদ্বারা ব্যবহার করা, চালনা করা। **3.** To control; to manage; as, the boy is hard to *handle*; শাসন করা, দমন করা; শাসন সংরক্ষণ করা। **4.** To deal with; as, to *handle* a person roughly or kindly; ব্যবহার করা। **5.** To treat of, as a theme or subject; আলোচনা করা। **6.** To deal, or trade, in; ব্যবসায় করা। **To handle roughly** or **kindly**— To treat as a person in a rough manner or kindly; কঠোর ব্যবহার করা, সদয়ভাবে ব্যবহার করা। **To handle without mittens** — To treat without superficial gentleness; রূঢ় ব্যবহার করা, কঠোর ব্যবহার করা।

hăn'-dle (-dl), *n.* **1.** That part of a vessel, instrument, etc. which is held in the hand when used; হাতল, বাঁট, বসরু। **2.** The fact that may be taken advantage of; "I would not give this *handle* to calumny"; যে বিষয়ের সুবিধা গ্রহণ করা যাইতে পারে, সুযোগ। **A handle to one's name**—A title; উপাধি, খেতাব। **The handle of the face**—(*Facet.*) The nose; (কৌতুকচ্ছলে) নাসিকা। **To give a handle to**— To furnish an occasion; সুযোগ দেওয়া। **To go off the handle**— (*Slang*) To die; (ইতর ভাষায়) শিঙ্গা ফুঁকা, পটল তোলা, অক্কা পাওয়া।

hănd'-sĕl, hăn—, *n.* & *v. t.* **1.** A new year's gift; the first present sent to a woman on her wedding day; নববর্ষের উপহার; কোন স্ত্রীলোকের বিবাহ উপলক্ষে প্রেরিত প্রথম উপহার। **2.** First money received for the sale of goods in the morning; প্রাতের বউনীর টাকা। **3.** An earnest money; বায়নার টাকা। **4.** Foretaste; পূর্ব্বাস্বাদ। ***Verb t.*** **1.** To give a handsel to; নববর্ষের উপহার প্রদান করা, বিবাহোপলক্ষে সর্ব্বপ্রথম উপহার প্রদান করা। **2.** To inaugurate with some token of pleasure; as, to *handsel* a house with a banquet; প্রতিষ্ঠা করা। **3.** To use or do for the first time; সর্ব্বপ্রথম ব্যবহার করা, সর্ব্বপ্রথম করা।

hănd'-some (-sŭm), *adj.* **1.** Having a pleasing appearance; comely; সুন্দর, সুশ্রী, সুদর্শন, সুরূপ, শোভনাঙ্গ, রূপবান, সৌম্য, লাবণ্যবান। **2.** Liberal; generous; as, a *handsome* gift or treatment; উদার; বদান্য। **—ly,** *adv.* **—ness** *n.* **Handsome is that handsome does**—(*Prov.*) He who does good or noble things is really handsome; সুন্দর সে যে সুন্দর কাজ করে। **To do the handsome thing by another person**— To behave liberally towards him; তাহার সহিত উদার ব্যবহার করা।

hănd'-ȳ, *adj.* **1.** Near or ready to the hand; হাতের নিকট। **2.** Skilful in using the hand; dexterous; সিদ্ধহস্ত, হস্তপটু করদক্ষ; নিপুণ, চতুর, দক্ষ। **3.** Convenient to handle; as, a *handy* tool or book; হস্ত দ্বারা ব্যবহারের সুবিধাজনক। **—i-ly,** *adv.* **—i-ness,** *n.* **Handy dandy** — ছেলেদের ক্রীড়া বিশেষ—ইহাতে এক ছেলে অপর ছেলের হস্তে কোন্ জিনিষ লুকান আছে— তাহা বলিতে চেষ্টা করে, ছেলেদের টাক্কা-না-ফাক্কা খেলা। **Handy man**— One useful for odd jobs (esp. of sailor); যে ব্যক্তি টুকটাক কাজ করিয়া থাকে।

hăng, *v. t.* & *i.* (*p. t.* & *p. p.* HUNG or HANGED) **1.** To suspend, (often with *up, out, to, from*); as, to *hang* a thing *from* or *to* a hook; to tie up as meat, game, etc. for drying or flavour; লটকাইয়া রাখা, টাঙ্গাইয়া রাখা, বিলম্বিত করা, ঝুলান; মৃত জন্তুর দেহ শুষ্ক বা সুস্বাদ করার জন্য টাঙ্গাইয়া রাখা। **2.** To put to death by suspending by the neck, (here *p.t.* & *p. p.* HANGED); ফাঁসি দেওয়া, উদ্বন্ধন দ্বারা বধ করা। **3.** To decorate (with something); as, to *hang* a room with pictures; মণ্ডিত করা, সুসজ্জিত করা, ভূষিত করা। **4.** To cause to droop; as, to *hang* one's head (from shame etc.); অবনত করা, হেঁট করা, নত করা, নীচু করা। **5.** To attach as wallpaper etc.; লাগান। **6.** To fasten as on hinges, springs, etc.; as, to *hang* a door on hinges; কব্জা প্রভৃতির উপর লাগান। **7.** Sometimes used as an imprecation; as, *hang* it; কখন কখন অভিশাপ প্রদানে ব্যবহৃত হয়। ***Verb i.*** **1.** To be suspended; to dangle; বিলম্বিত হওয়া; ঝুলা। **2.** To depend; to rest, (with *on* or *upon*); as, a question *hangs on* a point; অবলম্বন করা; নির্ভর করা। **3.** To be executed on the gallows; ফাঁসি হওয়া। **4.** To lean; to incline; হেলিয়া থাকা; ঝুঁকিয়া থাকা। **5.** To appear threateningly; to impend; as, an evil *hangs* over a country; মাথার উপর

ঝুলা ; পতনোন্মুখ হওয়া। 6. To be in suspense ; to linger ; সন্দিগ্ধ অবস্থায় থাকা ; বিলম্ব করা, গড়িমসি করা, গয়ংগচ্ছ করা। 7. To adhere ; to cling ; "She *hung* on his arms" ; সংশ্লিষ্ট হওয়া ; লাগিয়া থাকা, জড়াইয়া থাকা। 8. To be in a state of attention, (with *on*) ; as, he *hung on* my words ; হাঁ করিয়া শোনা। **Hang-dog**—*n.* & *adj.* A base and degraded fellow ; নীচ প্রকৃতির লোক, নরপশু। (*Adj.*) Base ; low ; ইতর ; নীচ। **Hang-man**—One who executes criminals ; জল্লাদ, ঘাতক, দণ্ডপাশিক (কেণ্ডিঃ)। **Hang-nail** — Same as AGNAIL (which see). **Hang-them** — An imprecation ; খেংরা মার, ঝাঁটা মার। **Hang-you**—দূর তোর ভাল হোক। **A hang-dog look**—A guilty depressed look ; হত্যাকারীর মত চেহারা। **Not a hang**—(*Colloq.*) Not at all ; মোটেই নয়, আদবেই নয়। **To be hanged down and quartered**—To be disemboweled and cut into several pieces ; নাড়ীভুঁড়ি বহিষ্কৃত ও দেহ খণ্ড বিখণ্ড হওয়া। **To hang about**—To loiter about ; ঘুরা ফিরা করা, ঘুরিয়া বেড়ান। **To hang back**—To hesitate ; ইতস্ততঃ করা, দ্বিধা করা। **To hang behind** — To lag behind ; পাছে পড়িয়া থাকা। **To hang by a thread**—To be in a very precarious condition or position ; অতি সঙ্কটজনক অবস্থায় থাকা, মাথার উপর খড়্গ ঝুলা, ছিঁড়ে ছিঁড়ে অবস্থা হওয়া। **To hang down**—To bend down as one's head ; অবনত করা, হেঁট করা। **To hang down one's head**—To droop one's head ; ঘাড় হেঁট করা, অধোবদন হওয়া। **To hang fire**—To be slow in exploding ; as, the gun *hangs fire* ; আওয়াজ হইতে বিলম্ব হওয়া। (Hence) To hesitate ; to be slow ; to come to no decisive result ; ইতঃস্তত করা ; গড়িমসি করা ; পাকা-পাকি কিছু স্থির না হওয়া। To be wanting in life or spirit ; as, the play *hangs fire* ; নিস্তেজ হওয়া, নির্জ্জীব হওয়া, জীবন্তভাব না থাকা। **To hang heavy on**—(Of time) To be tediously slow ; (সময়) কাটে না কাটে না বোধ হওয়া। **To hang in chains**—To hang as a criminal's body in an iron frame, as a public spectacle ; জনসাধারণের দর্শনের জন্য ফাঁসিকাঠে নিহত ব্যক্তির মৃতদেহ লোহার কাঠামে ঝুলান। **To hang in the balance**—To be doubtful or in an uncertain or critical condition ; অতি সঙ্কটজনক অবস্থায় থাকা, যায় যায় হওয়া। **To hang off**—To hang back ; পশ্চাৎপদ হওয়া, অগ্রসর হইতে অনিচ্ছুক হওয়া। **To hang on**—To depend or rely on ; to attend carefully to ; to be persistent as a disease ; to stick closely ; নির্ভর করা ; মন দিয়া শোনা, হাঁ করিয়া শোনা ; অবহিত ভাবে শ্রবণ করা ; (রোগ সম্বন্ধে) না ছাড়া ; লাগিয়া থাকা, গলা জড়াইয়া ধরিয়া থাকা। **To hang on the lips**—To be charmed with eloquence ; বক্তৃতায় মুগ্ধ হওয়া। **To hang out**—*v. t.* & *i.* To suspend in the open air as from windows etc. ; to project ; ঝুলিয়া থাকা ; বহিরুদ্গত হওয়া, বহির্বিলম্বিত হওয়া। (*Verb i.*) To protrude downwards ; নীচের দিকে ঝুলিয়া থাকা। (*Slang*) To reside ; (ইতর ভাষায়) বাস করা। **To hang out the red flag**—To give signal of battle ; যুদ্ধের সঙ্কেত করা। **To hang out the white flag**—To give signal of submission ; বশ্যতাসূচক শ্বেতপতাকা উড্ডীন করা। **To hang over**—To be suspended above ; কোনও কিছুর উপরে ঝুলিয়া থাকা। To impend over ; আসন্ন হওয়া, মাথার উপরে ঝুলা। **To hang to**—To cling to ; জড়াইয়া ধরা। **To hang together**—To be coherent ; to be associated ; সুসম্বদ্ধ হওয়া ; সম্মিলিত হওয়া। **To hang up**—To suspend ; (*fig*) to postpone ; to put aside ; দোলায়মান রাখা ; (লক্ষণায়) স্থগিত রাখা ; ফেলিয়া রাখা। **To hang upon**—Same as TO HANG ON.

hăng, *n.* 1. A downward inclination, slope or bend ; নতি, প্রবণতা। 2. The mode or way in which a thing hangs ; যে ভাব বা প্রকারে কোন জিনিষ ঝুলিয়া থাকে। 3. Meaning ; knack ; as, to get the *hang* of ; অর্থ ; কল, কৌশল। **To get the hang of**—See HANG *n.* 3.

hăng'-êr, *n.* 1. One who hangs ; a hangman ; যে ব্যক্তি ঝুলায় ; জল্লাদ। 2. That from, or by, which a thing is suspended ; যাহাতে বা যাহা দ্বারা কিছু ঝুলান হয়। 3. A small sword originally hung from the belt ; ক্ষুদ্র বক্রাগ্র অসি বিশেষ। 4. A stroke with a double curve in writing ; লেখার একপ্রকার টানটোন (যে টানে দুইটী বক্র থাকে)। **Hanger on** — A dependent ; a follower ; আশ্রিত ব্যক্তি, আশ্রিত, পোষ্য, গলগ্রহ ; অনুবর্ত্তী।

hăng'-êr, *n.* A wood on the side of a steep hill ; দুরারোহ পর্ব্বত-পার্শ্বস্থ অরণ্য।

hăng'-ing, *n.* 1. Act of suspending ; ঝুলন, উদ্বন্ধন। 2. Execution by the halter ; ফাঁসি। 3. That which is hung, esp. a drapery etc. hung on the walls of a room about a bed etc., (*chiefly in plural*) ; ঝালর, কাপড়ের পর্দ্দা। **Hanging committee** — প্রদর্শনীতে ছবি টাঙ্গান সম্বন্ধে যে সমিতি নির্দ্ধারণ করিয়া থাকেন। **Hanging matter**—যে অপরাধের দরুণ প্রাণদণ্ড হইয়াছে। **Hanging gardens of Babylon**—See GARDEN.

hank (hăngk), *n.* **1.** A coil or skein of yarn or the like, esp. of a given length ; সুতার ফেটি বা গোছা। **2.** (*Naut.*) A ring of wood, iron or rope for fixing stay sails to stays ; (নৌ-বিদ্যা) যে কাঠ, লোহা বা দড়ার আংটা দ্বারা মাস্তুলের অবলম্বন রজ্জুর পাইল ঐ রজ্জুতে সংবদ্ধ করা হয়। **Hank for hank**—On equal terms ; সমান সর্ত্তে।

han′-kêr (hăng-), *v. i.* To long or desire eagerly, (with *after*) ; আকাঙ্ক্ষা করা, লালনা করা।

han′-kêr-ing (hăng-), *n.* A strong desire ; longing ; তীব্র বাসনা ; আকাঙ্ক্ষা, লালসা, মনস্তৃষ্ণা (উজ্জ্বলঃ), স্পৃহা।

han′-ky-pan′-kŷ (hăng-kî-păng-), *n.* **1.** Jugglery ; ভেল্কি। **2.** An underhand dealing ; তলে তলে দুষ্কর্ম্ম।

Hăn′-sârd, *n.* Printed report of the proceedings of the Parliament ; ব্রিটিশ পার্লেমেন্টের মুদ্রিত কার্য্য-বিবরণী। [এই বিবরণী ১৭৫৩—১৮২৮ খৃঃ অব্দ পর্য্যন্ত Luke Hansard নামক জনৈক ব্যক্তি মুদ্রণ করিয়া আসিতেছিলেন—এই হেতু এই নাম।] **–ize,** *v. t.* To remind as an M. P. of his former inconsistent remarks reported in the Hansard ; পার্লেমেন্টের কার্য্যবিবরণীতে মুদ্রিত উক্তির সহিত তাহার বর্ত্তমান উক্তির অসঙ্গতি রহিয়াছে—এই বিষয় পার্লেমেন্টের কোন সভ্যকে স্মরণ করাইয়া দেওয়া।

Hanse (hăns), *n.* **1.** (*Hist.*) A trading or merchant guild ; (ইতিহাস) ব্যবসায়ি-সংঘ, সার্থ, গণ। **2.** A political or commercial league of Germanic towns ; জর্ম্মণীর নগরী সমূহের রাজনৈতিক বা বাণিজ্যঘটিত সম্মেলন। **3.** The entrance fee of a guild ; ব্যবসায়ি-সমিতি প্রভৃতির প্রবেশ-দক্ষিণা।

Hăn-sē-ăt′-ic, *adj.* Relating to the league of German towns ; উল্লিখিত জর্ম্মণ নগর সমূহের বাণিজ্য ঘটিত সম্মেলন-সম্পর্কীয়।

hăn′-som (cab) (-sŭm), *n.* A two-wheeled cab, with the driver's seat elevated behind and the reins passing over the top ; একপ্রকার দুই চাকার হাল্‌কা গাড়ী,—এই গাড়ীর চালক পশ্চাদ্দিগস্থ উচ্চাসনে উপবিষ্ট থাকে এবং অশ্ব-রজ্জু গাড়ীর ছাদের উপর দিয়া আসিয়া থাকে। [১৮৩৪ খৃঃ অব্দে John A. Hansom কর্ত্তৃক উদ্ভাবিত হয়]।

hăp, *n.* **1.** (*Archaic*) Chance ; luck ; lot ; দৈব ; ভাগ্য ; অদৃষ্ট, কপাল। **2.** Casual or chance occurrence, (with *pl.*) ; দৈবঘটনা, আকস্মিক ঘটনা ;

hăp, *v. i.* (*Archaic*) To happen by chance ; দৈবযোগে ঘটা।

hăp′-hăz-ard (-êrd), *n., adj.* & *adv.* Chance ; দৈব। ***Adj.*** Accidental ; casual ; আকস্মিক ; নৈমিত্তিক, দৈবায়ত্ত, দৈবাধীন, দৈবাৎ-সংঘটিত। ***Adv.*** Casually ; দৈবাৎ, দৈবযোগে, কদাচিৎ। **–ly,** *adv.* **At** or **by haphazard** — By mere chance ; without design ; at random ; ঘটনাক্রমে ; দৈবক্রমে ; যথাতথা, যদৃচ্ছাক্রমে।

Hă′-pi, *n.* The personification of the Nile ; মূর্ত্তিমান নীল নদ।

hăp′-lĕss, *adj.* Unlucky ; unfortunate ; হতভাগ্য, অভাগা, দগ্ধভাল, ভাগ্যহীন ; দুর্ভাগা। **–ly,** *adv.*

hăp′-lŷ, *adv.* (*Archaic*) By chance ; perhaps ; দৈবক্রমে, দৈবযোগে, দৈববশে ; সম্ভবতঃ, বুঝি বা।

hăp-lŏg′-ră-phŷ, *n.* The mistake of writing once what should be written twice (*e. g., philogy* for *philology*) ; যাহা দুইবার লিখা উচিত ছিল তাহা একবার লিখন, একলিখন।

hăp′-pen (-pn), *v. i.* **1.** To occur by chance or otherwise ; to come to pass ; দৈবক্রমে ঘটা, সংঘটিত হওয়া ; ঘটা। **2.** To chance ; as, he *happened* to be at home ; ঘটনাক্রমে থাকা। **3.** To come by chance, (with *on* or *upon*) ; as, to *happen on* a lost article ; ঘটনাক্রমে পাওয়া।

hăp′-pŷ, *adj.* **1.** Fortunate ; lucky ; ভাগ্যবান ; সৌভাগ্যশালী। **2.** Enjoying pleasure or good ; contented ; joyous ; as, *happy* hours ; সুখী, সুখসম্পন্ন, প্রাপ্ত-সুখ ; সন্তুষ্ট, সদানন্দ ; আনন্দপূর্ণ, সুখময়। **3.** Apt ; felicitous ; as, a *happy* expression ; যথাযোগ্য, ঠিক, সময়োচিত ; সুষ্ঠু। **4.** Expressing happiness ; as, a *happy* smile ; আনন্দ-সূচক। **–pi-ly,** *adv.* **–pi-ness,** *n.* **Happy dispatch**—See DISPATCH. **Happy-go-lucky**—Improvident ; easy-going ; অপরিণামদর্শী ; আরাম-প্রিয়, শ্রমবিমুখ, দৃক্‌পাত শূন্য, কাছা-আল্‌গা (*colloq.*)। **Happy family**—বিভিন্ন জাতীয় এবং বিরুদ্ধ-প্রকৃতি জন্তুবর্গের একত্র সমাবেশ। **Happy the people whose annals are tiresome**—যে জাতির ইতিহাস যুদ্ধবিগ্রহাদির উদ্দীপনাপূর্ণ কাহিনীদ্বারা পূর্ণ সেই জাতিই সুখী।

hă′-ră-kĭ′-ri, *n.* Suicide by piercing the abdomen, practised in Japan by higher classes when in disgrace, sentenced to death, etc. ; জাপানের সম্ভ্রান্তবংশীয় ব্যক্তি দিগের উদরচ্ছেদ পূর্ব্বক আত্মহত্যা।

hă-rangue′ (-răng), *n., v. i.* & *t.* An address to an assembly ; a loud and vehement speech ; বক্তৃতা ; বাগাড়ম্বরপূর্ণ বক্তৃতা, গলাবাজি, বাক্‌প্রবন্ধ, সালঙ্কার ভাষণ। ***Verb i.*** To make a harangue ; গলাবাজি করা। ***Verb t.*** To address in a harangue ; as, to *harangue* an assembly ; বাগাড়ম্বরপূর্ণ বক্তৃতা করা।

hă′-răs, *n.* A horse-breeding station ; অশ্বশাবক উৎপাদনের স্থান।

hăr′-ăss, *v. t.* **1.** To worry ; to trouble ; জ্বালাতন করা, নাকাল করা, উত্ত্যক্ত করা, উৎপীড়ন করা ; উৎপাত করা। **2.** (*Mil.*) To worry and impede by repeated attacks ; বারংবার আক্রমণ করিয়া উত্ত্যক্ত করা বা প্রতিবন্ধক জন্মান। **–ment,** *n.*

hâr'-bin-gêr, *n.* & *v. t.* **1.** A forerunner ; a precursor ; অগ্রগামী সংবাদ বাহক ; অগ্রদূত । **2.** (*Formerly*) One sent before to provide lodgings for army, royal train, etc. ; (পূর্ব্বে) যে ব্যক্তি পূর্ব্বে যাইয়া সৈন্যদল, রাজা এবং তৎসহচরবর্গ প্রভৃতির বাসস্থানের বন্দোবস্ত করিত । ***Verb t.*** To announce the approach of ; to presage ; আগমন বার্ত্তা ঘোষণা করা ; পূর্ব্বাভাস দেওয়া ।

hâr'-bour, hâr'-bor (-bêr), *n., v. t.* & *i.* **1.** A shelter for ships ; a port or haven ; পোতাশ্রয়, পোতাধিষ্ঠান ; বন্দর । **2.** A refuge or shelter ; lodging ; আশ্রয়স্থলী ; আবাসস্থলী । ***Verb t.*** To afford shelter to ; as, to *harbour* a dacoit ; to entertain ; to cherish ; as, to *harbour* a thought (generally evil) ; আশ্রয় দেওয়া ; স্থান দেওয়া ; পোষণ করা । ***Verb i.*** To lodge for a time in a harbour ; to come to anchor in a harbour ; কিছুকাল পোতাশ্রয়ে বাস করা ; পোতাশ্রয়ে নোঙ্গর করিয়া থাকা । **—age,** *n.* A shelter ; a place of shelter ; আশ্রয় ; আশ্রয়স্থল । **Harbour-master**—পোতাশ্রয় রক্ষক ।

hârd, *adj.* & *adv.* **1.** Not easily penetrated : firm ; solid ; compact ; দুর্ভেদ্য ; দৃঢ়, কঠিন, শক্ত ; নিরেট ; সংহত । **2.** Difficult to understand or explain ; perplexing ; as, a *hard* problem ; দুর্ব্বোধ, কঠিন ; জটিল । **3.** Difficult to accomplish ; not easy ; arduous ; as, a *hard* task : a disease *hard* to cure ; দুঃসাধ্য, কঠিন ; দুরূহ ; শ্রমসাধ্য । **4.** Difficult to resist, manage or control ; অপ্রতিরোধ্য, দুর্নিবার, দুর্দ্দান্ত । **5.** Difficult to endure ; as, *hard* times ; rigorous ; severe, as winter etc. ; অসহনীয়, দুঃসহ ; কঠোর ; দারুণ । **6.** Unfeeling ; cruel ; strict ; as, a *hard* master : *hard* heart : *hard* word ; নির্ম্মম ; নিষ্ঠুর, ক্রূর ; কড়া । **7.** Harsh ; unpleasant to the eye or ear ; as, a *hard* style or face ; কর্কশ ; শ্রুতিকটু, কর্ণকটু, ঘোরদর্শন, কাটখোট্টা, কুরূপ । **8.** Miserly ; niggardly ; কৃপণ ; কঞ্জুষ । **9.** (*Slang*) Acid ; (ইতর-ভাষায়) টক, খাট্টা । **10.** High, as a price, market, etc. ; চড়া । **11.** Strenuous ; energetic ; violent ; as, *hard* fight, labour etc. : *hard* worker ; ঘোরতর ; সতেজ ; প্রচণ্ড, প্রবল । **12.** (*Pron.*) Abrupt in utterance, *c* in *cat* *g* in *go* etc. ; (উচ্চারণে) কর্কশ । ***Adv.*** **1.** Diligently ; earnestly ; vehemently ; violently ; as, he is working *hard* : it is raining *hard* ; পরিশ্রমের সহিত ; সাগ্রহে ; প্রচণ্ডভাবে ; প্রবলভাবে । **2.** Severely ; as, it bore *hard* on me ; গুরুতররূপে, কঠোরভাবে, নিদারুণভাবে । **3.** With difficulty ; অতি কষ্টে । **4.** Close or near ; as, to wait *hard* by ; নিকটে, কাছে, অদূরে । **5.** So as to be hard ; as, *hard* baked ; কঠিন হওয়ার জন্য । **Hard'-ness,** *n.* State or quality of being hard ; কাঠিন্য, কঠোরতা, অভেদ্যতা (সাঃ পঃ), দার্ঢ্য । **Hard bargain** — কড়াচুক্তি । **Hard-bitten**—একগুঁয়ে, কষ্টসহিষ্ণু । **Hard by**—Very near ; অতি নিকটে, খুব কাছে । **Hard-drinker**—নিত্য মদ্যপায়ী । **Hard-earned** — Earned with much toil ; কষ্টার্জ্জিত, বহু শ্রমার্জ্জিত, শ্রমোপার্জ্জিত, কষ্টোপার্জ্জিত । **Hard-favoured, Hard-featured**—কদর্য্যমূর্ত্তি, কদাকার, কাটখোট্টা । **Hard-fisted** — কঞ্জুষ, হাতকষা, বদ্ধ-মুষ্টি । **Hard-fought** — তুমুল । **Hard-gotten** — কষ্টার্জ্জিত । **Hard grained**—Having a close, firm grain, as an oak etc. ; মোটা, কসা আঁশওয়ালা । Unattractive ; grim ; অসুন্দর ; ঘোরদর্শন । **Hard-headed**—Practical ; sound in judgment ; not sentimental ; কার্য্যদর্শী, কেজো ; বিচারবুদ্ধিসম্পন্ন, ভাবাবেগশূন্য ভাবুকতাশূন্য । **Hard-hearted**—কঠিনান্তঃকরণ (কেণ্ডিঃ), পাষাণ-হৃদয়, কঠিনহৃদয়, নিষ্ঠুর-নির্দ্দয় । (*Hard-heartedly, adv. Hard-heartedness, n.*) **Hard labour**—কঠোর পরিশ্রমের সহিত কারাবাস । **Hard lines**—Harsh treatment ; unfortunate conditions ; কঠোর ব্যবহার ; দুর্ভাগ্যজনক অবস্থা । **Hard money, cash**—রোকড় টাকা, রোক টাকা, গিনি, টাকা প্রভৃতি । **Hard-mouthed**—Not easily controlled by the bit (said of a horse); দুর্দ্দমনীয়, দুর্দ্দম, দুর্দ্দম্য । **Hard-pressed**—প্রপীড়িত । **Hard shell**—Having a hard shell ; কঠিন আবরণ বিশিষ্ট । **Hard-set**—Beset with difficulty ; সঙ্কট-সঙ্কুল । Set so as to be hard or firm ; সুদৃঢ়ভাবে স্থাপিত । (*Fig.*) Rigid ; uncompromising ; কঠোর ; সন্ধিবিধানে পরাঙ্মুখ । **Hard-solder**—বজ্রসংঘাত (সাঃ পঃ) । **Hard-tack** — জাহাজের বিস্কুট । **Hard up**—In want, esp. of money ; টানাটানিতে, অর্থাভাবে, অর্থ-কষ্টে । (*Naut.*) As far as possible to windward ; (নৌবিদ্যা) যতদূর সম্ভবপর যেদিকে বায়ু প্রবাহিত হয় সেইদিকে । **Hard upon**—Close to ; অতি কাছে, সন্নিকটে । **Hard-ware**—Ironmongery ; লৌহনির্ম্মিত দ্রব্যাদি, লোহার জিনিষ । **Hard water**—খনিজ পদার্থময় জল—যাহা বস্ত্র ধৌত করার পক্ষে অযোগ্য । **Hard-wood**—মাজ কাঠ (সাঃ পঃ) । **Hard working** — Laborious ; industrious ; কঠোর পরিশ্রমী ; কঠোর শ্রমশীল । **A hard case**—An incorrigibly wicked man ; যে দুশ্চরিত্র ব্যক্তির আর সংশোধনের আশা নাই । **Hard and fast**—Strict, as rules ; বাঁধা-ধরা, বাঁধাবাঁধি, ধরা-বাঁধা । **Hard as the nether millstone**—Very hard ; unfeeling ; obdurate ; অতিশয় কঠিন ; নির্ম্মম ; পাষাণহৃদয় । **Hard of hearing**—কাণে খাট । **Hard up for**—At a loss for ; কিংকর্ত্তব্যবিমূঢ়,

উপায়ান্তরবিহীন। **It shall go hard but I will or if I do not**—I shall most surely; as, *It shall go hard but I will or if I do not* go with her; আমি নিশ্চিতই। **To be hard put to it**—To be in great difficulty; অত্যন্ত কষ্টে বা অভাবে পতিত হওয়া, অতিশয় সঙ্কটে পড়া। **To be hard upon one**—To treat one harshly; কাহার সহিত কঠোর ব্যবহার করা। **To die hard**—See DIE. **To go hard with one**—To prove to one's disadvantage; (কাহারও পক্ষে) বিশেষ কষ্টদায়ক হওয়া। **To run a person hard**—To pursue him closely; কাহারো পশ্চাদ্ধাবিত হওয়া। **To try hard**—To try strenuously; প্রাণপণ চেষ্টা করা।

hârd, *n.* A sloping road-way or jetty for landing; জাহাজ হইতে মালপত্র নামাইবার জন্য ক্রমনিম্ন পথ বা মঞ্চ।

hârd'-en (-n), *v. t.* & *i.* 1. To make hard or firm; as, to *harden* clay etc.; শক্ত করা, দৃঢ় করা, কঠিন করা। 2. To make callous; as, to *harden* one's heart; নির্মম করা। 3. To make hardy or robust; কষ্টসহ করা, বলিষ্ঠ করা। 4. To make obdurate in a course of action or state of mind; কঠোরচিত্ত করা। ***Verb i.*** 1. To become hard; as, mortar *hardens* by drying; শক্ত হওয়া, কঠিন হওয়া। 2. To become unfeeling or callous, (esp. in *p. p.*); নিষ্ঠুর হওয়া, নির্মম হওয়া। 3. To become robust; সুদৃঢ় হওয়া (যথা মাংসপেশী)। **–ened,** *p. p.* **Hardening of steel** — শস্ত্রপাণি (ব্রজঃ হিন্দুঃ)।

hâr'-di-hood, *n.* Boldness; impudence; audacity; সাহস; ধৃষ্টতা; প্রগল্‌ভতা।

hard'-ly, *adv.* 1. In a hard or difficult manner; with difficulty; অতিকষ্টে; কষ্টের সহিত। 2. Harshly; কঠোরভাবে, কর্কশভাবে। 3. Scarcely; কদাচিৎ, ক্বচিৎ, কালেভদ্রে। **Hardly earned**—কষ্টার্জ্জিত।

hârd'-ship, *n.* 1. Severe toil or suffering; privation; ক্লেশ, দুঃখ; কৃচ্ছ্র, কষ্ট। 2. Hardness of fate or circumstance; দুর্গতি, দুর্ভাগ্য, দুর্দ্দশা।

hârd'-y, *adj.* 1. Bold; rash; audacious; সাহসী; অসমসাহসী, হিতাহিত জ্ঞানহীন; দৃপ্ত, উদ্ধত। 2. Sturdy; capable of endurance; দৃঢ়িষ্ঠ; শ্রমসহিষ্ণু, কষ্টসহিষ্ণু, ক্লেশসহ (শুক্রঃ-বিনয়ঃ)। 3. Able to grow in the open throughout the year, as plants etc.; সারা বর্ষ ব্যাপিয়া মুক্ত স্থানে জন্মাইতে সমর্থ। **–i-ly,** *adv.* In a hardy manner; boldly; কঠোর ভাবে; সাহসের সহিত। **–i-ness,** *n.* **Half hardy** — (Of plants etc.) Requiring shelter in the winter only; (বৃক্ষাদি সম্বন্ধে) কেবলমাত্র শীতকালে আবরণ প্রয়োজনীয়। **Hardy annual**—One that may be sown or sows itself in the open; (*fig.*) a subject that comes up yearly; যে বর্ষজীবী উদ্ভিদ মুক্ত স্থানে জন্মিয়া থাকে বা জন্মান যাইতে পারে; (লক্ষণায়) যে বিষয় বর্ষে বর্ষে সমাগত হয়।

Hare-bell.

hāre, *n.* 1. A small timid animal with long ears, a short tail and a divided upper lip; শশক, খরগোস। 2. (*Cap.*) A constellation, ক্ষুদ্র তারাপ্রকোষ্ঠ বিশেষ। **Hare-bell**—নীলবর্ণ ঘণ্টাকৃতি পুষ্পপ্রসূ তরুবিশেষ। **Hare-brained**—Wild; rash; চঞ্চলমতি, অস্থিরচিত্ত; অবিমৃষ্যকারী। **Hare-lip**—ছিন্নোষ্ঠ, খণ্ডোষ্ঠ। **Hare-lipped**—Having the upper lip cleft like the hare; ছিন্নোষ্ঠ, ঠোঁট-কাটা, গন্না-কাটা। **Hare's-foot**—একপ্রকার গুল্ম, কাক-গাছ। A brush used by ladies for applying rouge; গোলাপী রংএর চূর্ণ মুখে মাখিবার জন্য স্ত্রীলোকদিগের বুরুশ বিশেষ। **First catch your hare**—(*Proverb*) One should make sure of getting a thing first before thinking of what to do with it; কালনেমির মত লঙ্কা ভাগ করিও না, (cf. গাছে কাঁঠাল গোঁফে তেল)। **Hare and hound** — বালকদিগের ক্রীড়া বিশেষ। **Mad as a March hare**—Mad as a hare in the breeding season; crazed; সঙ্গমঋতুতে শশকের মত মদমত্ত; উন্মত্ত। **To hold** (or **run**) **with the hare and run** (or **hunt**) **with the hounds, To run with hare and hounds**—To keep in with both sides; to play a double part; উভয় পক্ষের সহিত ভাব রাখা; চোরকে চুরি করিতে বলা ও গৃহস্থকে সজাগ থাকিতে বলা, বরের ঘরের পিসি কনের ঘরের মাসী হওয়া। **To make a hare of**—To make ridiculous; বিদ্রূপের পাত্র করা, উপহাসের পাত্র করা, হাস্যাস্পদ করা।

hā'-rĕm, –ăm, *n.* 1. The apartments of the female members in a Mohammedan dwelling house; শুদ্ধান্ত, স্ত্রীমহল, জেনানামহল, অন্তঃপুর, অন্দরমহল। 2. The occupants of the harem; অন্তঃপুরবাসিনী, অন্তঃপুরিকা। 3. (*Usu.* -AM) A Mohammedan sacred place; মুসলমানদিগের তীর্থস্থান।

hăr'-i-cot (-kö), *n.* 1. A ragout of meat (specially mutton and roots); তরকারী সহযোগে মাংসের ব্যঞ্জন। 2. A kind of bean (also called *haricot bean*); একপ্রকার শিম্বী।

hârk, *v. i.* & *t.* 1. To listen, (with *to*); শুনা। ***Verb t.*** To hear; to listen to; শুনা; কর্ণপাত করা। 2. Used imperatively; "*Hark* he knocks"; শোন! শোন! **Hark away, back, forward** or **off**—(Various calls to hounds in hunting) Go away, back, forward or off; দূরে যাও,

পশ্চাতে যাও, সম্মুখে যাও। To **hark back**—*v. i.* & *t.* To retrace course to find scent, (said of hounds) ; অনুসৃত জন্তুর ঘ্রাণ পাইবার জন্য পুনরায় প্রত্যাবৃত্ত হওয়া। (*Fig.*) To revert, as to a subject ; কোনও বিষয়ে প্রত্যাবর্ত্তন করা। (*Verb t.*) To recall (hounds) ; কুকুরকে ডাকিয়া ফিরাইয়া আনা।

hârl(e), *n.* **1.** A fibre of flax etc. ; a barb of feather ; আঁশ ; পালকের সূক্ষ্মরোম।

Hâr-lē'-ian (-ăn), *adj.* Of, or relating to, Robert Harley, Earl of Oxford (1661—1724), or his library ; অক্সফোর্ডের আর্ল রবার্ট হার্লী বা তদীয় পুস্তকাগার সম্বন্ধীয়।

Hâr'-lē-quin (-kwĭn), *n.* **1.** A character in Italian comedy ; a buffoon in a pantomime dressed in particoloured clothes who plays tricks to divert the audience ; মুখসধারী এবং চুমকি বসানো রং বেরঙ্গের পোষাক-পরা সংদার যাত্রার প্রধান সঙ্‌। **2.** A buffoon ; ভাঁড়, বিদূষক। **Harlequin duck**—চিত্রবিচিত্র পালক বিশিষ্ট উত্তর আমেরিকাদেশীয় হংস বিশেষ, চিত্রহংস।

hâr-lē-quin-āde' (-kwĭn-), *n.* The part of a pantomime in which the harlequin and clown play the principal parts ; the part of a harlequin ; সংদার যাত্রার যে প্রধান অংশে সং এবং বিদূষক মুখ্য ভূমিকা সকল অভিনয় করে ; সংদার যাত্রার প্রধান সঙ্‌।

hâr'-lŏt, *n.* & *v. i.* A prostitute ; বারাঙ্গনা, বেশ্যা, গণিকা, রূপাজীবা, পণ্যস্ত্রী, পণ্যাঙ্গনা, বারবধূ, বারযোষিৎ, বারবিলাসিনী, বারস্ত্রী, সাধারণী, সাধারণ স্ত্রী, সামান্যা স্ত্রী, সর্ব্ববল্লভা, অবিদ্যা। ***Verb i.*** To play the harlot ; ছেনালি করা।

hâr'-lŏt-rȳ, *n.* The practice of prostitution ; বেশ্যাবৃত্তি, বারাঙ্গনাবৃত্তি, গণিকাবৃত্তি, ভগবৃত্তি বেশ্যাজীবিকা, ভগজীবিকা।

hârm, *n.* & *v. t.* Injury ; hurt ; damage ; অনিষ্ট ; হানি ; অপকার, লোকসান, ক্ষতি। ***Verb t.*** To injure ; to damage ; অপকার করা ; ক্ষতি করা। **Harm'-ful,** *adj.* Injurious ; hurtful ; mischievous ; অনিষ্টজনক, ক্ষতিজনক ; হানিকর ; অপকারক। **Harm'-ful-ly,** *adv.* **Harm'-ful-ness,** *n.* **Harm'-less,** *adj.* **1.** (*Rare*) Free from harm ; অনপকারক। **2.** Causing no harm ; inoffensive ; অনপকারী ; নিরীহ।

hâr-măt'-tăn, *n.* A hot dry wind blowing to the Atlantic from the interior of Africa in December, January and February ; আফ্রিকার মধ্যস্থল হইতে ডিসেম্বর, জানুয়ারী এবং ফেব্রুয়ারী মাসে প্রবাহিত উষ্ণ এবং শুষ্ক বায়ু বিশেষ।

Hâr'-mō-ni-ă, *n.* The wife of Cadmus ; কেড্‌মাসের স্ত্রী — ইঁহার বিবাহ-সভায় দেবগণ উপস্থিত ছিলেন।

hâr-mŏn'-ic, *adj.* & *n.* **1.** Relating to harmony ; স্বরসঙ্গতি-সম্পর্কীয়, স্বরৈক্যসম্বন্ধী (কেণ্ডিঃ)। **2.** Concordant ; harmonious ; তানলয়-সঙ্গত ; সঙ্গতিবিশিষ্ট, শ্লিষ্ট (মূচ্ছঃ)। ***Noun.*** A less distinct tone accompanying a principal tone ; প্রধান স্বরের সহযোগী অপেক্ষাকৃত অস্পষ্ট স্বর। **–i-cal,** *adj.* **–i-cal-ly,** *adv.* **Harmonic analysis** — হরাত্মক বিশ্লেষণ (হিঃ কোঃ)। **Harmonic function**—হরাত্মক ফল (হিঃ কোঃ)। **Harmonic motion**—হরাত্মক গতি। **Harmonic pencil**—হরাত্মক সূচী। **Harmonic points**—হরাত্মক বিন্দু। **Harmonic Polar**—হরাত্মক ধ্রুব। **Harmonic progression**—A series of harmonic quantities ; হরাত্মক শ্রেণী (হিঃ কোঃ)। **Harmonic quantities**—যে সকল সংখ্যার হর সমূহ সমান্তর শ্রেঢ়ীতে আছে (যথা, ½, ⅓, ¼)। **Harmonic ratio**—হরাত্মক নিষ্পত্তি। **Harmonic resistance** — হরাত্মক প্রতিরোধ। **Harmonic section**—হরাত্মক খণ্ড (হিঃ কোঃ)। **Harmonic series**—হরাত্মক শ্রেণী (হিঃ কোঃ)। **Harmonic solid** — হরাত্মক ঘন (হিঃ কোঃ)। **Harmonic surface**—হরাত্মক পৃষ্ঠ (হিঃ কোঃ)। **Harmonic system**—হরাত্মক সম্প্রদায় (হিঃ কোঃ)। **Harmonic tones** — Tones produced by vibration of aliquot parts of strings etc. ; তন্ত্রী প্রভৃতির একাংশের স্পন্দন দ্বারা জাত স্বর সমূহ। **Harmonic triad**—স্বরত্রয় (হিঃ কোঃ)।

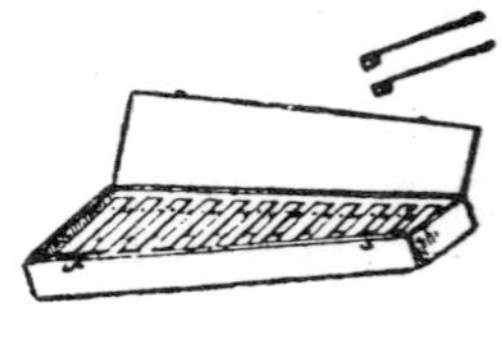

Harmonica

hâr-mŏn'-i-că, *n.* A musical instrument ; জলতরঙ্গ।

hâr-mŏn'-i-cŏn, *n.* A kind of musical instrument ; একপ্রকার বাদ্যযন্ত্র।

hâr-mō'-ni-ous (-ŭs), *adj.* **1.** Musically concordant ; sweet-sounding ; স্বরসঙ্গতি-বিশিষ্ট, তালশুদ্ধ, সমতাল, ঐকতানিক, মেলশুদ্ধ, তানলয়-বিশুদ্ধ ; সুশ্রাব্য, শ্রুতিমধুর, শ্রবণসুভগ, মধুর। **2.** Congruous ; forming an agreeable whole ; সঙ্গতিবিশিষ্ট ; সমঞ্জস। **3.** Free from dissent or discord ; as, a *harmonious* discussion or consent ; অনৈক্য বা বিরোধ শূন্য, নির্বিরোধ, নির্বিবাদ। **4.** (Of persons) Singing or playing tunefully ; (ব্যক্তি সম্পর্কে) তানলয়বিশুদ্ধভাবে গীতবাদ্যকারী।

hâr'-mō-nist, *n.* **1.** One skilled in musical harmony ; স্বরসঙ্গতিজ্ঞ। **2.** A harmonizer ; ঐক্য সংস্থাপক।

hâr-mō'-ni-ŭm, *n.* A musical instrument resembling a small organ ; একপ্রকার বাদ্যযন্ত্র, হার্ম্মোনিয়াম।

hâr'-mō-nīze, *v. t.* & *i.* **1.** To bring into harmony ; to cause to agree ; to reconcile ; ঐক্যস্থাপন করা ; মিলন সাধন করা, খাপ খাওয়ান ;

পুনর্ম্মিলিত করা। 2. To make agreeable in artistic effect; "The bluest skin that *harmonize* the whole"; সঙ্গতিবিশিষ্ট করা, ক্রমমিল করা। 3. (*Mus.*) To add harmony to; as, to *harmonize* a melody; (সঙ্গীত-শাস্ত্র) সুরের মিল করা। ***Verb i.*** 1. (*Mus.*) To form a concord; as, tones *harmonize* perfectly; সঙ্গতিবিশিষ্ট হওয়া, মিল হওয়া। 2. To agree in sense, sentiment, feeling, artistic effect; as, the colour do not *harmonize*; সঙ্গতিবিশিষ্ট হওয়া, সুসমঞ্জস হওয়া। **—ni·za'-tion**, *n.* **—niz-er**, *n.*

hâr-mŏ-nŏm'-ĕ-têr, *n.* An instrument for measuring the harmonic relations of notes; স্বরৈক্য সম্বন্ধ পরিমাপের যন্ত্র বিশেষ, স্বরৈক্যমান।

hâr'-mŏ-nŷ, *n.* **1.** Just adaptation of parts to a whole; agreement; সঙ্গতি; সমন্বয়, ক্রমমিল। **2.** Agreement in feeling, sentiment, etc.; peace; friendship; as, to live in *harmony*; ঐক্য, মিল; শান্তি; বন্ধুতা। **3.** (*Mus.*) Tuneful or melodious sound; combination of simultaneous notes into a chord; সুস্বর-লহরী, সুললিত স্বর, সুমধুর ধ্বনি; স্বর-সঙ্গতি, মেল, ঐকতান, রক্ত (cf. রক্তং নাম বেণুবীণাদিস্বরাণামেকীভাবঃ—নারদঃ)। **4.** A book seeking to harmonize parallel narratives etc., esp. of the four Gospels; যে পুস্তকে বিভিন্ন পুস্তকের অনুরূপ বৃত্তান্ত সমূহের (বিশেষতঃ খৃষ্টীয় সুসমাচার চতুষ্টয়োক্ত অনুরূপ কাহিনী সমূহের) সঙ্গতিসাধনের চেষ্টা করা হইয়াছে, সঙ্গতি-গ্রন্থ। **Pre-established harmony**—Leibenitzএর দর্শন-শাস্ত্রে চিৎ ও অচিতের (যথা আত্মা ও দেহের) মধ্যে উহাদের সৃষ্টির পূর্ব্বে প্রতিষ্ঠিত সঙ্গতি বা মিলন, পূর্ব্বপ্রতিষ্ঠিত-সঙ্গতি।

hâr'-nĕss, *n.* & *v. t.* **1.** The gear of a draught animal, esp. of a horse etc.; ঘোড়ার সাজ, অশ্বসজ্জা। **2.** (*Hist.*) Armour; (ইতিহাস) বর্ম্ম, সাঁজোয়া। **3.** An apparatus in a loom by which warp threads are shifted; 'ব' এবং তৎসংশ্লিষ্ট অংশ। ***Verb t.*** To put harness on; as, to *harness* a horse; ঘোড়ার সাজ পরান, অশ্ব সজ্জিত করা। **Harness cask**—জাহাজে লবণাক্ত মাংস রাখার জন্য ঢাকনিওয়ালা পিপা। **In harness**—In the routine of daily work; দৈনিক কার্য্যে নিযুক্ত, নিত্যনৈমিত্তিক কার্য্যে নিযুক্ত। **To die in harness** — See under DIE.

Knight in full harness.

hârp, *n.* A stringed musical instrument of triangular form played with the fingers; বহুতন্ত্রী-বিশিষ্ট ত্রিকোণবাদ্য-যন্ত্র বিশেষ, ত্রিভুজ-বীণা, ত্রিকোণ বীণ।

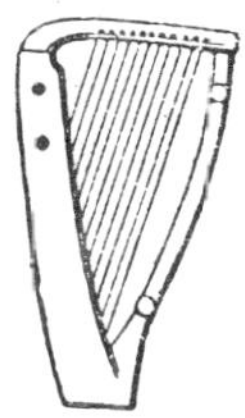
Anglo-Saxon harp.

hârp, *v. i.* **1.** To play on a harp; বীণা বাদন করা। **2.** To dwell *on* a subject tediously; এক বিষয় বিরক্তিজনকভাবে পুনঃ পুনঃ অবতারণা করা। **Harp'-er, Harp'-ist**, *ns.* A player on a harp; ত্রিকোণ বীণা বাদক। **To harp on the same string**—To dwell on one subject persistently; hence, to vex with one thing; একই কথা পুনঃ পুনঃ বলিয়া বিরক্ত করা; ঘ্যান্ ঘ্যান্ করা।

Hâr'-pies (-pîs), *n.* (*Pl.*) See HARPY.

hâr'-pōōn, *n.* & *v. t.* A spear for striking large fish like whale etc.; তিমি প্রভৃতি বৃহৎ মৎস্য বিঁধিবার জন্য একপ্রকার বর্শা বা টেঁটা। ***Verb t.***

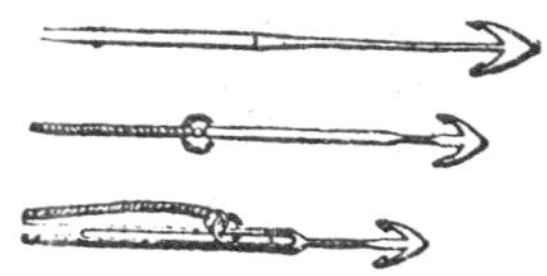
Harpoon.

To strike or catch with a harpoon; উক্তরূপ টেঁটাদ্বারা বিদ্ধ বা ধৃত করা। **Harpoon-gun**—টেঁটা ছুড়িবার জন্য কামান বিশেষ।

harp'-si-chŏrd, *n.* A harp-like obsolete stringed instrument of music; প্রাচীনকালে ব্যবহৃত ত্রিকোণ বীণার মত বাদ্য যন্ত্র বিশেষ।

Hâr'-pŷ, *n.* **1.** (*Gk. & Latin myth.*) A fabulous rapacious monster having the face of a woman and the body of a vulture; (গ্রীক ও রোমীয় পুরাণোক্ত) রাক্ষসী বিশেষ। ইহার বদন স্ত্রীলোকের মত ও শরীর শকুনির মত ছিল। **2.** A rapacious person; an extortioner; রাক্ষস, লোভী, পেটুক; পীড়ন-পূর্ব্বক অর্থশোষণ-কারী। **Harpy-eagle** — একপ্রকার বৃহদাকার ও বলবান ঈগল পক্ষী।

Harpy-eagle.

hâr'-que-bŭs (-kwĕ-), *n.* (*Hist.*) An old-fashioned portable gun or musket; (ইতিহাস) সাবেক কালের বন্দুক বিশেষ। **—ier'**, *n.* A soldier armed with a harquebus; উক্তপ্রকার বন্দুকধারী সৈনিক।

hăr'-ri-dăn, *n.* An odious old woman; a hag; a vixen; বৃদ্ধা, জরতী, বৃদ্ধা কুট্টনী; বুড়ী; উগ্রচণ্ডা নারী।

hăr'-ri-êr, *n.* **1.** A kind of hound for hunting hares; শশক শিকারের

জন্য একপ্রকার কুকুর। 2. (*Pl.*) A pack of these hounds with huntsmen; ঐরূপ কুকুর ও শিকারীর দল। 3. A kind of hawk; একপ্রকার বাজপক্ষী।

hăr'-ri-êr (-ĭ-), 1. One who harries; লুণ্ঠনকারী। 2. A kind of falcon; পানিডোবি (যোঃ)।

har'-row (hă-rö), *n.* An implement of agriculture set with teeth for breaking the clod;

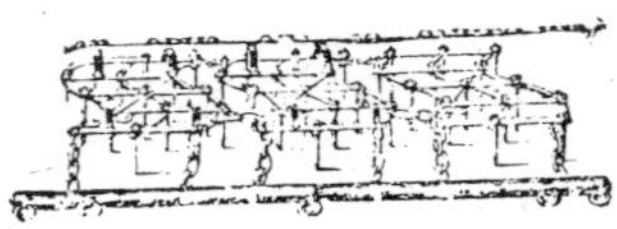

Harrow.

(বিলাতী) বিদা বা মই, কোটীশ (অঃ), লোষ্ট্রভেদন (ঐ), লোষ্ট্রঘ্ন (ঐ)। **Under the harrow** — In distress; দুর্দ্দশাগ্রস্ত।

har'-row (hă-rö), *v. t.* 1. To draw a harrow over, as a land; মৈ দেওয়া, বিদা দেওয়া। 2. To wound or lacerate; to torment; as, to *harrow* one's feelings or soul; ক্ষতবিক্ষত করা, ছিন্ন ভিন্ন করা; যন্ত্রণা দেওয়া, নির্যাতন করা। **–ing,** *adj.* Causing acute distress to the mind; heart-breaking; অরুন্তুদ, মর্ম্মান্তিক; হৃদয়বিদারক, মর্ম্মভেদী, মর্ম্মচ্ছেদী।

har'-row (hă-rö), *v. t.* To rob; to spoil, (used esp. in the phrase *to harrow hell*, said of Christ); লুণ্ঠন করা; কাড়িয়া লওয়া।

hăr'-rŷ (-ĭ), *v. t.* & *i.* 1. To plunder; to pillage; to ravage; as, to *harry* a land; লুণ্ঠন করা; লুঠপাট করা; উৎসন্ন করা, ছারখার করা। 2. To worry; to harass; উত্ত্যক্ত করা, জ্বালাতন করা; উৎপীড়ন করা, নির্যাতন করা। ***Verb i.*** To commit ravages; লুঠপাট করা।

hârsh, *adj.* 1. Grating or rough to the touch, taste, eye or ear; খরগাত্র, অস্নিগ্ধ, কটু, রুক্ষ, শ্রুতিকটু, কর্ক্কশ, কর্ণকঠোর, কর্ণকটু, কটকটে। 2. Offensive or repugnant to feelings or judgment; বিরক্তিকর, পরুষ। 3. Severe; unfeeling; cruel; ক্রূর, কঠোর; নির্ম্মম; নিষ্ঠুর। **Harsh'-ly,** *adv.* **Harsh'-ness,** *n.*

hârt, *n.* A stag; a male red deer esp. after the fifth year; হরিণ, মৃগ, কুরঙ্গ; বিশেষতঃ ৫ বৎসরের অধিক-বয়স্ক রক্তবর্ণ হরিণ, রক্তহরিণ। **Hart's tongue**—এক প্রকার পর্ণাঙ্গ। **A hart of ten**—যে মৃগের শৃঙ্গ দশটী শাখা-সমন্বিত।

hârts'-hŏrn, *n.* 1. The horn of a hart; the substance got from his horns; (formerly) the chief source of ammonia; মৃগশৃঙ্গ; মৃগ-শৃঙ্গ হইতে প্রাপ্ত পদার্থ বিশেষ; পূর্ব্বে উহা হইতে ক্ষারিণজল প্রস্তুত হইত। 2. A solution of ammonia (also called *spirit of hartshorn*); ক্ষারিণজল। **Spirit of hartshorn**—ক্ষারিণজল।

hâr'-ŭm–scâr'-ŭm, *adj.* & *n.* Rash; reckless; wild; অবিমৃষ্য-কারী; হঠকারী; অসভ্য, বন্য। ***Noun.*** A reckless person or conduct; অপরিণামদর্শী ব্যক্তি, হঠকারিতা।

hă-rŭs'-pĕx, –pĭce, *n.* (*Rom. Rel.*) A diviner or sooth-sayer of a class originally Etruscan, but early introduced into Rome though not as official priests of the State religion; (রোমীয় ধর্ম্ম) অলৌকিক উপায়ে ভবিষ্যৎ কথনক্ষম ব্যক্তি, নিমিত্তজ্ঞ (রঃ), দৈবজ্ঞ, জ্যোতির্ব্বিদ্।

hâr'-vĕst, *n.* & *v. t.* 1. The gathering or the season of gathering ripened crops or fruits; পক্কশস্য বা ফল সংগ্রহ, পক্ক শস্য বা ফল সংগ্রহের কাল, শস্যচ্ছেদন কাল, লব (Sans.)। 2. That which is reaped; the yield of any natural product in a season; সংগৃহীত শস্য অথবা বৃক্ষের ফল; কৃষিফল (মেঘঃ), ফসল। 3. (*Fig.*) The product of any action; কোন কার্য্যের ফল। ***Verb t.*** To reap or gather as any crop or result; শস্য কর্ত্তন অথবা সংগ্রহ করা, শস্যচ্ছেদন করা, দাওয়া (East Bengal)। **Harvest festival**—শস্য সংগ্রহ উপলক্ষে প্রদত্ত ভোজ। **Harvest-home**—শস্য গৃহজাত করার কাল; শস্য সংগ্রহ উপলক্ষে ভোজ বিশেষ, নবান্ন (আঃ বঃ)। **Harvest-month**—September; সেপ্টেম্বর মাস। **Harvest-moon**—হরিপদ সংক্রান্তির (২২শে ২৩শে সেপ্টেম্বর) কাছাকাছি পূর্ণিমা, সমোদয়কালিকচন্দ্র (হিঃ কোঃ)। **Harvest-house**—একপ্রকার ক্ষুদ্র মেঠো ইঁদুর। **Harvest-queen**—শস্য-দেবী, পৌষলক্ষ্মী। **Thanksgiving service for harvest** — ফসলের জন্য ভগবানকে ধন্যবাদ প্রদানার্থ উপাসনা।

hâr'-vĕst-êr, *n.* 1. One who harvests; শস্যসংগ্রহকারক, শস্য-চ্ছেদক। 2. A machine for reaping crops; শস্যচ্ছেদন যন্ত্র। 3. A harvest bug; একপ্রকার ছারপোকা বা মৎকুণ।

hăs, *3rd pers. sing. present ind. of* HAVE.

hăsh, *n.* 1. That which is hashed, *e. g.* meat etc.; a dish of hashed meat and vegetables; কুট্টিত মাংসাদি; কুটা মাংস ও তরিতরকারীর ব্যঞ্জন। 2. A new mixture of old things; পুরাতন জিনিষের নূতন মিশ্র। 3. A medley; "Make a strange *hash* of the story"; মিশ্র, পঞ্চমেল, পঞ্চশস্য।

hăsh, *v. t.* To cut into small pieces; to mince; to chop; as, to *hash* (up) meat; (*lit.* & *fig.*); টুকরা টুকরা করিয়া কাটা; কুচি কুচি করিয়া কাটা, কুটা, কুট্টিত করা; থোড়া। **To make a hash of**—To spoil in dealing with; নষ্ট করা। **To settle a person's hash**—To defeat one's object; to make an end of him; কাহারো উদ্দেশ্য ব্যর্থ করা; কাহারও দফারফা করা, নিকাশ করা।

hăsh'-ish (-ēsh), *n.* Leaves of the Indian hemp dried for smoking etc. ; ভাঙ্গ, সিদ্ধি, গাঁজা। **Hashish-smoker,** *n.* গাঁজাখোর।

hăs'-lĕt, hârs–, *ns.* A piece of meat to be roasted, such as the heart, liver, etc. of a hog ; পশুর (বিশেষতঃ শূকরের) ভাজিবার জন্য মাংসখণ্ড, যথা মেটে, কলিজা ইত্যাদি।

hăsp, *n.* & *v.t.* **1.** A fastening esp. a clasp that passes over a staple to be fastened by a padlock ; আঁকড়া। **2.** A spindle ; টাকুয়া, টাকু। **3.** A hank or skein of a yarn ; সূতার কেটি।

hăs'-sŏck, *n.* **1.** A thick mat or cushion for kneeling in a church ; উপাসনাকালে ধর্ম্মমন্দিরে জানু পাতিয়া উপবেশনের জন্য আসন বা গদিবিশেষ, কুশাসন। **2.** A tuft of bog grass etc. ; বিলজাত তৃণগুচ্ছ প্রভৃতি। **3.** (*In Kent*) A soft calcareous sand-stone ; (কেণ্ট প্রদেশে) একপ্রকার নরম চুণাপাথর।

hăs'-tāte, *adj.* Shaped like a spear ; as, a *hastate* leaf ; বল্লমাকৃতি, ত্রিশূলাকার।

hāste, *n.* & *v.i.* **1.** Speed; quickness; swiftness ; ত্বরা ; শীঘ্রতা ; ক্ষিপ্রতা। **2.** Hurry ; rashness ; ব্যস্ততা, তাড়াহুড়া ; হঠকারিতা। ***Verb i.*** To be quick ; to make haste ; ক্ষিপ্র হওয়া, সত্বর হওয়া ; তাড়াতাড়ি করা। **In haste**—With speed ; quickly ; ক্ষিপ্রতার সহিত ; তাড়াতাড়ি, শশব্যস্তভাবে। **In hot haste**— In very great haste ; খুব তাড়াতাড়ি, ব্যস্তসমস্ত হইয়া। **The more haste the less speed** — যত তাড়াতাড়ি করিতে যাওয়া যায় ততই বিলম্ব ঘটে। [cf. কর যদি তাড়াতাড়ি ভুলের হবে বাড়াবাড়ি]। **To make haste**—To hasten ; to be quick ; তাড়াতাড়ি করা ; ত্বরা করা।

hās'-ten (-n), *v. t.* & *i.* To cause to make haste ; to accelerate ; to expedite ; as, to *hasten* a person or work ; তাড়াতাড়ি করা ; ত্বরান্বিত করা ; দ্রুতগামী করা। ***Verb i.*** To make haste ; to hurry ; তাড়াতাড়ি করা ; ব্যস্তসমস্ত হওয়া।

hāst'-ȳ, *adj.* **1.** Speedy ; swift ; hurried ; as, a *hasty* retreat ; দ্রুত ; ত্বরিত, ক্ষিপ্র ; ব্যস্তসমস্ত। **2.** Precipitate ; rash ; inconsiderate ; as, a *hasty* conjecture ; হঠকারী ; অবিমৃষ্যকারী ; অবিবেচক। **3.** Irritable ; easily excited ; uttered or done in anger ; as, a *hasty* temper or word ; কোপন ; আশুক্রোধী ; উত্তেজনাবশে উচ্চারিত বা কৃত। **–i-ly,** *adv.* **1.** In haste ; speedily ; তাড়াতাড়ি ; দ্রুত, শীঘ্র। **2.** Precipitately ; rashly ; হঠকারিতার সহিত ; ভালমন্দ বিচার না করিয়া, অগ্রপশ্চাৎ চিন্তা না করিয়া। **–i-ness,** *n.* **Hasty pudding**—ময়দা অথবা যইএর আটা উষ্ণজল বা দুগ্ধের সহিত মিশ্রণপূর্ব্বক প্রস্তুত মণ্ড, পিষ্টক বিশেষ।

hăt, *n.* & *v. t.* **1.** A covering usually with a brim for the head ; সাহেবদিগের টুপি। **2.** A cardinal's hat ; his office (also called *red hat*) ; কার্ডিনালদিগের লোহিত বর্ণ টুপি ; কার্ডিনালের পদ। ***Verb t.*** To cover or provide with a hat ; টুপিদ্বারা ঢাকা, টুপি দেওয়া। **Hat'-ful,** *adj.* টুপি ভরা। **Hat'-less,** *adj.* টুপি শূন্য। **Hat'-ter,** *n.* টুপিওয়ালা, টুপিনির্ম্মাতা। **Hat-band**—টুপিবেষ্টনী। **Hat-block**—টুপির ফরমা। **Hat-mould**—টুপির ছাঁচ। **Hat-trick**—(ক্রীকেট ক্রীড়ায়) উপরি উপরি তিন বল দ্বারা তিন জনকে আউটকরণ ; বাজীকরের টুপীর খেলা ; বিলাতের প্রাকৃত সভায় (House of Commons) কেদারায় টুপি রাখিয়া আসন রক্ষা করিবার প্রণালী। **Opera-hat**—এক প্রকার চোঙ্গাকার টুপি — যাহা চাপ দেওয়ার পর পুনরায় পূর্ব্বাকার প্রাপ্ত হয়। **A bad hat**—নচ্ছার লোক, লক্ষ্মীছাড়া লোক। **A black hat** — অষ্ট্রেলিয়ার নবাগত ঔপনিবেশিক। **As black as my hat**—মিশ্‌মিশে কালো। **Hat in hand**—Servilely ; obsequiously ; দাসবৎ ; পা-চাটার মত, ধামাধরার মত। **Hats to be disposed of**—Lives lost ; বহুলোক নিহত। **Mad as a hatter** — Quite insane ; বদ্ধ পাগল। Very angry ; অগ্নিশর্ম্মা। **To be in a or the hat**—To be in a fix ; মুস্কিলে পড়া, ফাঁপরে পড়া। **To hang up one's hat in a house**—To make oneself quite at home in a house ; কোনও বাটীতে যাইয়া তাহাদের পরিবারের একজন হইয়া দাঁড়ান, বিশেষ মাখামাখি ভাব করিয়া তুলা, পরের বাড়ীতে নিজের বাড়ীর মত স্বচ্ছন্দতা বোধ করা। **To pass or send round the hat**—To beg for contributions ; চাঁদা সংগ্রহার্থ টুপি লইয়া ঘুরা। **Top high hat, Chimney pot hat**—চোঙ্গাকার রেশমী টুপি। **To raise the hat to one**—To salute one by raising the hat ; টুপি তুলিয়া অভিবাদন করা। **To take the hat off** — To salute by taking off the hat ; টুপি তুলিয়া অভিবাদন করা।

hatch (hăch), *v. t., i.* & *n.* **1.** To produce (young) from eggs by incubation ; to incubate as eggs ; তা দিয়া ডিম ফুটান ; ডিমে তা দেওয়া **2.** To contrive secretly ; as, to *hatch* a plot or mischief ; ষড়যন্ত্র পাকান। ***Verb i.*** **1.** To produce young from eggs by incubation ; তা দিয়া ডিম ফুটান। **2.** To produce young ; as, eggs *hatch* ; to come forth from the egg as young ; বাচ্চা ফুটান ; ডিম ফুটিয়া বাহির হওয়া। ***Noun.*** The act of hatching ; the chickens hatched at once ; (*fig.*) outcome ; তা দিয়া ডিম ফুটান, ডিমে তা দেওন ; এক কালে তা দিয়া ফুটানো মুরগীর ছানা সকল ; ফল, পরিণাম। **To count the chickens before they are hatched**—To depend too much on some future or uncertain event ; কালনেমির মত লঙ্কা ভাগ করা। [cf. গাছে কাঁটাল গোঁপে তেল, হাট না জমতেই মেড়া চার কড়া (East Bengal.)]

hatch (hăch), *n.* **1.** A lower half of a divided door ; দ্বিপাটিত দ্বারের নিম্নার্দ্ধ। **2.** (*Naut.*) An opening in a deck or hatchway ; a trap door covering this ; (নৌ-বিদ্যা) মাল নামাইবার জন্য জাহাজের পাটাতনের রন্ধ্র বিশেষ ; ঐ রন্ধ্র বন্ধ করার জন্য চোরা দরজা। **3.** A flood-gate : স্রোতোদ্বার। **Hatch-way** — An opening in a ship's deck for passage below ; জাহাজের উপর তল হইতে নীচের তলায় যাওয়ার জন্য রন্ধ্র। **Under hatches**— Below deck ; (*fig.*) brought low ; in distress or poverty; dead ; পাটাতনের নীচে ; (লক্ষণায়) পতিত, অধঃপতিত ; দুর্দ্দশাগ্রস্ত, দারিদ্র্যগ্রস্ত ; মৃত।

hatch (hăch), *v. t.* To close with a hatch ; চোরা দরজা দ্বারা বন্ধ করা।

hatch (hăch), *v. t.* & *n.* To mark as a surface with (esp. parallel) lines as in painting, engraving, etc. ; চিত্র, ক্ষোদাই, প্রভৃতির কাজে ফলকের উপর রেখা (বিশেষতঃ সমান্তরাল রেখা) সমূহ অঙ্কন করা। ***Noun.*** An engraved stroke or line ; উৎকীর্ণ রেখা।

hatch'-êr-ÿ (hăch-), *n.* A place for hatching fish ; মাছের ডিম ফুটাইবার স্থান, মৎস্যাণ্ডবাটিকা।

hatch'-ĕt (hăch-), *n.* A small axe used by one hand ; কুঠার, কুড়ালি, পরশু, টঙ্ক। **Hatched-faced**—টঙ্কাগ্রমুখ। **To bury the hatchet**—To put an end to hostilities ; to become friendly ; যুদ্ধে নিবৃত্ত হওয়া, সন্ধিস্থাপন করা ; বন্ধুভাবাপন্ন হওয়া। [উত্তর আমেরিকার আদিম অধিবাসিগণ শান্তিস্থাপনের পর রণপরশু ভূগর্ভে প্রোথিত করিত।] **To dig up the hatchet**—To renew hostilities ; পুনরায় যুদ্ধে প্রবৃত্ত হওয়া। **To take up the hatchet**—To declare war ; যুদ্ধে প্রবৃত্ত হওয়া। **To throw the hatchet** — To exaggerate ; to tell fabulous stories ; অতিরঞ্জিত করা ; আষাঢ়ে গল্প বলা, গল্প ফাঁদা। **To throw the helve after the hatchet** — To add new loss to those already incurred ; ক্ষতির উপর ক্ষতি হওয়া।

hatch'-mĕnt (hăch-), *n.* An escutcheon ; a kind of panel with the armorial bearings of a deceased person, placed in front of his hearse ; কুলচিহ্নাঙ্কিত চর্ম্ম ; মৃত ব্যক্তির কুলচিহ্নাঙ্কিত ফলক—যাহা তদীয় গৃহ সম্মুখে সম্বদ্ধ করিয়া রাখা হয়।

hāte, *v. t.* **1.** To dislike intensely ; ঘৃণা করা। **2.** To bear malice to ; দ্বেষ পোষণ করা। **Hat'-a-ble,** *adj.*

hāte, *n.* (*Chiefly Poet.*) Intense dislike ; hatred ; ঘৃণা ; জুগুপ্সা। **Hate'-ful,** *adj.* **1.** Exciting dislike or aversion ; odious ; ঘৃণাজনক ; গর্হিত, জুগুপ্সিত। **2.** Malignant ; দ্বেষজনক। **Hate'-ful-ly,** *adv.* **Hate'-ful-ness,** *n.* **Hat'-red,** *n.* Intense dislike ; strong aversion ; rancour ; ill will ; enmity ; ঘৃণা ; বিদ্বেষ ; বিরাগ ; অপ্রীতি ; শত্রুতা।

Hăth'-ŏr, *n.* The Egyptian goddess of beauty, love and joy ; মিসর দেশের সৌন্দর্য্য, প্রেম এবং আনন্দের অধিষ্ঠাত্রী দেবী।

hatti, *n.* A Turkish edict rendered irrevocable by being signed by the Sultan ; তুরস্ক সুলতানের ফরমান।

hau'-bêrk (hä-), *n.* A coat of mail ; বর্ম্ম, কবচ, সাঁজোয়া।

haugh (hä), *n.* A low lying alluvial land beside a river ; নদীনিকটস্থ পলি-পড়া ভূমি।

haugh'-tÿ (hä-), *adj.* **1.** Proud ; and disdainful ; arrogant ; overbearing ; উদ্ধত, দাম্ভিক, দৃপ্ত ; দুর্ব্বিনীত ; দুর্দ্ধর্ষ। **2.** Dignified ; grand ; মহিমান্বিত ; বিশাল, মহা। **–ti-ness,** *n.* State of being haughty ; arrogance ; ঔদ্ধত্য ; অবলেপ, দাম্ভিকতা। **–ti-ly,** *adv.* Disdainfully and proudly ; arrogantly ; দৃপ্তভাবে ; উদ্ধতভাবে।

haul (häl), *v. t., i.* & *n.* **1.** To pull or draw with force ; to drag ; সবলে টানা বা আকর্ষণ করা ; টানা। **2.** To pull, (with *at, upon*) ; as, to *haul at* a rope ; টানা। **3.** (Of wind) To shift ; (বাতাস-সম্পর্কে) পরিবর্ত্তিত হওয়া। ***Verb i.*** **1.** To change the course of a ship ; to sail in a certain course ; as, to *haul* along the coast ; জাহাজের মুখ ফিরান ; কোন বিশেষ দিকে চালান। ***Noun.*** **1.** Act of hauling ; a violent pull ; টান ; সবলে আকর্ষণ। **2.** A draught of a net ; as, 50 fish at a *haul* ; জালের টান। **3.** That which is caught or gained at once ; acquisition ; একবারে যাহা ধৃত হয় বা প্রাপ্ত হওয়া যায় ; প্রাপ্তি। **Haul'-age,** *n.* **To haul in with**—To sail close to the wind so as to approach an object more closely ; কোন পদার্থের নিকটবর্ত্তী হওয়ার জন্য বায়ুর প্রায় প্রতিকূলে জাহাজ চালান। **To haul off**—To sail close to the wind in order to avoid an object ; কোন পদার্থ হইতে দূরে সরিয়া যাওয়ার জন্য বায়ুর প্রতিকূলে জাহাজ চালান। **To haul over the coals**—তিরস্কার করা (see COAL)। **To haul round**—(Of the wind) To change course ; (বাতাস সম্পর্কে) গতি পরিবর্ত্তন হওয়া। **To haul the wind, To haul on, upon or to the wind**—To bring the ship round so as to sail close to the wind ; জাহাজ ঘুরাইয়া বায়ুর প্রায় প্রতিকূলে চালান।

haul'-ier (häl-yêr), *n.* One who hauls, esp. tubes in a coal mine to bottom of shaft ; যে ব্যক্তি কয়লার খনিতে কয়লা-ভরা গামলা সুড়ঙ্গের তলে টানিয়া নেয় বা ঠেলিয়া তুলে।

haulm (hälm), *n.* **1.** *(Collectively Sing.)* Stalks or stems of peas, beans, etc., used for thatching etc.; খড়। **2.** Stalk or stem; ডাঁটা।

haunch (hänsh), *n.* **1.** The part of the body between the last rib and the thigh; the hip; নিতম্ব দেশ; পাছা। **2.** (Of meats) The leg and loin, as of deer etc.; (মাংস সম্পর্কে) হরিণ প্রভৃতির পা এবং কটিদেশ, রাং। **3.** A part of an arch between the crown and the piers; খিলানের পার্শ্বভাগ।

haunt (hänt), *v. t., i.* & *n.* **1.** To visit frequently as a place; to frequent the company of (a person); সদাসর্ব্বদা যাতায়াত করা; সর্ব্বদা গতিবিধি করা। **2.** (Of thoughts, memories, etc.) To recur to (the mind etc.) frequently; পুনঃ পুনঃ মনে উদয় হওয়া; বারবার মনে পড়া। **3.** (*Usu in p. p.*) To visit or frequent as a ghost; (ভূতাদির পক্ষে) বাস করা, আশ্রয় করা। ***Verb i.*** To stay habitually; as, to *haunt in* or *about* a place or *with* a person; সচরাচর বাস করা। ***Noun.*** A place to which one often resorts; a lair or feeding place (of animals etc.); a den (of criminals); সর্ব্বদা গতিবিধির স্থান, শ্বাপদ শয্যা; পশুর আহারের স্থান; আড্ডা। **Haunt'-ed,** *p. adj.* Frequented by ghost; as, a *haunted* house; ভূতাশ্রিত, ভূতের। **Haunted house**—ভূতের বাড়ী।

haut'-boy (hō-), **hō'-boy, ō'-bue** (-boy), *ns.* **1.** A high-pitched wind instrument made of wood;

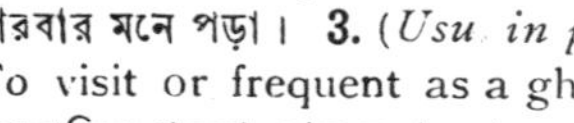

Hautboy.

একপ্রকার শানাই। **2.** A large species of strawberry; একপ্রকার বড় আকারের ষ্ট্রবেরী ফল।

hauteur, *n.* Haughtiness; pride; loftiness of manner; দর্প; গর্ব্ব; দেমাক।

haut-gout' (hō-gō), *n.* **1.** A high flavour; a taint; উগ্রস্বাদ; পচা।

Hă-văn'-ă, *n.* A kind of cigar manufactured at Havana or in Cuba; হ্যাভেনা চুরুট [হ্যাভেনা ও কিউবাতে প্রস্তুত হয়।]

have (hăv), *v. t.* & *i.* (*Pres. third pers. sing.* HAS; *past* HAD) **1.** To own; as, I *have* a book; থাকা, অধিকারে থাকা, অধিকারী হওয়া। **2.** To experience the existence of; as, to *have* a son, friend etc.; থাকা। **3.** To contain as a part or quality; as, this book *has* 100 pages: he *has* no thinking capacity; থাকা। **4.** To enjoy or suffer from; as, I *have* much pleasure: he *had* fever; ভোগ করা। **5.** To know; as, he *has* no Latin; জানা। **6.** To be burdened with; as, to *have* many things to do; to be compelled; as, I *have* to go there; চাপ থাকা; কোন কিছু করিতে বাধ্য হওয়া। **7.** To retain; to cherish; as, *have* this in mind; to hold or regard; as, to *have* one in reverence; to entertain in the mind; as, I *have* no doubt in this; ধারণ করা; পোষণ করা; গণ্য করা; মনে পোষণ করা। **8.** To show in action; to exercise; as, he *has* the audacity to say this; কার্য্যতঃ প্রদর্শন করা; চালনা করা। **9.** To perform; to carry on; to engage in; as, I *had* a quarrel with him; সম্পাদন করা; নির্ব্বাহ করা; প্রবৃত্ত হওয়া। **10.** To accept; to receive; to take; to take food, drink, etc.; গ্রহণ করা; প্রাপ্ত হওয়া, পাওয়া; পান করা, সেবন করা, ভোজন করা। **11.** To desire; as, I would not *have* thee die; ইচ্ছা করা। **12.** To procure; to effect; সংগ্রহ করা; সাধন করা, সম্পাদন করা। **13.** To demand or call for; "What would these madmen *have*"; চাওয়া, দাবী করা। **14.** To bring forth; to bear; উৎপাদন করা; ধারণ করা। **15.** To get the better of in an argument; to outwit; as, to *have* one in a retort; তর্কে জয়ী হওয়া; বুদ্ধিবলে পরাস্ত করা। **16.** To maintain; as, he will *have* it that there was no light; তর্কস্থলে সমর্থন করা। **17.** To cause to be; as, to *have* one shot; ঘটান। ***Verb i.*** To make attack, (with *at*); "*Have at* thee with a downright latin; আক্রমণ করা। **He had like to have**—He came near having; সে প্রায় পাইয়াছিল। **I had as lief**—I would as willingly; আমিও সেরূপ ইচ্ছার সহিত। **I had as well** or **better**—It would be quite as well or better for me to etc.; আমার পক্ষেও ততটা কিম্বা তার চেয়ে অধিক ভাল হইত। **I had better** or **rather go there**—I would act more wisely in going there; সেখানে গেলে আমার পক্ষে ভাল হইত। **I had him there**—I gained an advantage over him; তাহার উপর সুবিধা লাভ করিয়াছিলাম। **To have a care**—To take care; to be on one's guard; সাবধান হওয়া; হুসিয়ার হওয়া। **To have after** — To pursue or follow; পশ্চাদ্গমন করা, অনুগামী হওয়া। **To have an eye to**—To watch; চোখ রাখা, নজর রাখা। **To have at**—To assail; আক্রমণ করা। **To have at a thing**—To begin or attempt it; আরম্ভ করা, চেষ্টা করা। **To have at heart**—To desire (anything) earnestly; প্রাণে চাওয়া। **To have a try**—To make an attempt; চেষ্টা করা। **To have away** — To remove; সরান,

স্থানান্তরিত করা। **To have done**—To stop ; থামান। **To have in**—To contain ; ধারণ করা। **To have in the heart** — To purpose ; to intend to do ; ইচ্ছা করা ; কোন কাজ করিতে অভিপ্রায় করা, মনে মনে থাকা। **To have it**—To maintain ; as, he will *have it* that it is etc.; (মতাদি) ধরিয়া থাকা। To gain the advantage ; as, the Ayes *have it* ; সুবিধা লাভ করা। To receive a blow, punishment, etc. ; as, let him *have it* ; শাস্তি পাওয়া, সাজা পাওয়া, মার খাওয়া। **To have it out of a person**—To punish or retaliate on, a person ; শাস্তি দেওয়া, শোধ লওয়া, দাদ তোলা। **To have it out (with a person)** — To settle a dispute with him by discussion or contest ; to challenge (him) for an offence of which he has been guilty ; বিবাদ নিষ্পত্তি করা ; মীমাংসা করা, মিটমাট করা ; অভিযুক্ত করা। To finish it ; to enjoy the rest of it ; শেষ করা ; অবশিষ্টটুকু ভোগ করা। **To have on**—To wear ; পরিধান করা, পরা। **To have one out**—To engage (one) in a duel ; কাহাকেও দ্বন্দ্বযুদ্ধে প্রবৃত্ত করা। **To have out**—To cause to depart ; তাড়াইয়া দেওয়া। **To have rather**—To prefer ; অপেক্ষাকৃত ভাল মনে করা, সমধিক বরণীয় মনে করা। **To have up**—To cause to be brought before a court of justice ; আদালতে হাজির করা। **You have been had** — (*Slang*) You have been cheated ; তুমি ঠকিয়াছ।

have (hăv), *n.* (*Slang*) A swindler ; (ইতরভাষায়) জুয়োর।

hā′-ven (-vn), *n.* **1.** A harbour ; a port ; পোতাশ্রয় ; বন্দর। **2.** A shelter or refuge ; আশ্রয়, বিরামস্থলী, আশ্রয়স্থল।

hăv′-êr-săck, *n.* A bag of stout canvas for a soldier to carry in his rations ; সৈনিকদের রসদ নেওয়ার জন্য শক্ত ক্যাম্বিস কাপড়ের ঝুলি বা থলিয়া।

hăv′-ing, *n.* Act of possessing ; a thing possessed ; (*pl.*) possessions ; property ; অধিকার করণ ; অধিকৃত বস্তু; অধিকার; সম্পত্তি।

hăv′-ŏc, *n.* & *v. t.* General destruction ; devastation ; as, to play *havoc* among a people ; উচ্ছেদ, নাশ, বিনাশ, ধ্বংস, উৎসাদন ; ছারখার, উৎখাত। ***Verb t.*** To lay waste ; to devastate ; উজাড় করা ; ধ্বংস করা, উৎসন্ন করা, ছারখার করা। **To cry havoc**—To give signal for indiscriminate seizure of spoil, (now *fig.*) ; নির্ব্বিকার লুটপাট করার জন্য সৈন্যগণকে সঙ্কেত করা (বর্ত্তমানে লক্ষণায় ব্যবহৃত হয়)। **To make havoc of, To play havoc among**—To destroy or devastate ; উৎসন্ন করা, ছারখার করা।

haw (hä), *n.* **1.** (*Hist.*) A hedge ; an enclosure, esp. a yard ; (ইতিহাস) বৃতি ; বেষ্টিত স্থান, অঙ্গন। **2.** The hawthorn ; its fruit ; বনমঞ্জলি ; উহার ফল।

haw (hä), *n.* **1.** The third eyelid of a dog, horse, etc. ; অশ্ব, কুক্কুরাদির তৃতীয় অক্ষিপল্লব।

haw (hä), *v. i.* To speak with interruption and hesitation ; আম্‌তা আম্‌তা করিয়া বলা।

haw-haw′ (hä-hä), *n.* & *v. i.* A guffaw or boisterous laughter ; হোহো রবে হাস্য। ***Verb i.*** To laugh boisterously ; হোহো করিয়া হাসা।

hawk (häk), *n.*, *v. i.* & *t.* **1.** A bird of prey allied to the falcon ; বাজ পক্ষী, শশঘাতক (ভাব প্রঃ), শশঘাতী (সুশ্রুঃ)। **2.** A rapacious person ; পরস্বাপহারী ব্যক্তি। ***Verb i.* 1.** To catch birds with trained hawks ; শিক্ষিত বাজ পক্ষী ছাড়িয়া পক্ষী শিকার করা। **2.** To attack (*at*) like a hawk ; বাজ পক্ষীর মত আক্রমণ করা। ***Verb i.*** To attack like a hawk ; বাজ পক্ষীর মত আক্রমণ করা। **Hawk′-ish**, *adj.* **Hawk′-like**, *adj.* **Hawk-cuckoo** — চোখ-গেল-পাখী (যোঃ) পাপিয়া (প্রতিভা ১৩২২)। **Hawk-eyed**—Having a keen eye ; sharp-sighted ; শ্যেন-চক্ষু (রবীঃ) ; তীক্ষ্ণদর্শী, সূক্ষ্মদর্শী। **Hawk-nosed**—খগনাস, শুকনাস। **Hawk's bill**—একপ্রকার চিত্রকচ্ছপ। **To know a hawk from a handsaw** or **hern shaw**—To be clever ; চালাক হওয়া, সেয়ানা হওয়া।

hawk (häk), *v. i.* & *t.* To clear the throat with a noise ; গলা খেঁকানি দেওয়া। ***Verb t.*** To raise as phlegm by hawking, (usu. with *up*) ; খক্ খক্ করিয়া কাসিয়া কফ বাহির করা।

hawk (häk), *v. t.* To carry about for sale ; to peddle ; as, to *hawk* goods, (*lit.* & *fig.*) ; জিনিষ ফেরি করা ; জিনিষ হাঁকা।

hawk′-êr (häk-), *n.* A pedlar ; ফেরিওয়ালা।

hawse (häs), *n.* **1.** That part of a vessel's bow in which the hawse-holes for the cables are cut ; নঙ্গরের কাছি প্রবিষ্ট করার জন্য পোতাগ্রের যে অংশে ছিদ্র কাটা হয়। **2.** The space between a vessel's bows and her anchor ; নঙ্গরবদ্ধ জাহাজের অগ্রভাগ এবং নঙ্গরের মধ্যবর্ত্তী স্থান। **3.** The situation of the cables of a vessel when two anchors, port and starboard are used ; পোতাগ্রের উভয় পার্শ্ব হইতে নঙ্গর ফেলা হইলে জাহাজের কাছি সকল যে ভাবে থাকে। **Hawse-holes**—পোতাগ্রের উভয় পার্শ্বে নঙ্গরের রজ্জু প্রবিষ্ট করার জন্য ছিদ্র। **A foul hawse**—পরস্পরের সহিত জড়ানো কাছি। **To come in at the hawse-holes** — To enter the navy at the lowest grade ; সর্ব্বনিম্ন কর্ম্মচারিরূপে নৌ-বিভাগের কার্য্যে প্রবেশ করা।

haws'-êr (häs-) *n.* A large rope; a small cable now usually made of steel; জাহাজের কাছি; ক্ষুদ্র কাছি,—বর্তমানে সাধারণতঃ ইস্পাত দ্বারা তৈরি হয়।

haw'-thŏrn (hä-), *n.* A kind of thorny shrub with red, white or pink flower and small dark red berry; কণ্টকবহুল গুল্মবিশেষ (শ্বেত, রক্ত ও গোলাপী বর্ণের পুষ্প ও ঘোর লাল বর্ণের ক্ষুদ্র ক্ষুদ্র ফল হয়), বনমল্লিকা।

hay (hā), *n., v. t. & i.* Grass cut and dried for fodder; শুষ্ক ঘাস, খড়, শুষ্ক তৃণ। ***Verb t.*** 1. To supply with hay; to put as land under hay; শুষ্ক ঘাস জোগান; ক্ষেতে ঘাস জন্মান। 2. To make into hay; তৃণ শুষ্ক করা। ***Verb i.*** To make hay; তৃণ শুষ্ক করা। **Hay-cock**—শুষ্কতৃণস্তূপ, খড়ের গাদা। **Hay-fever, Hay-asthma**—ঘাসের গন্ধ হইতে জাত সর্দিজ্বর বা হাঁপানি, ওষধিগন্ধজ-জ্বর (হঃ চঃ)। **Hay-fork**—শুকনা ঘাস উল্টাইয়া দিবার জন্য বা বোনাই করার জন্য কাঁটা। **Hay-knife**—শুষ্ক ঘাস কাটিবার ছুরী। **Hay-loft** — খড়ের মাচান। **Hay-maker**—যে ব্যক্তি ঘাস শুকায়; ঘাস শুকাইবার জন্য যন্ত্র বিশেষ। **Hay-making**—ঘাস শুকাইবার কাজ। **Hay-rick, —stall**—খড়ের স্তূপ, ঘাসের গাদা। **Between hay and grass**—In an unformed state; অগঠিত অবস্থায়। **To look for a needle in a bottle** or **bundle of hay**—To try to find out a thing where it is not possible to find it out; খড়ের গাদায় সূচ খোঁজা। **To make hay**—To expose hay to the sun; রোদে খড় শুকান। **To make hay of**—To throw into confusion; লণ্ডভণ্ড করা। **To make hay while the sun shines**—To seize a favourable opportunity; সুযোগের সময় বা সময় থাকিতে নিজের কাজ গুছাইয়া লওয়া।

hay'-wărd (hā-), *n.* An officer of a parish etc. to look after hedges, enclosures, etc.; পল্লী প্রভৃতির বৃতি, বেষ্টিত স্থান প্রভৃতি পরিদর্শক কর্মচারি-বিশেষ।

hăz'-ard (-ĕrd), *n. & v. t.* 1. Chance; accident; অদৃষ্ট, দৈবঘটনা; দৈব। 2. Risk; danger; as, at the *hazard* of his life; ঝুঁকি; বিপদ্, সঙ্কট। 3. A game of chance played with dice; অক্ষক্রীড়া, দ্যূত ক্রীড়া। 4. Any kind of bad ground; নিকৃষ্ট ভূমি। 5. (*Billiard*) A stroke; as, a losing or winning *hazard*; (বিলিয়ার্ড খেলা) আঘাত। 6. (*Tennis*) One of the winning openings in a court; (আণ্টাল খেলায়) ক্রীড়াপ্রাঙ্গণস্থ মুক্ত বিজয় স্থান। 7. (In Ireland) A cab-stand; (আয়র্লণ্ডে) গাড়ীর আড্ডা। ***Verb t.*** 1. To expose to chance; to risk; সঙ্কটাপন্ন করা; বিপদাপন্ন করা। 2. To venture on; as, to *hazard* an opinion, statement, action, etc.; সাহস করিয়া বলা। **At all hazards**—At any risk; যতই বিপদ্ হউক না কেন তাহা অগ্রাহ্য করিয়া, সর্বপ্রকার বিপদ্ সত্ত্বেও। **To run the hazard**—To incur the risk; ঝুঁকি ঘাড়ে লওয়া।

hăz'-ard-ous (-ĕrd-ŭs), *adj.* 1. Exposed to hazard; risky; বিপৎসঙ্কুল, ঝুঁকিদার; সঙ্কট-সঙ্কুল। 2. Depending on chance; দৈবায়ত্ত, দৈবাধীন। **—ly**, *adv.* **—ness**, *n.*

hāze, *n. & v. t.* 1. Light mist; fog; কুয়াসা; কুজ্ঝটিকা। 2. (*Fig.*) Mental obscurity; confusion; অস্পষ্টতা; ঘোর। ***Verb t.*** To make hazy; কুজ্ঝটিকাচ্ছন্ন করা, ঘোরাল করা, অস্পষ্ট করা, ঝাপ্সা করা।

hāze, *v. t.* 1. (*Naut.*) To harass or annoy with overwork; (নৌবিদ্যা) অতিশয় খাটাইয়া উত্ত্যক্ত করা, জ্বালাতন করা। 2. (*U. S.*) To annoy by playing abusive tricks etc. upon; উত্ত্যক্ত করা, জ্বালাতন করা।

hā'-zel (-z'), *n.* 1. A kind of shrub or small tree; একপ্রকার ক্ষুদ্র বৃক্ষ, ফিন্দাক্ বা বিন্দাক (ওয়াট)। 2. Its wood; a stick of its wood; ঐ গাছের কাঠ; ঐ কাঠের লাঠি। 3. A reddish brown colour, esp. of eyes; পিঙ্গলবর্ণ (বিশেষতঃ চক্ষু-সম্পর্কে)। **—ly**, *adj.* 1. Abounding in, or covered with, hazel bushes; ফিন্দাক্ তরুবহুল, ফিন্দাক্ বৃক্ষ সমাচ্ছন্ন। 2. Light-brown; ফিকে বাদামী। **Hazel nut**—The nut of the hazel tree; ফিন্দাক্ বৃক্ষের ফল।

hăz'-ĕl-ine (-ĭn), *n.* An alcoholic extract from the Witch Hazel; ফিন্দাক জাতীয় বৃক্ষ বিশেষের পত্র ও বল্কলের নির্যাস হইতে প্রস্তুত মুখাদিতে মাখিবার জন্য স্নিগ্ধ অভ্যঞ্জন বিশেষ।

hā'-zȳ, *adj.* 1. Covered with haze; কুয়াসাচ্ছন্ন। 2. Obscure; vague; as, a *hazy* argument: a *hazy* mind; অস্পষ্ট; ঝাপ্সা, ঘোরাল। 3. Slightly drunk; ঈষৎ মাতাল। **—zi-ly**, *adv.* **—zi-ness**, *n.*

hē, *pron., n. & adj.* A male person or animal named before (*3rd pers., nom., sing., mas.*); তিনি, সে। ***Noun.*** (*Pl.* HES) A man; a male; "Good spouses to the shes and none at all to the *hes*"; মানুষ; পুরুষ। ***Adj.*** Masculine, as in *he*-goat; পুং।

head (hĕd), *n.* 1. The upper division of the human body; মস্তক, মাথা, শির, মুণ্ড, মৌলি, উত্তমাঙ্গ, বরাঙ্গ, শীর্ষ, তুণ্ড, মূর্দ্ধা। 2. The hair esp. when dressed; কেশ, বিশেষতঃ সুবিন্যস্ত কেশ। 3. The seat of intellect; the brain; the mental faculties; as, he has a good *head*; মস্তিষ্ক; বুদ্ধি; মাথা। 4. A ruler, chief or leader; the principal or headmaster of an institution; as, the *head* of a college or school; প্রধান, দলপতি, সর্দ্দার, অগ্রণী, নায়ক, নেতা; প্রধান শিক্ষক বা অধ্যক্ষ। 5. The place of honour or command; the most important position; the front; as, the *head* of a procession, army, etc. ; সম্মানের স্থান ; শীর্ষ স্থান ; অগ্রভাগ, সম্মুখ ভাগ। 6. A person ; as, wise *heads* ; ব্যক্তি। 7. Each one among many ; an individual, (*often used in a pl. sense*) ; as, a thousand *head* of cattle : give them Rs. 3 per *head* ; প্রতি ব্যক্তিটা ; জন। 8. The chief point of discourse ; আলোচনার মুখ্য বিষয়। 9. A title ; a heading ; a category ; উপাধি ; শীর্ষলিপি ; শ্রেণী। 10. A source ; as, the *head* of a river ; মূল, উৎপত্তি স্থান। 11. Highest point of anything ; পরাকাষ্ঠা, সর্ব্বোচ্চ সীমা। 12. Culminating point or crisis ; চরম সীমা, সঙ্কট-কাল। 13. A thing like a head in form or position ; আকার বা অবস্থানে মস্তকবৎ বস্তু। 14. Top ; as, the *head* of a mast, staircase, etc. ; অগ্রভাগ। 15. The compact mass of leaves or flowers at the top of a stem ; বৃন্তাগ্রস্থ সংহত পত্র বা পুষ্পগুচ্ছ। 16. The part of a lake at which a river enters it ; হ্রদের যে ভাগে নদী উহাতে প্রবেশ করে। 17. The froth on beer etc. ; cream on the top of milk ; বীয়র প্রভৃতি মদ্যের ফেনা বা গাজলা ; দুধের সর। 18. Image of head on one side of a coin ; টাকা প্রভৃতির উপরে মুদ্রিত মাথা। 19. That end of a bed at which one's head rests ; শিয়র। 20. The bow of a ship ; পোতাগ্র, জাহাজের আগা গলুই। 21. The antlers of a deer ; মৃগশৃঙ্গ। 22. The matured part of a boil etc. ; ফোঁড়া প্রভৃতির মুখ। 23. A quantity of water kept at a height for a mill etc. ; the pressure of a confined body of stream etc. ; কল প্রভৃতির জন্য উচ্চ স্থানে সঞ্চিত জলরাশি ; রুদ্ধ প্রবাহ প্রভৃতির চাপ। 24. A promontory or headland ; অন্তরীপ। 25. The front part of a plough holding the share ; লাঙ্গলের যে অংশে ফাল নিবদ্ধ থাকে। **Head'-ed**, *adj.* Furnished with a head (commonly as denoting intellectual faculties) ; as, a clear-*headed* man ; মস্তকবিশিষ্ট, মাথাওয়ালা। **Head'-less**, *adj.* 1. Having no head ; মস্তকহীন, বিশিরস্ক, অশিরস্ক। 2. Having no brains ; foolish ; মস্তকহীন ; বুদ্ধিহীন। **Headache**—Pain in the head ; শিরোবেদনা, মাথাব্যথা, শীর্ষবেদনা, শিরঃপীড়া, মস্তকশূল, কপাল-শূল। **Head-achy**—শিরঃপীড়াগ্রস্ত, শিরোবেদনাজনক। **Head-band** — শিরোবেষ্টনী, শিরোবন্ধনী, কানপট্টী। **Head-dress**—শিরোবস্ত্র, শিরস্ক, শিরস্ত্রাণ, উষ্ণীষ, পাগড়ী, শিরোভূষণ, মস্তকাবরণ, শিরোভূষা, টুপি, শিরোবেষ্টন। **Head-fast**—জাহাজ বা নৌকার আগা বাঁধিবার কাছি। **Head-gear**—A hat or cap ; a head-dress ; মস্তকাবরণ ; শিরোভূষণ। **Head-hunting**--বোর্ণিও দ্বীপের Dyaks জাতীয় লোকদিগের মধ্যে মনুষ্য-মস্তক সংগ্রহের জন্য হঠাৎ আক্রমণের প্রথা। **Head-land**—অন্তরীপ, টেক, ভূশলাকা (কেপ্‌ডিঃ) ; ক্ষেত্রের কোন কোণের অকর্ষিত ভূমিখণ্ড। **Head-light**—পোত, বাষ্পীয় শকট, প্রভৃতির সম্মুখভাগের আলোক। **Head-line**—(পত্রাদির) শীর্ষ রেখা ; সংবাদ পত্রের প্রবন্ধাদির শীর্ষনাম বা উপশীর্ষনাম। **Head-long** — *adv.* & *adj.* With the head foremost ; precipitately ; rashly ; হুমড়ি খেয়ে, মুখ থুবড়ে ; উদ্দাম বেগে ; বেপরওয়া ভাবে, অবিবেচনাপূর্ব্বক। (*Adj.*) Plunging head foremost ; as, a *headlong* dive ; মাথা নীচু করিয়া। Precipitate ; impetuous ; rash ; as, *headlong* folly ; বেগে অধঃপতনশীল ; উদ্দাম ; হিতাহিতবিচারশূন্য, কাণ্ডজ্ঞানহীন। **Head-man**—প্রধান লোক, সর্দ্দার, মণ্ডল, মোড়ল, নেতা, মাতব্বর। **Head-master, —mistress** — বিদ্যালয়ের প্রধান শিক্ষক ; (*Fem.* প্রধান শিক্ষয়িত্রী)। **Head-money** — পলাতক অপরাধীর মস্তকের জন্য পুরস্কার। **Head-most**—Foremost ; শীর্ষস্থানীয়, সর্ব্বাগ্রগামী (কেপ্‌ডিঃ)। **Head-piece**—A helmet ; উষ্ণীষ, পাগড়ী। Intellect ; a man of intellect ; বুদ্ধি ; মাথাওয়ালা লোক, বুদ্ধিমান ব্যক্তি। Ornamental engraving at the head of a chapter or of a page ; কোন পরিচ্ছেদ বা পৃষ্ঠার শীর্ষভাগের শোভাজনক চিত্র। **Head-quarters**—(১) সেনাপতির বাসস্থান ; যে স্থান হইতে আদেশাদি প্রচারিত হয়, মুখ্যনিবেশ, সদর মোকাম, সদর ; মুখ্য নিবেশস্থ কর্ম্মচারিবর্গ। (২) প্রধান কর্ম্মক্ষেত্র। **Heads-man**—An executioner ; জল্লাদ, ঘাতক। A man in command of a whaling boat ; তিমি মাছ শিকারের নৌকার প্রধান চালক। **Head-spring**—The fountain-head or chief source of a stream etc. ; source ; as, the *head-spring* of our belief ; উৎপত্তি, উৎস ; উৎপত্তিস্থল। **Head-stall**—অশ্বাদির লাগাম বা গলরজ্জুর যে অংশ মাথায় লাগান হয়। **Head-stock**—(*Mach.*) A bearing or pedestal for a revolving or moving part ; (যন্ত্রবিজ্ঞান) আবর্ত্তনশীল বা গতিশীল অংশের জন্য ঘর্ষণবেগ নিবারক ব্যবস্থা। **Head-stone**—The chief or corner-stone (*lit.* & *fig.*) ; প্রাচীর কোণের অংশ স্বরূপ প্রস্তরখণ্ড, কোণপ্রস্তর। **Headstone**—The stone at the head of a grave ; সমাধিশীর্ষ প্রস্তর। **Head-strong**—Self-willed ; obstinate ; as, a *headstrong* boy ; উগ্রমস্তিষ্ক ; মগড়া, একগুঁয়ে, একরোখা। (*Headstrongness, n.*) **Head-tire**—শিরোবস্ত্র ; শিরোভূষা। **Head-way**—The progress or rate of progress of a ship in motion ; hence, progress of any kind ; জাহাজের অগ্রগতি ; পুরোবর্ত্তন, অগ্রগতি। (*Arch.*) The space overhead ; মাথার উপরের স্থান। **Head-wind**—A wind opposite a ship's course ; প্রতিকূলবায়ু, সম্মুখবায়ু, সম্মুখবাত। **Head-work**—Mental labour ; মানসিক শ্রম, মাথার খাটুনি।

Better be the head of an ass than the tail of a horse—বড় লোকের পা হওয়ার চাইতে ছোট লোকের মাথা হওয়া ভাল। **By head and shoulders**—By force; সবলে। Considerably, (*lit.* & *fig.*); as, taller *by head and shoulders*; (কাঁধ ও মাথা যতটা); অনেকটা। **By the head**—(*Naut.*) Laden too deeply at the forepart; (*fig.*) slightly drunk; মাথাভারি; আধ-মাতাল। **By the head and ears**—Forcibly (esp. of dragging in a story); সবলে। **From head to foot**—From top to toe; all over the person; আপাদমস্তক, আপাদশির; সর্ব্বশরীরে, সর্ব্বাঙ্গে। **Head and front**—The outstanding and important part; the chief point; প্রধান অংশ; আসল কথা, সার বিষয়। **Head and shoulders**—By the height of the head and shoulders; এক মাথা ও কাঁধের উচ্চতা। **Head first or foremost**—With the head foremost (of a fall, plunge, etc.); (*fig.*) precipitately; হুমড়ি খেয়ে; (লক্ষণায়) উদ্দাম বেগে। **Head of a comet**—কেতু-শিখা (হিঃ কোঃ)। **Head over heels**—Topsy turvy; hurriedly; মুখ থুবড়ে, ডিগবাজী খাইয়া; ব্যস্ত ভাবে। **Heads or tails**—চিৎ না উপড়, এপিঠ না ওপিঠ, চিৎ না ভুট। **Off one's head**—Crazy; ক্ষিপ্ত, উন্মত্ত, বিকৃত-মস্তিষ্ক। **Out of one's own head**—From one's own mind, imagination or invention; নিজের মাথা হইতে। **Over head and ears**—Completely; as, *over head and ears* in debt; সম্পূর্ণরূপে। **Over one's head**—Above one; কাহারও মাথার উপরে। (Of time) Past; (সময় সম্পর্কে) অতীত। Beyond one's comprehension; as, he talks *over our heads*; বুদ্ধির অতীত, ধারণার অতীত। Neglecting the prior claim of one in promotion etc.; as, he promoted me *over his head*; অগ্রগণ্য দাবী উপেক্ষা করিয়া। **The head-end of a bed**—শিয়র, শিথান। **To beat one's head off**—To beat him out and out or thoroughly; সম্পূর্ণরূপে পরাজিত করা। **To buy or sell a property over one's head**—To buy or sell it without consulting the occupants; কোন সম্পত্তির দখলকারকে জিজ্ঞাসা না করিয়া সেই সম্পত্তি ক্রয় বা বিক্রয় করা। **To carry a high head**—To be proud; মাথা উঁচু করিয়া চলা। **To eat his head off**—(Of a horse) See under EAT. **To gain, get or gather head**—To gain strength or force; শক্তি বা বল লাভ করা। **To give the head**—To give freedom or license (to); as, *to give the head* to a horse; স্বাধীনতা দেওয়া, যথেচ্ছাভাবে চলিতে দেওয়া, রাশ ছাড়িয়া দেওয়া। **To grow or come to a head**—To ripen; to approach completion; to come to a crisis; পাকিয়া উঠা; সম্পন্ন হইয়া আসা; চরম অবস্থায় আসা। **To have a head on one's shoulders**—To possess judgment and discretion; বিচারবুদ্ধি-সম্পন্ন হওয়া। **To hit the nail on the head**—To guess aright; to do the right thing; ঠিক অনুমান করা; ঠিক কাজ করা; **To keep one's head**—To keep calm; মাথা ঠিক রাখা, স্থির থাকা, ধৈর্য্যাবলম্বন করিয়া থাকা। **To keep one's head above water**—(*Fig.*) To keep out of debt; (লক্ষণায়) অঋণী থাকা। **To lay heads together**—To consult together; একত্র মন্ত্রণা করা, কয়েক জন মিলিয়া পরামর্শ করা। **To let a man have his head**—To allow him to have freedom; কাহাকেও স্বাধীনতা দেওয়া। **To lose one's head**—To be beheaded; শিরশ্ছেদ হওয়া। To be confused; মাথা ঘুরিয়া যাওয়া বিভ্রান্ত হওয়া, ভ্যাবাচ্যাকা লাগা। **To make head**—To press forward; ঠেলিয়া অগ্রসর হওয়া। **To make head against**—To resist successfully; বাধা দেওয়া, প্রতিরোধ করা। **To make head or tail of**—To understand; বুঝিতে পারা। **To make neither head nor tail of anything**—To be unable to understand it; মাথামুণ্ডু কিছুই না বুঝিতে পারা। **To put a thing into one's head**—To suggest it to one; কাহারও মাথায় ঢুকাইয়া দেওয়া। **To put out of one's head**—To forget; to remove the thought of; ভুলিয়া যাওয়া; মন হইতে দূর করা। **To take it into one's head**—To conceive a sudden idea or notion of it; হঠাৎ মনে উদয় হওয়া, হঠাৎ খেয়াল চাপা। **To talk a person's head off**—To weary him with talk; পচাল পাড়িয়া হয়রান করা। **To turn one's head**—মাথা ঘুরাইয়া দেওয়া।

head (hĕd), *v. t.* & *i.* **1.** To act as a head to; to be as a head of; কোন কিছুর মস্তকস্বরূপ হওয়া; মস্তকস্বরূপ থাকা। **2.** To furnish with a head; মস্তকবিশিষ্ট করা। **3.** To lead; to direct, as, to *head* an expedition or a company; নেতৃত্ব করা; পরিচালনা করা। **4.** To go in front of; to oppose; কোন কিছুর সম্মুখবর্ত্তী হওয়া; প্রতিরোধ করা, বাধা দেওয়া। **5.** To cut off the top of (trees, etc.); অগ্রভাগ ছেদন করা। **6.** To be at the head of; as, to *head* a list; শীর্ষস্থান অধিকার করা। **7.** To excel; অতিক্রম করা, ছাড়াইয়া যাওয়া। **8.** To go round the head or source of (a stream or other body of water); উৎপত্তি স্থল পরিক্রম করা। **9.** To hit with the head; as, to *head* a foot ball; মস্তকদ্বারা আঘাত করা।

10. (*Obs.*) To behead ; (অপ্রঃ) শিরশ্ছেদ করা, মাথা কাটা। ***Verb i.*** 1. To form a head ; as, these cabbages will not *head* ; মাথা বাঁধা। 2. To go in a certain direction ; as, a ship *heads* for a place ; to tend ; যাওয়া ; উন্মুখ হওয়া। 3. To come to a head, as a boil etc. ; পাকিয়া উঠা, মুখ তুলিয়া উঠা। **To head back, off**—To get ahead of so as to turn back aside ; পশ্চাদ্দিকে ফিরিয়া একপার্শ্বে সরিবার জন্য কাহারো বা কোন কিছুর অগ্রবর্তী হওয়া।

head'-êr (hĕd-), *n.* 1. One who puts a head on anything, *e. g.* a cask etc. ; যে ব্যক্তি কোন কিছুতে মাথা বা ডালা লাগায়। 2. A fall or plunge head foremost, as while riding a bicycle or in bathing ; as, to take a *header* (*colloq.*) ; হুমড়িখেয়ে পড়ন, মুখ থুবড়ে পড়ন, অবমূর্দ্ধপাত। 3. A brick or stone laid with the end in the face of a wall, (*opp.* to a STRETCHER) ; যে ইষ্টক বা প্রস্তর খণ্ডের প্রান্ত প্রাচীরে স্থাপিত করা হয়।

head'-ing (hĕd-), *n.* 1. A title etc. at the top of a page ; শীর্ষনাম, শিরোনাম। 2. Hitting a football with the head ; মস্তক দ্বারা পাদগোলক তাড়ন। 3. A horizontal passage in preparation for a tunnel ; সুড়ঙ্গের জন্য নির্ম্মানাধীন ভূমির সহিত সমান্তরাল পথ।

head'-ŷ (hĕd-), *adj.* 1. Wilful ; violent ; impetuous ; as, to grow *heady* : a *heady* current ; একগুঁয়ে ; উগ্র; উগ্র-প্রকৃতি, হঠকারী, অবিমৃষ্যকারী ; প্রচণ্ড, উদ্দাম। 2. Intoxicating, as a liquor; মত্ততাজনক, নেশাজনক। **—i-ly,** *adv.* **—i-ness,** *n.*

heal (hēl), *v. t.* & *i.* 1. To make hale or sound ; to cure ; as, to *heal* one of a disease : to *heal* a disease or wound ; আরোগ্য করা, আরাম করা ; নিরাময় করা, সুস্থ করা। 2. To remedy or repair ; as, time *heals* grief ; to reconcile ; as, to *heal* dissensions ; প্রতীকার করা ; মিটান, মিটমাট করা, মীমাংসা করা। 3. To make pure ; "*Heal* me with your pardon" ; শুদ্ধ করা, পবিত্র করা। ***Verb i.*** To become sound or whole as a sick person, wound, etc. ; আরোগ্য হওয়া, আরাম হওয়া, সারিয়া উঠা। **Heal'-a-ble,** *adj.* **Heal'-er,** *n.* **Heal-all**—A universal remedy ; সর্ব্বৌষধি, সর্ব্বরোগহর ঔষধ। **The healing art**—চিকিৎসা-বিদ্যা, আরোগ্য-শাস্ত্র, আয়ুর্ব্বেদশাস্ত্র।

heald (hēld), *n.* Same as HEDDLE.

health (hĕlth), *n.* 1. Soundness of body, mind or soul ; condition of body ; as, good or bad *health* ; স্বাস্থ্য ; সুস্থতা, নীরোগতা। 2. A wish of health and happiness, in pledging a person in a toast ; a toast ; স্বাস্থ্যকামনা ; কোন ব্যক্তির স্বাস্থ্যকামনার জন্য ভোজ্য মদ্যসিক্ত রুটিকা-খণ্ড। **Bill of health** — See BILL. **Health-officer, Officer of health**—স্বাস্থ্য-পরিদর্শক কর্ম্মচারী, স্বাস্থ্যরক্ষক।

health'-fûl (hĕlth-), *adj.* 1. Tending to promote health ; wholesome ; as, a *healthful* climate ; স্বাস্থ্য-জনক ; স্বাস্থ্যকর, আরোগ্যপ্রদ, আরোগ্য-বর্দ্ধক, হিতকর, অনাময়ক্ষম। 2. (*Rare*) Full of, or enjoying, health ; (কচিদ্ ব্যবহৃত) স্বাস্থ্যপূর্ণ, সুস্থ। 3. Conducive to moral or spiritual welfare ; আধ্যাত্মিক মঙ্গলজনক। **—ly,** *adv.* **—ness,** *n.*

health'-ŷ (hĕlth-), *adj.* 1. Enjoying good health ; sound ; সুস্থ ; নিরাময়। 2. Conducive to health ; salutary ; as, *healthy* exercise or climate ; স্বাস্থ্যজনক ; স্বাস্থ্যকর। 3. Evincing health ; as, a *healthy* pulse ; স্বাস্থ্যসূচক। **—i-ly,** *adv.* **—i-ness,** *n.* **Healthy ulcer**—শুদ্ধ ব্রণ (সাঃ পঃ)।

heap (hēp), *n.* 1. A group of things lying one on another ; a pile ; as, a *heap* of earth or stones ; স্তূপ, রাশি ; গাদা, ঢিবি, উচ্চয়, চয়, পুঞ্জ, কাঁড়ি। 2. A crowd or large number (*colloq.*) ; as, a *heap* of people ; দল, সংঘ, সমূহ, সমবায়, সমুচ্চয়, বৃন্দ, বহুসংখ্যা। **He is heaps better**—He is much better ; সে আগের চাইতে ঢের ভাল। **To strike all of a heap**—To prostrate mentally ; অভিভূত করা।

heap (hēp), *v. t.* 1. To pile in a heap, (with *up*, *together*) ; as, to *heap up* earth ; to amass ; to accumulate ; as, to *heap up* treasures : "*Heaped* on her terms of disgrace" ; স্তূপীকৃত করা, রাশীকৃত করা ; পুঞ্জীভূত করা ; সঞ্চিত করা। 2. To load (carts, persons, etc. *with* goods, benefits etc.) ; বোঝাই করা, ভারাক্রান্ত করা।

hear (hēr), *v. t.* & *i.* 1. To perceive with the ear ; শোনা, শ্রবণ করা। 2. To listen to ; as, to *hear* him out to the end ; কর্ণপাত করা। 3. To try in a court of justice ; as, to *hear* a case ; মোকদ্দমার বিচার করা। 4. To accede to the demand or wishes of ; to grant as a prayer or request ; কাহারও ইচ্ছা পুরণ করা ; প্রার্থনা পুরণ করা। 5. To learn or come to know ; জানা, অবগত হওয়া। 6. (*Obs.*) To obey ; (অপ্রঃ) মানা, মান্য করা। ***Verb i.*** 1. To have the sense or faculty of perceiving sound ; শ্রবণশক্তি-সম্পন্ন হওয়া। 2. To listen ; to attend ; as, he *hears* with solicitude ; কর্ণপাত করা ; কাণ দেওয়া। 3. To be informed, (usu. followed by *that*, *of*, *about*) ; as, I have *heard of* such a man ; অবগত হওয়া, লোকমুখে শোনা। 4. An imperative expression of approbation or cheering (often ironical) ;

as, *hear! hear!* ঐ শোন! ঐ শোন! **Hear'-a-ble,** *adj.* **Hear'-er,** *n.* শ্রবণকর্ত্তা, শ্রোতা। **Hear! hear!**—An exclamation indicating either admiration, acquiescence, indignation or derision; ক্রোধ, প্রশংসা, ঘৃণা, বা সম্মতিসূচক চীৎকার, শোন! শোন! **He will hear of this**—He will be reprimanded for it; সে ইহার জন্য ধমক খাইবে। **He will not hear of it**—He will not entertain the notion of it; সে এই কথা মনেও স্থান দিবে না। **To hear a bird sing**—(*Colloq.*) To receive private communication; (চলিত ভাষায়) গোপনীয় সংবাদ প্রাপ্ত হওয়া। **To hear tell of**—(*Slang*) To hear by report; to learn; (ইতর ভাষায়) লোক মুখে শোনা; জানিতে পারা।

hear'-ing (hër-), *n.* **1.** Act of perceiving sound; শ্রবণ, আকর্ণন। **2.** Perception of sound by ear; as, my *hearing* is good; শ্রবণশক্তি, শ্রুতিশক্তি। **3.** Audience; as, I could not obtain a *hearing* from him; কর্ণ প্রদান। **4.** A judicial trial of a suit; মোকদ্দমার শুনানি, দর্শন (মিতঃ)। **5.** Reach of the ear; as, he was not within *hearing*; শ্রবণবিষয়, শ্রবণসীমা, শ্রুতিযোগ্য দূরত্ব, শ্রুতিসীমা। **6.** A scolding; a lecture (*colloq.*); তিরস্কার, ভৎর্সনা (cf. বেশ দু'কথা শুনাইয়া দেওয়া); বক্তৃতা (চলিত ভাষায়)। **Give him a fair hearing**—Listen impartially to him; নিরপেক্ষভাবে শ্রবণ কর। **Within hearing**—Near enough to be heard; শ্রুতিসীমার মধ্যে।

hear'-ken (hâr-kn), *v. i.* To listen to; কর্ণপাত করা।

hear'-say (hër-sā), *n.* Report; rumour; জনশ্রুতি; জনরব। **Hearsay evidence**—জনশ্রুতিমূলক প্রমাণ, যথাশ্রুত প্রমাণ।

hearse (hêrs), *n.* A carriage for conveying the dead to the grave; শবযান, প্রেতরথ, প্রেতশকট (সায়ন)। **Hearse-cloth**—শবযানাচ্ছাদন বস্ত্র।

heart (hârt), *n.* **1.** (*Anat.*) An organ keeping up the circulation of blood; হৃৎপিণ্ড, রক্তাশয় (হঃ চঃ)। **2.** The seat of emotions esp. of love; as, to give or lose one's *heart*; affection; as, he has no *heart*: মর্ম্মস্থান, হৃদয়, মরম (কবিতায়), হিয়া (ঐ), অন্তঃকরণ; স্নেহ, প্রীতি, করুণাদি ভাব, হৃদয় (যথা—সে হৃদয়হীন)। **3.** Breast; বক্ষঃ, বুক। **4.** Mind; soul; মন; আত্মা। **5.** Courage; spirit; as, to pluck up or take *heart*: to lose *heart*; সাহস, কলিজা, বুকের পাটা, বুকের ছাতা; উৎসাহ। **6.** (*Obs.*) Disposition; (অপ্রঃ) স্বভাব। **7.** The central part esp. of a tree; মধ্যবর্ত্তী অংশ (বিশেষতঃ বৃক্ষের)। **8.** Vital or most essential part; secret meaning; as, Wordsworth goes to the very *heart* of things; মরম, মর্ম্ম; গূঢ়ার্থ। **9.** Fertility; as, keep the land in *heart*; উর্ব্বরতা। **10.** A thing like a heart in shape; হৃৎপিণ্ডাকৃতি বস্তু। **11.** One of a suit of cards marked with heart-shaped figures in red; (*pl.*) the suit itself; হরতন; হরতনের তাস। **12.** A term of affectionate address; as, dear or sweet *heart*; প্রাণ (যথা, আমার প্রাণ, প্রাণপ্রতিম, প্রাণাধিক)। **Heart'-ed,** *adj.* In heart; as, kind or hard *hearted*; অন্তঃকরণবিশিষ্ট। **Heart'-less,** *adj.* **1.** Without a heart; spiritless; হৃৎপিণ্ডহীন; উদ্যমহীন। **2.** Pitiless; cruel; হৃদয়হীন, নির্দ্দয়; ক্রূর। **Heart'-less-ly,** *adv.* **Heart'-less-ness,** *n.* **Heart-ache**—হৃদয়বেদনা, মর্ম্মবেদনা, মর্ম্মব্যথা, মনস্তাপ, হৃদয়সন্তাপ, মনোদুঃখ, চিন্তাজ্বর। **Heart-beat**—A pulsation of the heart; ধুকধুকি, হৃদয়-স্পন্দন, দুরুদুরু। **Heart-blood, Heart's-blood**—Blood of the heart; life blood; হৃদয়ের-রক্ত, বুকের রক্ত; হৃচ্ছোণিত। **Heart-break**—মনোভঙ্গ। **Heart-breaking**—Causing heartbreak; হৃদয়-বিদারক, মর্ম্মভেদী, হৃদয়ভেদী। **Heart broken**—Intensely afflicted or grieved; ভগ্নহৃদয়। **Heartburn**—অগ্নিমান্দ্য সহকারে আমাশয়ের উপরের মুখে উত্তাপ ও অস্বচ্ছন্দতা অনুভব (হঃ চঃ), বুকজ্বালা, হৃদ্দাহ, অম্লপিত্ত (কেণ্ডিঃ), হৃদ্রোগ (ঐ)। **Heart-burning**—গাত্রদাহ, গাত্রজ্বালা, মর্ম্মজ্বালা; অন্তর্দাহ, মর্ম্মসন্তাপ, আক্রোশ। **Heart-disease**—হৃদরোগ, বক্ষঃপীড়া (আয়ুঃ রসঃ)। **Heart-easing**—চিত্ত-প্রশামক, মানসিক শান্তিপ্রদায়ক। **Heart-felt**—অকৃত্রিম, আন্তরিক, হৃদয়ানুভূত, হৃদ্য (কেণ্ডিঃ)। **Heart-pea**—ইঙ্গুদী। **Heart-rending**—Distressing; হৃদয়ভেদী, মর্ম্মচ্ছেদী, মর্ম্মভেদী, হৃদয়-বিদারক। **Heart-searching**—মর্ম্মানুসন্ধায়ী। **Heartsease**—এক-প্রকার গুল্ম। **Heart-shaped**—হৃৎপিণ্ডাকৃতি। **Heart-sick**—Sick at heart; despondent; আর্ত্তহৃদয়; নিরাশ। **Heart-sore**—হৃদয়ক্ষত। **Heart-stealing, -alluring**—চিত্তচোর। **Heart-stirring**—প্রাণ-চঞ্চলকর, প্রাণোন্মাদী, হৃদয়হারী। **Heart strings**—হৃদয়তন্ত্রী। **Heart-whole**—Undismayed; sincere; not in love; ভয়রহিত; সরল, অকৃত্রিম; কাহারো প্রেমে পতিত নয়। **Heart-wood**—বৃক্ষের সার। **After on'es own heart**—To one's own liking; মনের মতন, পুসন্দ সই। **At heart**—In one's inmost feelings; really; as, he is *at heart* a good man; অন্তরের অন্তরতম প্রদেশে; বাস্তবিক পক্ষে। **By heart**—In or from memory; as, to learn or say *by heart*; মুখস্থ, কণ্ঠস্থ। **From one's heart**—Sincerely; অকপটচিত্তে। **Heart and hand**—Enthusiastically; মনে-প্রাণে। **Heart and soul**—With all one's energy; with the utmost earnestness; মনেপ্রাণে; সর্ব্বান্তঃকরণে, সর্ব্বপ্রযত্নে। **Heart of oak**—সাহসী, কর্ম্মঠ লোক—বিশেষতঃ ইংরেজ জাতির। **His heart is in the right place**—He means well; তাঁহার মনের গতি ভাল। **His heart sank into his boots**—He became disheartened or discouraged; সে দমিয়া গিয়াছিল। **In heart**—In good spirits; স্ফূর্ত্তিতে। **In one's heart**—Secretly; গোপনে। **In one's heart of hearts**—In one's inmost feelings; in the inmost heart; প্রাণে প্রাণে; অন্তরের অন্তরতম প্রদেশে, অন্তরের অন্তঃপুরে (রবীঃ)। **It does my heart good**—It rejoices me; ইহাতে আমার প্রাণে আনন্দ হয়। **Near** or **nearest one's heart**—প্রিয়তম, প্রাণপ্রতিম। **Out of heart**—In poor condition, as a piece of land; অনুর্ব্বর। In low spirit; স্ফূর্ত্তিহীন, উৎসাহশূন্য। **Right** or **left heart**—The right or left side of the organ heart; হৃৎ পিণ্ডের বাম বা দাক্ষণ পার্শ্ব। **Searchings of the heart**—Misgivings; সন্দেহ, অবিশ্বাস। **Smoker's heart**—ধূমপান হেতু হৃৎপিণ্ডের রোগ। **To break one's heart**—*v. t.* & *i.* To overwhelm a person with sorrow; হৃদয়-ভগ্ন করা, বুক ভাঙ্গা। (*Verb i.*) To die of disappointment; ভগ্নমনোরথ হইয়া মৃত্যুমুখে পতিত হওয়া। **To carry** or **wear one's heart upon one's sleeve**—To lack proper reserve; to show one's feeling etc. openly; মনের ভাব প্রকাশ করা; প্রকাশ্যে হৃদয়াবেগ প্রদর্শন করা। **To cry one's heart out**—To cry violently; উচ্চৈঃস্বরে চীৎকার করা। **To eat one's heart out**—To pine away from vexation etc.; বিরক্তি, মনস্তাপ প্রভৃতির দরুন দিন দিন শীর্ণ হওয়া। **To find in one's heart**—To be willing or ready to do something; কোন কাজ করিতে ইচ্ছুক বা প্রস্তুত হওয়া। **To get** or **learn by heart**—To commit to memory; মুখস্থ করা, কণ্ঠস্থ করা। **To have a thing at heart**—To purpose or plan; মনে মনে ইচ্ছা থাকা। **To have in the heart**—To be deeply interested in it; কোন বিষয়ে গভীর অনুরাগ থাকা। **To have one's heart in one's boots**—To be greatly depressed esp. by terror; (ভয়ে) মুহ্যমান হওয়া। **To have one's heart in one's mouth**—To be violently alarmed at or startled; ভয়ে থরহরি কাঁপা, অতিশয় চমকিত হওয়া। **To have the heart**—To be hard-hearted enough (to do); ততটা কঠিনচিত্ত হওয়া। **To lay a thing to heart**—To think it over seriously; কোন বিষয়ে গভীরভাবে চিন্তা করা। **To lose heart**—To become discouraged; নিরুৎসাহ হওয়া, ভগ্নাশ হওয়া, বলভরসা হারান। **To lose one's heart**—To fall in love; প্রেমে পড়া। **To make the heart bleed**—To cause extreme pain or anguish; বক্ষ বিদীর্ণ করা, বুক ফাটান। **To one's heart's content**—To one's utmost satisfaction; আশ মিটাইয়া। **To set the heart at rest**—To become easy in mind; খাতিরজমা থাকা, নিশ্চিন্ত থাকা। **To set the heart upon**—To desire earnestly; প্রাণে চাওয়া, মন প্রাণ সমর্পণ করা। **To take a thing to heart**—To feel deeply pained about anything; মনে লাগা, প্রাণে বাজা, প্রাণে লাগা। **To take heart (of grace)**—To pluck up courage; to feel encouraged; সাহসে বুক বাঁধা; উৎসাহিত বোধ করা। **With all one's heart**—Very earnestly or sincerely; সর্ব্বান্তঃকরণে, মনে প্রাণে।

heart'-en (hârt-n), *v. t.* & *i.* To encourage; to cheer, (often with *on, up*); উৎসাহিত করা; আনন্দিত করা। ***Verb i.*** To cheer up; প্রোৎসাহিত করা।

hearth (hârth), *n.* **1.** The floor of a fire-place; গৃহমধ্যস্থ অগ্নিসেবনস্থলীর ভিত্তি-ভূমি, অগ্নিসেবনস্থলীর তলদেশ। **2.** The house or family; as, household talk and phrases of the *hearth*; গৃহ, পরিবার। **Hearth-rug**—অগ্নিসেবনস্থলীর সম্মুখে যে কম্বল বিছান হয়। **Hearth-stone**—যে চ্যাপ্টা প্রস্তরখণ্ডদ্বারা অগ্নিসেবনস্থলীর ভিত্তিভূমি গঠিত হয়; অগ্নিসেবনস্থলীর ভিত্তিভূমি প্রভৃতি ধবলীকরণের জন্য কোমল প্রস্তর বিশেষ।

heart'-i-lŷ (hârt-), *adv.* **1.** With all the heart; sincerely; সর্ব্বান্তঃকরণে; সরলভাবে, অকপটভাবে। **2.** With zeal or courage; willingly; as, he *heartily* assisted the prince; সোৎসাহে, নির্ভীক ভাবে; সাগ্রহে। **3.** With good appetite; as, to eat *heartily*; রুচির সহিত। **4.** Very; as, *heartily* sick of it; ভারি, অত্যন্ত।

heart'-ŷ (hârt-), *adj.* & *n.* **1.** Cordial; sincere; as, a *hearty* welcome or feeling; আন্তরিক, প্রাণভরা, হৃদ্গত; অকৃত্রিম, সহৃদয়, অকপট, নিষ্কপট, অমায়িক। **2.** Strong; vigorous; as, a *hearty* man; বলবান; বীর্য্যবান, তেজস্বী, সতেজ। **3.** Abundant; as, a *hearty* meal; প্রচুর, ভুরি। ***Noun.*** (*Pl.*) Address to sailors; as, my *hearties*; নাবিকদিগকে সম্বোধনে ব্যবহৃত হয়। **—i-ness,** *n.*

heat (hēt) *n.* **1.** A form of energy manifested in the effects of fire, the sun's rays or friction; তাপ, উত্তাপ, উষ্মা, উষ্ণতা। **2.** A sensation produced by this; a perception of this; আঁচ (*colloq.*), গুমট, গরমী; তাপানুভব। **3.** High temperature; as, the *heat* of body in fever;

hot weather ; উচ্চ তাপের মাত্রা ; গ্রীষ্মকাল, গরমের দিন, গুমটকাল, গরম (cf. গরমের ছুটী)। 4. Flush ; "It has raised *heat* of their faces" ; গণ্ডদেশের অরুণিমা, কপোলরাগ। 5. (*In forging*) A single exposure to the fire ; as, give the iron another *heat* ; (হাতুড়ি প্রভৃতি দ্বারা পিটিয়া গড়নে) আগুনে দেওন। 6. Vehemence ; rage ; as, the *heat* of battle ; প্রচণ্ডতা, উচ্চণ্ডতা, চণ্ডতা ; প্রবলতা। 7. A single effort ; as, at a *heat* ; a race or contest ; as, a trial of final *heat* ; একবার চেষ্টা, দম (কেন্ডিঃ) ; (ঘোড়দৌড়) প্রতিদ্বন্দ্বিতা। 8. Agitation of mind ; warmth of feeling ; anger ; ক্ষোভ, সন্তাপ ; আবেগপ্রাবল্য, উত্তেজনা ; ক্রোধ, রাগ। 9. Animation, as in discourse ; ardour ; as, the *heat* of debate ; সজীবতা ; আগ্রহ, উৎসাহ। 10. Sexual excitement of animals during the breeding season ; সঙ্গমঋতুতে জন্তুর কামোত্তেজনা, গরম, মদ। 11. Pungency of flavour ; as, the *heat* of the ginger ; ঝাল, ঝাঁঝ। **Animal heat**—জঠরানল (ব্রজঃ হিন্দু), ঔদর্য্য (ঐ)। **Atomic heat**—পরমাণুতাপ (হিঃ কোঃ)। **Heat appoplexy**—সর্দ্দিগর্ম্মি। **Heat fluid**—তাপদ্রব (হিঃ কোঃ)। **Heat rays**—তাপকিরণ (হিঃ কোঃ)। **Heat spot**—কোন বস্তুর উপরিভাগস্থ যে স্থানে তাপানুভব হয়, তাপবিন্দু। **Heat wave**—তাপোর্ম্মি। **Intense heat**—খরপাক (সাঃ পঃ)। **Latent heat**—কঠিন বস্তুকে তরল বা বাষ্পীয় অথবা তরল বস্তুকে বাষ্পীয় পদার্থে পরিণত করিতে যে পরিমাণ তাপের আবশ্যক হয়, প্রচ্ছন্ন তাপ, অনুভূত তাপ। **Mild heat**—মধ্যপাক (সাঃ পঃ), মৃদুপাক (ঐ)। **Prickly-heat**—ঘর্ম্মচর্চ্চিকা, ঘামাচি। **Red-heat, white heat**—যেরূপ উত্তাপে ধাতু প্রভৃতি রক্ত বা শ্বেতবর্ণ ধারণ করে। **Specific heat**—কোন নির্দ্দিষ্ট বস্তুর তাপ নির্দ্দিষ্ট মাত্রা পর্য্যন্ত বর্দ্ধিত করার জন্য যে পরিমাণ তাপের আবশ্যক, আপেক্ষিক তাপ (হিঃ কোঃ)। **(Trial) heats**—যে ঘোড়দৌড় বা প্রতিযোগিতার ক্রীড়ায় বিজয়ী অশ্বাদি চরম দৌড় প্রভৃতিতে প্রতিযোগিতা করে।

heat (hēt), *v. t. & i.* 1. To communicate heat to ; to make hot ; as, to *heat* an oven or an iron ; তাপসঞ্চার করা ; গরম করা, উত্তপ্ত করা, তাতান। 2. To inflame ; as, to *heat* the blood ; উদ্দীপ্ত করা। 3. To excite with passion or desire ; উত্তেজিত করা, কোপজ্বলিত করা। ***Verb i.*** 1. To grow hot or warm ; as, the iron *heats* slowly ; গরম হওয়া, উষ্ণ হওয়া। 2. (*Fig.*) To become excited or inflamed ; উদ্দীপ্ত হওয়া, উত্তেজিত হওয়া। **Heat'-ed-ly,** *adv.* **Heat'-er,** *n.* One that heats ; a contrivance as a stove etc. for heating ; উষ্ণকারক ; চুল্লী প্রভৃতি। **To heat in a crucible**—ভাবনা করা (সাঃ পঃ)।

heath (hēth), *n.* 1. A shrub esp. of the genus *Erica* ; গুল্ম বিশেষ। 2. Open area overgrown with heath ; a waste tract of land ; as, the *heaths* of Straffordshire ; উক্ত গুল্মাবৃত ভূমি ; অকর্ষিত ভূমি, পতিত জায়গা। **Heath'-y,** *adj.* **Heath-bell** — উক্ত গুল্মের পুষ্প। **Heath-berry**—বিভিন্ন প্রকার ক্ষুদ্র ফল। **Heath-cock**—কপিঞ্জল পক্ষী (মঃ উঃ)।

hea'-then (hē-), *adj. & n.* 1. Neither Jewish, Christian, nor Moslem ; pagan ; irreligious ; অ-খৃষ্টান, অ-ইহুদী বা অ-মুসলমান ; পৌত্তলিক, মূর্ত্তিপূজক ; কাফের, বিধর্ম্মী, ম্লেচ্ছ (হিঃ কোঃ), পাষণ্ড, অপধর্ম্মসেবী। 2. Unenlightened ; barbarous ; অসভ্য ; বর্ব্বর। ***Noun.*** 1. A person who is neither a Jew, Christian nor a Moslem ; an idolater ; যে ব্যক্তি ইহুদী, মুসলমান বা খৃষ্টীয়ান নহে ; পৌত্তলিক, পুত্তলিকাপূজক, মূর্ত্তিপূজক, প্রতিমাপূজক। 2. An unenlightened person ; অসভ্য ব্যক্তি, অশিক্ষিত লোক। **—dom,** *n.* **—ish,** *adj.* **—ish-ly,** *adv.* **—ish-ness,** *n.* **—ry,** *n.* 1. Heathenism ; পৌত্তলিকতা। 2. Heathens collectively ; প্রতিমাপূজকগণ। **—ism,** *n.* 1. Paganism ; পৌত্তলিকতা, মূর্ত্তিপূজা। 2. Barbarism ; অসভ্যতা। **—ize,** *v. t. & i.* To render or become heathen ; পৌত্তলিক করা বা হওয়া।

heath'-êr (hěth-), *n.* Same as HEATH which see. **Heather-bell**—গুল্মবিশেষ ; উক্ত গুল্মের পুষ্প। **Heather-mixture**—মিশ্রবর্ণে রঞ্জিত বস্ত্র বিশেষ। **To set the heather on fire**—To create a disturbance ; লঙ্কাকাণ্ড ঘটান, হাঙ্গামা বাঁধান। **To take to the heather**—To become an outlaw ; নরহত্যাদি গুরুতর অপরাধ করিয়া ফেরার হওয়া।

heave (hēv), *v. t. & i.* (*p. t. & p. p.* HEAVED or HOVE) 1. To lift or raise with exertion ; সবলে উত্তোলিত করা। 2. To cause to swell, as the breast or bosom ; ফুলান, স্ফীত করা। 3. To utter with effort ; as, to *heave* a sigh, groan etc. ; কষ্টে উচ্চারণ করা, কষ্টে ফেলা বা মোচন করা। 4. (*Geol. & mining*) To displace ; as, a vein or stratum *heaves* another ; (ভূবিদ্যা ও খনির কাজ) স্থানান্তরিত করা, স্থানভ্রষ্ট করা, স্থানচ্যুত করা। 5. (*Naut. & colloq.*) To cast or throw ; as, to *heave* a stone or the lead in sounding ; (নৌ-বিদ্যা ও চলিত ভাষায়) নিক্ষেপ করা, ফেলা। 6. (*Naut.*) To haul or haul up by rope etc. ; as, to *heave* a ship ahead : to *heave up* an anchor ; (নৌবিদ্যা) কাছি দ্বারা টানা, কাছিদ্বারা টানিয়া তোলা। ***Verb i.*** 1. To rise with alternate falling, as waves etc. ; পর্য্যায়ক্রমে উঠা নামা। 2. To rise or swell up ; উন্নমিত হওয়া, উচ্ছ্বসিত হওয়া, স্ফীত হওয়া, ফুলিয়া উঠা। 3. To pant ; as, he *heaves* for breath ; কষ্টে শ্বাস

ফেলা, হাঁসফাঁস করা। **4.** To make an effort to vomit; বমনের চেষ্টা করা। **5.** To pull; as, to *heave* at a rope etc.; টানা। **Heave ho**—The cry of sailors in heaving an anchor up; উঠাও। **To heave down**—To turn as ship over on one side for cleaning etc.; পরিষ্কারাদি করার জন্য জাহাজ কাত করিয়া রাখা। **To heave in sight**—To become visible; দৃষ্টিগোচর হওয়া, নয়নগোচর হওয়া, দৃষ্টিপথবর্ত্তী হওয়া। **To heave to**—To stop the progress of (a ship) esp. by bringing her into the wind; (জাহাজ) থামান, বিশেষতঃ অগ্রভাগ বায়ুর অভিমুখীন করিয়া জাহাজ থামান।

heave (hēv), *n.* **1.** Raising something with effort; সবলে উত্তোলন। **2.** A swelling; a rising (and falling) as of waves etc.; স্ফীতি; (তরঙ্গাদির) উত্থানপতন। **3.** A rising of the heart; a sigh; বক্ষস্ফীতি; দীর্ঘনিশ্বাস। **4.** (*Mining*) A displacement of the strata or mineral vein by a dislocation; (খনির কাজ) স্তরচ্যুতি, স্তরভ্রংশ। **5.** (*Pl.*) A disease of horses; অশ্বরোগ বিশেষ।

heav′-en (hĕv-n), *n.* **1.** The sky; the firmament; (*in prose now usu. pl.*); আকাশ, খ, গগন, বিমান, নভঃ, ব্যোম, অম্বর, দিগন্তর; অন্তরীক্ষ, নভোমণ্ডল, গগনমণ্ডল, নক্ষত্রমণ্ডল, খগোল, তারামণ্ডল, তারাঙ্গণ, তারাপথ, ঊর্দ্ধলোক, ঘনাশ্রয়। **2.** The abode of God and of His angels; স্বর্গ, অমরাবতী, অমৃতলোক, দেবধাম, ত্রিদিব, ত্রিদশালয়, স্বর্লোক, সুরপুরী, ইন্দ্রপুরী, দিব্যধাম, সুরলোক, উত্তমলোক, দিব্যলোক, দেবলোক, পরলোক, পুণ্যলোক। **3.** The Supreme Being; God; as, it is *Heaven's* will; পরমপুরুষ; ঈশ্বর, ভগবান। **4.** The state or place of supreme happiness; as, a *heaven* of delight; পরমানন্দধাম, পরমানন্দ, আনন্দঘন অবস্থা। **—ward,** *adj.* & *adv.* **—wards,** *adv.* **Heaven-born**—স্বর্গজাত, স্বর্গজ, স্বর্গোৎপন্ন। **Heaven-born service**—(রঙ্গচ্ছলে) ভারতীয় সিভিল সার্ভিস। **Heaven-directed**—Pointing to the sky; গগনাভিমুখীন, উন্মুখ। Directed by Heaven; ঈশ্বরনির্দ্দিষ্ট। **Heaven-gifted**—দেবদত্ত, ঈশ্বরদত্ত। **Heaven-kissing**—নভোলিহ, আকাশচুম্বী, গগনচুম্বী, অভ্রংলিহ (রঃ)। **Heaven-sent**—দৈবিক, ঈশ্বরপ্রেরিত। **By heavens**—ঈশ্বরের নামে। **Good heavens**—হা ঈশ্বর, হা পরমেশ্বর। **In the seventh heaven**—In a state of supreme bliss; সপ্তম স্বর্গে। **The heaven of heavens, The seventh heaven**—The highest heaven; a place or state of supreme bliss; সপ্তমস্বর্গ, ধ্রুবলোক; পরমানন্দধাম, আনন্দঘন অবস্থা।

heav′-en-lȳ (hĕv-n-), *adj.* **1.** Of, or relating to, heaven; divine; celestial; গগনস্থ, অন্তরীক্ষস্থ, আকাশমণ্ডলসম্বন্ধী, স্বর্গীয়; দিব্য; অপার্থিব। **2.** Of the sky; as, *heavenly* bodies; আকাশিক, আকাশসম্বন্ধীয়। **3.** Supremely excellent; দিব্য, দিব্যি (*colloq.*), পরমোত্তম। **—li-ness,** *n.* **Heavenly minded**—Holy; devout; ধর্ম্মনিষ্ঠ, পরমার্থবুদ্ধি, পরমার্থদৃষ্টি, পরমার্থনিষ্ঠ, পরমার্থিক; ঈশ্বরভক্ত।

heav′-ȳ (hĕv-), *adj.*, *n.* & *adv.* **1.** Weighty; ponderous; as, a *heavy* stone; of high specific gravity; as, gold is a *heavy* metal; গুরু, ভারি; গুরুভার; উচ্চ আপেক্ষিক গুরুত্বসম্পন্ন। **2.** Weighty, because abundant; as, a *heavy* crop; প্রচুর। **3.** Oppressive; afflicting; grievous; as, *heavy* taxes: a *heavy* fate; দুর্ব্বহ; কষ্টজনক; গুরুতর। **4.** Laden with what is weighty; গুরুভারাক্রান্ত, গুরুভার প্রপীড়িত। **5.** Slow; as, a *heavy* gait: a *heavy* style of writing; ধীর, মন্থর, মন্দগামী। **6.** Doleful; as, *heavy* notes of woe; বিষাদপূর্ণ। **7.** Drowsy; spiritless; নিদ্রাতুর, তন্দ্রাতুর; নির্জ্জীব, নিস্তেজ, জড়। **8.** Loud; deep; as, *heavy* thunder or noise; উচ্চ-নিনাদী; গুরুগম্ভীর, গুরুগুরু। **9.** Violent; as, a *heavy* sea or storm; প্রবল, প্রচণ্ড। **10.** Overcast; gloomy; as, a *heavy* sky; মেঘাচ্ছন্ন; তিমিরাচ্ছন্ন, অন্ধকার। **11.** Cloggy; clayey; as, a *heavy* road; প্রতিবন্ধকপূর্ণ; কর্দ্দমাক্ত, পঙ্কিল, কর্দ্দমময়। **12.** Not properly raised or made light; as, a *heavy* bread; উপযুক্তরূপ ফুলান বা হাল্কা করা হয় নাই এরূপ। **13.** Not easily digested; as, *heavy* food; গুরুপাক। **14.** Strong; as, a *heavy* wine or ale; তেজাল, উগ্র। **15.** Difficult; as, a *heavy* task; কঠিন। **16.** (*Theatre*) Serious; grave; as, a *heavy* villain; (নাটকে) গুরুতর, ভয়ঙ্কর; ঘোর, ভয়ানক। **17.** (*Mil.*) Carrying heavy arms; (সামরিক শাস্ত্র) গুরুভার অস্ত্রধারী। **18.** (Of guns etc.) Of the larger kind; (কামান সম্বন্ধে) বৃহৎ। **19.** Sad, as news; বিষাদজনক, শোকাবহ, খেদজনক। **20.** Despondent; grieved; as, a *heavy* heart; নিরাশ, ভগ্নমনোরথ; শোকাকুল। ***Noun.*** (*Pl.*—with *the*) Dragoon Guards; the heavy cavalry; অশ্বারোহী সৈন্য বিশেষ; গুরুভার অস্ত্রধারী অশ্বারোহী সৈন্য। ***Adv.*** Heavily (*now chiefly used in compounds*); as, *heavy*-laden; গুরুভাবে। **—i-ly,** *adv.* **1.** In a heavy manner; as, to be *heavily* loaded; ভারিরূপে, গুরুভাবে। **2.** Slowly and laboriously; মন্দ মন্দ, শনৈঃ শনৈঃ, আস্তে আস্তে। **3.** Forcibly; severely; as, to be *heavily* punished; বলপ্রকাশপূর্ব্বক; কঠোরভাবে, গুরুতররূপে। **—i-ness,** *n.* **1.** Weight; ভার। **2.** Drowsiness; dullness; তন্দ্রাবিষ্টতা; মান্দ্য, অলসাঙ্গতা। **3.** Gloom; বিষাদ। **4.** Oppressiveness; পীড়াদায়কতা, দুর্ব্বহতা। **Heavy-armed**—গুরুভার অস্ত্র বা বর্ম্মধারী।

Heavy-artillery—গুরুভার কামান ; দুর্গাদি অবরোধ কালে সমুদ্রোপকূলে স্থাপিত গুরুভার কামান ; যে সকল গোলন্দাজ সৈন্য গুরুভার কামান চালায়। **Heavy cavalry** — Same as HEAVY. *n.* **Heavy fire**—অবিশ্রান্ত এবং ধ্বংসজনক গোলাগুলি বৃষ্টি। **Heavy-handed**—আনাড়ী, গোব্দা। **Heavy-headed**—জড়বুদ্ধি, নির্ব্বোধ, স্থূলবুদ্ধি। **Heavy-hearted**—বিষণ্ণ, দুর্ম্মনাঃ, দুঃখভারপীড়িত। **Heavy-laden**—Loaded or laden heavily ; গুরুভারাক্রান্ত। Oppressed ; উৎপীড়িত, ভারব্যাকুল (কেঙিঃ)। **Heavy-metal** — বৃহৎ কামান বা গোলা ; (লক্ষণায়) দুর্দ্ধর্ব শত্রু। **Heavy-spar**—একপ্রকার শ্বেতবর্ণ রঞ্জন বস্তু। **Heavy-weight** — সাধারণ অপেক্ষা অধিকতর ভারী বা গুরুভারবস্তু বহনকারী অশ্ব, অশ্বারোহী, মুষ্টি-যোদ্ধা, প্রভৃতি। **Heavy-witted** — Dull ; স্থূলবুদ্ধি (কেঙিঃ)। **Heavier than air-ship** — যে আকাশযান প্রধানতঃ যন্ত্র বলে উত্থিত হয়, বিমানপোত। **Heavy in** or **on hand** — (Of horse) Bearing or hanging on bit ; (*fig.*) dull ; awkward ; hard to entertain ; (অশ্ব-সম্বন্ধে) খলীনের উপর বিলম্বমান ; (লক্ষণায়) হীন বুদ্ধি ; কদাকার ; দুস্তোষ্য। **It lies heavy**—It makes its weight felt ; ইহা পাষাণের মত চাপিয়া রহিয়াছে। **Time hangs heavy** — Time passes slowly ; সময় আর কাটে না। **The Heavies**—See HEAVY. *n.*

hĕb'-dŏ-măd, *n.* A week (esp. with ref. to *Dan.* ix. 27.) ; সপ্তাহ।

hĕb-dŏm'-ă-dăl, *adj.* Weekly ; সাপ্তাহিক। **Hebdomadal Council**—(*Oxf. Uni.*) অক্সফোর্ড বিশ্ববিদ্যালয়ের কার্য্য নির্ব্বাহক সমিতি [প্রতি সপ্তাহে একবার এই সমিতির অধিবেশন হয়]।

Hē'-bē, *n.* **1.** (*Gr. myth.*) The goddess of youth, daughter of Jupiter and Juno and the cup-bearer of Olympus ; (গ্রীক পুরাণ) যৌবনের অধিষ্ঠাত্রী দেবী। ইনি দেবরাজ জুপিটারের দুহিতা। দেবী জুনো ইঁহার জননী। Hebe স্বর্গধামে দেবগণের সুরা পরিবেষণ করিয়া থাকেন। **2.** (*Facet.*) A barmaid ; (কৌতুকচ্ছলে) সুরা-বিপণীর পরিচারিকা, সুরাপরিবেষণ-কারিণী।

hĕb'-ē-tāte, *v. t.* & *i.* To make dull ; to stupify, as, to *hebetate* the intellectual faculties ; মন্দীভূত করা ; আড়ষ্ট করা। ***Verb i.*** To become dull ; মন্দীভূত হওয়া।

Hē-brā'-ic, *adj.* Of, or pertaining to, the Hebrews or their language ; ইহুদীজাতীয়, হিব্রুভাষা-সম্পর্কীয়। **—i-cal-ly,** *adv.*

Hē'-brā-ĭsm, *n.* **1.** A Hebrew idiom or expression ; হিব্রু ভাষার রীতিসিদ্ধ প্রয়োগ, হিব্রুভাষানুসারিণী বাকপদ্ধতি। **2.** Hebrew system of thought or religion ; Hebrew custom ; হিব্রু চিন্তা প্রণালী, হিব্রুধর্ম্ম ; হিব্রু আচারপদ্ধতি। **3.** The type or character of the Hebrews ; হিব্রু-প্রকৃতি। **—is'-tic,** *adj.* Pertaining to, or resembling, the Hebrew language or idiom ; হিব্রু ভাষা বা উহার রীতিসিদ্ধ প্রয়োগ-সম্পর্কীয় বা তদ্বৎ। **—is'-ti-cal-ly,** *adv.* **—ize,** *v. t.* & *i.* To make or become Hebrew ; to speak Hebrew ; হিব্রুস্বভাবাপন্ন করা বা হওয়া ; হিব্রু ভাষায় কথা বলা।

Hē'-brā-ist, *n.* **1.** A Hebrew scholar ; হিব্রু সাহিত্যে সুপণ্ডিত ব্যক্তি। **2.** An adherent of Hebrew religion ; হিব্রুধর্ম্মাবলম্বী।

Hē'-brew (-brō), *n.* & *adj.* **1.** An Israelite ; a Jew ; এস্রায়েলবাসী ; ইহুদী। **2.** The ancient language of the Hebrews ; প্রাচীন হিব্রু ভাষা। **3.** (*Colloq.*) An unintelligible speech ; (চলিত ভাষায়) অবোধগম্য ভাষা। ***Adj.*** Of, or pertaining to, the Hebrews or their language ; হিব্রুজাতি বা হিব্রু-ভাষা সম্পর্কীয়। **Hebrew-wise** — (Of writing) From right to left ; (লিপি সম্বন্ধে) দক্ষিণ হইতে বামে। **Epistle to the Hebrews**—বাইবেলের নব নিয়মের অন্তর্গত পুস্তক বিশেষ।

Hĕc'-ă-tē, *n.* রাত্রি, অন্ধকার, যাদু, ইন্দ্রজাল, প্রভৃতির অধিষ্ঠাত্রী গ্রীকপুরাণোক্ত দেবী—এই দেবী ভূতপ্রেত পিশাচাদির অধিশ্বরী ছিলেন।

hĕc'-ă-tomb (-tōm), *n.* **1.** (*Gr. antiq.*) A sacrifice of a hundred oxen ; (গ্রীক প্রত্নতত্ত্ব) শতবৃষবলি, শতগোমেধ। **2.** A great sacrifice of victims ; বহুপ্রাণিহত্যা, সংহারযজ্ঞ।

hĕck, *n.* A contrivance for catching fish made in the form of a lattice work or grating ; মাছ ধরার আটল্।

hĕc'-kle (-l), *v. t.* & *n.* **1.** To dress with a hackle ; as, to *heckle* flax, hemp etc. ; শণ বা পাট আঁচড়ান। **2.** To catechize severely ; প্রশ্নের উপর প্রশ্ন জিজ্ঞাসা করা। ***Noun.*** A flax comb of steel ; শণ বা পাট আঁচড়াইবার কাঁটা।

hĕc'-tāre, *n.* A French measure equal to 2·471 acres ; ফরাসীদেশের ভূমির মাপ বিশেষ (২·৪৭১ একর)।

hĕc'-tic, *adj.* & *n.* **1.** Slow but long continued so as to impair the strength and cause ; wasting away ; as, a *hectic* type of disease ; মৃদুমন্দ অথচ দীর্ঘস্থায়ী ; ক্ষয়কারী, ক্ষয়জনক। **2.** Affected with hectic fever ; consumptive ; as, a *hectic* patient ; বিলেপি-জ্বরাক্রান্ত ; ক্ষয়রোগাক্রান্ত। **3.** Morbidly flushed, (*lit.* & *fig.*) ; রোগারক্ত, রোগারুণ। ***Noun.*** **1.** Hectic fever ; a hectic patient ; বিলেপী জ্বর ; বিলেপিজ্বরাক্রান্ত ব্যক্তি। **2.** A hectic flush ; বিলেপিজ্বরজনিত কপোলরাগ। **Hectic fever** — শারীরিক যন্ত্রাদির পুরাতন রোগজনিত দীর্ঘকালস্থায়ী মন্দ মন্দ জ্বর (হঃ চঃ), বিলেপী জ্বর (ঐ), প্রলেপক জ্বর (ঐ), জ্বরক্ষয়ী (সাঃ পঃ)। **Hectic-flush**—(ভৈষজ্য-শাস্ত্র) বিলেপিজ্বররোগগ্রস্ত ব্যক্তির গণ্ডদেশের অস্বাভাবিক অরুণিমা।

hĕc'-tō-grăm, —gramme (-grăm), *ns.* A measure of 100 grams ;

১০০ গ্রাম [কিঞ্চিদধিক ৩½ আউন্স, প্রায় অর্দ্ধ পোয়া।]

hêc'-tŏ-grăph, *n.* An apparatus for multiplying copies; পত্রাদির বহু অনুলিপি প্রস্তুতের জন্য যন্ত্র বিশেষ, অনুলিপি যন্ত্র।

hĕc'-tŏ-me-têr (-mā-), *n.* A measure of length equal to 100 metres; ১০০ মিটার।

hĕc'-tor (-têr), *n., v. t. & i.* A bully; a blustering fellow; ধুমধামকারী; তর্জ্জন গর্জ্জনকারী। ***Verb t.*** To bully; to treat insolently; তর্জ্জনগর্জ্জন করা; উদ্ধত ব্যবহার করা। ***Verb i.*** To bluster; তর্জ্জন গর্জ্জন করা।

Hĕc'-tor (-têr), *n.* The eldest son of Priam and Hecuba; Priam এবং Hecubaর জ্যেষ্ঠ পুত্র। ইনি ট্রয়ের যুদ্ধে ট্রোজানদের পক্ষে সর্ব্বশ্রেষ্ঠ বীর ছিলেন। ইনি Achilles কর্ত্তৃক যুদ্ধে নিহত হন।

Hĕc'-ū-bá, *n.* Wife of Priam, king of Troy; ট্রয়রাজ প্রায়ামের পত্নী। ট্রয় নগরী গ্রীকগণকর্ত্তৃক অধিকৃত হইলে পর Hecuba বন্দিনীরূপে Thrace প্রদেশে নীতা হন। Hecuba তৎপুত্র Polydorusএর হত্যার প্রতিশোধস্বরূপ Polymestorএর চক্ষুরুৎপাটন এবং তদীয় সন্তানগণকে নিধন করেন। রাজা Agamemnon Hecubaকে মার্জ্জনা করেন, কিন্তু, অল্পদিন পর Hecuba কুক্কুটী দেহ প্রাপ্তা হইয়া সমুদ্রে লম্ফ প্রদান করেন।

hĕd'-dle (-l), *n.* (*Pl.—Weaving*) Series of vertical chords or wires, each having in the middle a loop to receive a warp thread, and passing round and between parallel bars; (বয়ন-বিদ্যা) তাঁতের ব্যবস্থা বিশেষ—যদ্দ্বারা টানার সুতা পর্য্যায়ক্রমে উঠিয়া ও নামিয়া উহাদের ভিতর দিয়া পড়েনের সুতা চালাইবার জন্য মাকুর পথ খোলসা করিয়া দেয়, ব, বোয়া (ঢাকা)।

hedge (hĕj), **1.** A fence formed of bushes or plants growing closely together; গুল্ম বা অনুচ্চ বৃক্ষের বেড়া, বেড়া, বৃতি। **2.** A barrier (*lit. & fig.*); প্রতিবন্ধক। **3.** (*Betting*) The act or means of hedging; উভয় দিকে বাজী রাখা। **Dead hedge** — শুষ্ক গাছগাছড়ার বেড়া। **Hedge-bill** or **hedging bill**—বেড়ার ডাল পালা ছাঁটিবার জন্য কাটারি। **Hedge-born**—হীনবংশজ ব্যক্তি, অন্ত্যজ, ছোটলোক, ইতর ব্যক্তি। **Hedge-creeper** — নীচাশয় ব্যক্তি।

Hedge-hog.

Hedge-hog—কাঁটাচুয়া (সাঃ পঃ)। The prickly seed-vessel of some plants; সকণ্টক বীজকোষ। A person hard to get on with; রুক্ষ-প্রকৃতি ব্যক্তি। A kind of dredging machine; নদ্যাদির গর্ভ হইতে কর্দ্দমোত্তলনের জন্য একপ্রকার আকর্ষিণী। **Hedge-hoggy** — *adj.* Of the nature of hedge-hog; কাঁটাচুয়ার মত। Difficult to get on with as a person; রুক্ষ-স্বভাব। **Hedge-knife**—গাছ পালার গোড়ার ডালপালা ছাঁটিবার ছুরি। **Hedge-marriage**—গোপনপরিণয়, গন্ধর্ব্ববিবাহ। **Hedge-priest**—মূর্খ ধর্ম্মযাজক। **Hedge-row**—বেড়ার জন্য গুল্মের সারি। **Hedge-school**—আয়র্লণ্ডে খোলা মাঠে গাছ গাছড়ার বেড়ার নীচে যে পাঠশালা বসে; গ্রাম্য পাঠশালা। **Hedge-sparrow** — ক্ষুদ্র গায়কপক্ষি-বিশেষ। **Quickest hedge**—A hedge of living trees; সজীববৃক্ষের বেড়া।

hedge (hĕj), *v. t. & i.* **1.** To inclose or fence with a hedge; as, to *hedge* a field or garden; বেড়া দেওয়া, বৃতিবেষ্টিত করা। **2.** To obstruct, as a road with a barrier (usually with *up*); অবরোধ করা। **3.** To surround for defence; to protect; শত্রুর আক্রমণ হইতে রক্ষার্থ পরিবেষ্টিত করা; রক্ষা করা। **4.** To safeguard oneself against loss etc. (on bet etc.) by making compensatory arrangements, on the other side; অন্য পক্ষের সহিত ক্ষতিপূরণ জনক বন্দোবস্ত করিয়া (বাজি প্রভৃতিতে) ক্ষতির হাত এড়ান। ***Verb i.*** **1.** To make or trim hedges; বেড়া প্রস্তুত করা, বৃতি নির্ম্মাণ করা, বেড়ার ডালপালা ছাঁটা। **2.** To skulk; to dodge; ভয়ে বা কোনরূপ মন্দ অভিপ্রায়ে লুকাইয়া থাকা; চাতুরীপূর্ব্বক এড়ান। **3.** (*Betting*) To protect one's self from loss by betting on both sides; উভয় দিকে বাজি রাখিয়া ক্ষতির হাত এড়ান। **Hedg'-er,** *n.* **To hedge a bet**—To bet on both sides, thus guarding against loss; ক্ষতির হাত এড়াইবার জন্য উভয় দিকে বাজি রাখা।

hē-dŏn'-ic, *adj. & n.* Pertaining to pleasure; সুখসম্বন্ধীয়। ***Noun.*** (*Pl.*) That branch of moral philosophy that treats of the relation of duty to pleasure; the doctrine of pleasure; নীতিবিজ্ঞানের যে বিভাগে সুখ ও কর্ত্তব্যের সম্বন্ধবিষয়ক আলোচনা থাকে; সুখবাদ, সুখদুঃখবিদ্যা (হিঃ কোঃ)।

hē'-dŏn-ĭsm, *n.* (*Ethics*) The doctrine that pleasure is the chief good; (নীতিবিজ্ঞান) সুখই মানবের শ্রেয় বস্তু—এইরূপ মতবাদ, সুখ-প্রয়োজনতাবাদ (হিঃ কোঃ)। [সুখ বা আনন্দলাভই মানবের শ্রেষ্ঠ আদর্শ। চার্ব্বাক, এপিকিউরিয়া প্রভৃতির মতে আত্মসুখ অথবা ক্ষণস্থায়ী ইন্দ্রিয়সুখ মানবের একমাত্র শ্রেয় বস্তু। এই মত Egoistic Hedonism বা আত্মতন্ত্রসুখবাদ নামে অভিহিত হয়। আবার Hume, Bentham প্রভৃতি নব্য নীতিবিজ্ঞানবিদ্‌গণের মতানুসারে সমাজের অথবা অধিকতম লোকের প্রভূততম সুখ সাধনের চেষ্টাই পরমানন্দপ্রদ বিষয়। এই মতবাদকে Universal Hedonism বা বিশ্বসুখবাদ

আখ্যা প্রদান করা হইয়া থাকে। *See* J. Watson, *Hedonistic Theories*, 1895.] **–do-nis'-tic,** *adj.* Same as HEDONIC. **–ist,** *n.* A believer in Hedonism ; সুখপ্রয়োজনতাবাদী।

Hedychium coronarium — দুলাল চাঁপা (বেলঃ)।

Hedyotis Burmanniana — ক্ষেত পাঁপড়া (বেলঃ)।

heed (hēd), *v. t.* & *n.* To regard with care ; to take notice of ; অবধান করা, মনোযোগ দেওয়া ; গ্রাহ্য করা, প্রণিধান করা। ***Noun.*** Care ; tention ; notice ; as, to take *ed* : to pay or give *heed* to ; অবধান, সাবধানতা ; মনোযোগ ; প্রণিধান। **Heed'-ful,** *adj.* Attentive ; cautious ; watchful ; অবহিত, মনোযোগী ; সাবধান ; সতর্ক। **Heed'-ful-ly,** *adv.* **Heed'-ful-ness,** *n.* **Heed'-less,** *adj.* Inattentive ; অমনোযোগী, অনবহিত, অসতর্ক, অসাবধান। **Heed'-less-ly,** *adv.* **Heed-less-ness,** *n.* **To pay** or **give heed to**—To attend to ; মনোযোগ দেওয়া, প্রণিধান করা।

hee'-haw (hē-hä), *n.* The bray of an ass ; a loud laugh ; গর্দ্দভের চীৎকার, রাসভ রব ; হো হো রবে হাস্য।

heel (hēl), *n.* **1.** The hinder part of the foot in man or quadrupeds ; (*pl.*—of quadrupeds) the hinder feet ; পায়ের গোড়ালি, গুড়মুড়া ; (বহুবচনে) জন্তুর পিছনের পা। **2.** The part of a shoe, socks, etc. that supports or covers the heel ; জুতা মোজা প্রভৃতির গোড়ালি। **3.** Something shaped like heel in shape or position ; a knob ; গুল্ফাকৃতি বস্তু, গুল্ফবৎ অবস্থিত বস্তু ; উদ্গত কঠিন অংশ। **4.** A spur ; অশ্বারোহীর পাদুকাসংলগ্ন কাঁটা। **5.** The latter or concluding part of anything ; the remainder ; as, the *heel* of a leaf or of session ; পরবর্ত্তী অংশ, শেষ অংশ ; অবশিষ্ট। **Achilles'-heel**—একমাত্র ভেদ্য অংশ [cf. দুর্য্যোধনের উরু ; গ্রীকবীর Achilles এর পায়ের গোড়ালি ভিন্ন দেহের অপরাংশ অস্ত্র দ্বারা অভেদ্য ছিল]। **Heel-ball**—কঠিন মোম ও প্রদীপের কালীর মিশ্র বিশেষ—যদ্দ্বারা মুচিগণ জুতা পালিস করে। **Heel-tap** — (*Shoe-making*) A thickness of leather in the heel ; গোড়ালির চামড়া। Liquor left at the bottom of a glass ; সুরাপানের পর গেলাসের নীচে যে সামান্য মদ্য অবশিষ্ট থাকে। **At heel, At, on** or **upon one's heels** — Close behind one ; as, hungry want is *at my heels* ; পদে পদে। **Down** or **out at heel** — Having the heels of one's shoes or stockings worn out ; slovenly ; in poor circumstances ; গোড়ালি ছেঁড়া-মোজা-পরা ; নোংরা ; দুরবস্থাপন্ন। **Heel-and-toe** — With proper walking as opposed to running ; গমন ভঙ্গী। **Heels over head, Head over heels** — Upside down ; hence, in a rash inconsiderate manner ; মাথা নীচের দিকে ও পা উপরের দিকে ; হঠকারিতার সহিত। **Neck and heels**—(*Colloq.*) The whole body ; (চলিত ভাষায়) আপাদমস্তক, সর্ব্বাঙ্গ। **To be carried with the heels foremost**—To be carried as a corpse ; শববৎ বাহিত হওয়া। **To come** or **follow upon the heels of**—To follow closely ; পশ্চাদনুসরণ করা। **To cool one's heels**—To have to wait rather too long or tediously when calling upon a great personage ; কোন বড় লোকের সহিত দেখা করিতে যাইয়া অপেক্ষা করিতে করিতে পায় ব্যথা ধরা। **To have** or **get the heels of another** — To outrun him ; কোন ব্যক্তিকে দৌড়াইয়া পিছে ফেলা। **To heel**—(Of dog) Close behind ; under control ; পশ্চাৎ পশ্চাৎ ; পদানত। **To kick one's heels**—To stand waiting ; দাঁড়াইয়া অপেক্ষা করা। **To kick up the heels**—To die ; মরা, অক্কা পাওয়া, পটল তোলা। **To lay** or **clap by the heels**—To imprison ; to put under arrest ; to prostrate ; কারারুদ্ধ করা ; গ্রেপ্তার করা ; পদানত করা। **To show a clean** or **light pair of heels, To take to one's heels**—To run away or flee ; চম্পট দেওয়া, পিট্টান দেওয়া, সট্‌কান। **To show the heels**—To run off ; দৌড়িয়া পালান ; ভোঁদৌড় দেওয়া। **To show the heels to**—To outstrip ; অতিক্রম করা, ছাড়াইয়া যাওয়া, পিছে ফেলা। **To tread upon one's heels** — To pursue one closely ; পশ্চাৎ পশ্চাৎ যাওয়া। **To turn on one's heel**—To turn sharply round ; হঠাৎ ঘুরিয়া দাঁড়ান।

heel (hēl), *v. i.* & *t.* **1.** To touch grouud with the heel, as in dancing ; পায়ের গোড়ালি দ্বারা ভূমি স্পর্শ করা। **2.** (*Football*) To kick the ball backward out of a scrummage, (with *out*) ; (পাদগোলক ক্রীড়ায়) পদাঘাত করিয়া ধ্বস্তাধ্বস্তির স্থান হইতে পশ্চাদ্দিকে কন্দুক চালিত করা। ***Verb t.*** **1.** To add a heel to ; as, to *heel* a shoe ; জুতার গোড়ালি লাগান। **2.** To chase or follow closely ; as, to *heel* a thief ; পশ্চাদনুসরণ করা, পশ্চাদ্ধাবিত হওয়া, পাছু পাছু ছুটা। **3.** (*Golf*) To strike as, a ball with the *heel* of a club ; (গোল্‌ফ ক্রীড়ায়) তাড়নদণ্ডের গোড়ালিদ্বারা কন্দুক আঘাত করা।

heel (hēl), *v.i., t.* & *n.* (Of a ship) To incline to one side ; জাহাজ এক পার্শ্বে কা'ত করা বা হওয়া। ***Noun.*** Inclination of a ship to one side ; জাহাজ এক পার্শ্বে কা'ত হওন।

hĕft, *n.* & *v.t.* **1.** Weight (*colloq.—U. S.*) ভার। **2.** (*Dial.*) The act of heaving or lifting ; push ; as, with violent *hefts* ; (উপভাষায়) জোরে তোলন ; ঠেলা। ***Verb t.*** To heave up, esp. to judge weight ; তোলা (বিশেষতঃ গুরুত্ব নির্ণয়ের জন্য)।

hĕ-gĕm′-ŏ-nŷ, *n.* Leadership; preponderance of one state among others; নেতৃত্ব; এক রাজ্যের উপর অপর রাজ্যের প্রভুত্ব। **Heg-e-mon′-ic,** *adj.* Leading; ruling; supreme; নেতৃস্থানীয়; শাসনকারী; সর্ব্বপ্রধান।

hĕg′-i-ră, *n.* **1.** The flight of Mohammed from Mecca to Medina; the Mohammedan era reckoned from 622 A. D., the date of Mohammed's flight; হজরৎ মহম্মদের মক্কা হইতে মদিনায় পলায়ন; মহম্মদীয় অব্দ, হিজিরা [মক্কানগরী হইতে হজরত মহম্মদের পলায়ন দিবস—১৬ই জুলাই ৬২২ খৃঃ অব্দ। এই তারিখ হইতে মহম্মদীয় বৎসর গণিত হইয়া থাকে]।

Heh, *n.* The Egyptian god of eternity; মিসর দেশের অনন্ত দেবতা,—এই দেবতার মস্তক ভেকের মত চিত্রিত হইয়া থাকে।

heif′-êr (hĕf-) *n.* A young cow; বৎসতরী, বক্না গাভী।

heigh (hī), *interj.* An exclamation of encouragement or inquiry; বেশ! বেশ, বা! বা, এঁ।

heigh′-hō (hī-), *interj.* An exclamation expressing disappointment and uneasiness; আহা! আহা, হায়রে।

height (hīt), *n.* **1.** Altitude; the measurement from base to top; elevation; as, the *height* of a tower; উচ্চতা, তুঙ্গতা; উৎসেধ; উচ্ছ্রায়। **2.** An eminence; an elevated ground; as, Alpine *heights*; উচ্চস্থলী; উন্নতভূভাগ, উচ্চভূমি। **3.** The utmost degree; as, the *height* of folly; চরমমাত্রা। **4.** A high point or position; "Critics who reach classical *heights*"; উচ্চস্থান, পরাকাষ্ঠা। **5.** The top; শীর্ষভাগ। **At its height**—At the highest point or degree; as, her glory was *at its height*; পরাকাষ্ঠায়, চরম মাত্রায়।

height′-en (hīt-n), *v. t.* & *i.* **1.** To make high or higher; to elevate; উচ্চ করা, উচ্চতর করা; উন্নীত করা। **2.** To increase; to intensify; as, to *heighten* our confusion; to inflate; as, to *heighten* a story or description; বৃদ্ধি করা, বাড়ান; প্রবলতর করা; স্ফীত করা। **3.** To make brighter, as a tint etc.; উজ্জ্বলতর করা, অধিকতর দীপ্তিশালী করা। ***Verb i.*** To rise, (usu. *fig.*); বৃদ্ধি পাওয়া।

hei′-nous (hā-nŭs), *adj.* Hateful; odious; atrocious; as, a *heinous* crime; ঘৃণ্য; জঘন্য; ঘোর, ঘোরতর, ভয়ঙ্কর। **—ly,** *adv.* **—ness** *n.*

heir (ãr), *n.* One who succeeds or is to succeed another in the possession of property etc.; an inheritor; উত্তরাধিকারী; দায়াদ। **Heir′-dom,** *n.* Succession by inheritance; উত্তরাধিকার। **Heir′-ess,** *n.* (*Fem.*) **Heir′-less,** *adj.* Without an heir; উত্তরাধিকারিহীন, অদায়ক (দেবলঃ), দায়াদশূন্য (বিবাদ), বেওয়ারিস, লাওয়ারিস। **Heir′-ship,** *n.* The state or right of an heir; উত্তরাধিকারিত্ব, উত্তরাধিকার। **Heir apparent** — আসন্ন উত্তরাধিকারী, প্রকৃত উত্তরাধিকারী। **Heir-at-law**—আইনতঃ উত্তরাধিকারী। **Heir-in-tail**—পুত্রপৌত্রাদিক্রমে কেবলমাত্র ভোগ দখলের জন্য প্রাপ্ত সম্পত্তির উত্তরাধিকারী। **Heir-loom** — উত্তরাধিকারসূত্রে প্রাপ্ত আসবাবপত্র বা অস্থাবর সম্পত্তি। **Heir-male** — পুরুষ উত্তরাধিকারি পরম্পরাসূত্রে প্রাপ্ত সম্পত্তির উত্তরাধিকারী। **Heir-presumptive** — যে উত্তরাধিকারীর উত্তরাধিকারস্বত্ব নিকটতর উত্তরাধিকারীর জন্ম হইলে লোপ হইয়া যায়।

hĕj′-i-rā, *n.* Same as HEGIRA.

Hĕl, *n.* The goddess of the Scandinavian Hades; নোর্স পুরাণোক্ত নরক রাজ্যের অধিশ্বরী।

Hĕl′-ĕn, *n.* The heroine of the Trojan war and the most beautiful of women; ট্রয় যুদ্ধের নায়িকা লাবণ্যললামভূতা হেলেন। Helen, Zeus এবং Ledaর নন্দিনী এবং Castor ও Polluxএর ভগিনী। বহু ব্যক্তি অসামান্য রূপলাবণ্যশালিনী Helenএর পরিণয়প্রার্থী হওয়াতে সকলের সম্মতি অনুসারে স্থিরীকৃত হইল যে Helen স্বয়ং বিবাহার্থী যুবকগণের মধ্যে একজনকে বরণ করিবেন। Helen Menelausকে বরণ করেন, কিন্তু কিছুদিন পর ট্রয়ের রাজকুমার Parisএর প্রেমে পড়িয়া Helen তাহার সহিত ট্রয়ে পলাইয়া যান। এই ব্যাপারই বিশ্ববিখ্যাত ট্রোজান যুদ্ধের কারণ। Parisএর মৃত্যুর পর Helen তদীয় ভ্রাতা Deiphobusকে পতিত্বে বরণ করেন এবং ট্রয় নগরী ধ্বংসের পর তিনি মিসর প্রভৃতি নানা দেশ পর্য্যটনান্তে Menelausএর সহিত Sparta নগরীতে প্রত্যাবর্ত্তন করেন।

Hĕl′-ĕ-nŭs, *n.* Son of Priam and Hecuba; ট্রয়রাজ Priamএর পুত্র। ইনি দিব্যদৃষ্টিসম্পন্ন ছিলেন। ইনি বিভীষণের মত স্বজাতিপক্ষ পরিত্যাগ পূর্ব্বক গ্রীকদিগের সহিত যোগদান করেন।

hē-lī′-ă-căl, *adj.* Coincident with the rising or setting of the sun (applied to the rising of a star just before and to its setting just after the sun); সূর্য্যের উদয়াস্তের সহিত ঐক্যবিশিষ্ট [সূর্য্যের অব্যবহিত পূর্ব্বে উদীয়মান ও অব্যবহিত পরে অস্তগমনশীল তারাসম্বন্ধে প্রয়োগ হয়], প্রকাশমণ্ডলীয় (হিঃ কোঃ), সূর্য্যকেন্দ্রক (ঐ)। **Heliacal longitude**—সূর্য্যকেন্দ্রক ভুজ (হিঃ কোঃ)।

Heliadæ, *n.* The progeny of the sun (Helios); সূর্য্যপুত্রগণ। ইহাদের ভ্রাতা Phaetonএর মৃত্যুর পর তাহারা শোকে অভিভূত হইয়া এরূপ করুণ ক্রন্দন করেন যে দেবতারা করুণাপরবশ হইয়া তাহাদিগকে পপলার বৃক্ষে এবং তাহাদের অশ্রুবিন্দু তৃণস্ফটিকে (amber) পরিবর্ত্তিত করেন।

hē-li-ăn′-thŭs, *n.* The sun flower genus of plants; সূর্য্যমুখীজাতীয় ফুল। ***Helianthus Annuus*** — সূর্য্যমুখী (বেলঃ)।

hĕl′-ĭ-căl, *adj.* Spiral ; as, a *helical* spring ; ঘুরানিয়া, পেঁচানিয়া। **–coid, –coi′-dal,** *adjs.* Spiral ; আবর্ত্তাকার।

Hĕl′-ĭ-cŏn, *n.* A mountain in Boeotia in Greece, which is sacred to the Muses ; a source of poetic inspiration ; গ্রীসদেশের অন্তঃপাতী Boeotia নামক স্থানের বাগ্দেবীগণনিষেবিত গিরিবিশেষ ; কবিত্ব-নির্ঝর। **–co′-ni-an,** *adj.*

hē-li-ō-cĕn-tric, *adj.* Relating to the sun as centre ; সূর্য্যকেন্দ্রক (জিঃ), রবিকেন্দ্রক (সাঃ পঃ), হেলিকেন্দ্রিক (ঐ), হেলিকেন্দ্রীয় (ঐ)। **Heliocentric motion**—মন্দস্ফুট গতি (সাঃ পঃ)। **Heliocentric place of superior planets** — মন্দস্ফুটস্থান (সাঃ পঃ)।

hē′-li-ō-chrō-mȳ, *n.* The art of producing photographs in natural colours ; স্বাভাবিকবর্ণে আলোকচিত্র উৎপাদনের কলা, রঙ্গিনছায়চিত্রণ (হিঃ কোঃ)।

hē′-li-ō-grăph, *n.* & *v. t.* **1.** A picture taken by heliography ; a photograph; সূর্য্যকিরণ দ্বারা গৃহীত চিত্র ; আলোকচিত্র। **2.** An instrument for taking photographs of the sun ; সূর্য্যের আলোকচিত্রগ্রহণার্থ যন্ত্র-বিশেষ, সূর্য্যচ্ছায়াচিত্রণ যন্ত্র (হিঃ কোঃ), ছায়াচিত্র (ঐ)। **3.** An apparatus for telegraphing by means of the sun's rays ; দর্পণে প্রতিবিম্বিত সূর্য্যরশ্মির সাহায্যে সংবাদপ্রেরণের জন্য যন্ত্রবিশেষ, আলোকবার্ত্তাবহ, প্রকাশসঙ্কেত-যন্ত্র। ***Verb t.*** **1.** To send message by means of the sun's rays ; সূর্য্যরশ্মির সাহায্যে সংবাদ প্রেরণ করা। **2.** To photograph by heliography ; সূর্য্যরশ্মির সাহায্যে আলোকচিত্র উৎপাদন করা। **–og′-ra-phy,** *n.* Photography; আলোকচিত্রগ্রহণবিদ্যা।

hē-li-ŏl′-ă-trȳ, *n.* Sun worship ; সূর্য্যপূজা।

Hē-li-ŏp′-ō-lis, *n.* The city of the sun ; সূর্য্যনগরী। [(ক) নিম্ন মিসরের নগরী বিশেষ। এই নগরী সূর্য্যপূজার প্রধান কেন্দ্র ছিল। ইহার অপর নাম On বা Annu. এই নগরীতে সূর্য্যদেব Ram নামে পূজিত হইতেন। (খ) সিরিয়ার অন্তর্গত Baalbekএর গ্রীক নাম।

Hē′-li-ōs, *n.* The sun god ; গ্রীক পুরাণোক্ত সূর্য্যদেব। [ইঁহার পিতার নাম Hyperion এবং জননীর নাম Thea. গ্রীক পুরাণানুসারে সূর্য্য অশ্বচতুষ্টয়বাহিত অগ্নিময় রথে প্রভাতকালে উদয়াচল প্রাসাদ হইতে যাত্রা করিয়া সন্ধ্যাকালে অস্তাচল প্রাসাদে বিশ্রাম করেন।]

hē′-li-ō-scōpe, *n.* (*Astron.*) A telescope or instrument for observing the sun without injury to the eyes ; (জ্যোতির্বিজ্ঞান) সূর্য্যদর্শনের জন্য দূরবীক্ষণ যন্ত্র বিশেষ ; সূর্য্যদর্শন (হিঃ কোঃ), সূর্য্যদর্শন যন্ত্র (ঐ), রবিবীক্ষণ।

hē-li-ō′-sis, *n.* **1.** (*Bot.*) Spots produced on leaves by the concentration of the rays of the sun through glass etc. ; (উদ্ভিদ্-বিদ্যা) কাচ প্রভৃতির ভিতর দিয়া সূর্য্য-কিরণ কেন্দ্রীভূত করিয়া পত্রের উপর বিন্দু উৎপাদন। **2.** Sunstroke ; সর্দ্দিগর্ম্মি।

hē′-li-ō-trōpe, *n.* **1.** A garden plant of the genus heliotropium ; a light blue colour ; মৃদু নীলবর্ণ পুষ্পপ্রসূ উদ্যানরোপিত তরু বিশেষ, হাতীশুঁড়া ; মৃদুনীল বর্ণ। **2.** (*Mining*) Blood-stone ; লোহিত বর্ণ ফুট্‌ফুট্ বিন্দুবিশিষ্ট গাঢ় হরিদ্বর্ণ মণিবিশেষ। **3.** An instrument for making signals to an observer at a distance by means of sun's rays thrown from a mirror ; দর্পণে প্রতিবিম্বিত সূর্য্যালোকের সাহায্যে সংবাদ প্রেরণের যন্ত্র, সায়নযন্ত্র (হিঃ কোঃ)। **–ot′-ro-pism,** *n.* The tendency of plants and flowers to turn in a particular way under the influence of light ; বৃক্ষাদির সূর্য্য বা আলোকের অভিমুখীন হওয়ার আসক্তি বা প্রবণতা, অভিমুখত্বশক্তি (হিঃ কোঃ), রুক্মুখবৃদ্ধি (সাঃ পঃ)। **–trop′-ic,** *adj.* Tending to turn in a particular way under the influence of light ; আলোকের প্রভাবে কোন বিশেষ দিকে উন্মুখ।

hē′-li-ŭm, *n.* A gaseous element discovered in the atmosphere of the sun ; একপ্রকার বাষ্পীয় মূল পদার্থ [সূর্য্যে বর্ত্তমান আছে বলিয়া ১৮৬৮ খৃষ্টাব্দে Lockyer কর্ত্তৃক অনুমিত হয় এবং Ramsay কর্ত্তৃক ১৮৯৫ খৃষ্ট অব্দে পৃথিবীতে Heliumএর অস্তিত্ব আবিষ্কৃত হয়।]

hē′-lix, *n.* **1.** A spiral line as of wire in a coil ; a spiral thing ; পেঁচালো রেখা, কুণ্ডলী ; কুণ্ডলিত বস্তু। **2.** (*Anat.*) The whole extent of the external border of the ear ; (শারীর-সংস্থান বিদ্যা) কর্ণের বহিঃপ্রান্ত। **3.** (*Zool.*) A genus of snails ; (জন্তু-বিদ্যা) এক জাতীয় শম্বুক। **4.** (*Arch.*) Spiral ornament ; (স্থাপত্য-বিজ্ঞান) আবর্ত্তিতাকার ভূষা।

hĕll, *n.* **1.** The place of the dead or of souls after death ; নরক, নিরয়, যমপুরী, যমালয়, অধোভুবন। **2.** The abode of evil spirits ; ভূতপ্রেতাদির আবাসস্থলী, প্রমথালয় (অঃ)। **3.** The place or state of misery or wickedness ; torment ; "Within him *hell*" ; দুর্গতি ভোগের স্থান নরকভোগ, নরক যন্ত্রণা। **4.** The infernal powers ; শয়তান ও তদীয় অনুচরগণ। **5.** A place resembling hell ; a prison ; নরকতুল্য স্থান ; কারাগার। **Hell′-ish,** *adj.* **1.** Pertaining to hell ; infernal ; নরকসম্বন্ধীয় ; নারকীয়। **2.** Detestable ; ঘৃণ্য, জুগুপ্সিত। **Hell′-ish-ly,** *adv.* **Hell′-ish-ness,** *n.* **Hell′-ward,** *adv.* Toward hell ; নরকাভিমুখে। **Hell-born**—Of hellish origin ; নরকজাত। **Hell-cat**—বিদ্বেষ পরায়ণা স্ত্রীলোক, রায়বাঘিনী। **Hell-fire**—নরকাগ্নি, নরকানল। **Hell-gate**—নরকের প্রবেশদ্বার, নরকতোরণ। **Hell-hound** — শয়তান। **Hell-weed**—বিভিন্ন প্রকার গুল্মের নাম। **A hell of noise**—Considerable noise ; মহাকলরব ; কিলকিলা। **Better to reign in hell than to serve in heaven**—স্বর্গে দাসত্ব অপেক্ষা নরকে রাজত্ব ভাল। **Go to hell**—জাহান্নমে যাও, রসাতলে যাও।

hĕl'-lĕ-bōre, *n.* **1.** The name of various plants formerly used as a cure for insanity ; উন্মাদরোগের ঔষধস্বরূপ ব্যবহৃত বিভিন্ন প্রকার গুল্মের নাম। **2.** (*Bot.*) A species including the Christmas rose ; কটুকী, কটী (দ্রব্য), কটু রোহিণী (ঐ), রোহিণী।

Hĕl'-lĕn, *n.* The mythical ancestor of all the Grecian races ; গ্রীস দেশের বিভিন্ন জাতির পূর্ব্বপুরুষ।

Hĕl'-lene (-lĕn), *n.* A Greek ; গ্রীসদেশীয় লোক। **—len'-ic,** *adj.* Grecian ; গ্রীসদেশীয়।

Hĕl'-lĕn-ĭsm, *n.* **1.** An idiom or construction of the Greek language ; গ্রীকভাষার রীতিসিদ্ধ প্রয়োগ, গ্রীকভাষায় বাক্য রচনা। **2.** Imitation of the Greeks ; গ্রীকদিগের অনুকরণ। **3.** Grecian culture ; গ্রীসদেশীয় সভ্যতা। **4.** The Greek race or nationality ; গ্রীক বংশ, গ্রীক জাতি। **—ize,** *v. i.* & *t.* To speak the Greek language ; to play the Greek ; গ্রীক ভাষায় কাথাপকথন করা ; গ্রীসদেশবাসীর মত চলা বা আচরণ করা। (*Verb t.*) To give a Greek form to ; as, to *hellenize* a word ; গ্রীক আকার প্রদান করা।

Hĕl'-lĕn-ĭst, *n.* **1.** A follower of the Greeks in language ; ভাষা বিষয়ে গ্রীকদিগের অনুসরণকারী। **2.** A Greek scholar ; গ্রীক ভাষায় সুপণ্ডিত ব্যক্তি। **—is'-tic,** *adj.*

hĕl'-lō, *n.* & *v.* Same as HALLO.

hĕlm, *n.* & *v. t.* **1.** (*Naut.*) The instrument by which a ship is steered ; হাইল, কর্ণ। **2.** Administration ; guidance, as, the *helm* of the commonwealth ; শাসন ; পরিচালন। **3.** An administrator ; a guide ; as, the *helms* of the state ; শাসক ; পরিচালক, কাণ্ডারী। ***Verb t.*** **1.** To steer ; (*fig.*) to direct or guide ; হাইল ঘুরাইয়া চালান ; (লক্ষণায়) পরিচালনা করা, নির্ব্বাহ করা। **Helmsman**—Steersman ; কর্ণধার, কাণ্ডারী, কর্ণগ্রাহ, সুখানী (of a steamer). **To put down the helm**—হাইল ঘুরাইয়া যে দিক হইতে বাতাস বহে সে দিকে জাহাজ ফিরান। **To put up the helm** — হাইল ঘুরাইয়া বায়ু প্রবাহ হইতে রক্ষিত পার্শ্বের অভিমুখে জাহাজ ফিরান।

hĕlm *n.* **1.** (*Archaic*) A helmet ; (অপ্রঃ) শিরস্ত্র, শিরস্ত্রাণ। **2.** A heavy cloud lying on the brow of a mountain ; গিরিচূড়াগ্রস্থ ঘন জলদ-পটল।

hĕl'-mĕt, *n.* **1.** (*Armour*) A defensive covering for the head ; শিরস্ত্রাণ, শিরস্ক, শিরস্ত্র, শির্ষণ্য, শীর্ষত্রাণ। **2.** A hat of cork, felt etc. for use in hot

Helmets.

climate ; গ্রীষ্মপ্রধান দেশে ব্যবহারের উপযোগী কাক (cork), নেমদা (felt) প্রভৃতির টুপি। **3.** A thing resembling a helmet in form, position, etc. ; শিরস্ত্রাকার বস্তু। **4.** (*Chem.*) The top of a retort ; বকযন্ত্রের শীর্ষভাগ। **—ed,** *adj.* Wearing a helmet ; শিরস্কধারী।

hĕl'-mĭnth, *n.* A worm, esp. intestinal ; ক্রিমি। **—min'-thic,** *adj.* ক্রিমিনিঃসারক, ক্রিমিঘ্ন। **—min'-thoid,** *adj.* Worm-like ; ক্রিমিবৎ। **—min-thol'-o-gy,** *n.* The study of worms ; ক্রিমিতত্ত্ব।

hĕl'-ŏt, *n.* **1.** (*Hist.*) A slave in ancient Sparta ; (ইতিহাস) প্রাচীন স্পার্টার ক্রীতদাস। **2.** A slave or serf ; ক্রীতদাস, চিরদাস। **—ism,** *n.* **—ize,** *v. t.* **—ry,** *n.*

hĕlp, *v. t.* **1.** To assist ; সাহায্য করা, সহায়তা করা। **2.** To change for the better ; to remedy ; as, it cannot be *helped* ; উৎকর্ষ সাধন করা ; প্রতীকার করা। **3.** To prevent ; to avoid ; as, I can't *help* it ; বারণ করা ; পরিহার করা, না করিয়া পারা। **4.** To distribute, as food at a meal ; পরিবেষণ করা। **Help'-ing,** *n.* **1.** Act of helping ; সাহায্যকরণ। **2.** A portion of food served ; পরিবেষিত অন্নব্যঞ্জনাদির অংশ। **It cannot be helped**—না করিয়া উদ্ধার নাই, এর কোন চারা নাই, না করিয়া পারার যো নাই। **So help me God**—(In invocation or oath) As I speak the truth ; as I keep my word ; আমি যেমন সত্য কথা বলিলাম ; আমি যেমন আমার সত্য রক্ষা করিলাম। **To help forward**—To assist in making progress ; অগ্রসর করা, আগুয়ান করা। **To help off**—To remove by help ; সাহায্য করিয়া দূর করা। **To help on**—To forward ; to advance or promote ; অগ্রসর করা ; শ্রীবৃদ্ধি করা, উন্নতিসাধন করা। **To help out**—To aid in finishing a task ; to aid in getting out (of difficulty) ; কোন কার্য্যসাধনে সহায়তা করা ; কোন সঙ্কট হইতে উদ্ধারের সাহায্য করা। **To help over**—To enable to surmount ; (বিপদ্‌ প্রভৃতি) অতিক্রমে সাহায্য করা। **To help to**—To serve with ; as, to *help* one *to* soup ; পরিবেষণ করা। **To help up**—To raise ; to support ; উত্তোলিত করা ; ধরিয়া রাখা।

hĕlp, *n.* **1.** Aid or assistance ; the person or thing furnishing aid ; সাহায্য, সহায়তা, আনুকূল্য ; সাহায্যকারী ব্যক্তি বা বস্তু। **2.** Remedy or escape ; as, there is no *help* for it ; প্রতীকার, পরিত্রাণ,

উদ্ধার, চারা। 3. A domestic servant (*U. S.*) ; (মার্কিণযুক্ত রাজ্যে) গৃহভৃত্য। 4. A portion of food served ; পরিবেষিত অন্নব্যঞ্জনাদির অংশ। **Help'-ful,** *adj.* Giving aid ; useful ; serviceable ; সহায়তাকারী, সাহায্যদ ; প্রয়োজনীয় ; কার্য্যোপযোগী। **Help'-ful-ness,** *n.* **Help'-less** *adj.* 1. Destitute of help ; unable to help oneself ; as, a *helpless* infant ; সহায়হীন, নিঃসহায়, অসহায়, নিরুপায় ; নাচার, পরাধীন-শরীর (কেন্ডিঃ)। **Help'-less-ly,** *adv.* **Help'-less-ness,** *n.* **Help-mate**—জীবন সঙ্গী, জীবন সঙ্গিনী। **Help-meet**—A wife ; a helpmate ; সহধর্ম্মিণী, জীবনসঙ্গিনী। **A lady help**—সহচরী। **Mother's help**—ধাত্রী।

hĕl'-têr-skĕl'-têr, *adv., adj. & n.* In a confused hurry ; ব্যস্ত-সমস্ত ভাবে, তাড়াহুড়া করিয়া। ***Adj.*** Characterised by such hurry ; ব্যস্তসমস্ত। ***Noun.*** Disordered haste ; তাড়াহুড়া।

helve (hĕlv), *n.* The handle of a tool or weapon ; হাতল, বাঁট।

Hĕl-vĕ'-tian (-shăn), *adj. & n.* Pertaining to Switzerland or its inhabitants ; সুইজরল্যাণ্ড বা তদ্দেশের অধিবাসিসম্পর্কীয়। ***Noun.*** A Swiss ; সুইজারল্যাণ্ডবাসী।

hĕm, *n. & v. t.* The border of a cloth or garment (esp. a border) doubled down and sewed ; মৌজি, মুড়ি, হাঁসিয়া, দশা (আঃ বঃ)। ***Verb t.*** To fold and sew down the edge of ; as, to *hem* a handkerchief ; মুড়ি সেলাই করা। **To hem in, about, round**—To confine or enclose ; পরিবেষ্টিত করা।

hĕm, *n., interj. & v. i.* An utterance of the voice *hem* to express hesitation or call attention ; হুম্। ***Interj.*** A sound calling attention or expressing hesitation ; হুম্, হুঁ। ***Verb i.*** To utter the sound *hem* ; to hesitate in speaking ; to clear the throat ; হুম্ শব্দ উচ্চারণ করা ; কথা বলিতে ইতস্ততঃ করা, এঁ এঁ করা, আম্‌তা আম্‌তা করা ; গলা খেঁকারী দেওয়া।

hē-măt'-ic, *adj. & n.* Same as HAEMATIC.

hĕm-ĭ-ăn-ŏp'-sĭ-ă, *n.* Half blindedness ; অর্দ্ধদৃষ্টিরোগ, অর্দ্ধদৃষ্টি (হিঃ কোঃ) [এই রোগে দৃষ্ট বস্তুর অর্দ্ধাংশমাত্র দেখা যায়]।

hĕm-ĭ-crā'-nĭ-ă, *n.* Headache confined to one side of the head ; আধকপালে মাথা ব্যথা, অর্দ্ধশিরঃশূল, অর্দ্ধকপালী (সাঃ পঃ), অর্দ্ধাবভেদক (ঐ)।

hĕm-ĭ-dĕs'-mŭs, *n.* A kind of Asiatic shrub ; অনন্তমূল (জাহিঃ)।

hĕm-ĭ-ō'-pĭ-ă, *n.* Same as HEMIANOPSIA.

hĕm-ĭ-plē'-gĭ-ă, *n.* Paralysis of one side of the body ; অর্দ্ধ অঙ্গের পক্ষাঘাত, অর্দ্ধাঙ্গবাত, পক্ষবধ (হঃ চঃ), অর্দ্ধাঙ্গ (সাঃ পঃ), একাঙ্গবাত (ঐ), পক্ষবাত।

hĕm'-ĭ-sphēre, *n.* 1. A half sphere ; অর্দ্ধগোলক, অর্দ্ধগোল। 2. Half of the celestial or terrestrial globe ; ভূমণ্ডলের অর্দ্ধাংশ, অর্দ্ধ-ভূমণ্ডল, গোলার্দ্ধ, কপাল (সুঃ সিঃ)। **–spher'-ic, –spher'-i-cal,** *adjs.* **Eastern hemisphere**—পূর্ব্বগোলার্দ্ধ (ইয়ুরোপ, এসিয়া, আফ্রিকা ও অষ্ট্রেলিয়া ইহার অন্তর্গত)। **Magdeburg hemispheres**—পিত্তলনির্ম্মিত (পানপাত্রাকৃতি) গোলার্দ্ধদ্বয়। ইহাদের একটা অপরটার উপরে রাখিয়া অভ্যন্তরস্থ বায়ু নিষ্কাশিত করা হইলে ইহারা পরস্পরের সহিত দৃঢ়ভাবে সংশ্লিষ্ট হইয়া থাকে। এই যন্ত্র দ্বারা ভূবায়ুর চাপ প্রদর্শিত হইয়া থাকে। [জর্ম্মণীর অন্তঃপাতী Magdeburg নগরবাসী Otto Von Guericke নামক জনৈক বৈজ্ঞানিক ১৬৫০ খৃষ্টাব্দে বায়ুচাপপ্রদর্শক উদ্ভাবন করেন], বায়ুচাপ প্রদর্শক, বায়ুভারপ্রদর্শক যন্ত্র (হিঃ কোঃ)। **Northern and Southern hemispheres**—বিষুব রেখা দ্বারা বিভক্ত পৃথিবীর অর্দ্ধাংশদ্বয়। **Western hemisphere** — পশ্চিম গোলার্দ্ধ (উভয় আমেরিকা ও ওশেনিয়ার কিয়দংশ ইহার অন্তর্গত)।

hĕm'-ĭ-stich, *n.* Half a poetic line or verse ; কবিতার অর্দ্ধ পংক্তি বা চরণ।

hĕm'-lŏck, *n.* 1. An umbelliferous plant whose leaves and roots are poisonous ; poisonous potion got from this ; এক-প্রকার বিষাক্ত গুল্ম, কিরদাম্‌না (পার্শী), খোরাসানি আজো-য়ান (ঐ) ; উক্ত গুল্মের পত্র ও মূলের নির্যাস হইতে প্রস্তুত বিষাক্ত পেয় দ্রব্য। [গ্রীস দেশীয় দার্শনিক সক্রেতিস এই গুল্মের বিষাক্ত নির্যাসপানে প্রাণত্যাগ করিতে বাধ্য হন।]

Hemlock.

hĕm'-ŏr-rhage (-āj), *n.* Same as HAEMORRHAGE (which see).

hĕmp, *n.* 1. A plant with a fibrous bark used for cordage etc. ; শণ। 2. The fibre of this plant ; শণের আঁশ বা তন্তু। 3. Rope for hanging ; ফাঁসির রজ্জু। 4. Bhang or hashish ; ভাঙ্গ, গাঁজা, সিদ্ধি।

Hemp.

hĕmp'-en (-n), *adj.* Made of, or like, hemp ; শণনির্ম্মিত, শাণ। **Hempen-collar, –caudle**—ফাঁসীর রজ্জু। **Hempen-widow**—যে বিধবার স্বামীর ফাঁসি হইয়াছে।

hĕm'-stitch (-stĭch), *v. t & n.* To ornament by hemstitch ; as, to *hemstitch* a handkerchief ; রুমালাদির কিনারা হইতে কয়েকটী সুতা তুলিয়া একপ্রকার সৌখীন সেলাই করা। ***Noun.*** A kind of stitch in needle work ; উক্তরূপ সেলাই।

hĕn, *n.* **1.** The female of the domestic fowl; the female of other species of birds; as, the gray *hen*; মোরগী, কুক্কুটী; মাদী পাখী। **Hen'-ny,** *adj.* & *n.* Hen-like; মুরগীর মত, কুক্কুটীবৎ। (*Noun*) A hen-like cock; কুক্কুটীবৎ কুক্কুট। **Hen-bane**—খোরাসানী যমানী (দ্রব্যঃ); খোরাসানী যমানী হইতে প্রাপ্ত ঔষধ বিশেষ। **Hen-coop**—গৃহ পালিত কুক্কুটের জন্য বৃহৎ পিঞ্জর। **Hen-hearted**—ভীরু, কাপুরুষ। **Hen-hussy**—যে ব্যক্তি স্ত্রীলোকের ব্যাপারে হস্তক্ষেপ করে। **Hen-pecked** — স্ত্রৈণ, স্ত্রী-নির্জ্জিত, স্ত্রীজিত, স্ত্রীবশ্য (পক্ষতঃ), **Hen-roost**—যে স্থানে কুক্কুটগণ রাত্রিকালে বিশ্রাম করে, কুক্কুট-নিলয়। **Water hen**—ডাহুকী। **Like a hen on a hot girdle**—Very restless; অত্যন্ত ছট্‌ফটে। **To sell one's hens on a rainy day**—To sell at a disadvantage or foolishly; নির্ব্বোধের মত বেচা।

hence (hĕns), *adv.* **1.** (*Archaic*) From this place; এই স্থান হইতে। **2.** From this time; as, a week *hence*; এই সময় হইতে, এখন হইতে। **3.** As a result from this; "Learn courage *hence*"; ইহা হইতে, ইহার ফলে। **4.** From this reason; therefore; এই হেতু; সুতরাং, অতএব। **Go hence**—Go from this place; die; এই স্থান হইতে প্রস্থান কর; মর। **Hence**—Go away; ভাগো, দূর হও। **Henceforth, –forward**—From this time forward; in future; অদ্যাবধি, এখন হইতে; ভবিষ্যতে। **Hence with it**—Take it away; ইহা লইয়া যাও।

hench'-măn (hĕnsh-), *n.* **1.** (*Hist.*) A squire or page; (ইতিহাস) নাইটের সহচর বা ভৃত্য। **2.** The chief servant of a Highland chief; হাইল্যাণ্ডের সর্দ্দারের প্রধান ভৃত্য। **3.** A trusty follower; বিশ্বস্ত অনুচর। **4.** A political supporter; রাজনীতিক্ষেত্রে সাহায্যকারী।

hĕn-dĕc'-ă-gŏn, *n.* A plane figure of eleven sides; একাদশাস্র ক্ষেত্র।

hĕn-dĕc-ă-sȳl'-lă-ble (-bl), *n.* A metrical line or verse of eleven syllables; একাদশ শব্দাংশবিশিষ্ট কবিতার চরণ। **–lab'-ic,** *adj.* & *n.*

hĕn-dī'-ă-dȳs, *n.* A figure in which the same idea is presented by two words; একপ্রকার অলঙ্কার—যাহাতে একই ভাব দুইটী বাক্য দ্বারা প্রকাশিত হয়।

hĕn'-nă, *n.* **1.** A shrub, the leaves of which yield an orange dye; মেঁদি। **2.** The paste made of the powdered leaves of the plant used in the East for dyeing nails etc.; হেনা পত্রের চূর্ণ হইতে প্রস্তুত পিণ্ড বিশেষ—যদ্দ্বারা মুসলমানগণ নখ প্রভৃতি রঞ্জিত করিয়া থাকে।

hĕn'-ō-thē-ĭsm, *n.* The worship of one deity as supreme among others; একপ্রকার ধর্ম্মমত যাহাতে প্রতি দেবতাকে স্বতন্ত্রভাবে একমাত্র উপাস্য দেব বলিয়া আবাহন করা হয়, একদেববাদ (হিঃ কোঃ)। [Max Muller এই শব্দটী গঠন করেন। See *Hibbert Lectures*, 1878, p. 230.]

hē-păt'-ic, *adj.* **1.** Of, or pertaining to, the liver; good for the liver; যকৃতসম্বন্ধীয়; যকৃতের পক্ষে হিতকর। **2.** Of the colour of the liver; যকৃতবর্ণ। **Hep-a-ti-za'-tion,** *n.* **Hep'-a-tize,** *v. t.* To convert into liver substance; as, *hepatized* lungs; যকৃতপদার্থে পরিণত করা।

hĕp-ă-tī'-tis, *n.* (*Med.*) Inflammation of the liver; যকৃতপ্রদাহ।

hĕp-ă-tŏg'-ē-nous (-nŭs), *adj.* Originating in the liver; যকৃতে জাত।

hĕp'-tăd, *n.* The sum or number or a group of seven; সপ্ত, সপ্তবন্ধক (হিঃ কোঃ)।

hĕp'-tă-glŏt, *adj.* & *n.* Containing or using seven languages; সপ্তভাষাত্মক, সপ্তভাষায় লিখিত। *Noun.* A book in seven languages; সপ্তভাষায় লিখিত পুস্তক।

hĕp'-tă-gŏn, *n.* A plane figure of seven sides; সপ্তাস্র ক্ষেত্র, সপ্তভুজ। **–tag'-o-nal,** *adj.*

hĕp'-tăr-ch-ȳ, *n.* A government by seven rulers; a country under seven rulers; সপ্ত নৃপতিকর্ত্তৃক শাসন, সপ্তশাসন (আঃ বঃ); সপ্ত নৃপতিকর্ত্তৃক শাসিত দেশ। [৫ম হইতে ৯ম শতাব্দী পর্য্যন্ত ইংলণ্ড দেশ Wessex, Sussex, Kent, East Anglia, Mercia এবং Northumbria এই সপ্তরাজ্যে বিভক্ত ছিল।]

hĕp'-tă-teuch (-tūk), *n.* A book consisting of seven books; সপ্তখণ্ডাত্মক পুস্তক।

hêr, *Pron.* (*Obj.* & *Poss. case of* SHE).

Hē'-ră, *n.* The queen of Heaven; দেবরাজ Zeusএর ভগ্নী এবং পত্নী। তিনি বায়ুমণ্ডলের উপর আধিপত্য বিস্তার করিতেন। ঋতুদেবী Horae এবং রামধনুর অধিষ্ঠাত্রী দেবী Iris Heraর সহচরী ছিলেন।

Heracleidae, *n.* The descendants of Heracles; হার্কিউলিজের বংশধরগণ।

Heracles, *n.* Same as HERCULES (which see.)

hĕr'-ăld, *n.* & *v. t.* **1.** An officer whose business was to proclaim war or peace, bear messages or to arrange state ceremonials etc.; (পূর্ব্বে) রাজকীয় সংবাদঘোষণাকারী এবং উৎসবাদির বন্দোবস্তকারী [রাজ-কর্ম্মচারী, অভিক্রোশক। **2.** An officer who settled questions of precedence and recorded names and pedigrees of those entitled to armorial bearings; যে কর্ম্মচারী মধ্যযুগে knightদিগের আদবকায়দা, প্রভৃতির প্রণালী নির্দ্ধারণ এবং সম্ভ্রান্ত-বংশীয় ব্যক্তিগণের কুলজি এবং কুলমর্য্যাদা-সূচক চিহ্নসমূহ রক্ষা করিতেন। **3.** A

Herald in official dress.

messenger ; a forerunner ; বাহক, দূত, বার্ত্তাবহ ; অগ্রদূত। **4.** (Sometimes used as a title of a newspaper) ; কোন কোন সংবাদ-পত্রের নাম। ***Verb t.*** To proclaim the approach of ; to introduce ; আগমন বার্ত্তা ঘোষণা করা ; উপস্থিত করা। **He-ral'-dic,** *adj.* **—ry,** *n.* **1.** The art or science of recording genealogies etc. ; কুলবিদ্যা, কুলাদর্শ। **2.** Armorial bearings ; আভিজাতিক চিহ্ন, কুলচিহ্ন। **3.** Heraldic pomp or ceremony ; কুলাচার্য্যগণের সমারোহ বা ক্রিয়াকাণ্ড। **Heralds' College**—কুলাচার্য্য মণ্ডলী।

hĕrb, *n.* **1.** A plant, the stem of which is not woody and dies down to the ground after flowering ; যে গাছের কাণ্ড কাষ্ঠময় নহে অথবা যাহা পুষ্পিত হওয়ার পর শুকাইয়া যায়, ওষধি। **2.** A plant the leaves of which are used as food, medicine, scent or flavour ; যে গাছের পাতা আহার করা হয় অথবা ঔষধ বা গন্ধদ্রব্য প্রস্তুতে ব্যবহৃত হয়,—গাছগাছড়া। **Her-ba'-ceous,** *adj.* Pertaining to, like, or of the nature of, herbs; ওষধিধর্ম্মা, ওষধি সম্বন্ধীয়। **Her-bif'-er-ous,** *adj.* Bearing herbs ; ওষধি উৎপাদক। **Her-biv'-o-rous,** *adj.* Eating or living on vegetables ; নিরামিষভোজী, তৃণভোজী। **Herb'-less,** *adj.* **Herb'-y,** *adj.* Having the nature of, pertaining to, or covered over with, herbs ; ওষধিধর্ম্মা, ওষধি সম্বন্ধীয়, ওষধি সমাবৃত। **Pot-herb**—শাক।

hêrb'-āge, *n.* **1.** Herbs collectively; grass pasture ; ওষধি সমূহ; গোচারণ মাঠ। **2.** The foliage and young stems of herbaceous plants ; কোমল উদ্ভিদের পত্র এবং ডগা। **3.** (*Law*) An easement of pasturage on another ground ; অন্যের ভূমিতে গোচারণের ব্যবহার-স্বত্ব।

hêrb'-ăl, *adj.* & *n.* Of, or pertaining to, herbs ; ওষধিসম্বন্ধীয়। ***Noun.*** A book containing descriptions of herbs ; ওষধিসম্বন্ধীয় পুস্তক, ওষধিকল্প (কেভিঃ)। **—ist,** *n.* **1.** A person skilled in plants ; ওষধিতত্ত্বজ্ঞ, ওষধিবেত্তা। **2.** A collector or dealer in medicinal herbs ; যে ব্যক্তি ঔষধ প্রস্তুতের (ভেষজ) গাছগাছড়া বিক্রয় করে, ওষধি সংগ্রাহক।

hêr-bā'-ri-ŭm, *n.* **1.** A collection of dried plants systematically arranged ; প্রণালীবদ্ধভাবে সজ্জিত শুষ্ক উদ্ভিদ সমূহ **2.** A book or case for preserving such a collection ; শুষ্ক উদ্ভিদ রক্ষার জন্য পুস্তক বা আধার। **3.** A building or room for keeping it in ; শুষ্ক উদ্ভিদ শালা, ওষধিশালা।

hêrb'-ă-rŷ, *n.* (*Obs.*) A garden of herbs or vegetables ; (অপ্রঃ) ভৈষজ্যোদ্যান, গাছগাছড়ার বাগান।

hêr'-bŏ-rīze, *v. i.* To seek for plants for scientific study ; to botanize ; উদ্ভিদ বিজ্ঞান বিষয়ে শিক্ষা লাভের জন্য গাছগাছড়া অন্বেষণ করা ; উদ্ভিদবিদ্যার অনুশীলন করা। **—rist,** *n.* Same as HERBALIST (which see). **—ri-za'-tion,** *n.*

Hêr'-cū-lēs, *n.* **1.** (*Gr. Myth.*) A hero of extraordinary strength, said to have accomplished twelve labours ; গ্রীক পুরাণে বর্ণিত মহা বলশালী বীর—ইনি দ্বাদশটী অতি-কৃচ্ছ্রসাধ্য কর্ম্ম সম্পাদন করেন, যথা :—(১) নীমিয়ার (Nemea) সিংহ বধ ; (২) লার্নিয়ার (Lernea) বিলবাসী নবশিরা সর্প বধ ; (৩) আর্কেডিয়ার (Arcadia) হরিণ বন্দীকরণ ; (৪) এরিমেন্থিয়ার (Erymanthia) শূকর বধ ; (৫) রাজা Augeasএর মলভূয়িষ্ঠ অশ্বশালা পরিষ্করণ ; (৬) Stymphalis হ্রদের নরমাংসাশী পক্ষিগণের নিধন ; (৭) Crete দ্বীপের ষণ্ড বন্দীকরণ ; (৮) Thrace বাসী Diomedesএর অশ্ব বন্দীকরণ ; (৯) স্ত্রীরাজ্যের রাণী Hippolyteর চন্দ্রহার হরণ ; (১০) Geryon নামক দৈত্যের ষণ্ডসমূহ বন্দীকরণ; (১১) Hesperides ভগিনীত্রয় কর্ত্তৃক রক্ষিত সুবর্ণময় সেওফল হরণ ; (১২) যমপুরী হইতে Cerberus নামক ত্রিশিরা কুক্কুর আনয়ন। [কোন কোন প্রত্নতত্ত্ববিদ্ হার্কিউলিজ্‌কে হরিকুলেশ বা বলরামের সহিত অভিন্ন বলিয়া মনে করেন।] **2.** A very strong man ; মহাবলশালী ব্যক্তি, কলির ভীম। **3.** A constellation in the northern hemisphere ; উত্তর গোলার্দ্ধের তারা-প্রকোষ্ঠ বিশেষ। **—cu'-le-an,** *adj.* **1.** Of, or pertaining to, Hercules ; হার্কিউলেস সম্বন্ধীয়। **2.** Very great ; difficult ; as, a *Herculean* task ; বিরাট ; কৃচ্ছ্রসাধ্য। **Hercules-beetle**—একপ্রকার বৃহৎ গোবরে পোকা (প্রায় ৬ ইঞ্চি লম্বা হইয়া থাকে)। **Hercules' choice**—ঐহিক সুখভোগ উপেক্ষা করত কর্ত্তব্যের অনুসরণ করিলে তাহার পুরস্কার স্বরূপ যে অমরত্ব লাভ করা যায়। **Hercules' club**—গুরুভার লগুড় (cf. ভীমের গদা)। **Hercules powder** — খনির কার্য্যে ব্যবহৃত বিস্ফোরক পদার্থ বিশেষ। **Pillars of Hercules** — See PILLAR.

hêrd, *n., v. i.* & *t.* **1.** A number of beasts feeding or driven together ; as, a *herd* of cattle ; পশুর পাল, যূথ, বৃন্দ। **2.** A crowd of common people ; a rabble ; as, a vulgar *herd* ; সাধারণ লোকের দল ; ইতর জনতা, ইতর লোকের ভিড়। ***Verb i.*** **1.** To go in a herd ; as, sheep *herd* in many hills ; দলবদ্ধ হইয়া চলা, যূথবদ্ধ হইয়া চলা। **2.** (*Fig.*) To associate or become one of any party ; as, I will *herd* among his friends ; (লক্ষণায়) দলে মিশা, দলভুক্ত হওয়া। ***Verb t.*** To form or put into a herd ; to tend, as sheep or cattle ; দলবদ্ধ করা, যূথবদ্ধ করা ; পালন করা। **Herd book** — গোমেষাদি বা শূকরের বংশবৃত্তান্তসম্বন্ধীয় পুস্তক। **Herdsman**—রাখাল, গোপাল, পশুপ, গোপালক,

পশুরক্ষক, গোপ। **Herdswoman**—গোপী, গোয়ালিনী, গোপিকা।

hērd, *n.* One who herds cattle etc.; a herdsman (*esp. with a word prefixed*; as, cow*herd*); গোপাল, গোপালক; পশুপালক।

here (hēr), *adv.* & *n.* **1.** In this place; as, behold *here* am I; এই স্থানে। **2.** Hitner; as, come *here*; এখানে। **3.** In this life or state; as, happy *here* and more happy hereafter; ইহলোকে, ইহকালে, ইহজীবনে। **4.** At this point; now; as, *here* cease thy questions; এই জায়গায়; এখন। **5.** In this matter; এই বিষয়ে। ***Noun.*** This place or point; as, from or to *here*; এই স্থান, অত্র। **Here-about(s)** — Somewhere about this place; আশে পাশে কোথায়ও। **Hereafter**—*adv.* & *n.* After this (or later on); in future; in the world to come; অতঃপর, অনন্তর; ভবিষ্যতে; পরলোকে। (*Noun*) A future existence or state; as, it is heaven that points out an *hereafter*; পারলৌকিক জীবন, পরত্র, পরকাল, পরলোক। **Hereat**—At, or by reason of, this; এই হেতু, এই কারণে, এই নিমিত্ত, এজন্য। **Hereby**—By means of this; ইহাদ্বারা, এই উপায়ে। **Herein**—In this (place or book etc.); এই স্থানে বা পুস্তকের এই জায়গায়। **Hereinafter** — In the following part of this (document, speech, etc.); এই দলীল, বক্তৃতা প্রভৃতির পরবর্ত্তী অংশে। **Hereof**—(*Archaic*) Of this; as a result of this; (অপ্রঃ) এই বিষয়ে; ইহার পরিণামে, ইহার ফলে। **Hereon**—On or upon this; ইহাতে, ইহার উপর। **Hereto**—(*Archaic*) To this matter; till this time; এই বিষয় পর্য্যন্ত; এই সময় পর্য্যন্ত, এযাবৎ। **Heretofore**—Formerly; up to this time; ইতঃপূর্ব্বে; এই সময় পর্য্যন্ত, এযাবৎ। **Hereunder**—Below this (in book etc.); ইহার নীচে। **Hereunto**—To this point or time; এই স্থানে, এই সময়ে। **Hereupon**—After this; in consequence of this; ইহার পর; ইহার ফলে। **Herewith**—With this; এতৎসঙ্গে। **Here and there** — In various places; as, footsteps *here and there*; স্থানে স্থানে, এখানে সেখানে। **Here's for you**—Here is something for you; এই জিনিষটী তোমার জন্য **Here's to you**—I drink to your good health; আমি তোমার স্বাস্থ্যকামনায় মদ্যপান করিতেছি। **Here you are**—Here is what you want; এই যে (তুমি যাহা চাও)। **I don't belong here**—আমি এই জায়গার লোক না। **Neither here nor there**—Of no importance; irrelevant; বিশেষ দরকারী নয়; অপ্রাসঙ্গিক।

hē-rĕd'-i-tā-ble (-bl), *adj.* Capable of being inherited; উত্তরাধিকারসূত্রে প্রাপ্য। **—bil'-i-ty,** *n.*

hĕr-ē-dit'-ā-mĕnt, *n.* **1.** Any species of property that may be inherited; a real property; দায়, উত্তরাধিকার সূত্রে প্রাপ্য সম্পত্তি; স্থাবর সম্পত্তি, ভূসম্পত্তি। **2.** Inheritance; উত্তরাধিকার।

hē-rĕd-i-tā'-ri-ăn, *n.* A person holding the doctrine of heredity; যে ব্যক্তি সন্তানে কৌলিক গুণ সংক্রমিত হয় বলিয়া বিশ্বাস করে, কুলসংক্রমণবাদী।

hē-rĕd'-i-tā-rȳ, *adj.* **1.** Descending by inheritance; as, a *hereditary* estate; কুলক্রমাগত, বংশপরম্পরাগত, মূলাগত (মঃ সং), মৌরুসী, কৌলিক। **2.** Transmitted from parent to offspring; as, *hereditary* pride or disease; কৌলিক, বংশজ, পুরুষানুক্রমিক, অনুবৃত্ত (অভিঃ), বংশগত। **3.** Of, or relating to, inheritance; উত্তরাধিকারসম্বন্ধীয়। **—ri-ly,** *adv.* **—ri-ness,** *n.*

hē-rĕd'-i-tȳ, *n.* **1.** Hereditary character or quality; কৌলিক স্বভাব বা গুণ, বংশপরম্পরা (হিঃ কোঃ)। **2.** The tendency of like to beget like; মনুষ্যাদির আত্মগুণানুরূপ সন্তানজননের প্রবৃত্তি, অনুবৃত্তি (অভিঃ), বংশানুক্রম (সাঃ পঃ), কুলসংক্রমণ (ঐ)। **—tism,** *n.* The doctrine of heredity; কুলসংক্রমণবাদ।

hĕr-ē-si-ârch, *n.* A leader in heresy; অপধর্ম্মসেবিগণের নেতা, পাষণ্ডশিরোমণি।

hĕr'-ĕ-sȳ, *n.* **1.** (*Theol.*) Opinion contrary to the orthodox doctrines of the Christian church; (ধর্ম্মশাস্ত্র) খৃষ্টীয় ধর্ম্মসংঘের চিরপ্রতিষ্ঠিত মতের বিরোধী মত, অপধর্ম্ম, উপধর্ম্ম, পাষণ্ডমার্গ। **2.** A doctrine at variance with established principles; as, a moral *heresy*; প্রচলিত ধর্ম্ম বা নীতির বিরোধী মত, উপমত। **—si-ol'-o-gy,** *n.* The history of heresies; পাষণ্ডমার্গসম্বন্ধীয় ইতিহাস।

hĕr'-ĕ-tic, *n.* The upholder of a heresy; পাষণ্ডী (বৃঃ সং), পাষণ্ডধর্ম্মী (সাঃ পঃ)। **He-ret'-i-cal,** *adj.* Containing, or pertaining to, heresy; পাষণ্ডতাপূর্ণ, পাষণ্ডতাসম্বন্ধীয়।

hĕr'-i-ŏt, *n.* (*Law*) A chattel or payment given to the lord of a fee on the decease of the tenant or vassal; (আইন) প্রজার মৃত্যুর পর ভূস্বামীকে প্রদত্ত গবাদিপশু, আসবাবপত্র বা অন্য কোন রূপ অস্থাবর সম্পত্তি।

hĕr'-it-ā-ble (-bl), *adj.* Capable of inheriting or taking by descent; উত্তরাধিকারসূত্রে প্রাপ্য। **—age,** *n.* **1.** That which is, or may be, inherited; inheritance; (*fig.*) lot, portion or condition by birth; উত্তরাধিকারসূত্রে প্রাপ্ত বা প্রাপ্য সম্পত্তি; উত্তরাধিকার; (লক্ষণায়) মানুষ যে অবস্থার মধ্যে বা যেরূপ অদৃষ্ট লইয়া জন্মগ্রহণ করে। **2.** The ancient Israelites; the Christian church; প্রাচীন এশ্রায়েলগণ; খৃষ্টীয় ধর্ম্মসংঘ। **—bly,** *adv.*

hĕr'-i-tor (-tĕr), *n.* An inheritor; উত্তরাধিকারী।

hêrl, *n.* Same as HARL.

hêr-măph′-rö-dīte, *n.* & *adj* 1. A human being or animal with both male and female organs or characteristics ; উভলিঙ্গ মানব বা পশু, ষণ্ড, অর্দ্ধনারী নর। 2. (*Bot.*) A plant in which the same flower has both stamens and pistils ; (উদ্ভিদ্-বিদ্যা) যে বৃক্ষের একই পুষ্পে পুংকেশর ও স্ত্রীকেশর আছে, দ্বিলিঙ্গ (সাঃ পঃ), উভলিঙ্গ। 3. An individual and thing in which opposite qualities are combined ; বিরুদ্ধধর্ম্মাশ্রিত ব্যক্তি বা বস্তু। 4. A ship with characteristics of two kinds of craft ; দ্বিবিধপোতের বিশেষত্ব সমন্বিত পোত। *Adj.* Combining both sexes or opposite qualities ; উভলিঙ্গ, উভলিঙ্গাত্মক, স্ত্রীপুং চিহ্নসমন্বিত। **–dit′-ic, –dit′-i-cal,** *adjs.* **–dit-ism,** *n.* The union of the two sexes in one body ; দ্বিলিঙ্গত্ব, উভলিঙ্গত্ব।

Hêr-măph-rö-dī′-tŭs, *n.* Son of Hermes and Aphrodite; Salmacis উৎসের পরী Hermaphroditusএর প্রেমে পতিত হইয়া প্রেমিকের সহিত চিরবন্ধনে সংবদ্ধ হইবার জন্য দেবগণের নিকট কাতর ভাবে প্রার্থনা করায় তাহারা প্রেমিক প্রেমিকার দেহ একত্র সংযুক্ত করিয়া দিয়াছিলেন।

hêr-mē-neu′-tic (-nü-), *adj.* & *n.* Of, or pertaining to, interpretation ; explanatory ; ব্যাখ্যাসম্বন্ধীয় ; অর্থ-প্রকাশক। *Noun.* (*Pl.*) Interpretation (esp. of the Scripture) ; ব্যাখ্যা, ভাষ্য, টীকা, ব্যাখ্যান, বিবৃতি শ্রুতিশব্দার্থ মীমাংসা (হিঃ কোঃ)। **–ti-cal,** *adj.*

Hermes.

Hêr′-mēs, *n.* 1. (*Gr. myth.*) Mercury, the messenger of the gods and god of science, eloquence, etc.; (গ্রীক পুরাণ) দেবতাদিগের বার্ত্তাবহ এবং বিজ্ঞান, বাগ্মিতা, প্রভৃতির অধিষ্ঠাতা। **Hermes Trismegistus**—(Thrice-Great) ; প্রাচীন মিসরীয় দেবতা Thothএর নব প্লেটোনিক দার্শনিকগণ প্রদত্ত নাম। এই দেবতা নানাপ্রকার গুহ্যতত্ত্ব ও তান্ত্রিকরহস্য ব্যক্ত করেন।

hêr-mĕt′-ic, –i-căl, *adjs.* 1. Of, or pertaining to, alchemy ; magical ; কিমিয়াবিদ্যাসম্বন্ধীয় ; ঐন্দ্রজালিক। 2. Perfectly closed and air-tight ; দৃঢ়নিরুদ্ধ, বায়ুপ্রবেশ পথহীন। **–i-cal-ly,** *adv.* 1. Chemically ; রাসায়নিকভাবে। 2. By means of fusion ; closely ; as, a vessel *hermetically* sealed ; গালাইয়া ; দৃঢ়রূপে। **Hermetic art**—Alchemy ; কিমিয়াবিদ্যা। **Hermetically sealed**—বায়ু প্রবেশের পথ শূন্য করিয়া রুদ্ধ, দৃঢ়রুদ্ধ।

hêr′-mit, *n.* A person retiring from society and living in solitude ; a recluse ; an ascetic ; সাধু, উদাসীন, যতি, বিজনবাসী ব্যক্তি ; বনবাসী; সন্ন্যাসী, তপস্বী, তাপস। **–age,** *n.* 1. A hermit's abode ; a secluded residence ; আশ্রম, তপোবন ; বিজননিবাস, বিজনকুটীর, বিজনভবন। 2. A kind of French wine produced near Valence ; একপ্রকার ফরাসী দেশীয় মদিরা। **Hermit-crab**—এক প্রকার কর্কট—যাহারা উহাদের দেহের খোলশূন্য পশ্চাদ্‌ভাগ রক্ষা করিবার নিমিত্ত শঙ্খ শম্বুকাদির পরিত্যক্ত খোলে বাস করিয়া থাকে, যতিকর্কট।

hêr′-nĭ-ă, *n.* The protrusion of an organ or part of an organ through an interstice in the wall of its natural cavity ; a rupture ; শরীরের কোন যন্ত্র বা যন্ত্রাংশের স্বাভাবিক গহ্বর হইতে বিচ্যুতি ও বহির্গমন ; অন্ত্রবৃদ্ধি। **–al, –ry,** *adjs.* **–ot′-o-my,** *n.* (*Med.*) A cutting for the cure or relief of hernia ; (ভৈষজ্য-শাস্ত্র) অন্ত্রবৃদ্ধি কর্ত্তন।

hêrn′-shaw (-shä), *n.* See HERONSHAW.

Hē′-rö, *n.* 1. A kind of demigod in ancient Greek mythology ; (প্রাচীন গ্রীক পুরাণ) নরদেব, অর্দ্ধদেব। 2. (*l. c.*) A man of distinguished valour etc. ; a great warrior ; one admired for noble achievements and qualities ; বীর ; সুবিখ্যাত যোদ্ধা ; শূর। 3. The principal character in a novel, play or poem ; নায়ক। **Hero-worship**—বীরপূজা ; মহাপুরুষার্চ্চন (হিঃ কোঃ)।

Hĕ′-rŏd, *n.* Herod, the Great, king of the Jews ; ইহুদীদিগের রাজা। ইনি যীশুখৃষ্টের সমসাময়িক ছিলেন। ইনি কংসের মত দৈববাণী শুনিয়া বহু শিশু হত্যা করেন। **To out-herod Herod** — To surpass Herod in cruelty ; নিষ্ঠুরতায় কংসকেও অতিক্রম করা।

hē-rö′-ic, *adj.* & *n.* 1. Pertaining to, or becoming a hero ; as, *heroic* valour ; *heroic* death ; বীরসম্বন্ধীয়, বীরোচিত। 2. Having the qualities of a hero ; bold ; as, the *heroic* son of Priam ; শৌর্য্যসম্পন্ন, বীর্য্যবান্; সাহসী। 3. Relating the achievements of heroes ; as, a *heroic* poetry ; বীরগণের অবদানসম্বন্ধীয়। 4. Grand or high-flown, as language ; বীররসাত্মক। *Noun.* 1. A heroic verse or poem ; বীররসাত্মক কবিতা বা কাব্য। 2. (*Pl.*) High-flown language or sentiments ; (বহুবচনে) বীররসাত্মক ভাষা বা ভাব। **–i-cal-ly,** *adv.* **Heroic poetry**—নরদেবগণের কাহিনীপূর্ণ কবিতা। **Heroic verse**—বীররসাত্মক কবিতা। **The heroic age**—(গ্রীক ইতিহাস ও পুরাণ) যে যুগে নরদেবগণ বাস করিতেন।

hē-rö-i-cŏm′-ic, *adj.* Combining the heroic and the ludicrous ; বীর ও হাস্যরসের সমাবেশ পূর্ণ।

hē-rö′-i-fȳ, *v. t.* To make a hero of, or heroic; বীর করা, বীরতুল্য করা।

hĕr′-ō-ine (-ĭn), 1. (*Gr. myth.*) A demi-goddess ; (গ্রীকপুরাণ) নরদেবী।

2. A woman of heroic spirit; বীরাঙ্গনা, বীরবালা, বীরনারী। 3. The principal female character in a poem etc.; নায়িকা।

hĕr'-ō-ĭsm, *n.* The qualities of a hero; bravery; heroic conduct; বীরত্ব; শৌর্য্য; বীরোচিত আচরণ।

hē'-rō-īze, *v. t.* & *i.* To make a hero of; to make heroic; বীর করিয়া তোলা; বীরোচিত করা। ***Verb i.*** To play the hero; বীরত্ব প্রদর্শন করা।

hĕr'-on (-ŭn), **hêrn,** *ns.* A large screaming water fowl with long

European heron.

necks and legs; বক, কঙ্ক। **–ry,** *n.* A place where herons breed; কঙ্কনিলয়। **Heron shaw**—কঙ্কশাবক, বকশাবক।

hêr'-pēs, *n.* A kind of skin disease with patches of distinct vesicles; প্রদাহিত চর্ম্মের উপর রসপূর্ণ ক্ষুদ্র ক্ষুদ্র পীড়কার অসমস্তবক বিশিষ্ট চর্ম্মরোগ বিশেষ, ইন্দ্রবিদ্ধ (হঃ চঃ), পামা (সাঃ পঃ), বিসর্প (কেণ্ডিঃ), দদ্রু (ঐ)। **–pet'-ic,** *adj.* দদ্রুরোগী।

hêr-pē-tŏl'-ō-ġȳ, *n.* The natural history of reptiles; সর্পজাতীয় জীব জন্তুর বিবরণ। **–gist,** *n.* One versed in herpetology; সর্প জাতীয় জীববর্গ-তত্ত্বজ্ঞ।

Herr, *n.* The German term of address equivalent to Mr.; জর্ম্মণ ভাষায় ইংরাজী Mr. শব্দের প্রতিশব্দ।

hĕr'-rĭng (-ing), *n.* A well known sea-fish; একপ্রকার সামুদ্রিক মৎস্য। **Herring-bone**—*n.* & *v. t.* হেরিং মৎস্যের মেরুদণ্ডের অনুরূপ সেলাই। (*Arch.*) A zigzag arrangement of stones or tiles; (স্থপতি-বিজ্ঞান) <<< এইরূপ গাঁথুনি। (*Verb t.*) To work with herring-bone stitch; to mark with a herring bone pattern; হেরিং মৎস্যের মেরুদণ্ডের অনুকরণে সেলাই করা; হেরিং মৎস্যের মেরুদণ্ডের মত নমুনা তোলা। **Herring-pond**—North Atlantic ocean; উত্তর অতলান্তিক মহাসাগর। **Kippered herring**—শুষ্কীকৃত হেরিং মৎস্য। **Red-herring**—ধোঁয়াদ্বারা শুষ্কীকৃত হেরিং মৎস্য। **Neither fish, flesh, nor good red herring**—See FISH.

Herrn'-hût-êr (hĕrn-), *n.* One of the Moravians; মোরেভিয়ান সম্প্রদায়ভুক্ত ব্যক্তি।

hêrs, *Pron.* (*Poss. case of* SHE) Of, or belonging to, her; as, it is *hers*; (it is a double genetive and cannot be joined to a noun); তাহার (স্ত্রীবাচক)।

hêr'-sĕlf, *Pron.* An emphatic and reflexive form of *she* and *her*; তিনি নিজে, সে স্বয়ং; তাহাকে। **By herself**—একাকিনী। **She is not herself**—She is not in her normal state; তিনি (সেই স্ত্রীলোক) প্রকৃতিস্থ নহেন।

Hêr'-sĭ-lĭ-ă, *n.* Wife of Romulus; রমিউল্যাসের পত্নী।

Hē'-sĭ-ŏd, *n.* An early Greek poet; প্রাচীন গ্রীক কবি। ইনি "Theogonia" নামক গ্রন্থে গ্রীকদেবদেবীগণের কাহিনী বর্ণন করিয়াছেন।

hĕs'-ĭ-tănt, *adj.* Not prompt in deciding; hesitating; irresolute; দ্বিধাকারী; সংশয়াকুল; অস্থিরমতি। **–tance,** *n.* **–tan-cy,** *n.* Indecision; scruple; সংশয়; দ্বিধা।

hĕs'-ĭ-tāte, *v. i.* **1.** To pause in deciding; to scruple; সংশয় করা, ইতস্ততঃ করা, সঙ্কোচ করা, সংশয় দোলায় দোলায়মান হওয়া; দ্বিধা করা। **2.** To stammer; তোতলান। **–tat-ing-ly,** *adv.* **–ta'-tion,** *n.* **1.** The act of hesitating; doubt; সংশয় করণ; দ্বিধা, কুণ্ঠা, সংশয়, সন্দেহ। **2.** A faltering in speech; তোতলামি। **–ta-tive,** *adj.*

Hĕs-pē'-rĭ-ăn, *adj.* (*Poet.*) Occidental; western; প্রতীচ্য; পাশ্চাত্য, অপরান্ত।

Hĕs'-pĕr-ĭ-dēs, *n.* The guardians of the golden apples. They dwelt in the far west, at the confines of ocean; গ্রীক উপকথায় উক্ত ভগিনীত্রয়—ইঁহারা পৃথিবীর সুদূর পশ্চিম প্রান্তস্থ উদ্যানে স্বর্ণময় সেওফল রক্ষা করিতেন।

hĕs'-pêr-ĭs, *n.* A genus of plants; এক জাতীয় গুল্ম।

hĕs-pêr-ŏr'-nĭs, *n.* An American genus of fossil birds; আমেরিকা দেশে প্রাপ্ত এক জাতীয় শিলীভূত পক্ষী।

Hĕs'-pêr-ŭs, *n.* Venus; the evening star; শুক্র; শুক তারা, সন্ধ্যা তারা, সাঁঝের তারা।

Hes'-si-ăn (hĕ-shĭ-), *adj.* & *n.* Relating to Hesse in Germany; জর্ম্মণীর অন্তঃপাতী হেসী নামক স্থান সম্বন্ধীয়। ***Noun.*** **1.** A native of Hesse in Germany; জর্ম্মণীর অন্তঃপাতী হেসী নামক স্থানের অধিবাসী। **2.** (*Pl.*) Hessian boots; (বহুবচনে) একপ্রকার লম্বা বুট জুতা [সর্ব্বপ্রথম Hesse নামক স্থানের অধিবাসিগণ ব্যবহার করিয়াছিল বলিয়া এই নাম]। **3.** A strong coarse cloth of hemp or jute; পাট অথবা শণের চট। **Hessian boot**—Same as HESSIAN *n.* 2. **Hessian fly**—একপ্রকার কীট—যাহার কীড়া গোধূম নষ্ট করে।

hĕst, *n.* (*Archaic*) Command; order; "At thy *hest*"; (অপ্রঃ) আদেশ; আজ্ঞা।

Hĕs'-tĭ-ă, *n.* The Vesta of the Romans; রোমানদিগের গার্হস্থ্যাগ্নির

অধিষ্ঠাত্রী দেবী। এই দেবী চিরকৌমার্য্য-ব্রতাবলম্বিনী ছিলেন। ইনি সর্ব্বপ্রকার পারিবারিক সুখশান্তি প্রদাত্রীরূপে গণ্যা হইতেন।

hĕ-tae'-ră (-tē-), **-tai'-ră** (-tĭ-), *ns.* **1.** (*Gr. antiq.*) A female paramour (they were often singers and dancers); প্রাচীন গ্রীসের বিদুষী এবং নৃত্যগীত প্রভৃতি নানা ললিত কলাভিজ্ঞা বারাঙ্গনা। [Lasthenia নাম্নী বিদুষী বারাঙ্গনা সুবিখ্যাত গ্রীক দার্শনিক প্লেতোর নিকট দর্শনশাস্ত্র শিক্ষা করিয়াছিল। Leontion নাম্নী অপর একজন গ্রীক চার্ব্বাক Epicurusএর শিষ্যা ছিল। Periclesএর প্রণয়িনী সুপণ্ডিতা Aspasia সক্রেতিস প্রভৃতি দার্শনিকগণের সহিত গভীর অধ্যাত্মতত্ত্ব সমূহ আলোচনা করিতেন। (cf. our বসন্তসেনা, লক্ষহীরা, চিন্তামণি!) *See* Limburg-Browers *Histoire de la Civilisation morable et religieuse des Grecs*]. **2.** A harlot; বেশ্যা। **—rism,** *n.* **1.** Concubinage; বেশ্যাবৃত্তি। **2.** The primitvie state of society in which all the women of a tribe were held in common; সমাজের যে প্রাচীন অবস্থায় বিবাহপ্রথা প্রচলিত ছিল না এবং রমণীগণ সাধারণের উপভোগ্যা ছিল, জাতিপত্নীত্ব।

hĕt'-ĕr-ŏ-clīte, *adj.* & *n.* **1.** Irregularly declined or inflected; as, a *heteroclite* noun; বিকল্পে সাধিত বা বিভক্তি প্রদত্ত, উদ্দামরূপ (আঃ বঃ), বিধিভঞ্জক (কেণ্ডিঃ)। **2.** (*Fig.*) Irregular; abnormal; অনিয়মিত; নিয়মবিরুদ্ধ। ***Noun.*** **1.** (*Gram.*) A heteroclite word or noun; বিকল্পে সাধিত বা বিভক্তি প্রদত্ত শব্দ। **2.** Anything or person deviating from the ordinary rule. সাধারণ নিয়মের ব্যভিচারী বস্তু বা ব্যক্তি।

hĕt'-ĕr-ŏ-dŏx, *adj.* **1.** (*Theol.*) Contrary to established opinions; not orthodox; as, a *heterodox* opinion; (ধর্ম্ম-শাস্ত্র) প্রচলিত মতের বিরোধী, প্রচলিত মতের বিরুদ্ধাচারী, অপথগামী, বামমার্গানুযায়ী, বামমার্গী, বামাচারী, ইতর পথাবলম্বী (হিঃ কোঃ); ধর্ম্মবিরুদ্ধ। **2.** Holding heterodox opinions, as a person; প্রচলিত মতের বিরুদ্ধাচারী। **—y,** *n.* The holding of heterodox opinions; heresy; প্রচলিত মতের বিরুদ্ধাচার, ধর্ম্মবিরুদ্ধতা, ইতরপথাবলম্বিতা (হিঃ কোঃ); পাষণ্ডতা, অপধর্ম্মসেবিতা।

hĕt-ĕr-ŏ-ğē'-nē-ous (-ŭs), *adj.* **1.** Of a different kind of nature; dissimilar; composed of different elements; বিজাতীয়, ইতরাবয়ব (হিঃ কোঃ); বিসদৃশ; বিবিধজাতিক, অনেকজাতিক, পৃথগ্‌বিধ। **2.** (*Math.*) Of different kinds so as to be incommensurable; ইতরাবয়ব (হিঃ কোঃ)। **—ly,** *adv.* **—ne'-i-ty, —ness,** *ns.* The quality of being heterogeneous; বিজাতীয়তা, বৈজাত্য, অনেকজাতিত্ব, ভিন্নত্ব, বিবিধজাতিত্ব, বৈগুণ্য, বৈবর্ণ্য।

hĕt-ĕr-ŏ-ğĕn'-ĕ-sis, *n.* **1.** Spontaneous generation; abiogenesis; স্বতঃজনন; আজীবোৎপত্তি। **2.** Origination of a being otherwise than from a parent of the same kind; ভিন্ন জাতীয় জনকজননী হইতে উদ্ভব। **—ge-net'-ic,** *adj.*

hĕt-ĕr-ŏg'-ră-phȳ, *n.* Incorrect or inconsistent spelling; অশুদ্ধ এবং অসংলগ্ন বর্ণবিন্যাস। **—o-graph'-ic,** *adj.*

hĕt-ĕr-ŏ-mŏr'-phĭc, *adj.* Having dissimilar forms; ভিন্নরূপ, ভিন্নাকৃতি। **—phism,** *n.*

hĕt-ĕr-ŏn'-ŏ-mȳ, *n.* **1.** Subordination to the law of another (*opp. to autonomy*); পরায়ত্তশাসন, পরাধীনতা, পরতন্ত্রতা। **2.** (*Metaph.*) The law imposed on us from without; (তত্ত্ব-বিদ্যা) বহির্জগৎ হইতে যে নিয়মনিচয় আমাদের উপর চাপান হয়। **3.** (*Biol.*) State or quality of being heteronomous; (জীব-বিজ্ঞান) পরাধীনতা। **—mous,** *adj.* **1.** Subject to external law (*opp. to autonomous*); বাহ্য নিয়মের অধীন। **2.** Subject to different laws; বিধিসমূহের অধীন।

hĕt-ĕr-ŏ-path'-ic, *adj.* **1.** Allopathic; বিষমচিকিৎসাবিধান সম্পর্কীয়। **2.** Differing in effect; ভিন্নরূপ ফলপ্রদ, বিজাতীয় (ব্রজঃ হিন্দুঃ)।

hĕt'-măn, *n.* (*Polish*) The title of a chief or general of the Cossacks; কসাকদিগের সর্দ্দার বা সেনাপতি।

heu-ris'-tic (hū-), *adj.* Serving to discover; guiding in finding out; আবিষ্কারে সাহায্যকারী; আবিষ্কারে পথপ্রদর্শক।

hew (hū), *v. t.* & *i.* **1.** To cut or fell with an axe etc. (usu. followed by *down, off, away, asunder, to pieces* etc.); as, to *hew down* an oak tree; ছেদন করা, চেলা করা। **2.** To form or shape with a sharp instrument; ধারাল যন্ত্র দ্বারা গঠন করা, কাটিয়া গড়া। ***Verb i.*** To deal blows with a cutting instrument, (with *at, among* etc.); কুঠার প্রভৃতি দ্বারা আঘাত করা। **To hew one's way** — To make a way for oneself by hewing; বৃক্ষাদি ছেদনপূর্ব্বক পথ পরিষ্কার করা।

hew'-ĕr (hū-), *n.* One who hews; one who cuts coal from seams; ছেদক, ছেদনকারী; যে ব্যক্তি স্তর হইতে কয়লা কাটে। **Hewers of wood and drawers of water** — Drudges; জল তোলা, কাঠ কাটা ইত্যাদি হীনকার্য্যে নিযুক্ত ব্যক্তিগণ।

hĕx'-ă-chŏrd, *n.* (*Mus.*) A diatonic series of six notes or tones; (সঙ্গীত-শাস্ত্র) ষড়জগ্রাম।

hĕx'-ă-gŏn, *n.* A figure with six sides; ষট্‌কোণ ক্ষেত্র, ষড়ভুজ, ষড়স্র ক্ষেত্র। **—ag'-o-nal,** *adj.* Pertaining to a hexagon; ষট্‌কৌণিক।

hĕx-ă-hē'-drŏn, *n.* A solid body of six sides or faces; ষড়স্র ঘনক্ষেত্র, ষড়্‌ফলক (হিঃ কোঃ)। **—dral,** *adj.*

hĕx-ăm'-ĕ-tĕr, *n.* A verse or poetic line of six feet, consisting chiefly of dactyls and spondees ; ষট্‌পদ কবিতাপংক্তি, ষট্‌পংক্তি। **–a-met'-ric** *adj.* **–trist** *n.*

hĕx'-ă-plă *n.* An edition of the Bible in six versions in parallel columns ; ছয় সমান্তরাল স্তম্ভে ছয় বিভিন্ন ভাষায় অনুবাদ সম্বলিত বাইবেলের সংস্করণ।

hĕx'-ă-pŏd, *n.* & *adj.* An animal with six feet ; ষট্‌পদ জন্তু। ***Adj.*** Having six feet ; ষট্‌পদ বিশিষ্ট।

hey (hā), *interj.* An exclamation calling attention or denoting joy, surprise or interrogation ; ওহে! শোন! কি মজা!

hey' day hā-dā, *interj.* An exclamation of joy, surprise, etc. : হায় কি মজা! হায় কি হলো! একি!

hey'-day hā-dā), *n.* Full bloom : height ; flush : as, the *hey day* of youth ; prosperity : পূর্ণ বিকাশ ; পরাকাষ্ঠা, চরমসীমা ; নবীনতা, সমৃদ্ধি **Heyday of youth**—পূর্ণ যৌবন, ভরা যৌবন, প্রৌঢ় যৌবন।

hī, *interj.* An expression to call attention ; ওহে!

hī-ā'-tŭs, *n.* **1.** (*Rare*) A gap ; an opening : ফাঁক ; ছিদ্র। **2.** A break in a series, account, writing, etc. : a missing link : হিসাব প্রভৃতিতে ফাঁক বা শূন্য স্থান ; কোন শ্রেণী বা পরম্পরা সম্পূর্ণ করিতে হইলে যেটী আবশ্যক। **3.** (*Gram.*) The coming together of two vowels in successive syllables or words : (ব্যাকরণ) ক্রমিক শব্দাংশ বা শব্দদ্বয়ের স্বরবর্ণযুগলের সম্মিলন, সন্ধিবিশ্লেষ (সাঃ পঃ), সন্ধিভঙ্গ (আঃ বঃ)।

hī'-bêr-nāte, *v. i.* **1.** (Of animals) To pass the winter in a torpid state ; (সর্প, ভেক, বাদুড়, ভল্লুক, প্রভৃতি জন্তুর পক্ষে) শীতকাল জড়ভাবে অতিবাহিত করা। **2.** (Of persons) To winter in a mild climate ; (মনুষ্যের পক্ষে) নাতিশীতোষ্ণ স্থানে শীতকাল অতিবাহিত করা। **3.** (*Fig.*) To remain inactive ; (লক্ষণায়) জড় থাকা, নিশ্চেষ্ট থাকা, নিরুদ্যম হওয়া, তন্দ্রিত হওয়া। **–nal, –nant,** *adjs.* **–na'-tion,** *n.* **1.** Act of hibernating ; হিমশয়ন (সাঃ পঃ), শীতস্বাপ (হিঃ কোঃ)।

Hī-bêr'-ni-ăn, *adj.* & *n.* Of, or pertaining to, Hibernia or Ireland; আয়র্লণ্ডসম্বন্ধীয়। ***Noun.*** A native of Ireland ; আয়র্লণ্ডের অধিবাসী। **–cism,** *n.* An idiom peculiar to the Irish ; an Irish bull ; আইরিশ ভাষার রীতিসিদ্ধ প্রয়োগ ; আয়র্লণ্ডের ষাঁড়।

hī-bis'-cŭs, *n.* A genus of beautifully flowered mallows ; জবা, স্থলপদ্ম প্রভৃতি পুষ্পের সাধারণ নাম। ***Edible hibiscus***—ঢেঁড়স। ***Hibiscus cannabinus***—মেস্তা পাট (বেলঃ)। ***Hibiscus mutabilis*** — স্থলপদ্ম (বেলঃ)। ***Hibiscus rosa-sinensis***—জবা (বেলঃ)। ***Hibiscus sabdariffa*** — মেস্তা (বেলঃ)।

hic'-cup (-ŭp), *n.*, *v. i.* & *t.* A spasmodic affection of the diaphragm and glottis producing a sudden sound ; হিক্কা, হেঁচকি। ***Verb i.*** To have a hiccup : হিক্কা উঠা। ***Verb t.*** To say or bring out with hiccups ; হেঁচকি দিতে দিতে বলা বা বাহির করা।

hicjacet, (L. = *here lies*) An epitaph [শব্দানুযায়ী অর্থ,—এই স্থানে নিদ্রিত] সমাধিস্তম্ভের উপর উৎকীর্ণ লিপি, সমাধিলিপি।

hick'-ō-rȳ, *n.* **1.** An American tree of the walnut family valuable for timber : উত্তর আমেরিকার আখরোট জাতীয় বৃক্ষবিশেষ। **2.** Wood or stick of this tree ; ঐ বৃক্ষের কাঠ বা উহা হইতে প্রস্তুত যষ্টি।

hid (*P. t.* & *p. p.* of HIDE.)

hī-dăl'-gō, *n.* A Spanish nobleman of the lowest class ; স্পেনদেশীয় সর্ব্বনিম্নশ্রেণীর সম্ভ্রান্তপুরুষ।

hīde, *n.* & *v. t.* **1.** The skin of an animal, either raw or dressed ; চর্ম্ম, চামড়া, কৃত্তি। **2.** (*Facet.*) The human skin ; as, to save one's own *hide* ; (রঙ্গচ্ছলে) মনুষ্য-চর্ম্ম। ***Verb t.*** (*Colloq.*) To whip or flog ; (চলিত ভাষায়) বেত্রান, বেত মারা, কষাঘাত করা। **Hide-bound**—With the hide adhering closely to the body as an animal ; চর্ম্ম দেহে দৃঢ়সংবদ্ধ, দৃঢ়সংবদ্ধচর্ম্ম। Having the bark so close as to impede the growth, as a tree ; বল্কল কাষ্ঠে দৃঢ়সংবদ্ধ, দৃঢ়বদ্ধ-বল্কল। (*Fig.*) Obstinate and bigoted ; narrow-minded ; (লক্ষণায়) গোঁড়া এবং এক গুঁয়ে ; সঙ্কীর্ণমনাঃ।

hīde, *v. t.* & *i.* **1.** To conceal ; to put out of view ; লুকান, লুক্কায়িত করা ; দৃষ্টিপথের অন্তরাল করা। **2.** To keep secret ; as, he *hid* the fact from me ; ছাপান, গোপন রাখা। **3.** To obstruct the view of ; as, a hill *hides* the sea ; দৃষ্টিপথ রোধ করা। ***Verb i.*** To conceal oneself ; to be withdrawn from sight ; লুক্কায়িত হওয়া ; দৃষ্টিপথের অন্তরাল হওয়া, গা ঢাকা দেওয়া। **Hid'-den,** *p. p.* Concealed ; unknown ; obscure ; লুক্কায়িত, অপ্রকাশ, গুপ্ত, গূঢ়, প্রচ্ছন্ন ; অজ্ঞাত ; অস্পষ্ট। **Hide-and-seek**—লুকোচুরি খেলা। **Hide-away**—*n.* & *adj.* A fugitive ; পলাতক। (*Adj.*) That hides away ; সংগোপনকারী। **To hide one's head**—To keep out of sight from shame etc. ; লজ্জা বা অপমানে মাথা হেঁট করা, লজ্জায় বা অপমানে অধোবদন হওয়া, লাজ বা অপমানে মুখ লুকান।

hīde', *n.* (*Hist.*) A certain portion of land about 120 acres ; (ইতিহাস) প্রায় ১২০ একর পরিমিত ভূমি।

hid'-ē-ous (-ŭs), *adj.* **1.** Frightful ; revolting to the senses or feelings ; repulsive ; as, a *hideous* monster ; ভয়ঙ্কর, ভীষণ ; বিকট,

বীভৎস; বিকৃত, বিকৃতাকার, দুষমন্ (*colloq*)। **2.** Detestable; odious; ঘৃণ্য; জঘন্য। **—ly,** *adv.* **—ness,** *n.*

hĭd'-ing, *n.* Act of hiding; concealment; state of being hidden; as, he is in *hiding*; সংগোপন; প্রচ্ছাদন; প্রচ্ছন্নাবস্থিতি। **Hiding-place**—A place of concealment; লুকাইবার স্থান। **To be in hiding**—To remain hidden; as, he is in *hiding*; লুক্কায়িত থাকা।

hĭd'-ing, *n.* (*Colloq.*) A thrashing; a flogging; (চলিত-ভাষায়) বেত্রাঘাত; কষাঘাত।

hie (hī), *v.i.* (*Poet.*) To go quickly; (কবিতায়) শীঘ্র যাওয়া, ত্বরা করিয়া যাওয়া।

hī'-êr-ârch, *n.* A ruler in sacred matters; archbishop; as, princely *hierarchs*; ধর্ম্মসংক্রান্ত বিষয়ের নায়ক; প্রধান ধর্ম্মাধ্যক্ষ, প্রধান ধর্ম্মনায়ক, ধর্ম্মাধীশ (আঃ বঃ), মুখ্য আচার্য্য (কেণ্ডিঃ)।

hī'-êr-ârch-ȳ, *n.* **1.** Each of the three divisions of angels; the angels collectively; দেবদূতগণের বিভাগত্রয়ের অন্যতম; দেবদূতবৃন্দ। **2.** Rule or government of priests; যাজক-তন্ত্র, ধর্ম্মাধীশতন্ত্র। **3.** A body of ecclesiastical rulers organised in successive grades; পদমর্যাদানুক্রমে শ্রেণীবদ্ধ যাজকসমাজ। **4.** Any graded organization; পদমর্যাদানুক্রমে শ্রেণীবদ্ধ সমাজ। **—ar'-chic, —ar'-chi-cal,** *adjs.* **—chism,** *n.*

hī-êr-ăt'-ic, *adj.* **1.** Pertaining to priests; consecrated to sacred uses; যাজকসম্পর্কীয়; দেবকার্য্যে উৎসর্গীকৃত। **2.** Designating a style of writing used by the ancient Egyptian priests; প্রাচীন মিশর দেশীয় পুরোহিতগণের লিপিপ্রণালী-সম্পর্কীয়।

hī-êr-ŏc'-ră-cȳ, *n.* Goverment by priests; যাজকতন্ত্র।

hī'-êr-ŏ-glȳph, *n.* **1.** A figure of an object standing for a word, syllable or sound, as used in ancient Egyptian and other writing; প্রাচীন মিশর বাসিগণের চিত্রাক্ষর, চিত্রবর্ণ (আঃ বঃ) [ইহাতে পশু, পক্ষী, পুষ্পাদি দ্বারা শব্দ, শব্দাংশ, অক্ষর বা ভাব প্রকাশ করা হইত]। **2.** Any figure having a hidden or mysterious significance; any unintelligible character or mark; গুহ্য বা রহস্যপূর্ণ অর্থসূচক চিত্র; দুর্ব্বোধ অক্ষর বা চিহ্ন।

hī-êr-ŏ-glȳph'-ic, —ĭ-căl, *adj.* & *n.* **1.** Symbolical; as, *hieroglyphic* writing; সাঙ্কেতিক। **2.** Relating to, written in, or resembling hieroglyphs; not decipherable; as, a *hieroglyphic* scrawl; চিত্রাক্ষর সম্পর্কীয়, চিত্রাক্ষরে লিখিত, চিত্রাক্ষরবৎ; অক্ষররহস্যভেদাযোগ্য। ***Noun.*** (*Pl.*) Hieroglyphs; চিত্রাক্ষর, দুষ্পাঠ্য লিপি, সাঙ্কেতিক চিত্র সাঙ্কেতিকাক্ষর। **—i-cal-ly,** *adv.*

hī'-êr-ŏ-grăm', *n.* A form of sacred writing; পবিত্র লিপি বিশেষ।

hī-êr-ŏl'-á-trȳ, *n.* The worship of saints; সিদ্ধপুরুষ পূজা।

hī'-êr-ŏl'-ŏ-gȳ, *n.* Sacred literature or lore; ধর্ম্মশাস্ত্র।

hī-êr'-ŏ-phănt, *n.* **1.** (*Gk. antiq.*) One who teaches the mysteries of religion; ধর্ম্ম সম্বন্ধীয় নিগূঢ় রহস্যের শিক্ষাদাতা। **2.** An expounnder of the sacred mysteries; ধর্ম্ম সম্বন্ধীয় নিগূঢ় রহস্যের ব্যাখ্যাতা। **—phan'-tic,** *adj.*

hig'-gle (-l), To chaffer; to be tedious and nice in bargaining; দর কষাকষি করা; দরদস্তুর করা, কচ্লা কচ্লি করা।

hig'-gle-dy-pig'-gle-dȳ (hĭ-gl-dĭ-pĭ-gl-), *adv.*, *adj.* & *n.* In confusion; topsy-turvy (*colloq.*); এলোমেলো; উলটপালট। ***Adj.*** Confused; এলোমেলো। ***Noun.*** Utter confusion; মহা বিশৃঙ্খলা, লণ্ডভণ্ড।

high (hī), *adj.*, *adv.* & *n.* **1.** Lofty; tall; elevated; as, a *high* mountain; উচ্চ, তুঙ্গ, উচ্ছ্রিত, ঊর্দ্ধ; প্রাংশু, দীর্ঘাকৃতি; উন্নত। **2.** Elevated or exalted in quality; difficult or abstruse; as, *high* speculation; সমুন্নত, মহান্; কঠিন, জটিল, দুর্ব্বোধ, দুর্জ্ঞেয়। **3.** Elevated in rank or condition; noble; as, *high* birth; সম্ভ্রান্ত, কুলীন, অভিজাত; উচ্চপদস্থ। **4.** (Of officers) Chief; as, *High* Admiral; প্রধান, মুখ্য। **5.** Strong; violent; as, a *high* wind; প্রবল; প্রচণ্ড। **6.** Far advanced; as, *high* noon; অধিকদূর অগ্রসর। **7.** Proud; arrogant; angry; as, *high* looks or words; দৃপ্ত, দাম্ভিক; উদ্ধত; ক্রুদ্ধ, চটা। **8.** Costly; dear; as, to hold goods at a *high* price; চড়া; মহার্ঘ, উচ্চ। **9.** Luxurious; as, *high* feeding; ভোগবিলাসপূর্ণ, ভোগবিলাসসাধক। **10.** Extreme in opinion; as, a *high* Tory; চরমপন্থী। **11.** Intense; extreme, as, heat, temperature, etc.; তীব্র; নিতান্ত। **12.** Loud; sharp; as, a *high* sound or note; উচ্চ; চড়া। **13.** Hilarious; as, *high* spirits; হর্ষোৎফুল্ল। **14.** Deep; vivid, as a colour; গাঢ়, ঘন; সজীব। **15.** (*Cookery*) Slightly tainted, as meat or game; strong scented; rich; as, *high* seasonings; (রন্ধনবিদ্যা) ঈষৎ পচা; উগ্রগন্ধ; মসলাদার। ***Adv.*** **1.** At, or to, a great altitude; far up; অনেক উচ্চে; বহু ঊর্দ্ধে। **2.** In, or to, a great degree; অতিশয়, অতিমাত্রায়, মহা। **3.** At, or to, a high pitch; as, to sing *high*; চড়া স্বরে। **4.** At a high price; উচ্চ মূল্যে। ***Noun.*** **1.** (*Obs.* or *Scot.*) An elevated place or region; উচ্চ স্থান, ঊর্দ্ধলোক। **2.** (*Card-playing*) The highest card dealt or drawn; (তাসখেলা) সর্ব্বোচ্চ তাস। **3.** People of rank or high station; as, *high* and low; সম্ভ্রান্ত সমাজ, অভিজাত সমাজ। **High altar**—খৃষ্টীয় ধর্ম্মমন্দিরের প্রধান বেদী। **High art**—উচ্চাঙ্গের লিপি, চিত্র, ভাস্কর্য্য বা সঙ্গীত। **High blooded**—উচ্চবংশজ, উচ্চকুলোদ্ভব।

High-blower—যে অশ্ব সশব্দে নাসিকা বিধূনন করে। **High-born**—Of high or noble birth; উচ্চবংশজ, অভিজাত, উচ্চকুলোদ্ভব; কুলীন। **High-bred** — অভিজাত, কুলীন। **High Church**—*adj.* & *n.* Belonging to that section of the Episcopal Church that maintains the highest notions respecting Episcopacy, the priesthood, sacraments, etc.; ধর্ম্মাধ্যক্ষশাসিত ধর্ম্মসংঘের যে বিভাগে ধর্ম্মাধ্যক্ষ-শাসনতন্ত্র, যাজকসমাজ, সংস্কার, প্রভৃতি সম্পর্কে উচ্চ ধারণা পোষণ করা হইয়া থাকে তদন্তর্ভুক্ত। (*Noun*) A party within the Church of England which exalts the authority of the Episcopate, priesthood, etc.; ইংলণ্ডের রাজবিধিদ্বারা প্রতিষ্ঠিত ধর্ম্মসংঘান্তর্গত সম্প্রদায় বিশেষ—যাহা ধর্ম্মাধ্যক্ষ, যাজকসমাজ, প্রভৃতির কর্ত্তৃত্বের প্রতি বিশেষ সম্মান প্রদর্শন করিয়া থাকে। **High-coloured**—সমুজ্জ্বল বর্ণে রঞ্জিত, অতিরঞ্জিত; বিচিত্র। **High Court**—সর্ব্বোচ্চ ধর্ম্মাধিকরণ, উচ্চতম আদালত। **High day**—ছুটীর দিন; পর্ব্বদিন, উৎসবদিবস, পর্ব্বাহ। **High-falutin(g)**—*adj.* & *n.* Bombastic; বাগাড়ম্বরপূর্ণ, শব্দাড়ম্বরপূর্ণ। (*Noun*) High-flown language; বাগাড়ম্বরপূর্ণ ভাষা, শব্দচ্ছটাবিশিষ্ট ভাষা। **High-flier, -flyer**—উৎকট ধারণাপূর্ণ ব্যক্তি; উচ্চাভিলাষী ব্যক্তি। **High-flying** — উচ্চাভিলাষী, উৎকট ধারণাপূর্ণ। **High-flown**—উৎকট; শব্দাড়ম্বরপূর্ণ, শব্দচ্ছটাপূর্ণ। **High-handed** — Overbearing; arbitrary; প্রভুত্বকারী, উৎপীড়ক, জুলুমকারী; যথেচ্ছাচারী। *High-handedness, n.* জুলুম, জবরদস্তি। **High-hearted**—সাহসপূর্ণ। **High jinks**—See JINK. **Highlander**—An inhabitant (esp. the Scotch) of Highlands; স্কটলেণ্ডের পার্ব্বত্যপ্রদেশের অধিবাসী, স্কটলেণ্ডের পার্ব্বত্য অঞ্চলের অধিবাসী, লেংটা গোরা। **Highlands**—A mountainous district; as, the *Highlands* of Scotland; পার্ব্বত্য প্রদেশ, শৈলাঞ্চল। **High latitude**—Far from the equator—বিষুব রেখা হইতে দূরবর্ত্তী। **High life**—The style of living of the fashionable classes; বড়লোকের চাল। The upper classes collectively; সম্ভ্রান্ত সম্প্রদায়। **High mass**—বিশেষ ঘটনা উপলক্ষে ধূপদীপবাদ্য সহকারে রোমান ক্যাথলিক ধর্ম্মসংঘে যে খৃষ্টের অন্তিমভোজন স্মৃতি-পর্ব্ব অনুষ্ঠিত হয়। **High-mettled**—অতিতেজস্বী, মহাতেজস্বী, মহাসত্ত্ব, মহাতেজা। **High-minded**—Of morally lofty character; উন্নতমনাঃ, উচ্চমনাঃ, মহামনাঃ, উদারচেতা, মহামতি। *High-mindedness, n.* **High-necked**—এরূপভাবে কাটা যাহাতে গলা ও কাঁধ ঢাকা যায়। **High-pitched**—Acute in pitch; as, a *highpitched* sound; উচ্চ গ্রামে বাঁধা, জিল। Steep; as, a *highpitched* roof; খাড়া। (*Fig.*) Of lofty or exalted character; (লক্ষণায়) উন্নতচরিত্র, উন্নতপ্রকৃতি। **High pressure**—Having or involving a pressure exceeding that of the atmosphere; as, a *high-pressure* steam; বায়ুমণ্ডলের চাপ অপেক্ষা অধিকতর চাপ প্রয়োগকারী। (*Fig.*) Intense; urgent; as, a *high-pressure* business; (লক্ষণায়) তীব্র; জরুরি। **High-priced**—বহুমূল্য। **High-priest**—প্রধান পুরোহিত, মহাযাজক (বিশেষতঃ ইহুদিগণের)। **High-principled**—উন্নত নীতিজ্ঞানসম্পন্ন, উন্নত ধর্ম্মবুদ্ধিসম্পন্ন। **High road**—A main road; (*fig.*) the ordinary direct course (of action etc.); প্রধান রাস্তা, রাজপথ, রাজমার্গ, রথ্যা, মহাপথ; (লক্ষণায়) সোজাপথ। **High seas**—The open sea; the ocean beyond the limit of 3 miles from the coast; বাহির দরিয়া; উপকূল হইতে ৩ মাইল সীমার বাহিরের সাগর। **High souled**—মহাপ্রাণ, মহদন্তঃকরণ, মহাত্মা। **High-sounding**—Pompous; noisy; as, *high-sounding* words; লম্বাচওড়া, বাগাড়ম্বরপূর্ণ; উচ্চনিনাদী। **High-spirited**—অতি তেজস্বী, মহাতেজাঃ। **High-stepper**—যে অশ্ব পা উচ্চে তুলিয়া কদমে চলে। **High strung**—উচ্চ গ্রামে বাঁধা; অতি তেজস্বী, তীব্রসংবেদনশক্তিসম্পন্ন। **High table**—কলেজের ফেলোগণের জন্য মেজ। **High tea** — যে চা-পান বা সান্ধ্য-ভোজন কালে মাংস পরিবেসিত হয়। **High-tide** — যে জোয়ারের জল সাধারণ জোয়ার অপেক্ষা অধিক উঠিয়া থাকে। Holiday; ছুটীর দিন। **High-toned**—High in tone or sound; as, a *high-toned* instrument; জিল স্বর বিশিষ্ট। Noble; high-principled; as, a *high-toned*; character; মহান্; উন্নতনীতিজ্ঞান সম্পন্ন। **High treason**—রাজা বা রাজ্যের বিরুদ্ধে ষড়যন্ত্র। **High water**—পুরা জোয়ারের সময়; জোয়ারের ঊর্দ্ধ সীমা, বেলোর্দ্ধ সীমা (সাঃ পঃ)। **High water mark**—The line of the shore to which the waters reach at high water; পুরা জোয়ারের সময় যে রেখা পর্য্যন্ত জল উঠে, বেলোর্দ্ধসীমা চিহ্ন; উন্নতি বা উৎকর্ষের চরম সীমা। **High-way**—A public road; রাজপথ, রাজমার্গ, মহাপথ, প্রধান পথ, রথ্যা। **Highway-man**—রাহাজান, ঠেঙ্গাড়িয়া, বাটপাটচ্চর, পান্থমুষ (মিতঃ)। **Highway robbery**—রাহাজানি। **High words**—চড়া কথা। **A high hand**—Power; triumph; as, the children went out with *a high hand*; arrogance; as, they ruled the kingdom with *a high hand*; শক্তি; জয়োল্লাস; ঔদ্ধত্য। **A high time**—(*Colloq.*) A time of special jollity or enthusiasm; (চলিত ভাষায়) বিশেষ স্ফূর্তি বা উৎসাহের সময়। **A high opinion of**—A very favourable opinion of; উচ্চ মত, উচ্চ ধারণা। **From on high** — From heaven or a high place; স্বর্গ হইতে, ঊর্দ্ধলোক হইতে, উচ্চস্থান হইতে। **High and dry**—Out of the water; as, the retreating tide has left the ship *high and dry* ; ডাঙ্গার উপর। (*Fig.*) Out of the current of events ; as, a *high and dry* officer ; (লক্ষণায়) সাময়িক ঘটনাপ্রবাহ অস্পৃষ্ট। **High and low**—Rich and poor ; people of all conditions ; ভদ্রেতর, আপামর সাধারণ, উত্তমাধম ; আবালবৃদ্ধবনিতা। **High and mighty**—Arrogant ; উদ্ধত, দৃপ্ত। **In high feather**—In high spirits ; happy ; উৎফুল্লচিত্ত ; প্রফুল্ল। **On high** — In or to heaven ; ঊর্দ্ধলোকে, স্বর্গে, স্বর্গাভিমুখে। **On the high ropes**—(*Colloq.*) In an elated or excited mood ; (চলিত ভাষায়) খুব স্ফূর্তিতে, উল্লাসে। **To be on the high horse, To ride the high horse** — To be arrogant ; উদ্ধত হওয়া, কর্তৃত্ব ফলান। **To run high**—(Of the sea) To have strong current with high tide ; পুরা জোয়ার হওয়া। (*Fig.*) (Of feelings) To manifest themselves forcibly ; (লক্ষণায়) (আবেগাদি সম্পর্কে) প্রবলভাবে উচ্ছ্বসিত হওয়া। **With a high hand** — Arrogantly ; উদ্ধতভাবে, জুলুম করিয়া, জবরদস্তি করিয়া।

high'-lў (hī-), *adj.* **1.** In a high degree ; as, *highly* amusing ; অতিমাত্রায়, অতিশয়, অতীব, অত্যন্ত। **2.** Honourably ; favourably ; as, think or speak *highly* of ; সম্মানের সহিত, সসম্মানে ; অনুকূলভাবে। **Highly seasoned**—Rich or spicy ; প্রচুর মসলাদার।

high'-nĕss (hī-), *n.* **1.** The state of being high ; loftiness (used where *height* is not idiomatic) ; as, the *highness* of his character ; উচ্চতা, সমুন্নতি ; উন্নত ভাব। **2.** A title of honour given to princes or oher persons of similar rank ; as, His Royal *Highness* ; নৃপতি বা তত্তুল্য ব্যক্তিগণের সম্ভ্রমসূচক উপাধি।

hight (hīt) *p. p.* (*Archaic and poet.*) Called or named ; (অপ্রঃ বা কবিতায়) অভিহিত।

hi-lā'-ri-ous (-ŭs), *adj.* Joyous ; mirthful ; merry ; আনন্দপূর্ণ ; হর্ষোৎফুল্ল ; উল্লাসপূর্ণ। **—lar'-i-ty,** *n.* Cheerfulness ; mirth ; হর্ষ, আহ্লাদ ; উল্লাস, প্রফুল্লতা, রঙ্গভঙ্গ। **—ly,** *adv.* **—ness** *n.*

hill, *n.* & *v. t.* **1.** A natural elevation of less size than a mountain ; ক্ষুদ্র পর্বত, পাহাড়, গিরি, শৈল, অচল, ভূধর, অদ্রি, সানুমান, মহীধর। **2.** A heap ; a mound ; as, a dung-*hill* ; an ant *hill* ; স্তূপ ; ঢিবি। ***Verb t.*** **1.** To form into a hill, mound, etc. ; ঢিবি করা, পাহাড় গঠন করা। **2.** To raise earth about (plants) ; গাছের চারিদিকে মাটীর আল বাঁধা। **Hill'-i-ness,** *n.* **Hill'-y,** *adj.* Abounding with hills ; as, a *hilly* country ; পাহাড়ময়, পাহাড়ে।

hil'-lō, —loa (-lō), *interj.* Often used in hailing distant persons or in expressing surprise at meeting ; অহে ! অহো !

hill'-ŏck, *n.* A small hill or mound ; ক্ষুদ্র পাহাড়, ঢিবি।

hilt, *n.* & *v. t.* A handle especially of a sword or dagger ; বাঁট, মুষ্টি, ৎসরু, খড়্গমুষ্টি। ***Verb t.*** To furnish with a hilt ; as, to *hilt* a sword ; বাঁট লাগান। **Up to the hilt**—Completely ; পুরাপুরি, আমূল, সমস্তটা, সম্পূর্ণরূপে।

hi'-lŭm (L), *n.* (*Bot.*) The eye of a bean or other seed ; বীজের চোক, বীজক্ষত (সাঃ পঃ)।

him, *Pron.* (*Objective case* of HE.) Colloquially used also as a subject ; as, you are worse than *him* ; তাহাকে ; (চলিত ভাষায়) সে।

him-sĕlf', *Pron.* The emphatic and reflexive form of *he* and *him* ; সে নিজে, স্বয়ং, খোদ তাহাকেই। **He is not himself**—He is not in the normal state of body or mind ; সে প্রকৃতিস্থ নহে (cf. "সই আমি কি আমাতে আছি")।

hīnd, *n.* & *adj.* The female of the stag or red deer ; হরিণী, কুরঙ্গী, মৃগী, মৃগবধূ, রক্তহরিণী।

hīnd, *n.* **1.** A farm servant or skilled workman ; কৃষিক্ষেত্রের মজুর, নিপুণ শ্রমজীবী। **2.** (*Colloq.*) A rustic ; a boor ; (চলিত ভাষায়) গেঁয়ে লোক ; চাষা, বর্ব্বর।

hīnd, *adj.* In the rear ; pertaining to the part behind ; as, the *hind* legs ; পশ্চাদ্‌বর্ত্তী ; পশ্চাদ্‌ভাগ সম্বন্ধীয়। **Hind'-most,** (*Superl. degree*) Furthest behind ; last ; অতি পশ্চাতে ; সর্ব্বশেষ।

hīnd'-êr, *adj.* Same as HIND.

hin'-dêr, *v. t.* To prevent ; to interrupt ; to impede ; (often followed by *from*) ; বাধা দেওয়া, বারণ করা, নিবারণ করা, নিষেধ করা, প্রতিষেধ করা ; প্রতিরোধ করা ; ব্যাঘাত করা, অবরোধ করা।

hin'-drance (-drăns), *n.* Act of hindering ; obstruction ; an impediment ; নিবারণ, প্রতিষেধ ; বারণ, নিষেধ, বাধাপ্রদান ; প্রতিরোধ ; অবরোধ, নিরোধ, ব্যাঘাত, অন্তরায়, বাধা, প্রতিবন্ধক, বিঘ্ন।

hinge (hĭnj), *n.*, *v. t.* & *i.* **1.** The hook or joint on which a door or lid hangs and turns ; "The gate ... on golden *hinges* turning" ; কব্জা। **2.** The joint of a bivalve shell ; দ্বিপুটক ঝিনুকাদির সন্ধিস্থল। **3.** (*Fig.*) A central principle ; that on which anything turns or depends ; as, the argument was the *hinge* on which the question turned ; মূলনীতি ; মূলকেন্দ্র। ***Verb t.*** To furnish with hinges ; as, to *hinge* a gate ; কব্জা লাগান। ***Verb i.*** To turn as on a hinge ; to depend ; as, the question *hinges* on this point ; কব্জার উপর ঘুরা ; নির্ভর করা। **Hinged,** *adj.* Furnished with hinges ; কব্জাওয়ালা। **Hinge-less,** *adj.*

Off the hinges—In disordered state of body or mind; in disorder; বিক্ষুব্ধ, উদ্বেজিত, ভগ্নস্বাস্থ্য; এলোমেলোভাবে, স্থানচ্যুত, উলটপালট।

hin'-ný, *n.* A mule; খচ্চর, অশ্বতর।

hin'-ný, -nie (-nĭ), *n.* (Corrupted form of HONEY) Darling; প্রিয়, দয়িত।

hint, *n., v. t. & i.* A distant allusion; an intimation; a suggestion, ইঙ্গিত, ইসারা, সঙ্কেত; আভাস; আঁচ। ***Verb t.*** To bring to notice by a slight mention; to suggest indirectly; ইঙ্গিতে বলা; ইঙ্গিত করা, ঠারেঠোরে বলা। ***Verb i.*** To make a hint or indirect allusion; ইঙ্গিত করা, আঁচ দেওয়া। **To hint at**—To give a hint of; to allude to; আঁচ দেওয়া, আভাস দেওয়া; ইঙ্গিত করা।

hinterland, *n.* A district behind a coast or river's banks; সমুদ্রোপকূল বা নদীতীরের পশ্চাদ্বর্ত্তী প্রদেশ।

hip, *n. & v. t.* **1.** The fleshy projecting part of the thigh; the haunch; নিতম্ব, শ্রোণি, দাবনা; কটি। **2.** (*Arch.*) The external angle formed by the meeting sides of a roof; ছাদের পার্শ্বদ্বয়ের সংযোগে উৎপন্ন বহিঃকোণ। **Hipped,** *adj.* Having hips, (esp. in compounds); as, larger-*hipped*; শ্রোণি-বিশিষ্ট। **Hip-bath**—নাভি হইতে উরু পর্য্যন্ত স্নান, কটিস্নান (হঃ চঃ)। **Hip-bone**—শ্রোণিফলক। **Hip-joint disease**—উরুসন্ধির একপ্রকার পুরাতন রোগ—এই রোগে সাধারণতঃ যুবকদিগের উপাস্থিতে এবং বালকদিগের উরুর অস্থির মাথায় ক্ষত থাকে (ডাঃ হরিপ্রসাদ চক্রবর্ত্তী), কটি-কাগ। **Hip-joint**—(শারীর-সংস্থান-বিদ্যা) কুঁচকি, উরু-সন্ধি, বঙ্ক্ষণ-সন্ধি (হঃ চঃ)। **Hip and thigh**—নির্দ্দয়ভাবে। **To have on the hip**—To get an advantage over some one; as, to *have a person on the hip*; কায়দায় পাওয়া, বাগে পাওয়া। **To smite hip and thigh**—To overthrow completely; সম্পূর্ণরূপে উৎসাদিত করা।

hip, *interj.* An expression introducing a united cheer; as, *hip, hip,* hurrah! জয়! জয়! জয়!

hip, hĕp, *ns.* The fruit of the dog-rose or wild brier; একপ্রকার কণ্টকাকীর্ণ আরণ্য গুল্মের ফল।

hip, hÿp, *ns.* Hypochondria; the blues; বিষাদরোগ; স্ফূর্ত্তিহীনতা।

hip, *v. t.* To make low spirited; স্ফূর্ত্তিহীন করা, বিরস করা। **Hipped,** *adj.* Low spirited; বিষণ্ণ, ম্লান, স্ফূর্ত্তিহীন, বিরস।

hīpe, *v. t. & n.* To throw in a particular manner (*in wrestling*); (মল্লযুদ্ধে) বিশেষ একভাবে ভূপাতিত করা। ***Noun.*** Such a throw; ঐ প্রকার অবপাতন।

hip-pö-căm'-pŭs, *n.* (*Pl.* -PI) **1.** A name of small fishes having the head and foreparts horselike

Hippocampus.

in form; এক জাতীয় ক্ষুদ্রকায় অশ্বমুখ মৎস্য বিশেষ, অশ্বকুঞ্চিক (আঃ বঃ)। **2.** (*Class. myth.*) A sea-horse with two feet and a body ending in the tail of a dolphin or other fish which drew the car of Neptune and other deities; (রোমীয় ও গ্রীক পুরাণ) ক্ষুদ্র তিমি প্রভৃতি মৎস্যের মত লাঙ্গুলবিশিষ্ট দ্বিপদ সামুদ্রিক অশ্ব-বিশেষ—যে বরুণ এবং অন্যান্য সাগরদেবতাগণের রথ টানিত, সাগরাশ্ব। **3.** (*Anat.*) Two ridges of white matter in each lateral ventricle of the brain, (the larger being called the *hippocampus major* and the smaller *hippocampus minor*); (শারীর-সংস্থান বিদ্যা) (মস্তিষ্ক পার্শ্ব-কোঠদ্বয়ের নলাকার মৎস্যের ন্যায়) কুণ্ডলীদ্বয়।

Hip-pö-cĕn'-taur (-tär), *n.* (*Myth.*) A fabulous monster, half-horse and half man; (গ্রীক পুরাণ) দৈত্য বিশেষ, অশ্বাসুর।

hip'-pö-crăs, *n.* A medicinal drink of wine and spices and other ingredients; লবঙ্গ, এলাচ, দারুচিনি প্রভৃতি দ্বারা সুবাসিত সুরা।

Hip'-pö-crene (-krēn, krē-nē), *n.* A sacred fountain in Mount Helicon in Boeotia; Boeotia প্রদেশের Helicon পর্ব্বতস্থ পবিত্র উৎস বিশেষ। ইহা বাগ্দেবীগণের নামে উৎসর্গীকৃত হইয়াছিল। সপক্ষ অশ্ব Pegasus এর খুরাঘাতে এই উৎস সৃষ্ট হইয়াছিল বলিয়া প্রসিদ্ধ।

hip'-pö-drōme, *n.* **1.** (*Gr. & Rom. antiq.*) A racecourse for horses and chariots; (গ্রীক ও রোমীয় প্রত্নতত্ত্ব) অশ্বরথাদির দৌড়-চক্র, রথাচর্য্যাস্থলী। **2.** A circus; সার্কাস।

hip'-pö-griff, -grÿph, *ns.* A fabulous animal, half horse and half griffin; a winged horse; একপ্রকার দৈত্য,—ইহার অর্দ্ধদেহ অশ্বাকৃতি এবং অপরার্দ্ধ গৃধ্রাকৃতি, শ্যেন-ঘোটক (আঃ বঃ); সপক্ষ অশ্ব।

Hip-pŏl'-ÿ-tē, *n.* Queen of the Amazons; স্ত্রীরাজ্যের রাণী। ইনি Hercules কর্ত্তৃক নিহতা হন।

Hip-pŏl'-ÿ-tŭs, *n.* Son of Theseus and Hippolyte; Theseus এবং Hippolyteএর পুত্র। বিমাতা Phaedra সপত্নী-পুত্র Hyppolytus এর সৌন্দর্য্যে মুগ্ধ হইয়া তাহার নিকট প্রণয় যাচ্‌ঞা করেন। Hyppolytus বিমাতার মনস্কামনা পূর্ণ না করাতে সেই পামরী Hippolytus তাহাকে কুপথে পরিচালিত করিতে চেষ্টা করিয়াছে এইরূপ মিথ্যা অভিযোগপূর্ণ একখানা পত্র রাখিয়া উদ্বন্ধনে প্রাণত্যাগ করে। Theseus তদীয় পিতা সাগররাজ Poseidonকে Hippolytus এর বধের জন্য অনুরোধ করেন। একদিবস Hippolytus সমুদ্র তীরে

রথারোহণে ভ্রমণ করিতেছেন এমন কালে বারীন্দ্র Poseidon সমুদ্র হইতে একটী বৃষ প্রেরণ করেন। সেই ভীষণাকৃতি বৃষভকে দেখিবা মাত্র Hippolytus এর রথাশ্ব সকল সন্ত্রস্ত ভাবে অশ্ব-রশ্মি ছিন্ন করিয়া পলাইল এবং Hippolytus রথ হইতে উৎক্ষিপ্ত হইয়া নিহত হইলেন।

hĭp·pŏph′-ă-ġȳ, *n.* The practice of feeding on horse flesh ; অশ্বমাংস ভোজন।

hĭp·pō-pŏt′-ă-mŭs, *n.* A large pachydermatous animal, inhabiting the Nile and other rivers in Africa ; the river-horse ;

Hippopotamus.

আফ্রিকাদেশীয় নীলনদ এবং অন্যান্য নদীবাসী স্থূলচর্ম্মা বৃহৎকায় জন্তু বিশেষ ; নদীঘোটক (সাঃ পঃ), জলঘোটক।

hir′-cīne (hêr-), *adj.* Goat-like esp. in smell ; lustful ; ছাগবৎ, অজগন্ধা ; ছাগবৃত্ত, কামুক।

hīre, *v. t.* **1.** To procure for temporary use at a certain price ; as, to *hire* a farm for a year ; ভাড়া করা। **2.** To engage in service for wages ; as, to *hire* a servant for a month ; মজুরী দিয়া নিযুক্ত করা। **3.** To let (usu. with *out*) ; as, he *hired out* his horse ; ভাড়া দেওয়া। **Hir′-a-ble,** *adj.*

hīre, *n.* **1.** The price paid for the temporary use of anything ; wages ; rent ; ভাড়া, কেরায়া ; বেতন, মজুরি, পারিশ্রমিক ; খাজানা। **2.** Act of hiring or fact of being hired ; ভাড়া করণ, ভাড়া। **3.** (*Fig.*) Reward ; recompense : ...."make her hand the *hire* of this Savoyard" ; (লক্ষণায়) পুরস্কার ; প্রতিদান। **Hire′-less,** *adj.* **Hire purchase, Hire-system**—যে প্রণালীতে নির্দ্দিষ্ট সংখ্যক বার টাকা প্রদান করা হইলে ভাড়া-করা জিনিষ কোন ব্যক্তির নিজস্ব হয়। **On hire**—ভাড়া দেওয়ার জন্য প্রস্তুত।

hīre′-lĭng, *n.* One who serves for hire or wages (*often contemptuously*) ; as, lewed *hirelings* ; যে ব্যক্তি বেতন লইয়া কাজ করে, বেতনভোগী চাকর, বেতনের চাকর।

hir′-sūte (hêr-), *adj.* **1.** Having rough hair ; hairy ; shaggy ; খররোমা ; রোমশ, লোমশ ; ঝাকড়ামাকড়া। **2.** (*Bot.*) Having long stiffish hair ; (উদ্ভিদ-বিদ্যা) খররোমা (সাঃ পঃ)। **3.** (*Zool.*) Covered with hair-like feathers ; as, the *hirsute* feet of a bird ; (প্রাণি-বিদ্যা) লোমবৎ পালকবিশিষ্ট। **4.** (*Fig.*) Rough ; untrimmed ; আবড়োখাবড়ো ; উস্কোখুস্কো। **—ness,** *n.*

hĭs, *Pron.* (*Possessive case of* HE) ; তাহার, তদীয়।

hĭs′-pĭd, *adj.* **1.** (*Bot. & Zool.*) Beset with stiff bristles or hairs ; কণ্টকরোমা (সাঃ পঃ)। **2.** Bristly ; shaggy ; কণ্টকাকীর্ণ, শূকবিশিষ্ট, সকণ্টক ; ঝাকড়ামাকড়া।

hĭss, *v. i., t. & n.* **1.** To make a sound like that of the letter *S* in contempt or disapprobation ; as, the merchants shall *hiss* at thee ; to emit a similar sound, as a goose or serpent ; হিস্‌হিস্ শব্দ করা ; ফোঁস ফোঁস করা। **2.** To pass with a sibilant sound ; to whizz ; as, the arrow *hissed* as it flew ; সোঁ করিয়া ছুটা ; হুস্ করিয়া ছুটা। ***Verb t.*** **1.** To condemn or show dislike of by hissing ; as, the spectators *hissed* him off the stage ; টিট্‌কারী দেওয়া, ধিক্কার দেওয়া। **2.** To utter with a hissing sound ; as, he *hissed* the words out ; হিস্ হিস্ করিয়া উচ্চারণ করা। ***Noun.*** **1.** A sound like that of the letter *S* expressing dislike and contempt ; হিস্ হিস্ শব্দ, সোঁ শব্দ, ধিক ধিক, ছি ছি, টিটকারী। **2.** Any similar sound, as of a serpent or goose ; ফোঁস ফোঁসানি, প্যাঁক প্যাঁক। **To hiss off (the stage), away, down etc.**—To drive off (the stage), away, down, etc. by hisses ; as, the audience *hissed* him *away* from the stage ; টিটকারী দিয়া বাহির করা।

hĭst, *interj.* A word used to call attention, command silence or incite dogs etc. ; চুপ ! চুপ ! শোন ! শোন ! থাম।

hĭs-tō-gĕn′-ĕ-sĭs, —tŏġ′-ĕ-nȳ, *ns.* The formation and development of the organic tissues ; শারীরিক বিধানতন্তুসমূহের গঠন বা বৃদ্ধি। **-ge-net′-ic,** *adj.*

hĭs-tŏl′-ō-ġȳ, *n.* The science of animal and vegetable tissues ; জৈব এবং উদ্ভিদ বিধানতন্তুবিষয়ক বিজ্ঞান, শরীরের বিধানতন্তুর অণুবীক্ষণ-দৃষ্ট নির্ম্মাণতত্ত্ব, বিধানতন্তুবিদ্যা। **—gist,** *n.* One versed in histology ; বিধানতন্তুতত্ত্ববিৎ। **—to-log′-i-cal,** *adj.*

hĭs-tō′-ri-an, *n.* **1.** A writer or compiler of history ; ইতিহাস লেখক, ঐতিহাসিক, ইতিহাসরচক। **2.** (*Rare*) A person well versed in history ; (অপ্রঃ) ইতিহাসবেত্তা (কৃঞ্চঃ), ইতিহাসজ্ঞ।

his-tō-ri ăt·ĕd, *adj.* Decorated with figures of men or animals ; as, a *historiated* capital letter ; মনুষ্যজীবজন্তুর প্রতিকৃতিদ্বারা সমলঙ্কৃত।

his-tŏr′-ic, —i-căl, *adjs.* **1.** Of, pertaining to, or connected with, history ; ঐতিহাসিক, ইতিহাসসম্পর্কীয়, ইতিহাসবিষয়ক। **2.** Noted or celebrated, in history, (in this sense *historic* is now the more usual form) ; ইতিহাসপ্রসিদ্ধ, ইতিহাসবিখ্যাত। **—i-cal-ly,** *adv.* In the manner of history ; ঐতিহাসিক ভাবে. **Historic-**

al method — অনুশীলনের প্রণালী বিশেষ—যাহাতে কোন বিষয়ের ঐতিহাসিক ক্রম-বিকাশ আলোচনা করা হইয়া থাকে। **Historical painting** —ঐতিহাসিক ঘটনাবলীর চিত্রাঙ্কণ। **Historic present**—(ব্যাকরণ) ঐতিহাসিক ঘটনা বর্ণনে অতীত কালের পরিবর্ত্তে ব্যবহৃত বর্ত্তমান কাল। **Historic sense**—যে বৃত্তি দ্বারা ঐতিহাসিক ঘটনাবলীর মর্ম্ম-কথা ক্ষিপ্র হৃদয়ঙ্গম হয় এবং উহাদের সমুজ্জ্বল চিত্র মানসপটে প্রতিবিম্বিত হইয়া থাকে। **Historic tenses**—অতীত ঘটনা সম্বন্ধে যে সকল কাল ব্যবহৃত হয়।

hĭs-tō-rĭ-ŏg′-ră-phêr, *n.* A writer of history; an official historian appointed in a court etc.; ইতিহাসলেখক; রাজসভাদিতে নিযুক্ত ঐতিহাসিক। **—o-graph′-ic, —o-graph′-i-cal,** *adjs.* **—phy,** *n.* The art or employment of writing history; the writing of history; ইতিহাস রচনা বিদ্যা, ইতিহাসবিরচন কার্য্য; ইতিহাস রচনা, ইতিহাস প্রণয়ন।

hĭs′-tō-rȳ, *n.* **1.** The record of important public events etc.; ইতিহাস, ইতিবৃত্ত, ইতিকথা, (কেঙিঃ), পুরাবৃত্ত (ঐ)। **2.** A systematic account or study of the origin and progress of a nation or state; কোন জাতি বা রাষ্ট্রের উৎপত্তি বিকাশ সম্বন্ধে ধারাবাহিক বিবরণ। **3.** The branch of knowledge dealing with past events; ইতিহাস-শাস্ত্র। **4.** The aggregate of past events in general; প্রাচীন ঘটনাবলী। **5.** A systematic account of existing things, as animals or plants etc. (also called *natural history*); জীবজন্তু বা উদ্ভিদের ধারাবাহিক বিবরণ। **6.** A historical play; ঐতিহাসিক নাটক। **Ancient history**—প্রাচীন কাল হইতে আরম্ভ করিয়া রোম নগরীর পতন পর্য্যন্ত (৪৭৬ খৃঃ অব্দ) পৃথিবীর ইতিহাস, প্রাচীন ইতিহাস। **Mediaeval history** — রোম নগরীর পতন হইতে পঞ্চদশ শতাব্দীর শেষ পর্য্যন্ত ইয়ুরোপের ইতিহাস, মধ্যযুগের ইতিহাস। **Modern history** — ষোড়শ শতাব্দী হইতে আরম্ভ করিয়া বর্ত্তমান কাল পর্য্যন্ত জগতের ইতিহাস, বর্ত্তমান ইতিহাস, আধুনিক ইতিহাস। **Natural history**—(পূর্ব্বে) জীবজন্তু, উদ্ভিদ্ এবং খনিজ পদার্থ সম্বন্ধে ধারাবাহিক আলোচনা (পূর্ব্বে জীববিজ্ঞান, ভূবিদ্যা, রসায়ন প্রভৃতি শাস্ত্র ইহার অন্তর্ভুক্ত ছিল), প্রাকৃতিক ইতিহাস; (বর্ত্তমানে) জীবজন্তুর বিবরণ, জীবজন্তুর ইতিহাস। **Profane history**—সাংসারিক ব্যাপারের ইতিহাস (অর্থাৎ বাইবেলে বর্ণিত ঘটনা সমূহের আলোচনামূলক ইতিহাস নহে)।

hĭs′-trĭ-ŏn, *n.* An actor; অভিনেতা, নট।

hĭs-trĭ-ŏn′-ic, *adj.* & *n.* **1.** Relating to the stage or stage players; রঙ্গমঞ্চসম্বন্ধীয়, নট বা নটী-সম্বন্ধীয়। **2.** (*Fig.*) Hypocritical; (লক্ষণায়) কপট, ভণ্ড, ছদ্ম। ***Noun.*** **1.** An actor; অভিনেতা, নট। **2.** (*Pl.*) Dramatic representation; pretence; নাট্যাভিনয়; ছল, ব্যপদেশ। **—i-cal-ly,** *adv.* **—i-cism,** *n.* Stage playing; the histrionic art; নাট্যাভিনয়; নাট্যকলা।

hĭs′-trĭ-ō-nĭsm, *n.* Same as HISTRIONICISM.

hĭt, *v. t., i.* & *n.* **1.** To strike with a blow or missile; আঘাত করা, প্রহার করা। **2.** To give or deliver; as, to *hit* a blow: to *hit* a person a blow; দেওয়া। **3.** To reach or attain; পাওয়া, প্রাপ্ত হওয়া। **4.** To light upon; to guess; as, thou hast *hit* it; ঠাওরান; আন্দাজ করা, অনুমান করা। **5.** To suit or agree with; "Too bright to *hit* the sense of human sight;" মিলা, খাপ খাওয়া। **6.** To imitate to a nicety; as, to *hit* the exact colour of the human face in painting; সূক্ষ্মভাবে অনুকরণ করা। **7.** (*Fig.*) To affect sensisbly; to wound; as, the taunt *hit* him hard; মর্ম্মে আঘাত করা; ঘা দেওয়া। **8.** (*Backgammon*) To replace by a piece belonging to the opposing player; (ব্যাক্‌গ্যামন ক্রীড়ায়) প্রতিদ্বন্দ্বী ক্রীড়কের গুটিকা দ্বারা স্থান পূরণ করা। ***Verb i.*** **1.** To strike; to come in contact forcibly, (usu. followed by *against, on*); as, the bodies *hit against* one another; ঠক্কর লাগা, ধাক্কা লাগা, উপহত হওয়া; সংঘৃষ্ট হওয়া, ঠুকাঠুকি হওয়া। **2.** To reach what was aimed at; as, to *hit upon* the thing; অভীষ্ট লাভ করা, উদ্দিষ্ট বস্তু প্রাপ্ত হওয়া। **3.** (*Obs.*) To suit; (অপ্রঃ) মিলা, খাপ খাওয়া। ***Noun.*** **1.** A blow or stroke; a collision; ঘা, আঘাত, প্রহার; ঠক্কর। **2.** A lucky chance; a successful attempt; "Each lucky *hit*"; দৈবক্রমে সফল আঘাত; সফল চেষ্টা। **3.** A striking expression or turn of thought; a remark of a sarcastic nature; চমকপ্রদ উক্তি বা চিন্তা; শ্লেষোক্তি, ব্যঙ্গোক্তি। **A hard hit**—A severe blow; a sharp taunt; গুরুতর আঘাত; তীব্র শ্লেষ। **A lucky hit**—See HIT. *n.* 2. **To hit it off (with together)**—To agree (with, together); as, I *hit it off with* him; মিলা; **To hit off**—To imitate or reproduce to a nicety; সূক্ষ্মভাবে অনুকরণ করা, প্রায় অভিন্নরূপে পুনরুৎপাদন করা। **To hit on or upon**—To light upon; to guess; to discover; as, none of them *hit upon* the art; ঠাওরান; আন্দাজ করা; আবিষ্কার করা। **To hit out**—To deal vigorous blows; as, to *hit out* a man; to strike out with the fists; বেদম প্রহার করা; ঘুষি মারা। **To hit the (right) nail on the head**—To guess right; to say a thing in the right way; ঠিক অনুমান করা, ঠাহর করা; ঠিকভাবে বলা।

hitch (hĭch), *v. t.* & *i.* **1.** To fasten, hook or yoke; as, to *hitch* a rope : to *hitch* a horse ; বাঁধা, আঁকড়া দিয়া আঁটা, যোজনা করা। **2.** To move with hitches or jerks ; as, he *hitched* his chair nearer ; হেঁচকা টান দিয়া সরান। **3.** To contrive ; to bring as a thing (into a story etc.) ; কৌশলক্রমে গড়া ; গল্প ফাঁদা। ***Verb i.*** **1.** To move by jerks or with stops ; as, to *hitch* along ; হেঁচকাইয়া হেঁচকাইয়া চলা, থমকিয়া থমকিয়া চলা। **2.** To be entangled, hooked, etc. ; to cling ; জড়াইয়া যাওয়া, গাঁথিয়া যাওয়া ; লাগিয়া থাকা। **3.** To hit the legs together in going as a horse ; চলিবার সময় ঘোড়ার পায়ে পায়ে টক্কর লাগা। **To hitch up**—To raise with a jerk ; ঝিঁকা মারিয়া তোলা। To fasten up ; বাঁধা।

hitch (hĭch), *n.* **1.** A sudden pull or push ; a jerk ; হেঁচকা টান ; ঝিঁকা। **2.** A stoppage ; impediment ; obstruction ; প্রতিবন্ধক ; বাধা, বিঘ্ন ; বাঁধ, আটক, খট্‌কা। **3.** (*Naut.*) A knot or noose in a rope which can be readily undone ; as, a clove *hitch* ; (নৌ-বিদ্যা) গলাসি গাইট।

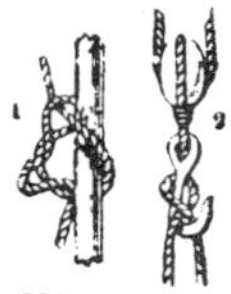

Hitch knot ; 1. timber hitch : 2. blackwall hitch.

hith'-ĕr, *adv.* To this place ; as, come *hither* : bring *hither* ; এখানে, এইস্থানে, হেথায়। **Hitherto**—Up to this time ; এ পর্য্যন্ত, এযাবৎ, অদ্যাবধি। **Hither-ward**—(*Archaic*) Towards this place ; (অপ্রঃ) এদিকে। **Hither and thither**—In various directions ; here and there ; ইতস্ততঃ ; এদিকে সেদিকে, এথা ওথা।

hīve, *n., v. t.* & *i.* **1.** A box or receptacle for the habitation of honey bees ; মৌমাছির বাসের জন্ম পেটক বা ঝুড়ি, অলিগৃহ, দ্বিরেফভবন, মধুপভবন, কৃত্রিম মধুমক্ষিকালয়। **2.** The bees of one hive ; a swarm of bees ; এক পেটকের মৌমাছিগণ ; মৌমাছির ঝাঁক, অলিপংক্তি,

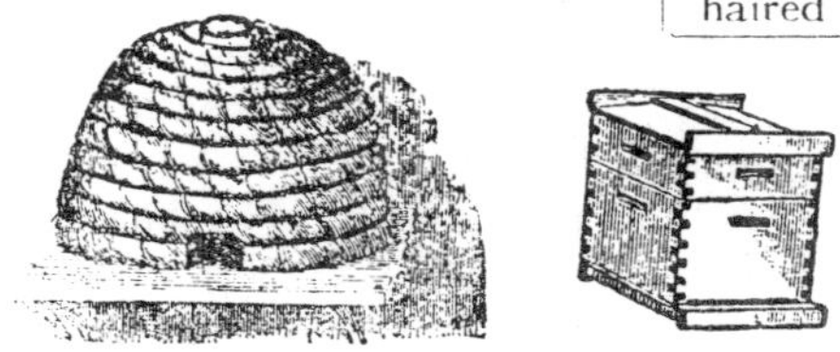

Old and modern style of hives.

মধুকর-শ্রেণী, দ্বিরেফমালা। **3.** (*Fig.*) A place swarming with busy occupants ; (লক্ষণায়) কর্ম্মব্যস্ত লোক-সমাকুল স্থান, কর্ম্মকোলাহলপূর্ণ স্থান। ***Verb t.*** **1.** To place in a hive ; as, to *hive* bees ; (*fig.*) to house as a person snugly ; মধুপ-ভবনে স্থাপন করা ; আরাম-জনক গৃহে বাস করিতে দেওয়া। **2.** To store up in a hive, as honey ; to lay up in store ; "*Hiving* wisdom with each studious year" ; মধুপ-ভবনে সঞ্চিত করা ; সঞ্চয় করিয়া রাখা। ***Verb i.*** To enter a hive ; to lodge or live together like bees ; দ্বিরেফভবনে প্রবেশ করা ; মৌমাছির মত একত্র বাস করা।

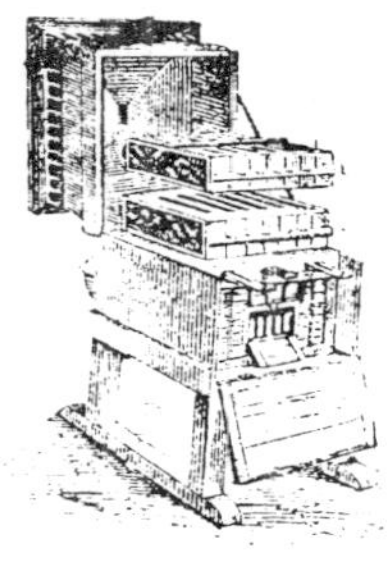

Neighbour's Improved Bee-hive.

hīves, *n.* (*Pl.*) **1.** An eruptive skin disease ; জলবসন্তের অনুরূপ রোগ-বিশেষ। **2.** Inflammation of the bowels, larynx, etc. ; অন্ত্র, কণ্ঠনালী, প্রভৃতির প্রদাহ, স্বরঘ্ন (হঃ চঃ)।

hō, *interj.* **1.** A call to excite attention ; as, what noise there *ho!* ওহে! শোন! **2.** A cry of surprise, admiration, triumph or decision ; অহো!

hoar (hör), *adj.* & *n.* **1.** White ; greyish-white ; সাদা, শ্বেত, শুভ্র, শুক্ল, ধবল, সিত ; ধূসর। **2.** Grey-haired ; white with age ; as, a matron grave and *hoar* ; পক্ককেশ, শুভ্রকেশ, পলিতকেশ ; বার্দ্ধক্য-ধবলিত। ***Noun.*** **1.** Hoariness ; শুভ্রতা, শুক্লতা। **2.** Hoar frost ; ঘনীভূত শিশির, তুষারকণা, শজল (সাঃ পঃ), খবাষ্প (ঐ)। **Hoar frost**—See HOAR *n.* 2. **Hoar stone** — প্রাচীন কালীন সীমাপ্রস্তর।

hoard (hörd), *n.* & *v. t.* A store ; a hidden stock ; a treasure ; as, a *hoard* of money ; ভাণ্ডার, গুপ্তভাণ্ডার ; ধনরাশি। ***Verb t.*** **1.** To store ; to amass and deposit in secret ; as, to *hoard* up money or wealth ; ভাণ্ডারজাত করা ; গোপনে সঞ্চয় করিয়া রাখা। **2.** (*Fig.*) To cherish or treasure *up* (esp. in the heart) ; সযত্নে পোষণ করা, সযত্নে হৃদয়ে ধারণ করা।

hoard'-ĭng (hörd-), *n.* A screen of boards inclosing a house and materials while builders are at work, (often used for posting bills) ; গৃহ নির্ম্মাণ বা মেরামত করার কালে উহার চতুর্দ্দিকে যে তক্তার বেড়া দেওয়া হয়। [এইরূপ বেড়াতে সাধারণতঃ বিজ্ঞাপন লাগান হয়।]

hoar'-hound (hör-hownd), *n.* A plant of a whitish appearance, used as a tonic ; একপ্রকার তিক্তাস্বাদ গুল্ম।

hoarse (hörse), *adj.* **1.** Having a harsh grating voice ; গলা-ভাঙ্গা, ভগ্নস্বর। **2.** Harsh ; rough ; husky ; as, a *hoarse* voice ; কর্কশ ; রুক্ষ ; ভগ্ন। **Hoarse'-ly,** *adv.* **Hoars'-en,** *v. t.* & *i.* To make or become hoarse ; স্বরভঙ্গ জন্মান বা জন্মা। **Hoarse'-ness,** *n.* Harshness or roughness of voice or sound; স্বরভেদ (সাঃ পঃ), স্বরভঙ্গ। **To cry hoarse**—চেঁচাইয়া গলা ভাঙ্গা।

hoar'-ȳ (hör-), *adj.* **1.** White or whitish; as, *hoary* willows; শ্বেত, শুভ্র, ধবল, শুক্ল, সিত, শ্বেতাভ। **2.** White or grey with age; as, a *hoary* head; grey-haired; venerable, as a person; জরা-ধবলিত; পলিতকেশ, শুক্লকেশ, ধবলকেশ, পক্ককেশ; মাননীয়, নমস্য। **3.** (*Bot.*) Covered with short hairs; ক্ষুদ্র ক্ষুদ্র শ্বেতরোমাবৃত। **4.** Remote in time past; as, *hoary* antiquity; সুদূর।

hoax (hōx), *v. t.* & *n.* To deceive by way of joke; to play a trick upon for sport; ধোঁকা দেওয়া, ফাঁকি দেওয়া; চাতুরী খেলা। ***Noun.*** A deceptive trick; a practical joke; ঠকামি, ফাঁকি, ছলনা, ধোঁকা; ক্রিয়া দ্বারা ঠাট্টা, পরিহাসমূলক কার্য্য।

hŏb, *n.* **1.** The projecting nave of a wheel; উদ্গত চক্রনাভি। **2.** The part of a grate on which things are placed in order to be kept warm; অগ্নিসেবনস্থলীর পার্শ্বের তাক — যথায় জিনিষপত্র গরম করার জন্য রক্ষিত হয়। **3.** A pin or peg used in quoits; a game in which these are used; চাক্‌তি খেলায় ব্যবহৃত শলাকা; চাক্‌তি খেলা। **4.** The runner of a sledge; যে দীর্ঘাকৃতি কাষ্ঠফলক সকলের উপর বরফ-চলা গাড়ী চলে তাহার একটী। **5.** A hobnail; বুটজুতার তলার জন্য একপ্রকার বড় মাথাওয়ালা পেরেক।

hŏb'-ble (-bl), *v. i.* & *t.* **1.** To walk lamely or awkwardly; to limp; to halt; খোঁড়াইয়া চলা, নেঙ্গড়াইয়া চলা; নেঙ্গচাইয়া চলা। **2.** (*Fig.*) To speak or act haltingly; ঠেকিয়া ঠেকিয়া বলা বা করা। ***Verb t.*** **1.** To cause to limp; খোঁড়াইয়া চলিতে বাধ্য করা। **2.** To fasten loosely the legs of (a horse) to prevent it from straying; to tie as legs thus; অশ্ব বিপথে না যাইতে পারে তজ্জন্য উহার দুই পা শিথিল ভাবে বাঁধা; ঐরূপে পা বাঁধা। ***Noun.*** An awkward limping gait; নেঙড়ানি, নেঙচানি। **2.** A clog or fetter for hobbling a horse; ঘোঁড়ার দুই পা বাঁধিবার জন্য শিকল বা আটক। **3.** A perplexing or awkward situation; গোল, খট্‌কা, গোলমাল।

hŏb'-ble-dē-hoy (-bl-), **hŏb'-băd—, hōb-bĕd—,** *ns.* A gawky youth, between boyhood and manhood; হাবাগোবা যুবা। **—hoy'-hood, —hoy'-ism,** *ns.* **—hoy'-ish,** *adj.*

hŏb'-bȳ, *n.* A small species of falcon; একপ্রকার ক্ষুদ্রজাতীয় বাজ পক্ষী।

hŏb'-bȳ, *n.* **1.** Any favourite object, plan or pursuit; সখের বিষয়, প্রিয় বিষয়, খেয়াল, ব্যসন (আঃ বঃ)। **2.** (*Archaic*) A small horse; (অপ্রঃ) ক্ষুদ্র অশ্ব। **3.** (*Hist.*) An early form of bicycle; (ইতিহাস) একপ্রকার প্রাচীন ধরণের দ্বিচক্রযান। **To ride a hobby**—To pursue a favourite object eagerly; সখের বিষয়ের অনুসরণ করা। **To ride a hobby horse**—To follow a favourite pursuit; কোন প্রিয় বিষয়ের অনুসরণ করা। **To ride a hobby to death** — To weary people utterly with one's peculiar notions on a subject; কোন বিষয়ের পুনঃ পুনঃ আলোচনা করিয়া লোককে অবসাদগ্রস্ত করা।

hŏb'-bȳ-hōrse, *n.* **1.** A wicker horse used in morris-dance etc.; নৃত্য বিশেষে ব্যবহৃত বংশ বেত্রাদি নির্ম্মিত অশ্ব। **2.** A stick or figure of a horse on which boys ride; লাঠি কিম্বা কাঠের ঘোড়া — যাহা ছেলেরা চড়িয়া থাকে। **3.** A rocking horse; দোল খাইবার জন্য ছেলেদের কাঠের ঘোড়া। **4.** A wooden horse on a merry-go-round; মেলায় ছাতা প্রভৃতিতে টাঙ্গানো কাঠের ঘোড়া— যাহার উপর চড়িয়া ছেলেরা ঘুরিয়া থাকে। **5.** Any favourite object or pursuit, (*now rare*); সখের বিষয় প্রিয় বিষয় (অধুনা অপ্রঃ)।

hŏb'-gŏb-lin, *n.* A mischievous sprite; an imp; a bugbear; দুষ্ট ভূত; ছোট ভূত; জুজু।

hŏb'-nail (-nāl), **1.** A large-headed nail for studding the soles of boots; বুট জুতার তলায় লাগাইবার জন্য একপ্রকার বড় মাথাওয়ালা পেরেক। **2.** A clownish person; a rustic; হাবাগোবা লোক; চাষাভুষা লোক পাড়াগেঁয়ে ভূত। **—nailed,** *adj.* Furnished or marked with hob-nails; বড় মাথাওয়ালা পেরেকে আঁটা। **Hob-nailed liver**—মাথামোটা পেরেকের মত উদ্গত অংশ-বিশিষ্ট যকৃত।

hŏb'-nŏb, *v. i.* **1.** To drink together familiarly; এক বৈঠকে মদ্য পান করা। **2.** To associate familiarly (with); ইয়ারকি করা।

Hŏb'-son's choice (-snz), *n.* See under CHOICE.

hock (hŏk), *n.* **1.** (In an animal) The joint between the knee and the fetlock; (জন্তুতে) জানু এবং অশ্বপদের পশ্চাদ্‌ভাগস্থ অংশের সন্ধি। **2.** (In man) The posterior part of the knee-joint; (মনুষ্যে) জানু-সন্ধির পশ্চাদ্‌বর্ত্তী অংশ।

hock (hŏk), *n.* A German white wine; জর্ম্মণ দেশীয় শ্বেতবর্ণ মদিরা বিশেষ।

hock'-ey (hŏk-ĭ), *n.* **1.** A game at ball played with curved clubs between goals; একপ্রকার ক্রীড়া—যাহা কন্দুক এবং বক্রাগ্র দণ্ড দ্বারা খেলিতে হয়। **2.** (*U. S.*) The stick used by the players; (মার্কিণ যুক্ত রাজ্য) উক্ত ক্রীড়ায় ব্যবহৃত যষ্টি।

hō'-cŭs, *v. t.* **1.** To impose upon; to cheat; ধোঁকা দেওয়া; প্রতারণা করা। **2.** To drug, as a liquor; বিষ বা নিদ্রাজনক ঔষধ মিশ্রিত করা। **3.** To supply with drugged liquor; বিষ বা নিদ্রাজনক ঔষধমিশ্রিত সুরা প্রদান করা।

hō'-cŭs-pō'-cŭs, *n., v. t.* & *i.* **1.** A juggler's trick; an imposition ; deception ; ভোজবাজি ; ধাঁধা, ভেল্কি ; ধোকা। 2. One of the words used by jugglers in playing tricks ; যাদুকরের লাগ্‌ভেল্‌কী-লাগ্‌ প্রভৃতি শব্দ, লাগ্‌ ধাঁধা লাগ্‌। ***Verb t.*** To play tricks on ; চালাকি করা, ধাঁধা লাগান। ***Verb i.*** To juggle ; ভোজবাজি দেখান।

hŏd, *n.* **1.** A kind of trough borne on the shoulder for carrying bricks and mortar ; একপ্রকার লম্বা দাণ্ডাওয়ালা বাক্স বা আধার—যাহা কাঁধে করিয়া রাজমজুরগণ ইট, সুরকী নেয়। **2.** A coal scuttle ; কয়লার আধার। **Hodman**—A labourer for carrying a hod ; রাজমজুর জোগাড়ে, তাগাড়িয়া, জোগালিয়া। (*Fig.*) A mechanical worker ; a literary hack ; কারিগর, মিস্ত্রি ; যে ব্যক্তি বেতন লইয়া পুস্তকাদি লিখে।

hŏd′-den (-dn), *n.* (*Scot.*) A coarse woollen cloth ; একপ্রকার মোটা পশমী কাপড়। **Hodden-grey, Grey hodden**—A coarse rustic garb ; চাষাভূষা লোকদিগের একপ্রকার মোটা পশমী কাপড়।

hodge (hŏj), *n.* A rustic or clown ; পাড়াগেঁয়ে লোক, চাষাভূষা লোক।

hodge′-podge (hŏj-pŏj), *n.* Same as HOTCH-POTCH which see.

hō-dĭ-êr′-năl, *adj.* Of, or pertaining to, the present day ; বর্ত্তমানকালীন।

hō-dŏm′-ĕ-têr, ŏd–ŏm′–, *ns.* An automatic instrument for measuring the distance travelled by a wheeled vehicle ; একপ্রকার স্বয়ংবহ যন্ত্র—যদ্দারা শকটাদি কতটা স্থান অতিক্রম করিয়াছে তাহা পরিমাপ করা যায়, শকট-পথমান যন্ত্র।

hoe (hō), *n., v. t. & i.* **1.** An instrument for cutting up weeds and loosening the earth ; নিড়ানি। ***Verb t.*** To cut, dig or clean with a hoe ; to weed ; to loosen, as earth ; as, to *hoe* the earth in a garden : to *hoe* corn (to clear from weeds) ; নিড়ানিদ্বারা কাটা, নিড়ানি দ্বারা খুঁড়া, নিড়ানিদ্বারা পরিষ্কার করা ; নিড়ান ; নিড়ানি দ্বারা মাটী খুঁড়া। ***Verb i.*** To use a hoe ; নিড়ানি দ্বারা কাজ করা। **A hard or long row to hoe**—কোনরূপ শ্রমসাধ্য কার্য্য সম্পাদন করিতে হইবে।

hŏg, *n.* **1.** A swine ; a castrated boar ; শূকর, বরাহ ; ছিন্নমুষ্ক শূকর। **2.** (*Dial.*) A young sheep that has not been shorn ; (উপভাষায়) যে মেষশাবকের রোম কর্ত্তিত হয় নাই। **3.** A filthy or gluttonous fellow ; নোংরা লোক, লোভী লোক। **4.** (*Naut.*) A sort of scrubbing broom for scraping a ship's bottom under water ; (নৌবিদ্যা) জাহাজের জলতলস্থ তলদেশ মার্জ্জনের জন্য মার্জ্জনী বিশেষ। **Hog′-gish,** *adj.* Swinish ; filthy ; selfish ; শূকরবৎ ; নোংরা ; স্বার্থপর। **Hog′-gish-ly,** *adv.* **Hog′-gish-ness,** *n.* **Hog′-like,** *adj.* **Hog′-ling,** *n.* A young hog ; শূকরশাবক। **Hog or Hog's-back**—ন্যুব্জ-পৃষ্ঠ। A ridge of a hill having this shape ; শূকরের পৃষ্ঠবৎ পাহাড়ের আল। **Hog-fish**—সকণ্টকমস্তক মৎস্যবিশেষ। **Hog-mane**—ঘোড়ার ঘাড়ের ছাটা লোম, অশ্বকেশর। **Hog-plum**—আমড়া, আম্রাট, অম্রাতক (বেলঃ)। **Hogg's-pudding**—নানা প্রকার মাংসের পুর দেওয়া শূকরের অন্ত্র। **Hog-reeve, Hog-constable**—যূথভ্রষ্ট শূকরের রক্ষণাবেক্ষণের ভারপ্রাপ্ত কর্ম্মচারী। **Hog-wash**—মদের ভাঁটি, রন্ধনশালা, প্রভৃতির ময়লা আবর্জ্জনা ইত্যাদি—যাহা শূকরগণ ভোজন করিয়া থাকে। **Hog-weed (Spreading)**—পুনর্ণবা (থোরা)। **A hog in armour**—অমার্জ্জিত এবং কর্কশ-স্বভাব ব্যক্তি, বনমানুষ, শূয়র। **To bring one's hog to a fine market**—To make a complete mess of something ; কোন বিষয়ে গোলমাল করিয়া ফেলা, একেবারে খিচুড়ি পাকিয়ে ফেলা। **To go the whole hog**—To do a thing thoroughly ; কোন কাজ সম্পূর্ণভাবে করা।

hŏg, *v. t. & i.* **1.** To raise (back etc.) archwise in the centre ; ন্যুব্জ করা। **2.** To cut short like bristles ; as, to *hog* the mane of a horse ; ছাঁটা। **3.** (*Naut.*) To scrub with a hog or scrubbing broom ; (নৌবিদ্যা) শক্ত বুরুষ দ্বারা ঘষিয়া মাজিয়া পরিষ্কার করা। ***Verb i.*** To rise in the centre like a hog's back ; মধ্যদেশ শূকরের পৃষ্ঠের মত হইয়া উঠা, ন্যুব্জ হইয়া উঠা।

hŏg′-get (-ĕt), *n.* **1.** A boar of the second year ; দুই বৎসর বয়স্ক শূকরশাবক। **2.** A yearling sheep or colt ; এক বৎসর বয়স্ক মেষশাবক বা অশ্বশাবক।

hŏg′-gin (-ĭn), *n.* Sifted gravel ; চালুনিতে চালা কাঁকর।

hŏgs′-head (-hĕd), *n.* **1.** A large cask of indefinite size ; বড় পিপা। **2.** A measure of capacity containing $52\frac{1}{2}$ imperial gallons, (*abbr. hhd.*) ; তরল পদার্থের পরিমাণ বিশেষ ($৫২\frac{১}{২}$ ইম্পিরিয়েল গেলন)।

hoick(s) (hoyk), *interj.* An expression used to incite hounds ; লে ! লে !

hoist (hoyst), *v. t. & n.* To lift ; to raise with tackle ; as, to *hoist* a sail or flag ; তোলা, উত্তোলিত করা ; দড়াদড়ী দ্বারা তোলা। ***Noun.*** 1. The act of raising ; উত্তোলন, তোলন। **2.** The apparatus for lifting goods ; মালপত্র উত্তোলনের জন্য যন্ত্র-বিশেষ, উত্তোলন-যন্ত্র, উন্নমনযন্ত্র, ভারোত্তলন যন্ত্র। **3.** (*Naut.*) The height of a sail or flag or the extent to which it may be hoisted ; as, give the sail more *hoist* ; (নৌবিদ্যা) পতাকা বা পালের উচ্চতা অথবা উহারা যতদূর পর্য্যন্ত উত্তোলিত হইতে পারে।

hoist (hoyst), *p. p.* **Hoist with his own petard**—Blown up by his own bomb ; ruined by his own devices against others ; নিজের বোমা দ্বারা উড়িয়া গিয়াছে ; পরের জন্য

ফাঁদ পাতিয়া সেই ফাঁদে নিজে পতিত হইয়া ধ্বংসপ্রাপ্ত [cf. পরের জন্য গর্ত্ত খোঁড়ে আপনি তায় পড়ে মরে, ফাঁদ পেতে ফাঁদে পড়া]।

hoi'-ty–toi'-ty (hōy-tĭ-tōy-tĭ), *n. adj.* & *interj.* Riotous or giddy conduct; উচ্ছৃঙ্খলতা। ***Adj.*** **1.** Thoughtless; haughty; frolicsome; as, *hoity-toity* spirits; চিন্তাশক্তিহীন; উদ্ধত; ক্রীড়াপর, ক্রীড়াশীল। **2.** Petulant; খিটখিটে। ***Interj.*** An exclamation of surprise or disapprobation with some degree of contempt; বা! বেশ!

hö'-key–po'-key (-kĭ-pö-kĭ), *n.* **1.** Cheap ice-cream peddled in the street; কুল্পী বরফ, মালাই বরফ। **2.** Hocus-pocus; লাগ ভেল্কি লাগ, লাগ ধাঁধা লাগ।

hōld, *v. t., i.* & *n.* **1.** To have in the grasp; as, to *hold* a sword, pen or candle; to sustain; ধারণ করা, ধরিয়া রাখা; পড়িতে না দেওয়া। **2.** To contain; (জিনিষ) ধরা, আঁটা। **3.** To keep possession of; to keep forcibly; to defend; as, the troops *held* their station; অধিকার বজায় রাখা; বলপূর্ব্বক রক্ষা করা; রক্ষা করা। **4.** To occupy; as, to *hold* office, title or place; অধিকার করা। **5.** To conduct; to celebrate; as, to *hold* a meeting or feast; to bring about officially; as, to *hold* a court or committee; পরিচালনা করা, সম্পন্ন করা; অনুষ্ঠান করা; অধিবেশন করা। **6.** To prosecute; as, to *hold* an argument or debate; করিতে থাকা, চালাইতে থাকা, অনুসরণ করা। **7.** To detain; to arrest the attention of; "She found herself *held* by his eyes"; থামান, নিরোধ করা; চিত্ত নিবদ্ধ করা। **8.** To keep in a particular place or condition; "He was *held* at bay"; কোন নির্দ্দিষ্ট স্থানে বা অবস্থায় রাখা। **9.** To maintain as an opinion; to persist in, as a purpose; পোষণ করা; ধরিয়া থাকা, অটল থাকা। **10.** To restrain; as, *hold* your tongue; সংযত করা। **11.** To regard; to esteem; to judge; to decide, as a judicial enquiry; মান্য করা; সমাদর করা; বিচার করা, নিষ্পত্তি করা। **12.** To bear or manage in a certain way; to keep in a certain position or attitude; as, he *holds* his rifle very awkwardly; কোন বিশেষ ভাবে বহন বা পরিচালনা করা; কোন বিশেষ ভঙ্গীতে রাখা। **13.** To make (a person) adhere (to); as, to *hold* one *to* his words; কোন বিষয়ে নিষ্ঠ, পরায়ণ বা অনুরক্ত রাখা। **14.** To use; as, to *hold* insolent language; ব্যবহার করা। **15.** To entertain specified feeling towards; as, to *hold* one in contempt etc.; কাহার প্রতি কোন বিশেষ ভাব পোষণ করা। ***Verb i.*** **1.** To maintain a grasp on; to cling; (*archaic*) to stop; "*Hold*! enough"—*Shaks.*; ধরিয়া রাখা; লাগিয়া থাকা; (অপ্রঃ) থামা। **2.** To remain firm or fixed; to remain unbroken; as, he cannot *hold* any longer: I think the rope will *hold*; অটল থাকা, স্থির থাকা; ভাঙ্গিয়া না পড়া, অটুট থাকা, অক্ষুণ্ণ থাকা। **3.** To last; to continue; to persist; "While our obedience *holds*"—*Milton*; স্থায়ী হওয়া; চলিতে থাকা; টিঁকিয়া থাকা, অটল থাকা। **4.** To refrain; to restrain oneself; "His heart...*held* from weeping"; বিরত হওয়া; সংযত করা, চাপিয়া রাখা। **5.** To remain attached; to adhere (often with *to, for, with* and *by*); as, to *hold to* the one and despise the other; আসক্ত থাকা, অনুরক্ত থাকা; নিষ্ঠ থাকা, পরায়ণ থাকা। **6.** To be valid; to apply; as, the law *holds* good in both cases; বৈধ হওয়া, সিদ্ধ হওয়া; প্রযোজ্য হওয়া, খাটা। **7.** To keep going; as, he *holds*, on his way; চলিতে থাকা। **8.** To derive right or titles; as, petty barons *holding* under the greater barons; স্বত্ব বা অধিকার প্রাপ্ত হওয়া। ***Noun.*** **1.** A grasp with the hand; (*lit.* & *fig.*) the act of holding; (often used with the verbs *lay, get, keep* and *take*); as, to take *hold* of one's hands; ধরণ, মুষ্টি-গ্রাহ; ধারণ। **2.** Authority to seize or keep; claim; "The law hath yet another *hold* on you"—*Shaks.*; influence; as, to have a *hold* on one; ধরিবার বা রাখিবার ক্ষমতা; দাবী, দাওয়া; প্রভাব। **3.** A place of confinement; custody; prison; as, he is in the mighty *hold* of Bolingbroke; অবরোধ স্থল; জিম্মা, হেপাজৎ; কারাগার। **4.** That which supports; means of support; অবলম্বন; অবলম্বনের উপায়। **5.** A fortified place; a fort; "Besieged the *hold* that could not long defend;" সুরক্ষিত স্থান; দুর্গ, কোট। **Hold-all**—একপ্রকার ব্যাগ। **Hold-back**—Check; hindrance; obstacle; as, the only *hold-back* is the affection; বাধা, অন্তরায়; বিঘ্ন; প্রতিবন্ধক। **Hold-fast**—A firm grasp; that which holds fast; a clinch or clamp; দৃঢ়মুষ্টি; যদ্দারা দৃঢ়ভাবে ধরা যায়; আঁকড়া। **Hold hard**—Stop (imperative); থাম! **Neither to hold nor to bind**—(*Colloq.*) Uncontrollably enraged; এত রাগিয়াছে যে তাহাকে ধরিয়া বা বাঁধিয়া রাখা যায় না। **To have a hold on**—To have influence over; কাহারো উপর প্রভাব থাকা। **To hold a brief for**—To act as a pleader for; কাহারো পক্ষে ওকালতি করা। **To hold a candle to**—To aid or countenance (that which is wrong); to be compared with; সাহায্য করা, অন্যায় কাজ সমর্থন করা; তুলনীয় হওয়া, তুলনার যোগ্য হওয়া। **To hold** or **set a candle to the devil**—কোনরূপ দুষ্কর্ম্মে সহায়তা করা। **To hold a round table**—To proclaim or hold a grand tournament; মহাক্রীড়াযুদ্ধ ঘোষণা করা, মহাক্রীড়াযুদ্ধের অনুষ্ঠান করা। **To hold at arm's length**—To keep at a distance; not to allow to close in; দূরে থাকা; কাছে ঘেঁষিতে না দেওয়া। **To hold at bay**—To prevent from closing in or attacking; as, he *held* the enemy *at bay* with his bayonet; শত্রুকে নিকটে আসিতে বা আক্রমণ করিতে না দেওয়া। **To hold a wager**—To stake or hazard a wager; বাজি রাখা, পণ রাখা। **To hold back**—*v. t.* & *i.* To restrain; সংযত করা। (*Verb i.*) To hesitate; to refrain; ইতস্ততঃ করা, দ্বিধা করা; নিবৃত্ত থাকা, বিরত থাকা। **To hold by** or **to**—To adhere to as a purpose, choice, etc.; লাগিয়া থাকা, ধরিয়া থাকা। **To hold by the button**—To detain in conversation to weariness; to be in terms of familiarity with; কোন ব্যক্তিকে আটক করিয়া কথাবার্ত্তা বলিতে বলিতে বিরক্তি বা অবসাদ জন্মান; কাহারও সহিত অন্তরঙ্গতা থাকা। **To hold forth**—To put forward; to show; to speak publicly; উপস্থাপিত করা; প্রদর্শন করা; প্রকাশ্যে বলা। **To hold good, To hold true**—To be true; to be well applicable; as, the same rule *holds good* in politics; স্থির থাকা, অবিচলিত থাকা; সুপ্রযোজ্য হওয়া। **To hold in**—To keep in check; to restrain; as, *to hold in* one's passions; সংযত রাখা; দমন করা, নিরোধ করা। **To hold in check**—To restrain; সংযত রাখা, দমন করিয়া রাখা। **To hold in play**—To keep fully occupied with secondary matters while the attention is diverted from the main point of issue; মূল বিষয় হইতে অপসৃত করিয়া অবান্তর বিষয়ে ব্যাপৃত রাখা। **To hold off**—*v. i.* To keep at a distance; to delay; দূরে রাখা; বিলম্ব করা, দেরী করা। **To hold on**—To persist in something; to continue; (*colloq.* imperative), stop; লাগিয়া থাকা; চালান; (চলিত ভাষায়) থাম, দাঁড়াও। **To hold one in hand**—To amuse in order to gain some advantage; কোন রূপ সুবিধালাভের জন্য চিত্তবিনোদন করা। **To hold one's breath**—To cease breathing for a short time (through fear etc.); ক্ষণকালের জন্য নিশ্বাস বন্ধ করিয়া রাখা। **To hold one's hand high**—To behave proudly; মাথা উঁচু করিয়া চলা, গর্ব্বিত ভাব প্রদর্শন করা। **To hold one's ground**—To keep up one's position against opponents; স্বস্থান রক্ষা করা। **To hold one's hand**—To forbear; to refrain from doing anything; নিবৃত্ত হওয়া, ক্ষান্ত হওয়া; বিরত থাকা। **To hold one's head above water**—Not to sink; not to be overwhelmed; ডুবিয়া না যাওয়া; অভিভূত না হওয়া। **To hold one's nose to the grindstone**—To oppress one; পেষণ করা, তক্তাচাপা দেওয়া। **To hold one's own**—Not to give way; to stand one's ground; স্থান ছাড়িয়া না দেওয়া, না হটিয়া যাওয়া; স্বস্থান রক্ষা করা, নিজের কোট বজায় রাখা। **To hold one's peace, tongue** or **voice**—To keep silence; not to speak; চুপ থাকা, নীরব থাকা; কথা না বলা। **To hold on one's way**—To keep going; পথ ধরিয়া চলিতে থাকা। **To hold on to**—To cling to; লাগিয়া থাকা, ধরিয়া থাকা। **To hold out**—*v. t.* & *i.* To extend; to offer; as, fortune *holds out* these to you as rewards; বিস্তার করা, ছড়ান; প্রদান করা। To endure; to be able to stand; to keep up to the end; সহা, সহ্য করা; টিঁকিয়া থাকিতে সমর্থ হওয়া; শেষ পর্য্যন্ত টিঁকিয়া থাকা। (*Verb i.*) Not to yield or give way; to endure; to last; as, it can no longer *hold out*; বশ্যতাস্বীকার না করা; স্থায়ী হওয়া; টিঁকিয়া থাকা। **To hold over**—To postpone; as, the application was *held over* for consideration; স্থগিত রাখা, মুলতবী রাখা। (*Law*—of a lessee) To keep possession of land after the expiration of his term; (আইন—পাট্টাদারের পক্ষে) নির্দ্দিষ্ট সময় অতীত হওয়ার পরও ভূমি নিজের দখলে রাখা। **To hold the cards in one's own hands**—(*Prov.*) পরমুখাপ্রেক্ষী না হওয়া, নিজের উপর কর্ত্তৃত্ব থাকা। **To hold to bail**—To bind by bail; জামিনে আবদ্ধ করা। **To hold together**—*v. t.* & *i.* To cause to cohere; সংযোগ করা, সংশ্লিষ্ট করা। (*Verb i.*) To remain united; to be joined; সংযুক্ত থাকা; সংযুক্ত হওয়া। **To hold up**—*v. t.* & *i.* To raise; as, *to hold up* one's head; to support; to sustain; "Gold *holds up* its price still;" to display; as, he was *held up* as an example; to check; to halt; as, *hold up* your horses; to stop and rob on high way, (*U. S.*); উঠান, তোলা, উত্তোলন করা; ধারণ করা, ধরিয়া রাখা; রক্ষা করা, না পড়া, পূর্ব্ববৎ থাকা; প্রদর্শন করা; নিরোধ করা, দমন করা; থামা, থামান; আটক করিয়া রাহাজানি করা (মার্কিণ-যুক্তরাজ্যে)। (*Verb i.*) To hold out; as to *hold up* under misfortune; টিঁকিয়া থাকা, স্থির থাকা। To keep up; not to fall (an address to a horse); দাঁড়াইয়া থাকা; না পড়া। To keep from raining; বৃষ্টি হইতে রক্ষা করা।

To hold up one's head—To maintain one's dignity or cheerfulness ; মাথা উচু করিয়া রাখা, স্বীয় গৌরব বা চিত্তের প্রফুল্লতা অক্ষুণ্ণ রাখা। **To hold water** — To be sound ; to endure trial ; as, his statements will not *hold water* ; অভ্রান্ত হওয়া, সঙ্গতিবিশিষ্ট হওয়া ; পরীক্ষায় টেঁকা, পরীক্ষাসহ হওয়া, পরীক্ষায় উতরান। **To hold with**—To take sides with ; to approve of ; দুই পক্ষের এক পক্ষ অবলম্বন করা ; অনুমোদন করা। **To hold with the hare and run with the hounds**—See HARE.

hōld, *n.* The whole cavity in ship below the deck ; জাহাজের খোল।

hōld'-ėr, *n.* **1.** One that holds something ; a contrivance to hold something ; as, a pen-*holder* ; ধারক ; কোন কিছু ধরার জন্য কৌশল। **2.** A tenant ; প্রজা, রায়ৎ, জোতদার।

hōld'-ing, *n.* **1.** The act of grasping or retaining ; ধরণ। **2.** A farm or other estate held of a superior ; a tenure ; তালুক ; জোত। **3.** That which binds, holds or influences ; যদ্দারা কোন কিছু বাঁধা বা ধরা যায় অথবা প্রভাবিত হয়।

hōle, *n.* **1.** A cavity ; an opening in a solid body ; a hollow place ; an aperture ; as, the wall is full of *holes* ; গহ্বর ; গর্ত্ত ; ফাঁক ; ছিদ্র, রন্ধ্র। **2.** The burrow of an animal ; বিবর, গর্ত্ত। **3.** A mean abode ; a low dark lodging ; হীন বাসস্থান ; অন্ধকূপ। **Hol'-ey,** *adj.* Having a hole or holes ; রন্ধ্র-বিশিষ্ট, রন্ধ্রবহুল। **Hole and corner** — Underhand ; clandestine ; as, a *hole and corner* policy ; গুপ্ত, তলে তলে সাধিত ; গোপন। **A round** (or **square**) **peg in a square** (or **round**) **hole**—A person not fitted for his place ; পদের অনুপযোগী ব্যক্তি। **Full of holes**—শতচ্ছিদ্র (কেঁডিঃ)। **In a hole**—In a difficult position ; সঙ্কটে। **To make a hole in**—To use a large amount of ; বহু পরিমাণ জিনিষ ব্যবহার করা। **To pick holes in**—To find fault with ; "Any one can *pick holes in* the university system of teaching and examination" ; দোষ ধরা, ছিদ্রান্বেষণ করা, খুঁত ধরা।

hōle, *v. t.* & *i.* **1.** To cut, dig or make a hole or holes in ; গর্ত্ত করা। **2.** To make (a shaft, tunnel, etc.) ; (সুড়ঙ্গ প্রভৃতি) খনন করা। **3.** To drive into a hole ; as, to *hole* an animal or a golf-ball ; গর্ত্তে ফেলা। ***Verb i.*** To get into a hole ; গর্ত্তে পড়া।

hŏl'-i-day (-dā), *n.* **1.** A holy or sacred day, (now usu. *holy day*) ; পবিত্র দিন। **2.** A day of exemption from labour ; a day of recreation and amusement ; ছুটীর দিন, বন্ধের দিন ; বিশ্রাম ও আমোদের দিন। **3.** (*Pl.*) A time or period of recreation ; "Summer *holidays*" ; ছুটীর কাল, ছুটী, অনধ্যায় (*school holiday*)। **Holiday clothes**—Gay clothes ; উৎসবোচিত বেশ, উৎসববেশ, তোলা কাপড়। **Holiday speeches** — Fine but empty phrases ; শ্রুতিমধুর অথচ শূন্যগর্ভ বাক্যাবলী। **Holiday task**—ছুটীর সময় বাড়ীতে করিবার জন্য ছেলেদিগকে যে কাজ দেওয়া হয়। **To make holiday** — To cease from work ; বিশ্রাম করা।

hō'-li-ly̆, *adv.* In a holy manner ; পবিত্রভাবে, পূতভাবে।

hō'-li-nĕss, *n.* The state or quality of being holy or sinless ; sanctity ; পবিত্রতা, শুদ্ধতা, অপাপবিদ্ধতা-মনঃশুদ্ধিতা, অন্তঃশুচিতা, নিষ্পাপতা, পাপরাহিত্য, অন্তঃপাবিত্র্য ; শুচিতা। **Holiness, His Holiness**—A title of the Pope ; রোমের ধর্ম্মসম্রাট্ পোপের উপাধি।

hŏl'-lă, *interj.* An exclamation to one at a distance in order to call attention or in answer, (see HOLLO) ; ঐ শোন !

Hŏl'-lănd, *n.* A province of Northern Netherlands ; the kingdom of the Netherlands ; উত্তর নেদারলেণ্ডস্‌এর প্রদেশ-বিশেষ ; নেদারল্যাণ্ডস্ রাজ্য। **—er,** *n.* **1.** A Dutchman ; ওলন্দাজ। **2.** A linen fabric ; একপ্রকার ক্ষৌম বস্ত্র।

Hŏl'-lănds, *n.* **1.** Gin made in Holland ; হল্যাণ্ডদেশে প্রস্তুত সরাপ। **2.** Grain-spirit made in Holland ; হল্যাণ্ড দেশে প্রস্তুত যবসুরা বিশেষ।

hŏl'-lō, *interj.* & *n.* An exclamation calling attention ; ওহে শোন ! হাবে ! ***Noun.*** A loud cry ; a halloo ; হলা হলা শব্দ ; লে লে শব্দ।

hŏl'-lō, —low (-lö), **—lă, —loa** (-lö), *v. i.* & *t.* To exclaim ; to call to hounds ; চীৎকার করা ; লে লে শব্দে কুকুরকে লেলান। ***Verb t.*** To shout, as words ; চীৎকার করিয়া বলা।

hŏl'-low (-lö), *adj., adv.* & *n.* **1.** Having an empty space within ; as, a *hollow* tree ; not solid ; ফাঁকা, ফাঁপা, শূন্য গর্ভ, সুবির ; অসংহত। **2.** Concave ; sunken ; as, a *hollow* eye ; বক্রোদর, সংবৃতমধ্য ; কোটর-গত, কোটর-প্রবিষ্ট, বসা। **3.** Deep ; low ; muffled ; as, a *hollow* roar ; গভীর ; ধীর, অনুচ্চ ; মন্দীভূত। **4.** Insincere ; deceitful ; false ; as, a *hollow* heart ; empty ; vain, as a victory ; অসরল, কুটিল ; ছলনাপর ; কৃত্রিম ; অসার ; নিষ্ফল। **5.** Hungry ; "I am feeling pretty *hollow*" ; শূন্যোদর, ক্ষুধিত, ক্ষুধার্ত্ত। ***Adv.*** Completely ; as, beaten *hollow* ; সম্পূর্ণরূপে, একেবারে। ***Noun.*** **1.** A hole ; a cavern ; a cavity ; as, the *hollow* of a tree ; গর্ত্ত, বিবর ; কোটর ; গহ্বর। **2.** A valley ; any depression in a body ; a channel ; as, forests grew upon the barren *hollows* ; উপত্যকা ; নিম্নস্থান ; খাত। **—ly,** *adv.* **—ness,** *n.*

Hollow brick—(বায়ু চলাচল ও তাপ সঞ্চারের জন্য) সরন্ধ্র ইষ্টক। **Hollow-eyed** — কোটরগত-নয়ন, কোটরপ্রবিষ্ট-চক্ষুঃ। **Hollow hearted** — Insincere ; faithless ; কপট, খল ; অবিশ্বাসী। **Hollow square**—শূন্য-মধ্য চতুরস্রাকারে সজ্জিত সৈন্য শ্রেণী। **Hollow-ware** — কড়াই, কেটলী, প্রভৃতি। **Hollow of the hand**—করপুট। **To beat hollow**—To defeat completely ; সম্পূর্ণরূপে পরাভূত করা, পর্য্যুদস্ত করা।

Hollow bricks.

hŏl′-low (-lō), *v. t.* To make hollow by digging : to excavate ; as, trees rudely *hollowed* ; to bend into a hollow or concave shape : খনন করিয়া শূন্য-গর্ভ করা, খুঁদিয়া ফাঁকা করা ; খনন করা ; কটাহ প্রভৃতির মত বাঁকান।

hŏl′-lȳ, *n.* An evergreen shrub with glossy leaves and red berries ; রক্তবর্ণফলপ্রসূ মসৃণ-পর্ণ চিরশ্যামল গুল্ম বিশেষ, সদাহরিতা (আঃ বঃ)।

hŏl′-lȳ-hŏck, *n.* A tall biennial plant of the mallow family ; নানাবর্ণ পুষ্পপ্রসূ দীর্ঘ তরুবিশেষ, চিত্রসেবতী (আঃ বঃ) ।

holm, holme (hōlm, or hōm), *ns.* **1.** An islet in a river or near the mainland : নদীমধ্যস্থ দ্বীপ, উপকূলান্তিকস্থ দ্বীপ। **2.** A rich flat land beside a river ; নদীপার্শ্ববর্ত্তী সমতল উর্ব্বর ভূমি।

holm (hōlm or hōm), *n.* A common evergreen oak of Europe (usu. *holm-oak*) ; ইয়ুরোপীয় চিরহরিৎ ওক বৃক্ষ বিশেষ।

hŏl′-ō-caust (-kăst), *n.* **1.** A burnt sacrifice of which the whole was consumed by fire ; নিঃশেষরূপে হোমানলে ভস্মীভূত হব্য দ্রব্য, হুত, হোম। **2.** A complete or thorough sacrifice or destruction of life esp. by fire etc. ; "...a *holocaust* of thirteen hundred persons in a church" ; বধযজ্ঞ, কালানলগ্রাস, অগ্নি হোম, খাণ্ডবদাহ।

hŏl′-ō-grăph, *n.* & *adj.* A document wholly written by the person from whom it proceeds ; দলীলসম্পাদনকারীর স্বহস্তলিখিত দলীল। ***Adj.*** Written, as a deed wholly by the person in whose name it appears ; দলীলসম্পাদনকারীর স্বহস্তলিখিত।

hŏl-ō-hē′-drăl, *adj.* (Of crystal) ; Having all the planes required by complete symmetry ; (স্ফটিকের পক্ষে) সর্ব্বাবয়বসম্পন্ন।

hŏl-ō-mē-tăb′-ō-lă, *n.* Insects undergoing complete metamorphosis ; পূর্ণরূপান্তরপ্রাপী কীট।

hŏl′-ō-phōte, *n.* (In light-house etc.) An apparatus for making available all the light of a lamp ; (আলোক মন্দির প্রভৃতিতে) প্রদীপের সমস্ত আলো কার্য্যে লাগাইবার জন্য যন্ত্র বিশেষ, সর্ব্বালোকসঞ্চায়ক।

hōl′-stêr, *n.* A leathern case for a pistol carried at the saddle or worn on the belt ; পিস্তল রাখার জন্য চামড়ার থলি—যাহা ঘোড়ার জিনে লাগান হয় কিম্বা পেটীতে বাঁধা হইয়া থাকে।

hōlt, *n.* (*Poet*) A wood or woody hill ; a grove ; (কবিতায়) বন, বনময়গিরি, বনবহুলগিরি ; উপবন, কুঞ্জবন।

hō′-lȳ, *adj.* & *n.* **1.** Set apart to the worship of God or a sacred use ; sacred ; pure ; as, *holy* priesthood ; দেবার্চ্চনার উদ্দেশ্যে রক্ষিত ; পবিত্র, পূত, পুণ্য ; শুদ্ধ, শুচি, মেধ্য, বিশুদ্ধ। **2.** Pertaining to God ; divine ; "Shed over the world Thy *holy* light" ; ঐশ্বরিক ; দিব্য, স্বর্গীয়। **3.** Morally and spiritually perfect ; pious ; guiltless ; as, a *holy* thought ; পূতচরিত্র, সাধু, সজ্জন, পবিত্রাত্মা ; পুণ্যবান ; নিষ্পাপ। ***Noun.*** A holy thing ; পবিত্র বস্তু। **—li-ly**, *adv.* **—li-ness**, *n.* **Holy City**—পবিত্রনগরী, পুণ্যনগরী, পুণ্যপুরী, যথা—কাশী, জেরুজেলেম, মক্কা। **Holy-Coat**—যীশুখ্রীষ্টের অনসেলাই কোর্ত্তা [ইহা জর্ম্মাণীর অন্তঃপাতী দ্রাক্ষালতাচ্ছাদিত-গিরিমালাবেষ্টিত Treves নদীর তীরস্থ ভজনমন্দিরে রক্ষিত আছে।] **Holy Communion** — The EUCHARIST (which see.) **Holy Cross**—পবিত্র ক্রুশ। **Holy Cross day**—যীশুখ্রীষ্টের ক্রুশের প্রতি সম্মানপ্রদর্শনার্থ ১৪ই সেপ্টেম্বর তারিখে অনুষ্ঠিত খৃষ্টীয় পর্ব্ব বিশেষ। **Holy-day**—A religious festival ; পর্ব্ব, পুণ্যদিন, পর্ব্বাহ। A holiday ; ছুটীর দিন। **Holy-Family** — যীশুখ্রীষ্ট এবং তদীয় পিতামাতার প্রতিকৃতিযুক্ত চিত্র, পবিত্র পরিবার। **Holy-Ghost, -Spirit**—The Divine spirit ; the third person in the Trinity ; পবিত্র আত্মা ; খৃষ্টীয় ত্রিমূর্ত্তির তৃতীয় ব্যক্তি। **Holy-grail**—See GRAIL. **Holy-Land** — West Palestine esp. Judaea ; প্যালেষ্টাইনদেশের পশ্চিমাঞ্চল, বিশেষতঃ জুডিয়া ; পুণ্যস্থল, পুণ্যভূমি, পুণ্যদেশ, ধর্ম্মক্ষেত্র, পুণ্যক্ষেত্র। **Holy Office**—See INQUISITION. **Holy orders** — খৃষ্টীয় যাজকসমাজ। **Holy quest** — পবিত্র পানপাত্রের অন্বেষণ। (See HOLY GRAIL under GRAIL). **Holy Roman Empire** — Theodosius কর্তৃক ৩৯৫ খৃঃ অব্দে রোমসাম্রাজ্য পশ্চিম অথবা ল্যাটিন এবং পূর্ব্ব অথবা গ্রীকসাম্রাজ্যে বিভক্ত হয়। পূর্ব্ব সাম্রাজ্য ১৪৫৩ খৃঃ অব্দ পর্য্যন্ত স্থায়ী থাকে এবং পশ্চিম সাম্রাজ্য ৪৭৬ খৃঃ অব্দে বিলুপ্ত হওয়ার পর আবার Charlemagne কর্তৃক ৮০০ খৃঃ অব্দে পুনঃ প্রতিষ্ঠিত হয়। এই সাম্রাজ্য Holy Roman Empire নামে পরিচিত এবং ইহা ১৮০৬ খৃঃ পর্য্যন্ত বর্ত্তমান ছিল। **Holy Rood**—রোমান ক্যাথলিক ভজনালয়ের যাজকবৃন্দের উপবেশনস্থলীর উপরিস্থ ক্রুশ। **Holyrood**—স্কটল্যাণ্ডের নৃপতিবৃন্দের রাজপ্রাসাদ। **Holy-Saturday**—ঈষ্টার পর্ব্বের অব্যবহিত পূর্ব্ববর্ত্তী শনিবার। **Holy-see** — রোমীয় ধর্ম্ম-সম্রাটের শ্রীপাট। **Holy-Thursday** — Ascension Day ; খৃষ্টের

স্বর্গারোহণ দিবস। Thursday in the Holy Week ; ঈষ্টারের পূর্ব্ব সপ্তাহের বৃহস্পতিবার। **Holy-war**—মুসলমানদিগের হস্ত হইতে জেরুজেলেম নগরীর উদ্ধারসাধনার্থ ধর্ম্মযুদ্ধ। **Holy water**—পবিত্রবারি, শান্তিজল (এভেলন)। **Holy Week**—ইষ্টার পর্ব্বের পূর্ব্ববর্ত্তী সপ্তাহ। **Holy Writ** — শাস্ত্র, বাইবেল, বেদ, কোরাণ। **Holy of holies**—The inner chamber of the sanctuary in a Jewish temple ; ইহুদীদিগের দেবমন্দিরের গর্ভগৃহ, গর্ভগৃহ (হ্যাভেঃ)। (*Fig.*) The innermost shrine ; (লক্ষণায়) সর্ব্বাভ্যন্তরস্থ পীঠ।

hŏ'-lȳ-stōne, *n.* & *v. t.* A sandstone used to scrub the decks of ships ; জাহাজের পাটাতন ঘষিয়া মাজিয়া পরিষ্কার করার জন্য একপ্রকার বেলে পাথর। ***Verb t.*** To scrub with a holystone ; ঐরূপ পাথর দ্বারা ঘষিয়া মাজিয়া পরিষ্কার করা।

hōm, *n.* A sacred plant of ancient Persians and Parsees ; its juice ; সোমলতা ; সোমরস [প্রাচীন পারসীকগণ 'সোমকে' 'হোম' কহিত।]

hŏm'-āge, *n.* **1.** Act of fealty to a sovereign or superior lord ; a formal acknowledgment of allegiance ; রাজা কিম্বা জমিদারের নিকট বশ্যতাস্বীকারসূচক প্রতিজ্ঞা ; বশ্যতাস্বীকার। **2.** Obeisance ; dutiful respect or reverence ; অভিবাদন, রাজাভিবন্দন ; শ্রদ্ধা, সমাদর।

hōme, *n., adj., adv., v. t.* & *i.* **1.** One's own abode ; the habitual abode or residence of one's family ; one's birth place ; as, there is no place like *home* ; বাটী, বাড়ী, ভবন, গৃহ, আলয়, ধাম ; স্বগৃহ, নিজধাম নিজালয় ; জন্মস্থান। **2.** One's own country ; "Our old *home* (England)"—*Hawthorne* ; স্বদেশ, জন্মভূমি, দেশমাতৃকা। **3.** (*Fig.*) The place where a thing is native or most common ; the seat ; as, the *home* of the pine (লক্ষণায়) জন্মস্থান ; জন্মনিকেতন। **4.** A place of refuge and rest for the destitute ; as, a *home* for outcasts ; আশ্রয়স্থল, অনাথাশ্রম, দরিদ্রনিবাস। **5.** (*Game*) The goal ; (ক্রীড়ায়) চরমগম্যস্থল। ***Adj.*** **1.** Pertaining to, or connected with, one's dwelling or country ; domestic ; as *home*-affairs : *home* comforts ; produced in one's own country ; not foreign ; as, *home* manufactures ; গার্হস্থ্য ; গৃহপালিত ; স্বদেশজাত, স্বদেশ-প্রস্তুত ; স্বদেশী। **2.** Severe ; poignant ; pointed ; as, a *home* thrust ; তীব্র ; মর্ম্মচ্ছেদী ; তীক্ষ্ণ। ***Adv.*** **1.** To one's country or home ; as, to go or come *home* ; স্বদেশে ; স্বগৃহে। **2.** To the point ; to the desired place or distance ; as, to drive a nail *home* ; মর্ম্মে মর্ম্মে ; ঈপ্সিত স্থানে, ইচ্ছানুরূপ দূরে। **3.** Closely ; close ; as, to come *home* to men's business ; নিকট ; কাছে। ***Verb t.*** To furnish a person with a home ; গৃহ প্রদান করা। ***Verb i.*** To go home, as pigeons ; গৃহে যাওয়া, গৃহাগত হওয়া। **Home'-less,** *adj.* Destitute of home ; গৃহহীন, গৃহহারা, অনাশ্রয়, নিরাশ্রয়। **Home'-like,** *adj.* Like a home ; cheerful ; বাটীর মত ; উৎফুল্ল। **Home-born**—Native ; natural ; স্বদেশজাত, গৃহজাত, গৃহপ্রস্তুত; স্বাভাবিক। Pertaining to the home or family ; as, *home-born* happiness ; গার্হস্থ্য, পারিবারিক। **Home-bound**—গৃহগামী, স্বদেশগামী। **Home-bred**—গৃহ-নির্ম্মিত, গৃহপ্রস্তুত, গৃহজ। Unpolished ; rude ; plain ; as, *homebred* youths ; অমার্জ্জিত ; রূঢ় ; সাদাসিধা। **Home-coming**—গৃহাগমন। **Home-department**—শাসনতন্ত্রের গার্হস্থ্য বিভাগ, স্বরাষ্ট্রবিভাগ। **Home-farm**—গৃহসন্নিহিত কৃষিক্ষেত্র। **Home-felt**—মর্ম্মে মর্ম্মে অনুভূত। **Home-keeping** — গৃহে অবস্থান। **Home-made**—গৃহ-প্রস্তুত, স্বদেশ-প্রস্তুত, ঘরগড়া। **Home Office**—স্বরাষ্ট্রসচিবের কার্য্যালয়। **Home-Rule**—স্বায়ত্তশাসন। **Home-sick**—গৃহে প্রত্যাগমনের জন্য কাতর, ঘরমুখো গৃহচেতা। *Home-sickness, n.* **Home-spun**—*adj.* & *n.* Spun or wrought at home ; as, *home-spun* country goods ; ঘরে বুনা। Plain in manner or style ; rude ; as, a *home-spun* proverb ; সাদাসিধা, সাদামাঠা ; রূঢ়। (*Noun*) Cloth made at home ; ঘরে বুনা কাপড়, গৃহপ্রস্তুত বস্ত্র। **Home stall**—A homestead ; a mansion house ; বাটী, বাস্তু ; জমিদারের বাড়ী। **Homestead** — A house with the adjoining grounds and buildings ; the seat of a family ; বসতবাটী ; ভদ্রাসন, বাসভূমি (মিতঃ)। A farm ; কৃষিক্ষেত্র। **Home-ward**—*adv.* & *adj.* Towards home ; বাটীর দিকে। (*Adj.*) In the direction of home ; গৃহাভিমুখী। **Home-ward-bound**—(Of ships) Preparing to go home ; (জাহাজের পক্ষে) স্বদেশপ্রত্যাগমনের জন্য প্রস্তুত। **Home-wards**—*adv.* Towards home ; গৃহাভিমুখে। **A home thrust**—An expression or repartee which deals a severe blow to one's heart ; মর্ম্মচ্ছেদী বাক্য, আঁতে ঘা। **An at home**—An evening party ; সান্ধ্যসম্মিলনী, সান্ধ্যপ্রীতি-সম্মিলনী। **At home** — In one's own house or native land ; as, peace abroad and *at home* ; স্বগৃহে, স্বদেশে। Conversant ; familiar (with *in* or *on*) ; as, he is not *at home in* or *on* that subject ; জ্ঞাতসার ; পারদর্শী, ব্যুৎপন্ন, সুপরিজ্ঞাত। Accessible to callers ; as, he is not *at home* ; (তাহার সহিত দেখা হবে না)। At one's ease ; as, I feel quite *at home* in your house ; গৃহাগত ব্যক্তিগণের দর্শনীয়, স্বচ্ছন্দচিত্ত। **He is home** — He is arrived at home ; তিনি বাটীতে পৌঁছিয়াছেন। **One's long home**—চিরবিরামস্থলী, সমাধিভবন। **The long**

or **last home** — The grave; অন্তিমভবন, কবর। **To be at home to people** — To be ready to receive visitors; গৃহাগত ব্যক্তিগণের সহিত দেখা করার জন্য প্রস্তুত থাকা। **To bring a charge home to a person**—To convict him of it; কোন অপরাধের জন্য কাহাকেও শাস্তি দেওয়ান। **To bring a thing home to people**—To say something interesting to people; লোকের নিকট কৌতূহলজনক কোন কিছু বলা, মজার কথা বলা। **To bring home to**—To prove conclusively; to impress upon; সুনিশ্চিত রূপে প্রমাণ করা; হৃদয়ঙ্গম করান, হৃদ্‌বোধ করান। **To bring oneself home**—To recover what has been previously lost; হারান জিনিষ পুনরায় পাওয়া। **To come home to a person**—To touch him deeply; হৃদয়ঙ্গম হওয়া, হৃদ্বোধ হওয়া। **To eat out of house and home**—To live at the expense of another so as to ruin him; কাহারও ঘাড়ে খাওয়া পরার ব্যয় চাপাইয়া তাহার ভিটায় ঘুঘু চরান। **To make oneself at home**—To be as free and unrestrained as when in one's own house; নিজ বাটীর মত স্বচ্ছন্দ বোধ করা, বাঁধ বাঁধ না ঠেকা। **To pay home**—To strike to the quick; to retaliate; আঁতে ঘা দেওয়া; প্রতিশোধ নেওয়া, দাদ তোলা।

hōme'-lȳ, *adj.* **1.** Of plain features; not handsome; as, a *homely* face; সাদামাঠা; অসুন্দর। **2.** Unpretending; simple; plain; সরল; সোজা; সাদাসিধা, ঘরোয়া (যথা ঘরোয়া ভাষা—ভারতী, চৈত্র ১৩২২), ঘরো। **—li-ness,** *n.*

hō-mē-ŏp'-ă-thȳ *n.* A system of curing disease by small quantities of drugs which excite symptoms similar to those of the disease; সুস্থ শরীরে বিষমাত্রায় যে ঔষধে যে লক্ষণ প্রকাশ পায় অল্পমাত্রায় সেই ঔষধে সেই রোগ আরোগ্য হয়—এই প্রকার চিকিৎসা-পদ্ধতি, সদৃশ-চিকিৎসাবিধান, সদৃশ চিকিৎসা (হঃ চঃ), সদৃশমত (ঐ)। **Ho'-me-o-path,** *n.* One who practises homeopathy; সদৃশচিকিৎসক। **—o-path'-ic,** *adj.* **—o-path'-i-cal-ly,** *adv.* **—thist,** *n.* A practitioner or believer in homeopathy; সদৃশ চিকিৎসা প্রণালীতে বিশ্বাসী ব্যক্তি, সদৃশ চিকিৎসক।

hō'-mêr, *n.* A home-going pigeon; গৃহগামী কপোত।

Hō'-mêr, *n.* The great epic poet of ancient Greece; প্রাচীন গ্রীসের কবিগুরু। ইনি Iliad নামক মহাকাব্য রচনা করেন। Homer অন্ধ ছিলেন বলিয়া কথিত আছে।

Hō-mêr'-ic, *adj.* Pertaining to Homer, the great Greek poet; or to his poetry; resembling his verse; প্রাচীন গ্রীক কবিগুরু হোমার বা তৎরচিত কবিতা সম্বন্ধীয়; হোমরের কবিতার অনুরূপ।

hŏm'-i-çīde, *n.* **1.** Man-slaughter; নরহত্যা, খুন, নরবধ। **2.** One who kills another; নরহত্যাকারী, নরঘ্ন, নরহন্তা, মনুষ্যহত্যাকারী, খুনী। **—cid-al,** *adj.* Murderous; মানুষঘাতী, নরহত্যাঘটিত।

hŏm-i-lĕt'-ic, *adj.* & *n.* Pertaining to homilies; ধর্ম্মোপদেশসম্পর্কীয়। *Noun.* (*Pl.*) The art of preaching; ধর্ম্মপ্রচারবিদ্যা।

hŏm'-i-lȳ, *n.* **1.** A sermon; ধর্ম্মোপদেশ। **2.** A tedious moral discourse or admonition; অবসাদজনক নৈতিক উপদেশ।

hōm'-ing, *adj.* Going home; (of a pigeon) trained to fly home; গৃহগামী; (কপোত পক্ষে) গৃহাভিমুখে উড্ডয়নের জন্য শিক্ষিত।

hŏm'-i-nȳ, *n.* Coarsely ground maize boiled with water or milk for food; ভুট্টার সাতুর পায়স বা মণ্ড।

hō'-mō, *n.* The animal man; মনুষ্যরূপ জন্তু।

hō-mō-çĕn'-tric, *adj.* Having the same centre; এককেন্দ্রিক।

hō-moe-op'-ă-thȳ (-mē-), *n.* See HOMEOPATHY.

hō-mŏg'-ă-mous (-mŭs), *adj.* (*Bot.*) Having the same essential parts of fructification; ফলোৎপাদনের জন্য সমরূপ মৌলিক অংশসমন্বিত, সমজম্পতী (সাঃ পঃ)।

hō-mō-ġē'-nē-ous (-ŭs), *adj.* **1.** Of the same kind; consisting of similar parts or elements; uniform; as, *homogeneous* bodies; একজাতিক, সমজাতিক (হিঃ কোঃ), সজাতীয়, একধর্ম্মক, সমধর্ম্মক, অনুগুণ, সবর্ণ (ঐ); সদৃশ অংশ বা অবয়বসম্পন্ন; সমরূপ, একরূপ, সমাকার (রাঃ সুঃ ত্রিঃ)। **2.** (*Algebra*) Having the same number of factors of a given kind; as, *homogeneous* polynomial; (বীজগণিত) নির্দ্দিষ্ট জাতীয় সমসংখ্যক গুণ্যগুণাবয়ব সম্পন্ন, সমঘাতিক (হিঃ কোঃ)। **—ly,** *adv.* **—ness, —ne'-i-ty,** *ns.* Sameness of nature or kind; সাজাত্য, সাধর্ম্ম্য, সমজাততা (সাঃ পঃ), সমজাতিতা (হিঃ কোঃ), একরূপতা, আনুগুণ্য, সমঘাততা (হিঃ কোঃ)।

hō-mō-ġē-nĕt'-ic, *adj.* (*Biol.*) Having common descent or origin; (জীব-বিজ্ঞান) একমূলজ, একপিতৃজ।

hō-mŏg'-ĕ-nȳ, *n.* (*Biol.*) Similarity due to common descent; (জীব-বিজ্ঞান) সাজাত্যহেতু সাদৃশ্য, সমজনি (হিঃ কোঃ)।

hō-moi-ou'-si-ăn (-moy-ow-), *adj.* & *n.* Pertaining to the Homoiousians or their belief; similar in essence; সাদৃশ্যবাদিগণ-সম্পর্কীয়; সমপ্রকৃতিক। *Noun.* A person believing that the nature of Christ is not the same with, but only similar to, that of the Father; খৃষ্ট-প্রকৃতি পিতা ঈশ্বরের প্রকৃতির সহিত অভেদ নয়, কিন্তু ঈশ্বর প্রকৃতির অনুরূপ—যাঁহারা এরূপ মত পোষণ করেন, সাদৃশ্যবাদী।

hŏ-mŏl′-ŏ-gāte, *v. t.* (*Scot.*) To approve of ; to ratify ; as, the court *homologates* a proceeding ; (স্কটলণ্ডে) অনুমোদন করা ; বলবৎ করা। **–ga′-tion,** *n.*

hŏ-mŏl′-ŏ-ğize, *n.* & *v. t.* To correspond ; অনুরূপ হওয়া, সমসংস্থান হওয়া। ***Verb t.*** To make homologous : অনুরূপ করা।

hŏ-mŏl′-ŏ-gous (-gŭs), *adj.* **1.** Having the same relation, relative position etc. ; corresponding ; অভিন্নসম্বন্ধ, আপেক্ষিক অবস্থিতি, প্রভৃতি সম্পন্ন ; অনুরূপ, সমমূলক (হিঃ কোঃ), সমকারণক (ঐ)। **2.** (*Biol.*) Corresponding in type or structure ; (জীব-বিজ্ঞান) সমসংস্থান (সাঃ পঃ), তুল্যজাতীয় (হিঃ কোঃ), সমধর্ম্মী (ঐ), সমশ্রেণীক (ঐ)। **3.** (*Chem.*) Characterized by homology ; (রসায়ন-শাস্ত্র) অনুরূপাত্মক। **Homologous sides**—তুল্যজাতীয় ভুজ (হিঃ কোঃ)।

hŏm′-ŏ-logue (-lŏg), *n.* That which is homologous ; অনুরূপবস্তু, সমসংস্থিত বস্তু [যথা, মনুষ্যের বাহু, মৎস্যের বুকের পাখ্‌না, এবং পক্ষীর পক্ষ]।

hŏ-mŏl′-ŏ-ğy, *n.* Sameness of relation ; correspondence ; as, the *homology* of similar polygons ; (*Biol.*) affinity of structure and not of form or use ; (*Chem.*) correspondence of substances belonging to the same type ; সমসংস্থিতি, সমধর্ম্মতা, আনুগুণ্য ; অনুরূপতা ; (জীব-বিজ্ঞান) সংস্থানসাম্য ; (রসায়ন-শাস্ত্র) একজাতীয় পদার্থ সমূহের মধ্যে সামঞ্জস্য। **–mo-log′-i-cal,** *adj.* **–mo-log′-i-cal-ly,** *adv.*

hŏm′-ŏ-nўm, *n.* **1.** A word having the same sound as another but a different meaning (as, the noun *bear* and the verb *bear*) ; সমধ্বনিবিশিষ্ট ভিন্নার্থক শব্দ। **2.** A namesake ; সমনামধারী ব্যক্তি বা বস্তু। **Ho-mon′-y-mous, –nym′-ic,** *adjs.* **1.** Having the same name or designation ; এক নাম বা উপাধিবিশিষ্ট। **Ho-mon′-y-mous-ly,** *adv.*

hō-mō-ou′-sĭ-ăn (-ōw-), **hō-mou′-sĭ-ăn** (-mōw), *adj.* & *n.* Pertaining to the Homousians or the doctrine they hold ; অভেদবাদিগণ সম্পর্কীয়, অভেদবাদ সম্পর্কীয়। ***Noun.*** A person who holds that the nature of the Father and the Son is the same, (opp. to *Homoiousian*) ; খৃষ্ট-প্রকৃতি পিতা ঈশ্বরের প্রকৃতি হইতে অভিন্ন—যাঁহারা এই মত পোষণ করেন, অভেদবাদী।

hŏm′-ŏ-phōne, *n.* **1.** A letter or symbol denoting the same sound as another ; সমধ্বনিসূচক বর্ণ বা চিহ্ন। **2.** A word having the same sound as another, but differing in meaning or origin ; ভিন্নার্থ বা ভিন্নধাতুজ সমধ্বনিবিশিষ্ট শব্দ।

hō-mŏph-ŏ-nў, *n.* **1.** Sameness of sound ; ধ্বনিসাম্য। **2.** (*Mus.*) Unison ; (সঙ্গীত-শাস্ত্র) সমস্বর, একতান।

hō-mō-plăs′-tic, *adj.* Similar in form or general structure ; একাকৃতি, সমরূপ, সমগঠন।

hŏm′-ŏ-tўpe, *n.* A part or organ of an animal corresponding to another part or organ ; as, one arm is the *homotype* of the other ; কোন জন্তুর অঙ্গের অনুরূপ অঙ্গ।

hō-mun′-cūle (-mŭng-), **–cle** (-kl), *n.* A manikin ; a dwarf ; মানবক ; বামন, খর্ব্বকায় ব্যক্তি।

hōm′-ў, *adj.* Like home ; suggesting home ; গৃহতুল্য ; গৃহসূচক, গৃহব্যঞ্জক, গৃহদ্যোতক।

hōne, *n.* & *v. t.* A whetstone esp. for razors ; a stone of which such whetstones are made ; শাণ, শাণোপল, শাণাশ্ম ; যে পাথর হইতে শাণ তৈয়ারী হয়। ***Verb t.*** To sharpen, as a razor on a hone ; শাণ দেওয়া।

hon′-ĕst (ŏn-), *adj.* **1.** Upright ; truthful ; not false ; sincere ; just ; as, an *honest* man : an *honest* business or conduct ; সাধু, সৎ, সাত্ত্বিক ; সত্যসন্ধ ; অকৃত্রিম ; সরল, অকপট, নিষ্কপট ; ন্যায়বান, ন্যায়পরায়ণ, ন্যায়নিষ্ঠ। **2.** (*Archaic*—of women) chaste ; virtuous ; as, wives may be merry and yet *honest* too ; (অপ্রঃ—স্ত্রীসম্পর্কে) সতী, সাধ্বী ; পুণ্যশীলা, পুণ্যবতী। **3.** Genuine ; unadulterated ; as, *honest* goods ; সাঁচ্চা ; খাঁটি। **4.** Fair ; straightforward ; free from fraud ; as, *honest* dealing ; সাধু ; অকপট, অকৈতব। **5.** Gained or earned by fair means ; "To earn an *honest* shilling" ; সদুপায়ে অর্জ্জিত। **6.** Frank ; open ; সরল ; উদার। **–ly,** *adv.* **To make an honest woman of**—To marry, where the woman was dishonoured first ; কোন স্ত্রীলোকের ধর্ম্ম নষ্ট করার পর তাহাকে বিবাহ করা। **To turn** or **earn an honest penny**—To gain by fair means ; সৎপথে থাকিয়া অর্থোপার্জ্জন করা, সদুপায়ে অর্থার্জ্জন করা।

hon′-ĕs-tў (ŏn-), *n.* **1.** The state of being honest ; uprightness ; sincerity ; truthfulness ; integrity ; সাধুতা ; ন্যায়পরতা ; সরলতা ; সত্যবাদিতা ; আর্জ্জব। **2.** (*Obs.*) Chastity, modesty (*Shaks*) ; সতীত্ব ; ব্রীড়া। **3.** (*Bot.*) A small flowering plant ; (উদ্ভিদ্‌-বিদ্যা) একপ্রকার ক্ষুদ্র পুষ্পপ্রসূ গুল্ম।

hon′-ey (hŭn-ĭ), *n.* **1.** A sweet thick fluid collected by bees from flowers ; মধু, মৌ, কুসুমাসব, ক্ষৌদ্র (সাঃ পঃ), পুষ্পনির্যাস, পুষ্পাসব, মাক্ষিক। **2.** Sweetness of language ; as, the *honey* of his language ; মাধুর্য্য, মধুরতা, লালিত্য। **3.** A term of endearment (esp. applied to a female) ; a sweet one or darling ; মধুময়ী ; দুলাল। **–eyed, –ied,** *adjs.* **1.** Containing honey ; sweetened as with honey ; sweet ; as, *honeyed* words ; মধুপূর্ণ ;

মধুমাখা, মধুময় ; মধুর। **Honey-bag**—মধুমক্ষিকার মধু-কোষ। **Honey-bee**—মধুমক্ষিকা, মৌমাছি, দ্বিরেফ, ভৃঙ্গ, অলি। **Honey bird** — ফুলটীকী (যোঃ)। **Honey-bush** — কামিনী (গোরী)। **Honey-buzzard**—একপ্রকার পাখী—ইহারা মৌমাছি, বোলতা, প্রভৃতি আহার করিয়া জীবন ধারণ করে। **Honey-comb**—*n.* & *v.t.* A mass of waxy cells formed by bees for storing their honey ; মধুচক্র, মৌচাক, মধুক্রম, ক্ষৌদ্র-পটল (রঃ), মধুজালক (শিশুঃ) ; মধুকোষ। Anything having little cells like a honey-comb ; মৌচাকের মত ক্ষুদ্র ক্ষুদ্র গর্ত্ত বিশিষ্ট বস্তু। An ornamental or other work arranged like a honey-comb ; পোষাক প্রভৃতির উপর মধুচক্রের অনুরূপ শোভাসাধক শিল্পকার্য্য। (*Verb t.*) To fill with cells or cavities ; to mark with a honey-comb pattern ; কোষ বা গর্ত্ত দ্বারা পরিপূর্ণ করা ; মধুচক্রের অনুরূপ শিল্প দ্বারা শোভিত করা। **Honey-dew**—A sugary substance found on the leaves of trees and other plants ; বৃক্ষের কাণ্ড ও পত্রে প্রাপ্ত মধুবৎ সুমিষ্ট বস্তু। An ideally sweet substance ; অমৃত। A sort of tobacco moistened with molasses ; একপ্রকার গুড়-মাখা তামাক।

Honey-eater.

Honey-eater, Honey-sucker—একজাতীয় পক্ষী। **Honey-moon**—*n.* & *v. i.* The first month after marriage, commonly spent in travelling by the couple ; বিবাহের প্রথম মাস—এই সময় নবপরিণীত দম্পতী যুগল দেশপর্য্যটনে যাপন করিয়া থাকে, মধুচন্দ্র (প্রভাত)। (*Verb i.*) To spend the honey-moon (*in* or *at* a place) ; নববিবাহিত দম্পতী যুগল কর্ত্তৃক কোন স্থানে বিবাহের প্রথম মাস যাপন করা। **Honey-mouthed**—Having a honeyed mouth or speech ; মধুরভাষী, মিষ্টভাষী, প্রিয়বাদী, প্রিয়ংবদ। **Honey-suckle**—A beautiful flowering and climbing shrub ; একপ্রকার পীতপুষ্প-প্রসবিনী লতা, মধুলতিকা (আঃ বঃ)। **Honey-sweet**—Sweet as honey ; মধুবৎ স্বাদু, মধুর, মধুময়। **Honey-tongued** — Having a honeyed tongue or speech ; মধুরভাষী, মিষ্টভাষী। **Virgin honey**—See under VIRGIN.

hŏng, *n.* A Chinese factory or warehouse ; a foreign mercantile establishment in China or Japan ; চীনদেশীয় কুঠি বা আড়ৎ ; চীন বা জাপানে বিদেশীয় বাণিজ্যশালা।

hon-o-rā′-ri-ŭm (ŏn-ō-), *n.* (*Pl.* -UMS, -A) A fee to a professional man for his services ; ফিস্, পারিশ্রমিক, দক্ষিণা।

hon′-or-ă-rȳ (ŏn-ēr-), *adj.* 1. Done or conferred as a sign of honour ; as, *honorary* services : *honorary* degree ; সাম্মানিক, সম্মানসূচক, প্রতিষ্ঠাসূচক। 2. Having a title or office without performing services or receiving a reward ; as, an *honorary* member of a society ; অবৈতনিক। 3. Depending on honour ; not enforceable by law as an obligation ; মর্য্যাদা-বুদ্ধির উপর নির্ভরশীল ; অবাধ্যতা-জনক।

hon-or-if′-ic (ŏn-ēr-), *adj.* & *n.* Conferring honour ; implying respect, as an expression ; সম্মানজনক ; সম্মানসূচক। ***Noun.*** An expression denoting respect ; সম্মানসূচক বাক্য।

hon′-our, hon′-or (ŏn-ēr), *n.* 1. Respect ; reverence ; high estimation ; সম্মান, মান ; শ্রদ্ধা, মর্য্যাদা (কেভিঃ) ; সমাদর। 2. Dignity ; nobleness of mind ; integrity ; সম্ভ্রম, মর্য্যাদা ; মহানুভবতা, সত্ত্ববৃত্তি (কেভিঃ), সত্ত্বাশক্তি (ঐ), সত্ত্বশীলতা, (ঐ) ; সাধুতা। 3. Chastity ; self-respect ; as, she forgot *honour* and virtue ; সতীত্ব ; আত্মমর্য্যাদা। 4. Exalted place or position ; high rank ; উচ্চপদ ; উচ্চপদবী। 5. Glory ; fame ; good name ; as, his *honour* is unsullied ; যশ ; কীর্ত্তি ; সুখ্যাতি, সুনাম। 6. A nice sense of what is right and just ; "It (*honour*) is the first sense of justice"—*Wordsworth* ; সূক্ষ্ম ন্যায়-অন্যায় বোধ। 7. A mark of respect ; as, to wear an *honour* on one's breast ; সম্মানচিহ্ন, গৌরবচিহ্ন। 8. A glory ; ornament ; as, he is an *honour* to his nation ; গৌরব ; ভূষা, অলঙ্কার। 9. (*Pl.*) Academic distinction ; as, to pass with *honours* in a subject ; কোন পরীক্ষায় বিশেষ কৃতিত্বের সহিত উত্তীর্ণ হইলে যে গৌরব প্রদান করা হয়, সম্মান। 10. A title of respect or distinction to a judge or other official ; as, His *Honour* the Mayor ; বিচারক প্রভৃতির সম্মানসূচক উপাধি। 11. (*Whist.*) One of the four highest trump cards, *viz.* the ace, king, queen or jack ; (বিন্তি খেলায়) রঙ্গের টেক্কা, সাহেব, বিবি, গোলাম। 12. (*Pl.*) Civilities paid, as at an entertainment ; ভোজ প্রভৃতিতে অভ্যাগত ব্যক্তিগণকে যে শিষ্টাচার প্রদর্শন করা হয়। **Honour-bright**—A kind of interjectional minor oath or appeal to honour ; সত্য সত্য বলিতেছি ! সত্যি ! **Military honours**—সৈনিক কর্ম্মচারীর অন্ত্যেষ্টি ক্রিয়াকালে সৈন্যগণ যে সম্মান প্রদর্শন করিয়া থাকে ; রাজা বা উচ্চপদস্থ রাজপুরুষগণকে (পতাকা নামাইয়া, ব্যাণ্ড বাজাইয়া অথবা তোপধ্বনি করিয়া) সৈন্যগণ যে সম্মান প্রদর্শন করিয়া থাকে, সামরিক-সম্মান। **A debt of honour**—দ্যুতক্রীড়া প্রভৃতিতে বাজি হারিয়া

যে ঋণ করা হয়, এবং যাহা মোকদ্দমা করিয়া আদায় করা যায় না; যে ঋণের জন্য কোনরূপ খত দেওয়া হয় নাই এবং কেবল ন্যায়বুদ্ধি প্রণোদিত হইয়া যাহা শোধ করা হয়। **An affair of honour**—A dispute to be decided by a duel; a single combat; যে বিরোধ দ্বন্দ্বযুদ্ধ দ্বারা মীমাংসা করিতে হইবে; দ্বন্দ্বযুদ্ধ। **A point of honour**—কর্ত্তব্যবোধ হইতে যে দ্বিধা উপজাত হয়। **Bound in honour (to do)**—সত্যবাক্যদ্বারা আবদ্ধ। **For (the) honour (of)**—যাহার নামে হুণ্ডী দেওয়া হইয়াছে সে রীতিমত প্রতিবাদ করিয়া হুণ্ডীর টাকা দিতে অস্বীকার করিলে, তৃতীয় ব্যক্তি কর্ত্তৃক হুণ্ডী দাতার বা হুণ্ডীর পৃষ্ঠে নাম-স্বাক্ষরকারীর বাজারসম্ভ্রম রাখার জন্য হুণ্ডীগ্রহণ বা হুণ্ডীর টাকা প্রদান। **Honours of war**—শত্রুহস্তে নগর-দুর্গ সমর্পণকারী সৈন্যকে পতাকা উড়াইয়া, ভেরী বাজাইয়া, এবং অস্ত্রশস্ত্র লইয়া বহির্গমনের জন্য অনুমতি। **In honour of**—In celebration of; সম্মানার্থ। **Last or funeral honours**—Observances of respect at funeral; অন্ত্যেষ্টি ক্রিয়াকালে সম্মান প্রদর্শন। **Laws of honour**—সম্ভ্রান্ত জনোচিত আচরণের প্রচলিত প্রথাসম্মত নিয়ম। **Maid of honour**—A lady in the service of a queen or princess; রাণী বা রাজকুমারীর সহচরী। A kind of cheese cake; একপ্রকার পনীরের পিঠা। **Sense of honour**—Sense of respect or dignity; গৌরববোধ, মর্য্যাদাবোধ, মর্য্যাদা-বুদ্ধি। Sense of duty; কর্ত্তব্যবোধ, কর্ত্তব্য-বুদ্ধি। **The honours rested with him**—He was the most successful; সে সর্ব্বাপেক্ষা অধিক কৃতকার্য্য হইয়াছিল। **To be on one's honour to do etc.**—To be under moral obligation to do etc.; সত্যবদ্ধ হওয়া। **To do honour to** — To show respect to; to reflect credit on; সম্মান প্রদর্শন করা; গৌরবের বিষয় হওয়া। **To do the honours of**—To show civility and attention to guests in the manner of a host; as, *to do one the honours of* the table, a house, etc.; গৃহাগত অতিথির প্রতি শিষ্টাচার প্রদর্শন করা, অভ্যাগতের প্রতি গৃহস্বামীর কর্ত্তব্য পালন করা। **Upon my honour**—আমি সত্য সত্য বলিতেছি, আমি নিজের মান পণ করিয়া বলিতেছি। **Word of honour**—সত্যবাক্য।

hon'-our (ŏn-êr), *v. t.* **1.** To respect highly; to revere; to hold in high esteem; as, to *honour* one's parents; উচ্চ সম্মান করা; সম্মান করা; শ্রদ্ধা করা, সমাদর করা। **2.** To bestow honour upon; to glorify; সম্মানজনক উপাধি প্রদান করা; গৌরবান্বিত করা, মহিমান্বিত করা। **3.** (*Com.*) To accept and pay when due; as, to *honour* a bill; (বাণিজ্য) (হুণ্ডী) গ্রহণ করা এবং নিরূপিতকালে টাকা প্রদান করা।

hon'-our-a-ble (ŏn-êr-ă-bl), *adj.* **1.** Worthy of honour; illustrious or noble; as, an *honourable* family; মাননীয়, মান্য, সম্মানার্হ; সুপ্রসিদ্ধ, সম্ভ্রান্ত। **2.** Actuated by principles of honour; upright; as, an *honourable* man; মর্য্যাদাবুদ্ধি-প্রণোদিত; সাধু, সজ্জন। **3.** Fair; not base; not reproachable; as, the *honourable* motive; সৎ; অহীন; অনিন্দ্য। **4.** A title of respect (applied to the children of peers below the rank of Marquess, the Maids of Honour, Justices of High Court, Lords of Session, members of Government or Executive Councils in India and Colonies); সম্ভ্রান্তপুরুষগণের পুত্রকন্যা, রাণীর সহচরী, হাইকোর্টের বিচারপতি, এবং ভারতীয় ব্যবস্থাপক সভার সদস্যগণের সম্মানসূচক উপাধি, মাননীয়। **5.** Consistent with honour or reputation; as, to capitulate on *honourable* terms; coferring honour; সম্মান বা সুখ্যাতিজনক; সম্মানপ্রদ, সম্মানকর, গৌরবজনক। **6.** Performed or accompanied with marks of honour and respect; as, an *honourable* burial; সম্মান এবং শ্রদ্ধাসূচক অনুষ্ঠানের সহিত সম্পাদিত। **—bly**, *adv.* With honour; সম্মানের সহিত, সসম্মানে। **Most Honourable**—মার্কুইস্, অর্ডার অব বাথ্ ও প্রিভি কাউন্সিলের নামের পূর্ব্বে ব্যবহৃত—মহামান্যবর। **Right Honourable**—মার্কুইসের নিম্নতর সম্ভ্রান্ত পুরুষগণ, প্রিভি কাউন্সিলের সভ্য, প্রভৃতির নামের পূর্ব্বে ব্যবহৃত উপাধি।

hood, *n.* & *v. t.* **1.** A covering for the head and neck; a cowl;

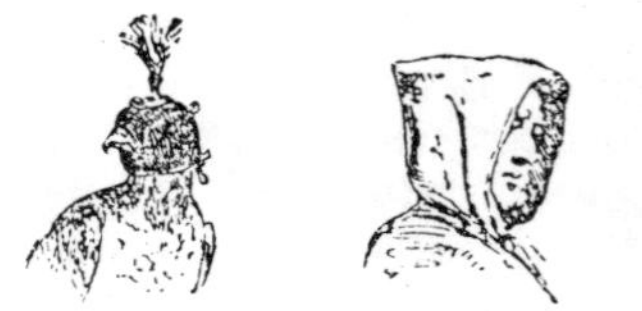

Hood for hawk. Monk's hood.

মস্তক ও গলদেশের আবরণ-বস্ত্র, অবগুণ্ঠন; খৃষ্টীয় সন্ন্যাসিগণের পরিচ্ছদ-সংলগ্ন মস্তক ও কণ্ঠাবরণ বস্ত্র। **2.** (*University*) An ornamental badge worn over a gown etc. to indicate a degree; (বিশ্ববিদ্যালয়) গাউন প্রভৃতির উপরে পরিহিত উপাধি-নির্দ্দেশক চিহ্ন। **3.** A leather covering for a hawk's head; বাজপক্ষীর মস্তকের জন্য চর্ম্মনির্ম্মিত আবরণ। **4.** A folding roof for a carriage; গাড়ীর ছত্রী, ছাউনী। **5.** The expanded head of a serpent (Indian); ফণা। ***Verb t.*** **1.** To cover with a hood; অবগুণ্ঠনাবৃত করা। **Hood'-ed**, *adj.* **1.** Covered or furnished with a hood or hood-like thing; ছত্রীওয়ালা, ছাউনীওয়ালা। **2.** Hood-shaped; with a hood-like crest or expansion of the head; অবগুণ্ঠনাকৃতি, ছাউনির আকার; মস্তকে অবগুণ্ঠনের মত চূড়াবিশিষ্ট, ফণাবিশিষ্ট। **—ie, y**, *adjs.* **Hoodie crow**—The hooded crow; সচূড় কাক। **Hood-man-blind**—কাণামাছি খেলা।

hood'-wink (-wĭngk), *v. t.* To blindfold; to impose on; to deceive; as, *hood-winked* with kindness; চোখ বাঁধা; চোখে ধূলি দেওয়া; প্রতারণা করা, ছলনা করা, মাথায় হাত বুলান।

hoof, *n., v. t. & i.* **1.** The horny substance on the feet of certain animals, *e. g.* horses etc.; খুর, ক্ষুর। **2.** (*Facet.*) A human foot; (রঙ্গচ্ছলে) মানুষের পা (cf. তোমার খুরে নমস্কার)। **3.** (In some phrases) A hoofed animal; "Not a *hoof* be left"; খুরবিশিষ্ট জন্তু, খুরান্বিত জন্তু, খুরী। ***Verb t.*** To strike with a hoof; (of a person) to kick out; খুর দ্বারা আঘাত করা; (ব্যক্তি সম্পর্কে) লাথি দিয়া বাহির করা। ***Verb i.*** To walk, (sometimes with *it*); হাঁটিয়া চলা। **Hoof'-ed,** *adj.* **Hoof-bound**—খঞ্জ। **Hoof-mark** — ক্ষুর-চিহ্ন। **Hoof-pad**—এক পায়ের সহিত অন্য পায়ের ঠক্কর না লাগে এজন্য যে গদী ব্যবহার করা হয়। **Hoof-pick**—খুর হইতে পাথর খসাইবার জন্য কাঁটা। **To beat** or **pad the hoof**—To walk about; বেড়াইয়া বেড়ান।

hook, *n.* **1.** A piece of metal bent into a curve for catching, holding or sustaining anything; অঙ্কুশ, আঁকড়া, ডুমনা, ছিটকিনী। **2.** A barbed bent piece of wire for catching fish, (also *fish-hook*); বড়শী, বড়িশ। **3.** A trap; a snare (*fig.*); ফাঁদ; পাশ, কল। **4.** A curved instrument for cutting grass etc.; a sickle; দা, কাটারী; কাস্তে। **5.** That part of a hinge on which a door or gate hangs and turns; কব্জার যে অংশের উপর দ্বার বা কপাট ঘুরিয়া থাকে। **6.** A sharp bend as in a river; নদী প্রভৃতির সূক্ষ্মাগ্র বাঁক। **7.** A projecting point of land; as, the *hook* of Holland; বহিরুদ্গত ভূখণ্ড। **Hooked,** *adj.* Hookshaped; furnished with a hook; বড়িশাকৃতি, বড়িশাকার; বড়িশসমন্বিত। **Hook-and-eye**—পোষাক আঁটিবার কৌশল-বিশেষ,—যাহাতে কুর্ত্তার এক কিনারার একটী আঁকড়া অপর কিনারায় ঐটী আটকাইবার জন্য একটী ছিদ্র থাকে। **Hook-nose(d)**—শুক নাসা, শুকনাস, খগ নাসা, খগনাস। **Hook-pin**—বক্রাগ্র পেরেক-বিশেষ। **By hook** or **by crook**—By fair means or foul; যে প্রকারেই হউক, যে কোন প্রকারে। **On one's own hook** — (*Slang*) On one's own responsibility; (ইতর ভাষায়) নিজের ঘাড়ের উপর। **To drop off the hooks** — (*Slang*) To die; (ইতর ভাষায়) শিঙ্গা ফুঁকা, পটল তোলা। **To hook it**—(*Slang*) To decamp; to make off; চম্পট দেওয়া; সরিয়া পড়া, পিট্টান দেওয়া, সট্‌কান।

hook, *v. t. & i.* **1.** To catch, hold or fasten with a hook; as, to *hook* fish etc.; to secure; বড়শী বা আঁকড়া দ্বারা ধরা, বিঁধা বা আটক করা; আটকান। **2.** To seize or draw (as) with a hook; to drag; বড়শী, আঁকড়া প্রভৃতি দ্বারা ধরা বা ধরিয়া টানা; টানা। **3.** To steal; চুরি করা। **4.** (*Golf*) To drive a (ball) widely to the left; (গোল্‌ফ ক্রীড়ায়) কন্দুক বামে তাড়িত করা। ***Verb i.*** **1.** To join (*on*); to fit *on*; "He *hooked on* to my arm"; সংযোগ করা; লগ্ন করা। **2.** To bend; বক্র করা, বাঁকান। **To hook on, in,** or **up etc.**—To attach with a hook; আঁকড়াদ্বারা লাগান, বড়শীদ্বারা লাগান। **Hook'-er,** *n.* One who, or that which, hooks; যে ব্যক্তি বড়শী প্রভৃতি দ্বারা বিঁধে বা আটক করে; যাহা আঁকড়াইয়া ধরে।

hook'-ĕr, *n.* A two-masted Dutch vessel; a small fishing smack; হলাণ্ডদেশীয় দ্বি-মাস্তুল পোত-বিশেষ; ক্ষুদ্র জেলে নৌকা।

hoo'-li-găn, *n.* One of a gang of street rouges; গুণ্ডা [লণ্ডন নগরীর Hooligan নামক জনৈক গুণ্ডার সর্দ্দারের নাম হইতে গৃহীত।] **—ism,** *n.*

hoop, *n. & v. t.* **1.** A band of wood or metal used to confine the staves of casks, tubs, etc.; পিপার বেড় বা হালি। **2.** A circle of elastic material for expanding the skirt of a lady's dress; স্ত্রীলোকের ঘাগরা ফুলাইবার জন্য এক-প্রকার স্থিতিস্থাপক পদার্থের চক্র। **3.** Anything resembling a hoop; a ring; চক্রাকার বস্তু; আংটা। **4.** A large ring of wood or metal which children trundle in the street; ছেলে মেয়েরা যে লোহা বা কাঠের চাকা রাস্তায় গড়াইয়া খেলিয়া থাকে। **5.** An iron arch used in croquet; ক্রীড়া বিশেষে ব্যবহৃত তোরণাকৃতি লৌহখণ্ড। ***Verb t.*** **1.** To bind or fasten with hoops; as, to *hoop* a barrel; (পিপায়) হালি লাগান। **2.** To encircle; to surround; বেষ্টিত করা; বলয়িত করা।

Hoop-costume.

Hoop-costume — স্থিতিস্থাপক পদার্থ-রচিত চক্রদ্বারা পরিস্ফীত পরিচ্ছদ। **Hoop petticoat**—স্থিতিস্থাপক পদার্থ-নির্ম্মিত চক্রদ্বারা প্রসারিত স্ত্রীলোকের অধোবাস।

hoop, *v. i. & n.* To utter a loud cry; চীৎকার করা। ***Noun.*** A shout or whoop; চীৎকার। **Hooping cough**—ঘুংড়ি কাসি।

hoop'-oe (-ö), *n.* A beautiful bird with a crest generally found in South Europe; নানাবর্ণপালকশোভিত দক্ষিণ ইয়ুরোপবাসী সচূড় পক্ষি-বিশেষ।

hoot, *v. i., t. & n.* **1.** To shout in contempt, (with *at*); as, to 'hoot *at* a bad speaker; টিট্‌কারী দেওয়া, ধিক্কার দেওয়া। **2.** To cry as an owl; পেচকের মত চীৎকার করা। **3.** To sound as a steam whistle; জাহাজের চোঙ্গা প্রভৃতির মত বাজা। ***Verb t.*** To assail (persons etc.) with derisive cries or shouts; to drive *out* or *away* by hooting; টিটকারী দেওয়া; টিটকারী দিয়া তাড়াইয়া দেওয়া। ***Noun.*** **1.** A loud inarticulate shout, esp. a scornful derisive cry; টিট্‌কারী, ধিক্কার। **2.** The cry of an owl; পেচকের চীৎকার, পেচকরব। **Hoot'-er,** *n.* One who, or that which, hoots; a siren; a steam whistle etc.; যে ব্যক্তি টিটকারী দেয়; জলপরী; জাহাজের চোঙ্গা প্রভৃতি।

hoove (hōōv), *n.* A disease of cattle and sheep with inflammation of the stomach; গোমহিষাদির পাকস্থলীর প্রদাহজনক রোগ বিশেষ।

Hop.

hŏp, *n., v. t. & i.* **1.** A climbing plant with a long twining stalk; একপ্রকার লতা। **2.** (*Pl.*) Ripe cones of the hop much used in brewing, to give a bitter taste; উক্ত লতার পক্ব ফল—যদ্দ্বারা যবসুরা প্রভৃতি তিক্তাস্বাদ করা হয়। ***Verb t.*** **1.** To mix with hops; হপ লতার পাকা ফলের রস মিশান। **2.** To bear hops; হপ লতায় ফল ধরা। ***Verb i.*** To gather hops; হপ লতার ফল সংগ্রহ করা। **Hop-bind, -bine**—হপ লতার ডাঁটা। **Hop-flea**—হপ লতা-নাশক কীট। **Hop-fly**—হপ লতার অনিষ্টকারী সূক্ষ্ম কীটবিশেষ। **Hop-garden** — হপ লতার ক্ষেত্র। **Hop-picker**—হপ লতার ফল সংগ্রহকারী, হপ ফল সংগ্রাহক যন্ত্র। **Hop-pillow**—হপ-ভরা বালিশ। [ইহার নিদ্রাজনক গুণ আছে বলিয়া প্রসিদ্ধি আছে।] **Hop-pocket**—হপ ফল রাখার জন্য মোটা ছালা। **Hop-pole**—হপলতার অবলম্বন স্বরূপ ক্ষুদ্র যষ্টি। **Hop-yard**—হপক্ষেত্র।

hŏp, *v. i., t. & n.* **1.** To leap on one leg; to skip as a bird; এক পায়ে লাফ দেওয়া; পাখীর মত লাফান। **2.** (*Colloq.*) To dance; (চলিত ভাষায়) নাচা। **3.** To limp; খোঁড়াইয়া চলা, নেংড়াইয়া চলা। ***Verb t.*** To hop over; as, to *hop* a ditch; লাফাইয়া পার হওয়া। ***Noun.*** **1.** A spring; a leap on one leg; লম্ফ; এক পায়ে লাফ, একপদ-লম্ফ। **2.** (*Colloq.*) A dance; নাচ। **Hop-o'-my-thumb**—A dwarf; a pigmy; বামন; বালখিল্য। **Hopscotch**—একপ্রকার খেলা—যাহাতে ছেলে মেয়েরা মাটীর উপর আঁকা রেখা সকল এক পায়ে লাফ দিয়া পার হয়, বিছু খেলা, গঙ্গা খেলা। **Hop, skip (or step), and jump**—একপ্রকার মল্ল-ক্রীড়া—যাহাতে ক্রীড়কগণ যথাক্রমে এক পায়ে লম্ফ, দীর্ঘপদক্ষেপ ও উভয় পায়ে লম্ফ দিয়া যথাসম্ভব অধিক স্থান অতিক্রম করে। **To hop, To hop off**—(*Slang*) To die; (ইতর ভাষায়) শিঙ্গা ফুঁকা। **To hop the twig**—(*Slang*) To depart or go off suddenly; ঝাঁ করিয়া চলিয়া যাওয়া।

hōpe, *n.* **1.** A desire of some good with a slight expectation of obtaining it; confidence; "*Hope* is the encouragement given to desire"; আশা, ভরসা; বিশ্বাস। **2.** Trust or confidence; বিশ্বাস। **3.** Ground or source of hope; আশার কারণ, আশার হেতু। **4.** An object of hope; "Lavinia is thine elder brother's *hope*"—*Shaks.*; আশার স্থল, আশার পাত্র। **Hope'-ful,** *adj. & n.* Full of hope; expectant; inspiring hope; promising; as, a *hopeful* prospect: a *hopeful* youth; আশাপূর্ণ; আশান্বিত; আশাপ্রদ; আশাজনক। ***Noun.*** A promising boy or girl (often *ironically*); as, young *hopefuls*; যে বালক বা বালিকা ভবিষ্যতে উন্নতি-লাভ করিবে বলিয়া আশা করা যায়, আশার স্থল বালক বা বালিকা (প্রায়শঃ অবজ্ঞাচ্ছলে)। **Hope'-ful-ly,** *adv.* **Hope'-ful-ness,** *n.* **Hope'-less,** *adj.* Destitute of hope; admitting no hope; as, a *hopeless* case; আশাহীন, নিরাশ, ভরসাশূন্য, হতাশ; আশার কারণ শূন্য। **Hope'-less-ly,** *adv.* **Hope'-less-ness** *n.* **Forlorn hope**—See FORLORN.

hōpe, *v. i. & t.* **1.** To entertain hope (usu. followed by *for*); as, to *hope for* good success; আশা করা, ভরসা করা। **2.** To have confidence; বিশ্বাস থাকা। ***Verb t.*** To desire with some expectation of attainment; আশা করা, ভরসা করা। **To hope against hope**—To hope even where there is no ground of hope; আশার কারণ না থাকা সত্ত্বেও আশা করা।

hŏp'-līte, *n.* **1.** A heavy armed foot soldiers of ancient Greece; প্রাচীন গ্রীসের গুরুভার অস্ত্রধারী পদাতিক।

hŏp'-pêr, *n.* **1.** One who hops; যে ব্যক্তি এক পায়ে লাফ দেয়, একপদ লম্ফকারী। **2.** (*Pl.*) A child's game; ছেলেদের ক্রীড়া বিশেষ। **3.** (*Mach.*) A chute or receptacle for feeding any material to a machine; ময়দার কল প্রভৃতির মুখপাত্র। **4.** A hopping insect esp. a flea etc.; একপ্রকার লম্ফকারী কীট। **5.** A boat carrying away mud etc. from a dredging machine and discharging it; তলকর্ষণী হইতে কর্দ্দমরাশি প্রভৃতি যে নৌকায় উঠাইয়া ফেলা হয়।

hŏp'-pêr, *n.* One that picks hops; যে ব্যক্তি হপ ফল সংগ্রহ করে।

hŏp'-ple (-pl), *v. t. & n.* **1.** To tie loosely the feet of (a horse or cow); অশ্ব বা গাভীর পা সকল ঢিলা ভাবে বাঁধা। **2.** (*Fig.*) To entangle or fetter;

জড়িত করা, শৃঙ্খলিত করা। *Noun.* A fetter for the legs of horses or other animals ; অশ্ব বা অন্য জন্তুর পদবন্ধনী।

Horae, n. The goddesses of order, justice, and of the unalterable march of natural time ; ন্যায়, শৃঙ্খলা, ও সময়ের অধিষ্ঠাত্রী দেবীত্রয়। Thallo (বাসন্তী দেবী), Carpo (পৌষ লক্ষ্মী—the goddess of the harvest). এবং Ausco।

Hor-Amen, n. An Egyptian deity ; প্রাচীন মিসর দেশের দেবতা বিশেষ।

hö'-ră-rȳ, *adj.* **1.** Pertaining to an hour ; occuring every hour ; ঘণ্টা সম্বন্ধীয় ; প্রতি ঘণ্টায় সংঘটিত।

Hō-rā'-ti-ăn (-shî-), *adj.* Of, or pertaining to, Horace, the Latin poet or like his style ; প্রাচীন রোম নগরবাসী কবি হোরেস বা তদীয় রচনা-রীতি সম্পর্কীয়।

hörde, *n.* **1.** A tribe or clan of Asiatic or other nomads ; a gang ; যাযাবর জাতি, যাযাবর বংশ ; দল। **2.** A crowd ; সংঘ।

höre'-hound (-hōwnd), **hoar-** (hör-), *n.* **1.** A plant with bitter aromatic juice used for coughs etc. ; other similar herbs ; একপ্রকার তিক্তাস্বাদ গুল্ম ; অন্যান্য অনুরূপ ঔষধি সমূহ।

hŏ-rī'-zŏn, *n.* **1.** The circular line formed by the apparent meeting of the earth and sky ; চক্রবাল, দিগ্বলয়, ক্ষিতিজ, দিঙ্‌মণ্ডল, দিগন্ত। **2.** (*Astron.*) A plane passing through the eye of a spectator and at right angles to the vertical at a given place ; (জ্যোতির্বিজ্ঞান) হরিজ (সাঃ পঃ), কুজবৃত্ত (ঐ), ক্ষিতিবৃত্ত (ঐ), হোরাচক্র (ভারতী ১৩২১), আকাশকক্ষা (কেণ্ডিঃ), গগনান্তরাল (বিশ্বঃ)। **3.** (*Fig.*) The range or limit of mental perception or experience ; (লক্ষণায়) অভিজ্ঞতা বা মানসপ্রত্যক্ষের প্রসর বা সীমা। **Apparent, sensible, visible** or **physical horizon**—যে সূচীক্ষেত্রের চূড়া দ্রষ্টার চক্ষুস্থানীয় তৎসহ ভূপৃষ্ঠের সংস্পর্শ দ্বারা উপজাত বৃত্ত, আপাতচক্রবাল, দৃশ্যচক্রবাল (হিঃ কোঃ), দৃশ্যক্ষিতিজ (ঐ), দৃশ্য দিঙ্‌মণ্ডল (ঐ)। **Celestial, rational, astronomical** or **true horizon**—আকাশমণ্ডলের কোন স্থানের আপাতচক্রবালের সহিত সমান্তরাল সুবৃহৎ বৃত্ত বিশেষ—ইহার ধরাতল পৃথিবীর কেন্দ্র ভেদ করিয়া থাকে, খগোলগর্ভক্ষিতিজ (হিঃ কোঃ)।

hŏr-ī-zŏn'-tăl, *adj.* & *n.* **1.** Of, or pertaining to, the horizon ; as, *horizontal* misty air ; চক্রবাল-সম্পর্কীয়, ক্ষিতিজ-সম্পর্কীয়। **2.** At, or near, the horizon ; চক্রবালস্থ, চক্রবাল সন্নিহিত। **3.** Parallel to the horizon ; level ; as, a *horizontal* line or surface ; চক্রবালের সহিত সমতল বা সমান্তরাল, ক্ষিতিজ-সমান্তরাল ; সমতল। **4.** (Of machinery etc.) Having the parts working in a horizontal direction ; (যন্ত্রাদি-সম্পর্কে) চক্রবালের সমান্তরাল দিকে ক্রিয়াশীল যন্ত্রাংশসমূহ সমন্বিত। **5.** Measured or contained in a plane of the horizon ; as, a *horizontal* distance চক্রবালের ধরাতলের (plane) অন্তর্ভূত। **—ly** *adv.* **—tal'-i-ty,** *n.* **Horizontal-plane**—ক্ষিতিজ ক্ষেত্র (হিঃ কোঃ), ক্ষিতিজধরাতল (ঐ)।

Hormzd, n. A God among the Zoroastrians ; পারসীকদিগের ঈশ্বরদ্বয়ের মধ্যে কল্যাণময় ঈশ্বর।

hŏrn, *n.* **1.** The hard substance projecting from the head of certain animals, as oxen etc. ; শৃঙ্গ, শিং, বিষাণ। **2.** Anything made of, or resembling a horn ; শৃঙ্গ-নির্ম্মিত দ্রব্য, শৃঙ্গবৎ বস্তু। **3.** A wind instrument of music ; শিঙ্গা, বিষাণ, শৃঙ্গবেণু, কাহলা (cf. কাহলাঃ পূরয়াঞ্চক্রুঃ—ভট্টিকাব্য ১৪শ সর্গ ৩ শ্লোক)। **4.** A drinking cup or powder flask, made of horn ; শৃঙ্গনির্ম্মিত পানপাত্র বা বারুদদান। **5.** The antlers of a deer ; মৃগশৃঙ্গ, হরিণের শিং। **6.** The material of which horns are composed ; শৃঙ্গের উপাদান বস্তু। **7.** An extremity of the moon when waxing or waning ; ক্ষীয়মাণ বা বর্দ্ধমান চন্দ্রের প্রান্ত সিনিবালী। **8.** An arm or branch of a bay or river ; শাখানদী, উপসাগর-শাখা। **9.** Either alternative of a dilemma ; উভয়সঙ্কটের অন্যতর। **10.** (*Bible*) A symbol of strength, glory, etc. ; "The Lord is the *horn* of my salvation" ; the sign of a cuckold ; (বাইবেল) শক্তি, মহিমা, প্রভৃতির চিহ্ন ; কুলটাপতির চিহ্ন। **Horn'-ful, Horn'-less** *adjs.* **Horn-bar**—গাড়ীর এড়োকাঠ। **Horn-beak**—একপ্রকার মৎস্য **Horn-beam**—একপ্রকার গাছ—ইহার কাঠ খুব শক্ত ও বেড়ার বিশেষ উপযোগী। **Hornbill**—ধনেশ পাখী (যোঃ) **Horn-bug**—উত্তর আমেরিকার একপ্রকার গোবরে পোকা। **Horned horse** — ষণ্ডাকৃতি কৃষ্ণসার মৃগবিশেষ। **Horned** or **horn-owl** — একপ্রকার পেচক—ইহাদের মস্তক শৃঙ্গাকৃত পালক গুচ্ছে শোভিত বলিয়া এই নাম, শৃঙ্গপেচক। **Horn-mad** — (অপ্রঃ) বদ্ধপাগল। **Horn-plate** — বাষ্পীয়শকটের চক্রদণ্ড-রক্ষক। **Horn-stone** — একপ্রকার চকমাক পাথর। **Horn wood sorrel**—আমরুল শাক (বনঃ)। **His horn is exalted**—He is happy and proud ; সে আনন্দে ও গর্ব্বে স্ফীত। **Horn of plenty**—Cornucopia—the symbol of plenty held by Ceres in her left arm ; সমৃদ্ধি ও প্রাচুর্য্যের নিদর্শন ; লক্ষ্মীর ভাণ্ডার, লক্ষ্মীর ঝাঁপি, লক্ষ্মীর খুঁচি [গ্রীকদিগের লক্ষ্মীদেবীর হস্তে ফলপুষ্পপূর্ণ শৃঙ্গ শোভা পাইয়া থাকে]। **The horns of a dilemma**—See under DILEMMA. **To be on** or **between the horns of a dilemma**—To be in an extreme difficulty from which there seems to be no way of escape; উভয় সঙ্কটে পড়া। **To draw in one's horns**—To restrain one's ardour; to draw back; সংযত করা; সরিয়া পড়া, লেজ গুটান। **To lift up the horn**—To exalt oneself; to show resistence; মাথা উঁচু করা; ঘাড় বাঁকাইয়া দাঁড়ান। **To lower one's horns**—To humiliate oneself; to condescend; মাথা নীচু করা, মাথা হেঁট করা, অধোবদন হওয়া; হীনতা স্বীকার করা। **To show one's horns**—To exhibit signs of a devilish nature; শয়তানি প্রকৃতি প্রদর্শন করা। **To take the bull by the horns**—See BULL.

hŏrn, *v. t.* **1.** To furnish with horns, (*usu. used in p. p.*); সশৃঙ্গ করা, শৃঙ্গসমন্বিত করা, শৃঙ্গবিশিষ্ট করা। **2.** To adjust as the frame of a ship at right angles to the line of keel; জাহাজের প্রধান তলকাষ্ঠের (পানিতরাস) সহিত সমকোণ উৎপাদন পূর্ব্বক (জাহাজের কাঠাম) সংযোগ করা। **3.** To gore with the horns; শৃঙ্গাঘাতে বিদ্ধ করা।

hŏrn′-blende (-blĕnd), *n.* A mineral of various colours, found in granite and other igneous rocks that contain quartz; নানা-বর্ণের খনিজ পদার্থ বিশেষ।

hŏrn′-êr, *n.* **1.** A blower of horns; শৃঙ্গবাদক, বিষাণবাদক। **2.** A maker of horn spoons, combs, etc.; শিঙ্গের চামচ, চিরুণী প্রভৃতি নির্ম্মাতা।

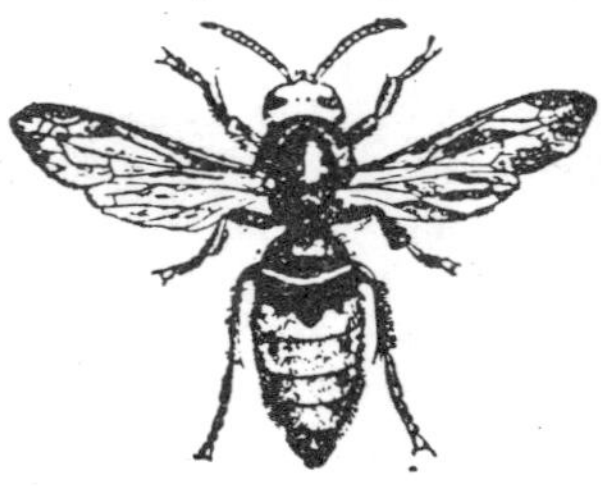

Hornet (female).

hŏr′-nĕt, *n.* A species of wasp so called from its horns; ভীমরুল, সারঙ্গ (ব্রজঃ হিন্দুঃ)। **To bring or raise a hornet's nest about one's ears**—To stir up a host of enemies against oneself; বহু-লোককে শত্রু করিয়া তোলা, ভীমরুলের চাক ঘেঁটান।

hŏrn′-pīpe, *n.* **1.** An old type of wind instrument; একপ্রকার সাবেক ধরণের বাঁশী। **2.** A lively air; a dance usually of a single person (popular amongst sailors); সতেজ স্বর; একপ্রকার নৃত্য।

hŏrn′-ȳ, *adj.* **1.** Made of, or like, horn; as, the *horny* coat of the eye; শৃঙ্গনির্ম্মিত, শার্ঙ্গ, শৃঙ্গীয়। **2.** Hard; callous; as, a *horny* fist; কঠিন; কড়াযুক্ত, বেদনাবোধ-শূন্য। **3.** Having, or abounding in, horns or horn-like projections; শৃঙ্গবিশিষ্ট, সশৃঙ্গ, শৃঙ্গবহুল। **—i-ness**, *n.*

hŏr′-ŏ-loge (-lŏj), *n.* A time-piece of any kind; a clock or dial; কালমান যন্ত্র, কালসাধন যন্ত্র (সুঃ সিঃ); ঘড়ী, সূর্য্যঘড়ী। **Ho-rol′-o-gist, Ho-rol′-o-ger**, *ns.* Maker of clocks, watches, etc.; ঘটিকাযন্ত্র-নির্ম্মাতা।

hŏ-rŏl′-ŏ-ḡȳ, *n.* The science of measuring time or the art of constructing clocks, watches, etc.; কালমানযন্ত্র বিদ্যা, কালজ্ঞান (সুঃ সিঃ), কালপরিমাণবিদ্যা, ঘটিকা-নির্ম্মাণ বিদ্যা, কালপরিমিতি, হোরা-শাস্ত্র (সাঃ পঃ)। **Hor-o-log′-ic, Hor-o-log′-i-cal**, *adjs.*

hŏ-rŏp′-têr, *n.* An aggregate of points seen single in any given position of the eye; যে বিন্দুসমুচ্চয় বিশেষ অবস্থানে অবস্থিত চক্ষুতে একটীমাত্র বিন্দুর ন্যায় প্রতিভাত হয়।

hŏr′-ŏ-scōpe, *n.* **1.** An observation of the heavens at the hour of a person's birth, by which the astrologer predicts the events of his life; কোন ব্যক্তির জীবনের শুভাশুভ কথনের জন্য তদীয় জন্মকালীন গ্রহাদির অবস্থার পরিদর্শন। **2.** A scheme of the twelve signs of the zodiac showing the disposition of the heavens at a particular moment; জন্মকুণ্ডলী, কুণ্ডলী, গ্রহকুণ্ডলী জাতপত্র, জন্মপত্রিকা, কোষ্ঠী, ঠিকুজি। **—scop′-ic, —scop′-i-cal**, *adjs.* **To cast a horoscope**—জন্মপত্রিকা প্রস্তুত করা, কোষ্ঠী প্রস্তুত করা।

hŏr′-rĕnt, *adj.* (*Poet.*) Standing on end; bristling; খাড়া; কণ্টকিত।

hŏr′-ri-ble (-bl), *adj.* **1.** Exciting horror; terrific; hedious; as, a *horrible* sight; ভীষণ; ভয়ঙ্কর, লোমহর্ষণ, ঘোর, করাল; বিকট, ভৈরব, বীভৎস। **2.** (*Colloq.*) Excessive; unpleasant; as, a *horrible* noise or weather; মহা, অত্যন্ত; অপ্রীতিকর। **—bly**, *adj.* **—ness**, *n.*

hŏr′-rid, *adj.* **1.** Dreadful; terrible; লোমহর্ষণ; ভয়ঙ্কর, ভয়াবহ, ঘোর, রৌদ্র, দারুণ। **2.** (*Archaic*) Rough or rugged; bristling; (অপ্রঃ) কর্কশ, আব্‌ড়োখাব্‌ড়ো; কণ্টকিত। **3.** (*Colloq.*) Excessively unpleasant; (চলিত ভাষায়) বীভৎস। **—ly**, *adv.* **—ness**, *n.*

hŏr′-rĭ-fȳ, *v. t.* To strike with horror; to shock; ভীত করা, ভয়াপ্লুত করা, ভয়ার্ত্ত করা; ভয়স্তম্ভিত করা। **—fi-ca′-tion**, *n.* **—rif′-ic**, *adj.*

hŏr-rip-i-lā′-tion, *n.* A bristling of the hair resulting from disease, terror, chillness, etc.; রোমহর্ষ, রোমাঞ্চ, লোমাঞ্চ, রোমপুলক, ত্বগঙ্কুর, পুলক, গা-কাঁটা, রোমোদ্গম, রোমহর্ষণ, লোমহর্ষণ।

hŏr′-ror (-rêr), *n.* **1.** (*Med.*) A shuddering as in a feverish fit; (ভৈষজ্যশাস্ত্র) গাত্রকম্প, কাঁপুনি। **2.** A feeling of dread and abhorrence; a terrified shuddering; বিভীষিকা; ভয়প্রকম্প, থরহরি। **3.** That which excites horror; যদ্দ্বারা বিভীষিকা উদ্রিক্ত হয়। **Horror struck** — বিভীষিকাগ্রস্ত, ভয়চকিত (কেঃ হিঃ), ভয়গ্রস্ত (ঐ)। **The**

horrors—Extreme depression ; a spasm or spasms of horror as in delirium tremens ; অতিশয় অবসাদের ভাব ; অতিরিক্তমাদক সেবন জনিত কম্পরোগ। **A chamber of horrors**—A place full of horror ; বিভীষিকাপূর্ণ স্থান।

hors (*F.*) *adv.* & *prep.* Outside ; as, *hors* concours ; বাহিরে। **Hors concours**—(Of an exhibit) Not competing for a prize ; যাহা প্রদর্শনীতে প্রদর্শিত দ্রব্যের তালিকাভুক্ত নয়। **Hors de combat**—Out of fight ; disabled ; যুদ্ধের বাহিরে ; যুদ্ধার্থ অকর্ম্মণ্য, অশক্ত বা অক্ষম। **Hors d'œuvre**—আচার, মোরব্বা প্রভৃতি রুচিকর দ্রব্য—যাহা ভোজনের পূর্ব্বে বিভিন্ন ব্যঞ্জন পরিবেষণের অবকাশকালে প্রদত্ত হয়।

horse (hŏrs), *n.* **1.** A well-known quadruped with flowing mane and tail ; a stallion or gelding ;

Horse.

a, muzzle ; *b*, gullet ; *c*, crest ; *d*, withers ; *e*, chest ; *f*, loins ; *g g*, girth ; *h*, hip or ilium ; *i*, croup ; *k*, haunch or quarters ; *l*, thigh ; *m*, hock ; *n*, shank or cannon ; *o*, fetlock ; *p*, pastern ; *q*, shoulder-bone or scapula ; *r*, elbow ; *s*, fore-thigh or arm ; *t*, knee ; *u*, coronet ; *v*, hoof ; *w*, point of hock ; *x*, ham-string ; *z z*, height.

অশ্ব, ঘোড়া, ঘোটক, তুরগ, তুরঙ্গ, তুরঙ্গম, হয়, বাহ, তাজি (আরব), অচ্ছিন্নমুষ্ক জননাশ্ব, বাজী, ছিন্নমুষ্ক অশ্ব, আখ্তা ঘোড়া। **2.** (*Collectively*) Cavalry ; as, a regiment of *horse* ; (সংঘবাচক ভাবে) অশ্বারোহী সৈন্য, সাদী সৈন্য। **3.** A sea-horse ; সিন্ধুঘোটক। **4.** That by which something is supported ; as, clothes-*horse* ; আলম্বন, ধারক। **5.** A vaulting block in a gymnasium ; ব্যায়ামযন্ত্র বিশেষ। **6.** (*Mining*) A mass of earthy matter occurring as an obstruction in a vein ; (খনির কাজ) পাষাণাদির মধ্যস্থ ধাতু প্রভৃতির অবরোধক মৃত্তিকাময় পদার্থ। **7.** (*Naut.*) A rope or iron bar in various uses ; (নৌ-বিদ্যা) বিভিন্ন কার্য্যের জন্য রজ্জু বা লৌহখণ্ড। **Horse'-less,** *adj.* **Horse artillery**—হাল্কা ময়দানী কামান এবং উহার অশ্বারোহী গোলন্দাজ সৈন্য। **Horse-back** — অশ্বপৃষ্ঠ। **Horse-block** — অশ্বারোহণের জন্য কাষ্ঠ বা প্রস্তর রচিত ক্ষুদ্র মঞ্চ, অশ্ব মঞ্চ। **Horse-boat**—অশ্ববহনের জন্য নৌকা বা অশ্ব দ্বারা চালিত নৌকা। **Horse-box**—অশ্ববহনের জন্য বাষ্পীয়শকটমালার অন্তর্গত শকট ; জাহাজের মধ্যে অশ্ব রাখার স্থান ; (রঙ্গচ্ছলে) খৃষ্টীয় ধর্ম্মমন্দিরস্থ বৃহৎ পারিবারিক আসন। **Horse-boy**—আস্তাবলের কার্য্যে নিযুক্ত বালক। **Horse-breaker**—যে ব্যক্তি ঘোড়াকে গাড়ী চালাইতে বা সওয়ার লইতে শিক্ষা দেয়। **Horse-chestnut** — একপ্রকার ফল ; ঐ ফলের গাছ। **Horse-cloth**—অশ্বপৃষ্ঠাবরণবস্ত্র, (অশ্ব) পৃষ্ঠাবগুণ্ঠন বস্ত্র (কুমারঃ)। **Horse-coper**—অশ্ব-ব্যবসায়ী, অশ্ব-বিক্রয়ী। **Horse doctor** — অশ্ববৈদ্য, অশ্বচিকিৎসক, শালিহোত্রজ্ঞ বৈদ্য। **Horse drench**—ঘোড়ার জন্য এক মাত্রা ঔষধ। **Horse-faced**—দীর্ঘ-বদন। **Horse-flesh**—অশ্বমাংস ; অশ্বসমূহ। **Horse-fly**—অশ্বদংশ, ধেনুমক্ষিকা। **Horse gram**—কুর্ত্তি কালাই (নৃত্যাঃ), কুলথ (বেলঃ)। **Horse Guards**—Horse soldiers employed as guards ; the third cavalry brigade of the English army forming a part of the Household troops ; the head-quarters of such a cavalry at Whitehall in London ; the military authorities at the head of an army ; অশ্বারোহী রক্ষি-সৈন্য ; ইংলণ্ডীয় গার্হস্থ্য সৈন্যের তৃতীয় অশ্বারোহী বাহিনী (*Brigade*) ; লণ্ডননগরীস্থ Whitehall নামক স্থান, যথায় উক্ত বাহিনীর সেনাপতি বাস করেন, সৈন্যদলের নায়ক স্বরূপ সামরিক কর্ম্মচারিবর্গ। **Horse-hair**—ঘোড়ার ঘাড়ের বা লেজের লোম, অশ্বলোম, বালামচি। **Horse-knacker**—যে ব্যক্তি বধ করার জন্য শীর্ণকায় অশ্ব সকল ক্রয় করে। **Horse-latitudes**—উত্তর অতলান্তিক মহাসাগরের নির্ব্বাত অংশ বিশেষ। **Horse-laugh**—অট্ট হাস্য, খল খল হাস্য, খক্ খক্ হাস্য বিশেষ। **Horse-leech**—বৃহৎ জলৌকা বিশেষ ; (অপ্রঃ) অস্ত্র চিকিৎসক ; অতৃপ্ত ব্যক্তি। **Horse-litter**—দ্বিঘোটক-বাহিত খট্টা। **Horse-man**—A skilled rider on horse-back ; a mounted soldier ; অশ্বারোহণনিপুণ ব্যক্তি, অশ্বারোহণপটু ব্যক্তি, অশ্বারোহণকুশল ব্যক্তি ; সাদী, তুরঙ্গসাদী, অশ্বারোহী সৈনিক। **Horseman-ship**—The art and the skill in riding on horseback ; অশ্বারোহণ-কৌশল, অশ্বারোহণ-পটুতা, অশ্বারোহণ-নৈপুণ্য, অশ্বারোহণবিদ্যা। **Horse-marine**—An imaginary soldier the name of which is often used to play a joke on the innocent ; a man out of his element, as a horse-soldier in a sea-fight ; কল্পিত সৈন্য ; স্বাভাবিক আবাস হইতে ভ্রষ্ট ব্যক্তি—যথা, জল-ছাড়া মীন। **Horse-mill**—অশ্বচালিত কল। **Horse-nail** — ঘোড়ার নাল বাঁধিবার পেরেক। **Horse-pistol**—একপ্রকার বৃহৎ পিস্তল। **Horse-play**—Boisterous play ; কোলাহলপূর্ণ ক্রীড়া। **Horse-pond** — অশ্ব ধৌত করণার্থ পুষ্করিণী ; (চলিত ভাষায়) যে পুষ্করিণীতে দুষ্ট লোককে চোবানি দেওয়া যায়। **Horse-power (H. P.)**—The power a horse can exert or its equivalent ; অশ্ব-শক্তি। (*Mech.*) A unit of power numerically equal to a rate of 33,000 foot pounds of work per minute ; (যন্ত্র-বিজ্ঞান) বাষ্পীয় যন্ত্রাদির শক্তির একক বিশেষ, অশ্ববল [৩৩,০০০ পাউণ্ড

ওজনের জিনিষ এক মিনিটে এক ফুট উচ্চে তুলিতে যতটা শক্তির আবশ্যক হয়]। **Horse-race**—ঘোড়দৌড়। **Horse radish**—সজিনা, সাজনা (ওয়াট)। **Horse-sense**—(মার্কিণ যুক্তরাজ্যে) পাকা বৈষয়িক লোক। **Horse-shoe**—ঘোড়ার নাল। **Horse-tail**—অশ্বপুচ্ছ; (তুরস্ক দেশের পাশাগণের পতাকা-চিহ্ন স্বরূপ ব্যবহৃত হয়); একপ্রকার পত্রহীন বৃক্ষ। **Horse-way**—ঘোড়া চলার উপযোগী পথ। **Horse-whip**—*n.* & *v. t.* A whip for driving horses; চাবুক। (*Verb t.*) To strike with a horse-whip; to lash; চাবুক মারা, চাবকান; বেত মারা। **Horsewoman**—A woman who rides on horse-back; অশ্বারোহণকারিণী। **Light horse**—Lightly armed mounted soldiers; লঘু অস্ত্রধারী অশ্বারোহী সৈন্য। **One-horse** — (American) Petty; mean; (আমেরিকায় ব্যবহৃত) হীন; নীচ। **A dark horse**—(ঘোড়দৌড়ে) যে ঘোড়ার গুণাগুণ সম্বন্ধে জনসাধারণ অবগত নহে। **A willing horse is worked the most**—যে সয় তার পিঠে সবাই চাপায়। **Many a ragged colt may make a good horse**—অনেক গবাই কালে গোবর্দ্ধন বাবু হয়। **On horse back**—Mounted on the back of a horse; অশ্বারূঢ়। **They cannot draw** or **set horses together** — They cannot agree together; তাহারা একমত হইতে পারে না। **To eat, work, like a horse**—To eat, work, much; খুব খাওয়া, খুব কাজ করা। **To flog** or **mount on a dead horse**—To try to work up excitement about a threadbare subject; পুরাতন বিষয়ে কৌতূহল উদ্রেকের চেষ্টা করা; পণ্ডশ্রম করা। **To grin through a horse-collar**—To practise elementary humour; চাষার মত গাদি করা। **To horse**—(*A command*) Mount your horse; ঘোড়ায় চড়। **To look a gift horse in the mouth**—To find fault with a gift; ভিক্ষার চাল কাঁড়া আর আঁকাড়া। **To mount** or **ride the high horse**—To put on airs; জাঁক দেখান, উদ্ধতভাব প্রদর্শন করা। **To put the cart before the horse**—See CART. **To take horse**—To mount on horse-back; অশ্বারোহণ করা। **To work the dead horse**—To do work which has been paid in advance; অগ্রিম টাকা পাইয়া কাজ করা। **When the horse** or **steed is stolen lock the stable-door**—চোর পালালে বুদ্ধি বাড়ে।

horse (hŏrs), *v. t.* & *i.* **1.** To provide, as a person or vehicle with a horse or horses; "Being better *horsed* outrode me"; অশ্ব প্রদান করা, ঘোড়া যুতা। **2.** To take or carry on the back; পিঠে লওয়া, পৃষ্ঠে বহন করা। **3.** To place on the back of another to be flogged; to flog; বেত মারার জন্য অন্য লোকের পিঠে রাখা; বেত মারা। **4.** (*Obs.*) To bestride; (অপ্রঃ) চড়িয়া বসা। ***Verb i.*** To get on horseback; to mount on horseback; ঘোড়ায় চড়া; অশ্বপৃষ্ঠে আরূঢ় হওয়া।

hŏrs'-ȳ, *adj.* **1.** Pertaining to, or concerned with, a horse; addicted to horses or horse racing; ঘোটক-সম্বন্ধীয়, অশ্বসংক্রান্ত; ঘোটকানুরক্ত, ঘোড়দৌড়ে অনুরক্ত। **2.** Characteristic of the dress, language, task, etc. of the groom or jockey; as, a *horsy* talk; ঘোড়ার সহিস বা ঘোড়সওয়ারের পোষাক, ভাষা বা রুচির অনুরূপ।

hŏr'-tă-tive (-tĭv), *adj.* Exhortative; giving, or tending to give, advice; উপদেশাত্মক, উপদেশ-গর্ভ; উপদেশপ্রদ। **—to-ry**, *adj.*

hŏr'-ti-cŭl-tūre, *n.* The art of cultivating gardens; উদ্যানবিদ্যা, উদ্যানরচনাবিদ্যা, উদ্যানকর্ম্ম (কেঙিঃ)। **—cul'-tur-al**, *adj.* **—cul'-tur-ist**, *n.* One who practises horticulture; উদ্যানরচক।

hortus siccus (*L.*), *n.* A collection of dried plants; a herbarium; শুষ্ক উদ্ভিদ-সংগ্রহ; শুষ্ক উদ্ভিদ-গৃহ।

Hō'-rŭs, *n.* One of the gods of Egypt; প্রাচীন মিসরের দেবতা বিশেষ।

hō-săn'-nă, *n.* (*Gk. Pl.*) An exclamation of praise to God or a prayer for blessings (*Matt.* XXI. 9, 15 etc.); স্তোত্র বিশেষ।

hōse, *n.* & *v. t.* **1.** Stockings; socks; মোজা; অনুপদীনা। **2.** Close-fitting breeches or trousers reaching to the knees; জাঙ্গিয়া। **3.** A flexible pipe for watering plants; গাছে জল দেওয়ার জন্য একপ্রকার স্থিতিস্থাপক নল। ***Verb t.*** **1.** To provide with a hose; মোজা প্রদান করা। **2.** To water with a hose; স্থিতিস্থাপক নল দ্বারা গাছে জল দেওয়া।

hō'-si-ėr, *n.* One who deals in hose or stockings, socks, etc.; মোজা, গেঞ্জি, প্রভৃতি বিক্রেতা। **—y**, *n.* Stockings in general; মোজা, গেঞ্জি প্রভৃতি। **2.** The business of a hosier; মোজা, গেঞ্জি প্রভৃতির ব্যবসায়। **3.** A factory where hosiery is made; মোজা, গেঞ্জি, প্রভৃতির কারখানা।

hŏs'-piece (-pīs), *n.* **1.** A house of entertainment for travellers esp. one kept by a member of a religious order; পথিকাশ্রম, বিশেষতঃ যাজকগণকর্তৃক পরিচালিত পান্থশালা। **2.** A home for the sick or destitute; রুগ্নাশ্রম, অনাথাশ্রম।

hŏs'-pi-tă-ble (-bl), *adj.* **1.** Receiving, or entertaining, strangers and guests with kindness; অতিথি-সৎকারপরায়ণ, আতিথেয়, অতিথিপূজক, অতিথিসৎকারী, অতিথিপ্রিয়, অতিথি-বৎসল, আতিথ্যতৎপর, আতিথ্যাসক্ত। **2.** Generous; liberal; as, *hospitable* rites; সদাশয়; উদার, বদান্য। **—bly**, *adv.* **—ness**, *n.*

hŏs′-pi-tăl, *n.* **1.** An institution for the reception and careful treatment of the sick or the wounded; রুগ্নাবাস (রবীঃ), হাঁসপাতাল, আরোগ্যশালা (পালি সাহিত্য)। **2.** A charitable institution for the education etc. of the young; as, Christ's *Hospital* (a school in London); বালকগণের শিক্ষার্থ অবৈতনিক বিদ্যালয় প্রভৃতি। **3.** (*Hist.*) A hospice; (ইতিহাস) পথিকাশ্রম। **Hospital-fever**—হাঁসপাতালের রোগীদিগের দূষিত শ্বাসপ্রশ্বাস হইতে জাত সংক্রামক জ্বর। **Hospital Saturday, -Sunday**—যে শনিবার বা রবিবার স্থানীয় রুগ্নাবাসের রোগিগণের জন্য রাজপথে (শনিবার) বা ভজনালয়ে (রবিবার) ভিক্ষা করা হয়। **To walk the hospitals** — (চিকিৎসক বা চিকিৎসাবিদ্যা শিক্ষার্থিগণের পক্ষে) চিকিৎসাবিদ্যাশিক্ষার্থ বা শিক্ষাদানার্থ রুগ্নাবাসে গমন করা।

hŏs′-pi-tăl-ism, *n.* **1.** Hospital system or practice; রুগ্নাবাসব্যবস্থা। **2.** Bad hygiene due to careless conduct of hospitals; অসতর্কভাবে রুগ্নাবাসের কার্য্য পরিচালন জনিত স্বাস্থ্যহীনতা।

hŏs-pi-tăl′-i-tȳ, *n.* Reception or entertainment of strangers without reward; as, given to *hospitality*; আতিথ্য, আতিথেয়তা, অতিথিসেবা, অতিথিসৎকার, অতিথিপূজন।

hŏs′-pi-tăl-(l)er (-ĕr), *n.* **1.** One of a charitable brotherhood for the care of the sick in hospitals; রুগ্নাবাসের রোগিগণের শুশ্রূষার জন্য পরহিতব্রত ভ্রাতৃমণ্ডলীর সভ্য। **2.** A chaplain (in some London hospitals); লণ্ডননগরীর কোন কোন রুগ্নাবাসের পুরোহিত। **3.** One of an order of military monks called Knights of St. John of Jerusalem, Knights of Malta etc.; সামরিক সন্ন্যাসিসম্প্রদায় বিশেষ ভুক্ত ব্যক্তি—পীড়িত ও অসহায় ব্যক্তিগণের আশ্রয়ের জন্য মাল্টা, জেরুজেলেম, প্রভৃতি, স্থানে এই সম্প্রদায়ের আশ্রম প্রতিষ্ঠিত হইয়াছিল।

hŏs′-pŏ-dâr, *n.* (Formerly the title of the princes of Moldavia and Wallachia) Lord; প্রভু।

hōst, *n.* (*R. C. Church*) The consecrated bread of the Eucharist; খৃষ্টের অন্তিম ভোজন ক্রিয়ানুষ্ঠানের উৎসর্গীকৃত রুটী।

hōst, *n.* **1.** One who entertains a stranger or guest at his house; an inn-keeper; অতিথিসেবক, ভোজদাতা; সরাইদার। **2.** (*Bible*) An animal or plant on which another lives, as a parasite; (বাইবেল) যে জন্তু বা উদ্ভিদের উপর অপর জন্তু বা উদ্ভিদ পরাঙ্গপুষ্টজীব বা পরগাছা স্বরূপ জন্মে। **To reckon without one's host** — To come to conclusions without taking into consideration some important circumstance of the case; কোন ঘটনার প্রধান বিষয় সম্বন্ধে বিবেচনা না করিয়াই তৎসম্পর্কে কোন সিদ্ধান্তে উপনীত হওয়া [যেমন সরাইএর অধিকারীর সহিত পরামর্শ না করিয়াই সরাইয়ে কত দেনা হইয়াছে তাহার হিসাব করা। cf. দশম স্থায়]।

hōst, *n.* **1.** (*Archaic*) An army; "A *host* so great as covered all the field"; (অপ্রঃ) সৈন্যদল, চমূ। **2.** A large number; multitude; "A *host* of golden daffodils"; বহুসংখ্যা; গণ, বৃন্দ, ফৌজ (*colloq.*)। **He is a host in himself**—He is one of great strength, skill or resources within himself; তিনি একাই একশ। **A host or hosts of heaven**—The sun, the moon and the stars; সূর্য্য, চন্দ্র, তারকা। Angels; দেবদূতগণ। **Lord of hosts**—(*Bible*) God of armies or of battles; (বাইবেল) রণেশ্বর, চমূপতি।

hŏs′-tāge, *n.* A person given to another as a pledge or security; pledge; security; যে ব্যক্তি জামিন বা প্রতিভূরূপে অন্য ব্যক্তির নিকট রক্ষিত হয়; বন্ধক; জামিন, প্রতিভূ। **A hostage to fortune**—A person or thing that one may lose; a man's wife and children etc.; নশ্বর বস্তু; কোন ব্যক্তির স্ত্রীপুত্র, কন্যা, প্রভৃতি।

hŏs′-tĕl, *n.* **1.** (*Archaic*) An inn; (অপ্রঃ) সরাই। **2.** A residence for university students; ছাত্রাবাস।

hŏs′-tĕl-rȳ, *n.* (*Archaic*) An inn; সরাই।

hōst′-ĕss, *n.* *Fem.* of HOST (which see.) অতিথিসেবিকা, ভোজনদাত্রী, আতিথ্যকারিণী।

hŏs′-tīle, *adj.* **1.** Belonging to an enemy; inimical; unfriendly; as, a *hostile* force or intention; শত্রুসম্বন্ধীয়; শত্রুভাবাপন্ন, বৈরভাবাপন্ন; অবন্ধুভাবাপন্ন, বিরোধী। **2.** Adverse; opposed; "*Hostile* principles"; প্রতিকূল; বিরুদ্ধ, বিরোধী। **—ly**, *adv.*

hŏs-tĭl′-i-tȳ, *n.* **1.** The state of being hostile; enmity; state of warfare; শত্রুভাবাপন্নতা, প্রাতিকূল্য; শত্রুতা; যুদ্ধাবস্থা। **2.** A hostile deed; (*pl.*) acts of warfare; as, to carry on *hostilities* with humanity; শত্রুতার কার্য্য; যুদ্ধকার্য্য, যুদ্ধব্যাপার, যুদ্ধবিগ্রহ। **3.** Opposition in thought, principle, etc.; বিরোধ।

hos′-tler (ŏs-lêr), *n.* Same as OSLER.

hŏt, *adj.* & *adv.* **1.** Very warm; characterized by unusual heat; as, *hot* air or water: *hot* climate; উষ্ণ, গরম; উত্তপ্ত। **2.** Feeling heat; producing the sensation of heat; as, *hot* fever; উষ্ণতাসংবেদনশীল; উষ্ণতাজনক। **3.** Eager; ardent; passionate; fiery; as, youth is *hot* and bold; angry; "After some *hot* words"; আগ্রহান্বিত; উত্তেজিত; উচ্চণ্ড; জ্বলন্ত; ক্রুদ্ধ। **4.** Violent; raging; "Plague grows *hot* in the city"; প্রবল; প্রচণ্ড। **5.** Lustful;

(of an animal) in heat ; কামজ্বর-পীড়িত, কামাতুর ; (জন্তু-সম্পর্কে) গরম, মদমত্ত । **6.** Pungent ; biting ; as, *hot* as mustard ; ঝাল, ঝাঁঝাল ; তীক্ষ্ণ (মরিচং কটুকং তীক্ষ্ণং—ভাবপ্রকাশঃ), কটু । **7.** Fresh ; recent ; টাট্‌কা ; গরম গরম, নূতন । **8.** (*Hunting*) Strong ; as, *hot* scent ; (মৃগয়া) উগ্র, তীব্র । ***Adv.*** Hotly ; eagerly ; angrily ; উত্তপ্ত-ভাবে ; আগ্রহান্বিতভাবে ; ক্রুদ্ধভাবে, গরম হইয়া । **Hot'-ly,** *adv.* **Hot'-ness,** *n.* **Hot-bed**—A glass-covered bed of earth heated for bringing forward plants rapidly ; বৃক্ষগুল্মাদি দ্রুত-বর্দ্ধনের জন্য গাঁজলা উৎপাদক সারদ্বারা উষ্ণীকৃত কাচসমাচ্ছাদিত (covered) উষ্ণক্ষেত্র । (*Fig.*) Any place favourable to rapid growth ; as, a *hot-bed* of vice (পাপ-ক্ষেত্র) ; (লক্ষণায়) দ্রুতবর্দ্ধনের পক্ষে অনুকূল ক্ষেত্র । **Hotblast**—চুল্লীর উত্তাপ বৃদ্ধির জন্য তদভ্যন্তরে তাড়িত উষ্ণ বাত্যাপ্রবাহ । **Hot-blooded**—চণ্ডপ্রকৃতি, চটা-মেজাজী ; ক্রোধোদ্দীপ্ত । **Hot-brained, -headed**—উষ্ণমস্তিষ্ক । **Hot-cockles**—কাণা মাছি । **Hot-flue**—শুষ্কীকরণার্থ গৃহ । **Hot-foot** — Quickly ; ত্বরিতপদে, ক্ষিপ্রপদে । **Hot-head** — উষ্ণমস্তিষ্ক ব্যক্তি । **Hot-house**—অকালে কিম্বা শীতপ্রধান দেশে তরুগুল্মাদি উৎপাদনের জন্য উষ্ণীকৃত গৃহ, কাচের ঘর (প্রবোধ), তপ্তাগার (আঃ বঃ) । **Hot-mouthed**—Headstrong ; মাথা-পাগলা, দুর্দ্দমনীয় । **Hot-pot**--আলু ও মাংসের কোর্ম্মা । **Hot-press**—*n.* & *v. t.* A press of glazed boards and hot metal plates for smoothing papers or cloth ; কাগজ, কাপড়, প্রভৃতি তাপ ও চাপদ্বারা মসৃণ করার জন্য চাপ-যন্ত্র বিশেষ, তপ্তযন্ত্র । (*Verb t.*) To press (paper etc.) in this to produce a glossy surface ; তপ্তযন্ত্রদ্বারা চাপ দেওয়া । **Hot-short**—উষ্ণাবস্থায় ভঙ্গপ্রবণ (যেমন লৌহ) । **Hot-spirited**—উষ্ণপ্রকৃতি । **Hot-spring** — উষ্ণপ্রস্রবণ, সীতাকুণ্ড (সাঃ পঃ), গরম ঝরণা (হিঃ কোঃ) । **Hot-spur**—A rash person (the surname of Sir H. Percy, d.1403) ; বেপরওয়া লোক । **Hot-tempered**—গরম মেজাজী । **Hot trod**—প্রাচীন কালে (ইংলণ্ড ও স্কটলণ্ডের) সীমান্ত প্রদেশে উদ্দামভাবে লুণ্ঠনাভিযানকারি-গণের অনুসরণ । **Hot-water**—(*Fig.*) Trouble ; disgrace ; (লক্ষণায়) কষ্ট, ঝঞ্ঝাট, দুঃখ ; অপমান । **Hot-well**—A spring of naturally hot water ; উষ্ণজলের কূপ, উষ্ণকূপ । A reservoir in a condensing steam engine ; সংহননকারক বাষ্পীয় যন্ত্রের কুণ্ড বিশেষ । **Give it him hot**—Chastise or reprimand him severely ; তাহাকে খুব শাসাইয়া দেও, কঠোর শাস্তি দেও । **Hot and hot**—Served as soon as cooked ; as, *hot and hot* food ; গরম গরম । **In hot haste**—তাড়াতাড়ি । **In hot water**—In trouble or difficulty ; ঝঞ্ঝাটে বা সঙ্কটে । **To make it** or **the place too hot for,** or **to hold, him**—To make it impossible for him to stay there ; তাহার পক্ষে টিঁকিয়া থাকা অসম্ভব করা, তাহার পক্ষে অতিষ্ঠ করিয়া তোলা ।

hŏt, *v. t.* (*Vulg.*) To heat ; (ইতর ভাষায়) গরম করা ।

hotch'-potch (hŏch-pŏch), **-pŏt,** *n.* **1.** A dish of mixed ingredients ; a hodge-podge ; a medley ; খিচুড়ী ; জগাখিচুড়ী ; সপ্তমিশ্র । **2.** (*Law*) A blending of property esp. of intestate parents for equality of division ; (আইন) অকৃতচরমপত্র পিতামাতার সম্পত্তি সমাংশে বিভাগের জন্য সংমিশ্রণ ।

hō'-tĕl, *n.* A house for entertaining strangers and travellers ; an inn, esp. a large one ; পান্থশালা, ভোজনাগার, ভোজনালয়, পথিকাশ্রম ; সরাই, বৃহৎ সরাই । ***Hotel de ville***—(*F.*) A town-hall ; নগরীর সভা-গৃহ । ***Hotel Dieu***—(*F.*) A hospital ; রুগ্নাবাস ।

Hŏt'-ten-tŏt (-n-), *n.* One of a savage race of South Africa ; (*fig.*) a person of inferior intellect and culture ; দক্ষিণ আফ্রিকার অসভ্য জাতি বিশেষ ; (লক্ষণায়) বর্ব্বর ।

hough (hŏk), *n.* & *v. t.* The hock of animal ; পশু-জঙ্ঘা । ***Verb t.*** To hamstring ; জঙ্ঘার শিরা কাটা । **Hough'-er,** *n.*

hound (hownd), *n.* **1.** A dog used in hunting ; শিকারী কুকুর । **2.** A mean contemptible fellow ; নীচ-লোক, শ্বপচ, হীনলোক । **3.** A player who follows scent in the game of hare and hounds ; ক্রীড়া বিশেষ—যে ক্রীড়ায় ক্রীড়ক কোনরূপ সূত্র ধরিয়া অপরের অনুসরণ করে । **Hound'-ish,** *adj.* **Hound's tongue**—একপ্রকার গুল্ম, কুক্কুর-জিহ্বা । **Master of hounds**—শিকারী কুকুর দলের রক্ষক । **The hounds** — A pack of foxhounds ; শিকারী কুকুরের দল ।

hound (hownd), *v. t.* **1.** To set on in chase ; as, to *hound* a dog at a hare ; to urge (a person) *on* ; as, to *hound* a man on the pursuer ; শিকারী কুকুর লেলাইয়া দেওয়া ; উৎসাহিত করিয়া আগুয়ান করা । **2.** To hunt or chase with hounds ; (*fig.*) to pursue unrelentingly ; as, to be *hounded* by creditors ; শিকারী কুকুরের সাহায্যে শিকার করা ; (লক্ষণায়) নির্দ্দয়ভাবে অনুসরণ করা ।

hour (owr), *n.* **1.** 60 minutes or the 24th part of a day ; এক ঘণ্টা, ঘটিকা । **2.** The time indicated by a clock etc. ; as, at what *hour* shall we meet ; ঘড়ী দ্বারা নির্দ্দিষ্ট সময়, টা । **3.** A time or occasion ; as, the man for the *hour* ; সময়, উপলক্ষ । **4.** (*Pl.*) Fixed time for daily work ; as, office *hours* are 10 to 3 ; দৈনিক কার্য্যের জন্য নিরূপিত সময় । **5.** (*Pl.*) The times of the day set for prayers ; certain prayers to be repeated at such times ; উপাসনার জন্য নির্দ্দিষ্ট সময় ; ঐরূপ সময়ের নির্দ্দিষ্ট উপাসনা। 6. (*Astron.*) 15° of the longitude ; (জ্যোতির্বিজ্ঞান) দ্রাঘিমার ১৫ অংশ। **Hour'-ly,** *adj.* & *adv.* Happening, or done, every hour ; frequent ; continual ; প্রতি ঘণ্টায় সংঘটিত, প্রতি ঘণ্টায় সম্পাদিত ; সতত ; অবিরত, নিরবচ্ছিন্ন। (*Adv.*) Continually ; frequently ; every hour ; as, it was *hourly* renewed ; সতত, সর্ব্বদা ; অনবরত ; প্রতি ঘণ্টায়, ঘণ্টায় ঘণ্টায়। **Hour-angle** — কোন স্থানের দ্রাঘিমা এবং নির্দ্দিষ্ট জ্যোতিষ্কভেদকারী হোরাবৃত্তের মধ্যবর্ত্তী কোণ, নতকাল (স্থঃ সিঃ), লম্বনঘটিকা (সাঃ পঃ)। **Hour-circle**—আকাশমণ্ডলে কল্পিত বৃহৎ বৃত্ত বিশেষ—যাহা মেরুদ্বয় ভেদ করিয়া যায়, হোরাবৃত্ত (স্থঃ সিঃ), হোরানাড়ীমণ্ডল (হিঃ কোঃ)। **Hour-glass**—একপ্রকার ঘটিকা যন্ত্র,—যাহাতে একটী কাচপাত্রের নিম্নস্থ অপর পাত্রে বালুকাকণা সকল পতিত হইয়া সময় নির্দ্দেশ করে, বালুকাযন্ত্র, বালুঘড়ী (হিঃ কোঃ), ঘটিযন্ত্র, ঘটিকা, লম্বনঘটিকা (সাঃ পঃ)। **Hour-hand**—ঘণ্টার কাঁটা। **Hour-line**—হোরারেখা (হিঃ কোঃ)। **Hour-plate** — ঘড়ী বা টেঁকঘড়ীর মুখপট্ট। **At the eleventh hour** — At the last moment possible ; শেষ মুহূর্ত্তে, অন্তিম মুহূর্ত্তে **In a good or evil hour**—Luckily or unluckily ; শুভ বা অশুভ মুহূর্ত্তে, শুভ বা অশুভক্ষণে। **The man or question of the hour**—The man or question of the present time ; বর্ত্তমান সময়ের বিশেষ প্রয়োজনীয় প্রশ্ন বা বিশেষ প্রসিদ্ধ ব্যক্তি। **The small hours**—1, 2 etc. A. M., *i. e.* the early hours in the morning ; রাত্রি ১টা ২টা প্রভৃতি, অর্থাৎ শেষ রাত্রে। **To keep bad or late hours**—To go to bed and rise late ; দেরীতে নিদ্রা যাওয়া ও দেরীতে জাগা। **To keep good, early or regular hours**—To go to bed and rise early or regularly ; সকাল সকাল নিদ্রা যাওয়া, ও সকাল সকাল উঠা।

hou'-ri (how-), *n.* **1.** A nymph of the Mohammedan paradise ; মুসলমানদিগের স্বর্গের অপ্সরা, স্বর্গাঙ্গনা, দিব্যাঙ্গনা। **2.** A very beautiful woman ; পরম রূপবতী স্ত্রী, লাবণ্যললামভূতা ললনা, ডানাকাটা পরী।

house (hows), *n.* **1.** A building for the habitation or use of man ; a mansion ; a place of abode ; গৃহ, ভবন, ঘর, বাসা, বাড়ী ; প্রাসাদ; বাস-স্থান। **2.** A building for keeping animals, goods, etc. ; পশুশালা, মালঘর, প্রভৃতি। **3.** A public house ; an inn ; পানাগার ; সরাই। **4.** A family esp. noble one ; as, the *house* of Hanover ; পরিবার, বিশেষতঃ সম্ভ্রান্ত পরিবার, বড়ঘর। **5.** A trading establishment ; (*colloq.* with *the*) Stock Exchange of London ; ব্যবসায়নিকেতন, বাণিজ্যাগার, বাণিজ্যশালা ; লণ্ডন নগরীর কোম্পানীর কাগজ ক্রয় বিক্রয়ের স্থান। **6.** The members of a family ; "One that feared God with all his *house*" ; পরিবারবর্গ, পরিজনবর্গ। **7.** A religious fraternity or its place of abode ; ধর্ম্মভ্রাতৃসংঘ, আশ্রম, সজ্বারাম, বিহার। **8.** A legislative body of men, as, the *House* of Commons or Lords ; a quorum of legislative body ; as, the government failed to keep a *house* ; the building or chamber where it meets ; পার্লেমেণ্ট বা ব্যবস্থাপক সভার সভ্যগণ ; ন্যূনকল্পে যত জন সভ্য উপস্থিত থাকিলে পার্লেমেণ্ট মহাসভা প্রভৃতির অধিবেশন হইতে পারে ; পার্লেমেণ্ট প্রভৃতির সভাগৃহ। **9.** A boarding house or the students in it collectively ; ছাত্রাবাস, ছাত্রাবাসের ছাত্রবৃন্দ। **10.** A theatre ; an audience of such a place ; as, the play draws a good *house* ; রঙ্গালয় ; রঙ্গালয়ের দর্শকবৃন্দ। **11.** (*Astrol.*) One of the twelve divisions of the heavens ; (ফলিত জ্যোতিষ) গৃহ। **House'-ful, -less,** *adjs.* **House-agent**—বাটীর দালাল। **House-boat** — বাসোপযোগী নৌকা, আবাসতরী। **House-breaker**—সিঁদেল চোর, কপাটঘ্ন, গৃহভেদক (কেঙিঃ), সন্ধিভেত্তা (ঐ) ; পুরাতন গৃহ ধ্বংসকরণার্থ নিযুক্ত ব্যক্তি। **House-breaking**—সন্ধিচৌর্য্য। **House-dog**—গৃহরক্ষক কুক্কুর। **House-duty, -tax**—A tax paid on inhabited houses ; বাটীর কর। **House-father**—গৃহস্বামী, গৃহকর্ত্তা, গৃহস্থ, গৃহপতি ; কোন সম্প্রদায়ের

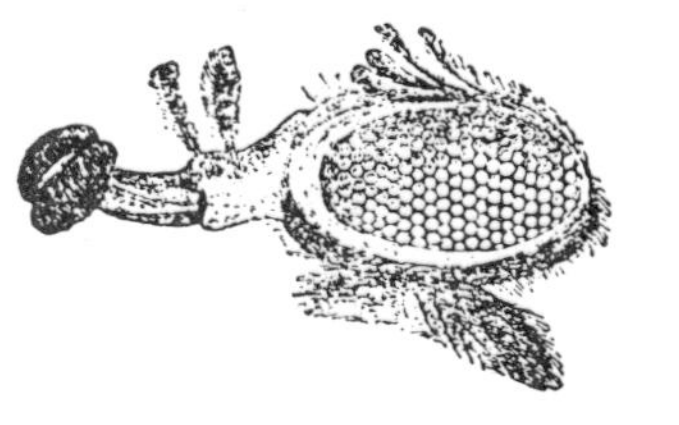

Head of house fly (magnified.)

কর্ত্তা। **House-fly**—মাছি। **House-keeper**—A female who has the chief care of the house ; গৃহকার্য্যের তত্ত্বাবধায়িকা, গৃহিণী, গিন্নি। A person in charge of a house, office, etc. ; গৃহরক্ষক, গৃহপাল (মঃ ভাঃ)। **House-keeping**—গৃহস্থালী, গৃহিণীপনা, ঘরকন্না ঘরসংসার, গৃহস্থধর্ম্ম। **House-leek**—গৃহের ছাদ ও প্রাচীরে জাত এক প্রকার পাটলপুষ্পপ্রসূ গুল্ম, কুতৃণ। **House-maid**—গৃহদাসী। **House maid's knee**—ভিজা মেঝের উপর হাঁটু পাতিয়া বসার দরুণ মালাইচাকির (knee-cap) প্রদাহ। **House-master**—ছাত্রাবাসের অধ্যক্ষ। **House-mate**—এক-গৃহবাসী। **House mother**—গৃহিণী, গিন্নি, গৃহকর্ত্রী। **House-rent**—বাড়ীর খাজানা, বাড়ীভাড়া। **House-room**—গৃহে বাসোপযোগী স্থান। **House-steward**—বড়লোকের বাড়ীর দেওয়ান। **House-surgeon, -physician**—আরোগ্যশালা প্রভৃতিতে বাসকারী চিকিৎসক। **House-warming**—গৃহপ্রবেশ, গৃহপ্রবেশোৎসব। **House**

and home—ঘর বাড়ী। **He hath eaten me out of house and home**—See under EAT. **House of call**—যে বাটীতে কোন বিশেষ কার্য্যে পারদর্শী শ্রমজীবিগণ সম্মিলিত হয় এবং যথায় যাইয়া যাহাদের ঐরূপ লোকের আবশ্যক তাহারা উহাদিগকে কার্য্যে নিযুক্ত করে। **House of correction**—A jail; সংশোধনাগার। **House of God, prayer** or **worship**—ধর্ম্মমন্দির, দেবালয়, গির্জ্জা, ভজনালয়। **House of ill fame**—বেশ্যালয়, বারাঙ্গনা-ভবন, গণিকানিকেতন। **House to house**—Carried on from house to house; বাড়ী বাড়ী, ঘরে ঘরে। **Like a house on fire**—With astonishing rapidity; vigorously; আশ্চর্য্য ক্ষিপ্রতার সহিত; সতেজে। **The house**—(*Colloq.*) See HOUSE 5. (Also) The House of Parliament; পার্লেমেন্ট সভাগৃহ। The work-house; দরিদ্রশালা। **To bring down the house**—To draw forth a universal burst of praise as in a theatre; রঙ্গালয় প্রভৃতিতে সর্ব্বজনীন সাধুবাদ লাভ করা। **To cry from the house-tops** — যতদূর সম্ভবপর প্রকাশ্যভাবে ঘোষণা বা প্রচার করা। **To keep a good house**—To keep up a plentifully supplied table; প্রচুর ভোজ্যপেয়ের ব্যবস্থা রাখা। **To keep house**—To maintain a separate establishment; পৃথক সংসার রাখা। To manage domestic affairs; গৃহস্থালী করা, ঘরকন্না দেখা। **To keep open house**—আগন্তুক মাত্রকেই পানভোজনাদি দ্বারা আপ্যায়িত করা। **To keep the house**—Not to go outdoors; বাড়ীর ভিতর থাকা, বাটীর বাহিরে না যাওয়া। **To make a House**—To secure presence of 40 members in the House of Commons; বিলাতের প্রাকৃত সভায় ৪০ জন সভ্যের উপস্থিতি নিশ্চিত করা। **To throw the house out of the windows**—To throw all things into confusion from exuberance of spirits; লণ্ডভণ্ড করা।

house (hōwz), *v. t.* & *i.* **1.** To put or receive into a house; to protect by covering; to shelter; গৃহে রাখা, গৃহে গ্রহণ করা; আবরণ দ্বারা রক্ষা করা; আশ্রয় প্রদান করা। **2.** (*Naut.*) To place in a secure position; as, to *house* guns, etc.; (নৌ-বিদ্যা) সুরক্ষিত স্থানে স্থাপন করা। ***Verb i.*** To take shelter; to reside; আশ্রয় গ্রহণ করা; বাস করা।

house'-hŏld (hōws-), *n.* & *adj.* **1.** The member of a family; a domestic establishment; পরিবার-বর্গ, পরিজনবর্গ; সংসার, পরিবার। **2.** (*Pl.*) The second quality of flour; ২ নং ময়দা। ***Adj.*** Pertaining to the house and family; as, *household* affairs; গার্হস্থ্য, পারিবারিক। **Household gods**—(*Rom. antiq.*) Presiding deities of the household, Lares and Penates; (রোমীয় প্রত্নতত্ত্ব) Lares এবং Penates নামক দেবতাদ্বয়, গৃহ-দেবতা, কুলদেবতা। Essentials of home life; গার্হস্থ্যজীবনের সারবস্তু। **Household suffrage**—পার্লেমেন্টের সভ্যনির্ব্বাচনের জন্য গৃহস্বামীর মত প্রদানের ক্ষমতা। **Household-troops**—রাজার শরীর-রক্ষী সৈন্য। **Household word**—A familiar word or name; অতি প্রচলিত শব্দ বা নাম, চলতি কথা, যে কথা প্রত্যেকের মুখে শোনা যায়।

house'-hŏld-ėr (hōws-), *n.* **1.** The chief of a household; গৃহস্থ, গৃহস্বামী, গৃহকর্ত্তা, গৃহপতি, গৃহী, গৃহস্থাশ্রমী। **2.** One who occupies a house as his own dwelling; বাটীর মালিক।

house'-wife (hōws-, or hŭz-zĭf); *n.* (*Pl.* HOUSEWIVES) **1.** The mistress of a family; a female domestic manager; গৃহিণী, গিন্নী, গৃহকর্ত্রী, গৃহস্বামিনী; গৃহকার্য্যের তত্ত্বাবধায়িকা। **2.** (*Pl. huzzif*) A small case for articles of female work; সূচ, আলপিন, কাঁচি, প্রভৃতি রাখার ক্ষুদ্র আধার। **—ly,** *adj.* Skilful in domestic management; relating to, or befitting a housewife; thrifty; গৃহকর্ম্মনিপুণ; গৃহিণীসম্বন্ধীয়, গৃহিণীসমুচিত; মিতব্যয়ী। **—wif-er-y,** *n.* Domestic economy; house keeping; গৃহিণীপনা, ঘরকন্না; গৃহকর্ম্ম।

hous'-ing (hōwz-), *n.* An ornamental covering for a horse; a saddle-cloth; কারুকার্য্যশোভিত অশ্বাবরণবস্ত্র, আস্তরণ; জিনপোষ।

Hou-yhnhnm (hōw-ĭnm), *n.* A horse with human characteristics (*in Gulliver's Travels*); মানবধর্ম্মা অশ্ব।

Hŏv'-ă, *n.* A number of the dominant native people of Madagascar; মাদাগাস্কার দ্বীপের প্রধান আদিম জাতি বিশেষের লোক।

hōve, *p. t.* & *p. p.* of HEAVE.

hŏv'-ĕl, *n.* **1.** An open shed for cattle etc.; চালা। **2.** A mean dwelling; a hut or cottage; কুঁড়ে ঘর; কুটীর। **3.** A conical building enclosing a porcelain oven or kiln; চীনামাটীর চুল্লীর আবরণ-স্বরূপ মোচাকার গৃহ।

hŏv'-ĕl-ler (-ėr), *n.* An unlicensed boatman, esp. one who assists in saving life and property from a wreck; অপ্রাপ্ত-সনন্দ নৌচালক—বিশেষতঃ জাহাজডুবি কালে যে নাবিক লোকের প্রাণ ও সম্পত্তি রক্ষাকল্পে সাহায্য করে।

hŏv'-ėr, *v. i.* & *n.* **1.** To remain fluttering (*over* or *about* a place or object); পক্ষসঞ্চালন বা পক্ষ-বিস্তার পূর্ব্বক শূন্যমার্গে অবস্থান করা। **2.** To loiter about; as, he was found *hovering* about a place; ইতঃস্তত ঘুরিয়া বেড়ান। **3.** To be in suspense; সংশয়দোলায় দোলায়মান হওয়া। ***Noun.*** The state of suspense; সংশয়াকুলভাব।

hōw, *adv.* & *n.* **1.** In what manner or way; কেমন করিয়া, কি

প্রকারে, কিরূপে, কি উপায়ে। **2.** To what degree or extent ; as, *how* love I thy law ; কি পরিমাণে, কত। **3.** In what state or condition ; as, *how* are you ? ; কি ভাবে, কি অবস্থায়। **4.** By what name or title ; as, *how* art thou called ? ; কি নামে, কি উপাধিতে। **5.** At what price ; as, *how* is corn ? ; কত মূল্যে। ***Noun.*** The way in which ; as, the *how* ; পন্থা, উপায়। **Howbeit**—(*Archaic*) Nevertheless ; তথাপি। **However**—In whatever manner, way or degree ; to whatever extent ; nevertheless ; yet ; notwithstanding ; যে রূপেই হউক, যে উপায়েই হউক ; যতদূর হউক ; পরন্তু, অথচ ; তথাপি ; তৎসত্ত্বেও। **Howsoever**—In whatever manner; to what extent soever ; যে রূপেই হউক ; যতদূর হউক। **How-d'ye-do**—In an embarassing situation ; সঙ্কটে, ঝঞ্ঝাটে। **How's that**—(ক্রীকেট ক্রীড়ায়) সে আউট হইয়াছে কি না ? **How far**—কত দূর। **How now**—What is the meaning of this ; ইহার অর্থ কি ? **How so**—How can you show that to be so ; ইহা যে এরূপ তাহা তুমি কিরূপে প্রমাণ করিবে। **The how and the why** — The manner and the cause ; কেন এবং কি প্রকার।

Howdah

how'-dah (-dă), *n.* Seat usually with canopy, on elephant's back ; হাওদা।

how-itz-êr (-its-), *n.* A short gun for the horizontal firing of shells with small charges ; সোজাসুজি গোলা ছুড়িবার জন্য একপ্রকার খাটো কামান, খর্ব্ব-কামান।

howl, *v. i.* & *t.* **1.** To yell or cry as a wolf or dog ; কুকুর, নেকড়ে বাঘের মত চীৎকার করা, ফেউ ফেউ করা, হাউ মাউ করা, ঘেউ ঘেউ করা। **2.** To utter a painful cry ; to wail ; চীৎকার করা ; আর্ত্তনাদ করা। **3.** To utter a cry of derision ; অবজ্ঞাসূচক চীৎকার করা। ***Verb t.*** To utter words etc. with howling ; হাউ মাউ করিয়া কথা বলা।

howl, *n.* **1.** A doleful cry of a dog or wolf ; খেউ খেউ, ঘেউ ঘেউ। **2.** A long loud cry of distress ; a wail ; চীৎকার ; আর্ত্তনাদ। **3.** A yell of derision ; হাউ মাউ।

howl'-êr, *n.* **1.** One who howls ; চীৎকারকারী। **2.** A South American monkey ; দক্ষিণ আমেরিকার বানর বিশেষ। **3.** (*Slang*) A glaring blunder ; (ইতর ভাষায়) মস্ত ভুল। **To come a howler** — (*Slang*) To come to grief ; (ইতর ভাষায়) কষ্টে পড়া ;

howl'-ĕt, *n.* (*Dial.*) An owl ; (উপভাষায়) পেচক।

howl'-ing, *adj.* **1.** That howls ; as, a *howling* wolf ; চীৎকারকারী। **2.** (*Slang*) Glaring ; extreme ; as, a *howling* shame ; (ইতরভাষায়) ডাহা, ঘোরতর ; নিতান্ত। **Howling monkey**—উলুক। **Howling wilderness**—(*Bible*) Dreary wilderness ; বিজন প্রদেশ, মরু প্রদেশ।

hoy, *n.* A small coasting vessel usually rigged as a sloop ; এক প্রকার উপকূলগামী পোত।

hoy, *interj.* An exclamation for calling attention or driving beasts ; লে, থাম, হোই।

hoy'-ă, *n.* A genus of plants with pink or white flowers ; এক জাতীয় শ্বেত ও পাটল পুষ্পপ্রসূ গুল্ম।

hoy'-den (-dn), *n.* A boisterous girl ; উদ্দাম-প্রকৃতি বালিকা, গেছো মেয়ে। **—hood, —ism,** *ns.* **—ish,** *adj.*

hŭb, *n.* **1.** The nave of a wheel ; চক্রনাভি। **2.** (*Fig.*) The central part of interest etc. ; (লক্ষণায়) কৌতুহলাদির কেন্দ্রস্থল। **3.** (*Dial.*) The hilt of a weapon ; (উপভাষায়) খড়্গাদির বাঁট, হাতল, মুষ্টি। **4.** A mark at which quoits etc. are cast ; যে লক্ষ্যের অভিমুখে ক্রীড়া-চক্র প্রভৃতি নিক্ষিপ্ত হয়। **The hub (centre) of the universe** — Boston ; বোষ্টন নগরী।

Hubble-bubble.

hŭb, hŭb'-bȳ, *ns.* (*Colloq.*) A husband ; (চলতি ভাষায়) ভাতার।

hŭb'-ble–bub'-ble (-l—bŭb-l), *n.* **1.** A tobacco pipe in which the smoke passes through water making a bubbling sound ; গুড়গুড়ি, হুঁকা কল্কি। **2.** A bubbling noise ; a confused talk ; গর্‌গর্ শব্দ, গোল ; গোলমাল, সোর।

hŭb'-bŭb *n.* **1.** A confused noise ; tumult ; uproar ; riot ; গোলমাল ; গোলযোগ ; সোরগোল, কোলাহল, হিড়িক; হাঙ্গামা,হল্লা। **2.** A confused yelling of war cry ; রণকোলাহল।

hŭb'-bŭ-boo, hŭb'-bă-boo, *ns.* Same as HUBBUB.

hŭck'-ă-băck, *n.* A kind of coarse linen for towels etc. ; তোয়ালে প্রভৃতির জন্য একপ্রকার মোটা কাপড়।

hŭck-le (-l), *n.* **1.** The haunch ; the hip ; নিতম্ব ; পাছা। **2.** A part projecting like the hip ; নিতম্ববৎ উদ্গত অংশ। **Huckle-back(ed)**—Hump-back(ed) ; কুব্জ। **Huckle-bone**—শ্রোণিফলক।

hŭck'-le-ber-ry (-l-bĕr-i), *n.* A North American shrub with blue berries ; its fruit ; উত্তর আমেরিকার গুল্মবিশেষ ; ঐ গুল্মের ফল।

hŭck'-stêr, *n., v. i.* & *t.* **1.** A retailer of small articles ; a hawker ; ক্ষুদ্রপণ্যবিক্রয়ী ; ফেরিওয়ালা। **2.** A mean mercenary fellow ; হীন অর্থগৃধ্নু লোক। ***Verb i.*** To deal in small articles ; to haggle ; ক্ষুদ্র পণ্যের ব্যবসায় করা ; দর কষাকষি করা। ***Verb t.*** **1.** To hawk or peddle ; to make a matter of bargain (*lit.* & *fig.*) ; as, to *huckster* one's honour ; ফেরি করা ; ক্রয় বিক্রয়ের বিষয়ীভূত করা, কেনা বেচার জিনিষ করা। **2.** To adulterate ; ভেজাল দেওয়া। **–er, –stress,** (*fem.*), **–y,** *ns.*

hŭd'-dle (-l), *v. t., i.* & *n.* **1.** To crowd or heap (things etc.) together in confusion ; বিশৃঙ্খলভাবে ঠাসিয়া বা গাদা করিয়া রাখা। **2.** To do hastily or imperfectly ; as, to *huddle up* a work ; to put on hastily as clothes ; তাড়াতাড়ি বা আধা খেচড়াভাবে করা ; তাড়াতাড়ি পরা। **3.** To draw (oneself) into a contracted heap ; "He lay as he fell, all *huddled* up" ; মাংসপিণ্ডবৎ করা। **4.** (*Dial.*) To embrace ; (উপভাষায়) বুকে লওয়া। ***Verb i.*** To press or crowd together promiscuously ; এলোমেলোভাবে ঠাসিয়া থাকা। ***Noun.*** A confused mass ; confusion ; disorder ; as, a *huddle* of ideas ; বিশৃঙ্খলভাবে রক্ষিত জিনিষ ; গোলমাল ; বিশৃঙ্খলা।

Hū-di-brăs'-tic, *adj.* In the style or meter of Hudibras, the mock-heroic poem of Butler, published in 1663—78 ; Hudibras নামক কৃত্রিম বীররসাত্মক কাব্যের ছন্দঃ বা রচনা-পদ্ধতির অনুকারী।

hue (hū), *n.* **1.** Colour ; tint ; রঙ্গ, বর্ণ, রাগ ; বর্ণের আভা। **2.** A compound colour in which one of the primaries predominates ; যে মিশ্রবর্ণে কোন এক মূল বর্ণের আভা বিশেষভাবে পরিস্ফুট হয়। **Hued,** *adj.* Having a hue ; as, bright *hued* ; রঞ্জিত।

hue (hū), *n.* A shouting ; a clamour (obs. except in *hue and cry*) ; গণ্ডগোল ; (অপ্রঃ) কোলাহল। **Hue and cry**—A clamour of pursuit or assault ; an outcry ; আক্রমণ বা অনুসরণের জন্য চীৎকার ; হৈ চৈ, চীৎকার। A written proclamation for the capture of a criminal ; অপরাধী ব্যক্তিকে ধৃত করণার্থ ঘোষণা পত্র। (*Formerly*) An official gazette publishing information as to crimes and criminals ; পূর্ব্বে যে সরকারী পত্রিকায় অপরাধ বা অপরাধি-সম্বন্ধে জ্ঞাতব্য বিবরণ প্রকাশিত হইত।

hŭff, *v. t.* & *i.* **1.** To bully ; to chide or treat with insolence ; তর্জ্জন গর্জ্জন করা, শাসান ; তিরস্কার করা, উদ্ধতভাবে ব্যবহার করা। **2.** To offend ; মনঃক্ষুণ্ণ করা। ***Verb i.*** To take offence ; দোষ নেওয়া। **2.** (*Obs.*) To bluster ; (অপ্রঃ) তর্জ্জন গর্জ্জন করা। **3.** (*Obs.*) To swell up ; (অপ্রঃ) ফুলিয়া উঠা।

hŭff, *n.* A fit of anger or petulance ; "Left the place in a *huff*" ; রাগ, রোষ, মন্যু, খিট্‌মিটেমি। **Huff'-i-ly, Huff'-ish-ly,** *advs.* **Huff'-i-ness, Huff'-ish-ness,** *ns.* **Huff'-ish, Huff'-y,** *adjs.* **In a huff**—রাগের মাথায়। **To take huff**—To take offence ; দোষ গ্রহণ করা, মনঃক্ষুণ্ণ হওয়া।

hŭg, *v. t.* & *n.* **1.** To embrace closely and fondly ; "And *hugged* me in his arms" ; নিবিড় আলিঙ্গন করা, বুকে চাপিয়া ধরা, গাঢ় আলিঙ্গন পাশে বদ্ধ করা, প্রেমালিঙ্গন করা। **2.** To exhibit fondness for a person ; কাহারও প্রতি অনুরাগ বা আদর প্রদর্শন করা। **3.** To cling to ; to cherish ; as, to *hug* a prejudice etc. ; লাগিয়া থাকা ; পোষণ করা। **4.** (Of a bear) To squeeze between the forelegs as a man etc. ; (ভল্লুকের পক্ষে) সম্মুখের দুই পা দ্বারা ধরিয়া চাপ দেওয়া। **5.** (*Naut.*) To keep close to ; as, to *hug* the land ; (নৌ-বিদ্যা) নিকটে থাকা, কাছে কাছে থাকা। ***Noun.*** A close embrace or clasp ; a grip in wrestling ; নিবিড় আলিঙ্গন, গাঢ় আলিঙ্গন, কণ্ঠাশ্লেষ ; এক প্রকার কুস্তির পেঁচ। **To hug one's self (on, for, etc.)**—To congratulate one's self (on etc.) ; to chuckle with satisfaction ; অভিনন্দিত করা ; মনের আনন্দে মুখ টিপিয়া হাসা। **To hug the shore**—See HUG *v. t.* 5.

hūge *adj.* Very large ; of immense size ; enormous ; as, a *huge* mountain ; great (of immaterial things) ; as, a *huge* difference ; প্রকাণ্ড, বিশাল, বিরাট, মহান্, বিপুল ; প্রকাণ্ডকায়, অতিকায়, বিশালাকৃতি ; মহাপ্রমাণ ; মহা। **Huge'-ly,** *adv.* Enormously ; very much ; সুবিশালভাবে ; অতিশয়, অত্যন্ত। **Huge'-ness,** *n.*

hūge'-ous (-ŭs), *adj.* (*Usu. humourous*) Huge ; (কৌতুকচ্ছলে) প্রকাণ্ড।

hŭg'-gêr–mŭg'-gêr, *n., adj. adv., v. t.* & *i.* Secrecy ; ঢাক ঢাক গুড় গুড়। ***Adj.*** **1.** Secret ; গোপনীয়। **2.** Confused ; disorderly ; as *hugger-mugger* doings ; বিশৃঙ্খল ; এলোমেলো। ***Adv.*** **1.** Confusedly ; এলোমেলোভাবে। **2.** In secret ; চুপ্‌ সাড়ে, ঢাক ঢাক গুড় গুড় ভাবে, চুপে চাপে। ***Verb t.*** To conceal ; to hush up ; গোপন করা ; চাপা দেওয়া। ***Verb i.*** To proceed in secret ; চুপি চুপি অগ্রসর হওয়া।

hŭg'-gêr-ÿ, *n.* The practice of courting an attorney etc. for employment ; এটর্ণি প্রভৃতিকে নিযুক্ত করার জন্য খোসামুদ করণ।

Hū'-gue-nŏt (-gĕ-), *n.* (*Hist.*) A French protestant of the 16th and 17th centuries ; (ইতিহাস) ষোড়শ ও সপ্তদশ শতাব্দীর ফরাসী প্রোটেষ্টেণ্ট বা নব্যতান্ত্রিক খৃষ্টীয়ান। [১৫৭২ খৃঃ অব্দে ফরাসীরাজ নবম চার্লসের আদেশে এই সম্প্রদায়ের সমস্ত নরনারী নিহত হয়। এই

লোমহর্ষণ হত্যাকাণ্ড ইতিহাসে Massacre of St. Bartholomew নামে প্রসিদ্ধ।]

hŭlk, *n.* **1.** The body of an old vessel ; পুরাতন জাহাজের খোল। **2.** A heavy unwieldy ship ; বৃহৎ গুরুভার জাহাজ। **3.** (*Fig.*) A big unwieldy fellow; a bulky mass (of anything) ; (লক্ষণায়) বৃহৎকায় ব্যক্তি ; কদাকার এবং প্রকাণ্ড স্তূপ।

hŭlk'-ing, *adj.* Bulky ; clumsy ; প্রকাণ্ড ; কদাকার।

hŭll, *n.* & *v. t.* **1.** The husk or outer covering esp. of a fruit, pease, bean, etc. ; খোসা, তুষ। **2.** (*Fig.*) A covering ; (লক্ষণায়) ঢাক্‌নি। ***Verb t.*** To stirp the hull off ; খোসা ছাড়ান।

hŭll, *n.* & *v. t.* The frame or body of a vessel ; জাহাজের খোল। ***Verb t.*** To pierce the hull of (a ship) with a cannon ball ; কামানের গোলা দ্বারা জাহাজের খোল ভেদ করা। **Hull down**—এত দূরে যে জাহাজের খোল অদৃশ্য।

hŭl-lă-bă-lōō', *n.* An uproar ; চীৎকার, হল্লা, হৈ হৈ, রৈ রৈ শব্দ।

hŭl'-lō, –loa' (-lö), *interj.* An expression calling attention ; ঐ, ওহে।

hŭm, *v. i.* & *t.* **1.** To make buzzing sound as a bee or spinning top etc. ; গুঞ্জন করা, গুণ্ গুণ্ করা, ভন্ ভন্ করা। **2.** To make a low inarticulate vocal sound esp. from hesitation etc. ; এঁ, ওঁ, তা করা, আম্‌তা আম্‌তা করা। **3.** To sing with closed lips ; গুণ্ গুণ্ স্বরে গান করা। **4.** (*Colloq.*) To be very active ; to be all astir ; as, to make things *hum* : (চলিত ভাষায়) চটপটে হওয়া; উঠিয়া পড়িয়া লাগা। ***Verb t.*** To sing or utter with closed lips ; as, to *hum* a tune ; গুণ্ গুণ্ স্বরে গান করা বা বলা। **To hum and haw**—To hesitate in speaking ; কথা বলিতে বলিতে এঁ, ওঁ, তা করা, আম্‌তা আম্‌তা করা। **To make things hum**—See HUM *v. i.* 4.

hŭm, *n.* **1.** The noise of bees etc. ; গুঞ্জন, গুণ্ গুণ্ শব্দ, ভন্ ভন্। **2.** Any inarticulate droning sound ; as, the *hum* of industry ; অব্যক্ত ধ্বনি। **3.** A humming sound of hesitation, applause or surprise ; এঁ, ওঁ, তা, আম্‌তা আম্‌তা, বাঃ বাঃ, হুঁ।

hŭm, *n.* (*Slang*) A sham ; a hoax ; (ইতর ভাষায়) ফাঁকি ; ধোঁকা।

hŭm, *interj.* A sound with a pause implying doubt, dissent, etc. ; হুঁ, হুম্।

hü'-măn, *adj.* & *n.* Belonging, or relating, to man or mankind ; having or showing the qualities of a man ; as, a *human* voice : he is more or less than *human* ; মানবীয়, মানুষী, মানবত্বসূচক; মানবোচিত গুণসম্পন্ন, মনুষ্যধর্ম্মী, মনুষ্যধর্ম্মক। ***Noun.*** (*Humorous*) A human being ; (কৌতুকচ্ছলে) মানুষ। **–ly,** *adv.* **1.** In a human manner ; from the human point of view ; মানবীয় ভাবে ; মানবত্বের দিক্ হইতে। **2.** With human feelings or kindness ; মানবসুলভ দয়া ও সমবেদনার সহিত।

hü-māne', *adj.* **1.** Kind ; benevolent ; as, *humane* inclinations ; সদয়, দয়ালু, কারুণিক, করুণাত্মক, করুণহৃদয়, সহৃদয় ; হিতজনক, লোকোপকারজনক, হিতকর, কল্যাণজনক। **2.** Refining ; elegant ; as, *humane* studies ; রুচিমার্জ্জক ; সুকুমার। **–ly,** *adv.* **–ness,** *n.* **Humane society**—জলমগ্ন ব্যক্তিগণের উদ্ধারের জন্য সম্প্রদায় বিশেষ, জলোদ্ধারসমিতি।

hü'-măn-ĭsm, *n.* **1.** Human nature or disposition ; মানবপ্রকৃতি, মানবস্বভাব, মানবত্ব। **2.** Devotion to human interests ; মানবীয় ব্যাপারে অনুরাগ। **3.** A system of thought etc. concerned with human (not divine) interests and with the human race (not the individual) ; যে দর্শনশাস্ত্রে কেবল মানবীয় ব্যাপার (ঐশ্বরিক বিষয় নয়) এবং মানবজাতির (ব্যক্তিবিশেষের নয়) স্বার্থ-সম্পর্কে আলোচিত হয়, মানবত্ববাদ (হিঃ কোঃ), মানবীয়বাদ (ঐ)। **4.** Polite learning esp. that of the humanists ; সুকুমার বিদ্যা।

hü'-măn-ist, *n.* **1.** One who studies human nature or human affairs ; যে ব্যক্তি মানবপ্রকৃতি বা মানবীয় ব্যাপার সম্বন্ধে আলোচনা করে, মানবতত্ত্বজ্ঞ। **2.** An advocate of philosophical humanism ; মানবত্ববাদী। **3.** A student of Greek and Roman literature and antiquities ; রোমীয় ও গ্রীক সাহিত্য ও প্রত্নতত্ত্ব অনুশীলনকারী। **–is'-tic,** *adj.*

hü-măn-i-tā'-ri-ăn, *n.* & *adj.* **1.** One who denies the divinity of Christ and believes him to be a mere man ; an advocate of humanism ; যীশুখৃষ্টের দেবত্বে অবিশ্বাসী ব্যক্তি ; মানবত্ববাদী, মনুষ্যৈকবাদী (হিঃ কোঃ)। **2.** A philanthrophist ; বিশ্ব-হিতৈষী, বিশ্ব-প্রেমিক। ***Adj.*** **1.** Holding, or pertaining to, the views of the humanitarians ; মানবত্ববাদ সম্বন্ধীয়, মানবত্ববাদী। **2.** Benevolent ; লোকহিতৈষী, পরহিতব্রত, লোকোপকারজনক। **–ism,** *n.* The system or principles of the humanitarians ; মানবত্ববাদ (হিঃ কোঃ), মানবীয়বাদ (ঐ)।

hü-măn'-i-tȳ, **1.** The human nature ; মানবপ্রকৃতি, মানবধর্ম্ম, মানবস্বভাব, মানবতা, মানবিকতা। **2.** (*Pl.*) Human characteristics and attributes ; মানবের বিশেষত্ব বা মানবীয় গুণরাজি, মনুষ্যত্ব (হিঃ কোঃ)। **3.** The human race ; মানবজাতি, বিশ্বমানব (রবীঃ), মহামানব (ঐ)। **4.** Benevolence ; tenderness ; লোকহিত, বিশ্বপ্রেম, মানবপ্রেম, জনদয়া, লোকদয়া, আনৃশংস্য ; কোমলতা। **5.** (*Pl.*) Benevolent acts ; হিতজনক কার্য্য। **6.** (*Pl.*, with *the*) The branch of polite learning, esp. the Latin and Greek classics ; সুকুমার বিদ্যা, বিশেষতঃ প্রাচীন গ্রীক ও রোমের সাহিত্য ও প্রত্নতত্ত্ব। **The humanities**—গ্রীক ও ল্যাটিন সাহিত্য, সুকুমার সাহিত্য (রচনা, কবিতা, উপন্যাস, অলঙ্কারশাস্ত্র প্রভৃতি) ; (স্কটলণ্ডে) ল্যাটিন সাহিত্য। **The Religion of Humanity** — যে ধর্ম্ম সর্ব্বপ্রকার অতীন্দ্রিয় ব্যাপার অগ্রাহ্য করিয়া প্রধানতঃ মানব জাতির কল্যাণ বৃদ্ধির চেষ্টায় ব্যাপৃত থাকে, মানবত্ব ধর্ম্ম। ফরাসী দার্শনিক Augustus Comte এই ধর্ম্মের প্রবর্ত্তক।

hū'-măn-īze, *v. t.* & *i.* **1.** To render human ; to give a human character to ; মানবত্ব প্রদান করা ; মানব-প্রকৃতিবিশিষ্ট করা, মানবধর্ম্মাক্রান্ত করা। **2.** To render humane or kind ; দয়াবান করা, কোমলহৃদয় করা, দয়ার্দ্র করা। ***Verb i.*** To become human ; to become civilized ; মানবত্ব প্রাপ্ত হওয়া ; সভ্যতা প্রাপ্ত হওয়া। **–i-za'-tion,** *n.*

hū'-măn-kīnd, *n.* Mankind ; মানবজাতি, বিশ্বমানব।

hŭm'-ble (-bl), *adj.* & *v. t.* **1.** Thinking lowly of one's self ; not proud ; modest ; "Wisdom is *humble* that he knows no more" ; বিনম্র, নিরভিমান ; বিনীত ; সবিনয়, বিনয়সম্পন্ন। **2.** Low ; not magnificent ; as, a *humble* cottage ; দীন ; সামান্য, ক্ষুদ্র। ***Verb t.*** **1.** To bring low ; to abase ; to humiliate ; as, to *humble* a marshal ; অবমানিত করা ; হীন করা ; অবনত করা, হৃতগর্ব্ব করা। **2.** To make humble, modest or submissive, (*often reflexively*) ; as, *humble* yourselves under the mighty hand of God ; বিনম্র করা, বিনীত করা, বিনয়নম্র করা। **–bly,** *adv.* Lowly ; modestly ; submissively ; নতভাবে ; বিনীতভাবে, বিনম্রভাবে, বিনয়নম্রভাবে ; অনুগতভাবে। **–ness,** *n.* **Humble-plant**—এক-প্রকার লজ্জাবতী লতা। **To eat humble pie**—See under EAT. **Your humble servant**—(Used formally esp. in subscribing letters) ; আপনার বিনয়াবনত ভৃত্য, আপনার অনুগত ভৃত্য।

Male humble bee.

hŭm'-ble-bee (-bl-bē), *n.* The bumble bee ; ভোমরা, ভ্রমর, ভৃঙ্গ।

hŭm'-bŭg, *n., v.t.* & *i.* **1.** A fraud ; sham ; "A mere catchpenny *humbug*" ; জুয়াচুরি ; ফাঁকি, ধোঁকা। **2.** Pretence ; deception ; ছলনা ; প্রতারণা। **3.** An impostor ; প্রতারক, জুয়োচোর। **4.** (Used *interjectionally*) Nonsense ; পাগল আর কি। ***Verb t.*** To deceive ; to hoax ; প্রতারণা করা ; ধোঁকা দেওয়া। ***Verb i.*** To be, or behave, like a humbug ; প্রতারকের মত হওয়া, প্রতারকের মত আচরণ করা। **–ger-y,** *n.*

hŭm'-drŭm, *adj., n.* & *v. i.* Monotonous ; commonplace ; "A *humdrum* evening" ; একঘেয়ে, একটানা, একসুরা ; নীরস, নূতনত্বহীন। ***Noun.*** Monotony ; dullness ; as, dissatisfied with *humdrum* ; একঘেয়ে ভাব ; নীরসতা। ***Verb i.*** To proceed in a humdrum way ; একঘেয়েভাবে চলা বা বলিয়া যাওয়া। **–ness,** *n.*

hū'-mêr-ăl, *adj.* Of, or relating to, the humerus or shoulder ; প্রগণ্ডাস্থি-সম্বন্ধীয়।

hū'-mêr-ŭs, *n.* The bone of the upper part of the arm ; বাহুর বৃহত্তর অস্থি, প্রগণ্ডাস্থি (সাঃ পঃ)।

hū'-mid, *adj.* Moist ; damp ; আর্দ্র, ভিজা, সিক্ত ; স্যাঁতস্যেঁতে। **–mid'-i-fy,** *v. t.* **–mid'-i-ty,** *n.* Moisture ; dampness ; রস ; আর্দ্রতা।

hū-mil'-i-āte, *v. t.* To lower the dignity or self-respect of ; to humble ; to mortify ; as, to *humiliate* slaves ; অবনত করা, হৃতগর্ব্ব করা ; নত করা ; হীন করা, মর্যাদা হানি করা, পরাভব করা। **–at-ing,** *adj.* Lowering one's dignity or self-respect ; abasing ; mortifying ; অপমানজনক, মর্য্যাদাহানিকর ; হীনতাজনক ; পরাভবজনক। **–a'-tion,** *n.* The act of humiliating ; the state of being humiliated ; অবমাননা ; পরাভব, মর্য্যাদাহানি, নিগ্রহ।

hū'-mil'-i-tȳ, *n.* **1.** The quality of being humble ; meekness ; বিনম্রতা, নিরভিমানিতা ; বিনয়-নতি, বশ্যতা, নম্রতা, নিরহঙ্কারতা, দীনতা। **2.** An act of submission ; "With these *humilities* they satisfied the young king" ; অনুগত ব্যক্তির কার্য্য। **3.** Humble condition ; হীনাবস্থা।

hŭm'-ming (ing), *adj.* **1.** Murmuring ; buzzing ; গুঞ্জনরত ; গুঞ্জৎ। **2.** (*Colloq.*) Vigorous ; energetic ; as, a *humming* knock on the head ; (চলতি ভাষায়) সতেজ ; সজোর। **Humming-bird** — পক্ষী বিশেষ—যাহার পক্ষবিধূননে একপ্রকার গুঞ্জনধ্বনি উৎপন্ন হয়। **Humming top**—যে লাটিম ভন্ ভন্ করিয়া ঘুরে।

hŭm'-mŏck, *n.* A hillock ; a rising ground, esp. in a swamp etc. ; ক্ষুদ্র পাহাড় ; ঢিবি। **–y,** *adj.*

hū'-mor-ăl (-mêr), *adj.* Pertaining to the humour of the body ; as, a *humoral* fever ; শরীরস্থ রসাদি সম্বন্ধীয়, কফপিত্তাত্মক, কফপিত্তাদিজ। **–ism,** *n.* Same as HUMORAL PATHOLOGY. **–ist,** *n.* **–is'-tic,** *adj.* **Humoral pathology**—শরীরস্থ তরল পদার্থের বিকৃতি সকল রোগের কারণ—এই মত।

hū'-mor-ist (-mêr), *n.* A comical person ; a wag ; a humorous talker, actor or writer ; পরিহাসরসিক ব্যক্তি ; ফচকে লোক, ইয়ার ; হাস্যরসিক বক্তা, লেখক, বা অভিনেতা। **–is-tic,** *adj.*

hū'-mor-ous (-mêr-ŭs), *adj.* Full of humour ; exciting laughter ;

facetious ; funny ; রসিকতাপূর্ণ, সরস ; হাস্যোদ্দীপক ; রঙ্গরসময়, রঙ্গপূর্ণ ; কৌতুকপূর্ণ, কৌতুকপ্রিয়। **—ly,** *adv.* **—ness,** *n.*

hŭ′-mour (-mêr), *n.* **1.** The state of mind ; temper ; mood ; as, to be in a bad *humour* ; মনের গতি ; মেজাজ, প্রকৃতি ; ভাব। **2.** Inclination ; "In the *humour* for fighting" ; caprice ; whim ; "To please a *humour*" ; আসক্তি ; খেয়াল, মর্জ্জি ; সখ। **3.** Facetiousness ; comicality ; রসিকতা, রঙ্গপ্রিয়তা ; কৌতুকপ্রিয়তা। **4.** The faculty of perceiving the ludicrous : droll imagination ; রসিকতাবোধ ; আজব কল্পনা। **5.** (*Hist.*) One of the cardinal humours ; বায়ু, পিত্ত বা শ্লেষ্মা, দোষ (ঠাকুর) [প্রাচীন ইয়ুরোপীয় শারীর বিজ্ঞানানুসারে দোষ চারিটী—যথা রক্ত, শ্লেষ্মা, পীত পিত্ত (choler) এবং কৃষ্ণ পিত্ত (melancholy or black bile)। ভারতীয় বৈদ্যগ্রন্থ মতে দোষ তিনটী—বায়ু, পিত্ত, শ্লেষ্মা।] **6.** A morbid animal fluid ; শরীরস্থ দূষিত রস, রস (সাঃ পঃ)। **—less,** *adj.* **—moured,** *adj.* **Aqueous** or **vitreous humour**—চক্ষুর স্বচ্ছ তরল অংশ। **Bad** or **ill humours**—বদ্ মেজাজ। **Cardinal humours**—See HUMOUR *n.* 5. **Good-humour** — Good temper ; খোস মেজাজ। **Out of humour**—Displeased ; মেজাজ ভাল নয়।

hŭ′-mour (-mêr), *v. t.* **1.** To soothe by compliance ; to gratify ; to indulge ; as, to *humour* a person, taste or temper ; মনোরঞ্জন করা, মন যোগান ; তুষ্ট করা, খুসী করা ; ছন্দানুবর্ত্তন করা। **2.** To adapt oneself to ; as, an actor *humours* his part ; উপযোগী করা।

hŭ′-mour-some (-mêr-sŭm), *adj.* Capricious ; petulant ; চঞ্চলচিত্ত ; খিট্‌খিটে। **—ness,** *n.*

hŭmp, *n.* & *v. t.* **1.** A protuberance esp. that caused by a crooked back ; as, the *hump* of a camel ; কুঁজ, ককুদ, ঝুঁট, অংসকূট। **2.** A mound of earth etc. ; মাটীর ঢিবি। **3.** (*Slang*) A fit of depression ; as, it gives me the *hump* ; (ইতরভাষায়) স্ফূর্ত্তিহীনতা, অবসাদ। ***Verb t.*** **1.** To make humped or humpshaped ; কুব্জ করা। **2.** To annoy ; to depress ; বিরক্ত করা ; দমাইয়া দেওয়া। **Humped,** *adj.* **Hump′-less, Hump′-y,** *adjs.* **Hump-back**—A back with a hump ; কুব্জ। A person with a hump-back ; কুব্জপৃষ্ঠ ব্যক্তি। **Hump-backed**—কুব্জ, ন্যুব্জ-দেহ।

hŭmph, *interj.* & *v. t.* An expression of doubt or dissatisfaction ; হুঁ, হুম্। ***Verb t.*** To utter this ; হুঁ করা।

hŭmp′-tў-dŭmp′-tў, *n.* **1.** A short dumpy person ; হৃষ্টপুষ্ট এবং খর্ব্বকায় ব্যক্তি। **2.** A person or thing that once overthrown or shattered cannot be restored (in allusion to *Humpty-dumpty*, meaning an egg in a well-known nursery rhyme) ; যে জিনিষ বা ব্যক্তি একবার হাতছাড়া বা নষ্ট হইলে আর ফিরিয়া পাইবার যো থাকে না।

hū′-mŭs, *n.* A vegetable mould ; সারমাটী (সাঃ পঃ)।

Hŭn, *n.* **1.** One of a powerful nomad race of Asia who invaded and ravaged Europe in the 4th and 5th centuries ; এশিয়া দেশীয় যাযাবর জাতি বিশেষ — ইহারা চতুর্থ ও পঞ্চম শতাব্দিতে ইয়ুরোপ আক্রমণ ও বিধ্বস্ত করিয়াছিল, হূণ (মঃ ভাঃ)। **2.** (*Derisively*) The Germans ; (অবজ্ঞাচ্ছলে) জার্ম্মাণ।

hunch (hŭnsh), *n.* **1.** A hump ; কুঁজ। **2.** A lump ; a thick piece ; as, a *hunch* of bread ; তাল, পিণ্ড ; পুরু টুকরা। **Hunch-back(ed)**—Hump-back(ed) ; কুব্জ, কুব্জক।

hunch (hŭnsh), *v. t.* **1.** To bend into a hump, (with *up, out*) ; to bend convexly ; কুব্জ করা ; ন্যুব্জ করা। **2.** (*Dial.*) To push or thrust ; "(The dog) *hunching* his person heavily against her" ; (উপভাষায়) ঠেলা দেওয়া, ধাক্কা দেওয়া।

hŭn′-drĕd, *n.* & *adj.* **1.** The number of ten times ten ; শত, একশ। **2.** A large number ; (also *hundred and one*) বৃহৎ সংখ্যা। **3.** A hundred pounds (of money) ; ১০০ এক শত পাউণ্ড মুদ্রা। **4.** (*Hist.*) A division of a country in England, supposed originally to contain 100 families ; (ইতিহাস) ইংলণ্ডের পরগণা। ***Adj.*** Ten times ten ; শত, শত সংখ্যক। **—fold,** *n.* A hundred times as much or as many ; শতগুণিত। **—dredth,** *adj.* & *n.* **1.** Next in order to the ninety-ninth ; শততম। **2.** Forming one of a hundred equal parts of anything ; শতাংশিত। (*Noun.*) **1.** One of a hundred equal parts ; শতাংশের এক অংশ। **2.** That coming next after the ninety-ninth ; শততম বস্তু বা ব্যক্তি। **Chiltern hundreds**—See under CHILTERN HUNDREDS. **Great** or **long hundred**—120 ; ১২০। **Hundredweight**—112 lbs avoirdupois, (*abbr. cwt.*) ; ১১২ পাউণ্ড। **Hundred and one**—See HUNDRED *n.* 2. **Not a hundred miles off** or **from**—Here ; very near ; এই খানে ; অতি নিকটে।

hŭng, *p. t.* & *p. p.* of HANG.

hun′-gêr (hŭng-), *n.* **1.** An uneasy sensation occasioned by the want of food ; ক্ষুধা, বুভুক্ষা, জঠরজ্বালা। **2.** (*Fig.*) Strong desire *for* or *after* anything ; as, a *hunger for* gold ; তীব্র লালসা, প্রবল স্পৃহা। **Hunger is the best sauce**—ক্ষুধা পেলে পাটকিলে কামড়।

hun′-gêr (hŭng-), *v. i.* & *t.* **1.** To feel hunger ; ক্ষুধা বোধ করা, ক্ষিধে পাওয়া। **2.** To long (*for* and *after*) ; as, to *hunger after* righteousness ; প্রবল আকাঙ্ক্ষা হওয়া, প্রবল স্পৃহা হওয়া। ***Verb t.*** To famish ; to starve (a man etc. into submission *out of* a place etc.) ; দুর্ভিক্ষপীড়িত করা, অনশনক্লিষ্ট করা ; অনাহারে রাখা।

hŭn'-grȳ (hŭng-), *adj.* **1.** Feeling hunger ; ক্ষুধিত, ক্ষুধার্ত্ত, ক্ষুধাতুর, বুভুক্ষিত, ক্ষুৎপীড়িত, ক্ষুধান্বিত, ক্ষুধাবিষ্ট, ক্ষুধাকুল, ক্ষুধাগ্রস্ত, ক্ষুধাক্রান্ত। **2.** (*Fig.*) Having an eager desire ; greedy ; "*Hungry* for intellectual food" ; প্রবলস্পৃহান্বিত ; লুব্ধ, লোলুপ। **3.** Indicating hunger ; lean ; as, a *hungry* look ; ক্ষুধাসূচক ; কৃশ, কাহিল। **4.** Causing or inducing hunger ; as, a *hungry* air ; ক্ষুধাজনক, ক্ষুধাবর্দ্ধক। **5.** Poor ; unfertile ; as, a *hungry* soil ; উৎপাদিকাশক্তি হীন ; অনুর্ব্বর। **–grily,** *adv.* **–griness,** *n.*

hunk (hŭngk), *n.* A large lump or piece ; as, a *hunk* of bread ; a hunch ; বৃহৎখণ্ড ; কুঁজ, ককুদ।

hunks (hŭngks), *n.* A miser ; কৃপণ।

hŭnt, *v. i., t. & n.* **1.** To pursue or chase wild animals or game ; as, to *hunt* for venison ; শিকার করা, মৃগয়া করা। **2.** To seek, (with *for* and *after*) ; he after honour *hunts*, I after love; খুঁজা, অন্বেষণ করা। ***Verb t.*** **1.** To pursue for prey or sport ; as, to *hunt* deer ; শিকারের জন্য অনুসরণ করা। **2.** To search after, (with *up*) ; as, to *hunt up* the facts ; to find out by seeking ; as, to *hunt out* evidences ; অনুসন্ধান করা ; অনুসন্ধান করিয়া বাহির করা। **3.** To pursue animals over ; as, he *hunts* the woods ; জন্তুর অনুসরণ করা। **4.** To drive ; to chase, (with *down, from, away*) ; as, to *hunt down* a criminal ; তাড়ান ; অনুসরণ করা, পশ্চাদ্ধাবিত হওয়া। **5.** To use or manage in the chase; as, he *hunts* a pack of hounds ; শিকারে ব্যবহার করা বা আয়ত্তে রাখা। ***Noun.*** **1.** Act of chasing wild animals or game ; search ; as, the *hunt* is up ; মৃগয়া, শিকার ; অন্বেষণ। **2.** A hunting district ; মৃগয়া ভূমি। **3.** A number of persons hunting with hounds ; কুকুর লইয়া শিকার করে এরূপ শিকারীর দল। **To hunt down**—To pursue or search for until killed, captured or found ; না ধরা, না পাওয়া, বা না বিনাশ করা পর্য্যন্ত অনুসরণ করা। **To hunt out**—To find out by search ; খুঁজিয়া বাহির করা, তল্লাস করিয়া পাওয়া। **To hunt up**—To search for ; অন্বেষণ করা।

hŭnt'-êr, *n.* **1.** One who hunts ; শিকারী, ব্যাধ, লুব্ধক, মৃগয়াকারী। **2.** A horse used in hunting ; মৃগয়ায় ব্যবহৃত অশ্ব। **3.** A seeker after anything ; as, a fortune-*hunter* ; অন্বেষণকারী, অন্বেষী। **4.** A hunting watch whose face is protected with a metal case ; ধাতুর ঢাকনিওয়ালা টেঁকঘড়ি [এইরূপ ধাতুর ঢাকনির মধ্যদেশে গোলাকৃতি কাচখণ্ড থাকিলে তাহাকে *half-hunter* কহে]।

hŭnt'-ing, *n.* The pursuit or chase of wild game ; মৃগয়া, শিকার। **Hunting box**—মৃগয়ার জন্য অস্থায়ী আবাস-বাটীকা। **Hunting crop**—মৃগয়া-ক্ষেত্রে ব্যবহৃত ক্ষুদ্র চাবুক। **Hunting ground**—A place or region for hunting, (often *fig.*) ; as, the library was his favourite *hunting ground* ; মৃগয়াস্থলী, শিকারের জায়গা, মৃগয়াভূমি, মৃগয়াক্ষেত্র [প্রায়শঃ লক্ষণায় ব্যবহৃত হয়]। **Hunting horn**—শিকারীর শিঙ্গা। **Hunting song**—মৃগয়াসঙ্গীত, শিকারের গান। **Hunting tide**—মৃগয়াকাল। **Happy-hunting ground(s)**—The paradise of the Red Indians ; the future state ; a good place for hunting (*often fig.*) ; লাল আমেরিকানগণের স্বর্গ ; পরকাল ; উত্তম মৃগয়ার স্থান (প্রায়শঃ লক্ষণায়)।

hŭnts'-măn, *n.* **1.** A hunter ; মৃগয়াজীবী, শিকারী। **2.** A servant in charge of the hunting hounds ; শিকারী কুকুরের তত্ত্বাবধানকারী ভৃত্য।

hur'-dle (hêr-dl), *n. & v. t.* **1.** A movable rectangular frame of twigs or sticks interlaced for temporary fence etc ; অস্থায়ী বেড়ার জন্য জাফরি। **2.** A wooden barrier to be jumped over in a hurdle race ; লাফ দিয়া পার হইবার জন্য কাঠের বেড়া। **3.** (*Hist.*) A frame on which criminals were drawn to the place of execution ; (ইতিহাস) একপ্রকার ঠাট বা কাঠাম,—যাহার উপর বসাইয়া পূর্ব্বে অপরাধীদিগকে বধ্যভূমিতে নেওয়া হইত। ***Verb t.*** To enclose with hurdles ; জাফরি দ্বারা বেড়া দেওয়া। **–dler,** *n.* One who makes hurdles or runs in a hurdle race ; যে ব্যক্তি কাঠের জাফরির বেড়া দেয় অথবা দৌড়ে লাফ দিয়া জাফরির বেড়া ডিঙ্গাইয়া যায়। **Hurdle-race**—একপ্রকার দৌড়—যাহাতে (মনুষ্য কিম্বা অশ্বকে) জাফরির বেড়া উল্লঙ্ঘন করিতে হয়।

Hurdy-gurdy.

hur'-dy-gur-dy (hêr-dî-gêr-dî), *n.* A stringed instrument of music ; তন্ত্রী-বিশিষ্ট বাদ্যযন্ত্র বিশেষ।

hurl (hêrl), *v. t. & n.* **1.** To send whirling through the air ; to throw with violence ; (*lit. & fig.*) ; as, to *hurl* a stone or lance : "Raised to power and *hurled* from it" ; নিক্ষেপ করা, ক্ষেপণ করা ; সবলে নিক্ষেপ করা, ছোড়া। **2.** To emit or utter with vehemence ; as, to *hurl* an invective ; to dart, as a ray, glance, etc. ; প্রবল বেগে নির্গত করা, ক্ষেপণ করা ; হানা, নির্গত

করা। ***Noun.*** Act of hurling ; a violent throw ; ক্ষেপণ, ক্ষেপ ; সবেগে নিক্ষেপ।

hurl'-ey (hêrl-ĭ), *n.* The game of hockey or the stick used in it ; হকি খেলা ; হকি খেলার যষ্টি।

hurl'-y̆ (hêrl-), *n.* (*Archaic*) Noise ; confusion ; গোলমাল ; গোলযোগ।

hurl'-y—burl'-y (hêrl-ĭ-bêrl-ĭ), *n.* Tumult ; commotion ; গোলমাল, হড়বড়ি, হল্লা ; তুমুল বিভ্রাট।

hur-rah' (hû-râ), **—ray'** (-rā), *interj., n. & v. i.* An exclamation of joy or approbation ; উল্লাস বা প্রশংসাসূচক ধ্বনি, জয় ! জয় ! ***Noun.*** A shout of joy sounding like this ; a cheer ; আনন্দ-ধ্বনি ; জয়ধ্বনি। ***Verb i.*** To utter hurrahs ; জয়ধ্বনি করা।

hŭr'-ri-cāne (-ĭ-), *n.* A storm with extremely violent wind ; a tempest (*lit. & fig.*) ; as, a *hurricane* of cheers or of shells ; ঝঞ্ঝা, প্রভঞ্জন ; প্রবল ঝটিকা, চণ্ডবাত, ঝঞ্ঝানিল। **Hurricane-bird**—এক প্রকার পক্ষী। **Hurricane-deck**—যাত্রী জাহাজের উপরের হাল্‌কা পাটাতন। **Hurricane-lamp**—বাত্যারোধক দীপ।

hŭr'-ry̆ (-ĭ), *n.* **1.** Immoderate or undue haste ; eagerness ; as, to be in a *hurry* ; (with *no* or *any*) need for haste ; "Is there any *hurry* ?" ; তাড়াতাড়ি, সত্বরতা, তাড়াহুড়া, ছুটাছুটি ; ব্যস্ত-সমস্তভাব, শশব্যস্তভাব, সম্ভ্রম (Sans.)। **2.** (*Rare*) Hasty motion ; rush ; "*Hurry* of hoofs in a village street" ; (ক্বচিদ্ ব্যবহৃত) ক্ষিপ্রগতি ; হুড়মুড়। **In a hurry**—In haste or urgent haste ; তাড়াতাড়ি করিয়া, শশব্যস্তভাবে, অস্তেব্যস্তে, ব্যস্তসমস্ত ভাবে। **To be in no hurry**—(*Colloq.*) To have plenty of time ; (চলিত ভাষায়) বিশেষ তাড়াতাড়ি না থাকা।

hŭr'-ry (-ĭ), *v. t. & i.* **1.** To carry or drive hastily ; "My master was *hurried* away to a prison" ; তাড়াতাড়ি নেওয়া, তাড়াতাড়ি চালান। **2.** To urge impetuously to some activity ; প্রচণ্ডভাবে তাড়িত করা। **3.** To hasten unduly ; "You need not *hurry* yourself" ; তাড়াহুড়া করা। ***Verb i.*** To move or act with undue haste ; as, let us *hurry* ; তাড়াতাড়ি করা, তাড়াতাড়ি চলা, ব্যস্তসমস্ত ভাবে গমন করা। **—ried-ly,** *adv.* In a hurried manner ; তাড়াতাড়ি, সত্বর। **—ried-ness,** *n.* **To hurry up**—To make haste ; তাড়াতাড়ি করা।

hur'-ry-skur-ry (hŭr-i-skŭr-i), *adv., adj., n. & v.i.* (In) disorderly haste ; তাড়াহুড়া, অস্তব্যস্ত, ব্যস্ত-সমস্ত, দৌড়াদৌড়ি ধূমধাম। ***Verb i.*** To proceed in a hurry-skurry way ; ব্যস্তসমস্তভাবে অগ্রসর হওয়া।

hurst (hêrst), *n.* **1.** A wooded eminence or hillock ; a wood ; ক্ষুদ্রশৈল ; বন। **2.** A sand bank in a sea etc. ; সমুদ্র প্রভৃতির বালুকাতট, কচ্ছ, বালিয়াড়ি।

hurt (hêrt), *n.* **1.** A wound ; a bruise ; আঘাত, ঘা, চোট, জখম ; কালশিরা। **2.** Harm ; damage ; injury ; as, you do me yet but *hurt* ; অনিষ্ট ; ক্ষতি ; অপকার। **Hurt'-ful,** *adj.* Causing hurt ; detrimental ; injurious ; অনিষ্টজনক, অপকারজনক ; হানিকারক ; ক্ষতিজনক। **Hurt'-ful-ly,** *adv.* **Hurt'-ful-ness,** *n.* **Hurt'-less,** *adj.*

hurt (hêrt), *v. t. & i.* **1.** To cause physical injury or pain ; আঘাত করা। **2.** To injure ; to damage ; as, virtue may be assailed but never *hurt* ; অনিষ্ট করা, ক্ষতি করা ; অপকার করা। **3.** To wound the feelings of ; to distress ; as, he was much *hurt* by the insult ; মনে আঘাত দেওয়া, মনে ব্যথা দেওয়া, মনঃপীড়া দেওয়া ; পীড়া দেওয়া, সন্তপ্ত করা। ***Verb i.*** **1.** To be hurtful ; অনিষ্টজনক হওয়া। **2.** (*Colloq.*) To suffer injury or pain ; "Does your hand still *hurt*" ; (চলিত ভাষায়) কষ্ট বা ব্যথা বোধ করা।

hur'-tle (hêr-tl), *v. t., i. & n.* **1.** To strike or dash against ; ঠোকাঠুকি করান, ঠক্কর লাগান। **2.** To throw or hurl violently ; সজোরে নিক্ষেপ করা, সবলে ক্ষেপণ করা। ***Verb i.*** **1.** (*Archaic*) To dash together with noise ; to clash (*against*) ; (অপ্রঃ) ঠক্কর লাগা। ঠোকাঠুকি লাগা। **2.** To move violently or with a chattering sound ; to rattle ; "Thundering *hurtles* in the heavens" ; ঠক্ ঠক্ শব্দ করিয়া চলা ; ঠক্ ঠক্ করা। ***Noun.*** Act of hurtling ; a clashing sound ; a rattle ; ঠোকাঠুকিকরণ ; ঠক্ ঠক্ শব্দ ; ঠক্কর, ঠোকাঠুকি।

hŭs'-bănd, *n.* **1.** A married man—the correlative of wife ; as, a bad or good *husband* ; স্বামী, পতি, ভর্ত্তা, ভাতার (*colloq.*), উপযন্তা (রঃ)। **2.** (*Archaic*) An economist ; (অপ্রঃ) মিতব্যয়ী। **—hood, —ship,** *ns.* **—like,** *adj.* **Husband's tea**—অতি নিস্তেজ চা। **Ship-husband**—জাহাজ বন্দরে থাকিলে যে নাবিক জাহাজ ছাড়িয়া তীরে যায় না। **The husband's boat**—যে নৌকা প্রতি শনিবার লণ্ডন নগরী হইতে গ্রীষ্মের কয়েক মাস মারগেটের নিকটবর্ত্তী গৃহস্থদিগকে মারগেটে পৌঁছাইয়া দেয়।

hŭs'-bănd, *v. t.* **1.** To manage with economy ; মিতব্যয়িতার সহিত চালান। **2.** (*Archaic*) To cultivate ; (অপ্রঃ) চাষ করা। **3.** (*Poet.*) To supply with a husband ; পতি দান করা। **4.** (*Rare*) To marry, as a woman ; বিবাহ করা।

hŭs'-bănd-măn, *n.* A farmer ; কৃষক, চাষা, কৃষাণ, কৃষীবল (আঃ বঃ), কৃষিজীবী।

hŭs'-bănd-ry̆, *n.* **1.** Agriculture ; farming ; কৃষিকার্য্য ; কৃষি, কৃষিকর্ম্ম। **2.** Management of the household ; economy ; as, good or bad *husbandry* ; গার্হস্থ্যব্যবস্থা ; গৃহস্থালী। 3. Wise or careful management ; thrift ; সুপরিচালনা, সুব্যবস্থা ; মিতব্যয়।

hŭsh, *n.* Stillness ; silence ; "The *hush* of night ;" নীরবতা, নিস্তব্ধতা ; বিজনতা। **Hush-money**—কোন বিষয় গোপন রাখিবার জন্য যে টাকা দেওয়া হয়, কোন ব্যক্তির মুখ বন্ধ করার জন্য তাহাকে যে ঘুষ দেওয়া হয়।

hŭsh, *v. t., i. & interj.* To silence ; to make quiet ; as, to *hush* the noisy crowd ; মৌন করা, নীরব করা ; নিস্তব্ধ করা, শান্ত করা। ***Verb i.*** To keep silent ; নীরব থাকা, মৌনী থাকা, তুষ্ণীম্ভাব অবলম্বন করা। ***Interj.*** Silence ! be still ! চুপ্ চুপ্ ! আস্তে আস্তে ! **To hush up**—To suppress ; as, *hush up* the affair ; চাপা দেওয়া, চাপিয়া রাখা, গাপ করা।

hŭsh'-ă-bȳ, *interj.* A lullaby used to lull a child ; ছেলেদের ঘুম-পাড়ানো গান।

hŭsk, *n. & v. t.* 1. A dry thin covering of a fruit or seed ; rind ; (*fig.*) worthless outer covering ; তুষ, ছাল ; খোসা, চোকলা ; (লক্ষণায়) অসার বাহ্যাবরণ। 2. A disease of cattle ; গোমহিষাদির রোগ বিশেষ। ***Verb t.*** To remove the husk from ; as, to *husk* Indian corn ; ভানা, কাঁড়া, খোসা ছাড়ান।

hŭsk'-ȳ, *adj.* 1. Pertaining to, full of, or resembling, husk ; তুষ সম্বন্ধীয়, তুষপূর্ণ, তুষযুক্ত, সতুষ, তুষবৎ। 2. Harsh ; hoarse ; as, a *husky* voice ; কর্কশ ; ভাঙ্গা। **Hus'-ki-ly,** *adv.* **Hus'-ki-ness,** *n.*

hŭs-sar' (-âr), *n.* A light armed cavalry soldier (originally a national cavalry soldier of Hungary) ; লঘু অস্ত্রধারী অশ্বারোহী সৈন্য।

hŭs'-sif, *n.* A case for holding needles, thimbles, thread, etc. ; সূচ, সূতা, অঙ্গুস্তানা প্রভৃতি রাখার আধার।

Hŭss'-ite, *n.* A follower of the Bohemian reformer John Huss, flourishing in the 15th century ; বোহেমিয়ার ধর্ম্মসংস্কারক John Huss এর মতাবলম্বী।

hŭs'-sȳ, *n.* 1. A woman of worthless character ; a loose wench ; হীনস্বভাবা নারী ; দুষ্টা নারী, ছেনাল। 2. A pert girl ; প্রগল্ভা বালিকা।

hŭs'-tings, *n.* 1. A platform on which the candidates for Parliament were formerly nominated ; (পূর্ব্বে) যে মঞ্চের উপর পার্লেমেন্টের সভ্যগণ নির্ব্বাচিত হইতেন। 2. The proceedings at an election ; নির্ব্বাচন-কার্য্য। 3. An old court held in the Guildhall of London ; লণ্ডন নগরীর সভাভবনে যে প্রাচীন বিচারালয়ের অধিবেশন হইত।

hŭs'-tle (-l), *v. t., i. & n.* 1. To push rudely ; to jostle ; to thrust roughly ; as, to *hustle* a person out of a room ; সবলে ধাক্কা দেওয়া ; রূঢ় ভাবে ধাক্কা দেওয়া ; ঠেলিয়া বাহির করা। 2. To impel or urge roughly ; as, he was *hustled* into doing it ; রূঢ় ভাবে প্রণোদিত করা বা অগ্রসর করা। ***Verb i.*** 1. To push or crowd ; ঠেলা দেওয়া, ভিড় করা। 2. To push one's way ; ভিড় ঠেলিয়া পথ করা। 3. To move or act with haste ; to hurry ; ছুটাছুটি করা ; তাড়াহুড়া করা। ***Noun.*** Act of hustling ; ঠেলাঠেলি, ধাক্কাধাক্কি।

African huts.

hŭt, *n., v. t. & i.* 1. A small or mean house ; কুটীর, কুঁড়ে ঘর, পর্ণশালা। 2. (*Mil.*) A small temporary dwelling for troops ; (সামরিক শাস্ত্র) সৈন্যদিগের জন্য অস্থায়ী কুটীর। ***Verb t.*** To place in huts ; as, to *hut* troops in winter quarters ; সৈন্যদিগকে অস্থায়ী কুটীরে বাস করিতে দেওয়া। ***Verb i.*** To live in a hut ; কুটীরে বাস করা, কুঁড়ে ঘরে বাস করা।

hŭt'-mĕnt, *n.* Accommodation or lodging in hut ; কুটীরবাস।

hutch (hŭch), *n.* 1. A box or chest in which things are stored ; বাক্স, সিন্দুক। 2. A coop for rabbits etc. ; শশকাদির জন্য বাক্সের আকার খাঁচা। 3. A hut ; a small house ; কুটীর ; কুঁড়ে ঘর। 4. (*Mining*) A jig for washing ore ; a truck used in mining etc. ; (খনির কাজ) খনিজ বিমিশ্র ধাতু ধৌত করার জন্য আধার বিশেষ ; যে বাক্সে করিয়া খনি হইতে কয়লা প্রভৃতি তোলা হয়।

hŭz-zä', *interj., n., v. i. & t.* An exclamation of exultation or applause ; জয় ! জয় ! ***Noun.*** The cry huzza ; a cheer ; হুজ্জা শব্দ ; উল্লসিত ধ্বনি, জয়রব, জয়ধ্বনি। ***Verb i.*** To cry huzza ; জয়ধ্বনি করা। ***Verb t.*** To receive or greet with huzzas ; জয় জয় শব্দে অভ্যর্থনা করা।

hȳ'-ă-cinth, *n.* 1. A bulbous-rooted flowering plant of many varieties with flowers of diverse colours esp. purplish blue ; রজনীগন্ধাকৃতি নানাবর্ণ (বিশেষতঃ, লোহিতাভনীল) সুগন্ধি-পুষ্পপ্রসূ কন্দজ গুল্ম-শ্রেণী বিশেষ। [গ্রীক পুরাণানুসারে সূর্য্যদেবতা Apollo কর্ত্তৃক নিহত Hyacinthus এর রুধির হইতে এই বৃক্ষ জাত হইয়াছিল]। 2. A purplish blue colour; লোহিতাভনীলবর্ণ। **3.** An orange variety of zircon; a gem; একপ্রকার কমলা রঙ্গের গোমেদ মণি; মণি। **—cin'-thine,** *adj.* **1.** Belonging to, or resembling, the hyacinth; উক্তপুষ্পসম্বন্ধীয়, উক্ত পুষ্প সদৃশ। **2.** Curled like hyacinth flower; very beautiful; উক্ত পুষ্পবৎ কুঞ্চিত (কেশ); অতি মনোহর, অতি সুন্দর। **Water hyacinth**—বিলাতীপানা।

Hȳ'-ă-dēs, *n.* (*Pl.*) A cluster of stars near Pleiades কৃত্তিকার নিকটস্থ নক্ষত্রপুঞ্জ, রোহিণী (সাঃ পঃ)।

hȳ-æ'-nă (-ē-), Same as HYENA. ***Hyaena strata*** — নেকড়ে বাঘ (বেলঃ)।

hȳ'-ă-line (-lĭn), *adj.* & *n.* Glass-like; transparent; কাচবৎ; স্বচ্ছ। ***Noun.*** **1.** (*Poet.*) The clear sky, the smooth sea, etc.; (কবিতায়) স্বচ্ছ গগন, নির্ম্মলাকাশ, মসৃণ সাগর প্রভৃতি। **2.** (*Zool.* & *Physiol.*) Hyaline cartilage; (প্রাণিবিদ্যা ও শারীর বিজ্ঞান) বিকাশাবস্থায় কোষস্থ (cell) অর্দ্ধস্বচ্ছ পদার্থ (হঃ চঃ)।

hȳ'-ă-lite, *n.* A colourless variety of opal; একপ্রকার অবর্ণ উপল মণি।

hȳ'-ă-loid (-lo̅yd), *adj.* & *n.* Transparent; glassy; স্বচ্ছ; কাচবৎ। ***Noun.*** (*Anat.*) Hyaloid membrane which is transparent and envelops the vitreous humour of the eye; (শারীরসংস্থান-বিদ্যা) চক্ষুর কাচবৎ পর্দ্দা।

hȳ'-brid, *n.* & *adj.* **1.** An animal or plant produced from two different species; সঙ্কর, দোঁ-আশলা। **2.** A person of mixed nationality; বিভিন্ন জাতীয় স্ত্রী পুরুষের সংসর্গ-জাত সন্তান, জাতি-সঙ্কর। **3.** A word composed of elements from different languages: যে শব্দের বিভিন্ন অংশ বিভিন্ন ভাষা হইতে গৃহীত হইয়াছে, সঙ্করশব্দ। **4.** (*Fig.*) Anything of heterogeneous composition; (লক্ষণায়) মিশ্রবস্তু, বিবিধজাতিক বস্তু। ***Adj.*** **1.** Mongrel; produced from different species; as, a plant of *hybrid* nature; সঙ্কর, বর্ণসঙ্কর; দোঁ-আশলা। **2.** Derived from unlike sources; heterogeneous; মিশ্রজ; বিজাতীয়। **—brid'-i-ty,** *n.* **—ism,** *n.* Cross-breeding; state of being hybrid; সঙ্করোৎপাদন; সাঙ্কর্য্য।

hȳ'-brid-īze (*or* hī-) *v. t.* & *i.* To produce hybrids; to cause to interbreed; সঙ্কর উৎপাদন করা; বিভিন্ন জাতীয় স্ত্রী পুরুষ বা উদ্ভিদের সংযোগে সঙ্কর উৎপাদন করা। ***Verb i.*** To interbreed as an animal or plant; সঙ্কর উৎপাদন হওয়া। **—iz-a-ble,** *adj.* **—i-za'-tion,** *n.* The act of hybridizing; সঙ্করোৎপাদন। **Hybrid-bill** — (পার্লেমেণ্ট) সরকারী এবং বে-সরকারী বিধির সংমিশ্রণাত্মক বিধি, [ঐরূপবিধি যে বৈঠকে আলোচিত হয় তাহার কতক সভ্য পার্লেমেণ্টের প্রাকৃত সভাকর্ত্তৃক (সরকারী বিধির স্থলে) এবং কতক সভ্য নির্ব্বাচনসমিতি কর্ত্তৃক (বে-সরকারী বিধির স্থলে) নির্ব্বাচিত হয়], মিশ্রবিধি।

hȳ'-dă-tid, *n.* (*Pathol.*) A watery cyst or vesicle sometimes found in the animal bodies; (নিদান-শাস্ত্র) শোথাদি রোগে শরীরে অবর্ণ তরল পদার্থ-পূর্ণ যে স্বচ্ছ থলি উৎপন্ন হয়।

Hȳ'-dră, *n.* **1.** (*Gk. myth.*) A serpent with hundred heads which grew again when cut off; (গ্রীক পুরাণ) শতশীর্ষ সর্প বিশেষ—ইহার মস্তক ছিন্ন হইলে পুনরায় তৎস্থানে নূতন মস্তক জাত হইত, শতশীর্ষ নাগ। **2.** (*Fig.*) Any evil; a thing hard to extirpate; অনিষ্টকর বিষয়; যে অনিষ্টকর বিষয়ের মূলোচ্ছেদ করা অসম্ভব, রক্তবীজের বংশ। **3.** A water-serpent; জলবাসী সর্প। **4.** A genus of fresh-water polyps; নদ্যাদির জলজাত একজাতীয় নিম্নস্তরের কীট। **Hydra-headed**—Many headed; (of a difficulty etc.) going on increasing as it is combated; বহু-শীর্ষ; (বিপদ, সঙ্কট প্রভৃতি সম্পর্কে) রক্তবীজের বংশের মত। **Hydra-headed multitude**—The rabble; ইতর জনতা।

hȳ'-lră'-gogue (-gŏg), *n.* A very powerful purgative জোলাপ, রেচক (ঠাকুরঃ)।

hȳ-drăn'-gē-ă, *n.* A genus of shrubby plants with large heads of showy flowers; একজাতীয় উজ্জ্বল বর্ণ পুষ্পপ্রসূ গুল্ম।

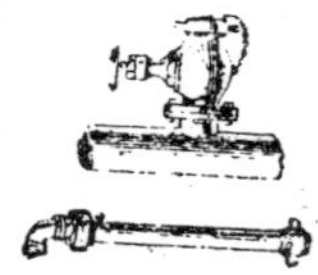

Hydrant.

hȳ'-drănt, *n.* A pipe by which water is drawn from a main pipe; জলের কলের প্রধান নল হইতে জলাকর্ষণের জন্য নল বিশেষ।

hȳ'-drāte, *n.* & *v. t.* (*Chem.*) A compound formed by the union of water with an element or another compound; (রসায়ন শাস্ত্র) জলের সহিত কোন মৌলিক বা যৌগিক পদার্থের সংযোগে উৎপন্ন মিশ্র-পদার্থ। ***Verb t.*** (*Chem.*) To combine with water; (রসায়নশাস্ত্র) জলের সহিত সংমিশ্রিত করা। **—dra'-tion,** *n.*

hȳ-drau'-lic (-drā-) *adj.* & *n.* **1.** Pertaining to hydraulics; conveying water; চলজ্জলবিজ্ঞান-সম্বন্ধীয়, জঙ্গমজলবিদ্যাবিষয়ক (কেভিঃ); জলবাহী। **2.** Operated by water-power; as, a *hydraulic* crane; জলশক্তিদ্বারা চালিত। **3.** Hardening or setting under water; as, *hydraulic* cement; জলসংস্পর্শে কাঠিন্যপ্রাপী। ***Noun.*** (*Pl.*) The science of conveyance of liquids, through pipes etc., esp. as motive power; চলজ্জলবিজ্ঞান, দ্রব-গতিবিজ্ঞান, তরলবেগগণিত (হিঃ কোঃ), জঙ্গমজল বিদ্যা (কেভিঃ), চলজলবিদ্যা (ঐ)। **—li-cal-ly,** *adv.* **Hydraulic cement**—যে গাঁথুনির মসলা জল লাগিলে কঠিন হয়। **Hydraulic lift** — জলশক্তি দ্বারা চালিত

ভারোত্তোলন-যন্ত্র, জলোত্থাপক (হিঃ কোঃ)। **Hydraulic press** — জলীয়শক্তিদ্বারা

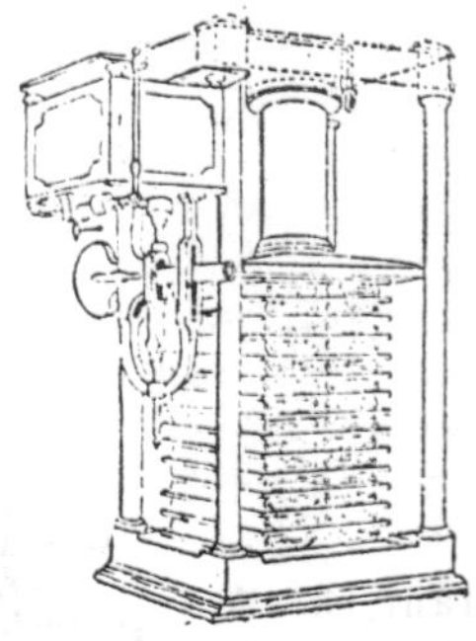

Hydraulic or Bramah press.

পরিচালিত চাপযন্ত্র, জলপীড়নযন্ত্র (হিঃ কোঃ), জলচাপ যন্ত্র। **Hydraulic-ram**—যে যন্ত্র সাহায্যে পতনশীল জলপ্রবাহের গুরুত্ব বা বেগ দ্বারা উহার কতক অংশ সবেগে ঊর্দ্ধে উৎক্ষিপ্ত হইয়া থাকে।

hȳ'-dric, *adj.* Pertaining to, or containing hydrogen ; as, *hydric-*oxide ; উদজান সম্বন্ধীয়, উজ্জনক (হিঃ কোঃ)।

hȳ'-drīde, *n.* A chemical compound of hydrogen and a metal or some base ; উদজন বাষ্প এবং কোন ধাতু বা ভস্মের রাসায়নিক সংমিশ্রণ।

hȳ'-drō, *n.* A hydropathic establishment ; জলচিকিৎসাগার।

hȳ-drō-câr'-bŏn, *n.* A compound of hydrogen and carbon ; উদজান বাষ্প ও অঙ্গারকের মিশ্র।

hȳ'-drō-cele (-sēl), *n.* Dropsy of the scrotum or the testicle ; অন্ত্রবৃদ্ধি, কুরণ্ড, কোষবৃদ্ধি, জলদোষ, বৃদ্ধি (সুশ্রুঃ), জলকোষ শোথ (ঐ), জলজবৃদ্ধি রোগ (হঃ চঃ)।

hȳ-drō-cĕph'-ă-lŭs, *n.* Water in the head ; dropsy of the brain ; মস্তিষ্কে জলসঞ্চার, শিরোগতজল (সাঃ পঃ), মস্তকশোথ। **–lous, –phal'-ic,** *adjs.*

hȳ-drō-chlō'-rĭc, *adj.* Compounded of hydrogen and chlorine ; উদজান এবং হরিণ বাষ্প মিশ্রিত। **Hydrochloric acid** — লৌহদ্রাব (সাঃ পঃ), সূচিদ্রাব (ঐ), লবণকাম্লজল (ঐ)।

hȳ-drō-cȳ-ăn'-ĭc, *adj.* Containing hydrogen and cyanogen ; উদজানবাষ্প এবং সমাঙ্গারকযবক্ষারযান মিশ্র, সমন্বিক। **Hydrocyanic acid**—অতি সাংঘাতিক বিষ বিশেষ।

hȳ-drō-dȳ-năm'-ĭcs, *n.* The science which treats of forces acting upon or exerted by fluids ; জল বা অন্যবিধ তরল পদার্থের গতি-বিজ্ঞান, জলবেগ-গণিত (হিঃ কোঃ), জলগতি-বিদ্যা (ঐ), উদকস্থিতিশাস্ত্র (কেঙ্গিঃ)। **–ic, –i-cal,** *adjs.* Pertaining to the force or pressure of water ; জলবলসম্বন্ধীয়, জলচাপসম্বন্ধীয়।

hȳ-drō-ē-lĕc'-trĭc, *adj.* Pertaining to the evolution of electricity by the use of water or steam ; জল বা বাষ্প ক্রিয়াজনিত তড়িদ্‌বিকাশসম্বন্ধীয়, আর্দ্রবৈদ্যুত (হিঃ কোঃ)।

hȳ-drō-flū-ŏr'-ĭc-ăc-ĭd, *n.* A colourless, mobile volatile liquid, very corrosive in its action ; দন্তদ্রাব (সাঃ পঃ)।

hȳ'-drō-gĕn, *n.* The gaseous elementary substance which combined with oxygen forms water ; উদজান বাষ্প, জলজান বাষ্প, উদজনক, অবজনন (আঃ বঃ)। [১৭৬৬ খৃঃ অব্দে Cavendish কর্ত্তৃক আবিষ্কৃত হয়। Hydrogen এই নাম ফরাসী রাসায়নিকগণ কর্ত্তৃক প্রদত্ত হয়।] **–drog'-e-nous,** *adj.*

hȳ'-drō-gĕn-āte, *v. t.* To combine with hydrogen ; উদজান বাষ্পের সহিত মিশ্রিত করা।

hȳ'-drō-gĕn-īze, *v. t.* To hydrogenate ; উদজান বাষ্পের সহিত সংমিশ্রিত করা।

hȳ-drŏg'-ră-phȳ, *n.* The science which treats of the measurement and description of seas, lakes, etc. ; হ্রদ, সাগর, নদী, প্রভৃতির পরিমাপ এবং বর্ণন বিষয়ক বিজ্ঞান, সমুদ্রমাপক (হিঃ কোঃ)। **–dro-graph'-ic, –dro-graph'-i-cal,** *adjs.* **–pher,** *n.*

hȳ'-droid (-droȳd), *adj.* & *n.* (*Zool.*) Allied to, or resembling, the hydra ; (জন্তু বিজ্ঞান) নিম্নস্তরের জীববর্গ বিশেষের মত। ***Noun.*** (*Zool.*) An animal like the hydra ; নিম্নস্তরের জীববর্গ বিশেষ।

hȳ-drō-kĭ-nĕt'-ĭcs, *n.* A branch of hydro-dynamics ; জলগতি-বিজ্ঞানের শাখাবিশেষ। **–ic,** *adj.* Pertaining to the motions of fluids ; তরল পদার্থের গতি সম্বন্ধীয়।

hȳ-drŏl'-ō-ġȳ, *n.* The science of the properties and laws etc. of water ; জলবিজ্ঞান (হিঃ কোঃ)।

hȳ-drō-mā'-nĭ-ă, *n.* An insatiable craving for water ; বহুমূত্রাদি রোগে প্রবল জলতৃষ্ণা।

hȳ-drō-mē-chăn'-ĭcs, *n.* The mechanics of liquids ; জলযন্ত্র-বিজ্ঞান।

hȳ'-drō-mĕl, *n.* A liquor made of honey and water ; মধু ও জলের মিশ্র। **Vinous hydromel**—(also *mead*) মধু হইতে প্রস্তুত মদিরা, মাধ্বী।

hȳ-drŏm'-ē-tēr, *n.* **1.** An instrument for finding specific gravity of liquids (sometimes of solids also) ; তরল পদার্থের (সময় সময় কঠিন পদার্থেরও) আপেক্ষিক গুরুত্ব নির্ণায়ক যন্ত্র, দ্রবমাপ (আঃ বঃ), ঘনত্বমাপক (হিঃ কোঃ), বিশিষ্ট গুরুত্ব মাপক (ঐ), জলগুরুত্বমাপক (ঐ)। **2.** An instrument for measuring the velocity or force of a current ; a current gauge ; প্রবাহের বল বা গতিবেগমাপক যন্ত্র ; প্রবাহমাপক। **–dro-met'-ric,** *adj.* **–try,** *n.*

Hydrometer.

hȳ-drō-păth'-ĭc, *adj.* & *n.* Relating to hydropathy ; জলচিকিৎসা-সম্পর্কীয়। ***Noun.*** A hydropathic establishment ; জলচিকিৎসাগার।

hȳ-drŏp'-ă-thȳ, *n.* The treatment of disease by cold water ; the water-cure ; শীতল জল বাহ্য ও আভ্যন্তরিক প্রয়োগ দ্বারা যাবতীয়

রোগের চিকিৎসার প্রণালী বিশেষ, জল-চিকিৎসাপ্রণালী (বিশ্বঃ); জলোপচার (কেভিঃ)। **—thist,** *n.* A person practising hydropathy; জল-চিকিৎসক।

hȳ'-drö-phāne, *n.* A variety of opal made transparent by immersion in water; জলকান্তমণি, ভীষ্মমণি।

hȳ-drö-phŏ'-bi-ȧ, *n.* A morbid and unnatural dread of water; rabies from the bite of a mad dog; জলাতঙ্ক, জলত্রাস (সুশ্রুঃ); ক্ষিপ্ত কুকুরাদির দংশন জনিত রোগ, ক্ষিপ্তশ্বদংশ-রোগ।

hȳ'-drö-phōne, *n.* An instrument for detecting by sound the flow of water in a pipe; ধ্বনিদ্বারা নলের ভিতর জলের প্রবাহ নির্ণয় করার জন্য যন্ত্র বিশেষ।

hȳ'-drö-phȳte, *n.* An aquatic plant; একপ্রকার জলজ উদ্ভিদ্।

hȳ-drŏp'-ic, *adj.* Dropsical; resembling dropsy; শোথরোগাক্রান্ত; শোথবৎ।

hȳ'-drö-plāne, *n.* **1.** A motor-boat; যন্ত্রশক্তিচালিত দ্রুতগামী নৌকা। **2.** A boat with planes which can rise or sink when going ahead; একপ্রকার নৌকা,—যাহা জলের উপর উড়িতে পারে এবং আবশ্যক মত জলে নিমজ্জিত করা যায়, জলাকাশযান।

hȳ'-drŏp-sȳ, *n.* Dropsy; শোথ।

hȳ'-drö-scōpe, *n.* (*Hist.*) A kind of water-clock; (ইতিহাস) এক প্রকার জলঘড়ী।

hȳ'-drö-stăt, *n.* An electrical device for detecting pressure of water; জলের সত্তা নির্ণয়ের জন্য তাড়িত-যন্ত্র বিশেষ।

hȳ-drö-stăt'-ic, *adj.* & *n.* Relating to hydrostatics; তরল পদার্থের স্থিতিবিজ্ঞানসম্পর্কীয়। ***Noun.*** (*Pl.*) The science of the pressure and equilibrium of liquids at rest; তরল পদার্থের স্থিতিবিজ্ঞান, জলগণিত (হিঃ কোঃ), স্থিরজল বিজ্ঞান, অচলজলবিদ্যা, জলস্থিতি বিদ্যা (হিঃ কোঃ), উদকস্থিতিশাস্ত্র (কেভিঃ)। **—i-cal,** *adv.* **Hydrostatic balance**—জলের ভিতর কোন দ্রব্য মাপিয়া উহার আপেক্ষিক গুরুত্ব নিরূপণের জন্য তুলাযন্ত্র বিশেষ, জল-তুলা যন্ত্র। **Hydrostatic bellows**—তরল পদার্থের চাপ সর্ব্বদিকে সমরূপ এই তত্ত্ব প্রদর্শনের জন্য বায়ুপ্রবেশপথরুদ্ধ ভস্ত্রাকার আধারে লম্বভাবে সম্বদ্ধ নল সমন্বিত যন্ত্র বিশেষ। **Hydrostatic paradox**—অচল জল বিজ্ঞানের তত্ত্ব বিশেষ—ইহা এই যে, যতই অল্প পরিমাণ জল হউক না কেন উহা যতদূর ভারি দ্রব্য হউক না কেন তাহার সহিত সমতুলিত করা যাইতে পারে; অথবা সর্ব্বদিকে তরল পদার্থের চাপের সমতা সম্বন্ধীয় নিয়ম। **Hydrostatic or Bramah's press**—Same as HYDRAULIC PRESS (which see.)

hȳ-drö-thêr'-ȧ-pȳ, *n.* Same as HYDROPATHY which see.

hȳ-drö-thêr'-măl, *adj.* Pertaining to the action of heated water in bringing about changes in the earth's crust; ভূপঞ্জরের বিকৃতি সাধনে উষ্ণ জলের ক্রিয়া-সম্বন্ধীয়।

hȳ-drö-thō'-rax, *n.* Dropsy in the thorax or chest; বক্ষঃস্থলে শোথ, উরোগত জল।

hȳ-drŏt'-rö-pĭsm, *n.* (Of plants) Tendency to turn to, or from, moisture; জলোন্মুখতা, জলবিমুখতা, জলানুগমন (সাঃ পঃ)।

hȳ'-drous (-drŭs), *adj.* **1.** Watery; জলীয়। **2.** (*Chem.*) Containing water; (রসায়ন শাস্ত্র) জলযুক্ত, উদকময় (হিঃ কোঃ)।

hȳ-drö-zō'-ȧ, *n.* (*Pl., sing.* -zoon), A class of animals including some polyps; নিম্নস্তরের জীববর্গবিশেষ।

hȳ-ē'-nȧ, —æ'- (-ē-), *ns.* **1.** A carnivorous quadruped of the dog kind; তরক্ষু, গো বাঘা, হেঁাদড় (সাঃ পঃ), মৃগাদন (আঃ বঃ)। **2.** A cruel or treacherous person; নিষ্ঠুর ব্যক্তি, বিশ্বাসঘাতক ব্যক্তি। **Striped hyena**—একপ্রকার চিত্রিত তরক্ষু—ইহার চীৎকার পৈশাচিক হাস্যের সহিত তুলিত হয়।

hȳ-ē-tŏg'-rȧ-phȳ, *n.* The science of the distribution of rain; বৃষ্টি-সংবিভাগ-বিজ্ঞান।

hȳ-ē-tŏm'-ĕ-têr, *n.* A rain gauge; বৃষ্টিমান যন্ত্র, বর্ষমান যন্ত্র।

Hȳ-gē'-ia (-yȧ), *n.* The goddess of health, the daughter of Aesculapius; বৈদ্যদেবতা Aesculapiusএর কন্যা—স্বাস্থ্যের অধিষ্ঠাত্রী দেবী, স্বাস্থ্যদেবী। **—ian,** *adj.* Relating to health and its preservation; স্বাস্থ্যসম্বন্ধীয়, স্বাস্থ্যরক্ষা সম্পর্কীয়, শরীরপালন সম্পর্কীয়।

hȳ'-gi-ene (-ēn), *n.* A system of principle designed for the promotion of health; sanitary science; স্বাস্থ্যবিদ্যা, স্বাস্থ্যতত্ত্ব; স্বাস্থ্য-বিজ্ঞান। **—en'-ic, —en'-i-căl,** *adjs.* **—en'-i-cal-ly,** *adv.* **—en'-ics,** *n.* The science of health; স্বাস্থ্য-বিজ্ঞান। **—ist,** *n.* One versed in hygiene; স্বাস্থ্যবিজ্ঞানবিদ্, স্বাস্থ্যতত্ত্বজ্ঞ।

hȳ-grŏl'-ö-ğȳ, *n.* That branch of science which treats of the humidity of the atmosphere etc.; বায়ুমণ্ডল প্রভৃতির আর্দ্রতা সম্বন্ধীয় বিজ্ঞান, বাষ্পবিজ্ঞান।

hȳ-grŏm'-ĕ-têr, *n.* An instrument for measuring the moisture of the atmosphere; বাষ্পমানযন্ত্র, সিক্ততামান, আর্দ্রতামাপক যন্ত্র, ক্লেদমাপক (হিঃ কোঃ)। **—gro-met'-ric,** *adj.* **—try,** *n.* The art of measuring the degree of moisture in the air or atmosphere; সিক্ততা-মান-বিদ্যা, আর্দ্রতামানবিদ্যা, ক্লেদমিতি (হিঃ কোঃ)।

hȳ'-grö-scōpe, *n.* An instrument for indicating, but not measuring the humidity of the atmosphere; সিক্ততাদর্শক, আর্দ্রতাদর্শক, ক্লেদসূচক (হিঃ কোঃ)। **—scop'-ic,** *adj.* **1.** Of, or pertaining to, hygroscope; সিক্ততাদর্শকযন্ত্র সম্বন্ধীয়। **2.** (Of bodies) Sensitive to moisture; সিক্ততা-সংবেদক। **Hygroscopic substance**—আর্দ্রতাগ্রাহী পদার্থ (হিঃ কোঃ)।

hȳ′-lic, *adj.* Of, or pertaining to, matter ; material ; জড়বস্তুসম্বন্ধীয় ; জড়ীয় ।

hȳ′-lō-thē-ĭsm, *n.* The doctrine that God and matter are identical ; ঈশ্বর ও জড়পদার্থ অভিন্ন—এইরূপ মতবাদ, জড়েশ্বরাভেদবাদ । **–ist,** *n.* The holder of this doctrine ; জড়েশ্বরাভেদবাদী । **–is′-tic,** *adj.*

hȳ-lō-zō′-ism, *n.* The doctrine that all matter is endowed with life ; জড়চৈতন্যবাদ, প্রকৃতিচেতনাবাদ (হিঃ কোঃ) । **–ist,** *n.*

Hȳ′-mĕn, *n.* (*Gr. & Rom. myth.*) The God of marriage ; (গ্রীক পুরাণোক্ত সুরাদেবতা ব্যাকাস ও রতি দেবী ভিনাসের পুত্র) বিবাহদেবতা, ভগদেবতা (cf. our প্রজাপতি) । **–me-ne′-al,** *adj.* Relating to marriage ; বিবাহসম্বন্ধীয় । **–me-ne′-al-ly,** *adv.*

hȳ′-mĕn, *n.* (*Anat.*) A thin membrane partially closing the virginal vagina ; (শারীর-সংস্থান বিদ্যা) কুমারীদিগের যোনিমুখ আবরক অর্দ্ধচন্দ্রাকার ঝিল্লী-বিশেষ, সতীচ্ছদ (জাহিঃ), সতীদেবী (হঃ চঃ) ।

hȳ-mĕn-ŏp′-têr-ă, *n.* (*Pl.*) An order of insects having four membranous wings ; ঝিল্লিময় পক্ষ চতুষ্টয় বিশিষ্ট কীটবর্গ । **–al, –ous,** *adjs.*

hymn (hĭm), *n., v. t. & i.* A song or ode in praise, honour or adoration of God or some deity ; a song of praise ; ঈশ্বরস্তুতি, ঈশ্বরস্তোত্র, ভগবৎস্তোত্র, সূক্ত, স্তব, উক্ত (বেদান্ত); স্তুতি, স্তব-সঙ্গীত (রবীঃ), ভজন, স্তবগান । ***Verb t.*** To worship by hymns ; to praise or celebrate in song ; স্তবদ্বারা অর্চ্চনা করা ; স্তবগান করা, স্তুতিগান করা । ***Verb i.*** To sing in praise or adoration ; স্তবগান করা । **Hym′-nic,** *adj.* **Hym′-nist,** *n.* A writer of hymns ; স্তোত্ররচক ।

hȳm′-năl, *adj. & n.* Pertaining to hymns ; স্তোত্রসম্বন্ধীয় । ***Noun.*** A hymn book ; স্তোত্রসংগ্রহ । **–na-ry,** *adj.*

hȳm′-nō-dȳ, *n.* **1.** Act of singing hymns ; স্তোত্র গান । **2.** Hymns collectively ; স্তবমালা । **3.** The study or composition of hymns ; স্তবপাঠ, স্তোত্র রচনা । **–dist,** *n.*

hȳm-nŏg′-ră-phêr, *n.* One who composes hymns ; স্তোত্ররচক ।

hȳm-nŏl-ŏ-ġȳ, *n.* **1.** The composition of rhymes ; স্তোত্ররচনা, স্তব রচনা । **2.** The study or science of hymns ; স্তবশাস্ত্র, স্তবাধ্যয়ন । **–gist,** *n.* **–no-log′-ic,** *adj.*

hȳ′-oid (-ŏyd), *adj. & n.* **1.** Pertaining to the bone at the base of the tongue ; জিহ্বামূলাস্থি সম্বন্ধীয় । ***Noun.*** The tongue-bone situated between the chin and the thyroid cartilage, (also *hyoid-bone*) ; স্বরযন্ত্র ও জিহ্বার মধ্যবর্ত্তী U অক্ষরের আকার অস্থি, জিহ্বামূলাস্থি (হঃ চঃ) ।

hȳp, *n.* Hypochondria ; বিষাদ রোগ ।

hȳp-ae(e)′-thrăl (-ē) *adj.* Having no roof ; open air ; ছাদশূন্য ; অনাবৃত স্থানের ।

hȳp-ăl′-lă-ġē, *n.* (*Gram. & Rhet.*) A figure consisting of an interchange in the syntactic relationship between two terms, (*e. g., apply the wound to water* for *apply water to the wound*) ; (ব্যাকরণ ও অলঙ্কার-শাস্ত্র) শব্দালঙ্কার বিশেষ—যাহাতে বাক্যের পদান্বয়-যোজনা পরিবর্ত্তন করা হয় ।

hȳ-pêr-aes-thē′-sĭ-ă (-ĕs-), *n.* Morbid sensitiveness of the nerves or nerve centres ; স্নায়ু বা স্নায়ু-কেন্দ্রের অস্বাভাবিক সংবেদনশক্তি, অতিরিক্ত স্পর্শশক্তি (হঃ চঃ) ।

hȳ-pêr′-bă-tŏn, *n.* (*Gram.*) A figurative construction inverting the natural order of words and sentences ; (ব্যাকরণ) একপ্রকার অলঙ্কার—যাহাতে শব্দ বা বাক্য সমূহের স্বাভাবিক ক্রমবিন্যাসের বিপর্য্যয় করা হয়, ক্রমবিপর্য্যয় ।

hȳ-pêr′-bō-lă, *n.* (*Geom.*) A curve formed by a section of a cone when the cutting plane makes a larger angle with the base than the side of the cone makes ; (জ্যামিতি) অতিপরবলয় (সূঃ সিঃ), অতিক্ষেত্র, উদ্‌বৃত্ত (আঃ বঃ), অতিবৃত্ত (ঐ), অপাস্ত (হিঃ কোঃ) । **–bol′-ic,** *adj.*

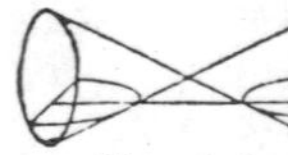

Hyperbola.

hȳ-pêr′-bō-lē, *n.* (*Rhet.*) A figure of speech which goes much beyond the truth ; an exaggerated statement ; (অলঙ্কার-শাস্ত্র) অত্যুক্তি অলঙ্কার, অতিশয়োক্তি (কাব্য-দর্শন) ; পুষ্পিত বা পল্লবিত উক্তি, অতিরঞ্জিত উক্তি । **–bol′-i-cal,** *adj.* অতিশয়োক্তি বিশিষ্ট (কেম্ভিঃ), অতিশয়োক্তিসূচক (ঐ) । **–bol′-i-cal-ly,** *adv.* **–lism, –list,** *ns.*

hȳ-pêr-bŏ′-rē-ăn, *adj. & n.* Of, or pertaining to, the extreme north of the earth or (*colloq.*) of a country ; পৃথিবীর নিতান্ত উত্তরাঞ্চল সম্বন্ধীয়, (চলিত ভাষায়) কোন দেশের উত্তরসীমান্তবর্ত্তী প্রদেশসম্বন্ধীয় । ***Noun.*** **1.** (*Gr. myth.*) One of a race who lived beyond the north wind ; (গ্রীক পুরাণ) পৃথিবীর উত্তর প্রান্তবাসী জাতিবিশেষের লোক । **2.** An inhabitant of the extreme north ; (*fig.*) one who lives in a northerly clime ; নিতান্ত উত্তরাঞ্চলবাসী লোক ; (লক্ষণায়) উত্তরদেশীয় লোক ।

hȳ-pêr-căt-ă-lĕc′-tic, *adj.* (*Pros.*) Having a syllable or two beyond the regular measure ; as, a *hypercatalectic* verse ; অধ্যক্ষর (আঃ বঃ) ।

hȳ-pêr-crit′-i-căl, *adj.* Over-critical ; "*Hypercritical* readers" ; captious ; অতিরিক্তসমালোচনাকারী ; ছিদ্রান্বেষী, দোষদর্শী । **–cism,** *n.* অতিচিকিৎসা (কেম্ভিঃ) । **–cize,** *v. t. & i.* **–ly,** *adv.*

hȳ-pêr-mĕt′-ric, –ri-căl, *adjs.* (Of a verse) Having a redundant syllable ; redundant, as a syllable ; (কবিতার চরণ) অতিরিক্ত শব্দাংশবিশিষ্ট ; অতিরিক্ত (শব্দাংশ) ।

hȳ-pêr-mĕ-trö'-pi-ă, *n.* Morbid long-sightedness as opp. to *myopia* ; রোগজনিত দূরদৃষ্টি। **–trop'-ic,** *adj.*

hȳ-pêr-phȳs'-i-căl, *adj.* Supernatural ; অতিপ্রাকৃত, অলৌকিক।

hȳ'-pêr-sthene (-sthĕn), *n.* A greenish grey mineral allied to hornblende ; একপ্রকার হরিদ্বর্ণ খনিজ পদার্থ।

hȳ-pêr'-trö-phȳ, *n.* The excessive growth of an organ or part of the body from excessive nutrition ; কোন শারীরিক যন্ত্রের অস্বাভাবিক বিবর্দ্ধন, অতিপুষ্টি (হিঃ কোঃ), অতিবৃদ্ধি (ঐ)। **–troph'-ic, –phied,** *adjs.*

hȳp-ĕ'-thrăl, *n.* See HYPAETHRAL.

hȳ'-phĕn, *n.* & *v.t.* A sign (-) joining two syllables or words ; a short pause between syllables in speaking ; সংযোগ চিহ্ন ; কথা বলিবার সময় শব্দাংশ সংযোগের মধ্যে ক্ষণিক বিরাম। *Verb t.* To connect with, or separate by, a hyphen ; as, to *hyphen* words etc. ; সংযোগ-চিহ্ন দ্বারা সংযুক্ত বা পৃথক করা।

hȳp-nŏl'-ö-ḡȳ, *n.* The study of the phenomena of sleep ; a treatise on sleep ; নিদ্রাতত্ত্ব ; নিদ্রা সম্বন্ধীয় পুস্তক।

hȳp-nō'-sis, *n.* Sleep artificially produced ; the hypnotic state ; যোগনিদ্রা ; সম্মোহাবস্থা, সমাধি (হিঃ কোঃ)।

hȳp-nŏt'-ic, *adj.* & *n.* **1.** Inducing sleep ; নিদ্রাজনক। **2.** Of, or pertaining to, hypnotism ; as, an *hypnotic* condition ; যোগনিদ্রাসম্বন্ধীয়, সম্মোহনবিদ্যা সম্বন্ধীয়। *Noun.* **1.** A thing that induces sleep ; নিদ্রাজনক, ঔষধ, নিদ্রক (ঠাকুর)। **2.** A person under the influence of hypnotism ; সম্মোহিত ব্যক্তি, যোগনিদ্রাচ্ছন্ন ব্যক্তি, যোগনিদ্রাভিভূত ব্যক্তি।

hȳp'-nō-tism, *n.* A sleep-like condition produced by artificial means ; the production of such sleep ; যোগনিদ্রা ; সম্মোহন (হিঃ কোঃ)। [ইহা একরূপ কৃত্রিম উপায়ে সঞ্জাত নিদ্রা—এইরূপ ব্যক্তির ইন্দ্রিয় ও মনোবৃত্তিসমূহ অপর ব্যক্তির সম্পূর্ণ কর্তৃত্বাধীন হইয়া পড়ে ও তাহার ইঙ্গিতে সেই যোগনিদ্রাভিভূত ব্যক্তি যন্ত্রপুত্তলিকাবৎ কার্য্য করিয়া থাকে।] **–tist,** *n.* **–tize,** *v.t.* To subject to hypnotism ; to induce hypnotism in ; যোগনিদ্রাভিভূত করা, সম্মোহিত করা ; মুগ্ধ ও আচ্ছন্ন করা।

hȳ-pō-brăn'-chi-ăl, *adj.* Situated under the gills ; কানকোর নীচে স্থিত।

hȳp'-ö-caust (-cäst), *n.* (*Rom. antiq.*) A vaulted chamber for heating baths or dwelling rooms ; গৃহতলস্থ শূন্যগর্ভ স্থান—যথায় গৃহ বা স্নানাগার উত্তপ্ত করার উদ্দেশ্যে চুল্লীর উত্তাপ সঞ্চিত রাখা হইত।

hȳp-ö-chŏn'-dri-ă, *n.* Melancholy ; morbid state of depression ; বিষাদরোগ ; অবসাদ বায়ু (হঃ চঃ) ; [প্রকৃত পীড়ার অবর্ত্তমানেও পীড়ার কল্পনা ও স্বাস্থ্য সম্বন্ধে সর্ব্বদা উৎকট ভাবনা এই রোগের লক্ষণ।] **–dri'-a-sis,** *n.*

hȳp-ö-chŏn'-dri-ăc, *adj.* & *n.* **1.** Of, or pertaining to, hypochondria ; বিষাদরোগসম্বন্ধীয়। **2.** Affected with hypochondria ; বিষাদরোগগ্রস্ত, অবসাদবায়ুগ্রস্ত। *Noun.* A person affected with hypochondria ; বিষাদরোগগ্রস্ত ব্যক্তি অবসাদবায়ুগ্রস্ত ব্যক্তি। **-dri'-a-cal,** *adj.* **–dri'-a-cal-ly,** *adv.*

hȳ-pŏc'-ri-sȳ, *n.* A feigning to be what one is not ; a pretence to virtue or goodness ; dissimulation ; কপটতা ; ভণ্ডামি, ভক্তবিটলামি, মর্কটবৈরাগ্য (হঃ চঃ), মুখোসপরাধর্ম্ম (জিঃ) ; কপটাচরণ।

hȳp'-ö-crite (-krĭt), *n.* One who practises hypocrisy ; a dissembler ; ভক্তবিটল, বকধার্ম্মিক, ধর্ম্মধ্বজী, বৈড়ালব্রতিক ; ভণ্ড, কপট। **–crit'-i-cal,** *adj.* **–crit'-i-cal-ly,** *adv.*

hȳ-pō-cȳ'-cloid (-kloyd), *n.* A curve generated by the movement of a curve upon the concave side of another fixed curve ; কোন স্থির বক্র রেখার পৃষ্ঠের উপর অপর বক্ররেখার গতিদ্বারা সৃষ্ট বক্র।

hȳ-pō-dêr'-mic, *adj.* **1.** (*Anat.*) Relating to the parts under the skin ; lying under the skin ; (শারীর সংস্থান বিদ্যা) অধস্তকসম্বন্ধীয় ; চর্ম্মনিম্নস্থ, অধস্ত্বগ। **2.** (Of medicines etc.) Introduced beneath the skin, as an injection etc. ; (ঔষধাদি সম্বন্ধে) চর্ম্মাভ্যন্তরে প্রবিষ্ট। **–mi-cal-ly,** *adv.* **Hypodermic injection**—চর্ম্মের নিম্নে সূচী পিচকারী-দ্বারা প্রবিষ্ট ঔষধ। **Hypodermic syringe**—চর্ম্মের নীচে পিচকারী দেওয়ার জন্য সূচীমুখ ক্ষুদ্র কাচের পিচকারী বিশেষ।

hȳ-pō-găs'-tri-ŭm, *n.* (*Anat.*) The lowest region of the abdomen ; (শারীর-সংস্থান বিদ্যা) পিউবিস্ অর্থাৎ মণিপুর হইতে নাভীর তিন অঙ্গুলী নিম্ন পর্য্যন্ত উদরের নিম্নভাগ (ডাঃ হরিপ্রসাদ চক্রবর্ত্তী), উদরনিম্নপ্রদেশ (হঃ চঃ), বস্তি (কেভিঃ), উত্তরবস্তি (ঐ), নাভ্যধোভাগ (ঐ), উপস্থোর্দ্ধভাগ (ঐ)।

hȳp-ö-ḡĕ'-ăl, –ḡĕ'-ăn, *adjs.* Under-ground ; ভূনিম্নস্থ, অন্তর্ভৌম, ভূগর্ভস্থ।

hȳp'-ö-gene (-jĕn), *adj.* Formed beneath the earth's surface ; as, a *hypogene* rock ; ভূনিম্নে রচিত।

hȳp-ö-ḡĕ'-ŭm, *n.* (*Pl.* -GEA) An under-ground chamber ; অন্তর্ভৌম কক্ষ, ভূগর্ভস্থ কক্ষ।

hȳ-pō-glŏs'-săl, *adj.* & *n.* (Of nerves) Under the tongue ; (স্নায়ু সম্বন্ধে) জিহ্বামূলস্থ। *Noun.* A motor nerve of the tongue ; জিহ্বানিম্নস্নায়ু (হঃ চঃ), নবমযুগ্ম স্নায়ু (ঐ)।

hȳ-pŏg'-ȳ-nous (-nŭs), *adj.* (*Bot.*) Placed below the pistils or ovary ; (উদ্ভিদ্ বিদ্যা) গর্ভাশয় বা বীজাধারের নিম্নে রক্ষিত, অবজাত (সাঃ পঃ)।

hȳ'-pō-năs-tȳ, *n.* (*Bot.*) The tendency in plant organs to grow more rapidly on the underside ; (উদ্ভিদ্ বিদ্যা) বৃক্ষাদির অঙ্গের অধোদিকে অধিকতর দ্রুতভাবে বৃদ্ধির উন্মুখতা, অধোবৃদ্ধি (সাঃ পঃ)।

hȳ-pö-phŏs′-phite, –phāte, *ns.* A salt of hypophosphorous acid ; বহুল পরিমাণ ফুস্ফুরক বিশিষ্ট রাসায়নিক পদার্থদ্বয়। [বলকারক ঔষধ স্বরূপ ব্যবহৃত হয়।]

hȳ-pŏs′-tă-sis, (*Pl.* -SES) **1.** (*Med.*) Excess of blood in the organs of a body ; sediment, as that of the urine ; (ভৈষজ্য শাস্ত্র) কোন শারীরিক যন্ত্রে অত্যধিক রক্তসঞ্চয় ; মূত্রাদির তলানি। **2.** (*Metaph.*) That which lies at the basis or foundation of anything ; (তত্ত্ব-বিদ্যা) মূলবস্তু, মূলতত্ত্ব, বীজ। **3.** (*Theol.*) A term used to denote the distinct personal existence of each Person in the Trinity ; ঈশ্বর, যীশুখৃষ্ট, পবিত্রাত্মার স্বতন্ত্র ব্যক্তিত্বসূচক শব্দ, ব্যূহ (ব্রজঃ বৈষ্ণঃ)। **–po-stat′-ic, –po-stat′-i-cal,** *adjs.* **–po-stat′-i-cal-ly,** *adv.* **–tize, –size,** *v. t.* To make into, or regard as, a distinct substance or person ; to impersonate ; "*Hypostatized* as divine persons" ; (ঈশ্বর, যীশুখ্রীষ্ট বা পবিত্র আত্মাকে) স্বতন্ত্র করা, স্বতন্ত্র ব্যক্তি বলিয়া গণ্য করা ; ব্যক্তিত্বারোপ করা।

hȳp′-ö-stȳle, *adj.* & *n.* Supported on pillars ; স্তম্ভোপরি রক্ষিত। ***Noun.*** That which is supported on pillars ; স্তম্ভোপরি স্থাপিত বস্তু।

hȳ-pŏt′-ĕ-nūse, *n.* The side opposite to the right angle of a triangle ; সমকোণী ত্রিভুজের দীর্ঘতম বাহু, কর্ণ।

hȳ-pŏth′-ĕc, *n.* (*Law*) The legal right or security which a creditor has over goods belonging to the debtor ; (আইন) অধমর্ণের স্থাবর সম্পত্তির উপর উত্তমর্ণের যে আইন সঙ্গত অধিকার বা দাওয়া থাকে। **–e-ca-ry,** *adj.* Of, or pertaining to, an hypothec or mortgage ; বন্ধক সম্বন্ধীয়।

hȳ-pŏth′-ĕ-cāte, *v. t.* To mortgage ; to pledge, as a security ; বন্ধক দেওয়া ; দায়বদ্ধ করা। **–ca′-tion,** *n.*

hȳ-pŏth′-ĕ-sis, *n.* **1.** A proposition assumed for the purpose of argument ; কল্পনা (ব্রজঃ হিন্দুঃ), অনুভব, অভ্যুপগম-সিদ্ধান্ত (হিঃ কোঃ), কল্পিতার্থ (ঐ), অনুমিতি (কেঙিঃ), অভ্যুপগম। **2.** A groundless assumption ; অমূলক অনুমান। **–po-thet′-ic, –po-thet′-i-cal,** *adjs.* কল্পনাত্মক (হিঃ কোঃ), আনুমানিক (ঐ), অভ্যুপগত (ঐ), অনুমানসিদ্ধ। **–po-thet′-i-cal-ly,** *adv.* **–size,** *v. i.* & *t.* To form a hypothesis ; কল্পনা করা। ***Verb t.*** To assume ; অনুমান করা, ধরিয়া লওয়া। **Hypothetical ethics**—সাপেক্ষনীতি (হিঃ কোঃ)। **Hypothetical imperative**—সাপেক্ষ বিধি (হিঃ কোঃ)।

hȳ-pö-tră-chē′-li-ŭm, *n.* The lower part of the capital of a column ; বোধিকার নিম্নাংশ।

hȳp-sŏm′-ĕ-têr, *n.* An instrument for determining altitudes ; উচ্চতামান। **–so-met′-ric, –so-met′-ri-cal,** *adjs.* Relating to hypsometry ; উচ্চতামানসম্বন্ধীয়। **–try,** *n.* The art or science of measuring altitudes ; উচ্চতামিতি।

hȳ′-răx, *n.* A genus of rabbit-like quadrupeds ; শশকাকৃতি চতুষ্পদ জীবশ্রেণী।

hȳ′-sŏn, *n.* A Chinese green tea ; চীনদেশীয় সবুজ চা।

hȳ-spȳ′, I– (ī-), *n.* A kind of hide-and-seek ; এক প্রকার লুকোচুরি খেলা।

hȳs′-sŏp, *n.* **1.** (*Bot.*) A kind of aromatic herb ; (উদ্ভিদ্ বিদ্যা) সুরভি গুল্মবিশেষ। **2.** (*Bible*) A plant whose twigs were used for sprinkling in Jewish rites ; a bunch of this plant used in purification ; (বাইবেল) একপ্রকার গুল্ম—যাহার কচি ডগাদ্বারা ইহুদীদিগের পূজাদিতে শান্তি জল ছড়াইয়া দেওয়া হইত; ঐ গুল্মের গুচ্ছ—যাহা শোধন ক্রিয়ায় ব্যবহৃত হয়।

hȳs-têr-ăl′-gi-ă, *n.* (*Med.*) Pain in the uterus ; (ভৈষজ্য-শাস্ত্র) জরায়ুর বেদনা, জরায়ু-শূল।

hȳs-têr-ĕc′-tŏ-mȳ, *n.* (*Surg.*) Excision of the uterus ; (অস্ত্রোপচার-বিদ্যা) জরায়ুচ্ছেদন।

hȳs-tē′-ri-ă, *n.* A nervous affection chiefly attacking women characterized by laughing and crying, convulsive struggling, sense of suffocation, etc. ; স্ত্রীলোকদিগের একপ্রকার আবেশিক ও আক্ষেপিক রোগ—ইহাতে হাস্য, ক্রন্দন, শ্বাসরোধ অনুভবাদি লক্ষণ অথবা অন্যান্য লক্ষণের সাদৃশ্য থাকে, মূর্চ্ছারোগ, ক্ষোভোন্মাদ।

hȳs-têr′-ic, *adj.* & *n.* Relating to hysteria ; মূর্চ্ছারোগসংক্রান্ত। ***Noun.*** (*Pl.*) Hysterical fits ; মূর্চ্ছার আক্রমণ। **–i-cal,** *adj.* Pertaining to, or affected with, hysterics ; morbidly emotional; মূর্চ্ছারোগাক্রান্ত, বায়ুরোগগ্রস্ত ; উৎকটভাবপ্রবণ। **–i-cal-ly,** *adv.*

hȳs-têr-ŏl′-ŏ-ġȳ, *n.* A treatise on the uterus ; জরায়ুসম্বন্ধীয় পুস্তক।

hȳs′-tĕr-ŏn-prŏt′-êr-ŏn, *n.* (*Gram.*) A figure of speech in which the word that should follow comes first ; an inversion of natural or logical order ; (ব্যাকরণ) একপ্রকার অলঙ্কার যাহাতে যে শব্দ পরে আসিবে তাহা পূর্ব্বে আসিয়া থাকে ; স্বাভাবিক ক্রমবিপর্য্যয়, হেতুসাধ্যবিবর্ত্ত (হিঃ কোঃ)।

hȳs-têr-ŏp′-ă-thȳ, *n.* **1.** Any disease of uterus ; জরায়ুর রোগ। **2.** Hysteria ; মূর্চ্ছা বায়ু।

hȳs-têr-ŏ′-pĕx-ȳ, *n.* (*Surg.*) An operation for fixing the uterus in position ; জরায়ু স্বস্থানস্থ করার জন্য অস্ত্রোপচার।

hȳs-tĕr-ŏt′-ŏ-mȳ, *n.* The operation of cutting into the uterus ; dissection of the womb ; জরায়ুচ্ছেদ (হঃ চঃ) ; গর্ভব্যবচ্ছেদ।

Hystrix Leucura—শজারু (বেলঃ)।

I

I, *n.* The ninth letter of the English alphabet ; ইংরাজী বর্ণমালার নবম অক্ষর।

I (ī), *pron.* & *n.* The pronoun of the first person in the nominative case ; আমি। ***Noun.*** (*Metaph.* with *the*) The ego ; অহং, আত্মা। **The I**—See I, *n.*

Iacchus, *n.* The reborn Dionysius ; ইনি পূর্ব্বজন্মে সুরাদেবতা Dionysius ছিলেন। Dionysiusএর মৃত্যুর পর Athene দেবী তদীয় হৃৎপিণ্ড দেবরাজ Zeusকে প্রদান করেন। Zeus উহা গলাধঃকরণ পূর্ব্বক Iacchusকে জন্মদান করেন।

ī'-ămb, *n.* Same as IAMBUS.

ī-ăm'-bĭc, *adj.* & *n.* Consisting of iambic feet ; প্রথম শব্দাংশ লঘু ও পরবর্ত্তী শব্দাংশ গুরু—এইরূপ শব্দাংশ-দ্বয়বিশিষ্ট। ***Noun.*** **1.** An iambic foot ; যে কবিতার চরণের প্রথম শব্দাংশ লঘু ও পরবর্ত্তী শব্দাংশ গুরু। **2.** A verse consisting of two syllables, the first short and the second long ; প্রথম শব্দাংশ লঘু ও পরবর্ত্তী শব্দাংশ গুরু—এইরূপ চরণবিশিষ্ট শ্লোক, ধ্বজ (মঃ উঃ), আদিলঘুদ্বিক (আঃ বঃ)।

ī-ăm'-bŭs, *n.* (*Pl.* -BUSES) A metrical foot consisting of a short syllable followed by a long one ; যে কবিতার চরণের প্রথম শব্দাংশ লঘু ও পরবর্ত্তী শব্দাংশ গুরু, আদিলঘুদ্বিক (আঃ বঃ)।

Iapetus, *n.* Titan of the Greek mythology ; গ্রীক পুরাণোক্ত দৈত্য-বিশেষ। Atlas ও Prometheus এই দৈত্যের পুত্র।

ī-ăt'-rĭc, –rĭ-căl, *adjs.* Pertaining to medicines or medical men ; ভৈষজ্য, বৈদ্যসম্পর্কীয়, চিকিৎসক-সম্পর্কীয়।

I-bē'-rĭ-ăn (ī-), *adj.* & *n.* **1.** Pertaining to ancient Iberia, comprising Spain and Portugal ; প্রাচীন আইবিরিয়া (স্পেন ও পর্ত্তুগাল) সম্পর্কীয়। **2.** Relating to Spain and Portugal unitedly ; যুক্ত স্পেন ও পর্ত্তুগাল সম্বন্ধীয়। ***Noun.*** An inhabitant or the language of ancient Iberia ; প্রাচীন আইবিরিয়ার ভাষা বা অধিবাসী।

ī'-bĕx, *n.* (*Pl.* -ES) A kind of wild goat of the Alps etc. with large recurved horns ; দ্বিরাবর্ত্তিত শৃঙ্গবিশিষ্ট পার্ব্বত্য ছাগ বিশেষ।

ĭ-bī'-dĕm, *adv.* (*abbr. ib., ibid.*) In the same book, chapter, passage, etc. ; সেই খণ্ড, পরিচ্ছেদ বা অংশ প্রভৃতিতে, তথায়।

ī'-bĭs, *n.* (*Pl.* -ES), A grallatorial bird allied to the stork ; বকজাতীয়

Ibis.

জলচর পক্ষী বিশেষ। **Sacred ibis**—A kind of ibis ; প্রাচীন মিসরবাসিগণ কর্ত্তৃক সম্পূজিত বকজাতীয়-পক্ষি বিশেষ।

I-că'-rĭ-ŭs (ī-), *n.* An Athenian who was taught the art of cultivation of the vine by Dionysius ; জনৈক এথেন্সবাসী। Dionysius ইহাকে দ্রাক্ষার চাষ সম্বন্ধে শিক্ষা প্রদান করেন। Icarius সকলকে নির্ব্বিচারে দ্রাক্ষা চাষের কৌশল শিক্ষা দিতে লাগিলেন। নিকটবর্ত্তী স্থানের মেষপালকগণ ঐ দ্রাক্ষাজাত সুরাপানে মত্ত হইয়া মনে করিল যে Icarius তাহাদিগকে বিষ পান করাইয়াছে—তাহারা এই বিশ্বাসের বশবর্ত্তী হইয়া তাহাকে হত্যা করিল। Icariusএর কন্যা Erigone পিতার মৃত্যুতে শোকোন্মত্তা হইয়া উদ্বন্ধনে প্রাণত্যাগ করেন।

I-că'-rŭs (ī-), *n.* The son of Dædalus ; গ্রীক শিল্পী Dædalusএর পুত্র। পিতা পুত্র একসঙ্গে কৃত্রিম পক্ষ সংযোজন পূর্ব্বক Crete দ্বীপ হইতে পলায়ন করে। Dædalus সূর্য্য হইতে দূরে উড়িতে উপদেশ দান করে ; কিন্তু পুত্র পিতার কথায় কর্ণপাত না করিয়া সূর্য্যের সন্নিকটবর্ত্তী ঊর্দ্ধাকাশে উড্ডীন হওয়াতে যে মোমদ্বারা তদীয় পক্ষ স্কন্ধের সহিত সংযুক্ত করা হইয়াছিল তাহা গলিয়া গেল এবং Icarus আকাশ হইতে সাগরে পতিত হয়। সমুদ্রের যে অংশে Icarus পতিত হইয়াছিল—তাহা Icarian সাগর নাম প্রাপ্ত হয়।

ice (īs), *n.* Frozen water ; বরফ, হিমানী, তুষার, তুহিনশর্করা (রাঃ তঃ), হিমশিলা (সাঃ পঃ)। **Ice-age**—তুষার যুগ [যে যুগে ইয়ুরোপ ও উত্তর আমেরিকার অধিকাংশ তুষারাচ্ছন্ন ছিল]। **Ice-axe** — আল্পস্ পর্ব্বতারোহিগণ পর্ব্বতের সানুদেশে সোপান কাটিবার জন্য যে এক-প্রকার কুঠার ব্যবহার করে। **Ice-bag**—(ভৈষজ্য শাস্ত্র) চূর্ণীকৃত বরফপূর্ণ রবারের থলিয়া [ঐরূপ থলিয়াদ্বারা রোগাক্রান্ত

ব্যক্তির মস্তকে চাপ দেওয়া হয়]। **Ice-berg**—A vast body of ice floating

Ice-berg.

in the ocean ; (*fig.*) an unemotional person ; প্রবমান তুষার স্তূপ, হিমশৈল, তুষারগিরি, হিমপ্লব ; (লক্ষণায়) আবেগশূন্য ব্যক্তি, হিমপুত্তলিকা, বরফের পুতুল। **Ice blink** — বরফস্তূপের প্রতিফলন জনিত দিক্‌চক্রবালের চতুঃপার্শ্ববিসারী ধবলিমা। **Ice-boat**—বরফের উপর চলার উপযোগী নৌকা বিশেষ ; নদী প্রভৃতির উপরিস্থ বরফ ভাঙ্গিবার জন্য নৌকা বিশেষ। **Ice-bound**—হিমানীবদ্ধ। **Ice-cold** — হিমশীতল, তুষারশীতল, হিমানীশীতল, বরফের মত ঠাণ্ডা। **Ice-cream**—মালাই বরফ, কুল্পি বরফ। **Ice-fall**—ঘনীভূত জলপ্রপাত সদৃশ তুষারনদীর সরলোন্নত অংশ, তুষারপ্রপাত। **Ice-field** — তুষারক্ষেত্র [বিশেষতঃ মেরুসন্নিহিত প্রদেশের সুবিস্তীর্ণ

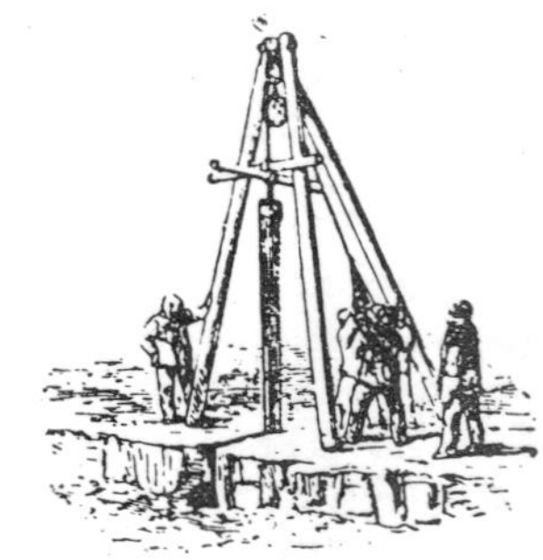

Ice-saw at work.

তুষারক্ষেত্র]। **Ice-house**—A building for storing ice ; a house made of ice ; তুষারসঞ্চয়গৃহ ; হিমানীরচিত গৃহ, তুষারগৃহ। **Ice-man** — One skilled in travelling upon ice ; বরফের উপর হাঁটিতে নিপুণ ব্যক্তি। A dealer in, or maker of, ice ; বরফ ব্যবসায়ী, বরফ প্রস্তুতকারী। **Ice-machine**—বরফের কল। **Ice-pudding** — একপ্রকার জমাট্-করা পিঠা। **Ice-saw**—জমাট পুকুর প্রভৃতির বরফ কাটার জন্য একপ্রকার লম্বা করাত। **Ice-water**—বরফগলা জল, বরফ জল। **To break the ice**—কোনও অপ্রীতিকর বিষয়ে প্রথম প্রথম কথা বলিতে যে বাঁধ বাঁধ ঠেকে তাহা দূর করিয়া কথা পাড়া।

īce, *v. t.* **1.** To cover with ice ; তুষারাবৃত করা, হিমানীমণ্ডিত করা, তুষারাচ্ছন্ন করা। **2.** To chill as with ice ; to freeze ; হিমানী প্রভৃতি দ্বারা শীতল করা ; জমাট বাঁধান, জমান। **3.** To cover (cake etc.) with concreted sugar etc. ; পিষ্টক প্রভৃতি দোবারা চিনিদ্বারা আবৃত করা। **Iced,** *adj.* Covered with ice ; তুষারাবৃত।

Ice'-lănd (īs-), *n.* An island between Norway and Greenland ; নরওয়ে ও গ্রীনল্যাণ্ডের মধ্যবর্ত্তী দ্বীপবিশেষ, হিমানীদ্বীপ। **—er,** *n.* **—lan'-dic,** *adj.* & *n.* Of, or relating to, Iceland ; হিমানীদ্বীপসম্বন্ধীয়। ***Noun.*** The language of Iceland ; হিমানীদ্বীপের ভাষা।

ich-neu'-mŏn (-nū-), *n.* An animal like a weasel noted for destroying crocodiles' eggs ; বেজি, নকুল। **Ichneumon fly**—এক জাতীয় ক্ষুদ্র পতঙ্গ।

ich-nŏg'-ră-phy̆, *n.* The art of drawing ground plans, maps, etc. ; মানচিত্রাদি অঙ্কন বিদ্যা। **—no-graph'-ic, —no-graph'-i-cal,** *adjs.*

Ichnocarpus frutescens — শ্যামালতা (বেলঃ)।

ī'-chŏr, *n.* **1** (*Gr. myth.*) The fluid flowing like blood in veins of gods ; (গ্রীকপুরাণ) দেবগণের ধমনীতে প্রবাহিত শোণিতবৎ পদার্থ বিশেষ, দেবশোণিত। **2.** A thin, acrid watery discharge from an ulcer, wound, etc. ; ক্ষতাদি হইতে নিঃসৃত জলবৎ দূষিত স্রাব, রসানি, কলতানি, পূযশোণিত। **3.** A thin watery discharge from elephant's skin etc. ; গজমদ, মদ, দান।

ich-thy̆-ŏg'-ră-phy̆, *n.* A treatise, or description, on fishes ; মৎস্যবিবরণ। **—pher,** *n.*

ich'-thy̆-oid (-ŏyd), *adj* & *n.* Resembling a fish ; মৎস্যবৎ, মীনসদৃশ। ***Noun.*** A vertebrate of the fish type ; মৎস্যজাতীয় মেরুদণ্ডী প্রাণী।

ich-thy̆-ŏl'-ă-try̆, *n.* Fish worship ; মৎস্যপূজা, মৎস্যার্চ্চনা।

ich'-thy̆-ō-līte, *n.* A fossil fish ; শিলীভূত মৎস্য।

ich-thy̆-ŏl'-ō-ğy̆, *n.* The natural history of fishes ; মৎস্যতত্ত্ব, মৎস্যবিদ্যা, মৎস্যবর্ণন। **—gist,** *n.* **—o-log'-i-cal,** *adj.*

ich-thy̆-ŏph'-ă-gous (-gŭs), *adj.* Eating, or subsisting on, fish ; মৎস্যভোজী, মৎস্যাশী, মৎস্যখাদক, মৎস্যভক্ষক, মৎস্যাহারী। **—gist, —gy,** *ns.* The practice of eating fish ; মৎস্যভোজন, মৎস্যাহার।

ich-thy̆-ō-sau'-rŭs (-sä-), *n.* An extinct marine reptile ; অধুনালুপ্ত সামুদ্রিক সরীসৃপ, মৎস্যমকর (মঃ ইঃ)।

ich-thy̆-ō'-sis, *n.* A disease in which the skin becomes rough, thick and scaly ; একপ্রকার চর্ম্মরোগ—যাহাতে চর্ম্ম মৎস্যের ন্যায় কঠিন ও শুষ্ক আঁইসদ্বারা পূর্ণ হয়, মীন বল্কিকা (হুঃ চঃ)। **—ot'-ic,** *adj.*

ī'-ci-cle (-kl), *n.* A hanging, tapering piece of ice formed by the freezing of dropping water ; হিমকণিকা, বরফকণা, হিমবিন্দু, হিমানীকণা।

ic'-ing, *n.* A coating of concreted sugar etc. ; দোবারা চিনি প্রভৃতির আচ্ছাদন।

ī'-cŏn, *n.* **1.** An image ; a portrait or statue ; মূর্ত্তি ; বিগ্রহ, প্রতিমা, প্রতিকৃতি, ঠাকুর। **2.** (East Church) A painting etc. of a sacred personage ; *e.g.*, Virgin Mary etc. ; (রুশিয়া

প্রভৃতি দেশে) কুমারী মেরী প্রভৃতির প্রতিকৃতি। **-con'-ic,** *adj.* Relating to an image etc. ; sculptured as a statue according to a conventional type ; মূর্ত্তি প্রভৃতি সম্বন্ধীয় ; রীতিসিদ্ধ আদর্শানুযায়ী ক্ষোদিত।

ī-cŏn'-ŏ-clăsm, *n.* The image breaking (*lit.* & *fig.*); মূর্ত্তিভঙ্গ, প্রতিমাভঙ্গ, দেবতাপ্রতিমাভঙ্গ।

ī-cŏn'-ŏ-clăst, *n.* **1.** A destroyer of idols ; one of a party who opposed the use of idols in the 8th and 9th centuries ; মূর্ত্তিভঞ্জক, প্রতিমাভঞ্জক (মঃ ইঃ), প্রতিমাভঙ্গকারী ; প্রতিমাপূজাবিরোধী। **2.** (*Fig.*) One who assails cherished beliefs ; (লক্ষণায়) যে ব্যক্তি অন্যের চিরপোষিত বিশ্বাসের উপর অযথা আক্রমণ করে, ধর্ম্মবিশ্বাসভঙ্গকারী। **-clas'-tic,** *adj.*

ī-cō-nŏg'-ră-phȳ, *n.* The art of representation by pictures or images ; illustration of a subject by drawing of figures ; মূর্ত্তিশিল্প, প্রতিকৃতি বিদ্যা ; চিত্রাদি দ্বারা সুস্পষ্টীকরণ। **-con-o-graph'-ic,** *adj.* **-ra-pher,** *n.*

ī-cō-nŏl'-ă-trȳ, *n.* The worship of images ; মূর্ত্তিপূজা, প্রতিমাপূজা। **-a-ter,** *n.* The worshipper of icons ; মূর্ত্তিপূজক।

ī-cō-nŏl'-ŏ-ġȳ, *n.* The science of icons ; মূর্ত্তিবিজ্ঞান, প্রতিমাতত্ত্ব।

ī-cŏ-să-hē'-drŏn, *n.* (*Geom.*) A solid bounded by twenty sides ; বিংশতিপার্শ্ববিশিষ্ট ঘনক্ষেত্র, বিংশতিফলক (হিঃ কোঃ)।

ĭc'-tŭs, *n.* Rhythmical or metrical stress ; (সঙ্গীতের বা তালের) ছন্দের জোর।

ī'-çȳ, *adj.* **1.** Relating to, or abounding in, ice ; coverd with ice ; very cold ; হিমানীসম্বন্ধীয়, হিমপ্রচুর ; হিমানীসমাবৃত, তুষারাবৃত ; হিমশীতল, তুষারশীতল, বরফের মত ঠাণ্ডা। **2.** (*Fig.*) Characterized by coolness, as manner, speech, etc. ; (লক্ষণায়) অনুরাগশূন্য, প্রীতিশূন্য, আবেগহীন, উদাস। **-ci-ly,** *adj.* **-ci-ness,** *n.*

ĭd, *n.* (*Bot.*) A unit of germ-plasm ; (জীব-বিজ্ঞান) বীজ বা কললের একক।

I-dă (ī-), *n.* **1.** A mountain range in Asia Minor ; এশিয়া মাইনরের অন্তঃপাতী শৈলশ্রেণী। এই পর্ব্বতের উচ্চ চূড়ায় Cybele দেবীর মন্দির নির্ম্মিত হইয়াছিল। **2.** A mountain in Crete ; ক্রীটদ্বীপস্থ পর্ব্বত বিশেষ—এই গিরির গুহায় দেবরাজ Zeus শিশুকালে পালিত হইয়াছিলেন।

I'-dăs (ī-), *n.* The son of Aphareus and Arne ; Aphareus এবং Arneর পুত্র। Idas এবং Apollo উভয়েই Marpessa নাম্নী সুন্দরীর প্রণয়প্রার্থী ছিলেন। Idas সুন্দরী Marpessaকে লইয়া পলায়ন করেন। ইহাতে Apollo ক্রোধাবিষ্ট হইয়া Idasএর পশ্চাদ্ধাবিত হন। তিনি Idasকে প্রাপ্ত হইয়া তাহার সহিত সংগ্রামে প্রবৃত্ত হইলেন। এমন সময়ে দেবরাজ Zeus আসিয়া এইরূপ মীমাংসা করেন যে Marpessa উভয়ের মধ্যে যাঁহাকে অভিরুচি পতিত্বে নির্ব্বাচন করিবে। চিরতরুণ অমর দেবতা Apollo মানবী Marpessa বৃদ্ধা হইলে পাছে তাহার প্রতি বিরাগ প্রদর্শন করেন—ইহা ভাবিয়া Idasকেই পতিত্বে বরণ করিলেন।

īde, *n.* A fish of the carp family ; রোহিতজাতীয় মৎস্য-বিশেষ।

ī-dē'-ă, *n.* **1.** An image of anything formed in the mind ; a conception ; কল্পনা ; ধারণা, প্রত্যয়। **2.** A notion ; a thought ; a way of thinking ; "Western *ideas* making progress" ; ভাব, ভাবনা, (হিঃ কোঃ), প্রত্যয় (ঐ), বুদ্ধি (ঐ), সংস্কার ; চিন্তা ; চিন্তাপ্রণালী। **3.** An archetype or pattern ; a plan or purpose of action ; an intention ; a design ; মূল আদর্শ ; কার্য্যের উদ্দেশ্য বা পরিকল্পনা ; অভিপ্রায় ; উদ্দেশ্য, মতলব, অভিসন্ধি। **4.** Vague belief ; "I had no *idea* you would be flooded" ; অস্পষ্ট বিশ্বাস। **5.** (*Philos., Descartes* & *Locke*) The immediate object of thought or mental perception ; (দেকার্তে, লক, প্রভৃতি) চিন্তা বা মানসপ্রত্যক্ষের অব্যবহিত বিষয়। **6.** (*Kant.*) A conception of reason that transcends all experience ; (ক্যাণ্ট) ভূয়োদর্শনলব্ধ জ্ঞানের অতীত প্রত্যয়সমূহ। **7.** (*Platonic*) An eternally existing pattern of which individual things in any class are imperfect copies ; (প্লেটো) স্থূল জগতের প্রতি বস্তু যে আদর্শীভূত নিত্য বস্তুর অসম্পূর্ণ প্রতিরূপ, কোন বস্তুর স্বরূপ বা নিত্যরূপ। **-aed, -a'd,** *adjs.* Having an idea or ideas ; significant ; "A flood of *idea'd* words" ; ভাবযুক্ত ; ভাবসূচক, ভাবব্যঞ্জক। **-less,** *adj.* **Idea-force**—ভাবনাশক্তি (হিঃ কোঃ)।

ī-dē'-ăl, *adj.* & *n.* **1.** Existing in idea ; visionary ; unreal ; কাল্পনিক, মনঃকল্পিত, মনোগত, চিন্তাগত, মানসিক ; ভাবপ্রধান (হিঃ কোঃ) ; অবাস্তব। **2.** Fit for a model ; faultless or perfect ; as, *ideal* beauty ; আদর্শযোগ্য, আদর্শস্থানীয় ; নির্দ্দোষ, অনবদ্য, সর্ব্বাঙ্গসুন্দর। **3.** Of, or relating to, Platonic ideas ; নিত্য আদর্শ সম্পর্কীয়। **4.** Embodying or symbolising an idea ; as, an *ideal* representation ; ভাবাত্মক, ভাবসূচক, ভাবপ্রধান (হিঃ কোঃ)। ***Noun.*** A perfect type ; a standard of perfection ; নমুনা (হিঃ কোঃ), প্রতিভাস (ঐ) ; আদর্শ। **-ly,** *adv.*

ī-dē-ăl'-ĭsm, *n.* **1.** (*Phil.*) The system of thought in which the object of external perception is held to consist of ideas ; (দর্শনশাস্ত্র) যে চিন্তাপ্রণালীতে বাহ্য বস্তু নিচয় ভাবমাত্র অর্থাৎ মূর্তসত্তা বিরহিত বলিয়া গণ্য করা হইয়া থাকে, ভাববাদ, বাহ্যশূন্যবাদ, প্রত্যয়াত্মকবাদ (হিঃ কোঃ), চিদাত্মকবাদ (ঐ), ভাবপ্রাধান্যবাদ (ঐ)। [আমি একটী বৃক্ষ দেখিতেছি। মনস্তত্ত্ববিৎ বলিতেছেন—এই বৃক্ষ দর্শনের অন্তরালে তিনটী বিষয় নিহিত আছে—বৃক্ষের দৃষ্ট ও স্বরূপ মূর্ত্তি এবং মন যাহা এই বৃক্ষের

দৃষ্টরূপ প্রত্যক্ষ করিতেছে। Fichte বলিতেছেন যে, কেবলমাত্র আমিই বর্ত্তমান আছি। বৃক্ষের দৃষ্ট ও স্বরূপ এই উভয় মূর্ত্তিই অভিন্ন, এবং এই উভয় রূপ আমার মনেরই রূপান্তর ; ইহার নাম *Subjective idealism* (বিষয়িগত-ভাববাদ)। Schelling বলিতেছেন, বৃক্ষ ও আমার অহং বা জীবাত্মা তুল্য-পরিমাণে বাস্তব ও চিদাত্মক ; কিন্তু উহারা উভয়েই সেই নির্ব্বিশেষ পরমসত্তার প্রকাশ ভিন্ন আর কিছুই নহে। ইহার নাম বিষয়গতভাববাদ (*Objective idealism*)। Hegel বলিতেছেন যে উপরিউক্ত সকল তত্ত্বনিরূপণই অলীক। এই বৃক্ষদর্শন-রূপব্যাপারে বাস্তববস্তু কেবলমাত্র দুইটী—"প্রত্যয়" এবং "সম্বন্ধ"। "অহং" এবং "বৃক্ষ" এই দুইটী পদ সেই সম্বন্ধেরই দুইটী পদ এবং ইহাদের বাস্তবত্ব "সম্বন্ধ"রূপ নিত্যসত্য বস্তুর উপর প্রতিষ্ঠিত ; ইহার নাম নির্ব্বিশেষ ভাববাদ (*Absolute idealism*) *G. H. Lewis.*]। **2.** Ideal representation of things ; imaginative treatment of a subject in art or literature ; বস্তুর ভাবমূর্ত্তি প্রদর্শন, চিন্মূর্ত্তিপ্রকটন ; (শিল্প বা সাহিত্যে) ভাবাঙ্গস্ফুরণ। **—ist,** *n.* **1.** An adherent of the doctrine of idealism ; ভাববাদী (এপিঃ), অধ্যাত্ম-বাদী, বাহ্যশূন্যবাদী। **2.** An artist or writer who treats a subject imaginatively ; ভাবাঙ্গস্ফুরণপন্থী, চিদ্বস্তুবিকাশপন্থী। **3.** One who follows after ideals ; আদর্শের অনুসরণকারী। **—is'-tic,** *adj.* **—i-za'-tion,** *n.* The act of idealizing ; ভাবাঙ্গস্ফুরণ (নারায়ণ), আদর্শী-করণ (হিঃ কোঃ)। **—ize,** *v. t.* & *i.* To make ideal ; to represent in an ideal form ; আদর্শস্বরূপ করা ; ভাবমূর্ত্তি প্রদর্শন করা, চিন্মূর্ত্তি প্রকটন করা, ভাবাঙ্গস্ফুরণ করা। ***Verb i.*** To conceive or form an ideal ; আদর্শ ধারণা বা গঠন করা, মানসসৃষ্টি করা।

ī-dē-ăl'-ĭ-tȳ, *n.* **1.** The quality of being ideal ; আদর্শত্ব। **2.** (*Phrenol.*) The conceptive faculty ; (মস্তিষ্ক-সামুদ্রিক) ভাবাঙ্গস্ফুরণ বৃত্তি।

ī-dē'-āte, *v. t.* & *i.* To conceive or imagine ; কল্পনা করা, ধারণা করা। ***Verb i.*** To form ideas ; ধারণা করা। **—a'-tion,** *n.* The act of ideating ; প্রত্যয়ণ (হিঃ কোঃ), অবধারণ (ঐ)। **—a-tion'-al,** *adj.*

idee fixe, *n.* A fixed idea dominating in the mind ; monomania ; বদ্ধমূল ধারণা ; একবিষয়োন্মাদ।

idem, *pron or adj.* (abbr. *id*) The same ; the same as above ; সেই ; উপরে যাহা তাহাই।

ī-dĕn'-tic, *adj.* **1.** Identical ; একই, অনন্য, অভিন্ন, একরূপ। **2.** (*Diplom.*) Designating an action or expression in which two or more governments follow precisely the same course or employ the same form ; as, an *identic* note ; (কূটরাজনীতি) যে কার্য্য বা মতাদি প্রকাশে দুই বা ততোধিক শাসনতন্ত্র একই পন্থা বা পদ্ধতি অবলম্বন করে তৎসূচক।

ī-dĕn'-tĭ-căl, *adj.* **1.** The very same ; as, the *identical* person or thing ; একই, অভিন্ন, অনন্য, অভেদ, স্বরূপ (হিঃ কোঃ), তদ্রূপী (ঐ)। **2.** Exactly alike or equal ; অভিন্ন, অনন্য, অভেদ, নির্ব্বিশেষ, তদ্রূপ। **3.** (*Log.* & *Math.*) Expressing an identity ; as, 'man is man' is an *identical* proposition ; (তর্ক-বিজ্ঞান ও গণিত-শাস্ত্র) অভিন্নতাবাচক, তাদাত্ম্যসূচক। **—ly,** *adv.*

ī-dĕn'-tĭ-fȳ, *v. t.* **1.** To make identical (*with*) ; to treat as the same ; as, to *identify* one's interest with those of another ; অভিন্ন করা ; অভিন্ন বলিয়া গণ্য করা, তাদাত্ম্য প্রদর্শন করা। **2.** To associate (oneself etc.) inseparably (*with* a party, policy etc.) ; অবিচ্ছেদ্য ভাবে সম্মিলিত হওয়া। **3.** To ascertain or prove to be the same ; as, to *identify* stolen goods ; অভিন্ন বস্তু বা ব্যক্তি রূপে নির্ণয় বা সপ্রমাণ করা। **—fi-a-ble,** *adj.* **—fi-ca'-tion,** *n.* The act of identifying ; state of being identified ; অভেদত্বপ্রতিপাদন, সনাক্ত-করণ, নিশানদিহী। **To identify oneself with**—See IDENTIFY *v.* 2.

ī-dĕn'-tĭ-tȳ, *n.* **1.** Sameness ; oneness ; অভিন্নতা, অভেদত্ব, অনন্যভাব, তদ্রূপতা, একরূপতা, একতা, সমানতা, অনন্যতা, স্বরূপতা, সমত্ব (বিশ্বঃ) ; একত্ব, ঐক্য, তাদাত্ম্য (বেদান্তঃ)। **2.** Individuality ; personality ; "He doubted his own *identity*" ; ব্যক্তিস্বাতন্ত্র্য ; ব্যক্তিত্ব, পৃথগাত্মতা, পুরুষবিধত্ব। **3.** (*Math.*) An identical equation ; (গণিতশাস্ত্র) সরূপ সমীকরণ। **Identity in difference**—অচিন্ত্য ভেদাভেদ (ব্রজঃ বৈষ্ণঃ)। **Identity Philosophy** — বিষয়িবিষয়ৈকতাবাদ (হিঃ কোঃ)। **Law of identity**—তাদাত্ম্য নিয়ম।

ĭ'-dē-ō-grăm, —grăph, *ns.* A character symbolizing the idea of a thing without expressing the name ; যে অক্ষর বা চিহ্ন দ্বারা কোন বস্তুর নাম প্রকাশিত না হইয়া ভাবমূর্ত্তি সূচিত হয়, চিত্রলিপি (হিঃ কোঃ), চিত্রাক্ষর। **—graph'-ic, —graph'-i-cal,** *adjs.* **—og'-ra-phy,** *n.*

ī-dē-ŏl'-ō-ġȳ, *n.* **1.** The science of ideas ; ভাব-বিজ্ঞান, ভাবনা-শাস্ত্র (হিঃ কোঃ), প্রত্যয়বিদ্যা (ঐ)। **2.** Idle theorizing ; অলস সিদ্ধান্ত করণ। **—gist,** *n.* **1.** One versed in ideology ; ভাবতত্ত্বজ্ঞ। **2.** A theorist ; a visionary ; কল্পনাপ্রিয় ব্যক্তি ; স্বপ্নাবিষ্ট ব্যক্তি। **—o-log'-i-cal,** *adj.*

ides (īdz), *n.* (*Rom. antiq.*) (*Pl.*) The fifteenth day of March, May, July and October, and thirteenth day of other months ; মার্চ্চ, মে, জুলাই ও অক্টোবর মাসের ১৫ই তারিখ ও অন্যান্য মাসের ১৩ই তারিখ, মধ্যদিন (আঃ বঃ)।

id est, (abbr. *i. e.*) That is to say ; অর্থাৎ।

ĭd'-ĭ-ō-çȳ, *n.* Extreme mental imbecility ; মানসিক জড়তা, জড়বুদ্ধিতা, জড়বুদ্ধিত্ব।

id′-i-ō-grăph, *n.* A signature ; a trade mark ; স্বাক্ষর; ব্যবসায় চিহ্ন।

id′-i-ŏm, *n.* **1.** The language peculiar to a people or to a country ; কোন জাতি বা দেশের বিশেষ ভাষা। **2.** The specific character of a language ; "....attempt to maintain *idiom*" : কোন ভাষার বিশিষ্ট প্রকৃতি, বাগ্‌ধারা, বাক্‌পদ্ধতি, বাক্যরীতি, শব্দগ্রন্থন পদ্ধতি (ভাঃ বিঃ)। **3.** A form of expression peculiar to a language ; কোন ভাষার রীতিসিদ্ধ প্রয়োগ, কোন ভাষার বিশেষত্বদ্যোতক প্রয়োগ।

id-i-ō-măt′-ic, *adj.* **1.** Pertaining to, or conforming to, idiom ; vernacular ; colloquial ; "........ *idiomatic* German words" ; কোন ভাষার বাক্‌পদ্ধতি-সম্বন্ধীয়, কোন ভাষার রীতিসিদ্ধ প্রয়োগ সম্বন্ধীয় ; দেশীয় ; চলিত, চল্‌তি।

id-i-ŏp′-ă-thȳ, *n.* **1.** A peculiar characteristic; বিশিষ্টপ্রকৃতি, বিশেষত্ব। **2.** A primary disease ; মূল রোগ।

id-i-ō-păth′-ic, *adj.* Primary ; অন্য কোন পূর্ব্ববর্ত্তী রোগাদি হইতে অনুৎপন্ন, স্বয়স্তূত, মূলীভূত (রোগ)। **–i-cal-ly,** *adv.*

id-i-ō-sȳn′-cră-sȳ, *n.* **1.** Peculiarity of temperament, view or disposition belonging to a person ; ব্যক্তিগত প্রকৃতি, মত বা স্বভাবের ব্যক্তিগত বৈশিষ্ট্য, ব্যক্তিগত ভাব, আত্মভাব, বিশেষ প্রকৃতি, প্রকৃতিবিশিষ্টতা, প্রকৃতিবিশেষতা (হিঃ কোঃ)। **2.** (*Med.*) The physical constitution peculiar to an individual; (ভৈষজ্য শাস্ত্র) ধাতুবৈষম্য, দেহপ্রকৃতি, ধাত [কোন ঔষধ বা পদার্থ দ্বারা সাধারণের যে প্রকার ফল দর্শে, ধাতুবৈষম্য-বশতঃ ব্যক্তিভেদে তদ্বিপরীত ফল দৃষ্ট হয়]। **3.** A mode of expression peculiar to an author ; কোন গ্রন্থকারের বিশিষ্ট প্রয়োগ। **–crat′-ic,** *adj.*

id′-i-ŏt, *n.* A person of weak or defective intellect ; an utter fool ; জড়বুদ্ধি, জড়মতি, জড়ধী ; বেকুব, জন্মমূঢ়, অকাট মূর্খ। **–ot′-ic, –ot′-i-cal,** *adj.* **–ot′-i-cal-ly,** *adv.*

ī′-dle (-dl), *adj., v. t. & i.* **1.** Worthless ; ineffective ; useless ; trifling ; as, *idle* thought or word ; অসার ; নিষ্ফল ; নিরর্থক ; তুচ্ছ, অকিঞ্চিৎকর, নগণ্য। **2.** Groundless ; as, *idle* hopes ; ভিত্তিহীন, অমূলক। **3.** Unemployed ; doing nothing ; as, *idle* workmen ; বেকার ; নিষ্কর্ম্মা, অকর্ম্মা, অকর্ম্মণ্য। **4.** Inactive ; নিষ্ক্রিয় ; নিশ্চেষ্ট। **5.** Lazy ; slothful; অলস ; কুড়ে। *Verb t.* To pass in idleness, (with *away*) ; as, to *idle away* time ; আলস্যে কাটান। *Verb i.* To spend time in idleness ; আলস্যে সময় কাটান। **–ness** *n.* **1.** Uselessness ; triviality ; "The *idleness* of the proceedings" ; নিরর্থকতা; তুচ্ছতা, নগণ্যতা। **2.** Slothfulness ; inactivity ; আলস্য, অলসতা; কুড়েমি। **–dler,** *n.* One who spends time in inaction ; a lazy person ; নিষ্কর্ম্মা লোক, অকর্ম্মা লোক ; অলস লোক। **–dly,** *adv.* Lazily ; vainly ; অলসভাবে, নিষ্কর্ম্মার

Idle wheel.

মত ; নিরর্থক, বৃথা, অনর্থক। **Idle wheel**—দন্তুর চক্রদ্বয়ের মধ্যদেশে স্থাপিত যে দন্তুর চক্র দ্বারা একটীর গতি অপরটীতে সঞ্চারিত হয়, অলস-চক্র। **Idly-busy**—Busy to no purpose ; বাজে কাজে ব্যস্ত।

ī′-dlesse (-dlĕs), *n.* Idleness ; আলস্য, কুড়েমি।

ī′-dŏl, *n.* **1.** An image of a deity as an object of worship ; a false god ; প্রতিমা, বিগ্রহ, মূর্ত্তি, ঠাকুর, দেবতা (হিঃ কোঃ) ; অলীক দেবতা। **2.** An object of passionate devotion ; a person or thing greatly loved or adored ; নয়নপুত্তলী, স্নেহের পুত্তলী, প্রাণের দেবতা ; প্রাণেশ্বর, প্রাণেশ্বরী, পরাণপুত্তলী। **3.** A phantom ; "I looked upon that ugly *idol* (his image) in the glass ; ছায়ামূর্ত্তি। **4.** (*Logic*) A false notion or conception ; ভুল ধারণা, ভ্রম, ভ্রমাত্মক সংস্কার। **Idol-worship**—মূর্ত্তিপূজা, প্রতিমাপূজা। **Idols of the cave**—(*Idola specus*) সংসারত্যাগী ব্যক্তিসুলভ ভ্রান্তবিশ্বাস। **Idols of the forum** or **market place**—(*Idola fori*) ভাষা বা সামাজিক সম্মিলন হইতে জাত ভ্রান্ত বিশ্বাস, গড্ডলিকা। **Idols of the theatre**—(*Idola theatri*) বিভিন্ন নাট্যতত্ত্বের মত হইতে উপজাত ভ্রান্তি। **Idols of the tribe**—(*Idola tribus*) মানব প্রকৃতিসুলভ ভ্রান্ত বিশ্বাস।

ī-dŏl′-ă-têr, *n.* **1.** An idol-worshipper ; মূর্ত্তিপূজক, পৌত্তলিক, প্রতিমাপূজক, দেবপূজক। **2.** A great admirer (of) ; স্তাবক। **–trous,** *adj.* **–trous-ly,** *adv.* **–try,** *n.* **1.** The worship of idols ; প্রতিমাপূজা, মূর্ত্তিপূজা, দেবপূজা। **2.** Excessive attachment or veneration for anything ; পূজা, পরমানুরাগ, পরমপ্রেম।

ī′-dŏl-īze, *v. t.* **1.** To make an idol of ; to worship as an idol ; দেববিগ্রহবৎ করা ; প্রতিমাবৎ পূজা করা। **2.** To adore or love in excess ; প্রাণের দেবতা বা প্রাণের দেবীরূপে পূজা করা, পরাণ পুত্তলীর মত আদর করা। *Verb i.* To practise idolatry ; প্রতিমাপূজা করা। **–i-za′-tion** *n.*

ī-dō′-lŭm, *n.* (*Pl.* -LA) **1.** A mental image or idea ; মানসমূর্ত্তি, চিন্মূর্ত্তি, ভাব। **2.** (*Logic*) A fallacy ; (তর্কবিজ্ঞান) অপসিদ্ধান্ত।

ī′-dȳl, –dȳll, *ns.* **1.** A short poem dealing with a pastoral life or scenery ; ক্ষুদ্র কবিতা, গোষ্ঠগাথা, গোষ্ঠগীতি, গ্রাম্যগাথা। **2.** An episode or series of events suitable for an idyll ; গ্রাম্য গাথার উপযোগী ঘটনাবলী। **–dyl′-lic,** *adj.* **–dyl′-li-cal-ly,** *adv.* **–ist,** *n.* Of, or relating to, idylls ; pastoral ; পল্লীগাথাসম্পর্কীয়, পল্লীজীবন বা পল্লীদৃশ্যবিষয়ক। **–ize,** *v. t.* To make idyllic ; পল্লীজীবন বা পল্লীসৌন্দর্য্য চিত্রণ দ্বারা মাধুর্য্যময় করা।

if, *conj.* & *n.* **1.** On condition that ; granting or supposing that ; যদি, যদ্যপি, যদিস্যাৎ ; যদিও, যদিচ, যদিবা। **2.** Whether ; as, try *if* you can do it ; কি না। **3.** Whenever ; as, *if* I feel any doubt I enquire ; যখনই। ***Noun.*** Condition ; supposition ; as, there are too many *ifs* in the way ; অবস্থা ; অনুমান। **As if**—As the case would be if ; যেন। **As if you did not know** — You know quite well ; যেন তুমি জান না। **Even if**—যদ্যপি। **If not**—If a thing is, be or were not ; যদি না থাকে বা থাকিত, না হইলে, নচেৎ। **If you please**—Please don't suppose the contrary ; আপনি অন্যরূপ ভাবিবেন না।

ig′-nĕ-ous (-ŭs), *adj.* **1.** Pertaining to, or containing, fire ; fiery ; অগ্নিগর্ভ, আগ্নেয়, বহ্নিময় ; অগ্নিসদৃশ, অগ্নিতুল্য। **2.** Produced by the action of fire ; (*Geol.*) produced by volcanic agency, as rocks etc. ; অগ্ন্যদ্ভূত ; (ভূ-বিদ্যা) আগ্নেয়গিরির ক্রিয়া দ্বারা উৎপন্ন। **Igneous rock**—See IGNEOUS, 2.

ig-nĕs′-cĕnt, *adj.* Emitting sparks of fire ; inflammatory ; অগ্নিস্ফুলিঙ্গ নিঃসারী ; প্রদাহজনক।

ig′-nis-făt′-ū-ŭs, *n.* **1.** Phosphorescent light appearing in the night over marshy grounds, also called *will-o'-the-wisp* ; আলেয়া, পিশাচদীপিকা পেত্নীর আলো, আলেয়ার আলো। **2.** A delusive hope or aim ; মায়ামরীচিকা, আশার ছলনা, আলেয়ার আলো।

ig-nīte′, *v. t.* & *i* **1.** To kindle ; to set on fire ; প্রজ্বালিত করা, জ্বালান ; আগুন ধরাইয়া দেওয়া। **2.** To heat strongly ; উত্তপ্ত করা। **3.** (*Chem.*) To heat to the point of combustion or chemical change ; (রসায়ন-শাস্ত্র) প্রজ্বালন বা রাসায়নিকপরিবর্ত্তনের মাত্রা পর্য্যন্ত উত্তপ্ত করা। ***Verb i.*** To take fire ; আগুন ধরা। **—nit′-a-ble,** *adj.* **—ni′-tion,** *n.*

ig-nō′-ble (-bl), *adj.* **1.** Of low family or birth ; not illustrious ; common ; হীনবংশ, নীচবংশসম্ভূত, নীচবংশোদ্ভব, হীনকুলজাত, প্রাকৃত, নীচবর্ণ ; অপ্রসিদ্ধ ; সাধারণ। **2.** Mean ; dishonourable ; হীন, নীচ, হেয়, নিকৃষ্ট, ইতর ; অখ্যাতিজনক, অপযশস্কর। **—bly,** *adv.* Basely ; নীচভাবে। **—ness,** *n.* Meanness ; নীচতা, হীনতা, ইতরামি।

ig-nō-min′-i-ous (-us), *adj.* **1.** Dishonourable ; shameful ; অপমানজনক, অখ্যাতিজনক, অপযশস্কর ; লজ্জাস্কর। **2.** Infamous ; despicable ; জঘন্য, হেয়, ঘৃণ্য ; অবজ্ঞেয়। **—ly,** *adv.* অপমানজনকরূপে।

ig′-nō-min-ȳ, *n.* **1.** Disgrace ; infamy ; অপমান, লাঞ্ছনা ; অখ্যাতি, কলঙ্ক, অপযশ। **2.** An infamous act or conduct ; লজ্জাজনক কার্য্য ; জঘন্য আচরণ।

ig-nō-rā′-mŭs, *n.* (*Pl.* -MUSES) An ignorant person ; a vain pretender to knowledge ; অজ্ঞব্যক্তি, মূঢ়, মূর্খ ; জ্ঞানাভিমানী মূর্খ, পণ্ডিতম্মন্য।

ig′-nō-rance (-răns), *n.* State of being ignorant ; want of knowledge ; অজ্ঞতা ; বিদ্যাহীনতা, অবিদ্যা, (বেদান্ত), অজ্ঞান (ন্যায় সূত্র)।

ig′-nō-rănt, *adj.* **1.** Destitute of knowledge ; অবোধ, মূর্খ, বিদ্যাহীন, অজ্ঞ, অপণ্ডিত। **2.** Uninformed ; অপরিজ্ঞাত, অপ্রাপ্তজ্ঞান, অনভিজ্ঞ। **3.** Unaware, (with *of* or *in*) ; as, to be ignorant *of* or *in* a subject, *of* a fact etc. ; অজ্ঞাত, অবিদিত। **—ly,** *adv.*

Ignoratio Elenchi — An argument that appears to refute the opponent while actually disproving something not advanced by him ; (তর্ক বিজ্ঞান) তর্কবিজ্ঞানের হেত্বাভাস—যাহাতে দৃষ্টতঃ প্রতিপক্ষের যুক্তি খণ্ডন করিতে যাইয়া তদীয় প্রকৃত উক্তি হইতে ভিন্ন উক্তির খণ্ডন করা হয় ; খণ্ডনানভিজ্ঞতা (হিঃ কোঃ), তর্কাভাস (ঐ)।

ig-nōre′, *v. t.* **1.** To refuse to take notice of ; to disregard wilfully ; নগণ্য মনে করা ; তাচ্ছিল্য করা, অগ্রাহ্য করা, উপেক্ষা করা। **2.** To set aside or reject as false or ungrounded ; as, the Grand Jury *ignored* the bill of indictment ; বাতিল করা, রদ করা, রহিত করা, মিথ্যা বা অমূলক বলিয়া অগ্রাহ্য করা।

Ignotum per ignotius—The explanation of the unknown by the still less unknown ; অধিকতর অজ্ঞাত বিষয় দ্বারা কোন অজ্ঞাত বিষয়ের ব্যাখ্যা করণ।

Iguana.

ī-gua′-nă (-gwâ-), *n.* An American reptile of the lizard family ; গোধা, গোসাপ।

ī-guan′-ō-dŏn (-gwân-), *n.* An extinct huge herbivorous lizard ; একপ্রকার অধুনালুপ্ত বৃহৎ গিরগিটী।

IHS—An abbr. for Jesus ; যীশুখ্রীষ্ট।

il′-ē-ŭm, *n.* (*Pl.* -IA) The large division of the small intestine ; ক্ষুদ্রান্ত্রের তৃতীয়াংশ, জড়িতান্ত্র (হঃ চঃ)।

il′-ē-ŭs, *n.* (*Med.*) An intestinal disorder marked by constipation griping pains etc. ; (ভৈষজ্য শাস্ত্র) অন্ত্রশূল (হঃ চঃ), অন্ত্রাবরোধ (ঐ)।

ī′-lĕx, *n.* (*Pl.* -LEXES), **1.** The holm-oak or evergreen oak ; একপ্রকার চিরহরিত ওক বৃক্ষ। **2.** (*Bot.*) A genus of plants including the common holly ; (উদ্ভিদ্ বিদ্যা) এক জাতীয় বৃক্ষ।

il'-i-ăc, *adj.* Of, or relating to, the flank or flank-bone ; পঞ্জর ও কুঁচকির মধ্যবর্ত্তী উদরাংশ সম্বন্ধীয়। **Iliac passion**—মল ও বমন সংযুক্ত অন্ত্রাবরোধ, উদাবর্ত্ত (সুশ্রুঃ)। **The iliac region**—শ্রোণিপ্রদেশ, পঞ্জর ও কুঁচকির মধ্যবর্ত্তী উদরাংশ।

Il'-i-ăd (ĭl-), *n.* **1.** The Epic poem attributed to Homer and describing the siege of Troy ; গ্রীক কবি হোমার রচিত মহাকাব্য। **2.** (*Fig.*) Long series, as of woe ; (লক্ষণায়) লহরী।

ilk, *adj.* (*Scot.*) Same (*rare*) ; একই, অনন্য (কচিদ্‌ব্যবহৃত)। **That ilk**—(*Vulg.*) That family, class or set ; ঐ শ্রেণী, ঐ দল, ঐ পরিবার।

ill, *adj. n.* & *adv.* **1.** Morally bad ; as, *ill* fame ; মন্দ, কু, বদ্। **2.** Unfriendly ; adverse ; harsh ; cruel ; as, *ill* feeling or treatment ; অমিত্র ; প্রতিকূল ; কর্কশ ; নিষ্ঠুর। **3.** Sick ; unwell ; পীড়িত, কাতর, রুগ্ন ; অসুস্থ। **4.** Defective ; faulty ; as, *ill* management ; মন্দ, ত্রুটিযুক্ত ; সদোষ। **5.** Miserable or wretched ; disastrous ; as, *ill* fate ; দুঃ, দুঃস্থ ; দুর্দ্দশাজনক। **6.** Improper, as manners or conduct ; অসঙ্গত, অবিধেয়, অনুচিত। **7.** Imperfect as success ; অসম্পূর্ণ। **8.** Harmful ; as, *ill* weeds grow apace ; অনিষ্টজনক। **9.** (*Archaic*) Difficult ; (অপ্রঃ) কঠিন। ***Noun.*** **1.** An evil ; the opposite of good ; মন্দ ; অশুভ। **2.** (*Pl.*) Misfortunes ; calamities ; দুর্ভাগ্য, দুর্দ্দৈব ; বিপদ্। **3.** Harm ; mischief ; ক্ষতি ; অনিষ্ট, অপকার। **4.** (*Chiefly Scot.*) A disease ; (প্রধানতঃ স্কটলণ্ডে) রোগ। ***Adv.*** **1.** Badly ; মন্দভাবে, কদর্য্যভাবে। **2.** Unfavourably ; unpropitiously ; "It would have gone *ill* with these players" ; প্রতিকূলভাবে ; অশুভভাবে। **3.** Improperly ; scarcely ; as, *ill* provided ; অনুচিতভাবে, অসম্পূর্ণভাবে ; অসম্যগ্‌ভাবে। **Ill-advised**—Imprudent ; অবিবেচক, অপরিণামদর্শী। **Ill-advisedly**—অবিবেচনার সহিত। **Ill-affected**—Not well disposed ; অপ্রসন্ন। **Ill-behaved**—Not well behaved ; দুর্বিনীত, দুঃশীল, অশিষ্ট, দুরাচার, দুর্বৃত্ত। **Ill-being**—অকল্যাণ, অশ্রেয়ঃ, অহিত, অকুশল। **Ill-blood, Ill-will**—Enmity ; strife ; শত্রুতা ; দ্বেষ, অপ্রীতি, রেষারেষি, চটাচটি, কলহ। **Ill-boding**—Inauspicious ; অশুভ, অমঙ্গলসূচক, অপায়া (*colloq.*)। **Ill-bred**—Badly brought up ; rude ; অশিষ্ট, অসভ্য, দুর্বৃত্ত, অবিনয়ী, দুর্বিনীত ; রূঢ়। **Ill-breeding** — Want of good breeding ; bad manners ; অশিষ্টতা, অভদ্রতা ; অশিষ্টাচার। **Ill-conditioned**—In a bad condition ; দুরবস্থাপন্ন। Of evil disposition ; দুঃশীল, বদ্‌মেজাজী। **Ill-defined**—Not distinct ; অস্পষ্ট, অনির্দ্দিষ্ট, অনিরূপিত। **Ill-disposed**—Disposed to evil ; malevolent ; পাপবুদ্ধি, দুষ্টবুদ্ধি ; বিদ্বেষপূর্ণ। Unfavourably disposed (towards) ; বিরূপ, প্রতিকূল, অপ্রসন্ন। **Ill-fame** — Bad repute ; অখ্যাতি, বদনাম, অপযশ, কলঙ্ক। **Ill-fated**—Destined to bad fortune ; bringing bad fortune ; দুর্ভাগ্য, হতভাগ্য, অভাগা ; দুর্ভাগ্যজনক। **Ill-favoured**—Deformed ; ugly ; displeasing ; objectionable ; কদাকার, শ্রীভ্রষ্ট ; কুৎসিত, বিশ্রী ; দুর্মনা ; অপ্রীতিকর। **Ill-feeling**—Malice ; animosity ; মনোমালিন্য ; রেষারেষি, বিদ্বেষ। **Ill-got**—Procured by bad means ; অসদুপায়ে অর্জ্জিত। **Ill-gotten**—অন্যায়ার্জ্জিত, অন্যায়লব্ধ। **Ill-humour or temper** — Bad or morose temper ; বদ্‌মেজাজ, খারাপ মেজাজ। **Ill-humoured** — Bad-tempered ; বদ্‌মেজাজী। **Ill-judged**—Unwise ; অবিজ্ঞ, জ্ঞানহীন, মূঢ়। **Ill-luck**—দুরদৃষ্ট, দুর্ভাগ্য, পোড়াকপাল (*clloq.*)। **Ill-mannered** — Unmannerly ; rude ; অভদ্র, অসভ্য, বেআদব, দুর্বিনীত ; রূঢ়। **Ill-nature** — Sullenness ; খিট্‌খিটে স্বভাব, বদ্‌মেজাজ। **Ill-natured** — Peevish ; churlish ; খিট্‌খিটে ; পাড়াগেঁয়ে। **Ill-off**—In poor circumstances ; দুরবস্থাপন্ন, দুঃস্থ। **Ill-omened**—Attended by bad omens ; অশুভ, দুর্নিমিত্ত সূচক, কুলক্ষণাক্রান্ত, অনিষ্টশকুন। **Ill-starred**—Born under an evil star ; unlucky ; অশুভনক্ষত্রজাত ; মন্দভাগ্য, হতভাগ্য, দৈবোপহত, হতদৈব। **Ill-temper** — বদ্‌মেজাজ, দুষ্টবৃত্তি, অসদ্বৃত্তি। **Ill-tempered**—বদ্‌মেজাজী, অপ্রসন্ন, বিরস ; খিট্‌খিটে ; রুক্ষস্বভাব, রুখা ; (শরীরের পিত্ত, শ্লেষ্মা প্রভৃতি সম্বন্ধে) যথানুপাতে সম্মিলিত নয় ; অসুস্থ। **Ill-trained** — দুর্বিনীত (কেভিঃ), অশিষ্ট (ঐ)। **Ill-turn**—Harm ; অপকার, অনিষ্ট, অহিত। **A house of ill fame**—A house where bad persons meet for illicit intercourse ; বেশ্যালয়, বারাঙ্গনাগার, গণিকালয়। **Ill at ease**—Uneasy ; uncomfortable ; অস্থিতর মতি, অস্থির-চিত্ত ; অস্বচ্ছন্দ, অসুখী। **Ill got ill spent**—পাপের ধন প্রায়শ্চিত্তে যায়। **Ill news runs apace**—Bad news spreads quickly ; কুসংবাদ বাতাসের আগে যায়। **It's an ill wind that blows nobody good**—There are no events which are misfortunes to all concerned ; এমন কোন ঘটনা নাই যাহাতে সকলেরই অপকার হইয়া থাকে। **To do ill turn to a person**—To do harm to him or his interests ; কাহারো অনিষ্ট করা, কাহারো অনুপকার করা, কাহারো স্বার্থহানি করা। **To feel ill at ease**—To feel uneasy ; কেমন কেমন বোধ করা, অস্বচ্ছন্দতা বোধ করা, অসোয়াস্তি বোধ করা। **To go ill with**—To result in misfortune or danger ; দুর্ভাগ্যজনক হওয়া, বিপজ্জনক হওয়া। **To speak ill of**—To speak something unfavourable of ; দুর্নাম করা। **To take it ill**—To be offended at it ; রুষ্ট হওয়া, ক্ষুব্ধ হওয়া, বিরক্ত হওয়া।

il-lā'-tion, *n.* Act of inferring from premises ; deduction ; conclusion ; সিদ্ধান্ত ; নিগমন ; অনুমান, (হিঃ কোঃ) ; তর্ক (ঐ)।

il'-lā-tive (-tiv), *adj.* Pertaining to, or introducing an illation or inference ; as, an *illative* word ; inferential ; আনুমানিক, অনুমানবাচক ; অনুমানাত্মক। **—ly,** *adv.* **Illative conjunctions**—Such as, *then, therefore,* etc. ; সিদ্ধান্তবাচক অব্যয়, *then, therefore* ইত্যাদি। **Illative conversion** — আনুমানিক পরিবর্ত্তন (হিঃ কোঃ)। **Illative sense**—আনুমানিক অর্থ।

il-lē'-găl, *adj.* Contrary to law ; unlawful ; অবৈধ, বিধিবিরুদ্ধ ; আইনবিরুদ্ধ, বে-আইনী, ব্যবহারবিরুদ্ধ স্মৃতিবিরুদ্ধ, অস্মার্ত্ত। **—gal'-i-ty,** *n.* Unlawfulness : বিধিবিরুদ্ধতা, অবৈধতা। **—ly,** *adv.* Unlawfully ; অবৈধরূপে, বিধিবিরুদ্ধভাবে, বে-আইনীভাবে।

il-lĕg'-i-ble (-bl), *adj.* Not legible ; that cannot be read ; indistinct ; দুষ্পাঠ্য, দুষ্পঠনীয় ; পঠনাশক্য ; অস্পষ্ট। **—bil'-i-ty,** *n.* The sate of being illegible ; অপাঠ্যতা, অস্পষ্টতা, অস্পষ্টাক্ষরত্ব। **—bly,** *adv.*

il-le-ğit'-i-mate, *adj. n.* **1.** Unlawful ; improper ; spurious ; "*Illegitimate* curiosity" ; অবৈধ ; অন্যায় ; অসঙ্গত, অনুচিত, অকৃত। **2.** Unlawfully begotten ; bastard ; জারজ, বিজন্মা ; অনৌরস, ব্যভিচারজ, অধর্ম্মজাত, অদম্পত্যুৎপন্ন, অদম্পত্যুদ্ভব, অদম্পতীজাত, অবিধিজাত, অশাস্ত্রজাত, অন্তোৎপন্ন, অসতীপ্রসূত, উপস্ত্রীসুত। **3.** Illogical ; not correctly deduced ; ন্যায়বিরুদ্ধ, যুক্তিবিরুদ্ধ ; প্রমাণাসিদ্ধ (কেভিঃ), অশুদ্ধরূপে উপপাদিত। **4.** Abnormal ; "*Illegitimate* plants" ; অস্বাভাবিক, কিম্ভূতকিমাকার। **—ly,** *adv.* **—ma-cy,** *n.* The state of being illegitimate ; জারজতা।

il-le-ğit'-i-māte, *v. t.* To declare illegitimate ; জারজ বলিয়া ঘোষণা করা। **—ma'-tion,** *n.*

il-lib'-ĕr-ăl, *adj.* **1.** Not liberal ; অনুদার। **2.** Lacking culture or good breeding ; mean ; vulgar ; sordid ; অসভ্য, অশিষ্ট ; নীচ ; গ্রাম্য ; হীন। **3.** Narrow-minded ; সংকীর্ণমনাঃ, ক্ষুদ্রচেতাঃ, ক্ষুদ্রমনঃ। **4.** Niggardly ; কৃপণ, অমুক্তহস্ত, অবদান্য, অদানশীল, ব্যয়কুণ্ঠ। **—al'-i-ty,** *n.* **1.** State of being illiberal ; অবদান্যতা (কেভিঃ), কার্পণ্য (মঃ ইঃ), অনৌদার্য্য (ঐ)। **2.** Narrowness of mind ; meanness ; সঙ্কীর্ণতা, অনুদারতা ; নীচতা। **3.** Niggardliness ; কার্পণ্য। **—ly,** *adv.*

il-lic'-it, *adj.* Unlawful ; forbidden by law or custom ; অবৈধ, বিধিবিরুদ্ধ ; নিষিদ্ধ, ব্যবহারবিরুদ্ধ, অব্যাবহারিক। **—ly,** *adv.* **—ness,** *n.* **Illicit process**—অনুচিত প্রক্রিয়া (হিঃ কোঃ)।

il-lim'-it-ă-ble (-bl), *adj.* Limitless ; boundless ; অপরিসীম ; অসীম, নিঃসীম, অপ্রমেয়, অনন্ত। **—bil'-i-ty, —ness,** *ns.* **—bly,** *adv.*

il-lit'-ĕr-āte, *adj.* Unlettered ; uneducated ; unable to read ; বর্ণজ্ঞানহীন, নিরক্ষর, অনক্ষর, অক্ষরশূন্য ; অনধীত, মূর্খ, অশিক্ষিত, বিদ্যাশূন্য, অবিদ্বান, অপণ্ডিত ; পঠনাক্ষম। **—a-cy,** *n.* Ignorance ; inability to read or write ; অজ্ঞতা ; নিরক্ষরতা, বর্ণজ্ঞানহীনতা। **—ly,** *adv.* **—ness,** *n.*

ill'-nĕss, *n.* Disease ; sickness ; রোগ, পীড়া, অসুখ ; ব্যাধি, ব্যামোহ।

il-lŏg'-i-căl, *adj.* Contrary to the rules of sound reasoning ; প্রমাণাসিদ্ধ, ন্যায়বিরুদ্ধ (হিঃ কোঃ), তর্কবিরুদ্ধ (ঐ), ন্যায়শাস্ত্র বিরুদ্ধ, অসঙ্গত, অযৌক্তিক, যুক্তিবিরুদ্ধ, অযুক্তিসিদ্ধ। **—cal'-i-ty,** *n.* **—ly,** *adv.* **—ness,** *n.*

il-lūme', *v. t.* (*Poet.*) To make bright ; to illuminate, (*lit.* & *fig*) ; (কবিতায়) উজ্জ্বল করা ; আলোকিত করা, দীপ্ত করা, উদ্ভাসিত করা।

il-lū'-mi-nănt, *n.* That which affords light ; উদ্ভাসক।

il-lū'-mi-nāte, *v. t.* **1.** To light up ; to brighten ; আলোকিত করা, উজ্জ্বল করা, উদ্ভাসিত করা ; প্রদীপিত করা, প্রভাভাসিত করা। **2.** (*Fig.*) To enlighten spiritually or mentally ; (লক্ষণায়) জ্ঞানালোক প্রদান করা, আধ্যাত্মিক আলোক দ্বারা উদ্ভাসিত করা। **3.** To decorate as a building etc. with light ; উৎসবাদি উপলক্ষে আলোক দ্বারা সজ্জিত করা, দীপমালা দ্বারা সজ্জিত করা। **4.** To throw light upon ; to elucidate ; বিশদ করা ; সহজবোধ্য করা, সুখবোধ্য করা। **5.** To adorn as an initial letter, in a manuscript etc. with gold, silver, and brilliant colours ; পুঁথির আদ্যক্ষর, শব্দ, প্রভৃতি সমুজ্জ্বলবর্ণে রঞ্জিত করা, হস্তলিপির পুঁথির আদ্যক্ষর স্বর্ণ, রজত প্রভৃতি নানা দীপ্ত বর্ণে রঞ্জিত করা। **6.** To make resplendant ; "Self-sacrifice *illuminated* by love" ; সমুজ্জ্বল করা, প্রভাময় করা। **—na'-tion,** *n.* **1.** The act of giving light ; দ্যোতন, প্রকাশন, দীপন, উদ্ভাসন, উদ্দ্যোতন। **2.** Intellectual light or knowledge ; প্রতিভাদীপ্তি, জ্ঞানালোক। **3.** Spiritual enlightenment ; divine inspiration ; revelation ; মোহান্ধকারনাশ, তত্ত্বপ্রকাশ ; ভগবৎ প্রেরণা ; ঐশ্বরিক প্রত্যাদেশ। **4.** Festive decoration with lights ; (উৎসবাদি উপলক্ষে) দীপমালাদি দ্বারা মণ্ডন। **5.** (*Pl.*) Lights or designs formed by lamps etc. ; দীপালী, দীপমালা, অগ্নিক্রীড়া, রোশনাই। **6.** Adorning letter, manuscripts, etc. with brilliant colours, flourishes etc. ; অক্ষর, হস্তলিপি, প্রভৃতি উজ্জ্বলবর্ণ দ্বারা রঞ্জন। **7.** A coloured drawing or figure etc. used in a manuscript page ; হস্তলিখিত পুস্তকের পাতার পত্রে নানাদীপ্ত বর্ণে অঙ্কিত রেখাচিত্রাদি। **—na-tive,** *adj.* **—na-tor,** *n.* **1.** An illuminating agent ; উদ্ভাসক, দীপ্তিপ্রদায়ক, দীপক, প্রদীপক, দ্যুতিকর। 2. A mental or spiritual enlightener ; জ্ঞানালোক-প্রদাতা, তত্ত্বজ্ঞানদাতা, গুরু। 3. One who decorates manuscript etc. ; হস্তলিখিত পুঁথির আদ্যক্ষরাদি রঞ্জক, পত্ররঞ্জক (মঃ ইঃ।

il-lü′-mi-nä′-ti, *n.* (*Pl.*) 1. A secret society founded by Weishaupt in 1776, holding deistic and republican principles and orgainsed like freemasons ; গুপ্ত-সমিতি বিশেষ। 2. Persons affecting to possess extraordinary knowledge ; যাহারা অসাধারণ জ্ঞানী বলিয়া ভাণ করে। 3. (*Cap., Eccl. Hist.*) A sect which sprang esp. in Spain about the year 1575. Their principal doctrine was that, by means of prayer, they had attained to so perfect a state as to have no need of ordinances, sacraments, etc. ; ১৫৭৫ খৃঃ অব্দে স্পেন দেশে উদ্ভূত ধর্ম্মসম্প্রদায় বিশেষ—এই সম্প্রদায়ের সভ্যগণ আপনা-দিগকে চরম আধ্যাত্মিক উন্নতির অধিকারী এই জ্ঞানে তাহাদের পক্ষে কোন প্রকার দীক্ষা, সংস্কার অনুষ্ঠানাদির আবশ্যকতা আছে বলিয়া মনে করিতেন না। 4. (*Cap.*) An obscure sect of French Familists, which arose in Picardy in 1634. ; Picardyতে ১৬৩৪ খৃষ্টাব্দে উদ্ভূত নগণ্য ধর্ম্মসম্প্রদায় বিশেষ। 5. (*Cap.*) Same as ROSICRUSIANS (which see). 6. (*Cap.*) The Mystic's Quietists and Hesychasts ; ধ্যানরসিক, রাজ-যোগী প্রভৃতি। **–nism, –nist**, *ns.*

il-lü′-mine (-mĭn), *v.t.* 1. To light up ; to brighten ; উজ্জ্বল করা ; দীপ্ত করা। 2. To enlighten spiritually ; মোহান্ধকার নাশ করা, অজ্ঞানতিমির বিদূরিত করা।

il-lü′-sion, *n.* 1. Deception ; delusion ; মায়া ; ভ্রান্তি, ভ্রম, প্রপঞ্চ, মিথ্যা প্রত্যয়, অবিদ্যা, মোহ, বিভ্রম, আভাস, অধ্যাস, যোগমায়া, বিপর্য্যয় (হিঃ কোঃ), বিবর্ত্ত (ঐ)। 2. An unreal visual appearance ; মরীচিকা, মৃগ-তৃষ্ণিকা। 3. Sensual perception of an external object involving a false belief ; বাহ্যবস্তু সম্বন্ধে মিথ্যা প্রত্যয়। 4. A tulle ; একপ্রকার সূক্ষ্ম রেশমী জাল। **–ist**, *n.* 1. A producer of illusions ; a conjurer ; মায়াবী ; যাদুকর, ঐন্দ্রজালিক। 2. One who disbelieves in objective existence ; মায়াবাদী। **Illusion tactia**—স্পর্শমায়া (হিঃ কোঃ)। **Visual illusion**—দৃষ্টিমায়া (হিঃ কোঃ), দৃশ্যমায়া (ঐ)।

il-lü′-sive (-sĭv), **–sŏ-rȳ**, *adjs.* Deceptive ; unreal ; মিথ্যা, প্রবঞ্চনা-ময়, মায়াময়, ভ্রান্তিজনক, অলীক, মায়িক, ভ্রমাত্মক, মায়ারূপ ; অপ্রকৃত, অবাস্তব। **–ly, –ri-ly**, *advs.* **–ness, –ri-ness**, *ns.*

il-lŭs′-trāte, *v. t.* 1. To make clear ; to elucidate ; সুবোধ্য করা, সুস্পষ্ট করা ; বিশদ করা, সুখবোধ্য করা। 2. To explain by means of examples, pictures, etc. ; উদাহরণাদি দ্বারা বুঝাইয়া দেওয়া। 3. To ornament as a book, newspaper, etc. with elucidating designs ; চিত্রাদি দ্বারা শোভিত করা। **–tra′-tion**, *n.* 1. Act of illustrating ; elucidation ; সুস্পষ্টীকরণ ; বিশদীকরণ। 2. That which illustrates ; an example ; উদাহরণ ; দৃষ্টান্ত। 3. A picture or design to illustrate a book etc. ; চিত্র, ছবি। **–tra-tive**, *adj.* Serving to explain or exemplify ; সুখবোধ্য, উদাহরণ-স্থলীয়, প্রকাশক, উদ্দেশক। **–tra-tive-ly**, *adv.* **–tra-tor**, *n.*

il-lŭs′-tri-ous (-ŭs), *adj.* 1. Eminent ; famous ; distinguished ; renowned ; বিখ্যাত, খ্যাতনামা, নামজাদা ; প্রসিদ্ধ ; লব্ধপ্রতিষ্ঠ ; পুণ্যশ্লোক। **–ly**, *adv.* **–ness**, *n.* Greatness ; fame ; glory ; মহানুভবতা, মহত্ব ; খ্যাতি ; গৌরব।

im′-āge, *n.* 1. A likeness ; a statue, esp. of a saint etc. ; idol ; প্রতিমূর্ত্তি, প্রতিরূপ, প্রতিকায়, প্রতিকৃতি ; পুতুল ; বিগ্রহ, প্রতীক (ছান্দোগ্য)। 2. Form ; semblance ; "We grow into the *image* of what we love" ; রূপ ; আভাস। 3. A picture drawn by fancy ; a conception ; an idea ; মানসচিত্র, কাল্পনিক চিত্র ; ধারণা ; ভাব। 4. The figure of an object produced by reflection from a mirror or refraction through lens ; প্রতিবিম্ব, প্রতিচ্ছায়া, ছায়া। 5. Counterpart ; as, he is the very *image* of his father ; প্রতিরূপ। 6. Embodiment ; type ; as, she is the *image* of piety ; প্রতিমূর্ত্তি ; আদর্শ। 7. (*Rhet.*) A simile or metaphor ; (অলঙ্কার-শাস্ত্র) রূপক, উপমা। **–less**, *adj.* **Image-breaker** — An iconoclast ; প্রতিমাভঙ্গ-কারী, মূর্ত্তিভঞ্জক। **Image-maker, –graver** — A sculptor ; ভাস্কর। **Image-worshipper**—An idolator ; প্রতিমাপূজক, পৌত্তলিক, মূর্ত্তি-পূজক। **Mental image**—মানসিক চিত্র (হিঃ কোঃ), মনঃকল্পনা। **Real image**—বাস্তবিক প্রতিরূপ (হিঃ কোঃ)। **Virtual image** — অদৃষ্ট প্রতিরূপ (হিঃ কোঃ)।

im′-āge, *v. t.* 1. To make an image of ; to represent or portray ; মূর্ত্তি প্রস্তুত করা ; মূর্ত্তিদ্বারা প্রদর্শন করা। 2. To reflect or mirror ; প্রতিফলিত করা, প্রতিবিম্বিত করা। 3. To imagine ; কল্পনা করা। 4. To describe in a graphic manner ; সুচিত্রিত করা, সজীব বর্ণনা করা। 5. To typify ; to symbolize ; "Oh stream ! Thou *imagest* my life" ; চিহ্ন বা আদর্শদ্বারা প্রদর্শন করা ; চিহ্নদ্বারা প্রকাশ করা। **–a-ble**, *adj.*

im′-āg-ĕ-rȳ, *n.* 1. Images collectively ; মূর্ত্তিসমূহ। 2. Statuary ; ভাস্কর্য্য, মূর্ত্তিশিল্প। 3. Mental images collectively ; "Like a dream's dim *imagery*" ; মানসপ্রতিমাসমূহ, মানস-সৃষ্টি, কল্পনাসৃষ্টি, মনঃসৃষ্টি। 4. Rhetorical figures ; রূপক, উপমাদি, অলঙ্কার।

im-ăg′-i-nă-ble (-bl), *adj.* Capable of being imagined ; কল্পনার যোগ্য, কল্পনীয়, কল্পিতব্য, বিভাবনীয়, বোধগম্য। **–bly,** *adv.*

im-ăg′-i-năl, *adj.* Of, or pertaining to, an insect imago ; কীটের চরমরূপ প্রজাপতি সম্বন্ধীয়।

im·ăg′-i-nă-rŷ, *adj.* **1.** Fancied ; visionary ; not real ; কল্পিত, কাল্পনিক, কল্পনাপ্রসূত, সঙ্কল্পজ, স্বকপোলকল্পিত, কল্পনাসিদ্ধ ; মনঃকল্পিত, মানসিক, কল্পনাসিদ্ধ ; অবাস্তব, অবাস্তবিক। **2.** (*Math.*) Having no real existence but assumed to exist for a special purpose ; as, an *imaginary* quantity ; (গণিতশাস্ত্র) যাহার কোন বাস্তব সত্তা নাই কিন্তু যাহা কোন বিশেষ উদ্দেশ্যের জন্য গৃহীত হয়—এরূপ, কাল্পনিক (হিঃ কোঃ)। **–ri-ly,** *adv.*

im-ăg-i-nā′-tion, *n.* **1.** The faculty of the mind by which new combinations of ideas are formed ; fancy ; কল্পনাশক্তি ; কল্পনা। **2.** The act of imagining ; conception ; কল্পনা করণ ; ধারণা। **3.** That which is imagined ; an idea ; কল্পনা, কল্পিত বিষয় ; ভাব।

im-ăg′-i-na-tive (-tĭv), *adj.* Of, or relating to, imagination ; কল্পনাসম্বন্ধীয়। **2.** Given to imagination ; proceeding from, or characterised by, imagination ; কল্পনাপ্রিয়, কল্পনাপটু, কল্পনাকুশল, কল্পনাচতুর ; কল্পনাসম্ভূত, কল্পনাত্মক। **–ly,** *adv.* **–ness,** *n.*

im-ăg′-ine (-ĭn), *v. t.* & *i.* **1.** To form a mental image of ; to conceive ; কল্পনা করা ; ধারণা করা। **2.** (*Rare*) To scheme ; to devise ; (অপ্রঃ) মতলব করা ; ধারণা করা। **3.** To guess or conjecture ; as, I can't *imagine* what he is doing ; to suppose ; অনুমান করা, আন্দাজ করা, ঠাওরা ; মনে করা।

i-mā′-gō, *n.* (*Pl.* -GINES, -GOS) **1.** The last or perfect stage of an insect after all metamorphoses, *e. g.,* a butterfly ; সর্ব্বপ্রকার রূপান্তরের পর কীটের অন্তিম বা চরম রূপ, যথা, প্রজাপতি, পতঙ্গাবস্থান (সাঃ পঃ)।

i-mâm′, i-maum′ (-mäm), *ns.* **1.** One officiating as priest of a Mohammedan mosque ; ইমাম। **2.** The title given to various Mohammedan leaders ; ভিন্ন ভিন্ন মুসলমান সরদারদিগের উপাধি।

im′-bĕ-cile (-sēl), *adj.* & *n.* **1.** Feeble-minded ; stupid ; idiotic ; জড়বুদ্ধি, দুর্ব্বলচিত্ত, জড়ধী ; বোকা, আহাম্মক ; জড়মতি। **2.** Physically weak or feeble ; দুর্ব্বল, অক্ষম, শক্তিহীন, অশক্ত, ক্ষীণ। ***Noun.*** A person weak in intellect ; জড়বুদ্ধি ব্যক্তি, হীনবুদ্ধি ব্যক্তি। **–cil′-i-ty,** *n.* **1.** Mental weakness ; silliness ; folly ; মানসিক দুর্ব্বলতা, বুদ্ধিদৌর্ব্বল্য (হিঃ কোঃ) ; জড়বুদ্ধিতা ; নির্ব্বুদ্ধিতা। **2.** Physical weakness ; debility ; দৌর্ব্বল্য ; শক্তিহীনতা। **3.** Incapacity ; inability ; "Its *imbecility* to restrain us" ; অক্ষমতা ; অপারগতা। **–ly,** *adv.*

im-bībe′, *v. t.* **1.** To drink as a liquid ; to inhale as air etc. ; to absorb as a moisture ; পান করা ; শ্বাসগ্রহণ করা ; শোষণ করা। **2.** To take into the mind and retain ; to assimilate ; as, to *imbibe* a principle or idea ; মনোমধ্যে গ্রহণ ও পোষণ করা, হৃদয়ে ধারণ করা ; হৃদয়ঙ্গম করা। **–bi-ba′-tion,** *n.*

im′-bri-cāte, *v. t.* & *i.* To lay or place, so as to overlap like roof-tiles ; as, to *imbricate* leaves or scales of fish ; টালির ন্যায় একটীর কিনারা অপরটীর উপর রাখিয়া সাজান। ***Verb i.*** To lie overlapping like tiles ; টালির মত একটীর কিনারা অপরটীর উপর থাকা। **–cate, –ca-tive,** *adjs.* Overlapping like tiles ; টালির মত একটীর কিনারা অপরটীর উপর রক্ষিত। **–ca′-tion,** *n.*

Imbricated flower bud.

im-brō′-glio (-lyō), *n.* **1.** A confused mass or heap ; এলোমেলোভাবে সজ্জিত বস্তুর স্তূপ, হযবরল। **2.** A complicated situation esp. dramatic or political ; a serious misunderstanding ; "No household *imbroglios*" ; নাটকীয় কিম্বা রাজনীতিকব্যাপারের জটিল অবস্থা ; গুরুতর বিসম্বাদ।

im-brue′ (-brô), *v. t.* To dye or stain as one's hand, sword, etc. *in* or *with* blood, slaughter, etc. ; শোণিতসিক্ত করা, রুধিররঞ্জিত করা, রক্তরঞ্জিত করা, কলঙ্কিত করা। **–ment,** *n.*

im-brute′ (-brôt), **ĕm-,** *v. t.* To make brutal or bestial ; পশুবৎ করা, পশুভাবাপন্ন করা।

im-bue′ (-bü), *v. t.* **1.** To saturate ; to tinge or dye ; সিক্ত করা, আর্দ্র করা ; রঞ্জিত করা। **2.** To imbue, as with blood, etc. ; রক্তাদিদ্বারা রঞ্জিত করা। **3.** To permeate or pervade ; to inspire ; as, to *imbue* young minds with good principles ; পরিব্যাপ্ত করা, আচ্ছন্ন করা ; অনুপ্রাণিত করা।

im′-i-tāte, *v. t.* **1.** To follow as a model or example ; to copy ; অনুকরণ করা ; নকল করা। **2.** To mimic ; ভেঙ্চান। **3.** To be or appear like ; "A lathe painted to *imitate* iron" ; কোন কিছুর মত হওয়া বা প্রতিভাত হওয়া। **–ta-ble,** *adj.* Capable of being imitated ; অনুকরণীয়, অনুকরণযোগ্য। **–ta-bil′-i-ty, –ta-tor,** *ns.*

im-i-tā′-tion, *n.* & *adj.* **1.** The act of imitating ; অনুকরণ, অনুবর্ত্তন। **2.** A copy or artificial likeness ; অনুকৃতি, নকল, প্রতিরূপ, অনুরূপ, প্রতিমান। ***Adj.*** Counterfeit ; as, *imitation* leather ; নকল, কৃত্রিম, ঝুঁটা।

im′-i-tā-tive (-tĭv), *adj.* **1.** Imitating; inclined to imitate ; অনুকারী,

গতানুগতিক, অনুসারী, অনুগামী, অনুবর্ত্তী; অনুকরণপ্রবণ, অনুকরণশীল, অনুকরণস্বভাব। 2. Done or formed after a model; আদর্শানুরূপগঠিত বা সম্পাদিত। 3. Counterfeit; "...... *imitative* jewellery"; নকল, কৃত্রিম, ঝুঁটা। **—ly,** *adv.* **—ness,** *n.* **Imitative arts**—Paintings and sculpture; অনুকরণাত্মক শিল্প—ভাস্কর্য্য ও চিত্রবিদ্যা। **Imitative word**—*e. g.* fizz etc.; ধ্বন্যাত্মক শব্দ।

im-măc'-ū-lāte, *adj.* 1. Spotless; clean; pure; নিষ্কলঙ্ক, নিখুঁত; নির্ম্মল, অনবদ্য, নিষ্কলুষ, বিমল, অমল; পবিত্র, শুদ্ধ, পরিশুদ্ধ। 2. Without fault, (*often ironical*); নির্দ্দোষ। 3. (*Bot.* & *Zool.*) Without coloured spots; (উদ্ভিদ বিদ্যা ও জন্তু বিদ্যা) রঞ্জিতবিন্দুবিহীন। **—la-cy,** *n.* **—ly,** *adv.* **—ness,** *n.* **Immaculate Conception**—(*R. C. C.*) (রোমানক্যাথলিক ধর্ম্ম-সংঘ) মানবজাতির আদিম পাপ হইতে নির্ম্মুক্ত অবস্থায় যীশুজননী মেরীর গর্ভধারণ, অপৌরুষেয় গর্ভাধান (হিঃ কোঃ)।

im'-mă-nĕnt, *adj.* 1. Remaining within; intrinsic; inherent; অন্তরস্থ; অন্তর্নিহিত, অন্তর্মুখী (বিশ্বঃ); অন্তর্ভব, অনুস্যূত, ওতপ্রোত। 2. (Of God) Permanently pervading the universe; (পরমেশ্বর সম্বন্ধে) সর্ব্বগত, সর্ব্বব্যাপী। **—nence, —nen-cy,** *ns.* The condition or quality of being immanent; inherence; অনুস্যূততা, অন্তর্ভাব, বিভুতা, ব্যাপিতা, ওতপ্রোততা; অন্তর্নিহিত্ব।

im-mă-tē'-ri-ăl, *adj.* 1. Incorporeal; spiritual; অশরীরী, নিরবয়ব, অভৌতিক, অমূর্ত্ত (ব্রজঃ হিন্দু), অমূর্তিমান্, অদেহী, অপাঞ্চভৌতিক, অমাত্রক (হিঃ কোঃ); আধ্যাত্মিক, চিন্ময়। 2. Unimportant; as, it is wholly *immaterial* whether he does so or not; অনাবশ্যক, অসার, অকিঞ্চিৎকর। **—al'-i-ty,** *n.* **—ism,** *n.* The doctrine that matter does not exist in itself apart from perception; জড়বস্তুর আমাদের অনুভূতিনিরপেক্ষ স্বতন্ত্র সত্তা নাই—এইরূপ মতবাদ, তন্মাত্রনস্তিত্ববাদ (হিঃ কোঃ)। **—ist,** *n.* One who believes in this doctrine; তন্মাত্রনস্তিত্ববাদী। **—ize,** *v. t.* To render immaterial; অমূর্ত্ত করা, অজড় করা, অশরীরী করা।

im-mă-tūre', *adj.* Unripe; undevolped; not mature; not perfect or complete; কাঁচা, অপরিপক্ক; কমপোক্ত (*colloq.*); অপরিণত, অপ্রৌঢ়; অপূর্ণ, অসম্পূর্ণ। **—ly,** *adv.* **—tu'-ri-ty,** *n.*

im-meas'-ur-a-ble (-mĕz-ŭr-ă-ble), *adj.* Incapable of being measured; immense; অমেয়, অপরিমেয়, অপ্রমেয়, অপরিসীম, অপরিমিত; বিশাল, অমিত। **—bil'-i-ty,** *n.* **—bly,** *adv.*

im-mē'-di-āte, *n.* 1. Proximate; without anything intervening; নিকটস্থ; অব্যবহিত, ব্যবধানরহিত, অনন্তর (হিঃ কোঃ)। 2. (Of time) Near; without delay; as, the *immediate* future or reply; (সময়-সম্পর্কে) নিকটবর্ত্তী; অবিলম্বিত। 3. Direct, as a relation, action, etc.; সাক্ষাৎ, প্রত্যক্ষ, অপরোক্ষ। 4. Nearest; next; as, my *immediate* neighbour; নিকটতম; অব্যবহিত পরবর্ত্তী। **—a-cy,** *n.* **—ly,** *adv.* 1. Proximately; directly; সন্নিকটে; সাক্ষাৎভাবে। 2. Without delay; instantly; at once; promptly; অগোণে, অবিলম্বে; তৎক্ষণাৎ; চটপট্ করিয়া, কালবিলম্ব না করিয়া; হাতে হাতে। **—ness,** *n.* **Immediate consequence** — সদ্যঃপ্রসূত পরিণাম, হাতেহাতে ফল, সদ্যঃফল (বৃঃ সং), তাৎকালিক ফল। **Immediate inference**—See INFERENCE.

im-mĕm'-ŏ-ră-ble (-bl), *adj.* Not worth remembering; স্মরণাযোগ্য, অস্মর্য্য, অস্মরণীয়।

im-mĕ-mō'-ri-ăl, *adj.* Beyond the reach of memory; indefinitely ancient; স্মরণাতীত, স্মৃতিকালাতীত অস্মার্ত্ত; অতি প্রাচীন। **—ly,** *adv.* **Immemorial custom** — শাশ্বত আচার (মঃ সং), পারম্পর্য্যাগত আচার। **Immemorial time**—স্মরণাতীত কাল, আবহমান কাল (জিঃ), অস্মার্ত্তকাল (মিতঃ)। **From time immemorial**—From time beyond memory or out of mind; আবহমান কাল ধরিয়া, মান্ধাতার আমল হইতে, স্মরণাতীত কাল হইতে।

im-mense' (-mĕns), *adj.* 1. (*Rare*) Immeasurable; অপরিমেয়, অপ্রমেয়, অমিত। 2. Vast; huge; বিস্তীর্ণ, বহুদূরব্যাপী; বিপুল, বিরাট, প্রকাণ্ড। 3. (*Slang*) Exceedingly good; "The poem turned out something *immense*"; তোফা, খাসা, চমৎকার (ইতর ভাষায়)। **—ly,** *adv.* 1. To an inmense degree; hugely; অমিতরূপে; বিরাটভাবে। 2. (*Colloq.*) Very much; (চলিত ভাষায়) বেজায়, ঘোর। **—men'-si-ty, —ness,** *ns.* 1. Vastness; greatness; infinity; বিশালতা; মহত্ব (হিঃ কোঃ), বৃহত্ব (ঐ); অনন্ততা, অসীমতা। 2. An immense amount or quantity; "Save an *immensity* of searcher's time"; অমিত পরিমাণ। 3. (*Pl.*) Immense or infinite beings or things; "Trust the heavenly *immensities*"; (বহুবচন) প্রকাণ্ড বস্তু, বিরাটকায় দেবযোনি সমূহ।

im-mĕn'-sū-ră-ble (-bl), *adj.* Immeasurable; অমিত, অপরিমেয়, অপ্রমেয়। **—bil'-i-ty,** *n.*

im-merge' (-mêrj), *v. t.* (*Now rare*) To plunge into or under a fluid; to dip; নিমগ্ন করা; ডুবান।

im-merse' (-mêrs), *v. t.* 1. To dip; to plunge, as in a liquid; নিমজ্জিত করা; জলমগ্ন করা, ডুবান। 2. To baptise by immersion; জলাবগাহন পূর্ব্বক ধর্ম্মে দীক্ষিত করা। 3. To bury or imbed *in* other things; "A traveller *immersed* to the waist *in* the jaws of a fissure" ; জলভিন্ন অন্য বস্তুতে প্রোথিত করা। **4.** To engage or involve deeply (as in debt, difficulties, thought, etc.) ; নিমগ্ন করা, জড়িত করা। **—mersed,** *adj.* **1.** Plunged ; নিমগ্ন, নিমজ্জিত। **2.** Deeply occupied ; entangled ; অভিনিবিষ্ট, নিমগ্ন ; জড়িত। **To be immersed in thought**—See IMMERSE *v.* 4.

im-mêr′-sion, *n.* **1.** The act of immersing ; বিসর্জ্জন, মজ্জন, নিমজ্জন, অবগাহন। **2.** (*Fig.*) The state of being deeply engaged ; absorption ; তদ্‌গতচিত্ততা, অভিনিবেশতা, অনন্যমনস্কতা ; ধ্যাননিমগ্নতা, তন্ময়তা। **2.** Baptism by immersion ; (খৃষ্টীয় ধর্ম্ম) জলাবগাহনান্ত দীক্ষা, জলসংস্কার, অবগাহনসংস্কার। **3.** (*Astron.*) Disappearance of a celestial body behind another or in its shadow ; (জ্যোতির্বিজ্ঞান) কোন জ্যোতিষ্কের পশ্চাদ্দেশে বা উহার ছায়ায় অপর জ্যোতিষ্কের অদর্শন, (জ্যোতিষ্কের) নিমীলনকাল (সূঃ সিঃ), যুতিভেদ (হিঃ কোঃ), নিমীলন (ঐ), নিমজ্জন (ঐ)।

im-mĕ-thŏd′-i-căl, *adj.* Without method or order ; irregular ; confused ; ব্যবস্থারহিত, বিশৃঙ্খল ; অক্রমিক, নিরন্বয়, অনিয়মিত, অব্যবস্থিত ; এলোমেলো। **—ly,** *adv.*

im′-mi-grāte, *v. i. & t.* To remove into a foreign country for permanent residence ; স্থায়িভাবে বসবাসের জন্য বিদেশে গমন করা। ***Verb t.*** To introduce as a settler or settlers ; স্থায়িভাবে বসবাসের উদ্দেশ্যে আনয়ন করা। **—grant,** *adj.* & *n.* Immigrating ; বসবাসের উদ্দেশ্যে আগমনকারী, পরদেশী (হিঃ কোঃ)। (*Noun*) One who immigrates (correlative of *emigrant*) ; যে ব্যক্তি বসবাসের উদ্দেশ্যে স্বদেশত্যাগপূর্ব্বক বিদেশে গমন করে, অধিপ্রবাসী। **—gra′-tion,** *n.* The act of immigrating ; স্থায়িভাবে বসবাসস্থাপনের জন্য বিদেশ গমন, অধিপ্রবাস, পরদেশবাস (হিঃ কোঃ), দেশান্তরাধিবাসন।

im′-mi-nĕnt, *adj.* Near at hand ; ready to befall one as a danger ; impending ; নিকটবর্ত্তী ; পতনোন্মুখ ; আসন্ন, আগতপ্রায়, আসন্নোপস্থিত। **—ly,** *adv.* **—nence,** *n.*

im-mis′-ci-ble (-ĭ-bl), *adj.* Not capable of being mixed ; অমিশ্রণীয়, অমেল, অমিলনীয়। **—bil′-i-ty,** *n.* **—bly,** *adv.*

im-mit′-i-gā-ble (-bl), *adj.* Not capable of being mitigated or softened ; অদমনীয়, অনুপশাম্য, অশাম্য। **—bly,** *adv.*

im-mix′-tūre, *n.* Act of mixing up ; state of being involved *in* something ; "To avoid an *immixture* in political strife" : সংমিশ্রণ ; মিশন।

im-mō′-bile (-bîl) *adj.* Immovable ; fixed (loosely) ; motionless ; অচল, স্থাবর, অজঙ্গম ; (শিথিলভাবে) সংবদ্ধ ; নিশ্চল। **—bil′-i-ty,** *n.* The state of being immobile ; স্থাবরভাব, অচলভাব, স্থাবরধর্ম্ম, নিশ্চলত্ব, অচলত্ব, স্থাবরত্ব।

im-mō′-bi-līze, *v. t.* **1.** To make immobile ; to fix immovably ; অচল করা ; স্থির করা, অটল করা। **2.** To render (troops etc.) incapable of being mobilized ; সৈন্য দল প্রভৃতিকে যুদ্ধার্থ প্রস্তুত করার জন্য অশক্ত করা। **3.** To withdraw as a specie from circulation holding it against bank notes ; মুদ্রা প্রভৃতি প্রচলন হইতে তুলিয়া আনা। **—li-za′-tion,** *n.*

im-mŏd′-êr-āte, *adj.* Exceeding just or usual limits ; excessive ; অত্যধিক, অপরিমিত ; অমিত, অতিরিক্ত। **—a′-tion, —ness,** *ns.* Extravagance ; excess ; অমিতাচার ; আধিক্য, অতিশয্য।

im-mŏd′-ĕst, *adj.* **1.** Indecent ; indelicate or lewd ; as, *immodest* picture ; অশ্লীল ; ভদ্রতাবিরুদ্ধ, কুৎসিত। **2.** Arrogant ; forward ; impudent ; উচ্ছৃঙ্খল, অবিনীত, দুর্বিনীত, গোঁয়ার ; প্রগল্‌ভ ; ধৃষ্ট। **—es-ty,** *n.* **1.** Want of modesty ; arrogance ; impudence ; লজ্জাহীনতা, নির্ল্লজ্জতা, লজ্জাভাব ; ঔদ্ধত্য ; প্রগল্‌ভতা, ধৃষ্টতা। **2.** Indecency ; অশ্লীলতা। **—ly,** *adv.*

im-mō′-lāte, *v. t.* To offer in sacrifice ; to kill as a sacrificial victim ; (*fig*) to sacrifice ; বলিদানার্থ উৎসর্গ করা ; বলি দেওয়া ; (লক্ষণায়) বলিদান করা। **—la′-tion,** *n.* **1.** Act of immolating ; বলিদান, উৎসর্গ, বধ, হনন। **2.** A sacrifice ; বলি। **—la-tor,** *n.* One who offers in sacrifice ; ঘাতক।

im-mŏr′-ăl, *adj.* Inconsistent with rectitude or moral purity ; vicious ; wicked ; dishonest ; licentious ; নীতি-বিগর্হিত, নীতদুষ্ট ; পাপজনক, পাপী ; অসৎ ; অসাধু ; ভ্রষ্ট, দুশ্চরিত্র, লম্পট, দুরাচারী (হিঃ কোঃ)। **—mo-ral′-i-ty,** *n.* **1.** The quality of being immoral ; দুর্নীতিপরায়ণতা, দুশ্চরিত্রতা, নীতিবিরুদ্ধতা, পাপ, অপবিত্রতা, নীতিদুষ্টতা, ব্যভিচার। **2.** An immoral act or practice ; পাপকাজ, পাপাচার, নীতিবিরুদ্ধ কাজ।

im-mŏr′-tăl, *adj.* & *n.* **1.** Undying ; imperishable ; unfading ; অমৃত, অমরণীয়, অজরামর, অমর (হিঃ কোঃ), অতিমৃত্যু (ছান্দোগ্য) ; অবিনাশী (ঐ), অবিনশ্বর ; অক্ষয়, অক্ষয্য, অম্লান। **2.** Famous for all time ; never to be forgotten ; চিরপ্রসিদ্ধ, চিরস্মরণীয় ; অমরকীর্ত্তি। **3.** Heavenly ; divine ; "Our souls have sight of that *immortal* sea which brought us hither" ; স্বর্গীয় ; দিব্য। **4.** (*Colloq.*) Lasting long ; constant ; "An *immortal* body of six thousand brave English.... to be continually recruited" ; (চলিত ভাষায়) দীর্ঘস্থায়ী ; নিত্য। ***Noun.*** **1.** One exempt from death ; (*pl.*) gods of classical mythology ; অমর ; অমরগণ, দেবগণ। **2.** The royal bodyguard of ancient Persia ; প্রাচীন পারস্যদেশের রাজকীয় রক্ষি-সৈন্য।

–i-za′-tion, *n.* **–ize**, *v. t.* **1.** To cause to live or exist for ever; অমর করা, চিরস্থায়ী করা। **2.** To perpetuate; চিরস্মরণীয় করা। **3.** To bestow enduring fame upon; অনন্তকীর্তি প্রদান করা, অমরকীর্তি প্রদান করা। **–tal′-i-ty**, *n.* **1.** The quality or state of being immortal; perpetuity; অমরতা, অবিনশ্বরতা, অমরত্ব; অবিনাশিত্ব, চিরস্থায়িতা। **2.** Lasting fame; "Shakespeare's *immortality* is secure"; অমরকীর্তি, অবিনশ্বর কীর্তি, অনন্তকীর্তি, অমরত্ব। **Immortal flowers**—অমর কুসুম।

im-mŏr′-tăl-lȳ, *adv.* **1.** Eternally; everlastingly; অনন্তকালের জন্য; চিরস্থায়িরূপে। **2.** (*Colloq.*) To an excessive degree; infinitely; (চলিতভাষায়) অত্যন্ত; সীমাহীনরূপে।

im-mŏr-telle′ (-tĕl), *adj.* & *n.* The everlasting (flower); অনন্তকালস্থায়ী (পুষ্প)।

im-môv′-ă-ble (-bl), *adj.* & *n.* **1.** Incapable of being moved; fixed; motionless; স্থাবর; দৃঢ়বদ্ধ; অচল, অটল, নিশ্চল। **2.** Unchangeable; "Words kept *immovable* ever"; অপরিবর্তনীয়। **3.** Steadfast; unyielding, as an opinion, purpose, etc.; স্থির; অচল, ধ্রুব। **4.** Emotionless; impassive, as countenance etc.; আবেগশূন্য; অসাড়, সুখদুঃখসংবেদনাক্ষম। **5.** Permanent, as property etc.; চিরস্থায়ী, মৌরসী। ***Noun.*** (*Pl.*) Lands and things adherent thereto, as buildings, trees, etc.; স্থাবর সম্পত্তি। **–bil′-i-ty**, **–ness**, *ns.* **–bly**, *adv.* **Immovable property** — See IMMOVABLE *adj.* 5.

im-müne′, *adj.* & *n.* Free or protected from poison, contagion, etc.; মুক্ত, অব্যাহতিপ্রাপ্ত, বিমুক্ত। ***Noun.*** An immune person or animal; মুক্তিপ্রাপ্ত ব্যক্তি বা জন্তু।

im-mü′-ni-ty, *n.* **1.** Exemption from any charge, obligation, tax, etc.; a particular privilege; অব্যাহতি, মুক্তি; বিশেষ অধিকার, ক্ষমতা। **2.** Freedom; as, *immunity* from error; মুক্তি। **3.** Security against contagion etc., (with *from*); সংক্রামক পীড়াদি হইতে নিষ্কিয়তা। **–mun-i-za′-tion**, *n.* **mun′-ize**, *v. t.* To render immune *against* contagion etc.; সংক্রামক পীড়াদি হইতে নিরাপদ করা, নিষ্কিয় করা।

im-müre′, *v. t.* **1.** To imprison; to inclose within walls; অবরুদ্ধ করা; কারারুদ্ধ করা। **2.** To shut (one's way) up; রোধ করা, বন্ধ করা। **3.** To entomb within a wall; as, to *immure* a heretic; প্রাচীর গাত্রমধ্যে সমাহিত করা, প্রাচীরের মধ্যে গাঁথিয়া ফেলা। **–ment**, *n.* Imprisonment; confinement; কারাবরোধ; আটক।

im-mü′-tă-ble (-bl), *adj.* Unchangeable; unalterable; invariable; অপরিবর্তনীয়, অপরিবর্তনশীল; নির্বিকল্প (কেন্ডিঃ), অবিক্রিয় (ঐ), অবিকার্য; নিত্য। **–bil′-i-ty**, **–bly**, *adv.*

imp, *n.* **1.** A young devil; a little devil; শয়তানের বাচ্চা; ছোট ভূত। **2.** A mischievous child; দুরন্ত বালক, দুষ্ট ছেলে।

imp, *v. t.* **1.** (*Jocularly*) To mend a deficient wing etc. by inserting a new feather; (কৌতুকচ্ছলে) পালক প্রবিষ্ট করিয়া অপূর্ণ পক্ষ সারা। **2.** (*Rare*) To enlarge; (অপ্রঃ) বৃদ্ধি করা। **To imp the wings of a bird**—To strengthen its flight; পক্ষীর উড্ডয়ন-শক্তি বৃদ্ধি করা।

im′-păct, *n.* A striking *against* or *on*; collision; অভিঘাত (ব্রজঃ হিন্দু), নোদন (ঐ), সংঘাত, উপঘাত, আঘাত, প্রতিঘাত; সংঘট্ট, টক্কর।

im-păct′, *v. t.* To press firmly together; to fix firmly, (with *in*, *into*); অভিহত করা; দৃঢ়রূপে সংবদ্ধ করা।

im-pair′ (-pār), *v. t.* To diminish in quantity, value, etc.; to deteriorate; to injure; to weaken; হ্রাস করা; হীন করা, অপকৃষ্ট করা, নষ্ট করা, হানি করা, বিকল করা; দুর্বল করা, ক্ষীণ করা। **–ment**, *n.* Impairing; state of being impaired; injury; ক্ষয়ণ, ন্যূনীকরণ; অপকৃষ্টতা; ক্ষতি।

im-pāle′, *v. t.* **1.** To pierce with a pale or stake as a form of capital punishment, torture, etc.; শূলবিদ্ধ করা, শূলে দেওয়া, শূলারোপণ করা। **2.** (*Rare*) To enclose, surround or fence in with stakes; খোটা দ্বারা বেড়া দেওয়া। **3.** (*Herald.*) To join as two coats of arms by placing them side by side on one shield separated by a vertical line down the middle; (কুলবিদ্যা) এক ঢালের উপর পাশাপাশি রাখিয়া এবং লম্ব-রেখা দ্বারা মধ্যদেশ পৃথক করিয়া কুলচিহ্নদ্বয় প্রভৃতি সংযুক্ত করা। **–ment**, *n.* The act of impaling; শূলারোপণ, শূলাধিরোপণ।

im-păl′-pă-ble (-bl), *adj.* **1.** Imperceptible to the touch; intangible; extremely fine; as, an *impalpable* gas or powder; স্পর্শ দ্বারা অননুভবনীয়, স্পর্শাশক্য; স্পর্শেন্দ্রিয়াতীত, ইন্দ্রিয়াগ্রাহ্য; অতিশয় সূক্ষ্ম। **2.** Not easily apprehensible; দুর্বোধ, দুরবগম্য। **–bil′-i-ty**, *n.* **–bly**, *adv.*

im-păl′-ü-dism, *n.* A morbid state with a tendency to intermittent fever and enlargement of the spleen usually found among the inhabitants of marshes; একপ্রকার ম্যালেরিয়ার অবস্থা।

im-pa′-nāte, *adj.* (Of Christ's body) Embodied in bread esp. of the Eucharist; (খৃষ্টদেহ সম্বন্ধে) রুটিতে (বিশেষতঃ অন্তিমভোজনের স্মৃতি অনুষ্ঠানের রুটিতে) বর্তমান। **–na′-tion**, *n.*

im-păn'-ĕl, *v. t.* Same as EMPANEL.

im-păr'-ă-dīse, ĕm-, *v. t.* **1.** To bring into a state of supreme happiness; to transport; পরমানন্দময় করা; স্বর্গসুখ প্রদান করা। **2.** To convert or make into a paradise, as a place, state, etc.; স্বর্গে পরিণত করা, স্বর্গরাজ্য করিয়া তুলা।

im-păr-i-sȳl-lăb'-ic, *adj.* & *n.* (*Gr.* & *Latin Gram.*) Consisting of more syllables in the genitive than in the nominative, as a noun; (গ্রীক ও ল্যাটিন ব্যাকরণ) কর্তৃকারক অপেক্ষা সম্বন্ধ কারকে অধিকতর শব্দাংশ বিশিষ্ট, অসমানাক্ষর (মঃ ইঃ)। ***Noun.*** Such a noun; ঐরূপ বিশেষ্য।

im-păr'-i-tȳ, *n.* Inequality; অসমতা, বৈষম্য, অসাম্য।

im-pârk', *v. t.* **1.** To enclose or confine, as beasts in a park; বৃতি-বেষ্টিত কাননে বদ্ধ করা। **2.** To enclose as lands for a park; মৃগয়া-কাননের জন্য বেষ্টিত করা। **—par-ka'-tion**, *n.*

im-pârt', *v. t.* **1.** To bestow a part of; to give; অংশ প্রদান করা; দান করা। **2.** To communicate; to tell; as, to *impart* a news to a person; জ্ঞাপন করা; বলা। **—ment**, **—par-ta'-tion**, *ns.*

im-pâr'-tial (-shăl), *adj.* Unprejudiced; just; fair; disinterested; অপক্ষপাতী, পক্ষপাতশূন্য, নিরপেক্ষ, সমদর্শী, উভয় সাধারণ (মঃ ইঃ), নিষ্পক্ষপাতী (ঐ); ন্যায়পরায়ণ; ন্যায্য; নিঃস্বার্থ। **—ly**, *adv.* নিরপেক্ষভাবে। **—ness**, **—ti-al'-i-ty**, *ns.* The quality of being impartial; justness, disinterestedness; অপক্ষপাতিত্ব, অপক্ষপাতিতা, নিরপেক্ষতা, সমদর্শিতা; ন্যায়পরতা; নিঃস্বার্থপরতা।

im-părt'-i-ble (-bl), *adj.* Incapable of being partitioned; indivisible; অবিভাজ্য; অনংশনীয়।

im-păss'-ă-ble (-bl), *adj.* Incapable of being traversed; অগম্য, অনতিক্রমনীয়, অপার, অতার্য্য, দুস্তর, দুরত্যয়, দুর্লঙ্ঘ্য, অলঙ্ঘনীয়, অলঙ্ঘ্য, দুর্গম, দুস্তর, দুরুত্তর, আচর (হরিঃ), অগম (মঃ ভাঃ)। **—bil'-i-ty**, **—ness**, *ns.* অলঙ্ঘ্যতা, দুর্লঙ্ঘ্যতা, অগম্যতা, দৌস্তর্য্য। **—bly**, *adv.*

impasse, (*F.*), *n.* **1.** Impassable road or way; a blind alley; দুর্গম পথ; বন্ধ গলি। **2.** (*Fig.*) A position from which there is no way of escape; (লক্ষণায়) যে অবস্থা হইতে আর পরিত্রাণের উপায় নাই।

im-păs'-si-ble (-ĭ-bl), *adj.* **1.** Incable of suffering; not subject to suffering; কষ্টভোগে অসমর্থ; কষ্টভোগের অনধীন। **2.** Unfeeling; impassive; insensible; "*Impassible* before victory, before danger etc."; অসাড়; অদুঃখজ্ঞ ক্লেশদুঃখাদিহীন (মঃ ইঃ), সংবেদনশূন্য; চেতনাহীন, অচেতন। **—bil'-i-ty**, **—ness**, *ns.* **—bly**, *adv.*

im-pas'-sion (-pă-), *v. t.* To arouse the passions or feelings of; to excite strongly; ক্রোধোদ্রেক করা; উত্তেজিত করা। **—a-ble**, *adj.* Excitable; উত্তেজনীয়যোগ্য, ক্রোধোদ্রেকযোগ্য। **—ate**, *v. t.* To arouse the passions of; উত্তেজিত করা, রোষোদ্দীপ্ত করা, ক্রোধোদ্দীপ্ত করা। **—sioned**, *adj.* Excited; ardent; প্রচণ্ড, উদ্দীপ্ত, উত্তেজিত, ক্রোধান্বিত, কোপপ্রজ্বলিত; আগ্রহান্বিত।

im'-păs--sive (-ĭv), *adj.* **1.** Deficient in, or devoid of, feeling or emotion; apathetic; serene; আবেগশূন্য; উদাসীন; ধীর, অচল, স্থির, প্রশান্ত, গম্ভীর। **2.** Not liable to suffering; "The *impassive* soul"; অদুঃখভোগাধীন। **3.** Insensible; unconscious; চেতনাশূন্য, অচেতন, বিচেতন; সংজ্ঞাশূন্য, সংজ্ঞাহীন। **—ly**, *adv.* **—ness**, *n.* **—siv'-i-ty**, *n.*

im-păste', *v. t.* **1.** To make into a paste; মণ্ডে পরিণত করা, লেই করা। **2.** To inclose in, or as in, a paste; লেই বা তদ্বৎ কোন কিছু দ্বারা আবৃত করা। **3.** (*Painting*) To lay on, as colours thickly and boldly; ঘনভাবে রং লাগান, রংএর লেপ দেওয়া।

im-păs'-tō, *n.* (*Painting*) Laying on of colour thickly; (চিত্রবিদ্যা) ঘনভাবে বর্ণসন্নিবেশ।

im-pā'-tient (-shĕnt), *adj.* **1.** Uneasy; restless; eagerly longing; as, he is *impatient* to go; অস্থির; অধীর, অকালসহ, ধৈর্য্যহীন; উতলা, উতরোল (প্রাঃ সাঃ); উৎকণ্ঠাকুল। **2.** Not bearing with composure; intolerant (*of*); as, he is *impatient of* restraint; অধীর; অসহিষ্ণু। **—ly**, *adv.* অধীরভাবে। **—tience**, *n.* **1.** Restlessness; fretfulness; restless or eager longing; চঞ্চলতা, চাঞ্চল্য, অস্থিরতা, অধৈর্য্য, অসহিষ্ণুতা; বিক্ষোভ; উৎকণ্ঠা।

im-pawn' (-pän), *v. t.* **1.** To pledge as security; to pawn; বাঁধা দেওয়া, বন্ধক দেওয়া; রেহান দেওয়া। **2.** (*Fig.*) To pledge or plight; (লক্ষণায়) প্রতিজ্ঞাবদ্ধ হওয়া, সত্যবদ্ধ হওয়া, কথা দেওয়া।

im-pay'-a-ble (-pā-ă-bl), *adj.* **1.** That which cannot be paid or discharged; "*Impayable* obligations"; অপরিশোধ্য। **2.** Priceless; অমূল্য, অনর্ঘ। **3.** (*Colloq.*) Going beyond ordinary limits; "For they (notes) are *impayable*"; (চলিত ভাষায়) মাত্রাছাড়া।

im-peach' (-pēch), *v. t.* **1.** To charge with a crime; to accuse (*of*); দোষারোপ করা; অভিযুক্ত করা। **2.** To challenge; to call in question; to disparage; "...... her character (was) *impeached*"; আপত্তি উত্থাপন করা; প্রশ্ন উঠান; সন্দেহ প্রকাশ করা, হতাদর করা। **3.** To find fault with (a thing); দোষ ধরা। **4.** To bring a charge of treason or other high crime against before a competent tribunal; উপযুক্ত আদালতে কোন ব্যক্তিকে রাজদ্রোহাদি গুরুতর অপরাধে অভিযুক্ত

করা। **–a-ble,** *adj.* Liable to impeachment; chargeable; অভিযোগার্হ; দোষারোপণীয়। **–ment,** *n.* 1. Act of impeaching; a calling in question; reproach; অভিযোগস্থাপন; সন্দেহপ্রকাশ; তিরস্কার। 2. Accusation (esp. *facet.*); "The cigarette denied the soft *impeachment*"; অভিযোগ। 3. Accusation and prosecution for treason etc. before a competent tribunal; রাজদ্রোহাদি গুরুতর অপরাধের জন্ম অভিযোগ।

im-pĕc′-ca-ble (-ă-bl), *adj.* 1. Not liable to sin; নিষ্পাপ, পাপসম্ভাবনাতীত, অসম্ভাব্যপাপ, পাপাতীত, অপাপবিদ্ধ। 2. (Of things) Free from error; অভ্রান্ত। **–bil′-i-ty,** *n.* **–bly,** *adv.* **–cant,** *adj.*

im-pē-cü′-ni-ous (-ŭs), *adj.* Having no money; poor; অর্থশূন্য, নির্ধন, নিঃস্ব, নিঃসম্বল; অকিঞ্চন; দরিদ্র, দীন, কাঙ্গাল। **–os′-i-ty,** *n.* State of being without money; poverty; নির্ধনতা, নিঃস্বতা; দারিদ্র্য, দীনতা।

im-pēd′-ance (-ăns), *n.* (*Electr.*) Virtual resistance due to self-induction in an electrified body; (তাড়িত-বিদ্যা) তাড়িতসঞ্চারিত পদার্থে আত্ম-তাড়িতপ্রবর্তনহেতু কার্য্যতঃ যে বাধা উপজাত হয়।

im-pede′ (-pēd), *v. t.* To hinder or obstruct; প্রতিরোধ করা, বাধা দেওয়া, প্রতিবন্ধক দেওয়া, ব্যাঘাত করা, প্রতিহত করা, গতিরোধ করা।

im-pĕd′-i-mĕnt, *n.* 1. Hindrance; that which impedes; an obstruction; প্রতিবন্ধক, বাধা; বিঘ্ন, আটক, প্রতিষ্টম্ভ, অন্তরায়; ব্যাঘাত, লেঠা (*colloq.*)। 2. A stammer etc. as in one's speech; তোতলামি, বাক্‌স্খলন। 3. (*Pl.*—also *L. impedimente*) Baggage, as of an army etc.; সৈন্যদলের তল্পীতল্পা। **–men′-tal,** *adj.* **Impediment in speech**—বাক্‌জড়তা, বাক্‌স্খলন।

im-pĕl′, *v. t.* 1. To urge; to instigate; to force; "......what *impels* me to speak"; চালিত করা, উত্তেজিত করা; প্ররোচিত করা, প্রণোদিত করা; অনুপ্রাণিত করা। 2. To drive forward; to propel; ঠেলিয়া অগ্রসর করা; অগ্রে চালিত করা। **–lent,** *adj.* & *n.* **–ler,** *n.*

im-pĕnd′, *v. i.* 1. To be suspended (*over*); ঝুলা, দোদুল্যমান হওয়া। 2. (*Fig*) To hang threateningly (*over*); (লক্ষণায়) মাথার উপর ঝুলা। 3. To be imminent; প্রত্যাসন্ন হওয়া, ঘনাইয়া আসা, আসন্নবর্ত্তী হওয়া, সন্নিকৃষ্ট হওয়া। **–ence, –en-cy,** *ns.* **–ent, –ing,** *adjs.* 1. Overhanging; দোদুল্যমান। 2. Imminent; পতিষ্যমাণ, পতনোন্মুখ, আসন্ন, প্রত্যাসন্ন।

im-pĕn′-ē-tră-ble (-bl), *adj.* 1. That cannot be pierced; impervious; (*Natural Philos.*) preventing another body from occupying the same space at the same time; অভেদনীয়, ভেদনাশক্য, অবেধনীয় (কেঃিঃ), নির্ভেদ্য (ঐ), অভেদ্য; (পদার্থবিজ্ঞান) অপ্রবেশ্য। 2. Incomprehensible; inscrutable; unfathomable; as, an *inpenetrable* mystery; দুর্ব্বোধ, দুর্জ্ঞেয়; জটিল; অনবগাহ্য, গহন, দুরবগাহ। 3. Inaccessible; unimpressible; as, an *impenetrable* mind or heart; দুর্গম; অবিচলনীয়। **–bil′-i-ty, –ness,** *ns.* The state of being impenetrable; অভেদ্যতা, অনবগাহ্যতা। **–bly,** *adv.*

im-pĕn′-ē-trāte, *v. t.* To penetrate deeply or thoroughly; গভীর ভাবে প্রবেশ করা।

im-pĕn′-i-tĕnt, *n.* Not penitent or repentant; অননুতপ্ত, অপশ্চাত্তাপী। **–ly,** *adv.* **–tence, –ten-cy,** *ns.* The state of being impenitent; অননুতাপ, অনুতাপ-রাহিত্য।

im-pĕn′-nate (-āte), *adj.* Wingless; having too short wings for flight; পক্ষহীন; উড্ডয়নের পক্ষে অনুপযোগী ক্ষুদ্র পক্ষসম্পন্ন।

im-pĕr′-ă-tive (-tĭv), *adj.* & *n.* 1. Commanding; authoritative; peremptory; অনুজ্ঞাপ্রকাশক, অনুজ্ঞাব্যঞ্জক; প্রভুত্বব্যঞ্জক; দৃঢ়াজ্ঞাসূচক, অলঙ্ঘনীয়। 2. Obligatory; compulsory; urgent; as, an *imperative* duty or necessity; অবশ্যপালনীয়, অবশ্যকর্ত্তব্য; অবশ্যমাননীয়; জরুরি। 3. (*Gram.*) Expressive of command, entreaty, advice or exhortation; as, the *imperative* mood; অনুজ্ঞা, অনুনয়, আদেশ বা উপদেশবাচক, অনুজ্ঞাবাচক, অনুজ্ঞাত্মক। *Noun.* (*Gram.*) The imperative mood; ধাতুর রূপ বিশেষ, লোট্, অনুজ্ঞা। **–ly,** *adv.* **–ness,** *n.* **–ti′-val,** *adj.*

im-pē-rā′-tŏr, *n.* 1. (*Rom. hist.*) Commander; (রোমীয় ইতিহাস) প্রাচীন রোমের-রণবিজয়ী অধিনায়কগণের উপাধি বিশেষ। 2. A commander; a leader; an emperor; সেনাপতি, রণনায়ক; অধিনায়ক; সম্রাট্। **–to′-ri-al,** *adj.*

im-pêr-cĕp′-ti-ble (-bl), *adj.* 1. That cannot be perceived; not discernible; ইন্দ্রিয়ের অগোচর, অপ্রত্যক্ষ, ইন্দ্রিয়াগোচর, ইন্দ্রিয়াগ্রাহ্য, ইন্দ্রিয়াজ্ঞেয়, অতীন্দ্রিয়, ইন্দ্রিয়াতীত, ইন্দ্রিয়াবিষয়, অপ্রত্যক্ষ; অননুভবনীয়, অবিভাবনীয়, অগোচর (হিঃ কোঃ), অসংবেদ্য (ঐ)। 2. Extremely slight; as, *imperceptible* changes; অতিসূক্ষ্ম। **–bil′-i-ty, –ness,** *ns.* **–bly,** *adv.* In an imperceptible manner or degree; অজ্ঞাতসারে, অননুভূতরূপে, অপ্রত্যক্ষভাবে, অজ্ঞাতে।

im-pêr-cĕp′-tive (-tĭv), *adj.* Same as IMPERCIPIENT.

im-pêr-cĭp′-i-ĕnt, *adj.* Not perceiving; lacking perception; অপ্রত্যক্ষকারী; প্রত্যক্ষহীন।

im-pêr′-fĕct, *adj.* & *n.* 1. Not fully formed, made or done; incomplete; deficient; অপূর্ণ

অনিষ্পন্ন ; অসমাপ্ত, অসম্পন্ন ; খুঁতযুক্ত, ত্রুটিযুক্ত। 2. Defective ; faulty ; "So *imperfect* a creature as man" ; ন্যূন, হীন, বিকল, বিকলাঙ্গ, ন্যূনাঙ্গ ; সদোষ। 3. (*Gram.*) Denoting an action going on but not completed ; as, an *imperfect* tense ; অসমাপক, অসমাপিকা। *Noun.* An imperfect tense ; ভূতকাল, লঙ্ (in Sanskrit Grammar only)। **–ly,** *adv.* In an imperfect manner ; অসম্পূর্ণরূপে। **Imperfect figure**—অপূর্ণরূপ (হিঃ কোঃ)। **Imperfect induction**—অপূর্ণ আগমন (হিঃ কোঃ)। **Imperfect tense**—See IMPERFECT *adj.* 3.

im-pêr-fĕc′-tion, *n.* **1.** State of being imperfect ; incompleteness ; অসম্পূর্ণতা ; অপূর্ণতা, বৈকল্য। **2.** Faultiness ; দোষযুক্ততা, সদোষতা। **3.** A fault ; a blemish ; দোষ ; খুঁত, ত্রুটি।

im-pêr′-fö-rāte, *adj.* **1.** Not perforated ; having no holes or apertures ; অচ্ছিদ্র ; ছিদ্রহীন, নীরন্ধ্র, রন্ধ্রহীন, অবিদ্ধ, নিচ্ছিদ্র। **2.** (*Anat.*) Without the normal opening, as a part of a body ; (শারীর-সংস্থানবিদ্যা) দেহের স্বাভাবিক দ্বারাদির রন্ধ্র বা মুখহীন। **3.** (Of a sheet of stamp) Without rows of openings separating individual stamps ; (of a single stamp) with the margin entire ; (ডাক টিকেটের পাতা সম্বন্ধে) সচ্ছিদ্র রেখাহীন ; (একটী ডাক টিকিট সম্বন্ধে) অখণ্ড প্রান্তবিশিষ্ট।

im-pē′-ri-ăl, *adj.* & *n.* **1.** Pertaining to an empire or an emperor ; সাম্রাজ্যসম্বন্ধীয়, সম্রাটসম্বন্ধীয় অধিরাজিক, সার্ব্বভৌমিক, সার্ব্বভৌমরাজ্যসম্বন্ধীয়, সাম্রাজিক। **2.** Of, or relating to, a sovereign state as being independent and supreme over colonies etc. ; স্বাধীন এবং উপনিবেশ প্রভৃতির উপর আধিপত্য বিস্তারকারী রাজ্যসম্বন্ধীয়। **3.** Of, or relating to, Great Britain as distinct from its constituent kingdoms etc. ; গ্রেটব্রিটেন সম্পর্কীয়। **4.** Royal ; supreme in authority ; majestic ; রাজকীয়, বাদসাহী ; একচ্ছত্র ; মহিমান্বিত। **5.** Magnificent ; of special excellence ; "*Imperial* diet" ; জাঁকালো, জমকালো, জাঁকজমকশালী, বিশেষ উৎকর্ষসম্পন্ন। **6.** (Of superior or special size (22″ × 32″) ; as, *Imperial* paper; বিশেষ আকারের, বৃহদায়তন। **7.** Designating weights and measures established by law to be used in the United Kingdom (Great Britain and Ireland) ; as, an *imperial* acre ; গ্রেট ব্রিটেন এবং আয়র্লণ্ডের রাজবিধিদ্বারা স্থিরীকৃত তুলামান। *Noun.* **1.** A tuft of hair worn on the lower lip (from its use by Napolean III.) ; অধরের নিম্নস্থ শ্মশ্রুগুচ্ছ। **2.** A baggage-case on the top of a travelling carriage ; যাত্রি শকটের উপরিস্থ মাল রাখার আধার। **3.** Anything of unusual size or excellence, as paper, etc. ; অসাধারণ আয়তন বা উৎকর্ষ সম্পন্ন বস্তু। **4.** A Russian gold coin worth 15 roubles ; রুষদেশীয় স্বর্ণমুদ্রা বিশেষ (ইহার মূল্য ১৫ রুবল)। **–ly,** *adv.* **Imperial-city**—Rome ; রোম নগরী। **Imperial-federation** — ব্রিটিশ সাম্রাজ্যের বিভিন্ন অংশের ইংলণ্ড ও পরস্পরের সহিত মৈত্রী বন্ধন। **Imperial-paper**—See IMPERIAL *adj.* 6. **Imperial weights and measures** — ব্রিটিশ পার্লেমেণ্ট কর্তৃক অনুমোদিত তুলামান।

im-pē′-ri-ăl-ĭsm, *n.* **1.** The power or government of an emperor ; সার্ব্বভৌমশাসন, সম্রাটের ক্ষমতা, সাম্রাজ্যতন্ত্র। **2.** The policy or practice of seeking the extension of the British Empire where commerce demands the protection of the flag ; বাণিজ্য প্রসারের জন্য যে স্থান ব্রিটিশ পতাকার অধীন করা আবশ্যক—তথায় ব্রিটিশসাম্রাজ্য বিস্তারের নীতি, সাম্রাজ্যপ্রসার নীতি। **3.** The policy or practice of uniting the different parts of the British Empire for purposes of warlike defence, internal commerce, etc. ; অন্তর্বাণিজ্য, যুদ্ধকালে স্বদেশ রক্ষা, প্রভৃতির জন্য ব্রিটিশসাম্রাজ্যের বিভিন্ন অংশের ঘনিষ্ঠ সংযোগ সাধনের নীতি। **4.** Belief in the value of colonies and dependencies ; উপনিবেশ, অধীনরাজ্য সমূহের উপকারিতা সম্বন্ধে বিশ্বাস। **–is′-tic,** *adj.* **–ize,** *v. t.* To make imperial ; to cause to be, or belong to, an empire ; সাম্রাজ্যে পরিণত করা ; সাম্রাজ্যভুক্ত করা।

im-pē′-ri-ăl-ist, *n.* **1.** A subject or supporter of an emperor or empire ; সম্রাটের প্রজা, সাম্রাজ্যের পক্ষপাতী। **2.** An advocate of imperial rule esp. an adherent of the Bonaparte family ; সম্রাটকর্তৃক শাসনের পক্ষপাতী, বিশেষতঃ নেপোলিয়ান বোনাপার্টের পরিবারের পক্ষপাতী ব্যক্তি। **3.** An advocate of imperialism in British politics ; সাম্রাজ্যবাদী।

im-pĕr′-il, *v. t.* To bring into peril ; to endanger ; বিপদাপন্ন করা, সঙ্কটাপন্ন করা ; বিপদ্‌গ্রস্ত করা।

im-pē′-ri-ous (-ŭs), **1.** Haughty ; arrogant ; domineering ; উদ্ধত ; দাম্ভিক, গর্ব্বিত, দৃপ্ত ; প্রভুত্বকারী, প্রভুত্বপরায়ণ। **2.** Imperative ; urgent ; as, *imperious* need ; প্রভুত্বজ্ঞাপক ; জরুরী। **–ly,** *adv.* **–ness,** *n.*

im-pĕr-ish-ă-bil′-i-tỹ, *n.* Indestructibility ; everlastingness ; অবিনশ্বরতা ; চিরস্থায়িতা।

im-pĕr′-ish-ă-ble (-bl), *adj.* Indestructible ; everlasting ; অবিনশ্বর, অক্ষয্য, অবিনাশী, অক্ষর, অচ্যুত, অক্ষয়, অনশ্বর, অজরামর, অনাশ্য (মঃ ইঃ) ; চিরস্থায়ী। **–bly,** *adv.* **–ness,** *n.*

imperium, *n.* (*Lat.*) Absolute or supreme power ; empire ; অনিয়ন্ত্রিত ক্ষমতা ; সাম্রাজ্য। ***Imperium in imperio***—অন্যের অধিকারের ভিতর অনিয়ন্ত্রিত অধিকার।

im-pêr'-mă-nĕnt, *adj.* Not permanent; অচিরস্থায়ী, অস্থায়ী, অনিত্য, অশাশ্বত, অধ্রুব। **—nence,** *n.* অচিরস্থায়িতা, অস্থায়িতা, অনিত্যতা।

im-pêr'-mē-ă-ble (-bl), *adj.* **1.** Impassable; অবেধ্য, দুর্ভেদ্য, দুষ্প্রবেশ্য, অবেধনীয়। **2.** (*Phys.*) Not allowing the passage of fluids through its substance; as, India-rubber is *impermeable* to water or to air; (পদার্থবিদ্যা) দ্রবাগম্য, দ্রবরোধক, দ্রবাভেদ্য, জলাভেদ্য। **—bil'-i-ty, —ness,** *ns.* The state of being impermeable; দ্রবাগম্যতা, দ্রবাভেদ্যতা, অপ্রবেশ্যতা, অভেদ্যত্ব। **—bly,** *adv.*

im-pêr-mis'-si-ble (-i-bl), *adj.* Not permissible; অননুমন্তব্য।

im-pêr-scrip'-ti-ble (-bl) *adj.* Unwritten; not recorded; as, an *imperscriptible* right; অলিখিত; অলিপিবদ্ধ।

im-pêr'-sŏn-ăl, *adj.* **1.** Having no personality; অপৌরুষেয়, অব্যক্তিক, মূর্ত্তিহীন। **2.** Without personal reference or connection; "*Impersonal* considerations of public duty"; ব্যক্তিসম্পর্ক বা উল্লেখশূন্য। **3.** (*Gram.*) Denoting the action of an unspecified agent; as, an *impersonal* verb (*e. g.* it *rains*); অনির্দ্দিষ্ট কর্ত্তার কার্য্য সূচক, অকর্তৃক। **—al'-i-ty,** *n.* The state of being impersonal; অপৌরুষেয়ত্ব। **—ly,** *adv.* **Impersonal verb**—One used only in 3rd person singular; কেবলমাত্র প্রথম পুরুষের একবচনে ব্যবহৃত ক্রিয়া, ভাববাচ্য।

im-pêr'-sŏn-āte, *v. t.* **1.** To represent in a personal or bodily form; to personify; "The conscience of the community is *impersonated* in its government"; to typify; ব্যক্তিত্ব আরোপ করা, মানবধর্ম্ম আরোপ করা; মূর্ত্তিমান করা; আদর্শ দ্বারা প্রদর্শন করা। **2.** To personate; to act; as, to *impersonate* a character; অন্য কেহ স্বরূপ কার্য্য করা; কাজ করা। **—a'-tion,** *n.* Act of impersonating; representation in a bodily form; personification; মানবধর্ম্মারোপ; মূর্ত্তিমানকরণ; অন্য কেহ স্বরূপ কার্য্যকরণ। **—a-tive,** *adj.* **—a-tor,** *n.*

im-pêr-sŏn'-i-fȳ, *v. t.* To represent in personal form; ব্যক্তিত্ব আরোপ করা।

im-pêr'-ti-nĕnt, *adj.* **1.** Out of place; irrelevant; absurd; অপ্রযোজ্য; অপ্রাসঙ্গিক, অবান্তর; অসঙ্গত, অসম্ভব। **2.** Insolent; saucy; pert; intrusive; উদ্ধত; ধৃষ্ট, বে-আদব; প্রগল্ভ, জ্যাঠা; অনধিকারচর্চ্চা, ফাজিল। **—nence, —nen-cy,** *n.* **1.** Irrelevance; absurdity; an irrelevant fact or matter; "*Impertinence* of forms"; অপ্রাসঙ্গিকতা; অসঙ্গতি; অপ্রাসঙ্গিক বিষয়। **2.** Rudeness; incivility; insolence; intrusiveness; রূঢ়তা; অসভ্যতা; ধৃষ্টতা, বে-আদবি, ধাষ্টর্য; জ্যাঠামি, অনধিকারচর্চ্চা, ফাজলামি। **3.** An impertinent act; ধৃষ্টতার কার্য্য। **—ly,** *adv.*

im-pêr-turb'-a-ble (-têrb-ă-bl), *adj.* Incapable of being disturbed or agitated; calm; serene; অক্ষোভ্য, অক্ষোভণীয়, নির্ব্বিকার, অবিচলিত; স্থির, ধীর, নিত্য; শান্ত, প্রশান্ত। **—bil'-i-ty, —ness,** *ns.* The state of being imperturbable; অক্ষোভ্যতা, অবিক্ষুব্ধতা। **—bly,** *adv.*

im-pêr'-vi-ous (-ŭs), *adj.* **1.** Not pervious; not to be penetrated; not admitting passage (to); অভেদ্য; ভেদনাযোগ্য, ভেদনাশক্য; অগম্য, অপ্রবেশ্য, অপ্রবেশনীয়, দুষ্প্রবেশ। **2.** (*Fig.*) Deaf; as, *impervious* to argument; (লক্ষণায়) বধির। **—ly,** *adv.* **—ness,** *n.* **Impervious to argument**—See IMPERVIOUS, 2.

im-pĕ-tī'-gō, *n.* (*Med.*) A pustular eruption; পীতবর্ণ পীড়কার উপর আঁইশের ন্যায় মামড়ি ও কণ্ডুয়ন বিশিষ্ট চর্ম্মরোগ, চর্ম্মদল (সাঃ পঃ)। **—tig'-i-nous,** *adj.*

im'-pĕ-trāte, *v. t.* **1.** (*Theol.*) To obtain by request or entreaty; (ধর্ম্মশাস্ত্র) অনুনয় বিনয় দ্বারা প্রাপ্ত হওয়া, কাকুতিমিনতি করিয়া পাওয়া। **2.** (*Rare*) To ask for; চাওয়া। **—tra'-tion,** *n.* **—tra-to-ry,** *adj.* Containing, or expressing, entreaty; অনুনয়সূচক, মিনতিসূচক।

im-pĕt-ū-ŏs'-i-tȳ, *n* **1.** State of being impetuous; fury; vehemence; প্রচণ্ডতা; উগ্রতা; তীব্রতা। **2.** An impetuous movement, act or impulse; সংরম্ভ, রভস, বেগ।

im-pĕt'-ū-ous (-ŭs), *adj.* **1.** Rushing or moving with violence or rapidity; furious; violent; বেগবান বেগগামী; উত্তাল, চণ্ড, প্রচণ্ড; প্রবল, উদ্দাম, রৌদ্র, দুর্দ্দান্ত, সরভস। **2.** Hasty; rashly energetic; passionate; "His affection was as *impetuous* as his wrath"; হঠকারী; উচ্চণ্ড, গোঁয়ার গোবিন্দ; প্রবলানুরাগপূর্ণ। **—ly,** *adv.* **—ness** *n.*

im'-pĕ-tŭs, *n.* **1.** Force with which a body moves; চলদ্বস্তুর বেগ, ধাক্কা (জিঃ)। **2.** (*Fig.*) Impulse; vigour; stimulus; as, to give an *impetus* to the mind; প্রেরণা, নোদনা, প্ররোচনা; তেজ; উত্তেজনা।

im'-pey-an—pheas'-ant (-pī-ăn-fĕz-ănt), *n.* A kind of pheasant of Southern Kashmir (named 1787 after Lady Impey who tried to naturalize the bird in England); দক্ষিণ কাশ্মীরের পক্ষি-বিশেষ।

im'-pi (-pē), *n.* A body of Kafir warriors; কাফির যোদ্ধৃদল।

im-pī'-ĕ-tȳ, *n.* **1.** Want of piety; ungodliness; ভক্তিহীনতা, অধর্ম্ম, অধার্ম্মিকতা; পাষণ্ডতা, পাষণ্ডবুদ্ধি, নাস্তিকতা। **2.** An impious or irreligious act; পাপকাজ, অধর্ম্মাচরণ। **3.** Irreverence; undutifulness; "A gross insolence of filial *impiety*" ; অভক্তি, অশ্রদ্ধা ; অকর্ত্তব্যপরায়ণতা।

im-pinge′ (-pĭnj), *v. t.* & *i.* To clash or strike (*t.* & *i.*) *on* or *upon* ; আহত হওয়া, আঘাত করা, ঘা দেওয়া, ঠক্কর দেওয়া, অভিহত হওয়া। ***Verb i.*** To encroach (*on* or *upon*) ; "...*impinging on* the province of the reviewers" ; অনধিকার প্রবেশ করা, চড়াও করা। **—ment,** *n.*

im′-pĭ-ous (-ŭs), *adj.* Irreligious ; irreverent ; profane ; অধার্ম্মিক, অধর্ম্মনিষ্ঠ, পাপিষ্ঠ, পাষণ্ড ; ভক্তিহীন ; দেবনিন্দক, দেবদ্বেষী। **—ly,** *adv.* **—ness,** *n.*

ĭmp′-ish, *adj.* Of, relating to, or resembling, an imp ; শয়তানী। **—ly,** *adv.* **—ness,** *n.*

im-pĭt′-ē-ous (-ŭs), *adj.* (*Poet.*) Pitiless ; (কবিতায়) নিষ্করুণ, নির্দ্দয়, নিষ্ঠুর।

im-plā′-că-ble (-bl), *adj.* Not to be appeased ; inexorable ; as, *implacable* enmity or anger ; অশাম্য, অনারাধ্য, দুষ্প্রসাদ, দুঃশাম্য, অপ্রশাম্য, দুস্তোষণীয়, দুঃপ্রসাদ্য (কেঙিঃ) ; (in enmity) বদ্ধবৈর, দুরনুমেয়। **—bil′-i-ty, —ness,** *ns.* **—bly,** *adv.*

im-plă′-cĕn-tăl, *adj.* (*Zool.*) Having no placenta ; (জন্তু-বিজ্ঞান) জরায়ু-কুসুমশূন্য।

im-plănt′, *v. t.* **1.** To insert or infix (*in*) ; পোতা, প্রোথিত করা। **2.** To instil or inculcate thoroughly ; as, to *implant* a principle, idea etc. in a person or his mind" ; অন্তর্নিবিষ্ট করা, মুদ্রিত করা। **3.** To plant as a ground etc. ; রোপণ করা। **—plan-ta′-tion,** *n.*

im-plead′ (-plēd), *v. t.* (*Rare*) To institute or prosecute a suit at law ; (অপ্রঃ) মোকদ্দমা করা, মামলা করা, মোকদ্দমা চালান।

im-pledge′ (-plĕj), *v. t.* To pledge or pawn ; বন্ধক দেওয়া, রেহান দেওয়া, পুরু রাখা, বাঁধা দেওয়া।

im′-plē-mĕnt, *n.* **1.** A tool or instrument (*esp. in pl.*) ; যন্ত্র, হাতিয়ার। **2.** An article of furniture, dress, etc. ; "He left for an *implement* of his house...a costly table" ; আসবাবদ্রব্য, পোষাক, প্রভৃতি। **3.** (*Pl.*) Things serving as equipment or outfit, as household furniture, ecclesiastical vestments, wearing apparel, etc. ; "They...bear the *implements* of the mass" ; সাজসজ্জা। **4.** (*Scot. Law*) Fulfilment or performance ; (স্কটলণ্ডের আইন) সম্পাদন, পালন।

im′-plē-mĕnt, *v. t.* (*Scot. Law*) **1.** To fulfil or perform as a contract or engagement ; (স্কটলণ্ডের আইন) পূরণ করা, সম্পাদন করা। **2.** To fill up or supplement ; "Projects for *implementing* wages by Pauper relief" ; পূরণ করা, কোন কিছু যোগ করিয়া পূর্ণ করা। **3.** To provide with implements or tools ; যন্ত্র বা হাতিয়ার দেওয়া।

im-plē′-tion, *n.* The act of filling ; the state of being full ; পূরণ ; পরিপূর্ণতা।

im-plī′-ā-ble (-bl), *adj.* (*Rare*) Not pliable ; (ক্বচিদ্ ব্যবহৃত) অনমনীয়।

im′-plĭ-cāte, *v. t.* **1.** To interweave ; to entangle ; সংগ্রথিত করা ; জড়িত করা। **2.** To involve or imply as an inference ; সংসৃষ্ট করা, লিপ্ত করা, সূচিত করা। **3.** To involve deeply or unfavourably ; as, to *implicate* a person in a crime etc. ; জড়ান, পেঁচান। **4.** (*Pass.*) To be affected in the action of something ; "The brain is *implicated* in insanity ; আক্রান্ত হওয়া। **—ca-ted,** *p. p.* Entwined ; involved ; বিজড়িত ; লিপ্ত, জড়িত, সংসৃষ্ট। **—ca′-tion,** *n.* **1.** The act of implicating ; the state of being implicated ; বিজড়ন ; বিজড়িতাবস্থা। **2.** Act of implying ; state of being implied ; an inference ; সূচনা ; ফলিতার্থ, ধ্বনি, ব্যঙ্গ্যার্থ, ধ্বনিতার্থ, লক্ষ্যার্থ, লক্ষিত, অনুমান, অর্থাপত্তি। **—ca-tive,** *adj.* **—ca-tive-ly,** *adv.* **By implication**—By what is implied ; by natural inference ; প্রকারান্তরে ; আভাসে, অনুমান দ্বারা।

im′-plĭ-cāte, *n.* A thing implied ; সূচিত বিষয়, ধ্বনি।

im-plĭc′-it, *adj.* **1.** Implied ; স্পষ্টভাবে উক্ত না হইলেও বোধগম্য, সূচিত, অধ্যাহৃত (হিঃ কোঃ)। **2.** Virtually contained (in) ; potential ; undeveloped ; "Conceptions that lay *implicit* in it" ; কার্য্যতঃ অন্তর্ভুক্ত ; প্রচ্ছন্ন ; অনুদ্ভূত, অবিকশিত। **3.** Relying entirely on another ; unquestioning ; unreserved ; as, *implicit* confidence ; সম্পূর্ণ নির্ভরশীল ; নিশ্চিত ; অসঙ্কুচিতচিত্ত। **—ly,** *adv.* **1.** Unreservedly ; unquestioningly ; অসঙ্কুচিতচিত্তে ; বিনাবাক্যব্যয়ে। **2.** Impliedly ; লক্ষিত ভাবে। **—ness,** *n.*

im-plōre′, *v. t.* To beg earnestly for ; as, to *implore* favour or aid ; to entreat ; as, to *implore* a person to do something ; সানুনয় প্রার্থনা করা, যাচ্ঞা করা ; কাকুতি মিনতি করা, সবিনয় প্রার্থনা করা। **—plor′-ing,** *adj.* Beseeching ; entreating ; অনুনয়সূচক ; মিনতিজ্ঞাপক। **—plor′-ing-ly,** *adv.* **—plor′-ing-ness,** *n.*

im-plŭ′-vĭ-ŭm, *n.* (*Rom. antiq.*) A cistern or basin in the court of a Roman house to receive rain water from an open space in the roof ; (রোমীয় প্রত্নতত্ত্ব) প্রাচীন রোমবাসীদের গৃহপ্রাঙ্গণস্থ বৃষ্টিজলসঞ্চয়ের জন্য কুণ্ড।

im-plȳ′, *v. t.* **1.** To involve the truth or existence of when not expressly stated ; to include virtually ; as, war *implies* fighting ; স্পষ্টরূপে উক্ত না হইলেও কোন কিছুর সত্য বা সত্তা অন্তর্ভুক্ত করা ;

কার্য্যতঃ অঙ্গীভূত করা। 2. To express indirectly; to suggest; to hint; পরোক্ষভাবে অর্থ প্রকাশ করা; সূচনা করা; জ্ঞাপন করা। 3. To mean; বুঝান। **—plied,** *adj.* Contained or stated by implication; উপলক্ষিত, নিহিত, প্রকারান্তরে উক্ত, অর্থসিদ্ধ, ফলিত, লক্ষিত, ধ্বনিত। **—pli'-ed-ly,** *adv.*

im-pŏck'-ĕt, *v. t.* To put into one's pocket; জেবে রাখা।

im-pō-līte', *adj.* Not of polished manner; uncivil; rude; অসভ্য, ইতর; অভব্য, অশিষ্ট; রূঢ়, রুক্ষ, দুর্বিনীত। **—ly,** *adv.* **—ness,** *n.*

im-pŏl'-i-tic, *adj.* Not politic; unwise; inexpedient; দুর্নীত, অশিষ্ট; অবিজ্ঞ, অনভিজ্ঞ, অবিবেকী, অদূরদর্শী, অপরিণামদর্শী; অযৌক্তিক, অসঙ্গত, অবিধেয়। **—cy,** *n.* Bad policy; inexpediency; দুর্নীতি, কুরীতি; অযৌক্তিকতা। **—ly,** *adv.*

im-pŏn'-dêr-ă-ble (-bl), *adj.* & *n.* (*Phys.*) Without weight; very light; (পদার্থ-বিজ্ঞান) ভারহীন; অতি লঘু, অতি সূক্ষ্ম। ***Noun.*** (*Phys.*) An imponderable substance; (পদার্থ বিজ্ঞান) ভারহীন পদার্থ। **—a-bil'-i-ty, —ness** *ns.* The state of being imponderable; ভারশূন্যতা, ভারহীনতা।

im-pō'-nĕnt, *adj.* & *n.* That imposes; ছলনাকারী। ***Noun.*** A person who imposes; প্রতারক।

im-pōrt', *v. t.* & *n.* 1. To carry, bring from abroad (*into*); as, to *import* goods *into* a country; আমদানী করা, দেশান্তর হইতে আনয়ন করা। 2. To signify; to imply; অর্থ প্রকাশ করা, বুঝান; সূচনা করা, দ্যোতন করা। 3. To express or state; "An inscription *importing* 'that it was erected by Pope' etc."; প্রকাশ করা, বিবৃত করা। 4. To be of consequence to; to concern; as, questions that *import* us nearly; গুরুত্ব-বিশিষ্ট হওয়া; সংস্রব থাকা। ***Noun.*** 1. What is implied; meaning; সূচিত অর্থ, ধ্বনি, ভাবার্থ; মর্ম্ম, অভিপ্রায়, অর্থ (হিঃ কোঃ), অর্থব্যাপ্তি (ঐ), অভিধেয়। 2. Importance; গুরুত্ব, প্রয়োজনীয়তা, কার্য্যগুরুত্ব, সার্থকতা। 3. (*Usu. Pl.*) Merchandize imported; বিদেশ হইতে আনীত পণ্যদ্রব্য, আমদানীদ্রব্য। 4. Act of importing goods etc.; importation; দেশান্তর হইতে আনয়ন; আমদানীকরণ। **—a-ble,** *adj.* Capable of being imported, as goods etc.; আমদানীযোগ্য। **—a-bil'-i-ty, —por-ta'-tion,** *ns.* 1. The act of bringing goods etc. into a country; আমদানীকরণ। 2. That which is imported; আমদানী মাল। **—er,** *n.* One who imports goods etc.; আমদানীকারী।

im-pŏr'-tănt, *adj.* 1. Carrying with it great consequences; significant; weighty; গুরুত্ববিশিষ্ট, গরীয়ান, সারবান; গূঢ়ার্থপ্রকাশক; গুরুতর। 2. Ostentatious; pompous; as, an *important* manner; আড়ম্বরপূর্ণ; জাঁকাল। **—ly,** *adv.* **—tance,** *n.* State of being important; significance; গুরুত্ব; সার্থকতা। 2. Dignity; "A family...of some *importance*"; গৌরব, খ্যাতি, মর্য্যাদা, সম্ভ্রম। 3. Pompousness; "With *importance* every rite is done"; ধূমধড়কা, আড়ম্বর, ঘটা।

im-pŏr'-tū-nate, *adj.* Troublesomely urgent in request or demand; persistently solicitous; নির্ব্বন্ধাতিশয়যুক্ত, নির্ব্বন্ধশীল, অতিযাচক, অতিপ্রার্থক, নাছোড়বান্দা। **—ly,** *adv.* **—tu'-ni-ty,** *n.* Pressing or persistent solicitation; নির্ব্বন্ধাতিশয়, নির্ব্বন্ধাতিশয্য।

im-pŏr-tūne', *v. t.* To request or solicit with urgency; to urge with troublesome application; নির্ব্বন্ধাতিশয় সহকারে প্রার্থনা করা; সনির্ব্বন্ধ অনুরোধ করা।

im-pōse' *v. t.* & *i.* 1. (*Archaic*) To lay or place (a thing) *upon*; (অপ্রঃ) স্থাপন করা, ন্যস্ত করা। 2. To levy or inflict as a tax, penalty, duty, etc., (with *on* or *upon*); ধার্য্য করা, বসান। 3. (*Printing*) To arrange the pages for printing and prepare the form for the press; (মুদ্রণ) মুদ্রণের পূর্ব্বে মুদ্রাক্ষর-বিন্যস্তপৃষ্ঠাসমূহ সাজান, ফরমা সজান। 4. To palm or pass off; as, to *impose* inferior goods *upon* one; ঠকান, ফাঁকি দিয়া চালাইয়া দেওয়া। ***Verb i.*** 1. To exert an influence (*on* or *upon* a person) by a striking character or appearance; ভড়ক দেখাইয়া (কোন লোকের উপর) প্রভাব বিস্তার করা। 2. To cheat or deceive, (with *on* or *upon*); প্রতারণা করা, ঠকান, ভোগা দেওয়া। **—pos'-ing,** *adj.* Impressing; commanding; as, an *imposing* air or spectacle; হৃদয়গ্রাহী, চিত্তাকর্ষক, ভাবগম্ভীর; প্রভুত্বকারী। **—pos'-ing-ly,** *adv.* **—pos'-ing-ness,** *n.* **To impose upon (a person)**—To take advantage of (a person); to cheat or deceive; সুবিধা বা সুযোগ গ্রহণ করা; প্রতারণা করা, ঠকান।

im-pō-ŝi'-tion, *n.* 1. The act of imposing; স্থাপন, নির্দ্ধারণ। 2. That which is imposed; tax; duty; যাহা স্থাপিত বা নির্দ্ধারিত করা হয়; কর; শুল্ক। 3. Cheating; fraud; প্রতারণা, প্রবঞ্চনা; জুয়াচুরি। 4. (*Eccl.*) Laying on of hands (in ordination etc.); (যাজকীয়-শাস্ত্র) যাজক পদে নিয়োগকালে হস্তন্যাস। 5. An exercise enjoined on students at school as a punishment; ছেলেদের উপর শাস্তিস্বরূপ যে অতিরিক্ত পাঠ চাপান হয়।

im-pŏs'-si-ble (-i-bl), *adj.* 1. Not possible; impracticable; unattainable; অসম্ভব, অসম্ভাবনীয় অসম্ভাব্য; অসাধ্য; অপ্রাপ্য। 2. Not easy or convenient; অসুবিধাজনক। 3. (*Colloq.*) Intolerable; as, an

(ঐ)। **Log-cabin**—প্রকাণ্ড প্রকাণ্ড কাঠের কুঁদা সাজাইয়া নির্ম্মিত গৃহ। **Log-line**—পোতগতিমাপক যন্ত্রের প্রব। **Log-roll** — পোড়াইবার বা বোঝাই করার জন্য কুঁদাকাঠ গড়ানে বা জড়করণে সাহায্য করা; পরস্পরকে সাহায্য প্রদান করিতে হইবে এই সর্ত্তে দুই ব্যক্তির সংযোগ হওয়া; দুই গ্রন্থকার কর্তৃক পরস্পরের রচনার প্রশংসা করা। (Hence) **Log-rolling,** *n.* **Log wood** — আমেরিকা দেশীয় বৃক্ষ বিশেষ; ঐ বৃক্ষের কাষ্ঠ — যাহা রঞ্জনকার্য্যে ব্যবহৃত হয়, কুচন্দন **In the log** — Unhewn; চেলা করা নয় **Roll my log and I'll roll yours**—If you help me I shall help you: তুমি আমাকে সাহায্য করিলে আমিও তোমাকে সাহায্য করিব। **To float, fall or lie like a log**—To do so in a helpless or stunned state; অসহায় অবস্থায় পড়া, স্রোতের কাষ্ঠের মত ভাসিয়া যাওয়া **To sail by the log**—To calculate a ship's position by it পোতগতিবেগমাপক যন্ত্রদ্বারা জাহাজের অবস্থানস্থল গণনা করিয়া ঠিক করা।

im-pŏs'-tor (-tĕr), A deceiver under a false character; a swindler; প্রতারক, প্রবঞ্চক; শঠ, ধূর্ত্ত, জুয়াচোর, বুজরুগ, ভণ্ড। **—ship,** *n.* প্রতারণা, প্রবঞ্চনা, ছলনা। **—trous,** *adj.*

im-pŏs'-tūre, *n.* Cheating; fraudulent deception; প্রতারণা, ছলনা, বঞ্চনা, শাঠ্য; বুজরুগি।

im'-pŏ-tĕnt, *adj.* Weak; feeble; deficient in capacity; wholly lacking in sexual power; দুর্ব্বল, শক্তিহীন; হীনসামর্থ্য, হীনবল; নির্ব্বীর্য্য, অক্ষম, অসমর্থ; ক্লীব, নষ্টবীর্য্য, সুরতাশক্ত, পুরুষত্ববিহীন, ভগ্নধ্বজ, গতবীর্য্য, অপৌরষ, প্রজননাশক্ত, পুংশক্তিহীন, নিষ্পুরুষ। **—ly,** *adv.*

im'-pŏ-tĕn-cy̆, —tence (tĕns), *ns.* 1. Weakness; feebleness; inability; দৌর্ব্বল্য, বৈকল্য; দুর্ব্বলতা; অসমর্থতা, অক্ষমতা, শক্তিহীনতা, ক্লৈব্য (গীতা)। 2. Complete absence of procreative or sexual powers (usu. of males); পুরুষত্বহীনতা, ক্লীবতা, ধ্বজভঙ্গ।

im-pound' (-pownd), *v. t.* 1. To shut up (cattle) as in a pound; খোঁয়াড়ে আবদ্ধ করা। 2. To confine or shut in; "How to *impound* the rebels:" to *impound* water for distribution; আবদ্ধ করা, আটক করা, অবরুদ্ধ করা। 3. To seize and hold in the custody of law as a document etc; to confiscate; অধিকার করা; বাজেয়াপ্ত করা।

im-pŏv'-ĕr-ish, *v. t.* 1. To make poor; দরিদ্র করা, নিঃস্ব করা। 2. To exhaust the resources, fertility or strength of; as, to *impoverish* land, blood or mind; নিঃশেষিত করা, অনুর্ব্বর করা, দুর্ব্বল করা, শক্তিহীন করা, ক্ষীণ করা।

im-prăc'-ti-că-ble (-bl), *adj.* 1. Not practicable; practically impossible; অসাধ্য, দুষ্কর, দুষ্করণীয়, অসাধনীয়, দুঃসাধ্য; কার্য্যতঃ অসম্ভব। 2. Unmanagable, as a person or thing; অদম্য, দুর্দ্দান্ত, অনায়ত্ত, 3. Impassable, as a road, country, etc.; অগম্য, দুর্গম। **—bil'-i-ty, —ness,** *ns.* The state of being impracticable; দুঃসাধ্যতা, অসাধ্যতা, দৌষ্কর্য্য। **—bly,** *adv.*

im'-prĕ-cāte, *v. t.* 1. To call down or invoke as a curse, calamity, etc. (*upon*); অমঙ্গল প্রার্থনা করা, অনিষ্টপাতের জন্য আকাঙ্ক্ষা করা। 2. (*Rare*) To curse; (ক্বচিদ্ ব্যবহৃত) অভিসম্পাত দেওয়া, শাপ দেওয়া। **—ca'-tion,** *n.* The act of imprecating; a curse; অমঙ্গল প্রার্থনা; শাপ, অভিশাপ। **—ca-to-ry,** *adj.*

im-prĕg'-nă-ble (-bl), *adj.* 1. That cannot be taken by force; able to resist attack; as, an *impregnable* fortress; দুর্জ্জেয়, অজেয়; অপ্রবেশ্য, অভেদ্য। 2. (*Fig.*) Invincible or proof against attack; "*Impregnable* truth"; (লক্ষণায়) দুর্জ্জেয়, অপরাজেয়, অকাট্য।

im-prĕg'-nāte, *v. t.* 1. To make pregnant; গর্ভবতী করা, সসত্ত্বা করা, অন্তঃসত্ত্বা করা, গর্ভস্থাপন করা, গর্ভাধান করা। 2. (*Biol.*) To fertilize; to fecundate; (জীব-বিজ্ঞান) ডিম্ব নিষেক করা; গর্ভসঞ্চার করা। 3. To fill or saturate (*with*); পূর্ণ করা, সম্পূরিত করা, অভিসিক্ত করা। 4. To fill or imbue (*with*) thoughts, feelings or moral qualities etc.; পরিপূরিত করা, অনুপ্রাণিত করা। **—na'-tion,** *n.* 1. The act of impregnating; the state of being impregnated; বংশরক্ষণ (সাঃ পঃ), গর্ভোৎপাদন, গর্ভাধান, গর্ভস্থাপন; গর্ভাবস্থা। 2. Fertilization; fecundation; ডিম্ব নিষেক, নিষেক (সাঃ পঃ); গর্ভসঞ্চার, গর্ভাধান। 3. Saturation; নিষেক, অনুপ্রবেশন। 4. That with which anything is impregnated; "These *impregnations* seemed...equally colourless and bright"; যদ্দারা কোন কিছুর গর্ভসঞ্চার হয় বা কোন কিছু নিষিক্ত বা পরিপূরিত হয়।

im-prĕg'-nāte, *adj.* 1. Pregnant (*lit.* & *fig.*); গর্ভবতী, অন্তঃসত্ত্বা। 2. Imbued; saturated or filled (*with*); "......Palestine *impregnate with* this life divine"; সম্পূরিত; পরিপূরিত।

im-pre-să'-ri-ŏ (-prā-), *n.* The manager or conductor of an opera or concert company; গীতিনাট্য বা ঐকতান বাদকদলের কর্ম্মকর্ত্তা বা পরিচালক।

im-pre-scrip'-ti-ble (-bl), *adj.* Not subject to prescription; incapable of being legally taken away as a right; আবহমানকাল ব্যবহারের অনধীন; আইনতঃ রহিত করার অযোগ্য।

im-prĕss', *v. t.* 1. To stamp or press (*upon, on*); to imprint; as, to *impress* or mark *on* something; মুদ্রিত করা; ছাপ দেওয়া।

2. To set a mark upon *with* a stamp etc., (*lit.* & *fig.*) ; as, he *impressed* her hand *with* kisses ; অঙ্কিত করা, মুদ্রিত করা। 3. To fix or inculcate deeply ; to imprint ; as, to *impress* an idea *on* a person or his mind ; গভীরভাবে অঙ্কিত করা ; মুদ্রিত করা। 4. To make an impression upon ; to affect deeply or forcibly ; as, he tried to *impress* me with his importance ; মনে ছাপ দেওয়া ; মনোমধ্যে গভীরভাবে অঙ্কিত করা। **—i-ble,** *adj.* Capable of being impressed ; susceptible ; sensitive to impression ; মুদ্রাঙ্কগ্রহণোপযোগী ; সংবেদনশীল ; বিচলনীয়। **—i-ble-ness,** *n.*

im'-prĕss, *n.* 1. The act of impressing or marking ; মুদ্রণ, চিহ্নিত করণ। 2 Mark made by a seal, stamp, etc. ; মোহর, চিহ্ন, মুদ্রা, ছাপ। 3. (*Fig.*) A distinctive or characteristic mark ; as, the work bore the *impress* of a great artist ; বিশেষত্বদ্যোতক চিহ্ন বা লক্ষণ, ব্যক্তিগত ছাপ।

im-prĕss', *v. t.* 1. To compel (men) to serve in army or navy ; কোন ব্যক্তিকে সেনা বা নৌ বিভাগে কার্য্য করিতে বাধ্য করা, বেগার ধরা। 2. To seize as goods etc. by authority for public service ; সরকারী কাজের জন্য উচ্চকর্ম্মচারীর আদেশে মালপত্র অধিকার করা। 3. To enlist or utilize as a thing in argument etc. ; "They *impressed* a small school to assist in the performances" ; সাহায্য বা সহযোগিতা প্রাপ্ত হওয়া, ব্যবহার করা। **—ment,** *n.*

im-pres'-sion (-prŏ-), *n* 1. The act of impressing a mark etc. ; মুদ্রিত করণ, মুদ্রণ। 2. That which is impressed ; a stamp or mark ; মুদ্রিত বস্তু ; মোহর, চিহ্ন, ছাপ। 3. Influence or effect produced on the senses or mind ; as, it made no *impression* on his mind ; মনের উপর ছাপ, মন বা ইন্দ্রিয়ের উপর প্রভাব, সংস্কার (বেদান্ত), ধারণা, প্রতিপত্তি (হিঃ কোঃ), প্রতীতি (ঐ), রসপ্রতিপত্তি (ঐ)। 4. An indistinct notion, remembrance or belief ; as, that was my *impression* ; অস্ফুট ভাব, অস্ফুট স্মৃতি, ক্ষীণ-বিশ্বাস। 5. A printed copy from a type or engraved block etc. ; মুদ্রাক্ষর, চিত্রফলক, প্রভৃতির মুদ্রিত প্রতিলিপি। 6. The printing of the number of copies forming one edition of a book ; an edition ; এক সংস্করণের সমস্ত পুস্তক মুদ্রণ ; সংস্করণ।

im-pres'-sion-ă-ble (-prĕ-shŭn-a-bl), *adj.* Capable of being impressed ; susceptible of impression ; easily influenced ; as, an *impressionable* person ; মুদ্রণযোগ্য, অঙ্কনযোগ্য ; সংবেদনশীল ; আশুবিচলিত। **—bil'-i-ty, —ness,** *ns.*

im-pres'-sion-ism (-prĕ-), *n.* The method of painting or writing with broad simplicity and little attention to detail ; "A touch of literary *impressionism*" ; খুঁটিনাটি বিষয়ের দিকে মনোযোগ না দিয়া স্পষ্ট ও সাদাসিধা ভাবে রচনা বা চিত্রাঙ্কণের প্রণালী বিশেষ। **—ist,** *n.* **—is'-tic,** *adj.*

im-prĕs'-sive (-iv), *adj.* Having power to impress ; exciting or tending to excite deep feeling ; হৃদয়গ্রাহী, মর্ম্মস্পর্শী, হৃদয়স্পর্শী, হৃদয়হারী ; গভীর ভাবোদ্দীপক। **—ly,** *adv.* **—ness,** *n.* The state of being impressive ; হৃদয়হারিতা, হৃদয়গ্রাহিতা।

im'-prĕst, *n.* An advance of money to a person by the goverment to be used in a state business ; দাদন।

imprimatur, *n.* (*L.—Let it be printed*) 1. Licence to print or publish a book or paper ; গ্রন্থ বা সংবাদপত্র প্রকাশন বা মুদ্রাঙ্কণের অনুমতি বা অধিকার, মুদ্রাঙ্কণাধিকার, গ্রন্থ-প্রকাশাধিকার। 2. (*Fig.*) Sanction ; (লক্ষণায়) অনুমতি।

imprimis, *adj.* In the first place ; প্রথমতঃ।

im-print', *v. t.* 1. To mark by pressure ; to stamp ; as, to *imprint* a footstep on sand ; চিহ্নিত করা, অঙ্কিত করা ; মুদ্রিত করা। 2. To impress as an idea etc., *on*, or *in* the mind, memory, etc. ; মনোমধ্যে দৃঢ়বদ্ধ করা। 3. To stamp or impress (something *with* a figure) ; "A land never before *imprinted* by the foot of man" ; মুদ্রিত করা, চিহ্নিত করা, অঙ্কিত করা।

im'-print, *n.* 1. A stamp or impression (*lit.* & *fig.*) ; মুদ্রা, মোহর, ছাপ। 2. The name of the printer or publisher with the time and place of publication of a book printed on the title page ; গ্রন্থপরিচয়পৃষ্ঠায় গ্রন্থমুদ্রণের স্থান, কাল ও প্রকাশকের নাম। **Publisher's** or **printer's imprint**—See IMPRINT, *n.* 2.

im-pris'-ŏn, *v. t.* 1. To put into prison or jail ; কারারুদ্ধ করা, কয়েদ করা। 2. (*Fig.*) To confine or shut up ; "Try to *imprison* the resistless wind" ; অবরুদ্ধ করা, আটক করা, বন্দী করা, নিরোধ করা। **—ment,** *n.* The act of imprisoning or the state of being imprisoned ; confinement ; কয়েদকরণ, নিরোধন, কারাবন্ধন ; কারাবাস, কয়েদ, অবরোধ।

im-prŏb'-ă-ble (-bl), *adj.* Unlikely ; not likely to happen or to be true ; অসম্ভব ; দুর্ঘট, অঘটনীয়। **—bil'-i-ty,** *n.* 1. Quality of being improbable ; unlikelihood ; অভাবনীয়তা ; অসম্ভাব্যতা। 2. An improbable event or result ; অভাবনীয় ঘটনা বা ফল। **—bly,** *adv.* **—ness,** *n.*

im-prŏb'-i-ty, *n.* Dishonesty ; অসাধুতা।

im-prŏmp'-tū, *adv., adj.* & *n.* Off hand ; extempore ; (*both adv.* & *adj.*) ; তাৎক্ষণিক ; প্রত্যুৎপন্ন;

অচিন্তিতপূর্ব্ব, উপস্থিতমত, সময়স্ফূর্ত্ত, পূর্ব্ববিচাররহিত। ***Noun.*** An extempore composition or address ; উপস্থিত রচনা, উপস্থিত বক্তৃতা।

im-prŏp'-ẽr, *adj.* **1.** Unsuitable ; unfit ; as, an *improper* medicine ; অনুপযুক্ত, অনুপযোগী, অযৌক্তিক; অনুচিত, অবিধেয়, অযুক্ত। **2.** Inaccurate, erroneous ; wrong ; as, an *improper* conclusion ; অঠিক ; ভ্রমপূর্ণ ; অশুদ্ধ। **3.** (*Arith.*) Not properly so called, as a fraction (one with a numerator greater than the denominator) ; (পাটীগণিত) অপ্রকৃত। **4.** Indecorous ; indecent ; as, *improper* language ; অশিষ্ট ; অশ্লীল। **–ly,** *adv.* In an improper manner ; অন্যায়ভাবে। **Improper fraction**—যে সকল ভগ্নাংশের হর অপেক্ষা লব বৃহত্তর, অপ্রকৃত ভগ্নাংশ।

im-prō'-pri-āte, *v. t.* & *adj.* **1.** (*Obs.*) To appropriate to one's self ; আত্মসাৎ করা। **2.** To place (ecclesiastical property etc.) in the hands of a layman ; দেবোত্তর বা যাজকোত্তর সম্পত্তি যাজকসম্প্রদায় বহির্ভূত ব্যক্তির হস্তে অর্পণ করা। ***Adj.*** Impropriated as a benefice etc. ; যাজকসম্প্রদায় বহির্ভূত ব্যক্তির হস্তে সমর্পিত। **–a'-tion,** *n.* **–a-tor,** *n.* A layman in possession of church property ; যাজকীয় সম্পত্তির স্বত্বস্বামিত্ব প্রাপ্ত যাজকসম্প্রদায় বহির্ভূত ব্যক্তি।

im-prō-prī'-ĕ-tȳ, *n.* **1.** Incorrectness ; inaccuracy ; ভ্রমাত্মকতা ; অশুদ্ধি। **2.** Unfitness ; অনুপযুক্ততা, অনুপযোগিতা। **3.** Unseemliness ; indecency ; অশোভনতা, অনৌচিত্য ; অশ্লীলতা। **4.** An improper act or expression ; as, a moral *impropriety* ; অনুচিত ব্যবহার, অনুচিতবাক্য।

im-prôv'-ă-ble (-bl), *adj.* Capable of being improved ; susceptible of improvement ; উন্নতিযোগ্য ; উৎকর্ষসাধনীয়। **–bil'-i-ty, –ness,** *ns.* **–bly,** *adv.*

im-prôve', *v. t.* & *i.* **1.** To make better ; to ameliorate ; উৎকর্ষ সাধন করা ; উন্নতি সাধন করা, শ্রীবৃদ্ধি করা। **2.** To use or employ to good purpose ; as, to *improve* the opportunity or occasion ; সদুদ্দেশ্যে ব্যবহার বা নিয়োগ করা। **3.** To turn (*into* something better) by improving ; উৎকর্ষ সম্পাদন দ্বারা শ্রেষ্ঠতর করা। **4.** To correct ; to mend ; সংশোধন করা ; পরিশোধিত করা। ***Verb i.*** **1.** To grow better ; উন্নতি লাভ করা, শ্রীবৃদ্ধি প্রাপ্ত হওয়া। **2.** To make something better ; as, to *improve* upon a thing ; উৎকর্ষ সাধন করা। **–ment,** *n.* The act of improving ; advancement or progress ; amelioration ; উন্নতি সাধন, উন্নয়ন ; উন্নতি, উৎকর্ষ, শ্রীবৃদ্ধি। **To improve away**—To get rid of by improvements ; উৎকর্ষসাধন দ্বারা নিষ্কৃতি পাওয়া। **To improve the occasion** — To draw some moral lesson from an event which has occured ; কোন ঘটনা হইতে নৈতিক শিক্ষা লাভ করা। **To improve upon**—See IMPROVE, *v. i.* 2.

im-prôv'-ẽr, *n.* **1.** One who, or that which, improves ; উৎকর্ষসাধক, শ্রীবৃদ্ধিকারক। **2.** One who works at a trade for low wages or none to improve his skill ; যে ব্যক্তি কোনরূপ ব্যবসায়াদিতে অধিকতর পারদর্শিতা লাভের জন্য বিনা বেতনে বা অল্প বেতনে কাজ করে। **3.** (*Dressing*) A learner in dress-making ; যে ব্যক্তি পরিচ্ছদ প্রস্তুতের কার্য্য শিক্ষা করে।

im'-prŏv'-i-dĕnt, *adj.* Not provident ; wanting foresight ; heedless ; thriftless ; অপরিণামদর্শী ; অদূরদর্শী ; অবিবেচক ; অমিতব্যয়ী, অপব্যয়ী। **–dence,** *n.* Want of foresight or thrift ; অপরিণামদর্শিতা, অমিতব্যয়িতা। **–ly,** *adv.*

im-prō-vīse' (*or* -vēz), *v. t.* & *i.* **1.** To compose or recite, as a verse, music, etc. without previous preparation ; উপস্থিত মত (কবিতা) রচনা বা আবৃত্তি করা। **2.** To provide or get up off hand ; "A tent *improvised* this morning" ; তৎক্ষণাৎ প্রস্তুত করা। ***Verb i.*** To compose or utter a verse, music, etc. extempone ; উপস্থিত মত রচনা করা, না ভাবিয়া চিন্তিয়া রচনা করা, উপস্থিত মত গান বা আবৃত্তি করা। **–prov-i-sa'-tion,** *n.* **1.** The act of improvising a composition etc. ; উপস্থিত মত রচনা করণ বা বক্তৃতা প্রদান। **2.** That which is improvised ; উপস্থিত বক্তৃতা, রচনা, গান, প্রভৃতি। **–prov'-i-sa-tor, –vis'-er, –prov-(v)i-sa-to'-re,** *ns.* One who composes extempore ; উপস্থিত রচনাকারী। **–prov-i-sa-to'-ri-al, –prov'-i-sa-to-ry,** *adjs.* **–pro(v)-vi-sa-trice',** *n.* (*Fem.*)

im-pru'-dĕnt(-prô-), *adj.* Not prudent ; indiscreet ; rash ; অবিবেচক, বিবেচনাশূন্য ; অসমীক্ষ্যকারী ; হঠকারী, অবিমৃষ্যকারী। **–dence,** *n.* State of being imprudent ; indiscretion ; a rash act ; অবিবেকিতা ; বিবেচনাহীনতা ; হঠকারিতা। **–ly,** *adv.* Injudiciously ; rashly ; অবিবেকের মত ; হঠকারিতার সহিত।

im'-pū-dence (-dĕns), *n.* The quality of being impudent ; insolence ; effrontery ; want of modesty ; ধৃষ্টতা, হঠকারিতা ; অসমীক্ষ্যকারিতা, অবিমৃশ্যকারিতা প্রগল্‌ভতা ; ঔদ্ধত্য ; নির্লজ্জতা।

im'-pū-dĕnt, *adj.* Impertinent ; shamelessly forward ; brazen-aced ; rude ; উদ্ধত, প্রগল্‌ভ ; ধৃষ্ট ; নির্লজ্জ ; রূঢ়, দুর্বিনীত। **–ly,** *adv.* In an impudent manner ; impertinently ; ধৃষ্টতার সহিত ; বে-আদবের মত।

im-pū-dĭc'-i-tȳ, *n.* Immodesty ; shamelessness ; প্রগল্‌ভতা ; নির্লজ্জতা, ধৃষ্টতা।

im-pugn′ (-pūn), *v. t.* To attack by words or arguments ; to contradict ; to call in question ; as, to *impugn* a statement or opinion ; বাক্য বা যুক্তিদ্বারা আক্রমণ করা ; প্রতিবাদ করা ; কোন উক্তির বিরুদ্ধে প্রশ্ন উত্থাপন করা, বিপ্রপত্তি করা । **–a-ble,** *adj.* Capable of being impugned ; প্রতিবাদযোগ্য । **–ment,** *n.*

im′-pū′-is-sant (-ănt), *adj.* Powerless ; impotent ; feeble ; অক্ষম, অশক্ত ; পুরুষত্বহীন, ক্লীব ; ক্ষীণ, দুর্ব্বল। **–sance,** *n.* State of being impuissant ; দুর্ব্বলতা, ক্ষীণতা, শক্তিহীনতা, দৌর্ব্বল্য ।

im′-pūlse (-pŭls), *n.* **1.** The act of impelling ; push ; তাড়না, নোদনা, নোদন (ব্রজঃ হিন্দু) ; ধাক্কা । **2.** The effect of an impelling force ; impetus ; অভিঘাতবলের ক্রিয়া ; ধাক্কা, অভিঘাত (ব্রজঃ হিন্দু) । **3.** *(Dynamics)* A great force suddenly communicated *e. g.* blow of a hammer ; the product of the average value of force multiplied by the time during which it acts ; (গতিবিজ্ঞান) সহসা সঞ্চারিত মহাবল, অভিঘাতবল, পরিবর্ত্তক বল (হিঃ কোঃ) ; বলের গড়পড়তা মান এবং যে সময় ব্যাপিয়া বল ক্রিয়া করে তাহার গুণফল । **4.** Mental incitement ; আবেগ (হিঃ কোঃ), মানসিক উত্তেজনা । **5.** Hasty inclination ; as, to be guided by an *impulse* ; হঠাৎ ঝোঁক ।

im-pŭl′-sion, *n.* **1.** Same as IMPULSE I. **2.** Mental impulse ; প্রেরণা । **3.** Impetus , ধাক্কা ।

im-pŭl′-sive (-sĭv), *adj.* **1.** Tending to impel ; প্রণোদক, আবেগী (হিঃ কোঃ), উত্তেজক । **2.** Actuated by impulse, as a person, conduct, etc. ; সাময়িক উত্তেজনাপ্রণোদিত, সাময়িক উত্তেজনা বশে কার্য্যকারী । **–ly,** *adv.* **–ness,** *n.*

im-pū′-ni-ty, *n.* Exemption from injury, loss or punishment ; অক্ষতি, অপীড়া, শাস্তি হইতে অব্যাহতি, দণ্ডমুক্তি, রেহাই । **With impunity**—Without any punishment or penalty ; বিনা দণ্ডে, বিনা শাস্তিতে ।

im-pūre′, *adj.* **1.** Not pure ; dirty ; সমল ; অপরিষ্কার, নোংরা । **2.** Mixed with extraneous substance ; adulterated ; সমল ; ভেজাল, অবিশুদ্ধ । **3.** Unholy ; অপবিত্র, অশুচি, অমেধ্য, অপূত, অশুদ্ধ । **4.** Unchaste ; obscene ; অসৎ, ভ্রষ্ট, অসাধ্বী ; অশ্লীল । **5.** (Of a colour) Mixed with another colour ; (বর্ণ-সম্বন্ধে) অন্য বর্ণের সহিত মিশ্রিত । **–ly,** *adv.* **–ness, –pu′-ri-ty,** *ns.* **1.** The state of being impure ; dirtiness ; অপবিত্রতা, অবিশুদ্ধতা ; সমলতা । **2.** Adulteration ; ভেজাল দেওন । **3.** That which renders anything impure ; a foul matter ; খাইদ, ভেজাল ; দূষিত পদার্থ, মল ।

im-pūte′, *v. t.* **1.** To attribute or ascribe ; as, to *impute* a fault to a person ; আরোপ করা, নির্দ্দেশ করা । **–put-a-bil′-i-ty, –put′-a-ble-ness,** *ns.* **–put′-a-ble,** *adj.* Capable of being imputed ; আরোপণীয়, আরোপ্য । **–put′-a-tive,** *adj.* Imputable ; given to imputation ; আরোপণযোগ্য ; আরোপণপ্রবণ । **–put′-a-tive-ly,** *adv.*

im-pū-tā′-tion, *n.* **1.** Act of imputing ; ascription ; anything imputed ; আরোপণ ; নির্দ্দেশ ; আরোপিত বিষয় । **2.** Censure ; reproach ; তিরস্কার ; ভৎর্সনা ।

in, *prep. & adv.* Denoting presence or situation in place, time or circumstances ; within ; during ; inside ; by or through ; স্থান, কাল বা অবস্থায় স্থিতি বা অবস্থান নির্দ্দেশক অব্যয় ; এ, তে, যাবৎ, ধরিয়া ; মধ্যে ; ভিতরে ; দ্বারা, ভিতর দিয়া । ***Adv.*** Within or inside some place ; indoors ; as, is he *in* ; অভ্যন্তরে, ভিতরে ; বাটীর ভিতরে। **In a bad way**—In a condition not prosperous or happy ; মন্দ অবস্থায় দুর্দ্দশাগ্রস্ত, দুরবস্থাপন্ন । **In a box, In the seeds, In a fix, In a pickle**—In difficulty ; ফাঁপরে, সঙ্কটে, মুস্কিলে । **In a crack**—Instantly ; চট্ করিয়া, যস্ করিয়া । **In all**—সর্ব্বসাকল্যে, মোটে । **In and for itself**—স্বতঃ (হিঃ কোঃ), স্বয়ম্ (ঐ), স্বলক্ষণতঃ (ঐ) । **In an instant**—In a moment ; ক্ষণকাল মধ্যে, মুহূর্ত্ত মধ্যে, ক্ষণেকে । **In and out**—Now in now out ; কখন ভিতরে কখন বাহিরে । **In any case**—At any rate ; যাহাই ঘটুক না কেন । **In a small way**—On a petty scale ; সামান্য রকমে, সামান্যভাবে । **In as much as**—Since ; because ; কেননা ; যেহেতু । **In a word**—In short সংক্ষেপে, এক কথায় । **In black and white**—In writing or printing ; কাগজে কলমে । **In brief**—In short ; in a few words ; সংক্ষেপে ; অল্প কথায় । **In bulk**—In a mass ; এক থোকে, থাউকো । **In case**—If ; যদি, যদিস্যাৎ । **In company**—In society ; বন্ধুসংঘে, সমাজে । **In days gone by**—In former times ; পূর্ব্বকালে, অতীত দিবসে, পুরাকালে । **In deep water**—In a perilous position ; বিষম সঙ্কটে, গভীর সমুদ্রে । **In detail**—Part by part ; সবিস্তারে । **Indoors or within doors**—Within the house ; ঘরের ভিতরে । ***In esse***—In actual existence ; ভাবতঃ, বস্তুতঃ, বুদ্ধিতঃ । **In exchange**—In return ; বিনিময়ে, পরিবর্ত্তে, বদলে । ***In extremis***—At the point of death ; মুমূর্ষু অবস্থাপন্ন, অন্তিম দশায়, দশম দশায়, মৃত্যুমুখে । **In fact** — Practically ; কার্য্যতঃ বস্তুতঃ, ফলতঃ । ***In flagrante delicto***—In the very act of guilt ; হাতে নাতে । **In fine**—At last ; অবশেষে । **In for**—Involved in ; as, we are *in for* a severe storm ; ঝঞ্ঝাটে পতিত । **In for it**—In a crictial situation ; সঙ্কটাপন্ন অবস্থায় । **In haste**—In a hurry ; সত্বর, তাড়াতাড়ি, ব্যস্তসমস্ত ভাবে, শশব্যস্তে । **In itself**—Apart from all else

আপনা আপনি, স্বয়ং। **In kind**—In produce or some kind of commodity as distinguished from the general representative of value, that is money; শস্য বা অন্য কোন দ্রব্যের বিনিময়ে। **In lieu of**—In place of; instead of; স্থলে; পরিবর্ত্তে। ***In loco parentis***—In the place of a parent; পিতা কিম্বা মাতার স্থানে। ***In medias res***—Right into the middle of a subject; কোন বিষয়ের ঠিক মধ্যভাগে। ***In memoriam***—In memory of; স্মৃতিতে। **In no time, In less than no time**—Without delay; অবিলম্বে, দেখিতে দেখিতে, চক্ষুর পলকে। ***In nubibus***—In the clouds; not in actual existence; মেঘলোকে; আকাশ কুসুমের কুঞ্জবনে (রবীঃ)। **In one's name**—On the authority of; কাহারও দোহাই দিয়া। **In one's teens**—Between thirteen and nineteen; তের হইতে উনিশ বৎসর কালে। **In order**—In regular arrangement; শ্রেণীবদ্ধভাবে। In proper state; যথাযথভাবে, সুসম্বদ্ধভাবে। **In part**—Partly; আংশিকভাবে, অংশতঃ। ***In posse***—Potentially (opp. to *in esse*) অব্যক্তভাবে, সম্ভবতঃ (হিঃ কোঃ)। ***In re***—Really; বাস্তবিক পক্ষে, ভাবতঃ; (হিঃ কোঃ), বুদ্ধিতঃ (ঐ), বস্তুতঃ (ঐ)। **In short**—Briefly; সংক্ষেপে। ***In situ***—In its (original) place; স্বস্থানে। **In so far as, In as far as**—In such measures; এতদূর পর্য্যন্ত যে, এই পরিমাণ যে। **In spite of**—Notwithstanding; সত্ত্বেও। ***In statu quo***—In the same state (as before); তদবস্থায়, পূর্ব্বাবস্থায়। ***In terrorem***—As a warning; সতর্কতার জন্য, সাবধান করার জন্য। **In that**—Since; because; যেহেতু; এই কারণে যে। **In the dark**—In darkness; অন্ধকারে। Ignorant; অজ্ঞ। **In the full swing of**—In the full exercise of; পুরাদমে চলার সময়। **In the least**—In the smallest degree; বিন্দুমাত্র, লেশমাত্র, কণামাত্র। **In the long run**—In the final result; অবশেষে, চরমে। **In the mean time**—Meanwhile; ইত্যবসরে, ইতিমধ্যে। **In the name of**—In behalf of; কাহারও পক্ষে। **In the night**—Unexpectedly; সহসা, হঠাৎ, অপ্রত্যাশিতরূপে। **In the same boat**—In the same situation; সমাবস্থাপন্ন। **In the sweat of one's brow**—By very hard labour; মাথার ঘাম পায়ে ফেলিয়া। **In time**—In due time; যথাকালে, যথাসময়ে। ***In toto***—Completely; সম্পূর্ণরূপে। **In two twos**—With as little delay as possible; যথাসম্ভব শীঘ্র, যত সত্বর সম্ভব। **In use**—In employment; in customary practice; ব্যবহৃত; প্রচলিত। **In vain**—Without effect; বৃথা, নিরর্থক, নিষ্ফল, অনর্থক। **In with it**—Put or take it in; ইহা ভিতরে রাখ বা লইয়া যাও। **The train, boat or summer is in**—The train, boat etc. have arrived; গাড়ী, নৌকা, প্রভৃতি পৌঁছিয়াছে। **To be in**—To be at home; to be in office; as, the liberals are *in*; বাটীতে থাকা; সরকারী কার্য্যের ভার থাকা। **To be (or keep) in with**—To be close or near; সন্নিকটে থাকা। To be on terms of friendship; to secure and retain favour of; বন্ধুত্বসূত্রে বাস করা; অনুগ্রহভাজন হওয়া। **To breed in and in**—To breed among the members of the same family; সজাতীয় জন্তুর মধ্যে পরস্পরের সংযোগে শাবক উৎপাদন করা। **To burn, cut or rub in**—To burn, cut or rub (a thing) so as to penetrate into another; পুড়িয়া, কাটিয়া বা ঘষিয়া ঢুকান। **To come in**—To enter; ভিতরে আসা। **To keep one's hand in**—To retain one's skill by practice; অভ্যাস দ্বারা হাত ঠিক রাখা। **To keep the fire in**—To keep it burning; অগ্নি প্রজ্বালিত রাখা। **To put a notice in**—To put it into a paper; কাগজে বিজ্ঞাপন দেওয়া।

in, *adj.* & *n.* Internal; as, the *in* part, living inside; as, an *in*-patient; অভ্যন্তর; অভ্যন্তরবাসী। ***Noun.*** 1. (*Pol., pl.*) The party in office; "Everything the *ins* do"; (রাজনীতি) যে দল শাসনতন্ত্র পরিচালনা করে। 2. (*Pl.*) Nooks or corners; অলিগলি, কোণাকাণাচ। 3. (*Pl.*) Details, as of a proceeding; বিস্তৃত বিবরণ। **Ins and outs**—Nooks and corners; turnings in and out, as in a road, course of action, etc.; the details of any matter; অলিগলি; কোণাকাণাচ; নাড়ীনক্ষত্র।

in-ă-bil′-i-tў, *n.* State of being unable; want of power, capacity or means; অক্ষমতা; অসামর্থ্য, অশক্তি, অশক্যতা, শক্তিহীনতা।

in-ăc-cĕs′-si-ble (-ĭ-bl), *adj.* That cannot be reached or obtained; unapproachable; as, an *inaccessible* place or person; অগম্য, দুরারোহ, দুরাসদ, দুর্লভ, দুর্গম; দুরাপ, অনধিগম্য, দুর্নিরীক্ষ্য। **–bil′-i-ty, –ness,** *ns.* State of being inaccessible; অগম্যতা, দুষ্প্রাপ্যতা, দুর্গমতা। **–bly,** *adv.*

in-ăc′-cū-rāte, *adj.* Not accurate; not exact or correct; অযথার্থ; অঠিক, ভ্রমপূর্ণ, অশুদ্ধ, সপ্রমাদ। **–racy,** *n.* 1. Want of accuracy or exactness; ভ্রান্তি, অশুদ্ধি, অযাথার্থ্য। 2. Mistake; an error; ভ্রম; দোষ, ত্রুটি, অশুদ্ধি, ভুল। **–ly,** *adv.*

In-ăc′-lĭ-ŭs (ĭn-), *n.* The son of Oceanus, and father of Jo; Joএর পিতা এবং Oceanus এর পুত্র, ইনি Argosএর সর্ব্বপ্রথম ভূপতি ছিলেন।

জ্ঞাপন করা; ব্যক্ত করা। **—ma'-tion,** *n.* Act of intimating; the thing intimated; declaration; a hint; জ্ঞাপন, বিজ্ঞাপিত বিষয়; ঘোষণা, প্রচার, ইঙ্গিত, আভাস। **Intimate relation** — সমবায় (হিঃ কোঃ) ঘনসম্বন্ধ (ঐ)।

in-tim'-i-date, *v. t.* To make timid; to inspire with fear; to deter with threats; to cow; ভীত করা, ভয়ার্ত্ত করা; ভয়বিহ্বল করা, সন্ত্রস্ত করা; ভয়প্রদর্শনে নিবৃত্ত করা; ভয় দেখাইয়া দাবাইয়া রাখা। **—da'-tion,** *n.* Act of intimidating; the state of being intimidated; সন্ত্রাসন, ভয়প্রদর্শন; ভয়যুক্ততা, ভয়বিহ্বলতা। **—da-tor,** *n.*

in-tim'-i-ty, *n.* Inwardness; privacy; আভ্যন্তরতা; গোপনীয়তা।

in-tit'-ūle, *v. t.* **1.** To give a title to or entitle, as a legislative or

in-ad-mis'-si-ble (-ĭ-bl), *adj.* Not admissible; not to be admitted or allowed; অগ্রাহ্য, অস্বীকরণীয়, অগ্রহণীয়; অস্বীকার্য্য, অননুমোদনীয়। **—bil'-i-ty,** *n.* The state of being inadmissible; অগ্রহণীয়তা, অননুমোদনীয়তা। **—bly,** *adv.*

in-ad-vêrt'-ence (-ĕns), **—ĕn-cy,** *ns.* **1.** The state of being inadvertent; inattention; negligence; প্রমাদ, অনবধানতা; অমনোযোগিতা; অপ্রণিধানতা; অবহেলা। **2.** An oversight; a mistake; ভুল; প্রমাদ, ভ্রম। **—ent,** *adj.* **1.** Heedless; careless; inattentive; অনবধান, অনবহিত; অসাবধান; অমনযোগী। **2.** (Of an action) Unintentional; অনিচ্ছাকৃত। **—ent-ly,** *adv.* In an inadvertent manner; অনবধানহেতু, ভুলক্রমে। **Through inadvertence**—ভুলক্রমে, অনবধানতা বশতঃ।

in-ăl'-ĭ-ĕn-ă-ble (-bl), *adj.* Incapable of being transferred to another; অবিচ্ছেদ্য, অনন্তদেয়, অনন্তসমর্পণীয়, হস্তান্তরাযোগ্য। **—bil'-i-ty, —ness,** *ns.* **—bly,** *adv.*

being intolerent; অসহিষ্ণুতা, অসহনশীলতা, অক্ষান্তি, ধর্ম্মবিষয়ে পরমতসহনাক্ষমতা।

in-tomb' (-tōm), *v. t.* (Obs. form of ENTOMB).

in'-tō-nate, *v. i. & t.* Same as, INTONE which see.

in-tō-nā'-tion, *n.* **1.** Reciting in a singing voice; তানলয়সহকারে আবৃত্তি। **2.** Modulation of the voice; স্বরকম্পন, স্বরভঙ্গী, মূর্চ্ছনা, নাদপদ্ধতি, স্বরলয়, স্বরভেদ। **3.** Utterance or production of musical tones; স্বরসাধন।

in-tōne', *v. t. & i.* **1.** To chant, as a psalm, prayer, etc.; সুর করিয়া পাঠ করা, তানলয় বিশুদ্ধ ভাবে গান করা, সুর করিয়া আবৃত্তি করা। **2.** To utter with a particular tone; বিশেষ সুরে উচ্চারণ করা।

in-tŏx'-i-cănt, *adj. & n.* Intoxi-

as, a tree is *inanimate*; নিষ্প্রাণ, অচেতন; জড়। **2.** Spiritless; dull; নিস্তেজ, নিৰ্ব্বীর্য্য, নির্জীব; ঢিলা। **—ly,** *adv.* **—ness, —ma'-tion,** *ns.* **Inanimate nature** or **world**—That which is outside the animate world; জড়প্রকৃতি, জড়জগৎ (জিঃ)। **Inanimate object** — A lifeless thing; অচেতন পদার্থ, জড় বস্তু। **Animate and inaminate** — চেতনাচেতন।

in-ă-ni'-tion, *n.* Emptiness; exhaustion from want of food; "Feeble from *inanition*"; শূন্যতা; উদররিক্ততা, অনশনজনিত অবসাদ, শূন্যোদরতা।

in-ăp-peal'-a-ble (-pēl-ă-bl), *adj.* Not to be appealed against; উচ্চ আদালতে পুনর্ব্বিচারের অযোগ্য।

in-ăp-peas'-a-ble (-pēz-ă-bl), *adj.* Not capable of being appeased; দুস্তোষ্য, অপরিতোষণীয়।

in-ăp'-pli-că-ble (-bl), *adj.* Not capable of being applied; unsuitable; অপ্রযোজ্য; অযোগ্য, অনুপযোগী। **—bil'-i-ty, —ness,** *ns.*

in-tră'-dŏs, *n.* The interior curve of an arch; খিলানের আভ্যন্তরিক বক্রিমা।

in-trăn'-si-gĕnt, *adj. & n.* Uncompromising or irreconcilable esp. in politics; মীমাংসাপরাঙ্মুখ, অশাম্য। ***Noun.*** An uncompromising republican; চরমগণতন্ত্রানুরাগী।

in-trăn'-si-tive (-tiv), (*Eng. Gram.*) Not transitive; অকর্ম্মক। **—ly,** *adv.* **Intransitive verb**—অকর্ম্মক ক্রিয়া।

in'-trănt, *adj. & n.* Entering; penetrating; প্রবেশকারী; বিভেদী। ***Noun.*** One who enters specially upon a college, an association, etc.; উচ্চতম বিদ্যালয়, পরিষৎ, প্রভৃতিতে প্রবেশকারী ব্যক্তি।

in-trĕnch', *v. t. & i.* **1.** To fortify with a ditch and parapet; গড় বা অগম্য।

in-ăp-prō'-pri-āte, *adj.* Not appropriate; unsuitable; অনুপযুক্ত, অনুপযোগী; অসঙ্গত, বেমানান। **—ly,** *adv.* **—ness,** *n.*

in-ăpt', *adj.* Unfit; unsuitable; unskilful; অনুপযোগী; অনুপযুক্ত, অযোগ্য; অপটু, অনিপুণ। **—i-tude, —ness,** *ns.* Unfitness; unskilfulness; অনুপযুক্ততা, অনুপযোগিতা; অনিপুণতা, অপটুতা, অপাটব। **—ly,** *adv.* unfitly; unskilfully; অনুপযুক্তরূপে; অপটুভাবে।

in-ârch', *v. t.* To graft by connecting scion and stock while both are growing on their own roots; জোড় কলম বাঁধা। **—ing,** *n.* A method of grafting by approach; জোড় কলম করণ।

Inarching.

in-ârm', *v. t.* (*Poet.*) To embrace; (কবিতায়) ভুজপাশে বাঁধা, বাহুযুগলদ্বারা বেষ্টন করা।

in-âr-tic'-ü-lāte, *adj.* **1.** Not articulate ; not uttered distinctly as a sound ; ধ্বনিরূপ (হিঃ কোঃ), অব্যক্ত, কল, অস্ফুট ; অস্পষ্টোচ্চারিত, অস্পষ্টাক্ষর, অব্যক্তাক্ষর। **2.** Unable to speak distinctly ; dumb ; "*Inarticulate* with rage and grief" ; স্পষ্ট উচ্চারণে অশক্ত, রুদ্ধবাক্ ; মূক। **3.** (*Zool.*) Not jointed ; (জন্তুবিজ্ঞান) অগ্রন্থিল। **—ly,** *adv.* Indistinctly ; অস্পষ্টরূপে। **—ness,** *n.*

in-âr-ti-fi'-cial (-shăl), *adj.* **1.** Not artificial ; natural ; artless ; অকৃত্রিম, অকাল্পনিক, নৈসর্গিক, অকৃতক ; স্বভাবিক ; সরল, অকপট। **2.** Inartistic ; clumsy ; as, an *inartificial* style ; কলাকৌশলহীন ; অমার্জ্জিত। **—ly,** *adv.*

in-âr-tis'-tic, *adj.* Not conforming to the principles of art ; unskilled in art ; কলাশাস্ত্রসম্মত নিয়মবিরোধী ; কলাকৌশলহীন। **—ti-cal-ly,** *adv.*

in-ăs-mŭch', *adv.* (Used with *as* meaning since or because) ; যেহেতু, কারণ, কেননা।

in-ăt-tên'-tion, *n.* **1.** Want of attention ; heedlessness ; neglect ; অমনোযোগ, অনাবিষ্টচিত্ততা, অনাসক্তচিত্ততা ; অনবধানতা ; তাচ্ছিল্য, অবহেলা, উপেক্ষা। **2.** Want of courteous attention ; "*Inattention* of the Indians to the female" ; শিষ্টাচারের অভাব। **—tive,** *adj.* Heedless ; careless ; neglectful ; অমনোযোগী, অনাবিষ্ট ; অনবহিত, অসাবধান, অবহেলাকারী, তাচ্ছিল্যকারী, উপেক্ষাকারী। **—tive-ly,** *adv.* Without attention ; negligently ; অনবধানপূর্ব্বক ; অবহেলা করিয়া। **—tive-ness,** *n.*

in-au'-di-ble (-ä-dĭ-bl), *adj.* Incapable of being heard ; অশ্রাব্য, অশ্রবণীয়, শ্রবণাশক্য, শ্রুতির অগোচর। **—bil'-i-ty, —ness,** *ns.* **—bly,** *adv.*

in-au'-gü-răl (-ä-), *adj.* Of, or pertaining to, inauguration ; প্রারম্ভিক, প্রাথমিক, প্রতিষ্ঠাবিষয়ক। **Inaugural address**—One pronounced at an inauguration ; প্রারম্ভিক সম্ভাষণ, প্রারম্ভ বক্তৃতা, উদ্বোধন বক্তৃতা।

in-au'-gü-rāte (-ä-), *v. t.* **1.** To invest formally with an office ; অভিষিক্ত করা। **2.** To enter with ceremony upon, as an undertaking ; অনুষ্ঠানাদির পর কোন বিষয়ে প্রবৃত্ত হওয়া। **3.** To celebrate the first public use of, as a building etc. ; প্রতিষ্ঠা করা। **—ra'-tion,** *n.* Act of inaugurating ; state of being inaugurated ; অভিষেক, অভিষেচন, সংস্কার ; প্রতিষ্ঠা। **—ra-tor,** *n.* One who inaugurates ; প্রতিষ্ঠাতা, অভিষেককর্ত্তা। **—ra-to-ry.** *adj.* Pertaining to inauguration ; প্রারম্ভিক, উদ্বোধক।

in-aus-pi'-cious (-äs-pĭ-shŭs), *adj.* Not auspicious ; ill-omened ; unfavourable ; অশুভ, অশুভজনক, অভদ্র, দুর্লক্ষণ, অমঙ্গলজনক, অকল্যাণকর, অপায় ; দুর্লক্ষণযুক্ত, দুর্নিমিত্তসূচক ; প্রতিকূল।

in'-board (-börd), *adv.* & *adj.* Within the hull or interior of a ship ; জাহাজের ভিতর। ***Adj.*** Situated within, or towards the centre of, a vessel ; জাহাজের মধ্যভাগে স্থিত।

in'-bŏrn, *adj.* Implanted by nature ; innate ; as, an *inborn* quality ; প্রকৃতিগত, অন্তর্ভব, অন্তর্জনিত, অন্তর্জাত ; স্বাভাবিক, সহজাত, প্রকৃতিসিদ্ধ, নৈসর্গিক, নিসর্গজ, স্বভাবসুলভ।

in-breathe' (-brēth), *v. i.* **1.** To breathe in ; to inhale ; শ্বাস লওয়া ; শ্বাস গ্রহণ করা। **2.** To inspire ; অনুপ্রাণিত করা।

in'-brĕd, *adj.* Innate ; inborn ; অন্তর্জাত ; প্রকৃতিসিদ্ধ, স্বভাবসিদ্ধ।

in'-breed-ing (-brēd-), *n.* Breeding in and in ; এক জাতীয় পশুর সংসর্গে শাবক উৎপাদন।

In-că (ĭn-), *n.* A king or prince of Peru before its conquest by the Spaniards ; স্পেনদিগের বিজয়ের পূর্ব্বকালীন পেরুদেশের প্রাচীন রাজা।

in-căl'-cü-lă-ble (-bl), *adj.* **1.** Beyond calculation ; very great ; অগণ্য, অসংখ্য ; বিস্তর। **2.** Incapable of being reckoned or determined beforehand ; as, an *incalculable* position ; অভাবনীয়। **3.** Uncertain, as a temper etc. ; অনিশ্চিত। **—bil'-i-ty, —ness,** *ns.* **—bly,** *adv.*

in-căn-desce' (-dĕs), *v. i.* & *t.* **1.** To glow with heat ; তাপদীপ্ত হওয়া, তাপোজ্জ্বল হওয়া। ***Verb t.*** To cause to glow with heat ; তাপোজ্জ্বল করা, তাপোদ্দীপ্ত করা।

in-căn-dĕs'-cent (-ĕnt), *adj.* **1.** White or glowing with heat ; shining luminously ; উষ্ণজ্বলিত (হিঃ কোঃ), তাপপ্রদীপ্ত (ঐ), তাপোজ্জ্বল, তাপদীপ্ত, অত্যুত্তাপশুভ্র ; উজ্জ্বল, ভাস্বর। **2.** (Of electric or other light) Produced by the glowing of a filament etc. ; (বিজলী আলো, প্রভৃতি সম্পর্কে) অভ্যন্তরস্থ সূত্রবৎ সূক্ষ্ম তাপদীপ্ত তার হইতে উদ্ভূত। **—cence,** *n.* State of being incandescent ; তাপোজ্জ্বলতা। **Incandescent lamp**—(*Electric*) A lamp that is lighted by the incandescence of a filament ; যে বাতির অভ্যন্তরস্থ তাপদীপ্ত সূক্ষ্ম তার হইতে আলোক প্রসূত হয়।

Incandescent lamp.

in-căn-tā'-tion, *n.* **1.** The use of a magical formula ; the form of words used in sorcery ; মন্ত্রপ্রয়োগ ; যাদুমন্ত্র, মায়ামন্ত্র। **2.** A spell ; charm ; যাদু ; কুহক, মায়া।

in-cā'-pă-ble (-bl), *adj.* **1.** Not capable ; unable ; অশক্ত, অক্ষম, শক্তিহীন ; অসমর্থ। **2.** Not receptive ; not susceptible ; অগ্রহণক্ষম ;

অসংবেদনশীল। 3. Unable to take care of oneself; as, drunk and *incapable*; অবশ। **—bil'-i-ty, —ness**, *ns.* **—bly**, *adv.*

in-că-pā'-cious (-shŭs), *adj.* 1. Not capacious; narrow; অপ্রশস্ত, অবিশাল, অবিপুল; সঙ্কীর্ণ। 2. Unable to comprehend; foolish; অবোধ, অজ্ঞান; নির্ব্বোধ। **—ness**, *n.*

in-că-păc'-i-tāte, *v. t.* 1. To render incapable or unfit; to disqualify; অশক্ত করা, অপারগ করা; অযোগ্য করা। 2. To disqualify in law; আইনতঃ অযোগ্য করা। **—ta'-tion**, *n.*

ĭn-că-păc'-i-tȳ, *n.* 1. Inability; want of physical or mental power; অক্ষমতা, অপারগতা, অসমর্থতা; মানসিক শক্তিহীনতা, বুদ্ধিজাড্য, বুদ্ধিমান্দ্য, শক্তিবৈকল্য, অসামর্থ্য। 2. Legal disqualification; আইনতঃ অযোগ্যভাব, অক্ষমতা।

in-câr'-cĕr'-āte, *v. t.* To imprison; to confine; বন্দী করা; অবরুদ্ধ করা। **—a'-tion**, *n.* Imprisonment; confinement; কারাবরোধ; কারানিরোধ, অবরোধ। **—a-tor**, *n.*

in-câr'-nă-dīne, *adj.* & *v. t.* (*Poet.*) Flesh-coloured; reddish; (কবিতায়) মাংসবর্ণ; রক্তাভ। ***Verb t.*** (*Poet.*) To dye red or of a flesh colour; রক্তবর্ণে রঞ্জিত করা, মাংসবর্ণে রঞ্জিত করা।

in-câr'-nāte, *adj.* Invested with flesh; embodied in human nature and form; as, a devil *incarnate*; দেহধারী, শরীরধারী, শরীরী; দেহধৃত, মনুষ্যমূর্ত্তিতে আবিভূর্ত, মূর্ত্তিমান, মূর্ত্তিধর, দেহগত, বিগ্রহবান, বিগ্রহী, কায়বান, মূর্ত্ত, শরীরবদ্ধ, অবতীর্ণ, আবিভূর্ত, দেহভৃৎ, বপুষ্মান, শরীরগত গৃহীতশরীর অবরুদ্ধদেহ। ***Verb t.*** 1. To embody in flesh; শরীরধারী করা, বিগ্রহবান করা। 2. To give a concrete form; to realize; as, to *incarnate* an idea; মূর্ত্ত করা; বাস্তব করা। 3. To be the living embodiment or type of; as, Luther *incarnates* the spirit of the revolution; জীবন্ত বিগ্রহ বা অবতার স্বরূপ হওয়া।

in-câr-nā'-tion, *n.* 1. Act of embodying in flesh or human form; state of being incarnate; as, the *incarnation* of God; দেহধারণ, শরীরগ্রহণ, শরীরধারণ, দেবতাদের মনুষ্যাকারে আবিভাব, অবতার, ভগবানের নরকলেবর ধারণ, নির্ম্মাণকায় ধারণ (বৌদ্ধ সাহিত্য); অবতারত্ব। 2. Impersonation; a living type; as, he is the *incarnation* of mischief; প্রতিমূর্ত্তি; অবতার, জীবন্ত আদর্শ।

in-cau'-tious (-kă-shŭs), *adj.* Not cautious or careful; rash; অসতর্ক, অসাবধান, অনবহিত, প্রমত্ত; হঠকারী, অবিমৃশ্যকারী **—ly**, *adv.* **—ness**, *n.*

in-cĕn'-dĭ-ă-rȳ, *adj.* & *n.* 1. Of, relating to, or guilty of, the malicious setting on fire of property; গৃহদাহাপরাধ সম্বন্ধী, গৃহদাহাপরাধে অভিযুক্ত। 2. (*Fig.*) Tending to excite quarrels; seditious; inflammatory; (লক্ষণায়) বিবাদানলপ্রজ্বালক; বিদ্রোহোত্তেজক, রাজদ্রোহপূর্ণ; উত্তেজনাপূর্ণ। ***Noun.*** 1. One that sets fire to a building etc. maliciously; গৃহাদিতে ঈর্ষাপূর্ব্বক অগ্নিপ্রদায়ক, গৃহদাহক, আগারদাহক, অগ্নিদ। 2. One who promotes factions or quarrels; an agitator; বিবাদানলপ্রজ্বালক; আন্দোলনকারী। **—rism**, *n.* The act or practice of an incendiary; আগারদাহিতা, গৃহদাহ। **Incendiary fire**—লাগানো আগুন। **Incendiary shell**—যে কামানের গোলা বিদীর্ণ হইয়া শত্রুর গৃহ, পোতপ্রভৃতিতে অগ্নিসংযোগ করে, অগ্নিবর্ষী গোলা।

in-cense' (-sĕns), *v. t.* To enrage; to incite; ক্রোধোদ্রেক করা, কোপজ্বলিত করা, কোপাবিষ্ট করা; উত্তেজিত করা, সঙ্কুক্ষিত করা। **—censed'**, *p. p.* Enraged; কোপজ্বলিত, রোষপ্রদীপ্ত, উত্তেজিত, প্রকোপিত।

in'-cense (-sĕns), *v. t.* 1. To fumigate with incense; ধূপধূনাদি দ্বারা সুবাসিত করা, ধূপসুরভিত করা, ধূপধূপিত করা। 2. To burn incense before, as a deity; দেবতার সম্মুখে ধূপ প্রজ্বালিত করা। 3. To perfume or scent; "Roses *incensed* the fresh air"; বাসিত করা, সুবাসিত করা, সুরভিত করা। **—sa'-tion**, *n.*

in'-cense (-sĕns), *n.* 1. Gum, spice, etc. producing perfume when burned; ধূপধূনাদি সুগন্ধি দ্রব্য, ধূপ, যক্ষধূপ, বহ্নিগন্ধ, সুগন্ধিক। 2. The perfume or smoke of gum, spices, etc. burned esp. in religious rites; দেবার্চ্চনাদিতে প্রজ্বালিত ধূপধূনাদির সুবাস, ধূপগন্ধ। 3. Any pleasant fragrance; সুগন্ধ, মনোরম সৌরভ। 4. Praise; flattery; প্রশংসা; চাটুবাক্য। **—cen-so-ry**, *n.* A vessel for burning incense; ধূপপাত্র, ধুনচি, ধুনী, ধূপতি, ধূপাধার, ধূপভাজন।

in-cĕn'-tive (-tĭv), *adj.* & *n.* 1. Inciting; encouraging stimulative; উত্তেজক, প্রবর্ত্তক, উদ্দীপক, উদ্বোধক, প্রযোজক; প্রোৎসাহক; প্রণোদক। ***Noun.*** That which incites to action; motive; provocation; উদ্দীপক, প্ররোচক (প্ররোচনা, প্রবর্ত্তনা, উদ্দীপনা; উত্তেজনা।

in-cĕpt', *v. i.* & *t.* (Camb. Univ.) To complete the taking of a degree; (কেম্ব্রিজ বিশ্ববিদ্যালয়) উপাধি গ্রহণ সমাপ্ত করা। ***Verb t.*** (*Biol.*) To take in; (জীববিজ্ঞান) গ্রহণ করা। **—çep'-tor**, *n.* One who incepts in a university; যে ব্যক্তি উপাধি গ্রহণ সমাপ্ত করে।

in-cĕp'-tion, *n.* 1. Beginning; commencement; প্রারম্ভ, আরম্ভ, সমারম্ভ; উপক্রম। 2. (Camb. Univ.) An act of incepting; (কেম্ব্রিজ বিশ্ববিদ্যালয় উপাধিগ্রহণ সমাপন।

in-cĕp'-tive (-tĭv), *adj.* & *n.* 1. Beginning; প্রাথমিক, প্রারম্ভিক।

2. (*Gram.*) Denoting the beginning of an action as a verb etc.; (ব্যাকরণ) কার্য্যের প্রারম্ভ সূচক ক্রিয়াপদ প্রভৃতি সূচক, আরম্ভোদ্বোধক। ***Noun.*** An inceptive verb; প্রারম্ভসূচকক্রিয়া।

in-cêr′-ti-tūde, *n.* Uncertainty; doubt; অনিশ্চয়, অনিশ্চিতত্ব; সংশয়, সন্দেহ।

in-cĕs′-sant (-ănt), *adj.* Unceasing; constant; continued; অবিরাম, বিরামবিহীন (রবীঃ), অশ্রান্ত, অবিশ্রান্ত; নিরবধি, নিরন্তর, অবিরত, সতত, নিত্য; নিয়ত, অনুক্ষণ, অনিবার, হরদম, অনবরত। **—ly,** *adv.* Unceasingly; continually; অনবরত, নিয়ত, নিরন্তর, নিরবধি; ক্রমাগত। **—ness, —san-cy,** *ns.*

in′-cĕst, *n.* Sexual intercourse within a prohibited degree of kindred; অগম্যাসম্ভোগ, গোত্রগমন, অগম্যাগমন (of men), অগম্যগমন (of women)। **—ces′-tu-ous,** *adj.* Guilty of incest; involving the crime of incest; অগম্যাগামী, অগম্যগ (বৃঃ সং); অগম্যাগমনাপরাধে সংসৃষ্ট। **—ces′-tu-ous-ly,** *adv.* **—ces′-tu-ous-ness,** *n.*

inch (ĭnsh), *n., v. t.* & *i.* **1.** Twelfth part of a foot; ইঞ্চি, এক ফুটের দ্বাদশ ভাগের এক ভাগ। **2.** The quantity of water which would cover a surface to the depth of an inch; as, two *inches* of rain; এক ইঞ্চি গভীর জল। **3.** A degree of atmospheric or other pressure that balances the weight of mercury one inch high in a barometer etc.; as, an atmospheric pressure of 30 *inches*; বায়ুচাপমান যন্ত্র প্রভৃতির এক ইঞ্চি উচ্চ পারদের ভার যে বায়ু প্রভৃতির চাপের মাত্রা দ্বারা সমতুলিত হয়। **4.** A small distance, degree or amount; সামান্য ব্যবধান, সামান্য দূরত্ব। **5.** (*Pl.*) Stature; "A fellow of his *inches*"; দেহের উচ্চতা। ***Verb t.*** To move by inches; ধীরে ধীরে অগ্রসর হওয়া। **Square or cubic inch**—বর্গ ইঞ্চি, ঘন ইঞ্চি। **By inches, Inch by inch**—Gradually; bit by bit; ধীরে ধীরে; ক্রমে ক্রমে, অল্পে অল্পে, শনৈঃ শনৈঃ, তিলে তিলে। **By inch of candle**—By auction; নিলামে। **Every inch** — Entirely; thoroughly; সর্ব্বাংশে, সর্ব্বতোভাবে; সম্পূর্ণরূপে। **Give him an inch and he'll take an ell**—বসতে পেলে শুতে চায়, দয়া করে দেয় নুণ, ভাত মারে দশ গুণ। **To die by inches**—To die bit by bit; তিলে তিলে মরা।

inch (ĭnsh), *n.* A small island (esp. Scotch); ক্ষুদ্র দ্বীপ।

inch′-êr (ĭnsh-), *n.* (In combination with a numerical prefix *e. g.* five or six-*incher*) Something of (so many) inches in length, diameter, etc.; দৈর্ঘ্য, ব্যাস প্রভৃতিতে নির্দ্দিষ্ট সংখ্যক ইঞ্চি।

in′-chō-āte, *adj.* & *v. t.* Recently begun; undeveloped; অচিরারব্ধ; অবিকাশপ্রাপ্ত, অবিকাশিত। ***Verb t.*** To begin; to initiate; আরম্ভ করা; প্রবর্ত্তন করা। **—a′-tion,** *n.* **—a-tive,** *adj.*

in′-ci-dence (-dĕns), *n.* **1.** The act of falling on or affecting; contact with a thing; "*Incidence* of divine thinking"; আপতন, অভিপতন; সংস্পর্শ। **2.** The falling of a ray of light or projectiles etc. on a surface; গোলা, কিরণ রেখা প্রভৃতির আপতন। **3.** The range of scope of an occurrence or influence; "The *incidence* of the plague was general"; কোন ঘটনা বা প্রভাবের প্রসর বা বিস্তার। **Angle of incidence**—আপতিত রেখা বা কিরণরশ্মি আপতন-বিন্দুতে উক্ত বিন্দু হইতে উত্থিত লম্বের সহিত যে কোণ উৎপাদন করে, আপতনকোণ (সাঃ পঃ)। **Incidence of taxation**—করভার (হিঃ কোঃ)। **What is the incidence of the tax** — On whom does it fall? কাহার উপর কর বসিল?

in′-ci-dĕnt, *adj.* **1.** Falling upon, as light; পতনশীল। **2.** Liable or apt to occur; naturally appertaining or belonging, (with *to*); "Disorders *incident to* a prosperous state"; সংঘটনশীল, আপতনশীল; স্বভাবতঃ সংসৃষ্ট, সহচর। **3.** (*Law*) Attaching (*to*); as, a privilege *incident to* a holding; (আইন) সংযুক্ত, সংসৃষ্ট।

in′-ci-dĕnt, *n.* **1.** An event or occurrence; ঘটনা, ব্যাপার। **2.** An incidental or subordinate event; দৈব ঘটনা, আকস্মিক ঘটনা। **3.** A distinct piece of action in a play or poem; "Plays......rich in stirring *incidents*"; কবিতা বা নাট্যের ঘটনা, প্রসঙ্গবাক্য। **4.** (*Law*) A privilege, burden, etc., commonly attaching to an office, estate, etc.; (আইন) কোন পদ, সম্পত্তি প্রভৃতির সহিত সংসৃষ্ট সুবিধা, দায়িত্ব, প্রভৃতি।

in-ci-dĕn′-tăl, *adj.* **1.** Casual; not primary or essential; as, an *incidental* conversation or expenses; কাদাচিৎক, প্রাসঙ্গিক, যাদৃচ্ছিক, নৈমিত্তিক; অপ্রধান। **2.** Liable to happen or follow, (with *to*); "Dangers *incidental to* pigsticking"; আপতনশীল, সংঘটনশীল, সহগামী। **—ly,** *adv.* Casually; কথাপ্রসঙ্গে, প্রসঙ্গক্রমে। **Incidental images, -colours**—চাক্ষুষ প্রতীতির অবর্ত্তমানেও যে মূর্ত্তি বা বর্ণরাজি প্রতিভাত হয়, গৌণমূর্ত্তি বা বর্ণরাজি।

in-cĭn′-êr-āte, *v. t.* To burn to ashes; to consume by fire; ভস্মীভূত করা; পোড়াইয়া ফেলা। **—a′-tion,** *n.* Burning to ashes; ভস্মীভূত করণ, ভস্মরাশীকরণ, ভস্মসাৎকরণ। **—a-tor,** *n.* A furnace for consuming anything; চুল্লী, চিতা।

in-cĭp′-i-ĕnt, *adj.* Beginning; in an initial stage; প্রারম্ভিক; প্রাথমিক, ঔপক্রমিক। **—ence, —en-cy,** *ns.* Commencement; incipient state;

প্রারম্ভ, সূত্রপাত; আদিম অবস্থা। **–ly,** *adv.*

in-cīse′, *v. t.* To cut in; to engrave; কর্ত্তন করা, ছেদন করা; খোদাই করা। **–ci′-sion, –cis-ure,** *ns.* **1.** The act of cutting into; কর্ত্তন। **2.** A cut; a gash; a notch; ছেদ; অস্ত্রাঘাতজনিত গভীর ক্ষত; খাঁজ। **–ci′-sive,** *adj.* Cutting; penetrating; sharp; acute; মর্ম্মচ্ছেদী; বিদারক; তীক্ষ্ণ; তীব্র। **–ci′-sive-ly,** *adv.* **–ci′-sor,** *n.* Cutting foretooth; কৃন্তনদন্ত, ছেদনদন্ত (প্রাঃ)। **Incised wound**—One caused by cutting; কর্ত্তিত ব্রণ, ছিন্ন ব্রণ (নিদানঃ)।

in-cīte′, *v. t.* To excite; to stir up; to instigate; উত্তেজিত করা, উদ্দীপ্ত করা; উৎসাহিত করা, প্রোৎসাহিত করা; প্ররোচিত করা। **–ment,** *n.* **1.** Act of inciting or instigating; উৎসাহ প্রদান, প্রেরণা, প্রণোদন, নোদন, প্ররোচনা। **2.** That which incites; stimulus or incentive; উত্তেজক; প্রবর্ত্তক। **–cit-a′-tion,** *n.* **1.** The act of inciting; উৎসাহদান, প্রবর্ত্তনা।

in-ci-vil′-i-tȳ, *n.* **1.** Want of courtesy; rudeness; অশিষ্টতা, অভদ্রতা, অসভ্যতা, বিনয়াপরাধ (বীরঃ), দুঃশীলতা (মঃ ইঃ); রূঢ়তা। **2.** An act of rudeness or ill-breeding; অশিষ্টাচার।

in′-ci-vism, *n.* Want of patriotism; unfriendliness to one's state or government; স্বদেশপ্রেমবিহীনতা; স্বদেশদ্রোহিতা।

in′-clear-ing (-clēr-), *n.* The amount payable by a bank on cheques etc. presented through the clearing house for settlement; মহাজনগণের চেক, হুণ্ডী প্রভৃতি বিনিময়ের কার্য্যালয় দ্বারা প্রদত্ত চেক হুণ্ডি প্রভৃতির বাবত প্রদেয় টাকা।

in-clĕm′-ĕnt, *adj.* Severe; stormy; very cold, as weather, climate etc.; ঘোর, দারুণ; ঝটিকাসঙ্কুল, ঝটিকাচ্ছন্ন; অতি শীতল। **–en-cy,** *n.* Roughness; storminess; বাত্যাসঙ্কুলতা; ঝটিকাসঙ্কুলতা, ঝটিকাবিক্ষুব্ধতা।

in-cli-na′-tion, *n.* **1.** The act of bending or leaning; হেলন, অবনমন। **2.** Slope; ঢাল, উৎসর্পিণী বা অপসর্পিণী ভূমি, প্রবণ ভূমি। **3.** Tendency of mind; propensity; liking; affection; "*Inclination* between a man and a woman"; ঝোঁক, প্রাবণ্য; প্রবণতা; প্রবৃত্তি, রুচি, অভিরুচি; স্নেহ, অনুরাগ। **4.** The angle between two lines or planes; রেখা বা ধরাতল যুগলের মধ্যবর্ত্তী কোণ। **Inclination of an orbit**—(*Astron.*) The angle at which the orbit meets the ecleptic; ক্রান্তিবৃত্ত এবং গ্রহকক্ষের সংযোগকোণ, অবনতি (সূঃ সিঃ)। **The inclination of a planet's orbit to the ecliptic**—পরমাপম (মঃ উঃ)।

in-clīne′, *v. t.* & *i.* **1.** To bend, as head, body, etc.; বক্র করা, অবনমিত করা। **2.** To turn; to dispose; as, to *incline* one's heart to do a thing; উন্মুখ করা; প্রবণ করা। To cause to lean from the vertical; প্রবণ করা, হেলান, কাত করা। ***Verb i.*** **1.** To lean or bend; আনত হওয়া, হেঁট হওয়া, প্রবণ হওয়া, হেলিয়া পড়া, ঝুঁকিয়া পড়া। **2.** To be disposed; ইচ্ছুক হওয়া। **3.** To have a tendency (*to*); "*Inclining to* corpulence; প্রবণ হওয়া। **4.** To deviate from the vertical; হেলিয়া থাকা। **-clin′-a ble,** *adj.* **1.** Capable of being inclined; অবনমনশীল। **2.** Disposed; propensed; ইচ্ছুক; প্রবৃত্ত। **3.** Favourable (*to*); as, *inclinable to* British interests; অনুকূল। **–clined′,** *adj.* **1.** Bent; বক্র। **2.** Sloping; গড়ানিয়া, প্রবণ। **3.** Disposed; প্রবৃত্ত, ইচ্ছুক, প্রবণ, উন্মুখ। **Inclined plane**—তির্য্যগ্‌ধরাতল (হিঃ কোঃ)। **To incline one's ear**—To listen favourably (*to*); সদয়ভাবে কর্ণপাত করা।

in-clīne′, *n.* An inclined plane; a slope; তির্য্যগ্‌ধরাতল; প্রবণভূমি।

in-clūde′, *v. t.* **1.** To confine; to shut in (usu. *p. p.*) অবরুদ্ধ করা; আবদ্ধ করা। **2.** To comprise; to contain; অন্তর্ভুক্ত করা, সামিল করা; অন্তর্নিবিষ্ট করা। **3.** To reckon or regard as so comprised; অন্তর্ভুক্ত বলিয়া গণ্য করা।

in-clū′-sion, *n.* The act of including or the state of being included; limitation; অন্তর্নিবিষ্টতা, অন্তর্ভাব (হিঃ কোঃ), অন্তর্নিবেশ; সীমাবন্ধন।

in-clū′-sive (-siv), *adj.* **1.** Comprising, (usu. with *of*); সহিত, সমেত, সহকারে, সায়, শুদ্ধ। **2.** Comprehensive; "A general *inclusive* term"; ব্যাপক। **–ly,** *adv.* **–ness,** *n.*

in-cŏg′-ni-tō, *adj.*, *adv.* & *n.* (*abbr.* spoken or written *incog.*) (*adj.* & *adv.*) In disguise; under an assumed name or character; ছদ্মবেশে, গুপ্তরূপ, প্রচ্ছন্নরূপ, অবরুদ্ধ (কোঽপি রাজসূনুরবরুদ্ধশ্চরন্—দশকুমারচরিত)। ***Noun.*** **1.** One concealed under disguise or assumed character; ছদ্মবেশধারী লোক। **2.** Disguise; as, his *incognito* was kept a secret; ছদ্মভাব। **–ta,** *n.* (*Fem.*)

in-cŏg′-ni-zi-ble (-bl), *adj.* Incapable of being recognized or distinguished; অপরিজ্ঞেয়, অপরিচেয়। **–zance,** *n.* Failure to recognize; অপরিজ্ঞেয়তা, অপরিচেয়তা। **–zant,** *adj.* Unware or unconscious, (with *of*); অজ্ঞাত, অপরিজ্ঞাত।

in-cō-hēr′-ĕnt, *adj.* **1.** Not connected; loose; অসংবদ্ধ, অসম্বদ্ধ, অসমঞ্জস, অযুতসিদ্ধ (ব্রজঃ হিন্দু); অসংলগ্ন। **2.** Incongruous; inconsistent; অসঙ্গত; বেখাপ্পা, খাপছাড়া, অগড়বগড়। **–ence, –en-cy,** *ns.* **1.** Want of coherence; অসংবদ্ধতা, অসংলগ্নতা। **2.** Incongruity; অসঙ্গতি।

–ly, *adv.* **Incoherent speech**—A disconnected speech; অসম্বদ্ধ প্রলাপ।

n-cŏm-bŭs′-ti-ble (-bl), *adj.* Not combustible; uninflammable; অদাহ্য; অদহনীয়, দহনাশক্য। **–bil′-i-ty, –ness,** *ns.* The state of being incombustible; অদাহ্যতা।

n′-come (-kŭm), *n.* The annual or periodical receipts of a person or corporation; revenue; আয়; রাজস্ব। **Income tax**—আয়কর।

in′-com-ĕr (-kŭm-), *n.* **1.** One who comes in; আগন্তুক, নবাগত ব্যক্তি। **2.** An immigrant; an intruder; দেশান্তর হইতে বসবাসের জন্য সমাগত ব্যক্তি; স্বয়মাগত ব্যক্তি, উপযাচক। **3.** One who succeeds another in office or position; যে ব্যক্তি অন্য ব্যক্তির স্থলে কোন কার্য্যে বা পদে নিযুক্ত হয়।

n′-com-ing (-kŭm-), *adj.* & *n.* **1.** Coming in; succeeding, as in office etc.; আগামী, আগন্তুক; কোন ব্যক্তির স্থলবর্ত্তী। **2.** Accruing, as profit etc.; উৎপন্ন। **3.** Coming in from abroad; immigrant; বিদেশাগত; বিদেশ হইতে বসবাসের জন্য আগত। ***Noun.*** **1.** Act of coming in; arrival; আগমন; উপস্থিতি। **2.** (*Pl.*) Outcome; revenue; ফল; রাজস্ব।

in-cŏm-mĕn′-sū-ră-ble (-bl), *adj.* **1.** Having no common measure; অসমগুণনীয়ক, অসমপরিমেয়, ভিন্নপরিমাপক, অতুল্যপরিমাণ, অপরিণামশীল (হিঃ কোঃ), অপরিচ্ছেদশীল। **2.** Surd; করণী। **3.** Not comparable in respect of magnitude or value; "The two states are *incommensurable*"; মূল্য বা পরিমাণসম্বন্ধে তুলনার অযোগ্য। **4.** Not worthy of being measured (*with*); "......life is *incommensurable with* infinity"; অপরিমেয়। **–bil′-i-ty,** *n.* **–bly,** *adv.*

in-cŏm-mĕn′-sū-rāte, *adj.* **1.** Incommensurable; অসমপরিমেয়, অপরিণামশীল (হিঃ কোঃ), অপরিচ্ছেদশীল (ঐ)। **2.** Disproportionate; inadequate, (with *to, with*); অসমঞ্জস; অপ্রচুর, অপ্রতুল। **–ly,** *adv.* **–ness,** *n.*

in-cŏm-mōde′, *v. t.* **1.** To give inconvenience or trouble to; to disturb; অসুবিধায় ফেলা, অসুবিধা জন্মান, কষ্ট দেওয়া; বিরক্ত করা। **2.** To hinder; বাধা দেওয়া। **–mo′-di-ous,** *adj.* Not commodious; unsuitable; inconvenient; uncomfortable; অবিস্তীর্ণ; অনুপযোগী, অনুপযুক্ত; অসুবিধাজনক; আরামহীন। **–mo′-di-ous-ly,** *adv.* **–mo′-di-ous-ness,** *n.*

in-cŏm-mū′-ni-că-ble (-bl), *adj.* Not communicative; reserved; অনালাপী, অনালাপপ্রিয়, অসামাজিক; চাপা, সংযতবাক্। **–bly,** *adv.* **–ness,** *n.*

in-cŏm-mūt′-ă-ble (-bl), *adj.* Not commutable; unchangeable; অবিনিময়যোগ্য অপ্রতিপণ্য; অপরিবর্ত্তনীয়। **–bil′-i-ty, –ness,** *ns.* **–bly,** *adv.*

in-cŏm-păct′, *adj.* Not compact; loosely put together; (esp. *fig.*); অসংহত; শিথিল, শ্লথ।

in-cŏm′-pă-ră-ble (-bl), **1.** Not comparable; matchless; অতুল, অনুপম, নিরুপম, অপ্রতিম; অদ্বিতীয়। **2.** Not suitable for comparison, (with *to, with*); তুলনার অযোগ্য। **–bly,** *adv.* **–ness,** *n.*

in-cŏm-păt′-i-ble (-bl), *adj.* **1.** Discordant; inconsistent; অসমঞ্জস, বিষম, অনৈক্যবিশিষ্ট, বিরুদ্ধ, বিসদৃশ, বিরুদ্ধধর্ম্মা; অসঙ্গত (হিঃ কোঃ)। **–bil′-i-ty, –ness,** *ns.* State of being incompatible; inconsistency; irreconcilableness; অসামঞ্জস্য, বিপ্রতিপত্তি (সর্ব্বঃ); অনৈক্য; বৈষম্য, পরস্পর বিরুদ্ধতা।

in-cŏm′-pĕ-tĕnt, *adj.* **1.** Wanting in adequate capacity, qualification, etc.; unable; inadequate; unfit; যথোচিত শক্তিশূন্য, যথোচিত যোগ্যতাহীন; অশক্ত, অক্ষম; অসম্পূর্ণ, অসম্যক; অযোগ্য, অনুপযুক্ত। **2.** Not legally qualified; আইনতঃ অযোগ্য। **–ly,** *adv.* **–tence, –ten-cy,** *ns.* The state of being incompetent; অযোগ্যতা, অক্ষমতা।

in-cŏm-plete′ (-plēt), *adj.* Not complete; imperfect; defective; অসমাপ্ত, অসম্পূর্ণ, অনিষ্পন্ন; অপূর্ণ; অঙ্গহীন। **–ly,** *adv.* Imperfectly; অসম্পূর্ণভাবে। **–ness, –ple′-tion,** *ns.* The state of being incomplete; অপূর্ণতা (হিঃ কোঃ)।

in-cŏm-prē-hĕn′-si-ble (-bl), *adj.* **1.** (Chiefly used in the Athanasian creed) Boundless; অসীম। **2.** Incapable of being understood; unintelligible; বুদ্ধির অতীত, বুদ্ধির অগোচর, অচিন্ত্য, অজ্ঞেয়, ইন্দ্রিয়াগোচর, অমনোগম্য, অগ্রাহ, অননুভবনীয়, বোধাতীত, অনধিগম্য, অগ্রাহ্য (হিঃ কোঃ), অবোধ্য; দুর্ব্বোধ, দুষ্পরিগ্রহ। **–bil′-i-ty, –ness,** *ns.* The state of being incomprehensible; unintelligibility; অচিন্তনীয়তা, অননুভবনীয়তা; দুষ্পরিগ্রহতা, অপরিজ্ঞেয়তা। **–bly,** *adv.*

in-cŏm-prē-hĕn′-sion, *n.* Failure to comprehend or understand; দুষ্পরিগ্রহ।

in-cŏm-prĕss′-i-ble (-bl), *adj.* Incapable of being compressed; অসঙ্কোচনীয়, অসংহরণীয়, আকুঞ্চনাশক্য। **–bil′-i-ty,** *n.* The state of being incompressible; অসঙ্কোচনীয়তা।

in-cŏm-pūt′-ă-ble (-bl), *adj.* That cannot be computed or reckoned; অসংখ্য, অগণ্য।

in-cŏn-ceiv′-a-ble (-sīv-ă-bl), *adj.* **1.** Incapable of being imagined; অকল্পনীয়, ধারণাতীত, বুদ্ধির অগম্য, অচিন্ত্য, অভাবনীয়, অবিভাব্য, ইন্দ্রিয়াগোচর। **2.** Incredible; very remarkable; as light moves with an *inconceivable* velocity; অবিশ্বাস্য; অতি বিস্ময়কর। **–bil′-i-ty, –ness,** *ns.* **–bly,** *adv.*

in-cŏn-clū′-sive (-sĭv), *adj.* Not decisive or convincing, as an argument, evidence etc. ; অসিদ্ধান্তকর, অপ্রামাণিক, পণ্ডনীয়, অনিশ্চায়ক, অনিশ্চয়াত্মক, অমীমাংসাত্মক, অনির্ণায়ক, অনিয়ামক, অপসিদ্ধান্তকারী। **–ly,** *adv.* In an inconclusive manner ; অনিশ্চায়কভাবে। **–ness,** *n.*

in-cŏn-dĕn′-să-ble (-bl), *adj.* Incapable of being condensed ; esp. that cannot be reduced to liquid or solid condition, as gas etc. ; অঘনীকরণীয় ; অসংহননীয়। **–bil′-i-ty,** *n.*

in-cŏn′-dīte, *adj.* Unpolished ; ill constructed ; unfinished, as a literary composition ; অপরিকর্ম্মীকৃত; কুগঠিত ; অসর্ব্বাঙ্গসম্পন্ন।

in-cŏn-fórm′-i-tÿ, *n.* **1.** Dissimilarity ; want of conformity, (with *to, with*) ; বৈসাদৃশ্য, অসাদৃশ্য ; অননুরূপতা। **2.** Refusal to conform to an established church ; রাজবিধিদ্বারা প্রতিষ্ঠিত ধর্ম্মসংঘের নিয়মাদি পালনে অসম্মতি।

in-con′-grû-ĕnt (-kŏng-), *adj.* Inconsistent ; disagreeing ; অসমঞ্জস, অসঙ্গত, বিষম ; অসম্বদ্ধ, অসংলগ্ন, বিরুদ্ধ।

in-con′-gru-ous (-kŏng-grû-ŭs), *adj.* **1.** Not congruous ; inconsistent ; disagreeing (*with*) ; অসম্বদ্ধ, অসংলগ্ন, অসমঞ্জস ; অনৈক্যবিশিষ্ট, সঙ্গতিশূন্য ; বিরুদ্ধ। **2.** Out of place ; absurd ; অনুপযোগী ; অযৌক্তিক। **–gru′-i-ty, –ness,** *ns.* The state of being incongruous ; inconsistency ; absurdity ; অসম্বদ্ধতা, অসংলগ্নতা ; অসঙ্গতি, অমিল ; অযৌক্তিকতা। **–ly,** *adv.*

in-cŏn-sĕc′-ū-tive (-tĭv), *adj.* Not succeeding in regular order ; inconsequent ; অধারাবাহিক ; অপৌর্ব্বাপর্য্যবিশিষ্ট। **–ly,** *adv.* **–ness,** *n.*

in-cŏn′-sĕ-quĕnt, *adj.* **1.** Illogical ; inconsistent ; ন্যায়বিরুদ্ধ, যুক্তিবিরুদ্ধ, অপসিদ্ধান্তিক ; অসঙ্গত। **2.** Disconnected ; irrelevant ; অসম্বদ্ধ, অসংলগ্ন ; অপ্রাসঙ্গিক। **–quence,** *n.* **1.** Want of logical sequence ; সিদ্ধান্তাভাব, অসিদ্ধান্ত, অনন্বয়। **2.** Inconsecutiveness ; irrelevance ; অপৌর্ব্বাপর্য্যতা ; অপ্রাসঙ্গিকতা। **–quen′-tial,** *adj.* Irrelevant ; unimportant ; of no consequence ; অপ্রাসঙ্গিক ; অপ্রয়োজনীয় ; তুচ্ছ, নগণ্য। **–quen′-tial-ly,** *adv.*

in-cŏn-sĭd′-êr-ă-ble (-bl), *adj.* Not worth considering ; of small value ; unimportant ; trivial ; অগণনীয়, অগণ্য ; সংসামান্য, উপেক্ষণীয়, অকিঞ্চিৎকর ; নগণ্য ; সামান্য, তুচ্ছ। **–bly,** *adv.* **–ness,** *n.* **Not inconsiderable**—Not trivial ; অসামান্য, অনল্প।

in-cŏn-sĭd′-êr-āte, *adj.* **1.** Not considerate ; thoughtless ; hasty ; বিচারহীন, অবিচারী, অবিবেচক ; অবিমৃশ্যকারী, অসমীক্ষ্যকারী, অপরিণামদর্শী ; চিন্তাশক্তিহীন। **2.** Not considering the feelings of others ; অন্যের মনে আঘাত লাগে কিনা তদ্বিষয়ে বিবেচনাহীন। **–a′-tion,** *n.* **–ly,** *adv.* Heedlessly ; imprudently ; অসতর্কভাবে ; অবিবেচকের মত, অসাবধানতার সহিত। **–ness,** *n.* The state of being inconsiderate ; অবিমৃশ্যকারিতা, অসমীক্ষ্যকারিতা।

in-cŏn-sĭst′-ĕnt, *adj.* **1.** Not consistent ; discordant ; incompatible (*with*) ; অসামঞ্জস্যবিশিষ্ট, বিরুদ্ধ, অসঙ্গত (হিঃ কোঃ), পরস্পরবিরুদ্ধ, সামঞ্জস্যহীন, অমিল, বিরোধী, পূর্ব্বাপরবিরুদ্ধ, বিপরীতধর্ম্মক ; অনৈক্যবিশিষ্ট ; সঙ্গতিহীন। **2.** Exhibiting inconsistency of thought or conduct ; fickle ; অব্যবস্থিতচিত্ত ; তরলমতি, চঞ্চলমতি, অস্থিরমতি। **3.** Without coherence of parts ; অযুতসিদ্ধ। **–en-cy,** *n.* **1.** A state of being inconsistent ; incongruity ; discrepancy ; অসামঞ্জস্য ; অসঙ্গতি ; বৈপরীত্য, অসাদৃশ্য, বিপর্য্যয়, অনন্বয়। **2.** Incongruity in action or conduct ; unsteadiness ; অসামঞ্জস্য ; চাঞ্চল্য, অস্থিরতা, অব্যবস্থিতচিত্ততা। **3.** Want of harmony in parts ; অসঙ্গতি, অসামঞ্জস্য। **–ly,** *adv.* **1.** Incongruously ; অসম্বদ্ধভাবে, অসংলগ্নভাবে। **2.** Without consistency of thought or conduct ; চিন্তা ও কার্য্যের সামঞ্জস্য বিনা।

in-cŏn-sōl′-ă-ble (-bl), *adj.* Incapable of being consoled, as a person, his grief, etc. ; অসান্ত্বনীয়, দুঃসান্ত্বনীয়, অবিনোদনীয়, দুর্ব্বিনোদ **–bly,** *adv.* **–ness,** *n.*

in-cŏn′-sō-nănt, *adj.* Not agreeing or harmonizing, (with *to*) ; অসমঞ্জস, বিরোধী, অসঙ্গত। **–nance,** *n.*

in-cŏn-spic′-ū-ous (-ŭs), *adj.* Not prominent or striking ; অপ্রকট অপ্রকাশ, অস্পষ্ট। **2.** (*Bot.*) Small, pale or green, as flowers ; (উদ্ভিদ-বিদ্যা) ক্ষুদ্র, বিবর্ণ বা সবুজ। **–ness,** *n.*

in-cŏn′-stănt, *adj.* **1.** Unsteady ; fickle ; পরিবর্ত্তনশীল, অব্যবস্থিতচিত্ত, চলচিত্ত, অনবস্থিত ; প্রকৃতিতরল, অস্থির, চপল, চঞ্চল, তরল। **2.** Variable ; irregular ; অনিত্য ; অনিয়মিত **–ly,** *adv.* **–stan-cy,** *n.* **1.** Want of constancy ; fickleness ; পরিবর্ত্তনশীলতা, অব্যবস্থিতচিত্ততা ; চঞ্চলতা, অস্থিরতা, চাপল্য। **2.** Mutability or variability ; অনিত্যতা।

in-cŏn-sŭm′-a-ble (-bl), *adj.* **1.** Incapable of being consumed by fire etc. ; অবিনশ্বর, অক্ষর, অক্ষয্য, অনাশ্য, অবিনাশ্য।

in-cŏn-tĕst′-ă-ble (-bl), *adj.* Indisputable ; undeniable ; অবিবদনীয়, অবিবাদ্য, নির্ব্বিবাদ, অসন্দিগ্ধ, অতর্কনীয়, অপ্রত্যাখ্যেয় ; অকাট্য, অখণ্ডনীয়, অবশ্যস্বীকার্য্য। **–bly,** *adv.*

in-cŏn′-ti-nĕnt, *adj.* **1.** Wanting self-restraint ; not restraining the sexual appetites ; unchaste ; lewd ; অসংযত, সংযমশূন্য ; অজিতেন্দ্রিয়, অযতেন্দ্রিয় ; ব্যভিচারী ; কামুক, লম্পট। **2.** Unable to restrain natural discharges ; ধারণাশক্তিহীন। **3.** Unable to retain or keep back, (*of*) ; "*Incontinent of* tongue" ; অশাসনক্ষম। **–nence,** *n.* **1.** State of being incontinent; lewdness; indulgence of lust; অসংযম, অধারণক্ষমতা, অজিতেন্দ্রিয়তা, ইন্দ্রিয়-পরতন্ত্রতা, ইন্দ্রিয়াসক্তি; লম্পটতা, লাম্পট্য; কামুকতা, দুশ্চরিত্রতা। 2. Inability to restrain or keep back, (with *of*); অসংযম। 3. Inability to retain natural discharges, as of urine etc.; ধারণাশক্তিহীনতা। **Incontinence of urine**—See INCONTINENCE 3.

in-cŏn′-ti-nĕnt-lŷ, *adv.* At once; immediately; তৎক্ষণাৎ; তন্মুহূর্ত্তে, অমনি।

in-cŏn-trōl′-la-ble (-ă-bl), *adj.* Uncontrollable; অদম্য, অসংযম্য। **—bly,** *adv.*

in-cŏn-trō-vêrt′-ĭ-ble (-bl), *adj.* Too clear to be called in question; indisputable; অবিবাদ্য, অখণ্ডনীয়, অপ্রত্যাখ্যেয়, অখণ্ড্য, অপরিবর্ত্তনীয়; (হিঃ কোঃ); অপ্রতিবাদ্য, অবিবদনীয়, অকাট্য, অবিতর্ক্য, অবিতর্কনীয়। **—bil′-i-ty, —ness,** *ns.* **—bly,** *adv.*

in-cŏn′-vĕn′-i-ĕnt, *adj.* Causing trouble or uneasiness; uncomfortable; disadvantageous; কষ্টকর, বিরক্তিকর, অসুখকর, ক্লেশকর, ক্লেশদ, দুঃখদ, পীড়াকর; আরামশূন্য; অসুবিধাজনক। **—ence,** *n.* & *v. t.* Disadvantage; that which gives trouble or uneasiness; অসুবিধা, অস্বাচ্ছন্দ্যতা, অস্বাচ্ছন্দ্য, বিরক্তি। ***Verb t.*** To put into inconvenience; অসুবিধায় ফেলা। **—ly,** *adv.* Disadvantageously; অসুবিধাজনকরূপে।

in-cŏn-vêrt′-ĭ-ble (-bl), *adj.* That cannot be converted; incapable of being exchanged, as paper money etc.; অপরিবর্ত্তনশীল, অপরিবর্ত্তনযোগ্য, অপরিবর্ত্তনীয়; অবিনিমেয়। **—bil′-i-ty,** *n.* **—bly,** *adv.*

in-cŏn-vin′-ĉi-ble (-bl), *adj.* Incapable of being convinced; অপরিবোধনীয়। **—bly,** *adv.*

in-cō-ŏr-dĭ-nā′-tion, *n.* Lack of harmonious adjustment or action; অসঙ্গতাবয়বতা, অসৌষ্ঠব, কার্য্যাসামঞ্জস্যাভাব, কার্য্যসঙ্গতিশূন্যতা, অসমন্বয় (হিঃ কোঃ)।

in-cŏr′-pō-rāte, *adj., v. t.* & *i.* 1. Constituted as a corporation, a company, etc.; সমবায়াদিরূপে গঠিত। 2. United in a corporation as persons; একীভূত, সম্মিলিত, দলবদ্ধ, সমবায়বদ্ধ, একীকৃত। ***Verb t.*** 1. To form into one body; to combine (*with* another thing); একাঙ্গীভূত করা; একত্র করা। 2. To unite as different ingredients esp. of gunpowder; মিশ্রিত করা। 3. To constitute as a legal corporation; আইনসঙ্গত সমবায়াদিরূপে গঠিত করা। 4. To embody or include; as, to *incorporate* another's ideas into one's book; অঙ্গীভূত করা, অন্তর্ভুক্ত করা। ***Verb i.*** To unite or become inconporated (*with*); সম্মিলিত হওয়া, অঙ্গীভূত হওয়া।

in-cŏr-pō-rā′-tion, *n.* 1. The act of incorporating or the state of being incorporated; সম্মিলন বা সম্মিলিতাবস্থা। 2. The union of different ingredients into one mass; বিভিন্ন উপাদানের একত্র মিশ্র, সংযোগ (মঃ ইঃ), সংমিশ্রণ (ঐ)। 3. Association; inclusion; সংহতি, সমবায়; অন্তর্নিবেশ। 4. (*Law*) The act of creating a corporation; আইনসঙ্গত সমবায় গঠন। 5. An incorporated society or company or corporation; সমবায়। **—cor′-po-ra-tive,** *adj.*

in-cŏr-pō′-rē-ăl, *adj.* 1. Not composed of matter; immaterial; অপার্থিব, অবিগ্রহ; অনঙ্গ, অদেহ, আধ্যাত্মিক, অভৌতিক, অজড়, অশরীরী, দেহশূন্য, নিরাকার, অদৈহিক, অদেহী, অমূর্ত্ত, বিদেহী। 2. Of, or relating to, immaterial being; অশরীরিসম্বন্ধীয়। 3. (*Law*) Not having physical existence as a hereditament; (আইন) জড়ীয় সত্তাহীন। **—al′-i-ty, —re′-i-ty,** *ns.* **—ly,** *adv.*

in-cŏr-rect′ (-ĕct), *adj.* 1. Not correct; improper; faulty, as a style etc.; অশুদ্ধ, অযথার্থ, ভুল, ভ্রমপূর্ণ, ভ্রমাত্মক; অযুক্ত, অসঙ্গত, অনুচিত; দোষযুক্ত। 2. Not exact; erroneous, as a statement etc.; অযথার্থ; ভ্রমাত্মক। 3. (Of a book) Not corrected for the press; অসংশোধিত। **—ly,** *adv.* In an incorrect manner; erroneously; অশুদ্ধরূপে, অযথার্থরূপে, অনুচিতভাবে; ভ্রমাত্মকভাবে। **—ness,** *n.* Inaccuracy; inexactness; অশুদ্ধতা; অযথার্থতা। **Incorrect knowledge**—অযথার্থজ্ঞান (হিঃ কোঃ), ভ্রম (ঐ)।

in-cŏr′-ri-gi-ble (-ĭ-jĭ-bl), *adj.* Bad or depraved beyond correction or reform; অশাসনীয়, অসংশোধনীয়, দুর্দ্দান্ত, অতি দুরন্ত। **—bil′-i-ty, —ness,** *ns.* **—bly,** *adv.*

in-cŏr-rupt′-ĭ-ble (-ŭpt-ĭ-bl), *adj.* 1. Incapable of decay; eternal; অবিনশ্বর, অক্ষয্য, অদূষনীয়, অবিকার্য্য; অনন্ত, সনাতন, শাশ্বত। 2. Incapable of being corrupted or bribed; অদূষ্য, অনুৎকোচবশ্য। **—bil′-i-ty,** *n.* State of being incorruptible; অদূষ্যতা, অবিকার্য্যতা। **—bly,** *adv.*

in-crăs′-sate (-āte), *adj.* (*Bot.* & *Zool.*) Thick or swollen in form; (উদ্ভিদ বিদ্যা ও প্রাণিবিজ্ঞান) স্থূলাকৃতি, স্ফীত, সান্দ্র, অসূক্ষ্ম।

in-crease′ (-krēs), *v. i.* & *t.* 1. To become greater; to grow; বর্দ্ধিত হওয়া, বাড়া, উপচিত হওয়া; বৃদ্ধি পাওয়া। 2. To become more numerous as by propagation; সংখ্যা বৃদ্ধি পাওয়া। 3. To grow or advance (*in* some quality etc.); "In and with wealth I *increase*"; বাড়া, উন্নতি করা। ***Verb t.*** 1. To augment; to add to; to enhance; বৃদ্ধি করা; বাড়ান; বর্দ্ধিত করা। 2. To intensify, as a quality; প্রগাঢ় করা। **—creas′-ing,** *adj.* **—creas′-ing-ly,** *adv.* More and more; অধিকতর।

in'crease (-krēs), *n.* **1.** Enlargement in size, number or degree; augmentation; বৃদ্ধি, প্রবৃদ্ধি, বর্দ্ধন, বিবর্দ্ধন; উপচয়। **2.** Multiplication as of men, animals or plants: production; offspring; সংখ্যাবৃদ্ধি; উৎপাদন; সন্তানসন্ততি। **3.** The amount increased; an increment; বৃদ্ধির পরিমাণ; বাড়তি। **4.** (*Archaic*) Crops; (অপ্রঃ) শস্য। **On the increase**—Increasing; বর্দ্ধিষ্ণু।

in-crĕd'-i-ble (-bl), *adj.* **1.** Not credible; surpassing belief; অবিশ্বাস্য; অশ্রদ্ধেয়, অপ্রত্যেয়, অসম্ভব, অতীতপ্রত্যয়। **2.** Surprising; অত্যাশ্চর্য্য। **—bil'-i-ty,** *n.* State of being incredible; অপ্রত্যয়তা, অবিশ্বাস্যতা, অত্যাশ্চর্য্যতা, অশ্রদ্ধেয়তা। **—bly,** *adv.*

in-crĕd'-ū-lous (-lŭs), *adj.* **1.** Unbelieving, (often with *of*); sceptical; অবিশ্বাসী, অশ্রদ্ধাবান, প্রত্যয়হীন; সন্দিগ্ধচিত্ত, সন্দিগ্ধমনাঃ। **2.** Indicating or prompted by disbelief, as a smile etc.; অবিশ্বাসসূচক, অবিশ্বাসপ্রসূত। **—cre-du'-li-ty** *n.* Scepticism; disbelief; সন্দিগ্ধচিত্ততা; প্রত্যয়হীনতা, অশ্রদ্ধা, অপ্রত্যয়, অবিশ্বাস, অপ্রতীতি, অপ্রত্যয়শীলতা। **—ly,** *adv.*

in'-crē-mĕnt, *n.* **1.** Augmentation; increase; বর্দ্ধন, বর্দ্ধিত করণ; বৃদ্ধি (হিঃ কোঃ), উন্নতি (ঐ), সমৃদ্ধি (ঐ), আধিক্য। **2.** Amount of increase; an addition; বৃদ্ধির পরিমাণ; বাড়তি। **3.** Profit; "His *increment* small"; লাভ। **4.** (*Math.*) The finite increase of a variable quantity; (গণিত শাস্ত্র) বৃদ্ধি।

in-crim'-i-nāte, *v. t.* To charge with a crime or fault; to involve in an accusation; দোষারোপ করা; অভিযোগে জড়িত করা। **—na-to-ry,** *adj.* Tending to incriminate; অভিযোগাত্মক। **—nat'-ing,** *adj.* Accusing; অভিযোগকারী।

in-crŭs-tā'-tion, *n.* **1.** Act of encrusting; কঠিন বস্তুদ্বারা বহির্দ্দেশ আচ্ছাদন। **2.** A crust or hard coating of anything; কঠিন বহিরাবরণ, বহিরাবেষ্টন। **3.** (*Arch.*) A facing of marble etc. on a building; (স্থপতি-বিজ্ঞান) অট্টালিকার সম্মুখভাগের উপর মর্ম্মর প্রস্তরাদির আবরণ। **4.** (*Fig.*) An accretion of habit; "A thin *incrustation* of vanity"; (লক্ষণায়) ক্রমশঃ বদ্ধমূল অভ্যাস। **5.** Scale; ক্ষতের উপরের মামড়ি।

in'-cū-bāte, *v. i.* & *t.* To sit on eggs for hatching them; তা দেওয়ার জন্য ডিমের উপর বসা। ***Verb t.*** To hatch as eggs by sitting on; ডিমে তা দেওয়া। **—ba'-tion,** *n.* **1.** The act of sitting on eggs to hatch them; ডিমে তা দেওন, অণ্ডপোষণ, অণ্ডভৃতি। **2.** (*Fig.*) Brooding, as of the Holy Ghost; "The mind became fruitful as by the *incubation* of the Holy Ghost; (লক্ষণায়) তাপসঞ্চার। **3.** The phase through which germs of a disease pass before the development of first symptoms; শরীরে কোন দোষ বা রোগ প্রবেশ ও তাহার স্পষ্ট লক্ষণ প্রকাশ এই উভয়ের মধ্যবর্ত্তী কাল, রোগের পূর্ব্বাবস্থা, প্রচ্ছন্নাবস্থা। **—ba-tive,** *adj.* **—cu'-ba-to-ry,** *adj.* **Artificial incubation**—কৃত্রিম উত্তাপ দ্বারা তা দেওন। **The period of incubation**—The period between the implanting of disease and development; রোগের বীজ প্রবেশ ও তদুৎপত্তির মধ্যবর্ত্তী সময়।

in'-cū-bā-tor (-tĕr), *n.* A machine for hatching eggs artificially, rearing aborted children or developing bacteria; কৃত্রিম তাপ দ্বারা ডিম ফুটাইবার জন্য অথবা অকালপ্রসূত সন্তান পালন বা জীবাণু উৎপাদনের জন্য যন্ত্র বিশেষ।

in'-cū-bŭs, *n.* **1.** An evil spirit supposed to descend on sleeping persons esp. to have sexual intercourse with women at sleep; গুমো, বোবা (East Bengal)। **2.** The nightmare; স্বপ্নে বুক-চাপ। **3.** Any person or thing oppressing like nightmare; প্রপীড়ক।

in-cŭl'-cāte, *v. t.* To urge or press persistently; to impress by frequent repetitions; as, to *inculcate* an idea or habit *upon* a person, mind; পুনঃ পুনঃ উপদেশ দ্বারা মনোমধ্যে অঙ্কিত করা; সংস্কার জন্মাইয়া দেওয়া, পুনঃ পুনঃ উপদেশ দ্বারা শিক্ষা দেওয়া। **—ca'-tion,** *n.*

in-cŭl'-pă-ble (-bl), *adj.* Faultless; blameless; নির্দ্দোষ, নিরপরাধ; নিষ্কলঙ্ক, অনিন্দ্য। **—bly,** *adv.* Blamelessly; নির্দ্দোষভাবে। **—ness,** *n.* The quality of inculpable; নিষ্কলঙ্কতা, নির্দ্দোষতা।

in'-cŭl-pāte, *v. t.* **1.** To blame; to accuse; দোষারোপ করা; অভিযুক্ত করা। **2.** To involve or implicate in a charge; অভিযোগ আরোপ করা, কোন অপরাধে জড়িত বা সংস্থষ্ট করা। **—cul'-pa-to-ry,** *adj.* Criminatory; অভিযোগাত্মক। **—pa'-tion,** *n.* Act of inculpating; অভিযোগারোপ।

in-cŭlt', *adj.* **1.** Inartistic, as a literary work etc.; কলাকৌশলহীন, গ্রাম্য। **2.** Coarse, as a person; অমার্জ্জিত, অসভ্য।

in-cŭm'-bĕnt, *adj.* **1.** Lying, or pressing, (with *on*); শয়ান, অর্দ্ধশায়িত। **2.** Resting or imposed as duty; obligatory, (used with *on* or *upon*); as, it is *incumbent on* you to inform him; অবশ্য-কর্ত্তব্য; অবশ্যপালনীয়।

in-cŭm'-bĕnt, *n.* A person who is in possession of a benefice or (rare) of any office; যাজকীয় বৃত্তিভোগী ব্যক্তি, ধর্ম্মবৃত্তিভোগী, স্থলাভিষিক্ত ব্যক্তি, স্থলবর্ত্তী ব্যক্তি। **—ben-cy,** *n.* **During one's incumbency**—কাহারো কার্য্যকালে।

in-cū-năb'-ū-lă, *n.* **1.** (*Pl.*) The earliest stages of a thing; কোন বস্তুর

আদিম অবস্থা সমূহ। **2.** (*Sing.* -LUM) A book printed before 1500 A. D.; ১৫০০ খৃষ্টাব্দের পূর্ব্বে মুদ্রিত পুস্তক।

in-cur′ (-kêr), *v. t.* To fall into; to become liable to; to bring on one's self; to contract; as, to *incur* a danger or debt; পতিত হওয়া; অধীন হওয়া; নিজের উপর আনা; গ্রস্ত হওয়া। **To incur debt, danger etc.**—বিপদ্‌গ্রস্ত হওয়া, ঋণগ্রস্ত হওয়া। **To incur the displeasure of**—To be an object of displeasure to; অপ্রীতিভাজন হওয়া, বিরাগভাজন হওয়া।

in-cür′-ă-ble (-bl), *adj.* & *n.* **1.** Incapable of being cured; অচিকিৎস্য, অচিকিৎসনীয়, নিরৌষধ, দুশ্চিকিৎস্য, নিরুপক্রম (চঃ), অসাধ্য (ঠাকুরঃ), অপ্রতিসমাধেয়, অনারোগ্য। **2** (*Fig.*) Beyond correction as faults etc.; অসংশোধনীয়। ***Noun.*** One suffering from incurable disease; অসাধ্য রোগগ্রস্ত ব্যক্তি। **—bil′-i-ty, —ness,** *ns.* **—bly,** *adv.*

in-cü′-ri-ous (-ŭs), *adj.* **1.** Destitute of curiosity; indifferent; কৌতূহলশূন্য, অকুতুহলী, অনুৎসুক; উদাসীন। **2.** Inattentive; careless; অমনোযোগী, অনুৎসুক; অসতর্ক, উদাসীন। **—ly,** *adv.* **—ness, —os′-i-ty,** *ns.*

in-cur′-sion (-kêr-), *n.* Hostile inroad or invasions; sudden attack; উপদ্রব, উপপ্লব, আক্রমণ; আকস্মিক আক্রমণ। **—sive,** *adj.* Invasive; আক্রমণাত্মক।

in-cur′-vāte (-kêr-), *v. t.* To bend; to curve inwards; বাঁকান; ভিতরের দিকে বক্র করা। **—va′-tion,** *n.*

in-curve′ (-kêrv), *v. t.* **1.** To curve; বক্র করা। **2.** To bend inwards (esp. in *p. p.*); বক্রীভূত করা। **—cur-va′-tion,** *n.*

in′-cŭs (-ing-), *n.* A small bone of the ear receiving vibrations from the malleus; কর্ণের ক্ষুদ্র অস্থি বিশেষ।

in-cuse′ (-küz), *adj.*, *v. t.* & *n.* Struck or stamped in, as an impression on a coin; মুদ্রিত। ***Verb t.*** To impress by stamping as a figure etc.; to mark as a coin with an impressed figure etc.; ছাপ দেওয়া; মুদ্রিত করা। ***Noun.*** Such an impression; মুদ্রা, ছাপ।

in-debt′-ĕd (-dĕt-), *adj.* **1.** Being in debt; ঋণগ্রস্ত, ঋণী। **2.** Obliged by something received; ঋণবদ্ধ, অনুগৃহীত, উপকৃত, উপকারবদ্ধ। **—ness,** *n.* The state of being indebted; ঋণগ্রস্ততা।

in-dē′-cĕnt, *adj.* Unseemly; obscene; immodest; অভদ্র; অশ্লীল, অশ্রাব্য, অকথ্য; অবিনীত। **–cen-cy,** *n.* **1.** Obscenity; want of decency; অশ্লীলতা; অভব্যতা, অভদ্রতা। **2.** An indecent act or word; অশ্লীলবাক্য, লজ্জাজনক কার্য্য। **—ly,** *adv.* In an indecent manner, অভদ্রভাবে, অশ্লীলভাবে।

in-dē-cĭd′-ū-ous (-ŭs), *adj.* (Of leaves) Not deciduous; (of trees, plants) evergreen; (পত্র সম্পর্কে) অপরিণতাবস্থায় পতনশালী; (বৃক্ষ-সম্বন্ধে) চিরশ্যামল।

in-dē-cī′-phêr-ă-ble (-bl), *adj.* Incapable of being deciphered; অরহস্যোদ্ভেদক্ষম।

in-dē-cĭ′-sion, *n.* Want of decision; hesitation; অনিশ্চয়তা; সন্দিগ্ধতা, দ্বিধা।

in-dē-cī′-sive (-sĭv), *adj.* **1.** Not decisive; inconclusive, as a contest etc.; অনিশ্চিত, অনিশ্চায়ক, অনির্ণীত, অনির্ণায়ক; অসিদ্ধান্তিত। **2.** Irresolute; hesitating; অস্থিরমতি; সংশয়কারী, দ্বিধাকারী। **—ly,** *adv.* **—ness,** *n.*

in-dē-clĭn′-ă-ble (-bl), *adj.* & *n.* Not declinable; not varied by inflection; অপরিবর্ত্তনীয়; অবিকারী, অবিভক্তিক, অব্যয়াত্মক, অব্যয়রূপ। ***Noun.*** An indeclinable word; অব্যয় শব্দ। **Indeclinable compound**—অব্যয়ীভাব।

in-dē-cŏm-pōs′-ă-ble (-bl), *adj.* Incapable of being composed or resolved into constituents; অবিশ্লেষণীয়। **—ness,** *n.*

in-dē-cō′-rous (-rŭs), *adj.* Unbecoming; improper; অশোভন, অশিষ্ট, শিষ্টাচারবিরুদ্ধ, অভদ্র, বিনয়বিরুদ্ধ; অনুচিত অসঙ্গত, অন্যায্য। **—ly,** *adv.*

in-dē-cō′-rŭm, *n.* **1.** Want of decorum; impropriety of behavionr; মর্য্যাদাতিক্রম, বিনয়বিরোধ, শিষ্টাচারাতিক্রম, অশোভনতা; অনৌচিত্য। **2.** An unbecoming act or proceeding; অনুচিত কার্য্য।

in-deed′ (-dēd), *adv.* **1.** In fact; really; প্রকৃতপক্ষে, বাস্তবিক পক্ষে; যথার্থই বটে, নিশ্চয়ই, বস্তুতঃ। **2.** Emphasising an affirmation or negation; as, yes *indeed*: no *indeed*; দৃঢ়তাসূচক, প্রশ্নবোধক ও আশ্চর্য্যবোধক রূপে ব্যবহৃত। **3.** Denoting concession or admission; as, there are *indeed* expectations; স্বীকৃতিসূচক। **4.** (*Interrogative*) Is it so? তাই কি? **5.** (As an *interjection*) Expressing irony, contempt, surprise, etc.; "Oh *indeed* what a wonderful thing...!"; বটে। **Indeed and indeed** — (*Colloq.*) Really and truly; (চলিত ভাষায়), তাই তাই, সত্য সত্য।

in-dē-făt′-i-gă-ble (-bl), *adj.* Incapable of being fatigued; untiring or unremitting; persevering; অপরিশ্রান্ত, শ্রান্তিহীন, অশ্রান্ত; অক্লিষ্টকর্ম্মা, অতীন্দ্রিত, অখিন্ন; অধ্যবসায়ী। **—bil′-i-ty, —ness,** *ns.* **—bly,** *adv.* Untiringly; perseveringly; অবিশ্রান্তরূপে, অক্লান্তরূপে; অধ্যবসায়ের সহিত।

in-dē-fea′-si-ble, (-fē-zĭ-bl), *adj.* That cannot be defeated or done away with, as a right etc.; অলোপ্য, অলোপনীয়, অপরাজেয়, অখণ্ডনীয়, অচ্ছেদ্য। **—bil′-i-ty,** *n*

—bly, *adv.* **Indefeasible right**—A right that cannot be anulled or forfeited ; অখণ্ড্য অধিকার।

in-dē-fĕct′-i-ble (-bl), *adj.* Not liable to defect, failure or decay ; faultless ; unfailing ; অক্ষয়, অবিকার, অবিকার্য্য ; নির্দ্দোষ, নিখুঁত, ত্রুটিহীন ; অব্যর্থ।

in-dē-fĕn′-si-ble (-bl), *adj.* Not capable of being defended ; unjustifiable ; অরক্ষণীয়, অসমর্থনীয় ; অপ্রতিপাদ্য, অপ্রতিপাদনীয়, অব্যবস্থাপনীয়। **—bil′-i-ty,** *n.* অরক্ষণীয়তা, অসমর্থনীয়তা। **—bly,** *adv.*

in-dē-fīn′-ā-ble (-bl), Incapable of being defined or described ; অনির্দ্দেশ্য, অবর্ণনীয়, অনিরূপণীয়, অনির্ব্বচনীয়। **—bly,** *adv.*

in-dĕf′-i-nite (-nĭt), *adj.* 1. Not definite ; uncertain ; vague ; অনিরূপিত, অনবধারিত ; অনিশ্চিত, অনিয়ত (হিঃ কোঃ), অনির্দ্দিষ্ট ; অস্পষ্ট, অব্যক্ত। 2. Unlimited ; অসীম। 3. (*Gram.*) Not defining or determining the person, thing or time, as an article, adjective, pronoun etc. ; *e. g.*, *an*, *any*, *few* etc. ; (ব্যাকরণ) অনির্দ্দেশবাচক। **—ly,** *adv.* In an indefinite manner ; অনির্দ্দিষ্টরূপে, অনিশ্চিতরূপে। **—ness, —fin′-i-tude,** *ns.* The state of being indefinite ; অনির্দ্দিষ্টতা, অনিশ্চয়তা। **Indefinite article**—(*Gram.*) The word *a* or *an* used adjectively to denote one of a class or number without specifying it ; অনির্দ্দেশবাচক অব্যয় শব্দ (*a* এবং *an*)। **Indefinite proposition**—অনিশ্চিত প্রতিজ্ঞা (হিঃ কোঃ), অনিশ্চিত বাক্য (ঐ)। **Indefinite term**—অনিশ্চিত সংজ্ঞা (হিঃ কোঃ)।

in-dē-his′-cent (-ĕnt), *adj.* (*Bot.*) Not dehiscent ; (উদ্ভিদ-বিদ্যা) আস্ফোটনশীল (সাঃ পঃ)।

in-dĕl′-i-ble (-bl), *adj.* Incapable of being blotted out or effaced, as a mark, stain, ink etc. ; (also *fig.*) ; as, an *indelible* disgrace ; অনপনেয়, অমোচনীয়, অমার্জ্য, দুরপনেয়। **—bil′-i-ty, —ness,** *ns.* **—bly,** *adv.*

in-dĕl′-i-cāte, *adj.* 1. Coarse ; unrefined ; শিষ্টাচারবিরুদ্ধ, অভদ্রোচিত ; অমার্জ্জিত, গ্রাম্য। 2. Somewhat immodest ; লজ্জাজনক। 3. Tactless ; "*Indelicate* greediness might disgust the benefactor" ; কার্য্যকৌশলহীন। **—ca-cy,** *n.* Want of delicacy ; rudeness ; coarseness ; অমার্জ্জিত ভাব ; অভদ্রতা, অসভ্যতা ; অশ্লীলতা। **—ly,** *adv.*

in-dĕm′-ni-fȳ, *v. t.* 1. To secure against loss or damage ; to protect (*from*) ; (ক্ষতি, অনিষ্ট প্রভৃতি হইতে) রক্ষা করা ; রক্ষা করা। 2. To compensate ; ক্ষতিপূরণ করা। **—fi-ca′-tion,** *n.* 1. The act of indemnifying ; ক্ষতিপূরণ। 2. That which indemnifies ; ক্ষতিপূরণকর বস্তু।

in-dĕm′-ni′-tȳ, *n.* 1. Security against loss, damage, etc. ; ক্ষতি অনিষ্ট প্রভৃতি হইতে রক্ষা। 2. (*Law*) Immunity from penalties etc. incurred ; (আইন) দণ্ড হইতে অব্যাহতি, দণ্ডনিস্তার (হিঃ কোঃ), দণ্ডনিষ্কৃতি। 3. Compensation for loss or injury ; ক্ষতিপূরণ, ক্ষতিনিষ্কৃতি। 4. A sum paid by way of compensation, esp. a sum exacted by a victorious belligerent as a condition of peace ; ক্ষতিপূরণ স্বরূপ প্রদত্ত অর্থ, বিজয়ী জাতি কর্ত্তৃক বিজিত দেশ হইতে সন্ধির সর্ত্তস্বরূপ যে ক্ষতিপূরণের টাকা আদায় করা হয়। **Indemnity-bond**—ক্ষতিপূরণের অঙ্গীকারপত্র, ক্ষতি হইতে রক্ষা করার খত, ক্ষতিপূরণপত্র, হানিপূরণপত্র।

in-dē-mŏn′-strā-ble (-bl), *adj.* Incapable of being demonstrated ; a primary truth ; অপ্রতিপাদ্য, অনুপপাদনীয়, অপ্রামাণ্য ; স্বতঃসিদ্ধ।

in-dĕnt′, *v. t., i.* & *n.* 1. To cut into toothlike notches ; খাঁজ কাটা, দন্তবিশিষ্ট করা, দন্তুরিত করা। 2. To divide as a document drawn up in duplicate into two parts with a zigzag line ; to draw up as a document etc. in duplicate ; দুই অনুরূপ অংশবিশিষ্ট রসিদ চেক প্রভৃতি আঁকাবাঁকা রেখা দ্বারা বিভক্ত করা ; দুই অনুরূপ অংশে (দলীল প্রভৃতি) মুসাবিদা করা। 3. (*Print*) To set in, as a line etc. from the margin to mark new paragraph ; (মুদ্রণ-কার্য্য) নূতন অনুচ্ছেদের প্রারম্ভে পার্শ্বের দিকে কতকটা স্থান ফাঁক রাখিয়া পংক্তি আরম্ভ করা। 4. (*Com.*) To order as goods by an indent ; (বাণিজ্য) কোন মাল সরবরাহের জন্য লিখিত আদেশ দেওয়া। 5. (*Obs.*) To bind by a contract ; (অপ্রঃ) চুক্তিবদ্ধ করা। 6. To cut into (a board) for dovetailing ; to join in this way ; খাঁজে খাঁজে জোড়া দেওয়ার জন্য (তক্তায়) খাঁজ কাটা ; খাঁজে খাঁজে জোড়া দেওয়া। *Verb i.* 1. To be notched or dented ; খাঁজবিশিষ্ট হওয়া, দন্তুরিত হওয়া। 2. To make out a written order in duplicate ; to make a requisition ; as, to *indent on* or *upon* a person for a thing ; অনুরূপ দুই প্রস্থ কাগজে লিখিয়া ফরমায়েস দেওয়া ; ফরমাইস দেওয়া। *Noun.* 1. A cut or notch in the margin ; খাঁজ, দাঁত। 2. Indenture ; চুক্তিপত্র, একরারনামা। 3. Order for goods etc. to England from abroad ; বিদেশ হইতে ইংলণ্ডে মালপত্রাদি সরবরাহের জন্য আদেশ। 4. An official requisition or order for supplies ; সরকারী মালপত্র সরবরাহের জন্য লিখিত আদেশ।

in-dĕnt′, *v. t.* 1. To form (a dent) in ; খাঁজ কাটা। 2. To impress as a mark etc. মুদ্রিত করা।

in-dĕnt′, *n.* A dent or depression ; খাঁজ, টোল।

in-dĕn-tā'-tion, *n.* **1.** The act of indenting; state of being indented; খাঁজ কাটন; দন্তুরতা। **2.** A notch; a deep recess in a coast line; খাঁজ; গভীর ভাবে পশ্চাদ্দিকে অপসৃত উপকূল-রেখা। **3.** (*Print.*) Same as INDENTION below.

in-dĕn'-tion, *n.* **1.** Act of indenting a line in printing; (মুদ্রণ) নূতন অনুচ্ছেদের প্রারম্ভে পার্শ্বের দিকে কতকটা স্থান বাদ দিয়া পংক্তি আরম্ভ করণ। **2.** Same as INDENTATION.

in-dĕn'-tūre, *n.* & *v. t.* **1.** Act of indenting; a notch; খাঁজকাটন; খাঁজ। **2.** The contract or sealed agreement by which an apprentice is bound to his master; শিক্ষানবীশের চুক্তি-পত্র, অঙ্গীকারপত্র, কবারনামা, প্রতিজ্ঞাপত্র। **3.** An official or formal list; a certificate; সরকারী বা রীতিসম্মত তালিকা; নিদর্শনপত্র। ***Verb t.*** To bind as an apprentice by indentures; শিক্ষানবীশকে চুক্তিপত্র দ্বারা আবদ্ধ করা। **To take up one's indentures**—To receive the indenture back on completion of service; কার্য্য সমাপ্তির পর চুক্তিপত্র ফিরাইয়া নেওয়া।

in-dē-pĕnd'-ence (-ĕns), **-ĕn-cȳ,** *ns.* **1.** (*-ence only*) State of being independent; স্বাধীনতা, স্বাতন্ত্র্য, মুক্তি, স্বতন্ত্রতা, স্বৈরতা, আত্মতন্ত্রতা। **2.** An independent income; স্বাধীন আয়। **3.** (*-ency*) Same as CONGREGATIONALISM. **4.** (*-ency*) An independent State; স্বাধীনরাজ্য।

in-dē-pĕnd'-ĕnt, *adj.* & *n.* **1.** Free; not subject to external control; not subordinate; স্বতন্ত্র (হিঃ কোঃ), নিস্তন্ত্র (ঐ), আত্মতন্ত্র, স্বাধীন, মুক্ত, অপরবশ, অপরাধীন, অনধীন, অপরতন্ত্র, অনন্যাধীন, স্বায়ত্ত, অনায়ত্ত। **2.** Affording a comfortable livelihood, as a means; not requiring to earn one's livelihood, as a person: সুখ-স্বাচ্ছন্দ্যজনক জীবিকাপ্রদ; জীবিকার্জ্জনের প্রয়োজনীয়তাহীন। **3.** Not depending on something else for revalidity, efficiency, as proof, search, etc.; প্রামাণিকতাদি সম্বন্ধে অনন্যাধীন। **4.** (*Eccl., cap.*) Same as CONGREGATIONAL. **5.** Exclusive; irrespective, (with *of*); "Quite *independent of* regard to the feelings of others"; একান্ত, অনন্যসাধারণ; নিরপেক্ষ, নির্ব্বিশেষ। **6.** Not subject to bias or influence, as a person or spirit; unconstrained, as manner etc.; নিরপেক্ষ, পক্ষপাতশূন্য; অবাধ, স্বচ্ছন্দ, সহজ, সলীল। **7.** Refusing to be under obligation to others; আত্মতন্ত্র, স্বৈরবৃত্তি, যাদৃচ্ছিক, স্বাধীন। ***Noun.*** **1.** (*Eccl.*) Same as CONGREGATIONALIST. **2.** (*Politics, arts* etc.) One acting independently of any party; (রাজনীতি, শিল্পকলা, প্রভৃতিতে) স্বতন্ত্র। **3.** As a title of a newspaper; as, New-York *Independent*; সংবাদপত্রের উপাধি বিশেষ। **-ly,** *adv.* **1.** In an independent manner; without bias or influence; স্বাধীনভাবে; নিরপেক্ষ ভাবে। **2.** Irrespectively (*of*); নির্ব্বিশেষে, নিরপেক্ষভাবে। **Independent income**—স্থায়ী আয়।

in-dē-scrīb'-ă-ble (-bl), *adj.* Incapable of being described; অবর্ণনীয়, অনির্ব্বচনীয়, বর্ণনাতীত, শব্দাতীত (কেঞ্জিঃ)। **2.** Vague; অবিশেষ (ব্রজঃ হিন্দু), অস্পষ্ট। **-bil'-i-ty,** *n.* **-bly,** *adv.*

in-dē-strŭct'-i-ble (-bl), *adj.* Incapable of being destroyed; অবিধ্বংসী, অবিনশ্বর, অনশ্বর, অবিনাশ্য, অবিনাশী, অক্ষয়, অক্ষয্য, অনাশ্য, অব্যয়, অজর। **-bil'-i-ty, -ness,** *ns.* অবিনশ্বরতা, অনশ্বরতা, অবিনাশত্ব (হিঃ কোঃ)। **-bly,** *adv.*

in-dē-têr'-mi-nă-ble (-bl), *adj.* **1.** That cannot be ascertained or settled; অনির্ণেয়, অনিশ্চেয়, দুর্নিরূপণীয়, অনবধারণীয়। **-bly,** *adv.*

in-dē-têr'-mi-nāte, *adj.* **1.** Not certain or fixed; indefinite; অনিশ্চিত, অনির্দ্ধারিত, অনিরূপিত; অনিয়মিত, অব্যবস্থিত। **2.** Vague, as word, statement, etc.; অস্পষ্ট। **3.** (*Math.*) Not limited to a fixed value or values, as a quantity; (গণিত-শাস্ত্র) নির্দ্দিষ্ট মান বা মানসমূহে সীমাবদ্ধ নয়।

in-dē-têr-mi-nā'-tion, *n.* **1.** Want of determination; an unsettled or wavering state of the mind; সঙ্কল্লাভাব; অব্যবস্থিতচিত্ততা, অস্থিরতা। **2.** State of being indeterminate as a quantity etc.; অনিরূপিত অবস্থা।

in-dē-têr'-min-ism, *n.* (*Metaph.*) The theory that human action is not necessarily determined by motives but is to some extent free; (তত্ত্ব-বিদ্যা) মানবের কর্ম্ম অবশ্যম্ভাবিরূপে উদ্দেশ্য দ্বারা নিরূপিত হয় না, কিন্তু কতক পরিমাণে স্বাধীন—এইরূপ মতবাদ, অনিয়তিবাদ (হিঃ কোঃ)।

in'-dĕx, *n.* & *v. t.* (*Pl.* -ES, -DICES) **1.** The fore-finger; তর্জ্জনী। **2.** A part of an instrument indicating measurements etc.; a pointer; the hand of a clock, watch etc.; যন্ত্রের যে অংশদ্বারা মাপ প্রভৃতি সূচিত হয়; প্রদর্শক, সূচক, জ্ঞাপক, নির্দ্দেশক (হিঃ কোঃ), অনুদেশক; ঘড়ির কাঁটা। **3.** An alphabetical list of subjects etc. treated of in a book usually put at the end; সূচীপত্র, অনুক্রমণিকা। **4.** (*Obs.*) A table of contents prefixed to a book; (অপ্রঃ) সূচীপত্র, নির্ঘণ্ট। **5.** A guiding principle; "One of the *indices* to the solution of the question"; সমাধাননির্দ্দেশক সূত্র। **6.** A sign or indication (*of* something); চিহ্ন, লক্ষণ, সূচনা। **7.** Exponent; (বীজগণিতাদির) কোনও রাশির ঘাত-চিহ্ন, কূটক (সাঃ পঃ), ঘাত (হিঃ কোঃ)। ***Verb t.*** To put into an index; to furnish, as a book with index (usu. in p. p.); সূচীপত্রে সন্নিবিষ্ট করা; সূচীপত্র সমন্বিত করা। —less, adj. Index expurgatories—কোন পুস্তকের পরিবর্জ্জিত আপত্তিজনক অংশ সমূহের তালিকা। Refractive-index—বক্রাংশ সংখ্যা (হিঃ কোঃ)। The Index — রোমান ক্যাথলিক সম্প্রদায়ের অপাঠ্য পুস্তকাবলী।

In'-di-ă (ĭn-), n. A country in the south of Asia; ভারতবর্ষ। **Further India** — খাস ভারতবর্ষ ও চীনদেশের মধ্যবর্ত্তী দেশ (ব্রহ্মদেশ, শ্যাম, আনাম, প্রভৃতি)। **Indiaman**—ভারতীয় বাণিজ্যে নিযুক্ত অর্ণবপোত। **India Office**—লণ্ডননগরীস্থ ভারত সাম্রাজ্য শাসন বিষয়ক কার্য্যালয়। **India paper**—একপ্রকার মসৃণ এবং হাল্কা কাগজ। **India-rubber** — রবার। **East India company**—যে ইংরাজ বণিক-সম্প্রদায় ষোড়শ শতাব্দীতে ইংলণ্ডের রাণী এলিজেবেথের নিকট হইতে সনন্দ লইয়া ভারতবর্ষে বাণিজ্য করিতে আসিয়াছিল।

In'-di-ăn (ĭn-), adj. & n. **1.** Of, or relating to, India; ভারতীয়, ভারত-জাত। **2.** Of, or relating to, the aboriginal inhabitants of America and West Indies; আমেরিকার ও পশ্চিমভারতীয় দ্বীপপুঞ্জের আদিম নিবাসি-সম্বন্ধীয়। ***Noun.*** **1.** A native of India; ভারতবাসী। **2.** One of the aborigines of America or West Indies; আমেরিকা বা পশ্চিম ভারতীয় দ্বীপপুঞ্জের অধিবাসী। **3.** A European esp. an Englishman who resides or resided in India; ভারতপ্রবাসী ইংরাজ, ভারতবর্ষে বাস করিয়াছে এরূপ ইংরাজ। **—ize,** v. t. To make Indian in character, habit, etc.; ভারতীয় ভাবাপন্ন করা। **East Indian**—An inhabitant of India; ভারতবাসী। **Indian club**—মুগুর। **Indian corn, —maize**—জনার (যোঃ)। **Indian file**—See under FILE. **India(n) ink**—চীন ও জাপানদেশে প্রস্তুত কৃষ্ণবর্ণ রঞ্জক পদার্থ। **Indian meal**—জনারের আটা। **Indian summer**—মার্কিণ যুক্তরাজ্যে শরদ্ ঋতুর শেষভাগে সুখময় উষ্ণকাল। **Red Indian**—One of the aborigines of America; আমেরিকার আদিম নিবাসী, লাল ইণ্ডিয়ান। **West Indian**—পশ্চিম ভারতীয় দ্বীপপুঞ্জের অধিবাসী।

in'-di-cāte, v. t. **1.** To point out; to show; নির্দ্দেশ করা, সূচিত করা, জ্ঞাপন করা; প্রদর্শন করা। **2.** To suggest as a remedy or course of treatment; প্রতিকার বা চিকিৎসার পন্থা বা উপায়স্বরূপ নির্দ্দেশ করা। **3.** To betoken; সূচনা করা। **—ca'-tion,** n. **1.** Act of pointing out; a hint or suggestion; প্রদর্শন, দ্যোতন, সূচন, প্রকাশন, ব্যঞ্জন; নির্দ্দেশ, উদ্দেশ, ইঙ্গিত, সঙ্কেত। **2.** A mark, sign or symptom; চিহ্ন, লক্ষণ, লিঙ্গ, অভিজ্ঞান, সংজ্ঞা, নিশান (কেঙিঃ)। **3.** A suggestion as to the treatment of a disease, derived from a symptom observed; রোগের কোন বিশেষ লক্ষণ পর্য্যবেক্ষণ হইতে চিকিৎসা-সম্বন্ধে নির্দ্দেশ।

in-dic'-ă-tive (-tĭv), adj. & n. **1.** Pointing out; giving intimation (of); suggestive; প্রদর্শক, দর্শক, সূচক, বোধক; নির্দ্দেশক (হিঃ কোঃ), ব্যঞ্জক; ব্যঞ্জনাপূর্ণ, অভিব্যঞ্জক। **2.** (Gram.) Applied to that mood of a verb which affirms, denies or interrogates; ধাতুরূপ বিশেষ সম্বন্ধীয়। ***Noun.*** The Indicative mood; ধাতুরূপ বিশেষ। **—ly,** adv. **Indicative mood** — See INDICATIVE, adj. 2.

in'-di-cā-tor (-tĕr), n. **1.** One who or that which indicates or points out; প্রদর্শক, জ্ঞাপক, সূচক, দ্যোতক, প্রকাশক (হিঃ কোঃ), নির্দ্দেশক, বোধক। **2.** A recording instrument of various kinds; নানাপ্রকার নির্দ্দেশক যন্ত্রের নাম। **—to-ry,** adj. Showing; indicative; signifying; প্রদর্শক; সূচনাত্মক; নির্দ্দেশাত্মক।

indicium, (L.), n. (Pl. -CIA) A sign or indication; সূচনা, লক্ষণ।

in-dict' (-dīt), v. t. To charge with a crime esp. by a legal process; অপরাধী করা, অভিযুক্ত করা। **—a-ble,** adj. Liable to indictment as an offender or offence; সমভিযোজ্য, অভিযোক্তব্য, অভিযোজ্য, অভিযোজনীয়।

in-dic'-tion, n. **1.** A fiscal period of 15 years fixed by Constantine the Great of Rome; রোম সম্রাট কন্ষ্টেন্টাইন দি গ্রেট কর্ত্তৃক নির্দ্ধারিত পঞ্চদশবর্ষব্যাপী রাজস্বসংক্রান্ত কাল। **2.** Assessment of property-tax by Roman Emperors at the beginning of each fifteen years; প্রতি পঞ্চদশবর্ষের প্রারম্ভে রোম সম্রাটগণ কর্ত্তৃক সম্পত্তির উপর কর নির্দ্ধারণ। **3.** The tax thus levied; ঐরূপে সংগৃহীত কর। **4.** Proclamation; ঘোষণা।

in-dict'-mĕnt (-dīt-), n. **1.** Act of accusing formally; a formal accusation preferred to and presented by a Grand Jury; অভিযোগস্থাপন; গ্র্যাণ্ডজুরির নিকট যে রীতিসম্মত অভিযোগ করা হয় এবং যাহা তাহারা বিচারকের নিকট উপস্থাপিত করেন। **2.** The legal document containing the charges; অভিযোগপত্র, অভিযোগলেখ। **Bill of indictment**—(জুরিকর্ত্তৃক) অনুমোদিত অভিযোগ।

In'-dies (ĭn-dĭz), n. (Also *East Indies*) India, Further India and the islands beyond; ভারতবর্ষ, তন্নিকটবর্ত্তী দ্বীপসমূহ এবং শ্যাম, আনাম, ব্রহ্ম প্রভৃতি। **West Indies**—পশ্চিম ভারতীয় দ্বীপপুঞ্জ।

in-dif-fer-ence (-ĕns), n. **1.** Neutrality; impartiality; নিরপেক্ষতা, অপক্ষপাতিতা; সমদৃষ্টি (হিঃ কোঃ), সমপক্ষতা, তাটস্থ্য। **2.** Inattentiveness; absence of interest; apathy; অমনোযোগিতা; অনুৎসাহ; ঔদাসীন্য, উদাসীনতা, ঔদাস্য, উপেক্ষা। **3.** Mediocrity; মধ্যবিধভাব। **4.** Unimportance; অকিঞ্চিৎকরত্ব, নগণ্যতা। **5.** Want of difference or distinction; অবৈষম্য, প্রভেদবিহীনতা।

—en-cy, *n.* Same as INDIFFERENCE 5.

in-dif'-fêr-ĕnt, *adj.* & *n.* **1.** Neutral ; impartial ; নিরপেক্ষ, সমদৃষ্টি, নির্লিপ্ত, তটস্থ ; অপক্ষপাতী, সমভাবাপন্ন। **2.** Feeling no inclination for or against ; apathetic, (with *to*) ; অনাসক্ত, উদাস, তটস্থ ; উদাসীন। **3.** Mediocre ; মাঝারি, মধ্যবিধ। **4.** Rather bad (frequently preceded by *very*) ; "With *very indifferent* success" ; কতকটা মন্দ। **5.** Neutral in chemical, electrical or magnetic quality ; রাসায়নিক, বৈদ্যুতিক বা চৌম্বকক্রিয়া সম্বন্ধে নিষ্ক্রিয়। **6.** Without importance or significance, (with *to*) ; গুরুত্বহীন, অকিঞ্চিৎকর। **—ly,** *adv.* Impartially ; without concern ; tolerably ; নিরপেক্ষভাবে ; উদাসীনভাবে ; একরূপ।

in-dif'-fêr-ĕnt-ĭsm, *n.* **1.** The spirit of indifference ; ঔদাসীন্য, উদাসীনতা। **2.** Absence of zeal or interest in religious matters ; ধর্ম্মবিষয়ে উদাসীনতা। **—ist,** *n.*

in'-di-gence (-jĕns), *n.* Penury ; poverty ; নিঃস্বতা, দৈন্য, নির্ধনতা ; দরিদ্রতা, দারিদ্র্য। **—gent,** *adj.* Needy ; poor ; অন্নসংস্থানহীন ; নিঃস্ব, দরিদ্র, নির্ধন, কাঙ্গাল, গরীব, অকিঞ্চন। **—gent-ly,** *adv.*

in'-di-gene (-jēn), *n.* A native ; কোন দেশের অধিবাসী।

in-dig'-ĕ-nous (-nŭs), *adj.* **1.** Native ; not foreign or exotic, as a plant ; স্বদেশী, দেশীয় ; দেশজ, স্বদেশজাত, স্বদেশজ, স্বদেশোদ্ভব। **2.** (*Fig.*) Inborn ; innate ; "Emotions *indigenous* to the mind" ; (লক্ষণায়) অন্তর্জাত ; অন্তর্নিহিত।

in-di-gĕst'-ĕd *adj.* **1.** Not arranged ; shapeless, as facts etc. ; অশৃঙ্খলাবদ্ধ, অজাতব্যবস্থ (কেণ্ডিঃ), অব্যবস্থিত (ঐ) ; বিকৃত। **2.** Ill-considered, as a judgment etc. ; অসুবিবেচিত। **3.** Not having undergone digestion, as food ; অজীর্ণ। **—i-bil'-i-ty, —i-ble-ness,** *ns.* অপরিপক্কতা, বদ্‌হজম, অজীর্ণ। **—i-ble,** *adj.* Not to be easily disgested, (*lit.* & *fig.*) ; গুরুপাক।

in-di-gĕs'-tion (-tyŏn), *n.* **1.** Difficulty of digestion ; dyspepsia ; বদ্‌হজম ; মন্দাগ্নি, অগ্নিমান্দ্য। **2.** State or condition of being indigested, (*lit.* & *fig.*) ; অজীর্ণতা। **—tive,** *adj.* Suffering indigestion ; dyspeptic ; অজীর্ণগ্রস্ত ; অজীর্ণ রোগাক্রান্ত।

in-dign' (-dīn), *adj.* (*Archaic*) Unworthy ; (অপ্রঃ) অযোগ্য।

in-dig'-nănt, *adj.* Affected with anger and disdain ; wrathful ; সমন্যু, জাতামর্ষ ; ক্রোধান্বিত, ক্রুদ্ধ, রুষ্ট, কোপজ্বলিত, রোষাবিষ্ট। **—ly,** *adv.*

in-dig'-nā'-tion, *n.* Anger excited by what is unworthy or base ; anger mixed with contempt ; মন্যু ; অমর্ষ (দশঃ), কোপ, রোষ। **Indignation meeting**—কোন অত্যাচার বা অবিচারের বিরুদ্ধে রোষপ্রকাশার্থ সভা, ক্রোধ-সভা।

in-dig'-ni-tȳ, *n.* Unworthy treatment ; a slight or insult ; অযোগ্য-ব্যবহার ; অবমাননা, হেলা, অবজ্ঞা।

in'-di-go, *n.* **1.** A blue powdered dye-stuff obtained from plants of the genus indigofera ; নীল, নীলী, নীলিকা, নীলবড়ী, অক্লিকা (মঃ উঃ)। **2.** An indigo plant ; নীলগাছ, মধুপর্ণিকা (মঃ ইঃ), নীলপুষ্পিকা (ঐ)। **—go-tic,** *adj.* Pertaining to, or derived from, indigo ; নীলসম্বন্ধীয়, নীলোদ্ভব, নীলজাত। **Black indigo**—কাল নীল (হিঃ কোঃ)। **Blue indigo**—শ্যাম নীল (হিঃ কোঃ)। **Brown indigo**—কপিল নীল (হিঃ কোঃ)। **Green indigo**—হরিত নীল (হিঃ কোঃ)। **Indigo blue**—Deep blue-violet ; গাঢ় নীলাভ ধূমল, নীলীনীল (সাঃ পঃ)। **Indigo factory**—নীলকুঠি। **Indigo planter**—নীলকর। **Indigo vat**—নীলপাচন ভাণ্ড, নীলসন্ধান ভাণ্ড। **Indigo white**—নীল হইতে প্রাপ্ত শ্বেতবর্ণ স্ফটিকবৎ পদার্থ। **Purple indigo**—বেগুনী নীল (হিঃ কোঃ)। **Red indigo**—রক্তনীল, লোহিতনীল (হিঃ কোঃ)। **White indigo**—শ্বেত নীল (হিঃ কোঃ)।

Indigo plant.

in-di-gŏf'-ĕr-ă, *n.* A plant from which indigo is obtained ; নীল গাছ।

in-di-rĕct' *adj.* **1.** Not direct ; crooked, oblique, as a road etc. ; অসরল, অনৃজু (কেণ্ডিঃ) ; আঁকাবাঁকা, বক্র। **2.** Not directly aimed at, as a result etc. ; অপ্রত্যক্ষ, পরোক্ষ, গৌণ, অসাক্ষাৎ। **3.** Unfair ; dishonest ; "*Indirect* dealing" ; অসাধু ; অনৃজু, কুটিল। **4.** Roundabout, as a question or answer ; ঘুরালো। **-ly,** *adv.* In an indirect manner ; বক্রভাবে, অপ্রত্যক্ষরূপে, অসংভাবে, প্রকারান্তরে, পাকে প্রকারে। **--ness,** *n.* **Indirect evidence** or **testimony**—অনুমিত প্রমাণ, আনুষঙ্গিক প্রমাণ, পরোক্ষ প্রমাণ। **Indirect object**—গৌণ কর্ম্ম। **Indirect proof**—কোন বিষয়ের বিরুদ্ধমতাদির অসত্যতা প্রতিপাদনপূর্ব্বক তদ্বিষয়ের প্রমাণ। **Indirect speech** or **narration**—প্রথম পুরুষোক্তি। **Indirect tax**—পরোক্ষ কর। **Indirect vision**—আনুষঙ্গিক দর্শন (হিঃ কোঃ)।

in-di-rĕc'-tion, *n.* **1.** Oblique or roundabout means ; "By *indirections* find directions out" ; ঘুরপেঁচ, পরোক্ষ উপায়। **2.** Deceit or trickery ; ছলনা, চাতুরী।

in-dĭs-cern'-i-ble (-zĕrn-ĭ-bl), *adj.* Imperceptible ; incapable of being discerned or distinguished from another ; অননুভবনীয় ; ইন্দ্রিয়াতীত, দুর্লক্ষ্য, ইন্দ্রিয়াগোচর, অতি সূক্ষ্ম, অলক্ষ্য, অদৃশ্য ; প্রভেদনিরূপণাযোগ্য। ***Noun.*** An indiscernible thing ; অলক্ষ্য বস্তু। **—bly,** *adv.* **—ness,** *n.*

in-dis-cêrp′-ti-ble (-bl-), *adj.* Not subject to dissolution ; not destructible by dissolution of parts ; অভেদ্য, অচ্ছেদ্য, অচ্ছেদনীয় ; অংশসমূহের বিশ্লেষণ দ্বারা অবিনাশ্য । **—bil′-i-ty, —ness,** *ns.*

in-dis′-ĉi-pline (-plin), *n.* Want of discipline or order ; শাসনাভাব, শিক্ষাভাব । **—plin-a-ble,** *adj.*

in-dis-creet′ (-krēt), *adj.* Injudicious ; imprudent ; অপরিণামদর্শী, অবিচারশীল, অবিবেকী ; অবিবেচক । **—cre′-tion,** *n.* **1.** Want of discretion ; imprudence ; বিচারাভাব, বিচারশূন্যতা ; অবিজ্ঞতা, অসমীক্ষা, অবিবেচনা । **2.** Unwise conduct ; অবিবেচনার কার্য্য । **—ly,** *adv.* Injudiciously ; অবিবেচকের মত । **—ness,** *n.*

in-dis-crete′ (-krēt), *adj.* Compact ; homogeneous ; সংহত ; অভিন্ন, অপৃথক, অবিভক্ত (হিঃ কোঃ), সমরূপ ।

in-dis-crim′-i-nāte, *adj.* **1.** Promiscuous ; confused ; অবিচারিত, অবিবেচিত, অবিভেদী, নির্ব্বিশেষ ; বিশৃঙ্খল । **2.** Not distinguishing or making discrimination ; "His *indiscriminate* admirers" ; নির্ব্বিশেষ (হিঃ কোঃ) । **—ly,** *adv.* Without discrimination or distinction ; ইতর বিশেষ না করিয়া, নির্ব্বিশেষে, নির্ব্বিচারে । **—na′-tion,** *n.* Want of discrimination, distinction or discernment ; অবিবেক, বিচারাভাব, বিবেচনাভাব, ভেদরাহিত্য, অপক্ষপাত । **—na-tive,** *adj.*

in-dis-pĕn′-sā-ble (-bl), *adj.* **1.** Incapable of being dispensed with ; absolutely necessary ; অপরিহার্য্য, অনিবার্য্য ; অত্যাবশ্যক । **2.** (*Law*) That cannot be set aside, as a law, duty, etc. ; (আইন) অনন্যথাসিদ্ধ । **—bil′-i-ty, —ness,** *ns.* **—bly,** *adv.* In an indispensable manner ; unavoidably ; অপরিহার্য্যরূপে, অত্যাবশ্যকরূপে ।

in-dis-pōse′, *v. t.* **1.** To render unfit or unable ; to disqualify ; অনুপযুক্ত করা, অসমর্থ করা, অক্ষম করা ; অযোগ্য করা । **2.** To make somewhat ill, (usu. in *p. p.*) ; অসুস্থ করা । **3.** To disincline ; to render averse ; অপ্রবৃত্তি জন্মান ; বীতস্পৃহ করা, বীতরাগ করা, পরাঙ্মুখ করা । **—posed′,** *adj.* **1.** Unwilling ; averse ; অনিচ্ছুক ; বীতস্পৃহ, বীতরাগ । **2.** Slightly ill ; অসুস্থ ।

in-dis-pō-si′-tion, *n.* **1.** Illness ; slight disorder or ailment ; পীড়া ; অসুখ । **2.** Disinclination ; aversion ; বিতৃষ্ণা, অনিচ্ছা, অপ্রবৃত্তি, অরুচি ; বীতস্পৃহা, বিরাগ, অপ্রীতি ।

in-dis′-pū-tā-ble (-bl), *adj.* Not disputable ; incontrovertible ; certain ; অবিবাদ্য, অবিবদনীয়, অপ্রতিবাদ্য, নির্ব্বিবাদ, অবিসংবাদী, অখণ্ডনীয় ; অবিচারণীয়, অবিতর্কনীয়, অবিতর্ক্য, অপ্রত্যাখ্যেয় ; ধ্রুব, সত্য, অবশ্যস্বীকার্য্য, সুনিশ্চিত । **—bil′-i-ty, —ness,** *ns.* **—bly,** *adv.* Incontrovertibly ; অখণ্ডনীয়রূপে, নির্ব্বিবাদে, নিশ্চয়তার সহিত, সুনিশ্চিতভাবে ।

in-dis′-sō-lū-ble (-bl), *adj.* **1.** Incapable of being dissolved or decomposed ; অদ্রবণীয়, অগলনীয়, অবিদ্রাব্য, অদ্রাব্য, অবিলয়নীয়, অবিশ্লেষণীয় । **2.** Not to be broken or violated, as a bond or league ; lasting ; stable ; অবিচ্ছেদ্য, অলঙ্ঘ্য, অনতিক্রমণীয় ; চিরস্থায়ী ; সুদৃঢ় । **—bil′-i-ty, —ness,** *ns.* **—bly,** *adv.*

in-dis-tinct′ (-tingkt), *adj.* Not distinct ; not clear ; obscure ; faint ; অবিস্পষ্ট, অস্পষ্ট, অস্ফুট ; অপরিষ্কার, অপরিস্ফুট ; ঝাপ্‌সা, ঘোরাল ; মৃদু । **—ly,** *adv.* In an indistinct manner ; অস্পষ্টরূপে, অব্যক্তরূপে । **—ness,** *n.* State of being indistinct ; confusion ; uncertainty ; অপরিস্ফুটতা ; অস্পষ্টতা ; অনিশ্চয়তা । **—tinc′-tive,** *adj.* Not distinctive ; অবিশেষ, অসাধারণ । **—tinc′-tive-ly,** *adv.*

in-dis-tin′-guish-a-ble (-ting-gwish-ă-ble), *adj.* **1.** Incapable of being distinguished ; অপ্রভেদ্য, অবিজ্ঞেয়, ইতরবিশেষ করণাযোগ্য । **2.** Imperceptible ; অবিজ্ঞেয়, অদৃষ্টিগোচর, অপ্রত্যক্ষ । **—bly,** *adv.*

in-dis-trib′-ūt-ă-ble (-bl), *adj.* Not distributable ; অবিতরণীয় ।

in-dīte′, *v. t.* **1.** To compose ; to write ; as, to *indite* a poem, speech or letter ; রচনা করা ; লেখা, প্রণয়ন করা ।

in-di-vêrt′-i-ble (-bl), *adj.* Not to be diverted or turned aside ; অবিচলনীয় । **—bly,** *adv.*

in-di-vid′-ū-ăl, *adj.* & *n.* **1.** Single ; singular ; particular (opp. to *general*) ; এক ; একমাত্র, অদ্বিতীয় ; অব্যাপক । **2.** Distinctive ; of a peculiar character ; বিশিষ্ট ; বিশিষ্টপ্রকৃতিসম্পন্ন, বিশিষ্টপ্রাকৃতিক । **3.** Relating, or peculiar, to a particular person or things ; characteristic of an individual ; ব্যক্তি সম্পর্কীয় ; ব্যক্তিগত । ***Noun.*** **1.** A single member of a class ; একমাত্র জন্তু, বস্তু বা ব্যক্তি, ব্যষ্টিগত জন্তু, বস্তু বা ব্যক্তি । **2.** A single human being as opp. to *society, family* ; (*vulg.*) a person ; ব্যক্তি, জন ; (ইতর ভাষায়) লোক । **Individual property**—ব্যক্তিগত সম্পত্তি ।

in-di-vid′-ū-ăl-ism, *n.* **1.** Selfishness ; egoism ; স্বার্থপরতা ; অহংবাদ, স্বস্বার্থবাদ (হিঃ কোঃ) । **2.** A social theory favouring free action of the individual ; সমাজতত্ত্বসম্বন্ধীয় মতবাদ বিশেষ—যাহাতে কোন ব্যক্তির ব্যক্তিগত কার্য্যে রাষ্ট্রের হস্তক্ষেপের অধিকার আছে বলিয়া স্বীকৃত হয় না, ব্যক্তিসাম্যবাদ, ব্যক্তিস্বাতন্ত্র্যবাদ (হিঃ কোঃ), ব্যক্তিবাদ । **—ist,** *n.* **—is′-tic,** *adj.*

in-di-vid-ū-ăl′-i-tŷ, *n.* **1.** State of being individual ; separate existence ; ব্যক্তিত্ব, একত্ব (হিঃ কোঃ), পৃথগাত্মকতা, ব্যষ্টি ; ব্যক্তিগত স্বাতন্ত্র্য, স্বাতন্ত্র্য । **2.** Individual or distinctive character ; "The Puritan *individuality*" ; ব্যক্তিগত

স্বভাব, ব্যক্তিগত বৈশিষ্ট্য। 3. (*Pl.*) Individual characteristics ; ব্যক্তিগত বিশেষত্ব।

in-di-vid′-ū-ăl-īze, *v. t.* 1. To make individual in character ; ব্যক্তিভাবাপন্ন করা। 2. To specify or particularize ; বিশেষিত করা, বিশেষ ভাবে নির্দ্দেশ করা। **–i-za′-tion,** *n.*

in-di-vid′-ū-ăl-ly̆, *adv.* 1. In an individual manner or capacity ; in a distinctive way ; পৃথক্‌ভাবে; স্বতন্ত্রভাবে, বিশিষ্টরূপে। 3. Personally ; as, this affair affects me *individually* ; ব্যক্তিগতভাবে।

in-di-vid′-ū-āte, *v. t.* 1. To give individuality to ; ব্যক্তিত্ব প্রদান করা। 2. To form into an individual ; ব্যক্তিস্বরূপ করা। **–a′-tion,** *n.* The act of individuating ; ব্যক্তীকরণ (হিঃ কোঃ), উপাধান (ঐ)।

in-di-vis′-i-ble (-bl), *adj.* & *n.* Not divisible ; not separable into parts ; অবিভাজ্য, অভাজ্য ; অপৃথক্‌করণীয়, অবিভেদ্য। ***Noun.*** An infinitely small particle or quantity ; সূক্ষ্মকণিকা বা ক্ষুদ্র রাশি। **–bil′-i-ty, –ness,** *ns.* The state of being indivisible ; অভাজ্যতা। **–bly,** *adv.*

In′-dō- (în-), A prefix signifying Indian ; ভারতবর্ষীয়বোধক উপসর্গ। **Indo-Aryans**—Aryans of, or in, India ; ভারতীয় আর্য্যগণ, য়ুরো-ভারতীয় (প্রবাসী ১৩২২), ভারতবাসী আর্য্যগণ। **Indo-Chinese** — The Chinese of Further India ; ব্রহ্ম, শ্যাম, আনাম, প্রভৃতি দেশবাসী চীনদেশীয় লোক। **Indo-European, –Germanic** — Aryan ; applied to the class of languages spoken over greater part of Europe and Asia as far as Northern India ; আর্য্য ; গ্রীক, ল্যাটীন, সংস্কৃত, প্রভৃতি—ইয়ুরোপ ও ভারতবর্ষে ব্যবহৃত ভাষাসম্বন্ধে প্রযোজ্য।

in-dŏc′-ile (*or* -il), *adj.* Not docile or teachable ; intractable ; অদম্য, অবশীকরণীয়, দুঃশাস্য অনয়াত্ত ; অবিনেয়। **–do-cil′-i-ty,** *n.*

in-dŏc′-tri-nāte, *v. t.* To instruct in any doctrine ; to teach ; কোনও তত্ত্ব শিক্ষা দেওয়া ; শিক্ষা দেওয়া। **–na′-tion,** *n.*

in′-dō-lĕnt, *adj.* 1. Lazy ; inactive ; অলস, শ্রমবিমুখ, কার্য্যপরাঙ্মুখ, কুড়ে ; উদ্যমহীন, জড়, নিশ্চেষ্ট। 2. (*Med.*) Causing little or no pain as a tumour etc. ; বেদনাশূন্য, অল্প বেদনাজনক। **–lence,** *n.* Laziness ; আলস্য, শ্রমবিমুখতা, কর্ম্মপরাঙ্মুখতা, নিরুদ্যম। **–ly,** *adv.*

in-dŏm′-i-tă-ble (-bl), *adj.* Not to be subdued ; unyielding ; stubbornly persistent ; অবশ্য, অদম্য, দুর্দ্দান্ত, দুরবগ্রহ ; অজেয় ; দুর্দ্দম, দুর্দ্দম্য, অপ্রতিহন্তব্য। **–bly,** *adv.*

in′-door (-dōr), *adj.* 1. Done, performed or situated, indoors ; গৃহাভ্যন্তরস্থ, গৃহাভ্যন্তরে সম্পাদিত। 2. Within the workhouse ; as, *indoor* relief ; দরিদ্রশালার অভ্যন্তরস্থ। **Indoor-games**—যে সকল খেলা ঘরে বসিয়া খেলা যায়—যথা তাস, পাশা প্রভৃতি। **Indoor-patient**—যে সকল রোগী রুগ্নাবাসে থাকিয়া চিকিৎসিত হয়।

in-doors′ (-dōrz), *adv.* Within a house or under cover ; গৃহাভ্যন্তরে, আড়ালে।

in-dŏr-să′-tion, *n.* Act of endorsing ; পৃষ্ঠে লিখন।

in-dorse′ (-dŏrs), *v. t.* Same as ENDORSE.

in-dŏr-see′ (-sē), *n.* The person to whom a note or bill is endorsed ; যে ব্যক্তির অনুকূলে কোন নোট বা হুণ্ডীর পৃষ্ঠে লিখা হয়।

in′-draught (-drăft), **–drăft,** *n.* 1. Drawing or pulling in ; অন্তর্গ্রাহ। 2. An inward flow or current, as of air, water, etc. ; অন্তর্ব্বাহ।

in′-dri, *n.* A lemurine animal of Madagascar ; মাডাগাস্কার দ্বীপের কপিজাতীয় জন্তুবিশেষ।

in-dū′-bi-ous (-ŭs), *adj.* (*Rare*) Not doubtful ; certain ; অসংশয়িত, অসন্দিগ্ধ ; ধ্রুব, নিশ্চিত।

in-dū′-bi-tă-ble (-bl), *adj.* Not doubtful ; certain ; নিঃসন্দিগ্ধ, অসন্দিগ্ধ, নিঃসন্দেহ ; ধ্রুব, সুনিশ্চিত। **–bly,** *adv.* **–ness,** *n.*

in-dūce′, *v. t.* 1. To prevail on or persuade ; প্রবর্ত্তিত করা, প্রণোদিত করা, প্ররোচিত করা, মত লওয়ান, প্রবৃত্তি জন্মান। 2. To cause ; to bring on ; as, a fever *induced* by exposure ; সংঘটিত করা ; উৎপাদন করা। 3. To conclude or infer as an inference from particulars ; অনুমান করা, সিদ্ধান্ত করা, ব্যাপ্তি-সাধন করা। 4. (*Elec.*) To produce by induction as a current ; (তাড়িত-বিজ্ঞান) প্রবর্ত্তনদ্বারা উৎপাদন করা।

in-dūce′-mĕnt, *n.* That which induces ; something attractive leading one on *to* action etc. ; প্রবর্ত্তক, প্রবৃত্তিসাধক ; প্ররোচনা, প্রবর্ত্তনা, প্রলোভন। **Words of inducement**—Persuasive words; প্রলোভন বাক্য, প্ররোচনা বাক্য।

in-dŭct′, *v. t.* 1. To introduce formally as to a benefice ; to install, as into a seat, room, etc. ; যাজকীয় পদ প্রভৃতিতে যথারীতি আসীন করা ; প্রতিষ্ঠিত করান, পদাসীন করা। 2. To bring in ; to introduce ; to initiate, (with *to, into*) ; প্রবর্ত্তিত করা ; উপস্থিত করা ; দীক্ষিত করা।

in-dŭc′-tile (-tĭl), *adj.* Not ductile ; অপ্রসার্য্য, অতাণ্ডব।

in-dŭc′-tion, *n.* 1. (*Rare*) Introduction ; entrance ; commencement ; (অপ্রঃ) আমুখ ; প্রবেশ ; প্রারম্ভ। 2. The formal introduction to an office esp. of a clergyman ; কোন পদে বিশেষতঃ যাজকীয় পদে স্থাপন, নবপদপ্রবেশকরণ। 3. (*Logic*) The act or process of reasoning from particular instances to genenral conclusions ; an inducative inference ; বিশেষ বিশেষ দৃষ্টান্ত হইতে সাধারণ

সিদ্ধান্তে উপনীত হওয়ার যুক্তিপ্রণালী, যে যুক্তিপ্রণালীর সাহায্যে কোন শ্রেণী-ভুক্ত এক বা ততোধিক ব্যক্তি বা বস্তুর সম্পর্কে যাহা নির্ণীত হইয়াছে তাহা সমস্ত শ্রেণীর পক্ষে সিদ্ধান্ত বা অনুমান করা হয়, ব্যাপ্তি-নিশ্চয়, ব্যাপ্তিগ্রহ, ব্যাপ্তিসিদ্ধান্ত (বিশ্বঃ), অনুমান (হিঃ কোঃ), পরীক্ষা-প্রসূত অনুমান (ঐ), অনুগম (ঐ), উপপাদন (হিঃ কোঃ), ব্যাপ্তিসাধন (ঐ)। **4.** (*Elect. magnet.*) The transfer of an electric or magnetic state from an electrified or magnatized body to one not so, by proximity without contact ; কোন তড়িন্ময় বা চৌম্বক ধর্ম্মাক্রান্ত বস্তু হইতে সংস্পর্শ বিনা নৈকট্যদ্বারা চৌম্বক বা তড়িন্ময় অবস্থা অতড়িন্ময় বা অচৌম্বকধর্ম্মাক্রান্ত অপর বস্তুতে পরিবর্ত্তন, তাড়িতপ্রবর্ত্তন (*electric*), প্রবর্ত্তন (সাঃ পঃ), চৌম্বক-প্রবর্ত্তন (*magnetic*)। **Induction coil**—An apparatus for producing electric currents by induction ; প্রবর্ত্তন দ্বারা তাড়িতপ্রবাহ উৎপাদনের জন্য যন্ত্র বিশেষ, প্রবর্ত্তনকুণ্ডলী। **Magnetic induction** — চুম্বকীয় উপপাদন (হিঃ কোঃ)। **Mutual induction**—দ্বৈতপ্রবর্ত্তন (সাঃ পঃ), পরস্পরপ্রবর্ত্তন (ঐ)।

in-dŭc'-tive (-tĭv), *adj.* **1.** Of, relating to, or based on, logical induction as a reasoning, etc. ; ব্যাপ্তিসাধনসম্বন্ধীয়, ব্যাপ্তিমূলক, উপপাদনীয় (হিঃ কোঃ), আনুমানিক (ঐ)। **2.** Of, or relating to, electric or magnetic induction ; তাড়িত বা চুম্বকপ্রবর্ত্তন সম্বন্ধীয়। **—ly,** *adv.* **—ness,** *n.* **Inductive logic**—ব্যাপ্তিমূলক তর্কশাস্ত্র, ব্যাপ্তিবাদ (হিঃ কোঃ), আগমনশাস্ত্র (ঐ)। **Inductive method**—বিশেষ হইতে সামান্যে উপনীত হইবার প্রণালী, আরোহপ্রণালী, ব্যাপ্তিমূলক প্রণালী। **Inductive science** — ব্যাপ্তিমূলক প্রণালীর উপর প্রতিষ্ঠিত বিজ্ঞান। **Inductive syllogism** — ব্যাপ্ত্যনুমান (হিঃ কোঃ)।

in-dŭc'-tor (-têr), *n.* **1.** A part of an electric induction apparatus ; তাড়িতপ্রবর্ত্তন যন্ত্রের অংশবিশেষ, উপপাদক (হিঃ কোঃ)। **2.** The person who inducts a clergyman to a benefice ; যাজকপদে প্রতিষ্ঠাতা।

in-dulge' (-dŭlj), *v. t.* & *i.* **1.** To give free course to ; not to restrain ; as, to *indulge* a desire ; প্রশ্রয় দেওয়া, আস্কারা দেওয়া ; বাধা না দেওয়া। **2.** To gratify by compliance ; to humour ; as, to *indulge* a boy *in* whims ; ইচ্ছাপূরণ করিয়া খুসী করা ; মনোরঞ্জন করা। ***Verb i.*** To gratify one's appetites or desires freely (*in*) ; অসংযতভাবে ইন্দ্রিয়বৃত্তি চরিতার্থ করা।

in-dŭl'-gence (-jĕns), *n.* **1.** The act of indulging ; gratification, (with *in*) ; প্রশ্রয়, আস্কারা, আদর ; বিনোদন, সংরঞ্জন। **2.** A favour or privilege granted ; অনুগ্রহ, অধিকার। **3.** Habitual indulging of one's desires, (also *self-indulgence*) ; ইন্দ্রিয়াদির সেবা। **4.** (*Rom. Cath. Ch.*) Remission of the penance attached to certain sins after sacramental absolution ; (রোমান ক্যাথলিক ধর্ম্মসংঘ) প্রায়শ্চিত্ত হইতে অব্যাহতি প্রদান। **Declaration of Indulgence**—ধর্ম্ম-সম্বন্ধে স্বাধীনতা ঘোষণা—বিশেষতঃ ১৬৭২ খৃঃ অব্দে দ্বিতীয় চার্লসের সময় এবং ১৬৮৭ খৃঃ অব্দে দ্বিতীয় জেমসের সময়ে ধর্ম্মসম্বন্ধীয় ব্যাপারে স্বাধীনতা ঘোষণা।

in-dŭl'-genced (-jĕnst), *p.p.* (*R. C. Church*—of prayer, material objects etc.) Procuring indulgence to the user ; "*Indulgenced* prayers for souls" ; প্রায়শ্চিত্তমোচন সাধক।

in-dŭl'-gĕnt, *adj.* Prone to indulge ; compliant ; lenient ; প্রশ্রয়-দায়ক, প্রশ্রয়শীল ; অনুগ্রাহী, বিনয়গ্রাহী, বিনেয়, প্রিয়কারী ; অনুগ্রহশীল, সদয়। **—ly,** *adv.*

in-dŭlt', *n.* (*R. C. Church*) A dispensation granted by the Pope ; পোপকর্ত্তৃক প্রায়শ্চিত্ত হইতে অব্যাহতি প্রদান।

in'-dū-rāte, *adj.* **1.** (*Rare*) Hardened ; not soft ; (কচিদ্ ব্যবহৃত) কঠিনীভূত, দৃঢ়ীভূত ; শক্ত। **2.** (*Rare*) Rendered callous ; (কচিদ্ ব্যবহৃত) নির্ম্মমীভূত।

in'-dū-rāte, *v. t.* & *i.* **1.** To make hard ; শক্ত করা, কঠিন করা। **2.** To make unfeeling or callous ; নির্ম্মম করা, বেদনাবোধশূন্য করা, অসাড় করা। ***Verb i.*** **1.** To grow hard ; অসাড় হওয়া, বেদনাবোধশূন্য হওয়া। **2.** To become fixed or inveterate ; বদ্ধমূল হওয়া। **—ra'-tion,** *n.* **—ra-tive,** *adj.*

in-dū'-si-ŭm, *n.* (*Pl.* -SIA) **1.** (*Bot.*) An outgrowth of the leaf covering the sorus or fruit-cluster of a fern ; (উদ্ভিদ্ বিদ্যা) মণ্ডলছত্র (সাঃ পঃ), মণ্ডলচ্ছদ (ঐ)। **2.** Collection of hairs enclosing the stigma of some flowers ; কোন কোন পুষ্পের চিহ্নাবরক রোমগুচ্ছ। **3.** (*Zool.*) The larval case of an insect ; (জন্তু-বিদ্যা) পতঙ্গের কৃমির আধার।

in-dŭs'-tri-ăl, *adj.* & *n.* Of, or relating to, industries ; pertaining to the products of industry ; শ্রমশিল্প সম্বন্ধীয় ; শ্রমশিল্পজাত দ্রব্যাদি সম্বন্ধীয়। ***Noun.*** **1.** A person engaged in industrial pursuits ; কৃষি, শিল্প, প্রভৃতি কার্য্যে নিযুক্ত ব্যক্তি। **2.** (*Pl.*) Shares in a joint-stock industrial enterprise ; কৃষিশিল্পসংক্রান্ত সমবায়ের অংশ সমূহ। **—ism,** *n.* A social organization or system founded on, or made with reference to, industrial occupations ; কৃষিশিল্প প্রভৃতি ব্যবসায়ের উপর বা তৎসম্পর্কে প্রতিষ্ঠিত সমাজব্যবস্থা বা পদ্ধতি। **—ist,** *n.* One engaged in, or connected with, industrial occupations ; a worker or manufacturer ; কৃষিশিল্প প্রভৃতি ব্যবসায়ে নিযুক্ত বা তৎসংসৃষ্ট ব্যক্তি ; শ্রমজীবী, শিল্পী। **—ize,** *v. t.* To make industrial ; to occupy or organize industrially ; শ্রমশিল্পাত্মক

করা ; শ্রমশিল্পাত্মক ভাবে ব্যবস্থাবদ্ধ করা। **—ly,** *adv.* **Industrial exhibition**—কৃষিশিল্প প্রদর্শনী। **Industrial school**—যে বিদ্যালয়ে উপেক্ষিত বালক-বালিকাগণ সাধারণ শিক্ষার সঙ্গে সঙ্গে জীবিকানির্ব্বাহোপযোগী কোন প্রকার শিল্প শিক্ষা করিয়া থাকে, শিল্পবিদ্যালয়।

in-dŭs'-tri-ous (-ŭs), *adj.* Laborious ; diligent ; hard-working ; পরিশ্রমী, শ্রমানুরাগী ; কর্ম্মানুরাগী, উদ্যোগী, কর্ম্মিষ্ঠ, কর্ম্মঠ, কর্ম্মনিষ্ঠ, কর্ম্মশীল, কার্য্যনিষ্ঠ, অতন্দ্রিত, অনলস ; কঠোর পরিশ্রমী। **—ly,** *adv.* **—ness,** *n.*

in'-dŭs-trȳ, *n.* **1.** Diligence ; শ্রম, যত্ন, পরিশ্রম, কর্ম্মশীলতা। **2.** Systematic labour or habitual employment in useful work ; প্রণালীবদ্ধ শ্রম, কার্য্যকরী ব্যবসায়ে নিত্য নিযুক্তি। **3.** A branch of manufacture or trade ; as, sugar-*industry* ; শ্রমশিল্প বা ব্যবসায়ের শাখা।

in-dwĕll', *v. t.* & *i.* To dwell in or abide within, (usu. *fig.*) ; as, a spirit *indwells* a body ; ভিতরে বাস করা। ***Verb i.*** To dwell (*in*) ; বাস করা। **In'-dwell-er,** *n.* An inhabitant ; অধিবাসী।

in-ē'-bri-ănt, *adj.* & *n.* Intoxicating ; মত্ততাজনক। ***Noun.*** That which inebriates ; মাদক (ঠাকুর:)।

in-ē'-bri-āte, *v. t.* **1.** To make drunk ; to intoxicate ; প্রমত্ত বা মাতাল করা ; মত্ততা জন্মান। **2.** (*Fig.*) To disorder the sense of ; to stupify ; (লক্ষণায়) বুদ্ধিভ্রষ্ট করা, বুদ্ধিলোপ করা ; হতবুদ্ধি করা। **—a'-tion,** *n.* Intoxication, (*lit.* & *fig.*) ; মত্ততাজনন, মত্ততা।

in-ē'-bri-āte, *adj.* & *n.* Drunk ; intoxicated ; (*fig.*) stupefied ; সুরামত্ত ; প্রমত্ত ; (লক্ষণায়) বুদ্ধিভ্রষ্ট। ***Noun.*** A habitual drunkard ; নিয়ত সুরাসেবী। **—bri'-e-ty,** *n.* Intoxication ; habit of drunkenness ; মত্ততা ; পানদোষ।

in-ĕd'-i-ble (-bl), *adj.* Unfit to be eaten ; অভক্ষ্য, অখাদ্য, অভোজ্য। **—bil'-i-ty,** *n.*

in-ĕd'-it-ĕd, *adj.* Unpublished ; published without editorial alterations ; অপ্রকাশিত ; অসম্পাদিত।

in-ĕf'-fa-ble (-ă-bl), *adj.* Unutterable ; indescribable ; অব্যক্ত ; অনির্ব্বচনীয়, অকথনীয়, অবর্ণনীয়, শব্দাতীত। **—bil'-i-ty,** *n.* The state of being ineffable ; অব্যক্ততা, অবর্ণনীয়তা। **—bly,** *adv.*

in-ĕf-face'-ă-ble (-bl), *adj.* Incapable of being effaced ; অনপনেয়, অমোচ্য, অবিলোপনীয়, অলোপনীয়। **—bly,** *adv.*

in-ĕf-fĕc'-tive (-tiv), *adj.* **1.** Not producing the intended effect ; অকার্য্যকর, ব্যর্থ, নিষ্ফল, বিফল, মোঘ, নিরর্থক। **2.** Wanting in artistic merit ; কলাকৌশলহীন। **3.** (Of a person) Inefficient ; অকর্ম্মণ্য। **—ly,** *adv.* **—ness,** *n.* The state of being ineffective ; নিষ্ফলতা, অকার্য্যকরতা, ব্যর্থতা, বিফলতা।

in-ĕf-fĕc'-tū-ăl, *adj.* Not effectual ; without effect ; fruitless ; নিষ্ফল, অফলজনক ; ব্যর্থ ; বিফল। **—ly,** *adv.* **—ness, —al'-i-ty,** *ns.*

in-ĕf-fi-ca'-cious (-shŭs), *adj.* (Of remedy etc.) Not producing the desired effect ; not efficacious ; অভীষ্ট-ফলপ্রদানাক্ষম ; মোঘ, অফলপ্রদ। **—ef'-fi-ca-cy, —ness,** *ns.* Want of efficacy ; অভীষ্ট ফলপ্রদানাভাব, ব্যর্থতা, নিষ্ফলতা। **—ly,** *adv.* Not efficaciously ; ব্যর্থভাবে।

in-ĕf-fi'-cien-cȳ (-shĕn), *n.* Want of efficiency ; incapacity ; ineffectiveness ; অযোগ্যতা ; অপারগতা, অসামর্থ্য ; নিষ্ফলতা, বিফলতা।

in-ĕf-fi'-cient (-shĕnt), *adj.* **1.** Not efficient or well qualified ; incompetent ; গুণবিহীন, অনুপযুক্ত, অক্ষম, অপারগ ; অযোগ্য, অনুপযুক্ত। **2.** Ineffective ; not producing the desired effect ; বিফল ; অভীষ্ট ফলপ্রদানাক্ষম। **—ly,** *adv.*

in-ē-lăs'-tic, *adj.* **1.** Not elastic ; wanting in elasticity ; অস্থিতিস্থাপক ; অসঙ্কোচনীয়। **2.** (*Fig.*) Unadaptable ; as, Buddhism did not seem to be *inelastic* ; (লক্ষণায়) অনুপযোগী। **—tic'-i-ty,** *n.*

in-ĕl'-ē-gance (-găns), **—găn-cȳ,** *ns.* **1.** Want of elegance ; want of beauty, refinement or polish in language, manners, etc. ; অলাবণ্য, অমাধুর্য্য, অচারুতা, অকমনীয়তা ; সৌন্দর্য্যাভাব, শোভাহীনতা, শোভারাহিত্য, অমার্জ্জিত ভাব। **2.** Anything inelegant ; as, *inelegancies* of style ; অশোভন বস্তু।

in-ĕl'-ē-gănt, *adj.* **1.** Ungraceful ; unrefined ; unpolished ; কমনীয়তাশূন্য, চারুতাবিহীন, মাধুর্য্যবিহীন, অসুন্দর, অশোভন ; সুরুচিবহির্ভূত ; অমার্জ্জিত। **—ly,** *adv.* In an inelegant manner ; অশোভনভাবে, অমার্জ্জিতভাবে।

in-ĕl'-i-gi-ble (-bl), *adj.* Not capable, or worthy, of being elected or chosen ; অনির্ব্বাচনযোগ্য, অমনোনয়নযোগ্য, অযোগ্য, অনধিকারী। **—bil'-i-ty,** *n.* State of being ineligible ; অযোগ্যতা, অনধিকারিতা। **—bly,** *adv.*

in-ĕl'-ō-quĕnt, *adj.* Not eloquent ; অবাগ্মী, বাক্পটুতাহীন। **—ly,** *adv.*

in-ē-lūc'-tā-ble (-bl), *adj.* Inevitable ; অপরিহার্য্য, অনিবার্য্য।

in-ĕpt', *adj.* **1.** (*Archaic*) Unfit ; unsuitable ; অযোগ্য ; অনুপযুক্ত, অনুপযোগী। **2.** Absurd ; foolish ; অসঙ্গত, অযৌক্তিক, অযুক্ত ; নির্ব্বুদ্ধিতাপ্রসূত। **3.** Inappropriate ; out of place ; অনুপযোগী ; বেমানান। **—i-tude,** *n.* **1.** State of being inept ; unsuitableness ; incapacity ; অযোগ্যতা ; অনুপযোগিতা ; অক্ষমতা। **2.** Silliness ; a foolish act or remark ; নির্ব্বুদ্ধিতা ; নির্ব্বোধোচিত উক্তি বা আচরণ। **—ly,** *adv.* **—ness,** *n.*

in-ĕ-qual′-i-tў (-kwŏl-), *n.* **1.** Want of equality; difference; dissimilarity; অসমতা, অসাম্য, অসমানতা; বৈষম্য, পার্থক্য; অতুল্যতা (হিঃ কোঃ), বিষমতা (ঐ), বৈভিন্ন্য, বিভিন্নতা, অসাদৃশ্য, বৈসাদৃশ্য। **2.** Unevenness, as of a surface; বন্ধুরতা, উচ্চাবচতা। **3.** Changeableness; inconstancy; পরিবর্তনশীলতা, পরিবর্তনীয়তা; অস্থিরতা। **4.** (*Astron.*) Deviation from uniformity in the motion of a heavenly body; (জ্যোতিবিজ্ঞান) জ্যোতিষ্কের গতিবৈষম্য, বিষমতা (হিঃ কোঃ)।

in-ē-qui-lăt′-ĕr-ăl (-kwî-), *adj.* Having unequal sides; বিষমবাহু।

in-eq′-ui-ta-ble (-ĕk-wî-tă-bl), *adj.* Unfair; not just; অনুচিত; অন্যায়। **bly,** *adv.*

in-eq′-ui-tў (-ĕk-wî-), *n.* **1.** Want of equity; unfairness; অবিচার; অন্যায় বিচার, অসাধুতা। **2.** An unfair matter or action; অন্যায় কার্য্য, অন্যায়।

in-ē-răd′-i-că-ble (-bl), *adj.* Incapable of being eradicated or rooted out; অনুন্মূলনীয়। **—bly,** *adv.*

in-êr′-ra-ble (-ă-bl), *adj.* Not liable to err; unerring; অভ্রান্তিশীল, ভ্রমাযোগ্য; অভ্রান্ত।

in-êr′-răn-cў, —ra-bil′-i-tў (-ă-), *ns.* Freedom from error; ভ্রান্তিমুক্তি। **—rant,** *adj.* Unerring; অভ্রান্ত।

in-êrt′, *adj.* **1.** Without natural power of action, motion or resistance; জড়, অচেতন, নিশ্চল। **2.** Without active chemical or other properties; সক্রিয় রাসায়নিক বা অন্যবিধ কর্ম্মবিহীন, নিষ্ক্রিয় (ব্রজ: হিন্দু)। **3.** Sluggish; inactive; slow; dull; অলস, কুঁড়ে; নিশ্চেষ্ট, নিষ্ক্রিয়, জড়, অচেষ্ট; মন্থর, মন্দগামী, অত্বরিত, অক্ষিপ্র; ঢিলা। **—ly,** *adv.* **—ness,** *n.* State of being inert; sluggishness; জড়তা, জাড্য; অলসতা, ঢিলামি।

in-êr′-ti-ă (-shî-), *n.* **1.** The inherent property of matter by which it tends to remain for ever at rest or in motion when moving; চলৎ অথবা নিশ্চল বস্তুর তদবস্থায় স্থিতিপ্রবণতা, জড়তা (হিঃ কোঃ), জড়ত্ব (হিঃ কোঃ), অকর্ম্মত্ব (ঐ)। **2.** Want of energy; sluggishness; sloth; জড়তা, জড়িমা (রবীঃ), জাড্য; আলস্য, নিৰ্জ্জীবতা, নিশ্চেষ্টতা, মান্দ্য; অনুদ্যোগ, তামসিক নিশ্চেষ্টতা, তমোগুণ।

in-ĕr′-ū-dīte, *adj.* Unlearned; ignorant; অশিক্ষিত, অবিদ্বান, অপণ্ডিত (হিঃ কোঃ); অজ্ঞ, মূর্খ।

in-ĕs-căp′-ă-ble (-bl), *adj.* Not to be escaped; inevitable; অপরিহার্য্য, অপরিত্যাজ্য; অনিবার্য্য, অবশ্যম্ভাবী।

in-ĕs-sĕn′-tial (-shăl), *adj.* Not essential or indespensable; immaterial; অপ্রধান, অসারভূত; অনাবশ্যক।

in-ĕs′-ti-mă-ble (-bl), *adj.* **1.** Too great to be estimated; priceless; অপরিমেয়, অগণ্য, অনিরূপ্য; অমূল্য, অনর্ঘ্য। **2.** Excellent; অত্যুৎকৃষ্ট, পরমোত্তম, অত্যুত্তম। **—bly,** *adv.* In an inestimable manner; অপরিমেয়রূপে।

in-ĕv′-i-tă-ble (-bl), *adj.* Unavoidable; certain to take place; অনিবার্য্য, অপরিহার্য্য, অবর্জ্জনীয়; অবশ্যম্ভাবী, ভবিতব্য, নিশ্চিত। **—bil′-i-ty, —ness,** *ns.* The quality of being inevitable; অপরিহার্য্যতা, অনিবার্য্যতা, অবশ্যম্ভাবিত্ব, ভবিতব্যতা। **—bly,** *adv.* Unavoidably; অনিবার্য্যরূপে, নিশ্চয়ই, অবশ্যম্ভাবিরূপে। **The inevitable**—That which is sure to happen; অবশ্যম্ভাবী বিষয়।

in-ex-ăct′ (-ĕgz-), *adj.* **1.** Not precisely correct or true; inaccurate; অযথার্থ; অশুদ্ধ, অঠিক। **2.** Not rigorous or careful as reason etc.; অকঠোর। **—i tude, —ness,** *ns.* **—ly,** *adv.*

in-ĕx-cit′-a-ble (-ĭt-ă-bl), *adj.* Not susceptible of excitement; অনুত্তেজনীয়, অক্ষোভনীয়, অক্ষোভ্য।

in-ĕx-cūs′-ă-ble (-bl), *adj.* Not justifiable; unpardonable; অসমর্থনীয়; অমার্জ্জনীয়, অক্ষমণীয়, অক্ষন্তব্য, অক্ষমার্হ, অক্ষমাযোগ্য। **—bly,** *adv.* **—ness,** *n.*

in-ĕx′-ē-cūt-ă-ble (-bl), *adj.* Incapable of being executed or performed; অসাধ্য, দুষ্কর।

in-ex-haust′-i-ble (-ĕgz-hăst-î-bl), *adj.* **1.** That cannot be exhausted, consumed or spent; অনিঃশেষণীয়, অক্ষয়, অফুরন্ত, অক্ষয়ণীয়, অশক্যক্ষয়, অব্যয়. **2.** Incapable of being worn out as a person, his energy, etc.; অক্ষয্য। **—bil′-i-ty, —ness,** *ns.* **—bly,** *adv.*

in-ex-ist′-ĕnt (-ĕgz-), *adj.* Indwelling; inherent; অন্তরস্থ, হৃদয়স্থ, হৃৎস্থিত; সহজাত, অন্তর্নিহিত।

in-ĕx′-ō-ră-ble (-bl), *adj.* Not to be persuaded by entreaty or prayer; relentless; দৃঢ়চিত্ত, নাছোড়বান্দা, নানুরোধ্য, দুরারাধ্য, অনারাধ্য, অপ্রসাদ্য, অপ্রাসদনীয়, অননুনেয়, অবিনেয়; নির্দ্দয়, নিষ্ঠুর, পাষাণহৃদয়, কঠোরহৃদয়, নির্ম্মম। **—bly,** *adv.* **—ness,** *n.*

in ĕx-pĕct′-ănt, *adj.* Not expectant; অপ্রত্যাশী, অপ্রতিক্ষাকারী।

in-ĕx-pē′-di-ĕnt, *adj.* Not expedient; not advisable or judicious; অসঙ্গত, অনুচিত, অনুপযোগী, অযোগ্য, অযুক্ত; অপরামর্শসিদ্ধ, অযৌক্তিক। **—ence, —en-cy,** *ns.* State or quality of being inexpedient; অনুপযোগিতা, অনৌচিত্য, অপরামর্শসিদ্ধতা, অযৌক্তিকতা।

in-ĕx-pĕn′-sive (-sîv), *adj.* Not expensive; cheap; অমহার্ঘ; সস্তা, সুলভ।

in-ĕx-pē′-ri-ence (-ĕns), *n.* Want of experience; অননুভূতি, অননুভব, অনভিজ্ঞতা, অল্পদর্শিতা, অপক্কবুদ্ধিতা, অপরিপক্কতা। **—enced,** *adj.* Not experienced; অনভিজ্ঞ, অভূয়োদর্শী, অল্পদর্শী, অপরিপক্কবুদ্ধি।

in-ĕx-pêrt′, *adj.* Unskilled; অনিপুণ, অদক্ষ, অপটু, আনাড়ী, অকুশল, অবিদগ্ধ। **—ly,** *adv.* **—ness,** *n.*

in-ĕx′-pi-ă-ble (-bl), *adj.* 1. That cannot be expiated or atoned for; প্রায়শ্চিত্তাতীত, অমার্জ্জনীয়। 2. (Of resentment etc.) Implacable; (ক্রোধ সম্পর্কে) অশাম্য। **—bly,** *adv.* **—ness,** *n.*

in-ĕx′-pli-că-ble (-bl), *adj.* That cannot be explained; unaccountable; mysterious; অব্যাখ্যেয়, অব্যাখ্যাতব্য; দুর্ব্বোধ; রহস্যপূর্ণ। **—bil′-i-ty, —ness,** *ns.* **—bly,** *adv.*

in-ĕx-plĭc′-ĭt, *adj.* Not clearly expressed; vague; অস্পষ্ট, অপরিস্ফুট; অনির্দ্দিষ্ট। **—ly** *adv.* **ness,** *n.*

in-ĕx-plōr′-ā-ble (-bl), *adj.* That cannot be explored or discovered; অনাবিষ্করণীয়।

in-ĕx-plō′-sive (-siv), *adj.* Not explosive; অস্ফোটনশীল।

in-ĕx-prĕss′-i-ble (-bl) *adj.* & *n.* Incapable of being expressed in words; indescribable; অপ্রকাশনীয়, অনিবেদ্য, অনির্ব্বাচ্য, অনাখ্যেয়; বাক্যাতীত, অনির্ব্বচনীয়, অবর্ণনীয়, অকথ্য। **—bly** *adv.*

in-ĕx-prĕs′-sive (-ĭv), *adj.* Not expressive or significant; wanting in expression; অপ্রকাশক, অবাচক; দ্যোতনাহীন। **—ness,** *n.* **—ly,** *adv.*

in-ĕx-pug′-na-ble (-pū-nă-bl), *adj.* 1. Impregnable; unconquerable; অভেদ্য; অজেয়। 2. (*Fig.*) Incapable of being overthrown; stable; "*Impregnable* argument or dignity"; (লক্ষণায়) অখণ্ডনীয়, অকাট্য; অটল।

in-ĕx-tĕn′-si-ble (-bl), *adj.* Not extensible; অপ্রসার্য্য, অপ্রসরণার্হ (হিঃ কোঃ)।

in-ĕx-tin′-guish-a-ble (-tĭng-gwĭsh-ă-bl), *adj.* Incapable of being extinguished or quenched, (*lit.* & *fig.*); অনির্ব্বাপ্য, অনির্ব্বাণীয়, অনির্ব্বাণযোগ্য, অনাশনীয়।

in-ĕx′-tri-că-ble (-bl), *adj.* 1. From which one cannot escape; as, to get into an *inextricable* danger; অলঙ্ঘ্য, অনুদ্ধরণীয়, অমোচ্য, অনুদ্ধার্য্য, দুস্তর, দুস্তর্য্য, জটিল। 2. Incapable of being disentangled or solved, as a knot, problem, etc.; অমোচনীয়, অসমাধানযোগ্য।

in-făl′-li-bi-lism (-ĭ-), *n.* The dogma of Pope's infallibility; পোপের অভ্রান্ততা বাদ। **—list,** *n.* An adherent of this view; পোপের অভ্রান্ততাবাদী।

in-făl′-li-ble (-ĭ-bl), *adj.* 1. Incapable of erring; unerring; ভ্রমাতীত, স্খলনাতীত, ভ্রমাযোগ্য, অভ্রান্তিধর্ম্মা, অস্খলিতমতি, প্রমাদাতীত; অভ্রান্ত। 2. Not liable to fail; certain; as, *infallible* remedy, proof, etc.; অবিপ্লুতধী (হিঃ কোঃ), অমোঘ, অব্যর্থ; সংশয়াতীত, সুনিশ্চিত, ধ্রুব। **—bil′-i-ty, —ness,** *ns.* Inerribility; unfailing certainty; অভ্রান্তি; অমোঘত্ব, অচ্যুততা (হিঃ কোঃ)। **—bly,** *adv.* Unerringly; unfailingly; অব্যর্থরূপে, অভ্রান্তরূপে; নিশ্চিতরূপে, ধ্রুবরূপে।

in′-fă-mous (-mŭs), *adj.* 1. Of ill repute; notoriously vile; detestable; দুর্ণামগ্রস্ত, অপযশস্কর, অকীর্ত্তিকর; জঘন্য, গর্হিত; ঘৃণ্য, জুগুপ্সিত, ঘৃণিত, নিন্দার্হ। 2. Branded with infamy by the conviction of a crime; কারাবাসাদিজনিত কলঙ্কলিপ্ত। **—ly,** *adv.* With infamy; detestably; অপযশস্করভাবে; জঘন্য ভাবে। **—mize,** *v. t.* To make infamous; to defame; দুর্ণামগ্রস্ত করা, কলঙ্কিত করা; মানহানি করা। **—my, —ness,** *ns.* 1. Ill fame; public disgrace; অখ্যাতি, অপযশ; অসম্মান, কলঙ্ক, দুর্ণাম, অকীর্ত্তি, কুখ্যাতি, লোকাপবাদ (কৃঃ), বদ্‌নাম। 2. Shameful vileness; as, the *infamy* of an act; জঘন্যতা।

in′-fănt, *n.* & *adj.* 1. A babe; a child under 7 years of age; শিশু, বাল; ৭ বৎসরের অপেক্ষা কম বয়সের শিশু। 2. A minor; one under the age of 21 years; নাবালক, অপ্রাপ্ত ব্যবহার (কেঃঃ), অজ্ঞাত ব্যবহার (ঐ); ২১ বৎসরের নিম্নবয়স্ক ব্যক্তি। *Adj.* 1. Of, or pertaining to, infancy; tender; not mature; শৈশবকালীন, শৈশবকালসম্বন্ধীয়; কোমল; কচি, তরুণ, অপরিপক্ক, কাঁচা। 2. Intended for young children; as, *infant* school; শিশুদিগের জন্য অভিপ্রেত। **—fan-cy,** *n.* 1. The state or period of being an infant; childhood; শৈশবাবস্থা; শৈশব, বাল্য, বাল্যাবস্থা, শিশুকাল। 2. The first beginning or early state of anything; minority (to the end of one's 21st year); প্রারম্ভ, প্রথমাবস্থা; নাবালকত্ব। **—fan-tile, —fan-tine,** *adjs.* Of, or relating to, infants or infancy; childish; শৈশবকালীন, শিশুসম্বন্ধীয়; বালসুলভ, শৈশবসুলভ। **Treatment of infants**—কুমারভৃত্য (উদয়)।

in-făn′-tā, *n.* Daughter of the king and queen of Spain and Portugal esp. the eldest, who is not heir to the throne; স্পেন বা পর্টুগালের রাজপুত্রী—বিশেষতঃ সিংহাসনের উত্তরাধিকারিণী নন—এরূপ জ্যেষ্ঠা রাজকুমারী।

in-fan′-te (tā), *n.* A son of the king and queen of Spain or Portugal, except the eldest, being the heir-apparent; স্পেন বা পর্টুগাল রাজ্যের (জ্যেষ্ঠ ভিন্ন) রাজপুত্র।

in-făn′-ti-cīde, *n.* 1. Murder of a new-born child (esp. with mother's consent); (বিশেষতঃ মাতার মতানুসারে) নবজাত বালহত্যা, শিশুহত্যা, বালঘাত, বালবধ, শিশুবধ। 2. Custom of killing infants; নবজাতশিশুবধপ্রথা। 3. One who kills infants; শিশুঘাতক, শিশুবিনাশকারী, বালহন্তা, বালহিংসক। **—cid-al,** *adj.* Of, or pertaining to, infanticide; practising infanticide; শিশুহত্যাসম্বন্ধীয়; শিশুঘাতী, শিশুহত্যায় লিপ্ত, শিশুহত্যার অপরাধী।

in′-făn-try̆, *n.* Foot-soldiers; পদাতিক সৈন্য, পত্তি। **Infantry man**—পদাতিক সৈন্য। **Mounted**

infantry—যে সকল পদাতিক সৈন্য অশ্বপৃষ্ঠে এক স্থান হইতে অন্য স্থানে গমন করে, অশ্বারূঢ় পদাতিক।

in-făt′-ū-āte, *v. t.* **1.** To make foolish ; to affect with utter folly ; বিমূঢ় করা ; হতজ্ঞান করা, বুদ্ধিলোপ করা, হতবুদ্ধি করা, বুদ্ধিভ্রংশ করা। **2.** To inspire with extravagant passion ; প্রেমমুগ্ধ করা, প্রমত্ত করা, বিমুগ্ধ করা, বিমোহিত করা, সম্মোহিত করা। **—at-ed,** *adj.* Besotted ; inspired with foolish passion ; প্রমত্ত, বিমুগ্ধ ; বিমূঢ়। **—at-ed-ly,** *adv.* **—a′-tion,** *n.* Act of infatuating ; state of being infatuated ; an extravagant foolish passion ; মোহজনন ; হতবুদ্ধিতা, মূঢ়তা, নষ্টবিবেকতা, জ্ঞানভ্রংশতা, মোহাবিষ্টতা ; মোহ।

in-fea′-si-ble (-fē-zĭ-bl), *adj.* Impracticable ; অসাধ্য, দুষ্কর, দুঃসাধ্য, অশক্য। **—ness,** *n.* The quality of being infeasible ; অসাধ্যতা, দুষ্করতা, দুঃসাধ্যতা, অশক্যতা।

in-fĕct′, *v. t.* **1.** To taint or contaminate as air etc., with germs of disease etc. ; সংক্রামক ব্যাধির বীজ দ্বারা দূষিত করা, রোগসংক্রমিত করা। **2.** To communicate infection to ; as, to *infect* a person with a disease ; সংক্রামক-ব্যাধি সঞ্চার করা। **3.** (*Fig.*) To corrupt ; to contaminate ; দূষিত করা ; বিষাক্ত করা, কলুষিত করা। **4.** To imbue with an opinion, belief, etc. ; অনুরঞ্জিত করা, অনুসিক্ত করা। **5.** (Of feelings) To seize upon ; "Her gaiety *infected* him" ; অভিভূত করা। **—fec′-tive,** *adj.* **—fec-tiv′-i-ty, —fec′-tive-ness,** *ns.*

in-fĕc′-tion, *n.* **1.** The act of infecting ; communication of disease through air or water ; সঞ্চার ; বায়ু বা কীটাণুসহযোগে ব্যাধিসংক্রমণ, রোগসংক্রমণ। **2.** That which infects ; সংক্রামক। **3.** An infectious disease ; an epidemic ; সংক্রামক ব্যাধি ; ব্যাপক রোগ। **4.** Moral contamination ; নৈতিক অপবিত্রতা, কলুষ, কল্মষ। **5.** Diffusive influence of sympathy, example, etc. ; "The *infection* of his poetic enthusiasm" ; দৃষ্টান্ত, সমবেদনা, প্রভৃতির সঞ্চারী প্রভাব।

in-fĕc′-tious (-shŭs), *adj.* **1.** Capable of infecting with disease ; communicable by infection ; pestilential ; সংক্রামক ; সাংক্রামিক ; স্পর্শসঞ্চারী (cf. আময়ঃ স্পর্শসঞ্চারী—রাজতরঙ্গিণী)। **2.** Corrupting ; demoralizing ; দূষণ ; দুর্নীতিজনক। **3.** (Of emotions) Capable of being easily diffused ; catching ; as, *infectious* mirth ; আশু সম্প্রসারণশীল ; সংক্রামক। **—ly,** *adv.* **—ness,** *n.*

in-fē-li-cĭf′-ic, *adj.* Productive of unhappiness ; নিরানন্দজনক।

in-fē-lĭc′-i-tous (-tus), *adj.* **1.** Not happy ; unfortunate ; নিরানন্দ ; অকল্যাণকর, অকুশলকর। **2.** Not appropriate ; not well said or expressed, as a remark etc. ; অস্থষ্ঠু ; অকালোচিত, অসময়োচিত।

in-fē-lĭc′-i-tȳ, *n.* **1.** Unhappiness ; misery ; misfortune ; অসুখ, অকল্যাণ, দুর্ভাগ্য, অকুশলতা, অশ্রেয়স্, অক্ষেম ; দুঃখ, দুর্দশা ; দুর্ভাগ্য। **2.** Inappropriateness ; unsuitableness of expression etc. ; অসুষ্ঠুতা ; অনুপযোগিতা। **3.** An act, word, expression etc. which are infelicitious ; as, *infelicities* of speech ; অসুষ্ঠু প্রয়োগ, অকালোচিত কার্য্য বা উক্তি।

in-fêr′, *v. t.* **1.** To derive by deduction or induction ; to conclude ; সিদ্ধান্ত করা, অনুমান করা ; উপপাদন করা। **2.** To imply ; সূচনা করা। **—a-ble,** *adj.* Capable of being inferred ; অনুমেয়, উপপাদ্য।

in′-fêr-ence (-ĕns), *n.* **1.** The act or process of inferring ; তর্ক (হিঃ কোঃ), অনুমান (সাঃ পঃ), অন্বীক্ষা (হিঃ দঃ), অনুমিতি, নিগমন, তর্কসিদ্ধান্ত, অনুমানসিদ্ধান্ত। **2.** That which is inferred ; অনুমিত বিষয়। **—en′-tial,** *adj.* Deduced or deducible by inference ; অনুমেয়, উপপাদ্য। **—en′-tial-ly,** *adv.* **Immediate inference**—নিরপেক্ষানুমান (সাঃ পঃ)। **Mediate inference**—সাপেক্ষানুমান (সাঃ পঃ)।

in-fē′-rĭ-or (-ĕr), *adj.* & *n.* **1.** Situated below ; নিম্নস্থ, অধঃস্থ। **2.** Lower in rank, degree, quality, etc. (*to*) ; হীনতর, নিকৃষ্ট, অপকৃষ্ট, ন্যূন, অপর (হিঃ কোঃ)। **3.** Of no great value or excellence ; bad or poor ; "So *inferior* an acquaintance" ; অপকৃষ্ট, নিকৃষ্ট ; হীন, লঘু। **4.** (*Bot.*—of calyx) Below ovary ; (of ovary) below calyx ; (উদ্ভিদ্‌বিদ্যা) গর্ভাশয় বা ডিম্বকোষের নিম্নস্থ ; পুষ্পচ্ছদ বা পুষ্পকুণ্ডের নিম্নস্থ।

Inferior ovary.

5. (Of a planet) Nearer the sun than the earth ; (গ্রহসম্পর্কে) পৃথিবী হইতে যত দূরবর্ত্তী সূর্য্য হইতে তদপেক্ষা অল্পতর দূরবর্ত্তী, লঘু (হিঃ কোঃ)। **6.** (*Print.*) Standing at the bottom of ordinary letter, as in B_1, C_n 2 and *n* are *inferiors* ; (মুদ্রণ) সাধারণ অক্ষরের নিম্নে অবস্থিত। ***Noun.*** One inferior to another ; as, my or his *inferiors* ; পদমর্য্যাদা প্রভৃতিতে নিম্নতর ব্যক্তি। **—ly,** *adv.* **—or′-i-ty,** *n.* The state of being inferior ; হীনতা, অপকৃষ্টতা, অকপর্দ, অপরত্ব (হিঃ কোঃ)। **Inferior planets**—লঘুগ্রহ।

in-fêr′-năl, *adj.* **1.** Of, or relating to, the lower regions or hell ; অধোভুবনসম্বন্ধীয়, যমালয়সম্বন্ধীয়। **2.** Hellish ; devilish ; নরকসম্বন্ধীয়, নারকীয় ; পৈশাচিক। **3.** Detestable ; as, *infernal* mystery ; *infernal* fool ; জঘন্য। **—ly,** *adv.* **—nal′-i-ty,** *n.* **Infernal machine**—বোমা প্রভৃতি।

in-fêr′-nŏ, *n.* Hell (esp. referring to Dante's *Divine Comedy*) ; নরক।

in-fêr′-ra-ble (-ă-bl), *adj.* Same as INFERABLE.; অনুমেয় (হিঃ কোঃ), অনুমানসাধ্য (ঐ), তর্কণীয় (ঐ)।

in-fêr′-tîle (*or*-tîl), *adj.* Not fertile ; barren ; অনুর্ব্বর, অনুৎপাদী, অশস্যপ্রদ ; অফলপ্রসূ, বন্ধ্যা, নিষ্ফল, অফলপ্রদ, অল্পফল। **—til′-i-ty,** *n.*

in-fést′, *v. t.* To trouble greatly by frequency of presence ; to swarm in or about (a place); as, a sea *infested* with pirates; উত্ত্যক্ত করা, প্রপীড়িত করা, উপপ্লুত করা, উপদ্রুত করা ; আকীর্ণ করা। **—fes-ta′-tion,** *n.*

in-feu-dā′-tion (-fü-), *n.* Act of putting one in possession of an estate in fee ; যাজকোত্তর সম্পত্তির অধিকার প্রধান। **Infeudation of tithes** — Granting of tithes to laymen ; সাধারণ লোককে যাজকদিগের প্রাপ্য আয় বা উৎপাদিত শস্যের দশমাংশ প্রদান।

in-fib-ü-lā′-tion, *n.* Fastening of the sexual organs with a clasp to prevent copultation ; সঙ্গম প্রতিরোধের জন্য কুড়ুপ (আঁকড়া) দ্বারা স্ত্রী বা পুং জননেন্দ্রিয় বন্ধন বা নিরোধ।

in′-fi-dĕl, *adj.* & *n.* Not believing in religion ; of, or relating to, the unbelievers ; অবিশ্বাসী, নাস্তিকধর্ম্মী, বিধর্ম্মী, নিঃশ্রদ্ধ (হিঃ কোঃ) ; অবিশ্বাসিজনগণ সম্বন্ধীয়। ***Noun.*** **1.** One who does not believe in religion ; নাস্তিক, ধর্ম্মদ্বেষী। **2.** (*Hist.*) Heathen; a non-Christian ; প্রচলিত ধর্ম্মে অবিশ্বাসী ব্যক্তি, পৌত্তলিক ; খৃষ্টধর্ম্মে অবিশ্বাসী ব্যক্তি। **3.** (From Jewish or Mohammedan point of view) A disbeliever in the true religion ; সত্যধর্ম্মে অবিশ্বাসী, কাফের। **4.** One who does not believe in something specified ; as, a political *infidel* ; অবিশ্বাসী। **—del′-i-ty,** *n.* **1.** Want of faith in Christianity ; খৃষ্টধর্ম্মে অনাস্থা, খৃষ্টধর্ম্মে অবিশ্বাস। **2.** Unfaithfulness, esp. in marriage ; (স্বামীর পক্ষে) অন্য রমণীর সহিত ব্যভিচার, পারদারিকতা, পারদার্য্য, (পত্নীর পক্ষে) অপাতিব্রত্য, অসাধ্বীত্ব, জারকর্ম্ম। **—ize,** *v.t.* & *i.* To render infidel ; নাস্তিক করা।

in′-field (-fēld), *n.* A field near a farmhouse ; arable land ; কৃষিবাটীকার নিকটবর্ত্তী ক্ষেত্র; কর্ষণযোগ্য ভূমি।

in-fil′-têr, *v. t.* To filter in or through ; ছাঁকা।

in-fil′-trāte, *v. t.* & *i.* **1.** To cause to pass *through* or *into* as in filtering ; ছাঁকিবার সময় অনুপ্রবিষ্ট করা। **2.** To infuse or permeate as by filtration ; অনুপ্রবিষ্ট করা, পরিব্যাপ্ত করা। ***Verb i.*** To pass through or into a substance by filtration ; ছাঁকিবার কালে অনুপ্রবিষ্ট হওয়া। **—tra′-tion,** *n.*

in′-fi-nite (-nît), *adj.* & *n.* **1.** Unlimited ; boundless ; অসীম, অনাদ্যন্ত, অনন্ত (হিঃ কোঃ) ; অপার, অশেষ, অপরিমিত (মঃ ইঃ), অপ্রমেয় (ঐ), অমিত (হিঃ কোঃ), অপরিচ্ছিন্ন (ঐ)। **2.** Exceedingly great ; vast ; immense ; বিরাট; বিশাল; বিস্তীর্ণ। ***Noun.*** **1.** (*Cap.*, with *the*) God ; অনন্তদেব। **2.** (With *the*) Infinite space ; অসীম বা অনন্ত বস্তু, ভুমা। **3.** (With *pl. noun.*) Innumerable ; "*Infinite* pigs" ; অসংখ্য, অগণ্য। **4.** (*Gram.*—of parts of verbs) Not limited by number or person *e. g.* infinitive, gerund, etc. ; (ব্যাকরণ—ক্রিয়ার অংশসমূহ সম্পর্কে) বচন বা পুরুষদ্বারা অপরিচ্ছিন্ন। **—ly,** *adv.* **—ness,** *n.*

in-fin-i-tĕs′-i-măl, *adj.* & *n.* Infinitely or indefinitely small ; অতিসূক্ষ্ম, অনন্তসূক্ষ্ম, অণীয়ান (হিঃ কোঃ), অত্যন্তসূক্ষ্ম, আণুবীক্ষণিক। ***Noun.*** An infinitesimal amount or quanity ; অতি ক্ষুদ্র সংখ্যা। **—ly,** *adv.*

in-fin′-i-tive (-tîv), *adj.* & *n.* (*Gram.*—Of a mood or form of verb) Expressing the verbal notion without predicating it of any subject, *e. g. to see* etc. ; (ব্যাকরণ) কোন কর্ত্তার উদ্দেশ্যে অনুক্ত ক্রিয়াসূচক, ভাববাচক। ***Noun.*** The infinitive mood or form of a verb ; সাধারণরূপ (মঃ ইঃ), সামান্যরূপ (ঐ)। **—ti′-val,** *adj.*

in-fin′-i-tüde, —tŷ, *ns.* **1.** State of being infinite ; boundlessness ; immensity ; সীমাহীনতা, অপ্রমেয়তা (মঃ ইঃ) ; অবধিহীনতা (ঐ), অনন্ততা (হিঃ কোঃ), অসীমত্ব (ঐ) ; অপরিমিততা, বিশালতা। **2.** A boundless extent, amount or number, (with *of*) ; অনন্ত বিস্তার, অনন্তসংখ্যা। **3.** (Only *-ty, Math.*) An infinite quantity (symbol ∞) ; অনন্তসংখ্যা।

in-firm′ (-fêrm), *adj.* **1.** Weak ; feeble, esp. due to age ; দুর্ব্বল, ক্ষীণবল, ক্ষীণ, শিথিলশক্তি, অল্পবীর্য্য, অসমর্থ, ক্ষীণসত্ত্ব ; জরাতুর, জরাগ্রস্ত, জরাপরিণত, জরাজীর্ণ, অশক্ত, অক্ষম। **2.** Irresolute ; wavering ; "He was *infirm* of purpose" ; দুর্ব্বলমনাঃ, অকৃতসংকল্প, অস্থিরমতি ; অব্যবস্থিতচিত্ত, দ্বিধাকারী। **—fir′-mi-ty,** *n.* **1.** State of being infirm ; feebleness ; অল্পশক্তিত্ব, হীনশক্তিত্ব ; দৌর্ব্বল্য, ক্ষীণতা, জরাজীর্ণতা। **2.** A malady ; রোগ, পীড়া। **3.** Weakness of mind or resolution ; দুর্ব্বলচিত্ততা, চিত্তদৌর্ব্বল্য, হৃদয়দৌর্ব্বল্য, অদৃঢ়চিত্ততা। **4.** A failing ; a defect ; as, a man should bear his friend's *infirmities* ; ত্রুটী, দোষ ; কসুর, খুঁত, অপূর্ণতা। **—ly,** *adv.*

in-fir′-mā-rŷ (-fêr-), *n.* **1.** A hospital ; রুগ্নাবাস, আরোগ্যশালা, চিকিৎসালয়। **2.** The sick quarters in a work-house, school or other institutions ; দরিদ্রশালা, বিদ্যালয়, প্রভৃতির রুগ্নাবাস।

in-fix′, *v. t.* **1.** To set in or fix by piercing ; বসান, দৃঢ়সংলগ্ন করা, পোতা। **2.** To inculcate; to impress; as, to *infix* a fact in the memory or mind ; মনোমধ্যে প্রবিষ্ট করা ; মনোমধ্যে মুদ্রিত করা। 3. (*Gram.*) To insert as an infix in a word ; (ব্যাকরণ) কোন শব্দের মধ্যে আকার বা রূপান্তরপ্রদ অংশ অন্তর্নিবিষ্ট করা।

in'-fix, *n.* (*Gram.*) A formative or modifying element inserted in a word ; (ব্যাকরণ) কোন শব্দের মধ্যে অন্তর্নিবিষ্ট আকার বা রূপান্তরপ্রদ শব্দ।

in-flame', *v.t.* & *i.* **1.** To set ablaze ; to kindle ; জ্বালান ; প্রজ্বালিত করা। **2.** To redden as if with flame ; "The red sky *inflames* the river" ; অগ্নিশিখাবৎ লোহিত করা। **3.** To kindle or excite passionately ; সন্ধুক্ষিত করা, উত্তেজিত করা, উদ্দীপিত করা। **4.** To enrage ; কোপ-জ্বলিত করা, রোষপ্রজ্বলিত করা। **5.** To raise to a feverish or morbid heat, as body, blood, etc. ; to make morbidly red and swollen ; as, to *inflame* the eyes with crying ; উত্তপ্ত করা, সন্তাপিত করা ; প্রদাহিত করা, লাল করা ও ফুলান। **6.** To aggravate ; as, to *inflame* an existing animosity ; বর্দ্ধিত করা। ***Verb i.*** **1.** To burst into flame ; জ্বলিয়া উঠা। **2.** To become excited or angered ; উত্তেজিত বা ক্রুদ্ধ হওয়া, কোপজ্বলিত হওয়া। **3.** To become morbidly inflamed ; প্রদাহিত হওয়া। **—flamed',** *adj.*

in-flăm'-ma-ble (-ă-bl), *adj* & *n.* **1.** Capable of being easily set on fire ; combustible ; আশুজ্বলনীয় ; দাহ্য, প্রজ্বলনশীল, দহনশীল, দহনীয়। **2.** Easily excited ; সহজে উত্তেজিত, আশুক্রোধী। ***Noun.*** An inflammable substance ; দাহ্যবস্তু। **—bil'-i-ty, —ness,** *ns.* **—bly,** *adv.*

in-flăm-ma'-tion (-ā-), *n.* **1.** The act of inflaming ; state of being inflamed ; প্রজ্বলন, দাহ, দাহন, উদ্দীপন, দীপন, তাপন, সন্তাপন প্রদীপন ; প্রদীপ্ততা, উদ্দীপ্ততা, সন্তপ্ততা। **2.** The morbid state of a part of the body characterised by heat, swelling, pain and redness ; প্রদাহ। **3.** Violent excitement ; তীব্র উত্তেজনা।

in-flăm'-ma-tŏ-rȳ (-ă-), *adj.* **1.** (*Obs.*) Tending to inflame or kindle ; (অপ্রঃ) প্রদীপনশীল, দাহক, তাপক, বিদাহী। **2.** Tending to excite passion or desire (often in a bad sense) ; seditious ; ক্রোধোদ্দীপক, উত্তেজক, উত্তেজনাপূর্ণ ; বিদ্রোহোত্তেজক। **3.** Relating, or tending, to the inflammation of the body ; প্রাদাহিক, তাপকারক, তাপজনক। **Inflammatory fever**—প্রদাহজ্বর।

in-flate' *v. t.* & *i.* **1.** To swell with air or gas ; to distend ; বায়ু দ্বারা স্ফীত করা ; স্ফীত করা। **2.** To swell or elate with pride etc. ; ফুলাইয়া তোলা, ফুলান, ফাঁপাইয়া তোলা। **3.** To increase artificially as price etc. ; কৃত্রিম উপায়ে বৃদ্ধি করা। ***Verb i.*** To distend ; স্ফীত হওয়া। **—flat'-ed,** *p. p.* **1.** Swollen by air or gas ; বাতপূরিত, বায়ুস্ফীত। **2.** Bombastic, as language etc. ; বাগাড়ম্বরপূর্ণ, শব্দাড়ম্বরপূর্ণ। **—fla'-tion,** *n.* **1.** Distention ; প্রসর, স্ফীতি। **2.** Vanity ; গর্ব্ব, বড়াই। **3.** Undue expansion or increase in paper money, price, etc. ; নোট, মূল্য, প্রভৃতির অত্যধিক প্রচার বা বৃদ্ধি।

in-flĕct', *v. t.* **1.** To bend or curve ; বক্র করা, বাঁকান। **2.** (*Gram.*) To vary in the terminations ; (*mus.*) to modulate, as the voice ; (ব্যাকরণ) ধাতুরূপ করা, পদসাধন করা, বিভক্তি করা, সাধন করা ; (সঙ্গীত-শাস্ত্র) মূর্চ্ছনা দেওয়া।

in-flĕc'-tion, in-flĕx'-ion (flĕk-shŏn), *n.* **1.** Act of inflecting ; a bend ; a curve ; বক্রীভবন ; মোড় ; বাঁক। **2.** Modulation of voice ; মূর্চ্ছনা। **3.** Grammatical variation of nouns, verbs, etc. ; বিভক্তি, শব্দরূপ, ধাতুরূপ। **4.** An inflected form of a word ; the inflectional suffix or element ; বিভক্তি বা প্রত্যয়যুক্ত শব্দ ; বিভক্তি, (noun inflection)। **5.** (*Geom.*) Change of curvature from convex to concave ; (জ্যামিতি) বহির্বর্তুল বক্র সংবৃত্তমধ্য বক্রে পরিবর্তন। **—al,** *adj.* Of, or relating to, grammatical inflection ; রূপান্তর সম্বন্ধীয়।

in-flĕc'-tive (-tiv), *adj.* (*Gram.*) Relating to, or subject to, inflection ; রূপান্তর সম্বন্ধীয়, ধাতুরূপসাধ্য।

in-flĕx'-i-ble (-bl), *adj.* **1.** That cannot be bent ; অনমনীয়, নমনাশক্য। **2.** (*Fig.*) Unbending ; rigid ; inexorable ; (লক্ষণায়) অনম্র ; কঠিন, শক্ত, দৃঢ় ; দৃঢ়সঙ্কল্প। **—bil'-i-ty,** *n.* **—bly,** *adv.* The quality of being inflexible ; অনমনীয়তা, সুদৃঢ়তা।

in-flict', *v. t.* To lay on, as a stroke, blow or wound ; to cause to be borne ; to impose ; as, to *inflict* punishment, suffering, loss etc. on a person ; বসান ; বহন করান ; প্রয়োগ করা, বিধান করা। **—a-ble,** *adj.* **—flic'-tion,** *n.* **1.** Act of inflicting or imposing ; বিধান, প্রয়োগ। **2.** That which is inflicted, as punishment, pain, etc. ; বিহিত দণ্ড।

in-flō-rĕs'-cence (-sĕns), *n.* **1.** The process of flowering (*lit.* & *fig.*) ; পুষ্পবিকাশপ্রণালী। **2.** (*Bot.*) The general arrangement of flowers on an axis ; (উদ্ভিদ্-বিদ্যা) পুষ্প-বিন্যাস (সাঃ পঃ)। **3.** Flowers collectively of a plant ; কোন বৃক্ষের পুষ্পপুঞ্জ।

in'-flow (-flō), *n.* The act of flowing in ; influx ; মধ্যে প্রবহণ ; প্রবাহ। **—ing,** *adj.* & *n.*

in'-flū-ence (-ĕns), *n.* & *v. t.* **1.** (*Astron.*) The supposed flowing from stars of an ethereal fluid affecting character and destiny of men ; (জ্যোতির্বিজ্ঞান) গ্রহের প্রভাব,

গ্রহাবেশ। **2.** Action exercised invisibly or insensibly (*upon*); as, to be under the *influence* of religious zeal; credit; প্রভাব, অনুভাব (হিঃ কোঃ); খ্যাতি, প্রতিষ্ঠা, প্রতিপত্তি। **3.** Ascendant or moral power; control; as, to have *influnce over* or *with* a person; প্রভাব; কর্তৃত্ব। **4.** Something that exerts influence; an influential person; প্রভাববিস্তারক বস্তু; প্রভাবশালী ব্যক্তি। **5.** (*Elec.*) Induction; (তাড়িত-বিদ্যা) তাড়িতপ্রবর্তন। ***Verb t.*** **1.** To exercise influence upon; প্রভাববিস্তার করা, প্রভাবিত করা। **2.** To move or induce by influence; to affect; বিচলিত করা; বিকার উৎপাদন করা। **Latent influence**—গুপ্তপ্রভাব (হিঃ কোঃ) গুপ্তগুণ (ঐ)। **Under the influence of**—See INFLUENCE 2. **Planetary influence**—See INFLUENCE 1.

in'-flü-ěnt, *adj.* & *n.* **1.** Flowing in, (*lit.* & *fig.*); অন্তঃপ্রবাহী। ***Noun.*** A tributary or affluent; শাখানদী, উপনদী।

in-flü-ěn'-tial (-shăl), *adj.* Having or exerting influence; ক্ষমতাসম্পন্ন, প্রতিষ্ঠাসম্পন্ন, প্রতিপত্তিশালী, প্রভাবশালী। **—ly,** *adv.*

in-flü-ěn'-ză, *n.* **1.** An epidemic catarrh; প্রবল সর্দ্দি হইতে জাত ব্যাপক জ্বররোগ বিশেষ, বহুব্যাপক প্রতিশ্যায় (হঃ চঃ), পিনস (ঐ)। **2.** (*Fig.*) A mental or commercial epidemic; ব্যাপক মানসিক বিকার, দেশব্যাপী বাণিজ্য সংক্রান্ত বিশৃঙ্খলা।

in'-flŭx, *n.* **1.** Act of flowing in, esp. of a stream etc. into a river; আগম, প্রবাহ, প্রস্রবণ। **2.** Inpouring as of men, things, etc. *into* a place; আমদানী।

in-fŏrm', *v. t.* & *i. n.* **1.** To tell; to acquaint; as, to *inform* one of a thing; সংবাদ দেওয়া; জ্ঞাত করা, বিদিত করা, জানান। **2.** To animate; to inspire; as, to *inform* one with a principle; জীবনসঞ্চার করা; অনুপ্রাণিত করা। ***Verb i.*** To bring a charge (*against*); কাহারো বিরুদ্ধে অভিযোগ উপস্থাপিত করা। **—ant,** *n.* One who gives information; an informer; সংবাদদাতা, বিজ্ঞাপক; গোয়েন্দা। **—er,** *n.* **1.** One who informs; বিজ্ঞাপক। **2.** One who informs against another; one who informs a magistrate of a violation of a law, (also called a *common informer*); বিজ্ঞাপক; গোয়েন্দা, গুপ্তচর, সূচক (শুক্রঃ ন্নিনয়ঃ)।

in-fŏr'-măl, *adj.* Not according to due form; irregular; without ceremony or formality; unusual; রীতিবিরুদ্ধ, অশাস্ত্র, বিধিবিরুদ্ধ; অনিয়মিত: লৌকিকতাশূন্য; অপ্রচলিত। **—mal'-i-ty,** *n.* State of being informal; বিধিবিরুদ্ধতা, নিয়মবিরুদ্ধতা, নিয়মব্যতিক্রম, বিধিব্যতিক্রম।

in-fŏr-mā'-tion, *n.* **1.** Act of informing; জ্ঞাপন, সংবাদপ্রদান। **2.** Intelligence; news; সংবাদ, সমাচার; বৃত্তান্ত, সন্দেশ, খবর, বার্ত্তা। **3.** A charge or accusation lodged with a magistrate or court; আদালতে উপস্থাপিত অভিযোগ। **—al,** *adj.*

in-fŏrm'-ă-tive (-tĭv), *adj.* Imparting knowledge; শিক্ষাপ্রদ। **—to-ry,** *adj.* Full of information; imparting instruction; নানাতথ্যসম্বলিত; শিক্ষাপ্রদ।

in-formed' (-fŏrmd), *adj.* Having information; instructed; educated; intelligent; as, well or ill *informed* public; বিজ্ঞাপিত, বিদিত, অবগত; শিক্ষাপ্রাপ্ত; শিক্ষিত; বুদ্ধিমান।

in'-fră, *adv.* Below; beneath; further on (esp. in a book); as, see *infra* (see below); নীচে; নিম্নে; আরও পরে। **Infra-sensible**—অতীন্দ্রিয়।

in-frăc'-tion, *n.* Violation; breach; লঙ্ঘন, ব্যতিক্রম; ভঙ্গ।

in-fră-dig', (*Abbr.* of *L. infra dignitatem*) *pred. adj.* Beneath one's dignity; undignified; কাহারো পক্ষে অগৌরবজনক; অমর্য্যাদাজনক।

in-frē'-quěnt, *adj.* **1.** Seldom occurring; rare; কচিদ্দৃষ্ট, কদাচিৎ সংঘটিত, কাদাচিৎক; অসতত, অপৌনঃপুনিক। **2.** Occurring or placed at wide distances apart; as, *infrequent* openings in a wall; অনেক দূরে দূরে স্থাপিত। **—ly,** *adv.* Rarely; কদাচিৎ, কালেভদ্রে, কচিৎ। **—quen-cy,** *n.* Uncommonness; rarity; অসাধারণত্ব; বিরলতা।

in-fringe' (-frĭnj), *v. t.* To break or violate as a law, contract, etc.; ভঙ্গ করা, লঙ্ঘন করা, অমান্য করা। **—ment,** *n.* Violation; breach; লঙ্ঘন, ব্যতিক্রম; ভঙ্গ।

in-frŭc'-tü-ous (-ŭs), *adj.* **1.** Not fruitful; barren; অফলপ্রসূ; অবন্ধ্য, অনুৎপাদক, উষর। **2.** (*Fig.*) Fruitless; (লক্ষণায়) নিষ্ফল।

in'-fü-lă, *n.* (*Rom. antiq.*) A fillet worn as a badge of priestly, sacrificial or royal consecration; (রোমীয় প্রত্নতত্ত্ব) পৌরোহিত্য, যজ্ঞকার্য্য বা রাজপদে দীক্ষা বা অভিষেকের চিহ্নস্বরূপ শিরোবন্ধনী।

Infula.

in-fŭn-dĭb'-ü-lar (-lêr), *adj.* Funnel-shaped; ফুঁদেলের আকার।

in-fü'-ri-āte, *v. t.* & *adj.* To render furious; to enrage; রাগান্বিত করা, ক্রোধান্ধ করা; ক্রোধবিক্ষিপ্ত করা, ক্রোধোন্মত্ত করা। ***Adj.*** Enraged; maddened; ক্রুদ্ধ; উন্মত্ত, ক্ষিপ্ত। **—a'-tion,** *n.*

in-füse', *v. t.* **1.** To pour in or into; ঢালা বা ঢালিয়া দেওয়া। **2.** (*Fig.*) To instill as life, spirit or quality etc. *into*; to inculcate; অনুপ্রবিষ্ট করা, নিষেক করা, সঞ্চারিত করা, অন্তর্নিবিষ্ট করা; পুনঃ পুনঃ উপদেশ দ্বারা মনোমধ্যে অঙ্কিত করা। **3.** To steep in a liquid without boiling for extracting useful qualities ; as, to *infuse* herb, tea, etc. ; সার বাহির করার জন্য তরল পদার্থে ভিজাইয়া রাখা, ভাবনা করা। **—fus′-er,** *n.*

in-fū′-si-ble (bl), *adj.* **1.** Not capable of being fused or dissolved ; অদ্রবণীয়, অগলনীয়, অদ্রাব্য। **—bil′-i-ty,** *n.*

in-fū′-sion (-zŭn), *n.* **1.** Act of infusing (*lit.* & *fig.*) ; অনুপ্রবেশ, নিষেক। **2.** The steeping in water of some substance to extract its virtues ; a liquid extract thus obtained ; (ভাবনা (যোঃ) ; শীতকষায় (বনঃ), ফান্ট (ঠাকুরঃ), রস (হিঃ কোঃ), আরক (ঐ)। **3.** A tincture ; an admixture ; আসব ; মিশ্র। **4.** (*Surg.*) Injection : (অস্ত্রোপচারবিদ্যা) পিচকারী দ্বারা চর্ম্মাভ্যন্তরে ঔষধ প্রক্ষেপ, পিচকারীকরণ।

in-fū-sō′-ri-ă, *n.* A class of minute microscopic animals found in organic infusions ; কষায়কীট (সাঃ পঃ), সূক্ষ্মদেহী। **—al,** *adj.* Relat-

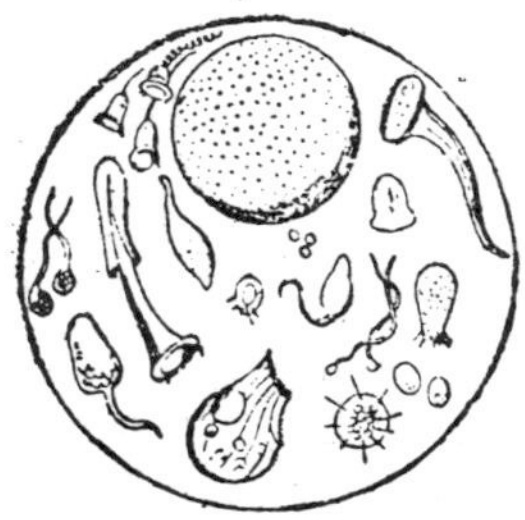

Magnified drop of water, showing infusoria.

ing, or pertaining, to infusoria ; কষ। **—an, —fu′-so-ry,** *adj.* & *n.* Same as INFUSORIAL. (*Noun*) One of the infusoria ; সূক্ষ্ম কীট।

in′-găth-ĕr-ing, *n.* Act of gathering in ; collecting of harvest ; সঞ্চয়, সংগ্রহ ; শস্যসংগ্রহ।

in-gĕm′-i-nāte, *v. t.* To repeat or reiterate ; আবৃত্তি করা, পুনরায় বলা।

in-gĕn′-i-ous (-ŭs), *adj.* **1.** Apt in contriving ; clever ; skilful ; দক্ষ, চতুর ; নিপুণ ; পটু। **2.** Skilfully contrived ; নিপুণভাবে উদ্ভাবিত। **—ly,** *adv.* In an ingenious manner ; cleverly ; নিপুণতার সহিত ; চতুরতার সহিত, দক্ষতার সহিত। **—ness,** *n.*

ingenue, (*F.*), *n.* An ingenuous girl or woman ; an actress representing such a person ; চতুরা রমণী, চতুরা বালিকা, চালাক মেয়ে ; যে অভিনেত্রী চতুরা রমণীর ভূমিকা অভিনয় করে।

in-gē-nū′-i-tȳ, *n.* **1.** Power of invention ; skill or cleverness in devising ; উদ্ভাবনশক্তি, উদ্ভাবন ক্ষমতা ; বুদ্ধিকৌশল, হেকমৎ, চাতুর্য্য, দক্ষতা, নিপুণতা। **2.** Cleverness of design or contrivance ; as, *ingenuity* of a plan ; গঠন-কৌশল, নির্ম্মাণ-কৌশল, রচনাকৌশল। **3.** An ingenious device or contrivance ; কল, কৌশল।

in-gĕn′-ū-ous (-ŭs), *adj.* **1.** Frank ; candid ; সরল, উদার ; অকপট, সাদা, শুভ্রচিত্ত। **2.** Innocent ; artless ; অমায়িক ; অকপট। **—ly,** *adv.*

in-gĕst′, *v. t.* To throw or take into the stomach, as food ; পাকস্থলীর মধ্যে গ্রহণ বা নিক্ষেপ করা, আহার করা। **—ges′-tion,** *n.* The act of ingesting ; আহরণ (সাঃ পঃ)। **—ges′-tive,** *adj.* Having the function of taking in food ; খাদ্যগ্রাহী।

in′-gle (ĭng-gl), *n.* Fire ; a fire on the hearth ; অগ্নি ; গৃহমধ্যস্থ অগ্নিকুণ্ডের জ্বলন্ত অগ্নি। **Ingle-corner—** CHIMNEY CORNER (which see).

in-glō′-ri-ous (-ŭs), *adj.* **1.** Not glorious ; obscure ; গৌরবহীন, খ্যাতিহীন ; অপ্রসিদ্ধ, অজ্ঞাত। **2.** Disgraceful ; shameful ; ignominious ; অপমানজনক, অগৌরবজনক ; লজ্জাকর ; অকীর্ত্তিকর, কলঙ্কজনক। **—ly,** *adv.* **—ness,** *n.*

in′-gō-ing, *adj.* & *n.* Going in ; অন্তর্গামী। ***Noun.*** Act of going in ; অন্তঃপ্রবেশ।

in′-gŏt, *n.* A mass of gold, silver, steel, etc. cast in a mould ; ছাঁচে ঢালিয়া গড়া স্বর্ণ, রৌপ্য বা ইস্পাতের পিণ্ড, ধাতুপিণ্ড, শিলা (হিঃ কোঃ)।

in-grain′ (-grān), *v. t.* See ENGRAIN.

in′-grain (-grān), *adj.* **1.** (*Dyeing*) Dyed in grain ; (রঞ্জন-বিদ্যা) কাঁচা অবস্থায় রঞ্জিত। **2.** Ingrained ; innate ; inherent ; "The *ingrain* humanity of his soul" ; অন্তর্নিহিত ; প্রকৃতিসিদ্ধ ; মজ্জাগত।

in′-grained (-grānd), *adj.* **1.** Deep-rooted ; inherent ; inveterate ; as, *ingrained* prejudice ; বদ্ধমূল ; প্রকৃতিসিদ্ধ, অন্তর্নিহিত ; মজ্জাগত। **2.** Thorough ; as, he is an *ingrained* sceptic ; পাকা, পুরা, ডাহা, বদ্ধ। **—grain′-ed-ly,** *adv.*

in′-grāte, *adj.* & *n.* (*Archaic*) Ungrateful (person) ; অকৃতজ্ঞ (ব্যক্তি) কৃতঘ্ন (ব্যক্তি)।

in-grā′-ti-āte (-shi), *v. t.* (Used *reflexively*) To bring into favour (*with*) ; অনুগ্রহভাজন করা, প্রীতিভাজন করা। **—at-ing-ly,** *adv.*

in-grăt′-i-tūde, *n.* Want of gratitude ; unthankfulness ; অকৃতজ্ঞতা ; কৃতঘ্নতা, নিমকহারামী (*colloq.*)।

in-gră-vĕs′-cent (-ĕnt), *adj.* (*Med.*) Gradually growing worse as a disease ; (ভৈষজ্য-শাস্ত্র) ক্রমশঃ মন্দের দিকে অগ্রসর। **—cence,** *n.*

in-grē′-di-ĕnt, *n.* A component part of a mixture ; an element or constituent ; মিশ্রপদার্থের উপদানীভূত বস্তু ; উপকরণ, অঙ্গ, অবয়ব (হিঃ কোঃ), সাধন (হিঃ কোঃ)।

in′-grĕss, *n.* **1.** The act of entering ; প্রবেশ, সমাবেশ, আগম। **2.** Right of entrance; প্রবেশাধিকার, **3.** (*Obs.*) The entrance of the sun into a sign of the zodiac ; (জ্যোতির্বিজ্ঞান) সংক্রান্তিকাল (হিঃ কোঃ), ভুমাপ্রবেশকাল (ঐ)।

in′-grow-ing (-grō-), *adj.* Growing inwards; অন্তর্বর্দ্ধী। **—growth,** *n.* Act of growing inwards ; that which grows inwards ; অন্তর্বর্দ্ধন ; অন্তর্বর্দ্ধী বস্তু। **Ingrowing nail**—যে নখের প্রান্ত নিকটবর্ত্তী মাংস পর্য্যন্ত বিস্তৃত হইয়া প্রদাহ, যন্ত্রণা, ইত্যাদি উৎপাদন করে।

in'-gui-năl (-gwĭ-), *adj.* Of, or pertaining to, the groins ; বঙ্ক্ষণ বা কুঁচকি সম্বন্ধীয় বা তৎপ্রদেশস্থ।

in-gŭlf', *v. t.* Same as ENGULF.

in-gur'-gĭ-tāte (-gêr-), *v. t.* **1.** To swallow or drink greedily ; পেটুকের মত গলাধঃকরণ করা, ঢক্ ঢক্ করিয়া পান করা। **2.** (*Fig.*) To swallow up as in a gulf ; গ্রাস করা। **—ta'-tion,** *n.*

in-hăb'-it, *v. t.* **1.** To live or dwell in ; to occupy, as a house, city, etc., (*lit.* & *fig.*) ; "The echo *inhabited* the valley" ; বাস করা, বসতি করা ; অধিকার করা। **—a-ble,** *adj.* Habitable ; বাসযোগ্য, নিবসনীয়। **—an-cy,** *n.* **1.** The act of inhabiting ; residence ; বাসকরণ, নিবসন ; বসতি, নিলয়, নিবাস। **—ant,** *n.* One who resides permanently in a place ; স্থায়ী অধিবাসী, নিবাসী (হিঃ কোঃ)। **—i-ta'-tion,** *n.* Act of inhabiting ; বাস, নিবসন।

in-hāle', *v. t.* To breathe in ; to draw into the lungs ; as, to *inhale* air, smoke of tobacco etc. ; নিশ্বাস গ্রহণ করা, শ্বাস লওয়া ; ফুসফুসের ভিতর নেওয়া। **—ha-la'-tion,** *n.* The act of inhaling ; that which is inhaled ; নিশ্বাসগ্রহণ, অন্তর্শ্বসন (হিঃ কোঃ), নিঃশ্বসন ; নিশ্বাস দ্বারা গৃহীত বস্তু।

in-hāl'-ēr, *n.* **1.** One who inhales ; নিশ্বাসগ্রহণকারী। **2.** An apparatus for inhaling any vapour or volatile substance for medicinal purposes etc. ; ফুসফুসে বাষ্পীয় কিম্বা জলীয়পদার্থ প্রবেশ করাইবার যন্ত্র-বিশেষ, ধূম বা বাষ্পাদি নিশ্বসনার্থ যন্ত্র-বিশেষ, শ্বসনযন্ত্র। **3.** A contrivance to filter as air ; a respiratory apparatus for divers ; বায়ু প্রভৃতি শোধনের জন্য যন্ত্র-বিশেষ ; ডুবুরীগণের নিশ্বাস গ্রহণের যন্ত্র।

in-hâr-mŏn'-ic, —i-căl, *adjs.* Not harmonic ; discordant ; তানলয়শূন্য ; বিস্বর, বেসুর।

in-hâr-mō'-ni-ous (-ŭs), *adj.* Not harmonious ; unmusical ; discordant ; অমিল, অনৈক্য বিশিষ্ট, বিরুদ্ধভাবপন্ন ; শ্রুতিকটু ; বেসুর, অসঙ্গত।

in-here' (-hēr), *v. i.* **1.** To exist ; to belong (*in*) ; as, a quality *inheres in* a person ; থাকা, অবস্থিত থাকা ; অন্তর্ভূত হওয়া। **2.** To be vested or inherent (*in* a person) as a right etc. ; অর্পিত হওয়া। **3.** (*Obs.*) To cleave (*to*) ; লাগিয়া থাকা, সংসক্ত হওয়া। **—her'-ence,** *n.* Act of inhering ; state of being inherent ; permanent existence, as of a quality etc. in a subject ; অধিষ্ঠান ; অন্তঃস্থিতি, সমবায় (হিঃ কোঃ) ; নিত্যসম্বন্ধ। **—her'-ent,** *adj.* **1.** (*Obs.*) Sticking fast ; দৃঢ়সংলগ্ন, দৃঢ়সম্পৃক্ত। **2.** Innate ; natural ; সহবর্ত্তী, সহজ, সহজাত, অন্তর্নিহিত, সামবায়িক ; স্বাভাবিক, স্বভাবসুলভ, স্বভাবসিদ্ধ, প্রকৃতিসিদ্ধ। **3.** Inalienable ; permanently existing, as a right, privilege, etc. ; অবিভেদ্য ; নিত্যসম্বন্ধ বিশিষ্ট, নিত্যবর্ত্তমান। **—her'-ent-ly,** *adv.* **—her'-ing,** Same as INHERENT.

in-hĕr'-it, *v. t.* & *i.* **1.** To take by descent from an ancestor as property etc. ; উত্তরাধিকারিরূপে পূর্ব্বপুরুষ হইতে প্রাপ্ত হওয়া। **2.** To be an heir to ; উত্তরাধিকারী হওয়া। **3.** To have by nature from a progenitor ; as, he *inherits* a strong constitution etc. ; পূর্ব্বপুরুষ হইতে স্বভাবতঃ প্রাপ্ত হওয়া। ***Verb i.*** To take property or rights by inheritance ; উত্তরাধিকারসূত্রে অধিকার করা। **—a-bil'-i-ty,** *n.* **—a-ble,** *adj.* **1.** Capable of being inherited ; উত্তরাধিকারসূত্রে প্রাপ্য। **2.** Entitled to succeed to property by legal right ; উত্তরাধিকারসূত্রে পাইবার অধিকারী।

in-hĕr'-it-ance (-ăns), *n.* **1.** The act of inheriting ; উত্তরাধিকারসূত্রে প্রাপ্ত হওন। **2.** A thing or property that is inherited (*lit.* & *fig.*) ; উত্তরাধিকারসূত্রে প্রাপ্ত বিষয় বা সম্পত্তি। **Right of inheritance**—Right to inherit property etc. from ancestors ; উত্তরাধিকার, দায় (হিঃ কোঃ)।

in-hĕr-i-tor (-têr), *n.* One who inherits ; উত্তরাধিকারী। **—tress, —trix,** *ns.* (*fem.*)

in-hē'-sion (-zŭn), *n.* Act of inhering ; inherence ; অধিষ্ঠান ; অন্তঃস্থিতি, অধিস্থিতি।

in-hib'-it, *v. t.* **1.** To prohibit ; as, to *inhibit* a person *from* doing something ; নিবারণ করা, নিষেধ করা, প্রতিষেধ করা। **2.** To hinder ; to check or restrain ; বাধা দেওয়া ; দমন করা। **3.** To forbid as an ecclesiastic to exercise clerical functions ; কোন যাজককে অযাজকীয় কার্য্য সম্পাদন করিতে নিষেধ করা। **—hi-bi'-tion,** *n.* Act of inhibiting ; prohibition ; স্তম্ভন (হিঃ কোঃ), নিষেধ, নিবারণ ; প্রতিষেধ, নিরোধ (ভক্তিঃ)। **—i-to-ry,** *adj.* Prohibitory ; নিষেধক, নিষেধাত্মক।

in-hŏs'-pi-tă-ble (-bl), *adj.* **1.** Not hospitable ; আতিথ্যবিমুখ, অনাতিথেয়, আতিথেয়তাশূন্য, আতিথেয়তাবিমুখ, অতিথিপরাঙ্মুখ, অভ্যাগতদ্বেষী। **2.** Affording no shelter or entertainment, as a desert etc. ; আশ্রয়শূন্য। **—bly,** *adv.* **—ness, —tal'-i-ty,** *ns.* The state of being inhospitable ; want of hospitality ; আতিথ্যবিমুখতা, অনাতিথেয়তা, অতিথিদ্বেষ, অভ্যাগতদ্বেষ, অতিথ্যনাদর ; আতিথ্যাভাব।

in-hū'-măn, *adj.* Brutal ; barbarous ; cruel ; পশুবৎ, পাশব, অমানুষিক ; বর্ব্বরোচিত ; নিষ্ঠুর, ক্রূর, নৃশংস, নির্দ্দয়। **—ly,** *adv.* In an inhuman manner ; নির্দ্দয়রূপে,

পশুবৎ, অমানুষিকরূপে। **—man′-i-ty,** *n.* Cruelty; নিষ্ঠুরতা, ক্রূরতা, অমানুষিকতা।

in-hūme′, *v. t.* To bury; to inter; সমাহিত করা, গোর দেওয়া; প্রোথিত করা। **—hu-ma′-tion,** *n.* Burial; সমাধি।

in-im′-i-căl, *adj.* **1.** Hostile; unfriendly (with *to*); প্রতিকূল, অননুকূল; বৈরভাবাপন্ন, পরিপন্থী, দ্বেষী (in compound)। **2.** Hurtful; injurious (*to*); পীড়াদায়ক; অনিষ্টজনক। **—cal′-i-ty,** *n.* Hostility; শত্রুতা। **—ly,** *adv.*

in-im′-i-tă-ble (-bl), *adj.* Incapable of being imitated or copied; matchless; অননুকরণীয়; অনুপম, অতুল, অপ্রতিম, অদ্বিতীয়। **—bil′-i-ty, —ness,** *ns.* **—bly,** *adv.*

in-iq′-ui-tў (-ĭk-wĭ-),*n.* **1.** Absence of righteousness or rectitude; wickedness; gross injustice; as, *iniquity* of bribery; অধার্ম্মিকতা, অন্যায়াচরণ; অসাধুতা; অবিচার, অন্যায়। **2.** (*Usu. pl.*) An iniquitous act; পাপকার্য্য, দোষের কার্য্য। **—tous,** *adj.* Unrighteous; unjust; wicked; অধার্ম্মিক; ন্যায়বিরুদ্ধ; দুষ্ট, অসাধু। **—tous-ly,** *adv.* In an unjust or iniquitous manner; অন্যায়রূপে।

in-i′-tial (-shăl), *adj., n.* & *v. t.* Pertaining to, existing, or occurring at, the beginning; as, *initial* symptoms of a disease; প্রাথমিক, আদ্য, প্রারম্ভিক, আদি। ***Noun.*** The initial letter of a word (esp. *pl.*); the first letters of a person's name or surname; কোন শব্দের আদ্যক্ষর; কোন লোকের নাম বা উপনামের আদ্যক্ষর সমূহ। ***Verb t.*** To mark or sign with initials; নামের আদ্যক্ষর লিখিয়া স্বাক্ষর করা। **—ly,** *adv.* In an initial way; at the beginning; আদৌ; প্রথমে।

in-i′-ti āte (-shĭ-), *v. t.* **1.** To commence or begin; to originate; to set afoot; আরম্ভ করা; উদ্ভব করা; প্রবর্ত্তন করা। **2.** To admit with introductory rites or forms, as *into* a sect, society, social or religious status etc.; যথারীতি (সমাজে) গ্রহণ করা, দীক্ষিত করা, দীক্ষা দান করা। **3.** To instruct in the rudiments or principles; as, to *initiate in* the elements of a science; মূলসূত্র শিক্ষা দেওয়া, দীক্ষিত করা। **—at-ed,** *adj.* **1.** Commenced; আরব্ধ। **2.** Admitted into some society, religion, etc.; যথারীতি কোন সমাজে বা ধর্ম্মে গৃহীত, দীক্ষিত। **—a′-tion,** *n.* Act of initiating; beginning; formal introduction; আরম্ভণ (হিঃ কোঃ), দীক্ষাপ্রদান, অভ্যন্তরীকরণ (দশঃ), আরম্ভ, প্রারম্ভ; দীক্ষা, সংস্কার, মন্ত্রোপদেশ। **—a-tor,** *n.* One who initiates; প্রবর্ত্তক, দীক্ষাদাতা। **—a-to-ry,** *adj.* Initial; introductory; আদ্য, প্রাথমিক, প্রথম প্রবর্ত্তনশীল, প্রারম্ভসূচক, মৌলিক; আরম্ভক, প্রারম্ভিক। **—a′-trix,** *n.* (Fem.)

in-i′-ti-āte (-shĭ-) *adj.* & *n.* **1.** (One) who is initiated; দীক্ষিত (ব্যক্তি)। **2.** Serving to initiate into some society or some branch of study; দীক্ষাদায়ক।

in-i′-ti-ā-tive (-shĭ-ā-tĭv), *adj.* & *n.* Initiatory; originating; প্রাথমিক; আরম্ভক, প্রারম্ভক। ***Noun.*** **1.** First step; beginning; origination; as, the *initiatives* of good things to come; lead; as to take the *initiative*; সূত্রপাত; প্রারম্ভ; উৎপত্তি; নেতৃত্ব। **2.** The right or power of initiating or originating something; as, to have the *initiative* with respect to a measure; কোন নূতন বিষয় প্রবর্ত্তন করিবার ক্ষমতা বা অধিকার, প্রবর্ত্তনাধিকার। **3.** The right of a citizen or citizens outside the legislature, to originate legislation, as in Switzerland; ব্যবস্থাপক সভার সভ্য নয় এমন নাগরিক বা নাগরিক বৃন্দের নববিধি প্রবর্ত্তনাধিকার। **To take the initiative**—To take the lead; to make the first step; নেতৃত্ব গ্রহণ করা, পথপ্রদর্শন করা; প্রথম আরম্ভ করা, সূত্রপাত করা।

initio, (*L.*), *adv.* (abbr. *init.*) At the beginning (with reference to a passage in a book etc.); প্রথমে, প্রারম্ভে।

in-jĕct′, *v. t.* **1.** To throw or drive in by means of a syringe; as, to *inject* fluid or medicine into a cavity, stomach, etc.; অন্তর্নিক্ষেপ করা, মধ্যে প্রবিষ্ট করা, পিচকারী করা। **2.** (*Anat.*) To fill; as, to *inject* a vessel or cavity with a fluid; (শারীর-সংস্থান-বিদ্যা) তরল পদার্থ দ্বারা (পিচকারী প্রভৃতির সাহায্যে) পূর্ণ করা। **—jec′-tor,** *n.* **1.** One that injects; a device to inject water into the boilers of a steam-engine; অন্তঃপ্রক্ষেপক; বাষ্পীয় যন্ত্রের বাষ্পজনকের ভিতর জল প্রক্ষেপের জন্য যন্ত্র-বিশেষ।

in-jĕc′-tion, *n.* **1.** Act of injecting; অন্তর্নিক্ষেপ, পিচকারী করণ। **2.** That which is injected; a liquid medicine injected; অন্তঃপ্রবিষ্ট বস্তু; পিচকারী প্রভৃতির সাহায্যে অন্তঃপ্রবিষ্ট তরল ঔষধ। **Injection engine**—যে কলে শীতল জলধারা প্রক্ষেপ দ্বারা বাষ্প ঘনীভূত করা হয়।

in-jū-di′-cious (-shŭs), *adj.* **1.** Unwise; imprudent; rash; অবিবেচক, বিবেচনাশূন্য, অবিজ্ঞ, অবিচক্ষণ; বিবেচনারহিত, বিচারমূঢ়, পরিণামদৃষ্টিহীন, অপরিণামদর্শী; হঠকারী, অবিমৃষ্যকারী। **2.** Ill-judged, as a measure etc.; অবিবেচনাসিদ্ধ, অসুবিবেচিত। **—ly,** *adv.* In an injudicious manner; অবিবেচিতভাবে, হঠকারিতার সহিত। **—ness,** *n.*

in-junc′-tion (-jŭngk-), *n.* **1.** Act of enjoining; an authoritative order; precept; admonition; আজ্ঞা, নিষেধাজ্ঞা; আদেশ, নিদেশ; উপদেশ, বিধান, বিধি; মৃদু ভর্ৎসনা। **2.** A judicial process compelling a person to do or not to do something ; আদালতের নিষেধাজ্ঞা।

in′-jure (-jêr), *v. t.* **1.** To do wrong to ; অপকার করা, ক্ষতি করা, অনিষ্ট করা। **2.** To hurt or harm ; to impair ; as, to *injure* health ; হানি করা, পীড়া দেওয়া ; নষ্ট করা। **–jured,** *adj.* **1.** Wronged ; offended ; অপকৃত ; ব্যথিত, পীড়িত। **2.** Hurt ; impaired ; আহত ; নষ্ট। **–jur-er,** *n.*

in-jü′-ri-ous (-ŭs), *adj.* **1.** Harmful ; detrimental ; mischievous ; অনিষ্টকর, ক্ষতিজনক, পীড়াকর ; অপকারক, অহিতকারী, হানিকর, অহিতজনক ; অনিষ্টকারী। **2.** Insulting ; calumnious, as language etc. ; অপমানজনক ; অপবাদগর্ভ, গ্লানিজনক। **–ly,** *adv.* **–ness,** *n.*

in′-jü-rŷ, *n.* **1.** Hurt ; harm ; damage ; আঘাত ; হানি, অপকার, অনিষ্ট, পীড়া, অহিত ; ক্ষতি। **2.** A wrongful act or treatment ; অহিতজনক কার্য্য, অন্যায় ব্যবহার।

in-jŭs′-tice (-tĭs), *n.* Unfairness ; iniquity ; অবিচার, অন্যায় ; অন্যায্যতা, ন্যায়বিরুদ্ধতা। **You do him an injustice**—You judge him unfairly ; তুমি তাহার প্রতি অবিচার করিতেছ।

ink (ĭngk), *n.* & *v. t.* **1.** A coloured liquid usually black for writing, printing, etc. ; কালি, মসী, মলিনাম্বু, মসীজল। **2.** A black liquid ejected by cuttlefish from the bladder ; সমুদ্রজিভ্ মৎস্যের পট্‌কা হইতে প্রক্ষিপ্ত কৃষ্ণবর্ণ তরলপদার্থ। ***Verb t.*** **1.** To blacken, daub or colour with ink ; কৃষ্ণবর্ণ করা, কালিমালিপ্ত করা, মসীলিপ্ত করা, কৃষ্ণবর্ণে রঞ্জিত করা। **2.** (*Print.*) To cover as types etc. with ink for printing ; (মুদ্রণ) হরফে কালি লাগান। **Ink′-i-ness,** *n.* **Ink′-less,** *adj.* **Ink′-y,** *adj.* Black ; resembling ink ; blackend with ink ; কৃষ্ণবর্ণ ; মসীবৎ, মসীকৃষ্ণ ; মসীলিপ্ত, মসীরঞ্জিত। **Ink-bag** — কোন কোন মৎস্যের দেহাভ্যন্তরস্থ কৃষ্ণবর্ণপদার্থপূর্ণ কোষ। **Ink-bottle, –pot**—কালীর বোতল, দোয়াত, মসীপাত্র, মসীভাজন, মস্যাধার। **Ink-stand**—A stand for holding one or more ink bottles, often with a tray or rest for pens etc. ; দোয়াত রাখার জন্য আধার, কলমস্থান (আঃ বঃ), লিপিসজ্জাপাত্র, লেখসাধনপাত্র। An ink-pot ; দোয়াত, মসিপাত্র, মস্যাধার। **Printer's** or **printing ink** — ছাপার কালি। **Sympathetic** or **invisible ink**—অদৃশ্য কালি, গুপ্ত কালি (হিঃ কোঃ)। **To sling ink**—(*Slang*) To write ; to earn one's bread by writing ; (ইতর ভাষায়) লিখা ; লেখকের ব্যবসায় দ্বারা জীবিকার্জ্জন করা।

ink′-êr (ĭngk-), *n.* **1.** An instrument in telegraphy, recording messages in ink ; তাড়িতবার্ত্তাবহ সংসৃষ্ট যন্ত্র-বিশেষ—যদ্দ্বারা সংবাদ কালিতে লিখিত হয়, মসিলেখক। **2.** A roller which inks the type ; যে ডলনা দ্বারা হরফে কালি লাগান হয়।

ink′-ling (-ingk-), *n.* A hint ; a slight knowledge or intimation, (with *of*) ; ইঙ্গিত ; সঙ্কেত, টের, আভাস।

in-lāce′, *v. t.* Same as ENLACE.

in′-lănd, *n., adj.* & *adv.* The interior of a land or country ; অন্তর্দেশ। ***Adj.*** **1.** Remote from the sea or border ; interior ; as, an *inland* town ; সমুদ্র হইতে দূরবর্ত্তী ; দেশমধ্যবর্ত্তী, মধ্যদেশীয়। **2.** Carried on within a country ; domestic ; as, *inland* trade ; আন্তর্দেশীক ; দেশীয়, দৈশিক, স্বদেশীয়। ***Adv.*** In, or towards, the interior of a country ; অন্তর্দেশে, দেশাভ্যন্তরাভিমুখে। **–er,** *n.* One who lives inland ; অন্তর্দ্দেশবাসী। **–ish,** *adj.* Relating to the interior of a country ; of an inland nature or character ; অন্তর্দ্দেশীয় ; অন্তর্দ্দেশীয়-ভাবাপন্ন। **Inland duty**—অন্তর্দেশীয় শুল্ক। **Inland sea**—দেশাভ্যন্তরস্থ সাগর, অন্তঃস্থলসমুদ্র (সাঃ পঃ)।

in′-lay (-lā), *n.* Inlaid work ; pieces of wood, ivory, etc. inlaid ; খচিত কার্য্য ; হস্তিদন্ত প্রভৃতির খণ্ড—যদ্দ্বারা খচিত করা হইয়াছে।

in-lay′ (-lā), *v. t.* **1.** To set in or insert (one thing *in* another) so as to make their surfaces even ; অন্তর্নিবদ্ধ করা, খচিত করা, অবনদ্ধ করা। **2.** To insert, as a page, plate etc. in a space cut in a larger, stouter page etc. ; অন্তর্নিবিষ্ট করা। **–laid′,** *adj.* Ornamented with insertions ; as, *inlaid* with pearls (মুক্তাখচিত) ; পরিখচিত, খচিত, অন্তর্নিবদ্ধ, অবনদ্ধ (বলয়াবনদ্ধতাম্রাশ্মঃ—শিশুঃ) ; প্রতিবদ্ধ, প্রণিহিত (মঃ ইঃ), পরিত, পিনদ্ধ।

in′-lĕt, *n.* **1.** A small recess in a shore or creek ; ক্ষুদ্র উপসাগর, খাড়ি, সমুদ্রবঙ্ক, বঙ্ক। **2.** An opening or passage for entrance ; প্রবেশ-দ্বার, প্রবেশপথ, প্রবেশমার্গ। **3.** An inserted material ; অন্তর্নিবদ্ধ বস্তু।

in′-lī-êr, *n.* (*Geo.*) An underlying formation completely covered by the overlying one ; (ভূবিদ্যা) নিম্নস্তর।

in-loco, (*L.*), In the proper or natural place ; যথাস্থানে।

in′-lŷ, *adv.* (*Poet.*) Inwardly ; deeply ; in the heart ; অভ্যন্তরে ; গভীররূপে, মর্ম্মে মর্ম্মে ; হৃদয়ে। **–ing,** *adj.* Lying inside ; মধ্যস্থিত।

in′-māte, *n.* & *adj.* An occupant of a house ; a fellow-lodger ; গৃহবাসী, পরিজন, অন্তর্জন (ললিত) ; সহবাসী, সহস্থায়ী, একগৃহবাসী, একগৃহস্থায়ী।

in-mĕsh′, *v. t.* Same as ENMESH.

in′-mōst, *adj.* **1.** Most inward ; furthest within ; অন্তরস্থ, গূঢ়তম ; অন্তরতম (রবীঃ), অন্তস্তম (ঐ)। **2.** (*Fig.*) Deepest as thought etc. ; গভীরতম। **Inmost recess**—অন্তরতম প্রদেশ।

inn, *n.* A public house for lodging and entertainment of travellers ; a hotel ; পান্থনিবাস, পথিকশালা,

পথিকাবাস, পথিকাশ্রম, পান্থাবাস; সরাইখানা, চটী, উত্তরণশালা। **Inn-keeper**—One who keeps an inn; পান্থনিবাসাধিকারী, সরাইওয়ালা, সরাইদার। **Inns of chancery**—The buildings in London formerly used for residence of law-students; societies occupying these; লণ্ডননগরীস্থ প্রাচীন অট্টালিকাশ্রেণী—পূর্ব্বে আইনশিক্ষার্থী ছাত্রগণকর্তৃক ব্যবহৃত হইত; উক্ত অট্টালিকায় অধিষ্ঠিত সম্মিলনী সমূহ। **Inns of court**—Inner Temple, Middle Temple, Lincoln's inn, Gray's inn নামক লণ্ডন নগরীস্থ ব্যবহারজীবিসম্প্রদায় চতুষ্টয়। The sets of buildings belonging to these societies; উক্ত ব্যবহারজীবিসম্প্রদায় চতুষ্টয়ের অট্টালিকাশ্রেণী।

in'-nāte, *adj.* Inborn; natural; native; প্রকৃতিজাত, অন্তর্জাত, দেহভূত, অন্তর্ভব, অন্তরুৎপন্ন (হিঃ কোঃ); সহজাত, স্বাভাবিক; স্বভাবসিদ্ধ। **–ly,** *adv.* **–ness,** *n.* **Innate ideas**—প্রত্যক্ষাদি নিরপেক্ষ সহজাত সংস্কার (মনোভাব)।

in-nāv'-i-gā-ble (-bl), *adj.* Not navigable; অনাব্য, অনৌতার্য্য, নাবাগম্য। **–bly,** *adv.*

in'-nêr, *adj.* & *n.* **1.** Further in; interior; internal; অন্তরতর; অন্তর্ব্বর্ত্তী, আন্তর; আভ্যন্তর; অভ্যন্তরস্থ, অন্তরস্থ, মধ্যস্থ। **2.** (*Fig.*) More intimate; as, the *inner* circle of his friends; (লক্ষণায়) অন্তরঙ্গ। **3.** Not obvious; as, the *inner* meaning; অন্তর্নিহিত। ***Noun.*** The division of a target next outside the centre; the shot that strikes this; লক্ষ্যের কেন্দ্রবিন্দুর অব্যবহিত বহির্দেশস্থ বিভাগবিশেষ; যে গুলি দ্বারা উক্ত স্থান আহত হয়। **–most,** *n.* Inmost; অন্তরতম (মঃ ইঃ)। **Inner-apartment**—অন্তঃপুর, অন্দরমহল, অন্তর্গৃহ, অন্তর্ভবন, শুদ্ধান্ত। **Inner body**—অতিবাহিক দেহ (হিঃ কোঃ), লিঙ্গদেহ, সূক্ষ্মদেহ। **Inner-man**—The soul or mind; আত্মাপুরুষ। (*Facet.*) Stomach; as, he refreshed his *inner man*; (রঙ্গচ্ছলে) পাকস্থলী। **Inner organ**—অন্তঃকরণ (হিঃ কোঃ)। **Inner self**—অন্তরাত্মা (হিঃ কোঃ)।

in-nėr'-vāte, *v. t.* To supply with nerve force or nerves, as an organ etc.; স্নায়বিক বল প্রদান করা। **–va'-tion,** *n.* Act of innervating; nervous action or stimulation; স্নায়বিক বলপ্রদান; স্নায়বিকক্রিয়া, স্নায়বিক বেদনা, যন্ত্রসংবেদন (হিঃ কোঃ), নাড়ী সংবেদন (ঐ)।

in-nerve' (-nêrv), *v. t.* To give nerve to; to invigorate or animate; স্নায়বিকশক্তি প্রদান করা; সতেজ করা, সবল করা।

in'-ning (-ing), *n.* **1.** Harvesting; শস্যসংগ্রহ। **2.** (*Pl.*) The turn or time of a player or of a side at the bat; ক্রিকেট খেলায় ব্যক্তিবিশেষের বা পক্ষবিশেষের ব্যাট ধরার পালা বা সময়। **3.** (*Pl.*) Lands recovered from the sea; সিকস্তি জমি। **4.** (*Fig.*) The time during which a person or a party is in power; (লক্ষণায়) প্রভাবকাল, অভ্যুদয়কাল।

in'-nö-cence (-sĕns), *n.* **1.** The state of being innocent; harmlessness; নির্দ্দোষিতা, নিষ্কলঙ্কতা, অপরাধহীনতা, শুদ্ধমতিত্ব, অনবদ্যতা, নিরপরাধতা; অনপকারিতা। **2.** Freedom from moral wrong; purity; সাধুতা; বিশুদ্ধতা, পবিত্রতা, নির্ম্মলতা। **3.** Simplicity; artlessness; foolishness; সরলতা; অকপটতা, মুগ্ধতা; নির্ব্বুদ্ধিতা।

in'-nö-cĕnt, *adj.* & *n.* **1.** Morally pure; sinless, সাধু, বিমলচিত্ত, শুভ্রচিত্ত, অকৃষ্ণকর্ম্মা, শুচিকর্ম্মা, শুদ্ধশীল, শুদ্ধস্বভাব, সিতমনাঃ; নিষ্পাপ। **2.** Free from the guilt of any crime; নির্দ্দোষ, নিরপরাধ। **3.** Simple; guileless; সরল; অকপট। **4.** Harmless; innocuous as a remedy etc.; অনপকারী। **5.** Not contraband as goods, etc.; অনিষিদ্ধ, অবিজোড়। ***Noun.* 1.** An innocent person; নির্দ্দোষ লোক। **2.** A simple or guileless person; an idiot; নিরীহ লোক, সোজা লোক; বোকা। **–ly,** *adv.* In an innocent manner; নির্দ্দোষভাবে, অকপট চিত্তে, সরল ভাবে, নিরীহ ভাবে। **Innocents' Day**—ইহুদিরাজ হিরোদের আদেশে সংঘটিত শিশুহত্যাস্মরণার্থ ২৮শে ডিসেম্বর দিবসে অনুষ্ঠিত পর্ব্ববিশেষ। **Massacre of the innocents**—(ক) ইহুদীরাজ হিরোদের আদেশে বেথেলহেম নগরের শিশুনিধন। (খ) (পার্লেমেন্টের অবর ভাষায়) পার্লেমেন্টের অধিবেশনকালের অবসানে সময়াভাবপ্রযুক্ত গভর্ণমেণ্টকর্তৃক প্রস্তাবিত আইন পরিত্যাগ।

in-nŏc'-ü-ous (-ŭs), *adj.* Harmless; producing no ill effect; অনপকারী; অক্ষতিজনক, অহানিকর। **–ly,** *adv.* Harmlessly; নির্দ্দোষভাবে, অনপকারপূর্ব্বক। **–no-cu'-i-ty, –ness,** *ns.*

in-nŏm'-i-nāte, *adj.* Having no name; unnamed; অনামধেয়; নামহীন। **Innominate-bone**—The hip-bone; নিতম্বাস্থি।

in'-nö-vāte, *v. t.* & *i.* (*Rare*) To introduce as a novelty; (ক্কাচিৎ ব্যবহৃত) নুতন নুতন রীতি বা নব্যপ্রথা প্রবর্ত্তন করা। ***Verb i.*** To introduce novelties; to make changes (*in*); as, every man is not fit to *innovate*; নুতন বিষয় প্রবর্ত্তন করা; কোন পরিবর্ত্তন সাধন করা, নুতন কিছু করা। **–va'-tion,** *n.* **1.** Act of innovating; introduction of something new; নব্যভাবপ্রবর্ত্তন; নব্যপ্রথা প্রবর্ত্তন, নবব্যবহারস্থাপন, নুতনরীতি স্থাপন, নবীনাচারস্থাপন। **2.** A change effected by innovating; something newly introduced; নব্যধারাস্থাপন জনিত পরিবর্ত্তন; নবপ্রবর্ত্তিত বিষয়, নবরীতি, নবমার্গ। **–va-tor,** *n.* One who innovates; সংস্কারপ্রবর্ত্তক, নব্যপ্রথাপ্রবর্ত্তক, নবরীতিস্থাপক, নুতন ব্যবহারস্থাপক, নবব্যবহারপ্রবর্ত্তক। **–va-tor-y,** *adj.*

in-nox'-i-ous (-ŏk-shŭs), *adj.* Harmless; নির্দ্দোষ, অনপকারী,

অনপকারক। **—ly,** *adv.* Harmlessly; guiltlessly; অপকার না করিয়া; নির্দ্দোষরূপে। **—ness,** *n.*

in-nü-ĕn'-dō, *n.* & *v. i.* An oblique hint; an insinuation; allusive reference usually deprecatory; বক্রোক্তি, ভঙ্গ্যুক্তি, পর্য্যায়োক্তি; ঠার; ইঙ্গিত। ***Verb i.*** To make innuendoes; ইঙ্গিত করা, বক্রোক্তি করা, ঠারেঠুরে বলা।

in-nü'-mêr-ă-ble (-bl), *adj.* Incapable of being numbered or counted; countless; অগণনীয়; অসংখ্য, অগণ্য, অগণিতব্য, অসংখ্যেয় (জিঃ), সংখ্যাতীত, গণনাতীত, অগণিত। **-bil'-i-ty, —ness,** *ns.*

in-nü-trĭ'-tion, *n.* Want of nutrition; failure of nourishment; পোষণাভাব; অপুষ্টি। **—tious,** *adj.* Not nutritious; অপুষ্টিকর, অপুষ্টিদ, অপৌষ্টিক।

in-ŏb-sêrv'-ance (-ăns), *n.* **1.** Heedlessness; inattention; অসতর্কতা, অসাবধানতা; অমনোযোগিতা। **2.** Non-observance, as of law etc.; অপ্রতিপালন। **—ant,** *adj.*

in-ŏc-cü-pā'-tion, *n.* Want of occupation; অধিকাররাহিত্য, অনধিকৃতাবস্থা।

in-ŏc'-ü-lă-ble (-bl), *adj.* **1.** Capable of being communicated by inoculation; সংক্রামণযোগ্য। **2.** Capable of being inoculated; টীকার যোগ্য। **3.** That may communicate a disease as virus etc.; রোগ সংক্রামণযোগ্য। **—bil'-i-ty,** *n.*

in-ŏc'-ü-lāte, *v. t.* **1.** To communicate a milder form of a disease to (a person etc.) to safeguard him against its attacks; to implant a disease (*on* or *into* a person) in this way; চর্ম্মভেদপূর্ব্বক সংক্রামকরোগাদির বীজ (পূয) অন্তশরীরে প্রবেশ করাইয়া সেই রোগ উৎপাদন করা, টিকা দেওয়া; ঐ উপায়ে রোগ উৎপাদন করা। **2.** To insert as a bud or scion in a plant for growth on the new stock; চোক কলম করা, অপর বৃক্ষে বর্দ্ধনের জন্য কোন বৃক্ষের চোক বা প্ররোহ তাহাতে প্রবিষ্ট করা। **—la'-tion,** *n.* **1.** The act of inoculating trees or plants; টিপ্পনী (প্রবোধঃ)। **2.** The act or practice of inoculating a disease; নৃমসূর্য্যাধান (অর্থাৎ নরবীজে টিকাদান)। **—la-tor,** *n.* One who inoculates; টিকাদার। **—la-tive,** *adj.*

in-ō'-dor-ous (-dêr-ŭs), *adj.* Scentless; having no odour or smell; নির্গন্ধ; গন্ধহীন, গন্ধশূন্য; বাসহীন।

in-ŏf-fĕn'-sive (-sĭv), *adj.* **1.** Unobjectionable; giving no offence; অনাপত্তিজনক; অদ্রোহশীল, অদ্বেষ্টা, অদ্রোহী, অনুপদ্রবকারী। **2.** Harmless; নির্দ্দোষ, অনপকারী।

in-ŏf-fĭ'-cious (-shŭs), *adj.* **1.** Void of office or function; inoperative; কার্য্যহীন; অকার্য্যকর, অকার্য্যকারী। **2.** (*Law*) Contrary to moral duty; as, *inofficious* treatment; কর্ত্তব্যবিরুদ্ধ।

in-ŏp'-êr-ă-tive (-tĭv), *adj.* Not operative; not producing or taking effect; নিষ্ফল; অফলদায়ক, অকার্য্যকর, অকার্য্যসাধক।

in-ŏp-pŏr-tüne', *adj.* Not opportune; unseasonable; অনাসময়িক, অকালোচিত; অসময়োচিত। **—ly,** *adv.* Unseasonably; অকালোচিতভাবে। **—ness,** *n.*

in-ŏr'-di-nāte, *adj.* **1.** Irregular; disorderly; অনিয়মিত; বিশৃঙ্খল। **2.** Excessive; immoderate; অতিরিক্ত; অপরিমিত, অত্যন্ত, অতীব, অত্যধিক। **3.** Intemperate; অমিতাচারী। **—ly,** *adv.* Disorderly; immoderately; অনিয়মিতরূপে; অপরিমিতভাবে। **—ness,** *n.*

in-ŏr-găn'-ic, *adj.* **1.** Devoid of the organized physical structure of a living being; inanimate; প্রাণিদেহের মত ব্যবস্থাবদ্ধ গঠনবিহীন, নিরঙ্গ (হিঃ কোঃ), নিরবয়ব, অপ্রাণী; জড় (হিঃ কোঃ), অচেতন (ঐ) নির্জ্জীব (ঐ)। **2.** Not arising by natural growth; অস্বভাবজ, অনিসর্গজ। **3.** (*Chem.*) Not entering into the composition of organized bodies, as elements, compounds etc.; অজৈব। **Inorganic bodies**—খনিজ পদার্থ। **Inorganic Chemistry**—See CHEMISTRY.

in-ŏr-găn-i-zā'-tion, *n.* Want of organization; অব্যবস্থাবদ্ধতা।

in-ŏr-nāte', *adj.* Not ornate; not decorated; অনলঙ্কৃত; অবিভূষিত, ভূষাহীন, অনাভরণ, নিরাভরণ।

in-ŏs'-cü-lāte, *v. i.* & *t.* **1.** To unite by contact; to have connection terminally; as, one vein or artery *inosculates* with another; সংস্পর্শ বা সম্প্রবেশ দ্বারা যুক্ত হওয়া, দুই মুখ একত্র হইয়া জোড়া লাগা, সংলগ্ন হওয়া; দুই রক্তবহা নাড়ীর প্রান্তভাগ সংস্পর্শ বা সম্প্রবেশ দ্বারা একীভূত হওয়া, পরস্পরের প্রান্তদেশে সংযুক্ত হওয়া। **2.** To interjoin; to join closely as fibres etc.; পরস্পর সংগ্রথিত হওয়া; দৃঢ়ভাবে সংযুক্ত হওয়া। **3.** (*Fig.*) To blend; (লক্ষণায়) সংমিশ্রিত করা। ***Verb t.*** To unite (fibres etc.) closely; দৃঢ়ভাবে সংযুক্ত করা। **—la'-tion,** *n.* Act of inosculating; union; connection; সম্মিলন; সংযোগ; অগ্রদ্বয়সন্ধি পার্শ্বদ্বয়সংযোগ।

in'-pour-ing (-pŏr-), *adj.* & *n.* Pouring in; অন্তর্বর্ষী। ***Noun.*** Act of pouring in; বর্ষণ।

in'-quĕst, *n.* **1.** Judicial inquiry especially held before a jury; বিচারঘটিত অনুসন্ধান, ব্যবহারপরীক্ষা, ব্যবহারদর্শন। **2.** A coroner's inquest; অপমৃত্যুপরীক্ষা, অপমৃত্যুকারণবিচার, অপমৃত্যুবৃত্তান্তবিচার। **3.** A jury; (now esp.) a coroner's jury; জুরি; বিশেষতঃ শবপরীক্ষক কর্ম্মচারীর জুরী। **4.** (*Obs.*) Search; inquiry; (অপ্রঃ) অনুসন্ধান; তদন্ত, তদারক। **Coroner's inquest**—শবপরীক্ষক কর্ম্মচারী

কর্ত্তৃক মৃত্যুর কারণ নির্দ্দেশার্থ অনুসন্ধান। **Grand inquest**—Same as GRAND JURY (which see.) **Great, last inquest**—The last judgment; খৃষ্টীয় ও মহম্মদীয় ধর্ম্মোক্ত অন্তিমবিচার।

ĭn-quī′-ĕ-tūde, *n.* **1.** Disturbed state; uneasiness of mind or body; অশান্তি, বিক্ষুব্ধতা, অশান্তচিত্ততা, উদ্বিগ্নতা; শারীরিক বা মানসিক অস্বাচ্ছন্দ্য বা উদ্বেগ, ব্যাকুলতা। **2.** (*Pl.*) Disquieting or anxious thoughts; দুশ্চিন্তা, ব্যাকুলতা, অস্থৈর্য্য, বৈক্লব্য।

ĭn-quīre′, ĕn–, *v. i.* & *t.* **1.** To seek for information by asking questions; as, to *inquire* of a person *about* or *after* a thing etc.; অনুসন্ধান করা; খোঁজ নেওয়া, তল্লাস করা, জিজ্ঞাসা করা, সংবাদ নেওয়া। **2.** To make investigation; to search, (with *into*); as, to *inquire into* a matter; তদন্ত করা, তদারক করা; অনুসন্ধান করা। ***Verb t.*** To ask about; as, he *inquired* the way; to request to be told, as one's name etc.; জিজ্ঞাসা করা; বলিবার জন্য অনুরোধ করা। **–quir′-ing,** *adj.* Disposed to inquire; curious; as, an *inquiring* mind; অনুসন্ধিৎসু, জিজ্ঞাসু, অনুসন্ধানশীল; কুতূহলী। **–quir′-ing-ly,** *adv.* **To inquire about one's health** — To ask about one's health; কাহারও স্বাস্থ্যসম্বন্ধে খবর নেওয়া। **To inquire after a thing** — To search after (it); কোন বিষয়ে অনুসন্ধান করা। **To inquire after or for a person**—To inquire about his welfare etc.; to ask how he is; কাহারো কুশলপ্রশ্ন জিজ্ঞাসা করা; সে কেমন আছে জিজ্ঞাসা করা। **To inquire into a matter** — To investigate it; তদন্ত করা, অনুসন্ধান করা। **To inquire of a person**—To ask a person (about anything); কাহাকে কোন বিষয়ে প্রশ্ন বা জিজ্ঞাসা করা।

ĭn-quīr′-ў, –ĕn–, *ns.* **1.** The act of inquiring; search; investigation; অনুসন্ধান; তদন্ত, তদারক; গবেষণা, সমীক্ষা (হিঃ কোঃ), তত্ত্বানুসন্ধান। **2.** A question; query; প্রশ্ন; পৃচ্ছা, জিজ্ঞাসা। **Court of inquiry**—কোন সৈনিককর্ম্মচারীর বিরুদ্ধে অভিযোগের বিচারার্থ যে আদালত বসে। **To make inquiries (about)**—To ask (about); (কোন বিষয়) প্রশ্ন করা।

ĭn-quĭ-sĭ′-tion, *n.* **1.** Inquiry; investigation; অনুসন্ধান, অন্বেষণ; তত্ত্বানুসন্ধান, সমীক্ষণ (মঃ ইঃ)। **2.** Official or judicial inquiry; সরকারী-তদন্ত বা পরীক্ষা, বিচারবিভাগীয় অনুসন্ধান। **3.** (*Cap.*, with *the* prefixed) A court or tribunal in the Roman Catholic Church to punish heresy; রোমান ক্যাথলিক ধর্ম্মমতের বিরুদ্ধবাদিগণের বিচারের জন্য যাজকীয় ধর্ম্মাধিকরণবিশেষ, পাষণ্ডসংযমসভা (আঃ বঃ)। [উক্তরূপ ধর্ম্মাধিকরণ পোপ নবম গ্রেগরী কর্ত্তৃক ১২৩৩ খৃঃ অব্দে প্রতিষ্ঠিত হয়। প্রথমতঃ প্রতি যাজকপল্লীতে কতিপয় সম্ভ্রান্ত ব্যক্তি ও পল্লী পুরোহিত দ্বারা এক একটী সমিতি গঠিত হইয়াছিল। ঐ সমিতির সভ্যগণ প্রচলিত ধর্ম্মের বিরুদ্ধবাদিগণকে বিশপের নিকট উপস্থিত করিত। অল্পকাল পরে বিশপদিগের পরিবর্ত্তে বিভিন্ন সন্ন্যাসিসম্প্রদায় হইতে পাষণ্ডদলনকারিগণ (Inquisitors) নিযুক্ত হইতেন; এই সকল পাষণ্ডদলনকারিগণের আদেশে অপধর্ম্ম-সেবিগণের উপর অমানুষিক অত্যাচার করা হইত। তাহাদের অনেককেই জলন্ত অনলে দগ্ধ করিয়া বধ করা হইত। স্পেনদেশে পাষণ্ডসংযমসভা বিশেষ প্রভাব-শালী হইয়া উঠিয়াছিল।] **–al,** *adj.* Relating to inquisition; পাষণ্ডসংযম-সম্বন্ধীয়। **The inquisition**—See INQUISITION, 3.

ĭn-quĭs′-ĭ-tive (-tĭv), *adj.* Given to inquiry; disposed to ask questions; curious; অনুসন্ধিৎসু। জিজ্ঞাসু; কৌতূহলপরায়ণ, কৌতূহলী। **–ly,** *adv.* In an inquisitive manner; অনুসন্ধিৎসা সহকারে, জিজ্ঞাসু ভাবে। **–ness,** *n.* The state of being inquisitve; curiosity; অনু-সন্ধিৎসা, অনুসন্ধানশীলতা; কৌতূহল।

ĭn-quĭs′-ĭ-tor (-tėr), *n.* **1.** An official inquirer; সরকারী তদন্তকারী। **2.** (*R. C. C.*) An officer of the Inquisition; প্রচলিত রোমান ক্যাথলিক ধর্ম্মমতভ্রষ্ট ব্যক্তিগণের বিচারার্থ ধর্ম্মাধিকরণের অন্যতম বিচারক, পাষণ্ড-নিয়ামক (আঃ বঃ)।

ĭn-quĭs-ĭ-tō′-rĭ-ăl, *adj.* **1.** Offensively enquiring or prying; অতি-জিজ্ঞাসু, অন্যায়ানুসন্ধিৎসু। **2.** Pertaining to the official inquisitors; পাষণ্ডনিয়ামকগণ সম্পর্কীয়। **–ly,** *adv.* In an inquisitorial manner; অতি-পরীক্ষা পূর্ব্বক, অত্যন্ত সন্ধান পূর্ব্বক।

ĭn′-road (-rōd), *n.* **1.** A sudden hostile incursion; raid; অকস্মাৎ আক্রমণ; লুণ্ঠনের উদ্দেশ্যে আক্রমণ, উপদ্রব, অভিদ্রব, উপপ্লব। **2.** (*Fig.*) Forcible entrance or encroachment; বলপূর্ব্বক প্রবেশ।

ĭn′-rŭsh, *n.* A rush inwards; অন্তঃপ্রবাহ।

ĭn-săl′-ĭ-vāte, *v. t.* To mix with saliva, as food in eating; লালার সহিত মিশ্রিত করা, লালাসিক্ত করা। **–va′-tion,** *n.*

ĭn-să-lū′-brĭ-ous (-ŭs), *adj.* Unhealthy; unwholesome; as, an *insalubrious* place or climate; অস্বাস্থ্যকর; স্বাস্থ্যহানিকর, অস্বাস্থ্যজনক। **–ty,** *n.*

ĭn-sāne′, *adj.* **1.** Mad; deranged in mind; পাগল, উন্মাদ, উন্মত্ত; বিকৃতমনাঃ, ছন্নমতি, নষ্টবুদ্ধি, বিক্ষিপ্তবুদ্ধি, ভ্রষ্টবুদ্ধি, নষ্টমতি, বিকৃতমস্তিষ্ক, বাউড়া, (*coloq.*), বিকৃতমতি। **2.** Senseless; impractical, as an attempt, plan, etc.; নিরর্থক; অকার্য্যকর। **–ly,** *adv.* In an insane manner; উন্মত্তভাবে।

ĭn-săn′-ĭ-tă-rў, *adj.* Not sanitary; unhealthy; অস্বাস্থ্যকর; অস্বাস্থ্যজনক।

ĭn-săn′-ĭ-tў, *n.* Madness; unsoundness of mind; উন্মত্ততা, বিক্ষিপ্ততা (হিঃ কোঃ); বাতুলতা, বিকৃত-মস্তিষ্কতা, মতিবিভ্রম।

in-să'-ti-a-ble (-shî-ă-bl), *adj.* Incapable of being satisfied ; inordinately greedy (*of*) ; "*Insatiable of* glory" ; অতোষণীয়, অতর্পণীয়, অতৃপ্য ; অতিলোভী, অতিলুব্ধ, লোলুপ। **—bil'-i-tŷ,** *n.* **—bly,** *adv.* In an insatiable manner ; অতৃপ্তরূপে।

in-să'-ti-āte (-shî-), *adj.* Insatiable ; never satisfied ; "*Insatiate of* battle" ; অতর্পণীয়, অতোষণীয় ; অতৃপ্ত।

in-scrībe', *v. t.* **1.** To write or engrave ; as, to *inscribe* words etc. *in* or *on* stone, metal, paper etc. ; উৎকীর্ণ করা, ক্ষোদিত করা, বর্ণাঙ্কিত করা, অক্ষরাঙ্কিত করা। **2.** To mark, as a stone etc. with letters or words ; ক্ষোদিত করা, অক্ষরাদি উৎকীর্ণ করা। **3.** To dedicate ; as, to *inscribe* an ode to a friend ; উৎসর্গ করা। **4.** To imprint deeply ; as, to *inscribe* a sentence on the memory ; গভীররূপে অঙ্কিত করা, গভীরভাবে মুদ্রিত করা। **5.** To enroll ; as, to *inscribe* one's name in the visitor's book ; ভুক্ত করা। **6.** (*Geom.*) To draw within so as to meet yet not cut the boundaries ; as, to *inscribe* a triangle in a circle ; (জ্যামিতি) অনর্গত করা, একটী ক্ষেত্রের মধ্যে অপর একটী ক্ষেত্র এরূপভাবে অঙ্কিত করা যাহাতে শেষোক্ত ক্ষেত্র প্রথমোক্ত ক্ষেত্রের সীমারেখা স্পর্শ করিবে কিন্তু ছেদন করিবে না। **7.** (*Commr.*) To register the names of the holders of stocks etc., (*often in p. p.*) ; as, *inscribed* stock ; (বাণিজ্য) কোম্পানীর কাগজ প্রভৃতির ক্রেতার নাম খাতায় ভুক্ত করা ; **—scrib'-a-ble,** *adj.*

in-scrip'-tion, *n.* **1.** Act of inscribing ; ক্ষোদন। **2.** That which is inscribed ; words engraved ; as, *inscriptions* on monuments etc. ; উৎকীর্ণ অক্ষরাদি ; পাষাণলেখ, উৎকীর্ণলিপি, শিলালিপি, শিলালেখ, তাম্রলিপি, তাম্রলেখ, লেখ (হিঃ কোঃ)। **3.** An address or dedication as of a book to a person ; গ্রন্থাদির উৎসর্গপত্র, উৎসর্গলিপি। **4.** Act of inscribing loans or securities ; (*pl.*) inscribed stocks ; কোম্পানীর কাগজ, ঋণের অংশ প্রভৃতির ক্রেতার নাম খাতায় ভুক্তকরণ ; যে সকল কোম্পানীর কাগজ প্রভৃতির ক্রেতার নাম খাতায় ভুক্ত করা হইয়াছে। [ঐরূপ কোম্পানীর কাগজ প্রভৃতির ক্রেতাকে কোনরূপ নিদর্শন পত্র (certificate) দেওয়া হয় না। তাহার কোম্পানীর কাগজ হস্তান্তরিত করিতে হইলে—যাহার নিকট হস্তান্তরিত করা হয়—সেই ব্যক্তির নাম পূর্ব্বাধিকারীর নামের স্থানে বহিতে লিখা হয়।]

in-scrū'-tă-ble (-bl), *adj.* Impenetrable to investigation ; unintelligible ; wholly mysterious ; দুষ্প্রবেশ, দুর্ভেদ্য, দুর্জ্ঞেয়, অজ্ঞেয় ; বোধাতীত, বোধাগম্য, অবোধগম্য, ইন্দ্রিয়াগোচর, দুর্ব্বোধ, অনধিগম্য, দুরধিগম্য ; রহস্যপূর্ণ, রহস্যাচ্ছন্ন, রহস্যাবৃত, রহস্যময়, নিগূঢ়, গহন। **—bil'-i-ty, —ness,** *ns.* The quality of being inscrutable ; দুর্ব্বোধতা, অজ্ঞেয়ত্ব, অনধিগম্যতা, রহস্যপূর্ণতা। **—bly** *adv.*

in'-sĕct, *n.* **1.** A small invertebrate animal with a body divided into segments and several pairs of legs ; পোকা, কীট, পতঙ্গ। **2.** An insignificant person or creature : নগণ্য লোক বা প্রাণী। **Insect powder**—কীটনাশক চূর্ণ।

Figure showing the part of an insect. Beetle—*a*, head ; *b*, thorax ; *c*, abdomen ; *dd*, elytra or wing cases ; *ee*, wings ; *ff*, antennæ.

in-sĕc'-tā'-ri-ŭm, *n.* A place for keeping insects ; কীটরক্ষার্থ স্থান।

in-sĕc'-ti-cīde, *n.* Insect-killer ; a preparation used to kill insects ; কীটনাশক ; কীটনাশক চূর্ণ-বিশেষ। **—cid'-al,** *adj.*

in-sĕc-tiv'-ŏ-ră, *n.* (*Pl.*) Mammals feeding principally on insects ; কীটভুকজন্তুসমূহ, কীটাদিবর্গ, পতঙ্গভুক (সাঃ পঃ)।

in-sĕc'-ti-vōre, *n.* A member of the insectivora ; কীটভুক জন্তু।

in-sĕc-tiv'-ŏ-rous (-rŭs), *adj.* Living upon insects ; relating to the insectivora : পতঙ্গভোজী, কীটভুক ; পতঙ্গভোজী সম্পর্কীয়।

in-sĕc-tŏl'-ŏ-gŷ, *n.* Science of insects ; কীট-বিজ্ঞান, কীট-তত্ত্ব, কীট-বিদ্যা।

in-sĕ-cūre', *adj.* **1.** Not safe ; exposed to danger or loss ; অনিরাপদ, বিপদসঙ্কুল, বিঘ্নসঙ্কুল ; অসুরক্ষিত। **2.** Liable to give way, as ice, ground etc. ; বসিয়া যাইতে পারে এরূপ, তলগমনশীল। **—cu'-ri-ty,** *n.* The state of being insecure ; want of safety ; hazard ; বিপৎসঙ্কুলতা, বিঘ্নসঙ্কুলতা ; অনির্ব্বিঘ্নতা ; সঙ্কট।

in-sĕm'-i-nāte, *v. t.* To sow ; as, to *inseminate* seeds in a field, (*also fig.*) ; বপন করা। **—na'-tion,** *n.*

in-sĕn'-sāte, *adj.* **1.** Destitute of sense ; stupid ; বুদ্ধিহীন, জ্ঞানহীন, মূঢ় ; জড়বুদ্ধি। **2.** Wanting sensibility ; unfeeling ; সংজ্ঞাহীন, বিচেতন, অচেতন, লুপ্তচেতন ; অসাড়, সংবেদনশূন্য। **—ly,** *adv.*

in-sĕn-si-bil'-i-tŷ, *n.* **1.** The state of being insensible ; unconsciousness ; swoon ; সংবেদনশূন্যতা, অচৈতন্য ; স্পন্দহীনতা, জড়তা, জাড্য, নষ্টেন্দ্রিয়তা, লুপ্ততা (সুশ্রুঃ) ; মূর্চ্ছা, ইন্দ্রিয়সুপ্তি, ইন্দ্রিয়স্বাপ। **2.** Lack of feeling or emotion ; সংবেদনশূন্যতা (হি. কোঃ), আবেগহীনতা। **3.** Indifference (*to*) ; ঔদাসীন্য, উদাসীনতা।

in-sĕn'-si-ble (-bl), *adj.* **1.** Wanting physical sensibility ; as, the injury rendered that limb *insensible* ; অনুভবশক্তিশূন্য, বোধশক্তিহীন, অচেতন, বিচেতন, বিগতচেতন,

নষ্টেন্দ্রিয়, সুপ্তেন্দ্রিয়, স্পর্শানভিজ্ঞ ; অবেদনাক্ত (রুগ্ন)। 2. Inappreciable ; imperceptible ; as, *insensible* motion ; ইন্দ্রিয়াগোচর, অতীন্দ্রিয় ; অননুভবনীয়। 3. Void of feeling ; indifferent ; callous ; as, *insensible* fear or love ; রাগহীন ; উদাসীন ; অসাড়, অনুভবহীন। 4. Unconscious ; অচেতন, বিচেতন, লুপ্তচেতন, বিগতচেতন। 5. Unaware *(of)* ; as, he is *insensible of* his danger ; অজ্ঞাত, অপরিজ্ঞাত। **—bly,** *adv.* In an insensible manner ; imperceptively ; অননুভবনীয়রূপে ; অজ্ঞাতসারে, অলক্ষিতে। **Insensible (to)**—Indifferent *(to)* ; উদাসীন।

in-sĕn′-si-tive (-tiv), *adj.* 1. Not sensitive (to touch, sight, light etc.) ; অনুভূতিহীন, বোধহীন। 2. Not mentally or morally sensitive ; not quick to feel ; as, *insensitive* nature ; সাড়াহীন, সাড়াশূন্য ; ক্ষিপ্রসংবেদনশূন্য। **—ness,** *n.* The quality of being insensitive ; সংবেদনশূন্যতা, অনুভূতিহীনতা, অচেতনতা, বিচেতনতা।

in-sĕn′-ti-ĕnt (-shi-), *adj.* Inanimate ; জড়, অনুভূতিশূন্য, অচেতন, সংজ্ঞাশূন্য, বেহুস।

in-sĕp′-ă-ră-ble (-bl), *adj.* & *n.* 1. Incapable of being separated ; অবিচ্ছেদ্য, অবিয়োজ্য, অবিভাজ্য, নিত্যসম্বন্ধ, সহভাব, সার্ব্ব, নিত্যসহবর্ত্তী, অদ্বৈধীকরণীয়, অপৃথক্করণীয়। ***Noun.*** An inseparable person or thing esp. a friend ; অবিচ্ছেদ্য ব্যক্তি বা বস্তু। **—bil′-i-ty,** *n.* **—bly,** *adv.* In an inseparable manner ; অবিচ্ছেদ্যভাবে, অবিয়োজ্যভাবে। **Inseparable accident** — অবিশ্লেষ্য উপাধি (হিঃ কোঃ)। **Inseparable prefix**—*(Gram.)* One that cannot be used separately ; (ব্যাকরণ) অবিচ্ছেদ্য উপসর্গ। **Inseparable relation**—সমবায়িসম্বন্ধ, সমবায়িকরণ।

in-sêrt′, *v. t.* 1. To place in ; to put or thrust in or into ; নিবেশিত করা ; অন্তর্নিবিষ্ট করা। 2. To introduce ; to include ; as, to *insert* a word in a composition ; প্রবেশ করান ; সন্নিবিষ্ট করা।

in-sêr′-tion, *n.* 1. Act of inserting ; state of being inserted ; সন্নিবেশন, অন্তস্থাপন, অন্তর্নিবেশন ; অন্তর্নিবিষ্টতা। 2. That which is inserted ; অন্তর্নিবিষ্ট বস্তু। 3. Embroidery or ornamental needle work inserted into plain material ; as, a lace *insertion* ; সাদা জমির উপর চিকণের কাজ। 4. *(Anat.)* A mode of attachment of muscle, organ etc. ; (শারীর-সংস্থানবিদ্যা) পেশী, দৈহিক যন্ত্র প্রভৃতির সংযোগপ্রণালী বিশেষ।

in′-sĕt, *n.* 1. One or more extra pages inserted in a sheet or book ; পুস্তকাদিতে সন্নিবিষ্ট এক বা ততোধিক অতিরিক্ত পৃষ্ঠা। 2. A small map, illustration, etc. set in the border of a larger one ; বৃহত্তর চিত্র বা মানচিত্রের প্রান্তদেশে সন্নিবিষ্ট ক্ষুদ্রচিত্র বা মানচিত্র। 3. A piece of cloth inserted into a dress ; পরিচ্ছদের অভ্যন্তরে অন্তর্নিবিষ্ট বস্ত্রখণ্ড।

in-sĕt′, *v. t.* To insert or fix in (a sheet etc.) ; মধ্যে সংস্থাপিত করা, অন্তর্নিবিষ্ট করা।

in′-shōre, *adj.* & *adv.* Near or moving towards the shore ; তীরান্তিকস্থ, তীরসন্নিহিত, তীরাভিমুখী। ***Adv.*** Towards the shore ; close to shore ; তীরাভিমুখে ; তীরসন্নিকটে। **Inshore of** — Nearer to the shore than ; তীর হইতে অপেক্ষাকৃত অল্প দূরবর্ত্তী।

in-sīde′, *n., adv.* & *prep.* 1. *(in′-side)* The interior ; the internal part ; অভ্যন্তর ; মধ্যভাগ, অভ্যন্তরভাগ। 2. The inner side or surface ; (of a foot-path) the side next to the wall or away from a road ; অভ্যন্তরভাগ, ভিতরের দিক, মধ্যভাগ ; (পদপথ সম্বন্ধে) প্রাচীরের অব্যবহিত নিকটবর্ত্তী পার্শ্ব। 3. *(in-side′)* *(Colloq.)* The stomach and bowels ; (চলিতভাষায়) পাকস্থলী এবং নাড়িভূঁড়ি, আঁতড়ি। 4. An inside passenger in a coach etc. ; গাড়ী প্রভৃতির অভ্যন্তরভাগের আরোহী। ***Adv.*** *(in-side′)* On or in the inside ; as, go *inside* ; মধ্যভাগে, অভ্যন্তরে। ***Prep.*** Within ; as, *inside* a house ; অভ্যন্তরে। **Inside of a week**—In less than a week ; এক সপ্তাহের মধ্যে। **The inside of a week**—The middle part of a week ; সপ্তাহের মধ্যভাগ। **To get the inside track of anything** — To understand its working ; ভিতরের ব্যাপার বুঝিতে পারা। **Turned inside out**—Turned so that the inner side becomes outer ; ওলট-পালট, বিপর্য্যস্ত।

in′-sīde, *adj.* Situated within or inside ; internal ; as, the *inside* passenger ; the *inside* decoration ; অভ্যন্তরস্থ ; মধ্যগত, অভ্যন্তরীণ, আভ্যন্তর।

in-sīd′-êr, *n.* 1. A person inside ; a member of a society, organization etc., (cf. *outsider*) ; অভ্যন্তরস্থ ব্যক্তি ; কোন সম্প্রদায়ের সভ্য। 2. One who is in the secret of something ; যে ব্যক্তি ভিতরের কথা জানে, ভিতরের লোক, অন্তরঙ্গ ব্যক্তি।

in-sĭd′-i-ous (-ŭs), *adj.* 1. Deceitful ; treacherous ; wily ; crafty ; প্রবঞ্চক, ধূর্ত্ত ; বিশ্বাসঘাতক ; শঠ, ফন্দীবাজ, ফেরেববাজ ; চালাক, মতলববাজ। 2. Proceeding secretly as a disease ; অলক্ষিতে প্রবেশকারী। **—ly,** *adv.* In an insidious manner ; treacherously ; কপটভাবে, অতর্কিতভাবে ; বিশ্বাসঘাতকের মত। **—ness,** *n.* কাপট্য, কূটতা, বঞ্চকত্ব।

in′-sight (-sīt), *n.* Deep inspection or view ; the faculty of seeing deeply ; as, an *insight into* character ; সম্যগ্দর্শন, অবেক্ষণ ; অন্তর্দৃষ্টি, সূক্ষ্মদৃষ্টি।

in-sig'-ni-ă, *n.* **1.** Badge ; distinguishing marks of office, honour, etc. ; চিহ্ন, লক্ষণ, ব্যঞ্জন ; পদবীসূচক চিহ্ন। **2.** (*Fig.*) Marks indicative of anything ; লক্ষণ, চিহ্ন। **Insignia of royalty**—ছত্রচামরাদি, রাজচিহ্ন, রাজলক্ষণ।

in-sig-nif'-i-cănt, *adj.* **1.** Not significant ; meaningless ; অর্থশূন্য, অর্থবিহীন ; নিরর্থক। **2.** Of no importance ; trifling ; গুরুত্ববিহীন, সামান্য, অল্পপ্রভাব, তুচ্ছ, নগণ্য, অকিঞ্চিৎকর। **3.** Contemptible ; হেয়, অবজ্ঞেয়। **—cance, —can-cy,** *ns.* **1.** (*-cance* only) State of being insignificant ; want of significance or meaning ; অর্থশূন্যতা, নিরর্থকতা ; অর্থহীনতা। **2.** Unimportance ; contemptibility ; তুচ্ছতা, নগণ্যতা, স্তোকতা, গুরুত্বহীনতা ; অকিঞ্চিৎকরত্ব ; হেয়তা। **—ly,** *adv.*

in-sin-cere' (-sēr), *adj.* Not sincere ; false ; hypocritical ; কুটিল, অসরল ; কৃত্রিম ; কপট, লোকদেখানিয়া। **—cer'-i-ty,** *n.* Want of sincerity ; dissimulation ; hypocrisy ; ভণ্ডামি, কপটতা, কাপট্য ; অসরলতা ; কুটিলতা। **—ly,** *adv.* In an insincere manner ; কপটভাবে, অসরলভাবে।

in-sin'-ū-āte *v. t.* **1.** To introduce slowly or subtly ; as, to *insinuate* oneself into a place, favour or office ; অল্পে অল্পে প্রবিষ্ট করান, ধীরে ধীরে প্রবেশ করান, অলক্ষিতে প্রবেশ করান। **2.** To infuse or instil subtly or imperceptibly ; "Wisdom was to be *insinuated* not enforced" ; অলক্ষিতে সঞ্চার করা, অজ্ঞাতসারে সঞ্চার করা। **3.** To hint indirectly ; to suggest ; সঙ্কেত করা, ইঙ্গিত করা ; ইসারায় বলা, সঙ্কেতে বলা, আঁচ দেওয়া, ঠারেঠুরে বলা। **—a-ting-ly,** *adv.* By insinuation ; সঙ্কেতে, ইঙ্গিতে। **—a'-tion,** *n.* The act of insinuating ; that which is insinuated ; ইঙ্গিতে উল্লেখ, ভঙ্গিভাষণ ; বক্রোক্তি। **—a-tive,** *adj.* **—a-tor,** *n.*

in-sip'-id, *adj.* **1.** Tasteless ; without flavour ; নিরাস্বাদ, স্বাদহীন, নিঃস্বাদ, নীরস, রসহীন, পান্‌সে (*colloq.*), ভস্‌কা (*colloq.*) ; গন্ধহীন। **2.** Wanting spirit or life ; uninteresting ; নিস্তেজ, নিৰ্জীব ; নীরস। **—pid'-i-ty, —ness,** *ns.* The state of being insipid ; নীরসতা, বৈরস্য, স্বাদহীনতা। **—ly,** *adv.*

in-sist', *v. i.* **1.** To be persistent or pressing ; as, he *insisted* on immediate payment ; জেদ করা, দৃঢ়তা সহকারে বলা। **2.** To dwell at length or with emphasis (*on, upon*) ; as, he *insisted* on this point ; বহুক্ষণ বলা, নির্ব্বন্ধসহকারে বলা, জোরের সহিত বলা। **3.** To maintain positively ; as, he *insisted* on his innocence ; দৃঢ়তার সহিত সমর্থন করা। **—ence, —en-cy,** *ns.* The act of insisting ; জেদ্, পণ, কোট্, নির্ব্বন্ধাতিশয়। **—ly,** *adv.* In an insistent manner ; জেদের সহিত, নির্ব্বন্ধাতিশয় সহকারে।

in-sō-bri'-ē-tȳ, *n.* Want of sobriety ; intemperance ; drunkenness ; অসংযম ; অমিতাচার ; সুরাপানজনিত মত্ততা, পানাসক্তি, পানদোষ, মদ্যপানাসক্তি।

in-sŏ-lā'-tion, *n.* **1.** Exposure of things to the sun for dryinig ; sunstroke ; রৌদ্রে শুষ্কীকরণ ; সর্দ্দিগর্ম্মি। **2.** (*Med.*) Treatment of a disease by sun baths ; রৌদ্রস্নান দ্বারা রোগ চিকিৎসা।

in'-sŏ-lĕnt, *adj.* **1.** Overbearing ; haughty ; contemptuous ; দৃপ্ত, দাম্ভিক ; উদ্ধত, প্রগল্‌ভ, ধৃষ্ট ; অবজ্ঞাকারী। **2.** Insulting ; as, *insolent* words or behaviour ; অপমানজনক, অপমানসূচক। **—lence,** *n.* The state of being insolent ; দৃপ্ততা, দাম্ভিকতা, প্রগল্‌ভতা, ঔদ্ধত্য, ধৃষ্টতা, ধাষ্ট্য। **—ly,** *adv.* In an insolent manner ; গর্ব্বিতভাবে, দৃপ্তভাবে, উদ্ধতভাবে। **What insolence**—কি আস্পর্দ্ধা ! কি এত বড় কথা !

in-sŏl'-ū-ble (-bl), *adj.* **1.** Incapable of being solved or explained ; অসমাধানযোগ্য। **2.** Incapable of being dissolved ; অদ্রবণীয়, অদ্রাব্য, অগলনীয়। **—bil'-i-ty, —ness,** *ns.* **—bly,** *adv.*

in-sŏl'-vĕnt, *adj.* & *n.* **1.** Not solvent ; unable to pay the debts ঋণপরিশোধার্থ অপর্য্যাপ্ত বা অক্ষম ; দেউলিয়া, পরিক্ষীণ (মঃ সং), ঋণশোধনাক্ষম। **2.** Relating to an insolvent person ; as, an *insolvent* law ; দেউলিয়া ব্যক্তিসম্বন্ধীয়। ***Noun.*** An insolvent person ; দেউলিয়া ব্যক্তি, যোত্রহীন ব্যক্তি। **—ven-cy** *n.* The state ; of being insolvent ; ঋণ পরিশোধে অক্ষমতা, যোত্রহীনতা।

in-sŏm'-ni-ă, *n,* Sleeplessness ; নিদ্রাভাব, নিদ্রাহীনতা, অনিদ্রা, অস্বাপ, অস্বাপরোগ (হিঃ কোঃ), জাগররোগ।

in-sō-mŭch', *conj.* To such an extent (that) ; এই পর্য্যন্ত (যে)।

insouciant, (*F.*) *adj.* Careless ; unconcerned ; indifferent ; অনবধান ; ভ্রূক্ষেপহীন ; উদাসীন। ***Insouciance,*** *n.*

in-spăn', *v. t.* To yoke as oxen etc. to a vehicle ; যুগবদ্ধ করা, যোতা।

in-spĕct', *v. t.* **1.** To view closely or critically ; to scrutinize ; পরিদর্শন করা ; পুঙ্খানুপুঙ্খরূপে পরীক্ষা করা। **2.** To examine officially ; সরকারী কর্ম্মচারিরূপে পরিদর্শন করা। **—spec'-tion,** *n.* The act of inspecting ; পরিদর্শন, অন্বেক্ষণ (মঃ ভাঃ)। **—spec'-tor,** *n.* **1.** One who inspects ; পরিদর্শক, তত্ত্বাবধায়ক, তদারককারী, নিরীক্ষক (মঃ ইঃ)। **2.** An officer to examine into and report upon the working of a department or institution ; অবেক্ষক, পরিদর্শক, কার্য্যদর্শী, অধ্যক্ষ, কার্য্যাধ্যক্ষ। **3.** A police officer ranking next below a superintendent and above a sergeant;

পরিদর্শনকারী পুলিসকর্ম্মচারী বিশেষ। **–spec′-to-ral, –spec′-to-ri-al,** *adjs.* **–spec′-tor-ship,** *n.*

in-spĕc′-tŏr-āte, *n.* **1.** The office or function of an inspector; পরিদর্শকের পদ বা কার্য্য। **2.** A body of inspectors; পরিদর্শকবর্গ। **3.** The jurisdiction of an inspector, esp. in Greenland; পরিদর্শকের এলাকা।

in-spi-ra′-tion, *n.* **1.** The drawing in of breath (opp. to *expiration*); act of inspiring; state of being inspired; শ্বাসগ্রহণ, পূরক (এভেলন) অপান (ডিউসেন), অন্তঃশ্বসন (সাঃ পঃ) অনুপ্রাণনা; অনুপ্রাণন। **2.** Divine influence, esp. that by which the sacred writers were instructed; প্রত্যাদেশ, দৈবপ্রভাব, ঈশ্বরপ্রেরণা, (হিঃ কোঃ), ভগবৎপ্রেরণা। **3.** An inspired thought, idea, etc.; "They poured grave *inspiration*"; ঈশ্বর-চিন্তা, ভাবপ্রেরিত, প্রভৃতি। **4.** An inspiring principle; প্রেরণা। **–al,** *adj.* Pertaining to inspiration; অনুপ্রাণনসম্বন্ধীয়। **–ism,** *n.* **–ist,** *n.* One who holds the doctrine of inspiration; দৈবপ্রত্যাদেশে বিশ্বাসবান।

in′-spi-ra-tor (-tĕr), *n.* A kind of respirator; নিঃশ্বাসবায়ু শোধনের জন্য যন্ত্র-বিশেষ। **–spir′-a-to-ry,** *adj.* Of, or pertaining to, inspiration or inhalation; শ্বাসগ্রহণসম্বন্ধীয়।

in-spīre′, *v. t.* **1.** To inhale; শ্বাস গ্রহণ করা। **2.** To infuse *into* a person or mind; to create; as, to *inspire* a feeling *in* or *into* a person; মনোমধ্যে সঞ্চার করা; জন্মান। **3.** To give inspiration to; to animate; as, to *inspire* a child *with* sentiments of virtue; প্রেরণা দেওয়া; অনুপ্রাণিত করা। **4.** To influence or actuate by divine or supernatural energy; দৈবভাবে অনুপ্রাণিত করা, অলৌকিক শক্তি দ্বারা অনুপ্রাণিত করা। **–spired′,** *p. p.* Having received inspiration; প্রত্যাদিষ্ট, ঈশ্বরপ্রেরিত, প্রত্যাদেশপ্রাপ্ত। **Inspired idiot**—কবি গোল্ডস্মিথ। **An inspired article**—কোন প্রভাবশালী ব্যক্তির ইঙ্গিতে লিখিত প্রবন্ধ।

in-spir′-it, *v. t.* To infuse life or spirit into; to animate; to encourage; প্রাণ অথবা তেজ সঞ্চারিত করা; অনুপ্রাণিত করা, উত্তেজিত করা, উদ্দীপিত করা; প্রোৎসাহিত করা। **–ing,** *adj.* Animating; invigorating; উত্তেজক; অনুপ্রাণক।

in-spis′-sate (-āt), *v. t.* To thicken; to condense by evaporation; ঘন করা; ঘনীভূত করা, গাঢ় করা। **–sa′-tion,** *n.* **Inspissated milk**—ক্ষীরোত্তর, ঘনীভূত দুগ্ধ।

in-stā-bil′-i-tȳ, *n.* **1.** Want of stability or firmness; অস্থৈর্য্য, অধৃতি, অদৃঢ়তা, অনবস্থিতি, চঞ্চলতা, অস্থায়িত্ব। **2.** (*Fig.*) Inconstancy; fickleness, as of character etc.; স্থায়িত্বের অভাব, অস্থিরতা, চপলতা; চাঞ্চল্য, অনিত্যতা, অব্যবস্থিতচিত্ততা।

in-stall′, *v. t.* **1.** To place in any office, rank, etc. with due ceremony; কোন পদে প্রতিষ্ঠিত করা, পদাসীন করা, অভিষিক্ত করা, যথাবিধি প্রতিষ্ঠা করা। **2.** To establish one or oneself in a place, condition etc.; স্থাপিত করা, প্রতিষ্ঠিত করা, অভিষিক্ত করা। **3.** To set up or fix in a position for use, as a lighting or heating apparatus; যথাস্থানে স্থাপন করা। **–stal′-lant,** *adj.* & *n.* Installing in any office, rank etc.; কোন পদে প্রতিষ্ঠাকারী। (*Noun*) One who installs; প্রতিষ্ঠাতা, অভিষেক-কর্ত্তা। **–stal-la′-tion,** *n.* **1.** Act of installing; formal establishment in any office or position; স্থাপন, প্রতিষ্ঠাপন; অভিষেক, প্রতিষ্ঠা। **2.** Placing in a position for use, as of lighting or heating apparatus etc.; a set of apparatus required for electric fitting in a house etc.; যথাস্থানে স্থাপন; কোন গৃহে বিজলী-বীজন ও প্রদীপ স্থাপনের জন্য প্রয়োজনীয় সরঞ্জাম।

in-stal(l)′-mĕnt, *n.* **1.** Each of several parts successively falling due, of a sum payable; এক এক কিস্তির টাকা, কিস্তি। **2.** (*Fig.*) One of several parts supplied at different times; (লক্ষণায়) কিস্তি। **By instalments**—কিস্তিতে কিস্তিতে, ভাগশঃ।

in′-stance (-stăns), *n.* & *v. t.* **1.** A case or example illustrating a general truth or statement; দৃষ্টান্ত, উদাহরণ, নিদর্শন (হিঃ কোঃ), স্থল। **2.** Request; as, at the *instance* of; অনুরোধ, উপরোধ, নির্ব্বন্ধ, প্রার্থনা। **3.** Suit; as, a court of the first *instance*; মোকদ্দমা। ***Verb t.*** To mention as an example; উদাহরণস্বরূপ উল্লেখ করা, দৃষ্টান্তস্বরূপ উল্লেখ করা। **–stan-cy,** *n.* Urgency; অত্যাবশ্যকতা, নির্ব্বন্ধাতিশয়। **At the instance of**—কাহারও উপরোধে, কাহারও অনুরোধে। **For instance**—যথা, দৃষ্টান্তস্বরূপ, দৃষ্টান্তস্থলে। **In the first instance**—In the first place; at the first stage of a proceeding; প্রথমতঃ; মোকদ্দমার প্রথম অবস্থায়।

in′-stănt, *adj.* **1.** Pressing; urgent; গুরুতর; অত্যাবশ্যক, জরুরী। **2.** Not deferred; immediate; as, the application gave *instant* relief; অব্যবহিত; আসন্ন। **3.** (*Abbr. inst.*) Of the current month; as, the 8th *inst.*; চলিত মাসের।

in′-stănt, *n.* **1.** A point of time; as, come this very *instant*; ক্ষণ। **2.** A very short space of time; a moment; "Every *instant* I expect him here"; তল্লক্ষণ; নিমেষ, মুহূর্ত্ত।

in-stăn-tā′-nē-ous (-ŭs), *adj.* **1.** Done or occurring in an instant; মুহূর্ত্ত মধ্যে কৃত বা সংঘটিত, তাৎক্ষণিক, সদ্য। **2.** Existence at a given instant; ক্ষণস্থায়ী, ক্ষণিক, ক্ষণমাত্রস্থায়ী,

ক্ষণমাত্রাবস্থায়ী। **—ly,** *adv.* In an instantaneous manner; ক্ষণস্থায়িভাবে, মুহূর্ত্তমধ্যে, তৎক্ষণাৎ, অবিলম্বে, ঝটিতি। **—ness,** *n.* **Instantaneous death**—তাৎক্ষণিক মৃত্যু, সদ্যোমৃত্যু। **In an instant**—মুহূর্ত্তমধ্যে, অবিলম্বে, ঝটিতি, তৎক্ষণাৎ, তন্মুহূর্ত্তে।

in'-stănt-lў, *adv.* Immediately; অচিরাৎ, অবিলম্বে, তৎক্ষণাৎ, ঝটিতি, তন্মুহূর্ত্তে।

in-stau-rā'-tion (-stä-), *n.* Restoration; renovation; সংস্কার; পুনর্নবীকরণ। **In'-stau-ra-tor,** *n.*

in-stead' (-stĕd), *adv.* **1.** In the place or room of as a substitute or alternative; পরিবর্ত্তে, বদলে, স্থানে, বিনিময়ে, স্থলে। **Instead of**—In place of; স্থানে, স্থলে, পরিবর্ত্তে।

in'-stĕp, *n.* **1.** The upper surface of the human foot between the toes and the ankle; পায়ের পাতার উপরিভাগ, পিণ্ডিকা (আঃ বিঃ), পাদোপরিভাগ পদাগ্র, পিচিণ্ডিকা। **2.** The part of a shoe, stocking, etc. covering the instep; মোজা বা জুতার যে অংশ দ্বারা পিণ্ডিকা আচ্ছাদিত হয়। **3.** A thing shaped like the instep; পিণ্ডিকাকার বস্তু।

in'-sti-gate, *v. t.* **1.** To urge forward; to incite; as, to *instigate* one to a crime; প্রণোদিত করা; উদ্দীপিত করা, উত্তেজিত করা, কুকর্ম্মে প্ররোচিত করা, উৎসাহিত করা, প্রোৎসাহিত করা। **2.** To foment or provoke as a revolt etc.; উদ্দীপ্ত করা। **—ga'-tion,** *n.* Act of instigating; প্রণোদন, উদ্দীপন, প্রচোদন, প্ররোচনা, প্রবর্ত্তনা, আদীপন, উৎসাহপ্রদান, প্রোৎসাহন। **—gator,** *n.* One who instigates or incites; প্রণোদক, উত্তেজক, কুকার্য্যে উৎসাহদাতা।

in-stil(l)', *v. t.* **1.** To pour in by drops; বিন্দু বিন্দু করিয়া ফেলা। **2.** To infuse slowly or gradually; as, he *instilled* his malice into thousands; আস্তে আস্তে বা ক্রমে ক্রমে সঞ্চারিত করা। **—la'-tion, —ment,** *ns.* Act of instilling; that which is instilled; বিন্দু বিন্দু করিয়া সঞ্চারণ বা পাতন; আস্তে আস্তে বা ক্রমে ক্রমে সঞ্চারিত বস্তু।

in'-stinct (-stingkt), *n.* **1.** Natural impulse, esp. in lower animals to do what is necessary for existence etc. independently of any conscious design; ইতর প্রাণীর বুদ্ধি, সহজজ্ঞান, স্বাভাবিকজ্ঞান, প্রাকৃতিকবুদ্ধি, নৈসর্গিকবুদ্ধি (হিঃ কোঃ), সহজক্রিয়া, সহজাতবুদ্ধি, অঙ্গস্বভাব। **2.** Innate tendency or inclination; "Edward by *instinct* was a law-giver; স্বাভাবিকপ্রবৃত্তি, প্রকৃতিগতপ্রবৃত্তি, স্বাভাবিক রুচি। **3.** Intuition; unconscious skill; হৃৎস্থিত সহজ জ্ঞান, স্বাভাবিক জ্ঞান, আত্মপ্রত্যয়, বোধি (হিঃ কোঃ); অজ্ঞাতসারে বর্ত্তমান নৈপুণ্য।

in-stinct' (-stingkt), *pred. adj.* Imbued or charged *with* life, force etc., "Digressions *instinct* with meaning to his audiences"; অনুপ্রাণিত, পরিপূরিত, ভরপুর, পরিব্যাপ্ত।

in-stinc'-tive (-stĭng-tĭv), *adj.* Derived from, or prompted by, instinct or natural impulse; প্রকৃতিনিষ্ঠ, স্বভাবসিদ্ধ, প্রকৃতিসিদ্ধ, স্বভাবপ্রেরিত, সহজজ্ঞানপ্রযুক্ত, সহজজ্ঞানসিদ্ধ, স্বাভাবিক। **—ly,** *adv.*

in'-sti-tūte, *n.* & *v. t.* **1.** (*Pl.*) A comprehensive summary of legal principles and decisions; as, the *institutes* of Manu; ব্যবস্থা শাস্ত্রের মূলতত্ত্ব বা মীমাংসার বিস্তৃতসার, ব্যবস্থা, বিধান, নিয়ম, শাস্ত্রবিধান, সংহিতা। **2.** An organization or society for the promotion of learning, science, etc.; বিদ্যালোচনা, সাহিত্য, প্রভৃতির উৎকর্ষ সাধনার্থ সমাজ বা প্রতিষ্ঠান। **3.** A building used by such a society etc.; ঐরূপ প্রতিষ্ঠান প্রভৃতির মন্দির। *Verb t.* **1.** To establish; to set up, as a court etc.; প্রতিষ্ঠিত করা; স্থাপিত করা, প্রতিষ্ঠাপিত করা। **2.** To initiate or set on foot; as, to *institute* an enquiry: to *institute* a suit; প্রবর্ত্তন করা, আরম্ভ করা, রুজু করা, দায়ের করা, স্থাপন করা। **3.** To invest with the spiritua charge of benefice; যাজকীয় অধিকার প্রদান করা।

in-sti-tū'-tion, *n.* **1.** Act of instituting; প্রতিষ্ঠা, স্থাপন, সংস্থাপন, সংস্থান। **2.** A society or organization for the promotion of some public object, *e. g.* a school, college, hospital etc.; as, a literary or charitable *institution*; a building used by such a society; প্রতিষ্ঠান, সভা (হিঃ কোঃ), লোকসাধারণের উন্নতি বিধায়িনী সমাজ, পরিষৎ, বিদ্যালয়, প্রভৃতি; কোন প্রতিষ্ঠানের গৃহ। **3.** An established law, custom or practice; অচলপ্রতিষ্ঠ বিধি, প্রথা বা আচার, বিধি, ব্যবস্থা, বিধান। **4.** The investing of (a clergyman) with the spiritual charge of a benefice; (যাজককে) কোন স্থানের আধ্যাত্মিক ভার প্রদান। **5.** (*Colloq.*) A familiar practice or object; "He is one of the *institutions* of the place"; (চলিত-ভাষায়) প্রচলিত রীতি, ধারা, সুপরিচিত বস্তু। **—al,** *adj.* Pertaining to an institution; প্রতিষ্ঠানসম্বন্ধীয়।

in-strŭct', *v. t.* **1.** To teach; শিক্ষা-দেওয়া, উপদেশ দেওয়া, শিখান। **2.** To give information to; as, a client *instructs* a solicitor; সংবাদ দেওয়া, জ্ঞাপন করা, জানান, অবগত করান। **3.** To command; to direct; as, the judge *instructs* the jury; আদেশ দেওয়া; অনুজ্ঞা করা। **4.** To apprise; to inform; "Observations *instruct* me that ..."; অবগত করা; জ্ঞাপন করা, জ্ঞাত করা, সংবাদ দেওয়া, বিদিত করা।

–struc′-tor, *n.* One who instructs; শিক্ষক, উপাধ্যায়, শিক্ষাগুরু, আচার্য্য, উপদেশক, উপদেষ্টা, অধ্যাপক। **–struc′-tress** (*Fem.*) শিক্ষাদাত্রী, অধ্যাপিকা (ঐ)।

in-strŭc′-tion, *n.* **1.** The act of instructing or teaching; a precept or lesson; শিক্ষাদান, উপদেশ প্রদান; উপদেশ, শিক্ষা, বিধি, বিধান। **2.** (*Pl.*) Directions; orders; আজ্ঞা, নিদেশ, অনুজ্ঞা; আদেশ। **–al,** *adj.* Educational; শিক্ষাসম্বন্ধীয়, শিক্ষা-সংক্রান্ত। **–tive,** *adj.* Serving to instruct; conveying a lesson; উপদেশাত্মক, জ্ঞানগর্ভ; উপদেশপ্রদ, শিক্ষাপ্রদ। **–tive-ly,** *adv.* In an instructive way; উপদেশাত্মকভাবে, শিক্ষাচ্ছলে। **–tive-ness,** *n.*

in′-strū′-mĕnt, *n.* **1.** That by which any work is performed; a tool; an implement; যদ্দ্বারা কোন কার্য্য সম্পন্ন হয়, উপায়, সাধন, উপকরণ (হিঃ কোঃ), হেতু, কারণ; যন্ত্র; হাতিয়ার। **2.** A contrivance for producing musical sounds; বাদ্যযন্ত্র। **3.** A document; a legal deed; দলিল; দস্তাবেজ। **4.** A person used as a tool; an agent; means; যন্ত্রস্বরূপ ব্যক্তি; কার্য্যকারক; উপায়। **A musical instrument**—See INSTRUMENT, 2. **Wind instrument** — বায়ুবাদ্য (হিঃ কোঃ)।

in-strū′-mĕn′-tăl, *adj.* **1.** Serving as an instrument or means; helpful; কার্য্যসাধক, প্রয়োজক, কার্য্যসাধনোপায় বা যন্ত্রস্বরূপ; সাহায্যকারী, সহায়। **2.** Of, or relating to, a tool or implement; যন্ত্রসম্বন্ধীয়। **3.** Pertaining to, or produced on, an instrument; as, *instrumental* music; বাদ্যযন্ত্রসম্বন্ধীয়, তৎকৃত, বাদ্যসিদ্ধ, বাদ্যোৎপন্ন। **4.** (*Gram.*, of a case) Denoting means or agency; (ব্যাকরণ) করণসম্বন্ধীয়। **–ist,** *n.* One who plays upon a musical instrument; বাদক। **–ly,** *adv.* In an instrumental way; যান্ত্রিকভাবে। **The instrumental case** — See INSTRUMENTAL 4. করণকারক।

in-strū-mĕn-tăl′-i-tў, *n.* Agency; medium; means; as, by the *instrumentality* of; কর্তৃত্ব, কারকত্ব, সাধকত্ব; মধ্যস্থতা; উপায়। **By the instrumentality of**—By means of; with the help of; দ্বারা; সাহায্যে।

in-strū-mĕn-ta′-tion, *n.* **1.** Agency; instrumentality; কর্তৃত্ব; সাধকত্ব। **2.** (*Mus.*) The composition or arrangement of music for instruments esp. the orchestra; বাদ্যযন্ত্রের জন্য গীত বাদ্যাদিতে রচনা বা বিন্যাস। **3.** (*Surgery*) Operation with an instrument; (অস্ত্রোপচার-বিদ্যা) অস্ত্রোপচার।

in-sŭb-ôr′-di-nate, *adj.* Not submissive to authority; disobedient; rebellious; অবশীভূত; অবাধ্য; বিদ্রোহী। **–na′-tion,** *n.* Disobedience; অবাধ্যতা।

in-sŭb-stăn′-tial (-shăl), *adj.* **1.** Not real or substantial; অবাস্তব, অসার। **2.** Wanting in solidity; frail; অসার, সত্ত্বহীন, নিঃসত্ত্ব; দুর্ব্বল। **–ti-al′-i-ty,** *n.*

in-sŭf′-fêr-ă-ble (-bl), *adj.* Intolerable; unbearable, as insolence etc.; অসহ্য; অসহনীয়, দুঃসহ, সহনাতীত। **–bly,** *adv.*

in-sŭf-fi′-cient (-shĕnt), *adj.* Not enough; inadequate; অপ্রচুর, অযথেষ্ট, অযোগ্য; অপর্য্যাপ্ত। **–cien-cy,** *n.* Inadequacy; অপ্রাচুর্য্য, ন্যূনতা। **–ly,** *adv.* Inadequately; অপর্য্যাপ্তরূপে।

in′-sŭf-flāte, *v. t.* **1.** To blow or breathe as air, gas etc., into a cavity of the body etc.; শরীরগহ্বরে বায়ু, বাষ্প, ঔষধের সূক্ষ্মচূর্ণ ফুৎকারদ্বারা প্রবেশ করান। **–fla′-tion,** *n.* **1.** Act of blowing or breathing on or into; বায়ু, বাষ্প বা ঔষধের সূক্ষ্মচূর্ণ ফুৎকার দ্বারা শরীর গহ্বরে প্রবেশ, শ্বাসপ্রক্ষেপণ, শ্বাসন্যাস। **2.** (*Ec.*) Act of breathing on a person, a rite of exorcism; (যাজকীয় শাস্ত্র) ভূত ছাড়াইবার জন্য কাহারও উপর শ্বাস ফেলন। **–fla-tor,** *n.* An instrument for blowing air into the lungs or injecting powder etc. into a cavity, wound etc.; ফুসফুসে বায়ু প্রবিষ্ট করার অথবা শরীরগহ্বর বা আহত স্থানে চূর্ণ প্রভৃতি প্রক্ষেপের জন্য যন্ত্রবিশেষ, প্রক্ষেপক।

in′-sū-lar (-lĕr), *adj.* **1.** Of, or pertaining to, or of the nature of, an island; দ্বীপসংক্রান্ত বা তৎসম্বন্ধীয়, দ্বৈপ্য। **2.** Like islanders; narrow-minded; illiberal; as, *insular* prejudices; দ্বীপবাসিবৎ; সংকীর্ণমনাঃ; অনুদার। **–ism,** *n.* State of being insular or narrowminded; অনুদারতা, সংকীর্ণচিত্ততা। **–lar′-i-ty,** *n.* **1.** State of being an island; দ্বীপাকারত্ব, দ্বীপরূপতা, দ্বৈপত্ব। **3.** Narrowness of mind; "The *insularity* of the average Briton"; সঙ্কীর্ণচিত্ততা, অনুদারতা। **–ly,** *adv.*

in′-sū-lāte, *v. t.* **1.** To make an island of; as, to *insulate* a ground; দ্বীপে পরিণত করা, দ্বীপাকার করা। **2.** To isolate, as a person or thing; পৃথক স্থানে সন্নিবিষ্ট করা, বিচ্ছিন্ন করা, বিশ্লিষ্ট করা। **3.** (*Phys.*) To cut off from conducting bodies the interposition of non-conductors so as to prevent transfer of electricity or heat; (পদার্থ-বিদ্যা) অপরিচালক পদার্থের বেষ্টনদ্বারা তাড়িত অথবা উত্তাপের বহিঃসঞ্চালনপথ রুদ্ধ করা। **–la-ted,** *adj.* বিন্যস্ত (হিঃ কোঃ), রোধিত (ঐ)। **–la′-tion,** *n.* The act of insulating; isolation; পৃথকীকরণ; অনন্যসংযোগ, রোধন (হিঃ কোঃ)। **–la-tor,** *n.* **1.** One who

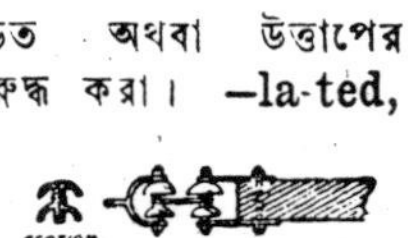

Telegraph wire insulators.

that which insulates ; রোধক (ইঃ কোঃ), বিদ্যুদ্‌রোধক (ঐ)। **2.** (*Elec. & thermotics*) A non-conductor ; অপরিচালক পদার্থ। **Insulating bodies**—রোধকপদার্থ (হিঃ কোঃ)।

in′-sŭlt, *n.* A gross affront ; an insulting word or act ; অপমান, অবমাননা, মর্য্যাদাতিক্রম, অবজ্ঞা ; অপমানসূচক বাক্য বা কার্য্য, অপমান-বাক্য। **To add insult to injury**—To aggravate the wrong already done to a person ; কাটা ঘায়ে নুণের ছিটা দেওয়া, পেঁয়াজ পয়জার করা।

in-sŭlt′, *v. t.* **1.** To treat with abuse or contempt ; to affront ; অপমান করা ; অবমাননা করা, মর্য্যাদা লঙ্ঘন করা। **–ing,** *adj.* That which insults ; অপমানকারী, অপমান-জনক। **–ing-ly,** *adv.* In an insulting manner ; অপমানজনকভাবে।

in-sū′-pêr-ă-ble (-bl), *adj.* Insurmountable ; incapable of being overcome ; দুর্লঙ্ঘ্য, অলঙ্ঘনীয়, অনতিক্রমনীয়, দুস্তর ; অনধিগম্য দুরধিগম্য, দুঃসাধ্য, অজেয়। **–bil′-i-ty,** *n.* **–bly,** *adv.* In an insuperable manner ; অনতিক্রমণীয়ভাবে, দুর্লঙ্ঘ্যরূপে।

in-sŭp-pôrt-ă-ble (-bl), *adj.* Unbearable ; দুর্ব্বহ, অসহ্য, অসহনীয়, দুঃসহ, দুর্ব্বিসহ। **–bly,** *adv.* In an insupportable way ; অসহনীয়রূপে।

in-sur′-ance (-shôr-ăns), *n.* **1.** Act of insuring ; the contract by which one engages for a stipulated premium to make up a loss which another may sustain ; বিমা বা ক্ষতিপূরণার্থ বন্দোবস্ত-করণ, বীমাকরণ ; বীমা। **2.** Sum paid for insuring property, life etc. ; premium ; বীমার জন্য দেয় টাকা ; বীমার কিস্তির টাকা। **Life insurance**—জীবন বীমা।

in-sur′-ănt (-shôr-), *n.* The person to whom an insurance policy is issued ; বীমাকারী।

in-sure′ (-shôr), *v. t.* **1.** To ensure ; to secure ; as, to *insure* safety to any one ; সুনিশ্চিত করা ; নিরাপদ্ করা। **2.** To secure against a possible loss or damage at a given rate of premium ; as, to *insure* life, property, etc. ; বীমা করা। **–sur′-a-ble,** *adj.* Capable of being insured against loss, damage, etc. ; বীমাযোগ্য। **The insured**—যাহার অনুকূলে বীমা করা হয়।

in-sur′-êr (-shôr-), *n.* One who insures property etc. ; an underwriter ; বীমাকারী ; বীমাব্যবসায়ী।

in-sur′-gĕnt (-sêr-), *adj.* & *n.* **1.** Rebellious ; rising in revolt against lawful authority ; as, the *insurgent* provinces ; বিদ্রোহী ; রাজদ্রোহী, রাজবিরোধী। **2.** (Of the sea) Rushing in ; (সমুদ্র সম্বন্ধে) প্রচণ্ডবেগে ধাবমান। ***Noun.*** A rebel ; বিদ্রোহী ব্যক্তি। **–gen-cy,** *n.* An insurrection ; বিদ্রোহ।

in-sur-mount′-a-ble (-sêr-mownt-ă-bl), *adj.* Not surmountable; insuperable ; দুরতিক্রম, দুস্তর, অনুল্লঙ্ঘনীয়, দুরুত্তর, অনুত্তীর্য্য, দুরারোহ, দুস্তর, অনারোহ, অনতিক্রম্য ; অলঙ্ঘ্য। **–bly,** *adv.* In a manner not to be overcome ; অনতিক্রমণীয় ভাবে।

in-sur-rĕc-tion (-sêr-), *n.* **1.** Act of rising against civil or political authority ; রাজবিদ্রোহ। **2.** A revolt ; an incipient rebellion ; প্রজাক্ষোভ, বিদ্রোহ ; বিদ্রোহের সূচনা। **–al,** *adj.* Pertaining to insurrection ; rebellious ; বিদ্রোহ সংক্রান্ত, রাজদ্রোহ সংক্রান্ত ; বিদ্রোহাচারী, বিদ্রোহী। **–ist,** *n.* One who favours insurrection ; বিদ্রোহানুরাগী।

in-sŭs-cĕp′-ti-ble (-bl), *adj.* Not susceptible ; incapable of being moved or affected, (followed by *of, to*) ; as, a mind *insusceptible to* folly ; অবিচলনীয়, অবিকার্য্য ; অসাড়, বেদনাবোধশূন্য, সংবেদনশূন্য। **–bil′-i-ty,** *n.*

in-tăct′, *adj.* Untouched by anything harmful ; entire ; unimpaired ; ক্ষতিকর কোন কিছুদ্বারা অস্পৃষ্ট ; অবিকল, অক্ষুণ্ণ, অটুট, নিটুট, টন্‌টনে, বজায়, অখণ্ড ; অক্ষত, অবিকৃত, অক্ষীণ, অভগ্ন।

in-tagl′-i-ā-tĕd (-tăl-), *adj.* Covered or engraved on the surface, as a stone etc. ; ক্ষোদিত, উৎকীর্ণ।

in-tagl′-io (-tăl-), (*It.*) *n.* & *v. t.* **1.** A cutting or engraving ; an engraved design ; ক্ষোদন, অঙ্কন ; ক্ষোদিত নক্সা। **2.** The art or process of engraving on stone or other hard materials ; প্রস্তর বা অন্য কঠিন পদার্থের উপর ক্ষোদন। **3.** A gem with incised design as distinguished from a *cameo* ; ক্ষোদিত মণি, উৎকীর্ণ মণি। ***Verb t.*** To engrave as stone or figure ; ক্ষোদিত করা।

in′-take, *n.* **1.** (*Chiefly Scot.*) The place where water is taken into a pipe etc. ; নলের মুখ। **2.** The air-way in a mine ; খনির বায়ু প্রবেশ-পথ। **3.** The abrupt narrowing or contraction in a tube, stocking, etc. ; নল, মোজা, প্রভৃতির আকস্মিক কুঞ্চন। **4.** A taking in ; the amount taken in ; গ্রহণ ; গৃহীত বস্তুর পরিমাণ।

in-tăn′-gi-ble (-bl), *adj.* **1.** Incapable of being touched ; impalpable ; অস্পৃশ্য ; স্পর্শাজ্ঞেয়, স্পর্শবোধাতীত, স্পর্শদ্বারা অজ্ঞেয়, সূক্ষ্ম, অননুভবনীয়। **2.** Incapable of being grasped mentally; "*Intangible* argument"; দুর্গ্রহ, দুর্বোধ। **–bil′-i-ty,** *n.* The state of being intangible; অস্পৃশ্যতা, অননুভবনীয়তা। **–bly,** *adv.*

in′-tē-gêr, *n.* **1.** A whole number as opposed to a fraction ; পূর্ণ সংখ্যা, অখণ্ড সংখ্যা, অখণ্ড রাশি, অভগ্ন রাশি, পূর্ণাঙ্ক (মঃ উঃ)। **2.** A thing complete in itself ; অখণ্ড বস্তু।

in′-tĕ-grăl, *adj.* & *n.* **1.** Of, or relating to, a whole ; forming a necessary part of a whole ; constituent ; as, an *integral* part ; সামগ্রিক ; সম্পূরক বা অপরিহার্য্য অংশ গঠনকারী ; উপাদানমূলক। **2.** Complete ; entire ; পূর্ণ ; সমগ্র, গোটা, আস্ত, অখণ্ড, অভগ্ন, পূর্ণ (হিঃ কোঃ), সাবয়ব (ঐ), অবয়বরূপ (ঐ), অভিন্ন, (ঐ), চল (ঐ)। **3.** Pertaining to an integer ; not fractional ; অখণ্ডসংখ্যা সংক্রান্ত ; অখণ্ড। ***Noun.*** **1.** (*Rare*) An entire thing ; a whole (কচিদ্-ব্যবহৃত) আস্ত জিনিষ ; সমগ্র বস্তু। **2.** (*Math.*) A whole number ; (গণিতশাস্ত্র) পূর্ণ সংখ্যা। **–gral′-i-ty,** *n.* **–ly,** *adv.* Completely ; wholly ; entirely ; সম্পূর্ণভাবে ; সমগ্রভাবে ; পুরাপুরি। **Integral calculus**—See under CALCULUS.

in′-tĕ-grănt, *adj.* Component ; forming a part of a whole ; পূর্ণতা-সাধক, সম্পূরক, পূর্ণতার অংশীভূত।

in′-tĕ-grāte, *adj.* & *v. t.* Composed of parts ; whole ; complete ; অংশসমন্বিত ; সমগ্র ; সম্পূর্ণ। ***Verb t.*** **1.** To complete by addition of parts as an imperfect thing ; পূর্ণাঙ্গ করা, সম্পূর্ণ করা, পূর্ণতাসম্পাদন করা। **2.** To unite as parts into a whole ; অংশ সংযোজনপূর্ব্বক পূর্ণ করা। **3.** (*Math.*) To find the integral of ; (গণিতশাস্ত্র) অখণ্ডসংখ্যা বাহির করা। **4.** To indicate the whole of ; to give the sum or total of ; সমগ্র প্রদর্শন করা, পূর্ণভাবে প্রদর্শন করা ; সমষ্টি বা যোগফল প্রদান করা। **–gra′-tion,** *n.* Act of making whole ; completion ; সমগ্রতাসম্পাদন, পূর্ণতাপাদন, উপচয় (হিঃ কোঃ), একত্রীভাব (ঐ) ; সমাপ্তি **gra-tive,** *adj.* **gra-tor,** *n.* Thet which integrates ; একীকারক, পূর্ণতাপাদক।

in-tĕg′-ri-tў, *n.* **1.** Entirety ; wholeness ; পূর্ণতা, সমগ্রতা, সাকল্য ; অখণ্ডতা, অন্যূনতা। **2.** Honesty ; rectitude ; সাধুতা ; ন্যায়নিষ্ঠা, ন্যায়পরতা, ধার্ম্মিকতা, পবিত্রতা। **3.** Unimpaired state ; soundness ; অক্ষত বা অক্ষুণ্ণ অবস্থা ; অটুটতা।

in-tĕg′-ū-mĕnt, *n.* A husk, rind, skin or other usually natural covering ; খোসা, ছাল, বল্কল, ত্বক্, বেষ্টন (ভাবঃ), আবেষ্টন, কঞ্চুক, আচ্ছাদন, আবরণ। **–men′-ta-ry,** *adj.* Composed of, or belonging to, integuments ; কোষিক।

in-tĕl′-lĕct, *n.* **1.** The knowing or reasoning faculty ; the power of thought ; understanding ; জ্ঞান বা বোধশক্তি, প্রজ্ঞা, চিৎ, চিচ্ছক্তি ; বিচারশক্তি ; বুদ্ধিবৃত্তি, মেধা, ধী, মনীষা। **2.** A person of intellect ; intellectual persons collectively ; বুদ্ধিমান ব্যক্তি ; মনিষিবর্গ।

in-tĕl-lĕc′-tion, *n.* The act or process of understanding ; apprehension of ideas, as opp. to *imagination* ; বুদ্ধিক্রিয়া (হিঃ কোঃ), বুদ্ধিব্যাপার (ঐ) ; ভাববোধ। **–tive,** *adj.* Intellectual ; intelligent ; বুদ্ধিসম্বন্ধীয়, মানসিক, বুদ্ধিমান, প্রতিভাশালী।

in-tĕl′-lĕc-tū-ăl, *adj.* & *n.* **1.** Relating to, produced by, or requiring the exercise of, the intellect ; mental ; বুদ্ধিসম্বন্ধীয়, বুদ্ধিবিষয়ক (হিঃ কোঃ), বুদ্ধি দ্বারা অনুষ্ঠিত বা সম্পাদ্য, জ্ঞানবিষয়ক ; মানসিক। **2.** Having intellect or power of understanding ; বুদ্ধিমান, প্রতিভাশালী, ধীমান, মনীষাসম্পন্ন। ***Noun.*** A person having intellect ; an enlightened person ; বুদ্ধিমান ব্যক্তি ; সুসভ্য ও সুশিক্ষিত ব্যক্তি। **–al′-i-ty,** *n.* Quality of being intellectual ; প্রতিভাশালিতা, মানসতা। **–i-za′-tion,** *n.* **–ize,** *v. t.* **1.** To express or discuss intellectually ; as, sentiment is *intellectualized* emotion ; বুদ্ধির সহিত প্রকাশ বা আলোচনা করা। **2.** To give an intellectual character or aspcct to ; as, to *intellectualize* life ; to endow with intellect ; চিন্ময় করা, চিদ্গুণ সম্পন্ন করা, চিদাত্মক করা ; প্রতিভাসম্পন্ন করা। **–ly,** *adv.* In an intellectual manner ; জ্ঞানতঃ, বুদ্ধিপূর্ব্বক। **Intellectual faculty**—ধীশক্তি (মঃ ইঃ)।

in-tĕl-lĕc′-tū-ăl-ĭsm, *n.* **1.** The doctrine that knowledge is derived from pure reason ; শুদ্ধ প্রজ্ঞা হইতে জ্ঞান উদ্ভূত হয় — এইরূপ মতবাদ, জ্ঞানপ্রাধান্যবাদ (হিঃ কোঃ), তত্ত্বজ্ঞেয়তাবাদ (ঐ)। **2.** The exercise of the intellect alone ; কেবলমাত্র বুদ্ধিবৃত্তি পরিচালনা। **–ist,** *n.* **1.** One who overrates the importance of understanding ; যে ব্যক্তি বুদ্ধির গুরুত্ব অতিরিক্তমাত্রায় গণ্য করে। **2.** An adherent of intellectualism ; জ্ঞানপ্রাধান্যবাদী, তত্ত্বজ্ঞেয়তাবাদী।

in-tĕl′-li-gence (-jĕns), *n.* **1.** The faculty of understanding ; the intellect ; বুদ্ধি, বিজ্ঞতা (হিঃ কোঃ), মনীষা (ঐ), প্রজ্ঞা, জ্ঞান, মেধা ; চিচ্ছক্তি, চেতনা, বুদ্ধিসত্তা, চৈতন্য (ব্রজঃ হিন্দু)। **2.** (Of persons and animals) Quickness of apprehension ; sagacity ; ক্ষিপ্রগ্রাহিতা ; বুদ্ধিমত্তা। **3.** An intelligent or rational being ; বুদ্ধিমান ব্যক্তি, বুদ্ধিমান জীব, বিচার-বুদ্ধিসম্পন্ন ব্যক্তি। **4.** News ; information ; সংবাদ ; খবর, বার্ত্তা, সমাচার, সন্দেশ, বৃত্তান্ত। **–gen′-tial,** *adj.* Intellectual ; মানসিক, বুদ্ধিসংক্রান্ত।

in-tĕl′-li-genc-ĕr (-jĕns-), *n.* **1.** A messenger ; an informant ; বার্ত্তাবহ ; চর। **2.** A spy ; গুপ্তচর।

in-tĕl′-li-gĕnt, *adj.* Endowed with the faculty of understanding ; marked by intelligence ; as, an *intelligent* answer ; সুধী, সুবুদ্ধি, ধীমান, প্রাজ্ঞ, মনিষী, মনীষাসম্পন্ন, মতিমান, সুবুদ্ধি ; বুদ্ধিপরিচায়ক। **–ly,** *adv.* In an intelligent manner ; বুদ্ধিমত্তার সহিত।

in-tĕl′-li-gĭ-ble (-bl), *adj.* **1.** Capable of being understood ; clear ; বোধগম্য, জ্ঞেয়, বুদ্ধিগ্রাহ্য, সুগম ; বিশদ, সুস্পষ্ট, প্রাঞ্জল। **2.** (*Philos.*)

Capable of being apprehended only by the intellect and not by the senses; (দর্শন-শাস্ত্র) কেবলমাত্র বুদ্ধি দ্বারা জ্ঞেয়, বুদ্ধৈকজ্ঞেয়। **—bil′-i-ty,** *n.* State of being intelligible; perspicuity; বোধগম্যতা; সুস্পষ্টতা, বিশদতা, প্রাঞ্জলতা। **—bly,** *adv.*

in-tĕm′-pêr-āte, *adj.* **1.** Immoderate; unbridled; অমিতাচারী; অসংযমী, অসংযমশীল। **2.** Indulging any appetite or passion to excess; অমিতাচারী। **3.** Addicted to drinking; পানাসক্ত, মদ্যপায়ী। **—ance,** *n.* **1.** State of being intemperate; অমিতাচারিত্ব। **2.** Excessive indulgence in drinking; অত্যধিক পানাসক্তি, অতিপান। **3.** An intemperate act; অমিতাচার, অমিতাচারিত্ব। **—ly,** *adv.* Immoderately; অপরিমিতরূপে।

in-tĕnd′, *v. t.* **1.** To design or plan; to purpose; অভিপ্রায় করা, মতলব করা, সংকল্প করা; ইচ্ছা করা, উদ্দেশ্য করা। **2.** To mean; as, what exactly do you *intend* by the word?; বুঝা। **3.** To destine for a purpose; as, he *intended* his son for the bar; পূর্ব্ব হইতেই নিরূপিত করা, নির্দ্দিষ্ট করা। **—ed,** *adj.* Designed; meant; সঙ্কল্পিত, ঈপ্সিত; সূচিত, অভিপ্রেত।

in-tĕnd′-ănt, *n.* A superintendent or manager of public business etc.; তত্ত্বাবধায়ক, অধ্যক্ষ, কার্য্যপরিদর্শক, কার্য্যপরিদর্শী। **—an-cy,** *n.*

in-tĕnd′-ĕd, *n.* & *adj.* An affianced lover; বাগ্‌দত্ত বর বা বাগ্‌দত্তা কন্যা। ***Adj.*** See under INTEND.

in-tend′-mĕnt, *n.* The true meaning or intention of law; আইনের প্রকৃত অর্থ বা মর্ম্ম, অভিপ্রায়, আশয়।

in-tense′ (-tĕns) *adj.* **1.** Very eager or earnest, as a feeling or act; প্রগাঢ়, গাঢ়। **2.** Extreme in degree; vehement; violent; as, *intense* heat, passion, pain etc.; নিতান্ত; ঘোর, উগ্র, নিদারুণ, তীব্র, প্রগাঢ়, সান্দ্র; প্রচণ্ড, প্রবল। **3.** Very deep as a colour; অতি গাঢ় বা ঘন। **4.** Having some characteristic quality in a very high degree; intensely bright, hot, etc.; as, an *intense* star: an *intense* sky; অতিমাত্রায় কোন বিশিষ্ট গুণ সমন্বিত; তীব্রোজ্জ্বল, গাঢ়োষ্ণ। **5.** Feeling or susceptible to intense emotion, as a person; প্রবলাবেগপ্রবণ। **—ly,** *adv.* In an intense degree or manner; গাঢ়রূপে, প্রচণ্ডরূপে, নিরতিশয়। **—ness, —ten′-si-ty,** *ns.* State of being intense; extreme degree; keenness; আতিশয্য, প্রাখর্য্য; উগ্রতা, তীব্রতা, প্রচণ্ডতা, প্রগাঢ়তা, সান্দ্রতা; প্রাবল্য, অত্যন্ততা, তীক্ষ্ণতা।

in-tĕn′-si-fȳ, *v. t.* & *i.* To render intense; as, to *intensify* heat; উগ্র করা, প্রখর করা, প্রবল করা, ঘনাইয়া তোলা। ***Verb i.*** To become intense; উগ্র বা প্রখর হওয়া, সান্দ্রীভূত হওয়া। **—fi-ca′-tion,** *n.*

in-tĕn′-sion, *n.* **1.** Energetic exercise of the mind or will; বুদ্ধি বা ইচ্ছাশক্তির সতেজ পরিচালনা। **2.** High degree or intensity of a quality, opp. to *extension* (width of range); প্রকর্ষ, প্রকৃষ্টতা, গুণোৎকর্ষ। **3.** (*Logic*) The collective attributes of a general notion; a connotation; (তর্ক-বিজ্ঞান) সামান্য প্রত্যয়ের গুণ সমুচ্চয়, সামান্যবিধান; অর্থব্যাপ্তি।

in-tĕn′-sive (-sĭv), *adj.* **1.** Of, or pertaining to, intensity; intense; প্রগাঢ়তাসম্বন্ধীয়; প্রগাঢ়, তীব্র, তীক্ষ্ণ (ব্রজঃ হিন্দু)। **2.** (*Gram.*) Giving or expressing force or emphasis; আতিশয্যবাচক, উৎকর্ষজ্ঞাপক। **3.** (*Econ.*) Serving to increase the production of a given area; as, an *intensive* method; (অর্থশাস্ত্র) নির্দ্দিষ্ট পরিমাণ ভূমির উৎপাদনবৃদ্ধিকর। **—ly,** *adv.*

in-tĕnt′, *adj.* & *n.* **1.** Strictly attentive; resolved; bent; as, mind *intent* on self-improvement; eagerly occupied (*on*); অত্যন্ত মনোযোগী, নিবিষ্টচিত্ত, একাগ্রচিত্ত, অবধানপর, অভিনিবিষ্ট, সমাহিত, অনন্যচিত্ত, আসক্ত, আসক্তচিত্ত; দৃঢ়প্রতিজ্ঞ, কৃতসংকল্প; প্রবৃত্ত, প্রবণ; নিরত। **2.** Earnest; eager, as a faculty, look etc.; আগ্রহান্বিত, আগ্রহপূর্ণ; ব্যগ্র। ***Noun.*** An intention; purpose; ইচ্ছা, অভিসন্ধি; উদ্দেশ্য, অভিপ্রায় (হিঃ কোঃ), আশয় (ঐ), সন্ধান (ঐ)। **—ly,** *adv.* In an intent manner; as, the eyes *intently* fixed; একাগ্রচিত্তে, অভিনিবিষ্টভাবে, সাভিনিবেশ, নিবিষ্টভাবে অনন্যমনে। **—ness,** *n.* The state of being intent; একাগ্রতা, অনন্যমনস্কতা, অভিনিবেশ। **To all intents and purposes**—Practically; কার্য্যতঃ, বস্তুতঃ, ফলতঃ, সর্ব্বথা।

in-tĕn′-tion, *n.* **1.** Act of intending; ঈপ্সন। **2.** That which is intended; a purpose; meaning; অভিপ্রেত বিষয়, ঈপ্সিত বস্তু; উদ্দেশ্য; সন্ধান (হিঃ কোঃ), অভিসন্ধি (ঐ); আশয়, অভিপ্রায়। **3.** An end or aim; উদ্দেশ্য, লক্ষ্য। **4.** (*Logic*) A conception; (তর্ক-বিজ্ঞান) সমবধারণ (হিঃ কোঃ)। **5.** (*Pl., colloq.*) A purpose as to marriage; (চলিত ভাষায়) বিবাহ সম্পর্কে অভিপ্রায়। **First intention**—(*Med.*) Healing of a wound without granulation by immediate reunion of parts; (ভৈষজ্যশাস্ত্র) মাংসাঙ্কুর উৎপাদন বিনা অবিলম্বে ক্ষতসংযোজন। (*Logic, Pl.*) Primiray conceptions of things (as, a tree, an oak); বস্তুর প্রাথমিক ধারণা, পদার্থ সম্পর্কীয় প্রথম সংস্কার (যথা বৃক্ষ, ওকবৃক্ষ)। **Second intention**—(*Med.*) Healing of a wound by granulation; পূয, মাংসাঙ্কুর, ও ত্বগোৎপাদন দ্বারা ক্ষতারোগ্য। (*Logic, Pl.*) Secondary conceptions (*e. g.* difference, identity, etc.); গৌণ ধারণা, (যথা বৈভিন্ন্য, অভিন্নতা প্রভৃতি)।

in-tĕn′-tion-ăl, *adj.* **1.** Relating to intention; অভিপ্রায়সম্পর্কীয়। **2.** Done on purpose; designed; intended; ইচ্ছাকৃত; সঙ্কল্পিত; অভিপ্রেত। **–ly,** *adv.* Purposely; স্বেচ্ছার সহিত, উদ্দেশ্য পূর্ব্বক।

in-tĕr′, *v. t.* To bury; সমাহিত করা, কবর দেওয়া, সমাধিস্থ করা, গোর দেওয়া। **–ment,** *n.* Burial; সমাধি।

inter, (*L*), *prep.* Amid; between; মধ্যে; ভিতরে। ***Inter alia*** — Amongst other things; অন্যান্য বিষয়ের মধ্যে। **Inter-atomic**—পরমাণবান্তরিক (হিঃ কোঃ)। **Inter-molecular** — অণবান্তরিক (হিঃ কোঃ)। ***Inter nos***—Between ourselves; আমাদের মধ্যে। ***Inter se***—Between themselves; তাহাদের মধ্যে।

in′-tĕr-ăct, *n.* **1.** An interval between two acts of a drama; নাটকের অঙ্কদ্বয়ের মধ্যে অবকাশ।

in-tĕr-ăct′, *v. i.* To act on each other; পরস্পরের উপর ক্রিয়া করা, অন্যোন্যের উপর ক্রিয়া করা। **–ac′-tion,** *n.* Reciprocal action; পারস্পরিকক্রিয়া (হিঃ কোঃ), অন্যোন্যক্রিয়া (ঐ)। **–ac′-tive,** *adj.* Acting on each other; পরস্পরের প্রতি ক্রিয়াশীল, অন্যোন্যের উপর ক্রিয়াকারী।

in-tĕr-bĕd′, *v. t.* To embed as a thing between others; অন্যান্য বস্তু সমূহের মধ্যে স্থাপন করা।

in-tĕr-blĕnd′, *v. t.* & *i.* To blend or mingle; সংমিশ্রিত করা। ***Verb i.*** To blend with each other; সংমিশ্রিত হওয়া।

in-tĕr-breed′ (-brēd′), *v. t.* & *i.* To cross-breed; বিভিন্ন জাতীয় প্রাণী বা উদ্ভিদের সম্মিলনে সঙ্কর বা মিশ্রজাতি উৎপন্ন করা। ***Verb i.*** To breed together; বিভিন্ন জাতীয় প্রাণী বা উদ্ভিদের পক্ষে পরস্পরের সংসর্গে জাতি-সঙ্কর উৎপাদন করা।

in-tĕr′-că-lă-rȳ, *adj.* **1.** Inserted or introduced among others; as, an *intercalary* verse; অন্যান্যের মধ্যে সন্নিবিষ্ট। **2.** Inserted among others in the calendar; as, an *intercalary* day or month; (of a year) having such additions; সৌর এবং সাধারণ বর্ষের সামঞ্জস্য বিধানের জন্য পঞ্জিকায় অন্যান্যের মধ্যে সন্নিবিষ্ট; (বর্ষ সম্পর্কে) ঐরূপ সংযোজনবিশিষ্ট, অধিক (নীলঃ)। **Intercalary month**—মলমাস, অধিমাস, অসংক্রান্ত (হর্ষঃ), অসংক্রান্তি মাস (ঐ)।

in-tĕr′-că-lāte, *v. t.* **1.** To insert among others specially in a calendar; অন্যান্যের মধ্যে সন্নিবিষ্ট করা, বিশেষতঃ পঞ্জিকায় অতিরিক্তভাবে সন্নিবিষ্ট করা। **2.** (*Geol.*) To introduce as a layer between layers of other materials; বিভিন্ন স্তরের মধ্যে নিবেশিত করা। **–la′-tion,** *n.*

in-tĕr-cede′ (-sēd), *v. i.* To plead on behalf of another, (followed by *with* & *for*); as, to *intercede with* one *for* another; কাহারও জন্য অনুরোধ করা, উপরোধ করা।

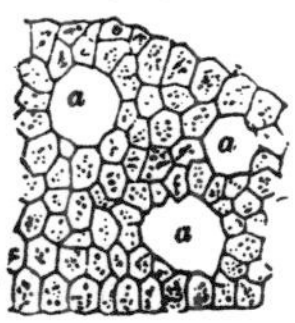

a a, intercellular spaces.

in-tĕr-cĕl′-lū-lar (-lĕr), *adj.* Situated between or among cells; কোষমধ্যবর্ত্তী।

in-tĕr-cĕpt′, *v. t.* **1.** To seize or catch on the way; as, to *intercept* a person, a letter, etc.; পথে আটক করা, গতিরোধ করা, গতিভঙ্গ করা, গতিবিচ্ছেদ করা। **2.** To obstruct the course or progress of, as light etc.; গতিরোধ করা। **3.** To stop or check; থামান, বাধা দেওয়া, আটক করা। **4.** (*Math.*) To include between; as, a line *intercepted* between the points A & B; মধ্যবর্ত্তী করা। **–cep′-tor, –cep′-tion,** *ns.* **–cep′-tive,** *adj.* Intercepting; tending to intercept; প্রতিবন্ধকজনক; গতিরোধাত্মক।

in-tĕr-ces′-sion (-sĕ-), *n.* Act of interceding, esp. by prayer etc.; a prayer for another; অনুনয়; অনুরোধ, উপরোধ। **–sor,** *n.* **–so′-ri-al, –so′-ry,** *adjs.*

in-tĕr′-chănge, *n.* **1.** Exchange between two persons; বিনিময়, অদলবদল, আদানপ্রদান, ব্যতিহার (হিঃ কোঃ)। **2.** Alternate sucession; as, the *interchange* of light and darkness; পর্য্যায়, পরম্পরানুগমন।

in-tĕr-chănge′, *v. t.* **1.** To exchange mutually; বিনিময় করা, অদলবদল করা। **2.** To put each in the place of the other; as, to *interchange* two things; একটীকে অপরটীর স্থানে রাখা। **3.** To alternate; as, to *interchange* cares with pleasures; পরম্পরানুগামী করা, পর্য্যায়গামী করা। **–a-bil′-i-ty, –a-ble-ness,** *ns.* **–a-ble,** *adj.* **1.** Admitting of exchange; বিনিময়-যোগ্য, পরিবর্ত্তনসহ, পরিবর্ত্তনীয়।

in-tĕr-cŏl-lē′-gĭ-āte, *adj.* Existing or carried on in colleges or universities; কলেজ বা বিশ্ববিদ্যালয়ে বর্ত্তমান বা সম্পাদিত।

in-tĕr-cŏ-lō′-nĭ-ăl, *adj.* Existing or carried on between or among colonies; উপনিবেশ সমূহের মধ্যে বর্ত্তমান বা প্রচলিত, আন্তঃঔপনিবেশিক।

in-tĕr-cŏm-mū-nĭ-cāte′, *v. i.* To communicate mutually; to have mutual intercourse; পরস্পরের মধ্যে যোগাযোগ রাখা; পরস্পরের মধ্যে যোগাযোগ থাকা। **–ca′-tion,** *n.* Mutual communication; পরস্পর যোগাযোগ।

in-tĕr-cŏm-mūn′-i-ŏn, *n.* **1.** Mutual intimate intercourse; পরস্পরের মধ্যে যোগাযোগ। **2.** Mutual action or relation; অন্যোন্যসম্বন্ধ, পারস্পরিক ক্রিয়া।

in-tĕr-cŏm-mū′-nĭ-tȳ, *n.* State of being common to different parties; বিভিন্ন দলে সাধারণাধিকারিত্ব। **2.** Having things in common; সাধারণাধিকার।

etc., to keep it open ; (ভৈষজ্য-শাস্ত্র) অভ্যন্তরে নল প্রবিষ্ট করিয়া কণ্ঠনালী প্রভৃতি উন্মুক্ত রাখা। **–ba′-tion,** *n.*

in′-tü-it, *v. t.* & *i.* To know or apprehend by intuition ; সহজ-জ্ঞান দ্বারা জানা, আত্মপ্রত্যয় দ্বারা উপলব্ধি করা। *Verb i.* To receive knowledge intuitively ; আত্মপ্রত্যয় দ্বারা জ্ঞানলাভ করা।

in-tü-i′-tion, *n.* **1.** The immediate apprehension by the mind or by sense without reasoning ; স্বানুভূতি, আত্মপ্রত্যয়, অনুভব (শুক্রঃ বিনয়ঃ)। **2.** A quick or ready insight ; ক্ষিপ্র অন্তর্দৃষ্টি। **3.** Innate or instinctive knowledge ; হৃৎস্থিত সহজ ও অখণ্ডবুদ্ধি, স্বভাবসিদ্ধ জ্ঞান, সহজ-জ্ঞান, বোধি (হিঃ দঃ), বিচারনিরপেক্ষ-জ্ঞান, প্রমাণনিরপেক্ষজ্ঞান, সহজোপলব্ধ জ্ঞান, প্রত্যক্ষজ্ঞান (হিঃ কোঃ), প্রতিভা (ঐ), স্ফূর্ত্তি (ঐ), সাহজিক জ্ঞান, অন্তর্জ্ঞান, তাৎকালিকজ্ঞান, অপ্রামাণিক জ্ঞান, অযত্ন-সম্ভূত জ্ঞান [Kant বোধিকে তিন ভাগে বিভক্ত করিয়াছেন :—(১) Empirical intuition—সবিচারা নির্ব্বিকল্প প্রজ্ঞা। (২) Pure intuition—শুদ্ধ অনুভব (যথা দেশ, কাল)। (৩) Intellectual intuition—নির্ব্বিচারা নির্ব্বিকল্প প্রজ্ঞা]। [নীতিবিজ্ঞানে Intuition শব্দ দ্বারা বিশিষ্ট নৈতিকবৃত্তি বা ইন্দ্রিয়জনিত স্বভাবসিদ্ধ ন্যায়ান্যায়াবধারণ বুঝায়।] **–al, –tu′-i-tive,** *adjs.* Of, or relating to intuition ; possessing or perceived by intuition ; বোধি-সম্পর্কীয় ; সহজসিদ্ধ, অন্তর্জ্ঞানোপলব্ধ, সহজজ্ঞানোপলব্ধ প্রমাণনিরপেক্ষজ্ঞেয়, সহজজ্ঞেয়, নির্ব্বিচার, নৈসর্গিক (হিঃ কোঃ), সাক্ষাৎ (ঐ), অপরোক্ষ (ঐ), আত্ম-প্রত্যয়সিদ্ধ। **–al-ly,** *adv.* **–ism,** *n.* Same as INTUITIONALISM. **–ist,** *n.* **Empirical intuition**—সবিচারা নির্ব্বিকল্পপ্রজ্ঞা (ব্রজঃ হিন্দু)। **Intellectual intuition**—নির্ব্বিচারা নির্ব্বিকল্প প্রজ্ঞা (ব্রজঃ হিন্দু)। **Intuitional ethics** — নৈসর্গিক নীতিবাদ (হিঃ কোঃ)। **Intuitive knowledge**—সবিকল্প প্রজ্ঞা, সহজজ্ঞান (হিঃ কোঃ), প্রত্যক্ষজ্ঞান (ঐ)।

in-tü-i′-tion-ăl-ĭsm, *n.* The doctrine that the perception of truth is by intuition ; হৃৎস্থিত সহজ ও অখণ্ড বুদ্ধি দ্বারা সত্য উপলব্ধি হয় — এইরূপ মতবাদ, সহজজ্ঞানবাদ (হিঃ কোঃ), নৈসর্গিকবাদ (ঐ)।

in-tü′-i-tiv-ĭsm, *n.* The doctrine that the ideas of right and wrong are intuitive ; ন্যায়ান্যায়বুদ্ধি সহজ-বুদ্ধি জাত—এইরূপ মতবাদ। **–ist,** *n.*

in-tü-mĕs′-cĕnt (-ĕnt), *adj.* Swelling up ; স্ফীতিশীল। **–cence,** *n.* A swelling ; স্ফীতি, শোথ (মঃ ইঃ)।

in-tŭs-sŭs-cĕp′-tion, *n.* **1.** The reception of one part within another ; একাংশে অন্যাংশের গ্রহণ। **2.** The withdrawal of one portion of the intestine within another ; অন্ত্রের একাংশে অন্যাংশের প্রতিগ্রহণ, অন্ত্রপ্রবেশ (হঃ চঃ)। **3.** The act of taking in foreign matter by a living organism and its conversion into organic tissue ; সজীব শরীরে বাহ্য বস্তুর অন্তর্গ্রহণ এবং উহার জৈব বিধানতন্তুতে পরিবর্ত্তন।

in-unc′-tion (-ŭngk-), *n.* Act of smearing or rubbing with oil ; তৈলমর্দ্দন।

in′-ŭn-dāte, *v. t.* **1.** To cover with flood ; to flood ; to overflow ; as, the river *inundates* the town ; বন্যাপ্লাবিত করা, জলব্যাপ্ত করা ; প্লাবিত করা ; আপ্লাবিত করা। **2.** (*Fig.*) To fill with an overflowing abundance ; পরিপ্লাবিত করা। **–da′-tion,** *n.* **1.** The act of inundating ; a flood ; প্লাবন ; জলপ্লাবন, বন্যা, তোয়বিপ্লব, সলিলোপ্লব, জলপ্রলয়, জলোচ্ছ্বাস। **2.** An overflowing abundance ; ছড়াছড়ি।

in-ur-bāne′ (-êr-), *adj.* Uncivil ; unpolished ; rude ; অসভ্য, অশিষ্ট, অভদ্র ; গ্রাম্য, অমার্জ্জিত ; রূঢ়। **–ban′-i-ty,** *n.* Want of urbanity ; rudeness ; গ্রাম্যতা, অসভ্যতা, অভদ্রতা, অবিনয়, অশিষ্টতা ; রূঢ়তা।

in-üre′, ĕn–, *v. t.* To accustom ; to habituate ; to harden ; অভ্যস্ত করা ; স্বভাবগত করা ; অভ্যাস দ্বারা কষ্টসহিষ্ণু করা। **–ment,** *n.* Practice ; অভ্যাস। **Inured to hardship**—Habituated to hardship ; কঠোরতায় অভ্যস্ত, কষ্ট সহনে অভ্যস্ত।

in-urn′ (-êrn), *v. t.* **1.** To put in an urn as the ashes of the dead ; (মৃতদেহের ভস্মাবশেষ) পাত্রে রাখা। **2.** To bury ; সমাহিত করা, গোর দেওয়া।

in-ü-tĭl′-i-tў, *n.* Uselessness ; unprofitableness ; অব্যবহার্য্যতা ; নিরর্থকতা, ব্যর্থতা, বিফলতা। **–u′-tile,** *adj.* Useless ; অব্যবহার্য্য, নিরর্থক।

in-vāde′, *v. t.* **1.** To enter with hostile intentions ; আপতিত হওয়া। **2.** To infringe ; to encroach on as rights etc. ; লঙ্ঘন করা, ভঙ্গ করা ; চড়াও করা, অনধিকার প্রবেশ করা। **3.** To affect injuriously as a wound, disease, feeling, etc. ; উপদ্রুত করা। **–vad′-er,** *n.* One who invades ; an intruder ; আক্রমণকারী, আক্রামক, দেশাক্রামক ; অনধিকার প্রবেশকারী।

in-văg′-i-nāte, *v.t.* **1.** To sheathe ; পরদা, চামড়া, প্রভৃতির ভিতরে প্রবিষ্ট করা। **2.** To introvert as a tubular sheath ; নলাকার আবরণের ভিতরের দিক উল্টাইয়া বাহিরে আনা, অন্তঃপরিবর্ত্ত করা। **–na′-tion,** *n.*

in′-vă-lid (-lēd), *adj.* & *n.* **1.** Feeble or infirm from illness ; enfeebled by injury ; রুগ্ন, রোগজীর্ণ ; রোগশীর্ণ। *Noun.* Such a person ; রুগ্নব্যক্তি, রোগশীর্ণ ব্যক্তি। **–hood, –ism,** *ns.*

in-văl′-id, *adj.* Not valid ; having no legal effect or force ; অসিদ্ধ, অবৈধ ; অন্যায্য।

in′-vă-lid (-lēd), *v. t.* & *i.* **1.** To make invalid or infirm by illness (*usu. in pass. voice*) ; রুগ্ন করা,

blend with each other ; পরস্পর মিলিত হওয়া। **–fu′-sion,** *n.*

in′-têr-im, *n., adj.* & *adv.* The mean time ; মধ্যবর্তী কাল, মধ্য সময়, মধ্যকাল, অন্তর্গতকাল, অন্তরিতকাল, কালান্তর। ***Adj.* 1.** Temporary ; provisional; অস্থায়ী; সাময়িক। **2.** (Of time) Intervening ; (সময় সম্পর্কে) মধ্যবর্তী। ***Adv.*** In the mean time ; ইতঃমধ্যে, ইত্যবসরে। **An interim order**—মোকদ্দমার বিচার শেষ হওয়ার পূর্ব্বে যে হুকুম দেওয়া হয়।

in-tē′-ri-or (-êr), *adj.* & *n.* **1.** Internal ; situated within ; আভ্যন্তর ; মধ্যস্থিত। **2.** Remote from the frontier or coast ; inland ; সীমান্ত বা সাগরোপকূল হইতে দূরবর্ত্তী ; ভূমধ্যস্থ, ধরণীমধ্যস্থ। **3.** Domestic ; গার্হস্থ্য। **4.** Mental or spiritual ; inward ; মানস, অধ্যাত্ম, অন্তরস্থ, আন্তরিক ; ভিতরকার। ***Noun.* 1.** The internal part of a thing ; the inside ; অভ্যন্তরভাগ, মধ্যভাগ ; গর্ভ। **2.** The inland part of a country, island, etc. ; দেশ, দ্বীপ, প্রভৃতির অন্তঃপ্রদেশ। **3.** The inside of a building or room ; অট্টালিকা বা কক্ষের অভ্যন্তর ভাগ। **4.** The inner nature or character ; soul ; অন্তঃপ্রকৃতি, স্বভাব, অন্তর ; আত্মা। **5.** The internal affairs of a state or nation ; as, the minister of the *Interior* ; কোন রাষ্ট্র বা জাতির আভ্যন্তরিক ব্যাপার। **–ly,** *adv.* Inwardly ; internally ; ভিতরে ভিতরে ; অভ্যন্তরভাগে। **Interior planet**—অন্তর্গ্রহ (হিঃ জোঃ)।

in-têr-jā′-cěnt, *adj.* Lying or being between ; intermediate ; মধ্যবর্ত্তী ; মধ্যস্থিত।

in-têr-jěct′, *v. t.* **1.** To throw in between ; to interpose abruptly as a remark etc. ; প্রক্ষিপ্ত করা, মধ্যে ক্ষেপণ করা ; সহসা মন্তব্য করা। **2.** To remark as an interruption ; অন্তরায় জন্মাইবার উদ্দেশ্যে মন্তব্য করা।

in-têr-jěc′-tion, *n.* **1.** Act of interjecting ; মধ্যপ্রক্ষেপ, অন্তঃক্ষেপণ (মঃ ইঃ), মধ্যপ্রক্ষেপণ (ঐ)। **2.** A form of speech thrown in to express emotion or feeling ; হর্ষ, বিস্ময়াদিসূচক অব্যয়। **3.** An ejaculation or exclamation ; আবেগধ্বনি, হর্ষবিস্ময়াদিসূচক চীৎকার। **–al,** *adj.* Parenthetical ; pertaining to an interjection ; মধ্যে প্রক্ষিপ্ত ; হর্ষ, বিস্ময়াদিসূচক অব্যয়শব্দ সম্বন্ধীয়। **–al-ly,** *adv.* **–to-ry,** *adj.*

in-têr-lāce′, *v. t.* & *i.* **1.** To bind together intricately ; সংগ্রথিত করা। **2.** To intertwine or interweave, (often *fig.*) ; পরস্পরের সঙ্গে জড়িত করা, পরস্পরের সহিত গ্রথিত করা। **3.** To mix ; সংমিশ্রিত করা। ***Verb i.*** To be interwoven or intermixed ; to cross each other intricately ; সংগ্রথিত হওয়া ; পরস্পরের সহিত বিজড়িত হওয়া। **–ment,** *n.* Act of interlacing ; সংগ্রথন, পরস্পর মিলিত হওন।

in-têr-lăp′, *v.t.* Same as OVERLAP.

in-têr-lärd′, *v. t.* To mix or mingle (*with*) ; as, to *interlard* a writing or speech *with* foreign words ; মিশ্রিত করা।

in′-têr-leaf (-lēf), *n.* An extra leaf usually blank inserted among other leaves of a book ; পুস্তকের পত্রসমূহের মধ্যে নিবিষ্ট অতিরিক্ত পত্র (সাধারণতঃ সাদা)।

in-têr-leave′ (-lēv), *v. t.* To insert (usually blank) leaves in (a book), (also fig) ; পুস্তকের পত্রদ্বয়ের মধ্যে (সাধারণতঃ অলিখিত বা অমুদ্রিত) অতিরিক্ত পত্র সন্নিবেশ করা।

in-têr-līne′, *v. t.* To write or put between lines written or printed already ; to insert word between the lines of, as a document etc. ; মুদ্রিত বা লিখিত পংক্তি সমূহের মধ্যে লিখা বা সংযোগ করা ; দলীল প্রভৃতির পংক্তির মধ্যে শব্দ সন্নিবিষ্ট করা। **–lin-e-a′-tion,** *n.*

in-têr-link′ (-lĭngk), *v. t.* To link together ; সংগ্রথিত করা।

in-têr-lĭn′-ē-ar (-êr), *adj.* Written or printed between the lines ; পংক্তিদ্বয়ের মধ্যে লিখিত বা মুদ্রিত।

in-têr-lŏck′, *v. i.* & *t.* To unite or lock together by a series of connections ; পরস্পরের সঙ্গে মিলিত হওয়া বা জড়িত হওয়া। ***Verb t.* 1.** To lock or clasp within each other ; জড়াজড়ি করা, পরস্পরের সহিত জড়ান। **2.** (Railway) To arrange the connections of (switches, signals, etc.) so that one lever cannot be worked independently of the others ; (যে সকল টানারের সাহায্যে বাষ্পীয় শকট এক লৌহবর্ত্ম হইতে অপর লৌহবর্ত্মে স্থানান্তরিত করা হয় সে সকল এবং সঙ্কেতস্তম্ভ প্রভৃতির) এরূপভাবে সংযোগ-ব্যবস্থা করা যাহাতে একটী দণ্ডযন্ত্র চালনা করিতে হইলে অপরটাকেও চালিত করিতে হয়।

in-têr-lŏ-cū′-tion, *n.* A dialogue ; conversation ; কথোপকথন, আলাপন ; উত্তরপ্রত্যুত্তর, কথাবার্ত্তা, সংবাদ।

in-têr-lŏc′-ū-tor (-têr), *n.* One who takes part in a conversation ; কথোপকথনকারী। **–to-ry,** *adj.* **1.** Conversational ; কথোপকথনাত্মক। **2.** Spoken intermediately ; মধ্যভাগে কথিত। **–tress, –trix,** *ns.* (*Fem.*) **My interlocutor**—The person in conversation with me ; আমার সহিত কথোপকথনে প্রবৃত্ত ব্যক্তি।

in-têr-lōpe′, *v. i.* **1.** To traffic without a proper licence ; বিনানুমতিতে বাণিজ্য করা। **2.** To intrude (*upon*) ; অনধিকার প্রবেশ করা। **–lop′-er,** *n.* **1.** One who intrudes or interferes wrongfully esp. for his own profit ; যে ব্যক্তি অনধিকার প্রবেশ করে, যে ব্যক্তি অন্যায়ভাবে কোন বিষয়ে হস্তক্ষেপ করে, পরাধিকারমধ্যবর্ত্তী, অনধিকারী ব্যাপারী (হিঃ কোঃ)। **2.** (*Hist.*) An unauthorized trader ; (ইতিহাস) যে ব্যক্তি বিনানুমতিতে ব্যবসায় করে।

in'-têr-lūde, *n.* **1.** A short pause or performance dramatic or musical between the acts of a play ; নাটকের অঙ্কদ্বয়ের মধ্যে সংক্ষিপ্ত অবকাশ বা নাট্য বা গীত, বিষ্কম্ভ (দশরূঃ), মধ্যরঙ্গ (আঃ বঃ)। **2.** An intervening time or space ; an event, amusing incident etc. interposed ; "Variegated with *interludes* of mirth" ; মধ্যবর্ত্তী সময়, মধ্যবর্ত্তী দেশ ; মধ্যবর্ত্তী ব্যাপার বা কৌতুকজনক বিষয়।

in-têr-măr'-riage (-ĭj), *n.* A marriage between two families, tribes etc. or between near relations ; দুই ভিন্ন পরিবার বা জাতির মধ্যে বিবাহ, অন্তর্বিবাহ, আদান-প্রদান, পরস্পর বিবাহ, অন্যোন্য বিবাহ, বিবাহব্যবহার।

in-têr-măr'-ry (-ĭ), *v. i.* To become connected by intermarriage as families, tribes, nations etc. ; অন্তর্বিবাহ করা, অন্তর্বিবাহদ্বারা সংযুক্ত করা।

in-têr-mĕd'-dle (-l), *v. i.* To meddle *with* or *in* the affairs of others ; to interfere ; অন্যের ব্যাপারে হস্তক্ষেপ করা; হস্তক্ষেপ করা।

in-têr-mē'-dĭ-ă-rӯ, *adj.* & *n.* **1.** Intermediate ; মধ্যবর্ত্তী। **2.** Acting as a mediating agent ; mediatory ; মধ্যস্থস্বরূপ কার্য্যকারী ; মধ্যস্থস্বরূপ। ***Noun.*** **1.** A go-between ; মধ্যস্থ ব্যক্তি। **2.** That which is intermediate; মধ্যবর্ত্তী বিষয়।

in-têr-mē'-dĭ-āte, *adj.* & *n.* Lying or being between two things with regard to time, space or order ; intervening ; মধ্যবর্ত্তী, অন্তর্ব্বর্ত্তী ; মধ্যস্থিত, অবান্তর (ছান্দোগ্য)। ***Noun.*** An intermediate thing ; মধ্যবর্ত্তী বস্তু। **—ly,** *adv.* **Intermediate state**—অন্তরাবস্থা। **Intermediate time**—কালান্তর।

in-têr-mē'-dĭ-āte, *v. i.* To come between ; to mediate, (with *between*) ; মধ্যবর্ত্তী হওয়া ; মধ্যস্থ হওয়া। **—a'-tion,** *n.* Mediation ; মধ্যবর্ত্তিতা, মধ্যস্থতা। **—a-tor,** *n.* A mediator ; মধ্যস্থ, শালিস।

in-têr-mē'-dĭ-ŭm, *n.* An intermediate agent or instrument ; a medium ; মধ্যবর্ত্তী ব্যক্তি বা যন্ত্র ; মধ্যবর্ত্তী পদার্থ।

in-têr'-mĕnt, *n.* The act of burying ; burial ; সমাহিত করণ ; সমাধি।

in-têr-mĕz'-zō, *n.* **1.** An interlude ; বিষ্কম্ভক, দুই অঙ্কের মধ্যবর্ত্তী চুটকী অংশ। **2.** A short musical composition of a light character ; নাটকের অঙ্কদ্বয়ের অবকাশের মধ্যকালে গেয় তরল সঙ্গীত, নাটকের দুই অঙ্কের মধ্যবর্ত্তী কালে যে চুটকী গান গাওয়া হয়।

in-têr-mī-grā'-tion, *n.* Reciprocal migration ; পরস্পরের দেশে যাইয়া বসবাস স্থাপন।

in-têr'-mĭn-ă-ble (-bl), *adj.* Boundless ; endless ; tediously long ; সীমাহীন, অসীম ; অনন্ত, অশেষ, নিরবধি ; অফুরন্ত। **—bly,** *adv.* Endlessly ; অসীমরূপে। **—ness,** *n.*

in-têr-mĭn'-gle (-mĭng-gl), *v. t.* & *i.* To mix together ; সংমিশ্রিত করা। ***Verb i.*** To be mixed or incorporated ; একত্র মিলিত বা মিশ্রিত হওয়া, সংমিশ্রিত হওয়া, সম্মিলিত হওয়া।

in-têr-mĭs'-sion (-mĭ-), *n.* Cessation for a time ; pause ; বিরতি, বিরাম, নিবৃত্তি ; ছেদ, অবকাশ। **Without intermission** — Without cessation ; অবিরাম, অবিশ্রান্ত, বিরামবিহীন।

in-têr-mĭt' *v. t.* & *i.* To cause to cease for a time ; to suspend ; কিছু সময়ের জন্য বিরত করা ; স্থগিত রাখা। ***Verb i.*** To cease for a time ; to be intermittent, as a fever etc ; কিছু সময় বিরত থাকা, সময় সময় স্থগিত হওয়া ; সবিরাম ভাবে বর্ত্তমান থাকা। **—tence,** *n.* Act of intermitting ; intermission ; বিরতি; বিরাম। **—tent,** *adj.* Coming and going at intervals, as fever ; সবিচ্ছেদ, সবিরাম, পর্য্যায়শীল, যাহা ছাড়িয়া ছাড়িয়া প্রকাশ পায়। **—tent-ly,** *adv.* **Intermittent fever**—সবিরামজ্বর।

in-têr-mĭx', *v. t.* & *i.* To mix together ; একত্র মিশ্রিত করা, সংমিশ্রিত করা। ***Verb i.*** To be intermingled ; সংমিশ্রিত হওয়া। **—ture,** *n.* Act of intermixing ; a mass formed by mixture ; মিশ্রিত করণ ; মিশ্রিত পদার্থ।

in-têr-mŭn'-dāne, *adj.* Being between worlds or orbs, as space etc. ; লোকান্তর্বর্ত্তী, ভুবনমধ্যস্থিত, জগন্মধ্যবর্ত্তী।

in-têr-mū'-răl, *adj.* Between walls ; প্রাচীরদ্বয়ের মধ্যবর্ত্তী, প্রাকারান্তর্বর্ত্তী, প্রাচীরান্তর্বর্ত্তী।

in-têrn', *v. t.* To oblige to reside within prescribed limits ; to confine within the limits of a country or place ; নির্দ্দিষ্ট চতুঃসীমার ভিতরে বাস করিতে বাধ্য করা ; কোন দেশ বা স্থানের চতুঃসীমার ভিতর আবদ্ধ করা, অন্তরাবদ্ধ করা, যুদ্ধকালে যে সকল সৈন্য কোন নির্লিপ্ত দেশে প্রবেশ করে তাহাদিগকে অস্ত্রশস্ত্র বিরহিত করিয়া তদ্দেশে বাস করিতে বাধ্য করা। **—ment,** *n.* The act of interning ; state of being interred ; কোন দেশ বা স্থানের চতুঃসীমার মধ্যে আবদ্ধকরণ ; অন্তরাবদ্ধতা।

in-têr'-năl, *adj. n.* **1.** Relating to the inside of a thing ; situated within ; interior ; আভ্যন্তরিক, অভ্যন্তরাবস্থ ; মধ্যবর্ত্তী ; অন্তরস্থ, অন্তর্বর্ত্তী। **2.** Inherent ; intrinsic ; স্বাভাবিক, অন্তর্জাত ; অন্তর্নিহিত, প্রকৃতিগত। **3.** Pertaining to the inner being or soul ; mental ; spiritual ; subjective ; আন্তরিক (হিঃ কোঃ) ; মানসিক ; অধ্যাত্ম ; বিষয়িগত। **4.** Relating to the domestic affairs of a country ; domestic ; কোন দেশের আভ্যন্তর ব্যাপারসম্বন্ধীয় ; গার্হস্থ্য। ***Noun.*** (*Pl.*) The intrinsic qualities ;

প্রকৃতিগত গুণসমূহ। **–ly,** *adv.* **1.** Inwardly ; মধ্যে, অভ্যন্তরে, অন্তরে অন্তরে, ভিতরে ভিতরে। **2.** Mentally ; spiritually ; মনে মনে ; আধ্যাত্মিক ভাবে। **–nal′-i-ty,** *n.* The state of being internal; আভ্যন্তরিকতা, আধ্যাত্মিকতা, আন্তরিকতা, অন্তর্ভাব। **Internal angle** — An interior angle ; মধ্যস্থিত কোণ। **Internal evidence** — Evidence derived from what is contained in the thing itself ; আভ্যন্তর প্রমাণ।

in-têr-nă′-tion-ăl, *adj.* & *n.* Relating to or common to nations ; relating to the intercourse of nations ; আন্তর্জাতিক ; জাতি-সমূহের পরস্পর ব্যবহার সম্বন্ধীয়, পরস্পরজন-সমূহসম্বন্ধী (হিঃ কোঃ)। ***Noun.*** **1.** (*Cap.*) The name of the society for promoting the interests of the industrial classes of all nations ; a member of that society ; পৃথিবীর সর্ব্বজাতীয় শ্রমশিল্পী-দিগের স্বার্থরক্ষার্থ প্রতিষ্ঠিত সমাজ বিশেষের নাম, নিখিলশ্রমশিল্পিহিত-সাধিনী সভা ; উক্ত সমাজের অন্যতম সভ্য। **2.** One who takes part in an international, usually athletic contest ; যে ব্যক্তি আন্তর্জাতিক প্রতিযোগিতা ক্রীড়া প্রভৃতিতে যোগদান করে। **–al′-i-ty,** *n.* **–ly,** *adv.* **International Working Men's Association** — See INTERNATIONAL, *n.* I.

in-têr-nă′-tion-ăl-ist, *n.* **1.** One versed in the principles of international law ; আন্তর্জাতিক আইনে অভিজ্ঞ ব্যক্তি। **2.** A member of the International Working Men's Association ; আন্তর্জাতিক শ্রমশিল্পি-সমাজের সভ্য বিশেষ। **–ism,** *n.* The principles or objects advocated by the internationalists ; আন্তর্জাতি শ্রমশিল্পি-সমাজের উদ্দেশ্য বা মূলতত্ত্ব, আন্তার্জতিকবাদ।

in-têr-nă′-tion-ăl-īze, *v. t.* To make international ; to bring under the combined protection of different nations, as a territory etc. ; আন্তর্জাতিক করা ; বিভিন্ন জাতির সম্মিলিত রক্ষণাধীন করা। **–i-za′-tion,** *n.*

in-têr-nē′-cīne, *adj.* Involving mutual destruction ; deadly as war etc. ; পরস্পরবিধ্বংসী ; সাংঘাতিক, মারাত্মক।

in′-têr-nōde, *n.* The interval or part between two nodes (in any sense) or between two joints ;

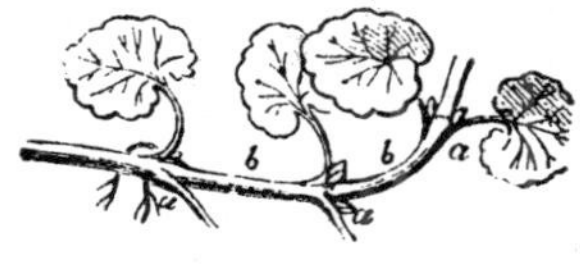

Branch of ground ivy.
a, nodes or joints ; *b*, internodes.

a segment ; অন্তঃপর্ব্ব (সাঃ পঃ) অস্থিমধ্য (সাঃ পঃ), গ্রন্থিদ্বয়মধ্য, পর্ব্বদ্বয়মধ্য ; খণ্ড।

in-têr-nŭn′-cial (-shăl), *adj.* **1.** Pertaining to an internuncio ; দূত সংক্রান্ত। **2.** Communicating between different parts of the system (of nerves) ; স্নায়ুমণ্ডলীর বিভিন্ন অংশে সঞ্চারী।

in-têr-nŭn′-ci-ō (-shĭ-), *n.* **1.** A messenger between two parties ; দূত, বার্ত্তাবহ। **2.** A representative of the Pope at a small foreign court ; ক্ষুদ্র বৈদেশিকরাজ-সভায় পোপের প্রতিনিধি। **3.** An envoy esp. the Austrian at Constantinople ; রাজদূত, বিশেষতঃ তুরস্ক রাজদরবারে অষ্ট্রিয়ার দূত।

in-têr-ŏs′-cū-lāte, *v. t.* **1.** To intermingle with each other ; সংমিশ্রিত করা। **2.** To form a connecting link between two arguments ; যুক্তিদ্বয়ের মধ্যে সংযোগ-শৃঙ্খল হওয়া। **–la′-tion,** *n.*

in-têr-pāge′, *v. t.* To print or insert on intermediate pages ; মধ্যবর্ত্তী পত্রে মুদ্রিত বা সন্নিবিষ্ট করা।

in-têr-pĕl′-lāte, *v. t.* To question formally as a minister or other officer as in a legislative council etc. ; ব্যবস্থাপক সভা প্রভৃতিতে প্রশ্ন করা। **–la′-tion,** *n.* Act of formally bringing into question a ministerial policy or action as in a legislative council etc. ; such a question ; ব্যবস্থাপক সভা প্রভৃতিতে প্রশ্নকরণ ; ব্যবস্থাপক সভা প্রভৃতির প্রশ্ন। **–la′-tor,** *n.*

in-têr-pĕn′-ē-trāte, *v. t.* & *i.* **1.** To penetrate thoroughly ; অন্তর্ভেদ করা। **2.** To penetrate mutually ; পরস্পর ভেদ করা। ***Verb i.*** To penetrate each other ; পরস্পর ভেদ করা। **–tra′-tion,** *n.* **–tra-tive,** *adj.*

in′-têr-play (-plā), *n.* Mutual action ; interaction ; অন্যোন্যের উপর ক্রিয়া ; অন্যোন্যক্রিয়া।

in-têr′-pō-lāte, *v. t.* **1.** To insert as a spurious word or passage in a book ; কোন পুস্তকে কোন অপ্রকৃত শব্দ বা অংশ যোগ করা, প্রক্ষিপ্ত করা। **2.** (*Math.*) To insert in a series an intermediate term ; (গণিতশাস্ত্র) কোন শ্রেঢ়ীতে মধ্যবর্ত্তী সংখ্যা অন্তর্নিবিষ্ট করা। **–la′-tion,** *n.* Act of introducing in a book etc. what is spurious ; something spurious introduced or inserted ; প্রক্ষেপ ; প্রক্ষিপ্ত বিষয়। **–la-tor,** *n.* One who interpolates ; প্রক্ষেপকারী।

in-têr-pōse′, *v. t.* & *i.* **1.** To place or insert *between* ; as, to *interpose* a screen *between* the light and the eye ; মধ্যে স্থাপিত করা, মধ্যবর্ত্তী করা। **2.** To introduce by way of interference ; as, to *interpose* an objection ; উপস্থাপিত করা। **3.** To say or pronounce as words etc. as an interruption ; কোনও কথা বলিয়া বা বাক্য উচ্চারণ করিয়া প্রতিবন্ধকতা জন্মান, কথার মাঝখানে কোন কথা

বলা। ***Verb i.*** **1.** To be, or come *between*; to intervene as between disputants etc.; মধ্যবর্ত্তী হওয়া বা মধ্যে আসা; মধ্যস্থ হওয়া। **2.** To interrupt; to make a digression; বাধা জন্মান; মূল বিষয় ছাড়িয়া অবান্তর বিষয় ধরা। **—pos′-al,** *n.* Interposition; intervention; মধ্যে স্থাপন; মধ্যবর্ত্তন, অন্তরস্থিত (সাঃ পঃ)।

in-têr-pō-ṡi′-tion, *n.* **1.** Act of interposing; interference; mediation; মধ্যে স্থাপন; হস্তক্ষেপ; মধ্যস্থতা, মাধ্যস্থ, শালিসী। **2.** The thing interposed; মধ্যে স্থাপিত বা প্রবিষ্ট বস্তু।

in-têr′-prĕt, *v. t.* & *i.* **1.** To explain the meaning of; to expound; to elucidate; to translate; অর্থপ্রকটন করা; ব্যাখ্যা করা; বিবৃত করা; অনুবাদ করা, ভাষান্তরিত করা, তরজমা করা। **2.** To understand or explain in a specified manner; as, we *interpret* as a threat; কোন বিশেষ ভাবে বুঝা বা বুঝান। **3.** To represent artistically; as, an actor *interprets* Hamlet; কলাকৌশলের সহিত অভিনয় করা। ***Verb i.*** To act as an interpreter; দ্বিভাষীর কাজ করা। **—a-ble,** *adj.* **—pre-ta′-tion** *n.* **1.** Act of interpreting; exposition; অর্থ প্রকটন; ব্যাখান, ব্যাখ্যা, টীকা। **2.** Oral translation, as by interpreters; মৌখিক অনুবাদ, অনুবাদন (হিঃ কোঃ)। **3.** The representation of a part in the stage; রঙ্গমঞ্চে কোন ভূমিকার অভিনয়। **—pre-ta-tive** *adj.*

in-têr′-prĕt-êr, *n.* One who interprets; one who translates orally between two parties; ব্যাখ্যাকারক, ব্যাখ্যাতা, বিবরণকর্ত্তা, অর্থপ্রবক্তা; দ্বিভাষী। **—pre-tress,** *n.* (*Fem.*) **—ship,** *n.*

in-têr-rĕg′-nŭm *n.* (*Pl.* -NA, -NUMS). **1.** The time between reigns; the period during which a throne is vacant, as between the end of a king's reign and the accession of the successor; দুই রাজত্বের মধ্যবর্ত্তী কাল; অরাজক কাল, অনায়ককাল, রাজদ্বয়মধ্যগত অরাজক কাল। **2.** A pause; an interval; as, one could be merry till bed-time without an *interregnum*; বিরাম; অবচ্ছেদ, অবকাশ।

in-têr-rē-lā′-tion, *n.* Mutual relation; correlation; অন্যোন্য-সম্পর্ক, পরস্পরসম্বন্ধ; অন্যোন্যসম্বন্ধ। **—ship,** *n.*

in-têr′-rō-gāte, *v. t.* & *i.* To question esp. formally; to examine by questions; প্রশ্ন করা; প্রশ্নদ্বারা পরীক্ষা করা। ***Verb i.*** To ask questions; প্রশ্ন জিজ্ঞাসা করা।

in-têr-rō-gā′-tion, *n.* Act of interrogating; a question put; প্রশ্নকরণ, পৃচ্ছন, প্রচ্ছন; প্রশ্ন, জিজ্ঞাসা, পৃচ্ছা। **Point, mark** or **note of interrogation** — প্রশ্নবোধক চিহ্ন।

in-têr-rŏg′-ȧ-tive (-tiv), *adj.* & *n.* **1.** Denoting a question; expressed in the form of a question; প্রশ্নসূচক, প্রশ্নবোধক; প্রশ্নাত্মক। **2.** (*Gram.*) Used in asking questions as pronouns etc.; প্রশ্নবোধক। ***Noun.*** (*Gram.*) A word used in asking questions, as, *who what,* etc.; প্রশ্নবোধক শব্দ। **—ly,** *adv.*

in-têr-rŏg′-ȧ-tō-rŷ, *adj.* & *n.* Implying a question or inquiry; প্রশ্নসূচক, প্রশ্নাত্মক। ***Noun.*** **1.** A question or set of questions; প্রশ্ন, প্রশ্নমালা। **2.** (*Law*) A formal question put to an accused person etc.; (আইন) অভিযুক্তব্যক্তিকে জিজ্ঞাসিত প্রশ্ন।

in-têr-rŭpt′, *v. t.* **1.** To stop or hinder by breaking in; বাধা দেওয়া, প্রতিবন্ধকতা জন্মান, অন্তরায় উপস্থিত করা। **2.** To break the continuity or uniformity of; ভঙ্গ করা, বিচ্ছিন্ন করা। **3.** To obstruct as view etc.; নিরোধ করা, ব্যাহত করা, প্রতিহত করা। **—ed-ly,** *adv.* **—er,** *n.*

in-têr-rŭp′-tion, *n.* **1.** Act of interrupting; the state of being interrupted; a break or breach; an obstruction; বাধাপ্রদান; বাধা, ব্যাঘাত, প্রতিবন্ধক, অন্তরায়; ভঙ্গ, বিচ্ছেদ; নিরোধ, প্রতিরোধ। **—to-ry,** *adj.*

in-têr-sĕct′, *v. t.* & *i.* To divide by passing through; to cut or cross mutually; ছেদন করা; পরস্পর ছেদন করা। ***Verb i.*** To cut or cross each other as lines etc.; পরস্পর কাটাকাটি বা ছেদ করা।

in-têr-sĕc′-tion, *n.* **1.** Act of intersecting; state of being intersected; পরস্পরছেদন, বিচ্ছেদ, পরস্পরছেদ; সম্পাত (আঃ বঃ), অন্তরখণ্ড (হিঃ (কাঃ); অন্যোন্যচ্ছিন্নতা। **2.** The point or line in which two lines or planes cut each other; রেখা-দ্বয় বা তলদ্বয়ের পরস্পর ছেদ-বিন্দু বা ছেদ-রেখা, ছেদবিন্দু, ছেদরেখা। **—al,** *adj.*

in-têr-sperse′ (-spêrs), *v. t.* **1.** To scatter or set here and there (*between* or *among* other things); (অন্য বস্তুর মধ্যে) ইতস্ততঃ বিক্ষিপ্ত করা, ছড়াইয়া দেওয়া, আস্তীর্ণ করা। **2.** To adorn or diversify *with* things set at intervals; as, to *intersperse* a book *with* pictures; মধ্যে মধ্যে বসাইয়া অলঙ্কৃত বা বৈচিত্র্য সম্পাদন করা। **—sper′-sion,** *n.*

in′-têr-stāte, *adj* (*Caps*) Pertaining to, or carried on between, different states; as, *interstate* commerce; (মার্কিণ যুক্ত রাজ্যে) বিভিন্নরাজ্যের পারস্পরিক সম্বন্ধ সংক্রান্ত, বিভিন্ন রাজ্যের মধ্যে নির্ব্বাহিত।

in-têr-stĕl′-lar (-lêr), *adj.* Between or among the stars, as space etc.; তারামণ্ডলান্তর্গত, তারাগণান্তবর্ত্তী, তারামণ্ডলমধ্যবর্ত্তী, সৌর-মণ্ডলের বহির্ভূত। **Interstellar space**—Space between stars; তারামধ্যাবকাশ (হিঃ কোঃ)।

in-têr′-stice (-stis), *n.* Intervening space; a crevice; a hole; অন্তরাল; ফাটা, ফাটল, ছিদ্র, রন্ধ্র।

in-têr-sti′-tial (-shăl), *adj.* Pertaining to, forming or containing interstices; ছিদ্রসম্বন্ধীয়, সচ্ছিদ্র, সরন্ধ্র।

in-têr-tĕx′-tūre, *n.* **1.** Act of interweaving; মিশ্র বুনন, পরস্পরগ্রন্থন, পরস্পরবুতি। **2.** That which is interwoven; একত্র বুনট বস্তু।

in-têr-trŏp′-i-căl, *adj.* Situated within the tropics; উষ্ণমণ্ডল-মধ্যবর্ত্তী।

in-têr-twīne, *v. t.* & *i.* To unite by twining or twisting; সংগ্রথিত করা, একত্র পাকান, জড়াজড়ি করা। ***Verb i.*** To become entwined; সংগ্রথিত হওয়া, পরস্পরগ্রথিত হওয়া। **—ment,** *n.*

in′-têr-văl, *n.* **1.** A space between things; as, the *interval* between two houses; ফাঁকা, অন্তর, ব্যবধান, অবচ্ছেদ, অন্তরাল (হিঃ কোঃ), অন্তর (ঐ), অবকাশ (ঐ)। **2.** Space of time between two points or events; a pause; a break; মধ্যকাল, অবকাশ, অবসর; বিরাম; বিচ্ছেদ। **3.** A brief space of time between two paroxysms of a disease, delirium, etc.; কোন রোগের প্রবল আক্রমণ বা প্রলাপ প্রভৃতির মধ্যবর্ত্তী বিরাম। **4.** (*Mus.*) Difference in gravity or acuteness between sounds; (সঙ্গীতশাস্ত্র) অন্তরা (মিউজিক)। **5.** Distance or difference between persons or things with respect to qualities; as, the *interval* between savegery and culture; গুণসম্পর্কে বৈভিন্ন্য বা দূরত্ব। **—val′-ic,** *adj.* **At intervals**—Now and then; here and there; মাঝে মাঝে, মধ্যে মধ্যে, সময় সময়; এখানে সেখানে।

in-têr-vene′ (-vēn), *v. i.* **1.** To come in as something extraneous; to lie between; as, the Mediterranean *intervenes* between Europe and Africa; মধ্যগত বা মধ্যবর্ত্তী হওয়া। **2.** To occur between points of time or events; দুই ঘটনা বা সময়ের মধ্যে ঘটা। **3.** To interpose or interfere; মধ্যে পড়া, হস্তক্ষেপ করা। **—ven′-i-ent,** *adj.* Coming between; মধ্যগামী। **—ven′-tion,** *n.* Act of intervening; interference; mediation; মধ্যে গমন; হস্তক্ষেপ; মধ্যস্থতা, মাধ্যস্থ।

in′-têr-view (-vū), *n.* & *v. t.* **1.** A meeting face to face; a conference; a conversation; সাক্ষাৎকার, পরস্পরদর্শন, অন্যোন্যদর্শন; মন্ত্রণা; আলাপ, কথাবার্ত্তা। **2.** A meeting of a reporter of a newspaper with a person from whom an information is sought; ব্যক্তি বিশেষের নিকট হইতে কোন সংবাদ সংগ্রহ করার জন্য তাহার সহিত পত্রিকার সংবাদ-দাতার সাক্ষাৎকার। ***Verb t.*** To have an interview with, esp. to get information for publication; সাক্ষাৎ করা, পত্রিকায় প্রকাশোপযোগী বিবরণ সংগ্রহের জন্য সাক্ষাৎ করা। **—er,** *n.* One who interviews; সাক্ষাৎ-কারী ব্যক্তি।

in-têr-volve′ (vŏlv), *v. t.* To roll up or wind (things) within each other; একত্র জড়াইয়া রাখা।

in-têr-weave′ (-wēv), *v. t.* **1.** To weave together; to intertwine; একত্র বুনা; সংগ্রথিত করা। **2.** To blend or unite intimately; সংমিশ্রিত করা, বিমিশ্রিত করা।

in-têr-wind′, *v. t.* & *i.* To wind together; to intertwine; একত্র জড়িত করা বা হওয়া, একত্র পাকাইয়া যাওয়া; সংগ্রথিত করা, সংগ্রথিত হওয়া।

in-tĕs′-tāte, *adj.* & *n.* **1.** Without having made a valid will; as, to die *intestate*; অকৃতচরমপত্র, চরমপত্রহীন। **2.** Not disposed of by will, as an estate; চরমপত্র দ্বারা অনর্পিত। ***Noun.*** A person who dies without making a valid will; অকৃতচরমপত্র ব্যক্তি। **—ta-cy,** *n.* **To die intestate**—To die without making a will; উইল না করিয়া মরা, চরমপত্র সম্পাদন না করিয়া মরা।

in-tĕs′-tīne, *adj.* Internal; domestic; civil; as, *intestine* war, struggle, etc.; অন্তর্ব্বর্ত্তী, আভ্যন্তর, অবাহ্য; গার্হস্থ্য; পৌরবর্গঘটিত। **Intestine quarrel** — গার্হস্থ্যবিগ্রহ, অন্তর্দ্রোহ।

in-tĕs′-tīne, *n.* (Usu. *Pl.*) The canal or tube that extends with convolutions from the stomach to the anus; the bowels; আমাশয় হইতে গুহ্যদ্বার পর্য্যন্ত প্রসারিত পরিপাক-ক্রিয়াসাধক নলাকার যন্ত্র; অন্ত্র, আঁতড়ি, নাড়ীভুঁড়ি। **—ti′-nal,** *adj.* Pertaining to the intestines; অন্ত্রসম্বন্ধীয়। **Large intestine**—বৃহদন্ত্র, মলাশয়। **Small intestine**—ক্ষুদ্রান্ত্র (হঃ চঃ), পক্বাশয় (ঐ), আমপক্বাশয় (ব্রজঃ হিন্দু)।

in′-ti-mă-cy̆, *n.* Close familiarity; nearness in friendship; ঘনিষ্ঠতা, সৌহৃদ্য, গাঢ় সৌহৃদ্য; অন্তরঙ্গতা, মাখামাখি, গলাগলি (*colloq.*)।

in′-ti-māte, *adj* & *n.* **1.** Innermost; intrinsic; essential; অন্তরতম; প্রকৃতিগত, স্বরূপগত; সারভূত, মূলীভূত। **2.** Close, as a connection; ঘনিষ্ঠ। **3.** Close in acquaintance; familiar; অন্তরঙ্গ; ঘনিষ্ঠ। **4.** Involving close union, as a mixture; গাঢ়সংযোগাত্মক। **5.** Recording emotions etc., as a diary; হৃদয়োচ্ছ্বাস প্রভৃতি জ্ঞাপক। ***Noun.*** An intimate friend; a confidant; সুহৃত্তম, অন্তরঙ্গ বন্ধু, প্রাণ-বন্ধু, পরাণবন্ধু (রবীঃ); নর্ম্মসখা। **—ly,** *adv.* In an intimate manner; ঘনিষ্ঠভাবে, দৃঢ়রূপে। **To be on intimate terms with anyone**—To be on friendly terms with anyone; কাহারো সহিত অন্তরঙ্গতা থাকা।

in′-ti-māte, *v. t.* **1.** To hint; to suggest; ইঙ্গিত করা; সূচিত করা, সূচনা করা। **2.** To announce; to state;

জ্ঞাপন করা; ব্যক্ত করা **—ma'-tion,** *n.* Act of intimating; the thing intimated; declaration; a hint; জ্ঞাপন; বিজ্ঞাপিত বিষয়; ঘোষণা, প্রচার; ইঙ্গিত, আভাস। **Intimate relation** — সমবায় (হিঃ কোঃ) ঘনসম্বন্ধ (ঐ)।

in-tim'-i-date, *v. t.* To make timid; to inspire with fear; to deter with threats; to cow; ভীত করা, ভয়ার্ত্ত করা; ভয়বিহ্বল করা, সন্ত্রস্ত করা; ভয়প্রদর্শনে নিবৃত্ত করা; ভয় দেখাইয়া দাবাইয়া রাখা। **—da'-tion,** *n.* Act of intimidating; the state of being intimidated; সন্ত্রাসন, ভয়প্রদর্শন; ভয়যুক্ততা, ভয়বিহ্বলতা। **—da-tor,** *n.*

in-tim'-i-ty, *n.* Inwardness; privacy; আভ্যন্তরতা; গোপনীয়তা।

in-tit'-ūle, *v. t.* **1.** To give a title to or entitle, as a legislative or parliamentary act; নাম দেওয়া, অভিহিত করা। **2.** To give a rightful claim to; অধিকারী করা, স্বত্ববান করা।

in'-tō, *prep.* **1.** To the inside of (It expresses motion or direction towards the inside of, or a change of condition); মধ্যে, অভ্যন্তরে, ভিতরে। **2.** (*Math.*) Denoting multiplication or the multiplicatory sign (×); পূরণবাচক, পূরণ চিহ্ন বাচক।

in'-toed (-tōd), *adj.* Having the toes turned inwards; পদাঙ্গুলী অন্তরাবর্ত্তিত।

in-tŏl'-ĕr-ă-ble (-bl), *adj.* Not capable of being endured; অসহ্য, দুর্ব্বিসহ, অবিসহ্য, দুর্ব্বহ। **—bly,** *adv.* Unbearably; অসহনীয়রূপে। **—ness,** *n.*

in-tŏl'-ĕr-ănt, *adj.* **1.** Not enduring; not able to endure, (with *of*); অসহিষ্ণু; অসহনক্ষম। **2.** Not tolerating difference of opinion or sentiment esp. in religious matters; ধর্ম্মবিষয়াদিতে পরমত সহনাক্ষম, অনুদার, গোঁড়া। **—ance,** *n.* State of being intolerent; অসহিষ্ণুতা, অসহনশীলতা, অক্ষান্তি, ধর্ম্মবিষয়ে পরমত-সহনাক্ষমতা।

in-tomb' (-tōm), *v. t.* (Obs. form of ENTOMB).

in'-tō-nāte, *v. i.* & *t.* Same as, INTONE which see.

in-tō-nā'-tion, *n.* **1.** Reciting in a singing voice; তানলয়সহকারে আবৃত্তি। **2.** Modulation of the voice; স্বরকম্পন, স্বরভঙ্গী, মূর্চ্ছনা, নাদপদ্ধতি, স্বরলয়, স্বরভেদ। **3.** Utterance or production of musical tones; স্বরসাধন।

in-tōne', *v. t.* & *i.* **1.** To chant, as a psalm, prayer, etc.; সুর করিয়া পাঠ করা, তানলয় বিশুদ্ধ ভাবে গান করা, সুর করিয়া আবৃত্তি করা। **2.** To utter with a particular tone; বিশেষ সুরে উচ্চারণ করা।

in-tŏx'-i-cănt, *adj.* & *n.* Intoxicating; মাদক, উন্মাদক, মাদকজনক। ***Noun.*** An intoxicating liquor or substance; মাদক দ্রব্য।

in-tŏx'-i-cāte, *v. t.* **1.** To make drunk, to inebriate; সুরাপান দ্বারা মাতাল করা; নেশা জন্মান, নেশাচ্ছন্ন করা। **2.** To excite beyond self-control; to elate excessively; প্রমত্ত বা উত্তেজিত করা; সাতিশয় উল্লসিত করা, মাতোয়ারা করা, বিভোর করা, মুগ্ধ ও আচ্ছন্ন করা। **—cat-ing,** *adj.* Producing intoxication; মাদক, মত্ততাজনক, উন্মাদক, উন্মদ। **—ca'-tion,** *n.* **1.** Act of intoxicating; drunkenness; মাদন, মত্ততাজনন; সুরাপানজনিত মত্ততা। **2.** Excessive excitement or elation; অতিরিক্ত উত্তেজনা বা উল্লাস।

in-trăc'-tă-ble (-bl), *adj.* **1.** Not tractable; perverse; refractory; দুঃসেব্য, অবশ্য, দুঃশাসন, দুঃশাস্য, দুঃশাম্য; অবিনেয়, দুর্দ্দান্ত, উচ্ছৃঙ্খল, বেআড়া; অদম্য, দুর্দ্দম। **2.** (Of things), Not easily dealt with; দুর্নিগ্রহ, দুরাধর্ষ, অনায়ত্ত। **—bil'-i-ty, —ness,** *ns.* **—tract'-a-bly,** *adv.*

in-tră'-dōs, *n.* The interior curve of an arch; খিলানের আভ্যন্তরিক বক্রিমা।

in-trăn'-si-gĕnt, *adj.* & *n.* Uncompromising or irreconcilable esp. in politics; মীমাংসাপরাঙ্মুখ, অশাম্য। ***Noun.*** An uncompromising republican; চরম-গণতন্ত্রানুরাগী।

in-trăn'-si-tive (-tiv), (*Eng. Gram.*) Not transitive; অকর্ম্মক। **—ly,** *adv.* **Intransitive verb**—অকর্ম্মক ক্রিয়া।

in' trănt, *adj.* & *n.* Entering; penetrating; প্রবেশকারী; বিভেদী। ***Noun.*** One who enters specially upon a college, an association, etc.; উচ্চতম বিদ্যালয়, পরিষৎ, প্রভৃতিতে প্রবেশকারী ব্যক্তি।

in-trĕnch', *v. t.* & *i.* **1.** To fortify with a ditch and parapet; গড় বা পরিখা দ্বারা সুরক্ষিত করা, গড়বন্দী করা। **2.** To furrow; নালী বা খাঁজ করা। **—trenched',** *p. a.* Provided with intrenchments; পরিখাপরিবেষ্টিত, পরিখাপরিবৃত।

in-trĕp'-id, *adj.* Not trembling with fear; brave; নির্ভয়, অভয়, অভীত, বিগতভয়, বিশঙ্ক, নিঃশঙ্ক, অকুতোভয়; সাহসী। **—ly,** *adv.* Fearlessly; নির্ভয়ে, নিঃশঙ্কচিত্তে। **—trepid'-i-ty,** *n.* Fearlessness; নির্ভীকতা, নির্ভয়তা, নিঃশঙ্কতা, অভয়, অভীতি।

in'-tri-ca-cy, *n.* **1.** The state of being intricate; complexity; জটিলতা, দুরূহতা, কাঠিন্য; অসরলতা, অসারল্য, ব্যস্ততা, সঙ্কুলতা। **2.** A perplexing difficulty; জটিলতা, পেঁচ, কুটিলতা, গোঁল, মুস্কিল, লটপট, নটখটি।

in'-tri-cate, *adj.* Entangled; involved; complicated; obscure; জটিল; লটপটে; পেঁচালো, অস্পষ্ট, অস্পষ্টার্থ, দুর্ব্বোধ। **—ly,** *adv.* In an intricate manner; জটিল ভাবে।

in-trigue' (-trig), *n.* & *v. i.* **1.** A plot to effect some purpose by secret artifice ; a conspiracy : কুমন্ত্রণা, জটিল চক্রান্ত; ষড়যন্ত্র, বৈদগ্ধ প্রয়োগ বিদগ্ধযোগ, কপটপ্রয়োগ, বিদগ্ধকল্পনা, কুযুক্তি, কপট প্রবন্ধ। **2.** An amour or liasion ; অবৈধপ্রণয়, প্রণয়চক্রান্ত, গুপ্তপ্রণয়, গুপ্তপ্রেম। *Verb i.* **1.** To form a secret plot ; to conspire ; চক্রান্ত বা ফন্দি করা ; বৈদগ্ধ প্রয়োগ করা, কপটপ্রবন্ধ করা, ষড়যন্ত্র করা। **2.** To carry on a secret and illicit love (*with*) ; প্রেম করা। **In′-tri-gant, In′-tri-guant,** *ns.* An intriguer ; ষড়যন্ত্রকারী। **—tri′-guer,** *n.* One who intrigues ; ষড়যন্ত্রকারী, বিদগ্ধনায়ক, বিদগ্ধপ্রয়োজক।

in-trin′-sic, *adj.* Internal ; essential ; real; as, the *intrinsic* value of gold ; অন্তর্নিহিত ; স্বরূপগত, স্বাভাবিক, প্রাকৃতিক, সাংসিদ্ধিক, সারভূত, সহজাত, স্বভাবজ, প্রকৃতিগত, প্রধান, মূলীভূত ; বাস্তব, প্রকৃত, সত্য, আসল, যথার্থ (হিঃ কোঃ)। **—si-cal-ly,** *adv.* Inherently ; essentially ; স্বরূপতঃ ; মূলতঃ, প্রকৃতরূপে, যথার্থভাবে, স্বভাবতঃ। **Intrinsic value**—প্রকৃত মূল্য বা মান, যথার্থ মূল্য বা মান।

in-trō-dūce′, *v. t.* **1.** To lead or bring in ; আনয়ন করা, উপস্থিত করা। **2.** To insert ; মধ্যে স্থাপন করা, অন্তর্নিবিষ্ট করা। **3.** To bring into use or practice, as a custom, a new fashion, etc. ; প্রবর্ত্তিত করা। **4.** To make known specially in formal manner ; as, to *introduce* a stranger to a person ; to present, as a young lady into society : পরিচিত করিয়া দেওয়া ; পরিচিত করান। **5.** To bring forward ; to present ; as, to *introduce* a subject with a preface ; উপস্থাপিত করা ; অবতারণা করা। **6.** To bring before parliament, as a bill etc. ; পার্লেমেন্ট মহাসভায় উপস্থিত করা। **7.** To instruct ; as, to *introduce* one *to* a poem ; উপদেশ দেওয়া। **8.** (Of a conjunction) To begin or open, as a sentence ; আরম্ভ করা। **—duc′-to-ry,** *adj.* Serving to introduce ; preliminary ; prefaratory ; as, an *introductory* discourse ; প্রারম্ভসূচক, মুখবন্ধস্বরূপ ; প্রাথমিক ; উপক্রমিক, প্রবেশিক (হিঃ কোঃ), আরম্ভক প্রস্তাবনারূপ।

in-trō-dŭc′-tion, *n.* **1.** The act of introducing ; প্রবর্ত্তন, প্রবেশন। **2.** Formal presentation or making known of one person to another ; পরিচিত করণ, অন্যোন্যপরিচয় করণ। **3.** Preliminary matter prefixed to a book ; a preface ; মুখবন্ধ, ভূমিকা ; প্রস্তাবনা (of a play), অবতরণিকা, গ্রন্থারম্ভ, প্রবেশিকা (হিঃ কোঃ), আমুখ (দশরূঃ), বামুখ। **4.** A treatise introductory to other treatise or subjects ; as, an *introduction* to English literature ; উপক্রমণিকা। **A letter of introduction**—পরিচয়পত্র।

in-trō′-it, *n.* (*Eccl.*) A short psalm or hymn sung while the priest proceeds to the altar to commence the Communion Service ; (যাজকীয় শাস্ত্র) অন্তিমভোজনোপাসনার্থ বেদীর অভিমুখে যাজক অগ্রসর হইলে যে সংক্ষিপ্ত স্তবসঙ্গীত গীত হয়।

in-trō-mit′, *v. t.* **1.** (*Archaic*) To introduce or insert ; অন্তর্নিবিষ্ট করা। **2.** To admit (*into*) ; প্রবিষ্ট করা, ঢুকান। **—mis′-sion,** *n.* **—tent,** *adj.*

in-trō-spĕct′, *v. i.* To look within ; to examine one's thoughts and feelings ; অন্তর্দর্শন করা ; স্বীয় চিন্তা ও ভাবসমূহ পরীক্ষা করা, স্বকীয় মনোভাবাদি পর্য্যালোচনা করা। **—spec′-tion,** *n.* Act of looking within ; examination of one's thoughts and feelings ; অন্তরালোকন, অন্তরাবলোকন, অন্তর্দর্শন ; আত্মপরীক্ষণ, অন্তর্দৃষ্টি (হিঃকোঃ), অন্তর্মুখতা (ঐ), প্রত্যগ্‌দৃষ্টি। **—spec′-tion-ist,** *n.* One given to introspection or to the introspective method of examining phenomena of mind ; অন্তর্দর্শী ব্যক্তি, যে ব্যক্তি অন্তর্দৃষ্টি ও মনোবৃত্তি সমূহের আলোচনা দ্বারা চিন্তা করিয়া থাকে। **—spec′-tive,** *adj.* Seeing inwardly ; examining one's thoughts and feelings ; অন্তর্দর্শী ; আত্মচিন্তাপরীক্ষক, অন্তর্মুখী। **—spec′-tive-ly,** *adv.* **—spec′-tive-ness,** *n.*

in-trō-vêrt′, *v. t.* **1.** To turn as thought, mind, etc., inwards upon itself ; অন্তর্মুখী করা। **2.** (*Zool.*) To draw in or invaginate as one tubular part within another ; (প্রাণি-বিদ্যা) ভিতরের দিকে আকর্ষণ করা। **—ver′-si-ble,** *adj.* **—ver′-sion,** *n.* **—ver′-sive,** *adj.* **—ver′-tive,** *adj.*

in-trude′ (-trôd), *v. t.* & *i.* **1.** To thrust or force as a thing (*into*) ; জোর করিয়া ঢুকান, বলপূর্ব্বক প্রবিষ্ট করা বা ঠেলিয়া দেওয়া। **2.** To force as opinion etc., *upon* a person ; জোর করিয়া চালান। *Verb i.* To force oneself in without leave or permission ; to come uninvited ; as, to *intrude into* a place, company, etc. or *upon* a person, in privacy, etc. ; অনাহূত ভাবে প্রবেশ করা, অনধিকারপ্রবেশ করা ; উপর-পড়া হইয়া আসা, উপযাচক হইয়া আসা। **—trud′-er,** *n.* One who intrudes ; স্বয়মাগত, উপর-পড়া, উপযাচক, অনাহূত প্রবেশক।

in-trū′-sion, *n.* **1.** Act of intruding or of forcing in ; সবলে প্রবেশন। **2.** Forcing oneself (*into* or *upon*) without welcome or permission ; অনাহূতপ্রবেশন, অনাহূতাগমন। **3.** (*Geol.*) The thrusting of molten rock into, or between, other rock-formations ; (ভু-বিদ্যা) পাষাণে বা পাষাণদ্বয়ের মধ্যে দ্রবীভূত পাষাণ সবলে প্রবেশন। **—sive,** *adj.* **—sive-ness,** *n.* **—sive-ly,** *adv.*

in′-tū-bāte, *v. t.* (*Med.*) To introduce a tube into, as a larynx etc., to keep it open ; (ভৈষজ্য-শাস্ত্র) অভ্যন্তরে নল প্রবিষ্ট করিয়া কণ্ঠনালী প্রভৃতি উন্মুক্ত রাখা। **—ba'-tion,** *n.*

in'-tü-it, *v. t.* & *i.* To know or apprehend by intuition ; সহজ-জ্ঞান দ্বারা জানা, আত্মপ্রত্যয় দ্বারা উপলব্ধি করা। ***Verb i.*** To receive knowledge intuitively ; আত্মপ্রত্যয় দ্বারা জ্ঞানলাভ করা।

in-tü-i'-tion, *n.* **1.** The immediate apprehension by the mind or by sense without reasoning ; স্বানুভূতি, আত্মপ্রত্যয়, অনুভব (শুক্রঃ বিনয়ঃ)। **2.** A quick or ready insight ; ক্ষিপ্র অন্তর্দৃষ্টি। **3.** Innate or instinctive knowledge ; হৃৎস্থিত সহজ ও অখণ্ডবুদ্ধি, স্বভাবসিদ্ধ জ্ঞান, সহজ-জ্ঞান, বোধি (হিঃ দঃ), বিচারনিরপেক্ষ-জ্ঞান, প্রমাণনিরপেক্ষজ্ঞান, সহজোপলব্ধ জ্ঞান, প্রত্যক্ষজ্ঞান (হিঃ কোঃ), প্রতিভা (ঐ), স্ফূর্ত্তি (ঐ), সাহজিক জ্ঞান, অন্তর্জ্ঞান, তাৎকালিকজ্ঞান, অপ্রামাণিক জ্ঞান, অযত্ন-সম্ভূত জ্ঞান [Kant বোধিকে তিন ভাগে বিভক্ত করিয়াছেন:—(১) Empirical intuition—সবিচারা নির্ব্বিকল্প প্রজ্ঞা। (২) Pure intuition—শুদ্ধ অনুভব (যথা দেশ, কাল)। (৩) Intellectual intuition—নির্ব্বিচারা নির্ব্বিকল্প প্রজ্ঞা]। [নীতি বিজ্ঞানে Intuition শব্দ দ্বারা বিশিষ্ট নৈতিকবৃত্তি বা ইন্দ্রিয়জনিত স্বভাবসিদ্ধ ন্যায়ান্যায়াবধারণ বুঝায়।] **—al, —tu'-i-tive,** *adjs.* Of, or relating to intuition ; possessing or perceived by intuition ; বোধি-সম্পর্কীয় ; সহজসিদ্ধ, অন্তর্জ্ঞানোপলব্ধ, সহজজ্ঞানোপলব্ধ প্রমাণনিরপেক্ষজ্ঞেয়, সহজজ্ঞেয়, নির্ব্বিচার, নৈসর্গিক (হিঃ কোঃ), সাক্ষাৎ (ঐ), অপরোক্ষ (ঐ), আত্ম-প্রত্যয়সিদ্ধ। **—al-ly,** *adv.* **—ism,** *n.* Same as INTUITIONALISM. **—ist,** *n.* **Empirical intuition**—সবিচারা নির্ব্বিকল্পপ্রজ্ঞা (ব্রজঃ হিন্দু)। **Intellectual intuition**—নির্ব্বিচারা নির্ব্বিকল্প প্রজ্ঞা (ব্রজঃ হিন্দু)। **Intuitional ethics** — নৈসর্গিক নীতিবাদ (হিঃ কোঃ)। **Intuitive knowledge**—সবিকল্প প্রজ্ঞা, সহজজ্ঞান (হিঃ কোঃ), প্রত্যক্ষজ্ঞান (ঐ)।

in-tü-i'-tion-ăl-ĭsm, *n.* The doctrine that the perception of truth is by intuition ; হৃৎস্থিত সহজ ও অখণ্ড বুদ্ধি দ্বারা সত্য উপলব্ধি হয় — এইরূপ মতবাদ, সহজজ্ঞানবাদ (হিঃ কোঃ), নৈসর্গিকবাদ (ঐ)।

in-tü'-i-tiv-ĭsm, *n.* The doctrine that the ideas of right and wrong are intuitive ; ন্যায়ান্যায়বুদ্ধি সহজ-বুদ্ধি জাত—এইরূপ মতবাদ। **—ist,** *n.*

in-tü-mĕs'-cĕnt (-ŏnt), *adj.* Swelling up ; স্ফীতিশীল। **—cence,** *n.* A swelling ; স্ফীতি, শোথ (মঃ ইঃ)।

in-tŭs-sŭs-cĕp'-tion, *n.* **1.** The reception of one part within another ; একাংশে অন্যাংশের গ্রহণ। **2.** The withdrawal of one portion of the intestine within another ; অন্ত্রের একাংশে অন্যাংশের প্রতিগ্রহণ, অন্ত্রপ্রবেশ (হঃ চঃ)। **3.** The act of taking in foreign matter by a living organism and its conversion into organic tissue ; সজীব শরীরে বাহ্য বস্তুর অন্তর্গ্রহণ এবং উহার জৈব বিধানতন্তুতে পরিবর্ত্তন।

in-unc'-tion (-ŭngk-), *n.* Act of smearing or rubbing with oil ; তৈলমর্দ্দন।

in'-ŭn-dāte, *v. t.* **1.** To cover with flood ; to flood ; to overflow ; as, the river *inundates* the town ; বন্যাপ্লাবিত করা, জলব্যাপ্ত করা ; প্লাবিত করা ; আপ্লাবিত করা। **2.** (*Fig.*) To fill with an overflowing abundance ; পরিপ্লাবিত করা। **—da'-tion,** *n.* **1.** The act of inundating ; a flood ; প্লাবন ; জলপ্লাবন, বন্যা, তোয়বিপ্লব, সলিলোপ্লব, জলপ্রলয়, জলোচ্ছ্বাস। **2.** An overflowing abundance ; ছড়াছড়ি।

in-ur-bāne' (-êr-), *adj.* Uncivil ; unpolished ; rude ; অসভ্য, অশিষ্ট, অভদ্র ; গ্রাম্য, অমার্জ্জিত ; রূঢ়। **—ban'-i-ty,** *n.* Want of urbanity ; rudeness ; গ্রাম্যতা, অসভ্যতা, অভদ্রতা, অবিনয়, অশিষ্টতা ; রূঢ়তা।

in-ūre', ĕn—, *v. t.* To accustom ; to habituate ; to harden ; অভ্যস্ত করা ; স্বভাবগত করা ; অভ্যাস দ্বারা কষ্টসহিষ্ণু করা। **—ment,** *n.* Practice ; অভ্যাস। **Inured to hardship**—Habituated to hardship ; কঠোরতায় অভ্যস্ত, কষ্ট সহনে অভ্যস্ত।

in-urn' (-êrn), *v. t.* **1.** To put in an urn as the ashes of the dead ; (মৃতদেহের ভস্মাবশেষ) পাত্রে রাখা। **2.** To bury ; সমাহিত করা, গোর দেওয়া।

in-ü-til'-i-tȳ, *n.* Uselessness ; unprofitableness ; অব্যবহার্য্যতা ; নিরর্থকতা, ব্যর্থতা, বিফলতা। **—u'-tile,** *adj.* Useless ; অব্যবহার্য্য, নিরর্থক।

in-vāde', *v. t.* **1.** To enter with hostile intentions ; আপতিত হওয়া। **2.** To infringe ; to encroach on as rights etc. ; লঙ্ঘন করা, ভঙ্গ করা ; চড়াও করা, অনধিকার প্রবেশ করা। **3.** To affect injuriously as a wound, disease, feeling, etc. ; উপদ্রুত করা। **—vad'-er,** *n.* One who invades ; an intruder ; আক্রমণকারী, আক্রামক, দেশাক্রামক ; অনধিকার প্রবেশকারী।

in-văg'-i-nāte, *v. t.* **1.** To sheathe ; পরদা, চামড়া, প্রভৃতির ভিতরে প্রবিষ্ট করা। **2.** To introvert as a tubular sheath ; নলাকার আবরণের ভিতরের দিক উল্টাইয়া বাহিরে আনা, অন্তঃপরিবর্ত্ত করা। **—na'-tion,** *n.*

in'-vă-lid (-lĕd, *adj.* & *n.* **1.** Feeble or infirm from illness ;

breath'-ing (brĕth-), *n.* & *adj.* **1.** Respiration ; শ্বাস-প্রশ্বাস, শ্বসন। **2.** Inspiration ; as, the *breathings* of the spirit ; অনুপ্রাণন। **3.** Air in gentle motion ; মন্দপবন, ধীরসমীর (গীতঃ)। **4.** Aspiration ; secret prayer ; as, earnest desires and *breathings* after that blessed state ; উচ্চাভিলাস, উচ্চাকাঙ্ক্ষা ; নিভৃত প্রার্থনা। **5.** Utterance ;

রোগশীর্ণ করা। 2. To regard as an invalid; to remove from active service on account of illness or injury; রুগ্ন বলিয়া গণ্য করা; পীড়া অথবা আঘাতপ্রাপ্তি হেতু যুদ্ধক্ষেত্র হইতে স্থানান্তরিত করা। *Verb i.* 1. To become an invalid; রুগ্ন হওয়া। 2. To be enlisted as an invalid; কার্য্যাক্ষম ব্যক্তিগণের তালিকাভুক্ত হওয়া।

in-văl′-i-dāte, *v. t.* To render invalid or of no effect; to make null and void; অকার্য্যকর করা; নিষ্ফল করা, বাতিল করা, নাকচ করা।

in-vă-lid′-i-tȳ, *n.* 1. Want of validity or of legal force; অসিদ্ধতা যোষতা, প্রভাবহীনতা, অবৈধতা। 2. Bodily infirmity; শারীরিক দৌর্ব্বল্য।

in-văl′-ü-ă-ble (-bl) *adj.* Precious above estimation; priceless; বহুমূল্য, অমূল্য; অনর্ঘ। **–bly,** *adv.*

in-vā′-ri-ă-ble (-bl), *adj.* 1. Not variable; unchangeable; always uniform; অপরিবর্ত্তনীয়; নিত্য, সতত (হিঃ কোঃ), নিত্যবর্ত্তী (ঐ), অবিকারী; (ঐ), অবিকার্য্য, নির্ব্বিকার, সনাতন, নিয়তএকরূপ। 2. (*Math.*) Constant; fixed; স্থির; ধ্রুব। **–bil′-i-ty, –ness,** *ns.* The quality of being invariable; অপরিবর্ত্তনীয়তা, নিয়তএকরূপতা, নিত্যতা, অবিকারিতা (হিঃ কোঃ)। **–bly,** *adv.*

in-vā′-sion, *n.* 1. The act of invading; a hostile inroad; আক্রমণ, প্রয়াণ; দেশাক্রমণ। 2. Encroachment; অনধিকার প্রবেশ, চড়াও। 3. The first attack of anything hurtful; as, the *invasion* of a disease; রোগের প্রথম বা উপক্রম অবস্থা। **–sive,** *adj.* Tending to invade; aggressive; আক্রমণশীল; চড়াওকারী।

in-věc′-tive (-tĭv), *adj.* & *n.* (*Rare*) Abusive; (কচিদ্ ব্যবহৃত) কটূক্তিময়, নিন্দাময়, গালিপূর্ণ। *Noun.* 1. A railing speech, abusive expression or writing; গালি, কটূক্তি, দুরুক্তি, নিন্দাবাক্য, নিন্দোক্তি, ভৎর্সনা, অপবাদ, পরিভাষণ, বাক্‌পারুষ্য, কুৎসাবাক্য। 2. A violent or harsh accusation; as, an *invective* against tyranny; তীব্র ভৎর্সনা, গঞ্জনা, তীব্র অভিযোগ।

in-veigh′ (-vā), *v. i.* To rail; to utter censorious language, (with *against*); গালাগালি করা; নিন্দা বা ভৎর্সনাসূচক বাক্য উচ্চারণ করা, গঞ্জনা করা।

in-vei′-gle (-vē-gl), *v. t.* 1. To entice; to allure; to seduce; প্রলুব্ধ করা, ভুলাইয়া কুপথগামী করা, বিপথগামী করা; ভুলান, প্রলোভনদ্বারা ভুলান; ফুসলান। 2. (*Obs.*) To ensnare; ফাঁদে ফেলা। **–ment,** *n.*

in-věnt′, *v. t.* 1. To devise or produce as something new; উদ্ভাবন করা। 2. To fabricate as a story etc.; রচনা করা। **–ven′-tive,** *adj.* 1. Able to invent; quick of contrivance; as, he had an *inventive* brain; উপায়জ্ঞ, উপায়ী, উদ্ভাবনপটু; উদ্ভাবনতৎপর। 2. Showing originality; as, an *inventive* art; উদ্ভাবনী। **–ven′-tive-ly,** *adv.* **–ven′-tive-ness, –ven′-tor,** *ns.* **–ven′-tress,** *n.* (*Fem.*) **Inventive power**—Power of invention; উদ্ভাবনীশক্তি। **Inventive faculty**—নির্ম্মাণশক্তি (হিঃ কোঃ)।

in-věn′-tion, *n.* 1. The act of inventing; devising; fabrication; উদ্ভাবন; পরিকল্পনা, নবকল্পনা (হিঃকোঃ); রচনা। 2. That which is invented; a contrivance; উদ্ভাবিত বিষয়; কৌশল, উদ্ভাবনা। 3. A fictitious statement or story; কাল্পনিক উক্তি, স্বকপোলকল্পিত উক্তি বা গল্প, মিথ্যাকল্পনা, মিথ্যাকল্পিত, মনঃসৃষ্টি। 4. The creative or imaginative faculty; inventiveness; উদ্ভাবনী শক্তি, রচনাশক্তি, কল্পনাশক্তি; উদ্ভাবনপটুতা। **Invention of the Cross**—রোম সম্রাট্ Constantineএর জননী Helenaর অনুচরগণ কর্ত্তৃক ৩২৬ খৃঃ অব্দে যীশুখৃষ্টের ক্রুশ আবিষ্কার। [ওরা মে এই ঘটনার স্মৃতিস্বরূপ উৎসব হইয়া থাকে।]

in′-věn-tŏ-rȳ, *n.* & *v. t.* 1. A detailed account or list of goods, chattels, etc.; জায়, ফর্দ্দ, অস্থাবরদ্রব্যসংখ্যা-পত্র, গৃহবস্তুপরিসংখ্যা। 2. The stock of goods that are, or may be, inventoried; জায়ে লিখিত মাল, যে সকল জিনিষের জায় করিতে হইবে। *Verb t.* To make an invenetory of; to insert in an inventory; জায় করা, ফর্দ্দ করা; তালিকাভুক্ত করা।

in-vē-răc′-i-tȳ, *n.* Untruthfulness; অসত্যবাদিতা, অনৃতত্ব।

in-verse′ (-vêrs), *adj.* & *n.* 1. Opposite in order, relation or position; inverted; উৎক্রম (হিঃ কোঃ), বিপরীত, উল্টা, বিলোম, ব্যত্যস্ত, ব্যতিক্রান্ত, প্রতীপ, বিপ্রতীপ; বিপর্য্যস্ত। 2. (*Math.*) Opposite in nature or effect; বিলোম। *Noun.* 1. That which is inverse; বিপরীত বস্তু। 2. Inverted state; বিপর্য্যস্ততা। **–ly** *adv.* In an inverse order or manner; বিপর্য্যস্তভাবে। **Inverse curve**—বিপরীত চক্র (হিঃকোঃ)। **Inverse proportion** — Proportion in a reverse order; ব্যত্যস্তানুপাত। **Inverse ratio**—বিষমানুপাত, ব্যস্তমান (হিঃ কোঃ)। **Inverse rule of three**—বিলোম ত্রৈরাশিক, ব্যস্ত ত্রৈরাশিক।

in-vêr′-sion, *n.* 1. The act of inverting; transposition; বিপর্য্যস্ত করণ; পর্য্যায়ব্যতিক্রম, বিপর্য্যয়, বৈলোম্য, বিপর্য্যাস (হিঃ কোঃ), ব্যুৎক্রম, ব্যত্যয়। 2. Reversal of position, relation or order; ক্রমবিপর্য্যয়, অবস্থান-বিপর্য্যয়, সম্বন্ধ-বিপর্য্যয়। 3. (*Gram.*) A change of the natural order of words; as, *of all vices impurity is one of the most detestable*, instead of *impurity is one of the most detestable of all vices*; (ব্যাকরণ) বাক্যে স্বাভাবিক শব্দবিন্যাসের পরিবর্ত্তন,

শব্দবিন্যাস বিপর্য্যয়। **4.** (*Math.*) A reversal of a ratio by interchanging the positions of the antecedent and the consequent ; আনুপাতিক সংখ্যা সমূহের এরূপ পর্য্যায়পরিবর্ত্তন যেন দ্বিতীয় প্রথমের স্থান এবং চতুর্থ পঞ্চমের স্থান অধিকার করে, উৎক্রমণ (হিঃ কোঃ)। **5.** (*Logic*) A form of immediate inference ; অন্তরাবর্ত্তন (সাঃ পঃ)। **Rule of inversion**—বিলোমক্রিয়া, উৎক্রমণ (হিঃ কোঃ), বিলোমবিধি (ঐ), ব্যস্তবিধি (ঐ)।

in-vêrt′, *v. t.* **1.** To turn upside down ; উল্টাইয়া ফেলা, বিপর্য্যস্ত করা, অধোমুখ করা (মঃ ইঃ)। **2.** To reverse the order or relation of ; ক্রমবিপর্য্যয় করা। **–ed**, *adj.* **1.** Turned upside down ; অধোমুখী-কৃত, অধঃকৃত, বিপর্য্যস্ত। **2.** Changed in order ; ক্রমবিপর্য্যস্ত। **Inverted commas**—উদ্ধার চিহ্ন।

in′-vêrt, *n.* (*Masonry*) An inverted arch ; বিপর্য্যস্ত তোরণ, যে তোরণের বক্রদিক নিম্নদেশে অবস্থিত থাকে।

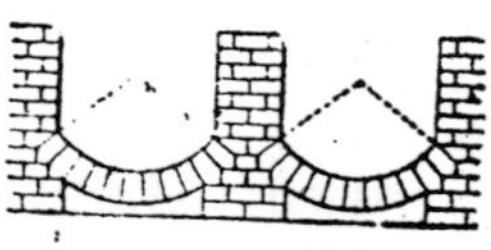

Inverted arches.

in-vêr′-tė-brate, *adj.* & *n.* **1.** (*Zool.*) Having no backbone or spinal chord ; মেরুদণ্ডহীন, অমেরুদণ্ডী। **2.** (*Fig.*) Wanting in firmness ; দৃঢ়তাশূন্য। *Noun.* **1.** An animal destitute of backbone; মেরুদণ্ডহীন প্রাণী, অমেরুপ্রাণী (সাঃ পঃ)। **2.** (*Fig.*) One lacking in firmness ; (লক্ষণায়) অদৃঢ়চিত্ত ব্যক্তি, দৃঢ়তাশূন্য ব্যক্তি।

in-vĕst′, *v. t.* & *i.* **1.** To clothe : to put garments on, (followed by *in* or *with*) ; as, to *invest* a person *with* or *in* a robe ; বস্ত্রাচ্ছাদিত করা ; পোষাক পরাইয়া দেওয়া। **2.** To clothe as with office or insignia of office ; to endow ; as, to *invest* with dignity, rank, etc. ; পদ বা ক্ষমতাদ্বারা অন্বিত করা, পদমর্য্যাদাদিদ্বারা ভূষিত করা, অধিকারে নিযুক্ত করা ; সম্পন্ন করা, সমন্বিত করা। **3.** To endue with qualities, a character, etc., (followed by *with*, *in* or *into*) ; গুণাদি সমন্বিত করা। **4.** To lay seige to ; as, to *invest* a town ; অবরোধ করা। **5.** To lay out as money in business etc. for income or profit ; নিয়োগ করা, খাটান, ধনপ্রয়োগ করা। ***Verb i.*** To make an investment ; as, to *invest* in stocks ; টাকা প্রভৃতি খাটান। **–ment**, *n.* (See below.) **–ves′-tor**, *n.*

in-vĕs′-ti-gate, *v. t.* To enquire into ; to make careful examination of ; অন্বেষণ করা, অনুসন্ধান করা ; সূক্ষ্মানুসন্ধান করা, পুঙ্খানুপুঙ্খরূপে পরীক্ষা করা। **–ga′-tion**, *n.* Act of investigating ; careful enquiry ; সূক্ষ্মানুসন্ধান ; গবেষণা। **–ga-tive**, *adj.* Characterised by, or inclined to, investigation ; অনুসন্ধানাত্মক, অনুসন্ধানতৎপর, অনুসন্ধিৎসু। **–ga-tor**, *n.* **–ga-to-ry**, *adj.* **Local investigation** — স্থানীয় অনুসন্ধান, সুরতহাল।

in-vĕs′-ti-tūre, *n.* **1.** Act or ceremony of giving possession of office, benefice, etc. ; পদ প্রভৃতির অধিকার প্রদান, প্রতিষ্ঠা, অভিষেক, প্রতিষ্ঠাপন, পদস্থাপন, অধিকার, অভিষেক, অভিষেচন। **2.** Act of clothing or covering ; that which clothes or covers ; আবরণ ; পরিচ্ছদ, আবরক। **3.** Endowment (*with* attributes or qualities) ; সমন্বিতকরণ।

in-vĕst′-mĕnt, *n.* **1.** The act of investing or clothing ; clothing or robes ; a covering or coating ; বস্ত্রাচ্ছাদন ; পরিচ্ছদ, পরিধান, পোষাক ; আবরণ, আচ্ছাদন। **2.** Act of besieging by an armed force ; অবরোধ, প্রতিরোধ, পরিবেষ্টন। **3.** The laying out of money or capital for profit ; the amount of money invested ; অর্থবিনিয়োগ, ধনবিনিয়োগ, অর্থপ্রয়োগ, ধনপ্রয়োগ, প্রয়োগ (মঃ সং) ; বিনিযুক্ত অর্থ।

in-vĕt′-ėr-āte, *adj.* **1.** Long established, as habits etc. ; বহুকালিক, পুরাতন। **2.** Deep-rooted, as an abuse ; deep-seated ; chronic, as a disease ; বদ্ধমূল, অচ্যুত ; দৃঢ়মূল। **3.** Habitual ; obstinate, as a drunkard, smoker etc. ; চিরাভ্যস্ত ; বদ্ধ। **–a-cy**, *n.* State of being inveterate ; obstinacy of any quality or state acquired by time ; বদ্ধমূলতা, দৃঢ়মূলতা ; চিরকালিকত্ব, বহুকালিকত্ব। **–ly**, *adv.* **Inveterate hatred**—বদ্ধবৈর, অচ্যুতবৈর।

in-vid′-i-ous (-ŭs), *adj.* **1.** Unjustly discriminating ; অন্যায়রূপে প্রভেদকারী, অন্যায় প্রভেদাত্মক। **2.** (Of a thing) Enviable ; fitted to excite ill feeling against the possessor ; as, *invidious* honour ; ঈর্ষণীয় ; ঈর্ষাজনক, ঈর্ষোৎপাদক, দ্বেষজনক, অসন্তোষোৎপাদক, মাৎসর্য্যজনক। **–ly**, *adv.* **–ness**, *n.*

in-vig′-i-late, *v. i.* To watch over students at examination ; পরীক্ষার সময় পরিক্ষার্থীদিগের উপর দৃষ্টি রাখা। **–la′tion**, **–la-tor**, *ns.*

in-vig′-ŏr-āte, *v. t.* To give vigour to ; to strengthen ; to animate ; সবল করা ; বলবর্দ্ধন করা, তেজোবর্দ্ধন করা ; সতেজ করা। **–at-ing**, *adj.* Strengthening ; animating ; সন্তোষদায়ক, বলকর, বলবর্দ্ধক, শক্তিকারক ; সতেজ, তেজস্কর, তেজোবৃদ্ধিকর। **–a′-tion**, *n.* Act of invigorating ; বলপ্রদান (ভাব প্রঃ)। **–a-tive**, *adj.* **–a-tor**, *n.*

in-vin′-ci-ble (-bl), *adj.* Unconquerable ; (*fig.*) insuperable ; as, *invincible* army or obstacle ; অজেয়, দুর্জ্জয়, অপরাজেয়, অপরাজেতব্য অপরাজিত ; অদম্য, অনভিভবনীয়,

অপ্রধৃষ্য। **—bil′-i-ty,** *n.* The quality of being invincible; অজেয়ত্ব, অনতিক্রমনীয়তা, অপরাজেয়তা। **—bly,** *adv.*

in-vī′-ō-lă-ble (-bl), *adj.* **1.** Not to be violated; অলঙ্ঘ্য, অলঙ্ঘনীয়, অনুল্লঙ্ঘনীয় অনতিক্রমণীয়, অনতিক্রম্য। **2.** To be kept sacredly free from profanation, infraction, etc. as laws, places etc.; অলঙ্ঘনীয়। **—bil′-i-ty,** *n.* State of being inviolable; অলঙ্ঘনীয়তা। **—bly,** *adv.*

in-vī′-ō-lāte, *adj.* **1.** Not violated; uninjured; unbroken; অলঙ্ঘিত; অক্ষত; অটুট, অভগ্ন, অখণ্ড, অভিন্ন। **2.** Not corrupted or profaned; pure; as, *inviolate* truth; অদূষিত; পবিত্র। **—la-cy, —ness,** *ns.* The state of being inviolate; অলঙ্ঘ্যতা, অদুষ্টতা। **—ly,** *adv.*

in-vis′-i-ble (-bl), *adj.* & *n.* **1.** Incapable of being seen; অদৃশ্য, অদর্শনীয়, অলক্ষ্য, অপ্রত্যক্ষ, অপ্রেক্ষণীয়। **2.** Not to be seen at a particular time; as, when I called she was *invisible*; সময় বিশেষে অদৃশ্য বা অলক্ষ্য। **3.** Too small to be seen; as, an *invisible* bird; চক্ষুরগ্রাহ্য, দর্শনাতীত, অচক্ষুর্বিষয়, দৃগগোচর, অপ্রেক্ষণীয়, দর্শনাতীত। **—bil′-i-ty, —ness,** *ns.* The state of being invisible; অদৃশ্যতা, অলক্ষ্যতা, অপ্রত্যক্ষতা। **—bly,** *adv.* In an invisible manner; অদৃশ্যভাবে। ***Noun.*** (With *the* prefixed) God; the invisible world; পরমেশ্বর; অদৃশ্য জগৎ। **Invisible ink**—অদৃশ্য কালি।

in-vīte′, *v. t.* & *n.* **1.** To request to do, or forbear from, some act; কোন কার্য্য করিতে বা কোন কার্য্য হইতে নিরস্ত হইতে অনুরোধ করা। **2.** To ask to entertainment; as, to *invite* to dinner; নিমন্ত্রণ করা, আমন্ত্রণ করা, আহ্বান করা। **3.** To allure; to attract; as, shady groves *invite* easy sleep; প্রলুব্ধ করা, চিত্তহরণ করা, মনোহরণ করা; আকর্ষণ করা। **4.** To give occasion for; to be open to; as, to *invite* criticism; সুযোগ প্রদান করা; উন্মুক্ত হওয়া। **5.** To solicit courteously, as suggestions, opinions, etc.; ভদ্রভাবে প্রার্থনা করা, সবিনয় প্রার্থনা করা, সাদরে আহ্বান করা। ***Noun.*** Invitation (*colloq.*); নিমন্ত্রণ। **—vi-ta′-tion,** *n.* **1.** The act of inviting; a bidding to an entertainment; আমন্ত্রণ; নিমন্ত্রণ। **2.** A written or spoken form by which one is invited; নিমন্ত্রণপত্র, আহ্বান। **3.** Attraction; inducement; আকর্ষণ; প্রলোভন। **—vit′-ing-ly,** *adv.* In an attracting manner; চিত্তাকর্ষকরূপে। **—vit′-ing-ness,** *n.* **—vit′-a-to-ry,** *adj.*

in-vō-cā′-tion, *n.* **1.** The act of invoking or calling upon God or deity in prayer; a prayer to a divine being; আবাহন, স্মরণ (হিঃ কোঃ); নামোচ্চারণ, নামগ্রহণ; প্রার্থনা। **2.** A prayer to the Muse for inspiration in a poem; মঙ্গলাচরণ। **3.** A spell or incantation used in conjuring; যাদুমন্ত্র। **—voc′-a-to-ry,** *adj.*

in′-voice (-voys), *n.* & *v. t.* **1.** A list of merchandise sent to a person with prices and charges annexed; প্রেরিত মালের চালান, বীজক। **2.** The lot of goods shipped or received; as, to receive a large *invoice* of goods; চালানি মাল। ***Verb t.*** To make an invoice of; to enter in an invoice; দ্রব্যজাতের বীজক তৈয়ার করা; বীজকে ভুক্ত করা।

in-vōke′, *v. t.* **1.** To address in prayer; to call on for aid etc.; as, to *invoke* God or His aid; আবাহন করা; সাহায্য প্রভৃতির জন্য আহ্বান করা। **2.** To call forth as a spirit by incantations; মন্ত্রবলে আহ্বান করা। **3.** To appeal to, as a person's authority for support; আহ্বান করা। **4.** To implore; to ask earnestly for; মিনতি করা, অনুনয় করা; সকাতরে প্রার্থনা করা।

in′-vō-lū-cre (-kêr), *n.* **1.** A covering; আবরণ। **2.** A whorl of bracts around a flower cluster; পুষ্পগুলস্থ অনিয়মিত পত্রাদির আবর্ত্ত।

in-vŏl′-ŭn-tā-rȳ, *adj.* **1.** Not voluntary; unintentional; অস্বেচ্ছ, অস্বেচ্ছাজাত, অনিচ্ছাপূর্ব্ব (হিঃ কোঃ); স্বেচ্ছাবিরুদ্ধ। **2.** Done unwillingly; reluctant, as submission etc.; অস্বেচ্ছাকৃত; অনিচ্ছুক। **—ri-ly,** *adv.* Unintentionally; অনিচ্ছার সহিত, অনিচ্ছাপূর্ব্বক। **—ri-ness,** *n.*

in′-vō-lūte, *adj.* & *n.* **1.** Intricate; entangled; জটিল; জড়িত, পেঁচাল। **2.** (*Bot.*) Rolled inwards from the edges, as a leaf; (উদ্ভিদ্-বিদ্যা) (পত্রাদি সম্পর্কে) প্রান্ত হইতে অভ্যন্তরাভিমুখে আবর্ত্তিত, দ্বিবর্ত্তিক (সাঃ পঃ)। **3.** Rolled or curled up spirally; পেঁচানো, কুণ্ডলিত। ***Noun.*** (*Geom.*) A curve traced by any point of a string when it is unwrapped from a given curve; (জ্যামিতি) কোন নির্দ্দিষ্ট চক্রের সহিত একটী সূত্র দৃঢ়ভাবে পেঁচাইয়া পরে উহা টান রাখিয়া খুলিলে উহার প্রতি বিন্দুদ্বারা যে এক একটী বক্র রচিত হয়, অনবলুত (হিঃ কোঃ), বক্রকেন্দ্রিক (ঐ)।

in-vō-lū′-tion, *n.* **1.** The act of involving; বিজড়ন। **2.** Entanglement; complication; something complicated; জড়িতাবস্থা; জটিলতা; জটিল বিষয়। **3.** A curling or turning inwards; a part so curled; অন্তরাবর্ত্তন; অন্তরাবর্ত্তিত অংশ। **4.** (*Math.*) The raising of a quantity to any power; (গণিত) কোন সংখ্যাকে যে কোন শক্তি পর্য্যন্ত বৃদ্ধি করণ, ঘাতাবেশ (সাঃ পঃ), ঘাতক্রিয়া (ঐ), ঘাতকর্ম্ম (কেঃডিঃ)।

in-volve′ (-vŏlv), *v. t.* **1.** To roll or fold up as one thing in another; to envelop completely; as, *involved* in darkness; জড়িত করা, আচ্ছাদিত করা, পরিবেষ্টিত করা; আবৃত করা, আচ্ছন্ন করা। 2. To wind or coil spirally; কুণ্ডলিত করা, পেঁচান। 3. To complicate; to make intricate; as, to *involve* a statement; জটিল করা; জড়িত করা। 4. To include (*in*); অন্তর্ভুক্ত করা। 5. To imply; as, it *involves* a contradiction; বুঝান, সূচনা করা। 6. To entangle; to embarrass; as, to *involve* a person in debt; to implicate, as in a crime etc.; বিজড়িত করা, ফাঁদে ফেলা; সংসৃষ্ট করা, লিপ্ত করা, জড়ান। 7. To absorb or occupy; as, *involved* in a deep study; নিমগ্ন করা, ব্যাপৃত করা। **—ment,** *n.* 1. The act of involving, or the state of being involved; বিজড়ন, বিজড়িতাবস্থা। 2. Financial difficulties; অর্থকষ্ট। 3. A complicated affair; গোলমেলে ব্যাপার।

in-vŭl'-nêr-ă-ble (-bl), *adj.* 1. Incapable of being wounded or hurt; অভেদ্য, অবেধ্য, অচ্ছেদ্য। 2. (*Fig.*) Irrefutable; unanswerable, as an argument etc.; অখণ্ডনীয়; দুরুত্তর। **—bly,** *adv.*

in'-ward (-wêrd), *adj.* & *n.* 1. Placed within; interior; অন্তঃস্থ, মধ্যবর্ত্তী; অন্তর্ব্বর্ত্তী, আভ্যন্তর। 2. Spiritual or mental; মানসিক, আন্তরিক, আধ্যাত্মিক। 3. Proceeding or directed towards the interior; অন্তর্জাত, অন্তর্মুখী। ***Noun.*** (*Pl.*) The entrails; অন্ত্র, নাড়িভুঁড়ি।

in'-ward(s) (-wêrds), *adv.* 1. Towards the inside; মধ্যদিকে, ভিতরের দিকে। 2. Into the mind; inwardly; as, to turn the attention *inwards*; মনোমধ্যে; অন্তরে।

in'-ward-lȳ (-wêrd-), *adv.* 1. Internally; towards the centre; অন্তরে, মধ্যে; কেন্দ্রের দিকে। 2. Spiritually; mentally; হৃদয়ে; মনে মনে, অন্তরে। 3. Not aloud; as, to speak *inwardly*; চুপে চুপে।

in'-ward-nĕss (-wêrd-), *n.* 1. Essential nature; as, the *inwardness* of conduct; মৌলিক প্রকৃতি। 2. State of being inward; আভ্যন্তরিকতা। 3. Heartiness; spirituality; আন্তরিকতা; আধ্যাত্মিকতা।

in-weave' (-wēv), **—ōn,** *v. t.* To weave in or together (*lit.* & *fig.*); মধ্যে বোনা, অন্তর্গ্রথিত করা, এক সঙ্গে বোনা বা গ্রথিত করা।

in-wrought' (-rôt), *p. p.* 1. Wrought or worked in or on a fabric as a pattern etc.; খচিত। 2. Wrought or adorned, as a fabric etc. with figures; কারুকার্য্যভূষিত, পরিখচিত। 3. (*Fig.*) Intimately blended (*with*); জড়িত, বিজড়িত।

in-yā'-lā, *n.* A South African antelope; দক্ষিণ আফ্রিকার কৃষ্ণসার মৃগ বিশেষ।

ī'-ō-dine (-dīn), *n.* A non-metallic element used in medicine and photography; ঔষধ প্রস্তুত এবং আলোক-চিত্রণে ব্যবহৃত অধাতব মূল পদার্থ বিশেষ, অরুণক, নীলীন (সাঃ পঃ), ধূম্রাশ্ম (আঃ বঃ), এতিন (মনীঃ)। **—dism,** *n.* A morbid state produced by the excessive use of iodine; অরুণক ব্যবহারে বিকৃত বা রুগ্ন অবস্থা। **—dize,** *v. t.* To treat with iodine; অরুণক দ্বারা চিকিৎসা করা। **—od'-ic,** *adj.*

ī-ō'-dō-fôrm, *n.* A compound of carbon, hydrogen and iodine used as an antiseptic; পচননিবারক গন্ধকবর্ণ উগ্রগন্ধ ঔষধ বিশেষ।

ī'-ō-līte, *n.* A mineral of a violet blue colour; ধূমলাভনীলবর্ণ খনিজ পদার্থ বিশেষ।

ī'-ŏn, *n.* One of the elements which pass to the poles in electrolysis; তাড়িত-প্রবাহজনিত রাসায়নিক বিশ্লেষণে মেরুদেশে আগত মৌলিক পদার্থ বিশেষ, কণা (সাঃ পঃ), অতিপরমাণু।

I-ō'-ni-ăn (ī-), *adj.* & *n.* Pertaining to Ionia or Ionians; গ্রীসের অন্তর্গত আইওনিয়া বাসিগণ বা বা তৎপ্রদেশ সংক্রান্ত, যাবনিক। ***Noun.*** A native of Ionia; আইওনিয়াবাসী, যূনানী, যবন। **Ionian mode**—(*Mus.*) Effiminate mode in ancient Greek music; প্রাচীন গ্রীক সঙ্গীতে স্ত্রীজনসুলভ রীতি।

I-ŏn'-ic (ī-), *adj.* Of, or pertaining to, Ionia; আইওনিয়া সংক্রান্ত। **Ionic dialect**—যাবনিক উপভাষা।

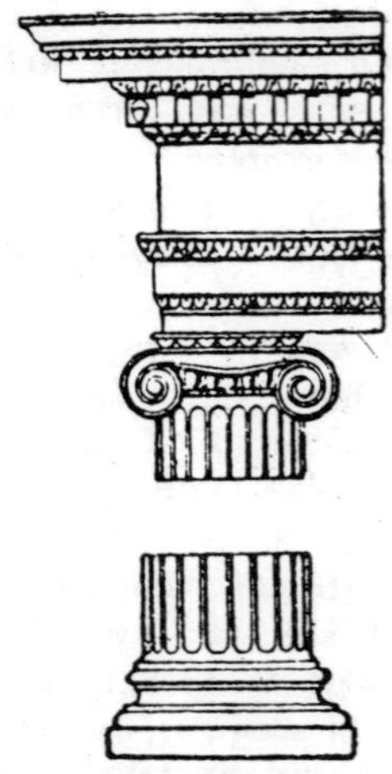

Ionic order.

Ionic order — গ্রীক স্থাপত্যরীতি বিশেষ—কুণ্ডলীবৎ স্তম্ভাগ্র এই রীতির বিশেষত্ব।

I-ō'-tă, *n.* 1. The ninth Greek letter corresponding to English *i.*; গ্রীক বর্ণমালার নবম অক্ষর। 2. A jot; বিন্দু, অণু, তিল, লেশ, বিন্দুবিসর্গ, বিন্দুমাত্র, তিলমাত্র, কণা, লবলেশ।

I-ō'-tă-cĭsm, *n.* 1. Frequent use of the letter or sound of *iota*; Iota অক্ষর বা ধ্বনির পুনঃ পুনঃ ব্যবহার। 2. Pronunciation of the Greek vowels like *iota* as *e*; Iotaর অনুরূপ গ্রীক স্বরবর্ণ সমূহের *e*এর মত উচ্চারণ।

I O U (ī-ō-ū), [I *owe you*] A paper having on it these letters followed by a sum of money and duly signed, serving as an acknowledgment of a debt ; কোন কাগজে এই বর্ণত্রয় লিখিয়া নাম স্বাক্ষর করিলে উক্ত দলীলে লিখিত টাকা স্বাক্ষরকারীর নিকট প্রাপ্য বলিয়া সাব্যস্ত হয়।

ip-ĕ-căc-ŭ-ăn'-ha (-ă), *n.* The root of a South American shrub used as an emetic and a purgative ; বমনকারক ও বিরেচক ঔষধরূপে ব্যবহৃত দক্ষিণ আমেরিকার গুল্ম বিশেষের মূল। (*Abbr. Ipecac.*)

ipse dixit, (*L.*), *n.* [*He himself* (*the master*) *said it*] Dogmatic assertion resting on bare authority ; [(প্রভু) স্বয়ং বলিয়াছেন] প্রভুত্বব্যঞ্জক উক্তি।

Ipomœa pes-capræ — ছাগল ক্ষুরী (বেলঃ)।

Ipomœa Turpethum—তুধ কল্‌মি (বেলঃ)।

Ipso facto, (*L.*), *adv.* By that very fact ; সেই বিষয়েই, সেই ঘটনাতেই।

irade, *n.* A written decree of the Sultan of Turkey ; তুরস্কের সুলতানের লিখিত হুকুম।

I-rā'-ni-ăn (ī-), *adj.* & *n.* Pertaining to Iran (Persia), its inhabitants or their language ; ইরাণীয়, পারস্যদেশীয়। ***Noun.*** A native of Iran ; ইরাণী, ইরাণবাসী।

ī-răs'-ci-ble (-ĭ-bl), *adj.* Prone to anger ; irritable ; আশুক্রোধী, সুলভকোপী, ক্রোধপ্রবণ, কোপনস্বভাব, রোষপরবশ, ক্রোধশীল, রোষপ্রবণ ; খিট্‌খিটে, চণ্ডস্বভাব। **—bil'-i-ty,** *n.* The state of being irascible ; irritability of temper ; রোষপরবশতা, কোপপ্রবণতা ; স্বভাবচণ্ডতা।

ī-rāte', *adj.* Angry ; enraged ; কুপিত ; ক্রুদ্ধ।

īre, *n.* (*Poet.*) Anger ; (কবিতায়) ক্রোধ, রোষ, কোপ। **Ire'-ful,** *adj.* **Ire'-ful-ly,** *adv.*

ī-rĕn'-ic', —i-căl, *adjs.* Pacific ; conciliatory ; peaceful ; শান্তিবিধায়ক ; মিলনসাধক ; শান্তিপূর্ণ।

ī-rĕn'-i-cŏn, *n.* A proposal for promoting peace especially in the church or between churches ; খৃষ্টীয় ধর্ম্মসংঘে বা ধর্ম্মসংঘসমূহের মধ্যে শান্তিবিধানার্থ প্রস্তাব।

īr-i-dĕs'-cent (-ĕnt), *adj.* **1.** Having or showing colours like that of the rainbow ; ইন্দ্রায়ুধসবর্ণ, ইন্দ্রায়ুধবর্ণ। **2.** Having a colour changing with position ; অবস্থান পরিবর্ত্তনে পরিবর্ত্তনকারী বর্ণবিশিষ্ট। **—cence,** *n.* The quality of being iridescent ; ইন্দ্রধনুবৎ বিভিন্ন বর্ণবিশিষ্টতা, ইন্দ্রায়ুধত্ব, ইন্দ্রচাপিত্ব।

ī-rĭd'-i-ŭm, *n.* A white metal of platinum group ; প্ল্যাটিনাম পর্য্যায়ভুক্ত শ্বেতবর্ণ ধাতু বিশেষ, হরিতক (সাঃ পঃ)।

ī'-ris, *n.* **1.** (*Anat.*) The coloured circle round the pupil of the eye ; চক্ষুর তারকার চতুর্দ্দিকস্থ রঞ্জিত মণ্ডল—যাহার ভিতরে তারা অবস্থিত থাকে, নেত্রতারকামণ্ডল, কনীনিকা মণ্ডল, কনীনিকাপরিধি, তারামণ্ডল, উপতারা। **2.** (*Class. myth., cap*) The goddess of the rainbow ; ইন্দ্রধনুর অধিষ্ঠাত্রী দেবী। **3.** The rainbow ; an appearance resembling the rainbow ; ইন্দ্রচাপ, রামধনু, ইন্দ্রায়ুধ, শক্রধনু, পুরন্দরধনু ; ইন্দ্রচাপসদৃশ দৃশ্য। **4.** The fleur-de-lis ; দশবাইচণ্ডী (প্রবোধ)। **5.** A kind of rock-crystal reflecting prismatic colours ; ইন্দ্রায়ুধবর্ণ প্রতিফলনকারী স্ফটিক প্রস্তর বিশেষ, ইন্দ্রায়ুধদ্যুতিবিস্তারী বিমলমণি বিশেষ।

I'-rish (ī-), *adj.* & *n.* Of, or pertaining to, Ireland or its people ; আয়র্লণ্ডদেশীয়, আয়র্লণ্ডবাসিগণ-সম্পর্কীয়। ***Noun.*** **1.** The language of Ireland ; আইরিশ ভাষা। **2.** (*Pl.* with *the*) The people of Ireland ; আয়র্লণ্ডবাসী, আইরিশজাতি। **—ism,** *n.* A mode of speaking peculiar to the Irish ; আইরিশদিগের ভাষার বিশেষ ধারা, ধরণ বা রীতি। **—ize,** *v. t.* To make Irish or Irish like ; আইরিশ ভাবাপন্ন করা, আয়র্লণ্ডবাসীর অনুরূপ করা। **Irish man, —woman** — Natives of Ireland ; আয়র্লণ্ডবাসী, আয়র্লণ্ডবাসিনী। **Irish stew**—কুচি কুচি করিয়া কাটা মাংস, আলু এবং পেঁয়াজের ঝোল।

irk (ērk), *v. t.* (*Archaic*) To give pain to ; to annoy ; to disgust ; as, it *irks* me ; কষ্ট দেওয়া, পীড়া দেওয়া, ব্যথা দেওয়া ; বিরক্ত করা ; ত্যক্ত করা।

irk'-some (ērk-sŭm), *adj.* Wearisome ; tedious ; পীড়াদায়ক, ক্লেশকর, খেদকর, ক্লেশদ, দুঃখদ, দুঃখকর ; বিরক্তিজনক, অবসাদকর, অবসাদজনক, শ্রমজনক। **—ly,** *adv.* **—ness,** *n.*

ī'-ron (-ērn), *n.* & *adj.* **1.** The most common and most useful metallic element used for tools etc. ; লৌহ, লোহা, অয়স, লোহক (সাঃ পঃ), স্বর্ণমারক (ঐ), তাটক (ঐ), তীক্ষ্ণঘন (ঐ), কাল (ঐ)। **2.** An instrument or utensil made of iron ; as, a smoothing *iron* ; লৌহনির্ম্মিত যন্ত্র বা পাত্রাদি। **3.** (*Pl.*) Fetters ; chains ; handcuffs ; নিগড়, লৌহবন্ধ, শৃঙ্খল ; হাতকড়ি, বেড়ী। **4.** Hardness ; strength ; inflexibility ; as, a man or rod of *iron* ; দৃঢ়তা, দার্ঢ্য ; শক্তি ; অনমনীয়তা। ***Adj.*** **1.** Of, or made of, iron ; as, an *iron* bar ; লৌহনির্ম্মিত, লৌহময়। **2.** Like iron in strength etc. ; robust ; লৌহতুল্য ; মহাবলশালী। **3.** Firm ; inflexible ; as, *iron* will ; merciless ; দৃঢ় ; অনমনীয় ; নিষ্ঠুর। **Cast-iron**—ঢালা লোহা, কান্তী লোহা (হিঃ কোঃ), কান্ত (সাঃ পঃ), কান্তলৌহ (ঐ), কৃষ্ণ (ঐ), কান্তভীক্ষ্ণ (ঐ), কাল লোহ (ঐ), চপলালয় (ঐ), বাজর (ঐ), ব্রাহণ (ঐ), রোমকান্ত (ঐ), তীক্ষ্ণ (ঐ)। **Iron-age**—কলিযুগ, তামস যুগ। **Iron-bark**—একপ্রকার বৃক্ষ। **Iron-bound** — লৌহবদ্ধ। Rock-bound, as a coast ; পাষাণবদ্ধ। Rigorous ; strict ; কঠিন ; কঠোর। **Iron-clad**—*adj* & *n.* Covered with iron plates ; লৌহ-পট্টাচ্ছাদিত। (*Noun*) A ship cased with

plates of iron ; লৌহপট্টাচ্ছাদিত

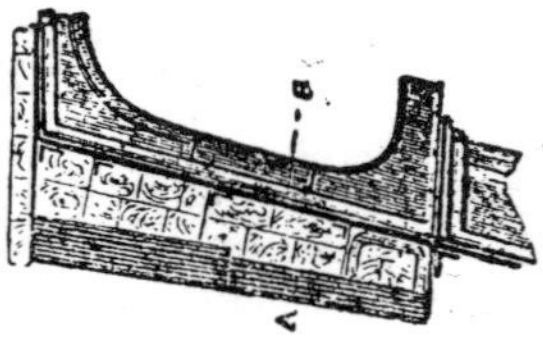

Section of an ironclad.
a, iron plating ; *b*, teak backing.

রণপোত। **Iron filings** — শস্ত্রচূর্ণ (অঃ), তীক্ষ্ণচূর্ণ (সাঃ পঃ), লৌহচূর্ণ লৌহকিট্ট, লোহজ। **Iron-fisted**—বজ্রমুষ্টি, লৌহমুষ্টি। **Iron foundry**—A place where iron castings are made ; কূপ্যশালা, সন্ধানী, লোহবিলয়ন শালা। **Iron green** — ধাতুকাসীস (সাঃ পঃ), বালুকাকাসীস (ঐ)। **Iron-grey**—*adj* & *n*. Of the colour of freshly broken iron ; সদ্যোভগ্ন লৌহবৎ বর্ণ। (*Noun*) The colour of iron just broken ; সদ্যোভগ্ন লৌহের বর্ণ। **Iron-hearted** — Hard-hearted ; অয়োহৃদয়, বজ্রহৃদয় (মঃ ইঃ)। **Iron horse**—A locomotive engine, also a bicycle or a tricycle ; বাষ্পীয় শকটের কল, দ্বিচক্রযান বা ত্রিচক্রযান। **Iron master**—A manufacturer of iron ; লৌহকার, অয়স্কার। **Iron monger**—One who deals in iron or hard-ware ; লৌহব্যবসায়ী, লোহারী, লৌহদ্রব্য বিক্রেতা, লৌহভাণ্ড বিক্রয়ী। **Iron mongery** — Hardware ; goods or articles of iron ; লৌহভাণ্ডাদি ; লৌহনির্ম্মিত দ্রব্যাদি, লোহার জিনিষ। A hardware store or shop ; লৌহনির্ম্মিত জিনিষের ভাণ্ডার, লোহার জিনিষ তৈয়ারের কারখানা, লোহার কারখানা। Iron monger's business ; লোহার ব্যবসায়। **Iron-mould**—A spot on cloth caused by iron-rust or ink stain ; কাপড়ে কালীর বা লোহার মরিচার দাগ। **Iron-ores**—Iron in crude form ; খনিজ বিমিশ্র লৌহ। **Iron pyrites**—সোণামুখী, স্বর্ণমক্ষিকা (খোরী)। **Iron-rust**—লোহার মরিচা, কিট্ট (সাঃ পঃ), লোহকিট্ট (ঐ), লোহমল (ঐ), মন্দুর (চক্রঃ)। **Ironsides**—Man of great bravery ; অতি সাহসী ব্যক্তি। (*Pl.*) Cromwell's troopers ; মধ্যযুগে ইংলণ্ডের রাষ্ট্রনায়ক ক্রমওয়েলের সৈন্যগণ। **Ironsmith** — A blacksmith ; কর্ম্মকার, লৌহকার, কামার। **Iron-stone** — A mineral into the composition of which iron largely enters ; লৌহময় খনিজ পদার্থ বিশেষ। (*Sing.* or *pl.*) Place where iron is melted and iron things are made ; লৌহ কারখানা। **Iron sulphate**—কাসীস (সাঃ পঃ), হরকাসীস (ঐ), হীরাকাসীস (ঐ)। **Iron wood**—A kind of hard wood ; একপ্রকার শক্ত কাঠ, লোহা কাঠ, নাগকেশর (খোরী)। **Iron-work**—Work in iron ; articles made of iron ; লোহার কাজ ; লৌহনির্ম্মিত দ্রব্য। **Magnetic iron** — চুম্বক লোহা (হিঃ কোঃ), কর্ষক (সাঃ পঃ), চুম্বক (ঐ)। **Malleable iron**—নরম লোহা (ঐ)। **Meteoric iron**—উল্কা লোহা (ঐ)। **Reduced iron**—স্বচ্ছ লোহা (হিঃ কোঃ)। **Steel iron** — তীক্ষ্ণ (সাঃ পঃ), কৃষ্ণ (ঐ)। **White iron** — শ্বেত লোহা (ঐ)। **Wrought iron**—পেটা লোহা, কুণ্ঠ (সাঃ পঃ), কড়ার (ঐ) মুণ্ড (ঐ), মুণ্ডক (ঐ)। **An inch of cold iron**—A strike with a dagger etc. ; ছুরিকা প্রভৃতির আঘাত। **In irons**—In fetters ; শৃঙ্খলিত, নিগড়িত। **Strike while the iron is hot**—(*Prov.*) Act while there is a good opportunity ; act energetically and promptly ; সুযোগ বুঝিয়া কাজ কর ; উৎসাহ বা তৎপরতার সহিত কার্য্য কর। **The iron entered into his soul**—(Mistranslation of Hebrew, *his person entered into the iron, i. e.* the fetters) His spirit was broken ; তাহার উৎসাহ ভঙ্গ হইয়াছিল, তাহার মন ভাঙ্গিয়া গিয়াছিল। **To be in irons**—শৃঙ্খলাবদ্ধ থাকা। **To have too many irons in the fire**—এক সঙ্গে অনেকগুলি কাজে হাত দেওয়া। **To rule with a rod of iron** — To rule tyrannically ; লৌহদণ্ড দ্বারা শাসন করা, কঠোর ভাবে শাসন করা।

ī-ron (-êrn), *v. t.* **1.** To smoothe with an instrument of iron ; ইস্ত্রি করা। **2.** To shackle with irons ; শৃঙ্খলিত করা। **3.** To fit, furnish, or cover, with iron ; লৌহপট্টাবৃত করা, লৌহ দ্বারা মোড়া।

ī-rŏn′-ic, –i-căl, *adjs.* **1.** Pertaining to, containing, or characterised by, irony ; as, an *ironical* remark ; ব্যঙ্গার্থক, শ্লেষাত্মক, বিদ্রূপাত্মক, ব্যঙ্গব্যঞ্জক। **2.** Addicted to the use of irony ; ব্যঙ্গপ্রিয়। **–i-cal-ly**, *adv.* **Ironical praise**—ব্যাজস্তুতি।

ī′-rŏn-ist, *adj.* One who uses irony ; বিদ্রূপকারী।

ī′-rō-nȳ, *n.* **1.** A mode of speech by which is expressed a sense contray to that which the speaker intends to convey ; an ironical expression ; শ্লেষ, ব্যাজোক্তি, ব্যঙ্গোক্তি ; রঙ্গব্যঙ্গ। **2.** Dissimulation ; কপটাচরণ। **3.** A state of affairs or events which is the reverse of what was or was to be expected ; অদৃষ্টের নিষ্ঠুর পরিহাস, বিধির বিড়ম্বনা। **Socratic irony**—Simulation of ignorance as means of confuting adversary ; প্রতিপক্ষকে তর্কে পরাভব করিবার জন্য অজ্ঞতার ভাণ। **Irony of fate**—অদৃষ্টের নিষ্ঠুর পরিহাস।

ī′-ron-ȳ (-ê.n-), *adj.* Of, or like, iron ; লৌহময়, লৌহবৎ, অয়োময়, লৌহিক।

ir-rā′-di-ănt, *adj.* Emitting rays of light ; shining brightly ; কিরণচ্ছটাবিকাশী ; উজ্জ্বল, প্রদীপ্ত, ভাস্বর। **–ance**, *n.*

ir-rā′-di-āte, *v. t.* **1.** To shed light ; to illuminate ; কিরণচ্ছটা প্রপাতিত করা ; আলোকিত করা, উদ্ভাসিত করা, দীপ্ত করা, প্রকাশমান

করা। 2. (*Fig.*) To enlighten intellectually; to throw light upon as a subject; (লক্ষণায়) জ্ঞানালোক প্রদান করা; প্রাঞ্জল করা, বিভাসিত করা, পরিষ্কার করা। 3. To brighten, as face etc. with joy, animation etc.; হর্ষোজ্জ্বল করা, দীপ্ত করা, স্পষ্ট করা, প্রাঞ্জল করা। **—a-tive,** *adj.* Illuminative; উদ্ভাসক।

ir-rā-di-ā'-tion, *n.* 1. Act of irradiating; illumination: brilliancy; প্রদ্যোতন, প্রকীরণ, কিরণচ্ছটাবিচ্ছুরণ, পরিস্ফুরণ, প্রকাশব্যাপার (হিঃ কোঃ), জ্যোতিবৃদ্ধি (ঐ), বিকাশন, দীপন, প্রদীপন উদ্দীপন, উজ্জ্বলন, দ্যোতন, প্রদ্যোতন উদ্ভাসন; আলোক; উজ্জ্বলতা, দীপ্তি। 2. (*Fig.*) Intellectual light or illumination; জ্ঞানালোক। 3. (*Opt.*) The apparent enlargement of a bright object seen upon a dark ground; (দৃষ্টি-বিজ্ঞান) অন্ধকার-তলভূমির উপর দৃষ্ট দীপ্ত পদার্থের আপাত-দৃশ্য বিস্তার।

ir-ră'-tion-al, *adj.* & *n.* 1. Not rational; void of reason or understanding; প্রজ্ঞাহীন, অবিবেকী, বুদ্ধিশূন্য, বুদ্ধিহীন, বিবেচনাশূন্য, অপরিভ্রামক (হিঃ কোঃ), অবিবেচক; বুদ্ধিবৃত্তিশূন্য, জ্ঞানশূন্য, জ্ঞানহীন, নির্ব্বুদ্ধি (হিঃ কোঃ)। 2. Not according to reason; absurd; অযৌক্তিক, অন্যায্য, ন্যায়বিরুদ্ধ, অযুক্তিসিদ্ধ, যুক্তিবিরুদ্ধ, যুক্তিবিচারবর্জ্জিত; অসঙ্গত, অসমঞ্জস। 3. (*Math.*—of roots) Not exactly expressible by integer or vulgar fraction; *e. g.* $\sqrt{2}$; (গণিত) পূর্ণ বা সামান্য ভগ্নাংশদ্বারা প্রকাশের অযোগ্য, করণীগত (হিঃ কোঃ)। ***Noun.*** An irrational number; surd; অখণ্ড সংখ্যায় প্রকাশের অযোগ্য রাশি; যে রাশি করণী চিহ্ন ($\sqrt{}$) ব্যতীত প্রকাশ হয় না, করণীগত রাশি। **—al'-i-ty,** *n.* The state of being irrational; অবিবেকিতা, অযৌক্তিকতা, বুদ্ধিহীনতা, জ্ঞানহীনতা, নির্ব্বুদ্ধিত্ব, অন্যায্যতা। **—ize,** *v. t.* To make irrational; অযুক্তিসিদ্ধ করা, অযৌক্তিক করা। **—ly,** *adv.* **Irrational quantity**—যে সংখ্যার বর্গমূল পূর্ণ সংখ্যা বা সামান্য ভগ্নাংশে প্রকাশ করা যায় না, করণীপদ।

ir-rē-claim'-a-ble (-clām-ă-bl), *adj.* Incapable of being reclaimed or reformed; অবিশোধ্য, অসংশোধনীয়, অশমনীয়, অশাম্য, অপ্রতিসমাধেয়, অসন্ধেয়। **—bly,** *adv.*

ir-rĕc'-ŏg-nīz-ă-ble (-bl), *adj.* Not recognizable; অপরিচেয়।

ir-rĕc-ŏn-cīl'-ă-ble (-bl), *adj.* & *n.* 1. Implacable, as an enemy; অসন্ধেয়, অসমাধেয়, অশমনীয়, অসাম্য, অপরিতোষণীয়, অপ্রতিসমাধেয়, অসন্ধাতব্য, অশমনীয়। 2. Inconsistent, as ideas etc.; অসমঞ্জস, অসঙ্গত, পরস্পরবিরুদ্ধ, অসদৃশ, অন্যোন্যবিপরীত। ***Noun.*** A implacable opponent of political measures etc.; রাষ্ট্রনৈতিক উপায় প্রভৃতির অপ্রশাম্য বিরোধী। **—bil'-i-ty, —ness,** *ns.* **—bly,** *adv.*

ir-rē-cov'-er-a-ble (-kŭv-ēr-ă-bl), *adj.* Irreparable, as losses etc.; অপুনরুদ্ধার্য্য, অসমাহার্য্য, অনারোগ্য, অপুনঃপ্রাপ্য, অপুনর্লভ্য, অপ্রতিকার্য্য। **—bly,** *adv.*

ir-rē-cū'-să-ble (-bl), *adj.* That cannot be refused acceptance; অপরিত্যাজ্য।

ir-rē-deem'-a-ble (-dēm-ă-bl), *adj.* 1. Not convertible in coin as paper money; মুদ্রায় পরিবর্ত্তনের অযোগ্য। 2. Not terminable by payment of the principal, as government annuities etc.; অপুনরুদ্ধার্য্য। 3. Irreclaimable; hopeless; অনোদ্ধার্য্য, অনুদ্ধরণীয়; আশাহীন। **—bly,** *adv.*

ir-rē-dĕn'-tist, *n.* An advocate of the recovery of all Italian speaking districts to Italy; যে সকল জেলায় ইতালীয় ভাষা কথিত হয় সে সকল ইতালী দেশভুক্ত করার জন্য অনুরাগী ব্যক্তি। **—tism,** *n.*

ir-re-dū'-ci-ble (-bl), *adj.* 1. Not reducible; incapable of being reduced (to a desired state); অপরিবর্ত্তনীয়; অকরণীয়। 2. (*Math.*) Incapable of being reduced to a simpler form; as, an *irreducible* formula; অধিকতর সরল আকারে অপরিবর্ত্তনীয়। **—bil'-i-ty,** *n.*

ir-rĕf'-ră-gă-ble (-bl), *adj.* Undeniable; indisputable, as an argument, statement, etc.; অপ্রত্যাখ্যেয়; অবিতর্কণীয়, অবিতর্ক্য, অখণ্ডনীয়। **—bly,** *adv.*

ir-rē-frăn'-gi-ble (-bl), *adj.* 1. Inviolable, as law etc.; অভঙ্গনীয়, অলঙ্ঘ্য, অপরিবর্ত্তনীয়। 2. (*Optics*) Not capable of being refracted; (দৃষ্টি-বিজ্ঞান) অতির্য্যগ্‌ গমনীয়।

ir-rē-fūt'-ă-ble (-bl), *adj.* Incapable of being refuted; অখণ্ডনীয়, অখণ্ড্য, খণ্ডনাশক্য। **—bil'-i-ty,** *n.* **—bly,** *adv.*

ir-rĕg'-ū-lar (-lêr), *adj.* & *n.* 1. Not regular; not according to rule; abnormal; অক্রমিক, ক্রমবিরুদ্ধ, ক্রমশূন্য, অনিয়মিত, অনিয়মিক; বিধিবিরুদ্ধ, বিধিভঙ্গক, বিধিহীন, অবৈধ, অবৈধিক, নিয়মবিরুদ্ধ, অযথাবিধি; অস্বাভাবিক, অপ্রাকৃতিক। 2. Not systematical; অপ্রণালীবদ্ধ, অব্যবস্থিত। 3. Uneven; as, *irregular* surface; অসম, বিষম, উচ্চাবচ। 4. Lawless, as a proceeding; অবৈধ, বে-আইনি, অবিধিসঙ্গত। 5. Disorderly; বিশৃঙ্খল। 6. Uneven in duration, order, etc.; অসম। 7. Unmethodical; অপ্রণালীসিদ্ধ, অপ্রণালীসঙ্গত, অনিয়মানুগত। 8. Not uniform; অসমভাবাপন্ন, অসমরূপ। 9. (*Gram.*) Not normally inflected; (ব্যাকরণ) নিপাতিত, নিপাতনীয়। 10. (Of troops) Not in regular service; (সৈন্য সম্বন্ধে) অনিয়মিতভাবে নিযুক্ত, অব্যবস্থিত। ***Noun.*** (*Pl.*) Troops not in regular service; অনিয়মিতভাবে নিযুক্ত সৈন্য। **—lar'-i-ty,** *n.* 1. State of being irregular; অবৈধত্ব, অনিয়মিকতা। 2. Deviation from rule or law; অনিয়ম, ব্যতিক্রম। 3. Unevenness; বিষমতা, বৈষম্য, অসমতা, উচ্চাবচতা। 4. Disorderliness; a disorderly act;

উচ্ছৃঙ্খলতা ; উচ্ছৃঙ্খল আচরণ। **—ly,** *adv.* In an irregular way; disorderly ; বিধিবিরুদ্ধভাবে, নিয়মবিরুদ্ধভাবে, অযথাবিধি, অনিয়মিত রূপে, অব্যবস্থিতভাবে ; উচ্ছৃঙ্খলতার সহিত। **Irregular troops**—See IRREGULAR, *n.* **Irregular verb**—That which does not take *d, ed* etc. to denote past tense ; যে সমস্ত ক্রিয়ার অতীতকালে *d, ed,* প্রভৃতি সংযুক্ত হয় না।

ir-rĕl′-ă-tive (-tĭv), *adj.* **1.** Not related ; unconnected, (with *to*) ; অসম্বন্ধ, নিঃসম্বন্ধ ; অসম্পৃক্ত, অনানুষঙ্গিক, অসংসৃষ্ট। **2.** Absolute ; নিরপেক্ষ। **—ly,** *adv.*

ir-rĕl′-ē-vănt, *adj.* Not relevant ; not to the point ; not applicable, (with *to*) ; as, testimony *irrelevant* to a case ; অপ্রাসঙ্গিক ; অসম্বন্ধ, প্রসঙ্গবাহ্য, অসংলগ্ন, বাজে ; অপ্রযোজ্য। **—vance, —van-cy,** *ns.* State of being irrelevant ; অপ্রাসঙ্গিকতা (হিঃ কোঃ), প্রসঙ্গবাহ্যতা, অসম্বন্ধতা, অপ্রযুক্তি। **—ly,** *adv.* **Irrelevant conclusion**—অপ্রাসঙ্গিক উপসংহার (হিঃ কোঃ)।

ĭr-rē-lĭ′gion (-jŏn), *n.* The state of being irreligious ; want, or disregard, of religion ; অধর্ম্মতা, বিধর্ম্মিতা, ধর্ম্মহীনতা ; ধর্ম্মৌদাসীন্য, ধর্ম্মদ্বেষিতা, সম্প্রদায়বিরোধ (হিঃ কোঃ)। **—gious,** *adj.* Destitute of religion ; profane ; as, *irreligious* speech ; ধর্ম্মহীন, অধর্ম্মী, ভ্রষ্টাচারী, অধার্ম্মিক, অধর্ম্মিষ্ঠ, অপবিত্র, দুষ্ট, অপুণ্য, অমেধ্য। **—gious-ly,** *adv.* **—ist,** *n.*

ir-rē-mē′-di-ă-ble (-bl), *adj.* Not to be redressed ; incurable ; অপ্রতিবিধেয়, নিষ্প্রতীকার (বাৎস্যঃ), অপ্রতীকার্য্য, অনুপায়, উপায়াতীত, দুরত্যয় ; অচিকিৎস্য, অসাধ্য। **—bly,** *adv.*

ir-rē-mis′-si-ble (-ĭ-bl), *adj.* Not remissible ; unpardonable, as sin; obligatory ; অমোচনীয় ; অক্ষন্তব্য, অমার্জ্জনীয়, অক্ষমার্হ, অক্ষমণীয় ; বাধ্যতাজনক, অবশ্যকরণীয়। **—bly,** *adv.*

ĭr-rē-môv′-ă-ble (-bl), *adj.* Incapable of being removed (esp. from office) ; অনপসারণীয়, অচল, স্থির, স্থায়ী। **—bil′-i-ly,** *n.* **—bly,** *adv.*

ĭr-rĕp′-ă-ră-ble (-bl), *adj.* Incapable of being rectified or compensated, as loss etc. ; অপ্রতিকার্য্য, অপ্রতিকরণীয়, অপূরণীয়, অনুদ্ধার্য্য, অপ্রতিকার। **—bly,** *adv.* **—ness,** *n.* **Irreparable loss**—(See IRREPARABLE) অপূরণযোগ্য ক্ষতি।

ĭr-rē-place′-a-ble (-plās-ă-bl), *adj.* Of which the loss cannot be supplied ; অপুনঃস্থাপনীয়।

ĭr-rĕp-rē-hĕn′-si-ble (-bl), *adj.* (*Rare*) Blameless ; (ক্বচিদ্ ব্যবহৃত) অনিন্দ্য।

ĭr-rē-prĕss′-i-ble (-bl), *adj.* & *n.* Not capable of being repressed or restrained, as joy etc. ; অদম্য, অনিবার্য্য, দুর্নিবার, অসংহরণীয়। ***Noun.*** (*Colloq.*) An irrepressible person ; দুর্দ্দান্ত ব্যক্তি। **—bly,** *adv.*

ir-rē-proach′-a-ble (-prōch-ă-bl), *adj.* Not reproachable ; free from blame or fault ; অনিন্দনীয়, অনিন্দ্য ; অনবদ্য, নিরবদ্য নিষ্কলঙ্ক। **—bil′-i-ty,** *n.* **—bly,** *adv.*

ĭr-rē-sist′-i-ble (-bl), *adj.* Incapable of being successfully resisted or opposed ; অনিবার্য্য, দুর্নিবার, দুরাধর্ষ, দুর্ব্বার, দুর্জ্জয়, অপ্রতিরোধনীয়, অপ্রতিকার্য্য। **—bil′-i-ty,** *n.* **—bly,** *adv.*

ĭr-rĕs′-ō-lūte *adj.* **1.** Not firm or constant in purpose ; undecided ; wavering ; hesitating ; অস্থিরচিত্ত, অস্থিরমতি, চঞ্চলমনাঃ, অদৃঢ়বুদ্ধি, অস্থিরবুদ্ধি, চঞ্চলবৃত্তি, অব্যবস্থিতচিত্ত ; দ্বিধাকারী ; সংশয়দোলায়িত ; অকৃতসংকল্প। **—ly,** *adv.* **—ness, —lu′-tion,** *ns.* Want of decision or firmness in purpose ; fluctuation of mind as in doubt ; অস্থিরচিত্ততা, অনিশ্চয়তা ; চলচিত্ততা, অনিষ্ঠা, সংকল্পাস্থৈর্য্য, চঞ্চলবুদ্ধি, চিত্তচাঞ্চল্য, অস্থিরবুদ্ধি, অস্থৈর্য্য।

ĭr-rē-sŏlv′-ă-ble (-bl), *adj.* **1.** Incapable of being solved as a problem ; অসমাধেয়, অসমাধানযোগ্য। **2.** Not separable into component parts ; অবিশ্লেষণীয়।

ir-rē-spĕc′-tive (-tĭv), *adj.* Without regard to something else ; নিঃসম্বন্ধ, নিরপেক্ষ, নির্ব্বিশেষ, অনপেক্ষ। **—ly,** *adv.* Without regard to something else ; independently (*of*) ; অনপেক্ষভাবে, নিরপেক্ষভাবে ; স্বাধীনভাবে, নির্ব্বিচারে। **Irrespective of** — (*Often used quasi-adverbially*) Not taking into account ; নির্ব্বিশেষে, নির্ব্বিচারে, বিচার না করিয়া।

ĭr-rē-spŏn′-si-ble (-bl), *adj.* **1.** Not responsible ; unreliable ; দায়িত্বহীন, দায়ী নয় ; বিশ্বাসের অযোগ্য। **2.** Acting or done without a sense of responsibility ; দায়িত্বজ্ঞানশূন্যভাবে কার্য্যকারী, দায়িত্বজ্ঞানশূন্যভাবে কৃত। **—bil′-i-ty,** *n.* The quality of being irresponsible ; দায়িত্বহীনতা। **—bly,** *adv.*

ir-rē-spŏn′-sive (-sĭv), *adj.* Not responsive ; not able or inclined to respond ; অনুত্তরদায়ী, অনুত্তরকারী ; অনুত্তরক্ষম, অনুত্তরপ্রবণ। **—ness,** *n.*

ĭr-rē-tĕn′-tive (-tĭv), *adj.* Not retentive ; as, an *irretentive* memory ; ধারণাক্ষম, ধারণাশক্তিহীন, অধারণপটু, অধারক। **—ness,** *n.*

ĭr-rē-triev′-a-ble (-trēv-ă-bl), *adj.* Irrecoverable ; irreparable, as loss etc. ; অপুনরুদ্ধার্য্য, অপুনঃপ্রাপ্য, অপ্রতিকার্য্য ; অপ্রতিসমাধেয়, অপূরণীয়। **—bil′-i-ty,** *n.* **—bly,** *adv.*

ĭr-rĕv′-ĕr-ĕnt, *adj.* Not reverent ; showing want of reverence ; ভক্তিহীন ; অশ্রদ্ধাপ্রদর্শক, অনাদরবুদ্ধি, অনাদরপ্রদর্শক, অবজ্ঞাকারী। **—ence,** *n.* The state of being irreverent ; অভক্তি, ভক্তিহীনতা, শ্রদ্ধাবিহীন। **—en′-tial,** *adj.* **—ly,** *adv.*

ĭr-rē-vêrs′-i-ble (-bl), *adj.* **1.** Incapable of being reversed, turned about or backwards ; as, an *irreversible* engine ; অপরাবর্ত্ত্য, অনিবর্ত্তনীয়। 2. Unalterable ; as, an *irreversible* sentence ; অপরিবর্ত্তনীয়। **–bil′-i-ty,** *n.* **–bly,** *adv.*

ir-rĕv′-ō-că-ble (-bl), *adj.* Incapable of being recalled or revoked ; unalterable ; as, *irrevocable* promise ; অনন্যথাকরণীয় ; অপরাবর্ত্ত্য, অপরিবর্ত্তনীয়, অনিবর্ত্ত্য (মিতঃ), অপরাবর্ত্ত্য। **–bil′-i-ty,** *n.* **–bly,** *adv.*

ir′-ri-gāte, *v. t.* **1.** (*Agri.*) To water, as a land by causing a stream to flow upon it ; (also of a stream) to supply (land) with water ; (কৃষি) প্রণালী কাটিয়া জল সরবরাহ করা ; (নদী পক্ষে ক্ষেত্রে) জল সরবরাহ করা। **2.** (*Med.*) To supply as a wound etc., with a constant flow of some liquid ; শরীরের কোন ক্ষত স্থান প্রভৃতিতে অবিরাম জলধারা প্রক্ষেপ করা। **3.** (*Fig.*) To refresh or make fruitful as with moisture ; "Her mind *irrigated* their minds" ; পুনরায় সতেজ করা, উর্ব্বরা করা। **–ga-ble,** *adj.* Capable of being irrigated ; জলসরবরাহযোগ্য। **–ga′-tion,** *n.* **1.** The act of irrigating ; the state of being irrigated ; জলপ্রণালী কাটিয়া জলসরবরাহ করণ, প্রণালিকাসিঞ্চন, জলসেচন ; জলসিক্ততা। **2.** Act of supplying land with water by means of channels or streams etc. ; জলপ্রণালীদ্বারা জলসরবরাহ করণ। **3.** (*Med.*) The application of a continuous stream or shower of some liquid to an affected part of the body, to allay inflammation or to cleanse an ulcer ; (ভৈষজ্য শাস্ত্র) শরীরের কোন স্থান অবিরত উপযুক্ত যন্ত্র দ্বারা বিন্দু বিন্দু করিয়া জল ধারা দ্বারা ভিজান (হঃ চঃ), ধারাস্নান (ঐ)। **–ga-tive,** *adj.* **–ga-tor,** *n.*

ir′-ri-tă-ble (-bl), *adj.* **1.** Easily irritated ; very susceptible of anger ; as, an *irritable* temper ; আশুক্রোধী, স্থূলভকোপী, শীঘ্রকোপী ; রোষপ্রবণ। **2.** (*Physiol.*) Responsive to stimuli as muscles, nerves etc. ; (শারীর বিজ্ঞান) উত্তেজনাপ্রবণ। **–bil′-i-ty,** *n.* **1.** State of being irritable ; ক্রোধপ্রবণতা (হিঃ কোঃ), আবেগশীলতা (ঐ), কোপপ্রবণতা, রোষপ্রবণতা, ক্রোধশীলতা, ক্রোধস্বভাব। **2.** (*Med.*) Susceptibility of irritation or excitement ; (ভৈষজ্য-শাস্ত্র) উপদাহিতা (হঃ চঃ), উদ্দীপনশীলতা (ঐ)। **–bly,** *adv.*

ir′-ri-tăn-cy̆, *n.* Irritation ; annoyance ; কোপ, গাত্রজ্বালা ; বিরক্তি।

ir′-ri-tăn cy̆, *n.* (*Law*) Rendering null and void ; the state of being null and void ; invalidity ; (আইন) বাতিলকরণ, রদকরণ ; বাতিল ; অবৈধতা।

ir′-ri-tănt, *adj.* & *n.* Producing irritation,usually physical ; উপদাহক, গাত্রজ্বালাকর, উদ্বেজক (হিঃ কোঃ), কোপজনক (ঐ)। ***Noun.*** An irritating substance or agency, (*lit.* & *fig.*) ; উত্তেজক বা প্রদাহজনক দ্রব্য।

ir′-ri-tāte, *v. t.* **1.** To provoke ; to annoy ; রাগান্বিত করা, ক্রোধাবিষ্ট করা ; বিরক্ত করা। **2.** To excite ; to produce an uneasy sensation in, as a bodily organ etc. ; উত্তেজিত করা ; জ্বালা বা প্রদাহ উৎপাদন করা, উপদাহ জন্মান। **3.** (*Physiol.*) To stimulate ; (শারীর-বিজ্ঞান) উত্তেজিত করা। **4.** (*Med.*) To excite heat and redness in ; as, to *irritate* a wound by a coarse bandage ; প্রদাহ জন্মান। **–tat-ing-ly,** *adv.* **–ta′-tion,** *n.* **1.** The act of irritating ; provocation ; ক্রোধোদ্দীপন, প্রকোপন ; ক্রোধ। **2.** (*Physiol.*) Stimulation ; (শারীর-বিজ্ঞান) উত্তেজনা। **3.** (*Med.*) Excitement of a tissue or organ ; (ভৈষজ্য শাস্ত্র) প্রদাহ, উত্তেজনা। **–ta-tive,** *adj.* **1.** Serving to excite ; as, an *irritative* agent ; ক্রোধোদ্দীপনশীল, উত্তেজক। **2.** Accompanied with irritation ; as, *irritative* fever (প্রদাহজ্বর) ; প্রদাহ সহকৃত।

ir′-ri-tāte, *v. t.* (*Law*) To make null and void ; (আইন) বাতিল করা, রদ করা।

ir-rŭp′-tion, *n.* A bursting in ; a violent entry ; a sudden invasion or incursion ; অভিধাবন ; বেগে-প্রবেশ, সহসা বলপূর্ব্বক প্রবেশ ; অভিযান, আক্রমণ, উপদ্রব, অবস্কন্দ।

ĭs, *v. t.* (The 3rd person sing. of the verb *be* in the Indicative Mood, Present Tense). **Isness**—অস্তিত্ব (হিঃ কোঃ), সত্তা।

Is-ă-bĕl′-lă (ĭz-) *adj.* & *n.* (*History doubtful*) Greyish-yellow ; ধূসরাভ পীত। ***Noun.*** A brownish yellow colour ; আকপিশ পীতবর্ণ। **–line,** *adj.*

ī-să-gŏg′-ic, *adj.* & *n.* Introductory ; প্রারম্ভসূচক। ***Noun.*** (*Pl.*) That part of the theological study introductory to the interpretation of the scripture ; ধর্ম্মশাস্ত্র ব্যাখ্যায় মুখবন্ধস্বরূপ ধর্ম্মশাস্ত্রের অংশ বিশেষ।

ī′-să-tin, *n.* (*Chem.*) A crystalline substance obtained by oxidizing indigo ; (রসায়নশাস্ত্র) জারিত নীল হইতে প্রাপ্ত স্ফটিকাকার পদার্থ বিশেষ।

is-chi-ăt′(ăd)-ic, *adj.* Pertaining to the hip ; sciatic ; শ্রোণি-সম্বন্ধীয় ; কটিবাতসম্বন্ধীয়, বস্তিশূল সম্বন্ধীয়।

Ish′-mă-ĕl (-ĭsh-), *n.* **1.** The son of Abraham by Hagar ; এব্রাহাম ও হেগারের পুত্র। **2.** An outcast ; one at war with the society ; সমাজচ্যুত ব্যক্তি ; সমাজদ্রোহী ব্যক্তি। [এব্রাহাম ও হেগারের পুত্র ইস্মায়েল সমাজদ্রোহী ছিল বলিয়া তদীয় বংশধরগণ উক্ত নামে পরিচিত হয়]। **–ite,** *n.* **1.** A descendant of Ishmael ; এব্রাহাম ও হেগারের পুত্র ইস্মায়েলের বংশধর। **2.** (*Fig.*) Same as ISHMAEL.

ī′-sin-glăss (-zĭng-), *n.* A semi-transparent gelatinous substance got from various species of fish called sturgeons ; ষ্টারজন নামক

মৎস্য হইতে প্রাপ্ত একপ্রকার ঈষৎ স্বচ্ছ শ্বেতাভ শিরিষ, ফৌষকুষ (আঃ বঃ), মৎস্যাস্ত্রজ, (ঐ), ঘনসার (ঐ), জিলেটিন (হিঃ কোঃ)।

I'-sis' (ī-), *n.* An Egyptian goddess of fecundity ; প্রাচীন মিসরের লক্ষ্মীদেবী। ইনি Osiris এর ভগ্নী এবং পত্নী ও Horusএর জননী ছিলেন। কথিত আছে, ইনি পতিহন্তা Setকে কারামুক্তি প্রদান করিলে পুত্র Horus Isisএর শিরশ্ছেদন পূর্ব্বক জননীর মস্তকের স্থানে একটী গোমুণ্ড সংযোজন করেন।

Is'-lăm (īz-), *n.* **1.** The religion of the Mahommedans ; Islamism ; মুসলমানধর্ম্ম ; ইসলামধর্ম্ম। **2.** The Mahommedan world ; মুসলমানরাজ্য। **–ism,** *n.* Mahommedanism ; মুসলমানধর্ম্ম। **–ite,** *n.* A Mahommedan ; মুসলমান। **–it'-ic,** *adj.* **–lam'-ic,** *adj.*

is'-lănd (ī-), *n.* & *v. t.* A tract of land surrounded by water and smaller than a continet ; দ্বীপ। **2.** (*Fig.*) Anything resembling an island ; a woodland surrounded by a prairie ; দ্বীপবৎ বা দ্বীপসদৃশ বস্তু ; বিস্তীর্ণ প্রান্তরপরিবৃত বনভূমি। **3.** (*Physiol.*) A detached portion of tissue or group of cells ; (শারীর-বিজ্ঞান) বিধানতন্তু বা অণুকোষপুঞ্জের বিচ্ছিন্ন অংশ। ***Verb t.*** **1.** To make an island of ; দ্বীপে পরিণত করা বা দ্বীপবৎ করা। **2.** To isolate ; বিচ্ছিন্ন বা অসংস্পৃষ্ট করা। **3.** To dot with or as with islands ; "Not a cloud...*islanded* the dark-blue deep"—*Southey* ; ক্ষুদ্র ক্ষুদ্র দ্বীপ বা দ্বীপবৎ বস্তু দ্বারা বৈচিত্র্য সম্পাদন করা। **–er,** *n.* One who lives in an island ; দ্বীপবাসী, দ্বৈপ্য, দ্বীপস্থ, দ্বীপনিবাসী। **Islands of the blessed**—(গ্রীকপুরাণ) পশ্চিমসাগরস্থ আনন্দদ্বীপপুঞ্জ যথায় সাধুদিগের আত্মা মরণান্তে সমানীত হয়।

isle (īl), *n.* **1.** An island (usu. with proper names, as, *isle* of Wight, British *isles*, etc.) ; দ্বীপ। **2.** (*Now. usu.*) A small island ; ক্ষুদ্রদ্বীপ।

is'-lĕt (ī-), *n.* **1.** A little island ; ক্ষুদ্র দ্বীপ। **2.** A spot within another of a different colour ; an isolated tract ; কোন দাগের মধ্যবর্ত্তী ভিন্ন রঙ্গের দাগ ; অনন্যসংলগ্ন বিচ্ছিন্ন স্থান।

ĭsm, *n.* A distinctive doctrine or theory etc. ; as, away with your *isms* and ologies ; বিশিষ্ট তত্ত্ব, মত বা সূত্র।

ī'-sō-bâr, *n.* A line on a map connecting places at which the mean height of the barometer at sea-level is the same ; যে সকল স্থানে সাগর ধরাতলে বায়ুচাপমানের গড়পড়তা উচ্চতা সমান—ঐ সকল স্থানসংযোজক মানচিত্রের রেখা বিশেষ, সমভাররেখা (সাঃ পঃ), সমচাপরেখা (ঐ)। **–ic,** *adj.* সমভারীয় (হিঃ কোঃ)।

ī-sō-chrō-măt'-ic, *adj.* Of the same colour ; সবর্ণ।

ī-sŏch'-rŏ-nous (-nŭs), *adj.* Of equal time ; performed in equal times ; vibrating uniformly as a pendulum ; সমকালীন ; সমকাল সম্পাদিত, সমগতিরেখীয় (হিঃ কোঃ) ; সমদোলনশীল।

ī sō-clī'-năl, *adj.* Having, or showing, equal magnetic inclination ; সমচুম্বকনতিবিশিষ্ট, সমচুম্বকনতিপ্রদর্শক। **Isoclinal lines**—সমাপাতরেখা (হিঃ কোঃ), সমচুম্বকরেখা (ঐ)।

ī-sō-gŏn'-ic, *adj.* Indicating equal angles ; তুল্যকোণনির্দ্দেশক। **–sog'-o-nal,** *adj.* Having equal angles ; সমকৌণিক। **Isogonic lines**—সমদিগ্‌রেখা (হিঃ কোঃ)।

ī'-sō-lāte, *v. t.* **1.** To place above or apart ; স্বতন্ত্র করা, বিচ্ছিন্ন করা, একাকী রাখা, অনন্যসংলগ্ন করা। **2.** (*Elec.*) To insulate ; (তাড়িতবিদ্যা) অপরিচালক পদার্থের বেষ্টন দ্বারা তাড়িত অথবা উত্তাপের বহিঃসঞ্চারপথ রুদ্ধ করা। **3.** (*Chem.*) To obtain (a substance) free from all its combinations ; (রসায়ন-শাস্ত্র) অবিমিশ্র ভাবে প্রাপ্ত হওয়া। **–lat-ed,** *adj.* Placed or standing alone ; separated ; solitary ; স্বতন্ত্র ; অনন্যসংলগ্ন ; একলা। **–la'-tion,** *n.* Act of isolating ; the state of being isolated ; loneliness ; স্বতন্ত্রীকরণ, পৃথকীকরণ ; অনন্যসংলগ্নতা, বিচ্ছিন্নতা, স্বতন্ত্রতা ; নির্জ্জনতা, বিজনতা। **–la-tor,** *n.*

ī-sō-mêr'-ic, *adj.* Composed of same elements in the same proportion by weight, but differently grouped ; সমাবয়বিক (হিঃ কোঃ)। **Isomeric change**—স্বাভাবিকপরিণাম (ব্রজঃ হিন্দু)।

ī-sō-mĕt'-ri-căl, *adj.* **1.** Of, pertaining to, or characterised by, the equality of measure ; সমমানসংক্রান্ত বা সমমানাত্মক, একমান, সমমাপক। **Isometrical projection**—তুল্যপ্রতিমা (হিঃ কোঃ)।

ī-sō-mŏr'-phĭsm, *n.* A similarity of crystalline form ; (রসায়ন-শাস্ত্র), সমস্ফাটিকরূপতা, সমাকৃতিত্ব (হিঃ কোঃ)।

ī-sŏn'-ō-mȳ, *n.* Equality of political rights and privileges ; রাষ্ট্রনৈতিকতুল্যাধিকার।

Isopod.

ī'-sō-pŏd, *n.* A crustacean usually having seven pairs of legs which are all similar in structure ; খোলবিশিষ্ট কীটবিশেষ—সচরাচর এই কীটের সাতজোড়া সমাকৃতি পা থাকে।

ī-sŏs'-cē-lēs, *adj.* Having two equal sides (said of a triangle) ; সমদ্বিবাহু, সমদ্বিপার্শ্ব। **Isosceles triangle**—দ্বিসম ত্রিভুজ, সমদ্বিবাহু ত্রিভুজ।

ī-sŏth'-êr-ăl, *adj.* & *n.* (Of a line) Joining places of same mean summer temperature ; সমগ্রীষ্মতাপযুক্ত স্থানসংযোজক। ***Noun.*** An isotheral line ; উক্ত প্রকার রেখা। **Isotheral line** — সমতাপরেখা (হিঃ কোঃ)।

ī'-sō-thĕrm, –thêr'-măl, *n.* & *adj.* An imaginary line on the earth's surface joining places of same mean annual temperature ; সমগ্রীষ্মরেখা, সমোষ্ণরেখা। *Adj.* Connecting places of the same mean annual temperature as a line ; সমোত্তাপগর্ভ, সমোষ্ণীয় (সাঃ পঃ), সমতাপক। **Isothermal line**—সমশীতোষ্ণরেখা (হিঃ কোঃ), সমৌষ্মিক রেখা (ঐ)। **Isothermal curve**—সমৌষ্মিক বক্র (হিঃ কোঃ।

Is'-rā-ĕl (ĭz-), **1.** The Jewish people ; ইহুদীজাতি। **2.** (*Fig.*) The chosen people of God ; the elect ; the Christian church ; the Christians collectively ; (লক্ষণায়) ঈশ্বরের প্রিয় জাতি ; ঈশ্বর কর্ত্তৃক মুক্তির জন্য নির্ব্বাচিত ব্যক্তিগণ ; খৃষ্টীয় ধর্ম্মসংঘ ; খৃষ্টধর্ম্মাবলম্বিগণ। **—ite,** *n.* A descendant of Israel or Jacob ; a Jew ; ইজ্রায়েল বা জ্যাকবের বংশধর ; ইহুদী। **—it-ish,** *adj.* Jewish ; ইহুদীজাতীয়।

is'-sue (ĭsh-ü), *n.* **1.** The act of passing out ; egress ; as, the *issue* of water from a pipe ; বহিঃসরণ, বহির্গমন, নিঃসরণ ; নির্গম, নিক্রমণ। **2.** An exit ; outlet or vent ; নির্গমনপথ, নিঃসরণপথ, নির্গমমার্গ, নির্গমপথ ; নির্গমদ্বার, ছিদ্র। **3.** The act of sending out ; delivery ; as, the *issue* of Bills of Exchange ; প্রচার, প্রচলন, জারি (*lāw*) ; মোচন। **4.** The whole quantity sent forth at one time ; the number of coins, notes, copies of a newspaper, etc. issued at one time ; একবারে প্রচারিত বা প্রকাশিত সমুদয় বস্তু ; একবারে প্রচারিত মুদ্রা, নোট বা সংবাদপত্র সমূহ। **5.** Progeny ; offspring ; a child or children ; as, to die without an *issue* ; বংশ ; অপত্য ; সন্তানসন্ততি। **6.** Produce, outcome or result ; event ; ফল ; পরিণাম। **7.** Discharge, as of blood ; ক্ষরণ, স্রাব। **8.** The mouth of a river নদীর মোহানা। **9.** Termination or end, as of a matter ; সমাপ্তি, অবসান, শেষফল। **10.** A point in debate or controversy ; তর্কের বিরোধীয় বিষয়, সংশয়হেতু, বাদবিষয়। **11.** (*Law*) The point or matter depending in a suit on which two parties join and put their cause to trial ; যে বিশেষ বিষয় লইয়া মোকদ্দমা হয়, বিচার্য্য বিষয়। **12.** (*Med.*) An artificial ulcer to promote secretion and discharge of pus ; পূযাদি নিঃসরণের জন্য উৎপাদিত কৃত্রিম ক্ষত, কৃত্রিমব্রণ, কৃত্রিমস্ফোটক, গুল। **—less,** *adj.* Childless ; নিঃসন্তান, অসন্তান, অপ্রজ, অনপত্য। **At issue**—In controversy ; at variance ; as, a point *at issue* ; persons *at issue* ; বিচার্য্য ; বিবদমান। **Issue of fact**—(*Law,* when the fact is denied) A point to be ascertained by a jury ; ঘটনামূলক বিচার্য্য বিষয়, বৃত্তান্তঘটিত ইসু। **Issue of law**—(When the application of the law is contested) A point to be determined by the court ; আইনঘটিত বিচার্য্য বিষয়, আইনঘটিত ইসু। **To join issue with**—To find fault with ; to dissent from ; to oppose ; দোষ ধরা ; ভিন্নমত হওয়া ; বাধা দেওয়া। **To join or take issue**—To take opposite sides in a matter in controversy ; বিবদমান বিষয়ে পরস্পরের বিপরীত পক্ষ অবলম্বন করা। To submit an issue jointly to a court for decision ; কোন বিশেষ বিচার্য্য বিষয় এক যোগে আদালতের মীমাংসার জন্য উপস্থাপিত করা। **To plead the general issue**—আরজীর সমুদয় কথা কিম্বা উহার অধিকাংশ একেবারে অস্বীকার করা।

is'-sue (ĭsh-ü), *v. i.* & *t.* **1.** To pass or flow out ; নির্গত হওয়া, নিঃসৃত হওয়া। **2.** To rush out ; to sally forth ; as, troops *issued* out of the fort ; দ্রুতগতিতে বহির্গত বা বেগে নিষ্ক্রান্ত হওয়া ; নিষ্ক্রমণ করা। **3.** To proceed, as from a source ; as, light *issues* from the sun ; নির্গত হওয়া বা আসা। **4.** To spring ; to be derived ; জন্মা ; উৎপন্ন হওয়া, উৎপাদিত হওয়া। **5.** To result (*from*) ; পরিণত হওয়া। **6.** To close ; to end (*in*) ; অবসান প্রাপ্ত হওয়া, শেষ হওয়া, সমাপ্ত হওয়া ; পর্য্যবসিত হওয়া। **7.** To be circulated or published ; প্রচারিত হওয়া, প্রচলিত হওয়া, প্রকাশিত হওয়া, বাহির হওয়া। ***Verb t.*** **1.** To circulate ; to publish, as notes, coins, newspapers etc. ; প্রচার করা, প্রচলিত করা ; প্রকাশ করা। **2.** To deliver for use ; as, to *issue* provisions ; প্রদান করা। **3.** To send out officially ; as, to *issue* an order ; যথারীতি প্রচার করা। **—su-a-ble,** *adj.* **—su-ance,** *n.* The act of giving out ; as, the *issuance* of an order ; প্রকাশ করণ।

isth'-mŭs (ĭst-), *n.* (*Pl.* -ES) **1.** A narrow piece of land by which two larger pieces of land are connected ; as, the *isthmus* of Panama ; যোজক, ভূকন্দর, সঙ্কটস্থল, স্থলসঙ্কট, ডমরুমধ্য। **2.** (*Anat.* & *Bot.*) A narrow part connecting two larger parts ; (শারীরসংস্থানবিদ্যা ও উদ্ভিদবিদ্যা) বৃহত্তর অংশদ্বয় সংযোজক সংকীর্ণ অংশ। **—mi-an,** *adj.*

is'-tle (-tl), *n.* A fibre used for cord etc. got from species of agave etc. ; আঁশ, তন্তু, রেশা।

it, *pron.* (Third person, neuter gender, singular number) **1.** The thing or the person in question ; as, what is *it* (that lies there) : who is *it* ; ইহা, যাহা, উহা, এই। **2.** It is used : (1) As an indefinite nominative to verbs called impersonal ; as, *it* rains ; *it* snows ; (2) generally at the beginning of a sentence pointing to what is about to be stated, named or mentioned ; as, *it* is I, be not afraid ;

(3) as a substitute for any noun of the neuter gender ; as, here is the book, take *it* home ; (4) as a substitute for such general terms as condition of things etc. ; as, how is *it* with the sick man ? ; (5) as an indefinite object after some transitive or intransitive verbs ; as, to earn *it* with a high hand : to lord *it* over.

ī'-tă-cĭsm, *n.* Pronunciation of Greek letter *eta* like *e* in the English word *be* ; গ্রীক অক্ষর etaর ইংরাজী *be* শব্দের *e* এর মত উচ্চারণ।

I-tăl'-ĭ-ăn (ĭ-), *adj.* & *n.* Of, or pertaining to, Italy ; ইতালীদেশীয়, ইতালীয়। *Noun.* **1.** A native of Italy; ইতালীবাসী। **2.** The language used in Italy ; ইতালীয় ভাষা। **—ism,** *n.* **1.** A word, phrase or idiom peculiar to the Italians ; ইতালীয় ভাষার রীতিসিদ্ধ প্রয়োগ। **2.** Attachment to, or sympathy for, Italy; ইতালীর প্রতি অনুরাগ বা সহানুভূতি। **—ize,** *v. t.* & *i.* **1.** To render Italian in any respect ; as, an Englishman *Italianized* ; ইতালীভাবাপন্ন করা। (*Verb i.*) To play the Italian ; to speak Italian ; ইতালীবাসীর মত ব্যবহার করা ; ইতালীয় ভাষায় কথা বলা। **Italian handwriting** — That which is now current in England, France, Italy etc. (opp. to *Gothic*) ; বর্ত্তমানে ইংলণ্ড, ফরাসী, ইতালী প্রভৃতি দেশে প্রচলিত হস্তাক্ষর। **Italian iron**— লেইস প্রভৃতি কুঞ্চিত করিবার জন্য একপ্রকার চোঙ্গাকার লৌহখণ্ড।

I-tăl'-ĭc (-ĭ-), *adj.* & *n.* Relating to ancient Italy (esp. as apart from Rome) ; প্রাচীন ইতালী সংক্রান্ত। *Noun.* (*Pl.*) Sloping letters ; টের্চ্চা অক্ষর, হেলান অক্ষর। **Italic type**—A kind of sloping type invented by Aldus Manutius about the year 1500 A. D. ; হেলান মুদ্রাক্ষর।

ĭ-tăl'-ĭ-cīze, *v. t.* To print in Italic character ; বক্রাক্ষরে মুদ্রিত করা, টের্চ্চা অক্ষরে ছাপান।

I-tăl'-ĭ-ōt (ĭ-), **—ōte,** *n.* & *adj.* A Greek inhabitant of South Italy ; দক্ষিণ-ইতালীস্থ গ্রীক উপনিবেশের অধিবাসী। *Adj.* **1.** Pertaining to the Greek colonies in South Italy ; দক্ষিণ ইতালীস্থ গ্রীক উপনিবেশ-সংক্রান্ত।

itch (ĭch), *n.* **1.** An uneasy sensation of irritation in the skin relieved by scratching or rubbing : কণ্ডূ, চুলকানি, কণ্ডূতি। **2.** An eruption of small vesicles caused by parasitic mite ; পাঁচড়া, কণ্ডূ। **3.** (*Fig.*) A constant teasing desire or hankering ; as, an *itch* for praise ; (লক্ষণায়) কণ্ডূয়ন (cf. রসনাকণ্ডূয়ন)। **Itch'-i-ness,** *n.* **Itch'-y,** *adj.* Affected with the itch ; of the nature of the itch ; কণ্ডূদ্বারা আক্রান্ত ; কণ্ডূবৎ। **Itch-mite**—কণ্ডূকীট।

itch (ĭch), *v. i.* **1.** To have an irritating sensation in the skin which inclines the person to scratch the part ; চুলকান, কণ্ডূয়ন করা। **2.** To have an uneasy craving ; to long (*for*) ; অধীরভাবে কামনা করা ; লালসা করা। **Itch'-ing,** *adj.* & *n.* **Itching palm** — A greed for gain ; অর্থলালসা।

ī'-tĕm, *n.* & *adv.* **1.** An article ; a separate particular in an account etc. ; as, the *items* in a bill ; বিষয় ; স্বতন্ত্র দফা। **2.** A scrap of news in a newspaper ; as, local *items* ; সংক্ষিপ্ত সংবাদ। *Adv.* Also ; likewise ; আরও ; তদ্রূপ। **Item by item**—দফায় দফায়।

it'-ĕr-āte, *v. t.* **1.** To utter, do or make, repeatedly ; to repeat ; বারবার করা, পুনঃ পুনঃ করা, পুনঃ পুনঃ বলা ; পুনরাবৃত্তি করা। **—ănce, —ăn-cy, —a'-tion** *ns.* Repetition ; পুনরাবৃত্তি, পুনরুক্তি। **—a-tive,** *adj.* Repeating ; পুনরুক্তিকারী, পুনরাবৃত্তিকারী।

ĭth-ȳ-phăl'-lĭc, *adj.* & *n.* **1.** Pertaining to the phallus carried in Bacchic festival ; সুরাদেবতা বেকাসের উৎসবোপলক্ষে বাহিত দেবলিঙ্গ-সম্বন্ধীয়। **2.** Composed in the metre used for Bacchic hymns ; সুরাদেবতা ব্যাকাসের স্তোত্রের ছন্দে রচিত। **3.** Indecent ; obscene ; অশ্লীল ; কুরুচিপূর্ণ। *Noun.* A poem in the metre used for Bacchic hymns ; a licentious poem ; সুরাদেবতা ব্যাকাসের স্তবের ছন্দে রচিত কবিতা ; অশ্লীল কবিতা, খেউড়।

ī-tĭn'-ĕr-ănt, *adj.* & *n.* **1.** Travelling or wandering from place to place ; ভ্রমণশীল, অটমান, পর্য্যটনশীল, ভ্রমণকারী। **2.** Travelling on circuit ; as, an *itinerant* judge ; বিচার-ব্যপদেশে ভ্রমণশীল। **3.** Preaching on circuit ; as, an *itinerant* preacher ; ধর্ম্মপ্রচার ব্যপদেশে পর্যটনশীল। *Noun.* **1.** One who itinerates from place to place, esp. in pursuannce of trade etc. ; ভ্রমণকারী, পর্য্যটক। **2.** A travelling preacher ; ভ্রমণকারী ধর্ম্মপ্রচারক। **—a-cy, —an-cy,** *ns.* **1.** A passing from place to place ; স্থানে স্থানে পর্য্যটন। **2.** A discharge of official duty involving frequent change of residence ; a body of persons who discharge such official duty ; স্থানে স্থানে ভ্রমণপূর্ব্বক সরকারী কার্য্য সম্পাদন : সরকারী কার্য্য উপলক্ষে স্থানে স্থানে ভ্রমণকারী কর্ম্মচারিগণ।

ī-tĭn'-ĕr-ă-rȳ, *n.* & *adj.* **1.** A course of travel ; a route ; ভ্রমণপথ ; পথ। **2.** An account of a travel or journey ; ভ্রমণ-বৃত্তান্ত, ভ্রমণবর্ণন, ভ্রমণকাহিনী। **3.** A road-book ; a guide-book ; ভ্রমণসম্বন্ধীয় জ্ঞাতব্য বিষয়াদি সম্বলিত পুস্তক ; দিগ্দর্শন পুস্তক। *Adj.* **1.** Of, or relating to, a journey or route ; ভ্রমণ বা

ভ্রমণ-পথসম্বন্ধীয়। **2.** Passing from place to place ; travelling ; পর্য্যটনশীল ; ভ্রমণশীল।

ī-tĭn'-êr-āte, *v. i.* **1.** To travel from place to place ; স্থানে স্থানে ভ্রমণ করা, পর্য্যটন করা। **2.** To travel preaching on a circuit ; ধর্ম্ম-প্রচার ব্যপদেশে ভ্রমণ করা। **–a'-tion,** *n.*

its, *pron.* (*Possessive form of it*)

it-sĕlf', *pron.* (*Reflexive form of it*) ; ইহাই। **By itself**—Alone ; আপনিই, একলা। **In itself**—Apart from its surroundings ; viewed in its essential qualities ; আপনাআপনি, স্বয়ং, নিজে ; নিজের প্রকৃতি অনুসারে।

ī'-vō-rȳ, *n.* **1.** The hard white substance composing the tusks of the elephant and of the sea-horse (walrus) etc. ; হাতীর দাঁত, গজদন্ত, হস্তিদন্ত, দ্বিরদরদ, দ্বিরদরদন (উজ্জ্বলঃ) সিন্ধুঘোটকের দাঁত। **2.** An article of ivory ; any carving executed in ivory ; হাতীর দাঁতের জিনিষ ; হস্তিদন্তের উপর খোদাই কাজ। **3.** (*Sing.* or *pl. slang*) Teeth ; as, to show one's *ivories* ; (ইতর ভাষায়) দাঁত। **4.** (*Slang pl.*) Dice ; billiard balls ; (ইতর ভাষায়) পাশা ; বিলিয়ার্ড ক্রীড়ায় ব্যবহৃত গোলক। **5.** Colour of ivory ; গজদন্তের বর্ণ। **6.** Something like ivory ; গজদন্তবৎ বস্তু। **Black ivory**—Negro slaves of Africa ; আফ্রিকার নিগ্রোজাতীয় ক্রীতদাস সমূহ। **Ivory-black** — A black powder or pigment obtained by calcining ivory ; দগ্ধ গজদন্ত হইতে প্রস্তুত কৃষ্ণবর্ণ চূর্ণক বা রঞ্জন পদার্থ। **Ivory-nut** — দক্ষিণ আমেরিকার তালজাতীয় বৃক্ষের ফল বিশেষ। **Ivory-palm**—বৃক্ষবিশেষ। **Vegetable-ivory** — দক্ষিণ আমেরিকার ফলবিশেষের মধ্যস্থ শ্বেতাংশ। **To show one's ivories**—দন্তরাজি বিকাশ করা, দন্তপাটি বিকাশ করা। **To wash one's ivories**—To drink ; মদ্যপান করা।

Ivy.

ī'-vȳ, *n.* An ever-green climbing plant with shining five-angled leaves ; দীপ্তবর্ণ পঞ্চকোণপত্রবিশিষ্ট চিরশ্যামল লতিকা-বিশেষ, আইভিলতা। **–vied,** *adj.* Overgrown or covered with ivy ; আইভিলতাচ্ছাদিত, আইভিলতাবগুণ্ঠিত। **Ivy-bush**—An ivy plant formerly hung over tavern doors, it being sacred to Bacchus, the God of wine ; শৌণ্ডিকালয়ের দ্বারে বিলম্বিত আইভি লতা। **Ivy-geranium** — আইভি পত্রবৎ পত্রবিশিষ্ট লতা-বিশেষ। **Ivy-mantled**—Same as IVIED (above.)

ĭx'-ĭ-ă, *n.* A genus of South African plants ; দক্ষিণ আফ্রিকা দেশীয় বৃক্ষ বিশেষ।

Ĭx'-ĭ-ŏn (ĭx-), *n.* The son of Phlegyas king of the Lapithæ ; Lapthæ রাজ Phlegyasএর পুত্র। Ixion Deïoneusএর কন্যা Diaর সহিত পরিণয়সূত্রে আবদ্ধ হন। বিবাহের অনতিকাল পরে ইনি স্বীয় শ্বশুর Deïoneusকে বধ করেন। এই অপরাধের জন্য ইনি সমাজকর্ত্তৃক পরিত্যক্ত হন। Zeus, Ixionএর প্রতি করুণাপরবশ হইয়া তাহাকে Olympus পর্ব্বতস্থ দেবলোকে লইয়া যান কিন্তু কৃতঘ্ন Ixion দেবরাজের পত্নী Hera দেবীর প্রণয়লাভের চেষ্টা করে। ইহাতে দেবরাজ Zeusএর প্রতিহিংসানল উদ্দীপ্ত হয়। তাঁহার আদেশে Hermes দেব তাহার হস্তপদ লৌহশৃঙ্খলদ্বারা একটী অবিরাম ঘূর্ণনশীল চক্রে সংবদ্ধ করেন। **The Ixion wheel**—See IXION.

iz'-ărd, *n.* A variety of the chamois found in the Pyrenees ; পিরিনিজ পর্ব্বতে দৃষ্ট শেময় ছাগ বিশেষ।

J

J, *n.* **1.** The tenth letter of the English alphabet ; ইংরাজী বর্ণমালার দশম অক্ষর। **2.** A broad pointed pen stamped with J (also called *J-pen*) ; মোটা ছাঁদে লিখার জন্য কলমের মুখ—ঐরূপ কলমের মুখের উপর J অক্ষর মুদ্রিত থাকে।

jă'-ăl–goat (-gōt), *n.* A kind of ibex of Abyssinia, Upper Egypt, etc. ; এবিশিনিয়া, উত্তর মিশর প্রভৃতি দেশীয় ছাগ বিশেষ।

jăb, *v. t.* & *n.* **1.** To poke roughly ; খোঁচা দেওয়া। **2.** To stab ; ছুরিকাঘাত করা, ছোরা মারা। **3.** To thrust something quickly (*into*) ; ফস্ করিয়া ঢুকান। ***Noun.*** An abrupt blow with a pointed thing or fist ; খোঁচা, ঘুষি।

jăb'-bêr, *v. t., i.* & *n.* To utter rapidly or indistinctly ; as, to *jabber* French ; অনর্থক কথা বলা, বাজে কথা বকা, বক্ বক্ করা। ***Verb i.* 1.** To speak nonsensically ; to gabble ; আবল তাবল বকা ; পচাল পাড়া, বিড়বিড় করিয়া বকা। **2.** To chatter, as monkeys etc. ; কিচিরমিচির করা। ***Noun.* 1.** Act of jabbering ; rapid indistinct talk ; gabble ; বক্ বক্ করণ ; বক্বক্ ; পচাল, আবল তাবল কথা। **2.** Chatter ; কিচিরমিচির।

jăb'-i-ru (-rō), *n.* A stork-like wading bird of America ; আমেরিকা দেশীয় এক জাতীয় পক্ষিবিশেষ—ইহারা জলে হাঁটিয়া চলে।

jăb-ō-răn'-di, *n.* The dried leaflets of a plant of Brazil ; ব্রাজিল দেশীয় বৃক্ষবিশেষের শুষ্ক পত্রক।

jă-bŏt', *n.* **1.** Ornamental frill on woman's bodice ; স্ত্রীলোকের জামার

উপর বেলদার কাজ। **2.** (*Hist.*) The frill on the bosom of a shirt worn by men; (ইতিহাস) পুরুষদের জামার উপর বেলদার কাজ।

jăc´-ă-nă, *n.* A tropical bird allied to the rails; জলপিপি (যোঃ)।

ja´-cinth, *n.* A gem of reddish orange colour; কমলাবর্ণ গোমেদ-মণিবিশেষ।

jăck, *n.* **1.** (*Cap.*) A familiar nick-name or substitute for John; John নামের অপভ্রংশ। **2.** (*Card-playing*) Knave; তাসের গোলাম। **3.** (*Often cap.*) A popular name for a sailor (called also a *Jack-tar* & *Jack-afloat*); নাবিক। **4.** (*Sometimes cap.*) A labourer; a doer of odd jobs; শ্রমজীবী; যে ব্যক্তি ঠিকা কাজ করে। **5.** A contrivance for turning a spit in roasting meat; মাংস ভাজার সময় শিক ঘুরাইবার জন্য কৌশল বিশেষ। **6.** A machine for lifting or moving heavy weight; গুরুভার দ্রব্য উত্তোলনের জন্য যন্ত্র বিশেষ, উত্তোলক-যন্ত্র। **7.** A contrivance for assisting a person in pulling off his boots; জুতা খোলার জন্য কল বিশেষ, পাদুকা নিষ্কাষণ যন্ত্র। **8.** Parts of various machines etc.; বিভিন্ন যন্ত্রের অংশ। **9.** A young or small pike; এক প্রকার মৎস্য, জলশূচি (মঃ ইঃ)। **10.** A travelling hawker, (also called *Cheap-Jack*); ফেরিওয়ালা। **11.** A man who climbs steeples etc. to do repair etc.; যে ব্যক্তি জীর্ণ-সংস্কারাদি করার জন্য গির্জ্জার চূড়া প্রভৃতিতে আরোহণ করে। **12.** The union jack; a flag on the bow-sprit of a ship; গ্রেট ব্রিটেন ও আয়র্লণ্ডের মিলিত জাতীয় পতাকা; পোতাগ্র হইতে প্রলম্বিত দণ্ডোপরিস্থ পতাকা, পোতাগ্রবহিঃপ্রলম্বী ধ্বজপট। **13.** A male of certain animals; কোন কোন জন্তুর নর (পুং জন্তু)। **Jack-a-dandy** — ফুলবাবু। **Jack-at-a-pinch**—One suddenly called upon to perform some duty (often applied to a clergyman); যে ব্যক্তি কোন কার্য্যসাধনের জন্য সহসা আহূত হয়। **Jack-boot**—ধীবর প্রভৃতির আজানু-উচ্চ বুট জুতা। **Jack-daw**—কাকজাতীয় পক্ষিবিশেষ—সচরাচর লোকে ইহাদিগকে পুষিয়া থাকে এবং ময়না প্রভৃতির মত মানুষের কথা অনুকরণ করিতে শিখে। **Jack frost** — মূর্ত্তিমান তুষার। **Jack-Horner** — Jack Horner নামক বালক যে পিঠা হইতে কিস্‌মিস্ খুঁটিয়া তুলিয়াছিল বলিয়া ছেলেদের ছড়ায় আছে। **Jack-in-office** — গর্ব্বিত ও উদ্ধত কর্ম্মচারী। **Jack-in-the-box**—এক-প্রকার খেলনার বাক্স—যাহা খুলিবা মাত্র একটী মূর্ত্তি লাফাইয়া উঠে। A kind of fire work; একপ্রকার আতস বাজী। **Jack-in-the-green**—ইংলণ্ডে ১লা মে দিবস বসন্তোৎসবোপলক্ষে শ্যামলপত্ররাজিদ্বারা সজ্জিত ধূমনির্গমনল-পরিমার্জ্জক বালক। **Jack Ketch**—জল্লাদ, যে ব্যক্তি ফাঁসি দেয়। **Jack-knife** — একপ্রকার বড় চাকু। **Jack of all trades**—সবজান্তা লোক, যে ব্যক্তি ইস্তক জুতা সেলাই লাগাৎ চণ্ডীপাঠ পর্য্যন্ত সব কাজ করিতে পারে। **Jack-o'-lantern**—আলেয়া, ভূতদীপিকা, ভূতের আলো, পেত্নীর আলো। **Jack-on-both-sides**—নির্লিপ্ত ব্যক্তি বা যে ব্যক্তি নির্লিপ্ত থাকিতে চেষ্টা করে। **Jack out-of-doors** — গৃহ-হীন ব্যক্তি। **Jack-pudding**—ভাঁড়, বিদূষক, বৈহাসিক। **Jack's-bean-stalk**—উপকথায় উক্ত শিম্বীর কাণ্ড,—যাহা এক রাত্রের মধ্যে বাড়িয়া স্বর্গে মাথা ঠেকাইয়াছিল। **Jack-snipe**—একপ্রকার ক্ষুদ্র জাতীয় কাদা-খোঁচা। **Jack-sprat** — বামন, বালখিল্য। **Jack-straw**— কুশপুত্তলিকা, খড়ের পুতুল। A man without property or influence; সম্পত্তি-হীন ব্যক্তি, খড়ের পুতুল। **Jack-tar**—A common sailor; সাধারণ নাবিক। **Lifting jack** — উত্তোলনযন্ত্র। **A Cheap Jack**—See JACK *n.* 10. **Before you could say Jack Robinson** — Very quickly or suddenly; মুখ হইতে কথা বাহির হইতে না হইতে। **Every man Jack**—Every individual; প্রতি ব্যক্তি। **Jack and Gill**—Proper names for any lad and lass, now used in various proverbial expressions; as, every *Jack* must have his *Gill*; যে কোন ছোঁড়া বা ছোঁড়ীর নাম (cf. রাজার রাণী, কাণার কাণী)। **Jack of all trades master of none**—সবজান্তা। [cf. সকল নৈবেদ্যে ঠোকর মারা।]

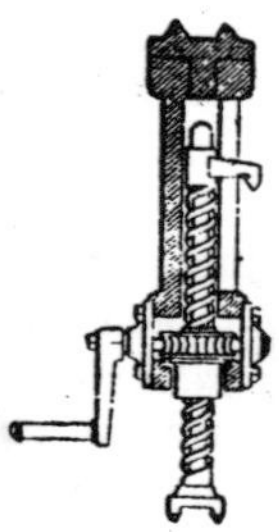
Lifting Jack.

jăck, *n.* An East Indian fruit like bread-fruit, but coarser; কণ্টকিফল, মহাফল, পনস।

jăck, *v. t.* & *i.* **1.** To hoist with a jack; উত্তোলন যন্ত্র দ্বারা তোলা। **2.** To do for; to ruin; নিকাশ করা; নাশ করা। **3.** (With *up*) To give up; to abandon, as an attempt; ত্যাগ করা; ছাড়িয়া দেওয়া। ***Verb i.*** To give up suddenly; হঠাৎ ত্যাগ করা।

jăck, *n.* (*Archaic*) A sleeveless tunic or jacket formerly worn by foot-soldiers; (অপ্রঃ) একপ্রকার হাতকাটা চোগা বা জামা যাহা পূর্ব্বে পদাতিক সৈন্যগণ ব্যবহার করিত। **2.** (Also *black jack*) A vessel for liquor; মদ্যপাত্র, মদ্যভাণ্ড।

jăck´-al, *n.* **1.** A wild animal,

Jackal.

closely allied to the dog, formerly supposed to hunt up a lion's prey for him ; শৃগাল, শেয়াল, শিবা, গোমায়ু, জম্বুক, জম্বুক, ফেরু, বঞ্চক, ক্রোষ্টা, খভীরু। 2. (*Fig.*) A person who does preparatory drudgery etc. ; (লক্ষণায়) যে ব্যক্তি প্রাথমিক শ্রমসাধ্য কার্য্য প্রভৃতি সম্পন্ন করে।

jăck'-ă-nāpes, *n.* 1. (*Archaic*) A monkey ; an ape ; বানর, বাঁদর, কপি ; হনুমান। 2. A coxcomb ; an impertinent fellow ; বক্কেশ্বর, ফুলবাবু ; ধৃষ্টলোক, বে-আদব লোক, দুর্বিনীত লোক। 3. A pert child ; বাঁদর ছেলে।

jăck'-ĕt, *n.* & *v.t.* 1. A sleeved outer garment for man or woman ; অঙ্গরাখা, কঞ্চুক, স্ত্রীলোকদিগের জ্যাকেট। 2. A natural covering or coat, *e. g.* sheep's fleece, skin of a potato etc. ; লোম, খোসা। 3. An outer covering round a boiler etc. for protection, keeping in heat etc. ; বাষ্পজননের বহিরাবরণ। ***Verb t.*** To cover with a jacket; কঞ্চুক দ্বারা আবৃত করা। **Eton jacket**—See under ETON. **Norfolk jacket**—See under NORFOLK. **To dust one's jacket**—To beat one ; উত্তম মধ্যম দেওয়া, আচ্ছা করিয়া পিটুনি দেওয়া।

Jā'-cŏb, *n.* 1. (*Bibl.*) A Hebrew patriarch, younger son of Isaac and Rebekah and father of the twelve patriarchs who were the reputed ancestors of the twelve tribes of Israel ; (বাইবেল) হিব্রুদিগের গোষ্ঠীপতি। 2. A ladder (*slang*) ; (ইতর ভাষায়) সিঁড়ী। **Jacob's ladder** — A kind of plant ; নীল ও শ্বেতপুষ্পপ্রসূ উদ্যানরোপিত গুল্মবিশেষ। (*Naut.*) A rope ladder with wooden steps ; (নৌ-বিদ্যা) কাঠের ধাপবিশিষ্ট দড়ীর সিঁড়ী। **Jacob's staff**—A surveyor's iron-shod rod used instead of a tripod ; জরীপকারীর লৌহ-বাঁধানো যষ্টি—যাহা ত্রিপদের পরিবর্ত্তে ব্যবহৃত হইত। An instrument for measuring heights and distances; উচ্চতা ও দূরত্ব মাপের জন্য যন্ত্র বিশেষ।

Jăc-ŏ-bē'-ăn, *adj.* 1. Of, or relating to, the reign of James I ; প্রথম জেম্‌সের রাজত্ব সম্বন্ধীয়। 2. Of, or relating to, St. James the Less ; কনিষ্ঠ সেন্ট জেমস্ সম্বন্ধীয়।

Jăc'-ŏ-bĭn, *n.* 1. A Dominican friar ; ডমিনিকান সম্প্রদায়ভুক্ত খৃষ্টীয় সন্ন্যাসী। 2. One of a society of revolutionists in France so called from their meeting in hall of the Jacobin convent ; sympathiser with the principles of this society ; an extreme radical ; ফরাসীবিপ্লববাদী সম্প্রদায় বিশেষের সভ্য ; বিপ্লবপন্থী ; চরমবিপ্লববাদী। **—bin'-ic, —bin'-i-cal,** *adjs.* **—ism,** *n.* **—ize,** *v. t.*

jăc'-ŏ-bĭn, *n.* A pigeon with reversed feathers on the back of the neck suggesting a cowl or hood ; ঝোটন-পায়রা।

Jăc'-ŏ-bīte, *n.* A partisan or adherent of James II after his abdication, or of his son the Pretender ; ইংলণ্ডেশ্বর দ্বিতীয় জেমস্ বা তদীয় পুত্রের পক্ষভুক্ত ব্যক্তি। **—bit'-i-cal,** *adj.* **—bit-ism,** *n.*

jă-cō'-bŭs, *n.* An English gold coin struck in the reign of James I worth 20-24*s.* ; প্রথম জেম্‌সের সময়ের ইংলণ্ডীয় স্বর্ণমুদ্রা।

jăc'-ŏ-nĕt, *n.* A cotton fabric, rather stouter than muslin originally made in India ; এক-প্রকার শক্ত মলমল কাপড়।

jacquerie, *n.* A rising or revolt of peasantry esp. that of 1357-58 in France ; কৃষক বিদ্রোহ, ১৩৫৭—৫৮ সনে ফরাসীদেশের কৃষক বিদ্রোহ।

jăc-tĭ-tā'-tion, *n.* 1. Boasting ; bragging ; "...*jactitation* about the...wealth of the Indies" ; দম্ভ ; বড়াই। 2. (*Med.*) Frequent tossing of the body ; restlessness ; আইঢাই ; শয্যাকণ্টকী, অত্যন্ত অ... 3. A twitching of a limb or muscle ; স্পন্দন, আক্ষেপ।

jăc'-ū-lāte, *v. t.* & *i.* (*Rare*) To dart ; (অপ্রঃ) নিক্ষেপ করা, ক্ষেপণ করা।

jāde, *n.* & *v. t.* 1. A mean or poor horse ; a tired horse ; অকর্ম্মণ্য ঘোটক, কদশ্ব ; ক্লান্ত অশ্ব। 2. A mean woman ; a wench (*used opprobriously or playfully*); হীনস্বভাবা নারী, বন্ধকী ; ছুঁড়ী। ***Verb t.*** (*Esp. in p. p.*) To wear out or exhaust with hard work ; হাড়ভাঙ্গা খাটুনী খাটাইয়া অবসন্ন করা, খিন্ন করা। **Jad'-ed,** *p. p.* Worn out ; খিন্ন, অবসন্ন, পরিক্লান্ত, পরিশ্রান্ত।

jāde, *n.* A dark green stone used for ornamental purposes ; গাঢ় সবুজবর্ণ মণি বিশেষ, পিলু, জসম।

jăg, *n.* 1. A sharp projection ; a sharp or ragged point of rock etc. ; সূক্ষ্মাগ্র উদ্গত অংশ ; পাষাণ-পর্ব্বতাদির সূক্ষ্মাগ্র অংশ। 2. A notch ; a denticulation ; খাঁজ ; দাঁত। **Jag'-gy,** *adj.* Abounding in jags ; notched ; uneven ; দাঁতাল, দন্তুর ; খাঁজবিশিষ্ট ; উচ্চাবচ।

jăg, *v. t.* 1. To notch ; খাঁজ কাটা, দন্তুরিত করা, দাঁতাল করিয়া কাটা। 2. To make rugged or uneven by cutting or tearing ; আবড়ো খাবড়ো করিয়া কাটা বা ছেঁড়া। **Jag'-ged,** *adj.* **Jag'-ged-ly,** *adv.* **Jag'-ged-ness,** *n.* **Jag'-ger,** *n.*

jăg'-ger-ȳ (-ĕr-), *n.* A kind of coarse sugar got from palm or palmyra sap ; তালের চিনি বা গুড়, দলুয়া।

jăg'-uar (-wâr), *n.* An American tiger allied to the **leopard** ; চিতাবাঘের মত আমেরিকা দেশীয় জন্তু বিশেষ।

Jah (jâ), *n.* Jehovah ; জিহোবা।

jail (jāl), **gaol** (jāl), *n.* & *v. t.* 1. Prison ; কারাগার, বন্ধনালয়, বন্দিশালা, কারা, কারাগৃহ, বন্দিগৃহ, বন্ধনাগার, কয়েদখানা, জেলখানা, শ্রীঘর

-লে)। 2. (*Without an article*) Confinement in prison; কারাবরোধ। ***Verb t.*** To put in prison; কারাগারে দেওয়া, জেলে দেওয়া। **Jail(gaol)′-er, –or,** *ns.* One who has charge of a jail or prisoner; জেলদারোগা, বন্দিপাল, কারাধ্যক্ষ, কারাগৃহাধিপতি, কারাগৃহাধ্যক্ষ। **Jail-(gaol)-bird**—A prisoner; one who has been long or frequently in prison; a habitual criminal; a rogue; কয়েদী; জেল খালাসী; পুরাতন কয়েদী। **Jail(gaol) –delivery** — Clearing of jail by trial of prisoners; হাজতে আবদ্ধ কয়েদীদিগের বিচার করিয়া জেল খালাস। **Jail(gaol)-fever**—Typhus fever formerly occurring in jails; এক-প্রকার স্পর্শসংক্রামক উৎকট অবিরাম জ্বর। **To break jail**—To escape from jail; জেল ভাঙ্গিয়া পলায়ন করা।

jăl′-ăp, *n.* A purgative drug got especially from the tuberous roots of a Mexican climbing plant; মেক্সিকো দেশীয় লতা বিশেষের মূল হইতে প্রাপ্ত বিরেচক ঔষধ বিশেষ, জুলাপ (হঃ চঃ) [Mexico দেশের Jalapa নামক নগরে হইতে সর্ব্বপ্রথম সমানীত হইয়াছিল বলিয়া এই নাম]।

jăm, *v. t., i.* & *n.* **1.** To press between two surfaces; to squeeze tight; to wedge in; চাপ দেওয়া; ঠাসা; ঠাসিয়া ভরা, ঠেলিয়া ঢুকান। **2.** To cause (a part of a machine) to be fixed so that it cannot work; (যন্ত্রের কোন অংশ যেন) না চলিতে পারে এরূপভাবে সংবদ্ধ করা। **3.** To crush or bruise; as, to *jam* a finger in a door; ছেঁচা। **4.** To block or obstruct as a passage etc. by crowding into it; ভিড় করিয়া পথরোধ করা। ***Verb i.*** To become tightly wedged; to stick fast; ঠাসিয়া লাগা; দৃঢ়রূপে সংলগ্ন হওয়া। ***Noun.*** **1.** Crush; a squeeze; a block; a crowded mass; নিষ্পেষণ, বিমর্দ্দন; নিষ্পীড়ন; আটক; ভিড়। **2.** The stopping of a machine by jamming; অংশ বিশেষ সংবদ্ধ করিয়া যন্ত্রের গতিরোধ।

jăm, *n.* **1.** A thick preserve of fruit boiled with sugar and water; মোরব্বা।

jamb (jăm), *n.* The side post of a doorway, window, etc.; esp. (*pl.*) stone sides or cheeks of a fireplace; দ্বার, বাতায়ন, প্রভৃতির পার্শ্বস্তম্ভ, দরজার বাজু; (বহুবচন) অগ্নিসেবনস্থলীর পাষাণবদ্ধ পার্শ্বভাগ।

Door way. *a.* jamb.

jăm′-bōōl, –bŭl, –bö-lä′-nä, *ns.* **1.** The Java plum; কালজাম। **2.** (Only **–bool, –bul**) A drug obtained from the bark and seeds of jambul used as a remedy for diabetes; কালজামের বাকল ও বীজ হইতে প্রাপ্ত বহুমূত্ররোগের ঔষধ বিশেষ।

jan′-gle (jăng-gl), *n., v. t.* & *i.* **1.** (*Archaic*) Noisy altercation; (অপ্রঃ) বচসা। **2.** A confused jangling; ঝন্ ঝন্ শব্দ, রণ্ রণ্, ঠন্ ঠন্ শব্দ। ***Verb t.*** **1.** To utter or speak discordantly or noisily; বেসুরা আওয়াজ করা বা হড়বড় করিয়া কথা বলা। **2.** To cause as a bell etc. to sound harshly or inharmoniously; ঝন্ ঝন্ করান, ঠন্ ঠন্ করান, বেসুর আওয়াজ করান। ***Verb i.*** **1.** To make a harsh noise; ঝন্ ঝন্ করা, ঠন্ ঠন্ করা। **2.** (*Archaic*) To quarrel in words; to wrangle; (অপ্রঃ) ঝগড়া হওয়া; বচসা হওয়া।

jăn′-i-tor (-têr), *n.* A door-keeper; a porter; দরোয়ান, দ্বারী, দ্বারপ, প্রতিহারী, দ্বাররক্ষক, দ্বারবান; মুটে।

jăn′-i-ză-rȳ, –is-să-rȳ, *ns.* **1.** A soldier of the old Turkish foot-guards (abolished in 1826); Turkish soldier; তুরস্কদেশীয় প্রাচীন পদাতিক রক্ষিসৈন্য (১৮২৬ খৃঃ অব্দে বিলুপ্ত হয়); তুর্কীসৈন্য। **2.** (*Fig.*) A personal instrument of tyranny; "A body of Janizaries ready... to carry out his personal will" (লক্ষণায়) অত্যাচারের যন্ত্র।

Jăn′-sĕn-ist, *n.* A follower of Cornelius Jansen, Roman Catholic bishop of Ypres in Flanders who upheld the doctrine of irresistible grace and denied the freedom of the will; ফ্লাণ্ডার্সের অন্তঃপাতী ইপ্রেস নগরীর ধর্ম্মাধ্যক্ষ Jansen এর মতাবলম্বী। **–ism,** *n.* The doctrine of the Jansenists; Jansen এর মতবাদ। **–is′-tic,** *adj.*

jâu′-tu (-tô), *n.* A machine for raising water to irrigate land, used in Bengal; ক্ষেত্রে সেচনের জল উত্তোলনের জন্য যন্ত্র বিশেষ।

Jăn′-ū-ă-rȳ, *n.* The first month of the year; ইংরাজী বর্ষের প্রথম মাস।

Jā′-nŭs, *n.* An ancient Italian God regarded as guardian of doors and gates; রোমানদিগের দ্বার-দেবতা—এই দেবতার দুইটী মুখ ছিল, উহার একটী মস্তক সম্মুখে ও একটী পশ্চাতে।

Jăp, *adj.* & *n.* (*Colloq.*) Japanese; (চলিত ভাষায়) জাপানী।

jā-păn′, *n.* **1.** (*Cap.*) The group of islands on the east coast of Asia; জাপান। **2.** A hard varnish esp. the kind brought originally from Japan; একপ্রকার কঠিন বার্নিশ—পূর্ব্বে জাপান হইতে আনীত হইত, জাপানী বার্নিশ। **3.** Work varnished or figured in Japanese style; জাপানীদিগের অনুকরণে বার্নিশ-করা বা মূর্ত্তি-আঁকা জিনিষ। **Jap-a-nese′,** *adj.* & *n.* Of, or relating to, Japan, its people or language; জাপানসম্বন্ধীয়, জাপানী, জাপানী লোক বা জাপানী ভাষা সম্বন্ধীয়। (*Noun*) **1.** A native of Japan; জাপানী লোক। **2.** The language of Japan; জাপানী ভাষা। **Jap a-nesque′,** *adj.*

Japanese in style or manner ; জাপানী ধরণের।

jă-păn′, *v. t.* **1.** To lacquer with japan ; জাপানী বার্ণিশ লাগান। **2.** To make black and glossy as with varnish ; চক্‌চকে কালো করা।

jāpe, *n.* & *v. i.* Jest ; তামাসা, পরিহাস, ঠাট্টা। ***Verb i.*** To jest or jeer ; ঠাট্টা করা, তামাসা করা, পরিহাস করা।

Jā-phĕt′-ic, *adj.* **1.** Of, or relating to, or descended from, Japhet son of Noah ; নোয়ার পুত্র জেফেট সম্বন্ধীয় বা তদ্‌বংশোদ্ভূত। **2.** Indo-European ; য়ুরো ভারতীয়।

Jā-pŏn′-ic, *adj.* Japanese ; জাপানী।

jâr, *n.* **1.** A rattling vibration of sound ; a harsh sound ; ঘর্ঘর শব্দ ; কর্কশ ধ্বনি, কর কর শব্দ। **2.** A thrill of the nerves or feelings etc. ; a shock ; পুলকস্পন্দন, আবেগকম্পন ; ধাক্কা। **3.** Discord ; quarrel ; conflict of opinion etc. ; অনৈক্য ; কলহ, ঠুকাঠুকি ; মতভেদ, মতদ্বৈধ।

jâr, *n.* A vessel as of earthenware or glass, of various shapes and dimensions ; কলস, ঘট, কুম্ভ, কাব্বা। **Jar′-ful**, *n.*

jâr, *v. i.* & *t.* **1.** To sound discordantly ; কর্কশ ধ্বনি করা। **2.** To shake or vibrate so as to cause a jarring sound ; to clatter ; ঘর্‌ ঘর্‌ করিয়া নাড়া বা ঝাঁকা ; খট্‌ খট্‌ করা, কড়মড় করা। **3.** To strike (*upon* or *against* an object) with a grating sound ; ঠুকাঠুকি লাগা, ঠেকর লাগা। **4.** To make a grating impression, as *upon* a person, his ear, nerves, feelings, etc. ; শ্রুতিকটু বোধ হওয়া, অপ্রীতিকর বোধ হওয়া। **5.** To clash ; to disagree ; to quarrel ; to wrangle ; as, our views do not *jar* ; সংঘর্ষ হওয়া ; অনৈক্য হওয়া, মতদ্বৈধ হওয়া ; কলহ হওয়া ; বচসা হওয়া। ***Verb t.*** **1.** To cause to shake or vibrate ; স্পন্দিত করা, কম্পিত করা। **2.** To cause to sound harshly ; ঘর্‌ ঘর্‌ করান। **3.** To affect painfully ; to shock ; ব্যথা দেওয়া ; ধাক্কা দেওয়া। **Jar′-ring**, *adj.* **Jar′-ring-ly**, *adv.*

jâr, *n.* A term only in the phrase **on the jar**—Ajar or partly open, as a door ; ঈষদুন্মুক্ত।

Jardin des plantes, (*F.*) *n.* (*Garden of plants*) The celebrated botanical garden in Paris ; উদ্ভিদ্‌-বিদ্যা অনুশীলনের জন্য উদ্যান (বিশেষতঃ প্যারীনগরীস্থ উক্তপ্রকার উদ্যান)।

jardiniere, (*F.*) *n.* An ornamental pot or stand for display of growing flowers, plants, etc. ; কারুকার্য্যখচিত পুষ্পপাত্র।

jâr′-gŏn, *n.* **1.** Confused unintelligible language ; gibberish ; অর্থহীন প্রলাপ ; হড়বড়ানি, হযবরল। **2.** A barbarous or outlandish language or a dialect ; অপভাষা, বর্ব্বরভাষা, রাক্ষসীভাষা, পিশাচভাষা। **3.** A form of speech full of unintelligible terms ; as, metaphysical *jargon* ; দুর্ব্বোধ শব্দবহুল বক্তৃতা। **4.** Twittering of birds ; কিচিরমিচির, কাকলী। **–ize**, *v. t.* & *i.* To utter jargon ; দুর্ব্বোধ বাক্য উচ্চারণ করা।

jâr′-gŏn, –gōōn′, *n.* A variety of zircon ; একপ্রকার গোমেদ মণি।

jâr-gō-nelle′ (-nĕl), *n.* An early ripening variety of pear ; একপ্রকার সেওফল।

jarl (yârl), *n.* (*Hist.*) A Danish or Norse chieftain or headman ; (ইতিহাস) ডেনমার্ক বা নরওয়েদেশীয় সর্দ্দার।

jăr′-rah (-ră), *n.* A durable timber of West Australian mahogany gum tree ; পশ্চিম অষ্ট্রেলিয়ার দীর্ঘকাল স্থায়ী কাঠ বিশেষ। [এই কাঠ গৃহতলাদি আচ্ছাদনার্থ বহুল পরিমাণে ব্যবহৃত হইয়া থাকে।]

jâr′-vey (-vĭ), *n.* The driver of a hackney carriage or an Irish car ; গাড়োয়ান।

jăs′-min(e) (-mĭn), **jĕs′-sa-min(e)** (-ă-mĭn), *ns.* A genus of plants bearing white or yellowish flowers ; যূঁই, স্বর্ণ যূঁই, বেল, চামেলী, প্রভৃতি পুষ্পের সাধারণ নাম। **Arabian jasmine**—কুন্দ, মল্লিকা, বসন্ত। **Double flowered jasmine**—নবমালিকা, রাইবেলা। **Greybone jasmine**—টগর। **Night jasmine**–শিউলি, শেফালিকা। **Single jasmine**—খ'য়ে বেলা, মতিয়া বেলা। **Spanish** or **Cataline jasmine**—চামেলি। **Spanish jasmine**—গুলঞ্চ, গুলাচি। **Tuscany jasmine**—বৃত্তমল্লিকা। **Yellow jasmine**—হেমপুষ্পিকা।

Jasminun angustifolium—কাননমল্লিকা (বেলঃ), বনমল্লিকা (ঐ)।

Jasminum arborescens—বড় কুন্দ (বেলঃ)।

Jasminum auriculatum—যূঁই (বেলঃ)।

Jasminum chrysanthemum—হেমপুষ্পিকা (বেলঃ)।

Jasminum grandiflorum—চামেলি (বেলঃ), জাতি (ঐ)।

Jasminum heterophyllum—কুন্দ (বেলঃ)।

Jasminum sambac—বেলা (বেলঃ) মতিয়া (ঐ), নবমল্লিকা (ঐ)।

Jăs′-ŏn, *n.* The son of Æson, king of Iolchus, in Thessaly ; থেসেলী প্রদেশের Iolchus এর রাজা Æson এর পুত্র। ইনি খুল্লতাত Pelias কর্ত্তৃক পিতৃসিংহাসন হইতে বঞ্চিত হইয়া Chirou নামক দৈত্যের নিকট প্রেরিত হন। Jason সাবালক হইলে তিনি খুল্লতাতের নিকট পিতৃরাজ্যের দাবী করেন। Pelias সুবর্ণ মেষলোম আনার সর্ত্তে জেসনকে রাজ্য প্রদানে স্বীকৃত হন। জেসন বহু বিপৎ অতিক্রমপূর্ব্বক কলসিস্‌ দ্বীপ হইতে সুবর্ণ মেষলোমসহ স্বদেশে প্রত্যাবৃত্ত হন। দেশে আসিয়া জেসন দেখিলেন যে দুষ্ট Pelias তাহার পিতাকে নিধন করিয়াছে। জেসন তদীয়

পত্নী মায়াবিনী Medea কে পিতৃহন্তার উপর প্রতিশোধ নেওয়ার জন্য আদেশ করেন। Medea Pelias এর কন্যাদিগকে বলিলেন যে তিনি তাহাদের বৃদ্ধ পিতাকে নবযৌবন প্রদান করিতে পারেন। তাহার প্রস্তাবে কন্যাগণ নবযৌবন প্রদানের উদ্দেশ্যে পিতাকে কটাহে সিদ্ধ করিতে লাগিলেন। শেষ মুহূর্ত্তে Medea সাহায্য করিতে বিরতা হইলে Pelias বিনষ্ট হন। এই অপরাধের দরুণ Pelias এর পুত্র Acartus, Jason ও Medea কে রাজ্য হইতে নির্ব্বাসিত করেন। তাহারা Corinth এ গমন করেন; তথায় জেসন Medea কে পরিত্যাগ করিয়া রাজকন্যা Cracusa কে বিবাহ করেন। Medea Creusa কে বিষলিপ্ত পরিচ্ছদ প্রদান করেন। ঐ পরিচ্ছদ পরিধান করা মাত্র Creusa দগ্ধ হইয়া জীবনলীলা সাঙ্গ করেন। কেহ কেহ বলেন Medea ও Jason এর পুনর্ম্মিলন হইয়াছিল।

Jatropha curcas—বাগ ভেরেণ্ডা (বেলঃ)।

jăs′-pĕr, *n.* An opaque variety of quartz; একপ্রকার মূল্যবান স্ফটিক প্রস্তর, জাস্‌প্‌ং। (সচরাচর রক্ত, পীত ও কপিশবর্ণের দৃষ্ট হয়।)

jaun′-dice (jän-dĭs), *n.* & *v. t.* **1.** A disease in its most common form characterized by yellowness of the skin and eyes, loss of appetite etc.; কামলা, পাণ্ডুরোগ, নেবা, পাণ্ডুর, হলীমক (সুশ্রুঃ) পাণ্ডুক (সাঃ পঃ), পাণ্ডুল (ঐ), কমলবন্ধ (ঐ)। **2.** (*Fig.*) A state of disordered feeling or judgment etc.; anything which disorders the judgment; (লক্ষণায়) বুদ্ধিবিকৃতি, বিচারবুদ্ধিবিকৃতি; যদ্দ্বারা বিচারবুদ্ধি বিকৃত হয়। ***Verb t.*** **1.** To affect with jaundice; কামলা রোগ দ্বারা আক্রান্ত করা। **2.** (*Fig. usu. p. p.*) To affect with envy, jealousy, prejudice, etc. as a person or judgment; ঈর্ষান্বিত করা, পূর্ব্বসংস্কার দ্বারা বিকৃত করা। **Jaundiced eye**—Prejudiced eye; পক্ষপাতদুষ্ট দৃষ্টি। **All things look yellow to a jaundiced eye**—চোখের দোষে সব হলদে।

Jaunt (jânt), *n.* & *v. i.* A short excursion for pleasure; a short journey; ভ্রমণ, বিহার, বিহরণ; পর্য্যটন, পরিভ্রমণ, সফর (*colloq.*)। ***Verb i.*** To make an excursion or journey esp. for pleasure; বিহার করা, প্রমোদভ্রমণ করা, পর্য্যটন করা, পরিভ্রমণ করা।

jaun′-tў (-jân-), *adj.* **1.** Having an air of easy sprightliness; affecting airy self-satisfaction; সলীল, লীলাপূর্ণ; লঘুচিত্ত, স্বচ্ছন্দচিত্ত। **2.** (*Obs.*) Stylish; চটকদার। **—ti-ly,** *adv.* **—ti-ness,** *n.*

jăve′-lin, *n.* A light spear; a dart; বর্শা, বল্লম, শড়কি, শূল; শক্তি, শল্য।

jaw (jä), *n.*, *v. i.* & *t.* The bones of the mouth in which the teeth are fixed; চোয়াল, হনু, চিবুক। **2.** (*Fig.*) Anything resembling the jaw of an animal in form or in action; as, the *jaw* of death; (লক্ষণায়) আকারে অথবা ক্রিয়ায় জন্তুর চোয়ালের মত কোন কিছু। **3.** (*Pl.—colloq.*) Loquacity; as, hold your *jaw*; a sermonizing talk; a lecture; (চলিত ভাষায়) বাচালতা; সাধুগিরি; বক্তৃতা। **4.** (*Pl.*) The mouth; (বহুবচনে) মুখ। **5.** Impudent talk; scolding; বাক্‌পারুষ্য; বকুনি, গঞ্জনা। **6.** The narrow mouth of a valley or channel etc.; প্রণালী বা উপত্যকার সংকীর্ণ মুখ। ***Verb i.*** To speak or talk; আলাপ করা, কথা বলা, বকিয়া যাওয়া। ***Verb t.*** To scold; মুখ করা, বকুনি দেওয়া, মুখঝামটা দেওয়া। **Jaw-bone**—চোয়ালের হাড়, চিবুকাস্থি, হন্বাস্থি। **Jaw-breaker**—(*Colloq.*) A word hard to pronounce; (চলিত ভাষায়) দুরুচ্চার্য্য শব্দ, দাঁত-ভাঙ্গা শব্দ। **Jaw of death**—মৃত্যুমুখ, অন্তকানন। **Locked jaw**—হনুগ্রহ, হনুস্তম্ভ। **Lower jaw**—অধোহনু (সাঃ পঃ)। **Upper jaw**—ঊর্দ্ধহনু (সাঃ পঃ)। **Hold** or **stop your jaw**—(*Colloq.*) Be quiet; (চলিতভাষায়) মুখ সামলাও।

jay (jā), *n.* A noisy chattering European bird of brilliant plumage, allied to the crows; ইয়ুরোপদেশীয় উজ্জ্বলবর্ণ পক্ষপরিশোভিত কাকজাতীয় পক্ষি-বিশেষ, চাষপক্ষী, কিকিদীবি, নীলকণ্ঠ, মনিকণ্ঠ (কেভিঃ)। **2.** (*Fig.*) An impertinent chatterer; a simpleton; (লক্ষণায়) প্রগল্‌ভ বাচাল; বোকা। **Blue jay**—নীলকণ্ঠ

Common jay. European jay.

jeal′-ous (jĕl-ŭs), *adj.* **1.** Solicitous for preservation as of rights etc.; (সম্পত্তি প্রভৃতি রক্ষার জন্য) আগ্রহবান, আগ্রহান্বিত। **2.** Apprehensive regarding the love or good-will (*of* wife, husband, lover, friend, etc.); (স্ত্রী, স্বামী বা বন্ধুর) প্রীতি বা প্রণয় সম্বন্ধে শঙ্কাকুল, প্রীতিব্যত্যয়াশঙ্কী, প্রীতিব্যভিচারাশঙ্কী, প্রেমসংশয়ী, (a husband of a wife) পরপুরুষাশঙ্কী, পরপুরুষশঙ্কিত, জারশঙ্কিত, (a wife of a husband) পরস্ত্রীশঙ্কিনী। **3.** Apprehensive (of the supposed rival); (কল্পিত প্রতিদ্বন্দ্বিসম্বন্ধে) শঙ্কিত বা শঙ্কাকুল, অন্যশুভদ্বেষী। **4.** Envious (*of*); ঈর্ষাপরায়ণ, ঈর্ষী, দ্বেষী, পরশ্রীকাতর, সমৎসর, অসূয়ক, পরোৎকর্ষাশঙ্কী, পরোৎকর্ষদ্বেষী, পরোৎকর্ষাসহ, অন্যশুভাশঙ্কী, পরোৎকর্ষাসূয়ক। **5.** Vigilant or exact in scrutiny etc., as enquiry, supervision, etc.; সূক্ষ্মানুসন্ধায়ী। 6. (*Bibl.*) Intolerant of unfaithfulness (of God); (বাইবেল) অবিশ্বাসীর প্রতি অসহিষ্ণু, নাস্তিকদ্বেষী। **—ly,** *adv.* 1. In a jealous manner; ঈর্ষার সহিত। 2. With apprehension of rivalry or of loss or damage; প্রতিদ্বন্দ্বিতা প্রভৃতি সম্পর্কে শঙ্কাকুলচিত্তে।

jeal'-ous-ў (jŏl-ŭs-), *n.* 1. Quality or state of being jealous; painful apprehension of rivalry or of infidelity of wife, husband, etc.; ঈর্ষান্বিত ভাব; (প্রণয়াদি ব্যাপারে) শঙ্কাকুলতা, প্রেমসংশয়, প্রীতিব্যত্যয়াশঙ্কা, প্রেমশঙ্কা, (husband of a wife) পরপুরুষাশঙ্কা, জারশঙ্কা (ঐ), (wife of a husband) পরস্ত্রীশঙ্কা। 2. Envy; দ্বেষ, ঈর্ষা, মাৎসর্য্য, পরশ্রীকাতরতা, পরোৎকর্ষাসূয়া, পরোৎকর্ষাশঙ্কা। 3. Vigilant care; earnest solicitude; সাবধানতা, সাবহিতত্ব; সকাতর প্রার্থনা।

jean (jān), *n.* A twilled cotton cloth; একপ্রকার টের্চ্চা বুনা সুতার কাপড়, জীন কাপড়। **Jean Crapaud**—ফরাসীগণের উপনাম। **Satin jean**—একপ্রকার কার্পাস বস্ত্র,—যাহার উপরিভাগ মসৃণ থাকে, জীন সাটীন।

jĕd'-dart (-ârt), *adj.* [From Jedburgh in the South of Scotland.] **Jeddart** or **jedwood justice**—স্কটলণ্ডের স্থান বিশেষে প্রচলিত বিধিবিশেষ—যদনুসারে অপরাধীকে ফাঁসী দিবার পর তাহার অপরাধের বিচার করা হইত।

jeer (jēr), *n., v. t. & i.* A scoff; a taunt; jest; ব্যঙ্গ, অবহাস; উপহাস, বিদ্রূপ, শ্লেষ; ঠাট্টা। ***Verb t.*** To deride; to mock at; উপহাস করা, ব্যঙ্গ করা; বিদ্রূপ করা। ***Verb i.*** To utter sarcastic or scoffing reflection, (with *at*); ব্যঙ্গোক্তি করা, ঠাট্টা করা, চিড়ান।

jeer (jēr), *n.* (*Naut. usu pl.*) An assemblage or combination of tackle for hoisting and lowering lower yards; (নৌ বিদ্যা) নিম্নতর পালিদণ্ড নামাইবার বা তুলিবার জন্য রজ্জু-সংহতি বা রজ্জু-সম্মিলন।

Jē-hō'-vah (-vȧ), *n.* The principal name of God in the Old Testament; ইহুদীদিগের ঈশ্বর, জিহোবা।

Jē-hō'-vist, *n.* The author of those passages of the Old Testament in which God is called Jehovah; বাইবেলের প্রাচীন নিয়মের যে অংশ সমূহে ঈশ্বরকে জিহোবা বলিয়া অভিহিত করা হইয়াছে ঐ সকল অংশের রচয়িতা। **—vic,** *adj.*

Jē'-hū, *n.* (*Facet.*) A driver, esp. a furious or fast driver; (রঙ্গচ্ছলে) চালক, বিশেষতঃ যে ব্যক্তি প্রচণ্ডবেগে শকট চালনা করে। [See 2 *Kings* ix. 20].

jē-jūne', *adj.* 1. Void of substance; শুষ্ক, শূন্যগর্ভ, অন্তঃসারশূন্য, নিঃসত্ত্ব, রুক্ষ। 2. Meagre; scanty; as, *jejune* diet; স্বল্প; সামান্য, অপ্রচুর। 3. Void of interest in satisfying, as a narrative; নীরস, রসহীন, হীনরস। 4. (Of land) Barren; (মৃত্তিকা সম্বন্ধে) অনুর্ব্বর। **—ly,** *adv.* **—ness,** *n.* The quality of being jejune; শুষ্কতা, রুক্ষতা, রসরাহিত্য, রসাভাব, নীরসতা।

jĕl'-lў, *n., v. t. & i.* 1. A transparent substance obtained by decoction from skin, bone, etc; জন্তুর হাড়, চামড়া প্রভৃতি সিদ্ধ করিয়া যে কাথ প্রস্তুত হয়। 2. The thickened juice of fruit boiled with sugar; ফলাদির রস চিনির শিরায় ফুটাইয়া যে গাঢ় জিনিষ প্রস্তুত হয়, জেলি। 3. Anything coagulated into a viscous and glutinous state; আটালো চটচটে জিনিষ, শ্যানদ্রব্য। ***Verb t.*** 1. To bring to the consistency of jelly; to coagulate; জেলির মত গাঢ় করা; জমান। ***Verb i.*** To become gelatinous; to congeal; আটালো হওয়া, চট্‌চটে হওয়া; জমিয়া যাওয়া। **Jelly-fish** — সামুদ্রিক মৎস্য। **To beat to j**[elly] মেরে পাট পাট করা, মেরে ধূনে [ফেলা], কাঁচক বধ করা।

Jelly fish.

jĕm'-my (-ĭ-), *n.* 1. A short crow-bar used by burglars; সিঁধেল চোরদিগের একপ্রকার শাবল। 2. A sheep's head used for food; রন্ধিত মেষমুণ্ড।

je ne sais quoi, (*F.*—*I know not what*), *n.* An indescribable something; অবর্ণনীয় বিষয়।

jĕn'-nĕt, *n.* A small Spanish horse; স্পেনদেশীয় খর্ব্বকায় অশ্ব।

jĕn'-nĕt-ing, *n.* A variety of early apple; মরসুমের প্রথমভাগে পক্ব একপ্রকার সেওফল।

jĕn'-nў, *n.* 1. A machine for spinning; একপ্রকার চরকা। 2. A locomotive crane; বাষ্পবলে চালিত উত্তোলনযন্ত্র। 3. A stroke at billiard; বিলিয়ার্ড খেলায় আঘাত। 4. (*Derisively*) A man who concerns himself with purely feminine matters; (অবজ্ঞাচ্ছলে) যে ব্যক্তি স্ত্রীলোকদিগের বিষয় লইয়া ব্যাপৃত থাকে। 5. Used as a prefix to denote a female animal; as, *jenny*-ass; মাদী।

jeop'-ȧrd-īze (-jĕp-), *v. t.* To endanger; বিপদাপন্ন করা, বিপদ্‌গ্রস্ত করা, সঙ্কটে ফেলা, সঙ্কটাপন্ন করা।

jeop'-ȧrd-ў (jĕp-), *n.* Danger; peril; বিপদ্, দায়; সঙ্কট।

jē-quir'-i-tў (-kwĭr-), Indian twining shrub with parti-coloured seeds used for ornament and in medicine; গুঞ্জা লতা।

jĕr-bō'-ȧ, *n.* A small rodent resembling a mouse, but with long hind legs; মূষিকবৎ জন্তু বিশেষ।

jĕr-ē-mī'-ȧd, *n.* A doleful complaint; lamentation; [from Jeremiah, the prophet—alluding to the lamentations of Jeremiah in the Old Testament]; আক্ষেপোক্তি, কাতরোক্তি; বিলাপ, খেদ, হাহাকার।

wooden or metal bar extending from one support to another as in fences, staircases, etc. ; গরাদ, গড়া। 2. A fence ; a railing ; বেড়া ; কাঠগড়া। 3. An iron bar or continuous line of bars গোপন স্থানে যাওয়া। [Chelmsfordএর সন্নিকটবর্ত্তী জমিদার বাড়ীকে Jericho কহিত। এই বাটী অষ্টম হেনরীর বিলাস-ভবন ছিল। এই রাজা রাজবেশ্যাগণের আলিঙ্গনসুখ ভোগের জন্য নির্জ্জন কক্ষে গমন করিলে সভাসদ্‌গণ বলিতেন *He is gone to Jericho.*] **Go to Jericho with you, I wish he had been at Jericho**—গোল্লায় যাও, সে চুলোয় যাউক ইহাই আমি চাই।

jĕ-rid′ (-rēd), **—reed′** (-rēd), *n.* **1.** A javelin used by horsemen in Moslem communities ; বল্লম, বর্শা। **2.** A game in which it is used ; ঐরূপ বর্শাদ্বারা একপ্রকার খেলা।

jêrk, *n., v. t.* & *i.* **1.** A short sudden pull, thrust, push or twitch ; a jolt ; as, a *jerk* of the elbow ; হেঁচকা, ঝিঁকা ; ঝাঁকুনি। **2.** An involuntary spasmodic muscular movement ; খেঁচুনি। **3.** (*Pl.*) Spasmodic movements of limbs or face esp. from religious excitement ; আক্ষেপ বা অঙ্গগ্রহ, বিশেষতঃ ধর্ম্মোত্তেজনাজনিত অঙ্গগ্রহ, অঙ্গমোটন (প্রাঃ সাঃ)। **Jerk′-i-ly,** *adv.* **Jerk′-i-ness,** *n.* **Jerk′-y,** *adj.*

jêrk, *v. t.* & *i.* **1.** To pull, thrust or twist with a jerk ; as, to *jerk* a coat ; ঝিঁকা মারা, হেঁচকিয়া টানা, ঝাঁকুনি দেওয়া। **2.** To throw with a quick motion ; হেঁচকা মারিয়া ফেলা। ***Verb i.*** To move with a jerk ; হেঁচকিয়া চলা।

jêrk, *v. t.* To cut into long slices and dry in the sun ; as to *jerk* beef ; লম্বা লম্বা ফালি করিয়া কাটিয়া রৌদ্রে শুকান।

jêr′-kin, *n.* (*Hist.*) A jacket or a short coat of leather ; (ইতিহাস) এক প্রকার চামড়ার জামা।

jĕr′-ry (-ĭ), *n.* A low beer shop (also *jerry-shop*) ; নিম্নশ্রেণীর বীয়র মদ্যের দোকান।

jĕr′-ry (-ĭ), *adj.* Flimsy ; অন্তঃসার-শূন্য। **Jerry-build**—*v. t.* To build cheaply and unsubstantially as with cheap or insufficient materials; নিকৃষ্ট বা অপ্রচুর উপকরণ দ্বারা সস্তায় নির্ম্মাণ করা। *Jerry-builder, Jerry-buildings, ns. Jerry-built, adj.* **Jerry-shop, Tom and jerry shop**—যে মদের দোকানে কেবলমাত্র বীয়র মদ বিক্রীত হয়। **Jerry-work**—নিকৃষ্ট ধরের কাজ।

jêr′-sey (-zĭ), *n.* **1.** A woollen knitted close-fitting tunic, esp. as worn in athletic sports ; a similar garment worn as underdervest ; খেলোয়াড়দিগের একপ্রকার আঁটসাঁট পশমী জামা ; পশমী গঞ্জি। **2.** A knitted close-fitting jacket worn by women ; স্ত্রীলোকদিগের একপ্রকার আঁটসাঁট বুনা জামা। **3.** (*Cap.*) An island in the English Channel ; ব্রিটীশপ্রণালীমধ্যস্থ দ্বীপ-বিশেষ। **4.** A cow from the island of Jersey ; জারসি দ্বীপ হইতে সমানীত গাভী।

Jĕ-rü′-să-lĕm, *n.* The chief city of Palestine, intimately associated with the glory of the Jewish nation and with the life and death of Jesus Christ ; জেরুশেলেম নগরী। **Jerusalem pony**—An ass ; গর্দ্দভ।

jĕss, *n.* & *v. t.* A short strap of leather, silk, etc. round the legs of a hawk used in falconry ; বাজপক্ষীর পা বাঁধিবার জন্য চামড়ার বা পশমের রজ্জু। ***Verb t.*** To attach jesses to (a hawk) ; বাজ-পক্ষীর পা ঐরূপ রজ্জু দ্বারা বাঁধা।

jes′-sa-min(e) (-ă-mĭn), *n.* See JASMIN(E).

jĕs′-sē, *n.* (*Hist.*) A large branching candlestick used in churches ; (ইতিহাস) খৃষ্টীয়ভজনালয়ে ব্যবহৃত শাখাবিশিষ্ট বৃহৎ দীপপাদপ।

jĕs′-sie (-sĭ), *n.* Used only in the phrase **to give a man jessie**—To beat or thrash a man soundly ; উত্তম মধ্যম দেওয়া, মেরে পাট পাট করা।

jĕst, *n.* **1.** A jeering or satirical remark ; a piece of banter or railery ; a taunt ; a joke ; পরিহাস, পরিহাসোক্তি, বিনোদোক্তি (কেঃ), বিনোদভাষণ (ঐ) ; ফষ্টি ; ঠাট্টা ; বিদ্রূপ। **2.** Fun ; as, in *jest* ; কৌতুক, রহস্য, রঙ্গরস, রঙ্গব্যঙ্গ। **3.** An object of derision ; as, a standing *jest* ; অবজ্ঞার পাত্র, বিনোদাস্পদ (কেঃ), বিনোদপাত্র (ঐ), উপহাসপাত্র (ঐ), উপহাসাস্পদ (ঐ)। **Jest-book**—A book of jests ; হাসির বই। **In jest**—Not seriously ; রহস্যচ্ছলে, তামাসা করিয়া, পরিহাসচ্ছলে।

jĕst, *v. i.* **1.** To joke ; তামাসা করা। **2.** To scoff or jeer ; to utter gibes ; পরিহাস করা ; ব্যঙ্গ করা। **3.** To speak or act in a trifling manner ; ছেলেমি করা, ছেবলামি করা, ছেলেমি করিয়া বলা। **Jest′-ing-ly,** *adv.*

jĕst′-ēr, *n.* **1.** One who jests esp. a buffoon or merry-andrew ; পরিহাসরসিক, ভাঁড়, বিদূষক, বৈহাসিক। **2.** A joker ; ঠাট্টাবাজ, কৌতুককারী।

Jĕs′-ū-ĭt, *n.* A member of the famous religious order, The Society of Jesus, founded in 1533 by Ignatius Loyola ; ১৫৩৩ খৃঃ অব্দে Ignatius Loyola কর্ত্তৃক প্রতিষ্ঠিত খৃষ্টীয় সম্প্রদায় বিশেষের সভ্য। **2.** A crafty deceitful person ; a prevaricator ; "Yourself are more a *jesuit* than he, nay worse than any of that crew" ; শঠ লোক, ধূর্ত্ত লোক, প্রবঞ্চক লোক ; সত্যের অপলাপকারী। **—ism, —ry,** *ns.* **—it′-ic, —it′-i-cal,** *adjs.* **—it′-i-cal-ly,** *adv.* **—ize,** *v.t.* & *i.* **Jesuit's bark**—Peruvian bark ; সিন্‌কোনা বৃক্ষের বল্কল—যাহা হইতে কুইনাইন প্রস্তুত হয়। **Jesuits' nut**—পানি ফল।

jĕt′, *n.* & *adj.* **1.** A very compact velvet-black mineral of the nature of coal, susceptible of a good polish ; colour of this ; একপ্রকার কৃষ্ণবর্ণ কঠিন খনিজ পদার্থ ; [পালিস করিয়া নানারূপ অলঙ্কার প্রস্তুত হয়]; ঐ পদার্থের রং। **2.** Deep glossy black ; চক্‌ চকে কালো। ***Adj.*** **1.** Of the colour of jet ; made of jet ; উক্ত খনিজ পদার্থের বর্ণ-বিশিষ্ট ; উক্ত পদার্থ হইতে প্রস্তুত। **2.** Black as jet (also *jet-black*) ; ঘনকৃষ্ণ। **Jet-black**—Black as jet : deep black ; মিশ্‌মিশে কালো, চক্‌চকে কালো, কালো কিট কিটে ; ঘনকৃষ্ণ।

jĕt, *n.* **1.** A shooting forth or spouting ; a gush, as of water or gas from a pipe or of fire from an orifice etc. ; ফিন্‌কি দিয়া ছুটন ; ফিন্‌কি, ধারা (হিঃ কোঃ)। **2.** A spout or nozzle for emitting a jet of gas, water or the like ; জল, বাষ্প প্রভৃতির ধারা নির্গমের জন্য মুখনল।

jĕt, *v. t.* & *i.* To emit in a stream ; ফিন্‌কি দিয়া ছুটা। ***Verb i.*** To shoot forth ; to spurt ; as, water *jets* from the earth ; ফিন্‌কি দিয়া ছুটা ; উৎসারিত হওয়া, উৎক্ষিপ্ত হওয়া।

jĕt′-săm, *n.* Goods thrown overboard from a ship to lighten it, specifically such goods when washed ashore ; জাহাজ পাতলা করার জন্য উহা হইতে যে সকল মালপত্র জলে নিক্ষিপ্ত হয়, বিশেষতঃ ঐ সকল মালপত্র যখন তীরে আসিয়া লাগে।

jĕt′-tĭ-sŏn, *n.* & *v.t.* The throwing of goods overboard in order to lighten a ship in distress ; বিপদগ্রস্ত জাহাজ হাল্‌কা করার জন্য উহা হইতে মালপত্র নিক্ষেপ। ***Verb t.*** To throw (goods) overboard to lighten a ship in distress ; বিপদাপন্ন জাহাজ হাল্‌কা করার জন্য উহা হইতে (মালপত্র) জলে নিক্ষেপ করা।

jĕt′-tȳ, *n.* **1.** A structure, as a pier or mole of wood or stone running out to defend a harbour or coast ; a landing pier ; পোতাশ্রয় বা উপকূল রক্ষার্থ কাঠ বা প্রস্তরপুঞ্জ ; জাহাজ হইতে মালপত্র নামাইবার জন্য মঞ্চ বা মাচা, ঘাট।

jeu (*F.*), *n.* Play ; diversion ; ক্রীড়া ; আমোদ। ***Jeu-de-mots***—Play on words ; pun ; শব্দশ্লেষ কাকুযমক ; দ্ব্যর্থক বাক্য। ***Jeu d'esprit***—Witty or humorous (usually literary) trifle ; সরস উক্তি, নর্মোক্তি।

Jew (jü), *n.* **1.** A person of the Hebrew race ; ইহুদী। **2.** An extortionate usurer ; সুদখোর। **3.** A trader driving hard bargains ; যে ব্যক্তি দর কষাকষি করে। **Jew′-ess**, *n.* (*Fem.*) **Jew′-ish**, *adj.* **Jew's ear** — একপ্রকার আহারোপযোগী ছত্রাক। [খৃষ্টের বিশ্বাসঘাতক শিষ্য Judas Iscariotএর কর্ণের তুল্য আকৃতি হেতু এবং Elder গাছে—যাহাতে উক্ত জুডাস উদ্বন্ধনে প্রাণত্যাগ করে — সচরাচর জাত হয় বলিয়া এই নাম।] **Jew's eye** — অমূল্যধন। [পূর্ব্বে খৃষ্টান ভূপতিগণ ইহুদীদিগের চক্ষু, দন্ত, প্রভৃতি উৎপাটন করিয়া অর্থ আদায় করিত।] **Jew's-harp** — একপ্রকার বীণা, মোরচাঙ্গ, মুখবাদ্য (কেভিঃ)। **Jew's mallow**—ললিতা পাট (ওয়াট), বনপাট (ঐ)।

jew (jü), *v. t.* (*Colloq.*) To cheat or overreach ; ঠকান, চোখে ধূলা দেওয়া, মাথায় হাত বুলান।

jew′-ĕl (jü-), *n.* & *v. t.* **1.** A personal ornament in which precious stones form a principal part রত্নখচিত অলঙ্কার। **2.** A precious stone ; মূল্যবান প্রস্তর, মণি, পাথর, মাণিক্য, রত্ন, চারুশিলা (অঃ)। **3.** A person or thing of great worth or highly prized ; a precious thing ; শ্রেষ্ঠ ব্যক্তি, রত্ন [cf. জাতৌ জাতৌ যদুৎকৃষ্ট তদ্রত্নমভিধীয়তে] ; মূল্যবান বস্তু। ***Verb t.*** To adorn or furnish with jewels ; মণিমণ্ডিত করা, রত্নখচিত করা, মণিমাণিক্য দ্বারা ভূষিত করা। **—er, —ler**, *ns.* One who makes or deals in jewels ; মণিকার (বাৎস্যঃ), রত্নজীবী, রত্নব্যবসায়ী, জহুরী। **—ler-y, —ry**, *ns.* **1.** Art or trade of a jeweller ; মণিরত্নের ব্যবসায়, জহুরীগিরি। **2.** Jewels collectively ; রত্নরাজি, মণিরত্নাদি গহনাগাটি। **Jewel-case**—রত্নপেটিকা, রত্নমঞ্জুষা, মণিমঞ্জুষা। **Jewel-house**—রত্নশালা, জহরীখানা। **Jeweller's gold**—৭৫ ভাগ সোণা ও ২৫ ভাগ তামার মিশ্র। **The Jewel house**—টাওয়ার অব লণ্ডনের যে কক্ষে ইংলণ্ডেশ্বরের রাজভূষাসমূহ রক্ষিত হয়।

jew′-ĭng (jü-), *n.* Wallets at the base of the beak in some domestic pigeons ; কোন কোন জাতীয় গৃহকপোতের চঞ্চুনিম্নস্থ ক্ষুদ্র কোষ।

Jew -rȳ (jü-), *n.* **1.** The Jewish race or people ; ইহুদী জাতি। **2.** (*Hist.*) Jews' quarter in a town etc. ; (ইতিহাস) নগরের যে অংশে ইহুদীগণ বাস করে, ইহুদীপল্লী, ইহুদী মহল্লা।

Jĕz′-ĕ-bĕl, *n.* **1.** A wicked, impudent or abandoned woman ; দুষ্টস্বভাবা প্রগল্‌ভা নারী, পরিত্যক্তা নারী [ইজ্রায়েলের রাজা Ahabএর পত্নী Jezebelএর নাম হইতে]। **2.** A woman who paints her face ; যে স্ত্রীলোক মুখে রঙ্‌ মাখে।

Jib-boom and rigging.
a, bowsprit ; *b*, jib-boom ; *c*, flying jib-boom ; *d*, sprit-sail yard ; *e*, martingale ; *f*, flying jib ; *g*, jib ; *h*, fore topmast staysail ; *i*, fore staysail.

jĭb, *n.* A triangular sail borne in front of the foremast in a ship, so called from its shifting of itself ; জাহাজের ত্রিকোণ পাইল। **Jib-boom** — উত্তোলন-যন্ত্রের উদ্গত বাহু ; পোতাগ্র হইতে প্রলম্বিত দণ্ডের প্রান্ত হইতে উদ্গত দণ্ড। **The cut of his jib**—His personal appearance ; তাহার দেহের গঠন।

jib, *v. t.* & *i.* (*Naut.*) To shift as a sail or yard from one side of a ship to the other ; পাইল বা পাইলদণ্ড জাহাজের এক পার্শ্ব হইতে অপর পার্শ্বে ফিরান। ***Verb i.*** To swing round as a sail etc. as in tacking ; পাইল প্রভৃতি জাহাজের এক পার্শ্ব হইতে অপর পার্শ্বে ফিরান।

jib, *v. i.* **1.** (Of horse etc.) To refuse to go on ; to move backward or sidewise instead of going on ; (অশ্বাদির পক্ষে) অগ্রসর হইতে অনিচ্ছা প্রকাশ করা ; অগ্রসর না হইয়া এক পার্শ্বে পশ্চাদ্দিকে সরা। **2.** (*Fig.*) To refuse to proceed in some action ; (লক্ষণায়) কোন কার্য্যে অগ্রসর হইতে অনিচ্ছা প্রকাশ করা। **Jib′-ber,** *n.* **To jib at**—To show repugnance to (a course, person) ; কাহারো প্রতি বিরাগ প্রদর্শন করা।

jib′-door (-dör), *n.* **1.** A disguised door ; ছদ্মদ্বার, কুটদ্বার।

jif′-fў, *n.* (*Colloq.*) An instant ; a very short time ; as, I will go in a *jiffy* ; (চলিত ভাষায়) মুহূর্ত্ত ; ক্ষণকাল। **In a jiffy**—In a very short time ; মুহূর্ত্ত মধ্যে, ক্ষণকালমধ্যে, পলকে।

jig, *n., v. i.* & *t.* **1.** A lively dance ; একপ্রকার উল্লাসপূর্ণ নৃত্য, উল্লাসনৃত্য। **2.** The music for this ; উক্ত নৃত্যের সহিত সঙ্গত বাদ্য। ***Verb i.*** **1.** To dance a jig ; উল্লাসনৃত্য করা। **2.** To move with vibrations or jerks ; হেলিয়া দুলিয়া চলা। ***Verb t.*** **1.** To give a jerky motion to ; ঝাঁকুনি দেওয়া, ঝিঁকা মারা। **2.** (*Mining*) To separate coarser and finer portions of (ore) by shaking it under water in a box with a perforated bottom ; (খনির কাজ) জলের নীচে সচ্ছিদ্রতল বাক্সে ঝাঁকিয়া খনিজ বিমিশ্র ধাতুর স্থূল ও সূক্ষ্ম অংশ পৃথক করা।

jig′-ger (-ёr), *n.* **1.** (*Naut.*) A small tackle consisting of a double and a single block with rope ; (নৌ-বিদ্যা) জাহাজের ক্ষুদ্র রজ্জু বিশেষ। **2.** A small sail ; a small vessel with this ; ক্ষুদ্র পাইল ; ক্ষুদ্র পাইলবিশিষ্ট নাতিবৃহৎ অর্ণবপোত। **3.** A kind of potter's wheel ; একপ্রকার কুলালচক্র। **4.** A miner who jigs ore ; যে খনির মজুর জলের তলে সচ্ছিদ্রতল বাক্সে ঝাঁকিয়া খনিজবিমিশ্র ধাতুর স্থূল ও সূক্ষ্ম অংশ পৃথক করে। **5.** One who dances a jig ; উল্লাস নৃত্যকারী।

jig′-ger (-ёr), *n.* The chigoe ; পশ্চিম ভারতীয় দ্বীপপুঞ্জের দংশমক্ষিকা বিশেষ।

jig′-gle (-gl), *v. t.* To jerk or shake lightly ; ঝাঁকুনি দেওয়া।

ji-hâd′, jё–, *n.* **1.** Religious war of Mahommedans against infidels ; বিধর্ম্মিগণের বিরুদ্ধে মুসলমানদিগের ধর্ম্মাভিযান, মুসলমানজনদিগের ধর্ম্মযুদ্ধ। **2.** (*Fig.*) Crusade for, or against, a doctrine etc. ; (লক্ষণায়) কোন মতের বিরুদ্ধে অভিযান।

jill, *n.* A young woman ; a sweetheart ; যুবতী ; প্রণয়িনী।

jilt, *n.* & *v. t.* A woman who first encourages a lover and then rejects him (rarely, a man treating a woman thus) ; যে স্ত্রীলোক প্রণয়িগণকে পূর্ব্বে আশ্বাস দিয়া পশ্চাৎ প্রত্যাখ্যান করে, বিপ্রলম্ভিকা, সঙ্কেতভাঙ্গগামিনী (কেণ্ডি) (ক্বচিৎ—যে পুরুষ প্রথমতঃ কোন রমণীকে আশ্বাস দিয়া পরে বঞ্চনা করে।) ***Verb t.*** To encourage and then reject a lover ; পূর্ব্বে আশ্বাস দিয়া পশ্চাৎ প্রণয়ীকে প্রত্যাখ্যান করা, প্রেম বিষয়ে এক পুরুষকে আশ্বাস দিয়া পরে অন্য পুরুষকে গ্রহণ করা।

jimp, *adj.* (*Scot.*) **1.** Graceful ; delicate ; slender ; ললিত, সুকুমার, সুঠাম ; তন্বী (*fem.*) ; ক্ষীণ, কৃশাঙ্গ। **2.** Scanty ; স্বল্প, অপ্রচুর।

jin′-gle (jĭng-gl), *n., v. i.* & *t.* **1.** A rattling or clinking sound, as of little bells or pieces of metals ; শিঞ্জা, শিঞ্জিত, ঝনৎকার, রুণু রুণু, ঝন্‌ঝনা, নিক্বণ। **2.** Repetition of same or similar sounds in words, esp. if designed to catch the attention ; অনুপ্রাস। **3.** A covered two-wheeled car used in Ireland and Australia ; আয়র্লণ্ড ও অষ্ট্রেলিয়ায় ব্যবহৃত দ্বিচক্রবিশিষ্ট আবৃত শকট। ***Verb i.*** **1.** To clink ; to sound with a tinkling metallic sound ; ঝন্ ঝন্ করা, রণ্ রণিয়া উঠা ; রুণু রুণু শব্দে বাজা, ঝন্ ঝন্ রবে বাজিয়া উঠা, শিঞ্জিত হওয়া। **2.** (Of a writing etc.) To be full of alliterations, rhymes, etc. ; (রচনা সম্বন্ধে) অনুপ্রাস, ছন্দের ঝঙ্কার প্রভৃতির প্রাচুর্য্য থাকা। ***Verb t.*** To cause to make a tinkling sound ; রণ্ রণ্ করা, ঝন্ ঝন্ করা, রুণু রুণু করা, শিঞ্জিত করা।

jin′-gō (jĭng-), *n.* & *adj.* **1.** A word used in asseveration ; as, by *jingo* : by the living *jingo* ! ; তোমার দিব্যি। **2.** A person clamorous for war or a warlike or aggressive policy, esp. that of Lord Beaconsfield in 1878 ; a blustering patriot ; যে ব্যক্তি যুদ্ধ বিগ্রহের জন্য বা পররাজ্যে অধিকার বিস্তারের জন্য আন্দোলন করে, যুদ্ধবিগ্রহপ্রিয় ব্যক্তি ; তর্জ্জনগর্জ্জনকারী স্বদেশভক্ত। ***Adj.*** Pertaining to, or characterised by, jingoism ; রণান্দোলনপ্রিয়তা সম্বন্ধীয়, পররাজ্যগ্রাসী। **—ism,** *n.* The policy or practice of the jingoes ; রণান্দোলনপ্রিয়তা, পররাজ্যগ্রাসপ্রিয়তা। **—ist,** *n.* **—is′-tic,** *adj.* **By (the living) jingo**—A form of asseveration ; তোমার দিব্য !

jink (jĭngk), *n.* **1.** (*Rare*) Sharp metallic sound of a coin or the like striking against a hard substance ; (টাকার) ঝন্ ঝন্, কন্ কন্। **2.** (*Slang*) Coins ; (ইতর ভাষায়) টাকা পয়সা।

jink (jĭngk) *n.* (*Pl.*) Boisterous sport or merry-making, chiefly in the phrase *high jinks* (see HIGH); কোলাহলপূর্ণ ক্রীড়া, আনন্দ কোলাহল।

jin-nee' (-nē), *n.* (*Pl.* JINU.) (In Mahommedan demonology) A spirit, lower than angels, able to appear in human and animal forms and having supernatural power over man ; জীন।

jin-rick'-shȧ, –rik'-i-shȧ, *ns.* A small two-wheeled hooded vehicle drawn by one or more men, used in Japan or other Eastern countries ; জাপান দেশীয় মানুষ-চালিত লঘু শকট বিশেষ।

jiu-jit'-sū (jū-), **–jūt'-sū,** *ns.* The Japanese art of wrestling ; জাপানী কুস্তি, জিউজিৎসু।

jŏb, *n.* **1.** An occasional piece of work ; a work done for hire or profit ; ফুরান কাজ ; টুমটাম্ ঠিকা কাজ। **2.** A public transaction in which duty or public interest is sacrificed for private advantage or gain ; দৃষ্টতঃ সাধারণের উপকারের জন্য কিন্তু কার্য্যতঃ ব্যক্তিগত স্বার্থসাধনের উদ্দেশ্যে যে কার্য্য করা যায়। **3.** (*Colloq.*) A situation ; (চলিত-ভাষায়) অবস্থা। **4.** Anything one has to do ; "To drive them out is...a difficult *job*" ; কার্য্য, কাজ। **5.** An affair or event fortunate or otherwise ; ব্যাপার, ঘটনা। **Bad job**—যে বিষয়ের জন্য বৃথা পরিশ্রম করা হইয়াছে, পণ্ডশ্রম। **Good** or **bad job**—Good or bad state of affairs ; ভাল বা মন্দ অবস্থা। **Job lot**—লাটে কেনা জিনিষ ; লাটে বিক্রীর জিনিষ। **Job-master**—যে ব্যক্তি গাড়ী বা ঘোড়া ভাড়া দেয়। **Job-work**—ফুরান কাজ, ঠিকা কাজ। **A job price**—সস্তা দাম। **To do a good** or **bad job**—To do in a good or bad way ; ভাল বা খারাপ ভাবে করা। **To do a person's job**—To ruin or kill one ; কাহারও দফারফা করা। **To pay a person by the job**—To pay him for each separate piece of work done ; ঠিকা হিসাবে বেতন দেওয়া।

jŏb, *v. i.* & *t.* **1.** To do occasional pieces of work for hire ; to work by the piece ; ফুরান কাজ করা ; ঠিকা কাজ করা। **2.** To buy and sell stock ; কোম্পানীর কাগজের দালালী করা। **3.** To seek private gain under pretence of public service ; জনসাধারণের উপকারজনক কার্য্য করার ছলে স্বীয়স্বার্থ সাধন করা। ***Verb t.*** **1.** To let out in separate portions to different contractors or workmen ; কোন কাজের ভিন্ন ভিন্ন অংশ ভিন্ন ভিন্ন ঠিকাদার বা মজুরকে ঠিকা দেওয়া। **2.** To let or hire by the job or for a period of service ; ঠিকা হিসাবে ভাড়া দেওয়া। **3.** To buy and sell as a broker ; দালালী করা। **4.** To deal corruptly with (a matter) ; (কোন বিষয়ে) দোষজনকভাবে করা। **Job'-ber,** *n.* **1.** One who jobs; যে ব্যক্তি ঠিকা কাজ করে। **2.** One who lets out and hires carriages etc. by the job ; যে ব্যক্তি গাড়ী বা ঘোড়া ভাড়া দেয়। **3.** One who deals in or dabbles in stocks ; কোম্পানীর কাগজের দালাল। **Job'-ber-y,** *n.* Act of jobbing ; conduct of matters of public trust or duty for private gain ; official corruption ; ঠিকা কাজ করণ ; (সাধারণের কার্য্য) ব্যক্তিগত স্বার্থ সাধনের উদ্দেশ্যে করণ; আফিসের কর্ম্মচারিগণের অন্যায়াচার। **To job off**—To sell cheaply ; সস্তা দরে বিক্রয় করা।

Jŏb, *n.* The patriarch whose story forms the Book of Job in the Old Testament ; বাইবেলের প্রাচীন নিয়মে উক্ত Job নামক বৃদ্ধ ব্যক্তি। ইনি অসীম কষ্ট ও যন্ত্রণার মধ্যে ধৈর্য্য ও সহিষ্ণুতা অক্ষুণ্ণ রাখিয়াছিলেন। **Job's comfort**—Expressions of sympathy which go rather to irritate than to soothe ; যে সমবেদনা প্রকাশে যন্ত্রণা উপশম না হইয়া বরঞ্চ আরও বৃদ্ধি পায়। **Job's comforter**—One who under the guise of comforter aggravates distress ; যে ব্যক্তি সান্ত্বনা প্রদানের ছলে যন্ত্রণা বৃদ্ধি করে। **Job's news**—News of calamities ; বিপদের সংবাদ, অশুভ সংবাদ, কুসংবাদ। **Job's post** — A bearer of bad news ; অশুভসংবাদবাহক, কুসংবাদদাতা। **Job's tears**—গড় গড়া (যোঃ), গবেধুকা (খোরী)। **The patience of Job** — Very great patience ; জবের মত সহিষ্ণুতা।

jŏb, *v. t., i.* & *n.* **1.** To stab slightly ; খোঁচা মারা, ঈষৎ বিদ্ধ করা। **2.** To hurt as a horse with the bit ; লাগামের লোহা দ্বারা অশ্বকে আহত করা। ***Verb i.*** To thrust (*at*) ; খোঁচা মারা। ***Noun.*** A sudden stab or prick ; a jerk of the bit ; খোঁচা ; খলীনের ঝাঁকুনি।

jō-ba'-tion, *n.* A scolding, esp. a long one ; তিরস্কার, গঞ্জনা।

jŏb'-ber-nowl (-êr-nōl), *n.* A stupid person ; a blockhead ; জড়ভরত, গোবর গণেশ ; জড়বুদ্ধি ব্যক্তি।

jŏck'-ey (-ĭ), *n.* **1.** A professional rider of horses in races ; (ঘোড়-দৌড়ের) সওয়ার। **2.** A lad ; an under-strapper ; বালক ; তাঁবেদার। **–dom, –ship,** *ns.* **Jockey club**—ঘোড়দৌড়ের নিয়মাদি প্রণয়নের জন্য সমিতি, বিশেষতঃ New Market সহরের ঘোড়দৌড় সমিতি।

jŏck'-ey (-ĭ), *v. t.* & *i.* **1.** To cheat ; to outwit ; প্রতারণা করা ; ঠকান, বুদ্ধিবলে পরাস্ত করা। **2.** To treat with trickery ; চাতুরী খেলান। **3.** To ride (a horse) in a race as a jockey ; (ঘোড়দৌড়ে) ঘোড়া

চড়া, সওয়ার হওয়া। ***Verb i.*** To cheat; প্রতারণা করা। **To jockey a person into or out of doing etc.**—To cheat a person into or out of doing etc.; কোন লোককে প্রতারণাপূর্ব্বক কোন কার্য্যে প্রবৃত্ত করা বা কোন কার্য্য হইতে নিবৃত্ত করা।

jŏck′-ō, *n.* A chimpanze; একপ্রকার বনমানুষ।

jō-cōse′, *adj.* Humorous; playful; waggish; পরিহাসপূর্ণ, সপরিহাস, হাস্যকর; ব্যঙ্গব্যঞ্জক, মজাদার, বহুরঙ্গপূর্ণ; রসিকতাপূর্ণ, রংদার। **—cos′-i-ty,** *n.* **—ly,** *adv.* Humorously; পরিহাসপূর্ব্বক, ব্যঙ্গচ্ছলে। **—ness,** *n.* State of being jocose; হাস্যকরতা, পরিহাসশীলতা।

jŏc′-ū-lar (-lêr), *adj.* **1.** Merry; mirthful; waggish; প্রফুল্ল; রঙ্গব্যঙ্গপূর্ণ, হাস্যপরিহাসপূর্ণ, প্রমোদপরিহাসপূর্ণ, রংদার, মজাদার, কৌতুকপূর্ণ, বিনোদাত্মক; ফচ্‌কে। **2.** Humorous; as, *jocular* expressions; হাস্যোদ্দীপক, হাসিতামাসাপূর্ণ। **—lar′-i-ty,** *n.* Mirth; humour; হাসিতামাসা, প্রমোদ, পরিহাস, রঙ্গভঙ্গ, রঙ্গরস, রঙ্গব্যঙ্গ; রসিকতা, কৌতুক। **—ly,** *adv.*

jŏc′-ŭnd, *adj.* **1.** Merry; sprightly; আমোদপূর্ণ, সরস; উৎফুল্ল, প্রফুল্লচিত্ত। **2.** Pleasant; মনোরম, মনোমদ। **Jo-cun′-di-ty,** *n.* Gaiety; sportiveness; আমোদপ্রমোদ, আমোদআহ্লাদ; প্রমোদতারল্য, লীলা খেলা। **—ly,** *adv.*

Joe-Mill′-êr (jō-), *n.* A jest book; a stale jest or joke [From Joseph Miller, a commedian, who died 1738 and whose name was attached to a jest book after his death].; হাসির বই; নূতনত্বহীন পরিহাস, নীরস ঠাট্টা।

jō′-ey (-ĭ), *n.* A young kangaroo; a young animal; কেঙ্গেরু শাবক; শাবক।

jŏg, *v. t., i. & n.* **1.** To push or shake as with the elbow or hand; to jostle; to nudge as a person esp. to arouse attention; হাত বা কনুই দ্বারা ধাক্কা বা ঠেলা দেওয়া; ধাক্কা দিয়া চলা, ভিড় ঠেলিয়া চলা; মনোযোগ আকর্ষণের জন্য কনুই দ্বারা ধাক্কা দেওয়া। **2.** To stimulate; as, to *jog* one's memory; উত্তেজিত করা, চেতান। ***Verb i.*** **1.** To trudge; to move slowly, leisurely or monotonously, (often with *on, along*); হাঁটিয়া চলা; আস্তে আস্তে চলা, গুঁড়িগুঁড়ি করিয়া চলা, একঘেয়েভাবে চলা, গজেন্দ্রগমনে চলা। **2.** To depart; to go on one's way; as, we must be *jogging*; প্রস্থান করা; নিজের পথ ধরিয়া চলা। **3.** To get through the time; to proceed; as, to *jog* on somehow: matters *jog* along; সময় কাটান; অগ্রসর হওয়া। ***Noun.*** **1.** A shake; a slight push; a nudge; নাড়া, ঝাঁকুনি; ঠেলা; ধাক্কা। **2.** Slow walk or trot; আস্তে আস্তে চলন, মৃদু কদম। **Jog-jog**—With a jogging motion or pace; আস্তে আস্তে, গুঁড়িগুঁড়ি করিয়া। **Jog-trot**—*n. & adj.* A slow regular trot; a slow monotonous way or course of action; মৃদু কদম; মামুলি প্রথার অনুসরণ, গতানুগতিকতা। (*Adj.*) Jogging; (*fig.*) monotonous; humdrum; আন্দোলনশীল; (লক্ষণায়) একঘেয়ে, একসুরা; নীরস, নূতনত্বহীন। **To be jogging**—To depart; প্রস্থান করা। **To jog another's memory** or **another's elbow**—To remind another of a promise or a duty apparently forgotten; বিস্মৃত বিষয় স্মরণ করাইয়া দেওয়া। **To jog on**—To proceed lazily and heavily; মৃদুমন্দ গতিতে চলা, গজেন্দ্র গমনে অগ্রসর হওয়া।

jŏg′-gle (-l), *v. t., i. & n.* To shake slightly; to jostle; নাড়া; ধাক্কা দেওয়া, ঠেলা মারা। ***Verb i.*** To move slightly; to totter; অল্প অগ্রসর হওয়া; টলা। ***Noun.*** A slight shake; ঝাঁকুনি।

jŏg′-gle (-l), *n. & v. t.* (*Arch.*) A joint between two bodies constructed so by means of jogs or notches as to prevent their gliding past each other; a similar joint held in place by means of pieces of stone or metal introduced into it; a notch in one of these two pieces or a projection in the other for this purpose; খাঁজ ও দন্তাকৃতি উদ্গত অংশের মিলনে একপ্রকার জোড়,—

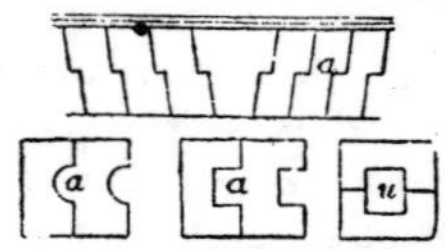

aa, Joggle joints: *n*, The last Joggle.

যাহাতে একটী খণ্ড অপর খণ্ড হইতে পিছলাইয়া যাইতে পারে না, কুলুপকাটা জোড়া; প্রস্তর বা ধাতুখণ্ডসমূহ ভিতরে প্রবিষ্ট করিয়া কঠিনীকৃত ঐরূপ জোড়া; ঐ জোড় দেওয়ার জন্য একখণ্ড কাঠ বা পাথরে খাঁজ ও অপর খণ্ডে দন্তাকৃতি উদ্গত অংশ। ***Verb t.*** To join by means of a joggle or joggles; ঐরূপ জোড়া দেওয়া।

Jō-hăn′-nine (-īn), *adj.* Pertaining to the apostle John or his writings; খৃষ্টশিষ্য John অথবা তদ্‌রচিত গ্রন্থাদি সম্পর্কীয়।

Jō-hăn′-nis-bêr-gêr (-ĭs-), *n.* A kind of white wine from Johannisberg, a village on the Rhine, Prussia; Rhine নদীর তীরবর্ত্তী Johannisberg নামক গ্রামে প্রস্তুত শ্বেতবর্ণ মদিরা।

John (jŏn), *n.* A masculine Christian name; কোন ব্যক্তির নাম। **John Bull**—The English nation; a typical English man [in Arbuthnot's satire *The History of John Bull*]; ইংরেজ জাতি; আদর্শ ইংরাজ। [Arbuthnot কৃত History of John Bull নামক ব্যঙ্গকাব্যের চরিত্র বিশেষের নাম হইতে গৃহীত।] **John-Bullism**—The typical English character ; আদর্শ ইংরেজ প্রকৃতি, ইঙ্গত্ব। **John Chinaman** — চীনদেশীয় লোক। **John Company** — ইষ্ট ইণ্ডিয়া কোম্পানী, কোম্পানী বাহাদুর। **John Doe and Richard Roe** — মোকদ্দমার বাদী ও প্রতিবাদীর কাল্পনিক নাম। **John O' Nokes and John o' Styles**— সাধারণ কৃষক। **John orderly**—নাচ তামাসায় সঙ্‌ প্রভৃতির প্রদর্শন শীঘ্র বন্ধ করার জন্য সঙ্কেত।

John'-i-ăn (-jŏn-), *adj.* & *n.* Of St. John's College, Cambridge; কেম্ব্রিজ নগরীর St. John's College সংক্রান্ত। ***Noun.*** A member or graduate of this college ; উক্ত কলেজের সভ্য বা উপাধিধারী।

John'-nȳ (jŏn-), *n.* **1.** A familiar diminutive of John ; John নামের ক্ষুদ্রতাবাচক রূপ। **2.** A fellow ; a chap ; a fashionable youngman of idle habits ; লোক ; ছোকরা ; ফুলবাবু। **Johnny cake**—ভুট্টার বা যবের ছাতুর পিঠা। **Johnny**

Johnny jump-up.

crapeau—ফরাসী। **Johnny jump-up** — একপ্রকার গুল্ম। **Johnny raw** — কাঁচালোক, আনাড়ী লোক ; নূতন লোক।

John-sō'-ni-ăn (jŏn-), *adj.* & *n.* **1.** Of, or pertaining to, Samuel Johnson, or his style ; বিখ্যাত সাহিত্যিক Samuel Johnson কিম্বা তদীয় রচনপদ্ধতি সম্বন্ধীয়। **2.** (*Fig.*) Pompous ; (লক্ষণায়) শব্দাড়ম্বরবহুল, বাগাড়ম্বরপূর্ণ। ***Noun.*** A follower of Dr. Johnson ; জনসনপন্থী। **–ism**, *n.* Johnsonian style or phrase; Johnsonএর ন্যায় রচনাপদ্ধতি বা বাক্যাংশ। **–son-ese'**, *n.* The language or style of Johnson ; an imitation of it ; Johnsonএর ভাষা বা রচনাপদ্ধতি ; Johnsonএর ভাষা বা রচনাপদ্ধতির অনুকরণ।

join (jōyn), *v. t., i.* & *n.* **1.** To put together ; to unite ; সংযুক্ত করা, সংযোগ করা, জোড় দেওয়া। **2.** (*Geom.*) To connect esp. by a straight line; (জ্যামিতি) সংযোগ করা। **3.** To unite in marriage, friendship, alliance, etc. ; বিবাহ, বন্ধুত্ব বা সন্ধি বন্ধনে বদ্ধ করা। **4.** To associate oneself with, as a club etc. ; যোগদান করা। **5.** To adjoin ; as, our farm *joins* her ; পাশাপাশি হওয়া, লাগালাগি হওয়া। **6.** To take or resume one's place in ; as, to *join* a regiment, company, etc. ; যোগ দেওয়া। **7.** To form, or construct, by uniting parts together ; as, to *join* a frame ; বিভিন্ন অংশ সংযোগপূর্ব্বক গঠন বা নির্ম্মাণ করা। ***Verb i.*** **1.** To come together ; to be united ; জোড়া লাগা, সংযোগ করা ; সংযুক্ত হওয়া, মিলিত হওয়া। **2.** To combine in some action or enterprise ; সম্মিলিত হওয়া। ***Noun.*** The line joining two points ; a point of junction ; সংযোগ-রেখা ; সংযোগ-বিন্দু। **To join battle**—To begin fighting ; যুদ্ধারম্ভ করা, যুদ্ধে প্রবৃত্ত হওয়া। **To join hands**—To clasp each other's hand ; to clasp one's hands together ; করপীড়ন করা, করমর্দ্দন করা ; যুক্তপাণি হওয়া, করজোড় করা, বদ্ধাঙ্গুলি হওয়া, যুক্তকর হওয়া। (*Fig.*) To combine in some action or enterprise, (followed by *with*) ; (লক্ষণায়) কোন কাযে যোগ দেওয়া, কোন দুঃসাহসিক কর্ম্মে যোগদান করা। **To join issue**—See under ISSUE. **To join one's standard**—To join one's forces with a view to fight for it ; যুদ্ধার্থে কাহারো পতাকাতে সম্মিলিত হওয়া। **To join the majority**—To die ; মরা, পরলোকগমন করা।

join'-dêr (jōyn-), *n.* (*Law*) A joining of parties as plaintiffs or defendants in a suit ; (আইন) কোন মোকদ্দমায় বাদী অথবা প্রতিবাদী উভয়পক্ষের সংযোগ।

join'-êr (jōyn-), *n.* **1.** One who joins ; সংযোজক। **2.** One who makes furniture, housefittings and other wood-work lighter than carpenter's; ছুতার মিস্ত্রী, তক্ষক।

join'-êr-ȳ (jōyn-), *n.* The work of a joiner ; ছুতার মিস্ত্রীর কাজ।

joint (jōynt), *n.* **1.** A place at which two things are joined together ; সন্ধিস্থল, সংযোগস্থল, গ্রন্থি (হিঃ কোঃ), সন্ধি (ঐ)। **2.** A structure by which two bones in animal body are fitted together ; গ্রন্থি, অস্থিগ্রন্থি, অস্থিসন্ধি, গাঁইট, জোড়। **3.** (*Bot.*) A knot ; the part from which leaves or branches grow ; পর্ব্ব ; গাঁইট। **4.** (*Geol.*) A fissure in a strata; (ভূবিদ্যা) স্তরমধ্যস্থ ফাটোল। **5.** One of the parts of which a body is composed ; খণ্ড। **6.** One of the parts of a carcass cut off by a butcher esp. as served at the table ; কসাই কর্ত্তৃক জবাই-করা জন্তুর কর্ত্তিত অংশ, বিশেষতঃ যাহা ভোজনকালে পরিবেষিত হয়। **7.** (*Slang*) A place of low resort for smoking etc. ; (ইতরভাষায়) আড্ডা। **Joint'-less,** *adj.* **Joint-stool**—ছুতার মিস্ত্রী কর্ত্তৃক সংযুক্ত অংশসমূহ রচিত ফলকাসন। **Out of joint** — Dislocated ; সন্ধিচ্যুত, গ্রন্থিচ্যুত। (*Fig.*) Out of order ; বিশৃঙ্খল। **To put one's nose out of joint**—To supplant, disconcert or frustrate him ; কাহাকে বিফলকাম করা, কাহার থোঁতা মুখ ভোঁতা করা।

joint (jo͞ynt), *adj.* **1.** Shared by two or more ; as, *joint* property ; held or done by two or more in conjunction, as an opinion, action, etc. ; অবিভক্ত, এজমালী ; যৌথ, অনেকস্বামিক। **2.** United ; combined ; as, *joint* force ; সমবেত ; সম্মিলিত, মিলিত। **3.** Having common interest in the same thing ; as, *joint* owners ; একই বস্তুতে অন্যের সহিত সমস্বার্থবিশিষ্ট, সহাধিকারী। **Joint′-ly,** *adv.* **Joint-property** — অবিভক্ত সম্পত্তি, এজমালী সম্পত্তি, সরিকানী সম্পত্তি, সাধারণ ধন (দায়:), সংসৃষ্টি ধন (মিতঃ)। **Joint-stock**—*n.* & *adj.* A capital divided into shares ; a common fund ; সম্মিলিত মূলধন ; সংযুক্ত মূলধন (হিঃ কোঃ), সাধারণ ভাণ্ডার। (*Adj*) Formed on the basis of a joint-stock, as a company, bank, etc. ; যৌথ। **During their joint lives**—When they are all alive ; তাহাদের জীবদ্দশায়।

joint (jo͞ynt), *v. t.* **1.** To connect by joins ; to prepare as boards etc. so as to fit together ; গ্রন্থিতে গ্রন্থিতে সংযোগ করা ; জোড়া লাগাইবার জন্য খাঁজ প্রভৃতি কাটিয়া কাষ্ঠফলকাদি প্রস্তুত করা। **2.** (*Rare*) To unite ; to combine ; (অপ্রঃ) সংযোগ করা ; সংযুক্ত করা। **3.** To provide with a joint or joints ; to articulate ; সন্ধিবিশিষ্ট করা ; সন্ধিবদ্ধ করা। **4.** To divide at a joint or into joints ; গ্রন্থিস্থলে বিভক্ত করা, গাঁইট ছাড়ান, সন্ধিভেদ করা, গ্রন্থিতে বিভক্ত করা, গ্রন্থিতে গ্রন্থিতে বিভক্ত করা। **5.** To fill up joints of (stone, brick-work, etc.) by mortar etc. ; (পাথর বা ইটের গাঁথুনির) জোড় চুণ সুর্কি প্রভৃতি দ্বারা পূর্ণ করা, জোড়পূর্ণ করা।

joint′-êr (jo͞ynt-), *n.* **1.** One that joints ; a plane for smoothing surfaces of pieces to be joined ; সংযোগকারী ; জোড়া দেওয়ার কাঠ পালিশ করার জন্য একপ্রকার রেঁদা। **2.** (*Masonry*) A bent piece of iron inserted to strengthen joints ; a tool for pointing joints ; (ইমারতের কাজ) জোড়া দৃঢ় করার জন্য অন্তঃপ্রবিষ্ট বক্র লৌহ খণ্ড ; বিলাতী মাটী বা মিশ্রিত চূণ সুর্কি প্রভৃতি দ্বারা জোড়া ভরিবার জন্য একপ্রকার যন্ত্র। **3.** A workman employed in jointing, esp. electric wire ; সন্ধিবন্ধনকারী, বিশেষতঃ বৈদ্যুতিক তারসংযোগকারী।

joint′-rĕss (jo͞ynt-), *n.* A widow who holds a jointure ; যে বিধবা পতিপ্রদত্ত সম্পত্তি আমরণ ভোগের অধিকার প্রাপ্ত হয়।

join′-tūre (jo͞yn-), *n.* & *v. t.* An estate joined to, or settled on, a woman at marriage, to be enjoyed after her husband's death, for her life ; স্বামীমরণোত্তর স্ত্রীর আমরণভোগার্থ সম্পত্তি, স্ত্রীধন (হিঃ কোঃ)। ***Verb t.*** To provide with a jointure, as a wife ; পতিকর্ত্তৃক তাহার মৃত্যুর পর আমরণ ভোগের জন্য ইচ্ছাপত্র দ্বারা পত্নীকে সম্পত্তি প্রদান করা।

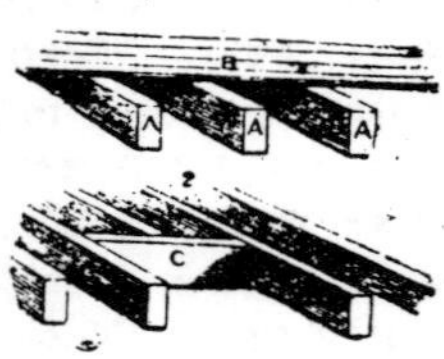

Joists.
1, *a a*, joists ; *b*, floor-boards ; 2, *c*, trimming-joist.

joist (jo͞yst), *n.* One of the parallel timbers stretched from wall to wall for floor boards to be nailed to ; কড়িকাঠ, লোহার কড়ি, আড়া, রুখা। **Joist′-ed** *adj.*

jōke, *n., v. i.* & *t.* **1.** Something said or done for exciting laughter ; jest ; witticism ; তামাসা, কৌতুক ; ঠাট্টা, পরিহাস, বিনোদোক্তি, বিনোদভাষণ ; রসিকতা। **2.** Something said or done in sport ; কৌতুকজনক কার্য্য বা উক্তি। **3.** A laughing stock ; an object of joking ; as, he is the *joke* of the town ; উপহাসাস্পদ, উপহাসের পাত্র ; পরিহাসের পাত্র। **4.** A ridiculous circumstance ; "The best *joke* of all was that I did not know my master's name" ; হাস্যকর অবস্থা। ***Verb i.*** To jest ; to make jokes ; পরিহাস করা ; কৌতুক করা, ঠাট্টা করা। ***Verb t.*** To make jokes upon ; to banter ; as, to *joke* a comrade ; কাহারো সহিত পরিহাস করা ; ঠাট্টা করা। **Jok′-ing-ly,** *adv.* **Jok′-y,** *adj.* **It is no joke**—এটা তামাসা নয়। **A practical joke**—See PRACTICAL.

jōk′-êr, *n.* **1.** One who jokes or jests ; পরিহাসকারী, ঠাট্টাবাজ, কৌতুককারী। **2.** (*Slang*) A fellow ; (ইতর ভাষায়) লোক। **3.** (*Cards*) An extra card sometimes added to the pack as in euchre, counting always as a trump and usually as the highest ; (তাস খেলায়) কোন প্রকার তাস খেলায় যে অতিরিক্ত তাস সর্ব্বদা রং বলিয়া গণ্য হয়।

jö′-kŭl(l), *n.* A snow-covered mountain in Iceland ; আইস্‌ল্যাণ্ড দ্বীপের তুষারাচ্ছাদিত পর্ব্বত।

jŏl′-li-fȳ, *v. t.* & *i.* To make or become jolly, আমোদপূর্ণ করা, আমোদপূর্ণ হওয়া। **—fi-ca′-tion,** *n.*

jŏl′-li-tȳ, *n.* Merry-making ; festivity ; হাসিখুসি, হাসিতামাসা, উল্লাস, রঙ্গরহস্য, উল্লাসবৃত্তি ; আমোদ-প্রমোদ।

jŏl′-lȳ, *adj.* & *adv.* **1.** Joyful ; আনন্দপূর্ণ। **2.** Jovial ; joyous ; merry ; সদানন্দ ; প্রফুল্ল, হৃষ্টচিত্ত ; আমুদিয়া। **3.** Slightly drunk ; ঈষৎ মাতাল। **4.** (*Colloq.*) Very pleasant ; excellent, as a person or thing ; (চলিত ভাষায়) অতি মনোরম ; চমৎকার। ***Adv.*** (*Colloq.*) Very ; as, he will be *jolly* savage ; (ইতর ভাষায়) ভারি, বেজায়, খুব। **—li-ly,** *adv.* Delightfully ; হর্ষের সহিত, সহর্ষে। **The jolly God** — Bacchus ; সুরাদেবতা। **The jolly Roger**—The pirate's flag ; জলদস্যুর পতাকা।

jŏl′-lȳ-boat (-bōt), *n.* A small clincker-built boat belonging

Jolly-boat.

to a ship, (also called *jolly*) ; জাহাজের ডিঙ্গি, জালি বোট, কেলিনৌকা।
jōlt, *v. t., i.* & *n.* **1.** To shake with sudden jerks, as in a carriage ; ঝাঁকুনি দেওয়া, আন্দোলিত করা। ***Verb i.*** (Of a carriage etc.) To move along with jerks as on a rough road ; ঝাঁকিয়া ঝাঁকিয়া চলা। ***Noun.*** A sudden shock or jerk ; ঝাঁকুনি, ধাক্কা, উদ্‌ঘাত (রঃ)। **Jolt′-y,** *adj.*
jōlt′-êr-head (-hĕd), *n.* A large clumsy head ; also, a dunce ; a blockhead ; বৃহৎ কদাকার মাথা ; মূর্খ; জড়মস্তিষ্ক।
Jō′-nah (-nȧ), *n.* **1.** (*Bible*) A Hebrew prophet ; জনৈক হিব্রু ভাববাদী। **2.** A person whose presence brings misfortune ; যে ব্যক্তির আগমনে দুর্ভাগ্য ও দুর্দ্দৈব ঘটে। **Jonah's gourd**—যে বস্তু অতিশয় দ্রুত বৃদ্ধি প্রাপ্ত হইয়া পরে অতি দ্রুত বিনষ্ট হয় [ভাববাদী Jonahকে আশ্রয় দেওয়ার জন্য এক প্রকাণ্ড কুষ্মাণ্ডলতা, এক রাত্রিতে অসম্ভবরূপে বৃদ্ধি প্রাপ্ত হইয়া অচিরেই বিশুষ্ক হইয়া গিয়াছিল]।
Jŏn′-ā-thăn, *n.* (Also, *Brother Jonathan*) The people of United States ; a typical citizen of United States, (From Jonathan Trumbull, governor of C nnecticut, U. S.] ; মার্কিণ যুক্তরাজ্যের অধিবাসিবৃন্দ ; মার্কিণ যুক্তরাজ্যের আদর্শ নাগরিক।
Jonesia Asoka—অশোক (বেলঃ)।
Jongleur, (*F.*), *n.* (*Hist.*) An itinerant ministrel ; (ইতিহাস) পর্য্যটনশীল চারণ।
jŏn′-quil, *n.* **1.** A plant of the genus Narcissus ; একপ্রকার গুল্ম। **2.** A light yellow colour like that of jonquil flowers ; উক্ত গুল্মের পুষ্পের মত মৃদু পীতবর্ণ। **Jonquil colour**—A pale yellow colour ; একপ্রকার মলিন পীতবর্ণ।
jŏr′-dăn, *n.* A chamber-pot ; শয়নকক্ষস্থ মূত্রভাণ্ড।
jor′-dăn-al′-mŏnds (-â-), *n.* Almonds imported from Malaya, (probably from *F. Jardin*-garden) ; মালয় দ্বীপ হইতে সমানীত বাদামসমূহ।
jō′-rŭm, *n.* (*Colloq.*) A large drinking vessel ; its contents, esp. punch ; (চলিত ভাষায়) বৃহৎ পানপাত্র ; উক্ত পানপাত্রের অভ্যন্তরস্থ মদিরা প্রভৃতি, বিশেষতঃ মদ্য, চিনি, দুগ্ধ ও লেবুর রসের মিশ্রণে প্রস্তুত পানীয় বিশেষ।
Jōs′-ĕph, *n.* **1.** A chaste person ; জিতেন্দ্রিয় ব্যক্তি, ব্রহ্মচর্য্যপরায়ণ ব্যক্তি। [যীশুখৃষ্টের জননী Joshepএর নাম হইতে গৃহীত।] **2.** (*l. c.*) A long outer garment worn by women in the 18th century ; অষ্টাদশ শতাব্দীতে ইংলণ্ডীয় মহিলাগণের পরিধেয় দীর্ঘ বহিঃপরিচ্ছদ বিশেষ।
jŏss, *n.* A Chinese idol ; চীনদেশীয় দেবমূর্ত্তি। **Joss-house**—A Chinese temple ; চীনদেশীয় দেবমন্দির। **Joss stick**—সুগন্ধি কাঠের গুড়া এবং মৃত্তিকা দ্বারা আবৃত কাঠি—যাহা চীনদেশে ধূপের পরিবর্ত্তে দেবমূর্ত্তির সম্মুখে পোড়ান হয়, চীনের ধূপ।
jŏs′-sêr, *n.* (*Slang*) A simpleton ; a fellow ; (ইতর ভাষায়) বোকা, হাবা ; লোক, বেটা।
jos′-tle (-l), *v. t., i.* & *n.* To push roughly or jarringly ; to elbow ; ধাক্কা দেওয়া ; ঠেলা মারা। ***Verb i.*** **1.** To hustle ; to push (against) ; to crowd ; ধাক্কা লাগা ; ঠেলা দেওয়া ; ভিড় করা। **2.** To struggle (*with* a person *for* a thing) ; ঠেলাঠেলি করা, ধাক্কাধাক্কি করা। ***Noun.*** An act of pushing or elbowing ; a collision ; encounter ; ঠেলা, ধাক্কা সংঘর্ষ ; হাতাহাতি।
jŏt, *n.* A little ; a whit (*usu. with a negative expressed or implied*) ; কণিকা, বিন্দুবিসর্গ, লেশ, তিল, অণুমাত্র।
jŏt, *v. t.* To write briefly or hastily, (usu. with *down*) ; টুকিয়া লওয়া।
jounce (jowns), *v. t.* & *i.* To bump ; to shake ; সজোরে ধাক্কা দেওয়া বা ধাক্কা খাওয়া ; ঝাঁকুনি খাওয়া, নাড়া, নড়া।
jour′-nal (jêr-), *n.* **1.** A diary ; an account of daily transactions and events ; a publication recording the transactions of a society ; দিনলিপি, রোজনামচা, দৈনন্দিনলিপি ; দৈনিকবহি ; কোন পরিষদের কার্য্যবিবরণী। **2.** (*Book-keeping*) A book in which the transactions of each day are entered in the order in which they occur ; যে হিসাব বহিতে প্রতি দিবসের ক্রয়বিক্রয়ের বিবরণ যথাক্রমে লিপিবদ্ধ হয়, জাবেদা বহি। **3.** A daily newspaper ; a periodical ; a magazine ; দৈনিক পত্রিকা, দিনিকা (বঃ দঃ নঃ) ; সাময়িক পত্র ; পত্রিকা, সঞ্চয়িকা (বঃ দঃ নঃ)। **4.** (*Naut.*) A log-book ; (নৌ-বিদ্যা) যে পুস্তকে চলনশীল জাহাজের গতিবেগ, বায়ুর বিভিন্ন অবস্থা এবং অপরাপর ঘটনা লিপিবদ্ধ হয়। **5.** (*Mach.*) That portion of a shaft, axle, etc. which turns in a bearing ; (যন্ত্র-বিজ্ঞান) গাড়ীর বোম, চাকার আল প্রভৃতির যে অংশ যন্ত্রের ঘর্ষণসহ অংশের ভিতর ঘূরিয়া থাকে। **—ese,** *n.* The style of language supposed to be characteristic of public journals ; সংবাদপত্রের ভাষা। **—ism,** *n.* The collection and periodical publication of current news ; the business of managing, editing or writing for journals or newspapers ; also journals or newspapers collectively ; সংবাদপত্রসম্পাদন ; সংবাদপত্রপরিচালন, সম্পাদকতা ; সংবাদপত্রসমূহ, সাময়িক

পত্রসমূহ। **–ist,** *n.* An editorial or other professional writer for a journal ; সংবাদপত্রের লেখক, পত্রিকালেখক, সংবাদপত্র সম্পাদক। **–is'-tic,** *adj.* Relating to journalism ; সংবাদপত্র-পরিচালন সম্পর্কীয়, সংবাদপত্র সম্বন্ধীয়। **–ize,** *v. t.* & *i.* **1.** (*Book-keeping*) To enter or record in a journal ; জাবেদা বহিতে তোলা। **2.** To enter or record in a private journal ; দৈনিক বহিতে তোলা। (*Verb i.*) **1.** To keep a private journal ; দৈনিকবহি রাখা। **2.** To do the work of a journalist ; সংবাদপত্র সম্পাদকের কার্য্য করা। **The Journals**—পার্লেমেণ্ট মহাসভার দৈনিক কার্য্যবিবরণী।

jour'-ney (jêr-nĭ), *n.* & *v. i.* **1.** The distance travelled in a specified time ; as, a day's *journey* ; কোন নির্দ্দিষ্ট সময়ে যে পরিমাণ স্থান অতিক্রম করা যায়, পথ। **2.** Travelling from one place to another ; tour ; ভ্রমণ ; পর্য্যটন, দেশভ্রমণ। **3.** (*Fig.*) The passage through life ; জীবন-যাত্রা। ***Verb i.*** To make a journey ; to travel from one place to another ; ভ্রমণ করা ; পর্য্যটন করা। **Journey** or **journey-clock** — (জ্যোতির্বিজ্ঞান) মানমন্দিরস্থ উপঘটিকা যন্ত্র। **Journey-man**—ঠিকা কারিগর ; (লক্ষণায়) বেতনের চাকর, ঠিকা লোক। **Journey work**—ঠিকা কারিগরের কাজ, ঠিকা লোকের কাজ।

joust (jôst), **jŭst,** *v. i.* & *n.* (Of knights etc.) To engage in a combat on horseback with lances ; বর্শাহস্তে অশ্বপৃষ্ঠে দ্বন্দ্বযুদ্ধে প্রবৃত্ত হওয়া। ***Noun.*** Such a combat ; অশ্বারোহী বীরযুগলের মধ্যে বর্শাদ্বারা যুদ্ধ।

Jōve, *n.* Jupiter ; প্রাচীন রোমানদিগের দেবরাজ। **By Jove**—A form of asseveration ; ঈশ্বরের নামে।

jō'-vi-ăl, *adj.* Gay ; merry ; joyous ; convivial ; প্রফুল্ল, উৎফুল্ল ; সোল্লাস, সদানন্দ ; আমুদিয়া ; আমোদজনক। **–al'-i-ty,** *n.* **–ly,** *adv.*

Jō'-vi-ăn, *adj.* **1.** Of, pertaining to, or like Jove or Jupiter ; দেবরাজ Jove সম্বন্ধীয়। **2.** Relating to the planet Jupiter ; বৃহস্পতিগ্রহ-সম্বন্ধীয়।

jowl, *n.* **1.** A jaw ; a jaw-bone ; চোয়াল, হনু ; হন্বস্থি, চোয়ালের হাড়। **2.** The cheek ; গণ্ড, গাল। **3.** The dewlap of cattle ; the crop of a bird ; গবাদির গলকম্বল ; পাখীর গলার থলি। **4.** The head and adjacent parts of a salmon or other fish ; স্যামন বা অন্যান্য মাছের মুড়া। **Cheek by jowl**—See under CHEEK.

joy, *n.* **1.** Vivid emotion of pleasure ; gladness ; আনন্দ, হর্ষ, সন্তোষ, উল্লাস, প্রমোদ, পরিতোষ ; আহ্লাদ, সুখ। **2.** That which causes happiness or delight ; "A thing of beauty is a *joy* forever" ; আনন্দজনক বিষয়। **Joy'-ful,** *adj.* Full of joy ; causing joy ; very glad ; আনন্দপূর্ণ, সহর্ষ, আনন্দযুক্ত, হর্ষান্বিত, হৃষ্ট, আনন্দিত, প্রফুল্ল, হর্ষাত্মক, আনন্দময়, সানন্দ ; আনন্দজনক, আনন্দপ্রদ, হর্ষপ্রদ ; অতিশয় আনন্দিত, আনন্দপ্লুত। **Joy'-ful ly, Joy'-less-ly, Joy'-ous-ly,** *advs.* **Joy'-ful-ness, Joy'-less-ness, Joy'-ous-ness,** *ns.* **Joy'-less,** *adj.* Not having or causing joy ; নিরানন্দ, ম্লান, বিষণ্ণ। **Joy'-ous,** *adj.* Gay ; merry ; affording joy ; সানন্দ ; সহর্ষ ; আনন্দজনক। **Joy-bells** — উৎসব উপলক্ষে বাদিত ঘণ্টাসমূহ। **Outburst of joy**—আনন্দোচ্ছ্বাস।

joy, *v. i.* & *t.* (*Chiefly poet.*) To rejoice ; আনন্দ করা। ***Verb t.*** gladden ; সুখী করা, আহ্লাদিত করা।

ju'-bi-lāte (jōō-), *v. i.* To exult ; to rejoice ; to make demonstrations of joy ; উল্লসিত হওয়া ; হর্ষোৎফুল্ল হওয়া ; আনন্দ প্রকাশ করা। **–lance, –la'-tion,** *ns.* **–lant,** *adj.* Shouting with joy ; exulting ; আনন্দধ্বনিকারী, জয়শব্দোচ্চারী, জয়শব্দকারী ; উল্লাসপূর্ণ, হর্ষোৎফুল্ল, আমোদমত্ত। **–lant-ly,** *adv.*

jū-bi-la'-tē, *n.* **1.** The hundredth psalm—so called from the opening word in the Latin version ; শততম ধর্ম্ম সংগীত। **2.** An outburst of joy or triumph ; আনন্দোচ্ছ্বাস, বিজয়োল্লাস।

ju'-bi-lee (jōō-bĭ-lē), *n.* **1.** (*Jewish Hist.*) The year of emancipation and restoration kept every 50 years according to *Lev.* xxv ; (ইহুদীদিগের ইতিহাস) ইহুদীদিগের দাসত্ব-মোচন ও স্বদেশপ্রত্যাগমনের স্মৃতিউৎসব—যাহা প্রতি পঞ্চাশত্তম বৎসরে অনুষ্ঠিত হয়। **2.** (*R. C. C.*) A year of remission of the penal consequences of sin proclaimed formerly at intervals but now at any time ; (রোমান ক্যাথলিক ধর্ম্মসংঘ) পোপকর্তৃক বিঘোষিত পাপ-পরিণাম মুক্তির বৎসর। **3.** The fiftieth anniversary ; পঞ্চাশত্তম সাম্বৎসরিক উৎসব। **4.** Any season or occasion of rejoicing ; আনন্দোৎসবকাল। **5.** Exhultant joy ; আনন্দোল্লাস, আনন্দোচ্ছ্বাস। **Diamond jubilee**—Sixtieth year of the reign of Queen Victoria ; Queen Victoriaর রাজত্বের ষষ্টিতম সাম্বৎসরিক উৎসব। **Silver jubilee**—পঞ্চবিংশতিতম সাম্বৎসরিক উৎসব।

Jū'-dā-ism, *n.* The Jewish religious system or policy ; ইহুদীদিগের ধর্ম্ম নীতি। **–ist,** *n.* A follower of Judaism ; ইহুদীধর্ম্মাবলম্বী। **–ize,** *v. i.* & *t.* To follow Jewish customs or rites ; ইহুদীদিগের আচার-পদ্ধতি অনুসরণ করা। (*Verb t.*) To make Jewish ; ইহুদীভাবাপন্ন করা।

jū'-dās, *n.* **1.** (*Cap.*) The disciple who betrayed Christ ; যীশুখৃষ্টের বিশ্বাসঘাতক শিষ্য জুডাস। **2.** Hence (*fig.*) an infamous traitor ; (অতএব লক্ষণায়) জঘন্য বিশ্বাসঘাতক। **3.** A peephole, as in a door or wall ; দরজা বা প্রাচীরে উঁকি দেওয়ার জন্য ছিদ্র। **Judas colour (ed)** — (Of beard etc.) Red ; (শ্মশ্রু প্রভৃতি সম্পর্কে) রক্তবর্ণ, লাল। **Judas kiss**—কপট-চুম্বন। [জুডাস যীশুকে চুম্বন করিয়া শত্রুদিগের নিকট তাঁহাকে পরিচিত করে।]

Judenhetze, *n.* Persecution of the Jews ; ইহুদীদিগের উপর নির্য্যাতন।

judge (jŭj), *n.* A public officer invested with authority to determine litigated questions ; বিচারক, বিচারকর্ত্তা, জজ, প্রাড্‌বিবাক, ন্যায়াধীশ, ধর্ম্মাধ্যক্ষ, নির্ণেতা (হিঃ কোঃ), নির্ণায়ক (ঐ)। **2.** (Of God) Supreme arbiter ; (ঈশ্বর সম্বন্ধে) বিধাতা। **3.** (*Jewish Hist.*) One of the magistrates with civil and military powers, governing Israel after Joshua's death ; (ইহুদী ইতিহাস) Joshuaর মৃত্যুর পর সামরিক এবং পৌরবর্গঘটিত ক্ষমতাসম্পন্ন যে শাসনকর্ত্তৃগণ এস্রায়েল রাজ্য শাসন করিতেন—তাহাদের অন্যতম। **4.** A person who decides a question ; an umpire ; যে ব্যক্তি কোন প্রশ্ন মীমাংসা করে ; মধ্যস্থ, সালীশ। **5.** A connoiseur ; a critic ; as, I am no *judge* of that ; গুণদোষজ্ঞ, রসজ্ঞ, দোষ-গুণ-বিচারক, সমজদার ; সমালোচক। **Judge'-ship,** *n.*

judge (jŭj), *v. t.* & *i.* **1.** To pass a sentence or judgment upon ; to try ; as, to *judge* a person or case ; to determine or decide as a question ; দণ্ডাজ্ঞা প্রচার করা, রায় দেওয়া ; বিচার করা ; নির্ণয় করা, নিষ্পত্তি করা ; মীমাংসা করা। **2.** To decide judicially ; to decree or order ; as, he *judged* that the estate belonged to the plaintiff ; বিচার করা ; বিধান করা, আদেশ দেওয়া। **3.** To criticize ; to censure ; "*Judge* not that ye be not *judged*" ; সমালোচনা করা, দোষগুণ বিচার করা ; তিরস্কার করা। **4.** To estimate, as a person by his deed etc. ; to conclude ; to think ; to consider ; as, to *judge* a person or thing to be etc. ; নির্দ্ধারণ বা অনুমান করা ; সিদ্ধান্ত করা ; ভাবা ; বিবেচনা করা। ***Verb i.*** **1.** To act as a judge ; to pronounce judgment ; as, he was present on the bench but could not *judge* in the case ; বিচারকের কার্য্য করা ; বিচারাজ্ঞা প্রদান করা। **2.** To arbitrate ; সালিশী করা, মধ্যস্থ করা। **3.** To criticize ; "Forbear to *judge*, for we are sinners all" ; সমালোচনা করা, দোষগুণের বিচার করা। **4.** To form an opinion or judgment, (often with *of*) ; মত গঠন করা, সিদ্ধান্তে উপনীত হওয়া।

judg'-măt-ic, —i-căl (jŭj-), *adjs.* (*Colloq.*) Judicious ; discerning ; (চলিত-ভাষায়) বিচারবুদ্ধিসম্পন্ন; সূক্ষ্মদর্শী। **—i-cal-ly,** *adv.*

judg'-mĕnt (jŭj-), **judge'-mĕnt** (jŭj-), *ns.* **1.** The sentence of a court of justice ; রায়, বিচারনিষ্পত্তি, হুকুম, জয়পত্র (শুক্রঃ বিনয়)। **2.** Misfortune or calamity viewed as a providential punishment ; as, it is a *judgment* on you for getting up late ; দুর্দ্দৈব, দুর্ঘটনা, দৈবদুর্ব্বিপাক। **3.** Opinion ; decision ; "She, in my *judgment*, was as fair as you" ; মত ; মীমাংসা, নির্ণয় (শুক্রঃ বিনয়)। **4.** (*Log.*) A proposition ; (তর্ক-বিজ্ঞান) বাক্য, অবগতি (সাঃ পঃ), বাক্যার্থ (হিঃ কোঃ)। **5.** Criticism ; সমালোচনা। **6.** The faculty of judging rightly or justly ; discernment ; good sense ; দোষগুণবিচারক্ষমতা, বিচারশক্তি, বিবেচনাশক্তি, নির্ণয় (হিঃ কোঃ), গুণদোষজ্ঞতা ; সূক্ষ্মবিচার ; বিবেচনা, অবধারণ (শুক্রঃ বিনয়)। **Judgment creditor**—ডিক্রীপ্রাপ্ত মহাজন, ডিক্রীদার। **Judgment-day** —শেষবিচার দিন (জিঃ), অন্তিমবিচার দিবস, রোজ কেয়ামৎ (মুসলমান ধর্ম্মশাস্ত্র)। [খৃষ্টীয় ও মুসলমান শাস্ত্রানুসারে যে দিবস ঈশ্বর সমস্ত লোকের বিচার করিয়া—পুণ্যবানদিগের জন্য অনন্ত স্বর্গ ও পাপীদিগের চিরনিরয় বাসের ব্যবস্থা করিবেন।] **Judgment debt**—যে দেনা আদায়ের জন্য আদালতের ডিক্রী পাওয়া গিয়াছে। **Judgment-hall**—ন্যায়সভা (কেণ্ডিঃ), ধর্ম্মসভা (ঐ)। **Judgment-seat**—The seat of a judge ; a court or tribunal ; বিচারাসন, ধর্ম্মাসন (মঃ সং), ন্যায়াসন ; ধর্ম্মাধিকরণ। **Judgment by default**—আদালতে উপস্থিত না হওয়ার দরুণ কোন লোকের প্রতিকূলে যে রায় দেওয়া হয়। **The last judgment** — The judgment by God at the end of the world ; যুগপ্রলয়ের পর ঈশ্বর কর্ত্তৃক মানবাত্মার বিচার, অন্তিমবিচার, কেয়ামৎ।

jü'-di-că-türe, *n.* **1.** Administration of justice ; বিচার-বিধান, ব্যবহার, ন্যায়দর্শনাধিকার, ন্যায়াধিকার, ধর্ম্মাধিকার। **2.** Judges collectively ; a court of justice ; বিচারকবর্গ, ন্যায়াধীশ ; বিচারালয়, ধর্ম্মাধিকরণ। **3.** The authority or jurisdiction of a judge or court ; a judge's term of office ; বিচারকের ক্ষমতা বা এলেকা ; বিচারকের কার্য্যকাল।

jü-di'-cial (-shăl), *adj.* **1.** Pertaining, or appropriate, to courts of justice or to a judge thereof ; ordered or enforced by a court, as a sale etc. ; বিচারালয়সম্বন্ধীয়, বিচারক-সম্বন্ধীয়, বিচারকসমুচিত, ব্যবহারিক, ব্যবহার বিষয়ক, ন্যায়সম্বন্ধী (হিঃ কোঃ) ; আদালত কর্ত্তৃক আদিষ্ট। **2.** Having the function of judgment ; as, a *judicial* assembly ; বিচারক্ষমতা-সম্পন্ন। **3.** Impartial ; নিরপেক্ষ, অপক্ষপাতদুষ্ট। **—ly,** *adv.* **Judicial murder**—Legal but unjust death sentence; যে মৃত্যুদণ্ড বিধিসঙ্গত হইলেও ন্যায়তঃ সমর্থনীয় নহে। **Judicial separation**—Separation of husband and wife by a judicial sentence ; আদালতের আদেশে পতিপত্নীর স্বতন্ত্রভাবে অবস্থান।

jŭ-di′-ci-ā-ry (-shī-), *adj.* & *n.* (*Obs.*) Of, or pertaining to, courts of justice or a judge thereof ; (অপ্রঃ) বিচারালয়-সম্বন্ধীয়, বিচারক-সম্বন্ধীয়। ***Noun.*** The system of courts of justice ; judges collectively ; বিচারালয়ের ব্যবস্থা ; বিচারকবর্গ।

jŭ-dī′-cious (-shŭs), *adj.* Sensible ; prudent ; wise ; sagacious ; সদ্বিবেচক, প্রাজ্ঞ ; উচিতজ্ঞ ; বিজ্ঞ, জ্ঞানী ; তীক্ষ্ণবুদ্ধিসম্পন্ন। **—ly,** *adv.* **—ness,** *n.* The quality of being judicious ; বিবেকিতা।

jŭg, *v. t.* **1.** To boil or stew, as a hare etc. in a jug or jar (*usu.* in *p. p.*) ; হাতলওয়ালা পেট-মোটা ও গলা সরু পাত্রে সিদ্ধ করা। **2.** (*Archaic*) To imprison ; (অপ্রঃ) জেলে পুরা।

jŭg, *n.* **1.** A deep vessel with a handle on one side and often with a spout ; a pitcher ; ঘট, ঘটী, কমণ্ডলু ; কুঁজা, ঘড়া। **2.** (*Slang*) A prison (also *stone-jug*) ; (ইতর ভাষায়) জেল, শ্রীঘর, হরিণবাড়ী, শ্বশুরবাড়ী। **Jug′-ful,** *n.*

jŭg, *v. i.* & *n.* (Of a nightingale etc.) To utter a sound represented by this word ; জগ্ জগ্ ধ্বনি করা। ***Noun.*** This sound ; জগ্ জগ্ ধ্বনি।

ju′-gāte, *adj.* (*Bot.*) Having leaflets in pairs ; (উদ্ভিদ্-বিদ্যা) যুগ্মপত্রসমন্বিত।

jŭg′-gins (-īns), *n.* (*Slang*) A simpleton ; (ইতরভাষায়) হাবা, গোবরগণেশ।

jŭg′-gle (-l), *v. t., i.* & *n.* **1.** To deceive by trick or artifice ; to cheat (*out of* something) ; ভেল্কী লাগান, ধাঁধা লাগান ; প্রতারণা করা, ধোঁকা দেওয়া। **2.** To perform juggling tricks with ; as, to *juggle* knives ; কোন কিছু দ্বারা ভোজবাজী দেখান। ***Verb i.*** **1.** To play conjuring tricks ; ভোজবাজী দেখান, ইন্দ্রজাল প্রদর্শন করা, ভানুমতীর খেলা দেখান। **2.** To practise artifice or imposture (*with*) ; ধোঁকা দেওয়া, চালাকি খেলা। ***Noun.*** **1.** A trick of magic, sleight of hand, etc. ; ভোজবাজী, ভোজবিদ্যা, ভানুমতীর বাজী, ভানুমতীর খেলা ; হাতের চালাকি, হস্তকৌশল। **2.** An act of deception ; fraud ; ছলনা, ভেল্কী, প্রতারণা ; জুয়াচুরি, ফেরেব, ছল। **To juggle with**—To deceive (a person) ; to misrepresent (facts) ; ধোঁকা দেওয়া, ধাঁধা লাগান, চোখে ধূলি দেওয়া ; অসত্য বর্ণনা করা।

jŭg′-gler (-lêr), *n.* **1.** One who practises or exhibits tricks by sleight of hand ; a conjurer ; ঐন্দ্রজালিক ; বাজীকর, মায়াজীবী। **2.** An impostor ; জুয়াচোর, ভণ্ড, প্রতারক। **—y,** *n.* **1.** The art or feats of a juggler ; sleight of hand ; ভোজবাজী, ভোজবিদ্যা, ইন্দ্রজাল, ভানুমতীর খেলা ; হস্তলাঘব, হাতের সাফাই। **2.** Imposture ; জুয়াচুরি, শাঠ্য, ফেরেব, ছল।

jŭ′-gŭ-lar (-lêr), *adj.* & *n.* **1.** (*Anat.*) Of, or relating to, the neck or throat ; (শারীর-সংস্থান-বিদ্যা) গ্রীবাদেশীয়, গ্রৈব, কণ্ঠ-সম্বন্ধীয়। **2.** (Of a fish) Having the ventral fins in front of the pectoral ; (মৎস্য-সম্পর্কে) পেটের পাখ্না বুকের পাখ্নার সম্মুখে স্থিত। ***Noun.*** A jugular vein ; মাতৃকাশিরা। **Jugular veins**—গ্রীবাদেশীয় বৃহৎ শিরা (হঃ চঃ), মাতৃকাশিরা (ঐ)।

jŭ′-gŭ-lāte, *v. t.* **1.** To kill or slay ; বিনাশ করা, বধ করা। **2.** (*Fig.*) To stop the course of (a disease) by a powerful remedy etc. ; (লক্ষণায়) শক্তিশালী ঔষধ প্রভৃতি দ্বারা (রোগের) বেগরোধ করা।

jŭ′-gŭ-lŭm, *n.* The lower throat of a bird ; পক্ষীর নিম্নতর কণ্ঠ।

juice (jūs), *n.* **1.** The liquid part of vegetables or fruits ; রস, রসদ্রব, নির্যাস, সুধা। **2.** The fluid content of animal body or substance ; (*pl.*) the bodily humours ; জীবদেহস্থ তরল পদার্থ, রস ; (বহুবচনে) বায়ু, পিত্ত, শ্লেষ্মা, প্রভৃতি। **3.** (*Fig.*) The essence or spirit of anything ; (লক্ষণায়) সার। **Juice′-less,** *adj.* **Juc′-i-ness,** *n.* **Juic′-y,** *adj.* **1.** Abounding with juice ; succulent ; রসাল ; সরস, টুস্‌টুসে (*colloq.*)। **2.** (*Colloq.*) Interesting ; "His *juicy* way of teaching" ; (চলিত ভাষায়) সরস। **3.** Wet, as a weather ; আর্দ্র, ভিজা, সিক্ত। **4.** (*Art., Slang*) Having a rich colouring suggestive of a moist surface ; "*Juicy* landscape" ; (ললিত-কলার ইতর ভাষায়) আর্দ্রভূপৃষ্ঠের দীপ্ত বর্ণব্যঞ্জনাসম্পন্ন।

ju-ju, *n.* **1.** A charm or fetish of the west African tribes ; পশ্চিম আফ্রিকার অসভ্যজাতিদিগের যাদু বা পিশাচাশ্রিত বৃক্ষ, পাষাণ, প্রভৃতি, মন্ত্রপূত দ্রব্য, মাদুলী, প্রভৃতি যাদুদ্রব্য। **2.** The ban or interdiction effected by this ; ঐরূপ যাদুদ্রব্যের সাহায্যে যে বাধা বা প্রতিষেধ দেওয়া হয়।

jŭ′-jūbe, *n.* **1.** A genus of spiny shrubs or small trees ; the fruit of this ; কুল গাছ ; কুল ফল, বদর, বদরিকা, বদরী ফল। **2.** A lozenge made of gelatine and flavoured with, or in imitation of, jujubes ; বদরী ফলের আকার বা উক্ত ফলদ্বারা সুরভীকৃত চিনির মিঠাই।

jŭ′-jŭt-sŭ, *n.* See JIUJUTSU.

jŭ′-lĕp, *adj.* **1.** A refreshing drink, esp. a sweet one used as a vehicle for a medicine ; ক্লান্তিনিবারক পানীয়, ঔষধের অনুপান স্বরূপ ব্যবহৃত মিষ্ট পানীয়। **2.** Medicated drink, as stimulant etc. ; ঔষধমিশ্রিত উত্তেজক পানীয়।

Jūl′-i-ăn (l-), *adj.* Relating to, or derived from, Julius Caesar ; জুলিয়াস সীজরসম্বন্ধীয়, জুলিয়াস্ সীজর হইতে সমুদ্ভূত। **Julian calendar**—জুলিয়াস সীজর দ্বারা প্রবর্তিত পঞ্জিকা।

julienne (*F.*), *n.* A soup of vegetables cooked in meat-broth; মাংসের সুরুয়াতে রন্ধিত শাকসব্জীর ঝোল।

Jū-lȳ', *n.* The seventh month of the year called after Julius Caesar, who was born in this month; ইংরাজী বৎসরের সপ্তম মাস।

jŭm'-ble (bl), *v. i.* & *t.* To mix confusedly; to move in a confused or agitated way; এলোমেলোভাবে মিশান; ত্রস্ত ও ব্যস্তসমস্তভাবে চলা। ***Verb t.*** To mix *up* in confusion; to confuse; এলোমেলোভাবে মিশান; এলেমেলো করা।

jŭm'-ble (-bl), *n.* **1.** A mass or collection without order; a medley; as, a *jumble* of words; a disorder or muddle; বিশৃঙ্খলভাবে বিক্ষিপ্ত বস্তুসমূহ; খিচুড়ী, হ য ব র ল; গোলমাল, বিশৃঙ্খলা। **2.** A jolting; ঝাঁকুনি। **Jum'-bly,** *adj.* **Jumble-sale** — বাজার প্রভৃতিতে নানাপ্রকার সস্তা মাল নীলামে বিক্রয়। **Jumble-shop**—যে দোকানে হরেক রকম জিনিষ বিক্রীত হয়।

jŭm'-bō, *n.* & *adj.* **1.** A big clumsy person, animal or thing; esp. (with *cap.*), the famous elephant in the London Zoological Gardens; বিপুলকায় ব্যক্তি, অতিকায় জন্তু, প্রকাণ্ডবস্তু; লণ্ডন নগরীর পশুশালার সুবিখ্যাত Jumbo নামক হস্তী। **2.** A notably successful person; বিশেষ কৃতকার্য্য ব্যক্তি। ***Adj.*** Very large; অতিপ্রকাণ্ড, বিপুল, বিশাল।

jŭmp, *n.* **1.** A bound; a spring from the ground; লম্ফ, ঝম্প; উল্লম্ফন। **2.** The space or place traversed by a leap; as, a *jump* of 12 feet; লম্ফ দ্বারা অতিক্রান্ত স্থান। **3.** A start caused by a shock or excitement; (*pl.*) the delirium tremens; চমৎকম্পন, গাত্রমোটন; (বহুবচন) অতিরিক্ত মাদকদ্রব্য সেবন অথবা উহা হইতে বিরতিবশতঃ অনিদ্রা ও কম্পসংযুক্ত প্রলাপরোগ। **4.** Abrupt rise in amount, price, value etc.; হঠাৎ মূল্যবৃদ্ধি, চড়তি। **5.** A gap, as in a series, argument, etc.; "There is a *jump* in the logic here"; যুক্তিপরম্পরার মধ্যে ফাঁক। **Jump'-i-ness,** *n.* **Jum'-py,** *adj.* **The jumps**—Delirium tremens (See JUMP *n.* 3.)

jŭmp, *v. i.* & *t.* **1.** To spring from ground etc.; to leap or bound; লম্ফপ্রদান করা, লাফ দেওয়া; ঝাঁপান। **2.** To bounce; to jolt; to start with a jerk from excitement, shock, etc; as, to *jump* for joy; ঝুপ্ করিয়া লাফ দেওয়া; ঝাঁকিয়া চলা; চমকিয়া কাঁপিয়া উঠা। **3.** To tally; to coincide; to agree, (generally followed by *with*); "It *jumps* with my humonr"; খাপ খাওয়া; মিলা, মিল হওয়া; ঐক্য হওয়া। **4.** To come (*to*) or arrive (*at*) hastily; as, to *jump* to a conclusion; দ্রুত উপনীত হওয়া। **5.** (*Fig.*) To accept suddenly or eagerly, as an offer, (with *at*); (লক্ষণায়) তাড়াতাড়ি সাগ্রহে গ্রহণ করা, লাফাইয়া ধরা। ***Verb t.*** **1.** To pass over or across by a spring or leap; as, to *jump* a stream; উল্লঙ্ঘন করা, লাফ দিয়া পার হওয়া, ডিঙ্গাইয়া যাওয়া, টপ্‌কান। **2.** (Of railway carriage etc.) To leave (the line); (বাষ্পীয় শকট-সম্বন্ধে) বর্ত্মচ্যুত হওয়া। **3.** To cause to jump; as, he *jumped* his horse across the ditch; লাফ দেওয়ান। **4.** To come down upon and seize; to pounce upon; আপতিত হইয়া ধরা; ছোঁ মারা। **5.** To cook (potato etc.) in a frying pan occasionally shaking them, (*usu. in p. p.*); মাঝে মাঝে নাড়িয়া (গোলআলু প্রভৃতি) চাটুতে পাক করা। **6.** To startle, as a man or his nerves; আবেগকম্পিত করা, চমকান, আক্ষেপ, খিঁচুনি, প্রভৃতি উৎপাদন করা। **7.** To skip over; to pass by as a subject or a part of a book etc.; উপেক্ষা করিয়া চলিয়া যাওয়া; ছাড়িয়া যাওয়া। **8.** To steal a march upon; "To *jump* the Transvaal"; অলক্ষিতে অতিক্রম করিয়া যাওয়া। **Jump'-a-ble,** *adj.* **To jump a claim**—To seize upon a piece of land called a claim by force or in the absence of the previous occupier; পূর্ব্ব অধিবাসীর অনুপস্থিতিতে কোন জমি অধিকার করিয়া বসা, বলপূর্ব্বক কোন জমি দখল করা। **To jump at** — To come to, or arrive at, hastily, as a conclusion etc.; তাড়াতাড়ি উপনীত হওয়া। To accept eagerly an offer etc.; সাগ্রহে গ্রহণ করা। **To jump down**—*v. i.* & *t.* To fall down by a leap; লাফাইয়া পড়া, ঝাঁপাইয়া পড়া। (*Verb t.*) To help a boy to jump down; নীচে লাফাইয়া পড়িতে বালককে সাহায্য করা। **To jump on** or **upon**—To spring upon; লাফাইয়া পড়া। To attack as an offender etc. crushingly with word or act.; কোন ব্যক্তিকে সাংঘাতিক ভাবে আক্রমণ করা (বাক্যে বা কার্য্যে)। **To jump over**—To leap over; লাফ দিয়া পার হওয়া, ডিঙ্গাইয়া যাওয়া, টপ্‌কান। **To jump (over) the broomstick**—To marry in an informal way; রীতিবিরুদ্ধভাবে বিবাহ করা, গন্ধর্ব্ব বিবাহ করা।

jŭmp'-ər, *n.* **1.** One who jumps; লম্ফপ্রদানকারী। **2.** One of a Christian sect in Wales who jumps while worshipping; ওয়েল্‌স্ প্রদেশের খৃষ্টীয় ধর্ম্মসম্প্রদায়বিশেষ ভুক্ত ব্যক্তি, উপাসনাকালে যাহাদের অঙ্গে আক্ষেপ, খিঁচুনি, প্রভৃতি হইয়া থাকে, গাত্রমোটন-কারী। **3.** A rope made fast to keep yard, mast etc. from jumping; মাস্তুল, পালিদণ্ড প্রভৃতি যাহাতে লাফাইয়া না উঠে তজ্জন্য যে রজ্জু ব্যবহৃত হয়। **4.** A jumping insect; লম্ফপ্রদানকারী কীট। **5.** A long iron chisel; লোহার লম্বা বাটালি।

jŭmp′-ėr, *n.* A loose outer jacket of canvas etc. worn by sailors etc.; জাহাজের মাল্লাদের ঢিলা জামা।

jŭmp′-ing, *adj.* Leaping or bounding; উল্লম্ফনশীল। **Jumping bean**—আমেরিকার উষ্ণমণ্ডলজাত শিম্বীর বীজবিশেষ—অভ্যন্তররুদ্ধ পোকার সঞ্চালন হেতু এই বীজ ইতস্ততঃ লাফাইতে থাকে।

junc′-tion (jŭngk-), *n.* **1.** Act of joining; union; as, *junction* of two armies; সংযোজন; যোজন, সংযোগ, সংগতি, সমাগম, সংসর্গ। **2.** A joint; a meeting place; specifically the place where lines of railway meet or cross; সন্ধি, জোড়; সংযোগস্থল, মিলনস্থল, সঙ্গম; বিশেষতঃ বিভিন্নস্থানগামী লৌহবর্ত্ম সমূহের সংযোগস্থল, জংশন।

junc′-tūre (jŭngk-), *n.* **1.** A joining; union; সংযোজন; যোগ। **2.** The place where two bodies or things are joined; সংযোগস্থল। **3.** Concurrence of events; a critical time or state of affairs; a crisis; as, at this *juncture*; ঘটনাসম্মিলন; সঙ্কটকাল; গুরুতর সময়।

Jūne, *n.* The sixth month of the year [from Junius, the name of Roman gens.]; ইংরাজী বর্ষের ষষ্ঠ মাস।

jun′-gle (jŭng-gl), *n.* **1.** A land covered with thick brush-wood etc.; জঙ্গল, বন, অরণ্য, কানন, কান্তার, অটবী। **2.** (*Fig.*) A wild tangled mass; "...*jungle* of disconnected precedents"; (লক্ষণায়) জঙ্গল। **3.** (*Slang—Stock-Exchange*) The West-African share-market; পশ্চিম আফ্রিকার কোম্পানীর কাগজের বাজার। **–gled,** *adj.* **–gly,** *adj.* Abounding with jungles; জঙ্গলময়। **Jungle-cat** — খাটাস (লিডেকার)। **Jungle fever** — একপ্রকার গুরুতর ম্যালেরিয়া বা অবিরাম জ্বর।

jūn′-i-or (-ėr), *adj.* & *n.* **1.** The younger (esp. of son having the same name as father, or of the younger of two boys of the same surname in a school; abbr. *jun.*, *jr.*); কনিষ্ঠ, অনুজ। **2.** Of lower standing; of lower position; as, a *junior* partner or counsel; অপেক্ষাকৃত অল্প অভিজ্ঞ; নিম্নপদস্থ, কর্ম্মকনিষ্ঠ। ***Noun.*** **1.** One who is younger; বয়ঃকনিষ্ঠ ব্যক্তি। **2.** One who is of lower standing or position, as at the bar etc.: ওকালতি প্রভৃতি ব্যবসায়ে অপেক্ষাকৃত অল্প অভিজ্ঞ ব্যক্তি। **–or′-i-ty,** *n.*

jūn′-i-or-āte (-ėr-), *n.* (*R. C. Church*) A two-year course of instruction for Jesuits in preparation for the priesthood; যীশুইটদিগের যাজকত্ব প্রাপ্তির জন্য দুই বৎসরব্যাপী শিক্ষা লাভ।

jū′-ni-pêr, *n.* An evergreen shrub, the berries of which yield an oil used in medicine and in

Juniper.

making gin; একপ্রকার চিরহরিত গুল্ম—এই গুল্মের ফল ঔষধস্বরূপ এবং জিন-সরাপ প্রস্তুতে ব্যবহৃত হয়, হপুষ (খোরী)।

junk′ (jŭngk), *n.* & *v. t.* **1.** Pieces of old cable or cordage used for making mat, oakum, etc.; পুরাতন কাছির টুকরা। **2.** Lump; chunk; পিণ্ড; স্থূল খণ্ড। **3.** (*Naut.*) Salt-beef supplied to vessels; (নৌবিদ্যা) জাহাজে যে লবণাক্ত মাংস সরবরাহ করা হয়। ***Verb t.*** To divide into pieces or chunks; স্থূল খণ্ডে বিভক্ত করা।

junk (jŭngk), *n.* A flat-bottomed sailing vessel used in Chinese seas; একপ্রকার প্রশস্ততল চীনদেশীয় পোত।

Chinese junk.

সারস, বক, বলাকা, দীর্ঘজঙ্ঘ (মঃ ইঃ), ক্রৌঞ্চ। **2.** A machine for raising and removing heavy goods; ভারোত্তলনযন্ত্র। **3.** A siphon; বক্রনলিকা। **4.** An overhanging tube for supplying a tender with water, (also *water-crane*); বাষ্পীয় শকটের সহিত সংলগ্ন জলবাহিশকটে জল যোগাইবার জন্য বক্রনল বিশেষ। **Crane fly** — Daddy-longlegs; একপ্রকার মক্ষিকা। **Crane's bill** — একজাতীয় নানাপ্রকার গুল্মের সাধারণ নাম।

crāne, *v. t.* & *i.* **1.** To lift by or as by a crane; ভারোত্তলন যন্ত্রদ্বারা উত্তোলন করা, ভারোত্তলন যন্ত্রবৎ উত্তোলন করা। **2.** To stretch (the neck) like a crane, (also *Verb i.*); বকের মত গলা বাড়াইয়া দেওয়া। **To crane at**—To shrink from a danger or difficulty; বিপদ্ বা সঙ্কটদর্শনে ভয়ে সঙ্কুচিত হইয়া সরিয়া আসা।

crā-ni-ŏl′-ŏ-ġy, *n.* The science of the human skull, esp. its conformation in connexion with the separate faculties and properties of the mind; করোটি-বিজ্ঞান, কপালবিদ্যা (হিঃ কোঃ), কপাল-সামুদ্রিক, কপাল-শাস্ত্র।

crā′-ni-ŭm, *n.* **1.** Bones enclosing the brain; মস্তিষ্ক-পরিবেষ্টক অস্থি-সমূহ, শিরঃকপাল (সাঃ পঃ)। **2.** The skull; করোটী, কর্পর (মঃ ইঃ)। **–al,** *adj.*

jupe (*F.*), *n.* A woman's skirt ; স্ত্রীলোকের বহির্বাস,—যাহা কটির নীচে পরিহিত হয়।

Jü'-pi-têr, *n.* **1.** (*Rom: myth.*) The supreme Roman deity ; রোমীয় দেবরাজ। **2.** The largest planet of the solar system ; বৃহস্পতি, অঙ্গিরস (বৃহৎ), সুরগুরু (ঐ), বাচস্পতি (ঐ), ইজ্য (ঐ), জীবগুরু, অমররাজমন্ত্রী। **Jupiter Pluvius**—The god of rain ; বৃষ্টিদেবতা, পর্জ্জন্য, মেঘবাহন, জীমূতবাহন।

jü'-răl, *adj.* **1.** Of, or pertaining to, law ; আইনসম্বন্ধীয়, ঋতসম্বন্ধী (হিঃ কোঃ)। **2.** (*Moral Philos.*) Of, or relating to, rights and obligations ; (নীতি-বিজ্ঞান) অধিকার বা কর্ত্তব্যসম্বন্ধীয়।

jü-răs'-sic, *adj.* **1.** Of, or relating to, the Jura mountains between France and Switzerland ; ফ্রান্স ও সুইজারল্যাণ্ডের মধ্যবর্ত্তী Jura পর্ব্বতসম্বন্ধীয়। **2.** (*Geol.*) Marked by the prevalence of oolitic limestone ; (ভূবিদ্যা) মৎস্য ডিম্বাকৃতি দানাদার চূর্ণ প্রস্তর বিশিষ্ট।

jü'-răt, *n.* **1.** A municipal officer similar to an alderman ; মিউনিসিপ্যাল কর্ম্মচারি-বিশেষ। **2.** A magistrate for life in the Channel Islands ; ব্রিটীশপ্রণালীর দ্বীপপুঞ্জের শাসনকর্ত্তা।

jü-rid'-i-căl, *adj.* **1.** Of, or relating to, the administration of justice ; legal ; বিচারকার্য্যসম্বন্ধীয় ; আইন সম্বন্ধীয়, ব্যবহারিক। **2.** Pertaining to a judge ; বিচারক-সম্পর্কীয়।

jü-ris-cŏn'-sült, *n.* A man learned in law, esp. civil law ; a jurist ; ব্যবহারশাস্ত্রজ্ঞ, ধর্ম্মশাস্ত্রজ্ঞ ; স্মার্ত্ত।

jü-ris-dic'-tion, *n.* **1.** Administration of justice ; legal authority ; বিচারকার্য্য ; আইনসঙ্গত ক্ষমতা, বৈধ ক্ষমতা। **2.** Authority in general ; control ; প্রভুত্ব, অধিকার, সীমা (হিঃ কোঃ) ; কর্ত্তৃত্ব। **3.** The sphere or extent of judicial or administrative authority ; the territory over which it extends ; বিচারক বা শাসনকর্ত্তার অধিকারের ক্ষেত্র বা প্রসর ; এলাকা, সহরদ্দ, হুদ্দা। **—al,** *adj.*

jü-ris-pru'-dence (-prô-dŏns), *n.* **1.** The science or philosophy of human law ; ব্যবস্থাবিজ্ঞান, ব্যবহারশাস্ত্র, ব্যবহারবিদ্যা, ব্যবস্থাশাস্ত্র, নিয়মশাস্ত্র (হিঃ কোঃ), স্মৃতিশাস্ত্র (ঐ)। **2.** A body or system of law ; as, medical *jurisprudence* ; ব্যবস্থাপদ্ধতি। **3.** Skill in law ; as, men of *jurisprudence* ; ব্যবস্থাশাস্ত্রে পারদর্শিতা। **—dent,** *adj.* & *n.* Skilled in law ; ব্যবস্থাশাস্ত্রজ্ঞ, ধর্ম্মশাস্ত্রজ্ঞ। (*Noun.*) One versed in jurisprudence ; ব্যবহারশাস্ত্রবিদ্ পণ্ডিত। **—den'-tial,** *adj.*

jü'-rist, *n.* **1.** One versed in law ; ব্যবহারশাস্ত্রবিদ্, ধর্ম্মশাস্ত্রী, ব্যবহারজ্ঞ (ব্যঃ মাঃ), ব্যবহারধর্ম্মজ্ঞ (আঃ বঃ), ব্যবস্থাশাস্ত্রবিৎ। **2.** A writer on law ; আইন পুস্তক লেখক, ব্যবস্থাশাস্ত্র সম্বন্ধীয় গ্রন্থ লেখক। **3.** A university law student ; a graduate in law ; বিশ্ববিদ্যালয়ের আইনশিক্ষার্থী ছাত্র ; ব্যবস্থাশাস্ত্রে উপাধিধারী। **—ris'-tic, —ris'-ti-cal,** *adjs.* **—ris'-ti-cal-ly,** *adv.*

jü'-ror (-rêr), *n.* **1.** A member of a jury ; a jury man ; বিচারালয়ে বিচারকের সহিত যাঁহারা ঘটনার সত্যাসত্য নির্ণয় করেন তাঁহাদের অন্যতম, জুরি ; সভাসদ্ (ব্যঃ মাঃ)। **2.** One who takes oath, esp. of allegiance ; যে ব্যক্তি শপথ গ্রহণ করে, বিশেষতঃ যে ব্যক্তি রাজভক্তির শপথ গ্রহণ করে।

jü'-ry̆, *n.* **1.** A body of men sworn to render verdict on a question submitted to them in the court of justice ; বিচারালয়ে বিচারকের সহিত যাঁহারা ঘটনার সত্যাসত্য নির্ণয় করেন (যোঃ), সভ্যসমূহ, সভাসদ্ বর্গ (cf. সভ্যাঃ—মিতঃ)। **2.** A body of persons selected for awarding prizes at an exhibition or competition ; প্রদর্শনী বা প্রতিযোগিতার ক্রীড়ায় কে কে পুরস্কার পাইবার যোগ্য তাহা নির্দ্ধারণের জন্য মনোনীত ব্যক্তি-বর্গ। **Grand jury**—See GRAND. **Jury-box** — বিচারালয়ে সভাসদগণের উপবেশনার্থ বৃতিবেষ্টিত স্থান। **Jury-man** — A member of a jury ; সভ্য, সভাসদ্। **Jury-mast**—ভগ্ন বা নষ্ট মাস্তুলের স্থানে যে অস্থায়ী মাস্তুল প্রবিষ্ট করান হয়। **Special jury**—যে সকল সভাসদ্ কোন বিশেষ তালিকা হইতে নির্ব্বাচিত হন। **Trial, common** or **petty jury**—যে দ্বাদশ জন সভাসদ্ কোন দেওয়ানী কি ফৌজদারী মোকদ্দমা সংক্রান্ত কোন বৃত্তান্ত বা হালাৎএর চূড়ান্ত নিষ্পত্তি করিয়া এক বাক্যে তাঁহাদের অভিমত প্রকাশ করেন।

jŭst, *adj.* **1.** Equitable ; impartial ; as, a *just* man or conduct ; বিচারসঙ্গত, ন্যায়সঙ্গত, ন্যায্য, ন্যায়শীল, যথার্থ (হিঃ কোঃ), ন্যায়পরায়ণ, ন্যায়নিষ্ঠ, ন্যায়পর, ন্যায়ানুসারী, ন্যায়ানুবর্ত্তী, ন্যায়ানুযায়ী ; নিরপেক্ষ। **2.** Deserved ; as, a *just* reward, treatment, etc. ; ন্যায্য, সমুচিত। **3.** Well-founded ; reasonable ; as, a *just* suspicion, fear, etc. ; সুপ্রতিষ্ঠিত ; যুক্তি-সঙ্গত, যুক্তিযুক্ত। **4.** True ; fit ; proper ; প্রকৃত ; উপযুক্ত ; সমীচীন, সঙ্গত। **Just'-ly,** *adv.* **Just'-ness,** *n.*

jŭst, *adv.* **1.** Exactly ; as, *just* at that spot ; ঠিক। **2.** Barely ; scarcely ; as, he *just* missed the train ; কষ্টেসৃষ্টে, কোনপ্রকারে ; প্রায় সেই মুহূর্ত্তে। **3.** Now but a moment ago ; as, I have *just* seen him pass ; এখন, এইমাত্র, সবে, সবেমাত্র। **4.** (*Colloq.*) Positively ; quite ; as, this is *just* splendid ; (চলিত ভাষায়) বাস্তবিক, যথার্থই ; সম্পূর্ণ। **Just now**—At this moment ; a little time ago ; এই মুহূর্ত্তে, এই মাত্র ; অল্পক্ষণ হইল। **Just so**—Exactly so ; তাইতো, বটে তো। **Just then**—Exactly then ; এমন সময়ে, ঠিক এমন সময়ে।

jŭst, *n.* See JOUST.
jŭs'-tice (-tĭs), *n.* **1.** The quality of being just; just conduct; rectitude; ন্যায়পরায়ণতা, ন্যায়নিষ্ঠা, ন্যায়বিচার, ন্যায্যতা; ন্যায়াচরণ; সাধুতা। **2.** Conformity to fact, reason or truth; fairness; impartiality; সত্যপরায়ণতা, যুক্তিযুক্ততা, যৌক্তিকতা, যুক্তিসিদ্ধতা; ন্যায্যতা; অপক্ষপাত। **3.** Administration of law; exercise of authority in maintenance of right; as, where *justice* is not, the fertilest land becomes barren; ন্যায়বিচার, ন্যায় (হিঃ কোঃ); স্বত্ব বা অধিকাররক্ষার্থ ক্ষমতার পরিচালনা। **4.** A judge (in England and India) or judge of the Supreme Court of Judicature; ইংলণ্ড বা ভারতের সর্ব্বোচ্চ আদালতের বিচারক, বিচারপতি, হাইকোর্টের বিচারপতি। **5.** Judicial proceedings; as, a Court of Justice; বিচার। **–ship,** *n.* The office or function of a judge; বিচারকের কার্য্য বা পদ। **A Court of Justice**—A law-court or a tribunal; ধর্ম্মাধিকরণ, বিচারালয়। **In justice to**—Wishing to treat fairly; doing justice to; সুবিচার করিতে ইচ্ছুক হইয়া; নিরপেক্ষ ভাবে বলিতে হইলে, ন্যায়বিচার করিতে হইলে। **Justice of the Peace (J. P.)**—An inferior magistrate appointed to preserve peace in a country, town, etc.; নিম্নশ্রেণীর শান্তিরক্ষক এবং বিচারক—ইনি ক্ষুদ্র ক্ষুদ্র মোকদ্দমার বিচার, গুরুতর মোকদ্দমা উচ্চতর আদালতে বিচারার্থ প্রেরণ এবং অন্যান্য ক্ষমতা পরিচালন করিয়া থাকেন। **To do justice to**—To treat fairly; to show due appreciation of; কাহারও প্রতি সুবিচার করা; যথোচিত গুণ-গ্রহণ করা। **To do one justice**—To exhibit one's good qualities or good looks; নিজের সদ্‌গুণ বা সৌন্দর্য্য প্রকাশ করা। **To do oneself justice**—To perform worthily of one's abilities; স্বীয় ক্ষমতার অনুরূপ সম্পাদন করা।
jŭs-tĭ'-ci-a-ble (-shĭ-ă-bl), *adj.* & *n.* Liable to trial in a court of justice; subject to jurisdiction; বিচারযোগ্য; এলাকার অধীন। ***Noun.*** One subject to the jurisdiction (*of* another); কোন ব্যক্তির কর্তৃত্বাধীন ব্যক্তি।
jŭs-tĭ'-ci-ar (-shĭ-êr), *n.* A chief political and judicial officer under the Norman and early Plantagenet kings; নর্ম্মাণ এবং প্ল্যান্টাজেনেট নৃপতিগণের অধীন প্রধান বিচারক বা রাজনীতিক কর্ম্মচারী।
jŭs-tĭ'-ci-ă-rȳ (-shĭ-), *n.* & *adj.* **1.** One who administers justice; বিচারক, ন্যায়াধ্যক্ষ, ন্যায়াধীশ, ধর্ম্মাধ্যক্ষ। **2.** Same as JUSTICIAR (which see.) ***Adj.*** Of, or relating to, the administration of justice; বিচার-কার্য্যসম্বন্ধীয়।
jŭs'-tĭ-fȳ, *v. t.* **1.** To prove or show to be just; to vindicate; ন্যায্যতা প্রতিপাদন করা, ন্যায্যতা প্রদর্শন করা; সমর্থন করা। **2.** (Of circumstances) To be such as to vindicate; সমর্থনকারী হওয়া। **3.** To afford adequate grounds for (conduct, claim etc.); যথোচিত কারণ হওয়া। **4.** To declare free from guilt or blame; "I cannot *justify* whom the law condemns"; পাপনির্ম্মুক্ত বলিয়া ঘোষণা করা, দোষমুক্ত বলিয়া ঘোষণা করা। **5.** (*Theol.*) To declare free from penalty of sin on the ground of Christ's righteousness or of the infusion of grace; (খৃষ্টীয় শাস্ত্র) খ্রীষ্টের সাধুতা অথবা ঈশ্বরের করুণাপ্রকাশ হেতু পাপের দণ্ডভোগ হইতে মুক্ত বলিয়া ঘোষণা করা। **6.** To make good; to corroborate, as a statement etc.; বজায় রাখা, স্থিরতর করা; প্রতিষ্ঠিত করা, দৃঢ় করা, বলবৎ করা। **7.** To adjust; (esp. in printing) to space out the line of type in the composing stick properly; ঠিকঠাক করা; (বিশেষতঃ মুদ্রণে) হরফ সাজাইবার আধারে অক্ষরের পংক্তিসমূহ অবকাশ-সাধক সীসকফলক দ্বারা পূর্ণ করা। **–fi-a-bil'-i-ty,** *n.* **–fi-a-ble,** *adj.* Capable of being justified; warrantable; excusable; ন্যায্যতা প্রতিপাদনযোগ্য, দোষনিরাকরণার্হ; সমর্থনীয়; মার্জ্জনীয়, ক্ষমার্হ। **–fi-a-bly,** *adv.* **–fi-ca'-tion,** *n.* **1.** Act of justifying; vindicating; ন্যায্যতাপ্রতিপাদন, ন্যায়ীকরণ, দোষমোচন, দোষনিরাকরণ, ঔচিত্যসাধন (হিঃ কোঃ); সমর্থন। **2.** Remission of sin; পাপক্ষমা, পাপমুক্তি। **3.** Adjustment esp. (in printing) of type by spacing it so as to make it exactly fill a line; ঠিকঠাক করণ, বিশেষতঃ হরফ সাজাইবার আধারে অক্ষরের পংক্তিসমূহ অবকাশ-সাধক সীসকফলক প্রভৃতি দ্বারা পূরণ। **–fi-ca-tive, –fi-ca-to-ry,** *adjs.* **–fi-er,** *n.* **Justifiable homicide**—আত্মরক্ষার্থ অথবা ঘোরতর অপরাধজনক কার্য্যে বাধা দিবার জন্য নরহত্যা। **Justification by faith**—ঈশ্বরের করুণার প্রতি আস্থা স্থাপন দ্বারা পাপমুক্তি। **To justify bail**—To show by oath of a person furnishing a bail that he is pecuniarily qualified; জামিনদাতার জামিনের টাকা দিবার সঙ্গতি আছে—তৎসম্বন্ধে শপথ করিয়া বলা।
jŭt, *n.* & *v. i.* A projection or protruding point; প্রলম্বন, উদ্গতি, উদ্গতবিন্দু। ***Verb i.*** To project; to protrude, (with *out*, *forth*, etc.); উদ্গত হওয়া, প্রলম্বিত হওয়া; বহিরুদ্গত হওয়া।
jūte, *n.* A fibre from the bark of certain plants chiefly imported from Bengal, used for canvas, cordage, etc.; পাট।
Jūte, *n.* One of a Low German tribe who invaded Britain in the 5th and 6th centuries; জর্ম্মণ দেশীয় জাতিবিশেষের

লোক—ইহারা পঞ্চম এবং ষষ্ঠ শতাব্দীতে ব্রিটিশ-দ্বীপ আক্রমণ করিয়াছিল।

jü-vĕ-nĕs′-cence (-ĕns), *n.* State of being young; youth; তারুণ্য; নবযৌবন, যৌবনাবস্থা। **—cent,** *adj.*

jü′-vĕ-nīle, *adj.* & *n.* **1.** Young; youthful; তরুণবয়স্ক; বাল্য, বালকোচিত। **2.** Suitable for or characteristic of, youth; as, *juvenile* sports; বালকোচিত, বালস্বভাবসুলভ। ***Noun.*** A young person; তরুণবয়স্ক ব্যক্তি। **—ly,** *adv.* **—nil′-i-ty,** *n.*

jŭx-tă-pōse′, *v. t.* To place side by side; একটীর পার্শ্বে অপরটী রাখা, পাশাপাশি রাখা।

jŭx-tă-pō-si′-tion, *n.* A placing, or being placed, near or side by side; সংযোগ (ব্রজঃ হিন্দু), সন্নিধান, সান্নিধ্য, সন্নিকর্ষ, নিকটসংস্থিতি, সন্নিধি (হিঃ কোঃ), উপশ্লেষ (ঐ)। **—al,** *adj.*

K

K, *n.* **1.** The eleventh letter of the English alphabet; ইংরাজী বর্ণমালার একাদশ অক্ষর। **2.** The Roman numeral = 250; ২৫০। **3.** (*Chem.—cap.*) Potassium; পটাসিয়াম ধাতু, পত্রক (সাঃ পঃ)।

kaa′-mă (kâ-), *n.* A kind of South African antelope; দক্ষিণ আফ্রিকার কৃষ্ণসার মৃগবিশেষ।

kăb′-ă-lă, *n.* See CABALA.

kăd′-dish (-ĭsh), *n.* A portion of the daily ritual of the synagogue; ইহুদীদিগের ধর্ম্মসভার দৈনিক আচারানুষ্ঠানের অংশ বিশেষ।

kă′-dī (*or* kā-), *n.* See CADI.

Kăf′-fir (-êr), **Kă′-fir** (-fêr), **Căf′-fre** (-êr), *ns.* **1.** The name of a tribe living between Cape Colony and Natal in South Africa; দক্ষিণ আফ্রিকার আদিম অধিবাসী। **2.** A native of Kafiristan; এসিয়ার অন্তর্গত কাফ্রিস্থানের অধিবাসী। **3.** A name given to certain infidel races by the Mahommedans; কাফের। **4.** (*Pl.*) South-African mine shares; দক্ষিণ আফ্রিকার খনির অংশ। **Kaffir-bread**—দক্ষিণ আফ্রিকার বৃক্ষবিশেষের কোমল মজ্জা—যাহা তদ্দেশবাসিগণ আহার করিয়া থাকে; ঐ বৃক্ষ। **Kaffir-corn**—জোয়ার।

kăf′-tăn, *n.* A long vest worn in Turkey and Egypt; মিশর, তুরস্ক প্রভৃতি দেশের মুসলমানদিগের ব্যবহৃত জামা (see CAFTAN)।

Kaftan robe.

kă′-gō, *n.* A kind of Japanese palanquin; একপ্রকার জাপানী পালকী।

kail (kāl), *n.* See KALE.

Kai′-sĕr (kī-), *n.* **1.** An emperor especially of Germany; সম্রাট্, জর্ম্মণ সম্রাট্। [জর্ম্মণ ভাষায় Kaiser শব্দ ল্যাটিন Caesar শব্দের প্রতিরূপ।] **2.** (*Hist.*) The head of the Holy Roman Empire; (ইতিহাস) পবিত্র রোমসাম্রাজ্যের নায়ক। **—ship,** *n.*

kajawah, *n.* A pannier used in pairs on camels and mules; খচ্চরের পিঠে যে ঝুড়ি জোড়ায় জোড়ায় চাপান হয়।

kāle, kail (kāl), *ns.* **1.** A kind of cabbage with curled or wrinkled leaves; একপ্রকার বাঁধা কপি—এই জাতীয় কপির পাতাগুলি কোঁকড়ানো থাকে **2.** A broth or soup of kale; any vegetable soup; ঐ কপির ঝোল; তরকারীর ঝোল। **Kale, Kail-yard** — তরিতরকারীর বাগান। **Kale, Kail-yard school**—স্কটলণ্ডের যে সকল লেখকসম্প্রদায়ের উপন্যাসাদিতে পল্লীজীবনের দৈনন্দিন ঘটনাবলীর বর্ণনা থাকে। **Kale, Kail-yard novelist**—যে ঔপন্যাসিক স্কটলণ্ডের পল্লীজীবন চিত্রিত করিয়া থাকেন এবং যাহার উপন্যাসে বহুল পরিমাণে তদ্দেশের প্রাদেশিক শব্দ ব্যবহৃত হয়।

kă-lei′-dō-scōpe (-lī-), *n.* **1.** A tube through which are seen symmetrical figures produced by reflections of pieces of coloured glass and varied by the rotation of the tube; যে নলের ভিতর নানা বর্ণের কাচখণ্ডের প্রতিফলন দ্বারা উৎপাদিত নানাবিধ রমণীয় চিত্র পরিদৃষ্ট হয়, বহুরূপদর্শক (হিঃ কোঃ), বৈচিত্র্যদর্শক (প্রবাসী ১৩২২)। **2.** (*Fig.*) A constantly changing group; (লক্ষণায়) নিয়তপরিবর্ত্তনশীল নানাবর্ণসমুজ্জ্বল বস্তুপরম্পরা। **—scop′-ic, —scop′-i-cal,** *adjs.* **—scop′-i-cal-ly,** *adv.*

kā-lī, *n.* Glasswort, a prickly shrub, the ashes of which are used in making glass; কণ্টকাকীর্ণ গুল্ম বিশেষ — উহার ভস্ম কাচ প্রস্তুতে ব্যবহৃত হয়।

kăl-i-ăn′, *n.* A Persian form of the hookah ; পারস্যদেশের হুঁকা।

kă′-lŏng, *n.* A fruit bat or flying fox of Malay ; মালয় দ্বীপের বাদুড় বা চামচিকা বিশেষ।

kă-mă′-lă, *n.* An orange-red powder got from the capsules of an East Indian tree, (it is used for dyeing silks etc.) ; মান্দ্রাজ দেশের তরু-বিশেষ হইতে প্রাপ্ত কমলাবর্ণের রঞ্জকপদার্থ, কমলাগুঁড়ি (দ্রব্যগুণ)।

kami, *n.* **1.** A God in Japanese religion ; জাপানীদিগের দেবতা। **2.** A Japanese title of governors ; জাপানদেশের শাসনকর্ত্তার উপাধি।

kămp-tū′-li-cŏn, *n.* A floor-cloth composed of cork, India-rubber, etc. ; কাক, রবার, প্রভৃতি দ্বারা প্রস্তুত গৃহতলাচ্ছাদনবস্ত্র।

kan-gă-rōō′ (kăng-), *n.* **1.** A large marsupial mammal found in Australia, with long and strongly developed hind legs and great

Kangaroo.

leaping power ; অষ্ট্রেলিয়াদেশীয় জন্তু বিশেষ—উহার পশ্চাতের পদদ্বয় দীর্ঘ ও সুপুষ্ট এবং শাবকদিগের আশ্রয়ের জন্য উদরে একটী থলি আছে, কেঙ্গারু। **2.** (*Pl.*, *Slang*) West Australian mining shares ; dealers in these ; (ইতর ভাষায়) পশ্চিম-আফ্রিকার খনির অংশ ; উহার ব্যবসায়ী। **Kangaroo-grass**—A valuable Australian fodder grass; পশুদিগের খাদ্যোপযোগী অষ্ট্রেলিয়াদেশীয় মূল্যবান তৃণবিশেষ। **Kangaroo-rat** — অষ্ট্রেলিয়াদেশীয় দ্বিগর্ভকোষ ক্ষুদ্র জন্তুবিশেষ।

kă-nōōn′, *n.* A kind of harp with 50 to 60 strings ; ৫০ হইতে ৬০ পর্য্যন্ত তন্ত্রীবিশিষ্ট একপ্রকার বীণা।

Kănt′-i-ăn, *adj.* Of, or pertaining to, Immanuel Kant, the German philosopher or his philosophy ; জর্ম্মণ দার্শনিক ইম্যানুয়েল ক্যাণ্ট সম্পর্কীয়। **—ism,** *n.*

kă′-ō-lin, —line (-lin), *n.* A fine white clay used in making porecelain ; চীনা মাটী প্রস্তুতের জন্য একপ্রকার সূক্ষ্ম সাদা বালি। **—ize,** *v. t.* To convert as feldspar as into kaolin ; ঐরূপ বালুকায় পরিণত করা।

kapellmeister, *n.* The leader or conductor of a chapel, choir or orchestra ; খৃষ্টীয় ভজনালয় বা নাট্যমন্দিরের বাদকদলের নায়ক।

kă′-pŏk, *n.* A fine cotton wool investing the seeds of a certain tree, used for stuffing cushions ; শ্বেতশিমুল।

Ka′-ră-īte, *n.* One of a Jewish sect rejecting Rabbinical tradition and interpreting scriptures literally ; ইহুদী সম্প্রদায় বিশেষ—এই সম্প্রদায় ইহুদী শাস্ত্রকারগণের পরম্পরাগত ব্যাখ্যা অগ্রাহ্য করিয়া খৃষ্টীয় ধর্ম্মশাস্ত্র সমূহের শব্দার্থানুযায়ী ব্যাখ্যা করিতেন।

kă-rōō′, kăr-rōō′ (-ōō), *ns.* One of the elevated dry table-lands of South Africa (waterless in dry season) ; দক্ষিণ আফ্রিকার মালভূমি। **The Great Karoo**—One in Cape Colony ; কেপ্ কলনির অন্তর্গত সুবিস্তীর্ণ মালভূমি।

kă-rŏss′, *n.* A garment or rug of animal skins worn by South-African natives ; দক্ষিণ আফ্রিকার আদিমনিবাসিগণ কর্ত্তৃক পরিহিত পশু-চর্ম্মে প্রস্তুত পরিচ্ছদ বা কম্বল।

kăr′-tĕl, *n.* A wooden bed used in waggons in South-Africa ; দক্ষিণ আফ্রিকার শকটে ব্যবহৃত একপ্রকার কাঠময় শয্যা।

kăr-tĕll′, *n.* See CARTEL.

kă-tăb′-ō-lĭsm, *n.* (*Biol.*) Destructive metabolism ; (জীব-বিজ্ঞান) শরীরের প্রাণপঙ্কের মধ্যে (protoplasm) অনবরত যে বিশ্লেষণক্রিয়া হইয়া থাকে, প্রতিলোমপরিণাম (সাঃ পঃ), ধ্বংসক্রিয়া (ঐ), প্রতিবলনক্ষয় (হিঃ কোঃ)।

kăt′-i-ŏn, *n.* The element or elements of an electrolyte which in electro-chemical decompositions appear at the negative pole or cathode ; তাড়িদ্বিশ্লেষণ ক্রিয়াদ্বারা বিশ্লিষ্ট বস্তুর যে উপাদান বা উপাদানসমূহ বিয়োগাত্মক প্রান্তে আবির্ভূত হয়, কুকণা (সাঃ পঃ), বিকণা (ঐ)।

kă′-tȳ-dĭd, *n.* A large insect of America ; আমেরিকাদেশীয় বৃহৎ পতঙ্গ বিশেষ।

kau′-ri (kow-), *n.* A timber tree of New Zealand ; নবজিলণ্ড-দ্বীপের বৃক্ষবিশেষ।

kă′-vă, *n.* A shrub of Polynesia ; a beverage made from its roots ; পলিনিশিয়ার গুল্ম-বিশেষ ; উহা হইতে প্রস্তুত শ্রান্তিনিবারক পানীয়।

kă-văss′, *n.* An armed constable ; a government servant or courier in Turkey ; সশস্ত্র কনষ্টেবল ; তুরস্ক-দেশের অশ্বারোহী দূত বা সরকারী কর্ম্মচারী।

kay′-ăk (kā-), *n.* A light boat in Greenland made of a light wooden frame covered with seal-skin ; সীল মৎস্যের চামড়ায় মোড়া গ্রীনল্যাণ্ড দ্বীপের একপ্রকার হাল্কা কাঠের নৌকা।

ke′-ă (kā-), *n.* A New Zealand parrot that kills sheep for their kidney fat ; নবজিলাণ্ড দ্বীপের শুক-পক্ষিবিশেষ—ইহারা মেষের মূত্রাশয়সংলগ্ন মেদ ভক্ষণের জন্য উহাদিগকে বধ করে।

kĕck, *v. i.* To retch ; to make sound, as if about to vomit ; বমন চেষ্টা করা ; ওয়াক্ ওয়াক্ করা। **To keck at**—To eject (food) with loathing ; বমি করিয়া ফেলা।

kedge (kĕj), *n., v. i.* & *t.* **A small anchor for keeping a ship steady**

and for warping her, (also called a *kedge-anchor*) ; ক্ষুদ্র নঙ্গর, জাহাজ ঘুরাইবার জন্য ক্ষুদ্র নঙ্গর। ***Verb i.*** To warp a ship by a hawser attached to a kedge ; (of a ship) to move by means of kedging ; উক্ত ক্ষুদ্র নোঙ্গরে বদ্ধ রজ্জুর সাহায্যে জাহাজ ঘুরান ; (জাহাজের পক্ষে) ঐরূপ ক্ষুদ্র নোঙ্গরে বদ্ধ রজ্জুর সাহায্যে ঘুরা। ***Verb t.*** To warp (turn the course of) a ship by means of a kedge ; উক্ত ক্ষুদ্র নোঙ্গরে বদ্ধ রজ্জুর সাহায্যে জাহাজ ঘুরান।

kedg'-er-ee (kĕj-êr-ë), (Hindustani *khichri*) *n.* **1.** An Indian dish of rice, cooked with butter, split pulse etc. ; খিচুড়ী। **2.** A European dish of fish, rice, eggs, etc. ; মৎস্য, তণ্ডুল, ডিম্ব, প্রভৃতির সহযোগে প্রস্তুত খাদ্যবিশেষ, বিলাতী খিচুড়ী।

keel (kēl), *n.* & *v. t.* The principal timber in a ship or boat, extending from stem to stern along the bottom ; the corresponding part composed of iron-plates in iron vessels ; জাহাজের প্রধান তলকাঠ, পানিতরাস, তরীদল (সাঃ পঃ) ; লৌহময় পোতের তরীদল। **2.** (*Poet*) A ship ; (কবিতায়) জাহাজ, পোত। ***Verb t.*** To turn as a ship keel upwards ; জাহাজ উল্টান। **Keel'-less,** *adj.* **False keel**—পানিতরাস রক্ষার জন্য উহার তলায় যে দ্বিতীয় পানিতরাস সংবদ্ধ করা হয়। **Keel-blocks**—নির্ম্মাণের বা মেরামতের সময় যে কাষ্ঠখণ্ড সকলের উপর পানিতরাস রক্ষিত হয়। **To keel haul**—To punish a person by hauling him under the keel of a ship by ropes ; কোন লোককে জাহাজের পানিতরাসের উপর টানিয়া শাস্তি দেওয়া। **To keel over** — *v. t.* & *i.* To capsize (*lit.* & *fig.*) উল্টান, বিপর্য্যস্ত করা। (*Verb i.*) To fall suddenly as in a swoon ; হঠাৎ মূর্চ্ছিত হইয়া পড়া।

keel (kēl), *n.* **1.** A flat-bottomed ship esp. a kind used on the Tyne for carrying coal from Newcastle ; Newcastle হইতে কয়লা বহন করার জন্য পোত বিশেষ। **2.** The quantity of coal carried in a keel ; ঐরূপ জাহাজে যে পরিমাণ কয়লা লওয়া হয়।

keen (kēn), *adj.* **1.** Having sharp edge or point ; sharp ; তীক্ষ্ণাগ্র ; তীক্ষ্ণ, তীব্র, প্রখর, খরধার, শাণিত, ধারাল। **2.** Piercing ; penetrating ; severe ; as, *keen* satire ; তীক্ষ্ণ ; মর্ম্মভেদী ; তীব্র। **3.** (Of cold) Intense ; প্রবল, দারুণ (হিঃ কোঃ)। **4.** (Of pain) Acute ; bitter ; (যন্ত্রণাসম্বন্ধে) নিদারুণ ; মর্ম্মান্তিক। **5.** Eager ; ardent, (of a person, desire, interest, etc.) ; ব্যগ্র, উৎসাহী, প্রোৎসাহী, উৎসুক ; আগ্রহান্বিত, আগ্রহবান। **6.** Highly sensitive ; sharp (of sight, smell, etc.) ; তীব্র সংবেদনশীল ; সূক্ষ্ম, তীক্ষ্ণ। **7.** Vivid, shrill or strong, as light, sound etc. ; সতেজ, প্রবল, তীব্র। **8.** Intellectually acute ; shrewd ; as, *keen* wits ; তীক্ষ্ণবুদ্ধি, সূক্ষ্মবুদ্ধি, প্রখরবুদ্ধি, কুশাগ্রবুদ্ধি, তীব্রবুদ্ধি (হিঃ কোঃ), কুশাগ্রমতি (ঐ) ; চালাক। **Keen'-ly,** *adv.* **Keen'-ness,** *n.* **Keen edged**—Sharp ; তীক্ষ্ণধার, খরধার। **Keen-eyed**—Sharp-sighted ; তীক্ষ্ণদর্শী, সূক্ষ্মদর্শী। **Keen-set**—Eager ; ardent, (with *for*) ; উৎকণ্ঠিত ; আগ্রহপূর্ণ। **Keen of a job**—(*Slang*) Eager for work ; (ইতর ভাষায়) কাজের জন্য ব্যগ্র।

keen (kēn), *n., v. i.* & *t.* An Irish funeral song with wailing ; আয়র্লণ্ড দেশীয় শ্মশানসঙ্গীত। ***Verb i.*** To wail with the keen ; শ্মশানসঙ্গীত গাইয়া বিলাপ করা। ***Verb t.*** To bewail (a person) thus ; to utter in a wailing tone ; বিলাপ করা ; বিলাপসূচক স্বরে উচ্চারণ করা।

keep (kēp), *v. t.* & *i.* **1.** To hold ; to retain in one's possession or power ; to guard or protect, as a town, fort, etc. ; রাখা ; আয়ত্তে রাখা ; রক্ষা করা। **2.** To cause to remain in a given position or situation ; to maintain ; to preserve ; কোন বিশেষ অবস্থায় রাখা ; পালন করা ; রক্ষা করা। **3.** To have in custody ; to take charge ; জিম্মায় রাখা ; ভারগ্রহণ করা। **4.** Not to reveal or betray, as a secret ; গুপ্ত কথা প্রকাশ না করা, গোপন রাখা। **5.** To record accounts or events in ; as, to *keep* books, a diary, etc. ; বহিতে লিখিয়া রাখা। **6.** To conduct ; to manage ; as, to *keep* a hotel ; পরিচালনা করা, চালান ; নির্ব্বাহ করা। **7.** To support ; to supply with the necessaries of life ; as, to *keep* family ; ভরণপোষণ করা ; জীবনযাত্রার উপযোগী দ্রব্যসামগ্রী সরবরাহ করা। **8.** To have in one's service ; to have and maintain ; as, to *keep* a servant, mistress, etc. ; কাহারো অধীনে নিযুক্ত করা ; রাখিয়া ভরণপোষণ করা। **9.** To hold to ; to maintain ; as, to *keep* silence : to *keep* possession ; ধরিয়া থাকা ; রক্ষা করা। **10.** To remain in ; as, to *keep* one's house, room, bed, etc. ; ভিতরে থাকা, মধ্যে অবস্থান করা। **11.** To be faithful to ; to perform ; as, to *keep* one's promise or word ; নিষ্ঠ থাকা ; সম্পাদন করা, পালন করা, রক্ষা করা। **12.** To solemnize ; to celebrate ; যথাবিধি অনুষ্ঠান করা ; উৎসবাদির অনুষ্ঠান করা। **13.** To retain one's place in (the saddle, the field, the stage, etc.) against opposition ; রক্ষা করা। **14.** To have as commodity etc. habitually in stock for sale ; বিক্রয়ের জন্য সদা সর্ব্বদা রাখা। **15.** To continue to follow as a way or course ; কোন পথ ধরিয়া চলা। **16.** To restrain as a person, thing, etc., from doing etc. ; দমন করা, নিরোধ করা

Verb i. **1.** To remain in a splendid condition ; as, to *keep* in good health ; ভাল থাকা। **2.** To remain, as indoors etc. ; বাটীতে থাকা। **3.** To last ; to remain in good condition, as food etc. ; টেঁকা, স্থায়ী হওয়া ; তাজা থাকা, টাট্‌কা থাকা। **4.** (*Colloq.*) To reside ; to lodge ; "Knock at his study where they say he *keeps*" ; (চলিত ভাষায়) বাস করা ; থাকা। **5.** To have rooms at college (esp. Cambridge) ; কলেজে বাসের জন্য কোঠা থাকা (বিশেষতঃ কেম্ব্রিজ)। **6.** To continue ; as, to *keep* to the right ; ক্রমাগত চলা, চলিতে থাকা। **To keep abreast of**—To advance at the same pace with ; not to fall behind ; সমগতিতে অগ্রসর হওয়া, সমভাবে চলা ; পিছাইয়া না পড়া। **To keep alive**—To preserve from extinction ; to keep in action ; জীবিত রাখা, জীবিত রাখা ; চলিত অবস্থায় রাখা। **To keep aloof**—To remain at a distance ; তফাৎ থাকা, দূরে থাকা। **To keep an eye to** or **on**—To watch ; দৃষ্টি রাখা, চোখ রাখা। **To keep a stiff upper lip**—To keep up one's courage ; সাহস রাখা, সাহসে বুক বাঁধিয়া রাখা। **To keep at**—To work persistently at ; কোন কাজে লাগিয়া থাকা, উঠিয়া পড়িয়া লাগা। **To keep at it**—*v. t.* & *i.* To continue hard at work ; কঠোর পরিশ্রমের সহিত কাজ করিতে থাকা। (*Verb i.*) To keep hard at work ; কাজে লাগিয়া থাকা। **To keep away**—To remain absent ; অনুপস্থিত থাকা। **To keep back**—To reserve ; সরাইয়া রাখা, হাতে রাখা, সঞ্চিত রাখা। To restrain; to prevent from ; to withhold ; সংযত রাখা ; নিবারণ করা ; নিবৃত্ত করা, চাপিয়া রাখা। **To keep body and soul together**—To keep alive; to keep from starving ; জীবিত থাকা ; কায়ক্লেশে দিনপাত করা। **To keep clear of**—To keep free from ; to avoid ; মুক্ত রাখা ; পরিহার করা। **To keep company**—To be a lover ; to court ; প্রণয়ী হওয়া ; বিবাহার্থ প্রেম যাচ্ঞা করা। **To keep company with**—To associate with ; to frequent the society of ; সংসর্গ করা ; সঙ্গ করা। **To keep countenance** or **in countenance**—To lend moral support to ; নৈতিকসাহায্য প্রদান করা। **To keep down**—To restrain ; to control ; সংযত করা, চাপিয়া রাখা ; দমন করা। **To keep from**—*v. i.* & *t.* To abstain from ; বিরত থাকা, ক্ষান্ত থাকা, নিবৃত্ত থাকা। (*Verb t.*) To restrain from ; সংযত থাকা। **To keep good** or **bad hours**—To go to bed or rise habitually early or late ; সকাল সকাল অথবা বিলম্বে নিদ্রা যাওয়া বা ঘুম হইতে উঠা। **To keep hold of**—To retain ; ধরিয়া রাখা। **To keep house**—See under HOUSE. **To keep in**—*v. t.* & *i.* To prevent from escaping ; to conceal ; to restrain ; to cofine (a pupil) in the school-room after school hours ; to cause to remain burning, as a fire ; পলায়নে বাধা দেওয়া ; লুকান ; আটক করা ; বিদ্যালয়ের ছুটীর পর (কোন ছাত্রকে) কয়েদ রাখা ; জ্বালিয়া রাখা। (*Verb i.*) To remain indoors ; বাটীতে থাকা। **To keep in with**—To be on good terms with ; কাহারও সহিত ভাল ভাব থাকা। **To keep in view**—To have in view ; to fix one's aim or attention in a certain direction ; লক্ষ্য রাখা ; কোনদিকে লক্ষ্য রাখা, মনোযোগ দেওয়া। **To keep late hours**—To go to bed late ; অধিক রাত্রি পর্য্যন্ত জাগা। **To keep off**—To hold at a distance ; to prevent from coming near ; দূরে রাখা ; নিকটে আসিতে না দেওয়া। **To keep on**—To continue at anything ; not to leave off ; কোন বিষয় ধরিয়া থাকা, চালান ; ছাড়িয়া না দেওয়া। **To keep one going**—To keep one well supported or in constant work ; সর্ব্বদা কাজ দিয়া রাখা। **To keep one's countenance**—To hide one's emotion ; to preserve one's gravity ; মনের ভাব (হর্ষ শোকাদি) গোপন রাখা ; গাম্ভীর্য্য রক্ষা করা। **To keep oneself to oneself**—To avoid society ; অনালাপী হওয়া, অমিশুক হওয়া। **To keep oneself within proper limits**—Not to exceed proper limits ; to act with propriety or discretion ; সঙ্গত সীমা লঙ্ঘন না করা, নিজকে সামলান ; ঔচিত্য বা সদ্বিবেচনার সীমা লঙ্ঘন না করা। **To keep one's feet**—Not to fall ; না পড়া। **To keep one's hand in**—To keep oneself in practice ; কোন কাজে হাত ঠিক রাখা, হাত বজায় রাখা, কোন কাজে অভ্যাস রাখা। **To keep one's head above water**—To keep out of debt ; দেনায় ডুবিয়া না যাওয়া। **To keep one's** or **one's own counsel**—To keep one's thought etc. secret ; পেটের কথা পেটে রাখা, গুপ্ত কথা প্রকাশ না করা। **To keep one's powder dry**—To be ready for action ; কার্য্যের জন্য প্রস্তুত থাকা। **To keep one's word**—To be true to one's promise ; অঙ্গীকার পালন করা, কথা রাখা, বাক্য রক্ষা করা। **To keep on foot**—To maintain, as a standing army etc. ; ব্যয় নির্ব্বাহ করা। **To keep on friendly terms**—To remain friendly ; বন্ধুভাবে থাকা। **To keep open house**—See HOUSE. **To keep out**—To exclude ; to prevent from occupying ; বাদ দেওয়া, বর্জ্জন করা ; অধিকার করিতে না দেওয়া। **To keep pace with**—To go along with ; সমানে সমানে চলা, পিছাইয়া না পড়া।

To keep term—To reside during a term of the English university ; ইংলণ্ডের কোন বিশ্ববিদ্যালয়ে নির্দ্দিষ্ট কাল বাস করিয়া অধ্যয়ন করা। **To keep the fight**—To continue to fight ; যুদ্ধ করিতে থাকা। **To keep the pot boiling**—To defray family expenses ; পারিবারিক ব্যয় নির্ব্বাহ করা, হাঁড়ী চালান। **To keep the wolf from the door**—To satisfy hunger ; ক্ষুন্নিবৃত্তি করা, ক্ষুধানলে আহুতি প্রদান করা। **To keep to**—To adhere to ; to stick closely to ; not to neglect ; সংলগ্ন থাকা ; লাগিয়া থাকা ; অবহেলা না করা ; **To keep to oneself**—To hold secret ; গোপন রাখা, পেটের ভিতর রাখা। **To keep touch**—To maintain connection ; সংশ্রব রাখা, সম্পর্ক রাখা। **To keep under**—To oppress ; to subdue ; to hold in restraint ; অত্যাচার করা ; দমন করা ; চাপিয়া রাখা। **To keep up**—To continue ; to retain one's strength or spirit ; to prevent from falling ; as, *to keep up* the price of goods ; to support ; to maintain ; to keep from retiring to rest ; চালান ; শক্তি ও তেজ অক্ষুণ্ণ রাখা ; পড়িতে না দেওয়া ; রক্ষা করা ; পালন করা ; ঘুমাইতে না দেওয়া। **To keep up appearances**—See under APPEARANCE. **To keep up with**—To keep pace with ; সমান ভাবে অগ্রসর হওয়া, পিছাইয়া না পড়া।

keep (kēp), *n.* **1.** (*Hist.*) A stronghold ; the donjon ; (ইতিহাস) দুর্গ ; দুর্গাভ্যন্তরস্থ সুদৃঢ় স্থান—যথায় বন্দীদিগকে রুদ্ধ করা হইত। **2.** Maintenance ; food for maintenance ; as, to earn one's *keep* ; ভরণপোষণ ; খোরপোষ।

keep'-êr (kēp-), *n.* **1.** One who keeps ; one who holds or has possession of ; a guard ; রক্ষক ; অধিকারী ; প্রহরী। **2.** One who has the care, custody and charge of a thing etc. ; জিম্মাদার, রক্ষক, তত্ত্বাবধায়ক, পালক। **3.** One who remains or keeps in a position ; যে ব্যক্তি কোন বিশেষ অবস্থায় অবস্থান করিয়া থাকে। **4.** A lunatic's attendant ; উন্মাদগ্রস্ত ব্যক্তির রক্ষক। **5.** A ring that keeps a larger one especially a wedding ring on the finger ; যে অঙ্গুরীয়ক দ্বারা বৃহত্তর অঙ্গুরীয়ক অঙ্গুলীতে রক্ষিত হয়, রক্ষকাঙ্গুরীয়ক। **Keeper of the Great seal**—The officer of the state who keeps the great seal ; the Lord Chancellor ; যে রাজকর্ম্মচারী রাজ্যের প্রধান প্রধান মুদ্রা (মোহর) রক্ষা করিয়া থাকেন ; লর্ড চেন্সেলার।

keep'-ing (kēp-), *n.* **1.** A hold or retaining ; রক্ষণ। **2.** Custody ; charge ; guardianship ; জিম্মা ; ভার ; অভিভাবকতা। **3.** Maintenance ; support ; তত্ত্বাবধান, রক্ষণাবেক্ষণ ; ভরণপোষণ। **4.** Conformity ; consistency ; harmony ; ঐক্য, মিল ; সামঞ্জস্য ; সঙ্গতি। **5.** (*Attributive*) Fit for keeping as some apples etc. ; রক্ষণোপযোগী। **In or out of keeping with**—In or out of harmony with ; বেমিল, অনৈক্যবিশিষ্ট, বেমানানসই।

keep'-sake (kēp-), *n.* A thing kept or given to be kept, for the sake of the giver ; a token of friendship ; বন্ধুত্বের নিদর্শনস্বরূপ প্রদত্ত বা রক্ষিত বস্তু ; বন্ধুত্বের স্মৃতি-চিহ্ন।

kef, keif, kief, *ns.* **1.** A drowsy state produced by bhang etc. ; ভাঙ্গ প্রভৃতির নেশা। **2.** Indian hemp etc. ; গাঁজা, ভাঙ্গ। **3.** The enjoyment of idleness ; আলস্যসম্ভোগ।

kĕg, *n.* A small cask or barrel ; ক্ষুদ্র পিপা (উহাতে সাধারণতঃ ১০ গেলন অপেক্ষা কম জিনিষ ধরে)।

kĕlp, *n.* **1.** A large seaweed ; একপ্রকার সামুদ্রিক শৈবাল। **2.** The calcined ashes of the seaweed from which carbonate of soda is obtained (formerly used in making soap and glass) ; সামুদ্রিক শৈবালের ভস্ম [পূর্ব্বে উহার ক্ষারে কাচ, সাবান, প্রভৃতি প্রস্তুত হইত]।

kĕl'-pie (-pi), **–pȳ,** *ns.* (*Scotch myth.*) A malignant water-spirit in the form of a horse ; স্কটলণ্ডদেশীয় উপকথায় বর্ণিত জলবাসী অশ্বাকৃতি উপদেবতা।

kĕl'-sŏn, keel'-sŏn (kĕl-), *ns.* A longitudinal piece of timber above the floor-timbers binding them to the keel ; জাহাজের পানিতরাসের উপরে স্থাপিত কাষ্ঠ—যদ্দারা মেঝের তক্তাগুলি পানিতরাসের সহিত সংবদ্ধ করা হয়।

kĕmp, *n.* Coarse hair in wool ; পশমের ভিতর মোটা রোম। **Kemp'-y,** *adj.*

kĕn, *v. t.* & *n.* To know ; to recognize at sight ; জানা, বিদিত থাকা, অবগত থাকা ; দেখিয়া চিনিতে পারা। ***Noun.*** Range of sight or knowledge ; cognizance ; as, in, out of or beyond one's *ken* ; জ্ঞান বা দৃষ্টির সীমা ; জ্ঞানগোচর, দৃষ্টিগোচর।

kĕn'-dăl (green), *n.* A kind of green coarse cloth ; একপ্রকার সবুজ বর্ণের মোটা কাপড়।

kĕn'-nĕl, *n., v. i.* & *t.* **1.** A house for dogs ; কুকুরের ঘর, কুক্কুরাগার, কুক্কুরশালা, শ্বশালা, শ্বানশালা। **2.** A pack of hounds ; কুকুরের দল। **3.** (*Obs.*) The hole of a fox ; (অপ্রঃ) শৃগালের গর্ত্ত। **4.** A mean dwelling ; নিকৃষ্ট আবাস, হীন বাসস্থান। ***Verb i.*** To lie or dwell in a kennel, as a dog ; (*contemptuously of a person*) to lodge ; কুকুরের ঘরে শুইয়া থাকা বা বাস করা ; (অবজ্ঞাচ্ছলে) বাস করা। ***Verb t.*** To keep or confine in a kennel ; to put into a kennel ; কুকুরের ঘরে আবদ্ধ রাখা ; কুকুরের ঘরে রাখা।

kĕn'-nĕl, *n.* The water-course of a street ; a gutter ; পয়ঃপ্রণালী, নর্দ্দমা।

kē-nō'-sis, *n.* (*Theol.*) Renunciation of the divine nature, at least partly, by Christ, in the incarnation ; (খৃষ্টীয় ধর্ম্ম শাস্ত্র) অবতীর্ণ যীশুখৃষ্টের অন্ততঃ আংশিকরূপে দেবপ্রকৃতি-বর্জ্জন। **—not′-ic,** *adj.* **—not′-i-cism,** *n.*

Kĕnt′-ish, *adj.* Of, or relating to, Kent ; ইংলণ্ডের অন্তঃপাতী কেণ্ট প্রদেশসম্পর্কীয়। **Kentish fire**—See FIRE. **Kentish rag**—কেণ্ট প্রদেশে প্রাপ্ত একপ্রকার কঠিন চূর্ণ প্রস্তর।

kĕp′-ī, *n.* A French military cap with a horizontal peak ; শয়ান চূড়াবিশিষ্ট ফরাসীদেশীয় সামরিক টুপি বিশেষ।

kĕ-răm′-ic, *adj.* See CERAMIC.

kĕr′-ă-tōse, *adj.* Containing horn-like fibres as a sponge etc. ; শৃঙ্গবৎ অংশুবিশিষ্ট।

kêrb, *n.* An edging of stone etc. bordering a raised path, pavement, etc. ; উচ্চপথ, তলপত্তন, প্রভৃতির পার্শ্ব-প্রস্তরশ্রেণী।

kêr′-chief (-chĕf), *n.* **1.** A piece of cloth used to cover the head ; অবগুণ্ঠনবস্ত্র। **2.** A covering for the neck, shoulder, etc. ; গলদেশে পরিধেয় বস্ত্র খণ্ড। **3.** (*Poet.*) A handkerchief ; (কবিতায়) রুমাল। **—chiefed,** *p. p.*

kêrf, *n.* **1.** (*Rare*) Act of cutting ; a cut or stroke ; (কচিদ্ ব্যবহৃত) কর্ত্তন ; আঘাত, অস্ত্রক্ষত। **2.** A notch or slit made in anything by cutting esp. by a saw ; করাত প্রভৃতি দ্বারা যে জুলি বা খাঁজ কাটা হয়। **3.** The cut-end of a felled tree ; ছেদিত বৃক্ষের ছিন্ন প্রান্ত।

kêr′-mĕs, *n.* **1.** The pregnant female of an insect ; গর্ভবতী স্ত্রী কীট। **2.** A red dye stuff consisting of the dried bodies of these insects ; কোন কোন কীটের দেহাবশেষ হইতে প্রাপ্ত রক্তবর্ণ রঞ্জক পদার্থ।

kermis, *n.* A periodical fair in Holland etc. ; হলণ্ড দেশের মেলা।

kêrn, kerne (kêrn), *n.* **1.** (*Hist.*) A light-armed foot soldier of Ireland ; (ইতিহাস) আয়র্লণ্ড দেশের লঘুঅস্ত্রধারী পদাতিক সৈন্য। **2.** A peasant : a boor ; চাষাড়ে লোক ; বর্ব্বর।

kêr′-nĕl, *n.* **1.** The edible softer substance within the hard shell of nuts or stone-fruits ; বাদাম, নারিকেল প্রভৃতি ফলের শাঁস, শস্য (সাঃ পঃ)। **2.** The body of a seed within husk ; a whole grain of a cereal as of wheat etc. ; তুষ ছাড়াইলে বীজের যে অংশ অবশিষ্ট থাকে ; বীজশস্য (সাঃ পঃ)। **3.** The central or essential part of anything ; a core ; a nucleus ; কোন জিনিষের মজ্জা ; মধ্যাংশ, সার ; কেন্দ্র, মধ্যবিন্দু।

kĕr′-ō-sene (-sēn), *n.* A lamp-oil from petroleum etc. ; কেরোসিন তৈল।

kêr′-sey (-zĭ), *n.* A kind of coarse woollen cloth ; একপ্রকার মোটা পশমী কাপড়।

kêr′-sey-mere (-zĭ-mēr), *n.* **1.** A twilled woollen cloth made from finest wool ; একপ্রকার টেৰ্চ্চা-বুনা সূক্ষ্ম পশমী বস্ত্র। **2.** (*Pl.*) Trouser of this ; ঐ কাপড়ের পাজামা।

kĕs′-trĕl, *n.* A small European hawk ; ইয়ুরোপদেশীয় ক্ষুদ্র বাজপক্ষী।

Ketch.

ketch (kĕch), *n.* A small two-masted coasting vessel ; একপ্রকার ক্ষুদ্র দ্বিমাস্তুল উপকূলগামী পোত।

ketch′-ŭp (kĕch-), *n.* A kind of sauce made from mushrooms, tomatoes, etc. ; ছত্রাক, বিলাতি বেগুণ, প্রভৃতি দ্বারা প্রস্তুত একপ্রকার চাটনি, আচার।

kĕt′-tle (-l), *n.* A vessel of metal with a spout and a handle for boiling liquids ; জল প্রভৃতি উত্তপ্ত করার জন্য ধাতবপাত্র বিশেষ, কেটলি। **2.** An oval pan for boiling fish ; মৎস্য সিদ্ধ করিবার জন্য একপ্রকার ডিম্বাকার পাত্র। **—ful,** *n.* **Kettle-holder**—বস্ত্র, মাদুর, প্রভৃতির খণ্ড,—যদ্দ্বারা তপ্ত কেটলীর হাতল ধরা হয়। **A pretty kettle of fish** — An awkward state of affairs ; গোলমেলে ব্যাপার।

kĕt′-tle-drŭm (-l), *n.* **1.** A drum made of a hollow brass or copper hemisphere and covered with parchment ; টিকারা, ডঙ্কা, নাগারা, দামামা, দুন্দুভি, ভেরী, আনক, পটহ। **2.** (*Colloq.*) Tea-party held in the afternoon ; (চলিতভাষায়) অপরাহ্ণ বেলার চা-পান সম্মিলনী। **—mer,** *n.* A player of kettledrums ; ভেরীবাদক।

kĕv′-ĕl, *n.* (*Naut.*) A strong cleat or peg to which certain ropes are belayed ; (নৌ-বিদ্যা) সুদৃঢ় কীলক বিশেষ—যাহাতে জাহাজের কোন কোন রজ্জু জড়াইয়া বাঁধা হয়।

key (kē), *n.* **1.** An instrument for shutting or opening a lock ; চাবি, কুঞ্চিকা (সঃ উঃ), অঙ্কুট (ঐ) তালিকা, তালা। **2.** The middle stone of an arch ; খিলানের মধ্যপ্রস্তর, চাবিপাথর। **3.** That which affords or prevents entrance, control or possession etc. ; as, the *key* of a line of defence ; যদ্দ্বারা কোন স্থানে প্রবেশ করিতে পারা যায়, অথবা যাহা কোন স্থানের প্রবেশপথ রুদ্ধ করে, কিম্বা যদ্দ্বারা কোন কিছু অধিকার বা কোন কিছুর উপর আধিপত্য বিস্তার করা যায়। **4.** That which explains a mystery ; a solution ; explanation ; যদ্দ্বারা কোন রহস্যের উদ্ভেদ কিম্বা কোন প্রশ্ন সমাধান হয় ; সমাধান, সমস্যাপূরণ ; ব্যাখ্যা পুস্তক, অর্থ, অর্থপুস্তক, বোধিনী। **5.** A translation of a foreign book ; বিদেশীয় পুস্তকের অনুবাদ। **6.** A book of solution of mathematical problems, exercise, etc.; গণিতের প্রশ্ন-সমাধান পুস্তক। 7. (*Mus.*) A lever in musical instrument for producing notes; the fundamental note or tone in a piece of music; (সঙ্গীত-শাস্ত্র) বাদ্যযন্ত্রের চাবি; গানের প্রধান সুর। 8. (*Mus.*) A system of notes based on their relation to a particular key-note; (সঙ্গীতশাস্ত্র) কোন বিশেষ প্রধান সুরের সহিত সম্পর্কের উপর প্রতিষ্ঠিত সুরমালা। 9. The tone or style of thought or expression; as, his writings are all in the same *key*; চিন্তাপ্রণালী বা বাক্য-বিন্যাসের ধারা বা প্রকৃতি, সুর। 10. An instrument for grasping screws, pegs, nuts, etc.; an instrument for winding clock or watch; সাঁড়াশী; ঘড়ীর চাবী। 11. A dentist's rotary extracting instrument; ঘূর্ণ্যমান দন্তোৎপাটন যন্ত্র। 12. A lever in a typewriter etc., to be pressed by finger; টাইপ রাইটারের চাবি। **Key'-less**, *adj.* **False key**—পরচাবি। **Gold-key**—ইংলণ্ডের রাজপ্রাসাদের কর্ম্মচারিবিশেষের চিহ্ন। **Golden, silver key** — Money used as bribe; ঘুষের টাকা। **Key-board** — পিয়ানো প্রভৃতি বাদ্য-যন্ত্রের চাবির সারি। **Key-bugle**—চাবিওয়ালা রণশিঙ্গা। **Key-hole**—চাবির ছিদ্র। **Key-note**—The fundamental note of a piece of music; প্রধান সুর। (*Fig.*) The prevailing idea or the controlling thought; (লক্ষণায়) প্রধানভাব, মুলভাব, নিয়ামকচিন্তা। **Key-ring**—চাবি রাখার আংটা। **Key-stone**—খিলানের মধ্যপ্রস্তর; (লক্ষণায়) মূলতত্ত্ব; প্রধান উপাদান। **Key-stone-state**—পেনসিল্‌ভেনিয়া। **Power of the keys**—যাজকীয় ক্ষমতা। **St. Peter's keys**—পোপের পদগৌরব-চিহ্নস্বরূপ পরস্পরের উপর আড়ভাবে স্থিত চাবিদ্বয়। **The key of a position**—See KEY 3. **To get** or **have the key of the street**—To be shut out for the night; to be homeless; বাটীর তালা বন্ধ থাকা হেতু সারারাত্রি রাজপথে যাপন করিতে বাধ্য হওয়া; মাথা গুঁজিবার স্থান না পাওয়া, নিরাশ্রয় হওয়া।

key (kē), *v. t.* 1. To furnish or fasten with key; to secure or fasten firmly; চাবি দ্বারা বন্ধ করা; দৃঢ়বদ্ধ করা। 2. To regulate the pitch of the strings of (a piano etc.); সুর বাঁধা। **To key up**—To stimulale; উত্তেজিত করা।

key (kē), *n.* A low island or roof; অনুচ্চ দ্বীপ বা সাগরশৈল।

kha'-ki (kă-), *adj.* & *n.* Of a dull brownish yellow or drab colour; বাদামী রংএর, খাকী রংএর। ***Noun.*** A kind of khaki cloth; a uniform of khaki used in the British army; একপ্রকার খাকী কাপড়; সৈনিকের পোষাকের জন্য খাকী কাপড়।

khan (kăn), *n.* 1. The title of rulers and officials in Central Asia, Afghanistan, etc.; মধ্য এশিয়া, আফগানিস্থান, প্রভৃতির শাসনকর্ত্তা বা রাজকর্ম্মচারীর উপাধি বিশেষ। 2. (*Hist.*) The supreme rulers of Mogol, Tartar and Turkish tribes, as well as emperor of China in the middle ages; (ইতিহাস) তাতার, মোগল, ও তুর্কিজাতিসমূহের সর্ব্বপ্রধান শাসন-কর্ত্তা, মধ্যযুগের চীন সম্রাট্।

Interior of a khan.

khan (kăn), *n.* An eastern inn; a caravanserai or resthouse; সরাই; পান্থনিবাস।

Khe-dive' (kĕ-dēv), *n.* A title granted by the Sultan of Turkey to the viceroy or ruler of Egypt; মিশরাধিপতির উপাধি, খেদিব। **-div'-al, -di'-vi-al** *adjs.*

khodmutgar, *n.* A male servant who waits at table (India); খিদমদ্‌গার।

khutbah, *n.* A Mohammedan prayer delivered in the mosques on Fridays; মুসলমানদিগের জুম্মা বারের নমাজ।

kib'-ble (-l), *v. t.* To bruise or grind corsely; সাতু করা।

kibe, *n.* A crack in the flesh caused by cold; an ulcerated chilblain esp. on the heel: শীতের দরুণ হাত পায় ফাটা; ক্ষতরিশিষ্ট বিপাদিকা, ক্ষতবিশিষ্ট নীহারস্ফোট, পাদস্ফোট। **To tread on one's kibes**—To hurt one's feelings; কাহারো মনে আঘাত দেওয়া।

kiblah, keblah, *ns.* The point towards which Mohammedans turn at prayer *i. e.* towards the temple at Mecca; মুসলমানেরা নমাজ পড়িবার সময় যে দিকে মুখ করে অর্থাৎ মক্কার মসজিদের দিকে—পশ্চিমদিকে।

ki'-bŏsh, *n.* 1. (*Slang*) Nonsense; পাগল আর কি! 2. The proper style or fashion; উপযুক্ত রীতি বা পদ্ধতি। **To put the kibosh on**—To do for; to knock on the head; নিকাশ করা; মাথায় ঘা দেওয়া।

kick, *v. t.* & *i.* 1. To strike, thrust or hit with the foot; to drive or move by kicking; পদাঘাত করা, লাথিমারা; পদাঘাতে তাড়িত করা। 2. To strike in recoil as a gun when fired; (বন্দুক কামানাদির পক্ষে) আওয়াজ হওয়ার পর পশ্চাদ্দিকে ধাক্কা মারা। 3. To drive with force and contempt, (with *out, down-stairs*); জোর করিয়া বাহির করা, অপমান করিয়া তাড়াইয়া দেওয়া। ***Verb i.*** 1. To strike out with the foot as a horse etc.; পদাঘাত করা, চাইট মারা। 2. To show opposition, annoyance or dislike, (with *at, against*); প্রতিকূলভাব প্রকাশ করা, বিরাগ বা অপ্রীতি প্রকাশ করা। 3. To recoil, as a gun, when fired; (বন্দুকাদির পক্ষে) পশ্চাদ্দিকে ধাক্কা মারা। **Kick'-er,** *n.* One that kicks, esp. a horse given to kicking; পদাঘাতকারী, বিশেষতঃ পদাঘাতকারী অশ্ব। **Kick off**—পাদগোলক ক্রীড়ায় কন্দুকে প্রথম পদাঘাত। **To kick against the pricks**—To kick against something sharp or piercing; to resist to one's own hurt; ধারাল বা সূক্ষ্ম কোন কিছুতে লাথি মারা; নিজে আহত হইয়া বাধা দেওয়া। **To kick at or against**—See KICK *v. i.* 2. **To kick off**—To throw off as shoes by kicking etc.; লাথি প্রভৃতি মারিয়া জুতা প্রভৃতি ফেলিয়া দেওয়া। (Foot-ball) To give the first kick; (পাদগোলক ক্রীড়ায়) প্রথম পদাঘাত করা। **To kick one's heels**—See under HEEL. **To kick out, downstairs** — See KICK *v. t.* 3. **To kick over the traces**—To become insubordinate; শাসনের বাহির হইয়া উঠা। **To kick the beam**—To fly up and strike the beam, (said of the lighter scale of a balance); hence, to be found wanting in weight; (অল্পভার দরুণ) তুলাদণ্ডে ধাক্কা মারা; লঘুতর বলিয়া গণ্য হওয়া। **To kick the bucket** — (*Slang*) To die; মরা, কুপোকাৎ হওয়া, অক্কা পাওয়া, শিঙ্গা ফুঁকা, পটল তোলা। **To kick up**—To raise dust; to create a noise or disturbance; ধূলি উড়ান; হাঙ্গামা বা গোলমাল বাঁধান। **To kick up a row** or **shindy**—To make a disturbance; গোলমাল বাঁধান।

kick, *n.* **1.** A striking or thrust with the foot; পদাঘাত, লাথি, পদপ্রহার। 2. Recoil of gun when fired; (বন্দুকাদির আওয়াজের পর) পশ্চাদ্দিকে ধাক্কা। **A drop kick**—See under DROP. **Good or bad kick**—(*Foot-ball*) A good or bad kicker; (পাদগোলক ক্রীড়ায়) ভাল বা মন্দ পাদপ্রহারকারী। **To get more kicks than halfpence**—To get more harshness than kindness; পয়সা যত পাওয়া যায় তার চেয়ে বেশী লাথি ঝাঁটা খাওয়া।

kick, *n.* An indentation in the bottom of a glass bottle diminishing the internal capacity; কাচের বোতলের নীচের কোটর—যদ্দারা ইহার ধারণশক্তি হ্রাস প্রাপ্ত হয়।

kick'-shaw (-shä), *n.* **1.** Any trumpery thing; a toy; a trifle: আজব জিনিষ; খেলনা; ফুটকি নাটকি জিনিষ। **2.** A fancy dish; a tit-bit; বিচিত্র ব্যঞ্জন; রসনাতৃপ্তিকর খাদ্য।

kid, *n., v. t.* & *i.* **1.** A young of a goat; ছাগলছানা, ছাগশিশু, ছাগশাবক, অজশিশু। 2. A leather made from the skin of a kid; ছাগশিশুর চর্ম্ম—যাহা হইতে দস্তানা প্রস্তুত হয়। **3.** (*Slang*) A child esp. a boy; ছোট শিশু, বালক। **4.** (*Pl.*) Gloves of kid leather; ছাগশিশুর চর্ম্মের দস্তানা। ***Verb t. & i.*** **1.** To bring forth a kid or young goat; ছাগশিশু প্রসব করা, ছাগলের প্রসব হওয়া। **Kid'-dy, Kid'-ling,** *ns.* **1.** A little kid; ক্ষুদ্র ছাগশিশু। **2.** A little child; কচি ছেলে। **Kid-glove** — Made of kid leather; (*attributively*) overdainty; free from roughness; ছাগশাবকের চর্ম্ম দ্বারা প্রস্তুত; অতিরিক্ত সূক্ষ্মবিচারী, উৎকটবিচারী; মোলায়েম। **The kids or kid**—যুগ্ম নক্ষত্র বিশেষ। **With kid-gloves** — In a gentle manner; মৃদুভাবে, সুকোমল ভাবে, সন্তর্পণে।

kid, *n.* **1.** A small wooden tub or vessel, especially a sailor's mess-tub; কাঠের ক্ষুদ্র গামলা।

kid, *n.* A fagot; a bundle of sticks; জ্বালানি কাঠের আঁটি; সলার আঁটি।

kid, *v. t.* & *n.* To hoax or humbug; ধোঁকা দেওয়া, প্রতারণা করা। ***Noun.*** A humbug; প্রতারক।

Kid'-der-min-stêr (-êr-), *n.* A town in Worcestershire; উরস্টারসায়ারের নগরবিশেষ। **Kidderminster carpet**—একপ্রকার গালিচা।

kid'-dle (-dl), *n.* A kind of barrier, set in a stream to catch fish; মৎস্য ধরিবার জন্য নদীতে যে বেড়া দেওয়া হয়।

kid'-năp, *v. t.* **1.** To steal (a child); to carry off by illegal force, as a human being; ছেলে চুরি করা; বলপূর্ব্বক মনুষ্য হরণ করা, মানুষ চুরি করা। **—per,** *n.* One who kidnaps; মনুষ্যচোর, ছেলেধরা। **—ping,** *n.*

kid'-ney (-nĭ), *n.* **1.** One of the two oblong flattened glands in the abdominal cavity of mammals, birds, etc. which secrete the urine; a urinary gland; মূত্র-পিণ্ড (জাহিঃ), বৃক্ক (ভাবঃ); মূত্রাশয়, মূত্রগ্রন্থি। 2. Temperament; disposition; স্বভাব, ধাত; মানসিক ভাব, মেজাজ। 3. Sort or kind; প্রকার, রকম। **Kidney-bean**—মুগ, মাষ। **Kidney potato**—নৈনিতাল আলু। **Kidney-vetch**—ঢেঁড়স। **A man of that kidney**—*i. e.* of that temperament; ঐরূপ প্রকৃতির।

kief (kĕf), *n.* See KEF.

kier (kēr), *n.* A large vat in which goods are boiled, bleached, etc.; বৃহৎ পাত্র বিশেষ।

kil'-dêr-kin, *n.* **1.** A cask for liquids containing 16 or 18 gallons; ১৬ অথবা ১৮ গ্যালন ধরে এরূপ তরল পদার্থ রাখিবার পিপা। **2.** A liquid measure of 18 gallons; তরল পদার্থের মাপ—১৮ গেলন।

kill, *v. t., i.* & *n.* **1.** To put to death; to slay; to bring about the death of; খুন করা, সংহার করা, নিকাশ করা (*colloq.*); হত্যা করা, বধ

কর, মারিয়া ফেলা। **2.** To slaughter for food; খাদ্যের জন্য বধ করা। **3.** To quell or suppress; to put an end to, as a feeling etc.; দমন করা; ঠাণ্ডা করা, নির্ব্বাণ করা। **4.** To neutralize; as, alkali *kills* acid; ক্রিয়া বা শক্তি নষ্ট করা। **5.** To defeat, as a Parliamentary bill; (পার্লিয়ামেন্টে প্রস্তাবিত আইন) বিধিবদ্ধ হইতে না দেওয়া। **6.** To destroy the vitality of, as a seed, plant, etc.; জীবনীশক্তি নষ্ট করা। **7.** To represent (a character in a fiction etc.) as dead; (নাটকাদিতে) বধ করা। **8.** To consume as time; সময় কাটান, কাল কাটান। **9.** To overwhelm; as, to *kill* a person with admiration; অভিভূত করা, বিহ্বল করা। **10.** (*Lawn-tennis*) To play (a ball) so hard that it cannot be returned; এরূপ জোরে বলে আঘাত করা যে ফিরাইয়া দিতে পারা যায় না। **11.** (*Football*) To stop dead, as a ball; থামান। ***Verb i.*** **1.** To commit murder or slaughter; হত্যা করা। **2.** To yield good or much meat when slaughtered as pigs; প্রচুর মাংস হওয়া। ***Noun.*** **1.** Act of killing; বধ, হনন। **2.** An animal killed, esp. as game; শিকারে হত জন্তু। **Kill′-er,** *n.* One that kills; হত্যাকারী, ঘাতক। **Kill′-ing,** *n.* & *adj.* Slaying or slaughtering; হত্যা, বধ। (*Adj.*) **1.** Destructive; deadly; প্রাণান্তক; প্রাণঘাতী, মারাত্মক, সাংঘাতিক। **2.** Overpowering; exhausting; "The *killing* part of the day's work"; অভিভবকারী; অবসন্নতাজনক। **3.** Completely fascinating; "*Killing* attire"; চিত্তবিমোহন। **Kill′-ing-ly,** *adv.* **Kill-devil**—(*Angling*) An artificial bait made to spin in water; একপ্রকার কৃত্রিম টোপ। **Kill-joy**—One who throws gloom over a social enjoyment; যে ব্যক্তি কোন সভা বা সম্মিলনীতে উপস্থিত হইলে সকলের আনন্দ এবং উৎসাহ নষ্ট হয়। **Kill-time**—*adj.* & *n.* Meant to kill time; সময়-ক্ষেপের জন্য অভিপ্রেত। (*Noun*) An occupation intended to kill time; কালক্ষেপণোযোগী কার্য্য। **Killing of gold**—হেমমারণ (সাঃ পঃ)। **Killing of metal**—মারণ (সাঃ পঃ)। **Killing of silver**—রৌপ্যমারণ (সাঃ পঃ)। **To kill by inches**—To kill gradually by torture; তিলে তিলে মারা। **To kill off**—To exterminate; ধ্বংস করা, উচ্ছেদ করা, নির্ম্মূল করা। **To kill one's man**—To fight a duel with fatal result to one's opponent; দ্বন্দ্বযুদ্ধে প্রতিদ্বন্দ্বীকে বধ করা। **To kill time**—To consume time; কাল হরণ করা, সময় কাটান, কাল কাটান। **To kill two birds with one stone**—To accomplish two objects at the same time by one effort; এক ঢিলে দুই পাখী মারা, ঘটি কেনা গঙ্গাস্নান করা, রথ দেখা কলা বেচা, এক লাঠিতে সাত সাপ মারা। **To kill with kindness**—To harm fatally with mistaken kindness; অতি মাত্রায় আদর করিয়া সর্ব্বনাশ করা।

kiln (kĭl), *n.* A large furnace or oven for burning, baking or drying bricks, pottery, etc.; (ইটের) পাঁজা, পোয়ান, ভাঁটি, আপাক। **Brick-kiln**—A kiln for burning bricks; ইটের পাঁজা।

kil′-ŏ-grăm, –gramme (-grăm), *ns.* A French measure of weight being 1000 grammes or 2·205 lbs. avoirdupois; ফরাসী ওজনের পরিমাণ বিশেষ, প্রায় এক সের।

kil′-ŏ-li-têr, –tre (-têr), *ns.* A measure equal to a cubic meter or 1000 litres (35·31 cubic ft.); পরিমাণ বিশেষ।

kil′-ŏ-mĕ-têr, –tre (-têr), *ns.* A measure of length being 1000 metres (3280·89 ft. or about $\frac{5}{8}$ ths. of a mile); ফরাসী দূরত্বের মান বিশেষ (প্রায় $\frac{5}{8}$ মাইল)। **–met′-ric, –met′-ri-cal,** *adjs.*

kilt, *n.* A kind of short petticoat worn by men in the Highlands of Scotland; নেংটা গোরাদের এক প্রকার জাঙ্গিয়া।

kilt, *v. t.* **1.** To tuck up (skirts) round the body; কোমরে গুটাইয়া রাখা। **2.** To lay in plaits like a kilt; নেংটা গোরাদের জাঙ্গিয়ার মত ভাঁজে ভাঁজে ঝুলিয়া পড়া।

ki-mö′-nö, *n.* A long Japanese robe with sleeves; জাপানী পুরুষ ও মেয়েদের ঢিলা জামা—ইহার আস্তিন অতিশয় ঢিলা থাকে এবং ইহা চওড়া ফিতা দ্বারা কোমরে বাঁধা হয়।

kin *n.* & *adj.* **1.** Ancestral stock; family; জ্ঞাতিগোষ্ঠী; বংশ, কুল। **2.** One's relatives collectively; জ্ঞাতিবর্গ, কুটুম্ববর্গ। **3.** Affinity, relation or connection by blood; kindred (in character); সম্পর্ক; রক্তগত সম্পর্ক। ***Adj.*** Related; akin; সম্পর্কবিশিষ্ট; সজাতীয়। **Kin′-less,** *adj.* Having no kin or kindred relations; সম্পর্কশূন্য, জ্ঞাতিশূন্য। **Kith and kin**—One's relations; স্বজাতি, কুটুম্ব। **Near of kin**—Closely related; নিকট সম্পর্কীয়। **Of kin**—Akin; related by blood or in character; স্বজাতীয়; নিকট সম্পর্কীয়, গোত্রজ (হিঃ কোঃ)।

kin′-chin, *n.* (*Thieves' slang*) A child; (চোরদিগের ভাষায়) শিশু, বাচ্চা। **Kinchin lay**—কার্য্যে প্রেরিত বালক-বালিকাদিগের অর্থ অপহরণ।

kin′-cŏb (kĭngk-), *n.* A rich Indian silken stuff embroidered with gold and silver thread; কিংখাপ বস্ত্র।

kīnd, *n.* **1.** Race; genus; natural group as of animals, plants, etc.; বর্গ, গণ; জাতি; শ্রেণী। **2.** Sort, class or variety; ভেদ, প্রকার, রকম, বিধ, প্রকৃতি, ধারা, রূপ। **3.** (*Archaic*) Nature; style; way or fashion; as, they act after their *kind*;

(অপ্রঃ) প্রকৃতি ; রীতি ; ধরণ। 4. Character ; quality ; as, they differ in *kind* not in degree ; স্বভাব, প্রকৃতি ; রকম। **In a kind** — (*Archaic*) In a way ; to some extent ; একরূপ ; কিয়ৎ পরিমাণে, কতক পরিমাণে। **In kind**—In produce or commodities as opposed to money ; as, to pay one *in kind* ; উৎপন্ন দ্রব্য দ্বারা, ফসল দ্বারা, পণ্যদ্রব্য দ্বারা। **Kind of** — *Adv.* (*Colloq.*) To some extent ; as, I *kind of* expected it ; (চলিত ভাষায়) কতকটা। **Nothing of the kind**—Not at all like it ; একবারেই এর মত নয়, মোটেই এর মতন নয়। **Repay his insolence in kind**—উদ্ধত ব্যবহারের পরিবর্তে উদ্ধত ব্যবহার করিও।

kīnd, *adj.* **1.** Benevolent ; humane ; sympathetic ; সদয়, দয়ালু, দয়াবান ; কৃপাশীল, কৃপাবিশিষ্ট, কারুণিক, অনুকম্পাপরায়ণ, লোকহিতেচ্ছু ; সমবেদনাপূর্ণ, দরদী। **2.** Friendly in one's conduct (to a person etc.) ; বন্ধুভাবাপন্ন। **3.** (*Rare*) Affectionate ; (ক্বচিদ্-ব্যবহৃত) মমতাশীল, স্নেহশীল। **Kind'-ness,** *n.* **1.** State of being kind ; benevolence ; দয়ালুতা ; অনুগ্রহ, পরোপকার (হিঃ কোঃ)। **2.** A kind act ; দয়ার কার্য্য। **Kind-hearted**—Having a kind heart ; সদয়হৃদয়, দয়ার্দ্রচিত্ত, হৃদয়ালু, হৃদয়বান, সুহৃদয়।

kīnd'-lȳ, *adv.* & *adj.* Benevolently ; favourably ; সদয়ভাবে ; অনুগ্রহ সহকারে। ***Adj.*** **1.** Benevolent or kind ; দয়ালু, সদয়, দয়ার্দ্র। **2.** Mild, genial or agreeable, as a climate, surroundings, etc. ; শান্ত, মৃদু, অনুগ্র। **3.** (*Archaic*) Native born ; as, a *kindly* Scot ; (অপ্রঃ) স্বদেশজ। **–li-ness,** *n.* **–li-ly,** *adv.*

kĭn'-dêr-gär-ten (-tn), *n.* An infant school for developing minds of children by object-lessons, toys, games, etc. ; খেলনা, ক্রীড়া, গান ও বস্তুপাঠ দ্বারা শিশুদিগের মনোবৃত্তি পরিস্ফুরণের জন্য বিদ্যালয়-বিশেষ, বাল্যোদ্যান (হিঃ কোঃ), কুমার-কানন [জর্ম্মণ ভাষায় *Kindergarten* শব্দের অর্থ "শিশুর বাগান"।] **–ism,** *n.* The Kindergarten system ; খেলনা, ক্রীড়া, গান প্রভৃতির সাহায্যে শিশুদিগের মনোবৃত্তি পরিস্ফুরণের প্রণালী, বাল্যোদ্যাননীতি [জর্ম্মণ দেশীয় সুপ্রসিদ্ধ শিক্ষানীতিবিৎ Friedrich Froebel (১৭৮২–১৮৫২) এইরূপ শিক্ষানীতি উদ্ভাবিত করেন]।

kĭn'-dle (-dl), *v. t.* & *i.* **1.** To set on fire ; to light ; as, to *kindle* a fire or substance ; আগুনে পোড়ান ; জ্বালান, প্রজ্বালিত করা। **2.** (*Fig.*) To inflame as the passions ; to rouse ; to excite or stir up action or emotion ; উত্তেজিত করা, উদ্দীপিত করা ; সন্ধুক্ষিত করা, সন্দীপিত করা ; কার্য্যে প্রণোদিত করা। **3.** To make bright or glowing, (sometimes with *up*) ; "Costumes *kindled up* with scarlet" ; উজ্জ্বল করা, দীপ্ত করা, দীপ্তিমান করা। ***Verb i.*** **1.** To take fire ; to burst into flame ; আগুন লাগা ; জ্বলিয়া উঠা। **2.** (*Fig.*) To become excited or animated ; to glow with passion etc. ; (লক্ষণায়) উত্তেজিত হওয়া, উদ্দীপিত হওয়া ; উদ্দীপ্ত হওয়া। **3.** To become glowing or bright ; "His eyes *kindled*" ; জ্বলিয়া উঠা।

kĭn'-drĕd, *n.* & *adj.* **1.** Relationship by blood or marriage ; জ্ঞাতিত্ব, কুটুম্বত্ব, গোত্রসম্বন্ধ। **2.** Relatives collectively ; আত্মীয়, বান্ধব, কুটুম্ববর্গ, বন্ধুবর্গ, বন্ধুজন। **3.** (*Rare*) Family ; race ; (অপ্রঃ) পরিবার ; বংশ। **4.** Resemblance in character ; প্রকৃতি-সাদৃশ্য। ***Adj.*** **1.** Related by blood ; রক্তগতসম্পর্কবিশিষ্ট, গোত্রজ, একগোত্রজ, সগোত্র, সবর্ণ। **2.** Allied ; connected ; similar ; as, frost and *kindred* phenomena ; সজাতীয়, সমপ্রকৃতিক ; সংসৃষ্ট ; সদৃশ, সমতুল।

kīne, *n. pl.* of cow which see.

kĭn-ē-măt'-ics, *n.* (*Pl.*) The science of motion considered abstractly without reference to the forces producing it ; গতি-বিজ্ঞান। **–ic, –i-cal,** *adjs.* Of, or relating to, that motion or science ; গতিবিজ্ঞান সম্বন্ধীয়।

kĭn-ĕ-măt'-ö-grăph, cĭn-ĕ–, *ns.* A contrivance or arrangement for projecting in rapid succession on a screen a numerous series of instantaneous photographs taken at intervals giving a moving representation of the original scene ; ক্ষণে ক্ষণে গৃহীত বহুসংখ্যক তাৎক্ষণিক আলোকচিত্রপরম্পরা যবনিকায় প্রক্ষেপ দ্বারা মূল দৃশ্যের সচল প্রতিরূপ প্রদর্শনের জন্য যান্ত্রিক কৌশল বা ব্যবস্থা বিশেষ, চলচ্চিত্রবীক্ষণযন্ত্র। **–ic,** *adj.*

kī-nĕt'-ics, *n.* That branch of dynamics which treats of forces causing or changing motion in bodies ; গতি-বিজ্ঞান, গতি-শাস্ত্র (সাঃ পঃ), গমনসম্বন্ধীয়বিদ্যা (হিঃ কোঃ)। **–ic, –i-cal,** *adjs.* Of, relating or due to, motion ; গতিবিজ্ঞানসম্বন্ধীয়, গতিসম্বন্ধীয়, গতিগত, গত্যুৎপাদক, গতিজনিত, গতিকারক (হিঃ কোঃ)। **Kinetic energy** — গমনশীলশক্তি (হিঃ কোঃ)। [See under ENERGY.] **Kinetic theory of heat or of gases**—The theory that heat or the gaseous state is due to motion of particles ; উত্তাপ বা বাষ্পীয় অবস্থা কণিকা-সমূহের গতিদ্বারা উৎপন্ন হয়—এইরূপ মতবাদ।

kĭng, *n.* **1.** The male sovereign of a state or nation ; a monarch ; রাজা, নৃপতি, নরপতি ; পৃথিবীপতি, ভূপ, ভূপাল, ভূপতি, ক্ষিতিপতি, ধরণীপাল, অবনীপতি, ক্ষিতিপাল, মহীপাল, মহীপতি, ছত্রপতি, নরেন্দ্র, নরেশ্বর, নরাধিপ, লোকপাল। **2.** A playing card having the picture of a king ; তাসের সাহেব।

3. The principal piece in the game of chess; দাবাখেলার রাজা। 4. A crowned man in the game of draughts; শতরঞ্চ ক্রীড়ার অনুরূপ ক্রীড়াবিশেষের রাজা। 5. One holding a pre-eminent position or rank; the best kind; as, the *king* of beasts, fruits, etc.; শ্রেষ্ঠ ব্যক্তি; শ্রেষ্ঠ জিনিষ। 6. A great merchant etc.; as, a railway *king*; বড় সওদাগর প্রভৃতি, শ্রেষ্ঠিরাজ। **King′-less,** *adj.* Without a king; অরাজক। **King′-like,** *adjs.* Suitable to a king; royal; regal; noble; like a king; রাজোচিত, রাজযোগ্য, রাজার্হ, নৃপতোচিত; বাদশাহী; রাজকীয়; মহৎ; রাজতুল্য। **King′-li-ness,** *n.* **King′-ling,** *n.* **King′-ly,** **King′-ship,** *n.* **King-at-arms** or **King of Arms**—কুলাচার্য্য মণ্ডলীর অধ্যক্ষত্রয়ের অন্যতম। **King-bird** — একপ্রকার নন্দন পক্ষী। **King-bolt**—প্রধান বল্টু। **King-crab** — একপ্রকার বৃহদাকার কর্কট। **King-craft**—রাজ্যশাসনকৌশল, রাষ্ট্রনীতি। **King-cup**—একপ্রকার পুষ্প। **Kingfisher**—

King Crab.

Kingfisher.

মাছরাঙ্গা পাখী, মৎস্যরঙ্গ, মনীচক। **King-Log**—One who becomes first popular and then unpopular; [From a story in Æsop's Fables which relates that the frogs praying to Jupiter for a king he threw down a log among them, which made a satisfactory ruler till the frogs recovered from their fright and discovered his real nature. They therefore entreated Jupiter for another king, whereupon he sent them a stork who devoured them.]; যে ব্যক্তি প্রথম জনপ্রিয় হইয়া অবশেষে জনসাধারণের বিরাগভাজন হইয়া উঠে। **King-maker**—যে ব্যক্তি যাহাকে অভিরুচি তাহাকে রাজসিংহাসনে বসাইয়া থাকে—বিশেষতঃ Henry IIএর সময়ের Earl of Warwick। **King-post**—ঢালু ছাদের মধ্যের খুঁটি—যাহার এক প্রান্ত ছাদের সংযোগ স্থলে অপর প্রান্ত প্রাচীরদ্বয় সংযোজক কড়ি কাষ্ঠের উপরস্থিত থাকে, রাজ-স্তম্ভ। **King's Bench**—ইংলণ্ডের উচ্চতম আদালত। **King's bishop, knight, rook**—গজ (পিল), ঘোটক এবং রথ বা নৌকা। **King's English**—বিশুদ্ধ ইংরাজী। **King's** or **queen's evidence**—রাজসাক্ষী। **King's evil**—Scrofula; গলগণ্ড, গণ্ডমালা। **King's speech**—See under SPEECH. **King of kings**—The almighty God; সর্ব্বশক্তিমান ঈশ্বর। A title of some Eastern kings; রাজাধিরাজ, রাজরাজেশ্বর, রাজরাজ, রাজাধিপ, রাজেন্দ্র। **King of the Castle**—A child's game; ছেলেদের ক্রীড়া। **The king of beasts** — The lion; পশুরাজ, সিংহ, মৃগেন্দ্র, মৃগরাজ। **The king of birds**—The eagle; উৎক্রোশ পক্ষী। **The king of forests**—ওকবৃক্ষ। **The king of metals**—Gold; স্বর্ণ। **The king of terrors**—মৃত্যু। **To be unwilling to call the king one's cousin**—To be in a state of elation; উল্লসিত হওয়া।

king, *v. t.* & *i.* To make a king of; to raise to royalty; রাজপদে অধিষ্ঠিত করা; রাজপদে উন্নীত করা। ***Verb i.*** To act or govern as king; রাজ্যশাসন করা।

king′-dom (-dŭm), *n.* **1.** The state or government of a monarch; the territory of a king; রাজ্য, রাজ্যাধিকার; রাষ্ট্র। **2.** The sphere where one has dominion or control; a domain; "The *kingdom* of her thoughts"; অধিকার; এলেকা। **3.** One of the three great divisions of Natural History, as, the animal, vegetable and mineral *kingdoms*; জন্তু, উদ্ভিদ ও খনিজ এই তিন প্রধান বিভাগের অন্যতম, সৃষ্টি, সর্গ (হিঃ কোঃ)। **4.** The spiritual reign of God or its sphere; ভগবানের আধ্যাত্মিক রাজত্ব বা অধিকার। **Kingdom-come**—(*Slang*) The next world (From the clause *Thy Kingdom come* in the Lord's Prayer); (ইতর ভাষায়) পরলোক। **Monarchical kingdom** — এক-রাজসত্তাক (কেণ্ডিঃ)। **Sub-kingdom** — অবান্তরসর্গ (হিঃ কোঃ)। **The animal kingdom**—জীবজাতি, জীবগণ, জীবকোটি। **The mineral kingdom**—ধাতুজাতি, ধাতুগণ, ধাতুকোটি। **The vegetable kingdom**—বনস্পতি জাতি, বনস্পতিগণ, বনস্পতিকোটি, উদ্ভিজ্জকোটি।

king′-lĕt, *n.* **1.** A petty king; ক্ষুদ্র রাজা। **2.** A golden crested bird; স্বর্ণচূড় পক্ষিবিশেষ।

kink (kingk), *n.*, *v. i.* & *t.* **1.** A twist or curl in a string, rope or thread etc.; দড়ি বা রশির জট বা গাঁইট। **2.** An unreasonable or obstinate notion; a crotchet or whim; অযৌক্তিক বা একগুঁয়ে ধারণা, সংস্কার; খেয়াল। ***Verb i.*** (Of a rope etc.) To form a kink; জট লাগান, জড়াইয়া যাওয়া। ***Verb t.*** To cause (a rope etc.) to form a kink; to twist; জট লাগান; জড়ান। **Kink′-y,** *adj.*

kī′-nō, *n.* The dark red dried juice of certain plants resembling catechu used in medicine and tanning) ; পিয়াশাল (যোঃ), পীতসার (দ্রব্যগুণ)।

kins'-folk (-fök), *n.* (*Pl., literary*) Relations by blood ; kindred : ঘনিষ্ঠ আত্মীয়গণ, কুটুম্বগণ, জ্ঞাতিবর্গ, রক্তগত সম্পর্কীয় ব্যক্তিগণ ; স্বগণ।

kin'-ship, *n.* **1.** Relationship by blood ; জ্ঞাতিত্ব, সগোত্রতা। **2.** Similarity or alliance in character ; প্রকৃতিসাদৃশ্য, স্বভাবসাদৃশ্য।

kins'-man, *n.* (*Now chiefly literary*) One related by blood ; একবংশজ, সগোত্র, গোত্রবন্ধু, গোত্রপুরুষ, জ্ঞাতি, সমানোদক। **—woman,** *n.* (*fem*).

ki-ösk', *n.* **1.** A light open pavilion in Turkey and Persia ; তুরস্ক এবং পারস্যদেশের উদ্যানমণ্ডপ বা নিদাঘমন্দির। **2.** A small shop or structure for the sale of newspapers etc. ; খবরের কাগজ, মিষ্টদ্রব্য, তামাক, প্রভৃতি বিক্রয়ের জন্য কারুকার্য্যখচিত ক্ষুদ্র কুটীর, চারুকুটীর।

kip, *n.* The hide of a young or small beast ; leather made from this ; পশুশাবকের চর্ম্ম ; পশুশাবকের শোধিত চর্ম্ম।

kip, *n.* (*Slang*) An ordinary lodging house ; a lodging ; a bed ; সাধারণ বাসাবাড়ী ; বাসা ; বিছানা।

kip'-per (-êr), *n.* & *v. t.* **1.** A male salmon after spawning ; ডিম্ব নিষেকের পর স্যামন মৎস্য। **2.** A salmon or herring split open, seasoned and dried or smoked ; লোণামাছ, (বিশেষতঃ) লবণমিশ্রিত এবং শুষ্কীকৃত স্যামন ও হেরিং মৎস্য। ***Verb t.*** To cure or preserve salmon, herring, etc. by splitting open, seasoning and drying etc. ; স্যামন ও হেরিং প্রভৃতি মৎস্য শুষ্ক এবং লবণাক্ত করা।

kirk, *n.* **1.** (Scot. & Northern England) A church ; গির্জ্জাঘর, স্কট্‌লণ্ডের গির্জ্জা। **2.** (*In English, usu. cap.*) The Church of Scotland as opposed to the Church of England or to the Episcopal Church of Scotland ; স্কট্‌লণ্ডের ধর্ম্মসংঘ। **Kirkman—**A member of the Kirk of Scotland ; স্কট্‌লণ্ডের ধর্ম্মসংঘভুক্ত ব্যক্তি। **Kirk-session—**স্কট্‌লণ্ডের ধর্ম্মসংঘের নিম্নতম বিচারালয়।

Kirsch'-(was-sêr) (kërsh-vâs-), *n.* A spirit distilled from the fermented juice of wild berries ; একপ্রকার মদ্য।

kir'-tle (kêr-tl), *n.* **1.** (*Archaic*) Woman's gown or outer petticoat ; (অপ্রঃ) স্ত্রীলোকের ঘাগরা। **2.** A man's tunic or coat ; পুরুষের ঢিলা জামা। **—tled,** *p. p.*

kiss, *n.* **1.** A caress or salute given with the lips ; চুম্বন। **2.** (*Billiard*) Contact between moving balls ; গতিশীল কন্দুকসমূহের সংস্পর্শ। **3.** A kind of sugar-plum ; একপ্রকার চিনির মিঠাই।

kiss, *v. t.* & *i.* **1.** To touch with the lips especially as marks of affection, greeting or reverence ; to caress with the lips ; চুমো খাওয়া ; চুম্বন করা। **2.** (*Fig.*) To touch lightly ; "...the wind gently *kissed* the trees" ; মৃদুস্পর্শ করা। **3.** (*Billiard*) To touch as balls ; (বিলিয়ার্ড খেলায়—কন্দুক সম্পর্কে) পরস্পরের সহিত ঠক্কর লাগা। ***Verb i.*** **1.** To salute or caress one another with the lips : as, *kiss* and be friends ; চুম্বন করা। **2.** (*Billiard*) To come in slight contact as two balls ; (বিলিয়ার্ডখেলা) কন্দুকদ্বয় পরস্পরের সহিত ঠক্কর লাগা। **Kiss'-a-ble,** *adj.* **Kiss'-a-bly,** *adv.* **Kiss'-ing,** *adj.* Saluting or caressing with the lips ; চুম্ব্যমান, চুম্বনশীল, চুম্বী। **Kissing crust—**সেঁকার সময় যেস্থানে একটী পাঁউরুটী অপরটীতে স্পর্শ লাগিয়াছিল—তথাকার যে কোমল ছিল্কা। **Kissing kind—**চুম্বন করিতে পারে ততটা সদয় বা বন্ধুভাবাপন্ন ; স্নেহবন্ধনে আবদ্ধ। **Kissing strings—**চিবুকের নিম্নে টুপীর যে ফিতা বাঁধা হয়। **Kiss-me-quick—**A kind of flower-plant ; the pansy ; একপ্রকার পুষ্পবৃক্ষ ; নানাবর্ণপুষ্পপ্রসূ উদ্যানতরুবিশেষ। A small bonnet ; স্ত্রীলোকের ক্ষুদ্র টুপী। **Kiss-in-the-ring** — বালকবালিকাদিগের ক্রীড়াবিশেষ—যাহাতে বালক বালিকাকে বা বালিকা বালককে চুম্বন করে। **To kiss and be friends** — To be reconciled ; পুনর্ম্মিলিত হওয়া। **To kiss away—**To remove tears with kisses ; চুম্বন দ্বারা অশ্রুবিন্দু দূর করা। **To kiss hands or the hand—**To kiss the hand of sovereign etc., as a ceremonial salutation on an appointment to, or retirement from, high office ; কোন উচ্চপদ গ্রহণ বা পরিত্যাগ কালে রাজা বা রাণীর করচুম্বন করা। **To kiss the book—**To kiss the Bible (New Testament) in taking oath ; শপথ গ্রহণ কালে বাইবেল চুম্বন করা। **To kiss the dust—**To yield or submit abjectly ; to be slain ; পদানত হওয়া ; নিহত হওয়া। **To kiss the ground** — To prostrate oneself in token of homage ; to be brought low ; সাষ্টাঙ্গে প্রণিপাত করা, ভূমিষ্ঠ হওয়া, প্রণাম করা ; পদানত করা। **To kiss the rod—**To accept chastisement or punishment submissively ; অবনত মস্তকে দণ্ড গ্রহণ করা।

kit, *n.* **1.** A small wooden tub or pail for various purposes such as holding fish, butter, etc. ; কাঠের ক্ষুদ্র গামলা। **2.** A soldier's knapsack or the articles in it ; সৈনিকের ঝুলি, সৈনিকের ঝুলির জিনিষ। **3.** The personal equipment or necessaries as packed up for travelling etc. ; পথিকের বোঁচকা, আসবাব, সরঞ্জাম। **4.** A workman's especially shoe-maker's outfit ; কারিগরের যন্ত্রপাতি, বিশেষতঃ চর্ম্মকারের যন্ত্রাদি। **5.** A box or bag containing necessaries or tools ; যন্ত্রাদি বা

আবশ্যকীয় দ্রব্যাদি রাখিবার বাক্স বা ঝুলি। **Kit-bag**—সৈনিক ও ভ্রমণকারিগণের সঙ্গীয় জিনিষপত্র নেওয়ার জন্য চামড়ার ব্যাগ।

kit, *n.* (*Now rare*) A small fiddle used by a dancing master; (কচিদ্‌ব্যবহৃত) নৃত্যশিক্ষকের ক্ষুদ্র বেহালা।

kit, *n.* A contraction of KITTEN.

kit′-căt, *n.* **1.** (Also *Kit-cat club*) The club of the Whig politicians founded under James II [From Kit (Christopher) Cat or Catling, the keeper of a pie-house where the club met]; রাজা দ্বিতীয় জেম্‌সের সময় প্রতিষ্ঠিত উদারনীতিকগণের সভা। **2.** A member of that club; উক্ত সভার সভ্য। **3.** (Also *kit-cat portrait*) A portrait of less than half length in which the hands are shown; অর্দ্ধায়তন প্রতিকৃতি—যাহাতে হস্ত প্রদর্শিত হয়।

kitch′-ĕn (kich-), *n.* A room where food is cooked; পাকঘর, পাকশালা, রন্ধনশালা, হেঁসেল, রসবতী, মহানস। **—er,** *n.* **1.** A person employed in a kitchen esp. in a monastery; পাচক, বিশেষতঃ মঠের রন্ধনশালার পাচক, সূপকার। **2.** A cooking range; রন্ধনচুল্লীবিশেষ। **Kitchen-garden**—তরিতরকারীর বাগান, শাকসব্জীর বাগান, শাকবাটিকা (আঃ বঃ)। **Kitchen-maid** — রন্ধনশালার পরিচারিকা। **Kitchen-stuff**—রন্ধন দ্রব্য।

kite, *n., v. i. & t.* **1.** A bird of prey of the falcon family; চিল, শ্যেন। **2.** A rapacious person; a sharper or rogue; লুব্ধক, দুর্বৃত্ত; ধড়িবাজ, জুয়াচোর। **3.** A light frame covered with paper for flying in the air; ঘুড়ি। **4.** (*Pl.*) The lightest and the loftiest sails set only in light wind; নৌকা বা জাহাজের সর্ব্বাপেক্ষা লঘু ও উচ্চ পাইল। **5.** (*Commer. slang*) An accomodation bill; সিফারসি হুণ্ডী। ***Verb i.*** **1.** To fly or soar like a kite; চিলের মত উড়া, ঘুড়ীর মত উড়া। **2.** To get money or credit by kites; সিফার্সি হুণ্ডী দ্বারা টাকা পাওয়া বা বাজারসম্ভ্রম রক্ষা করা। ***Verb t.*** **1.** To cause to soar like a kite; ঘুড়ীর মত উড়ান। **2.** (*Commer.*) To convert into kites; সিফার্সি হুণ্ডীতে পরিণত করা। **To fly a kite**—(*Fig.*) To make experiment to gauge public opinion; (লক্ষণায়) জনসাধারণের মতামত নির্ণয়ের জন্য পরীক্ষা করা। To sustain one's credit by obtaining accomodation bill; সিফার্সি হুণ্ডী দ্বারা বাজারসম্ভ্রম বজায় রাখা।

kith, *n.* Friends and relatives collectively (used only in the phrase *Kith and kin*=Acquaintances, friends and relatives.); আত্মীয়গণ, বন্ধুবর্গ, বন্ধুবান্ধব, কুটুম্বগণ।

kit′-ten (-n), *n., v. t. & i.* **1.** A young cat; বিড়াল-ছানা, মার্জ্জার-শাবক। **2.** A skittish young girl; চঞ্চলপ্রকৃতি বালিকা, প্রকৃতিতরলা বালিকা। ***Verb t. & i.*** To bring forth (kittens); বিড়ালছানা প্রসব করা। **-ish,** *adj.* Like a kitten; frolicsome; মার্জ্জারশাবকবৎ; ক্রীড়াতৎপর, ক্রীড়াকৌতুকপ্রিয়, কেলিকলাপর।

kit′-tle (-l), *adj.* Ticklish; difficult to manage; troublesome; সুড়সুড়ে; দুর্দ্দান্ত, অদম্য; বিরক্তিকর। **Kittle-cattle, Kittle-cattle to shoe** — অদম্যব্যক্তি দুর্দ্দান্তলোক।

kit-tûl′, ki-tōōl′, *ns.* A kind of palm; a strong fibre got from its leaf-stalks; একপ্রকার তাল জাতীয় বৃক্ষ; এই বৃক্ষের পত্রবৃন্ত হইতে প্রাপ্ত সুদৃঢ় অংশু।

kit′-tŷ, *n.* A pet name for a kitten; বিড়াল ছানা।

klĕpt, *n.* **1.** A Greek, who after the Turkish conquest of Greece (15th century) maintained independence in the mountains; তুরস্ক কর্ত্তৃক (পঞ্চদশ শতাব্দীতে) গ্রীস্ বিজয়ের পর Klept নামীয় যে একজন গ্রীক্ পার্ব্বত্য প্রদেশে অবস্থানপূর্ব্বক স্বাধীনতা রক্ষা করিয়াছিল। **2.** A brigand; দস্যু।

klĕp-tō-mā′-nĭ-ȧ, *n.* An irresistible desire of stealing in persons not tempted to it by need; mania for stealing; কোনরূপ অভাবগ্রস্ত নয় এরূপ ব্যক্তির পক্ষে অদমনীয় চৌর্য্য প্রবৃত্তি; চৌর্য্যোন্মাদ। **—ac,** *n.* A person affected with kleptomania; চৌর্য্যোন্মত্ত ব্যক্তি।

klipspringer, *n.* A small graceful South-African antelope; দক্ষিণ আফ্রিকার একপ্রকার ললিতবপু-কৃষ্ণসারমৃগ।

klōōf, *n.* A ravine or deep narrow valley in South Africa; দক্ষিণ আফ্রিকার সঙ্কীর্ণ গিরিবর্ত্ম বা উপত্যকা।

knack (năk), *n.* **1.** Facility in performance or doing something; dexterity; কার্য্যকৌশল; নিপুণতা, নৈপুণ্য, পটুতা, চাতুরী, বুদ্ধিকৌশল। **2.** An ingenious device; কল, কৌশল। **3.** A habit or trick of action or speech etc.; বাক্‌ভঙ্গী, বাক্‌কৌশল, কর্ম্মকৌশল। **4.** A petty contrivance; (obs.) a toy; a trifle; ফন্দি; (অপ্রঃ) খেলনা; ফটকি নাটকী। **Knack′-y,** *adj.*

knack′-ĕr (-năk), *n.* **1.** One who buys or slaughters old or useless horses; যে ব্যক্তি বৃদ্ধ এবং অকর্ম্মণ্য অশ্ব ক্রয় বা বধ করে। **2.** One who buys old houses etc. for the materials; যে ব্যক্তি কাষ্ঠ, ইষ্টক প্রভৃতি উপাদানের জন্য পুরাতন গৃহ ক্রয় করে। **—y,** *n.* The yard of a knacker (*sense* 1); বৃদ্ধ বা অকর্ম্মণ্য অশ্ব বধকারী বা ক্রয়কারীর অঙ্গন।

knag (năg), *n.* A knot in wood; the base of a branch; কাঠের গাঁইট, গ্রন্থি; শাখার মূল। **Knag′-ged, Knag′-gy,** *adjs.* Knotty; rough; গ্রন্থিল; উচ্চাবচ, বন্ধুর, অসমান।

knap (năp), *n.* (*Dial.*) The top or crest of hill; hill or rising ground; (উপভাষায়) পাহাড়ের চূড়া; পাহাড় বা উন্নত ভূমি।

knap (năp), *v. t.* & *i.* **1.** To break as flints for roads with a hammer; to break with blows; হাতুড়ি দ্বারা (রাস্তার জন্য) পাথর প্রভৃতি ভাঙ্গা; বারবার আঘাত করিয়া ভাঙ্গা। **2.** (*Bibl.—dial.*) To knock or rap; to snap: ধাক্কা দেওয়া, ঠক্ ঠক্ করা; পটাস্ করিয়া ফুটান। **Knap'-per,** *n.*

knap'-săck (năp-), *n.* A canvas or leather bag used by soldiers and travellers for carrying necessaries; সৈনিক ও ভ্রমণকারিগণের চামড়া বা ক্যাম্বিসের থলি, ঝোলা।

knap'-weed (năp-wēd), *n.* A kind of weed; একপ্রকার আগাছা।

knar (nâr), *n.* Knot or burr in wood; কাষ্ঠ-গ্রন্থি, কাঠের গাঁইট।

knave (nāv), *n.* **1.** A petty rascal; a rogue; a villain; deceitful fellow; ধূর্ত্ত, শঠ; প্রবঞ্চক; ধড়িবাজ, দুর্ব্বৃত্ত; প্রতারক, জুয়াচোর। **2.** A playing card having the picture of a soldier or servant painted on it; তাসের গোলাম। **knav'-er-y,** *n.* The practice of a knave; dishonesty; নষ্টামি, ধূর্ত্তামি; অসাধুতা। **Knav'-ish,** *adj.* Dishonest; villainous; অসাধু; দুর্ব্বৃত্ত। **Knav'-ish-ly,** *adv.* **Knav'-ish-ness,** *n.* **A knave of hearts**—A flirt; হাবভাবময়ী নারী।

knead (nēd), *v. t.* **1.** To work up as flour, clay, etc. into dough by pressing etc., usu. with hands; to make (bread, pottery, etc.) in this way; ডলা, ঠাসা, মাখা, চটকান, মলা, ছানা; ডলিয়া রুটী, মাটীর পাত্র প্রভৃতি গড়া। **2.** (*Fig.*) To blend, incorporate or weld together; সংমিশ্রিত করা, ছানিয়া মিশান। **3.** To operate on muscles etc.; শরীর ডলা। **Knead'-a-ble,** *adj.* **Knead'-er,** *n.* **Knead'-ing** *n.* **Kneading trough**—A wooden trough in which dough is kneaded; বারকোস বা কাঠের দ্রোণি।

knee (nē), *n.* **1.** The joint between the thigh and the leg-bones in man; the corresponding part in animals; জানু, হাঁটু; জন্তুর জানুদেশ। **2.** Something resembling this in shape or position; a piece of iron or timber with an angular bend; আকার বা অবস্থানে জানুবৎ কোন কিছু; কোণাকৃতি লৌহ বা কাষ্ঠখণ্ড, কোণাচি। **3.** The part of a garment covering the knee; পরিচ্ছদের জানুদেশ আবরক অংশ। **Knee-breeches**—জাঙ্গিয়া। **Knee-cap, Knee-pan**—জানুসন্ধির সম্মুখস্থ ন্যুব্জাকৃতি অস্থি, মালাইচাকি, জানুফলক (সাঃ পঃ)। A strong covering protecting the knee; জানুত্রাণ। **Knee-deep** — So deep as to reach the knees; এক হাঁটু। **Knee-hole table**—একপ্রকার লিখিবার মেজ—যাহার দুই পার্শ্বের দেরাজের মধ্যে জানু রাখার জন্য ফাঁক থাকে। **Knee-joint**—জানুসন্ধি। **Knee-swell**—হারমোনিয়াম প্রভৃতিতে বায়ু প্রবেশ নিয়মনের জন্য জানু দ্বারা চালিত দস্তর যন্ত্র বিশেষ। **Week-kneed**—দুর্ব্বলপ্রকৃতি, দুর্ব্বলচিত্ত। **On one's knees**—Kneeling in supplication, worship, etc.; হাঁটু গাড়িয়া, জানু পাতিয়া, প্রণতজানু হইয়া। **To bring one to his knees**— To reduce one to submission; পদানত করা, বশীভূত করা। **To bow the knee before**—To submit to; বশ্যতাস্বীকার করা। **To bow the knee to Baal**—To conform to the prevailing worship of the day; প্রচলিত পূজানুষ্ঠানাদির অনুসরণ করা। **To give a knee to**—To act as a second to; একপ্রকার মল্লযুদ্ধে একপক্ষের অনুচর হওয়া।

knee (nē), *v. t.* **1.** To touch with the knee; জানুদ্বারা স্পর্শ করা। **2.** (*Carpentry*) To fasten with the knees (*sense 2 n.*); লৌহ বা কাঠের কোণাচি দ্বারা আটকান। **3.** To cause (trousers etc.) to bulge out at the knee; (পায়জামা প্রভৃতি) হাঁটুর দিকে ফুলান।

kneel (nēl), *v. i.* To bend the knee; to fall on the knees, esp. in supplication or reverence (to person); প্রণতজানু হওয়া; জানু পাতিয়া বসা, হাঁটু গাড়িয়া বসা। **Kneeled, Knelt,** *p. p.* **Kneel'-er,** *n.*

knell (nĕl), **1.** The sound of a bell esp. when rung at a death or funeral; মৃত্যুকালীন ঘণ্টাধ্বনি, মৃত্যু-সূচক ঘণ্টাধ্বনি, প্রেতনয়নকালিক ঘণ্টাধ্বনি। **2.** (*Fig.*) An announcement, event, etc. regarded as an omen of death or extinction; মৃত্যু বা বিলোপের পূর্ব্বাভাসস্বরূপ বিবেচিত ঘোষণা, ঘটনা, প্রভৃতি।

knell (nĕl), *v. i.* & *t.* **1.** To sound or ring as bell esp. at death or funeral; ঘণ্টাবাদন করা, মৃত্যু বা অন্ত্যেষ্টি ক্রিয়াকালে ঘণ্টাবাদন করা। **2.** (*Archaic.*) To give forth a doleful sound; (অপ্রঃ) শোকসূচক ধ্বনি করা। **3.** To sound as a warning or evil omen; সাবধানতা-সূচক বা দুর্নিমিত্তজ্ঞাপক ধ্বনি করা। ***Verb t.*** To proclaim, as by a knell; to summon, as by a knell; ঘণ্টাবাদন দ্বারা ঘোষণা করা; মৃত্যুসূচক ঘণ্টাধ্বনি দ্বারা আহ্বান করা।

knick'-êr-bŏck-êr, *n.* (*pl., colloq.*) A kind of loose knee-breeches gathered in at the knee (*abbr. knickers*); একপ্রকার ঢিলা পাজামা—যাহা সরু ফিতা দ্বারা ঠিক হাঁটুর নীচে বাঁধা হয়। [Washington Irving কৃত *History of New York* এর কল্পিত গ্রন্থকার Diedrich Knickerbocker এর নাম হইতে গৃহীত, উক্ত Knickerbocker ওলন্দাজ ছিলেন। ওলন্দাজেরা ঐরূপ পাজামা পরে বলিয়া ইহার নাম Knickerbocker।]

knick'-knack (nĭk-năk), **nick'-năck,** *ns.* **1.** A light dainty article as of furniture, dress or food; ফটকি নাটকি জিনিষ। **2.** A trifle or gimcrack ; a gewgaw ; তুচ্ছ জিনিষ, অকিঞ্চিৎকর দ্রব্য, খেলনা ; অল্পমূল্যের চটকদার জিনিষ। **—er-y,** *n.* **—ish',** *adj.*

knife (nīf), *n.* & *v. t.* **1.** A cutting instrument consisting of a thin blade of steel ; a dagger ; ছুরী, ছুরিকা, চাকু ; ছোরা। **2.** A knife-like weapon ; a short sword etc. ; কর্ত্তরিকা ; কৃপাণিকা। **3.** A blade or cutting tool forming part of a machine ; (কোন যন্ত্রের) ছেদনকারক অংশ। ***Verb t.*** To cut or stab with a knife ; ছুরী দ্বারা কাটা বা বিদ্ধ করা, ছুরী মারা। **Knife-blade**—ছুরীর ফলা। **Knife-board**—যে ফলকের উপর ছুরী পরিষ্কার করা হয়। **Knife-boy**—ভোজন কালে ব্যবহৃত ছুরী পরিষ্কার করার জন্য নিযুক্ত ছোকরা চাকর। **Knife-edge**—The edge of a knife ; ছুরীর ধারাল পার্শ্ব। A sharp steel wedge serving as the axis of a balance, pendulum, etc. ; তুলাদণ্ড, দোলনফলক প্রভৃতির অক্ষদণ্ডস্বরূপ ইস্পাতের কীলক (কাজল)। **Knife-grinder** — ছুরী শানওয়ালা। **Knife-machine**—ছুরী পরিষ্কার করার যন্ত্র। **Knife-rest**—ভোজনকালে ছুরী কাঁটা রাখিবার আধার। **Before you can say knife**—Very quickly or suddenly ; মুখ হইতে কথা বাহির হইতে না হইতে, চট্ করিয়া, ধাঁ করিয়া। **To have a horror of the knife**—To have a fear for surgical operations ; অস্ত্রচিকিৎসাভয় করা। **To play a good knife and fork**—To eat heartily ; পরিতোষপূর্ব্বক ভোজন করা। **War to the knife**—Mortal combat ; relentless war ; প্রাণান্তকর সমর ; নির্ম্মম যুদ্ধ।

knight (nīt), *n.* **1.** (In feudal times) A man of noble birth, who after serving as page and squire is raised to an honourable military rank, by a king etc. ; (মধ্যযুগে) সম্ভ্রান্তবংশোদ্ভব অশ্বারোহী বীরপুরুষ, ভট। **2.** A military follower ; especially one devoted to the service of a lady as an attendant or champion in war or tournament ; সামরিক সহচর ; যে-ব্যক্তি যুদ্ধ বা ক্রীড়াযুদ্ধে বা কোন মহিলার সমর্থক বা সহচররূপে ব্রতী হয়, নারীমর্য্যাদা-রক্ষক।

Knight.

3. One on whom a corresponding dignity with the title *Sir* is conferred for his personal merit or services to the crown or country ; বেরোনেটের নিম্নতর উপাধিধারী ব্যক্তি। [এই উপাধিধারী ব্যক্তিগণের নামের পূর্ব্বে *Sir* শব্দ সংযোজিত হয়।] **4.** (*Hist.*) One representing a shire or county in parliament, (also *knight of the shire*) ; (ইতিহাস) পার্লেমেন্টে কোন জেলা বা প্রদেশের প্রতিনিধি। **5.** A piece in game of chess, usually with a horse's head ; দাবা খেলার ঘোড়া, ঘোটক। ***Verb t.*** To dub or create (one) a knight ; to confer knight-hood on ; ভট সমাজভুক্ত করা ; নাইট উপাধি প্রদান করা। **Knight'-age,** *n.* A list and account of knights ; ভটসমাজ, নাইটশ্রেণী বা সম্প্রদায়। **Knight'-hood,** *n.* **Knight'-like,** *adj.* **Knight'-ly,** *adv.* (*Poet.*) **Knight'-ly,** *adj.* **1.** Of, or pertaining to, a knight ; chivalrous ; আদর্শ ভট-সম্বন্ধীয় ; ভটোচিত। **2.** Consisting of knights ; as, *knightly* order ; ভটগঠিত। **Carpet knight** or **Knight of the carpetry**—বৈঠকী বীর, তালপাতার সিপাই। **Knight-errant**—A knight who travelled in search of adventures ; (*fig.*) a person of chivalrous or quixotic spirit ; মধ্যযুগে যে সকল সম্ভ্রান্ত বংশীয় অশ্বারোহী বীরপুরুষ বীরোচিত দুঃসাহসিক কার্য্যের অন্বেষণে এবং আর্ত্ত ও দুর্ব্বলের রক্ষার্থ পর্য্যটন করিতেন ; (লক্ষণায়) শূর, উৎকট খেয়ালপরবশ ব্যক্তি। **Knight-errantry**—The practice or conduct of a knight-errant (*lit.* & *fig.*) ; ভটের কার্য্য বা বৃত্তি। **Knight-service**—(*Hist.*) The tenure of lands on condition of performing military service ; (ইতিহাস) সৈনিক বিভাগে কাজ করার সর্ত্তে ভূমি ভোগ দখল। **Knight's fee**—নাইট উপাধি প্রদানকালে কোন ব্যক্তিকে যে পরিমাণ ভূমি দেওয়া হয়। **Knight of Industry**—A sharper ; জুয়াচোর, প্রবঞ্চক। **Knight of the Garter** — See GARTER. **Knight of the Order of the Golden Fleece**—A lawyer ; ব্যবহারজীবী। **Knight of the pestle**—An apothecary ; ঔষধ-প্রস্তুতকারী। **Knight of the post**—মিথ্যা সাক্ষ্য প্রদান করিয়া জীবিকার্জ্জনকারী। **Knights of the Rainbow**—Livery servants ; নানাবর্ণের পরিচ্ছদ-পরিহিত ভৃত্যগণ। **Knight of the road**—A high-way man ; রাহাজান। **Knights of the Round Table**—রাজা আর্থারের সহচর সম্ভ্রান্তবংশীয় বীরবৃন্দ [ইঁহারা এক গোলাকার মেজের চতুর্দ্দিকে উপবেশন করিতেন।] **Knight of the shire**—See KNIGHT, *n.* 4. **Knight of the shears**—A tailor ; দরজী। **Knight of the stick**—A compositor ; মুদ্রাযন্ত্রের অক্ষরবিন্যাসক। **Knight of the whip**—A coachman ; কোচোয়ান, গাড়োয়ান।

knit (nit), *v. t.* & *i.* **1.** To form as a textile fabric by interlacing a yarn or thread ; as, to *knit* stockings ; বুনা। **2.** To unite closely ; to join or cause to grow together, as bones etc. ; সংযোগ করা, মিলান ; একত্র করা ; একত্রবর্দ্ধিত হইতে দেওয়া। **3.** To contract (one's brow) in wrinkles ; কুঞ্চিত করা। **4.** (*Fig.*) To unite intimately by marriage, common interest, etc. ; ঘনিষ্ঠরূপে সংযোগ করা। **5.** To make close, firm or hard ; to compact ; as, a well-*knit* frame ; নিবিড় বা কঠিন করা ; সংহত করা। ***Verb i.*** **1.** To weave by making loops and knots ; বুনা। **2.** To grow together ; to be united closely ; একত্র বর্দ্ধিত হওয়া ; দৃঢ়রূপে সংশ্লিষ্ট হওয়া। **3.** To unite intimately by marriage, common interest, etc. ; বিবাহ প্রভৃতি দ্বারা ঘনিষ্ঠভাবে সংযোগ করা। **4.** To become close, firm or compact ; "Limbs *knit* into force" ; দৃঢ়, নিবিড় বা সংহত হওয়া। **To knit one's brows**—See KNIT *v. t.* 3. **To knit up**—To repair by knitting ; বুনিয়া সারা। (*Fig.*) To close up ; to conclude (argument) ; গুছাইয়া লওয়া ; সমাধা করা, শেষ করা।

knit′-ting (nît-îng), *n.* **1.** Act of one who knits ; বুনন। **2.** A net-work or fabric formed by, or in the process of, knitting ; বুনাট কাজ, বুনা হইতেছে এরূপ কাজ। **Knitting-needle** — মোজা প্রভৃতি বুনিবার শলা।

knit′-tle (nît-l), *n.* (*Naut.*) A small line composed of yarn used on board-ship ; (নৌ বিদ্যা) ক্ষুদ্র রশি।

knob (nŏb), *n., v. t.* & *i.* **1.** A rounded protuberance, esp. at the end or surface of a thing ; a boss ; a lump ; বর্ত্তুলাকৃতি উদ্গত অংশ—বিশেষতঃ কোন বস্তুর অগ্র বা উপরিভাগস্থ বর্ত্তুলাকৃতি উদ্গত অংশ ; স্ফীতাংশ, টোপ ; পিণ্ড। **2.** A round handle for a door, drawer, etc. ; দরজা, দেরাজ, প্রভৃতির গোল হাতল। **3.** A small lump of sugar etc. চিনি প্রভৃতির ক্ষুদ্রপিণ্ড, খণ্ড, ডেলা। **4.** (*Slang*) Head (*usu. nob*) ; (ইতরভাষায়) মুণ্ড। ***Verb t.*** To furnish with knobs ; টোপবিশিষ্ট করা। ***Verb i.*** To grow into knobs ; to bulge *out* ; টোপদিয়া উঠা ; ফুলিয়া উঠা। **Knob′-bi-ness**, *n.* **Knob′-by,** *adj.* **Knob-latch**—গোল হাতল ঘুরাইয়া যে দরজার খিল খোলা বা লাগান যায়।

knob′-ble (nŏb-l), *n.* A little nob ; ক্ষুদ্র টোপ।

knock (nŏk), *v. t., i.* & *n.* **1.** To give a blow to ; to strike ; ধাক্কা দেওয়া ; আঘাত করা, টক্কর দেওয়া। **2.** To make a strong impression on ; as, what *knocks* me is his impudence ; মনে ধাক্কা লাগা। **3.** To drive *in* or *out* etc. by striking ; ধাক্কা দিয়া ঢুকান বা বাহির করা। **4.** To strike against, as a door for admittance ; ঢুকিবার জন্য দরজাদিতে আঘাত করা। **5.** To rouse as a person from sleep etc. by knocking at his door ; as, he asked to be *knocked* at 7 O'clock ; দরজায় খট্‌খট্ করিয়া কাহাকে ঘুম হইতে জাগান। ***Verb i.*** **1.** To strike a sharp blow ; to rap upon a door for admittance, (with *at*) ; ধাক্কা মারা ; দরজায় খট্‌খট্ করা। **2.** To clash ; to collide ; ধাক্কা লাগা ; টক্কর লাগা। **3.** (*Mech.*) To rattle on account of parts being loose and striking each other ; (যন্ত্রাদি সম্বন্ধে) কোন কোন অংশ শিথিল হওয়ার দরুণ পরস্পরের সহিত টক্কর লাগিয়া খট্‌খট্ করা। ***Noun.*** A blow ; a rap, esp. at door etc. ; আঘাত, ঘা, ধাক্কা ; দরজায় খট্‌খট্ শব্দ। **Knock-about**—*adj.* & *n.* Boisterous ; noisy (*theatrical slang*) ; কোলাহলকারী ; কোলাহলপূর্ণ (রঙ্গমঞ্চের ইতর ভাষায়) Wandering irregularly ; টোটোবাজ। Suitable for travelling or rough use, as clothes ; মোটা, শক্ত। (*Noun*) (*Theatrical slang*) A noisy performance or performer ; (রঙ্গমঞ্চের ইতরভাষায়) কোলাহলপূর্ণ অভিনয়, কোলাহলকারী অভিনেতা। **Knock-down**—*adj.* & *n.* Such as to fall to the ground ; (*fig.*) overwhelming ; ভূপাতনকারী ; (লক্ষণায়) অভিভবকারী। Designating the price below which an article will not be disposed of by the auctioneer ; যে মূল্যের কমে কোন জিনিষ নীলামে বিক্রয় করা হইবে না—তন্নির্দ্দেশক। (*Noun*) That which knocks one down ; something overpowering or overwhelming, *e. g.* a strong liquor ; যদ্দারা কোন ব্যক্তি ধরাশায়ী হয় ; বিহ্বলতাজনক বা অভিভবকারী বস্তু। A free fight ; as, let us have a *knock-down* ; মারামারি। **Knock-kneed**—বক্রজানুক, সংহতজানুক, চলিবার সময় ঠোকাঠুকি লাগে—এরূপ জানুবিশিষ্ট। A *knock-kneed woman*—বিকটা (বাংস্যঃ)। **Knock-knees**—চলিবার সময় যে জানুদ্বয় পরস্পরের সহিত ঠোকাঠুকি লাগে, সংহতজানু। **Knock-out**—*adj.* & *n.* Disabling as a blow ; অকর্ম্মণ্যকর। (*Noun*) One of the bidders in collusion at an auction ; such a sale or auction ; নীলামে অল্পমূল্যে জিনিষ কেনার জন্য যে সকল লোক জোট বাঁধে তাহাদের অন্যতম ; ঐরূপ নীলাম। **A knock-down argument**—Irresistible or overwhelming argument ; অকাট্য যুক্তি, অখণ্ডনীয় যুক্তি। **A knock-down blow**—See KNOCK-DOWN *adj.* 1. **To knock about**—*v. t.* & *i.* To strike repeatedly ; to treat roughly ; পুনঃ পুনঃ আঘাত করা ; কর্কশ ব্যবহার করা, রূঢ় ব্যবহার করা। (*Verb i.*) To roam about ; to lead an irregular life ; ইতস্ততঃ ঘুরিয়া বেড়ান, এদিক ওদিক ঘুরা, টোঁ টোঁ করিয়া ঘুরা ; অব্যবস্থিত জীবন যাপন করা। **To knock (a person) on the head**—To kill or stun him by blows on the head ; মাথায় আঘাত করিয়া মারিয়া ফেলা বা স্তব্ধতা জন্মান। (*Fig.*) To put an end to (a scheme) etc. ; (লক্ষণায়) কোন (সঙ্কল্প বা কল্পনা) শেষ করিয়া ফেলা। **To knock a person's head off**—(*Fig.*) To surpass him easily ; (লক্ষণায়) কোন ব্যক্তিকে অনায়াসে

অতিক্রম করা। **To knock down**—To prostrate by a blow ; আঘাত করিয়া ভূতলশায়ী করা, ধরাশায়ী করা। To cause to succumb ; বিনাশ করা। To dispose of an article to a bidder by a knock with the hammer ; হাতুড়ির আঘাতে নীলামের ডাক শেষ করিয়া যাহার ডাক সর্ব্বোচ্চ তাহাকে জিনিষ দেওয়া। (*Colloq.*) To call upon (a person for a song etc.) ; (চলিত-ভাষায়) অনুরোধ করা। (*Colloq.*) To lower effectively as prices etc. ; (চলিত ভাষায়) কার্য্যতঃ মূল্যাদি হ্রাস করা। **To knock head**—To kotow ; ভূমিষ্ঠ হইয়া প্রণাম করা, মাথা ঠুকিয়া প্রণাম করা। **To knock off**—To strike off with blows ; আঘাত দ্বারা বিচ্ছিন্ন করা। (*Trans. & intrans.*) To leave (off work) ; কাজ বন্ধ করা। To accomplish (business) hastily; (কাজ) তাড়াতাড়ি শেষ করিয়া ফেলা। To deduct (a sum from the price or bill) ; মূল্য বা ক্রীত জিনিষের হিসাব হইতে কিছু কাটিয়া দেওয়া। To prepare ; প্রস্তুত করা। **To knock one's head against**—To strike with one's head ; (*fig.*) to hurt oneself by coming into collision with unfavourable facts or conditions ; মাথা ঠুকা ; প্রতিকূল অবস্থার সংঘর্ষে আসিয়া প্রতিহত হওয়া। **To knock out**—To force out by blows ; আঘাত করিয়া বাহির করিয়া ফেলা। (*Fig.*) To vanquish ; to overcome ; (লক্ষণায়) পরাস্ত করা ; পরাজিত করা। To loose scent, as a hound in fox-hunting ; শিকারের সন্ধান হারান। **To knock out of time**—To disable as a pugilist so that he cannot respond to call of time ; মল্লযোদ্ধাকে এরূপভাবে অকর্ম্মণ্য করা যাহাতে সে সময়মত পুনরায় যুদ্ধে প্রবৃত্ত হইতে পারে না। (*Colloq.*) To make hastily, as a plan etc. ; (চলিত ভাষায়) তাড়াতাড়ি কোন কল্পনা করা। **To knock the bottom out of**—To render invalid as an argument ; অপ্রামাণিক করা, নিষ্প্রমাণ করা। **To knock together**—To put together hastily ; তাড়াতাড়ি জোড়াতাড়া দেওয়া। **To knock under**—To submit ; to yield to ; অধীনতাস্বীকার করা, হার মানা ; বশ্যতা স্বীকার করা। **To knock up**—To drive upwards or fasten up by knocking ; মারিয়া বন্ধ করা, উপরের দিকে ঠেলিয়া দেওয়া। To arouse by knocking at door ; দরজায় খট্ খট্ করিয়া জাগান। (*Trans. & Intrans.*) To exhaust with fatigue ; to be worn out ; পরিশ্রান্ত হওয়া, পরিশ্রান্ত করা ; অবসন্ন হওয়া। To make or arrange hastily ; তাড়াতাড়ি কোন কাজ করা, তাড়াতাড়ি গোছান। To score (runs) at cricket ; ক্রীকেট খেলায় রন করা।

knock'-ĕr (nŏk-), *n.* **1.** One who, or that which, knocks ; a kind of hammer hinged to a door to knock with for admittance ; যে ব্যক্তি ঘা বা ধাক্কা দেয়, যাহা দ্বারা ঘা বা ধাক্কা দেওয়া হয় ; দ্বারে ঘা দিবার জন্য কব্জা দ্বারা দ্বারের সহিত আঁটা হাতুড়ি বিশেষ, দ্বার-তাড়নী। **2.** A goblin supposed to dwell in mines and indicate presence of ore by knocking ; খনিবাসী ভূত বিশেষ।

knol'-kohl (kŏl-kōl), *n. Brassica oleracea caulorapa* ; ওলকপি।

knoll (nōl), *n.* A small round hill ; a mound ; the top or crown of a hill ; ক্ষুদ্র গোলাকৃতি পাহাড় ; মাটীর ঢিবি ; পাহাড়ের চূড়া।

knoll (nōl), *v. t. & i.* **1.** (*Archaic*) To ring (a bell) ; (অপ্রঃ) ঘণ্টা বাজান। **2.** To toll out as hours ; ঘণ্টা বাজান। **3.** To summon by the sound of a bell ; ঘণ্টা বাজাইয়া আহ্বান করা। ***Verb i.*** To sound as a bell ; ঘণ্টা বাদিত হওয়া।

knop (nŏp), *n.* A knob ; a bud of flower ; a bunch ; স্ফীতাংশ, উদ্গত বর্ত্তুল ; কুসুমকলিকা ; গুচ্ছ, স্তবক।

knot (nŏt), *n., v. t. & i.* **1.** Intertwining of the parts of one or more cords, ropes, etc. to fasten them together or to another object ; a tie in a rope etc. ; সূত্রগ্রন্থি ;

Knots.

গাঁইট। **2.** An ornamental tie or bunch of ribbon or the like ; শোভাজনক ফিতার গুচ্ছ। **3.** A bond ; as, the marriage or wedding *knot* ; বন্ধন। **4.** Anything like a knot in form ; গ্রন্থিবৎ কোন কিছু। **5.** A hard lump in an animal body ; আঁব। **6.** The hard part of a tree where the branch shoots out ; গ্রন্থি, গাঁইট। **7.** A protuberance or excrescence in the tissue of a plant ; বৃক্ষকাণ্ডের স্ফীত বা উদ্গত অংশ। **8.** A group or cluster of things or persons ; সংহতি, সমষ্টি, দল, গুচ্ছ, পুঞ্জ। **9.** A difficult or intricate question ; a problem ; বিষম সমস্যা, জটিল বিষয়, খট্কা, ফের, গোল, পেঁচ ; সমস্যা। **10.** The central point in a problem or plot of a story etc ; কোন সমস্যা বা গল্পের আখ্যানবস্তু প্রভৃতির প্রধান অংশ বা সারভাগ। **11.** A division of a ship's log-line as a measure of speed ; জাহাজের গতিবেগ পরিমাপক রজ্জুর

Car-man—Carter ; শকটচালক। **The car festival**—রথযাত্রা।

ă-răb'-i-doe (-dē), *n. pl.* A large family of beekes ; গোবরে পোকার "বর্গ" বিশেষ।

ăr'-ă-bīne, *n.* See CARBINE.

ăr-ă-bi-neer', —nier' (-nēr), *n.* A soldier armed with a carbine ; ক্ষুদ্র বন্দুকধারী সৈনিক [৬ সংখ্যক Dragoon Guards সৈন্যদলকে *Carabineers* বলা হয়।]

পেঁচান। *Verb i.* 1. To form knot or knots; to become knotted; গ্রন্থির আকার হইয়া উঠা; গাঁইট বাঁধা, গাঁইট পড়া, গ্রন্থিল হওয়া, গ্রন্থিবিশিষ্ট হওয়া। 2. To knit knots for a fringe; ঝালর প্রভৃতির জন্য গ্রন্থি বুনা। **Knot′-less,** *adj.* **Knot′-ted,** *adj.* Having a knot or full of knots; গ্রন্থিল, গ্রন্থিযুক্ত। **Knot′-ting,** *n.* 1. Tying a knot; গ্রন্থিবন্ধন। 2. The knitting of knots for fancy work; a fancy work done by knitting; ঝালর প্রভৃতির জন্য গ্রন্থিবুনন; বোনা ঝালর, প্রভৃতি। **Knot′-ti-ness,** *n.* **Knot′-ty,** *adj.* 1. Full of knots; hard; rugged; গ্রন্থিল, গ্রন্থিময়, গ্রন্থিবিশিষ্ট; কঠিন; বন্ধুর, আবড়োখাবড়ো। 2. Difficult; intricate; puzzling; as, a *knotty* subject, question or point; কঠিন, দুরূহ; জটিল, পেঁচালো; গোলমেলে, হতবুদ্ধিতাজনক। **Gordian knot**—See under GORDIAN. **Knot work**—Ornamental work representing or consisting of intertwined cords; পরস্পরের সহিত সংগ্রথিত রজ্জুবৎ বা তদনুকরণে রচিত শোভাসাধক কারুকার্য্য। A fancy needle work; এক প্রকার চিকণের কাজ। **Porter's knot**—মুটের মাথার বিঁড়া। **Surgeon's knot**—দৃঢ় সূত্র দ্বারা ছিন্ন ধমনী বাঁধিবার কালে অস্ত্রচিকিৎসকগণকর্ত্তৃক যে সমচতুষ্কোণ গ্রন্থি ব্যবহৃত হয়। **To seek for a knot in a rush**—To seek for something that does not exist; অশ্বডিম্বের অন্বেষণ করা।

knout (nowt), *n.* & *v. t.* A kind of whip for flogging criminals formerly in Russia; একপ্রকার কষা—যদ্দ্বারা পূর্ব্বে রুষদেশে অপরাধীদিগকে শাস্তি দেওয়া হইত। *Verb t.* To flog with a knout; ঐরূপ কষা দ্বারা আঘাত করা।

know (nō), *v. t.* & *i.* 1. To perceive or apprehend as familiar; to recognize; জানা; চিনা। 2. To be acquainted with, as a place, thing, person, etc.; পরিচিত থাকা। 3. To be cognizant of; to be aware of; as, to *know* a fact; বিদিত থাকা, পরিজ্ঞাত থাকা; অবগত থাকা। 4. To be versed or skilled in, as a language, science, etc.; ব্যুৎপন্ন হওয়া, পারদর্শী হওয়া। 5. To have personal experience of, as pain, fear, etc.; অবগত থাকা। 6. To be on intimate terms with; অন্তরঙ্গ থাকা। *Verb i.* 1. To have understanding or knowledge; জ্ঞান থাকা, জানা। 2. To feel confident; কৃতনিশ্চয় হওয়া। **Know-a-bil′-i-ty, Know′-a-ble-ness,** *ns.* **Know′-a-ble,** *adj.* That can be known; জ্ঞেয়, বিজ্ঞেয়, জ্ঞাতব্য, বেদনীয়, বেদ্য, জ্ঞানগম্য, বুদ্ধিগম্য, পরিচয়গম্য। **Know′-er,** *n.* One who knows; জ্ঞাতা (হিঃ কোঃ), বিজ্ঞাতা, বেত্তা। **Know′-ing,** *adj.* 1. Well-informed; ব্যুৎপন্ন, জ্ঞাতসার, পারদর্শী। 2. Artful; cunning; wide awake; চতুর; চালাক; সজাগ। 3. (*Colloq.*) Stylish; smart; as, a *knowing* hat; চটকদার; চোস্ত। **Know′-ing-ly,** *adv.* In a knowing manner; consciously; intentionally; জ্ঞানপূর্ব্বক, জ্ঞানতঃ; জ্ঞাতভাবে; ইচ্ছাপূর্ব্বক। **Know′-ing-ness,** *n.* **Know-all**—One who thinks he knows all; সবজান্তা লোক। **Know-nothing**—An ignorant person; অজ্ঞ লোক। Agnostic; অজ্ঞেয়তাবাদী। **Know-nothingism** — The practice of wilful ignorance; অজ্ঞতার ভাণ। The doctrine of agnostics; অজ্ঞেয়তাবাদ। **All one knows**—All one can; সাধ্যানুরূপ। (*Adv.*) To the utmost of one's power; যথাসাধ্য। **I know better (than that)**—I am too well-informed of the facts to believe that; আমি ঐ বিষয় এমন ভালরূপে জানি যে আমার পক্ষে ইহা বিশ্বাস করা সম্ভবপর নয়। **Not that I know of**—Not so far as I know; আমি যতদূর জানি ততদূর নয়। **To know about**—To have information about; কোন ঘটনা সম্পর্কে অবগত থাকা। **To know better than**—To be too discreet to do; সে এতটা সদ্বিবেচক যে তাহার পক্ষে করা সম্ভব নয়। **To know how to** — To have knowledge of the process of doing something; কোন কিছু করার প্রক্রিয়া জানা। **To know of**—To be aware of; অবগত থাকা, বিদিত থাকা। **To know on what side one's bread is buttered**—To be fully alive to one's interest; নিজের বুঝ ষোল আনা বুঝা। **To Know the ropes**—See ROPE. **To know what one is about** — To be prudent and foresighted; বিজ্ঞ হওয়া, দূরদর্শী হওয়া। **To know what's what**—To have proper knowledge of the world; to be wide awake; সংসারাভিজ্ঞ হওয়া; সজাগ থাকা, হুঁসিয়ার থাকা।

know (nō), *n.* (*Colloq.*) Knowledge (chiefly in the phrase *in the know*); জ্ঞাতসারতা। **In the know**—Knowing the thing in question or what is not generally known; জ্ঞাতসার, ভিতরের কথা জ্ঞাত।

knowl′-edge (nŏl-ĕj), *n.* 1. The act of knowing; acquaintance; familiarity gained by experience; as, the *knowledge* of a person, thing or fact; জ্ঞাত হওন, বেদন; পরিচয়; পরিজ্ঞান। 2. That which is known; জ্ঞাত বিষয় বা বস্তু, জ্ঞান। 3. One's scope of information; as, to come to one's *knowledge*; অবগতি, জ্ঞানের সীমা, গোচর। 4. Theoretical or practical understanding (of a subject, language, etc.); উপপত্তিক বা ক্রিয়াসিদ্ধ জ্ঞান। 5. Information acquired by study; learning; notice; অধ্যয়নলব্ধ জ্ঞান; বিদ্যা, পাণ্ডিত্য; গোচর। **Divine or spiritual knowledge**—ব্রহ্মজ্ঞান,

ব্রহ্মবিদ্যা, তত্ত্বজ্ঞান, আত্মজ্ঞান, আত্মবিদ্যা, অধ্যাত্মজ্ঞান, অধ্যাত্মবিদ্যা, পরমার্থজ্ঞান, পরমার্থবিদ্যা, জ্ঞানবিদ্যা। **Not to my knowledge** — Not so far as I know ; আমি যতদূর জানি না। **To one's knowledge**—So far as one knows ; যতদূর কেহ জানে।

known (-nön), *p. p.* Understood ; familiar ; জ্ঞাত, বিদিত, উপলব্ধ ; পরিজ্ঞাত।

knuck'-le (nŭk-l), *n., v.t.* & *i.* **1.** The joint of a finger esp. at its base ; অঙ্গুলীর পর্ব্ব বা গ্রন্থি, অঙ্গুলি-সন্ধি। **2.** The knee joint of a quadruped ; a joint of meat consisting of this and the adjacent parts ; চতুষ্পদ জন্তুর জানু-সন্ধি ; চতুষ্পদ জন্তুর জানুসন্ধি ও তৎসন্নিহিত অংশ সমূহের মাংস খণ্ড। **3.** A metal instrument with points worn to protect the hand from injury in striking ; আঘাত করার জন্য ধাতুময় করত্রাণ। ***Verb t.*** To strike or press with the knuckle ; to pommel ; ঘুষি মারা ; মুষ্ট্যাঘাত করা। ***Verb i.*** **1.** To place knuckles on the ground in playing at marbles ; মার্ব্বেল খেলার সময় অঙ্গুলি-সন্ধি ভূমিতে স্থাপন করা। **2.** To submit or yield, (with *down* or *under*) ; বশ্যতাস্বীকার করা, হারমানা, পরাজয় স্বীকার করা। **Knuckle-bone**—A bone forming the knuckle esp. of a sheep or the like ; (*pl.*) the game played with such bones ; মেষ প্রভৃতির জানুসন্ধির অস্থি ; ঐ সকল অস্থির সাহায্যে ক্রীড়া বিশেষ। **Knuckle duster**—Same as KNUCKLE *n.* 3. **To knuckle down** or **under**—See KNUCKLE *v. i.* 2. **To rap a man's knuckles**—To give a sharp reproof ; তীব্র তিরস্কার করা, খুব একচোট বকুনি দেওয়া।

knur(r) (nêr), *n.* **1.** A knot in wood ; a hard excrescence, concretion or swelling as in a tree trunk, stone, etc. ; বৃক্ষের গাঁইট ; বৃক্ষত্বকের স্ফীতাংশ। **2.** A wooden ball used in a North country game ; কাষ্ঠময় ক্রীড়াকন্দুক।

knurl (nêrl), *n.* **1.** A knob ; a nodule ; a knot ; গোলাকৃতি উদ্গতাংশ ; পিণ্ড, তাল ; গাঁইট। **2.** A small bead or ridge esp. one of a series worked upon a metal surface for ornamentation etc. ; গুলিকা, টোপ। **Knurled**, *adj.*

kō-â'-lă, *n.* (Native name) A marsupial tailless animal of

Koala.

Australia also called *bear* or *native bear* ; অষ্ট্রেলিয়া দেশীয় লাঙ্গুল-হীন উপজঠরী জন্তু বিশেষ।

kō'-bōld, *n.* A domestic or familiar spirit ; an underground spirit in mines etc. ; অপদেবতা ; খনিবাসী ভূত।

kō'-dăk, *n.* & *v. t.* A small photographic camera to take instantaneous pictures ; তাৎক্ষণিক আলোকচিত্র গ্রহণের জন্য ক্ষুদ্র যন্ত্র-বিশেষ ***Verb t.*** **1.** To photograph with kodak ; উক্ত প্রকার

Kodak.

যন্ত্রদ্বারা আলোকচিত্র গ্রহণ করা। **2.** To catch quickly ; to describe vividly ; as, to *kodak* a scene or ক্ষণিক দর্শন করা ; সজীব বর্ণনা জীবন্ত ভাবে চিত্রিত করা।

kō'-ēl, *n.* A kind of cuckoo India, Australia, etc. ; কোকিল, পরভৃত, পিক।

kohl (kōl), *n.* A black pigment used in the East to darken eyelids etc. কজ্জল, কাজল, অঞ্জন।

kohl'-ra-bi (kōl-râ-bē), *n.* A kind of cabbage with a turnip shaped stem ; ওলকপি।

Koo'-doo, ku'-du (kô-dô), *ns.* A large white striped spiral horned South-African antelope ; দক্ষিণ আফ্রিকার মৃগ-বিশেষ—ইহার শিং পেঁচানো এবং গায়ে সাদা সাদা ডোরা থাকে।

kō'-pĕck, cō'—, *ns.* A Russian copper coin ; রুষদেশীয় তাম্র মুদ্রা বিশেষ [মূল্য প্রায় দেড় পয়সা।]

kŏp'-je (-ĭ), *n.* (S. Africa) A small hill ; (দক্ষিণ আফ্রিকা) ক্ষুদ্র পাহাড়

kō'-shêr, *adj.* & *n.* According to Jewish law, as a food, shop, etc. ; ইহুদী বিধানানুযায়ী। ***Noun.*** Kosher food or shop ; ইহুদী বিধানানুযায়ী খাদ্য বা দোকান।

kō-tow', *n.* & *v. i.* **1.** (In China) The practice of touching the ground with the forehead as a sign of worship or of salutation to the Emperor ; (চীনদেশে) প্রণাম, প্রণিপাত, দণ্ডবৎ। **2.** An act of obsequious respect ; হীন চাটুকারিতা-সূচক সম্মান। ***Verb i.*** To perform the kotow ; to act obsequiously ; ভূমিষ্ঠ হইয়া প্রণাম করা ; গড়াগড়ি দেওয়া।

kour'-băsh (koor-), **koor'—**, *ns.* A hide whip as an instrument of punishment in Turkey and Egypt ; চর্ম্মনির্ম্মিত কষা বিশেষ।

kraal (krâl, kräl), *n.* **1.** A South-African village or collection of huts enclosed by fence ; দক্ষিণ আফ্রিকার বৃতিবেষ্টিত গ্রাম বা কুটীর-শ্রেণী। **2.** An enclosure or pen sheep or cattle; গো, মহিষ ভৃতির জন্য বৃতিবেষ্টিত স্থান।

-kĕn, *n.* A fabulous Scandinavian sea-monster; স্ক্যাণ্ডিনেভিয়ার বিকটাকার কাল্পনিক সামুদ্রিক জন্তু।

kran(t)z, *n.* (*S.-Afr.*) Precipitous overhanging wall of rocks; দুরারোহ বা উর্দ্ধে প্রলম্বমান পাষাণ প্রাচীর।

krĕm′-lin, *n.* The citadel of a Russian town or city, esp. that of Moscow with the Imperial palace etc.; রুষিয়ার নগরদুর্গ, বিশেষতঃ মস্কোনগরীর দুর্গ।

kreut′-zer (krŏĭt-sêr), *n.* A small silver or copper coin formerly current in Austria and Germany; জর্ম্মণী বা অষ্ট্রিয়ার প্রাচীন মুদ্রা বিশেষ।

kriegspiel, *n.* A game in which blocks representing troops etc. are moved about on maps; ক্রীড়া বিশেষ—যাহাতে মানচিত্রের উপর সৈন্যাদির প্রতিরূপস্বরূপ গুটিকা চালিত হয়।

krone, *n.* **1.** A silver coin of Norway, Sweden and Denmark = 1s. 1½d.; নরওয়ে, সুইডেন ও ডেনমার্কের রৌপ্য মুদ্রা বিশেষ। **2.** An Austrian silver coin worth 10*d.*; a German gold coin; অষ্ট্রিয়ার রৌপ্য-মুদ্রা বিশেষ; জর্ম্মণীর স্বর্ণমুদ্রা বিশেষ।

krўp′-tŏn, *n.* (*Chem.*) A gas discovered by Ramsay in 1898; (রসায়ন শাস্ত্র) একপ্রকার বাষ্প।

kū′-dŏs, *n.* Glory; fame; renown; যশ; খ্যাতি; গৌরব।

kultur, *n.* A German word corresponding to *culture*; সভ্যতা। *Kultur-kampt*—Culture war; সভ্যতাবিকাশ সমর। [এই শব্দ প্রথমতঃ রাজকীয় পদে নিয়োগ এবং শিক্ষা সম্বন্ধীয় বিষয় লইয়া (১৮৭৩ খৃঃ অব্দে) যাজক সমাজ ও জর্ম্মণ শাসনতন্ত্রের যে বিরোধের সূত্রপাত হয় — তৎসম্পর্কে ব্যবহৃত হইয়াছিল। বর্ত্তমানে যুদ্ধ দ্বারা জর্ম্মণ সভ্যতা বিস্তারের যে ধূঁয়া উঠিয়াছে তাহা *Kultur* নামে অভিহিত হইতেছে।]

kursaal, *n.* A building for visitors esp. at health resorts in Germany; জর্ম্মণীর স্বাস্থ্যজনক স্থানের যাত্রিনিবাস।

kvass, *n.* The rye-beer used in Russia; রুষদেশের মদ্য বিশেষ।

kў′-ăn-īze, *v. t.* To preserve (timber, wood) from decay by steeping in a solution of corrosive sublimate; রসকর্পূর মিশ্রিত জলে ভিজাইয়া কাষ্ঠের পচন নিবারণ করা।

kў′-lō, *n.* One of a breed of Scotch cattle; স্কটলণ্ডের একজাতীয় গোমেষাদি পশু।

kўr′-ĭ-ē—ē-lei′-sŏn (-lĭ-), *n.* **1.** The words of a short petition used in the Eastern and Roman Churches esp. at the beginning of the Mass; a musical setting of these words; গ্রীক ও রোমান ক্যাথলিক ধর্ম্মসংঘের সংক্ষিপ্ত প্রার্থনা বিশেষ; ঐ প্রার্থনার স্বরলিপি। **2.** The response in the Anglican church to the ten commandments (as, *Lord have mercy on us etc.*); দশাদেশের প্রত্যেক আদেশ আবৃত্তির পর (kyrie eleison "ঈশ্বর আমাদের কৃপা করুণ" এই বাক্য উচ্চারণপূর্ব্বক সাড়া দেওন।]

Kyrle society—(With *The*) One founded in 1878 by John Kyrle for decorating the walls of hospitals, cottages, etc. and for improving the artistic taste of the poorer classes; (উদ্যান, ঐক্যতান, সঙ্গীত এবং শিল্পভূষাদিশোভিত গৃহের ব্যবস্থা দ্বারা) দরিদ্র ব্যক্তিগণের জীবনের আনন্দ বৃদ্ধি করার উদ্দেশ্যে প্রতিষ্ঠিত সমাজ বিশেষ। John Kyrle (১৬৩৭—১৭২৪) নামক জনৈক লোক-হিতৈষী ব্যক্তি এই সম্প্রদায়ের প্রতিষ্ঠাতা।

L

L, *n.* **1.** The twelfth letter of the English alphabet; ইংরাজী বর্ণমালার দ্বাদশ অক্ষর। **2.** A Roman numeral equal to 50; রোমীয় সংখ্যা ৫০। **3.** Something shaped like L; L অক্ষরাকৃতি পদার্থ। **4.** A right-angled pipe-fitting used in connecting two pipes at right angles; সমকোণী নলসন্ধি, যদ্দ্বারা নলদ্বয় সমকোণ উৎপাদনপূর্ব্বক সংযুক্ত করা হয়।

lâ, *n.* (*Mus.*) The sixth of the seven sounds in the diatonic scale; স্বরগ্রামের অন্তর্গত ষষ্ঠ স্বর, ধা।

laa′-gêr (lă-), *n., v. t. & i.* In South Africa a camp, esp. one with a defensive barrier of waggons; দক্ষিণ আফ্রিকার শিবির, বিশেষতঃ শকটবেষ্টিত শিবির। ***Verb t.*** To form as waggons into a laager; to encamp as persons in a laager; শকটশ্রেণী দ্বারা শিবির বেষ্টিত করা; শকটবেষ্টিত শিবিরে বাস করিতে দেওয়া। ***Verb i.*** To encamp; শিবির সন্নিবেশ করা।

lăb′-ă-rŭm, *n.* **1.** A Roman military standard adopted by Constantine the Great with Christian symbol added to it; রোমান সম্রাট্ কনষ্টেণ্টাইন কর্ত্তৃক গৃহীত খৃষ্টীয়চিহ্ন সংযুক্ত রণপতাকা। **2.** A symbolical banner or standard; সাঙ্কেতিক ধ্বজা।

lăb′-dă-cĭsm, *n.* See LAMDACISM.

lăb-ĕ-făc′-tion, *n.* A decay; downfall; "The *labefaction* of all"; ক্ষয়; অধঃপতন।

lā′-bel (-bl), *n.* & *v. t.* **1.** A slip of paper, cardboard, metal, etc. affixed to something and indicating in writing its nature, owner, name, destination etc.; অঙ্কপত্র, অঙ্কপট্ট, টিকিট, ল্যাবেল, লেপপত্র। **2.** (*Fig.*) A short classifying phrase or name applied to persons etc.; (লক্ষণায়) সংক্ষিপ্ত শ্রেণীবাচক বাক্য বা নাম। **3.** An adhesive stamp; টিকিট। **4.** (*Arch.*) A projecting moulding over doorways, windows, etc.; (স্থপতিবিজ্ঞান) দ্বার, বাতায়ন প্রভৃতির উপরিস্থ উদ্গাত ভূষা। ***Verb t.*** **1.** To affix or attach a label to; টিকিট মারা। **2.** To assign to a category; "To *label* Byron...as a rhetorician only"; কোন বিশেষ শ্রেণীতে নির্দ্দেশ করা।

Labeo bata—বাটা (গুপ্তঃ)।

Labeo boga—ভাঙ্গন বাটা (গুপ্তঃ)।

Labeo calbasu—কালবাউস (গুপ্তঃ)।

Labeo gonius—ঘনিয়া (গুপ্তঃ)।

Labeo nandina—নান্দিম (গুপ্তঃ)।

Labeo rohita—রুই (গুপ্তঃ)।

lā′-bĭ-ăl, *adj.* & *n.* **1.** Of, or pertaining to, the lips; ওষ্ঠসম্বন্ধীয়, ওষ্ঠজ। **2.** (*Phonetic*) Uttered chiefly by the lips as a sound, letter, etc.; ওষ্ঠ দ্বারা উচ্চারিত, ঔষ্ঠ্য, ওষ্ঠোচ্চারিত। **3.** (*Zool.*) Of, relating to, like, or serving as, a lip or labium etc.; (জন্তু-বিদ্যা) ওষ্ঠসম্বন্ধীয়, ওষ্ঠকার্য্যসাধক, ওষ্ঠবৎ। ***Noun.*** **1.** A labial sound, consonant or vowel; ওষ্ঠ উচ্চারণ, ওষ্ঠবর্ণ। **2.** (*Zool.*) A labial scale or plate, as of a reptile; (প্রাণিবিদ্যা) ওষ্ঠপট্ট বা শল্ক। **—ism,** *n.* **—i-za′-tion,** *n.* **—ize,** *v. t.* To make labial: to utter labially; ওষ্ঠ্য করা; ওষ্ঠের সাহায্যে উচ্চারণ করা। **—ly,** *adv.*

lā′-bĭ-āte, *adj.* & *n.* **1.** (*Bot.*) Having the corolla or calyx divided into two parts suggesting lips; (উদ্ভিদ বিদ্যা) হরিদ্বর্ণ পুষ্পাচ্ছাদন বা গর্ভদল ওষ্ঠাধরের মত বিভিন্ন। **2.** (*Bot.* & *Zool.*) Resembling a lip or labium; (প্রাণিবিদ্যা ও উদ্ভিদ বিদ্যা) ওষ্ঠবৎ। ***Noun.*** A labiate plant; যে বৃক্ষের পুষ্পের হরিদ্বর্ণ আচ্ছাদন বা গর্ভদল ওষ্ঠাধরের মত বিভিন্ন থাকে।

Labiate Corolla.

lā′-bile (-bĭl), *adj.* (*Phys.* & *Chem.*) Unstable; prone to undergo displacement or change; (পদার্থ-বিদ্যা, রসায়নশাস্ত্র প্রভৃতি) অস্থির; স্থানচ্যুতিপ্রবণ, পরিবর্ত্তনপ্রবণ।

lā′-bĭ-ŭm, *n.* (*Pl.* -BIA) **1.** (*Usu. Pl.*) The fold(s) of integument at the opening of the vulva; স্ত্রীলোকের বাহ্যজননেন্দ্রিয়ে ওষ্ঠাধরবৎ অংশ, ভগোষ্ঠ (হঃ চঃ)। **2.** (*Bot.*) The lower lip of a labiate corolla; ওষ্ঠাধরবৎ ভিন্ন হরিদ্বর্ণ পুষ্পাচ্ছাদন বা গর্ভদলের অধরসন্নিভ অংশ।

Lablab cultratum—শিম (বেলঃ)।

Lablab vulgare—বনশিম (বেলঃ)।

lăb′-ŏ-ră-tŏ-rў, *n.* **1.** (Originally) The work-room of a chemist; (now) a room or building for experiment in Chemistry, Physics etc.; a building for manufacturing chemicals, etc.; (পূর্ব্বে) রাসায়নিক পরীক্ষাগার, রসশালা, রসায়নশালা (হিঃ কোঃ); (অধুনা) বৈজ্ঞানিক-পরীক্ষাগার, বীক্ষণাগার; রাসায়নিক পদার্থ প্রস্তুতের গৃহ। **2.** (*Fig.*) A place where something is prepared or some operation is performed; "A notion turned out of the *laboratory* of the mind"; (লক্ষণায়) নির্ম্মাণাগার, ক্রিয়াস্থলী। **—to′-ri-al,** *adj.*

lă-bō′-ri-ous (-ŭs), *adj.* **1.** Toilsome; শ্রমজনক, পরিশ্রমসাধ্য, আয়াসকর, শ্রমসাধ্য, কষ্টসাধ্য। **2.** Industrious; hard-working; পরিশ্রমী; শ্রমসহিষ্ণু, কষ্টসহিষ্ণু। **3.** Not facile or fluent as a style etc.; লীলাপ্রবাহহীন, আয়াসসাধ্য। **—ly,** *adv.* In a laborious manner; পরিশ্রমসহকারে, শ্রমপূর্ব্বক, সপ্রয়াস, আয়াসপূর্ব্বক। **—ness,** *n.*

lā′-bour (-bêr), **—bor** (-bêr), *ns.* **1.** Physical or mental toil; exertion; পরিশ্রম, শ্রম, মেহনৎ; উদ্যোগ, প্রযত্ন, আয়াস, প্রয়াস। **2.** Exertion or toil directed to supplying the wants of society; labourers in the aggregate (opp. to *capital*); শ্রম; শ্রমজীবিসমাজ। **3.** A task; as, a Herculean *labour*; অর্পিত কার্য্যভার। **4.** The pains or pangs of childbirth; প্রসববেদনা, প্রসূতিবেদনা, গর্ভবেদনা, গর্ভযন্ত্রণা। **Forced labour**—বেগার (কেম্ব্রিঃ)। **Hard labour**—Hard toil; কঠোর পরিশ্রম। **Herculean labour** or **Labour of Hercules**—One needing enormous strength etc.; যে কার্য্য সম্পাদনে ভীমবলের আবশ্যক হয়। **Labour-market**—চাহিদার অনুপাতে বেকার শ্রমজীবী সরবরাহ। **Labour organization**—কারিগরগণের ব্যবস্থা। **Lost labour**—Fruitless effort; নিষ্ফল প্রয়াস, নিষ্ফল চেষ্টা। **Productive labour**—উৎপাদকশ্রম (হিঃ কোঃ)। **Skilled labour**—কারিগরি (হিঃ কোঃ)। **Unproductive labour** — অনুৎপাদক শ্রম। **A labour of love**—A work undertaken spontaneously and gratuitously; প্রীতির খাটুনি, স্বতঃপ্রবৃত্ত হইয়া প্রীতিপূর্ব্বক যে কার্য্য করা হয়। **Twelve labours of Hercules**—See under HERCULES.

lā′-bour (-bêr), *v. i.* & *t.* **1.** To undergo or engage in labour; to toil; পরিশ্রম কর; মেহনৎ করা। **2.** To strive or endeavour strenuously; চেষ্টা করা, উদ্যোগ করা। **3.** To proceed with difficulty; as, wheels *labour* in the sand; কষ্টে অগ্রসর হওয়া। **4.** To be troubled or distressed; as, her *labouring* heart; to be impeded, as with prejudice etc.; as, to *labour under* a mistake; to suffer, (with *under*); কষ্ট পাওয়া, সন্তপ্ত হওয়া; বাধাপ্রাপ্ত হওয়া; কষ্ট ভোগ করা। 5. (*Naut.*) To pitch and roll heavily as a ship; (নৌবিদ্যা) প্রবলভাবে আন্দোলিত হওয়া। ***Verb t.*** 1. (*Archaic* or *poetry*) To till; to cultivate; (অপ্রঃ এবং পদ্যে) চাষ করা; কর্ষণ করা। 2. To work out in detail; to elaborate or treat at length; as, to *labour* a point or question; সবিস্তারে বর্ণনা করা; বিস্তৃত ভাবে আলোচনা করা। **—boured,** *adj.* 1. Produced or accomplished with labour; শ্রমসিদ্ধ, আয়াসসিদ্ধ, যত্নসিদ্ধ, কষ্টসিদ্ধ। 2. Much elaborated; not spontaneous; বিস্তারে বিবৃত বা আলোচিত; অস্বতঃস্ফূর্ত্ত। **—er,** *n.* One doing for wages that requires strength or patience rather than skill; শ্রমিক, শ্রমজীবী, কর্ম্মজীবী (বিক্রঃ), মজুর। **A labouring man**—শ্রমজীবী।

lā'-brĕt, *n.* A piece of bone, shell, etc. inserted into the lip by savage people as ornament; অসভ্য ব্যক্তিগণের ওষ্ঠের ভিতর নিবিষ্ট ভূষাস্বরূপ অস্থি বা শুক্তি খণ্ড।

lă-bur'-nŭm (-bêr-), *n.* A small tree with cluster of yellow flowers; পীতপুষ্পস্তবকশোভী ক্ষুদ্র বৃক্ষবিশেষ, (Indian) সোঁদাল (কানাই)।

lăb'-ÿ-rinth, *n.* 1. An edifice or place full of intricacies or winding passages which render it difficult to find the way through or about; a maze; গোলকধাঁধা; চক্রব্যূহ। 2. Any intricate or tortuous arrangement; গোলকধাঁধার ব্যাপার। 3. An inextricable or entangled state of affairs; বিষম সমস্যা, লটখট, নটখট। 4. (*Anat.*) The complex cavity of internal ear; কর্ণমধ্যস্থ গহ্বর সমূহ। **—rin'-thine,** *adj.* Pertaining to, or like, a labyrinth; winding; intricate; perplexing; গোলকধাঁধা সম্বন্ধীয়, গোলকধাঁধাবৎ; পেঁচাল; জটিল; অতি গহন।

lăb-ÿ-rin'-thō-dŏn, *n.* An extinct gigantic amphibian with labyrinthine teeth; অধুনালুপ্ত বৃহৎকায় জন্তু বিশেষ। **—dont,** *n.* & *adj.* Same as LABYRINTHODON. (*Adj.*) with labyrinthine teeth; গহন দন্তরাজি সমন্বিত।

lăc, *n.* 1. A dark red resinous substance produced by insects on trees and used in dyeing; গালা, লা, লাক্ষা, জতু, অলক্ত, অলক্তক, যাবক, যাব। 2. Ware coated with lac; লাক্ষাচ্ছাদিত পাত্র। **Lac-dye**—আলতা, অলক্ত রস, অলক্ত, অলক্তক।

lāce, *n., v. t.* & *i.* 1. A cord or leather strip for fastening or tightening boots or some part of dress; ফিতা, জরি, লেইস। 2. An ornamental cord or braid for trimming men's coats, uniform, etc.; শোভাসাধক রজ্জু, সূত্রজাল। 3. A fine open fabric of linen, cotton, silk or metal threads usually with inwrought patterns; সূক্ষ্মতন্তু-নির্ম্মিত বস্ত্রাঞ্চল, জাল, জালক, সূত্রজাল, জরির ফিতা। ***Verb t.*** 1. To fasten or tighten with a lace; to pass as a cord etc. through; ফিতা দ্বারা বাঁধা; ফিতা, দড়ি প্রভৃতি লাগান। 2. To adorn with trim with lace; ফিতা দ্বারা সুশোভিত করা। 3. To compress the waist of by tightening stay-laces; কাঁচুলির ফিতা আঁটিয়া কোমর সরু করা। 4. To interlace or embroider with thread etc.; ফিতা লাগান, চিকণ প্রভৃতির কাজ করা, জরীর কাজ করা। 5. To diversify (flowers with *streaks* of colour); নানাবর্ণের ডোরা দ্বারা পুষ্প সমূহের বৈচিত্র্যসম্পাদন করা। 6. To lash; to beat; "If I meet thee I will *lace* thee roundly"; চাবুক মারা, কষাঘাত করা; প্রহার করা। 7. To flavour as milk, beer, etc. *with* spirit; বীয়র প্রভৃতি সুরা সংযোগে দুগ্ধ সুস্বাদু ও সুগন্ধ করা। ***Verb i.*** 1. To admit of being fastened or tightened with lace; ফিতা দ্বারা বাঁধিবার উপযোগী করা। 2. To compress one's waist by lacing; কাঁচুলির ফিতাদ্বারা আঁটিয়া কোমর সরু করা। **Lac'-y,** *adj.* Resembling lace; ফিতার মত। **Lace-boot**—ফিতা দ্বারা বাঁধা হয় এরূপ বুট জুতা। **Lace-frame**—ফিতা তৈরী করার কল। **Lace-glass**—ফিতার মত নমুনায় শোভিত ভেনিস নগরীতে প্রস্তুত কাচ। **Lace-man**—যে ব্যক্তি লেইস বিক্রয় করে। **Lace-pillow**—লেইস তৈয়ার করার সময় স্ত্রীলোকেরা কোলের উপর যে গদী রাখে। **I will lace your jacket for you**—I will beat you; আমি তোমাকে মেরে পাট পাট করিব।

lăc'-êr-āte, *v. t.* & *adj.* 1. To tear; to rend; to mangle; ছিন্ন ভিন্ন করা; ছিঁড়িয়া ফেলা, ছেঁড়া; বিদারণ করা, চিরা। 2. To afflict; to distress (heart or feeling); ব্যথিত করা, সন্তপ্ত করা; (হৃদয়) বিদীর্ণ করা। ***Adj.*** Torn or mangled; harrowed; ছিন্নভিন্ন; বিদীর্ণ। **—a-ble,** *adj.* **—a'-tion,** *n.* 1. Act of lacerating; ছেদন, ভেদন, বিপাটন, বিদারণ। 2. The breach or wound made by rending; ছেদনজনিত দাগ বা ক্ষত, ছিদ্র। **—a-tive,** *adj.* Lacerating; harrowing; ছিন্নভিন্নকারী, ছেদক; বিদারক।

lă-cêr'-ti-ăn (-shĭ), **—tīne,** *adjs.* Of, or relating to, lizards; lizard-like; কৃকলাসসম্বন্ধীয়; কৃকলাসতুল্য।

lāc-ĕt', *n.* A work made of braid or tape shaped into a design with lace stitches; একপ্রকার ফিতা।

lăch'-ĕs, *n.* 1. (*Law*) Negligence in doing a duty; undue delay in asserting a right etc.; (আইন)

কর্ত্তব্য কার্য্যে অবহেলা, ত্রুটী, কসুর, গাফিলী দাবী উপস্থাপনে অনুচিত বিলম্ব। 2. Culpable negligence ; অপরাধ-জনক ত্রুটী।

Lăch'-ĕ-sis, *n.* The Fate who spins life's thread ; যে ভাগ্যদেবী জীবনের সূতা কাটে এবং তৎসঙ্গে সঙ্গে জীবনের ভাবী ঘটনাবলীর চিত্র বয়ন করিয়া থাকে। উহার ভগিনী Clotho চরকী ধরিয়া রাখে এবং আয়ু ফুরাইলে অপর ভগ্নী Atropos সূত্র ছেদন করিয়া ফেলে।

Lăch'-rȳ-mă–Chris'-ti, *n.* (*Lit. Christ's tears*) A strong sweet red wine of South Italy ; (শব্দানুযায়ী—খৃষ্টের অশ্রু) দক্ষিণ ইতালীর লোহিতবর্ণ সুমিষ্ট উগ্র মদিরা বিশেষ।

lăch'-rȳ-măl, *adj.* **1.** Of, relating to, or for tears ; অশ্রুসম্বন্ধীয়। **2.** (*Anat.*) Pertaining to, or situated near, the organs producing tears ; অশ্রুস্রাবী গ্রন্থিসম্বন্ধীয়, উক্ত গ্রন্থির অস্তিকস্থ।

lăch-rȳ-mā'-tion, *n.* A flow of tears ; অশ্রুপাত, অশ্রুবর্ষণ। **Lachrymal gland** — অশ্রুস্রাবী গ্রন্থি, অশ্রু গ্রন্থি।

lăch'-rȳ-mă-tō-ry, *adj.* & *n.* Of, or producing tears ; designed to contain tears as a vase ; অশ্রুসম্বন্ধী, অশ্রুজনক, অশ্রুৎপাদক, অশ্রুবাহক ; অশ্রুরক্ষার্থ অভিপ্রেত।

Lachrymatory.

Noun. **1.** A lachrymal vase *i. e.* one intended for holding tears ; অশ্রুপাত্র। **2.** (*Anat. Pl.*) Lachrymal organs ; অশ্রুস্রাবী দৈহিক যন্ত্র সমূহ। **Lachrymatory shell**—অশ্রুজনক গোলা।

lăch'-rȳ-mōse, *adj.* Full of tears ; tearful ; given to weeping ; সাশ্রু, অশ্রুপূর্ণ, অশ্রুময় ; অশ্রুপ্লুত, বাষ্পাকুল ; অশ্রুপাতপ্রবণ। **—ly,** *adv.*

laǒ'-ing, *n.* **1.** A fastening with a lace or cord through eyelet holes ; জুতা, প্রভৃতি ফিতাদ্বারা বাঁধন। **2.** A cord used in fastening ; বন্ধনরজ্জু।

lă-cin'-i-āte, —āt-ĕd. *adjs.* (*Bot. & Zool.*) Cut into deep irregular lobes ; (উদ্ভিদ্-বিদ্যা ও জন্তু-বিদ্যা) ঝালরিত (সাঃ পঃ), অঙ্কলিত (ঐ)।

lăck, *v. i., t.* & *n.* **1.** To be in want ; বিহীন হওয়া, হীন হওয়া, রহিত হওয়া। **2.** To be wanting, (now usually in *p. p.*) ; as, to be *lacking* in strength ; বিরহিত হওয়া, অপ্রতুল হওয়া, শূন্য হওয়া। *Verb t.* To want ; to be destitute of ; not to have or possess ; অভাব থাকা ; বর্জ্জিত হওয়া ; কিছু না থাকা। *Noun.* Want ; need ; deficiency ; অভাব, অপ্রতুল, কমী ; দরকার, প্রয়োজন, আবশ্যক ; ন্যূনতা। **Lack-brain** — মস্তিষ্কহীন ব্যক্তি। **Lack-land**—ভূমিশূন্য ব্যক্তি। **Lack-lustre** — অনুজ্জ্বল, নিষ্প্রভ, দীপ্তিহীন, কান্তিহীন, নিস্তেজ, মন্দকান্তি, মন্দপ্রভ। **For lack of**—Owing to the want or absence of ; অভাবে, অনুপস্থিতি হেতু। **No lack of**—Plenty of ; প্রচুর।

lăck-ă-dai'-ṡi-căl (-dā-), *adj.* **1.** Affectedly pensive or languishing ; কপটচিন্তামগ্ন বা ভাবতন্ময়িত। **2.** Given to airs and graces ; ভড়ংদার। **3.** Languishly sentimental ; ভাবালস। **—ly,** *adv.* **—ness,** *n.*

lăck'-ey (-ĭ), **lăc'-quey** (-ĭ), *n.* & *v. t.* **1.** A foot-man or foot-boy ; a liveried male servant ; পাইক, খিদ্‌মগার, নফর, পার্শ্বানুচর ; তকমাপরা ভৃত্য, চোপদার। **2.** A servile follower ; a toady ; পা-চাটা ; ধামা-ধরা। *Verb t.* To dance attendance on ; to wait upon ; হাঁটাহাঁটি করা, উমেদারী করা ; পরিচর্য্যা করা।

Lă-cō'-ni-ăn, *adj.* & *n.* Of Laconia, a division of Greece ; গ্রীস দেশের লেকোনিয়া নামক বিভাগ সম্বন্ধীয়। *Noun.* An inhabitant of Laconia ; Spartan ; লেকোনিয়ার অধিবাসী ; Sparta দেশীয় লোক।

lă-cŏn'-ic, *adj.* **1.** Expressing much in few words after the manner of Laconians or Spartans ; brief and pithy ; sententious ; স্পার্টা বা লেকোনিয়ার অধিবাসীর মত অল্পকথায় বহুভাব প্রকাশকারী ; সংক্ষিপ্ত অথচ সারবান ; অল্পাক্ষরগ্রথিত, সারগর্ভ, সংক্ষিপ্ত, সংক্ষিপ্তোক্তি, অল্পশব্দক, মিত। **2.** Given to such speech or style ; স্বল্পাক্ষর বাক্যকথনশীল। **—i-cal-ly,** *adv.* Briefly ; সংক্ষেপে, অল্পকথায়।

lăc'-ō-niṡm, lă-cŏn'-i-ciṡm, *ns.* A concise style ; a brief pithy expression ; স্বল্পাক্ষর বাক্য, পরিমিতোক্তি সঙ্কলিতোক্তি, সংক্ষিপ্তোক্তি, সংক্ষেপোক্তি ; অল্পাক্ষরগ্রথিত বাক্য।

lăc'-quer (-ĕr), **lăck'-ĕr,** *n.* & *v. t.* **1.** A varnish consisting of a solution of shellac in alchohol, used esp. as a coating for brass etc. ; সুরাবীর্য্যে গালানো লাক্ষার বার্নিস, কোপল। **2.** A resinous varnish (usually Japanese) for coating wood etc. ; articles of wood etc. coated with lacquer ; রোগন ; লাক্ষা দ্বারা আচ্ছাদিত কাষ্ঠপাত্রাদি। *Verb t.* To varnish or coat with lacquer ; রোগন দ্বারা বার্নিস করা।

lă-crosse' (-krŏs), *n.* A Canadian game of ball like hockey, played with a kind of battledore called a crosse ; কেনেডাবাসিগণের ক্রীড়া বিশেষ।

lăc'-tă-gogue (-gŏg), *adj.* & *n.* (A medicine) adapted to produce a flow of milk ; স্তন্যজনক (ঔষধ)।

lăc'-tāte, *n.* (*Chem.*) A salt of lactic acid ; (রসায়নশাস্ত্র) দুগ্ধাম্লের লবণক।

lăc-tā'-tion *n.* **1.** Act of giving suck ; স্তন্যপ্রদান। **2.** The secreting of milk ; স্তন্যক্ষরণ।

lăc'-tē-ăl, *adj.* & *n.* **1.** Of, pertaining to, or resembling milk ; milky ; দুগ্ধসম্পর্কীয় ; দুগ্ধবৎ। **2.** Conveying chyle or other milky fluids ; অন্নরস বা অপর দুগ্ধবৎ তরল-পদার্থবাহী, অন্নরসবাহক, অন্নরসচালক। ***Noun.*** (*Pl.*) Vessels conveying the chyle from the intestines to the thoracic duct ; অন্নরসবাহী নাড়ীসমূহ, অন্নরসবাহিনী, অন্নরসবাহী সূক্ষ্মসূক্ষ্ম নল।

lăc-tĕs′-cence (-ĕns), *n.* **1.** Milky appearance ; milkiness : দুগ্ধবৎবর্ণ ; দুগ্ধবত্তা। **2.** Milk-like juice ; দুধের মত সাদা রস।

lăc-tĕs′-cent (-ĕnt), *adj.* Producing milky juice as a plant ; milky ; দুগ্ধবৎ-রসোৎপাদক ; দুগ্ধবৎ।

lăc′-tic, *adj.* (*Chem.*) Pertaining to milk ; procured from sour milk or whey as an acid ; দুগ্ধ সম্বন্ধীয় ; দধি বা ছানার জল হইতে উৎপন্ন। **Lactic-acid**—দুগ্ধোৎপন্ন অম্ল বিশেষ, দুগ্ধাম্ল (হঃ চঃ)।

lăc-tĭf′-êr-ous (-ŭs), *adj.* Producing milk or white juice ; দুগ্ধোৎপাদক বা দুগ্ধবৎ শুভ্ররসোৎপাদক।

lăc′-tĭ-fūge, *n.* A medicine which checks the flow of milk ; দুগ্ধস্রাব-নিরোধক ঔষধ।

lăc-tŏm′-ĕ-têr, lăc′-tō-scōpe, *ns.* An instrument for testing the purity of milk ; দুগ্ধের বিশুদ্ধতা পরীক্ষার জন্য যন্ত্র বিশেষ, দুগ্ধমান (খাঃ), দুগ্ধবীক্ষণ (ঐ), দুগ্ধপরীক্ষক (হিঃ কোঃ)।

lăc′-tōse, *n.* Sugar of milk ; দুগ্ধ-শর্করা, ক্ষীরশর্করা।

lăc′-tō-scōpe, *n.* Same as LACTOMETER (which see.)

lă-cū′-nă, *n.* (*Pl.* -NAC, -NAS) **1.** A small missing portion ; a gap ; a hiatus ; ক্ষুদ্র হারান অংশ, ক্ষুদ্র ফাঁক ; শূন্যস্থান। **2.** A cavity in bone or tissue etc. ; চর্ম্ম, ঝিল্লি বা অস্থিস্থিত ক্ষুদ্র গহ্বর (হঃ চঃ)। **Lac′-u-na-ry, –nal, –nar, –nose,** *adjs.*

lă-cŭs′-trīne, *adj.* Of, or pertaining to, lakes ; growing or inhabiting in lakes ; হ্রদসম্বন্ধীয় ; হ্রদজ, হ্রদে প্রাপ্ত, হ্রদবাসী, হ্রদচর। **Lacustrine age**—যে যুগে লোকে হ্রদোপরিস্থ ক্ষুদ্র ক্ষুদ্র দ্বীপ মধ্যে বা হ্রদতীরে মঞ্চোপরি আবাস-ভবন নির্ম্মাণ করিত।

lăd, *n.* A stripling ; a young man or boy ; a young fellow ; a fellow ; বালক ; ছোকরা, যুবক ; ছোঁড়া ; বেটা।

lăd′-dêr, *n.* **1.** A frame of wood or metal or rope consisting of two long upright pieces connected by a set of steps or cross-pieces (also called *rungs*) ; সোপান, সিঁড়ী, মই, অধিরোহিণী, নিঃশ্রয়ণী, আরোহিণী। **2.** (*Fig.*) A means of rising to eminence or attaining an object ; (লক্ষণায়) উন্নতিসোপান। **Ladder-dredge** — মইএর আকার শিকলে সংযুক্ত দ্রোণিশ্রেণীযুক্ত তলকর্ষিণী বিশেষ। **Ladder-stitch**—একপ্রকার সেলাই। **To kick down ladder** — To abandon friends etc. that have helped one to rise ; যে বন্ধু প্রভৃতির সাহায্যে উন্নতি লাভ করা হইয়াছে, তাহাদিগকে ত্যাগ করা।

lăd′-die (-ĭ), *n.* A young lad ; বালক, ছেলে।

lāde, *v. t.* To load ; to put a cargo or load on or in ; as, to *lade* a ship ; to ship (goods) as cargo ; বোঝাই করা ; জাহাজাদিতে মাল বোঝাই করা। **Lad′-en,** *p. adj.* **1.** Loaded (*with*) ; ভারাক্রান্ত। **2.** Painfully burdened (*with* sin, sorrow etc.) ; প্রপীড়িত, ক্লিষ্ট। **Lad′-ing,** *n.* **1.** The act of lading or loading ; বোঝাই করণ। **2.** That which constitutes a cargo ; load ; freight ; বোঝাই-মাল ; ভার, বোঝা ; বোঝাই মালের ভাড়া। **Bill of lading**—See BILL.

lă-di-dă′, *n.* (*Slang*) A dandy ; a swell ; (ইতর ভাষায়) খোস পোষাকী বাবু, নবকার্ত্তিক ; কেতাদুরস্ত লোক।

lā′-dle (-dl), *n.* & *v. t.* A large spoon for transferring liquids ; দর্ব্বী, হাতা। ***Verb t.*** To transfer, as a liquid with a ladle, from one vessel to another ; হাতা দ্বারা এক পাত্র হইতে অন্য পাত্রে তরল পদার্থ স্থানান্তরিত করা। **–ful,** *n.* As much as fills a ladle ; এক হাতা পরিমাণ।

lā′-dȳ, *n.* **1.** (*Obs.*) The female head or mistress of a household ; গৃহিণী, গিন্নী, কর্ত্তাঠাকুরাণী, গৃহকর্ত্রী। **2.** A woman having rule or authority (correlative to *lord*) ; as, the *lady* of the manor ; সম্ভ্রান্তমহিলা। **3.** A woman of good breeding, education and refined manners (correlative to *gentleman*) ; ভদ্রমহিলা, সভ্যাস্ত্রী। **4.** (*Courteously*) A woman ; কুলস্ত্রী, কুলাঙ্গনা কুলবধূ, কুলজা, কুলীনা, (mohammedan) বিবি, বেগম। **5.** A woman to whom one is devoted ; a sweetheart ; a love ; প্রেয়সী ; প্রণয়িনী ; প্রেমিকা। **6.** (*Archaic or vulg.*) Wife ; (অপ্রঃ বা ইতর ভাষায়) স্ত্রী। **7.** A title of the wives of knights and all degrees above them and of the daughters of a nobleman not lower than an earl ; নাইট এবং তদূর্দ্ধতর উপাধিধারিগণের পত্নী এবং আর্ল এবং তদূর্দ্ধতর উপাধিধারী সম্ভ্রান্তপুরুষগণের কন্যার উপাধি, সম্ভ্রান্তমহিলা, আর্য্যা, দেবী।

Lady-bird.

Lady-bird, –cow, –fly, –bug, –clock—পদ্মী পোকা (যোঃ), ইন্দ্রগোপ (প্রবাসী ১৩১৯), পদ্মকীট (নৃত্যঃ), শক্রকীট, তাম্রকৃমি (কেঙিঃ)। **Lady-bountiful** — দানশীলা গৃহিণী। **Lady-chair**—আহত ব্যক্তি প্রভৃতিকে বহনের জন্য দুই ব্যক্তির সংগ্রথিত হস্তদ্বারা রচিত আসন। **Lady-chapel**—কুমারী মেরীর নামে উৎসর্গীকৃত ক্ষুদ্র মন্দির। **Lady-clerk, –doctor, –dog, etc.** — মেয়ে কেরাণী, মেয়ে ডাক্তার, মাদী কুকুর, ইত্যাদি। **Lady-Day**—যে দিবস খৃষ্টজননী কুমারী মেরীর নিকট খৃষ্টের অবতরণবার্ত্তা বিঘোষিত

হইয়াছিল, ২৫শে মার্চ্চ। **Lady-in-waiting**—রাণীর সখী বা সহচরী। **Lady killer**—স্ত্রীজনমোহন, স্ত্রীচিত্তহারী, রমণীজনবিনাশক, রমণীমনোমোহিন, স্ত্রীচিত্তচোর, রমণীমনচোরা। **Lady-love**—প্রণয়িনী, প্রেয়সী, প্রেমিকা, প্রিয়া, কান্তা। **Ladies' gallery**—ভদ্রমহিলাগণের উপবেশনের জন্য বিশেষভাবে রক্ষিত পার্লেমেন্টের প্রাকৃতসভাগৃহের আসনশ্রেণী। **Lady's bedstraw**—একপ্রকার গুল্ম। **Lady's companion**—A small bag for needles, thread, etc.; সূচ, সূতা, প্রভৃতি রাখার জন্য ক্ষুদ্র থলিয়া। **Lady's finger**—ঢেঁড়স। A piece of confectionery; একপ্রকার মিঠাই। **Lady's maid** — প্রসাধিকা (রঃ), অলঙ্কত্র (মঃ সং)। **Lady's man**—যে ব্যক্তি সর্ব্বদা রমণীসমাজে যাতায়াত করে। **My lady**—আর্য্যে! দেবি! **Our Lady**—খৃষ্টজননী কুমারী মেরী। **Painted lady**—একজাতীয় প্রজাপতি।

lā'-dy̆-fy̆, –di-fī, *v. t.* To make a lady of; to call lady; সম্ভ্রান্ত মহিলাসমাজভুক্ত করা; দেবী বা আর্য্যা বলিয়া সম্বোধন করা। **–fied,** *p p.* Having the airs of a fine lady; মাজ্জিতরুচি মহিলার ভঙ্গি-পূর্ণ।

lā'-dy̆-līke, *adj.* **1.** Like a lady in manners; befitting a lady; সম্ভ্রান্তমহিলাসুলভ; ভদ্রমহিলোচিত। **2.** Feeble; effiminate; দুর্ব্বল; স্ত্রীজনসুলভ, মেয়েলী।

lā'-dy̆-ship, *n.* **1.** The rank, position, or personality of a lady; সম্ভ্রান্তমহিলার পদবী, পদমর্য্যাদা বা ব্যক্তিত্ব। **2.** Used as a title with *her, your*, etc. in respectful mention, of or address to, a titular lady; as, *your* or *her ladyship*; সম্ভ্রান্তমহিলার সহিত বা তৎসম্বন্ধে কথা বলার কালে সম্মানসূচক উপাধিস্বরূপ ব্যবহৃত শব্দ।

Laeradh, *n.* The tree round the trunk of which the hall of Valhalla was supposed to have been built; Laerdah নামক বৃক্ষ—যাহার চতুঃপার্শ্বে মৃতবীরগণের প্রমোদপ্রাসাদ Valhalla নির্ম্মিত হইয়াছিল।

Lā-ēr'-tēs, *n.* The father of Odysseus; Odysseusএর পিতা।

Læs-try̆g-ō-ni-ăn (lĕs-), *n.* A cannibal folk whom Odysseus encountered on the east coast of Sicily; সিসিলী দ্বীপের উপকূলের প্রাচীন নরমাংসভোজী জাতি বিশেষ।

l(a)ev'-ū-lōse (lĕv-), *n.* Fruit-sugar; ফলশর্করা।

lăg, *v. i.* & *n.* **1.** To walk or move too slowly; to fall behind; to linger; আস্তে আস্তে চলা, মন্থরগতিতে চলা; পিছাইয়া পড়া; বিলম্ব করা, দেরী করা। ***Noun.*** (*Phys.*) Retardation in current or movement; the amount of this; স্রোতঃ কিম্বা গতির বিলম্ব; ঐ বিলম্বের পরিমাণ। **Lag'-gard,** *adj.* & *n.* Slow; lagging; ঢিলা; বিলম্বকারী, দীর্ঘসূত্রী। (*Noun*) One who lags; a loiterer; গেঁতো; বিলম্বকারী ব্যক্তি, ঢিলালোক। **Lag'-ger,** *n.* **Lag'-ging,** *adj.* Slow in movement; loitering; মৃদুগামী, মন্থরগামী, মন্দগামী; বিলম্বকারী। **Lag of tide**—Same as RETARDATION OF TIDE.

lăg, *v. t.* & *n.* **1.** To send to penal servitude; কঠোরপরিশ্রমসহকৃত কারাদণ্ড বিধান করা। **2.** To apprehend or arrest; গ্রেপ্তার করা, ধরা।

lăg, *n.* & *v. t.* A stave or strip of wood or felt used esp. as a non-conducting cover of boilers etc., বাষ্পস্থালী প্রভৃতির উপর [কাঠের বা নেমদার (felt)] অপরিচালক আবরণ। ***Verb t.*** To case with lags; কাঠ বা নেমদা দ্বারা আবৃত করা। **Lag'-ging,** *n.*

lā'-găn, *n.* (*Law*) The goods or wreckage lying on the bed of the sea; (আইন) সমুদ্রগর্ভে স্থিত মালপত্র বা ভগ্নপোতাদির ধ্বংসাবশেষ।

Lagenaria vulgaris — লাউ (বেলঃ)।

lâ'-gêr, –beer (-bēr), *n.s.* A kind of light beer made originally in Germany; একপ্রকার পাতলা বীয়র।

Lager strœmia Reginæ—অর্জ্জুন (বেলঃ)।

lă-gōon', –gūne', *n.* **1.** A shallow sheet of water connected with the sea; সাগরের সহিত সংযুক্ত স্বল্পপরিসর জলরাশি, উপহ্রদ (সাঃ পঃ), লগুন (ইং কোঃ)। **2.** An enclosed stretch of water in an atoll; প্রবালবলয়বেষ্টিত জলরাশি, বদ্ধজল (সাঃ পঃ)।

lā'-ic, *adj.* & *n.* Of, or pertaining to, the laity or layman; secular; temporal; অযাজকীয়; লৌকিক; বৈষয়িক, ঐহিক। ***Noun.*** A layman; অযাজক, গৃহস্থ। **–i-ci-za'-tion,** *n.* **–i-cize,** *v. t.* To render laic or lay; to commit as a school etc. to the direction of laymen; to throw, as office etc to laymen; অযাজকীয়ভাবাপন্ন করা; বিদ্যালয় প্রভৃতি অযাজকসমাজভুক্ত লোকের হস্তে সমর্পণ করা; পদ প্রভৃতি অযাজক সমাজভুক্ত লোকের প্রাপ্য করা।

laid (lād), *p. p.* of LAY. **Laid up**—Bed-ridden; শয্যাগত, শয্যাশায়ী।

lain (lān), *p. p.* of LIE.

lair (lār), *n., v. i.* & *t.* **1.** A bed or resting place of a wild beast; শ্বাপদশয্যা, পশুর গুহা, গহ্বর আবাসগুহা। **2.** A place for animals to lie or rest; পশুর শয়ন বা বিশ্রামের স্থান, শ্বাপদস্থান। **3.** A shed for cattle on the way to market; বাজারের পথে গো মহিষাদির বিশ্রামের জন্য চালা। ***Verb i.*** To go to, or lie in a lair; (বন্যজন্তুর) গহ্বরে গমন করা বা শয়ন করা। ***Verb t.*** To place or put in a lair; (হিংস্রজন্তুকে) শ্বাপদশয্যায় রাখা।

laird (lārd) *n.* (In Scotland) A landowner; স্কটলণ্ডের ভূম্যধিকারী বা বাড়ীওয়ালা। **Laird'-ship,** *n.*

Lā'-is, *n.* An accomplished or beautiful courtesan [from the name of two famous Greek hetæræ]; গুণালঙ্কৃতা গণিকা, রূপবতী বারাঙ্গনা, সুন্দরী গণিকা [প্রাচীন গ্রীসে Lais নাম্নী দুইজন পরমা সুন্দরী বারাঙ্গনা বাস করিত। প্রথমা Lais Corinth নগরবাসিনী ছিল। দ্বিতীয়া Lais প্রেমিকের সহিত Thessalyতে যায়। তথাকার রমণীগণ তাহার অপরূপ লাবণ্যে ঈর্ষ্যাকুলা হইয়া তাহাকে Aphrodite (রতীদেবীর) মন্দিরে প্রস্তরবর্ষণে বিনাশ করে।]

laissez-aller (*F.*), *n.* Lack of restraint; unconstrained freedom; স্বৈরতা; পূর্ণস্বাধীনতা।

laissez faire, *n.* A letting alone; governmental non-interference with the free action of the individual esp. in commerce; হস্তক্ষেপ না করণ, যথেচ্ছভাবে কার্য্য করিতে দেওন, যথেষ্ট প্রবর্ত্ততা (হিঃ কোঃ); সামাজিক বা ব্যবসায়াদি বিষয়ে গভর্ণমেণ্টের নির্লিপ্ততা।

lā'-i-tȳ, *n.* **1.** The state of being layman; অযাজকত্ব। **2.** The people as distinguished from the clergy; laymen collectively; যাজকশ্রেণী বহির্ভূত ব্যক্তিগণ; গৃহস্থবর্গ, গৃহস্থসমাজ। **3.** Unprofessional people; those outside any particular learned profession; অব্যবসায়ী লোক; ওকালতি, ডাক্তারি, প্রভৃতি কোন বিশেষ ব্যবসায়ের বহির্ভূত লোক।

lāke, *n.* A large sheet or expanse of water wholly surrounded by land; হ্রদ, সরোবর, সরসী, জলাশয়, বাপী, দীর্ঘিকা, ঝিল (হিঃ কোঃ), পুষ্করিণী। **Lake'-less,** *adj.* **Lake'-let,** *n.* A little lake; ক্ষুদ্র ঝিল (হিঃ কোঃ), ক্ষুদ্রহ্রদ। **Lake-dweller**—হ্রদাবাসবাসী। [প্রাগৈতিহাসিক যুগে যে সকল লোক হ্রদোপরিনির্ম্মিত ভবনে বাস করিত।] **Lake-dwellings**—হ্রদাবাস, জলটুঙ্গি, হ্রদোপরিনির্ম্মিত ভবন। **Lake-land, Lake-country** — Westmoreland, Cumberland প্রভৃতি স্থানের হ্রদবহুল গিরিরাজিশোভিত প্রকৃতির লীলানিকেতন। **Lake-poets**—Southey এবং Wordsworth — যাঁহারা বৎসরের অধিকাংশ কাল ইংলণ্ডের অন্তঃপাতী Cumberland এবং Westmoreland এর হ্রদবহুল

Ancient lake-dwellings restored.

শৈলাঞ্চলে বাস করিতেন। **The Great Lake**—অতলান্তিক মহাসাগর। **The Great Lakes**—Superior, Huron, Michigan, Erie এবং Ontario প্রভৃতি ক্যানেডা এবং মার্কিন যুক্তরাজ্যের সীমান্তস্থলবর্ত্তী হ্রদসমূহ।

lāke, *n.* A crimson pigment originally made from lac now from different combinations; অলক্তক বর্ণ।

lăl-lā'-tion, *n.* Same as LAMBDACISM.

lăm, *v. t.* & *i.* (*Slang*) To beat or thrash hard with cane etc.; (ইতর ভাষায়) চাবকান।

lâ'-mâ, *n.* A Tibetan Buddhist priest; তিব্বতদেশীয় বৌদ্ধপুরোহিত, লামা। **–ism, –ist,** *ns.* **Dalai** or **Grand-Lama**—তিব্বত দেশের প্রধান লামা। **Teshu-Lama** — মঙ্গোলিয়ার সর্ব্বপ্রধান লামা পুরোহিত।

lâ'-mâ-sêr-rȳ, *n.* A monastery or convent of lamas; তিব্বতের লামাদিগের মঠ।

lamb (lăm), *n., v. t.* & *i.* **1.** The young of a sheep; the flesh of the young sheep as food; মেষশাবক; কচি ভেড়ার মাংস, মেষশাবকের মাংস। **2.** An innocent and gentle person; নিরীহ লোক, ভাল মানুষ, গো-বেচারা। ***Verb t.*** **1.** (*Pass.*) To be brought forth as lambs; মেষশাবক প্রসূত হওয়া। **2.** To tend as ewes at lambing time; আসন্নপ্রসবা মেষীকে পরিচর্য্যা করা। ***Verb i.*** To bring forth lambs; মেষশাবক প্রসব করা। **Lamb'-hood,** *n.* **Lamb'-kin,** *n.* A young lamb; ছোট ভেড়া। **Lamb'-like,** *adj.* Like a lamb; gentle or meek; মেষবৎ; শান্ত, নম্র, মৃদুস্বভাব, মৃদুশীল। **Lamb's skin**—মেষ-চর্ম্ম। **As well be hanged for a sheep as for a lamb**—Sin boldly; নির্ভীকচিত্তে পাপ করিতে থাক। **A wolf** or **fox in lamb's skin**—A hypocrite; মেষ চর্ম্মাবৃত ব্যাঘ্র, ভণ্ড। **The Lamb** or **the Lamb of God**—The Saviour Christ; পরিত্রাতা যীশুখৃষ্ট।

lamb'-dâ (lăm-), *n.* The Greek letter corresponding to *L*; ইংরাজী *L* অক্ষরের অনুরূপ গ্রীক অক্ষর।

la(m)b'-dâ-cĭsm (lăm-), *n.* The defective pronunciation of the letter *r* as *l*; র স্থানে ল উচ্চারণ।

lamb'-doid (lăm-doyd), **–doi'-dâl** (-doy-), *adjs.* Lambda-shaped; উক্ত অক্ষরাকৃতি। **Lambdoid suture**—যে সীবনি-সন্ধিদ্বারা করোটির ঊর্দ্ধভাগস্থ অস্থিসমূহ করোটীর পশ্চাদ্দেশীয় অস্থির সহিত সংযুক্ত থাকে।

lăm'-bĕnt, *adj.* **1.** Touching lightly (as with the lips); (of light, flame, etc.) flickering; twinkling; মৃদুস্পর্শী; মিটমিটকারী; টিমটিমকারী। **2.** Softly radiant, as sky, eyes, etc.; মৃদুপ্রভ, মৃদুজ্জ্বল, স্নিগ্ধোজ্জ্বল, স্নিগ্ধপ্রভ। **3.** Gently brilliant, as wits, style, etc.; শান্তোজ্জ্বল। **–ben-cy,** *n.* **–ly,** *adv.*

lăm'-bre-quin (-bêr-kĭn), *n.* A piece of drapery over the top of a door or window or hung from a mantlepiece; দ্বার বা বাতায়নের উপরিভাগস্থ বস্ত্রখণ্ড, অগ্নিসেবনস্থলীর তাক হইতে দোদুল্যমান বস্ত্রখণ্ড।

lāme, *adj.* & *v. t.* **1.** Crippled or disabled in a limb, (esp. a foot or leg); limping; খঞ্জ, পঙ্গু, বিকলাঙ্গ;

খোঁড়া। **2.** Defective; imperfect; unsatisfactory, as an argument, excuse, etc.; দোষযুক্ত; অসম্পূর্ণ, বিকল; অসন্তোষজনক। **3.** Halting; not smooth, as a metre etc.; গতি-বিকল; আয়াসসিদ্ধ। ***Verb t.*** To make lame; to cripple; (*lit* & *fig.*); খোঁড়া করা, পঙ্গু করা, খঞ্জ করা; অক্ষম করা, বিকল করা। **Lame′-ly,** *adv.* **Lame′-ness,** *n.* State of being lame; defectiveness; পঙ্গুতা, খঞ্জতা; অসম্পূর্ণতা। **Lam′-ish,** *adj.* **Lame excuse** — Unsatisfactory excuse; বাজে ওজর, খঞ্জ আপত্তি। **Lame of** or **in one leg**— Crippled in one leg; এক পা খোঁড়া।

lă-mĕl′-lă, *n.* (*Pl.* -LAE) A thin plate, scale, layer or film esp. of a bone or tissue; অস্থি প্রভৃতির সূক্ষ্ম স্তর বা ফলক। **Lam′-el-late, Lam′-el-lose, –lar,** *adjs.*

lă-mĕnt′, *n., v. t.* & *i.* **1.** Expression of grief or sorrow; lamentation; শোক প্রকাশ; বিলাপ, খেদ, পরিদেবন, কাতরোক্তি। **2.** A dirge; শোকগাথা। ***Verb t.*** To mourn for; to express grief for; to regret; to deplore; বিলাপ করা; শোচনা করা; আক্ষেপ করা; খেদ করা। ***Verb i.*** To weep, (often with *for* or *over*); to wail; to express sorrow; ক্রন্দন করা, রোদন করা; খেদ করা; শোক করা। **–ed,** *p. adj.* Mourned for (conventionally of the dead); as, the late *lamented*; পরলোকগত।

lăm′-ĕn-tă-ble (-bl), **1.** *adj.* (*Archaic*) Doleful; mournful; (অপ্রঃ) সকরুণ, শোচনীয়; দুঃখজনক, শোকপূর্ণ, শোকাবহ, খেদজনক। **2.** Pitiable; deplorable; শোকযোগ্য, শোচনার্হ, শোকার্হ; খেদাস্পদ, শোকাস্পদ, শোচনীয়, শোকপূর্ণ। **–bly,** *adv.*

lăm-ĕn-tā′-tion, *n.* **1.** Act of lamenting; expression of sorrow; cries of grief; a wailing; আক্রন্দন, বিলপন; শোকপ্রকাশ, খেদোক্তি, কাতরোক্তি; হাহাকার; খেদ, আক্ষেপ, বিলাপ। **2.** (*Cap., pl.*) A book of the Old Testament ascribed to the prophet Jeremiah (*Abbr. Lam.*); বাইবেলের প্রাচীন নিয়মের অন্তর্গত পুস্তকবিশেষ।

lā′-mĭ-ă, *n.* (*Rom. myth.*) A monster in woman's shape devouring human beings and sucking children's blood; রাক্ষসী, ডাইনী, ডাকিনী।

lamina, (*L.*), *n.* (*Pl.* -AE) **1.** A thin plate or scale; a layer or coat lying over another; পাতলা পাত, পত্র (কেভিঃ), কল্ক, পাতলা আঁইস; সূক্ষ্মস্তর। **2.** The broad part or blade of a leaf; পত্রের প্রশস্ত অংশ, পত্রভাগ (সাঃ পঃ)। **3.** A thin plate of metal or bone; হাড় বা ধাতুর পাতলা পাত। ***Laminar, Laminose,*** *adjs.*

lăm′-i-nāte, *v. t.* & *i.* **1.** To form (metal) into thin plates by beating or rolling; পিটিয়া বা বেলনাদ্বারা ডলিয়া পাতলা পাত করা। **2.** To split into layer or leaves; স্তরে স্তরে বিভক্ত করা। **3.** To [illegible]y with metal plates; ধাতুর পাত দ্বারা আচ্ছাদিত করা। **4.** To construct or make by placing layer on layer; "Method of *laminating* steel"; স্তরের উপর স্তর সাজাইয়া রচনা বা নির্ম্মাণ **Lam′-i-nate,** *adj.* **–na′-tion,** *n.*

Lăm′-măs, *n.* The first day of Aug st, formerly observed as the harvest-festival; ১লা আগষ্ট—পূর্ব্বে ঐ দিবসে নবান্ন উৎসব অনুষ্ঠিত হইত। **Lat**[illegible] **Lammas**—A non-existent day, a day that will never come; অবর্ত্তমান দিন; যে দিন কখনও আসিবে না।

lăm′-mêr-gei-êr (-gī-), **lăm′-mêr-gey-êr** (-gī-), *n.* The bearded vulture, the largest European bird of prey; ইয়ুরোপদেশীয় বৃহৎ গৃধ্র বিশেষ।

lămp, *n., v. t.* & *i.* **1.** A vessel with oil to be burnt by means of a wick; any device for supplying artificial light; আলোকাধার; প্রদীপ, দীপ, বাতি, বর্ত্তি, গৃহমণি (অঃ)। **2.** A glass vessel containing candle or other artificial light; লণ্ঠন। **3.** (*Fig.*) The sun, moon or a star; "*Lamps* of glory begemm'd the sky"; (লক্ষণায়) চন্দ্র, সূর্য্য, তারা, নভোমণি (sun)। **4.** (*Fig.*) Anything which enlightens intellectually or morally; a source of hope; (লক্ষণায়) পুণ্যালোক, জ্ঞানদীপ, জ্ঞানালোক; আশার আলো। ***Verb t.*** To furnish with lamps; to illuminate; দীপমালাসমন্বিত করা, দীপমালাশোভিত করা; আলোকিত করা, প্রদীপ্ত করা। ***Verb i.*** To shine; দীপ্তি পাওয়া। **Lamp′-less,** *adj.* **Lamp-black**—প্রদীপের কালি, দীপকজ্জল, ভূষা, কজ্জল, কাজল, দীপকীট্ট। **Lamp-burner**—দীপের জ্বালামুখ। **Lamp-chimney, Lamp-glass**—প্রদীপের কাচময় আবরণ, চিম্‌নি। **Lamp-light** — প্রদীপের আলো দীপালোক, দীপপ্রকাশ, দীপপ্রভা। **Lamp-lighter** — রাজপথের দীপ, প্রজ্বালক। **Lamp-post** — রাজপথের-আলোকস্তম্ভ, দীপস্তম্ভ (অঃ)। **Lamp-stand**—দীপবৃক্ষ, পিলসুজ, দীপগাছা, দীপপাদপ, শিখাতরু, জোৎস্নাবৃক্ষ (অঃ)। **Like a lamp-lighter** — With speed; দ্রুতবেগে, চকিতে। **The lamp of phoebus** — (*Poet.*) The sun; সূর্য্য, দিনমণি। **To smell of the lamp**—To betray signs of nocturnal study; গভীর রাত্রব্যাপী অধ্যয়নের লক্ষণ প্রদর্শন করা। To be laborious in style etc.; বিশেষ আয়াসের সহিত সম্পাদিত হওয়া। **To pass** or **hand on the lamp**— To do one's part in advancing knowledge, a cause, etc.; জ্ঞানালোক বিস্তারাদি কার্য্যে সাহায্য করা।

lăm′-păs, *n.* A kind of horse-disease with a swelling in the roof of the mouth ; অশ্বের মুখ-স্ফীতি রোগবিশেষ।

lăm'-păs, *n.* A flowered fabric of silk etc. ; ফুলতোলা রেশমী কাপড়।

Lampetie, *n.* A daughter of Helios ; সূর্যনন্দিনী।

lăm'-pi-ŏn, *n.* A kind of small lamp as used at illumination ; একপ্রকার ক্ষুদ্র প্রদীপ।

lăm-poon', *n.* & *v. t.* A virulent or scurrilous personal satire in writing ; ব্যঙ্গব্যঞ্জক বা বিদ্রূপাত্মক রচনা, ব্যঙ্গকবিতা। ***Verb t.*** To write a lampoon against ; (কাহারও নামে) তীব্র শ্লেষাত্মক রচনা বা প্রবন্ধ লিখা। **—er, —ist,** *ns.* One who writes a lampoon ; (কাহারও নামে) ব্যঙ্গব্যঞ্জক রচনা লিখক।

lăm'-prey (-prĭ), *n.* An eel-like scaleless fish ; বাইন মাছের মত একপ্রকার মাছ।

lăm'-pў-ris, *n.* A firefly ; জোনি-পোকা (যোঃ), খদ্যোত।

lance (lăns), *n.* **1.** A weapon with a long wooden shaft or handle and a steel blade or head ; বল্লম, বড়শা, কুন্ত (cf. Latin *contus*), শক্তি, তোমর, শূল, শেল। **2.** A long spear used by whalers and fishermen ; এক প্রকার লম্বা টেঁটা। **3.** A cavalry soldier armed with a lance ; বড়শাধারী অশ্বারোহী সৈন্য। **Lance-snake** — আমেরিকা দেশীয় ভয়ঙ্কর বিষধর সর্প-বিশেষ। **Lance-wood**— উত্তর আমেরিকার একপ্রকার সুদৃঢ় স্থিতিস্থাপক কাষ্ঠ।

lance (lăns), *v. t.* **1.** To pierce with a lance or any sharp pointed instrument ; বল্লম বা অন্য কোনরূপ তীক্ষাগ্র অস্ত্র দ্বারা বিদ্ধ করা। **2.** (*Slang*) To cut open with a lancet ; ছুরিকা দ্বারা কাটা, অস্ত্র করা। **3.** (*Poet.*) To hurl or fling ; to launch ; (কবিতায়) নিক্ষেপ করা, ছোড়া ; ক্ষেপণ করা।

lance'-lĕt (lăns-), *n.* A fish-like animal ; মৎস্যবৎ জন্তু বিশেষ।

lăn'-cē-ō-lāte, *adj.* Shaped like a spear-head ; tapering towards ends ; as, a *lanceolate* leaf ; বল্লমাগ্রাকৃতি, শূলাগ্রবৎ ; ক্রমসূক্ষ্মাগ্র।

lanc'-êr (lăns-), *n.* **1.** A cavalry soldier armed with a lance ; বড়শাধারী অশ্বারোহী সৈনিক। **2.** (*Pl.*) A kind of dance ; music for this ; একপ্রকার নৃত্য ; ঐরূপ নৃত্যের সহ সঙ্গতবাদ।

lăn'-cĕt, *n.* **1.** A sharp pointed and two-edged surgical instrument ; রক্তমোক্ষণ ও স্ফোটকাদি ছেদনার্থ সূক্ষ্মমুখ দ্বিধার শস্ত্র-বিশেষ, ছুরিকা, শলাকা (সুশ্রুঃ)। **2.** (Also *lancet-arch, -window*) ; সূক্ষ্মাগ্র-বাতায়ন, সূক্ষ্মশীর্ষ বাতায়ন।

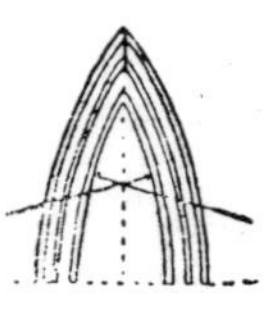

Lancet-arch.

lăn'-ci-nāt-ing, *adj.* Piercing ; (applied to shooting pains) ধারাল শস্ত্রবিদ্ধবৎ (হঃ চঃ)।

lănd, *n.* **1.** The solid part of the surface of the earth ; পৃথিবীর স্থলভাগ। **2.** A definite portion of the surface of the globe ; a country ; a state ; a nation ; দেশ বা প্রদেশ ; দেশ ; রাজ্য, রাষ্ট্র ; জাতি। **3.** Ground ; soil ; ভূমি, ডাঙ্গা ; মৃত্তিকা, মাটি। **4.** Landed property ; ভূসম্পত্তি, জমিদারী। **5.** (*Agri., English*) A strip of land marked by deep furrows ; সুগভীর লাঙ্গলপদ্ধতি দ্বারা চিহ্নিত ভূখণ্ড **Land'-less,** *adj.* **Land'-ward,** *adv.* & *adj.* Toward the land ; স্থলাভিমুখে। (*Adj.*) Lying toward the land ; inland ; স্থলাভিমুখে অবস্থিত ; সমুদ্র হইতে দূরবর্তী। **Land'-wards,** *adv.* **Arable land**—কর্ষণযোগ্য ভূমি, ক্ষেত্রভূমি। **Fallow** or **waste land**—পতিত জমি, অনাবাদী ভূমি। **Good** or **bad landfall**— সমুদ্র যাত্রায় গণনার অনুরূপ বা বিপরীত ভূমি প্রাপ্তি। **Happy land** or **land of bliss**—সুখাবতী (জিঃ), আনন্দভূমি। **Land-agent** — ভূ-সম্পত্তি বিক্রয়াদি কার্য্যের দালাল। **Land-agency,** *n.* **Land-bank**—ভূ-সম্পত্তি বন্ধক রাখিয়া যে ধনাগার হইতে নোট দেওয়া হয়। **Land-breeze, —wind**—স্থল হইতে সাগরাভিমুখে প্রবাহিত বায়ু, স্থলবায়ু, ভূমিবায়ু। **Land-crab** — স্থলকর্কট। **Landfall**—An approach to land for the first time on a voyage ; সমুদ্রযাত্রায় প্রথম ভূমির সমীপাগমন। **Land-fish** — ডাঙ্গার মাছ ; যে ব্যক্তি স্বীয় স্বভাবের বিরুদ্ধে কাজ করে। **Land-force**—(Generally *forces*) ; স্থলসৈন্য, স্থলবল। **Land-grabber**—যে ব্যক্তি আয়র্লণ্ডের প্রজা উচ্ছেদ হইলে পর তাহার ভূমি অধিকার করে। **Land-herd** — স্থলচর জন্তুর দল। **Land-holder**—ভূস্বামী, জমিদার, মিরাসদার। **Land-hunger** — ভূ-সম্পত্তি অর্জ্জনের জন্য লোলুপতা, ভূমিবুভুক্ষা, ভূবুভুক্ষা। **Land-hungry**—ভূবুভুক্ষিত। **Land-jobber**—ভূসম্পত্তি ব্যবসায়ী। **Land-lady**—A woman who has tenants ; ভূম্যধিকারিণী, ভূস্বামিনী। The mistress of an inn, boarding house, lodging house, etc. ; সরাইএর কর্ত্রী, বাড়ীওয়ালী। **Land-laws**—ভূসম্পত্তিসম্বন্ধীয় আইন। **Land-locked** — ভূ-বেষ্টিত, ভূ-প্রতিরক্ষিত, ভূপ্রতিরুদ্ধ। **Landlord**—The owner of lands having tenants under him ; ভূস্বামী, জমিদার, ভূম্যধিকারী। The master of an inn or boarding house etc. ; সরাইস্বামী, পান্থশালার অধিকারী, বাড়ীওয়ালা। **Land-loper**— ভবঘুরে। **Land-lubber**—জাহাজ বা সমুদ্র সম্বন্ধে অনভিজ্ঞ ব্যক্তি। **Land-mark**—An object marking the boundaries of a country, state, etc. ; দেশ, সম্পত্তি, প্রভৃতির সীমানির্দ্দেশক বস্তু, ক্ষেত্রসীমাচিহ্ন, সীমাচিহ্ন। Any conspicuous object in a locality ; "The house is......the......*land-mark* of the......neighbourhood" ; কোন স্থানের বিশেষ লক্ষ্যের বিষয়ীভূত

বস্তু। An object or event marking a turning point or a stage; সীমা নির্দ্দেশক বিষয় বা ঘটনা, অবস্থান্তর নির্দ্দেশক বিষয় বা ঘটনা। **Land-measure** — ক্ষেত্র পরিমাণ, ভূমিতি, ভূমানপদ্ধতি। **Land-owner** — ভূম্যধিকারী, জমিদার। **Land pirate**—রাহাজান। **Land-revenue**—মাল গুজারি (হিঃ কোঃ), ভূমিরাজস্ব। **Land service**—সৈনিক বিভাগ। **Land-shark**—যে জুয়াচোর সমুদ্রতীরে নাবিকদিগের পয়সা কড়ি ঠকাইয়া নেয়। **Land-sick**—(জাহাজ সম্পর্কে) নৈকট্য হেতু ভূমি দ্বারা প্রতিহত গতি। **Land-slide** — (*U. S.*) An overwhelming political defeat; (মার্কিণ যুক্ত রাজ্য) রাজনীতিক ব্যাপারে ভীষণ পরাজয়। **Landslip**—ভূমিপাত (সাঃ পঃ), পাহাড়ধসা (ঐ), ভূপাত। **Landsman** — স্থলবাসী; অনাবিক। A novice in seamanship; নাবিকের কর্ম্মে নূতন ব্রতী। **Land-spout**—ঘূর্ণিবায়ু বা বৃষ্টিপাতকালে স্থলে মোচাকার মেঘের অবতরণ, স্থলস্তম্ভ। **Land-steward**—জমিদারের নায়েব। **Land-swell**—তীরের নিকটবর্ত্তী স্থানে সাগরের তরঙ্গান্দোলন। **Land-tax** — tax on land; ভূমিকর। **How the land lies**—What is the state of affairs; ব্যাপারটা কি? **Land of cakes**—স্কটলণ্ড (ঐ দেশের লোকেরা সচরাচর যইএর পিষ্টক ভোজন করে বলিয়া এই নাম)। **Land of the leal** — Heaven; স্বর্গ, ত্রিদিব, অমরাবতী। **Land of the living**—present life; ইহকাল। **To make the land**—To come in sight of the land as the ship approaches; it; জাহাজ হইতে উপকূল দর্শন করা।

lănd, *v. t. & i.* **1.** To set on the land; to disembark; তীরে নামাইয়া দেওয়া; জাহাজ হইতে নামান। **2.** To bring to land, as fish; to win, as a prize; ডাঙ্গায় তোলা; লাভ করা। **3.** To set down from a vehicle; কোন যান হইতে নামান। **4.** To bring to a certain place or position; as, to be *landed* in mud: to *land* one in difficulties; কোন স্থানে বা অবস্থায় আনা। **5.** To bring (the horse) to the winning post; অশ্বকে জয়স্তম্ভের নিকট আনা। **6.** To deal (a person a blow etc.); as, I have *landed* him one in the eye; কাহাকেও ঘুষি প্রভৃতি মারা। ***Verb i.*** **1.** To go ashore; to disembark; to come to shore, as a boat or ship; তীরে যাওয়া; জাহাজাদি হইতে নামা; জাহাজ নৌকা ইত্যাদি তীরে লাগা। **2.** To arrive at a place or stage in a journey etc.; কোন স্থানে পৌঁছা। **3.** To alight; অবতরণ করা, নামা। **4.** (*Jockey*) To come in first or win as a horse; (ঘোড়দৌড়ের সওয়ার) প্রথম আসা, জয়লাভ করা।

lăn'-dau (-dä), *n.* A four-wheeled coach or carriage whose top, divided into two sections, can be

Landau.

raised and thrown back; একপ্রকার চারি চাকার গাড়ী—ইহার ছই দুইভাগে বিভক্ত—যাহার একটী গুটাইয়া রাখিলে অপরটী মেলিয়া রাখা যায়, ল্যাণ্ডো।

lăn-dau-lĕt' (-dö-), *n.* A small landau; ক্ষুদ্র ল্যাণ্ডো গাড়ী।

lănd'-ĕd, *adj.* **1.** Having an estate in land; as, a *landed* proprietor; ভূসম্পত্তিশালী। **2.** Consisting of land; as, *landed* property; ভূ-সম্পত্তিবিশিষ্ট। **The landed interest**—কোন সমাজের ভূম্যধিকারি সমাজ, জমিদার সম্প্রদায়।

lănd'-ing *n.* **1.** Act of landing or causing to land; উত্তরণ, অবতরণ, অবতারণ। **2.** Place of landing, (also *landing-place*); ঘাট, পারঘাটা, উঠানঘাটা, অবতরণস্থান, জলাবতরণস্থান। **3.** A resting place or platform between two flights of stairs; সোপানশ্রেণীদ্বয়ের মধ্যবর্ত্তী মঞ্চ বা বিরামস্থলী। **Landing-net**—বড়শীতে বিদ্ধ মৎস্য ডাঙ্গায় তোলার জন্য জাল। **Landing-stage**—যে প্লবমান মঞ্চের উপর জাহাজের যাত্রিগণ অবতরণ করে বা মাল নামান হইয়া থাকে।

lănd'-lōrd-ĭsm, *n.* A system of holding land by the landlord receiving fixed rents from tenants (esp. depreciatively of the Irish system); advocacy of this system; যে পদ্ধতি অনুসারে ভূস্বামিগণ প্রজাগণ হইতে ভূমি ভোগের নির্দ্দিষ্ট খাজানা পাইয়া থাকেন; ঐরূপ পদ্ধতি সমর্থন।

lănd-ŏc'-ră-çy̆, *n.* The landed class; ভূম্যধিকারিসম্প্রদায়, জমিদারশ্রেণী। **Land'-o-crat,** *n.*

lănd'-scape, *n.* **1.** A piece of country scenery; inland natural scenery; পল্লীর নৈসর্গিক দৃশ্য; দেশ-মধ্যস্থ প্রাকৃতিক দৃশ্য। **2.** A picture of inland scenery; representation of landscape in painting; পল্লীর প্রাকৃতিক দৃশ্যের চিত্র; নিসর্গ চিত্র (মন্মথ)। **—scap-ist,** *n.* Same as LANDSCAPE PAINTER. **Landscape-gardening**—প্রাকৃতিক দৃশ্যের অনুকরণে উদ্যানরচনা। **—gardener,** *n.* **Landscape-marble**—বৃক্ষবৎ চিহ্নাঙ্কিত মর্ম্মর প্রস্তর, দ্রুমমর্ম্মরপ্রস্তর। **Landscape-painter**—One who paints natural scenery; প্রাকৃতিকদৃশ্যচিত্রকর, নিসর্গ-চিত্রকর।

landsturm, (*Ger.*) *n.* (In Germany etc.) A general levy in time of war, of men outside the army, navy and landwehr; (জর্ম্মণি প্রভৃতি দেশে) স্থলসৈন্য, নৌসৈন্য ও কেবল যুদ্ধকালে নিরবচ্ছিন্ন ভাবে সৈনাবিভাগে কার্য্যকারী ব্যক্তিগণের বহির্ভূত জনগণ হইতে সংগৃহীত সৈন্য।

land-tag (*Ger.*), *n.* A legislative body of a German State; জর্ম্মণ-রাজ্যের ব্যবস্থাপক সভা।

landwehr, (*Ger.*) *n.* (In Germany etc.) That part of the army which serves continuously only during war ; (জর্ম্মণি প্রভৃতি দেশে) সৈন্যদলের যে অংশ কেবল যুদ্ধকালে নিরবচ্ছিন্নভাবে কার্য্য করে।

lāne, *n.* **1.** A narrow way or street ; a narrow way between hedges etc. ; সঙ্কীর্ণ পথ ; জঙ্গলের মধ্যস্থিত অপ্রশস্ত পথ। **2.** A passage made or left between lines of persons ; লোকের সারির মধ্যে কৃত বা স্থিত সঙ্কীর্ণ পথ বা গলি। **3.** A route prescribed for ocean steamers ; সমুদ্রগামীপোতের জন্য নির্দ্দিষ্ট পথ। **Blind-lane**—বন্ধগলি। **The Lane**—লণ্ডন নগরীর ড্রুরি লেইন ; উক্ত গলিতে অবস্থিত রঙ্গালয়। **The red lane**—কণ্ঠ।

lăng'-sȳne', *adv.* & *n.* (*Scot.* = *long since*) In the old days; long ago ; পুরাকালে ; বহুদিন গত হইল। ***Noun.*** The old days ; পূর্ব্বকাল, পুরাকাল।

lan'-guage (lăng-gwāj), *n.* **1.** The expression of thought by articulate sounds or words ; a mode of expression peculiar to a country, nation, etc. ; অর্থযুক্ত বাক্য দ্বারা মনোভাব প্রকাশ ; ভাষা। **2.** A mode of expressing ideas ; as, finger-*language* ; মনোভাব প্রকাশের উপায় বিশেষ। **3.** A body of words and their use ; শব্দসমূহ ও তাহাদের ব্যবহার। **4.** The faculty of speech ; বাক্‌শক্তি। **5.** A person's style of expressing himself ; as, it is in his *language* so and so ; ব্যক্তিবিশেষের মনোভাব প্রকাশের প্রণালী। **6.** Words appropriate to, or especially employed in, any branch of knowledge ; as, the *language* of Chemistry ; বিদ্যার কোন বিশেষ শাখার ভাষা। **7.** The literary style ; the wording ; as, the *language* of an essay or document ; রচনার ভাষা ; শব্দব্যবহারপ্রণালী। **Bad** or **vulgar language**—কুৎসিত ভাষা, অশ্লীল ভাষা, অপভাষা। **Dead-language** — মৃত বা অপ্রচলিত ভাষা। **Finger-language**—অঙ্গুলিসঙ্কেত দ্বারা মনোভাব প্রকাশ, অঙ্গুলি-ভাষা। **Language-master** — ভাষাশিক্ষক, বিশেষতঃ বৈদেশিক ভাষা শিক্ষাদাতা। **Living-language**—কথিত বা চলিত ভাষা। **Strong-language**—তীব্র ভাষা। **Language of flowers**—কুসুমসমূহ দ্বারা মনোভাব প্রকাশের পদ্ধতিবিশেষ।

lan'-guid (lăng-gwĭd), *adj.* **1.** Drooping or flagging from exhaustion ; spiritless ; গ্লানিযুক্ত, অবসন্ন, অবসাদিত, নিস্তেজ ; অলসাঙ্গ (উজ্জ্বলঃ), মন্থরাঙ্গ (ঐ), মদালস, শ্লথাঙ্গ, সতন্দ্র, খিন্ন। **2.** Sluggish ; apathetic ; ঢিলা, ঢিমা, মন্থর, অলস ; উদাসীন, বিরাগী। **3.** Not vivid ; uninteresting, as a style etc. ; নিস্তেজ, ম্রিয়মাণ, নির্জ্জীব ; নীরস। **–ly,** *adv.* **–ness,** *n.* State of being languid ; অলসাঙ্গতা, মন্থরাঙ্গতা, শ্লথাঙ্গতা, নির্জ্জীবতা, মান্দ্য, গ্লানি, ম্লানিমা, ঔদাসীন্য। **A woman with languid looks**—অলসেক্ষণা, মদিরাক্ষী।

lan'-guish (lăng-gwĭsh), *v. i.* **1.** To become languid, faint or feeble ; to lose vitality or animation ; অলসাঙ্গ হওয়া, শিথিলাঙ্গ হওয়া, মন্থরাঙ্গ হওয়া ; দুর্ব্বল হওয়া, নিস্তেজ হওয়া, নির্জ্জীব হওয়া। **2.** To live under enfeebling or depressing conditions ; to droop or pine, (often with *for*) ; অবসাদজনক অবস্থার ভিতর বাস করা ; খিন্ন হওয়া, পরিক্ষীণ হওয়া, ম্রিয়মাণ হওয়া। **3.** To grow slack ; to lose force or intensity ; to fade ; ঢিলা হওয়া, শিথিল হওয়া ; নিস্তেজ হওয়া, নির্জ্জীব হওয়া ; শুকাইয়া যাওয়া, পরিম্লান হওয়া। **4.** To assume an expression of weariness or tender grief or emotion ; "When a visitor comes in she smiles and *languishes*" ; অলসাঙ্গ হওয়া, মদালসা হওয়া, সকরুণ আবেগ, ক্লান্তি বা পরিক্লান্তির ভাব প্রদর্শন করা। **–ing,** *adj.* **1.** Pining ; ক্ষীয়মাণ। **2.** Expressing a sentimental emotion ; amorously pensive ; ভাবাবেগব্যঞ্জক ; মদালস, অনঙ্গবাণখিন্নমানস, মদনমদালস, মদনভাবনাকুল। **–ing-ly,** *adv.* **–ment,** *n.*

lan'-guor (lăng-gwêr), *n.* **1.** The state of being languid or faint ; fatigue ; অলসাঙ্গতা, অবসন্নতা ; ক্লান্তি। **2.** Lassitude ; want of alertness ; শ্লথাঙ্গতা, অঙ্গাবসাদ (হিঃ কোঃ), শিথিলতা (ঐ), মন্থরাঙ্গতা, অঙ্গগ্লানি (চন্দ্রঃ), খেদ ; নির্জ্জীবতা, নিস্তেজতা। **3.** Softness or tenderness of mood etc. ; সকরুণভাব। **4.** State of being slack or dull ; drooping ; শিথিলতা, মান্দ্য ; ম্লানিমা। **5.** (Of sky etc.) Oppressive stillness ; (আকাশাদি সম্পর্কে) অবসাদজনক নিস্তব্ধতা। **–ous,** *adj.* **–ous-ly,** *adv.*

lā'-ni-ā-rȳ, *adj.* & *n.* Fitted for tearing ; canine ; ছেদনকারী ; শৌবন। ***Noun.*** A canine teeth ; শ্বদন্ত।

lă-nĭf'-êr-ous (-ŭs), **–nig'–,** *adjs.* Bearing wool ; পশম উৎপাদী।

lank (lăngk), *adj.* **1.** Shrunken ; slender ; tall and lean ; বলিকুঞ্চিত ; কৃশ, ক্ষীণ, কাহিল ; ঢেঙ্গা। **2.** Long and flaccid ; as, *lank* grass ; লম্বা এবং থলথলিয়া। **3.** Without curl or wave, as hair ; অকুঞ্চিত।

lank'-ȳ (lăngk-), *adj.* Ungracefully lean and long or tall, (as persons, limbs, etc.) ; ঢেঙ্গা, একহারা। **–i-ness,** *n.*

lăn'-nêr, lăn'-nêr-ĕt, *ns.* **1.** A kind of hawk or falcon ; the female of the species ; (*-et* only) the male of the lanner ; একপ্রকার বাজপক্ষী ; ঐ জাতীয় স্ত্রী পক্ষিণী ; ঐ জাতীয় পুং পক্ষী।

lăn'-ŏ-lĭn, –line (-lĭn), *ns.* Extract from sheep's wool as basis of ointment ; মলম প্রস্তুতের জন্য মেষের পশম হইতে নিষ্কর্ষিত নির্যাস বিশেষ।

lăns'-que-nĕt (-kĕ), *n.* A game at cards of German origin একপ্রকার তাসখেলা।

lăn'-têrn, *n.* **1.** A transparent case for holding and sometimes carrying a light ; লণ্ঠন, ফানুস, প্রচ্ছন্নপ্রদীপ, আবৃতদীপ। **2.** The light-chamber of a lighthouse ; আলোকমঞ্চের আলোককক্ষ। **3.** A small structure on the top of a dome or room with glazed sides to admit light ; আলোক-প্রবেশের জন্য গুম্বজ বা কক্ষের উপরিস্থ কাচসমাচ্ছাদিতপার্শ্ব ক্ষুদ্র কক্ষবিশেষ। **4.** The luminous proboscis of the lantern-fly ; দীপমক্ষিকার জ্যোতির্ম্ময় শুণ্ড (শুঁড়)। **5.** A magic-lantern ; যাদুপ্রদীপ, ম্যাজিক লণ্ঠন। **—ist,** *n.* One who uses a magic lantern ; ম্যাজিকলণ্ঠনওয়ালা। **Chinese-lantern**—চীনের ফানুস। **Dark-lantern** — চোরালণ্ঠন, গুপ্তপ্রদীপ। **Lantern-fly**—খদ্যোত। **Lantern-jaws**—দীর্ঘহনু। **Lantern-jawed**—দীর্ঘহনুবিশিষ্ট, ক্ষীণবদন (আঃ বঃ)। **Magic-lantern** — See under MAGIC.

lăn'-thă-nŭm, *n.* (*Chem.*) A rare element discovered in 1839-41 ; (রসায়ন শাস্ত্র) ১৮৩৯—৪১ খৃঃ অব্দে আবিষ্কৃত দুষ্প্রাপ্য মূলপদার্থ বিশেষ।

lănt'-hôrn (-êrn) *n.* Same as LANTERN.

lăn'-yârd, *n.* A short piece of rope for fastening something in ships ; জাহাজে কোন কিছু বাঁধিবার জন্য ক্ষুদ্র রজ্জুখণ্ড।

Lā-ŏc'-ō-ŏn, *n.* Priest of Apollo at Troy ; ট্রয় নগরীস্থ এপলোদেবের মন্দিরের পুরোহিত। ইনি ট্রয় যুদ্ধে শত্রু-পক্ষকর্তৃক প্রেরিত কাষ্ঠময় অশ্ব নগর-প্রাচীরের বাহিরে রাখার জন্য ট্রয়বাসিগণকে অনুরোধ করেন ; কিন্তু তাহারা এই অনুরোধ কার্য্যে পরিণত করার পূর্ব্বেই সমুদ্র হইতে দুই প্রকাণ্ড সর্প উত্থিত হইয়া Laocoon ও তাঁহার পুত্রগণকে বিনাশ করে।

Lā-ŏd-ă-mī'-ă, *n.* Daughter of Acastus ; Acastusএর কন্যা। ইনি মৃত পতির প্রেতাত্মার সহিত কথা বলিবার জন্য দেবতাদিগকে আরাধনা করেন। দেবতাগণ তাঁহার প্রার্থনা পূরণ করেন। Laodamia পরলোকগত পতির সহিত সাক্ষাতের পর তাঁহার সঙ্গে সঙ্গে দেহত্যাগ করিয়া পতীর সঙ্গিনী হন।

lā-ŏd-ĭ-cē'-ăn, *adj.* & *n.* Lukewarm esp. in religion and politics ; [From Laodicea, a city in Asia Minor] ; ধর্ম্ম বা রাজনীতি সংক্রান্ত বিষয়ে উদাসীন (ব্যক্তি)।

Lă-ŏm'-ĕ-dŏn, *n.* The king of Troy and father of Priam ; ট্রয়রাজ Priamএর পিতা। দেবরাজ Zeus, বরুণদেব Poseidon এবং সূর্য্যদেব এপলোকে Laomedonএর অধীনে কার্য্য করার জন্য আদেশ দেন। ইহাদের এক জনকে তিনি ট্রয়ের প্রাচীর নির্ম্মাণ ও অপর জনকে পশুচারণ কার্য্যে নিযুক্ত করেন। Laomedon দেবতাদ্বয়ের বেতন প্রদানে অস্বীকৃত হইলে বরুণদেব Poseidon, Laomedonএর রাজ্য বন্যা-প্লাবিত করেন। এক বিকটাকার সামুদ্রিক-জীব তাঁহার রাজ্যে নানারূপ উপদ্রব করিতে থাকে। রাজা প্রতি বৎসর ঐ দানবকে এক একটী কুমারী প্রদান করিবেন এই অঙ্গীকারে আবদ্ধ হইয়া ঐ বিকট সামুদ্রিক জীবের অত্যাচার হইতে প্রজাগণকে রক্ষা করেন। এই অঙ্গীকার অনুসারে রাজকন্যা Hesione সামুদ্রিক দৈত্যের নিকট প্রেরিতা হন।

lăp, *n.* **1.** The loose lower part of a garment, saddle, etc. ; the front portion of the skirt ; পরিচ্ছদ, ঘোড়ার জিন প্রভৃতির নিম্নাংশ ; কোঁচড়। **2.** The knees up to waist of one sitting with dress ; (*fig.*) a place of rearing and fostering ; as, in the *lap* of fortune or luxury ; অঙ্ক, ক্রোড়, উৎসঙ্গ, কোল ; (লক্ষণায়) ক্রোড়। **3.** A lobe of the ear ; কাণের লতি, কর্ণলতিকা। **4.** A hollow among hills ; পর্ব্বতকন্দর, পর্ব্বত-গহ্বর, গুহা। **Lap'-ful,** *n.* **Lap-dog**—ক্রোড়কুক্কুর, অঙ্ককুক্কুর। **Lap-stone**—মুচী যে পাথরের উপর রাখিয়া চামড়া পিটায়। **In the lap of luxury**—In luxury ; ভোগবিলাসিতার ক্রোড়ে।

lăp, *v. t.* & *i.* **1.** To coil, fold or wrap round or about ; জড়ান, আবৃত করা, পাট করা, তহ করা, কুণ্ডলী পাকান, গুটান, ভাঁজ করা। **2.** To enfold *in* wraps etc. ; মোড়া। **3.** To surround ; to clothe (round) ; "Now peace *laps* her round" ; পরিবেষ্টন করা, পরিবৃত করা ; সজ্জিত করা। **4.** To wrap up caressingly (esp. *in passive*) ; as, *lapped* in luxury ; আদরে জড়াইয়া ধরা। **4.** To make to overlap as a valve, roof-slate, etc. ; একটীর কিনারার উপর অপরটী রাখা বা সাজান। ***Verb i.*** **1.** To be spread or laid *over* ; to project *over* something ; উপরে বিস্তৃত হওয়া ; কোন কিছুর উপরে উদ্গত হওয়া। **2.** To overlap or lie over something in part (as slates on a roof) ; একটীর উপর অপরটী আংশিক ভাবে থাকা।

lăp, *n.* **1.** The overlapping part of a thing ; the measure or amount of such overlapping ; কোন বস্তুর যে অংশ অপর বস্তুর উপর উদ্গত থাকে ; ঐরূপ উদ্গত অংশের পরিমাণ। **2.** One circuit in a race-course ; এক চক্কর। **3.** A layer or sheet of cotton etc. wound round a roller ; ডলনায় জড়ানো কাপড়ের একভাঁজ। **4.** A single turn of rope, silk or thread, etc. round a drum or reel ; নাটাই প্রভৃতিতে জড়ানো পশম বা রজ্জুর এক পাক **Lap-streak**—A CLINKER-BUILT boat (which see).

lăp, *n.* & *v. t.* A rotating disk of lead, leather, etc. for polishing gem or metal ; মণি, ধাতু, প্রভৃতি পালিস করার জন্য একপ্রকার শানযন্ত্র। ***Verb t.*** To polish with lap ; শান পালিস করা।

lăp, *v. t., i.* & *n.* **1.** To drink up (liquid) with the tongue ; চক্ চক্ করিয়া পান করা। **2.** To consume greedily as a liquid, (with *up* or *down*) ; চক্ চক্ করিয়া পান

করা। 3. (Of water, wave, etc.) To flow against or beat upon (the shore) with a lapping sound; চলচ্ছল ছলচ্ছল শব্দে তীরে প্রতিহত হওয়া। *Verb i.* 1. To take up liquid with the tongue; চক্ চক্ করিয়া পান করা। 2. To make a sound as of licking; জিহ্বা দ্বারা চক্ চক্ শব্দ করা। *Noun.* 1. A liquid food for dogs; কুকুরের তরল খাদ্য। 2. Act of lapping; a lick with the tongue; চক্ চক্ করিয়া পান করণ; লেহন। 3. The sound of water rippling against a beach etc.; সৈকতে প্রতিহত জলরাশির চলচ্ছল ছলচ্ছল ধ্বনি।

lă-pĕl′, *n.* The part of the breast of a coat which is folded back; কোর্ত্তার বুকের যে অংশ উল্টাইয়া ভাঁজ করা থাকে। **—pelled′**, *p. adj.*

lăp′-i-cīde, *n.* A stone-cutter; one who cuts inscriptions on stones; পাষাণচ্ছেদক; যে ব্যক্তি শিলালিপি উৎকীর্ণ করে।

lăp′-i-dă-rȳ, *adj.* & *n.* 1. Pertaining to, or concerned with, stones; প্রস্তরসম্বন্ধীয়, পাষাণ-সংক্রান্ত। 2. Engraved on stones; পাষাণ-ফলকে উৎকীর্ণ। 3. Pertaining to, or suitable for, inscriptions, as a style etc.; শিলালিপিসম্বন্ধীয়, শিলালিপিসমুচিত। *Noun.* A cutter of precious stones; one who polishes or engraves gems; মণিকার, রত্নকার; রত্নসম্মার্জ্জক, মণিপরিষ্কারক, রত্নপরিষ্কারক, মণিক্ষোদক। **Lapidary-style**—সমাধিস্তম্ভের শিলালেখের উপযোগী রচনারীতি।

lăp′-i-dāte, *v. t.* To throw stones at; to stone to death; কাহারও উপর প্রস্তর নিক্ষেপ করা; প্রস্তরবর্ষণে নিহত করা। **—da′-tion**, *n.*

lă-pid′-i-fȳ *v. i.* To convert into stone; to petrify; প্রস্তরে পরিণত করা; পাষাণীভূত করা, শিলীভূত করা। **—fi-ca′-tion**, *n.* Petrifaction; প্রস্তরীকরণ, পাষাণীকরণ।

lā-pis-lăz′-ū-lī, *n.* 1. A bright blue pigment; একপ্রকার গাঢ় নীলবর্ণ রঞ্জকপদার্থ। 2. A stone of a rich azure blue, much valued for ornamental purposes; গাঢ় নীলবর্ণের মূল্যবান প্রস্তর বিশেষ, লাজবর্দ্দ, রাজাবর্ত্ত, নীলোপল (আ: বঃ), অসিতাশ্ম, বৈদুর্য্যমণি (শুক্র বিনয়ঃ), সুনীলক, অসিতোপল।

Lăpp, *n.* & *adj.* One of a dwarfish race of North Scandinavia; their language; ল্যাপলেণ্ডবাসী; ল্যাপলেণ্ডবাসিদিগের ভাষা। *Adj.* 1. Of, or pertaining to, the Lapps or their language; ল্যাপজাতি বা তাহাদের ভাষাসম্বন্ধীয়। **Lapp′-ish**, *n.* & *adj.* The language of the Lapps; ল্যাপজাতির ভাষা। (*Adj.*) Same as LAPP. **Lap-land**—The country of Lapps; ল্যাপল্যাণ্ড। **Lap-lander**—A Lapp; ল্যাপল্যাণ্ডবাসী।

lăp′-pet (-ĕt), *n.* 1. Small decorative flap or fold in a garment etc.; পরিচ্ছদের ঝালর বা ঝুলানো অংশ, টুপি বা শিরস্ত্রাণের ঝালর। 2. A lapel; কোর্ত্তার বুকের যে অংশ উল্টাইয়া ভাঁজ করা যায়। 3. A lap of flesh; a lobe of the ear etc.; মাংসের ফালি; কর্ণলতিকা। 4. A streamer of a lady's head-dress; ইয়ুরোপীয় মহিলার টুপীর ঝালর। **—ed**, *p. adj.*

Lăp-pō′-nĭ-an, *adj.* & *n.* Same as LAPP.

lapse (lăps), *n.* 1. A slip of memory, tongue or pen; slight mistake; (লিখন কথনের) ভ্রম বা ত্রুটি; সামান্য ভুল, প্রমাদ। 2. Moral slip; a failing in duty; a fault; নীতিভ্রংশ; কর্ত্তব্যে ত্রুটি; অপরাধ। 3. A slipping or falling away as *from* faith etc.; স্খলন, পদস্খলন, ভ্রংশ, চ্যুতি, স্খলিত। 4. A decline to a lower state; "A *lapse* of the high powers of the soul"; পতন, অবনতি। 5. A passage or interval (of time); ক্রম (cf. কালক্রম), অত্যয়। 6. A gentle flow (as of water); ধীরপ্রবাহ, মৃদুপ্রবাহ। 7. The termination or failure of a right or privilege through disuse; ভোগ না করা হেতু অধিকারাদি বিলোপ, স্বত্বচ্যুতি, খেলাপ। **Lapse of memory**—স্মৃতিভ্রংশ। **Lapse of time**—See LAPSE *n.* 5.

lapse (lăps), *v. i.* 1. To pass away slowly; to slide or glide; to subside; ধীরে ধীরে চলিয়া যাওয়া, মৃদুমন্দ গতিতে চলিয়া যাওয়া; অবাধে বহিয়া যাওয়া; প্রশমিত হওয়া। 2. To slip in moral conduct; to fall from virtue; to fail in duty; নীতিপথ হইতে স্খলিত হওয়া; ধর্ম্মভ্রষ্ট হওয়া, পদস্খলন হওয়া; কর্ত্তব্যভ্রষ্ট হওয়া। 3. To fall *back* or *away* as *into* some previous or inferior state; পূর্ব্বাবস্থা প্রাপ্ত হওয়া, পুনরায় নিকৃষ্ট অবস্থায় পতিত হওয়া। 4. To pass from one *to* another or some estate, right, etc. become void as by failure of conditions, heirs, etc.; (সম্পত্তি) স্বত্বাধিকারীর কর্ত্তব্যে ত্রুটী, অনবধান বা উত্তরাধিকারীর অভাব বশতঃ হস্তান্তরিত হওয়া, বাতিল হওয়া, ব্যর্থ হওয়া, খেলাপ হওয়া, বাজেয়াপ্ত হওয়া বা সরকারে খাস হওয়া। **Lapsed**, *p. p.* Ineffectual; having undergone a lapse; forfeited; as, a *lapsed* policy; ব্যর্থ; বাতিল; বাজেয়াপ্ত।

lapsus (*L.*), *n.* A slip; প্রমাদ, ভ্রম, ত্রুটী। ***Lapsus calami***—A slip of the pen; লিপিপ্রমাদ, কলমের ভুল। ***Laspus linguae***—A slip of the tongue; বলার ভুল, জিহ্বার দোষ, বাগ্দোষ।

Lă-pū′-tăn, *adj.* & *n.* 1. Of, or relating to, Laputa, a flying island in Swift's *Gulliver's Travels*; গালিভারের ভ্রমণবৃত্তান্ত নামক পুস্তকে বর্ণিত উড্ডয়নশীল ল্যাপুটা দ্বীপসম্বন্ধীয়। 2. Preposterous; visionary; absurd; অস্বাভাবিক, অযৌক্তিক; কাল্পনিক; অসম্ভব। *Noun.* An inhabitant of Laputa; ল্যাপুটা দ্বীপের অধিবাসী।

lăp'-wing, *n.* A small handsome bird ; the peewit ; তিত্তির (বয়েস), তিতই (ডেওয়ার) টিট্টিভ, পঙ্কক্রীড় ।

lâr, *n.* (*Pl.* -ES). **1.** The household deity of the ancient Romans ; (প্রাচীন রোমকদিগের) গৃহাধিষ্ঠাত্রীদেবী, গৃহদেবী । **2.** (*Pl.* LARS) The white-handed gibbon of Burma ; ব্রহ্মদেশের শ্বেতহস্ত উল্লুক । **The Lares and Penates, The Lares**—The home ; বাটী ।

lâr'-board (-bōrd), *n.* & *adj.* (*Naut.*) The left-hand side of a ship, (now replaced by *port*) ; জাহাজের বাম-পার্শ্ব । ***Adj.*** Pertaining to the left-hand side of a ship ; জাহাজের বামপার্শ্বসম্বন্ধীয় ।

lâr'-cĕ-nȳ, *n.* A legal term for stealing ; theft ; চুরি ; চৌর্য্য, চৌর্য্যকর্ম্ম, স্তেয় । **—ner, —nist,** *ns.* A thief ; চোর, তস্কর, কুম্ভিল । **—nous,** *adj.* Thievish ; চৌর্য্যাসক্ত । **—nous-ly,** *adv.* **Grand larceny**—(In England) Theft of property of the value of one shilling or more ; এক শিলিং বা অধিক মূল্যের দ্রব্য চুরি । **Petty larceny** — এক শিলিং বা তাহার কম মূল্যের দ্রব্য চুরি, সামান্য চুরি ।

Larch.

lârch, *n.* A tall cone-bearing tree ; its wood ; দেবদারুজাতীয় বৃক্ষ বিশেষ ; ইহার কাষ্ঠ ।

lârd, *n.* & *v. t.* The internal part of the abodomen of pigs separated from the flesh and melted ; শূকরের বস্তিদেশের চর্ব্বি, শূকরমেদ । ***Verb t.*** **1.** To apply lard to ; to smear or mix with lard ; চর্ব্বি লাগান, চর্ব্বি মাখান ; চর্ব্বির সহিত মিশ্রিত করা । **2.** To stuff with bacon ; to insert strips of bacon in (meat) before cooking ; শূকরের মাংসে পুর দেওয়া ; রন্ধনের পূর্ব্বে মাংসে শূকর মাংসের খণ্ড সমূহ প্রবিষ্ট করা । **3.** (*Fig.*) To garnish as talk, writing, etc. with metaphors, foreign words, etc. ; উপমা, রূপক, বিদেশীয় শব্দাদি দ্বারা বাক্য, রচনা প্রভৃতি অলঙ্কৃত করা । **Lard'-er,** *n.* A room or closet where meat etc. is kept ; মাংসাগার, মাংস রক্ষণ প্রকোষ্ঠ, ভক্ষ্য মাংসাগার । **Lard'-y,** *adj.* Containing, or resembling, lard ; শূকরমেদযুক্ত, শূকরমেদসদৃশ ।

lâr-dā'-ceous (-shŭs), *adj.* (*Med.*) Lard-like ; (ভৈষজ্য শাস্ত্র) শূকরমেদবৎ, শূকরবসাবৎ ।

lâr'-dȳ – dâr'-dȳ, *adj.* (*Slang*) Languidly or affectedly dandyish ; "When the *lardy-dardy* swells are present" ; (ইতরভাষায়) বাবুয়ানির বাহার দেখানিয়া, আলস্যে জরজর, ফুলবাবুটীর মত ।

Lāres, *n.* See LAR.

lâr'-dŏn, lâr-dōon', *ns.* A bit or strip of bacon used in larding ; মাংসের মধ্যে পুরিবার জন্য শূকরমাংসখণ্ড ।

large (lârj), *adj.* & *n.* **1.** Great in size, quantity, number, capacity, etc. ; bulky ; as, a *large* supply of provision ; বড়, বৃহৎ, বিশাল, প্রকাণ্ড, মস্ত, বৃহদায়তন, বিরাট, বিপুল, বিশাল ; মহা, অতিকায় ; প্রকাণ্ড । **2.** Extensive ; comprehensive, as powers, discretion, etc. ; বিস্তৃত, বিস্তীর্ণ ; ব্যাপক । **3.** (*Archaic*) Generous ; kindly ; munificent ; liberal ; (অপ্রঃ) বদান্য ; সদয় ; প্রশস্ত, উদার ; মুক্তহস্ত । **4.** (Of artistic treatment) Free ; broad ; "In his colouring he was *large* and general" ; স্বাধীন ; সুপরিস্ফুট । **5.** (With agent nouns) On a large scale ; "A *large* planter" ; বড় দরের । **6.** (Of a speech or manner) Pompous ; imposing ; "And said in a *large* way" ; জাঁকালো, শব্দাড়ম্বরপূর্ণ ; গুরুগম্ভীর । ***Noun.*** (Now only with *at* and *in* (see below.) **Larg'-en,** *v.t.* & *i.* (*Poet.*) To make or grow large ; (কবিতায়) বাড়া, বাড়ান, বৃহত্তর হওয়া, বৃহত্তর করা । **Large'-ly,** *adv.* **1.** Diffusely ; widely ; extensively ; বিস্তৃতভাবে ; ব্যাপকভাবে ; বিস্তীর্ণভাবে । **2.** To a great extent ; as, it is *largely* due to that ; অনেক পরিমাণে, অনেকাংশে, বহুল-পরিমাণ । **Large'-ness,** *n.* **1.** The state of being large ; প্রকাণ্ডতা, বিশালতা, মহত্ত্ব, বৃহত্ত্ব, বিস্তীর্ণতা । **2.** Liberality ; উদারতা, বদান্যতা, প্রশস্ততা, ঔদার্য্য । **Larg'-ish,** *adj.* **Large-handed** — Open handed ; liberal ; মুক্তহস্ত ; বদান্য । *Large-handedness, n.* **Large-hearted**—Kind ; generous ; দয়ালু ; উদারমনাঃ, প্রশস্তমনাঃ । *Large-heartedness,* ***n.*** **Large-minded** — Liberal ; not narrow-minded ; উদারমনাঃ ; প্রশস্তচিত্ত । *Large mindedness,* ***n.*** **A gentleman at large** — See GENTLEMAN. **At large** — At liberty ; free ; স্বাধীন ; মুক্ত । At full length ; with details ; as a body or whole ; as, the people *at large* ; সবিস্তারে, বিস্তৃতভাবে ; খুঁটিনাটি সকল বিষয় উল্লেখ করিয়া ; সাধারণভাবে । Without particularizing ; সাধারণ ভাবে, বিশেষভাবে কাহাকে লক্ষ্য না করিয়া । **In large**—On a large scale (opp. to *in little*) ; বিরাটভাবে । **Large of limb**—বৃহৎ হস্তপদ-বিশিষ্ট ।

lâr'-gess(e) (-jĕs), *n.* A present ; a gift or donation ; বকশীস্ ; দান পারিতোষিক, পরিতোষ্য (শুক্রঃ বিনয়) ।

lâr'-ĭ-ăt, *n.* A long rope used in catching or picketting horses etc. ; ঘোড়া ধরিবার জন্য বা খোঁটায় বাঁধিবার জন্য লম্বা দড়ী ।

Lark.

lärk, lă'-vêr-ŏck, *ns.* A small singing bird esp. the sky-lark ;

ভরত পক্ষী, ভারুই পাখী, ভরদ্বাজ পক্ষী। **Lark heel, Lark-spur**—একপ্রকার গুল্ম। **Sky-lark**—See under SKY. **When the sky falls we shall catch larks**—সাত মণ তেলও পুড়বে না রাধাও নাচবে না।

lärk, *n.* & *v. i.* A sport; a frolic; an amusing incident; ক্রীড়া, খেলা, কেলি, লীলা; ক্রীড়াকৌতুক; আমোদজনক ঘটনা। ***Verb i.*** To play tricks; to sport or frolic; চাতুরী খেলা; ক্রীড়াকৌতুক করা, কেলি করা, ক্রীড়া করা। **Lark'-y,** *adj.* Frolicsome; sportive; ক্রীড়াতৎপর, ক্রীড়াশীল, সলীল। **To have larks**—To be boyishly trickish; ছেলেখেলা করা; বালসুলভ ক্রীড়াকৌতুক করা।

lăr'-ri-kin, *n.* A street rowdy, usually young; গুণ্ডা।

lăr'-ŭm, *n.* (*Archaic*) Same as ALARUM.

Lă-rŭn'-dă, *n.* An ancient Roman deity of the under-world; রোমীয় পুরাণোক্ত অধোভুবনের দেবীবিশেষ।

lâr'-vă, *n.* (*Pl.* -VÆ) **1.** An insect in its caterpillar or grub state after issuing from the egg; কৃমি, কীটপোত (হিঃ কোঃ), পোকা। **2.** An immature form of other animals that undergo metamorphosis; অন্যান্যরূপান্তরগ্রাহী প্রাণীর আদ্যরূপ। **—val,** *adj.*

lă-rÿn'-gê-ăl, —ăn, *adj.* Relating to, or used on, the larynx; স্বরযন্ত্রসম্বন্ধীয়, স্বরযন্ত্রে ব্যবহৃত। **Laryngeal-plexus**—বিশুদ্ধপদ্ম (বামন)।

lăr-ÿn-gī'-tis, *n.* (*Med.*) Inflammation of the larynx; (ভৈষজ্যশাস্ত্র) স্বরযন্ত্রপ্রদাহ।

lăr-yn-gŏl'-ŏ-ḡÿ (-ĭng-), *n.* That branch of the medical science which treats of the larynx and its diseases; ভৈষজ্যশাস্ত্রের স্বরযন্ত্র ও স্বরযন্ত্র-সংক্রান্ত রোগ-সম্বন্ধীয় শাখা।

lă-ryn'-gŏ-scōpe (-rĭng), *n.* A mirror apparatus for examining the larynx; স্বরযন্ত্রপরীক্ষার্থ দর্পণযন্ত্র।

lăr-ÿn-gŏt-ŏ-mÿ, *n.* The cutting into the larynx from without to assist respiration; শ্বাসরোধাদি রোগে স্বরযন্ত্রচ্ছেদ।

lar'-ynx (-ĭngks), *n.* A cavity in the throat holding the vocal chords; কণ্ঠনালীর ঊর্দ্ধভাগ, স্বরযন্ত্র। **La-ryn'-gic,** *adj.*

lăs-cĭv'-ĭ-ous (-ŭs), *adj.* **1.** Lustful; wanton; lewd; কামী, কামাতুর, স্ত্রীব্যসনী, স্ত্রীলম্পট, কামপ্রবণ; লোচ্চা; কামুক, কামাসক্ত, ইন্দ্রিয়পরায়ণ রতিলম্পট। **2.** Exciting to lust; কামোদ্দীপক। **—ly,** *adv.* **—ness,** *n.*

lăsh, *n.* **1.** A stroke with a whip etc.; the thong of a whip; a whip; চাবুকাঘাত, কষাঘাত; চাবুকের চর্ম্মরজ্জু বা রজ্জু; চাবুক, কষা। **2.** A sarcasm or cutting remark; a goading influnce; ব্যঙ্গোক্তি, বিদ্রূপবাণ; তাড়না। **3.** The eye-lash; অক্ষিপক্ষ্ম। **Lash'-less,** *adj.* **Eye-lash** — See under EYE. **The lash**—বেত্রাঘাত, বেত্রদণ্ড।

lăsh, *v. i.* & *t.* **1.** To move a limb, tail, etc. suddenly; লাঙ্গুল, হস্তপদ, প্রভৃতি হঠাৎ সঞ্চালিত করা। **2.** To rush vehemently; to pour as rain, tears, etc.; (of light) to flash; প্রচণ্ডবেগে ধাবিত হওয়া; বর্ষিত হওয়া; (আলোক) স্ফুরিত হওয়া। **3.** To strike forcibly (*at*); (*fig.*) to direct censure etc. (*at*); সজোরে আঘাত করা; তিরস্কারবাক্য প্রয়োগ করা। **4.** To strike or kick (*out*) vigorously, as a horse etc.; সজোরে আঘাত করা বা লাথি মারা। **5.** To break (*out*) into excess, strong language, etc.; "Forbear *lashing out* into free expressions"; to squander one's substance, (with *out*); অতি মাত্রায় চড়া; অপব্যয়-করা। ***Verb t.*** **1.** To strike with a lash; to whip; to flog; চাবুকদ্বারা মারা; কষাঘাত করা; বেত্রাঘাত করা। **2.** To strike forcibly; (of waves) to beat upon; as, the big waves *lash* the shore; সজোরে আঘাত করা; ক্রমাগত আঘাত করিতে থাকা। **3.** To castigate in words; to censure severely; to satirize; তীব্র ভাষায় তিরস্কার করা; তীব্র তিরস্কার করা; বিদ্রূপ করা। **4.** To tie, fasten (*to* something) with a rope or cord, (with *down*, *on*, *together*); দড়ী বা সূতলিদ্বারা বন্ধন করা। **To lash out**—See LASH, *v. i.* 4 & 5.

lăsh'-êr, *n.* **1.** One who lashes; বেত্রাঘাতকারী। **2.** The water rushing over the weir; the weir or the pool receiving water over it; আলি বা জাঙ্গালের উপর দিয়া প্রচণ্ডবেগে ধাবমান জলরাশি; বাঁধ জাঙ্গাল, জাঙ্গালের উপর দিয়া ছুটিয়া যে নালায় জল পড়ে।

lash'-ing, *n.* **1.** The act of whipping; বেত্রাঘাত, চাবুক লাগান। **2.** A rope for binding; বন্ধনরজ্জু। **3.** Chastisement; পিটুনি।

lăs'-prĭng, *n.* A young salmon; স্যামন মাছের বাচ্চা।

lasque (lăsk), *n.* A flat or ill-formed diamond; চ্যাপ্টা অথবা কুগঠিত হীরা।

lăss, *n.* (*Fem.* of LAD) A girl; a young woman; a sweetheart; "The shepherd and his *lass*"; বালিকা, বালা; কুমারী, যুবতী, তরুণী; প্রণয়িনী, প্রেয়সী।

lăs'-sie (-ĭ), *n.* A lass or girl; ছোট মেয়ে, ছোট বালিকা।

lăs'-sĭ-tūde (-ĭ), *n.* Langour of body or mind; disinclination to exert oneself; weariness; শিথিলাঙ্গতা, অঙ্গাবসাদ (হিঃ কোঃ), শিথিলতা (ঐ), শ্লথাঙ্গতা, মন্থরাঙ্গতা, অঙ্গগ্লানি, অঙ্গশৈথিল্য, তন্দ্রালসভাব, তন্দ্রাজড়িমা, অবসাদ; গ্লানি, খেদ; শ্রান্তি।

lăs'-sŏ, *n.* & *v. t.* **1.** A long rope or cord with a noose used in America for catching wild horses, cattle, etc.; বন্য ঘোটক, গো মহিষাদি ধরিবার জন্য ফাঁসযুক্ত লম্বা দড়ী, পাশবন্ধ। ***Verb t.*** To catch with lasso ; পাশবন্ধ দ্বারা অশ্ব প্রভৃতি ধৃত করা।

Lasso.

lăst, *n.* A wooden model or mould of the foot on which boots and shoes are made or formed ; জুতা তৈয়ার করার জন্য কাঠের ফর্ম্মা বা ছাঁচ। **The cobbler must stick to his last** — আদার ব্যাপারীর জাহাজের খবর নিয়ে কাজ নাই। **To stick to one's last**—Not to interfere with matters one does not understand; অনধিকারচর্চ্চা না করা।

lăst, *n.* A commercial measure or weight varying with place and goods ; দেশ ও বস্তুভেদে বিভিন্ন পরিমাণ বিশেষ।

lăst, *adj., n.* & *adv.* **1.** Coming after all others ; final ; সর্ব্বশেষ ; অন্তিম, চরম, অন্ত্য। **2.** Next before the present ; as, *last* Tuesday or week ; বিগত, গত। **3.** Lowest ; of least estimation ; as, the *last* prize ; সর্ব্বনিম্ন ; সর্ব্বশেষ। **4.** Most unlikely or unwilling ; least suitable ; as, he should be the *last* man to do it : the *last* thing to try ; সবচেয়ে অসম্ভব, সবচেয়ে নারাজ ; সর্ব্বাপেক্ষা অনুপযোগী। **5.** Belonging to the end esp. of life or the world ; অন্তিম। **6.** Definite ; conclusive ; as, he has said his *last* word on the subject ; চরম, চূড়ান্ত। **7.** Only remaining; as, the *last* resource ; কেবলমাত্র অবশিষ্ট। **8.** Utmost ; supreme ; highest in degree ; as, matters of *last* importance ; চরম ; পরম ; সর্ব্বোচ্চ। ***Noun.*** **1.** A person or thing mentioned last ; শেষোক্ত ব্যক্তি। **2.** The end ; death ; অন্ত, জীবনান্ত ; মৃত্যু। **3.** Last mention ; as, I shall never hear the *last* of it ; শেষবার উল্লেখ। ***Adv.*** **1.** After all others ; as, he was mentioned *last* ; সর্ব্বশেষে, সকলের পরে। **2.** On the last occasion ; as, I saw him *last* in London ; শেষবার। **3.** In the last place ; finally ; অবশেষে ; চরমে, অন্তিমে। **Last'-ly,** *adv.* In the last place ; finally ; শেষে, পরিশেষে, অবশেষে ; চরমে, অন্তিমে, আখেরে। **Last day**—খৃষ্টীয় ও মহম্মদীয় শাস্ত্রোক্ত অন্তিমবিচার দিবস, রোজকেয়ামত (মুসলমানশাস্ত্র)। **At last**—In the end ; in conclusion ; after much delay ; শেষে, অবশেষে ; চরমে, অন্তিমে ; বহু বিলম্বে, বহুকাল পর। **At the last gasp**—At the point of death ; নাভিশ্বাসের অবস্থায়, অন্তিম অবস্থায়, মুমূর্ষু অবস্থায়, এখন তখন (*colloq.*), মর মর (*colloq.*)। **I said in my last**—(*Ellipt.*) I said in my last letter ; আমি পূর্ব্বের পত্রে লিখিয়াছিলাম। **Last but not least**—Last in order of mention or occurrence but not of importance ; সর্ব্বশেষে উল্লেখ করা হইলেও বা ঘটিলেও গুরুত্বে অল্প নয়। **Last but one**—Last excepting one ; সর্ব্বশেষটীর অব্যবহিত, উপান্ত্য, পূর্ব্ববর্ত্তী। **Mrs.—'s last**—(*Ellipt.*) Her last baby ; তাহার শেষ সন্তান। **On one's last legs**—Near death or end ; মরণোন্মুখ, ধ্বংসোন্মুখ। **The four last things**—Death, judgment, heaven and hell ; মৃত্যু, অন্তিমবিচার, স্বর্গ, নরক। **The last cast**—The last chance ; শেষ ভরসা। **To breathe one's last**—To die ; প্রাণত্যাগ করা, প্রাণবায়ু মোচন করা। **To hear one's last**—(*Ellipt.*) To hear one's last joke ; কাহার শেষ ব্যঙ্গোক্তি শ্রবণ করা। **To put the last hand to**—(*Obs.*) To give the finishing touch to ; (অপ্রঃ) শেষ চানকান দেওয়া। **To the last**—To the end ; till death ; শেষ পর্য্যন্ত ; আমরণ।

lăst, *v. i., t.* & *n.* To continue in time ; to endure ; to remain unexhausted, adequate or alive ; স্থায়ী থাকা, টিঁকিয়াথাকা ; স্থায়ী হওয়া ; অখিন্ন থাকা, যথেষ্ট হওয়া, জীবিত থাকা। ***Verb t.*** To suffice ; as, it will *last* me six months ; প্রচুর হওয়া, যথেষ্ট হওয়া। ***Noun.*** Staying power or stamina ; সহনক্ষমতা, ধৃতি।

lăst'-ing, *adj.* & *n.* Durable ; permanent ; enduring ; টেঁকসই, মজবুত ; চিরস্থায়ী, ধ্রুব ; স্থায়ী। ***Noun.*** A kind of durable cloth ; একপ্রকার মজবুত কাপড়। **—ly,** *adv.* **—ness,** *n.*

Lăt-ă-ki'-ă (-kē), *n.* A kind of Turkish tobacco ; তুরস্কদেশীয় তাম্রকূট বিশেষ।

latch (lăch), *n.* & *v. t.* A door or gate fastening consisting of hinge-bolt and catch ; a small spring-lock for a front door opened from the outside by means of a key ; খিল, অর্গল, হুড়কা ; সদর দরজার স্প্রিংএর তালা—যাহা বাহির হইতে চাবি দ্বারা খোলা যায়। ***Verb t.*** To fasten with a latch ; অর্গলবদ্ধ করা, খিল দেওয়া। **On the latch**—Fastened by a latch only ; অর্গলবদ্ধ।

latch'-ĕt (lăch-), *n.* (*Bibl.*) A string or buckle for fastening a shoe ; জুতার ফিতা।

lāte, *adj.* & *n.* **1.** Coming after due or proper time ; slow ; tardy ; বিলম্বাগত; ধীর ; মন্থর, বিলম্বিত, চিরাগত। **2.** Far on in day or night ; as, *late* hours ; দিন বা রাত্রির অধিকাংশ অতীত, বেলাতীত। **3.** Long-delayed ; not early ; as, a *late* crop : a *late* spring ; অতিবিলম্বিত ; অশীঘ্র। **4.** Lately deceased or gone out of office ; as, the *late* Head master ; not long past ; of recent date ; as the *late* floods ; ভূতপূর্ব্ব, পূর্ব্বতন ; সম্প্রতিসংঘটিত, অচিরগত ; অধুনাতন, ইদানীন্তন। **5.** Keeping late hours ; অধিক রাত্রি জাগরণশীল। ***Noun.*** Only in *of late* (see below). **Late'-ly,** *adv.* Not long ago ; recently ; in recent times ; অনতিপূর্ব্বে ; ইদানীন্তন; সম্প্রতি, ইদানীং, অধুনা। **Late'-ness,** *n.* **Lat'-er,** *adj.* & *adv.* Comp. degree of LATE. **Lat'-est,** *adj.* & *adv.* Supl. degree of LATE. **Lat'-ish,** *adj.* & *adv.* Somewhat late ; কতকটা বিলম্বিত। **Late-fee**—কোন নির্দ্দিষ্ট স্থানের ডাকের ব্যাগ বন্ধ হওয়ার পর চিঠি ডাকে দিলে, ঐ চিঠির জন্য যে অতিরিক্ত মাশুল দিতে হয়। **Late hours**—Hours after the usual time for rising or going to bed ; প্রভাতে শয্যাত্যাগ করার ও রাত্রে নিদ্রা যাওয়ার নিরূপিত সময়ের পরবর্ত্তীকাল। **At a late hour**—Late ; বিলম্বে, দেরিতে, গোণে। **Late in the day**—Too late ; অতি বিলম্বে। **Of late**—Recently ; সম্প্রতি, ইদানীং। **Of late years**—In the last few years ; বিগত কয়েক বৎসরের মধ্যে। **To keep late hours at night**—To sit up late at night ; রাত্রি জাগরণ করা। **Too late**—অতি বিলম্বিত।

lāte, *adv.* **1.** After the proper or usual time ; far on in time ; as, soon or *late* ; নিয়মিত বা উপযুক্ত সময়ের পরে ; বিলম্বে, দেরীতে, গোণে। **2.** At or till a late hour ; অনেক দেরীতে, অনেক বিলম্বে। **3.** (*Poet.*) Recently ; lately ; সম্প্রতি, ইদানীং ; অল্পদিন হইল। **4.** Formerly but not now ; as, his own room, *late* the chaplain's ; ইতঃপূর্ব্বে। **5.** Relatively near the end of a historical period etc. ; as, traces remained so *late* as the Stuart times ; কোন ঐতিহাসিক কালের অপেক্ষাকৃত প্রায় শেষ ভাগে।

lāt'-en (-n), *v. t.* & *i.* To make or become late ; বিলম্ব করা, বিলম্ব হওয়া।

lā'-tĕnt', *adj.* **1.** Not visible or apparent ; dormant ; অদৃশ্য, অপ্রকট ; অনুদ্ভূত (হিঃ কোঃ), প্রচ্ছন্ন, নিষ্ক্রিয়, সুপ্ত, গুপ্ত, গূঢ়, নিগূঢ়। **—ly,** *adv.* In a latent manner ; not openly ; গুপ্তভাবে, অদৃশ্যভাবে, প্রচ্ছন্নভাবে ; অপ্রকাশ্যে। **—ten-cy,** *n.* State of being latent ; প্রচ্ছন্নাবস্থান, অনুদ্বোধ (হিঃ কোঃ), অব্যক্ততা (ঐ), সম্ভাব্যাবস্থা (ঐ), তিরোভাব (ঐ), অন্তর্ভাব (ঐ)। **Latent energy** — Dormant energy ; প্রচ্ছন্নশক্তি, অনুদ্ভূতশক্তি। **Latent heat**—অনুদ্ভূত তাপ (হিঃ কোঃ), গূঢ়তাপ (সাঃ পঃ), প্রচ্ছন্নতাপ (ঐ)। **Latent period**—অনুদ্বোধাবকাশ (হিঃ কোঃ)। **Latent period of a disease**—যে সময় ব্যাপিয়া কোন রোগ বাহিরে প্রকাশ পায় না, কিন্তু, শরীরের ভিতর প্রচ্ছন্নভাবে বিদ্যমান থাকে।

lăt'-ĕr-ăl, *adj.* & *n.* Of, at, towards or from, the side ; পার্শ্বসম্বন্ধীয়, পার্শ্বাভিমুখীন, পার্শ্বস্থ, পার্শ্বিক (হিঃ কোঃ), পার্শ্বোত্থিত, পার্শ্ববর্ত্তী। ***Noun.*** A lateral or side part, member, or object ; a lateral shoot, branch, etc. ; পার্শ্বভাগ, পার্শ্বভাগস্থ ব্যক্তি বা বস্তু ; পার্শ্ব-মুকুল, পার্শ্ব-শাখা **—ly,** *adv.* Sideways ; sidewise ; পাশাপাশি ; পার্শ্বের দিকে। **Lateral branch of a family**—A branch descended from the brother or sister in the direct line ; ভগ্নী বা ভ্রাতার পুত্র, পৌত্রাদি। **Lateral section**—পার্শ্বিক ছিদ্র (হিঃ কোঃ)। **Lateral surface**—পার্শ্বিকপৃষ্ঠ (ঐ)।

Lăt'-ĕr-ăn, *n.* & *adj.* The cathedral church of St. John Lateran in Rome, being the highest in rank of all churches in the Catholic world [From the Lateran family possessing a palace near the said church] ; রোমনগরীস্থ রোমান ক্যাথলিক জগতের সর্ব্বশ্রেষ্ঠ ধর্ম্মমন্দির।

lăt'-ĕr-īte, *n.* A clay-like sandstone of a reddish or brick colour found in India ; মাকড়া পাথর (যোঃ), মাকড়া (ঐ)।

Lates calcarifer—ভেটকী (গুপ্তঃ)।

lā'-tĕx, *n.* (*Bot.*) A milky juice of plants ; (উদ্ভিদ্-বিদ্যা) দুগ্ধবৎ বৃক্ষ-নির্যাস।

lâth, *n.* & *v. t.* A long thin narrow strip of wood esp. used to support tiles, slates or plastering ; কাঠের পাতলা পাত, বাতা, বাঁখারি। ***Verb t.*** To provide (wall, ceiling, etc.) with laths ; কাঠের বাতা লাগান। **Lath'-ing,** *n.* **Lath'-y,** *adj.* Thin, as a person, animal, etc. ; পাতলা। **A person as thin as a lath**—A very thin person ; তালপাতার সিপাহী, কঙ্কালসার ব্যক্তি।

lāthe, *n.* **1.** A machine by which articles of wood, metal, ivory, etc. are turned and cut into a smooth round form ; কুঁদযন্ত্র, কুন্দ, ভ্রমি, ভ্রমিযন্ত্র। **2.** (Also *potter's lathe*) A potter's wheel ; কুমারের চাক, কুলালচক্র। **Lathe-bearer, —carrier, —dog**—যে কল দ্বারা কোন বস্তু কুঁদে আটকান হয়। **Lathe-bed**—কুঁদের বাট।

lăth'-ĕr, *n.*, *v. t.* & *i.* **1.** Foam or froth made by soap and water ; সাবানের ফেনা। **2.** Frothy sweat of a horse ; অশ্বের সফেন ঘর্ম্ম। ***Verb t.*** To cover or spread over with lather as the chin for shaving etc. ; ক্ষৌর কার্য্যের সময়ে গালে সাবানের ফেনা মাখান। ***Verb i.*** **1.** To form a foam (of soap) ; সাবানের ফেনা করা। **2.** To become frothy as a horse ; (অশ্বাদির পক্ষে) ঘর্ম্মাক্তকলেবর হওয়া। **3.** To beat or thrash ; মারা, প্রহার করা, পিটুনি দেওয়া। **—ing,** *n.* **—y,** *adj.* Covered with lather ; frothy ; সাবানের ফেনা যুক্ত ; সফেন।

lat-ĭ-fŭn'-dĭ-ă, *n.* (*Pl.*) Large landed estates ; বিস্তীর্ণ ভূ-সম্পত্তি।

Lăt′-in, *adj.* & *n.* **1.** Of, or pertaining to, Latium (a district of Italy) or to ancient Latins; ইতালীর অন্তর্গত ল্যাটিয়াম্ নামক জেলাসম্পর্কীয়, প্রাচীন ল্যাটীনজাতিসম্পর্কীয়। **2.** Pertaining to, like, or composed in, the language of the ancient Latins or Romans; ল্যাটিন ভাষা-সম্বন্ধীয়, ল্যাটিনভাষাবৎ, ল্যাটিন ভাষায় রচিত। **3.** Of, or relating to, the Catholic church; রোমান ক্যাথলিক ধর্ম্মসংঘসম্বন্ধীয়। **4.** Speaking one of the languages descended from Latin; relating to the peoples speaking Latin; ল্যাটিন ভাষা হইতে উদ্ভূত ভাষা-বিশেষ ভাষী; ল্যাটিনভাষাভাষী লোকগণ সম্পর্কীয়। ***Noun.*** **1.** A native or inhabitant of Latium; প্রাচীন ল্যাটিয়াম্ নগরের অধিবাসী। **2.** The language of the ancient Romans; প্রাচীন রোমকদিগের ভাষা। **—ism,** *n.* A Latin idiom; ল্যাটিন ভাষার রীতিসিদ্ধ প্রয়োগ। **—ist** *n.* one versed in Latin; ল্যাটিন ভাষাভিজ্ঞ ব্যক্তি, ল্যাটিন ভাষায় সুপণ্ডিত ব্যক্তি। **—less,** *adj.* Ignorant of Latin; ল্যাটিন ভাষানভিজ্ঞ। **Classical Latin**—রোমনগরীর শ্রেষ্ঠ গ্রন্থকারগণের গ্রন্থের ল্যাটিন ভাষা। **Dog Latin**—নিকৃষ্ট ল্যাটিন। **Late Latin**—প্রায় ১৭৫ খৃঃ অব্দ হইতে—৬০০ খৃঃ অব্দ পর্য্যন্ত সময়ের ল্যাটিন ভাষা। **Latin-Church** — রোমানক্যাথলিক ধর্ম্মসংঘ। **Mediæval Latin**—৬০০ খৃঃ অব্দ হইতে ১৫০০ খৃঃ অব্দ পর্য্যন্ত সময়ের ল্যাটিন ভাষা। **Modern Latin**—প্রায় ১৫০০ খৃঃ অব্দের পরবর্ত্তী ল্যাটিন ভাষা। **Old Latin**—প্রায় খৃঃ পূঃ ৭৫ অব্দের পূর্ব্ববর্ত্তী ল্যাটিন ভাষা। **Thieve's Latin**—চোরের সাঙ্কেতিক ভাষা। **The Latin peoples**—ফ্রান্স, স্পেন, পর্ত্তুগাল ও ইতালী প্রভৃতি দেশের অধিবাসিগণ।

Latine, (*L*) *adv.* In Latin; ল্যাটিন ভাষায়।

Lă-tin′-i-tў, *n.* **1.** The purity of Latin style or idiom; ল্যাটিন রচনাপদ্ধতি বা বাগ্‌ধারার বিশুদ্ধতা। **2.** Ths style of writing Latin; ল্যাটিন রচনাপদ্ধতি।

Lăt′-in-īze, *v. t.* & *i.* **1.** To give Latin forms to; to render into Latin; ল্যাটিন আকার প্রদান করা; ল্যাটিন ভাষায় অনুবাদ করা। **2.** To make conformable to the ideas and customs of the ancient Romans, Latin peoples or the Latin Church; প্রাচীন রোমক, ল্যাটিয়ামের অধিবাসী ও রোমানক্যাথলিক-দিগের ভাব ও আচার পদ্ধতির অনুযায়ী করা। ***Verb i.*** To use Latin idioms and phrases; ল্যাটিন ভাষার বাক্য বা রীতিসিদ্ধ শব্দ প্রয়োগ করা।

Lā-tī′-nŭs, *n.* The father of Lavinia; ল্যাটিয়ামের রাজা Laviniaর পিতা। Æneus ইহার কন্যা Laviniaকে বিবাহ করেন।

lăt′-i-tūde, *n.* **1.** (*Jocularly*) Breadth; width; as, a hat with great *latitude* of brim; (রঙ্গচ্ছলে) প্রস্থ; বিস্তার, পরিসর। **2.** (*Rare*) Extent; scope; (অপ্রঃ) বিস্তর; প্রসর। **3.** Freedom from narrow restrictions; liberality of interpretation; independence of action, thought or opinion; "Extremest *latitude* in theology; উদারতা; ব্যাখ্যার উদারতা; কার্য্য, চিন্তা বা মতের স্বাধীনতা। **4.** (*Geog.*) The angular distance measured on a meridian; the distance of a place North or South from the equator measured on a meridian; (ভূগোল) দ্রাঘিমার উপর পরিমিত কৌণিক দূরত্ব, অক্ষ (সাঃ পঃ); নিরক্ষবৃত্ত হইতে উত্তর বা দক্ষিণে দিকে কোন স্থানের দূরত্ব, নিরক্ষান্তর, অক্ষাংশ (সাঃ পঃ), পর (ঐ), ধ্রুব (ঐ)। **5.** (*Usu. Pl.*) Regions marked by their latitudes; as, cold *latitude*; নিরক্ষান্তর দ্বারা চিহ্নিত দেশসমূহ। **6.** (*Astron.*) The angular distance of a heavenly body from ecliptic; (জ্যোতির্বিজ্ঞান) ক্রান্তিবলয় হইতে কোন জ্যোতিষ্কের কৌণিক দূরত্ব, খগোলীয় অক্ষাংশ, শর (সাঃ পঃ), বিক্ষেপ (ঐ), ক্ষেপ (ঐ), অস্পষ্টশর (ঐ)। **—tu′-di-nal,** *adj.* Of, or relating to, the geographical latitude; নিরক্ষান্তর সম্পর্কীয়। **A degree of latitude**—অক্ষাংশ, অক্ষভাগ (প্রায় ৬০ সামুদ্রিক মাইল বা ৬৯½ মাইল)। **Apparent latitude**—স্পষ্টবিক্ষেপ। **Argument of the latitude**—অক্ষ-কর্ণ (কঃ), অক্ষকেন্দ্র (সাঃ পঃ), পতন-কেন্দ্র (ঐ), বিক্ষেপকেন্দ্র (ঐ)। **Ascending latitude** — আরোহীশর (হিঃ কোঃ। **Celestial latitude**—খগোলীয় অক্ষাংশ (হিঃ কোঃ), খগোলীয় শর (ঐ)। **Circle or parallels of latitude**—নিরক্ষবৃত্তের সমান্তরাল এবং ঐ বৃত্ত হইতে ক্রমশঃ দশ দশ অংশ দূরে কল্পিত ক্ষুদ্র ক্ষুদ্র বৃত্ত, অক্ষবৃত্ত, অক্ষাংশবৃত্ত, স্বদেশ-মধ্যপরিধি, স্পষ্টভূপরিধি (সাঃ পঃ), অক্ষাংশীয় সমান্তরালবৃত্ত, সমাক্ষবৃত্ত, শরসমানান্তর (সূর্য্য বিঃ)। **Geographical latitude** — ভৌগোলিকশর (হিঃ কোঃ), অক্ষাংশ (ঐ)। **Heliocentric latitude** — সূর্য্যকেন্দ্রকশর (হিঃ কোঃ)। **Northern latitude** — উত্তরাক্ষদেশ (সূর্য্য বিঃ)। **Polar latitude**—শর (সাঃ পঃ), ক্ষেপ (ঐ), বিক্ষেপ (ঐ), স্পষ্টশর (ঐ)। **The complement of latitude**—লম্ব, লম্বক।

lăt-i-tū-di-nā′-ri-ăn, *adj.* & *n.* Liberal in religious belief; tolerant of variations in opinion or doctrine; ধর্ম্মমত সম্বন্ধে উদার; মতসম্বন্ধে শিথিল, শিথিল-ধর্ম্মভক্ত (আঃবঃ), নানা মত সহিষ্ণু। ***Noun.*** **1.** One who is liberal in religious views; one not strictly orthodox; স্বাধীন মতাবলম্বী, উদারধর্ম্মমতাবলম্বী; যাহার ধর্ম্ম বিষয়ে গোঁড়ামি নাই। **—ism,** *n.* Freedom of opinion in the theology; free-thinking; ধর্ম্ম-সম্বন্ধে মতের উদারতা, মতশৈথিল্য, অঙ্গীকার বিস্তৃতি (হিঃ কোঃ); স্বাধীন চিন্তা।

Latona, *n.* See LETO.

lă-trine′ (-trēn), *n.* (*Usu. Pl.*) A privy esp. in a camp, hospital or the like ; মলমূত্রাদি ত্যাগের স্থান, পাইখানা, বিশেষতঃ সেনানিবাশ, রুগ্নাবাস, প্রভৃতির পাইখানা।

lăt′-ten (-n), *n.* & *adj.* (*Archaic*) A mixed yellow metal either same as, or like, brass ; (অপ্রঃ) পিত্তল বা পিত্তলবৎ ধাতু বিশেষ। ***Adj.*** Of, or relating to, this mixed metal ; উক্ত ধাতু সম্পর্কীয়।

lăt′-ter (-ėr), *adj.* **1.** (*Archaic*) Later; "*Latter* flowers" ; (অপ্রঃ) পরবর্ত্তী, শেষের। **2.** Second-mentioned ; শেষোক্ত। **3.** Belonging, or pertaining to, the end of a period, world, etc. ; অন্ত্য। **–ly,** *adv.* **1.** Of late ; recently ; ইদানীং ; সম্প্রতি। **2.** Towards the end of some period of life ; শেষভাগে। **Latter-day**—Modern ; আধুনিক, বর্ত্তমান। **Latter-end**—Death ; মৃত্যু। **In these latter days**—At this late period of the world's history ; পৃথিবীর ইতিহাসের উত্তরকালে। **The latter**—(*Ellipt.*) The second mentioned thing or person ; শেষোক্ত ব্যক্তি বা বস্তু।

lăt′-tice (-ĭs), *n.* & *v. t.* **1.** A structure of cross laths, rods or bars with openings ; a window, gate, etc. with a lattice ; জাফরি, জাল, জালকর্ম্ম, জালক, গবাক্ষজাল ; গবাক্ষ। **2.** Laths arranged crosswise (also *lattice work*) ; ঝরকা, জাফরি। ***Verb t.*** To furnish with a lattice, (with *up* or *over*) ; জাফরী বসান। **–ticed,** *p. p.* **–tic-ing,** *n.* **Lattice-bridge**—যে সেতুর স্তম্ভের মধ্যবর্ত্তী অংশে জাফরী বসান থাকে। **Lattice leaf, Lattice-plant**—জাফরির আকার পাতা ; জালকবৎ পত্র-বিশিষ্ট জলজ গুল্মবিশেষ। **Lattice window**—One with a lattice ; one composed of small diamond-shaped panes set in lead-work ; জালগবাক্ষ (কথাঃ সঃ) ; জালাক্ষ, জালমার্গ (আঃ বঃ)। **Lattice work**—A work made of lattices ; lattices collectively ; জাফরীর কাজ, জালির কাজ, জালিকর্ম্ম ; জাফরি সমূহ।

Lattice.

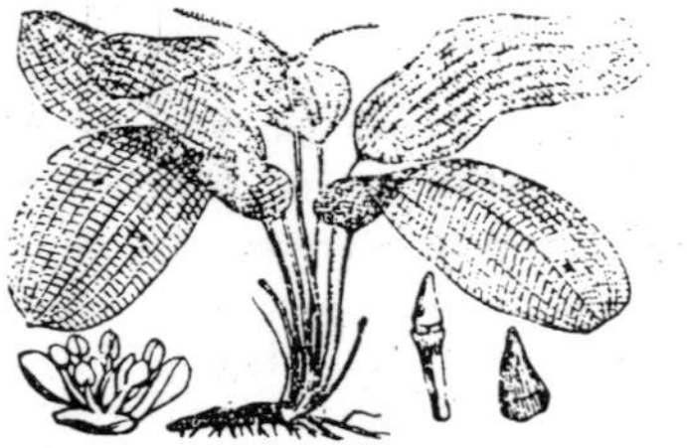

Lattice-leaf.

laud (läd), *n.* & *v. t.* **1.** (*Rare except in hymns*) Praise ; exaltation ; প্রশংসা ; স্তব। **2.** A song or hymn of praise; স্তব, স্তোত্র। **3.** (*Pl.*) The first of the day-hours of the church ; রোমান ক্যাথলিক ধর্ম্মসংঘের উপাসনা করার জন্য নির্দ্দিষ্ট সাত ঘণ্টার মধ্যে প্রথম ঘণ্টা। ***Verb t.*** To praise ; স্তুতি করা, প্রশংসা করা, গুণকীর্ত্তন করা। **Laud-a-bil′-i-ty,** *n.* **Laud′-a-ble,** *adj.* **1.** Deserving praise ; praise-worthy ; প্রশংসনীয় ; শ্লাঘ্য, প্রশস্ত, স্তুত্য, কীর্ত্তনীয়, স্তবনীয়, বন্দ্য, গেয়, শ্লাঘনীয়, শ্লাঘ্য, স্তবার্হ। **2.** (*Med.*) Sound, as pus etc. ; সুস্থ। **Laud′-a-bly,** *adv.*

lau-dā′-tion (lä-), *n.* Commending ; praise ; গুণকীর্ত্তন ; প্রশংসা, স্তুতি। **Laud′-a-tive, Laud′-a-to-ry,** *adjs.* Relating to, or expressing, praise ; প্রশংসাসম্বন্ধীয়, স্তুত্যাত্মক, স্তবনাত্মক, স্তুতিপ্রদ। **Laud′-a-tor,** *n.*

lau′-dă-nŭm (lä-), *n.* Opium prepared in spirit of wine ; tincture of opium ; অহিফেনারিষ্ট ; অহিফেনের আরক, অহিফেনরস (আঃ বঃ)।

Laudator temporis acti, (*L.*) *n.* One who prefers the good days ; যে ব্যক্তি প্রাচীন কালের সুখময় দিন বরণীয় মনে করে।

laugh (lâf), *v. i., t.* & *n.* **1.** To make the noise and exhibit the features which by sudden mirth etc. creates ; হাস্য করা, হাসা। **2.** (With *at*) To ridicule ; উপহাস করা, বিদ্রূপ করা। **3.** (Of inanimate things) To appear gay, lively, or pleasant ; "Thus...plateau *laughs* with verdure" ; (বস্তু সম্বন্ধে) উৎফুল্ল, সতেজ বা মনোরম দেখান। ***Verb t.*** **1.** To utter or express by laughter ; হাসির দ্বারা প্রকাশ করা। **2.** To hold up, as a person *to* scorn ; হাস্যাস্পদ করা। **3.** To get (one *out of* habit etc.) by ridicule ; ঠাট্টা করিয়া (কোন অভ্যাস) ছাড়ান। ***Noun.*** **1.** Act of laughing ; the expression of mirth, joy, ridicule etc. ; sound made in laughing ; হাসন ; হাস্য, হসিত, হাস ; হাসির শব্দ, হি হি, হো হো। **2.** A person's manner of laughing ; কোন লোকের হাসির ধরণ। **Laugh′-a-ble,** *adj.* Exciting laughter ; amusing ; ludicrous ; হাস্যজনক, হাস্যকর, হাস্যোদ্দীপক, মজার, বিদ্রূপাত্মক। **Laugh′-a-bly,** *adv.* **Laugh′-er,** *n.* **He laughs best who laughs last**—A warning against premature exultation ; যে জেতে সেই হাসে ; ঘুঁটে পোড়ে গোবর হাসে তোমার একদিন আছে শেষে; যত হাসি তত কান্না বলে গেছে রাম শর্ম্মা। **To have** or **get the laugh of**—To turn the tables on assailant ; অপরকে হারাইয়া উপহাস করিতে সমর্থ হওয়া ; পড়তা উল্টাইয়া দেওয়া। **To join in the laugh**—To take banter good humouredly ; কেহ ঠাট্টা করিলে রাগ না হইয়া খোসমেজাজে হাসিতে যোগ দেওয়া। **To laugh a person, opinion, etc. out of court**—To deprive of a hearing by ridicule ; হাসিয়া

উড়াইয়া দেওয়া। **To laugh at**—To make an object of laughter ; to ridicule ; হাস্যাস্পদ করা ; উপহাস করা। **To laugh away**—To dismiss (a subject) with a laughter ; হাসিয়া উড়াইয়া দেওয়া। To while away (time) with jests ; হাসি তামাসায় সময় কাটান। **To laugh down**—To silence with laughter ; হাসিয়া নিরস্ত করা, হাসিয়া চুপ করান। **To laugh in one's sleeve**—To laugh inwardly ; to be secretly amused ; মুখ চাপিয়া হাসা, মুখ টিপিয়া হাসা, মনে মনে হাসা ; মনে মনে আমোদ বোধ করা। **To laugh on the wrong side of the mouth**—To have revulsion from joy or amusement to tears or sorrow ; to be humiliated ; হাসি তামাসার পর সহসা ভাব পরিবর্তন হইয়া বিষণ্ণ হওয়া বা অশ্রুজল নির্গত হওয়া ; গর্ব্ব খর্ব্ব হওয়া, জাঁকজাড়ি ভেঙ্গে যাওয়া। **To laugh out of the other corner** or **side of the mouth**—To be made to feel vexation ; to have the laugh turned against a jeering person ; বিরক্তি উৎপাদন করা, মনস্তাপ জন্মান ; বিদ্রূপকারী ব্যক্তিকে বিদ্রূপভাজন করা। **To laugh over**—To discuss with laughter ; কোন বিষয় লইয়া হাসা। **To laugh to scorn**—To deride ; to treat with mockery ; বিদ্রূপের হাসি হাসা ; বিদ্রূপ করা।

laugh'-ing (lâf-), *adj.* & *n.* Fit to be treated, or accompanied, with laughter ; as, it is no *laughing* matter ; হাসির উপযুক্ত, হাসির সহিত। ***Noun.*** Act of one who laughs ; হাসন, হাস্য, হাসি, হসিত। **Laughing-gas** — একপ্রকার বাষ্প—ইহা নিশ্বাসের সহিত টানিলে হাসি পায়। **Laughing stock** — An object of ridicule ; উপহাসাস্পদ ব্যক্তি, হাসির পাত্র। **No laughing matter**—A serious thing ; not a fit subject for laughing ; গুরুতর বিষয় ; হাসির কথা নয়, হাসির বিষয় নয়।

laugh-têr (lâf-), *n.* The act or sound of laughing ; হাস্য, হাস্যরব, হসিত, হাসি। **Homeric laughter**—অট্টহাস্য।

launce (lâns), *n.* The sand-eel ; একপ্রকার বাইন মাছ।

launch (lânsh), *v. t*, *i.* & *n.* **1.** To throw ; to hurl ; to discharge ; as, to *launch* a dat, blow or censure ; নিক্ষেপ করা ; মোচন করা, ছুড়িয়া মারা ; ক্ষেপণ করা। **2.** To set afloat, as a ship ; জলে ভাসান। **3.** To start on a career ; to send off on a new course ; নূতন পথে চালান ; নূতন কার্য্যে ব্রতী করা। ***Verb i.*** **1.** (*Lit.* & *fig.*) To set out as upon sea, (with *forth*, *out*) ; "To *launch out* beyond Sicily" ; (শব্দানুযায়ী ও লক্ষণায়) জলে ভাসা। **2.** To go *forth* or *out* on an enterprise ; দুঃসাহসিক কর্ম্মসাধনে যাত্রা করা। **3.** To burst *out into* expense, strong languag etc. ; "Slow to *launch out into* expense" ; হঠাৎ নামা, হঠাৎ প্রকাশ করা। ***Noun.*** The act or process of launching a ship or boat ; জাহাজ বা নৌকা জলে ভাসান বা ভাসাইবার প্রণালী। **To be launched into eternity**—To die ; অনন্তের যাত্রী হওয়া।

launch (lânsh), *n.* **1.** The largest flat-bottomed boat carried by a man-of-war ; রণপোতসংলগ্ন বৃহত্তম তরণী। **2.** A large electric or steam-boat for passangers, pleasure trips, etc. ; বিদ্যুৎ বা বাষ্পবলে চালিত বৃহৎ তরী, প্রমোদপোত।

laun'-drĕss (lân-), *n.* **1.** A woman who washes and dresses linen etc. ; ধোপানী, রজকী, রজকিনী (not strictly grammatical, used by poets ; cf. তুমি রজকিনী হরের ঘরনী তুমি হও মাতৃপিতৃ) রজিকা; (পর্ণিঃ)। **2.** A caretaker of chambers in the London Inns of Court ; বিলাতে ব্যবহারজীবিগণের সম্মিলন-গৃহের রক্ষক।

laun-drȳ (lân-), *n.* An establishment for washing linen etc. ; ধোপাখানা, ধোলাইখানা, ধোপাখলা, রজকালয়, ধাবনশালা, রজকগৃহ।

lau'-rē-âte (lä-), *adj.* & *n.* **1.** Crowned or decked with laurels ; লরেলপত্ররচিতমুকুটশোভিত, লরেলপত্রভূষিত। **2.** Composed of laurels, as a wreath ; লরেলপত্ররচিত। **3.** Worthy of laurels or honour, as a poet, or for eloquence etc. ; লরেলপত্ররচিতমুকুটপ্রাপ্তির যোগ্য, সম্মানার্হ। ***Noun.*** **1.** A poet-laureate ; "Rabindra Nath Tagore is the *Poet-laureate* of India" ; রাজকবি, কবিসম্রাট্। **Poet-laureate**—রাজকবি। **Poet-laureate ship**, *n.*

lau'-rĕl (lä-), *n.* & *v. t.* **1.** A shrub with glossy leaves esp. the bay tree ; its foliage as an emblem of victory or distinction in poetry ; স্নিগ্ধশ্যামলপত্রশোভিত গুল্মবিশেষ ; উক্ত পত্ররচিত মাল্য বা মুকুট, যাহা কবি বা বীরশ্রেষ্ঠগণকে সম্মানস্বরূপ প্রদত্ত হইত। **2.** A crown or wreath of laurel ; hence, honour ; distinction ; (us. in *pl.*) ; লরেলপত্ররচিত মুকুট বা মালিকা ; মান, গৌরব ; খ্যাতি। ***Verb t.*** To wreath with laurel ; বিজয়মাল্যে বিভূষিত করা, বিজয়মুকুট পরান। **Laurel-bottle** — কীটবধের জন্য লরেলপত্রপূর্ণ বোতল। **To look to one's laurels**—To beware of losing pre-eminence ; প্রাধান্য নষ্ট না হয় তদ্বিষয়ে সাবধান হওয়া, বিজয়মুকুট হৃত না হয় তজ্জন্য সাবধান হওয়া। **To reap** or **win laurels**—To gain distinction or fame ; বিজয়মুকুট লাভ করা, বিজয়মাল্য প্রাপ্ত হওয়া। **To rest on one's laurels**—To cease to strive for further glory ; সমধিক গৌরবলাভের চেষ্টায় বিরত হওয়া।

lau'-rŭs(rĕs)-tī-nŭs (lä-), *n.* An evergreen shrub with white flowers ; শ্বেতপুষ্পপ্রসূ চিরশ্যামল তরু-বিশেষ।

lâ'-vă, *n.* **1.** The melted rock discharged by a volcano, that flows down its sides ; this material solidified by cooling ; আগ্নেয়োদ্গার, ধাতুস্রব (সাঃ পঃ), গিরিনিস্রব, লাবা (হিঃ কোঃ), জ্বালামুখীনির্গতদ্রব (কেঙিঃ) ; কঠিনীভূত ধাতুস্রব। **2.** A kind of lava ; a bed of lava ; একপ্রকার ধাতুস্রব ; ধাতুস্রবস্তর।

lă-vā'-tion, *n.* Washing ; ধাবন, প্রক্ষালন।

lăv'-ă-tŏ-rȳ, *n.* **1.** (*Archaic*) A vessel for washing ; (অপ্রঃ) প্রক্ষালনপাত্র। **2.** A room or place for washing the hands and face often with water-closets ; প্রক্ষালনাগার।

lāve, *v. t.* (*Poet.*) **1.** To wash ; to bathe ; (কবিতায়) ধৌত করা, প্রক্ষালন করা ; স্নান করান। **2.** (Of streams) To wash against ; to flow along ; বিধৌত করা ; প্রবাহিত হওয়া।

āve'-mĕnt, *n.* (*Med.*) An injection ; (ভৈষজ্যশাস্ত্র) পিচকারী দ্বারা ঔষধ প্রবিষ্ট করণ, ইনজেকশন।

lăv'-ĕn-dêr, *n., adj.* & *v. t.* **1.** An aromatic plant cultivated for perfume ; একপ্রকার সুগন্ধি গুল্ম—ইহার পত্র ও পুষ্প হইতে গন্ধদ্রব্য প্রস্তুত করা হয়, ল্যাভেণ্ডার ফুলের গাছ। **2.** Its flowers and stalks laid among linen etc. to preserve them from moths etc. ; কীট প্রভৃতি হইতে বস্ত্রাদি রক্ষার জন্য উহাদের মধ্যে রক্ষিত ল্যাভেণ্ডার পুষ্প বা উহার বৃন্ত। **3.** A pale purplish colour like that of lavender flower ; ল্যাভেণ্ডার পুষ্পের মত আলোহিত নীলবর্ণ। ***Adj.*** Of the colour of lavender flowers ; ল্যাভেণ্ডারপুষ্পবর্ণ। ***Verb t.*** To perfume with lavender ; to put lavender among ; ল্যাভেণ্ডারপুষ্প দ্বারা সুবাসিত করা ; ল্যাভেণ্ডারপুষ্প সন্নিবিষ্ট করা। **Lavender water**—ল্যাভেণ্ডার। [সুরাবীর্য্য (alchohol), ল্যাভেণ্ডার তৈল ও অম্বরীর (ambergris) সংমিশ্রণে প্রস্তুত]। **To lay up in lavender**—(*Fig.*) To put aside for future use ; (লক্ষণায়) তুলিয়া রাখা।

lā'-vêr, *n.* **1.** (*Bibl.*) A vessel for Jewish priests' ablutions ; (বাইবেল) ইহুদী পুরোহিতগণের প্রক্ষালন-পাত্র। **2.** (*Archaic*) A fountain basin ; a font ; (অপ্রঃ) প্রস্তরকুণ্ড ; বৃহৎ জলপাত্র ; প্রক্ষালনপাত্র। **3.** The baptismal font ; দীক্ষাজলভাণ্ড।

lāv'-êr-ŏck, *n.* Same as LARK.

Lă-vĭn'-ĭ-a, *n.* Daughter of Latinus ; ল্যাটিনাসের কন্যা। Æneas ইহাকে বিবাহ করেন।

lăv'-ĭsh, *adj.* & *v. t.* **1.** Expending or bestowing profusely ; prodigal ; extravagant ; as, he is *lavish* of money or praise : *lavish* in gifts to holy places ; অতিব্যয়ী ; অমিতব্যয়ী ; অপব্যয়ী। **2.** Expended or produced profusely ; overabundant ; as, *lavish* expenditures ; অতিরিক্ত, অপরিমিত ; অত্যধিক, অসংযত। ***Verb t.*** To bestow or spend profusely (money, admiration etc.) ; to squander ; মুক্তহস্তে ব্যয় করা, ঢালিয়া দেওয়া ; অপরিমিত ব্যয় করা। **—ly**, *adv.* Profusely ; অপরিমিতভাবে, যথেষ্ট পরিমাণে। **—ment, —ness**, *ns.* অমিতব্যয়িতা, অমিতব্যয়।

law (lä), *n.* **1.** A rule of action prescribed or recognised as binding by authority ; আইন, বিধি। **2.** The body of such rules or statutes ; আইনসমূহ, বিধানমালা। **3.** The controlling influence of laws ; as, necessity has no *law*: *law* and order ; অনুশাসন। **4.** Legal science ; jurisprudence ; as, men learned in the *law* ; সমগ্র ব্যবস্থাশাস্ত্র, বিধিশাস্ত্র ; ব্যবস্থাবিজ্ঞান, ব্যবহারবিজ্ঞান। **5.** The laws concerning a particular department ; as, the *law* of evidence ; ব্যবস্থাশাস্ত্রের বিশেষ বিভাগ। **6.** The legal profession ; as, bred to the *law* ; ব্যবহারজীবীর ব্যবসায়। **7.** Judicial remedy ; litigation ; law courts ; as, to go to *law* ; বিধিসঙ্গত প্রতীকার, মোকদ্দমা, মামলা ; বিচারালয়। **8.** Legal learning or knowledge ; ব্যবহার শাস্ত্রে পাণ্ডিত্য, বিধিশাস্ত্রসম্বন্ধীয় জ্ঞান। **9.** Binding injunctions ; as, to give the *law* to ; বিধান। **10.** A rule or rules of procedure ; a principle or maxim ; as, the *laws* of poetry ; কার্য্যপদ্ধতি, নিয়ম ; নীতি, মূলসূত্র। **11.** The precepts contained in the Pentateuch ; the Mosaic dispensation ; বাইবেলের প্রাচীন নিয়মের প্রথম পঞ্চম পুস্তক ; মুসার বিধান। **12.** (Also *natural law*) A statement or formula invariably observed in natural phenomena ; নৈসর্গিকনিয়ম। **13.** (*Sport*) Allowance or start given to a hunted animal or weak competitor ; hence, indulgence ; respite ; "Never grant one inch of *law* to blasphemies ; মৃগয়ায় অনুসৃত জন্তু বা হীন প্রতিযোগীকে যে সুবিধা দেওয়া হয় ; প্রশ্রয়, আস্কারা ; বিরাম, অবকাশ। **14.** (*Math.*) The rule or principle on which a series etc. depends (গণিত-শাস্ত্র) যে নিয়ম বা মূলসূত্রের উপর শ্রেঢ়ী প্রভৃতি নির্ভর করে, সিদ্ধান্ত (হিঃ কোঃ), ক্রিয়া, নিয়ম। **Case-law**—নজিরী আইন। **Civil-law**—দেওয়ানী আইন। **Criminal-law**—ফৌজদারী আইন, ফৌজদারী দণ্ডবিধি, দণ্ডবিধি, দণ্ডনীতি। **Law-abiding**—Obedient to law ; আইনের বশবর্ত্তী, আইনপালনকারী। **Law-abiding-ness**, *n.* **Law-book** — আইনের বহি, নজীর। **Law-breaker**—One who violates law ; বিধিভঙ্গকারী। **Law-calf** — একপ্রকার সাদা মোটা চামড়ার বাঁধাই আইনের পুস্তক ; আইনের পুস্তক বাঁধাইবার জন্য একপ্রকার অরঞ্জিত চর্ম্ম। **Law-giver**—ব্যবস্থাপক,

বিধিস্থাপক, বিধিপ্রবর্ত্তক, স্মৃতিকার। **Law-list**—আইন এবং আইনব্যবসায়িগণসংক্রান্ত যাবতীয় জ্ঞাতব্যবিবরণ-সম্বলিত প্রতি বর্ষে প্রকাশিত পুস্তক। **Law-lord**—পার্লেমেণ্টের লর্ড সভার যে সভ্যের আইনসম্বন্ধীয় বিষয়ে সাহায্য করার যোগ্যতা আছে। **Law-maker**—ব্যবস্থাশাস্ত্রপ্রণেতা, ব্যবস্থাকারক। **Law-merchant** or **commercial law**—বাণিজ্যসংক্রান্ত আইন। **Law-officer**—ব্যবহারজীবী রাজকর্ম্মচারী; এটর্নী অথবা সলিসিটার জেনারেল। **Law-stationer**—উকীল মোক্তারের ব্যবহারোপযোগী কাগজপত্রবিক্রেতা। **Law-suit**—মামলা মোকদ্দমা। **Law-term**—Word or expression used in law; আইনের পারিভাষিক শব্দ। A period appointed for the sitting of law-courts; বিচারালয় খোলা থাকার নির্দ্দিষ্ট কাল। **Law writer** — আইন পুস্তকলিখক, ব্যবস্থাশাস্ত্রকারক। **Martial law**—See under MARTIAL. **Moral laws**—নৈতিকবিধি, নৈতিক নিয়ম। **Poor-laws**—সরকারী ব্যয়ে দরিদ্রগণের ভরণ-পোষণের জন্য আইন। **A law of the Medes and the Persians**—An unalterable law; অখণ্ডনীয় বিধি, অপরিবর্ত্তনীয় আইন, ভীষ্মের প্রতিজ্ঞা। **Avogadro's law**—চাপ ও তাপ তুল্য হইলে সমায়তন বিভিন্ন বাষ্পের পরমাণু-সংখ্যা সমান থাকে—এই নিয়ম। **Boyle's law**—রবার্ট বয়েল কর্ত্তৃক ১৬৬২ খৃঃ অব্দে প্রচারিত বৈজ্ঞানিকতত্ত্ববিশেষ। তত্ত্বটী এই:—(তাপ অপরিবর্ত্তিত থাকিলে) কোন নির্দ্দিষ্ট বাষ্পের আয়তন চাপের সহিত উৎক্রমভাবে (inversely) পরিবর্ত্তিত হয়। অর্থাৎ চাপ দ্বিগুণিত করিলে বাষ্পের আয়তন পূর্ব্বায়তনের অর্দ্ধেক এবং চতুর্গুণ করিলে পূর্ব্বায়তনের চতুর্থাংশ হইয়া থাকে। **Charles's laws**—Alex. César Charles (1746-1823) কর্ত্তৃক আবিষ্কৃত নিয়ম বিশেষ। নিয়মটী এই:—শতাঙ্কিত তাপমান যন্ত্রে পারদের (centigrade thermometer) প্রতি এক এক অংশ (degree) উত্থানের সঙ্গে সঙ্গে শূন্য বিন্দুতে কোন বাষ্পের যে আয়তন থাকে তাহা ·০০৩৬৬ বৃদ্ধি প্রাপ্ত হয়। **Code of laws**—ধর্ম্মসংহিতা, ধর্ম্মশাস্ত্র, ব্যবহারবিধি। **Dulong and Petit's law**—প্রাত রাসায়নিক মূলপদার্থের পারমাণবিক তাপ প্রায় তুল্য—এই নিয়ম। **Grassman's law**—জর্ম্মণদেশীয় ভাষাবিজ্ঞান-বিদ্ Grassman কর্ত্তৃক ১৮৬০ খৃঃ অব্দে আবিষ্কৃত নিয়ম বিশেষ। নিয়মটী এই:—আদিম আর্য্যগণের ভাষার কোন শব্দের একই শব্দাংশে (syllable) বা ক্রমিক শব্দাংশসমূহে *f*, *th* বা *ch* উচ্চারণ-মূলক অক্ষর থাকিলে সংস্কৃত ভাষায় উহারা যথাক্রমে *b*, *d*, *g* উচ্চারণমূলক অক্ষরে (media) এবং গ্রীকভাষায় *p*, *t*, *k* উচ্চারণমূলক অক্ষরে (tenuis) পরিবর্ত্তিত হয়। **Gresham's law**—Sir Thomas Gresham কর্ত্তৃক আবিষ্কৃত অর্থনীতি-শাস্ত্রসম্বন্ধীয় তত্ত্ববিশেষ। তত্ত্বটা এই—উৎকৃষ্ট ও অপকৃষ্ট উভয় প্রকার মুদ্রা এক সময়ে প্রচলিত থাকিলে, উৎকৃষ্ট মুদ্রাগুলি বিদেশে রপ্তানী হওয়া হেতু এবং লোকে সঞ্চয় করিয়া রাখার দরুণ ফলে কেবলমাত্র অপকৃষ্ট মুদ্রাগুলি দেশে প্রচলিত থাকে। **Grimm's law**—জর্ম্মণদেশীয় সুবিখ্যাত ভাষাবিজ্ঞানবিদ্ জেকব গ্রীমকর্ত্তৃক আবিষ্কৃত নিয়ম। গ্রীমের মতে আর্য্যগণের আদিম ভাষা হইতে বিকাশপ্রাপ্ত ভাষাসকলের স্বর ও ব্যঞ্জনবর্ণসমূহ এক নির্দ্দিষ্ট নিয়মানুসারে পরিবর্ত্তিত হইয়াছে। নিয়মটী এই:—আদিম আর্য্যভাষার *bh*, *dh*, *gh* (voiced aspirates) পরিণামে টিউটনিক ভাষায় b, d, g তে (voiced stops or mediæ); *b*, *d*, *g*, p, t, k, তে এবং *p*, *t*, *k* (unvoiced stops or tenues) f, p, এবং h (unvoiced spirants) এ পরিবর্ত্তিত হইয়াছে। যথা:—

SANS.	GOTH.	ENG.
dh rudhir (রুধির)	rands	red
p pad (পদ)	fôtus	feet

Kepler's laws—(*Astron.*)—সুপ্রসিদ্ধ জর্ম্মণ জ্যোতির্ব্বিৎ কেপলার কর্ত্তৃক আবিষ্কৃত নিয়মত্রয়, যথা:—(১) গ্রহগণ বৃত্তাভাসাকৃতি কক্ষায় (*elliptical orbit*) সূর্য্যকে প্রদক্ষিণ করে। এই বৃত্তাভাসক্ষেত্রের একটী নাভিতে সূর্য্যের কেন্দ্র অবস্থিত আছে। (২) প্রতিগ্রহ এরূপভাবে আবর্ত্তিত হয় যে, উহা হইতে সূর্য্য পর্য্যন্ত কোন রেখা টানিলে ঐ রেখা সমান সময়ে সমান স্থান অতিক্রম করে। (৩) গ্রহদ্বয়ের আবর্ত্তনকালের বর্গের অনুপাত উহাদের মধ্যম অন্তরের (mean distance) অর্থাৎ সূর্য্য হইতে ঐ আবর্ত্তনশীল গ্রহদ্বয়ের ক্রমপরিবর্ত্তনশীল দূরত্বের মধ্যম অন্তর = ইহাদের বৃত্তাভাসাকার কক্ষার (orbit) অর্দ্ধ মুখ্য অক্ষ (semi-major axis) ঘনের অনুপাতের সমান হইয়া থাকে। **Law of continuity**—সাতত্য-নিয়ম (হিঃ কোঃ)। **Law of contradiction**—ব্যাবর্ত্তনন্যায় (হিঃ কোঃ), বিরোধন্যায় (ঐ)। **Law of excluded middle**—মধ্যস্থাভাবন্যায় (হিঃ কোঃ)। **Law of identity**—তদাত্ম্যন্যায় (হিঃ কোঃ)। **Law of parsimony**—লাঘবন্যায় (হিঃ কোঃ)। **Law of relativity**—সাপেক্ষন্যায় (হিঃ কোঃ)। **Law of the conditioned** — প্রতিবন্ধন্যায়। **Laws of association** — স্মৃতিসাহচর্য্য নিয়ম, উদ্দীপনবিভাব (সৌন্দর্য্য) (Also see ASSOCIATION OF IDEAS under ASSOCIATION.) **Laws of nations**—আন্তর্জাতিক বিধি। **Laws of nature** or **natural laws** — প্রাকৃতিক নিয়ম, নৈসর্গিক নিয়ম। **Necessity has no law**—See NECESSITY. **The law of the land** — দেশের আইন। **To give the law to**—To impose one's will upon; কাহারো উপর নিজের ইচ্ছা খাটান। **To have** or **take the law of a person**—To sue a person in a court of law; কাহারো বিরুদ্ধে মোকদ্দমা করা। **To lay down the law**—To talk authoritatively; to hector; প্রভুত্ব-সহকারে বলা; তর্জ্জন গর্জ্জন করা। **To take the law into one's own hands**—To redress one's wrong by force; নিজের বিচার নিজে করা।

law'-fûl (lā-), *adj.* Allowed by law; appointed or qualified by law; legal; legitimate, as a child etc.; আইনসঙ্গত; বিধিসঙ্গত; বৈধ, ন্যায্য, যথার্থ; অজারজ। **–ly**, *adv.* In a lawful manner; legally; বৈধভাবে, ন্যায়সঙ্গতরূপে, যথাযোগ্যভাবে,

আইনানুসারে, আইনতঃ। **—ness,** *n.* **Lawful age**—সাবালকের বয়স।

law, laws (lä, läs), *interj.* An interjection denoting astonishment ; এ কি !

law'-lĕss (lä-), *adj.* **1.** (Of a country etc.) Where there is no law ; আইনবহির্ভূত। **2.** Regardless for, or disobedient to, law ; uncontrolled by law : unruly ; licentious ; নীতি বা সামাজিক নিয়মবিরুদ্ধ ; উচ্ছৃঙ্খল ; দুরাচার, আচারভ্রষ্ট, আচারহীন, দুর্ব্বৃত্ত ; লম্পট, লোচ্চা, ব্যভিচারপরায়ণ। **—ly,** *adv.* In a lawless manner ; বে-আইনি ভাবে, ব্যবস্থাবিরুদ্ধ ভাবে। **—ness,** *n.* The state of being lawless ; অরাজকতা, উচ্ছৃঙ্খলতা, আচারভ্রষ্টতা, ব্যভিচার, নিয়মাতিক্রম।

lawn (län), *n.* **1.** (*Archaic*) An open space between woods ; a glade ; (অপ্রঃ) বনমধ্যস্থ উন্মুক্ত স্থান ; বনবীথি। **2.** A grass-covered land ; a piece of pleasure-ground or garden covered with close-mown grass ; তৃণাচ্ছাদিত সমতলভূমি ; তৃণশোভিত প্রমোদোদ্যান, তৃণবীথিকা (প্রবোধঃ), তৃণমণ্ডল (ঐ)। **Lawn'-y,** *adj.* **Lawn-mower**—ঘাসকাটা কল।

Lawn-mower.

Lawn-sprinkler—গৃহপ্রাঙ্গণের তৃণভূমিতে জলসিঞ্চন করিবার যন্ত্র। **Lawn-tennis**—আণ্ডা খেলা।

lawn (län), *n.* A sort of fine linen or cambric used especially for bishops' sleeves ; একপ্রকার সূক্ষ্ম ক্ষৌম বস্ত্র, অংশুক, দুকূল। **Lawn'-y,** *adj.*

law'-yĕr (lä-), *n.* **1.** One versed in the laws ; আইনজ্ঞ, ধর্ম্মজ্ঞ, ধর্ম্মশাস্ত্রজ্ঞ। **2.** One who practises law ; an attorney ; a solicitor ; ব্যবহারজীবী; এটর্নী; উকীল। **Penang-lawyer**—পিনাং দ্বীপজাত গুবাকজাতীয় বৃক্ষবিশেষের কাষ্ঠ হইতে প্রস্তুত যষ্টি।

lăx, *adj.* **1.** (*Rare*) Loose ; not compact ; porous ; (অপ্রঃ) শিথিল, শ্লথ, আল্‌গা ; বিরল ; সচ্ছিদ্র। **2.** Not strict or stringent ; slack ; negligent ; careless ; vague ; স্খলৎচিত্ত, স্খলনশীল ; অকঠোর ; অনবহিত, অমনোযোগী ; অসাবধান ; অস্পষ্ট। **Lax'-i-ty,** *n.* The state of being lax ; want of strictness ; শিথিলতা ; শৈথিল্য। **Lax'-ly,** *adv.*

lax'-ă-tive (-tĭv), *adj.* & *n.* (*Med.*) Having the power of loosening the bowels ; (ভৈষজ্য-শাস্ত্র) বিরেচক, সারক (ভাব প্রঃ), মৃদুভেদক (সাঃ পঃ)। ***Noun.*** A gentle purgative ; মৃদু বিরেচক ঔষধ, সারক ঔষধ, ছেদন (ঠাকুরঃ)।

lay (lā), *n.* **1.** A short lyric or narrative poem meant to be sung ; a ballad ; নীতিকবিতা ; গাথা। **2.** A song or poem ; a bird's song ; গীতিকবিতা ; বিহঙ্গকাকলী।

lay (lā), *v. t., i.* & *n.* **1.** To cause to lie down ; to prostrate ; শায়িত করা ; ভূপাতিত করা। **2.** To place in a recumbent position ; as, to *lay* to sleep ; to put or set down ; to deposit ; as, to *lay* a body in the grave ; শায়িতভাবে রাখা ; স্থাপন করা ; শায়িত রাখা। **3.** To cast or beat down ; as, the wind *lays* crops ; পাতিত করা, ভাঙ্গিয়া ফেলা। **4.** To calm ; to cause to subside ; to allay ; as, to *lay* the dust or one's fears ; শান্ত করা ; প্রশমিত করা ; লাঘব করা। **5.** To deposit as wager ; to stake ; to risk ; গচ্ছিত রাখা ; পণ করা ; ঝুঁকি লওয়া। **6.** (Of hen etc.) To produce, as eggs ; ডিম পাড়া। **7.** To impose, as a tax, burden, punishment, etc. ; ধার্য্য করা, নির্দ্ধারণ করা, বসান, চাপান, বিধান করা। **8.** To impute ; as, to *lay* a fault to one's charge or at one's door ; to cast as a blame *on* or *upon* a person ; আরোপ করা, ভার অর্পণ করা, ভার চাপান, প্রয়োগ করা, লাগান। **9.** To place ; to apply ; to set ; as, to *lay* heads together : to *lay* a hound on the scent ; স্থাপন করা ; প্রয়োগ করা ; লাগাইয়া দেওয়া, ধরাইয়া দেওয়া। **10.** To point ; to aim ; as, to *lay* a gun ; নির্দ্দেশ করা ; লক্ষ্য করা। **11.** To present or put forward ; as, to *lay* claim to something ; to place or submit as a fact, question *before* a person for consideration ; উপস্থাপিত করা ; পেশ করা। **12.** To locate ; as, the scene of the tale was *laid* in London ; কোন স্থানে স্থাপন করা। **13.** To put into a certain condition or state ; as, to *lay* waste a region ; কোন নির্দ্দিষ্ট অবস্থায় আনা। **14.** To place in a certain position ; as, the horse *laid* his ears back ; কোন বিশেষ ভাবে রাখা। **15.** To fix *at* a certain sum ; as, the suitor *lays* the damages at 300 rupees ; নির্দ্দিষ্টসংখ্যক টাকা স্থির করা। **16.** To bring as a stick etc. down (*on*) ; to inflict blows ; বসান ; লাগান, প্রয়োগ করা। **17.** To represent (some evil) as a consequent on some cause ; আরোপ করা। **18.** To make, as a rope etc., by twisting yarn etc. ; রজ্জু প্রভৃতি পাকান। **19.** To prepare ; to arrange ; to devise ; as, to *lay* a meal, plan, plot, etc. ; প্রস্তুত করা ; সাজান, সজ্জিত করা ; উদ্ভাবন করা। **20.** To spread or put on a surface in layers ; as, to *lay* colour ; to coat or cover ; as, to *lay* a surface with carpet, metal or straw ; লাগান, লেপন করা ; আবৃত করা, আচ্ছাদিত করা,

মণ্ডিত করা। ***Verb i.*** **1.** To produce eggs ; ডিম পাড়া। **2.** To lay a wager ; to bet ; বাজি রাখা ; বাজি ধরা, পণ রাখা। **3.** To attack vigorously ; প্রচণ্ডভাবে আক্রমণ করা। **4.** (*Vulg.*) To lie ; (ইতর ভাষায়) শায়িত থাকা, পড়িয়া থাকা। **5.** (*Naut.*) To lie in a specified position ; as, to *lay* at anchor ; কোন বিশেষভাবে অবস্থান করা। ***Noun.*** **1.** (*Slang*) A line of activity or business ; a job ; a pursuit ; (ইতর ভাষায়) কার্য্যপ্রণালী ; ঠিকা কাজ ; পেশা, ব্যবসায়। **2.** The direction or amount of twist in rope-strands ; রজ্জুর গুণের পাকের দিক বা পরিমাণ। **3.** The way or position in which a thing lies ; as, the *lay* of a country etc. ; অবস্থানভঙ্গী। **The kid** or **kinchin lay**—শিশুদিগের নিকট হইতে টাকা পয়সা বা অলঙ্কার কাড়িয়া লওন। **To be laid up**—See under LAID. **To lay about one**—To deal one blows on all sides ; সর্ব্বাঙ্গে প্রহার করা। **To lay apart**—To set apart ; পৃথক করিয়া রাখা। **To lay aside** or **by**—To put off or away ; to discard ; to abandon ; to put apart for future use ; to cease to use, practise or think of ; ফেলিয়া রাখা ; অগ্রাহ্য করা ; পরিত্যাগ করা ; তুলিয়া রাখা ; ব্যবহারে নিবৃত্ত হওয়া, বিরত হওয়া, কোন বিষয়ে আর না ভাবা। **To lay at**—To endeavour to strike ; আঘাত করিতে চেষ্টা করা। **To lay bare**—To make bare ; to disclose ; প্রকাশ করা, উদ্ঘাটন করা ; ব্যক্ত করা, খুলিয়া বলা। **To lay before**—To submit to, as plans ; to exhibit ; উপস্থাপিত করা, পেশ করা ; প্রদর্শন করা। **To lay down**—To put on the ground ; ভূতলে স্থাপন করা To give up ; to resign ; as, to *lay down* hopes, office, etc. ; ছাড়িয়া দেওয়া ; ত্যাগ করা। To set down on paper as a chart etc. ; অঙ্কিত করা। To formulate, as a principle etc. ; to prescribe, as a course of action ; সূত্রাকারে নিবদ্ধ করা ; কার্য্যপ্রণালী নিরূপিত করা। To store as wine in a cellar ; সঞ্চিত করা, ভাণ্ডারজাত করা। To sacrifice as one's life etc. ; উৎসর্গ করা, বলিদান করা। To convert, as land into pasture ; to put (*in, under, to, with,* grass) ; as, land *laid down under* grass ; পরিণত করা ; (ঘাস প্রভৃতি) লাগান। To construct, as roads, railways, ship, etc. ; রাজপথ, অর্ণবযান, লৌহবর্ত্ম, প্রভৃতি নির্ম্মাণ করা। To pay or wager as money ; পণ রাখা, বাজির টাকা দেওয়া। **To lay down one's arms**—To surrender ; শত্রুর হাতে আত্মসমর্পণ করা। **To lay down the law**—To talk authoritatively (See under LAW.) **To lay fast by the heels**—To confine ; to put in prison ; অবরুদ্ধ করা ; কারারুদ্ধ করা। **To lay hands on**—To seize ; to appropriate ; বলপূর্ব্বক অধিকার করা ; আত্মসাৎ করা। **To lay hands on oneself**—To commit suicide ; আত্মহত্যা করা। **To lay heads together**—To consult together ; to deliberate ; একত্র মিলিয়া পরামর্শ করা ; চিন্তা করা। **To lay hold of, on**—To seize ; বলপূর্ব্বক অধিকার করা। **To lay in**—To collect and store ; সঞ্চয় করিয়া ভাণ্ডারে রাখা, ভাণ্ডারজাত করা। **To lay it on**—To exaggerate ; অতিরঞ্জিত করা। **To lay it on thick** or **with a trowel**—To use obvious flattery ; তৈলমর্দ্দন করা। **To lay low**—To bring down ; to humble ; to bury ; নত করা ; পদানত করা ; সমাহিত করা, গোর দেওয়া, কবর দেওয়া। **To lay off**—To cast aside ; ত্যাগ করা, ফেলিয়া দেওয়া। **To lay on**—To impose as tax, penalty, etc. ; ধার্য্য করা, বসান। To deal blows ; to inflict (blows) ; ঘা বসান, ঘা লাগান ; ঘা দেওয়া। To apply a coating of ; to paint ; লেপন করা ; রং লাগান। To provide pipes etc. (supplying gas water, etc.) ; নল, চুঙ্গী, প্রভৃতি বসান। To put, as hounds on scent ; ধরাইয়া দেওয়া। **To lay one's bones**—To be buried *in* a specified place ; নিরূপিত স্থানে সমাধিস্থ হওয়া। **To lay oneself down** — To lie down ; শায়িত হওয়া। **To lay oneself out for**—To exert oneself greatly ; কোন ব্যাপারে যথাসাধ্য শক্তিপ্রয়োগ করা। **To lay oneself out to do** — To put forth one's best efforts to do ; কোন বিষয়ে যথাসাধ্য শক্তিপ্রয়োগ করা, প্রাণপণ চেষ্টা করা। **To lay oneself to**—To expose oneself to ; আস্পদ করা, ভাজন করা। **To lay one's hopes on**—To value highly ; অতিশয় মূল্যবান মনে করা। **To lay open**—To make bare ; to show ; to expose ; প্রকাশ করা ; দেখান, প্রদর্শন করা ; উদ্ঘাটন করা। **To lay out**—To expose to view ; to spread ; প্রকাশ করা, উদ্ঘাটন করা ; বিস্তার করা, বিন্যাস করা। To prepare (body) for burial ; কবর দেওয়ার জন্য মৃতদেহ প্রস্তুত করা। To expend or invest as money ; ব্যয় করা, প্রয়োগ করা, খাটান। To map out or dispose of (garden, grounds, etc.) according to a plan ; আদর্শ অনুযায়ী বিন্যাস করা। (*Reflex.*) To take pains to do ; as, to *lay oneself out* to do a thing ; উপায় অবলম্বন করা। (*Slang*) To kill ; (ইতর ভাষায়) মারিয়া ফেলা, কুপোকাৎ করা। **To lay siege to**—To besiege ; (*fig.*) to importune ; অবরোধ করা ; (লক্ষণায়) অবিরত প্রার্থনা করা। **To lay the corner-stone**—To make a regular beginning ; সূত্রপাত করা, রীতিমত আরম্ভ করা। **To lay the dust**—To put down the dust by water etc. ; জল প্রভৃতি

ছিটাইয়া ধুলি উড়া বন্ধ করা। **To lay the land**—(*Naut.*) To cause the land to disappear below the horizon by sailing away from it ; ভূমি হইতে বহুদূর সমুদ্রে অগ্রসর হওয়া হেতু চক্রবালের নিম্নে স্থলভাগ অদৃশ্য হওয়া। **To lay to**—To stop advance ; পথরোধ করা, অগ্রসর হইতে না দেওয়া। To be sure of ; কৃতনিশ্চয় হওয়া। **To lay together**—To collect ; to bring to one place ; সংগ্রহ করা ; একত্র করা, জড় করা। **To lay to heart**—To consider earnestly ; to feel deeply ; গভীর ভাবে চিন্তা করা ; মর্ম্মে মর্ম্মে অনুভব করা। **To lay** (as faults etc.) **to one's charge**—To impute it to one ; দোষারোপ করা। **To lay to sleep** or **rest** — (*Fig.*) To bury ; (লক্ষণায়) চিরনিদ্রা বা চিরবিরামের ব্যবস্থা করা। **To lay under**—To subject to ; অধীন করা। **To lay up**—To store ; to save (money etc.) ; সঞ্চয় করা ; টাকা জমান। (*Pass.*) To confine to one's bed or room for a time ; শয্যাশায়ী করা, শয্যাগত করা। **To lay upon**—To wager upon ; বাজি রাখা। **To lay up store for a rainy day**—To store for bad times ; অসময়ের সংস্থান করা। **To lay violent hands on**—To murder ; হত্যা করা, খুন করা। **To lay wager**—See LAY *v. t.* 5. **To lay wait for**—To lie in ambush for ; (শত্রুর প্রতীক্ষায়) জঙ্গলে লুকাইয়া থাকা, ওৎ পাতিয়া থাকা। **To lay waste**—To destroy ; to make desolate ; ধ্বংস করা ; জনশূন্য করা, উজাড় করা। **To lay weight, stress, emphasis on** — To emphasize ; to treat as important ; জোর দেওয়া ; গুরুত্ববিশিষ্ট বলিয়া গণ্য করা, গুরুতর মনে করা।

lay (lā), *adj.* **1.** Of, or pertaining to, the laity, as distinct from the clergy ; not clerical ; সাধারণ লোকসম্বন্ধীয়, প্রাকৃতলোকসম্বন্ধীয় ; অযাজকীয়। **2.** Unprofessional ; unexpert (esp. with reference to law or medicine) ; আনাড়ী, অব্যুৎপন্ন ; ডাক্তারী, ওকালতী, প্রভৃতি ব্যবসায়ের বহির্ভূত। **3.** (*Cards*) Other than trump ; রঙ ভিন্ন অন্য তাসের। **Lay brother, sister**—যে পুরুষ বা নারী কোন মঠে রীতিমত প্রতিজ্ঞাগ্রহণের পর গৃহীত হয় এবং যাহাদিগকে মঠে কেবল শারীরিক শ্রমের কার্য্য করিতে হয় এবং সাধনভজনাদি করিতে হয় না। **Lay-clerk**—মহাধর্ম্মমন্দিরের গায়ক ; যাজকপল্লীর কেরাণী। **Lay-lord**—পার্লেমেণ্টের লর্ড সভার যে সভ্যের আইন সম্বন্ধীয় বিষয়ে সাহায্য করার যোগ্যতা নাই। **Layman** — One of the laity as distinct from clergy ; সাধারণ লোক, বৈষয়িক লোক, প্রাকৃত লোক, গৃহস্থ, অযাজকসমাজভুক্ত লোক। A non-expert in regard to some profession, art or science (esp. law or medicine) ; ব্যবসায়, বিজ্ঞান, চিকিৎসা, আইনশাস্ত্রে, বা কলাবিজ্ঞানে অব্যুৎপন্ন ব্যক্তি। **Lay-reader** — উপাসনাদি কার্য্যে অধিকারী অযাজকসমাজভুক্ত ব্যক্তি।

lay'-ēr (lā-), *n. v. t.* & *i.* **1.** One who, or that which, lays ; স্থাপক, যে ডিম পাড়িয়া থাকে। **2.** A stratum ; a coating, as of paint ; স্তর, পরদা, তবক, পুট, পরত ; রঙ্গের এক পোঁচ, লেপ, আস্তর। **3.** A shoot or twig of a plant fastened into earth or laid under ground to strike root while attached to the parent stock ; দাবাকলম (প্রবোধ)।

Layering.

4. (*Pl.*) Patches of laid corn ; ভূপতিত শস্যের স্তর। **5.** An oyster bed ; শুক্তির স্তর। ***Verb t.*** **1.** To propagate by bending the shoots of a living stem into the soil ; দাবা কলম করা। ***Verb i.*** (Of corn) To be laid flat by the weakness of growth ; (শস্য সম্বন্ধে) নিস্তেজভাবে বৃদ্ধি পাওয়ার দরুন মাটিতে পতিত হওয়া। **—ered,** *adj.*

layette, *n.* A complete outfit of clothing, blankets, etc. for a newborn infant ; নবজাত শিশুর কাপড়চোপড়, কম্বল, প্রভৃতি।

lay'-fig-ūre (lā-), *n.* **1.** A jointed wooden figure which can be placed in any attitude used by artists for arranging draperies on etc. ; মনুষ্যমূর্ত্তি — এই মূর্ত্তি যে কোনপ্রকার ভঙ্গীতে স্থাপন করা যাইতে পারে এবং ইহা চিত্রকরগণের কাষ্ঠনির্ম্মিত পরিচ্ছদাদি দ্বারা সজ্জিত হইলে প্রতিমূর্ত্তির বেশবিন্যাস অঙ্কনের আদর্শস্বরূপ হইয়া থাকে।

Lay-figure

2. An unimportant person ; a nonentity ; ক্রীড়াপুত্তলিকা ; খড়ের পুতুল, কাঠের পুতুল। **3.** A fictitious character in a novel ; উপন্যাসোক্ত ব্যক্তি।

lay'-lŏck (lā-), *n.* (*Dial.*) Same as LILAC.

lay'-stall (lā-stäl), *n.* A refuse heap ; আস্তাকুড়।

lā'-zar (-zēr), *n.* (*Archaic*) A poor person inflicted with a loathsome disease ; a leper ; ঘৃণাজনক এবং দুষ্ট সংক্রামক পীড়াগ্রস্ত ব্যক্তি ; কুষ্ঠরোগী, কুষ্ঠী, পাপরোগী, কুষ্ঠরোগগ্রস্ত ব্যক্তি, পাপরোগগ্রস্ত ব্যক্তি। **Lazar-house**—A lazaretto ; কুষ্ঠিশালা, কুষ্ঠাশ্রম।

lăz-ă-rĕt'-tō, lăz-ă-rĕt', *ns.* **1.** A public hospital for poor diseased persons esp. lepers ; কুষ্ঠাশ্রম। **2.** A building or ship for performing quarantine in ; যাহাদের দ্বারা সংক্রামক রোগ ব্যাপ্ত হইতে পারে এরূপ লোককে বন্দর হইতে পৃথক করিয়া রাখিবার গৃহ বা পোত।

Lăz′-ă-rŭs, *n.* A poor or diseased man; a beggar; a leprous beggar, [From Lazarus (Luke xxvi, 20)]. দরিদ্র ব্যক্তি, ব্যাধিগ্রস্ত ব্যক্তি ; ভিক্ষুক ; কুষ্ঠগ্রস্ত ভিক্ষুক।

lāze, *v. i., t. & n.* **1.** (*Colloq.*) To be lazy ; (চলিত ভাষায়) আলস্যপরায়ণ হওয়া, কুঁড়ে হওয়া। ***Verb t.*** To pass (time) away in idleness ; আলস্যে সময় কাটান। ***Noun.*** A lazy time ; অবসর সময়।

lăz′-ū-lī, *n.* Same as LAPIS LAZULI.

lā′-zȳ, *adj., v. i. & t.* **1.** Indolent ; idle ; অলস, কুঁড়ে, জড়, শ্রমবিমুখ ; নিরুদ্যোগী, ঢিলা, নিষ্ক্রিয়, নিরুদ্যম, তন্দ্রিত, তন্দ্রাতুর। **2.** Appropriate to, or inducing, indolence ; আলস্যজনক, অলসসমুচিত। ***Verb i. & t.*** Same as LAZE. **–zi-ly,** *adv.* In a lazy manner ; sluggishly ; অলসভাবে ; মন্থরভাবে, জড়ভাবে। **–zi-ness,** *n.* Indolence ; sloth ; আলস্য, অলসতা ; জড়তা, মন্দতা, মান্দ্য, জাড্য, তন্দ্রালুতা, কুঁড়েমি। **Lazy-bed**—গোল আলু বপনের জন্য দুই দিকে খাত-কাটা প্রায় ৬ ফিট আইল। **Lazy-bones**—A lazy person ; অলস লোক, কুঁড়ে লোক। **Lazy-pinion**—Same as IDLE-WHEEL which see. **Lazy-tongs**—পরস্পর সংযুক্ত শলাকাসমূহরচিত চতুষ্কোণ সন্দংশ-শ্রেণী দ্বারা রচিত সন্দংশ—যাহা ইচ্ছা মত বহুদূর পর্য্যন্ত প্রসারিত করা যায় এবং যদ্দ্বারা দূরস্থিত পদার্থ সমূহ ধরিয়া তোলা হয়।

lea (lē), *n.* (*Poet.*) A meadow ; a grassy land ; (কবিতায়) প্রান্তর, মাঠ ; তৃণাবৃত ভূমি, শাদ্বলভূমি, হরিদ্বর্ণ তৃণভূমি।

lea (lē), *n.* A measure of yarn (300, 200, 120 and 80 yds. in different districts) ; সূতার মাপ বিশেষ (স্থানভেদে ৩০০, ২০০, ১২০ ও ৮০ গজ হইয়া থাকে)।

leach (lēch), *v. t.* **1.** To cause as a liquid to percolate through some material ; as, to *leach* water through ashes ; কোন কিছু দিয়া পরিস্রাবিত করা, চোয়ান। **2.** To subject to the action of percolating water etc. ; as, to *leach* ashes or ore ; পরিস্রাবী জল প্রভৃতির ক্রিয়ার অধীন করা। **3.** To take *away, out* by percolation ; পরিস্রবণ দ্বারা বিদূরিত করা।

lead (lĕd), *n., v. t. & i.* **1.** A well-known soft and heavy metal ; সীসা, সীস, সীসক, নাগ (রঃ রঃ সঃ), অহি, (সাঃ পঃ), অন্তরুপ্য (ঐ), ভুজঙ্গম (ঐ), পন্নগ (ঐ), ধাতুভঙ্গ (ঐ), বিনত (ঐ)। **2.** A plummet or mass of lead used in sounding water ; সমুদ্রের গভীরতা মাপিবার জন্য সীস-খণ্ড। **3.** A thin plate of type-metal used to separate lines in printing ; মুদ্রণে পংক্তি পৃথক করার জন্য পংক্তিদ্বয়ের মধ্যে নিবিষ্ট সীসক ফলক, লেড্। **4.** (*Pl.*) Sheets of lead for covering roofs ; a flat roof covered by lead ; ছাদ আবৃত করার জন্য সীসার পাত ; সীসার পাত দ্বারা আচ্ছাদিত সমতল ছাদ। **5.** (*Pl.*) Lead framing for panes of painted windows ; চিত্রিত বাতায়ন প্রভৃতির কাচফলকের কাঠামস্বরূপ সীসক। ***Verb t.*** **1.** To cover with lead ; to fit or frame (panes) with lead ; সীসকাবৃত করা, সীসকমণ্ডিত করা ; সীসা দ্বারা জানালার কাচ লাগান, জানালার কাঠে সীসার ফ্রেম বা কাঠাম লাগান। **2.** To widen the space between lines in printing with thin plates of lead ; মুদ্রাঙ্কণে সীসার পাতলা পাত দ্বারা পংক্তিদ্বয়ের মধ্যে ফাঁক করা। ***Verb i.*** (Of a gun-barrel) To become foul with a coating of lead ; বন্দুকের নাল সীসার লেপ পড়িয়া মলিন হওয়া। **Lead′-less,** *adj.* **Black-lead**—কৃষ্ণসীস। **Lead-colic**—সীসজনিত শূল বেদনা। **Lead-comb**—সীসার চিরুণী [ইহা দ্বারা আঁচড়াইয়া ইংরাজেরা চুল কাল করিয়া থাকেন]। **Lead-line**—ওলন দড়ী, মান-সূত্র। **Lead-pencil**—কাঠ পেন্সিল, সীসার লেখনী। **Lead-poisoning** — শরীরের ভিতর সীসার প্রবেশ হেতু যে বিষক্রিয়া হইয়া থাকে, সীসকজনিত বিষক্রিয়া। **Leads-man**—সমুদ্রজলের গভীরতা পরিমাপক নাবিক। **Lead sulphide**—নীলাঞ্জন (সাঃ পঃ), সৌবীরাঞ্জন (ঐ)। **Lead-work** — জলের কল প্রভৃতির নল মেরামতের কাজ, জানালা প্রভৃতিতে কাচ লাগাইবার কাজ। **Lead-works**—সীসার কারখানা। **Lead-wort** — চিত্রমূল, চিত্রক (কেঙিঃ)। **Red-lead**—সিন্দূর, নাগসম্ভব। **White lead**—সফেদা।

lead (lēd), *v. t. & i.* **1.** To guide or conduct esp. by going before ; to show the way to ; পথ দেখাইয়া নেওয়া ; চালিত করা। **2.** To guide by the hand or physical connection as a person ; to conduct as an animal by a halter etc. ; চালিত করা ; চালান। **3.** To compel to go with one ; as, to *lead* one captive ; ধরিয়া নেওয়া। **4.** To direct ; to instruct ; to bring by argument etc. as *to* a conclusion ; to induce *to* do ; পরিচালিত করা ; শিক্ষা দেওয়া ; যুক্তি দ্বারা কোন সিদ্ধান্তে উপনীত করা ; কোন কার্য্যে প্রবর্ত্তিত করা, প্ররোচিত করা, প্রবৃত্তি জন্মান। **5.** (Of a commander etc.) To direct the movements of (an army etc.) ; সৈন্য চালনা করা। **6.** (Of a road etc.) To serve as a passage for ; to guide ; (পথ প্রভৃতি সম্পর্কে) চলিবার উপযোগী হওয়া ; চালিত করা। **7.** To make (rope, water, etc.) go through pulley, channel, etc. ; চালান। **8.** To pass ; to spend ; as, to *lead* a miserable life ; যাপন করা ; অতিবাহিত করা, কাটান। **9.** (Cards) To begin a game ; as, to *lead* trumps or heart ; খেলা। **10.** To direct by example ; as, to *lead* a band or chorus ; to take the first place in, as a dance etc. ; পরিচালিত করা ; নৃত্য প্রভৃতিতে প্রথম স্থান অধিকার করা। **11.** To set as a fashion etc. ; to be the director of ; as, to *lead* a party in the Houses of Parliament ; ফ্যাসন বা নূতন ধারা প্রবর্ত্তন করা; পরিচালক হওয়া। 12. To be the leading counsel (in a case etc.) ; কোন মোকদ্দমায় প্রধান কৌঁসুলীর কাজ করা। ***Verb i.*** 1. To go before and guide ; to be first ; to go first at some point in a race; as, who *leads* now ; পথপ্রদর্শন করা : প্রথম হওয়া : ঘোড়দৌড়ে কোন এক সময়ে সর্ব্বাগ্রবর্ত্তী হওয়া। 2. To be chief or commander ; নায়ক হওয়া, নেতা হওয়া। 3. To take or hold the chief place ; প্রধান স্থান গ্রহণ বা অধিকার করা। 4. To tend or reach in a certain direction, (with *to*) ; as, the path *leads to* the mill ; to have as result ; as, gambling *leads to* other vices ; উন্মুখ হওয়া, কোন নির্দ্দিষ্ট স্থান পর্য্যন্ত যাওয়া ; ফলস্বরূপ হওয়া। **Lead'-a-ble,** *adj.* **A led captain**—A hanger-on ; a toady; গলগ্রহ ব্যক্তি; চাটুকার, পাচাটা, ধামাধরা। **To lead astray**—To mislead ; to induce to evil ; কুপথগামী করা, কুপথে লইয়া যাওয়া, বিপথগামী করা ; কুকার্য্যে প্রবৃত্তি দেওয়া। **To lead away**—(Usually *Passive*) To induce to follow unthinkingly ; মূঢ়বৎ অনুসরণে প্রবৃত্ত করা। **To lead a woman to the altar**—To marry; বিবাহ করা। **To lead by the nose**—To induce to do unconsciously all one wishes ; নাকে দড়ী দিয়া চালাইয়া নেওয়া, যথেচ্ছভাবে চালিত করা। **To lead captive**—To take away as prisoner ; বন্দী করিয়া লইয়া যাওয়া। **To lead off** or **out**—To begin ; to take the start in anything ; আরম্ভ করা ; কোন কার্য্যে প্রথম পথপ্রদর্শন করা। **To lead on**—To persuade to go on ; to entice into going further than was intended ; ভুলাইয়া নিয়া যাওয়া ; ফুসলাইয়া অনেক দূরে নিয়া আসা। **To lead one a dance** or **a fine dance** — To give one much unnecessary trouble to secure his end ; উদ্দেশ্য সাধনের জন্য অযথা অনেক কষ্ট দেওয়া। **To lead one a life**—To worry him constantly ; অষ্টপ্রহর জ্বালাতন করা। **To lead the way**—To go first and show the way ; to act as guide ; অগ্রগামী হইয়া পথপ্রদর্শন করা ; পথপ্রদর্শক হওয়া। **To lead up a ball**—(Of an important couple) To start the ball by commencing to dance ; (প্রধান নর্ত্তক নর্ত্তকীর পক্ষে) নৃত্য আরম্ভ করিয়া বল নাচের উদ্বোধন করা। **To lead up to**—To prepare for anything by steps or degrees ; to direct conversation towards (a subject) ; ক্রমেক্রমে বা শনৈঃশনৈঃ কোন বিষয়ের জন্য প্রস্তুত হওয়া ; কোন বিষয়ে কথা পাড়া। (*Cards*) To play a card to bring out (a card from another player) ; (তাস) খেলা।

lead (lĕd), *n.* 1. Direction given by going before ; guidance ; example ; পথপ্রদর্শন ; চালনা ; দৃষ্টান্ত। 2. Leadership ; as, to take the *lead* ; নেতৃত্ব, নায়কতা, শীর্ষস্থান। 3. An artificial water-way as to a mill ; কলকারখানার পয়ঃপ্রণালী, জলের নালা। 4. A channel in ice-field ; হিমানীক্ষেত্রের প্রণালী। 5. A string etc. for leading dogs ; কুকুরের গলায় বাঁধিবার দড়া প্রভৃতি। 6. (*Cards*) The act or right of playing first ; (তাসখেলায়) প্রথম খেলা বা প্রথম খেলার অধিকার। 7. (*Theatre*) A chief part ; one who plays this ; নাটকের প্রধান ভূমিকা ; যে ব্যক্তি উক্ত ভূমিকা অভিনয় করে। **Lead-off**—Commencement ; আরম্ভ, প্রারম্ভ। **To follow the lead of**—To follow the example of ; কাহারো দৃষ্টান্ত অনুসরণ করা। **To give one a lead**—To encourage one by doing a thing, esp. leaping a fence first in hunting ; নিজে দৃষ্টান্ত প্রদর্শন করত প্রোৎসাহিত করা, বিশেষতঃ মৃগয়ায় প্রথম বৃতি উল্লঙ্ঘন পূর্ব্বক প্রোৎসাহিত করা। **To take the lead**—নেতৃত্ব গ্রহণ করা।

lead'-en (lĕd-n), *adj.* 1. Made of lead ; of the nature of lead ; সীসকনির্ম্মিত ; সীসকবৎ, সীসময়। 2. Heavy ; sluggish ; burdensome ; ভারি ; মন্থর, ঢিলা ; দুর্ব্বহ। 3. Inert ; spiritless ; unfeeling ; নিষ্ক্রিয়, জড় ; নির্জ্জীব, নিস্তেজ ; হৃদয়হীন, নির্ম্মম। 4. Of the colour of lead ; সীসবর্ণ। **Leaden-limbs**—Heavy or burdensome limbs ; ভারি হাত পা। **Leaden-hearted** -- পাষাণহৃদয় **Leaden-sword**—Useless sword ; অব্যবহার্য্য তরবারী। **Sleep's leaden sceptre**—The stupefying power of sleep ; ঘোর নিদ্রার আবেশ।

lead'-êr (lĕd-), *n.* 1. One who, or that which, leads or conducts ; a guide ; পথপ্রদর্শক ; চালক। 2. A chief ; a commander ; a captain ; নায়ক, অগ্রণী ; নেতা, অধিনায়ক ; সর্দ্দার, দলপতি, চাঁই, মোড়ল, অধ্যক্ষ, মুখপাত্র। 3. A leading counsel in a case etc. ; মোকদ্দমা প্রভৃতিতে নিযুক্ত সর্ব্বপ্রধান কৌঁশুলি। 4. A horse placed in advance of others ; one of the forward pair of horses ; শকট প্রভৃতিতে সংযোজিত অশ্বসমূহের অগ্রে স্থাপিত অশ্ব ; অগ্রগামী অশ্বযুগলের অন্যতর। 5. The principal editorial article in a newspaper ; সংবাদপত্রের সম্পাদকলিখিত প্রধান প্রবন্ধ, সম্পাদকীয় প্রবন্ধ, খবরের কাগজের প্রধান প্রবন্ধ, মুখ্য প্রবন্ধ। 6. (*Printing*) A line of dots or dashes to guide the eye ; মুদ্রাঙ্কণে ক্ষুদ্র ক্ষুদ্র বিন্দু বা ক্ষুদ্র ক্ষুদ্র সরলরেখাদ্বারা রচিত রেখা। 7. (*Mus.*) A performer who leads a band in music ; বাদকদলের নায়ক। 8. A shoot growing at the apex of a stem ; কাণ্ডের শিখরে জাত প্ররোহ। 9. A tendon or sinew ; মহাশিরা। **—less,** *adj.* **—ship,** *n.* The office of a leader ; নায়কের পদ, নেতৃত্ব, অধিনায়কত্ব।

lead-er-ette′ (lĕd-êr-ĕt), *n.* A short editorial paragraph in the same type as the leader in a newspaper ; সম্পাদকীয় মন্তব্য।

lead′-ing (lēd-) *adj.* 1. Chief ; principal ; most important ; guiding ; controlling ; প্রধান, শ্রেষ্ঠ, মুখ্য ; সর্ব্বপ্রধান, শীর্ষস্থানীয় ; অতি প্রয়োজনীয় ; পরিচালক ; নিয়ামক। **Leading-article**—An editorial article in a newspaper ; সংবাদপত্রের প্রধান প্রবন্ধ, সম্পাদকীয় প্রবন্ধ, মুখ্য প্রবন্ধ। (*Commr.*) An article of trade sold at low price to attract customers for other things ; (বাণিজ্য) অন্যান্য জিনিষের ক্রেতা জোটাইবার জন্য যে বাণিজ্যদ্রব্য অল্প মূল্যে বিক্রীত হয়। **Leading-case**—যে মোকদ্দমা দ্বারা অন্য মোকদ্দমার বিচারের স্থবিধা হয়, নজীর। **Leading lady, –man**—নাটকের প্রধান অভিনেতা বা অভিনেত্রী। **Leading principle**—সিদ্ধান্ত (হিঃ কোঃ), প্রমাণ (ঐ)। **Leading question**—A question which suggests a certain answer which the questioner desires to get ; যে প্রশ্নে প্রকারান্তর উত্তর নির্দ্দেশ করিয়া দেওয়া হয়।

lead′-ing (lēd-), *n.* Act of one that leads ; পরিচালন। **Leading-business**—প্রধান অভিনেতা, সাধারণতঃ যে সকল ভূমিকা গ্রহণ করে। **Leading rein**—অশ্বের প্রধান বল্গা। **Men of light and leading** — গণ্যমান্য ব্যক্তিগণ (Also see LIGHT)।

leaf (lēf), *n.* & *v. i.* (*Pl.* LEAVES.) 1. An expanded deciduous organ of a plant ; as, the fall of the *leaf* ; পাতা, পত্র, বৃক্ষপত্র, পর্ণ, বিটপ। 2. A petal ; ফুলের পাঁপড়ি, দল, পলাশ (as in পদ্মপলাশলোচন)। 3. Leaves of tobacco or tea ; চা বা তামাকের পাতা। 4. A folded sheet in a book containing two pages one on each side ; পুস্তকের পাতা। 5. A very thin sheet of gold, silver, etc. or of marble, talc, etc. ; সোনা রূপা প্রভৃতির পাত। 6. A hinged part or flap of a door, table, shutter, bridge, etc. ; কপাট প্রভৃতির পাট। 7. One of the teeth of a pinion ; ক্ষুদ্র চাকার দাঁত। ***Verb i.*** To put forth leaves ; পত্র উদ্গত হওয়া, পত্র উদ্গত করা, পাতা বাহির হওয়া। **Leaf′-age,** *n.* Leaves collectively ; abundance of leaves ; পত্রগুচ্ছ ; পত্রপ্রাচুর্য্য। **Leaf′-less,** *adj.* Without leaf ; পত্রহীন, নিষ্পত্র, নিষ্পর্ণ, অপত্র, পর্ণশূন্য। **Leaf′-less-ness,** *n.* **Leaf′-i-ness,** *n.* পর্ণবাহুল্য, পত্রপ্রাচুর্য্য। **Leaf′-y,** *adj.* With, or full of, leaves ; পর্ণবহুল, পর্ণপ্রচুর, পর্ণময়। **Leaf-brass**—A brass foil ; পিত্তলপত্র। **Leaf-bud** — পত্রকোরক, পত্রকুট্মল, পত্রমুকুল (সাঃ পঃ), পত্রকলিকা (ঐ)। **Leaf-mould**—পাতার সার, পাতাসার। **Leaf-stalk**—পত্রের ডাঁটা, পত্রবৃন্ত। **The fall of the leaf**—The autumn ; পত্রপতন কাল, শরদ্ ঋতু। **To be in leaf**—To bear leaves ; পত্রধারণ হওয়া, পত্রসমন্বিত হওয়া। **To take a leaf out of one's book**—To follow the example of some one ; to imitate one ; কাহারো দৃষ্টান্ত অনুসরণ করা ; কাহারো অনুকরণ করা। **To turn over a new leaf**—To adopt a different and better line of conduct · নবজীবন আরম্ভ করা।

leaf′[illegible] -), *n.* 1. A little [illegible] [illegible]ত্র, পত্রক। 2. A printed sheet of pa[illegible] but not stitched esp. for free distribution ; মুদ্রিত ক্ষুদ্র কাগজ।

league (lēg), *n.* A measure of road-distance varying in different countries (usually being 3 miles) ; দূরত্বের পরিমাণ বিশেষ—প্রায় দেড় ক্রোশ, (সমুদ্রপথে প্রায় ৩॥৹ মাইল)।

league (lēg), *n., v. t.* & *i.* An alliance or combination of states, individuals, etc. for mutual aid or defence or for prosecution of common interests etc. ; the parties to it collectively ; a covenant ; পরস্পরের সাহায্য বা স্বার্থসংরক্ষণাদির জন্য দুই বা ততোধিক জাতি অথবা ব্যক্তির যোগ, ঐক্য বা মিলন, সংঘবৃত্তি ; সংঘবদ্ধ ব্যক্তি বা জাতিসমূহ ; চুক্তি, পণ। ***Verb t.*** To join in a league ; পরস্পরের সাহায্য বা স্বার্থসংরক্ষণার্থ মিলিত করা, সঙ্ঘবদ্ধ করা। ***Verb i.*** To form a league ; পরস্পর সাহায্যার্থ সম্মিলিত হওয়া, সঙ্ঘবদ্ধ হওয়া। **Leagued,** *adj.* United in a league (*with, together*) ; সঙ্ঘবদ্ধ। **In league with**—Allied with ; সঙ্ঘবদ্ধ।

lea′-guer (lē-gêr), *n.* A member of a league ; চক্রী, সঙ্ঘভুক্ত ব্যক্তি।

lea′-guer (lē-gêr), *n.* (*Archaic*) A camp esp. of a besieging army ; a siege ; অবরোধকারী সৈন্যদলের শিবির ; অবরোধ।

leak (lēk), *n.* & *v. i.* A crack ; a crevice or hole in a vessel that admits water or permits it to pass out ; ছিদ্র, ফাটা, ফাটল ; ফুটা—যাহার মধ্য দিয়া জল বা তরল পদার্থ যাতায়াত করিতে পারে, (নৌকাদি সম্বন্ধে) বাইনচাল। ***Verb i.*** 1. To let any fluid into, or out of, a vessel through a leak ; (of liquid) to pass gradually in or out through a leak ; ছিদ্র বা ফাটা দিয়া জলাদি প্রবেশ করিতে বা নির্গত হইতে দেওয়া ; ফোঁটা ফোঁটা করিয়া প্রবেশ করা বা বাহির হওয়া, চুয়ান, চুয়াইয়া বাহির হওয়া, (নৌকাদি-সম্বন্ধে) বাইনচাল হওয়া। 2. (Of secrets etc.) To transpire ; to be divulged gradually, (with *out*) ; গুপ্তকথা অল্পে অল্পে বাহির হইয়া পড়া ; আস্তে আস্তে প্রকাশ হইয়া পড়া। **Leak′-i-ness,** *n.* **Leak′-y,** *adj.* 1. Having a leak or leaks ; ছিদ্রযুক্ত, সচ্ছিদ্র, ছিদ্রবহুল, সরন্ধ্র, রন্ধ্রপূর্ণ, রন্ধ্রবহুল। 2. Incontinent of urine ; মূত্রধারণাক্ষম। 3. Apt to give out secrets ; গুপ্তকথা প্রকাশপ্রবণ।

To spring a leak — To be found to have a leak ; ফুটা হওয়া, বাইনচাল হওয়া।

leak′-āge (lĕk-), *n.* **1.** A leaking ; চুয়ান, চুয়াইয়া পড়ন। **2.** The quantity of liquid that enters or issues by leaking; ছিদ্র পথে প্রবিষ্ট বা নিঃসৃত তরল পদার্থের পরিমাণ। **3.** An allowance for loss by leaking ; (নৌকা বা পাত্র প্রভৃতিতে) ছিদ্র হওয়ার দরুণ জিনিষের ক্ষতির জন্য যে বাদসাদ দেওয়া হইয়া থাকে।

leal (lēl), *adj.* (*Scot.* & *lit.*) Loyal; true; faithful ; বিশ্বস্ত ; নিষ্ঠ ; বিশ্বাসী। **Land of the leal**—See under LAND.

lean (lēn), *v. i., t.* & *n.* **1.** To bend one's body *against* or *on* something for support etc. ; (of a thing) to lie in a sloping position *against* or *on* something ; আনত হওয়া, হেলিয়া পড়া, কোন জিনিষের উপর ভর দেওয়া ; ঠেস দিয়া থাকা। **2.** To incline from a vertical position ; হেলান দেওয়া, হেলিয়া থাকা, হেলিয়া পড়া। **3.** To depend for consolation, comfort and the like, (usu. with *on* or *upon*) : সান্ত্বনা বা প্রবোধের জন্য কাহারও উপর নির্ভর করা। **4.** To tend to mercy etc. ; to be partial (*to* a cause, opinion or person) ; দয়া প্রভৃতি বৃত্তির প্রবণ হওয়া ; কোন বিষয়ে পক্ষপাতযুক্ত হওয়া, কোন বিষয়ে ঝোঁক থাকা, ঝুঁকিয়া পড়া, হেলিয়া পড়া। **5.** To incline the body, (*back, forward, over, towards,* etc.) ; পশ্চাতে, সামনে বা কোন দিকে হেলিয়া থাকা। ***Verb t.*** To cause to lean ; to incline ; to support ; হেলানোভাবে রাখা ; আনত করা ; ঠেস দিয়া রাখা। ***Noun.*** Inclination ; slope ; আনত হওন, প্রবণতা ; ঢালু, আনতি। **Lean′-ing,** *n.* Inclining ; inclination ; tendency ; bias ; প্রবণতা ; ঝোঁক ; প্রবৃত্তি ; পক্ষপাত। **Leaning tower** — লীনস্তম্ভ (ভারতী ১৩১৯)। **Lean-to**—যে ঘরের চালা অপর ঘরের প্রাচীরে হেলানো থাকে। **To lean upon**—To incline upon ; to depend or rest upon ; হেলিয়া থাকা ; নির্ভর করা, অবলম্বন করা, সংশ্রিত হওয়া। (*Mil.*) To have as protection on a flank ; (সামরিক শাস্ত্র) পার্শ্বভাগ রক্ষা করা।

lean (lēn), *adj.* & *n.* **1.** Wanting flesh ; not plump ; thin ; কাহিল, ক্ষীণ, শীর্ণ, কৃশ ; অপুষ্ট ; পাতলা, একহারা, তনু। **2.** Of poor quality ; scant ; innutritious ; as, a *lean* harvest, diet, etc. ; নিকৃষ্ট ; অপ্রচুর, সামান্য ; অপুষ্টিকর। **3.** (Of meat) Containing little fat, chiefly of muscle ; স্বল্পমেদযুক্ত। **4.** Unremunerative, as wages etc. ; অলাভজনক। ***Noun.*** The muscular part of meat, without fat ; মাংসের পেশীময় অংশ। **Lean′-ness,** *n.* State of being lean ; meagreness ; কৃশতা, কার্শ্য, কৃশাঙ্গতা, শীর্ণতা, তনুতা, ক্ষীণতা। **Lean-type**—একপ্রকার সূক্ষ্ম হরফ। **Lean-wit′ted**—Of little sense ; ক্ষীণবুদ্ধি, অল্পবুদ্ধি, মন্দধী। **Lean years** — Years of scarcity ; আকালের বছর।

Lē′-ăn-dêr, *n.* A beautiful young-man of Abydos who loved Hero ; প্রাচীন Abydos নগরবাসী জনৈক রূপবান যুবক। ইনি Sestos নগরবাসিনী রতিদেবীর পূজারিণী H[illegible] প্রেমে পতিত হন। Leander [illegible] Dardene[illegible] প্রণালী সন্তরণে অতিক্রম করিয়া প্রণয়িনীর সহিত মিলিত হইতেন। এক ঝটিকাচ্ছন্ন রাত্রে Leander প্রেমিকার সহিত মিলনের জন্য Dardenelles প্রণালী অতিক্রম করিতে যাইয়া প্রাণ হারান। Hero প্রেমিকের মৃত্যুসংবাদ শুনিবা মাত্র উচ্চ বুরুজ হইতে পড়িয়া প্রাণত্যাগ করেন।

leap (lēp), *v. i.* & *t.* **1.** (*Usd still in poetry or dignified language*) To spring or rise from the ground ; to jump ; লাফাইয়া উঠা লাফান, লাফ দেওয়া, লম্ফ দেওয়া। **2.** (Of things) To move with a spring or bound ; লম্ফ দেওয়া। **3.** To spring from the water, as fish ; জল হইতে লাফাইয়া উঠা। **4.** (Of the heart) To beat vigorously ; to throb ; ধুক্ ধুক্ করা ; দুরু দুরু করা। ***Verb t.*** **1.** To pass over by a jump ; টপ্‌কান্‌, ডিঙ্গাইয়া যাওয়া, লাফাইয়া পার হওয়া। **2.** To cause (one's horse) to take a leap ; লাফ দেওয়ান। **3.** (Of a beast) To cover or copulate with ; (পশুর সম্পর্কে) সঙ্গম করা। **Leap′-er,** *n.* **Leap frog**—*n.* & *v. i.* বালকদিগের ভেকলম্ফ ক্রীড়া, ঘাড়েচড়াচড়ি খেলা। (*Verb i.*) To perform such vault (*over*) ; ঐরূপ ক্রীড়ায় লম্ফ দেওয়া।

leap (lēp), *n.* **1.** Act of leaping ; a jump ; লম্ফ, লাফ ; ঝম্প। **2.** A leaping place ; something to be leaped over ; the place or distance leaped ; লম্ফের স্থান ; যাহা লাফাইয়া পার হইতে হয় ; লম্ফদ্বারা অতিক্রান্ত স্থান, লম্ফদ্বারা অতিক্রান্ত দূরত্ব। **3.** Copulation with a female beast ; (পশুর) সঙ্গম। **Leap-day**—29th February ; ২৯শে ফেব্রুয়ারী। **Leap-year**—৩৬৬ দিনের বৎসর — এইরূপ বৎসরে ফেব্রুয়ারী মাস ২৯ দিনে হয়, অধিবর্ষ (হিঃ কোঃ), প্লবকবর্ষ (সাঃ পঃ), পরিবৎসর (ঐ), অধিকদিনবৎসর (কেম্ভিঃ)। **A leap in the dark**—A hazardous attempt of doubtful consequence ; অন্ধকারে লম্ফ প্রদান, ফলাফল অনিশ্চিত এরূপ সঙ্কটসঙ্কুল কার্য্যে প্রবৃত্ত হওন। **By leaps and bounds**—With startlingly rapid progress ; অতিদ্রুত, লম্ফে ঝম্পে।

learn (lêrn), *v. t.* & *i.* **1.** To gain knowledge of, or skill in, by study, instruction or experience ; to fix in the mind ; শিক্ষা করা, শিখা, অভ্যাস করা, বিদ্যাভ্যাস করা ; মনে গাঁথিয়া রাখা। **2.** To commit to memory ; as, to *learn* by rote ; মুখস্থ করা, কণ্ঠস্থ করা। **3.** To get information about ; to ascertain ;

অবগত হওয়া; নির্ণয় করা, নিরূপণ করা। *Verb i.* **1.** To gain knowledge; to be aware; জ্ঞান লাভ করা; অবগত হওয়া, বিদিত হওয়া। **2.** To receive instruction; উপদেশ লাভ করা। **Learn'-a-ble,** *adj.* **Learn'-er,** *n.* One who learns; a pupil; শিক্ষার্থী, বিদ্যার্থী; ছাত্র। **To learn by heart** or **rote** — To commit to memory; কণ্ঠস্থ করা।

learn'-ĕd (lêrn-), *adj.* **1.** Having much information obtained by study; deeply read; erudite; সুশিক্ষিত; বিদ্বান, অধ্যয়নসম্পন্ন, লব্ধবিদ্য, শিক্ষিত, কৃতবিদ্য, অধীত, বহুবিদ্য, ব্যুৎপন্ন; বহুজ্ঞ, বহুশ্রুত; কোবিদ, পণ্ডিত। **2.** Showing profound knowledge; containing learning; গভীরপাণ্ডিত্যসূচক; পাণ্ডিত্যপূর্ণ। **3.** Well-informed (*in*); as, *learned in* the law; (conventionally courteous mention of a lawyer in the House of Commons, law-courts etc.); বুৎপন্ন, সুপণ্ডিত; বিচারালয় প্রভৃতিতে শিষ্টাচারের অনুরোধে ব্যবহারজীবিগণ সম্পর্কে ব্যবহৃত হয়। **4.** Studied or pursued by learned men, as a language; introduced by learned men, as words in a language; পণ্ডিতগণ দ্বারা অধীত বা অনুসৃত; পণ্ডিতগণ কর্তৃক প্রবর্তিত, পণ্ডিতী। **—ly,** *adj.* **—ness,** *n.* **The learned**—Learned men; men of erudition; scholars; পণ্ডিতমণ্ডলী; কৃতবিদ্যসমাজ, শিক্ষিতসমাজ, বিদ্বজ্জনমণ্ডলী; পণ্ডিতসমাজ, সারস্বতসমাজ, বুধমণ্ডলী।

learn'-ing (lêrn-), *n.* **1.** Acquisition of knowledge, skill, etc.; বিদ্যালাভ, নৈপুণ্যলাভ, বিদ্যার্জ্জন। **2.** The possession of knowledge got by study; acquired knowledge; erudition; education; বিদ্যালাভ; অধ্যয়নলব্ধ জ্ঞান; বিদ্যা, ব্যুৎপত্তি, পাণ্ডিত্য; শিক্ষা। **Book-learning**—পুস্তকগতবিদ্যা, পুঁথিগতবিদ্যা, কেতাবীবিদ্যা। **A man of learning**—A man of erudition; পণ্ডিত ব্যক্তি, সুবিদ্বান ব্যক্তি। **The new learning**—ষোড়শ শতাব্দীতে ইংলণ্ডে প্রাচীন গ্রীক ও ল্যাটিন ভাষা চর্চ্চার পুনরুজ্জীবন।

lease (lēs), *n.* & *v. t.* A contract for conveying lands, houses, etc. in consideration of rent; পাট্টা। *Verb t.* **1.** To grant by lease; to let; জোত জমা বিলি করা, পাট্টা দেওয়া; ভাড়া দেওয়া। **2.** To take lease of; ইজারা নেওয়া। **Lease'-hold**—*n.* A tenure by lease; land held under a lease; পত্তনি; পত্তনি বা ইজারা মহাল। **Lease holder** — *n.* One who holds land under lease; ইজারাদার, পাট্টাদার। **A new lease of life**—A prospect of living due to recovered health or removal of anxiety etc.; নব জীবনলাভ, রোগান্তে স্বাস্থ্য লাভ, উৎকণ্ঠাদির অপগমে নবজীবন লাভ, পুনর্জ্জন্ম।

lease (lēs), *n.* **1.** The plane in which the warp threads cross; this system of crossing; টানার সূতার যে স্থান ব্যাপিয়া পড়েনের সূতা অতিক্রম করে; টানার সূতার অতিক্রমণ। **2.** (*Weaving*) Same as LEASH, *n.* 3.

leash (lēsh), *n.* & *v. t.* **1.** A thong or cord by which a hawk or dog is held; শিকারী কুকুরাদির চর্ম্মবন্ধ, শিকারী পক্ষীর বন্ধনরজ্জু। **2.** A set of three hounds, foxes, hares, etc.; ত্রিসংখ্যক জন্তু। **3.** A string with a loop at the end for lifting warp threads in a loom; প্রান্তদেশে ফাঁশবিশিষ্ট রজ্জু বিশেষ,—যদ্দ্বারা তাঁতের টানার সূতা তোলা হয়। *Verb t.* To bind, hold or connect with a leash; বাঁধা, একত্র করিয়া বাঁধা, রজ্জুবদ্ধ করা। **To hold in leash**—To control; সংযত করা।

leas'-ing (lēs-), *n.* (*Bibl.*) Lying; a lie; falsehood; মিথ্যাকথন; মিথ্যা কথা; মিথ্যাবাদ।

least (lēst), *adj.*, *n.* & *adv.* (*Used as the superlative of little*) Smallest; slightest; most unimportant; অত্যল্প, ক্ষুদ্রতম; অল্পিষ্ঠ, অল্পতম; সামান্যতম। *Noun.* The least amount or degree; ক্ষুদ্রতম পরিমাণ, অল্পতম মাত্রা। *Adv.* In the smallest or the lowest degree; অত্যল্পপরিমাণে, ক্ষুদ্রতম পরিমাণে। **At least** — At all events; at the lowest degree; on the lowest estimate; অন্ততঃ, নিতান্তপক্ষে; ন্যূনকল্পে; নিদান পক্ষে, কম পক্ষেও, নিদেন। **At the least**—At the lowest estimate or computation; নিতান্তপক্ষে। **In the least**—In the smallest degree; at all; কিছুমাত্র, লেশমাত্র; সামান্য মাত্রও। **The least said the soonest mended**—It is prudent to speak little; অল্প কথা বলাই উচিত। **To say the least of it**—To put the case moderately; নিতান্ত কম করিয়া বলিলেও।

leat (lēt), *n.* An open watercourse leading to a mill etc.; কারখানা প্রভৃতিতে জল সরবরাহের জন্য অনাবৃত পয়ঃপ্রণালী।

leath'-ĕr (lĕth-), *n.* & *v. t.* **1.** The skin of an animal dressed and prepared for use; শোধিতচর্ম্ম, পরিষ্কৃত চামড়া। **2.** An article, or part of one, made of leather; a thong; চর্ম্মনির্ম্মিত দ্রব্য; চামড়ার দোয়াল, চর্ম্মরজ্জু। **3.** (*Slang*) A cricket ball or foot-ball; (*pl.*) leggings or breeches; ক্রীকেট খেলার বল, পাদগোলক; পাদাবরণ, জঙ্ঘাত্রাণ, জাঙ্গিয়া। **4.** (*Slang*) Skin; as, to lose *leather*, (to suffer abrasion); (ইতর ভাষায়) চামড়া, ছাল। *Verb t.* **1.** To cover with leather; চর্ম্মাবৃত করা। **2.** To beat with a thong of leather; চর্ম্মরজ্জুদ্বারা আঘাত করা। **—ern,** *adj.* Consisting of leather; made of leather; চর্ম্মময়;

চর্ম্মনির্ম্মিত। **–ette'**, *n.* A fabric of cloth and paper in imitation of leather ; কাগজ ও কাপড়দ্বারা তৈরী কৃত্রিম চামড়া। **–ing**, *n.* **1.** Act of forming or furnishing with leather ; চর্ম্ম দ্বারা আচ্ছাদন, চর্ম্ম দ্বারা গঠন। **2.** Flogging ; বেত্রাঘাত। **–y**, *adj.* Like leather ; tough ; চর্ম্মবৎ ; দৃঢ়, কড়া, চিমড়া। **Leather-back**—একপ্রকার চিত্র কচ্ছপ। **Leather-dresser** — চর্ম্মকার, চর্ম্মসংস্কারক। **Leather-head** — A block-head ; নির্ব্বোধ, বোকা। **Leather-hunting**—(*Cricket*) Fielding ; (ক্রিকেট ক্রীড়ায়) মাঠে দাঁড়াইয়া কন্দুক থামান বা লুফিয়া ধরণ। **Leather-jacket**—কঠিন-চর্ম্ম মৎস্যবিশেষ। **Leather-knife**—চামড়া কাটিবার জন্য বাঁকা ছুরী। **Leather-neck**—(*A sailor's slang*) A soldier ; (নাবিকদিগের ইতরভাষায়) সৈনিক। **Leather-trunk**—চর্ম্মপেটিকা। **Leather-wood**—দৃঢ়বল্কল বৃক্ষ বিশেষ। **Patent leather** — চক্‌চকে কাল চামড়া। **Leather and prunella**—Unessential thing ; worthless stuff ; অপ্রধান জিনিষ ; অসার বস্তু, অকেজো জিনিষ, বাজে জিনিষ। **Nothing like leather**—One's own goods will serve all purposes ; নিজের জিনিষে সব কাজ চলে।

leath'-er-oid (lĕth-ẽr-ōyd), *n.* Cotton-paper chemically treated and resembling raw hide ; কৃত্রিম চর্ম্ম।

leave (lēv), *n.* **1.** Permission ; অনুমতি, আজ্ঞা, অনুজ্ঞা। **2.** Permission to be absent from duty ; a period for which it lasts ; বিদায়, ছুটী ; বিদায়কাল। **Leave-breaker**—যে নাবিক বিদায়ের অতিরিক্ত কাল কার্য্য হইতে অনুপস্থিত থাকে। **Leave-taking**—বিদায়গ্রহণ। **By your leave**—A form of apology for taking liberty, making any unwelcome tatement etc. (esp. a porter's formula for asking persons to make way for him or his load) ; আপনার অনুমতি হইলে। **Leave of absence** — Same as LEAVE *n.* 2. **On leave** — Absent from duty with permission from authority ; ছুটীতে। **To take (one's) leave (of)** — To bid farewell (to) ; বিদায় গ্রহণ করা, বিদায় লওয়া।

leave (lēv), *v. t.* & *i.* **1.** To allow or cause to remain ; to go away without taking ; to bequeath ; থাকিতে দেওয়া ; ত্যাগ করিয়া যাওয়া, ছাড়িয়া যাওয়া ; (উত্তরাধিকারীকে) দিয়া যাওয়া। **2.** To abstain from ; to desist from ; to let continue ; ক্ষান্ত হওয়া ; বিরত হওয়া, নিরস্ত হওয়া, থামা ; চলিতে দেওয়া। **3.** To abandon ; to forsake ; to quit ; to go away from ; পরিত্যাগ করা ; পরিবর্জ্জন করা ; ত্যাগ করা ; চলিয়া যাওয়া, প্রস্থান করা। **4.** To allow to remain in a specified state ; as, this *leaves* one cool ; রাখা। **5.** To submit ; to refer for decision etc.,(with *to*) ; as, nothing was *left to* accident ; অর্পণ করা, সমর্পণ করা ; নির্দ্দেশ করা। **6.** To deposit or entrust to be sent, delivered, etc. ; as, I *leave* it with you or in your house ; গচ্ছিত রাখা, বিশ্বাসপূর্ব্বক ন্যস্ত রাখা। **7.** To allow (person or thing) to do something without interference ; করিতে দেওয়া। **8.** To pass as an object so as to keep it in a specified direction ; as, he *left* the house on the right ; রাখিয়া চলা। **9.** To cease to reside at (a place) or to belong to (a school, society, etc.) ; ত্যাগ করা। ***Verb i.*** To depart ; as, we *leave* tomorrow ; প্রস্থান করা, চলিয়া যাওয়া। **He will be well left**—He will be well provided for by legacy etc. ; ভরণপোষণের যথেষ্ট সম্পত্তি উইল করিয়া রাখিয়া মরিবে। **(I) leave it to you sir**—Fix my pay yourself ; আমার বেতন আপনি ঠিক করুন। **It leaves much to be desired**—It is unsatisfactory ; ইহা সন্তোষজনক নহে। **Leave him to himself**—Do not try to control him ; তাহাকে ইচ্ছামত চলিতে দাও। **Leave it aside**—ও থাক্ না। **This leaves me cool** — It does not excite me ; ইহাতে আমি উত্তেজিত হই নাই। **To get left**—(*Colloq.*) To be deserted or worsted ; পরিত্যক্ত হওয়া, পরাভূত হওয়া। **To leave alone** — To let remain undisturbed ; not to interfere with ; শান্তিতে থাকিতে দেওয়া ; না ঘাঁটান। **To leave behind**—To go away without ; to pass ; ছাড়িয়া যাওয়া, ফেলিয়া যাওয়া ; পশ্চাতে রাখিয়া যাওয়া, পার হইয়া যাওয়া, অতিক্রম করা। **To leave hold of**—To cease holding ; মুঠা ছাড়িয়া দেওয়া। **To leave in the dark**—To conceal information from ; লুকাইয়া রাখা, প্রকাশ না করা। **To leave in the lurch**—To leave in a forlorn state, without help ; সঙ্কটে ফেলিয়া যাওয়া, অসহায় অবস্থায় ফেলিয়া যাওয়া, বিপন্ন অবস্থায় পরিত্যাগ করিয়া যাওয়া। **To leave off**—To desist from ; to stop ; to cease wearing or using ; to come to or make an end ; নিবৃত্ত হওয়া, নিরস্ত হওয়া, বিরত হওয়া ; থামা ; ব্যবহার না করা ; শেষ হওয়া, শেষ করা। **To leave out** — To omit ; বাদ দেওয়া, ছাড়িয়া দেওয়া বর্জ্জন করা, উল্লেখ না করা। **To leave out in the cold** — To neglect ; not to allow to participate in anything ; অবহেলা করা ; উপেক্ষা করা, অনাদর করা, কোন ব্যাপারে যোগদান করিতে না দেওয়া। **To leave over**—To let stand over for the time ; আপাততঃ স্থগিত রাখা। **To leave to one's self**—To let one be alone ; to cease caring for one ; (কাহাকে) নিজের ইচ্ছামত কাজ করিতে দেওয়া ; কাহারো সম্বন্ধে আর তত্ত্বাবধান না নেওয়া। **To leave undone** — To let remain unfinished ; অসমাপ্ত রাখা, অসম্পন্ন রাখা।

leaved (lēvd), *adj.* 1. (*Rāre*) With leaves ; (কচিদ্ ব্যবহৃত) সপত্র। 2. Having leaves ; as, one-*leaved* : red-*leaved* ; পত্র-সমন্বিত।

leav'-en (lĕv-n), *n.* & *v. t.* 1. A substance that produces fermentation as in dough ; তাড়ির বীজ, খমীর, কিম্বা কাদম্বরী বীজ। 2. (*Fig.*) A spreading or transforming influence ; an admixture or element that modifies or tempers the whole ; as, a *leaven* of wit ; (লক্ষণায়) বিস্তারক বা বিকারজনক প্রভাব ; আভাস, আমেজ। ***Verb t.*** 1. To mix or ferment (dough) with leaven ; খমীরের সহিত মিশান, খমীর মিশাইয়া গাঁজাইয়া তোলা। 2. (*Fig.*) To permeate and transform ; to modify *with* tempering element ; "When this revelation has had time to *leaven* the city" ; পরিব্যাপ্ত হইয়া বিকার উৎপাদন করা ; প্রশামক বস্তু দ্বারা প্রশমিত করা। **The old leaven**—Traces of unregenerate state ; ভগবানের সহিত অপ্রীতির ভাবের চিহ্ন।

leav'-ings (lēv-), *n.* (*Pl.*) Things left ; remnant ; পরিত্যক্ত জিনিষ ; উদ্বর্ত্ত, অবশেষ, অবশিষ্টাংশ, (of food) উচ্ছিষ্ট, উচ্ছিষ্টান্ন, ভুক্তাবশেষ।

lĕch'-êr, *n.* 1. (*Archaic*) A man given to lewdness ; fornicator ; (অপ্রঃ) লম্পট, কামাসক্ত ; লোচ্চা, রণ্ডাবাজ। **—ous,** *adj.* **—ous-ly,** *adv.* **—ous-ness,** *n.* **—y,** *n.* Debauchery ; লাম্পট্য, লোচ্চামি।

lĕc'-têrn, *n.* A reading or singing desk in a church ; খৃষ্টীয় ধর্ম্মমন্দিরস্থ পাঠমঞ্চ বা গীতমঞ্চ।

lĕc'-tion-ā-rȳ, *n.* A portion or list of portions of Scripture appointed to be read at the divine service ; উপাসনাকালে পাঠের জন্য নির্দ্দিষ্ট বাইবেল হইতে উদ্ধৃত অংশ সমূহ বা উহাদের তালিকা।

lĕc'-tūre, *n., v. i.* & *t.* 1. A discourse read or delivered on any subject ; বক্তৃতা। 2. A methodical discourse intended for instruction ; as, a *lecture* on history in a college ; অধ্যাপনার জন্য অভিপ্রেত প্রণালীবদ্ধ ব্যাখান বা নিবন্ধ। 3. Admonition ; reprimand ; reproof ; as, to read one a *lecture* ; তিরস্কার ; ধিগ্‌দণ্ড, বাগ্‌দণ্ড, বাগ্‌শাসন ; ভৎর্সনা। ***Verb i.*** To read or deliver a lecture or lectures (on) a subject ; বক্তৃতা প্রদান করা, বক্তৃতা পাঠ করা। ***Verb t.*** 1. To give a lecture to ; to instruct or entertain, as a class etc. by lecture ; বক্তৃতা প্রদান করা, বক্তৃতাচ্ছলে শিক্ষা দেওয়া, অধ্যাপনা করা ; 2. To admonish ; to reprimand ; তিরস্কার করা ; ভৎর্সনা করা। **—ship,** *n.* The office of a lecturer ; a course of lectures or the foundation ; অধ্যাপকত্ব, প্রবক্তৃত্ব ; বক্তৃতাবলী, বক্তৃতার জন্য প্রদত্ত বৃত্তি। **—tur-er,** *n.* One who lectures ; a professor or instructor in a college etc. ; বক্তা ; অধ্যাপক। **Lecture-room**—বক্তৃতাগৃহ, বক্তৃতামন্দির, অধ্যাপনকক্ষ। **To read one a lecture** — To reprove him ; তিরস্কার করা, কড়াকড়া দু কথা শুনাইয়া দেওয়া।

Lē'-dă, *n.* A daughter of Thesetices and wife of Tyndareus, king of Sparta ; স্পার্টার রাজা Tindareusএর পত্নী। দেবরাজ Jupiter রাজহংসের রূপ ধারণ করিয়া Ledar সহিত বিবাহ করেন। এই মিলনের ফলে Leda দুইটী ডিম্ব প্রসব করে ; তাহার একটী হইতে Castor ও Pollux ও অপরটী হইতে Helen জন্মগ্রহণ করে।

ledge (lĕj), *n.* 1. A narrow horizontal surface projected from wall ; a shelf ; প্রাচীরাদির উদ্গত অংশ ; তাক। 2. A projection on the side of a rock etc. resembling a shelf ; পাষাণ, পর্ব্বত প্রভৃতির তাকের আকার উদ্গত অংশ। 3. A stratum of metal-bearing rock ; ধাতুগর্ভপাষাণের স্তর **Ledged,** *adj.* **Ledg'-y,** *adj.* Abounding in ledges ; উদ্গত শিলাফলকবহুল, স্তরবহুল।

ledg'-êr (lĕj-), *n.* & *adj.* 1. The principal book of accounts among merchants, in which a summary of all other books are entered ; (মহাজনের) খতিয়ান, পাকা খাতা। 2. A horizontal piece of timber to support the platform of scaffolding ; কোন মঞ্চ বা সোপান-শ্রেণীর অবলম্বনস্বরূপ শায়িত কাষ্ঠখণ্ড। 3. A large flat grave-stone ; সুবৃহৎ সমতল প্রস্তর খণ্ড। 4. (Also *Ledger-bait*) A fishing bait fixed in one place ; একস্থানে নিবদ্ধ টোপ।

lee (lē), *n.* & *adj.* 1. (Also *Lee-side*) The quarter toward which the wind blows (opp. to *windward* or *weather-side*) ; যে দিকে বায়ু প্রবাহিত হয়। 2. Shelter or protection ; as, under the *lee* of Turkish guns ; আশ্রয়, রক্ষণ। ***Adj.*** Of, or pertaining to, the side opposite to that against which the wind blows ; জাহাজের যে পার্শ্বে বায়ু প্রবাহিত হয় তদ্বিপরীত পার্শ্বসম্বন্ধীয়। **Lee-shore**—যে তীরের দিকে বাতাস প্রবাহিত হয়। **Lee-tide**—বায়ুপ্রবাহের অভিমুখীন স্রোত **Lee-way** — নির্ব্বাত দিকে পার্শ্বিক জাহাজের গতি। **The lee-side of a ship**—The side sheltered from the wind ; জাহাজের যে পার্শ্বে বায়ু প্রবাহিত হয় না, জাহাজের নির্ব্বাতপার্শ্ব। **To make up a lee-way**—(*Fig.*) To struggle out of a bad position ; (লক্ষণায়) প্রতিকূল অবস্থার সহিত সংগ্রাম করিয়া উন্নতির দিকে অগ্রসর হওয়া। **Under the lee of**—Under the shelter or protection of ; আশ্রয়ে, রক্ষণাধীনে।

leech (lēch), *n.* (*Archaic, poet.* or *jocular*) ; A physician ; a healer ; (অপ্রঃ, কবিতায় ও রঙ্গচ্ছলে) চিকিৎসক ;

ভিষক্, বৈদ্য। **Leech-craft**—চিকিৎসা বিদ্যা।

leech (lēch), *n.* **1.** An aquatic blood sucking worm-like animal especially the kind that is used medicinally for bleeding ; জলৌকা, জোঁক, রক্তশোষক, রক্তপ। **2.** (*Fig.*) A person who sucks profit of others ; যে ব্যক্তি পরের অর্থ শোষণ করে, রক্তশোষক। **To stick like a leech**—To stick persistently ; জোঁকের মত লাগিয়া থাকা।

leech (lēch), *n.* The perpendicular or sloping side of a sail ; পাইলের খাড়া বা প্রবণ পার্শ্ব।

leek (lēk), *n.* **1.** A culinary vegetable allied to the onion ; পেঁয়াজ জাতীয় একপ্রকার গুল্ম। **2.** This as the national badge of the Welsh ; ওয়েলস্‌দিগের জাতীয় চিহ্নস্বরূপ উক্ত গুল্ম। **To eat or swallow the leek** — To pocket an affront ; to retract one's words ; অপমান সহ্য করা ; কিল খাইয়া কিল চুরী করা, প্রত্যাহার করা।

leer (lēr), *v. i.* & *n.* To cast a sidelong, lustful, or malign look ; কটাক্ষক্ষেপ করা ; চোখ ঠারা, অপাঙ্গ-বিক্ষেপ করা, কটাক্ষ-ক্ষেপণ করা, আড় চোখে চাওয়া। ***Noun.*** A sidelong glance with sly or lascivious expression ; অপাঙ্গ-দৃষ্টি, কটাক্ষ, নয়নবাণ, অপাঙ্গবীক্ষণ, কটাক্ষক্ষেপণ, অপাঙ্গদর্শন। **Leer'-ing-ly,** *adv.* With a leering look ; চোক ঠারিয়া, অপাঙ্গদৃষ্টি করিয়া।

leer (lēr), *n.* An oven in which glassware is annealed ; কাচপাত্র প্রভৃতি তপ্তশীতল করার জন্য চুল্লী।

leer'-ȳ (lēr-), *adj.* (*Slang*) Knowing ; sly ; (ইতর ভাষায়) জ্ঞাতসার ; ধূর্ত্ত।

lees (lēz), *n.* (*Pl.*) **1.** Sediment of wine etc. ; তলানি, গাদ, কিট্ট, শিটা, কাইট। **2.** Refuse ; basest part ; পরিত্যক্ত অংশ, জঞ্জাল নিকৃষ্ট অংশ।

lee'-ward (lē-wêrd or lū wêrd), *adj.*, *n.* & *adv.* Pertaining to, or in, the direction towards which the wind blows ; যে দিকে বায়ু প্রবাহিত হয়—তৎসম্বন্ধীয় যে দিকে বায়ু প্রবাহিত হয় সেই দিকের। ***Noun.*** This direction ; as, to the *leeward* ; যে দিকে বায়ুপ্রবাহিত হয়। ***Adv.*** Toward the lee ; যে দিকে বায়ু প্রবাহিত হয় তদভিমুখে। **—most,** *adj.*

lee'-ward-lȳ (lē-wêrd- or lū-wêrd-), *adj.* (Of a ship) Tending to fall to leeward (opp. to *weatherly*) ; (জাহাজ সম্পর্কে) যে দিকে বায়ু প্রবাহিত হয় তদভিমুখে পতন প্রবণ।

lĕft, *adj.*, *adv.* & *n.* **1.** Denoting the part opposed to the right of the body ; বাম, বাঁ, সব্য। **2.** Situated nearer to the left hand than to the right ; বামদিকে অবস্থিত। ***Adv.*** On, or towards, the left side ; বাম পার্শ্বে, বাম ভাগে, বাম দিকে। ***Noun.*** **1.** The side opposite to the right ; the left hand ; "Trying to push his *left* in Sharkey's face" ; বাম পার্শ্ব, বাঁ দিক ; বাম হস্ত, সব্যপাণি। **2.** The left wing of an army ; সৈন্য দলের বাম পার্শ্ব। **3.** The members of a legislative body on the left of the president ; the liberal or democratic party whose representatives occupy those seats ; ব্যবস্থাপক সভার সভাপতির বাম পার্শ্বে উপবিষ্ট সভ্যগণ ; উদারনৈতিক বা গণতন্ত্রানুরাগী সভ্যবর্গ—যাহারা বাম পার্শ্বস্থ আসনশ্রেণীতে উপবেশন করে। **4.** The advanced or innovating section of philosophical school, religious sect, etc. ; দার্শনিক সমাজ বা ধর্ম্মসম্প্রদায় প্রভৃতির উন্নত বা নূতন রীতিপ্রবর্ত্তনকারী ব্যক্তিগণ (cf. বামাচারী), নবপন্থিগণ। **Left'-most,** *adj.* Furthest off on the left ; অতিশয় বামদিকে। **Left'-ward,** *adj.* & *adv.* Toward, or on, the left side ; বামপার্শ্বস্থ বামভাগে। **Left'-wards** *adj.* **Left-turn**—One that makes one's face as one's left side did before ; যেরূপ আবর্ত্তনে পূর্ব্বে যেখানে বামপার্শ্ব ছিল তথায় মুখ ঘুরাইয়া আনিতে হয়, বামপার্শ্বাবর্ত্তন। **The left bank of a river**—নদীর স্রোত যে দিকে বহে সেই দিকে মুখ করিয়া দাঁড়াইলে যে তীর বামভাগে থাকে। **Over the left**—Implying that the contrary of what is said, is to be understood ; যাহা বলা হইয়াছে তাহার বিপরীত বুঝিতে হইবে এইরূপ বুঝায়।

lĕft'-hănd, *n.* & *adj.* **1.** The hand opposite to the right ; বামহস্ত, বাঁ হাত, বামকর, বামপাণি, সব্যহস্ত। **2.** The region or direction nearer the left hand ; বাম হাতের নিকটবর্ত্তী স্থান, বাঁ দিক। ***Adj.*** **1.** Situated on the left-hand side ; nearer the left hand than the right ; বামপার্শ্বে অবস্থিত ; দক্ষিণ হস্ত অপেক্ষা বামহস্তের অধিকতর নিকটবর্ত্তী। **2.** Using, done, or delivered with the left hand ; as, a *left-hand* blow ; বামহস্তসেবী, বামহস্তকৃত, বামহস্তদ্বারা সম্পাদিত, বাম হস্তদ্বারা অর্পিত। **Lefthand blow**—See LEFT-HAND *adj.* 2. **Left-hand man**—বাঁ দিকের ব্যক্তি। **Left hand rope** — ঘড়ীর কাঁটার গতির বিপরীত দিকে পাক দিয়া যে রজ্জু প্রস্তুত করা হয়। **On the lefthand**—Irregularly ; অনিয়মিত-ভাবে। **On the lefthand of**—On the left-hand side relatively to ; অপেক্ষাকৃত বামদিকে। **To marry with the lefthand**—To marry morganatically ; হীন বংশে বিবাহ করা। [যেরূপ বিবাহ দ্বারা স্ত্রী বা তদীয় সন্তান স্বামীর উপাধি বা বিষয়সম্পত্তি উত্তরাধিকারসূত্রে পাইতে পারে না।]

lĕft'-hănd-ĕd, *adj.* **1.** Having the left-hand more serviceable and dexterous than the right ; ন্যাটা, নেঙা, ড্যাবরা, সব্যসাচী। **2.** Clumsy ; awkward ; কদাকার ; কুৎসিত। **3.** Ambiguous ; insincere ; as, a *left-handed* compliment ; দ্ব্যর্থক ; অকপট, অসরল। **4.** Morganatic, as marriage (see MORGANATIC). [জর্ম্মণীতে এরূপ বিবাহে বর কন্যাকে বামহস্ত প্রদান করিতেন।] **5.** Done, or delivered, with the left hand, as an act, blow, etc.; adapted for use of the left hand, as an implement; বামহস্ত সম্পাদিত, বমহস্তদ্বারা নিক্ষিপ্ত, বামহস্ত দ্বারা প্রদত্ত; বামহস্ত দ্বারা ব্যবহারের উপযোগী। **6.** (*Archaic*) Inauspicious; sinister; (অপ্রঃ) অশুভ; অপায়া, অমঙ্গল-সূচক। **7.** Contra-clockwise as a twist etc.; ঘড়ীর কাঁটার গতির বিপরীত দিকে। **—ly,** *adv.* **—ness,** *n.* State or quality of being left-handed; সব্যসাচিতা (হিঃ কোঃ)। **Left-handed compliment** — স্তুতিচ্ছলে নিন্দা, ব্যাজস্তুতি। **A left-handed oath**—যে প্রতিজ্ঞাপালন সম্বন্ধে বাধ্যবাধকতা নাই।

lĕft′-hănd-ĕr, *n.* A left-handed person or blow; সব্যহস্ত ব্যক্তি, বামহস্তের আঘাত।

lĕg, *n., v. i., & t.* **1.** One of the limbs of man or other animals used for walking or running; পদ, পা, চরণ। **2.** (*In ship-building etc.*) A bar or pole serving as a support, prop, etc.; ঠেকো। **3.** A support of a chair, table or bed; পায়া। **4.** The part of any article of clothing which covers the leg; পাজামা প্রভৃতির পা। **5.** (*In cricket*) That part of the field to the left of, and behind, the batsman as he faces the bowler; ব্যাটধারীর বাম এবং পশ্চাদ্‌ভাগস্থ স্থান। **6.** A fieldsman in his specific position; as, a short or long *leg* etc.; যে ব্যক্তি খেলার মাঠে নির্দ্দিষ্ট স্থানে দাঁড়াইয়া বল থামায় বা লুফিয়া থাকে। **7.** The leg of an animal as food; কসাই কর্ত্তৃক কর্ত্তিত জন্তুর ঠ্যাং। **8.** (Also *black-leg*) A swindler; জুয়ারী, ঠগ। **9.** One branch of a forked object; one limb of a compass; দ্বি-শাখ বস্তুর অন্যতর শাখা; বৃত্তাদি অঙ্কনের যন্ত্রের অন্যতম পদ। **10.** (*Archaic*) An obeisance; a bow; (অপ্রঃ) প্রণতি, প্রণিপাত; প্রণাম। **11.** A side of a triangle other than the base; ত্রিভুজের বাহু। **12.** An artificial leg; as, a cork or wooden *leg*; কৃত্রিম পদ। **13.** (*Naut.*) The run made by a vessel on a single tack; (নৌ-বিদ্যা) এক যাত্রায় জাহাজ যে পরিমাণ স্থান অতিক্রম করে। ***Verb i.*** To walk or run, (with *it*); হাঁটা, দৌড়া। ***Verb t.*** To propel, as a boat by means of legs; পা দ্বারা চালান। **Leg′-ged,** *adj.* Having legs; পদবিশিষ্ট। **Leg′-ger,** *n.* **Leg′-i-ness,** *n.* **Leg′-less,** *adj.* **Leg′-gy,** *adj.* Long-legged, lanky-legged, as a boy, colt, puppy, etc.; লম্বপদ, দীর্ঘপদ, ক্ষীণ-পদ। **Leg-guard**—জঙ্ঘাত্রাণ। **Leg-rest**—উপবিষ্ট রুগ্ন ব্যক্তির জন্য পাদপীঠ। **A leg-of-mutton sail, sleeve**—A sail or sleeve shaped like leg of mutton; কসাইর কাটা ভেড়ার পার মত আকৃতি বিশিষ্ট পাইল বা আস্তিন। **All legs** — Over-grown; অতি বর্দ্ধিত। **Good sea-legs**—Capacity of not being affected by sea-sickness; সমুদ্র-পীড়া দ্বারা আক্রান্ত না হওয়ার ক্ষমতা। **In high leg**—In great excitement; অতিশয় উত্তেজিত। **Leg before wicket**—(Abbr. *l. b. w.*) Illegal stopping of the cricket ball by a batsman's legs; ব্যাটধারী কর্ত্তৃক পা-দ্বারা অন্যায় মতে বল আটক করণ। **On one's last legs**—Near death or end; মরণোন্মুখ, মুমূর্ষু, পতনোন্মুখ, শেষ অবস্থায়। **On one's legs** or (*Jocul.*) **hind legs**—Standing to make speech: well enough to go about; in prosperous or established state; বক্তৃতা প্রদানের জন্য দণ্ডায়মান; বর্ত্তমানে বাহিরে যাইয়া বেড়াইতে পারে—এরূপ সুস্থ; সমৃদ্ধ অবস্থায়, সুপ্রতিষ্ঠিত। **To fall on one's legs**—To be fortunate or successful; সৌভাগ্যশালী হওয়া, কৃতকার্য্য হওয়া, সফলমনোরথ হওয়া। **To feel** or **find one's legs**—To get power of walking or standing; দাঁড়াইবার বা হাঁটিবার শক্তি লাভ করা। **To give a leg-bail**—To escape from custody; to decamp; পলায়ন করা; ভাগা, চম্পট দেওয়া, পিট্টান দেওয়া। **To give a leg to**—To assist by supporting the leg; to help; পায়ের ভর রাখিতে দিয়া সাহায্য করা; সাহায্য করা। **To give a leg up**—To assist in riding a horse by supporting the leg; পায়ের ভর রাখিতে দিয়া ঘোড়ায় চড়িতে সাহায্য করা। **To give one a leg up**—To help him to mount a horse or get over an obstacle material or immaterial; বাধা বিঘ্ন অতিক্রমে সাহায্য করা। **To have not a leg to stand on**—To be at the end of one's resources or strength; not to be able to support thesis by any facts or sound reason; দাঁড়াইবার স্থান না থাকা; যুক্তি তর্ক দ্বারা স্বীয় নিবন্ধ সমর্থনে অসমর্থ হওয়া। **To keep one's legs**—Not to fall; পতিত না হওয়া, না পড়া। **To make a leg** — (*Archaic*) To make a bow; প্রণাম করা। **To pull one's legs**—To befool him; বোকা সাজান। **To put one's best legs foremost** — To walk as fast as possible; খুব দ্রুত চলা। **To shake a leg**—To dance; নৃত্য করা। **To stand on one's own legs**—To be self-reliant or independent; আত্মনির্ভরশীল হওয়া, নিজের পায়ে ভর করিয়া দাঁড়ান, নিজের পায়ের উপর দাঁড়ান। **To stretch one's legs** — To take walking exercise; হাঁটিয়া বেড়ান, পায়চারি করা। **To walk one off his legs**—To tire him out in walking; হাঁটাইয়া হাঁটাইয়া হয়রান করা।

lĕg′-ă-çy̆, *n.* A gift of money or property by will; that which is left or bequeathed; a bequest; ইচ্ছাপত্রদ্বারা প্রদত্ত ধন, উইল ক্রমে দত্ত বস্তু বা ধন; পূর্ব্বপুরুষের মৃত্যুজনিত প্রাপ্ত সম্পত্তি; উত্তরাধিকার সূত্রে প্রাপ্ত সম্পত্তি, উত্তরদান (হিঃ কোঃ)। **Legacy-hunter**—যে ব্যক্তি তোষামোদ দ্বারা কাহারও অনুগ্রহ লাভ করিয়া ইচ্ছাপত্রে তাহার নামে কিছু লিখাইয়া লইতে চেষ্টা করে।

lē′-găl, *adj.* **1.** Of, relating to, or based on, law; included in law; as, *legal* authority; আইনসম্বন্ধীয় স্মার্ত্ত, বিধিমূলক, ব্যবহারিক; বিধিভুক্ত। **2.** Permitted by, or in conformity with, law; lawful; আইনানুমোদিত, স্মৃতিশাস্ত্রসম্মত, ব্যবহারবিধিসম্মত, ব্যবহারবিধিপ্রোক্ত, রাজ্যনিয়মানুমত, রাজ্যনিয়মসম্মত, বিধিসিদ্ধ, বৈধ; আইনসঙ্গত। **3.** Enforced, protected or recognized, by law distinguished from *equity*; বিধিশাস্ত্রবিহিত, ব্যবহারবিধিপ্রোক্ত, বিধিরক্ষিত। **4.** Required, or appointed, by law; বিবিশাস্ত্রবিহিত, বিধিনির্দ্দিষ্ট। **5.** (*Theol.*) Relating, or according, to the Mosaic law; of, or relating to, salvation by works, not faith; মুসার বিধানসম্বন্ধীয়, মুসার বিধানানুমোদিত; কর্ম্মমার্গী, কর্ম্মমার্গাশ্রয়ী, কর্ম্মমার্গাবলম্বী। **–i-za′-tion**, *n.* **–ize**, *v. t.* To make legal or lawful; বিধিসিদ্ধ বা আইনসঙ্গত করা, বৈধ করা, আইনানুমোদিত করা। **–ly**, *adv.* Lawfully; আইনানুযায়ী, আইনানুসারে, আইনতঃ। **Legal tender**—যে মুদ্রা দায়িকের নিকট হইতে মহাজন গ্রহণ করিতে বাধ্য।

lē′-găl-ĭsm, *n.* **1.** Strict adherence to law; বিধিপরায়ণতা, ব্যবস্থানুরক্তি, বিধিশাস্ত্রনিষ্ঠা। **2.** (*Theol.*) The doctrine of adhering to the law as opposed to the Gospel; the doctrine of justification by works; (খৃষ্টীয় ধর্ম্মশাস্ত্র) খৃষ্টীয় সুসমাচারের পরিবর্ত্তে মুসার বিধানের প্রতি আনুরক্তি; কর্ম্মযোগ। **3.** A disposition to exalt the importance of law or formula; সূত্র বা বিধির গুরুত্ব বৃদ্ধির জন্য প্রবণতা।

lē-găl′-ĭ-ty̆, *n.* **1.** State of being legal; lawfulness; স্মৃতিশাস্ত্রানুযায়িতা, ব্যবহারবিধানানুযায়িতা, ধর্ম্মশাস্ত্রানুসারিতা, বিধিসিদ্ধতা। **2.** (*Theol.*) Same as LEGALISM.

lē′-găl-ĭst, *n.* **1.** One who advocates strict conformity to law; কঠোর বিধিসঙ্গতভাবে চলিবার পক্ষপাতী। **2.** (*Theol.*) An advocate of legalism; কর্ম্মমার্গী।

lĕg′-āte, *n.* **1.** An ecclesiastic representing the Pope; পোপের প্রতিনিধি। **2.** (*Archaic*) An ambassador or delegate; (অপ্রঃ) রাজদূত, প্রতিনিধি। **–a-tive**, *adj.* Of, or pertaining to, a legate; দূতসম্পর্কীয়। **–ship**, *n.*

lē-gāte′, *v. t.* To bequeath; as, give and *legate*; ইচ্ছাপত্রদ্বারা দান করা। **–ga′-tor**, *n.*

lĕg-ā-tee′ (-tē), *n.* One to whom a legacy is bequeathed; অন্যের ইচ্ছাপত্রদ্বারা প্রাপ্তসম্পত্তির অধিকারী, উত্তরাধিকারী।

lē-gā′-tion, *n.* **1.** The sending of a person or persons as a legate or deputy; প্রতিনিধিস্বরূপ প্রেরণ, দূতপ্রেরণ বা নিয়োগ। **2.** A diplomatic minister and his suite; an embassy; বৈদেশিক রাজদূত এবং তদীয় সহচরগণ; দৌত্যকর্ম্ম। **3.** The official residence of a diplomatic minister; বৈদেশিক দূতাবাস। **4.** Legateship; পোপের প্রতিনিধিত্ব।

lē-gä′-tō, *adj.* & *adv.* (*A musical direction*) Smoothly connected; without breaks; কোমলভাবে সংযুক্ত; অভগ্ন।

lĕg′-ĕnd, *n.* **1.** (*Hist.*) A collection of the lives of saints or of similar stories; (ইতিহাস) খৃষ্টীয় সিদ্ধপুরুষদের জীবনী-সংগ্রহ। **2.** A story coming down from the past; a tradition; a myth; আখ্যান, উপাখ্যান, পুরাবৃত্ত, পুরাকাহিনী, পৌরাণিক আখ্যায়িকা, প্রাচীন গল্প, কথাপ্রবন্ধ; লোককথা, কিম্বদন্তী, উপকথা। **3.** An inscription or motto on a medal or coin or heraldic shield; কোন পদক বা মুদ্রার উপর বলয়াকারে উৎকীর্ণ লিপি বা সংক্ষিপ্ত বচন। **–ry**, *n.* Legends collectively; উপকথা সমূহ। **The Legend** or **golden Legend**—ত্রয়োদশ শতাব্দীতে রচিত সিদ্ধপুরুষ-জীবনীসংগ্রহ।

lĕg′-ĕnd-ă-ry̆, *adj.* & *n.* **1.** Pertaining to, or consisting of, legends; fabulous; mythical; উপকথাসম্বন্ধীয়, অনৈতিহাসিক (কৃত্রিমঃ); অবাস্তব, কাল্পনিক; পৌরাণিক। ***Noun.*** A writer of legends; উপন্যাস-লেখক।

lĕg′-ēr-dē-main (-mān), *n.* **1.** A sleight of hand; conjuring tricks; jugglery; হাতের কৌশল, হাতের চালাকি, হাতের সাফাই; ইন্দ্রজাল; ভোজবাজী, যাদুবিদ্যা। **2.** An artful deception or trick; sophistry; চালাকি, চাতুরী; কুতর্ক।

lĕg′-ging (-ĭng), *n.* (*Usu. pl.*) A covering of leather etc. for the leg, usually up to the knee; চর্ম্মাদি নির্ম্মিত পাদচ্ছদ, জঙ্ঘাত্রাণ।

lĕg′-hōrn, *n.* **1.** A plaiting of straw for hats and bonnets, [imported from Leghorn in Italy]; টুপি তৈরীর জন্য বুনট-করা খড়। **2.** A kind of domestic owl; একপ্রকার গৃহপালিকুক্কুট।

lĕg′-ĭ-ble (-bl), *adj.* (Said of handwriting or print) Capable of being easily read or deciphered; clear; সুখপাঠ্য, সুপাঠ্য, পঠনযোগ্য, পঠনশক্য; পরিষ্কার। **–bil′-i-ty**, *n* The state or quality of being legible; সুখপাঠ্যতা, সুপাঠ্যতা। **–bly**, *adv.* In a legible manner; clearly; সুপাঠ্যরূপে; পরিষ্কার রূপে।

lē′-gion (-jŏn), *n.* **1.** A body of soldiers among the ancien Romans in number from 3000 to

6000 ; প্রাচীন রোমের সৈন্যদল—যাহাতে ৩০০০ হইতে ৬০০০ পর্য্যন্ত যোদ্ধা থাকিত। **2.** A military force ; an army ; সেনাদল, সৈন্যদল ; চমূ, ফৌজ, বাহিনী, সৈন্য, সেনা। **3.** A vast host, multitude or number ; বহুসংখ্যা, সমূহ, ফৌজ, বৃন্দ, নিবহ। **—gioned,** *adj.* (*Poet.*) **Foreign legion** — A body of foreign volunteers esp. in the French army ; ফরাসী সৈন্য মধ্যে বিদেশী স্বেচ্ছাসেবক সৈন্য। **Legion of Honour**—ফরাসী দেশের সামরিক বা অন্য বিভাগে প্রশংসাজনক কার্য্যের জন্য প্রদত্ত উপাধি বিশেষ। ১৮০২ খৃঃ অব্দে নেপোলিয়নের সময় প্রবর্ত্তিত হয়। **Their name is Legion**—They are numberless (*Mark*) ; বহুসংখ্যক, অসংখ্য, অগণিত।

lē'-gion-ā-rȳ (-jŏn), *adj.* & *n.* Of, or relating to, a legion or legions ; রোমীয় বাহিনী সম্বন্ধীয়। ***Noun.*** A soldier of a legion ; রোমীয় বাহিনীভুক্ত ব্যক্তি।

lĕg'-is-lāte, *v. i.* To make or enact law or laws ; to bring forward laws ; ব্যবস্থাবিধান করা, ব্যবস্থাবদ্ধ করা, বিধিবদ্ধ করা ; আইন উপস্থাপিত করা। **—la'-tion,** *n.* Enactment of laws ; the laws enacted ; ব্যবস্থাবিধান, ব্যবস্থাপন, নিয়মনির্ম্মাণ (হিঃ কোঃ), নিয়মস্থাপনা, বিধিব্যবস্থা, বিধিস্থাপনা ; আইন, বিধিব্যবস্থা।

lĕg'-is-lā-tive (-tĭv), *adj.* Making, or having the power to make, a law or laws ; of, or pertaining to, the enacting of laws ; ব্যবস্থাপক, নিয়মস্থাপক, বিধিস্থাপক ; আইনপ্রণয়নসম্বন্ধীয়। **—ly,** *adv.*

lĕg'-is-lā-tor (-tĕr), *n.* A law-giver ; a member of a legislative body ; আইনপ্রণয়নকর্ত্তা, নিয়মস্থাপক, বিধিস্থাপক ; ব্যবস্থাপক সভার সভ্য। **—late,** *v.i.* To make or enact a law or laws ; আইনপ্রণয়ন করা, বিধিস্থাপন করা। **—tress,** *n.* (*Fem.*)

lĕg'-is-lā-tūre, *n.* The body of men invested with power to make and repeal laws ; ব্যবস্থাপক সভা।

lē'-gist, *n.* One skilled, or versed in law ; আইনজ্ঞ।

lē-git'-i-māte, *adj.* & *v. t.* **1.** Lawful ; proper ; regular ; conforming to a recognized standard ; "*Legitimate* delivery" : "*Legitimate* English classics" ; বিধিসঙ্গত, আইনানুমোদিত ; বিহিত, ন্যায্য, বৈধ, ধর্ম্ম্য ; নির্দ্দিষ্ট মানের অনুযায়ী। **2.** Born in lawful wedlock ; বিবাহিতা স্ত্রীর গর্ভজাত, ঔরসজাত, বিবাহজাত, ধর্ম্মপত্নীজ। **3.** Based upon a hereditary right, as a sovereign's title ; কৌলিক-অধিকারমূলক, পুরুষপরম্পরাগত অধিকার-মূলক। **4.** Reasonable ; logically admissible ; as, a *legitimate* reasoning or inference ; valid ; যুক্তিযুক্ত, যথান্যায়, ন্যায্য (হিঃ কোঃ), ধর্ম্ম্য (ঐ), যুক্তিসঙ্গত ; তর্কসিদ্ধ ; অখণ্ডনীয়। ***Verb t.*** **1.** To make legitimate by decree, enactment or proof ; বিধিসঙ্গত করা, বৈধ করা। **2.** To render as a bastard legitimate, by legal means ; জারজ সন্তানকে বৈধ উপায়ে ঔরসজাত পুত্রের অধিকার দেওয়া। **3.** To justify or serve as justification for ; ন্যায্যতা প্রতিপাদন করা। **—ly,** *adv.* In a legitimate manner ; বিধিসঙ্গতরূপে, বৈধভাবে, ন্যায্যরূপে। **—ma-cy,** *n.* **1.** The state or quality of being legitimate ; বৈধতা, বিধিসিদ্ধতা। **2.** The state of being born in wedlock ; বিশুদ্ধজন্মত্ব, বৈধজন্মতা, ধর্ম্মপত্নীজত্ব। **—ma'-tion,** *n.* The act of rendering legitimate ; বৈধকরণ। **—ma-tize,** *v. t.* To legitimate ; esp. to render legitimate as a bastard by legal means ; বিধিসঙ্গত করা, বৈধ করা, বিধিসিদ্ধ করা ; জারজ সন্তানকে বিধিসঙ্গত উপায়ে ঔরসজাত পুত্রের অধিকার প্রদান করা। **The legitimate drama**—শেক্ষপীয়র বা অন্য নাট্যকারের সর্ব্বজনসমাদৃত নাট্যসমূহ।

lē-git'-i-mism, *n.* The principles of legitimists; বৈধ অধিকার সমর্থননীতি।

lē-git'-i-mist, *n.* & *adj.* One who supports a sovereign or pretender whose claim is based on hereditary right ; যে ব্যক্তি রাজা বা রাজসিংহাসনপ্রার্থীর পুরুষপরম্পরাগত অধিকারমূলক দাবী সমর্থন করে, ন্যায্যাধিকার-সমর্থক। ***Adj.*** Of, or pertaining to, the legitimist ; ন্যায্যাধিকারসমর্থন-সম্পর্কীয়।

lē-git'-i-mīze, *v. t.* Same as LEGITIMATIZE which see under LEGITIMATE.

lĕg'-ūme, lē-gū'-mĕn, *ns.* **1.** A seed-vessel of two valves ; a pod ; দুই খোলায় বিভক্ত বীজকোষ বা শুঁটি ; শিম্বি, শুঁটি, খাঁড়া। **2.** The fruit or seed of a leguminous plant, as pulse, peas, beans, etc. ; শিম্বী, মটরশুঁটি। **3.** A vegetable used for food ; তরকারী, আনাজ।

lē-gū'-mi-nous (-nŭs), *adj.* Of, relating to, or like pulse ; bearing legumen or pods ; মটরকলাই সম্বন্ধীয়, মটরকলাইযুক্ত, দ্বিদলজাতীয়, দ্বিদলান্তর্গত ; বীজকোষপ্রসূ, শুঁটীধারী।

leis'-tĕr (lĕs-), *n.* & *v. t.* A pronged spear for striking salmon etc. ; মৎস্য মারিবার বর্শা, টেঁটা। ***Verb t.*** To spear (fish) with this ; বর্শাদ্বারা মৎস্য বিদ্ধ করা।

lei'-sūre (lē-), *n.* & *adj.* Freedom from occupation ; vacant time ; time at one's own disposal ; convenient opportunity ; অবকাশ, অবসর, বিশ্রাম ; ফুরসৎ (*colloq.*) ; অবসরকাল, অবসর সময় ; সুবিধা। ***Adj.*** Unemployed ; free ; as, *leisure* hours ; মুক্ত ; স্বাধীন। **—less,** *adj.* **—sured,** *adj.* Having leisure ; অবকাশযুক্ত। **At leisure**—*Adj.* & *adv.* Not occupied ; অবসর। (*Adv.*) Deliberately ; without hurry ; ভাবিয়া চিন্তিয়া ; তাড়াতাড়ি না করিয়া। **At one's leisure**—When one has time ; কাহারও অবকাশকালে, বিশ্রামের সময়ে, অবসর মত। **To wait one's leisure**—To wait till he has leisure ; কেহ অবসর না হওয়া পর্য্যন্ত অপেক্ষা করা।

lei′-süre-lў (lē-), *adj.* & *adv.* Having leisure; acting, or done at leisure; not hurried; deliberate; অবসরযুক্ত, সাবকাশ; অবসরকালে কৃত; অত্বরিত, অক্ষিপ্র, অশীঘ্র; সুচিন্তিত। ***Adv.*** Deliberately; without haste; ভাবিয়া চিন্তিয়া, ধীরে সুস্থে, মন্দ মন্দ, শনৈঃ শনৈঃ; তাড়াতাড়ি না করিয়া, তাড়াহুড়া না করিয়া। **–li-ness,** *n.*

leit-motif, *n.* (*Mus.*) A theme or passage associated with a certain person, situation or sentiment; (সঙ্গীত-শাস্ত্র) কোন ব্যক্তি, অবস্থা বা ভাবের সহিত সম্পৃক্ত বিষয় বা গ্রন্থাংশ।

lĕm′-ăn, *n.* **1.** (*Archaic*) A lover either male or female; a paramour; প্রণয়িনী, প্রণয়ী; জার, উপপতি, লাং (*slang*)। **2.** (*In later use*) An unlawful mistress; উপপত্নী।

lĕm′-mă, *n.* (*Pl.* -MATA) **1.** An assumed or demonstrated proposition used in argument or proof; পূর্ব্বগৃহীতসিদ্ধান্ত, উপপ্রতিজ্ঞা (হিঃ কোঃ), অবলম্বন (হিঃ কোঃ)। **2.** The argument or subject of a composition, annotation, etc., prefixed as heading; শীর্ষ-লিপি স্বরূপ পূর্ব্বে সন্নিবিষ্ট রচনা, টীকা প্রভৃতির সংক্ষিপ্ত সার। **3.** A motto appended to a picture etc.; আলেখ্যাদির নিম্নে সংযোজিত ক্ষুদ্র সারবান বাক্য।

lĕm′-ming (-ĭng), *n.* A small arctic rodent; উত্তর মহাসাগরের সন্নিকটপ্রদেশবাসী মূষিক বিশেষ।

Lemming.

lĕm′-nă, *n.* A very small genus of aquatic herbs; গুঁড়ি পানা।

lĕm′-ŏn, *n.* **1.** An acid fruit resembling the orange; গোড়া লেবু, জম্বীর, জম্বীরফল, নিম্ব (মঃ উঃ) নিম্বক। **2.** The tree bearing this fruit; লেবু গাছ। **3.** A pale-yellow colour; পাকা লেবুর রঙ্গ, মলিন পীতবর্ণ। **–ade′,** *n.* A beverage, usually aerated, consisting of lemon-juice mixed with water and sweetened; লেবুর রস বা লেবুর তৈল দ্বারা সুবাসিত কার্ব্বনিক এসিড বাষ্প সম্পূরিত পানীয় বিশেষ, মিঠাপানি, লেমনেড, নিম্বকফলপানক (ভাবঃ প্রঃ), নিম্বুপানক, জম্বীরজল (আঃ বঃ)। **–y,** *adj.* Having a lemon flavour; লেবুর গন্ধযুক্ত, নিম্বকগন্ধী। **Lemon-drop**—Sugar-plum flavoured with lemon; লেবু দ্বারা সুবাসিত চিনির মিঠাই বিশেষ। **Lemon-grass** — গন্ধবেণা, গন্ধতৃণ, (এই ঘাসের গন্ধ লেবুর মত)। **Lemon kali**—সোডা, তিন্তীড়িকাম্ল (Tartaric acid) ও জলের সংমিশ্রণে প্রস্তুত বুদ্বুদায়মান পানীয় বিশেষ। **Lemon-plant** — জম্বীরগন্ধী চারু তরুবিশেষ। **Lemon-squash**—লেবুর রস ও বিলাতি পানি (Soda water) সংমিশ্রণে প্রস্তুত পানীয়বিশেষ। **Lemon-squeezer**—লেবুর রস বাহির করিবার চাপকলবিশেষ। **Lemon-yellow**—পাকা লেবুর রং।

lĕm′-ŏn, *n.* (Usu. *Lemon-dale Lemon-sole*) A kind of flat fish; একপ্রকার চ্যাপ্টা মাছ।

lē′-mur (-mêr), *n.* A nocturnal mammal, esp. of Madagascar, allied to monkeys, but having a pointed muzzle; বানরজাতীয় নিশাচর জন্তু-বিশেষ। **Lem′-u-rine, Lem′-u-roid,** *adjs.* Like, or pertaining to, the lemurs; উক্ত জন্তু সদৃশ, উক্ত জন্তু সম্বন্ধীয়।

lĕnd, *v. t.* **1.** To grant the temporary use of something on condition of the return of the same or its equivalent; as, to *lend* a book, flour, etc.; অল্পকালের জন্য ব্যবহার করিতে দেওয়া, ধার দেওয়া, কর্জ্জ দেওয়া। **2.** To bestow; to contribute; as, to *lend* aid or assistance; প্রদান করা, দেওয়া; অর্পণ করা। **3.** To let out at interest, as money; (of libraries) to let out (books) for hire; সুদে ধার দেওয়া; (পুস্তকালয় সম্পর্কে) চাঁদা লইয়া পুস্তক দেওয়া। **4.** To accommodate (one-self or itself) to; as, he *lends* himself to illusory hopes; ঢালিয়া দেওয়া, উপযোগী করে। **Lend′-a-ble,** *adj.* **Lend′-er,** *n.* One who lends; উত্তমর্ণ, ঋণদাতা, মহাজন **Lend′-ing,** *n.* The act of giving in loan; ঋণদান, কর্জ্জদেওন। **Lending library**—যে পুস্তকালয় হইতে চাঁদাদাতাদিগকে বাড়ীতে পাঠ করিবার জন্য পুস্তক দেওয়া হয়। **A thing lends itself to**—It is serviceable for; কার্য্যোপযোগী। **To lend ear, To lend an ear, To lend one's ears**—To listen; কর্ণপাত করা, মনোযোগপূর্ব্বক শুনা। **To lend a hand** or **helping hand** — To assist or help; সাহায্য করা।

lĕngth, *n.* The longest measure of any object in distinction from breadth and thickness from end to end; দৈর্ঘ্য, দীর্ঘতা। **2.** Extent in space or time; duration from a beginning to an end; as, the *length* of a speech; বিস্তার; স্থিতিকাল। **3.** The distance to which a thing extends; as, at arm's *length*; (কোন বস্তুর) বিস্তৃতি, আয়তি। **4.** Detail; degree; as, he will not go to the *length* of asserting; খুঁটিনাটি; মাত্রা। **5.** (*Prosody*) The time occupied in uttering a vowel or syllable; the quality of a vowel as long or short; স্বরবর্ণ বা শব্দাংশ উচ্চারণ করিতে যে সময় লাগে; স্বরবর্ণের দীর্ঘতা বা হ্রস্বতা। **6.** (*Cricket*) The distance for a bowled ball to go before it hits the ground; (ক্রীকেট ক্রীড়ায়) ভূমিতে প্রতিহত হইবার পূর্ব্বে নিক্ষিপ্ত কন্দুক যতটা স্থান অতিক্রম করে। **7.** A piece of cloth etc. of a certain length ; নির্দ্দিষ্ট দৈর্ঘ্যের বস্ত্রখণ্ড। 8. A long stretch or extent ; "He brandishes his pliant *length* of whip" ; দীর্ঘপ্রসর, পাল্লা। **Length'-ways**, *adv.* Lengthwise ; দৈর্ঘ্যে। **Length'-wise**, *adv.* & *adj.* In the direction of the length ; লম্বালম্বি। **At arm's length**—As far away as an arm can reach ; বাহু যতদূর ছড়ান যায় ততদূরে। **At full, great** or **some length** — In detail ; সবিস্তারে। **At full length**—In detail ; সবিস্তারে। Lying with the body fully extended ; শরীর যতদূর সম্ভব ছড়াইয়া শায়িত। **At length**—In detail ; without curtailment ; সবিস্তারে ; সংক্ষেপ না করিয়া। At the end or conclusion ; after a long period ; পরিশেষে, অবশেষে, উপসংহারে ; বহুকাল পরে, বহুদিন পর। **To go to great lengths, To go to all lengths** — To use extreme efforts ; প্রাণপণ চেষ্টা করা। **To go to the length of**—To proceed so far as ; এতদূর পর্য্যন্ত অগ্রসর হওয়া যে। **To keep one at arm's length** — To avoid intimacy with him ; কাহারও সহিত ঘনিষ্ঠতা না করা, কাহাকেও দূরে রাখা।

lĕngth'-en (-n), *v. t.* & *i.* 1. To make longer in extent or duration ; বর্দ্ধিত করা, লম্বা করা। 2. To make long as a vowel ; দীর্ঘ করা *Verb i.* To become longer ; দীর্ঘতর হওয়া, বর্দ্ধিত হওয়া।

lĕngth'-ÿ, *adj.* Not brief or short ; rather too long ; prolix ; tedious ; as, a *lengthy* speech, writing, style, speaker, etc. ; লম্বা ; সুদীর্ঘ ; বাগ্বহুল ; বিরক্তিকর। **—i-ly**, *adv.* In a lengthy manner ; বহুবিস্তৃতরূপে, সবিস্তারে। **—i-ness**, *n.*

lē'-ni-ĕnt, *adj.* 1. Not rigorous or severe ; gentle ; clement ; tolerant ; অকঠোর ; মৃদু, কোমল, সৌম্য, অনুগ্র ; দয়াশীল, সদয় ; অনুগ্রহপরায়ণ। 2. (*Archaic*) Assuasive ; softening ; প্রশামক ; মৃদুতাজনক। **—ence, —en-cy**, *ns.* The quality or state of being lenient ; clemency ; মৃদুতা, অকঠোরতা, শমক, উপশমক ; সদয়ভাব, দয়ার্দ্রভাব। **—ly**, *adv.*

lĕn'-i-tive (-tîv-), *adj.* & *n.* Assuasive ; soothing, as a drug, appliance, etc. ; প্রশামক ; স্নিগ্ধকারক, প্রদাহপ্রশামক। *Noun.* 1. A lenitive medicine or appliance ; যন্ত্রণানিবারক ঔষধ, প্রদাহনিবারক ঔষধ। 2. A palliative ; উপশামক। **—ness**, *n.*

lĕn'-i-tÿ, *n.* Gentleness ; mildness ; mercifulness ; a merciful or lenient act ; নম্রতা, মৃদুতা, অপরুষত্ব ; কোমলতা, মৃদুতা ; দয়া, কৃপাপরায়ণতা ; দয়ার কার্য্য।

lē'-nō, *n.* A kind of cotton used for window curtains, caps, etc. ; জানালার পর্দ্দা প্রভৃতির জন্য একপ্রকার সূক্ষ্ম কার্পাস বস্ত্র।

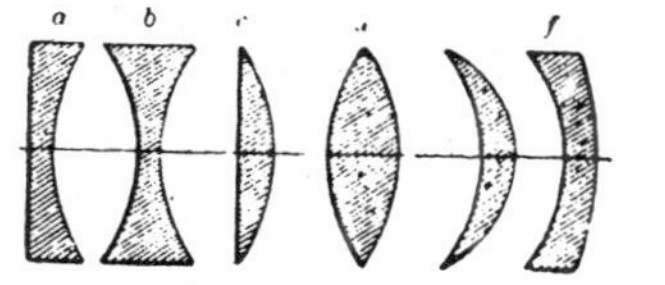

Lenses.

a, Plano-concave ; *b*, Double-concave ; *c*, Plano-convex ; *d*, Double-convex ; *e*, Meniscus ; *f*, Concavo-convex.

lĕns, *n.* (*Pl.* LENSES) 1. A transparent substance, usually glass with both sides curved or one side curved and one flat for concentrating or dispersing light-rays ; যে কাচখণ্ডের এক বা উভয় পার্শ্ব মধ্যোন্নত থাকে এবং যৎসাহায্যে আলোকরশ্মিসমূহ কেন্দ্রীভূত কিম্বা বিকেন্দ্রীভূত করা যায়, তাল (হিঃ কোঃ), বীক্ষণকাচ (আঃ বঃ), কাচপুটক, পরকলা। 2. A combination of lenses used in photography ; আলোকচিত্র গ্রহণে ব্যবহৃত কাচপুটক শ্রেণী। 3. The crystalline lens (see under CRYSTALLINE). **Lensed**, *adj.* **Lens'-less**, *adj.* **Concave lens** — নতোদর লেন্স (হিঃ কোঃ)। **Convex-lens**—উন্নতোদর লেন্স (হিঃ কোঃ)। **Crossed lens**-দ্বয়োন্নতোদরতাল (হিঃ কোঃ)। **Multiplying lens**—বহুচিত্রতাল (হিঃ কোঃ)। **Aperture of a lens**—লেন্সব্যাস (হিঃ কোঃ)।

lĕnt, *n.* 1. An annual feast and penitence of forty days from Ash-Wednesday till Easter in commemoration of the forty days' fast by Christ in the wilderness ; খৃষ্টীয় ধর্ম্ম-সংঘে ঈষ্টার পর্ব্বের পূর্ব্ববর্ত্তী উপবাসকাল। [Irenaens এর সময় ঈষ্টার পর্ব্বের পূর্ব্বে চল্লিশ ঘণ্টাকাল উপবাসব্রত পালন করা হইত। খৃষ্টীয় তৃতীয় শতাব্দীতে Alexandriaতে খৃষ্টানগণ ঈষ্টারপর্ব্বের পূর্ববর্ত্তী সারা সপ্তাহ উপবাস করিতেন। খৃষ্টীয় চতুর্থ শতাব্দীতে এই উপবাসকাল বৃদ্ধি হইয়া চল্লিশদিবসব্যাপী হয়।] 2. (*Pl.*, At Cambridge) The boat-races in lent ; লেণ্ট পর্ব্বের সময়ের বাইচ খেলা। **Lent-lily**—The daffodil ; ইংলণ্ডদেশীয় পীতবর্ণ পুষ্পবিশেষ। **Lent-term**—বিশ্ববিদ্যালয়ের যে দুইটী দীর্ঘ বন্ধের মধ্যবর্ত্তীকালে lent পর্ব্ব পড়ে।

lĕnt, *p. t.* & *p. p.* of LEND.

lĕnt'-ĕn, *adj.* 1. Of, or pertaining to, the fast called lent ; suitable to, or used in, lent ; খৃষ্টের চল্লিশদিবস ব্যাপী উপবাসসম্বন্ধীয় ; ঐ উপবাসোপযোগী, ঐ উপবাসে ব্যবহৃত। 2. Sparing ; meagre ; dismal ; as, *lenten* diet ; অপ্রচুর ; সামান্য, যৎকিঞ্চিৎ, আড়ম্বরশূন্য ; নিরানন্দজনক। **Lenten-face** — Dismal look ; অপ্রসন্নদৃষ্টি, বিরস বদন। **Lenten-fare**—মাংসবিহীন ভোজন।

lĕn-tic'-ū-lar (-lĕr), *adj.* 1. Resembling a lentil or lens in shape ; double convex ; মসূরাকৃতি, মসূরাকার, কাচপটকাকৃতি ; দ্বিবহির্বর্ত্তুল, দ্বিনুব্জ। 2. Of, or relating to, the lens of the eye ; অক্ষিমুকুরবৎ।

lĕn'-til, *n.* A leguminous plant or its seed grown for food ; মসূর, মঙ্গল্যক (ভাবঃ প্রঃ), ব্রীহিকাঞ্চন (অঃ)।

lĕn′-tisk, *n.* The mastic tree; রুমিমস্তকীর গাছ।

lĕn′-ti-tūde, *n.* Sluggishness; ঢিলামি, কর্ম্মকুণ্ঠতা, মান্দ্য, জড়তা।

lĕn′-toid (-toyd), *adj.* Lens-shaped; কাচপুটকাকার।

Lē′-ō, *n.* The Lion; the fifth sign of the Zodiac; সিংহরাশি; রাশিচক্রের পঞ্চম রাশি।

Lē′-ō-nid, *n.* One of the meteors which seem to radiate from the constellation Lion; সিংহ রাশি হইতে বিকীর্য্যমান বলিয়া প্রতীয়মান উল্কা রাশির অন্যতম।

lē′-ō-nīne, *adj.* Relating to, or characteristic of, a lion; lion-like; সিংহসম্বন্ধীয়, সিংহধর্ম্মক; সিংহবৎ, সিংহসদৃশ, মৃগেন্দ্রবৎ।

Lē′-ō-nīne, *adj.* & *n.* Of, relating to, or made by, a person named Leo (one of the fifteen popes so called); Leo নামধেয় ব্যক্তি সম্পর্কীয় বা তৎকৃত। ***Noun.*** A Leonine line or verse: (See below.) **Leonine City**—রোমের যে অংশে পোপের প্রাসাদ Vatican অবস্থিত আছে **Leonine verse**—মধ্যযুগের লাটিন কবিতার পংক্তি-বিশেষ—যাহাতে পংক্তির অন্ত্যভাগের সহিত মধ্যভাগের মিল থাকে।

leop′-ărd (lĕp-), *n.* A large carnivorous animal with a spotted skin; the panther: চিতাবাঘ, চিত্রক, উপব্যাঘ্র; চিতা। **2.** (*Her.*) A lion passant guardant as in arms of England; (কুল-বিদ্যা) বর্ম্মাদিতে অঙ্কিত ভ্রমনশীল এবং চিত্রব্যাঘ্রের মত চতুর্দ্দিকে পরিভ্রমণ-কারী সিংহ। **3.** (*Attri.*) Spotted like

Leopard.

the leopard; as, the *leopard* cat, frog, etc.; চিতাবাঘের মত চিত্রবিচিত্রিত, ফুটফুট দাগ বিশিষ্ট। **—ess,** *n.* (*Fem.*) **Black leopard**—চিতাবাঘ। **Hunting leopard**—চিতা। **Can the leopard change his spots**—One's character persists; স্বভাব যায় না ম'লে ইজ্জত যায় না ধু'লে।

lĕp′-ēr, *n.* A person affected with leprosy; কুষ্ঠরোগী, কুষ্ঠী, কুষ্ঠপীড়িত ব্যক্তি। **Leper asylum**—কুষ্ঠাশ্রম, কুষ্ঠনিবাস।

lĕp-i-dŏp′-tēr-ă, *n.* (*Pl.*) The order of insects including butterflies and moths; শল্কপক্ষক ষট্পদ পতঙ্গ জাতি, সরেণুপত্রী (সাঃ পঃ)। **—ist,** *n.* One who studies the lepidoptera: সরেণুপাত্রতত্ত্বানুসন্ধায়ী। **—ous,** *adj.* Relating to this order; ঐ প্রকার পতঙ্গবর্গসম্বন্ধীয়।

lĕp-i-dō-sau′-ri-ăn (-sä-), *n.* (*Zool.*) Squamata (order of reptiles); অপদী (সাঃ পঃ)।

Lepidosiren.

lĕ-pi-dō sī′-rĕn, *n.* One of the Amazon mud-fishes; এক জাতীয় মৎস্য।

lĕp-i-dō′-tŭs, *n.* A genus of fishes; শল্কময় (সাঃ পঃ)।

lĕp′-rō-sȳ, *n.* **1.** A foul cutaneous disease characterized by dusky red or livid tubercles on the face and extremities; কুষ্ঠ রোগ, মহাব্যাধি, মহারোগ, পাপরোগ। **2.** Moral corruption or contagion; "Idleness is a moral *leprosy*"; নীতিদুষ্টতা, দুর্নীতির সংক্রামক বীজ, পাপরোগ। **White leprosy**—শ্বেত কুষ্ঠ, শ্বিত্র।

lĕp′-rous (-rŭs), *adj.* Relating to, or like, leprosy; infected with leprosy; কুষ্ঠব্যাধিসম্বন্ধীয়, কুষ্ঠরোগসদৃশ; কুষ্ঠরোগাক্রান্ত, কুষ্ঠী।

lĕp-tō-dăc′-tyl, *n.* & *adj.* A bird having long slender toes; দীর্ঘ এবং ক্ষীণাঙ্গুলিবিশিষ্ট পক্ষী। ***Adj.*** With long slender toes; ক্ষুদ্র এবং কোমল অঙ্গুলিবিশিষ্ট।

Leptoptilos Javanica—চন্দনা (বেলঃ), চান্দিয়ারী (ঐ), মদনচোর (ঐ), মদনটিকী (ঐ)।

Lepus Indicus—খরগোশ (বেলঃ)।

Lĕs′-bi-ăn, *adj.* Of, or relating to, Lesbos, an island of the Grecian Archipelego; গ্রীসীয় দ্বীপপুঞ্জের অন্তর্গত লেস্‌বস্ নামক দ্বীপ-সম্বন্ধীয়। **Lesbian-vice**—Same as SAPPHISM (which see.)

lese—măj′-ĕs-tȳ (lēz-), (*Fr., lese majesty*), *n.* (*Civil law*) Treason; রাজদ্রোহমূলক অপরাধ, রাজাপমান (হিঃ কোঃ)।

lē′-sion, *n.* **1.** A wound; injury; damage; আঘাত, ক্ষত; ক্ষতি, হানি; অনিষ্ট, অপকার। **2.** A morbid change in the exercise of functions or texture of organs; শারীরিক যন্ত্রাদির বিকৃতি।

lĕss, *adj., prep., n.* & *adv.* (Serves as comparative of LITTLE) **1.** Smaller, (opp. to *greater*); ক্ষুদ্রতর, অল্পতর, তত বৃহৎ নয়। **2.** Of small quantity or amount; not so much, (opp. to *more*); অল্প; কম। **3.** Of lower station or rank (*rare except in—No less a person than*: *James the Less*); নিম্নতর পদবীর, নিম্নপদস্থ। ***Prep.*** Subtracting or deducting; as, 10 *less* 4; বাদ, বিয়োগ। ***Noun.*** A smaller amount, quantity or number; as, cannot take *less*: in *less* than no time (*i. e.* very quickly): অল্পতর পরিমাণ বা সংখ্যা। ***Adv.*** In a smaller or lower degree; to a smaller extent; (often *none the less*: *no less*: *not the less*); অল্পতর মাত্রায়; অল্পতর পরিমাণে। **In less than no time**—(*Jocul.*) Very quickly; soon; চক্ষুর পলকে; নিমেষে, দেখিতে দেখিতে। **May your shadows**

never be less — May you not grow thin ; ঈশ্বর করুণ তোমার শরীরটী যেন শীর্ণ না হয়। **Nothing less**—See NOTHING. **To expect nothing less than an attack**—To expect no attack at all, (here *less, adv.*) ; কোনরূপ আক্রমণের প্রত্যাশা না করা। To expect an attack and no milder procedure, (here *less noun.*) ; আক্রমণ অপেক্ষা কম কিছুর প্রত্যাশা না করা।

lĕs-see′ (-sē), *n.* One who is granted or holds a lease ; পাট্টাদার, পাট্টাগ্রহীতা, যে ব্যক্তি পাট্টা করিয়া লয়। **—ship,** *n.*

lĕss′-en (-n), *v. t.* & *i.* To make less ; to diminish ; অল্পতর করা, ন্যূন করা ; হ্রাস করা, হীন করা। ***Verb i.*** To become less ; to decrease ; অল্পতর হওয়া, হ্রাস হওয়া, ন্যূন হওয়া ; কমা, সঙ্কুচিত হওয়া।

lĕs′-son (-n), *n.* & *v. t.* **1.** A portion of a book etc. to be learnt by a pupil ; পাঠ, পড়া, পাঠনা, ছাত্রের দৈনিক পাঠ, নিপাঠ। **2.** That which is learnt or taught at one time ; the time assigned to it ; (*pl.*) systematic instruction in a subject ; as, to take or give *lessons* in history ; যাহা একবারে পঠিত বা শিক্ষাদান হয় ; ঐরূপ পঠন বা পাঠনে যে সময় লাগে ; কোন বিষয়ে প্রণালীবদ্ধ ভাবে শিক্ষাদান। **3.** A portion of Scripture appointed to be read in divine service ; উপাসনাকালে পঠিতব্য ধর্ম্ম-গ্রন্থাংশ। **4.** An occurrence or example serving as an encouragement or warning ; "He (Christ) is also their *lesson*" ; শিক্ষার স্থল। **5.** Reproof ; rebuke ; তিরস্কার ; ভৎসনা, গঞ্জনা। ***Verb t.*** To teach ; to give a lesson to ; to admonish or rebuke ; শিক্ষা দেওয়া ; পাঠ দেওয়া ; তিরস্কার করা, ভৎসনা করা।

lĕs′-sŏr, *n.* A person who gives a lease ; যে ব্যক্তি ইজারা বা পত্তনি দেয়, যে ব্যক্তি পাট্টা করিয়া দেয়, পট্টদাতা।

lĕst, *conj.* That—not ; for fear that ; in order that—not ; এই আশঙ্কায়, অন্যথায় ; পাছে, কি না জানি ; যদি না।

lĕt, *v. t., i. aux.* & *n.* **1.** To permit to ; to allow to ; as, to *let* him go ; to cause to ; as, *let* him know ; ক্ষমতা বা স্বাধীনতা দেওয়া ; কোন কাজ করিতে বাধা না দেওয়া ; দেওয়া। **2.** To make escape ; as, to *let* liquid, air or blood ; রন্ধ্রপথে নির্গত হইতে দেওয়া, ছিদ্রপথে বহির্গত হইতে দেওয়া। **3.** To grant possession and use of for rent or hire ; ভাড়া দেওয়া। ***Verb i.*** To be leased or let ; as, the rooms *let* well ; ভাড়া দেওয়া। ***Aux.*** Used imperatively with 1st and 3rd persons in exhortations, commands, assumptions and permissions ; as, *let* us pray : *let* him do it at once : *let* ABC be a triangle : *let* him do as he likes ; অনুজ্ঞা, উপদেশ, অনুমতিতে উত্তম পুরুষ ও প্রথম পুরুষে ব্যবহৃত হয়। ***Noun.*** A letting for hire or rent ; ভাড়া দেওন। **Let down**—*n.* Disappointment ; নৈরাশ্য, মনোভঙ্গ। Something undesirable (esp. in cricket not being caught etc. when there is a chance) ; অপ্রিয় বিষয় (বিশেষতঃ ক্রীকেট ক্রীড়ার বল লুফার সুযোগ স্বত্ত্বেও বিফল চেষ্টা)। **Let off**—*n.* State of being allowed to escape ; মুক্তি। **A house to let**—One offered for rent ; ভাড়া দেওয়া যাইবে। **Let alone**—(*Imperative*) Not to mention, much less or more ; রেখে দাও, দূরে থাক। **Let alone to do**—He may be trusted to do ; তাহার হস্তে এই কার্য্যের ভার ন্যস্ত করা যাইতে পারে। **Let be**—No matter ; থাকুক। **Let him down gently**—Avoid humiliating him abruptly ; তাহাকে কর্কশ ভাবে অপমান করিও না। **To let alone** — To refrain from interfering with ; to leave ; হস্তক্ষেপ না করা, যে অবস্থায় আছে সেই অবস্থায় থাকিতে দেওয়া, না ঘাঁটান ; ছাড়িয়া দেওয়া, ত্যাগ করা। **To let be**—Not to interfere with ; not to attend to or do ; as, *let* me *be* : *let* it *be* ; হস্তক্ষেপ না করা ; কোন বিষয়ের প্রতি দৃষ্টি না করা, কোন কিছু না করা। **To let blood**—To open a vein and suffer the blood to flow ; রক্তমোক্ষণ করা। **To let down**—To lower ; to disappoint ; নামাইয়া দেওয়া ; নিরাশ করা। **To let fall**—To drop intentionally or by accident, (*lit.* & *fig.*) ; ইচ্ছাপূর্ব্বক ফেলিয়া দেওয়া বা অকস্মাৎ ফেলিয়া দেওয়া, বলিয়া ফেলা, মুখ হইতে হঠাৎ বাহির করিয়া ফেলা। (*Geom.*) To draw as a perpendicular from an outside point on or upon a line ; বহিঃস্থিত বিন্দু হইতে কোন রেখার উপর লম্ব টানা। **To let fly** or **drive**—To discharge forcibly as a missile etc. ; to aim a blow ; মোচন করা, নিক্ষেপ করা, ছোড়া ; সন্ধান করা। **To let go**—To release ; to set at liberty ; to lose or relinquish hold of ; "If once the heart *lets go* of the faith" ; to dismiss from thought ; to cease to restrain ; মুক্তি দেওয়া ; ছাড়িয়া দেওয়া ; ঢিল দেওয়া, শিথিল করা ; মন হইতে দূর করা ; যথেচ্ছভাবে চলিতে দেওয়া। **To let go of anything**—See TO LET GO. **To let in**—To allow to enter ; to admit or open door to ; to insert into the surface of something ; প্রবেশ করিতে দেওয়া ; প্রবিষ্ট করা, দ্বার খুলিয়া প্রবেশ করিতে দেওয়া ; বসান। **To let into**—*v. t.* & *i.* To admit to ; to insert into the surface of ; প্রবেশ করিতে দেওয়া ; বসান, ঢুকান। To make acquainted with (secret etc.) ; গোপনীয় কথা বা রহস্য অবগত করান। (*Verb i.*) To assail with blow or words ; পিটুনি দেওয়া, বাক্যবাণে বিদ্ধ

করা। **To Let loose**—To set free; to unchain, as a dog etc.; মুক্ত করা ছাড়িয়া দেওয়া; শৃঙ্খলমুক্ত করা, শিকল খুলে দেওয়া। **To let loose on**—To set on; to allow to fall upon; লেলিয়ে দেওয়া; আপতিত হইতে দেওয়া। **To let off**—To allow to escape or pass away as a fluid, fumes, etc.; পলাইতে দেওয়া, নির্গত হইতে দেওয়া, নিঃসৃত হইতে দেওয়া। Not to punish or compel; to let go *with* light punishment; বিনাদণ্ডে ছাড়িয়া দেওয়া, বাধ্য না করা; সামান্য কিছু শাস্তি দিয়া ছাড়িয়া দেওয়া। To discharge as an arrow, joke, etc.; to fire, as a gun; ছোঁড়া, নিক্ষেপ করা; আওয়াজ করা। To excuse as from punishment, payment, etc.; as, *let him off* the penalty; রেহাই দেওয়া, নিষ্কৃতি দেওয়া। **To let on**—(*Slang*) To peach; to reveal secret; (ইতরভাষায়) সহাপরাধীর বিরুদ্ধে গোপনে সংবাদ দেওয়া; গুপ্তকথা প্রকাশ করা। (*Slang*) To pretend; ভাণ করা। **To let one alone to do**—He may be trusted to do; তাহার হস্তে কার্য্যের ভার ন্যস্ত করা যাইতে পারে। **To let one have one's head**—See under HEAD. **To let one in**—To involve in loss or difficulty; বিপদে জড়িত করা, ক্ষতিগ্রস্ত করা। **To let oneself go**—To yield to enthusiasm, impulse, etc.; আবেগ, উৎসাহ প্রভৃতিতে. গা ঢালিয়া দেওয়া। **To let out**—*v. t.* & *i.* To open door for exit to; to allow (person) to escape; to divulge; বাহির হইতে দেওয়ার জন্য দরজা খোলা; পলাইতে দেওয়া; প্রকাশ করা, ব্যক্ত করা। To put out to hire; ভাড়ার জন্য দেওয়া। To loosen as garment etc.; ঢিলা করা। (*Verb i.*) To strike out with the fist; to lash out with heels; to use strong language; ঘুষি মারা, কিল মারা; পদাঘাত করা; কড়া কথা শুনান। **To let slide**—To allow to pass unnoticed; অলক্ষিতে বা অজ্ঞাতসারে চলিয়া যাইতে দেওয়া। **To let slip**—To loose from lash; to miss, as an opportunity etc.; গলবন্ধনী খুলিয়া ছাড়িয়া দেওয়া; সুবিধা হারান। **To let the cat out of the bag**—See under CAT. **To let well alone**—Not to interfere where everything is already satisfatory; যেমনটী আছে তেমনটী থাকিতে দেওয়া।

lĕt, *v. t.* & *n.* **1.** (*Archaic*) To hinder; to impede; (অপ্রঃ) বাধা দেওয়া; গতিরোধ করা, বিঘ্ন জন্মান। ***Noun.*** **1.** (*Archaic*) A hindrance; an obstacle; (অপ্রঃ) বাধা, প্রতিবন্ধক; বিঘ্ন, অন্তরায়। **2.** (*Rackets* etc.) Obstruction of a ball in certain ways requiring it to be served again; কোন কোন নির্দ্দিষ্ট কন্দুক প্রতিরোধ।

lē′-thăl, *adj.* Mortal; causing or sufficient to cause death; fatal; মারাত্মক, প্রাণনাশক, প্রাণহারক; প্রাণহর, মৃত্যুজনক; সাংঘাতিক। **Lethal chamber** — যন্ত্রণা না দিয়া পশুবধ করার জন্য কক্ষ, নির্বেদন বধকক্ষ।

lĕth′-âr-ġy̆, *n.* **1.** Morbid drowsiness; profound unnatural slumber; নিদ্রালসতা, তন্দ্রা, নিদ্রালুতা, তন্দ্রালুতা; অস্বাভাবিক নিদ্রাচ্ছন্নতা। **2.** Inert or apathetic state; dullness; want of interest and energy; অবসাদ; জড়তা, জাড্য; নিশ্চেষ্টতা, আলস্য। **–gic, –gi-cal,** *adjs.* **–gi-cal-ly,** *adv.*

lĕth′-âr-ġize, *v. t.* To make lethargic; নিদ্রাপরবশ করা, অবসাদগ্রস্ত করা, জড় করা, নিদ্রালস করা. নিশ্চেষ্ট করা, তন্দ্রালস করা।

Lē′-thē, *n.* **1.** A river of Hades whose waters, when drunk, caused forgetfulness of the past; গ্রীক-পুরাণোক্ত নরকরাজ্যের নদী বিশেষ—ইহার জলপানে পূর্ব্বস্মৃতি বিলুপ্ত হইত। **2.** Oblivion; forgetfulness; বিস্মরণ; বিস্মৃতি। **–the′-an,** *adj.* Of, or relating to, Lethe; inducing forgetfulness or oblivion; উক্ত নদী সম্বন্ধীয়; বিস্মৃতিজনক, বিস্মারক, স্মৃতি-লোপকর, স্মৃতিহারক।

lē′-thē-ŏn, *n.* Sulphuric ether used as an anæsthetic; এক-প্রকার স্পর্শবোধ লোপকর ঔষধ।

Lē′-tō, Lă-tō′-nă, *n.* The daughter of Coeus, the Titan, and Phœbe; Coeus এর কন্যা। দেবরাজ জুপিটার ইহার প্রেমে বদ্ধ হন। জুপিটারের ঔরসে ইহার গর্ভে Apollo দেব ও Artemis দেবী জন্মগ্রহণ করেন।

lĕt′-ter (-ēr), *n.* & *v. t.* **1.** A mark or character used as the representative of a sound; an alphabetic symbol; অক্ষর; বর্ণ, মাত্রিকা (এভেলন)। **2.** An epistle; (*pl.*) an epistle of the legal or formal kind; as, *letters* patent; চিঠি, পত্র, লিপি, লেখ, পত্রিকা; আইন-ব্যাপার সংক্রান্ত বা রীতিসিদ্ধ লিপি। **3.** The literal statement or meaning; exact terms of a statement; as, to follow one's command to the *letter*; অক্ষরে অক্ষরে প্রকৃত অর্থ, শব্দার্থ, বাচ্যার্থ, পদার্থ, প্রথমিকার্থ, অক্ষরার্থ; কোন উক্তির অবিকল শব্দসমূহ। **4.** (*Print.*) A single type or character; also types collectively; (ছাপিবার) হরফ, অক্ষর, অক্ষরমুদ্রা; মুদ্রাক্ষরসমূহ। **5.** (*Pl.*) Learning; literature; erudition; as, a man of *letters*; the profession of *letters*; authorship; বিদ্যা, পাণ্ডিত্য; সাহিত্য; বিদ্যাবত্তা; গ্রন্থকর্ত্তৃত্ব। **6.** (*Pl.*) Writings; inscription; (*obs.* except in *proof before letters*); লিখন; ক্ষোদিত লিপি। ***Verb t.*** **1.** To impress title etc. on (a book-cover); to impress or inscribe with letters; to classify with letters; (প্রচ্ছদপটে) পুস্তকের নামাদি মুদ্রিত করা; অক্ষর মুদ্রিত বা ক্ষোদিত করা, অক্ষরাঙ্কিত করা, অক্ষরচিহ্নিত করা; অক্ষর দ্বারা শ্রেণী-বিভাগ করা। **–ing,** *n.* **1.** The act of marking or impressing with letters, as by cutting or painting ; অক্ষরাঙ্কন, অক্ষর ক্ষোদন। 2. The letters impressed ; অঙ্কিত বা ক্ষোদিত অক্ষরাবলী। **–tered**, *adj.* Versed in literature or science ; literate ; educated ; বিজ্ঞানবিদ্, পণ্ডিত, কৃতবিদ্য, বিদ্বান ; লিখনপঠনক্ষম; শিক্ষিত। **Dead-letter**—One not delivered for want of the addressee ; মালিকের ঠিকানা না পাওয়ায় যে চিঠি বিলি করা হয় নাই। An obsolete law etc.; অপ্রচলিত আইন প্রভৃতি। **Letter-balance**—A balance for ascertaining postage of letters ; (ডাকমাশুল ঠিক করিবার জন্য) চিঠি ওজনের নিক্তি। **Letter-book** — চিঠির নকল বহি। **Letter-bound**—অক্ষরে অক্ষরে আদেশ পালনপর। **Letter-box**—চিঠির বাক্স। **Letter carrier**—ডাকহরকরা, ডাকপিয়ন। **Letter-case**—যে পুস্তকে পত্রের নকল রাখা হয়। **Letter-clip**—চিঠি আটকাইবার আঁকড়া। **Letter-founder**—যে ছাপার অক্ষর ঢালাই করে, অক্ষরঢালাইকর। **Letter-lock**—এক প্রকার তালা—যাহা উপরিস্থ কতকগুলি অক্ষর মিলাইয়া মালিকের জ্ঞাত কোন বিশেষ শব্দ গঠন করিলে খোলা যায়। **Letter-paper**—ডাক কাগজ, চিঠির কাগজ। **Letter-perfect**—(*Theatre*) Knowing one's part to the letter ; (নাট্য) নিজের ভূমিকা উত্তমরূপে কণ্ঠস্থ। **Letter-press** — মুদ্রিত অক্ষর বা শব্দসমূহ [পুস্তকের ছবি প্রভৃতি ব্যতিরিক্ত পঠনীয় অংশ সম্বন্ধে সচরাচর ব্যবহৃত হয়।]; পত্রের প্রতিলিপি তুলিবার জন্য যন্ত্র। **Letter-sorter**—ডাকঘর প্রভৃতিতে যে ব্যক্তি চিঠি ঠিকানা অনুসারে বাছিয়া শ্রেণীবদ্ধ করে। **Letters-patent**—See PATENT. **Letter-weight**—কাগজপত্র চাপা দিয়া রাখিবার জন্য ভারি দ্রব্য, কাগজচাপা। **Letter-worship**—কোন আদেশ বা বিধির শব্দের প্রতি অনুচিত অনুরাগ। **Letter-writer**—One who writes letters ; a book giving instruction in writing letters ; পত্রলেখক; যে পুস্তক পাঠে পত্র লিখা শিক্ষা করা যায়, পত্রাবলী, পত্রকৌমুদী। **Red-letter-day**—See under RED. **Common wealth** or **republic of letters**—Authors as a body; গ্রন্থকারসম্প্রদায়, গ্রন্থকারসমাজ। **Letter of advice**—যে পত্রে মাল প্রেরণ প্রভৃতির সংবাদ দেওয়া হয়। **Letter of attorney**—Same as POWER OF ATTORNEY (which see under ATTORNEY.) **Letter of the law**—আইন বা দলীলের আক্ষরিক বা শব্দানুগত অর্থ। **Man of letters**—Scholar; author; পণ্ডিত, কৃতবিদ্যব্যক্তি; গ্রন্থকার, সাহিত্যিক। **To the letter**—With adherence to every detail; অক্ষরে অক্ষরে, ঠিক, যথার্থ।

Lĕt′-tic (-îc), *adj.* & *n.* 1. Of, or pertaining to, the Letts (a branch of the Slavic family) ; of, or relating to, the languages including Lettish, Lithuanian and Old Prussian ; লেট্ বা লেটীস্ জাতি সম্বন্ধীয় ; লেট, লিথুনিয়ান এবং প্রাচীন প্রুশিয়ান ভাষাসম্পর্কীয়। ***Noun.*** The Letts ; their language ; লেট্ জাতি ; ঐ জাতির ভাষা।

Let′-tish (-îsh), *adj.* & *n.* Of, or relating to, the Letts ; লেট্ জাতি সম্বন্ধীয়। ***Noun.*** The language of the Letts ; ঐ জাতির ভাষা।

lĕt′-tuce (-îs), *n.* A garden-herb with crisp leaves much used as salad ; উদ্যানরোপিত শাকবিশেষ, কাজু (প্রবোধ), সালাদ (ঐ)।

leu′-cō-cȳle (lü-), *n.* A white or colourless blood corpuscle ; শ্বেতবর্ণ বা অবর্ণ রক্তকণিকা।

leu-co-cy-th(a)e′-mi-ă (lü-cö-sî-thë-), *n.* A disease in which the white corpuscles of the blood are largely increased in numbers, and there is enlargement of the spleen ; একপ্রকার রোগ — যাহাতে রক্তে শ্বেতকণিকাধিক্য ও লোহিতকণিকার হ্রাস এবং প্লীহা বৃদ্ধি পায়।

leu-cō-dêr′-mă (lü-), *n.* (*Med.*) Abnormal whiteness of the skin in spots ; শ্বেতকুষ্ঠ (হঃ চঃ), ধবল (ঐ), শ্বিত্র।

leu-cō′-mă (lü-), *n.* A white opacity of the cornea of the eye ; চক্ষুর কনীনিকার শ্বেতবর্ণ অস্বচ্ছতা।

leu-cŏp′-ă-thȳ (lü-), *n.* The state of an albino ; ধবল (হঃ চঃ)। See ALBINO.

leu-cor-rhoe′-ă (lü-cö-rë-), *n.* A morbid discharge of a white or yellowish mucus from the female genital organs ; স্ত্রীজননেন্দ্রিয় হইতে শুভ্র বা ঈষৎ পীতবর্ণ স্রাব নিঃসরণ, শ্বেতপ্রদর।

Leu-cŏth′-ö-ë (lü-), *n.* Daughter of a king of Babylon ; বেবিলনের জনৈকা রাজকন্যা। Apollo দেব ইহার প্রণয়প্রার্থী হওয়াতে ইনি ভূগর্ভে জীবন্ত সমাহিতা হন। Apollo ইহাকে একটী গুল্মে পরিণত করেন।

Lĕ-văn̆t′, *n.* 1. The Eastern part of the Mediterranean with its islands and neighbouring countries (*lit.* the point where the sun rises; the east) ; ভূমধ্যসাগরের পূর্ব্বাংশ এবং তৎসন্নিহিত দ্বীপপুঞ্জ এবং দেশসমূহ ; [শব্দানুযায়ী সূর্য্যোদয়ের দিক, পূর্ব্বদিক বা দেশ]।

lĕ-văn̆t′, *v. i.* To run away without paying debts ; to abscond, esp. with betting losses unpaid ; ধার পরিশোধ না করিয়া পলাইয়া যাওয়া; জুয়াখেলার বাজি হারিয়া টাকা না দিয়া পলাইয়া যাওয়া।

lĕ-văn̆t′-ĕr, *n.* 1. An eastern wind blowing up the Mediterranean ; ভূমধ্যসাগরোপরিপ্রবাহিত পূর্ব্ববাতাস। 2. An inhabitant of the Levant ; ভূমধ্যসাগরের পূর্ব্বদিকস্থ দেশসমূহের অধিবাসী।

lĕ-văn̆t′-îne (*or* **tē**), *adj.* & *n.* Of, relating, or trading to, the Levant ; ল্যাভাণ্ট সম্বন্ধীয়, ঐ দেশের ব্যবসায়কারী। ***Noun.*** An inhabitant of the Levant ; ভূমধ্যসাগরের পূর্ব্বদেশবাসী, ল্যাভাণ্টবাসী। **Levant nut**—কাকমারী (খোরী), কাকফল (ঐ)।

lĕ-vā′-tor (-têr), *n.* 1. (*Anat.*) A muscle that raises some part, as the lip, eye, etc. (also *muscle levator*) ; (শারীরসংস্থানবিদ্যা) যে পেশীর ক্রিয়ায় অঙ্গাদি উত্তোলিত হয়, উত্তোলকপেশী (হঃ চঃ)।

lĕv'-ee (-ē), *n.* 1. (*Formerly*) The reception of visitors by a person on rising from the bed ; প্রাভাতিক সম্মিলনী, প্রাভাতিক সম্বর্দ্ধনা-সভা, প্রভাতী মজলিস বা দরবার, দর্শকমেল (আঃ বঃ)। 2. (In Great Britain and Ireland) An assembly held by a sovereign or his representative at which men only are received ; (গ্রেট্ ব্রিটেন এবং আয়র্লণ্ডে) রাজা কিম্বা রাজপ্রতিনিধির অপরাহ্নকালীন সম্বর্দ্ধনা-সভা — যাহাতে কেবল পুরুষগণের প্রবেশাধিকার আছে। 3. A miscellaneous assembly or gathering of visitors ; নানাপ্রকার লোকের সম্মিলন।

lĕv'-ĕl, *n., adj.* & *v. t.* 1. An instrument for finding a horizontal line or plane ; সমতলতা পরীক্ষণার্থ যন্ত্রবিশেষ, লেবেল (সাঃ পঃ)। 2. A horizontal plane ; সমস্থল (হিঃ কোঃ), সমতল। 3. A surface without inequalities ; a flat country ; সমধরাতল (হিঃ কোঃ) ; সমদেশ, সমভূমি। 4. A position, place or standard in social, moral or intellectual matters ; "We must place English and Norman writers on a *level*" ; সামাজিক, নৈতিক বা মানসিক ব্যাপারে স্থান, পদবী বা আদর্শ। *Adj.* 1. Horizontal ; সমান, চৌরস (হিঃ কোঃ), জলসম (শংকু)। 2. Of the same rank, grade or condition ; as, they are now *level* with me ; সমপদস্থ, সমাবস্থ, সমশ্রেণীস্থ। 3. Of even, equable or uniform quality, style, temper, etc. ; "A leisured and *level* life" ; নিয়ত একরূপ স্বভাবসম্পন্ন, সমগুণসম্পন্ন। *Verb t.* 1. To make level or horizontal ; to make even or uniform ; সমতল করা, সমান করা ; চোলাই করা। 2. To bring to a same level or plane (*lit.* & *fig.*), (often with *up* or *down*) ; সমপদস্থ করা, সমাবস্থায় আনা, সমতল করা। 3. To aim horizontally ; to direct ; as, to *level* a gun, missile, remark, etc. (*at, against*) ; তাক করা ; নিশানা করা। 4. To lay low ; to overthrow ; as, to *level* a house *to* or *with*, the ground or *in* the dust ; পাতিত করা, ভূমিসাৎ করা ; উচ্ছেদ করা, ধ্বংস করা। 5. (*Rare*) To knock down, as a person ; (কদাচিদ্ব্যবহৃত) ধাক্কা দিয়া ফেলা। 6. To abolish as distinctions ; (ভেদ বা বৈষম্য) দূর করা। **—ly,** *adv.* **—ness,** *n.* **Level crossing**—যে স্থানে কোন রাস্তা বা লৌহবর্ত্ম কিম্বা লৌহবর্ত্মদ্বয় সমতল হইয়া পরস্পরকে ছেদন করে।

Spirit-level.

Spirit-level—সুরাসূত্র (See under SPIRIT). **Carpenter's level, Mason's level**—থামাল যন্ত্র, একখণ্ড সোজা কাষ্ঠফলকে সংলগ্ন বুদ্বুদবিশিষ্ট কাচযন্ত্র। **Surveyor's level**—ভূমির সমতলতা পরীক্ষার জন্য সুরাসূত্র (Spirit Level) সংবদ্ধ দূরবীক্ষণযন্ত্রবিশেষ। **On a level with**—In the same horizontal plane as ; সমতল। **To do one's level best**—To try one's utmost ; যথাসাধ্য চেষ্টা করা, প্রাণপণ চেষ্টা করা। **To find one's level**—To reach the right place with regard to others ; পারিপার্শ্বিক ব্যক্তিগণের সম্পর্কে নিজের যথোপযুক্ত স্থান প্রাপ্ত হওয়া। **To have one's head level**—To be prudent or discreet ; সদ্বিবেচক হওয়া, সুবিবেচনাশীল হওয়া। **To level down** — To bring down to the same level with other things ; নিম্নতর বস্তুর সহিত সমতল করা। **To level up**—To raise to the same level with other things ; নিম্নতর বস্তুকে উচ্চতর বস্তুসমূহের সহিত সমতল করা। **Water finds its level**—পরস্পরের মধ্যে তরল পদার্থ অবাধ চলাচলের সুবিধা আছে—এইরূপ দুইটী পাত্রে কোন তরল পদার্থ রাখিলে উভয় পাত্রের তরল পদার্থের উচ্চতা সমান হইয়া থাকে।

lĕv'-ĕl-ler (-ĕr), *n.* 1. One who, or that which, levels ; সমতলকারী, উচ্চাবচতানাশক। 2. One who wishes to destroy all social distinction ; an advocate of equality ; যে ব্যক্তি সর্ব্বপ্রকার সামাজিক বৈষম্য দূরীভূত করিয়া সাম্যসংস্থাপন করিতে চায়, সমতাসংস্থাপক, উচ্চনীচভাব বিঘাতক ; সমতাসমর্থক, সাম্যবাদী।

lĕv'-ĕl-ling (-ĭng), *n.* 1. The act of making level or reducing to a level ; চৌরস করণ, সমীকরণ, চোলাই করণ। 2. The process of ascertaining the different elevations of objects on the surface of the earth ; ভূপৃষ্ঠস্থ পদার্থ সমূহের বিভিন্ন উচ্চতা নিরূপণ। **Levelling pole, rod, staff**—A graduated rod or staff used in connection with a spirit level and telescope for measuring difference of level between points ; ভূমিমাপক যন্ত্র-বিশেষ।

lē'-vĕr, *n., v. i.* & *t.* 1. A bar used to raise or dislodge heavy weights ; a crowbar ; উত্তোলন-দণ্ড ; ঠেকো, চাড়া। 2. (*Mech.*) A bar turning on a support called the fulcrum and acted on at two other points by two forces, power applied and weight ; (যন্ত্রবিজ্ঞান) দণ্ডযন্ত্র। 3. A watch having a vibrating lever to connect the action of the escape wheel with that of the balance ; একপ্রকার টেঁক ঘড়ী। 4. A piece to open or close the barrel of a breech-loading firearm ; আগ্নেয়াস্ত্রের নালী খোলা বা বন্ধ করার জন্য খণ্ড বিশেষ। *Verb i.* To use lever ; উত্তোলনদণ্ড ব্যবহার করা। *Verb t.* To raise, move or act on with a lever, (with *along, away, out, over, up*) ; চাড়াইয়া তোলা, দণ্ডযন্ত্রের সাহায্যে তোলা।

lĕ'-vêr-āge, *n.* 1. The action or method of applying a lever; the mechanical advantage gained by the use of a lever; the power of a lever; দণ্ডযন্ত্রের কার্য্য, দণ্ডযন্ত্র ব্যবহারপ্রণালী, দণ্ডযন্ত্রের দ্বারা লব্ধ সুবিধা। 2. A set or system of levers; দণ্ডযন্ত্রশ্রেণী। 3. Means of accomplishing a purpose; power; influence; "Putting additional *leverage* into his hands"; উদ্দেশ্য সাধনের উপায়; ক্ষমতা; প্রভাব।

lever de rideau, (*F.*), *n.* (*Theatre*) A curtain-raiser, *i. e.* a short opening piece; (রঙ্গালয়) সংক্ষিপ্ত প্রারম্ভিক বক্তৃতা।

lĕv'-êr-ĕt, *n.* A hare in its first year; খরগোসের বাচ্চা, এক বৎসর বয়স্ক শশক, শশশাবক।

lē-vī'-ā-thăn, *n.* 1. (*Bibl.*) A large sea monster; (বাইবেল) মহাকায় জলজন্তু-বিশেষ, তিমিঙ্গিল (আঃ বঃ)। 2. A huge ship; বৃহৎ অর্ণবযান। 3. Something huge and formidable of its kind; প্রকাণ্ড বা বৃহদাকার পদার্থ। 4 A person of formidable ability, power or wealth; অতিমানুষ শক্তি বা ক্ষমতাসম্পন্ন ব্যক্তি, প্রভূত অর্থশালী ব্যক্তি (টাকার জাহাজ, বিদ্যার জাহাজ)।

lĕv'-ĭ-gāte, *v. t.* To make smooth by reducing to a fine powder to make a smooth paste of; সূক্ষ্মচূর্ণে পরিণত করা; লেই করা। **—ga'-tion,** *n.*

lĕv'-in, *n.* (*Poet.*) Lightning or its flash; (কবিতায়) বিজলী, চপলা, চপলচমক, বিদ্যুৎস্ফুরণ।

lĕv'-i-rāte, *n.* The Jewish custom by which a dead man's brother or next of kin had to marry his widow; প্রাচীন ইহুদীদিগের মধ্যে প্রচলিত বিবাহপদ্ধতি—ইহাতে কোন নিঃসন্তান বিধবা নারীর সহিত তদীয় মৃতস্বামীর নিকটতম আত্মীয়ের বিবাহ বিহিত হইত। **—rat'-ic, —rat'-i cal,** *adjs.*

lĕv'-ĭ-tāte, *v. t.* & *i.* 1. (A term used by the spiritualist.) To cause to float in the air; শূন্যে উত্থিত করা। ***Verb i.*** To rise and float in the air; শূন্যে উত্থিত হওয়া। **—ta'-tion,** *n.* 1. Act of levitating or rising in virtue of lightness; শূন্যোত্থান। 2. Rising or raising a body from the ground by spiritualistic means; যোগবলে শূন্যোত্থান, শূন্যমার্গে উত্তোলন, লঘিমা।

Lē'-vīte, *n.* One of the tribe or family of Levi, one of the twelve sons of Jacob; an assistant to the Jewish priests; লেভির বংশধর বিশেষ—এই বংশ হইতে প্রাচীনকালে ইহুদী পুরোহিতদিগের সহকারী সংগ্রহ হইত; ইহুদী পুরোহিতের সহকারী নিম্নশ্রেণীর যাজক।

Lē-vit'-ĭ-căl, *adj.* 1. Of, or pertaining to, or connected with, the Levites; লিভাইটসম্বন্ধীয়, সংক্রান্ত বা বিষয়ক। 2. Of, or relating to, Levites' ritual; লেভাইটদের পূজানুষ্ঠানসম্বন্ধীয়। 3. Of, or relating to, Leviticus; প্রাচীন নিয়মের তৃতীয় খণ্ড অনুযায়ী। **—cism,** *n.*

Lē-vit'-ĭ-cŭs, *n.* (*Abbr. Lev.*) The Third Book of the Old Testament with the Levitical laws and rituals; বাইবেলের প্রাচীন নিয়মের তৃতীয় পুস্তক বা খণ্ড—যাহাতে ইহুদীদিগের পূজানুষ্ঠানাদির বিষয় লিখিত আছে, ইহুদীদিগের স্মৃতিশাস্ত্র।

lĕv'-ĭ-tȳ, *n.* (*Rare*) 1. Lightness of weight; (কচিদ্‌ব্যবহৃত) লঘুতা, লঘিমা, লঘুত্ব, ভারহীনতা। 2. Lack of gravity or thought; frivolity; unseasonable jocularity; গাম্ভীর্য্যরাহিত্য, চিন্তাশূন্যতা; চাপল্য, চঞ্চলতা, হালকামি, পাতলামি, ছেব্‌লামি, ফচ্‌কেমি; অসময়োচিত আমোদপ্রমোদ। 3. Fickleness: inconstancy; লঘুচিত্ততা, চিত্তচপলতা; অস্থিরতা। 4. Light manners or behaviour; চরিত্রের লঘুতা।

lĕv'-ȳ, *n.* & *v. t.* 1. The act of enlisting troops for war; যুদ্ধার্থ সৈন্যসংগ্রহ। 2. Collecting of assessment, tax, etc.; করসংগ্রহ, করধার্য্য করণ। 3. Amount of tax etc. levied or number of men enrolled; সংগৃহীত বস্তু, করাদি, বা সৈন্যদল। ***Verb t.*** 1. To raise as contribution, taxes, etc.; to impose by authority as a toll etc.; চাঁদা বা কর সংগ্রহ করা; কর, রাজস্ব বা শুল্ক নির্দ্ধারণ করা। 2. To raise, as a sum by execution or other legal process on a person's goods; ক্রোক পরওয়ানা জারি করিয়া টাকা আদায় করা। 3. To enlist as soldier or army; সৈন্যদলভুক্ত করা 4. To collect men and munitions for; to proceed to, make as, to *levy* war *on, upon* or *against* a country or nation; (যুদ্ধার্থ) লোকজন এবং সমরসরঞ্জাম সংগ্রহ করা; কোন কার্য্যে অগ্রসর হওয়া। **—i-a-ble,** *adj.* Capable of being levied as a tax, duty etc.; নির্দ্ধারণযোগ্য, সংগ্রহযোগ্য। **Levy in mass**—সৈনিকবিভাগে ভুক্ত করিবার জন্য দেশের সমস্ত কার্য্যক্ষম ব্যক্তিক আহ্বান।

lewd (lūd), *adj.* 1. (*Bibl.*) Base; bad worthless; (বাইবেল) নীচ, হেয়, অধম; মন্দ; অসার। 2. Lustful; lascivious; unchaste; indecent; লম্পট কামুক কামাসক্ত, কামপরায়ণ; রতিলম্পট, রতিলালসাপূর্ণ, ইন্দ্রিয়পরায়ণ, স্ত্রীলম্পট, স্ত্রীব্যসনী; অসৎ, ভ্রষ্ট; অশ্লীল। **Lewd'-ly,** *adv.* **Lewd'-ness,** *n.* Unlawful indulgence of lust; lasciviousness; লাম্পট্য, লম্পটতা; কামাসক্তি।

lew'-is (lū-), *n.* An iron contrivance for raising heavy blocks of stone; প্রকাণ্ড ভারী প্রস্তরখণ্ড উত্তোলনের জন্য লৌহনির্ম্মিত যন্ত্রবিশেষ।

lĕx'-ĭ-căl, *adj.* 1. Of, or pertaining to, a lexicon, শব্দকোষসম্বন্ধীয়,

অভিধানসম্বন্ধীয়, আভিধানিক। 2. Relating to the vocabulary of a language (opp. to *grammatical*) ; কোন ভাষার শব্দকোষবিষয়ক। **–ly,** *adv.*

lĕx-ĭ-cŏg′-ră-phêr, *n.* One who writes, or compiles, a dictionary : অভিধানপ্রণেতা, শব্দকোষসঙ্কলক, অভিধানকার, কোষকার, কোষকর্ত্তা, অভিধানকর্ত্তা।

lĕx-ĭ-cŏg′-ră-phȳ. *n.* The art of compiling a dictionary ; dictionary-making ; অভিধানপ্রণয়ন, কোষপ্রণয়ন, শব্দকোষরচনা ; শব্দকোষকরণ। **–co-graph′-i-cal,** *adj.* Of, or pertaining to, lexicography ; অভিধানসঙ্কলনঘটিত, শব্দকোষপ্রণয়নবিষয়ক।

lĕx-ĭ-cŏl′-ŏ-ġȳ, *n.* The science of words, their derivation and signification etc. ; শব্দবিজ্ঞান। **–gist,** *n.*

lĕx′-ĭ-cŏn, *n.* A dictionary ; esp. a dictionary of the Greek, Hebrew, Syriac or Arabic language ; অভিধান, শব্দকোষ, কোষ ; বিশেষতঃ গ্রীক, ইহুদী, সিরিক বা আরবী ভাষার অভিধান।

lĕx-ĭg′-ră-phȳ, *n.* A system of writing in which each character represents a word, as that of the Chinese ; লিপি প্রণালী বিশেষ—যাহাতে প্রতি অক্ষর দ্বারা এক একটী শব্দ বুঝায়।

lex non scripta, (*L.*) *n.* The unwritten or common law of the land ; দেশের প্রচলিত অলিখিত আইন।

lex scripta, (*L.*), *n.* Written law of a country ; কোন দেশের লিখিত আইন।

lex talionis (*L.*), *n.* The law of retaliation ; an eye for an eye ; তুল্য প্রতিশোধমূলক আইন ; তোমার একটী চক্ষু উৎপাটন করিলে তুমিও তাহার একটী চক্ষু উৎপাটন করিতে পার—এই নীতিমূলক আইন।

Ley′-den (lĭ-dn), *n.* A Dutch city ; হলণ্ডের নগরবিশেষ। **Leyden-jar, –phial**—A glass-jar or bottle

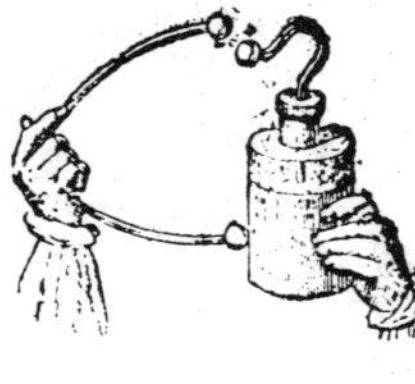

Leyden-jar and phial.

for accumulating electricity (so named from its having been invented at Leyden) ; তাড়িত সঞ্চয়ের জন্য কাচনির্ম্মিত ঘটবিশেষ, লিডেনজার (হিঃ কোঃ)। [হলাণ্ড দেশের অন্তঃপাতী Leyden নামক সহরে সর্ব্বপ্রথম নির্ম্মিত হইয়াছিল বলিয়া এই নাম]। **Leyden-battery** — বিদ্যুদ্‌দনটমালা, বিদ্যুৎকুম্ভ (সাঃ পঃ), কুম্ভ (ঐ), লিডেনভাণ্ড (ঐ)।

lī-ă-bĭl′-ĭ-tȳ, *n.* **1.** The state of being liable ; responsibility ; দায়িত্ব ; বাধ্যতা, অধীনত্ব। **2.** What one is liable for ; (*pl.*) pecuniary obligations or debts ; যাহার জন্য কেহ দায়ী থাকে, যাহা করিতে বাধ্য ; অধমর্ণতা, জিম্মাদারী (হিঃ কোঃ), দায়, ঋণ (হিঃ কোঃ)। **Limited liability**—কোন যৌথকারবারের অংশীদারদের অংশের অনুপাতে দেনার জন্য দায়িত্ব, দায়সীমাবদ্ধতা। **Assets and liabilities** — One's dues and debts ; দেনা পাওনা।

lī′-ă-ble (-bl), *adj.* **1.** Legally bound ; responsible ; answerable (*for*) ; দায়ী ; বাধ্য ; জবাবদিহী। **2.** Subject (*to* tax or penalty) ; অধীন, (অর্হ in comp.)। **3.** Exposed (*to*) ; likely *to* do, or suffer, something undesirable ; as, *liable* to slip : *liable* to accident ; অধীন ; প্রবণ, শীল (in comp.)। **–ness,** *n.*

li-ai-son′ (lē-ā-zn), *n.* **1.** An illicit intimacy between a man and a woman ; স্ত্রী পুরুষের অবৈধ প্রেম, আসনাই, কুসম্বন্ধ, গুপ্তপ্রণয়, গুপ্তপ্রেম, অবৈধ প্রেম। **2.** (*In French*) The joining of ordinary silent final consonant to a following word beginning with a vowel or silent *h* ; (ফরাসী ভাষায়) শব্দের অন্ত্যস্থিত অনুচ্চারিত ব্যঞ্জনবর্ণের আদ্যবর্ণ স্বর বা অনুচ্চারিত *h* এরূপ শব্দের সহিত সংযোগ।

li-â′-nâ (lē-), **–nē,** *ns.* A name for the climbing and twining plants in tropical forests ; আমেরিকাদেশীয় লতা বিশেষ।

lī′-ar (-êr), *n.* One who tells a lie or lies ; মিথ্যুক, মিথ্যাবাদী, অনৃতভাষী, মৃষাবাদী, অসত্যবক্তা।

lī′-ăs, *n.* **1.** The blue limestone rock of some of the South-Western countries ; ইয়ুরোপের দক্ষিণপশ্চিমভাগস্থ কোন কোন দেশে প্রাপ্ত নীলবর্ণ চূর্ণ প্রস্তর। **2.** (*Geol.*) The blue argillaceous limestone containing a great deal of fossils ; (ভূতত্ত্ব) শিলীভূত জন্তুদেহ বা অস্থিপঞ্জরময় নীলবর্ণ মৃন্ময় চূর্ণ প্রস্তর। **–as′-sic,** *adj.* Of, or relating to, the lias formation ; উক্ত প্রকার চূর্ণপ্রস্তর গঠন সম্বন্ধীয়।

lī-bā′-tion, *n.* **1.** The pouring of a liquid usually wine in honour of some deity ; a drink-offering to a god ; দেবোদ্দেশ্যে মদ্যাদি প্রদান ; উদকনিষেক, তর্পণোদক, দেবোদ্দেশ্যে পেয় নিষেক। **2.** (*Joc.*) Potation ; (কৌতুকচ্ছলে) চুমুক, ঢোক।

lī′-bĕl, *n.* & *v. t.* **1.** (*Civil and Eccl. law*) A written statement of a plaintiff's allegations ; বিবাদীর বিরুদ্ধে বাদীর লিখিত দরখাস্ত বা অভিযোগপত্র। **2.** (*Law*) Any published defamatory statement ; act of publishing it ; মানহানিকর প্রবন্ধাদি, অপবাদলেখ, নিন্দাপত্র ; মানহানিজনক বিষয় প্রচার বা প্রকাশ। **3.** A false and defamatory statement in conversation ; অপবাদ, কুৎসা, পরিবাদ। **4.** A representation etc. that conveys an unjustly unfavourable impression about a person or thing, (with *on*) ; as, this photograph is a *libel* on Miss Y. ; যে প্রতিকৃতি, প্রতিরূপ বা প্রতিমূর্ত্তি প্রভৃতি দ্বারা কোন ব্যক্তি বা বস্তু সম্বন্ধে অনুচিতরূপে প্রতিকূল ধারণা জন্মে। ***Verb t.*** **1.** To defame by a libel ; কুৎসা-প্রচার করা, মানহানি করা। **2.** (*Law*) To publish a libel against ; মানহানিকর প্রবন্ধাদি প্রকাশ করা। **3.** (*Eccl. & Admiralty*) To bring a suit against ; as, to *libel* a person or ship etc. ; কাহারও বিরুদ্ধে মোকদ্দমা করা। **—lant,** *n.* One who brings a charge in an ecclesiastical or admiralty court ; যে ব্যক্তি যাজকীয় বা নৌবিভাগীয় বিচারালয়ে কাহারো বিরুদ্ধে মোকদ্দমা করে। **—lee',** *n.* One against whom a libel is filed by a libellant ; যে ব্যক্তির বিরুদ্ধে যাজকীয় বা নৌবিভাগীয় বিচারালয়ে মোকদ্দমা রুজু করা হয়। **—ler,** *n.* One who publishes libels ; a lampooner ; মানহানিকারী, কুৎসাপ্রচারক ; অপবাদকারী। **—list,** *n.* **—lous,** *adj.* Containing a libel ; defamatory ; অপবাদপূর্ণ ; কুৎসাজনক। **—ly,** *adv.*

Lī'-bêr, *n.* A Roman name for Dionysius ; রোমীয় সুরাদেবতা।

lĭb'-êr-ăl, *adj.* & *n.* **1.** Becoming or befitting a gentleman (*rare except in liberal education*) ; ভদ্রোচিত। **2.** Generous ; open-handed ; munificent ; as, a *liberal* man ; বদান্য ; মুক্তহস্ত ; উদারহস্ত, দানশীল, দানশূর, দানশৌণ্ড। **3.** Ample ; abundant ; profuse ; as, a *liberal* flow of water ; প্রচুর ; পর্য্যাপ্ত অজস্র ; যথেষ্ট, অত্যধিক। **4.** Not rigorous or literal ; free ; as, a *liberal* interpretation of law ; যথাযথ নহে, অবিকল নহে ; অনাক্ষরিক। **5.** Broad-minded ; candid ; unprejudiced ; as, a *liberal* examiner ; প্রশস্তমনাঃ ; উদারচেতা, সরল, অমায়িক, অকপট ; সংস্কারশূন্য। **6.** (*Pol.*) Favourable to democratic reforms and abolition of privileges, (*opp.* to *conservative*) ; উদারনৈতিক। ***Noun.*** A member of the liberal party, esp. British ; উদারনৈতিক সম্প্রদায়ের সভ্য। **—ism,** *n.* The principles of the Liberal party ; liberal principles in politics or theology ; উদারনৈতিক সম্প্রদায়ের মত ; ধর্ম্মশাস্ত্র সম্বন্ধে উদার মত, রাজনীতিক মতৌদার্য্য, স্বাতন্ত্র্যবাদ (হিঃ কোঃ)। **—ist,** *n.* & *adj.* A liberal ; উদারনৈতিক। **—is'-tic,** *adj.* Of, relating to, or characterized by, liberalism ; উদারনীতি-সম্বন্ধীয়, উদারনৈতিক। **—i-za'-tion,** *n.* **—ize,** *v. t.* & *i.* To make liberal ; to free from narrowness or bigotry ; to enlarge ; উদারভাবাপন্ন করা ; সংকীর্ণতাবিমুক্ত করা, গোঁড়ামি দূর করা, চিত্তের প্রসার বৃদ্ধি করা ; বৃদ্ধি করা। (*Verb i.*) (*Rare*) To be or become liberal ; উদারভাবাপন্ন হওয়া। **—ly,** *adv.* **Liberal-conservative** — রক্ষণশীল সম্প্রদায়ের যে সভ্য শাসনসংস্কারের বিরোধী নহেন। **Liberal-education**—যে শিক্ষা দ্বারা মনের বিস্তার হয়, উদারশিক্ষা, অশিল্প বা অব্যবসায়সংক্রান্ত শিক্ষা। **Liberal-party**—See under PARTY. **Liberal-unionist**—উদারনৈতিক সম্প্রদায়ের যে সকল সভ্য আয়র্লণ্ডে স্বায়ত্তশাসন-প্রতিষ্ঠার বিরোধী হইয়া ১৮৬৬ খৃঃ অব্দে উক্ত দল পরিত্যাগপূর্ব্বক রক্ষণশীল-সম্প্রদায়ে যোগদান করেন।

lĭb-êr-ăl'-ĭ-tȳ, *n.* **1.** Bounty ; munificence ; generosity ; বদান্যতা, দানশীলতা ; দাতৃত্ব, মুক্তহস্তত্ব, মুক্তহস্ততা ; ঔদার্য্য, উদারতা। **2.** Lack of prejudice or bigotry ; breadth of mind ; নিরপেক্ষতা ; চিত্তের প্রসার।

lĭb'-êr-āte, *v. t.* **1.** To free ; to set at liberty, (with *from*) ; বন্ধনমুক্ত করা, দাসত্ব হইতে মুক্ত করা ; স্বাধীনতা প্রদান করা। **2.** (*Chem.*) To free as gases etc. from combination ; (রসায়ন-শাস্ত্র) পৃথক করা, বিশ্লিষ্ট করা। **—a-tor,** *n.* A deliverer ; মুক্তিদাতা, উদ্ধারকর্ত্তা, স্বাধীনতা প্রদাতা।

lĭ-bêr-ā'-tion, *n.* **1.** Setting free from restraint or confinement ; release ; দাসত্ব মোচন, স্বাধীনতা প্রদান, মুক্তিদান, উদ্ধার ; বিমোচন। **2.** Salvation ; নিঃশ্রেয়স, ক্ষেম (বেদান্ত), অপবর্গ (ঐ), মোক্ষ, মুক্তি (হিঃ কোঃ), কৈবল্য। **—ism,** *n.* The principle of the liberationists ; রাষ্ট্রাধীনতা বিমুক্তি। **—ist,** *n.* A sympathizer with the Liberation Society ; রাষ্ট্রাধীনতা বিমোচনবাদী। **Liberation Society**—রাষ্ট্র বা শাসনতন্ত্রের পৃষ্ঠপোষকতা অথবা কর্তৃত্বাধীন হইতে ধর্ম্মকে মুক্তিদানের উদ্দেশ্যে প্রতিষ্ঠিত সম্প্রদায়বিশেষ। এই সম্প্রদায়ের অপর নাম British Anti-state Church Association. **Liberation of energy**—উপষ্টম্ভ (ব্রজঃ হিন্দু), অবষ্টম্ভ (ঐ)।

lĭb-êr-tā'-rĭ-ăn, *adj.* & *n.* Believing in, relating to, the doctrine of free will, (*opp.* to *necessitarian*) ; স্বাধীন ইচ্ছায় বিশ্বাসী, স্বাধীনইচ্ছাবাদিসম্বন্ধীয়। ***Noun.*** **1.** A believer in the doctrine of free-will ; স্বাধীন ইচ্ছাবাদী। **2.** An advocate of liberty ; জনসাধারণের স্বাধীনতার পক্ষপাতী। **—ism,** *n.*

Liberte, equalite, fraternite—সাম্য, মৈত্রী, স্বাধীনতা।

lĭ-bêr'-tĭ-cīde, *n.* & *adj.* A destroyer of liberty ; স্বাধীনতাবিনাশক। ***Adj.*** Destructive of liberty ; স্বাধীনতাবিনাশী।

lĭb'-êr-tīne, *n.* & *adj.* **1.** A free-thinker on religion ; ধর্ম্ম সম্বন্ধে প্রত্যাদেশবাদবিরোধী, ধর্ম্ম বিষয়ে স্বাধীন-চিন্তাকারী। **2.** A profligate or licentious man ; স্বেচ্ছাচারী, লম্পট, রতিক্রিয়ারত, কামুক, লোচ্চা। ***Adj.*** **1.** Free-thinking in religion ; স্বাধীনচিন্তাকারী। **2.** Dissolute ; profligate ; লম্পট, কামাসক্ত ; দুশ্চরিত্র, ব্যভিচারপরায়ণ। **—tin-age,** *n.* **—tin-ism,** *n.* **1.** Freethinking in religion ; ধর্ম্ম সম্বন্ধে স্বাধীন চিন্তা।

2. Practice or conduct of a licentious man : লাম্পট্য, ব্যভিচার, লোচ্চামি। **Chartered libertine**—A person allowed to do as he pleases ; যে ব্যক্তিকে যথেচ্ছাচার করিতে দেওয়া হয়।

lib'-êr-tȳ, *n.* **1.** The state of being free from captivity, imprisonment, slavery or despotic control ; স্বাধীনতা, মুক্তি, স্বতন্ত্রতা, স্বাতন্ত্র্য, স্বায়ত্ততা, স্বেচ্ছাচারিতা, অদাস্য। **2.** Power to do as one pleases ; leave ; as, *liberty* to come or go ; যথেচ্ছভাবে কার্য্য করার ক্ষমতা ; অনুমতি। **3.** (*Philos.*) Freedom from control of necessity or fate ; (দর্শন শাস্ত্র) ভবিতব্যতা বা আবশ্যকতা হইতে নির্মুক্তি, স্ববশতা, আত্মবশতা, স্বাতন্ত্র্য, অদৃষ্টানধীনতা (কেভিঃ), অদৈবাধীনতা (ঐ)। **4.** A setting aside of the rules of etiquette etc. ; a licence ; as, to take the *liberty* to do or of doing ; শিষ্টাচারের নিয়ম লঙ্ঘন, অমর্য্যাদা, মর্য্যাদাতিক্রম, মর্য্যাদাতিচার ; অধিকার। **5.** A privilege granted by a sovereign to the subjects ; রাজদত্ত বিশেষ অধিকার। **6.** (*Pl.*) Rights or immunities enjoyed by grant or by prescription ; প্রদত্ত ক্ষমতা। **7.** A freedom from despotic rule personified ; as, *Liberty*, Equality, Fraternity ; স্বাধীনতাদেবী। **Civil-liberty** — পৌরস্বাধীনতা। **Liberty-hall**—See under HALL. **Moral-liberty** — নৈতিক দায়িত্বের পক্ষে অপরিহার্য্য ন্যায়ান্যায় নির্ব্বাচন স্বাধীনতা, নৈতিক স্বাধীনতা। **Natural-liberty**—নৈসর্গিক স্বাধীনতা, মানবের সহজ স্বাধীনতা—যাহার দরুণ সে কোন পার্থিব শক্তির অধীন হইতে প্রস্তুত নহে। **Political liberty** — রাজনৈতিক স্বাধীনতা, জাতীয় স্বাধীনতা। **At liberty**—Unconfined ; free ; স্বাধীন, মুক্ত ; অবারিত। At leisure ; disengaged ; অবসর ; কার্য্যবিরত। Having the right to do ; as, you are quite *at liberty* to do this ; ক্ষমতাবান। **Cap of liberty**—See CAP. **Liberty of the press**—মুদ্রাযন্ত্রের স্বাধীনতা। **The liberty of conscience**—ধর্ম্মমত সম্বন্ধে স্বাধীনতা। **To be at liberty to do**—To have the right to do ; কোন কাজ করার স্বাধীনতা থাকা। **To set at liberty**—To set free ; মুক্তি প্রদান করা। **To take liberties**—To be unduly familiar (*with*) ; to deal freely *with* rules or facts ; শিষ্টাচার বা ভদ্রতার নিয়ম লঙ্ঘন বা কোন মান্য ব্যক্তির মর্য্যাদা রক্ষা না করিয়া অনুচিত ভাবে মেশা বা কথা বলা। **To take the liberty to do** or **of doing**—To go so far beyond the bounds of civility or propriety as to do etc. ; শিষ্টাচার বা ঔচিত্যের সীমা লঙ্ঘন করিয়া কোন কথা বলা বা কাজ করা।

lĭ-bid'-i-nous (-nŭs), *adj.* Lustful ; lewd ; কামাসক্ত, লম্পট ; রতিক্রিয়ারত, কামুক, কামরসিক। **—ly,** *adv.* **—nist,** *n.* A lewd person ; কামুক ব্যক্তি।

lī'-brā, *n.* (*Pl.*-BRAE) (*Astron.-cap.*) **1.** The Balance ; the seventh sign of the zodiac ; তুলারাশি ; রাশিচক্রের সপ্তম রাশি। **2.** Pound-weight (used only in abbr. lb ; as 5 lb, 10 lb) ; এক পাউণ্ড ওজনের সাঙ্কেতিক চিহ্ন। **3.** Pound sterling (used in abbr. £. *s. d.*) ; পাউণ্ড মুদ্রার সাঙ্কেতিক চিহ্ন।

lī-brā'-rĭ-ăn, *n.* The custodian of a library ; গ্রন্থরক্ষক, পুস্তকালয়াধ্যক্ষ, পুস্তকশালাধিকারী, পুস্তকশালাধ্যক্ষ, পুস্তকশালাধিপতি। **—ship,** *n.*

lī'-brā-rȳ, *n.* **1.** A room or building devoted to a collection of books ; গ্রন্থসংগ্রহাগার, গ্রন্থসংগ্রহকক্ষ। **2.** A writing and reading room in a house ; কোন বাড়ীর লিখাপড়া করিবার গৃহ, পাঠকক্ষ। **3.** A collection of books for use by the public or members of some society ; a public institution charged with the care of such collection of books ; as, a city *library* ; পুস্তকসংগ্রহ, গ্রন্থসংগ্রহ ; পুস্তকালয়, পুস্তকাগার, গ্রন্থাগার, গ্রন্থকুটীর, সংগ্রহাগার, **4.** A collection of books belonging to a private person ; কোন ব্যক্তিবিশেষের সংগৃহীত পুস্তকাবলী। **5.** A series of books of some similarity issued by a publisher ; কোন প্রকাশক কর্ত্তৃক প্রকাশিত কতিপয় বিষয়ে সাদৃশ্যবিশিষ্ট পুস্তকাবলী। **6.** Books used by, or familiar to, an author ; কোন গ্রন্থকারের সর্ব্বদা ব্যবহৃত বা প্রিয় গ্রন্থসমূহ। **Circulating library**—See CIRCULATING. **Free library**—যে পুস্তকালয়ে জনসাধারণ বিনা ব্যয়ে পাঠ করিতে পারে। **Lending library**—যে পুস্তকালয় হইতে চাঁদা দিয়া বা না দিয়া বাটীতে পুস্তক নেওয়া যায়। **Library-edition** — কোন পুস্তকের গ্রন্থাগারে রক্ষণোপযোগী সংস্করণ। **Reference library** — One in which a book may be consulted ; যে পুস্তকাগারে বসিয়া পুস্তক পড়া যায়। **Walking library**—বিদ্যাসাগর।

lī'-brate, *v. i.* To be poised ; to balance ; to waver ; to quiver ; সমতুল হওয়া ; তুলিত হওয়া ; ঈষৎ দোলায়মান হওয়া, দোদুল্যমান হওয়া, ঈষদান্দোলিত হওয়া ; কম্পিত হওয়া। **—bra'-tion,** *n.* The act of oscillating or balancing ; equipoise ; ঈষদান্দোলন, তুলামান ; ভারসাম্য। **—bra-to-ry,** *adj.* Oscillating ; moving like a balance ; দোদুল্যমান ; তুলাদণ্ডের ন্যায় দোদুল্যমান। **Diurnal libration**—দৈনিকদর্শনস্থিতি (হিঃ কোঃ)। **Libration of the moon**—যে আপাত প্রতীয়মান (স্ফুট) দোলনবশতঃ চন্দ্রবিম্বের প্রান্তসন্নিহিত অংশসমূহ পর্য্যায়ক্রমে দৃশ্য ও অদৃশ্য হইয়া থাকে, চন্দ্রদর্শনস্থিতি (হিঃ কোঃ), পরিলম্বন (সাঃ পঃ), আলম্বন (ঐ), দোলন (সূর্য্য বিঃ), তুলামান (প্রঃ রসঃ)।

li-brĕt'-tō (lē-), *n.* (*Pl.*-TI) **1.** The text or words of an opera or long musical work ; গীতিনাট্যাদির মূলগ্রন্থ বা মূলগ্রন্থস্থ শব্দাবলী। **—tist.** *n.* The writer of a libretto or librettos ; গীতিনাট্য লেখক।

Lib′-ȳ-ăn, *adj.* & *n.* **1.** Of, or relating to, Libya, the ancient name of a large district in the North of Africa ; লিবিয়া প্রদেশ সম্বন্ধীয়। **2.** (*Poet.*) African ; (কবিতায়) আফ্রিকাদেশীয়। **3.** Of, or relating to, the Berber language or the Hamitic languages spoken in this area; বারবার ভাষাসম্বন্ধীয়, বারবারির শৈলাঞ্চলের অধিবাসীদের ভাষাসম্বন্ধীয়। ***Noun.*** An inhabitant of Libya; the Libyan language ; লিবিয়ার অধিবাসী ; লিবিয়ার ভাষা।

lice, *n.* See LOUSE.

lī′-cence (-sŏns), *n.* **1.** Leave ; permission ; অনুমতি ; অনুজ্ঞা। **2.** A formal permission from proper authorities to do particular acts, to print something, to preach, to carry on some trade (esp that in alcoholic liquor), etc. ; a document embodying such permission ; বিশেষ অধিকার ; সনন্দ। **3.** A university certificate of competence in some faculty ; বিশ্ববিদ্যালয়ের উপাধিপত্র। **4.** Excess of liberty ; abuse of freedom ; disregard of law or propriety ; স্বেচ্ছাচারিতা, কামাচার ; উচ্ছৃঙ্খলতা, স্বৈরাচার ; ভদ্রতা বা শোভনতার অমর্য্যাদা, মর্য্যাদাতিক্রম, স্বৈরবিসর্পণ (বাংস্তঃ)। **5.** A writer's or artist's irregularity in grammar, metre, perspective, etc. ; as, poetic *licence* ; আর্ষপ্রয়োগ, লিখক, কবি বা চিত্রকরগণের ছন্দঃ, ব্যাকরণ, পরিপ্রেক্ষিত সম্পর্কে নিরঙ্কুশতা। **6.** Profligacy ; licentiousness ; ভ্রষ্টাচার ; লাম্পট্য।

lī′-cense (-sŏns), **—cence** (-sŏns), *v. t.* **1.** To give authority or permission to do any act or carry on any business, profession, etc. by a formal licence ; to give licence to ; সনন্দ প্রদান করা ; যথেচ্ছভাবে চলিতে দেওয়া। **2.** To authorize the use of (premises) for certain purpose ; কোন বিশেষ উদ্দেশ্যে গৃহাদি ব্যবহার করিতে অনুমতি দেওয়া। **3.** To authorize publication of (books etc.) or performance of (a play) ; পুস্তক প্রকাশ বা নাটকাদি অভিনয়ের অনুমতি দেওয়া। **4.** (In *p. p.*) To give complete freedom to ; as, a *licensed* satirist ; পূর্ণ স্বাধীনতা প্রদান করা। **5.** (*Rare*) To allow *to* do something ; (কচিদ্ব্যবহৃত) কোন কার্য্য করিতে অনুমতি দেওয়া। **—censed,** *adj.* Permitted by authority ; দত্তাধিকার, প্রাপ্তানুমতি, সনদী (কেঙিঃ)। **—censee′,** *n.* The holder of a licence ; সনন্দপ্রাপ্ত ব্যক্তি। **—cens-er,** *n.* One who grants a licence ; সনন্দদাতা। **Licensed home**—মদের দোকান। **A licensed murderer**—যে অনভিজ্ঞ চিকিৎসকের হস্তে বহু রোগী নিহত হয়। **Licenser of the press** or **of plays**—পুস্তকাদি প্রকাশ বা নাটকাদি অভিনয় সম্বন্ধে অনুমতিদাতা কর্ম্মচারী।

lī-cĕn′-ti-āte (-shī-), *n.* **1.** One holding a license, esp. one granted by a university or other degree-conferring body, (abbr. *L.* as part of a title); as, L. M. S. (*Licentiate* in Medicine and Surgery) ; প্রাপ্তাধিকার ব্যক্তি, সনন্দ-প্রাপ্ত ব্যক্তি, বিশ্ববিদ্যালয়ের উপাধিপ্রাপ্ত ব্যক্তি, সনদী (কেঙিঃ), সনদওয়ালা (ঐ)। **2.** A licensed preacher not yet having appointment esp. in the Presbyterian Church ; প্রচারকের পদে এপর্য্যন্ত নিযুক্ত নয় কিন্তু ধর্ম্ম প্রচারের জন্য বিশেষ অধিকারপ্রাপ্ত প্রচারক।

lī-cĕn′-tious (-shŭs), *adj.* **1.** Using too much license or freedom ; unrestrained by accepted rules esp. of grammar or style ; ব্যভিচারী, স্বৈরী, স্বেচ্ছাচারী, কামাচারী, উচ্ছৃঙ্খল, অনিয়মসংযত, নিরঙ্কুশ। **2.** Libertine ; lewd ; লম্পট, দুর্নীতিপরায়ণ, লোচ্চা, ভ্রষ্ট ; কামুক, রত্যাসক্ত, ব্যসনাসক্ত। **—ly,** *adv* **—ness,** *n.*

lich, lȳch, lȳke, *ns.* (*Obs.*) Corpse ; (অপ্রঃ) শব, মৃতদেহ। **Lich-gate, Lych-gate**—বাহকের আগমন সময় পর্য্যন্ত শবাধার রাখিবার নিমিত্ত গির্জ্জা সংলগ্ন ছাদবিশিষ্ট তোরণ। **Lich-house, Lych-house**—শবগৃহ। **Lich-owl, Lych-owl**—কাল পেঁচা। **Lich-stone, Lych-stone**—গির্জাসংলগ্ন শবগৃহে শবাধার রাখিবার শিলা। **Lyke-wake**—শব চৌকি দেওয়ার জন্য রাত্রি জাগরণ।

lī′-chĕn, *n.* **1.** One of an order of cryptogamic plants without stem and leaves growing on the bark of trees, on rocks etc. ; শৈবাল (ব্রজঃ হিন্দু), শিলাবাক। **2.** A skin-disease with reddish eruption ; একপ্রকার চর্ম্মরোগ যাহাতে রক্তবর্ণ পীড়কা জন্মে। **—chened,** *adj.* With lichens (plants) growing on the surface ; শৈবালাচ্ছিত। **—ous,** *adj.* **1.** Covered with, or abounding in, lichens ; শৈবালাচ্ছাদিত, শেওলা-পড়া, শৈবালপূর্ণ। **2.** (*Med.*) Characteristic of, belonging to, lichen ; (ভৈষজ্য-শাস্ত্র) রক্তবর্ণ পীড়কা-বিশিষ্ট চর্ম্মরোগ সম্বন্ধীয়।

lī-chĕn-ŏl′-ŏ-gȳ, *n.* That branch of Botany which deals with lichens ; শৈবালতত্ত্ব।

lĭc′-it, *adj.* Lawful ; legal ; legitimate ; বৈধ ; বিধিসম্মত ; বিধিসঙ্গত, বিহিত। **—ly,** *adv.*

lick, *v. t., i.* & *n.* **1.** To pass the tongue over to taste, to moisten, etc. ; as, the dog *licks* his master's hand ; চাটা, লেহন করা। **2.** To take in with the tongue ; to take up or off by licking ; to cleanse with the tongue ; as, the dog *licks* the wound ; চাটিয়া খাওয়া চাটিয়া উঠান ; চাটিয়া পরিষ্কার করা। **3.** (Of waves etc.) To play over (coast etc.) like a tongue ; (of flames etc.) to consume in passing; "Flames *licked* up everything in their path of destruction"; আস্তে আস্তে গেলিয়া যাওয়া; ভস্মসাৎ করিয়া চলা। **4.** (*Slang*) To beat; to flog; to chastise; as, to *lick* a person or a fault out of him; (ইতর ভাষায়) মারা, পিটুনি দেওয়া; বেত মারা; সাজা দেওয়া। **5.** To conquer; to beat in fight or competition; to excel; জয় করা; হারাইয়া দেওয়া; অতিক্রম করা। **6.** To surpass comprehension of; as, it *licks* me; বুদ্ধির অগোচর হওয়া, বুদ্ধির অতীত হওয়া। ***Verb i.*** (*Slang*) To go; to hasten; as, as hard as he could *lick*; (ইতরভাষায়) যাওয়া; তাড়াতাড়ি করা, ত্বরা করা। ***Noun.*** **1.** Act of licking; লেহন, চাটন। **2.** A place where wild animals resort for salt (also *salt-lick*); যে স্থানে বন্য পশু সমূহ লবণলেহনের জন্য সমাগত হয়, লবণলেহনস্থল। **3.** A strike or blow with a stick etc.; লাঠি প্রভৃতির আঘাত। **4.** (*Slang*) Pace; as, at a great *lick*: at full *lick*; (ইতর ভাষায়) পদক্ষেপ, গতি। **Lick-spittle**—পা-চাটা, ধামাধরা। **This licks me**—(*Slang*) I cannot explain it; (ইতরভাষায়) আমি ইহা বুঝাইতে পারি না। **To lick into shape**—To mould; to give proper form to; গড়িয়া তোলা; যথোচিত অবয়ববিশিষ্ট করা। [ভল্লুক শাবক কিম্ভূতকিমাকার মাংসপিণ্ডবৎ জন্মে এবং ভল্লুকীগণ লেহন করিয়া উহাকে অবয়ববিশিষ্ট করে এই প্রাচীন বিশ্বাস হইতে এই বাক্যটী উদ্ভূত হইয়াছে।] **To lick one's chops** or **lips**—To do so in relish or in anticipation of food; ভোজ্যবস্তুর রসাস্বাদন করিয়া ওষ্ঠ লেহন করা, ভোজ্য বস্তুর আশায় ওষ্ঠ লেহন করা। **To lick one's shoes**—To show servility to him; পদলেহন করা, পা চাটা। **To lick the dust**—To be vanquished; to be slain; পরাস্ত হওয়া, পরাভূত হওয়া; নিহত হওয়া। To cringe servilely to gain favour; অনুগ্রহলাভের আশায় অতি হীনভাবে তোষামোদ করা। **To lick the spittle of**—To fawn upon servilely; to court meanly; ঘৃণিতভাবে তোষামোদ করা; পা চাটা, পদলেহন করা। **To lick up**—To consume; নষ্ট করা, ধ্বংস করা।

lick'-êr-ish, liq'-uor-ish (lĭk-êr-), *adj.* **1.** Fond of dainty fare; মুখরোচক আহারলিপ্সু, সুস্বাদু ভোজ্যপ্রিয়, ভোজনবিলাসী, সুখাদ্যপ্রিয়। **2.** Eager to swallow; greedy; desirous; গৃধ্নু, লোভী; পেটুক; ভোগোৎসুক। **3.** Lecherous; lustful; লম্পট, কামুক; রতিরসিক।

lic'-ŏ-rice (-rĭs), *n.* Same as LIQUORICE.

lic'-ŏ-rous (-rŭs), *adj.* Same as LICKERISH.

lic'-tor (-têr), *n.* (*Rom. antiq.*) An officer attending the Roman magistrates bearing an axe and rods; প্রাচীন রোমের শাসনবিভাগীয় উচ্চপদস্থ কর্ম্মচারিগণের অগ্রগামী দণ্ডগুচ্ছ ও কুঠারধারী অনুচর।

lid, *n.* **1.** A hinged or detached cover for the opening of a vessel, box, etc.; আবরণ, ঢাকনী, শরাব, ডালা, পিধান। **2.** The cover of the eye; চক্ষুর পাতা, চক্ষুর আবরণ, অক্ষিপত্র, নেত্রচ্ছদ। **3.** (*Bot. Conch.*) Operculum; ঢাকনী, শরাব। **Lid'-ded,** *adj.* **Lid'-less,** *adj.* Having no lid; আবরণ শূন্য, ঢাকনীবিহীন।

lie (lī), *n.* **1.** An intentional untrue statement; অনৃত, মিথ্যা কথা, অসত্য কথা, মিথ্যোক্তি। **2.** An imposture; a false belief; a mistaken conviction; as, to worship or maintain a *lie*; প্রতারণা, ছলনা; মিথ্যা প্রতীতি; ভ্রান্ত ধারণা। **White lie** — সদুদ্দেশ্যমূলক মিথ্যা বাক্য। **A lie out of whole cloth**—ডাহা মিথ্যা কথা। **To give one the lie**—To accuse him of lying; মিথ্যাবাদী বলিয়া অভিযুক্ত করা। **To give the lie to (supposition etc.)**—To serve to show its falsity; to belie it; মিথ্যা কথা আরোপ করা; অসত্য বা মিথ্যা বলিয়া সপ্রমাণ করা। **To tell a lie**—To make a false statement; মিথ্যা কথা বলা।

lie (lī), *v. i.* & *t.* To utter false word with intent to deceive; to tell a lie or lies; মিথ্যা কথা বলা; অসত্য বলা। ***Verb t.*** **1.** To take away as reputation by lying; to get, as a person or oneself *into* or *out of* by lying; মিথ্যা বলিয়া খ্যাতি প্রভৃতি নষ্ট করা; মিথ্যা বলিয়া নিজকে বা অপর কাহাকে কোন কিছুতে ফেলা বা কোন কিছু হইতে রক্ষা পাওয়া। **2.** To deceive; ঠকান, প্রতারণা করা, ছলনা করা। **To lie like a gas-meter**—To tell lies freely; অনর্গল মিথ্যা কথা বলা।

lie (lī), *v. i.* **1.** To occupy or rest in a more or less horizontal position; to be prostrate; শায়িত হওয়া; ধরাশায়ী হওয়া। **2.** To be in the grave (of a dead); সমাহিত হওয়া, কবরে শায়িত হওয়া। **3.** To assume a lying or inclining position, (usu. with *down*, *back*); as, the watchful traveller *lay down* again; শয়ন করা, শুইয়া থাকা। **4.** To be in a specified state; as, to *lie* in prison: to *lie* helpless, idle, etc.; নির্দ্দিষ্ট অবস্থায় থাকা। **5.** To have sexual intercourse (*with*); রতিক্রিয়া হওয়া। **6.** To be posted or encamped in a specified place, (said of troops); নির্দ্দিষ্ট স্থানে ছাউনি করা, তাঁবু ফেলা। **7.** (Of inanimate things) To remain more or less horizontally; অল্প বা অধিক শয়ানভাবে থাকা। **8.** To be stored up in specified place; as, the money *lies* at the bank; নির্দ্দিষ্ট স্থানে সঞ্চিত বা গচ্ছিত থাকা। **9.** (Of inanimate things) To remain in specified state; to be situated; as, the land *lies* waste, barren: Ireland *lies* west of England ; নির্দ্দিষ্ট স্থানে থাকা ; অবস্থান করা। **10.** To be exposed to view ; as, to *lie* on the surface : to *lie* open ; প্রকাশ্যে থাকা, চোখের উপর থাকা। **11.** (Of road) To lead *by, along, among, through,* etc. ; as, the road *lay by* the church ; (পথ সম্পর্কে) কিনারা দিয়া, মধ্য দিয়া, পাশ দিয়া যাওয়া। **12.** (Of ship) To be stationed as at anchor etc. ; (জাহাজ) নোঙ্গর করিয়া থাকা। **13.** To exist ; to depend ; to reside ; to be arranged or related in some position or manner ; as, all our hope *lies* in watchfulness : he knows where his interest *lies* ; বর্ত্তমান থাকা : নির্ভর করা : বাস করা ; কোন প্রকারে সম্পর্কান্বিত হওয়া। **14.** (*Law*) To be admissible or sustainable ; as, an appeal *lies* in this case ; গ্রাহ্য হওয়া, চলা। **Lie-abed**—A late riser ; বিলম্বে শয্যাত্যাগকারী। **A lying-in hospital**—আসন্নপ্রসবা স্ত্রীলোকগণের জন্য রুগ্নাবাস, প্রসূতি চিকিৎসাগার (হঃ চঃ)। **As far as in one lies**—As far as is practicable for him ; তাহার পক্ষে যতদূর সাধ্য। **Let the sleeping dogs lie**—Avoid mooting debatable questions ; বিবদনীয় বিষয় উত্থাপন করিও না। **To lie along**—To be extended at full length ; সটান হইয়া পড়া। **To lie along the shore**—(*Naut.*) To keep a course parallel to the land ; (নৌবিদ্যা) ভূমির সহিত সমান্তরালভাবে চলা। **To lie at**—To tease ; to importune ; বিরক্ত করা, ক্ষেপান ; পুনঃ পুনঃ যাচ্ঞা বা অসঙ্গত-প্রার্থনা দ্বারা বিরক্ত করা। **To lie at one's door**—To be imputable or chargeable to (one) ; as, the blame *lies at your door* ; কাহারো ঘাড়ে চাপানের যোগ্য হওয়া, কাহারো উপর আরোপিত হওয়ার যোগ্য হওয়া। **To lie at one's heart**—To be a source or object of anxiety, care or desire ; কামনা, উৎকণ্ঠা বা তত্ত্বাবধানের বিষয় হওয়া, প্রাণের জিনিষ হওয়া। **To lie at the mercy of**—To be in the power of ; to depend on ; কাহারও অধীনে থাকা ; কাহারও উপর নির্ভর করা। **To lie at the root of**—To be the true cause or source of ; মূলে থাকা। **To lie between**—To be limited to ; as, the choice *lies between* two courses ; সীমাবদ্ধ হওয়া। **To lie by**—To remain with ; as, he has the papers still *lying by* him ; to keep quiet or retired ; পড়িয়া থাকা ; চুপ থাকা, নীরব থাকা, নিরিবিলি থাকা। **To lie down** — To go to rest (*colloq.*) ; (চলিত ভাষায়) বিশ্রাম করিতে যাওয়া। To submit abjectly to defeat or disappointment ; to yield without further struggle ; পায়ে লুটাইয়া পড়া, পায় পড়া, গড়াইয়া পড়া ; পদানত হওয়া। **To lie fallow**—পতিত থাকা, অনাবাদী থাকা। **To lie hard** or **heavy**—To press or weigh ; to bear hard ; চাপিয়া পড়া ; চাপ দেওয়া। **To lie in**—To be in a child-bed ; আঁতুড় ঘরে থাকা। **To lie in a nutshell**—To be capable of brief statement or explanation ; সংক্ষেপে বর্ণনীয় হওয়া, অতি অল্প কথায় বলিতে পারা। **To lie in the way** — To be an obstacle or impediment ; বাধাস্বরূপ হওয়া, প্রতিবন্ধক হওয়া, পথরোধ করা। **To lie in wait**—To watch or wait in ambush or concealment ; to watch for an opportunity to attack ; আড়ি পাতিয়া থাকা। কাহাকেও আক্রমণ করার উদ্দেশ্যে ওৎ পাতিয়া থাকা। **To lie low**—See under LOW. **To lie off**—(*Naut.*) To stand some distance from shore or other ship ; (নৌ-বিদ্যা) তীর বা অন্য জাহাজ হইতে কিছু দূরে থাকা। **To lie on one's hand**—To remain unsold or undisposed of, (also *to lie on hand*) ; হাতে থাকা, অবিক্রীত অবস্থায় পড়িয়া থাকা। To hang heavily ; as, time *lies on one's hand* ; দুর্ব্বহ হওয়া, ভারবোধ হওয়া, আর যেন কাটে না এরূপ বোধ হওয়া। **To lie on one's oars**—To be idle ; to cease work ; অলস হওয়া ; কার্য্য-নিরত হওয়া। **To lie on the bed one has made** — See under BED. **To lie on the head of**—To be imputed to ; আরোপ-যোগ্য হওয়া। **To lie over** — To be deferred as payment etc. ; to be postponed ; অনাদায়ী থাকা ; পড়িয়া থাকা, বিথুলত থাকা। **To lie to**—(*Naut.*) To be checked or stopped in her course ; (নৌবিদ্যা) গতিরোধ হওয়া। **To lie to one's work**—To work energetically ; সোৎসাহে কার্য্য করা। **To lie under**—To be subject to ; to be oppressed by ; অধীনে থাকা ; উৎপীড়িত হওয়া। **To lie up**—To be in, or go into, retirement ; to take to one's bed or room ; (of a ship) to go into dock ; বিশ্রাম লওয়া, অবসর লওয়া ; শয্যার আশ্রয় গ্রহণ করা, নিজ কক্ষে যাওয়া ; (পোত সম্পর্কে) পোতাশ্রয়ে যাওয়া। **To lie upon**—To be incumbent upon ; to depend upon ; অবশ্যপালনীয় হওয়া ; নির্ভর করা। **To lie with**—To lodge or sleep with ; একত্র বাস করা, একত্র শয়ন করা। To have sexual intercourse with ; রতিক্রিয়া হওয়া, সঙ্গম হওয়া। To belong to ; to depend on ; as, it *lies with* you to remedy the mistake ; অধিকার থাকা ; নির্ভর করা।

lie (lī), *n.* **1.** The position, manner or direction in which anything lies ; অবস্থানের ভঙ্গী, দিক্ বা প্রণালী। **2.** A place where beast, bird or fish is accustomed to lie ; পশু, পক্ষী বা মৎস্যের শয়নস্থান।

lied, *n.* (*Pl.* ADLIEER) German song or poem of the ballad kind ; জর্ম্মণ গাথা।

lief (lēf), *adv.* Gladly ; willingly ; (*Rare,* except in, *I would as lief do something etc.*) ; আনন্দের সহিত, সানন্দে ; ইচ্ছাপূর্ব্বক, ইচ্ছার সহিত।

liege (lēj), *adj.* & *n.* **1.** Having right or claim to feudal service or allegiance ; as, a *liege*-lord ; প্রজার বশ্যতা ও সেবার অধিকারী। **2.** Bound to feudal service and allegiance, as to a liege-lord ; ভূস্বামীর কাজে বশ্যতা স্বীকারে বাধ্য। ***Noun.*** **1.** A lord or superior to whom one owes feudal service and allegiance ; ভূস্বামী, প্রভু, রাজা। **2.** (*Usu. Pl.*) A vassal or subject doing feudal service or allegiance to a superior ; প্রজা, রায়ত। **Liege-lord**—ভূস্বামী। **Liegeman**—A vassal or subject ; রায়ত, প্রজা।

lī'-ĕn, *n.* (*Law*) The right of possession over the property of another until some claim or due is satisfied ; (আইন) সম্পত্তি যাহার দখলে আছে তাহার কোন দাওয়ার পরিশোধ না হওয়া পর্য্যন্ত ঐ সম্পত্তি দখলে রাখার অধিকার, দাবী, দাওয়া।

li-erne' (lē-ĕrn), *n.* A branch rib introduced between the principal ribs of a groined arch ; কোণাকৃতি শীর্ষ তোরণের প্রধান আশ্রয়বক্রদ্বয়ের মধ্যে নিবিষ্ট শাখা আশ্রয়-বক্র।

lieu (lü), *n.* Place ; stead ; (used only in the phrase *in lieu of*= instead of) ; স্থল, জায়গা ; অনুকল্প।

lieu-tĕn'-ant (lĕf-), *n.* **1.** A deputy or substitute acting for a superior ; as, the Lieutenant of the Towers ; প্রতিনিধি। **2.** A commissioned officer next below a captain in the army or next below a commander in the navy ; সেনানী বিশেষ—সেনাবিভাগে Captain এবং নৌবিভাগে Commander এর অব্যবহিত নিম্নবর্ত্তী কর্ম্মচারী। **–ant'-cy,** *n.* The office, rank or position of a lieutenant ; উক্ত কর্ম্মচারীর কার্য্য বা পদ। **Lieutenant colonel** — কর্ণেলের অব্যবহিত নিম্নবর্ত্তী এবং কাপ্তেনের অব্যবহিত উর্দ্ধতন সামরিক কর্ম্মচারী **Lieutenant-colonelcy**—লেপ্টেনান্ট কর্ণেলের পদ। **Lieutenant general** — জেনারেলের অব্যবহিত নিম্নবর্ত্তী এবং মেজর জেনারেলের অব্যবহিত উর্দ্ধতন কর্ম্মচারী। **Lieutenant-governor**—ছোট লাট। *Lieutenant-governorship, n.*

Lif and Lifthrasir—The Adam and Eve of the Norse myths ; স্কেণ্ডেনেভিয়ার পুরাণোক্ত আদম ও ঈভ—যাহারা দেবগণের ধ্বংসের পর নবজগতে পুনরায় আবির্ভূত হয়।

life, *n.* **1.** The existence on earth of a human being ; state of being alive ; জীবন, জীবিত, জীবিতকাল, প্রাণ ; জীবদ্দশা। **2.** The period from birth to death, from birth to this time or from this time to death ; আজীবন, আমরণ। **3.** A person ; a living being ; as, many *lives* were lost ; living beings or organisms and their motion ; as, very little *life* to be seen ; ব্যক্তি ; প্রাণী, জীব ; প্রাণিবর্গ, জীবগণ, শরীরী **4.** The living form or model ; as, a picture taken from the *life* ; জীবন্তবিগ্রহ, জীবন্ত প্রতিরূপ, সজীবমূর্ত্তি। **5.** Animation ; spirit ; vivacity ; as, he has no *life* in him ; a poem without *life* : সজীবতা ; শক্তি ; তেজ। **6.** Conscious existence ; as, spiritual *life* ; জীবন। **7.** A fresh start after a narrowly-escaped death, (*lit.* & *fig.*) ; as, cats have nine *lives* ; চুলেচুলে মৃত্যুর হাত হইতে রক্ষা পাইয়া নবজীবনারম্ভ। **8.** A mode or manner of living with respect to conditions, circumstances, etc. ; as, the *life* of Indians ; জীবনযাত্রা, জীবনযাপনপ্রণালী। **9.** Animating influence ; a person or thing that imparts life, vigour, spirit, etc. ; as, he was the *life* of the party : you have touched the *life* of our design ; প্রাণপ্রদশক্তি ; প্রাণপ্রদ ব্যক্তি বা বস্তু। **10.** Active part of existence ; business and pleasures of the world ; as, see *life* (mix freely with others) ; জীবনের রাজসিক অংশ ; সাংসারিক ব্যাপার ও সুখভোগ। **11.** The history of the life of a person ; a biography ; as, Abbot's *life* of Napolean ; জীবনচরিত, জীবনী ; জীবনবৃত্তান্ত। **12.** Something dear to one ; darling one ; প্রাণপ্রতিম ব্যক্তি, প্রাণ ; জীবন পরাণ-বঁধু। [cf. ত্বমসি মে জীবনং।] **13.** (*Commer.*) A person considered as the object of a policy of insurance ; as, a good or bad *life* ; (বাণিজ্য) বীমার যোগ্য ব্যক্তি। **14.** (*Theol.*) Salvation ; regenerate state ; (ধর্ম্মশাস্ত্র) মুক্তি ; নবজীবন। **Life'-less,** *adj.* **1.** Deprived of life ; dead ; গতপ্রাণ, বিগতজীবিত, প্রাণহীন, গতায়ু, গতচেষ্ট, নিষ্প্রাণ, প্রাণবিরহিত ; মৃত। **2.** Inanimate ; অচেতন। **3.** Destitute of vigour or spirit ; dull ; inactive ; মন্দতেজাঃ, নির্জ্জীব ; নিস্তেজ ; নিশ্চেষ্ট, অক্রিয়, নিষ্ক্রিয়। **Life'-less-ly,** *adv.* **Life'-less-ness,** *n.* **Life'-like,** *adj.* Like a living person ; true to the life ; জীবিতবৎ, সজীববৎ ; জীবন্ত। **Life annuity**—See ANNUITY. **Life-assurance**—Same as LIFE INSURANCE. **Life-belt**—শোলা প্রভৃতি হাল্কা জিনিষে তৈয়ারী কটিবন্ধ—যাহার সাহায্যে অল্প আয়াসে জলে ভাসা যায়। **Life-blood**—The blood necessary to life ; (*fig.*) that which gives strength and energy ; an involuntary twitching (quiver) of the lip or eyelid ; হৃদয়শোণিত ; (লক্ষণায়) সঞ্জীবনী শক্তি ; ওষ্ঠ বা অক্ষিপত্রের স্বতঃস্পন্দন। **Life-boat**—A boat designed for saving ship-wrecked people ; ঝড়ের সময় প্রাণরক্ষার্থ

বিশেষভাবে গঠিত নৌকা, জীবনতরী **Life-breath** — Inspiring influence ;

Life-boat.
1. longitudinal section ; 2. section amidship ; *aa*, air-cases at stem and sides ; *bb*, tubes for escape of water shipped ; *cc*, longitudinal cases packed with cork beneath the deck.

sustaining principle ; অনুপ্রাণনশীল প্রভাব ; জীবনীশক্তি। **Life-buoy**—See under BUOY ; জীবনপ্লব, বয়া। **Life-estate** — যে সম্পত্তিতে কোন ব্যক্তির জীবনস্বত্ব আছে। **Life-giving**—That gives, sustains, restores physical or spiritual life ; inspirating ; invigorating ; জীবনপ্রদ, প্রাণপ্রদ, অধ্যাত্মশক্তিসঞ্চারক ; প্রাণদায়ক ; শক্তি-সঞ্চারক। **Life-guard** — জীবন রক্ষক সেনা, তৈনাতি সেনা, শরীররক্ষী সৈন্য। **Life-Guards** — ইংলণ্ডেশ্বরের প্রাসাদ রক্ষার্থ অশ্বারোহী সেনা পল্টনদ্বয়। **Life-interest**—জীবনস্বত্ব **Life-jacket**—Same as LIFE-BELT. **Life-line**—প্রবল ঝটিকার সময়ে নাবিকদিগের ধরার জন্য জাহাজের পাটাতনের যে কোন স্থল হইতে প্রসারিত রজ্জু। A rope attached to a life-buoy to assist a person to grasp it ; জলনিমজ্জনোন্মুখ ব্যক্তির ধরার জন্য জীবনপ্লবসংলগ্ন রজ্জু, জীবনরজ্জু। **Life-long**—Continued for life ; যাবজ্জীবন, জন্মাবচ্ছিন্ন, আজীবন, আমরণ। **Life-member**—আজীবন সদস্য। **Life-office** — An office for life-insurance ; জীবনবীমার কার্য্যালয়। **Life-peerage**—জীবিতকাল পর্য্যন্ত ভোগ্য সম্ভ্রমসূচক উপাধি। **Life-preserver** — An invention, as a buoyant belt or jacket, for the preservation of life in case of shipwreck ; জলমগ্ন জাহাজ হইতে উদ্ধারের জন্য প্লবনশীল কোর্ত্তা, কোমরবন্ধ প্রভৃতি। A short stick with a loaded head for defence ; আত্মরক্ষার জন্য মাথাভারি লাঠি। **Life-raft**—জলমগ্ন জাহাজের আরোহিগণের জীবনরক্ষার ভেলা। **Life-rocket**—একপ্রকার হাউই বাজী—বিপন্ন জাহাজের সহিত সমুদ্রতীরস্থ জনগণের সংযোগস্থাপনের জন্য এইরূপ হাউই বাজীর সহিত একটা রজ্জু বাঁধিয়া দেওয়া হয়। **Life-school**—যে চিত্রবিদ্যালয় বা চিত্রাঙ্কণকক্ষে চিত্রশিল্পিগণ জীবন্ত মনুষ্যাদির আদর্শ অবলম্বনে চিত্র করিয়া থাকে। **Life-size** — *Adj.* Of the size of the person or object represented ; পূর্ণায়তন। **Life-spring** — The source of life ; জীবনের উৎস। **Life-table** — বিভিন্ন বয়সের ব্যক্তিগণের সম্ভাবিত জীবিতকালের তালিকা। **Life-time** — জীবিতকাল, জীবদ্দশা। **Life-work** — জীবনব্যাপী কার্য্য, জীবনের কাজ। **A cat has nine lives** — See CAT. **A matter of life and death** — Something on which it depends whether one shall live or die ; a critical thing ; a very serious matter ; জীবনমরণের সমস্যা; জীবনমরণের ব্যাপার; অতি গুরুতর ব্যাপার। **As large as life**—Life-size ; (*facet.*) in person ; as, here he is *as large as life* ; পূর্ণায়তন ; (কৌতুকচ্ছলে) সশরীরে। **Come bring, to life**—To recover or cause to recover from swoon ; চৈতন্য সম্পাদিত হওয়া, চৈতন্য লাভ করা, চৈতন্য সম্পাদন করা। **Expectation of life**—The average period that a person at a specified age may expect to live ; কোন নির্দ্দিষ্ট বয়সের লোক গড়পড়তা যত কাল বাঁচিবার আশা রাখে। **For life**—Until death ; আজীবন, আমরণ। **For my life, For the life of me** — Even if my life depended on it ; আমার জীবন পণ করিয়াও, আমার প্রাণ গেলেও। **For one's life, For dear life** — To escape death ; জীবনরক্ষার জন্য, প্রাণরক্ষার জন্য। **Great sacrifice of human life** — Great loss of human life ; বহুলোকক্ষয়। **High life below stairs**—প্রভু বা মনীব বাহিরে গেলে যে আমোদপ্রমোদ ও রঙ্গরস করার অবসর পাওয়া যায়। **Life and death struggle** — জীবনমরণ সংগ্রাম। **Long or short lived**—Living for a long or short time ; দীর্ঘায়ু, অল্পায়ু। **My life**—(*Vocative*) A term of endearment ; আমার প্রাণ, প্রাণনাথ, প্রাণেশ, প্রাণেশ্বর। **The batsman was given a life**—অর্থাৎ ব্যাটধারীকে আউট করার বিশেষ সুযোগ হারাইয়া তাহাকে পূর্ব্ববৎ খেলিতে দেওয়া হইল। **To bear a charmed life**—See CHARM. **To have no regard for human life**—To kill many persons cruelly ; নিষ্ঠুরভাবে বহুলোক হত্যা করা। **To lose one's life**—To be deprived of one's life ; প্রাণ হারান। **To seek the life of**—To seek to kill ; প্রাণনাশের চেষ্টা করা। **To the life**—Exactly like a living person or thing ; ঠিক জীবন্ত ব্যক্তি বা বস্তুর মত। **Upon my life** — A form of asseveration ; আমার দিব্যি।

lif'-ĕr, *n.* (*Slang*) One sentenced to penal servitude for life ; such a sentence ; (ইতর ভাষায়) যাবজ্জীবনের জন্য কঠোর পরিশ্রমের সহিত কারাদণ্ড প্রাপ্ত ব্যক্তি ; যাবজ্জীবনের জন্য কঠোর পরিশ্রমের সহিত কারাদণ্ড।

lift, *v. t., i.* & *n.* **1.** To raise from a lower to a higher position ; to hoist ; as, to *lift* one's hand or heart ; উত্তোলিত করা, উত্তোলন করা ; উঠান। **2.** To direct upwards, as eye, face, etc. ; উপরের দিকে ফিরান, ঊর্দ্ধে প্রেরিত করা। **3.** To exalt ; to elevate to a higher plane of thought and feeling ; as, to *lift* one's heart in prayer ; উন্নীত করা ; উন্নয়ন করা। **4.** To have on high ; as, the church *lifts* its spire ; ঊর্দ্ধে থাকা। **5.** To steal, as cattle ; গোমহিষাদি চুরি করা। **6.** To remove, as tents etc. ; তাঁবু প্রভৃতি তুলিয়া ফেলা, উঠান। **7.** To take in the way of plagiarism, as a passage, information, etc.

কোন পুস্তক হইতে চুরি করিয়া নেওয়া। **8.** To dig up (potatoes); আলু প্রভৃতি মাটার নীচ হইতে তোলা, উঠান। **9.** To hit, as a ball into the air; খেলার বল জোরে আঘাত করিয়া অনেক উপরে তোলা। ***Verb i.*** **1.** To try to raise something; কোন বস্তু উঠাইতে চেষ্টা করা। **2.** (Of ship afloat) to raise on wave; তরঙ্গের উপর উত্থিত হওয়া। **3.** (Of cloud, fog, darkness) To rise; to disappear; (মেঘ, কুয়াসা, অন্ধকার প্রভৃতি) কাটিয়া যাওয়া; অদৃশ্য হওয়া। **4.** (Of floor) To swell upwards; to warp; উপরের দিকে স্ফীত হইয়া উঠা; ফাঁপিয়া উঠা। ***Noun.*** **1.** Act of lifting or raising; উত্থাপন, উত্তোলন, উন্নয়ন। **2.** Assistance in lifting; as, to give one a *lift* in a wagon; উত্তোলনে সাহায্য। **3.** An apparatus for raising or lowering people or things to other floor of a house; a hoisting machine; একতালা হইতে দ্বিতলে মাল, মানুষ প্রভৃতি উত্তোলন করিবার যন্ত্র; উত্তোলনযন্ত্র। **4.** A layer of leather in the boot-heel; বুট জুতার গোড়ালীর চামড়ার পাত। **5.** An elevation or rise in the ground; মৃত্তিকার স্ফীতি, উত্থান। **Lifting bridge**—জাহাজাদি নীচ দিয়া পার হইতে পারে এরূপ একপ্রকার টানা পুল। **To lift a hand against one** — To strike (him); কাহারও গায়ে হাত তোলা। **To lift one's hand**—To take an oath; শপথ গ্রহণ করা। **To lift up another's head**—(*Bibl.*) To restore the liberty or dignity; পুনঃ স্বাধীনতা প্রদান করা, পূর্ব্বগৌরবে প্রতিষ্ঠিত করা। **To lift up** or **lift one's hands**—To raise the hands in prayer; উপাসনার সময় হাত উর্দ্ধে তোলা। **To lift up one's head**—To recover vigour after prostration; to rejoice; পীড়াবসানে প্রাপ্তবল হওয়া, মাথা তুলিতে পারা; আনন্দ করা। **To lift (up) one's heart**—See LIFT *v. t.* 3. **To lift up one's heel (against)**—To treat with insolence or contempt; to kick; উদ্ধতভাবে বা ঘৃণার সহিত ব্যবহার করা; পদাঘাত করা। **To lift up one's horn**—To be ambitious or proud; অহঙ্কারী বা গর্ব্বিত হওয়া, উচ্চাভিলাষী হওয়া। **To lift up one's voice** or **a cry**—To cry aloud; চীৎকার করা, উচ্চৈঃস্বরে ডাকা। **To lift up the eyes** or **face** — To look with confidence; চক্ষু বা মুখ তুলিয়া চাওয়া। **To lift up the feet**—To come quickly to one's help; কাহারও সাহায্যার্থ ক্ষিপ্রপদে আগমন করা।

lig′-ă-mĕnt, *n.* **1.** (*Archaic*) A tie or band; বন্ধনী, পটি। **2.** (*Anat.*) A tough band of flexible fibrous tissue binding bones together; any membranous fold supporting or retaining an organ in place; অস্থিবন্ধ, সন্ধিবন্ধ, বন্ধনী, শ্বেতবর্ণ তন্তুগুচ্ছময় শরীরের এক প্রকার নির্ম্মাণ উপাদান—ইহা দ্বারা সন্ধি পরিবেষ্টিত ও অস্থি সংযুক্ত থাকে; বন্ধনী। **–men-tal, –men-ta-ry, –men-tous,** *adjs.* Composing a ligament; of the nature of a ligament; সংযোজক ঝিল্লিময়; সংযোজক ঝিল্লিবৎ।

li-gāte′, *v. t.* (*Surg.*) To tie up bleeding artery etc.; গলদ্‌রক্ত ধমনী বাঁধিয়া দেওয়া। **–ga′-tion,** *n.*

lig′-ă-tūre, *n.* & *v. t.* **1.** Anything that binds or unites; a bond; যাহা দ্বারা বাঁধা যায়; বন্ধনী। **2.** A band or cord used to tie up bleeding artery etc.; a wire or thread used in removing tumours; রক্তবহা ধমনীর মুখ বাঁধিবার জন্য সূত্র বা বন্ধনবস্ত্র, বস্ত্রপটি, রক্তস্রাব নিবারণের জন্য রক্তবহা নাড়ী বাঁধিবার নিমিত্ত দৃঢ় সূত্র, রেশম প্রভৃতি; অর্ব্বুদ প্রভৃতি অপাসারণের জন্য তার বা সূত্র। **3.** The act of binding or tying; বন্ধন ক্রিয়া, বন্ধন। **4.** (*Print.*) A type consisting of two or more letters joined together; (মুদ্রাঙ্কণে) দুই বা ততোধিক সংযুক্ত অক্ষর, দ্বিত্ব অক্ষর। **5.** (*Mus.*) A line connecting notes; (সঙ্গীত-শাস্ত্র) স্বরবন্ধনী। ***Verb t.*** To bind with a ligature; বন্ধনীদ্বারা বাঁধা।

light (lĭt), *n.* **1.** That agent or force in nature by which objects are rendered visible; আলোক। **2.** A condition of space in which sight is possible, (opp. to *darkness*); প্রকাশ। **3.** Appearance of brightness; জ্যোতিঃ, তেজঃ, দীপ্তি, দ্যুতি, আলো, প্রকাশ, প্রভা। **4.** The sensation aroused by the stimulation of the optic nerve; রূপবহা স্নায়ুর উত্তেজনা দ্বারা উদ্বুদ্ধ অনুভূতি বা সংবেদন। **5.** The amount of illumination in a place; as, the picture hung in a good *light*; কোন স্থানের দীপ্তির পরিমাণ। **6.** Sparkle or vivacity in a person's eyes; "An eye without *light*"; নয়নের দীপ্তি, চোখের আলো, অক্ষিপ্রভা। **7.** Aspect; the point of view; as, to put things in the right *light*; ভাব, আকার; যে দিক হইতে কোন বস্তু দেখা যায়, যে ভাবে কোন বিষয় বিবেচনা করা হয়, দৃষ্টি। **8.** The sun's rays; day-light; day; day-break; সূর্য্যরশ্মি, সূর্য্যকিরণ; দিবালোক, দিনের আলো; দিন; উষাকাল, অরুণোদয়। **9.** The state of being exposed; public view; as, to bring or come to *light*; দৃশ্যমানতা, লোকপ্রকাশতা, লোকপ্রসিদ্ধি; লোকসাধারণের দৃষ্টি। **10.** (*Slang, pl.*) Eyes; চোখ। **11.** A source of light; the sun or other heavenly body; an ignited candle, lamp or the like; a beacon lamp esp. of ship or light-house; a light-house; আলোকের উৎপত্তিস্থল; সূর্য্য, জ্যোতিষ্কসমূহ; দীপ, প্রদীপ; সঙ্কেতদীপ, আলোকমঞ্চের প্রদীপ; আলোকমঞ্চ। **12.** (*Poet.*) Eye-sight; (কবিতায়) দৃষ্টিশক্তি, দর্শনশক্তি। **13.** (*Fig.*) An eminent person or luminary ; as, the shining *lights* of the age ; (লক্ষণায়) প্রখ্যাতনামা ব্যক্তি, জ্যোতিষ্ক। **14.** Mental illumination ; elucidation ; as, to throw *light* upon ; enlightenment ; as, a man of superior *light* ; সুস্পষ্টবোধ ; আলোক ; জ্ঞানালোক। **15.** A window or opening in a wall for the admission of light ; sky light ; a compartment of a window ; a pane in a window, greenhouse, etc. ; গবাক্ষ, বাতায়ন ; আলোকমার্গ ; বাতায়নের প্রকোষ্ঠ ; বাতায়ন, হরিৎমন্দির, প্রভৃতির কাচফলক। **16.** (*Pl.*) Facts or discoveries serving to explain a subject ; explanation ; as, we have many new *lights* upon it since then ; কোন বিষয়ের ব্যাখ্যানুকূল তথ্য ; ব্যাখ্যা। **17.** (*Pl.*) Mental powers of an individual ; as, to do one's best according to one's *lights* ; (কাহারও) মানসিক শক্তি। **18.** (*Theol.*) The brightness of heaven ; the illumination of the soul by divine truth ; ত্রিদিবজ্যোতিঃ ; ঐশ্বরিক সত্য দ্বারা আত্মার উদ্ভাসন। **19.** (*Painting*) The more illuminated part of a picture, (opp. to *shade*) ; (চিত্রবিদ্যা) চিত্রের আলোকিত অংশ। **20.** (*Law*) The natural light unobstructed by erections ; a right to it ; (আইন) প্রতিবেশীর প্রাচীর প্রভৃতি দ্বারা প্রতিরুদ্ধ নৈসর্গিক আলোক ; ঐরূপ আলোক পাওয়ার অধিকার। **21.** Flame or spark serving to ignite ; as, to strike a *light* ; প্রজ্বালক শিখা বা স্ফুলিঙ্গ, অগ্নিকণা। **22.** Something used for igniting ; taper, matches, etc. ; প্রজ্বালক দ্রব্য ; ক্ষুদ্র মোমবাতি, দিয়াশলাই প্রভৃতি। **Light'-less,** *adj.* Without light ; dark ; আলোকহীন ; অন্ধকারাচ্ছন্ন। **Inner light, Divine light**—দিব্যজ্যোতিঃ, আধ্যাত্মিক আলোক। **Light-due** or **duty**—আলোকমঞ্চ ও আলোকপোতের ব্যয়-নির্ব্বাহার্থ জাহাজ সকল হইতে যে মাশুল লওয়া হয়। **Light-house**—রাত্রিকালে সমুদ্রগামী জাহাজের পথপ্রদর্শনের জন্য উপকূলের উচ্চভূমিতে নির্মিত শীর্ষদেশে শক্তিশালী আলোকসমন্বিত বুরুজ বা গৃহ, বাতিঘর, দীপগৃহ, আলোকমন্দির, আলোকমঞ্চ, প্রকাশস্তম্ভ। **Light-keeper**—আলোকমঞ্চের তত্ত্বাবধায়ক। **Light-ship** — সাগরপৃষ্ঠস্থিত অর্ণবযানের পথপ্রদর্শক বা বিপৎসঙ্কেত সূচনার জন্য প্রদীপসমন্বিত পোত, আলোকপোত। **Northern lights**—Aurora Borealis ; সুমেরুজ্যোতি, উদীচিউষা। **A man of light and leading**—See under LEADING. **Between the lights**—In the twilight ; প্রদোষে বা সন্ধ্যাকালে। **Between two lights**—Under cover of darkness ; ঘনান্ধকারে। **By the light of nature**—Without the aid of revelation or teaching ; শিক্ষা বা প্রত্যাদেশের সাহায্য ব্যতিরেকে, স্বভাবদত্ত-বুদ্ধির সাহায্যে। **In the light of**—With the help afforded by (some fact etc.) ; (কোন তথ্য প্রভৃতি দ্বারা) প্রদত্ত সাহায্যে। In the aspect or character of ; ভাবে, রূপে। **In the light of these facts**—With the help given by them ; এই সকল তথ্যের সাহায্যে। **Light of nature**—নৈসর্গিক (প্রাকৃতিক, স্বাভাবিক, সহজ) বুদ্ধি (বিকাশ, প্রকাশ, স্ফূর্ত্তি) (হিঃ কোঃ)। **Sensation of light**—প্রকাশ সংবেদন (হিঃ কোঃ), দৃশ্যসংবেদন (ঐ)। **The light of one's countenance**—*i. e.* his favour, approving presence (*often used ironically*) ; অনুগ্রহ, কৃপাকটাক্ষ, অনুগ্রদৃষ্টি। **The light of one's eyes**—His beloved person ; নয়নতারা, চক্ষুর মণি, নয়নের আলো। **To bring to light**—To disclose or make known ; প্রকাশ করিয়া দেওয়া, প্রকাশ করা। **To come to light** — To be revealed or known ; প্রকাশিত হওয়া, সর্ব্বজনগোচর হওয়া। **To place a thing in a good light** — To represent it favourably ; কোন বিষয় ভাল ভাবে প্রদর্শন করা। **To see the light**—To be born (*lit.* & *fig.*) ; as, the book never *saw the light* ; জন্ম নেওয়া, ভূমিষ্ঠ হওয়া, দৃষ্টিগোচর হওয়া, প্রকাশিত হওয়া। **To strike a light**—To produce a flame or spark with a match etc. ; দিয়াশলাই প্রভৃতি ঠুকিয়া আলো জ্বালা। **To stand in one's light**—To deprive him of light ; (*fig.*) to prejudice his chances ; আলোক হইতে বঞ্চিত করা ; (লক্ষণায়) কাহারো উদ্দেশ্যসিদ্ধির ব্যাঘাত করা। **To stand in one's own light**—To frustrate one's own purpose or wishes ; নিজের উদ্দেশ্য ব্যর্থ করা। **To throw** or **shed light upon**—To help to explain ; বিশদ করা, প্রাঞ্জল করা।

light (līt), *adj.* **1.** Well provided with lights ; bright ; not dark or obscure ; আলোকপূর্ণ, আলোকময় ; উজ্জ্বল ; পরিষ্কার। **2.** Not deep as to colour ; pale in colour (often prefixed to adjectives and nouns of colour) : as, *light* blue ; পাতলা ; ফিঁকে, ফিঁকা।

light (līt), *v. t.* & *i.* **1.** To burn ; to ignite ; to kindle (often with *up*) ; পোড়ান ; অগ্নিসংযোগ করা ; জ্বালাইয়া দেওয়া, প্রজ্বালিত করা। **2.** To give light to (room, street, etc.) ; দীপ্তি প্রদান করা, প্রদীপ্ত করা, আলো দেওয়া, আলোকিত করা, উজ্জ্বলিত করা। **3.** To brighten or animate, as eyes, face, etc. ; উদ্ভাসিত করা, উদ্দীপ্ত করা। **4.** To show the way to, with a light ; to attend with a light ; কাহাকে আলো ধরিয়া পথ দেখাইয়া দেওয়া ; আলো লইয়া সঙ্গে যাওয়া। ***Verb i.*** **1.** To be ignited ; as, the match will not *light* ; জ্বলা, প্রজ্বলিত হওয়া। **2.** To be illuminated ; আলোকিত হওয়া, দ্যোতিত হওয়া, উজ্জ্বলিত হওয়া। **3.** (Of eyes, face, etc.) ; To brighten with animation ; উদ্ভাসিত হওয়া, দীপ্তি পাওয়া।

light (līt), *adj.* & *adv.* **1.** Having little weight; not heavy; লঘু, হাল্কা; পাতলা। **2.** Deficient in weight as a coin, sovereign, etc.; কম ওজনের। **3.** Of small specific gravity; অল্প আপেক্ষিক গুরুত্ববিশিষ্ট। **4.** Not burdensome; easily borne or done; as, *light* tax, punishment, task, etc.; সহজে বহনীয়; অনায়াসে বাহিত বা সাধিত। **5.** Slight; unimportant; trivial; as, a *light* error; সামান্য; অকিঞ্চিৎকর; তুচ্ছ, নগণ্য। **6.** Not dense or tenacious; porous; sandy; as, *light* soil: *light* bread; অঘন, ঝিরঝিরে; সচ্ছিদ্র; বালুকাময়। **7.** Intended for a small load; carrying a small load or weight; as, a *light*-ship, horseman, infantry, etc.; অল্পভারমালবাহী। **8.** Not looking heavy or massive; elegant; as, a *light* building or spire; অস্থূলদর্শন, নাতিস্থূলাকৃতি; সুচারু, সুদৃশ্য, শোভনদর্শন। **9.** Not heavy or violent in movement, action, etc.; as, *light* touch, wind, etc.; সলীল, মৃদু, লীলাগতি। **10.** Easy of digestion; as, *light* food; not strong; as, *light* wine or beer; লঘুপাক, সুপাচ্য, সুখপাচ্য; তেজাল বা উগ্র নহে, কড়া নয়। **11.** (Of syllable) Unemphatic; গুরুউচ্চারণযোগ্য নহে। **12.** Wanton; unchaste (esp. of women or their conduct); তরলস্বভাব; অসতী, ভ্রষ্ট। **13.** Nimble; quick-moving; as, *light* heels: he is *light* of foot; ক্ষিপ্র, চটুল, চপল; দ্রুতগতি, শীঘ্রগামী। **14.** Fickle; inconstant; as, a girl's *light* fancy; চঞ্চল, চপল; অস্থির, লঘুচিত্ত, লঘুপ্রকৃতি, তরলচিত্ত। **15.** Aimed at or aiming at entertainment merely; as, *light* literature or writer; তরল। **16.** Frivolous: thoughtless; jesting; as, a *light* person, mind, jest, etc.; হাল্কা, তরল; চুটকী; ফচকে। **17.** (Of sleep) Not profound; স্বল্প। **18.** Free from sorrow; buoyant; cheerful; as, a *light* heart; আনন্দময়; স্ফূর্তিময়, উৎফুল্ল; প্রফুল্ল। **19.** Delirious, (now only in *light-headed, light-headedness*); প্রলাপী। ***Adv.*** In a light manner; পাতলাভাবে, হাল্কারূপে, তরলভাবে। **Light′-ly,** *adv.* **1.** In a light manner; easily; হাল্কাভাবে; সহজে, স্বচ্ছন্দে, অনায়াসে। **2.** Cheerfully; উৎফুল্লচিত্তে। **3.** Nimbly; চটুলভাবে। **Light′-ness,** *n.* **Light-air**—চুটকী সুর। **Light-armed**—লঘু অস্ত্রশস্ত্রে বা সাজসজ্জায় সজ্জিত। **Light coin**—See LIGHT *adj.* 2. **Light-eater**—স্বল্পাহারী। **Light engine**—যে ইঞ্জিন গাড়ী টানে না। **Light-fingers**—Those good at stealing; অপহরণতৎপর, চৌর্য্যবিদ্যাবিশারদ। **Light-fingered**—Addicted to petty thefts; thievish. (a term applied to pick-pockets; চৌর্য্যপটু; হাতটান। **Lightfoot**—Nimble; চটুল, চপল। **Light-footed**—Nimble in running or dancing; active; চটুলচরণ; কর্মঠ, কার্যতৎপর, চটপটে। **Light hand**—(*Fig.*) Tactful management; (লক্ষণায়) বুদ্ধিকৌশলসহকারে পরিচালন। *Light-handed, adj. Light-handedness, n.* **Light-headed**—Thoughtless; unsteady; dizzy; delirious; চিন্তাশূন্য; চঞ্চল; অস্থিরচিত্ত, তরলমস্তিষ্ক; প্রলাপী, বিকৃতমতি। *Light headedness, n.* **Light-hearted**—Free from grief or anxiety; gay; cheerful; নিরুদ্বিগ্ন, চিন্তাভাবনারহিত, ভাবনাহীন; হৃষ্টচিত্ত; প্রফুল্ল, উৎফুল্ল, স্ফূর্তিযুক্ত, সানন্দ, আনন্দময়, প্রফুল্লচিত্ত। **Light-heeled**—দ্রুতপদ, চটুলচরণ। **Light horse**—লঘু অস্ত্রশস্ত্রে সজ্জিত অশ্বারোহী। **Light literature**—See LIGHT *adj.* 15. **Light-minded**—Thoughtless; not grave; frivolous; লঘুমনাঃ, চিন্তাশূন্য; গাম্ভীর্যহীন; হাল্কা, ছেবলা। *Light-mindedness, n.* **Light railway** — অল্প ওজনের মাল বা অল্প লোক বহনের উপযোগী লৌহবর্ত্ম। **Light-refreshment**—জলযোগ। **Light-skirts**—A woman of light character তরলস্বভাবা নারী, চপলা রমণী। **Light-weight** — *adj.* ১০ ষ্টোন অপেক্ষা অল্প ওজনের। **Light weight** — *n.* ১০ ষ্টোন অপেক্ষা অল্প ওজনের মাল বা বস্তু। **Light-wood** — সরল কাঠ। **Light come light go**—What is easily gained is soon (easily) lost; যাহা সহজে পাওয়া যায় তাহা সহজে খোয়ান যায়। **Light of carriage**—Loose in conduct; স্খলিতচরিত্র। **Light-o'-love** — A fickle, wanton woman; a harlot; ব্যভিচারিণী, স্খলিতচরিত্রা নারী; গণিকা, বেশ্যা। **To make light of**—To treat as of little consequence; লঘু জ্ঞান করা, সামান্য জ্ঞান করা, তুচ্ছ জ্ঞান করা, উড়াইয়া দেওয়া।

light (līt), *v. t.* & *i.* (*Naut.*) To haul or move as a rope etc.; (নৌবিদ্যা) কাছি প্রভৃতি সবলে টানা। ***Verb i.*** **1.** (*Archaic*) To alight; to come down; (অপ্রঃ) অবতরণ করা; নামা। **2.** To happen; to come by chance, (with *on, upon*); দৈবক্রমে ঘটা; ঘটনাক্রমে আসা।

light′-en (līt-n), *v. t.* & *i.* **1.** To reduce the load of (a ship etc.); মাল নামাইয়া জাহাজাদি হাল্কা করা। **2.** To relieve; to cheer; as, to *lighten* the heart; হৃদয়ের ভার কমান, লাঘব করা; উল্লসিত করা, উৎফুল্ল করা। **3.** To reduce in weight; (*fig.*) to mitigate; to grow lighter; ভার কমাইয়া দেওয়া, ভার লাঘব করা; (লক্ষণায়) উপশম করা; অপেক্ষাকৃত পাতলা হওয়া, লঘুতর হওয়া। ***Verb i.*** (Of a ship) To become light by the reduction of its load; কতক মাল কমান হেতু হালকা হওয়া। **2.** (Of heart) To get relief; উপশম বোধ করা, দুঃখলাঘব হওয়া, আরাম বোধ করা। **3.** To grow less heavy; হালকা হওয়া, পাতলা হওয়া। **4.** (*Obs.*) To alight; to descend; as, Oh

Lord, let thy mercy *lighten* upon us ; (অপ্রঃ) নামা ; পতিত হওয়া, অবতরণ করা।

light'-en (lĭt-n), *v. t.* & *i.* **1.** To shed light upon ; to brighten ; to illuminate ; আলোকপাত করা ; আলোকিত করা, উজ্জ্বল করা, দীপ্তি প্রদান করা ; দীপ্ত করা। ***Verb i.*** **1.** To grow bright (said of eyes, face, sky, etc.) ; to shine ; to flash ; উজ্জ্বল হইয়া উঠা ; জ্বলিয়া উঠা, উদ্ভাসিত হওয়া ; দীপ্ত হইয়া উঠা। **2.** To display a flash or flashes of lightning, as the sky, clouds ; বিদ্যুৎ বিকাশ করা, বিদ্যুৎ ঝলসিয়া উঠা, বিদ্যুৎ চমকান, বিদ্যুৎস্ফুরণ হওয়া। **It is lightening** — There is flashes of lightning ; বিদ্যুৎস্ফুরণ হইতেছে, বিজলী চমকিতেছে।

light'-êr (lĭt-), *n.* & *v. t.* **1.** One who, or that which, lights or kindles ; প্রজ্বালক। **2.** A flat-bottomed boat used in loading and unloading ships ; জাহাজের মাল তোলা ও জাহাজ হইতে মাল খালাস করার জন্য একপ্রকার নৌকা। ***Verb t.*** To convey goods by a lighter to, or from, a shore ; ঐরূপ নৌকা দ্বারা জাহাজ হইতে তীরে মাল নেওয়া অথবা তীর হইতে জাহাজে মাল উঠান। **—age,** *n.*

light'-ish (lĭt-), *adj.* **1.** Somewhat light or bright ; ঈষদুজ্জ্বল, অল্পোজ্জ্বল, মন্দপ্রভ। **2.** Somewhat light or less heavy ; ঈষৎ লঘু।

light'-ning (lĭt-), *n.* A sudden vivid flash in the atmosphere due to discharge of electricity ; বিদ্যুৎ, বিজলী, ক্ষণপ্রভা, তড়িৎ, সৌদামিনী, চপলা, চঞ্চলা, দামিনী, ক্ষণরুচি (উজ্জ্বলঃ), অচিরদ্যুতি, অচিরপ্রভা, ক্ষণদ্যুতি, অচিরাংশু, বিজুরী (In old poems) ইরম্মদ, চিলমীলিকা (সাঃ পঃ)। [other less used Sanskrit names :—মেঘজ্যোতিঃ, মেঘবহ্নি, মেঘদীপ, ঘনজ্বালা, ক্ষণিকা, নীলাঞ্জনা, ছটাভা, রোহিণী, মহোল্কা, ঐরাবতী, অনুভা, অশুভা, বজ্রস্ফুলিঙ্গ, শম্পা, সম্পা, চটুলা, হ্রাদিনী, শতহ্রদা।] **Forked, chain** or **chained lightning**— আঁকাবাঁকা বিদ্যুৎ, বৃক্ষশাখার মত বিভক্ত বিদ্যুৎ, বিদ্যুল্লতা, তড়িল্লতা। **Lightning rod, —conductor**— জাহাজের মাস্তুলাগ্রে বা অট্টালিকার প্রকট অংশে প্রোথিত ধাতবদণ্ড বা তার—যদ্দ্বারা বিদ্যুৎ সমুদ্রে বা পৃথিবীর ভিতর পরিচালিত হয়, বিদ্যুৎপরিচালকদণ্ড, বিজলীশূল, তাড়িতদণ্ড (সাঃ পঃ)। **Lightning speed**—Greatest speed ; বিদ্যুদ্বেগ, ইরম্মদবেগ (মেঘঃ)। **Sheet lightning** — ব্যাপ্তদ্যুতিসমন্বিত বিদ্যুৎস্ফুরণ, ব্যাপ্তবিদ্যুৎ। **Summer** or **heat lightning** — বজ্রগর্জ্জনবিহীন ব্যাপ্ত বিদ্যুৎ। **Flash of lightning**— Vivid display of lightning ; চপলাচমক, বিদ্যুৎস্ফুরণ, বিজলীচমক, বিদ্যুদুন্মেষ (মেঘঃ), বিদ্যুৎকম্প, বিদ্যুদ্বল্লী, বিদ্যুদ্দাম (flash of forked lightning)। **Like lightning**— With the greatest conceivable speed ; তড়িদ্বেগে, বিদ্যুদ্বেগে।

lights (lĭts), *n.* (*Pl.*) The lungs of animals, such as sheep, pigs, etc., used as food for cats and dogs ; কুকুর বিড়ালের ভোজনের জন্য ভেড়া শূকর প্রভৃতির ফুসফুস্‌।

light'-some (lĭt-sŭm), *adj.* **1.** Light ; graceful ; elegant in appearance ; লঘু ; কমনীয়, সুচারু, মাধুর্য্যময়, ললিত ; শোভনদর্শন। **2.** Gay ; merry ; হৃষ্ট, প্রফুল্ল ; আনন্দদায়ক। **—ly,** *adv.* **—ness,** *n.*

light-some (-lĭt-sŭm), *adj.* (*Rare*) Giving light ; luminous ; bright ; (অপ্রঃ) আলোকপ্রদ ; উজ্জ্বল ; দীপ্ত।

lig'-nē-ous (-ŭs), *adj.* Woody ; wooden ; কাষ্ঠময়, দারুময় কাষ্ঠবৎ ; কাষ্ঠনির্ম্মিত।

lig'-ni-fȳ, *v. t.* & *i.* To turn or convert into wood ; কাষ্ঠে পরিণত করা, দারুময় করা। ***Verb i.*** To become wood ; কাষ্ঠ হওয়া, কাষ্ঠে পরিণত হওয়া। **—fi-ca'-tion,** *n.* **—nif'-er-ous, —ni-form,** *adjs.*

lig'-nīte, *n.* Fossil wood converted into a kind of coal ; একপ্রকার কয়লায় পরিণত শিলীভূত কাষ্ঠ।

lig'-nŭm-vī'-tae (-tē), *n.* A tree of the genus guaiacum ; একপ্রকার বৃক্ষ।

lig'-ū-lāte, *adj.* (*Bot.*) Like a strap or band in shape ; ফিতা বা দোয়ালের মত।

līke, *adj., prep., adv., conj.* & *n.* **1.** Similar ; as, he is very *like* his brother ; সদৃশ, সম, অনুরূপ, মত, মতন, নিভ, প্রতিম, সান্নভ। **2.** Equal in quality, quantity or degree ; same ; সমগুণ, সমসংখ্যক ; তুল্য, সমতুল। **3.** Resembling ; such as ; as, there is nothing *like* leather ; অনুরূপ, মত ; সদৃশ। **4.** Characteristic of ; as, such behaviour was just *like* him ; প্রকৃতির অনুরূপ। **5.** Resembling the original ; as, the portrait is not all *like* ; মূল চিত্রের অনুরূপ। **6.** In a promising state ; disposed to ; inclined toward ; as, this looks *like* lasting ; I feel *like* taking a walk ; আশাজনক অবস্থায় স্থিত ; উন্মুখ ; প্রবণ। **7.** (*Archaic* & *colloq.*) Likely to ; as, I had *like* to have done ; সম্ভবতঃ। ***Prep.*** In the manner of ; to the same degree as ; as, I cannot do it *like* you ; তদনুরূপ ; মত। ***Adv.*** **1.** (*Archaic*) In the same manner as ; similarly ; সেইভাবে, তদনুরূপ। **2.** Probably, (*rare* except in *very like, like enough*) ; সম্ভবতঃ। **3.** (*Vulg.*) So to speak ; as, by way of argument *like* ; (ইতর ভাষায়) বলিতে গেলে। ***Conj.*** (*Vulg.*) As ; as, snow falls *like* in January ; (ইতর ভাষায়) যেমন। ***Noun.*** **1.** An exact counterpart ; an equal ; a similar thing or person ; সাদৃশ্য, প্রতিরূপ ; সমকক্ষ ব্যক্তি ; সদৃশ ব্যক্তি বা বস্তু। **2.** A thing or things of the same kind ; as, he will not do the *like* again; এক জাতীয় বস্তু। 3. (*Golf*) The stroke that equalizes the number of strokes played by each side; যে আঘাত দ্বারা প্রতিপক্ষের সংখ্যা সমান হয়। **Like-signs**—(*Algebra*) Both positive or both negative signs; উভয়ই যোগ বা উভয়ই বিয়োগ চিহ্ন। **And the like**—Etcetera; ইত্যাদি, প্রভৃতি, প্রমুখ। **Do as you like**—Do as you choose or please; তোমার যাহা খুশী কর। **I had like to have done**—I was likely to have done; আমি সম্ভবতঃ করিয়া ফেলিতাম। **In a like manner**—In a similar manner; তদনুরূপ, তদ্রূপ। **Like a shot**—Without demur; willingly; regardless of consequences; অসঙ্কুচিত চিত্তে, দ্বিধা না করিয়া; ইচ্ছাপূর্ব্বক; ফলাফল চিন্তা না করিয়া, অগ্রপশ্চাৎ না ভাবিয়া। **Like cures like**—বিষস্য বিষমৌষধম্। **Like draws like**—যোগ্যং যোগ্যেন যুজ্যতে, যে যেমন তার জোটেও তেমন। **Like father like son**—যেমন বাপ তেমন ছেলে, বাপকা বেটা। **Like man like wife**—যেমন দেবা তেমনি দেবী। **Like master like man**—যেমন মনিব তেমন চাকর, যেমন গুরু তেমন চেলা। **Like saint like offering**—যেমনি চুলোমুখো দেবতা তেমনি পাঁশের নৈবেদ্য। **Likes and dislikes**—অনুরাগ বিরাগ। **Nothing like as good**—Not nearly; প্রায় ঐরূপ নয়। **Some thing like a day**—(*With stress on like*) Remarkably fine or otherwise satisfactory; আশ্চর্য সুন্দর বা অন্য প্রকারে সন্তোষজনক। **Something like Rs. 1000**—Nearly or about Rs. 1000; প্রায় হাজার টাকা। **That is like your impudence**—That is characteristic of your impudence; ইহা তোমার মত ধৃষ্ট লোকের পক্ষে স্বাভাবিক। **The likes of me**—(*Colloq.*) Persons so humble as I; (চলিত ভাষায়) আমার মত অধম লোক। 2. (*Rarely*) To make like *to*; (কদাচিদ্ব্যবহৃত) অনুরূপ করা।

līke′-nĕss, *n.* 1. State of being like; resemblance; অনুরূপতা; সাদৃশ্য, সারূপ্য, সমরূপতা, আনুগুণ্য। 2. Guise; as, an enemy in *likeness* of a friend; আকার, মূর্তি, রূপ, স্বরূপ। 3. A representation; a copy; a portrait; প্রতিরূপ; প্রতিলিপি; প্রতিকৃতি। 4. A person or thing having the exact appearance of another; as, he is a *likeness* of his father; অবিকল দুইটী বস্তু বা ব্যক্তি।

līke′-wīse, *adv.* & *conj.* 1. (*Bibl.*) In like manner; তদ্রূপে। 2. Moreover; too; তথা, আরও, অপরঞ্চ; অধিক, ও।

likin, *n.* (*Chinese*) A provincial transit duty in China; চীনদেশের প্রাদেশিক শুল্ক-বিশেষ।

līk′-ing, *n.* 1. What one likes; his taste; as, is it to your *liking*?; পসন্দ; অভিরুচি, রুচি, অনুরাগ। 2. Desire; fondness; fancy, (with *for*); as, to have a *liking* for a person or thing; ইচ্ছা, স্পৃহা, অভিরুচি; অনুরাগ; সখ।

lī′-lăc, *n.* & *adj.* 1. A shrub with fragrant white or bluish flowers; শ্বেত অথবা আনীল-লোহিত সুরভিপুষ্পপ্রসূ গুল্মবিশেষ। 2. A light purplish colour; আনীললোহিত বর্ণ। ***Adj.*** Of this colour; আনীল-লোহিতবর্ণবিশিষ্ট। **Persian lilac**—মহানীম, ঘোড়ানীম।

lil-i-ā′-ceous (-shŭs), *adj.* Pertaining to, or like, lilies; of the lily kind; স্থলকুমুদসম্বন্ধীয়, স্থলকুমুদবৎ, স্থলকুমুদজাতীয়।

Lil-li-pu′-tian (-i-pü-shăn), *adj.* & *n.* Small like the inhabitants of Lilliput; pigmy; diminutive; বালখিল্যবৎ, বামনাকৃতি; অঙ্গুষ্ঠপ্রমাণ, অঙ্গুষ্ঠমাত্রক; বামনমূর্তি। ***Noun.*** A member of the diminutive race of beings

ছদ্মপথ বা ভিক্ষুণী-সংঘে পরিণত করা। **—tered, —tral**, *adjs.* **The cloister**—The monastic life; আশ্রম-জীবন, খৃষ্টীয় মঠবাসীর জীবন।

cloke (klōk), *n.* & *v. t.* See CLOAK.

clŏ′-nŭs, *n.* A spasm with violent successive muscular contractions and relaxations; একপ্রকার আক্ষেপ রোগ। **Clon′-ic**, *adj.* (opp. to *tonic.*)

cloop, *n.* & *v. i.* The sound made by drawing a cork from a bottle; বোতলের মুখ হইতে কাক বা ছিপি (কর্ক) টানিয়া লইলে যে শব্দ হয়। ***Verb i.*** To make this sound; উক্তপ্রকার শব্দ করা।

clōse, *adj.* & *adv.* 1. Shut fast; as, a *close* carriage; রুদ্ধ। 2. Enclosed; confined; narrow; as, *close* alleys, prison: *close* confinement; প্রাচীরবেষ্টিত; আবদ্ধ; সংকীর্ণ। 3. Hidden; concealed; as, *close* sins, plots; secret; secluded; as, *close* caverns; গুপ্ত; লুক্কায়িত; গোপন; নির্জ্জন। 4. Confined; stifling (said of air, weather, etc.); আবদ্ধ; শ্বাসরোধকর। 5. Reserved; reticent; as, he was, too *close* to name his circumstances; অনালাপী; মৌনী, বাগ্‌যত। 6. Stingy; niggardly; ব্যয়কুণ্ঠ; কৃপণ। 7. Dense or compact; without interstices or vacuities; as, *close* writing; ঘন, নিবিড়; নীরন্ধ্র, সঙ্কাপিত। 8. Intimate; confidential; as, *close* friend; অন্তরঙ্গ; বিশ্বস্ত। 9. Fitting tightly or exactly; as, *close* cap, bonnet, etc.; আঁটসাট। 10. Exact; to the point; as, *close* translation; accurate; careful; as, *close* observer, reasoning; strict; minute; as, *close* examination, attention, etc.; ঠিক; যথার্থ; প্রামাণিক; সযত্ন; সঠিক; পুঙ্খানুপুঙ্খ। 11. Very near; immediately adjoining; (followed by *to*); অতি নিকটবর্ত্তী; আসন্ন। 12. Leaving no gaps or weak skins in lime and water ; চামড়া প্রভৃতি চূণের জলে ডুবাইয়া রাখা। **Lime′-less,** *adj.* **Lim′-y,** *adj.* **1.** Viscous ; sticky ; আটালো ; চট্‌চটে। **2.** Containing lime ; resembling lime ; চূর্ণমিশ্রিত; চূর্ণবৎ, চূর্ণসদৃশ, চূণগর্ভ। **Birdlime**—See BIRD. **Lime-burner**—চূর্ণ প্রস্তুত করিবার জন্য যে ব্যক্তি চূণাপাথর পোড়ায়, চূর্ণকার, চুনুরী। **Lime-cast** — চূণের লেপ। **Lime-floor**—পাকা মেঝে। **Lime-kiln**—চূণ পোড়াইবার পোয়ান, চূণাভাটী, চূণভট্টি। **Lime-light**—An intense white light got by heating a cylinder of lime in any hydrogen-flame ; চূণাপাথরের চোঙ্গ অম্লজলজানের (oxy-hydrogen) শিখায় পোড়াইলে যে তীব্রোজ্জ্বল শ্বেতবর্ণের আলোক উৎপন্ন হয়, চূর্ণালোক, লাইমলাইট (হিঃ কোঃ)। That part of the stage where limelight is cast while an important action is progressing ; hence, full glare of public light ; রঙ্গমঞ্চের যে অংশে চূর্ণালোক প্রপাতিত হয় এবং যথায় কোন বিশেষ দৃশ্য অভিনীত হইয়া থাকে ; লোকসাধারণের সমক্ষে সুপ্রকট ভাবে অবস্থান। **Lime-pit**—চূর্ণময়-গর্ত,—যথায় লোম ছাড়াইবার চামড়া ডুবাইয়া রাখা হয়। **Limestone**—চূর্ণপ্রস্তর, চূণাপাথর, চূর্ণোপল। **Lime-twig**—পাখী ধরার জন্য আটা মাখানো ক্ষুদ্র ডাল। **Lime-wash**—চূণের আস্তর, চূণকাম। **Lime-water**—চূণের জল, ক্ষারজল (সাঃ পঃ)। **Quick-lime**—See under QUICK.

līme, *n.* A fruit smaller and more acid than lemon ; কাগজিলেবু (যোঃ)। **Lime-juice**—লেবুর রস, লুঙ্গাম্বু (সাঃ পঃ)।

līme, *n.* A kind of ornamental tree, (also *lime-tree*) ; এক প্রকার সুদৃশ্য বৃক্ষ (ইহার পাতা হৃৎতনের মত ও ফুল সকল সুরভি এবং পীতবর্ণ)।

lī′-mĕn, *n.* (*Psychol.*) The limit below which a given stimulus is not perceptible ; the minimum of nerve excitation required to produce sensation ; (মনস্তত্ত্ব) যে সীমার নীচে কোন নির্দ্দিষ্ট উত্তেজনা অনুভবগম্য নয় ; কোনরূপ অনুভূতি উৎপাদনের জন্য যে অল্পতম স্নায়বিক উত্তেজনার আবশ্যক হয়। **—i-nal,** *adj.*

lĭm′-it, *n.* **1.** A boundary ; a border ; a terminal point ; সীমা ; প্রান্ত ; অবধি (ব্রজঃ হিন্দুঃ), অবচ্ছেদ, পরিসীমা, পরিমিতি (হিঃ কোঃ)। **2.** The bound that may not or cannot be passed ; as, to transgress *limits* ; অনতিক্রম্য সীমা। **—less,** *adj.* Without limit ; অসীম, সীমাবিহীন, অপার। **Superior, inferior limit** — Earliest and latest possible date ; largest and smallest possible or permissible amount ; যতদূর সম্ভব পূর্ব্ববর্ত্তী বা পরবর্ত্তী তারিখ ; বৃহত্তম বা ক্ষুদ্রতম সংখ্যা বা পরিমাণ, ঊর্দ্ধতম বা নিম্নতম সীমা। **Without limit**—Unlimited ; অসীম, সীমাবিহীন।

lĭm′-it, *v. t.* **1.** To apply limit to ; to set bounds to ; to restrict to ; as, to *limit* the issue of paper money ; সীমাবদ্ধ করা ; সীমানির্দ্দেশ করা, পরিমিতি করা ; সংযত করা, পরিচ্ছিন্ন করা। **2.** To act as a limit to ; সীমাস্বরূপ হওয়া। **—ed,** *pp.* **1.** Bounded ; confined ; restricted ; সসীম ; সীমাবদ্ধ ; অবরুদ্ধ, পরিবদ্ধ, (ব্রজঃ হিন্দু) পরিচ্ছিন্ন, অবচ্ছিন্ন, নির্দ্দিষ্ট। **2.** Scanty ; স্বল্প, সামান্য। **Limited-company**—A company in which the liability of each share-holder is limited to the amount of his stock or shares ; যে কোম্পানীর দায় সীমাবদ্ধ (অর্থাৎ যে কোম্পানীর অংশীদারগণ স্ব স্ব অংশের অনুপাতে কোম্পানীর ঋণের জন্য দায়ী থাকে)। **Limited-mail** — যে ডাক গাড়ীতে কেবল মাত্র নির্দ্দিষ্ট সংখ্যক যাত্রী লওয়া হয়। **Limited-monarchy**—নিয়মতন্ত্র-রাজ্য (সাঃ পঃ)। **Limiting value**—অন্তিমমান (হিঃ কোঃ)।

lĭm-ĭ-tā′-rĭ-ăn, *n.* & *adj.* One who holds that only a limited part of mankind is to be saved ; মানবজাতির নির্দ্দিষ্ট অংশমাত্র মুক্তি পাইবে এইরূপ মতাবলম্বী। ***Adj.*** Of, or relating to, the doctrine held by a limitarian ; উক্তমতসম্বন্ধীয়।

lĭm′-ĭ-tă-rȳ, *adj.* **1.** Restrained within, or subject to, limits ; সীমাবদ্ধ। **2.** Of, pertaining to, or serving as, a boundary ; সীমাসম্বন্ধীয়, সীমাস্বরূপ।

lĭm-ĭ-tā′-tion, *n.* **1.** The act of limiting or bounding ; the limited condition ; disability ; as, the *limitations* of thought ; সীমাবন্ধন, সীমাবধারণ ; সীমাবদ্ধাবস্থা, নির্দ্দিষ্ট অবস্থা, সময়াবধি (হিঃ কোঃ) ; অক্ষমতা, অসামর্থ্য, অপারগতা। **2.** A limiting rule or circumstance ; "This *limitation* made by parliament" ; নিরূপিত নিয়ম। **3.** (*Law*) Certain period limited by law beyond which an action must not be brought and an estate or law is not to continue ; মিয়াদ, তমাদির কাল। **Limitation-act**—তমাদিবিষয়ক আইন, তমাদির আইন, কালস্থাপনবিধি। **Barred by limitation**—তমাদি, খারিজ। **He has his limitations** — He is not talented in all directions ; তাহার প্রতিভা সর্ব্বতোমুখী নহে। **Statute of limitation** — Same as LIMITATION ACT above. **To know one's own limitation**—To know the limits of one's own abilities ; নিজের ক্ষমতার সীমা অবগত থাকা।

lĭm′-ĭ-trō-phē, *adj.* (Of a district etc.) On the border or frontier ; adjacent (*to*) ; প্রান্তবর্ত্তী, সীমান্তদেশবর্ত্তী ; সন্নিহিত।

limn (lĭm), *v. t.* (*Archaic*) To depict ; to portray ; to draw ; (অপ্রঃ) বর্ণিত করা ; চিত্রিত করা ; অঙ্কিত করা।

To fan into blaze or **flame**—To kindle by fanning; বাতাস দিয়া জ্বালান, অগ্নিশিখা উদ্দীপ্ত করা। **To fan the flame**—To increase excitement etc.; উত্তেজনা বৃদ্ধি করা।

fȧ-nӑt′-ic, *adj.* & *n.* Filled with excessive and mistaken enthusiasm, esp in religion; ধর্ম্মোন্মত্ত, উৎকট ধার্ম্মিক। ***Noun.*** A person excessively enthusiastic, esp. in religion; a visionary zealot; ধর্ম্মোন্মত্ত ব্যক্তি; স্বপ্নাবিষ্ট ব্যক্তি, গোঁড়া। **—i-cal,** *adj.* Unreasonably zealous; উৎকট আগ্রহবান। **—i-cal-ly,** *adv.* **—i-cism,** *n.* Wild and excessive enthusiasm, esp. in religion; ধর্ম্মোন্মাদ। **—i-cize,** *v. t.* & *i.* To make fanatical; ধর্ম্মোন্মত্ত করা। (*Verb i.*) To act as a fanatic; ধর্ম্মোন্মত্তের মত কার্য্য করা।

fӑn′-ci-ėr, *n.* **1.** One who is governed by fancy; খেয়াল-পরবশ ব্যক্তি। **2.** One who has special liking for, or interest in, certain objects, as birds, dogs, etc.; যে ব্যক্তির কোন বিশেষ জন্তু প্রভৃতির জন্য সখ বা প্রীতি আছে।

fӑn′-cy̆, *n.* & *adj.* **1.** That faculty of the mind by which it forms an image or representation of anything not present; imagination; কল্পনাবৃত্তি, কল্পনাশক্তি; কল্পনা। **2.** An image or representation thus formed in the mind; a conception; a thought; কল্পনা; ধারণা; চিন্তা। **3.** An arbitrary notion or supposition; caprice; as, that's a mere *fancy*; খেয়াল; বাহানা, মর্জ্জি। **4.** Inclination; liking; as, to take a *fancy* for a thing; আসক্তি; রুচি। **5.** (*Collectively*, with *the*) Those who have a certain hobby; (সংঘবাচকভাবে) কোন বিষয়ের জন্য একান্ত সখ আছে এরূপ লোকের সমবায়। ***Adj.*** **1.** Pleasing to the fancy or caprice; as, *fancy* goods or articles; মনোহারী, পসন্দসই, বিচিত্র। **2.** Above real value; extravagant; as, a *fancy* price; প্রকৃত মূল্যের অতিরিক্ত; অসম্ভব, কাল্পনিক। **3.** Whimsical; irregular; "A display of *fancy* shooting"; খেয়াল-পরবশ; অব্যবস্থিত। **4.** Based on imagination; as, a *fancy* picture; কল্পনামূলক, কাল্পনিক। **5.** Bred for particular points of beauty etc.; as, *fancy* pigeons; বিশেষ গুণ, সৌন্দর্য্য প্রভৃতির জন্য পালিত, সখের। **6.** Particoloured; as, a *fancy* flower; বিচিত্র-বর্ণ। **—ci-ful,** *adj.* **1.** Guided by fancy; full of fancy; খেয়ালপরবশ; কাল্পনিক। **2.** Imaginary; unreal; "Spake at shadows *fanciful* and vain"; কাল্পনিক; অবাস্তব। **2.** Fantastically designed; peculiarly shaped; as, a *fanciful* head-dress; অপরূপভাবে কল্পিত; সৃষ্টিছাড়া রকমের। **—ci-less,** *adj.* **Fancy-ball**—যে নৃত্যোৎসবের নর্ত্তক-নর্ত্তকীগণ কোন বিশেষ যুগ, জাতি বা ঐতিহাসিক ব্যক্তির অনুকরণে বিচিত্র পরিচ্ছদ পরিধান করে। **Fancy dress** — উক্তরূপ নৃত্যোৎসবে পরিহিত পরিচ্ছদ। **Fancy dog etc.** — See FANCY, *adj.* 5. **Fancy-fair**—See FAIR. **Fancy franchise** — জটিল অথবা খামখেয়ালভাবে যোগ্যতার উপর প্রতিষ্ঠিত নির্ব্বাচনক্ষমতা। **Fancy-free**—অপ্রণয়বদ্ধ। **Fancy goods**—সখের জিনিষ, মনোহারী জিনিষ। **Fancy man** — A sweet heart; প্রণয়ী; যে ব্যক্তি বেশ্যার অর্থে জীবনধারণ করে, পিরীতের লাং (ইতর ভাষায়)। **Fancy picture**—See FANCY, *adj.* 4. **Fancy-sick**—বিকৃতমতি; প্রণয়পীড়িত। **Fancy work** — শোভাসাধক সূচীকর্ম্ম। **The fancy**—মল্লক্রীড়কগণ, বিশেষতঃ মুষ্টিযুদ্ধকারিগণ। **To catch the fancy of**—To please; খুসী করা, সুখ দেওয়া। **To take** or **have a fancy to, for** — To have a liking or fondness for সখ থাকা।

fӑn′-cy̆, *v. t.* & *i.* **1.** To form a conception of; to imagine; ধারণা করা; কল্পনা করা। **2.** To like; to be pleased with; "Which (face) I could *fancy* more than any other"; পসন্দ করা; ভাল লাগা। **3.** To be inclined to think; to suppose; ভাবা; অনুমান করা, বোধ করা, মনে করা। **4.** To believe without sufficient evidence; "He *fancies* he was welcome"; উপযুক্ত প্রমাণাভাবে বিশ্বাস করা। ***Verb i.*** To imagine; to suppose without proof; কল্পনা করা; ভাবা। **—ci-er,** *n.* Which see.

fӑn-dan′-gle (-dӑng-gl), *n.* Fantastic ornament; nonsense; কিম্ভূত কিমাকার অলঙ্কার; আজগুবি কথা।

fӑn′-dan′-gō (-dӑng-), *n.* **1.** A lively Spanish dance; স্পেনদেশীয় নৃত্যবিশেষ। **2.** The time for this; উক্ত নৃত্যের সময়।

fāne, *n.* A temple, (*poetic*); (কবিতায়) মন্দির, দেবালয়, দেবমন্দির।

fӑn′-fare (-fâr), *n.* A flourish of trumpets or bugles; তূরী বা শিঙ্গার ধ্বনি।

fӑn′-fȧ-rŏn, *n.* One who uses bravado; a braggart; আস্ফালনকারী; দম্ভকারী।

fӑn-fȧ-rŏn-āde′, *n.* **1.** Vain boasting; ostentation; গর্ব্ব, বড়াই; আস্ফালন, জাঁক, ধুমধাম। **2.** Same as FANFARE (which see).

fӑng, *n.* **1.** The canine tooth of some beasts, as dogs, wolves, etc.; the venom tooth of a serpent; কুকুর, নেকড়ে বাঘ, প্রভৃতির শোবন দন্ত; সর্পের বিষ-দাঁত। **2.** The root of a tooth; দন্তমূল। **3.** The tang

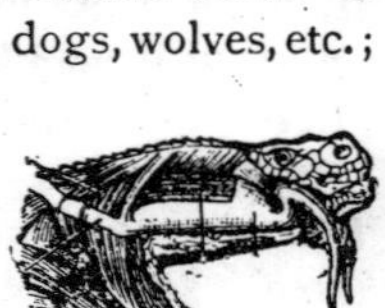

Fangs of Rattle snake.

lim'-nêr, *n.* (*Archaic*) One who draws or paints pictures ; (অপ্রঃ) চিত্রকর, পটুয়া।

lim-nŏl'-ŏ-ġy̆, *n.* A study of the physical phenomena of lakes ; a study of the pond-life ; হ্রদের প্রাকৃতিকদৃশ্য অধ্যয়ন ; দীর্ঘিকা প্রভৃতিতে স্থিত প্রাণিসমূহের জীবন অধ্যয়ন।

lī-mō'-sis, *n.* (*Med.*) An excessive and morbid hunger ; (ভৈষজ্যশাস্ত্র) পীড়াজনিত বুভুক্ষা, উৎকট ক্ষুধা।

limp, *v. i.* & *n.* To walk lamely ; (of verse) to halt ; খোঁড়াইয়া চলা, নেংচান, খোঁড়ান ; (কবিতার চরণসম্বন্ধে) অঙ্গহীন হওয়া। ***Noun.*** A lame walk ; a halt in walking ; খোঁড়াইতে খোঁড়াইতে চলন, খঞ্জগতি ; গতিভঙ্গ। **Limp'-ing-ly,** *adv.*

limp, *adj.* **1.** Flexible ; flaccid ; নমনীয়, ঢিলা, শিথিল ; ভস্‌কা, থল্‌থলিয়া। **2.** (Of book-bindings) Not stiffened with mill-board ; (পুস্তক বাঁধাই) নরম মলাটযুক্ত। **3.** (*Fig.*) Lacking strength or energy ; হীনবল, নিস্তেজ। **Limp'-ly,** *adv.* **Limp'-ness,** *n.*

lim-pĕt', *n.* A marine mollusc with tent-shaped shell ; তাঁবুর আকৃতি শম্বুক — যাহারা স্রোতঃমধ্যবর্তী পাষাণে দৃঢ়ভাবে লাগিয়া থাকে, গুগলি।

lim'-pĭd, *adj.* Clear ; transparent ; pellucid (said of liquids, atmosphere, eyes, literary style, etc.) ; পরিষ্কার, বিশুদ্ধ, নির্মল ; স্বচ্ছ ; বিমল, পরিচ্ছন্ন, টলটলে, প্রাঞ্জল (তরল পদার্থ, বায়ু, চক্ষু, সাহিত্য, রচনারীতিসম্বন্ধে ব্যবহৃত হয়)। **—ly,** *adv.* **—pid'-i-ty, —ness,** *ns.* Clearness ; transparency ; বিশুদ্ধতা, পরিচ্ছন্নতা ; স্বচ্ছতা।

limp'-kin, *n.* A kind of bird ; পক্ষিবিশেষ।

lin'-āge, *n.* **1.** The number of lines in a printed matter ; মুদ্রিত পংক্তির সংখ্যা। **2.** The payment according to linage ; পংক্তি হিসাবে বেতন প্রদান।

lin'-ă-mĕnt, *n.* (*Surg.*) Lint ; lint made into a tent for insertion into wounds ; শণের সূত্র চাঁছিয়া লইয়া ক্ষত প্রভৃতিতে দিবার জন্য যে কোমল বস্ত্রের ন্যায় পদার্থ প্রস্তুত হয় ; ক্ষতাদিতে অন্তর্নিবিষ্ট করার জন্য তাঁবুর আকারে ভাঁজ-করা ঐরূপ বস্ত্র খণ্ড।

linch'-pin (līnsh-), *n.* **1.** A pin used to keep a wheel on the axle-tree ; চাকার খিলকাঠি, অক্ষাগ্রকীলক (আঃ বঃ), অণি (ঐ)।

linc'-ture (lĭngk-tūr), **linc'-tŭs** (lĭngk-), *n.* A medicine to be taken by licking with the tongue ; অবলেহ, কাশাদি রোগে ব্যবহার্য্য সুমিষ্ট গাঢ় ঔষধ বিশেষ।

lin'-dĕn, *n.* The lime-tree (see LIME, *n.*)

līne, *n.* A fine long flax separated from the tow ; সূক্ষ্ম শণসূত্র।

līne, *n.* **1.** A string or cord ; a rope ; রজ্জু ; দড়ি। **2.** A wire or cable for telegraph or telephone ; the route traversed by the cable ; তাড়িতবার্তাবহ বা দূরশ্রবণযন্ত্রের তার, তাড়িতবার্তা প্রেরণের জন্য সমুদ্রতলগামী ধাতবরজ্জু ; ঐরূপ তারের পথ, তারপথ। **3.** A cord or string with fish-hooks ; বড়শীর সূতা। **4.** A measuring or levelling cord etc. ; as, plumb-*line* ; ভূমিমানরজ্জু, ওলন দড়ী। **5.** (*Pl.*) One's lot in life (*Ps.* xvi. 6. (with reference to marking out land for a dwelling house) ; as, my brother's *lines* are fallen unto him in pleasant places : অদৃষ্ট, কপাল, ভাগ্য। **6.** A rule or canon, (*obs.* except in *line upon line*, *Ps.* xxviii 10) ; বিধি, নিয়ম। **7.** A long thread-like mark traced on a surface ; (কোন বস্তুর) উপর চিহ্নিত সূত্রবৎ রেখা। **8.** A mark limiting a court or ground or special parts of them ; কোন অঙ্গন অথবা ক্রীড়াঙ্গনের সীমা নির্দ্দেশক রেখা, উহাদের বিশেষ বিভাগের সীমানির্দ্দেশক রেখা। **9.** Anything resembling a long traced mark ; a thin furrow or marking on the face or hands ; "Filled his brow with *lines* and wrinkles" ; অঙ্কিত দীর্ঘ রেখাবৎ কোন কিছু (যেমন সীতা বা লাঙ্গলপদ্ধতি) ; ললাট বা করতলের রেখা। **10.** (*Math.*) A magnitude, either straight or curve which has length but no breadth or thickness ; (গণিতশাস্ত্র) রেখা। **11.** The course or track followed by a moving point ; as, the arrow descended in a curved *line* ; কোন গতিশীল বিন্দুকর্তৃক অনুসৃত পথ **12.** The equator (with *the* prefixed) ; বিষুব-রেখা। **13.** A straight line ; as, go as straight as a *line* ; সরলরেখা। **14.** Outline ; contour ; lineament ; as, the *lines* of a face ; প্রান্তরেখা ; বাহ্যরেখা ; মুখাবয়ব। **15.** A limit ; boundary ; as, to draw the *line* ; সীমা ; সীমারেখা। **16** (*Pl.*) A plan or method of making or doing something ; কার্য্যপদ্ধতি, নির্ম্মাণপদ্ধতি, গঠনপদ্ধতি। **17.** A measure of length, one-twelfth of an inch ; দৈর্ঘ্যের পরিমাণবিশেষ, এক ইঞ্চির দ্বাদশাংশ। **18.** A row of persons or objects ; শ্রেণী বা সারি, পংক্তি। **19.** (*Mil.*) A trench or rampart ; (*pl.*) a row of tents or huts in a camp ; a connected series of field-works ; (সামরিক শাস্ত্র) পরিখা, প্রাকার ; (বহুবচন) সেনানিবেশের তাঁবু বা কুটীরশ্রেণী ; পরস্পরের সহিত সংযুক্ত পরিখা, উপদুর্গ, প্রভৃতির শ্রেণী। **20.** A straight row of soldiers drawn up in an extended front, (opp. to *column*) ; যুদ্ধার্থ সজ্জিত সৈন্যপংক্তি, দণ্ডব্যূহ। **21.** (*Navy*) An arrangement of ships abreast ; পাশাপাশি ভাবে পোতবিন্যাস। **22.** A single verse of poetry ; (*pl.*) a poem ; কবিতার পংক্তি, পদ, চরণ ; (বহুবচন) কবিতা। **23.** A number

অন্তরাবর্ত্তিত।

in-tŏl′-ĕr-ă-ble (-bl), *adj.* Not capable of being endured; অসহ্য, দুর্বিসহ, অবিসহ্য, দুর্ব্বহ। **—bly,** *adv.* Unbearably; অসহনীয়রূপে। **—ness,** *n.*

in-tŏl′-ĕr-ănt, *adj.* **1.** Not enduring; not able to endure, (with *of*); অসহিষ্ণু; অসহনক্ষম। **2.** Not tolerating difference of opinion or sentiment esp. in religious matters; ধর্ম্মবিষয়াদিতে পরমত সহনাক্ষম, অনুদার, গোঁড়া। **—ance,** *n.* State of

tion, *n.* **1.** Act of intoxicating; drunkenness; মাদন, মত্ততাজনন; সুরাপানজনিত মত্ততা। **2.** Excessive excitement or elation; অতিরিক্ত উত্তেজনা বা উল্লাস।

in-trăc′-tă-ble (-bl), *adj.* **1.** Not tractable; perverse; refractory; দুঃসেব্য, অবশ্য, দুঃশাসন, দুঃশাস্য, দুঃশাম্য; অবিনেয়, দুর্দ্দান্ত, উচ্ছৃঙ্খল, বে-আড়া; অদম্য, দুর্দ্দম। **2.** (Of things), Not easily dealt with; দুর্নিগ্রহ, দুরাধর্ষ, অনায়ত্ত। **—bil′-i-ty, —ness,** *ns.* **—tract′-a-bly,** *adv.*

in′-tri-ca-cy̆, *n.* **1.** The state of being intricate; complexity; জটিলতা, দুরূহতা, কাঠিন্য; অসরলতা, অসারল্য, ব্যস্ততা, সঙ্কুলতা। **2.** A perplexing difficulty; জটিলতা, পেঁচ, কুটিলতা, গোঁ, মুস্কিল, লটপট, নটখটি।

in′-tri-cate, *adj.* Entangled; involved; complicated; obscure; জটিল; লটপটে; পেঁচালো, অস্পষ্ট, অস্পষ্টার্থ, দুর্ব্বোধ। **—ly,** *adv.* In an intricate manner; জটিল ভাবে।

in-trigue′ (-trīg), *n.* & *v. i.* **1.** A plot to effect some purpose by

অভিনেয় অংশের (ভূমিকার) শব্দসমূহ। **28.** A connected series of public conveyances (steamers, omnibuses etc.) plying regularly between certain places; as, the City Coast *line*; নির্দ্দিষ্ট স্থান হইতে স্থানান্তরে নিয়মিত রূপে যাতায়াতকারী যাত্রিবাহী পোতাদির শ্রেণী। **29.** A chronological series of persons or things; as, I shall show you a long *line* of heroes; ব্যক্তি বা বস্তু সমূহের কালানুক্রমিক শ্রেণী, পরম্পরাগত ব্যক্তি বা বস্তু সমূহ। **30.** A series or succession of ascendants or descendants; lineage; family; as, he comes of a good *line*; পুরুষ-পরম্পরা, বংশপরম্পরা, পুরুষানুক্রম, কুল-পরম্পরা, বংশাবলী; বংশ; পরিবার। **31.** A direction, course or track; as, a *line* of march; গতি, দিক্, গমনপথ। **32.** The single track of a railway; as, up or down *line*; a railway; as, the main-*line*: a branch *line*; কোন লৌহবর্ত্মের একটী বর্ত্ম; লৌহবর্ত্ম; লৌহবর্ত্মের শাখা। **33.** A course of conduct, thought, occupation or policy, etc.; as, to follow this *line* of thought; কার্য্যপ্রণালী, চিন্তার গতি, অনুষ্ঠিত কার্য্যের লক্ষ্য, চিন্তাপ্রণালী, আচরণপদ্ধতি। **34.** A department of activity; a branch of business; as, something out of one's *line*; কর্ম্মের বিভাগ; কাজ বা ব্যবসায়ের শাখা। **35.** (*Commerce*)

চিত্র, রেখাচিত্র। **Ling-filling**—হস্তলিখিত পুঁথি প্রভৃতিতে পংক্তির শেষ ভাগের ফাঁকা জায়গায় টান টোন বা চিত্রাদি। **Line-firing**—সারিবন্দিভাবে সজ্জিত সৈন্যের গুলিবর্ষণ। **Line-fishing**—Fishing with a fishing-line (opp. to *net-fishing*); বড়শীর দ্বারা মৎস্যশিকার। **Line man**—টেলিগ্রাফ ও টেলিফোঁর তার বা রেলওয়ের রাস্তা মেরামত করার কার্য্যে নিযুক্ত ব্যক্তি। **All along the line** — In every particular; সর্ব্বাংশে, সর্ব্বতোভাবে। **A picture hung on the line**—যে চিত্র এরূপভাবে টাঙ্গানো হয় যাহাতে ইহার কেন্দ্রস্থল দ্রষ্টার চক্ষুর সহিত প্রায় সমতল থাকে। **By rule and line** — With precision; সঠিকভাবে, নির্ভুলভাবে। **Line of affection** — বিবাহরেখা। **Line of battle**—See under BATTLE. **Line of beauty**—Line with two opposite curves like elongated S; সৌন্দর্য্যরেখা (〜 ইত্যাকার রেখা)। **Line of collimation** — অক্ষরেখা (হিঃ কোঃ)। **Line of direction**—দিগ্‌রেখা (হিঃ কোঃ)। **Line of fate, Line of satan (or the fate line)**—ঊর্দ্ধরেখা। **Line of grace**—Same as LINE OF BEAUTY above. **Line of head (or head line)**—বুদ্ধিরেখা (হিন্দুমতে মাতৃরেখা)। **Line of heart (or heart line)**—হৃদয়রেখা (হিন্দুমতে অনুরেখা)। **Line of life** — (*Palmistry*) আয়ুরেখা,

line—(*Army*) The regular numbered regiments (not Guards, Engineers or Artillery); (সৈন্যদল) স্থায়ী পল্টনসমূহ। **The lines are fallen to me in pleasant places**—I am fortunate in worldly surroundings (Ps. xvii. 6); আমি সাংসারিক ব্যাপারে সৌভাগ্যবান। **To bring into line** — To induce to do so; কোন কাজে প্রবৃত্ত করা। **To come into line**—To agree or co-operate; একমত হওয়া, একযোগে কার্য্য করা। **To give a person line enough** — To let a person go his own way for a time in order to check or secure him later (like a hooked-fish that swims away with the line); পরে স্ববশে আনিবে বা বাধা দিবে এই উদ্দেশ্যে কোন লোককে কিছু কালের জন্য ইচ্ছামত চলিতে দেওয়া। **To read between the lines**—See READ.

līne, *v. t.* & *i.* **1.** To mark with a line or lines; as, to *line* a copy-book; রেখা টানা, রেখাঙ্কিত করা, রেখাচিহ্নিত করা, রেখান্বিত করা, রেখাপাত করা। **2.** To cover with lines; as, a face *lined* with pain; রেখাময় করা। **3.** To place troops etc. along, as a road, hedge, etc.; to form a line along; as, the troops *lined* the pass; সৈন্যশ্রেণী

the health of; স্বাস্থ্যকামনায় মদ্য পান করা। **To look up**—To search for, or find out, by looking, as a word in a dictionary or a fact in a book of reference; খোঁজা, খুঁজিয়া দেখা, দেখিয়া বাহির করা। (*Colloq.*) To call upon, as a person; to raise eyes; (চলিত ভাষায়) সাক্ষাৎ করা; চোখ তুলিয়া চাওয়া, উপরের দিকে তাকান। **To look upon**—To regard as; to regard *with* a specified feeling; দেখা, ভাবা; গণ্য করা। **To look up to**—To respect; মান্য করা, সম্মান করা। **To look well** or **ill**—To seem to be in good or bad health; (of things) to seem to be going well or ill; সুস্থ বা অসুস্থ দেখান; (বস্তু-সম্পর্কে) ভাল চলিতেছে বলিয়া বোধ হওয়া, ভাল চলিতেছে না বলিয়া বোধ হওয়া। **Will have a look in**—(*Sports*) Will come near winning and perhaps win; (ক্রীড়ায়) প্রায় জয় লাভ করিবে এবং হয় ত জয়ী হইবে। **Will not look at**—Refuses to take; scorns; rejects; গ্রহণ করিতে অস্বীকার করে; অবজ্ঞা করে; অগ্রাহ্য করে।

Loom for weaving carpet.

lōōm, *n.* **1.** A machine by which thread is woven into a fabric; বস্ত্রবয়নযন্ত্র, তাঁত। **2.** The shaft of an oar or the part which is within the boat in rowing; দাঁড়ের বাঁট বা দাঁড় টানিবার সময় উহার যে অংশ নৌকার ভিতর থাকে। **Fly-shuttle loom**—ঠকঠকি তাঁত। **Power-loom**—কলের তাঁত।

lōōm, *v. i.* & *n.* **1.** To appear larger than the real size and indistinctly as a ship at sea; to appear faintly; ঝাপ্সা এবং প্রকৃত আকার হইতে বৃহত্তর প্রতীয়মান হওয়া (যেমন সমুদ্রোপরি জাহাজ); অস্পষ্টভাবে দৃশ্য হওয়া, ঝাপ্সা দেখান। **2.** (*Fig.*) To appear in an impressively great form; "On no occasion does he *loom* so high"; (লক্ষণায়) বিরাটরূপে আবির্ভূত হওয়া। ***Noun.*** The vague first appearance of land at sea; সমুদ্র হইতে স্থলের প্রথম অস্পষ্ট দর্শন।

lōōm, *n.* An auk, guillemot or puffin; একপ্রকার পাখী।

lōōn, *n.* (*Scot.* & *Archaic*) **1.** Scamp; a worthless fellow; an idler; (স্কটলণ্ডে ব্যবহৃত, অপ্রঃ) পাজি, দুর্বৃত্ত, বদমাইস, নরাধম, হারামজাদা; অকর্মণ্য লোক; অলসলোক। **2.** A lad; ছেলে, ছোঁড়া।

lōōn, *n.* A kind of diving water-bird; পানিকৌড়ী, ডুবরী পক্ষী।

lōōn′-ȳ, lŭn′–, *n.* & *adj.* (*Vulg.*) Lunatic; (ইতর ভাষায়) পাগলা, ক্ষেপা।

lōōp, *n., v. t.* & *i.* **1.** The figure produced by a curve or bent string that crosses itself; a noose; রজ্জুর বেড়, পুঁটে-ঘরা, গলাসি; ফাঁশ। **2.** A fold of cord or ribbon serving as an ornament as on a uniform; রজ্জু বা ফিতার শোভাসাধক পুঁট। **3.** A ring or curved piece of metal as handle; আংটা বা ধাতুনির্ম্মিত বক্র হাতল। **4.** A railway or telegraph line that diverges from the main line and joins it again (also *loop-line*); প্রধান লৌহবর্ত্মের যে অংশ উহা হইতে দূরে সরিয়া পুনরায় উহাতে মিলিত হয়। ***Verb t.*** **1.** To form (strings etc.) into a loop or loops; রজ্জুদ্বারা ফাঁস তৈয়ার করা, পুঁটে-ঘরা করা। **2.** To fasten *up* or join *together* with a loop or loops; গলাসি দ্বারা বাঁধা বা সংযোগ করা। **3.** To ornament with loops; শোভাসাধক রজ্জুক ফিতার পুঁটদ্বারা ভূষিত করা। **4.** To place within a loop; গলাসির মধ্যে রাখা। ***Verb i.*** To form a loop or loops; ফাঁস হওয়া। **Looping the loop**—দ্বিচক্রযানারোহীর পক্ষে ঋজুভাবে অবস্থিত চক্রোপরি আবর্ত্তন।

lōōp, *n.* (*Rare*) An opening or loop-hole; (অপ্রঃ) ছিদ্র, ফাঁক, রন্ধ্র।

lōōp′-ėr, *n.* **1.** A caterpillar of geometer moths; একপ্রকার তসরে পোকার লম্বা কীড়া। **2.** A contrivance in sewing-machine etc. for making loops; পুঁটে-ঘরা তৈয়ার করার জন্য সেলাই কলের কৌশল-বিশেষ।

lōōp′-hōle, *n.* & *v. t.* **1.** A small vertical opening in the walls for shooting or looking through or to admit light or air; (দুর্গ-বা জাহাজে) কামানাদি দাগিবার বা আলোকাদি প্রবেশের জন্য প্রাচীর-গাত্রস্থ রন্ধ্র। **2.** A hole affording means of escape; an outlet; means of evading a rule etc.; পলাইবার পথ; নির্গমপথ, নির্গমরন্ধ্র; কোন নিয়ম প্রভৃতি এড়াইবার উপায়, প্রতি-প্রসব। ***Verb t.*** To make loop-holes in, as walls etc.; প্রাচীরাদির গাত্রে রন্ধ্র করা।

loose (lōōs), *adj.* **1.** Untied; not fastened or confined; as, the *loose* sheets of paper; আঁবাধা; আল্‌গা। **2.** Released from bonds or restraint; অসংযত, বন্ধনমুক্ত। **3.** Not rigidly fixed; as, to have a screw *loose*; শ্লথ, শিথিল, ফস্‌কা, স্রস্ত, স্রংসিত, গলিত, বিগলিত। **4.** Not tight; slack; as, a *loose* garment; আঁটা নহে; ঢিলা। **5.** Having partial freedom of movement etc.; as, *loose* end; আংশিক ভাবে অবাধ-গতি। **6.** Not dense or compact; composed of loose particles; not serried; as, a *loose* soil: *loose* fabric; বিরল, অঘন; ঝিরঝিরে; ফাকফাক। **7.** (*Chem.*) Uncombined; (রসায়ন-শাস্ত্র) অমিশ্রিত। **8.** Inaccurate; indefinite; vague; incorrect; as, a *loose* statement: *loose* ideas; অঠিক; অনির্দ্দিষ্ট; অস্পষ্ট; ভ্রমাত্মক। **9.** Not close or faithful, as translation; আক্ষরিক নহে, অনবিকল। **10.** Ungrammatical; not precise; as, a *loose* style; ব্যাকরণদুষ্ট,

6. To be slow to move or act; to delay; চলিতে বিলম্ব করা, কার্য্যে বিলম্ব করা, চিরক্রিয় হওয়া; বিলম্ব করা। ***Verb t.*** To pass as time *away* in delays; বিলম্ব করিয়া কালক্ষয় করা, গড়িমসি করিয়া সময় নষ্ট করা। **–er,** *n.* **–ing,** *adj.* Delaying; protracted; দীর্ঘসূত্র, চিরক্রিয়, চিরায়মান, মন্দায়মান; চিরস্থায়ী, দীর্ঘকালীন, চিরকালীন। **–ing-ly,** *adv.*

lingerie, (*F.*), *n.* Linen articles; stock of these; ক্ষৌমবস্ত্র; ক্ষৌমবস্ত্রভাণ্ডার।

lin′-gō (lĭng-), *n.* (A contemptuous term for) a foreign language; a language peculiar to a subject or class of people; (অবজ্ঞাচ্ছলে) বিদেশী ভাষা; কোন বিষয় বা কোন শ্রেণীর লোকের পক্ষে বিশেষ উপযোগী ভাষা।

lin′-gua-fran′-că (lĭng-gwă-frăngk-), *n,* **1.** A mixture of the languages of Italy, France, Greece and Spain used in the Levant; ইতালীয়, ফরাসী, গ্রীক এবং স্পেনিস্ ভাষার সংমিশ্রণে উৎপন্ন মিশ্র ভাষা। **2.** Any mixed or other language serving as a medium between different peoples; বিভিন্ন ভাষাভাষী লোকের মধ্যে পরস্পরের মনোভাব আদান-প্রদানের জন্য মিশ্র অথবা অনুরূপ ভাষা, সাধারণ ভাষা।

lin′-gual (lĭng-gwăl), *adj.* & *n.* **1.** Of, or pertaining to, the tongue; জিহ্বাসম্বন্ধীয়, জৈহ্বিক। **2.** (*Phon.*) Pronounced with the tongue, as a sound etc.; জিহ্বোচ্চারিত। **3.** Of, or relating to, lauguages; ভাষাসম্পর্কীয়। ***Noun.*** (*Phon.*) A lingual sound or letter; জিহ্বামূলীয় বর্ণ বা ধ্বনি। **–ize,** *v. t.* (*Phon.*) To make lingual; জিহ্বামূলীয় করা।

lin′-gui-fórm (lĭng-gwĭ-), *adj.* (*Bot., Anat., Zool.*) Shaped like the tongue; জিহ্বাকার, জিহ্বাকৃতি।

lin′-guist (lĭng-gwĭst), *n.* One knowing several languages; বহুভাষাবিৎ, বিবিধভাষাবিৎ, পণ্ডিত, ভাষাবিদ, ভাষাপ্রবীণ, ভাষাপণ্ডিত, বহুভাষাভিজ্ঞব্যক্তি, বহুভাষাবেত্তা, অনেকভাষাজ্ঞ। **–guis′-tic,** *adj.* **1.** Of, or relating to, languages; ভাষাসম্বন্ধীয়। **2.** Of, or pertaining to, the study of languages; বিবিধভাষাধ্যয়নসম্পর্কীয়। **–guis′-ti-cal-ly,** *adv.* **Linguistic science**—ভাষাশাস্ত্র।

lin′-gū-lāte (lĭng-), *adj.* Shaped like a tongue; রসনাকৃতি, জিহ্বাকৃতি।

lin-guo-dĕn′-tăl (lĭng-gwō-), *adj.* Made with the tongue and teeth, as a sound; (ধ্বনিসম্বন্ধে) দন্ত্য-জিহ্বামূলীয়।

lĭn′-ĭ-mĕnt, *n.* A liquid preparation thinner than ointment applied by rubbing; an embrocation; মালিস, পাতলা মলম, তরল প্রলেপ, উদ্বর্ত্তন (ঠাকুরঃ), স্নেহন (সাঃ পঃ), উপদেহ (ঐ); দ্রবমর্দ্দনৌষধ।

link (lĭngk), *n., v. t.* & *i.* **1.** A single ring or division of a chain; শিকলের কড়া। **2.** (As a measure) The $\frac{1}{100}$th part of a surveying chain = 7·92 inches; (মাপের পরিমাণে) জরীপশিকলের শতাংশের একাংশ। **3.** A loop in knitting; (বুনন কাজে) সুতার একটী ফাঁস। **4.** A person or thing that unites others; a tie or bond; a part of a connected series; as, a *link* of brother-hood: the missing *link*; সংযোগসাধক ব্যক্তি বা বস্তু; বন্ধন; পরস্পরসংযুক্ত বস্তুপরম্পরার অংশ। **5.** A sleeve-link; কোমরবন্ধ প্রভৃতি আটকাইবার জন্য জোড় বোতাম। ***Verb t.*** **1.** To connect or join *together* or *to*; একত্র সংবদ্ধ করা, সংযোজন করা। **2.** To clasp or join; as, to *link* hand or an arm in arm; সংযোগ করা, সংগ্রথিত করা। ***Verb i.*** To be connected or joined; সংযুক্ত হওয়া, সম্মিলিত হওয়া। **Link′-age,** *n.* **Linked battalions** — সৈন্যদলের বিভাগদ্বয়—যাহারা একটী দেশে থাকে এবং উহা হইতে বিদেশে যুদ্ধনিরত অপর দলের জন্য সৈন্য প্রেরিত হইয়া থাকে। **Missing-link**—See MISSING.

link (lĭngk), *n.* A torch made of pitch and tow used formerly; পূর্ব্বকালের এক প্রকার মশাল **Link-boy, –man**—মশালধারী বালক, মশালচী।

links (lĭngks), *n.* **1.** (*Pl.*) A level or undulating sandy ground along the sea-shore; সমুদ্রতীরস্থ সমতল বা উচ্চাবচ বালুকাভূমি। **2.** A ground for the game of golf, (often resembling that of the preceding sense); গল্‌ফ্ খেলার ময়দান।

linn, *n.* (*Chiefly Scot.*) **1.** A waterfall; জলপ্রপাত। **2.** A poo below it; জলপ্রপাতের নিম্নস্থ প্রবাহিণী। **3.** A steep ravine; a precipice; সঙ্কীর্ণ গিরিবর্ত্ম; সমুন্নত পর্ব্বতপার্শ্ব।

Lin-n(a)e′-ăn (-nē-), *adj.* & Of, or pertaining to, Linnæus, the celebrated Swedish botanist or to his stystem of classifying plants and animals; সুইডেনদেশীয় সুপ্রসিদ্ধ উদ্ভিদ্‌বিজ্ঞানবিৎ পণ্ডিত লিনিয়াস্ বা তৎপ্রবর্ত্তিত উদ্ভিদ্ ও জন্তুর শ্রেণী-বিভাগ সম্পর্কীয়। ***Noun.*** A follower or advocate of Linnæus or his system; উদ্ভিদ্‌বিজ্ঞানবিদ্ লিনিয়াসের সমর্থক বা অনুসরণকারী।

Linnet.

lin′-nĕt, *n.* A small singing bird; গায়ক পক্ষিবিশেষ।

lī-nō-'lē-ŭm, *n.* A kind of floor-cloth of canvas with a thick coating of oxidized linseed oil ; গৃহতলাচ্ছাদনের জন্য একপ্রকার কাম্বিস বিশেষ। **—umed,** *adj.*

lin'-ō-tȳpe, *n.* A type-setting machine which produces castings, each of which corresponds to a

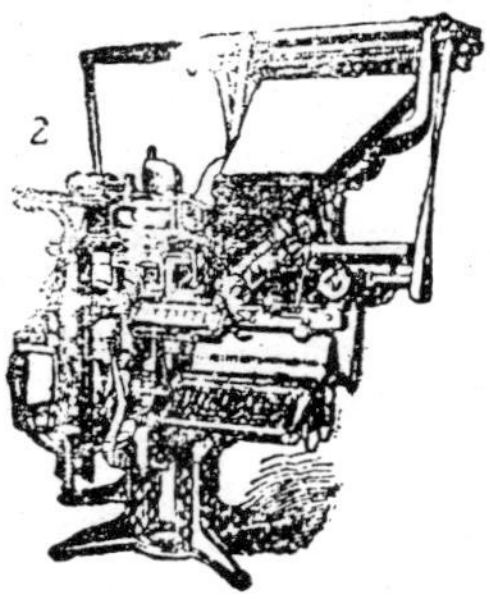

Linotype machine.

line of separate types ; হস্ত দ্বারা মুদ্রণের হরফ এক একটী করিয়া বিন্যস্ত করার পরিবর্ত্তে যে যন্ত্রের সাহায্যে পংক্তিতে পংক্তিতে ঢালাই করিয়া বিন্যাস করা হয়, মুদ্রাক্ষরপংক্তিজনক।

lin'-săng, *n.* A civet cat of Borneo and Java ; যবদ্বীপ ও বোর্নিওর গন্ধগোকুলা বিশেষ।

lin'-seed (-sēd), *n.* The seed of flax (also *lintseed*) ; তিসি, মসিনা, উমাবীজ (কেন্দ্রিঃ), অতসীবীজ (ঐ)। **Linseed-cake**—তিসির খইল। **Linseed-meal** — তিসির গুঁড়া, তিসির আটা। **Linseed-oil**—তিসির তৈল। **Linseed poultice**—তিসির পুলটিস্।

lin'-sey—wool'-sey (lĭn-sĭ—wŭl-sĭ), *n.* Cloth made of linen and wool or wool and cotton; শণসূত্র ও পশম মিশ্রণে প্রস্তুত বস্ত্র, পশম ও কার্পাসের মিশ্রণে প্রস্তুত বস্ত্র।

lint, *n.* Linen scraped into a soft substance for dressing wounds ; শণের সূত্র চাঁছিয়া লইয়া ক্ষত প্রভৃতিতে দিবার জন্য যে কোমল বস্ত্রের ন্যায় বস্তু প্রস্তুত হয়।

সৃষ্টিছাড়া, জাতিরূপাপচারী। **—ly,** *adv.* **—mal'-i-ty,** *n.* **1.** The state or quality of being abnormal ; irregularity ; নিয়মবিরুদ্ধতা, অনৈসর্গিকতা ; অনিয়মিতত্ব। **2.** Something abnormal ; অস্বাভাবিক পদার্থ, কিম্ভূতকিমাকার জীব বা বস্তু, বিকট জীব। **—mi-ty,** *n.* Irregularity ; deformity ; monstrosity ; স্বভাববিরুদ্ধতা ; বিরূপতা, অঙ্গবিকৃতি ; বিকটতা।

ă-board' (-bōrd), *adv.* & *prep.* **1.** Within a ship or boat or in a train ; জাহাজে, নৌকায় বা রেলগাড়ীতে। **2.** Alongside ; পাশাপাশি। ***Prep.*** On board of ; জাহাজোপরি। **He fell aboard of me**—He abused me ; সে আমাকে গালাগালি করিয়াছিল। *(Naut.)* **To fall aboard**—To strike against another ship ; (নৌ-বিদ্যা) অন্য জাহাজের সহিত ধাক্কা লাগা। **To go aboard**—To embark ; জাহাজ, নৌকা প্রভৃতিতে আরোহণ করা। **To keep the land aboard**—তীরের নিকটে নিকটে থাকা। **To lay (a ship) aboard**—যুদ্ধের জন্য নিজ জাহাজ অন্য জাহাজের পাশাপাশি রাখা।

ă-bōde', *n.* **1.** Dwelling-place ; residence ; বাসস্থান, বসতি ; আবাসস্থান (আঃ মঠ), আবাসভবন, অধিষ্ঠান (ইন্দিঃ)। **2.** Stay ; as, he fled away without *abode* ; অবস্থান।

ă-bŏl'-ish, *v. t.* To do away with ; as, to *abolish* laws, customs or institutions ; to annul ; উঠাইয়া দেওয়া, তুলিয়া দেওয়া, রহিত করা, বাতিল করা ; ধ্বংস করা, very brave ; সিংহতুল্য ; সিংহহৃদয়। **Lion-hearted**—Fearless ; brave ; নির্ভীক ; সাহসী। **Lion's provider**—সিংহের আহারসংগ্রহকারী অর্থাৎ শৃগাল। **Lion's share** — The largest or the best part ; বৃহত্তম বা শ্রেষ্ঠ অংশ, প্রধান ভাগ। **A (great) lion**—A popular or conspicuous person ; সর্ব্বজনপ্রিয় ব্যক্তি, সর্ব্বজনমান্য ব্যক্তি। **A lion in the way** or **path**—An obstacle or danger,esp. imaginary; কর্ম্মপথে প্রতিবন্ধক বা বিপদ্, বিশেষতঃ কাল্পনিক বিপদ্। **Do not rouse the sleeping lion**—ঘুমন্ত বাঘকে জাগাইও না। **The British Lion**—The British nation ; ইংরাজজাতি। **To put one's head into the lion's mouth**—To get into a perilous position ; সাপের মাথায় হাত দেওয়া, সিংহের মুখে মাথা ঢুকান। **To put on lion's skin**—To make a false assumption of courage ; মিথ্যা সাহস দেখান, সাহসের ভাণ করা। **To see, show the lions**—To see, show the sights worth seeing in town etc. (from the custom of showing country visitors the lions in the Tower of London) ; নগরের আশ্চর্য্য দৃশ্যাবলী দেখা বা দেখান। **To twist the lion's tails**—To defy or insult England ; সিংহের লাঙ্গুল মোচড়ান, ব্রিটিশ সিংহকে তুচ্ছ বা অপমান করা।

lī'-ŏn-īze, *v. t.* & *i.* **1.** To visit or show the objects of interest of (a place); কোন স্থানের আশ্চর্য্য বস্তু বা কৌতূহলজনক পদার্থ দর্শন বা প্রদর্শন করা। **2.** To treat (a person) as a lion or celebrity ; বড়লোক বলিয়া গণ্য করা। ***Verb i.*** To see the interesting objects ; কোন স্থানের চমকপ্রদ বস্তু দর্শন করা। **—ism,** *n.* Lionizing ; state of being treated as a lion or celebrity কোন স্থানের কৌতূহলজনক দ্রব্যপ্রদর্শন; বীরকেশরিসমুচিত অভ্যর্থনাপ্রাপ্তি।

lĭp, *n.* & *v. t.* **1.** One of the fleshy edges of the opening of the mouth ; অধর, ওষ্ঠ, ঠোঁট। **2.** The edge or border of anything, *e. g.* of a cup, vessel, cavity, wound, etc. ; ধার, কিনারা, প্রান্ত। **3.** (*Slang*) Saucy or impudent talk ; (গ্রাম্যভাষায়) বে-আদবি কথা, উদ্ধত বাক্য। ***Verb t.*** **1.** To touch with the lips ; to apply the lips to ; to kiss ; ওষ্ঠাধর দ্বারা স্পর্শ করা ; ওষ্ঠাধর স্থাপন করা ; চুম্বন করা। 2. (Of water) To lap or lave ; (জলসম্পর্কে) বিধৌত করা। 3. To utter softly ; চুপে চুপে বলা। **Lip'-less,** *adj.* **Cherry lip**—বিম্বোষ্ঠ। **Lip-comfort** — মৌখিক সান্ত্বনা। **Lip-deep** — Superficial ; insincere ; উপরি উপরি, ভাসা ভাসা, মৌখিক ; কপট। **Lip-deep words**—দন্তকথা (গুজরাটী সাহিত্য)। **Lip-devotion** — মৌখিক ভক্তি, মৌখিক অনুরাগ। **Lip-homage**—Insincere homage ; কপট ভক্তি, মৌখিক বশ্যতা বা সম্মান। **Lip-language, read-ing, speaking, etc.**—মূক এবং বধিরদিগের দ্বারা অথবা তাহাদের শিক্ষার জন্য নিঃশব্দে ওষ্ঠাধরসঞ্চালন, ওষ্ঠ-ভাষা। **Lip-loyalty** — মৌখিক রাজভক্তি। **Lip-salve**—ঠোঁটের ঘায়ের মলম, ওষ্ঠাঞ্জন। (*Fig.*) Flattery ; চাটুক্তি, তোষামোদ। **Lip-service**—মৌখিক সেবা। **Lip-wisdom** — পুস্তকগতবিদ্যা। **Lip-work** — জল্পনা কল্পনা। **Lower or under lip**—অধর। **Upper-lip**—ওষ্ঠ। **Stiff under lip**—সহিষ্ণুতা ; একগুঁয়েমি। **The word escaped his lips**—It was uttered thoughtlessly ; মুখ হইতে অজ্ঞাতসারে বাহির হইয়া পড়িয়াছিল, মুখ ফসকিয়া বাহির হইয়াছিল। **To bite one's lip**—To press the lips between the teeth in anger ; to repress emotion or to stifle laugh ; (also see BITE.) ক্রোধে ওষ্ঠাধর দংশন করা ; ওষ্ঠ চাপিয়া আবেগ রুদ্ধ করা বা হাসি বন্ধ করা। **To curl one's lip**—To do so in scorn ; ঘৃণায় ওষ্ঠ কুঞ্চিত করা। **To hang on one's lip**—To listen to his every word in reverence ; শ্রদ্ধাপূর্ব্বক কাহারও প্রত্যেকটী কথা শোনা। **To hang the lip**—To look vexed ; ঠোঁট ফুলান। **To keep or carry a stiff upper lip**—To keep one's courage ; না দমিয়া যাওয়া। To be hard or obstinate ; ঠেঁটা হওয়া। **To lick or smack one's lips**—To do so in enjoyment or in anticipation of food, (also *fig.*) ; ভোজনের আশায় বা সুখাদ্য ভোজন করিতে করিতে ওষ্ঠ লেহন করা। **To make a lip**—To have an angry or mocking expression of face ; ক্রোধব্যঞ্জক বা বিদ্রূপসূচক মুখভঙ্গী করা।

lip'-lĕt, *n.* A little lip ; ক্ষুদ্র ওষ্ঠ।

li-pŏg'-ră-phȳ, *n.* Same as HAPLOGRAPHY.

lī-pō'-mă, *n.* A tumour formed of fatty tissues ; মেদার্ব্বুদ।

lĭp'-pêr, *n.* (*Naut.*) A slight roughness or ruffling of the sea : (নৌ-বিদ্যা) সমুদ্রের ঈষৎ উত্তরঙ্গতা।

lī'-quāte, *v. t.* To separate or purify as metals by liquifying ; তরলতাপাদন করিয়া ধাতু প্রভৃতি বিশুদ্ধ করা। **–qua'-tion,** *n.*

liq'-ue-fȳ (lĭk-wĕ-), *v. t.* & *i.* To convert into a liquid condition ; to melt ; তরল করা ; গালান, বিগলিত করা, বিদ্রাবিত করা, দ্রবীভূত করা। ***Verb i.*** To become liquid ; তরল হওয়া, দ্রবীভূত হওয়া, গলা। **–fa'-cient,** *adj.* & *n.* Serving to liquify ; তরলতাপাদক। ***Noun.*** 1. Something serving to liquify ; দ্রাবক, বিদ্রাবক। 2. (*Med.*) An agent supposed to have power to liquify solid deposits ; (ভৈষজ্যশাস্ত্র) তরলতাপাদক বস্তু। **–fac'-tion,** *n.* The act of liquefying ; the state of being liquefied ; বিদ্রাবণ, তরলীকরণ, দ্রবীকরণ, দ্রবীভবন, দ্রাবণ, বিলয়ন, তরলতাপাত (সাঃ পঃ) ; দ্রবত্ব দ্রাবিতত্ব, দ্রাবিতাবস্থা। **–fac'-tive,** *adj.* **–fi-a-ble,** *adj.* Capable of being liquefied ; দ্রাবণযোগ্য। **–fi-er,** *n.*

lĭ-quĕs'-cĕnt, *adj.* Becoming or tending to become liquid ; গলনশীল।

lĭ-queur' (-kür), *n.* 1. A strong alcoholic beverage sweetened and flavoured with aromatic substances ; সুরামিশ্রিত সুমিষ্ট এবং সুগন্ধ পানীয় বিশেষ। 2. A mixture of alcohol or wine and sugar for flavouring champagne ; শ্যাম্পেন সুবাসিত করার জন্য সুরাবীর্য্য, মদিরা এবং চিনির মিশ্র বিশেষ। **Liqueur glass**—অতি ক্ষুদ্র পানপাত্র। **Liqueur frame or stand**—সরাপ বা পানীয় দ্রব্য রাখার জন্য ক্ষুদ্র তাক বা বৈঠক।

liq'-uid (lĭk-wĭd), *adj.* & *n.* 1. Composed of particles that flow freely like water ; not solid or gaseous ; তরল ; দ্রব। 2. Watery ; "Plough the *liquid* plain" ; জলবৎ, জলীয়। 3. Transparent, translucent or bright, like water or wine ; as, *liquid* lustre eyes, air or sky ; জল বা মদিরার মত স্বচ্ছ, অর্দ্ধস্বচ্ছ বা উজ্জ্বল। 4. Flowing smooth ; not grating as a melody or sound ; pronounced easily ; vowel-like ; not guttural ; as, *l* & *r* are *liquid* letters ; সুললিত ; শ্রুতিসুখদ, শ্রবণসুখদ, শ্রবণসুভগ ; অনায়াসে উচ্চারিত ; সুখোচ্চার্য্য ; স্বরবর্ণবৎ ; কণ্ঠোচ্চারিত নহে। 5. Unstable ; as, *liquid* convictions or principles ; অব্যবস্থিত, অস্থির, চঞ্চল, অধীর। 6. (Of assets and securites etc.) Easily convertible into cash ; সহজে রোক টাকায় পরিবর্ত্তনীয়। ***Noun.*** 1. A liquid substance ; তরল পদার্থ, দ্রব পদার্থ, দ্রব দ্রব্য। 2. A letter which has a smooth flowing sound ; as, *l, m, n, r* ; অনায়াসে উচ্চারিত বর্ণ। **–ize,** *v. t.* To make liquid ; তরল করা, দ্রব করা। **–ly,** *adv.* **–ness, Li-quid'-i-ty,** *ns.* The state of being liquid ; দ্রবত্ব, তরলত্ব, তরলতা। **Liquid amber**—একপ্রকার বৃক্ষ—যাহার নির্যাস ঔষধে ব্যবহৃত হয় [এই বৃক্ষের নির্যাসের নাম কপি তৈল]। **Liquid letters**—ইংরাজী *l r,* এবং কখন কখন *m* ও *n.* **Liquid-measure**—ভেঁড়ো মাপ। **To have liquid convictions**—See LIQUID *adj.* 5.

liq'-ui-dāte (lĭk-wĭ-), *v. t.* & *i.* 1. To pay off as a debt ; ঋণ পরিশোধ করা, দেনা চুকাইয়া দেওয়া। 2. To wind up ; to ascertain the liabilities and apportion the assets of (a company, firm, etc.) ; কারবার গুটাইয়া ফেলা ; কোন কোম্পানীর দায় নিরূপণ করা ও কোম্পানীর সম্পত্তি অংশানুরূপ বণ্টন করা। *Verb i.* (Of a company etc.) To be wound up in this way ; (কোম্পানী সম্পর্কে) গুটান। **–da'-tion,** *n.* **1.** The act of settling or paying off ; ঋণ পরিশোধ বা ঋণ পরিশোধের বন্দোবস্ত করণ। **2.** The act of winding up, as a firm or company by clearing up its money affairs ; (কারবার) গুটানি, ব্যবসায়োত্তলন। **–da-tor,** *n.* An official appointed to conduct the liquidation or winding up of a firm or company ; কোন কারবার গুটাইয়া ঋণ পরিশোধের বন্দোবস্ত করার জন্য নিযুক্ত কর্ম্মচারী। **Liquidated damages** — যে ক্ষতির পরিমাণ আদালতে নির্দ্দিষ্ট হইয়াছে। **To go into liquidation**—To have the affairs (of a firm or company wound up) ; to become bankrupt ; হিসাব নিকাশ করিয়া (দেনা পাওনা মিটাইয়া) কারবার তুলিয়া ফেলা, কারবার গুটাইয়া ফেলা ; দাউলিয়া হওয়া।

liq'-uor (lĭk-êr), *n., v. t.* & *i.* **1.** (*Somewhat rare*) Any liquid substance, as water, milk, etc. ; তরল পদার্থ। **2.** A beverage ; পানীয়, আসব। **3.** The liquid constituent of a secretion ; the liquid product of a chemical operation ; রস ; রাসায়নিক ক্রিয়ার ফলে উৎপন্ন তরল পদার্থ। **4.** A liquid used as a wash ; প্রক্ষালনে ব্যবহৃত তরল পদার্থ। **5.** Water used in brewing ; মদ্য চোলাই করার জন্য ব্যবহৃত জল। **6.** Water in which food has been boiled ; যে জলে খাদ্যদ্রব্য সিদ্ধ করা হইয়াছে। (*Pharmacy, pr.* lĭk-) A solution of a medicinal substance in water ; as, *liquor* ammoniæ etc.; (ঔষধালয়) জলমিশ্রিত ঔষধ, ঔষধজল। *Verb t.* **1.** To dress with grease or oil, as leather, shoe, etc. ; জুতা প্রভৃতিতে তৈল বা চর্ব্বি মাখান। **2.** To steep (malt etc.) in water ; (কলা-বেরুণ যব প্রভৃতি) জলে ভিজান। *Verb i.* **1.** (*Slang*) To drink alcoholic liquor, (often with *up*) ; (ইতরভাষায়) মদ্য পান করা, সুরা পান করা। **Malt liquor**—Ale, beer, porter, etc. ; যবসুরা। **Liquor shop** — মদের দোকান, মদিরাগৃহ, শৌণ্ডিকালয়, মদ্যবিপণি। **Spirituous liquor**—সুরাসার, শরাব, মদ, মদ্য, মদিরা, সুরা, শীধু। **A liquor-(up)**—(*Slang*) Taking of liquor as refreshment ; (ইতর ভাষায়) শ্রান্তি-নিবারণের জন্য সুরাপান। **To be in liquor** — To be intoxicated ; মাতাল হওয়া।

liq'-uor-ice (lĭk-êr-ĭs), **lic'-or-ice** (-êr-ĭs), *ns.* **1.** A kind of European plant ; its root ; যষ্টিমধু গাছ ; যষ্টিমধু। **2.** A black substance used in medicine and as sweetmeat made from the root of this plant ; যষ্টিমধু গাছের শিকড় হইতে প্রস্তুত কৃষ্ণবর্ণ পদার্থ—যাহা ঔষধ এবং মিষ্ট দ্রব্যরূপে ব্যবহৃত হয়।

liq'-uor-ish (lĭk-êr-), *adj.* Fond of liquor ; মদ্যপ্রিয়। **–ly,** *adv.* **–ness,** *n.*

li'-ră (lē-) *n.* (*Pl. lire, liras, abbr. L.*) An Italian silver coin and monetary unit equivalent to about 10*d.* ; ইতালী দেশীয় রৌপ্য-মুদ্রা বিশেষ—মূল্য দশ আনা।

lisp, *v. i., t.* & *n.* **1.** To pronounce the sibilant letters (S & Z) imperfectly as in pronouncing *th* for *s* ; "স" কে "থ" র মত উচ্চারণ করা। **2.** (Of a child) To speak with imperfect pronunciation ; শিশুর মত কথা বলা, অর্দ্ধস্ফুটস্বরে কথা বলা, আধো আধো স্বরে কথা বলা। *Verb t.* To say with a lisp, (often with *out*) ; অর্দ্ধস্ফুটস্বরে বলা। *Noun.* **1.** Lisping sound or pronunciation ; আধোআধো কথা, অস্ফুট উচ্চারণ, বালভাষিত। **2.** Rippling of waters, rustling of leaves ; তরঙ্গের কুলুকুলু ধ্বনি, পত্রমর্ম্মর। **Lisp'-ing,** *adj.* **Lisp'-ing-ly,** *adv.*

lis'-som(e) (-sŭm), *adj.* Supple ; flexible ; lithe ; agile ; নমনীয় ; কোমল, নরম ; চঞ্চল, চটুল ; দ্রুত, ক্ষিপ্র, চটপটে। **–ness,** *n.*

list, *n., v. t.* & *i.* **1.** The border or selvage of a cloth (usu. of different material) ; বস্ত্রপ্রান্ত, কাপড়ের পাড়, ডোরা। **2.** Selvages ; the material of which the selvage cloth consits ; as, to line edges of door with *lists* ; ঐরূপ পাড় সকল ; ঐরূপ কাপড়ের পাড় যে বস্তু দ্বারা তৈরি হয়। **3.** (*Pl.*) The palisades enclosing a tilting ground ; (*fig.*) a scene of contest ; as, to enter the *lists*; (বহুবচন) রঙ্গভূমির বৃতি; (লক্ষণায়) রঙ্গাঙ্গন, রঙ্গভূমি, মল্লভূমি, আখড়া ; সংগ্রামক্ষেত্র। **4.** A register or catalogue ; একজাতীয় বস্তু বা বস্তু সমূহের নামের তালিকা, ফর্দ্দ, নির্ঘণ্ট, ফিরিস্তি, জায়। *Verb t.* **1.** To insert in a list or catalogue ; তালিকাভুক্ত করা। **2.** To cover with a list or a strip of cloth ; as, to *list* a door ; দরজায় কাপড়ের পাড় বা ফিতা লাগান। *Verb i.* (*Rare* or *vulg.*) To enlist in the army or navy ; সৈন্যদলভুক্ত করা, নৌবাহিনী ভুক্ত করা। **List'-ing,** *n.* The selvage of cloth ; কাপড়ের পাড়। **Active list**—নৌ বা স্থলসৈন্য-বিভাগের যে সকল সৈন্য যুদ্ধের জন্য আহূত হইতে পারে—তাহাদের তালিকা। **Civil-list** — See under CIVIL. **Free list**—যে সকল লোককে বিনা টিকিটে রঙ্গালয়ে প্রবেশ করিতে দিতে হইবে তাহাদের তালিকা। **To enter the lists against**—To challenge or to accept the challenge of usually to controversy ; যুদ্ধের

আমন্ত্রণ গ্রহণ করা, রণে প্রবৃত্ত হওয়া, তর্কযুদ্ধে আহ্বান করা, তর্কযুদ্ধের আমন্ত্রণ গ্রহণ করা।

list, *v. i.* (*Archaic*) To desire; to choose; to like or please; as, the wind blew where it *listed*; (অপ্রঃ) ইচ্ছা করা; পসন্দ করা; খুসী হওয়া।

list, *n.* & *v. i.* Inclination to one side as of a ship, building, fence, etc.; জাহাজাদির এক পার্শ্বে আনতি। ***Verb i.*** To lean over to one side as a ship etc.; জাহাজাদির পক্ষে এক পার্শ্বে কাৎ হওয়া।

list, *v. i.* & *t.* (*Arch.*) To give ear; to listen; (অপ্রঃ) কান দেওয়া, কর্ণপাত করা; শুনা। ***Verb t.*** (*Archaic*) To listen to; (অপ্রঃ) কান দিয়া শুনা, মনোযোগপূর্ব্বক শুনা।

lis'-tĕl, *n.* (*Aricht.*) A narrow fillet; (স্থপতিবিজ্ঞান) স্বল্লায়ত কম্প বা বন্ধনী (স্নাঃ রাঃ)।

lis'-ten (-n), *v. i.* & *t.* **1.** To give ear; to hear a person speaking attentively; কান দেওয়া; কাহারো কথা মন দিয়া শুনা, কর্ণপাত করা। **2.** To yield to advice, request or temptation; as, *listen* not to temptation; উপদেশ, উপরোধ বা প্রলোভনে কর্ণপাত করা। ***Verb t.*** (*Archaic*) To give ear to; কোন বিষয়ে কান বা মন দেওয়া। **–er**, *n.* One who listens; শ্রবণকর্ত্তা, শ্রোতা।

lis'-têr-ine (-în), *n.* An antiseptic solution; পচননিবারক তরল ঔষধ বিশেষ।

lis'-têr-îze, *v. t.* To treat (a wound) on the antiseptic methods introduced by Sir Joseph Lister, an English surgeon; সুপ্রসিদ্ধ অস্ত্রচিকিৎসক Sir Joseph Listerএর প্রবর্ত্তিত পচননিবারক প্রণালীমতে ক্ষত প্রভৃতির চিকিৎসা করা। **–te'-ri an**, *adj.* Of, or relating to, the system of Lord Lister's antiseptic surgery; উক্ত প্রণালী সম্বন্ধীয়।

list'-lĕss, *adj.* Indifferent; uninterested; languid; weary; উৎসাহশূন্য, নিরুৎসাহ, আস্থাহীন; উদাস, উদাসীন, নিস্পৃহ, স্পৃহাশূন্য; নিরুদ্যম, নিষ্ক্রিয়, অলসাঙ্গ, অবসন্ন, ক্লান্ত, পরিশ্রান্ত। **–ly**, *adv.* **–ness**, *n.*

lit, *pt.* & *pp.* of LIGHT.

lit'-ă-nŷ, *n.* A series of invocations, supplications, etc. for use in the church-services or processions, recited by the clergy and responded to usually in repeated formulas by the people; উপাসনাকালীন প্রার্থনাবিশেষ, সূক্ত। **Litany-desk, –stool**—যে হেলানো মেজ বা ছোট টুলের সামনে সূক্ত আবৃত্তিকারী জানু পাতিয়া বসিয়া থাকে।

li-tchi' (lē-chē), *n.* (Also *lichi*) **1.** A kind of fruit-tree grown in Bengal; লিচুগাছ [এই ফল সর্ব্বপ্রথম চীনদেশ হইতে ভারতবর্ষে আনীত হয়]। **2.** The fruit of that tree; লিচু ফল।

lit'-êr-ă-cŷ, *n.* Ability to read and write; লিখনপঠনক্ষমতা, বর্ণজ্ঞান, বর্ণপরিচয়।

literæ humaniores (*L.*), *n.* (*Abbr. Lit. Hum.*) Polite letters esp. as a name of a classical school or examination for B. A. degree at Oxford; সুকুমার সাহিত্য, বিশেষ ভাবে ল্যাটিন ও গ্রীক সাহিত্য অধ্যাপনের বিদ্যালয়, অক্সফোর্ড বিশ্ববিদ্যালয়ের বি, এ পরীক্ষা।

lit'-êr-ăl, *adj.* & *n.* **1.** According to, or following, the letter, exact words or text: as, *literal* translation; আক্ষরিক, শব্দানুযায়ী, ঠিক, যথাযথ, অবিকল, অন্বর্থ, মূলশব্দানুসারী, মূলশব্দানুযায়ী, যথাশব্দ, মূলপদানুসারী। **2.** Of, relating to, or expressed by, a letter or letters of the alphabet; অক্ষরসম্বন্ধীয়, অক্ষর বা অক্ষর সমূহ দ্বারা প্রকাশিত। **3.** Not figurative or metaphorical; as, *literal* interpretation; আক্ষরিক, মূলার্থক, মুখ্যার্থক, অরূপক। **4.** Prosaic; unimaginative, as a person গদ্যময়; অকল্পনারসিক। **5.** Not exaggerated; as, *literal* transformation; যথাযথ। ***Noun.*** A misprint of a letter; "A large number of *literals*"; মুদ্রাকরপ্রমাদ, ছাপার ভুল। **–al'-i-ty**, *n.* **–ism**, *n* **1.** The practice or theory of following the letter as in translation etc.; tendency to adopt the literal sense; (অনুবাদাদিতে) আক্ষরিকতা; শব্দানুযায়ী অর্থগ্রহণ প্রবণতা। **2.** (*Arts*) Extreme realism in portrayal; (কলাশাস্ত্র) আলেখ্যাদি চিত্রণে চরমনিসর্গনিষ্ঠা। **–ist**, *n.* **–ly**, *adv.* In a literal manner; word for word; মূলশব্দানুরূপ, যথামূলশব্দ, মূলশব্দপ্রমাণ; কথায় কথায়। **Literal error** — A misprint; মুদ্রাকরপ্রমাদ। **Literal translation**—অনুবাদ, আক্ষরিক অনুবাদ, কথায় কথায় তরজমা।

lit'-êr-ăl-îze, *v. t.* To understand or interpret literally, as a metaphor etc.; উপমা, অলঙ্কার প্রভৃতি মূল অর্থে ধরা, কথায় কথায় ব্যাখ্যা করা।

literarum doctor (*L.*), *n.* Doctor of literature (as a University degree); সাহিত্যে বিশ্ববিদ্যালয়ের "ডাক্তার" উপাধি।

lit'-êr-ă-rŷ, *adj.* **1.** Of, or pertaining to, letters, literature or polite learning, etc.; সাহিত্য সম্বন্ধীয়, বিদ্বজ্জনবিষয়ক, সুকুমারসাহিত্যসম্বন্ধীয়। **2.** Versed in, or occupied with, literature; connected with literature or learned men; সাহিত্যচর্চ্চাশীল, সাহিত্যিক, সাহিত্যানুশীলনরত; সাহিত্য-সংক্রান্ত, বিদ্বজ্জনসংক্রান্ত, সাহিত্যিক সমাজসংক্রান্ত। **–ri-ly**, *adv.* **–ri-ness**, *n.* **Literary man**—A man of letters; সাহিত্যিক। **Literary property** — গ্রন্থাদি প্রকাশের অনন্যসাধারণ অধিকার; যে সকল পুস্তক প্রভৃতি প্রচারে কাহারো অনন্যসাধারণ অধিকার রহিয়াছে।

Literary history of a thing—সাহিত্যে ঐ বিষয়ের আলোচনার ইতিহাস।

lit′-êr-āte, *adj.* & *n.* Instructed in, or acquainted with, literature; esp. able to read and write; শিক্ষিত; লিখনপঠনক্ষম, বর্ণজ্ঞানসম্পন্ন। ***Noun.*** **1.** A learned or literary person; one who can read and write; সাহিত্যিক, বিদ্বান ব্যক্তি; লিখনপঠনক্ষম ব্যক্তি। **2.** A man admitted to the Anglican orders without any university degree; এংলিকান ধর্ম্ম সম্প্রদায়ে গৃহীত বিশ্ববিদ্যালয়ের উপাধিবিহীন ব্যক্তি, এংলিকান সম্প্রদায়ভুক্ত ব্যক্তি।

literati, (*L.*), *n.* (*Pl.*) (Sing. *literatus*) Men of letters; the learned; সাহিত্যিক সমাজ, বিদ্বৎসমাজ; শিক্ষিতসম্প্রদায়, পণ্ডিতমণ্ডলী, বিদ্বদ্‌বৃন্দ, বিবুধমণ্ডলী।

literatim, (*L.*) *adv.* Letter for letter; literally; অক্ষরে অক্ষরে; কথায় কথায়, অবিকল।

lit′-êr-ā-tor (-têr), *n.* A literary man; সাহিত্যিক।

lit′-êr-ă-türe, *n.* **1.** Production of literary work; the literary profession; গ্রন্থরচনা; সাহিত্যিকবৃত্তি। **2.** The writings of a country or period; সাহিত্য। **3.** The class of writings distinguished for beauty of style or expression; as, light *literature*; সুকুমার সাহিত্য। **4.** The books or writings treating of a subject; কোন বিষয় সম্বন্ধীয় গ্রন্থ বা প্রবন্ধসমূহ। **5.** (*Colloq.*) The printed matter; (চলিত-ভাষায়) মুদ্রিত বিষয়। **Light literature**—তরল সাহিত্য। **Polite literature** — সুকুমার সাহিত্য।

lith-arge (-ârj), *n.* Protoxide of lead; মুদ্রাশঙ্খ (যোঃ), সীসভস্ম (আয়ু রসঃ)।

lithe, *adj.* Supple; pliant; flexible; কোমল; নরম, নম্র; নমনীয়। **Lithe′-ness,** *n.* **Lithe′-some,** *adj.*

lith′-i-ă, *n.* Oxide of the metal lithium; অম্লজানজারিত লোহিতক। **Lithia-water** — গেঁটেবাত রোগের ঔষধস্বরূপ ব্যবহৃত খনিজমিশ্রিত নির্ঝর-বারিবিশেষ।

lith′-ic, *adj.* **1.** Of, or pertaining to, stone; as, *lithic* architecture; প্রস্তরসম্বন্ধীয়। **2.** (*Med.*) Of, or pertaining to, the formation of stone in the bladder; অশ্মরী-সম্বন্ধীয়।

lith′-ic, *adj.* (*Chem.*) Of, or relating to lithium; (রসায়ন শাস্ত্র) লিথিয়াম ধাতুসম্বন্ধীয়।

lith′-i-ŭm, *n.* A metallic element of the alkaline group; রজতবর্ণ ধাতুবিশেষ, লোহিতক (সাঃ পঃ)।

lith′-ō-clăst, *n.* (*Surg.*) An instrument for crushing stones in the bladder; (অস্ত্রোপচার বিদ্যা) অশ্মরীচূর্ণক।

lith′-ō-grăph, *n.* & *v. t.* A print from a drawing on stone; প্রস্তরফলক হইতে গৃহীত কাগজে ছাপ, শিলাক্ষর (বেণীঃ), প্রস্তরলেখ (আঃ বঃ), যে শিলাফলকোপরি চিত্রাদি ক্ষোদন পূর্ব্বক উহা কাগজে মুদ্রিত হয়। ***Verb t.*** To print by lithography; উক্ত প্রকারে মুদ্রিত করা।

li-thŏg′-ră-phy̆, *n.* The art of writing or drawing on a special kind of stone and of producing impression therefrom on paper; প্রস্তরলেখবিদ্যা, শিলাক্ষর বিদ্যা। **—pher,** *n.* **Lith-o-graph′-ic,** *adj.* **Lithographic-stone** — প্রস্তরলেখ প্রস্তুতের উপযোগী প্রস্তর।

li-thŏl′-ō-ğy̆, *n.* **1.** The science of the nature and composition of stones and rocks; প্রস্তরবিজ্ঞান। **2.** A treatise on calculi; মানব মূত্রাশয়, বৃক্ক প্রভৃতিতে উৎপন্ন প্রস্তর সম্বন্ধীয় গ্রন্থ। **Lith-o′-log-i-cal,** *adj.*

lith′-ō-marge (-mârj), *n.* (*Min.*) A smooth compact variety of common kaolin; (খনিজবিদ্যা) চিকণ মাটী (যোঃ)।

lith-ŏn-trip′-tic, *adj.* & *n.* Breaking up stone in the bladder; অশ্মরীচূর্ণকারী, অশ্মরীঘ্ন, অশ্মরীহর, মূত্রাশ্মনাশক। ***Noun.*** A lithontriptic medicine; অশ্মরীচূর্ণকর ঔষধ।

lith′-ō-phy̆te, *n.* **1.** Any one of the polyps whose substance is stony or hard, as corals; শুণ্ডাল-দেহী (polyps) প্রাণিসমূহের অন্যতম—যাহাদের দেহ প্রস্তরবৎ বা সুকঠিন:—যথা, প্রবালকীট। (See POLYPS.) **2.** (*Bot.*) A plant that grows on stone; (উদ্ভিদ্‌-বিদ্যা) শিলাজ উদ্ভিদ্‌।

li-thŏt′-ō-my̆, *n.* The operation of cutting for stone in the bladder; অস্ত্রোপচার ক্রিয়া দ্বারা মূত্রাশয় হইতে প্রস্তর বহিষ্করণ, অশ্মরীচ্ছেদ, মূত্রাশ্মরীচ্ছেদ। **Lith-o-tom′-ic, Lith-o-tom′-i-cal** *adjs.* **—mist,** *n.* **—mize,** *v. t.* To perform lithotomy on: অশ্মরীচ্ছেদন করা।

lith′-ō-trīte, lith′-ō-trī-tor (-têr), *ns.* An apparatus for crushing a stone in the bladder; অশ্মরী চূর্ণ করিবার যন্ত্র, অশ্মরীচূর্ণক।

li-thŏt′-ri-ty̆, *n.* The operation of breaking stone in the bladder into small pieces that can be passed through the urethra; অশ্মরীচূর্ণন। **—tist,** *n.* **—tize,** *v. t.* To subject to lithotrity; মূত্রাশয়ের প্রস্তর খণ্ডে খণ্ডে ভাঙ্গিয়া মূত্রপথে বাহির করা, অশ্মরীচূর্ণ করা।

lit′-i-gāte, *v. i.* & *t.* To go to law; to be a party to a lawsuit; মামলা করা, মোকদ্দমা করা, আদালতের আশ্রয় গ্রহণ করা; মোকদ্দমায় কোন পক্ষ হওয়া। ***Verb t.*** To contest in law; as, to *litigate* a cause for point; মোকদ্দমার বিষয়ীভূত করা। **—ga-ble,** *adj.* That may be contested in law; মোকদ্দমাযোগ্য। **—gant,** *adj.* & *n.* Engaged in a lawsuit; মোকদ্দমায় নিযুক্ত, বিবদমান, ব্যবহারিক, ব্যবহারী। (*Noun*) A person engaged in law-suit; মোকদ্দমাকারী

ব্যক্তি। **—ga′-tion,** *n.* Act of litigating; a lawsuit; মামলাকরণ; মামলা, মোকদ্দমা, বিবাদ (ব্যাঃ মাঃ)।

li-ti′-gious (-jŭs), **1.** Inclined to, or fond of, litigation; মামলাবাজ, মোকদ্দমাপ্রিয়। **2.** Disputable at law; offering matter for law-suit; মোকদ্দমা দ্বারা বিবদনীয়; মোকদ্দমাযোগ্য। **3.** Of, or relating to, litigations; মোকদ্দমা-সম্বন্ধীয়। **—ly,** *adv.* **—ness,** *n.*

lit′-mŭs, *n.* (*Chem.*) A dye-stuff obtained from certain lichens; কোন কোন জাতীয় শিলাবাক্ হইতে প্রাপ্ত নীলবর্ণ রঞ্জকপদার্থবিশেষ, লিট্মাস (হিঃ কোঃ)। **Blue litmus**—নীলা লিট্মাস্ (হিঃ কোঃ)। **Litmus paper**—দ্রাবকের অস্তিত্ব নির্ণয়ার্থ উক্ত নীলবর্ণ রঞ্জকপদার্থ দ্বারা রঞ্জিত কাগজ, লিট্মাস্ কাগজ (হিঃ কোঃ)। [এইরূপ কাগজ সামান্য মাত্র দ্রাবকের সংস্পর্শে লোহিত বর্ণ ধারণ করে।] **Red litmus**—লাল লিট্মাস্ (হিঃ কোঃ)।

li′-tö-tēs, *n.* (*Rhet.*) An affirmation made indirectly by the negation of its contrary; as, a citizen of no mean city=of an illustrious city; (অলঙ্কার-শাস্ত্র) কোন বাক্যের বিপরীত বাক্যের প্রত্যাখ্যান দ্বারা পরোক্ষ ভাবে উক্ত বাক্য দৃঢ়ীকরণ, বিপরীতনিষেধাত্মক অলঙ্কার।

li′-tre (lē-tr), *n.* The unit of the French measure of capacity equal to 61·028 cubic inches; ফরাসীদেশীয় শুষ্ক এবং তরল দ্রব্যের পরিমাণ বিশেষ।

Litter.

lit′-tĕr, *n., v. t. & i.* **1.** A frame containing a bed shut in by curtains and used for carrying passengers; শিবিকা, তাঞ্জাম, ডুলি, মাফা। **2.** A frame-work with a couch for transporting the sick or the wounded; পীড়িত বা আহত ব্যক্তিকে স্থানান্তরিত করিবার খাট বা খাটুলি। **3.** Straw, hay, etc. used as bedding, esp. for animals; খড়, বিচালি বা তৃণরচিত পশুশয্যা, পশুর তৃণশয্যা। **4.** Straw and dung of a farmyard; কৃষিবাটীকার খড়, গোময় প্রভৃতি আবর্জ্জনা, তৃণ, বিচালি, গোবর, প্রভৃতি। **5.** Disorderly accumulation of papers etc.; scattered rubbish; এলোমেলো ভাবে ছড়ান কাগজ, প্রভৃতি; বিক্ষিপ্ত জঞ্জাল। **6.** Disorder or untidiness; as, a room in a state of *litter*; এলোমেলো ভাব, অপরিচ্ছন্নতা। **7.** The young brought forth at a birth; একেবারে প্রসূত শাবক সমূহ। ***Verb t.*** **1.** To provide (horse, cattle, etc.) with litter or bedding of straw etc., (often with *down*); পশুর শয়নের জন্য বিচালি প্রভৃতি বিছাইয়া দেওয়া। **2.** To cover with litter or straw etc., as a floor, stable, etc., (usu. with *down*); ঘর, মেঝে, বা আস্তাবলে বিচালি বিছান। **3.** To strew with scattered articles; to make untidy, as a place; ইতস্ততঃ বিক্ষিপ্ত দ্রব্য দ্বারা আস্তীর্ণ করা; নোঙ্গরা করা, অপরিচ্ছন্ন করা। **4.** To scatter in disorder; এলোমেলোভাবে ছড়ান। **5.** To give birth to (whelps etc.); ছানা প্রসব করা, বাচ্চা দেওয়া। ***Verb i.*** To produce a litter or young; শাবক প্রসব করা, বাচ্চা দেওয়া।

litterateur (*F.*), *n.* A literary man; সাহিত্যসেবী ব্যক্তি, সাহিত্য-ব্যবসায়ী ব্যক্তি, সাহিত্যিক।

lit′-tle (-l), *adj., n. & adv.* **1.** Small in size or extent; ক্ষুদ্র, ছোট, অল্প। **2.** Short in duration; as, a *little* sleep; খানিক, সামান্য, অল্প। **3.** Small in quantity or amount; পরিমাণে অল্প, অল্পস্বল্প, কিঞ্চিৎ, ঈষৎ, সামান্য, অনধিক, স্তোক, খানিক। **4.** Trivial; unimportant; as, a *little* difficulty; তুচ্ছ; সামান্য, অকিঞ্চিৎকর। **5.** Illiberal; contemptible; as, the *little* cunning of the *little* minds; অনুদার, সঙ্কীর্ণ; তুচ্ছ, হেয়। **6.** Weak; inconsiderable; slight; as, a *little* effort or attention; দুর্ব্বল; অল্প; কিঞ্চিৎ। **7.** Of smaller or smallest size; as, the *little* finger; ক্ষুদ্রতম, কনিষ্ঠ। **8.** The young; as, the *little* Joneses; ছোট, কনিষ্ঠ। ***Noun.*** **1.** A small amount, time, distance or the like; as, for, or after, a *little*; অল্পমাত্র, অল্প পরিমাণ, অল্প সময়, সামান্য দূর। **2.** A small scale; as, one's picture in *little*; ক্ষুদ্র আকার। ***Adv.*** **1.** To a small extent only; as, I like him *little*; অল্প পরিমাণে, সামান্য পরিমাণে। **2.** Not at all; as, he *little* knows etc; মোটেই না। **—ness,** *n.* The state of being little; ক্ষুদ্রতা। **Little Bear**—লঘু সপ্তর্ষি (হিঃ কোঃ)। **Little Englands** — গ্রেট ব্রিটেনের উপনিবেশ বা অধীনদেশ সমূহের দায়িত্ব সঙ্কোচ করিতে হইবে—যাঁহারা এই মত পোষণ করেন। **Little Englandism**—That principle; ঐরূপ মত। **Little finger** — কনিষ্ঠাঙ্গুলি, কড়ে আঙুল। **Little-go** — (*Colloq.*) See GO. **A little**—*adv.* To a small degree; rather; somewhat; অল্প পরিমাণে, সামান্য পরিমাণে; বরং; কিছু। (*Adj.*) Some; কতক। **A little man** or **woman**—A boy or girl; বালক বা বালিকা। **In little**—On a small scale; অল্প মাত্রায়। **Little by little, By little and little**—By degrees; gradually; আস্তে আস্তে, শনৈঃ শনৈঃ; ক্রমে ক্রমে, অল্পে অল্পে। **Not a little** — Considerably; সামান্য নয়, অতিমাত্রায়, নিরতিশয়। **The little Joneses**—The children of Jones ; জোন্সের ছেলে মেয়েরা। **The little people**— Fairies ; পরী।

lit′-tō-ral, *adj.* & *n.* Of, relating to, or on, the shore ; সমুদ্রকূলবর্ত্তী, সাগরকূলসংক্রান্ত, সাগরতীরবর্ত্তী, তটস্থ, তীরস্থ। ***Noun.*** A strip of land lying along the shore ; উপকূল-ভূমি, সাগরতীরভূমি, সৈকত (সাঃ পঃ)। **Littoral zone**—জোয়ার ভাঁটার সীমার মধ্যবর্ত্তী স্থান।

lit′-ur-ġy (-ẽr-), *n.* 1. A ritual or established formulas for public worship ; নির্দ্ধারিত বা নিরূপিত উপাসনাপদ্ধতি। 2. The book of Common Prayer ; উপাসনাপুস্তক, নির্দ্ধারিত উপাসনাপদ্ধতিলিখিত সাধারণের ব্যবহার্য্য পুস্তক, স্তোত্রপদ্ধতি, স্তোত্রমালা, সূক্তসমষ্টি। 3. (In the Eastern Church) Mass ; Holy Communion ; রোমান ক্যাথলিক অনুষ্ঠান বিশেষ ; অধ্যাত্মযোগ। 4. (In ancient Greece) Public office or duty performed gratuitously by the rich Athenians ; (প্রাচীন গ্রীসে) এথেন্স নগরের ধনী অধিবাসিগণ কর্ত্তৃক সম্পাদিত অবৈতনিক সরকারী কার্য্য। **Li-tur′-gi-cal**, *adj.* **Li-tur′-gi-cal-ly**, *adv.*

liv′-a-ble (-bl), *adj.* 1. (Of house room, climate, etc.) Fit or suitable to live in ; বাসোপযোগী, অধিষ্ঠান-যোগ্য, আবাসযোগ্য। 2. Such as can be lived, as a life etc. ; (জীবন সম্বন্ধে) জীবনধারণযোগ্য, জীবন-ধারণোপযোগী। 3. Companionable ; easy to live with ; সহচরোপযোগী ; সামাজিক, মৈত্রেয়। **—ness**, *n.*

līve, *adj.* 1. Having life ; alive ; জীবিত, জীবন্ত ; সজীব, জ্যান্ত (colloq.) 2. (*Joc.*) Actual ; not pretended or pictured or toy ; as, a real *live* burglar or steam-engine ; (কৌতুকচ্ছলে) সত্যিকার ; প্রকৃত, বাস্তব। 3. Full of power, energy or importance ; of current interest or moment ; as, a *live* issue or otpic ; শক্তি বা বীর্য্যসম্পন্ন, তেজোগর্ভ, সাময়িক কৌতুহলোদ্দীপক গুরুত্ব বিশিষ্ট। 4. Glowing ; ignited ; জ্বলন্ত ; প্রজ্বলিত। 5. (Of shell, match, wire) Unkindled ; charged with electricity ; অপ্রজ্বালিত ; তাড়িত-প্রবাহসম্পূরিত। 6. Glowing or burning as embers ; (*fig.*) ardent, as hatred etc. ; জ্বলন্ত ; (লক্ষণায়) বিজাতীয়। 7. (Of rocks) Not detached ; forming part of the earth's frame ; (প্রস্তরাদি সম্বন্ধে) অবিচ্ছিন্ন, সংশ্লিষ্ট ; ভূপঞ্জরের অংশীভূত। 8. Having, or imparting, motion ; as, a *live* wheel or spindle ; গতিশীল, গতি-প্রদায়ক, গতিসঞ্চারক। **Live bait**—মাছ ধরিবার জন্য জ্যান্ত মাছ বা কীটের টোপ। **Live-coal**—জ্বলদঙ্গার, জ্বলন্ত কয়লা। **Live oak**—আমেরিকাদেশীয় শ্যামল তরুবিশেষ। **Live stock**—যে সকল গৃহপালিত পশু গৃহস্থের চাষবাসের কার্য্যে ব্যবহৃত হয়, জীবধন (অঃ), চর্ম্মধন (কেঃঃ)। **Live well**—জেলে ডিঙ্গিতে মৎস্য জীবিত রাখিবার জন্য কুণ্ড।

live (lĭv), *v. i.* & *t.* 1. To be alive ; to have animal or vegetable life ; জীবিত থাকা, বাঁচিয়া থাকা, প্রাণধারণ করা ; জান্তব বা উদ্ভিজ্জ জীবন থাকা। 2. To reside ; to dwell ; বসতি করা, বাস করা ; অবস্থান করা। 3. To pass life or time in a certain manner ; as, to *live* honestly or like a saint ; চলা, ব্যবহার করা, যাপন করা, থাকা। 4. To continue alive ; to have one's life prolonged ; as, that patient cannot *live* ; বাঁচিয়া থাকা ; আয়ুবৃদ্ধি পাওয়া। 5. To subsist, (with *on* or *upon*) ; as, horses *live on* grass ; to depend (*on* or *upon*) for maintenance ; as, he *lives upon* his wife or her earnings etc. ; to be supported as by one's labour, wit, etc. ; আহার করিয়া প্রাণধারণ করা, উদরনির্ব্বাহ করা ; জীবিকার জন্য নির্ভর করা ; নিজের শ্রম, বুদ্ধি প্রভৃতি দ্বারা জীবিকার্জ্জন করা। 6. (*Fig.*) To sustain one's position or repute *on* or *upon* ; as, he lives *upon* his name ; (লক্ষণায়) কোন কিছুর উপর নির্ভর করত স্বীয় পদগৌরব বা খ্যাতি রক্ষা করা। 7. To enjoy or use one's life intensely ; "*Living* up to the last days of his life" ; পূর্ণমাত্রায় জীবনের সুখ ভোগ করা। 8. (Of things) To survive ; to last ; as, his memory *lives* ; অপেক্ষাকৃত অধিককাল স্থায়ী থাকা ; টি'কিয়া থাকা। ***Verb t.*** 1. To lead, pass or spend ; as, to *live* a happy life ; অতিবাহিত করা, কাটান, যাপন করা 2. To act in conformity to ; as to *live* the Gospel ; (কোন কিছুর) অনুসারে কাজ করা। 3. To express in one's life ; as, to *live* poetry ; কাহারও জীবনে ব্যক্ত করা। **To live a life**—See LIVE *v. t.* I. **To live by**—To get livelihood etc. (by one's wit etc.) ; জীবিকাদি অর্জ্জন করা। **To live down** — To live so as to subdue or overcome as scandal etc. ; to prove false by the course of one's life ; এরূপভাবে বাস করা যাহাতে কোন নিন্দা বা অপবাদ অমূলক বলিয়া প্রতিপন্ন হয় ; নিজের আচরণ দ্বারা নিন্দা বা অপবাদ মিথ্যা বলিয়া সপ্রমাণ করা, পরবর্ত্তী আচরণ দ্বারা কোন-রূপ অন্যায় কার্য্যের স্মৃতি লোপ করা। **To live from hand to mouth**—ডাইনে আনতে বাঁয়ে কুলায় না। (See also under HAND.) **To live on** or **upon**—To subsist or feed on ; কোন কিছু আহার করিয়া জীবনধারণ করা। To depend on (another or another's income etc.) for maintenance ; জীবিকার জন্য কাহারো উপর নির্ভর করা, কাহারো গলগ্রহ হইয়া থাকা। **To live out the night**—To live through it ; রাত্রি ব্যাপিয়া জীবিত থাকা। **To live under**—To be a tenant to ; প্রজা হইয়া থাকা। **To live up to**—To rule one's life according to some standard ; কোন আদর্শ অনুযায়ী জীবন নিয়মিত করা।

To live up to anything — To make oneself worthy of an excellent thing by one's life ; এরূপভাবে জীবন যাপন করা যাহাতে কোন উৎকৃষ্ট বস্তু লাভের যোগ্য হওয়া যায়। **To live with**—To dwell or to be a lodger with ; একত্র বাস করা, এক বাসায় থাকা। To cohabit with ; সহবাস করা, সঙ্গম করা।

lived (lîvd), *adj.* Having life (used in compounds) ; as, long-*lived* ; আয়ুষ্মান (সমাসে ব্যবহৃত হয়)।

live'-li-hood, *n.* Means of living ; subsistence ; sustenance ; জীবনোপায় ; জীবিকা ; উপজীবিকা।

live'-lŏng (lîv-), *adj.* Whole ; long in passing ; দীর্ঘকালব্যাপী, দীর্ঘকাল-স্থায়ী, বহুক্ষণস্থায়ী, দীর্ঘকালিক ; বিরক্তিকর, আর যেন কাটে না এরূপ। **Live-long day** — The whole day ; সমস্তটা দিন, সারাদিন, দীর্ঘদিবস।

live'-lŷ, *adj.* **1.** Life-like ; vivid ; as, a *lively* description ; বাস্তব, জীবন্তবৎ ; সজীব। **2.** Full of life ; vigorous ; energetic ; active ; enlivening ; fresh ; interesting ; keen ; স্ফূর্ত্তিযুক্ত, প্রাণবান, প্রাণপূর্ণ, আনন্দপূর্ণ ; সতেজ ; উৎসাহপূর্ণ ; জীবনপ্রদ, প্রাণপ্রদ ; নবীন ; আমোদপ্রদ। **3.** (Of colour) Bright ; (বর্ণ সম্বন্ধে) দীপ্ত। **4.** Gay ; sprightly ; as, he was *lively* in conversation ; প্রফুল্ল, উৎফুল্ল ; উল্লসিত, উল্লাসপূর্ণ। **5.** (Of boat etc.) Rising lightly to the waves ; (নৌকাদি সম্বন্ধে) তরঙ্গসঙ্গে মৃদুমন্দভাবে উত্থানশীল। **6.** (*Joc.*) Exciting ; dangerous ; as, the police had a *lively* tune ; (কৌতুকচ্ছলে) উত্তেজনাপূর্ণ ; সঙ্কটপূর্ণ, বিপৎসঙ্কুল। **—li-ly**, *adv.* **—li-ness,** *n.* The state of being lively or energetic ; sprightliness ; vivacity ; animation ; briskness ; সতেজতা ; উল্লাস, স্ফূর্ত্তি ; সজীবতা, তেজস্বিতা, হৃষ্টতা, প্রফুল্লতা, উল্লাস, প্রহর্ষ ; উৎফুল্লতা, প্রসন্নতা ; ক্ষিপ্রতা, চটুলতা।

līv'-en (-n), *v. t.* & *i.* To enliven ; to cheer up ; সজীব করা, অনুপ্রাণিত করা ; উৎফুল্ল করা, প্রফুল্ল করা।

liv'-êr, *n.* **1.** A large organ in all vertebrates secreting bile ; যকৃত (শিরার রক্ত পরিষ্কারক এবং পিত্ত-নিঃসারক যন্ত্র), পিত্তাশয়। **2.** (*Archaic*) Liver, as the seat of emotion as, hot *liver*, (*i. e.* passionate or amorous temperament ; কাম বা ক্রোধপ্রধান প্রকৃতি) ; কাম ক্রোধাদির স্থান। **3.** A disease of the liver (also *liver-complaint*) ; যকৃদ্‌রোগ। **4.** (Also *liver-colour*) Dark reddish brown ; গাঢ় রক্তপিঙ্গল বর্ণ। **5.** The flesh of liver used as food ; মেটে। **—ish,** *adj.* Having liver trouble ; যকৃদ্‌রোগপীড়িত। **—less,** *adj.* **Liver-complaint**—যকৃতের পীড়া। **Liver-line** — মণিবন্ধ হইতে আরম্ভ হইয়া অনামিকার মূলদেশ পর্য্যন্ত বিস্তৃত রেখা, স্বাস্থ্যরেখা। **Liver-wing** — The right wing of a cooked fowl under which liver is tucked ; (*joc.*) the right arm ; রন্ধিত মোরগের ডাহিন পাখা—যাহার নীচে ইহার মেটে ঢুকাইয়া দেওয়া হয় ; (কৌতুকচ্ছলে) দক্ষিণ বাহু। **Liver-wort** — যকৃতের পীড়ায় ব্যবহৃত গুল্ম-বিশেষ। **White, lily, pigeon, milk, —livered** — Cowardly ভীরু, কাপুরুষ।

liv'-êr, *n.* **1.** One who lives ; a dweller ; বাসকারী ; বাসিন্দা। **2.** One who lives in a specified way ; as, a free *liver* ; যে ব্যক্তি কোন নির্দ্দিষ্ট নিয়মানুসারে জীবনযাপন করে। **Fast liver**—অপব্যয়ী লম্পট ব্যক্তি। **Free liver**—ভোজনবিলাসী, ঔদরিক। **Good liver**—A virtuous person, (also a *free-liver*) ; ধর্ম্মনিষ্ঠ ব্যক্তি। **Loose-liver**—A dissolute person ; ইন্দ্রিয়পরায়ণ ব্যক্তি, চরিত্রভ্রষ্ট ব্যক্তি।

liv'-êr-ŷ, *n.* **1.** (*Hist.*) An allowance of food or clothing delivered over to a family, servants, relatives, etc. ; (ইতিহাস) পরিবার, ভৃত্য বা অধীন ব্যক্তিদিগকে প্রদত্ত পোষাক পরিচ্ছদ, খাদ্যসম্ভার প্রভৃতি। **2.** An allowance of provender for horses ; অশ্বাদির জন্য শুষ্ক তৃণ বা বিচালি। **3.** The uniform worn by a member of a city company or by the male servants of a person o position ; নগরের কোন সম্প্রদায়বিশেষভুক্ত ব্যক্তিদিগের ব্যবহৃত নির্দ্দিষ্ট পোষাক অথবা কোন সম্ভ্রান্ত ব্যক্তির ভৃত্যদিগের পরিহিত নির্দ্দিষ্ট পরিচ্ছদ। **4.** Characteristic dress or outward appearance ; as, birds in their winter *livery* ; বিশিষ্ট পরিচ্ছদ, বাহ্য শোভা। **5.** The membership of a city company ; as, to take up one's *livery* (*i. e.* to become a livery-man) ; নগরের কোন বিশেষ সম্প্রদায়ের সভ্য। **6.** (*Law*) The delivery of legal possession of property ; a writ allowing this ; (আইনে) কোন সম্পত্তিতে আইনতঃ অধিকার প্রদান ; বৈধ অধিকার প্রদানের দলীল। **—ied,** *adj.* **Livery-company** — লণ্ডন নগরের সম্প্রদায় বিশেষ (যাহাদের পূর্ব্বে নির্দ্দিষ্ট পরিচ্ছদ ছিল)। **Liveryman** — নির্দ্দিষ্ট পরিচ্ছদধারী লোক ; নগরীর কোন বিশিষ্ট সম্প্রদায়ের সভ্য ; আড়গড়াওয়ালা, আড়গড়ার চাকর। **Livery-servant**—চোপদার, তকমাপরা ভৃত্য। **Livery-stable** — আড়গড়া। **At livery**—নিরূপিত বেতনে (মালিকের) অশ্বাদির পরিচর্য্যা করা ও আহারাদি যোগান। **In or out of livery**—Attired in livery or in plain clothes, as a person ; বিশিষ্ট পরিচ্ছদ পরিহিত। **Keeper of or attendant in a livery stable** — আড়গড়ার চাকর, আড়গড়াওয়ালা। **To keep at livery**—To keep for the owner and feed and groom for a fixed charge ; নির্দ্দিষ্ট হারে টাকা লইয়া অশ্বাদির পরিচর্য্যা করা। **To sue one's livery**—To bring a suit as heir in a court of wards to get possession ; সম্পত্তিতে অধিকার পাওয়ার জন্য কোর্ট অব্ ওয়ার্ডসের নামে নালিস করা।

liv'-id, *adj.* Black and blue ; of bluish leaden colour ; discoloured as flesh by bruise ; নীলকৃষ্ণ ; সীসবর্ণ, শ্যাব বর্ণ ; (আঘাতের দরুণ) বিবর্ণ, কালশিরা-পড়া। **—ly,** *adv.* **Li-vid'-i-ty,** *n.*

liv'-ing, *adj.* **1.** Having life ; জীবন্ত, সজীব। **2.** Now existent ; as, no man *living* could do better ; বর্ত্তমান। **3.** Active ; vigorous (said of the states of mind) : as, *living* faith ; কর্ম্মঠ ; সতেজ, প্রাণপূর্ণ। **4.** Exact ; as, a *living* picture ; জীবিতবৎ, অবিকল। **5.** Issuing continually ; flowing ; as, *living* water : *living* spring, (opp. to *stagnant*) ; নিঃস্রাবী ; প্রবহমাণ। **6.** Ignited ; burning ; as, *living* coal ; জ্বলন্ত ; প্রজ্বলিত। **7.** Still in vernacular use ; as, *living* language ; ব্যবহৃত, প্রচলিত। **—ly,** *adv.* **Living death**—State of hopeless misery ; জীবন্মৃত অবস্থা। **Living language**—প্রচলিত ভাষা। **Living matter**—সজীব দ্রব্য (হিঃ কোঃ)। **Living water**—চিরপ্রবহমাণ জল। **In the land of the living**—Alive ; জীবিত। **The living**—Those who are now alive ; জীবিত ব্যক্তিগণ। **Within living memory**—*i. e.* that of persons still alive ; জীবিত ব্যক্তিদের স্মরণকাল মধ্যে।

liv'-ing, *n.* **1.** Act of being in life ; জীবনধারণ। **2.** Means of subsistence; livelihood; জীবনোপায়; উপজীবিকা। **3.** The benefice of a clergyman ; ধর্ম্মযাজকের বৃত্তি বা উপস্বত্ব। **Good living**—Luxurious feeding ; ষোড়শোপচারে ভোজন। **Living-room**—বসিবার ঘর, বৈঠকখানা। **Living wage**—যে বেতনে কোন কারিকর ও তাহার পরিবারস্থ ব্যক্তিগণ স্বচ্ছন্দে গ্রাসাচ্ছদনের ব্যয় নির্ব্বাহ করিতে পারে। **Plain living and high thinking** — সাদাসিধা ভাবে থাকিয়া উচ্চ চিন্তায় জীবন যাপন।

livre, *n.* An old French money of account = 20 sous, about the value of a franc ; ফরাসী দেশের হিসাবে লিখিত সাবেক মুদ্রা বিশেষ—মূল্য এক ফ্রাঙ্ক,—প্রায় দশ আনা।

lix-iv'-i-āte, *v. t.* To separate (a substance) into soluble and insoluble constituents by percolation of water ; জলের ভিতর চুয়াইয়া দ্রবণীয় ও অদ্রবণীয় অংশে পৃথক করা। **—a'-tion,** *n.* The process of lixiviating ; কাষ্ঠের ভস্ম জল দ্বারা ধৌত করিয়া লবণ ক্ষারাদি প্রস্তুতপ্রক্রিয়া।

liz'-ard (-ĕrd), *n.* **1.** A kind of reptile ; জেঠী, গৃহগোধা, জ্যেষ্ঠি, টিকটিকি, কৃকলাশ। **2.** A variety of the domestic canary ; একপ্রকার সুন্দর বিচিত্রবর্ণের পক্ষিবিশেষ। **A house lizard**—গৃহগোধিকা।

'll, Contraction of *will,* as in I'll, he'll, etc.

lla'-mâ (lâ- or -lyâ-), *n.* **1.** A South-American ruminant allied to the camel, but smaller and

Llama.

without a hump; দক্ষিণআমেরিকার উষ্ট্রজাতীয় জীববিশেষ—ইহারা উষ্ট্রের অপেক্ষা অনেক খর্ব্ব এবং ইহাদের পিঠে ককুদ থাকে না। **2.** Its hair; the material made of its hair ; ঐ জন্তুর লোম ; ঐ জন্তুর লোম দ্বারা প্রস্তুত কম্বল প্রভৃতি।

Lloyds (loydz), *n.* An incorporated society of marine underwriters in London, [From the 17th-century coffee-house established by Edward Lloyd] ; নৌ-বিভাগের যাবতীয় কার্য্যকারী লণ্ডননগরীস্থ বিধিবদ্ধ সমাজ। **Lloyd's list** — যে সংবাদপত্রে সামুদ্রিক বিষয়সংক্রান্ত সংবাদ প্রকাশিত হয়। **Lloyd's register**—প্রতিবর্ষে প্রকাশিত সমুদ্রগামী পোতসমূহের শ্রেণী বিভাগাত্মক তালিকা, পোততালিকা।

lō, *interj.* (*Archaic*) Look ; behold ; (অপ্রঃ) দেখ, দেখ ; ঐ দেখ।

loach (lōch), *n.* A small fresh-water fish used as food ; নদীচর সুখাদ্য ক্ষুদ্র মৎস্য বিশেষ।

load (lōd), *n.* **1.** What is or to be carried ; a burden ; বোঝাই, পসরা ; ভার, বোঝা, মোট। **2.** A cargo ; as, a cart-*load* ; জাহাজে বোঝাই মাল। **3.** The recognized unit in measure or weight of certain substances ; as, the *loads* of wheat and oats are respectively 40 and 80 bushels ; যে পরিমাণ বোঝা একবারে নেওয়া যায়, কোন কোন বস্তুর পরিমাণ বা ওজন করিবার জন্য নিরূপিত মান বা নিরিখ। **4.** That which oppresses the mind ; a burden, as of responsibility, care, grief, etc. ; মনঃপীড়াদায়ক বিষয় ; দায়িত্বভার, শোকভার, চিন্তাভার। **5.** The charge of a firearm ; as, a *load* of powder ; বন্দুকাদিতে যে পরিমাণ বারুদ একবারে ভরা যায়। **6.** (*Mech.*) Resistance overcome by a machine or prime mover as by a dynamo or a steam-engine ; (যন্ত্রবিজ্ঞান) বাষ্পীয়যন্ত্র, তাড়িতোৎপাদক যন্ত্র প্রভৃতি দ্বারা অতিক্রান্ত বাধা। **7.** (*Pl., colloq.*) Plenty, heaps or lots of ; আতিশয্য, বাহুল্য, প্রাচুর্য্য, ঢিবি, স্তূপ। **Load-displacement**—মালবোঝাই জাহাজ দ্বারা যে পরিমাণ জল স্থানচ্যুত হয়, মাল বোঝাই জাহাজ যে পরিমাণ গভীর জলে চলে। **Loadstar, Lodestar** — ধ্রুবনক্ষত্র ; (লক্ষণায়) ধ্রুবতারা (cf. তোমারেই

করিয়াছি জীবনেরই ধ্রুবতারা)। **Loadstone, Lodestone**—The magnetic oxide of iron; a piece of it used as magnet; (*fig.*) a thing that attracts; অয়স্কান্ত, চুম্বকপাথর, চুম্বকলৌহ, অয়োমণি কান্তপাষাণ, চপলালয় (সাঃ পঃ), কর্ষক (সাঃ পঃ); চুম্বক; (লক্ষণায়) আকর্ষক বস্তু, লোহচুম্বক (ঐ)। **All lay load on the willing horse**—যে সয় তার পিঠে সবাই চাপায়। **A load of sorrow**—দুঃখভার।

load (lōd), *v. t.* & *i.* **1.** To lay a load on, in, or aboard; as, to *load* a person, beast, vehicle or ship; ভার চাপান, মাল চাপান। **2.** To place, as a cargo aboard ship, on vehicle etc.; ভার চাপান, বোঝাই করা। **3.** To add weight to; as, stomach *loaded* with food; to increase the weight of with lead, as a cane etc.; ভারাক্রান্ত করা, প্রপীড়িত করা; ভার বৃদ্ধি করা। **4.** To charge as firearms; (বন্দুক, কামান) গুলিবারুদ ভরা, ঠাসা, গাদান। **5.** To adulterate; as, to *load* sugar or wine; ভেজাল দেওয়া। **6.** (*Fig.*) To supply or assail overwhelmingly *with*; as, to *load* one *with* gifts, praise, abuse, etc.; (লক্ষণায়) পূরণ করা, পর্য্যাপ্ত পরিমাণে দেওয়া। **7.** (*fig.*) To weigh down or encumber; to oppress; "Lest so stern a solitude *load*...thy being"; (লক্ষণায়) ভারাক্রান্ত করা; প্রপীড়িত করা। **8.** (Life insurance) To add extra charge to (premium) for special reasons; বিশেষ কারণে বীমার কিস্তির টাকার উপর অতিরিক্ত টাকা চাপান। ***Verb i.*** **1.** To fill with load or passengers, as a vehicle; ভর্ত্তি করা। **2.** To take load aboard; মাল লওয়া, বোঝাই হওয়া। **3.** To charge a firearm with a load; বন্দুকাদিতে বারুদগুলি ভরা বা গাদা। **4.** (Stock Exchange) To buy heavily of stock; প্রচুর পরিমাণে কোম্পানীর কাগজ ক্রয় করা। **Load'-ed,** *adj.* Burdened; charged; ভারাক্রান্ত, ভারপ্রপীড়িত; গুলিবারুদ দ্বারা পুরিত। **Load'-er,** *n.* **1.** One that loads; বোঝাইকারী ব্যক্তি। **2.** An attendant loading a sportsman's guns; শিকারীদের বন্দুক ভরিবার লোক। **3.** A machine for loading a gun, waggon, etc.; বন্দুকাদি গাদিবার যন্ত্র, শকট প্রভৃতি ভর্ত্তি করার যন্ত্র। **4.** (*With a qualification*) A gun loaded in a particular way; as, a breech, muzzle or single-*loader*; বিশেষভাবে গাদিলে যে বন্দুকে গুলি বারুদ ভরা যায়। **Load'-ing,** *n.* **1.** Act of one that loads; বোঝাই করণ। **2.** (Life insurance) An amount added to the net premium for some reasons; কোন বিশেষ কারণে বীমার কিস্তির নিট টাকার উপর যে অতিরিক্ত টাকা চাপান হয়। **Loaded-dice**—পাশভারী পাশা।

loaf (lōf), *n.* (*Pl.* LOAVES) **1.** A regularly-shaped mass of bread formed by the baker; পাঁউরুটী, রুটী। **2.** A conical moulded mass of sugar, (also *sugar-loaf*); মোচাকার শর্করার স্তূপ, চিনির তাল। **3.** A roundish head of cabbage or lettuce; বাঁধাকপি বা সালাদের গোলাকৃতি মাথা। **Loaf-sugar**—মোচাকৃতি শর্করাখণ্ড। **Sugar-loaf**—See LOAF *n.* 2. **Half a loaf is better than no bread**—নেই মামার চেয়ে কাণা মামাও ভাল। **Loaves and fishes** — Pecuniary advantages; emoluments; (alluding to the miracle of feeding the people and the Saviour's charge that some of them followed him only for a selfish purpose—*John* vi. 26); আর্থিক সুবিধা; চাকুরীর টাকা।

loaf (lōf), *v. i., t.* & *n.* To lounge; to idle away one's time; বৃথা ঘুরিয়া বেড়ান; আলস্যে সময় কাটান, টোঁ টোঁ করিয়া বেড়ান। ***Verb t.*** To spend (time) idly (with *away*); আলস্যে সময় কাটান, বৃথা কালক্ষয় করা, টোঁ টোঁ করিয়া ঘুরা। ***Noun.*** Act of loafing; as, to go to have a, or on the, *loaf*; টোঁ টোঁ করিয়া ঘুরণ। **Loaf'-er,** One who loafs; বৃথা ভ্রমণকারী, ভবঘুরে, যে ব্যক্তি রাস্তায় রাস্তায় ঘুরিয়া বেড়ায়।

loaf (lōf), **loave** (lōv), *v. i.* (Of cabbages etc.) To form a loaf or head; (বাঁধাকপি প্রভৃতি) গোলাকার মাথা বাঁধিয়া উঠা।

loam (lōm), *n.* **1.** A clay moistened with water to form a paste; a mixture of moistened clay and sand with chopped straw etc. used in making bricks etc.; পঙ্কিলমৃত্তিকা, কাদা; ইষ্টক প্রভৃতি প্রস্তুত করিবার জন্য পাঁক, বালি ও টুকরা টুকরা খড় মিশ্রিত মাটী, তৈয়ারী মাটী ছাঁচের মাটী। **2.** A fertile soil chiefly of clay and sand with admixtuture of decayed vegetable matter; বালুকা ও ক্ষয়প্রাপ্ত বৃক্ষাদি মিশ্রিত পঙ্কিলমাটী, দোঁয়াস মাটী, ফাঁসমাটী। **Loam'-y,** *adj.* **Loamy sand**—এঁশো বালি, ফাঁসমাটী।

loan (lōn), *n.* & *v. t.* **1.** That which is lent; esp. a sum of money lent at interest; ঋণ, কর্জ্জ, ধার, দেনা; ঋণস্বরূপ প্রদত্ত অর্থ। **2.** The act of lending; ঋণদান, কর্জ্জদান। **3.** Money contribution from individuals or public bodies, to State expenses acknowledged as a debt; সরকারী ঋণ। **4.** Something, as a custom, word, etc. borrowed by one people from another; এক জাতি কর্ত্তৃক গৃহীত অপর জাতির ভাষা, ব্যবহার, প্রভৃতি। ***Verb t.*** To lend (*used chiefly in U. S.*) ধার দেওয়া, কর্জ্জ দেওয়া (প্রধানতঃ মার্কিণ যুক্তরাজ্যে ব্যবহৃত)। **Loan'-a-ble,** *adj.* **Loan-ee',** **Loan'-er,** *ns.* **Loan-collection**—প্রদর্শনীর জন্য ধার করিয়া

ছবি-সংগ্রহ। **Loan-holder**—কোম্পানীর কাগজের অধিকারী; বন্ধকগ্রহীতা। **Loan-office**—ঋণদানকার্য্যালয়। **Loan-society**—যে সমিতির সভ্যগণ সমিতির ধনভাণ্ডারে নিয়মিত চাঁদা দিয়া আবশ্যক মত ঐ ভাণ্ডার হইতে টাকা কর্জ্জ নিতে পারে, সমবায় ঋণদানসমিতি।

loath (lōth), **lōth**, *adjs.* Averse; reluctant; unwilling; বিরক্ত, নারাজ; পরাঙ্মুখ, বিমুখ; অনিচ্ছুক, অসম্মত। **Nothing loath**—Quite willing or willingly; খুব ইচ্ছুক, ইচ্ছাপূর্ব্বক। **Loath-to-depart**—বিদায় সঙ্গীত।

loathe (lōth), *v. t.* To have extreme disgust at; to abominate; বিজাতীয় ঘৃণা করা; দ্বেষ করা। **Loath'-ing**, *n.* Extreme disgust; abhorrence; detestation; বিজাতীয় ঘৃণা; জুগুপ্সা; বিরাগ, বিতৃষ্ণা। **Loath'-ing-ly**, *adv.*

loath'-ly (lōth-), *adv.* (*Archaic & lit*) Same as LOATHSOME. **—li-ness**, *n.*

loath'-some (lōth-sŭm), *adj.* Nauseating or disgusting; offensive to the senses; repulsive; odious; ঘৃণার্হ, ন্যক্কারজনক; বীভৎস, ঘৃণাজনক; জঘন্য, জুগুপ্সিত। **—ly**, *adv.* **—ness**, *n.*

lŏb, *v. i., t. & n.* To walk, run or move heavily or clumsily or slowly, (often *along*); ধীরে ধীরে চলা, ঝিমাইয়া ঝিমাইয়া চলা, গজেন্দ্রগমনে চলা। ***Verb t.* 1.** To throw or toss as a ball with a slow or high-pitched motion; (*cricket*) to bowl underhand; আস্তে আস্তে বা অতি জোরে ক্রীড়াকন্দুক নিক্ষেপ বা উৎক্ষেপণ করা; (ক্রীকেট ক্রীড়ায়) করতল উপরের দিকে রাখিয়া এবং হাত সোজাভাবে ঝুলাইয়া কন্দুক ক্ষেপণ করা। **2.** (*Lawn-tennis*) To strike the ball high over into the end of the court; (আন্টাল খেলায়) অতি জোরে আঘাত করিয়া ক্রীড়াভূমির শেষ প্রান্তে কন্দুক নিক্ষেপ করা। ***Noun.* 1.** (*At cricket*) A slow underhand ball; (ক্রীকেট ক্রীড়ায়) করতল উপরের দিকে রাখিয়া এবং হাত সোজাভাবে ঝুলাইয়া কন্দুক ক্ষেপণ। **2.** (*Lawn-tennis*) A ball sent high in the air; (আন্টাল খেলায়) ঊর্দ্ধে উৎক্ষিপ্ত কন্দুক।

lō'-bāte, *adj.* (*Nat. Hist.*) Having lobes; (প্রাকৃতিক ইতিহাস) কর্ণলতিকা-বিশিষ্ট। **—ba'-tion**, *n.* State of being lobed; a lobe; কর্ণলতিকা-বিশিষ্টতা; কর্ণলতা।

lŏb'-bȳ, *n., v. t. & i.* **1.** A porch; an entrance-hall; দরদালান, উপশালা, দেউড়ি, দ্বারমণ্ডপ, উপগৃহ, উপপ্রকোষ্ঠ; প্রবেশশালা। **2.** (In the House of Commons etc.) A large hall open to the public used esp. for interviews between members and outsiders; one of the two corridors to which the members retire to vote; (পার্লেমেন্টের প্রাকৃত-সভা প্রভৃতিতে) যে প্রকাণ্ড কক্ষে বাহিরের লোকের প্রবেশাধিকার আছে, বিশেষতঃ যে কক্ষে সভ্যগণ বাহিরের লোকের সহিত দেখা করিতে পারেন, সাধারণ-কক্ষ; পার্লেমেন্টের যে দুই দরদালানে ভোট দিবার জন্য সভ্যগণ সমবেত হন তাহাদের অন্যতর। ***Verb t.*** To procure the passage of, as a bill, measure, etc. by means of lobby interviews; to influence, as a legislator in the same way; পার্লেমেন্টের সাধারণ কক্ষে সভ্যগণের সহিত দেখা সাক্ষাৎ করিয়া কোন আইনের পাণ্ডুলিপি ঐ সভায় বিধিবদ্ধ করাইবার পর উহা লর্ড সভায় প্রেরণের ব্যবস্থা করা; পার্লেমেন্টের সাধারণকক্ষে দেখা করিয়া কোন ব্যবস্থাকারককে প্রভাবিত করা। ***Verb i.*** To frequent the lobby of a legislative assembly to influence the members' votes; to solicit the votes of members; কোন ব্যবস্থাপকসভার সভ্যগণকে প্রভাবিত করার উদ্দেশ্যে ঐ সভার সাধারণকক্ষে নিয়ত গতিবিধি করা; সভ্যগণের ভোট প্রার্থনা করা। **—ist**, *n.* One frequenting the lobby of a legislature; a journalist frequenting the lobby of the House of Commons; যে ব্যক্তি পার্লেমেন্টের সাধারণকক্ষে নিয়ত গতিবিধি করে; যে সংবাদদাতা পার্লেমেন্টের প্রাকৃতসভার সাধারণকক্ষে নিয়ত গতিবিধি করে।

lōbe, *n.* **1.** A round projecting part as of the liver, lungs, brain, etc.; যকৃত, ফুসফুস, মস্তিষ্ক প্রভৃতি যন্ত্রাদির গোলাকার উদ্গতাংশ। **2.** The lower soft part of the ear; কর্ণের নিম্নস্থিত দোদুল্যমান অংশ, কর্ণলতা, কর্ণবল্লী। **3.** (*Bot.*) A rounded projection or division of a leaf etc.; (উদ্ভিদ্‌বিদ্যা) কোন পত্রের গোলাকৃতি উদ্গত অংশ বা বিভাগ, কর্ণ (সাঃ পঃ)। **Lobed, Lobe'-less**, *adjs.* **Lob'-u-lar**, *adj.* **Lob'-ule**, *n.* A small lobe; ক্ষুদ্র উদ্গত গোলাকার অংশ। **Lobe of ear**—See LOBE *n.* 2.

lō-bē'-lĭ-ȧ, *n.* A kind of plant; এক প্রকার গুল্ম।

lŏb'-lŏl-lȳ-măn, —boy, *ns.* (*Naut.*) A surgeon's attendant on ship-board; (নৌবিদ্যা) জাহাজের অস্ত্র-চিকিৎসকের অনুচর।

lŏb'-scouse (-skows), *n.* A sailor's dish of meat, vegetables, bread, etc.; (নাবিকদের জন্য) মাংস, শাকসব্জী, রুটী প্রভৃতির ঘণ্ট।

lŏb'-stêr, *n.* **1.** A large ten-footed edible crustacean; its flesh as food; বড় চিংড়ী, গলদা চিংড়ী; গলদা চিংড়ীর মাংস। **2.** (*Contempt.*) A British soldier; (অবজ্ঞাচ্ছলে) গোরা সৈন্য। **Lobster-pot**—গলদা চিংড়ী আটকাইবার আঁটল।

lŏb'-worm (-wêrm), *n.* A large earth-worm used as a fishing bait; একপ্রকার বড় কেঁচো (ইহা বড়শীর টোপস্বরূপ ব্যবহৃত হয়)।

lō'-căl, lō-căle', *ns.* A scene or locality of operations or events; ঘটনাস্থান, ক্রিয়াস্থলী।

lō'-căl, *adj. & n.* **1.** Relating to a place; as, *local* habitation, situation, etc.; স্থানসম্বন্ধীয়, দেশসম্বন্ধীয়,

স্থানিক। **2.** Belonging to, existing in, or peculiar to, a certain place or places; as, *local* time or custom; কোন নির্দ্দিষ্ট স্থানের অন্তর্গত, কোন নির্দিষ্ট স্থানে বর্ত্তমান বা অবস্থিত, এক-দেশিক, একস্থানিক, বিশেষস্থানিক, বিশেষ-দেশীয়, স্থানবিশেষে প্রচলিত, একস্থানস্থ। **3.** Relating to what is local; not general; স্থানিক; অব্যাপক। **4.** Affecting, or confined to, a part and not the whole, as a disease; একাঙ্গীন (হঃ চঃ), স্থানিক। **5.** (*Math.*) Of, or relating to, a locus; (গণিত-শাস্ত্র) বিন্দুপথসম্পর্কীয়। **6.** For delivery in this town or district (written on the cover of a letter as a warning to post office officials); স্থানীয়। ***Noun.*** **1.** An inhabitant of a particular locality; a professional man of a particular place or district; কোন বিশেষ স্থানের লোক; কোন বিশেষ জেলার ব্যবসায়ী লোক **2.** (*In a newspaper*) An item of local news; local news collectively; খবরের কাগজের স্থানীয় সংবাদ; স্থানীয় সংবাদ-সমূহ। **3.** A train serving the stations of a district; এক জেলার অন্তর্গত বিভিন্ন ষ্টেশনে যে রেলগাড়ী যাতায়াত করে। **4.** Postage stamp current in a particular district; কোন বিশেষ জেলায় প্রচলিত ডাক টিকিট। **5.** (*Pl.*) Local examination(s); "Preparing for university *locals*"; স্থানীয় পরীক্ষা (See below)। **—ly,** *adv.* In a local manner; স্থানীয় ভাবে, স্থান-বিষয়ে, স্থানে, দেশে। **Local-board** — কতিপয় শাসনসংক্রান্ত কার্য্য নির্ব্বাহার্থ সমিতি, স্থানীয় সমিতি, লোকেল-বোর্ড। **Local examination**—বিশ্ববিদ্যালয়ের পরীক্ষকসমিতি কর্ত্তৃক বিভিন্ন স্থানে গৃহীত পরীক্ষা বিশেষ। এই পরীক্ষোত্তীর্ণ ছাত্র ও ছাত্রীদিগকে পরীক্ষক-সমিতি কর্ত্তৃক নিদর্শন পত্র (certificate) দেওয়া হয়। **Local-government**—স্থানীয় লোকদিগের দ্বারা কোন নগর প্রভৃতির শাসনকার্য্য পরিচালন; বিকেন্দ্রী-করণ; প্রাদেশিক শাসনতন্ত্র (in India)। **Local-investigation**—See INVESTIGATION. **Local option, —veto**—কোন স্থানে মদের দোকান খোলা হইবে কি না তদ্বিষয়ে স্থানীয় অধিবাসিগণের মতামত গ্রহণে মীমাংসা করার বাধ্যবাধকতা বা অধিকার। **Local-time**—কোন স্থানের সূর্য্যোদয় হইতে যে সময় নিরূপিত করা হয়, স্থানীয়কাল। **Local-usage** — স্থানীয়প্রথা, দেশাচার, দেশপ্রথা।

lō'-căl-ĭsm, *n.* **1.** Affection for a place; limitation of ideas etc. resulting from this; বিশেষ স্থানের প্রতি অনুরাগ বা আসক্তি, প্রাদেশিকতা; স্থান বিশেষের প্রতি অনুরাগ হেতু চিন্তা বা মনোভাবের সঙ্কীর্ণতা। **2.** Favouring of what is local; স্থানীয় জিনিষের প্রতি অনুরাগ বা সমাদর। **3.** A local idiom, custom, etc.; দেশ বা স্থান বিশেষে প্রচলিত বাগ্‌ধারা, আচার অনুষ্ঠান, প্রভৃতি।

lō-căl'-ĭ-tȳ, *n.* **1.** The position of a thing; the geographical place or situation as of a plant or mineral; স্থান, জায়গা; দেশাবস্থান, স্থানবিচ্ছিন্নতা। **2.** A site or scene of something; as, it happened in that *locality*; স্থান, স্থল। **3.** (*Phrenol.*) The faculty of remembering places and their relative positions; (মস্তিষ্ক সামুদ্রিক) স্থান সমূহ ও ইহাদের আপেক্ষিক অবস্থান স্মরণ রাখার বৃত্তি।

lō'-căl-īze, *v. t.* **1.** To fix in, or assign to, a definite place; স্থান-নির্দ্দেশ করা। **2.** To make local; স্থানীয় করা, স্থানিক করা। **3.** To attach to particular districts; to decentralize; বিশেষ জেলায় নির্দ্দেশ করা; বিকেন্দ্রীভূত করা। **4.** To concentrate, as attention *upon* a spot etc.; (স্থান বিশেষে) মনোনিবেশ করা, (কোন স্থান প্রভৃতিতে) একাগ্রচিত্ত হওয়া। **—iz-a-ble,** *adj.* **—i-za'-tion,** *n.* The act of localizing: স্থাননির্দ্দেশ (হিঃ কোঃ), স্থাননিশ্চয়ন, স্থানারোপণ।

lō'-cāte, *v. t.* **1.** (*U. S.*) To set or establish in a place; (*Pass.*) to be situated; "Where I am now *located*"; কোন স্থানে স্থাপিত বা প্রতিষ্ঠিত করা; অবস্থিত হওয়া। **2.** To state the locality of; to discover the exact place of; as, to *locate* the enemy; সঠিক স্থান নির্দ্দেশ করা; সঠিক স্থান নির্দ্ধারণ করা। **—ca'-tion,** *n.* Locating; state of being located; place; স্থাননির্দ্দেশ, স্থাননিশ্চয়ন, স্থানারোপণ, নিবেশন; অবস্থিতি, প্রতিষ্ঠা; স্থান, জায়গা, স্থিতি।

lŏc'-ă-tive (-tĭv), *adj.* & *n.* (*Gram.*) Designating a case; denoting a place where; (ব্যাকরণ) অধিকরণকারক সম্বন্ধীয়; স্থাননির্দ্দেশক। ***Noun.*** (*Gram.*) The locative case; (ব্যাকরণ) অধিকরণ কারক।

lŏch, *n.* A Scotch lake; a land-locked arm of the sea; (স্কটলণ্ডের) হ্রদ, ঝিল; ভূবেষ্টিত সাগরবাহু।

lŏck, *n.* **1.** A tuft or ringlet of hair; a tress; কেশপাশ, কেশগুচ্ছ, অলকগুচ্ছ; চুলের গোছা। **2.** (*Pl.*) The hair of the head; (বহুবচনে) কেশরাশি, কুন্তলকলাপ, চিকুররাশি। **3.** A tuft of wool, cotton, flax, etc.: পশম বা কার্পাসের গুচ্ছ। **Locked.** *adj.*

lŏck, *n.* **1.** An appliance for fastening doors, lids, drawers, etc.; কুলুপ, তালা। **2.** An appliance to keep a wheel from revolving or slewing; চক্রগতিরোধক যন্ত্র। **3.** The mechanism by which a fire-arm is discharged; বন্দুক কামানাদি ছুড়িবার বা দাগিবার কল। **4.** An enclosure in a canal with gates at each end, used in raising or lowering boats, as they pass from one level to another; খালের কপাটকল। **5.** A fastening together; সংবন্ধন। **6.** (*Engineering*) An antechamber giving access to a chamber in which work is carried on in compressed air ; (পূর্ত্তকর্ম্ম) যে উপপ্রকোষ্ঠ হইতে যে কক্ষে সঙ্কাপিত বায়ুতে কাজ হইতেছে তথায় যাওয়া যায়। 7. Same as LOCK-HOSPITAL (which see below.) **Lock'-less,** *adj.* **Lock-fast**—তালাদ্বারা বদ্ধ। **Lock-hospital** — উপদংশ রোগীদের জন্য রুগ্নাবাস। **Locksman**—খালের কপাটকল রক্ষক। **Locksmith** — তালা চাবি প্রস্তুত বা মেরামতকারী (কর্ম্মকার)। **Under lock and key**—তালাদ্বারা আট্‌কানো, কুলুপ-আঁটা।

lŏck, *v. t.* & *i.* 1. To fasten, as a door, box, etc. with a lock to shut up, as a house ; তালা দেওয়া, কুলুপ দেওয়া ; বন্ধ করা। 2. To shut up or confine as a person or thing, (with *up, in, into*) ; তালা দিয়া রাখা, আটক করা। 3. To link together ; to embrace closely ; as, to *lock* hand in hand ; সংবদ্ধ করা, গ্রথিত করা ; গাঢ় আলিঙ্গনপাশে বদ্ধ করা। 4. (Canals) To furnish

Lock in a canal.

with locks ; (খাল প্রভৃতিতে) কপাটকল দেওয়া। 5. (*Fig.*) To store inaccessibly, (with *up, away*) ; as, facts *locked up* in hieroglyphics ; (লক্ষণায়) অনধিগম্য স্থানে সঞ্চিত করা। 6. To move (a boat) up and down a lock ; কপাটকলের উজান ও ভাঁটিতে নৌকা চালান। 7. To keep *out* by locking door as a worker etc. ; দরজায় তালা দিয়া ব...র রাখা। 8. To close fast ; to fasten by fitting of corresponding parts ; to entangle ; দৃঢ়ভাবে রুদ্ধ করা, পরস্পরের অনুরূপ অংশসমূহ আটকাইয়া সংবদ্ধ করা ; জড়িত করা। 9. To hold inactive ; as, the senses are *locked* in sleep ; নিষ্ক্রিয় অবস্থায় রাখা। ***Verb i.*** 1. To become locked or fast ; দৃঢ়বদ্ধ হওয়া। 2. To unite closely by mutual insertion of parts ; অনুরূপ অংশ সমূহ আট্‌কাইয়া দেওয়ায় দৃঢ়সংবদ্ধ হওয়া। 3. (*Mil.*—Of the rear rank) To march so close to the front rank that the feet overlap ; সম্মুখের দলের এতটা নিকটে পা ফেলা—যাহাতে পশ্চাতের দলের লোকের পা সম্মুখের দলের লোকের পায়ের পাশে পড়ে। 4. (Of a vehicle) To permit the fore-wheels to swivel round freely in turning ; (of the wheels) to have freedom of motion ; (শকট-সম্পর্কে) সম্মুখের চক্রদ্বয়কে অনায়াসে ঘুরিতে দেওয়া ; অনায়াসে ঘুরা। 5. (Of a boat etc.) To pass through a lock in a canal ; (নৌকা প্রভৃতি সম্পর্কে) খালের কপাটকল অতিক্রম করিয়া যাওয়া। **Lock-chain**—চক্রবন্ধন শৃঙ্খল **Lock-jaw Locked-jaw**—দাঁত কপাটি দাঁতাপল, চোয়ালধরা রোগ, হনুস্তম্ভ (হঃ চঃ)। **Lock-out**—Act of locking out ; refusal of the employer to furnish work to employee, used as a means of coercion ; দরজায় তালা বন্ধ করিয়া বাহিরে রাখন ; কলের মজুরদিগকে কাজ দিতে মনীবের অস্বীকার। **Lock-up**—Locking up schools etc. for night ; time for this ; রাত্রিতে বিদ্যালয় প্রভৃতি বন্ধ করণ ; রাত্রিতে বিদ্যালয় প্রভৃতি বন্ধ করিবার সময়। A house or room for temporary detention of prisoners ; হাজত, গারদঘর, কয়েদখানা, ফাটক। Unrealizable state of invested capital or amount of capital locked up ; মূলধনের অনাদায়যোগ্য অবস্থা, অনাদায়ী মূলধন। (*Attrib.*) That can be locked up ; as, a *lock-up* coach-house ; তালাদ্বারা বন্ধ করার উপযোগী। **To lock the stable door after the steed is stolen**—To be cautions when it is too late ; চোর পালাইলে বুদ্ধি বাড়ে, কিং গতে সলিলে সেতুবন্ধনেন, নির্ব্বাপিত দীপে তৈল প্রদান করা।

lŏck'-āge, *n.* 1. Materials for locks in a canal ; the works which form the lock in a canal ; খালের বাঁধ নির্ম্মাণের উপাদান বা তন্নির্ম্মাণ-কার্য্য। 2. The amount of rise or fall effected by canal-locks ; খালে কপাটকলের দরুণ জলের উত্থান-পতনের পরিমাণ। 3. Toll paid for passing through canal locks ; খালের কপাটকল পার হইবার জন্য শুল্ক।

lŏck'-ẽr, *n.* 1. One that locks ; তালাবন্ধনকারী। 2. A drawer, cupboard or chest that may be locked, esp. one for individual use, as in a cricket pavilion or schoolroom ; তালাদ্বারা বন্ধ করিয়া রাখা যাইতে পারে এরূপ দেরাজ, তাক বা সিন্দুক, বিশেষতঃ ক্রীকেট ক্রীড়ার প্রাঙ্গণের মণ্ডপ বা বিদ্যালয়কক্ষে ব্যক্তি বিশেষের ব্যবহারের জন্য দেরাজ বা সিন্দুক 3. (*Naut.*) A chest or compartment for clothes, stores, ammunitions, etc. ; (নৌবিদ্যা) পোষাক, গুলিগোলা, প্রভৃতি রাখিবার কামরা বা সিন্দুক। **Not a shot in the locker**—Not a penny in the pocket ; হাতে একটীও পয়সা নাই।

lŏck'-ĕt, *n.* 1. A case of gold or silver for holding a portrait, a lock of hair, etc., usually hung from the neck ; প্রতিকৃতি, কেশগুচ্ছ প্রভৃতি রক্ষার্থ স্বর্ণ বা রজতরচিত আধার, দোলক, ধুকধুকি। 2. A metal plate or band on a scabbard ; অসিকোষের উপরিস্থিত ধাতব ফলকবন্ধনী।

loco citato, (*L.*), *n.* (*abbr. l. c.*) In the passage already quoted ; পূর্ব্বোদ্ধৃত বাক্যে।

Cocculus cordifolius — গুলঞ্চ (বেলঃ), কন্দগুরুচি।
Cocculus Indicus — কাকমারী (বেলঃ)।

cŏc′-cŭs, *n.* (*Bot.*) One of the carpels or seed vessels of a dry fruit ; (উদ্ভিদ্-বিদ্যা) শুষ্কফলের কিঞ্জলক বা বীজাধারের কোন একটী, গুটিকাফল (সাঃ পঃ)।

Coccystes, *n.* A genus of birds, family Cucelidæ, sub-family Cuculidæ ; চাতকাদি। *Coccystes melanoleucos*—চাতক (যোঃ)।

cŏc′-cŷx, *n.* (*Anat.*) The lower bone of the vertebral column ; পৃষ্ঠবংশের অধঃপ্রান্তস্থ ত্রিকোণাস্থি, কোকিলচঞ্চু অস্থি, চঞ্চ্বস্থি। **—cyg′-e-al,** *adj.*

cō′-chin, *n.* A breed of large domestic fowls (from Cochin-China) : একপ্রকা। গৃহপালিত কুক্কুট।

প্রধান ব্যক্তি, চাঁই ; সর্দ্দার। **5.** A tap ; নল, নালী। **6.** The indicator of a balance ; নিক্তির কাঁটা। **7.** The hammer in the lock of a fire-arm ; বন্দুকের ঘোড়া। **Cock-boat**—জাহাজের ডিঙ্গী, ক্ষুদ্র নৌকা। **Cock-brained**—লঘুমস্তিষ্ক। **Cock-crowing**—ঊষাকাল। **Cock-eyed**—টেরা। **Cock-fighting, Cock-fight**—কুক্কুটযুদ্ধ (বাৎস্যঃ)। **Cock's-comb**—কুক্কুটশিখা, শ্বেতমুর্গা (গোরী), মোরগজটা (প্রবোধ)। **Cock-a-hoop** or **Cock on the hoop**—Triumphant ; exulting ; বিজয়োল্লাসপূর্ণ ; হর্ষোৎফুল্ল, দৃপ্ত। **At or on full cock**—(ছুড়িবার পূর্ব্বে) বন্দুকের ঘোড়া উঠান। **Cock and bull story**—আষাঢ়ে গল্প, গাঁজাখুরি গল্প। **Cock of the school**—The leader in games, fighting, etc. ; যে বালক

knock into a cock or cocked hat—To be out of shape or recognition ; পরিচয় করিতে পারা যায় না এরূপ হওয়া।

cock (kŏk), *v. t.* & *i.* **1.** To set erect or upright ; খাড়া করিয়া রাখা। **2.** To place, as the hat, on one side of the head ; টুপি প্রভৃতি মাথার একপার্শ্বে টেরছা করিয়া স্থাপন করা। **3.** To turn or set up with an air of pertness ; টুপি প্রভৃতি মস্তকের একপার্শ্বে টের্চ্ছা-করিয়া উদ্ধতব্যঞ্জকভাবে পরা। **4.** To draw the hammer of (a fire-arm) fully back and set it for firing ; বন্দুক প্রভৃতির ঘোড়া পশ্চাদ্দিকে টানিয়া ছুড়িবার জন্য প্রস্তুত করা। ***Verb i.*** To strut ; to swagger ; গর্ব্বিতভাবে চলা ; গর্ব্বভরে হেলিয়া দুলিয়া চলা। **To cock the ears**—To prick

locomotive organs ; গত্যুৎপাদক, গতিশক্তিজনক, গতিসহায়ক। ***Noun.*** **1.** A locomotive engine ; গতিশীল বাষ্পীয়যন্ত্র, রেলগাড়ীর কল। **2.** (*Slang*—*Pl.*) Legs. ; as, use your *locomotives* ; (ইতর ভাষায়) দুই পা। **3.** A locomotive animal ; গতিশক্তিবিশিষ্ট জন্তু, চলনক্ষম জীব। **Locomotive engine**—See LOCOMOTIVE *n.* I. **A locomotive person** — নিয়ত পর্য্যটনশীল ব্যক্তি। **Use your locomotives**—(*Slang*) See LOCOMOTIVE *n.* 2.

lō-cō-mō′-tŏr, *n.* & *adj.* A person or thing capable of locomotion ; গমনশীল ব্যক্তি বা বস্তু। ***Adj.*** Of, or relating to, locomotion ; গতি বা গমনসম্বন্ধীয়।

lō-cō-mō′-tō-rȳ, *adj.* Of, relating to, or possessing locomotion ; গতিসম্বন্ধীয়, গমনশক্তিক।

lō′-cŭm-tē′-nĕns, *n.* One acting for another ; a deputy or substitute (esp. for a doctor or clergyman) ; যে ব্যক্তি অন্যের পরিবর্ত্তে অল্পকালের জন্য কাজ করে ; প্রতিনিধি, প্রতিভূ, স্থলবর্ত্তী ব্যক্তি, কায়েম, মোকাম

স্বীকৃত স্থান বা পদ। The right to intervene, to appear in court, etc. ; হস্তক্ষেপের অধিকার, আদালতে উপস্থিত হওয়ার অধিকার।

lō′-cŭst, *n.* **1.** A winged insect migrating in vast hords and destructive to vegetation ; পঙ্গ (সাঃ পঃ), শলভ, শরভ। **2.** (*Fig.*) A person of devouring or destructive propensities ; (লক্ষণায়) সর্ব্বগ্রাসী বা সর্ব্বনাশকারী ব্যক্তি। **3.** The carob-tree ; its fruit ; একপ্রকার বৃক্ষ ; উহার ফল। **Locust-bird, -eater**—

Locust tree.

পঙ্গভুক্ পক্ষী। **Locust-tree**—See LOCUST 3.

lodge (lŏj), *n.* **1.** A small house ; a hut or cottage in a park or in connection with a large house ; ক্ষুদ্র গৃহ ; কুটীর, পর্ণশালা, কুঁড়েঘর, উপগৃহ, নগরোদ্যানস্থ ক্ষুদ্র মণ্ডপ। **2.** A shelter for the gatekeeper or porter of an institution, factory, etc. ; প্রতিষ্ঠান, শিল্পশালা, প্রভৃতির দ্বারবানের জন্য ক্ষুদ্র গৃহ। **3.** (Freemasons etc.) A place of meeting for the members of a local branch ; as, Freemasons' *lodge* ; the members of such a branch ; ফ্রী-মেসন সম্প্রদায়ের সভাগণের মিলনমন্দির ; ফ্রী-মেসন সম্প্রদায়ের সভ্যমণ্ডলী। **4.** The residence of the head of a college at Cambridge ; কেম্ব্রিজ বিশ্ববিদ্যালয়ের অন্তর্গত কোন মহাবিদ্যালয়ের অধ্যক্ষের আবাসভবন। **5.** The lair of a beaver or otter ; বীবর অথবা উদ্বিড়ালের বাসগহ্বর। . A North American Indian's tent or wigwam ; উত্তর আমেরিকার আদিমবাসীর (চর্ম্মাদি নির্ম্মিত) সূক্ষ্মাগ্র কুটীর বা তাঁবু। **Grand lodge** — ফ্রিমেসন বা তদনুরূপ সম্প্রদায়ের পরিচালক সভা।

lodge (lŏj), *v. t.* & *i.* **1.** To provide with a temporary place longer being susceptible to sense impressions it can contemplate divine mysteries; trance; ভাবসমাধি, ভাবোন্মাদ ; রসোন্মত্ততা (রবীঃ), সংরাধ (বেদান্ত), আনন্দময় দশা (বিশ্বঃ)। 3. (*Med.*) A morbid condition of nervous system marked by mental exaltation, suspension of voluntary motion, etc.; (ভৈষজ্য-শাস্ত্র) হর্ষোন্মাদ (হঃ চঃ), রসোন্মাদ (ঐ)। **—size,** *v. t.* & *i.* To throw or go into ecstasies; হর্ষাবিষ্ট করা, রসোন্মত্ত হওয়া। **—stat′-ic,** *adj.* Pertaining to ecstasy; causing ecstasy; in a state of ecstasy; হর্ষাবেশ-সম্বন্ধীয়; উল্লাসকর, রসোন্মাদজনক; রসোন্মত্ত, হর্ষাবিষ্ট। **—stat′-i-cal-ly,** *adv.*

ĕc′-tŏ, in combination as **Ecto-blast**—কোষের বহিস্তর। **Ecto-derm**—জন্তু বা উদ্ভিদের বহিশ্চর্ম্ম বা বহিস্তর। **Ecto-parasite** — জন্তুর শরীরের বহির্ভাগবাসী পরজীবী (চাটুয়া) কীটবিশেষ। **Ecto-plasm**—প্রাণীজীবের

Rag-baby—ন্যাকড়ার পুতুল। **Rag-bag**—ন্যাকড়া প্রভৃতি রাখার জন্য থলিয়া। **Rag-bolt**—*n.* & *v. i.* An iron-pin with barbs on its shank to retain it in its place; একপ্রকার বল্টু। (*Verb i.*) To join together with this; এইরূপ বল্টু দ্বারা জোড়া দেওয়া। **Rag-fair**—Houndsditch নামক স্থানে পুরাতন পোষাকের বাজার। **Rag-paper**—ন্যাকড়া হইতে তৈরি কাগজ। **Ragtag, Ragtag and bobtail**—Ragged people; the rabble; the mob; ন্যাকড়াপরা লোকজন; ইতর সমাজ; ইতর লোকের জনতা। **Rag-wheel**—স্বিচক্রযান প্রভৃতির দন্তুর চক্র। **Rag-wort**—একপ্রকার গুল্ম। **In rags**—Torn; ছেঁড়া, ছিন্ন। In old clothes; ন্যাকড়া-পরা, জীর্ণবস্ত্র-পরিহিত। **It was cooked to rags**—It was cooked till it fell to pieces; টুকরা টুকরা হইয়া ছাড়িয়া যায় এমতভাবে সিদ্ধ করা হইয়াছিল। ...*n.* 1. A kind of roofing-

an eddy; পাক দেওয়া, ঘুরা, ঘূর্ণিত হওয়া; আবর্ত্তিত করা, ঘূর্ণিত করা। **Eddy current** — (*Elect.*) An induced electric current circulating wholly within a mass of metal; আবর্ত্তন-প্রবাহ (সাঃ পঃ)।

e-del-weiss (ā-dl-vīs), *n.* An Alpine plant with white flowers growing in rocky places; শ্বেতপুষ্পপ্রসূ বৃক্ষ বিশেষ।

E′-dĕn (ē-), *n.* The garden where Adam and Eve lived before their fall; paradise; a place of pleasure; a state of bliss; যে সুরম্য উদ্যানে আদি মানব আদম ও তদীয় পত্নী ইভ বাস করিতেন, স্বর্গোদ্যান, নন্দন কানন; স্বর্গ; প্রমোদ নিকেতন, আনন্দ নিকেতন; আনন্দময় দশা।

ē-dĕn′-tāte, *n.* & *adj.* A toothless animal; দন্তহীন প্রাণী, অদন্তক প্রাণী। ***Adj.*** Not possessing teeth or incisor; দন্তহীন, অদন্তক, কৃন্তন দন্তহীন।

edge (ĕj), *n., v. t.* & *i.* **1.** Sharp

a wind, sea, fire, etc.; প্রকোপ, উগ্রতা, প্রচণ্ডতা। **3.** Vehemence as of desire, emotion, suffering, etc.; as, the *rage* of hunger, প্রচণ্ডতা, তীব্রতা। **4.** Extreme desire or passion (*for*); তীব্র বাসনা, তীব্র লালসা, প্রবল স্পৃহা। **5.** An object of eager desire or enthusiasm; as, open-air cure is (all) the *rage*; প্রবল বাসনার বিষয়ীভূত বস্তু, ধূম (আঃ মঠ)। 6. Poetic, prophetic or martial ardour; enthusiasm; excitement; কাব্যোন্মাদ, রণোন্মাদ, ভাবোন্মাদ, দিব্যোন্মাদ; উৎসাহ; উত্তেজনা।

rage (rāj), *v. i.* **1.** To be furious with anger; to speak violently or madly; to storm; ক্রোধোন্মত্ত হওয়া, ক্রোধাবিষ্ট হওয়া; ক্রোধোন্মত্তভাবে বা ক্ষিপ্তভাবে কথা বলা; তর্জ্জন গর্জ্জন করা, ধমকান। 2. (Of wind, sea, battle, feeling, pain, etc.) To be violent or furious; to be at the height;

ক্ষুদ্র ক্ষুদ্র বৃক্ষশ্রেণী, খরঞ্জা (প্রবোধ)। **2.** A border or fringe; কিনারা, পাইড়, মগজি, ঝালর, হাসিয়া। **Edge′-less,** *adj.* Not sharp; blunt; obtuse; অধারাল; ভোঁতা; স্থুল। **Edge′-ways** or **—wise.** *adv.* Sidewise; with the edge foremost; পাশাপাশি; কিনারার দিকে। **Edge** or **edged tool**—ধারাল অস্ত্র। **Edging shears**—তৃণভূমির প্রান্ত ছাঁটিবার জন্য কাঁচি। **To be on edge**—To be anxious; উদগ্রীব হওয়া। **To get a word in edgeways**—To get one in a talkative person's silent interval; বাচাল ব্যক্তির কথার অবকাশের মধ্যে অতি কষ্টে একটী কথা পাড়া। **To play with edge-tools**—To play with what is dangerous; শাণিত অস্ত্র লইয়া ক্রীড়া করা, সাপ লইয়া ক্রীড়া করা। **To set the teeth on edge**—To cause unpleasant sensation in the teeth, (also *fig*); দাঁত সিড়সিড় করান। **To take the**

adv. **—ness,** *n.* **Ragged robbin**—রক্তবর্ণ পুষ্পপ্রসূ আরণ্য গুল্মবিশেষ। **Ragged school**—দরিদ্র বালকদিগের জন্য অবৈতনিক বিদ্যালয়।

ră-gout′ (-gō), *n.* & *v. t.* A dish of meat stewed and highly seasoned; মাংসের কালিয়া। ***Verb t.*** To make a ragout of (meat); (মাংসের) কালিয়া রাঁধা।

raid (rād), *n., v. i.* & *t.* **1.** A hostile incursion, especially of mounted men; a foray; অশ্বারোহী দস্যু প্রভৃতির আকস্মিক আক্রমণ; লুণ্ঠনের উদ্দেশ্যে সহসা আক্রমণ। **2.** A sudden attack or invasion as for arrest, seizing property etc.; as, a *raid* of the police upon a suspected house; পুলিসের আকস্মিক অভিযান। ***Verb i.*** To make a raid; লুণ্ঠনের উদ্দেশ্যে হঠাৎ আক্রমণ করা। ***Verb t.*** To make a raid on or into; লুণ্ঠনের উদ্দেশ্যে হঠাৎ আক্রমণ করা, খানাতল্লাসি প্রভৃতির জন্য হঠাৎ অভিযান

wonder, (how, why, etc.) ; আশ্চর্য্যান্বিত হওয়া, বিস্ময়াবিষ্ট হওয়া বিস্ময়স্তম্ভিত হওয়া, অবাক হওয়া, বিস্ময়াপন্ন হওয়া ; আশ্চর্য্য হওয়া।
Marvel of Peru—কৃষ্ণকেলি (যোঃ)।
mâr'-vĕl -lous (-ŭs), *adj.* **1.** Astonishing ; wonderful ; আশ্চর্য্যজনক, অপরূপ, আশ্চর্য্য ; বিস্ময়কর, বিস্ময়জনক, বিস্ময়োৎপাদক, অদ্ভুত। **2.** Strange ; incredible ; অদ্ভুত, অপরূপ ; অবিশ্বাস্য। **—ly,** *adv.* **—ness,** *n.* The **marvellous**—(Opp. to *the probable*) ; অলৌকিক ব্যাপার, অতিপ্রাকৃতব্যাপার, তাজ্জবব্যাপার।
măs'-cŏt, *n.* A person or thing that brings good luck ; সৌভাগ্যজনক ব্যক্তি বা বস্তু, শকুন (মঃ উঃ)।
măs'-cū-line (-lĭn), *adj.* & *n.* **1.** Of the male sex ; male ; পুংজাতীয় ; পুরুষজাতীয়। **2.** Manly ; vigorous ; robust ; পুরুষোচিত, পৌরুষসম্পন্ন ; বলবান, শৌর্য্যশালী ; বলিষ্ঠ। **3.** (Of woman) Having qualities appropriate to man ; bold ; forward ; পুরুষোচিতগুণসম্পন্ন ; সাহসী ; অগ্রসর। **4.** (*Gram.*) Denoting nouns which are names of males ; পুংলিঙ্গবাচক। ***Noun.*** The masculine gender ; a word of this gender ; পুংলিঙ্গ ; পুংলিঙ্গবাচক শব্দ। **—lin'-i-ty, —ness,** *ns.* পুরুষস্বভাব, পুরুষবৃত্তি, পুংপ্রকৃতি।
Masculine gender—পুংলিঙ্গ।
măsh, *n.* **1.** A mixture of ground malt and warm water yielding wort ; অঙ্কুরোদ্গাত যবের চূর্ণ এবং উষ্ণ জলের মিশ্র। **2.** A mixture of boiled grain, bran, etc. for feeding horses, cattle, etc. ; অশ্বাদির খাদ্যের জন্য জলে সিদ্ধ করা ভূষি প্রভৃতি। **3.** A soft pulp made by crushing, mixing with water etc. ; মণ্ড কাই, লেই। **4.** A confused mixture ; জবাখিচুড়ী। **ash tube**—অঙ্কুরোদ্গাতযবচূর্ণ এবং উষ্ণজল সংমিশ্রণের জন্য চোঙ্গ বিশেষ।
măsh, *v. t.* **1.** To mix malt with hot water ; উষ্ণজলের সহিত অঙ্কুরোদ্গাত যবচূর্ণ সংমিশ্রিত করা। **2.** To crush ; to pound ; to pulp ; চূর্ণ করা ; কুট্টিত করা, থেঁতলান ; লেই করা, মণ্ড করা। **3.** To reduce as potatoes etc. to uniform mass by crushing ; (আলু প্রভৃতি নিষ্পেষণ করিয়া) তাল বা পিণ্ডবৎ করা।
măsh, *v. t.* & *n.* (*Slang*) To gain the affections of ; to fascinate ; (ইতর ভাষায়) স্নেহ ও প্রীতিলাভ করা ; বিমুগ্ধ করা। ***Noun.*** A person on whom one of the opposite sex is mashed ; প্রেমোন্মত্ত পুরুষ, প্রেমোন্মাদিনী নারী। **To be mashed on** — To have sentimental admiration for ; to be struck with love for another ; আবেগবিমিশ্র শ্রদ্ধা, প্রেম ও বিস্ময়পূর্ণ হওয়া ; প্রেমোন্মত্ত হওয়া। **To make one's mash**—To get a devoted admirer ; একনিষ্ঠ স্তাবক প্রাপ্ত হওয়া।
măsh'-er, *n.* A fop posing as a lady-killer ; রমণীবিঘাতক নাগর, রমণীমনোহর পুরুষ, নারীচিত্তচোর।
măsh'-ie (-ĭ), **măsh'-ȳ,** *ns.* An iron golf-club ; গোল্‌ফ ক্রীড়ার জন্য লৌহময় দণ্ড।
măsk, *n.* **1.** A covering for the face for disguise or for protection ; as, a dancer's or fencer's *mask* ; a masked person ; মুখস, ছদ্মমুখ (আঃ বঃ), কৃত্রিমমুখ, ছদ্মাস্য ; মুখসপরা লোক। **2.** (*Fig.*) A disguise ; a pretence ; as to throw off the *mask* ; (লক্ষণায়) ছদ্মবেশ ; ছল, কূট, ছদ্ম। **3.** A hollow figure of human head worn by the Greek and Roman actors ; প্রাচীন গ্রীক এবং রোমান নাট্যকারগণ কর্তৃক ব্যবহৃত মুখস। **4.** A representation or impression of a person's face in any material, as wax, clay, plaster, etc. ; মোম, এঁটেল মাটী প্রভৃতি দ্বারা রচিত মনুষ্যমুখ বা মুখের ছাপ। **5.** A festive entertainment in which all wear masks ; যে উৎসবে সকলে মুখস পরিধান করে। **6.** A face or head of a fox ; শৃগালমুণ্ড, শিবামুণ্ড।
măsk, *v. t.* **1.** To cover as a face with a mask ; মুখস পরা, কৃত্রিম মুখস দ্বারা মুখ আচ্ছাদিত করা, মুখসাবৃত করা। **2.** (*Pass.*) To be disguised with mask ; মুখস ধারণে আত্মগোপন করা। **3.** (*Mil.*) To conceal as a force, battery, etc. from enemy's sight ; to keep in check, as an army etc. by watching it with a sufficient force ; (সামরিক শাস্ত্র) সৈন্য, কামানশ্রেণী প্রভৃতি প্রচ্ছন্ন রাখা ; প্রচুর সৈন্যদ্বারা পর্য্যবেক্ষণপূর্ব্বক (শত্রুসৈন্য) বাধা দিয়া রাখা। **4.** To disguise as feelings etc. ; আত্মগোপন করা। **A masked ball**—যে বল নাচে নর্ত্তক নর্ত্তকীগণ মুখস পরিয়া থাকে।
mā'-son (-sn), *n.* & *v. t.* **1.** A builder in stone or brick ; a worker in stone ; রাজমিস্ত্রী, রাজশিল্পী, লেপকার, সুধাজীবী ; স্থপতি। **2.** (*Cap.*) A member of the society of Freemasons ; ইয়ুরোপীয় তান্ত্রিক গুপ্তসভা বিশেষের সভ্য। ***Verb t.*** To build or strengthen with masonry ; ইষ্টক প্রভৃতির গাঁথনি দ্বারা নির্ম্মাণ বা সুদৃঢ় করা। **—ry,** *n.* **1.** The art and occupation of a mason (*rare*) ; স্থাপত্যকর্ম্ম (কচিদ্ব্যবহৃত)। **2.** The work of a mason ; stonework ; রাজমিস্ত্রীর কাজ ; ইমারতী কাজ। **3.** The institution or mysteries of freemasons ; ফ্রিমেসন সম্প্রদায়ের প্রতিষ্ঠান বা গুহ্যতত্ত্ব। **—son'-ic,** *adj.* Relating to freemasons or freemasonry ; ফ্রিমেসনসম্প্রদায়সম্পর্কীয়, উক্ত সম্প্রদায়ের ক্রিয়াকলাপ সম্পর্কীয়।
Mă-sō'-ră, Măs-sō'-rah (-ră), *ns.* The Hebrew tradition as to the correct form of the text of the scriptures ; খৃষ্টীয় বাইবেলের বিশুদ্ধ পাঠ সম্বন্ধে হিব্রু পরম্পরাগত বাক্য।
Măs'-s(ō)-rīte, —rete (-rēt), *ns.* A Jewish scholar contributing to the Massora ; বাইবেলের বিশুদ্ধ পাঠ নির্দ্ধারক ইহুদী পণ্ডিত। **—ret'-ic,** *adj.*

lŏ′-gie (-jē), *n.* Zinc ornament looking like jewel used in theatre; নাট্যশালায় ব্যবহৃত দস্তানির্ম্মিত অলঙ্কার—যাহা মণিরত্নের মত দেখায়।

lŏg′-i-ŏn, *n.* (*Pl.* -A) A saying of Jesus not recorded in Gospels but preserved elsewhere; খৃষ্টীয় সুসমাচারগ্রন্থে লিপিবদ্ধ হয় নাই—অথচ অন্যত্র সংরক্ষিত যীশুর উক্তি।

lō-ğis′-tics, *n.* (*Pl.*) The art of moving and squaring troops; সৈন্যচালনবিদ্যা, সৈন্যসন্নিবেশবিদ্যা, ব্যূহরচনাবিদ্যা।

lŏg′-ō-grăm, *n.* A sign or character representing a word in shorthand; a word-letter; রেখাক্ষর বর্ণমালায় কোন শব্দের সাঙ্কেতিক চিহ্ন; একাক্ষরশব্দ।

lŏg′-ō-grăph, *n.* **1.** Same as LOGOGRAM. **2.** Same as LOGOTYPE.

lō-gŏg′-ră-phêr, *n.* **1.** (*Gk. antiq.*) One of the prose historians before Herodotus; হিরোডোটাসের পূর্ব্ববর্ত্তী গল্পইতিহাসলেখক। **2.** (*Gk. antiq.*) Professional speech-writer; প্রাচীন গ্রীসদেশের বক্তৃতালিখন ব্যবসায়ী।

lō-gŏg′-ră-phȳ, *n.* Use of logotypes in printing; মুদ্রাঙ্কণে বহ্বাক্ষরক্ষোদিত অক্ষরফলকের ব্যবহার।

lŏg′-ō-grĭph, *n.* A kind of anagrammatic word-puzzle; এক-প্রকার অক্ষর-বিপর্য্যয় মূলক ধাঁধা।

lō-gŏm′-ă-chȳ, *n.* A contention about words; a controversy turning on merely verbal points; শব্দ সম্বন্ধে বিতণ্ডা, শব্দবিবাদ; কেবল শব্দগত বিষয় লইয়া বাদানুবাদ।

lŏg-ō-mā′-nĭ-ă, *n.* (*Med.*) Morbid talkativeness; বাচালতা রোগ।

lŏg′-ŏs, *n.* (*No. pl.*) The Divine Word or the Second Person of the Trinity; শব্দব্রহ্ম, প্রজ্ঞঃ (এপিঃ), ঈশ্বর (হিঃ কোঃ)।

lŏg′-ō-tȳpe, *n.* (*Print.*) A single type, containing two or more letters; মুদ্রাঙ্কণে দুই বা ততোধিক অক্ষরক্ষোদিত অক্ষরফলক।

loin (loin), *n.* **1.** (*Pl.*) The part of body on either side between the false ribs and the haunch bones; কোমর, কটি, শ্রোণি, মাজা (*colloq.*)। **2.** The joint of meat that includes the vertebrae of the loins; মেরুদণ্ডের নিম্নভাগের মাংস। **Loin-cloth**—কটিবাস, কৌপিন। **Fruit** or **child of,** or **sprung from, one's loins**—One's begotten offspring; ঔরসজাত সন্তান। **To gird up one's loins**—To prepare for energetic action (journey etc.); কোমর বাঁধিয়া লাগা, বদ্ধপরিকর হওয়া।

loir (loir), *n.* A large European dormouse; ইয়ুরোপদেশীয় বৃহৎকায় বৃক্ষমূষিক।

loi′-têr (loi-), *v. i.* & *t.* To linger on the way; to hang about; to saunter; to travel slowly and idly; গৌণ করা, বিলম্ব করা, গড়িমসি করা; এদিক ওদিক ঘুরিয়া বেড়ান; টোঁ টোঁ করিয়া বেড়ান; ধীরমন্থর গতিতে চলা। ***Verb t.*** To pass time *away* in loitering; গড়িমসি করিয়া বৃথা সময় নষ্ট করা। **—er,** *n.* **—ing-ly,** *adv.*

Lö′-ki, *n.* A Scandinavian God; স্কেণ্ডেনেভিয়ার পুরাণোক্ত দেবতা বিশেষ। দুর্ভাগ্যবশতঃ কোন দুষ্টা নারীর হৃৎপিণ্ড ভক্ষণ করাতে ইনি কতিপয় বিকট জীব প্রসব করেন। দেবতাদিগের মন্ত্রণাসভায় অনাহূতভাবে প্রবেশ করার অপরাধে ইনি দেবগণকর্ত্তৃক এক কুণ্ডে নিক্ষিপ্ত হন।

lŏll, *v. t.* & *i.* **1.** To hang (one's tongue) *out*; জিহ্বা লক্ লক্ করা, জিহ্বা লোলিত করা। **2.** To let or cause to rest lazily, as one's head, limbs, etc.; অলস ভাবে ঠেস দিয়া রাখা। ***Verb i.*** **1.** To act lazily or indolently; to stand, sit or recline in lazy attitude; গা ছাড়া ভাবে কাজ করা; অলস ভাবে পড়িয়া থাকা, গা ছাড়িয়া দাঁড়ান, বসা, বা হেলান দেওয়া, ঠেস দেওয়া। **2.** To hang *out* from the mouth, as the tongue of on animal; (জিহ্বা মুখ হইতে বাহির হইয়া ঝুলিয়া পড়া, জিহ্বা লক্ লক্ করা। **Loll′-ing-ly,** *adv.*

Lŏl′-lard (-ârd), *n.* One of the 14th century followers of Wyclif in England or who held opinions like his; ইংলণ্ডের (ধর্ম্মসংস্কারক) Wyclifএর শিষ্য বা তন্মতাবলম্বী। **—ism,** *n.* The principle of the Lollards; উক্ত সম্প্রদায়ের মত।

lŏl′-li-pŏp (-ĭ), (*Usu. pl.*) A kind of sugar-plum; sweets; চিনির লাড্ডু; মিঠাই, মিষ্টদ্রব্যবিশেষ।

lŏl′-lop (-ŏp-), *v. i.* (*Colloq.*) To proceed in an ungainly lounging way; (চলিত ভাষায়) অজগরের মত চলা।

Lŏm′-bârd, *n.* & *adj.* **1.** A native of Lombardy, in Italy; ইটালীর অন্তঃপাতী লমবার্ডি প্রদেশের অধিবাসী। **2.** One of the 6th century Germanic conquerors of Italy; লম্বার্ডজাতীয় লোক [এই জাতি ৬ষ্ঠ শতাব্দীতে ইতালী জয় করিয়াছিল।] ***Adj.*** Of, or relating to, Lombardy or its natives; লমবার্ড সম্বন্ধীয়, লম্বার্ডির অধিবাসী সম্বন্ধীয়। **—bard′-ic,** *adj.* **Lombard street**—লণ্ডননগরীর রাজপথবিশেষ—এই স্থানে পূর্ব্বে লমবার্ডি প্রদেশবাসী বহু মহাজন বাস করিত, বর্ত্তমানে ঐ রাস্তার উপর লণ্ডননগরীর অনেক প্রধান কুঠি অবস্থিত আছে; রোম নগরীর কাগজ প্রভৃতি ক্রয় বিক্রয়ের স্থান.

Lon′-don (lŭn-dŭn), *Attrib. adj.* Of, or relating to, London; লণ্ডন-সম্পর্কীয়। **—er,** *n.* A native or citizen of London; লণ্ডননগরীর অধিবাসী। **—ism,** *n.* A mode of speaking peculiar to London; লণ্ডননগরীতে প্রচলিত বাক্যরীতি **—ize,** *v. t.* **London ivy**—লণ্ডননগরীর ধূম বা কুজ্‌ঝটিকা। **London smoke**—নিষ্প্রভ ধূসর বর্ণ। **London particular**—লণ্ডননগরীতে বিশেষভাবে দৃষ্ট একপ্রকার কুজ্‌ঝটিকা। **London-pride** — লণ্ডননগরীতে জাত শিলাজ গুল্মবিশেষ।

lōne, *Attrib. adj.* **1.** (Short for *alone*) Solitary ; companionless ; unfrequented ; uninhabited ; lonely ; একাকী, একলা ; সহচরশূন্য, সাথীহীন, নিঃসঙ্গ ; নিভৃত, নির্জ্জন ; জনমানবশূন্য ; বিজন। **2.** Feeling or making feel lonely ; নিঃসঙ্গভাবপীড়িত, নিঃসঙ্গভাবজনক। **3.** (Of woman) Single or widowed ; অনূঢ়া বা বিধবা। **Lone'-some,** *adj.* Solitary ; নির্জ্জন, বিজন। **Lone'-some-ly,** *adv.* **Lone'-someness,** *n.*

lōne'-lȳ, *adj.* **1.** Solitary ; secluded ; companionless ; একাকী ; নির্জ্জন, নিভৃত, বিজন, জনশূন্য ; সহচরশূন্য। **2.** Unfrequented ; জনমানবহীন, মনুষ্যসমাগমশূন্য। **—li-ness,** *n.*

lŏng, *adj.* & *n.* **1.** Of great extent from end to end ; extended ; লম্বা ; দীর্ঘ। **2.** (*Colloq.*) Tall ; as, *long* Tom (a gun of great length or range) ; (চলিতভাষায়) দীর্ঘ। **3.** Having a great duration ; not brief ; tedious ; as, *long* hours of watching : দীর্ঘকালব্যাপী, দীর্ঘ; বিলম্বিত, মন্থর, মৃদুগামী। **4.** Coming after an extended interval ; distant in time ; as, a *long* custom or memory ; বহুকাল পর আগত, দীর্ঘ কালাগত; দূরবর্ত্তী। **5.** Having a specified length or duration ; as, a yard *long* : a vacation two months *long* ; নির্দ্দিষ্ট পরিমাণ দীর্ঘ। **6.** Far-reaching ; extensive ; acting at a distance ; as, *long* sight ; সুদূরপ্রসারিত; বহুদূরবিস্তৃত ; দূর হইতে কার্য্যকারী। **7.** Somewhat random ; as, a *long* guess or inference ; যদৃচ্ছাপ্রসূত, যদৃচ্ছাক্রমে কৃত। **8.** Expressed by many ciphers or consisting of many individuals ; as, *long* figure : *long* family ; containing many items, as, a list etc. ; বহুশূন্যদ্বারা প্রকাশিত, বহুব্যক্তিসমন্বিত ; বহুবিষয় বা প্রকরণসমন্বিত। **9.** Of elongated shape ; দীর্ঘাকৃতি। **10.** Of greater length or quantity than the standard ; as, a *long* dozen (=13) : a *long* hundred (=120) ; সাধারণ আদর্শ অপেক্ষা অধিকতর দীর্ঘ বা অধিক সংখ্যক। **11.** (*Pros.*) (Of a vowel or syllable) Of a relatively great duration ; (ছন্দঃশাস্ত্র) গুরু। *Noun.* **1.** A long interval or period ; as, I shall see you before *long* : I shall not be away for *long* ; দীর্ঘকাল, দীর্ঘ অন্তর ; দীর্ঘ অবকাশ। **2.** A long syllable ; দীর্ঘ শব্দাংশ। **3.** A long vacation ; সুদীর্ঘ ছুটী। **Long'-ish,** *adj.* Somewhat long ; লম্বাটে। **Long'-ways, Long'-wise,** *advs.* Lengthwise ; লম্বালম্বি। **Long arm**—ভুজদণ্ড, ভুজযষ্টি। **Long-armed**—*adj.* লম্বহস্ত, আজানুলম্বিতভুজ, আজানুলম্বিতবাহু। **Long bill** — লম্বা বিল। **Long-bill** — A kind of bird esp. snipe ; একপ্রকার পক্ষী, বিশেষতঃ কাদাখোঁচা। **Long-boat**—পালের জাহাজের বৃহত্তম নৌকা। **Long-bow**—যে ধনুক হইতে হস্তের সাহায্যে দীর্ঘ সপক্ষ বাণ নিক্ষিপ্ত হয়। **Long breathed**—বহুক্ষণ শ্বাসরোধে সমর্থ। **Long-cloth** — লংক্লথ। **Long dated** — বহুদিবস পরের তারিখযুক্ত। **Long-day**—বহুদূরবর্ত্তী কাল। **Long ears**—Stupidity, as of ass ; গর্দ্দভবৎ নির্ব্বুদ্ধিতা। **Long-eared,** *adj.* লম্বকর্ণ। **Long face** — Dismal face ; অপ্রফুল্ল মুখ, অপ্রসন্ন বদন। **Long-faced,** *adj.* দীর্ঘমুখ। **Long family** — যে পরিবারে বহু ছেলে মেয়ে আছে। **Long field**—Same as LONG OFF or ON. A part of the ground behind the bowler ; কন্দুক-ক্ষেপকের পশ্চাদ্বর্ত্তী ভূমির অংশবিশেষ। **Long finger**—The second finger ; তর্জ্জনী। **Long firm**—একদল প্রবঞ্চক—যাহারা দোকান খুলিয়া মালপত্রের দাম না দিয়া অন্যত্র পলাইয়া যায়। **Longhand**—(opp. to *shorthand*) ; সাধারণ হাতে লিখিবার প্রণালী। **Long head**—A head of more than average length ; (*fig.*) shrewdness or foresight ; sagacity ; বড় মাথা ; (লক্ষণায়) দূরদৃষ্টিসম্পন্নতা ; বুদ্ধিমত্তা, তীক্ষ্ণদৃষ্টি। *Long-headed, adj. Long headedness, n.* **Long-home**—The grave ; অন্তিম শয্যা, সমাধি। **Long-jump**—লম্বালম্বি লম্ফ। **Long-lived**—দীর্ঘায়ুঃ, দীর্ঘজীবী, চিরায়ুঃ, চিরজীবী, আয়ুষ্মান, চিরঞ্জীব। **Long measure**—Miles, yards, inches, etc. ; মাইল, গজ, ইঞ্চি প্রভৃতি। **Long off, on** — A man fielding at the bowler's left, right, rear ; কন্দুকক্ষেপকের বামে, দক্ষিণে বা পশ্চাতে থাকিয়া যে ব্যক্তি কন্দুক থামায় বা লুফিয়া ধরে। **Long Parliament**—১ম চার্লস কর্ত্তৃক আহূত পার্লেমেণ্ট সভা (১৬৪০—১৬৬০)। **Long pepper**—পিপুল। **Long-pig**—নরমাংসাশী অসভ্য জাতিগণের ভোজের জন্য নিহত মনুষ্য। **Long-robe** — ব্যবহারজীবিগণের পরিচ্ছদ। **Long-service** — বহু বৎসরের জন্য সেনাবিভাগের কার্য্য গ্রহণ। **Longshanks**—পাদযষ্টি; দীর্ঘপাদ পক্ষিবিশেষ। **Long-sight**—One seeing distant objects ; (*fig.*) penetration ; foresight ; যে ব্যক্তি অতি দূরবর্ত্তী বস্তু দেখিতে পারে, দূরদর্শী ; (লক্ষণায়) সূক্ষ্মদৃষ্টি ; দূরদর্শিতা। *Long-sighted, adj.* দীর্ঘদর্শী, দূরদর্শী, দীর্ঘদৃষ্টি। *Long-sightedness, n.* (*lit.* & *fig.*) **Long-stop** — উইকেট রক্ষকের অব্যবহিত পশ্চাতে থাকিয়া যে ব্যক্তি বল থামায় বা লুফিয়া থাকে। (*Verb i.*) To field there ; উইকেট রক্ষকের অব্যবহিত পশ্চাতে থাকিয়া বল থামান বা লুফিয়া ধরা। **Long-sufferance**—Forbearance ; patience ; ধৈর্য্য ; সহিষ্ণুতা। **Long-suffering**—চিরসহিষ্ণু। **Long suit**—কোন হাতে এক জাতের অনেক তাস। **Long-tongued** — Loquacious ; prating ; talkative ; বাচাল ; বাবদুক, মুখর ; বহুভাষী। **Long-vacation** — বিচারালয়, বিশ্ববিদ্যালয় প্রভৃতির গ্রীষ্মাবকাশ। **Long-wind**—The capacity for running without rest or (*fig.*) for talking or writing at tedious length ; লম্বাদম, বহুক্ষণ কাজ করিবার শক্তি, বহুক্ষণ কথা বলিবার বা লিখিবার শক্তি। *Long-winded, adj.* অবসাদজনকরূপে দীর্ঘ ; সুদীর্ঘকালে ক্ষয়কারী। *Long-winded-ness, n.* **A long dozen**—13 ; ১৩। **At or in the long run**—In the end ; after vicissitudes ; eventually ; চরমে, অন্তিমে ; অবশেষে ; পরিণামে। **At longest**—To mention the most distant date possible ; যতদূর সম্ভব দূরবর্ত্তী তারিখ। **By a long chalk**—Very considerably ; নিরতিশয়। **Ere long**—Before long ; soon ; সত্বর, অচিরে ; শীঘ্র। **For long**—For a considerable period of time ; দীর্ঘ কালের জন্য, দীর্ঘ সময়ের জন্য। **Gentle-man of the long robe**—Lawyers ; ব্যবহারজীবিবর্গ। **Longs and shorts**—কবিতার চরণ, বিশেষতঃ, ল্যাটিন কবিতার চরণ। **The long and short of it**—The sum and substance of it ; the total upshot ; মোট কথা, স্থূল কথা ; (কোন বিষয়ের) সংক্ষিপ্ত বিবরণ। **The long and short of the story is**—স্থূল কথা এই যে। **To draw or pull the long bow**—See BOW. **To have a long arm**—To be able to make one's power felt far ; বহু দূরবর্ত্তী স্থানে নিজের ভুজবল বিস্তার করিতে পারা। **To make a long arm**—To reach out the arm for something esp. at the table ; কোন কিছুর জন্য হাত বাড়ান। **To make a long nose** — Same as TO COCK A SNOOK (which see under SNOOK **To pull a long face**—See PULL. **To take long views** — To consider remote effects ; সুদূর পরিণামের বিষয় বিবেচনা করা।

lŏng, *adv.* 1. To a great extent in space or time ; for a long time ; অনেক দূর বা অনেকক্ষণ পর্য্যন্ত; বহুক্ষণ ব্যাপিয়া, দীর্ঘ সময়ের জন্য, সুদীর্ঘকালের জন্য। 2. Throughout an extent of time specified ; as, all day *long* ; কোন নির্দ্দিষ্ট পরিমাণ কাল ব্যাপিয়া। 3. By a long time ; as, *long* before the foundation of Rome : *long* ago ; বহুকাল পূর্ব্বে বা পরে, বহুদিন পূর্ব্বে। 4. (Comparative with *any, no, much*) After an implied point of time ; as, not to wait any *longer* ; লক্ষিত সময়ের পর। **Long ago**—*adj.* & *n.* Belonging to the distant past ; সুদূর অতীত কালের। (*Noun*) The distant past ; সুদূর অতীত। **Long drawn (out)**—অতিমাত্রায় প্রবর্দ্ধিত, অতিশয় দীর্ঘীকৃত। **Long-liver**—One who lives long ; দীর্ঘজীবী লোক। **Long-practised**—চিরাভ্যস্ত। **Long-standing** — দীর্ঘকালাগত। **Long suffering**—*n.* & *adj.* দীর্ঘকালসহন, দীর্ঘকালসহিষ্ণু, চিরসহিষ্ণু। **No longer**—Not henceforth or formerly ; আর নয়। **Not to be long for this world**—To have a short time to live; আর অধিক দিন বাঁচিবে না, আয়ু ফুরাইয়া আসিয়াছে। **So long as, As long as**—Till ; provided that ; যে পর্য্যন্ত, যতক্ষণ নয় ; এরূপ হইলে। **To be long doing or in doing**—To take a long time to do ; করিতে অনেক সময় লাগা, বহু সময়সাপেক্ষ হওয়া।

lŏng, *v. i.* To desire earnestly or eagerly ; to wish vehemently ; (*usu. follwed by an infinitive* or *for*) ; অতিশয় আকাঙ্ক্ষা করা, স্পৃহা করা ; লোলুপ হওয়া। **Long'-ing** *n.* A craving or unnatural appetite ; আকাঙ্ক্ষা, স্পৃহা, বাসনা, লালসা, অভিলাষ। **Long'-ing-ly,** *adv.* **Longing of a pregnant woman** — গর্ভিনীর অভিলাষ, দোহদ (রঃ)।

lon'-găn (lŏng-), *n.* A kind of pulpy fruit ; the tree bearing this ; আঁস ফল (ফার্ম্মিঃ) ; আঁসফলের গাছ।

lŏn-gë'-văl, -gae'- (-gë-), *adjs.* Long-lived ; দীর্ঘায়ুঃ, চিরঞ্জীবী, চিরায়ুঃ, আয়ুষ্মান্।

lŏn-gĕv'-ĭ-tў, *n.* Long life ; দীর্ঘজীবন, দীর্ঘায়ুস্ত্ব, দীর্ঘায়ুষ্য, চিরায়ুষ্য, চিরঞ্জীবিত্ব।

lŏn-gĭm'-ă-nous (-nŭs), *adj.* Having long hands ; দীর্ঘবাহু, দীর্ঘভুজ।

lŏn-gĭm'-ĕ-tў, *n.* The measurement of distances or lengths ; দূরত্ব বা দীর্ঘত্বের পরিমাণ, দূরত্বমিতি, দূরত্বমাপন, দৈর্ঘ্যমাপন।

lŏn'-gĭ-tūde, *n.* 1. Length ; দৈর্ঘ্য, লম্বাই (বর্ত্তমানে কৌতুকচ্ছলে ব্যবহৃত হয়)। 2. (*Geog.*) The distance of a place east or west from a given meridian (abbr. *long.*) ; (ভূগোল) কোন নির্দ্দিষ্ট দ্রাঘিমা হইতে কোন স্থানের পূর্ব্ব বা পশ্চিম দিকের দ্রাঘিমাবচ্ছিন্ন নিরক্ষদূরতা, দ্রাঘিমান্তর, দেশান্তর (হিঃ কোঃ)। 3. (*Astron.*) The angular distance reckoned eastward on the ecliptic from the vernal equinox to the ecliptic meridian passing through the point or body ; (জ্যোতির্বিজ্ঞান) ভুজাংশ (হিঃ কোঃ), ধ্রুবক (সাঃ পঃ), খেট (ঐ), ভুক্তি (ঐ), গ্রহ (ঐ), ভাগ (celestial longitude for planets), অপবৃত্তাংশ (ঐ), খগোলীয়দেশান্তর (হিঃ কোঃ), খগোলীয়ভুজাংশ (ঐ)। **Geographical longitude** — ভৌগোলিক ভুজাংশ (হিঃ কোঃ), ভৌগোলিকদেশান্তর (ঐ)। **Heliocentric longitude** — সূর্য্যকেন্দ্রকভুজাংশ (হিঃ কোঃ)। **Jovecentric longitude**—গুরুকেন্দ্রক ভুজাংশ (হিঃ কোঃ)। **Longitude of perihelion**—রবিনীচ অক্ষাংশ (হিঃ কোঃ)। **Terrestrial longitude in arc**—তুলাংশ (সাঃ পঃ)। **Terrestrial longitude in space**—দেশান্তরযোজন (সাঃ পঃ)। **Terrestrial longitude in time**—দেশান্তর ঘটিকা (সাঃ পঃ)। **A dergree of longitude**—রেখাংশ (কেম্ভিঃ)।

lŏn-gĭ-tū'-dĭ-năl, *adj.* 1. Of, pertaining to, or in length ;

দৈর্ঘ্যসম্বন্ধীয়, দৈর্ঘ্যবিষয়ক, লম্বাকার, দৈর্ঘিক (সাঃ পঃ)। 2. Running lengthwise ; অনুদৈর্ঘ্য। 3. Of, or relating to, longitude : দ্রাঘিমান্তর সম্বন্ধীয়, খগোলীয়দেশান্তর-সম্বন্ধীয় **—ly,** *adv.*

lŏng'-shōre, *adj.* Existing, found, or employed, on the shore ; frequenting the shore ; সমুদ্রতীরস্থিত সমুদ্রতীরে প্রাপ্ত, সমুদ্রতীরে নিযুক্ত ; তীরচর **Longshore man**—জাহাজ বোঝাইর কার্য্যে নিযুক্ত লোক ; সমুদ্রতীরে থাকিয়া মৎস্য শিকারের কার্য্যে নিযুক্ত ব্যক্তি।

loo, *n.* & *v. t.* **1.** A game of cards ; একপ্রকার তাস খেলা **2.** A stake or penalty at loo ; ঐরূপ তাস খেলার পণ বা নিয়মভঙ্গের জন্য শাস্তি। ***Verb t.*** To beat in the game of loo ; ঐরূপ তাস খেলায় হারাইয়া দেওয়া।

loo'-bȳ, *n.* An awkward silly fellow ; গোবর গণেশ।

loo'-fah (-fă), **—fá, lŭf'-fá,** *ns.* The sponge-like fibrous interior of a kind of gourd used as a flesh-brush ; স্নানকালে শরীর পরিষ্কার করার জন্য ঝিঙ্গা, ধুন্দুল প্রভৃতির শুষ্ক অভ্যন্তর ভাগ।

lo͝ok, *v. i., t.* & *n.* **1.** To direct or turn the eyes (*at*) ; to use one's sight ; দেখা, দৃষ্টি করা, দর্শন করা, অবলোকন করা ; চক্ষু ফিরান, তাকান। **2.** To gaze in wonder or surprise ; to stare ; বিস্ময়স্তিমিতনেত্রে দৃষ্টিপাত করা ; বিস্ময়ে হাঁ করিয়া একদৃষ্টে চাহিয়া থাকা। **3.** (*Fig.*) To apply the mind ; to pay attention *at* and consider ; as, the way of *looking* at things ; to enquire ; as, when one *looks* deeper ; (লক্ষণায়) মন দেওয়া ; বিবেচনা করা, অবধান করা, অভিনিবেশ পূর্ব্বক বিবেচনা করা ; অনুসন্ধান করা। **4.** To ascertain or observe by sight ; as, *look* where they go ; দৃষ্টি দ্বারা লক্ষ্য বা নির্ণয় করা। **5.** To face ; to front ; as, the gate that *looks* towards the north ; সম্মুখীন হওয়া, সম্মুখবর্ত্তী হওয়া, অভিমুখীন হওয়া। **6.** To seem ; as, the patient *looks* better ; দেখান, প্রতীয়মান হওয়া, বোধ হওয়া, লাগা, মনে হওয়া। **7.** To tend ; to point ; as, this statement *looks* to be true ; উন্মুখ করা ; সূচনা করা, নির্দ্দেশ করা। **8.** To take care ; as, *look* that you do not fall ; দেখা, সাবধান হওয়া, সতর্ক হওয়া (দেখিও যেন না পড়)। **9.** To expect ; as, we *look* to profit by the investment ; প্রতীক্ষা করা, প্রত্যাশা করা। **10.** To turn or resort (*to*) ; as, we *look to* a friend for help ; ফিরা, আশ্রয় নেওয়া। ***Verb t.*** **1.** To turn the eyes towards ; to see ; চক্ষু ফিরান ; তাকান। **2.** To express by a look ; as, to *look* compassion or death ; to influence or subdue by looks ; দৃষ্টি দ্বারা প্রকাশ করা ; দৃষ্টি দ্বারা অভিভূত করা বা প্রভাবিত করা। **3.** To inspect or examine ; to contemplate ; পরিদর্শন করা, পরীক্ষা করা ; চিন্তা করা। ***Noun.*** **1.** The act of looking ; glance ; as, a kind, scornful *look* ; অবেক্ষণ, প্রেক্ষণ, অবলোকন, দৃষ্টিপাত, দর্শন, পেখন (*poet.*), চকিতদৃষ্টি, ঈষদ্দৃষ্টি। **2.** Appearance or expression of the countenance ; personal aspect ; as, a proud or defiant *look* ; মুখাবয়ব, মুখাকৃতি ; হাবভাব। **3.** (Of things) Appearance ; aspect ; as, the house has a gloomy *look* ; আকার, আকৃতি ; দৃষ্টি, ভাব, ভঙ্গী। **Look'-er,** *n.* One who looks ; দ্রষ্টা। **Look'-ing,** *n.* Using eyesight ; দর্শন, অবলোকন। **Good looks**—Beauty ; সৌন্দর্য্য। **Looker on**—An onlooker ; a spectator ; দর্শক ; দ্রষ্টা। **Look-in**—A short call or visit ; সাক্ষাৎ। **Looking-glass**—A mirror ; মুকুর, আয়না, আর্শি, দর্পণ, আদর্শ। **Look-out**—A careful watch or looking for any object or event ; as, to keep a good *look-out* ; চৌকি, পাহারা। The post or place of observation ; অবেক্ষণ-স্থলী, অবেক্ষণ-মঞ্চ। A man or party or boat stationed to look out ; পাহারায় নিযুক্ত ব্যক্তি বা ব্যক্তিগণ, পাহারায় ব্যবহৃত বস্তু (যথা নৌকা)। A view or prospect ; দৃশ্য। Prospect of luck ; as, it is a bad *look-out* for him ; ভাগ্যফল, কপাল। A person's own concern ; as, that is his *look-out* ; ব্যক্তিগত বিষয়, ভাবনার বিষয়। **Fair to look at**—Fair in outward appearance ; দেখিতে সুন্দর। **Look before you leap**—Avoid precipitate action ; দেখিয়া শুনিয়া লম্ফ দিও, অবিমৃষ্যকারীর মত কোন কাজ করিও না, সাবধানের বিনাশ নাই, অবস্থা বুঝে ব্যবস্থা কর। **Look here**—(*Imper.*) Pay attention ; শোন, মন দেও। **Look lively** or **alive**—Be alert ; be quick ; হুঁসিয়ার হও ; তৎপর হও। **Look you**—(*Imper.*) Observe ; mind ; দেখ ; শোন। **That is your look-out**—See under LOOK-OUT. **The house looks to the east**—It faces the east ; পূর্ব্বমুখীন। **To look about**—To look on all sides ; to be on the watch ; to be on search for ; চারিদিকে দেখা ; সতর্ক হওয়া, সাবধান হওয়া, হুঁসিয়ার হওয়া ; অনুসন্ধান করা। **To look about one**—To examine one's surroundings ; চারিদিকে ভাল করিয়া দেখা। To be vigilant ; হুসিয়ার থাকা, সতর্ক থাকা। To take time to form plans ; মতলব আটিবার জন্য সময় নেওয়া। **To look a fool**—To seem to be a fool ; নির্ব্বোধের মত দেখান। **To look after**—To follow with the eye ; to seek for ; to attend to ; to take care of ; as, to *look after* children ; চক্ষু দ্বারা অনুসরণ করা ; অনুসন্ধান করা ; তত্ত্বাবধান করা ; যত্ন নেওয়া। To expect ; প্রত্যাশা করা। **To look ahead**—(Of a rower)

To turn round and see where he is going (esp. imperative); (দাঁড়বাহকের পক্ষে) মুখ ফিরাইয়া কোথায় যাইতেছে দেখা। **To look a person up**—To visit him; কোন ব্যক্তির সহিত সাক্ষাৎ করা। **To look as if**—To suggest by appearance the belief that; যেন দেখান। **To look at**—To direct the eyes so as to see; to examine; to consider; as, to *look at* a question impartially; চক্ষু ফিরান, দেখা, অবলোকন করা, দৃষ্টিপাত করা; পরীক্ষা করা; বিবেচনা করা। **To look at him etc.**—Judging by his looks; তাহার চেহারা দেখিয়া বিচার করিলে। **To look back**—To be half-hearted about an enterprise one has begun; to turn one's thoughts *upon* or *to* something past; to cease to progress; আরব্ধকার্য্য সম্বন্ধে ভগ্নোৎসাহ হওয়া; গত বিষয়ের চিন্তা করা; অগ্রসরে বিরত হওয়া। **To look black**—To frown; to have a threatening appearance; ভ্রূকুটী করা, চোক পাকান; ক্রোধ-ব্যঞ্জক দৃষ্টিপাত করা। **To look blue**—See under BLUE. **To look daggers**—See DAGGER. **To look down**—To subdue with a look; চোক পাকাইয়া দাবাইয়া দেওয়া। (*Commer.*) To sink in price; দাম কমা। **To look down on or upon**—To despise; to treat with contempt; to consider oneself superior to; ঘৃণা করা, অবজ্ঞা করা; তুচ্ছতাচ্ছিল্য করা; নিজকে অন্য হইতে শ্রেষ্ঠ জ্ঞান করা। **To look for**—To expect; to be on the watch for; to search for; প্রত্যাশা করা; প্রতীক্ষা করা; অন্বেষণ করা। **To look for a needle in a bottle (bundle) of hay**—To engage in a hopeless search; ঘাসের গাদায় সূচ খোঁজা, অসাধ্যসাধনে নিযুক্ত হওয়া। **To look forward to**—To anticipate (with pleasure); (উৎফুল্লচিত্তে) প্রত্যাশা করা। **To look in**—To make short visit or call; দেখাশুনা করিয়া আসা। **To look in the face**—To meet with boldness or at close quarters; সাহসের সহিত সম্মুখীন হওয়া। **To look into**—To inspect closely; to examine the inside of, as a box etc.; to dip into (a book); to investigate; পুঙ্খানুপুঙ্খরূপে পরীক্ষা করা, তন্ন তন্ন করিয়া দেখা; কোন কিছুর অভ্যন্তর পরীক্ষা করা; মগ্ন হওয়া, নিবিষ্ট হওয়া; অনুসন্ধান করা। **To look in upon**—To visit informally; অনিয়মিত ভাবে সাক্ষাৎ করা। **To look like**—To seem to be; to threaten to be; to promise to be; as, it *looks like* biting or winning; প্রতিভাত হওয়া, বোধ হওয়া মনে হওয়া, দেখান, অনুমিত হওয়া, প্রতীয়মান হওয়া; আশঙ্কার কারণ হওয়া; আশ্বাস দেওয়া। **To look on**—To regard *as*; ভাবা, গণ্য করা। To regard *with* distrust; সন্দেহের চোখে দেখা। To be a mere spectator; দ্রষ্টামাত্র হওয়া। **To look oneself again**—To seem recovered; রোগমুক্ত বলিয়া বোধ হওয়া। **To look one up and down**—To scrutinize him keenly or contemptuously; পুঙ্খানুপুঙ্খরূপে দেখা, অবজ্ঞার সহিত দেখা। **To look on with**—To read from a book etc. at the same time as (another person); পুস্তক প্রভৃতি হইতে এক সময়ে পাঠ করা। **To look out**—To be on the watch or vigilant; to direct eyes or put head out of a window etc.; সতর্ক থাকা, সাবধান হওয়া; জানালা দিয়া তাকান, জানালা দিয়া মাথা বাহির করা। (*Commer.*) To improve in price or prosperity; to be in demand; মূল্য বৃদ্ধি হওয়া, সমৃদ্ধতর হওয়া; চাহিদা থাকা। To select by inspection; মনোনীত করা, পসন্দ করা। To be prepared *for* squalls ঝঞ্ঝার জন্য প্রস্তুত হওয়া। To have or afford outlook *on, over* etc.; উপর দিয়া দৃশ্যমান হওয়া, দৃশ্যমান করা। **To look out for**—To search for; তল্লাস করা, অনুসন্ধান করা। **To look over**—To inspect; to examine part by part or one by one; পরিদর্শন করা; অংশে অংশে বা একে একে পরীক্ষা করা। To overlook or pardon; উপেক্ষা করা, মার্জ্জনা করা। To read over; উপর উপর দেখিয়া যাওয়া, চোখ বুলাইয়া যাওয়া। **To look sharp**—To lose no time; to bestir oneself; (*originally*) to keep strict watch; সময় নষ্ট না করা; স্ফূর্ত্তি করা, তাড়াতাড়ি করা, তৎপর হওয়া; কড়া পাহারা রাখা। **To look sharp after**—To watch carefully; চোখে চোখে রাখা, কড়া পাহাড়া রাখা। **To look thin**—To appear thin; কৃশ বলিয়া বোধ হওয়া, কাহিল বলিয়া বোধ হওয়া। **To look through**—To direct eyes through, as a window etc.; to penetrate with the eye or the understanding; to observe or inspect minutely or exhaustively; to glance through, as a book; to be visible through; as, his greed *looks* through his eyes; ভিতর দিয়া দেখা; ভেদ করা; পুঙ্খানুপুঙ্খরূপে পরিদর্শন করা; চোখ বুলাইয়া যাওয়া; কোন আবরণে ভিতর দিয়া দৃশ্যমান হওয়া। **To look through coloured spectacles**—To view things not as they are but distorted by one's own prejudices; কোন বস্তু ঠিক যেমনটী তেমনটী না দেখিয়া নিজের সংস্কার দ্বারা বিকৃত করিয়া দেখা। **To look to**—To take care of; to be careful about; to depend on for; to consider; to expect; to count on; to aim at; তত্ত্বাবধান নেওয়া; সাবধান হওয়া, সতর্ক হওয়া; নির্ভর করা; বিবেচনা করা; প্রত্যাশা করা; পরিগণনা করা; লক্ষ্য করা। **To look to be**—To seem; দেখান, বোধ হওয়া, প্রতিভাত হওয়া। **To look towards**—(*Colloq.*) To drink the health of; স্বাস্থ্যকামনায় মদ্য পান করা। **To look up**—To search for, or find out, by looking, as a word in a dictionary or a fact in a book of reference; খোঁজা, খুঁজিয়া দেখা, দেখিয়া বাহির করা। (*Colloq.*) To call upon, as a person; to raise eyes; (চলিত ভাষায়) সাক্ষাৎ করা; চোখ তুলিয়া চাওয়া, উপরের দিকে তাকান। **To look upon**—To regard as; to regard *with* a specified feeling; দেখা, ভাবা; গণ্য করা। **To look up to**—To respect; মান্য করা, সম্মান করা। **To look well or ill**—To seem to be in good or bad health; (of things) to seem to be going well or ill; সুস্থ বা অসুস্থ দেখান; (বস্তু-সম্পর্কে) ভাল চলিতেছে বলিয়া বোধ হওয়া, ভাল চলিতেছে না বলিয়া বোধ হওয়া। **Will have a look in**—(*Sports*) Will come near winning and perhaps win; (ক্রীড়ায়) প্রায় জয় লাভ করিবে এবং হয় ত জয়ী হইবে। **Will not look at**—Refuses to take; scorns; rejects; গ্রহণ করিতে অস্বীকার করে; অবজ্ঞা করে; অগ্রাহ্য করে।

Loom for weaving carpet.

lōōm, *n.* **1.** A machine by which thread is woven into a fabric; বস্ত্রবয়নযন্ত্র, তাঁত। **2.** The shaft of an oar or the part which is within the boat in rowing; দাঁড়ের বাঁট বা দাঁড় টানিবার সময় উহার যে অংশ নৌকার ভিতর থাকে। **Fly-shuttle loom**—ঠকঠকি তাঁত। **Power-loom**—কলের তাঁত।

lōōm, *v. i.* & *n.* **1.** To appear larger than the real size and indistinctly as a ship at sea; to appear faintly; ঝাপ্সা এবং প্রকৃত আকার হইতে বৃহত্তর প্রতীয়মান হওয়া (যেমন সমুদ্রোপরি জাহাজ); অস্পষ্টভাবে দৃশ্য হওয়া, ঝাপ্সা দেখান। **2.** (*Fig.*) To appear in an impressively great form; "On no occasion does he *loom* so high"; (লক্ষণায়) বিরাটরূপে আবির্ভূত হওয়া। ***Noun.*** The vague first appearance of land at sea; সমুদ্র হইতে স্থলের প্রথম অস্পষ্ট দর্শন।

lōōm, *n.* An auk, guillemot or puffin; একপ্রকার পাখী।

lōōn, *n.* (*Scot.* & *Archaic*) **1.** Scamp; a worthless fellow; an idler; (স্কটলণ্ডে ব্যবহৃত, অপ্রঃ) পাজি, দুর্বৃত্ত, বদমাইস, নরাধম, হারামজাদা; অকর্মণ্য লোক; অলসলোক। **2.** A lad; ছেলে, ছোঁড়া।

lōōn, *n.* A kind of diving water-bird; পানিকৌড়ী, ডুবরী পক্ষী।

lōōn'-ȳ, lŭn'—, *n.* & *adj.* (*Vulg.*) Lunatic; (ইতর ভাষায়) পাগলা, ক্ষেপা।

lōōp, *n., v. t.* & *i.* **1.** The figure produced by a curve or bent string that crosses itself; a noose; রজ্জুর বেড়, পুঁটে-ঘরা, গলাসি; ফাঁশ। **2.** A fold of cord or ribbon serving as an ornament as on a uniform; রজ্জু বা ফিতার শোভাসাধক পুঁট। **3.** A ring or curved piece of metal as handle; আংটা বা ধাতুনির্ম্মিত বক্র হাতল। **4.** A railway or telegraph line that diverges from the main line and joins it again (also *loop-line*); প্রধান লৌহবর্ত্মের যে অংশ উহা হইতে দূরে সরিয়া পুনরায় উহাতে মিলিত হয়। ***Verb t.*** **1.** To form (strings etc.) into a loop or loops; রজ্জুদ্বারা ফাঁস তৈয়ার করা, পুঁটে-ঘরা করা। **2.** To fasten *up* or join *together* with a loop or loops; গলাসি দ্বারা বাঁধা বা সংযোগ করা। **3.** To ornament with loops; শোভাসাধক রজ্জুক ফিতার পুঁটদ্বারা ভূষিত করা। **4.** To place within a loop; গলাসির মধ্যে রাখা। ***Verb i.*** To form a loop or loops; ফাঁস হওয়া। **Looping the loop**—দ্বিচক্রযানারোহীর পক্ষে ঋজুভাবে অবস্থিত চক্রোপরি আবর্ত্তন।

lōōp, *n.* (*Rare*) An opening or loop-hole; (অপ্রঃ) ছিদ্র, ফাঁক, রন্ধ্র।

lōōp'-êr, *n.* **1.** A caterpillar of geometer moths; একপ্রকার তসরে পোকার লম্বা কীড়া। **2.** A contrivance in sewing-machine etc. for making loops; পুঁটে-ঘরা তৈয়ার করার জন্য সেলাই কলের কৌশল-বিশেষ।

lōōp'-hōle, *n.* & *v. t.* **1.** A small vertical opening in the walls for shooting or looking through or to admit light or air; (দুর্গ-বা জাহাজে) কামানাদি দাগিবার বা আলোকাদি প্রবেশের জন্য প্রাচীর-গাত্রস্থ রন্ধ্র। **2.** A hole affording means of escape; an outlet; means of evading a rule etc.; পলাইবার পথ; নির্গমপথ, নির্গমরন্ধ্র; কোন নিয়ম প্রভৃতি এড়াইবার উপায়, প্রতি-প্রসব। ***Verb t.*** To make loop-holes in, as walls etc.; প্রাচীরাদির গাত্রে রন্ধ্র করা।

loose (lōōs), *adj.* **1.** Untied; not fastened or confined; as, the *loose* sheets of paper; আঁবাধা; আল্গা। **2.** Released from bonds or restraint; অসংযত, বন্ধনমুক্ত। **3.** Not rigidly fixed; as, to have a screw *loose*; শ্লথ, শিথিল, ফস্কা, স্রস্ত, স্রংসিত, গলিত, বিগলিত। **4.** Not tight; slack; as, a *loose* garment; আঁটা নহে; ঢিলা। **5.** Having partial freedom of movement etc.; as, *loose* end; আংশিক ভাবে অবাধ-গতি। **6.** Not dense or compact; composed of loose particles; not serried; as, a *loose* soil: *loose* fabric; বিরল, অঘন; ঝিরঝিরে; ফাকফাক। **7.** (*Chem.*) Uncombined; (রসায়ন-শাস্ত্র) অমিশ্রিত। **8.** Inaccurate; indefinite; vague; incorrect; as, a *loose* statement: *loose* ideas; অঠিক; অনির্দ্দিষ্ট; অস্পষ্ট; ভ্রমাত্মক। **9.** Not close or faithful, as translation; আক্ষরিক নহে, অনবিকল। **10.** Ungrammatical; not precise; as, a *loose* style; ব্যাকরণদুষ্ট,

অসাধু ; অসুষ্ঠু প্রয়োগকুশল। 11. Incontinent ; dissolute ; unchaste ; lewd ; অসংযতেন্দ্রিয় ; স্খলিতচরিত্র, নষ্ট, ভ্রষ্ট, উচ্ছৃঙ্খল ; অসত, ব্যভিচারিণী ; লোচ্চা, স্ত্রীব্যসনী, ব্যভিচারী। 2. Lax ; not costive ; as, *loose* bowels ; পাতলা ; অকঠিন। 3. Wanton in speech ; consisting of obscene language ; as, a *loose* epistle ; অশ্লীলভাষী ; অশ্লীলতাদুষ্ট। **Loose′-ly,** *adv.* 1. In a loose manner ; laxly ; slackly ; শিথিলভাবে ; ঢিলাভাবে ; শ্লথভাবে। 2. Dissolutely ; উচ্ছৃঙ্খল ভাবে। **Loose′-ness,** *n.* 1. State of being loose ; slackness ; শিথিলতা, শৈথিল্য, অধৃতি ; ঢিলামি। 2. Dissoluteness ; লাম্পট্য, চরিত্রহীনতা। 3. Diarrhœa ; পেটের পীড়া, গ্রহণী, উদরাময়। **Loos′-ish,** *adj.* **Loose bowels**—উদরাময়ের ভাব। **Loose box**—যে আস্তাবলে ঘোড়া ইচ্ছামত চলাফেরা করিতে পারে। **Loose build** or **make**—বিশ্রী গঠন। **Loose colour** — কাঁচা রং। **Loose** or **loosely flowing, —fitting**—ঢিলাভাবে ঝুলানো, ঢিলাভাবে লাগানো। **Loose-handwriting**—Straggling handwriting ; বিশৃঙ্খল এবং ফাঁক ফাঁক হাতের লেখা। **Loose-order**—ফাঁক ফাঁক সৈন্য সন্নিবেশ। **Loose tongue**—বাচাল, মুখর। **A loose fish**—A dissolute person ; ভ্রষ্টচরিত্র ব্যক্তি, লোচ্চা, লম্পট। **At a loose end**—নির্দ্দিষ্ট বৃত্তিহীন। **A tile** or **slate loose**—A disordered brain ; বিকৃত-মস্তিষ্ক। **On the loose**—Dissipated ; ভ্রষ্টচরিত্র, স্খলিতচরিত্র। **To break loose**—To escape from confinement ; জেল ভাঙ্গিয়া পালান। **To let loose**—To set at liberty ; to free from restraint ; ছাড়িয়া দেওয়া, মুক্তি দেওয়া ; বন্ধনমুক্তি দেওয়া। **To play fast and loose**—See under FAST.

lōose, *v. t., i.* & *n.* 1. To release ; to let loose ; to free from any constraint ; as, wine *loosed* his tongue ; মুক্ত করা, খালাস দেওয়া ; ছাড়িয়া দেওয়া ; বন্ধনমুক্ত করা। 2. To untie or unbound ; to undo ; as, to *loose* a knot, fetters, hair of head etc. ; গ্রন্থিমোচন করা, বন্ধনমোচন করা ; আল্‌গা করা, খুলা। 3. To detach from moorings ; নোঙ্গরাদি হইতে বিচ্ছিন্ন করা, নোঙ্গর তুলিয়া নেওয়া। 4. To discharge an arrow etc. ; শরনিক্ষেপ করা, শর ত্যাগ করা, অস্ত্র মোচন করা। 5. To slacken (now only in the phrase *to loose hold*) ; ঢিলা করা, শিথিল করা, বিস্রস্ত করা আল্‌গা করা। ***Verb i.*** To shoot ; ক্ষেপণ করা, ছোঁড়া। ***Noun.*** Vent ; free expression ; as, to give *loose* or a *loose* to one's feelings ; প্রকাশ ; অনর্গল ভাবে মনোভাব প্রকাশ।

lōos′-en (-n), *v. t.* & *i.* 1. To make loose ; to make less tight for firm ; ঢিলা করা, আল্‌গা করা ; শ্লথ করা। 2. To free from constraint, as a person's tongue ; আটক ভাঙ্গা, সঙ্কোচ হইতে মুক্ত করা, কুণ্ঠা দূর করা। 3. To relieve (bowels) from costiveness or (cough) from dryness ; কোষ্ঠকাঠিন্য দূর করা, শুক্‌না সর্দ্দি তরল করা। 4. To relax as discipline etc. ; (শাসনের কঠোরতা) শিথিল করা, ঢিল দেওয়া। ***Verb i.*** To become loose ; আল্‌গা হওয়া, ঢিলা হওয়া, শিথিল হওয়া, শ্লথ হওয়া, বিস্রস্ত হওয়া।

lōose′-strife, *n.* Two kinds of herbaceous plants (one golden or yellow and the other red or purple) ; বর্ষজীবী গুল্মদ্বয় (উদ্ভিদের মধ্যে একটী পীত বা শ্বেতবর্ণ অপরটী লোহিত কিম্বা নীলারুণবর্ণ)।

lōot, *n., v. t.* & *i.* 1. Spoil ; booty ; esp. that taken of an enemy ; লুণ্ঠন ; লুণ্ঠিত দ্রব্য, লুঠের মাল ; বিশেষভাবে শত্রু হইতে লুণ্ঠিত দ্রব্য। 2. Gains of corrupt officials ; উৎকোচগ্রাহী রাজকর্ম্মচারিগণের অবৈধ লাভ। ***Verb t.*** 1. To plunder or sack, as a city etc. ; লুণ্ঠন করা, নগরাদি লুঠপাট করা। 2. To carry off as loot ; লুঠিয়া নেওয়া। ***Verb i.*** To plunder ; to sack ; লুণ্ঠন করা, লুঠপাট করা ; লুঠতরাজ করা। **Loot′-er,** *n.*

lŏp, *n., v. t.* & *i.* The small branches and twigs of trees ; trimmings ; ক্ষুদ্র ডাল, শাখা, প্রভৃতি, ছোট ছোট ডালপালা ; কাটছাঁট। ***Verb t.*** 1. To cut off branches, twigs, etc. from, as a tree ; to trim ; ডালপালা কাটিয়া বা ছাঁটিয়া দেওয়া ; কাটাছাঁটা। 2. To strip a tree of (branches etc.), (with *off, away*) ; বৃক্ষাদির ডালপালা কাটিয়া ফেলা। 3. To cut off, as the head or limbs of a person ; কাটিয়া ফেলা। ***Verb i.*** To perform the act of lopping or trimming (*at*) ; ছেদন করা, ডালপালা কাটা বা ছাঁটা। **Lop′-pings,** *n.* (*Pl.*) That which is cut off ; small branches lopped off ; trimmings ; ছিন্ন অংশ, ছিন্ন ভাগ ; কাটা ডালপালা ; কাটছাঁট। **Lop and top, Lop and crop**—ছাঁটা ডালপালা।

lŏp, *v. i., t.* & *n.* 1. To hang limply ; to be pendent ; আল্‌গা ভাবে ঝুলিয়া পড়া ; ঝুলা, লম্বমান হওয়া, দোলায়মান হওয়া। 2. To move or act lazily or slouchily ; অলসের মত চলা বা কাজ করা, জড়ভাবের মত চলা বা কাজ করা, জড়বৎ চলা। 3. Same as LOPE. ***Verb t.*** To let, as ears hang down ; ঝুলিতে দেওয়া। ***Noun.*** A lop-eared rabbit ; নতকর্ণ শশক। **Lop-ear**—A kind of rabbit ; একপ্রকার শশক। **Lop-eared**—নতকর্ণ। **Lop-ears**—Drooping ears ; নতকর্ণ।

lŏp, *v. i.* & *n.* (Of water) To break in short lumpy waves ; (জল সম্পর্কে) তরঙ্গভঙ্গ হওয়া। ***Noun.*** Such wavy condition of water ; তরঙ্গভঙ্গতা।

lōpe, *v. i.* & *n.* To run with a lope (esp. of animals) ; লাফাইয়া লাফাইয়া চলা। ***Noun.*** A long bounding stride, as of animals ; দীর্ঘ লম্ফ।

lŏp'-sīd-ĕd, *adj.* Inclining to one side; as, a *lop-sided* ship; একপার্শ্বে প্রবণ, একপার্শ্বে আনত বা পতনশীল। **—ly,** *adv.* **—ness,** *n.*

lō-qua'-cious (-kwā shŭs), *adj.* **1.** Talkative; garrulous; বাচাল, বহুভাষী; মুখর, বাবদুক, জল্পাক। **2.** (Of birds, water, etc.) Chattering; babbling; কিচ্‌মিচ্ শব্দকারী; কলকলনিনাদী, কুলুকুলুনাদী। **—ly,** *adv.* **—ness, —quac'-i-ty,** *ns.* Talkativeness; বাচালতা, বহুভাষিতা, মুখরতা, ফড়ফড়ানি (*colloq.*)।

lō'-quat (kwăt), *n.* A Chinese and Japanese fruit-tree, naturalized in S. Europe, Australia, etc.; its fruit; লকেট ফলের গাছ; লকেট ফল।

loquitur, (*L.*), *v. i.* (Abbr. *loq.*) He or she speaks; (used as a stage-direction or notice to a reader); সে (পুরুষ বা স্ত্রী) বলিতেছে।

lŏr, lŏr', *n.* (*Vulg.*) A form of lord used as an interjection; (ইতর ভাষায়) প্রভু।

lō-răn'-thŭs, *n.* A large genus of plants; গুল্মবিশেষ।

lŏr'-chă, *n.* A light vessel of European build but rigged like a Chinese Junk; চীনদেশীয় পোতের ন্যায় পাইলমাস্তুলাদিযুক্ত ইয়ুরোপে নির্ম্মিত লঘু তরীবিশেষ।

lŏrd, *n., v. i.* & *t.* **1.** A master; a sovereign; a ruler; a chief; a prince; প্রভু, কর্ত্তা, নাথ; অধিপতি, অধীশ, অধীপ, অধীশ্বর, নরপতি, নরনাথ, নরেশ, নরাধিপ, রাজ্যাধিপ, শাসনকর্ত্তা; নায়ক, নেতা; রাজকুমার, রাজপুত্র। **2.** (*Poet.*) Owner or proprietor; (কবিতায়) স্বামী, অধিকারী। **3.** A magnate in some trade; as, jute *lords*: cotton *lords*; বড় দরের ব্যবসায়ী। **4.** (*Poet.*) A husband; (কবিতায়) স্বামী, পতি, ভর্ত্তা। **5.** (*Cap.*) The Supreme Being; as, *Lord* knows how it came about; Jesus Christ; as, our *Lord*; পরমেশ্বর; যীশুখৃষ্ট। **6.** The proprietor of a feudal land; as, the *lord* of the manor; সামন্তভূম্যধিকারী। **7.** (*Astrol.*) A planet having dominant power or influence; (ফলিতজ্যোতিষ) প্রবল গ্রহ, তুঙ্গগ্রহ। **8.** A titled nobleman; উপাধিধারী সম্ভ্রান্তব্যক্তি। **9.** A British title applied to peers, younger sons of dukes and marquises and the eldest sons of earls; ইংলণ্ডের সম্ভ্রান্তসম্প্রদায়ভুক্ত ব্যক্তি, ডিউক ও মাকুইসগণের জ্যেষ্ঠেতর পুত্র ও আর্লের জ্যেষ্ঠপুত্রের উপাধি। **10.** An honorary title bestowed on certain high officials; as, *Lord* Mayor; কোন কোন উচ্চ রাজপুরুষগণের সম্মানসূচক উপাধি। **11.** (*Pl.,* with *the*) Temporal and spiritual peers of parliament; পার্লেমেণ্ট মহাসভার অভিজাতশ্রেণীর ও উচ্চ যাজকসম্প্রদায়ের সভ্যগণ। ***Verb i.*** To play the lord over; to domineer; প্রভুত্ব করা; আধিপত্য করা, কর্ত্তৃত্ব ফলান। ***Verb t.*** To raise to the peerage; to confer the title of lord upon; অভিজাতসম্প্রদায়ে উন্নীত করা; লর্ড উপাধি প্রদান করা। **Lord'-less,** *adj.* **Lord'-ling,** *n.* A petty lord; ক্ষুদ্র লর্ড উপাধিধারী ব্যক্তি। **Lord-ol'-a-try,** *n.* Adoration or worship of nobility; অভিজাতসম্প্রদায়ের পূজা, অভিজাত পূজা। **Lord High Chancellor**—See under CHANCELLOR. **Lord-in-waiting** — রাণীর সম্ভ্রান্তবংশীয় অনুচর। **Lord Lieuten ant**—আয়র্লণ্ডের রাজপ্রতিনিধি। **Lord Lieutenancy** *n.* **Lords spiritual** — পার্লেমেণ্ট মহাসভার আঢ্য বিভাগের সভ্য, মহাধর্ম্মাধ্যক্ষ (Archbishop) এবং ধর্ম্মাধ্যক্ষগণ (Bishops). **Lords temporal**—পার্লেমেণ্টমহাসভার আঢ্য বিভাগের সম্ভ্রান্তবংশীয় সভ্যগণ। **Drunk as** or **swear like a lord**—Drunk or swear excessively; অতিমাত্রায় মাতাল, অতিমাত্রায় অপভাষা প্রয়োগ করা। **House of Lords**—পার্লেমেণ্ট মহাসভার আঢ্য বিভাগ, লর্ড-সভা। **In the year of our Lord** — খৃষ্টাব্দে। **Lord have mercy, Lord bless me** or **us** or **my soul** or **you**—ঈশ্বর কৃপা করুন। **Lord of Lords**—The Lord; যীশুখৃষ্ট (cf. our মহাপ্রভু)। **Lord of the Bed-chamber**—ইংলণ্ডেশ্বরের সম্ভ্রান্তবংশীয় অনুচর। **Lord's day**—রবিবার। **Lords of creation** — (*Jocul.*) Men as opposed to women; (কৌতুকচ্ছলে) পুরুষ জাতি। **Lord's prayer**—যীশুখৃষ্টের প্রার্থনা। **Lord's supper** -- খৃষ্টের শেষভোজন স্মারক অনুষ্ঠান, অন্তিমভোজনানুষ্ঠান। **Lord's table** — খৃষ্টীয় ধর্ম্মমন্দিরের বেদী; খৃষ্টের শেষ নৈশভোজনস্মারক অনুষ্ঠান। **My lord**—উচ্চ সম্ভ্রান্ত ব্যক্তিদিগের এবং ধর্ম্মাধিকরণের বিচারকদিগের সম্বোধনে ব্যবহৃত শব্দ, দেব, স্বামিন্, প্রভো, নাথ। **To live** or **treat like a lord**—To fare or entertain sumptuously; রাজার হালে থাকা, জাঁকালো ভাবে ভোজ প্রদান করা। **To lord it over**—To domineer over; প্রভুত্ব করা, কর্ত্তৃত্ব করা।

lŏrd'-lȳ, *adj.* **1.** Fit for, or belonging to, a lord; grand; magnificent; সম্ভ্রান্তজনসম্বন্ধীয়, আভিজাতিক; জাঁকাল, জমকাল; সমারোহপূর্ণ। **2.** Haughty; imperious; insolent; disdainful; গর্ব্বিত, দৃপ্ত, প্রভুত্বপরায়ণ, দাম্ভিক; ধৃষ্ট, উদ্ধত; অবজ্ঞাপূর্ণ। **—li-ness,** *n.*

lŏrd'-ship, *n.* **1.** The rank or position of a lord, (with *his, your*); a title applied to a lord (except a duke or archbishop who is called *his* or *your grace*) or a judge; সম্ভ্রান্ত ব্যক্তিদিগের পদ বা পদগৌরব; ডিউক বা আর্কবিশপ ব্যতীত সম্ভ্রান্ত সম্প্রদায়ের ব্যক্তিগণ ও বিচারক সম্পর্কে প্রযোজ্য উপাধি। **2.** Dominion; authority; rule, (with *of* or *over*); অধিকার;

আধিপত্য, স্বামিত্ব, প্রভুত্ব, ঐশ্বর্য্য (এভেলন); শাসন। 3. Domain; estate; জমিদারী, এলাকা; সম্পত্তি, অধিকারভুক্ত স্থান।

lōre, *n.* **1.** (*Archaic*) Learning; erudition; (অপ্রঃ) জ্ঞান, বিদ্যা, শিক্ষা; পাণ্ডিত্য, বৈদুষ্য, বিদ্যাবত্তা। **2.** (*Archaic*) A doctrine; (অপ্রঃ) মত। **3.** The whole body of traditions and facts on a subject; as, a ghost, fairy or folk *lore*; কোন বিষয়ের (প্রচলিত) পরম্পরাগত কথা এবং তথ্যসমূহ।

lōre *n.* The space between the eye and bill in birds, and between the eye and nostril in snakes; (পক্ষীর) চক্ষু এবং চঞ্চুর মধ্যবর্ত্তী এবং সর্পের চক্ষু এবং নাসারন্ধ্রের মধ্যবর্ত্তী স্থান। **Lo′-ral,** *adj.*

lorgnette (*L.*), *n.* **1.** A pair of eye-glasses with a long handle; লম্বা হাতলযুক্ত এক জোড়া চসমা। **2.** An opera-glass (also *lorgnon*); ক্ষুদ্র দূরবীক্ষণ যন্ত্র।

lŏr′-i-cāte, *adj.* (*Zool.*) Having defensive armour of bone, plates, scales, etc.; শঙ্ক বা খোল প্রভৃতি দ্বারা আচ্ছাদিত, শল্কী, খোলকী, বর্ম্মধারী।

lō′-ris, *n.* A small tailless nocturnal climbing Cingalese mammal; সিংহল দ্বীপের ক্ষুদ্র, লাঙ্গুলবিহীন, নিশাচর চতুষ্কর স্তন্যদায়ী জন্তুবিশেষ।

lŏrn, *adj.* (*Poet* & *joc.*) Desolate; forlorn; lonely; (কবিতায় ও কৌতুকচ্ছলে) জনশূন্য; অসহায়, আশ্রয়হীন, অনাথ, নিরাশ্রয়; একাকী।

lŏr′-ry (-i), *n.* **1.** A long flat wagon without sides; পার্শ্বহীন মালগাড়ী। **2.** A truck used in railways and tramways; রেল এবং ট্রামের পার্শ্বহীন মালগাড়ী।

lō′-rȳ, *n.* An oriental bird of the parrot family with brilliant plumage; নানাবর্ণসমুজ্জ্বল পালকশোভিত শুকজাতীয় পক্ষি-বিশেষ।

lose (lôz), *v. t.* & *i.* **1.** To be deprived of; to cease to possess by negligence, accident, etc.; বঞ্চিত হওয়া; হারান, খোয়ান। **2.** To suffer loss by death or final separation of; as, to *lose* a son or friend; হারান। **3.** To miss so as not to be able to find, as one's way; to fail to keep in sight; to fail to follow mentally; as, to *lose* the thread of a discourse; হারাইয়া ফেলা; দৃষ্টিপথে রাখিতে অক্ষম হওয়া; অনুধাবনে বিফল হওয়া। **4.** To spend uselessly (time, opportunities, pains); to waste; নষ্ট করা, কালক্ষয় করা, কালক্ষেপ করা, অপব্যয় করা; অপচয় করা, নাশ করা, উড়াইয়া দেওয়া। **5.** To fail to obtain, catch, see or hear; as, to *lose* one's train; to *lose* a word or remark; পাইতে অক্ষম হওয়া, ধরিতে না পারা, দেখিতে না পাওয়া, শুনিতে না পাওয়া। **6.** To be defeated in; as, to *lose* a game, battle, lawsuit, etc.; to fail to gain or win as a stake; পরাস্ত হওয়া; হারিয়া যাওয়া। **7.** To cause the loss of; to cost; as, it *lost* you your place; হানির কারণ হওয়া; ব্যয় করান। **8.** (*Reflexively* & *Pass.*) To cause to lose one's way or bearings; as, he *lost* himself in the wilds; to be engrossed or obscured (*in*); as, he was *lost* in contemplation; the peak was *lost* in the clouds; দিগ্‌ভ্রান্ত করা, দিশেহারা করা; নিবিষ্ট হওয়া, মগ্ন হওয়া, ডুবিয়া থাকা, ঝাপ্সা হওয়া। **9.** (*Pass.*) To perish; to die or be dead; to disappear; as, the ship and all hands were *lost*; ধ্বংসমুখে পতিত হওয়া; মরা, প্রাণত্যাগ করা, জীবন নষ্ট হওয়া; অদৃশ্য হওয়া, অন্তর্হিত হওয়া। ***Verb i.*** **1.** To suffer loss or detriment; to incur disadvantage; to be the worse off in money or otherwise by transaction etc.; as, the publisher *lost* by it; হানি হওয়া, ক্ষতিভোগ করা; অসুবিধায় পড়া; কোন ব্যাপারে অর্থহানি হওয়া বা অন্য কোন প্রকার ঝঞ্চাটে পড়া। **2.** To suffer loss of military strength; as, the army *lost* heavily; বহু সৈন্যাদি ক্ষয় হওয়া, সামরিক শক্তিহানি হওয়া। **Los′-a-ble,** *adj.* **Losing hazard**—See under HAZARD. **A losing game**—One in which defeat seems inevitable; যে ব্যাপারে পরাজয় সুনিশ্চিত। **A lost soul**—A damned soul; নারকী। **He cannot play a losing game**—He loses heart or temper in it; এই বিষয়ে সে নিরুৎসাহ হয় বা তাহার ধৈর্য্যচ্যুতি হয়। **I have lost my cold**—I have got rid of it; আমার সর্দ্দি আরাম হইয়াছে। **Lost to**—Insensible to; বোধশূন্য, সংজ্ঞাহীন, অচেতন। **To be lost upon**—To fail to influence or draw the attention of; প্রভাব বিস্তার করিতে না পারা, মনোযোগ আকর্ষণ করিতে না পারা। **To lose a patient**—(Of a doctor) Not to be able to save his life; to be left by him for another doctor; রোগীর জীবন রক্ষা করিতে না পারা; রোগী হারান (অর্থাৎ রোগীর অন্য ডাক্তারের চিকিৎসাধীন হওয়া)। **To lose caste**—To be no longer welcomed in respectable houses; ভদ্রসমাজে প্রবেশাধিকার হইতে বঞ্চিত হওয়া। **To lose ground**—To fall behind; to fail to keep position; to decline; পিছু পড়া; হটিয়া যাওয়া; অধোগামী হওয়া। **To lose heart**—To lose courage; সাহস হারান, ভীত হওয়া, নিরুৎসাহ হওয়া। **To lose interest**—(Of a person) To cease to be interested; (of a thing) to cease to interest; (ব্যক্তি সম্পর্কে) কোন বিষয়ে কৌতুহলপ্রদর্শনে বিরত হওয়া; (বস্তু সম্পর্কে) কৌতুহল উদ্রিক্ত না করা। **To lose one's head**—To lose the use of one's good sense or judgment ; হতবুদ্ধি হওয়া, দিশাহারা হওয়া, ভেবাচেকা খাওয়া, মাথা ঘুরিয়া যাওয়া। **To lose one's self**—To become bewildered ; to have the rational powers temporarily suspended ; হতবুদ্ধি হওয়া, আত্মহারা হওয়া। **To lose one's way**—To miss so as not to find it ; পথ হারান। **To lose patience** — To become impatient ; ধৈর্য্যলুপ্ত হওয়া, ধৈর্য্য হারান, অধীর হওয়া। **To lose sight of** — To disappear from view ; দৃষ্টিপথের বহির্ভূত হওয়া। **To lose temper** — To be angry ; রাগিয়া উঠা, রাগান্বিত হওয়া, চটিয়া উঠা। **To lose the day**—To be defeated ; পরাজিত হওয়া, পরাস্ত হওয়া।

lö'-sĕl, *n.* (*Archaic*) A worthless person ; a profligate ; a ne'er-do-well ; নিষ্কর্ম্মালোক ; লম্পট, ব্যভিচারী ; হতচ্ছাড়া।

lōs'-ĕr, *n.* **1.** One who loses ; ক্ষতিগ্রস্ত ব্যক্তি । **2.** A person or horse that loses a race etc. ; যে ব্যক্তি বা ঘোড়া দৌড় প্রভৃতিতে হারিয়া থাকে।

lŏss, *n.* **1.** The act of losing or the state of being lost ; ক্ষয়, নাশ। **2.** A person, thing or amount lost ; হারান জিনিষ, হৃত দ্রব্য, ক্ষতির পরিমাণ। **3.** Detriment or disadvantage resulting from loss ; ক্ষতি, লোকসান, হানি। **4.** A failure to win or gain ; as, *loss* of a race or battle ; পরাজয়। **Loss of life**—প্রাণনাশ, প্রাণবিয়োগ, প্রাণহানি। **To be at a loss**—To be puzzled ; to be in a state of hesitation or uncertainty ; দিশেহারা হওয়া ; কিংকর্ত্তব্যবিমূঢ় হওয়া, হতভম্ব হওয়া।

lŏst, *adj.* **1.** Not to be found ; missing ; as, a *lost* book or sheep ; হৃত ; হারানো। **2.** No longer held or possessed ; as, a *lost* limb ; নষ্ট। **3.** Not gained or won ; as, a *lost* battle ; পরাজয়প্রাপ্ত। **4.** Merged or engrossed (*in*) ; as, to be *lost* in meditation ; নিবিষ্ট, মগ্ন, তদ্গতচিত্ত। **5.** Wasted ; squandered ; অপব্যয়িত ; অপচয়প্রাপ্ত। **6.** Ruined or destroyed, either physically or morally ; as, a ship *lost* at sea : a *lost* soul ; বিনষ্ট, নষ্ট, ধ্বংসপ্রাপ্ত। **7.** Insensible ; as, *lost* to shame ; অনুভবশক্তিহীন, বোধহীন, সাড়াশূন্য। **Lost to all sense of shame**—Shameless ; নির্লজ্জ। **Lost to sight**—No longer visible ; অন্তর্হিত, দৃষ্টিপথ-বহির্ভূত।

lŏt, *n.* & *v. t.* **1.** Fate which falls to one ; fortune ; condition : ভাগ্য, অদৃষ্ট, দৈবদশা ; নিয়তি, কপাল ; অবস্থা। **2.** Anything (as a die, pebble, ball or slip of paper) used in determining a question by the chance fall or choice of one or more of them ; as, to cast or draw *lots* ; যাহা কিছু দ্বারা দৈবনির্দ্দেশ করা যায়, ভাগ্যনির্দ্দেশক কোন বস্তু। **3.** This method of deciding fate ; choice resulting from it ; as, to decide by *lot* : the *lot* fell upon me ; ঐরূপে ভাগ্যনির্দ্দেশ ; ঐরূপ নির্দ্দেশের ফলে যাহা নির্ব্বাচিত হয়। **4.** That which falls to a person by lot ; a share ; "Neither part nor *lot* in this matter" ; যাহা কোন লোকের ভাগ্যে পড়ে ; হিস্যা, অংশ, ভাগ। **5.** A tax, duty, etc. ; as, scot and *lot* ; কর, শুল্ক, প্রভৃতি। **6.** A plot or allotment of land ; as, a building *lot* in a city ; স্বতন্ত্র ভূমিখণ্ড, এক কিতা জমি, ভূমিখণ্ড। **7.** An article or set of articles offered separately at sale ; an item at auction ; as, a *lot* of stationery ; পৃথগ্‌ভাবে নীলামে বিক্রয়ার্থ বস্তু বা বস্তুসমূহ, এক লাটে বিক্রয়ের জন্য বস্তুসমূহ ; নীলামের এক দফা জিনিষ। **8.** A number of persons or things of the same kind or somehow associated ; একজাতীয় বা কোনরূপ সম্বন্ধবিশিষ্ট ব্যক্তি বা বস্তু সমূহ। **9.** A considerable quantity or number ; বহুসংখ্যা বা পরিমাণ। *Verb t.* To divide by lots ; as, to *lot* out land : to *lot* goods for the market ; ভূমি বা দ্রব্যাদি বিক্রয়ার্থ পৃথক পৃথক করা। **A bad lot**—A disreputable or vicious person ; দুশ্চরিত্র ব্যক্তি, পামর, দুরাচার, দুর্জ্জন। **The lot** — The whole number or quantity ; সমস্তটা, সবগুলি। **To cast or draw lots** — To throw dice or use some other contrivance to settle a matter ; পাশা ফেলিয়া ভাগ্য স্থির করা, গুলি বাঁট করা। **To lot on** or **upon**—(*Colloq. U. S.*) To reckon upon ; to expect with pleasure ; (মার্কিন যুক্তরাজ্যের চলিত ভাষায়) নির্ভর করা, ভরসা বাঁধা, মুখ চাহিয়া থাকা ; কোন কিছু পাওয়া যাইবে বলিয়া নিশ্চয় আশা করা। **To throw** or **cast in one's lot with**—See CAST.

lōth, *adj.* See LOATH.

Lō-thā'-rĭ-ō, *n.* (A character in Rowe's *Fair Penitent*) A seducer of females ; a libertine or rake ; যে ব্যক্তি স্ত্রীলোককে ভুলাইয়া কুপথগামিনী করে ; লম্পট, কামুক, ইন্দ্রিয়পরায়ণ।

lō'-tion, *n.* **1.** A liquid preparation applied externally to heal wound, to cure skin disease or to clear complexion etc. ; বাহ্যপ্রয়োগার্থ তরল ঔষধ, প্রোত (ঠাকুরঃ), ধাবন (হঃ চঃ), অভ্যঞ্জন (সাঃ পঃ)। **2.** (*Slang*) An alcoholic drink ; (ইতর ভাষায়) আসব।

lŏt'-tĕr-y̆, *n.* **1.** A scheme for distributing prizes by lot or chance among purchasers of tickets ; চিঠি খেলা, সুরতি খেলা, ভাগ্য-পরীক্ষার খেলা। **2.** (*Fig.*) An affair of chance ; (লক্ষণায়) ভাগ্যপরীক্ষার ব্যাপার। **Lottery-wheel** — ক্ষুদ্র পেটকসমন্বিত চক্র বিশেষ—যাহা ঘুরাইয়া টিকিটের অনুরূপ সংখ্যাচিহ্নিত চিরকুট সকলের ভাঁজ নষ্ট হয়।

lŏt′-tō, *n.* A game of chance played with numbered disks and cards ; সংখ্যা-চিহ্নিত চাকতি ও তাসের সাহায্যে একপ্রকার স্বরতি খেলা।
lō′-tŭs, *n.* **1.** (*Gk. legend*) A plant, the fruit of which was fabled to cause forgetfulness of the past and distaste for active life ; (গ্রীক উপকথায়) একপ্রকার বৃক্ষ—যাহার ফলভক্ষণে লোকের

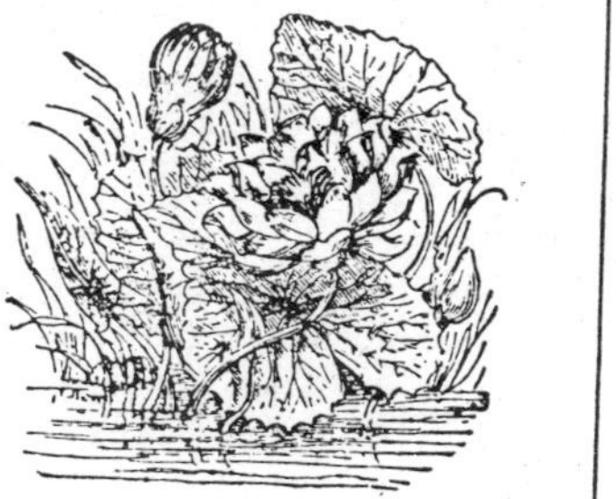

Lotus.

গত জীবনের স্মৃতি বিলুপ্ত হইত এবং কর্ম্মে অপ্রবৃত্তি জন্মিত। **2.** A name for the Egyptian or Asiatic water-lily ; পদ্ম, কমল, পঙ্কজ, অরবিন্দ, নলিন, সরসিজ, সরোজ, জলজ, নীরজ, বারিজ, বনজ, সরসীরুহ, শতদল, রাজীব (red), কোকনদ (red), সরোরুহ, কুবলয় (blue), ইন্দীবর (blue), উৎপল (blue), পুণ্ডরীক (white), সহস্রপত্র, শতপত্র, কুশেশয়, তামরস, পঙ্কেরুহ, পুষ্কর, অম্বুরুহ, অম্বুজ, অম্ভোরুহ, ইন্দিরালয়, অম্ভোজ, বিসপ্রসূন, রমাপ্রিয়, শ্রীপর্ণ [The plant as distinguished from the flower, also assemblage of lotus flowers], নলিনী, মৃণালিনী, সরোজিনী, কমলিনী, পদ্মিনী। **3.** (*Bot., cap.*) A large genus of plants ; (উদ্ভিদ-বিদ্যা) পদ্মজাতীয় উদ্ভিদ। **Lotus-eater**—A person given to indolent enjoyment or luxurious dreaminess ; পদ্মভুক্‌, আলস্যপরায়ণ ব্যক্তি, সুখতন্দ্রালস ব্যক্তি। **Lotus eating,** *adj.* & *n.* **Lotus-film**—পদ্মের মৃণাল। **Lotus-land**—ভোগের দেশ, অলস আমোদপ্রমোদের দেশ, বিলাসভূমি। **Lotus-stalk**—পদ্মনাল।

loud (lowd), *adj.* & *adv.* **1.** Having, or making, a great sound ; উচ্চনিনাদী, মহাধ্বনিক, মহাধ্বনিকর, মহানাদী। **2.** Strikingly audible, as a sound, noise, etc. ; ভীমনাদী, উচ্চরবকারী, তীব্রগর্জ্জনকারী। **3.** Clamorous ; boisterous ; noisy ; চীৎকারকারী ; কোলাহলকারী, কলরবকারী ; কোলাহলপূর্ণ। **4.** (Of colour, dress, pattern, manners) Obtrusive ; ostentatious ; showy ; (বর্ণ, পরিচ্ছদ, নমুনা, রীতিনীতি সম্বন্ধে) নেত্রাকর্ষক ; আড়ম্বরপূর্ণ ; জাঁকজমকপূর্ণ, চটকদার। ***Adv.*** Loudly ; as, do not talk so *loud* ; উচ্চৈঃস্বরে, উচ্চরবে, মহাশব্দে। **Loud′-en,** *v. i.* To become loud ; উচ্চনিনাদী হওয়া। **Loud′-ish,** *adj.* **Loud′-ly,** *adv.* With great sound or noise ; clamorously ; মহারবে, উচ্চৈঃস্বরে, চেঁচাইয়া ; কোলাহল সহকারে। **Loud′-ness,** *n.*
lough (lŏk), *n.* (*Anglo-Irish*) A lake ; an arm of the sea ; (*loch* শব্দের আইরিশ আকার) হ্রদ; সাগর-শাখা।
louis-d'or, (*F.*) *n.* A French gold coin of about 20 francs from Louis XIII to Louis XVI ; ফরাসী স্বর্ণমুদ্রা বিশেষ—মূল্য ২০ ফ্রাঙ্ক।
lounge (lownj), *v. i., t.* & *n.* **1.** To act or move lazily ; to saunter ; অলসভাবে ঘুরিয়া বেড়ান; বেড়াইয়া বেড়ান, বৃথা ঘুরিয়া বেড়ান। **2.** To spend time lazily ; অলসভাবে সময় কাটান। **3.** To loll ; to recline ; অলসভাবে হেলান দেওয়া ; ঠেস দেওয়া, ঠেস দিয়া বসা। ***Verb t.*** To idle away, as time ; আলস্যে কাটান। ***Noun.*** **1.** An idle gait or stroll ; a spell of saunter or lounging ; অলসগতি ; অলসভাবে ভ্রমণ। **2.** A place of lounging ; অলসভাবে বেড়াইবার স্থান। **3.** A sofa or deep chair ; একপ্রকার আরাম কেদারা। **Loung′-er,** *n.* **Loung′-ing-ly,** *adv.*
louse (lows), *n.* (*Pl.* LICE) A parasitic insect infesting human hair and skin ; উকুণ, উৎকুণ, কেশকীট, যূক। **Lous′-i-ness,** *n.* **Lous′-y,** *adj.*
lout (lowt), *n.* A clown or awkward fellow ; a bumpkin ; কদাকার অসভ্য ব্যক্তি, চাষা ; নীচলোক, পাড়াগেঁয়ে লোক। **Lout′-ish,** *adj.* **Lout′-ish-ly,** *adv.*
lout (lowt), *v. i.* **1.** (*Archaic*) To bow or make obeisance ; (অপ্র:) প্রণাম করা, প্রণিপাত করা।
lou′-vêr (lô-), **—vre** (-vêr), *ns.* **1.** An open turret on roofs, to allow the smoke or air in ; ছাদের ধূমনির্গম বা বায়ুপ্রবেশপথ। **2.** An arrangement of boards or slips of glass to admit air or exclude rain, (also *louver-boards*) ; গৃহের ভিতর বৃষ্টির জল প্রবেশ না করিতে পারে অথচ বাতাসের চলাচল হইতে পারে তদুপযোগী কাষ্ঠ বা কাচফলকরচিত ব্যবস্থাবিশেষ। **—vered,** *adj.* **Louver window**—A window with louver boards (see LOUVER 2.)
lov′-a-ble (lŭv-ă-bl), *adj.* Worthy of love ; amiable ; প্রীতিপ্রদ, প্রীতিজনক ; প্রেয়, প্রিয়, কমনীয়, মনোরম। **—bly,** *adv.* **—ness,** *n.*
lov′-āge (lŭv-), *n.* A kind of herb ; যবাণী গাছ।
love (lŭv), *n.* **1.** Warm affection ; fond attachment ; strong liking (*of, for, to* or *towards* persons and *for* or *to* thing) ; স্নেহ, ভালবাসা, আসক্তি ; অনুরক্তি, অনুরাগ ; প্রীতি ; প্রেম, মমতা, প্রণয়, প্রীতিভাব, প্রেমভাব, স্নেহভাব। **2.** Sexual affection or passion or desire ; relation between sweethearts ; a love affair ; as, *loves* of gods ; কাম, রাগ, শৃঙ্গার, শৃঙ্গাররস, রতিভাব, মদন ; প্রেমিকপ্রেমিকার সম্বন্ধ, স্ত্রীপুরুষপ্রেম, স্ত্রীপুরুষের প্রেম ভাব ; প্রণয়ব্যাপার। **3.** (*Cap.*) Cupid, the god of love, (a representation of Cupid or of naked winged child) ; প্রণয়দেবতা, রতিপতি, পুষ্পধন্বা, কন্দর্প, স্মর, কামদেব, মার, মন্মথ, প্রদ্যুম্ন, মীনকেতন,

অনঙ্গ, মনসিজ, অতনু। 4. Beloved one ; a sweetheart ; প্রণয়পাত্র, প্রণয়াস্পদ, প্রেমাস্পদ ; প্রণয়ী, প্রেমিক, প্রেমিকা। 5. (*Colloq.*) A delightful person or a pretty thing ; as, he is an old *love* ; (চলিতভাষায়) প্রিয়জন, প্রিয়বস্তু। 6. (*Games*) No score ; nothing ; nil ; as, he won the match by three sets to *love* ; (ক্রীড়ায়) কোন জয়াঙ্ক নয় ; কিছুই নয় ; শূন্য। **Love′-less,** *adj.* Unloving ; unloved ; unattractive ; স্নেহমমতাশূন্য ; প্রেমহীন ; অসুন্দর। **Love′-less-ly,** *adv.* **Love′-less-ness,** *n.* **Love′-y,** *n.* **Love′-wor-thy,** *adj.* Worthy of love ; প্রেমযোগ্য। **Love′-wor-thi-ness,** *n.* **Love-affair**—Amour ; প্রণয়ব্যাপার। **Love all**—(*Sports*) Neither side has scored ; ক্রীড়ায় কোন পক্ষই জয়াঙ্ক লাভ করিতে পারে নাই। **Love apple**—বিলাতী বেগুন। **Love-begotten** — জারজ। **Love-bird**—শুক জাতীয় ক্ষুদ্র পক্ষিবিশেষ—ইহার সাথীর মৃত্যু হইলে ইহা শোকে দিন দিন শীর্ণ হইয়া প্রাণত্যাগ করে। **Love-charm**—বশীকরণের ঔষধ, বশীকরণের চূর্ণ। **Love-child** — জারজ সন্তান। **Love-game**—যে ক্রীড়ায় পরাজিত ব্যক্তি কোন জয়াঙ্ক লাভ করে নাই। **Love-in-a-mist**—Fennel-flower ; মৌরীর ফুল। **Love-in-idleness**—Heart's ease ; আরাম, মনের সুখ। **Love-juice**—প্রণয়বর্দ্ধক রস। **Love-knot**—প্রণয়চিহ্নস্বরূপ গ্রন্থি, প্রণয়গ্রন্থি, গাঁইট-চূড়া। **Love-letter** — প্রণয়পত্র, প্রীতিপত্র, প্রেমলিপি, প্রেমপত্র, মদনলেখ (শকুঃ), অনঙ্গলেখ (ঐ)। **Love-lock**—কর্ণপ্রান্তে লম্বিত কেশগুচ্ছ [রাজ্ঞী এলিজাবেথ ও প্রথম জেম্‌সের সময়ে ফুলবাবুগণ ঐরূপ চুল রাখিত।] **Love-lorn**—Pinining with love; deserted by one's lover; প্রণয়পীড়িত, প্রেমশীল ; প্রেমিকপরিত্যক্ত। **Love-making**—Making of love ; প্রেম করণ। **Love-marriage** — ভালবাসা হইতে বিবাহ, প্রিয়বিবাহ, প্রীতিবিবাহ। **Love-shaft**—মদনবাণ, স্মরশর, কন্দর্পবাণ, মদনশর। **Love-sick** — বিরহরোগী, কামবিহ্বল, প্রণয়-পীড়িত, কামার্ত্ত, মন্মথমথিত। **Love-song**—প্রেমসঙ্গীত, প্রণয়সঙ্গীত। **Love-story**—প্রেমকাহিনী। **Love-token**—প্রণয়চিহ্ন, প্রেমনিদর্শন। **Love-tryst**—প্রেমাভিসার (গীতাঞ্জঃ)। **My love**—প্রেয়সি, আমার প্রাণ, প্রিয়তম, প্রাণেশ্বর, প্রাণবল্লভ, প্রাণপতি। **A labour of love** — See LABOUR. **A love-match**—প্রণয়ঘটিত বিবাহ, প্রীতি-বিবাহ। **For love or money**—By any means ; as, he cannot get it *for love or money* ; যে কোন উপায়ে। **For the love of**—For the sake, or in name, of esp. in adjurations, জন্য, খাতিরে, নামে। **In love**—Enamoured ; প্রেমবিহ্বল, প্রেমমুগ্ধ। **In love with**—Enamoured of ; fond of (pursuit, thing, etc.) ; প্রণয়মুগ্ধ, প্রেমাসক্ত ; অনুরাগী, অনুরক্ত। **Love in a cottage**—Marriage on insufficient means ; দরিদ্র অবস্থায় বিবাহ। **There is no love lost between them** — They dislike each other ; (*obs.*) they love one another sincerely ; তাহারা পরস্পরকে অপ্রীতি করে ; (অপ্রঃ) তাহারা পরস্পরকে অকপটচিত্তে ভালবাসে। **To give love to**—To convey affectionate message to ; প্রীতিসম্ভাষণ প্রদান করা, ভালবাসা জানান। **To make love to**—To court ; to woo ; কাহারও প্রীতি লাভের চেষ্টা করা; বিবাহের উদ্দেশ্যে প্রেমোপাসনা করা। **To play for love**—To play for the pleasure of it, not for stakes ; খেলার জন্য খেলা—কোনরূপ বাজির টাকা লাভের জন্য নয়।

love (lŭv), *v. t.* & *i.* **1.** To bear love to ; to be in love with ; to be fond of ; as, to *love* one's children : to *love* one's country ; ভালবাসা থাকা, স্নেহ থাকা ; প্রেম হওয়া ; অনুরাগী হওয়া। **2.** To delight in ; to be pleased with ; to be addicted to ; আনন্দিত হওয়া ; সন্তুষ্ট হওয়া ; আসক্ত হওয়া। ***Verb i.*** To be in love ; অনুরক্ত হওয়া। **Lord love you**—An exclamation of surprise at a person's mistake ; হরিবোল।

Love′-lāce (lŭv-), *n.* A well-mannered libertine ; an accomplished rake ; (a character in Richardson's *Clarissa Harlowe*) ; নাগর ; বিদগ্ধ।

love′-lȳ (lŭv-), *adj.* Charmingly beautiful ; মনোমুগ্ধকর, সুরম্য, মনোজ্ঞ, অভিরাম, লাবণ্যবান, লাবণ্যশালী, ললিত, মনোরম, মুগ্ধ, সুভগ, সুচারু, সুদর্শন, [cf. মুগ্ধবধূ (রঃ)।] **2.** (*Colloq.*) Delightful ; very pleasing ; intensely amusing ; (চলিত ভাষায়) ললিত, কমনীয়, কান্ত ; রমনীয়, সুমধুর ; মনোমদ। **–li-ly,** *adv.* **–li-ness,** *n.* The quality of being lovely ; রমনীয়তা, সুচারুতা, মাধুরী, কান্তি, কমনীয়তা, লাবণ্য, লালিত্য, মনোহারিতা, প্রিয়করত্ব, মুগ্ধত্ব।

lov′-êr (lŭv), *n.* **1.** A female's sweetheart or wooer ; (*pl.*) a pair in love ; প্রেমিক, রমণ, চিত্তচোর, প্রণয়াস্পদ (উজ্জ্বলঃ), প্রণয়ী, বঁধু, প্রিয় কান্ত, নায়ক, দয়িত, বল্লভ ; (বহুবচন) প্রেমিকপ্রেমিকা, প্রণয়ীযুগল। **2.** A paramour or gallant ; উপপতি বা উপপত্নী, নাগর, জার। **3.** One who has a strong liking for a thing, action or idea ; as, a *lover* of books ; ভক্ত, অনুরাগী, পক্ষপাতী। **–less, –like,** *adj.* **–ly,** *adj.* & *adv.* **Lover's knot** — Same as LOVE-KNOT which see. **Journey of a lover**—অভিসার (গীতাঞ্জঃ)।

lov′-ing (lŭv-), *adj.* **1.** Affectionate ; fond ; প্রেমময়, ভক্তিপূর্ণ, সস্নেহ ; প্রেমপূর্ণ, স্নেহময়, সপ্রেম। **2.** Manifesting, or proceeding from, love ; amorous ; স্নেহব্যঞ্জক, প্রেমব্যঞ্জক, প্রণয়জাত ; কামজ। **–ly,** *adv.* **–ness,** *n.* **Loving cup**—দুই বা ততোধিক হাতল বিশিষ্ট কারুকার্য্যশোভিত সুবৃহৎ পানপাত্র-বিশেষ। **Our loving**

subjects — A formula of royal proclamation ; আমাদের প্রিয় প্রজাবৃন্দ। [রাজকীয় ঘোষণাপত্রে প্রজার সম্পর্কে ব্যবহৃত বাক্য।] **Your loving friend etc.**—A formula in concluding letters ; তোমার প্রিয়বন্ধু (পত্রের শেষে ব্যবহৃত হয়)।

low (lö), *adj.* & *adv.* **1.** Not high, tall or elevated ; depressed ; as, *low* ground ; অনুচ্চ, অনুন্নত ; নীচু, নিম্ন। **2.** Not rising to the usual height ; as, *low* stature : *low* forehead ; খর্ব্ব, খাটো। **3.** Near the horizon ; as, the sun is *low* at four O' clock in winter ; অস্তমান, অস্তাচলচূড়াবলম্বী, চক্রবালসন্নিহিত। **4.** Not much above sea-level ; as, *low* tide ; সাগরপৃষ্ঠ হইতে অধিক উপরে নয়। **5.** Beneath the ordinary value ; cheap ; as, *low* price ; *low* wages ; স্বল্পমূল্য ; সুলভ, সস্তা। **6.** Not shrill ; not loud ; as, a *low* note or voice ; মৃদু ; অনুচ্চ, ক্ষীণ। **7.** Recent ; as, belongs to a *lower* date ; আধুনিক। **8.** Numerically small ; as, a *low* number ; ক্ষুদ্র, স্বল্প। **9.** Depressed ; dejected ; as, *low* spirits ; বিমর্ষ ; বিষণ্ণ, খিন্ন, উদাসীন, অবসন্ন, বিমনাঃ। **10.** Humble in rank or position ; as, the *lower* classes ; হীন, নিম্ন। **11.** Mean ; vulgar ; base ; degraded ; as, a person of *low* mind ; নীচ ; গ্রাম্য ; অধম, অপকৃষ্ট, জঘন্য, হীন ; ইতর, হেয়, অবজ্ঞেয়। **12.** Not sublime ; commonplace ; little civilized ; as, a person of *low* mind ; গরিমাহীন ; সাধারণ ; অনুন্নত। **13.** Moderate ; not intense ; as, a *low* fever ; মৃদু ; সামান্য, অল্প। **14.** Nearly exhausted or empty, as, a liquid, receptacle or (*fig.*) purse or money ; শূন্যপ্রায়। **15.** Not rich or nourishing ; plain ; as, *low* diet ; মসলাযুক্ত বা পুষ্টিকর নয় ; সাদাসিধা। **16.** Of small degree ; as, a *low* temperature or power ; মৃদু। **17.** Holding low church doctrines ; নিম্নসংঘের মতাবলম্বী। **18.** Deficient in vital energy ; weak ; as, made *low* by sickness ; নিস্তেজ, নির্জ্জীব ; দুর্ব্বল, ক্ষীণ। *Adv.* **1.** In or to mean or low position ; as, it *hangs* low ; নিম্নে, নীচে। **2.** Humbly ; নম্রভাবে, বিনীত ভাবে, বিনম্র ভাবে, দীন ভাবে, মৃদু ভাবে, শান্ত ভাবে। **3.** On low diet ; লঘু পথ্যে। **4.** With a depressed voice or tone ; মৃদুস্বরে, চুপে চুপে, অনুচ্চস্বরে। **5.** In subjection, poverty or disgrace ; as, to be brought *low* by oppression ; হীনাবস্থায়, অবনতির দশায়। **6.** For small stakes ; as, to play *low* ; সামান্য পণ রাখিয়া। **7.** Late ; as, find it as *low* as the 19th century ; পরবর্ত্তী কালে। **Low'-ish,** *adj.* Somewhat low ; কতকটা নীচ। **Low'-ness,** *n.* State of being low ; অনুচ্চতা, নিম্নতা, হীনতা, লঘুত্ব, খর্ব্বতা। **Low-born**—Of mean birth ; নীচকুলোদ্ভব, অন্ত্যজ, হীনবংশজাত, নীচকুলজাত, হীনকুলপ্রসূত, অবরবর্ণজ। **Low-bred** — অন্ত্যজ, নীচ, ইতর। **Low-Church**—ইংলণ্ডীয় ধর্ম্মসংঘের অন্তর্ভুক্ত সম্প্রদায়বিশেষ—এই সম্প্রদায়ে ধর্ম্মাধ্যক্ষ (bishop) ও অন্যান্য পুরোহিতদিগের ক্ষমতা, দীক্ষাদি সংস্কারের প্রকৃতিসিদ্ধ গুণ এবং ক্রিয়ানুষ্ঠানাদির বিশেষ গৌরব করা হয় না। **Low comedy**—যে মিলনান্ত নাটকের বিষয় বা রচনাপ্রণালী প্রহসনের কাছাকাছি হইয়া থাকে। **Low-diet**—লঘুপথ্য। **Low down**—*adv.* Far down ; in mean or ungenerous way ; অনেক ভাটিতে, অনেক নীচে ; হীনভাবে, অনুদারভাবে। **Low dress**—যে পোষাক পরিলে কণ্ঠ, স্কন্ধ ও বক্ষের কিয়দংশ দৃষ্ট হয়। **Lower boy**—নীচের শ্রেণীর ছাত্র। **Lower class**—(*Noun*) নিম্নশ্রেণী, অনুন্নতশ্রেণী। (*Adj.*) Pertaining to persons of the humble rank ; নিম্নশ্রেণীর, অনুন্নতশ্রেণীর। **Lower-critic**—One of the verbal or textual kind ; শাব্দিক সমালোচক। (Sc *Lower criticism, n.*) **Lower-lip**—নিম্নোষ্ঠ। **Lower propensities**—ইতর প্রবৃত্তি, নিকৃষ্ট প্রবৃত্তি। **Lower world**—The earth ; nether world ; মর্ত্ত্যভূমি, পৃথিবী ; অধোলোক, নরক, পাতাল। **Lowland**—*n.* & *adj.* (*Usu. pl.*) Low-lying country ; নিম্নভূমি, নিম্নদেশ, সমতট (সাঃ পঃ)। (*Adj.*) Of, relating to, or in, this ; নিম্নভূমিসম্বন্ধীয়। **Lowland** — *adj.* Of, relating to, or in the Low-lands of Scotland ; স্কটলণ্ডের নিম্নভূমিসম্বন্ধীয়, স্কটলণ্ডের নিম্নভূমিতে স্থিত। **Low-Lands**—স্কটলণ্ডদেশের অপেক্ষাকৃত নিম্নভূমি। **Low-latitudes**—বিষুবরেখার নিকটবর্ত্তী অক্ষাংশসমূহ। **Low life**—Humble life ; হীনজীবন। **Low-lived** — হীনজীবনযাপনকারী। **Low-minded**—Mean-hearted ; নীচমনাঃ, হীনচেতাঃ। **Low-pitch**—Low key or tone ; slight angular elevation of a roof ; নিম্ন গ্রাম ; ছাদের ঈষৎ কোণাকৃতি উচ্চতা। **Low-pitched,** *adj.* **Low relief**—See RELIEF. **Low-spirited** — Dejected ; বিমর্ষ, বিষণ্ণ, সবিষাদ, দুর্ম্মনাঃ, উদাসবৃত্তি। **Low spirits**—Dejected spirits ; বিমর্ষভাব, উৎসাহশূন্যতা, উদ্যমবিহীনতা। **Low Sunday, Week**—ঈষ্টার পর্ব্বের অব্যবহিত পরবর্ত্তী রবিবার বা সপ্তাহ। **Low tide** or **water**—ভাটারকালীন সর্ব্বনিম্ন জলসীমা, পুরা ভাঁটা ; পুরা ভাঁটার কাল। **Low-water mark** — Lowest point reached by ebb-tide, (also *fig.*) ; ভাঁটার সময় জল যে দাগ পর্য্যন্ত নামে ; (লক্ষণায়) ভাঁটার অবস্থা [cf. তাহার যৌবনে ভাঁটা পড়িয়াছে]। **At lowest**—To mention the least possible amount etc. ; কম পক্ষেও। **High and low**—Every one ; ভদ্রেতর সকলেই, আপামরসাধারণ। **I have low opinion of him**—I do not estimate highly ; তাহার সম্বন্ধে আমি বড় উচ্চ মত পোষণ করি না। **In low**

water — Out of funds etc.; অর্থসঙ্কটে, দীন অবস্থায়। **To bring low** — To depress; to reduce in health, wealth or position; হতোৎসাহ করা, অবনত করা; হৃতগৌরব করা, হীন করা। **To collar low**—(*Foot-ball*) To catch at or below waist; (পাদগোলক ক্রীড়ায়) কোমরে বা কোমরের নীচে ধরা। **To lay low**—To overthrow; ধ্বংস করা, উচ্ছন্ন করা। To inter; সমাধিস্থ করা, সমাহিত করা, গোর দেওয়া। **To lie low**—To be prostrate or dead; to crouch; to keep quiet or hidden; সটান হইয়া পড়া, মরা; গুটি-সুটি মারা; চুপ করিয়া থাকা, লুকাইয়া থাকা। **To play it low down** or **low upon**—To treat scurvily; ইতরজনোচিত ব্যবহার করা।

low (lö), *v. i., t.* & *n.* To make the loud noise as of a cow or ox; to bellow; হাম্বারব করা; ষাঁড়ের মত গর্জ্জন করা। ***Verb t.*** To say or utter *forth* with lowing sound; ষাঁড়ের মত চেঁচাইয়া বলা। ***Noun.*** A cow's cry; গাভীর ডাক, হাম্বা রব।

low'-ĕr (lö-), *v. t.* & *i.* **1.** To let down or bring down; as, to *lower* a sail or boat; নামাইয়া দেওয়া, নামান, নোয়ান। **2.** To diminish the height of; as, to *lower* a wall; নীচু করা। **3.** To reduce or humble; to degrade; as, to *lower* one's ambition; নীচু করা, খর্ব্ব করা, হেঁট করা; অবনত করা। **4.** To diminish (price etc.); হ্রাস করা, কমান। **5.** To reduce in intensity, strength, pitch, etc.; শক্তি হ্রাস করা, তেজোহানি করা, শক্তিক্ষয় করা, প্রশমিত করা। **6.** To reduce the bodily condition of; as, a *lowering* diet; কৃশ করা। ***Verb i.*** **1.** To sink; to descend; to slope downwards; হ্রাস হওয়া; অবনত হওয়া; ঢালু হওয়া। **2.** To bring down sail etc.; to let down obat etc.; পাইল নামান; জাহাজ হইতে ডিঙ্গি নামান। **3.** (Of price) To become low; (দর) নামা। **4.** To become low in intensity, pitch, etc.; (তীব্রতা) হ্রাস পাওয়া।

low'-ĕr, lour (lowr), *v. i.* & *n.* **1.** To frown or scowl; to look sullen (*on, upon,* at); ভ্রূকুটী করা, ভ্রূভঙ্গী করা, চোক পাকান, রোষকষায়িত লোচনে দৃষ্টিপাত করা; অপ্রসন্ন দেখান। **2.** (Of clouds, sky, storm) To be dark and threatening; ঘনঘটাচ্ছন্ন হওয়া, মেঘাচ্ছন্ন হওয়া। ***Noun.*** **1.** Scowl; a frowning; ভ্রূকুটী, রোষকটাক্ষ; চোকপাকানি। **2.** Gloominess of sky, aspect of weather, etc.; মেঘাচ্ছন্নতা, ঘনঘটাচ্ছন্নতা। **—ing,** *adj.* **1.** Frowning; রোষকষায়িত, ভ্রূকুটি-কুটিল। **2.** Dark and threatening; ঘনঘটাচ্ছন্ন। **—ing-ly,** *adv.*

low'-lȳ (lö-), *adj.* & *adv.* Humble; modest; unpretending; বিনম্র, বিনীত; বিনয়ী, নম্র; নিরভিমান। ***Adv.*** In a low manner; বিনীতভাবে, শান্তভাবে, বিনম্রভাবে। **—li-ly,** *adv.* **—li-ness,** *n.*

loy'-ăl, *adj.* & *n.* **1.** Faithful to duty, love, etc.; কর্ত্তব্যপরায়ণ, অনুরক্ত, অনুগত, বিশ্বস্ত, আস্থাবান, নিষ্ঠ। **2.** Faithful to sovereign, government or mother-country; unswerving in allegiance; রাজভক্ত, স্বদেশভক্ত, প্রভুভক্ত, স্বপ্রভুভক্ত; একনিষ্ঠ। **3.** Of, pertaining to, or showing, loyalty; রাজভক্তিসম্পর্কীয়, রাজভক্তিসূচক। ***Noun.*** A person who remains loyal in time of disaffection; রাজ্যবিপ্লবকালে যে ব্যক্তির রাজভক্তি অক্ষুণ্ণ থাকে। **—ism,** *n.* **—ist,** *n.* A person who adheres to his sovereign or constituted authority; রাজভক্ত প্রজা। **—ize,** *v. t.* To make loyal; রাজভক্ত করা। **—ly,** *adv.* Faithfully; বিশ্বস্তভাবে। **—ty,** *n.* State of being loyal; রাজভক্তি, অনুরাগ, বিশ্বস্ততা, নিষ্ঠা, আনুগত্য।

lŏz'-enge (-ĕnj), *n.* **1.** A figure of four equal sides with two acute and two obtuse angles; a diamond figure especially as a bearing in heraldry; দুইটী সূক্ষ্ম এবং দুইটী স্থূলকোণ বিশিষ্ট সমচতুর্ভুজ ক্ষেত্র; রুহিতনের আকার চিহ্ন, বিশেষতঃ কুলচিহ্ন। **2.** A small cake of flavoured sugar, medicine, meat-essence, etc. to be dissolved in mouth; সুরভিত চিনি, ঔষধ, মাংসসার প্রভৃতি দ্বারা প্রস্তুত সুমিষ্ট চোষ্য, দ্রব্যবিশেষ, লজঞ্জুস। **3.** A small diamond-shaped pane of glass; রুহিতনের আকার জানালার কাচ। **4.** A diamond-shaped facet of cut gem; কর্ত্তিত মণির বরফির আকার পল। **—enged,** *adj.* **1.** Framed into lozenge; বরফির আকারে গঠিত। **2.** With lozenge panes; (দরজা জানালা প্রভৃতি) বরফির আকার কাচখণ্ড যুক্ত। **Lozenge-shaped**—Diamond shaped; বরফির আকার, রুহিতনের আকার।

£. s. d. (ĕl-ĕs-dē), *n.* Pounds, shillings and pence; money; পাউণ্ড, শিলিং এবং পেন্স; টাকা কড়ি। **L. S. Deism** — Money-worship; ধনপূজা।

lŭb'-ber (-ĕr), *n.* **1.** A big clumsy stupid fellow; a lout; হাঁদা, গোবর গণেশ; স্থূলবুদ্ধি ব্যক্তি। **2.** A clumsy unskilled seaman; আনাড়ী নাবিক। **—like,** *adj.* **—li-ness,** *n.* **—ly,** *adj.* & *adv.*

lū'-bri-cāte, *v. t.* **1.** To make smooth or slippery; মসৃণ করা, পিচ্ছিল করা, তেল্‌তেলে করা। **2.** To minimize friction of (machinery) with grease etc. (also *fig.*); চর্ব্বি মাখাইয়া (যন্ত্রাদির) ঘর্ষণজনিত ক্ষয় নিবারণ করা। **—cant,** *adj.* & *n.* Lubricating; পিচ্ছিল। (*Noun*) A substance, as oil, grease, etc. used in lubricating machines etc.; যন্ত্রাদিতে মাখাইবার জন্য তৈল, বসা, প্রভৃতি, অভ্যঞ্জন, চর্ব্বি। **—ca'-tion,** *n.*

Act of lubricating; স্নেহন (চঃ), স্নিগ্ধীকরণ, তৈলাদি দ্বারা অভিমর্দ্দন, চিক্কনীকরণ। **—ca-tor,** *n.* One who, or that which, lubricates; যে ব্যক্তি চর্ব্বি প্রভৃতি মাখায়, যাহা দ্বারা চর্ব্বি প্রভৃতি মাখান যায়। An oil cup attached to a machine; যন্ত্র-সংলগ্ন তৈল-পাত্র।

lü-bric'-i-ty, *n.* **1.** Smoothness; oiliness; as, *lubricity* of oil; মসৃণতা, স্নিগ্ধতা, স্নৈগ্ধ্য; তৈলাক্ততা, চিকনাই, চিক্কণতা। **2.** (*Fig.*) Slipperiness; as, the *lubricity* of fortune; (লক্ষণায়) অস্থিরতা, চঞ্চলতা। **3.** Lewdness; incontinence; "Wantonness and *lubricity*"; কামুকতা, লাম্পট্য; লোচ্চামি, কামপ্রবণতা, অজিতেন্দ্রিয়তা। **Lu'-bri-cious, Lu'-bri-cous,** *adjs.*

Lü'-căn, *adj.* Of, or relating to, St. Luke; সেণ্ট্ লুকসম্পর্কীয়।

lüce, *n.* A pike fish esp. when full grown; মৎস্যবিশেষ।

lü'-cĕnt, *adj.* Shining; bright; translucent; উজ্জ্বল, দীপ্তিমান; আলোকময়, ভাস্বর; অর্দ্ধস্বচ্ছ। **—cen-cy,** *n.*

lü-cẽrn', lü-cerne' (-sẽrn), *ns.* A kind of plant used for fodder; গবাদির খাদ্যোপযোগী তৃণবিশেষ [পারস্য ভাষায় রিস্ক, সাস্ত।]

Lü-ci-ăn'-ic, *adj.* After the manner of Lucian, a writer of Greek satirical dialogues: witty and scoffing; পরিহাসরসিক গ্রীক-সাহিত্যিক লুসিয়ানের অনুরূপ; ব্যঙ্গ-ব্যঞ্জক, রসিকতাপূর্ণ, বিদ্রূপাত্মক।

lü'-cid *adj.* **1.** (*Poet.*) Shining; bright; as, the *lucid* orbs of heaven; উজ্জ্বল, দীপ্তিমান; তেজোময়, আলোকময়, আভাময়। **2.** Clear; transparent; as, *lucid* stream s; নির্ম্মল, বিমল, অমল, সুপ্রভ; স্বচ্ছ। **3.** (*Fig.*) Easily understood; pellucid, as a style, reasoning, etc.; (লক্ষণায়) বিশদ, স্পষ্টার্থ, অনায়াসবোধ্য, সুখবোধ্য, প্রসাদগুণবিশিষ্ট, প্রাঞ্জল। **—cid'-i-ty,** *n.* State of being lucid: clearness; intelligibility: দীপ্তি, উজ্জ্বলতা; নির্ম্মলতা; বৈশদ্য (হিঃ কোঃ), অনায়াসবোধ্যতা, সুখবোধ্যতা, স্পষ্টতা, প্রাসাদগুণ্য, অর্থব্যক্তি, প্রাঞ্জলতা। **—ly,** *adv.* **Lucid interval**—উন্মত্ত ব্যক্তি মধ্যে মধ্যে যে সময় প্রকৃতিস্থ থাকে; গোলযোগ হাঙ্গামার মধ্যে শান্তিপূর্ণ কাল।

Lü'-ci-fêr, *n.* **1.** The morning star; the Venus appearing as such; প্রভাততারা; শুকতারা। **2.** The chief rebel angel Satan; the devil; শয়তান; দায়াবল। **3.** (*l. c.*) A match ignitible by friction, (also *lucifer-match*); দিয়াশলাই, দীপশলাকা।

lü-cif'-ü-gous (-gŭs), *n.* Shunning day-light; দিবালোকপরিহারী।

lŭck, *n.* **1.** A casual event, good or ill affecting one's interests; chance; fate; fortune; দৈবঘটনা, দৈব, দৈবযোগ; অদৃষ্ট, নসিব (*colloq.*); কপাল, নিয়তি; ভাগ্য। **2.** Good fortune, success due to chance; সৌভাগ্য; শুভাদৃষ্ট। **Luck'-less,** *adj.* Without luck; ভাগ্যহীন, মন্দভাগ্য, দুর্ভাগ্য, হতভাগ্য, অভাগা, দুর্ভাগা। **Luck'-less-ly,** *adv.* **Luck'-less-ness,** *n.* **Bad or ill luck**—দুর্ভাগ্য, দুরদৃষ্ট, পোড়া কপাল, দুর্দ্দৈব (*colloq.*)। **Good luck**—সৌভাগ্য। **Luck-money, —penny**—সৌভাগ্যের জন্য রক্ষিত মুদ্রা; বিক্রেতা ক্রেতাকে যে অর্থ প্রত্যর্পণ করে (বিশেষতঃ গবাদি বিক্রয় কালে)। **Worse-luck**—(*Parenthetically*) Unfortunately for me or us; দুর্ভাগ্যবশতঃ, কপালের দোষে। **As luck would have it**—Unfortunately; দুর্ভাগ্যবশতঃ। **Bad luck to him**—A form of imprecation; তাহার কপাল পুড়ুক। **Down on on'es luck**—Dispirited by misfortune; temporarily unfortunate; দৈবোপহত; দুঃসময়ে পতিত। **For luck**—To bring good; সৌভাগ্যের জন্য। **Just my luck**—I am unlucky as usual; আমার ভাগ্যে যেরূপ সচরাচর ঘটিয়া থাকে। **To have the luck to**—To be fortunate enough to; এরূপ ভাগ্যবান্ যে। **To try one's luck**—To make a venture in anything; কোন বিষয়ে সাহসে ভর করিয়া প্রবৃত্ত হওয়া, অদৃষ্ট পরীক্ষা করা।

lŭck'-i-lȳ, *adv.* **1.** (*Rare as an ordinary adv.*) By luck; সৌভাগ্যক্রমে, সৌভাগ্যবশে। **2.** (*Used as a qualification of a sentence or clause*) Fortunately; as, *luckily* for me I was wrong; সৌভাগ্যক্রমে।

lŭck'-ȳ, *adj.* **1.** Fortunate; meeting with good luck or good success; সুভগ, সৌভাগ্যশালী; ভাগ্যবান, লক্ষ্মীমন্ত, পয়মন্ত, লক্ষ্মীবান। **2.** Presaging, bringing, good luck; auspicious; as, *lucky*-penny, -stone, -day; সৌভাগ্যসূচক, সৌভাগ্যজনক; শুভ, মঙ্গলজনক, কল্যাণজনক। **3.** Right by luck, as guess etc.; coming in the nick of time; দৈবক্রমে ঠিক; ঠিক সময়ে আগত। **Luck'-i-ness,** *n.* **You are a lucky dog**—A form of congratulation esp. to an accepted lover; অভিনন্দন বাক্যবিশেষ—বিশেষভাবে—পরিগৃহীত প্রেমিকের প্রতি।

lŭck'-ȳ, *n.* (*Slang*) **To cut or make one's lucky**—To decamp; (ইতর ভাষায়) পিট্টান দেওয়া, চম্পট দেওয়া।

lü'-cră-tive (-tiv), *adj.* Gainful; profitable; as, a *lucrative* business; লাভকর; লাভজনক। **—ly,** *adv.* **—ness,** *n.*

lü'-cre (-kẽr), *n.* Pecuniary profit; riches (*usu. in an ill-sense*); অর্থলাভ, ধনার্জ্জন লাভ, প্রাপ্তি; ধন দৌলত।

Lü-crē'-ti-ă (-shi-), *n.* **1.** (*Rom. legend*) The virtuous wife of Tarquinius Collatinus, who stabbed herself after being raped by Sextus Tarquinius; Tarquinius Collatinusএর পত্নী; Sextus Tarquinius ইঁহার সতীত্ব নষ্ট করিলে ইনি ছুরিকাঘাতে আত্মহত্যা করেন।

2. A model of chastity ; a virtuous woman ; আদর্শ সতী ; ধর্ম্মশীলা নারী, লক্ষ্মিস্বরূপিণী নারী।

lū'-cū-brāte, *v. i.* **1.** To study by lamp-light or at night ; দীপালোকে বা নিশাকালে অধ্যয়ন করা, রাত্রে পড়া। **2.** To express one's meditation in writing ; নিশীথচিন্তা লিপিবদ্ধ করা। **–bra'-tion,** *n.* **1.** Nocturnal study or meditation ; what is composed by night ; রাত্রিকালীন পাঠ, রাত্র্যধ্যয়ন, নিশাধ্যয়ন, নিশীথচিন্তা ; নিশীথরচনা। **2.** Any elaborate or pedantic literary work ; সুবিস্তৃত বা পাণ্ডিত্যপ্রকাশক গ্রন্থ। **–bra-tor,** *n.*

lū'-cū-lēnt, *adj.* (*Rare*) Clear ; convincing ; lucid ; as, a *luculent* proof or explanation ; (কচিদ্‌ব্যবহৃত) সুস্পষ্ট ; প্রত্যয়জনক ; বিশদ। **–ly,** *adv.*

lucus a non lucendo (*L.*), *n.* **1.** Paradoxical or absurd derivation ; উদ্ভট ব্যুৎপত্তি। **2.** Reference of effect to paradoxical cause ; explanation by contraries ; কোন কার্য্যের লোকসংস্কারবিরোধী কারণ নির্দ্দেশ ; বিরুদ্ধ বিষয় দ্বারা ব্যাখ্যান।

Lŭd, *n.* (*= Lord, vulgar or representing a hurried pronunciation*) হুজুর।

Lŭd'-dīte, *n.* & *adj.* One of a band of mechanics, who for six years (1811—17) tried to prevent the use of labour-saving machinery by breaking it, burning factories etc. ; যে সকল লোক (১৮১১—১৭) পর্য্যন্ত ছয় বৎসর কাল কলকারখানাদি ভগ্ন করিয়া কলের প্রচলন বন্ধ করার জন্য চেষ্টা করিয়াছিল—তাহাদের অন্যতম, যন্ত্রভঞ্জক। ***Adj.*** Of, or relating to, this band ; যন্ত্রভঞ্জক সমিতি সম্পর্কীয়।

lū'-dī-crous (-krŭs), *adj.* Ridiculous ; exciting laughter ; deserving derision ; absurd ; বিদ্রূপাত্মক ; হাস্যোদ্দীপক, হাস্যজনক হাস্যকর, পরিহাসের ; পরিহাস্য, অবহাস্য ; অসঙ্গত, যুক্তিবিরুদ্ধ, যুক্তিবিরোধী। **–ly,** *adv.* **–ness,** *n.*

lues, *n.* **1.** Any pestilential or contagious disease ; contagion ; মহামারী, সংক্রামক রোগ ; স্পর্শাক্রামক-বিষ। **2.** Syphillis (also *lues venerea*) ; উপদংশ। ***Luetic,*** *adj.* Affected with syphillis ; উপদংশ-রোগাক্রান্ত।

lŭff, *n., v. i.* & *t.* **1.** (*Naut.*) The weather-part of a fore-and-aft sail ; (নৌবিদ্যা) জাহাজের লম্বালম্বি দিকে টাঙ্গানো পাইলের বাত্যাভিমুখীন অংশ। **2.** The broadest part of a ship's bow where the sides begin to curve in ; পোতপার্শ্বের প্রশস্ততম অংশ—যে স্থান হইতে পার্শ্বদ্বয় বক্র হইতে আরম্ভ করে। ***Verb i.*** To bring the head of a vessel nearer to the wind ; জাহাজের অগ্রভাগ বাতাসের দিকে ঘুরান। ***Verb t.*** **1.** To bring the head of (a ship) nearer the wind ; জাহাজের অগ্রভাগ বাতাসের দিকে ফিরান। **2.** To turn (the helm) so as to effect this ; হাইল ঘুরাইয়া জাহাজের অগ্রভাগ বাত্যাভিমুখীন করা, বাতাসের মুখে ধরা। **3.** (*Yacht-racing*) To get the windward side of (an opponent) ; প্রতিপক্ষের তরীর বাত্যাভিমুখীন পার্শ্বে যাওয়া। **Luffing-match**—প্রতিপক্ষের তরীর বাত্যাভিমুখীন পার্শ্বে যাইবার জন্য প্রবল প্রতিযোগিতা।

Luffa amra—তিতা ধুঁধুল (বেলঃ)।

Luffa foetida—ঝিঙ্গা (বেলঃ)।

lŭg, *v. t., i.* & *n.* **1.** To drag or haul, as a heavy object with effort or force ; ভারী বস্তু সজোরে টানিয়া লইয়া যাওয়া, অতি কষ্টে টানা। **2.** To introduce in a forced or unnatural manner, (with *in* or *into*) ; as, to *lug* a story *into* a conversation ; কষ্টকল্পিত বা অস্বাভাবিকভাবে অবতারণা করা। **3.** To force along as a person ; বলপূর্ব্বক টানিয়া লইয়া যাওয়া। ***Verb i.*** To pull hard (*at*) ; সজোরে টানা। ***Noun.*** A hard pull ; সজোরে হেঁচকা টান। **In lug**—Pawned ; বন্ধক-দেওয়া। **To lug in**—See LUG *v. t.* 2.

lŭg, *n.* Same as LUG-SAIL (below).

lŭg, *n.* A marine worm used as a bait ; বড়শীর টোপস্বরূপ ব্যবহৃত সামুদ্রিক কীট-বিশেষ।

lŭg'-gage (-āj), *n.* A traveller's baggage, boxes, portmanteaus, etc. ; পথিক বা পর্য্যটকের আসবাব, বোঁচ্‌কা বুঁচ্‌কি, বাক্স, পেটারা, প্রভৃতি, যাত্রীর মাল, তল্পীতল্পা। **Luggage-van**—যাত্রীর সঙ্গীয় মালপত্র বহনের জন্য গাড়ী।

lŭg'-ger (-ēr), *n.* A vessel with four-cornered sails set fore and aft ; একপ্রকার ক্ষুদ্র পোত—যাহার আগা ও পাছায় চতুষ্কোণ পাইল টাঙ্গানো থাকে।

lŭg'-sail (-sāl), *n.* A four-cornered sail bent upon a yard that hangs obliquely to the mast ; মাস্তুলের উপর তির্য্যগ্‌ভাবে লম্বিত পাইল দণ্ডে অবনমিত পাইল।

lū-gū'-bri-ous (-ŭs), *adj.* Doleful ; mournful ; শোকসূচক, শোচনীয়, শোকাবহ, শোকাত্মক ; বিষাদজনক, বিষাদাচ্ছন্ন, শোকসূচক। **–ly,** *adv.* **–ness,** *n.*

lūke'-wârm, *adj.* & *n.* **1.** Moderately warm ; tepid ; কবোষ্ণ, ঈষদুষ্ণ ; নিমগরম, মন্দোষ্ণ। **2.** Not ardent or zealous ; indifferent ; as, a *lukewarm* person etc. ; উদ্যমশূন্য, মন্দোৎসাহ, উৎসাহহীন ; উদাসীন, অনাসক্ত, আগ্রহশূন্য। ***Noun.*** A luke-warm person ; উদাসীন ব্যক্তি, উদ্যমশূন্য লোক। **–ly,** *adv.* **–ness,** *n.*

lŭll, *v. t., i.* & *n.* To soothe ; to sleep by sounds or caresses ; to quiet as a suspicion etc. (usu. *pass.*) ; to calm as a sea or storm ; সান্ত্বনা করা, সুস্থির করা ; গান বা সোহাগ

করিয়া ঘুম পাড়ান ; চুপ করা ; প্রশান্ত করা। ***Verb i.*** To subside ; to cease ; থামিয়া যাওয়া ; শান্ত হওয়া। ***Noun.* 1.** Intermission in storm, tumult or confusion ; (*lit* & *fig.*) ; বিরাম, আন্দোলনের বিরাম, প্রশান্তি, স্থিরতা, স্তব্ধতা।

lŭll'-ă-bȳ, *n.* & *v. t.* A soothing song to lull a child to sleep ; ঘুমপাড়ানো গান। ***Verb t.*** To sing to sleep ; গান গাহিয়া ঘুম পাড়ান।

lŭm-bā'-gō, *n.* A rheumatic pain in the loins ; কটিবাত। **–bag'-i-nous,** *adj.*

lŭm'-bâr, *adj.* & *n.* Of, relating to, or in the loins ; কটিদেশীয়, কটিদেশসম্বন্ধী, কটিদেশস্থ। ***Noun.*** An artery, vein, nerve or vertebra in the loins ; কোমরের ধমনী, শিরা, স্নায়ু, প্রভৃতি। **Lumbar region**—উপপর্শুকা (পঞ্জরাস্থির যে দশখানি বুকের হাড়ের সহিত সংযুক্ত নয়) ও উরুর অস্থির মধ্যবর্ত্তী স্থান, কটিদেশ। **Lumbar-vertebra**—কটিদেশীয় কশেরুকা।

lŭm'-bêr, *n., v. t.* & *i.* **1.** Disused articles of furniture etc. taking up rooms ; useless or refuse material ; cumbrous things ; অব্যবহার্য্য জিনিষ ; অকেজো জিনিষ ; আগড়বাগড়। **2.** Timber roughly prepared ; করাতে কাটা মোটা কাঠ। **3.** Superfluous flesh or fat অতিরিক্ত মাংস বা মেদ। ***Verb t.* 1.** To heap together as lumber ; to fill or encumber as a place or room, (often with *up, over*) ; বিশৃঙ্খল ভাবে বোঝাই করা ; বাজে জিনিষ দ্বারা (কোন স্থান বা কামরা) আবদ্ধ করা বা আটকাইয়া রাখা। ***Verb i.*** (In America) To cut timber in the forest and prepare it for the market ; জঙ্গলে কাঠ কাটিয়া বাজারে বিক্রীর উপযোগী করা। **–er,** *n.* One employed to cut and prepare lumber for the market ; কাঠুরিয়া। **Lumber-man**—করাতী। **Lumber mill**—করাতকল **Lumber-room**—বাজে বা অকেজো জিনিষ রাখার ঘর।

lŭm'-bêr, *v. i.* To move heavily, clumsily or noisily ; ধুপ ধাপ করিয়া চলা। **–ing-ly,** *adv.* **–some,** *adj.*

lŭm'-bri-căl, *adj.* & *n.* Resembling a worm ; as, the *lumbrical* muscles of the hand and feet ; ক্রিমিবৎ। ***Noun.*** (Also *lumbrical muscle*) One of muscles flexing fingers or toes ; হস্তপদাদির অঙ্গুলিসঙ্কোচক মাংসপেশী।

lū'-mi-nă-rȳ, *n.* **1.** One of the heavenly bodies that gives light, esp. the sun or the moon ; জ্যোতিষ্ক, প্রভাকর, অংশুমালী। **2.** A person intellectually, morally or spiritually eminent ; a person of light and leading ; উজ্জ্বল-রত্ন (cf. তিনি দেশের উজ্জ্বল রত্ন) ; গণ্যমান্য ব্যক্তি।

lū-mi-nif'-êr-ous (-ŭs), *adj.* Producing or transmitting light ; আলোকপ্রদ, আলোকসঞ্চারী।

lū'-mi-nous (-nŭs), *adj.* **1.** Shining ; emitting light ; bright ; দীপ্ত, প্রভাময়, উজ্জ্বল, তেজোময়, ভাস্বর ; চমকদার (হিঃ কোঃ), জগমগা (ঐ), আলোকসঞ্চারী ; দীপ্তিমান, অংশুমান্। **2.** Illuminated ; full of light, as a room ; আলোকিত ; আলোকময়, জ্যোতির্ম্ময়, জ্যোতিষ্মান্ (হিঃ কোঃ), প্রকাশমান (ঐ), ভাস্বর। **3.** Throwing light upon a subject ; as, a *luminous* statement or writer, etc. ; বিশদ, প্রকাশক (হিঃ কোঃ)। **–ly,** *adv.* **–ness, –nos'-i-ty,** *ns.* State of being luminous ; ঔজ্জ্বল্য, উজ্জ্বলতা, দীপ্তি, চমক (হিঃ কোঃ)। **Luminous paint**—ফুস্ফুরকময় রং বিশেষ—যদ্দ্বারা রঞ্জিত হইলে বস্তুসমূহ রাত্রিতে উজ্জ্বল দেখায়।

lŭmp, *n., v. t.* & *i.* **1.** A small, compact, shapeless mass ; ক্ষুদ্র তাল, পিণ্ড, ডেলা। **2.** A great quantity ; a heap ; স্তূপ, সংহতি, ঢিবি ; কাঁড়ি, রাশি, পুঞ্জ। **3.** The whole collection ; a lot ; সমস্তটা ; লাট। **4.** A mass of clay or dough ready for moulding or baking ; মাখা ময়দা বা তৈয়ারী কাদা। **5.** A protuberance ; an excrescent growth ; a swelling ; উচ্চাংশ; উদ্গতাংশ ; স্ফীতি। **6.** A dull, sluggish person ; হ্যাদা, গোবর-গণেশ। ***Verb t.* 1.** To form into a lump ; to throw into a mass ; to heap together ; to treat as all alike, (*together, in, with*, etc.) ; তাল পাকান, ডেলা পাকান ; পিণ্ডাকার করা বা হওয়া ; স্তূপীকৃত করা ; কোন প্রভেদ না রাখা, ভাজা খাজা এক করা, আলু কচু একদর দেওয়া। **2.** To take or regard as a whole ; to speak of collectively ; সামগ্রিক ভাবে গ্রহণ বা বিবেচনা করা ; সামুদয়িকভাবে বলা। ***Verb i.* 1.** To rise or collect into lumps ; ডেলা পাকান, তাল পাকান। **2.** To go heavily *along* ; to fall or sit heavily down ; ধুপধাপ করিয়া চলা ; ঢিপ্ করিয়া পড়া বা বসা। **Lump-sugar** — চিনির ডেলা, সিতাখণ্ড। **Lump-sum** — থোক টাকা। **A lump in the throat**—A feeling of pressure caused by emotion ; বাষ্পরুদ্ধকণ্ঠ, গদগদকণ্ঠ। **He is a lump of selfishness**—He is selfishness through and through ; সে হাড়ে হাড়ে স্বার্থপর। **In the lump**—Taking things as a whole ; in gross ; wholesale ; মোটের উপর, মোটামুটি ধরিয়া ; থোকে ; পাইকারী হিসাবে।

lŭmp, *n.* A kind of fish ; একপ্রকার মাছ।

lŭmp, *v. t.* To be displeased at ; অসন্তুষ্ট হওয়া। **To lump it**—To dislike any thing ; কোন জিনিষ অপসন্দ করা।

lŭmp'-êr, *n.* **1.** A labourer employed to load and unload cargoes ; জাহাজের কুলী। **2.** A middle man in contracting ; চুক্তির কাজের দালাল। **3.** A classifier who avoids minute subdivisions ; যে ব্যক্তি স্থূলভাবে শ্রেণীবিভাগ করে।

lŭmp'-ing, *adj.* (*Colloq.*) Bulky ; big ; plentiful ; স্থূল ; প্রকাণ্ড ; প্রচুর। **Lumping weight**—গুরুভার।

lŭmp'-ish *adj.* **1.** Heavy ; clumsy ; ভারী ; কদর্য্য। **2.** Dull ; stupid ; lazy ; নির্ব্বোধ ; স্থূলবুদ্ধি ; অলস, আলস্যপরায়ণ, জড়পিণ্ডবৎ, মাংসপিণ্ডবৎ। **–ish-ly,** *adv.* **–ish-ness,** *n.*

lŭmp'-ȳ, *adj.* **1.** Full of, or covered with lumps or small compact masses ; ডেলাবাঁধা, ক্ষুদ্র পিণ্ডবিশিষ্ট। **2.** (Of water) Choppy ; বাত্যাবিক্ষুব্ধ, উত্তরঙ্গ। **–i-ly,** *adv.* **–i-ness,** *n.*

Lü'-nȧ, *n.* The moon goddess ; (গ্রীকপুরাণোক্ত) চন্দ্রমাদেবী।

lü'-nȧ-cȳ, *n.* **1.** The state of being a lunatic ; insanity ; mental derangement ; বাতুলতা, ক্ষিপ্ততা ; বিক্ষিপ্ততা (হিঃ কোঃ), উন্মাদ ; মানসিক বিকৃতি। **2.** Great folly ; মহা নির্ব্বুদ্ধিতা। **Commissioner in lunacy** — উন্মাদরোগ পরিদর্শকমণ্ডলীর সভ্য। **Commission of lunacy**—কোন ব্যক্তির উন্মত্ততা সম্বন্ধে অনুসন্ধানের জন্য প্রদত্ত ক্ষমতা। **Master in lunacy**—কোন ব্যক্তি উন্মাদগ্রস্ত কি না—তদ্বিষয়ে যে রাজকর্ম্মচারী পরীক্ষা করিয়া থাকেন।

lü'-nar (-nẽr), *adj.* & *n.* **1.** Of, in, relating to, or resembling, the moon ; চান্দ্র, চন্দ্রসদৃশ, চান্দ্রমস, ঐন্দব, চন্দ্রমাসম্বন্ধী, চন্দ্রীয় (হিঃ কোঃ), চন্দ্রমণ্ডলস্থ। **2.** Measured by the revolutions of the moon ; as, a *lunar* month (*i. e.* interval between new moons—about $29\frac{1}{2}$ days) ; চন্দ্রের আবর্ত্তন দ্বারা পরিমিত, যথা চান্দ্রমাস। **3.** Lunate ; as, a *lunar* bone ; চন্দ্রকলাকৃতি। **4.** (Of light, glory, etc.) Pale ; feeble ; ম্লান, পাণ্ডুর ; ক্ষীণ, মন্দপ্রভ। **5.** Of, pertaining to, or containing silver (from alchemists' use of *luna* or moon for silver) ; as, *lunar* caustic ; রৌপ্যমিশ্রিত, রৌপ্যযুক্ত, রূপার। ***Noun.*** **1.** A lunar distance or observation ; সূর্য্য, গ্রহ বা তারা হইতে চন্দ্রের দূরত্ব, দ্রাঘিমা নির্ণয়ের জন্য চন্দ্র হইতে সূর্য্য অথবা গ্রহনক্ষত্রাদির দূরত্ব পর্য্যবেক্ষণ, চন্দ্রান্তর (হিঃ কোঃ)। **2.** A lunar bone ; মণিবন্ধস্থ চন্দ্রকলাকৃতি অস্থি। **Lunar bone**—See LUNAR *n.* 2. **Lunar caustic** — নেত্ররজত (হিঃ কোঃ)। **Lunar day** — তিথি। **Lunar distance** — চন্দ্রান্তর (হিঃ কোঃ), সূর্য্য গ্রহ বা তারা হইতে চন্দ্রের দূরত্ব। **Lunar-eclipse**—চন্দ্রগ্রহণ। **Lunar fever**—পাক্ষিক জ্বর। **Lunar herbs**—ওষধি সমূহ। **Lunar method**—চন্দ্র হইতে সূর্য্য অথবা গ্রহনক্ষত্রাদির দূরত্ব পর্য্যবেক্ষণ দ্বারা দ্রাঘিমা নির্ণয়ের পদ্ধতি-বিশেষ। **Lunar month**—চান্দ্রমাস। **Lunar observation**—See LUNAR *n.* 1. **Lunar politics**—See Unpractical questions — অকেজো প্রশ্ন। **Lunar rainbow**—চন্দ্রকিরণজনিত রামধনু। **Lunar-table**—চন্দ্রসারণী (হিঃ কোঃ)।

lü-na'-ri-ăn, *n.* **1.** A supposed inhabitant of the moon ; কল্পিত চন্দ্রলোকবাসী। **2.** An astronomer or navigator with special knowledge of the moon ; চন্দ্র সম্বন্ধে বিশেষজ্ঞ জ্যোতিষী বা নাবিক।

lü'-nāte, *adj.* (*Nat. Hist.*) Crescent-shaped ; as, a *lunate* leaf ; অর্দ্ধচন্দ্রাকৃতি, চন্দ্রকলাকৃতি চন্দ্রখণ্ডাকৃতি।

lü'-nȧ-tic, *adj.* & *n.* **1.** Insane or mad ; উন্মাদ, পাগল, ক্ষিপ্ত, বাতুল। **2.** (Of a person or act) Crazy ; foolish ; frantic ; উন্মাদ ; নির্ব্বোধ ; ক্রোধোন্মত্ত। ***Noun.*** **1.** A lunatic person ; a mad man ; ক্ষিপ্ত ব্যক্তি ; পাগল, উন্মাদ ব্যক্তি। **2.** A foolish or eccentric person ; বেকুব লোক, ছিটগ্রস্ত লোক, বাতিকগ্রস্ত ব্যক্তি। **Lunatic asylum** — ক্ষিপ্তনিবাস, পাগলা গারদ, বাতুলালয়, বাতুলাশ্রম, উন্মাদাগার।

lü-na'-tion, *n.* The time from one new moon to the next ; এক অমাবস্যা হইতে অন্য অমাবস্যা পর্য্যন্ত কাল, উত্তরকাল (সাঃ পঃ), চান্দ্রমাস।

lŭnch, *n., v. i.* & *t.* A light repast or refreshment taken between meals or between breakfast and dinner ; জলযোগ, প্রাতরাশ ও অপরাহ্নভোজনের মধ্যবর্ত্তী জলপান। ***Verb i.*** To take lunch ; জলযোগ করা। ***Verb t.*** To provide lunch for ; জল খাবার দেওয়া।

lŭnch'-eon (-ŏn), *n.* Same as LUNCH, *n.*

lūne, *n.* (*Geom.*) A figure in the form of a crescent bounded by two intersecting arcs of circles ; (জ্যামিতি) চন্দ্রখণ্ডাকার ক্ষেত্র।

lü-nette' (-nĕt-) *n.* **1.** An arched aperture for the admission of light in a concave ceiling ; আলোক প্রবেশের জন্য ন্যুব্জাকার ছাদের গাত্রস্থ অর্দ্ধচন্দ্রাকৃতি ছিদ্র। **2.** A semicircular space in a dome or ceiling decorated with painting ; গুম্বজ বা ভিতরের ছাদে চিত্রবিভূষিত

Lunette.

অর্দ্ধচন্দ্রাকৃতি স্থান। **3.** (*Fort.*) A small fortified work with an angular front ; উপদুর্গ বিশেষ। **4.** A flattened watch-glass ; ঘড়ীর চ্যাপ্টা কাচাবরণ। **5.** The hole in a guillotine for the victim's neck ; মুণ্ডচ্ছেদক যন্ত্রের ছিদ্র—যাহার ভিতর দণ্ডিত ব্যক্তির গলদেশ প্রবিষ্ট করা হয়।

lŭng, *n.* Either of the two organs of respiration in air-breathing animals ; বায়ুকোষ, ফুস্ ফুস্ যন্ত্র, ক্লোম। **Lunged, Lung'-less** *adjs.*

Good lungs—Strong voice ; চড়া-গলা। **Lung-power** — কণ্ঠস্বর বা ধ্বনির শক্তি। **Lungs of London etc.**—লণ্ডন প্রভৃতি বৃহৎ নগরীর মধ্যস্থিত বা সন্নিকটস্থ উন্মুক্ত স্থান। **Lungs of oak, Lung wort**—একজাতীয় গুল্ম ; ফুসফুস রোগে উপকারক বলিয়া কল্পিত শৈবাল বিশেষ। **At the top of one's lungs**—At the top of one's voice ; প্রাণপণে চেঁচাইয়া। **To cry one's lungs**—To try to cry aloud ; চেঁচাইতে চেষ্টা করা।

lunge (lŭnj), **longe** (lŭnj), *n.* & *v. t.* **1.** A long rope used to lead or guide a horse in training or exercise ; ঘোড়া বশীভূত করার জন্য দীর্ঘ রজ্জু-বিশেষ। **2.** A circular ground for training horses ; অশ্ব বশীভূত করার জন্য বৃত্তাকার ভূমি। ***Verb t.*** To exercise a horse with, or in, a lunge ; দীর্ঘ রজ্জু দ্বারা বাঁধিয়া চক্রাকার ভূমিতে ঘুরাইয়া অশ্বকে শিক্ষিত করা।

lunge (lŭnj), *n., v. i.* & *t.* **1.** A sudden thrust with a sword etc. especially in fencing ; তরবারী খেলায় হঠাৎ তরবারীদ্বারা খোঁচা দেওন। **2.** Act of plunging forward ; a rush ; সম্মুখে ধাবন ; বেগে ধাবন। ***Verb i.*** **1.** To make a sudden thrust, as with a sword ; সহসা অসির দ্বারা খোঁচা দেওয়া। **2.** To deliver a blow from the shoulder in boxing ; (মুষ্টিযুদ্ধে) স্কন্ধ হইতে ঘুষি মারা। **3.** To rush ; to move suddenly in some direction ; ধাবিত হওয়া ; সহসা কোন দিকে ধাবিত হওয়া। **4.** (Of a horse) To kick out ; (অশ্ব সম্বন্ধে) পদাঘাত করিয়া তাড়ান। ***Verb t.*** To drive (weapon, string, etc.) violently in some direction ; (অস্ত্রাদি) কোনদিকে সজোরে নিক্ষেপ করা।

lū-nī-sō'-lăr, *adj.* Resulting from the united action of, or relating to, the sun and the moon ; চন্দ্রসূর্য্যের সম্মিলিত কার্য্যসম্বন্ধীয়, চন্দ্রসূর্য্যসম্বন্ধীয়। **Lunisolar period or year**—যে নির্দ্দিষ্টকালের অন্তে অমাবস্যা, পূর্ণিমা এবং চন্দ্র ও সূর্য্যগ্রহণ একই পর্য্যায়ে পুনরাগত হয়। এই কালের পরিমাণ ৫৩২ বৎসর। **Lunisolar precession**—অয়নাংশভাগের যে অংশ চন্দ্র ও সূর্য্যের সম্মিলিত ক্রিয়ার উপর নির্ভর করে) চন্দ্রসৌরায়ণ ভাগ (হিঃ কোঃ)।

lū'-nū-lă, lū'-nūle, *n.* Anything crescent-shaped ; a lune ; চন্দ্রকলাকৃতি বস্তু ; চন্দ্রকলা, চন্দ্রখণ্ড।

lū'-pin(e) (-pĭn), *n.* **1.** A kind of plant ; একপ্রকার গুল্ম। **2.** (*Usu. pl.*) Seed of this ; ঐ গুল্মের বীজ।

lū'-pīne, *adj.* Of, or relating to, a wolf ; wolf-like ; বৃকসম্পর্কীয়, বৃকবৎ।

lū'-pŭs, *n.* An ulcerous disease of the skin ; মাংসক্ষয়কারক চর্ম্মরোগ-বিশেষ, বৃক (হঃ চঃ)। [নাসিকা ও মুখমণ্ডলের প্রসারণশীল রক্তপীড়কাবিশিষ্ট একপ্রকার রোগ। ডাঃ হরিপ্রসাদ চক্রবর্ত্তী।] **—pous, —poid**, *adjs.*

lurch (lêrch), *n.* & *v. i.* A sudden lean to one side as of a ship ; a stagger ; (জাহাজের) এক দিকে হেলন বা কা'ত হওন ; দোল, টলন। ***Verb i.*** To roll, sway to one side ; to stagger ; একদিকে গড়ান বা কাত হওয়া ; টলা, দোলা।

lurch (lêrch), *n.* **1.** (*Obs.*) An old game ; (অপ্রঃ) প্রাচীন ক্রীড়া বিশেষ। **2.** Difficulty or disadvantage (*obs.* except in *to leave one in the lurch*) ; সঙ্কট, অসুবিধা। **At lurch**—Hidden, usually for a bad purpose ; (অসদুদ্দেশ্যে) লুকায়িত। **To give a lurch**—To lie ; to deceive ; মিথ্যা কথা বলা ; প্রতারণা করা, ঠকান। **To leave in the lurch**—To desert (friend, ally, etc.) in difficulties ; বিপদে বা অসহায় অবস্থায় ফেলিয়া যাওয়া, পথে বসান, (বন্ধু, মিত্র প্রভৃতিকে) বিপদে ফেলিয়া চলিয়া যাওয়া।

lurch'-êr (lêrch-), *n.* **1.** A pilferer ; a swindler ; পাতি চোর, ছিঁচকে চোর ; জুয়াচোর। **2.** A spy ; গুপ্তচর, গোয়েন্দা। **3.** A cross-bred dog used esp. by poachers ; একপ্রকার দো-আঁসলা কুকুর।

lūre, *n.* & *v. t.* **1.** Something held to recall a trained hawk ; শিক্ষিত বাজপক্ষীকে পুনরায় আনার জন্য হাতে যে কোন কিছু ধরা হয়। **2.** Something used to entice ; a bait ; লোভানি ; প্রলোভন দ্রব্য। ***Verb t.*** **1.** To recall (hawk) with a lure ; কোন রূপ লোভানি দ্বারা বাজপক্ষীকে প্রত্যাবৃত্ত করা। **2.** To entice as a person or animal (usually with *away* or *into*) ; কোন ব্যক্তি বা জন্তুকে ভুলাইয়া নেওয়া, প্রলুব্ধ করা।

lū'-rid, *adj.* **1.** Pale yellow ; ghastly ; wan ; glaring ; gloomy ; dismal ; stormy ; terrible in colour or light ; ম্লানপীতবর্ণ ; ভীষণ, ভয়ঙ্কর, করাল ; বিবর্ণ, শীর্ণ, ফেঁকাসিয়া, পাঙ্গাসিয়া, পাণ্ডুর ; জ্বলজ্বল ; বিষাদমলিন ; অপ্রসন্ন ; ঝটিকাবিক্ষুব্ধ ; করালবর্ণ, করালদ্যুতি, রুদ্রদ্যুতি। **2.** Brown tinged with red ; আরক্ত কপিশবর্ণ। **—ly**, *adv.* **—ness**, *n.* **To cast a lurid light on facts or character**—To explain them in a terrible way ; কোন বিষয় ভয়োদ্দীপক ভাবে ব্যাখ্যা করা।

lurk (lêrk), *v. i.* & *n.* **1.** To lie hidden, (*in, under, abovt*, etc.) ; লুকাইয়া থাকা। **2.** To escape notice ; to exist unobserved ; to be latent ; দৃষ্টিপথে না পড়া ; অদৃশ্যে থাকা, অলক্ষিতে থাকা ; সুপ্ত বা লুক্কায়িত থাকা, প্রচ্ছন্ন থাকা। ***Noun.*** Same as LURKING PLACE. **A lurking place**—লুকাইবার স্থান, নিভৃত নিলয়।

lus'-cious (lŭsh-ŭs), *adj.* **1.** Very sweet ; delicious ; rich ; fragrant ; সুমিষ্ট, অতি মধুর ; রসাল ; সুমধুর, সুললিত ; সুরভি। **2.** Sweet to excess ; cloying ; অতিমধুর ; অতিমিষ্টতা হেতু বিস্বাদজনক। **3.** (Of language or literary style) Over-rich in sound, imagery or voluptuous suggestion ; (ভাষা বা রচনারীতি সম্বন্ধে) অতিরিক্ত কল্পনাত্মক, অনুপ্রাসবহুল ও উজ্জ্বলরসের ব্যঞ্জনাপূর্ণ। **—ly,** *adv.* **—ness,** *n.* State of being luscious ; লালিত্য, মাধুর্য্য।

lŭsh, *adj.* Luxuriant ; succulent, as grass or plants ; সতেজ ; সরস।

lŭsh, *n., v. t.* & *i.* Liquor or drink ; মদিরা, পানীয় দ্রব্য। ***Verb t.*** To give drink to ; পানীয় দ্রব্য প্রদান করা। ***Verb i.*** To drink ; পান করা, মদ্য পান করা।

lŭsh′-ȳ, *adj.* (*Slang*) Drunk ; (ইতর ভাষায়) মাতাল।

lŭst, *n.* & *v. i.* **1.** Depraved sexual desire ; concupiscence ; lascivious passion ; কামপ্রবৃত্তি, ইন্দ্রিয়াসক্তি, কামুকতা ; রমণেচ্ছা, রতিলালসা, আসঙ্গলিপ্সা ; কামাগ্নি, কামানল, মদনানল। **2.** Passionate enjoyment or desire, as of battle conquest, accumulation, applause; স্পৃহা, তৃষ্ণা, প্রবল আকাঙ্ক্ষা, লোলুপতা, অভিলাস, লিপ্সা, লালসা, ভোগবাসনা, ভোগলিপ্সা। **3.** (*Bibl.* & *Theo.*) A sensuous desire regarded as sinful ; কামক্রোধ লোভ মোহাদি, ষড় রিপু। ***Verb i.*** **1.** To have strong or excessive desire, (usu. *after* or *for*) ; প্রবল ইচ্ছা বা লালসা থাকা। **2.** To have carnal desire ; রমণেচ্ছু হওয়া, কামাতুর হওয়া।

Lust′-ful, *adj.* Inspired by sexual appetite; provoking to sensuality; libidinous ; lascivious ; মদনমত্ত, কামাতুর, কামাকুল, মদনবিহ্বল, কামার্ত্ত, মদনপরবশ ; কামোদ্দীপক, কামোত্তেজক, কামবর্দ্ধক ; কামাসক্ত, কামুক, কামী, কামপ্রবণ, কামান্ধ ; কামার্ত্ত, কামার্থী, রমণেচ্ছু, রতিলম্পট, স্ত্রীলম্পট, স্ত্রীরত, কামাভিলাষী, মদনেচ্ছু। **Lust′-ful-ness,** *n.*

lŭs′-trăl, *adj.* Relating to, or used in, ceremonial purification ; শুদ্ধি ক্রিয়ায় ব্যবহৃত।

lŭs′-trāte, *v. t.* To purify by expiatory sacrifice, ceremonial washing etc. ; প্রায়শ্চিত্ত, হোমাদি দ্বারা পাপক্ষয় বিধান করা, প্রায়শ্চিত্ত দ্বারা পরিশুদ্ধ করা, শুদ্ধি-বিধান করা। **—tra′-tion,** *n.* Purification by sacrifice ; পাবনশুদ্ধি, নীরাজন (lustration of arms)

lŭs′-tre (-tėr), *n.* & *v. t.* **1.** Gloss ; refulgence ; brightness ; brilliance ; radiant beauty ; কান্তি, তেজঃ, চাক্‌চিক্য ; দ্যুতি (হিঃ কোঃ) ; দীপ্তি, প্রভা, চমক (হিঃ বোঃ) ; বিভা, জ্যোতি ; উজ্জ্বলতা, দ্যুতিমত্তা, দীপ্তলাবণ্য, সমুজ্জ্বলশোভা। **2.** Splendour ; distinction ; as, to add *lustre* to : to throw or shed *lustre* on; গৌরববিভা ; খ্যাতি, মহিমা। **3.** A chandelier ; one of the prismatic glass pendant of it ; বেলওয়ারীর ঝাড় ; ঝাড়ের কলম। **4.** A fabric for ladie's dresses of wool and cotton having a highly finished lustrous surface ; মহিলাদিগের পোষাকের জন্য পশম ও সূতার তৈয়ারী একপ্রকার চক্‌চকে কাপড়। ***Verb t.*** To make or furnish with lustrous gloss (cloth, pottery, etc.) ; মাটীর বাসন, কাপড় প্রভৃতির উপরিভাগ চক্‌চকে করা। **—less,** *adj.* Without lustre ; দীপ্তিহীন। **—trous,** *adj.* Full of lustre ; bright ; shining ; glossy ; দ্যুতিপূর্ণ ; উজ্জ্বল ; দীপ্ত ; চক্‌চকে, জিল্লাদার। **—trous-ly,** *adv.*

lŭs′-tre (-tėr), *n.* Same as LUSTRUM.

lŭs′-trine (-trĭn), **lŭs′-trĭng,** *ns.* A glossy silk fabric ; একপ্রকার চক্‌চকে রেশমী কাপড়।

lŭs′-trŭm, *n.* (*Pl.* -TRA, -TRUMS) In ancient Rome, the purification of the people at the end of every five years ; hence, a period of 5 years ; প্রাচীন রোমানদিগের পঞ্চবার্ষিক প্রায়শ্চিত্ত বা পাপক্ষালন ; পঞ্চবর্ষকাল, পঞ্চযুগ (মঃ ভাঃ), পঞ্চবর্ষ।

lŭst′-ȳ, *adj.* **1.** Healthy and strong ; robust ; সবল, সুস্থ, দৃঢ়কায়, বলবান ; মাংসল। **2.** Vigorous ; lively ; সতেজ ; প্রাণপূর্ণ, প্রাণবান। **—i-hood, —i-ness,** *ns.* **—i-ly,** *adv.*

lusus naturae, *n.* A sport or freak of nature ; a strikingly abnormal production of nature ; প্রকৃতির খেয়াল ; বিকৃত বা অস্বাভাবিক সৃষ্টি, কিম্ভুতকিমাকার বস্তু।

Lute.

lūt′-ă-nist, *n.* A lute-player ; সারঙ্গ বা বীণাবাদক, বৈণিক।

lūte, *n.* A guitar-like instrument formerly much used in Europe ; বেহালাজাতীয় বাদ্যযন্ত্র-বিশেষ, বীণা, তম্বুরা [Other Sanskrit synonyms :—বিপঞ্চী, পরিবাদিনী, বল্লকী]। **A rift within the lute**—The first sign of coming discord or madness ; ভবিষ্যৎ গোলমালের প্রথম সূচনা, ভাবী উন্মাদরোগের প্রথম লক্ষণ।

lūte, *n.* & *v. t.* A clay or cement used to stop a hole, to make a joint airtight, to coat crucibles, etc. ; মৃত্তিকাদির প্রলেপ (জোড়া প্রভৃতির মুখ বন্ধ করার জন্য), লেই (হিঃ কোঃ)। ***Verb t.*** To close or coat with lute ; মৃত্তিকাদির প্রলেপ দেওয়া, মৃত্তিকা দ্বারা ছিদ্র বন্ধ করা। **Lut′-ing,** *n.*

lū′-tē-ous (-ŭs), *adj.* Of deep orange yellow ; গাঢ় জরদ রংএর, গাঢ় কমলাবর্ণ।

lūte′-strĭng, *n.* A lustrous silk fabric ; একপ্রকার চক্‌চকে রেশমী কাপড়।

Lū-tē′-ti-ăn (-shĭ-), *adj.* **1.** Parisian (from Lutetia, ancient name of Paris) ; প্যারী নগরী সম্বন্ধীয়।

Lū′-thêr-ăn, *adj.* & *n.* Of, or pertaining to, Martin Luther, or the church founded by him ; মার্টিন লুথার সম্বন্ধীয়, লুথারপ্রতিষ্ঠিত ধর্ম্ম-সংঘ সম্বন্ধীয়। ***Noun.*** An adherent of Luther or his church ; লুথারের অনুগামী, লুথারের মতের পক্ষপাতী ব্যক্তি, লুথারের শিষ্য। **-ism,** *n.* The doctrines of Luther or his church ; লুথার বা তৎকর্তৃক স্থাপিত ধর্ম্মসংঘের ধর্ম্মমত। **—ize,** *v. t.*

lū'-trȧ, *n.* Otter ; উদ্বিড়াল।

lŭx'-āte, *v. t.* To dislocate or displace as a joint etc. ; সন্ধিচ্যুত করা, স্থানচ্যুত করা, গ্রন্থিচ্যুত করা। **—a'-tion,** *n.* The act of luxating ; বিসন্ধীকরণ, অস্থি প্রভৃতির অবস্থান বিচ্যুতি, সন্ধিচ্যুতি, গ্রন্থি চ্যুতি।

luxe, (*F.*), *n.* Sumptuous quality or make (usu. preceded by *de*=of) ; as, articles *de luxe* ; জাঁকালো, জমকালো রকমের। ***Edition de luxe***—রাজসংস্করণ।

lux-ū'-ri-ănt (lŭgz-), *adj.* **1.** Exceedingly fertile (*lit.* & *fig.*) ; as, *luxuriant* soil or imagination ; অতিশয় উর্ব্বর (শব্দানুযায়ী ও লক্ষণায়)। **2.** Of exuberant growth ; rank ; abundant ; অতি বর্দ্ধনশীল ; সতেজ ; প্রচুর, অতিশয়, বহু, যথেষ্ট, ভূয়িষ্ঠ, বহুল। **3.** (Of literary style) Florid ; rich ; অতিশয় অলঙ্কৃত, পুষ্পিত ; অনুপ্রাসাদ বহুল। **—ance,** *n.* The state of being luxuriant ; অতিশয় উর্ব্বরতা ; প্রাচুর্য্য, বাহুল্য, ভূয়িষ্ঠতা। **—ly,** *adv.*

lux-ū'-ri-āte (lŭgz-), *v. i.* **1.** To live luxuriously ; ভোগবিলাসের মধ্যে বাস করা। **2.** To revel ; to enjoy oneself (*in* or *on*) ; ভোগবিলাস করা ; আমোদপ্রমোদ করা।

lux-u'-ri-ous (lŭgz-ū-rĭ-ŭs), *adj.* Given to luxury ; voluptuous ; very comfortable ; ইন্দ্রিয়সুখতৎপর, ভোগবিলাসানুরক্ত, ভোগাসক্ত, বিলাসী, বিলাসপ্রিয়, বিষয়সুখনিরত, ভোগী, বিষয়ভোগাভিলাষী, সুখভোগাসক্ত, সুখভোগপরায়ণ ; ইন্দ্রিয়সেবী, ভোগাসক্ত ; অতি সুখাবহ, অতি তৃপ্তিকর, অতি সুখদায়ক, অতিশয় আরামজনক। **—ly,** *adv.* In a luxurious manner ; ভোগবিলাসের ক্রোড়ে। **—ness,** *n.*

lux'-ū-rȳ (lŭgz-), *n.* **1.** A free indulgence in rich diet or costly dress, equipage, etc. ; luxurious living ; বিলাসিতা, বিলাসপ্রিয়তা, ভোগপরায়ণতা; ভোগবিলাস, ঐশ্বর্য্যসুখ কুমারঃ), বিষয়ভোগ, বিলাস (হিঃ কোঃ), সমৃদ্ধি (ঐ)। **2.** Anything gratifying to the senses ; an expensive rarity ; as, a raw fruit is a *luxury* ; ইন্দ্রিয়সুখজনকবস্তু ; বহুমূল্য দুষ্প্রাপ্যবস্তু। **3.** Luxuriousness ; ইন্দ্রিয়সুখতৎপরতা, ভোগবিলাসপ্রিয়তা, বিলাস (হিঃ কোঃ), আরাম (ঐ)। **Articles of luxury** — বিলাসদ্রব্য, বিলাসসামগ্রী, বিলাসোপকরণ, সুখোপভোগ্য বস্তু (হিঃ কোঃ)।

lȳ-căn'-thrō-pȳ *n.* **1.** The transformation of a witch into a wolf ; ডাইনীর বৃকরূপধারণ। **2.** A form of insanity in which the patient imagines himself to be a beast and imitates its actions ; একপ্রকার উন্মাদরোগ — যাহাতে রোগী নিজকে পশু বলিয়া কল্পনা করে ও পশুর অনুরূপ আচরণ করিয়া থাকে।

Lȳ-cā'-ōn, *n.* Son of Pelasgus, and king of Arcadia ; Pelasgusএর পুত্র এবং আর্কেডিয়ার রাজা। দেবরাজ Zeus আর্কেডিয়ায় আসিলে ইনি তাঁহাকে হত্যা করার জন্য চেষ্টিত হন এবং তাঁহার ভোজনের জন্য নরমাংসের ব্যঞ্জন প্রদান করেন ; কিন্তু Zeus উহাকে ও উহার পঞ্চাশৎ পুত্রকে বিনাশ করেন।

lycee, *n.* A French secondary school supported by the government ; ফরাসী দেশীয় সরকারী সাহায্যপ্রাপ্ত উচ্চবিদ্যালয়।

lȳ-cē'-ŭm, *n.* **1.** A garden at Athens in which Aristotle taught philosophy ; his philosophy and followers ; প্রাচীন এথেন্স নগরীর উদ্যান বিশেষ—এই উদ্যানে জ্ঞানগুরু আরিস্তোতল দর্শনশাস্ত্র অধ্যাপনা করিতেন ; আরিস্তোতলের দর্শন বা শিষ্যমণ্ডলী। **2.** A literary institution ; a lecture-hall ; a teaching place ; সাহিত্যসমাজ, সাহিত্যসভা, সাহিত্যপরিষৎ ; বক্তৃতাগৃহ ; শিক্ষানিকেতন।

lȳch, *n.* See LICH.

lȳch'-nis, *n.* A genus of plant ; একজাতীয় গুল্ম।

Lycopersicum esculentum—বিলাতী বেগুন (বেলঃ)।

lȳ'-cō-pŏd, —pō'-di-ŭm, *ns.* **1.** A genus of moss-like plants; শৈবাল জাতীয় উদ্ভিদ-বিশেষ। **2.** (*-podium* only) A powder made from lycopodium used as an absorbent in surgery and in making stage lightning ; ঐ বৃক্ষের পীতবর্ণ রেণু (spores)—যাহা ঘা প্রভৃতিতে রক্তশোষকরূপে এবং রঙ্গালয়ে বিদ্যুৎ উৎপাদনের জন্য ব্যবহৃত হইয়া থাকে, উদ্ভিজ্জগন্ধক, সমঙ্গ (সাঃ পঃ)।

Lycopod.

lȳdd'-īte, *n.* A powerful explosive chiefly of picric acid used in shells ; অতি শক্তিশালী বিস্ফোরক দ্রব্য বিশেষ (কামানের গোলাতে ব্যবহৃত হয়)।

Lȳd'-i-ăn, *adj.* & *n.* Of, or relating to, Lydia, an ancient division of Asia Minor or its inhabitants; এসিয়া মাইনরের প্রাচীন বিভাগ লিডিয়া বা তৎস্থানের অধিবাসিগণসম্পর্কীয়। ***Noun.*** An inhabitant of Lydia ; its language ; লিডিয়ার অধিবাসী ; লিডিয়ার ভাষা। **Lydian mode**—(সঙ্গীত শাস্ত্র) স্ত্রীজনসুলভ করুণভাবাত্মিকা রীতি, লীডিয় রীতি।

lye (lī), *n.* **1.** Water impregnated with alkaline salt imbibed from the ashes of wood ; ক্ষার-জল। **2.** A caustic alkaline solution esp. for washing ; any detergent ; বস্ত্রাদি ধৌত করার জন্য ক্ষারজল ; বিশোধক দ্রব্য।

lȳ'-ing, *n.* **1.** Act of one who lies ; শয়ন। **2.** A place to lie ; as, a dry or soft *lying* ; শয়নস্থান। **Lying in**—Being in child-birth ; প্রসবাবস্থা, সূতিকাবস্থা। **Lying in**

chamber or **room** — সূতিকাগৃহ, অরিষ্টগৃহ (রঃ)।

lȳ′-ing, *adj.* & *n.* Telling a lie or lies ; deceitful ; false ; মিথ্যাবাদী, অসত্যভাষী, অসত্যবক্তা, অনৃতভাষী; ছলনাপর ; কৃত্রিম, কপট। ***Noun.*** Telling a lie ; মিথ্যাভাষণ, মিথ্যাচরণ। **—ly,** *adv.*

lȳke′-wāke, *n.* A night watch kept over a dead body ; মৃতদেহের উপর রাত্রে যে পাহারা দেওয়া হয়।

lȳme′-grȧss, *n.* A kind of grass ; এক প্রকার ঘাস।

lȳmph, *n.* **1.** Pure water (*Poet.*) ; (কবিতায়) নির্ম্মল জল। **2.** (*Physiol.*) A colourless fluid in animal bodies ; (শারীর বিজ্ঞান) প্রাণিদেহস্থ স্বচ্ছ তরল পদার্থ, লসিকা, অস্‌কৃক্‌র, রস। **3.** An exudation from a sore etc. ; ক্ষতনিঃস্রাব, ঘায়ের কলতানি। **4.** (Also *vaccine lymph*) The matter taken from cow-pox vesicles and used in vaccination ; any other morbid matter for a similar purpose ; গোবসন্তবীজ ; বসন্ত বীজ। **—ous,** *adj.*

lȳm-phăt′-ic, *adj.* & *n.* **1.** Of, relating to, containing, or conveying lymph ; লসিকাসম্বন্ধীয়, লসিকাময়, লসিকাবাহী। **2.** Having a temperament lacking energy or indisposed to exertion or excitement ; (শ্লেষ্মাপ্রধান ধাতুর) অলস, মন্থর। ***Noun.*** A vessel conveying lymph ; লসিকাবাহী নাড়ী। **Lymphatic temperament**—শ্লেষ্মাপ্রধান ধাতু। [আলস্য, ক্ষীণ কল্পনাশক্তি উহার লক্ষণ।]

lȳn-cē′-ăn, *adj.* Relating to a lynx; sharp-sighted ; বন্যমার্জ্জারসম্বন্ধীয় ; তীক্ষ্ণ-দৃষ্টি, সূক্ষ্ম-দৃষ্টি।

lȳnch, *v. t.* To inflict punishment upon, esp. death, without the forms of law, as when a mob captures and hangs a suspected person ; আইন আদালতের অপেক্ষা না করিয়া শাস্তি প্রদান করা, বিশেষতঃ প্রাণদণ্ড প্রদান করা। **Judge-lynch**—কাল্পনিক দণ্ডদাতা। **Lynch-law**—(*cap.* or *l. c.*) — আইন আদালতের আশ্রয় না লইয়া, স্বয়ং অপরাধীকে শাস্তি-প্রদানের ব্যবস্থা, নিজের বিচার নিজে করার ব্যবস্থা [মার্কিণ যুক্তরাজ্যের Virginiaর অন্তঃপাতী Pidemont গ্রামবাসী Mr. James Lynch নামক জনৈক ন্যায়নিষ্ঠ ও সমদর্শী কৃষকের নাম হইতে গৃহীত বলিয়া কথিত। এই গ্রামের নিকট কোন বিচারালয় না থাকাতে ঐ গ্রাম ও পার্শ্ববর্ত্তী গ্রাম সমূহের অধিবাসিগণ James Lynchকে অপরাধিগণের দণ্ড-বিধানের জন্য মনোনীত করে।]

lynx (lĭngks), *n.* **1.** A kind of animal of the cat tribe with proverbially

Lynx.

keen sight ; একপ্রকার বন্য বিড়াল,—তীক্ষ্ণ দৃষ্টির জন্য প্রসিদ্ধ। **2.** Its fur ; ঐ জন্তুর লোম। **3.** (*Cap.*) One of the northern constellations ; উত্তরদিগ্‌বর্ত্তী তারাপ্রকোষ্ঠ বিশেষ। **Lynx-eyed**—Keen-sighted ; তীক্ষ্ণ-দৃষ্টিসম্পন্ন, সূক্ষ্মদৃষ্টি।

Lȳ-ŏn, *n.* (Also *Lyon King of Arms*) The chief herald of Scotland; স্কট্‌লণ্ডের সর্ব্বপ্রধান কুলাচার্য্য।

Lȳ′-rȧ, *n.* A northern constellation ; উদীচ্য তারাপ্রকোষ্ঠ বিশেষ, বীণামণ্ডল (বঃ দঃ নঃ)।

Lȳ′-rȧ-id, Lȳ′-rid, *ns.* (Usu. *pl.*) A meteor or meteors radiating from Lyra about 20th April ; ২০এ এপ্রিলের কাছাকাছি বীণামণ্ডল হইতে বিকিরণশীল উল্কা বা উল্কা সমূহ।

lȳ′-rāte, *adj.* (*Nat. Hist.*) Like the lyre in shape ; (প্রাকৃতিক ইতিহাস) সারঙ্গাকার (সাঃ পঃ)।

lȳre, *n.* A stringed musical instrument like the harp much used by the ancients ; বীণার ন্যায় একপ্রকার বাদ্যযন্ত্র, সারঙ্গ [প্রাচীন গ্রীকগণ কবিতা আবৃত্তি বা গান গাহিবা কালে এই যন্ত্র বাদন করিত। সর্ব্বপ্রথমে গ্রীক বীণাযন্ত্রের তিনটী তন্ত্রী ছিল, পরবর্ত্তী কালে গ্রীকগণ ইহাতে আরো চারিটী তন্ত্রী সংযোগ করিয়া ইহাকে সপ্ততন্ত্রীবিশিষ্ট করে, পরিশেষে তন্ত্রী সংখ্যা ষোড়শ পর্য্যন্ত বৃদ্ধি করা হয়।] **Lyr′-ist** *n.* **Lyre-bird**—প্রাচীন গ্রীস দেশীয় বীণাযন্ত্রবৎ পুচ্ছবিশিষ্ট বিহঙ্গ বিশেষ, বীণাবিহঙ্গ।

Lyre.

Lyre-bird.

lȳr′-ic, *adj.* & *n.* **1.** Of, relating to, or for, the lyre; বীণাযন্ত্র সম্বন্ধীয়। **2.** Suited or meant to be sung ; appropriate for song ; গেয় ; সঙ্গীতোপযোগী। **3.** (Of poem) Expressing a writer's own feelings, usually at no great length and in stanzas; (of a poet) writing such poetry ; রসপ্রধান, ভাবপ্রধান ; গীতি-কবিতারচক। ***Noun.*** **1.** A lyrical poem ; গীতিকবিতা। **2.** (*Pl.*) Ve[rse] in lyric poetry ; গাথা। **—i-cal,** *a[dj.]* **—i-cal-ly,** *adv.*

lȳr′-i-cĭsm, *n.* **1.** A lyric composition ; গীতিকবিতা। **2.** High-flown sentiments; আবেগপূর্ণ ভাবরাশি।

lȳ′-sis, *n.* The gradual abatement of a disease as distinguished from crisis ; রোগের উত্তেজনার হ্রাস।

lȳs′-sȧ, *n.* Hydrophobia ; জলাতঙ্ক রোগ।

THE MODERN ANGLO-BENGALI DICTIONARY

THE MODERN ANGLO BENGALI DICTIONARY

(In 6 Volumes)

(Volume- 4)

CHARUCHANDRA GUHA

Publications

KALPAZ PUBLICATIONS

DELHI - 1100052

THE MODERN ANGLO- BENGALI DICTIONARY

ISBN : 81-7835 - 484 - 5 (Set)
ISBN : 81 - 7835 - 488 - 8 (Vol. 4)

Rs. 4500 (Set)

CHARUCHANDRA GUHA

Published in 2007 in India by
Kalpaz Publications
C - 30, Satyawati Nagar,
Delhi - 110052
E-mail : kalpaz@hotmail.com

Laser Typesetting at : Tact Computer, Delhi
Printed at : Mehra Offset Press, Delhi

M

M, 1. The thirteenth letter of the English alphabet ; ইংরাজী বর্ণমালার ত্রয়োদশ অক্ষর। 2. A numeral standing for one thousand; ১০০০ জ্ঞাপক সংখ্যাচিহ্ন। **To have an M under the girdle**—To be courteous to address people by the title Mr. and Mrs. or Madam ; লোককে মিষ্টার, মিসিস্ বা ম্যাডেম (মহাশয়, মহাশয়া) প্রভৃতি শব্দে সম্বোধনপূর্ব্বক শিষ্টাচার দেখান।

mâ, *n.* (*Vulg.*) Mamma ; (ইতর ভাষায়) মা।

ma'am (mâm), *n.* Madam (*used in addressing ladies*) ; ভদ্রে, আর্য্যে।

Mab, *n.* The queen of the fairies ; পরীদিগের রাণী, পরীরাণী।

ma-cā'-bre (-bêr), *adj.* 1. Relating to, or suggesting, the dance of death ; মরণনৃত্যসম্বন্ধীয়, মরণনৃত্যব্যঞ্জক। 2. Grim ; বিকট, করাল। **Danse macabre**—Dance of death ; মরণনৃত্য।

mă-cā'-cō, *n.* A monkey of the genus Macacus ; মর্কট বিশেষ।

mă-cā'-cō, *n.* A kind of lemur (see LEMUR).

mă-cā'-cŭs, *n.* A genus of monkeys found in Asia and the East Indies ; একজাতীয় খর্ব্বপুচ্ছ কপি।

măc-ăd'-ăm, *adj.* & *n.* Made in the manner advocated by McAdam, as a road ; পাকা, খোয়া-বাঁধানো [আবিষ্কর্ত্তা McAdamএর নাম হইতে গৃহীত]। ***Noun.*** The small broken stones used in making such roads ; খোয়া, নুড়ি।

măc-ăd'-ăm-īze, *v. t.* To cover, as a road with small broken stones, which when consolidated form a firm surface ; to pave ; রাস্তায় খোয়া দেওয়া, পাথর দিয়া রাস্তা বাঁধা ; রাস্তা পাকা করা।

Macaroni.

măc-ă-rō'-nĭ, *n.* 1. A wheaten paste formed into long tubes used as food ; ইতালী দেশের চোঙ্গাকার পিষ্টক বিশেষ। 2. A kind of dandy in fashion in London about 1760 ; "Spruce *macaronis*" ; ১৭৬০ খৃঃ অব্দের প্রাচীন লণ্ডনের ফুলবাবু। **—nism**, *n.*

măc-ă-rŏn'-ĭc, *adj.* & *n.* 1. (*Obs.*) Pertaining to, or like, macaroni the food ; (অপ্রঃ) ইতালী দেশীয় চোঙ্গাকার পিষ্টকসম্বন্ধীয় বা তদ্বৎ। 2. Mixed ; medley ; মিশ্রিত ; খিচুড়ি-পাকানো। 3. Pertaining to the burlesque composition called macaronic; কৌতুকরচনাবিশেষসম্বন্ধীয়। ***Noun.*** (*Pl.*) Verses of burlesque form consisting of vernacular words Latinized or Latin words modernized ; ল্যাটিনের সহিত কথ্য ভাষার সংমিশ্রণে রচিত হাস্যরসাত্মক কবিতা বিশেষ।

măc-ă-rōōn', *n.* 1. A small cake composed chiefly of the white of eggs, almonds and sugar ; ডিম্বের শ্বেতভাগ, বাদাম ও চিনি দ্বারা প্রস্তুত ক্ষুদ্র মিষ্ট পিষ্টকবিশেষ।

mă-căs'-sâr (oil), *n.* A kind of oil for the hair, so called because originally obtained from Macassar, a district in Celebes ; সুগন্ধ কেশতৈল-বিশেষ, ম্যাকেসার অয়েল। [সর্ব্বপ্রথম Celebes দ্বীপের অন্তঃপাতী Macassar নামক স্থান হইতে আসিত বলিয়া এই নাম।]

mă-caw' (-kä), *n.* A beautiful bird of parrot tribe ; আমেরিকাদেশীয় শুকজাতীয় পক্ষি-বিশেষ।

mă-caw' (-kä), *n.* A kind of palm ; তালজাতীয় বৃক্ষবিশেষ।

măc-că-bē'-ăn, *adj.* Of the *Maccabees*, Jewish princes, who freed Judaea from the tyranny of Antiochus Epiphanes, 166 B. C. ; জুডিয়ার স্বাধীনতাপ্রদাতা ইহুদীরাজগণসম্বন্ধীয়।

măc'-că-bō̆y, —baw (-bä), *ns.* A kind of snuff ; নস্যবিশেষ।

māce, *n.* Dried outer covering of nutmeg ; জৈত্রী, জয়িত্রী, জাতিকোষ, জাতীপত্রী (বেলঃ)।

māce, *n.* 1. A staff used as an ensign of authority ; আঁশা-সোঁটা। 2. (*Hist.*) A wooden club ; (ইতিহাস) গদা, মুষল। 3. A stick used in bagatelle ; ক্রীড়া বিশেষে ব্যবহৃত দণ্ডবিশেষ।

māc'-êr, *n.* Same as MACE-BEARER. **Mace-bearer**—আঁশাসোঁটা-ধারী, চোপদার, আসাবরদার, ছড়ীবরদার, বেত্রধর, দণ্ডধারী।

măc′-êr-āte, *v. t.* & *i.* **1.** To soften by steeping in a liquid ; ভিজাইয়া নরম করা, পচান, ভাবনা দেওয়া, বিমর্দ্দন করা। **2.** To waste away by fasting ; উপবাসকৃশ করা, অনাহারকৃশ করা। *Verb i.* To undergo maceration or softening ; ভিজিয়া নরম হওয়া। **—a′-tion,** *n.* **1.** Act of macerating ; being macerated ; জল সেক দ্বারা কোমলীকরণ, আর্দ্রীকরণ ; ভাবনা। **2.** Wasting away ; being worn away ; কর্শন, ক্ষয়ন ; ক্ষীণীভবন।

Măch′-ĭ-ă-vĕl, *n.* An intriguer ; one practising duplicity in statecraft ; (From Machiavelli, an Italian writer and statesman) ; চক্রী ; কূটরাজনীতিবিদ্। [ফ্লোরেন্স নগরবাসী কূটরাজনীতিবিশারদ Machiavelliর (১৪৬৯—১৫২৭) নাম হইতে গৃহীত (cf. our চাণক্য)।] **—vel′-li-an** *adj.* Pertaining to Machiavelli, or to his principles ; politically cunning ; crafty ; ইতালীদেশীয় কূটরাজনীতিজ্ঞ মেকিয়াভেলি বা তদীয় নীতি বিষয়ক ; কূটনীতিজ্ঞ ; ধূর্ত্ত, চতুর, চক্রী, কৌশলী। **—vel′-ism, —vel′-li-an-ism,** *ns.* Political artifice and cunning ; কূটরাজনীতি।

mă-chic′-ō-lāte, *v. i.* To furnish a projecting parapet with openings between supporting corbels for dropping molten lead, stones, etc. on the assailants ; নিম্নস্থ আক্রমণকারিগণের উপর গলিত সীসক, প্রস্তর, প্রভৃতি বর্ষণের জন্য উদ্গত মঞ্চের তোড়া সকলের মধ্যে রন্ধ্র করা। **—la′-tion,** *n.* An opening between the corbels supporting a projecting parapet ; উদ্গতমঞ্চের অবলম্বনস্বরূপ তোড়াসমূহের মধ্যবর্ত্তী ছিদ্র বিশেষ।

mă-chi-cou′-lis (-shē-kō-lē), *n.* Same as MACHICOLATION.

măch′-ĭ-nāte, *v. i.* To lay plots ; to intrigue ; ষড়যন্ত্র করা ; চক্রান্ত করা। **—na′-tion,** *n.* **1.** The act of machinating ; চক্রান্ত করণ। **2.** A plot ; ষড়যন্ত্র, চক্রান্ত ; কূটপ্রবন্ধ, কূটমন্ত্র। **—na-tor,** *n.* One who machinates ; চক্রান্তকারী, চক্রী।

mă-chine′ (-shēn), *n* **1.** An apparatus, tool or contrivance ; as, a sewing-*machine* ; কল, যন্ত্র। **2.** A vehicle or conveyance ; a bicycle ; a tricycle ; an aeroplane ; যান, বাহন ; দ্বিচক্রযান ; ত্রিচক্রযান ; ব্যোমতরী। **3.** A person acting like a machine without intelligence or with unfailing regularity ; যন্ত্র, কলের পুতুল, যন্ত্র-পুত্তলিকা। **4.** (*Mech.*) An instrument transmitting force or directing its application ; as, a simple *machine* (*i. e.* one without parts, *e. g.* a lever) ; (যন্ত্র-বিজ্ঞান) যন্ত্র। **5.** A controlling organization of a political party (esp. in *U. S.*) ; কোন রাজনীতিক দলের পরিচালকসভা। **—chin′-ist,** *n.* **1.** A maker or controller of machines ; যন্ত্রনির্ম্মাতা, যন্ত্রচালক, যন্ত্রবিদ্যানিপুণ, যন্ত্রবিদ্, যন্ত্রকার। **2.** One working a sewing-machine etc. ; সেলাইএর কল ইত্যাদির চালক। **Machine-gun**—কলের কামান, যান্ত্রিক কামান। **Machine-made** — কলে তৈয়ারী, কলের। **Machine-man**—যন্ত্রচালক, বিশেষতঃ মুদ্রাযন্ত্র-চালক। **Machine-shop**—যন্ত্রনির্ম্মাণাগার।

mă-chin′-êr-ȳ (-shēn), **1.** Machines collectively ; যন্ত্রসমূহ, কলসামগ্রী (হিঃ কোঃ)। **2.** The working parts of a machine ; যন্ত্রের কার্য্যকরী অংশসমূহ, কলকব্জা। **3.** Contrivances, esp. supernatural persons and incidents used in literary works ; কৌশল ; পুস্তকাদিতে বর্ণিত অতিপ্রাকৃত ব্যক্তি বা ঘটনা সমূহ।

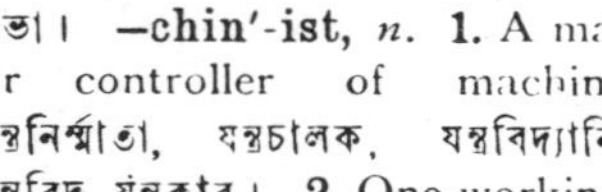

Mackerel.

măck′-êr-ĕl, *n.* An edible sea-fish ; আহারোপযোগী সামুদ্রিক মৎস্যবিশেষ। **Mackerel sky**—ক্ষুদ্র ক্ষুদ্র শুভ্রমেঘখণ্ড-বিচিত্রিত নভোমণ্ডল।

măck′-in-tŏsh, *n.* **1.** A water-proof material for garment—so called from the name of the inventor ; পোষাক প্রস্তুতের জন্য জলরোধক বস্ত্রবিশেষ [আবিষ্কর্ত্তা Mackintoshএর নাম হইতে গৃহীত।] **2.** A cloak or coat made of this ; ঐরূপ কাপড়ে তৈরী লম্বা কোর্ত্তা।

mă′-cle (-kl), *n.* **1.** Twin crystal ; যুগ্ম-স্ফটিক বিশেষ। **2.** A dark spot in a mineral ; কোন খনিজ পদার্থের গাত্রস্থ কৃষ্ণবিন্দু।

măc′-ră-mē, *n.* Fringe of knotted thread ; গ্রন্থিযুক্ত ঝালর।

măc-rō-cē-phăl′-ic, *adj.* Having a large or long head ; দীর্ঘমুণ্ডী।

măc′-rō-cŏsm, *n.* The great world ; the universe (as opp. to *microcosm*) ; ব্রহ্মাণ্ড [cf. যাহা আছে ভাণ্ডে তাহা আছে ব্রহ্মাণ্ডে], বিশ্বজগৎ, বিশ্ব-সংসার, মহাপ্রপঞ্চ, পিণ্ড (হিঃ কোঃ)। **—cos′-mic,** *adj.*

mă-crŏm′-ĕ-têr, *n.* An instrument for determining the size or distance for inaccessible objects ; অনধিগম্য বস্তুর দূরত্ব বা আয়তননির্ণায়ক-যন্ত্র, বিস্তারমাপক যন্ত্র (হিঃ কোঃ)।

mā′-crŏn, *n.* A sign placed over a vowel to show that it is long, as (-) in **ā** ; স্বরবর্ণের উপরিস্থ গুরু-উচ্চারণ নির্দ্দেশক চিহ্ন।

Macrones air—আইর (গুপ্তঃ)।

Macrones ccrsula — টেঙ্গরা (গুপ্তঃ)।

măc-rō-scŏp′-ic, *adj.* Visible to the naked eye (as opp. to *microscopic*) ; দূরবীক্ষণ, অণুবীক্ষণ, প্রভৃতি যন্ত্রের সাহায্য ব্যতিরেকে দর্শনযোগ্য।

măc′-ū-lă, *n.* (*Pl.* -LAE) **1.** A spot, esp. a permanent one on the skin ; মেচেতা, তিল। **2.** A dark spot on the surface of the sun ; সূর্য্যমণ্ডলস্থ কৃষ্ণবর্ণ চিহ্ন বা কলঙ্ক। **3.** A spot in a mineral ; খনিজ পদার্থের উপর দাগ। **—lar,** *adj.*

Spotted ; চিহ্নবিশিষ্ট, দাগযুক্ত। **–la′-tion,** *n.* A spot or mark ; দাগ, চিহ্ন, কলঙ্ক।

măd, *adj.* **1.** Disordered in intellect ; insane ; বিকৃতমস্তিষ্ক ; পাগল, বাতুল, ক্ষিপ্ত, উন্মাদ, ক্ষেপা, বায়ুগ্রস্ত, ভ্রষ্টবুদ্ধি, বিক্ষিপ্তমনস্ক, বিক্ষিপ্তমতি। **2.** Excited beyond self-control ; infatuated, (with *after, about, for, on*) ; as, he is *mad after* it ; উন্মত্ত, প্রমত্ত ; বিমুগ্ধ, পাগল। **3.** Proceeding from, or indicating, madness ; exceedingly foolish, as a person or act ; উন্মাদজনিত, উন্মাদ রোগসূচক ; বাতুলোচিত। **4.** Furious with rage, terror or disease ; rabid as an animal ; ক্রোধোন্মত্ত, উন্মদ, মদোদ্ধত, উদ্দাম, প্রমত্ত মদোগ্র ; ক্ষিপ্ত। **5.** (*Colloq.*) Vexed or annoyed ; as, I was rather *mad* at missing my train ; (চলিত ভাষায়) বিরক্ত। **6.** Extravagantly gay ; hilarious ; আনন্দোন্মত্ত, হর্ষপ্রমত্ত ; আনন্দাবিষ্ট। **Mad′-dish,** *adj.* Somewhat mad ; ক্ষেপাটিয়া, পাগলাটে। **Mad′-ling,** *n.* A mad man ; পাগল। **Mad′-ly,** *adv.* In a mad manner ; wildly ; উন্মত্তবৎ ; উদ্দামভাবে। **Mad′-ness,** *n.* Insanity ; wildness ; fury ; বাতুলতা, ক্ষেপামি, পাগলামি ; উদ্দাম ভাব ; ক্রোধোন্মত্ততা। **Madcap**—মাথাপাগলা লোক। **Mad-doctor**—উন্মাদরোগের চিকিৎসক। **Mad-house**—পাগলাগারদ, বাতুলাগার, বাতুলালয়। **Madman,–woman**—বাতুল, পাগলী। **Mad-wort**—ক্ষিপ্ত কুকুরের দংশনজনিত উন্মাদরোগের ঔষধস্বরূপ ব্যবহৃত গুল্মবিশেষ। **Like mad** — Furiously ; violently ; উন্মত্তবৎ ; উদ্দামভাবে, প্রচণ্ডভাবে। **As mad as a March hare**— Exceedingly mad ; বদ্ধ পাগল। **To go** or **run mad**— To become mad ; পাগল হওয়া। **To run** or **go mad after anything**—To become keenly eager for anything ; কোন কিছুর জন্য পাগল হওয়া।

măd, *v. t.* & *i.* (*Rare*) To make mad or insane ; (কচিদ্ ব্যবহৃত) পাগল করা, উন্মত্ত করা। ***Verb i.*** (*Rare*) To become mad ; to act madly ; as, the *madding* crowd ; (কচিদ্ ব্যবহৃত) পাগল হওয়া ; পাগলামি করা। **Mad′-ding,** *adj.* **1.** Acting madly ; ক্ষিপ্তবৎকার্য্যকারী। **2.** Maddening ; distracting ; উন্মাদক ; চিত্তবিক্ষেপকর।

măd′-ăm, *n.* A courteous form of address to a lady, esp. an elderly married one ; ভদ্রে, মহাশয়া, আর্য্যে।

madame (*F*), *n.* French form of MADAM.

măd-ă-pŏl′-lăm, *n.* A kind of cotton fabric ; একপ্রকার কার্পাস বস্ত্র, মাটাবালাম।

măd′-den (-n), *v. i.* & *t.* To make or become mad ; উন্মাদ করা ক্ষিপ্ত হওয়া। ***Verb t.*** To make mad ; to excite violently ; ক্ষিপ্ত করা ; ক্রোধোন্মত্ত করা, ক্ষেপাইয়া তোলা। **–ing,** *adj.* Causing madness ; উন্মাদক। **–ing-ly,** *adv.*

măd′-der (-êr), *n.* **1.** A climbing plant ; লতা বিশেষ। **2.** A dye got from it ; ঐ লতার শিকড় হইতে প্রাপ্ত রক্তবর্ণ রঞ্জক পদার্থ। **Indian madder**—মঞ্জিষ্ঠা।

Madder plant.

măde, *p. p.* of MAKE. নির্ম্মিত, রচিত গঠিত। **Made-dish**—বিভিন্ন উপকরণে প্রস্তুত ব্যঞ্জন। **Made-man**—যে ব্যক্তির জীবনে সফলতা সুনিশ্চিত। **Stoutly, loosely, powerfully, made**—Built or formed thus, as a person etc. ; দৃঢ়গঠিত, দৃঢ়কায়, শিথিলাঙ্গ।

Mă-dei′-ră (-dē-). *n.* A rich wine made in Madeira, an island in the Atlantic ; Madeira দ্বীপে প্রস্তুত মদিরাবিশেষ। **Madeira-cake**—একপ্রকার পিষ্টক।

mademoiselle, *n.* A courteous form of address applied to a French unmarried woman ; ফরাসীদেশে কুমারীগণের নামের পূর্ব্বে ব্যবহৃত শিষ্টাচারসূচক শব্দ [ইংরাজী Miss শব্দের প্রতিরূপ]।

mā′-di-ă, *n.* A plant allied to the sun-flower ; সূর্য্যমুখী জাতীয় পুষ্পতরুবিশেষ।

Mă-dŏn′-na (-ă) *n.* **1.** Virgin Mary ; কুমারী মেরী। **2.** Her picture or statue ; যীশুজননী কুমারী মেরীর চিত্র বা পাষাণ-মূর্ত্তি। **Madonna-lily** — শ্বেত স্থলকুমুদ, শাদা লিলি ফুল [মেডোনার চিত্রে ঐরূপ ফুল চিত্রিত হইয়া থাকে]।

măd′-rē-pōre, *n.* **1.** The common coral ; প্রবাল। **2.** An animal producing these ; প্রবাল কীট। **–por′-ic** *adj.* **–po′-ri-form,** *adj.*

măd′-ri-găl, *n.* **1.** A little amorous poem ; আদিরসাত্মক ক্ষুদ্র কবিতা। **2.** A pastoral song for several voices ; গোপগাথা, পল্লীগীতি। **–ga′-li-an,** *adj.*

mae-cē′-năs (mē-), *n.* A generous patron of literature and art ; (From Maecenas, the patron of Horace and Virgil) ; সাহিত্য বা ললিতকলার উদারচেতা পৃষ্ঠপোষক। [রোমনগরবাসী রাজনীতিবিশারদ Maecenasএর নাম হইতে গৃহীত। ইনি প্রাচীন রোমীয় কবি ভার্জ্জিলের বন্ধু ও পৃষ্ঠপোষক ছিলেন।]

mael′-strŏm (māl-), **1.** Accelerated whirlpool on the west coast of Norway ; নরওয়ে উপকূলের মহাবর্ত্ত। **2.** Any great whirlpool (*lit.* & *fig.*) ; (লক্ষণায়) মহাবর্ত্ত।

mae′-năd (mē-), *n.* A votaress of Bacchus ; সুরাদেবতার উপাসিকা।

maestoso, *adv.* (*It.*) (*Mus.*) Majestically ; (সঙ্গীত-শাস্ত্র) জমকালভাবে।

maestro, *n.* (*It.*) A musical master or composer; গীতবাদ্য-শিক্ষাদাতা, ওস্তাদ।

măf′-fick, *v. i.* To exult riotously; কোলাহল সহকারে আমোদ উল্লাস করা। [Mafeking শব্দ হইতে গৃহীত। ১৯০০ খৃষ্টাব্দে বুয়র যুদ্ধকালে উক্ত দুর্গ শত্রুর আসন্ন অধিকার হইতে রক্ষোপলক্ষে লণ্ডন নগরীতে যে আনন্দোৎসব হয় তৎস্মরণে এই শব্দটী গঠিত হইয়াছে।]

mā-fī′-ă, *n.* 1. (In Sicily) The popular hostility to law leading to refusal to bear witness in cases of crimes; বিধিবিদ্বেষ। 2. Those who share in this; বিধিবিদ্বেষী ব্যক্তিগণ।

măg, *n.* (*Slang*) A halfpenny; (ইতর ভাষায়) অর্দ্ধ পেনি।

măg-ă-zine′ (-zēn), *n.* 1. A store for arms, ammunition, and provision in time of war; শস্ত্রাগার, আয়ুধাগার, বারুদঘর, তোপখানা, অস্ত্রাগার। 2. The gunpowder room in a ship or fort; জাহাজ কিম্বা দুর্গের বারুদ ঘর। 3. A periodical publication containing compositions on various subjects; নানাপ্রকার প্রবন্ধ-সমন্বিত সাময়িকপত্র, সঞ্চয়না (বঃ দঃ নঃ) **Magazine gun** or **rifle** — এক প্রকার বন্দুক যাহাতে—নির্দ্দিষ্ট কোঠায় কার্ত্তুজ রাখিলে ইহার এক একটী আপনা আপনি বন্দুক ঘরায় আসিয়া লাগে, সুতরাং যাহাতে একবার কার্ত্তুজ ভরিলে পর পর অনেকবার আওয়াজ হয়।

măg′-dă-lene (-lĕn), **—lĕn**, *ns.* A reformed prostitute [From Mary Magdalene of Magdala, Luke viii, 2.]; যে গণিকা বেশ্যাবৃত্তি পরিত্যাগ পূর্ব্বক সৎপথ অবলম্বন করিয়াছে, সংশোধিতচরিত্রা গণিকা।

māge, *n.* (*Archaic*) A magician; a man of wisdom and learning; (অপ্রঃ) ঐন্দ্রজালিক; সুপণ্ডিত ব্যক্তি।

mă-gĕn′-tă, *n.* A colour between pink and red discovered soon after the battle of Magenta in North Italy (1859); মেজেণ্টা রং, পাটল।

măg′-got (-ŏt), *n.* 1. A worm or grub; কৃমি, পোকা, কীট। 2. Whim; caprice; as, a *maggot* in one's head; খেয়াল; মর্জ্জি। **—y**, *adj.* 1. Full of maggots; কৃমিসঙ্কুল।

mā′-gī, *n.* Priests of the ancient Persians; প্রাচীন পারসিক যাজক-মণ্ডলী। **—an**, *adj.* & *n.* 1. Of, or pertaining to, the magi; প্রাচীন পারসীক যাজকমণ্ডলী সম্পর্কীয়। 2. Magician; ঐন্দ্রজালিক, মায়াবী। (*Noun*) One of the magi; প্রাচীন পারসীক যাজক। **—an-ism**, *n.*

măg′-ic, *n.* & *adj.* 1. The pretended art of producing marvellous results by the aid of spirits or of the secret forces of nature; enchantment; sorcery; ইন্দ্রজাল, ভোজবিদ্যা; যাদু, মায়া, জাদু (হিঃ কোঃ); আসুরবিদ্যা, শাবরীবিদ্যা। 2. Inexplicable or remarkable influence producing wonderful results; ঐন্দ্রজালিক প্রভাব। *Adj.* 1. Of, or relating to, the art of magic; ইন্দ্রজালবিদ্যা সম্বন্ধীয়, ভোজবিদ্যাসম্বন্ধীয়। 2. Working, worked by, or as if, by magic; আভিচারিক, মায়িক, যাদুবিদ্যাদ্বারাকৃত। **—i-cal**, *adj.* Same as MAGIC. *adj.* **—i-cal-ly**, *adv.* **Black-magic**—আসুরী বিদ্যা, বামতন্ত্র (হিঃ কোঃ), বামোপচার (ঐ), অভিচার (ঐ), ভূতপ্রেতাদি অপদেবতার সাহায্যে ইন্দ্রজাল, শয়তানি ভোজবিদ্যা। **Magic-art**—মন্ত্র-বিদ্যা। **Magic-lantern**—যে প্রদীপের সাহায্যে ক্ষুদ্র ক্ষুদ্র চিত্র পর্দ্দার উপর বৃহদাকারে প্রতিফলিত করা যায়, যাদুপ্রদীপ। **Magic-square**—যে বর্গক্ষেত্র ক্ষুদ্রতর কতপয় বর্গক্ষেত্রে বিভক্ত করিলে সেই প্রকোষ্ঠ গুলিতে এরূপভাবে অঙ্কপাত করা যাহাতে ঐ অঙ্কগুলির যোগফল লম্বালম্ব, পাশাপাশি, অথবা কোণাকুণি ভাবে সমান হয়, বত্রিশেরঘর পূরণ। **Magic-wand**—ঐন্দ্রজালিক যষ্টি, যাদুদণ্ড, মায়াদণ্ড, মায়াযষ্টি। **White-magic** — নির্দ্দোষ ভোজবিদ্যা।

mă-gī-cian (-shăn), *n.* A wizard an enchanter; ঐন্দ্রজালিক; যাদুকর, যাদুগীর, মায়াবী, মায়াকার, মায়ী, মন্ত্রিক (শুক্রঃবিনয়)।

mă-gilp′, *n.* A vehicle used by oil-painters consisting of linseed oil and mastic varnish; তৈলচিত্রাঙ্কণ-কারীদিগের রঙ্গ গুলিবার জন্য তিসির তৈল ও রুমিমস্তকির মিশ্র।

măg-is-tē′-ri-ăl, *adj.* 1. Of, or pertaining to, a magistrate; conducted by him; মেজিস্ট্রেট সম্বন্ধীয়; মেজিস্ট্রেট দ্বারা পরিচালিত। 2. Invested with authority; ক্ষমতান্বিত। 3. Dictatorial; প্রভুত্বখ্যাপক। 4. Imperious; authoritative, as an opinion; উদ্ধত; প্রভুত্বজ্ঞাপক, প্রভুত্বব্যঞ্জক। **—ly**, *adv.*

măg′-is-trăl, *adj.* 1. Of, or relating to, a master or masters; as, the *magistral* staff of a school; প্রভু বা প্রভুগণ সম্বন্ধীয়। 2. Formulated for a particular case, as a medicine etc. (opp. to *officinal*); কোন বিশেষ রোগের জন্য গঠিত।

măg′-is-trāte, *n.* 1. A civil officer administering law; দণ্ডনায়ক, পুরাধ্যক্ষ, ন্যায়াধীশ, ধর্ম্মাধিকারী, ধর্ম্মাধ্যক্ষ। 2. Same as JUSTICE OF THE PEACE. **—ship**, *n.* **—tra-cy**, *n.* The office or dignity of a magistrate; the body of magistrates; দণ্ডনায়কের পদ বা মর্য্যাদা; দণ্ডনায়কসম্প্রদায়, ফৌজদারী বিচারকর্ত্তৃ-সম্প্রদায়। **—tra-ture**, *n.*

măg′-mă, *n.* 1. A crude mixture of mineral or organic matters in the state of a thin paste; খনিজ বা জৈব পদার্থের অশোধিত মণ্ডবৎ মিশ্র। 2. One of the supposed fluid strata under the solid crust of the earth; পৃথিবীর কঠিন আবরণের নিম্নস্থ কল্পিত দ্রব পদার্থের স্তর।

Măg-nă-chār′-tă, **—Câr′-tă**, *ns.* Great charter of English political liberty obtained from king John in 1215; ইংলণ্ডীয় প্রজাগণের রাজনৈতিক ও ব্যক্তিগত স্বাধীনতাসম্পর্কীয় প্রধান সনন্দ। ১২১৫ খৃঃ অব্দে রাজা

জনের নিকট হইতে ইহা গৃহীত হইয়াছিল, মহাসনন্দ।

măg-nă-nim′-i-tў̆, *n.* **1.** The quality of being magnanimous ; greatness of soul or mind ; মহানুভাব, উদারাত্মতা (হিঃ কোঃ), ঔদার্য্য, মহত্ব ; সদাশয়তা, মহানুভবতা ; মহাপ্রাণতা, মাহাত্ম্য। **2.** (*Pl.*) Instances of magnanimity ; "Aspire unto the calms and *magnanimities*..." ; মহানুভবতার কার্য্য। **—nan′-i-mous,** *adj.* Great of soul or mind ; noble ; above meanness or selfishness ; মহানুভাব, মহামনা, উদারচেতা, মহাত্মা, মহাপ্রাণ ; মহামতি, উদারচরিত, উন্নতচেতাঃ, উন্নতমনাঃ, মহৎ, মহাত্মা। **—nan′-i-mous-ly,** *adv.*

măg′-nāte, *n.* Great man ; wealthy or eminent man ; মহৎব্যক্তি ; ধনীলোক, বড়লোক, সম্ভ্রান্ত লোক, পদস্থব্যক্তি।

măg-nē′-si-ă (-shĭ-), *n.* **1.** A light white powder got by burning magnesium ; দগ্ধমগ্নক-চূর্ণ। [বিরেচক ঔষধরূপে ব্যবহৃত হয়।] **—an,** *adj.* **—sic,** *adj.* **Magnesic carbonate**—অঙ্গারকীয় মগ্ন।

măg-nē′-si-ŭm (-shĭ-), *n.* A white malleable metal ; একপ্রকার রজতশুভ্র ধাতু, মগ্ন (হিঃ কোঃ), মগ্নক (সাঃ পঃ)।

măg′-nĕt, *n.* **1.** Loadstone ; অয়স্কান্ত, চুম্বক, চুম্বকপ্রস্তর, আকর্ষকমণি। **2.** A bar of steel or iron to which

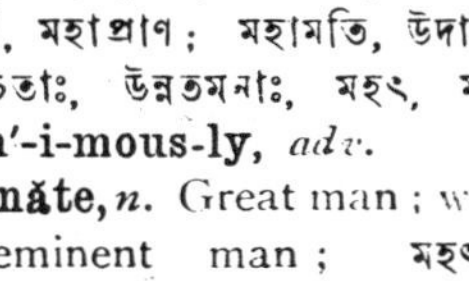

Magnet.

the properties of the loadstone have been imparted ; অয়স্কান্তমণির ধর্ম্মসঞ্চারিত লৌহ। **3.** (*Fig.*) Something that attracts ; (লক্ষণায়) আকর্ষকবস্তু, চুম্বক। **Artificial magnet**—কৃত্রিমচুম্বক (হিঃ কোঃ)। **Natural magnet**—স্বাভাবিক চুম্বক (হিঃ কোঃ), অকৃত্রিম চুম্বক (ঐ)।

măg-nĕt′-ic, *adj.* & *n.* Of, or pertaining to, the magnet ; possessing the properties of the magnet ; চৌম্বক, চুম্বকীয় ; চুম্বকধর্ম্মাক্রান্ত, চুম্বকধর্ম্মবিশিষ্ট, চুম্বকপ্রস্তরস্বভাব। **2.** Producing magnetism ; চুম্বকত্বজনক। **3.** Capable of being magnatized as a metal ; capable of being attracted by loadstone ; চুম্বকধর্ম্মগ্রাহী ; চুম্বক দ্বারা আকর্ষণীয়। **4.** (*Fig.*) Attractive ; (লক্ষণায়) আকর্ষক। **5.** Mesmeric ; যোগনিদ্রাসম্পর্কীয়। ***Noun.*** (*Pl.*) The science of magnetism ; চুম্বকবিদ্যা, চুম্বকবিজ্ঞান। **—i-cal-ly,** *adv.* **Magnetic attraction**—চুম্বকীয় আকর্ষণ (হিঃ কোঃ)।

măg′-nĕt-ĭsm, *n.* **1.** The properties of a magnet ; magnetic phenomena ; natural agency bringing about these ; চৌম্বকধর্ম্ম, চুম্বকশক্তি (হিঃ কোঃ), চুম্বকত্ব (ঐ) ; চৌম্বকব্যাপার ; যে সকল নৈসর্গিক শক্তি দ্বারা চৌম্বকীয় ব্যাপার সংঘটিত হয়। **2.** The science which treats of the properties of the magnet ; চুম্বকবিজ্ঞান। **3.** (*Fig.*) Attraction ; (লক্ষণায়) আকর্ষণ। **4.** Mesmerism ; মৈস্মরতত্ব। **—ist,** *n.* **Animal magnetism**—See MAGNETISM 4. **Personal magnetism**—ব্যক্তিত্বের আকর্ষণী শক্তি। **Terrestrial magnetism**—পৃথিবীর চৌম্বক গুণ, ভূচুম্বকত্ব।

măg′-nĕt-īte, *n.* Magnetic oxide of iron ; মুণ্ডলৌহ।

măg′-nĕt-īze, *v. t.* **1.** To supply with magnetic properties ; চুম্বকধর্ম্মাক্রান্ত করা। **2.** To attract as by a magnet, (*lit.* & *fig.*) ; চুম্বকের ন্যায় আকর্ষণ করা। **3.** To mesmerise ; যোগনিদ্রাভিভূত করা। **—i-za′-tion,** *n.*

măg-nĕt-ō-ē-lĕc-trĭc′-i-tў̆, *n.* Electricity produced by the action of magnets চুম্বকীয় বিদ্যুৎ (হিঃ কোঃ)।

măg-nĭf′-ic, *adj.* (*Archaic*) Splendid ; sublime ; (অপ্রঃ) জমকালো ; প্রশান্ত-গম্ভীর।

măg-nĭf′-i-căt, *n.* The song or hymn of the Virgin Mary in Luke I. 46-55, so called because it commences with this word ; যীশুজননী কুমারী মেরীর স্তোত্র।

măg-nĭf′-i-cĕnt, *adj.* **1.** Grand ; splendid ; pompous ; জমকালো ; জাঁকজমকশালী, চমৎকার ; আড়ম্বরপূর্ণ। **2.** Sumptuously constructed or adorned ; imposing ; জমকালোভাবে নির্ম্মিত বা সজ্জিত ; চিত্তাকর্ষক। **3.** (*Colloq.*) Fine ; excellent ; (চলিত ভাষায়) সুন্দর ; চমৎকার। **—cence,** *n.* Grandeur ; splendour ; জাঁকজমক, ঠাঁট, বৈভব ; শোভা, সমৃদ্ধি। **—ly,** *adv.*

măg-nĭf′-i-cō, *n.* **1.** A magnate of Venice ; ভেনিশ নগরীর সম্ভ্রান্ত ব্যক্তি। **2.** A person in an exalted position ; উচ্চপদস্থ ব্যক্তি।

măg′-ni-fў̆, *v. t.* **1.** To make great or greater in size ; to enlarge ; to exaggerate ; বর্দ্ধিত করা, বাড়াইয়া তোলা ; বড় করা ; বাড়াইয়া বলা, অত্যুক্তি করা। **2.** (*Archaic*) To increase ; (অপ্রঃ) বাড়ান। **3.** (*Archaic*) To extol ; (অপ্রঃ) অতি প্রশংসা করা। **—fi-ca′-tion,** *n.* **—fi-er,** *n.* **Magnifying glass** — যে উভয়পার্শ্বমধ্যোন্নত কাচখণ্ডের ভিতর দিয়া দেখিলে দ্রব্যের আয়তন বড় দেখায়, বৃহৎপ্রদর্শক তাল (হিঃ কোঃ), বিপুলদর্শক কাচ, আকারবর্দ্ধক কাচ। **To magnify one's self**—To show great pride ; অত্যধিক অহঙ্কার প্রদর্শন করা।

măg-nĭl′-ō-quĕnt, *adj.* **1.** Speaking loftily or pompously ; প্রগল্‌ভভাষী, শব্দাড়ম্বরবহুল। **2.** Boastful ; talking big ; গর্ব্বিত, অহঙ্কারী ; বাক্যবাগীশ। **—ly,** *adv.* **—quence,** *n.*

măg′-ni-tūde, *n.* **1.** Greatness ; as, the *magnitude* of mind ; বৃহত্ব, মহত্ব (হিঃ কোঃ), বিপুলত্ব, বিশালতা। **2.** Size ; bulk ; আয়তন, আকার ; পরিমাণ, ইয়ত্তা, পরিসর, আয়তি (সাঃ পঃ)। **3.** Importance ; গুরুত্ব। **First, seventh, etc. magnitude** — উজ্জ্বলতার মাত্রা অনুসারে

শ্রেণীবদ্ধ স্থির নক্ষত্রগণ। **Of the first magnitude** — Of the first importance ; সর্ব্বাগ্রগণ্য।

măg-nō'-li-ă, *n.* A genus of trees with beautiful foliage and flowers ; উত্তর আমেরিকার চাঁপা ফুলের গাছ। **Magnolia grandiflora**—জহরী চাঁপা (বোঃ)। **Red magnolia**—রক্তচম্পক। **White magnolia**—শ্বেতচম্পক।

măg'-nŭm, *n.* A bottle holding two quarts of wine etc. ; two quarts ; দুই কোয়ার্ট পরিমাণ তরল পদার্থ ধরে এরূপ বোতল ; দুই কোয়ার্ট। **Magnum opus**—See under OPUS.

măg'-nŭm-bō'-nŭm, *n.* **1.** A large oval plum ; একপ্রকার ডিম্বাকৃতি বৃহৎ বদরী ফল। **2.** A kind of potato ; একজাতীয় গোল আলু। **3.** A kind of large sized barrel pen ; একপ্রকার বড় আকারের চোঙ্গা বিশিষ্ট কলমের মুখ।

măg'-pie (-pī), *n.* **1.** A European bird with pied or coloured

Magpie.

feathers ; দৈয়াল (জাতীয়) পক্ষি-বিশেষ। **2.** A chatterer ; বকবককারী। **3.** A kind of pegion ; একপ্রকার কপোত। **4.** (*Mil.*) The outermost division but one of a target ; a shot striking this ; শরব্যের সর্ব্ব-বহির্ব্বর্ত্তী বিভাগের অব্যবহিত অন্তর্ব্বর্ত্তী বিভাগ ; ঐ স্থানে যে গুলি আঘাত করে। **Indian magpie** — হাঁড়ীচাঁচা। **Magpie robin**—দোয়েল (বোঃ), দয়াল (ঐ), দইয়াল (ঐ)।

măg'-ŭs, *n.* (*Pl.* MAGI), **1.** A priest of ancient Persia ; প্রাচীন পারস্যদেশের যাজক। **2.** A magician ; ঐন্দ্রজালিক, মায়াবী। **The (three) Magi** — পূর্ব্বদেশীয় যে জ্ঞানিত্রয় শিশু যীশুর নিকট উপহার লইয়া আসিয়াছিলেন।

Măg'-yâr, *n.* & *adj.* One of the prevailing race in Hungary ; their language ; হাঙ্গেরীদেশের জাতি বিশেষ ; তাহাদের ভাষা। ***Adj.*** Of, or relating to, these people or their language ; উক্ত জাতি কিম্বা তাহাদের ভাষাসম্পর্কীয়।

Mahdi, *n.* The great leader expected by the faithful Mohammedans, to appear in the last days ; ইমাম মেহেদি। [সচরাচর সুদানের (Soudan) বিদ্রোহিদলের নেতার সম্পর্কে ব্যবহৃত হয়।]

mahl'-stick (măl-), *n.* A rod used by artists as a rest for the hand in painting ; (also *maul-stick*) ; চিত্রাঙ্কণকালে চিত্রকরদের দক্ষিণ হস্ত স্থাপনের জন্য যষ্টি বিশেষ।

mă-hŏg'-ă-nȳ, *n.* **1.** A tree of tropical America ; মেহগ্নি বৃক্ষ। **2.** Its wood much used for furniture ; মেহগ্নি কাঠ। **3.** A dining table ; অপরাহ্ন-ভোজনের মেজ। **4.** The colour of mahogany ; reddish brown ; (often used *attributive-ly*) ; মেহগ্নি-বর্ণ ; রক্তাভ-পিঙ্গলবর্ণ।

Mā'-hound (-hownd), *n.* (*Archaic*) A contemptuous name for Mohammed ; (অপ্রঃ) মহম্মদের অবজ্ঞাসূচক নাম, মামুদ।

maid (mād), *n.* **1.** A girl ; virgin ; কন্যা, কন্যকা ; তরুণী, কুমারী, বালা। **2.** A female servant ; পরিচারিকা, দাসী। **Maid'-ish,** *adj.* **Maid'-y,** *adj.* **Maid-servant** — পরিচারিকা, দাসী। **Maid-of-all-work**—যে পরিচারিকা রন্ধনাদি যাবতীয় গৃহস্থালীর কার্য্য করিয়া থাকে। **Maid of honour** — রাণী বা রাজপুত্রীর অনূঢ়া সহচরী। **Old maid**—বর্ষীয়সী অনূঢ়া নারী।

maid'-en (mād-n), *n.* & *adj.* **1.** A maid or virgin ; কুমারী, কন্যা। **2.** A machine like the guillotine formerly used in Scotland for beheading criminals ; মৃত্যুদণ্ডে দণ্ডিত ব্যক্তিগণের শিরশ্ছেদের জন্য যন্ত্রবিশেষ। ***Adj.*** **1.** Pertaining to a virgin ; unmarried ; কুমারী-বিষয়ক ; অবিবাহিতা, অনূঢ়া। **2.** (*Fig.*) Unpolluted ; fresh ; (লক্ষণায়) অকলঙ্কিত ; তরুণ, অভিনব, টাট্কা, নবীন। **3.** (Of female animals) Uncoupled ; (স্ত্রী-জন্তু সম্পর্কে) অবিদ্ধযোনি। **4.** Having won a prize as a race-horse ; open to such horses as a race ; পুরস্কার-প্রাপ্ত ; পুরস্কার-প্রাপ্ত অশ্বের পক্ষে উন্মুক্ত। **5.** Grown from the seed, as a plant ; বীজ হইতে জাত। **6.** (*Cricket—of an over*) In which no run was scored ; (পাঁচ কি ছয়বার কন্দুক ক্ষেপের মধ্যে) অলব্ধ-জয়াঙ্ক। **7.** (Of soldiers, swords, etc.) Untried or unused ; অপরীক্ষিত, অব্যবহৃত। **—hood,** *n.* কৌমার্য্য, কৌমার। **—ish,** *adj.* **—like, —ly,** *adjs.* Becoming a maiden ; gentle ; modest ; কুমারী-জনোচিত ; শান্ত ; লজ্জাশীল। **Maiden-assize** — বিলাতের যে প্রব্রজনশীল প্রাদেশিক দায়রার আদালতের অধিবেশনে ফৌজদারী মামলা মোকদ্দমা থাকে না। **Maiden-fortress**—যে দুর্গ কখনই শত্রুর হস্তগত হয় নাই। **Maiden-**

Maiden-h[illegible]r.

hair—পাষাণফলকের [illegible] জাত এক প্রকার সুদৃশ্য পর্ণাঙ্গ, কালি [illegible] (বোঃ)।

Maiden-head—Virginity; কৌমার্য্য। **Maiden-name** — বিবাহিতা নারীর পিতৃবংশীয় নাম। **Maiden-speech**—সভাসমিতিতে সর্ব্বপ্রথম যে বক্তৃতা দেওয়া হয়। **Maiden-tongued** — কুমারী-কোমলকণ্ঠ। **Maiden over** — (*In cricket*) See MAIDEN 6.

mā-ieu'-tic (-ü-), *adj.* & *n* **1.** (Of Socratic method of inquiry) Serving to bring out from people the truth by continual questioning; প্রশ্নের উপর প্রশ্ন করিয়া কোন ব্যক্তির নিকট হইতে সত্য বাহির করণ। **2.** (*Rare*) Serving to assist child-birth; (অপ্রঃ) সন্তানপ্রসব সহায়ক। ***Noun.*** **1.** (*Pl.*) The Socratic method; সক্রেতিসের প্রণালী। **2.** Midwifery; ধাত্রীবিদ্যা।

mail (māl), *n.* Armour for the body formed of steel rings or network; armour generally; যুদ্ধে শরীররক্ষার্থ ইস্পাতের চক্র বা বলয়-সমন্বিত একপ্রকার জামা; বর্ম্ম, কবচ, সাঁজোয়া, বারবাণ, কঞ্চুক, কবচ, অক্ত।

mail (māl), *v. t.* To clothe in mail; বর্ম্মপরিহিত করা। **The mailed fist** — (*Fig.*) Physical strength; (লক্ষণায়) দৈহিক বল, শারীরিক শক্তি।

mail (māl), *n.* & *v. t.* **1.** A bag for the conveyance of letters etc.; the contents of such a bag; ডাকের ব্যাগ; ডাকের থলির মধ্যস্থ চিঠি পত্রাদি। **2.** The post esp. for foreign letters; ডাক, বৈদেশিক ডাক। **3.** The person, carriage or train, by which the mail is conveyed; যে লোক, গাড়ী বা ট্রেণ ডাক বহন করে, ডাক হর-করা, ডাকগাড়ী। ***Verb t.*** To send by mail, as letters etc.; ডাকে পাঠান। **Mail bag** — ডাকের ব্যাগ। **Mail boat**—ডাকের নৌকা। **Mail cart**—ডাক বহনের জন্ম গোযান। **Mail-catcher**—চলন্ত গাড়ীতে ডাকের থলি তুলিবার জন্ম একপ্রকার যন্ত্র। **Mail-coach**—(বর্ত্তমানে) ডাক বহনের জন্ম শকট; (পূর্ব্বে) ঘোড়ার গাড়ীর ডাক। **Mail-guard**—ডাকের ব্যাগের ভারপ্রাপ্ত কর্ম্মচারী। **Mail-train** — ডাক গাড়ী। **The mail**—ডাক।

maim (mām), *v. t.* To bruise; to mutilate; to cripple; (*lit.* & *fig.*); ছিন্নবিচ্ছিন্ন করা, ক্ষতবিক্ষত করা; অঙ্গচ্ছেদ করা; বিকলাঙ্গ করা, অঙ্গহীন করা, হীনাঙ্গ করা, বিকল করা, বিকলাঙ্গ করা, পঙ্গু করা। **Maimed,** *p. p.* Mutiltated; বিকলাঙ্গ, পঙ্গু নুলা, ঠুঁঠা।

main (mān), *n.* **1.** Might; strength; (only in *with might and main*); শক্তি; বল। **2.** (*Poet.*) The main or high sea; (কবিতায়) মহা সমুদ্র, তরঙ্গায়িতসাগর। **3.** (*Archaic*) Mainland or continent; মহাদেশ অথবা বৃহৎ দ্বীপ। **4.** The principal duct or pipe; as, a gas, water or electric light *main*; প্রধান নল। **Spanish main**—See under SPANISH. **In the main**—For the most part; প্রধানতঃ। **With might and main**—With all force or effort; প্রাণপণে, সর্ব্বপ্রযত্নে।

main (mān), *adj.* **1.** Chief; principal; first in importance; leading; প্রধান; মুখ্য; সর্ব্বাগ্রগণ্য; নেতৃস্থানীয়। **2.** Used with all one's might; as, by *main* force; প্রাণপণ বলে চালিত। **Main'-ly,** *adv.* Chiefly; principally; প্রধানতঃ, মুখ্যতঃ; মোটামুটি। **Main body** — The principal part of an army etc.; সৈন্যদল প্রভৃতির প্রধান ভাগ। **Main-deck**—জাহাজের প্রধান পাটাতন। **Mainland**—The principal land as opposed to an island; the continent; প্রধান ভূভাগ; মহাদেশ। **Main-line**—প্রধান লৌহবর্ত্ম। **Main-mast**—প্রধান মাস্তুল। **Main-sail**—জাহাজের সর্ব্বপ্রধান পাইল। **Main-sheet** — প্রধান মাস্তুল-সংলগ্ন রজ্জু। **Main-spring**—ঘড়ি প্রভৃতির প্রধান স্প্রীং বা দম। **Main-stay**—The rope extending from the top of the mainmast to the deck; প্রধান মাস্তুলের অগ্রভাগ হইতে পাটাতন পর্য্যন্ত বিস্তৃত দীর্ঘ রজ্জু। (*Fig.*) Main support; (লক্ষণায়) প্রধান অবলম্বন। **Main-stream**—মুখ্য প্রবাহ (হিঃ কোঃ)। **Main top**—প্রধান মাস্তুলের অগ্রভাগ। **Main-yard**—যে পাইলদণ্ডের উপর প্রধান পাইল প্রসারিত করা হয়। **The main guard** — The cavalry guard for a camp; শিবির-রক্ষী অশ্বারোহী সৈন্য। **To have an eye to the main chance**—To look to one's own interest; নিজের স্বার্থের দিকে দৃষ্টি রাখা। **To splice the main-brace**—(*Slang*) To drink freely; (ইতরভাষায়) দেদার মদ খাওয়া।

main-tain' (mān-tān), *v. t.* **1.** To keep in any state or condition; as, to *maintain* one in possession of a thing; কোন অবস্থায় বজায় রাখা। **2.** To carry on; to) keep up; চালান; বজায় রাখা। **3.** To uphold or back; to support; as, to *maintain* a cause, party; সমর্থন করা; পৃষ্ঠপোষণ করা। **4.** To furnish with means of subsistence; to support; as, to *maintain* life, oneself or children; জীবিকার সংস্থান করা; ভরণপোষণ-করা, প্রতিপালন করা। **5.** To keep or repair, as a road etc.; মেরামত করিয়া রাখা। **6.** To hold or defend, as a position etc.; রক্ষা করা, সংরক্ষণ করা। **7.** To affirm; to assert as true; দৃঢ়তার সহিত বলা; নিশ্চয় পূর্ব্বক বলা। **—a-ble,** *adj.* That can be maintained, supported or defended; সমর্থনীয়, সংধার্য্য, রক্ষণীয়।

main'-tĕ-năṅce (mān-), *n.* **1.** The act of maintaining, supporting or defending; রক্ষণ, প্রতিপালন, ভরণপোষণ, ধারণ (হিঃ কোঃ), ভরণ (ঐ), পোষণ (ঐ)। **2.** Means of support; জীবিকা, জীবনোপায়, ভৃতি। **Cap of maintenance**—See CAP.

maize (māz), *n.* The Indian corn (the plant or the grain) ; ভুট্টা, জনার, মক্কা জোয়ার।

Maize.

mai-zē′-nā (mā-), *n.* A food preparation of maize starch ; ভুট্টার আটা হইতে প্রস্তুত খাদ্য বিশেষ।

mǎj′-ĕs-tÿ, *n.* **1.** Stateliness ; grandeur ; প্রতাপ, রাজশ্রী, রাজপ্রতাপ, রাজগৌরব ; মহিমা, গরিমা, গৌরব, বিভূতি। **2.** Sovereign-power ; রাজপ্রতাপ। **3.** A title of king or other sovereigns ; as, His or Her Majesty ; রাজোপাধি। **4.** A representation of Christ or of God the Father enthroned with aureole ; খৃষ্ট অথবা পিতা ঈশ্বরের জ্যোতির্মণ্ডলমধ্যবর্ত্তী সিংহাসনাধিষ্ঠিত মূর্তি। **Ma-jes′-tic,** *adj.* Stately ; sublime ; imposing ; মহামহিম, ...াল, মহিমাব্যঞ্জক, মহিমান্বিত ; প্রবলপ্রতাপান্বিত, সুমহান্। **Ma-jes′-ti-cal-ly,** *adv.*

mā′-jor (-jĕr), *adj.* & *n.* **1.** Greater in number, quantity or size ; বৃহত্তর, অধিকতর, অধিকপরিমাণক, শ্রেষ্ঠতর, মুখ্যতর, প্রধান (হিঃ কোঃ), শ্রেষ্ঠ (ঐ)। **2.** Of full age ; পূর্ণবয়স্ক, প্রাপ্ত-বয়স্ক, প্রাপ্ত-ব্যবহার। **3.** (*Mus.*—Of intervals) Greater by half step than the minor ; as, a *major* third ; (of keys) in which a scale has a major third ; (সঙ্গীত-শাস্ত্র) সাগ্রামের ; (চাবি-সম্বন্ধে) সাগ্রামের এক হইতে তিন চিহ্নের মধ্যবর্ত্তী স্থানের। ***Noun.*** A person of full age ; সাবালক, প্রাপ্তবয়স্ক ব্যক্তি, বয়ঃপ্রাপ্ত ব্যক্তি, পূর্ণবয়স্ক ব্যক্তি। **Major-axis**—মুখ্য অক্ষ। **Major chord**—প্রধান পূর্ণজ্যা (হিঃ কোঃ)। **Major epilepsy**—পক্ষাঘাত রোগ। **Major domo**—রাজা বা জমীদার বাড়ীর দেওয়ান ; বাড়ীর নায়েব ; প্রধানমন্ত্রী। **Major-mode**—(সঙ্গীতশাস্ত্র) মধ্যগ্রাম। **Major part**—Majority ; অধিকাংশ। **Major premise** — That containing the major term ; ব্যাপ্তিবাক্য (হিঃ কোঃ), ব্যাপকপূর্ব্বাবয়ব (ঐ), অনুগমবাক্য (ঐ), উদাহরণ (ঐ)। **Major scale**—সাগ্রাম। **Major term**—(*Log.*) That enters into predicate of conclusion of syllogism ; (তর্কবিজ্ঞান) সাধ্য, ব্যাপকপদ। **Brown, Smith major**—ব্রাউন বা Smith ভ্রাতৃগণের মধ্যে জ্যেষ্ঠ বা বিদ্যালয়ে অগ্রে প্রবিষ্ট।

mā′-jor (-jĕr), *n.* An officer in rank between a captain and a lieutenant-colonel ; লেফ্‌টেনেন্ট কর্ণেল এবং কাপ্তেনের মধ্যবর্ত্তী সৈনিক কর্ম্মচারি, মেজর। **—ship,** *n.* The office of major ; মেজরের পদ। **Major-general**—লেফ্‌টেনেন্ট জেনারেলের অব্যবহিত নিম্নতর সামরিক কর্ম্মচারী।

mā-jŏr′-i-tÿ, *n.* **1.** The greater number ; more than half ; অধিকাংশ ; অর্দ্ধেকের বেশী। **2.** Full age ; সাবালকত্ব, প্রাপ্তবয়স্কতা। **3.** The rank or office of a major ; মেজরের পদ। **4.** The number by which votes cast on one side exceed those on the other ; দুই পক্ষের ভোট-সংখ্যার অন্তর। **Absolute majority of votes**—কোন সভ্যপদ প্রার্থিকর্ত্তৃক প্রাপ্ত ভোট—যাহা সমগ্র ভোট নির্ব্বাচক সংখ্যার অর্দ্ধেকের অধিক। **The majority, The great majority**—The dead ; মৃত ব্যক্তিগণ। **To go over to** or **join the majority**—To die ; মরা।

mā-jŭs′-cūle, *n.* & *adj.* A capital or uncial letter ; বড় হাতের অক্ষর, বড় অক্ষর। ***Adj.*** Large ; capital or uncial ; বড় ; বড় হাতের। **—cu-lar,** *adj.*

make, *v. t.* & *i.* **1.** To form ; to frame ; প্রস্তুত করা ; গঠন করা, নির্ম্মাণ করা। **2.** To produce ; to compose ; to perform or draw up ; as, to *make* a book, deed, etc. ; উৎপাদন করা ; রচনা করা ; সম্পাদন করা, মুসাবিদা করা। **3** To occasion ; to bring about, as a disturbance, noise, etc. ; উৎপাদন করা ; জন্মান। **4.** To prepare, as tea, coffee, etc. ; প্রস্তুত করা, তৈয়ার করা। **5.** To have or feel ; as, to *make* a doubt, scruple, etc. ; থাকা, বোধ করা। **6.** To establish ; to enact, as a rule, law, etc. ; স্থাপন করা, প্রতিষ্ঠা করা ; বিধান করা। **7.** To commit as a fault ; (দোষ) করা। **8.** To ascertain by reckoning, measuring, etc. ; গণিয়া বা মাপিয়া নির্ণয় করা। **9.** To amount to ; মোটে হওয়া। **10.** To serve or answer for ; as, this *makes* a pleasant reading ; কাজ করা। **11.** To compel or require ; as, he *made* me go ; বাধ্য করা, চাওয়া। **12.** To get together as a quorum etc. ; একত্র করা, সংগ্রহ করা। **13.** (*Naut.*) To come nearer or in sight of ; to arrive at ; (নৌ-বিদ্যা) আরো নিকটে আসা, দৃষ্টিপথে আসা ; পৌছা। **14.** To constitute ; as, one swallow does not *make* a summer ; প্রতিষ্ঠা করা। **15.** To be counted ; as, will you *make* one of the party ? ; সংখ্যাতে হওয়া। **16.** To turn out ; as, he will *make* a great man ; হইয়া উঠা, হইয়া পড়া। **17.** To acquire ; to gain, as money, a living, etc. ; লাভ করা ; অর্জ্জন করা, রোজগার, করা। **18.** (*Cards*) To play, as a card, to advantage ; to shuffle (cards) (তাস খেলা) সুবিধাজনকভাবে তাস খেলা ; তাস ভেস্তান, তাসা। **19.** To cause to be ; as, to *make* oneself a martyr ; করা। **20.** To convert (*into*) ; পরিণত করা। **21.** To think or consider to be ; as, I *make* it 5 miles ; মনে করা, ভাবা। **22.** To declare or wage, as war ; যুদ্ধাদি ঘোষণা করা, ...

প্রবৃত্ত হওয়া। **23.** To perform, as a bodily movement, a journey, etc. ; সম্পাদন করা। **24.** To travel over ; to pass over the distance of ; as, the ship *makes* 30 knots per hour ; ভ্রমণ করা ; স্থান অতিক্রম করা। ***Verb i.*** **1.** To go or proceed (towards) ; যাওয়া, অগ্রসর হওয়া। **2.** To contribute, (with *for* or *against*); as, it *makes* for his advantage ; আংশিকভাবে প্রদান করা। **3.** To act in a certain manner, (*sometimes with qualifying adjectives*) ; as, to *make* merry, bold, etc. ; কোন বিশেষ ভাবে কাজ করা। **4.** (Of a tide) To begin to ebb or flow ; ভাঁটা হওয়া, জোয়ার হওয়া। **Make-bate** — (*Archaic*) (অপ্রঃ) বিবাদসংঘটককারী। **Make-believe**—Pretence ছল, বাহানা, অছিলা, ভাণ। **Make-peace** — A peace-maker ; শান্তিসংস্থাপক। **Makeshift**—Temporary substitute or device ; সাময়িক উপায় বা কৌশল। **Make-up**—The way in which anything is arranged ; বিন্যাসপ্রণালী। Disguise of an actor ; cosmetics etc. used for this ; অভিনেতার ছদ্মবেশ ; উক্ত উদ্দেশ্য সাধনের জন্য মুখরাগ, দীর্ঘকেশ, প্রভৃতি। (*Adj.*) Arranged as types in columns or pages ; (মুদ্রাক্ষরসমূহ) স্তম্ভে স্তম্ভে বা পৃষ্ঠায় পৃষ্ঠায় বিন্যস্ত। **Makeweight** — small quantity added to make up weight, esp. a small candle, (also *fig.* of persons) ; পাল্লার দুই দিকের ওজন সমান করার জন্য যে ক্ষুদ্র ওজন যোগ করা হয়, কড়চা ; (*Fig.*) An unimportant point added to make a case seem stronger ; (লক্ষণায়) কোন বিষয় আরো দৃঢ় করার জন্য যে অপ্রয়োজনীয় বিষয় যোগ করা হয়। **To make a cat's paw of**—To make a dupe or tool of another ; ক্রীড়াপুত্তলি করা। **To make account of**—To esteem ; গণ্য করা। **To make a clean breast of**—To confess all ; to conceal nothing ; অকপটচিত্তে স্বীকার করা, অকপটে খুলিয়া বলা ; কোন কিছু গোপন না করা। **To make a clean sweep of**—To destroy wholesale ; একেবারে নষ্ট করা, উজাড় করা। **To make a dupe** or **tool of another**—কাহাকেও নিজের কার্য্যসাধনের যন্ত্র করা। **To make a figure** — To be conspicuous ; to become famous ; একজন হইয়া উঠা ; প্রসিদ্ধি লাভ করা। **To make a fool of**—To expose to ridicule : হাস্যাস্পদ করা, বোকা বানান। **To make a fortune**—To become wealthy ; সম্পত্তি করা, ধনশালী হওয়া। **To make after**—(*Archaic*) To follow ; to pursue ; (অপ্রঃ) অনুসরণ করা ; অনুগমন করা **To make against**—To be unfavourable: প্রতিকূল হওয়া। **To make allowance**—To make a deduction ; বাদ সাদ দিয়া লওয়া। **To make a man of**—To develop manly qualities ; মানুষ করা। **To make amends**—To make adequate compensation ; যথোচিত ক্ষতিপূরণ করা। **To make a mess of it** — To bungle ; to create confusion and make matters worse ; খিচুড়ি পাকান ; গোলমাল করিয়া ফেলা। **To make a mountain of a mole-hill**—To exaggerate ; তিলকে তাল করা। **To make a name for oneself**—To acquire fame or distinction ; নাম করা, খ্যাতি বা প্রসিদ্ধি লাভ করা। **To make an appointment**—To make an arrangement for a meeting ; সাক্ষাতের বন্দোবস্ত করা। **To make an ass of one's self**--To act foolishly ; নির্ব্বোধের ন্যায় কার্য্য করা। **To make a night of it**—To carry it (festivity etc.) on through the night ; রাত্রি ব্যাপিয়া করা। **To make a sensation**—To excite the feelings or interest of others ; হুজুগ উপস্থিত করা, হুলস্থুল বাধান, তুমল উত্তেজনা বা আন্দোলন সৃষ্টি করা। **To make as if** — To pretend or feign ; ভাণ করা, ছলনা করা। **To make assurance doubly sure**—To render as certain as possible ; যতদূর সম্ভব সুনিশ্চিত করা, পাকাপাকি করা। **To make at**—To run or go towards ; কোন কিছুর অভিমুখে বেগে ধাবিত হওয়া। **To make a virtue of necessity**—To do as graciously as possible something one is compelled to do ; See VIRTUE. **To make away**—To hasten away ; তাড়াতাড়ি যাওয়া। (*Obs.*) To alienate or transfer ; (অপ্রঃ) হস্তান্তর করা। **To make away with**—To put away ; to destroy ; to kill ; to squander ; সরাইয়া ফেলা ; নষ্ট করা ; সংহার করা ; অপব্যয় করা, উড়াইয়া দেওয়া। **To make away with oneself** — To commit suicide ; আত্মহত্যা করা। **To make bold**—To venture ; to dare ; সাহস করা ; সাহস করিয়া বলা। **To make bold with** — To venture to deal with ; কোন বিষয় আলোচনা করিতে সাহসী হওয়া। **To make both ends meet** — (See ENDS. **To make bricks with straw**—To work without sufficient materials ; যথোচিত উপকরণ বিনা কাজ করা। **To make choice of**—To choose ; পছন্দ করা। **To make common cause with**—To unite ; এক যোগ হওয়া, একজোট হওয়া। **To make default**—To fail to appear ; উপস্থিত হইতে না পারা। **To make eyes at**—To ogle at ; চোক ঠারা, কটাক্ষ ক্ষেপণ করা। **To make for**—To move towards ; to assail ; to confirm as a view ; to conduce to, as happiness, etc. ; অভিমুখে অগ্রসর হওয়া ; আক্রমণ করা ; দৃঢ় করা ; কারণ হওয়া। **To make free**

with—To use with freedom ; স্বচ্ছন্দে বা অকুণ্ঠিত চিত্তে ব্যবহার করা। **To make friends**—To be reconciled ; পুনর্ম্মিলিত হওয়া। **To make game** or **fun of**—To trifle ; to treat with ridicule ; তুচ্ছ-তাচ্ছিল্য করা ; হাস্যাস্পদ করা। **To make good**—See under GOOD. **To make head against**—To oppose successfully ; সফলভাবে প্রতিবাদ করা অথবা বাধা দেওয়া। **To make head way**—To progress ; উন্নতি করা। **To make it up** or **make up matter**—To be reconciled মিটমাট করা, পুনর্ম্মিলিত হওয়া। **To make light of, little of**—To regard as insignificant ; তুচ্ছ জ্ঞান করা, হেয় জ্ঞান করা। **To make merry**—To be jovial ; হৃষ্ট হওয়া। **To make mouths at**—To distort the mouth at ; to make faces at ; বিকৃত মুখভঙ্গী করা ; মুখ ভেঙ্গান। **To make much, little, the best, the most, etc. of**—To drive much, little, etc. advantage from ; to attach much, little, etc. importance to ; বেশী বা কম সুবিধা পাওয়া ; খুব গুরুতর মনে করা, সামান্য মনে করা। To treat with fondness or esteem ; আদর করা, সোহাগ করা। **To make neither head nor tail of**—To be unable to understand ; মাথামুণ্ড কিছুই বুঝিতে না পারা। **To make no doubt**—To have no doubt ; to be confident ; সন্দেহ না থাকা ; নিঃসন্দেহ হওয়া। **To make no secret of**—To declare openly ; প্রকাশ্যে বলা। **To make nothing of**—To trifle ; to understand nothing about ; সামান্য জ্ঞান করা ; কিছুই বুঝিতে না পারা। **To make of**—To account for ; কারণ প্রদর্শন করা। To understand ; as, I do not know what *of* it ; বুঝা। **To make off**—To run away (*with*) ; to decamp (*with*) ; লইয়া পলায়ন করা ; লইয়া চম্পট দেওয়া। To fatten as lambs for the market : বাজারে বিক্রয়ের জন্য মেষশাবক মেদস্বী করা। **To make one's blood boil**—To provoke one ; রাগান্বিত করা। **To make one's bread**—To earn livelihood ; জীবিকার্জ্জন করা। **To make one's hair stand on end**—To cause horripilation ; রোমাঞ্চিত করা। **To make one's way**—To proceed ; to succeed ; অগ্রসর হওয়া ; কৃতকার্য্য হওয়া। **To make or mar**—To cause success or ruin of ; হয় উন্নতি না হয় সর্ব্বনাশ করা। **To make out**—To discover ; to understand ; to decipher as a handwriting etc. ; to prove ; আবিষ্কার করা ; বুঝা, নির্ণয় করা ; সাঙ্কেতিক লিপির রহস্যোদ্ভেদ করা ; প্রমাণ করা, সাব্যস্ত করা। To get together with difficulty ; as, articles put in to *make out* a volume ; to make up as list, document, etc. ; কষ্টে সংগ্রহ করা ; প্রস্তুত করা। **To make over**—To transfer the possession of ; to convey or alienate ; হস্তান্তর করা ; অর্পণ করা। **To make political capital**—To turn to account ; কাজে লাগান। **To make room, place** or **way**—To give these for other ; জায়গা করা, স্থান করা। **To make sail** — To set sail ; পাল তুলিয়া রওনা হওয়া। **To make short work of** or **with**—To do rapidly or in a short time ; to make brief ; শীঘ্র করা ; সংক্ষেপে সারা। **To make sure**—To be certain of ; নিশ্চিত হওয়া। **To make sure of**—To consider as certain ; নিশ্চিত জ্ঞান করা। **To make the most of**—To use to the best advantage ; যতদূর সম্ভব সদ্ব্যবহার করা। **To make the mouth water**—To cause desire or longing ; লালায়িত করা, জিকের জল পড়া। **To make two bites of a cherry**—To do anything in parts and not thoroughly or at one stroke ; অল্প অল্প করিয়া করা। **To make up**—To fabricate or concoct, as a story ; গঠন করা, রচনা করা। To supply, as a deficiency ; to complete as, an amount, party etc. ; to compound ; to put together ; as, to *make up* a medicine ; অভাব পূরণ করা ; সম্পূর্ণ করা ; মিশ্রিত করা ; একত্র করা। To compensate ; ক্ষতিপূরণ করা। To reconcile ; পুনর্ম্মিলন করা, মিটমাট করা। To adjust ; to settle, as a dispute ; হিসাব ঠিক করা ; মিটাইয়া দেওয়া। To sew together, as a coat etc. ; to get together, as a company, sum of money, etc. ; সেলাই করা ; একত্র করা। To arrange in columns or pages as types ; to compile as a list, amount, document, etc. ; পৃষ্ঠায় পৃষ্ঠায় বা স্তম্ভে স্তম্ভে বিন্যাস করা ; সংগ্রহ করা, সঙ্কলন করা। To compose ; as, parts *make up* a whole ; to prepare, as an actor for his part by dressing, false hair etc. ; গঠন করা প্রস্তুত করা। To arrange, as marriage etc. ; ঠিক করা, স্থির করা। **To make up a quarrel**—To reconcile ; বিবাদ মিটান। **To make up for**—To compensate ; ক্ষতিপূরণ করা। **To mke up one's mind to** — To decide *to* (do) ; to resolve upon (a course) ; মন স্থির করা ; সঙ্কল্প করা। **To make up to**—To approach ; to pay court to ; অগ্রসর হওয়া ; বিবাহার্থ প্রেমোপাসনা করা। **To make way** — To progress ; অগ্রসর হওয়া। **To make water**—To void urine ; প্রস্রাব করা।

make, *n.* **1.** Mode of structure or composition ; form ; গঠন, গড়ন আকৃতি, আকার। **2.** Mental or moral disposition ; মনের ভাব, মনের গতি

3. (*Electr.*) The closing or completing of an electric circuit; (তাড়িত-বিদ্যা) তাড়িতবেষ্টনীসম্পূরণ। **American make** — আমেরিকায় নির্ম্মিত। **Is this your own make**—Is this made by you ?; ইহা কি তোমার হাতের তৈরী।

mak'-êr, *n.* One that makes; a creator; নির্ম্মাতা, নির্ম্মাণকারী; স্রষ্টা। **The Maker, Our Maker**—The Creator; স্রষ্টা, সৃষ্টিকর্ত্তা।

mak'-ing, *n.* **1.** Constructing or forming; গঠন, রচনা। **2.** (*Pl.*) Earning; income; রোজগার; আয় **3.** (*Pl.*) Essential qualities; as, he has the *makings* of a general; প্রকৃতিসিদ্ধ গুণসমূহ। **To be the making of**—To ensure success or favourable development of; সিদ্ধি বা সুবিকাশ সুনিশ্চিত করা।

Mă-lăc'-că, *n.* A district in Malay; a town there; মালয় দ্বীপের জেলা বিশেষ; ঐ জেলার নগর-বিশেষ। **Malacca cane**—ঐ জেলা হইতে আনীত বেতের ছড়ী।

măl'-ă-chite, *n.* **1.** A green carbonate of copper; হরিদ্বর্ণ খনিজপদার্থ-বিশেষ। **2.** A green dye-stuff; হরিদ্বর্ণ রঞ্জকদ্রব্য-বিশেষ।

măl-ă-cŏl'-ŏ-ġy, *n.* The branch of natural history that treats of the molluscs or soft-bodied animals; প্রাণিবিজ্ঞানের যে শাখায় শম্বুকাদির বিষয় আলোচিত হইয়া থাকে, শম্বুকতত্ত্ব। **—gist,** *n.*

măl-ăd-jŭst'-mĕnt, *n.* Bad adjustment; কুব্যবস্থা, অব্যবস্থা।

măl-ăd-min-is-trā'-tion, *n.* Bad management of affairs; কুশাসন।

măl-ă-droit' (-droyt), *adj.* Not dexterous; clumsy; অদক্ষ, অপটু, অকুশল; আনাড়ী। **—ly,** *adv.* **—ness,** *n.*

măl'-ă-dy, *n.* **1.** Illness; disease; পীড়া; রোগ, ব্যাধি, আময়। **2.** (*Fig.*) A moral or mental defect or disorder; (লক্ষণায়) মানসিক বা আধ্যাত্মিক ব্যাধি।

mă'-lă-fī'-dē, *adv.* & *adj.* In bad faith; প্রতারণাক্রমে, প্রবঞ্চনাপূর্ব্বক। *Adj.* Acting or done malafide; প্রতারণাক্রমে সংসাধিত বা সংসাধনকারী।

măl'-ă-gă, *n.* A wine imported from Malaga, a town in Spain; স্পেনদেশের অন্তঃপাতী মেলাগা নগরী হইতে সমানীত মদিরা।

măl-ă-găs'-y, *adj.* & *n.* Of, or pertaining to, Madagascar or its inhabitants; মাদাগাস্কার অথবা মাদাগাস্কারদ্বীপের অধিবাসিসম্পর্কীয়। *Noun.* A native of Madagascar; its language; মাদাগাস্কার দ্বীপের অধিবাসী; ঐ দ্বীপের ভাষা।

mă'-laise (-lāz), *n.* Uneasiness; a feeling of physical discomfort; অস্থিরতা; অসোয়াস্তি।

măl'-ă-pêrt, *adj.* & *n.* (*Archaic*) Forward; saucy; impudent; (অপ্রঃ) ধৃষ্ট; প্রগল্‌ভ; দুর্বিনীত। *Noun.* (*Archaic*) A saucy or impudent person; (অপ্রঃ) ধৃষ্টলোক, বে-আদব লোক। **—ly,** *adv.* **—ness,** *n.*

măl'-ă-prŏp(ism), *n.* A grotesque misuse of a word; কোন শব্দের উদ্ভট অপব্যবহার। **—prop'-i-an,** *adj.*

măl-ăp-rō-pos' (-pō), *adv.*, *adj.* & *n.* Inappositely; inopportunely; অস্থানে; অকালে, অসময়ে। *Adj.* Unreasonable; inopportune; অযৌক্তিক; অসময়োচিত, অকালোচিত, অপ্রাসঙ্গিক, অপ্রস্তুত। *Noun.* A thing inopportunely said, done or happening; অসময়োচিত উক্তি, অসময়োচিত কার্য্য বা ঘটনা।

mā'-lar (-lêr), *adj.* & *n.* Of or pertaining to, the cheek; গণ্ডদেশীয়, গণ্ডসম্বন্ধীয়। *Noun.* The bone forming the prominence of the cheek; গণ্ডাস্থি।

mă-lā'-ri-ă, *n.* **1.** A poisonous air emanating from marshy places, formerly supposed to produce fever etc.; সজলভূমি হইতে উত্থিত একপ্রকার বিষাক্ত বাষ্প, পুতিবাষ্প (হঃ চঃ), মারিবাত (আঃ বঃ)। **2.** A fever caused by mosquito bites conveying germs: মশকদংশনজনিত জ্বর-বিশেষ, ম্যালেরিয়া জ্বর। **—al, —an, —ous,** *adjs.*

Mă-lay' (-lā), *adj.* & *n.* Of, or pertaining to, the Malayas or its people; মালয়দ্বীপপুঞ্জ সম্বন্ধীয় অথবা মালয়বাসিগণ সম্পর্কীয়। *Noun.* A native or inhabitant of Malacca or of the Malay Archipelago; his language; মালাক্কা দ্বীপ বা মালয় দ্বীপপুঞ্জের অধিবাসী; মালাক্কা দ্বীপ বা মালয় দ্বীপপুঞ্জের ভাষা। **—an,** *adj.* & *n.*

Măl-ă-yă'-lăm, *n.* The language of Malabar; মালাবারের ভাষা, কেরল ভাষা।

măl'-cŏn-tĕnt, *adj.* & *n.* Discontented; dissatisfied, esp. in political matters; অসন্তুষ্ট; অতৃপ্ত, রাজনৈতিক ব্যাপারে অসন্তুষ্ট। *Noun.* One discontented; one inclined to rebellion; অসন্তুষ্ট ব্যক্তি; বিদ্রোহ-ভাবপ্রবণ ব্যক্তি।

male, *adj.* *n.* Masculine; of, or relating to, men or male animals; পুং (হিঃ কোঃ), পুমান্ (ঐ), পুং লঙ্গ (ঐ), মর্দ্দ, নর; পুংজাতীয়। *Noun.* One of the male sex; a male animal; পুংজন্তু; পুরুষ, মর্দ্দা, নর। **Male child**—Boy; পুত্রসন্তান, বেটাছেলে। **Male-rhymes**—যে ছন্দে অন্তিম শব্দাংশ সমূহের মিল থাকে। **Male-screw**—See under SCREW. **Male-species**—পুরুষজাতি।

măl-ĕ-dic'-tion, *n.* Curse; শাপ, অভিশাপ, অভিসম্পাত।

măl-ĕ-dic'-tŏ-ry, *adj.* Imprecatory; অভিশাপাত্মক।

măl-ĕ-făc'-tor (-têr), *n.* **1.** An evil-doer: অনিষ্টকারী, কুকর্ম্মী, দুষ্কর্ম্মী, অহিতকারী, দুষ্কর্ম্মান্বিত। **2.** A criminal; অপরাধী, দোষী। **—fac'-tion,** *n.* A crime; an offence; অপরাধ; দোষ।

mă-lĕf'-ic, *adj.* Doing mischief; producing evil; অনিষ্টকারী; অনিষ্টজনক, অহিতজনক, অকল্যাণকর, ক্রুর (বৃঃ সং)।

mă-lĕf′-i-cence (-sŏns), *n.* Evil doing : harmfulness ; অনিষ্ট করণ ; অনিষ্টকারিতা, অকল্যাণজনকতা। **—cent**, *adj.* **1.** Mischievous or hurtful to ; অনিষ্টকর, অপকারী, অশুভকারী। **2.** Criminal ; অপরাধাত্মক, অপরাধজনক, সাপরাধ।

mă-lĕv′-ō-lĕnt, *adj.* Wishing evil towards others ; spiteful ; malicious ; অশুভাকাঙ্ক্ষী, দুষ্টবুদ্ধি, দুর্ব্বুদ্ধি, অহিতকামী ; বিদ্বেষপরায়ণ, দ্রোহবুদ্ধি ; ঈর্ষ্যাপরায়ণ, অসূয়াপরবশ, হিংসাপরায়ণ। **—lence,** *n.* Spite malice ; বিদ্বেষ, দ্রোহ ; হিংসা, অসূয়া, ঈর্ষ্যা, পৈশুন্য, দ্বেষভাব, অশুভচিন্তন (হিঃ কোঃ), দুষ্টবুদ্ধি, কুভাব, অপকারেচ্ছা, অনিষ্টেচ্ছা।

măl-fea′-sance (-fē-zăns), *n.* (*Law*) Evil-doing ; esp. official misconduct ; (আইন) মন্দকর্ম্ম, দুষ্কর্ম্ম, কুকর্ম্ম ; বিশেষতঃ সরকারী কর্ম্মচারীর অন্যায়াচরণ। **—sant,** *adj.* & *n.* Evil-doing ; দুষ্কর্ম্মকারী। ***Noun.*** One who does evil ; a criminal ; অশুভকারী, দুষ্কর্ম্মকারী ; অপরাধী ব্যক্তি।

măl-fŏr-ma′-tion, *n.* Ill formation ; অঙ্গবিকৃতি, কুগঠন, বিকৃত গঠন, মন্দাকৃতি (জ্ঞাহিঃ)। **Mal′-formed,** *adj.*

ma′-lic, *adj.* (*Chem.*) Obtained from apples and other fruits as, *malic* acid ; (রসায়ন-শাস্ত্র) সেও বা অম্ল ফল হইতে প্রাপ্ত।

măl′-ice (-ĭs), *n.* **1.** Ill will ; spite ; intention to harm others ; মন্দ বুদ্ধি, দুষ্ট বুদ্ধি ; পৈশুন্য, দ্বেষভাব, অসূয়া, মৎসরতা, মাৎসর্য্য, ঈর্ষা, দ্বেষ, হিংসা ; অনিষ্টসাধন। **Ma-li′-cious** *adj.* Envious ; spiteful ; বিদ্বেষপরায়ণ, দ্রোহবুদ্ধি, দ্রোহশীল ; হিংসাপরায়ণ। **Ma-li′-cious-ly,** *adv.* Spitefully ; বিদ্বেষভাবে, দ্রোহবুদ্ধিতে। **Malice prepense**—See PREPENSE. **To bear malice (to)**—To have vindictive feelings (against) ; কাহারো প্রতি দ্রোহভাব পোষণ করা, কাহারো প্রতি বিদ্বেষভাব পোষণ করা।

mă-lign′ (-līn), *adj.* **1.** (*Rare*) Malicious ; (কচিদ্‌ব্যবহৃত) ঈর্ষাপরায়ণ, দ্রোহবুদ্ধি। **2.** (Of things) Unfavourable or injurious ; (বস্তু-সম্পর্কে) অশুভ, অকল্যাণজনক। **3.** (Of diseases) Malignant ; (রোগ সম্পর্কে) উৎকট, দুরারোগ্য। **—ly,** *adv.*

ma-lign′ (-līn), *v. t.* To defame : to slander ; মানহানি করা, অপমান করা ; অপবাদ দেওয়া, কলঙ্ক রটনা করা।

mă-lĭg′-nănt, *adj.* & *n.* **1.** Virulent ; dangerous to life ; as, *malignant* cholera ; উৎকট, মারাত্মক সাংঘাতিক, প্রাণহানিকর। **2.** Having or showing extreme malevolence উৎকটবিদ্বেষপরায়ণ, বিষহৃদয়, পিশুন। **3.** Harmful ; অনিষ্টজনক। **4.** (*Hist.*) Supporting Charles I. against the Parliament ; (ইতিহাস) পার্লেমেন্ট মহাসভার বিরুদ্ধে প্রথম চার্লসের সমর্থক। **5.** Hawing a babful influence ; অশুভ। ***Noun.*** (*Hist.*) An adherent of Charles I. ; প্রথম চার্লসের প্রতি অনুরাগী ব্যক্তি। **—nance, —nan-cy,** *ns.* **1.** Extreme malevolence ; চরম বিদ্বেষ। **2.** Virulence দুরারোগ্যতা।

mă-lĭg′-ni-tŷ, *n.* Malignancy : spite ; deadly quality ; দ্বেষ ; পৈশুন্য ; মারাত্মক গুণ।

măl-ĭn′-flū-ence (-ŏns), *n.* Evil influence ; কুপ্রভাব, অশুভ প্রভাব।

mă-lin′-gêr (-lĭng-), *v. t.* To feign or protract sickness in order to avoid duty, esp. military and naval ; কর্ত্তব্যকার্য্য পরিহারের উদ্দেশ্যে পীড়ার ভাণ করা, বিশেষতঃ সৈনিক বা নৌ-বিভাগের কার্য্য এড়াইবার অভিপ্রায়ে পীড়ার ভাণ করা।

mă′-lism, *n.* The doctrine that this world is bad ; পৃথিবী অমঙ্গলময়—এইরূপ মতবাদ।

măl′-i-son (-zn), *n.* (*Archaic*) Curse ; (অপ্রঃ) শাপ, অভিসম্পাত।

mall, *n.* **1.** (*Hist.*) The mallet used in the game of pall-mall ; the game itself ; an alley for it ; (ইতিহাস) ক্রীড়াবিশেষে ব্যবহৃত মুদ্গার ; ঐ ক্রীড়া ; ঐ ক্রীড়ার স্থান **2.** A public or shaded walk রাজপথ, স্নিগ্ধচ্ছায় রাজমার্গ।

Mallard.

măl′-lârd, *n.* **1.** A wild duck or drake ; its flesh ; বন্যহংস, বুনেহাঁস, নীলশীর (হিন্দীঃ হিউম) ; উহার মাংস।

măl′-lē-ă-ble (-bl), *adj.* **1.** Capable of being beaten out by hammering, as a metal ; ঘাতসহ, তাড়নবর্দ্ধনীয়। **2.** (*Fig.*) Pliable ; (লক্ষণায়) নমনীয়, সুখনম্য। **—bil′-i-ty,** *n.* Quality of being malleable ; ঘাতসহত্ব, তাড়নবর্দ্ধনীয়তা, উদ্বর্ত্তনক্ষমতা (হিঃ কোঃ), ঘনবর্দ্ধনীয়তা (ঐ), আঘাতবর্দ্ধনীয়তা (ঐ), তাড়নবর্দ্ধনীয়ত্ব।

măl′-lĕt, *n.* **1.** A small wooden hammer ; কাঠের ছোট মুগুর, ক্ষুদ্র কাষ্ঠমুদ্গার। **2.** A hammer for striking a croquet or polo ball ; ক্রীড়া বিশেষে ব্যবহৃত মুদ্গার।

malleus, (*L.*) *n.* An ear-bone transmitting vibrations of the tympanum to the incus ; কর্ণের অস্থিবিশেষ—যদ্দ্বারা কর্ণপটহের কম্পন কর্ণপটহমধ্যস্থ স্থূণাস্থিতে সঞ্চারিত হয়, মুদ্গরাস্থি (হঃ চ.)।

Mallow.

măl′-low (-lō), *n.* A genus of plants with downy leaves ; পালকর্

কোমল পত্রবিশিষ্ট গুল্মশ্রেণী-বিশেষ **Indian mallow**—বেড়েলা (দ্রব্যগুণ), অতিবলা (ঐ) ।

alm (mâm), *n.* **1.** A soft ime-stone ; একপ্রকার কোমল চূর্ণ-প্রস্তর । **2.** A loamy soil formed from the disintegration of this rock ; ঐরূপ প্রস্তরের বিশ্লেষণ হইতে উৎপন্ন ইষ্টকনির্ম্মাণোপযোগী মৃত্তিকা ।

ál-mai'-son (-mā-zn), *n.* A variety of the carnation ; একজাতীয় গুলনার ফুল ।

nalm'-sey (mâm-zî), *n.* **1.** A strong and sweet wine from Greece, Spain, etc. ; গ্রীস, স্পেন প্রভৃতি দেশ হইতে সমানীত একপ্রকার মিষ্ট এবং উগ্র মদিরা । **2.** A sort of grape ; এক প্রকার আঙ্গুর ।

nál-nü-tri'-tion, *n.* Bad or imperfect nutrition ; অপূর্ণপোষণ ।

măl-ō'-dour (-dêr), *n.* An offensive odour ; দুর্গন্ধ, পূতিগন্ধ । **—ous,** *adj.* Evil-smelling ; দুর্গন্ধ, পূতিগন্ধময় ।

măl-prăc'-tice (-tîs), *n.* **1.** Evil practice ; wrong-doing ; কুরীতি, অবৈধ কার্য্য, দুষ্ক্রিয়া, কদাচার ; কুক্রিয়া, অন্যায়াচরণ । **2.** (*Law*) The treatment of a patient by a physician in an improper or negligent way ; (আইন) অসঙ্গত উপায়ে বা অবহেলার সহিত চিকিৎসক কর্ত্তৃক রোগীর চিকিৎসা । **3.** (*Law*) Illegal conduct on the part of a trustee or professional man ; (আইন) ন্যাসরক্ষক বা ডাক্তার, উকীল, প্রভৃতির পক্ষে অবৈধ আচরণ । **—ti'-tion-er,** *n.*

măl-prē-sĕn-tā'-tion, *n.* (*Rare*) Abnormal presentation in childbirth ; (ক্বচিদ্ ব্যবহৃত) প্রসব সময়ে অপত্যপথে অস্বাভাবিকভাবে অঙ্গনির্গমন ।

malt, *n.*, *v. t.* & *i.* Barley or other grain steeped in water, till it germinates, and dried in a kiln used in brewing and distilling ; সুরাপ্রস্তুতের জন্য অঙ্কুরিত যব বা অন্য শস্য, কলা-বেরুনো যব । ***Verb t.*** To turn into malt as grain ; জলে ভিজাইয়া যব অঙ্কুরিত করা । ***Verb i.*** (Of seeds) To become malt ; (জলসিক্ত বীজের পক্ষে) অঙ্কুরিত হওয়া । **Malt-house**—অঙ্কুরিত যব প্রস্তুত বা রক্ষার জন্য গৃহ । **Malt-liquor**—যবসুরা । **Maltster, Malt-man**—যবসুরা প্রস্তুতকারী, শুঁড়ী । **Malt-worm** — (*Fig.*) Toper ; (লক্ষণায়) অতিশয় মদ্যপায়ী ব্যক্তি । **Extract of malt**—রোগীর আহারের জন্য অঙ্কুরিত যব হইতে নিষ্কাষিত সার ।

Măl-tese' (-tēz), *adj.* & *n.* Of, or relating to, Malta, an island in the Mediterranean ; মাল্টা দ্বীপ-সম্বন্ধীয় । ***Noun.*** A native of Malta ; the language of Malta ; মাল্টা দ্বীপের অধিবাসী ; মাল্টা দ্বীপের ভাষা । **Maltese cat, dog**—একপ্রকার সখের বিড়াল বা কুকুর ।

măl'-thă, *n.* A variety of cement ; একপ্রকার বিলাতী মাটী ।

măl-thü'-ŝi-ăn, *n.* & *adj.* A disciple of Malthus (died 1835) who advocated moral restraint as a means of checking the increase of population ; ম্যালথাসের শিষ্য । ***Adj.*** Relating to Malthus ; মেলথাস্ সম্বন্ধীয় । **—ism,** *n.* The theory upheld by Malthusians ; ম্যালথাসের মতবাদ । [Malthus এর মতে দেশের লোকসংখ্যা বৃদ্ধির অনুপাতে খাদ্যদ্রব্য বৃদ্ধি করা যাইতে পারে না । যদি দেশের অধিবাসিগণ ইন্দ্রিয়সংযম দ্বারা লোকসংখ্যা বৃদ্ধি নিরাকরণ না করে তবে, দেশব্যাপী দারিদ্র্য অপরিহার্য্য হইয়া উঠে । এরূপস্থলে দারিদ্র্য, পাপাচার, ও অন্যান্য দুর্গতিজনক কারণ দ্বারা লোকসংখ্যা বৃদ্ধি নিরাকৃত হয় ।]

malt'-ing, *n.* **1.** The act or process of making malt ; অঙ্কুরিত যব প্রস্তুত করণ । **2.** A MALT-HOUSE, which see.

malt'-ōse, *n.* (*Chem.*) A sugar formed from starch by the action of malt ; (রসায়ন-শাস্ত্র) অঙ্কুরিত যবের ক্রিয়াদ্বারা শ্বেতসার হইতে প্রস্তুত শর্করা-বিশেষ ।

măl-treat' (-trēt), *v. t.* To treat ill or roughly ; to abuse ; মন্দ ব্যবহার করা ; গালিমন্দ করা । **—ment,** *n.*

malt'-stêr, *n.* See under MALT.

măl-vā'-ceous (-shŭs), *adj.* Of, or relating to, the genus mallow ; বেড়েলা জাতীয় উদ্ভিদ সম্বন্ধীয় ।

măl-vêr-sā'-tion, *n.* **1.** Evil conduct ; fraudulent practice ; কদাচার, অসদাচরণ ; প্রবঞ্চনা । **2.** Corrupt administration (of public money etc.) ; জনসাধারণের অর্থের অপব্যবহার ।

măm'-ē-lŏn, *n.* A rounded hillock or elevation ; গোলাকৃতি ক্ষুদ্র শৈল ।

Măm'-ē-lūke, *n.* **1.** (*Hist.*) A member of a military body (orig. Caucasian slaves) that seized the throne of Egypt in 1254 ; (ইতিহাস) মিশরদেশীয় দাসসৈন্য — যাহারা ১২৫৪ খৃঃ অব্দে মিশর অধিকার করিয়াছিল । **2.** (In Mahommedan countries) A slave ; দাস, ক্রীতদাস ।

mă-mil'-lă, *n.* **1.** The nipple of a female breast ; চুচুক । **2.** An organ etc. shaped like this ; চুচুকাকৃতি অঙ্গ । **—late, —ted, —li-form, —ry,** *adjs.*

măm-(m)ă, *n.* **1.** Mother, chiefly used by young children ; মা ।

măm'-mă, *n.* (*Pl.* -MAE) **1.** A glandular organ, that secretes milk ; স্তন, পয়োধর । **2.** A corresponding non-secreting structure in the male ; পুরুষের স্তন । **—ry, —mif'-er-ous, —mi-form,** *adjs.*

măm'-măl, *n.* One of the mammalia ; স্তন্যদায়ী প্রাণী ।

măm-mā'-li-ă, *n.* (*Pl.*) The whole class of animals that suckle their young ; স্তন্যদায়ী প্রাণিগণ ।

măm-mā'-li-ăn, *adj.* & *n.* Of, or relating to, the mammalia ; স্তন্যদায়ী জীবগণসম্বন্ধীয় । ***Noun.*** One of the mammalia ; স্তন্যদায়ী প্রাণী ।

măm-mă-lif'-êr-ous (-ŭs), *adj.* (*Geol.*) Containing the remains of mammals ; (ভূবিদ্যা) স্তন্যদায়ী প্রাণিগণের দেহাবশেষপূর্ণ ।

măm-măl′-ŏ-ġy̆, *n.* The scientific knowledge of mammals ; স্তন্যদায়ি-প্রাণি-তত্ত্ব । **–gist**, *n.*

măm′-mee (-mē), *n.* An American tree yielding a large and nourishing fruit ; আমেরিকাদেশীয় ফলবৃক্ষ বিশেষ ।

măm′-mŏn, *n.* **1.** Riches regarded as idol or evil influence ; ধন । **2.** (*Cap.*) The god of riches ; কুবের, ধনাধিপ, ধনেশ্বর । **–ish**, *adj.* Devoted to money-getting ; অর্থোপার্জ্জনে রত, ধনার্থী । **–ism**, *n.* Devotion to gain ; ধনাগমাসক্তি, ধনাগমতৃষ্ণা, ধনস্পৃহা, ধনলালসা । **–ist, –ite**, *ns.* A person dovoted to the pursuit of riches ; a worldling ; ধনার্জ্জনরত ব্যক্তি, ঐহিকসর্ব্বস্ব ব্যক্তি ; বিষয়ানুরক্ত ব্যক্তি ।

măm′-mŏth, *n.* & *adj.* A large extinct species of elephant ; অধুনালুপ্ত এক জাতীয় অতিকায় হস্তী ।

Mammoth.

[হস্তীর সহিত এই জন্তুর প্রভেদ এই যে—ইহার শরীর ঘন লোমাচ্ছাদিত ও ইহার প্রায় ৮ ফিট দীর্ঘ দন্ত ঊর্দ্ধদিকে বক্রীভূত হইয়া ললাটাগ্রভাগে আবর্ত্তিত । এই জন্তুর দেহাবশেষ সাইবিরিয়া প্রভৃতি স্থানে বহুল পরিমাণে দৃষ্ট হয় ।] *Adj.* Very large ; সুবিশাল, সুবৃহৎ, প্রকাণ্ড, বিরাট, অতিকায়, বিপুল ।

măm′-my̆, *n.* Mother—a child's word ; মা ।

măn, *n.* **1.** A human being ; মনুষ্য, নর, মানব, মনুজ । **2.** A person ; as, no *man* : some *man* ; লোক, ব্যক্তি । **3.** Mankind ; as, *man* is mortal ; মানবজাতি । **4.** A grown-up male ; বয়ঃপ্রাপ্ত পুরুষ । **5.** A male attendant or servant ; ভৃত্য, চাকর । **6.** One having manly qualities ; as, be a *man* ; পুরুষোচিত গুণসম্পন্ন ব্যক্তি । **7.** A husband ; পতি, ভর্ত্তা, ভাতার (*colloq.*) । **8.** A piece used in playing chess or draughts ; দাবা প্রভৃতি খেলার বড়ে । **9.** (*Hist.*) A vassal ; (ইতিহাস) প্রজা । **10.** A workman ; as, the master locked out his *man* ; শ্রমজীবী, মজুর । **11.** (*Usu. pl.*) Common soldiers ; সাধারণ সৈনিক । **12.** (In combination) A ship ; as, a *man*-of-war ; জাহাজ । **Man′-ful**, *adj.* Full of manliness ; bold ; resolute ; পৌরুষসম্পন্ন ; সাহসী ; স্থির-প্রতিজ্ঞ, দৃঢ়প্রতিজ্ঞ । **Man′ ful-ly**, *adv.* Bravely ; সাহসের সহিত । **Man′-hood**, *n.* The state of being man ; manly quality ; courage ; বয়ঃপ্রাপ্তি ; পৌরুষ ; সাহস । **Man′-li-ness**, *n.* State of being manly ; bravery ; পৌরুষ ; বীর্য্য, সাহস । **Man′-ly**, *adj.* **1.** Becoming a man ; dignified ; brave ; পুরুষোচিত ; মর্য্যাদাবোধসম্পন্ন ; সাহসী । **2.** (Of a woman) Having qualities of a man ; (স্ত্রী সম্বন্ধে) পুরুষোচিত-গুণসম্পন্ন । **3.** (Of things) Befitting a man ; মানবোচিত । **Every man-jack**—All men, high or low ; আপামরসাধারণ, ভদ্রেতর সকলেই । **Inner man, Outer man**—অন্তরাত্মা ; (কৌতুকচ্ছলে) পাকস্থলী । **Little-man**—A young boy ; শিশু । **Man-about-town**—যে নিষ্কর্ম্মা খোস-পোষাকী বাবু নগরের রঙ্গালয় ও সভা-সমিতিতে ঘুরিয়া বেড়ায় । **Man-at-arms**—A soldier, esp. mounted and heavy armed ; সৈনিক, বিশেষতঃ গুরুভার অস্ত্রশস্ত্রে সজ্জিত সৈনিক । **Man-child**—পুত্র-সন্তান । **Man-eater**—নরখাদক, মানবাদ, মনুষ্যাদ, নরাশী, মনুষ্যভক্ষী ; ব্যাঘ্র ; দংশনশীল অশ্ব ; হাঙ্গর । **Man-eating** — মনুষ্যাদন, নরভক্ষণ । **Man-engine** — গভীর খনি হইতে লোক উঠাইবার জন্য ও খনিতে লোক নামাইবার জন্য যন্ত্র বিশেষ । **Man-Friday**—অনুচর ; সকলপ্রকার কার্য্য সম্পাদনের জন্য নিযুক্ত ভৃত্য [রবিন্সন ক্রুশোর ভৃত্য Fridayর নাম হইতে গৃহীত] । **Man-hole**—নর্দ্দমা বা মলকুণ্ডে প্রবেশের ছিদ্র । **Mankind**—মানবজাতি । **Man-of-war** — যুদ্ধ জাহাজ, রণপোত, রণতরী, মানোয়ারি জাহাজ । **Man-queller**—হত্যাকারী । **Man-slaughter** — নরহত্যা, খুন, মনুষ্যঘাত, মনুষ্যবধ, মনুষ্যহত্যা । **Man-trap**—অনধিকারী ব্যক্তিদিগকে আটকাইবার জন্য যন্ত্র-বিশেষ । **A man of Belial**—A wicked depraved person ; ভ্রষ্টচরিত্র ব্যক্তি । **A man of few words**—A man who does not talk much ; অল্পভাষী ব্যক্তি । **A man of war**—যোদ্ধৃপুরুষ । **As a man**—Viewed simply in regard to his personal qualities ; কেবলমাত্র তাহার ব্যক্তিগত চরিত্র সম্বন্ধে বিবেচনা করিলে । **He is a man of his word**—He is as good as his word ; তাহার যেই কথা সেই কাজ । **Man and boy**—(*adv.*) From boyhood upwards ; বাল্যকাল হইতে, আশৈশব । **Man in a thousand**—A man of rare excellence ; হাজারের মধ্যে একজন । **Man in the moon**—চন্দ্রমণ্ডলে দৃষ্ট কল্পিত ব্যক্তি ; কল্পিত ব্যক্তি, কল্পলোকবাসী ব্যক্তি । **Man of blood**—অত্যাচারী ব্যক্তি দৌরাত্ম্যকারী ব্যক্তি । **Man of business**—See under BUSINESS. **Man of his hands**—চতুর লোক, চালাক লোক । **Man of letters**—সাহিত্যিক, গ্রন্থকার । **Man of sin**—The devil ; শয়তান । **Man of straw**—Puppet or effigy ; one who has no substantial means ; worthless man ; খড়ের পুতুল ; অকিঞ্চন (কুমারঃ); নিষ্কর্ম্মা । **Man of the world**—পাকা বৈষয়িক লোক । **The**

man in the oak—ওকবৃক্ষবাসী ভূত। **The Sickman of Europe**—Turkey; তুরস্কদেশ। **To a man**—Without any one being left; সকলেই, একজনকেও বাদ না দিয়া। **To be one's own man**—To act independently; স্বাধীন ভাবে কার্য্য করা। **You'll be a man before your mother**—তুমি শীঘ্র শীঘ্র উন্নতি করিতে পারিবে। (বালকদিগকে উৎসাহ দানের জন্য বাক্য বিশেষ।)

măn, *v. t.* **1.** To supply with men as a ship or fort; লোক সরবরাহ করা, লোকসমন্বিত করা। **2.** To fortify the courage of (esp. oneself); "Having *manned* his soul with... reflections; হৃদয় দৃঢ় করা, হৃদয়ে বল প্রদান করা। **3.** To fill, as a post; কোন শূন্য পদে লোক নিযুক্ত করা। **4.** (*Naut.*) To post man at (the part of a ship); (নৌ-বিদ্যা) জাহাজের কোন অংশে নাবিক স্থাপন করা।

măn'-ă-cle (-kl), *n.* & *v. t.* (Usu. *pl.*) Handcuff; a fetter; (*lit.* & *fig.*) (সচরাচর বহুবচন) হাতকড়ি; শৃঙ্খল। ***Verb i.*** To put handcuffs on; হাতকড়ি দেওয়া, হাতকড়ি লাগান।

măn'-āge, *v. t.* & *i.* **1.** To handle; to wield, as a tool etc.; চালান; পরিচালন করা। **2.** To conduct (undertaking etc.); পরিচালন করা, নির্ব্বাহ করা। **3.** To administer; to control, as household, institution, state, etc.; পরিচালনা করা; তত্ত্বাবধান করা। **4.** To have the care of (cattle etc.); তত্ত্বাবধানের ভার থাকা। **5.** To subject (person, animal, etc.) to one's control; বশীভূত করা, দমন করা। **6.** To gain one's ends with (person) by flattery etc.; তোষামোদ করিয়া নিজের কাজ হাসিল করা। **7.** (With *can* or *be able to*) To make proper use of; to cope with; যথোচিত ব্যবহার করা; আঁটিয়া উঠা। **8.** To bring about; to contrive, (often *iron.*); as, he *managed* to muddle it; ঘটান; কৌশলক্রমে সাধন করা (প্রায়শঃ বিদ্রূপচ্ছলে)। ***Verb i.*** **1.** To conduct affairs; নির্ব্বাহ করা, পরিচালনা করা। **2.** To succeed in one's aim (often with inadequate material etc.): কৃতকার্য্য হওয়া, উদ্দেশ্যসিদ্ধ হওয়া, সিদ্ধকাম হওয়া, সফলকাম হওয়া। **—a-bil'-i-ty, —a-ble-ness,** *ns.* **—a-ble.** *adj.* That can be managed; governable; পরিচালনীয়, নির্ব্বোহোপযোগী; শাসনীয়, বশ্য। **—a-bly,** *adv.* **—ag-ing,** *adj.* Controlling; administering; পরিচালক; কার্য্যনির্ব্বাহক। **Managing committee**—পরিচালক সমিতি।

măn'-āge-měnt, *n.* **1.** Act of managing; administration; control; পরিচালন; কার্য্যনির্ব্বাহ; তত্ত্বাবধান। **2.** Trickery; as, talent for intrigue or *management*; চাতুরী, কৌশল। **3.** (With *the*) A body of managers; a body of directors; পরিচালকবর্গ; পরিরচালক সভা।

măn'-ăg-ěr, *n.* **1.** One who manages or controls a business, institution, etc.; কার্য্যাধ্যক্ষ, কর্ম্মকর্ত্তা, কর্ম্মাধ্যক্ষ, পরিচালক। **—a-ge'-ri-al,** *adj.* **—ess,** *n.* (*Fem.*) **—ship,** *n.*

Manatee or Sea-cow.

măn-ă-tee' (-tē), *n.* An aquatic mammal, also called the sea-cow; জলজন্তু বিশেষ।

mă-năv'-il-ins, mă-năv'-lins, *ns.* (*Pl. Slang*) Odds and ends, esp. of food; (ইতর ভাষায়) টুকিটাকি, ছিটছাট।

manche (*Fr.*), *n.* (*Obs.*) Sleeve; (অপ্রঃ) আস্তিন।

măn-chi-neel' (-nēl), *n.* A tree of tropical America with poisonous milky sap; শ্বেতবর্ণ বিষাক্ত নির্যাসস্রাবী আমেরিকার উষ্ণমণ্ডলজাত বৃক্ষবিশেষ।

măn-ĉĭ-pā'-tion, *n.* (In ancient Rome) A legal process of acquiring title to property by actual purchase; (প্রাচীন রোমে) ক্রীত সম্পত্তিতে স্বত্ব বা অধিকার লাভের জন্য আইনানুযায়ী কার্য্য। **—to-ry,** *adj.*

măn'-ĉĭ-ple (-pl), *n.* A steward or a purveyor esp. of a college or an inn of court; খাদ্যদ্রব্য সরবরাহকারী, বিশেষতঃ মহাবিদ্যালয় বা ব্যবহারজীবিপ্রতিষ্ঠানের খাদ্যদ্রব্যাদি সরবরাহকারী।

măn-dā'-mŭs, *n.* A command or writ issued by a higher Judiciary to a person, corporation or inferior court; নিম্ন আদালত বা কোন ব্যক্তিবিশেষ বা বিশেষরূপে কার্য্য করার জন্য ক্ষমতাপ্রাপ্ত আইনদ্বারা গঠিত সমবায়ের উপর যে পরোয়ানা জারি করা হয়।

măn'-dă-rin (-rēn), *n.* **1.** A European name for a Chinese official; চীনদেশীয় রাজকর্ম্মচারী। **2.** A nodding toy figure in Chinese costume; চীনদেশীয় পোষাক পরানো ক্রীড়াপুতুল।

măn'-dă-rin (-rēn), **—rine** (-rēn), *ns.* **1.** A Chinese species of orange; চীনদেশীয় কমলালেবু। **2.** Its colour; ঐ জাতীয় কমলালেবুর বর্ণ। **3.** A liqueur; সুরামিশ্রিত সুমিষ্ট এবং সুরভি পানীয়বিশেষ।

măn'-dă-tă-rў, *n.* (*Law.*) One with whom a mandate is made; (আইন) যাহার সহিত কোন কাজের চুক্তি করা হয়।

măn'-date, *n.* **1.** Judicial or legal command from a superior; হুকুমনামা, রাজাজ্ঞা, অনুশাসন, আজ্ঞালেখ, আজ্ঞা (হিঃ কোঃ)। **2.** (*Law*) A contract by which one employs another to do some service for him; (আইন) যে যুক্তি দ্বারা কোন ব্যক্তি অপর ব্যক্তিকে কোন কার্য্যের জন্য নিযুক্ত করে। **3.** A rescript of the pope; পোপের ব্যবস্থা। **4.** (*Political science*) Instructions supposed to be given by the electors to the parliament or any of its members; (রাজনীতি-শাস্ত্র) নির্ব্বাচকবৃন্দকর্তৃক পার্লেমেণ্ট বা পার্লেমেণ্টের কোন সভ্যকে যে উপদেশ দেওয়া হইয়াছে বলিয়া অনুমিত হয়। **5.** (*Poet.*) Command; (কবিতায়) আজ্ঞা, আদেশ।

măn'-dă-tŏ-rў, *adj.* & *n.* Of, relating to, or conveying, a command; আদেশাত্মক, আজ্ঞাসূচক, আজ্ঞাবোধক। ***Noun.*** Same as MANDATORY.

măn'-di-ble (-bl), *n.* **1.** A jaw, esp. the lower in mammals and fishes; চিবুক, চোয়াল; বিশেষতঃ মৎস্য ও স্তন্যদায়ী জন্তুগণের নিম্ন চিবুক, দংশনোষ্ঠ (সাঃ পঃ)। **2.** The upper or lower part of the beak of a bird; পক্ষীর চঞ্চুর উপর বা নীচের অংশ। **3.** The either half of the upper pair of jaws in insects; পতঙ্গের দংশনোষ্ঠের অর্দ্ধভাগ। **—dib-u-lar, —dib'-u-late,** *adjs.*

măn-dŏ'-lă, —ră, *n.* A large variety of mandolin; একপ্রকার বৃহদাকৃতি সারঙ্গবৎ বাদ্যযন্ত্র বিশেষ।

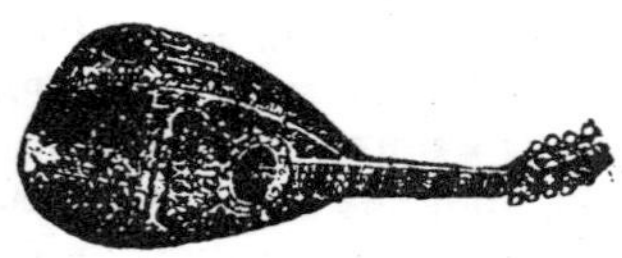

Mandolin.

măn'-dŏ-lin, —line (-lin), *ns.* A musical instrument somewhat like a guitar; একপ্রকার সারঙ্গ।

măn-drăg'-ŏ-ră, *n.* Same as MANDRAKE.

măn'-drāke, *n.* A narcotic poisonous plant with large roots, supposed to be like human form and to shriek like men when plucked; বৃহদাকার শিকড়বিশিষ্ট একপ্রকার নিদ্রাজনক বিষাক্ত গুল্ম, লক্ষণা (খোরী), লক্ষণাকন্দ (দ্রব্যগুণ), রক্তবিন্দু (ঐ), পুত্রদ (মঃ ইঃ)।

măn'-drĕl, —dril, *ns.* **1.** An axis or spindle usually cylindrical on which work is placed to be operated on; যে অক্ষদণ্ড বা ঘূর্ণনশীল শলাকার উপর রাখিয়া কোন জিনিষের উপর কাজ করা হয়। **2.** (*Dial.*) A miner's pick; (উপভাষায়) খনির কাজে ব্যবহৃত একপ্রকার গাঁতি। **3.** A piece of steel round which metals etc. may be cast, forged or otherwise shaped; যে ইস্পাত খণ্ডের চতুর্দ্দিকে ধাতু প্রভৃতি ঢালাই, পেটা বা অন্য কোনরূপে গড়া যায়।

măn'-drill, *n.* A large and hideous kind of baboon; একজাতীয় বৃহৎ বিকটদর্শন কপি।

măn'-dū-cāte, *v. t.* To chew or eat; চর্ব্বণ অথবা ভক্ষণ করা। **—ca'-tion,** *n.* **—ca-to-ry,** *adj.*

māne, *n.* **1.** The long hair on the neck of the horse, lion, etc.; সিংহাদির কেশর, সটা, অশ্বাদির ঘাড়ের লোম। **2.** (*Fig.*) The long hair of a person; "Her red rippling *mane* falling about her"; (লক্ষণায়) দীর্ঘ কেশ। **Maned,** *adj.* Having a mane; কেশরবিশিষ্ট। **Mane'-less,** *adj.* Without a mane; কেশরহীন।

***manege,* măn-ege'** (-āz), *n.* **1.** Art of horsemanship or of training horses; অশ্বারোহণবিদ্যা, অশ্বারোহণ-কৌশল, অশ্বশিক্ষাকৌশল। **2.** A riding academy; অশ্বারোহণ শিক্ষার বিদ্যালয়।

mā'-nēs, *n.* (*Pl.*) **1.** The spirits of departed ancestor; পিতৃপুরুষদের প্রেতাত্মা, প্রেত, পিতৃগণ। **2.** The shade of a departed person as an object of reverence; মৃত ব্যক্তির প্রেতাত্মা।

măn'-fŭl, *adj.* See under MAN.

măn'-gă-bey (-bi), *n.* A genus of African monkey; এক জাতীয় আফ্রিকা মহাদেশীয় বানর।

măn-gă-nese' (-nēz), *n.* (*Chem.*) A hard brittle metallic element of greyish white colour; (রসায়ন শাস্ত্র) দৃঢ়, ভঙ্গপ্রবণ এবং ধূসরাভ শুভ্র মূলপদার্থ বিশেষ, মঙ্গলক (সাঃ পঃ), মাঙ্গল (হিঃ কোঃ)। **—gan'-ic, —ne'-si-an,** *adjs.* **Black oxide of manganese,** or **Black manganese**—কাল মাঙ্গল (হিঃ কোঃ)। **Oxide of manganese**—(Also MANGANESE) কাচনির্ম্মাণে ব্যবহৃত কৃষ্ণবর্ণ খনিজ পদার্থ বিশেষ, দগ্ধমঙ্গলক।

mānge, *n.* **1.** A skin disease in horses, cattle, dogs, etc.; অশ্ব, গো, কুক্কুরাদির চর্ম্মরোগ। **2.** (Loosely) A dirty condition of the skin; চর্ম্মের মলিন অপরিচ্ছন্নতা। **Man'-gy,** *adj.*

man'-gel(-wur-zel) (măng-gl-wêr-zl), **man'-gold-wur-zel** (măng-gōld-wêr-zl), *n.* A kind of beet used for cattle; গবাদির খাদ্যস্বরূপ ব্যবহৃত একপ্রকার বীট পালং।

mān'-gêr, *n.* A trough or box in which food is placed for cattle and horses; অশ্বগবাদির ভোজনপাত্র, গামলা, দ্রোণি। **Dog in the manger**—যে ব্যক্তি কোন বস্তু নিজেও ভোগ করে না অথচ অন্যকেও ভোগ করিতে দেয় না।

man'-gle (măng-gl), *v. t.* **1.** To lacerate; to mutilate; to cut roughly so as to disfigure; ছিন্নভিন্ন করা, ছিন্নবিচ্ছিন্ন করা, খণ্ড খণ্ড করা, ক্ষতবিক্ষত করা; অঙ্গহীন করা; আব্‌ড়ো থাব্‌ড়ো করিয়া কাটা। **2.** (*Fig.*) To spoil or mutilate in doing or performing something; as, to *mangle* a piece of music or a recitation; (লক্ষণায়) অঙ্গহানি করা।

man'-gle (măng-gl), *n.* & *v. t.* A machine for smoothing washed cloth; ধৌতবস্ত্র মসৃণ করার জন্য যন্ত্র বিশেষ, বস্ত্রমার্জ্জনযন্ত্র। ***Verb t.*** To press or smooth in the mangle as clothes; ঐরূপ যন্ত্রে চাপ দিয়া মসৃণ করা, বস্ত্রমার্জ্জন যন্ত্র দ্বারা বস্ত্র মসৃণ করা। **—gler,** *n.*

man'-gŏ (măng-), *n.* An Indian fruit tree; its fruit; আম্রবৃক্ষ; আম্র, আম, চূত, আঁব, রসাল, সহকার (a very fragrant species)। [Some other synonyms :— মাকন্দ, মকরন্দ বসন্তদূত, কামবল্লভ, মদিরাসখ, কামশর, পিকবন্ধু,

পিকবল্লভ, কোকিলাবাস]। **Mango-fish**—তপ্‌সে মাছ, তপস্বী মৎস্য, তপস্যা মৎস্য। **Mango trick**—একপ্রকার ভোজবাজী — যাহাতে বাজীকর মাটীতে একটী আমের আঁটি পুঁতিয়া কয়েক ঘণ্টার মধ্যে গাছ জন্মাইয়া তাহাতে ফল ধরায়। **Mango-grove** — আম্রবন, (Panini viii-4-5.), আম্রকুঞ্জ, চূতকুঞ্জ।

măn′-gŏ-nĕl, *n.* (*Hist.*) An engine formerly used for throwing stones etc. ; (ইতিহাস) শত্রুসৈন্যের উপর প্রস্তরবর্ষণের জন্য যন্ত্রবিশেষ, পাষাণবর্ষক।

man′-go-steen (măng-gō-stēn), *n.* An East Indian tree bearing a delicious fruit ; this fruit ; বিলাতী গাবের গাছ ; ঐ গাছের ফল।

măn′-grōve, *n.* A tropical tree, the bark of which is used in tanning and medicines ; গরাণকাঠ (যোঃ), কামোডোরা (ওয়াট)।

Mangrove.

măn′-gy, *adj.* Infected with the mange ; squalid ; scabby ; ত্বগ্‌রোগী ; নোংরা ; মামড়িবিশিষ্ট। **–gi-ly,** *adv.* **–gi-ness,** *n.*

măn′-hood, *n.* See under MAN.

mā′-ni-ă, *n.* **1.** Madness ; insanity ; বাতুলতা ; উন্মত্ততা, উন্মাদ, উন্মত্তবায়ু। **2.** Excessive or unreasonable desire or enthusiasm (usu. with for) ; বাতিক।

mā′-ni-ăc, *adj.* & *n.* Affected with mania ; mad ; বাতিকগ্রস্ত ; উন্মাদ, পাগল। ***Noun.*** A raving lunatic ; উন্মত্ত ব্যক্তি। **–ni′-a-cal,** *adj.* **–ni′-a-cal-ly,** *adv.*

măn-i-chē′-ăn, –chae′– (-kē-), *adj.* & *n.* Of, or pertaining to, the Manichees or followers of Mani, a Persian of the third century ; ম্যানী প্রবর্ত্তিত ধর্ম্মমতানুবর্ত্তিসম্বন্ধীয়, পারস্যদেশীয় ম্যানী নামক ধর্ম্মপ্রবর্ত্তকের মতাবলম্বিগণ-সম্পর্কীয় [ম্যানী ২১৬ খৃঃ অব্দে তদীয় ধর্ম্মমত প্রচার করেন। ম্যানীর মতে পাপ ও পুণ্য যাবতীয় ব্যাপারের উপর আধিপত্য করিতেছে। ম্যানীর মতে মানবের দেহ শয়তান হইতে উদ্ভূত, কিন্তু তাহার আত্মা ঈশ্বরজ্যোতি হইতে জাত হইয়াছে। পাপ মানুষকে অনুক্ষণ অধঃপতনের পথে আকর্ষণ করিতেছে, অপরদিকে পুণ্য অর্থাৎ যীশুখৃষ্ট নিয়ত তাহার পরিত্রাণের চেষ্টা করিতেছেন। পারস্যের পুরোহিতগণ ম্যানীর পরম শত্রু হইয়া উঠে। পারস্য-রাজ প্রথম বারহাম ম্যানীকে পুরোহিত-দিগের হস্তে সমর্পণ করিলে উহারা তাঁহাকে ক্রুশে বিদ্ধ করত জীবন্ত অবস্থায় চর্ম্ম-নিষ্কাশণপূর্ব্বক হত্যা করে। ম্যানীর মত খৃষ্টীয় ত্রয়োদশ শতাব্দী পর্য্যন্ত বর্ত্তমান ছিল।] ***Noun.*** (Also *Manichee*) A believer in Manicheanism ; ম্যানীপ্রবর্ত্তিত ধর্ম্মমতে বিশ্বাসী ব্যক্তি **–ism,** *n.* The doctrines of the Manicheans ; ম্যানীপ্রবর্ত্তিত ধর্ম্মমত, শুভাশুভযুদ্ধবাদ (হিঃ কোঃ)।

măn′-i-cūre, *n.* & *v. t.* The care of hands and nails ; one whose occupation is to trim nails etc. of the hand ; হস্ত ও হস্তাঙ্গুলীর যত্ন ; যে ব্যক্তি নখ প্রভৃতি কাটিয়া ছাঁটিয়া বা ঘসিয়া মাজিয়া দেয়, নখপ্রসাধক, নখসম্মার্জ্জক। ***Verb t.*** To apply manicure treatment to, as nails ; নখ প্রভৃতি প্রসাধন বা সম্মার্জ্জন করা।

măn′-i-fĕst, *adj.* That can be easily seen by the eye or perceived by the mind ; clear ; apparent ; evident ; স্পষ্টদৃশ্যমান, প্রতীয়মান ; প্রকট, বিশদ, অভিব্যক্ত ; সুস্পষ্ট, প্রকাশমান, স্ফুট, ব্যক্ত, স্পষ্ট ; প্রকাশিত, প্রত্যক্ষ। **–ly,** *adv.*

măn′-i-fĕst *v. t.* & *i.* **1.** To make manifest to the eye or mind ; to exhibit ; to reveal ; প্রত্যক্ষগোচর করা, স্পষ্টপ্রদর্শন করা, প্রত্যক্ষীভূত করা, প্রত্যক্ষ-ভাবে দেখান ; প্রদর্শন করা ; প্রকাশ করা। **2.** To prove or evidence ; প্রমাণ করা। **3.** To record in a ship's mainfest ; জাহাজের মালের চালানে তোলা। ***Verb i.*** **1.** (Of government or political party) To make a public manifestation or public expression of opinion ; (শাসনতন্ত্র বা রাজনৈতিক দলের সম্পর্কে) প্রকাশ্যে ব্যক্ত করা, প্রকাশ্যে মত প্রচার করা। **2.** (Of a spirit or ghost) To appear ; (ভূত বা প্রেতাত্মাসম্পর্কে) আবির্ভূত হওয়া। **–fes-ta′-tion,** *n.* **1.** Act of disclosing what is dark or secret ; display ; revelation ; প্রত্যক্ষীকরণ, প্রকটীকরণ, প্রকাশন, স্ফুটীকরণ, স্পষ্টীকরণ, প্রদর্শন, প্রকটন, অভিব্যক্তি, অভিব্যঞ্জন, ব্যক্তকরণ ; অবভাস (বেদান্ত), আবির্ভাব (হিঃ কোঃ), ব্যক্তীভাব (ঐ); প্রকাশন। **2.** A public act on the part of a government intended as a display of its power and purpose ; a public collective action (*e. g.* a procession, public meeting, etc.) for drawing attention to the views of the orgainsers (*e. g.* a political party) ; শাসনতন্ত্রের ক্ষমতা বা উদ্দেশ্য প্রদর্শনের জন্য অনুষ্ঠিত প্রকাশ্য কার্য্য ; কোন রাজনীতিক দলের মতের প্রতি মনোযোগ আকর্ষণের জন্য প্রকাশ্য সমবেত কার্য্য—(যথা শোভাযাত্রা, সভা) চেষ্টিত (শুক্রঃ বিনয়)। **–fes′-ta-tive,** *adj.*

măn′-i-fĕst, *n.* **1.** (*Obs.*) An open or public statement ; (অপ্রঃ) প্রকাশ্য উক্তি, প্রকাশ্য বর্ণনা। **2.** A list or invoice of a ship's cargo for use of custom house officers ; জাহাজে প্রেরিত মালের চালান, জাহাজের বীজক (হিঃ কোঃ)।

măn-i-fĕs′-tō, *n.* A public written declaration of the intentions, opinions or motives of a sovereign, prince or other man ; প্রকাশ্য ঘোষণাপত্র, সাধারণ্যে প্রকাশিত বিজ্ঞাপন, প্রসিদ্ধিপত্র।

măn′-i-fōld, *adj.* **1.** Numerous and varied ; বিবিধ, নানাবিধ, বহুসংখ্যক, বহুবিধ, বহুপ্রকার, বহুগুণ। **2.** Having various forms, features, and applications, etc. ; as, a *manifold* flower ; নানাকৃতি বিশিষ্ট, বহুরূপ, অনেকরূপ, নানারূপ। **3.** Performing several functions at once ; entitled to the name on many grounds ; as, a *manifold* traitor ; এককালে কতিপয় কার্য্য-সম্পাদক ; বহু কারণে কোন নাম বা আখ্যা প্রাপ্তির যোগ্য। **—ly,** *adv.* **—ness,** *n.* **Manifold writer**—A carbon copying apparatus ; পত্রাদির প্রতিলিপি তোলার যন্ত্রবিশেষ।

măn′-i-fōld, *v. t.* To make many or several copies of (letters etc.), as by a mainfold writer ; একই পত্রের বিভিন্নপ্রকার প্রতিলিপি করা।

măn′-i-kin, *n.* **1.** A dwarf ; বামন, মাণবক। **2.** An artist's lay-figure, (see LAY-FIGURE). **3.** A model of human body for anatomical demonstration ; শারীর-সংস্থানবিদ্যা শিক্ষাদানের জন্য কৃত্রিম মনুষ্যদেহ। **4.** A small tropical American bird ; আমেরিকার উষ্ণমণ্ডল-বাসী ক্ষুদ্র পক্ষিবিশেষ।

Mă-nil′-lă, —ă, *n.* **1.** The capital of the Phillippine islands ; ফিলিপাইন দ্বীপপুঞ্জের রাজধানী। **2.** (Also *Manilla-hemp*) A material for ropes etc. ; রজ্জু প্রভৃতি প্রস্তুতের উপাদান-বিশেষ। **3.** Cheroot made in Manilla ; ম্যানিলা দ্বীপে প্রস্তুত চুরুট।

mă-nil′-lă, *n.* A ring worn upon the arm or wrist and used as a money by the African tribes ; আফ্রিকার আদিমনিবাসিগণের বাহু বা প্রকোষ্ঠে পরিহিত কঙ্কণবিশেষ—যাহা মুদ্রার পরিবর্ত্তে ব্যবহৃত হয়।

mă-nille′ (-nil), *n.* (*In some card games*) The second best trump ; in solo, the seven of trumps ; কোন কোন ক্রীড়ায় রংএর সর্ব্বোচ্চ তাসের পরবর্ত্তী তাস ; ক্রীড়া বিশেষে রংএর সাতা।

mă′-ni-ŏc, *n.* The cassava plant ; meal made from it ; শিমুল আলু গাছ ; শিমুল আলুর ময়দা।

măn′-i-ple (-pl), *n.* **1.** (*Rom. antiq.*) Subdivision of the legion containing 120 or 60 men ; (রোমীয় প্রত্নতত্ত্ব) রোমীয় সৈন্যদলের বিভাগ-বিশেষ। **2.** (*Eccl.*) An ornamental band or scarf worn on the left arm ; (যাজকীয়-শাস্ত্র) বামবাহুতে পরিহিত কারুকার্য্যশোভিত উত্তরীয় বা বস্ত্রবেষ্টনী। **Ma-nip′-u-lar,** *adj.*

mă-nip′-ū-lāte, *v. t.* **1.** To handle or treat, esp. with skill (material thing, question) ; হস্ত দ্বারা ব্যবহার করা, সুদক্ষভাবে আলোচনা করা। **2.** To manage artfully or fraudulently for one's own advantage ; as, to *manipulate* accounts ; সুকৌশলে বা চতুরতার সহিত নির্ব্বাহ করা, সুকৌশলে সাধন করা। **—la′-tion,** *n.* Act of manipulating ; use of the hands in an artistic or skilful manner ; হস্তদ্বারাসম্পাদন ; হস্তলাঘব, হস্তনৈপুণ্য, করকৌশল। **—la-tive, —la-to-ry,** *adjs.* Done by manipulation ; pertaining to manipulation ; হস্তচালনাদ্বারা সম্পাদিত ; হস্তচালনাসম্বন্ধীয়। **—la-tor,** *n.*

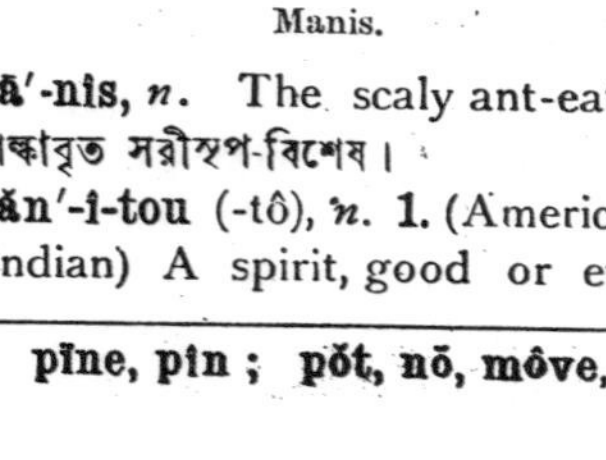

Manis.

mă′-nis, *n.* The scaly ant-eater ; শল্কাবৃত সরীসৃপ-বিশেষ।

măn′-i-tou (-tō), *n.* **1.** (American-Indian) A spirit, good or evil ; প্রেতাত্মা, ভূতশক্তি। **2.** Something with supernatural power ; অতি-প্রাকৃত শক্তিসম্পন্ন বস্তু।

măn-kīnd′, *n.* **1.** The human race ; মানবজাতি, মনুষ্যজন, বিশ্বজগৎ, জগজন (*Poet.*)। **2.** (*man′-*) The male sex ; পুরুষজাতি, নরজাতি।

măn′-līke, *adj.* **1.** Like a man ; মানববৎ **2.** (Of a woman) Mannish ; (নারীসম্বন্ধে) পুরুষস্বভাবা।

măn′-lȳ, *adj.* See under MAN.

măn′-nă, *n.* **1.** The food supplied to the Israelites in the wilderness of Arabia (*Exod.* xvi.) ; আরবদেশের অরণ্যভূমিতে পর্য্যটনকালে ইহুদীদিগকে ঈশ্বর যে খাদ্য প্রদান করেন। **2.** Spiritual nourishment as that of the Eucharist ; আধ্যাত্মিক পুষ্টিসাধক বস্তু। **3.** A sweet juice got from many trees ; কয়েকপ্রকার বৃক্ষের ক্ষীর বা নির্য্যাস, শিরখণ্ড। **—nif′-er-ous,** *adj.* **Manna-croup** — সুজি। **The manna of bamboo** — বংশলোচন, বংশক্ষীর।

măn′-nêr, *n.* **1.** The way in which anything is done or occurs ; প্রণালী, পদ্ধতি, রীতি। **2.** (*Pl.*) Modes of living ; conditions of society ; "The *manners* of the age" ; behaviour ; as, good or bad *manners* ; আচার, স্থিতিরীতি (হিঃ কোঃ) ; সামাজিক অবস্থা ; আচরণ। **3.** Deportment or outward bearing ; "His *manner* to women etc." ; আকারপ্রকার, ভাবভঙ্গী, চালচলন। **4.** (*Pl.*) Habits indicative of good breeding ; শিষ্টাচার, সৌজন্য। **5.** Style in art or literature ; রচনাপদ্ধতি, চিত্রণপদ্ধতি। **6.** (*Archaic*) Sort or kind ; (অপ্রঃ) প্রকার, রকম, জাতি। **7.** Mannerism (which see). **—less,** *adj.* Destitute of manners ; unmannerly ; শিষ্টাচারবিহীন ; অশিষ্ট, অভদ্র, অভব্য। **—li-ness,** *n.* **—ly,** *adj.* Showing good manners ; polite ; well-behaved ; শিষ্টাচারসম্পন্ন ; শিষ্ট, সভ্য ; বিনয়ী, ভদ্র। **—nered,** *adj*

Adverb of manner—যাহাতে কি প্রকারে কার্য্য করা হইল তাহা বলা বা জিজ্ঞাসা করা হয়। **All manner of**—Every kind of; সকল রকমের। **By no manner of means, Not by any manner of means**—Under no circumstances whatever; in no way; কিছুতেই না; কোনক্রমেই না। **In a manner**—To a certain degree; in some sense; কিয়ৎ পরিমাণে; কোনও অর্থে। **No manner of right**—No right at all; মোটেই কোন অধিকার নাই। **Shark's manners** — Rapacity; অত্যাচার, পীড়ন, দৌরাত্ম্য। **To make one's manners**—To salute a person on meeting by a bow, courtesy, etc.; কোন ব্যক্তির সহিত সাক্ষাৎ হইলে তাহাকে নমস্কার, প্রণিপাত বা অভিবাদন করা। **To the manner born**—(*Shakes.* Ham. I. IV. 15) Destined by birth to be subject to the custom; naturally fitted for the position etc.; কোন বিশেষ বংশ বা পরিবারে জন্মহেতু কোন বিশেষ আচার পালনে বাধ্য; আজন্ম-অভ্যস্ত কোন পদ প্রভৃতির জন্য স্বভাবতঃ উপযোগী।

măn'-nêr-ĭsm, *n.* An excessive adherence to a peculiar manner or style in art or literature; a characteristic peculiarity of action, expression, or artistic manipulation; কলা বা সাহিত্যে কোন বিশেষ রীতি বা পদ্ধতির প্রতি অতিরিক্ত নিষ্ঠা, উৎকট রীতি-প্রিয়তা; কার্য্য, উক্তি বা কলাকৌশলের বৈশিষ্ট্য, ঢপ। **—ist,** *n.* One addicted to mannerism; উৎকট রীতিপ্রিয়। **—is'-tic, —is'-ti-cal,** *adjs.*

măn'-nish (-ĭsh), *adj.* 1. Characteristic of, or resembling, a man; মানবপ্রকৃতিসিদ্ধ, মানবসদৃশ। 2. Masculine, as a woman; পুরুষস্বভাবা। **—ness,** *n.*

măn'-nite (-īt), *n.* (Also *mannite-sugar*) A substance got from manna; শিরখণ্ড হইতে প্রাপ্ত পদার্থ বিশেষ।

mă-nœu'-vre (-ô-vêr), *n., v. i.* & *t.* 1. A regulated movement of troops or ships of war; সৈন্যদল বা রণতরীশ্রেণীর কৃত্রিম যুদ্ধাভিনয় প্রদর্শন, যুদ্ধকৌশলপ্রদর্শন, কাওয়াৎ, যানকৌশল-প্রকার (কামঃ)। 2. A skilfully contrived plan; সুকৌশলোদ্ভাবিত পরিকল্পনা। 3. A deceptive or elusive movement; ভ্রান্তিজনক গতি, কূটগতি, ছল। ***Verb i.*** To perform a manœuvre; to employ stratagem or artifice; যুদ্ধাভিনয় প্রদর্শন করা; ছল, চাতুরী বা কৌশল প্রয়োগ করা। ***Verb t.*** 1. To cause to perform manœuvres; যুদ্ধাভিনয় প্রদর্শন করান। 2. To drive or entice, as a person or thing *into, out, away,* etc. by contrivance; "He... simply *manœuvred* the enemy *out* of position"; চাতুরী পূর্ব্বক আনা, তাড়িত করা, প্রলুব্ধ করিয়া আনা। 3. To manipulate adroitly; নিপুণতা সহকারে চালিত করা।

mă-nŏm'-ĕ-têr, *n.* An instrument for measuring the elastic force of gases; বাষ্পস্থিতিস্থাপক শক্তিমাপক, গ্যাসস্থিতিস্থাপকমিতি। **Man-o-met'-ric,** *adj.*

măn'-ŏr, *n.* The land belonging to a lord kept in his own position; তালুক, ভূসম্পত্তি, জমিদারী, খামার। **Ma-no'-ri-al,** *adj.* Pertaining to a manor; তালুক অথবা জমিদারী-সম্বন্ধীয়। **Manor-house, -seat** — ভূম্যধিকারী বা জমিদারের আবাসবাটী। **Lord of the manor**—জমিদার।

Mansard roof.

măn'-sård, *n.* (Also *mansard roof*) A roof having a break in the slope, the lower part being steeper than the upper (so called from the architect F. Mansard—1598-1666); একপ্রকার ছাদ—যাহার ঢালু অংশ দুই ভাগে বিভক্ত ও এই দুই ভাগের মধ্যে নিম্নের ভাগ উপরের ভাগ অপেক্ষা অধিকতর সরলোন্নত।

manse (măns), *n.* The residence of an ecclesiastic; esp. the house of a parish-minister in Scotland; ধর্ম্মযাজকের আবাসভবন; বিশেষতঃ স্কটলণ্ডের পল্লীযাজকের আবাসবাটী।

măn'-sion, *n.* 1. A large dwelling house; হর্ম্ম্য, মন্দির, সদ্ম, বেশ্ম, শালা, নিকেতন, বাসভবন। 2. (*Astrol.*) A house; (ফলিত-জ্যোতিষ) ভবন (বৃঃ সং), গৃহ। **Mansion house**—জমিদার বা ভূম্যধিকারীর ভবন, জমিদারবাড়ী; লর্ড মেয়রের সরকারী বাসভবন। **Lunar mansion**—নক্ষত্র।

măn'-tĕl, *n.* 1. (Also a *mantel shelf*) The shelf above a fire-place; গৃহমধ্যস্থ অগ্নিসেবনস্থলীর উপরিস্থ তাক। 2. (Also a *mantel-piece*) A structure of wood, marble, above and around a fireplace etc.; অগ্নিসেবনস্থলীর উপরিস্থ এবং চতুর্দ্দিকস্থ কাষ্ঠ বা মর্ম্মরপ্রস্তর প্রভৃতি রচিত মঞ্চ, অগ্নিস্থানপ্রাকার। **Mantel-board**—অগ্নিসেবনস্থলীর উপরিস্থ মঞ্চের উপর সংবদ্ধ তাক। **Mantel-tree**—অগ্নিসেবনস্থলীর দ্বারদেশে অনুপ্রস্থভাবে সংবদ্ধ দণ্ডবিশেষ।

măn'-tĕl-ĕt, măn'-tlĕt, *n.* 1. A kind of small mantel; একপ্রকার ক্ষুদ্র তাক। 2. A bullet-proof shelter; গুলি দ্বারা অভেদ্য আশ্রয়স্থলী।

măn'-tic, *adj.* Of, or relating to, divination; ভবিষ্যদ্বাণীসম্বন্ধীয়।

măn-til'-lă, *n.* 1. A small mantle, cape of silk, etc.; ক্ষুদ্র আবরণ। 2. A kind of large veil worn in Spain, Mexico, etc.; অবগুণ্ঠন বিশেষ।

măn'-tis, *n.* Orthopterous insect; গঙ্গাফড়িঙ্গ (সাঃ পঃ)। **Praying mantis**—একপ্রকার গঙ্গাফড়িঙ্গ—উহারা সম্মুখের পাদদ্বয় যুক্ত করিয়া রাখিলে প্রার্থনাকালীন যুক্তপাণির ভাব উপজাত হয়।

măn-tis'-sa (-ă), *n.* The decimal part of a logarithm; সংবর্গমানের দশমিক অংশ, অপূর্ণভাগ (হিঃ কোঃ)।

măn'-tle (-tl), *n., v. t.* & *i.* 1. A sleeveless cloak or loose outer garment for women ; স্ত্রীলোকের শ্লথ প্রাবরণ। **2.** (*Fig.*) A covering ; আচ্ছাদন, প্রাবরণ। **3.** A fragile lace-like tube fixed round a gas-jet to give incandescent light ; তাপপ্রদীপ্ত শুভ্রালোক উৎপাদনের জন্য গ্যাসের ধারার উপর যে ভঙ্গপ্রবণ জালবৎ টোপর দেওয়া হয়। ***Verb t.*** To cloak ; to cover, as with a mantle ; to conceal ; to disguise ; আচ্ছাদন করা ; আবৃত করা ; গোপন করা ; ছদ্মবেশ পরিহিত করা। ***Verb i.*** **1.** (Of liquids) To become covered with a coating ; to cream ; (তরলপদার্থ সম্বন্ধে) উপরে সরের মত পদার্থ পড়া ; সর পড়া। **2.** To rush to the face and impart a crimson glow, as blood ; (of face) to glow with a blush ; মুখমণ্ডলে উঠিয়া রক্তবর্ণ আভায় রঞ্জিত করা ; সরমের অরুণদীপ্তিতে বিভাসিত হওয়া, সরমারুণিমায় রঞ্জিত হওয়া। **To take the mantle and the ring**—(অপ্র:) চিরবৈধব্যব্রত গ্রহণ করা, ব্রহ্মচর্য্যব্রত গ্রহণ করা।

măn'-tü-ă, *n.* A lady's mantle or gown in the 17th and 18th centuries ; সপ্তদশ ও অষ্টাদশ শতাব্দীতে স্ত্রীলোকগণের ব্যবহৃত পেশোয়াজ-বিশেষ। **Mantua maker**—স্ত্রীপরিচ্ছদ প্রস্তুতকারী।

măn'-ü-ăl, *adj.* & *n.* Pertaining to the hand ; done, made, or used by the hand ; হস্তসম্বন্ধীয় ; হস্তকৃত, হস্তনির্ম্মিত, হস্তব্যবহৃত, হস্তসাধ্য। ***Noun.*** A small book for handy use ; হস্তদ্বারা ব্যবহারোপযোগী পুস্তক, সংক্ষিপ্তগ্রন্থ। **—ly,** *adv.* **Manual-alphabet** — মূক বধিরগণ কর্ত্তৃক কথোপকথনকালে অঙ্গুলী দ্বারা কৃত বর্ণমালা। **Manual exercise** — সৈনিকদিগকে অস্ত্রচালনা শিক্ষা দেওয়ার জন্য কাওয়াজ। **Manual fire-engine** — হস্ত দ্বারা চালিত দমকল। **Sign-manual**—See under SIGN.

măn-ü-făc'-tŏ-rȳ, *n.* A factory or place where goods are manufactured ; কারখানা, কলাভবন (হিঃ কোঃ), নির্ম্মাণশালা (ঐ), শিল্পগৃহ, শিল্পশালা, যন্ত্রগৃহ, শিল্পিশালা।

măn-ü-făc'-türe, *v. t.* **1.** To make as articles from raw materials by any means esp. on a large scale ; (*fig.—contemptuously of literary work*) ; নির্ম্মাণ করা, প্রস্তুত করা ; (লক্ষণায়—গ্রন্থাদিসম্বন্ধে অবজ্ঞাচ্ছলে) তৈয়ার করা। **2.** (*Fig.*) To fabricate as a story ; (লক্ষণায়) রচনা করা। **—tur-er,** *n.* One who manufactures ; নির্ম্মাতা, কারখানাওয়ালা (হিঃ কোঃ), কারিগর, শিল্পী।

măn-ü-făc'-türe, *n.* **1.** Act or process of manufacturing ; a branch of such industry ; as, woollen *manufacture* ; নির্ম্মাণ, নির্ম্মাণ-প্রণালী ; কোন শ্রমশিল্পের শাখা। **2.** (*Contempt.*) A mechanical production, as of literature etc. ; (অবজ্ঞাচ্ছলে) কলে তৈয়ারী রচনা, শুষ্ক প্রাণহীন নিয়মানুগত রচনা। **Of home** or **English manufacture**—স্বদেশে প্রস্তুত, ইংলণ্ডে প্রস্তুত।

măn-ü-mit', *v. t.* (*Hist.*) To release from slavery or bondage ; দাসত্ব হইতে মুক্তিদান করা, স্বাধীন করা। **—mis'-sion,** *n.* The act of manumitting ; স্বাধীনতাদান, মুক্তিদান, দাস্যমোচন, দাস্যমুক্তি।

mă-nüre', *n.* & *v. t.* Any substance applied to land to make it fertile ; সার। ***Verb t.*** To enrich (land) with any fertilizing substance (*lit* & *fig.*) ; সার দেওয়া। **—nu'-ri-al,** *adj.* **Animal manure** — প্রাণিসার (হিঃ কোঃ)। **Mineral manure** — খনিজসার। **Vegetable manure**—উদ্ভিজ্জসার।

măn'-ü-script, *adj.* & *n.* (*Abbr. Ms. pl. Mss.*) Written by the hand, as a book, document, etc. ; হস্তলিখিত। ***Noun.*** A book, document or paper written by the hand ; হস্তলিখিত পুস্তক বা কাগজ, পুঁথি। **—al,** *adj.*

măn'-ward (-wêrd), *adj.* Tending or directed towards man ; মনুষ্যাভিমুখীন।

Manx (măngks), *adj.* & *n.* Of, or pertaining to, the Isle of Man ; ম্যানদ্বীপ সম্বন্ধীয়। ***Noun.*** **1.** The language of the Isle of Man ; Manx people ; ম্যানদ্বীপের ভাষা ; ম্যানদ্বীপের লোক। **2.** A Manx cat ; ম্যানদ্বীপের বিড়াল। **Manx-cat** — ম্যানদ্বীপের পুচ্ছবিহীন মার্জ্জার। **Manx-man**—ম্যানদ্বীপের অধিবাসী।

man'-ȳ (mĕn-), *adj.* & *n.* [Comp. *more* ; sup. *most*] Numerous ; বহু, অনেক, বিস্তর, বহুতর, অনল্প, অনেক। ***Noun.*** Many persons ; a great number ; বহুলোক ; বৃহৎ সংখ্যা, বহুসংখ্যা। **Many coloured**—চিত্রবিচিত্র, নানাবর্ণ, নানারাগ, বহুবর্ণ। **Many-cornered**—বহুকোণ। **Many-fibred** — বহুতন্ত্রী। **Many-headed**—বহুমস্তক, বহুশিরস্ক, বহুমূর্দ্ধা। **Many-headed beast, —monster**—The populace ; ইতর লোকের জনতা। **Many-sided** — Having many sides, aspects, capabilities, etc. ; বহুপার্শ্ববিশিষ্ট, বহুমুখী। *Many sidedness, n.* **A great** or **good many**—A large or fair number ; বহুসংখ্যা। **In many ways**—In numerous ways ; বহুপ্রকারে, বহুধা, অনেক প্রকারে। **Many a time** — (*Poet, rhetor.*) Same as MANY TIMES ; (কবিতায়) বহুগুণ। **Many men many minds** — ভিন্নরুচির্হিলোকাঃ, নানা মুনির নানা মত। **Many times**—Often ; প্রায়শঃ, সর্ব্বদা, সচরাচর। **One too many**—Not wanted ; as, he finds himself *one too many* there ; অনাবশ্যক। **The many**—Multitude ; ভিড়, জনতা। **Too many** or **one too many**—Too powerful or crafty ; as, he was *too many* or *one too many* for us ; কাহারো সহিত তুলনায় অতিশয় ধূর্ত্ত বা শক্তিশালী।

Mä'-ō-rĭ *n.* A native of New Zealand ; his language ; নবজিলণ্ড দ্বীপের আদিম অধিবাসী ; উহাদের ভাষা।

măp, *n.* & *v. t.* A representation of the surface of the earth or of part of it or of the heavens on a paper etc. ; মানচিত্র, ভুচিত্র (কেন্ডিঃ), দেশচিত্র (ঐ), নক্‌সা (হিঃ কোঃ)। ***Verb t.*** **1.** To draw in the form of a map ; মানচিত্রাকারে অঙ্কিত করা। **2.** (*Fig.*) To describe clearly or sketch ; (লক্ষণায়) স্পষ্টভাবে বর্ণনা করা, নক্‌সা করা। **Map'-less,** *adj.* **To map out**—To plan or arrange in detail ; to represent or record in detail on, or as on, a map ; সবিস্তারে ব্যবস্থা, বন্দোবস্ত বা পরিকল্পনা করা ; সবিস্তারে প্রদর্শন বা লিপিবদ্ধ করা।

mā'-ple (-pl), *n.* **1.** A kind of tree grown for wood, sugar, etc. ; একপ্রকার বৃক্ষ—উহার রস হইতে চিনি প্রস্তুত হয়। **2.** The wood of this tree ; ঐ-বৃক্ষের কাষ্ঠ।

mâr, *v. t.* **1.** To injure, impair or ruin ; as, to make or *mar* ; ক্ষতি করা, হানি করা, নষ্ট করা। **2.** (*Archaic*) To mangle ; to disfigure : ক্ষত-বিক্ষত করা ; বিরূপ করা।

mâr'-â-bou (-bô), *n.* A large species of West African stork ; its downy feathers much used as trimming for hats ; a very white raw silk ; পশ্চিম আফ্রিকার হাড়গিলা জাতীয় পক্ষিবিশেষ ; ঐ পক্ষীর কোমল পালক—যাহা টুপিতে ব্যবহৃত হয় ; একপ্রকার অতি শ্বেতবর্ণ কাঁচা রেশম।

Marabou.

mâr'-â-bout (-bôt-), *n.* **1.** Mohammedan monk or hermit in Northern Africa ; উত্তর আফ্রিকার মুসলমান ফকির বা মোল্লা। **2.** A shrine over a marabout's grave ; ঐরূপ ফকিরের সমাধির উপর নির্ম্মিত দরগা।

mā-rā-schi'-nō (-skē-), *n.* A liqueur distilled from a black cherry ; কৃষ্ণবর্ণ চেরি ফল হইতে পরিস্রুত মদিরা-বিশেষ।

mă-răs'-mŭs, *n.* A wasting of flesh without any apparent disease ; atrophy ; প্রকাশ্য রোগ ব্যতিরেকে দেহক্ষয়, বিনা কারণে শরীর ক্ষয়, মাংসক্ষয় (হঃ চঃ) ; অঙ্গকৃশতা, সর্ব্বাঙ্গের শীর্ণতা। **—mic,** *adj.*

mā-raud' (-räd), *v. i.* & *t.* To rove in quest of plunder, (with *on*) : to go about pilfering লুণ্ঠনান্বেষণে বিচরণ করা ; নানা স্থানে ঘুরিয়া ছিঁচকে চুরি করা। ***Verb t.*** To plunder ; লুটপাট করা। **—er,** *n.* One who roves in quest of plunder or booty ; লুণ্ঠনোদ্দেশে বিচরণকারী।

mâr-â-ve'-di (-vā-dē), *n.* A copper-coin of Spain worth $\frac{1}{8}d.$; also, a gold-coin worth 14*s.* ; স্পেন দেশের ⅛ পেনি মূল্যের তাম্র-মুদ্রা ; ১৪ শিলিং মূল্যের স্বর্ণ মুদ্রা।

mâr'-ble (-bl), *n., adj.* & *v. t.* **1.** A species of limestone taking a high polish ; that which is made of marble ; মারবেল পাথর, মর্ম্মরোপল, শ্বেতপ্রস্তর, শ্বেতপাষাণ ; মর্ম্মরপ্রস্তর নির্ম্মিত দ্রব্য, শ্বেত পাথরের জিনিষ। **2.** That which is very hard, inflexible, smooth or cold like marble ; as, I pleaded in vain, he was *marble* ; মর্ম্মরপ্রস্তরবৎ কঠিন, মসৃণ বা শীতল বস্তু। **3.** A work of art, tombstone etc. of marble ; (*pl.*) collection of sculptures ; as, Elgin *marbles* ; মর্ম্মরপ্রস্তররচিত শিল্পদ্রব্য, সমাধিপ্রস্তর প্রভৃতি ; (বহুবচন) ক্ষোদিত মূর্ত্তি, স্তম্ভ, প্রভৃতির সংগ্রহ। **4.** A little ball of marble, clay, glass, etc. used by boys in play ; ছেলেদের খেলিবার ছোট গুলি, মারবল। ***Adj.*** **1.** Made of marble ; veined like marble ; মর্ম্মররচিত, মর্ম্মরময় ; মর্ম্মরপ্রস্তরবৎ শিরাবিশিষ্ট **2.** (*Fig.*) Hard ; inflexible ; smooth ; unfeeling ; (লক্ষণায়) কঠিন ; অনমনীয় ; মসৃণ ; নির্ম্মম। ***Verb t.*** To stain or colour, as paper, edges of books or soap, so as to look like variegated marble ; মর্ম্মরপ্রস্তরবৎ শিরাযুক্ত অথবা বিচিত্রিত করা। **—bly,** *adj.* Resembling marble ; মর্ম্মরনিভ। **Elgin-marbles** — See ELGIN. **Marble-edged**—পুস্তকের প্রান্তভাগ মর্ম্মরপ্রস্তরবৎ বিচিত্রিত। **Marble-hearted**—কঠিনহৃদয়, পাষাণহৃদয়, বজ্রহৃদয়। **Marble-plaster**—বজ্রলেপ (কেন্ডিঃ)। **Marble-paper**—চিত্রবিচিত্র মর্ম্মর প্রস্তরের অনুকরণে রঞ্জিত কাগজ, মারবেল কাগজ।

mârc, *n.* The refuse left after pressing out juice from a fruit ; কোন ফলের রস চাপ দিয়া বাহির করিয়া নিলে যে অব্যবহার্য্য অংশ অবশিষ্ট থাকে, ছিবড়া।

mâr'-că-site, *n.* A variety of pyrites ; স্বর্ণমাক্ষিক, স্বর্ণমুখী, স্বর্ণমাক্ষিক।

mâr-cĕs'-cent (-ĕnt), *adj.* Withering but not falling as a part of a plant ; পরিম্রিয়মাণ, শুষ্কপ্রায়। **—cence,** *n.*

mârch, *n.* **1.** (*Hist.*) A border ; boundary of a territory ; (ইতিহাস) প্রান্ত ; সীমান্ত। **2.** A tract of land (often debatable) between two countries ; দুই দেশের মধ্যবর্ত্তী (সচরাচর) বিবদমান ভূমি।

mârch, *v. i.* To border ; to be adjacent ; (with *upon, with*) ; সন্নিহিত হওয়া ; লাগাও হওয়া।

Mârch, *n.* (*Abbr.* MAR.) The third month of the year ; মার্চ্চ মাস। **March hare**— See under HARE.

mârch, *n., v. i.* & *t.* **1.** (*Mil.*) Advance or movement of troops ;

সৈন্যদের গমন, যুদ্ধযাত্রা, অভিযান, যান (অর্থঃ), প্রয়াণ। 2. A long toilsome walk; "Had a troublesome *march* to gain the top of it"; সুদীর্ঘ ক্লান্তিজনক পথ। 3. A piece of music fitted for marching of troops; সৈন্যযাত্রাকালোচিত বাদ্য। 4. The distance passed over by troops in a day; এক দিবসে সৈন্যদল যে পরিমাণ স্থান অতিক্রম করে। 5. A regular and uniform step of troops; as, a quick, slow or double *march*; কুচ। 6. Progress, as, of events, time, intellect or mind; অগ্রগতি, অগ্রগমন। ***Verb i.*** 1. To move in order, as soldiers (sometimes with *away, forth, past* or *out*); যুদ্ধযাত্রা করা, কুচ করা। 2. To walk in a grave or steady manner; গম্ভীরভাবে চলা; অকম্পিত পদে চলা। ***Verb t.*** To cause to march; কুচ করান। **A forced march**—যে অভিযানে সৈন্যগণকে সতেজে অগ্রে চালিত করা হয়। **Line of march**—Route of march; অভিযানপথ। **Rogue's march** — কোন সৈনিককে সৈন্যদল হইতে বহিষ্করণ কালে যে বিদ্রূপসূচক বাদ্য বাদিত হয়। **To march past**—(Of troops) To pass in marching by the side of, as a sovereign or reviewing officer; রাজা বা পরিদর্শনকারী কর্ম্মচারীর পার্শ্ব দিয়া কুচ করিয়া যাওয়া। **To steal a march upon**—See under STEAL.

mâr'-chion-ĕss (-shŭn-), *n.* 1. The wife or the widow of a marquis; মার্কুইস পত্নী, মার্কুইসের বিধবা স্ত্রী। 2. A woman holding a position like that of a marquis; মার্কুইস পত্নীর সমপদস্থা মহিলা।

mârch'-pāne, mâr'-zĭ-păn, *n.* A kind of sweet bread or biscuit; একপ্রকার মিষ্ট রুটি বা বিস্কুট।

mâr-cō'-nĭ-grăm, *n.* A message sent by Marconi's system of wireless telegraphy; মার্কণি কর্ত্তৃক উদ্ভাবিত অতার-তাড়িতবার্ত্তাবহযোগে প্রেরিত সংবাদ।

māre, *n.* The female of the horse; ঘোটকী, ঘোড়ী, বড়বা, হয়ী, বামী, অশ্বা, অশ্বিনী, তুরগী, তুরঙ্গিণী। **Mare's nest**—অশ্বডিম্ব, বকাণ্ডপ্রত্যাশা-ন্যায়। **Mare's tail**—অশ্বপুচ্ছবৎ গুল্ম-বিশেষ। **Shanks's mare**—দুই পা। **The grey mare is the better horse**—যে স্ত্রী স্বামীর উপর প্রভুত্ব করিয়া থাকে; স্বামী অপেক্ষা অধিকতর চতুরা স্ত্রী। **To find a mare's nest**—To discover something which turns out to be a hoax; অশ্বডিম্ব প্রাপ্ত হওয়া। **To make the mare go**—To display prosperity; to carry out undertakings; ঐশ্বর্য্যের আড়ম্বর প্রদর্শন করা; গৃহীত কার্য্য সম্পাদন করা।

mare, (*L.*), *n.* ***Mare clausum***—কোন বিশেষ দেশের অধিকারভুক্ত সাগর। ***Mare liberum***—সর্ব্ব-জাতির জন্য উন্মুক্ত সাগর।

mă-rĕm'-mă, *n.* A low marshy unhealthy region by the sea-shore; সাগরপার্শ্ববর্ত্তী অস্বাস্থ্যকর অনূপভূমি।

mâr'-gă-rine (-rīn), *n.* A legal term denoting all substances made in imitation of butter; কৃত্রিম মাখন।

mâr'-gay (-gā), *n.* A tiger-cat of South America; দক্ষিণ আমেরিকার আরণ্য মার্জ্জার বিশেষ।

marge (mârj), *n.* (*Poet.*) Same as MARGIN.

mâr'-gĭn, *n.* & *v. t.* 1. An edge; border; পার্শ্ব, তীর, কিনারা; প্রান্ত, সীমা, ধার। 2. The condition near the limit below or beyond which a thing ceases to be possible etc.; সম্ভাব্যতার সীমা। 3. The blank edge of a page of a book; পুস্তকের পৃষ্ঠার শাদা পার্শ্ব, পুস্তক-প্রান্ত। 4. Extra amount, as of time, money, etc.; প্রয়োজনাতিরিক্ত সময়, অর্থ, প্রভৃতি। 5. (*Commr.*) The difference between the cost and selling price of an article; (*Finance*) collateral security; (বাণিজ্য) কোন বস্তুর ক্রয়মূল্য এবং বিক্রেয় মূল্যের মধ্যে প্রভেদ (যাহা হইতে খরচ, লাভ প্রভৃতি পোষাইতে হয়); দালালের নিকট জামিনস্বরূপ গচ্ছিত অর্থ। ***Verb t.*** 1. To furnish with margins; to enter notes on the margin of; প্রান্তবিশিষ্ট করা; পুস্তকের পৃষ্ঠার কিনারায় টীকা, টিপ্পনী বা মন্তব্য লিখিয়া রাখা, পার্শ্ব-টিপ্পনী লিখা। 2. (*Finance*) To deposit margin on (a stock); দালালের নিকট অতিরিক্ত টাকা গচ্ছিত রাখা (যদ্দারা কোন ব্যক্তির অনুকূলে চুক্তি প্রভৃতি করার দরুণ যদি তাহার কোন ক্ষতি হয় তবে তাহা পোষাইতে পারে।) **—ate, —a-ted,** *adjs.* **—ise,** *v.t.* To furnish with marginal notes; পার্শ্ব-টিপ্পনী-সমন্বিত করা। **Margin of cultivation**—যে জমির আয় হইতে কষ্টেসৃষ্টে কেবলমাত্র মজুর খরচ ও মূলধনের সুদ পোষাইতে পারে কিন্তু খাজানা দেওয়ার সুবিধা হয় না তৎসম্পর্কে প্রযুক্ত।

mâr'-gĭn-ăl, *adj.* 1. Pertaining to, or written in, the margin; with marginal notes; প্রান্তসম্বন্ধীয়, পার্শ্ব-লিখিত; পার্শ্বটীকাসমন্বিত। 2. Of, relating to, or at the edge or border; প্রান্ত-সম্বন্ধীয়, সীমান্ত দেশবর্ত্তী, সীমান্ত সমীপবর্ত্তী। 3. (*Econ.*) That is close to the limit below or beyond which something ceases to be possible or desirable; as, *marginal* utility; (অর্থনীতি শাস্ত্র) যে সীমার ঊর্দ্ধে বা নিম্নে কোন বিষয় সম্ভবপর বা বাঞ্ছনীয় নহে — তৎসীমান্তবর্ত্তী। **—ly,** *adv.* **Marginal notes**—পার্শ্ব-টিপ্পনী।

mâr-gĭ-nā'-lĭ-ă, *n.* (*Pl.*) Notes written on the margin; পুস্তকের পার্শ্বস্থ টিপ্পনী সমূহ, পার্শ্বটিপ্পনী সমূহ।

mâr'-grāve, *n.* A title of a German noble man of rank equivalent to English marquis; জর্ম্মণী দেশের সম্ভ্রান্ত ব্যক্তির উপাধি বিশেষ। **—gra-vine,** *n.* (*Fem.*)

mâr′-gue-rite (-gĕ-rēt), *n.* The ox-eye daisy ; একপ্রকার পুষ্প।

mariage de convenance, (*F.*), *n.* Marriage contracted from prudential motives ; পরিণামে বৈষয়িক সুবিধা হইবে এই উদ্দেশ্যে যে বিবাহের অঙ্গীকারে আবদ্ধ হওয়া যায়।

Mā′-rĭ-ăn, *adj.* & *n.* **1.** Relating to the Virgin Mary ; কুমারী মেরী সম্বন্ধীয়। **2.** Relating to Queen Mary of England or of Scotland ; ইংলণ্ডের অথবা স্কটলণ্ডের রাজ্ঞী মেরী সম্বন্ধীয়। ***Noun.*** A follower of Mary, the Queen of Scotland ; স্কটলণ্ডের রাজ্ঞী মেরীর অনুবর্ত্তী ব্যক্তি।

mâr′-ĭd, *n.* (*Moham. myth.*) One of the most powerful class of jinn ; এক শ্রেণীর অতি শক্তিশালী জীন।

măr′-ĭ-gōld, *n.* A name for several plants with golden yellow blossoms ; গাঁদা, জারগুল, গুলজাফরী, (হিন্দী ও পার্সী ভাষায়)।

mâr-ĭ-nāde′, *n.* & *v. t.* A pickle containing wine, spices, etc. ; the meat or fish thus pickled ; মদ্য, মসলাদি দ্বারা রক্ষিত মৎস্য বা মাংস ; ঐরূপে যে মাংস বা মৎস্য তাজা রাখা হয়। ***Verb t.*** To pickle with marinade ; মদ্য মসলাদির সহযোগে তাজা রাখা বা আচার প্রস্তুত করা।

mă-rine′ (-rēn), *adj.* & *n.* **1.** Of, or belonging to, the sea ; সামুদ্রিক, সৈন্ধব, সামুদ্র, সমুদ্রীয়। **2.** Found in, or produced by, the sea ; for use at the sea ; as, *marine* barometer ; সমুদ্রপ্রাপ্ত, সমুদ্রজাত, অব্ধিজ, সমুদ্রজ, সমুদ্রোদ্ভব, সমুদ্রসম্ভব ; সমুদ্রে ব্যবহারের উপযোগী। **3.** Relating to naval affairs ; nautical ; নৌ-বিভাগীয়; নৌবিদ্যাসম্বন্ধীয়, নাবিকসম্বন্ধীয়। **4.** (Of soldiers) Serving on board a ship ; (সৈন্য সম্পর্কে) জাহাজে নিযুক্ত। ***Noun.*** **1.** A sea-soldier ; নৌসৈন্য। **2.** The collective shipping, fleet or navy of a country or state ; কোন দেশ বা রাষ্ট্রের নৌবল।

măr′-ĭ-nêr, *n.* A seaman or sailor ; নাবিক, পোতবাহ, জাহাজের মাল্লা। **Marine insurance**—জাহাজ বা জাহাজের মালের বীমা, সামুদ্রিক বীমা। **Marine soap**—নারিকেল তৈল হইতে প্রস্তুত একপ্রকার সাবান—যাহা সমুদ্রজলের সহিত মিশাইয়া ধৌত করার কার্য্যে ব্যবহার করা যাইতে পারে। **Marine-stores**—যে স্থানে পুরাতন জাহাজের জিনিষ (যথা, লৌহ, দড়াদড়ি, পাইল, খাদ্যদ্রব্য এবং অন্যান্য সাজসজ্জা) বিক্রীত হয় ; ঐ সমস্ত জিনিষ। **Master-mariner**—বাণিজ্য-পোতাধ্যক্ষ। **Mariner's compass**—See under COMPASS. **Tell that to the mariners**—An expression implying incredulity ; অবিশ্বাস-ব্যঞ্জক বাক্য।

Mā-rĭ-ŏl′-ă-trȳ, *n.* The worship of the Virgin Mary ; কুমারী মেরীর উপাসনা, মেরীদেবীর অর্চ্চনা।

măr-ĭ-ō-nette′ (-nĕt), *n.* A puppet worked by strings ; পুতুল নাচের পুতুল, যন্ত্রপুত্রক (রাঃ তঃ)। **Marionette show**—পুতুল নাচ।

măr′-ĭsh, *n.* & *adj.* (*Poet.*) Same as MARSH(Y) ; (কবিতায়) বিল।

Mā′-rĭst, *n.* A member of the R. C. Society of Mary ; রোমান ক্যাথলিক সম্প্রদায়-বিশেষের সভ্য।

măr′-ĭ-tăl, *adj.* **1.** Of, or pertaining to, marriage ; বিবাহ-সম্বন্ধীয়। **2.** Of, or relating to, a husband ; স্বামীসম্বন্ধীয়, ভর্ত্তৃসম্পর্কীয়। **—ly,** *adv.*

măr′-ĭ-tīme, *adj.* **1.** Pertaining to, or connected with, the sea ; সামুদ্রিক, সাগর-সংক্রান্ত। **2.** Situated, or found, near the sea ; সাগর-সন্নিহিত, সমুদ্রসমীপস্থ, সাগরসন্নিহিত দেশে প্রাপ্ত। **Maritime nations**—যে সকল জাতির সামুদ্রিক ব্যবসায় আছে।

mâr′-jō-răm, *n.* An aromatic plant used as a seasoning in cookery ; মরুয়াফল, মরুবক, সুরভিপত্রী।

mârk, *n.* & *v. t.* **1.** A visible sign or impression on something ; an affixed or impressed sign, seal, etc. ; লক্ষণ, চিহ্ন, নিশান, নিদর্শন, লাঞ্ছন, ব্যঞ্জন, অভিজ্ঞান, অঙ্ক, লিঙ্গ ; অঙ্কিত মোহর, ছাপ। **2.** A target or other object to be aimed at ; what one seeks to hit or reach ; a desired object ; শরব্য ; লক্ষ্য ; বাঞ্ছিত বস্তু, ঈপ্সিত বিষয়। **3.** A sign or indication as of quality, character, etc. ; চরিত্রলক্ষণ, গুণলক্ষণ। **4.** A trade-mark ; মালের উপর ব্যবসায়ীদের বিশিষ্ট চিহ্ন, ব্যবসায়-চিহ্ন। **5.** A cross etc. made by a person who cannot write his name ; ঢেড়া সহি। **6.** A written or printed symbol ; as, a *mark* of interrogation ; লিখিত বা মুদ্রিত সাঙ্কেতিক চিহ্ন। **7.** A unit of numerical award of merit in an examination ; পরীক্ষার নম্বর। **8.** Pre-eminence ; distinction ; as, to *make* one's *mark* ; প্রাধান্য, খ্যাতি ; প্রতিপত্তি, প্রতিষ্ঠা। **9.** The proper standard ; as, below or up to the *mark* ; উপযুক্ত সীমা। **10.** A scratch, scar, stain, etc. ; as, this pencil makes a fine *mark* ; অঙ্ক, আঁচড়, দাগ, ক্ষতচিহ্ন, কলঙ্কচিহ্ন। **11.** A line etc. that indicates position ; as, a flood-*mark* ; অবস্থান-নির্দ্দেশক রেখা প্রভৃতি। **12.** (*Hist.*) Tract of common land held by a community ; (ইতিহাস) কোন সম্প্রদায়ের সাধারণ অধিকারভুক্ত জমি। ***Verb t.*** **1.** To put a mark on (anything) by stamping, cutting, writing, etc. ; চিহ্নিত করা, দাগ কাটা, অঙ্কিত করা, দাগ দেওয়া। **2.** To put price figures on (articles) ; মূল্যাঙ্ক লিখিয়া রাখা। **3.** To indicate (a place on map, a length of syllable) by signs or marks ; মানচিত্রে কোন স্থান নির্দ্দেশ করা, কোন শব্দাংশ মাত্রাদ্বারা চিহ্নিত করা। **4.** To record as points gained in games ; কোন ক্রীড়ায় জয়াঙ্ক লিপিবদ্ধ করা। **5.** (*Pass.*) To furnish with natural marks ; as, *marked* with silver spots ; স্বাভাবিক চিহ্নে চিহ্নিত করা। **6.** To plan ; to trace out the boundary lines for, (with *out*) ; as, to *mark out* a course, ground, etc. ; নক্সা করা ; কোন কিছুর সীমান্ত রেখা অঙ্কিত করা। **7.** To destine (with *out*), as animals *marked out* for slaughter ; ভাগ্যে নির্দ্দিষ্ট করা। **8.** (*Lit.* & *fig.*) To separate by a mark or boundary, (with *off*) : চিহ্ন বা সীমারেখা দ্বারা পৃথক করা। **9.** To manifest as one's displeasure etc. *by* ; কোন উপায়ে কাহারও বিরক্তি প্রকাশ করা। **10.** To be a feature of ; to distinguish ; as, no triumph *marks* her manner ; বিশিষ্ট গুণ-স্বরূপ হওয়া ; প্রখ্যাত করা। **11.** To see or notice ; to pay heed to ; as, *mark* my words ; দেখা, লক্ষ্য করা ; অবধান করা। **12.** (*Hunting*) To observe and remember the spot of disappearance of (with *down*) ; যে স্থান হইতে অদর্শন হইয়াছে তাহা বিশেষরূপে লক্ষ্য করিয়া স্মরণ রাখা। **13.** (*Football*) To keep close to, as an opponent in order to hamper him ; (পাদগোলক ক্রীড়ায়) প্রতিপক্ষকে বাধা দিবার জন্য তাহার কাছে ঘেঁষিয়া থাকা। **Mark'-ed,** *adj.* Distinguished by a mark ; noticeable ; conspicuous ; as, a *marked* difference ; চিহ্নিত ; লক্ষ্য করার উপযোগী, অবধান-যোগ্য ; সুপ্রকট, সুস্পষ্ট। **Mark'-ed-ly,** *adv.* **Mark'-ed-ness,** *n.* **Trade-mark**—See MARK. *n.* 4. **A marked man**—সন্দেহের পাত্র, প্রতিহিংসার পাত্র। **Below** or **up to the mark**—Below or up to the standard ; নির্দ্দিষ্ট সীমার নীচে বা উপরে। **Beside** or **wide of the mark**—Not hitting the mark ; (*fig.*) not to the point ; লক্ষ্যত্যাগী ; (লক্ষণায়) অপ্রাসঙ্গিক। **(God) bless the mark**—A superstitious utterance originally used to avert evil ; ষাট, ষাট, ষাট। **(God) save the mark**—An invocation to God for mercy ; হে ঈশ্বর করুণা প্রকাশ কর। **Good** or **bad mark**—শিক্ষক, কারাধ্যক্ষ, প্রভৃতি কর্ত্তৃক খাতায় সৎ বা অসৎ আচরণের যে সাঙ্কেতিক চিহ্ন ব্যবহার করা হইয়া থাকে। **Mark of mouth**—অশ্ব দন্তে বয়সসূচক গর্ত্ত বা অবনমিত স্থান। **Of mark**—Famous ; noted ; বিখ্যাত, খ্যাতনামা, প্রথিতনামা ; প্রখ্যাত, লব্ধবর্ণ। **To make one's mark**—To gain distinction ; প্রতিষ্ঠা লাভ করা, খ্যাতি লাভ করা। **To mark out**—See MARK *v. t.* 6 & 7. **To mark time**—(*Mil.*) To lift and bring down feet alternately at the same rate as in marching ; কুচ করার কালে তালে তালে পা ফেলা।

mârk, *n.* **1.** A denomination of weight for gold and silver ; স্বর্ণরৌপ্যাদির মান বিশেষ—সচরাচর ৮ আউন্স। **2.** A German coin worth a littte less than a shilling ; জর্ম্মণীর রৌপ্যমুদ্রা—মূল্য প্রায় এক শিলিং।

mârk'-êr, *n.* **1.** One who marks ; চিহ্নকারক। **2.** One who records the score at games as in billiards ; যে ব্যক্তি ক্রীড়াদিতে জয়াঙ্ক লিপিবদ্ধ করে। **3.** One who marks down a game in hunting ; যে ব্যক্তি মৃগয়াতে পশুর অদর্শন স্থান লক্ষ্য করিয়া স্মরণ রাখে।

mâr'-kĕt, *n.* **1.** A gathering of people for purchase and sale of provisions etc. ; as, to hold a *market* at a place ; বাজার, হাট, হট্ট। **2.** The time for such gathering ; as, you must not bring your horse before the *market* ; বাজারের বেলা, হাটের সময়। **3.** An open place or a building where a market is held ; যে মুক্ত স্থানে বা অট্টালিকায় বাজার বসে, বাজারের স্থান। **4.** A demand, as for a commodity ; চাহিদা। **5.** The rate of purchase and sale ; as, the *market* fell ; বাজার দর। **6.** A seat of trade ; as, India is a *market* for English goods ; বাণিজ্যস্থলী। **Market day**—হাটবার, বাজারবার। **Market-garden**—যে বাগানে বাজারে বিক্রয়ের জন্য শাকশব্জী জন্মান হয়, তরিতরকারীর বাগান। **Market place**—হাটের স্থান, আপণ (শুক্রঃ বিনয়)। **Market town**—যে নগরে বাজার আছে। **Market price** or **value**—বাজার দর, বাজার ভাও। **The corn market**—শস্যের ব্যবসায়। **To bring one's eggs** or **hogs to a bad market**—To fail in one's schemes ; কাহারও সঙ্কল্প বা উদ্দেশ্য বিফল হওয়া। **To come into the market**—To be offered for sale ; বিক্রয়ের জন্য উপস্থাপিত হওয়া। **To make a market of**—(*Fig.*) To barter away ; (লক্ষণায়) বিনিময় করিয়া ফেলা। **To put on the market** — To offer for sale ; বিক্রয়ার্থ উপস্থিত করা।

mâr'-kĕt, *v. i.* & *t.* To buy and sell in a market ; বাজারে ক্রয় বিক্রয় করা, বাজার করা। ***Verb t.*** To offer for sale in a market ; বাজারে বিক্রয়ার্থ উপস্থিত করা। **—a-ble,** *adj.* Saleable ; পণ্য, বিক্রেয়। **—a-bly,** *adv.*

mâr'-kĕt-ing, *n.* **1.** The act of selling or purchasing in a market ; বাজার করণ। **2.** Commodities purchased ; বাজারে ক্রীত বস্তু, বাজার।

mârk'-ing, *n.* **1.** Putting a mark ; colouring of feathers, skin, etc. ; চিহ্নপ্রদান ; চর্ম্ম, পালক, প্রভৃতি রঞ্জন। **Marking-ink**—বস্ত্রাদির উপর স্থায়ী চিহ্ন বসাইবার জন্য কালি। **Marking nut** — ভেলা (খোরী), ভল্লাতক (ঐ)।

mârks'-măn, *n.* One skilful to hit a mark ; one who shoots well ; লক্ষ্যভেদনিপুণ ব্যক্তি ; লক্ষ্যবেধী, লক্ষ্যভেদক। **—ship,** *n.*

mârl, *n.* & *v. t.* A soil consisting of clay and carbonate of lime, valuable as a manure ;

চূণ এবং বালুকা মিশ্রিত সার মাটী, চূণমাঝারি (প্রবোধ)। ***Verb t.*** To overspread or manure with marl; চূণমাঝারি দ্বারা সার দেওয়া। **Marl'-y,** *adj.*

mâr'-line (-lĭn), *n.* **1.** (*Naut.*) A small line of two strands (used for winding round ropes and cables to prevent their being worn by rubbing); (নৌ:বিদ্যা) ঘর্ষণজনিত ক্ষয়নিবারণার্থ, কাছিতে জড়াইবার জন্য সরু দড়ি। **Marline-spike, Marlin-spike**—A pointed iron tool for separating strands of a rope in splicing; দুইটী রজ্জুর প্রান্ত একত্র পাকাইয়া জোড়া দেওয়ার কালে রজ্জুর গুণ পৃথক করার জন্য যে লৌহ সূচী ব্যবহৃত হয়।

mârl'-īte, *n.* A kind of marl resisting the action of the air; একপ্রকার সার মাটী—যাহা বায়ুর ক্রিয়া প্রতিরোধ করে।

mâr'-mȧ-lāde, *n.* A preserve made from various fruits, such as orange etc.; কমলালেবু প্রভৃতির মোরব্বা।

mâr'-mō-līte, *n.* A silicate of magnesia; ম্লান হরিদ্বর্ণ প্রস্তর বিশেষ।

mâr-mō'-rē-ăl, *adj.* (*Poet.*) Of, or like, marble; মর্ম্মরবৎ, মর্ম্মর-সদৃশ, শ্বেতপ্রস্তরময়।

Marmoset.

mâr'-mō-sĕt, *n.* A small tropical American monkey; আমেরিকার উষ্ণমণ্ডলবাসী ক্ষুদ্রকায় কপিবিশেষ।

mâr'-mŏt, *n.* **1.** A rodent of the squirrel family; কাঠবিড়াল জাতীয় জন্তুবিশেষ, গিরিমূষিক। **2.** A variety of bathing cap; একজাতীয় স্নানকালীন টুপী

Marmot.

Mâr'-ŏ-nīte, *n.* One of a Christian sect of Syria, dwelling in Lebanon; লেবাননবাসী খৃষ্টীয় ধর্ম্ম-সম্প্রদায় বিশেষ।

mȧ-rōōn', *adj.* & *n.* Of, or relating to, brownish crimson colour; পিঙ্গলাভরক্তবর্ণ। ***Noun.*** **1.** A brownish crimson or claret colour; পিঙ্গলাভ রক্তবর্ণ, কপিশবর্ণ, ইষ্টকবর্ণ। **2.** A fire-work exploding with loud report; একপ্রকার আতসবাজী—যাহা ভীষণ শব্দে বিদীর্ণ হয়।

mȧ-rōōn', *n., v. t.* & *i.* **1.** (In Dutch Guiana and West Indies) One of a class of Negroes, originally fugitive slaves, living in the mountains and forests; একশ্রেণীর কাফ্রী ক্রীতদাস—ইহারা প্রভু-গৃহ হইতে পলাইয়া অরণ্যে আশ্রয় গ্রহণ করিত। **2.** A person that is marooned; বিজনদ্বীপ বা সমুদ্রতীরে পরিত্যক্ত ব্যক্তি। ***Verb t.*** To land and leave on a desolate island or coast as punishment; (শাস্তিস্বরূপ) কাহাকে কোন বিজন দ্বীপ বা সমুদ্রতীরে পরিত্যাগ করা। ***Verb i.*** To idle; to hang about; আলস্যে কাল কাটান; কোন স্থানের নিকট দিয়া ঘুরিয়া বেড়ান।

mâr'-plŏt, *n.* One who mars or defeats a plot or design by interference where he has no right; অনধিকারে হস্তক্ষেপ করিয়া যে ব্যক্তি মন্ত্রণা বা অভিসন্ধি ব্যর্থ বা পণ্ড করে, মন্ত্রবিঘাতক, কার্য্য-বিঘাতক।

marque (mârk), *n.* **A letter** or **letters of marque** or **letters of marque and reprisal**—**1.** A license granted (by a sovereign) to a private person to fit out an armed vessel and employ it in the capture of the enemy's ships and merchandise; যুদ্ধকালে শত্রুপক্ষীয় জাহাজ আক্রমণপূর্ব্বক ঐ জাহাজ ধৃত বা উহার জিনিষপত্র লুটপাট করার জন্য (রাজা কর্ত্তৃক) স্বদেশীয় জাহাজের অধ্যক্ষকে প্রদত্ত অনুমতি পত্র। **2.** (*Sing.*) A private vessel carrying such a license; ঐরূপ অনুমতিপ্রাপ্ত বেসরকারী জাহাজ।

mâr'-quee (-kē), *n.* A large tent; বৃহৎ তাঁবু, বৃহৎ পটবেশ্ম, সেনা-নায়কের শিবির বা পটমণ্ডপ।

mâr'-quet-rȳ (-kĕt-), **–que-ter-ie,** (-kĕ-têr-ĭ), *ns.* Inlaid work; খচিত শিল্প, বিবিধ রঙ্গের কাষ্ঠ, অস্থি, গজদন্ত, প্রভৃতি খচিত শিল্প কার্য্য।

mâr'-quĭs, –quĕss, *ns.* (*Fem. marchioness.*) A title of nobility next below that of a duke; ডিউকের অব্যবহিত নিম্নপদস্থ সম্ভ্রান্ত উপাধি, মার্কুইস। **–ate,** *n.*

mâr-quise' (-kēz), *n.* **1.** (Of foreign nobility) A marchioness; মার্কুইস পত্নী। **2.** A finger-ring set with oval pointed cluster of gems; অণ্ডখণ্ডাকৃতি মণিগুচ্ছখচিত অঙ্গুরীয়ক।

mâr'-quois (-kwoyz), *n.* **Marquois scale** — সমদূরবর্ত্তী সমান্তরাল রেখাঙ্কনের জন্য যন্ত্র-বিশেষ।

mâr'-riage (-ĭj), *n.* **1.** Relation between husband and wife; wedlock; দাম্পত্যসম্বন্ধ; বিবাহ, বিয়ে (*colloq.*), উদ্বাহ, পরিণয়, পাণিগ্রহণ, দারপরিগ্রহ, পাণিপীড়। **2.** The act or ceremony of marrying; দারক্রিয়া, পাণিগ্রহণক্রিয়া, বিবাহানুষ্ঠান, বিবাহ-সংস্কার **3.** (*Fig.*) Intimate union; (লক্ষণায়) ঘনিষ্ঠ সংযোগ। **4.** (*Cards*) The combination of the king and queen of the same sort; ইস্তক। **–a-ble,** *adj.* **1.** Of an age to marry ; বিবাহযোগ্য। 2. Fit for marriage ; as *marriageable age* ; দারক্রিয়াযোগ্য, বিবাহযোগ্য, পরিণেয়, উদ্বাহ্য, বিবাহোচিত। **–a-ble-ness**, *n.* **Civil marriage**—রাজকর্ম্মচারিকর্তৃক সম্পাদিত ধর্ম্মানুষ্ঠানশূন্য বিবাহ। **Communal marriage**—যে ব্যবস্থানুসারে কোন ক্ষুদ্র সমাজের সকল পুরুষ সকল স্ত্রীর সহিত বিবাহিত বলিয়া গণ্য হয়, সংঘ-পরিণয়, গণবিবাহ। **Marriage articles**—সম্পত্তির উত্তরাধিকার এবং স্বত্ব সম্বন্ধে বিবাহের পূর্ব্বে চুক্তি। **Marriage-bed**—(*Fig.*) Marital intercourse ; (লক্ষণায়) স্বামীস্ত্রীর সহবাস। **Marriage-broker**—ঘটক। **Marriage contract**—বিবাহচুক্তি। **Marriage-favour**—বিবাহকালে পরিহিত শ্বেতবর্ণ ফিতার গ্রন্থি বা শ্বেতকুসুমগুচ্ছ। **Marriage lines**—A certificate of marriage ; বিবাহের নিদর্শনপত্র। **Marriage portion**—যৌতুক। **Marriage-string**—মঙ্গলসূত্র, সৌভাগ্যতন্তু, মাঙ্গল্যতন্তু। **Marriage settlement**—বিবাহের পূর্ব্বে যে ব্যবস্থা দ্বারা স্বামীর মৃত্যু ঘটিলে স্ত্রী এবং সন্তানের জন্য কতক ধনসম্পত্তি বন্দোবস্ত করিয়া দেওয়া হয়। **Secret marriage**—গুপ্ত পরিণয়, চোরিকা বিবাহ (মৃচ্ছঃ)। **To give or take in marriage** — বিবাহ দেওয়া বা বিবাহ করা।

măr′-ried (-ĭd), *adj.* Wedded; of, or relating to, a person or persons united in marriage ; as, *married* life ; বিবাহিত, কৃতবিবাহ, জাতবিবাহ ; বিবাহিত ব্যক্তি বা ব্যক্তিগণ-সম্পর্কীয়।

măr′-row (-ö), *n.* 1. The soft fatty substance in the cavities of bones ; মজ্জা, মেদ, অস্থিসার অস্থিস্নেহ, অস্থিমজ্জা, দেহসার। 2. The essence or the best part of anything ; as, pith and *marrow* ; সার, মজ্জা। **—less, —y**, *adjs.* **Marrow-bone**—One containing edible marrow ; (*facet., pl.*) knees ; আহারোপযোগী মজ্জাপূর্ণ অস্থি ; (কৌতুকচ্ছলে) হাঁটু। **Marrow (fat)**—A variety of large pea ; একজাতীয় বড় মটর। **Marrow-spoon**—অস্থির ভিতর হইতে মজ্জা বাহির করার জন্য চামচ বিশেষ। **Spinal marrow**—মেরুদণ্ডের মজ্জা। **Vegetable marrow**—কুষ্মাণ্ড।

mar′-rȳ (mă-), *v. t.* & *i.* 1. (Of priests etc.) To unite in wedlock ; বিবাহবন্ধনে স্ত্রীপুরুষকে সংযুক্ত করা, পরিণয়সূত্রে আবদ্ধ করা, বিবাহিত করা। 2. (Of parent or guardian) To give (son, daughter, etc.) in marriage ; বিবাহ দেওয়া, সম্প্রদান করা। 3. To take for husband or wife ; পতি বা পত্নীরূপে গ্রহণ করা, বিবাহ করা, দারপরিগ্রহ করা। 4. (*Fig.*) To unite intimately ; (লক্ষণায়) ঘনিষ্ঠভাবে সংযোগ করা। *Verb i.* To enter into the married state ; বিবাহিত হওয়া, পরিণীত হওয়া, বিবাহবন্ধনে বদ্ধ হওয়া, পরিণয়সূত্রে বদ্ধ হওয়া, পরিণীত হওয়া।

mar′-rȳ (mă-), *interj.* (*Archaic*) Expressing surprise, indignation, asseveration, etc. ; মাইরি।

Mârs, *n.* 1. (*Rom. religion*) The god of war ; রোমানদিগের রণদেবতা (cf. our কার্ত্তিকেয়)। 2. Warfare ; যুদ্ধবিগ্রহ। 3. The planet fourth in order of distance from the sun ; মঙ্গলগ্রহ, ক্ষিতিসুত, লোহিতাঙ্গ, কুজ (বৃঃ সং), ভৌম, অঙ্গারক, ভূমিজ, মহীসুত, লোহিত, লোহিতক, ঋণান্তক।

Mâr′-sâ-lă, *n.* A kind of wine from Marsala in Sicily ; সিসিলী দ্বীপের অন্তর্গত মার্সালা হইতে সমানীত মদ্য-বিশেষ।

Mâr-seilles (-sāls), *n.* 1. A seaport in the South of France ; ফরাসীদেশের দক্ষিণাংশস্থিত বন্দর-বিশেষ। 2. A kind of stiff cotton fabric (so named from its being first made there) ; একপ্রকার দৃঢ় কার্পাস বস্ত্র।

mârsh, *n.* A tract of low wet land ; a swamp ; কচ্ছভূমি, অনূপ; জলাভূমি, বদ্ধজলা, বিল। **Marsh′-i-ness**, *n.* **Marsh′-y**, *adj.* 1. Wet ; boggy ; আর্দ্র, ভিজা, সিক্ত স্যাঁতসেঁতে ; জলাটিয়া, জলাময়, বিলা। 2. Produced in marshes ; জলাজাত, বিলজাত। **Marsh fever**—ম্যালেরিয়া। **Marsh gas**—জলাভূমির দূষিত বাষ্প। **Marsh harrier**—মাঠ চিল (যোঃ)।

măr′-shăl, *n.* 1. An officer of high rank, arranging ceremonies, regulating the rank and order and directing the order of procession etc. ; উৎসব, শোভাযাত্রা, প্রভৃতির বন্দোবস্তকারী রাজকর্ম্মচারী। 2. A general officer of the highest rank in some foreign armies ; ইংলণ্ডব্যতিরিক্ত কোন কোন দেশে প্রধান সেনানায়ক। 3. Same as FIELD-MARSHAL which see. **–ship**, *n.* **Field-marshal**—See under FIELD. **Judge's-marshal**—ভ্রমণকারী বিচারকের কেরাণী।

mâr′-shăl, *v. t.* & *i.* 1. To arrange in due order (persons at feasts etc.), soldiers, facts, etc. ; যথাস্থানে সন্নিবিষ্ট করা, সুবিন্যস্ত করা। 2. To arrange in due order as different coats of arms in one escutcheon ; বিভিন্ন বংশের কুলমর্য্যাদার প্রাবরণ চিহ্নাদি এক ঢালের উপর যথাক্রমে সুবিন্যস্ত করা। 3. To conduct as a person ceremoniously into etc. ; কোন ব্যক্তিকে যথাবিহিত শিষ্টাচারের সহিত পথপ্রদর্শন করিয়া লইয়া যাওয়া। *Verb i.* To take up one's position ; যথাযোগ্য স্থানগ্রহণ করা, যথাবিধানে স্থাপিত হওয়া।

mâr-sü′-pi-ăl, *adj.* & *n.* 1. Of, relating to, or like a pouch ; as, *marsupial* muscle ; কোষসম্বন্ধীয়, কোষবৎ। 2. (Of animals) Having a pouch to carry the young; relating to the class of such animals ; দ্বিগর্ভ, উপজঠরী; কোষপায়ি-জন্তু-সম্পর্কীয়। *Noun.* An animal having a pouch in which to carry their young born imperfect ; যে চতুষ্পদ জন্তুর দেহ নবজাত অপূর্ণাঙ্গ শাবককে বহিয়া নিবার জন্য একটী

থলি থাকে, কোষপায়ী (অভিঃ), দ্বিগর্ভকোষ জন্তু, উপজঠরী জন্তু।

mârt, *n.* **1.** (*Poet.*) A market-place; ক্রয়বিক্রয়স্থলী, বাজার, বিক্রয়-স্থান। **2.** An auction room; নীলাম গৃহ। **3.** Emporium or a trade centre; আড়ং, আড়ঙ্গ, গঞ্জ, বাণিজ্যকেন্দ্র।

mâr-tĕl'-lō, *n.* **Martello-tower**—A small circular fort with very thick walls, built on the coast to prevent hostile landing; [From Mortella, a cape in Corsica]; উপকূলরক্ষার্থ গোলাকার বুরুজ।

Marten.

mâr'-tĕn, *n.* A weasel-like animal valued for its fur; বেজী-জাতীয় জন্তু বিশেষ।

mâr'-tial (-shăl), *adj.* **1.** Relating to, suitable for, appropriate to, warfare; যুদ্ধসম্বন্ধীয়, সামরিক, সাংগ্রামিক, সমরসংক্রান্ত, যুদ্ধোপযুক্ত। **2.** Brave; warlike; সাহসী; রণবীর, রণপ্রিয়, রণাসক্ত। **3.** (*Cap.*) Of, or relating to, the planet Mars; মঙ্গলগ্রহ-সম্বন্ধীয়। **—ize,** *v. t.* To render warlike; as to *martialize* a people; রণপ্রিয় করা, সমরাসক্ত করা। **—ly,** *adv.* **Court martial**—See under COURT. **Martial law** — সামরিক আইন, সামরিকবিধি। [যুদ্ধবিগ্রহাদিকালে বিশেষঘোষণা দ্বারা প্রচলিত সামরিক আইন—এইরূপ সামরিকশাসন ঘোষণার বলে সামরিক কর্ম্মচারিগণ বিচার ও শাসন-বিভাগের ভারগ্রহণ করে এবং প্রচলিত আইনের স্থলে কঠোর সামরিকবিধি প্রতিষ্ঠিত হইয়া থাকে।] **Martial-music**—রণবাদ্য।

Mâr'-tian (-shăn), *n.* An inhabitant of Mars; মঙ্গলগ্রহ নিবাসী।

mâr'-tin, *n.* (Also *house-martin*) **1.** A species of swallow building mud-nest on house walls etc.; গৃহপ্রাচীরের উপর কর্দ্দম-নীড় নির্ম্মাণকারী বাবুইজাতীয় পক্ষিবিশেষ, তালচঞ্চু পক্ষি-বিশেষ, আবাবিল (হিন্দী)। **2.** (*Cap.*, with *St.* prefixed) The name of the bishop of Tours in the 4th century; খৃষ্টীয় চতুর্থ শতাব্দীতে টুয়র্স নগরীর ধর্ম্মাধ্যক্ষের নাম। **St. Martin's day, Martinmas**—সেণ্ট মার্টিনের স্মৃতি-উৎসব দিবস (১১ নবেম্বর)।

mâr'-ti-nĕt, *n.* A military engine for throwing large stones; বৃহৎ প্রস্তরখণ্ড বর্ষণের জন্য যন্ত্রবিশেষ।

mâr-ti-nĕt', *n.* A strict disciplinarian, especially military or naval; সৈনিক অথবা নৌবিভাগে কঠোর-নিয়মানুবর্ত্তিতার পক্ষপাতী ব্যক্তি, নিয়ম-পরায়ণ ব্যক্তি [ফরাসীরাজ চতুর্দ্দশ লুইএর সৈন্যদলের অতি কঠোর নিয়মনিষ্ঠ কর্ম্মচারী Martinetএর নাম হইতে গৃহীত]। **—ism,** *n.* **—(t)ish,** *adjs.*

mâr'-tin-gāle, *n.* **1.** A strap fastened at one end to the nose-band, at the other end to the girth of a horse to prevent him rearing; পেটী, জেরবন্দ, পেশবন্ধ। **2.** A system of gambling in which one seeks to recoup for losses by increasing the stakes; একপ্রকার জুয়াখেলা—যাহাতে কোন বাজি হারিবার দরুণ যে ক্ষতি হইয়াছে তাহা পূরণের জন্য বাজি বাড়াইয়া ধরা হয়।

mârt'-lĕt, *n.* **1.** A swift; একপ্রকার পক্ষী। **2.** (*Herald.*) A bird without beak or feet; (কুলবিদ্যা) চঞ্চু বা চরণহীন পক্ষী।

mâr'-tyr (-tĕr), *n.* & *v. t.* **1.** One who suffers death or persecution on account of his religious beliefs or for any other great cause; যে ব্যক্তি ধর্ম্মবিশ্বাস বা অন্য কোন মহদুদ্দেশ্যে নিগ্রহ ভোগ করে বা আত্মবলিদান করে, আত্মোৎসর্গকারী, ধর্ম্মার্থ ত্যক্তপ্রাণ, ধর্ম্মার্থাপিতপ্রাণ। ***Verb t.*** To put to death as a martyr; to persecute; to torment; ধর্ম্মবিশ্বাসের জন্য হত্যা করা; অত্যাচার করা; নির্যাতন করা, পীড়ন করা। **—dom,** *n.* The death and sufferings of a martyr; persecution; স্বধর্ম্ম বা স্বমত রক্ষার্থ আত্মোৎসর্গ আত্মবলিদান; অত্যাচার, নিষ্পেষণ, নির্যাতন। **A martyr to gout etc.**—A constant sufferer from gout etc.; নিরবচ্ছিন্নভাবে গ্রন্থি-বাত প্রভৃতি রোগভোগকারী। **To make a martyr of oneself** — To sacrifice or pretend to sacrifice one's inclinations, for the sake of credit thus gained; সুনাম বা প্রতিষ্ঠা লাভের জন্য নিজের রুচি বা বাসনা বর্জ্জন করা বা বর্জ্জনের ভাণ করা।

mâr'-tyr-ize (-tĕr), *v. t.* To make a martyr of (oneself, a person); ধর্ম্ম বা সত্যের জন্য জীবন উৎসর্গ করা, আত্মবলিদান করা, ধর্ম্মার্থ জীবন বিসর্জ্জন দেওয়া, আত্মোৎসর্গ করা।

mâr-tyr-ŏl'-ă-trỹ (-tĕr-), *n* Worship of martyrs; আত্মবলিদান-কারিগণের অর্চ্চনা।

mâr-tyr-ŏl'-ō-ġỹ (-tĕr-), *n.* A list, register or history of martyrs; আত্মোৎসর্গকারিগণের তালিকা বা জীবনেতিহাস।

mâr-tyr'-ỹ (-tĕr-), *n.* A shrine or church erected in honour of a martyr; ধর্ম্মার্থত্যক্তজীবিত ব্যক্তি-গণের প্রতি সম্মানপ্রদর্শনের জন্য নির্ম্মিত ধর্ম্মমন্দির।

mâr'-vĕl, *n.* & *v. i.* **1.** A thing exciting wonder; a miracle; চমৎকার জিনিষ, চমকপ্রদ বস্তু, আশ্চর্য্য জিনিষ, আজব জিনিষ; অলৌকিক ব্যাপার, অতিপ্রাকৃত ঘটনা। **2.** A wonderful example of a quality etc.; কোন গুণ প্রভৃতির আশ্চর্য্য নিদর্শন। **3.** (*Archaic*) Astonishment; (অপ্রঃ) বিস্ময়। ***Verb i.*** To be struck with surprise, (*at, that*); to wonder, (how, why, etc.): আশ্চর্য্যান্বিত হওয়া, বিস্ময়াবিষ্ট হওয়া বিস্ময়স্তম্ভিত হওয়া, অবাক হওয়া, বিস্ময়াপন্ন হওয়া; আশ্চর্য্য হওয়া। **Marvel of Peru**—কৃষ্ণকেলি (যোঃ)।

mär'-vĕl-lous (-ŭs), *adj.* **1.** Astonishing; wonderful; আশ্চর্য্যজনক, অপরূপ, আশ্চর্য্য; বিস্ময়কর, বিস্ময়জনক, বিস্ময়োৎপাদক, অদ্ভুত। **2.** Strange; incredible; অদ্ভুত, অপরূপ; অবিশ্বাস্য। **–ly,** *adv.* **–ness,** *n.* **The marvellous**—(Opp. to *the probable*); অলৌকিক ব্যাপার, অতিপ্রাকৃতব্যাপার, তাজ্জবব্যাপার।

măs'-cŏt, *n.* A person or thing that brings good luck; সৌভাগ্যজনক ব্যক্তি বা বস্তু, শকুন (মঃ উঃ)।

măs'-cü-line (-lĭn), *adj.* & *n.* **1.** Of the male sex; male; পুংজাতীয়; পুরুষজাতীয়। **2.** Manly; vigorous; robust; পুরুষোচিত, পৌরুষসম্পন্ন; বলবান, শৌর্য্যশালী; বলিষ্ঠ। **3.** (Of woman) Having qualities appropriate to man; bold; forward; পুরুষোচিতগুণসম্পন্ন; সাহসী; অগ্রসর। **4.** (*Gram.*) Denoting nouns which are names of males; পুংলিঙ্গবাচক। ***Noun.*** The masculine gender; a word of this gender; পুংলিঙ্গ; পুংলিঙ্গবাচক শব্দ। **–lin'-i-ty, –ness,** *ns.* পুরুষস্বভাব, পুরুষবৃত্তি, পুংপ্রকৃতি। **Masculine gender**—পুংলিঙ্গ।

măsh, *n.* **1.** A mixture of ground malt and warm water yielding wort; অঙ্কুরোদ্গত যবের চূর্ণ এবং উষ্ণ জলের মিশ্র। **2.** A mixture of boiled grain, bran, etc. for feeding horses, cattle, etc.; অশ্বাদির খাদ্যের জন্য জলে সিদ্ধ করা ভুষি প্রভৃতি। **3.** A soft pulp made by crushing, mixing with water etc.; মণ্ড কাই, লেই। **4.** A confused mixture; জবাখিচুড়ী। **ash tube**—অঙ্কুরোদ্গতযবচূর্ণ এবং উষ্ণজল সংমিশ্রণের জন্য চোঙ্গ বিশেষ।

măsh, *v. t.* **1.** To mix malt with hot water; উষ্ণজলের সহিত অঙ্কুরোদ্গত যবচূর্ণ সংমিশ্রিত করা। **2.** To crush; to pound; to pulp; চূর্ণ করা; কুট্টিত করা, থেঁতলান; লেই করা, মণ্ড করা। **3.** To reduce as potatoes etc. to uniform mass by crushing; (আলু প্রভৃতি নিষ্পেষণ করিয়া) তাল বা পিণ্ডবৎ করা।

măsh, *v. t.* & *n.* (*Slang*) To gain the affections of; to fascinate; (ইতর ভাষায়) স্নেহ ও প্রীতিলাভ করা; বিমুগ্ধ করা। ***Noun.*** A person on whom one of the opposite sex is mashed; প্রেমোন্মত্ত পুরুষ, প্রেমোন্মাদিনী নারী। **To be mashed on** — To have sentimental admiration for; to be struck with love for another; আবেগবিমিশ্র শ্রদ্ধা, প্রেম ও বিস্ময়পূর্ণ হওয়া; প্রেমোন্মত্ত হওয়া। **To make one's mash**—To get a devoted admirer; একনিষ্ঠ স্তাবক প্রাপ্ত হওয়া।

măsh'-er, *n.* A fop posing as a lady-killer; রমণীবিঘাতক নাগর, রমণীমনোহর পুরুষ, নারীচিত্তচোর।

măsh'-ie (-ĭ), **măsh'-ÿ,** *ns.* An iron golf-club; গোল্‌ফ ক্রীড়ার জন্য লৌহময় দণ্ড।

măsk, *n.* **1.** A covering for the face for disguise or for protection; as, a dancer's or fencer's *mask*; a masked person; মুখস, ছদ্মমুখ (আঃ বঃ), কৃত্রিমমুখ, ছদ্মাস্য; মুখসপরা লোক। **2.** (*Fig.*) A disguise; a pretence; as to throw off the *mask*; (লক্ষণায়) ছদ্মবেশ; ছল, কূট, ছদ্ম। **3.** A hollow figure of human head worn by the Greek and Roman actors; প্রাচীন গ্রীক এবং রোমান নাট্যকারগণ কর্ত্তৃক ব্যবহৃত মুখস। **4.** A representation or impression of a person's face in any material, as wax, clay, plaster, etc.; মোম, এঁটেল মাটী প্রভৃতি দ্বারা রচিত মনুষ্যমুখ বা মুখের ছাপ। **5.** A festive entertainment in which all wear masks; যে উৎসবে সকলে মুখস পরিধান করে। **6.** A face or head of a fox; শৃগালমুণ্ড, শিবামুণ্ড।

măsk, *v. t.* **1.** To cover as a face with a mask; মুখস পরা, কৃত্রিম মুখস দ্বারা মুখ আচ্ছাদিত করা, মুখসাবৃত করা। **2.** (*Pass.*) To be disguised with mask; মুখস ধারণে আত্মগোপন করা। **3.** (*Mil.*) To conceal as a force, battery, etc. from enemy's sight; to keep in check, as an army etc. by watching it with a sufficient force; (সামরিক শাস্ত্র) সৈন্য, কামানশ্রেণী প্রভৃতি প্রচ্ছন্ন রাখা; প্রচুর সৈন্যদ্বারা পর্য্যবেক্ষণপূর্ব্বক (শত্রুসৈন্য) বাধা দিয়া রাখা। **4.** To disguise as feelings etc.; আত্মগোপন করা। **A masked ball**—যে বল নাচে নর্ত্তক নর্ত্তকীগণ মুখস পরিয়া থাকে।

mā'-son (-sn), *n.* & *v. t.* **1.** A builder in stone or brick; a worker in stone; রাজমিস্ত্রী, রাজশিল্পী, লেপকার, সুধাজীবী; স্থপতি। **2.** (*Cap.*) A member of the society of Freemasons; ইয়ুরোপীয় তান্ত্রিক গুপ্তসভা বিশেষের সভ্য। ***Verb t.*** To build or strengthen with masonry; ইষ্টক প্রভৃতির গাঁথনি দ্বারা নির্ম্মাণ বা সুদৃঢ় করা। **–ry,** *n.* **1.** The art and occupation of a mason (*rare*); স্থাপত্যকর্ম্ম (কচিদ্‌ব্যবহৃত)। **2.** The work of a mason; stonework; রাজমিস্ত্রীর কাজ; ইমারতী কাজ। **3.** The institution or mysteries of freemasons; ফ্রিমেসন সম্প্রদায়ের প্রতিষ্ঠান বা গুহ্যতত্ত্ব। **–son'-ic,** *adj.* Relating to freemasons or freemasonry; ফ্রিমেসনসম্প্রদায়সম্পর্কীয়, উক্ত সম্প্রদায়ের ক্রিয়াকলাপ সম্পর্কীয়।

Mă-sö'-ră, Măs-sö'-rah (-ră), *ns.* The Hebrew tradition as to the correct form of the text of the scriptures; খৃষ্টীয় বাইবেলের বিশুদ্ধ পাঠ সম্বন্ধে হিব্রু পরম্পরাগত বাক্য।

Măs'-s(ö)-rīte, –rete (-rēt), *ns.* A Jewish scholar contributing to the Massora; বাইবেলের বিশুদ্ধ পাঠ নির্দ্ধারক ইহুদী পণ্ডিত। **–ret'-ic,** *adj.*

masque (măsk), *n.* **1.** An amateur histrionic entertainment ; a masquerade ; একপ্রকার সখের নাটক ; মুখসধারী নর্ত্তকনর্ত্তকীগণের মজলিস। **2.** A drama acted at a masquerade ; মুখসধারী নর্ত্তকনর্ত্তকীগণ কর্ত্তৃক অভিনীত নাট্য।

măs-quer-āde′ (-kĕr-), *n. & v. i.* **1.** An assembly of persons wearing masks and amusing themselves with dancing ; মুখসধারী নর্ত্তক নর্ত্তকীগণের মজলিস। **2.** A false show ; a pretence ; ভাণ, ছদ্ম ; ছল। ***Verb i.*** **1.** To appear or go about in disguise ; ছদ্মবেশে উপস্থিত হওয়া, ছদ্মবেশে পর্য্যটন করা। **2.** To assume deceptive appearance ; ছদ্মবেশ ধারণ করা। **3.** To take part in a masquerade ; মুখসধারিগণের নাচের মজলিসে যোগদান করা।

măss, *n.* **1.** A celebration of the Eucharist ; রোমান ক্যাথলিক খৃষ্টান দিগের পর্ব্ববিশেষ—যাহাতে যীশুখৃষ্টের শেষ ভোজনের স্মৃতিস্বরূপ রুটী ও সুরা শোধিত করা হয়। **2.** The liturgy of the Eucharist ; a musical setting of certain parts of the liturgy ; শেষভোজনক্রিয়ার রুটী ও সুরা শোধন-সংস্পৃষ্ট পূজোপাসনাদি ; শেষভোজনক্রিয়া-সংস্পৃষ্ট স্তোত্রাদির সুর বাঁধন। **High mass**—See HIGH. **Low mass**—See LOW.

măss, *n., v. t. & i.* **1.** A body of matter of indefinite shape ; as, a *mass* of ore, metal, sand, etc. ; রাশি। **2.** A dense aggregation of objects ; as, a *mass* of fibres ; সংগ্রহ, সমবায়, পদার্থসমূহ (হিঃ কোঃ), নিবহ। **3.** A large quantity or number, (with *of*) ; কাঁড়ি, স্তূপ, পুঞ্জ। **4.** Bulk ; magnitude ; আকার, মাত্রা ; আয়তন। **5.** The main body ; the majority ; প্রধান ভাগ ; অধিকাংশ। **6.** (*Phys.*) The quantity of matter contained in a body ; (প্রাকৃতিক বিজ্ঞান) কোন বস্তুর পরিমাণ, জিনিষ (রাঃ সুঃ ত্রিঃ), সামগ্রী (সাঃ পঃ), বস্তুমান, জড়মান (সাঃ পঃ), বস্তুপরিমাণ, মাত্রা (হিঃ কোঃ), দ্রব্যমান (ঐ), পিণ্ডমাত্রা (ঐ)। **7.** Uninterrupted expanse, as of light etc. ; অবাধ-বিস্তার। ***Verb t.*** **1.** To form into a mass ; to bring together in masses : রাশীকৃত করা, পিণ্ডীভূত করা, পুঞ্জীভূত করা ; তাল পাকান। **2.** To concentrate as troops ; সমবেত করা। ***Verb i.*** To assemble in a mass ; জড় হওয়া। **Mass-meeting**—মহতী সভা (বিশেষতঃ রাজনীতিক আন্দোলনের জন্য)। **He is a mass of bruises**—তাহার সর্ব্বাঙ্গে কালশিরা পড়িয়াছে, তাহার সকল শরীরে চোট লাগিয়াছে। **In the mass**—In the aggregate ; সাকল্যে। **The masses**—The lower orders or the populace ; ভদ্রেতর জনগণ, জনসাধারণ, সাধারণ লোক, নিম্নশ্রেণী।

măs′-să-cre (-kêr), *n. & v. t.* A general slaughter ; a carnage ; হত্যাকাণ্ড ; বহুলোক হত্যা। ***Verb t.*** To slaughter ; to murder cruelly or violently ; বহু নরনারী নিধন করা ; নৃশংসভাবে হত্যা করা।

măs′-sage (-âz), *n. & v. t.* The process of kneading, rubbing, slapping, etc. of muscles and joints of a person's body to effect a cure ; অঙ্গসম্বাহন দ্বারা পীড়াদির (বৈজ্ঞানিক প্রণালীতে) চিকিৎসা। ***Verb t.*** To treat a part or person thus ; অঙ্গসংবাহন দ্বারা চিকিৎসা করা।

Masse, *n.* (*Billiards*) A stroke made with the cue held vertically ; (বিলিয়ার্ড ক্রীড়ায়) ক্রীড়াযষ্টি খাড়াভাবে ধরিয়া যে আঘাত করা হয়।

măs-seur′ (-ĕr), *n.* **1.** One who practises massage ; মর্দ্দনাদি দ্বারা চিকিৎসাকারী। **Mass′-er, –or,** *ns.* Same as MASSEUR.

măss′-ĭ-nĕss, *n.* The state or quality of being massy ; স্থূলতা, বৃহত্ব, স্থৌল্য।

măss′-ive (-ĭv), *adj.* **1.** Large and heavy ; solid and bulky ; স্থূলাকার, পিণ্ডাকার ; বৃহৎ এবং গুরুভার। **2.** (Of features, forehead, etc.) Large and bold ; স্থূল এবং সুপ্রকট। **3.** (*Fig.*) Substantial ; (লক্ষণায়) সারবান। **4.** (*Psychol.*) Having large volume or magnitude, as a sensation etc. বৃহদায়তন, প্রবল। **–ly,** *adv.* **–ness,** *n.* State of being massive : স্থূলত্ব, মহত্ব (ব্রজঃ হিন্দুঃ), স্থৌল্য।

măss′-ȳ, *adj.* Massive ; weighty ; solid ; স্থূল, বৃহৎ ; গুরুভার, পৃথুল ; নিরেট।

măst, *n. & v. t.* A long pole of timber, iron, etc. standing upright in a vessel and supporting the sails etc. ; গুণবৃক্ষ, মাস্তুল। ***Verb t.*** **1.** To punish as a sailor by sending him to the mast-head for a certain time : কোন নাবিককে কিছুকালের জন্য মাস্তুলাগ্রে উঠাইয়া শাস্তি দেওয়া। **2.** To raise (sail) to its position ; পাইল তোলা। **Mast′-ed,** *adj.* **Mast-head**—মাস্তুলাগ্র। **Mast-wood**—পুন্নাগ (যোঃ)। **To sail or serve before the mast**—To be an ordinary sailor ; সাধারণ নাবিক হওয়া। **Two years before the mast**—সাধারণ নাবিকরূপে দুই বৎসর।

măst, *n.* The fruit of the beech, oak, etc. esp. as food for swine ; শূকরাদির আহারের জন্য ওক, বীচ প্রভৃতি বৃক্ষের ফল।

măs′-tĕr, *n.* **1.** A person who controls or directs ; প্রভু, কর্ত্তা, স্বামী, অধিকারী, পতি, অধ্যক্ষ। **2.** An employer ; মনীব। **3.** The owner of a slave, dog, horse, etc. ; ক্রীতদাসের অধিকারী, দাস-স্বামী, অশ্ব-কুকুরাদির মালিক। **4.** The male head of a household ; বাড়ীর কর্ত্তা, গৃহস্বামী, গৃহপতি। **5.** One who has, or gets, the upper-hand ; as, we will see which of us is *master* ; প্রভু, কর্ত্তা।

6. A teacher in a school, (also *school-master*) ; বিদ্যালয়ের শিক্ষক। 7. A teacher in philosophy etc. ; দর্শনশাস্ত্রাদির অধ্যাপক। 8. (*Naut.*) The captain of a merchant-ship ; (নৌবিদ্যা) বাণিজ্যপোতাধ্যক্ষ। 9. A man eminently skilled in some occupation or art ; as, a *master* carpenter ; a great artist or a picture etc. by him ; কোন শিল্প বা ব্যবসায়বিশেষে নিপুণ ব্যক্তি ; শ্রেষ্ঠ চিত্রশিল্পী বা তৎকর্তৃক অঙ্কিত চিত্রাদি। 10. A word of address used before the name of boys ; কুমার। 11. The title of the head of some societies or institutions ; as, "The *Master* of the Templars" ; কোন সম্প্রদায় বা প্রতিষ্ঠানের অধ্যক্ষের উপাধি। 12. (*Attrib.*) Commanding ; superior ; as, a *master* mind ; প্রভুত্বকারী ; শ্রেষ্ঠ। **–dom, –hood,** *ns.* **–ful,** *adj.* Self-willed ; imperious ; স্বেচ্ছাচারী ; উদ্ধত, প্রভুত্বপরায়ণ। **–ful-ly,** *adv.* **–ful-ness,** *n.* **–less,** *adj.* **Master-at-arms** — সামরিক রণপোতে নিযুক্ত পুলিস কর্ম্মচারী। **Master builder**—প্রধান স্থপতি। **Master-hand**—সিদ্ধহস্ত ব্যক্তি। **Master-key** — যে চাবির সাহায্যে অনেক গুলি বিভিন্ন প্রকারের তালা খোলা যায়। **Master-mason**—A freemason who has passed the third degree ; ফ্রিমেসন সম্প্রদায়ের উচ্চশ্রেণীর সভ্য-বিশেষ। A superior or chief mason ; প্রধান মিস্ত্রী। **Master-mind**—যে ব্যক্তি বহুলোকের উপর প্রভাব বিস্তার করিতে পারে। **Master-piece**—সর্ব্বশ্রেষ্ঠ গ্রন্থ ; অত্যুৎকৃষ্ট শিল্পকার্য্য। **Master poet**—মহাকবি (গীতাঞ্জঃ)। **Master-stroke**—বাহাদুরির কাজ, অসাধারণ নৈপুণ্যের কর্ম্ম। **A passed master**—কোন বিশেষ বিষয়ে অভিজ্ঞ ব্যক্তি, বিশেষজ্ঞ। **Master of Arts**—(*Abbr.* M. A.) ; বিশ্ববিদ্যালয়ের এম্.এ উপাধিধারী। **Master of the Horse**—ইংলণ্ডেশ্বরের গার্হস্থ্যবিভাগের কর্ম্মচারিবিশেষ ; অশ্বাধ্যক্ষ। **The Master**—Christ ; যীশুখৃষ্ট (cf. our মহাপ্রভু)। **To be master of**—To have at one's disposal ; নিজের কর্তৃত্বাধীন থাকা। **To be master of one's self**—To have the control of one's passion ; স্বপ্রভু হওয়া, ইন্দ্রিয়জয়ী হওয়া, ইন্দ্রিয়াদি স্ববশে থাকা। **To be one's own master**—To be at liberty to act as one chooses ; স্বাধীনভাবে কাজ করিতে পারা। **To make oneself master of**—To acquire thorough knowledge of, or facility in, using ; বিশেষ নৈপুণ্য লাভ করা। **To serve two masters** — দুই প্রভুর সেবা করা (যাহাতে কাহাকেও সন্তুষ্ট করা যায় না)।

măs'-têr, *v. t.* 1. To overcome ; to defeat ; to bring into subjection ; to subdue ; পরাজয় করা ; পরাস্ত করা ; পরাভূত করা ; বশীভূত করা। 2. To acquire complete knowledge of (a subject) or facility in using (an instrument etc.) ; কোন বিষয়ে সম্পূর্ণ পারদর্শী হওয়া, সিদ্ধহস্ত হওয়া, সুনিপুণ হওয়া। 3. To rule or regulate as a master ; কর্তৃত্ব করা, প্রভুত্ব করা।

măs'-têr-lȳ, *adj.* Worthy of a master ; very skilful ; শ্রেষ্ঠশিল্পীসমুচিত, অতি সুনিপুণ, সুদক্ষ। **–li-ness,** *n.* **Masterly inactivity**—Prudent inactivity ; সদ্বিবেচনাপ্রসূত নিশ্চেষ্টতা।

măs'-têr-ship, *n.* 1. Dominion ; superiority ; প্রভুত্ব, আধিপত্য, কর্তৃত্ব, স্বামিত্ব ; শ্রেষ্ঠত্ব। 2. The office, function, etc. of a master, esp. in a school ; শিক্ষকতা।

măs'-têr-ȳ, *n.* 1. Sway ; dominion ; প্রভুত্ব ; শাসন। 2. Superiority ; upperhand, (with *the* prefixed) ; as, he gained the *mastery* in the end ; প্রাধান্য, শ্রেষ্ঠত্ব ; আধিপত্য। 3. Masterly skill ; দক্ষতা, সিদ্ধহস্ততা, সুনিপুণতা। 4. Masterly use or knowledge (*of* an instrument and subject) ; অতি পাণ্ডিত্য, অতি নৈপুণ্য, বৈশারদ্য।

măs'-tic *n.* 1. A gum or resin exuding from the bark of certain trees, and used for varnish ; বার্ণিসাদির কার্য্যে ব্যবহৃত বৃক্ষনির্যাসবিশেষ, রুমিমস্তকি। 2. The tree yielding this resinous substance ; রুমিমস্তকীর গাছ। 3. Any of various pasty cements ; আটালো বিলাতী মাটী। 4. A liquor flavoured with mastic used in Turkey and Greece ; রুমিমস্তকির দ্বারা সুবাসিত সুরা বিশেষ—যাহা তুরস্ক ও গ্রীসদেশে ব্যবহৃত হয়। 4. A yellowish colour ; আপীতবর্ণবিশেষ। **–tic'-ic,** *adj.*

măs'-ti-cāte, *v. t.* To grind with the teeth ; to chew, as food ; দন্তদ্বারা চর্ব্বণ করা ; চিবান। **–ca-ble,** *adj.* **–ca'-tion,** *n.* The act of masticating ; চর্ব্বণ, চর্ব্বণক্রিয়া, চর্ব্বণব্যাপার। **–ca-tor,** *n.* 1. One that masticates ; a machine for cutting meat into fine pieces for toothless people ; চর্ব্বণকারী ; দন্তহীন ব্যক্তিদিগের জন্য মাংস কুচি কুচি করিয়া কাটিবার যন্ত্রবিশেষ। 2. A machine for cutting leather, India rubber, etc. into fine pieces ; চামড়া, রবার প্রভৃতি অতি সরু সরু করিয়া কাটিবার জন্য যন্ত্রবিশেষ। **–ca-to-ry,** *adj.*

măs'-tiff, *n.* A large strong dog with drooping ears and pendulous lips ; ডালকুত্তা।

măs-tī'-tis, *n.* An inflammation of the female breast ; স্ত্রীলোকের স্তনের প্রদাহ, কুচপ্রদাহ।

măs'-tō-dŏn, *n.* A large extinct mammal like elephant ; অধুনালুপ্ত বৃহৎ মাতঙ্গবৎ জন্তু বিশেষ। [এই জন্তুর চর্ব্বন-দন্ত কুচাগ্রাকৃতি উদ্গত অংশবিশিষ্ট বলিয়া এই নাম।] অতিকায় মাতঙ্গ, ঐরাবত (অভিঃ), কুচদন্তী। **–don'-tic,** *adj.*

Măs'-tō-dȳ-ni-ă, –dȳ-nȳ, *ns.* Neuralgia of the female breast ; স্ত্রীলোকের স্তনপ্রদাহ, কুচপ্রদাহ।

măs'-toid (-toyd), *adj.* & *n.* (*Anat.*) Shaped like the female breast ;

(শারীরসংস্থান-বিদ্যা) স্তনাকৃতি, কুচাকৃতি। ***Noun.*** The mastoid process or bone ; স্তনবৃন্তের আকারে অস্থিপ্রভৃতির প্রবর্দ্ধন।

măs′-tur-bāte (-têr-), *v. i.* To practise self-abuse or self-pollution ; হস্তমৈথুন করা, খেঁচা (*colloq.*)। **—ba′-tion,** *n.* Onanism ; হস্তমৈথুন, আত্মদূষণ।

măt, *n.* **1.** A fabric of interwoven rushes, straw, twine, etc. for lying upon, packing furniture, etc. ; মাদুর, দরমা, চাটাই, চাটা, পাটি। **2.** A piece of such fabric used for cleaning shoes at the door ; পাপোষ। **3.** Anything growing thickly or closely interwoven ; as, a *mat* of weeds : a *mat* of hair ; জট, জটা।

măt, *v. t.* & *i.* **1.** To cover or furnish with mats ; চাটাই বা মাদুর দ্বারা আচ্ছাদিত বা সজ্জিত করা। **2.** To interweave into, or like, a mat ; to entangle ; as, *matted* hair ; চাটাই বা মাদুরের মত বোনা, চাটাই বা মাদুর বোনা ; জড়ান, জট পাকান। ***Verb i.*** To become interwoven or matted ; বিজড়িত হওয়া, জড়াইয়া যাওয়া, জট পাকাইয়া যাওয়া।

măt, *adj., n.* & *v. t.* **1.** (Of colours, surfaces, etc.) Dull ; lustreless ; চাক্‌চিক্যশূন্য, অনুজ্জ্বল ; নিষ্প্রভ, মন্দপ্রভ, মন্দদ্যুতি। ***Noun.*** **1.** An ornamental border of dead gold round a framed picture ; বাঁধানো চিত্রের চতুঃপার্শ্বস্থ অনুজ্জ্বল স্বর্ণ-রচিত কারুকার্য্যখচিত প্রান্তবেষ্টনী। **2.** A dull finish or appearance of unburnished gold ; অপরিকর্ম্মীকৃত স্বর্ণের মন্দাভা। **3.** A roughened groundwork ; বন্ধুরীকৃত তলদেশ। ***Verb t.*** **1.** To render mat or dull as gilding ; অনুজ্জ্বলভাবে গিল্টি করা। **2.** To frost, as glass ; (কাচ প্রভৃতির) উপরিভাগ তুষারবৎ করা। **Matted hair**—জটা।

măt′-ă-dōre, —dōr, *ns.* **1.** The man appointed to kill the bull in bull-fights ; বৃষযুদ্ধে যে ব্যক্তি বৃষবধ করিবার জন্য নিযুক্ত হয় [এই ব্যক্তি সুবেশে সজ্জিত হইয়া রঙ্গক্ষেত্রে অবতীর্ণ হয় এবং উহার দক্ষিণ হস্তে উলঙ্গ অসি এবং বাম হস্তে লোহিতবর্ণ পট্টখণ্ডসমন্বিত দণ্ড ধৃত থাকে। বৃষভ মল্লগণ-কর্ত্তৃক উপদ্রুত হইয়া উন্মত্তবৎ ধাবিত হইলে এই ব্যক্তি গম্ভীরভাবে অগ্রসর হইয়া উহার বামস্কন্ধাস্থির নিকটে তরবারি বসাইয়া দেয়।] **2.** One of the three principal cards at ombre and quadrille ; কোন কোন তাস খেলার অন্যতম প্রধান তাস। [ইস্কাপন ও চিড়িতনের টেক্কা ও গোলাম এবং রুহিতন ও হরতনের সাতা—এই সকল তাসকে খুনী তাস (murdering cards) বলে। কারণ উহারা আর সকল তাসকে জয় করিয়া লয়।]

Matadore.

match (măch), *n.* **1.** Anything easily kindled and used for lighting ; দিয়াশলাই, দীপশলাকা। **2.** A piece of wick, cord, etc. designed to burn at a uniform rate for firing cannon etc. ; কামান প্রভৃতিতে অগ্নিসংযোগের জন্য নিয়ত একরূপ বেগে প্রজ্বলনের জন্য নির্দ্দিষ্ট রজ্জু বা পলিতা। **Match-box** — দিয়াশলাইয়ের বাক্স। **Match-lock** — বন্দুকের বারুদ জ্বালাইবার জন্য দীপশলাকাসংযুক্ত কল ; ঐরূপ কলসংযুক্ত বন্দুক। **Match-wood** — A wood suitable for matches ; দিয়াশলাই প্রস্তুতের উপযোগী কাঠ। Minute splinters ; অতিশয় সরু চেলা, কাঠের কুচি।

match (măch), *n., v. t.* & *i.* **1.** A person able to cope with another ; an equal ; প্রতিদ্বন্দ্বী ; তুল্যবল ব্যক্তি, তুল্য প্রতিযোগী। **2.** A person equal to another in some quality ; as, we shall never see his *match* ; সমতুল্য ব্যক্তি, সমকক্ষ লোক, দোসর। **3.** A person or thing exactly like, or corresponding to, another ; অনুরূপ ব্যক্তি। **4.** A union of parties for contest of skill etc. ; as, a cricket *match* ; ক্রীকেট প্রভৃতি ক্রীড়ায় প্রতিযোগিতার জন্য বিভিন্ন দলের সম্মিলন, ম্যাচ। **5.** A matrimonial alliance ; বৈবাহিক সম্বন্ধ। **6.** One suitable to be gained in marriage (esp. as to rank or fortune) ; as, he is an excellent *match* ; অনুরূপ পাত্র বা কন্যা, যোগ্যবর, যোগ্যা কন্যা। ***Verb t.*** **1.** To prove a match or mate for ; to be able to compete with ; সমকক্ষ প্রমাণিত হওয়া ; প্রতিযোগিতা করিতে সমর্থ হওয়া। **2.** To place (a person or thing) in competetion *with* ; as, no history or antiquity can *match* his policies or his conduct ; তুল্যপ্রতিযোগিরূপে খাড়া করা, প্রতিযোগী করা। **3.** To set *against* as an equal ; to place in conflict *against* ; প্রতিদ্বন্দ্বী করা ; বিরুদ্ধে দণ্ডায়মান করা। **4.** To join (a person with another) in marriage ; বিবাহবন্ধনে বদ্ধ করা। **5.** To suit ; to correspond in quantity, quality, colour, etc., to ; as, the carpets *match* the wall-paper ; মানানসই করা, সংখ্যা, গুণ বা বর্ণে সামঞ্জস্য হওয়া, উপযোগী করা, অনুরূপ করা। **6.** To find material etc. that matches with another ; as, can you *match* me this silk ; কোন জিনিষের সহিত মানায় বা মানানসই হয় এরূপ জিনিষ যোগান। ***Verb i.*** **1.** To be of equal size, figure, colour, quality, etc. ; to correspond (*with*) ; তুল্যাকৃতি হওয়া, তুল্যবর্ণ হওয়া, তুল্যগুণ-সম্পন্ন হওয়া ; অনুরূপ হওয়া, উপযোগী হওয়া ; তুল্য হওয়া, উপযুক্ত হওয়া। **2.** To be united in marriage ; বিবাহ বন্ধনে বদ্ধ হওয়া, পরিণয়সূত্রে আবদ্ধ হওয়া। **Match′-less,** *adj.* Without an equal ; unequalled unrivalled ; সমকক্ষহীন ; অতুল, অনুপম, নিরুপম ; অদ্বিতীয়, অপ্রতিম । **Match'-less-ly,** *adv.* **Match-board**—যে ফলকের এক প্রান্তে খাঁজ এবং অপর প্রান্তে জিভি কাটা থাকে—যাহাতে ইহা সমরূপ ফলকে জোড়া লাগাইতে পারা যায়। **Match-joint**—জিভি-জোড়া । **Match-maker** — One who plans to bring about marriage, ঘটক। **Match-making**—ঘটকালি । **To be a match for**—To be able to cope with ; সমকক্ষ হওয়া, আঁটিয়া উঠিতে পারা । **To make a match**—To bring about matrimonial alliance ; বিবাহ সংঘটন করা ।

match'-et (măch-), *n.* A broad knife used in America ; আমেরিকায় ব্যবহৃত প্রশস্ত ছুরিকা ।

mate, *n.* **1.** A companion ; a comrade ; a fellow-worker ; সঙ্গী ; সহচর, সহকারী, সহবর্ত্তী, সাথী ; সহযোগী, সহকর্ম্মী । **2.** One of a wedded pair ; one of a pair, esp. of birds ; দম্পতীর একজন ; জীবনসঙ্গী, জীবনসঙ্গিনী ; জোড়ার একটী । **3.** A suitable partner in marriage ; যোগ্যবর বা যোগ্যা কন্যা । **4.** (*Naut.*) An officer in a merchant-vessel assisting the captain and commanding in his absence ; (নৌবিদ্যা) পোতাধ্যক্ষের অব্যবহিত নিম্নপদস্থ কর্ম্মচারী, জাহাজের মালিম । **5.** An assistant ; সহকারী । **6.** A match ; an equal ; সমকক্ষ ব্যক্তি ; সমতুল ব্যক্তি । **Mate'-less,** *adj.* Without or destitute of mate ; সঙ্গিহীন, সাথিহীন, জোড়ভাঙ্গা ।

māte, *v. t. & i.* **1.** To join in marriage ; to marry ; বিবাহ বন্ধনে বদ্ধ করা ; বিবাহ দেওয়া । **2.** To pair (birds) ; জোড়া বাঁধান । **3.** To treat as comparable (*with*) ; as, to *mate* one's words with deeds ; সমকক্ষ বলিয়া গণ্য করা, তুলনীয় বলিয়া গণ্য করা । ***Verb i.*** **1.** To marry ; (of birds etc.) to pair ; বিবাহ করা ; জোট বাঁধান । **2.** To keep company (*with*) ; সমভিব্যাহারী হওয়া, সঙ্গে থাকা ।

măte, *n. & v. t.* Check-mate in chess ; দাবাখেলায় কিস্তিমাৎ। ***Verb t.*** To check-mate ; কিস্তিমাৎ করা । **Stale mate**—See under STALE.

mäte, *n.* The Paraguay tea ; a shrub whose leaves are used extensively in South America as a substitute for tea ; একপ্রকার চা ; একপ্রকার গুল্ম—যাহার পাতা দক্ষিণ-আমেরিকায় চাএর পরিবর্ত্তে ব্যবহৃত হয় ।

matelote (*F.*), *n.* A dish of fish etc. with sauce of wine, onions, etc. ; মদ্য, পেঁয়াজের রস, প্রভৃতি মিশ্রিত মৎস্যাদির ব্যঞ্জন ।

mā'-tėr, *n.* **1.** (*School-slang*) A mother ; মা । **2.** The name of the two membranes that cover the brain—the dura-mater and pia-mater ; মস্তিষ্ক আবরক ঝিল্লীদ্বয় ; দৃঢ়মাতৃকা (হঃ চঃ) । ***Mater familias***—(*L.*) গৃহমাতা ।

mă-tē'-ri-ăl, *adj. & n.* **1.** Of, or pertaining to, matter ; corporeal ; as, *material* substance ; ভৌতিক, স্থূলময়, বস্তুগত ; কায়িক, শরীরী, মূর্ত্ত (ব্রজঃ হিন্দু), জড়, স্থূল (ঐ), পঞ্চভূতাত্মক । **2.** Relating to the bodily comforts, wants, interests, etc. ; as, the *material* well-being of a person ; শারীরিক, দৈহিক, দেহগত, বৈষয়িক । **3.** (Of conduct, point of view etc.) Unspiritual ; লৌকিক, অনাত্ম । **4.** Important ; essential (to) ; as, such as are most *material* to our present purpose ; অত্যাবশ্যক, অতি প্রয়োজনীয় ; অনিবার্য্য । **5.** (*Philos.*) Relating to the matter and not the form of reasoning ; যুক্তির মূল-বিষয়সম্বন্ধীয় । ***Noun.*** The substance or matter from which anything is made ; as, a raw *material* ; উপাদান, উপকরণ, মাল-মসল্লা, সাধন । **2.** The elements as of a substance ; মৌলিক পদার্থ, রূঢ় পদার্থ । **3.** Data of any sort ; as, *materials* for a biography ; উপকরণ, সামগ্রী । **4.** Stuff ; জিনিষ । **—al'-i-ty,** *n.* The quality of being material ; মূর্ত্তভাব, স্থৌল্য (বেদান্তঃ), ভৌতিকত্ব, পাঞ্চভৌতিকত্ব । **—ly,** *adv.* Not spiritually ; essentially ; অনাত্মভাবে ; বস্তুতঃ, সারতঃ, যথার্থতঃ, প্রধানতঃ, আসলে, বস্তুগত, মূলতঃ । **Material body** — অন্নময় কোষ, স্থূলশরীর । **Material cause** — সমবায়িকারণ (হিঃ কোঃ), উপাদান কারণ । **Material form** — চর্ম্মচক্ষু-দৃশ্য জড়মূর্ত্তি । **Material objects**—ভৌতিক পদার্থ (হিঃ কোঃ) । **Material prosperity**—সমৃদ্ধি । **Material world**—জড়জগৎ, স্থূলপ্রপঞ্চ, স্থূল জগৎ । **Raw material**—Unmanufactured material ; কাঁচা মাল । **Material theory of heat**—উত্তাপ জড়বস্তু বই আর কিছু নহে—এই মতবাদ ।

mă-tē'-ri-ăl-ism, *n.* **1.** The doctrine that nothing exists but matter and that consciousness and will are solely due to material agency ; জড়বস্তু ভিন্ন অন্য কিছুর সত্তা নাই,—মন, ইচ্ছা প্রভৃতিও জড়বস্তুর ক্রিয়াসঞ্জাত—এইরূপ দার্শনিক-মতবাদ, জড়বাদ, দেহাত্মবাদ, লোকায়তবাদ, বিষয়বাদ (আঃ বঃ), অনাত্মবাদ, চার্ব্বাক মত। **2.** (*Art.*) The tendency to give importance to material aspect of objects ; (কলাশাস্ত্র) বস্তুর জড়ীয় ভাবের উপর গুরুত্ব প্রদানের আসক্তি ।

mă-tē'-ri-ă-list, *n.* One who asserts that all existence is material ; জড়বাদী, দেহাত্মবাদী, চার্ব্বাকমতাবলম্বী, লোকায়তিক (বেদান্তঃ) । **—is'-tic, —is'-ti-cal,** *adjs.* **—is'-ti-cal-ly,** *adv.*

mă-tē'-ri-ăl-ize. *v. t. & i.* **1.** To render material ; to represent as material ; জড়ধর্ম্মান্বিত করা, শরীরধর্ম্মী করা ; জড়বস্তুরূপে বর্ণনা করা ; **2.** To cause, as spirits to appear in a bodily form ; প্রেতাত্মাকে স্থূল-শরীরে আবির্ভূত করা । **3.** To make iterialistic ; বিষয়াসক্ত করা, বিষয়ী রা। *Verb i.* 1. (Of spirits) o appear in bodily form ; become an actual fact ; (প্রেতাত্মা সম্বন্ধে) স্থূল শরীরে আবির্ভূত হয়া, জড়ীয় মূর্ত্তি পরিগ্রহ করা ; স্তব ঘটনায় পরিণত হওয়া। **—i-za′-on,** *n.* The act of materia-zing ; প্রেতাত্মাসম্বন্ধে মৃন্ময়তনুধারণ, জড়দেহধারণ।

ateria medica, (*L.*), *n.* **1.** The urative substances used in the actice of medicine ; ভৈষজ্য ব্যজাত, ভেষজদ্রব্য। **2.** That branch the medical science which eats of the nature and pro-erties of all the substances nployed in medicine ; ঔষধ ব্যের গুণজ্ঞাপক শাস্ত্র, ভৈষজ্যবিজ্ঞান, ষজ্যসংগ্রহ, ভৈষজ্যশাস্ত্র।

-teriel, (*F.*), *n.* The materials instruments employed in nction from the personnel men, as, the baggage, pro-ons, etc. of an army etc. ; ilable means ; দ্রব্যসম্ভার, সাজ-রঞ্জাম, যন্ত্রপাতি ; প্রযোজ্য উপায়।

-tĕr′-năl, *adj.* **1.** Of, or per-ing to, a mother ; মাতৃসম্বন্ধীয়, সংক্রান্ত, মাতৃ। **2.** Motherly ; oming a mother ; মাতৃবৎ ; তৃসমুচিত। **3.** Related on the other's side ; as, *maternal* cle ; মাতৃসম্পর্কীয়। **—ly,** *adv.* **-ty,** *n.* **1.** State of being a her ; motherhood ; motherli-ss ; মাতৃভাব ; মাতৃধর্ম্ম ; মাতৃত্ব। Same as MATERNITY HOSPITAL.

aternity hospital—যে আরোগ্যা-লয় গর্ভিণীদিগকে প্রসবের জন্য হয়, মাতৃনিকেতন।

-ĕ-măt′-ics, *n.* **1.** (*Pl.*, usu. **ted** as *sing.*) **1.** An abstract **nce** of space and number ; শাস্ত্র, গণিত, গণিতবিজ্ঞান, গণিত-শাস্ত্র, গণিতশাস্ত্র, সংখ্যাপরিমাণবিদ্যা। Same as MIXED OF APPLIED MATHEMATICS. **—i-cal,** *adj.* **1.** Of, or relating to, mathematics ; গণিতবিষয়ক, গণিতসম্বন্ধীয়, গণিতিক (হিঃ কোঃ), সংখ্যাপরিমাণবিদ্যাসম্বন্ধীয়। **2.** (Of proofs etc.) Rigorously precise ; অতিশয় সঠিক। **—i-cal-ly,** *adv.* **—ma-ti′-cian,** *n.* One versed in mathematics ; গণিতজ্ঞ, গণিতশাস্ত্রবিৎ, গণিতপণ্ডিত, গণিতবিশারদ, গণিত-কুশল।

matico, n. A Peruvian plant ; its leaves used in medicine as a styptic ; পেরুদেশীয় গুল্মবিশেষ ; ইহার পাতা [রক্তরোধক ঔষধ]।

măt′-in, *n.* **1.** (*Pl.*) Morning worship or service ; morning prayers ; প্রাতঃকালীন উপাসনা ; প্রাভাতিক প্রার্থনা, প্রভাতকরণীয় (শকুঃ), প্রাতর্ভজন। **2.** One of the canonical hours of the Roman Catholic Church ; রোমানক্যাথলিক ধর্ম্মসংঘের বিহিত উপাসনাকাল। **3.** (*Poet.*) The morning song of birds ; পক্ষীর প্রভাতসঙ্গীত, উষাকালীন বিহগকাকলী, প্রভাত-কাকলী।

măt-i-nee′ (-nā), *n.* Afternoon theatrical or musical performance ; অপরাহ্ণকালীন সঙ্গীত বা নাট্যাভিনয়।

măt′-răss, *n.* A long-necked glass vessel with a tapering neck used for distilling ; পরিস্রবণকার্য্যে ব্যবহৃত দীর্ঘগল, গোল বা অণ্ডাকৃতি কাচপাত্র-বিশেষ।

mā′-tri-ârch, *n.* (*Usu. facet.*) A woman corresponding in status to a patriarch ; বংশের আদিমাতা, কুলজননী।

mā′-tri-âr-chy̆, *n.* A social organization in which mother is the head of a family ; যে সমাজ-ব্যবস্থায় মাতা পরিবারের শীর্ষস্থানীয়া বলিয়া গণ্যা হন, স্ত্রীরাজ্য (হিঃ কোঃ), মাতৃরাজ্য (ঐ)। **—ar′-chal,** *adj.*

măt′-ri-cīde, *n.* One who kills his own mother ; the murder of one's own mother ; মাতৃহন্তা, মাতৃঘ্ন, মাতৃঘাতক, মাতৃঘাতী, মাতৃহ, (ছান্দোগ্য) ; মাতৃহত্যা, মাতৃবধ। **—ci-dal,** *adj.*

ma-tric′-ū-lāte, *v. t.* & *i.* To admit as a student to membership in a university ; বিশ্ববিদ্যালয়ে প্রবেশের অধিকারী করা। *Verb i.* To be thus admitted ; প্রবেশিকা পরীক্ষায় উত্তীর্ণ হইয়া বিশ্ববিদ্যালয়ে প্রবেশের অধিকারী হওয়া। **—la-ted,** *adj.* **—la′-tion,** *n.* **—la-to-ry,** *adj.* **Matriculation examination**—প্রবেশিকা পরীক্ষা।

măt′-ri-mō-ny̆, *n.* **1.** Wedlock ; marriage ; the married state ; বিবাহ, পরিণয় ; উদ্বাহ ; বিবাহিত অবস্থা। **2.** A kind of card game ; the combination of king and queen of trumps in some card games ; একপ্রকার তাস খেলা ; ইস্তক। **—mo′-ni-al,** *adj.* Nuptial ; hymeneal ; দাম্পত্য ; উদ্বাহসংক্রান্ত, ঔদ্বাহিক, বৈবাহিক। **—mo′-ni-al-ly,** *adv.* **Matrimonial alliance**—বৈবাহিক সম্বন্ধ।

mā′-trix, *n.* **1.** The womb ; জরায়ু, গর্ভাশয়। **2.** A place where anything is formed or developed ; যে স্থানে কিছু জন্মে বা পরিবর্দ্ধিত হয়। **3.** The formative part of an animal organ ; গর্ভকোষ, যোনি। **4.** The portion of rock in which gems etc. are embedded ; রত্নাদি দ্বারা অনুবিদ্ধ প্রস্তর খণ্ড। **5.** A mould in which type etc. is cast or shaped ; অক্ষর তৈরীর ছাঁচ **6.** (*Anat.* & *Biol.*) The intercellular substance of a tissue ; (জীব-বিজ্ঞান এবং শারীরসংস্থান বিদ্যা) বিধানতন্তুর কোষাণুর অভ্যন্তরস্থ পদার্থ।

mā′-trŏn, *n.* **1.** An elderly married woman ; বিবাহিতা প্রৌঢ়া নারী, বর্ষীয়সী নারী, গৃহিণী, গৃহকর্ত্রী, গিন্নি (*colloq.*), পুরস্ত্রী, পুরন্ধ্রী। **2.** A woman managing domestic affairs of a school, hospital, etc. ; বিদ্যালয়, আরোগ্যশালা, প্রভৃতির গৃহকর্ম্ম তত্ত্বাবধায়িকা। **—hood,** *n.* **Mat′-ron-age,** *n.* **1.** The collective body of matrons ; গৃহিণীগণ, পুরস্ত্রীবর্গ। 2. Matronly care or supervision ; গৃহিণীপণা। **—al, —ly,** *adjs.* Suitable to a matron ; grave ; motherly ; গৃহিণীসমুচিত ; গম্ভীর ; মাতৃবৎ। **—ship,** *n.* 1. The state or condition of a matron ; গৃহিণীত্ব। 2. The office of a matron as in a hospital, school, etc. ; আরোগ্যশালা, বিদ্যালয়, প্রভৃতির গৃহকর্ম্ম-তত্ত্বাবধায়িকার পদ।

măt-tă-mōre′, *n.* An underground dwelling or storehouse ; ভূগর্ভস্থ বাসস্থান বা ভাণ্ডার, অন্তর্ভৌম বাসগৃহ।

măt′-ter (-ėr), *n.* & *v. i.* 1. A substance or substances of which a physical thing is made ; বিষয় (হিঃ কোঃ), তন্মাত্র (ঐ), বীজ (ঐ), প্রকৃতি (ঐ), ভূত (ঐ), পদার্থ (ঐ), সাধন, সাধনভূত বস্তু, দ্রব্য, বস্তু, পদার্থ, উপাদান (বেদান্ত)। 2. Pus ; পুয, ক্লেদ, ক্ষতজ। 3. The physical substance as opposed to spirit, mind, etc. ; জড় পদার্থ, জড় বস্তু, অচিৎ (ব্রজঃ হিন্দু), স্থূলভূত (সাঃ পঃ), দৃশ্যস্পৃশ্য পদার্থ, পঞ্চভূতাত্মক বস্তু, সাকার পদার্থ, অনাত্মক বস্তু, মূর্ত্তবস্তু (হিঃ কোঃ), তন্মাত্র (হিঃ কোঃ)। 4. The subject or materials for writing, discourse or speech ; আলোচ্য বিষয়, চিন্তার বিষয়। 5. The contents or essence of a book, speech, etc. ; প্রবন্ধ বা বক্তৃতার সারমর্ম্ম, বিষয়, প্রকরণ, বৃত্তান্ত। 6. Cause or occasion (*of* or *for* complaint, regret, etc.) ; উপলক্ষ, নিমিত্ত, হেতু। 7. Consequence ; importance ; as, no *matter* when, how, etc. it happens ; ফল ; গুরুত্ব। 8. A thing or things ; as, printed *matter* ; বিষয় বা বিষয়সমূহ। 9. Affair ; business ; event ; as, observe how *matters* stand ; বিষয় ; ব্যাপার ; ঘটনা। 10. A thing (*usu. specified by a verbal noun*) ; as, no laughing *matter* : a hanging *matter* ; বিষয়, বস্তু। 11. A case ; a question ; as, it is a *matter* of habit ; বিষয় ; প্রশ্ন। *Verb i.* To be of importance ; to signify : (used with *it, this, that* or *what*) ; as, it does not *matter* how he does *it* ; গুরুত্ব বিশিষ্ট হওয়া ; ব্যক্ত করা, সূচিত করা। **Matter-of-course**—Phlegmatic ; indifferent ; cool ; শ্লেষ্মাপ্রধান ; উদাসীন ; অনুরাগশূন্য। **Matter-of-fact**—(*adj.*) Plain or common-place ; unimaginative ; prosaic ; সরল, সাধারণ, সাদাসিধা ; কবিত্ববর্জ্জিত ; গদ্যময়। **A matter of course**—A thing to be expected in natural course ; অবশ্যম্ভাবী ঘটনা, যাহা না ঘটিয়া যায় না। **Elementary matter**—কারণ। **Evolution of matter**—তান্মাত্রিক সৃষ্টি (সাঃ পঃ)। **For that matter** — For aught I know ; আমি যতদূর জানি। **For the matter of that**—So far as that is concerned ; তা ধরিতে গেলে। **In the matter of**—As regards ; বিষয়ে, সম্বন্ধে, সম্পর্কে। **It matters little** — তাতে আসে যায় না। **Matter of fact** — That which relates to the sphere of fact ; a real fact ; বাস্তব রাজ্যের বিষয় ; প্রকৃত ঘটনা, বাস্তব ঘটনা। (*Law*) A part of judicial inquiry concerned with the truth of alleged facts (*opp. to matter of law*) ; (আইন) বিচারের অংশ বিশেষ—যাহাতে আরোপিত বিষয় সমূহের সত্যতা সম্বন্ধে আলোচিত হয়। **No matter**—It is of no importance ; তাতে আসে যায় না। **Primary unevolved matter**—প্রধান (সর্ব্বঃ দঃ)। **That does not matter**—তাহাতে আসে যায় না। **To mend matters**—To better or improve the state of things ; কোন অবস্থার উন্নতি করা, কোন বিষয় সংশোধন করিয়া নেওয়া, কোন অবস্থা ভালভাবে দাঁড় করার জন্য চেষ্টা করিয়া কৃতকার্য্য হওয়া। **What is the matter (with)**—What is amiss (with) ? ; কি হলো ? কথাটা কি ব্যাপার কি ?

măt′-ting (-ĭng), *n.* 1. Covering with mats ; মাদুর বা দরমা দ্বারা আচ্ছাদন। 2. Materials for mats ; a fabric of hemp, straw, grass etc. as a covering etc. ; মাদুর দরমা প্রভৃতি বুনিবার উপাদান ; ঘরের মেঝে প্রভৃতি আচ্ছাদনের জন্য শণ, ঘাস, বিচালি প্রভৃতির মাদুর, দরমা, চাটাই, প্রভৃতি।

măt′-tŏck, *n.* A pick-axe with one or both of its ends broad for loosening hard soil ; খনিত্র, পাষাণদারণ।

măt′-trĕss, *n.* 1. A bed or support for bed stuffed with hair, straw, etc. ; (বিছানার) গদি, তোষক। 2. (Also a *spring-mattress*) A bed of springs stretched in a frame ; দমের গদি।

măt′-ū-rāte, *v. t.* 1. (*Rare*) To cause the ripeness or maturity of ; (কচিদ্ব্যবহৃত) পরিপক্ক অবস্থায় আনা, পরিণত অবস্থায় আনা, পরিপক্ক করা। 2. To promote the suppuration of (an abscess) ; পাকান। **Ma-tur′-tive,** *adj.* Conducing to suppuration ; পুযোৎপাদক। **—ra-tion,** *n.* 1. The formation of pus ; স্ফোটকাদিতে পুযোৎপাদন। 2. The ripening of a fruit ; পক্কতা, পরিপক্কতা। 3. Maturing ; development ; পরিপক্ক হওন ; বিকাশ।

mă-tūre′, *adj.* 1. Complete in natural development ; full grown ; ripe ; সুপরিণত ; পরিপক্ক পাকা, পক্ক, পোক্ত, ঝুনা (of a cocoanut). 2. Brought to completion ; perfected, as a plan etc. ; পূর্ণতাপ্রাপ্ত, সর্ব্বাঙ্গসম্পন্ন। 3. With fully developed powers of body and mind ; পূর্ণবিকাশপ্রাপ্ত শারীরিক ও মানসিক শক্তিবিশিষ্ট, পূর্ণাঙ্গ। 4. Due as a note or bill ; দেয়, প্রদেয়। **—ly,** *adv.* **—tu′-ri-ty, —ness,** *n.*

The state of being mature ; পরিণতাবস্থা, পরিপক্বতা, পক্কাবস্থা। **Mature deliberation**—Careful deliberation ; গভীর আলোচনা। **Mature plans**—Plans deliberately formed ; সুচিন্তিত কল্পনা।

mă-türe′, *v. t.* & *i.* **1.** To bring to perfect development or maturity ; to ripen ; পরিণত করা, পূর্ণতাসম্পাদন করা, সম্পূর্ণ করা, সমাপন করা ; সপক্ক করা, পরিপক্ক করা। 2. To perfect, as a plan etc. ; (কল্পনা, মতলব প্রভৃতি) সম্পূর্ণ করা, সর্ব্বাঙ্গসম্পন্ন করা। ***Verb i.*** **1.** To become mature or ripe; পরিণত হওয়া, পরিপুষ্ট হওয়া, সুপক্ক হওয়া, পোক্ত হওয়া। **2.** (Of a bill) To become due ; দেয় হওয়া, টাকা-পরিশোধের সময় উপস্থিত হওয়া।

mă-tü′-tĭ-năl, *adj.* Of, pertaining to, or occurring in the morning ; early ; প্রাতঃকালীন, প্রভাতী, প্রাভাতিক ; পৌব্বাহ্ণিক। **Mat′-u-tine**, *adj.* Same as MATUTINAL.

maud (mäd), *n.* **1.** A grey woollen plaid worn by shepherds in Scotland ; স্কটলণ্ডের রাখালগণের পরিধেয় ধূসরবর্ণ পশমী জানুত্রাণ। **2.** A travelling-rug like this ; ভ্রমণকারিগণের মোটা কম্বল।

maud′-lin (mäd-), *adj.* & *n.* **1.** Tearfully emotional ; mawkishly sentimental ; আবেগে অশ্রুপূর্ণ ; উৎকট ভাবপ্রবণ। **2.** Drunk enough to be emotionally silly ; সুরাপানবিমূঢ়, ঈষন্মত্ত। ***Noun.*** Mawkish sentiment ; উৎকটহৃদয়াবেগ, উৎকট হৃদয়োচ্ছ্বাস।

mau′-gre (mä-gĕr), *Prep.* (*Arch.*) In spite of ; (অপ্রঃ) স্বত্বেও।

maul (mäl), **mall**, *ns.* **1.** A heavy hammer, esp. for driving wedges ; গুরুভার কাষ্ঠমুদ্গর।

maul (mäl), *v. t.* **1.** To beat and bruise ; to wound coarsely ; as, he was *mauled* by a tiger ; প্রহার করিয়া ক্ষতবিক্ষত করা, ছিন্নবিছিন্ন করা ; আঘাত করা। **2.** To handle roughly or carelessly as a thing, subject, quotation etc. ; (কোন বস্তু, বিষয় বা উদ্ধৃত বাক্য) যদৃচ্ছভাবে ব্যবহার বা নাড়া চাড়া করা, কঠোর হস্তে তাড়না করা। **3.** To injure greatly by criticism ; সমালোচনা দ্বারা অতিশয় ক্ষতি করা।

maul′-stick (mäl-), *n.* A stick used by painters as a rest for the hand while working ; চিত্রাঙ্কণকালে চিত্রকরগণের হস্তের অবলম্বন দণ্ড।

maun′-dêr (män-), *v. i.* **1.** To move or act idly or listlessly ; জড়বৎ চলা বা কার্য্য করা। **2.** To talk in a dreamy or rambling manner ; স্বপ্নবিজড়িতস্বরে কথা বলা, অসংলগ্নভাবে কথা বলা, প্রলাপ বকা।

maun′-dy̆ (män-), *n.* **1.** The ceremony of washing the feet of the poor on Maundy Thursday ; গুড্ ফ্রাইডের পূর্ব্ববর্ত্তী বৃহস্পাতবারে দরিদ্রদের পদপ্রক্ষালনক্রিয়া, দীনপদপ্রক্ষালন ক্রিয়া। **2.** The distribution of alms on this occasion ; ঐ ক্রিয়া উপলক্ষে ভিক্ষা-প্রদান। **Maundy Thursday**—গুড্ ফ্রাইডের অব্যবাহত পূর্ব্বের বৃহস্পতিবার—যেদিন ইংলণ্ডেশ্বর গারিব দুঃখীদের ভিক্ষা প্রদান করেন। **Maundy-money** — দীনপদপ্রক্ষালন ক্রিয়োপলক্ষে প্রদত্ত অর্থ।

Mau′-sêr (mow-), *n.* A kind of rifle or pistol ; একপ্রকার রাইফেল বা পিস্তল। [জর্ম্মণ উদ্ভাবক মসারের নামানুসারে।]

mau-sō-lē′-ŭm (mä-), *n.* A magnificent tomb or monument ; জাঁকাল সমাধিমন্দির, স্মৃতি-স্তম্ভ, চৈত্য। [Caria র রাজা Mausolus এর সমাধির উপর তদীয় পত্নী Artemesia কর্ত্তৃক খৃঃ পূ চতুর্থ শতাব্দীতে যে সুবিশাল মন্দির নির্ম্মিত হয় তাহার নাম হইতে গৃহীত।]

mauvais, (*F.*), *adj.* **Mauvais sujet** — Black sheep ; rogue ; কুলকলঙ্ক ; দুর্ব্বৃত্ত।

mauvaise honte, (*F.*), *n.* **1.** False shame ; কৃত্রিম লজ্জা, কপট লজ্জা, জনলজ্জা। **2.** Painful diffidence ; হ্রী-যন্ত্রণা।

mauve (māv), *n.* & *adj.* **1.** A delicate purple, violet or lilac colour ; কমনীয় নীলারুণ বা আনীললোহিতবর্ণ। **2.** A dye stuff obtained by the oxidation of commercial aniline with Potassium dichromate ; একপ্রকার আনীল-লোহিতবর্ণ রঞ্জন-পদার্থ। ***Adj.*** Of, or relating to, the colour of this ; উক্ত বর্ণ-সম্বন্ধীয়, মৃদুনীলারুণ বর্ণের, ফিকে বেগুণে রঙ্গের।

ma′-vis, *n.* (*Poet.*) The European song-thrush ; (কবিতায়) এক প্রকার পাখী।

maw (mä), *n.* **1.** The stomach (*now used only of animals except humorously* or *in contempt*) ; পশুদিগের পাকস্থলী, (কৌতুকচ্ছলে) মনুষ্যের পাকস্থলী। **2.** (In birds) the craw ; পক্ষীর পাকস্থলী। **Maw-worm**—সূত্রবৎ ক্রিমি। A hypocrite, (From a character of this name in Bickerstaffe's *The Hypocrite*); ভণ্ড, কপট।

mawk′-ish (māk-), *adj.* **1.** Of sickly flavour ; loathsome ; nauseous ; রোগজনক-গন্ধবিশিষ্ট ; ঘৃণাজনক ; গুকারজনক। **2.** Weakly sentimental ; "The *mawkish* and unreal sentiment" ; দুর্ব্বলভাবপ্রবণ, ভাবাবেগপূর্ণ, ভাবোচ্ছ্বাসময়। **—ly**, *adv.* **—ness**, *n.*

maw′-seed (mä-sed), *n.* The seed of the opium poppy ; পোস্তদানা।

măx-il′-lă, *n.* (*Pl.* -LAE) (In animals and vertebrates) A jaw, esp. the upper one ; (জন্তু এবং মেরুদণ্ডী প্রাণি-সম্পর্কে) চোয়ালের অস্থি—বিশেষতঃ উপরের চোয়ালের হাড়, চর্ব্বনোষ্ঠ (সাঃ পঃ)। **Max′-il-la-ry, —li′-from**, *adjs.*

măx′-ĭm, *n.* **1.** A general truth derived from science or experience ; a principle ; সারসত্য, সূত্র, সর্ব্বতন্ত্রসিদ্ধান্ত (হিঃ কোঃ) ; মূলসূত্র। **2.** A rule of conduct ; নীতিতত্ত্ব, নীতিবিধান, ব্যবহারিক নীতি, প্রবচন, নয়, নীতিবাক্য, নীতকথা, ন্যায়, নীতিবচন।

măx'-im, *n.* (Often put for *maxim-gun*) A single barrelled quick-firing machine gun ; এক প্রকার দ্রুতবর্ষী কলের কামান। [মার্কিণ যুক্ত রাজ্যবাসী উদ্ভাবক Sir Hiram Stevens Maxim এর নাম হইতে গৃহীত।]

măx'-i-mīze, *v. t.* **1.** To increase or magnify to the highest degree ; চরমসীমা পর্য্যন্ত বর্দ্ধিত করা, অত্যন্ত বাড়াইয়া তোলা। **2.** To interpret as a doctrine etc., vigorously ; কোন মত, সিদ্ধান্ত, প্রভৃতি সতেজে ব্যাখ্যা করা। **—mi-za'-tion,** *n.*

măx'-i-mŭm, *n.* & *adj.* (*Pl.* -MA), The greatest quantity or magnitude ; উর্দ্ধসংখ্যা, সর্ব্বোচ্চ পরিমাণ, উর্দ্ধসীমা, পরমসীমা (হিঃ কোঃ), পরম (সাঃ পঃ)। ***Adj.*** Highest in quantity or degree ; as, *maximum* pressure ; (পরিমাণ) সর্ব্বাপেক্ষা অধিক, চরম, অধিকতম, পরাকাষ্ঠা, পরান্ত, ভূয়িষ্ঠ, অত্যন্ত। **Maximum thermometer**—যে তাপমান যন্ত্রে নির্দ্দিষ্ট সময়ের মধ্যে উর্দ্ধতম তাপমাত্রা নির্দ্দিষ্ট হয় ; মহত্তাপমাপক (হিঃ কোঃ)।

may (mā), *verb aux.* (*p. t. might*) **1.** Expressing possibility ; as, it *may* be true ; সম্ভাবনাসূচক। **2.** Expressing permission ; as, you *may* go ; অনুমতি সূচক। **3.** Expressing wish ; as, *may* you live to repent it ! ; ইচ্ছাসূচক। **4.** (*In questions*) Emphasizing uncertainty ; as, who *may* you be ; অনিশ্চয়তা প্রতিপাদক। **May be**—Perhaps ; সম্ভবতঃ, হয়ত।

may (mā), *n.* (*Poet.*) Maiden ; (কবিতায়) কুমারী।

may (mā), *n.* **1.** (*Cap.*) The fifth month of the year ; ইংরাজী বৎসরের পঞ্চম মাস, মে মাস। **2.** (*Fig.*) The early or gay part of life ; bloom ; prime ; (লক্ষণায়) নবযৌবন ; নবতারুণ্য ; যৌবনোন্মেষ। **3.** (*l. c.*) Hawthorn ; its blossom ; কণ্টকবহুল গুল্ম-বিশেষ ; ঐ গুল্মের শ্বেত, রক্ত বা গোলাবী বর্ণের ফুল। **4.** (*University cant, pl.*) May examination ; boat races held during May-week ; মে মাসের পরীক্ষা ; মে মাসের শেষ ভাগের বাইচ

Leaves, blossom and seeds of may-apple.

খেলা। **May apple**—আমেরিকা দেশীয় গুল্ম বিশেষ। **May-day**—May 1 ;

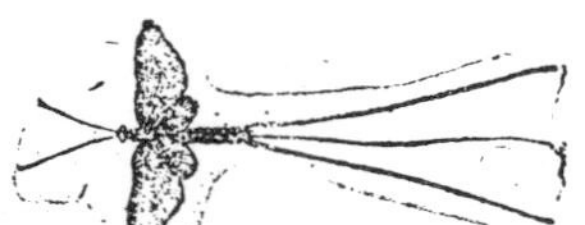

May-fly.

মে মাসের প্রথম দিন। **May-fly**—লেজাফড়িঙ্ (যোঃ)। **May-games**—মে মাসের প্রথম দিনের ক্রীড়াকৌতুকাদি। **May-pole** — চিত্রিত এবং কুসুমদামসজ্জিত দণ্ড-বিশেষ — এই দণ্ড ১লা মে দিবসের বসন্তোৎসবে প্রোথিত হয় এবং ইহার চতুর্দ্দিকে উৎসবকারিগণ নৃত্য করিয়া থাকে, মণ্ডলনৃত্যের জন্য সুসজ্জিত দণ্ড, মেনৃত্যযূপ (আঃ বঃ)। **May queen** or **Lady queen of the May**—মে মাসের প্রথম দিবসের উৎসবে যে বালিকাকে কুসুমভূষণে ভূষিত করা হয়, মে-রাণী। **May-week**—মে মাসের শেষ বা জুনের প্রথম ভাগ।

may-on-naise' (mā-ŏn-āz), *n.* A sauce of yolks of eggs and lemon-juice, etc. ; অণ্ডকুসুম, লেবুর রস প্রভৃতি মিশ্রিত (চিংড়ী মৎস্য প্রভৃতির) চাটনী।

may'-or (mā-ẽr), *n.* The head of the municipal corporation of a city or borough ; নগরাধ্যক্ষ, নগরপাল, পুরাধ্যক্ষ (শুক্রঃ বিনয়ঃ), পৌর (অর্থঃ)। **—al,** *adj.* **—al-ty,** *n.* The office or term of office of a mayor ; নগরাধ্যক্ষতা। **—ess,** *n.* (*Fem.*) The wife of a mayor ; পুরাধ্যক্ষপত্নী। **Lord mayor**—লণ্ডনের পুরাধ্যক্ষ।

măz'-ârd, *n.* **1.** A kind of small black cherry ; এক প্রকার ক্ষুদ্র কালো রঙ্গের চেরি ফল। **2.** (*Archaic*) Head ; face ; (অপ্রঃ) মাথা ; মুখ।

măz'-ă-rine' (-rēn), *n.* & *adj.* A deep blue colour ; গাঢ় নীলবর্ণ। ***Adj.*** Deep blue ; গাঢ়নীল, ঘন নীল।

Măz'-dă-ism, *n.* The Zoroastrian religion ; প্রাচীন পারসীক ধর্ম্ম।

māze, *n.* & *v. t.* **1.** A confusing network of paths ; a labyrinth ; দুর্নির্গম বর্ত্মজাল ; গোলকধাঁধা। **2.** A confused mass etc. ; "A tangled *maze* of bracken and briar" ; জটাজূটবৎ জটিল বস্তুপুঞ্জ। **3.** Perplexity ; bewilderment ; "...Reasoned high and found no end, in wandering *mazes* lost" ; হতবুদ্ধিতা ; বিভ্রান্তভাব। ***Verb t.*** To bewilder ; to confuse ; বিহ্বল করা, হতবুদ্ধি করা ; বিভ্রান্ত করা, আকুলিত করা, বিমূঢ় করা, দিশাহারা করা, কিংকর্তব্যবিমূঢ় করা। **Ma'-zi-ly,** *adv.* **Ma'-zi-ness,** *n.* **Ma'-zy,** *adj.* Winding ; perplexing ; intricate ; পেঁচানিয়া ; হতবুদ্ধিতাজনক ; গহন।

mē, *pron.* **1.** The objective case of *I* ; (*colloq.* also used subjectively ; as, it's only *me*) ; আমাকে।

mead (mēd), *n.* A fermented liquor of honey and water ; মধ্বাসব, মাধ্বী, মধুপানক।

mead'-ow (mĕd-ō), **mead** (mēd), (*Poet.*) *ns.* **1.** A grass-land, esp. used for hay ; তৃণাচ্ছাদিত ভূমি, গোচারণ স্থান, ময়দান, মাঠ, প্রান্তর। **2.** A low ground esp. near a river ; নিম্নভূমি, বিশেষতঃ নদীনিকটস্থ নিম্নভূমি। **—y,** *adj.*

mea′-gre (mē-gėr), *adj.* **1.** (Of persons etc.) lean ; thin ; কৃশ, কৃশাঙ্গ ; ক্ষীণ। **2.** Poor ; scanty ; barren ; নিকৃষ্ট, অপকৃষ্ট ; অপ্রচুর, সামান্য, স্বল্প ; অনুর্ব্বর। **3.** (Of style, composition, ideas, etc.) Wanting in fullness ; অপরিপূর্ণ। **–ly,** *adv.* **–ness,** *n.*

meal (mēl), *n.* **1.** The edible part of any grain or pulse ground to powder ; ছাতু, শক্তু, আটা।

meal (mēl), *n.* & *v. i.* **1.** The portion of food taken at one time ; an occasion of taking this ; এককালীন আহার, এককালীনভোজন ; আহারের সময় বা কাল, ভোজনবেলা। **2.** The quantity of milk given by a cow at a milking ; গরু এক একবারে যে পরিমাণ দুগ্ধ দেয়। ***Verb i.*** To eat a meal ; ভোজন করা। **Meal time** — ভোজনকাল, ভোজনবেলা।

meal′-y (mēl-), *adj.* **1.** Of, or relating to, a meal ; resembling or containing meal; এককালীন আহার সম্পর্কীয় ; শক্তুপূর্ণ, শক্তুসদৃশ। **2.** (Of boiled potatoes etc.) Dry and powdery ; (সিদ্ধ আলু সম্পর্কে) সহজে সাতুর মত চূর্ণ করা যায়—এরূপ। **3.** (Of horses) spotty ; (অশ্ব-সম্পর্কে) ফুট্ কুট্ দাগবিশিষ্ট। **4.** Pale as a complexion ; পাণ্ডুবর্ণ, ফেকাসিয়া, বিবর্ণ, পাঙ্গাসিয়া। **5.** Soft-spoken ; mealy-mouthed ; মৃদুভাষী ; মেনিমুখো। **–i-ness,** *n.* **Mealy bug** — Insect infesting vines etc. ; দ্রাক্ষানাশক কীট-বিশেষ। **Mealy-mouthed** — Soft-spoken ; unwilling to tell the truth in plain language ; মৃদুভাষী ; মেনিমুখো।

mean, (mēn), *adj.* **1.** Humble ; low ; as, of a *mean* parentage ; সামান্য, নীচ ; হীন, ক্ষুদ্র। **2.** Lowminded ; ignoble ; base ; as, a *mean* motive ; লঘুচেতাঃ, নীচমনাঃ, নীচাশয়, ক্ষুদ্রমনাঃ, ক্ষুদ্রান্তঃকরণ ; হেয় ; নীচ, ইতর, ছেঁচড়া। **3.** Inferior ; poor ; as, a man of *mean* capacity ; নিকৃষ্ট ; দরিদ্র। **4.** Contemptible ; despicable ; as, they are no *mean* foes ; হেয়, ঘৃণ্য ; অবজ্ঞেয়। **5.** Of poor quality ; as, *mean* fare ; যৎকিঞ্চিৎ, অকিঞ্চিৎকর। **6.** Penurious ; stingy ; as, *mean* hospitality ; ব্যয়কুণ্ঠ, কৃপণ ; কঞ্জুস। **Mean′-ly,** *adv.* **Mean′-ness,** *n.* **1.** State of being mean ; lowness ; নীচতা, নীচাশয়তা ; হীনতা, অধমতা। **2.** Baseness ; despicability ; ইতরতা ; অবমান্যতা। **Mean-spirited**—নীচমনাঃ, হীনচেতাঃ, লঘুচেতাঃ, ক্ষুদ্রমানস। **Mean white**—(ইতিহাস) মার্কিণযুক্তরাজ্যের দক্ষিণাংশবাসী ভূসম্পত্তিহীন শ্বেতাঙ্গ।

mean (mēn), *adj.* **1.** (*Math.*) Equally removed from two extremes ; average ; intermediate ; as, *mean* distance : *mean* motion ; (গণিতশাস্ত্র) উভয় প্রান্ত হইতে সমদূরবর্ত্তী ; গড়পড়তায় ; মধ্যবর্ত্তী, মধ্য (সাঃ পঃ), মধ্যম (ঐ), মধ্যস্থ (হিঃ কোঃ), মধ্যগত (ঐ)। **Mean density**—মধ্যমঘনতা (হিঃ কোঃ)। **Mean distance** — (জ্যোতির্বিজ্ঞান) মধ্যদূরত্ব, মধ্যম অন্তর (হিঃ কোঃ)। কোন গ্রহ সূর্য্যকে প্রদক্ষিণ করার কালে সূর্য্য হইতে বিভিন্ন সময়ে উহার যে বিভিন্ন দূরত্ব থাকে ঐ সকল দূরত্বের গড়কে মধ্যদূরত্ব কহে [এই মধ্যদূরত্ব বৃত্তাভাসাকার গ্রহকক্ষার (orbit) দীর্ঘাক্ষের অৰ্দ্ধেক এর (Semi-major axis of the orbit) সমান।] **Mean sun** — মধ্যম সূর্য্য (হিঃ কোঃ), বাস্তব সূর্য্য অসমগতিতে সঞ্চরমাণ হইয়া যে সময়ে সৌর অয়নমণ্ডল (ecliptic) রচনা করে বলিয়া প্রতিভাত হয়—উহার ঠিক সমপরিমাণ সময়ে যে অলীক সূর্য্য নিয়ত সমগতিতে সঞ্চরণপূর্ব্বক নাড়ীমণ্ডল (celestial equator) বিরচন করে বলিয়া কল্পিত হইয়া থাকে। ঐ অলীক সূর্য্য ঐরূপ গতিতে নাড়ী-মণ্ডলে সঞ্চরণপূর্ব্বক যে সময়ে উহার এক আহ্নিক গতি সমাপন করে ঐ কালকে মধ্য সৌরদিবস (mean solar day) কহে। **Mean obliquity**—মধ্যম পরক্রান্তি (হিঃ কোঃ) **Mean sidereal revolution**—মধ্যম নাক্ষত্রিক পরিক্রমণ (হিঃ কোঃ), মধ্যমনাক্ষত্রিক ভগণ (ঐ)। **Mean temperature**—মধ্যমতাপক্রম (হিঃ কোঃ)। **Meantime, meanwhile,** *ns.* & *advs.* The intervening time ; মধ্যবর্ত্তীকাল, মধ্যমকাল (হিঃ কোঃ)। (*Adv.*) In the intervening time ; অনন্তর, তদনন্তর, ইতিমধ্যে। **Mean tropical year** — মধ্যম সাবনবর্ষ (হিঃ কোঃ)। **In the mean time or while**—In the intervening time ; ইতিমধ্যে, ইত্যবসরে।

mean (mēn), *n.* **1.** The condition, quality, course equally removed from the two opposite extremes ; medium ; moderation ; as, the golden, happy *mean* ; মধ্যবর্ত্তী অবস্থা, মধ্যাবস্থা ; মধ্যবর্ত্তী বস্তু ; মধ্যপন্থা। **2.** (*Math.*) A term between the first and last terms of Arithmetical, geometrical etc. progression ; (গণিত) সমান্তর শ্রেঢ়ী ও সমগুণ শ্রেঢ়ীর প্রথম ও শেষ রাশির মধ্যবর্ত্তী রাশি। **3.** (*Pl., often treated as sing.*) That by which an end is attained ; as, it has been the *means* of extending our trade ; সাধন, উপায়। **4.** Pecuniary resources ; riches ; as, he lives beyond his *means* : a man of *means* ; আয়, সংস্থান ; সঙ্গতি, সম্পত্তি। **A golden or happy mean** — See GOLDEN. **A man of means**—A wealthy man ; সঙ্গতিপন্নলোক, সঙ্গতিশালী লোক, সম্পত্তিশালী ব্যক্তি। **By all means**—In every possible way ; at any cost ; certainly ; সর্ব্বপ্রকারে, সর্ব্বথা, সর্ব্বতোভাবে, সর্ব্বাংশে ; যে কোনরূপে ; নিশ্চয়ই, অবশ্যই, নিশ্চিত। **By fair means or foul** — (ভাল মন্দ) যে কোন উপায়েই হউক, সদুপায়েই হউক বা অসদুপায়েই হউক। **By means of**—By the instrumentality or help of ; দ্বারা, সাহায্যে। **By no means, By no manner of**

means — Not at all; certainly not; কিছুতেই নয়; নিশ্চয়ই না, কোন মতেই নয়। **He lives beyond his means**—সে আয়ের অতিরিক্ত ব্যয় করে। **Means of knowledge**—প্রমাণ (ন্যায়সূত্র)। **Means to an end**—কার্য্যসাধনোপায়।

mean (mēn), *v. t.* **1.** To intend; to purpose; as, he *means* mischief; অভিপ্রায় করা, মনে করা; ইচ্ছা করা, উদ্দেশ্য করা। **2.** To design or destine for an object; as, I *mean* it for a stopgag: he was *meant* (by Providence) for a soldier; অভিপ্রেত করা, ভাগ্যে নির্দ্দিষ্ট করা। **3.** To intend to convey or indicate; as, I *mean* his father; সূচনা করা, লক্ষ্য করা। **4.** To signify or import; as, the words do not really *mean* that; অর্থ প্রকাশ করা, বুঝান, মর্ম্ম প্রকাশ করা। **I mean you to go**—I am determined that you shall go; তুমি যাও এই আমার সংকল্প। **To mean well** or **kindly to** or **by**—To be kindly disposed towards; সদয় হওয়া, শুভানুধ্যায়ী হওয়া। **What do you mean by it**—How would you justify it; তুমি ইহা কিরূপে সমর্থন করিবে?

mē-ăn′-dĕr, *n.* & *v. i.* **1.** (*Pl.*) Sinuous windings of a river; নদীর আঁকাবাঁকা গতি। **2.** (*Pl.*) Winding paths or courses; (বহুবচন) আঁকাবাঁকা রাস্তা। **3.** (*Usu. Pl.*) A tortuous journey; আঁকাবাঁকা গতি। **4.** A fret work; একপ্রকার নকাশি কাজ। ***Verb i.*** **1.** To wander aimlessly or listlessly; উদ্দেশ্যবিহীন ভাবে ঘুরিয়া বেড়ান। **2.** (Of a stream) To wind about; নদী প্রভৃতির বক্র গতিতে চলা, ঘুরিয়া ফিরিয়া যাওয়া, আঁকিয়াবাঁকিয়া যাওয়া। **–dri′-an, –drous,** *adjs.*

mē-ăn′-drīne, *adj.* Full of windings (esp. of the genus of corals with surface like a human brain) আঁকাবাঁকা, পেঁচালো, কুটিল।

mean′-ing (mēn-), *n.* & *adj.* Design; signification; purport; তাৎপর্য্য, মানে, (*colloq.*) অর্থ; আশয়, অভিপ্রায়; ভাবার্থ, ফলিতার্থ। ***Adj.*** Expressive; significant; নির্দ্দেশক, ব্যঞ্জক, সূচক; গূঢ়ার্থপ্রকাশক, ইঙ্গিতময়। **–less,** *adj.* **–ly,** *adv.* **Well-meaning** — Having good intention; সদিচ্ছাসম্পন্ন, সদভিপ্রায়ানুরক্ত। **With meaning** — Significantly; সঙ্কেতগর্ব্বিতরূপে, গূঢ়ার্থসূচকভাবে।

mea′-sles (mē-zls), *n.* **1.** (*Pl.*) A contagious fever in man characterised by red pustules; these pustules; হামজ্বর; হাম, রোমান্তি, পণসিক। **2.** A disease of swine and cattle; গরু, শূকর প্রভৃতির একপ্রকার পীড়া। **–sly,** *adj.* **1.** Of, relating to, or affected with, measles; হামজ্বর-সম্বন্ধীয়, হামজ্বরাক্রান্ত। **2.** (*Slang*) Contemptible; worthless; (ইতর ভাষায়) হেয়, ঘৃণ্য, জঘন্য; অকর্ম্মণ্য।

meas′-ūre (mĕz-), *n.* **1.** The size or quantity determined by measuring; মাপ, মান (হিঃ কোঃ), পরিমাণ, আয়তন, বিস্তৃতি। **2.** A system of measurement; as, liquid, linear *measure*; পরিমাণপদ্ধতি। **3.** A vessel of standard capacity for dealing out liquids etc.; as, a pint *measure*; মাপের পাত্র বা চোঙ্গা, মাপিবার ভাঁড়। **4.** An instrument, as a rod, tape, etc. for measuring; মানদণ্ড বা মাপিবার ফিতা। **5.** A unit of measurement, *e.g.* a bushel; as, 20 *measures* of corn; শস্যাদি মাপিবার (নির্দ্দিষ্ট পরিমাণ বিশিষ্ট) ধামা বা পালি। **6.** (*Arith.*) A number or quantity contained in another an exact number of times; as, the greatest common *measure*; (গণিতে) অপবর্ত্তক, গুণনীয়ক। **7.** Something by which a thing can be computed; as, a chain's weakest link is the *measure* of its strength; মান, পরিমাপ। **8.** A prescribed extent or limit; as, beyond *measure*; নির্দ্দিষ্ট পরিমাণ, নির্দ্দিষ্ট সীমা, সীমা, ইয়ত্তা, পরিসীমা। **9.** A course of action; as, to take *measures*; কার্য্যপ্রণালী। **10.** Musical time; তাল, আবর্ত্ত (ক্রেমঃ), মাত্রা। **11.** A legislative enactment; বিধিবদ্ধ আইন। **12.** (*Archaic*) A dance; as, to tread a *measure*; (অপ্রঃ) নৃত্য। **–less,** *adj.* Without measure; boundless; vast; infinite; অপরিমিত, অমেয়, অপ্রমেয়, অপরিমেয়; অসীম; বিশাল; অনন্ত। **Above** or **beyond measure**—Excessively; অপ্রমেয়, অমেয়, অপরিমেয়। **In some measure** — In some degree; কতকাংশে, কিয়দংশে, কিয়ৎ-পরিমাণে। **To take measures**—See MEASURE *n.* 9. **To take one's measure**—To ascertain one's abilities or qualifications; to find out what one can or cannot do; কাহারো যোগ্যতা বা ক্ষমতা পরীক্ষা করা; কোন ব্যক্তি কি করিতে পারে বা না পারে তাহা নির্ণয় করা। To measure one for clothes; জামা তৈরীর জন্য কাহারও গায়ের মাপ লওয়া। **To take the measure of a man's foot**—To see what is his character; তাহার চরিত্র কিরূপ দেখা। **Within measure**—Moderately: পরিমিতরূপে।

meas′-ūre (mĕz-), *v. t.* & *i.* **1.** To ascertain the extent, quantity, or capacity of; hence, (*fig.*) to estimate; to value; পরিমাণ করা, মাপা, মাপ করা, ইয়ত্তা করা; (লক্ষণায়) আনুমানিক মূল্য নির্দ্ধারণ করা; মূল্যাঙ্কন করা। **2.** To ascertain size and proportions of a person for clothes; পোষাক তৈরির জন্য কাহারও গায়ের মাপ নেওয়া। **3.** To serve as the measure of; as, the thermometer *measures* changes of temperature; পরিমাপস্বরূপ হওয়া। **4.** To look as a person up and down (with one's eye); (কতটা শক্তি বা সামর্থ্য আছে তাহা জানিবার জন্য)

কাহারও সর্ব্বাঙ্গ নিরীক্ষণ করা। 5. To mark off as a line etc. of given length; নির্দ্দিষ্ট দৈর্ঘ্যের কোন রেখা চিহ্নিত করা। 6. To estimate with reference to a standard or measure; কোন মান বা আদর্শ সম্পর্কে মূল্যাবধারণ করা 7. (*Poet.*) To travel, as a distance etc.; "To *measure* kingdoms with his feeble steps"; (কবিতায়) পর্য্যটন করা। 8. To allot or distribute by measure; as, to *measure* a thing to a person; বাঁটিয়া দেওয়া, মাপিয়া দেওয়া। 9. To bring into competition with; as, he wishes to *measure* his strength with mine প্রতিযোগিতা করান। ***Verb i.*** 1. To be of certain size or quantity: as, the cloth *measures* 2 yards: মাপ হওয়া, পরিমিত হওয়া। 2. To measure something; কোন জিনিষ মাপা। **—ment,** *n.* Act of measuring; amount ascertained by measuring; পরিমাপ; মাপ। **—ur-a-ble,** *adj.* Capable of being measured; moderate; পরিমেয়; পরিমিত। **—ur-a-ble-ness,** *n.* **—ur-a-bly,** *adv.* **To measure one's length**—To fall prostrate; ধরাশায়ী হওয়া, সটান হইয়া পড়া। **To measure one's strength with**—(See MEASURE *v. t.* 9.) To ascertain by trial which is the stronger; সংগ্রামে শক্তি পরীক্ষা করা। **To measure swords with another**—To fight with another with swords; (*fig.*) to try one's strength with another; অসিযুদ্ধ করা; (লক্ষণায়) শক্তি পরীক্ষা করা।

meas'-ūred (mĕz-), *adj.* 1. Ascertained by measuring; পরিমিত। 2. Rhythmical; regular in movement; regulated; তালবদ্ধ, লয়বদ্ধ; সমগতিতে অগ্রসর; নিয়মিত। 3. Carefully weighed; as, he expressed himself in no *measured* terms; সুবিবেচিত, সুচিন্তিত।

meat (mēt), *n.* 1. Animal flesh used as food usually excluding fish and fowl; খাদ্যমাংস। 2. (*Archaic*) Food of any kind; (অপ্র:) খাদ্য। 3. (*Archaic*) Meal; as, before or after *meat*; (অপ্র:) আহার। **Meat'-y,** *adj.* 1. Of, or relating to, meat; full of meat; fleshy; মাংসসম্বন্ধীয়; মাংসপূর্ণ; মাংসল, মাংসযুক্ত। 2. (*Fig.*) Full of substance; (লক্ষণায়) সারযুক্ত, সারবান। **Green meat** — শাকসব্জী, তরীতরকারী। **Meat-safe**—(সচরাচর) তারের জালি দ্বারা আবৃত মাংস রাখার বাক্স। **Meat-offering** — (*Bibl.*) Sacrifice of flour and oil; (বাইবেল) তৈল এবং গোধূমচূর্ণদ্বারা হোম। **This was meat and drink to him**—It was a great pleasure to him; ইহা তাহার পক্ষে খুব আনন্দের বিষয় ছিল। **To sit at meat**—To sit at a table at meals; ভোজন করিতে বসা।

meatus, (*L.*) *n.*, (*Pl.* MEATUS, MEATUSES) (*Anat.*) A passage or canal in the body; নালী। **Auditory meatus**—কর্ণের নালী।

mē-c͟hăn'-ĭc, *n.* & *adj.* 1. An artisan; a handicraftsman; a skilled workman; one making or using machinery; শিল্পী, কারিগর; শিল্পকার; যন্ত্রী, যন্ত্রবিদ্ (ব্রজ: হিন্দু); যন্ত্রজ্ঞ (ঐ), যন্ত্রকৌশলী। 2. (*Pl.*) A branch of applied mathematics treating of the action of forces on bodies; (বহুবচন) মিশ্রগণিতের গতিশক্তি বা গতিবিজ্ঞান বিষয়ক শাখা। 3. (*Pl.*) The science of machinery; (বহুবচন) যন্ত্রবিজ্ঞান, যন্ত্রবিদ্যা। ***Adj.*** (Same as MECHANICAL, but little used).

mē-c͟hăn'-ĭ-căl, *adj.* 1. Of, or relating to, machines or mechanism; যন্ত্রসম্বন্ধী, যান্ত্রিক, যন্ত্রীয় বা শিল্পসম্বন্ধীয়, কলসম্বন্ধীয় (হিঃ কোঃ), যন্ত্রশাস্ত্রানুরূপ যন্ত্রবিদ্যানুসারী। 2. Of, or relating to, mechanics as a science; যন্ত্রবিজ্ঞানবিষয়ক, যন্ত্রশাস্ত্রসিদ্ধ, শিল্পশাস্ত্রপ্রসিদ্ধ। 3. Of the nature of handicraft; pertaining to artisans; করশিল্প প্রকৃতিক; শিল্পিসম্বন্ধীয়। 4. Working or made by machinery: as, *mechanical* products; যন্ত্র দ্বারা চালিত, যন্ত্র দ্বারা রচিত বা গঠিত, যন্ত্রকৃত। 5. Acting as a mere machine; doing or done without thought; lacking originality; done by the mere force of habit: যন্ত্রপুত্তলিকাবৎ কার্য্যকারী, কলের পুতুলের মত কার্য্যকারী; যন্ত্রবৎকার্য্যকারী বা কৃত; মৌলিকতাহীন, নূতনত্ববিহীন, বৈচিত্র্যহীন; অভ্যাসসিদ্ধ। 6. Automatic, as a telegraph or telephone; স্বয়ংক্রিয়, স্বয়ংবহ। 7. Acting by physical power; physical (often opp. to *chemical*); as, air is a *mechanical* mixture; ভৌতিক শক্তিসম্পাদিত; ভৌতিক। 8. Explaining phenomena by the assumption of mechanical action; as, the *mechanical* theory of the universe; জাগতিক ব্যাপার সমূহ জ্ঞানময় নিয়ন্তা ব্যতিরেকে কেবল প্রাকৃতিক বলে সংঘটিত বলিয়া ব্যাখ্যাকারী। **—ism,** *n.* **—ly,** *adv.* 1. In a mechanical manner; যন্ত্রবৎ। 2. Automatically; যন্ত্রচালিতবৎ, যন্ত্রপুত্তলিকাবৎ। **—ness,** *n.* **Mechanical contrivance** — কলকৌশল। **Mechanical drawing**—রুল, কম্পাস প্রভৃতির সাহায্যে অঙ্কিত চিত্র। **Mechanical mixture**—যে প্রকার মিশ্রে উপাদান সমূহের রূপান্তর হয় না, যৌগিকমিশ্রণ। **The mechanical powers**—সরল যন্ত্রাদি—যথা, (উত্তোলনার্থ) দণ্ডযন্ত্র, চাকা, চাকার আল, কাজলা, স্ক্রু, প্রভৃতি।

mĕch-ă-nĭ'-cian (-shăn), *n.* One skilled in constructing machinery; যন্ত্রাদিনির্ম্মাণকুশল, যন্ত্রনির্ম্মাণনিপুণ, যন্ত্রশাস্ত্রবেত্তা যন্ত্রবিদ্যাবেত্তা।

mĕc͟h'-ă-nĭsm, *n.* 1. The structure of a machine; the arrangement or relation of the parts of a machine; (*lit* & *fig.*); যন্ত্রের

গঠন; যন্ত্রাংশের যোজনা, যন্ত্রের বিভিন্ন অংশ সমূহের অন্যোন্য সম্বন্ধ। 2. Mechanical contrivance; যন্ত্রনির্ম্মাণ-কৌশল, কলকৌশল। 3. (*Arts*) Mechanical execution; technique; (ললিতকলা) শিল্পশাস্ত্রের নিয়মানুযায়ী গঠন; শিল্পকৌশল, কলা-কৌশল।

mĕch'-ă-nist, *n.* A mechanician; যন্ত্রনির্ম্মাতা, যন্ত্রনির্ম্মাণকৌশলী, যন্ত্রবিদ্যা-নিপুণ, যন্ত্রবিদ্যাবিশারদ, যান্ত্রিক। **—nize,** *v. t.* To give mechanical character to; যন্ত্রের ন্যায় প্রকৃতি দেওয়া, যন্ত্রের ন্যায় গঠন করা, যন্ত্রবৎ করা, যন্ত্রচালিতবৎ করা। **Mechanism of mind**—মনোযন্ত্র (হিঃ কোঃ), মনোযন্ত্রবাদ (হিঃ কোঃ)।

Mĕch'-lin, *n.* (Also *Mechlin lace*) A kind of fine lace made at Mechlin, in Belgium; বেলজিয়ামের অন্তর্গত মেকলিন নগরে প্রস্তুত একপ্রকার সুদৃশ্য লেইস্।

mē-cŏn'-ic, *adj.* Denoting a white crystalline acid obtained from opium; পোস্ত বা আফিম গাছ হইতে প্রাপ্ত একপ্রকার শাদা দানাদার দ্রাবক পদার্থসূচক।

mĕd'-ăl, *n.* A piece of metal, usually in the form of a coin, stamped with some figure, inscription or device as a memento or reward; পদক, প্রতিষ্ঠামুদ্রা, কীর্ত্তিমুদ্রা (কেণ্ডিঃ)। **—alled,** *adj.* Having received a medal as a reward; provided or decorated with a medal; পদকপ্রাপ্ত; পদকভূষিত। **—et,** *n.* A small medal; ক্ষুদ্র পদক। **—ist, —list,** *ns.* 1. An engraver or a designer of medals; পদকপ্রস্তুতকারী, পদকনির্ম্মাতা, পদকের নক্সাকারক। 2. One who has gained a medal as a reward; as, a gold *medalist*; পদকপ্রাপ্ত ব্যক্তি, পদকধারী। **Me-dal'-lic,** *adj.* **Me-dal'-lion,** *n.* 1. A large medal; বৃহৎ পদক। 2. Anything resembling a large medal, as a decorative panel or tablet, portrait, etc.; বৃহৎ পদক সদৃশ কোন কিছু। **The reverse of the medal**—The other side of the question; প্রশ্নের অপর দিক।

mĕd'-ăl-lur-ġy̆ (-ēr-), *n.* The art of making and striking medals and coins; পদকনির্ম্মাণ শিল্প।

mĕd'-dle (-l), *v. i.* To busy oneself improperly *with*; to interfere or interpose in; অন্যায়রূপে হস্তক্ষেপ করা, অপ্রয়োজনে হাত দেওয়া; ঘাঁটান, অনধিকার চর্চ্চা করা। **—dler,** *n.* One who meddles; an officious person; অকারণে হস্তক্ষেপ-কারী, অনধিকার চর্চ্চাকারী; উপযাচক। **—dling,** *adj.* Officious; unnecessarily busy in other men's affairs; অপরের বিষয়ে হস্তক্ষেপকারী; পরচর্চ্চাকারী। **—some,** *adj.* Officiously intrusive; অপ্রয়োজনে হস্তক্ষেপকারী, অনধিকারচর্চ্চী। **—someness,** *n.*

Medea, *n.* See JASON.

media, *n.* (*Pl.* MEDIAE) 1. Soft; mute (*b, d, g*); কোমল; অনুচ্চারিত। 2. The middle membrane of an artery or vessel; ধমনী অথবা রক্তরসাদিবহা নাড়ীর মধ্য-ঝিল্লী।

mē-di-ae'(e)-văl (-ē-), *adj.* Of, relating to, or imitating, the middle ages; মধ্যযুগসম্বন্ধীয়, মধ্য-যুগের। **—ism,** *n.* The spirit of the middle ages; devotion to the institutions and practices of the middle ages; মধ্যযুগের অন্তর্নিহিতভাব; মধ্যযুগের প্রতিষ্ঠান বা আচার-পদ্ধতির প্রতি নিষ্ঠা। **—ist,** *n.* One versed in the history of the middle ages; মধ্যযুগের ইতিহাস-বেত্তা। **—ize,** *v. t.* & *i.* **—ly,** *adv.*

mē'-di-ăl, *adj.* 1. Situated in the middle; middle; মধ্যস্থিত, মধ্যবর্ত্তী; মাঝামাঝি। 2. Of average dimensions; মধ্যবর্ত্তী আয়তনের, মাঝামাঝি আকারের। **—ly,** *adv.*

mē'-di-ăn, *adj.* & *n.* Being, or situated, in the middle; মধ্যস্থিত, মধ্যবর্ত্তী, মধ্যগত। ***Noun.*** The median artery, vein, nerve, etc.; মধ্যবর্ত্তী শিরা, ধমনী, নাড়ী, প্রভৃতি।

mē'-di-ănt, *n.* (*Mus.*) The third note above the key-note; অপন্যাস (ক্রেম)।

mē-di-ăs-ti'-nŭm, *n.* The space in the chest between the pleural sacs of the lungs; ফুস্‌ফুস্‌বেষ্ট-দ্বয়ের মধ্যবর্ত্তী বক্ষঃস্থলের মধ্যস্থান (ডাঃ হরিপ্রসাদ চক্রবর্ত্তী)।

mē'-di-āte, *adj.* 1. Acting as a means; not direct or immediate; উপায়স্বরূপ; পরোক্ষ, মধ্যগত (হিঃ কোঃ), সংব্যবধান (ঐ)। 2. Involving intermediate agency; মধ্যবর্ত্তী ব্যক্তির কর্ত্তৃত্বসাপেক্ষ। **—ly,** *adv.* **Mediate inference** — অনুমান (হিঃ কোঃ), ব্যবহিততর্ক (ঐ)।

mē'-di-āte, *v. i.* & *t.* 1. To form connecting link between; (দুই বস্তুর মধ্যে) সংযোগস্বরূপ হওয়া, সম্বন্ধ স্থাপন করা, দুই বস্তু সংযুক্ত করা। 2. To interpose *between* two persons or parties for reconciling them; মধ্যস্থতা করা। ***Verb t.*** To be the medium for bringing about (a result) or conveying (a gift etc.); উদ্দেশ্য সাধনার্থ মধ্যস্থ হওয়া। **—a'-tion,** *n.* 1. The act of mediating or coming between; intervention; মধ্যস্থালি, মধ্যবর্ত্তিত্ব, মধ্যস্থতা; ব্যবধান, ব্যবহিততা। 2. Entreaty for another; intercession; উপরোধ; অনুরোধ।

mē'-di-ă-tize, *v. t.* To annex as a small state to a larger one and yet allow its ruler to retain his princely rights; পূর্ব্ববর্ত্তী শাসনকর্ত্তার অধিকার অক্ষুণ্ণ রাখিয়া এবং তাহাকে শাসন-সংক্রান্ত কোন কোন কার্য্যের ভার প্রদান-পূর্ব্বক অপর রাজ্য প্রভৃতি স্বরাজ্যের অধীন করা। **—ti-za'-tion,** *n.*

mē'-di-ă-tor (-tēr), *n.* One who mediates, especially Christ; মধ্যস্থ, মীমাংসক, বিশেষতঃ যীশুখৃষ্ট। **—a'-trix, —tress,** (*Fem.*) *ns.*

—to'-ri-al, *adj.* **—to'-ri-al-ly,** *adv.* **—to-ry,** *adj.*

mĕd'-i-că-ble (-bl), *adj.* Capable of being medicated, cured or healed ; চিকিৎসাসাধ্য, সাধ্য।

mĕd'-i-căl, *adj.* & *n.* **1.** Pertaining to the art of healing diseases ; চিকিৎসাসংক্রান্ত, চিকিৎসাসম্বন্ধীয়, ঔষধীয়, চিকিৎসাবিদ্যাবিষয়ক, আয়ুর্বেদসম্বন্ধীয়। **2.** Relating to, or containing, medicine ; used in medicine ; as, the *medical* properties of plant ; ঔষধসংক্রান্ত, ভেষজ ; ঔষধরূপে ব্যবহৃত। **3.** Requiring medical and not surgical treatment ; ঔষধদ্বারা চিকিৎস্য, অস্ত্রপ্রয়োগের অনুপযোগী। ***Noun.*** A medical student ; চিকিৎসাশাস্ত্র শিক্ষার্থী ছাত্র। **—ly,** *adv.* **Medical jurisprudence**—অপরাধের বিচার বিষয়ে চিকিৎসাশাস্ত্রের তথ্য সমূহের প্রয়োগ সম্বন্ধীয় বিজ্ঞান। **Medical man**—চিকিৎসক, ভিষক।

mĕ-dic'-ă-mĕnt, *n.* Anything used for healing diseases ; ঔষধ, প্রলেপ, ভেষজ, ঔষধীয় দ্রব্য, ভেষজ-দ্রব্য।

mĕd'-i-căs-tĕr, *n.* A quack ; হাতুড়িয়া ডাক্তার।

mĕd'-i-cāte, *v. t.* **1.** To treat with medicine ; ঔষধ প্রয়োগ করা, ঔষধ প্রয়োগে চিকিৎসা করা। **2.** To impregnate with medicinal substance ; as, *medicated* water ; ঔষধদ্রব্য দ্বারা পরিপূরিত করা। **—ca'-tion,** *n.* Application of medicine ; ঔষধ-প্রয়োগ। **—ca-tive,** *adj.* Tending to cure or heal ; medicinal ; আরোগ্যজনক, আরোগ্যকারী ; ভৈষজ্য।

mĕ-dĭc'-i-năl, *adj.* **1.** Relating to medicine ; ঔষধীয়, ঔষধসম্বন্ধীয়, ভৈষজ্য। **2.** Containing healing properties ; আরোগ্যকর, রোগনাশক, রোগঘ্ন, রোগশমক, রোগহর, রোগান্তক।

mĕd'-i-cine (-sin), *n.* & *v. t.* **1.** The art and science of curing diseases, (opposed to *surgery and obstetrics*) ; ভৈষজ্য-শাস্ত্র, আয়ুর্বেদ, চিকিৎসাশাস্ত্র, কায়-চিকিৎসাতন্ত্র। **2.** Any substance, (especially one taken internally) used as a remedy for diseases ; ঔষধ, ভেষজ, দাওয়াই (*colloq.*), অষুধ (*colloq.*)। **3.** (Among savages) Spell ; charm ; fetish ; as, a *medicine*-man ; a magician ; a witch-doctor or excorciser ; যাদু, কুহক ; তুক, গুণ ; পিশাচাশ্রিত কাষ্ঠ, লোষ্ট্রাদি ; মায়াবী ; ভূতের ওজা। ***Verb t.*** To give medicine to ; to heal with medicine ; ঔষধ প্রদান করা ; ঔষধ দ্বারা আরোগ্য করা। **Medicine-chest**—ঔষধ-মঞ্জুষা।

mĕd'-i-cō, *n.* (*pl.* -cos.) Doctor ; চিকিৎসক, ভিষক্, বৈদ্য।

mĕd'-i-cō-lē'-găl, *adj.* চিকিৎসা-শাস্ত্রের তথ্যসমূহের সহিত অন্বিত আইন-সম্বন্ধীয়।

mē-di-ē'-văl, *adj.* See MEDIAEVAL.

mē'-di-ō-cre (-kĕr), *adj.* Of middling quality ; neither bad nor good ; indifferent ; as, a very *mediocre* poet ; মধ্যমরকমের, মাঝামাঝি, একরূপ, চলনসই ; একরকম। **—oc'-ri-ty,** *n.* **1.** A middle state or condition ; a moderate degree or rate ; মধ্যাবস্থা ; মাঝারি রকম, চলনসই রকম, মাঝারি গোছের। **2.** A person of middling talents or abilities ; "*Mediocrities* and respectabilities of every description" ; সাধারণগুণসম্পন্ন ব্যক্তি, বিশেষ প্রতিভাশূন্য ব্যক্তি।

mĕd'-i-tāte, *v. i.* & *t.* To dwell on anything especially religious in thought ; to cogitate, (with, *on, upon*) ; ধ্যান করা, তদ্গতচিত্তে চিন্তা করা ; অনুধ্যান করা। ***Verb t.*** To plan mentally ; to design ; as, to *meditate* war ; to think on ; সংকল্প করা ; কল্পনা করা ; চিন্তা করা। **—tat-ed,** *p.p.* Thought on ; planned on ; বিচিন্তিত ; সংকল্পিত, পরিকল্পিত। **—ta'-tion,** *n.* Serious contemplation ; close or continued thought ; reflection ; ধ্যান ; নিদিধ্যাসন (এভেলন) ; বিচিন্তন, সমাধান (হিঃ কোঃ)। **—ta-tive,** *adj.* Given to meditation ; expressing design ; ধ্যানগম্ভীর, ধ্যানপর, সমাহিত, ধ্যানপরায়ণ, ধ্যানশীল, ধ্যানতৎপর, ধ্যাননিষ্ঠ ; অভিসন্ধিসূচক। **—ta-tive-ly,** *adv.* **—ta-tive-ness,** *n.* **—tor,** *n.*

mĕd'-i-tĕr-ra'-nē-ăn (-ā-), *adj.* & *n.* **1.** Surrounded by, or in the midst of land ; (of land) remote from the coast ; ভূবলয়িত, ভূমধ্য ; (ভূমি-সম্বন্ধে) উপকূল হইতে দূরবর্ত্তী, মধ্যদেশীয়। **2.** (Of water surfaces) land-locked ; ভূবেষ্টিত। ***Noun.*** (*Cap.*) (Also *the Mediterranean Sea*) The sea separating Europe from Africa ; ভূমধ্যসাগর, ধরণী-মধ্যসাগর (রবীঃ)। **Mediterranean Sea**—See MEDITERRANEAN, *n.*

mē'-di-ŭm, *n.* & *adj.* (*pl.*-UMS.) **1.** That which lies in the middle ; the middle condition, degree, quality, etc. (*between* extremes); মধ্যবর্ত্তী বস্তু ; মধ্যাবস্থা, মধ্যমাত্রা, মধ্যস্থতা, মধ্যবৃত্তিতা (হিঃ কোঃ), মধ্যমপরিমাণ। **2.** A substance through which a force acts or an effect is transmitted ; as, air is the common *medium* of sound ; যে পদার্থের ভিতর দিয়া কোন বল ক্রিয়া করিয়া থাকে অথবা কোন ক্রিয়া সঞ্চারিত হয়, মধ্যস্থ (সাঃ পঃ), মধ্যগ (ঐ), ঘটক (ঐ), আকাশ (ঐ)। **3.** (*Fig.*) One's environment ; "The *medium* in which he (Burns) lived" ; (লক্ষণায়) প্রতিবেশ, পারিপার্শ্বিক অবস্থা, আবহাওয়া। **4.** An intermediate agency ; means ; "The Gazette is the best advertising *medium* in the country" ; instrumentality ; মধ্যবর্ত্তী কার্য্যকারক ; উপায়, দ্বার, পথ, মার্গ, বাহন, সাধন, নিমিত্তকত্ব, সাধকত্ব, কর্ত্তৃত্ব, কারকত্ব। **5.** A liquid vehicle with which pigments are mixed, *e. g.* oil, water ; যে তরল পদার্থের সাহায্যে রঞ্জকপদার্থ প্রভৃতি মিশ্রিত করা হয়, (যথা, তৈল, জল), আধানপদার্থ।

6. (In spiritualism) The person through whom spirits are said to make themselves seen or heard ; (প্রেত-তত্ত্ব) যে ব্যক্তিকে আশ্রয় করিয়া প্রেতাত্মা দর্শন দেয় বা কথা কহে, মাধ্যমিক। *Adj.* Intermediate between two degrees or amounts ; average : moderate ; as, *medium* size : *medium* strength : মধ্যবর্ত্তী; মাঝারি, পরিমিত। **–ism,** *n.* The practices of a spiritualistic medium ; মাধ্যমিকতা। **–ize,** *v. t.* To make a spiritualistic medium ; মাধ্যমিক করা। **Circulating medium**—টাকা, কড়ি, নোট প্রভৃতি। **Medium-sized**—মাঝারি, মধ্যায়তন। **Medium of exchange**—টাকা, নোট, বিনিময়হেতু।

mĕd'-lar (-lĕr), A fruit tree ; its fruit resembling an apple, and eaten when decayed ; একপ্রকার ফল বৃক্ষ ; ঐ বৃক্ষের ফল। [(হিন্দী) কোল]।

mĕd-ley (-lĭ), *n., adj.* & *v. t.* 1. heterogeneous mixture ; a jumble : এলোমেলোভাবে মিশ্রিত দ্রব্য ; খিচুড়ী 2. A mixed company ; নানাজাতীয় লোকের সংমিশ্রণ। 2. A mixed literary collection ; পঞ্চশস্য, পঞ্চমেল। *Adj.* Mixed ; motley ; mingled ; মিশ্র ; রং বেরংয়ের ; মিশ্রিত। *Verb t.* To make a medley of ; to mingle or intermix ; খিচুড়ী পাকান ; এলোমেলোভাবে মিশান।

Mĕ-dŏc', *n.* A kind of claret (red wine) from Medoc, a district in S.-W. France; ফরাসী দেশের দক্ষিণাঞ্চলস্থ ম্যাডক নামক স্থান হইতে সমানীত একপ্রকার লোহিতবর্ণ মদিরা।

medulla, (*L.*), *n.* 1. The marrow in the cavities of bones ; the spinal marrow ; মজ্জা; মেরুদণ্ডের মজ্জা, মেরু মজ্জা। 2. The inner substance of some organs, especially the kidney ; কোন কোন দৈহিকযন্ত্রের মধ্যস্থিত অংশ, বিশেষতঃ মূত্রাশয়ের মধ্যস্থিত পদার্থ। 3. The pith of mammalian hair ; স্তন্যদায়িজন্তুর রোমের অভ্যন্তরস্থ সারভাগ। 4. The pith of plants ; বৃক্ষের মজ্জা (মাইজ)। 5. Same as MEDULLA OBLONGATA. **Medulla oblongata** — গ্রীবাপৃষ্ঠের অভ্যন্তরস্থ মস্তিষ্কের অংশ, দীর্ঘীভূত মজ্জা (হঃ চঃ). অধিপতি (বিনয়ঃ), সহস্রদল পদ্ম (বামনঃ)।

mĕd'-ŭl-lă-rȳ, *adj.* 1. Pertaining to, consisting of, or resembling marrow or medulla oblongata ; মজ্জাসম্বন্ধীয়, মেরুমজ্জাসম্বন্ধীয়, দীর্ঘীভূত মজ্জাসম্বন্ধীয়, মজ্জাসদৃশ, মজ্জাময়। 2. Filled with spongy pith ; pithy ; শোষকবৎ মজ্জাপূর্ণ ; মজ্জাময়। **Medullary substance** — মস্তিষ্কের প্রধান অংশীভূত শ্বেতবর্ণ পদার্থ।

Mĕ-dū'-să, *n.* 1. (*Gr. Myth.*) One of the Gorgons, who had serpents for hair and turned lookers-on into stone ; (গ্রীকপুরাণ) গর্গন নাম্নী ফণি কুন্তলা দানবীত্রয়ের প্রধানতমা—ইহার করালবদনের পানে দৃষ্টিপাতমাত্র লোক পাষাণে পরিণত হইত। Perseus, Medusaকে সংহার করেন। 2. (*l. c.*) A jellyfish ; (প্রাণি-বিদ্যা) সামুদ্রিক মৎস্য-বিশেষ। **–sal, –san,** *adjs.* (*Zool.*) Relating to, or of the nature of, medusa ; (জন্তুবিদ্যা) সামুদ্রিক মৎস্য-বিশেষ সম্বন্ধীয়।

meed (mēd), *n.* 1. (*Poet.*) Reward or prize ; (কবিতায়) পুরস্কার, পারিতোষিক। 2. The merited portion of praise, honour, etc. ; "The office...to which the nobility looked as their *meed* of honour" ; সম্মান, প্রশংসা প্রভৃতির যথাযোগ্য অংশ।

meek (mēk), *adj.* 1. Piously humble ; submissive ; বিনীত, বিনম্র, বিনয়াবনত; শিষ্ট, নম্র, শান্ত। 2. Submitting tamely to injury etc. ; easily cowed or imposed upon ; বশ্য, সুবশ্য, নম্রপ্রকৃতি, মৃদুস্বভাব, দীনচেতা, নম্রশীল ; ভীরুস্বভাব, আশুপ্রতারিত। 3. Characterized by mildness or patience ; as, a *meek* answer : a *meek* face ; বিনয়-নম্র, ধীর, সহনশীল। **Meek'-ly,** *adv.* Gently ; submissively; humbly ; মৃদুভাবে; নম্রভাবে; বিনীতভাবে। **Meek'-ness,** *n.* Forbearance ; humility ; submission ; সহিষ্ণুতা, সহনশীলতা ; বিনয়নম্রতা ; বশ্যতা। **As meek as Moses**—গোবেচারা।

meer'-schaum (mēr-shŭm), *n.* 1. Silicate of magnesia, used for tobacco pipes ; সিন্ধুফেন, সমুদ্রফেন সাগরফেন (আঃ বঃ)। 2. A tobacco-pipe made of this mineral ; সাগর ফেন হইতে প্রস্তুত ধূমপান-নল।

meet (mēt), *adj.* Fit ; suitable ; proper ; as, it is *meet* that you should do it ; উপযুক্ত, যোগ্য ; উপযোগী ; উচিত, সমুচিত, বিহিত, সমীচীন, সঙ্গত। **Meet'-ly,** *adv.* **Meet'-ness,** *n.* The quality of being meet ; ঔচিত্য, সমীচীনতা।

meet (mēt), *v. t.* & *i.* 1. To come face to face with (a person coming from the opposite direction) ; সাক্ষাৎকার হওয়া। 2. To encounter in conflict ; to oppose in battle or duel ; as, they *met* the enemy and defeated them ; প্রতিরোধার্থ সম্মুখীন হওয়া ; যুদ্ধ বা দ্বন্দ্বযুদ্ধে সম্মুখীন হওয়া। 3. To come to be in company with ; to go to a place to receive a person, train, etc. ; as, to *meet* friends at a party : to *meet* a train at a junction ; সম্মিলিত হওয়া ; কোন ব্যক্তির সম্বর্দ্ধনা উপলক্ষে বা গাড়ী প্রভৃতি ধরিবার জন্য কোন স্থানে গমন করা। 4. (Of line, road, etc.) To join or intersect (another line etc.) ; যোগ করা, ছেদন করা। 5. To come by accident, or design into the company of ; ঘটনাক্রমে বা অভিসন্ধিপূর্ব্বক আসিয়া মিলিত হওয়া। 6. To experience ; to grapple with, (evils etc.) ; as, the eye *met* a horrid sight : to *meet* danger bravely ; অনুভব করা, ভোগ করা ; সংগ্রামকরা। 7. To satisfy or answer as a demand ; to come into conformity with ; to gratify, (a person, one's wishes) ; পূরণ করা, সন্তুষ্ট করা ; অনুসারী হওয়া ; চরিতার্থ

করা। 8. To pay (bill) at maturity; to discharge as a debt; (হুণ্ডীর টাকা) নির্দ্দিষ্ট তারিখে পরিশোধ করা; শোধ করা। *Verb i.* 1. To come together from different directions to join as lines; (of person) to come face to face; as, we *met* in the street; to come into contact বিভিন্নদিক হইতে আসিয়া মিলিত হওয়া; সংযুক্ত হওয়া; সামনাসামনি হওয়া, মুখোমুখী হওয়া; সম্মিলিত হওয়া। 2. To assemble together; to congregate; as, the Congress *meets* on the 27th Dec.; সম্মিলিত হওয়া অধিবেশন হওয়া। 3. To have an encounter; সম্মুখযুদ্ধ হওয়া। 4. (Of qualities) to unite in the same person; (গুণ সম্বন্ধে) একই ব্যক্তিতে সম্মিলন হওয়া। **To meet a person half-way**—To go half the distance between in order to meet (one); to come to compromise with; কাহারো সহিত মিলিত হওয়ার জন্য অর্দ্ধপথ যাওয়া; উভয় পক্ষে কিঞ্চিৎ ত্যাগ স্বীকার করিয়া মিটমাট করা। **To meet the eye or the ear**—To be visible or audible; দৃষ্টিগোচর হওয়া, দৃষ্টিপথবর্ত্তী হওয়া, দৃষ্টিপথারূঢ় হওয়া, নয়নগোচর হওয়া, নেত্রগোচর হওয়া, কর্ণগোচর হওয়া, শ্রুতিগোচর হওয়া, শ্রোত্রপথবর্ত্তী হওয়া, শ্রবণপথবর্ত্তী হওয়া, শ্রবণগোচর হওয়া। **To meet with**—To come across (a person, obstacles, etc.); দেখা সাক্ষাৎ হওয়া, সম্মুখীন হওয়া। To suffer unexpectedly; to experience; to undergo; as, to *meet with* a fall: to *meet with* a loss; অপ্রত্যাশিত ভাবে ভোগ করা; ভোগ করা; অধীন হওয়া। To encounter (*rare*); সম্মুখীন হওয়া।

meet (mēt), *n.* An assembling together of huntsmen and hounds for the hunt, or of men for athletic sport; মৃগয়ার্থ শিকারী ও কুক্কুরগণের সম্মিলন, মল্লক্রীড়ার্থ ব্যক্তিগণের সম্মিলন।

meet'-ing (mēt-), *n.* 1. Coming together; সম্মিলন। 2. An assembly; a public gathering; a convention; as, to address a *meeting*: the *meeting* of congress; সম্মিলন; সভা; সংসদ্। 3. A hostile encounter; a duel; যুদ্ধ; দ্বন্দ্বযুদ্ধ, দ্বৈরথ যুদ্ধ। 4. A junction; সংযোগ-স্থল। 5. An assembly for worship, (applied disparagingly to the assemblies of Dissenters); উপাসনাসভা। **Meeting-house**—উপাসনামণ্ডপ, (বিশেষতঃ) খৃষ্টীয় সম্প্রদায়-বিশেষের (Dissenter) উপাসনা মন্দির। **Meeting-place**—A place for meeting; সভাস্থলী।

mĕg-ă-cē-phăl'-ic, *adj.* Large headed; বৃহদ্‌মুণ্ডী, বিপুলশিরস্ক, মহাশিরা, মহামৌলি।

mĕg'-ă-lith, *n.* A large stone, especially one used as monument; বিশাল পাষাণ খণ্ড, বিশেষতঃ স্মৃতিস্তম্ভরূপে ব্যবহৃত পাষাণ খণ্ড। **-lith'-ic,** *adj.* Of, relating to, or made of, megaliths, (applied especially to ancient buildings or their remains); বিশাল প্রস্তরখণ্ডসম্পর্কীয়, বিশাল পাষাণখণ্ড বিনির্ম্মিত।

mĕg-ă-lō-mā'-ni-ă, *n.* Insanity of self-exaltation; a passion for doing great or grand things; গৌরবোন্মাদ, প্রতিষ্ঠোন্মাদ; মহৎকার্য্য সম্পাদনের জন্য উন্মাদনা।

Megalosaurus.

mĕg-ă-lō-sau'-rŭs (-sä-), *n.* A gigantic oolitic reptile of the dinosauria; অধুনালুপ্ত গোধা বিশেষ।

mĕg'-ă-phōne, *n.* An instrument for carrying sound a long distance; বহুদূরবর্ত্তী স্থানে শব্দবহনার্থ যন্ত্রবিশেষ, শব্দবাহকযন্ত্র [এই যন্ত্রের সাহায্যে

Megaphone.

শব্দ কয়েক মাইল দূরে নীত হয়। [Edison এই যন্ত্রের উদ্ভাবন কর্ত্তা।]

Mĕg'-ă-pŏd, -pode (-pōd), *n.* A genus of large-footed mound-

Megapode.

building birds; একজাতীয় বৃহৎপদবিশিষ্ট স্তূপনির্ম্মাণকারী পক্ষী।

mĕg'-ă-scōpe, *n.* A kind of magic-lantern; একপ্রকার যাদুপ্রদীপ। **-scop-ic,** *adj.* Visible to the naked eye; দূরবীক্ষণাদির সাহায্য ব্যতিরেকে দৃশ্য।

mĕ-găss', *n.* The residue after expression of sugar from cane; ইক্ষু নিষ্পেষিত করার পর যে ছিবড়া অবশিষ্ট থাকে, আকের ছিবড়া।

Megara, *n.* Wife of Heracles; হার্কিউলিসের পত্নী।

mĕg-ă-thē'-ri-ŭm, *n.* An extinct genus of huge herbivorous sloth-like animals ; অধুনালুপ্ত একজাতীয় তৃণভোজী বিপুলকায় জন্তু ।

mē-gĭlp', *n.* A gelatinous preparation usually of linseed oil and turpentine, used as a vehicle for oil-colours ; তৈলচিত্রের রং গুলিবার জন্য সাধারণতঃ তার্পিন ও তিসির তৈলের সংমিশ্রণে প্রস্তুত আধান দ্রব্য বিশেষ ।

mē'-grim, *n.* **1.** A severe headache usually on one side only ; আধকপালে মাথা ধরা, অর্দ্ধশিরঃশূল, অর্দ্ধশিরঃপীড়া, অর্দ্ধমস্তকশূল। **2.** A fancy ; a whim ; a freak ; সখ ; খেয়াল ; মর্জ্জি । **3.** (*Pl.*) Lowness of spirits ; vapours ; মানসিক অবসাদ, চিত্তগ্লানি ; একপ্রকার স্নায়বিক রোগ যাহাতে নানারূপ অস্পষ্ট মূর্ত্তি চোখের সামনে ভাসিতে থাকে। **4.** (*Pl.*) Staggers ; অশ্বাদির মস্তিষ্ক ও কশেরুকার রোগ বিশেষ ।

mei-ō'-sis (mī-), *n.* A rhetorical figure representing a thing less than it is ; litotes ; ন্যূনালঙ্কার, ন্যূনীকরণালঙ্কার ; বিরুদ্ধনিষেধকসমর্থন ।

Melampus, *n.* Son of Amythaon and brother of Bias ; Amythaonএর পুত্র এবং Biasএর ভ্রাতা । ইনি গ্রীসদেশে সুরাদেবতা Dionysusএর পূজা প্রবর্ত্তন করেন। ইনি গ্রীসদেশের আদি বৈদ্য এবং ভবিষ্যদ্বক্তৃরূপে প্রখ্যাত ।

mĕl-ăn-chō'-li-ă, *n.* (*Med.*) An emotional mental disease marked by extreme depression of spirits, ill-grounded fears etc. ; অবসাদ, উৎসাহ-শূন্যতা, অকারণভয়, প্রভৃতি লক্ষণাক্রান্ত মানসিক রোগ বিশেষ, বিষাদরোগ, বিষাদ, বিষাদ বায়ু ।

mĕl'-ăn-chō-lȳ, *n.* & *adj.* **1.** Continued depression of spirits ; gloominess ; নিত্যবিষণ্ণতা ; নির্ব্বেদ, মালিন্য, ম্লানিমা। **2.** Pensive sadness ; বিষাদ। ***Adj.*** **1.** (Of persons) Continually sad ; gloomy ; dejected ; সদাবিষণ্ণ ; বিষণ্ণ, বিরস, বিমর্ষ ; ম্লান। **2.** (Of things) Saddening ; depressing ; afflictive ; বিষাদজনক ; অবসাদজনক, চিত্তগ্লানিক : কষ্টজনক। **—chol'-ic,** *adj.* Given to, or liable to, melancholy ; depressed ; dejected ; বিষাদপ্রবণ ; দীনমনাঃ ; বিমর্ষ।

melange, (*F*) *n.* A mixture ; a medley ; মিশ্র ; খিচুড়ি।

Melanippe, *n.* Daughter of Chiron ; Chironএর কন্যা। Artemis ইহার প্রার্থনানুসারে বড়বারূপে পরিণত করিয়া ইহাকে নক্ষত্রপুঞ্জ মধ্যে সন্নিবিষ্ট করেন।

mĕl'-ă-nĭsm, *n.* Darkness of colour resulting from an abnormal development of black pigment in epidermis, hair, etc. (opp. of *albinism*) ; কেশ, ত্বক্ প্রভৃতির কৃষ্ণবর্ণ রঞ্জক পদার্থের অস্বাভাবিক বৃদ্ধি হেতু চর্ম্মের কৃষ্ণতা, কৃষ্ণ-চর্ম্মরোগ।

mĕl-ă-nŏch'-rō-ī, *n.* (*Anthrop*). A class of men with dark hair and pale complexion ; (Gr. *melas*=black & *khroa*=skin) ; একজাতীয় মানব যাহাদের কেশ কৃষ্ণবর্ণ ও মুখ পাণ্ডুবর্ণ।

mĕl-ă-nō'-sis, *n.* **1.** The morbid deposit of black matters in the tissues ; শরীরের বিধানতন্ত্র সমূহে রোগজনক কৃষ্ণবর্ণ পদার্থ সঞ্চয় । **2.** A black cancer; কৃষ্ণার্ব্বুদ। **—not'-ic,** *adj.*

melee, (*F*) *n.* **1.** A confused fight ; a skirmish ; হাঙ্গামা ; সংকুলযুদ্ধ। **2.** A lively debate ; প্রবল বাদানুবাদ।

mĕl'-ic, *adj.* (Of poem) Designed or meant to be sung ; গাহিবার জন্য অভিপ্রেত, গেয়।

mĕl'-ĭ-nīte, *n.* **1.** A kind of explosive invented in France ; ফরাসীদেশে উদ্ভাবিত একপ্রকার বিস্ফোরক পদার্থ। **2.** A yellow clayey material ; একপ্রকার পীতবর্ণ মৃন্ময় পদার্থ।

mĕl'-io-rāte (-yŏ), *v. t.* & *i.* To improve ; to make better ; উন্নতি সাধন করা ; উৎকর্ষ সম্পাদন করা। ***Verb i.*** To grow better ; উন্নততর হওয়া। **—rism,** *n.* The doctrine that the world may be improved by human efforts ; মানবের চেষ্টা দ্বারা পৃথিবীর উৎকর্ষ সম্পাদন করা যাইতে পারে—এইরূপ মতবাদ, উন্নতিবাদ (হিঃ কোঃ)। **—rist,** *n.*

mĕl-lĭf'-ĕr-ous (-ŭs), *adj.* Producing or bearing honey ; মধুপ্রদ, মধূৎপাদক, মধুজনক, মধূৎপাদী, মধুবহ।

mĕl-lĭf'-lū-ous (-ŭs), *adj.* Sweet as honey ; as, a *mellifluous* voice ; মধুর, মধুময়, সুমিষ্ট, শ্রুতিমধুর, মধুরাক্ষর। **—ence,** *n.* **—ent,** *adj.* Flowing as with honey ; মধুস্রাবী।

mĕl'-low (lō), *adj., v. t.* & *i.* **1.** Soft with ripeness ; as, a *mellow* apple ; পক্কতা হেতু কোমল। **2.** Well-matured, as, a vine ; সুপক্ক, সুপরিপক্ক। **3.** Not hard or rigid ; as a *mellow* soil ; কোমল, দোঁয়াস। **4.** Softened by age or experience ; as, a *mellow* character ; বার্দ্ধক্য বা অভিজ্ঞতা হেতু কোমল। **5.** Not harsh ; rich ; delicate ; (of sound, colour, light) ; মধুরকোমল ; সমুজ্জ্বল ; সুকুমার, মেদুর। **6.** Genial ; jovial ; সদালাপী, মিশুক ; সদানন্দ, উল্লাসময়। **7.** Partly intoxicated ; আধ মাতাল। ***Verb t. & i.*** To make or become mellow ; পাকান, সুপক্ক করা, সুপক্ক হওয়া। **—ly,** *adv.* **—ness,** *n.*

mē-lō'-dē-ŏn, —dĭ-ŏn, —dĭ-ŭm, *ns.* A kind of American organ ; an accordion ; আমেরিকাদেশীয় বাদ্যযন্ত্র বিশেষ ; বাজা।

mē-lō'-dĭ-ous (-ŭs), *adj.* Containing or characterized by melody ; sweet-sounding ; তানলয়-বিশুদ্ধ, মধুর, সুস্বর ; শ্রোত্রসুখকর, সুশ্রাব্য, মঞ্জুস্বন, শ্রুতিসুখকর, শ্রুতিমধুর, কল, সুখশ্রাব্য, মঞ্জুল, শ্রবণসুভগ, শ্রবণাভিরাম, শ্রোত্রমনোহর। **—ly,** *adv.* **—ness,** *n.*

mĕl′-ō-dist, *n.* A composer or singer of melodies ; শ্রুতিমধুর সঙ্গীতরচক, শ্রুতিমধুর সঙ্গীতগায়ক।

mĕl′-ō-dīze, *v. t.* & *i.* To compose or sing melodies ; শ্রুতিমধুর গান রচনা করা বা গাওয়া। ***Verb i.*** To make melodious ; শ্রুতিমধুর করা, সুশ্রাব্য করা।

mĕl-ō-drâ′-mȧ, *n.* **1.** A play of sensational nature with happy ending ; উত্তেজনাপূর্ণ মিলনান্ত নাটক। **2.** Language or behaviour suggestive of this ; ঐরূপ নাটকের উপযোগী ভাষা বা আচরণ। **3.** (Formerly) A drama with songs interspersed ; (পূর্ব্বে) গীতিনাট্য। **—dram′-a-tist,** *n.* **—dram′-a-tize,** *v. t.* **—mat′-ic,** *adj.* Relating to melodrama ; sensational ; উত্তেজনাপূর্ণ মিলনান্ত নাটকসম্বন্ধীয় ; উত্তেজনাপূর্ণ। **—mat′-i-cal-ly,** *adv.*

mĕl′-ō-dȳ, *n.* **1.** Sweet music ; সুতান, শ্রুতিমধুর গীত বাদ্য। **2.** Musical arrangement of words, especially in poetical composition ; শ্রুতিমধুর শব্দবিন্যাস, মধুরকোমলকান্ত পদবিন্যাস। **3.** An agreeable succession of single musical sounds ; শ্রুতিমধুরধ্বনিপ্রবাহ। **4.** The air or tune of a musical piece ; তান, মূর্চ্ছনা।

mĕl′-ŏn, *n.* A species of gourd ; তরমুজ। **Melon pumpkin**— মিষ্টকুমড়া, সফরিকুমড়া। **Musk-melon**— খরমুজ। **Sweet melon**—খরমুজ। **Water melon**—তরমুজ।

Melpomene, *n.* See MUSES.

mĕlt, *n.* **1.** A melted metal or other substance ; গালান ধাতু বা অন্য পদার্থ। **2.** The amount melted at a time ; একেবারে গালানো বস্তুর পরিমাণ। **On the melt**—In the process of melting ; দ্রবণ।

mĕlt, *v. i.* & *t.* **1.** To become liquefied by heat ; গালা, দ্রবীভূত হওয়া, বিদ্রাবিত হওয়া। **2.** To dissolve ; to disintegrate ; as, sugar *melts* in the mouth ; মিলাইয়া যাওয়া ; বিশ্লিষ্ট করা। **3.** (*Colloq.* — of a person) To suffer extreme heat ; (চলিত ভাষায়—কোন ব্যক্তি সম্পর্কে) উত্তাপে দগ্ধীভূত হওয়া। **4.** (Of cloud) To break into rain ; (মেঘ সম্পর্কে) বৃষ্টিধারা বর্ষিত হওয়া। **5.** To disappear or vanish, (with *away*) ; as, the clouds *melted* away ; অন্তর্হিত হওয়া, অদৃশ্য হওয়া, বিলীন হওয়া। **6.** To dwindle ; to waste away ; as, the resolution of the judges *melted* away ; হ্রাস হওয়া ; ক্ষয়প্রাপ্ত হওয়া। **7.** To become tender, mild or gentle ; "*Melting* with tenderness and mild compassion" ; কোমল হওয়া, দ্রবীভূত হওয়া। **8.** To be soft and liquid, as a sound ; শ্রুতিমধুর হওয়া, মধুরকোমল হওয়া, দ্রবময় হওয়া (see মাঃ মাঃ iii, 4.)। **9.** To pass imperceptibly *into* something else ; "Downs… that *melted* and faded *into* the sky" ; বিলীয়মান হওয়া। ***Verb t.*** To liquefy ; to dissolve ; as, to *melt* wax ; তরল করা ; দ্রব করা। **2.** To soften ; to render tender or gentle ; "Pity *melts* the mind to love" ; কোমল করা ; দ্রবীভূত করা। **3.** To cause to disappear, (with *away*) ; অদৃশ্য করা, বিলীন করা। **4.** To blend, as a colour or sound in or into another ; একটী অপরটীতে অননুভূতরূপে বিলীন করা। **Melt′-ing,** *p. adj.* & *n.* **1.** Dissolving ; গলিত। **2.** Tending to soften ; দ্রবণশীল। ***Noun.*** Act of dissolving ; দ্রবণ, দ্রাবণ, বিলয়ন, বিগালন, বিলায়ন। **Melt′-ing-ly,** *adv.* **Melting-pot**—ধাতু গালাইবার মুচী, মুষা, আবর্ত্তনী (আঃ বঃ)। **Melting point**—যে তাপাঙ্কে কঠিন বস্তু দ্রবীভূত হয়, দ্রবণাঙ্ক, গলনাঙ্ক। **To melt away**—See MELT, *v. i,* 5 & 6 & *v. t.* 3. **To put a question or subject into melting-pot**—To produce something for discussion ; কোন বিষয় আলোচনার জন্য উপস্থাপিত করা।

mĕm′-bĕr, *n.* **1.** (*Ant.*) A part or organ of the body, esp. a limb ; অঙ্গ, বিশেষতঃ হস্তপদাদি। **2.** A person belonging to an association, community, etc. ; সদস্য, সভাসদ, সভ্য। **3.** Any subordinate part of a building, order or composition, as a frieze, cornice or moulding ; অট্টালিকাদির অপ্রধান অংশ। **4.** (Short for) A member of parliament ; পার্লেমেণ্টের সদস্য। **5.** A part or branch of a political body ; কোন রাজনীতিক সমিতির শাখা বা অংশ। **6.** A part or clause of a sentence ; বাক্যাংশ। **7.** (*Math.*) Either of the two sides of an algebraic equation, connected by the sign of equality ; (গণিত-শাস্ত্র) সমীকরণের উভয়-পার্শ্বস্থ রাশির অন্যতর। **—less,** *adj.* **—ship,** *n.* **1.** The condition or status of a member of a society ; সভ্যত্ব, সভ্যপদ। **2.** The member or members in a particular body ; কোন সমিতি বা পরিষদের সভ্য বা সভ্যগণ।

mĕm′-brāne, *n.* **1.** A thin flexible texture in animal bodies or plants ; lining in an animal or vegetable body ; সূক্ষ্ম, কোমল জালবৎ ত্বক, অনুত্বক, ঝিল্লী ; জাল (সাঃ পঃ), জালক (ঐ)। **2.** A morbid formation in some diseases ; কোন কোন রোগে সঞ্জাত ঝিল্লী। **—bra-na′-ceous, —bra′-ne-ous, —bra-nous,** *adjs.* **False membrane** — উপজাত ঝিল্লী, কৃত্রিম ঝিল্লী। **Mucous membrane**—শ্লেষ্মা।

Memnon, *n.* In Greek legend, son of Eos ; (গ্রীকপুরাণ) উষাদেবীর পুত্র। ইনি ট্রয়ের যুদ্ধে Achilles কর্ত্তৃক নিহত হন। ইনি মিসররাজ Amenophis এর অভিন্ন বলিয়া বর্ণিত হইয়াছেন। ইহার সম্মানার্থ Thebes নগরীতে অতিকায় মূর্ত্তি সকল নির্ম্মিত হয় ; ইহার

একটী মূর্ত্তির মুখ হইতে প্রতি প্রভাতে প্রথম রবিকরস্পর্শে সুমধুর ধ্বনি নির্গত হইত।

mĕ-mĕn'-tō, *n.* (*Pl.* -TOES, -TOS) A hint, token, warning or memorial to awaken memory; a souvenir; স্মৃতিচিহ্ন; স্মারকচিহ্ন। **Memento mori**—(*L. Lit.* Remember, you must die) A warning or reminder of death; (*e. g.* a skull); (স্মরণ রাখিও তোমাকে মরিতে হইবে); মৃত্যুস্মারক কোন কিছু (যথা নরকপাল)।

mĕm'-ō, *n.* See MEMORANDUM.

mĕm'-oir (-ōyr, -wär), *n.* **1.** A written account of events; a history written from personal knowledge or memory; ঘটনা-বিবরণী; স্মরণলিপি, স্মৃতিরচনা; জীবন-স্মৃতি, চরিত। **2.** An autobiography; আত্মজীবনী, আত্মচরিত। **3.** A biography; জীবনী, জীবনচরিত। **4.** A record of investigations of any subject; কোন বিষয়ের গবেষণা-মূলক প্রবন্ধ; নিবন্ধ।

memorabilia, (*L*), *n.* (*Pl.*) Memorable things; স্মরণীয় বিষয়াবলী।

mĕm'-ō-ră-ble (-bl) *adj.* Deserving to be remembered; স্মরণীয়, স্মরণার্হ, স্মৃতিযোগ্য, স্মরণযোগ্য, স্মর্ত্তব্য। **—bil'-i-ty,** *n.* **—bly,** *adv.*

mĕm-ō-răn'-dŭm, *n.* (*Pl.* -DA, -DUMS.) **1.** A note to help the memory; স্মরণলিপি, স্মরণপত্র, স্মরণলেখ, স্মরণপত্রিকা, স্মারকলিপি। **2.** (*Law.*) A brief note of some transaction or the outline of an intended deed; (আইন) কোন ব্যাপারের সংক্ষিপ্তচুম্বক অথবা কোন দলীলের খসড়া। **3.** (*Diplomacy*) A summary of a question; justification of a course adopted; "The preparation of the Berlin *Memorandum*;" (কূটরাজনীতি) কোন প্রশ্নের সারমর্ম্ম; অবলম্বিত উপায়ের ন্যায্যতাপ্রতিপাদন। **4.** (*Commerce*) An informal letter without signature usually on paper headed '*memorandum*'; (বাণিজ্য) স্বাক্ষর বিহীন অরীতিসিদ্ধ পত্র, উপপত্র।

mĕ-mō'-ri-ăl, *adj.* & *n.* **1.** Serving to preserve memory; commemorative; as, a *memorial* building; স্মৃতিরক্ষাসাধক; স্মারক, স্মরণার্থক। **2.** Of, or relating to, memory; স্মৃতিসম্বন্ধীয়। ***Noun.*** That which preserves the memory of something; স্মারক বস্তু বা বিষয়, (যথা—প্রতিমূর্ত্তি, স্মৃতিস্তম্ভ, প্রভৃতি)। **2.** Chronicle (*usu. pl.*); ধারাবাহিক বৃত্তান্ত। **3.** A written representation; আবেদনপত্র, প্রার্থনাপত্র। **4.** (*Diplomacy*) Any of the various informal state papers; (কূটরাজনীতি) বিভিন্ন প্রকার অনিয়মিত রাষ্ট্রীয়কাগজ পত্রের কোন একটী। **—ist,** *n.* One who writes, signs, or presents a memorial; আবেদনকারী।

mĕ-mō'ri-ăl-īze, *v. t.* **1.** To commemorate; "To *memorialize* the five arches of the Pool of of Bethesda"; স্মৃতি চিরস্থায়ী করা, স্মৃতি জাগরূক রাখা। **2.** To present a memorial to; as, to *memorialize* a congress; আবেদনপত্র প্রদান করা।

Memoria technica, (*L*), *n.* A system or contrivance used to assist memory; স্মৃতিসহায়ক কৌশল বা ব্যবস্থা।

mĕm'-ō-rīze, *v. t.* (U. S.) To commit to memory; to record; "They neglect to *memorize* their conquest"; (মার্কিণ যুক্তরাজ্যে), মুখস্থ করা, কণ্ঠস্থ করা; স্মরণ রাখার উদ্দেশ্যে লিপিবদ্ধ করা।

mĕm'-ō-rȳ, *n.* **1.** Faculty of remembering; স্মৃতিশক্তি, স্মরণশক্তি, ধারণাশক্তি। **2.** Recollection; স্মৃতি, মেধা। **3.** Posthumous fame; as, his *memory* has been censured; মরণোত্তর খ্যাতি। **4.** The time within which past events can be, or are, remembered; as, within the *memory* of man; স্মরণকাল। **In memory of**—As a record of; in order to keep the memory of; স্মৃতিরক্ষার্থ; স্মরণার্থ।

mĕn'-ăce, *n.* **1.** A threat; ভীতি-প্রদর্শন, তর্জ্জন, ধমক, শাসানি। **2.** An impending evil; আসন্ন বিপদ্।

mĕn'-ăce, *v. t.* To threaten; as, to *menace* a country with war; ভয় প্রদর্শন করা। **—ac-ing,** *p. adj.* Threatening; ভীষণ, ভয়ঙ্কর, ভৈরব। **—ac-ing-ly,** *adv.*

menage, (*F.*), *n.* Domestic management; house-keeping; domestic establishment; গৃহস্থালী; গৃহকর্ম্ম, গৃহকার্য্য; পরিবার।

mĕ-năg'-êr-ie (-ĭ), *n.* **1.** A place where animals are kept esp. for exhibition; প্রদর্শনের জন্য যে স্থানে পশুদিগকে রাখা হয়, পশুবাটিকা। **2.** A collection of wild animals in cages etc.; প্রদর্শনার্থ সংগৃহীত পশুসমূহ, পশুসংগ্রহ, পশুপক্ষিসংগ্রহ।

mĕnd, *n.* Act of mending; a repaired place; as, there is a *mend* in his coat; মেরামত করণ, সারণ; সারা জায়গা। **On the mend**—আরোগ্যোন্মুখ, উন্নতির পথে অগ্রসর।

mĕnd, *v. t.* & *i.* **1.** To repair; as, to *mend* a road; মেরামত করা, সারান, জীর্ণসংস্কার করা। **2.** To correct; as, to *mend* one's ways; সংশোধন করা, শোধরান। **3.** To cut to regular shape; as, to *mend* a quill pen; (কলম প্রভৃতি) কাটা। **4.** To improve upon; "*Mend* the instance"; উৎকর্ষ সম্পাদন করা, সংস্কার করা। **5.** To quicken; as, *mend* your pace; দ্রুত করা। ***Verb i.*** To grow better; to improve; পূর্ব্বাপেক্ষা ভাল হওয়া; উৎকর্ষপ্রাপ্ত হওয়া। **To mend fire**—To add fuel to; অগ্নিতে ইন্ধন সংযোগ করা। **To mend or end**—To improve or abolish; হয় উৎকর্ষ সম্পাদন করা নয় বিলোপসাধন করা।

mĕn-dā'-cious (-shŭs), *adj.* Lying; as, a *mendacious* person; false;

as, a *mendacious* statement ; মিথ্যাবাদী, অনৃতভাষী, অসত্যভাষী ; মিথ্যা, অলীক । **—da'-cious-ly,** *adv.* **—dac'-i-ty,** *n.* Untruthfulness ; falsehood ; মিথ্যাবাদিত্ব, অনৃতবাদিত্ব, অনৃততা ; মিথ্যা কথা, মিথ্যাভাষণ ।

mĕn'-di-cănt, *adj.* & *n.* Begging ; as, *mendicant* friars (*i. e.* those living solely on alms) ; ভিক্ষোপজীবী, ভিক্ষাজীবী । ***Noun.*** A beggar ; ভিক্ষুক, পরিব্রাজক, শ্রমণ । **—can-cy, —dic'-i-ty,** *ns.* Begging ; ভৈক্ষ্য, ভিক্ষুকতা, ভিক্ষাবৃত্তি, যাজকবৃত্তি, ভিক্ষাটন, ভিক্ষাচর্য্যা ।

Mene maculta—চাঁদা (গুপ্তঃ) ।

mĕn-hā'-dĕn, *n.* A fish of the herring type ; একপ্রকার মৎস্য ।

mĕn'-hir (-ēr), *n.* An upright rough monumental stone; ঋজুভাবে প্রোথিত থরগাত্র স্মৃতিপ্রস্তর ।

mē'-ni-ăl, *adj.* & *n.* **1.** Low or servile as, service etc. ; নীচ । **2.** (*Contempt.*) ; Domestic, as a servant ; (অবজ্ঞাচ্ছলে) গৃহকার্য্যে নিযুক্ত ভৃত্য, চাকর, গৃহভৃত্য, ঘরচাকর, গৃহদাস । **—ly,** *adv.*

mē'-ninx, *n.* (Used in the *pl.*—MENINGES) Any of the three membranes enveloping brain and the spinal cord ; মস্তিষ্ক বা কশেরুকার আবরক ঝিল্লীত্রয়ের অন্যতম । **Men-in-gi'-tis** *n.* (*Med.*) ; Inflammation of the meninges ; মস্তিষ্ক ও কশেরুকার প্রদাহজনক উৎকট পীড়া, মস্তিষ্কঝিল্লীর প্রদাহ ।

mē-nis'-cŭs, *n.* **1.** A lens convex on one side and concave on the other ; যে কাচতালের এক পার্শ্ব মধ্যোন্নত ও অপর পার্শ্ব মধ্যানত । **2.** (*Math.*) A figure of crescent form ; (গণিত) অর্দ্ধচন্দ্রাকৃতি ক্ষেত্র । **—cate, —coid, Men-is-coi'-dal,** *adjs.* (*Bot.*) Resembling a meniscus in form ; (উদ্ভিদ্‌বিদ্যা) অর্দ্ধচন্দ্রাকৃতি ।

mē-nŏl'-ō-ġy̆, *n.* (*East Church*) A calendar with biographies of saints ; (গ্রীকধর্ম্মসঙ্ঘ) খৃষ্টীয় সিদ্ধপুরুষগণের জীবনীসম্বলিত পঞ্জিকা ।

mĕn'-ō-pause (-päz), (*Physiol.*) *n.* The period of natural cessation of menstruation, occurring usually between the ages of 45 and 50 ; (শারীর-বিজ্ঞান), রজোনিবৃত্তিকাল ।

mĕn-ŏr-rhoe'-ă (-rē-), *n.* Ordinary flow of the menses ; ঋতুস্রাব, রজোনির্গম ।

mĕn'-sēs, *n.* (*pl.*) The monthly discharge from the uterus ; ঋতু, স্ত্রীধর্ম্ম, নারীধর্ম্ম, আর্ত্তব, পুষ্প, কুসুম, রজঃ । **A woman in her menses**—ঋতুমতী, রজস্বলা, পুষ্পিণী ।

mĕn'-stru-ăl (-strô-), *adj.* **1.** Pertaining to the menses ; আর্ত্তব, স্ত্রীরজঃ সম্বন্ধীয় । **2.** (*Astron.*) Occurring once a month ; monthly ; (জ্যোতির্বিজ্ঞান) মাসিক ; প্রতিমাসিক **—ous,** *adj.* In menses ; ঋতুমতী, রজস্বলা, পুষ্পবতী, পুষ্পিণী, মলিনী, স্ত্রীধর্শ্মিণী, বৃষলী, আত্রেয়িকা, চাণ্ডালী (esp. of a woman in the first day of her menses), রজকী (a woman in the third day of her menses) (ভাব প্রঃ) ।

mĕn'-stru-āte (-strô-), *v. i.* To discharge the menses ; রজোনির্গত হওয়া, রজোস্রাব হওয়া । **—a'-tion,** *n.*

mĕn'-stru-ŭm (-strô-), *n.* (*pl.* -A) A solvent, (*lit.* & *fig.*); দ্রাবক পদার্থ, যে তরলপদার্থ দ্বারা কোন কঠিনপদার্থ দ্রবীভূত হয়, আবরণ, (ব্রজঃ হিন্দু), পুট (সাঃ পঃ) ।

mĕn'-sū-ră-ble (-bl), *adj.* **1.** Measurable ; having fixed limits ; পরিমেয়, প্রমেয়, মাপনীয়, মেয়, মাপনক্ষম ; সসীম । **2.** (*Mus.*) Having fixed rhythm ; নির্দ্দিষ্ট ছন্দোবদ্ধ ।

mĕn'-sū'-răl *adj.* **1.** Of, or pertaining to, measure; পরিমাণ-সম্বন্ধীয়, মানসম্বন্ধীয় । **2.** (*Mus.*) Same as MENSURABLE.

mĕn'-sū-rā'-tion, *n.* **1.** Act of measuring ; মাপন, পরিমাপ । **2.** (*Math.*) That branch of applied geometry giving the rules for finding lengths, areas and volume ; পরিমিতি, রেখাগণিত, ক্ষেত্রমিতি, ক্ষেত্রব্যবহার (লীলাঃ) ।

mĕn'-tăl, *adj.* Pertaining to the mind ; intellectual ; মানস, মনোময়, মানসিক, মনোজ ; চিত্তগত, মনোগত, চিদ্গত । **—ly,** *adv.* **—tal'-i-ty,** *n.* **1.** Mental power ; মানসিক শক্তি, ধীশক্তি । **2.** Mental cast or habit ; মানসপ্রকৃতি । **Mental alienation**—Insanity ; মানসিক বিকৃতি, উন্মাদরোগ। **Mental arithmetic** — মানসাঙ্ক । **Mental body**—মনোময়-কোষ, চিন্ময়-দেহ। **Mental-deficiency**—মস্তিষ্কের অসম্পূর্ণ পরিণতি। **Mental reservation**—See under RESERVATION. **Mental world**—মানসলোক ।

mĕn'-tăl, *adj.* Pertaining to the chin ; as, the *mental* nerve ; চিবুক-সম্বন্ধীয় ।

mĕn-tā'-tion, *n.* **1.** Mental function ; মানসিকবৃত্তি । **2.** State of mind ; মানসিক অবস্থা ।

Mentha sativa—পুদিনা (বেলঃ) ।

mĕn'-thŏl, *n.* A camphor-like substance got from the oil of peppermint ; পুদিনাসার [পুদিনার তৈল হইতে প্রস্তুত । দেখিতে কর্পূরের মত। ঘর্ষণে স্নায়ুমণ্ডলের বেদনা উপশম হয় ।]

mĕn'-tion, *n.* **1.** Naming, esp. incidentally (usu followed by *of*) ; as, to make *mention of* a thing ; উল্লেখ, উক্তি, নির্দ্দেশ । **2.** Short for HONOURABLE MENTION, (which see below). **Honourable mention**—প্রদর্শিত চিত্রাদির উৎকর্ষ এবং পরীক্ষায় অসাধারণ কৃতিত্বপ্রদর্শনের জন্য প্রদত্ত সম্মান, সসম্মান উল্লেখ ।

mĕn'-tion, *v. t.* To refer to ; to specify, esp. by name ; উল্লেখ করা ; নামোল্লেখ পূর্ব্বক নির্দ্দেশ করা । **Don't mention it**—ও কথা উল্লেখ করবেন না।

mĕn'-tŏr, *n.* An experienced and trusted adviser ; অভিজ্ঞ ও বিশ্বস্ত উপদেষ্টা [Ulyssesএর পুত্র যুবরাজ

Telemachus এর সুবিজ্ঞ উপদেশক Mentor এর নাম হইতে গৃহীত।]

měn′-u (-ōō), *n.* A list of the dishes of a banquet or meal; ভোজ্য-তালিকা।

Měph-is-tŏph′-ĕ-lēs, *n.* 1. The evil spirit to whom Faust sold his soul; যে দুষ্টাত্মার নিকট ফাষ্ট আত্মবিক্রয় করিয়াছিল। 2. (*Fig.*) A fiendish person; (লক্ষণায়) শয়তান। **–to-phe′-le-an, –to-phe′-li-an,** *adjs.*

mĕ-phī′-tis, *n.* A noxious or foul exhalation esp from the earth; a foul or poisonous stench; ভূমি হইতে উত্থিত পূতিগন্ধ; দুর্গন্ধ। **–phit′-ic,** *adj.*

mêr′-căn-tīle, *adj.* 1. Pertaining to trade; commercial; ব্যবসায়-সম্পর্কীয়, ব্যবসায়সংক্রান্ত, বাণিজ্য-সংক্রান্ত; সওদাগরী, আপণিক। 2. Mercenary; disposed for bargaining; "He is *mercantile*"; অর্থলোলুপ, অর্থপরবশ; দরকষাকষিতে অভ্যস্ত। **Mercantile theory**—অর্থই একমাত্র বিত্ত—এইরূপ মতবাদ। **Mercantile marine**—বাণিজ্যকার্য্যে নিযুক্ত পোত-সমূহ। **–til-ism, –til-ist,** *ns.*

mêr-cā′-tor (-têr), *n.* (See under PROJECTION).

mêr′-cĕ-nă-rȳ, *adj.* & *n.* 1. Working only for pay or reward; hired; বেতন বা পুরস্কারের জন্য কার্য্যকারী; ভাড়া করা। 2. Venal; moved by the love of money; as, a *mercenary* Judge; অর্থবশ, অর্থলোলুপ, ধনলুব্ধ; ধনলোভ-প্রণোদিত। ***Noun.*** A hired soldier; ভৃতক-সৈন্য, বেতনভোগী সৈন্য। **–ri-ness,** *n.*

mêr′-cĕr, *n.* 1. A dealer in textile fabrics, as silks and woollens; রেশমীবস্ত্র বিক্রেতা, কৌষেয়বিক্রয়ী, ঊর্ণাজীবী, কৌষেয়বণিক, দুকূলবিক্রয়ী। **–y,** *n.* A mercer's shop; রেশমী কাপড়ের দোকান।

mêr′-cĕr-īze, *v. t.* To treat (cotton fibre or fabrics) with a solution of caustic alkali for dyeing; (কার্পাসসূত্র বা বস্ত্র) রঞ্জিত করার জন্য দাহক্ষারজলদ্বারা অনুসিক্ত করা।

mêr′-chăn-dīse, *n.* The objects of commerce; wares; goods for sale; বাণিজ্যদ্রব্য; পণ্যদ্রব্য; বিক্রেয় জিনিষ।

mêr′-chănt, *n.* & *adj.* A wholesale trader, esp. with foreign countries; সওদাগর, সার্থবাহ, শ্রেষ্ঠী, ব্যবসায়ী, পণ্যাজীব, বণিক্। ***Adj.*** Commercial; as, a *merchant* city; বাণিজ্যসংক্রান্ত। **Merchantman, Merchant-ship** — বাণিজ্যপোত। **Merchant-prince** — A wealthy merchant; শ্রেষ্ঠিরাজ, পণ্যপতি। **Merchant-quarter**—শ্রেষ্ঠিচত্বর।

mêr′chănt-ă-ble (-bl), *adj.* Salable; marketable; বিক্রেয়; পণ্য।

mêr′-cĭ-fŭl, *adj.* Full of mercy; compassionate; humane; দয়ালু, সদয়, কৃপালু, কৃপাময়, করুণাময়, দয়াশীল, সকৃপ, কারুণিক, দয়াময়, দয়াবান, সকরুণ; সানুকম্প, কৃপাবীর (এভেলন); সহৃদয়। **–ly,** *adv.* In a merciful manner; সদয়ভাবে, অনুকম্পাপুরঃসর, সানুকম্প, দয়াপূর্ব্বক। **–ness,** *n.*

mêr′-cĭ-lĕss, *adj.* Showing no mercy; pitiless; নিষ্কৃপ, নির্ঘৃণ, নিষ্করুণ, নির্দ্দয়, অকরুণ; দয়াহীন, নিষ্ঠুর। **–ly,** *adv.* **–ness,** *n.*

mêr-cū′-ri-ăl, *adj.* & *n.* 1. Sprightly; ready-witted and volatile; fickle; উল্লাসময়; চপল, (cf. হে কৃষ্ণ! হে চপল!—কৃষ্ণকর্ণামৃত), তরল-প্রকৃতি, চঞ্চলপ্রকৃতি, প্রকৃতিতরল, অস্থির-মতি। 2. Relating to, or containing, mercury; পারদসম্বন্ধীয়, পারদগর্ভ, পারদাত্মক। 3. (*Cap.*) Of, or relating to, the planet Mercury; বুধগ্রহ, সম্বন্ধীয়। ***Noun.*** A preparation containing mercury; পারদমিশ্রিত ঔষধ। **–ism,** *n.* **–ize,** *v. t.* **–ly,** *adv.*

Mêr′-cū-ry, *n.* 1. The Roman god of eloquence, skill and thieving etc., messenger of gods; রোমীয়পুরাণোক্ত দেবলোকের বার্ত্তাবহ এবং বাগ্মিতা, চাতুর্য্য, চৌর্য্যবিদ্যা, প্রভৃতির অধিষ্ঠাতা দেবতা। 2. (*Astron.*) The planet nearest to the sun; (জ্যোতিবিজ্ঞান) বুধ, জ্ঞ (বৃঃ সং), সৌম্য (ঐ), শশিজ, রৌহিণেয়, তুঙ্গ, একাঙ্গ, শ্যামাঙ্গ, প্রহর্ষণ, পঞ্চার্চ্চিঃ। 3. (*Chem.*) (*l. c.*) Quicksilver; (রসায়ন-শাস্ত্র) পারদ, পারা, রস, চপল, সূত, রসরাজ, হরবীজ (তন্ত্র), মিশ্রক, সিদ্ধধাতু, রুদ্রজ, শিববীজ, যোগবাহী, দারদ, খলমূর্ত্তি, দেহদ, খেচর, অশোক, মুকুন্দ, মৃত্যুনাশক, রসনাথ, অমর। 4. (*l. c., facet.*) A carrier of tiding; a messenger; (কৌতুকচ্ছলে) সংবাদবাহক, সন্দেশহর; দূত। **–cu′-ric, –rous,** *adjs.* (*Chem.*) **Ash of mercury**—ভস্মসূত (রঃ রঃ সঃ প্রঃ)। **Black sulphide of mercury**—কজ্জলী। **Calx of mercury**—রসভস্ম। **Dead mercury** — মৃতসূতক (রঃ প্রঃ), নষ্টপিষ্ট (রঃ চূঃ প্রঃ)। **Fixation of mercury** — রসবন্ধন (রঃ রঃ সঃ প্রঃ)। **Killing of mercury** — পারদমারণ (রঃ রঃ সঃ প্রঃ)। **Mercuric bichloride** — রসপুষ্প (আয়ুঃ রসঃ)। **Perchloride of mercury**—রসপুষ্প (আয়ুঃ রসঃ)। **Pure mercury**—শুদ্ধসূত (রঃ রঃ সঃ প্রঃ), শোধিতরস (রঃ রঃ প্রঃ)। **Purification of mercury** — রসশোধন (সাঃ পঃ)। **Resublimate sulphide of mercury**—রসসিন্দুর, স্বর্ণসিন্দুর (আয়ুঃ রসঃ)। **Sublimate of mercury** — See SUBLIMATE. **Sulphate of mercury**—কজ্জলী। **Sulphide (red) of mercury**—স্বর্ণসিন্দুর (সাঃ পঃ), মকরধ্বজ (ঐ)।

mêr′-cȳ, *n.* 1. Disposition to pity and forgive, or spare; compassionateness; দয়া করুণা, কৃপা, ক্ষমা; অনুকম্পা, অভঃ (অর্থঃ), কারুণ্য (ভক্তি)। 2. A merciful act of God; a blessing; করুণার কার্য্য; কুশল, কল্যাণ। **An object of mercy**—কৃপাপাত্র, করুণার পাত্র। **At the mercy of**—Wholly in the power of ; কাহারও সম্পূর্ণ অধীনে। **Mercy-seat**—ইহুদীদের ধর্ম্মমন্দিরস্থ যে কাষ্ঠাধারে ধর্ম্মবিধিসমূহ রক্ষিত হয় তাহার স্বর্ণময় আচ্ছাদন। **Left to the tender mercies** — (*Facet.*) Exposed to probable rough handling by ; (রঙ্গচ্ছলে) কাহারো দ্বারা নিগৃহীত হইতে পারে—এরূপ অবস্থায় পরিত্যক্ত। **Mercy on me**—মাইরি। **Sisters of mercy** — রোগীর শুশ্রূষা ও দরিদ্রের সেবাকার্য্যে নিযুক্ত ধর্ম্মপ্রাণা নারীসম্প্রদায়, দয়াবতী ভগিনীসমাজ। **To cry mercy**—কৃপা ভিক্ষা করা, করুণা যাচ্ঞা করা।

mere (mër), *n.* **1.** A pool or lake ; সরসী, সরোবর, হ্রদ, জলাশয়। **2.** A marsh or fen ; বিল।

mere (mër), *adj.* Such and no more ; sole ; as, a *mere* child ; শুদ্ধ, কেবল, কেবলমাত্র, খালি ; একমাত্র। **—ly**, *adv.* Solely ; only ; কেবল, শুদ্ধ ; কেবলমাত্র। **Mere-right**—(আইন) দখল বিনা কেবলমাত্র স্বত্ব।

mĕr-ē-trī'-cious (-shŭs), *adj.* **1.** Pertaining to prostitutes ; libidinous ; বেশ্যাসম্বন্ধীয়, পণ্যাঙ্গনীয়, বারাঙ্গনীয় ; কামুক। **2.** (Of ornaments, literary style, etc.) ; Showily attractive ; "The style is gaudy and *meretricious*" ; কৃত্রিমশোভাময়, বাহ্যচাকচিক্যশালী, কৃত্রিমকারুকার্য্যময়, চটকদার। **—ly**, *adv.* **—ness**, *n.*

mêr-găn'-sêr, *n.* A diving fish-eating duck ; একপ্রকার হংস।

merge (mêrj), *v. t.* & *i.* **1.** To immerge ; to sink ; to absorb ; as, to *merge* a thing in another ; মগ্ন করা ; ডুবান, নিমজ্জিত করা ; লীন করা। **2.** (*Law*) To sink, as a title, interest, etc. in a greater one ; (আইন) উপাধি, স্বার্থ, প্রভৃতি, মহত্তর উপাধি প্রভৃতিতে বিলুপ্ত হওয়া। ***Verb i.*** To be sunk, swallowed or lost ; to be dissolved ; ডুবা, নিমজ্জিত হওয়া, লীন হওয়া, গ্রস্ত হওয়া ; মিলাইয়া যাওয়া।

mêr'-gence (-jĕns), *n.* Merging ; state of being merged ; নিমজ্জন ; নিমজ্জনাবস্থা।

mêrg'-êr, *n.* **1.** (*Law*) A merging or sinking of a title or estate in a greater one ; (আইন) কোন উপাধি বা সম্পত্তি বৃহত্তর সম্পত্তি বা উপাধিতে বিলয়ন। **2.** Same as MERGENCE.

mē-rĭd'-ĭ-ăn, *n.* & *adj.* **1.** (*Geog.*) An imaginary circle on the earth's surface passing through the poles and any given place ; as, the *meridian* of Greenwich ; (ভূগোল) যে সকল কল্পিত বৃত্তাকার রেখা মেরুদ্বয় ভেদপূর্ব্বক ভূগোলোকের চতুর্দ্দিকে ব্যাপ্ত আছে—তাহাদের অন্যতম, যাম্যোত্তর রেখা, মধ্যরেখা (সাঃ পঃ), যাম্যোত্তর (হিঃ কোঃ), বৃত্ত (ঐ)। **2.** (*Astron.*) A great circle of the celestial sphere passing through its poles and the zenith of a given place on the earth's surface ; (জ্যোতির্বিজ্ঞান) খগোলকের যে বৃহদ্বৃত্ত উহার উভয় মেরু ও ভূপৃষ্ঠের কোন নির্দ্দিষ্ট স্থানের খস্বস্তিক (zenith) অতিক্রম করিয়া ব্যাপ্ত থাকে, খগোলীয় যাম্যোত্তরবৃত্ত (হিঃ কোঃ), ধ্রুবপ্রোতবৃত্ত (সাঃ পঃ)। **3.** The point at which the sun or a star attains the highest altitude ; সূর্য্য বা নক্ষত্রের সর্ব্বোচ্চ উত্থান-বিন্দু। **4.** Hence, (*fig.*) the highest point ; the culmination ; prime ; as, the *meridian* of life ; (লক্ষণায়) সর্ব্বোচ্চসীমা ; পরাকাষ্ঠা ; পরমোৎকর্ষ। ***Adj.*** **1.** Of, or pertaining to, midday ; মাধ্যন্দিন, মাধ্যাহ্নিক। **2.** (*Fig.*) Of, or pertaining to, the culmination or highest point ; as, *meridian* splendour ; (লক্ষণায়) সর্ব্বোচ্চ, ঊর্দ্ধতম, উচ্চতম, পরম, চরম। **Calculated for the meridian of a place or people**—Calculated to suit the tastes etc. of a place or people ; কোন স্থান বা কোন জাতির রুচির উপযোগীকৃত। **First meridian**—প্রাথমিক দ্রাঘিমা (যাহা গ্রীণউইচ হইতে গণনা করা হয়)। **Meridian of a place**—স্বদেশ-রেখা, স্বরেখা। **Prime meridian**—ভূমধ্যরেখা (সাঃ পঃ), প্রধান যাম্যোত্তর-বৃত্ত, মধ্যরেখা (ঐ)।

mē-rĭd'-ĭ-ō-năl, *adj.* & *n.* **1.** Pertaining to a meridian ; যাম্যোত্তর-সম্বন্ধীয়। **2.** Southern ; দাক্ষিণাত্য, দক্ষিণদেশীয়, অবাচ্য। **3.** Of, or relating to, the South Europe or its inhabitants ; দক্ষিণইয়ুরোপ বা দক্ষিণইয়ুরোপের অধিবাসিগণ সম্পর্কীয়। ***Noun.*** An inhabitant of Southern Europe, esp. France ; দক্ষিণ-ইয়ুরোপের অধিবাসী, বিশেষতঃ ফরাসী দেশবাসী।

mē-ringue' (-răng), *n.* Confection of sugar and white of eggs etc. ; চিনি ও ডিম্বের শ্বেতভাগ প্রভৃতির সংমিশ্রণে প্রস্তুত মিষ্টদ্রব্যবিশেষ।

Merino sheep.

mē-rī'-nō (-rē-), *n.* **1.** A kind of Spanish sheep with fine wool ; (also *merino sheep*) ; স্পেনদেশীয় মেষবিশেষ। **2.** A fine woollen material originally made of merino-wool ; মেরুনা কাপড়। **3.** A fine woollen yarn ; একপ্রকার সূক্ষ্ম পশমী সূতা।

mĕr'-ĭt, *n.* & *v. t.* **1.** Quality of deserving well ; excellence ; worth ; as, a man of *merit* ; গুণ, সুকৃত, ধর্ম্ম (ব্রজঃ হিন্দু) ; উৎকর্ষ, গুণোৎকর্ষ, গুণপ্রকট, বিশিষ্টতা ; যোগ্যতা, পাত্রত্ব। **2.** (*Usu. pl.*) That which entitles one to reward or gratitude ; "His *merits*...laid up as a rich treasure" ; কৃতিত্ব। **3.** (*Law, pl.*) The intrinsic rights and wrongs of a case ; as, to judge a case on its *merits* ; (আইন) মোকদ্দমার দোষগুণ, কোন মোকদ্দমার মূল অবস্থা, কোন মোকদ্দমার ভাব ও মর্ম্ম। ***Verb t.*** To deserve (reward or punishment) ;

(দণ্ড বা পুরস্কারের) যোগ্য হওয়া, উপযুক্ত হওয়া। **In order of merit**—গুণানুসারে, যোগ্যতানুসারে। **To make a merit of**—To view, or represent as, meritorious, as one's own conduct ; প্রশংসনীয় বলিয়া দেখা বা প্রদর্শন করা। **To try a case on its merits**—মোকদ্দমার দোষগুণ বুঝিয়া বিচার করা।

mĕr-ĭ-tō'-rĭ-ous (-ŭs), *adj.* **1.** Deserving reward, honour or praise ; well-deserving ; পুরস্কারযোগ্য, সম্মানার্হ, প্রশংসার্হ, শ্লাঘ্য, গুণবান ; সুযোগ্য। **2.** (*Chiefly theol.*) Productive of merit ; "*Meritorious* observance" ; ধর্ম্মজনক, পুণ্যজনক। **—ly,** *adv.* **—ness,** *n.*

mêr'-lin, *n.* A small European falcon ; ইয়ুরোপমহাদেশীয় ক্ষুদ্র বাজপক্ষিবিশেষ।

mêr'-maid (-mād), *n.* A sea-woman having the head and body of a lovely woman to the waist ending in the tail of a fish ; শরীরের পূর্ব্বার্দ্ধ সুন্দরী রমণীর মত ও নিম্নার্দ্ধ মৎস্যবৎ, সাগর-নারী, জল-নারী, মৎস্য-নারী, মৎস্যাঙ্গনা, সাগরকুমারী, মৎস্যকুমারী, মৎস্যকন্যা।

Mermaid.

mêr'-măn, *n.* (Masculine of MERMAID) ; জলনর, জল-মানুষ, মৎস্য-পুরুষ।

mĕr'-ō-blăst, *n.* An ovum portion of which is directly germinal ; যে রজোডিম্ব অংশমাত্র সাক্ষাৎসম্বন্ধে শাবকের দেহ গঠনে প্রয়োজন হয়।

Mĕr-ō-vĭn'-gĭ-ăn, *adj.* & *n.* Pertaining to the first Frankish dynasty in Gaul or France founded by Clovis I ; প্রথম ক্লভিস-কর্ত্তৃক প্রতিষ্ঠিত গলদেশের প্রথম ফ্রাঙ্ক-রাজবংশসম্পর্কীয়। ***Noun.*** A king or member of this dynasty ; ঐ রাজবংশের রাজা বা ঐ রাজবংশীয় ব্যক্তি।

mĕr'-rĭ-mĕnt (-ĭ-), *n.* Mirthful enjoyment ; jollity ; noisy sport ; fun ; রঙ্গকৌতুক ; হাস্যপরিহাস, ক্রীড়াকৌতুক ; কোলাহলপূর্ণ ক্রীড়া ; মজা।

mĕr'-ry (-ĭ), *n.* A kind of black cherry ; একপ্রকার কৃষ্ণবর্ণ চেরী ফল।

mĕr'-ry (-ĭ), *adj.* **1.** Joyous, mirthful ; প্রফুল্ল, উল্লসিত, হৃষ্ট, সানন্দ, সোল্লাস, হৃষ্টমনাঃ ; সহর্ষ, মজাদার। **2.** Agreeable ; delightful ; as, the *merry* month of May ; রম্য ; রমণীয়, বিনোদক, মনোরম। **3.** Slightly tipsy ; "Mr. Verdon returning home pretty *merry*" ; অল্প মাতাল। **—ri-ly,** *adv.* Mirthfully ; in a merry manner ; সহর্ষে, সানন্দে ; সোল্লাসে। **—ri-ness,** *n.* **Merry-andrew**—ভাঁড়, বিদূষক, বৈহাসিক। **Merry-dancers**—মেরুজ্যোতিঃ, উদীচী উষা। **Merry England**—মনোরম ইংলণ্ড। **Merry-go-round**—বৃহৎ ছত্রের প্রান্ত হইতে লম্বিত কাষ্ঠময় অশ্বশ্রেণী—যাহার উপর চড়িয়া লোকে মেলায় ঘুরিয়া থাকে, নাগরদোলা। **Merry-making** — আনন্দোৎসব, আমোদোৎসব। **Merry-thought**—পক্ষীর কণ্ঠ ও বক্ষের মধ্যবর্ত্তী দ্বিশাখ অস্থি। (ক্রীড়াচ্ছলে এই অস্থির শাখা দুইটী ধরিয়া দুই ব্যক্তি সবলে টানিয়া থাকে—যাহার হাতের অস্থিশাখা ভাঙ্গিয়া যায় তাহার বিবাহ অগ্রে হইবে বলিয়া অনুমান করা হয়)। **The merry monarch**—২য় চার্লস। **To make merry**—To be festive ; আনন্দোৎসব করা, আমোদপ্রমোদ করা, আমোদ-আহ্লাদ করা। **To make merry over**—To make fun of ; কোন বিষয় লইয়া মজা বা কৌতুক করা।

mesalliance, (*F.*), *n.* Marriage with a person of inferior social position ; অপসম্বন্ধ।

mē-seems' (-sēmz), *v. i.* (*Archaic*) It seems to me ; (অপ্রঃ) আমার বোধ হয়, আমার মনে হয়।

mĕs-ĕm-brȳ-ăn'-thē-mŭm, *n.* A genus of succulent plants mostly belonging to South Africa ; এক জাতীয় রসপূর্ণ গুল্ম। **,৪-৭**

mĕs'-ĕn-têr-ȳ, *n.* A membrane in the cavity of the abdomen serving to retain the intestines and their appendages in a proper position ; উদরগহ্বরস্থ ঝিল্লীবিশেষ—যদ্দ্বারা অন্ত্রাদি যথাস্থানে অবস্থিত থাকে, মধ্যান্ত্র [উহা কটির কশেরুকায় নিবদ্ধ।] **—i'-tis,** *n.* (*Med.*) Inflammation of the mesentery ; (ভৈষজ্য-শাস্ত্র) মধ্যান্ত্রপ্রদাহ। **—ter'-ic,** *adj.*

mĕsh, *n.* **1.** The opening or space between the threads of a net ; জালের ছিদ্র, জালের ঘর। **2.** (*Pl.*) Network ; জালের কাজ, জালি, জালিকর্ম্ম। **3.** (*Fig.*) A snare ; as, to be caught in the *meshes* of law ; (লক্ষণায়) ফাঁদ, জাল। **4.** (*Pl.*) Interlaced structure in animal or vegetable bodies ; জীব বা উদ্ভিজ্জ দেহে জালবৎ ঝিল্লী প্রভৃতি। **In mesh** — (Of the teeth of wheels) Engaged ; (চক্রদন্ত সম্পর্কে) একের দন্ত অপরের দন্তে আবদ্ধ।

mĕsh, *v. t.* & *i.* **1.** (*Fig.*) To catch in a net ; (লক্ষণায়) জালে ফেলা। **2.** (*Fig.*) To entangle ; (লক্ষণায়) জালে জড়িত করা। ***Verb i.*** **1.** To become enmeshed ; জালে বদ্ধ হওয়া। **2.** (Of the teeth of wheels) To become engaged as with another piece of machinery ; (চক্রের দন্ত সম্বন্ধে) অপর যন্ত্রের অংশাদির সহিত বিজড়িত হওয়া।

mē'-sĭ-ăl, *adj.* Middle ; relating to, or directed towards, the middle line of a body ; মধ্য ; কোন বস্তুর মধ্যরেখাসম্বন্ধীয়, মধ্যরেখাভিমুখীন। **—ly,** *adv.*

mĕs'-mêr-ĭsm, *n.* **1.** Hypnotic state usually involving insensibility to pain and muscular rigidity, produced on a patient by the operator's influence over will and nervous system ; রোগীর ইচ্ছাশক্তি ও স্নায়ুমণ্ডলের উপর প্রভাব বিস্তার দ্বারা

উপজাত একপ্রকার যোগনিদ্রাবস্থা,—যাহাতে বেদনানুভব বিলুপ্ত হয় এবং শরীরের পেশীসমূহ দৃঢ় হইয়া উঠে। [এই প্রক্রিয়া অষ্ট্রিয়াদেশবাসী *Franz* (or *Friedrich-Anton*) *Mesmer* কর্তৃক ১৭৭২ খৃঃ অব্দে আবিষ্কৃত হয়।] মস্মরবিদ্যা, যোগনিদ্রা। 2. The doctrine concerning this; influence producing this; মেস্মরতত্ত্ব; যোগনিদ্রাজনকপ্রভাব। **—ist,** *n.* One who mesmerizes or believes in mesmerism. মেস্মরতত্ত্বজ্ঞ বা মেস্মরতত্ত্বে বিশ্বাসী ব্যক্তি। **—i-za'-tion,** *n.* **—ize,** *v. t.* To induce mesmerism; স্নায়ুমণ্ডলে বিকার জন্মাইয়া কৃত্রিম স্বপ্নাবস্থা উৎপাদন করা, যোগনিদ্রাবিষ্ট করা। **—mer'-ic,** *adj.*

mesne (mēn), *adj.* Intermediate; মধ্যবর্ত্তী, অন্তর্ব্বর্ত্তী, মধ্যস্থিত। **Mesne process**—মোকদ্দমা বিচারাধীন থাকার কালে যে সকল পরওয়ানা প্রভৃতি বাহির হয়। **Mesne profits**—ওয়াসিলাৎ।

mĕs'-ō-blăst, *n.* (*Physiol.*) The middle germ-layer of the embryo; (শারীর-বিজ্ঞান) আমগর্ভের অভ্যন্তরস্থ মধ্য জীবাঙ্কুর স্তর, মধ্য স্তর। **—blas'-tic,** *adj.*

mĕs'-ō-cârp, *n.* (*Bot.*) The middle of the three layers of a seed vessel; (উদ্ভিদ বিদ্যা) বীজকোষের স্তরত্রয়ের মধ্যবর্ত্তী স্তর, মধ্যফল (সাঃ পঃ)।

mĕs'-ō-dêrm, *n.* Same as MESOBLAST.

mĕs-ō-găs'-têr, *n.* A membrane attaching the stomach to the dorsal wall of the abdomen; যে ঝিল্লী দ্বারা পাকস্থলী উদরের পৃষ্ঠপ্রাচীরে সংলগ্ন থাকে।

mĕs-ō-lĭth'-ic, *adj.* Of, or relating to, the stone age between the palæolithic and the neolithic; প্রাচীন ও নব প্রস্তরযুগের মধ্যবর্ত্তী প্রস্তরযুগসম্বন্ধীয়। **Mesolithic-age**—কূর্ম্মযুগ (অভিঃ)।

mĕs'-ō-phȳll, *n.* (*Bot.*) The inner tissue of a leaf; (উদ্ভিদ বিদ্যা) পত্রের মধ্যাবধানতন্ত, পত্রান্তকলা (সাঃ পঃ)।

mĕs-ō-zō'-ic, *adj.* (*Geol.*) Of, or relating to, the second geological period; (ভূ-বিদ্যা) কূর্ম্মযুগ সম্বন্ধীয়। **Mesozoic age** — কূর্ম্মযুগ (অভিঃ)।

mĕss, *n.* **1.** A portion of liquid or soft food; তরল বা কোমল খাদ্যের অংশ। **2.** The food given to a beast at one time; পশুর একবারের খাদ্য। **3.** A disorderly mixture; medley; muddle; খিচুড়ি; এলোমেলোভাবে মিশ্রিত বস্তু; হ য ব র ল। **4.** Dirty or untidy state of things; বিশৃঙ্খলা, লণ্ডভণ্ড ব্যাপার। **5.** A number of persons who eat together; esp. a company of officers or men in the army or navy who take their meals together; একান্নমণ্ডলী, একপাকভোজী, একত্র ভোজনকারী, সহভোজিমণ্ডলী; বিশেষতঃ একান্নভোজী নৌ বা সামরিক বিভাগের কর্ম্মচারিমণ্ডলী। **6.** A meal so taken; as, to go to *mess*; সহভোজিব্যক্তিগণের ভোজন, গ্রাস। **Mess-jacket**—সহভোজিগণের পরিধেয় কোর্ত্তা। **Mess mate**—One of the same (*usu,* ship's) mess; সহভোজীব্যক্তিগণের অন্যতম, একান্ন (মঃ উঃ)। **To make a mess of**—To manage anything confusedly or clumsily; গোলযোগ পাকাইয়া তোলা, খিচুড়ি পাকান, গোলমাল করিয়া ফেলা।

mess, *v. t.* & *i.* **1.** To make a mess of; to make dirty or foul, as, a thing; গোলমাল করিয়া তোলা, গণ্ডগোল করা, ঘুলিয়ে দেওয়া; নোংরা করা। **2.** To supply with meals; "*Messing* me at his own table"; আহার প্রদান করা। ***Verb i.*** **1.** To eat together (with others), as in a mess; সহভোজন করা। **2.** To put thing in a disorderly state; বিশৃঙ্খলভাবে রাখা, এলোমেলো করিয়া রাখা। **3.** (*Slang*) To busy oneself in a untidy way; "Sydney was *messing away* at his nasty chemicals; (ইতর ভাষায়) নোংরা ভাবে করা। **To mess about**—To handle roughly; to confuse; রূঢ়ভাবে পীড়ন করা; বিভ্রান্ত করা।

mĕs'-săge, *n.* **1.** Oral or written communication from one person to another; সংবাদ, খবর, বার্ত্তা, সন্দেশ, সমাচার। **2.** A divinely inspired or revealed communication, as of a prophet; প্রত্যাদেশ, ভাববাণী, দেববাণী।

mĕs'-săge, *v. t.* **1.** To send, as a message; সংবাদপ্রদান করা। **2.** To transmit, as a sketch or plan by telegraphing etc.; নক্সা, রেখাচিত্র প্রভৃতি তাড়িত বার্ত্তাবহ প্রভৃতির সাহায্যে প্রেরণ করা।

mĕs'-sĕn-gĕr, *n.* **1.** One who bears a message; an official employed for carrying dispatches etc.; দূত, সংবাদবাহক, বার্ত্তাবহ, বার্ত্তাবাহক, অধ্বগ, সন্দেশহর, আজ্ঞপ্তিহর; সরকারী পত্রবাহক। **2.** (*Obs.*) A forerunner; (অপ্রঃ) অগ্রদূত। **3.** A person acting for the sheriff etc. in taking charge of the estate of the bankrupt; যে ব্যক্তি শেরিফের প্রতিনিধিরূপে দাউলিয়া ব্যক্তির সম্পত্তির ভার গ্রহণ করে। **4.** A cable used in weighing anchor; নোঙ্গর তোলার কার্য্যে ব্যবহৃত রজ্জু বিশেষ।

Mĕs-sī'-ah (-ă), *n.* **1.** The expected deliverer of the Jews; Christ the anointed; ইহুদীজাতির প্রত্যাশিত ত্রাণকর্ত্তা; অভিষিক্ত যীশুখৃষ্ট। **2.** A liberator of an oppressed people or country; প্রপীড়িত জাতি বা দেশের উদ্ধারকর্ত্তা। **—an'-ic,** *adj.* **—ship,** *n.*

Mĕs-si-dŏr', *n.* The tenth month of the French revolutionary calendar; ফরাসী বিপ্লবকারীদের পঞ্জিকার দশম মাস।

mĕs'-sieurs (-yĕrz), *n.* (*Abbr. Messrs*; *pl.* of MONSIEUR or MR.)

mĕs'-suage (-swāj), *n.* A dwelling house with adjacent building and land assigned to its use; বসতবাটী, ভদ্রাসনবাড়ী, বাস্তবাটী, গৃহবাটীকা।

mĕs-ti′-zō (-tē-), *n.* A Spanish or Portuguese half-caste; esp. offspring of a Spaniard or American Indian; আমেরিকার ফিরিঙ্গী বিশেষ; বিশেষতঃ স্পেনিয়ার্ড এবং আমেরিকার আদিমঅধিবাসীর সহযোগে জাত সন্তান।

mĕ-tăb′-ō-lă, *n.* (*Pl., Zool.*) The insects which undergo metamorphosis; রূপান্তরগ্রাহী পতঙ্গ।

mĕt-ă-bŏl′-ic, *adj.* (*Zool.* & *Biol.*) Of, or pertaining to, metamorphosis; changeable in form; (প্রাণি-বিদ্যা) রূপান্তরগ্রহণ-সম্বন্ধীয়; রূপান্তরগ্রহণীয়।

mĕ-tăb′-ō-lĭsm, *n.* **1.** (*Biol.*) The process by which nutritive material in a body is built up into living matter (*constructive metabolism*) or protoplasm is broken down into simpler substances (*destructive metabolism*); (জীববিজ্ঞান) দেহযন্ত্রের যে ক্রিয়ার ফলে দেহস্থ পুষ্টিজনক উপাদানসমূহ জৈবপদার্থে পরিণত হয় অথবা শরীরস্থ প্রাণপঙ্ক (protoplasm) বিশ্লিষ্ট হইয়া থাকে, পাক (ব্রজঃ হিন্দু), পরিণাম (সাঃ পঃ), গঠনভঞ্জন (ঐ), শরীরপরিবর্ত্ত (হিঃ কোঃ)। **2.** (*Zool.*) Complete metamorphosis; (জীববিজ্ঞান) পূর্ণ পরিবর্ত্তন (সাঃ পঃ), শরীরপরিবর্ত্তন (হিঃ কোঃ)। **—lize**, *v. t.*

mĕt-ă-căr′-pŭs, *n.* The part of the hand between the wrist and the fingers; অঙ্গুলী এবং মণিবন্ধের মধ্যবর্ত্তী হস্তের অংশ, করভ, পীলু, প্রপাণি।

mĕt′-ăge, *n.* Official measurement of coal; also the charge for it; সরকারী কর্ম্মচারী কর্ত্তৃক কয়লার মাপ; ঐরূপ মাপের জন্য দেয় টাকা।

mĕt-ă-gĕn′-ĕ-sis, *n.* A generation by the series of changes of individual form, through which certain animals pass from the egg to the perfect state; alternation of generation; ব্যক্তিগত আকৃতির পরিবর্ত্তন পরম্পরা দ্বারা জনন—যাহার ভিতর দিয়া কোন কোন প্রাণী ডিম্বাবস্থা হইতে পূর্ণাবস্থা প্রাপ্ত হয়; জননবিপর্য্যয়। **—ge-net′-ic**, *adj.*

mĕt′-ăl, *n.* & *v. t.* **1.** An elementary substance such as gold, silver etc. possessing a peculiar lustre, fusibility, etc.; ধাতু, লোহ (সাঃ পঃ), লোহক (ঐ)। **2.** A material used for making glass in molten state; কাচ প্রস্তুতের জন্য একপ্রকার দ্রবীভূত পদার্থ। **3.** (Also *road metal*) Stones broken small for roads; নুড়ি, খোয়া। ***Verb t.*** **1.** To cover or furnish with metals; as, to *metal* a ship's bottom; ধাতুর পাত দ্বারা মণ্ডিত বা আচ্ছাদিত করা। **2.** To mend as a road with metal; রাস্তা পাকা করা, খোয়া দ্বারা রাস্তা প্রভৃতি বাঁধা। **Base metals**—হীনধাতু (সাঃ পঃ), তাম্র, লৌহ, সীসক ও দস্তা। **Killing of metal**—জারণ (সাঃ পঃ)। **Noble or perfect metals** — সার লোহ (সাঃ পঃ), স্বর্ণ, রৌপ্য ও প্লাটিনাম, শ্রেষ্ঠধাতু। **Pure metal** — বিশুদ্ধ লোহ (সাঃ পঃ)। **Simple metal**—অকৃত্রিম লোহ (সাঃ পঃ)।

mĕ-tăl′-lic (-ĭc), *adj.* Of, or characteristic of, metals; as, *metallic* lustre or sound; ধাতব, ধাতু-সম্বন্ধীয়, ধাতুময়, ধাতুগুণক। **Metallic currency**—স্বর্ণ, রৌপ্য ও তাম্র মুদ্রা।

mĕ-tăl′-li-fórm (-ĭ-), *adj.* Having the form or properties of metals; ধাতুধর্ম্মা, ধাতুগুণক, ধাত্বাকৃতি।

mĕ-tăl′-li-fȳ (-ĭ-), *v. t.* To convert into metal; ধাতুতে পরিণত করা।

mĕt′-ăl-line (-ĭn-), *adj.* Consisting of, or containing, metal; as, *metalline* water; ধাতুময়, ধাতুগর্ভ

mĕt′-ăl-lize (-īz-), *v. t.* **1.** To make metallic; ধাতুগর্ভ করা, ধাতুময় করা। **2.** To vulcanize (rubber); গলিত গন্ধক মিশাইয়া রবর কঠিন করা। **—li-za′-tion**, *n.*

mĕt-ăl-log′-ră-phȳ (-ŏg-), *n.* The science of metals; ধাতুবিদ্যা, ধাতুবিজ্ঞান, ধাতুবিচার।

mĕt′-ăl-loid (-oyd), *adj.* & *n.* Having the form or appearance of metal; লোহাকৃতি, ধাতুবৎ। ***Noun.*** A non-metallic element; অধাতব পদার্থ।

mĕt′-ăl-lur-gȳ (-ĕr-), *n.* The art of working metals, esp. of separating metals from their ores by smelting; ধাতুক্রিয়া, ধাতুপ্রস্তুত-প্রক্রিয়া (আয়ুঃ রসঃ), ধাতুবিদ্যা, ধাতুশোধনবিদ্যা, ধাতুশোধন, ধাতুশোধনাদি-কলা, লোহশাস্ত্র (ব্রজঃ হিন্দু)। **—gist**, *n.* One skilled in, or practising, metallurgy; ধাতুবিদ্যাবিদ্, ধাতুবিদ্, ধাতুশোধক। **—lur′-gic, —lur′-gi-cal**, *adjs.* ধাতুসম্বন্ধী, ধাতুশোধনসম্বন্ধী।

mĕt′-ă-mere (-mēr), *n.* (*Zool.*) One of several similar segments of a body; (জন্তুবিদ্যা) দেহের অনুরূপ পর্ব্ব বা খণ্ড সমূহের অন্যতম।

mĕt-ă-mĕr′-ic, *adj.* **1.** (*Zool.*) Pertaining to a metamere; (জন্তুবিদ্যা) দেহের অনুরূপ পর্ব্ব বা খণ্ড সম্বন্ধীয়। **2.** (*Chem.*) Having the same chemical elements in the same proportion and atomic weight but different properties; (রসায়ন-শাস্ত্র) সমপারমাণবিক গুরুত্বসম্পন্ন একই মূলপদার্থ সমূহ সমানুপাতে বর্ত্তমান কিন্তু বিভিন্ন-ধর্ম্মক, বিধর্ম্মসবয়বিক (হিঃ কোঃ)।

mĕ-tăm′-ĕr-ĭsm, *n.* **1.** (*Zool.*) The state of being made of metameric sections; (জন্তুবিদ্যা) গ্রন্থিময়দেহত্ব। **2.** (*Chem.*) The state, or quality, of being metameric; (রসায়ন-শাস্ত্র) বিধর্ম্ম-সবয়বিকতা (হিঃ কোঃ)।

mĕt-ă-mŏr′-phic, *adj.* **1.** Of, or relating to, metamorphosis; changing the form or structure; variable; as, *metamorphic* action; পরিবর্ত্তনসম্বন্ধীয়; গঠনপ্রণালী পরিবর্ত্তক; পরিবর্ত্তনশীল। **2.** (*Geol.*) That has undergone transformation by natural agencies; (ভূ-বিদ্যা) নৈসর্গিক শক্তি সমূহ দ্বারা রূপান্তরিত। **—phism**, *n.*

mĕt-ă-mŏr′-phōse, *v. t.* 1. To change into a different form ; to transform ; "And earth was *metamorphosed* into man" ; রূপান্তরিত করা, আকারপরিবর্তন করা ; রূপপরিবর্তন করা। 2. To change the nature of ; প্রকৃতি পরিবর্তন করা।

mĕt-ă-mŏr′-phō-sis, *n.* 1. Change of form or shape ; transformation ; দেহান্তরাশ্রয় (জিঃ), শরীরপরিবৃত্তি (আঃ বঃ), রূপান্তর, আকারপরিবর্তন ; রূপভেদ, রূপপরিণাম, দেহান্তর, স্বরূপভেদ। 2. Changed form ; "I restore you to your old *metamorphosis*" ; পরিবর্তিত আকার, পরিবর্তিত রূপ। 3. Change of character, conditions, etc. ; প্রকৃতি পরিবর্তন, অবস্থান্তর।

mĕt′-ă-phor (-fẽr), *n.* 1. (*Rhet.*) A figure of speech in which a word or phrase literally denoting one thing is applied to another by way of suggesting a likeness ; (অলঙ্কারশাস্ত্র) রূপক, রূপকালঙ্কার, সারোপলক্ষণা (হিঃ কোঃ)। 2. An instance of this ; রূপকালঙ্কারের দৃষ্টান্ত। **—phor′-i-cal,** *adj.* **—phor′-i-cal-ly,** *adv.* **Mixed metaphor**—অসংলগ্ন রূপক সমূহের সংযোগ।

mĕt′-ă-phrāse, *n.* & *v. t.* A word-for-word translation ; কথায় কথায় অনুবাদ, আক্ষরিক অনুবাদ। ***Verb t.*** To put into other words ; অপর শব্দে প্রকাশ করা। **—phras′-tic,** *adj.*

mĕt-ă-phy̆s′-i-căl, *adj.* 1. Of, or relating to, metaphysics ; abstract or abstruse ; as, *metaphysical* reasoning ; অধ্যাত্মবিদ্যা-সম্বন্ধীয়, তত্ত্ববিজ্ঞানসম্বন্ধীয়, তত্ত্ববিদ্যা-সম্বন্ধীয় ; দুর্জ্ঞেয়, দুর্বোধ, জটিল। 2. Over-subtle ; too abstract ; "*Metaphysical* criticism" ; অতিসূক্ষ্ম ; অতিনিগূঢ়। 3. Incorporeal ; "That part of the pleasure is *metaphysical*" ; অশরীরী, চিন্ময়। 4. Preternatural or supernatural ; "Fate and *metaphysical* aid"; অলৌকিক, অতিপ্রাকৃত। 5. Imaginary ; as, *metaphysical* persons ; কাল্পনিক, কল্পনাপ্রসূত। **—ly,** *adv.* **Metaphysical idealism** — (দর্শনশাস্ত্র) এই বিশ্বসংসার মনেরই শরীরবদ্ধাবস্থা অথবা বাস্তবতা মূলতঃ জড়ধর্ম্মাক্রান্ত—এইরূপ মতবাদ।

mĕt-ă-phy̆s′-ics, *n.* 1. (*Pl.*) Theoretical philosophy of being and knowing ; তত্ত্ববিদ্যা, আত্মতত্ত্ববিদ্যা, আন্বীক্ষিকী, অধ্যাত্মবিদ্যা। 2. Philosophy of mind ; প্রজ্ঞানশাস্ত্র, মানসবিদ্যা। **—i-cal,** *adj.* Apertaining to metaphysics ; তত্ত্বজ্ঞান সম্বন্ধীয়। **—i-cize,** *v. t.* **—phy-si′-cian,** *n.* One versed in metaphysics ; তত্ত্ববিজ্ঞানবিৎ, আধ্যাত্মতত্ত্বজ্ঞ।

mĕt′-ă-plăsm, *n.* 1. (*Biol.*) That part of protoplasm that contains formative material ; (জীব বিজ্ঞান) প্রাণপঙ্কের যে ভাগে গঠনসাধক পদার্থ থাকে। 2. (*Gram.*) The change of a word by addition, removal or transposition of letters or syllables ; (ব্যাকরণ) শব্দ অথবা শব্দাংশের সংযোগ, বিয়োগ বা স্থান-বিপর্য্যয় দ্বারা কোন শব্দের পরিবর্তন।

mĕt-ă-pŏl′-i-tics, *n.* Theoretical political science, (*often contempt.*) ; ঔপপত্তিক রাজনীতি-বিজ্ঞান। **—po-lit′-i-cal,** *adj.* **—ti′-cian,** *n.*

mĕ-tăs′-tă-sis, *n.* 1. (*Physiol.* & *Med.*) Change in place of a disease, bodily function etc. ; শরীরের একস্থান হইতে অপর স্থানে রোগের সঞ্চার, স্থানবিকল্প (হিঃ কোঃ)। 2. (*Biol.*) Same as METABOLISM. **Met-a-stat′-ic,** *adj.*

mĕt-ă-târ′-sŭs, *n.* (*Anat.*) That part of the foot between the tarsus and the toes ; (শারীরসংস্থান বিদ্যা) গুল্ফ ও পদাঙ্গুলীর মধ্যবর্ত্তী স্থান। **—sal,** *adj.*

mĕ-tăth′-ĕ-sis, *n.* 1. (*Gram.*) Transposition, more especially of the letters, sounds or syllables of a word ; (ব্যাকরণ) বিপর্য্যয়, বিশেষতঃ কোন শব্দের অক্ষর, ধ্বনি বা শব্দাংশের বিপর্য্যয়, অক্ষর-বিপর্য্যয়, বর্ণব্যত্যয়। 2. (*Chem.*) Interchange of atoms between two molecules ; (রসায়নশাস্ত্র) অণুদ্বয়ের মধ্যে পরমাণু-বিপর্য্যয়।

metayage, (*F.*), *n.* The system of land tenure in which the farmer pays part (usu. half) of the produce as rent to the owner who furnishes stock and seed ; যে ব্যবস্থানুসারে কৃষক ভূস্বামীকে উৎপন্ন শস্যের অংশ (সাধারণতঃ অর্দ্ধেক) প্রদান করে এবং ভূস্বামী মূলধন ও বীজ প্রদান করেন।

metayer, (*F.*) *n.* A farmer who holds land on the metayage system ; যে কৃষক ভূস্বামীকে উৎপন্ন শস্যের অংশ (সাধারণতঃ অর্দ্ধেক) প্রদান করে, ভাগীদার (East Bengal)।

mete (mēt), *n.* Boundary, (*chiefly pl.*) ; as, in *metes* and bounds ; চতুঃসীমা।

mete (mēt), *v. t.* 1. (*Poet.*) To measure ; "By which his grace must *mete* the lives of others" ; (কবিতায়) পরিমাপ করা, পরিমাণ করা। 2. To distribute by measure, (often with *out*) ; as, to *mete out* reward or punishment ; ভাগ করিয়া দেওয়া, মাপিয়া দেওয়া। **Mete-wand, Mete-yard** — (লক্ষণায়) মানদণ্ড, গজকাঠি, মাপকাঠি। **To mete out**—See METE *v. t.* 2.

mĕt-ĕm-pir′-ic, (Also -ICS) *n.* 1. The philosophy of things that lie outside the sphere of knowledge derived from experience ; অতীন্দ্রিয় বিষয়াবলীসম্পর্কীয় দর্শন-শাস্ত্র। 2. A believer in this ; ইন্দ্রিয়াতীততত্ত্ববাদী। **—i-cal,** *adj.* **—i-cist,** *n.*

mĕ-temp-sy̆-chō′-sis (-tĕm-), *n.* Transmigration of the soul of a human being or an animal at death into another body of the same or different species ; পুনর্জন্ম,

দেহান্তরগমন, দেহান্তরাশ্রয়, জন্মান্তর, অন্যজন্ম, দেহান্তরপ্রাপ্তি। **—sist,** *n.*

mē'-tē-or (-êr), *n.* **1.** Any phenomenon in the atmosphere, esp. a shooting star or a meteoroid; উল্কা (সাঃ পঃ), কল্কক (ঐ), গোলক (ঐ), উল্কাপিণ্ড (সাঃ পঃ), উল্কাশ্ম (ঐ), উল্কাশিলা, অনলশিলা। **2.** (*Fig.*) Anything that for a time dazzles or strikes with wonder; "The *meteors* of fashion rise and fall"; (লক্ষণায়) যাহা অল্প সময়ের জন্য চক্ষু ঝলসাইয়া দেয় অথবা বিস্ময়াভিভূত করে, উল্কাচ্ছটা।

mē-tē-ŏr'-ic, *adj.* **1.** Of, or relating to, the atmosphere; dependant on atmospheric conditions; বায়ুমণ্ডলীয়; বায়ুমণ্ডলের অবস্থার উপর নির্ভরশীল। **2.** Of, or relating to, meteor; উল্কাসম্বন্ধীয়। **3.** (*Fig.*) Transiently or irregularly brilliant; rapid; as, swift *meteoric* fame; (লক্ষণায়) অচিরদ্যুতি, অস্থিরদ্যুতি, চঞ্চলপ্রভ; নক্ষত্রগতি।

mē'-tē-ŏr-īte (-êr-), *n.* A meteoric stone; উল্কাপ্রস্তর, উল্কা।

mē-tē-or'-ō-grăph (-êr-), *n.* An apparatus recording meteorological phenomena; ঝড়বৃষ্টি প্রভৃতির অবস্থা নির্ণায়ক-যন্ত্র, আবহমান।

mē'-tē-or-oid (-êr-oyd), *n.* (*Astron.*) A body moving through space resembling those which become meteors on entering the earth's atmosphere; (জ্যোতির্বিজ্ঞান) নির্বাত অন্তরীক্ষে বিবর্ত্তমান পিণ্ডবিশেষ—যাহা বায়ুমণ্ডলে প্রবেশ করিয়া উল্কায় পরিণত হয়। **—oi'-dal,** *adj.*

mē'-tē-or-ō-līte (-êr-), *n.* See METEORITE.

mē-tē-or-ŏl'-ō-ġy (-êr-), *n.* **1.** That department of physics which treats of the phenomena of the atmosphere as regards weather and climate; পদার্থবিদ্যার যে শাখায় দেশের জল, বৃষ্টি, ঝড়, বায়ু প্রভৃতির বিষয় আলোচিত হইয়া থাকে, বায়ুবিদ্যা, নভোবিদ্যা, আবহবিদ্যা, বায়ুবিজ্ঞান, বায়ুমণ্ডলবিদ্যা (সাঃ পঃ), বায়ুচক্রশাস্ত্র, অন্তরীক্ষবিদ্যা, পবনবিদ্যা। **2.** The atmospheric character as of a region; কোন স্থানের বায়ুমণ্ডলের অবস্থা। **—gist,** *n.* One versed in meteorology; আবহবিদ্যাবিৎ। **—o-log'-ic, —o-log'-i-cal,** *adjs.* **—o-log'-i-cal-ly,** *adv.*

mē'-têr, *n.* A person or thing that measures; an instrument for measuring the consumption of gas, water and electricity; মাপক, পরিমাপক; বাষ্প, জল বা তাড়িতের কতটা ব্যয় হইয়াছে তাহা যে যন্ত্রে মাপ হইয়া থাকে, মানযন্ত্র, মাননিরূপক।

mē-thinks' (-thĭngks), *v. i.* (Now *Archaic*) It seems to me; (বর্ত্তমানে অপ্রঃ) আমার বোধ হয়।

mĕth'-ŏd, *n.* **1.** Mode or manner of procedure, esp. in any branch of mental activity; as, a *method* of teaching; প্রণালী, পদ্ধতি, রীতি, প্রকার, ধারা, ব্যবস্থা, বিধান। **2.** Orderly arrangement of ideas; "Though this be madness, yet there's *method* in it"; সুশৃঙ্খলা, সুব্যবস্থা। **3.** Orderliness and regularity; habit of acting orderly and regularly; সুব্যবস্থা; সুব্যবস্থিতত্ব। **4.** (*Nat. Hist.*) A principle or system of classification; as, the *method* of Roy; (প্রাকৃতিক ইতিহাস) শ্রেণীবিভাগসূত্র, শ্রেণীবিভাগপদ্ধতি।

mē-thŏd'-ic, —i-căl, *adjs.* Systematic; orderly; as, a *methodical* treatise; প্রণালীসিদ্ধ, প্রণালীসম্মত, প্রণালীসঙ্গত, রীত্যনুগত, ব্যবস্থিত; সুশৃঙ্খল, নিয়মানুগত। **—i-cal-ly,** *adv.*

Mĕth'-ŏd-ist, *n.* **1.** A member of any of the several religious bodies originating in the evangelistic movement of Charles and John Wesley and George Whitefield; John Wesley কর্ত্তৃক প্রতিষ্ঠিত খৃষ্টীয়ান সম্প্রদায় বিশেষ—ইঁহারা ধর্ম্মবিষয়ে কঠোর নিয়মপ্রণালী পালন করেন, রীতি-ধ্বজ (আঃ বঃ), নৈষ্ঠিক খৃষ্টীয়ান। **2.** (*l. c.*) A person of strict religous views (*generally contempt*); (সাধারণতঃ অবজ্ঞাচ্ছলে) নিষ্ঠাচারী, নৈষ্ঠিক। **—is'-tic, —is'-ti-cal,** *adjs.* **—is'-ti-cal-ly,** *adv.*

mĕth'-ŏd-īze, *v. t.* To reduce to method; to arrange in order; ব্যবস্থাবদ্ধ করা, ব্যবস্থিত করা; শৃঙ্খলাবদ্ধ করা।

mĕth-ŏd-ŏl'-ō-ġy, *n.* The sceince of method or of classification; a discourse concerning method; ব্যবস্থাশাস্ত্র, পদ্ধতিবিদ্যা; পদ্ধতিসম্বন্ধীয় আলোচনা।

mĕth'-ўl, *n.* A hypothetical radical of wood spirit and its combinations; দারুসুরা প্রভৃতির কল্পিত মূল পদার্থ। **Me-thyl'-ic,** *adj.* **Methyl alcohol** — কাষ্ঠপরিস্রবণ হইতে বা অন্যান্য উপায়ে প্রাপ্ত লঘু, উদ্বায়ী এবং দাহ্য তরল পদার্থ বিশেষ।

mĕth'-ўl āte, *v. t.* (*Chem.*) To mix with methyl; as, *methylated* spirit; দারু-সুরার কল্পিত মূলপদার্থের সহিত মিশ্রিত করা। **Methylated spirit**—৯ ভাগ সুরাসার ও একভাগ দারু সুরার মিশ্র—ইহা প্রদীপে ও বার্ণিসাদির কার্য্যে ব্যবহৃত হয়, সুরামদ্যাক (হিঃ কোঃ)।

mē-tic'-ū-lous (-lŭs), *adj.* Finically scrupulous; "The *meticulous* civility of Addison"; খুঁত-খুঁতে, সূক্ষ্মবিচারী, অতিসূক্ষ্ম।

metier, (*F.*), *n.* One's trade, profession or line; ব্যবসায়, পেশা।

mē-tis', *n.* A half breed of European and American Indian parentage in Canada; আমেরিকা দেশীয় ফিরিঙ্গী।

Mē'-tis *n.* The personification of Prudence; দেবরাজ Zeusএর প্রথমা পত্নী প্রজ্ঞা দেবী। এই পত্নীর গর্ভজাত সন্তানের তেজঃ ও পরাক্রমে পিতার যশোগরিমা ম্লান হইবে এইরূপ ভবিষ্যদ্বাণী হওয়ায় Zeus পত্নী Metisকে মক্ষিকায় রূপান্তরিত করিয়া ভক্ষণ

and eagerly; to set to; as, *to fall to* work or working; to begin eating; তাড়াতাড়ি আগ্রহের সহিত আরম্ভ করা; প্রবৃত্ত হওয়া; আহার করিতে আরম্ভ করা, খাইতে সুরু করা। To come to blows; হাতাহাতি হওয়া, মারামারি লাগা। **To fall to one's lot**—To happen to one without his planning; ভাগ্যে ঘটা, অদৃষ্টে পতিত হওয়া। **To fall to the ground**—To come to nothing; to be abandoned, as a plan, project, etc.; পণ্ড হওয়া, নিষ্ফল হওয়া; পরিত্যক্ত হওয়া। **To fall under**—To come under or within the limit of; অন্তর্ভূত হওয়া। To become the subject of; as, it does not *fall under* human observation; বিষয়ীভূত হওয়া। To be ranged; as, it does not *fall under* this class; শ্রেণীভুক্ত হওয়া। **To fall under one's notice**—To be noticed by one; কাহারো চোখে পড়া, কাহারো লক্ষ্যের বিষয়ীভূত হওয়া। **To fall upon** (or **on**)—See TO FALL ON. To attack; আক্রমণ করা, আপতিত হওয়া। To have recourse to; আশ্রয় গ্রহণ করা, শরণ লওয়া। **To fall within**—To be included in; অন্তর্ভূত হওয়া। **Wicket falls**—The batsman is in the metric system of France, equal to 39·37 English inches; ফরাসীদেশে প্রচলিত দৈর্ঘ্যের পরিমাণের একক, ৩৯·৩৭ ইঞ্চির সমান। **—Met′-ric,** *adj.* **Metric system** — মাত্রিক রীতি।

mĕt′-ri-căl, *adj.* 1. Of, or relating to, or arranged in, metre; as, *metrical* composition; ছন্দোবদ্ধ, বৃত্তবদ্ধ। 2. Relating to, or involving, measurement; as, *metrical* geometry; পরিমাপসম্বন্ধীয়। **—ly,** *adv.*

mĕ-trŏl′-ŏ-ġy̆, *n.* The science or system of weights and measures; মানবিজ্ঞান। **Met′-ro-log-i-cal,** *adj.*

mĕt′-rŏ-nome, *n.* An instrument for marking exact time, esp.

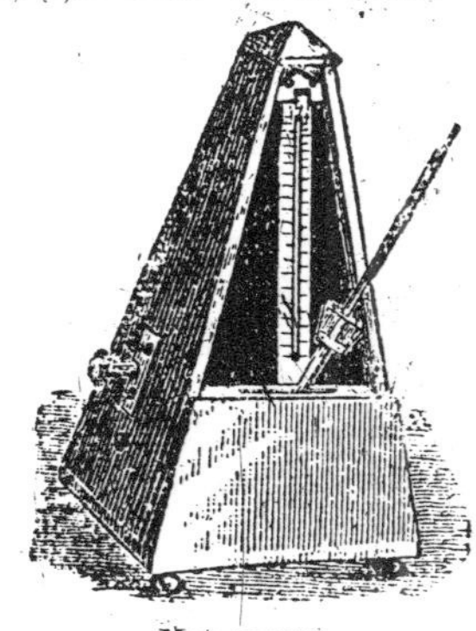

Metronome.

in music; তালমাপক, তালমাপনী। **—nom′-ic,** *adj.*

mĕ-trŏp′-ŏ-lis, *n.* 1. The chief city of a country; capital; কোন স্থানের প্রধান নগর; রাজধানী, রাজনগরী। 2. The see of a metropolitan bishop; পৌরাচার্য্যের শ্রীপাট। 3. The centre of activity; as, a *metropolis* of commerce; কর্ম্মকেন্দ্র। **The metropolis**—London; লণ্ডননগরী।

mĕt-rō-pŏl′-ĭ-tăn, *adj.* & *n.* 1. Of, or relating to, a metropolis; relating to the metropolis or London; রাজধানীসম্বন্ধীয়; লণ্ডননগরীসম্বন্ধীয়। 2. Of, or relating to, ecclesiastical metropolis; as, *metropolitan* bishops; পৌরাচার্য্যের শ্রীপাটসম্বন্ধীয়। ***Noun.*** An inhabitant of a metropolis; রাজধানীবাসী, পুরবাসী। **—ate,** *n.*

mĕt′-tle (-l), *n.* 1. Quality of temperament or disposition; natural ardour; courage; as, a gentleman of brave *mettle*; প্রকৃতি, স্বভাব, মেজাজ, ধাত, ধাতু; বীর্য্য, পরাক্রম, তেজ; সাহস। **—some,** *adj.* High-spirited; তেজস্বী, পরাক্রান্ত। **To be on one's mettle**—To be incited to do one's best; প্রাণপণ চেষ্টার জন্য উদ্দীপ্ত হওয়া।

meum, (*L.*) Mine; আমার। **Meum and Tuum**—Mine and thine (used to express rights of property); তোমার ও আমার। **To confound meum and Tuum**—পরদ্রব্য লোষ্ট্রবৎ জ্ঞান করা।

mew (mü), *n.* A gull, esp. the common European gull (also, *sea-mew*); সাগরবলাকা, সাগরকুক্কুট।

mew (mü), *n.* & *v. t.* A cage for hawks, esp. while moulting; বাজ পক্ষীর পিঞ্জর—বিশেষতঃ পক্ষমোচন কালে বাজপক্ষীকে যে পিঞ্জরে রাখা হয়। ***Verb t.*** 1. To keep (a hawk) in a mew; পক্ষমোচনকালে বাজপক্ষীকে পিঞ্জরে রাখা। 2. (*Fig.*) To shut up; to confine; (লক্ষণায়) রুদ্ধ করা; আটক করা।

mew (mü), *v. t.* (*Archaic*) To shed or cast as feathers; to moult; (said of hawks); (অপ্রঃ) পক্ষমোচন করা; পালক ফেলা।

mew (mü), *v. i.* & *n.* To cry as a cat or a sea bird; বিড়ালের মত মিউ মিউ করা। ***Noun.*** This cry esp. of a cat; মিউ মিউ শব্দ, ম্যাও ম্যাও।

mewl (mül), **müle,** *v. i.* 1. To cry feebly or whimper as an infant; শিশুর মত কাঁদা, প্যান প্যান করা। 2. To mew like a cat; বিড়ালের মত মিউ মিউ শব্দ করা।

mews (müz), *n. pl.* Stables; originally the royal stables in London so called because built where king's hawks were once mewed or cofined; আস্তাবল, অশ্বশালা, মন্দুরা; পূর্ব্বে লণ্ডননগরীস্থ রাজকীয় অশ্বশালা—যথায় এক সময়ে ইংলণ্ডেশ্বরের বাজ পক্ষিসমূহ রাখা হইত।

Mexicon poppy, *n.* শিয়ালকাঁটা (খোরী)।

mez′-za-nine (mĕt-ză-nēn), *n.* 1. (*Arch.*) A low story between two high ones, esp. between the ground floor and the story above; (স্থপতিবিজ্ঞান) উচ্চতর তলদ্বয়ের

মধ্যবর্ত্তী অনুচ্চ তল। 2. (*Theatr.*) A floor beneath the stage; (রঙ্গালয়) রঙ্গমঞ্চের নিম্নস্থ গৃহতল।

mez′-zō (mĕd-), *adv.* (*Mus.*) Half moderately; (সঙ্গীত-শাস্ত্র) মধ্যোচ্চ-ধ্বনিতে। **Mezzo-forte** — মধ্যোচ্চ। **Mezzo soprano**—মধ্যোচ্চ স্বর।

mez′-zō-tint (mĕd-), *n.* & *v. t.* 1. A manner of engraving on copper or steel by working on a surface previously roughened uniformly; ক্ষোদিতফলক প্রস্তুতের প্রণালীবিশেষ। [এই প্রণালীতে প্রথমতঃ তাম্র বা ইস্পাতের ফলকের উপরিভাগ অগ্রভাগ ক্ষুদ্র ক্ষুদ্র দাঁতের আকারে কাটা একপ্রকার বাটালির মত যন্ত্র দ্বারা উল্লেখন করা হয়। এইরূপ উল্লেখনের ফলে ফলকের উপর সর্ব্বত্র অতি ক্ষুদ্র ক্ষুদ্র অসংখ্য বিন্দু উত্থিত হয়। এমতাবস্থায় এই ফলক হইতে চিত্র তুলিলে এই চিত্রের সমস্ত স্থান সমভাবে কৃষ্ণচ্ছায়যুক্ত হইবে। এখন চিত্রের কোন কোন স্থান অল্পকৃষ্ণচ্ছায় করার আবশ্যক হইলে তাহা হইতে অন্য যন্ত্রদ্বারা বিন্দুগুলি তুলিয়া নিতে হয়। এই প্রণালী সর্ব্বপ্রথম ১ম চার্লসের সময় Prince Rupert কর্ত্তৃক প্রবর্ত্তিত হয়।] 2. An engraving so produced; ঐ প্রণালীতে ক্ষোদিত ফলক, বিন্দু ফলক। ***Verb t.*** To engrave in mezzotint; বিন্দু-ফলক খোদাই করা।

mi (mē), *n.* (*Mus.*) The third note of octave; (সঙ্গীতশাস্ত্র) গা।

mī-aow′, —aou′ (-ow) *n.* & *v. i.* The cry of a cat; মিউ মিউ শব্দ। ***Verb i.*** To make or imitate the cry of a cat; মিউ মিউ করা, ম্যাও ম্যাও করা।

mī-as′-mă, *n.* (*pl.* -MATA, -MATAS) Infectious or noxious emanation, esp. malaria; দূষিত স্থানে উৎপন্ন সংক্রামক রোগজনক বাষ্প বা বীজাণু, পূতি-বাষ্প, পূতিবাত। **—mal, —mat′-ic,** *adjs.*

mī-aul′ (-äl), *v. i.* To cry as a cat; মিউ মিউ করা, ম্যাও ম্যাও করা।

mī′-că, *n.* A mineral cleavable into thin shining elastic plates; অভ্র, অভ্রক, আভ, গগন (সাঃ পঃ) খেচর (ঐ), ব্যোম (রঃ রঃ সঃ প্র), স্বচ্ছপত্র, নির্ম্মল। **—ca′-ce-ous,** *adj.*

Mī′-chael (-kĕl), *n.* 1. An archangel; উচ্চশ্রেণীর দেবদূত বিশেষ। **Michaelmas**—সেণ্ট মাইকেলের স্মৃতি উৎসব—২৯শে সেপ্টেম্বর অনুষ্ঠিত হয়। **Order of St. Michael and St. George**—ইংলণ্ডীয় অসামরিক নাইট সম্প্রদায় বিশেষ।

mich′-ing, *p. a.* Skulking; hiding; আড়ালে স্থিত; লুক্কায়িত। **Miching mallecho**—Underhand mischief; তলে তলে ক্ষতিকরণ।

mick′-le (-l), *adj* & *n.* (*Archaic, Sc.*) Great; much; as, "A man of *mickle* might"; (অপ্রঃ) মহা; অত্যন্ত। ***Noun.*** A large amount; বহু পরিমাণ। **Many a little or pickle makes a mickle**—রাই কুড়িয়ে বেল।

mī′-crōbe, *n.* A microscopic organism; esp. a bacterium found wherever organic matter is in process of decomposition; জীবাণু; রোগজনকজীবাণু, জীবসূচী, অণুজীব (যোঃ)। **—cro′-bi-al,** *adj.* **—cro-bi-ol′-o-gy,** *n.*

mī-crō-cĕph′-ă-lous (-lŭs), *adj.* Having an abnormally small head; ক্ষুদ্র-মুণ্ডী। **—ce-phal′-ic,** *adj.* & *n.* Same as MICROCEPHALOUS. (*Noun*) A microcephalic person; ক্ষুদ্র-মুণ্ড ব্যক্তি।

mī′-crō-cŏsm, *n.* 1. Man viewed as an epitome of the universe ব্রহ্মাণ্ড, ভাণ্ড, পিণ্ড (এভেলন) [cf. যা আছে ভাণ্ডে তা আছে ব্রহ্মাণ্ডে; দেখেছি দেহপিণ্ড মাঝে নিখিল ব্রহ্মাণ্ডেরে—কবীর (সত্যেন্দ্র বাবুর অনুবাদ)]। 2. (*Humorous*) A community, institution, town, district, country, etc. regarded as an epitome of the world; (কৌতুকচ্ছলে) বিশ্বের প্রতিরূপ স্বরূপ বিবেচিত সম্প্রদায়, প্রতিষ্ঠান, নগর, জেলা, দেশ, প্রভৃতি। 3. A miniature representation (of); ক্ষুদ্র সংস্করণ, ক্ষুদ্র প্রতিরূপ। **—cos′-mic,** *adj.*

mī′-crō-phōne, *n.* An instrument to augment small sounds; যে যন্ত্রের সাহায্যে ক্ষীণ শব্দ উচ্চ বলিয়া প্রতীয়মান হয়, ধ্বনিবির্দ্ধক যন্ত্র।

mī′-crō-scōpe, *n.* An optical instrument consisting of a lens or of a combination of lenses for making enlarged or magnified images of minute objects: অণুবীক্ষণ, সূক্ষ্মদর্শক যন্ত্র, সূক্ষ্মদর্শক। **—scop′-ic,** *adj.* 1. Of, or relating to, the microscope; অণুবীক্ষণ সম্বন্ধীয়। 2. Too small to be visible without a microscope; অণুবীক্ষণদৃশ্য (কৃষঃ), অতি-সূক্ষ্ম, আণুবীক্ষণিক। **—scop′-i-cal,** *adj.* Same as MICROSCOPIC. **—scop′-i-cal-ly,** *adv.*

Microscope.

mī-crŏs′-cō-pȳ, *n.* Use of the microscope; অণুবীক্ষণব্যবহার। **—pist,** *n.*

mic-tū-rī′-tiŏn, *n.* 1. Desire to urinate; also a morbidly frequent desire to pass urine; মূত্রত্যাগের ইচ্ছা; প্রস্রাবের পীড়া। 2. (*Improp.*) Making water; (অপপ্রয়োগ) মূত্রত্যাগ।

mid, *adj.* At equal distance from extremes; as, *mid*-way; মধ্যবর্ত্তী। **Mid night**—নিশীথ, মধ্যরাত্র, অর্দ্ধরাত্র। **Mid-spoon**—মাঝারী আকারের চামচা। **Mid-way** — মধ্যপথ, অর্দ্ধপথ। **In mid air**—মধ্যাকাশে (পৃথিবী ও মেঘের মধ্যে)। **Mid-way between**—মধ্যস্থলে।

mid, *prep.* (*Poet.*) Amid; মধ্যে।

Midas, *n.* Son of Gordius and king of Phrygia; Gordius এর পুত্র এবং Phrygia দেশের রাজা।

ইনি Dionysius এর নিকট এই বর প্রার্থনা করেন যে ইনি যে বস্তু স্পর্শ করেন তাহা যেন তৎক্ষণাৎ স্বর্ণে পরিণত হয়। Dionysius অভীষ্ট বর প্রদান করিলে পর মিডাস খাদ্যস্পর্শ করিলে উহা অমনি স্বর্ণে পরিণত হইল—তাঁহার কন্যা তদীয় স্পর্শে স্বর্ণ প্রতিমায় রূপান্তরিতা হইল। Midas, Dionysius এর উপদেশানুসারে Pactolus নদীর উৎপত্তি, স্থানে স্নান করিয়া বরের প্রভাব হইতে মুক্ত হন। তদবধি Pactolus নদীর সৈকত স্বর্ণরেণুময় হইয়াছে বলিয়া প্রবাদ। মিডাস সম্বন্ধে আর একটী গল্প আছে। এক সময়ে Pan এবং Apollo দেব উভয়ে বংশিবাদন কৌশলে প্রতিযোগিতা করিতে যাইয়া মিডাসকে মধ্যস্থ নির্ব্বাচন করেন। Panকে শ্রেষ্ঠ বলিয়া মত প্রদান করায় Apollo দেবের শাপে মিডাসের কর্ণ গর্দ্দভের কর্ণে পবিণত হয়। কিন্তু একদিন তাহার ক্ষৌরকার ক্ষৌরক্রিয়া কালে টুপির নীচে মিডাসের গর্দ্দভকর্ণ দেখিতে পায়। সেই দিন হইতে এই গুপ্ত কথা প্রকাশ করার জন্য সেই নরসুন্দর এরূপ অধীর হইয়া পড়িল যে পরিশেষে সে ভূগর্ত্তে একটী গর্ত্ত করিয়া ঐ গর্ত্তের ভিতর চুপিচুপি বলিল "রাজা মিডাসের কান গাধার মত" এই কথা বলিয়া মৃত্তিকা দ্বারা গর্ত্তপূর্ণ করিয়া ফেলিল। কিন্তু অচিরে ঐ স্থানে একটী শরবৃক্ষ জাত হইয়া উহার পত্রমর্ম্মর দ্বারা মিডাসের গুপ্তরহস্য ব্যক্ত করিল।

mid'-day (-dā), *n.* The middle part of the day; noon; মধ্যাহ্ন; দ্বিপ্রহর, দুপুর।

mid'-den (-n), *n.* (*Dial.*) Dunghill; (উপভাষায়) গোময় স্তূপ।

mid'-dle (-l), *adj.* & *n.* 1. (Of member of group) So placed as to have same number of members on each side; as, the *middle* house in a row; মধ্যবর্ত্তী, মধ্যস্থিত। 2. Equally distant from the extremes; as, the *middle* point of a line; medium; as, a man of the *middle* size; মাঝামাঝি; মধ্য, মাঝারী। 3. Intermediate; as, *middle* space; মধ্যবর্ত্তী, ব্যবহিত। ***Noun.*** 1. The middle position; central portion; মধ্যস্থল; মধ্যভাগ। 2. The waist; কটিদেশ, মধ্যদেশ (মঃ ভাঃ), মধ্য (cf. মধ্যক্ষামা)। **Middle age**—মধ্য বয়স, প্রৌঢ় বয়স। **Middle aged** — প্রৌঢ়, মধ্যবয়স্ক, অর্দ্ধবয়স্ক, অর্দ্ধবৃদ্ধ। **Middle class**—মধ্যশ্রেণী, মধ্যবিত্তসম্প্রদায়। **Middle course, —way**—মধ্যপন্থা। **Middle distance**—চিত্রের সম্মুখ ও পশ্চাদ্ভূমির মধ্যবর্ত্তী স্থান। **Middle English**—See ENGLISH. **Middle finger**—মধ্যমা, মধ্যাঙ্গুলী। **Middle kingdom** — চীনদেশ। **Middleman**—যে ব্যক্তি কোন জিনিষের উৎপাদক, নির্ম্মাতা বা ব্যবসায়ীর নিকট হইতে জিনিষ ক্রয় করিয়া অপর ব্যবসায়ী বা ব্যবহারকারীর নিকট বিক্রয় করে, দালাল। **Middle passage**—আফ্রিকা ও পশ্চিম ভারতীয় দ্বীপপুঞ্জের মধ্যবর্ত্তী অতলান্তিক মহাসাগর। **Middle-sized**—মধ্যাকৃতি, মধ্যমাকৃতি, মধ্যমাকার। **Middle term**—(*Log.*) A term common to both premisses; (তর্কবিজ্ঞান) যে শব্দ ব্যাপ্তিবাক্যের (syllogism) উভয় হেতুবাক্যে (premisses) বর্ত্তমান থাকে, কিন্তু উপসংহারে (conclusion) থাকে না, মধ্যপদ, মধ্যমপদ, লিঙ্গ (হিঃ কোঃ), হেতু (ন্যাঃ পঃ)। **Middle watch** (*Naut.*) (নৌবিদ্যা) অর্দ্ধরাত্রি হইতে অপরাহ্ণ ৪টা পর্য্যন্ত পাহারা; ঐ সময়ে প্রহরায় নিযুক্ত ব্যক্তিগণ। **In the middle of**—While (doing); during (process); কোন কাজের মধ্যে; মাঝখানে। **The Middle Ages**—প্রাচীন যুগ ও আধুনিক যুগের মধ্যবর্ত্তী কাল, মধ্য যুগ। [হ্যালামের মতে ক্লভিসকর্ত্তৃক ফরাসীদেশ আক্রমণের বৎসর (৪৮৬ খৃঃ) হইতে ৮ম চার্লসকর্ত্তৃক নেপলস আক্রমণের বৎসর (১৪৯৫) পর্য্যন্ত কাল। সাধারণতঃ রোমনগরীর পতন হইতে সাহিত্য ও কলাপ্রতিভার পুনঃ প্রদীপ্তি (renaissance) পর্য্যন্ত কাল মধ্যযুগ বলিয়া গণনা করা হয়।] **The law of excluded middle**—মধ্যভাব-নিয়ম (ন্যাঃ পঃ)।

mid'-dle (-l), *v. t.* 1. To place in the middle; মধ্যভাগে স্থাপন করা। 2. (*Spec. in foot-ball*) To drive or kick (the ball) into the middle so that it may be kicked through the gaol; (বিশেষভাবে পাদগোলক ক্রীড়ায়) মধ্যভাগে (কন্দুক) তাড়িত করা। 3. (*Naut.*) To fold in the middle; (নৌবিদ্যা) মাঝখানে ভাঁজ করা।

mid'-dling (-lĭng), *adj.* & *adv.* 1. Of middle rank, state, size or quality; "A town of but *middling* size"; মাঝারি, মধ্যম, মধ্যবিধ, মাঝারিগোছের। 2. Moderately good; mediocre; as, a man of *middling* understanding; একপ্রকার; মধ্যম। ***Adv.*** 1. Moderately; as, *middling* good; একরূপ, একরকম 2. (*Colloq.*) Fairly well (in health); as, I am but *middling*; (চলিত ভাষায়) একরকম। **—ly,** *adv.*

mid'-dling (-lĭng), *n.* 1. (*Pl.*) Any of various commodities of medium quality; pins or needles of medium size; মাঝারি রকমের জিনিষ; মাঝারি আকারের সূচ বা আলপিন। 2. (*Pl.*) The coarser part of flour, intermediate between fine flour and bran ময়দার মোটা ভাগ।

Midgard, *n.* The Norse mythological name of the earth; নরওয়ে সুইডেনের পুরাণানুসারে পৃথিবীর নাম, মধ্যমলোক।

midge (mĭj), *n.* 1. A kind of gnat-like insect; মশক জাতীয় কীট বিশেষ। 2. A diminutive person; বামন, খর্ব্বকায়, বালখিল্য।

midg'-ĕt (mĭj-), *n.* A very small person, esp. when exhibited as curiosity; মাণবক, বালখিল্য, বিশেষতঃ প্রদর্শনীতে প্রদর্শিত ক্ষুদ্রকায় আজব মানুষ।

mid'-lănd, *n.* & *adj.* 1. The interior or central region of a country; মধ্যদেশ। 2. (With *the* prefixed) The middle countries of England; ইংলণ্ডের মধ্যভাগবর্ত্তী প্রদেশ সমূহ।

Adj. Of, or relating to, midland; মধ্যদেশসম্বন্ধীয়।

mid'-night (-nīt), *n.* **1.** The middle of the night; twelve O'clock at night; অৰ্দ্ধরাত্র (রঃ); মধ্যনিশা, মধ্যরাত্র। **2.** Deep darkness; ঘনান্ধকার, ঘনতমিস্রা। **To burn the midnight oil** — To study or work late at night; অধিক রাত্র পর্যান্ত অধ্যয়ন করা।

midrash, *n.* Ancient Jewish commentary on a part of the Hebrew scriptures; হিব্রু-ধর্ম্মশাস্ত্রের অংশ বিশেষের উপর প্রাচীন ইহুদীদের টীকা।

mid'-riff, *n.* Diaphragm (of the body); বক্ষোদর ব্যবধায়ক পেশী।

mid'-ship, *n.* Middle part of a ship or a boat; জাহাজ বা নৌকার মধ্যভাগ। **Midshipman** — (*Abbr. middy*) The rank between the naval cadet and sub-lieutenant; জাহাজের অধস্তন কর্ম্মচারিবিশেষ।

midst, *n., adv.* & *prep.* The middle; as, in the *midst* of the forest; মধ্য, মধ্যভাগ। *Adv.* In the middle; (only in the phrase, *first, midst and last*); মধ্যে। *Prep.* (*Poet.*) Amidst; "There I met my own love *midst* the golden corn"; (কবিতায়) মধ্যে। **In the midst of**—মধ্যে, মাঝে।

mid'-sŭm-mer (-ẽr), *n.* The middle of summer; the summer solstice about the 21st of June; মধ্যনিদাঘ, নিদাঘকালমধ্য; উত্তরায়ণ। **Midsummer day** — June 24; ২৪শে জুন। **Midsummer madness** — পাগলামির একশেষ, নেহাৎ পাগলামি।

mid'-wife, *n.* A woman who assists other women in childbirth; ধাত্রী, ধাই, সাধিকা, প্রসবকারিণী, প্রজননকুশলা স্ত্রী (সুশ্রুঃ)। **—ry,** *n.* Obsteterics; ধাত্রীবিদ্যা, গর্ভমোচন-বিদ্যা, কুমারভৃত্য, (রঃ), গর্ভাবেক্ষণ (সাঃ পঃ)।

mid'-wĭn-tẽr, *n.* The middle of winter; esp., winter solstice, December 21; মধ্যহেমন্ত; দক্ষিণায়ন।

mien (mēn), *n.* External air or manner of a person; bearing; as, a majestic *mien*; আকৃতি প্রকৃতি, আকারপ্রকার, বাহ্যরূপ, বহিরাকৃতি; ভাবস্বভাব, ভাবভঙ্গী, আকার, চাল।

miff, *n., v. i.* & *t.* (*Colloq.*) A petty quarrel; (চলিত ভাষায়) ঝগড়া। *Verb i.* **1.** To take offence (*with* or *at*); দোষ ধরা। **2.** (Of a plant) To wither; শুকাইয়া যাওয়া। *Verb t.* To offend; to displease; কষ্ট করা, মনঃক্ষুণ্ণ করা; অসন্তুষ্ট করা।

might (mīt), *n.* **1.** Great strength either physical or mental; শক্তি, ক্ষমতা, সামর্থ্য, পরাক্রম, বল। **2.** Power to accomplish one's purpose or desire; as, the doctrine that *might* makes right; জোর। **Might is right**—জোর যার মুলুক তার, লাঠি যার মাটি তার। **With might and main** — With all one's power; প্রাণপণে।

might'-ȳ (mīt-), *adj.* & *adv.* **1.** Having great mental or physical power; strong; বলশালী, বলবান, ক্ষমতাশালী, মহাবলী, পরাক্রমী; প্রবল পরাক্রান্ত, বলিষ্ঠ, দোর্দ্দণ্ডপ্রতাপশালী, শক্তিমান। **2.** Massive; bulky; "Giants of *mighty* bone"; গুরুভার; প্রকাণ্ড, বিশাল, বিরাট। **3.** (*Colloq.*) Great or considerable; "*Mighty* was their fuss about little things"; (চলিত ভাষায়) মহা, অতিশয়। *Adv.* In a great degree; very; as, *mighty* thoughtful; নিরতিশয়; অত্যন্ত, মহা। **—i-ly,** *adv.* **—i-ness,** *n.* **Mighty works** — (বাইবেল) অতিপ্রাকৃত ক্রিয়া, অলৌকিক ক্রিয়া।

mi'-gnon (mīn-yŏn), (*F.*) *adj.* Small and delicately formed; কচি।

mi-gnon-ette' (mīn-yŏn-ĕt), *n.* **1.** A plant bearing fragrnant greenish white flowers; হরিদাভ শ্বেত পুষ্পপ্রসূ তরু বিশেষ। **2.** The colour of the mignonette flower; a light green, হরিদাভ শ্বেতবর্ণ; ফিকে সবুজবর্ণ। **3.** A kind of lace and fine net; একপ্রকার লেইস বা সূক্ষ্ম জাল।

migraine, *n.* Same as MEGRIM.

mi'-grāte, *v. i.* **1.** To pass from one place (such as, country, town, college, house) to another; স্থানান্তরে গমন করা, একদেশ ত্যাগ করিয়া অপর দেশে গমন করা। **2.** (Of birds and fishes) To pass periodically from one region or climate to another for breeding or feeding; (পক্ষী এবং মৎস্য সম্বন্ধে) বিশেষ বিশেষ ঋতুতে একদেশ হইতে অন্য দেশে গমন করা, প্রব্রজন করা। **—grant,** *adj.* & *n.* Migrating; প্রব্রজনশীল। *Noun.* A migratory bird, person or animal; প্রব্রজনশীল বিহঙ্গ, ব্যক্তি বা জন্তু। **—gra'-tion,** *n.* Act of migrating; দেশান্তরগমন, পরদেশগমন, স্থানান্তরগমন (সাঃ পঃ), প্রব্রজন। **—gra'-tor,** *n.* One who migrates; দেশান্তরগামী ব্যক্তি, যাযাবর। **—gra-to-ry,** *adj.* **1.** Disposed to migrate; passing from one climate to another as birds etc.; প্রব্রজনশীল; যাযাবর, দেশান্তরগামী, স্থানান্তরগামী। **2.** Roving or wandering; ভ্রমণশীল, পর্য্যটনশীল।

mi-kā'-dō, *n.* The title of the Emperor of Japan; জাপান সম্রাটের উপাধি।

mīl'-āge, *n.* **1.** Aggregate number of miles travelled or used; অতিক্রান্ত মাইলের মোটসংখ্যা। **2.** A travelling allowance at a fixed rate per mile; মাইল প্রতি নির্দ্দিষ্ট হারে ভাতা।

Mil-ăn-ese' (-ēz), *adj.* & *n.* Of, or relating to, Milan, a city in Italy; ইটালীর অন্তঃপাতী মিলান নগরী-সম্বন্ধীয়। *Noun.* A native or inhabitant of Milan; মিলানের অধিবাসী। **The Milanese**—মিলানের প্রাচীন ডিউকের অধিকারভুক্ত স্থান।

milch, *adj.* Giving milk (now applied only to domestic animals) ; পয়স্বিনী, দুধাল, দুগ্ধবতী, ক্ষীরিণী, দোগ্ধ্রী। **Milch-cow**—One giving milk ; দুগ্ধবতী গাভী, ধেনু, দোহাগাই। (*Fig.*) A source of profit, esp. a person from whom money is easily drawn; (লক্ষণায়) ধনাগমের হেতু, বিশেষতঃ যে ব্যক্তির নিকট হইতে সহজে টাকা বাহির করা যাইতে পারে, কামধেনু।

mild, *adj.* 1. Tender or gentle in temper ; clement ; compassionate ; সৌম্য, মৃদু, ধীরপ্রকৃতি ; কোমলান্তঃকরণ, কোমলহৃদয় ; সদয়, দয়ার্দ্র, করুণাপূর্ণ। 2. Not severe ; as, *mild* punishment ; অকঠোর, অনুগ্র। 3. Not violent ; calm ; gentle ; as, a *mild* air or weather ; মৃদু, অনুগ্র ; শান্ত, ধীর ; সৌম্য, নম্র। 4. Operating gently ; as, a *mild* medicine ; মৃদু (আয়ুঃ রস)। 5. (Of food, tobacco etc.) Not sharp or strong in taste etc. ; (খাদ্য, তামাক, প্রভৃতি সম্পর্কে) অনুগ্র, কড়া নয়। 6. (Of beer) Not bitter ; not strongly flavoured with hops ; (যবসুরা সম্পর্কে) অতিক্ত ; অল্প হপ ফল মিশ্রণে মৃদু তিক্তীকৃত। 7. Lacking in energy or vivacity ; "*Mild* aspect" ; নিস্তেজ, নির্জ্জীব। **Mild'-en**, *v. t.* & *i.* To make mild or milder ; শান্ত করা, অনুগ্র করা। *Verb i.* To become mild or milder ; শান্ত হওয়া, মৃদু হওয়া। **Mild'-ly** *adv.* **Mild'-ness**, *n.* State of being mild ; gentleness ; clemency ; মৃদুতা, মার্দ্দব, কোমল-চিত্ততা ; সৌম্যতা, ধীরতা ; দয়ালুতা। **Mild steel**—এক প্রকার কোমল ঘাতসহ ইস্পাত। **Draw it mild**—Do not exaggerate ; অতিরঞ্জিত করিও না, রং চড়াইও না।

mil'-dew (-dū) *n., v. t.* & *i.* A disease on plants caused by the growth of minute fungi; ছেতো, চিতি, শুক্রকলঙ্ক। *Verb t.* & *i.* To taint or be tainted with mildew ; ছেতোধরা, চিতি পড়া চিতি ফেলান। **—y**, *adj.*

mile, *n.* 1. A measure in length in England now 1,760 yds. ; মাইল, অর্দ্ধ ক্রোশ। 2. A race extending over a mile's length ; এক মাইল ব্যাপী দৌড়চক্র। **Geographical** or **Nautical mile**—ভৌগোলিক মাইল, সামুদ্রিক মাইল (৬০৮০ ফিট)। **Mile-stone**—মাইলপ্রস্তর, অর্দ্ধক্রোশমান পাষাণ।

mil'-ėr, *n.* (*Colloq.*) A man or a horse qualified or trained to run a mile ; (চলিত ভাষায়) এক মাইল দৌড়াইতে পারে এরূপ শিক্ষাপ্রাপ্ত ঘোড়া অথবা মনুষ্য।

Mi-lė'-si-ăn, *adj.* & *n.* Of, or relating to, King Milesius of Spain ; Irish ; স্পেনরাজ মিলিসিয়াস্ সম্পর্কীয় (এই রাজার পুত্রদ্বয় খৃঃ পূঃ ১৩০০ অব্দে আয়র্লণ্ড বিজয় করিয়াছিলেন বলিয়া কথিত) ; আইরীস। *Noun.* An Irishman আয়র্লণ্ডের অধিবাসী।

mil'foil (-foyl), *n.* Common yarrow and other plants ; কয়েকপ্রকার বৃক্ষের সাধারণ নাম।

mil'-i-ă-rȳ, *adj.* Resembling, or of the size of, millet seeds ; as, *miliary* tubercle ; চীনারমত, চীনার আকার, শ্যামাকবীজবৎ, প্রিয়ঙ্গুবৎ। **Miliary fever**— চীনারমত ক্ষুদ্র ক্ষুদ্র পীড়কাবিশিষ্ট একপ্রকার চর্ম্মরোগ, প্রিয়ঙ্গু (হ্র চঃ), ঘামাচি।

mil'-i-tănt, *adj.* 1. Engaged in warfare, esp. spiritual ; as, church *militant* ; যুদ্ধরত, বিশেষতঃ অধ্যাত্মসমরত। 2. Combative; "The powers *militant*" ; সংগ্রামপ্রিয়, যুদ্ধপ্রিয় **Church militant**—পৃথিবীস্থ খৃষ্টীয় ধর্ম্মসংঘ — যাহা বিরুদ্ধাচারিগণের সহিত অনুক্ষণ সংগ্রামে রত আছে বলিয়া কল্পিত হইয়া থাকে। **—ly**, *adv.* **—tancy**, *n.*

mil'-i-tă-rĭsm, *n.* 1. Military spirit or tendencies ; an excessive attention to military affairs ; যুদ্ধপ্রিয়তা, যুদ্ধাসক্তি, সমরপ্রিয়তা ; যুদ্ধসংক্রান্ত ব্যাপারে অতিরিক্ত মনোযোগ। **—ri-za'-tion**, *n.* **—rize**, *v. t.* To train as a soldier ; to imbue with militarism ; যুদ্ধবিদ্যায় শিক্ষিত করা ; সামরিক ভাব দ্বারা অনুপ্রাণিত করা।

mil'-i-tă-rist, *n.* 1. A student of the military science ; যুদ্ধবিজ্ঞানশিক্ষার্থী, সামরিকশাস্ত্র শিক্ষার্থী, অস্ত্রবিদ্যাশিক্ষার্থী। 2. One who is imbued with the spirit of militarism ; সামরিক ভাব দ্বারা অনুপ্রাণিত ব্যক্তি।

mil'-i-tă-rȳ, *adj.* & *n.* 1. Of, or pertaining to, soldiers, arms or war ; সৈন্যসংক্রান্ত, অস্ত্রসংক্রান্ত, সামরিক, সমরসংক্রান্ত, যুদ্ধসংক্রান্ত। 2. Supported by armed force ; as, a *military* Government ; সশস্ত্র সৈন্যদ্বারা রক্ষিত। *Noun.* The soldiery ; সৈন্যবর্গ। **Military chest**—সৈন্যদলের ধনভাণ্ডার। **Military fever**—সন্নিপাত জ্বর। **Military law**—Same as MARTIAL-LAW. **Military testament**—সৈনিকের মৌখিক চরমপত্র।

mil'-i-tāte, *v. i.* 1. To take part in warfare ; যুদ্ধে যোগদান করা। 2. (*Fig.*) To contend ; "These are great questions, where great names *militate* against each other" ; (লক্ষণায়) সংগ্রাম করা। 3. (Of things, To have weight or effect ; to tell against ; as, the evidence *militates* against this opinion ; (বস্তুসম্পর্কে) কার্য্যকর হওয়া ; প্রতিকূল হওয়া।

mi-li'-tia (-shă), *n.* 1. Military force ; esp. a body of citizens enrolld as a regular military force ; সামরিক শক্তি ; বিশেষতঃ নাগরিকবৃন্দকর্ত্তৃক গঠিত নিয়মিত সৈন্যদল। 2. A branch of British military force formerly raised by the several counties, usu. by voluntary enlistment ; যে সকল ব্যক্তি পূর্ব্বে স্বদেশরক্ষার্থ স্বেচ্ছাপূর্ব্বক সৈন্যদলে ভুক্ত হইত, স্বদেশরক্ষী সৈন্য। **Militia-man**—স্বদেশ-রক্ষী সৈনিক।

milk, *n.* **1.** A white liquid secreted by female mammals for nourishment of their youngs ; দুগ্ধ, দুধ, গোরস, ক্ষীর, পয়ঃ, স্তন্য (mother's milk), পীযূষ (milk of a cow during the first 7 days after calving). [Also গব্য, অবদোহ, দোহ, উধস্য, উধস্ত, দোহজ, সোরজ।] **2.** A liquid resembling milk in appearance ; white juice of plants ; দুগ্ধবৎ তরল পদার্থ ; শ্বেতবর্ণ তরু নির্য্যাস, বৃক্ষক্ষীর। **Condensed-milk**—জমাট দুগ্ধ, ক্ষীরখণ্ড, মিষ্টি দুধ (যোঃ)। **Milk-abscess** — প্রসূতী দিগের স্তনব্রণ। **Milk-bush, Milk hedge**—লঙ্কাসীজ (বনঃ)। **Milk-fever**—প্রসূতীদিগের দুগ্ধস্রাবের পরবর্ত্তী বা সহবর্ত্তী জ্বর, ঠুনকো জ্বর। **Milk knot**—প্রদাহ বা দুগ্ধলোপবশতঃ স্তনের স্থানে স্থানে যে গ্রন্থি জন্মে। **Milk-leg** প্রসবান্তে জঙ্ঘাস্ফীতি রোগ। **Milk-maid**--A woman milking or working in a dairy ; গোপী, গোপিকা, গোয়ালিনী, আহিরিণী, আভীরী। **Milk-man**—গোয়াল, গোয়ালা, গোপ, আভীর, দুগ্ধবিক্রেতা, ক্ষীরবিক্রয়ী। **Milk-punch**—দুগ্ধ ও সুরাসার সহযোগে প্রস্তুত পানীয় বিশেষ। **Milk-scab or scall** — দুগ্ধকণ্ডু। **Milksop**—A spiritless man or youth ; নিস্তেজ লোক, কমজুরি লোক, নির্বীর্য্য লোক, মেদামারা লোক। **Milk sugar**—দুগ্ধ হইতে উৎপন্ন চিনি। **Milk-tooth**—দুধের দাঁত। **Milk-tree**—গোপাদপ। **Mlik-walk**—গোয়ালা যত দুরে দুগ্ধের জোগান দেয়। **Milk-white**—দুধেরমত শাদা, দুগ্ধবৎশ্বেত, দুগ্ধধবল, দুগ্ধফেনিভ। **Milk and honey** — ভোগবিলাসের প্রাচুর্য্য। **Milk-and-water** — *adj.* & *n.* Tasteless ; insipid ; feeble ; স্বাদহীন ; নীরস, পানসে ; ক্ষীণ। (*Noun*) What is insipid ; feeble or mawkish discourse or sentiment ; নীরস বিষয় ; দুর্ব্বল ভাবোচ্ছ্বাসপূর্ণ আলোচনা, দুর্ব্বল ভাবোচ্ছ্বাস। **Milk for babes**—শিশুসাহিত্য, শিশুর উপযোগী মত প্রভৃতি। **Milk of lime**—চুনের জল **The milk of human kindness** --স্বাভাবিক দয়াবৃত্তি, সমবেদনা, বদান্যতা। **This accounts for the milk in the cocoanut**—ইহা দ্বারা বিষয়টা পরিষ্কার হইল। **To cry over spilt milk**—To indulge in useless regrets ; বৃথা পরিতাপ করা, অপ্রতিবিধেয় বিষয়ের জন্য আক্ষেপ করা। (cf. গতস্য শোচনা নাস্তি)।

milk, *v. t.* **1.** To draw milk from ; দুধ দোয়া, গোদোহন করা। **2.** To compel to yield profit or advantage ; as, to *milk* a person ; দোহন করা। **3.** To steal the message from, as a telegraph or telephone wire ; টেলিগ্রাফ বা টেলিফোঁর তার হইতে খবর চুরি করা। **4.** To draw out the sap, venom, etc. from (a snake) ; সর্পাদি হইতে বিষ, রস প্রভৃতি নিষ্কর্ষণ করা। **To milk a telegram**—To make use of a telegram surreptitiously ; as, they receive their telegrams in cipher to avoid their being *milked* by rival journals ; গোপনে কোন তারের খবর জানিয়া লইয়া তাহার ব্যবহার করা। **To milk the ram or bull**—To engage in a hopeless enterprise ; বালি দিয়া সাগর বাঁধিতে চেষ্টা করা, অসম্ভব কার্য্যে প্রবৃত্ত হওয়া।

milk'-ỹ, *adj.* **1.** Pertaining to, resembling, or mixed with, milk ; whitish and turbid ; as, the water is *milky* ; দুগ্ধসম্বন্ধীয়, দুগ্ধবৎ, দুগ্ধমিশ্রিত ; সাদা, ঘোলা। **2.** Yielding milk, as an animal or plant ; দুগ্ধপ্রদ, ক্ষীরপ্রদ, দুধিয়া, শুভ্ররসপ্রদ। **3.** Gentle ; timorous ; effeminate ; "Has friendship such a faint *milky* heart" ; ধীর, শান্ত ; ভীরু ; ভেড়াকান্ত, কাপুরুষ। **—i-ness,** *n.* **Milky-way** — ছায়াপথ, সোমধারা (বঃ দঃ নঃ), নাগবীথী (সাঃ পঃ), স্বর্গঙ্গা, আকাশগঙ্গা, ব্যোমগঙ্গা।

mill, *n.* **1.** A machine or building fitted with machinery for manufacturing processes etc. ; as, a cotton *mill* ; কল, কলঘর (হিঃ কোঃ)। **2.** A building provided with machinery for grinding grain into flour ; ময়দা প্রভৃতির কলঘর। **3.** An apparatus for grinding corn or any solid substance to powder or pulp ; যাঁতা, পেষণযন্ত্র। **4.** Any of various machines which produces manufactured product or change the condition of raw material ; as, cotton *mill*, oil *mill* etc. : কল। **5.** A pugilistic encounter ; মুষ্টিযুদ্ধ। **Mill-dam**—কলের কাজে লাগাইবার জন্য স্রোতঃস্বিনীতে যে বাঁধ দেওয়া হয়, চক্রবন্ধ (আঃ বঃ)। **Mill-hand**—কলের মজুর। **Mill-race**—যে জলস্রোতঃ দ্বারা কলের চাকা ঘূর্ণিত হয়। **Millstone** — যাঁতার পাথর, শিলাপট্ট, যন্ত্রোপল। **Mill-wheel** — কল চালাইবার জন্য জলপ্রবাহি চালিত চক্র। **Millwright**—কলের নক্সাকার, কলনির্ম্মাতা। **Much water runs by the mill**—আমাদের অজ্ঞাতসারে অনেক ঘটনা ঘটিয়া যায়। **To bring grist to the mill**—To add to one's income or profits ; আয় বা লাভ বৃদ্ধি করা। **To bring more sacs to the mill** — যুক্তির উপর যুক্তি দেওয়া, ভারের উপর ভার দেওয়া। **To go or pass through the mill** — কোন বিষয়ে জ্ঞান বা কোন বিশেষ মানসিক অবস্থা লাভের জন্য কষ্ট, পরিশ্রম বা অভিজ্ঞতার ভিতর দিয়া যাওয়া। **To put through the mill**—To cause to pass through the mill ; কলের ভিতর দিয়া চালান। **To see far into a millstone**—(*Usu. iron.*) To be extraordinarily acute ; (প্রায়শঃ অবজ্ঞাচ্ছলে) অসাধারণ সূক্ষ্মবুদ্ধিসম্পন্ন হওয়া।

mill, *v. t.* & *i.* **1.** To pass (as, a cloth etc.) through a fulling mill ; চাপকলের (কাপড় প্রভৃতি) ভিতর দিয়া চালান। **2.** To grind ; to comminute ; পেষণ করা, পেষা ; চূর্ণ করা, গুঁড়া

করা।, **3.** To make a raised border on the edge and to put ridges and furrows on the rim of, as a coin ; also to stamp (a coin) ; টাকা প্রভৃতির কিনারায় চারিদিকে প্রান্তবেষ্টন রেখা তোলা, টাকা প্রভৃতির কিনারায় খাঁজ কাটা ; (টাঁকশালে) মুদ্রিত করা। **4.** To make frothy, as by churning or whipping ; as, *to mill* chocolate ; ফেনায়িত করা, ফেনিল করা। **5.** To beat or strike ; to fight ; প্রহার করা, আঘাত করা ; যুদ্ধ করা। ***Verb i.*** **1.** To swim under water (used of whales among whale-fishers) ; জলের নীচে সাঁতার দেওয়া (তিমি-মৎস্য সম্পর্কে)। **2.** To move in a circle, as a cattle upon a plain ; ঘুরা

mill, *n.* (*U. S.*) A money of account, being one thousandth part of a dollar ; ১ ডলারের সহস্র ভাগ,—যাহা কেবল হিসাবে ধরা হয় কিন্তু প্রকৃতপক্ষে যাহার কোন সত্তা নাই।

mil-lĕ-nā'-ri-ăn, *adj.* & *n.* Of, or pertaining to, thousand years ; of, or pertaining to, the millennium ; having faith in it ; সহস্রবার্ষিক ; খৃষ্টের সহস্রবর্ষব্যাপীরাজত্ব সম্বন্ধীয় ; খৃষ্টের সহস্রবর্ষব্যাপী রাজত্বে বিশ্বাসী। ***Noun.*** A believer in the millennium ; খৃষ্টের সহস্রবর্ষব্যাপী রাজত্বে বিশ্বাসী ব্যক্তি। **—ism,** *n.*

mil'-lĕ-nā-rȳ, *adj.* & *n.* **1.** Pertaining to, or consisting of, a thousand years ; সহস্রবার্ষিক, সহস্রবর্ষব্যাপী। **2.** Of, relating to, or beieving in the millennium ; খৃষ্টের সহস্রবর্ষব্যাপী রাজত্বসম্বন্ধীয়, খৃষ্টের সহস্রবর্ষব্যাপী রাজত্বে বিশ্বাসী। ***Noun.*** **1.** A period of one thousand years ; সহস্রবর্ষকাল। **2.** A MILLENARIAN. **3.** A thousandth anniversary or its celebration ; as, the King Alfred *millenary* ; সহস্রবার্ষিক স্মৃতি-উৎসব, সহস্রবার্ষিক অনুষ্ঠান।

mil-lĕn'-ni-ŭm (-ĭ-), *n.* **1.** Period of thousand years, esp. that of Christ's reign in person on the earth (*Rev.* xx. 1-5) ; সহস্রবর্ষ, বর্ষসহস্র, বিশেষতঃ যীশুখৃষ্ট সশরীরে ধরাধামে অবতীর্ণ হইয়া যে সহস্রবর্ষকাল পৃথিবীতে রাজত্ব করিবেন। **2.** (*Fig.*) A time or period of great happiness ; (লক্ষণায়) পরম সুখ ও শান্তি সমৃদ্ধির যুগ, সত্যযুগ, রামরাজ্য। **—ni-al,** *adj.*

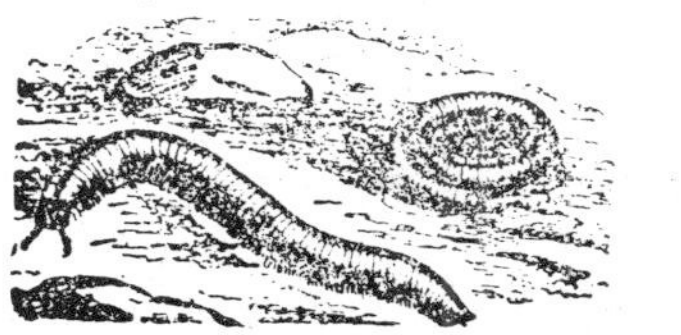

Millepede.

mil'-lĕ-pede (-pēd), *n.* An insect with numerous legs ; the wood-louse ; বহুপদী কীট ; কাষ্ঠ-মৎকুণ।

mill'-ĕr, *n.* **1.** One who owns, operates, or attends a corn-mill ; ময়দার কলের সত্ত্বাধিকারী, পেষণ-যন্ত্রচালক, শস্যপেষক, পেষণোপজীবী। **2.** A moth with white powdered wings ; শ্বেতচূর্ণময়পক্ষবিশিষ্ট পতঙ্গবিশেষ। **3.** A young spotted fly-catcher ; ফুট ফুট দাগবিশিষ্ট চোখদয়ালা পাখী। **Miller's thumb** — কয়েক প্রকার ক্ষুদ্র মৎস্যের সাধারণ নাম।

mil-lĕs'-i-măl, *adj.* & *n.* **1.** Thousandth ; consisting of thousandth parts ; সহস্র; সহস্রাংশাত্মক। ***Noun.*** A thousandth part ; সহস্রাংশ।

mil'-let (-ĕt), *n.* A kind of small grain of various speices used for food in many countries ; the plant bearing this ; চীনা, শ্যামাক, পলাল, রাজিকা, বাজরা, প্রিয়ঙ্গু (Italian millet), চীনাক (Indian millet) ; চীনা গাছ। **Kod millet**—কোদ্রব (ভাবঃ)। **Spiked millet**— কঙ্গু

mil'-li-ărd, *n.* A thousand millions ; শতকোটী।

mil'-li-nĕr (-ĭ-), *n.* A person (usu. a woman) who makes up bonnets and other dresses for women ; স্ত্রীলোকের টুপি, পোষাক প্রভৃতি প্রস্তুতকারী (সাধারণতঃ স্ত্রীলোক) **—y,** *n.* **Man-milliner**—(লক্ষণায়) সামান্য কাজে ব্যস্ত লোক।

mil'-lion (-yŏn), *n.* & *adj.* **1.** The number of ten hundred thousand or a thousand thousand ; নিযুত, দশলক্ষ, প্রযুত। **2.** A million pounds or dollars ; এক নিযুত পাউণ্ড বা ডলার। ***Adj.*** Numbering, or consisting of, a million ; নিযুতসংখ্যক। **—fold,** *adj.* & *adv.* **—lionth,** *adj.* & *n.* **The million**—The bulk of the population ; অধিকাংশ লোক।

mil-lion-aire' (-yŏn-âr), *n.* A man worth a million of money ; a person of great wealth ; লক্ষপতি, ক্রোড়পতি, লক্ষেশ, কোটীশ্বর ; ধনকুবের।

milor(d), *n.* French word for English lord or wealthy Englishman ; ইংলণ্ডের লর্ড বা ধনী ইংরেজের ফরাসী প্রতিশব্দ।

milt, *n.* & *v.t.* **1.** The roe or spawn of the male fishes ; পুং মৎস্যের ডিম্ব। **2.** The spleen ; প্লীহা। ***Verb t.*** To impregnate as the roe of the female fish ; স্ত্রী মৎস্যের ডিম্বে গর্ভাধান করা।

milt'-ĕr, *n.* A male fish in breeding time ; সঙ্গমঋতুর পুংমৎস্য।

Mil-tŏn'-ic, *adj.* Characteristic of, or pertaining to, Milton or his style ; মিল্টন সম্বন্ধীয়, মিল্টনের রচনা-সম্বন্ধীয়। **—to'-ni-an,** *adj.*

mime, *n.* & *v. i.* **1.** (*Gk.* or *Rom. Antiq.*) Simple farcical drama marked by mimicry ; প্রহসন। **2.** An actor in such performances ; প্রহসনের অভিনেতা। **3.** A buffoon ; a clown ; বিদূষক, বৈহাসিক ; ভাঁড়। ***Verb i.*** To play a part with mimic gesture and usually without words ; বিকৃত অঙ্গ-ভঙ্গীর সহিত কোন ভূমিকার অভিনয় করা।

mim'-ĕ-ō-grăph, *n.* An apparatus for making stencils of written pages from which many copies may be taken ; যে যন্ত্রের সাহায্যে কোন ফলকে কোন পত্রাদির প্রতিলিপি

অঙ্কিত হয় এবং যাহা হইতে বহু অনুলিপি গৃহীত হইতে পারে, অনুলিপিকা।

mī-mē'-sis, *n.* (*Biol.*) Same as MIMICRY 3.

mī-mĕt'-ic, *adj.* **1.** Apt to imitate; given to aping or mimicry; অনুকরণপ্রবণ; বিকৃতঅঙ্গভঙ্গীপ্রবণ। **2.** (*Biol.*) Characterized by mimicry (See MIMICRY 3.) **—i-cal-ly,** *adv.*

mĭm'-ic, *adj.* & *n.* **1.** Apt to imitate; অনুকরণপ্রবণ। **2.** Imitative, (*opposed to real*); as, a *mimic* king; ভণ্ড, জাল, নকল। ***Noun.*** A person skilled in ludicrous imitation; হাস্যোদ্দীপক অনুকরণকুশল ব্যক্তি।

mĭm'-ic, *v. t.* **1.** To ridicule by imitation; ভ্যাঙ্গচান। **2.** To copy or imitate very closely or servilely: as, he *mimicked* her walk: ব্যঙ্গচ্ছলে অনুকরণ করা, হীনভাবে অনুকরণ করা। **3.** (Of things) To resemble closely; সৌসাদৃশ্য থাকা, অনুরূপ হওয়া।

mĭm-ic'-rȳ, *n.* **1.** Act of mimicking; ludicrous imitation; an instance of this; নকল, অনুকরণ; হাস্যোদ্দীপক অনুকরণ; ভ্যাঙ্গচানি। **2.** At hing that mimics another; অনুকরণকারী, ব্যঙ্গাত্মক, অনুকরণকারী। **3.** (*Zool.*) The wonderful resemblance certain plants or animals exhibit to certain other plants or animals or to the natural objects in the midst of which they live; (জন্তুবিজ্ঞান) কোন কোন বৃক্ষ বা কীট পতঙ্গাদির নির্দিষ্ট বৃক্ষ, পতঙ্গাদি বা নিকটস্থ প্রাকৃতিক পদার্থনিচয়ের সহিত আশ্চর্য্য সাদৃশ্যপ্রদর্শন। (যথা—শত্রুর আগমনে কোন কোন কীট পত্র, শুষ্কবৃন্ত বা অন্য জীবের আকার ধারণ করে)।

mĭm-i-nȳ—pĭm'-i-nȳ, *adj.* Over-refined; finical; অতিরিক্ত মার্জ্জিত-রুচি; অতিরিক্ত সূক্ষ্ম-বিচারী, উৎকট-রুচি।

Mimir, *n.* A water giant of Norse mythology; নরওয়ে সুইডেনের পুরাণে উক্ত জলদৈত্য। এই দৈত্য Yggdrasill বৃক্ষনিম্নস্থ জ্ঞানবাপী রক্ষা করিত। এই বাপী জ্ঞান ও স্মৃতিশক্তির মূল নির্ঝর। Odin, Mimir দানবকে একটী চক্ষু প্রদান করিয়া একবার মাত্র ঐ বাপীর জলপান করিতে পারিয়াছিলেন। Mimir ঐ চক্ষু পানপাত্র রূপে ব্যবহার করিত।

mī-mō'-să, *n.* A genus of leguminous shrubs including the sensitive plant; লজ্জাবতী জাতীয় গুল্ম।

mī-ū'-lŭs, *n.* A genus of flowering shrubs, esp. the monkey-flower: একপ্রকার পুষ্প-প্রসূ গুল্ম।

mī'-nă, *n.* **1.** An ancient unit of weight used in Greece, Egypt etc.; গ্রীস, মিসর, প্রভৃতি দেশের প্রাচীন মান বিশেষের একক। **2.** A denomination of money in Greece about £4; গ্রীসদেশীয় মুদ্রা বিশেষ [প্রায় ৪ পাউণ্ড]।

mī'-nă, *n.* A kind of Eastern bird; ময়না।

mī-nā'-cious (-shŭs), *adj.* Threatening; menacing; ভয়প্রদ; ভীতিপ্রদ, ভয়প্রদর্শক। **—ly,** *adv.* **—nac'-i-ty,** *n.*

mī-năr', *n.* **1.** A lighthouse; আলোকমন্দির। **2.** A turret; ক্ষুদ্র বুরুজ, মিনার।

Minaret.

mĭn'-ă-rĕt, *n.* A slender lofty turret on a Mohammedan mosque from which the people are summoned to prayers; মসজিদের বুরুজ, মসজিদের চূড়া।

mĭn'-ă-tō-rȳ, *adj.* Threatening; menacing; ভয়প্রদ, ভীতিসঞ্চারক; ভয়প্রদর্শক, ভয়সূচক, ভীতিজনক।

mince (mĭns), *v. t.* & *i.* **1.** To cut or chop into very small pieces; as, to *mince* meat; কুচি কুচি করিয়া কাটা, খোড় কুচান, অতি কুচি কুচি করিয়া খোড়া। **2.** To moderate or restrain; as, to *mince* one's words; to utter, as words in an affectedly refined manner; সংযত করা; কৃত্রিম সুরুচির সহিত কথা বলা। ***Verb i.*** To walk with short steps or in an affected manner; "Hold up your head and *mince*"; গুড়ি গুড়ি করিয়া চলা, কৃত্রিম ভঙ্গী সহকারে চলা। **Minc'-ing-ly,** *adv.* In a mincing or affectedly nice manner; কৃত্রিম সৌষ্ঠবের সহিত। **Mince-meat**—খোড়কুচান মাংস; খোড়কুচান মাংস, চর্ব্বি, সেওফল, কিসমিস প্রভৃতির পুর। **Mince-pie**—A pie made of mince-meat; খোড়কুচান মাংসের পিঠা। **To make mince meat of**—To destroy as a person; খোড় কুচান, কাটিয়া কুচি কুচি করা। **Not to mince matters**—To speak outright; সোজাসুজি বলা, স্পষ্টাস্পষ্টি বলা, খোলাখুলি করিয়া বলা, লজ্জা বা ভদ্রতার জন্য সঙ্কোচ না করিয়া বলা।

mince (mĭns), *n.* Minced meat; কুচি কুচি করিয়া কাটা মাংস, খোড় কুচান মাংস।

mīnd, *n.* **1.** Remembrance; as, to keep in *mind*; মন, স্মৃতি। **2.** Sentiment; opinion; belief; "A fool uttereth all his *mind*"; মনোভাব; মত; বিশ্বাস। **3.** Direction of thought or desires; inclination; as, to set one's *mind on* something; মনের গতি; মনোরথ, রুচি, প্রবৃত্তি, মতি। **4.** Mental disposition; way of thinking or feeling; as, state of *mind* ; মনোভাব, মনের ভাবগতি ; চিন্তাপ্রণালী। **5.** Seat of consciousness, thought, volition and feeling ; মন, চিত্ত, মর্ম্ম, অন্তঃকরণ, মানস, মানসমন্দির (*poet.*) মর্ম্মপুর (*poet.*), মরম (*poet.*)। **6.** (*Psychol.*) The subject of consciousness or the soul considered as such a subject ; (মনোবিজ্ঞান) মন, দেহী। **7.** The intellectual powers as opposed to emotion and will ; "I fear, I am not in perfect *mind*"; চিত্তবৃত্তি, বুদ্ধিবৃত্তি। **8.** A person thought of with reference to his mental qualities; as, great *minds*; ধীমান ব্যক্তি। **9.** (*Philos.*) Spirit, as contrasted with matter ; চিৎ, অজড়। **Mind'-less,** *adj.* **1.** Unintelligent ; senseless ; মতিহীন, নির্ব্বোধ ; জ্ঞানহীন। **2.** Unmindful ; thoughtless ; অমনোযোগী, অন্যমনস্ক, অনবহিত ; ভাবনাহীন। **Absence of mind** — অন্যমনস্কতা। **Mind's eye**—মানসনেত্র, মনশ্চক্ষুঃ। **Presence of mind**—উপস্থিতবুদ্ধি, প্রত্যুৎপন্নমতিত্ব। **To be in two minds about a thing**—To be in doubt about it ; কোন বিষয়ে সন্দেহ থাকা। **To be of a** or **one mind**—To agree ; একমত হওয়া। **To be or go out of one's mind**—To lose one's reason or wits ; মতিচ্ছন্ন হওয়া, বিকৃতমস্তিষ্ক হওয়া, বিকৃতবুদ্ধি হওয়া। **To be of one's mind** — To agree in opinion with one ; একমত হওয়া, একচিত্ত হওয়া। **To change one's mind**—To change one's plan or purpose ; মত পরিবর্ত্তন করা, মন পরিবর্ত্তন করা। **To cross one's mind**—To occur to one's mind ; কাহারও মনে উদয় হওয়া, মনে পড়া। **To give a person a piece** or **bit of one's mind**—To give a person one's candid opinion ; কাহাকেও মুখের উপর ই কথা শুনাইয়া দেওয়া। To rebu তিরস্কার করা। **To give one's mind to**—To attend to, কোন বিষয়ে মন দেওয়া। **To go** or **pass out of mind**—To be forgotten ; বিস্মৃত হওয়া, ভুলিয়া যাওয়া। **To have a good** or **great mind to**—To be strongly disposed to ; খুব ইচ্ছুক হওয়া, প্রবল অভিলাষী হওয়া। **To have half a mind to**—To have a certain inclination ; কতকটা ইচ্ছা থাকা। **To have** or **keep in mind, To bring** or **call to mind**—To remember ; স্মরণ করা, মনে করা। **To know one's own mind**—To form or adhere to a decision ; কোন বিষয়ে স্থিরাসিদ্ধান্ত করা, কোন বিষয়ে মনঃস্থির করা বা দৃঢ়সংকল্প হওয়া। **To make up one's mind**—To resolve ; মন স্থির করা, সংকল্প করা। **To my mind**—As I think ; আমার যেরূপ মনে হয়, আমার মতে। **To one's mind**—As one would have it ; কাহারও মতে, কাহারও চক্ষে। **To put in mind of**—To remind ; স্মরণ করাইয়া দেওয়া, মনে করিয়া দেওয়া। **To set one's mind on**—To desire to attain ; কোন বিষয় লাভ করিতে চেষ্টা করা।

mĭnd, *v. t.* & *i.* **1.** To give heed to ; মন দেওয়া মনোযোগ দেওয়া, দৃক্‌পাত করা। **2.** To occupy oneself with ; as, to *mind* one's business ; মনোনিবেশ করা। **3.** To object to ; to dislike ; as, if you don't *mind* walking ; আপত্তি করা ; অপসন্দ করা। **4.** To remember or bear in mind (*chiefly imperative*) ; স্মরণ রাখা, মনে রাখা। **5.** To be careful about ; (*imperative*) to take care that ; as, *mind* you do it ; সতর্ক হওয়া ; সাবধান হওয়া। **6.** To have the charge of ; as, to *mind* a baby ; ভার লওয়া। ***Verb i.*** **1.** To be concerned or troubled ; to care ; (*in negative constructions*), as, never *mind* ; ভাবনা থাকা ; চিন্তা থাকা। **2.** To take care ; as, *mind* that he does not go away ; সাবধান হওয়া। **3.** To pay heed ; "Now, *mind*, mother, not a word about" , মন দেওয়া, সতর্ক থাকা। **Does not mind**—খেয়াল করেনা, দৃকপাত করে না। **Mind one's P's and Q's**—To be careful as to one's words or behaviour ; নিজের আচরণ বা কথাবার্ত্তা সম্বন্ধে সতর্ক হওয়া। **Mind your eye**—Be careful, or vigilant ; সাবধান হও, সতর্ক হও। **Mind your own business**—Attend to your own affairs leaving others alone ; নিজের চরকায় তেল দাও। **Never mind**—কুছপরওয়া নাই, চিন্তা নাই, ভাবনা নাই, রেখে দাও।

mīnd'-ĕd, *adj.* **1.** Disposed ; inclined ; "If men were *minded* to live virtuously" ; ইচ্ছুক, মনস্ক ; প্রবৃত্ত, উন্মুখ। **2.** Having (such) a mind ; as, high or small *minded* ; মনাঃ (in compound).

mīnd'-fŭl, *adj.* Regardful ; attentive ; (used with *of*); অবহিত, যত্নবান্‌, যত্নশীল ; মনোযোগী, সাবধান, সাবহিত। **—ly,** *adv.* **—ness,** *adj.*

mīne, *n.* **1.** An excavation in the earth for metal, coal, salt, etc. ; সুড়ঙ্গ (হিঃ কোঃ), আকর, খনি। **2.** (*Fig.*) A rich source ; an abundant store ; as, a *mine* of information ; (লক্ষণায়) খনি, আকর, (যথা রত্নাকর), ভাণ্ডার। **3.** Iron ore ; খনিজবিমিশ্র লৌহ। **4.** (*Mil.*) An excavation dug under a fortification to blow it up with gunpowder ; (সামরিক-শাস্ত্র) বারুদ প্রভৃতি দ্বারা দুর্গাদি উড়াইয়া দিবার জন্য তন্নিম্নে খনিত সুড়ঙ্গ, কুল্যা (আ: ব:)। **5.** (*Nav.*) A receptacle filled with dynamite and sunk or kept floating, esp. at the entrance to a harbour to destroy or impede the progress of hostile vessels ; শত্রুপক্ষীয় পোত ধ্বংস বা বাধা প্রদানের উদ্দেশ্যে জলে বিশেষতঃ পোতাশ্রয়ের প্রবেশদ্বারে

যে বিস্ফোরক দ্রব্যপূর্ণ কুম্ভ ডুবাইয়া বা ভাসাইয়া রাখা হয়, জলাশান, বিস্ফোরক কুম্ভ।

mīne, *v. t.* & *i.* **1.** To dig or burrow in earth ; খনন করা। **2.** To make as a hole underground ; to furnish with underground passages ; ভূগর্ভে গর্ত্ত করা ; সুড়ঙ্গ খনন করা, বিবর খনন করা। **3.** (*Fig.*) To undermine ; to sap ; (লক্ষণায়) অধঃখনন করা ; গোপনে ধ্বংস বা মূলোচ্ছেদ করা। **4.** (*Mil. & Nav.*) To lay a mine or mines under ; নিম্নে বিস্ফোরক দ্রব্যপূর্ণ ভাণ্ড বা ভাণ্ড সমূহ স্থাপন করা। **5.** To dig into as earth for ore or metal ; to get as metal from a mine ; ধাতু বা খনিজ বিমিশ্র ধাতুর জন্য ভূগর্ভে খনন করা ; খনি হইতে ধাতু প্রাপ্ত হওয়া। ***Verb i.*** **1.** To form a subterranean tunnel or hole (*obs.*) ; (অপ্রঃ) সুড়ঙ্গ খনন করা। **2.** To dig a mine for the purpose of obtaining minerals ; খনিজ পদার্থের জন্য খনি খনন করা।

mīne, *poss. pron.* & *adj.* Corresponding to *my* ; আমার, মম, মদীয়।

min'-êr, *n.* **1.** A worker in a mine ; খনক, আকরিক, খনিকর, বেলদার। **2.** A soldier whose duty is to lay mines ; যে সৈনিক দুর্গাদির নিম্নে বিস্ফোরকদ্রব্য স্থাপন করে।

min'-êr-ăl, *adj.* & *n.* **1.** Obtained from mines, as a substance ; খনিজ, আকরজ। **2.** Inorganic ; জড়, অজৈব। **3.** Impregnated with minerals, as water ; লৌহ, লবণ, প্রভৃতি খনিজ পদার্থ সম্পূরিত। ***Noun.*** **1.** A substance obtained by mining ; খনিজপদার্থ, আকরজ দ্রব্য, রস (রঃ রঃ সঃ প্রঃ), আকরিক (সাঃ পঃ)। **2.** Each of the species into which the inorganic substances are classified ; অজৈব পদার্থ সমূহ যে সকল শ্রেণীতে বিভক্ত করা যায় তাহাদের অন্যতম। **—i-za'-tion,** *n.* **—ize,** *v. t.* & *i.* **1.** To convert into an ore ; খনিজ-বিমিশ্র পদার্থে পরিণত করা। **2.** To petrify ; as *mineralized* leaves ; শিলীভূত করা। **3.** To impregnate with minerals as water খনিজ পদার্থ দ্বারা সম্পূরিত করা। ***Verb i.*** To engage in collecting minerals ; খনিজদ্রব্য সংগ্রহকার্যে নিযুক্ত হওয়া। **Mineral acids** — গন্ধক, যবক্ষার, প্রভৃতির দ্রাবক, খনিজ দ্রাবক। **Mineral oil**—কেরোসিনতৈল, খনিজ-তৈল (হিঃ কোঃ)। **Mineral stone**—গোরোচনা। **Mineral-water**—লৌহ, লবণ, প্রভৃতি খনিজ পদার্থ মিশ্রিত নির্ঝর-বারি (যাহা ঔষধ স্বরূপ ব্যবহৃত হয়) ; কৃত্রিম ঝরণার জল, বিশেষ ভাবে বিলাতী পানি (Soda-water) ; জিঞ্জার বীয়ার প্রভৃতি স্ফোটনশীল পানীয় দ্রব্য।

min-êr-ăl'-ō-ġȳ, *n.* The science of minerals ; খনিজবিদ্যা, ধাতুশাস্ত্র, গৈরিকবিদ্যা (সাঃ পঃ)। **—gist,** *n.* One versed in mineralogy ; ধাতুবিদ্যা বিশারদ, খনিজতত্ত্ববিৎ। **—og'-i-cal,** *adj.* **—og'-i-cal-ly,** *adv.*

Mi-nêr'-vă, *n.* (*Rom. Myth.*) The goddess of wisdom, liberal arts etc. ; গ্রীকপুরাণোক্ত বাণী দেবী। **Minerva-press** — ঊনবিংশ শতাব্দীর প্রথমভাগে লণ্ডন নগরীস্থ মুদ্রাযন্ত্রবিশেষ ; ঐ মুদ্রাযন্ত্র হইতে প্রকাশিত উৎকট ভাবোচ্ছ্বাসপূর্ণ উপন্যাসমালা।

min'-gle (mĭng-gl), *v. t.* & *i.* To mix or blend ; "Milk and blood being *mingled* both together" ; মিশ্রিত করা, মিশান, মিশা, মিশ্রিত হওয়া।

min'-i-āte, *v. t.* **1.** To paint or tinge with vermilion ; সিন্দুর দ্বারা রঞ্জিত করা, সিন্দুররঞ্জিত করা। **2.** To illuminate, as a manuscript ; হস্তলিপি প্রভৃতির আদ্যক্ষর স্বর্ণ, রজত বা নানাসমুজ্জ্বল বর্ণরাজিতে রঞ্জিত করা।

min'-i-ā-tūre *n., adj.* & *v. t.* **1.** A painting on a very small scale, on ivory, vellum or thick paper ; as, she had a *miniature* of her husband ; গজদন্ত, ধাতুফলক, স্থূলকাগজ প্রভৃতির উপর অঙ্কিত ক্ষুদ্র চিত্র। **2.** A picture in an illuminated manuscript ; নানাবর্ণচ্ছটামণ্ডিতাক্ষর প্রাচীন হস্তলিপির অন্তর্গত চিত্র। **3.** The art of painting miniatures ; ক্ষুদ্র চিত্রাঙ্কন-বিদ্যা। **4.** A greatly diminished size or scale ; as, a picture in *miniature* ; ক্ষুদ্র আয়তন, ক্ষুদ্র আকার। **5.** A reduced image ; হ্রস্বীকৃত মূর্ত্তি। ***Adj.*** Much reduced from reality ; on a small scale ; as, a *miniature* copy ; অতি ক্ষুদ্রাকারে অঙ্কিত ; ক্ষুদ্র আকারের। ***Verb t.*** To represent in miniature ; ক্ষুদ্রাকারে প্রদর্শন করা। **—tur-ist,** *n.* A maker of miniatures ; ক্ষুদ্র-চিত্রাঙ্কণকারী। **In miniature**—On a small scale ; ক্ষুদ্রাকারে।

min'-i-fȳ, *v. t.* To lessen in size or importance ; to represent as less important ; ক্ষুদ্রায়তন করা, গৌরব হ্রাস করা, খাটো করা, খর্ব্ব করা ; খাটোভাবে দেখান।

min'-i-kin, *n.* & *adj.* A diminutive creature ; ক্ষুদ্রাকৃতি জীব, বালখিল্য। ***Adj.*** **1.** Tiny ; very small or diminutive ; অতিক্ষুদ্র ; বালখিল্যবৎ। **2.** Affected ; mincing ; "*Minikin* duties of civily" ; কৃত্রিম ; চাল চলন ও কথাবার্ত্তায় কৃত্রিম সৌষ্ঠব প্রদর্শনকারী।

min'-im, *n.* **1.** (*Mus.*) A note equal in time to half a semibreve or two crotchets ; (সঙ্গীত শাস্ত্র) দীর্ঘস্বর (মঃ ইঃ)। **2.** A single downstroke of a pen, as any of the three in the letter *m* ; নীচের দিকে কলমের এক টান। **3.** A creature or thing of the smallest size or importance ; কণা, নগণ্য মানুষ জন্তু বা চুণো পুঁটি। **4.** One-sixtieth part of a fluid drachm ; এক তরল ড্রামের ষাট ভাগের এক ভাগ, বিন্দু, ফোঁটা। **Minim-glass** — একড্রামের অংশ বা ফোঁটা মাপিবার জন্য গ্লাস।

min'-i-măl, *adj.* Least ; smallest ; as, a *minimal* amount ক্ষুদ্রতম,

অল্পতম, অল্পিষ্ঠ। 2. Very minute; অতিসূক্ষ্ম।

min'-i-mize, *v. t.* To reduce to a minimum; to estimate at a minimum; যথাসম্ভব হ্রাস করা, খর্ব করা; যথাসম্ভব অল্প করিয়া ধরা। **—mi-za'-tion,** *n.*

min'-i-mum, *n.* (*Pl.* -MA) The smallest quantity or degree: অল্পতম সংখ্যা, অল্পতম পরিমাণ, ন্যূনতমসংখ্যা, অল্পতমমাত্রা, ন্যূনতম মাত্রা, অধঃসীমা, অধমসীমা (হিঃ কোঃ), সর্ব্বাল্প সংখ্যা। **Minimum thermometer**—একপ্রকার অঙ্কুশাকৃতি তাপমান যন্ত্র ইহার দক্ষিণ শাখা সম্পূর্ণ ও বাম শাখার অধিকাংশ সুরাবীর্য্যদ্বারা পূর্ণ থাকে। এই সুরাবীর্য্যের উপরিতলের টানে (surface tension) একটী ক্ষুদ্র প্রদর্শনী উহার নীচে সংলগ্ন থাকে। উত্তাপ বৃদ্ধি পাইলে সুরাবীর্য্য বাম শাখার নলের নিম্নদিকে ধাবিত হয় এবং প্রদর্শনীটি পশ্চাতে থাকিয়া ন্যূনতম তাপ মাত্রা সূচিত করে, নিম্ন তাপমান।

min'-i-mus *adj.* (In schools) Youngest of the name; as, Jones *minimus*; কোন বিশেষ নামধারী ছাত্রগণের মধ্যে বয়ঃকনিষ্ঠ।

min'-ion (-yŏn), *n.* 1. (*Contempt.*) A favourite child, animal, etc.; (অবজ্ঞাচ্ছলে) আলালের ঘরের দুলাল, আদরের জন্তু। 2. A slave; ক্রীতদাস। 3. (*Print.*) A size of type; একপ্রকার ক্ষুদ্রাকৃতি মুদ্রাক্ষর।

min'-ish, *v. t.* & *i.* 1. (*Archaic*) To reduce in power or influence; (অপ্রঃ) ক্ষমতা হ্রাস করা, শক্তি খর্ব্ব করা, প্রভাব হ্রাস করা। 2. To diminish: খর্ব্ব করা, হ্রাস করা, কমান। *Verb i.* To diminish; to lessen; হ্রাস হওয়া, খর্ব্ব হওয়া; কম হওয়া।

min'-is-ter, *n.* 1. An administrative chief of a department of State; মন্ত্রী, সচিব, অমাত্য, রাজমন্ত্রী। 2. A person employed in execution, as of a purpose, will, etc.; কোন কার্য্য নির্ব্বাহার্থ নিযুক্ত ব্যক্তি, কার্য্যসাধক, কার্য্যনির্ব্বাহক। 3. A diplomatic agent sent from one state to another; এক রাজ্য হইতে অপর রাজ্যে প্রেরিত কূটরাজনীতিবিশারদ প্রতিনিধি। 4. A pastor; a clergyman; যাজক; আচার্য্য, উপাধ্যায়। **Finance minister** — রাজস্বসচিব, সুমন্ত্রক (শুক্রঃ বিনয়)। **Prime minister**—প্রধানমন্ত্রী, প্রধানামাত্য, মহামন্ত্রী। **War minister**—সমরসচিব।

min'-is-ter, *v. t.* & *i.* 1. (*Obs.*) To administer or manage, as affairs; (অপ্রঃ) নির্ব্বাহ করা, পরিচালনা করা। 2. (*Archaic*) To furnish or supply; যোগান। *Verb i.* 1. To render aid; to be helpful or conducive; as, to *minister* to a person, cause, etc.; সাহায্য প্রদান করা; সহায়ক হওয়া, ফলোপধায়ক হওয়া। 2. To attend or serve; পরিচর্য্যা করা, সেবা করা। 3. To act as a minister of the church; যাজকের কার্য্য করা। **Ministering angel**—রক্ষাকারী দেবদূত, পরহিতব্রত ব্যক্তি, পরের দুঃখমোচন নিরত ব্যক্তি।

min'-is-te'-ri-al, *adj.* 1. Relating to the execution of law; বিধিব্যবস্থা নির্ব্বাহসম্বন্ধীয়, রাজবিধি নির্ব্বাহসম্বন্ধীয়। 2. Instrumental; contributive; "*Ministerial* intellectual culture"; কার্য্যসাধক, কারণীভূত; সহায়ক। 3. Of, or relating to, a minister of a State; মন্ত্রিসম্বন্ধীয়, রাজমন্ত্রিসম্বন্ধীয়। 4. Of, or relating to, the minister of the Gospel; যাজকসম্বন্ধীয়, উপাধ্যায়সম্বন্ধীয়। 5. Supporting the Ministry against the Opposition; প্রতিপক্ষের বিরুদ্ধে মন্ত্রিসমাজসমর্থক। **—ist,** *n.* A supporter of the ministry; মন্ত্রি-সমাজসমর্থক। **—ly,** *adv.* **Ministerial officer**—আমলা।

min-is-trā'-tion, *n.* 1. Act of ministering, esp. in religious matters; সম্পাদন, নির্ব্বাহ, বিশেষতঃ যাজকের কার্য্য সম্পাদন, যাজন। 2. Act of furnishing anything; as, *ministration* of food; সরবরাহ করণ।

Min'-is-trant, *adj.* & *n.* Ministering; সম্পাদনকারী, নির্ব্বাহকারী। *Noun.* One who ministers; সম্পাদক, নির্ব্বাহক। **Min'-is-tra-tive,** *adj.*

min'-is-trȳ, *n.* 1. The act of ministering; সম্পাদন, যাজন। 2. Instrumentality; কর্তৃত্ব। 3. The office or function of a minister; ecclesiastic or ambassadorial function; মন্ত্রিত্ব, সাচিব্য; যাজকতা, দৌত্য। 4. The body of ministers of a State; মন্ত্রিবর্গ, মন্ত্রিসমাজ, সচিবমণ্ডল। 5. The clergy; যাজকমণ্ডলী, যাজকসম্প্রদায়।

min'-i-ŭm, *n.* Red oxide of lead; মেটে সিন্দুর, সিন্দুর (হিঃ কোঃ)।

Minnow.

min'-now (-ō), *n.* A kind of small fish; ক্ষুদ্র মৎস্য বিশেষ। **Triton among the minnows**—One who seems great from the insignificance of those around him; বাঘ নাই বনে শেয়াল রাজা, নিরস্তপাদপে দেশে এরণ্ডোঽপি দ্রুমায়তে।

mī'-nŏr, *adj.* & *n.* 1. Lesser; inferior in bulk, degree, importance, etc.; as, a *minor* prophet or poet; ক্ষুদ্রতর, অল্প, অপ্রধান (হিঃ কোঃ); অল্পতর, অবর, লঘুতর। 2. (In school) The younger; as, Jones *minor*; (বিদ্যালয়ে) বয়ঃকনিষ্ঠ। 3. Absolutely small; petty; as, *minor* faults; অতিক্ষুদ্র; তুচ্ছ, সামান্য। *Noun.* 1. A Franciscan friar; ফ্রানসিস্‌ক্যান সম্প্রদায়ভুক্ত সন্ন্যাসী। 2. A person of either sex under age; নাবালক, নাবালিকা, অপ্রাপ্তবয়স্ক ব্যক্তি, অপ্রাপ্তব্যবহার ব্যক্তি। 3. Same as MINOR TERM or MINOR PREMISS. **Minor deity**—উপদেবতা। **Minor mode**—রাগিণী। **Minor premiss**—(*Log.*) The premiss of a syllogism in which the minor and middle terms are compared ; (তর্কবিজ্ঞান) সাবয়বক বাক্যের যে পুর্ব্বাবয়বে পক্ষ এবং হেতু তুলিত হইয়া থাকে, বাপ্যপুর্ব্বাবয়ব (হিঃ কোঃ), উপনয় (হিঃ কোঃ)। **Minor term**—(*Log.*) The subject of the conclusion of a categorical syllogism ; (তর্কবিজ্ঞান) পক্ষ, (সাঃ পঃ) ব্যাপ্যপদ।

mi-nŏr'-i-tȳ, *n.* **1.** State of being under age ; অপ্রাপ্তবয়স্কতা, নাবালকত্ব, অপ্রাপ্তব্যবহারতা, অপ্রাপ্তব্যবহারদশা। **2.** The smaller in number of two aggregates ; the party having the fewest votes ; as, the *minority* must be ruled by the majority ; অল্পসংখ্যা, অল্পতা, ন্যূনসংখ্যা, ন্যূনতা, অপ্রধানতা (হিঃ কোঃ) ; যে পক্ষের ভোটসংখ্যা অপেক্ষাকৃত অল্পতর। **3.** The number of votes cast for by the party called minority ; মতদাতৃগণের দুই দলের মধ্যে যে দলের সংখ্যা অল্পতর তাহাদের মত-সংখ্যা।

Mi'-nŏs, *n.* An ancient king of Crete ; ক্রীট দ্বীপের জনৈক প্রাচীন রাজা।

Min'-ō-taur (-tär), *n.* (*Greek myth.*) A fabulous monster, having the body of a man with the head of a bull and fed with human flesh, (with *the* prefixed) ; (গ্রীকপুরাণ) গ্রীক পুরাণোক্ত বৃষভমুণ্ড দানববিশেষ। এই দানব মনুষ্যমাংস ভক্ষণ করিত। ইহার ভোজনের জন্য প্রতিদিবস এথেন্স নগরী হইতে এক এক জন তরুণ যুবক বা যুবতী প্রেরিত হইত, বৃষভমুণ্ডদৈত্য বিশেষ, বৃষভাসুর, নরবৃষভ (আঃ বঃ)।

min'-stêr, *n.* **1.** A church of a monastery ; খৃষ্টীয় মঠের অন্তর্গত ভজনালয়। **2.** A large or important church ; প্রকাণ্ড ভজনালয়।

min'-strĕl *n.* **1.** One of a mediæval class of musical entertainers who sung or recited (often his own) poetry ; বন্দী, চারণ, ভাট, স্তুতিপাঠক, মাগধ, বৈতালিক, সূত। **2.** (*Hist.*) A person who entertained his patrons with singing, buffoonery, etc. ; (ইতিহাস) ভাঁড়, বিদূষক। **3.** (*Pl.*) A class of performers of negro songs and music with blacked faces in imitation of negroes ; একশ্রেণীর গায়ক যাহারা নিগ্রোদিগের মত মুখ কৃষ্ণবর্ণে রঞ্জিত করত নিগ্রো গানবাদ্য করে।

min'-strĕl-sȳ, *n.* **1.** The arts and occupation of ministrels ; মাগধবৃত্তি, চারণবৃত্তি। **2.** Collective body of ministrels ; বন্দিসমাজ, চারণসম্প্রদায়। **3.** Ministrel poetry ; চারণগাথা, ভাটের গান।

mint, *n.* **1.** A place where money is coined, usually by public authority ; টাকশাল, টঙ্ক-শালা। **2.** A place or source of invention etc. ; উদ্ভাবন প্রভৃতির স্থান, খনি। **3.** A vast sum or amount ; as, this cost a *mint* of money ; বিস্তর ধন, সাতরাজার ধন। **Mint-mark**—মুদ্রার উপর মুদ্রিত টঙ্কশালার বিশিষ্টচিহ্ন। **Mint-master** — টঙ্কশালাধ্যক্ষ, টঙ্কপতি। **Mint of money**—A large fortune ; সাতরাজার ধন।

mint, *v. t.* **1.** To make (coins) by stamping metal ; মুদ্রাপ্রস্তুত করা। **2.** (*Fig.*) To coin ; to fabricate ; to invent ; "Words, such as are daily *minted*" ; (লক্ষণায়) (নূতন শব্দ) গঠন করা ; রচনা করা ; উদ্ভাবন করা।

mint, *n.* Aromatic plant used in cookery ; পুদিনা।

mint'-āge, *n.* **1.** Act or process of coining money ; মুদ্রাপ্রস্তুত করণ। **2.** (*Fig.*) Fabrication or production ; (লক্ষণায়) রচনা, উৎপাদন। **3.** The product of a mint ; টাকশালায় তৈয়ারী মুদ্রা। **4.** The duty paid for coining ; মুদ্রা প্রস্তুতের জন্য দেয় শুল্ক।

min'-ū-ĕnd, *n.* (*Arith.*) The number or magnitude from which another number or magitude is to be subtracted ; (গণিতশাস্ত্র) যে রাশি হইতে অন্য রাশি বিয়োগ করা হয়।

min-ū-ĕt', *n.* A slow dance or music for it ; ধীর পদসঞ্চালনপূর্ব্বক নৃত্য বিশেষ বা ঐ নৃত্যোপযোগী বাদ্য।

mi'-nŭs, *quasi-prep* & *adj.* **1.** Decreased by ; as, seven *minus* four is equal to three ; ব্যবকলিত, ঋণিত। **2.** (*Colloq.* Deprived of ; without ; as, he left *minus* his pocket-book ; হীন, বিরহিত, বিহীন, ঋণ, ঊন। ***Adj.*** Negative ; as, a *minus* quantity ঋণাত্মক।

mi-nŭs'-cūle, *adj.* & *n.* Small, (applied to letters so called) ; ক্ষুদ্র। ***Noun.*** A small letter or character used in mediæval manuscripts ; মধ্যযুগের হস্তলিপিতে ব্যবহৃত ক্ষুদ্র অক্ষর।

min'-ute (-ĭt) *n.* **1.** One sixtieth of a degree ; মিনিট, কলা (হিঃ কোঃ)। **2.** A short time ; an instant ; "I go this *minute* to attend the king" ; মুহূর্ত্ত ; ক্ষণ, নিমেষ, নিমিষ। **3.** A note to preserve the memory of anything ; স্মরণলিপি। **4.** (*Pl.*) A brief summary of the proceedings of committee etc. ; সভা, সমিতি, প্রভৃতিতে আলোচিত বিষয়ের সংক্ষিপ্ত সার। **Minute-book**—যে পুস্তকে সভা, সমিতি, প্রভৃতিতে আলোচিত বিষয়ের সংক্ষিপ্তসার লিপিবদ্ধ করিয়া রাখা হয়, সভাবিবরণী। **Minute gun** — যে কামান প্রতি মিনিটে দাগা যায়। **Minute hand**—ঘড়ীর মিনিটের কাঁটা।

min'-ute (-ĭt), *v. t.* **1.** To ascertain the exact time of ; as, to *minute* the duration of an eclipse ; সঠিক কাল নির্ণয় করা। **2.** To set down in a short sketch or note ; as, to *minute* an agreement in writing ; to draft as a document ; সংক্ষেপে লিপিবদ্ধ করা ; মুসাবিদা করা। **To minute down**—To make a note of ; মন্তব্য করা।

mi-nūte', *adj.* **1.** Very small ; অতি ক্ষুদ্র, সূক্ষ্ম, অণুক, অণিষ্ঠ (হিঃ কোঃ)। **2.** Of very small importance ;

petty ; নগণ্য ; সামান্য, তুচ্ছ, অকিঞ্চিৎকর । 3. Accurate ; precise ; as, a *minute* observation ; সূক্ষ্ম ; সঠিক । **–ly,** *adv.* In a minute manner ; পুঙ্খানুপুঙ্খরূপে, পাতি পাতি করিয়া, সূক্ষ্মভাবে, তন্ন তন্ন করিয়া । **–ness,** *n.*

min′-ute-lȳ (-ĭt-), *adj.* & *adv.* Happening every minute ; প্রতি মিনিটে সংঘটিত । ***Adv.*** From minute to minute ; "*Minutely* proclaimed in thunder from heaven" ; মিনিটে মিনিটে ।

mi-nū′-ti-ă, (-shi-) *n.* (*Pl.* -AE) Precise or trivial detail ; খুঁটিনাটি ।

minx (mĭngks) *n.* A pert girl ; wanton woman or jade ; বেহায়া ছুঁড়ি, প্রগল্‌ভা বালিকা, গেছোমেয়ে ; ভ্রষ্টা নারী, ছেনাল ।

mī′-ō-cene (-sēn), *adj.* (*Geol.*) Of, or relating to, the middle division of tertiary strata ; (ভূ-বিদ্যা) মধ্যাধ্বনিক (সাঃ পঃ) ।

mĭr′-ă-cle (-kl), *n.* 1. A wonder or wonderful thing ; a marvel ; অলৌকিক বিষয় ; অপ্রাকৃত বস্তু । 2. A remarkable occurrence ; আশ্চর্য্য ঘটনা, অদ্ভুত ঘটনা ; অলৌকিক ঘটনা (হিঃ কোঃ), আশ্চর্য্যব্যাপার । 3. A supernatural act or event ; অতিপ্রাকৃতক্রিয়া, দৈবঘটনা (হিঃ কোঃ), অতিপ্রাকৃত ঘটনা । 4. A surpassing example, as of some quality ; as, a *miracle* of ingenuity or impudence ; অপূর্ব্ব দৃষ্টান্ত । 5. Same as MIRACLE PLAY. **A miracle play**—মধ্যযুগে অভিনীত যীশুখৃষ্ট অথবা খৃষ্টীয় সিদ্ধপুরুষগণের জীবনের ঘটনামূলক নাটক । **To a miracle**—Surprisingly well ; as, he fulfilled the requirements to a *miracle* ; অলৌকিকরূপে ।

mĭ-răc′-ū-lous (-lŭs), *adj.* 1. Supernatural ; অতিপ্রাকৃত, অলৌকিক, অতিমানুষ । 2. Marvellous ; wonderful ; অদ্ভুত ; আশ্চর্য্য, অপরূপ, পরমাশ্চর্য্য, অপ্রাকৃত । **–ly,** *adv.* **–ness,** *n.*

mĭ-rage′ (-râzh), *n.* Optical illusion ; esp. illusive appearance of a sheet of water in a desert etc., (*lit.* & *fig.*) ; দৃষ্টিভ্রম ; মরীচিকা, মায়ামরীচিকা, মৃগতৃষ্ণা, মৃগতৃষ্ণিকা, জলাভাস, গগননগর, গন্ধর্ব্বনগর, আতপোদক, মৃগজল (হিঃ কোঃ), মায়াজল মায়াবারি, মায়ারূপী ।

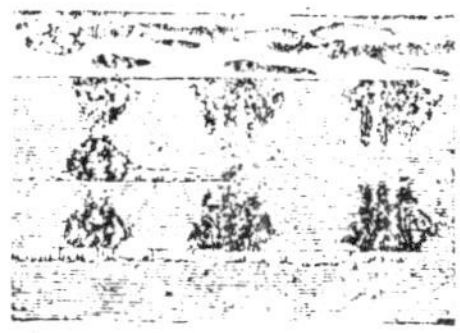

Mirage.

mīre, *n.* 1. Swampy earth ; হোড় । 2. Soft or deep mud ; dirt ; পঙ্ক, পাঁক, কর্দ্দম ; ময়লা । **To stick or find oneself in the mire**—To be involved in difficulties ; গোলে পড়া ।

mīre, *v. t.* & *i.* 1. To plunge or fix in mire ; as, to *mire* a horse ; কর্দ্দমমগ্ন করা, পঙ্কমগ্ন করা, পাঁকে আটকান । 2. (*Fig.*) To involve in difficulties ; (লক্ষণায়) গোলে ফেলা, ঝঞ্ঝাটে ফেলা । 3. To soil or defile with mire, (*lit.* & *fig.*) ; "Smirched thus and *mired* with infamy" ; ময়লা করা, কর্দ্দমলিপ্ত করা, পঙ্কলিপ্ত করা, পঙ্কিল করা । ***Verb i.*** To sink or stick in mire ; পাঁকে আটকাইয়া যাওয়া, পাঁকে ডুবিয়া যাওয়া ।

mĭr′-ror (-ēr), *n.* & *v. t.* 1. A looking glass ; আয়না, আর্শি, দর্পণ, আদর্শ, মুকুর, আত্মদর্শক । 2. (*Fig.*) A pattern ; an exemplar ; (লক্ষণায়) আদর্শ ; দৃষ্টান্ত । ***Verb t.*** To reflect as in a mirror ; প্রতিবিম্বিত করা, প্রতিফলিত করা ।

mirth (mêrth), *n.* Merriment ; হর্ষ, আনন্দ, উল্লাস, স্ফূর্ত্তি, আমোদ আহ্লাদ, হাসিতামাসা, রঙ্গরস, হাস্যবিনোদ, ক্রীড়াকৌতুক । **Mirth′-ful,** *adj.* Full of mirth ; joyous ; উৎফুল্ল, প্রফুল্ল, উল্লসিত ; সহর্ষ, হর্ষাকুল, হৃষ্ট, উল্লাসী । **Mirth′-ful-ly,** *adv.* **Mirth′-ful-ness,** *n.* **Mirth′-less,** *adj.*

mīr′-ȳ, *adj.* 1. Resembling mire ; muddy ; পঙ্কবৎ ; পঙ্কিল, মলিন, কর্দ্দমময়, পঙ্কময়, সকর্দ্দম, পঙ্কলিপ্ত, সপঙ্ক, পঙ্কক্লিন্ন, কর্দ্দমিত, পঙ্কদূষিত, পঙ্কাক্ত, পঙ্কদিগ্ধ । 2. (*Fig.*) Filthy ; vile ; "A *miry* business" ; (লক্ষণায়) জঘন্য ; কদর্য্য ।

mirza, *n.* A Persian title ; পারস্য-দেশের উপাধি বিশেষ, মির্জ্জা । [উপনামের পরে বসিলে "রাজপুত্র" ও পূর্ব্বে বসিলে "শ্রীযুক্ত" বুঝায় ।]

mis-ăd-vĕn′-tūre, *n.* Mischance ; misfortune ; a mishap ; দুর্ঘটনা, দুর্দ্দৈব, আপদ্ ; দুর্ভাগ্য, দুরদৃষ্ট, দুর্গতি ; অনিষ্টাপাত । **Homicide by misadventure**—(*Law*) Homicide by accident ; (আইন) দৈবকৃত নরহত্যা ।

mis-ăl-lī′-ance (-ăns), *n.* An improper alliance, esp. in marriage ; অপসম্বন্ধ, কুসম্বন্ধ, হীনসম্বন্ধ ।

mis′-ăn-thrōpe, *n.* A hater of mankind ; মনুষ্যদ্বেষী, নরদ্বেষী, জনশত্রু, জনদ্বেষ্টা, বিশ্বজনদ্রোহী, বিশ্বদ্রোহী, বিশ্ববিদ্বেষী, জনবৈরী । **–an′-thro-pist, –an′-thro-py,** *ns.* Hatred of mankind ; নরদ্বেষ, মানবদ্বেষ, বিশ্ববিদ্বেষ, জনদ্বেষ । **–an′-thro-pize,** *v. t.* & *i.* To make, or become, misanthrope ; নরদ্বেষী করা বা হওয়া । **–throp′-ic, –throp′-i-cal,** *adjs.* Hating mankind ; নরদ্বেষী ।

mis-ăp-plȳ′, *v. t.* To apply or use for a wrong purpose ; as, to *misapply* a name or fund ; অপব্যবহার করা, অপপ্রয়োগ করা । **–pli-ca′-tion,** *n.* Wrong use (esp. of funds) ; অপপ্রয়োগ, কুপ্রয়োগ, অপব্যবহার, অসৎপ্রয়োগ, অস্থানপ্রয়োগ, অন্যথাপ্রয়োগ ।

mis-ăp-prē-hĕnd′, *v. t.* To misunderstand ; ভুল বুঝা, ভ্রমপূর্ণ অর্থ গ্রহণ করা । **–hen′-sion,** *n.* The act of misapprehending ; অনর্থগ্রহণ, অন্যথাবোধ, অর্থবিপর্য্যাসকরণ । **–hen′-sive,** *adj.* **–hen′-sive-ly,** *adv.*

mis-ăp-prō′-pri-āte, *v. t.* To apply or appropriate wrongly ;

as, to *misappropriate* public money ; গচ্ছিত অর্থ আত্মসাৎ করা, তহবিল তছরুফ করা, স্থাপ্যাপহরণ করা। **—a'-tion,** *n.* The act of misappropriating ; গচ্ছিত অর্থ আত্মসাৎ করণ, তহবিল তছরুফ, স্থাপ্যাপহরণ।

mis-bĕ-come' (-kŭm), *v. t.* To suit ill ; not to befit or become ; ভালরূপে না মানান ; মানানসই না হওয়া, অযোগ্য হওয়া, অশোভন হওয়া।

mis-bĕ-gŏt'-ten (-tn), *adj.* Illegitimate ; bastard ; (*usu. a term of opprobrium*) ; বিজাত, বিজন্মা ; জারজ।

mis-bĕ-hāve', *v. t.* To conduct improperly ; অসঙ্গত ব্যবহার করা, অযুক্ত ব্যবহার করা, দুরাচরণ করা। **—hav'-iour,** *n.* Misconduct ; অসদাচরণ, অন্যায়াচরণ, অসঙ্গত ব্যবহার।

mis-bĕ-lief' (-lēf), *n.* **1.** Wrong belief in religious matter ; ভ্রান্ত-ধর্ম্মবিশ্বাস। **2.** False opinion or notion ; অলীকমত, মিথ্যা ধারণা। **—liev'-er,** *n.* **—liev'-ing.** *adj.*

mis-bĕ-seem' (-sēm), *v. t.* Same as MISBECOME.

mis-căl'-cū-lāte, *v. t.* To calculate wrongly ; to misjudge ; ভ্রান্ত গণনা করা ; অবিচার করা। **—la'-tion,** *n.* The act of miscalculating ; ভ্রান্ত গণনা, অবিচার।

mis-call', *v. t.* **1.** To call by a wrong name ; ভুল নামে ডাকা। **2.** (*Dial.*) To call (one) names ; (উপভাষায়) গালি দেওয়া।

mis-căr'-riage (-rĭj), *n.* **1.** Failure (of letter) to reach destination ; (চিঠি সম্বন্ধে) উদ্দিষ্ট স্থানে না পৌঁছন। **2.** Failure ; mistake ; non-success ; as, the criminal escaped by a *miscarriage* of justice : *miscarriage* of a scheme ; ব্যর্থতা, অসিদ্ধি, নিষ্ফলতা ; ভ্রান্তি ; অকৃতকার্য্যতা। **3.** Premature delivery ; গর্ভধারণের ছয় সপ্তাহের মধ্যে গর্ভস্রাব, গর্ভচ্যুতি, গর্ভপাত, অকালগর্ভ নিঃসরণ, পিণ্ডপাত। **Miscarriage of justice**—বিচার-বিভ্রাট, অন্যায়বিচার।

mis-căr'-rȳ, *v. i.* **1.** To fail ; to come to naught ; as, the business *miscarried* ; ব্যর্থ হওয়া ; পণ্ড হওয়া। **2.** To be delivered untimely (of child) ; গর্ভস্রাব হওয়া, গর্ভপাত হওয়া। **3.** (Of letters) To fail to reach destination ; "The Cardinal's letters to the Pope *miscarried*" ; (পত্র সম্পর্কে) উদ্দিষ্ট স্থানে না পৌঁছা।

mis-căst'-ing, *n.* **1.** Wrong addition, as of accounts ; ভুল যোগ। **2.** Bad casting, as of metal ; খারাপভাবে ঢালাই করণ।

mis-cĕ-gĕ-nā'-tion, *n.* An interbreeding of races, esp. the interbreeding of whites and negroes ; জাতিসঙ্কর উৎপাদন, কাফ্রী ও শ্বেতাঙ্গের সংযোগে সঙ্করসন্তানোৎপাদন।

mis-cĕl-lā'-nē-ă, *n.* Matters of various kinds, esp. literary miscellany ; বিবিধ বিষয়, বিবিধপ্রকার রচনা সংগ্রহ, নানাবিষয়ক রচনা সংগ্রহ, বিবিধ প্রবন্ধ।

mis-cĕl-lā'-nē-ous (-ŭs), *adj.* **1.** Mixed ; consisting of several kinds ; as, *miscellaneous* collection ; মিশ্রিত ; নানাপ্রকার, নানাবিধ, প্রকীর্ণ, নানাবিষয়ক। **2.** Having various qualities ; treating of various topics and subjects ; as, a *miscellaneous* writer ; নানাগুণ-সম্পন্ন ; নানাবিষয়ক, বিবিধবিষয়ক। **3.** (With *pl. noun*) Of various sorts ; হরেক রকমের। **—ly,** *adv.* **—ness,** *n.*

mis'-cĕl-lă-nȳ, *n.* **1.** A mixture of various things ; medley ; নানাদ্রব্যের মিশ্রণ ; খিচুড়ী। **2.** A collection of writing on different subjects ; নানাবিষয়ক রচনা-সংগ্রহ, বিবিধ রচনা-সংগ্রহ। **3.** A volume containing such writings ; নানাবিষয়কগ্রন্থ, প্রকীর্ণগ্রন্থ, বিবিধ প্রবন্ধ। **—nist,** *n.*

mis-chance' (-chăns), *n.* Ill luck ; an instance of it ; misfortune ; as, by *mischance* ; দুর্ভাগ্য ; দুর্ভাগ্য-জনক ঘটনা ; দুর্দ্দৈব, দুরদৃষ্ট। **By mischance**—দুর্দ্দৈববশতঃ, দুর্ভাগ্যক্রমে।

mis'-chief (-chĭf), *n.* **1.** Harm, or injury wrought by human or other agency ; হানি, ক্ষতি। **2.** A cause or source of evil, harm or vexation ; a worker of mischief ; "A curly-headed *mischief*" ; অনিষ্টের হেতু ; অনিষ্টকারী। **3.** Vexatious conduct, esp. of children ; বিরক্তিজনক আচরণ, দুষ্টামি, দুরন্তপনা। **Mischief-maker,** *n.* যে ব্যক্তি একের নিন্দা অপরের নিকট করিয়া উভয়ের মধ্যে মনোমালিন্যের সৃষ্টি করে, অনর্থ-সংঘটনকারী, সুহৃদ্ভেদকারী। **Mischief-making,** *n.* Fomenting discord esp. by talebearing ; ঐরূপভাবে মনোমালিন্যের সৃষ্টি, সুহৃদ্ভেদ। **The mischief of it is that etc.**—The annoying part of it is that etc. ; ইহাতে বিরক্তিজনক বিষয় এই যে। **To make mischief**—To create discord, esp. by talebearing ; মনোমালিন্যের সৃষ্টি করা, বিশেষতঃ কোন ব্যক্তির বিরুদ্ধে অপর ব্যক্তির কাছে কানাঘুষা করিয়া দুই ব্যক্তির মধ্যে বিরোধ বাঁধান। **To play the mischief with**—To cause great damage or injury to ; to ruin ; নিতান্ত ক্ষতিগ্রস্ত বা অনিষ্ট করা ; নাশ করা।

mis'-chie-vous (-chĭ-vŭs), *adj.* **1.** Harmful ; hurtful ; injurious ; "Most *mischievous* foul sin" ; ক্ষতিজনক, অপকারক, অহিতকারী, অনিষ্ট-কারী, অহিতজনক ; পীড়াজনক ; অনিষ্ট জনক, অনিষ্টকারক। **2.** Inclined to do harm ; annoying or troublesome in conduct ; as, a *mischievous* boy ; অপকারবুদ্ধি, দ্রোহবুদ্ধি ; দুরন্ত, দুষ্ট। **—ly,** *adv.* **—ness,** *n.*

mis'-ci-ble (-ĭ-bl), *adj.* Capable of being mixed with ; মিশ্রণীয়, মিশ্রণযোগ্য। **--bil'-i-ty,** *n.*

mis-cŏn-ceive' (-sēv), *v. t.* & *i.* To have a false notion or conception of; to misunderstand, as a word, person, etc.; মিথ্যা ধারণা করা, ভ্রান্ত ধারণা থাকা; ভুল বুঝা। ***Verb i.*** To have a false conception of; মিথ্যা ধারণা থাকা। **—cep'-tion**, *n.* False conception; ভ্রান্ত ধারণা, ভুল সংস্কার।

mis-cŏn'-dŭct, *n.* **1.** Improper conduct or behaviour, esp. adultery; অন্যায়াচরণ, অনাচার, অযুক্ত আচরণ, অন্যায়ব্যবহার, অসঙ্গত আচরণ, অসদাচরণ, দুর্নীতি, বিশেষতঃ ব্যভিচার। **2.** Mismanagement; "For *misconduct* of diplomatic affairs"; বেবন্দোবস্ত।

mis-cŏn-dŭct', *v. t.* & *reflex.* To mismanage; খারাপভাবে নির্ব্বাহ করা। ***Reflex.*** To misbehave অসঙ্গত আচরণ করা, অন্যায়ব্যবহার করা।

mis-cŏn'-strue (-strō), *v. t.* **1.** To interpret erroneously, esp. a word, action etc.; ভুল অর্থ করা, ভুল ব্যাখ্যা করা, ভ্রমপূর্ণ অর্থ করা, বিকৃত অর্থ করা। **2.** To mistake the meaning of, as a person; কাহারও অভিপ্রায় ভুল বুঝা। **—struc'-tion**, *n.* Wrong interpretation; অসঙ্গত ব্যাখ্যা, অযথার্থ ব্যাখ্যা।

mis-count' (-cownt), *n.* An erroneous counting, esp. of votes; ভ্রান্তগণনা, ভুলগণনা।

mis'-cre-ănt, *adj.* & *n.* **1.** Villainous; base; দুর্বৃত্ত, দুর্জ্জন, পামর, দুরাচার; দুরাত্মা, নীচ, পাজী, পাষণ্ডী। **2.** (*Archaic*) Heretical; (অপ্রঃ) অপধর্ম্ম-সেবী। ***Noun.*** **1.** A vile wretch; নরাধম, দুর্জ্জন। **2.** (*Archaic*) A heretic; an infidel; (অপ্রঃ) পাষণ্ডী; নাস্তিক।

mis-cre-ăt'-ĕd, *adj.* Formed improperly; misformed; (*often used as an abusive term*); কদাকার; কুগঠিত। **—a'-tion**, *n.*

mis-cue' (-cū), *n.* (*At billiards*) A failure to strike the ball properly with the cue; (বিলিয়ার্ড খেলায়) ক্রীড়াযষ্টি দ্বারা কন্দুক যথাযথরূপে তাড়নে অপারগতা।

mis-dāte', *v. t.* & *n.* To date erroneously; ভুল তারিখ দেওয়া। ***Noun.*** A wrong date; ভুল তারিখ।

mis-deal' (-dēl), *v. t.* & *i.* To deal improperly, as cards etc.; অন্যায়রূপে বাঁটা, গোলমাল করিয়া বাঁটা। ***Verb i.*** **1.** To behave improperly; অযুক্ত ব্যবহার করা, অসঙ্গত আচরণ করা। **2.** To make a wrong distribution of cards to the players; অন্যায়রূপে তাস বাঁটা।

mis-deed' (-dēd), *n.* An evil deed; a crime or offence; কুকার্য্য, দুষ্ক্রিয়া, কুক্রিয়া, অকার্য্য, দুষ্কৃতি, দুষ্কর্ম্ম, অপকর্ম্ম, কুকাজ; অপরাধ।

mis-deem' (-dēm), *v. t.* & *i.* (*Archaic, poet.*) **1.** To form a wrong opinion of; to misjudge; (অপ্রঃ বা কবিতায়) অন্যায় মত পোষণ করা; অবিচার করা। **2.** To mistake (for); ভুল করা। ***Verb i.*** To have, or form, a wrong opinion of; ভ্রান্তমত পোষণ করা, ভ্রান্ত ধারণা পোষণ করা।

mis-dē-mean'-ănt (-mēn-), *n.* A person convicted of misdemeanour; অন্যায়াচরণের জন্য দণ্ডিত ব্যক্তি।

mis-dē-mean'-our (-mēn-ĕr), *n.* **1.** Ill behaviour; evil conduct; দুশ্চরিত্রতা, দুরাচরণ, অসঙ্গত আচরণ; দুর্ব্যবহার, অসদাচরণ। **2.** (*Law.*) An offence of a less atrocious character than a crime; (আইন) লঘু অপরাধ।

mis-di-rĕct' *v. t.* To direct wrongly; বিপথে চালিত করা, ভ্রান্তপথে চালিত করা। **—rec'-tion**, *n.*

mis-dō'-ing, *n.* Misdeed; দুষ্ক্রিয়া, দুষ্কর্ম্ম, অপকর্ম্ম।

mis-doubt' (-dowt) *v. t.* & *i.* (*Archaic*) **1.** To have doubts as to the truth or existence of; (অপ্রঃ) কোন কিছুর সত্তা বা সত্যতা সম্বন্ধে সন্দেহ করা। **2.** To be suspicious about; to mistrust; "I do not *misdoubt* my wife"; কোন বিষয়ে সন্দেহ করা; অবিশ্বাস করা। ***Verb i.*** (*Archaic*) To suspect; (অপ্রঃ) সন্দেহ করা।

mise (mēz), *n.* (*Hist.*) Settlement by agreement; (ইতিহাস) মীমাংসা, মিটমাট।

mī'-sĕr, *n.* **1.** One having wealth but living miserably; কৃপণ, ব্যয়-কুণ্ঠ, কঞ্জুষ, অদাতা। **2.** An avaricious man; অর্থগৃধ্নু ব্যক্তি।

mī'-sĕr, *n.* A boring instrument for well-sinking; কূপখননার্থ যন্ত্রবিশেষ।

mĭs'-ĕr-ă-ble (-bl), *adj.* **1.** Very unhappy; wretched; pitiable; অতিদুঃখী; দুর্দ্দশাগ্রস্ত; দীন, করুণ। **2.** Causing misery or unhappiness; as, a *miserable* lot; দুঃখজনক, দুর্গতিজনক, দুর্দ্দশাজনক। **3.** Contemptible; mean; as, a ***miserable*** man; a *miserable* dinner; হেয়, ঘৃণ্য; নীচাশয়। **—bly**, *adv.*

misère, *n.* Same as MISERY 2.

mĭs-ē-rē'-rē, *n.* **1.** (*Eccl.*) The 51st psalm; (যাজকীয় শাস্ত্র) ৫১ সংখ্যক ধর্ম্ম-সংগীত। **2.** A cry for mercy; "The monotonous cry of *miserere* for the poor Irish"; দয়া কর।

mĭs'-ĕr-ĭ-cŏrd, *n.* **1.** A relaxation of the rule; নিয়ম শিথিল করণ। **2.** (*Eccl.*) A room in which some indulgences were allowed; খৃষ্টীয় মঠের কক্ষ-বিশেষ — যাহাতে পানাহার সম্পর্কে বিশেষ সুবিধাপ্রাপ্ত সন্ন্যাসিগণ ভোজন করিতেন। **3.** A narrow-bladed mediæval dagger used by a knight to give the death or "Mercy" stroke to a fallen adversary; মধ্যযুগে ব্যবহৃত একপ্রকার সরুফলার ছুরী—যদ্দ্বারা কোন নাইট পতিত শত্রুকে খতম ঘা দিত।

mī'-sĕr-lȳ, *adj.* Like a miser; stingy; কৃপণবৎ; ছেঁচড়া, কঞ্জুষ। **—li-ness**, *n.*

mis-'êr-ŷ, *n.* **1.** Wretchedness ; distress or unhappiness due to outword conditions, esp. to privation or poverty ; দুঃখ, দুর্দ্দশা, দুর্গতি ; দুরবস্থা, বিপত্তি। **2.** (*Cards, Colloq.*) A declaration by which a player engages to lose every trick ; (তাসখেলা) যে ঘোষণা দ্বারা কোন ক্রীড়ক সকল পিঠ হারিবে বলিয়া অঙ্গীকার করে।

mis-fea'-sance (-fē-zăns), *n.* (*Law*) Transgression, esp. the doing of a lawful act in a wrongful manner ; (আইন) অন্যায়, দোষ, ত্রুটি, বিশেষতঃ অন্যায়রূপে কোন আইনসঙ্গত কার্য্য করণ।

mis-fit', *n.* A dress that does not fit the person, it is meant for ; বেমানানসই পোষাক।

mis-fŏr'-tūne, *n.* Ill luck ; calamity ; দুর্ভাগ্য, দুর্দ্দৈব, বিপাক, মন্দভাগ্য ; বিপদ্, পোড়াকপাল (*colloq.*)। **Misfortune never comes alone**—বিপদ একা আসেনা।

mis-give' (-gĭv), *v. t.* To fill with doubt or suspicion ; সংশয়াকুল করা, আশঙ্কা বা উদ্বেগপূর্ণ করা।

mis-giv'-ing, *n.* Doubt ; mistrust ; সন্দেহ, শঙ্কা, আশঙ্কা; সংশয়, খটকা। **His mind misgives him**—His mind fills him with suspicion or foreboding *about* a thing ; তাহার মন আশঙ্কা ও উদ্বেগে পূর্ণ হয়।

mis-gov'-êrn (-gŭv-), *v. t.* To govern badly ; মন্দভাবে শাসন করা, কুশাসন করা। **–ment**, *n.* The act of misgoverning ; কুশাসন।

mis-guide' (-gīd), *v. t.* To guide wrongly ; to cause to err in thought or action ; (*chiefly in p. p.*) ; ভ্রান্তপথে পরিচালিত করা, কুপথে চালিত করা ; ভ্রান্তি জন্মান। **–guid'-ance**, *n.* **–guid'-ed**, *p. adj.* Misled ; ভ্রান্তপথে চালিত, বিপথগামী। **–guid'-ed-ly**, *adv.*

mis-hăn'-dle (-dl), *v. t.* To handle roughly or rudely ; নিগ্রহ করা।

mis-hăp', *n.* An unlucky accident ; দুর্ঘটনা, দুর্দ্দৈব, দৈব-দুর্ব্বিপাক, অনিষ্টাপাত, বিপত্তি।

mis-hear' (-hēr), *v. t.* & *i.* To hear amiss or imperfectly ; ভুল শোনা।

mish'-măsh, *n.* A medley ; jumble ; গোলমাল, বিশৃঙ্খলা ; হযবরল।

mish'-na(h) (-nă), *n.* The text of the Talmud ; তালমুদগ্রন্থের মূল। **–nic**, *adj.*

mis-in-fŏrm', *v. t.* To give wrong information to ; to mislead ; ভুল সংবাদ দেওয়া ; ভ্রান্তপথে পরিচালিত করা, বিপথে চালিত করা। **–for-ma'-tion**, *n.*

mis-in-têr'-prĕt, *v. t.* To interpret wrongly ; to make wrong inference from ; ভুল অর্থ করা, ভুল ব্যাখ্যা করা ; ভুল সিদ্ধান্ত করা। **–pre-ta'-tion**, *n.*

mis-judge' (-jŭj), *v. t.* & *i.* To judge erroneously ; to have false opinion of ; অন্যায় বিচার করা, অবিচার করা ; ভ্রান্তমত পোষণ করা। ***Verb i.*** To err in judging ; অবিচার করা।

mis-lay' (-lā), *v. t.* To lay in a place not recollected ; to lose ; as, to *mislay* one's hat ; অযথা স্থানে রাখা, বেঠিকানায় রাখা ; হারান।

mis-lead' (-lēd), *v. t.* **1.** To lead astray ; to guide into error ; ভ্রান্তপথে চালিত করা, বিপথগামী করা, উন্মার্গগামী করা ; বিপথে চালিত করা। **2.** To give wrong impression to ; ভ্রান্তসংস্কার জন্মান, ভ্রম জন্মান। **–ing**, *adj.*

mis-līke', *v. t.* (*Archaic*) To dislike ; (অপ্রঃ) অপছন্দ করা।

mis-măn'-āge, *v. t.* To manage ill or improperly ; খারাপভাবে নির্ব্বাহ করা। **–ment**, *n.* Bad management ; খারাপভাবে পরিচালনা, দুর্নির্ব্বাহ, বেবন্দোবস্ত, অব্যবস্থা।

mis-name', *v. t.* To call by a wrong name ; ভুল নামে ডাকা।

mis-nō'-mêr, *n.* **1.** Use of a wrong name ; ভুল নাম গ্রহণ। **2.** A wrong name ; ভুল নাম, মিথ্যানাম, অপনাম। **3.** Wrong use of a term ; কোন পদের অপপ্রয়োগ।

mi-sŏg'-ă-mŷ, *n.* Hatred of marriage ; বিবাহদ্বেষ, বিবাহবিদ্বেষ উদ্বাহদ্বেষ। **–mist**, *n.* One who hates marriage ; স্ত্রীদ্বেষী, বিবাহদ্বেষী, পরিণয়দ্বেষী।

mis-ŏ-gŷn'-ic, *adj.* Woman hating ; নারীবিদ্বেষী, স্ত্রীদ্বেষী।

mi-sŏg'-ŷ-nist, *n.* A hater of women ; নারীদ্বেষী, বনিতাদ্বেষী।

mi-sŏg'-ŷ-nŷ, *n.* Hatred of women ; স্ত্রীদ্বেষ, বনিতাদ্বেষ, নারীদ্বেষ।

mis-plăce', *v. t.* **1.** To put in a wrong place or hands ; অস্থানে রাখা। **2.** To set or place in an improper or unworthy objects ; as, he *misplaced* his confidence or affection ; অস্থানে রাখা, অযথা স্থানে রাখা, অপাত্রে ন্যস্ত করা। **–ment**, *n.*

mis-print', *n.* & *v. t.* A mistake in printing ; মুদ্রাকরপ্রমাদ, ছাপার ভুল, অশুদ্ধ ছাপা। ***Verb t.*** To print wrongly or incorrectly ; ভুল ছাপা করা, অশুদ্ধ ছাপা করা।

mis-pri'-sion (-zŏn), *n.* Wrong action or omission ; (now restricted to) conçealment of one's knowledge of treasonable designs etc. ; দুষ্কর্ম্ম, অন্যায়কর্ম্ম, অনবধানতা, ত্রুটী ; ষড়যন্ত্রমূলক অভিসন্ধি প্রভৃতি সম্বন্ধে অবগত হইয়া তাহা গোপন রাখন। **Misprision of treason** or **felony**—রাজার বিরুদ্ধে ষড়যন্ত্র কিংবা অন্য কোনরূপ গুরুতর অপরাধের বিষয় জানিয়া তাহা গোপন রাখন বা কর্ত্তৃপক্ষের কর্ণগোচর না করণ।

mis-pri'-sion (-zŏn), *n.* **1.** Contempt ; scorn ; অবজ্ঞা ; অশ্রদ্ধা। **2.** Failure to appreciate the value (of) ; মূল্যাবধারণাক্ষমতা।

mis-prize', *v. t.* **1.** To despise ; অশ্রদ্ধা করা, ঘৃণা করা। **2.** To undervalue ; তুচ্ছ মনে করা, হেয় জ্ঞান করা, হতাদর করা।

mis-prŏ-nounce′ (-nowns), *v. t.* To pronounce incorrectly ; অশুদ্ধ উচ্চারণ করা। **—nun-ci-a′-tion,** *n.*

mis-quōte′, *v. t.* To quote erroneously ; অযথার্থভাবে উদ্ধৃত করা, অযথার্থোদ্ধার করা। **—quo-ta′-tion,** *n.*

mis-read′ (-rĕd), *v. t.* To read amiss ; to interpret wrongly ; "The rich *misread* the signs of the times" ; ভুল পাঠ করা ; অযথার্থ ভাবে পাঠ করা, ভ্রান্ত ব্যাখ্যা করা।

mis-rĕp-rē-sĕnt′, *v. t.* To represent wrongly ; to give a false representation of ; ভ্রান্তভাবে বর্ণনা করা ; ভ্রান্তভাবে প্রদর্শন করা। **—sen-ta′-tion,** *n.* The act of misrepresenting ; মিথ্যাকথন, অন্যথাকথন, অযথার্থখ্যাপন, মিথ্যানিবেদন।

mis-rule′ (-rôl), *n.* Bad rule or government ; disorder ; কুশাসন ; বিশৃঙ্খলা। **Lord, Abbot** or **Master of misrule**—(ইতিহাস) খৃষ্টমাসের আমোদপ্রমোদের সভাপতি।

miss, *n.* **1.** Failure to hit or attain ; অকৃতকার্য্যতা, অসিদ্ধি, নিষ্ফলতা। **A miss is as good as a mile**—অকৃতকার্য্যতার ফল সর্ব্বত্রই সমান—তা অল্পের জন্যই হউক আর বেশীর জন্যই হউক। **To give a miss**—নিজের কন্দুক নিরাপদ্ রাখার জন্য লক্ষ্যীকৃত কন্দুকে আঘাত না করা।

miss, *v.t.* & *i.* **1.** To fail in hitting ; as, to *miss* the mark one shoots at ; লক্ষ্য ব্যর্থ হওয়া, লক্ষ্যচ্যুত হওয়া, লক্ষ্যভ্রষ্ট হওয়া, লাগাইতে না পারা। **2.** To fail to find, get, meet, catch, perceive, hear etc. ; as, to *miss* a train, remark etc. ; ধরিতে না পারা, খোয়ান, না পাওয়া, সাক্ষাৎ না হওয়া, শুনিতে না পাওয়া, বুঝিতে না পারা, ইত্যাদি। **3.** To lose ; as, to *miss* an opportunity ; হারান। **4.** To discover the absence, want or omission of ; to require ; as, to *miss* one's snuff-box ; অনুপস্থিতি, অভাব বা ত্রুটি সম্বন্ধে জ্ঞাত হওয়া ; আবশ্যক হওয়া। **5.** (Also with *out*) To omit, as words etc. in reading, writing etc. ; ছাড় দেওয়া। **6.** To fail to keep (appointment) or perform ; (প্রতিশ্রুতি) পালন করিতে না পারা, সম্পাদন করিতে না পারা। *Verb i.* **1.** To fail to strike what is aimed at ; লক্ষ্য ব্যর্থ হওয়া। **2.** To fail, as a person or his scheme ; "If they *miss* in their schemes" ; বিফলকাম হওয়া, ব্যর্থ-সংকল্প হওয়া। **To miss fire**—(Of gun) To fail to go off ; (বন্দুক সম্বন্ধে) আওয়াজ না হওয়া। (*Fig.*) To fail in one's objects ; (লক্ষণায়) উদ্দেশ্য ব্যর্থ হওয়া। **To miss one's tip**—To fail in one's plan or attempt ; সংকল্প ব্যর্থ হওয়া, বিফলপ্রযত্ন হওয়া। **To miss stays**—(*Naut.*) To fail in going about from one tack to another ; (নৌবিদ্যা) পাইল ফিরাইয়া জাহাজের মাথা ঘুরাইতে না পারা। (*Fig.*) To fail in any undertaking ; (লক্ষণায়) কোন বিষয়ে অকৃতকার্য্য হওয়া।

miss, *n.* **1.** A title of courtesy prefixed to the name of an unmarried girl or woman ; কুমারী। **2.** (*Usu. in contempt* or *playful*) A girl, esp. a school girl ; বালিকা, ছাত্রী। **Miss′-ish,** *adj.* Like, or characteristic of, a miss ; affected ; prim ; squeamish or sentimental ; কুমারীবৎ ; কৃত্রিম ; ফিটফাট ; খুঁতখুঁতে, ভাবপ্রবণ। **Mish′-ish-ness,** *n.*

mis′-sal (-ăl), *n.* The book containing the service of the Mass for the entire year ; a book of devotions ; রোমানক্যাথলিকগণের উপাসনা পুস্তক ; রোমক ধর্ম্মস্তোত্র সংহিতা।

mis′-sel (-ĕl), *n.* A kind of thrush that feeds on mistletoe berries, (also *missel-thrush*) ; এক প্রকার পক্ষী।

mis-shāp′-en (-n), *adj.* Having an ugly form ; deformed ; কদাকার, বিকৃতাকার, কুগঠিত, বিরূপ ; বিকৃতাকৃতি, কুরূপ, বেডৌল, বিকটাকৃতি।

mis′-sile (-ĭl), *adj.* & *n.* Capable of being thrown ; suitable for hurling ; ক্ষেপণীয়, ক্ষেপ্য। *Noun.* A weapon or projectile thrown, or to be thrown, with a hostile intention ; অস্ত্র, সায়ক, দিহ্যুত (মঃ উঃ)।

miss′-ing, *adj.* Absent from the place where it was expected to be found ; wanting ; lost ; as, there is a page *missing* ; নিরুদ্দিষ্ট ; অপূর্ণ ; হারানো, হৃত। **The missing link**—A creature between a man and a monkey ; মানুষ ও বানরের মধ্যবর্ত্তী জীব। (মানুষ বানরের বংশধর, এই মত প্রতিষ্ঠার জন্য যে জীবের আবিষ্কার আবশ্যক)। A thing lacking to complete a series ; কোন পর্য্যায় বা পরম্পরা-সম্পূরক বস্তু। **To be missing**—To be lost or wanting ; হারান, খোয়ান।

mis′-sion (mĭ-), *n.* **1.** A body of persons sent to a foreign country to conduct negotiations etc. ; সন্ধি প্রভৃতির কথাবার্ত্তা চালাইবার জন্য বিদেশে প্রেরিত ব্যক্তিবর্গ, দূতমণ্ডলী। **2.** A body sent out to spread a religion ; ধর্ম্মপ্রচারোদ্দেশ্যে প্রেরিত ব্যক্তিবর্গ। **3.** Any particular field of missionary enterprise ; ধর্ম্মপ্রচারকগণের প্রচারক্ষেত্র। **4.** A station or residence of missionaries ; ধর্ম্মপ্রচারকগণের বাসস্থলী বা আবাসভবন। **5.** An organization, usually including a church, established for the conversion and spiritual improvement of a certain district ; প্রচার-সমিতি। **6.** A course of services and sermons for this purpose ; প্রচার-সমিতির জন্য ধর্ম্মোপদেশ বা উপাসনা। **7.** A commission ; an errand, esp. political ; কোন বিশেষ কার্য্যসম্পাদনের জন্য প্রেরিত ব্যক্তিবর্গ ; সংবাদ বহনের উদ্দেশ্যে যাত্রা। **8.** Calling or vocation ; divinely appointed work in life ; as, he thinks his *mission* in life is to give lectures ; বৃত্তি ; জীবনের ব্রত।

mis'-sion-ă-rŷ (mĭ-), *adj.* & *n.* Of, or connected with, religious missions ; ধর্ম্মপ্রচারসংক্রান্ত, প্রচার-সম্বন্ধীয়। ***Noun.*** A person who is sent to propagate religion ; ধর্ম্মপ্রচারক। **Missionary box**—ধর্ম্ম-প্রচারের সাহায্যে অর্থপ্রদানের জন্য বাক্স।

mis'-sion-êr (mĭ-), *n.* A missionary ; an envoy, esp. one who has a charge of a mission ; ধর্ম্মপ্রচারক ; সন্দেশবহ, দূত।

mis'-sis (-ĭz), **—ŭs,** *ns.* (As used by servants) The mistress ; কর্ত্রী, ঠাকুরাণী। **The missis** or **missus**—(*Vulg., facet.*) One's own or another's wife ; (ইতরভাষায় বা রঙ্গচ্ছলে) গিন্নী।

mis'-sive (-sĭv), *adj.* & *n.* Specially sent or prepared to be sent ; as, letters *missive* ; বিশেষ ভাবে প্রেরিত বা প্রেরণের জন্য প্রস্তুত। ***Noun.*** A letter, especially an official one ; পত্র, সরকারী পত্র। **Letter(s) missive** — কোন ব্যক্তি বিশপ নির্ব্বাচন করিয়া কোন রাজা, ডীন বা যাজকমণ্ডলীকে যে পত্র বা পত্রসমূহ প্রেরণ করেন।

mis-spĕll', *v. t.* To spell wrongly ; ভুল বানান করা, বর্ণাশুদ্ধি করা।

mis-spĕnd', *v. t.* (*Usu. in p. p.*) To spend amiss or for wrong purposes ; to waste ; as, to *misspend* money ; অন্যায় কার্য্যে ব্যয় করা ; অপব্যয় করা, অন্যথা ব্যয় করা।

mis-stāte', *v. t.* To state wrongly or incorrectly ; অযথা বর্ণনা করা, মিথ্যা বর্ণনা করা, ভুল বর্ণনা করা। **—ment,** *n.*

mis'-sŷ, *n.* (*An affectionate, playful* or *contemptuous term for miss*) A young girl or miss ; বেটী।

mist, *n., v. i.* & *t.* **1.** Visible watery vapour ; কুহা, কুজ্ঝটিকা, কুহেলিকা, খবাষ্প, মেঘধূম্র, তুষার, শীকর। **2.** A haze or film before the eyes caused by tears ; চক্ষুর ঘোর, অশ্রুপাত জনিত চক্ষুর ঝাপ্সা ভাব। ***Verb i.*** To rain in very fine drops ; as, it *mists* ; to become dim or blurred ; as, one's eyes *mist* ; কুয়াসা পড়া ; অস্পষ্ট হওয়া, ঘোরালো হওয়া, ঝাপ্সা হওয়া। ***Verb t.*** To cover with or as with mist ; কুজ্ঝটিকাবৃত করা, কুহেলিকাচ্ছন্ন করা, কুয়াসার মত আবৃত করা। **Mist'-ful,** *adj.* **Mist'-like,** *adj.* & *adv.* Like mist ; কুজ্ঝটিকাবৎ। **Scotch-mist**—স্কটলণ্ডের গিরিমালায় সচরাচর দৃষ্ট ঘন কুজ্ঝটিকা।

mis-tāke', *n.* **1.** Misconception ; misapprehension ; ভ্রম, ভ্রান্তি, ভুল চুক ; ভ্রমপ্রমাদ, মতিভ্রম। **2.** A fault ; an error ; a wrong act done unintentionally ; দোষ, ভ্রম, ভ্রান্তি ; অশুদ্ধি, প্রমাদ ; অনিচ্ছাকৃত অন্যায়। **And no mistake**—Undoubtedly ; "For it was a cold night *and no mistake*" ; নিঃসন্দেহ, নিশ্চিতই।

mis-tāke', *v. t.* & *i.* **1.** To misapprehend the meaning or purpose of ; as, to *mistake* a remark ; ভুল বুঝা। **2.** To substitute wrongly in thought or perception ; as, to *mistake* one for another ; ভুল করা, ভ্রান্তি করা। ***Verb i.*** To err in opinion or judgment ; কোন মত প্রকাশে ভুল করা, বিচারে ভুল করা। **—tak'-a-ble,** *adj.* **—tak'-en,** *p. p.* Wrong in opinion or conception ; as, you are *mistaken* ; ill-judged ; as, *mistaken* kindness ; ভ্রান্ত ; অপবিচারিত। **—tak'-en-ly,** *adv.* **—tak'-en-ness,** *n.* **Mistaken kindness**—অপাত্রে ন্যস্ত দয়া। **There is no mistaking**—No one can help recognizing, as a person or fact etc. ; ভুল হইবার জো নাই। **You were mistaken**—তোমার ভুল হইয়াছে।

mis'-têr, *n.* & *v. t.* A title of address to a man, (written *Mr.*) or to a designation of occupation or office ; as, *Mr.* Jones, *Mr.* Speaker or Secretary ; ভদ্র লোকের নামের পূর্ব্বে ব্যবহৃত শব্দ, সংক্ষেপে Mr. লিখিত হয়। ***Verb t.*** To address as *Mr.* ; as, don't *mister* me ; মিষ্টার বলিয়া সম্বোধন করা।

mis'-ti-gris, *n.* **1.** (*Card*) A blank card or joker in a variety of poker ; কোন কোন তাসখেলায় শাদা বা অতিরিক্ত তাস। **2.** The card game poker ; একপ্রকার তাস খেলা।

mis-tīme', *v. t.* To time wrongly or improperly ; not to adapt to the time ; as, facts *mistimed* in a history ; ভুল সময় দেওয়া, অযথা সময় দেওয়া ; সময়ের উপযোগী না করা, অকালোপযোগী করা। **—timed',** *p. p.* Unseasonable ; ill-timed ; অসময়োচিত ; অকালোপযোগী।

mis'-tle toe (-l-tō), *n.* A parasitic plant growing on various trees, its fruits being used in making bird lime ; একপ্রকার চির-শ্যামল পরবৃক্ষাশ্রয়ী গুল্ম (এই পরগাছা ক্বচিৎ ওক বৃক্ষে জন্মিয়া থাকে), অমরবেল (Vedic Magazine 1897)। **Mistletoe berries** — কিসমিস কাওয়ালী (খোরী)। **Kissing under the mistletoe**—ইংলণ্ড এবং ইয়ুরোপের অপর কোন কোন স্থানে বড়দিনের আমোদ প্রমোদের সময় গৃহের ছাদ হইতে অমরবেলের (মিজলটো গুল্ম) ক্ষুদ্র শাখা টাঙ্গাইয়া রাখা হয়। কোন তরুণী ঐ শাখার নিম্ন দিয়া গমন করার কালে তাহাকে চুম্বন করা যাইতে পারে। এইরূপ চুম্বন দোষের বিষয় বলিয়া গণ্য হয় না। পরন্তু ইহা অতি আমোদের বিষয় বলিয়া বিবেচিত হয়।

mis'-trăl, *n.* A cold northerly wind in the Mediterranean provinces of France ; ফরাসীদেশের ভূমধ্যসাগর সন্নিহিত প্রদেশসমূহে প্রবাহিত শীত উত্তরানিল।

mis-trăns-late', *v. t.* To translate incorrectly ; অযথা অনুবাদ

করা, অযথা ভাষান্তরিত করা, ভুল তর্জ্জমা করা। **–la′-tion,** *n.*

mĭs′-trĕss, *n.* **1.** A woman having authority over servants or attendants ; কর্ত্রী, ঠাকুরাণী, প্রভুপত্নী। **2.** A female head of a household ; গৃহিণী, গেহেনী, গৃহকর্ত্রী, গৃহস্বামিনী। **3.** A concubine ; উপপত্নী, রক্ষিতা স্ত্রী। **4.** A female teacher ; শিক্ষয়িত্রী। **5.** A woman beloved and courted ; প্রেমিকা, প্রণয়িনী, হৃদয়েশ্বরী, প্রাণেশ্বরী, প্রেয়সী। **6.** A woman having thorough knowledge as of a subject ; কোন বিষয়ে বিশেষ ব্যুৎপত্তিশালিনী মহিলা। **7.** A title of address equivalent to *Mrs.* ; সম্বোধনসূচক উপাধি বিশেষ, "শ্রীমতী" শব্দের অনুরূপ। **–ship,** *n.* **Mistress of the Robes**—ইংলণ্ডেশ্বরীর পরিচ্ছদাগারের ভারপ্রাপ্তা মহিলা।

mis-trī′-ăl, *n.* A trial vitiated by some errors ; ভ্রান্ত বিচার।

mis-trûst′ *v. t.* & *n.* To have no trust or confidence in ; অবিশ্বাস করা, সন্দেহ করা, সন্দেহের চক্ষে দেখা। *Noun.* Doubt ; সন্দেহ, অবিশ্বাস। **–ful,** *adj.* Wanting in confidence ; distrustful ; সন্দেহাকুল ; অবিশ্বাসী। **–ful-ly,** *adv.* **–ful-ness,** *n.*

mist′-ȳ, *adj.* **1.** Relating to, or consisting of, mist ; overspread with mist ; as, *misty* rain, weather or mountains ; কুয়াসাসম্বন্ধীয়, কুয়াসাময় ; কুয়াসাচ্ছন্ন, কুজ্ঝটিকাময়। **2.** Indistinct in form or outline ; "The images *misty* and indistinct" ; অস্পষ্টাকৃতি। **3.** (*Fig.*) Vague ; indistinct ; as, a *misty* recollection ; (লক্ষণায়) ঝাপ্‌সা, ঘোরালো, ধোঁয়াটে ; অস্পষ্ট, অপরিস্ফুট। **–i-ly,** *adv.* **–i-ness,** *n.*

mis-ŭn-dêr-stănd′, *v. t.* & *i.* **1.** To understand wrongly ; to mistake ; ভুল বুঝা, ভ্রমাত্মক অর্থগ্রহণ করা ; ভুল করা। **2.** To misinterpret the words and actions of (a person) ; কোন ব্যক্তির কার্য্য বা বাক্যের কদর্থ করা, অযথা ব্যাখ্যা করা। *Verb i.* To misconceive ; ভ্রান্ত ধারণা করা। **–ing,** *n.* **1.** Misconception ; error ; অন্যথাবোধ, অন্যথাগ্রহণ ; ভুল, ভ্রান্তি। **2.** Disagreement ; dissension ; অবনিবনাও, অনৈক্য, অমিল, মতভেদ, মতান্তর ; বিরোধ, বিবাদ বিসম্বাদ।

mĭs-ūse′, *n.* **1.** Wrong or improper use ; misapplication ; অপব্যবহার ; অপপ্রয়োগ, কুপ্রয়োগ। **2.** Maltreatment ; দুর্ব্যবহার।

mĭs-ūše′, *v. t.* **1.** To use wrongly ; to apply to a wrong purpose ; অপব্যবহার করা ; অপপ্রয়োগ করা। **2.** To maltreat ; দুর্ব্যবহার করা, অসদ্ব্যবহার করা।

mīte, *n.* **1.** A small coin (orig. a small Flemish copper coin) ; specially half-farthing (see *Mark* xii 43) ; কপর্দ্দক, কড়ি ;

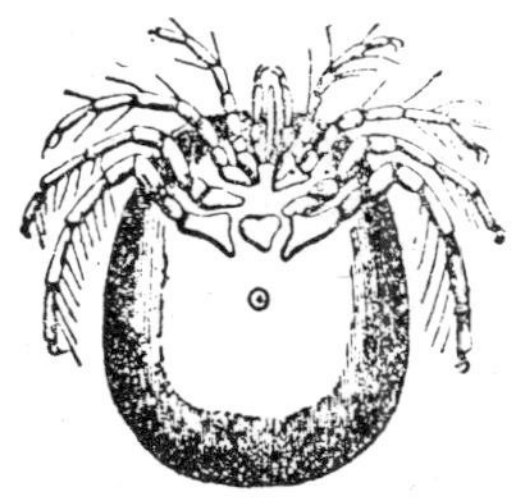

Mite greatly magnified.

বিশেষ অর্থে আধ ফার্দ্দিং। **2.** A small weight equal to one-twentieth of a grain ; অণু, লব, কণা। **3.** A small object or creature, esp. a child ; ছোট্ট জিনিষ, ছোট প্রাণী, কচি শিশু। **Not a mite**—(*Colloq.*) Not at all ; (চলিত ভাষায়) মোটেই না, আদবেই না। **One's mite**—The small amount which is all one can afford to contribute ; যথাসাধ্য ক্ষুদ্র দান।

Mĭth′-răs, –ră, *ns.* The Persian god identified with the sun ; প্রাচীন পারসীকদিগের সূর্য্যদেবতা। [প্রাচীন পারসীকগণের ভাষায় Mithras শব্দের অর্থ বন্ধু বা মিত্র। আমাদের বেদেও "মিত্র" নামক দেবতার উল্লেখ দৃষ্ট হয়। এই দেবতা দ্বাদশ আদিত্যের অন্যতম। বোধ হয় ভারতের "মিত্র" দেবতাই পারস্যদেশে Mithras নামে পূজিত হন। এই দেবতার উপাসনা ও তৎসংসৃষ্ট নিগূঢ় তান্ত্রিক অনুষ্ঠান ও রহস্য পূজা প্রাচীন গ্রীস ও রোমেও প্রচলিত হয়। ব্রিটিশ মিউজিয়ামে এই দেবতার যে মূর্ত্তি রক্ষিত হইয়াছে তাহা হইতে দৃষ্ট হয়—একটী মনোহর যুবক বৃষহননে নিরত, মুখখানি সুন্দরী তরুণীর মুখের মত লাবণ্যে ঢল ঢল। **–ra′-ic,** *adj.* **–ra-ism, –ra-ist,** *ns.*

mĭth′-ri-dāte, *n.* An antidote against poison ; বিষঘ্ন, বিষভঞ্জক। [এই বিষঘ্ন ঔষধ Pontusএর রাজা Mithridates কর্ত্তৃক ১২ রকম উপাদানে প্রস্তুত হইয়াছিল বলিয়া প্রসিদ্ধ।]

mith′-ri-dăt-īze, *v. t.* To produce mithridatism in ; ক্রমশঃ বর্দ্ধিত মাত্রায় কোন বিষাক্ত দ্রব্য ভোজন করাইয়া ঐরূপ বিষের ক্রিয়া হইতে রক্ষা করা। **–dat′-ic,** *adj.* **–da-tism,** *n.* (*Med.*) Immunity from a poison produced by using gradually increased doses of it ; (ভৈষজ্য-শাস্ত্র) ক্রমশঃ বর্দ্ধিত মাত্রায় কোন বিষাক্ত দ্রব্য ভোজনে সেই বিষের ক্রিয়া হইতে অব্যাহতি প্রাপ্তি। [Pontus এর অধিপতি Mithridates (মৃত খৃঃ পূঃ ৬৩) এই উপায় অবলম্বনে স্বীয় দেহ বিষক্রিয়া হইতে রক্ষা করিয়াছিলেন বলিয়া কথিত।]

mĭt′-i-gāte, *v. t.* **1.** To appease (anger etc.) ; প্রশান্ত করা। **2.** To render less severe or intense ; as, to *mitigate* punishment, pain, etc. ; to moderate ; as, to *mitigate* heat উপশম করা ; লাঘব করা। **–ga′-tion,** *n.* An act of mitigating ; alleviation ; প্রশমন, উপশমন, মৃদুকরণ, সান্ত্বন ; লাঘব। **–ga-to-ry,** *adj.*

mĭt′-i-gā-tive (-tĭv), *adj.* & *n.* Tending to mitigate ; alleviating ; প্রশামক, উপশামক ; লাঘবকর। *Noun.* A lenitive ; উপশামক ঔষধ।

mi-tra-illeuse′ (mē-tră-yêz), *n.* (*Mil.*) A many-barrelled breech-loading machine gun that can be the light *winks*; মিটমিট করা। *Verb t.* 1. To cause the eyes to wink; পলক ফেলান। 2. To affect or influence by winking; চোখ টিপিয়া কাহারো উপর ক্রিয়া করা। *Noun.* 1. The act of closing the eyelids quickly; পলক ফেলন। 2. No more time than is necessary to shut the eyes; পলক, নিমেষ। 3. A hint or sign given by shutting the eye with a significant cast; "Nod *wink* and laughter were over"; চোখের ইসারা। **Wink'-ing,** *n.* 1. Act of winking; নিমেষ ফেলন। 2. An instant; a twinkling; মুহূর্ত্ত; নিমেষ। **Forty winks**—(চলিতভাষায়) সামান্য ঘুম। **Like winking**—Quickly; নিমেষে। **To wink on**—Same as WINK *v. i.* 5. **To tap one the wink**—(*Slang*) To give him signal or intimation; ইসারা দেওয়া, চোখ টিপিয়া সঙ্কেত করা।

win'-kle (wing-kl), *n.* Same as PERIWINKLE.

win'-now (-nō), *v. t.* 1. To separate or drive the chaff from by means of wind; ঝাড়া, তুষ ছাড়ান। 2. To examine; to try, as for the purpose of separating truth from falsehood; to separate as bad from the good; "Bitter torture shall *winnow* the truth from falsehood"; পরীক্ষা করা; সত্য হইতে মিথ্যা বাছিয়া পৃথক করার জন্য চেষ্টা করা; ভাল জিনিষ হইতে মন্দ অংশ বাছিয়া ফেলা। 3. To beat with, or as with, wing; পক্ষ দ্বারা তাড়না করা। **—er,** *n.* **Winnowing-fan**—কুলা, কুলা, কুলা, সূর্প, শূর্প।

win'-some (-sŭm), *adj.* Charming; attractive; as, a *winsome* young lady; lively; রমণীয়, মনোহর; চিত্তাকর্ষক, বিমোহন, মুগ্ধকর; উৎফুল্ল। **—ly,** *adv.* **—ness,** *n.*

win'-tēr, *n., v. i.* & *t.* 1. The cold season of the year, commencing, astronomically, in the northern hemisphere, when the sun enters capricorn, or at the solstice about the 21st December, and ending at the equinox at March; শীতকাল, শিশিরসময়, তুষারকাল (কবিতায়)। 2. A year; as, a child of 12 *winters*; বয়স। 3. A period marked by dreariness or activity; "Life's autumn past, I stand on *winter's* verge"; জড়তা, আলস্যতা, দুর্দ্দশার কাল। 4. The part of a printing-press which sustains the carriage; মুদ্রাযন্ত্রের অংশ বিশেষ। *Verb i.* To hibernate; শীতকাল যাপন করা। *Verb t.* To keep or feed during the winter; শীতকালে পালন করা বা ভোজন করান। **Winter-garden**—শীতপ্রধান দেশে শীতকালে ফল-পুষ্পাদির বৃক্ষরোপণের জন্য কাচসমাচ্ছাদিত স্থান, শীতোদ্যান। **Winter-green**—একজাতীয় ক্ষুপ—যাহারা সারা শীতকাল ব্যাপিয়া সবুজবর্ণ থাকে, শীতহরিৎ। **Winter-lodge**—যে মুকুলাদি দ্বারা শীতকালে বৃক্ষের ভ্রূণ রক্ষিত হয়। **Winter quarters**—যে সেনানিবাসে সৈন্যগণ শীতকাল যাপন করে, শীতাবাস। **Winter-sleep**—Same as HIBERNATION.

win'-try, *adj.* 1. Cold; stormy; শীতল, ঠাণ্ডা; ঝটিকাচ্ছন্ন। 2. Cheerless; lacking warmth; as, a *wintry* smile; স্ফূর্ত্তিহীন, প্রাণশূন্য; নিরানন্দ, অপ্রফুল্ল।

Wipe, *v. t., i.* & *n.* 1. To rub with something soft for clearing; মুছা। 2. To rub off; to obliterate; as, to *wipe* out all traces of past affection; মুছিয়া উঠান; বিলুপ্ত করা, অপহৃত করা। 3. (*Slang*) To strike; to beat; (ইতর ভাষায়) আঘাত করা; প্রহার করা। *Verb i.* (*Colloq.*) To make a motion like that of wiping something as in striking (চলিত ভাষায়) কোন কিছু মুছিবার কালে যেরূপ ভাবে হস্ত-সঞ্চালন করিতে হয় তেমন ভাবে হস্ত চালনা করা। *Noun.* 1. The act of wiping; মুছন, মার্জ্জন, পরিমার্জ্জন। 2. (*Slang*) Handkerchief; (ইতরভাষায়) রুমাল। 3. (*Slang*) A blow or stroke; আঘাত। 4. (*Obs.*) Severe sarcasm; "To touch with a satiric *wipe*"; (অপ্রঃ) তীব্র বিদ্রূপ। 5. (*Obs.*) Brand; (অপ্রঃ) কলঙ্ক-চিহ্ন। **To wipe one's eyes**—To dry tears; চোখ মুছা, অশ্রু মুছিয়া ফেলা। (*Slang*) To get advantage over some one by anticipating him; কাহারো অগ্রে কোন কাজ করিয়া তাহার উপর সুবিধা লাভ করা। **To wipe out**—To annihilate; বিলুপ্ত করা। **To wipe the ground with**—To defeat utterly; সম্পূর্ণরূপে পরাজিত করা। **To wipe the nose of**—(ইতর ভাষায়) মাথায় হাত বুলান, ঠকান।

wire, *n., v. t.* & *i.* 1. Any metallic substance drawn to an even thread; তার। 2. A telegraph wire; a telegram; as, please send a *wire* to him to come here sharp; টেলিগ্রাফের তার; তাড়িতবার্ত্তা, তার। 3. (*Slang*) One who picks a woman's pocket; (ইতরভাষায়) যে ব্যক্তি স্ত্রীলোকের পকেট কাটে। 4. A string of musical instrument; a stringed musical instrument; বাদ্যযন্ত্রের তার; তন্ত্রীবিশিষ্ট বাদ্যযন্ত্র। 5. (*Scot.*) A knitting needle; বুনিবার শলা। 5. A wire fencing; তারের বেড়া। 6. The system of wires used to operate the puppetshow; the secret influence by which a political party or movement is controlled; as, to pull the *wires* for office; পুতুল নাচের পুতুল যে তার-শ্রেণী দ্বারা চালিত হয়; যে গুপ্ত প্রভাবে কোন রাজনীতিক দল বা আন্দোলন পরিচালিত হয়। *Verb t.* 1. To bind with wire; to provide with a wire; তার দ্বারা বাঁধা; তার লাগান। 2. To put upon wire; তার লাগান। 3. To telegraph; as he should be *wired* to come the place [illegible]তিনিধি, স্থলবর্ত্তী। **Vice-adm**[illegible]তীয় শ্রেণীর নৌ-সেনাধ্যক্ষ। [illegible]**-admirality**—তৃতীয় শ্রেণী[illegible]ধ্যক্ষের কার্য্যালয়। **Vice-chai**[illegible]পাধ্যক্ষ, প্রতিনিধি সভাপতি। [illegible]**ncellor**—বিশ্ববিদ্যালয়ের [illegible]পতি। **Vice-governor**[illegible] শাসনকর্ত্তা। **Vice-kin**[illegible]s VICEROY. **Vice-pre**[illegible]নিধি সভাপতি, প্রতিনিধি র[illegible] **principal**—উপাধ্যক্ষ, [illegible]ক্ষ। **Vice-queen**—[illegible]) Same as VICEREI[illegible]

vīce-gē′-[illegible] *adj.* & *n.* 1. Having, o[illegible]rcising delegated power; প্র[illegible]ধস্থানীয়, প্রতিনিধিস্থলীয়। 2. Acting by substitution ; প্রতিনিধিরূপে কার্য্যকারী। ***Noun.*** An officer who is deputed by a superior or by proper authority to exercise the power of another ; প্রতিনিধি কর্ম্মচারী। **—ren-cy**, *n.*

vī-cěn′-nĭ-ăl, *adj.* 1. Lasting twenty years ; বিংশতিবর্ষস্থায়ী। 2. Happening once in twenty years ; বিংশতিবর্ষ অন্তে সংঘটনশীল, বিংশতিবার্ষিক।

vīce′-reine (-rēn), *n.* The wife of a viceroy ; রাজপ্রতিনিধিপত্নী।

vīce′-roy, *n.* The governor of a country or kingdom who rules for the king ; রাজপ্রতিনিধি, বড়লাট, (ভারতে)। **—re′-gal,** *adj.* Pertaining to a viceroy ; রাজপ্রতিনিধিসম্বন্ধীয়। **—roy′-al** *adj.* **—roy′-al-ty** *n.*

vĭc′-ĭ-nage, *n.* 1. Neighbourhood; vicinity ; চতুঃপার্শ্ববর্ত্তী স্থান ; নিকটবর্ত্তী স্থান। 2. Relation of neighbours ; প্রতিবেশিগণের সহিত সম্পর্ক।

vĭ-cĭn′-ĭ-tў, *n.* 1. Quality or state of being near ; as, the *vicinity* of Calcutta ; নৈকট্য, সামীপ্য, সান্নিধ্য, সমীপতা। 2. Surrounding districts ; চতুঃপার্শ্ববর্ত্তী অঞ্চল। 3. Closeness of relation to ; নিকটসম্পর্কতা।

vĭ′-cious (-shŭs), *adj.* 1. Addicted to vice ; depraved ; wicked ; পাপাচাররত ; ভ্রষ্ট ; দুষ্ট, দুর্নীতিপরায়ণ, দুরাচার, দুর্বৃত্ত। 2. Contrary to moral principle or rectitude ; as, *vicious* examples ; নীতিবিগর্হিত, পাপপূর্ণ। 3. (Of language or style) Corrupt ; as, *vicious* ideas ; incorrect ; (ভাষা বা রচনা-রীতিসম্পর্কে) ব্যাকরণদুষ্ট ; অশুদ্ধ। 4. Noxious ; impure ; as, *vicious* air ; দূষিত ; অবিশুদ্ধ। 5. (Of a horse) Given to bad tricks ; as, a *vicious* horse ; পাজী, বদমায়েস। 6. (*Colloq.*) Spiteful ; as, a *vicious* accusation ; বিদ্বেষপূর্ণ। **—ly,** *adv.* **—ness,** *n.* **Vicious circle** or **syllogism**—Same as ARGUMENT IN A CIRCLE (See CIRCLE 10). **Vicious union**—(অস্ত্রোপচারবিদ্যা) ভগ্ন অস্থির প্রান্তসমূহ এরূপ ভাবে স্থাপন—যাহাতে দেহের বিকৃতি উৎপাদিত হয়।

vĭ-cĭs′-si-tūde (-ĭ-), *n.* Regular change or succession ; as, the *vicissitudes* of day and night ;

in the gratification of a passion or as a result of an event or circumstance ; as, a *victim* of ambition or jealous rage : a *victim* of pestilence ; কোন উদ্দেশ্য সাধনের জন্য বা কোনরূপ কামক্রোধাদির ফলে অথবা কোন ঘটনার ফলস্বরূপ প্রদত্ত ব্যক্তি বা বস্তুবলি। 3. One who is duped or cheated ; as, the *victim* of a gamble; প্রতারিত ব্যক্তি।

vĭc′-tĭm-īze, *v. t.* 1. To make a victim ; বলিদান করা। 2. To cheat; "He *victimized* a large number of gentlemen in Bombay"; প্রতারিত করা, প্রবঞ্চিত করা। **—i-za′-tion,** *n.*

vĭc′-tor (-têr), *n.* (*Fem.* VICTRESS) A conqueror ; জেতা, বিজেতা।

vĭc-tō′-rĭ-ȧ, *n.* 1. (*Cap.*) The Roman goddess of victory ; রোমকদিগের বিজয়া দেবী। 2. Same as VICTORIA REGIA 3. A low, light, four-wheeled carriage, with calash top, for two persons ; একপ্রকার হাল্কা চারি চাকার গাড়ী। 4. (*Cap.*) The name of the late Empress of India, grandmother of our present Emperor George V. ; ভারত সম্রাজ্ঞী ভিক্টোরিয়া। 5. Kind of domestic pigeons ; বিভিন্নজাতীয় গৃহকপোত। **Victoria Cross** (*Abbrev.* **V. C.**) — রণক্ষেত্রে অসাধারণ বীরত্ব প্রদর্শনের জন্য প্রদত্ত পদক বিশেষ। এই পদকের ফিতার বর্ণ স্থলসৈন্যদের পক্ষে লোহিত ও নৌসৈন্যদিগের পক্ষে নীলবর্ণ। এই পদকপ্রাপকগণ বৎসর ১০ পাঁচ (১০... টাকা) বৃত্তি পাইয়া থাকেন।

moans ; আর্ত্তধ্বনি করা। ***Verb t.*** 1. To bewail or deplore ; as, to *moan* a misfortune ; to lament for ; as, to *moan* a dead person ; শোচনা করা ; বিলাপ করা। 2. To utter with a moan or moans, as words, etc. ; কোঁকাইয়া বলা।

moat (mōt), *n.* & *v. t.* A ditch round a fortress, town, etc. ; পরিখা, গড়খাই, খাত। ***Verb t.*** To surround with, or as with moat ; পরিখাবেষ্টিত করা, গড়খাই করা।

bile people" ; তরলমতি, চঞ্চলমতি, চঞ্চলপ্রকৃতি, প্রকৃতিতরল ; অস্থিরচিত্ত, অব্যবস্থিতচিত্ত। 3. (Of troops) Capable of being easily moved from place to place ; অনায়াসে এক স্থান হইতে অপর স্থানে চালনীয়। **—bil′-i-ty,** *n.* 1. State of being mobile ; গতিক্ষমতা (হিঃ কোঃ), জঙ্গমতা, চঞ্চলতা, চপলত্ব (সাঃ পঃ), জঙ্গমত্ব (ঐ)। 2. Fickleness ; চঞ্চলপ্রকৃতি, রজোগুণ, অস্থিরমতিত্ব, অব্যবস্থিতচিত্ততা।

sham ; অলীক ; নকল, জাল, মেকি, ঝুটা ; ছদ্ম, কপট। **Mock-fight**—কৃত্রিম যুদ্ধ। **Mock-heroic,** *adj.* & *n.* Burlesquing heroic style ; as, *mock heroic* poem ; ব্যঙ্গবীররসাত্মক। (*Noun*) Burlesque imitation of the heroic style ; ব্যঙ্গবীররসাত্মক কবিতা।

mŏck, *v. t.* & *i.* 1. To deride ; to ridicule ; ঠাট্টা করা ; ব্যঙ্গ করা, বিদ্রূপ করা, উপহাস করা। 2. To defy contemptuously ; "*Mocking* the reality" ; তুচ্ছ করা। 3. To deceive to tantalize; to disappoint; as, to *mock* expectation; প্রতারণা করা: কোন আশা পূর্ণ হয় এমন সময় নিরাশ করা; নিরাশ করা। **4.** To deride by imitation; "He *mocks* all he sees and hears"; ভেঙ্গচান। ***Verb i.*** To scoff; to jeer; (with *at*); ঠাট্টা করা, বিদ্রূপ করা; ব্যঙ্গ করা। **Mock′-ing-ly,** *adv.*

Mocking-bird.

Mocking-bird — আমেরিকা দেশীয় হরবোলা পাখী, ভাষিপক্ষী।

mŏck′-êr-ŷ, *n.* **1.** Derision; ridicule; উপহাস; বিদ্রূপ। **2.** A subject or occasion of derision; বিদ্রূপের বিষয়, উপহাসের পাত্র। **3.** A false representation or appearance; contemptible imitation; "The *mockery* of a trial"; কৃত্রিম ভাব প্রদর্শন, কৃত্রিম ভঙ্গী; প্রহসন, বিড়ম্বনা। **4.** Ridiculously useless action; "*Mockery* of a mourning-coach"; হাস্যোদ্দীপক নিষ্ফল চেষ্টা।

mŏd′-ăl, *adj* **1.** Of, or pertaining to, a model or form; আকার সম্বন্ধীয়, আকারগত, রূপবিষয়ক, প্রকারবিষয়ক, প্রকারাত্মক (হিঃ কোঃ)। **2.** (*Gram.*) Of, or relating to, the mood of a verb; denoting manner; (ব্যাকরণ) ক্রিয়ার রূপসম্বন্ধীয়; প্রকারসূচক। **3.** (*Log.*, Of a proposition) Involving the affirmation of possibility, impossibility, necessity or contingency; (of a syllogism) containing such a proposition; (তর্কবিজ্ঞান—উপপাদ্য সম্পর্কে) সম্ভাব্যতা অসম্ভাব্যতা, অবশ্যম্ভাবিতা, অথবা নৈমিত্তিকতা সংসৃষ্ট; (অবয়বঘটিত বাক্য সম্পর্কে) উক্তরূপ উপপাদ্যসমন্বিত। **–ly,** *adv.* **Mo-dal′-i-ty,** *n.* **1.** (*Rare*) Quality or state of being modal; প্রকারতা, আকার (সৌন্দর্য)। **2.** (*Log.*) State of being a modal proposition or syllogism; (তর্কবিজ্ঞান) প্রকারাত্মক প্রতিজ্ঞাত্ব, অবয়বঘটিত বাক্যত্ব। **Modal legacy**—যে দানপত্র দ্বারা প্রদত্ত অর্থ বা সম্পত্তি কিরূপ ভাবে ব্যয়িত হইবে তাহা নির্দ্দিষ্ট করা হইয়া থাকে। **Modal proposition**—(তর্কবিজ্ঞান) যে প্রতিজ্ঞা দ্বারা কোনরূপ সীমা বা পরিমিতত্বের অধীনে কোন বিষয় নিশ্চিতরূপে কথিত হয় বা অঙ্গীকৃত হইয়া থাকে, প্রকারাত্মক প্রতিজ্ঞা।

mōde, *n.* **1.** Manner; method; way; as, a *mode* of speaking; রীতি, চাল; প্রণালী, পদ্ধতি, রকম, প্রকার; ধরণ, পন্থা। **2.** A prevailing custom or style; "There are *modes* where there are men"; প্রচলিত রীতি বা চালচলন। **3.** (*Mus.*) Each of the two classes (major and minor) of the keys; a kind of scale, as the Dorian, Ionian, etc.; (সঙ্গীত-শাস্ত্র) রাগ; একপ্রকার স্বরগ্রাম। **4.** (*Log.*) Character of a modal proposition; (তর্কবিজ্ঞান) প্রকারাত্মক প্রতিজ্ঞার প্রকৃতি। **Mode of teaching**—শিক্ষাপ্রণালী, অধ্যাপনাপ্রণালী। **The mode** — (*Archaic*) The fashion in dress etc.; (অপ্রঃ) পরিচ্ছদের রীতি বা ধরণ।

mŏd′-ĕl, *n.* **1.** A pattern of something to be made; as, the *model* of a building; নমুনা, আদর্শ। **2.** A figure in clay, wax, etc. to be reproduced in other material; মৃত্তিকা, মোম প্রভৃতি রচিতমূর্ত্তি, যাহার প্রতিরূপ অন্য জাতীয় পদার্থে গঠিত করিতে হয়। **3.** A style of a structure; design; "A church after the same model"; গঠনপদ্ধতি রচনাপদ্ধতি, পরিকল্পনা। **4.** An imitation or copy in miniature; ক্ষুদ্র প্রতিরূপ। **5.** A person or thing that serves as an example or imitation; আদর্শস্থানীয় ব্যক্তি, আদর্শীভূত বস্তু। **6.** (*Arts*) A person or thing serving as an artist's pattern; one whose profession is to pose for artists; "Living *models*"; (ললিত কলা) শিল্পীর আদর্শীভূত ব্যক্তি বা বস্তু; যে ব্যক্তি ভাস্কর, চিত্রকর প্রভৃতির অঙ্কণ বা গঠনের আদর্শরূপে নানাভঙ্গীতে উপবেশন করিয়া থাকে। **7.** A woman employed by dealers in costume or millinery to put on articles to show their effect to customers; পরিচ্ছদ বিক্রেতৃগণকর্ত্তৃক নিযুক্ত স্ত্রীলোক—যাহাকে পোষাক পরাইয়া ঐ পোষাক কেমন মানাইবে তাহা ক্রেতাদিগকে দেখান হয়। **8.** (*Attrib.*) Exemplary; ideally perfect; as, a *model* husband আদর্শস্থানীয়, আদর্শ (যথা—আদর্শ স্বামী)। **Model drawing**—আদর্শ চিত্রাঙ্কণ দ্রব্যাদিলিপি (বিবিধ-বিধান)। **Model school**—আদর্শ-বিদ্যালয়। **The New Model**—(১৬৪৪—১৬৪৮ খৃঃ অব্দ পার্লেমেণ্টের অধীন সৈন্যের পুনঃ সংস্থাপনের জন্য পরিকল্পনা। **Working model**—যে ক্ষুদ্র আদর্শযন্ত্র দ্বারা মূলযন্ত্রের গতি ও ক্রিয়া প্রদর্শিত হইয়া থাকে, কার্য্যকারী আদর্শ।

mŏd′-ĕl, *v. t. & i.* **1.** To shape in clay, wax, etc.; to mould; as, to *model* a figure; মোম, মৃত্তিকা, প্রভৃতি দ্বারা গঠন করা; ছাঁচে গড়া। **2.** To frame, as a document or argument, etc.; মুসাবিদা করা, খসড়া করা। **3.** To form a thing after, on, upon, a model; আদর্শানুসারে গঠন বা নির্ম্মাণ করা।

mŏd′-ē-nă, *n.* A deep purple colour; একপ্রকার ঘন নীলারুণ বর্ণ।

mŏd′-êr-āte, *adj.* & *n.* **1.** Temperate; not going to extremes; as, *moderate* in drinking; মিত,

লীলা, স্বচ্ছন্দাচার, অনাড়ষ্টতা। **—doned,** *adj.* Given up to vice ; profligate ; extremely wicked ; as, an *abandoned* villain ; পাপাসক্ত ; অভিত্যক্ত, উৎসৃষ্ট, ভ্রষ্টচরিত্র ; অতিশয় দুর্বৃত্ত বা দুরাচার। **—ment,** *n.* Total desertion ; state of being forsaken ; self-surrender ; careless freedom of manners ; একান্তভাবে পরিত্যাগ, সংত্যাগ ; বর্জ্জন ; আত্মবিসর্জ্জন ; স্বচ্ছন্দচারিতা, মেলামেশায় অনাড়ষ্টভাব। **Abandon one's self to**—Give up one's self to without attempt at restraint ; as, সংযত করা ; প্রশমিত করা। *Verb i.* 1. To become less violent, severe, rigorous or intense; পরিমিত হওয়া, প্রশমিত হওয়া, উপশম হওয়া, মন্দীভূত হওয়া। 2. To act as a moderator মধ্যস্থের কাজ করা, মধ্যস্থতা করা।

mŏd-êr-ā'-tion, *n.* 1. The act of moderating ; মিতাচার, পরিমিতাচার, যুক্ততা (হিঃ কোঃ), আহারবিহারনিয়ম, সমানবৃত্তি, সমবৃত্তি, নিয়তবৃত্তি। 2. State of being moderate ; পরিমিতবৃত্তি। 3. (*Oxf. Univer., pl.*) First public examination for the degree of B. A. (*abbr. Mods.*) ; (অক্সফোর্ড বিশ্ববিদ্যালয়) বি, এ, উপাধির জন্য প্রথম পরীক্ষা। **In moderation** — Moderately ; পরিমিতভাবে।

mŏd'-êr-ā-tor (-têr), *n.* 1. An arbitrator or mediator ; সালীশ, মধ্যস্থ। 2. The person who presides at a meeting or disputation ; সভাপতি, মুখপাত্র। 3. A president of meetings or courts in the Presbyterian churches ; খৃষ্টীয় ধর্ম্মসঙ্ঘ বিশেষের সভাধিবেশনে যে ব্যক্তি সভাপতির কার্য্য করেন। 4. One of the officers presiding over mathematical tripos at Cambridge ; কেম্ব্রিজের গণিতের ট্রাইপশ পরীক্ষায় যে কর্ম্মচারিদ্বয় অধ্যক্ষতা করেন তাঁহাদের অন্যতর। 5. An examiner for moderations ; অক্সফোর্ড বিশ্ববিদ্যালয়ে বি, এ, উপাধির জন্য প্রথম প্রকাশ্য পরীক্ষার প্রশ্নকর্ত্তা। **—ship,** *n.*

3. (*Law*) To do away with (nuisance) ; to frustrate by judicial sentence ; to quash (action) ; as, to *abate* a writ ; (আইন) অপসারিত করা ; বিচারাদেশ দ্বারা নিষ্ফল করা ; বিলোপ করা। ***Verb i.*** To decrease or become less in strength or violence ; to fall through ; to fail ; কমা, হ্রাস হওয়া, উপশমিত হওয়া ; ব্যর্থ হওয়া ; নিষ্ফল হওয়া।

ăb'-ā-tis, ăb'-ăt-tĭs, *n.* (*Fort.*) A defence made of felled trees with boughs pointing out- আধুনিকরীতি, নব্যরীতি। **—ist,** *n.* **—i-za'-tion,** *n.* **—ize,** *v. t.* & *i.* To make modern ; to cause to conform to modern usages or taste ; আধুনিক করা ; আধুনিক কালের রুচি ও রীতিনীতির উপযোগী করা। (*Verb i.*) (*Rare*) To adopt modern ways etc. ; আধুনিক রীতি প্রভৃতি গ্রহণ করা। **—ly,** *adv.* **—ness,** *n.* **Modern India**—বর্ত্তমান ভারত, আধুনিক ভারত।

mó-dêr'-ni-tȳ, *n.* 1. State of being modern ; আধুনিকতা। 2. Something modern ; আধুনিক বস্তু।

mŏd'-ĕst, *adj.* 1. Restrained by a sense of propriety ; not presumptuous or arrogant ; bashful ; সবিনয়, সব্রীড়, লজ্জান্বিত ; বিনীত, বিনম্র, বিনয়সম্পন্ন ; ব্রীড়ানম্র, হ্রীসম্পন্ন। 2. Decorous in conduct or bearing ; chaste ; "The blushing beauties of a *modest* maid" ; নম্রশীল ; সতী, সাধ্বী। 3. Not excessive ; as, a *modest* income ; unpretentious in appearance or style ; as, a *modest* mansion ; অতিরিক্ত নয় ; নাতিবৃহৎ, পরিমিত। **—es-ty,** *n.* 1. State of being modest ; bashfulness ; ব্রীড়ানম্রতা, বিনয়, হ্রী ; লজ্জাশীলতা। 2. Chastity ; সতীত্ব, পাতিব্রত্য। 3. Unpretentious character ; অমায়িকস্বভাব। **—ly,** *adv.* **—ness,** *n.* **To outrage the modesty**—লজ্জাশীলতা হানি করা।

mŏd'-ĭ-cŭm, *n.* A small quantity (of food etc.) ; যৎসামান্য, যৎকিঞ্চিৎ

mŏd'-i-fȳ, *v. t.* 1. To moderate ; to tone down ; পরিমিত করা, সংযত করা, প্রশমিত করা ; মন্দীভূত করা। 2. To make partial changes in ; as, to *modify* the terms of contract ; সামান্য পরিবর্ত্তন করা, কাটকুট দেওয়া, বাদসাদ দেওয়া, আংশিক পরিবর্ত্তন করা, রূপান্তর করা। 3. (*Gram.*) To limit or restrict the meaning of ; to qualify ; (ব্যাকরণ) অর্থ সীমাবদ্ধ করা ; গুণ আরোপ করা। **—fi-a-bil'-i-ty,** *n.* **—fi-a-ble,** *adj.* **—fi-ca'-tion,** *n.* The act of modifying ; বিকার, বিবর্ত্তন, বিক্রিয়া, রূপান্তর, রূপান্তরীকরণ। **—fi-ca-to-ry,** *adj.*

mō-dĭl'-lion (-yŏn), *n.* (*Arch.*) An ornamented bracket under the corona of the cornice of the

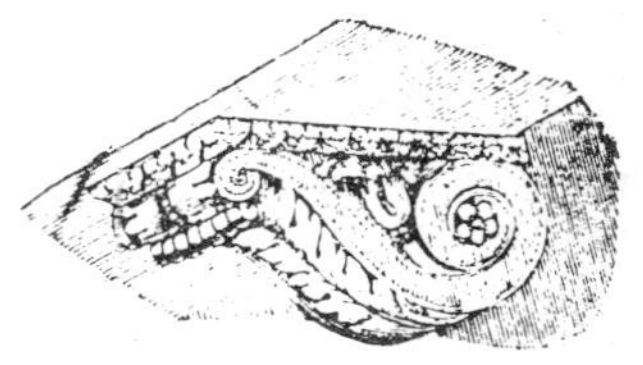

Modillion.

Corinthian and other orders ; কোরিন্থীয় বা অপর স্থাপত্যরীতিতে কার্ণিসের নীচের ভূষাবিশেষ।

mŏd'-ĭsh, *adj.* Observing the fashion ; fashionable ; as, a *modish* dress ; প্রচলিতপ্রথাসঙ্গত ; হালফ্যাসনের। **—ist,** *n.* (*Obs.*) **—ly,** *adv.* **—ness,** *n.*

mō-diste' (-dēst), *n.* A dress-maker or milliner ; পরিচ্ছদ প্রস্তুতকারী, স্ত্রীলোকের টুপি পোষাক প্রভৃতি প্রস্তুতকারিণী।

mŏd'-ū-lāte, *v. t.* & *i.* 1. To adjust ; to adapt ; ঠিকঠাক করা ; উপযোগী করা। 2. To vary in tone ; to attune to a certain key or pitch ; as, to *modulate* voice ;

স্বরবৈচিত্র্য সম্পাদন করা, স্বর পরিবর্তন করা, স্বরবিকৃত করা ; কোন বিশেষ স্বরে বাঁধা। *Verb i.* To pass (*from* one key *to* another) ; স্বরযোজনা করা। **—la'-tion,** *n.* Act of modulating ; স্বরযোজন (হিঃ কোঃ), স্বরভঙ্গী, মূর্চ্ছনা, স্বরসংক্রম (কৃষ্ণঃ), গিটগিরি। **—la-tor,** *n.*

mŏd'-ūle, *n.* **1.** A standard or unit for measuring ; মান। **2.** (*Arch.*) A measure for regulating the proportion of columns ; (স্থপতি-বিজ্ঞান) স্তম্ভের বিভিন্ন অংশের অনুপাতসূচক একক [স্তম্ভভিত্তির ব্যাসার্দ্ধ সাধারণতঃ এইরূপ—একক স্বরূপ ধরা হইয়া থাকে।]

mŏd'-ū-lŭs, *n.* (*Pl.* -LI) **1.** A constant multiplier, esp. for converting Napierian into common logarithms ; মধ্যগুণক (হিঃ কোঃ), নিত্যগুণক। **2.** (*Phys. & Mech.*) A constant indicating the relation between amount of physical effect and that of the force producing it ; কোন জড়ীয় ক্রিয়ার পরিমাণ ও ক্রিয়াজনক বলের পরিমাণের মধ্যে যে সম্বন্ধ তাহা যে নিত্য রাশিদ্বারা ব্যক্ত হয়।

modus, (*L.*), *n.* **1.** Mode ; manner ; রীতি, প্রকার; প্রণালী, ধরণ। **2.** (*Law*) Money-payment in lieu of tithe ; (আইন) উৎপন্ন শস্যের দশমাংশের পরিবর্ত্তে অর্থ প্রদান। ***Modus operandi***—কার্য্যপদ্ধতি, কার্য্যপ্রণালী। ***Modus vivendi***—জীবনযাত্রাপ্রণালী; বিরোধীয় বিষয় মীমাংসা না হওয়া পর্য্যন্ত সাময়িকভাবে কোন বিষয়ের বন্দোবস্ত।

mofette, (*F.*), *n.* An emanation of a noxious gas from a fissure in the earth ; this fissure ; পৃথিবীপৃষ্ঠস্থ বিদারিত স্থান হইতে দূষিত বাষ্প নির্গম ; ঐরূপ বিদারিত স্থান।

Mō-gŭl', *n.* & *adj.* **1.** A Mongol ; a follower or descendant of Baber, the founder of the Mogul Empire of India ; মোগল ; মোগল সম্রাট বাবরের বংশধর। **2.** (*Pl.*) Playing cards of the best quality ; উৎকৃষ্ট শ্রেণীর তাস। ***Adj.*** Pertaining to the Moguls or their empire in India ; মোগল-সম্বন্ধীয়, মোগলসাম্রাজ্য সম্বন্ধীয়। **The (Great or Grand) Mogul**—দিল্লীর সম্রাট, দিল্লীশ্বর।

mō'-hair (-hār), *n.* **1.** The long silky hair of the Angora goat ; এঙ্গোরা ছাগের লম্বা রেশমী রোম। **2.** A fine camlet made from this ; উক্ত রোম হইতে প্রস্তুত বস্ত্র।

Mō-hăm'-mĕd-ăn, *n.* & *adj.* A follower of Mohammed, the founder of the Moslem religion ; মুসলমান। ***Adj.*** Pertaining to Mohammed, or the religion, or institutions founded by him ; মহম্মদসম্বন্ধীয়, মুসলমানধর্ম্মসম্বন্ধী। **—ism,** *n.* The religion or the doctrines of Mohammed ; মুসলমানধর্ম্ম। **—ize,** *v. t.* To convert to Mohammedanism ; মুসলমান ধর্ম্মে দীক্ষিত করা।

Mō'-hawk (-hăk), *n.* A member of an American Indian tribe ; their language ; উত্তর আমেরিকার আদিম জাতিবিশেষের লোক ; ঐ লোকদের ভাষা।

Mō'-hŏck, *n.* (*Hist.*) One of the aristocratic ruffians who infested the streets of London during the latter part of the 18th century ; (ইতিহাস) যে সকল সম্ভ্রান্তবংশীয় গুণ্ডা অষ্টাদশ শতাব্দীর শেষভাগে লণ্ডনের রাজপথে ঘুরিয়া বেড়াইত—তাহাদের একজন।

mō'-hur (-hêr), *n.* An Indian gold coin worth 15 rupees ; মোহর।

moi'-dōre (mōy-), *n.* A Portuguese gold coin worth, a sum of, 27*s.* ; পর্ত্তুগালদেশীয় স্বর্ণ-মুদ্রাবিশেষ—এই মুদ্রার মূল্য ২৭ শিলিং অর্থাৎ প্রায় ২০॥০ টাকা।

moi'-ĕ-tȳ (mōy-), *n.* A half, esp. in legal use ; as, the *moiety* of a jury ; one of two parts ; অর্দ্ধ, অর্দ্ধভাগ, অর্দ্ধাংশ ; দুই অংশের অন্যতর।

moil (mōyl), *v. i.* To work hard ; to drudge ; as, to toil and *moil* ; কঠোর পরিশ্রম করা, অবিশ্রান্ত পরিশ্রম করা ; নীরস ও অবসাদজনক কাজ করা। **To moil with**—To make dirty with ; ময়লা করা।

moil (mōyl), *n.* Hard labour ; toil ; কঠোরশ্রম, অতিশ্রম, গুরুতর পরিশ্রম ; হাড়ভাঙ্গা খাটুনি।

Moirae, *n.* The personification of the Fates ; ভাগ্যদেবীত্রয়।

moire (mwär), *n.* **1.** Watered fabrics, usually silk ; a watered silk ; তরঙ্গবৎ রেখাচিহ্নিত বস্ত্র, বিশেষতঃ পট্টবস্ত্র; তরঙ্গাকার রেখাচিহ্নিত পট্টবস্ত্র। **2.** (*Orig.*) A kind of watered mohair ; (পূর্ব্বে) তরঙ্গাকার রেখা-চিহ্নিত বস্ত্র-বিশেষ।

moi-re' (mwä-rā), *adj.* & *n.* **1.** (Of silk) Watered ; (রেশম সম্বন্ধে) তরঙ্গাকার রেখা চিহ্নিত। **2.** (Of metals) Having watered or clouded appearance ; (ধাতুসম্পর্কে) তরঙ্গায়িত রেখা চিহ্নিত, মলিনপ্রভ। ***Noun.*** Watered or cloudy appearance ; তরঙ্গায়িত ভাব, ম্লানিমা।

moist (mōyst), *adj.* **1.** Moderately wet ; damp ; as, *moist* atmosphere ; rainy ; as, *moist* season ; আর্দ্র, সার্দ্র, সিক্ত ; স্যাঁতসেঁতে ; বাদলা। **2.** (Of a disease) Marked by a discharge of matter, phlegm, etc. ; "A cronic *moist* eczema" ; তরল, গলিত। **—ness,** *n.* আর্দ্রতা।

mois'-ten (mōys-n), *v. t.* & *i.* **1.** To make moist ; আর্দ্র করা, সিক্ত করা। **2.** To moisten with ; to soften with ; "It *moistened* not his executioner's heart with any pity" ; আর্দ্র করা ; দ্রবীভূত করা। ***Verb i.*** To become moist ; আর্দ্র হওয়া, সিক্ত হওয়া।

mois'-tūre (mōys-), *n.* **1.** (*Obs.*) State of being moist ; (অপ্রঃ) আর্দ্রতা। **2.** That which moistens ; water or other liquid diffused in small quantity through air and

সপ্তদশশতাব্দীতে ব্যবহৃত হারমোনিয়ামের ন্যায় একপ্রকার বাদ্যযন্ত্র। **—ly,** *adv.*

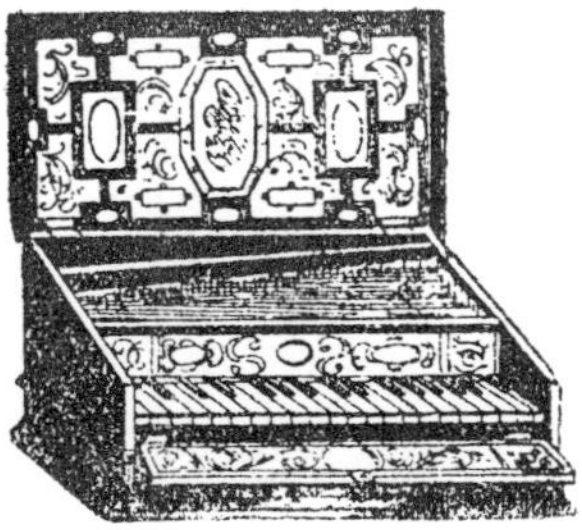

Virginal.

Virginal generation—Same as PARTHENOGENESIS. **Virginal membrane**—Same as HYMEN.

Vir-gin'-i-ă (vêr-), *n.* **1.** One of the states of the United States of America ; আমেরিকার যুক্তরাজ্যের অন্তর্গত ভার্জিনিয়া প্রদেশ। **2.** Tobacco grown in Virginia ; ভার্জিনিয়া প্রদেশে উৎপন্ন তাম্রকূট। **—an,** *adj.* & *n.* Pertaining to Virginia in America ; আমেরিকার অন্তর্গত ভার্জিনিয়াপ্রদেশসম্বন্ধীয়। *Noun.* A native of Virginia ; ভার্জিনিয়াবাসী। **Virginia creeper**—একপ্রকার আঙ্গুর লতা।

Vir'-gō (vêr-), *n.* **1.** A sign of the zodiac, which the sun enters about the twenty-second of August ; কন্যারাশি [Syn. পাথোল, যুবতী, কন্যা (যুবতিগে শশিনি প্রমদাজন প্রবলকেলিবিলাসকুতুহলৈঃ (কোষ্ঠীপ্রদীপ), অবলা, তন্বী) ।] **2.** A constellation ; চিত্রা, (L. VIRGIN).

vir-i-dĕs'-cĕnt, *adj.* Greenish ; tending to become green ; হরিদাভ; শ্যামায়মান, হরিতায়মান। **—cence,** *n.*

vi-rid'-i-ty, *n.* Greenness : verdure ; শ্যামলতা, শ্যামলিমা ; শ্যামশ্রী, শ্যামকান্তি।

vir'-ile (*or* -īl), *adj.* **1.** Pertaining to a man in his mature state ; not puerile or feminine ; "Man and all his *virile* virtues" ; পুরুষসম্বন্ধীয় ; পুরুষোচিত। **2.** Pertaining to procreative power : having procreative power ; as, *virile* power ; প্রজননশক্তিসম্বন্ধীয় ; সন্তানোৎপাদনক্ষম, প্রজননক্ষম। **3.** (Of style etc.) Having vigour ; as, a *virile* style ; ওজস্বী, তেজপূর্ণ। **—il'-i-ty,** *n.* **1.** The state of being virile ; পুরুষত্ব। **2.** The procreative power ; জননশক্তি, প্রজননশক্তি, সন্তানোৎপাদকশক্তি, রতিশক্তি। **3.** (Of style etc.) Vigour ; ওজস্বিতা।

vir-i-lĕs'-cĕnt, *adj.* (Of females) Assuming certain characteristics of the male in old age ; (স্ত্রীলোকসম্পর্কে) পরিণতবয়সে পুংধর্মগ্রাহিণী। **—cence,** *n.* The quality of being virilescent ; বৃদ্ধ বয়সে পুংলক্ষণগ্রাহিতা, পুংধর্মপ্রবণতা।

vi-rōle', *n.* Same as FERRULE (which see).

vī'-rōse, *n.* **1.** Poisonous ; বিষাক্ত। **2.** (*Bot.*) Emitting a fetid odour ; (উদ্ভিদ্‌বিদ্যা) পূতিগন্ধী।

vir-tu' (vêr-tō), *n.* **1.** Love of fine arts ; কলানুরাগ, চারুকলানুরাগ। **2.** Interest in curiosities ; কৌতুকসামগ্রীর প্রতি অনুরাগ, কৌতুকদ্রব্যানুরাগ। **3.** Objects of art or antiquity ; শিল্পদ্রব্য, প্রত্নদ্রব্য, কলাদ্রব্য। **4.** Excellence : চরমোৎকর্ষ, পরমোৎকর্ষ।

vir'-tū-ăl (vêr-), *adj.* **1.** In effect, though not in fact ; কার্যতঃ কিন্তু প্রকৃতপক্ষে নয়, বাস্তবিক (হিঃ কোঃ) । **2.** Having power of invisible efficacy without the material contact ; সূক্ষ্মশক্তিসম্পন্ন। **—al'-i-ty,** *n.* **—ly,** *adv.* In effect, though not in fact ; কার্যতঃ, ফলতঃ। **Virtual focus** — আলোকরশ্মিপুঞ্জের রেখাসমূহ বর্দ্ধিত হইলে যে বিন্দুতে সাম্মিলিত হইত, অদৃষ্টকেন্দ্র (হিঃ কোঃ) । **Virtual image** — See under IMAGE. **Virtual movement**—বাস্তবিক গতি (হিঃ কোঃ) । **Virtual velocity** or **displacement**—কোন বলের দিক পরিমাপ করিলে ঐ বল যে বিন্দু হইতে প্রয়োগ করা হয় তাহার যে সূক্ষ্ম ব্যতিক্রম হয়, সূক্ষ্মাতিচার। **Virtual velocity**—বাস্তবিক বেগ (হিঃ কোঃ) ।

vir'-tue (vêr-tū), *n.* **1.** Uprightness ; moral excellence ; good quality ; সাধুতা ; গুণ, পুণ্য, সুকৃত ; গুণ, সদ্গুণ। **2.** Chastity : "Angels had never the purpose to corrupt her ; only he hath made an assay of her *virtue*" ; সতীত্ব, ধর্ম্ম (cf. স্ত্রীলোকের ধর্ম্ম নষ্ট করা) । **3.** An inherent power or property ; as, the *virtue* of a drug ; efficacy ; ধর্ম্ম, গুণ ; কার্য্যকারিতা। **4.** The seventh order of angels ; দেবদূতগণের সপ্তম শ্রেণী। **—less,** *adj.* **—tu-ous,** *adj.* **1.** Morally good ; upright ; সাধু, সজ্জন, সুকৃতিমান ; পুণ্যবান, ধার্ম্মিক, পুণ্যাত্মা, ধর্ম্মশীল, ধর্ম্মিষ্ঠ। **2.** Showing moral rectitude ; as, *virtuous* act ; ধর্ম্ম্য, ধর্ম্মজনক, পুণ্যজনক। **3.** (Of woman) Chaste ; (স্ত্রীলোক সম্পর্কে) সতী, সাধ্বী। **—tu-ous-ness,** *n.* **By** or **in virtue of**—Through the authority of ; ক্ষমতায়, বলে। **Cardinal virtues** — See CARDINAL. **Seven principal virtues**—See SEVEN. **To make a virtue of necessity** — See NECESSITY.

vir-tū-ō'-sō (vêr-), *n.* **1.** A person skilled in the knowledge of fine arts, in antiquities, curiosities or the like ; কলাকোবিদ, বোদ্ধা, সমজদার, কলানাট্যজ্ঞ, রসজ্ঞ। **2.** A person skilled in the mechanical part of fine arts ; কোন ললিতকলার কলাশাস্ত্রানুযায়ী সম্পাদনরীতিতে পারদর্শী ব্যক্তি। **—si-ty,** *n.*

vir'-ū-lĕnt, *adj.* **1.** Very poisonous or venomous ; deadly ; অতিবিষাক্ত ; মারাত্মক, সাংঘাতিক। **2.** Extremely bitter, acrimonious or malignant ; উগ্র, প্রবল, বিদ্বেষদুষ্ট। **—lence, —len-cy,** *ns.* **1.** The quality or state of being extremely venomous ; অতিবিষাক্ততা। **2.** Extreme

mŏ'-mĕnt, *n.* 1. A minute portion of time ; an instant ; মুহূর্ত্ত, নিমেষ ; ক্ষণ। 2. Importance ; "Matter of some *moment*" ; গুরুত্ব। 3. (*Mech.*) Tendency or measure of tendency to produce motion, esp. about a point or axis ; (যন্ত্রবিজ্ঞান) গতিজননপ্রবণতা, গতিজননপ্রবণতার মাত্রা (বিশেষতঃ কোন বিন্দু বা অক্ষের চতুর্দ্দিকে)। 4. An essential or constituent element ; "The ethical *moment* is absent" ; উপাদান, মূল উপাদান। **—men'-tous,** *adj.* **—men'-tous-ly,** *adv.* **—men'-tous-ness,** *n.* **Am or was busy at the moment**—*i.e.* Just now or then ; এই মুহূর্ত্তে বা তখন বড় ব্যস্ত আছি বা ছিলাম। **Come here this moment**—এই মুহূর্ত্তে এখানে এস। **Critical moment**—সন্ধিক্ষণ সঙ্কটকাল। **Last moment**—চরমক্ষণ, চরমমুহূর্ত্ত, শেষমুহূর্ত্ত। **Men of the moment**—Men important at the moment ; ঐ সময়ে প্রভাবশালী ব্যক্তিবর্গ। **Of little, great or no moment**—See MOMENT 2. **One moment, Half a moment**—(*Ellipt.*) Wait a moment or half a moment ; একটু অপেক্ষা কর। **Pleasant for the moment**—আপাতমনোরম **Psychological moment**—পরম মুহূর্ত্ত, চরমক্ষণ। **The moment**—The time that affords an opportunity ; সুযোগের কাল। **Timed to the moment**—Timed very accurately ; সূক্ষ্মভাবে সময় নির্দ্দিষ্ট।

mō'-mĕn-tá-rŷ, *adj.* 1. Lasting only a moment ; ক্ষণিক, ক্ষণস্থায়ী, মুহূর্ত্তস্থায়ী। 2. (*Fig.*) Short-lived ; transitory ; (লক্ষণায়) অল্পকালস্থায়ী ; ক্ষণভঙ্গুর। **—ri-ly,** *adv.* Every moment ; for a moment ; প্রতিক্ষণ, অনুক্ষণ, প্রতিমুহূর্ত্তে ; মুহূর্ত্তের জন্য। **—ri-ness,** *n.* The state of being momentary ; ক্ষণিকতা, ক্ষণভঙ্গুরতা।

mō'-mĕnt-lŷ, *adv.* 1. From moment to moment; every moment; মুহূর্ত্তে মুহূর্ত্তে, ক্ষণে ক্ষণে ; প্রতিমুহূর্ত্তে। 2. For a moment ; মুহূর্ত্তের জন্য।

mō-mĕn'-tŭm, *n.* 1. (*Mech.*) The product of the mass and velocity of a body ; (যন্ত্র-বিজ্ঞান) কোন বস্তুর জড়-পরিমাণ ও গতিবেগের গুণফল, গতিপরিমাণ, বেগ (ব্রজঃ হিন্দু)। 2. Impetus gained by movement, (*lit.* & *fig.*); (শব্দানুযায়ী এবং লক্ষণায়) গতিবেগ।

Mŏ'-mŭs, *n.* 1. (*Gr. Myth.*) God of ridicule : (গ্রীকপুরাণ) বিদ্রূপ-দেবতা। 2. A fault-finder ; দোষদর্শী, পরচ্ছিদ্রানুসন্ধায়ী। **Daughter, disciple or son of Momus**—পরিহাসরসিক, বিদ্রূপরসিক।

mŏn'-ă-căl, —chăl, *adjs.* Monastic ; মঠসম্বন্ধীয়। **—chism,** *n.* Monastic life ; monasticism ; সন্ন্যাসাশ্রম ; তপস্বিতা।

mŏn'-ăd, *n.* 1. The number one ; a unit ; এক ; একক। 2. A simple primary element assumed by Leibnitz and other philosophers ; (লেইবনিজ প্রভৃতি দার্শনিকগণের মতে) সমস্ত পদার্থের অবিভাজ্য উপাদান, তন্মাত্র। [লেইবনিজের মতে Monad সমস্ত বস্তুর চরম উপাদান। Monad সমূহ অবিমিশ্র এবং বিভিন্ন monadএর গঠন একরূপ। ইহাদের মধ্যে কেবল গুণগত বৈষম্য দৃষ্ট হয়। Monadএর দ্বিবিধ গুণ আছে—অনুভূতি বা বিশ্ব-প্রতিবিম্বন শক্তি এবং বাসনা বা চেষ্টা। মানবের দেহ বিভিন্ন প্রকার monadএর সমবায়ে গঠিত—কিন্তু তাহার আত্মা একমাত্র monad দ্বারা গঠিত এবং ইহা তাহার সত্ত্বার কেন্দ্রস্বরূপ।] 3. (*Biol.*) Any minute simple organism or organic unit ; জীবাণু। 4. (*Chem.*) An element or radical which has the combining power of one atom of hydrogen ; (রসায়ন-শাস্ত্র) এক পরমাণু জলজানের সম্মিলনশক্তিসম্পন্ন মূল পদার্থ, একবন্ধন (হিঃ কোঃ)। **—ism,** *n.* The theory that the universe is a composite of monads ; তন্মাত্রবাদ। **Mo-nad'-ic, Mo-nad'-i-cal,** *adjs.*

mŏ-năn'-drous (-drŭs), *adj.* (*Bot.*) Having one stamen only ; (উদ্ভিদ্‌বিদ্যা) একপুংকেশর সম্পন্ন।

mŏ-năn'-drŷ, *n.* The custom of having one husband at a time ; একপতিত্ব।

mŏn'-ârch, *n.* 1. (*Early use*) The supreme governor of a state ; (*modern*) a sovereign whether king, queen, emperor, empress or the like ; (পূর্ব্বে) একরাজ, একচ্ছত্রাধিপতি, রাজচক্রবর্ত্তী ; (বর্ত্তমানে) রাজা, বা রাণী, সম্রাট বা সম্রাজ্ঞী। 2. One who, or that which, is superior to others of the same kind ; as, an oak is called the *monarch* of the forest ; অধিপতি, পতি, অধিপ। 3. A large red and black butterfly ; একপ্রকার বৃহৎ রক্ত-কৃষ্ণ প্রজাপতি।

mŏ-nâr'-chăl, *adj* Of, or pertaining to, a monarch ; imperial ; রাজসম্বন্ধীয় ; সম্রাট্‌সম্বন্ধীয়। **—chic, —chi-cal,** *adjs.* Same as MONARCHAL. **—chi-cal-ly,** *adv.* **—ly,** *adv.* **Monarchal form of government**—রাজতন্ত্র।

mŏn'-ârch-ĭsm, *n.* Monarchic government or principles or advocacy of them ; একচ্ছত্রশাসন, একচ্ছত্রশাসনানুরাগ। **—ist,** *n.*

mŏn'-ârch-ŷ, *n.* 1. Sovereignty of a single person ; একতন্ত্ররাজ্যপদ্ধতি, রাজতন্ত্র (সাঃ পঃ), একাধিপত্য, একচ্ছত্রাধিপত্য। 2. A state under a monarchical government ; রাজতন্ত্র শাসনাধীন রাজ্য। **Constitutional or limited monarchy** — See CONSTITUTIONAL GOVERNMENT.

mŏn'-ăs-tĕr-ŷ, *n.* A house for monks ; an abbey ; a convent ; বিহার, মঠ ; আয়তন ; আশ্রম।

mŏ-năs'-tic, *adj.* 1. Of, or pertaining to, monks or monasteries ; secluded from temporal concerns and devoted to religion ; "A life *monastic*" ;

punishment ; প্রতিহিংসাপরায়ণ, প্রতিজিঘাংসু, বৈরনির্য্যাতনপ্রবণ, বৈরসাধনতৎপর ; প্রতিহিংসা-সাধক, প্রতিজিঘিংসাত্মক। **—ly,** *adv.* **—ness,** *n.*

vine, *n.* & *v. i.* **1.** The climbing plant which produces the grapes of which there are several varieties; আঙ্গুরলতা, দ্রাক্ষালতা, দ্রাক্ষাবল্লী, দ্রাক্ষাব্রততী, দ্রাক্ষাবল্লরী [Syn. চারুগুচ্ছফলা, চারুফলা, কৃষ্ণা, প্রিয়ালা, তাপসপ্রিয়া, রসালা, অমৃতফলা।] [Arab. *kerm*; Egypt. *dips, dibs* ; Chenab. *dakhi, dehla* ।] **2.** Any plant that climbs like vine ; দ্রাক্ষার মত লতা। ***Verb i.*** To from a vine ; to grow after the manner of a vine ; আঙ্গুর লতা উৎপাদন করা ; আঙ্গুর লতার মত লতাইয়া দেওয়া। **Vin'-y,** *adj.* **Vine-borer**—একপ্রকার কীট। **Vine-clad** — দ্রাক্ষালতাচ্ছাদিত। **Vine-dresser** — যে ব্যক্তি দ্রাক্ষালতার চাষ করে।

vin'-ĕ-gar (-gêr), *n., adj.* & *v. t.* **1.** An acid liquor obtained from wine, cider, beer, etc. by acetous fermentation ; সির্কা [Syn. শুক্ত (ভাবঃ প্রঃ), তুষোদক (আয়ুঃ রসঃ), কাঞ্জিক (রঃ রঃ সঃ প্রঃ) ।] [Arab. *khull* ; It. *aceto* ; Fr. *vinaigre* ; Germ. *essig saure* ; Tam. *kadi* ; Teleg. *pulla millu* ; Russ. *ukzus* ; Sp. & Portng. *vinagre.*] **2.** Anything sour ; অম্লপদার্থ। ***Adj.*** Sour ; crabbed ; as, *vinegar* countenance ; কটুস্বভাব ; খিট্‌খিটে। ***Verb t.*** To apply vinegar to ; to make sour like vinegar ; সির্কা প্রয়োগ করা ; সির্কার মত কটু করা। **Aromatic vinegar** — কর্পূরাদি মিশ্রিত সির্কা। **Vinegar-Bible**—অক্সফোর্ডের Clarendon যন্ত্রে ১৭১৭ খৃষ্টাব্দে মুদ্রিত বাইবেলবিশেষ। ঐ বাইবেলের Luke xxii অধ্যায়ের শীর্ষে *vineyard* শব্দের স্থলে মুদ্রাকর প্রমাদবশতঃ *vinegar* শব্দ মুদ্রিত হইয়াছিল। **Vinegar-eel** — সির্কা প্রভৃতিতে প্রাপ্ত একপ্রকার ক্ষুদ্র পোকা। **Vinegar-plant**—একপ্রকার অন্তরুৎসেচনজনক আণুবীক্ষণিক ছত্রাক।

vin'-ĕr-ȳ, *n.* A kind of greenhouse in which vines are cultivated ; আঙ্গুর চাষের জন্য একপ্রকার হরিৎমন্দির।

vine'-yārd (vin-), *n.* A plantation of grape vines for producing grapes ; আঙ্গুরক্ষেত্র, দ্রাক্ষাক্ষেত্র, দ্রাক্ষাবাটিকা, দ্রাক্ষাবণ (হরিবংশ)।

vingt-(et-)un, *n.* A card game in which the object is to make the number or value of the pips on the cards, as nearly as 21 ; একপ্রকার তাসখেলা—যাহাতে ২১ ফোঁটা রাখিতে হয়।

vin'-i-cŭl-türe, *n.* Cultivation of vines ; আঙ্গুরের চাষ, দ্রাক্ষার চাষ।

vin-i-făc'-teur (-tür), *n.* An apparatus for making wine ; মদ্যপ্রস্তুতের জন্য যন্ত্রবিশেষ।

vi-nif'-ĕr-ous (-ŭs), *adj.* Producing wine ; as, a *viniferous* district ; মদিরাপ্রসূ।

vin-ŏm'-ĕ-têr, *n.* An apparatus for measuring the quantity of alcohol in wine ; মদ্যে কি পরিমাণ মদ্যসার আছে—তন্নির্ণয়ার্থ যন্ত্রবিশেষ।

vin ordinaire, *n.* A kind of cheap claret ; একপ্রকার সস্তা ক্লেরেট।

vi'-nous (-nŭs), *adj.* Pertaining to wine ; like wine ; having the qualities of wine ; মদ্যসম্বন্ধীয় ; মদ্যবৎ ; মদ্যধর্ম্মা।

vint, *v. t.* To make or prepare as wine ; মদ্যাদি প্রস্তুত করা।

vin'-tage, *n.* **1.** The produce of the vine for the season ; আঙ্গুরের ফসল। **2.** The time of gathering the crop of grapes ; আঙ্গুরের ফসল সংগ্রহকাল, আঙ্গুরের মরশুম। **Vintage-wines**—সুবৎসরের বাছাই আঙ্গুর হইতে প্রস্তুত উৎকৃষ্ট মদিরা।

vin'-tag-ĕr, *n.* A gatherer of grapes ; আঙ্গুরসংগ্রাহক, দ্রাক্ষাসংগ্রাহক।

vint'-nĕr, *n.* Wine-merchant ; মদ্যব্যবসায়ী।

vi-ŏl, *n.* A stringed musical instrument played with a bow of the same form as violin but larger ; একপ্রকার বৃহৎ বেহালা।

vi'-ŏ-lă, *n.* A kind of large violin ; একজাতীয় বৃহৎ বেহালা।

vi'-ŏ-lă, *n.* The violet genus of plants ; ভায়োলেটজাতীয়, গুল্মশ্রেণী।

vi'-ŏ-la'-ceous (-shŭs), *adj.* **1.** Of violet colour ; বেগুনে রংয়ের, ধূমলবর্ণ। **2.** Of the genus of violet flower ; ভায়োলেটজাতীয় গুল্মশ্রেণীসম্বন্ধীয়।

vi'-ŏ-late, *v. t.* **1.** To transgress ; লঙ্ঘন করা, ভঙ্গ করা। **2.** To commit rape upon ; সতীত্ব লঙ্ঘন করা, ধর্ম্ম নষ্ট করা, বলাৎকার করা। **3.** To desecrate ; অপবিত্র করা। **4.** To break in upon ; as, to *violate* a woman's privacy ; to disturb ; বলপূর্ব্বক প্রবেশ করা ; উত্ত্যক্ত করা। **—la-ble,** *adj.* **—la'-tion,** *n.* **1.** The act of one who violates ; লঙ্ঘন, ভঙ্গ। **2.** Rape ; সতীত্বলঙ্ঘন, বলাৎকার, ধর্ষণ, ধর্ম্মনষ্ট। **3.** The act of desecrating ; as, the *violation* of a temple ; অপবিত্রীকরণ। **—la-tor,** *n.*

vi'-ŏ-lence (-lĕns), *n.* **1.** The quality or state of being violent ; প্রাবল্য, প্রচণ্ডতা, উগ্রতা, প্রকোপ, তীব্রতা। **2.** Power exerted unjustly or illegally ; unjust force ; force employed against property, law, rights, or the like ; outrage ; injury ; hurt ; as, to do *violence* to one's person ; assault ; অন্যায়রূপে প্রযুক্ত ক্ষমতা ; অন্যায় পীড়ন ; অত্যাচার, দৌরাত্ম্য, জবরদস্তি, জুলুম ; বলপ্রয়োগ ; ক্ষতি ; আঘাত ; মারপিট। **3.** Rape ; বলাৎকার। **By violence** — By applying force ; বলপ্রয়োগে। **To do violence on**—To attack ; to murder ; আক্রমণ করা ; খুন করা। **To do violence to**—To cause injury to ; to outrage ; ধর্ষণ করা ; বলাৎকার করা। To apply force ; to hurt ; বলপ্রয়োগ করা ; আঘাত করা।

পীতজাতিসম্বন্ধীয়, পীতাঙ্গজাতিসম্পর্কীয়। 3. Designating a type of idiots like the Mongols; আদর্শমঙ্গোলিয়ানগণের অনুরূপ শারীরসাদৃশ্যসম্পন্ন জড়বুদ্ধি ব্যক্তিনির্দ্দেশক। *Noun.* 1. A number of the Mongolian race; মঙ্গোলীয়ান জাতীয় লোক। 2. A Mongol; মঙ্গোল জাতীয় লোক। 3. The language of the Mongols; মঙ্গোলদিগের ভাষা।

mŏn′-goose (-gōōs), **mŭn′-**, *n.* 1. An ichneumon of India often domesticated to destroy snakes; নকুল, নেউল, বেজী। 2. A kind of lemur; মাদাগাস্কর দ্বীপের কপিজাতীয় জন্তু বিশেষ।

mon′-grĕl, (mŭng-), *n.* & *adj.* 1. An animal of a mixed breed, esp. a dog; সঙ্কর জন্তু, বর্ণ সঙ্কর, খচ্চর, বিশেষতঃ সঙ্কর জাতীয় কুকুর। 2. A plant of a crossbreed; সঙ্কর জাতীয় উদ্ভিদ। 3. A person of a cross breed; বর্ণসঙ্কর। *Adj.* Of mixed breed, nature or character; সঙ্কর জাতীয়, গর্ভসংক্রমিত, মিশ্রজাতীয়। **—ism,** *n.* **—ize,** *v. t.* To render mongrel; বর্ণসঙ্কর করা, সঙ্কর করা। **—ly,** *adv.*

mō′-nĭ-ăl, *n,* Same as MULLION (which see)

mō-nĭl′-ĭ-fŏrm, *adj.* Like, or suggesting, a necklace or a string of beads; as, a *moniliform* root; মাল্যাকার, মালাকার (সাঃ পঃ)।

mŏn′-ĭsm, *n.* The doctrine that in the universe there is only a single element or principle from which everything developed, this single principle being either mind or matter; একমাত্র জড়ীয় বা চিদাত্মক মূলতত্ত্ব বা মূলভূত হইতে বিশ্বের যাবতীয় বস্তু বিকাশপ্রাপ্ত হইয়াছে এইরূপ মতবাদ। [অতএব জড়বাদ (materialism), সর্ব্বেশ্বরবাদ (pantheism), চিদাত্মকবাদ (idealism), অদ্বয়বাদেরই (monism) রূপান্তর] অদ্বৈতবাদ (এভেদন), অদ্বয়বাদ, ঐক্যবাদ

-less (A. S. *leas*) without as, useless, worthless, valueless, tenantless.

let (*el, le,* and *et*) diminution, little; as, eaglet, streamlet.

like (A. S. *lic*) like; as, warlike, saintlike, godlike.

ling (A.S.) little, young; as, darkling, codling, darling; sometimes depreciatory, as, hireling, groundling.

-ling, long (A. S. *lunga, linga*) *adv.* suffix, as, sidelong, darkling.

lock (A. S. *lac*) noun suffix; wedlock.

lock, lick (A. S. *leac*) a leek; garlic, hemlock.

ly (A.S. *lic*) like, as, lordly, friendly, kindly, manly.

meal (A. S. *mælum*) *adv.* suffix; as piecemeal.

men (L. *men*) state, that which; as, regimen, acumen.

ment (F. L. *mentum*) act or state of; as, treatment, excitement, advancement, nourishment.

mony (F. *monie,* L. *monium, monia*) act or state of; as, parsimony, testimony, matrimony.

most (*ma* and *est*) greatest; as, uppermost, endmost, topmost.

n, in participles, denoting possession; as, broken, hewn.

nd (A. S.) *ppr.* suffix; friend.

ness (A. S.) being or state of being; as, madness, blindness, kindness.

ock (A. S. *uc*) little; as, hillock.

oid, oidal (G. *oeides*) colloid.

om (A. S. *um*) old dative; as whilom.

on (L. *onem*) as felon.

on, one, oon (F. *on,* It. *one*) augmentative; as, balloon, flagon, trombone.

or (L.) one who; as, imitator, persecutor, author, factor.

ory (L. *orius*) belonging to or place where; as, olfactory, purgatory, prefatory, piscatory.

ose (L. *osus*) full of; as, verbose, jocose.

osity (L. *ositas*) abundance, state; as, verbosity, curiosity.

ot (F.) little; as, ballot, pivot;—(G. *otes*) one who; as, patriot, zealot.

our (F. *eur,* L. *or*) state of being; as, honour, favour.

ous (L. *us*) full of; as, prosperous, lustrous, nervous, dubious, fibrous.

ow, w (A. S. *u, we, wa*) meadow, sparrow, straw.

r, er, verb suffix; as, chatter, titter.

re (A. S.) place; as, here, there.

red (A. S. *ræd*) implying number; as, hundred.

red (A. S. *ræden,* rule) state, those who; as, kindred.

ric (A. S. *rice,* dominion) dominion, region; as, bishopric.

right (A. S. *riht*) as upright, downright.

ry, ery, (F. *rie, erie*) art, place; as, masonry, foundry: also the result of action; as, poetry; action; as, sorcery; condition; as, slavery; forming collective noun; as, infantry.

s (A. S. *es*) marking the genitive case.

se (A.S. *sian*) to make; as, cleanse.

ship (A. S. *scipe*) state or quality; as, hardship, friendship.

sis (G.) action or state; as, thesis.

some (A. S.) full of; as, tiresome, quarrelsome, gladsome.

son, son; as, Johnson.

ster (A. S. *estre*) agent or doer; as, punster, gamester.

stress (A. S.) as, songstress.

sy, se (G. *sis*) state; as, dropsy, eclipse.

t (L. *tus*) *adj.* and noun suffix; as, fact, exact.

t. for **th.** as, height.

up the chimney—Mortgage on a house ; বাড়ী বন্ধক। **To put his monkey up**—To enrage him ; রাগাইয়া তোলা। **To suck the monkey** — To drink rum out of cocoanuts ; নারিকেলের মালা হইতে সুরাপান করা। To suck liquor with a straw from casks ; পিপার ভিতর নল লাগাইয়া সুরা পান করা।

monk'-ish (mŭngk-), *adj.* Pertaining to monks ; monastic ; as, a *monkish* writer ; মঠবাসী সন্ন্যাসিসম্পর্কীয়, ভিক্ষুসম্পর্কীয়; মঠসম্বন্ধীয়।

mŏn'-ō–, A perfix signifying one, single, alone ; একবোধক উপসর্গ।

mŏn-ō-băs'-ĭc, *adj.* (*Chem.*) Having one base or atom of a base ; (রসায়ন-শাস্ত্র) কোন ভস্ম বা ভস্মের পরমাণুসম্বন্ধীয়।

mŏn-ō-câr'-pic, –pous (-pŭs), *adjs.* Bearing fruit but once and dying after fruiting ; এক বার মাত্র ফলপ্রসবকারী এবং ফলপ্রসবান্তে মরণশীল, এককিঞ্জল্ক (সাঃ পঃ)।

mŏn-ō-cĕph'-ă-lous (-lŭs), *adj.* Having but one head ; একশিরস্ক।

mŏn'-ō-chord, *n.* A musical instrument of one chord or string ; একতারা।

mŏn-ō-chrō-măt'-ic, *adj.* 1. Consisting of, or presenting, only one colour, as light ; একবর্ণাত্মক, একবর্ণপ্রদর্শী। 2. Executed in monochrome ; একবর্ণে চিত্রিত।

mŏn'-ō-chrōme, *n.* & *adj.* 1. A picture or painting executed in one hue ; একবর্ণে চিত্রিত চিত্র। 2. Art of executing these ; একবর্ণ-চিত্রণশিল্প। ***Adj.*** Having only one colour ; একবর্ণবিশিষ্ট, একরঙা।

mŏn'-ō-cle (-cl), *n.* A single eyeglass ; একচক্ষুর জন্য চশমা।

mŏn-ō-cŏt-ỹ-lē'-dŏn, *n.* A plant with single cotyledon ; একপর্ণিক (বিষঃ), একবীজপত্রিক, একপত্রোৎপত্তিক, একপত্রিক। **–ous**, *adj.*

mō-nŏc'-ră-cỹ, *n.* Government by a single person ; একতন্ত্ররাজ্য।

mō-nŏc'-ū-lar (-lêr), *adj.* Having only one eye ; একচক্ষু, একনেত্র, একলোচন, কানা।

mŏn'-ō-drâ-mă, *n.* A drama acted or intended to be acted by a single person ; এক ব্যক্তি দ্বারা অভিনীত বা অভিনয়ের জন্য অভিপ্রেত নাট্য।

mŏn'-ō-dỹ, *n.* 1. An ode sung only by one actor in a Greek tragedy ; গ্রীকদেশীয় বিয়োগান্ত নাট্যে একমাত্র অভিনেতা কর্তৃক গীত সঙ্গীত। 2. A poem expressing a mourner's lamentations for one's death ; বিলাপ-কবিতা, শোকগাথা। **–dist**, *n.* **Mo-nod'-ic**, *adj.*

mō-noe'-cious (-nē-shŭs), *adj.* 1. (*Bot.*) With male and female organs on the same plant ; (উদ্ভিদ্‌বিদ্যা) দ্বিলিঙ্গভাক (সাঃ পঃ)। 2. (*Zool.*) Hermaphrodite ; (জন্তুবিদ্যা) উভলিঙ্গ।

mō-nŏg'-ă-mỹ, *n.* 1. The practice of marrying only one at a time ; এক সময়ে এক স্ত্রী বিবাহ, একভার্য্যাপরিণয়, একবিবাহ (সাঃ পঃ) 2. (*Rare.*) The practice of marrying only once ; (কচিদ্ ব্যবহৃত) একভার্য্যাব্রত। 3. (*Zool.*) The habit of pairing with a single mate ; (জন্তুবিদ্যা) একমাত্র পুংজন্তুর সহিত সংসর্গের রীতি। **–mist**, *n.* **–mous**, *adj.*

mŏn-ō-gĕn'-ĕ-sis, *n.* Development of all beings from a single cell ; একমাত্র কোষ হইতে সকল সত্তাবান জীব বা বস্তুর উদ্ভব, এককোষোৎপত্তি। **–ge-net'-ic**, *adj.*

mō-nŏg'-ĕ-nỹ, *n.* Derivation of mankind from one pair of ancestors ; স্ত্রীপুরুষযুগ্ম হইতে মানবজাতির উদ্ভব।

mŏn'-ō-glŏt, *adj.* & *n.* Using only one language ; একভাষাভাষী। ***Noun.*** A person familiar with but one language ; একভাষাভাষী ব্যক্তি।

mŏn'-ō-grăm, *n.* A figure consisting of several letters, esp. one's initials, interwoven or written into one ; একত্র জড়িত অক্ষর সমূহ, বিশেষতঃ কোন ব্যক্তির নামের আদ্যক্ষর সমূহ, আদ্যক্ষরবন্ধ (আঃ বঃ)। **–mat'-ic**, *adj.*

mŏn'-ō-grăph, *n.* & *v. t.* An account or description of a single thing or a class of things ; একমাত্র বস্তু বা একশ্রেণীর বস্তু সমূহের বিবরণ, প্রকরণ (মঃ উঃ)। ***Verb t.*** To write a monograph on ; কোন বিষয়ে প্রকরণ লিখা। **–graph'-ic**, *adj.* **–graph'-i-cal-ly**, *adv.* **Mo-nog'-ra-pher, Mo-nog'-ra-phist**, *ns.*

mō-nŏg'-ỹ-nous (-nŭs), *adj.* (*Bot.*) Having only one pistil or stigma ; একমাত্র স্ত্রী বা পুংকেশরবিশিষ্ট।

mō-nŏg'-ỹ-nỹ, *n.* Practice of mating with only one female ; একমাত্র স্ত্রীর সহিত সংসর্গ। **–nist**, *n.*

mŏn-ō-ī-dē'-ĭsm, *n.* Concentration of mind on one idea, esp. as a form of monomania ; একাগ্রতা, বিশেষতঃ একবিষয়োন্মাদ।

mō-nŏl'-ă-trỹ, *n.* Worship of one God without denying others may exist ; একদেবার্চ্চনা।

mŏn'-ō-lĭth, *n.* A single stone or block of stones, esp. one of large size shaped into a pillar, statue or monument ; স্তম্ভাদির আকারে কর্ত্তিত প্রস্তরখণ্ড, একপাষাণস্তম্ভ, একপাষাণমূর্ত্তি। **–lith'-ic**, *adj.*

mŏn'-ō-logue (-lŏg), *n.* 1. A dramatic scene in which one person speaks by himself ; dramatic composition for a single performer ; নাটকের দৃশ্য বিশেষ—যাহাতে কোন ব্যক্তি স্বগতোক্তি করে; নাটকবিশেষ—যাহা একজন মাত্র নাট্যকার দ্বারা অভিনীত হয়। 2. Soliloquy ; একান্তকথন, স্বগতোক্তি। 3. A long talk or discourse by a single person in a company ; কোন সম্মিলনে এক ব্যক্তি কর্তৃক

দীর্ঘকালব্যাপী আলাপ বা আলোচনা। **logu-ist,** *n.*

mŏ-nŏl′-ŏ-ḡy̆, *n.* Habit of monopolizing a conversation; অপর লোককে কথা বলিতে না দিয়া সমস্ত আলাপ নিজের আয়ত্তীকরণ। **–gist,** *n.* **–gize,** *v. i.* **–no-log′-i-cal,** *adj.*

mŏn-ō-mā′-nĭ-ă, *n.* Insanity on one subject only; একবিষয়োন্মাদ, এক বিষয়ে চিত্তবিক্ষেপ, একাশ্রয়োন্মাদ (হঃ চঃ)। **–ni′-ac, –ni′-a-cal,** *adjs.*

mŏn-ō-mĕt′-ăl-ĭsm, *n.* Standard of currency based on one metal; কোন দেশে স্বর্ণ কিম্বা রৌপ্য এতদুভয়ের একতর ধাতুনির্ম্মিত মুদ্রার প্রচলন, একধাতু-পরিমাণবাদ। **–me-tal′-lic,** *adj.*

mŏ-nō′-mĭ-ăl, *n.* & *adj.* (*Algebra*) An expression consisting of one term; (বীজগণিত) একপদাত্মক রাশি। ***Adj.*** Consisting of one term; একপদাত্মক।

mŏn-ŏ-phy̑l′-lous (-ŭs), *adj.* (*Bot.*) Composed of a single leaf; (উদ্ভিদ্‌বিদ্যা) একপত্রিক (সাঃ পঃ)।

mŏ-nŏph′-y̆-site, *n.* (*Eccl.*) One who maintains that there is only one nature in the person of Christ; (যাজকীয় শাস্ত্র) যাহারা খৃষ্টে একমাত্র প্রকৃতি আছে বলিয়া মতপোষণ করে।

mŏn′-ŏ-plāne, *n.* A flying machine supported by a single aeroplane,

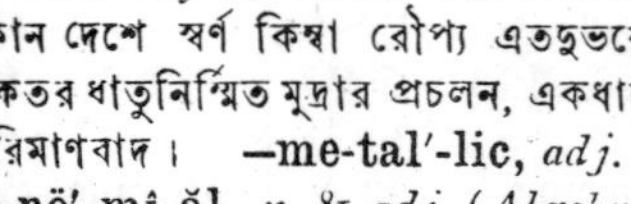

Monoplane.

একমাত্র সুবৃহৎ শয়ান অবলম্বনমঞ্চবিশিষ্ট "বায়ু-অপেক্ষা-গুরু" আকাশযান বিশেষ, একমঞ্চক।

mŏ-nŏp′-ŏ-list, *n.* One who has a monopoly (*of*); one who favours monopoly; একচেটিয়া ব্যবসায়ী, অনন্যসাধারণ ব্যবসায়ী; একচেটিয়া ব্যবসায়ের পক্ষপাতী ব্যক্তি।

mŏ-nŏp′-ŏ-līze, *v. t.* **1.** To obtain a monopoly of; to have full command of, for trade purposes; as, to *monopolize* a trade or commodity; অনন্যসাধারণ অধিকার লাভ করা; একচেটিয়া করা। **2.** (*Fig.*) To engross the whole of; as, to *monopolize* a conversation; (লক্ষণায়) স্বায়ত্তীভূত করা, নিজের আয়ত্ত করা, একচেটিয়া করা। **–li-za′-tion,** *n.*

mŏ-nŏp′-ŏ-ly̆, *n.* **1.** Exclusive possession of the trade in some commodity; একচেটিয়া ব্যবসায়, অনন্যসাধারণ অধিকার। **2.** A thing monopolized; as, in India opium is a *monopoly*; একচেটিয়া জিনিষ। **3.** (*Law*) A grant from the crown to an individual for the sole right to deal in anything; (আইন) কোন জিনিষের একচেটিয়া অধিকার, ইজারা মহাল। **4.** Exclusive possession, control, etc. (*of*); অনন্যসাধারণ অধিকার।

mŏn-ō-pŏl′-y̆-logue (-lŏg), *n.* An entertainment in which one performer plays many parts; যে নাট্যাদিতে এক ব্যক্তি বহু ভূমিকার অভিনয় করে।

mŏn′-ō-sy̆l-la-ble, (-ă-bl), *n.* A word of one syllable; একমাত্রাত্মক শব্দ। **–lab′-ic,** *adj.* Having one syllable; একস্বর। **–lab′-i-cal-ly,** *adv.* **–syl′-la-bism,** *n.* **–syl′-la-bize,** *v. t.* & *i.*

mŏn′-ō-thē-ĭsm, *n.* The doctrine that there is but one God; অদ্বৈতবাদ, একেশ্বরবাদ। **–ist,** *n.* One who believes that there is but one God; একেশ্বরবাদী, অদ্বৈতবাদী। **–is′-tic,** *adj.*

mŏn′-ō-tōne, *adj., n.* & *v. t.* Monotonous; একস্বর, অভিন্নস্বর। ***Noun.*** **1.** A sameness of sound; এক ঘেয়ে সুর, এক টানা সুর। **2.** Sameness of style in writing; এক ঘেয়ে রচনা, একসুরা রচনা। ***Verb t.*** To recite, speak or sing in an unvaried tone; একরকম সুরে গান করা, আবৃত্তি করা বা কথা বলা। **–ton′-ic,** *adj.*

mŏ-nŏt′-ŏ-nous (-nŭs), *adj.* **1.** Unvaried in tone or cadence; একস্বর। **2.** Wearisomely uniform; একসুরা, একঘেয়ে, একটানা। **–ly,** *adv.* **–ness,** *n.* **–nize,** *v. t.* **–ny,** *n.*

mŏn-ō-trē′-mă-tă, *n.* An order or sub-class of mammals called prototheria; সহবিন্মূত্ৰোৎসর্গী।

Mŏn-roe′-ĭsm (-rō-), *n.* Same as MONROE DOCTRINE (which see under DOCTRINE); **–ist,** *n.*

monseigneur, (*F.*), *n.* A French title given to eminent persons, esp. princes, cardinals, archbishops and bishops; ফরাসীদেশের রাজপুত্র এবং উচ্চশ্রেণীর ধর্ম্মাধ্যক্ষগণের সম্বোধনে ব্যবহৃত পদ।

monsieur, (*F.*) **1.** A title of courtesy in France, corresponding to Mr., (sometimes used by itself as a substitute for a name; as, did *monsieur* ring ?); ফরাসী দেশের ভদ্রলোকগণের সম্বোধনে ব্যবহৃত ইংরাজী Mr. শব্দের অনুরূপ উপাধি। **2.** A Frenchman; ফরাসী দেশীয় লোক। ***Monsieur de Paris***—জল্লাদ।

monsignor(e), (*F.*), *n.* The title of prelates, officers of the papal court and others; ফরাসীদেশীয় উচ্চযাজকগণ এবং পোপের দরবারের কর্ম্মচারিবৃন্দের সম্বোধনে ব্যবহৃত শব্দ।

mŏn-sōōn′, *n.* **1.** A periodical wind of the Indian Ocean; মৌশুমি (জিঃ), আগ্নেয় বায়ু, মলয়পবন (প্রঃ বাঃ), বায়ব্যবায়ু, কালবাত, আর্ত্তববায়ু (সাঃ পঃ) [এই বায়ু গ্রীষ্মকালে (wet monsoon) দক্ষিণপশ্চিম হইতে এবং শীতকালে (dry monsoon) উত্তরপূর্ব্ব হইতে প্রবাহিত হয়।] **2.** Similar winds with periodical changes; অনুরূপ বায়ু। **3.** The rainy season; বর্ষাকাল, প্রাবৃটকাল।

mŏn′-stẽr, *n.* & *adj.* **1.** An animal or plant of unnatural form or of great size ; a dwarfed or misshapen creature ; বিকটাকার জন্তু, বা উদ্ভিদ ; খর্ব্বকায় বা বিকৃতাকৃতি জন্তু, দৈত্য। 2. An imaginary figure compounded of incongruous elements, *e. g.* the centaur, sphinx, sagittary etc. ; বিকটাকার কাল্পনিক জীব। 3. Anything monstrous, esp. a person of unnatural or excessive ugliness, deformity, wickedness or cruelty ; বিকটাকৃতি বস্তু, কিম্ভূতকিমাকার বস্তু। ***Adj.*** Huge; বিরাট। **Monster-meeting**—বিরাট-সভা।

mŏn'-strance (-străns), *n.* (*R. C. Church,—Orig.*) Any receptacle in which sacred relics were exposed to view ; now, an open vessel in which the host is exposed ; (রোমান ক্যাথলিক ধর্ম্মসংঘ) পূর্ব্বে যে ভাণ্ডে সাধু-মহাপুরুষদিগের দেহাবশেষ বা স্মৃতি-নিদর্শন প্রদর্শিত হইত ; (বর্ত্তমানে) যে উন্মুক্ত পাত্রে খৃষ্টের অন্তিমভোজন ক্রিয়ার রুটিকা প্রদর্শিত হয়।

Monstrance.

mŏn-strŏs'-i-tȳ, *n.* 1. State of being monstrous ; a misshapen creature ; বিকটতা, বিরূপতা ; বিকৃতাঙ্গ-জীব, বিকৃতাকৃতি জীব। 2. An imaginary monster ; বিকৃতদর্শন কাল্পনিক জীব। 3. An extraordinary thing ; অসাধারণ বস্তু।

mŏn'-strous (-strŭs), *adj. & adv.* 1. Abnormal ; of unnatural form ; বিকট, বিরূপ, বিকৃতাঙ্গ (উজ্জ্বলঃ) ; সৃষ্টিছাড়া, কিম্ভূতকিমাকার, বিকৃতাকৃতি, ঘোরদর্শন। 2. Huge ; enormous ; outrageously absurd or wrong ; বিরাট, বিশাল ; রাক্ষুসে (cf. রাক্ষুসে বেগুণ); পৈশাচিক, বিকট। 3. Shocking ; frightful ; horrible ; বীভৎস ; বিভীষিকাপূর্ণ ; ভীষণ। ***Adv.*** (*Now colloq.*) Extremly ; as, *monstrous* good friends ; (বর্ত্তমানে চলিতভাষায়) ভয়ঙ্কর। **–ly,** *adv.* **–ness,** *n.*

mŏn'-tāne *adj.* Of, or pertaining to, or inhabiting, a mountainous country ; পার্ব্বত্যদেশসম্বন্ধীয়, পার্ব্বত্য-দেশবাসী।

mŏn'-te (-tā), *n.* A Spanish game of chance played with 45 cards ; স্পেনদেশীয় তাস ক্রীড়া বিশেষ।

month (mŭnth), *n.* 1. Any of the twelve portions into which the year is divided ; মাস। 2. A space of 28 days ; ২৮ দিন। **Lunar month**—চান্দ্রমাস, পক্ষদ্বয়। **Solar** or **calendar month** — সৌরমাস। **Month of Sundays**—অতিদীর্ঘকাল, অনির্দ্দিষ্ট কাল। **Month's mind**—A commemoration by a mass etc. of a deceased person, a month after death ; মাসান্তিক ঊর্দ্ধদেহিক ক্রিয়া প্রভৃতি। Inclination ; liking ; আসক্তি, অনুরাগ ; অভিরুচি। **This day month**—অদ্য হইতে একমাস।

month'-lȳ (mŭnth-), *adj., n. & adv.* 1. Performed in a month ; happening, recurring or published once a month ; একমাসে সম্পাদিত ; মাসিক, প্রতিমাসিক, মাসে মাসে সংঘটিত, মাসানুমাসিক। 2. Of, or pertaining to, the menses ; স্ত্রীলোকের ঋতুসম্বন্ধীয়, আর্ত্তব। ***Noun.*** 1. A magazine etc. published each month ; মাসিক পত্রিকা। 2. (*Pl.*) Menses ; স্ত্রীরজঃ, ঋতু। ***Adv.*** Once a month ; in every month ; মাসে মাসে ; প্রতি মাসে। **Monthly nurse**—ধাত্রী। **Monthly rose**—জবাফুল। [মাসে একবার ফোটে বলিয়া কল্পিত হয়।]

mŏn'-ti-cūle, *n.* 1. A hillock ; ছোট পাহাড়, ক্ষুদ্র শৈল, গণ্ডশৈল। 2. A small mound caused by volcanic eruption ; আগ্নেয় গিরির অগ্ন্যুৎপাত জনিত স্তূপ। 3. A very small eminence on the surface of an animal etc. ; জন্তু প্রভৃতির ক্ষুদ্র ককুদ।

mŏn'-ū-mĕnt, *n.* 1. A written record ; দলিল। 2. Anything that preserves the memory of a person or an event, as a building, pillar etc. ; a memorial erected over a grave ; কীর্ত্তি-স্তম্ভ, স্মৃতিস্তম্ভ ; সমাধিস্তম্ভ। 3. A notable example or instance ; as, this work is a *monument* of scholarship ; অত্যাশ্চর্য্য নিদর্শন। **The Monument**—লণ্ডননগরীর ১৬৬৬ খৃষ্টাব্দের ভীষণ অগ্নিকাণ্ডের স্মারকস্তম্ভ।

mŏn-ū-mĕn'-tăl, *adj.* 1. Of, or relating to, or serving as, a monument ; কীর্ত্তিস্তম্ভসম্বন্ধীয়, স্মৃতিস্তম্ভ-সম্বন্ধীয়, স্মৃতিস্তম্ভস্বরূপ। 2. Conspicuous and lasting ; impressive ; as, Gibbon's history is a *monumental* work ; অক্ষয়কীর্ত্তিস্তম্ভস্বরূপ ; হৃদয়গ্রাহী। 3. Stupendous ; as, *monumental* ignorance ; বিরাট, মহা, প্রকাণ্ড। **–ize,** *v. t.* **–ly,** *adv.*

mōō, *v. i. & n.* (Of cow and ox) To low ; হাম্বারব করা। ***Noun.*** The lowing of a cow or ox ; the sound moo ; গাভীর হাম্বারব ; "মূ" ধ্বনি।

mōōch, mouch (mowch), *v. t. & i.* (*Slang*) To loiter about ; (ইতর ভাষায়) ঘুরিয়া বেড়ান। ***Verb i.*** To steal ; চুরি করা।

mōōd, *n.* State of mind or feeling ; disposition ; temper of mind ; মনের গতি ; বৃত্তি (হিঃ কোঃ), ভাব ; মনোভাব, চিত্তের অবস্থা, মেজাজ। **In the mood**—Inclined ; প্রবণ, উন্মুখ। **In no mood**—Disinclined ; বিমুখ, পরাঙ্মুখ।

mōōd, *n.* 1. (*Gram.*) A form of the verb to express the mode or manner of an action or of a state of being ; (ব্যাকরণ) কোন কার্য্য বা অবস্থার প্রণালী বুঝাইবার জন্য ক্রিয়ার রূপবিশেষ, ক্রিয়ার রূপ। 2. (*Log.*)

Any of the classes into which each of the figures of a valid categorical syllogism is subdivided ; (তর্কবিজ্ঞান) প্রকার, রূপ, সংস্থান, ভাব (হিঃ কোঃ), বৃত্তি (ঐ) । 2. (*Mus.*) Mode ; (সঙ্গীতশাস্ত্র) রাগ ।

mōōd'-ȳ *adj.* Fretful ; gloomy ; sullen ; খিটখিটে ; বিষণ্ণ ; অপ্রসন্ন, মুখভার । **–i-ly,** *adv.* **–i-ness,** *n.* Quality or state of being moody ; বিষণ্ণতা, অপ্রসন্নতা, মুখভার ভাব ।

mōōn, *n.* **1.** The heavenly body next in conspicuousness to the sun ; চন্দ্র, চাঁদ, ইন্দু, বিধু, শশী, সুধাংশু, অব্জ, সুধা-কর, –দীধিতি, –রশ্মি ; শুভ্রাংশু, চন্দ্রমা, নিশা-পতি, –কর, –মণি, –কান্ত (কথাঃ সঃ) ; নক্ষত্রেশ, ক্ষপাকর, সোম, গ্লৌ, মৃগ-কেতন, –ধর, –লাঞ্ছন, –অঙ্ক ; কলানিধি, ওষধি-পতি, –ঈশ, –প ; শীত-রশ্মি, –অংশু, –দীধিতি, –মযূখ ; সিত-দীধিতি, –অংশু, –রশ্মি ; হিম-কর, –দীধিতি, –ধামা ; দ্বিজরাজ, রজনী-কর (মহাঃ), –রমণ (কথাঃ সঃ), –বর, –পতি ; শশ-ভৃত, –ধর, –অঙ্ক ; অনুষ্ণ-দীধিতি, –অংশু ; নক্ষত্র-নাথ, –রাজ (মঃ ভাঃ) ; নিশেশ, অমৃত-কর, –কিরণ, –দ্যুতি, –রশ্মি, অংশু ; উড়ু-প, –গণাধিপ, –নাথ, –পতি ; রোহিণী-পতি, –নাথ (বুদ্ধঃ), –কান্ত, –রমণ, –বল্লভ, –ঈশ (শিশুঃ) ; হরচূড়ামণি, কুমুদিনী-নায়ক (হিতঃ), –বধূবর (কাদঃ) ; কুমুদ-নাথ (কাদঃ), –বান্ধব ; তুষার-দ্যুতি, –রশ্মি, –অংশু, –কিরণ (কাদঃ), –কর ; তুহিন-কর, –কিরণ (কাদঃ), –গু (বৃঃ সঃ), –অংশু ; সিন্ধুনন্দন, ক্ষীরাব্ধিজ, তারা-রমণ (কাদঃ), –পতি, –অধিপ ; তারকা-রাজ, (কাদঃ), –ঈশ্বর (ঐ) ; শিবশেখর (মঃ উঃ), শিশির-কর (বৃঃ সঃ), –দীধিতি, –অংশু ; এণাঙ্ক, শ্বেতভানু (হরিঃ), নভোদীপ, –বাহন ; ভপতি, কৃত্তিকাভব, মাস (cf. পূর্ণমাসী), জ্যোৎস্নাবাপী (মঃ উঃ), গৌর, হরিণাঙ্ক (রাঃ তঃ), কুরঙ্গলাঞ্ছন । 2. A month ; as, this *moon* will last three days more ; মাস । 3. Any satellite or secondary planet ; as, the *moons* of Jupiter ; উপগ্রহ, চন্দ্র । **Moon'-less,** *adj.* **Full-moon**—পূর্ণচন্দ্র, পূর্ণিমা, পৌর্ণমাসী, রাকাশশধর, রাকেন্দু (cf. রাকেন্দুলালিত কৃষ্ণঃ কঃ) । **Moon-beam**—চন্দ্রকিরণ, শশিকিরণ, চন্দ্ররশ্মি, চন্দ্রপাদ, চন্দ্রমরীচি । **Mooncalf**—জড়ভরত, আজন্ম মূর্খ । **Moon face**—চন্দ্রমুখ, চন্দ্রবদন, পূর্ণেন্দুবদনা (*fem.*) । **Moonlight**—জ্যোৎস্না, কৌমুদী, চন্দ্রিকা, চন্দ্রালোক, চন্দ্রাতপ, চন্দ্রপ্রভা, শশিপ্রভা, চন্দ্রপ্রকাশ, অমৃততরঙ্গিণী (পঃ), মালতী (ঐ) । **Moon-light flitting**—বাড়ীভাড়ার টাকা পরিশোধে অসমর্থ হওয়ায় রাত্রে গোপনে আসবাবপত্রাদি স্থানান্তর করণ । **Moonlit** — চন্দ্রালোকিত, চন্দ্রিকাধৌত, চন্দ্রকিরণোদ্ভাসিত, চন্দ্রকিরণ-স্নাত, চন্দ্রিকায়াত । **Moonlit-night**—চন্দ্রালোকিত রজনী, জ্যোৎস্নাময়ী রাত্রি, জ্যোৎস্না, জ্যোৎস্নিকা । **Moon-plant**—সোমলতা । **Moon-shine**—Light of the moon ; চন্দ্রালোক, চন্দ্রপ্রভা, চন্দ্র-দীপ্তি । (*Fig.*) Pretence ; visionary talk or ideas ; (লক্ষণায়) ছল ; স্বপ্নপ্রলাপ, মায়ামরীচিকা, কল্পনা-কুসুম । Smuggled spiritis ; বিজোড়া মদ । **Moon-shiny,** *adj.* চন্দ্রালোকিত ; (লক্ষণায়) স্বপ্নাবিষ্ট । **Moon-stone**—চন্দ্রমণি, চন্দ্রকান্তমণি, বিধুপল (উজ্জ্বলঃ), চন্দ্রোপল, চন্দ্রিকাদ্রব, এণমণি (কুবলয়ঃ) । **Moon-struck**—মতিবিভ্রান্ত, বায়ুগ্রস্ত, পাগল, উন্মাদ, চন্দ্রাহত । **New moon**—অমাবস্যা । **A day of the moon**—তিথি । **Annual equation of moon**—দিগংশসংস্কার (সাঃ পঃ) । **A phase or digit of the moon**—চন্দ্রকলা, চন্দ্রলেখা । **Augmentation of moon**—বিম্বোপচিতি (সাঃ পঃ) । **Cusps of moon**—শৃঙ্গ । **Evection of moon**—তুঙ্গান্তরসংস্কার (সাঃ পঃ) । **Libration of moon** — পরিলম্বন (সাঃ পঃ), আলম্বন (ঐ) । **Line of the moon's mean anomaly**—চন্দ্রের মধ্যকেন্দ্রজ্যা (সূঃ সিঃ) । **Moon-culminating stars**—চন্দ্রগ্রস্ত তারা (সাঃ পঃ) । **Moon's-phases**—শুক্ল (সাঃ পঃ), শুক্লপরিবৃদ্ধি (ঐ) । **Old moon in new moon's arms**—শুক্ল প্রতিপদ হইতে শুক্লাষ্টমীর চন্দ্র—যখন চন্দ্রের অন্ধকার' অংশ ভূপ্রভা দ্বারা মৃদু আলোকিত হয় । **Once in a blue moon**—See under BLUE. **Shooting of moons**—Same as MOONLIGHT FLITTING. **The moon does not heed barking**—নীচ যদি উচ্চ ভাষে সুবুদ্ধি উড়ায় হাসে । **Variation of moon**—পাক্ষিক সংস্কার (সাঃ পঃ) ।

mōōn, *v. i.* & *t.* To act as if moon-struck ; to move or gaze listlessly *about*, *around* etc. ; পাগলের মত কাজ করা ; ফ্যাল ফ্যাল করিয়া তাকান, চারিদিকে চাওয়া । ***Verb t.*** To spend or idle *away* (time) in a listless manner ; আলস্যে সময় কাটান ।

mōōn'-ȳ, *adj.* **1.** Of, or like, the moon ; চন্দ্রবৎ, চন্দ্রপ্রতিম, ইন্দুনিভ । **2.** Listless ; dreamy ; অনবহিত ; কল্পনাপরবশ, স্বপ্নরাজ্যবিহারী ।

mōōr, *n.* **1.** A tract of marshy land overgrown with heath ; কচ্ছভূমি, জলা, অনূপদেশ । **2.** (In Cornwall) Waste land where tin is found ; (কর্ণওয়ালে) যে অনাবাদী ভূমিতে টিন (বঙ্গ) পাওয়া যায় । **Moor'-ish, Moor'-y,** *adjs.* **Moor-cock, moor-fowl, moor-game**—ডাহুক । **Moor-hen**—ডাহুকী । **Moor-land**—হাঁদার গুল্মাবৃত ভূমি । **Moor-stone**—একপ্রকার স্ফটিক প্রস্তর) ।

Mōōr, *n.* A native of Morocco or of neighbouring states ; মরক্কো ও তন্নিকটবর্তী রাজ্যসমূহের অধিবাসী । **Moor'-ish,** *adj.* **You cannot wash a black Moor white**—অঙ্গার শতধৌতেন মলিনত্বং ন মুঞ্চতি ।

mōōr, *v. t.* To confine or secure (a boat, ship, etc.) ; নৌকা প্রভৃতি ঘাটে বাঁধা । **Moor'-age,** *n.* **1.** Act of mooring ; a place for mooring ; নৌকা প্রভৃতি বাঁধন ; নৌকা প্রভৃতি বাঁধিবার স্থান । **2.** A charge for mooring ; নৌকাবন্ধনশুল্ক ।

mōōr'-ing, *n.* **1.** (*Usu. pl.*) Rope etc. with which a ship or boat is moored ; নৌকা, জাহাজ, প্রভৃতি বাঁধিবার কাছি । **2.** (*Pl.*) A place where a vessel is moored ; নৌবন্ধনস্থলী ।

moose' (mo͞os'), *n.* A North-American animal closely allied to the European elk; শম্বর। **Moose-deer**—শম্বর মৃগ।

moot, *n., adj., v. t.* & *i.* **1.** (*Eng. Hist.*) A meeting for discussion; সভা, মজলিস, বৈঠক। **2.** (*Law*) Students' discussion of a hypothetical case for practice; (আইন) আইনশিক্ষার্থী ছাত্রগণ কর্তৃক মোকদ্দমাপরিচালনসম্বন্ধে ব্যবহারিক জ্ঞানলাভের জন্য কল্পিত মোকদ্দমা সম্বন্ধে আলোচনা। ***Adj.*** Debated or debatable; as, a *moot* question; তর্কিত, বিতর্ক্য, বিবদনীয়, তর্কস্থলীয়। ***Verb t.*** **1.** To propose or bring up (question) for discussion; আলোচনার জন্য প্রস্তাব উপস্থাপিত করা। **2.** To discuss for practice, as in a mock court; মোকদ্দমাপরিচালনসম্বন্ধে ব্যবহারিক জ্ঞানলাভের জন্য কৃত্রিম আদালতে তৎসম্বন্ধে আলোচনা করা। ***Verb i.*** To argue or plead in a supposed case; কোন কল্পিত মোকদ্দমাসম্বন্ধে সওয়ালজবাব করা।

mŏp, *n.* **1.** A bundle of coarse yarn or cloth fastened at the end of a stick for cleaning floor etc.; also a smaller similar implement used in washing dishes etc.; ঝাড়ু, সম্মার্জনী; থালা প্রভৃতি পরিষ্কার করার জন্য মার্জনী। **2.** (*Fig.*) Something like a mop; entangled mass of hair; a person with this; (লক্ষণায়) ঝাড়ুর মত কোন কিছু; ঝাকড়ামাকড়া চুল; ঐরূপ চুলওয়ালা লোক। **Mop'-py,** *adj.* **Mop-head**—The head of a mop; ঝাড়ুর অগ্রভাগ (*Fig.*) A thick head of hair like a mop; a person with this; (লক্ষণায়) ঝাকড়ামাকড়া চুল; ঐরূপ চুলওয়ালা লোক।

mŏp, *v. t.* To rub or wipe with or as with a mop; as, to *mop* a floor; ঝাড়ু দেওয়া। **To mop the floor with**—To have and use overwhelming advantage of, as a combatant; প্রতিদ্বন্দ্বীর উপর খুব বেশী রকম সুবিধা থাকা ও তাহার ব্যবহার করা। **To mop up**—To wipe up; মুছিয়া ফেলা। (*Slang*) To absorb as profits etc.; (ইতর ভাষায়) শোষণ করা। To dispatch or make an end of; শেষ করা, নিকাশ করা।

mŏp, *v. i.* & *n.* To make a wry mouth; বিকৃত মুখভঙ্গী করা। ***Noun.*** Grimace; বিকৃতমুখভঙ্গী। **Mops and mows**—বিকৃত মুখভঙ্গী। **To mop and mow**—বিকট মুখভঙ্গী করা।

mōpe, *v. i., t.* & *n.* To be dull and spiritless; to be dejected; নিরুদ্যম হওয়া, অবসন্ন হওয়া, তন্দ্রাতুর হওয়া, ঝিমান; বিষাদক্লিষ্ট হওয়া, বিমর্ষ হওয়া, বিরস হওয়া। ***Verb t.*** (*Reflex. or passive*) To make spiritless, dejected or stupid; নিস্তেজ করা, বিমর্ষ করা, বিরস করা। ***Noun.*** A listless person; জড়, উদাসীন, নিরুৎসাহ বা তন্দ্রাতুর ব্যক্তি। **Mop'-ish,** *adj.* Given to, or characterized by, moping; নিরুদ্যম, উৎসাহহীন। **Mop'-ish-ly,** *adv.* **Mop'-ish-ness,** *n.* **The mopes**—Depression of spirits; চিত্তগ্লানি।

mō'-pōke, *n.* Same as MOREPORK.

mō-quette' (-kĕt), *n.* A material of wool and hemp or linen, used for carpets; গালিচা তৈয়ারীর সুতা।

mō-raine' (-rān), *n.* A continuous line of rocks and gravel along the edges of glaciers; তুষারনদীর তটদেশস্থ পাষাণ এবং কঙ্করের অবিচ্ছিন্ন রেখা।

mŏr'-ăl, *adj.* & *n.* **1.** Relating to right and wrong as determined by duty; as *moral* courage; নৈতিক, নীতিমূলক, নীতিবিষয়ক। **2.** (Of literary work etc.) Dealing with regulation of conduct; as, *moral* science; নীতিবিষয়ক। **3.** Practically sufficient; as, *moral* evidence; কার্য্যতঃ যথেষ্ট। **4.** Acting according to, or guided by, the laws of right and wrong; virtuous; just; as, a *moral* life; নীতিমার্গানুসারী; সৎ, সদাচারী, ধর্ম্মাচারী, সদাচারসম্পন্ন, সাধু, সদ্বৃত্ত, ধার্ম্মিক; ন্যায়নিষ্ঠ, ন্যায়বান, ন্যায়সঙ্গত। **5.** Based upon moral law; as, a *moral* right; নীতিমূলক, নৈতিক বিধির উপর প্রতিষ্ঠিত। ***Noun.*** **1.** Moral teaching of a story etc.; কোন গল্পের নীতি, নৈতিক উপদেশ। **2.** (*Pl.*) Moral habits esp. sexual conduct; সদাচার, নীতিধর্ম্ম, সংযতেন্দ্রিয়তা,—বিশেষতঃ ইন্দ্রিয়সংযম। **3.** Same as MORALE. **—ly,** *adv.* **Moral agent**—যে ব্যক্তি সদসৎ জ্ঞানের অধীন হইয়া কাজ করে। **Moral certainty**—এত অধিক সম্ভাবনা—যাহাতে কোনরূপ ন্যায়সঙ্গত সন্দেহ করা যাইতে পারে না। **Moral courage**—সৎসাহস, নৈতিক সাহস। **Moral defeat**—যে বিজয়ের পরিণাম কার্য্যতঃ পরাজয়ের তুল্য হইয়া থাকে, নৈতিক পরাজয়। **Moral faculty**—নৈতিকবৃত্তি। **Moral law**—নৈতিকবিধি। **Moral philosophy**—নীতিবিজ্ঞান, আচারশাস্ত্র (হিঃ কোঃ)। **Moral victory**—যে পরাজয়ের ফল কার্য্যতঃ জয়ের তুল্য, যেরূপ পরাজয়ে জয়ের তুল্য ফল লাভ করা যায়। **Moral virtues**—ন্যায়নিষ্ঠা, বিজ্ঞতা, মিতাচার, সহিষ্ণুতা ও বিশ্বস্ততা, আশা ও বদান্যতা। **The very moral of**—(*Vulg.*) The exact likeness of; (ইতর ভাষায়) ঠিক দোসর।

mō-rale' (-râl), *n.* Moral condition; state of the spirits as of body of troops as regards discipline, confidence, zeal, hope, etc.; as, the *morale* of the troops is excellent; নৈতিক অবস্থা; বিশ্বস্ততা, নিয়মানুবর্তিতা, আশা, উৎসাহ, প্রভৃতি সম্পর্কে (সৈন্যগণের) অবস্থা, সৈন্যগণের মানসিক অবস্থা, সৈন্যধর্ম্ম।

mŏr'-ăl-ĭsm, *n.* **1.** Inculcation of morality; moral teaching; নীতিশিক্ষাপ্রদান; নৈতিক উপদেশ। **2.** A moral maxim, saying, lesson or advice; নীতি, নীতিকথা, নৈতিক উপদেশ, নৈতিক শিক্ষা। **3.** Religion reduced to moral practice; নীতিমূলক ধর্ম্ম।

mŏr′-ăl-ist, *n.* 1. A teacher of morals ; a writer or lecturer on ethics ; নীতিশাস্ত্রের অধ্যাপক ; নীত্যুপদেশক, আচার উপদেশক (হিঃ কোঃ), নীতিবিজ্ঞানসম্বন্ধীয় গ্রন্থলেখক। 2. One practising morals ; one who leads a moral life ; সদাচারপরায়ণ, নীতিবান ; সদাচারমার্গী, নীতিমার্গাবলম্বী। **–is′-tic,** *adj.*

mö-răl′-i-tў, *n.* 1. Moral science ; নীতিবিজ্ঞান, নীতিশাস্ত্র। 2. Moral character or quality ; righteousness ; নৈতিক গুণ বা চরিত্র ; ধর্ম্ম, নীতিধর্ম্ম, সাধুতা, শীল, পবিত্রতা, নীতি, আচার (হিঃ কোঃ)। 3. (*Pl.*) Moral principles ; ethics ; নীতিতত্ত্ব ; নীতিবিজ্ঞান। 4. Act of moralizing ; নৈতিক উপদেশ প্রদান। 5. A particular system of morals ; as commercial *morality* ; নীতিশাস্ত্র সম্বন্ধীয় বিশিষ্ট পদ্ধতি। 6. (*Hist.*) A kind of Old English drama in which the characters represent virtues and vices ; নীতিশিক্ষাপ্রদ নাটকবিশেষ (ষোড়শ শতাব্দীতে ইংলণ্ডে অতিশয় জনপ্রিয় ছিল)।

mŏr′-ăl-īze, *v. i. & t.* To make moral reflections ; to talk morally ; as, to *moralize* on a subject ; নীতিমূলক মন্তব্য করা ; নৈতিক উপদেশ প্রদান করা। ***Verb t.*** 1. To interpret morally ; to draw a moral from ; "Did he not *moralize* this spectacle ?" ; নৈতিক ব্যাখ্যা করা ; নৈতিক উপদেশ প্রাপ্ত হওয়া। 2. To improve the morals of ; নৈতিক উৎকর্ষ সাধন করা। **–i-za′-tion,** *n.*

mö-r[illegible] *n.* A bog ; a marsh ; বিল, [illegible]মি ; অনূপদেশ, কচ্ছ।

mŏ′-răt[illegible] (*Hist.*) An ancient drink of honey flavoured with mulberries ; (ইতিহাস) প্রাচীনকালের লোকের পেয় তুঁত ফলদ্বারা সুরভিত মধু।

mŏr-ă-tō′-ri-ŭm, *n.* (*Law*) A period during which an obliger has a legal right to delay meeting an obligation, esp. such a period granted in an emergency, as to a bank or debtors generally ; (আইন) কোন চুক্তি প্রভৃতি দ্বারা আবদ্ধ ব্যক্তি (obliger) যে নির্দ্দিষ্ট কাল পর্য্যন্ত তাহার বাধ্যতা (obligation) পূরণ স্থগিত রাখার জন্য রাজবিধিপ্রদত্ত অধিকার প্রাপ্ত হইয়া থাকে, বিশেষতঃ যুদ্ধবিগ্রহাদি কালে ব্যাঙ্ক প্রভৃতি যে নির্দ্দিষ্ট কাল পর্য্যন্ত বিশেষ রাজবিধিবলে মুদ্রাদি প্রদান স্থগিত রাখিতে পারে।

Mö-rā′-vi-ăn, *adj. & n.* 1. Pertaining to Moravia, part of the Astro-Hungarian Empire ; অষ্ট্রো-হাঙ্গারিয়ান সাম্রাজ্যের অন্তর্ভুক্ত মরাভিয়া প্রদেশসম্বন্ধীয়। 2. Of the Protestant sect holding Hussite doctrines, founded in Saxony by Moravian emigrants ; মরাভিয়ান ঔপনিবেশিকগণ কর্ত্তৃক স্যাক্সনি প্রদেশে প্রতিষ্ঠিত রোমানক্যাথলিক ধর্ম্মবিরোধী সম্প্রদায়বিশেষ সম্পর্কীয়। ***Noun.*** 1. An inhabitant of Moravia ; মরাভিয়ার অধিবাসী। 2. A Moravian sect ; মরাভিয়ানসম্প্রদায়ভুক্ত লোক।

mŏr′-bid, *adj.* 1. Not sound and healthful ; sickly ; as, a *morbid* constitution ; অসুস্থ, রুগ্ন, রোগোন্মুখ (হিঃ কোঃ) ; ব্যাধিগ্রস্ত। 2. Of a gloomy or unwholesome nature ; "Her sick and *morbid* heart" ; বিষাদপীড়িত, দুঃখসন্তপ্ত। 3. Relating to disease ; as, *morbid* anatomy ; রোগসম্বন্ধীয়, পীড়াসম্বন্ধীয়। **–ly,** *adv.* **–ness,** *n.* **Morbid anatomy**—রুগ্নশরীরের বিকৃতি পরীক্ষাসম্বন্ধীয় শাস্ত্র।

mŏr-bi-dez′-za (-dĕt-să), *n.* 1. A soft delicate flesh-colouring ; সুকোমল মাংসবর্ণ। 2. (Of song or literary style) Soft delicacy ; সৌকুমার্য্য, লালিত্য।

mŏr-bid′-i-tў, *n.* 1. Morbid state or character ; রুগ্নতা, অসুস্থতা, অস্বাস্থ্য, রুগ্নাবস্থা। 2. Prevalence of disease (in a district) ; (কোন জেলায়) কোন রোগের প্রাদুর্ভাব।

mŏr-bif′-ic, *adj.* Causing disease ; রোগজনক, ব্যাধিপ্রদ।

mŏr-ceau′ (-sō), *n.* A short piece or passage of literary or musical composition ; ক্ষুদ্রপ্রবন্ধ, চুটকী গীত।

mŏr′-dănt, *adj. & n.* 1. Biting ; caustic ; sarcastic ; তীব্র ; কটু ; বিদ্রূপাত্মক। 2. Burning ; pungent ; জ্বলন্ত ; ঝাঁঝাল। 3. (*Dyeing & gilding*) Serving to fix a colouring matter or gold-leaf ; (রঞ্জন ও স্বর্ণাঙ্কণ কার্য্যে) রঞ্জকপদার্থ ও স্বর্ণপত্র লাগাইবার উপযোগী, রঙ্গসংস্থাপক, রাগবন্ধিনী (রঃ রঃ সঃ প্রঃ), রঙ্গবন্ধকারী (রঃ প্রঃ সুঃ প্রঃ)। ***Noun.*** (*Dyeing & gilding*) Mordant substance ; (রঞ্জন বা স্বর্ণাঙ্কণ) রঙ্গসংস্থাপক দ্রব্য। **–da′-cious,** *adj.* Caustic or biting ; কটু, মর্ম্মভুদ। **–dac′-i-ty,** *n.* Biting or sarcastic quality ; কটুতা, বিদ্রূপাত্মকতা। **–dan-cy,** *n.* State of being sarcastic ; sarcastic force ; বিদ্রূপাত্মকতা ; বিদ্রূপশক্তি।

mōre, *adj., n. & adv.* 1. Greater in quantity, amount or degree ; as, there is *more* truth in it than you think ; অধিকতর। 2. Additional ; আরো। ***Noun.*** 1. A greater quantity or number ; বেশী, অধিকতর পরিমাণ। 2. Something other and further ; আরো এবং অন্য কিছু। ***Adv.*** 1. In a greater degree ; অধিকতর পরিমাণে, অধিকতর মাত্রায়। 2. Again ; as, once *more* ; পুনরায়। **More and more**—With a continual increase ; ক্রমশঃ, অধিকতর, উত্তরোত্তর। **More by token**—In proof of this ; besides ; ইহার প্রমাণ স্বরূপ ; এতদ্ব্যতীত, আরো, অধিকন্তু। **More is meant than meets the ear**—যাহা শোনা হইল—ভিতরে এর চেয়ে অনেক বেশী কথা আছে। **More often than not**—Generally ; প্রায়শঃ, সচরাচর। **More or less**—In a greater or less degree ;

ন্যূনাধিক, কমবেশ, অল্প বিস্তর, অল্পাধিক। **More sinned against than sinning**—Rather wronged in a greater degree than wronging others ; অপরের যতটা উপদ্রব না জন্মায় অপর দ্বারা তদপেক্ষা অধিকতর উপদ্রুত। **More than a match for**—কোন ব্যক্তি অপেক্ষা শ্রেষ্ঠ বা অধিকতর বলশালী। **More than flesh and blood can bear**—Quite unbearable for a human being ; রক্তমাংসের শরীরে সহ্য হওয়া অসম্ভব। **More water glideth by the mill than wots the miller of**—গৃহস্থালীর ব্যাপারে এমন অনেক ঘটনা ঘটে যাহার বিন্দুবিসর্গও বাড়ীর কর্তা বা গৃহিণী জানিতে পারেন না। **Neither more nor less than absurd**—একেবারে অসম্ভব। **To be no more**—মরা। **What is more**—ইহা অপেক্ষা গুরুতর কিছু।

mō-reen′ (-rēn), *n.* A stout woollen stuff ; একপ্রকার স্থূল পশমী বস্ত্র।

mŏ-rĕl′, *n.* A kind of edible fungus ; একপ্রকার ভোজনোপযোগী ছত্রাক, খুম্ব (ফাঙ্গিঃ)।

mŏ-rĕl′, *n.* The plant nightshade ; কাকমারী জাতীয় গাছ।

mŏ-rĕl′-lō, *n.* A kind of cherry with a dark red skin ; একপ্রকার গাঢ়লোহিত ত্বগবিশিষ্ট চেরীফল।

mōre-ō′-vēr *adv.* Beyond what has been said ; further ; অপিচ, অধিকন্তু, বেশীর ভাগ ; আরো।

mōre′-pŏrk *n.* Kinds of birds ; বিভিন্নপ্রকারের পাখী। (Same as MOPOKE.)

Mō-resque′ (-rĕsk), *adj.* Moorish in style or design ; মুরদিগের স্থাপত্য-রীতি বা পরিকল্পনার অনুসারী।

mŏr-gă-năt′-ic, *adj.* Denoting a marriage of man with a woman of an inferior rank in which neither the latter nor her children enjoy the rank or inherit the possessions of her husband, though the children are legitimate ; নীচশ্রেণীর কোন স্ত্রীলোকের সহিত বিবাহ—যাহাতে স্ত্রী কিম্বা ঐ স্ত্রীর গর্ভজাত সন্তানগণ স্বামী কিম্বা পিতার উপাধি বা সম্পত্তির উত্তরাধিকারী হইতে পারে না, [এইরূপ বিবাহকে সচরাচর বাম-হস্ত পরিণয় (Left-handed marriage) কহে—কারণ বিবাহকালে স্বামী পত্নীকে বামহস্ত প্রদান করিয়া থাকে।] বামাচারবিবাহ (আঃ বঃ)।

morgue, (*F.*), *n.* A building (esp. one formerly in Paris) in which human bodies found dead are exposed for identification ; যে গৃহে মৃতাবস্থায় প্রাপ্ত অজ্ঞাত ব্যক্তিকে পরিচয়ার্থে রাখা হয়, শবব্যবচ্ছেদাগার, শবাগার।

morgue, (*F.*), *n.* Haughtiness, (esp. *morgue anglaise*) as is characteristic of the English ; উদ্ধতা, দাম্ভিকতা।

mŏr′-i-bŭnd, *adj.* In a dying state, (*lit. & fig.*) ; মুমূর্ষু, গতায়ু আসন্নমৃত্যু, মৃতকল্প।

Morion of the time of Queen Elizabeth.

mō′-r-i-ō-n, *n.* (*Hist.*) A helmet without beaver or visor ; মুখাবরণবিহীন শিরস্ত্রাণ।

Mŏr′-mŏn, *n.* **1.** A member of a sect founded in the United States in 1830 who practises polygamy (a latter-day saint); আমেরিকার যুক্তরাজ্যে প্রতিষ্ঠিত সম্প্রদায় বিশেষ—ইহাদের মধ্যে বহুবিবাহ প্রচলিত আছে। [এই সম্প্রদায়ের প্রতিষ্ঠাতার নাম Joseph Smith ; ইহাদের কেন্দ্রস্থল Utahএর অন্তর্গত Salt Lake নগরী। Book of Mormon ইহাদের ধর্ম্মগ্রন্থ। এই গ্রন্থ নিউইয়র্কের অন্তর্গত Palmyra নামক স্থানে ভূগর্ভে প্রাপ্ত স্বর্ণফলকোপরি অঙ্কিতলিপি হইতে ভগবৎ প্রত্যাদেশে Joseph Smith কর্তৃক অনূদিত বলিয়া প্রবাদ। Mormonগণ খৃষ্টের অনন্ত প্রায়শ্চিত্তে বিশ্বাসী এবং ইহাদের মতে সকল লোকেই খৃষ্টীয় সুসমাচারের বিধানসমূহ পালন দ্বারা মুক্তি লাভ করে]। **2.** A person who practises polygamy which is regarded as the chief feature of the sect ; বহুবিবাহকারী ব্যক্তি। **—ism**, *n.*

mŏrn, *n.* (*Poet.*) Morning ; (কবিতায়) প্রভাত, বিভাত, দিনমুখ, প্রাতঃকাল, প্রত্যূষ।

mŏrn′-ing, *n.* **1.** The first part of the day beginning at 12 O'clock at night and extending to 12 at noon ; প্রভাত, বিভাত, প্রত্যূষ, দিনমুখ, পূর্ব্বাহ্ণ, প্রাতঃকাল। **2.** (*Poet.*) Dawn ; (কবিতায়) ঊষাকাল, ভোর। **3.** (*Fig.*) The first or early part ; "O life, how pleasant is thy *morning* ; (লক্ষণায়) প্রভাত। **Good morning**—সুপ্রভাত, শুভপ্রভাত, [প্রাতঃকালীন অভিবাদন]। **The gray of the morning** — ঊষার ধূসরাভা। **The morn's morning**—(*Dial.*) To-morrow morning ; (উপভাষায়) আগামীকল্য প্রাতে।

mŏrn′-ing, *adj.* **1.** Of, or relating to, the first part of the day ; প্রভাত-সম্বন্ধীয়, প্রভাতকালীন, প্রভাতী। **2.** Used, or occurring, in the morning ; as, *morning* dress or prayer ; প্রাভাতিক, প্রাতঃকালিক। **Morning call**—অপরাহ্ণকালীন দেখাসাক্ষাৎ। **Morning draught** — প্রাতরাশের পূর্ব্বে পীত পানীয়। **Morning-glory**—একপ্রকার শ্বেত অথবা নীলারুণ বর্ণ পুষ্পপ্রসূ তরুবিশেষ, প্রভাতগরিমা (প্রবোধ)। **Morning star**—শুকতারা, প্রভাততারা, প্রভাতসূচক তারা। **Morning-time**—প্রাতঃকাল। **Morning-watch**—পূর্ব্বাহ্ণে ৪টা হইতে ৮টা পর্য্যন্ত প্রহর।

mō-rŏc′-co (-ō), *n.* A kind of leather prepared (orig. in Morocco now also in Europe) from goatskins ; একপ্রকার সংস্কৃত ছাগচর্ম্ম। **French morocco**—একপ্রকার ক্ষুদ্র দানাদার মরক্কোচর্ম্ম। **Levant morocco**—একপ্রকার উৎকৃষ্ট বড় দানাদার মরক্কোচর্ম্ম।

mō-rōse′, *adj.* Sullen ; ill humoured ; gloomy ; নিরানন্দ ; বদ-মেজাজী, খিট্‌খিটে ; বিষণ্ণ। **—ly**, *adv.* **—ness**, *n.*

Mŏr′-pheus (-fūs), *n.* (*Gk., Myth.*) God of sleep and dreams ; নিদ্রা ও স্বপ্নের অধিষ্ঠাতা দেবতা।

mŏr′-phi-ȧ, —phīne, *ns.* Alkaloid narcotic principle of opium, used to alleviate pain ; অহিফেনসার। **—phin-ism** *n.*

mŏr-phŏl′-ŏ-ġy̆, *n.* **1.** (*Biol.*) A science which treats of the forms of animals and plants : (জীব-বিজ্ঞান) জন্তু ও উদ্ভিদের অঙ্গ-বিন্যাসসম্বন্ধীয়বিদ্যা, শারীরতারতম্য-বিদ্যা, অঙ্গসংস্থানবিদ্যা, শরীরতুলনাশাস্ত্র (হিঃ কোঃ)। **2.** (*Philol.*) Study of the forms of words ; (ভাষাতত্ত্ব) ভাষার রূপ ও গঠন সম্বন্ধে আলোচনা। **—gist**, *n.* **—pho-log′-i-cal**, *adj.* **—pho-log′-i-cal-ly**, *adv.*

mŏr′-ris (-ĭs) *n.* & *adj.* A fantastic dance borrowed from the Moors by persons usually as characters in the Robin Hood legend, (also called *morris-dance*) ; মুরদিগের অনুকরণে নৃত্য বিশেষ। ***Adj.*** Pertaining to this dance ; মুরনৃত্যসম্পর্কীয়।

mŏr′-ris-tūbe (-ĭs-), *n.* A small-bore rifle barrel for insertion in a shotgun or rifle barrel to reduce the caliber ; বন্দুকের নলের মধ্যে লাগাইবার ক্ষুদ্ররন্ধ্র বিশিষ্ট নল।

mŏr′-row (-ō), *n.* **1.** The following day ; as, on the *morrow* ; কল্য, আগামী কল্য। **2.** The time immediately after the specified event ; as, on the *morrow* of a long war ; কোন বিশেষ ঘটনার অব্যবহিত পরবর্তী কাল। **To-morrow**—The day following the present ; আগামী কল্য। **Take no thought for the morrow**—জিভ দিয়াছেন যিনি আহার দিবেন তিনি।

morse (mŏrs), *n.* The walrus ; সিন্ধুঘোটক।

Morse (mŏrs), *adj.* Of the recording telegraph invented by S. F. B. Morse ; S. F. B. Morse কর্ত্তৃক উদ্ভাবিত তাড়িতবার্ত্তাবহ সম্বন্ধীয়।

mŏr′-sŏl, *n.* **1.** A mouthful ; a bite or bit (of food) ; একগ্রাস, একগাল, কবল ; এক কামড়। **2.** A small quantity ; a fragment ; অল্প পরিমাণ ; খণ্ড, টুকরা, অংশ।

mŏrt, *n.* A note sounded on horn at the death of a deer ; হরিণের মৃত্যুসূচক শৃঙ্গধ্বনি।

mŏrt, *n.* A salmon in its third year ; তিন বৎসর বয়স্ক স্যামনমৎস্য।

mŏr′-tăl, *adj.* & *n.* **1.** Subject to death ; destined to die ; as, man is *mortal* ; মর, নশ্বর, মৃত্যুবশ, প্রাণহর, মৃত্যুদ ; বিনাশশীল, অনিত্য, কালাধীন, মরণধর্ম্মী, মর্ত্ত্য, কালবশ, অন্তবান (গীতা)। **2.** Causing death ; deadly ; as, a *mortal* wound : *mortal* sin ; মৃত্যুজনক ; প্রাণঘাতী, প্রাণঘ্ন, মারাত্মক, ভীষণ, সাংঘাতিক। **3.** (Of battle) fought to the death ; (যুদ্ধ সম্পর্কে) প্রাণান্তকর, প্রাণান্তিক। **4.** Implacable ; as, a *mortal* enemy ; ঘোর, অদম্য, দুর্দ্দান্ত, দুষ্প্রসাদ। **5.** Human ; belonging to man who is mortal ; as, *mortal* wit or knowledge ; মানবীয় ; মরণশীল মানবসম্বন্ধীয়। **6.** Accompanying death ; as, *mortal* agony ; মরণকালীন। **7.** Extreme or very great ; as, in a *mortal* hurry ; অতিশয়, অত্যন্ত, নিরতিশয়। **8.** Wearisome ; tedious ; "Ten *mortal* years" ; ক্লান্তিজনক ; অবসাদ জনক। ***Noun.*** **1.** A being subject to death, esp. a human being ; মরণশীল জীব, বিশেষতঃ মানব, কালধর্ম্মক জীব। **2.** (*Facet.*) A person ; as, a thirsty *mortal* ; (কৌতুকচ্ছলে) ব্যক্তি। **—ly**, *adv.* **1.** In a fatal manner ; মারাত্মক-ভাবে। **2.** Severely or grievously ; as, *mortally* offended ; সাংঘাতিক ভাবে, গুরুতর রূপে।

mŏr-tăl′-ĭ-ty̆, *n.* **1.** Mortal nature or condition ; "I then did think on your *mortality*" ; মরণশীলতা, মরত্ব, নশ্বরত্ব, অনিত্যতা, মৃত্যুধর্ম্ম, মরণধর্ম্ম, মরণাধীনতা। **2.** Actual death of great numbers of men or beasts in a given time or area ; মড়ক। **3.** Death-rate ; কোন নগর বা দেশের লোকসংখ্যার অনুপাতে মৃত্যুর হার। **4.** The human race or nature ; মানবজাতি, মানবীয় প্রকৃতি, মনুষ্যত্ব। **5.** (*Rare*) Deadliness ; (ক্বচিদ্ ব্যবহৃত) মারাত্মক ভাব।

mŏr′-tar (-têr), *n.* & *v. t.* **1.** A strong vessel often in form of an inverted bell, in which substances are pounded or rubbed with a pestle ; উদূখল, খল, খল্ল। **2.** A short piece of ordnance, thick and wide, used for throwing bombs, shells, etc. ; বোমা, গোলা, প্রভৃতি নিক্ষেপের জন্য একপ্রকার কামান। **3.** A contrivance for throwing pyrotechnic bombs or shells ; আতসবাজীর বোমা ও গোলা নিক্ষেপের জন্য কৌশলবিশেষ। **4.** A mixture of lime, sand and water used as cement for building ; চুণ, বালি, এবং জল মিশ্রিত গাঁথুনির মসলা, তাগার, সুধাদ্রব (হঃ চঃ)। ***Verb t.*** To plaster or join with mortar ; চুণাবালির আস্তর করা, চুণা-বালির দ্বারা জোড় দেওয়া। **—less, —y**, *adjs.*

mort′-gāġe (mŏr-), *n.* A conveyance or pledge of property by a debtor to a creditor, as security for debt ; a deed effecting this ; বন্ধক, রেহান, আধি ; বন্ধকী খত। **Mortgage deed**—বন্ধকীখত, আধি (মঃ সং), আধিলেখ্য (আঃ বঃ)।

mort′-gāġe (mŏr-), *v. t.* **1.** To pledge (property) as security for debt ; বন্ধক দেওয়া, রেহান দেওয়া। **2.** To subject to a claim or obligation ; "I myself am *mortgaged* to thy will" ; কোন দাবী বা বাধ্যতার অধীন করা। **–ga-gee′**, *n.* The person to whom property is mortgaged ; বন্ধকগ্রহীতা, আধিধারী, ন্যাসধারী, আধিগ্রাহক (আঃ বঃ)। **–ga-gor′**, *n.* One who gives a mortgage ; বন্ধকদাতা, আধিদাতা।

mŏr′-tĭ-fȳ, *v. t.* & *i.* **1.** (*Obs.*) To destroy the vital functions of ; (অপ্রঃ) জীবনীক্রিয়া নষ্ট করা। **2.** To bring into subjection as the body, passions, etc. by discipline, self-denial, etc. ; দমন করা, সংযত করা, বশীভূত করা, নিগ্রহ করা। **3.** To humiliate ; to affect with vexation or chagrin ; to wound as feelings ; অবনত করা, পরাভব করা ; জ্বালাতন করা ; মর্ম্মাহত করা। ***Verb i.*** **1.** To practise penance from religious motives ; উগ্র তপস্যা করা, কৃচ্ছ্র করা, কঠোরসাধন করা। **2.** (Of the flesh) To gangrene ; (মাংস সম্পর্কে) পচিতে আরম্ভ করা। **–fi-ca-tion,** *n.* **1.** Act of mortifying ; state of being mortified ; নিগ্রহকরণ ; জীবিত প্রাণি-শরীরের কোন অংশের জীবনীশক্তির বিনাশ, চৈতন্যনাশ, জীবনীশক্তিনাশ **2.** Act of austerity, penance ; subjection of the appetites ; উগ্র তপস্যা, কৃচ্ছ্র, কঠোরতপশ্চর্য্যা ; ইন্দ্রিয়নিগ্রহ, ইন্দ্রিয় বশীকরণ, রিপু দমন। **3.** Humiliation ; the cause of humiliation, chagrin or vexation ; পরাভব, অভিভব, অভিমান, ব্যসন (কিরাতঃ) ; পরাভবের হেতু, বিরক্তির হেতু, কষ্টের কারণ। **4.** Gangrene ; necrosis ; জীবিত শরীরের পচনাবস্থা ; অস্থিনাশ। **–ing,** *adj.* **1.** Involving mortification of the natural desires and appetites ; ইন্দ্রিয়নিগ্রহজনক। **2.** Vexatious ; depressing ; বিরক্তিজনক ; অবসাদজনক, মনোভঙ্গকর।

mŏr′-tise, –tice (-tĭs), *n.* & *v. t.* **1.** A cavity made in a piece of timber to receive the tenon of another piece ; একখণ্ড কাষ্ঠের উদ্গাত অংশের সহিত সংযোজিত করার জন্য অপর কাষ্ঠখণ্ডে যে খাঁজ কাটা হয়। ***Verb t.*** To join or fasten securely, esp. by a tenon and mortise ; খাঁজে খাঁজে জোড়া দেওয়া।

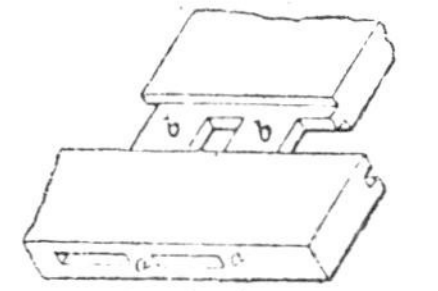

Mortise-joint. *a a*, Mortise ; *b b*, Tenon.

mŏrt′-main (-măn), *n.* (*Law*) Condition of lands and tenements held inalienably by ecclesiastical or other corporation ; (আইন) যাজকসংঘ বা অপর সমবায়ের চিরস্থায়ী বন্দোবস্তের অধীন সম্পত্তি, অস্খলিতভুক্তি (আঃ বঃ), সমবায়ভুক্তি (ঐ)। **In mortmain** — (*Fig.*) Under posthumous control ; (লক্ষণায়) মৃতব্যক্তির প্রভাবের অধীনে।

mŏr′-tū-ă-rȳ, *adj.* & *n.* Of, or relating to, the burial or death ; মৃত্যুসম্বন্ধীয়, সমাধিসম্বন্ধীয়, সমাধি-সংক্রান্ত। ***Noun.*** A building where dead bodies are kept for a time ; সৎকারের পূর্ব্বে যে গৃহে কিছুকালের জন্য শব রক্ষিত হয়, প্রেতগৃহ, শবাগার।

mō-ză′-ic, *adj.*, *n.* & *v. t.* Of, or relating to, mosaic ; চিত্রোপল-শিল্পসম্বন্ধীয়। ***Noun.*** **1.** (*Fine arts*) A surface decoration made by inlaying in patterns small pieces of variously coloured glass, stone, or other material ; also, the process of making it ; (ললিত কলা) একপ্রকার কারুকার্য্য—যাহাতে গৃহতল, প্রাচীরগাত্র, প্রভৃতি নানাবর্ণ কাচ, প্রস্তর, প্রভৃতির খণ্ডদ্বারা বিবিধ নমুনায় খচিত করা হয়, চিত্রোপলশিল্প [প্রাচীন রোমানগণের কালে এই শিল্পের চরমোৎকর্ষ সাধিত হয়"] ; উপলচিত্র-রচনাপ্রণালী। **2.** A picture or design in mosaic ; উপলচিত্র। **3.** (*Fig.*) Something resembling mosaic ; "In sweet *mosaic* she a story wrought" ; (লক্ষণায়) উপলচিত্রবৎ বস্তু। ***Verb t.*** To adorn with mosaics ; উপলচিত্রদ্বারা ভূষিত করা। **–i-cist,** *n.* **Mosaic gold**—অল্পমূল্যের অলঙ্কারাদি প্রস্তুতের জন্য একপ্রকার কৃত্রিম স্বর্ণ।

Mō-ză′-ic, *adj.* Of, or pertaining to, Moses, the leader of the Israelites or his writings and institutions ; ইহুদীদিগের ব্যবস্থাদাতা মুশাসম্বন্ধীয়, মুশার রচনা বা প্রতিষ্ঠান-সম্বন্ধীয়।

mō-să-sau′-rŭs (-sö), *n.* An extinct marine reptile first found near Maestricht on the Meuse ; অধুনা-লুপ্ত সামুদ্রিক সরীসৃপ বিশেষ।

mŏs-chă-tĕl′, *n.* A small plant with pale-green flowers and musky smell ; মৃগমদগন্ধী ম্লানহরিদ্বর্ণ ক্ষুদ্র পুষ্পপ্রসূ গুল্মবিশেষ।

Mŏs′-lĕm, Mŭs′-lĭm, *adj.* & *n.* Same as MOHAMMEDAN. **–ism,** *n.*

mosque (mŏsk), *n.* An Islamic place of public religious worship ; মসজিদ, দরগা।

mŏs-qui′-tō (-kē-), *n.* A stinging gnat or flay ; মশা, মশক। **Mosquito-craft**—একপ্রকার দ্রুতগামী লঘু এবং ক্ষুদ্র পোত। **Mosquito curtain, –net**—মশারি, নীশার (মঃ উঃ)।

mŏss *n.* & *v. t.* **1.** A bog ; a morass ; esp. a peat-bog ; ঝিল ; বিল ; বিশেষতঃ শুষ্ক দলপূর্ণ জলা-ভূমি। **2.** A kind of small herbaceous cryptogamous plants ; শিলাবল্ক, শৈবাল (ব্রজঃ হিন্দু), শেওলা। ***Verb t.*** **1.** To cover with a growth of moss ; শৈবালাচ্ছাদিত করা। **2.** To gather moss ; শৈবাল সংগ্রহ করা। **Moss′-i-ness,** *n.* **Moss′-y,** *adj.* Like moss ; শৈবালনিভ। **Moss-bunker**—Same as MENHADEN

Iceland moss.

Moss-grown—প্ররূঢ়শৈবাল, শৈবালাবৃত, শৈবালাচ্ছাদিত। **Moss-hag**—যে উচ্চাবচ ভূমি হইতে শুষ্ক শৈবাল তুলিয়া লওয়া হইয়াছে। **Moss-trooper**—সপ্তদশ শতাব্দীর ইংলণ্ড ও স্কটলণ্ডের সীমান্ত দেশের দস্যু। **A rolling stone gathers no moss**—ক্রমাগত এক ব্যবসায় ছাড়িয়া অন্য ব্যবসায় বা এক কাজ ছাড়িয়া অন্য কাজ ধরিলে কোনরূপ উন্নতি লাভ করা যায় না।

mōst, *adj., adv.* & *n.* Existing in greatest quantity or degree; নিরতিশয়, অত্যন্ত, বহুসংখ্যক। ***Adv.*** In the greatest or highest degree; অতিশয়, অত্যন্ত, অধিকতম। ***Noun.*** **1.** The greatest quantity or amount; as, this is the *most* I can do; সর্ব্বোচ্চ সংখ্যা বা পরিমাণ, পরাকাষ্ঠা। **2.** The greatest part or number; অধিকাংশ, অধিকসংখ্যা। **Most′-ly,** *adv.* Mainly; chiefly; generally speaking; প্রধানতঃ; মুখ্যতঃ; মোটের উপর বলিতে গেলে। **At (the) most**—বড় জোর, নিতান্ত পক্ষে, হদ্দমুদ্দ। **For the most part**—In the main; usually; প্রধানতঃ; সচরাচর। **Most an end**—(*Dial.*) Generally; all the time; (উপভাষায়) সাধারণতঃ, সচরাচর; সব সময়। **To make the most of**—To employ to the best advantage; to treat with the greatest consideration; to represent at the best or worst; যতদূর সম্ভব সুবিধা করিয়া লওয়া; বিশেষ সমাদর করা; অতিশয় ভাল বা মন্দভাবে প্রদর্শন করা।

mot (mō-), *n.* (*Pl.* MOTS, *pron.* MOZ) A witty saying; সরস উক্তি।

mōte *n.* **1.** A small particle of dust; anything proverbially small; ধূলিকণা, ত্রসরেণু (মঃ সং); কণিকা, রেণু, অণু। **2.** (*Cotton manu.*) A black spot on a yarn or woven cloth; কার্পাসসূত্র বা বস্ত্রে কৃষ্ণবর্ণ চিহ্ন। **A mote in (another's) eye**—A trifling fault if compared to one's own (*Math.* vii. 3); নিজের অপরাধের তুলনায় সামান্য মাত্র ত্রুটি।

mō-tĕt′, *n.* (*Mus.*) A short musical compostion of a sacred character: (সঙ্গীতশাস্ত্র) ক্ষুদ্র ধর্ম্মসংগীত।

mŏth, *n.* **1.** An insect mostly nocturnal allied to the butterfly, and breeding in cloth etc., (also *cloth-moth*); প্রজাপতি জাতীয় পতঙ্গবিশেষ, তসরে পোকা, ধেপসো পোকা ডাঁস, চোকরা।

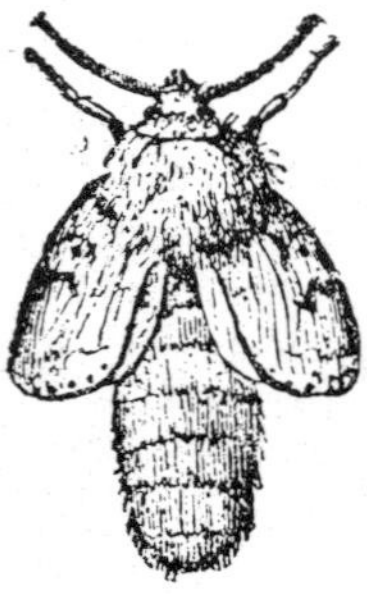

Moth just emerged.

2. Anything which gradually and silently eats, consumes or wastes any other thing; যদ্দ্বারা কোন জিনিষ তিলে তিলে ক্ষয় প্রাপ্ত হয়। **Moth′-y,** *adj.* **Moth-eaten**—কীটদষ্ট, পোকায় কাটা।

moth′-êr (mŭth-), *n.* **1.** A female parent; মাতা, মা, জননী, প্রসূতী, প্রসবিত্রী, প্রসবিনী, অম্বা, গর্ভধারিণী। **2.** Source of birth or origin; as, necessity is the *mother* of invention; যোনি, হেতু, মূল। **3.** A term of address for an elderly woman of the lower class: নিম্নশ্রেণীর বর্ষীয়সী স্ত্রীলোকের সম্বোধনে ব্যবহৃত শব্দ। **5.** An abbess or other female at the head of a religious or semi-religious institution; আশ্রম, মঠ, প্রভৃতির কর্ত্রী। **5.** Motherly affection; মাতৃস্নেহ। **6.** (*Archaic*) Hysteria; "O how this *mother* swells up toward my heart"; (অপ্রঃ) মূর্চ্ছাবায়ু, হিষ্টিরিয়া। **7.** (Also, *artificial mother*) A device or apparatus for rearing chickens; কুক্কুটশাবক পোষণের জন্য যন্ত্র-বিশেষ। **—hood** *n.* State of being a mother; জননীত্ব, মাতৃত্ব। **—less,** *adj.* Having no mother; অমাতৃক, মাতৃহীন। **—like,** *adj.* **—li-ness,** *n.* **—ly,** *adj.* Like, or becoming, a mother; maternal; affectionate; মাতৃসদৃশ, মাত্রোচিত; মাত্র্য; স্নেহপূর্ণ। **Artificial mother** — See MOTHER *n.* 7. **Mother Church**—দেশের আদিম ও প্রাচীন ধর্ম্ম-মন্দির—যাহা হইতে অন্যান্য ধর্ম্ম-মন্দির উদ্ভূত হয়। **Mother country** — জন্মভূমি, মাতৃভূমি, দেশমাতৃকা; ঔপনিবেশকগণের পক্ষে আদি বাসভূমি। **Mother earth** — মাতা বসুন্ধরা; (কৌতুকচ্ছলে) ভূমি। **Mother Hubbard**—ছেলেদের ছড়ায় উক্ত ব্যক্তিবিশেষ; একপ্রকার ঢিলা জামা। **Mother-in-law** — শ্বশ্রূ, শাশুড়ী। **Mother tongue, -language** — মাতৃভাষা, জাতিভাষা, জন্মভাষা (বিক্রঃ); মূল ভাষা। **Mother wit** — Natural wit; common sense; স্বাভাবিক বুদ্ধি, নৈসর্গিক বুদ্ধি; কাণ্ডজ্ঞান। **Does your mother know you're out?**—তুমি যে বাহির হইয়াছ তোমার মা জানেনত? [অর্থাৎ সে এমন শিশুপ্রকৃতির লোক যে পরের সাহায্য বিনা কোন বিষয়ে একপদও অগ্রসর হইতে পারে না।] **Every mother's son of you**—Every one of you; তোমাদের প্রত্যেক জন। **Mother Carey's chickens**—(নৌ-বিদ্যা) ক্ষুদ্র সাগরচর পক্ষি বিশেষ। **Mother of books**—গ্রন্থজননী এলেকজেণ্ড্রিয়া নগরী। [মুদ্রাযন্ত্র উদ্ভাবনের পূর্ব্বে এই নগরীর পুস্তকালয় পৃথিবীর মধ্যে বৃহত্তম ছিল।] **Mother of pearl** — কোন কোন শুক্তির স্নিগ্ধোজ্জ্বল বা ইন্দ্রায়ুধবর্ণ অন্তস্তর, ঝিনুক, শুক্তিবধূ (অঃ), মুক্তাস্ফোট। **Mother's apron strings** — মায়ের আঁচল (শিশুর আশ্রয়)।

moth′-êr (mŭth-), *v. t.* **1.** To protect as a mother; জননীর মত রক্ষা করা। **2.** To give birth to, (*usu. fig.*); as to *mother* a book; জন্মদান করা, উৎপাদন করা। **3.** To profess oneself to be the mother of, (*lit.* & *fig.*); as, to *mother* a child or a book; (লক্ষণায়) জননী বলিয়া প্রকাশ করা।

moth′-êr (mŭth-), *n.* A thick slimy substance that gathers in vinegar etc. ; সির্কাতে যে ঘন পিচ্ছিল পদার্থ জমাট হয়। **–y,** *adj.*

motif, (*F.*), *n.* **1.** (*In literature & fine arts*) A salient feature or element in a composition or work of art; (সাহিত্য এবং ললিতকলায়) কোন রচনা বা কাব্যের প্রধান বিশেষত্ব বা উপাদান। **2.** Ornament of lace etc. sewn separately on a dress ; পোষাকের উপর পৃথকভাবে স্যূত লেইস প্রভৃতির ভূষণ।

mō′-tile (-tĭl), *adj.* (*Zool. & Bot.*) Capable of motion ; (জন্তুবিদ্যা ও উদ্ভিদবিদ্যা) গমনক্ষম। **–til′-i-ty,** *n.*

mō′-tion, *n.* **1.** Act of moving ; change of place ; চলন ; গতি, গমন। **2.** Manner of walking etc. ; gait ; গমনভঙ্গী ; গতিভঙ্গী। **3.** Direction of movement ; course ; as, the direct *motion* of plantes is from west to east ; গতির দিক্ ; গমনপথ। **4.** A gesture ; a change of posture ; অঙ্গভঙ্গী, হাবভাব, অঙ্গবিক্ষেপ ; অবস্থানভঙ্গীর পরিবর্ত্তন। **5.** Inclination ; tendency ; "*Motions* of thought which elevate the will" ; ভাব, আসক্তি ; প্রবণতা। **6.** A proposal made ; particularly a proposition made in a deliberative assembly ; as a *motion* for introducing a bill ; প্রস্তাব; ব্যবস্থাপকসভা প্রভৃতিতে উপস্থাপিত প্রস্তাব। **7.** (*Law*) Application by a party etc. for a rule or order of the court ; আদালত হইতে রুল অথবা আদেশ জারির জন্য আবেদন, ছানি। **8.** (*Pl.*) Movements ; actions ; as, to watch one's *motion* ; গতিবিধি ; কার্য্যাবলী। **9.** (*Mech.*) A moving mechanism ; (যন্ত্রবিজ্ঞান) সচল যন্ত্র। **10.** (*Med.*) An evacuation of bowels ; দাস্ত, বাহ্য, রেচ। **–al,** *adj.* **–less,** *adj.* Without motion ; স্থাবর অচল, স্থাণু, স্তিমিত, স্থির, নিশ্চল, অনড় (পঃ পাঃ), নিষ্ক্রিয় (হিঃ কোঃ)। **Angular motion**—গতিলিপ্তিকা (সাঃ পঃ)। **Apparent or real motion**—স্ফুটগতি (সাঃ পঃ)। **Capillary motion**—অভিসর্পণ (ব্রজঃ হিন্দু)। **Daily motion**—কালগতি (সাঃ পঃ), ভুক্তি (ঐ)। **Direct motion**—অনুলোমগতি (সাঃ পঃ)। **Heliocentric motion**—মন্দস্পষ্টগতি (সাঃ পঃ)। **Mean motion**—মধ্যগতি (সাঃ পঃ)। **Retrograde motion** — বক্রগতি (সাঃ পঃ), বিলোমগতি (ঐ)। **Stationary motion** — বিকলাগতি (সাঃ পঃ)। **In motion**—Moving ; not at rest ; সচল ; চলৎ। **To put in motion** — To set going or moving ; চালান।

mō′-tion, *v. t. & i.* To direct by a sign or gesture ; to make gesture to direct a person ; ইঙ্গিত দ্বারা নির্দ্দেশ করা ; ইঙ্গিত করা, সঙ্কেত করা।

mō′-tive, (-tĭv) *adj. & n.* **1.** Causing motion ; having power or tending to move ; as, a *motive* argument ; গতিজনক, গত্যুৎপাদক, প্রবর্ত্তক, প্রয়োজক ; গমনক্ষম, গতিপ্রবণ। **2.** Concerned with movement ; গতিসংক্রান্ত। **3.** Relating to motive or motives ; হেতুসম্বন্ধীয়, উদ্দেশ্যসম্বন্ধীয়। ***Noun.*** **1.** That which incites to action, *e. g.* desire, fear, etc. ; object ; প্রবৃত্তি জনক বিষয়—ভয়, বাসনা প্রভৃতি, প্রয়োজক, নিমিত্তক, প্রবর্ত্তক ; উদ্দেশ্য, অভিপ্রায়, হেতু, প্রয়োজন। **2.** Same as MOTIF I. **Motive power** — গতিজনক শক্তি, বিশেষতঃ যন্ত্রচালক শক্তি, যথা বাষ্প, বিদ্যুৎ।

mŏt-ley (-lĭ), *adj. & n.* **1.** Variegated in colour ; চিত্রবিচিত্র, রং বেরঙের, নানারঙের। **2.** Of varied character ; as, a *motley* assembly ; বিভিন্নরকমের, বিভিন্ন প্রকৃতির। ***Noun.*** **1.** A dress of different colours, worn by a fool ; বিদূষকগণের পরিধেয় চিত্রবিচিত্র পরিচ্ছদ, ভাঁড়ের রংবেরঙের পোষাক। **2.** An incongruous mixture ; বিভিন্নপ্রকার দ্রব্যের মিশ্রণ। **To wear motley**—To play the fool ; ভাঁড়ামি করা।

mō′-tor (-têr), *n. & adj.* **1.** One that imparts motion ; a source of mechanical power ; গতিপ্রদায়ক ; যন্ত্রশক্তিজনক বস্তু। **2.** A machine supplying motive power for a carriage, vessel, etc. ; a motor car ; গাড়ী, জাহাজ, প্রভৃতির, গতিসঞ্চারকযন্ত্র ; হাওয়া গাড়ী। **3.** (*Anat.*) A muscle for moving a part of the body ; a nerve designed to excite muscular activity ; (শারীরসংস্থান বিদ্যা) দেহের কোন অংশ সঞ্চালনের জন্য পেশী, সঞ্চালকপেশী ; পৈশিকক্রিয়া উদ্দীপক শিরা। ***Adj.*** **1.** Causing, setting up, or imparting, motion ; গতিজনক, গতিসঞ্চারক, গতিপ্রদ, ক্রিয়াত্মক (হিঃ কোঃ)। **2.** (*Anat.*) Designed to excite the activity of the muscles, as a nerve ; পৈশিকক্রিয়া উদ্দীপনের জন্য অভিপ্রেত। **–ist,** *n.* A habitual driver in, or a traveller by, a motor ; হাওয়াগাড়ীর চালক বা আরোহী। **–y, –to′-rial,** *adjs.* (*Anat.*) Same as MOTOR. **Motor car**—হাওয়া গাড়ী। **Motor cycle**—তাড়িৎ কিম্বা বাষ্পশক্তিদ্বারা পরিচালিত দ্বিচক্রযান। **Motor tract at the bottom of the brain**—আজ্ঞাচক্র (ব্রজঃ হিন্দু)। **Volitional motor**—আজ্ঞাবহা (ব্রজঃ হিন্দু)।

mŏt′-tle (-l), *n. & v. t.* **1.** peculiarly blotched or spotted surface; ফুট ফুট দাগবিশিষ্ট উপরিভাগ, চিত্রবিচিত্র উপরিভাগ। **2.** (*Usu. pl.*) A coloured spot ; রঙ্গীন দাগ। **3.** A variegated woollen yarn ; একপ্রকার চিত্রবিচিত্র পশমী সূতা। ***Verb t.*** To mark with spots or blotches of different colours ; নানাবর্ণের ফুট ফুট বিন্দু বা দাগ দ্বারা চিত্রিত করা, চিত্রবিচিত্র করা। **–tled,** *p. adj.* Spotted, as a soap etc. ; ফুট ফুট দাগবিশিষ্ট, কর্ব্বুর।

mŏt'-tō, *n.* **1.** A sentence, phrase or word inscribed on anything as appropriate to, or indicative of, its character or use ; ক্ষুদ্র সারবান বাক্য, নীতিবাক্য। **2.** A maxim adopted as rule of conduct ; আদর্শ বাক্য। **3.** A quotatation prefixed to a book or chapter, suggestive of the subject matter ; পুস্তকের প্রারম্ভে বা কোন অধ্যায়ের শীর্ষভাগে উদ্ধৃত বাক্য—যাহা হইতে উক্ত পুস্তক বা পরিচ্ছেদের অন্তর্গত বিষয়ের আভাস পাওয়া যায়। **4.** (*Mus.*) A recurrent phrase ; (সঙ্গীতশাস্ত্র) পুনঃ পুনঃ আগত বাক্যাংশ। **Motto kisses**—বালক বালিকাদের আমোদ প্রমোদ ও প্রীতিসম্মিলনীতে ব্যবহৃত প্রেমকবিতা বা নীতিবাক্যসম্বলিত রঙ্গীন কাগজে মোড়া মিষ্টদ্রব্য।

mouf'-flon (môf-lŏn), *n.* A wild sheep of Corsica ; কর্সিকা দ্বীপের বন্য মেষ।

mou-jik' (mô-zĭk), **mu-zhik'** (mô-zĭk), *ns.* **1.** A Russian peasant ; রুশ কৃষক। **2.** A loose fur cape for ladies' wear ; স্ত্রীলোকদিগের জন্য লোমনির্ম্মিত একপ্রকার শ্লথ স্কন্ধাবরণ।

mould (möld), *n.* **1.** Loose or broken earth ; ঝুরা মাটী। **2.** The upper soil of cultivated land ; কর্ষিত ভূমির উপরের মাটী। **Mould'-y,** *adj.* Full of loose earth ; ঝুরা মাটী দ্বারা পূর্ণ। **Man of mould**—A mortal man ; নশ্বর মানব।

mould (möld), *n.* **1.** The matrix in which anything is cast and receives its form ; সাঁচ, সঞ্চক (নৈষঃ) ছেনি। **2.** That on which, or in accrordance with which, anything is modelled or formed ; ছাঁচ। **3.** A metal or earthenware vessel used to give shape to puddings etc ; also a pudding etc. so shaped ; পিঠা প্রভৃতির ছাঁচ ; ছাঁচে তৈরী পিঠা। **4.** (*Arch.*) A group of mouldings ; (স্থপতিবিজ্ঞান) বন্ধশ্রেণী। **5.** A form or shape, esp. of an animal body ; গঠন, আকৃতি, অবয়ব, গড়ন। **Mould candle**—ছাঁচে তৈয়ারী মোমবাতি। **Mould loft**—জাহাজ নির্ম্মাণস্থলীর যে কক্ষের তলে জাহাজের পূর্ণায়তন চিত্র বা নকল অঙ্কিত করা হয়। **Cast in heroic etc. mould**—Of heroic etc. character ; বীরপ্রকৃতিক।

mould (möld), *v. t.* **1.** To form in, or into, a particular shape ; to shape, (*lit.* & *fig.*) ; ছাঁচে গড়া ; গড়া। **2.** To shape (bread) into loaves ; পাঁউরুটি তৈয়ার করা।

mould (möld), *n.* A minute fungus which grows on bodies in a damp atmosphere ; ছাতা, চিতি। **Mould'-i-ness,** *n.* **Mould'-y,** *adj.* **1.** Overgrown with mould ; ছাতা-পড়া, চিতি-ধরা। **2.** (*Fig.*) Stale ; out of date ; (লক্ষণায়) বাসি, ভাপ্‌সা ; পুরাতন।

mould'-êr (möld-), *v. i.* To decay ; to dust ; to crumble *away* ; (*lit.* & *fig.*) ; "O how my friendships have *moulderd*" ; ক্ষয়প্রাপ্ত হওয়া ; ধূলিতে পরিণত হওয়া ; বিশীর্ণ হওয়া, ক্ষয়প্রাপ্ত হওয়া।

mould'-ing (möld-), *n.* **1.** Act of shaping according to a mould ; fashioning ; ছাঁচের অনুরূপে গঠন ; ছাঁচে গড়ন। **2.** Anything cast in a mould ; a moulded object ; যে কোন জিনিষ ছাঁচে ঢালা হয় ; ছাঁচে গড়া জিনিষ। **3.** (*Arch.*) A projection beyond a wall, column, etc. ; স্তম্ভ, প্রাচীর, প্রভৃতির উদ্গত ভূষা, বন্ধ (রাঃ রাঃ)। **Moulding board**—যে ফলকের উপর রুটির ময়দা ডলা হয়।

moulin, (*F.*), *n.* A deep and narrow cylindrical hole in a glacier into which a stream of water falls ; তুষারনদীর মধ্যস্থ সংকীর্ণ চোঙ্গাকার ছিদ্র—যাহাতে জলস্রোত পতিত হয়।

moult (mölt), *v. t., i.* & *n.* To shed and renew, as the hair, skin, feathers, etc. as an animal, bird etc., (*lit.* & *fig.*) ; (শব্দানুযায়ী ও লক্ষণায়) পক্ষমোচন করা, পক্ষত্যাগ করা। *Verb i.* (*Lit.* & *fig.*) To shed the hair, skin, feathers, etc. to be replaced by new growth ; লোম, চর্ম্ম বা পক্ষত্যাগ করা। *Noun.* The act of changing the feathers, etc. ; time of moulting ; পক্ষমোচন পক্ষত্যাগ ; পক্ষমোচন কাল।

mound (mownd), *n.* A ball of gold, etc. representing the earth, surmounting a crown etc. and used in heraldry ; কিরীটোপরিস্থ পৃথিবীর প্রতিরূপ স্বর্ণগোলক।

mound (mownd), *n.* & *v. t.* **1.** An artificial hill or earth ; a heap of earth on a grave ; মৃত্তিকাস্তূপ, মাটির ঢিপি ; কবরের উপরিস্থ মৃত্তিকা স্তূপ। **2.** A natural elevation ; a hillock ; টিলা ; গণ্ডশৈল। **3.** A bulwark ; a rampart ; বপ্র ; প্রাকার। *Verb t.* **1.** To inclose, fortify, with mounds ; প্রাকারবেষ্টিত করা, প্রাকার দ্বারা সুরক্ষিত করা। **2.** To heap up in mounds ; স্তূপীকৃত করা। **Mound-builder**—A pre-historic Indian race in North-America who erected mounds ; উত্তর আমেরিকার প্রাগৈতিহাসিক যুগের আদিম অধিবাসী—যাহারা স্তূপ নির্ম্মাণ করিত। A kind of bird depositing eggs in a heap ; একপ্রকার পক্ষী—যাহারা স্তূপাকারে ডিম্ব স্থাপন করে।

mount (mownt) *n.* **1.** A mountain or hill, (*abbr. Mt. often used before the name of mountain*) ; পর্ব্বত, পাহাড়, শৈল। **2.** (*Palmistry*) Fleshy prominence on the palm of the hand ; (করসামুদ্রিক) করতলস্থ উচ্চ মাংসল স্থান, ক্ষেত্র, স্থান।

mount (mownt), *v. i.* & *t.* **1.** To rise ; to ascend ; উঠা, উপরে উঠা ; উত্থিত হওয়া। **2.** (Of blood) To rise into cheeks ; (রক্ত সম্পর্কে) গণ্ডদেশে উঠা। **3.** To get *on* or *upon* anything, specifically on horseback ; আরোহণ করা, বিশেষতঃ ঘোড়ায় চড়া। **4.** To increase in amount ; as, debts *mount* fast ; পরিমাণে বৃদ্ধি

হওয়া। 5. To rise to a higher level of rank, power or intensity; উচ্চ পদবীতে অধিরূঢ় হওয়া, অধিকতর ক্ষমতা লাভ করা, প্রখরতার মাত্রা বৃদ্ধি পাওয়া। *Verb t.* 1. To get upon, as horse etc. for riding; আরোহণ করা, চড়া। 2. To put as a person on a horse etc.; আরূঢ় করা, চড়ান। 3. To put or place upon something elevated; as to *mount* a statue on a pedestal; অধিরূঢ় করা। 4. To furnish with horse; as to *mount* troops; অশ্ব জোগান। 5. To put on, or cover with, something necessary, useful, or ornamental; as, to *mount* a sword: to *mount* diamond: to *mount* a picture; বাঁধা, বসান। 6. To fix as an object on a microscope slide; অনুবীক্ষণ-যন্ত্রের কাচফলকের উপর কোন জিনিষ বসান। 7. To raise (guns) into position; কামান প্রভৃতি গাড়ী প্রভৃতিতে তোলা। 8. To put as a loom in working order; মেরামত করিয়া কাজের উপযোগী করা। 9. To put as a play on a stage; নাটকের অভিনয়ের উদ্যোগ বা ব্যবস্থা করা। 10. To put on or display oneself as wearing (an article of clothing); পোষাক পরা, পোষাকের বাহার দেখান। **To mount guard**—To act as a sentinel; পাহারা দেওয়া। **To mount the ass**—To become bankrupt; দাউলিয়া হওয়া। **To mount the cockade**—To become a soldier; সৈন্য হওয়া। **To mount the high horse**—To assume consequential airs; বড় লোকতা ফলান।

mount (mownt), *n.* 1. A card-board, etc. on which a drawing is placed; the margin of a card, picture etc. on which a drawing is mounted; যে পুরু কাগজ প্রভৃতির উপর কোন ছবি বসান হয়; ছবি, কার্ড, প্রভৃতির কিনারা। 2. Ornamental metal parts of various objects; বিভিন্ন দ্রব্যের ধাতুনির্ম্মিত শোভাসাধক ধাতব অংশ। 3. A horse, bicycle, etc. on which a person is mounted; ঘোড়া, দ্বিচক্রযান প্রভৃতি। 4. A horse provided for riding etc.; also a ride, esp. in a race; চড়ার জন্য দেওয়া ঘোড়া; অশ্বারোহণ, ঘোড়দৌড়ে ঘোড়া চড়ন।

moun'-tain (mown-tan *or* -tin), *n.* 1. A natural elevation of land larger than a hill; পর্ব্বত, গিরি, শৈল, অদ্রি, ভূধর, অচল, শিখরী, নগ, ধরণীধর, মহীধর, সানুমান (স্বেঃ), শিলোচ্চয়। 2. A large heap or pile; পর্ব্বত-প্রমাণ স্তূপ। 3. Malaga wine made from mountain grapes; পার্ব্বত্য দ্রাক্ষা হইতে প্রস্তুত মদিরা-বিশেষ। **Mountain ash**—A kind of tree; একপ্রকার বৃক্ষ। **Mountain chain**—পর্ব্বতশ্রেণী, গিরিশ্রেণী। **Mountain dew**—স্কটলণ্ডের হুইস্কি, গিরিমদিরা (আঃ বঃ)। **Mountain high**—As high as a mountain; পর্ব্বততুল্য উচ্চ। **Mountain-pass**—গিরিসঙ্কট। **Mountain sickness**—পর্ব্বতের উপরিস্থ লঘু বায়ুসেবনজনিত রোগবিশেষ। **If the mountain will not come to Mahomet, Mahomet must go to the mountain**—যে স্থলে বড় ছোটর কাছে না আসে সেই স্থলে ছোটকে বড়র কাছে অবশ্যই যাইতে হয়। **Mountain in labour producing a mouse**—অনেক গর্জ্জনের পর এক ফোঁটা বৃষ্টি। **Range of mountains**—গিরিজাল, পর্ব্বতশ্রেণী, কুলপর্ব্বত (আঃ বঃ)। **The mountain**—প্রথম ফরাসী বিপ্লবকালীন চরমপন্থী দল। [ইহারা সভাগৃহে উচ্চাসনে উপবেশন করিত বলিয়া উক্ত আখ্যা প্রাপ্ত হইয়াছে।] **To make a mountain of a mole hill**—তিলকে তাল করা, ছুঁচার বিষ্ঠায় পর্ব্বত করা। **Waves ran mountains high**—পর্ব্বতপ্রমাণ ঢেউ ছুটিয়াছিল।

moun-tain-eer' (mown-tin-ēr), *n.* 1. One who lives among mountains; a rustic; পার্ব্বতীয়, পর্ব্বতবাসী, শৈলাট, পাহাড়ীয়া লোক, পার্ব্বতীয় মনুষ্য; অসভ্য লোক। 2. One skilled in climbing up mountains; শৈলারোহণকুশলব্যক্তি। **—ing,** *n.*

moun'-tain-ous (mown-tin-ŭs), *adj.* 1. Containing, or abounding in, mountains; পার্ব্বত্য, পর্ব্বতময়, শৈলময়, পার্ব্বতীয়। 2. Huge; as, a *mountainous* heap; পর্ব্বতপ্রমাণ।

moun'-te-bank (mown-tĭ-băngk), *n.* 1. An itinerant quack who appeals to audience from a platform, and sells medicines therefrom; হাতুড়ে ডাক্তার, ওঝা, নাড়ী-টেপা, গো-বৈদ্য। 2. Charlatan; ভণ্ড। **—er-y,** *n.*

mourn (mörn), *v. i.* & *t.* 1. To show conventional signs of grief for a period after a person's death; কোন লোকের মৃত্যুর পর প্রথাসঙ্গত শোক-চিহ্ন প্রদর্শন করা। 2. To regret as *for* or *over* a person's death, loss, misfortune, etc.; শোচনা করা, দুঃখ করা, শোক করা, বিলাপ করা। *Verb t.* 1. To grieve for; to lament; as, to *mourn* a dead person or a thing; শোক করা, শোচনা করা; বিলাপ করা, আক্ষেপ করা।

mourn'-ĕr (mörn-), *n.* 1. One who mourns, esp. one who attends the funeral of a friend or relation; বিলাপকারী, বিশেষতঃ যে ব্যক্তি কোন বন্ধু বা আত্মীয়ের অন্ত্যেষ্টি ক্রিয়ায় যোগদান করে। 2. One hired to attend a funeral to mourn for the dead; মৃত ব্যক্তির অন্ত্যেষ্টি ক্রিয়া উপলক্ষে শোক করার জন্য অর্থপ্রদানে নিযুক্ত ব্যক্তি।

mourn'-fŭl (mörn-), *adj.* 1. Doleful; sorrowful; বিষাদপূর্ণ; দুঃখময়, শোকার্ত্ত, করুণ, শোকাবহ, খেদযুক্ত। 2. Causing sorrow; saddening; as, a *mournful news*; দুঃখজনক; বিষাদজনক। **—ly,** *adv.* Sorrowfully; দুঃখের সহিত। **—ness,** *n.*

mourn'-ing (mörn-), *n.* & *adj.* Act of sorrowing or expressing grief; esp. (wearing of) black clothes as a sign of this; শোককরণ, শোকপ্রকাশ; বিশেষতঃ শোকসূচক কৃষ্ণবস্ত্র, শোকবস্ত্র, শোকবস্ত্রধারণ। *Adj.* Grieving; শোকসূচক, শোককারী, শোকব্যঞ্জক। **Mourning-coach**—অন্ত্যেষ্টিক্রিয়াকালে ব্যবহৃত শকট, শ্মশান-শকট। **Mourning paper**—একপ্রকার চিঠির কাগজ—যাহার প্রান্তে কাল রঙ্গের রেখা থাকে। **Mourning ring**—যে অঙ্গুরীয়ক মৃত ব্যক্তির স্মৃতিচিহ্নস্বরূপ ধারণ করা হয়। **In mourning**—Wearing mourning dress; শোকবস্ত্রধারী।

mouse (mows), *n.* **1.** A small rodent quadruped inhabiting houses, fields, etc.; মূষিক, ইন্দুর, ইঁদুর। **2.** (*Slang*) A black eye; (ইতর ভাষায়) চক্ষুতে বা চক্ষুর নিকট প্রহারজনিত কালো দাগ। **Mous'-y,** *adj.* **1.** Like a mouse, its smell, colour, etc.; মূষিকবৎ, মূষিকগন্ধী, মূষিকবর্ণ। **2.** Infested with mice; মূষিকসঙ্কুল। **Mouse-colour**—মূষিকবর্ণ। **Mouse-ear**—কয়েক প্রকার গুল্মের সাধারণ নাম। **Mousetrap**—ইঁদুর ধরা কল, মূষিকবন্ধ, মূষিকগ্রহযন্ত্র। **To pour water on a drowned mouse**—মড়ার উপর খাঁড়ার ঘা দেওয়া।

mouse (mowz) *v. i.* & *t.* **1.** (Of cat or owl) To hunt or catch mice; (বিড়াল কিম্বা পেচক সম্বন্ধে) ইঁদুর ধরা বা শিকার করা। **2.** To search or watch industriously; পাঁতি পাঁতি করিয়া খুঁজা। *Verb i.* **1.** (*Obs.*) To handle as a cat does a mouse; "(Death) *mousing* the flesh of men"; (অপ্রঃ) বিড়াল যেমন ইন্দুরকে ধরিয়া উৎপীড়ন করে তেমন করা। **2.** To hunt as a cat does a mouse; বিড়াল যেমন ইন্দুর শিকার করে তেমন ভাবে শিকার করা। **3.** To search for patiently and carefully; তন্ন তন্ন করিয়া খুঁজা। **Mous'-er,** *n.* A catcher of mice, *e.g.* a cat, owl, etc.; ইন্দুরগ্রাহী—বিড়াল, পেচক প্রভৃতি।

mousse-line' (môs-lēn'), *n.* French muslin; ফরাসী দেশীয় মলমল কাপড়। **Mousseline-de-laine**—কার্পাস এবং পশমে তৈরী পোষাক প্রস্তুতের উপযোগী বস্ত্র।

mous-tache' (mŭs-tăsh), *n.* **1.** The long hair on a man's upper lip; গুম্ফ, গোঁফ। **2.** Similar hair round the mouth of some animals; বিড়াল প্রভৃতির গোঁফ। **Moustache cup**—দুগ্ধ পানকালে গোঁফ রক্ষার জন্য আংশিক আচ্ছাদন বিশিষ্ট বাটী।

mouth (mowth), *n.* **1.** An opening through which an animal receives food; মুখ, বক্ত্র, মুখগহ্বর, মুখবিবর। **2.** The part as of a river by which it meets the sea; নদীর মোহনা, নদীমুখ। **3.** The opening of a pitcher, bag, cave, furnace, etc.; কলস, থলিয়া, গহ্বর, প্রভৃতির মুখ। **4.** (Of a horse) Capability of being guided by the bit; খলীন দ্বারা চালিত হইবার ক্ষমতা। **5.** A person as a consumer of food; as, hunger of *mouths*; খাদক ব্যক্তি। **Mouth-ed,** *adj.* **Mouth'-ful,** *n.* As much as the mouth can hold; একগাল। **Mouth'-less,** *adj.* **Mouth-filling** — Bombastic; বাগাড়ম্বরপূর্ণ। **Mouth-friend**—কপট বন্ধু। **Mouth-organ**—শানাই প্রভৃতি বাদ্যযন্ত্র। **Mouthpiece** — The part of a musical instrument, pipe etc. which is put between the lips; শানাই প্রভৃতির মুখ। One speaking for others; মুখপাত্র। **By word of mouth**—Verbally; মুখের কথায়, মৌখিক ভাবে। **Down in the mouth**—Dejected or disappointed; বিমুখ, নিরাশ। **Mouth waters at**—মুখের লাল পড়ে, জিভের জল সরে। **This sounds strange in your mouth**—তোমার মুখে এই কথা আশ্চর্য্য শোনায়। **To give mouth**—(Of a dog) To bark; to bay; (কুকুর সম্বন্ধে) ঘেউ ঘেউ শব্দ করা; চীৎকার করা। **To laugh on the wrong side of one's mouth**—See LAUGH. **To make a wry mouth**—To grimace in sign of disapproval; মুখ-সিটকান। **To make mouths at**—ভেঙ্গচান, মুখভঙ্গী করা। **To put as a speech into a person's mouth**—To represent him as having made it; কেহ কোন উক্তি করিয়াছে বলিয়া বলা। **To put words into his mouth**—To tell him what to say; যাহা বলিতে হইবে তাহা তাহাকে বলিয়া দেওয়া। **To stop the mouth of**—To put to silence; চুপ করান। **To take the bread out of one's mouth**—To deprive him of the means of subsistence; কাহারো মুখের গ্রাস কাড়িয়া লওয়া। **To take the words out of a person's mouth**—To say what he was about to say; কাহারো মুখের কথা কাড়িয়া লওয়া। **Useless mouth** — One doinig nothing but requiring feeding; যে নিষ্কর্ম্মা লোক বসিয়া বসিয়া অন্ন ধ্বংস করে।

mouth (mowth), *v. t.* & *i.* **1.** To utter pompously or very distinctly; বাগাড়ম্বর করিয়া বলা, সুস্পষ্টভাবে বলা। **2.** To take into the mouth, as food etc.; to touch with the mouth; মুখে দেওয়া; মুখ দ্বারা স্পর্শ করা। **3.** To accustom as a horse to the bit and bridle; অশ্বকে বল্গা বা খলীন গ্রহণে অভ্যস্থ করা। *Verb i.* To grimace, esp. in contempt; মুখ সিটকান।

mouth'-y (mowth-), *adj.* **1.** Garrulous; railing; বাচাল; মুখর, কটূক্তিকারী। **2.** Bombastic; বাগাড়ম্বরপূর্ণ।

môv'-ă-ble (-bl), *adj.* & *n.* **1.** Capable of being moved; not fixed or stationary; as, a *movable* steam-engine; গমনশক্য; সচল, সক্রিয়, জঙ্গম (বেদান্তঃ), চটুল, চল, চর, চরিষ্ণু।

2. (Of property) That can be removed ; অস্থাবর। 3. Changing from one time to another ; as, *movable* feasts ; বিভিন্ন সময়ে অনুষ্ঠেয়। *Noun.* 1. An article of furniture as opposed to a fixture ; অস্থাবর দ্রব্য। 2. (*Pl.*) Personal property ; অস্থাবর সম্পত্তি। **–bil′-i-ty, –ness,** *ns.*

môve, *n.* 1. Act of moving of a piece, esp. at chess ; a player's turn to do this ; দাবা প্রভৃতি খেলায় চাল ; কোন খেলোয়াড়ের চাল দেওয়ার পালা। 2. A device or trick ; a step taken to secure an object ; চালাকি ; চাল (cf. চাল চালা)। **On the move** — Moving or stirring about ; সঞ্চরমাণ, চরিষ্ণু, চলন্ত, গতিশীল। Migrating : দেশান্তরগামী। **To make a move**— To go ; to rise and go from a dinner-table ; যাওয়া ; অপরাহ্ণ ভোজনের মেজ হইতে উঠিয়া যাওয়া।

môve, *v. t.* & *i.* 1. To change position of ; as, a horse *moves* a cart ; চালান। 2. To set in motion ; to stir ; as, the wind *moves* the reeds : to *move* one's head ; চালান ; চালনা করা, সঞ্চালিত করা। 3. To cause (bowels) to act ; (কোষ্ঠ.) খোলাসা করা। 4. (*Chess*) To transfer as a piece from one position to another ; চালা। 5. To touch pathetically ; to affect with any emotion ; as, the pitiful tale deeply *moved* them ; হৃদয়স্পর্শ করা, মর্ম্মস্পর্শ করা ; প্রাণ গলান, হৃদয় সঞ্চালিত করা, হৃদয় বিগলিত করা। 6. To prompt ; to incline ; প্রবৃত্ত করা ; প্রণোদিত করা, প্রবণ করা। 7. To propose ; specifically, to propose formally, as a motion, question, etc. in a deliberative assembly ; as, to *move* a resolution ; প্রস্তাব করা ; বিশেষতঃ ব্যবস্থাপক সভাদিতে প্রশ্ন করা। 8. To apply formally to, as a court etc. (*for*) ; বিচারকের নিকট যথারীতি আবেদন করা। *Verb i.* 1. To go or pass from place to place ; as, the ship *moves* rapidly ; একস্থান হইতে অন্য স্থানে গমন করা। 2. (*Fig.*) To progress ; to advance ; as, the action of the play *moves* slowly ; (লক্ষণায়) উন্নতি করা ; অগ্রসর হওয়া। 3. To make a move at chess ; দাবা খেলায় চাল দেওয়া। 4. To change residence ; বাসস্থান পরিবর্ত্তন করা, বাসান্তর করা। 5. To begin to act ; as, to *move* in a business ; কার্য্যে প্রবৃত্ত হওয়া। 6. To change posture as a person or part of the body ; সঞ্চালিত করা। 7. (Of the bowels) To have an evacuation ; দাস্ত হওয়া, বাহ্য হওয়া। 8. (Of inanimate things) To undergo change of position ; স্থানান্তরিত হওয়া। 9. To request or apply (*for*) ; প্রার্থনা করা, আবেদন করা। **Move-less,** *adj.* (*Rare*). **The spirit moves me**—I feel inclined (to do etc.) ; আমার প্রাণ চায়। **To be moved with**—To be touched painfully with ; বিগলিত হওয়া, দ্রবচিত্ত হওয়া। **To move about**—To do this often ; ঘুরা ফিরা করা। **To move heaven and earth**—To make every possible effort ; স্বর্গ মর্ত্ত্য পাতাল এক করা, স্বর্গ মর্ত্ত্য তোলপাড় করিয়া তোলা, প্রাণপণ চেষ্টা করা। **To move in**—To take possession of new abode ; নূতন বাসায় আসা। **To move on**—*v. t.* & *i.* পুলিশ প্রহরীর আদেশে সরান। (*Verb i., imper.*) সর [কোন লোক একস্থানে অধিকক্ষণ দাঁড়াইয়া থাকিলে পুলিশ প্রহরী "Move" বলিয়া তাহাকে সরিবার জন্য যে আদেশ দেয়।] **To move to tears**—বিগলিতাশ্রু করা।

môve′-mĕnt, *n.* 1. Act of moving ; state of being moved ; the course or process of changing place, position or posture ; চলন, গমন ; গতি ; স্থানপরিবর্ত্তন, ভঙ্গী পরিবর্ত্তন, অবস্থানপরিবর্ত্তন, গতিবিধি। 2. Military evolution ; সৈন্যের গতি। 3. Particular arrangement of the moving parts in a mechanism, esp. the wheelwork of a clock or watch ; কোন যন্ত্রের সচল অংশের, বিশেষতঃ ঘড়ী বা টেঁক্‌ঘড়ীর চক্রসমূহের বিশিষ্ট বিন্যাস। 4. (*Now rare*) Motion of the mind or feelings ; an impulse ; (অধুনা অপ্রঃ) ভাবগতিক ; প্রেরণা। 5. Manner or style of moving ; গমনভঙ্গী, চলনভঙ্গী। 6. (*Mus.*) Mode of progression as regards speed and rhythm ; also the main diyision of a musical work ; (সঙ্গীত-শাস্ত্র) ছন্দঃ বা দ্রুতত্ব সম্পর্কে গতিপ্রণালী ; সঙ্গীতের প্রধান বিভাগ। 7. An agitation in favour of some principle, policy or the like ; as, the prohibition of *movement* ; আন্দোলন। 8. Activity in market for some commodity ; কোন জিনিষের জন্য চাহিদা। 9. The development of poem, story, etc. ; গল্প, কবিতা প্রভৃতির ক্রমঃস্ফূর্ত্তি।

môv′-êr, *n.* A person or thing that moves ; esp. one who moves a proposal ; চালক, পরিচালক ; প্রস্তাবক, প্রস্তাবকারী। **Prime mover**—গতিশক্তির আদি কারণ (স্বাভাবিক বা যান্ত্রিক) ; প্রবর্ত্তক।

môv′-ing, *adj.* 1. Changing position or posture ; causing motion ; চলৎ, চরিষ্ণু, গতিশীল, সচল, সর (সাঃ পঃ), চল (ঐ) ; গতিজনক। 2. Touching ; মর্ম্মস্পর্শী, হৃদয়স্পর্শী, চিত্তোদ্বেলকর, চিত্তপ্রমাথী (রঃ)। **–ly,** *adv.*

mow (mō), *n.* A pile or mass of hay or sheaves of grain deposited in a barn ; also, the place in a barn for such a pile ; শুষ্কতৃণ, শস্যের আঁটি প্রভৃতির গাদা ; গোলাবাড়ীর যে স্থানে এরূপ গাদা রাখা হয়।

mōw, *n.* & *v. i.* A grimace ; as, mops and *mows* ; বিকৃত মুখভঙ্গী।

Verb i. To make grimaces; বিকৃত মুখভঙ্গী করা।

mow (mō), *v.t.* **1.** To cut down, as grass, with a scythe or machine; to cut the grass from, as a field; শস্যাদি কাটা, কর্ত্তন করা; ঘাস কাটা। **2.** To destroy sweepingly; to cut off or down in great numbers; as, the machine-guns *mowed* down the men in heaps; ব্যাপকভাবে ধ্বংস করা; বহুসংখ্যায় ছেদন বা ধ্বংস করা। **Mowing-machine**—শস্যচ্ছেদক যন্ত্র।

mow'-êr (mō-), *n.* One that mows; a mowing machine; শস্যচ্ছেদক; শস্যচ্ছেদক যন্ত্র।

mŏx'-ă, *n.* Any substance burnt on a diseased part, so as to produce a sore upon it; গেঁটেবাত প্রভৃতি রোগে রুগ্ন স্থানে যে জিনিষ পোড়াইয়া ক্ষত করা হয়। [কখন কখন চীনদেশীয় নাগদোনা (wormwood) গাছের তরুণ পত্র হইতে প্রস্তুত একপ্রকার পশমের মত কোমল পিণ্ডবৎ পদার্থ দ্বারা রোগদুষ্ট স্থান পোড়ান হয়]।

moy'-ă, *n.* Volcanic mud (so called locally in South America); আগ্নেয়গিরি হইতে উৎকীর্ণ মৃত্তিকা।

Mŏz-ăr'-ăb, *n.* (*Hist.*) A Christian Spaniard who lived in the parts of Spain under Moorish rule retaining his own liturgy; (ইতিহাস) স্পেনদেশের মুরদিগের অধিকৃত অংশের অধিবাসী স্পেনদেশীয় খৃষ্টান। **—a'-bic,** *adj.*

Mr. (mĭs-têr), *n.* See MISTER.

Mrs. (mĭ-sĭz), *n.* See MISTRESS.

mŭch, *adj., adv.* & *n.* Great in quantity, extent or duration; বহু, অনেক, অত্যন্ত, বিস্তর, প্রচুর প্রভূত, যথেষ্ট, ভূয়িষ্ঠ, অজস্র, জেয়াদা (*colloq.*), ভূরি। ***Adv.*** **1.** In a great degree; as, I *much* regret the mistake; far; as, *much* better; অত্যন্ত, অতিশয়, অতিমাত্র, অনেক; অনেকটা। **2.** By far; as, *much* the most likely; অনেক দূর। **3.** Pretty nearly; as, *much* of a size; প্রায়, অনেকাংশে। ***Noun.*** A great quantity; a great deal; বহুপরিমাণ; অতিমাত্রা, প্রাচুর্য্য, বাহুল্য। **Much'-ly,** *adv.* **Much'-ness,** *n.* Greatness in quantity or degree; আধিক্য, আতিশয্য, বহুত্ব, অনেকত্ব। **He is not much of a scholar**—He is not a good scholar; সে তত্তটা পণ্ডিত নহে। **Much at the same time**—Almost simultaneously; প্রায় সমসময়ে। **Much of a muchness**—Very similar; differing but slightly; সৌসাদৃশ্যসম্পন্ন; প্রায় অনুরূপ। **Much of a size**—About the same size; প্রায় সমায়তন। **To think or make much of**—বাড়াইয়া তোলা। **Too much for**—প্রতিদ্বন্দ্বী অপেক্ষা শ্রেষ্ঠতর।

mū'-cĭ-lăge, *n.* **1.** (*Bot.*) A gelatinous substance found in certain plants; (উদ্ভিদ্‌বিদ্যা) কোন কোন বৃক্ষে প্রাপ্ত একপ্রকার আটালো পদার্থ, লাসা (-হিঃ কোঃ)। **2.** Gum; গঁদ। **3.** A viscous fluid in animal bodies, as mucus; রক্ত বা স্নেহের জলীয় উপাদান। **—lag'-i-nous,** *adj.* Slimy; পিচ্ছিল। **—lag'-i-nous-—ness,** *n.* The state of being mucilaginous; পৈচ্ছিল্য।

mŭck, *n.* **1.** Dung in a moist state; manure; গলিত গোবর; সার। **2.** Dirt; ময়লা। **3.** (*Colloq.*) Something mean, vile or filthy; hence, a contemptuous term for money; (চলিত ভাষায়) নোংরা জিনিষ; (অবজ্ঞাচ্ছলে) টাকা পয়সা। **4.** (*Fig.*) A street arab; a money-grubber; (লক্ষণায়) গৃহহীন বালকবালিকা; অর্থপিশাচ। **Muck'-y,** *adj.*

mŭck, *v. t.* & *i.* **1.** To make dirty; ময়লা করা, নোংরা করা। **2.** To remove muck or dung from; সার অথবা গোবর স্থানান্তরিত করা। **3.** To manure with muck; গলিত গোবর দ্বারা সার দেওয়া। **4.** (*Slang*) To bungle, as a job; (ইতরভাষায়) নোংরা করা। ***Verb i.*** (*Slang*) To go aimlessly *about*; (ইতরভাষায়) উদ্দেশ্যবিহীনভাবে ঘুরা।

mŭck'-ĕr, *n.* (*Slang*) A heavy fall, (*lit.* & *fig.*); (ইতরভাষায়) ধপ্ করিয়া পড়ন (শব্দানুযায়ী এবং লক্ষণায়)। **To come a mucker**—To experience a mucker; to come utterly to grief; to ruin oneself; ধপাস্ করিয়া আছাড় খাওয়া; বিষম দুঃখে পড়া; নিজের সর্ব্বনাশ করা, কুপোকাৎ হওয়া। **To go a mucker**—To plunge into extravagance; অমিতাচারে গা ঢালিয়া দেওয়া।

mŭck'-êr, *n.* A canting hypocrite; ধর্ম্মধ্বজী, ভণ্ড। [Konigsberg নগরবাসী J .W. Ebel কর্ত্তৃক প্রতিষ্ঠিত সম্প্রদায়ের শিষ্যগণকে Mucker বলিত। Ebel ঘোরতর কুৎসিত ক্রিয়াকলাপের জন্য অভিযুক্ত হয়; কিন্তু অভিযোগ সপ্রমাণ না হওয়ায় সে মুক্তিলাভ করে]।

mū'-cous (-kŭs), *adj.* Of, pertaining to, resembling, or covered with, mucous; শ্লৈষ্মিক শ্লেষ্মাসদৃশ, শ্লেষ্মাবৃত। **Mucous membrane** — (শারীরসংস্থান-বিদ্যা) শরীরের অভ্যন্তরভাগের আবরণ বা শ্লেষ্মাস্রাবী ঝিল্লী, শৈষ্মিকত্বক, শ্লৈষ্মিক ঝিল্লী। **—cos'-i-ty,** *n.*

mū'-crō, *n.* (*Bot.* & *Zool.*) Pointed part or organ; (উদ্ভিদবিদ্যা এবং জন্তুবিদ্যা) সূক্ষ্মাগ্র অংশ বা অঙ্গ **—nate,** *adj.*

mū'-cŭs, *n.* **1.** A viscid slippery fluid secreted by mucous membranes; শ্লেষ্মা, শিক্‌নি, পোঁটা, ইন্দ্রিয়মল, কফাদি মল। **2.** A gumming substance found in plants; বৃক্ষাদিতে প্রাপ্ত গঁদের ন্যায় পদার্থ। **3.** A slimy substance exuded by some animals, esp. fishes; কোন কোন জন্তু, বিশেষতঃ মৎস্যাদির দেহ হইতে নিঃসৃত উজ্জ্বল পদার্থবিশেষ।

mŭd, *n.* **1.** Mire; কাদা, পঙ্ক, পাঁক, কর্দ্দম। **Mudguard**—আরোহীর গাত্রে

যাহাতে কর্দ্দমের ছিটা না লাগে, তজ্জন্য দ্বিচক্র যান প্রভৃতির চক্রোপরি যে ধাতু বা চর্ম্মনির্ম্মিত চক্রাবরণ সংলগ্ন করা হয়। **Mud-lark**—যে কুলি নর্দ্দমার কাদা পরিষ্কার করে; গৃহহীন বালকবালিকা। **Mud pie**—ছেলেদের তৈয়ারী মাটীর পিঠা। **Mud volcano**—যে আগ্নেয়গিরি হইতে মৃত্তিকা নিঃসৃত হয়। **To throw mud at**—To abuse; to speak evil of; গালাগালি করা; কুৎসা করা।

mū-där′, mä-, *ns.* An East-Indian shrub; আকন্দ, অর্ক, অলর্ক (*white mudar*), প্রতাপস [(*ib*) (ভাব প্রঃ)], ক্ষীরচ্ছদ, রশ্মিপতি।

mŭd′-dle (-dl), *n.* **1.** Disorder; a mess; বিশৃঙ্খলা, গোলমাল, বিভ্রাট; খিচুড়ী। **2.** Intellectual confusion; "We both grub on in a *muddle*"; বুদ্ধিবিভ্রাট, বুদ্ধিমোহ (রঃ), চিত্তবিভ্রম। **Muddle headed**—জড়বুদ্ধি। **Muddle headedness,** *n.* **To make a muddle of**—To bungle; গোল করিয়া ফেলা, খিচুড়ী পাকান।

mŭd′-dle (-l), *v. t.* & *i.* **1.** To bewilder; to intoxicate partially; আকুলিত করা, বিভ্রান্ত করা; সামান্য মাতাল করা। **2.** To mix blunderingly; to make a mess of; as, he *muddles* all he meddles with; গোল করিয়া ফেলা; গোলমাল করিয়া দেওয়া, ঘুলিয়ে দেওয়া। ***Verb i.*** To be in a confused state; বুদ্ধিবিভ্রান্ত হওয়া, বুদ্ধি ঘুলাইয়া যাওয়া। **To muddle on**—To get on in a haphazard way; যেমন তেমন করিয়া চলা। **To muddle through**—To attain one's end by no skill of one's own; যেমন তেমন ভাবে কাজ সারা।

mŭd′-dy (-ĭ), *adj.* & *v. t.* **1.** Abounding in, or besmeared with, mud; like mud; turbid; পঙ্কিল, সকর্দ্দম, সপঙ্ক; মৃত্তিকাবৎ; ঘোলা। **2.** Dull as a light; মন্দ, ঘোরালো, অস্পষ্ট। **3.** (Of voice) Thick; (স্বর সম্বন্ধে) গভীর। **4.** Confused in mind; stupid; "My intellect gets *muddy*"; বিভ্রান্তমতি; বুদ্ধিহীন। **5.** Obscure or confused, as a style, thought, etc.; ঘোরালো, অস্পষ্ট। ***Verb t.*** To soil with mud; to dirty; কর্দ্দমাক্ত করা, পঙ্কিল করা, পঙ্কদিগ্ধ করা; মলিন করা। **—di-ly,** *adv.* **—di-ness,** *n.*

mu-dir′ (mô-dür), *n.* The governor of an Egyptian province or a Turkish village; মিসরের প্রাদেশিক শাসনকর্ত্তা বা তুরস্কদেশের গ্রামাধ্যক্ষ।

Muezzin calling to prayer.

mû-ĕz′-zin, *n.* A Mohammedan who proclaims the hours of prayer from a minaret; মুজিন।

mŭff, *n.* A woman's warm covering for both hands in winter; শীতকালে স্ত্রীলোকের উভয় হস্ত ঢাকিবার পশমী কাপড়ের হস্তত্রাণ।

mŭff, *n.* & *v. t.* **1.** An awkward stupid fellow; হাবাগোবা লোক। **2.** Failure, esp. to catch ball at cricket, etc.; নিষ্ফলতা, ক্রীকেট্ প্রভৃতি খেলায় বল লুফায় ব্যর্থতা। ***Verb t.*** **1.** To handle or do awkwardly; আনাড়ীর মত চালান বা করা। **2.** To fail to catch, as a ball; লুফিতে অসমর্থ হওয়া। **Muf′-fish,** *adj.*

mŭf-fe-tee′ (-ĕ-tē), *n.* A wrister; a wristlet; একপ্রকার প্রকোষ্ঠাবরণ; বলয়, কঙ্কণ।

mŭf′-fin (-ĭn), *n.* A light round spongy cake, usually toasted and buttered; চাপাটী। **Muffin-belt**—চাপাটীবিক্রেতা যে ঘণ্টা বাজাইয়া চাপাটী বিক্রয় করে। **Muffin-man**—A seller of muffins; চাপাটীবিক্রেতা।

mŭf-fin-eer′ (-ĭn-ĕr), *n.* A small castor for sprinkling salt or sugar on muffins; চাপাটীতে লবণ অথবা চিনি ছিটাইয়া দিবার জন্য সচ্ছিদ্রাগ্র ক্ষুদ্র বোতল।

mŭf′-fle (-l), *n.* The thick part of the upper lip and nose of ruminants and rodents; রোমন্থক এবং দন্তুর জন্তুর ওষ্ঠ এবং নাসার স্থূল অংশ।

mŭf′-fle (-l), *n.* **1.** A leather glove for lunatics who tear clothes, etc.; যে সকল পাগল কাপড় ইত্যাদি ছিঁড়িয়া ফেলে তাহাদের জন্য চামড়ার দস্তানা। **2.** A boxing glove; মুষ্টিযোদ্ধার দস্তানা। **3.** A compartment or oven used for heating without exposing the contents to the direct action of the fire; সাক্ষাৎসম্পর্কে অগ্নির সংস্পর্শে না রাখিয়া উত্তপ্ত করার জন্য প্রকোষ্ঠ বা চুল্লীবিশেষ। **4.** A chamber in a kiln for baking pottery; পোয়াণের যে কোঠায় মৃন্ময় ভাণ্ডাদি অগ্নির সহিত সাক্ষাৎসম্পর্কে সংস্পৃষ্ট না করিয়া কঠিন করা হয়।

mŭf′-fle (-fl), *v. t.* **1.** To wrap up for warmth; গরম করার জন্য জড়ান। **2.** To prevent seeing, hearing or speaking by wraps bound about the head; অবগুণ্ঠিত করা। **3.** To wrap up as a bell, drum, oars, horses' hoofs etc. to deaden the sound; ধ্বনি মন্দীভূত করার জন্য ঘণ্টা, ঢাক, দাঁড়, প্রভৃতি বস্ত্রাদি দ্বারা আবৃত করা। **4.** To deaden, as a sound; মন্দীভূত করা।

mŭf′-fler (-lĕr), *n.* **1.** A wrap or cover worn for warmth usually round the neck, throat, etc; কণ্ঠাবরণবস্ত্র। **2.** A boxing glove; মুষ্টিযোদ্ধাদিগের দস্তানা। **3.** A stuffed glove; তুলা-ভরা দস্তানা। **4.** Something used to deaden a sound, esp. a pad of felt inserted between *views* of the landscape of this village ; চিত্র। 6. (*Law*) An inspection of a property in dispute, or of a place where a crime has been committed or of some object involved in a litigation by the jury previously to the trial of the case ; (আইন) কোন মোকদ্দমার বিচারে জুরিগণ কর্ত্তৃক বিরোধীয় সম্পত্তি বা ঘটনাস্থল বা মোকদ্দমার বিষয়ীভূত বস্তু পরিদর্শন। 7. Intention ; design ; as, will this meet your *views* ; aim ; "No man sets himself about anything but some *view* or other which serves for a reason" ; উদ্দেশ্য, অভিপ্রায় ; অভিসন্ধি ; লক্ষ্য। 8. Conception ; opinion ; as, to state one's *view* of a debated subject ; ধারণা ; মত, অভিমত। ***Verb t.*** 1. To survey with the eyes ; পরিদর্শন করা। 2. To examine with the mental eye ; to consider ; মনে মনে পুঙ্খানুপুঙ্খরূপে আলোচনা করা ; বিবেচনা করা। **View'-a-ble,** *adj.* That can be viewed ; দর্শনযোগ্য। **View-halloo**—শৃগাল ঝোঁপ হইতে বাহির হইলে পর শিকারীর চীৎকার। **View-point**—দর্শনের দিক। **Bird's eye view**—See under BIRD. **In one's view**—In one's opinion ; কাহারো মতে। **In view**—Within sight ; দৃষ্টিগোচর, দর্শনগোচর। **In view of**—In consideration of ; seeing the possibility of happening ; বিবেচনায়, বিবেচনা করিয়া ; ঘটিবে বুঝিয়া। **On view** — Exhibited before people ; লোকসাধারণের সমক্ষে প্রদর্শিত। **Point of view**—The aspect from which a question may be considered ; কোন প্রশ্ন যে দিক্ হইতে বিবেচনা করা যায়, দৃষ্টি (হিঃ কোঃ), দর্শন (ঐ), বিভাব। **Private view**—চিত্রপ্রদর্শনীতে প্রদর্শকের বন্ধু, সমালোচক, প্রভৃতির পরিদর্শন। **To be in view** — To be in sight ; দৃষ্টিপথে থাকা, নয়নগোচর থাকা। **To command the view**—See COMMAND. **To enter into one's view**—To accept one's opinion ; to agree with one ; কাহারো মত গ্রহণ করা ; কাহারো সহিত এক মত হওয়া। **To have in view**—To have aim towards something ; কোন বিষয়ের প্রতি লক্ষ্য থাকা। **To keep in view**—To keep one's aim ; লক্ষ্য রাখা, উদ্দেশ্য রাখা। **With a view to**—With the intention of ; with the view of ; in the hope of ; অভিপ্রায়ে ; উদ্দেশ্যে ; আশায়।

view'-y (vū-), *adj.* (*Colloq.*) Holding or prone to hold peculiar views ; faddy ; "Sheffield, on the other hand, without possessing any real view of things...was at this time fonder of hunting for views, and more in danger of taking up false ones, that is he was *viewey* in the bad sense of the word" ; উৎকট-মতাবলম্বী ; খেয়ালপরবশ।

vig'-il, *n.* 1. Keeping awake for religious exercises ; জাগরণ, নিশা-জাগরণ। 2. The eve before a feast or fast day, originally kept by watching through the night ; কোন উৎসবের পূর্ব্ববর্ত্তী দিবস বা অপরাহ্ণ। 3. Devotional watchings ; evening or nocturnal devotions ; "Their odes and *vigils* tuned" ; পূজোপাসনাদির জন্য রাত্রি জাগরণ, কোজাগরী ; সান্ধ্য বা নৈশ উপাসনা।

vig'-i-lance (-lăns), *n.* 1. Watchfulness ; caution ; circumspection ; সতর্কতা ; সাবধানতা ; অবহিতত্ব। 2. (*Med.*) Sleeplessness ; (চিকিৎসা-শাস্ত্র) অনিদ্রা। **—lant,** *adj.* Watchful ; cautious ; সতর্ক, সজাগ ; সাবধান, হুঁসিয়ার। **—lant-ly,** *adv.* **Vigilance committee** — কোন বেসরকারী শান্তিসংরক্ষণী সমিতি।

vi-gnette' (-nĕt *or* vin-yĕt), *n.* & *v. t.* 1. A running ornament of vine-leaves, tendrils and grapes used in gothic architecture ; গথিক স্থাপত্য ধারায় ব্যবহৃত দ্রাক্ষাপত্রাদির ভূষা। 2. Any small engraved embellishment for the illustration or decoration of the page of a book etc., not enclosed within a definite border ; পুস্তকের পৃষ্ঠায় মুদ্রিত প্রান্তরেখাবিহীন ক্ষুদ্র চিত্র-ভূষা। 3. A photographic portrait showing only head and shoulders the edges fading away insensibly to the background ; আলোকচিত্র দ্বারা গৃহীত মস্তক এবং স্কন্ধদেশের প্রতিকৃতি—যাহার প্রান্তভাগ ক্রমশঃ ক্ষীণ হইতে হইতে অজ্ঞাতভাবে, পশ্চাদ্ভূমিতে বিলীন হইয়া যায়। 4. Character sketch ; স্বভাবচিত্র। ***Verb t.*** To make a vignette of ; এরূপ ভাবে প্রতিকৃতি অঙ্কিত করা, যাহাতে কেবল মস্তক এবং স্কন্ধদেশ প্রদর্শিত হয় এবং নিম্নাংশ ক্রমশঃ বিলীন হইয়া যায়, কোন চিত্রফলকের বহির্ভাগ এরূপ ভাসা ভাসা ভাবে ক্ষোদা যাহাতে প্রান্তসমূহ অজ্ঞাতসারে পশ্চাদ্-ভূমিতে মিলাইয়া যায়। **—gnet'-ter,** *n.* An instrument for vignetting a photographic picture ; যে যন্ত্রের সাহায্যে আলোকচিত্রের নিম্নাংশ ক্রমশঃ বিলীন করা হয়। **—gnet-tist,** *n.*

vigoroso, *adv.* (*Mus.*) With vigour ; (সঙ্গীতশাস্ত্র) সতেজে।

vig'-our (-ŏr), *n.* 1. Active strength ; physical force ; energy ; vitality ; বল ; শক্তি ; তেজঃ, ওজঃ, বল, বীর্য্য ; জীবনীশক্তি। 2. Strength of mind ; intellectual force ; animation ; মনের বল ; মানসিক শক্তি ; সজীবতা। 3. Healthy growth ; as, the tree grows with *vigour* ; সতেজ বৃদ্ধি। 4. Vehemence ; "Have felt the *vigour* of his rage" ; প্রচণ্ডতা, প্রাবল্য। **—ous,** *adj.* 1. Possessing vigour ; full of physical strength ; শক্তিমান ; সবল, উর্জ্জস্বল, সবিক্রম, বলবান। 2. Energetic ; সতেজ, তেজস্বী। **—ous-ly,** *adv.* **—ous-ness,** *n.*

mŭl'-let (-ĕt), *n.* A name common to two groups of acanthopterygian fishes ; দুইজাতীয় মৎস্যের সাধারণ নাম।

mŭl-li-ga-taw'-nȳ (-ĭ-gă-tä-), *n.* An East-Indian curry soup made of chicken or other meat ; মুর্গী প্রভৃতির ঝোল।

mŭl'-li-grŭbs (-ĭ-), *n.* (*Pl.*) 1. Depression of spirits ; চিত্তগ্লানি, বিমর্ষভাব। 2. A griping of the intestines ; উদরশূল।

mŭl'-lion (-yŏn), *n.* (*Arch.*) A slender bar or pier forming a division between lights of windows, screens, etc. ; (স্থপতিবিজ্ঞান) পর্দ্দা, বাতায়নাদিবিভাজক কীলকবিশেষ, লম্ব (আঃ বঃ)। **—lion-ed,** *adj.* Furnished or divided with mullions ; বাতায়নবিভাজকলম্বসমন্বিত, বাতায়নবিভাজকলম্বদ্বারা বিভক্ত।

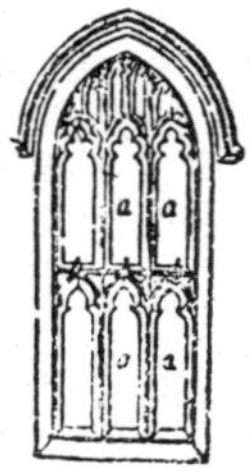

Mullioned window. *a a*, mullions ; *b b*, transom.

mŭl'-lock (-ŏk), *n.* 1. (*Austral., Mining*) Rock or earth bearing no gold ; refuse earth or rock from which gold has been extracted ; অস্বর্ণগর্ভ পাষাণ বা মৃত্তিকা ; যে মৃত্তিকা বা পাষাণ হইতে স্বর্ণ উঠাইয়া লওয়া হইয়াছে। 2. (*Dial.*) Rubbish ; (উপভাষায়) জঞ্জাল। 3. (*Dial.*) A muddle or mess ; (উপভাষায়) গোলমাল, বিশৃঙ্খলা।

mŭlsh, *n.* Same as MULCH. **Mulsh'-ing,** *n.* A covering of loose earth ; ঝুরা মাটীর আবরণ।

mŭl-tan'-gu-lar (-tăng-gü-lẽr), *adj.* Many-angled ; বহুকোণ, অনেকাস্র, বহ্বস্র।

mŭl-tē'-i-tȳ, *n.* Manifoldness ; নানাত্ব, বহুবিধত্ব, বহুগুণত্ব।

mŭl'-ti-, mŭlt-, *Pref.* A prefix signifying much or many ; several ; more than one ; বহুত্বজ্ঞাপক উপসর্গ ; কতিপয় ; বহু।

mŭl'-ti-col-our (-cŭl-ẽr), *adj.* Of many colours ; বিবিধবর্ণ, অনেকবর্ণ, নানাবর্ণ। **--oured,** *adj.*

mŭl-ti-fā'-ri-ous (-ŭs), *adj.* 1. Having great diversity or variety ; নানা, বহু, বহুবিধ, বহুপ্রকার, অনেকরূপ, নানাপ্রকার, বহুরূপ, বৈচিত্র্যপূর্ণ। 2. (*With a pl. noun*) Manifold ; various ; নানাবিধ ; বিবিধ। **—ly,** *adv.* **—ness,** *n.*

mŭl-ti-flō'-rous (-rŭs), *adj.* Bearing more than three flowers, as a stalk ; তিনের অধিক পুষ্পসম্পন্ন।

mŭl'-ti-fŏrm, *adj.* Having many forms ; of many kinds ; বহুরূপ ; নানাবিধ, অনেক প্রকারের। **—for'-mi-ty,** *n.*

mŭl-ti-nō'-mi-ăl, *adj.* & *n.* (*Algeb.*) (An expression) of more than two terms ; (বীজগণিত) বহুপদিক।

mŭl-tip'-ă-rous (-rŭs), *adj.* 1. Producing many or more than one at a time ; একসময়ে বহু বা একাধিকসংখ্যক উৎপাদক, অনেকোৎপাদী। 2. Of, or pertaining to, a woman bringing forth more than one child at a time ; এক সময়ে একাধিক সন্তানপ্রসবকারিণী, বহুপ্রসবা।

mŭl'-ti-pâr'-tīte, *adj.* Divided into many parts ; বহু অংশে বিভক্ত।

mŭl'-ti-ple (-pl), *adj.* & *n.* 1. Containing more than once or one ; having many parts or divisions ; বহুগুণিত ; বহু অংশ বা বিভাগবিশিষ্ট। 2. (*With a pl. noun*) Many and various ; বিবিধ, নানাবিধ। *Noun.* 1. (*Math.*) A quantity that contains another some number of times without remainder ; as, 14 is a *multiple* of 7 ; (গণিত-শাস্ত্র) গুণিতক, গুণনীয়ক, অপবর্ত্ত্য। **Least common multiple—** লঘিষ্ঠ সাধারণ গুণনীয়ক।

mŭl'-ti-plĕx, *adj.* Manifold ; complex ; of many elements ; বহুগুণিত ; জটিল ; বহু উপাদানবিশিষ্ট।

mŭl'-ti-plī-că-ble (-bl), *adj.* Multipliable ; গুণনীয়, গুণ্য।

mŭl-ti-plī-cănd', *n.* The quantity to be multiplied ; গুণনীয়, গুণ্য।

mŭl-ti-plī-cā'-tion, *n.* 1. The act of multiplying or increasing in number ; গুণীকরণ, বহুলীকরণ। 2. (*Math.*) The rule or process by which any given number or quantity is multiplied ; গুণন, পূরণ, অভ্যাস (সাঃ পঃ), হনন (ঐ), প্রত্যুৎপন্ন (ঐ), ঘাত। **Mul'-ti-pli-ca-tive,** *adj.* Tending, or having the power, to multiply ; গুণনশীল, গুণনক্ষম। **Cross multiplication —** বজ্রবধ (সাঃ পঃ), বজ্রাভ্যাস (ঐ), তির্য্যগ্‌গুণন, আড়গুণন। **Multiplication table—** পূরণের নামতা।

mŭl-ti-plĭc'-i-tȳ, *n.* State of being many ; a great number ; as, a *multiplicity* of thoughts ; বহুত্ব, নানাত্ব, বহুবিধত্ব, বৈশ্বরূপ্য, বহুতা (হিঃ কোঃ) ; বহুসংখ্যা।

mŭl'-ti-plī-ẽr, *n.* 1. One that multiplies ; esp. the quantity by which a multiplicand is multiplied ; বর্দ্ধক, বৃদ্ধিকারক ; গুণক। 2. (*Electr. & Magn.*) An instrument for multiplying the intensity of force, current, etc. so as to make it appreciable ; (তাড়িত এবং চুম্বকবিদ্যা) বল, তাড়িতপ্রবাহ, প্রভৃতির গাঢ়তা বৃদ্ধিপূর্ব্বক অনুভবগম্য করণার্থ যন্ত্রবিশেষ, গুণকযন্ত্র।

mŭl'-ti-plȳ, *v. t.* & *i.* 1. To increase in number ; as, to *multiply* evils ; সংখ্যাবৃদ্ধি করা। 2. To breed ; as, to *multiply* animals ; to propagate ; as, to *multiply* plants ; জন্মান ; বংশ বৃদ্ধি করা, বংশবিস্তার করা। 3. (*Math.*) To repeat as any given number or quantity as often as there are units in another number ; (গণিত-শাস্ত্র) গুণন করা, পূরণ করা। *Verb i.* To become numerous by procreation : বংশবৃদ্ধি হওয়া, বংশবিস্তার হওয়া, বংশবৃদ্ধি পাওয়া।

mŭl′-ti-tūde, *n.* **1.** Numerousness; বহুত্ব, অনেকত্ব, বাহুল্য। **2.** A great number, (with *of*) ; নিকর, সম্ভার, সমাহার, বহুত্ব, বৃন্দ, বহুতায়ত (হিঃ কোঃ), সমুচ্চয়, ব্রজ, সংঘ, গ্রাম, সমূহ, গণ, সংহতি, নিবহ, সংগ্রহ, বর্গ, পুঞ্জ, কুল, ওঘ, কদম্ব। **3.** A crowd ; an assembly ; ভিড়, জনতা, লোকারণ্য, জনস্রোত ; বহুজনসমাগম। **—tu′-di-nous,** *adj.* Manifold ; great in number ; অনেকরূপ, নানাবিধ (হিঃ কোঃ) ; বহুসংখ্যক, অনেকসংখ্যক। **—tu′-di-nous-ly,** *adv.* **—tu′-di-nous-ness,** *n.* **The multitude**—The populace ; ইতরজনগণ, প্রাকৃতজনগণ।

mŭl-ti-tūd′-i-nism, *n.* The principle that prefers interests of multitudes to those of individuals ; যে মতবাদ অনুসারে ব্যক্তির স্বার্থ অপেক্ষা বহুজনের স্বার্থ অধিকতর লক্ষ্যের বিষয় বলিয়া গণ্য করা হইয়া থাকে, বহুস্বার্থবাদ। **—nist,** *n.*

mŭl-tiv′-ō-căl, *adj.* & *n.* Susceptible of many meanings ; অনেকার্থক ; বিবিধার্থক, বহ্বর্থক। *Noun.* Such a word ; অনেকার্থক শব্দ।

mŭl-tŏc′-ū-lar (-lėr), *adj.* Having many eyes ; বহুনেত্র, অনেকনেত্র।

multum in parvo, (*L.*), *n.* Much in little ; (*attrib., with hyphen*) small but comprehensive ; অল্পেতে বহু ; ক্ষুদ্র অথচ ব্যাপক।

mŭl′-tūre, *n.* A toll or fee for the grinding of grain at a mill ; কলে গম প্রভৃতি পেষার জন্য যে শুল্ক লওয়া হয়, পেষণ-শুল্ক।

mŭm, *interj.* & *adj.* Silence ; চুপ! *Adj.* Silent ; নীরব, নিঃশব্দ, নিঝুম, নিথর।

mŭm, *v. i.* To act in a dumb show ; মূক অভিনয়ে অভিনয় করা।

mŭm, *n.* (*Hist.*) A species of beer originally made in Brunswick ; (ইতিহাস) একপ্রকার বীয়র মদ্য।

mŭm′-ble (-bl), *v. i., t.* & *n.* **1** To speak or utter indistinctly : মুখ চিবিয়ে কথা বলা, গজর গজর করা। **2.** To bite or chew, as one without teeth ; দন্তহীন ব্যক্তির মত দংশন বা চর্ব্বণ করা। *Noun.* Indistinct utterance ; অস্পষ্টভাষা।

Mŭm′-bō Jŭm′-bō, *n.* **1.** A god of certain negro tribes whose image is clad in fantastic clothing ; কোন কোন নীগ্রো গোষ্ঠীর দেবতাবিশেষ—যাহার মূর্ত্তি অদ্ভুত বেশে সজ্জিত করা হয়। **2.** (*Fig.*) Object of senseless veneration ; (লক্ষণায়) মূঢ় পূজার বিষয়ীভূত বস্তু।

mŭm′-chance (-chăns), *adj.* (*Archaic*) Silent ; tongue-tied ; (অপ্রঃ) নীরব ; রুদ্ধবাক।

mŭm′-mėr (-ėr), *n.* **1.** (*Contempt.*) A play-actor ; (অবজ্ঞাচ্ছলে) অভিনেতা। **2.** A masker ; a buffoon ; মুখসধারী ; ভাঁড়।

mŭm′-mer-ȳ (-ėr-), *n.* **1.** Performance of mummers ; buffoonery ; মুখসধারী অভিনেতৃগণের অভিনয় ; ভাঁড়ামি, মস্করামি। **2.** A farcical show ; rediculous ceremonial, esp. religious ; as, the *mummery* of a savage religion ; সং ; হাস্যোদ্দীপক অনুষ্ঠান।

mŭm′-mi-fȳ (-ĭ-), *v. t.* **1.** To embalm and dry for preserving, as a dead body ; পরিরক্ষণের জন্য গন্ধদ্রব্য দ্বারা অনুলেপন পূর্ব্বক শুষ্ক করা। **2.** (Of tissues and organs) To shrivel or dry up ; as *mummified* tisues ; মুষড়িয়া যাওয়া, বিশুষ্ক হওয়া। **—fi-ca′-tion,** *n.*

mŭm′-my (-ĭ), *n.* **1.** A dead body of a human being or animal embalmed as a preparation for burial ; সুগন্ধ ঔষধাদি দ্বারা পরিরক্ষিত শব, সুগন্ধরক্ষিত শব। [প্রাচীন মিশরবাসিগণ মনুষ্য এবং বৃষ, বানর, বিড়াল, মৎস্য, কুম্ভীর, প্রভৃতি উপাস্য জন্তু সমূহের মৃতদেহ রক্ষা করিত। নিম্নশ্রেণীর লোকদিগের দেহ লবণ ও অশোধিত ক্ষারের সাহায্যে শুষ্ক করা হইত। কিন্তু ধনীদিগের দেহ নানা উপায়ে পরিরক্ষিত হইত। সচরাচর নাসারন্ধ্রের পথে মস্তিষ্ক নিষ্কাশনান্তে উদরপার্শ্বের কতকাংশ ছেদনপূর্ব্বক নাড়িভুঁড়ি বাহির করিয়া ফেলিত। অতঃপর ক্ষৌরকার্য্যান্তে দেহটী উত্তমরূপে ধৌত করিয়া উহার অভ্যন্তরভাগ নানা সুগন্ধি দ্রব্য দ্বারা পরিপূরিত করার পর অশোধিত ক্ষার মাখিয়া উহা ঐ ক্ষারের ভিতর সাত দিন রাখিয়া রাখিত। তৎপর দেহটী নির্ধৌত করিয়া সুরভি বৃক্ষনির্য্যাসদ্বারা অনুলেপনপূর্ব্বক ক্ষৌমবস্ত্র দ্বারা বহুবার বিজড়িত করা হইত। অবশেষে ঐ বস্ত্রাবৃত দেহটী নানাভরণদ্বারা মণ্ডনান্তে কাষ্ঠময় আধারের ভিতর পুরিয়া প্রোথিত করা হইত।] **2.** A dried up body ; বিশুষ্ক দেহ। **3.** (*Obs.*) A kind of wax used in grafting ; (অপ্রঃ) কলম করার কাজে ব্যবহৃত একপ্রকার মোম। **4.** A pulpy substance or mass ; "...her face appeared to be smashed to a *mummy*" ; মণ্ডবৎ পদার্থ। **5.** A rich brown pigment ; একপ্রকার সমুজ্জ্বল কপিশবর্ণ রঞ্জক পদার্থ। **6.** One whose energies and affections are dried up ; শুষ্কহৃদয় ব্যক্তি। **To beat to a mummy**—To beat so as to reduce to a pulpy mass ; মেরে পাট পাট করা, মেরে খুনে দেওয়া, কীচক বধ করা।

mŭmp, *v. i.* **1.** To be silent and sulky ; to assume a demure expression ; অভিমান করা ; মান করা। **2.** To talk brokenly and feebly ; ভাঙ্গাভাঙ্গা স্বরে কথা বলা। **3.** To beg ; to go about begging ; যাচ্ঞা করা ; ভিক্ষা করিয়া ঘুরা। **Mump′-ing,** *adj.* **1.** Assuming a demure expression ; কপটবিনয়ী। **2.** Begging ; অনুনয়কারী, যাচ্ঞাকারী। **Mumping day**—২১শে ডিসেম্বর—যে দিবস দরিদ্রগণ দলবদ্ধ হইয়া ভিক্ষায় বাহির হইত।

mŭmps, *n.* (*Pl.* treated as *sing.*) **1.** A contagious swelling or inflammation of the parotid and sometimes of the other salivary glands ; কর্ণমূলস্ফীতি রোগ, পাষাণগর্দ্দভ (হঃ চঃ), ওন্দাবিবি (হঃ চঃ),

লালাশয় শোথ (আঃ বঃ)। **2.** Silent displeasure ; the sulks ; "He has the *mumps*" ; মান ; অভিমান ; অন্তঃক্রোধ। **Mump'-ish,** *adj.*

mŭnch, *v. t.* To chew audibly with the mouth shut and full ; কড় মড় করিয়া চর্ব্বণ করা।

Mŭn-chau'-sŏn (-chä-), *n.* **1.** The hero of an extravagant book of adventures written in English by R. E. Raspe, a German (d. 1797) ; গ্রন্থবিশেষের নায়ক। **2.** An extravagant story of marvellous exploit or adventure ; অদ্ভুত কাহিনীপূর্ণ গল্প।

mŭn'-dāne, *adj.* **1.** Of, or pertaining to, the world ; worldly ; as, *mundāne* affairs ; সাংসারিক, লৌকিক, ঐহিক, পার্থিব ; ইহলৌকিক। **2.** Of, or relating to, the universe ; বিশ্বসম্বন্ধীয়, জাগতিক, বিশ্বজাগতিক। **—ly,** *adv.* **—ness,** *n.*

mŭn-dun'-gŭs (-dŭng-), *n.* (*Archaic*) Bad-smelling tobacco ; (অপ্রঃ) দুর্গন্ধ তাম্রকূট।

mun'-gō (mŭng-), *n.* A kind of cloth similar to shoddy but of better quality ; পুরাতন বস্ত্রের সূত্র হইতে প্রস্তুত একপ্রকার ঠাসা বুনা কাপড়।

mū-nĭc'-i-păl, *adj.* Of, or pertaining to, the corporation or self-government of a town or city ; as, *municipal* rights ; কোন নগরী বা মহানগরীর স্বায়ত্তশাসনসম্বন্ধীয়, ম্যুনিসিপাল (হিঃ কোঃ)। **—ism,** *n.* Municipal condition or government ; the system or theory of municipal government ; স্বায়ত্তশাসন ; স্বায়ত্তশাসনপদ্ধতি, স্বায়ত্তশাসননীতি। **—ist,** *n.* **—ize,** *v. t.* **Municipal corporation**—স্বায়ত্তশাসনসমিতি। **Municipal law**—স্বায়ত্তশাসন সম্পর্কীয় আইন, ম্যুনিসিপালিটী আইন।

mū-nĭc-i-păl'-i-tȳ, *n.* **1.** A town, city or other district having powers of local self-government ; স্বায়ত্তশাসনের অধিকারপ্রাপ্ত নগরী, মহানগরী, প্রভৃতি, ম্যুনিসিপালিটী, ক্ষেমমণ্ডল (আঃ বঃ)। **2.** The governing body of this ; ম্যুনিসিপালিটীর পরিচালক সভা।

mū-nĭf'-i-cĕnt, *adj.* Liberal in giving ; generous ; bountiful ; বদান্য, মুক্তহস্ত, দানশৌণ্ড, দানশীল, দানশূর, দানবীর ; প্রশস্ত, ঔদার্য্য, প্রাশস্ত্য ; অতিদান, সত্র। **—cence,** *n.* Liberality ; generosity ; বদান্যতা, মুক্তহস্ততা ; দানশীলতা, দানশৌণ্ডতা। **—ly,** *adv.*

mū'-ni-mĕnt, *n.* **1.** (*Usu. Pl.*) A writing or document by which claims and rights are defended or maintained ; স্বত্ব, অধিকার, প্রভৃতি নির্দ্দেশক দলিলপত্র। **2.** (*Obs.*) Fortifying ; a fortification ; (অপ্রঃ) প্রাকার, পরিখা, দুর্গাদি দ্বারা সুরক্ষিত করণ ; দুর্গ প্রাকারাদি।

mū-ni'-tion, *n.* & *v. t.* (*Usu. Pl.*) Military stores ; ammunition ; materials used in war ; সামরিক দ্রব্যসম্ভার ; গোলাবারুদ, বোমা প্রভৃতি ; যুদ্ধসামগ্রী, যুদ্ধসম্ভার, রণদ্রব্য। ***Verb t.*** To provide with munitions ; সামরিক দ্রব্যসম্ভারের সংস্থান করা।

Munnin and Huggin, *n.* The ravens of Odin ; স্কেণ্ডেনেভিয়ান দেবরাজের বায়সদ্বয়। ইহারা সারাদিন পৃথিবী পর্য্যটন করিয়া রাত্রে পৃথিবীর সমাচার প্রভুর কর্ণগোচর করিত।

mŭn'-nion (-yŏn), *n.* Same as MULLION.

mŭnt'-jăk, *n.* A species of small Asiatic deer ; একজাতীয় ক্ষুদ্রকায় হরিণ।

mū'-rāge, *n.* (*Hist.*) A tax levied for building or repairing walls of towns ; (ইতিহাস) নগরপ্রাচীরের জীর্ণসংস্কার বা নির্ম্মাণের জন্য গৃহীত কর।

mū'-răl, *adj.* Of, or pertaining to, a wall ; being on, or in, a wall ; as, *mural* paintings ; a *mural* quadrant ; প্রাচীর সম্বন্ধীয় ; প্রাচীরোপরিস্থ, প্রাচীরমধ্যবর্ত্তী। **Mural crown**—(রোমীয় প্রত্নতত্ত্ব) অবরুদ্ধনগরীর প্রাচীর উল্লঙ্ঘনকারী প্রথম সৈনিককে যে বিজয়মালিকা প্রদান করা হইত। **Mural painting**—প্রাচীরগাত্রাঙ্কিত চিত্র।

Mū-ră-tō'-ri-ăn, *adj.* Of Muratori, the Italian scholar (died 1750) ; ইতালীদেশীয় শাস্ত্রজ্ঞ পণ্ডিত মিউরেটোরি সম্বন্ধীয়। **Muratorian canon**—Muratori কর্ত্তৃক স্বীকৃত ধর্ম্মবিধি। **Muratorian fragment**—Muratori কৃত অসম্পূর্ণ গ্রন্থ—যাহাতে বাইবেলের নবনিয়মের (New Testament) অন্তর্গত গ্রন্থ সমূহের তালিকা আছে।

mur'-dêr (mêr-), *n.* Homicide with malice aforethought ; বধ, নরহত্যা, খুন। **Murder**—খুন ! খুন ! **Murder in the first degree**—পূর্ব্বচিন্তিত নরহত্যা। **The murder is out**—The secret is no more unknown ; গুপ্ত কথা বাহির হইয়া পড়িয়াছে। **The murder will out**—A crime however secretely done must come to light sooner or later ; অপরাধ গোপন থাকেনা, চোরের দশ দিন গৃহস্থের একদিন, ধর্ম্মের ঢাক আপনি বাজে, পাপকর্ম্ম ছাপা থাকেনা। **To cry blue murder**—To make extravagant outcry ; হৈ রৈ করা, সোরগোল করা।

mur'-dêr (mêr-), *v. t.* **1.** To kill (human being) unlawfully with premeditated malice ; নরহত্যা করা, খুন করা। **2.** To kill wickedly or inhumanly ; হত্যা করা, নিহত করা, বধ করা। **3.** To mar by bad execution, mispronunciation etc. ; as, the actor *murdered* the part he had to play ; নাশ করা, মাটি করিয়া ফেলা। **—er,** *n.* One who commits a murder ; নরহন্তা, খুনী, হত্যাকারী, বধকারী, আততায়ী। **—ess,** *n.* (*Fem.*)

mur'-der-ous (mêr-dêr-ŭs), *adj.* Of, pertaining to, or involving, murder ; meditating murder ; bloody ; হত্যাজনক, হত্যাসংক্রান্ত, হত্যামূলক, প্রাণান্তক, প্রাণঘাতক,

মারাত্মক, জিঘাংসু, মানুষঘাতী; হত্যাচিন্তানিরত ; রক্তাক্ত, হিংস্র, হিংসক। **–ly,** *adv.*

müre, *v. t.* To inclose in walls; to confine, as in a prison; to shut *up* ; প্রাচীরের ভিতর রুদ্ধ করা ; কারারুদ্ধ করা ; রুদ্ধ করা, বদ্ধ করা।

mü'-rĕx, *n.* A kind of shell-fish yielding a purple dye; একজাতীয় শুক্তি—যাহা হইতে এক প্রকার নীলারুণবর্ণ রঞ্জকপদার্থ প্রাপ্ত হওয়া যায়।

mü'-ri-āte, *n.* (*Chem.*) A salt of muriatic acid; a chloride; (রসায়ন-শাস্ত্র) লোহদ্রাবকের লবণবিশেষ ; হরিণক বাষ্পের মিশ্র।

mü-ri-ăt'-ic, *adj.* (*Chem.*) Pertaining to, or designating, the acid now called hydrochloric acid; (রসায়ন শাস্ত্র) লোহদ্রাবকসম্বন্ধীয়। **Muriatic acid**—Same as HYDROCHLORIC ACID.

murk, mirk (mêrk), *adjs.* (*Archaic* & *poet.*) Dark; misty, as night, day or a place; (অপ্রঃ এবং কবিতায়) অন্ধকার ; কুজ্ঝটিকাচ্ছন্ন।

murk'-ŷ (mêrk-), *adj.* **1.** Dark; obscure; gloomy; অন্ধকার, তামস ; ঝাপ্সা, অনুজ্জ্বল ; তিমিরাচ্ছন্ন, অন্ধকারাচ্ছন্ন, তমসাবৃত। **2.** (Of darkness) Thick; (অন্ধকার সম্বন্ধে) ঘন, নিবিড়, সান্দ্র। **–i-ly,** *adv.* **–i-ness,** *n.*

mur'-mur (mêr-mêr), *n.* **1.** A low, confused and indistinct sound as that of running water; কলরোল, কলকল, কুলুকুলুধ্বনি, ঝঙ্কার, ছলছল শব্দ, গুঞ্জন, মর্মর, গুণ গুণ শব্দ। **2.** Subdued expression of discontent; a complaint or grumbling; গজরমজর; গজগজ। **3.** Softly or gently spoken word or speech; "His speech was the softest *murmur*"; মৃদুমধুর শব্দ বা ভাষা। **–ous,** *adj.* **–ous-ly,** *adv.*

mur'-mur (mêr-mêr), *v. i.* & *t.* **1.** To make a low continuous sound; কুলু কুলু নাদ করা, কুলুকুলু ধ্বনি করা, গুণ গুণ করা, গুঞ্জন করা। **2.** To express discontent; to grumble; (with *at* or *against*); গজগজ করা ; গজরমজর করা। ***Verb t.*** To utter in a low voice; as, to *murmur* tales; মৃদুস্বরে বলা। **–ing,** *adj.* & *n.*

mur'-phŷ (mêr-), *n.* (*Slang*) Potato; (ইতর ভাষায়) আলু।

mŭr'-rain (-ān), *n.* An infectious and fatal disease among cattle; গবাদির স্পর্শসংক্রামকরোগবিশেষ। **A murrain on you!**—A plague on you!; তুমি অধঃপাতে যাও।

mŭr'-rey (-ĭ), *adj.* & *n.* (*Archaic*) Of, or relating to, murrey; তুঁতফলের বর্ণসম্বন্ধীয়। ***Noun.*** The colour of a mulberry; a dark crimson red; তুঁতফলের রং ; একপ্রকার ঘনারুণ বর্ণ।

mŭr'-rhine (-ĭn), *adj.* (*Murra*, a substance of which precious vases etc. were made) Made of fluor-spar; স্ফটিকবিশেষ হইতে নির্মিত। **Murrhine glass**—স্ফটিকবিশেষ হইতে নির্মিত বাসনপত্র।

mŭs'-câ-dīne, *n.* A kind of musk-flavoured grape; মৃগনাভিগন্ধী দ্রাক্ষাফল বিশেষ।

mŭs'-câr-dīne, *n.* A disease of the silkworms caused by vegetable parasite; গুটিপোকার রোগবিশেষ।

mŭs'-căt, –că-tĕl', –că-dĕl', *ns.* **1.** A kind of rich wine from muscadines; মৃগমদগন্ধী দ্রাক্ষাফল হইতে প্রস্তুত সুরসাল সুরাবিশেষ। **2.** Same as MUSCADINE. **3.** (Only *-tel*) Raisin from muscadine; কস্তুরিগন্ধী দ্রাক্ষাফল হইতে প্রস্তুত কিসমিস।

mŭs'-cle (-l), *n.* **1.** Any of the contractile fibrous bands or bundles that produce movement in an animal body; মাংসপেশী, মাংসরজ্জু। **2.** The muscular part of a body; the chief constituent of flesh; দেহের পেশীময় অংশ ; মাংসের প্রধান উপাদান। **3.** (*Colloq.*) Muscular strength or development; as, to show one's *muscle* by lifting a weight; (চলিত ভাষায়) পৈশিকশক্তি, মাংসপেশীর পরিপুষ্টি। **–less,** *adj.* **Not to move a muscle**—To be perfectly motionless; নিঃস্পন্দ হওয়া, প্রস্তরপুত্তলিকাবৎ অবস্থান করা, চিত্রার্পিত মূর্তিবৎ অবস্থান করা।

mŭs-cŏl'-ŏ-ġŷ, *n.* That part of botany which investigates mosses; উদ্ভিদবিদ্যার শৈবালসম্বন্ধীয় শাখা, শৈবালবিজ্ঞান। **–gist,** *n.*

mŭs-cŏ-vā'-dŏ, *n.* Unrefined sugar got from the juice of sugar-cane; অশোধিত ইক্ষু-শর্করা।

Mŭs'-cŏ-vīte, *adj* & *n.* (*Archaic*) Russian; (অপ্রঃ) রুশদেশীয়। ***Noun.*** An inhabitant of Russia; রুশদেশবাসী।

mŭs'-cŏ'-vīte, *n.* Common mica; অভ্র।

Mŭs'-cŏ vŷ, *n.* (*Archaic*) Russia; (অপ্রঃ) রুশিয়া। **Muscovy duck**—একপ্রকার হংস, কস্তুরী-হংস।

mŭs'-cŭ-lar (-lêr), *adj.* **1.** Of, relating to, or affecting, the muscles; পেশীসম্বন্ধীয়, পৈশিক। **2.** Well-furnished with muscles; brawny; strong; powerful; as, a *muscular* body; পেশাল ; মাংসল ; বলবান্ ; শক্তিশালী। **–lar'-i-ty,** *n.* **Muscular Christianity**—Charles Kingsley প্রদর্শিত ধর্মজীবনের আদর্শ—তাঁহার মতে স্বাস্থ্যরক্ষাই ধর্মজীবনের প্রধান অঙ্গ।

mŭs'-cŭ-lă-tūre, *n.* The muscular system of a body or organ; পেশীজাল।

Mūse, *n.* **1.** (*Class. Myth.*) One of the nine goddesses who presided each over the nine liberal arts of the ancient Greeks; (গ্রীক পুরাণ) গ্রীক বাগ্‌দেবীগণের অন্যতমা। গ্রীক পুরাণানুসারে বাগ্‌দেবীর সংখ্যা নয়। (১) প্রস্থপূর্ণমঞ্জুষাধারিণী ইতিহাসবিদ্যার অধিষ্ঠাত্রী Clio দেবী। (২) গীতিকবিতার অধিষ্ঠাত্রী বেণুধারিণী Euterpe দেবী।

(৩) মিলনান্তনাট্যোচিত মেষপালকের যষ্টি অথবা আইভিপত্ররচিত মালিকা-ধারিণী গোষ্ঠগীতি ও মিলনান্তনাট্যের অধিষ্ঠাত্রী Thalia দেবী। (৪) বিয়োগান্ত-নাট্যোচিত মুখস, হার্কিউলিসের গদা অথবা অসিহস্তা বিয়োগান্তনাট্যের অধিষ্ঠাত্রী Melpomene দেবী। (৫) মিস্‌রাব এবং বীণাধারিণী সংঘনৃত্য ও সঙ্গীতের অধিষ্ঠাত্রী Terpsichore দেবী। (৬) বিদ্রূপাত্মক ভঙ্গী ও আদিরসাত্মক কবিতার অধিষ্ঠাত্রী বীণারঞ্জিতহস্তা Erato দেবী। (৭) স্তোত্রাদির অধিষ্ঠাত্রী ধ্যানোপবিষ্টা Polymnia অথবা Polyhymnia দেবী। (৮) জ্যোতির্বিজ্ঞানের অধিষ্ঠাত্রী Urania দেবী। ইনি করস্থিত যষ্টিদ্বারা একটা গোলক নির্দেশ করিতেছেন। (৯) মহাকাব্যের অধিষ্ঠাত্রী Calliope (or Calliopea) দেবী। ইঁহার হস্তে পুস্তক, কাগজ, ও অন্যান্য লেখ্যদ্রব্য শোভা পাইতেছে। **2.** (*l. c.*) Poet's inspiring goddess; a poet's genius; বাণী, বাগ্‌দেবী, সরস্বতী, বীণাপাণি, বাগ্‌দেবতা (গীতঃ), বিদ্যাদেবী; কবি-প্রতিভা। **3.** (*l. c., poet.*) A poet; (কবিতায়) কবি।

mūse, *v. i.* & *n.* **1.** To ponder; to think closely; (with *on*, *upon*); প্রগাঢ় চিন্তা করা, ভাবা; অনুধ্যান করা। **2** To gaze wonderingly or meditatively, as on a scene etc.; সবিস্ময়ে দৃষ্টিপাত করা, ধ্যানস্তিমিতনেত্রে নিরীক্ষণ করা। ***Noun.*** Absorbing thought; absence of mind; a fit of abstraction; প্রগাঢ় চিন্তা; অন্যমনস্কতা; অনুধ্যান, ধ্যান।

mū-sette' (-zět), *n.* **1.** A kind of bagpipe; একপ্রকার বাদ্য যন্ত্র। **2.** A simple pastoral melody; also, a kind of rustic dance; একপ্রকার গোষ্ঠগীতি; একপ্রকার পল্লীনৃত্য। **3.** A reed stop on an organ; অর্গেন নামক বাদ্যযন্ত্রের অংশবিশেষ।

mū-sē'-ŭm, *n.* A repository of natural, scientific, artistic and literary curiosities; যাদুঘর, আজব-খানা, চিত্রশালা, চিত্রশালিকা, কৌতুকাগার (আঃ বঃ), কৌতুকসংগ্রহালয়।

mŭsh, *n.* **1.** Anything soft and pulpy; কোমল শাঁস। **2.** (North-America) A kind of porridge; একপ্রকার সাতুর মণ্ড। **Mush'-i-ness,** *n.* **Mush'-y,** *adj.*

mŭsh, *n.* **1.** (*Slang*) An umbrella (ইতরভাষায়) ছাতা। **2.** A small cab-proprietor; ঘোড়ার গাড়ীর স্বত্বাধিকারী।

mŭsh'-rōōm, *n.* & *v. i.* **1.** An edible kind of fungus proverbial for rapid growth; ব্যাঙের ছাতা, ছত্রাক, ছত্র, শিলীন্ধ্র, অতিচ্ছত্র, [also পালঘ্ন (অঃ), দিলীর, মল্লিপত্র, উৰ্দ্ধ্বাঙ্গ।] **2.** (*Fig.*) An upstart; (লক্ষণায়) ভুঁইফোড়। **3.** (*Colloq.*) A straw hat for ladies; (চলিত ভাষায়) ভদ্রমহিলাদের খড়নির্ম্মিত টুপি। ***Verb i.*** **1.** To gather mushrooms; ব্যাঙের ছাতা সংগ্রহ করা। **2.** (Of bullet) To spread and flatten on striking on object; কোন পদার্থে আহত হইয়া ছড়াইয়া পড়া বা চ্যাপ্টা হওয়া।

mū'-sĭc, *n.* **1.** The science of harmonious sounds; সঙ্গীতশাস্ত্র, গন্ধর্ব্ববিদ্যা (মঃ ভাঃ), সুস্বরবিদ্যা। **2.** Melody or harmony; স্বরসঙ্গতি। **3.** Pleasant sound, *e. g.* song of a bird, murmur of a brook and the cry of a hound; শ্রোত্রমনোহরধ্বনি যথা—বিহগকাকলী, নদীর কুলু কুলু ধ্বনি। **Music-hall**—সঙ্গীতশালা, গন্ধর্ব্বশালা। **Music-school** — সঙ্গীতবিদ্যালয়। **Music of the spheres**—প্রাচীন গ্রীকদিগের মতে গ্রহাদির আবর্তনজনিত সুস্বরলহরী। **Rough music**—কোলাহল, কলরব, সোরগোল। **To face the music**—To face the consequences of one's actions; স্বকার্য্যের ফলাফল ভোগে প্রস্তুত হওয়া। **To set as a poem to music**—To furnish it with music to which it may be sung; সুর দেওয়া, সুরসংযোগ করা।

mū'-sĭ-căl, *adj.* **1.** Of, or pertaining to music; গীতবাদ্যসম্বন্ধীয়, সঙ্গীতবিদ্যাসম্বন্ধীয়। **2.** Melodious; harmonious; as, a *musical* voice; সুস্বর, শ্রুতিমধুর, শ্রবণসুভগ, সুশ্রাব্য; স্বরসঙ্গতিবিশিষ্ট। **3.** Fond of music; skilled in music; as, a *musical* coterie; গীতবাদ্যপ্রিয়; গীতবাদ্যবিশারদ। **4.** Accompanied by music; set to music; গীতবাদ্যসহকৃত; সুরে-বাঁধা। **—cal'-i-ty, —ness,** *ns.* **—ly,** *adv.* **Musical-box**—এক প্রকার বাদ্যযন্ত্র যাহা হইতে বিভিন্ন সুর উৎপাদিত করা যায়। **Musical glasses**—বিভিন্ন পরিমাণ জলপূর্ণ কাচপাত্রসমূহ রচিত বাদ্যযন্ত্র।

mū-sĭ'-ci-ăn (-shĭ-), *n.* One skilled in music; সঙ্গীতশাস্ত্রবিৎ, গান্ধর্ব্বজ্ঞ, বাদনবিদ্যাবেত্তা (কেশিঃ), গীতকোবিদ, বাদিত্রবাদক, গায়ক।

mŭsk, *n.* A strong-scented substance obtained from a cyst or bag near the navel of the musk-deer; কস্তুরী, কস্তুরিকা, মৃগনাভি, নাভি, মৃগমদ [also মৃগনাভিজ, মদ, কস্তুরিকাণ্ডজ, দর্প, গন্ধধূলি, গন্ধচেলিকা, যোজনগন্ধা, গন্ধশেখর, মৃগাণ্ডজ, মদার, মদাভ, বাতামোদা, ললিতা, মৃগদর্প, (বৃ সং), কামনীড়া, কুরঙ্গনাভি (নৈষঃ), এণমদ (ঐ)। **Musk'-y,** *adj.* Pertaining to musk; having the odour of musk; কাস্তুরিক; কস্তুরীগন্ধ। **Musk bag**—অণ্ড, মৃগাণ্ড, কস্তুরীমল্লিকা, মৃগমদবাস।] **Musk-cat** — Same as CIVET-CAT; a scented person; আতর, এসেন্সের গন্ধে ভরপুর ফুলবাবু। **Musk-deer**—কস্তুরিকা মৃগ, কস্তুরিকা কুরঙ্গ, কস্তুরী মৃগ, গন্ধমৃগ। **Musk-duck** — (also *Muscovy duck*); আমেরিকা ও অষ্ট্রেলিয়ার উষ্ণমণ্ডলবাসী হংসবিশেষ—এই জাতীয় হংসসমূহের দেহ হইতে মৃগমদগন্ধ নিঃসৃত হয়, কস্তুরীহংস। **Musk mallow**—লতাকস্তুরী, কালকস্তুরী, মৃগকদানা। **Musk-melon**—খরমুজ, খর্ব্বুজ (ভাবঃ প্রঃ)। **Musk-ox** — আমেরিকার উত্তরমেরুসন্নিহিত প্রদেশবাসী উগ্রমৃগমদগন্ধী রোমন্থক জন্তু-বিশেষ, কস্তুরী বৃষ। **Musk-rat**—গন্ধগোকুলা, গন্ধমূষিক, গন্ধমার্জ্জার,

ছুছুন্দরী, গন্ধনকুল, গন্ধাখু। **Musk-rose**—একপ্রকার মৃগমদগন্ধী গোলাপ। **Musk-shrew**—ছুঁচা। **Musk-tree, -wood**—মৃগমদগন্ধ তরু বা কাষ্ঠবিশেষ।

mŭs'-kĕt, *n.* A hand-gun used in war; পদাতিকসৈন্যের ব্যবহারের বন্দুক। **Musket-shot**—বন্দুক হইতে নিক্ষিপ্ত গুলি; উহার পাল্লা।

mŭs-kĕt-eer' (-ēr), *n.* A soldier armed with a musket; বন্দুকধারী সৈনিক।

mŭs'-kĕt-rȳ, *n.* **1.** Muskets collectively; বন্দুক সমূহ। **2.** The art of using muskets or troops armed with muskets; বন্দুক ব্যবহারের কৌশল, বন্দুকধারী যোদ্ধৃবৃন্দ।

mŭs'-lin, *n.* A fine thin cotton fabric; মলমল কাপড়, মসলিন। **-lined,** *adj.* **Fine muslin**—খাসা মলমল (As Dacca muslin), সূক্ষ্মদুকুল, সূক্ষ্মাংশুক। **Bit of muslin**—(*Colloq.*) A girl; a woman; (চলিত ভাষায়) বালিকা; স্ত্রীলোক।

mŭs-lin-ĕt', *n.* A kind of thick muslin; একপ্রকার স্থূল মলমল কাপড়।

mŭs'-mŏn, *n.* Same as MOUFFLON.

mŭs'-quash (-kwŏsh), *n.* A musk-rat; its fur; গন্ধগোকুলা; গন্ধগোকুলার লোম।

mŭs'-sel' (-ŏl), *n.* A marine bivalve shell-fish, used for food; আহারোপযোগী সামুদ্রিক শুক্তি, ঝিণুক (সাঃ পঃ)। **Mussel-plum**—একপ্রকার ঘন নীলারুণ বর্ণ আলুবোখারা।

mŭst, *n.* **1.** New wine; নবমদ্য। **2.** Grape juice before fermentation; অনুৎস্বেদিত দ্রাক্ষারস।

mŭst, *n.* Mould; state of being musty; ছাতা; ছাতা-পড়া অবস্থা।

mŭst, *adj.* & *n.* (Of male elephants and camels) In a state of frenzy; মদমত্ত, মদাবস্থ, মদকল, মদস্রাবী, মদোৎকট। ***Noun.*** The condition of frenzy; মদমত্ততা, মদাবস্থা।

mŭst, *v. auxl.* **1.** To be obliged *to*; to be necessitated *to*; as, a man *must* eat for nourishment; বাধ্য হওয়া; আবশ্যক হওয়া। **2.** To be sure *to*; নিশ্চিত হওয়া। **Must needs**—Necessarily; অবশ্যই।

mus-ta'-chi-ō (mŏs-tâ-shī-), *n.* (*Archaic*) Moustache; (অপ্রঃ) গোঁফ, গুম্ফ।

mŭs'-tăng, *n.* A wild horse found in Mexico, California, etc.; মেক্সিকো, কালিফর্ণিয়া, প্রভৃতি স্থানে প্রাপ্ত একপ্রকার বন্য অশ্ব।

mŭs'-tard (-tĕrd), *n.* **1.** A plant of the genus sinapis and its pungent seeds; সর্ষপ, সরিষা, রাই, [also সরিষক, কটুক, তন্তুভ, কদম্বক, তন্তুক, গৌর (white), সিদ্ধার্থ (*ib*), কটুতৈল (*ib*), কটুস্নেহ (*ib*), রাজিকা, (black), ক্ষুধাভিজনন (ঐ)], সরিষা গাছ। **2.** The condiment obtained from its seeds; সরিষাবাটা। **Mustard oil**—সরিষার তৈল, সর্ষপ-তৈল। **Mustard-pot**—ভোজন কালে ব্যবহৃত রাই সরিষার চূর্ণ রাখিবার পাত্র। **Wild-mustard**—হরহরিয়া, আদিত্যভক্ত।

mŭs'-têr, *n.* **1.** An assembling of men or troops, as for inspection, review, etc.; লোকসংগ্রহ, সৈন্যসংগ্রহ। **2.** An assembly; a collection; সম্মিলনী, সমিতি; সংগ্রহ। **Muster-book**—হাজিরা বহি। **Muster roll**—সাধারণ সৈন্য ও সৈনিককর্ম্মচারিগণের তালিকাপুস্তক, কোন জাহাজ কোম্পানীর অধীনে নিযুক্ত মাঝিমাল্লা ও নাবিককর্ম্মচারিগণের তালিকাপুস্তক। **To pass muster**—To be accepted as adequate; যথোচিত বলিয়া গৃহীত হওয়া।

mŭs'-têr, *v. t.* & *i.* **1.** To assemble, as men, troops, etc. for roll call, parade, inspection or the like; একত্র করা, জড় করা। **2.** To summon together; সমাহ্বান করা। **3.** To gather *up*, as strength, courage, thoughts, etc.; সঞ্চয় করা। ***Verb i.*** To come together; to assemble; একত্র হওয়া; জড় হওয়া, সম্মিলিত হওয়া। **To muster up courage**—To summon resolution; সাহসে বুক বাঁধা।

mŭs'-tȳ, *adj.* **1.** Mouldy; foul and fetid; ভাপসা; ছাতা-পড়া, ছেতোধরা, চিতেধরা, চিম্‌সা। **2.** (*Fig.*) Stale; antiquated; (লক্ষণায়) বাসি, পচা; সেকেলে। **-ti-ness,** *n.*

mū'-tă-ble (-bl), *adj.* **1.** Subject to change; পরিবর্তনশীল, পরিবৃত্তিশীল, বিকারী, পরিবর্তী, পরিণামপ্রবণ, পরিণামস্বভাবক, অনিয়ত, রূপান্তরগ্রাহী। **2.** Inconstant; fickle; অব্যবস্থিত; অস্থিরচিত্ত, অনবস্থিত, চঞ্চল। **-bil'-i-ty,** *n.* State of being mutable; পরিবৃত্তশীলতা, পরিবর্তনশীলতা, বিকারশীলতা, পরিণামশীলতা, অস্থিরচিত্ততা, চলচিত্ততা।

mū-tā'-tion, *n.* **1.** Act or process of changing; alteration; পরিবর্তন; রূপান্তর, পরিবৃত্তি। **2.** (*Biol.*) Change resulting in production of new species; (জীববিজ্ঞান) নব জাতি উৎপাদনজনিত পরিবর্তন, বিবর্তন (সাঃ পঃ), পরিবর্ত্ত (হিঃ কোঃ)। **Mutation suit**—খারিজ দাখিলের মোকদ্দমা, নামজারীর মোকদ্দমা।

Mutatis mutandis, (*L.*), *adv.* Necessary changes being made; আবশ্যক পরিবর্তন করাতে।

mūte, *adj.* & *n.* **1.** Silent; নীরব, মৌন, নিঃশব্দ। **2.** Dumb; also, unaccompanied by speech or sound; as, a *mute* boy: a *mute* appeal, বাক্‌শক্তিহীন; মূক। **3.** (*Gram.* and *Philol.*) Not pronounced, as a letter; stopped, as a consonant; (ব্যাকরণ এবং ভাষাবিজ্ঞান) অনুচ্চারিত; সাময়িকভাবে সম্পূর্ণরূপে শ্বাসরোধপূর্ব্বক উচ্চারিত (যথা *p, b, t, k*)। ***Noun.*** **1.** A dumb person; বোবা। **2.** (*Theatr.*) One whose part consists merely of dumb shows; (রঙ্গালয়ে) যে অভিনেতার কোন কথা বলিতে হয়না। **3.** A letter that represents no sound ; a mute consonant ; অনুচ্চারিত অক্ষর ; সাময়িকভাবে শ্বাস বা ওষ্ঠরসনাদিযন্ত্র রোধপূর্ব্বক উচ্চারিত ব্যঞ্জনবর্ণ (যথা *p, b, t, k*)। **4.** A hired mourner ; বেতনগ্রাহী বিলাপকারী। **5.** A dumb attendant in Turkey etc. ; তুরস্ক প্রভৃতি দেশে মূক অনুচর। **6.** (*Mus.*) A clip used for deadening the tone of a violin etc.; a pad for deadening the sound of a wind instrument ; (সঙ্গীত-শাস্ত্র) বেহালা প্রভৃতির ধ্বনি মন্দীভূত করার জন্য ব্যবহৃত আঁকড়াবিশেষ ; বংশী প্রভৃতির ধ্বনি মন্দীভূত করার জন্য ক্ষুদ্র গদি। **Mute′-ly,** *adv.* **Mute′-ness,** *n.* **Mute as a fish**—Entirely silent ; একেবারে নির্ব্বাক। **To stand mute of malice**—(*Law*) To refuse deliberately to plead ; (আইন) ইচ্ছাপূর্ব্বক মোকদ্দমার সওয়াল জবাব না করা।

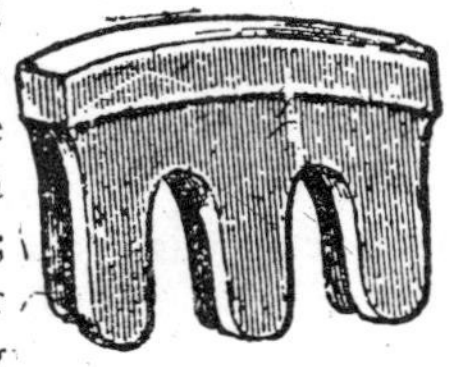

Mute of violin.

müte, *v. t.* To muffle or deaden the sound of, as a musical instrument etc. ; বেহালা প্রভৃতির ধ্বনি মন্দীভূত করা।

mü′-ti-lāte, *v. t.* **1.** To cut off a limb or essential part of ; to maim ; as, to *mutilate* a body : to *mutilate* a statue ; to destroy the use of, as a limb ; অঙ্গহীন করা, অঙ্গচ্ছেদন করা ; বিকল করা। **2.** To render, as a book imperfect by excision, etc. ; অঙ্গহীন করা। **–la′-tion,** *n.* The act of mutilating ; state of being mutilated ; removal of essential part; অঙ্গচ্ছেদন; অঙ্গহীনতা, ছিন্নাঙ্গতা, খণ্ডিতাঙ্গতা ; অঙ্গহানি। **–la-tor,** *n.*

mü-ti-neer′ (-nēr), *n.* One who mutinies ; বিদ্রোহী।

mü′-ti-nous (-nŭs), *adj.* Rebellious ; insubordinate ; বিদ্রোহী, বিদ্রোহভাবাপন্ন ; অবশীভূত, অদম্য। **–ly,** *adv.*

mü′-ti-nȳ, *n.* & *v. i.* An insurrection of soldiers or seamen against the authority of their commanders ; বিদ্রোহ, সৈন্যক্ষোভ। ***Verb i.*** To revolt ; বিদ্রোহী হওয়া। **Indian Mutiny**—সিপাহী বিদ্রোহ। **Mutiny Act**—বিদ্রোহবিষয়ক আইন।

mŭt′-ĭsm, *n.* The state of being mute or dumb ; silence ; মূকতা ; নীরবতা, নিঃশব্দতা।

mü′-tō-grăph *n.* & *v. t.* An apparatus for taking a series of photographs of moving objects ; সচল পদার্থের আলোকচিত্রমালাগ্রহণের জন্য যন্ত্রবিশেষ। ***Verb t.*** To portray with this ; ঐ যন্ত্রের সাহায্যে চিত্রিত করা।

mü′-tō-scōpe, *n.* An apparatus for exhibiting a scene recorded by a mutograph ; সচল বস্তুর চিত্র প্রদর্শনের জন্য যন্ত্রবিশেষ, চলচ্চিত্রদর্শক।

mŭt′-ter (-ēr), *v. i., t.* & *n.* **1.** To speak in very low voice ; বিড় বিড় করা। **2.** To grumble ; to murmur, (with *against, at*) ; গজর মজর করা ; গজগজ করা। ***Verb t.*** **1.** To utter in low tone ; as, to *mutter* threats ; বিড় বিড় করিয়া বলা। 2. (*Fig.*) To say in secret ; (লক্ষণায়) চুপে চুপে বলা। ***Noun.*** Act of muttering ; muttered words ; an obscure utterance ; বিড় বিড় করণ ; বিড় বিড় শব্দ ; অস্পষ্ট উক্তি।

mŭt′-ton (-n), *n.* **1.** The flesh of sheep, raw or dressed as food ; ভেড়ার মাংস, মেষমাংস, মেষামিষ (ভাঃ প্রঃ), রন্ধিত-মেষমাংস। **–y,** *adj.* **Mutton chop**—ভাজিবার জন্য মেরুদণ্ডের কতকাংশ সমেত ভেড়ার পাঁজরের মাংসখণ্ড, অন্যান্য স্থানের অনুরূপ মাংসখণ্ড, যথা কটির মাংসখণ্ড ; (ইতর ভাষায়) গালপাট্টা। **Mutton-headed**—জড়বুদ্ধি, গণ্ডমূর্খ। **Dead as mutton**—Quite dead ; সম্পূর্ণ মৃত। **To eat one's mutton**—কাহারো সহিত অপরাহ্লভোজন করা।

mü′-tü-ăl, *adj.* **1.** Reciprocal ; as, *mutual* love ; পরস্পর, ইতরেতর, অন্যোন্য, মিথ। **2.** Common to two or more persons ; conjoint ; as, *mutual* friend or effort ; দুই বা ততোধিক ব্যক্তির মধ্যে সাধারণ ; সম্মিলিত। **–al′-i-ty,** *n.* **–ly,** *adv.* Reciprocally ; পরস্পরে, অন্যোন্যে। **A mutual friend**—See MUTUAL. 2. **Mutual admiration society** — যে সম্প্রদায়ের প্রত্যেকে প্রত্যেককে অতি মাত্রায় প্রশংসা করে, অন্যোন্যগুণকীর্তন-সমিতি। **Mutual dependence**—ইতরেতরাশ্রয় (ব্রজঃ হিন্দু)। **Mutual terms**—(ব্যবসায়) যে সর্ত্ত দ্বারা টাকা প্রদানের স্থলে কার্য্যের বিনিময় করা হয়।

mü′-tü-ăl-ĭsm, *n.* The doctrine that mutual dependence is necessary to individual or social well-being ; ব্যক্তিগত বা সামাজিক শ্রেয়োলাভের জন্য অন্যোন্যের উপর নির্ভর আবশ্যক—এইরূপ মতবাদ, অন্যোন্যাশ্রয়বাদ (হিঃ কোঃ)। **–ist,** *n.* One holding the above doctrine ; অন্যোন্যাশ্রয়বাদী (হিঃ কোঃ)।

mü′-tüle, *n.* (*Arch.*) A projecting block under the corner of the Doric cornice ; (স্থপতি-বিজ্ঞান) ডোরীক স্থাপত্যরীতির অনুযায়ী প্রস্তরাগ্রের নিম্নস্থ উদ্গাত ভূষা।

mü′-zhik (-ĭk), *n.* See MOUJIK.

mŭzz′, *v. t.* (*Slang*) To render muzzy ; (ইতর ভাষায়) নিস্তেজ করা।

mŭz′-zle (-l), *n.* **1.** The projecting part of an animal's head including the nose and the mouth ; পশুর লম্বিত চিবুক ও নাসিকা। **2.** The open end of a fire-arm; আগ্নেয়াস্ত্রের উন্মুক্ত প্রান্ত বা মুখ। **3.** A fastening for an animal's mouth which hinders biting, eating, etc. ; পশুর মুখের জালতি, মুখবন্ধনী, মুখরোধনী। **Muzzle-loader**—যে বন্দুকের মুক্ত প্রান্ত দিয়া গুলি বারুদ ভরিতে হয়।

mŭz′-zle (-l), *v. t.* & *i.* **1.** To put a muzzle on, as an animal ; (*fig.*) to restrain from speech or action ; to silence ; "*Muzzling* an ambitious chief magistrate" ; পশুর মুখে জালতি দেওয়া ; (লক্ষণায়) মুখ বন্ধন করা, মুখরোধ করা ; চুপ করান। **2.** To root or grub with the muzzle or snout, (said, esp. of pigs) ; লম্বিত মুখাগ্রদ্বারা খুঁড়িয়া শিকড় প্রভৃতি উৎপাটন করা। **3.** To take in (sail) ; (পাইল) গুটাইয়া লওয়া। **4.** (*Dial.*) To drink greedily ; (উপভাষায়) লোলুপভাবে পান করা। ***Verb i.*** To bring the muzzle near ; লম্বিত মুখাগ্র নিকটে আনা।

mŭz′-zy (-ĭ), *adj.* **1.** Dull ; spiritless ; stupid ; ঢিমা ; নিস্তেজ, ম্যাদামারা ; জড়বুদ্ধি। **2.** Dazed or muddled, as with drink ; হতবুদ্ধি, বিভ্রান্ত। **–zi′-ly,** *adv.* **–zi-ness,** *n.*

mȳ, *Poss. adj.* Belonging to me ; আমার, মম, মদীয়। **My blood boils at this**—I feel highly indignant at it ; ইহাতে আমার রক্ত গরম হইয়া উঠিয়াছে, ইহাতে রাগে আমার গা কামড়াইতেছে। **My blood ran cold**—I was greatly terrorised ; ভয়ে আমার রক্ত জমাট হয়ে গেছিল। **My eye !**—A mild asseveration ; মাইরি ! সত্যি সত্যি ! আমার দিব্যি !

mȳ′-ăl-ĭsm, *n.* A kind of sorcery practised, esp. in the West Indies ; একপ্রকার যাদুবিদ্যা, বিশেষতঃ পশ্চিম-ভারতীয় দ্বীপপুঞ্জে প্রচলিত যাদুবিদ্যা।

mȳ′-all, *n.* A kind of Australian acacia having hard fragrant wood ; একজাতীয় অষ্ট্রেলিয়া দেশীয় কঠিন ও সুরভি দারু ; একেসিয়া বৃক্ষ।

mȳ-cē′-lĭ-ŭm, *n.* (*Bot.*) Mushroom spawn ; (উদ্ভিদবিদ্যা) ছত্র-তন্তু (সাঃ পঃ), জালতন্তু (ঐ)। **–al,** *adj.*

mȳ-cē-tō′-mă, *n.* A fungoid disease of the foot (or hand) ; একপ্রকার পাদরোগ। [ইহাতে পা বা হাত স্ফীত হয় ও তাহাতে মৎস্যের অণ্ডের ন্যায় ক্ষুদ্র ক্ষুদ্র থোপা থোপা গুটিকা জন্মে]।

mȳ-cŏl′-ō-ġȳ, *n.* The branch of Botany dealing with fungi ; ছত্রাকবিজ্ঞান, শিলীন্ধ্র তত্ত্ব। **–gist,** *n.*

mȳ-cō′-sĭs, *n.* Presence of fungus growth within the body ; disease caused by this ; দেহাভ্যন্তরে ছত্রাকবৎ বস্তুর বিদ্যমানতা ; উক্ত ছত্রাকজনিত রোগ-বিশেষ।

mȳ-ĕ-lī′-tĭs, *n.* Inflammation of the spinal cord ; মেরুদণ্ডের মজ্জা-প্রদাহ, মেরুমজ্জাপ্রদাহ।

mȳ′-lō-dŏn, *n.* An extinct edentate animal ; একপ্রকার অধুনালুপ্ত অদন্তী প্রাণী।

mȳ′-nă, *n.* An Indian bird ; ময়না। **Grey haired myna**—পাথই (বোঃ)।

mȳn′-heer′ (-hēr), *n.* A Dutchman ; ওলন্দাজ।

mȳ-ŏl′-ō-ġȳ, *n.* Science of muscles ; পেশীবিজ্ঞান।

mȳ′-ope (-ŏp), *n.* A short-sighted person ; অদূরদৃষ্টি ব্যক্তি, গজনেত্রী, গজদৃষ্টি। **–o′-pi-a, –o-py,** *ns.* Short sightedness ; অদূরদৃষ্টি (হঃ চঃ)। **–op′-ic,** *adj.*

mȳ-ō′-sĭs, *n.* Abnormal contraction of the pupil of the eye ; চক্ষুর তারার অস্বাভাবিক সঙ্কোচন। **–ot′-ic,** *adj.*

mȳ-ō-sī′-tĭs, *n.* Inflammation of the muscles ; পেশীপ্রদাহ।

mȳ′-ō-sōte, *n.* Same as FORGET-ME-NOT (which see.)

mȳ-ō-sō′-tĭs, *n.* Genus of small plants with blue pink or white flowers ; নীল, পাটল ও শ্বেতপুষ্পপ্রসূ ক্ষুদ্র গুল্ম বিশেষ।

mȳr′-ĭ-ăd, *n.* & *adj.* The number of ten-thousand ; a countless number ; অযুত, দশসহস্র ; অগণ্য সংখ্যা। ***Adj.*** Of indefinite number ; innumerable ; as, *myriad* stars ; অসংখ্য ; অগণ্য।

mȳr′-ĭ-ă-pŏd, *n.* & *adj.* A worm-shaped animal with many jointed legs ; বহুগ্রন্থিলপদসমন্বিত একপ্রকার কীটাকৃতি জন্তু, সহস্রপদী। ***Adj.*** With many legs ; of, or relating to, the centipedes and millepedes ; বহুপদী ; শতপদী বা সহস্রপদী জন্তু সম্বন্ধীয়।

mȳr-ĭ-ō-râ′-mă, *n.* **1.** A picture made of a number of separate sections capable of being combined in numerous ways so as to form different scenes ; বিভিন্ন খণ্ডাত্মক চিত্রবিশেষ—যাহার খণ্ডসমূহ বহুপ্রকারে সংযুক্ত করিয়া নানা প্রকার দৃশ্য গঠন করা যায়, বহুদৃশ্যকর। **2.** An entertainment consisting of a large number of views ; একপ্রকার আমোদ—যাহাতে বহুসংখ্যক দৃশ্য প্রদর্শিত হইয়া থাকে।

Myr′-mĭ-dŏn (mêr-), *n.* **1.** (*Gr. Myth.*) One of a fierce Thessalian tribe who accompanied Achilles, thier king, to the Trojan war ; (গ্রীকপুরাণ) Thessally প্রদেশ-বাসী দুর্দ্ধর্ষ জাতিবিশেষের লোক—যাহারা মহাবীর Achillesএর সহিত ট্রোজান যুদ্ধে গমন করিয়াছিল। **2.** (*l. c.*) A hired ruffian ; a base attendant ; ভাড়াটিয়া গুণ্ডা ; নীচজাতীয় অনুচর। **Myrmidon of the law** or **of the justice**—A policeman, bailiff, etc. ; পুলিশ কনেষ্টবল ; নাজীরের পেয়াদা, ক্রূরপরিচর (আঃ বঃ)।

mȳ-rŏb′-ă-lăn, *n.* A dried fruit from India used in dyeing, tanning, etc. ; হরীতকী। **Belleric myrobalan**—বহেড়া, বয়ড়া, [also বিভীতক, অক্ষ, ভূতবাস, কলিদ্রুম]। **Chebulic myrobalan**—হরীতকী, অভয়া, অমৃত, পূতনা, রোহিণী, জীবন্তী, অব্যথা, চেতকী, শ্রেয়সী, শিবা, বয়ঃস্থা, বিজয়া। **Emblic myrobalan**—আমলকী।

myrrh (mêr), *n.* Gum-resin used in perfumery, medicine and in incense ; গন্ধরস, রসগন্ধ, সমুদ্রগুগ্‌গুল, বোল, গন্ধবোল, হীরা [also সুরস, গোপরস, গোল, গান্ধার, জাতীরস, প্রাণ, পিণ্ড, শশ, রস]। **Myr′-rhic, Myrrh′-y,** *adjs.*

myr′-tle (mêr-tl), *n.* Shrub of evergreen leaves and fragrant flowers ; বিলাতী মেন্দী।

mȳ-sĕlf′, *pron.* Emphatic and reflexive form of *I* ; স্বয়ং, আপন। **I am not myself**—I am not in a normal state of body or mind ; আমি প্রকৃতিস্থ নহি।

mȳs′-tă-gogue (-gŏg), *n.* One who instructs in, or interprets, mysteries ; রহস্যাধ্যাপক, রহস্য-ব্যাখ্যাতা। **–gog′-ic, –gog′-i-cal,** *adjs.*

mȳs-tē′-ri-ous (-ŭs), *adj.* **1.** Wrapt in, or full of, mystery ; incomprehensible ; রহস্যপূর্ণ, রহস্যময়, রহস্যসমাচ্ছন্ন ; গুহ্য, দুর্ব্বোধ, জটিল, নিগূঢ়। **2.** (Of persons) Delighting in mystery ; one whose movements are mysterious ; রহস্যোল্লাসী; যে ব্যক্তির গতিবিধি রহস্যসমাচ্ছন্ন। **–ly,** *adv.* **–ness,** *n.*

mȳs′-tē-rȳ, *n.* **1.** A secret or inexplicable matter ; an enigma ; রহস্য ; ধাঁধা, প্রহেলিকা। **2.** State of being mysterious; obscurity ; as, to be wrapt in *mystery* ; রহস্যপূর্ণতা ; দুর্ব্বোধতা। **3.** A religious truth divinely revealed or beyond human reason ; নিগূঢ় তত্ত্ব। **4.** (*Pl.*) A sacred rite etc. esp. the Eucharist ; রহস্যানুষ্ঠান। **5.** (*Pl.*) Secret religious rites of Greeks, Romans, etc. ; রহস্যপূজা (এভেুলন), রোমীয় ও গ্রীসীয়দের তান্ত্রিক ক্রিয়াকলাপ। **6.** Same as MIRACLE PLAY. **Mystery play**—যাত্রা (মিউজিক)। **To make a mystery of**—To treat as a secret ; গুহ্য ব্যাপার করিয়া তোলা।

mȳs′-têr-ȳ, *n.* (*Archaic*) A trade, craft or calling ; (অপ্রঃ) ব্যবসায়, পেশা।

mȳs′-tic, *adj.* & *n.* **1.** Spiritually allegorical ; নিগূঢ়, রহস্যসমাচ্ছন্ন। **2.** Unknowable ; occult ; দুজ্ঞেয় ; গহন, নিগূঢ়। **3.** Involving some secret meaning ; mysterious and awe-inspiring ; গূঢ়াভিপ্রায়ক, গুহ্যঅর্থময় ; রহস্যসমাকুল, গুহ্যাতিগুহ্য। **4.** Of, or relating, to, mysticism ; মরমীপন্থাসম্বন্ধীয়। ***Noun.*** One who professes to have direct intercourse with the Spirit of God ; মরমী [মধ্যযুগে ভারতবর্ষে যে মুসলমান Mysticগণ প্রাদুর্ভূত হন, তাঁহাদিগকে মরমী বলিত।], ধ্যানরসিক (হীরেন্দ্র), ভাববাদী, ভাবযোগী। **–ti-cal,** *adj.* **–ti-cal-ly,** *adv.*

mȳs′-ti-cĭsm, *n.* **1.** Mystic quality or character ; রহস্যসমাচ্ছন্নতা, ধ্যানরসিকতা। **2.** Views in religion based on communion between man and God through spiritual perception ; মরমীপন্থা, মরমীবাদ, অপরোক্ষজ্ঞানবাদ, ভাবনাযোগ, ব্রহ্মসাক্ষাৎকারবাদ। **–cize,** *v. t.*

mȳs′-ti-fȳ, *v. t.* **1.** To make obscure or difficult to understand ; রহস্যাচ্ছন্ন করা, দুর্ব্বোধ করা, দুজ্ঞেয় করা, জটিল করা, গহন করা, নিগূঢ় করা। **2.** To perplex the mind of ; to bewilder ; হতবুদ্ধি করা, বিভ্রান্ত করা ; হতভম্ব করা। **′–fi-ca′-tion,** *n.*

mȳth, *n.* **1.** A fictitious narrative having an analogy more or less remote to some real event ; পৌরাণিকী কথা, পৌরাণিকী আখ্যায়িকা, পুরাবৃত্ত কথা। **2.** A fictitious person or thing ; কাল্পনিক ব্যক্তি বা বস্তু। **Myth′-ic, Myth′-i-cal,** *adjs.* **Myth′-i-cal-ly,** *adv.*

mȳth′-i-cize, *v. t.* To interpret mythically ; to treat as a myth ; পৌরাণিকভাবে ব্যাখ্যা করা ; পৌরাণিক আখ্যায়িকারূপে গণ্য করা। **–cism, –cist,** *ns.*

mȳ-thŏg′-ră-phêr, *n.* A writer of myths ; পৌরাণিক গল্পলেখক। **–phy,** *n.* Representation of myths in plastic art ; ভাস্কর্য্য প্রভৃতি পৌরাণিক চিত্রপ্রকটন, পুরাণাঙ্কণশিল্প।

mȳ-thŏl′-ŏ-ġȳ, *n.* **1.** The science of myths ; দেবতত্ত্ব, পুরাণ। **2.** A system of myths or fables, esp. with respect to a person or subject ; উপকথাপরম্পরা, বিশেষতঃ কোন ব্যক্তি বা বস্তুবিষয়ক উপকথাসমূহ। **–gist,** *n.* **–gize,** *v. t.* & *i.* To make mythical ; পৌরাণিক করা। ***Verb i.*** To relate a myth or myths ; to write a myth ; পৌরাণিকী গল্প বর্ণনা করা ; পৌরাণিকী গল্প রচনা করা।

mȳth-ŏ-lŏg′-ic, *adj.* Pertaining to mythology ; fabulous ; পুরাণসম্বন্ধীয়, পৌরাণিকী ; অবাস্তব। **–i-cal,** *adj.* **–i-cal-ly,** *adv.*

mȳth′-ŭs, *n.* Same as MYTH.

N

N, 1. The fourteenth letter of the English alphabet ; ইংরাজী বর্ণমালার চতুর্দ্দশ অক্ষর। **2.** (*In printing*) A unit of measurement, (freq. *en*) ; (মুদ্রণ) পরিমাপের একক বিশেষ। **3.** (*Math.*) An indefinite constant whole number ; (গণিত-শাস্ত্র) অনির্দ্দিষ্ট এবং অখণ্ড নিত্যসংখ্যা। **N-rays**—কোন কোন উত্তপ্ত বস্তু বা অন্যান্য পদার্থ হইতে যে কিরণবিকিরণ বা অংশুনিঃসরণ দ্বারা কোন দীপ্যমান বাষ্প বা কঠিনপদার্থের তাপমাত্রা বৃদ্ধি ব্যতিরেকেও ঔজ্জ্বল্য বর্দ্ধিত হয়, এন-রশ্মি। [M. Blond lot কর্ত্তৃক আবিষ্কৃত।] **To the nth**—(*Math.*)

To any required power; (*fig.*) to any extent; to the utmost; (গণিতশাস্ত্র) ইপ্সিত ঘাত পর্য্যন্ত; (লক্ষণায়) যে কোন পরিমাণ; চরম মাত্রায়।

năb, *v. t.* **1.** (*Slang*) To arrest; to seize, as a criminal; to catch in wrong-doing; (ইতরভাষায়) গ্রেপ্তার করা; ধরা; কুকার্য্য করার অবস্থায় ধরা। **2.** (*Obs.*) To snatch away; (অপ্রঃ) কাড়িয়া লওয়া।

nā'-bŏb, *n.* **1.** A deputy or governor under the Mogul Empire; নবাব। **2.** A wealthy luxurious person, esp. a European, returned from India or any far country with fortune; বিলাসী ধনীব্যক্তি, বিশেষতঃ ভারত বা কোন সুদূরদেশ হইতে প্রচুর ধনার্জ্জনান্তে প্রত্যাগত ব্যক্তি। **Nabob's vineyard**—(*Kings* I—10) Any property which is coveted by a rich neighbour; ধনী প্রতিবেশীর লোলুপদৃষ্টিতে পতিত সম্পত্তি।

năc'-ă-răt, *n.* A pale-red colour; একপ্রকার ম্লান লোহিতবর্ণ।

nā'-cre (-kėr), *n.* **1.** A pinna or sea-pen; সামুদ্রিক জীববিশেষ। **2.** Mother-of-pearl; a shellfish yielding this; মুক্তাস্ফোট; ঝিনুক। **—crous, —ous**, *adjs.*

nā'-dir (-dêr), *n.* **1.** The point of the celestial sphere directly under the observer, (*opp. to zenith*); আকাশমণ্ডলস্থ যে বিন্দু আমাদের পদের ঠিক নিম্নদিকে অবস্থিত, অধঃস্বস্তিক (হিঃ কোঃ), অধোবিন্দু, পাদবিন্দু, অধর (মঃ উঃ), অধরস্বস্তিক (ঐ), [আমাদের পদ হইতে পৃথিবীর কেন্দ্র ভেদ করিয়া রেখা টানিলে ঐ রেখা অধোবিন্দুতে আকাশমণ্ডল ছেদন করিয়া থাকে।] **2.** The lowest point; the time or place of greatest depression or degradation; as, the seventh century is the *nadir* of the human mind in Europe; অধঃসীমা; চরম পতন বা অবনতির কাল।

næ'-vŭs (nē-), **nē'—**, *ns.* A congenital mark on the skin; a birth-mark; জড়ুল, তিল, আঁচিল; জন্মদাগ।

năg, *n.* A small horse; a pony; (*colloq.*) any horse; ক্ষুদ্রকায় অশ্ব, ছোট ঘোড়া, অশ্বক; টাট্টু; (চলিত ভাষায়) ঘোড়া।

năg, *v. i.* & *t.* To scold pertinaciously; to find fault constantly; (often with *at*); খিট খিট করা; খিটিমিটি করা, খুঁত খুঁত করা। ***Verb t.*** To annoy persistently by petty fault-finding; খিটিমিটি করিয়া জ্বালাতন করা। **Nag'-ging**, *n.*

nā'-gŏr, *n.* A Senegal antelope; সেনিগেলদেশীয় কৃষ্ণসার মৃগ।

nā'-iad (-yăd), *n.* (*Class. Myth.*) A water-nymph; (রোমীয় ও গ্রীসীয় প্রত্নতত্ত্ব) জলদেবতা, জলপরী, নদী-দেবতা।

naif, *adj.* (*Rare*) Naive; as, a *naif* remark; (অপ্রঃ) সহজসরল।

nail (nāl), *n.* **1.** Horny covering at the end of the human fingers and toes; নখ, নখর, করজ (উজ্জ্বলঃ), কররুহ [also পাণিজ, পাণিরুহ, পুনর্নব, পুনর্ভব, কামাঙ্কুশ, করকণ্টক, করভূ, করশূক।] **2.** A claw; a talon; থাবা; নখর। **3.** (*Zool.*) The terminal horny plate on the beak of ducks and other allied birds; (জন্তু-বিজ্ঞান) হংসাদি পক্ষীর চঞ্চুর শৃঙ্গবৎপদার্থনির্ম্মিত প্রান্তফলক। **4.** A small pointed spike of metal driven into wood etc. for fastening purposes or to suspend articles from; প্রেক, পেরেক, গজাল, কীলক, শঙ্কু, শঙ্কুক। **Nailed**, *adj.* **Nail'-less**, *adj.* **Nail-brush**—নখমার্জ্জনী। **Nail-head** — স্থাপত্য-ভূষাবিশেষ। **Nail-print**—নখক্ষত, নখাঙ্ক (উজ্জ্বলঃ)। **Nail-scissors**—নখনিকৃন্তন, নখরঞ্জনী। **A nail in one's coffin**—Something regarded as likely to shorten one's life; as, a fit of anger is a *nail in your coffin*; যদ্দ্বারা শ্মশানযাত্রার কাল নিকটবর্ত্তী হয়। **Hard as nails**—In fine training; সুশিক্ষিত। **Nail fixed on the temple**—পূর্ব্বে রোম নগরীতে সর্ব্বসাধারণের বিপৎপাত নিবারণের জন্য জুপিটারের মন্দিরে যে পেরেক বসান হইত। **On the nail**—Without delay; চট্ করিয়া। In ready money; as, pay down *on the nail*; রোক টাকায়, নগদ টাকায়। **Right as nails**—Quite right; খুব ঠিক। **To fight tooth and nail**—To fight to the utmost; প্রাণপণে সংগ্রাম করা। **To hit the (right) nail on the head**—To come to a right conclusion; to propose or do the right thing; to hit the mark; ঠিক সিদ্ধান্তে উপনীত হওয়া; ঠিক কাজ করা, ঠিক বিষয় প্রস্তাব করা; ঠিক জায়গায় আঘাত করা।

nail (nāl), *v. t.* **1.** To fasten with nails; as, to *nail* board to the beams; প্রেক দ্বারা আঁটা। **2.** (*Fig.*) To hold or fix, as to an agreement etc.; (লক্ষণায়) ঠিক রাখা, অটল থাকা। **3.** To secure; to catch; as, to *nail* a person or a thing; হস্তগত করা; ধরা। **Nailed-up drama**—যে নাট্যের ঘটনাবলী অসংলগ্ন ভাবে সন্নিবিষ্ট। **To nail a lie**—To detect and expose it so as to put a stop to its currency; কোন মিথ্যা কথার প্রচার বন্ধ করার জন্য উহা ধরিয়া জনসমাজে প্রকাশ করিয়া দেওয়া। **To nail one's colours to the mast**—To refuse stubbornly to surrender; to stick obstinately to one's plans or opinions; আত্মসমর্পণ করিতে দৃঢ়ভাবে অস্বীকার করা [অর্থাৎ পতাকা পেরেক মারিয়া মাস্তুলে আঁটিয়া দিলে তাহা নত করিয়া বশ্যতা স্বীকার করা অসম্ভব হয়।]; নিজের কোট বজায় রাখা। **To nail to counter, barn-door** — To expose as spurious, vile; কৃত্রিম বা জঘন্য বলিয়া জনসমাজে প্রচার করা। **To nail up**—To close or affix at a height with nails; পেরেক মারিয়া উচ্চস্থানে আটকান বা বন্ধ করা।

nail′-ėr (nāl-), *n.* **1.** A nail-maker ; পেরেক নির্ম্মাণকারী, শঙ্কুনির্ম্মাতা। **2.** (*Slang*) Some one or something extremely good ; one very skilful (*at*) ; (ইতর ভাষায়) সবার সেরা লোক বা বস্তু, যারপর নাই ভাল লোক ; সুদক্ষ ব্যক্তি, সুনিপুণ ব্যক্তি। **–y,** *n.* A place where nails are made ; পেরেক নির্ম্মাণের স্থান, শঙ্কু-নির্ম্মাণস্থলী।

nail′-ing (nāl), *n.* **1.** Making nails ; শঙ্কুনির্ম্মাণ। **2.** (*Slang*) Splendid ; excellent ; (ইতর ভাষায়) তোফা, খাসা ; চমৎকার।

nain′-sook (nān-), *n.* (Hind. *nain, nayan*=eye and *sukh*= delight) A sort of jaconet muslin, plain or striped, originally made in India ; নয়নসুক কাপড়।

Nair-fish—ভেটকী মাছ।

nā-ive′ (-ēv), *adj.* Artless ; ingenuous ; unaffected ; simple ; সরল, সহজ ; ঋজু (হিঃ কোঃ), স্বভাব-সরল, অখল ; অকপট, অকৃত্রিম ; সাদাসিধা। **–ly,** *adv.* **–ty,** *n.* Same as NAIVETE.

naivete, (*F.*), *ns.* Artlessness ; the quality of native simplicity ; সহজসারল্য, স্বভাবসারল্য ; মুগ্ধতা।

nā′-kėd, *adj.* **1.** Unclothed ; nude ; bare ; as, a *naked* body ; বিবস্ত্র, বিবসন, অবাস, অবস্ত্র ; নগ্ন, উলঙ্গ, লেংটা, লেঙটা, দিগম্বর, দিগ্‌বসন ; অনাবৃত, অনাচ্ছাদিত। **2.** Defenceless ; "Behold my bosom *naked* to your sword" ; অরক্ষিত। **3.** (Of a sword or other weapon) Unsheathed ; উলঙ্গ, নিষ্কোষিত। **4.** Manifest ; plain ; as, *naked* truth ; স্পষ্ট ; প্রত্যক্ষ, সুপ্রকট। **5.** Devoid *of* ; destitute ; as, *naked* of comforts ; বিরহিত, বিহীন ; শূন্য, হীন, রিক্ত। **6.** Treeless ; leafless ; barren ; বৃক্ষহীন, তরুশূন্য, নিষ্পাদপ ; নিষ্পত্র, পত্রহীন ; অনুর্বর। **7.** (Of ground, rock, etc.) Exposed ; অনাবৃত। **8.** (Of rooms) Unfurnished ; (কক্ষ সম্বন্ধে) গৃহসজ্জাহীন, আসবাবশূন্য। **9.** Devoid of ornament or facing of any kind ; plain and bare ; নিরাভরণ, ভূষাহীন ; সাদামাটা, সাদাসিধা। **10.** (*Bot.*) Without pubescence ; destitute of enveloping parts ; (উদ্ভিদবিদ্যা) লোমময় আবরণহীন ; আবরক অংশবিহীন। **11.** (*Zool.*) Destitute of hair or scales ; (জন্তুবিদ্যা) নির্লোম, শল্কবিহীন। **12.** Mere ; simple ; as a *naked* command ; a *naked* belief ; শুদ্ধ ; কেবল। **13.** Unassisted ; as, a *naked* eye (without telescope etc.) ; খালি, সুধু। **–ly,** *adv.* **–ness,** *n.* State of being naked ; নগ্নত্ব, দিগম্বরত্ব, অনাবৃতত্ব। **Naked-bed**—যে শয্যায় কোন ব্যক্তি উলঙ্গ অবস্থায় শায়িত থাকে। **Naked bud**—নগ্নমুকুল (সাঃ পঃ)। **Naked eye**—সুধুচোখ, খালিচোখ (অর্থাৎ চসমা, দূরবীক্ষণাদির সাহায্য বিনা)। **Naked Lady, Naked Boys**—একপ্রকার কন্দজ গুল্ম—ইহার আরবী নাম সোরিঞ্জিন (Sorinjin)—ইহার বীজ ও শিকড় ঔষধাদিতে ব্যবহৃত হয়। **Naked truth**—খাঁটি সত্য। **Stark naked**—লেংটাদিগম্বর।

năm′-bȳ–păm′-bȳ, *adj.* & *n.* Affected ; insipid ; weakly sentimental ; "*Namby-pamby* madrigals of love" ; লোকদেখানিয়া ; নীরস ; ভাবপ্রবণ, ছিঁচকাঁদুনিয়া। ***Noun.*** A talk or writing of this kind ; কপট-ভাবোচ্ছ্বাসপূর্ণ রচনা। **–ism,** *n.* Weak or insipid sentimentality ; ভাবকালি, ছিঁচকাঁদুনিয়াভাব।

nāme, *n.* **1.** The title by which any person or thing is known or designated ; a designation ; a title ; নাম, নামধেয় ; সংজ্ঞা (হিঃ কোঃ), অভিধেয় ; উপাধি, আখ্যা। **2.** An opprobrious appellation ; abuse ; as, to call one *names* ; মন্দবাক্য ; গালি। **3.** A person as known, famed, or spoken of ; as, Nelson himself and many great *names* were there ; নামজাদা লোক, পরিচিত লোক। **4.** Family ; clan ; people ; পরিবার ; গোষ্ঠী ; জন। **5.** Fame or reputation ; "What men of *name* resort to him ?" ; সুখ্যাতি, সুনাম। **6.** Merely nominal existence, as, a friend in *name* ; নামে মাত্র স্থিতি। **7.** Calling to witness ; as, in Gods *name* ; নামে বলন, সাক্ষী করিয়া বলন। **8.** Authority ; behalf ; as, in one's own *name* (Independently) ; কর্ত্তৃত্ব ; পক্ষ। **Bad name**—বদনাম, দুর্নাম, অখ্যাতি, অপকীর্ত্তি। **Christian name**—See under CHRISTIAN. **Family name**—কুলনাম, গোত্র। **Good name**—সুনাম, সুখ্যাতি। **Name-child**—কাহারও নামানুসারে যে শিশুর নাম রাখা হয়। **Name-day**—যে খৃষ্টীয় সিদ্ধপুরুষ বা সিদ্ধিপ্রাপ্তা নারীর নামানুসারে কাহারো নাম রাখা হয়—তাহার দিন ; যে দিনে কোন শিশুর নামাকরণ করা হয়। **Name-part**—নাটকের যে ভূমিকার নামানুসারে নাটকের নামাকরণ করা হয়। **Name plate**—যে নামাঙ্কিত ধাতুফলক বাটীর প্রবেশদ্বারে সংবদ্ধ করা হয়, নামপট্ট, নামফলক। **Namesake**—একনামধারী ব্যক্তি, মিতা। **Proper name**—যে নামে কোন বিশেষ ব্যক্তি, বস্তু, স্থান, ইত্যাদি বুঝায়। **Another name for**—নামান্তর। **In name**—নামতঃ। **In the name of God**—By God ; ঈশ্বরের নামে। **Of or by the name of**—Called ; নামক। **To call a person names**—To speak disrespectfully to a person ; to abuse him ; নামখান্ত করে ডাকা ; গালি দেওয়া। **To call by name**—নাম ধরিয়া ডাকা। **To go by the name**—To pass under the name of ; কোন নামে পরিচিত হওয়া। **To have one's name up**—To be much spoken of ; খুব নাম হওয়া। **To keep one's name on or off the books**—To remain or cease to be a member of a college, club, etc. ; কোন সমিতি

মহাবিদ্যালয়, প্রভৃতিতে নাম রাখা বা নাম সমিতি প্রভৃতি হইতে তুলিয়া লওয়া। **To put one's name down for**—To apply as a candidate etc.; কোন চাকুরী প্রভৃতির জন্য আবেদন করা। **To take a name in vain**—To swear profanely by the name; to use a name lightly or profanely; অপবিত্র ভাব বা অশ্রদ্ধার সহিত নামগ্রহণ করা; নাম খান্ত করা।

nāme, *v. t.* **1.** To denominate; to designate by a particular word or words; নাম দেওয়া; আখ্যাত করা, অভিহিত করা। **2.** To call (a person or thing) by right name; ঠিক নামে ডাকা। **3.** To designate; to appoint; মনোনীত করা; নিযুক্ত করা। **4.** To mention by name; as, the person *named* in a document; নাম করিয়া উল্লেখ করা। **5.** To fix; as, to *name* a day for a wedding; নির্দ্দিষ্ট করা, স্থির করা। **6.** (*House of Commons—of a Speaker*) To mention as an M. P. as disobedient to the chair; (বিলাতে কমন্স সভায়) কোন সভ্য সভাপতির আদেশ মান্য করেন নাই বলিয়া উল্লেখ করা। **7.** To cite as an instance; দৃষ্টান্তস্বরূপ উল্লেখ করা। **Nam'-a-ble,** *adj.* **Not to be named on or in the same day with**—To be quite inferior to; কোন কিছু অপেক্ষা একেবারে নিকৃষ্টতর হওয়া। **To name the day**—(Of a woman) To fix the day for marriage; বিবাহের দিন স্থির করা। **To name the name of Christ**—To make profession of faith in him; খৃষ্টে বিশ্বাসী বলিয়া স্বীকার করা।

nāme'-lĕss, *adj.* **1.** Obscure; inglorious; "A *nameless* life I lead, a nameless death I'll die"; অপ্রসিদ্ধ; অগৌরবজনক। **2.** Not mentioned by name; anonymous; without a name; as, a *nameless* star; অনামক, নামহীন; বেনামী; নামশূন্য, অনভিধান। **3.** Left purposely in obscurtiy; as, a man who shall be a *nameless* person; অনুক্তনামা। **4.** Not specified by name; as, on the authority of one who shall be *nameless*; অনির্দ্দিষ্টনামা। **5.** Inexpressible; indefinable; "I have a *nameless* horror of the man"; অনির্ব্বচনীয়; অবর্ণনীয়। **6.** (Of altars, tombs, etc.) Bearing no name or inscription: (বেদী, সমাধি, প্রভৃতি সম্পর্কে) নাম বা উৎকীর্ণলিপিবিহীন। **7.** Abominable; loathsome; as, *nameless* vices; জঘন্য; বীভৎস।

nāme'-ly̆, *adv.* That is to say; videlicet; যথা; অর্থাৎ, উদাহরণ স্থলে।

năn-keen' (-kēn) *n.* **1.** A buff-coloured cotton cloth first made at Nankin in China; একপ্রকার বাদামীরংয়ের সূতী কাপড় (পূর্ব্বে) চীন দেশের নানকিন সহরে তৈরী হইত। **2.** (*Pl.*) Trousers of this; ঐ কাপড়ের পাজামা। **3.** Yellow or pale buff colour; পীতবর্ণ, হরিতকীবর্ণ।

năn'-ny̆ (-goat), *n.* A she-goat; ছাগল, ছাগী।

Năntz, *n.* (*Archaic*) Brandy; (অপ্রঃ) ব্রাণ্ডী। [ফরাসী দেশের অন্তঃপাতী Nantes সহর হইতে সমানীত।]

nā-ō-sau'-rŭs (-sä-), A genus of extinct reptiles; একজাতীয় অধুনালুপ্ত সরীসৃপ।

năp, *v. i* & *n.* To have a short sleep; to doze; স্বল্পনিদ্রা যাওয়া; ঝিমান, তন্দ্রানুভব করা। ***Noun.*** A short sleep; a doze, esp. by day; as, to take a *nap*; স্বল্পনিদ্রা; তন্দ্রা। **To take or catch one napping**—To find one asleep; to take one unawares; to detect one in negligence or error; কাহাকে ঘুমন্ত অবস্থায় পাওয়া; কাহাকে অতর্কিতভাবে আক্রমণ করা, অপ্রস্তুত অবস্থায় কাহাকেও আক্রমণ করা; কাহাকেও অবহেলায় বা ভুলভ্রান্তিতে ধরা।

năp, *n.* & *v. t.* **1.** The woolly substance on the surface of cloth, plants, etc.; আঁশ, ফুঁপি, এঁশো। **2.** A soft or downy surface; কোমল বা পালকবৎ উপরিভাগ। ***Verb t.*** To raise or put a nap on (cloth); কাপড়ে ফুঁপি তোলা। **Nap'-less,** *adj.*

năp, *n.* A card-game; একপ্রকার তাস খেলা। **To go nap**—(*Lit.* & *fig.*) To stake all the winnings; বাজি জিতিয়া যাহা পাওয়া হইয়াছে তৎসমুদয় পণ রাখা।

nāpe, *n.* The hind part of the neck; গ্রীবার পশ্চাদ্‌ভাগ, ঘাড়।

nā'-pêr-y̆, *n.* (*Scot.* & *Archaic*) Linen for domestic use, esp. at table; (স্কটলণ্ডে ব্যবহৃত—অপ্রঃ) পারিবারিক ব্যবহারের জন্য কাপড়।

naph'-thă (năp- *or* năf-), *n.* (*Old chem.*) A volatile, limpid, bituminous liquid of a strong peculiar odour and very inflammable; (প্রাচীন রসায়ন-শাস্ত্র) মেটে তৈল, গিরিতৈল, নফ্‌তা (হিঃ কোঃ)।

naph'-thă-līne (năp- *or* năf-), *n.* A white crystalline substance got in distilling coal-tar and used as disinfectant; আলকাতরা পরিস্রবণ-কালে প্রাপ্ত একপ্রকার শ্বেতবর্ণ স্ফটিকবৎ পদার্থ—যাহা রোগবীজাণুনাশকরূপে ব্যবহৃত হয়, নেফ্‌থেলিন। **—tha-lize,** *v. t.* To saturate or impregnate with naphtha; মেটেতৈলদ্বারা সম্পূরিত করা।

năp'-kin, *n.* **1.** (Also, *Table-napkin*) A little towel or small cloth, esp. one used at table for wiping the hands etc.; গামছা, গাত্রমার্জ্জনী, গাত্রপ্রক্ষণী। **2.** A small towel, esp. for nursery purposes; শিশুদের জন্য ক্ষুদ্র গামছা। **Napkin-ring**—যে কাষ্ঠ, গজদন্ত, প্রভৃতির বলয়ে ভোজনকালে ব্যবহৃত তোয়ালে জড়াইয়া রাখা হয়। **To lay up in a napkin**—To make no use of (*Luke* XIX, 20); কোন রূপ ব্যবহার না করা।

জীব। **3.** Failure of a project or action ; as, his attempt proved an *abortion* ; অসিদ্ধি, নিষ্ফলতা। **—bor′-tive,** *adj.* **1.** Born prematurely ; অকাল-প্রসূত। **2.** Fruitless unsuccessful ; as, an *abortive* attempt ; নিষ্ফল ; নিরর্থক। **3.** Imperfectly formed or developed ; rudimentary, as organs, etc. ; অপরিণত, অপুষ্টাঙ্গ ; প্রাথমিক। **—bor′-tive-ly,** *adv.* **—bor′-tive-ness,** *n.* **—ed,** *adj.* **1.** Untimely born ; undeveloped ; অকালপ্রসূত ; অপরিণত, অপুষ্টাঙ্গ। **2.** Rudimentary ; as, thorns are *aborted* branches মৌলিক, আদিম। **Criminal abortion**—Abortion by artificial means ; (ঘৃণা, লজ্জাদি ভয়ে) অপগর্ভপাত, অপরাধজনক গর্ভপাত, ভ্রূণহত্যা।

ă-bound′ (-bownd), *v.i.* To be in great plenty; to be copiously supplied—*(in, with)* ; as, to *abound with* provisions : tigers *abound in* the jungles of Bengal ; পর্য্যাপ্ত বা প্রচুর পরিমাণে থাকা ; ভূয়িষ্ঠ পরিমাণে বা বহুসংখ্যায় থাকা। **To abound in one's own sense**—To follow one's own judgment independently ; স্বাধীনভাবে স্বকীয় বিচারবুদ্ধি অনুসরণ করিয়া চলা।

ă-bout′ (-bowt), *prep.* & *adv.* **1.** Around ; as, look *about* you : bind them *about* thy neck ; চতুর্দ্দিকে, পরিতঃ, বেড়িয়া। **2.** Near to (in place, size, number, quality, etc.) ; as, *about* my stature (প্রায়) : *about* two thousand (ন্যূনাধিক); সন্নিকটে, প্রায়, কাছাকাছি, কমবেশ। **3.** By or on (one's person) ; as, I have no money *about* me ; সমীপে, কাছে, নিকটে, সঙ্গে। **4.** Here and there ; throughout ; as, pain lies all *about* the breast ; ইতস্ততঃ ; সর্ব্বত্র ব্যাপিয়া, জুড়িয়া। **5.** On account of ; touching ; concerning ; as, I know nothing *about* this ; জন্য ; বিষয়ে ; সম্পর্কে।

রোগ যাহাতে মাঝে মাঝে তন্দ্রালুতা জন্মে, স্বাপরোগ।

nâr-cō′-sis, *n.* **1.** The effect of a narcotic whether medicinal or poisonous ; নেশা, মাদকদ্রব্য-জনিত মত্ততা। **2.** The state of insensibility ; সংজ্ঞাহীনতা, নিস্‌সংবেদন (হিঃ কোঃ)।

nâr-cŏt′-ic, *adj.* & *n.* **1.** Having power to produce torpor, sleep, drowsiness, insensibility, etc. ; নিদ্রাজনক, নিদ্রাকারী অবশতাজনক, মাদক, সংবেদননাশক (হিঃ কোঃ), অবমোহন (চঃ)। **2.** Of, or relating to, narcosis ; মত্ততাসম্বন্ধীয়। **3.** (*Fig.*) Soporific ; as, a *narcotic* lecture ; (লক্ষণায়) নিদ্রাজনক, স্বাপজনক। *Noun.* **1.** A substance which induces sleep and insensibility ; যে ঔষধে নিদ্রা বা সংজ্ঞাহীনতা জন্মে। **2.** (*Fig.*) Something inducing sleep ; নিদ্রাজনক বিষয়। **—co′-tism, —co-ti-za′-tion, Nar′-co-tist,** *ns.* **Nar′-co-tize,** *v. t.* To render insensible with a narcotic ; to dull or deaden ; মাদকদ্রব্য দ্বারা সংজ্ঞাহীন করা ; অসাড় করা, আড়ষ্ট করা।

nârd, *n.* An aromatic balsam or ointment used by the ancients, derived from the plant of the same name ; জটামাংসী, জটিলা। *Nardosta-Chys*—জটামাংসী (বেলঃ)।

nâr′-ghi-lē (-gi-), *n.* An oriental apparatus for smoking tobacco ; hookah ; (From *nargil*=cocoanut) ; গুড়গুড়ি ; হুকা।

năr-rāte′ *v. t.* To relate ; to give an account of ; বিবৃত করা ; বর্ণনা করা। **—ra′-tor,** *n.*

năr-rā′-tion, *n.* **1.** Act of telling the particulars of an occurrence ; recital ; বর্ণন, কীর্ত্তন, কথন ; বিবৃতি, বর্ণনা। **2.** A story ; history ; গল্প, কথা ; ইতিবৃত্ত।

năr′-ra-tive (-ă-tiv), *n.* & *adj.* **1.** A tale ; a recital of facts etc. ; গল্প ; বর্ণনা, বৃত্তান্ত, আখ্যান (হিঃ কোঃ)। **2.** A particular style of composition ; রচনারীতি-বিশেষ। *Adj.* In the form of, or concerned with, narration ; বর্ণনা-সংক্রান্ত, বিবৃতিমূলক, বর্ণনাত্মক। **—ly,** *adv.*

năr′-row (-ō), *adj.*, *n.*, *v. i.* & *t.* **1.** Of little breadth ; not broad or wide ; অল্পপরিসর, স্বল্পপরিসর ; অপ্রশস্ত, অবিস্তৃত। **2.** Restricted ; limited ; সংকীর্ণ ; সঙ্কুচিত। **3.** Illiberal ; bigoted ; prejudiced ; self-centered ; mean ; niggardly ; অনুদার ; গোঁড়া ; সংস্কারদুষ্ট ; স্বার্থপর ; নীচ ; কৃপণ, হাতটান। **4.** With little margin ; as, a *narrow* escape ; চুলমাত্র। **5.** Accurate ; scrutinizing ; সঠিক ; পুঙ্খানুপুঙ্খ, সূক্ষ্ম। *Noun.* (*Usu. pl.*) The narrow part of a sound, strait, river, pass or street ; নদী, প্রণালী, গিরিসঙ্কট, রাজপথ, প্রভৃতির সংকীর্ণ অংশ। *Verb i.* To become narrower ; to lessen ; সংকীর্ণ হওয়া ; হ্রাস হওয়া। *Verb t.* **1.** To make narrower ; to diminish ; সংকীর্ণ করা ; হ্রাস করা। **2.** To contract in sentiment or views ; অনুদার করা, সঙ্কোচ করা। **3.** To limit ; সীমাবদ্ধ করা। **—ish,** *adj.* **—ly,** *adv.* **1.** In a narrow manner ; সংকীর্ণ ভাবে, অনুদারভাবে। **2.** Accurately ; carefully ; শুদ্ধরূপে ; সাবধানে। **3.** Illiberally ; strictly ; অনুদারভাবে ; কঠোরভাবে। **4.** Nearly ; by a little ; as, he *narrowly* escaped ; প্রায় ; অল্পের জন্য। **—ness,** *n.* **Narrow circumstances**—দারিদ্র্য, দুরবস্থা। **Narrow cloth**—যে কাপড়ের পরিসর ৫২ ইঞ্চির কম। **Narrow escape**—পুনর্যাত্রা, পুনর্জন্ম। **Narrow-gauge**—যে পাতা রেলদ্বয়ের মধ্যবর্ত্তী লৌহবর্ত্মের পরিসর ৪ ফিট ৮½ ইঞ্চি অপেক্ষা কম (পূর্ব্বে ৪ ফিট ৮½ ইঞ্চি পরিসর লৌহবর্ত্ম)। **Narrow goods**—চুল বাঁধিবার ফিতা প্রভৃতি। **Narrow-minded**—সংকীর্ণমনাঃ, সংকীর্ণচেতাঃ ; ক্ষুদ্রমনাঃ, অল্পচেতাঃ, ক্ষুদ্রচেতাঃ,

শুদ্রান্তঃকরণ; অনুদারচিত্ত। **Narrow mindedly,** *adv.* **Narrow mindedness,** *n.* **Narrow seas**—ইংলণ্ড ও আয়র্লণ্ডের প্রণালী। **Narrow vowels**—জিহ্বা এবং আলজিহ্বা টান করিয়া যে সকল স্বরবর্ণ উচ্চারিত হয়। **The narrow bed, cell, house** or **home**—কবর, সমাধি। **The narrow way**—ধর্ম্মপথ। **To have a narrow escape**—অল্পের জন্য বাঁচিয়া যাওয়া, মরিতে মরিতে বাঁচা।

nâr'-thĕx, *n.* A part of an early church railed off from the rest, to which penitents, catechumens and women were admitted; প্রাচীন খৃষ্টীয় গির্জ্জার গরাদেবেষ্টিত অংশবিশেষ—যথায় স্ত্রীগণ, অনুতপ্তজনগণ ও অশিক্ষিত বালকবালিকা বা পৌত্তলিকদিগের প্রবেশাধিকার ছিল।

nâr'-whăl, *n.* A cetaceous mammal found in the northern seas averaging from 12 to 20 feet in length; উত্তরসমুদ্রচর বৃহৎকায় জন্তুবিশেষ।

nā'-săl, *adj.* & *n.* **1.** Of, or relating to, the nose; নাসিকাসম্বন্ধীয়। **2.** Affected by, or sounded through, the nose; as, a *nasal* sound or voice; অনুনাসিক। ***Noun.*** **1.** (*Phon.*) An elementary sound uttered through, or partly through, the nose; (e. g. *m, n, ng*); অনুনাসিক উচ্চারণ। **2.** (*Anat.* & *Zool.*) A nasal bone, plate or scale: (জন্তুবিদ্যা ও শারীরসংস্থান-বিদ্যা) নাসিকার অস্থি, ফলক বা শল্ক। **—i-za'-tion,** *n.* **—ize,** *v. t.* & *i.* To render nasal; to speak nasally or through the nose; অনুনাসিক করা; নাসিকা দ্বারা উচ্চারিত করা। **—ly,** *adv.* **—sal'-i-ty,** *n.* **Nasal dot**—অনুস্বার, চন্দ্রবিন্দু (মহানির্ব্বাণ)। **Nasal organ**—নাসিকাযন্ত্র।

năs'-cent (ĕnt), *adj.* In the act of being born; beginning to exist or grow; জায়মান, উৎপাদ্যমান; উদ্ভাবী, বর্দ্ধিষ্ণু, বিকাশশীল, বর্দ্ধমান, ভূয়মান। **—cen-cy,** *n.*

nāse'-bĕr-ry (ĭ), *n.* A tree of the West Indies yielding Sapodilla plum; একপ্রকার ফলতরু।

năs-tur'-ti-ŭm (-têr-shĭ-), *n.* **1.**(*Bot.*) A genus of herbs including the watercress; (উদ্ভিদ্‌বিদ্যা) লুটপুটিয়া (watercress), হালিম (garden-cress) প্রভৃতি শাক। **2.** The Indian cress; গুণ (সিন্ধুদেশ), লুটপুটিয়া (বেলঃ)।

năs'-tȳ, *adj.* **1.** Very dirty or foul; filthy; কুৎসিত; জঘন্য, কদর্য্য। **2.** Obscene; indecent; অশ্লীল; কুরুচিপূর্ণ, কুৎসিত। **3.** Nauseous; disagreeable; objectionable; annoying; as, a *nasty* smell: cheap and *nasty* clothing; ন্যক্কারজনক; অপ্রীতিজনক; আপত্তিজনক; বিরক্তিকর। **4.** (Of weather etc.) Wet or stormy; বাদলা, ঝটিকাময়। **5.** Dangerous; bad; বিপজ্জনক; বদ্‌, খারাপ। **6.** (Of persons) Ill-natured; disagreeable; "...take delight in being *nasty* to a neighbour"; ব্যক্তিসম্পর্কে) দুষ্টপ্রকৃতি, দুঃশীল; অপ্রীতিকর। **—ti-ly,** *adv.* **—ti-ness,** *n.* **A nasty one**—ধাক্কা, ধমক; মুখঝামটা; যে আঘাত প্রভৃতিতে কেহ অক্ষম বা অকর্ম্মণ্য হয়।

nā'-tăl, *adj.* Of, relating to, or from, one's birth; জন্মসম্বন্ধীয়, জন্মবিষয়ক, জন্মগত।

nā-tăl'-i-tȳ, *n.* Brith-rate; লোকসংখ্যার অনুপাতে জন্মসংখ্যা।

nā'-tănt, *adj.* (*Bot.*) Floating; (উদ্ভিদ্‌বিদ্যা) ভাসমান, প্লবমান।

nă-tā'-tion, *n.* Swimming; সন্তরণ।

nā-tă-tō'-rĭ-ăl, nā'-tă-tō-rȳ, *adjs.* Swimming; pertaining, or adapted, to swimming; সন্তরণশীল; সন্তরণসম্বন্ধীয়, সন্তরণোপযোগী।

nā'-[illegible]s, *n., pl.* (*Anat.*) **1.** The buttocks; (শারীরসংস্থানবিদ্যা) নিতম্ব। **2.** See CORPORA QUADRIGEMINA.

nath(e)-lĕss (năth-), *adv.* (*Archaic*) Same as NEVERTHELESS.

nā'-tion, *n.* **1.** A people inhabiting a certain extent of territory and united by common political institutions; জাতি, লোক। **2.** (In mediaeval and some Scotch universities) A body of students from a particular country or district; (মধ্যযুগের বিশ্ববিদ্যালয় এবং স্কটলণ্ডের কোন কোন বিশ্ববিদ্যালয়ে) কোন বিশেষ দেশ বা জেলার ছাত্রদল। **—hood,** *n.* **Law of nation**—See under LAW. **Nation of gentlemen**—স্কচ্‌জাতি (George IV. ১৮২২ খৃঃ অব্দে স্কটলণ্ড দর্শনে গেলে পর তদ্দেশবা[illegible]কে ঐ আখ্যা প্রদান করেন।) **Nati[illegible] [illegible]hopkeepers**—বণিকের জাতি, দো[illegible]রের জাতি, ইংরেজ জাতি (নেপোলিয়ান অবজ্ঞাচ্ছলে ইংরেজদিগকে এই নামে অভিহিত করিতেন;। Samuel Adams নামক জনৈক স্বদেশপ্রেমিক আমেরিকান সর্ব্বপ্রথমে ইংরেজদিগকে এই আখ্যা প্রদান করেন বলিয়া কথিত আছে।) **The nations**—(বাইবেল) ইহুদী ব্যতিরিক্ত জাতি; পৃথিবীর লোকসমূহ।

nă'-tion-ăl, *adj.* & *n.* **1.** Pertaining to a nation; common to a whole people or race; জাতীয়, জাতিগত; রাষ্ট্রীয়। **2.** Characteristic of a nation; কোন জাতির স্বভাবগত। ***Noun.*** (*Pl., Diplomatic*) One's fellow-countrymen; স্বদেশবাসী। **—ly,** *adv.* **National anthem**—See ANTHEM. **National Artillery Association**—কামানচালনাবিদ্যার উৎকর্ষসাধনের জন্য ১৮৬১ খৃঃ অব্দে ইংলণ্ডদেশে স্থাপিত জাতীয় গোলন্দাজসমিতি। **National assembly**—কোন জাতির প্রতিনিধিগণ দ্বারা গঠিত সম্মিলনী; ধর্ম্মাধ্যক্ষগণের সংসদ্‌; ফরাসীদেশের রাষ্ট্রবিপ্লবকারিদলের প্রতিনিধিগণের সম্মিলনী (১৭৮৯—৯১)। **National Church**—রাজবিধিদ্বারা প্রতিষ্ঠিত ধর্ম্মসংঘ। **National Congress**—ভারতবর্ষের জাতীয় মহাসমিতি—১৮৮৪ খৃঃ অব্দে প্রতিষ্ঠিত। **National convention**—ফরাসীদেশে রাজতন্ত্রশাসনপদ্ধতির উচ্ছেদসাধন হইলে যে সমিতি ১৭৯২ খৃঃ অব্দের ২১ সেপ্টেম্বর

হইতে ১৭৯৫ খৃঃ অব্দের ২৬ অক্টোবর পর্য্যন্ত ফরাসীদেশের শাসনকার্য্য পরিচালনা করেন। **National Gallery**—লণ্ডন নগরীর বিশ্ববিখ্যাত চিত্রশালার নাম। এই প্রাসাদ Trafalgar Squareএর সন্নিকটে অবস্থিত। ইহাতে পৃথিবীর বহু প্রাচীন ও নবীন চিত্রকরের শ্রেষ্ঠ চিত্র রক্ষিত হইয়াছে। তন্মধ্যে Titianএর Venus বা রতীদেবী, Raphaelএর "Madonna degli Ansidei (১০½ লক্ষ টাকায় ক্রীত), Van Dyckএর Charles I. এবং Holbein's "Duchess of উল্লেখ-যোগ্য। **Nationa** -জাতীয় ঋণ, সরকারী ঋণ। **National flag**—জাতীয় পতাকা। **National Guard**—স্বদেশরক্ষী নাগরিক সৈন্য; ফরাসী রাষ্ট্রবিপ্লবকালে সংগঠিত নাগরিক সৈন্যদল। **National Insurance**—Mr. Lloyd George কর্তৃক প্রবর্তিত বিধি-বিশেষ। ১৯১২ সনে এই আইন বিধিবদ্ধ হয়। এই আইনের বিধানানুসারে যে সকল কর্ম্মচারীর বার্ষিক আয় ১৬০ পাউণ্ডের অনধিক কিম্বা যে সমস্ত ব্যক্তি শারীরিক পরিশ্রমদ্বারা বৎসরে ১৬০ পাউণ্ডের অধিক অর্জ্জন করে—তাহাদের প্রত্যেকেই রোগের জন্য বীমা করিতে বাধ্য। এই বীমার কিস্তির টাকা বীমাকারী, বীমাকারীর মনীব ও সরকার কর্তৃক নির্দ্দিষ্ট হারে প্রদেয়। বীমাকারিগণ রোগের সময় বিনাব্যয়ে চিকিৎসকের সাহায্য ও ভরণপোষণের খরচ পায়। রুগ্ন হইয়া বা অপর কারণে চিরদিনের জন্য অকর্ম্মণ্য হইলে, উহাদিগকে পেনসন দেওয়া হয়। স্ত্রীলোকদিগকে গর্ভাবস্থায় সাহায্য দেওয়া যায় এবং কেহ ক্ষয়রোগাদিতে পীড়িত হইয়া স্বাস্থ্যজনক স্থানে গেলে তাহার ব্যয়বহন করা হয়। **National law**—জাতীয়বিধান। **National Liberal Club** — ১৮৮৭ খৃঃ অব্দে প্রতিষ্ঠিত উদারনীতিকগণের সম্মিলনী বিশেষ। এই সম্মিলনী Thames নদীর তীরে অবস্থিত। ইহার প্রতি সভ্যের দেয় বার্ষিক চাঁদার পরিমাণ ৬ গিনি। **National Liberal Federation**—ইংলণ্ড ও ওয়েল্‌সের যাবতীয় উদারনীতিক সমিতিসমূহের সম্মিলন। **National Park**—অষ্ট্রেলিয়ার সিড্‌নীনগরীর সমীপবর্ত্তী ৫৭ মাইল ব্যাপী বিরাট উদ্যান। **National Physical Laboratory**—জাতীয়পদার্থবিজ্ঞানাগার। বৈজ্ঞানিকপরীক্ষালব্ধ ফলদ্বারা দেশের শ্রমশিল্পকে সাহায্যদানের জন্য ইহা ১৯০২ খৃঃ অব্দে ইংলণ্ডের অন্তঃপাতী Teddington নামক স্থানে স্থাপিত হয়। ইহার ৫টী বিভাগ আছে:—(১) Kew মানমন্দির বিভাগ। (২) পদার্থবিজ্ঞান বিভাগ। (৩) পূর্ত্তবিভাগ। (৪) ধাতুবিদ্যা বিভাগ। (৫) W. Froude জাতীয় জলকুণ্ড বিভাগ। **National Portrait Galleries**—ইতিহাসপ্রসিদ্ধ ব্যক্তিগণের প্রতিকৃতি রক্ষার জন্য গৃহ। লণ্ডন নগরীস্থ জাতীয় প্রতিকৃতিগৃহে ইংলণ্ডের রাজা ও ইতিহাসবিখ্যাত ব্যক্তিগণের প্রতিকৃতি রক্ষিত হইয়াছে। **National Society**—ইংলণ্ড দেশে ১৮১১ খৃষ্টাব্দে প্রতিষ্ঠিত দরিদ্রের শিক্ষোন্নতি বিধায়িনী সমিতি।

nă′-tion-ăl-ĭsm, *n.* **1.** State of being national; patriotic feeling, principles and efforts; স্বজাতিকতা, স্বাজাত্য; জাতিপ্রীতি, স্বদেশানুরাগ। **2.** Advocacy or policy of national independence, as of Ireland; জাতীয়স্বাধীনতা সমর্থন, জাতীয় স্বাধীনতা বিধান। **3.** A form of socialism advocating nationalizing industry; একপ্রকার সাম্যবাদ—যাহার সমর্থকগণ দেশের সমস্ত ভূমি, শ্রমশিল্প, লৌহবর্ত্ম, প্রভৃতি দেশের সমস্ত লোকের সাধারণ-সম্পত্তিতে পরিণত করিতে চায়। **4.** A national peculiarity, *e. g.* an idiom, trait or character; জাতীয়বিশেষত্ব। **—ist**, *n.* **1.** An advocate of, or a believer in, nationalism; স্বদেশানুরাগী, স্বদেশবৎসল **2.** (*Often cap.*) An advocate of national independence, as of Ireland; স্বরাজপন্থী। **3.** One advocating the nationalizing of industries; যে ব্যক্তি দেশের শ্রমশিল্পসমূহ দেশের সমস্ত লোকের সাধারণ সম্পত্তিতে পরিণত করিতে চায়।

nă-tion-ăl′-ĭ-tȳ, *n.* **1.** State of being national; national character; জাতীয়তা, স্বজাতিকতা, আভিজন্য (হিঃ কোঃ); জাতীয় প্রকৃতি **2.** National feeling; patriotism, স্বদেশানুরাগ; স্বদেশপ্রেম, দেশাভিমানিতা, দেশপ্রীতি। **3.** One's nation; কোন ব্যক্তির জাতি। **4.** A nation; জাতি। **5.** Existence as a sovereign-nation; স্বাধীনজাতিরূপে স্থিতি।

nă′-tion-ăl īze, *v. t.* **1.** To make national; জাতীয় করা, জাতীয়ভাবাপন্ন করা। **2.** To invest with the character of a nation; কোন জাতির বিশিষ্টপ্রকৃতি প্রদান করা। **3.** To naturalize (a foreigner); (বিদেশীয় লোককে) স্বদেশীয় রূপে পরিণত করা। **4.** To withdraw from private ownership and hand over to the nation at large; as, to *nationalize* the railways in a country; ব্যক্তিবিশেষের অধিকার হইতে বিচ্যুত করিয়া দেশের সমস্ত লোকের সাধারণ সম্পত্তিরূপে পরিণত করা। **—i-za′-tion**, *n.*

nā′-tive (-tĭv), *n.* **1.** One born, or whose parents are domiciled, in a place (*of*); অধিবাসী। **2.** One belonging to a non-European or imperfectly civilized or savage race; অ-ইয়ুরোপীয়, অসভ্য বা অর্দ্ধসভ্য জাতির লোক। **3.** (*Australia*) A white born in Australia; অষ্ট্রেলিয়ায় জাত শ্বেতাঙ্গ। **4.** An oyster raised in an artificial bed in British waters; ব্রিটনের নিকটবর্ত্তী সমুদ্রে কৃত্রিম স্তরে পালিত শুক্তি। **5.** An indigenous animal or plant; স্বদেশজ জন্তু বা উদ্ভিদ, দেশপ্রাকৃতিক (হিঃ কোঃ)। **6.** (*Astrol.*) One born under a particular sign or planet; (ফলিতজ্যোতিষ) জাতক।

nā-tive (-tĭv), *adj.* **1.** Innate; inborn; as, *native* genius; অন্তর্জাত, সহজ, সহজাত; প্রকৃতিসিদ্ধ, প্রকৃতিগত, স্বভাবসিদ্ধ। **2.** Relating to one's birth or the place or circumstances of one's birth; জন্মসম্পর্কীয়, জন্মস্থানসম্পর্কীয়, দেশীয়। **3.** Connected by birth; belonging to one by way of birth; as, *native*-land;

hence, natural; simple; জন্ম দ্বারা সংসৃষ্ট; জন্মগত অধিকারসূত্রে প্রাপ্ত; স্বাভাবিক, নৈসর্গিক; অকৃত্রিম, সরল। **4.** (Of metals etc.) Found in pure and uncombined state; বিশুদ্ধ এবং অবিমিশ্র অবস্থায় প্রাপ্ত, সহজ (রঃ রঃ সঃ প্রঃ)। **5.** Born in a particular place (esp. of non-Europeans); not exotic; কোন বিশেষ স্থানে জাত; দেশীয়, দেশজাত, স্বদেশজ। **6.** Of, or relating to, the natives of a particular place; কোন বিশেষ স্থানের অধিবাসিসম্বন্ধীয়। **—ly,** *adv.* **Native rock**—স্বস্থানে স্থিত পাষাণ।

nā'-tiv-ism, *n.* **1.** (*Philos.*) The doctrine that the mind possesses forms of thought or element of knowledge not derived from the sensation; (দর্শন-শাস্ত্র) মনের কতিপয় ইন্দ্রিয়জ সংবেদন-নিরপেক্ষ চিন্তার প্রকার বা জ্ঞানের মুলতত্ত্ব আছে—এইরূপ দার্শনিকবাদ, সহজজ্ঞানবাদ (হিঃ কোঃ)। **2.** (*Chiefly U. S.*) The policy or practice of protecting the interests of native residents against those of immigrants; (প্রধানতঃ মার্কিণযুক্তরাজ্যে) দেশবাসীর স্বার্থরক্ষার্থ অনুষ্ঠিত নীতি বা বিধান। **—ist,** *n.*

nā-tiv'-i-tȳ, *n.* **1.** (*Cap.*) Birth of Christ, the Virgin, or St. John the Baptist; খৃষ্ট, খৃষ্টজননী কুমারী মেরী, অথবা জন দি ব্যাপটিষ্টের জন্ম। **2.** (*Fine arts, cap.*) A picture or relief sculpture representing or symbolizing the early infancy of Christ; (ললিত-কলা) খৃষ্টের জন্মবিষয়ক চিত্র বা খৃষ্টের বাল্যলীলা অবলম্বনে খচিত উদ্গাত কারুকার্য্যশোভিত প্রস্তরাদি। **3.** (*Cap.*) Festival of Christ's Nativity; Christmas; খৃষ্টজন্মোৎসব; খৃষ্টমাস পর্ব্ব, বড়দিন। **4.** Birth; জন্ম, সম্ভব। **5.** (*Astrol.*) Horoscope; জন্মপত্রিকা, জন্মপত্র, কোষ্ঠী, জন্মকুণ্ডলী (হিঃ কোঃ)। **Sign of nativity**—জন্মলগ্ন, জন্মরাশি। **To cast one's nativity**—কোষ্ঠী তোলা।

nā'-trŏn, *n.* Native sesquicarbonate of soda; অশোধিত ক্ষার, সর্জ্জ, সর্জ্জিকাক্ষার, সর্জ্জিক্ষার (রঃ প্রঃ), কাপোত।

năt'-ter-jăck (-êr-), *n.* A species of toad abundant in various parts of Europe; ইয়ুরোপের বিভিন্ন স্থানে প্রাপ্ত একপ্রকার সোণাবেঙ্।

năt'-ty (-ĭ), *adj.* **1.** Finely neat and tidy; spruce; তকতকে, ঝকঝকে; পরিপাটি, ফিটফাট। **2.** Deft-handed; showing deftness; সিদ্ধহস্ত; নিপুণ, দক্ষ। **—ti-ly,** *adv.* **—ti-ness,** *n.*

năt'-ū-răl, *adj.* & *n.* **1.** Instinctive; innate; সহজ, সহজাত, প্রকৃতিসিদ্ধ, স্বভাবসিদ্ধ, প্রকৃতিগত, স্বভাবসুলভ, সাংসিদ্ধিক (মঃ ভাঃ), সংস্কারজাত; অন্তর্জাত, অন্তর্ভব, নৈসর্গিক (হিঃ কোঃ)। **2.** Constituted by nature; as, *natural* year; নৈসর্গিক, প্রাকৃতিক। **3.** Normal; not unusual, marvellous or miraculous; স্বাভাবিক; প্রাকৃত। **4.** Not enlightened or communicated by revelation; as, a *natural* man or religion; অপ্রত্যাদিষ্ট। **5.** Concerned with the physical uninverse; as, *natural* laws; নৈসর্গিক, প্রাকৃতিক (হিঃ কোঃ), স্বাভাবিক (ঐ)। **6.** Not artificial; existing naturally; as, *natural* heat; uncultivated, as vegetation or land; অকৃত্রিম; নিসর্গজ, স্বাভাবিক, স্বভাবজ; অকৃষ্ট। **7.** Lifelike; exact, as a painting, etc.; জীবিতবৎ; অবিকল। **8.** Simple; unaffected; easy; as, *natural* language; সরল; অকৃত্রিম; সহজ। **9.** Having the normal form; as, a *natural* fact; not disguised; "At home it is...... that we show the *natural* m n"; স্বাভাবিক রূপবিশিষ্ট; অছদ্মবেশী, অকপটবেশী। **10.** Not surprising; to be expected; as, it is quite *natural* that it should be so; অচমকপ্রদ; প্রত্যাশিত। **11.** Consonant with the nature or character of a person or thing; কোন ফাঁদ—যাহা পশ্বাদির উপর পতিত হয়। **The fall, The fall of man**—আদিমানব আদমের ঈশ্বরাদেশ লঙ্ঘন হেতু মানব জাতির মধ্যে প্রথম পাপের প্রবেশ। **The fall of the leaf** or **year**—যে ঋতুতে বৃক্ষ হইতে পত্র চ্যুত হয়, শরদৃতু। **To try a fall**—To try a bout at wrestling; কুস্তি লড়া।

fall'-ing, *p. adj.* & *n.* ভ্রংসমান, ভ্রশ্যমান, পতিষ্যমাণ। *Noun.* (*Med.*) Displacement of a part; as, the *falling* of the uterus; (ভৈষজ্য-শাস্ত্র) স্থানচ্যুতি। **Falling-off**—Degeneration; deterioration; decrease; অধঃপতন; অপকর্ষ; হ্রাস। **Fall-ness,** *n.* **Natural-born**—জন্মগত-বিশিষ্ট পদবী বা প্রকৃতিসম্পন্ন। **Natural day**—সূর্য্যোদয় হইতে সূর্য্যাস্ত পর্য্যন্ত কাল, সাবনদিন। **Natural death**—স্বাভাবিক মৃত্যু (অপমৃত্যু নয়)। **Natural history**—সমগ্র বিশ্ব (আকাশ এবং পৃথিবী সমেত) বর্ণন, প্রকৃতিবর্ণন (হিঃ কোঃ), প্রাণিবর্ণন (ঐ); সাধারণতঃ পৃথিবী ও তজ্জাত বস্তুসমূহের বিবরণ, কখনও কখনও প্রাণিজগতের বিবরণ, প্রাকৃতিক ইতিবৃত্ত। **Natural historian,** *n.* **Natural laws**—প্রাকৃতিক নিয়ম, নৈসর্গিক বিধান। **Natural note** or **key**—কড়ি বা কোমল নয়। **Natural obligation**—প্রাকৃতিক নিয়মনিচয়দ্বারা নিরূপিত দায়িত্ব, স্বাভাবিক বাধ্যতা (যথা—পুত্রের ভরণপোষণের জন্য পিতার দায়িত্ব)। **Natural order**—উদ্ভিদ্‌বিদ্যায় স্বাভাবিক বিভাগবিশেষ—যাহাতে সমস্ত অঙ্গের পর্য্যালোচনা দ্বারা উদ্ভিদের শ্রেণীবিভাগ করা হইয়া থাকে, প্রাকৃতিক-বিভাগ। **Natural philosophy**—পদার্থবিজ্ঞান, প্রকৃতি-বিদ্যা (হিঃ কোঃ), প্রকৃতিদর্শন (ঐ)। **Natural religion**—মানবের বুদ্ধি ও অভিজ্ঞতা হইতে প্রসূত প্রত্যাদেশ এবং অতিপ্রাকৃত-সাহায্যনিরপেক্ষ ধর্ম্ম, স্বাভাবিকধর্ম্ম (হিঃ কোঃ), সাধারণধর্ম্ম (ঐ)। **Natural science**—Same as NATURAL HISTORY (in its widest sense.) **Natural selection**—যে প্রাকৃতিক-বিধানে যোগ্যতম প্রাণী ও তরুলতাদির

সত্তা রক্ষা হইয়া থাকে, জীবনসংগ্রামজনিত প্রাকৃতিকনির্ব্বাচন, প্রাকৃতিকবরণ (হিঃ কোঃ)। **Natural son, child, brother**—জারজপুত্র প্রভৃতি। **Natural theology**—যে ধর্ম্মশাস্ত্রে ঐশ্বরিক প্রত্যাদেশ প্রভৃতি স্বীকৃত হয় না, কেবলমাত্র প্রকৃতি ও সৃষ্টিকৌশল হইতে ঈশ্বরসম্বন্ধীয় জ্ঞান লাভ করিতে হয়, প্রাকৃতব্রহ্মদর্শন, প্রাকৃততত্ত্ববিবেক, প্রাকৃতিকঈশ্বরবাদ (হিঃ কোঃ), সাধারণঈশ্বরবাদ (ঐ)। **One's natural life**—কোন ব্যক্তির আয়ু। **To come natural to**—কাহারো পক্ষে স্বাভাবিক কার্য্য হওয়া।

năt'-ū-răl-ism, *n.* **1.** Action or inclination based on natural instinct or desires; স্বাভাবিক প্রকৃতি বা বাসনামূলক কার্য্য বা প্রকৃতি। **2.** Moral or religious system on purely natural basis; স্বাভাবিক ভিত্তির উপর প্রতিষ্ঠিত নীতি বা ধর্ম্ম। **3.** (*Philos.*) The belief that there is no interference of any supernatural power in the universe; (দর্শনশাস্ত্র) বিশ্বজাগতিক ব্যাপারে কোন অপ্রাকৃত শক্তির হাত নাই—এইরূপ মতবাদ; প্রকৃতিবাদ (হিঃ কোঃ)। **4.** The theory that art or literature should conform to nature; realism; সাহিত্য এবং শিল্পকলা প্রকৃতির অনুসারী হইবে এইরূপ মতবাদ, অনুকৃতিকলাবাদ (হিঃ কোঃ); নিসর্গনিষ্ঠা, বস্তুতন্ত্রতা। **5.** Indifference to conventions; সংস্কারবিমুখতা।

năt'-ū-răl-ist, *n.* & *adj.* **1.** A student of animals or plants; জীবজন্তু ও উদ্ভিদতত্ত্ব অনুশীলনকারী, প্রাণিশাস্ত্রজ্ঞ (হিঃ কোঃ)। **2.** An adherent of naturalism in religion or philosophy; ধর্ম্ম বা দর্শনে নিসর্গপন্থী, স্বভাবপন্থী। ***Adj.*** Same as NATURALISTIC.

năt-ū-răl-is'-tic, *adj.* **1.** Pertaining, or according, to naturalism; নিসর্গপন্থাসম্বন্ধীয়, নিসর্গনিষ্ঠাসম্বন্ধীয়। **2.** Of, or relating to, natural history; প্রাকৃতিক ইতিবৃত্তিবিষয়ক। **—is'-ti-cal-ly,** *adv.*

năt'-ū-răl-īze, *v. t.* & *i.* **1.** To confer the rights of citizenship on, as an alien; পরদেশীয় ব্যক্তিকে কোন দেশের পৌরাধিকার প্রদান করা। **2.** To adopt (foreign word, custom, etc.); (বৈদেশিক শব্দ, রীতিনীতি, প্রভৃতি) গ্রহণ করা। **3.** To acclimatize; as, to *naturalize* an animal or plant; কোন স্থানের জলবায়ু সহনোপযোগী করা। **4.** To make natural; to free from conventions; স্বভাবসরল করা; সংস্কারবিমুক্ত করা। **5.** To free from the supernatural or miraculous; to place on a natural basis; অলৌকিক বা অপ্রাকৃত ভাব হইতে মুক্ত করা; নৈসর্গিক ভিত্তির উপর প্রতিষ্ঠিত করা। ***Verb i.*** **1.** To become naturalized; কোন দেশের পৌরাধিকার প্রাপ্ত হওয়া। **2.** To pursue the studies of a naturalist; প্রাকৃত ইতিহাস অধ্যয়ন করা। **3.** To explain phenomena by natural facts, agencies or laws to the exclusion of the supernatural; অলৌকিক বা অপ্রাকৃত কারণাদি নির্দ্দেশ ব্যতিরেকে নৈসর্গিক তথ্য, শক্তি বা নিয়মনিচয়ের সাহায্যে প্রাকৃতিক ঘটনা সমূহের ব্যাখ্যা করা। **—i-za'-tion,** *n.*

năt'-ū-răl-lȳ, *adv.* **1.** By nature; not by art or training; as, he is *naturally* honest; স্বভাবতঃ; প্রকৃতি নিসর্গতঃ, (শিল্প বা শিক্ষাদ্বারা নয়)। **2.** Spontaneously; without art or artificial treatment; as, this plant grows here *naturally*; স্বতঃ, আপনাআপনি; স্বচ্ছন্দভাবে। **3.** Of course; according to usual course of things; কাজেকাজেই; স্বাভাবিক নিয়মানুসারে। **4.** In a life-like manner; as, a *naturally* painted landscape; অবিকলভাবে।

nā'-tūre, *n.* **1.** The inherent qualities of any thing; intrinsic or inborn character; as, a human *nature*; a person of a specified character; as, sanguine *natures* do not feel this; প্রকৃতি (হিঃ কোঃ); অন্তঃপ্রকৃতি, স্বাভাবিক প্রকৃতি; কোন বিশেষ প্রকৃতির লোক। **2.** Kind; species; sort; "A dispute of this *nature* caused mischief; (of guns or shot) size; জাতি, রূপ; শ্রেণী; ধরণ; (কামান বা গোলাসম্বন্ধে) আয়তন। **3.** Inherent impulses determining character or action; সহজাতপ্রবৃত্তি। **4.** The vital powers, functions or needs; as, *nature* is exhausted; জীবনীশক্তি, জীবনীক্রিয়া, দেহ রক্ষার পক্ষে অপরিহার্য্য বিষয়। **5.** Powers and agencies producing the existing phenomena; physical phenomena, as a whole; as, all *nature* looks gay; the universe; প্রকৃতি, নিসর্গ, স্বভাব; জগদ্ব্যাপার; বিশ্বসংসার, বিশ্বজগৎ। **6.** Naturalness; spontaneity; স্বাভাবিকতা; স্বতঃস্ফূর্ত্তা। **Good nature, Ill nature** — সৎপ্রকৃতি, অসৎপ্রকৃতি। **Nature myth** — যে উপাখ্যানে প্রাকৃতিক ঘটনাসমূহ রূপকচ্ছলে বর্ণিত হইয়াছে। **Nature-printing**—ধাতুফলক দ্বয়ের মধ্যে চাপ দিয়া পাতা, লেইস্, প্রভৃতির ছাপ তোলার প্রণালী বিশেষ। [সাধারণতঃ একটী তামার ও অপরটী লোহার, এই দুইটী ফলকের মধ্যে পাতা প্রভৃতি রাখিয়া চাপ দিয়া সীসার ফলকের উপর ছাপ তোলা হয় ও পরে ঐ ফলক হইতে অনেক চিত্র মুদ্রিত করা যাইতে পারে।] **Nature spirit**—বৃক্ষাদিতে আশ্রিত অপদেবতা, দেবযোনি, আধিভৌতিক দেবতা (হিঃ কোঃ)। **Nature study**—বালকবালিকাগণ যাহাতে প্রাকৃতিক পদার্থনিচয় পর্য্যবেক্ষণে পুস্তকের সাহায্য বিনা সাক্ষাৎসম্বন্ধে জীব, জন্তু, বৃক্ষলতাদির প্রকৃতি ও বিশেষত্ব সম্বন্ধে জ্ঞান লাভ করিতে পারে—তদুদ্দেশ্যে প্রবর্ত্তিত আধুনিক শিক্ষাপ্রণালী বিশেষ। এই প্রণালী অনুসারে বিদ্যালয়ের প্রাঙ্গণে ছাত্রদের সাহায্যে উদ্যান রচনা করা হয়, এবং বিদ্যালয়ে মধুমক্ষিকা, গৃহপালিত পক্ষী, প্রভৃতি রক্ষিত হইয়া

থাকে। **Nature worship**—মূর্ত্ত প্রাকৃতিক পদার্থনিচয়ের (বৃক্ষ, প্রস্তর, সূর্য্য, চন্দ্র, নদী, পর্ব্বত, প্রভৃতির) পূজা, প্রকৃতিপূজা (হিঃ কোঃ)। **Against nature** — অস্বাভাবিক; নীতিবিরুদ্ধ। **Against** or **contrary to nature** — Miraculous(ly); প্রাকৃতিক, প্রাকৃতভাবে। **By nature**—স্বভাবতঃ। **Debt of nature**—Death; মৃত্যু। **In a state of nature**—উলঙ্গ, বিবসন, বিবস্ত্র। **In nature**—সত্য সত্য বিদ্যমান; বাস্তবিক পক্ষে; কুত্রাপি, কোথাও; মোটেও। **In the course of nature**—স্বাভাবিক নিয়মবশে। **Law of nature**—প্রাকৃতিক নিয়ম, নৈসর্গিক নিয়ম, স্বভাবের নিয়ম। **Paying the debt of nature**—ভবের বাজি ভোর করণ। **State of nature**—সমাজ-প্রতিষ্ঠার পূর্ব্বে মানবের অবস্থা; জন্তু বা উদ্ভিদের বন্যাবস্থা; উলঙ্গতা। **To ease or relieve nature**—মল বা মূত্র ত্যাগ করা।

Nauclea Cadamba—কদম্ব (বেলঃ)। ***Nauclea cordifolia***—কেলিকদম্ব (বেলঃ)।

naught (nät), *n.* & *pred. adj.* **1.** (*Archaic*) Nothing; (অপ্রঃ) কিছুই না। **2.** (*Arith.*) A cipher; (পাটীগণিত) শূন্য। ***Adj.*** Worthless; useless; অসার, নগণ্য; অনর্থক। **To come to naught**—বিফল হওয়া। **To set at naught**—অকিঞ্চিৎকর বলিয়া গণ্য করা, উড়াইয়া দেওয়া, তুচ্ছ করা; অবজ্ঞা করা।

naugh'-tȳ (nä-), *adj.* **1.** Wayward; disobedient; misbehaved; একগুঁয়ে; অবাধ্য; দুরন্ত, দুষ্ট, অবিনয়ী, দুর্ব্বিনীত। **2.** Morally bad; wicked; indecent; মন্দ; দুর্জ্জন; অশ্লীল। **–ti-ly,** *adv.* **–tiness,** *n.*

nau'-se-ă (nä-shē-), *n.* **1.** Seasickness; sickness with a desire to vomit; সমুদ্রগমনজনিত বমনরোগ; উৎক্লেদ, বিবমিষা, বমনপ্রবৃত্তি। **2.** Loathing or extreme disgust; জুগুপ্সা, বিতৃষ্ণা, ঘৃণাকার, গা-বমি।

nau'-se-āte (nä-shē-), *v. t.* & *i.* **1.** To reject (food) with loathing; বমনোদ্বেগবশতঃ প্রত্যাখ্যান করা। **2.** (*Fig.*) To abhor; to feel a strong aversion to something; (লক্ষণায়) ঘৃণা করা; বিতৃষ্ণা বোধ করা, বিরাগ বোধ করা। **3.** To affect with nausea; to cause to feel disgust; বমনোদ্বেগ দ্বারা আক্রান্ত করা; বিতৃষ্ণা জন্মান। ***Verb i.*** **1.** To feel nausea; বমি বমি বোধ করা, গা বমি বমি করা। **2.** To feel disgust; বিতৃষ্ণা বোধ করা। **–at-ing,** *adj.*

nau'-se-ous (nä-shē-ŭs), *adj.* **1.** Causing nausea; বমনজনক, উদ্বামক। **2.** Nasty; unpleasant to the taste or smell; বিশ্রী, জঘন্য; বিতৃষ্ণাজনক, অরুচিকর, অপ্রীতিকর। **3.** Disgusting; exciting abhorrence; বিরক্তিজনক, জুগুপ্সিত; ঘৃণাকারজনক, ঘৃণাজনক। **–ly,** *adv.* **–ness,** *n.*

nau'-ti-căl (nä-), *adj.* Of, or pertaining to, sea-men or navigation; maritime; naval; নাবিকসম্বন্ধীয়, নৌচালনসম্বন্ধীয়; সামুদ্রিক; নৌবিভাগীয়। **–ly,** *adv.* **Nautical almanac**—নাবিকদিগের জ্ঞাতব্যবিষয়সম্বলিত পঞ্জিকা, নাবিকপঞ্চাঙ্গ (হিঃ কোঃ), নাবিকপঞ্জিকা (আঃ বঃ), পঞ্চাঙ্গ (সূর্য্যঃ বিঃ)।

nau'-ti-lŭs (nä-), *n.* **1.** A genus of cephalopodous molluscs provided with membranous expansions by which they sail, (*paper nautilus*); একজাতীয় ত্বগাধার জীব। **2.** A cephalopod with chambered shell having nacreous septa, (*pearly nautilus*); একপ্রকার শম্বুকজাতীয় প্রাণী।

nā'-văl, *adj.* **1.** Of, pertaining to, or connected with, ships or a navy; পোতসংক্রান্ত, নৌবিভাগীয়, নাব্য। **2.** Consisting of, fought, or won, by, and based on, war vessels; রণপোতসমন্বিত, রণপোতবিজিত, সমরপোতমূলক। **–ly,** *adv.* **Naval officer**—নৌবিভাগের কর্ম্মচারী, নাবিক কর্ম্মচারী। **Naval stores**—নৌবিভাগের প্রয়োজনীয় দ্রব্যসম্ভার।

nāve, *n.* The hub or piece of wood, etc. in the centre of a wheel through which the axle passes; চক্রনাভি, নাভি।

nāve, *n.* The middle, or body of a church extending from the chancel or choir to the principal entrance; খৃষ্টীয় ধর্ম্মমন্দিরের মধ্যভাগ।

nā'-vel (-vl), *n.* **1.** A depression in the middle of the abdomen, marking the point of attachment of the umbilical cord; নাভি, নাই, নাভিকুণ্ড, উদরাবর্ত্ত। [also তুণ্ডি, তুন্দিকা, মধ্যবৃত্ত, অমর, অমলা, ভর্ম্ম, তুণ্ডিকা, নাভিকমল।] **2.** The central point of anything; মধ্যবিন্দু। **Naval orange**—একপ্রকার বড় আকারের কমলালেবু—যাহার উপরিভাগে নাভির আকার গর্ত্ত থাকে। **Navel-string** — নাভিনাল, নাল। **Navel-wort**—একজাতীয় গুল্ম।

nă-vic'-ū-lar (-lėr), *adj.* & *n.* **1.** Pertaining to, or resembling, a boat or ship; পোতসম্বন্ধীয়, নৌকাসম্বন্ধীয়, নৌকাকৃতি, নৌকাকার। **2.** (Of shrines and of parts of plants or body) Boat-shaped; cymbiform; scaphoid; নৌকাকৃতি; নাবাকার (সাঃ পঃ); নৌকাকার। ***Noun.*** A disease in horse's navicular bone, (also *Navicular disease*); অশ্বের নৌকাকৃতি অস্থির রোগ-বিশেষ। **Navicular bone**—হস্তের নৌকাকৃতি অস্থি (কচিদ্ ব্যবহৃত); পদের নৌকাকৃতি অস্থি।

năv'-i-gă-ble (-bl), *adj.* **1.** Affording passage to ships; নাব্য, নৌতার্য্য, নৌযান (রাঃ তঃ) নৌগম্য। **2.** (*Obs.*) Capable of being reached by navigable water; (অপ্রঃ) নদী প্রভৃতি দ্বারা পৌঁছা যায় এরূপ। **3.** (Of balloon) Dirigible; (ব্যোমযান) ইচ্ছানুরূপ চালনীয়। **4.** (Of ships) Fit for sailing; (জাহাজ সম্পর্কে) সমুদ্রগমনোপযোগী। **–bil'-i-ty,** *n.*

năv'-ĭ-gāte, *v. i.* & *t.* To sail or manage a vessel; to make a voyage; নৌচালন করা; সমুদ্রযাত্রা করা। *Verb t.* **1.** To sail over, up or down; জাহাজে চড়িয়া যাওয়া। **2.** To direct or manage, as a ship or flying-machine; জাহাজ অথবা আকাশযান চালান।

năv-ĭ-gā'-tion, *n.* **1.** Act of navigating; নৌবাহন, নৌচালন, নৌকানয়ন, নৌকাবাহন। **2.** The science or art of sailing or managing ships; seamanship; পোতচালনবিদ্যা; নৌচালনকৌশল। **3.** (*Rare*) A voyage; (কচিদ্-ব্যবহৃত) জলযাত্রা। **Aerial navigation** — আকাশমার্গে ব্যোমযান প্রভৃতি চালনা। **Inland navigation**—দেশের নদী, খাল, প্রভৃতিতে নৌচালন। **Navigation act** or **law**—পোতচালননিয়ামক বিধি, বিশেষতঃ ১৬৪৫ খৃঃ অব্দ হইতে আরম্ভ করিয়া গ্রেটব্রিটেন এবং উপনিবেশ সমূহের নৌস্বার্থ রক্ষার্থ যে সকল আইন বিধিবদ্ধ করা হয়—তাহার অন্যতম। **Navigation-coal**—জাহাজে ব্যবহারোপযোগী কয়লা।

năv'-ĭ-gā-tor (-tẽr), *n.* **1.** One charged with, or skilled in, navigation; also, a book teaching the art of navigation; নাবিক, নৌচালন-বিশারদ-ব্যক্তি, ক্ষেপণিক; নৌচালন-সম্বন্ধীয় পুস্তক। **2.** One who conducts exploration by sea; যে ব্যক্তি নূতন দেশ আবিষ্কার উদ্দেশ্যে সমুদ্রপথে পর্য্যটন করে। **3.** A NAVVY.

năv'-vy (-i), *n.* **1.** A labourer on canals, railroads, embankments, etc.; খাল, রেলপথ, বাঁধ, প্রভৃতিতে নিযুক্ত মজুর। **2.** (Also *steam-navvy*) A machine for digging out earth etc.; মৃত্তিকাদি খননোপযোগী যন্ত্রবিশেষ।

nā'-vy̆, *n.* **1.** (*Poet.*) A fleet; (কবিতায়) রণপোতশ্রেণী। **2.** The war vessels belonging to a nation, considered collectively; the officers serving in, or composing, the crews of the navy; কোন জাতির রণপোতবহর, নৌবল, নৌসাধন (রঃ); নৌবিভাগীয় কর্ম্মচারিবৃন্দ। **3.** Same as NAVY BLUE. **Navy bill** — নৌবিভাগের হুণ্ডী। **Navy blue**—*n.* & *adj.* The dark blue used in naval uniform; নৌকর্ম্মচারিদিগের পোষাকের ঘননীলবর্ণ। (*Adj.*) (*with hyphen*) Of, or relating to, this; ঐরূপ নীলবর্ণের, ঐরূপ নীলবর্ণ-সম্বন্ধীয়। **Navy league**—নৌবিভাগের কার্য্যে জাতীয় উৎসাহ উদ্দীপনের জন্য প্রতিষ্ঠিত সম্প্রদায়বিশেষ, নৌসমিতি। **Navy list** — নাবিক কর্ম্মচারিগণের তালিকা পুস্তক।

nă-wäb', *n.* **1.** (India) A Mohammedan ruler or nobleman; নবাব। **2.** A rich retired Anglo-Indian; অবসরপ্রাপ্ত ধনবান এংলোইণ্ডিয়ান।

nay (nā), *adv.* & *n.* **1.** No; না, নহে। **2.** Not only so; not this alone; কেবল এরূপ নয়; কেবল ইহা নয়। *Noun.* A denial or refusal; a negative vote; অস্বীকৃতি; না-বাচক মত। **He will not take nay**—সে না কথা শুনিবেনা। **Nay more**—অধিকন্তু, অধিকন্তু। **To say nay**—অস্বীকার করা; অগ্রাহ্য করা; প্রতিবাদ করা। **Yea and nay**—Shilly-shally; হাঁ না, দোটানা।

Năz-ă-rene' (-rēn), *n.* & *adj.* **1.** A native or inhabitant of Nazareth; esp. Jesus Christ; নেজারেথ নগরীর অধিবাসী (এই নগরীতে যীশুখৃষ্ট শৈশবকাল যাপন করেন); বিশেষতঃ যীশুখৃষ্ট। **2.** (In Jewish and Moham. use) A Christian; খৃষ্টান। **3.** (*Eccl. Hist.*) One of a sect of early Jewish-Christians who observed the law of Moses; মুসার বিধানপালনকারী প্রাচীন ইহুদী সম্প্রদায়-বিশেষ। *Adj.* Of, or pertaining to, these early Jewish Christians; ঐ সম্প্রদায় সম্বন্ধীয়।

Năz'-ă-rīte, *n.* A native of Nazareth; নেজারেথ নগরীর অধিবাসী।

Năz'-ă-rīte, *n.* Among the ancient Hebrews a consecrated person who abstained from using wine, cutting hair and touching corpse, (*Numb.* vi.); প্রাচীন হিব্রুদের সাধু ব্যক্তি—যিনি মদ্যপান, কেশচ্ছেদন ও শবস্পর্শ করিতেন না।

nāze, *n.* A promontory; অন্তরীপ।

neap (nēp), *adj.*, *n.* & *v. i.* Low; applied to those tides, which happen in the middle of the second and fourth quarters of the moon; মৃদু; মন্দ (জোয়ার); মরা (কটাল)। *Noun.* Neap-tide; মরাকটাল, মন্দ জোয়ার। *Verb i.* **1.** (Of a tide) To reach the point of neap-tide; (জোয়ারসম্বন্ধে) কটালের উচ্চতর সীমায় উঠা। **2.** (Of tides) To tend towards the neap; (জোয়ার সম্বন্ধে) মৃদু হওয়া। **3.** (Pass., of ship) To be prevented from getting off by neaping of tides; মরাকটালের দরুণ আটক থাকা। **Neap'-ed,** *adj.* (*Naut.*) See NEAP. *v.* 3. **Neap-tide**—See NEAP *noun.*

Nē-ă-pŏl'-ĭ-tăn, *adj.* & *n.* Of, or pertaining to, Naples in Italy; ইতালীর অন্তর্গত নেপলস্ নগরসম্বন্ধীয়। *Noun.* A native or inhabitant of Naples; নেপলস্ নগরবাসী। **Neapolitan ice**—একপ্রকার মালাই বরফ—যাহা বিভিন্ন রং বা স্বাদের স্তরে বিভক্ত থাকে; একপ্রকার মিঠাই—যাহা দেখিতে ঐরূপ মালাই বরফের মত। **Neapolitan violet**—একপ্রকার পুষ্প।

near (nēr), *adv.* & *prep.* **1.** Not far distant in time, space or degree; close at hand; উপান্ত, অন্তিক, প্রত্যাসন্ন; নিকটে, কাছে, সমীপে, সন্নিধানে, গোচরে, সকাশে। **2.** Almost, (now usually expressed by *nearly*); as, he was *near* dead with fright; প্রায়, কাছাকাছি। **3.** Closely; "An heir, and *near* allied unto the duke"; নিকটতমভাবে। **3.** Thriftily; parsimoniously; "I had lived, so *near*"; মিতব্যয়িতার সহিত; কৃপণের মত। *Prep.* At no great distance from ; close to ; অদূরে, অনতিদূরে ; নিকটে, কাছে। **Far and near**—সর্ব্বত্র। **Near at hand**—নিকটবর্ত্তী, সমীপবর্ত্তী, কাছাকাছি। **Near upon**—নিকটে। **To go or come near to do, To come or go near doing**—প্রায় করিয়া ফেলা।

near (nër), *adj.* 1. Closely related or allied by blood ; নিকটসম্পর্কীয়। 2. Intimate ; as, a *near* friend ; অন্তরঙ্গ, ঘনিষ্ঠ, নিকটতম। 3. Close at hand ; not distant in time ; নিকটবর্ত্তী, সমীপবর্ত্তী, সমীপস্থ, নিকটস্থ ; আসন্ন, সন্নিহিত, অদূরবর্ত্তী। 4. (Of animals, vehicles, etc.) Left ; as, the *near* side of a horse ; (জন্তু, গাড়ী, প্রভৃতি সম্পর্কে) বাম। 5. Direct ; as, the *nearest* way ; সোজা। 6. Close ; not free ; as, a *near* guess, escape, or translation ; কাছাকাছি, অল্পের জন্য ; আক্ষরিক। 7. Niggardly ; stingy ; কৃপণ ; কঞ্জুষ, হাতটান। **Near'-ish**, *adj.* Rather near ; অনেকটা নিকটে। **Near'-ness**, *n.* **Near east, Far east**—See under EAST. **Near-sighted** — অদূরদর্শী। **Near work**—যে কাজ চোক খুব নিকটে রাখিয়া করিতে হয়। **Near and dear**—অতি অন্তরঙ্গ। **The near side of a horse**—See NEAR *adj.* 3. **To be near**—কৃপণ হওয়া, ব্যয়কুণ্ঠ হওয়া।

near (nër), *v. i. & t.* To come near (*to*) ; to approach ; নিকটে আসা ; সন্নিহিত হওয়া।

Ne-ărc'-tic, *adj.* (*Zool.*) Of, or relating to, the arctic and temperate part of North America ; (জন্তু-বিজ্ঞান) উত্তর আমেরিকার মেরু বা সমশীতোষ্ণমণ্ডলের অন্তর্গত অংশ-সমূহ সম্বন্ধীয়।

near'-lȳ (nër-), *adv.* 1. Closely ; with careful scrutiny ; as, examine it *nearly* ; পুঙ্খানুপুঙ্খরূপে ; তন্ন তন্ন করিয়া। 2. Almost ; প্রায়, কাছাকাছি। 3. Intimately ; অন্তরঙ্গভাবে, ঘনিষ্ঠভাবে। **Not nearly**—কাছাকাছিও নয়।

neat (nēt), *n.* (*Sing. and collectively as pl.*) 1. An animal of the ox-kind ; বৃষজাতীয় জন্তু-বিশেষ। 2. (*Collect.*) Cattle ; গো মহিষাদি। **Neat-herd**—Cowherd ; গোপালক। **Neat house**—গোশালা। **Neat's-foot, Neat's-tongue** — খাদ্যস্বরূপ ব্যবহৃত বৃষভের পদ বা জিহ্বা। **Neat's-leather**—বৃষচর্ম্ম।

neat (nēt), *adj.* 1. Free from admixture ; (of liquor, esp. alcoholic) undiluted ; খাঁটী ; (মদ্য সম্বন্ধে) অজলমিশ্রিত। 2. Orderly and cleanly ; tidy ; nicely made ; as, a *neat* person, animal or furniture ; পরিষ্কার, পরিচ্ছন্ন ; ফিটফাট ; পরিপাটী, ঝর ঝরে। 3. Simply elegant ; chaste ; epigrammatic (said of style etc.) ; প্রাঞ্জল ; বিশুদ্ধ ; অল্পাক্ষরেগ্রথিত। 4. Dexterous ; clever ; cleverly executed ; as, a *neat* thief : a *neat* retort ; দক্ষ ; নিপুণ ; নিপুণভাবে সম্পন্ন। 5. Methodical ; সুশৃঙ্খল, গোছালো। **Neat'-ly**, *adv.* **Neat'-ness**, *n.* **Neat-handed**—নিপুণ ; দক্ষ। **Neat-handed Phillis**—যে বালিকা ভোজনকালে পরিবেষণ করে। **Neat as a band box**—তোলা কাপড়ের মত পরিষ্কার। **Neat as a pin** — তক তকে, ঝক ঝকে।

neath (nēth), *prep.* (*Poet.*) Beneath ; (কবিতায়) নীচে।

nĕb, *n.* 1. The beak of a bird ; চঞ্চু। 2. The nose ; a snout ; নাক ; লম্বিত মুখ। 3. (*Dial.*) The mouth ; (উপভাষায়) মুখ। 4. A tip, point or spout ; as, the *neb* of a screw ; সূক্ষ্মাগ্রভাগ, মুখ, মুখনল।

nĕb'-ū-lă, *n.* (*Pl.* -LÆ) 1. A white spot on the cornea causing defective sight ; ঈষৎ শুক্লমেঘের ন্যায় চক্ষুর তারকার একপ্রকার অস্বচ্ছতা, শুক্লপট, নীহারিকা (হঃ চঃ)। 2. (*Astron.*) A faint luminous patch made by a cluster of distant stars or by gaseous or stellar matter outside the solar system ; অতি দূরবর্ত্তী মেঘাকার নক্ষত্রপুঞ্জ, নীহারিকা।

nĕb'-ū-lar (-lēr), *adj.* Of, or pertaining to, nebula(e) ; নীহারিকা সম্বন্ধীয়। **Nebular theory or hypothesis**—Laplace এবং Sir William Herschel কর্ত্তৃক প্রবর্ত্তিত মতবাদ—এই মতানুসারে নীহারিকা তারাসমূহের আদিম অবস্থা, নীহারিকাবাদ, বাষ্পারম্ভবাদ (হিঃ কোঃ), নীহারিকাসিদ্ধান্ত (ঐ)।

nē-bū'-li-ŭm, *n.* An element whose existence in nebulæ is inferred from two characteristic green lines in their spectra ; নীহারিকায় বর্ত্তমান মূলপদার্থ বিশেষ—এই পদার্থের বর্ণচ্ছত্রে দৃষ্ট দুইটী হরিদ্বর্ণ রেখা হইতে নীহারিকায় ইহার সত্তা অনুমিত হয়।

nĕb'-ū-lous (-lŭs), *adj.* 1. (*Astron.*) Of, pertaining to, or resembling, nebula ; নীহারিকাসম্বন্ধীয়, নীহারিকাবৎ। 2. Cloud-like ; "*Nebulous* images" ; মেঘবৎ, মেঘতুল্য, নীহারপ্রতিম। 3. (*Fig.*) Hazy ; vague ; "*Nebulous* disquisition on religion" ; (লক্ষণায়) ঝাপ্সা, ঘোরালো ; অস্পষ্ট। 4. Clouded ; turbid ; "The *nebulous* ulcer" ; মলিন ; সমল। **-los'-i-ty**, *n.* **Nebulous star**—নীহারিকা-নক্ষত্র, উজ্জ্বল নাক্ষত্রিকগর্ভ বিন্দুবিশিষ্ট ক্ষুদ্র গোলাকৃতি নীহারিকা খণ্ড।

nĕc-ĕs-să'-ri-ăn, *n. & adj.* Same as NECESSITARIAN. **-ism**, *n.*

nĕc'-ĕs-să-ri-lȳ, *adv.* As a necessary result ; by necessity ; indispensably ; অবশ্যম্ভাবিফলস্বরূপ ; অবশ্য ; অপরিহার্য্যরূপে, অলঙ্ঘনীয়রূপে।

nĕc'-ĕs-să-rȳ, *adj. & n.* 1. Indispensable ; requisite ; অনিবার্য্য, অনন্যথাসিদ্ধ, অপরিহার্য্য ; আবশ্যক, প্রয়োজনীয়। 2. Not to be avoided ; inevitable ; অপরিহার্য্য ; অবশ্যম্ভাবী, অবশ্য ভবিতব্য। 3. Having no independent volition, as an agent ; determined by predestination ; inevitably produced by previous state of things ; involuntary ;

স্বাধীন-ইচ্ছাবিহীন ; বিধিবশ, দৈবাধীন ; বিধিকৃত ; অনিচ্ছাপ্রসূত। *Noun.* 1. That which is indispensable ; an essential or requisite; অপরিহার্য্য বস্তু ; আবশ্যক দ্রব্যসম্ভার, সরঞ্জাম। 2. (*Loosely*) A desirable thing not generally regarded as a luxury ; আবশ্যক বস্তু। 3. (*Slang*) That which is needful ; specifically, the necessary funds or money (with *the* prefixed) ; (ইতর ভাষায়) আবশ্যক বিষয়; বিশেষতঃ প্রয়োজনীয় অর্থ। **Necessary house**—A privy ; পায়খানা। **Necessary truths**—অপরিহার্য্য সত্য।

nē-cĕs-si-tā'-ri-ăn (-ĭ-), *adj.* & *n.* Denying free-will and maintaining that all action is determined by antecedent cause ; মানবীয় ইচ্ছার কোন প্রকার স্বাধীনতা নাই এবং মানবজীবনের যাবতীয় ব্যাপারই নিয়তির অলঙ্ঘনীয় বিধানে সংঘটিত হইয়া থাকে—এইরূপ মতবাদী, অদৃষ্টবাদী, দৈববাদী। *Noun.* A person of this opinion ; অদৃষ্টবাদী ব্যক্তি, নিয়তিবাদী ব্যক্তি। **—ism,** *n.*

nē-cĕs'-si-tāte (-ĭ-), *v. t.* 1. To make necessary ; to demand or involve as a condition or result ; প্রয়োজনীয় করা ; অবশ্যপালনীয় করা, অবশ্যকর্ত্তব্য করা। 2. (*Rare*) To force ; to compel ; (ক্বচিদ্ ব্যবহৃত) বলপ্রয়োগে বাধ্য করা ; বাধ্য করা।

nē-cĕs'-si-tous (-ĭ-tŭs), *adj.* Poor ; needy ; indigent ; দরিদ্র ; অভাবগ্রস্ত ; দীন, কাঙ্গাল।

nē-cĕs'-si-tȳ (-ĭ-), *n.* 1. Irresistible compulsion, either physical or moral ; fate ; আবশ্যকতা, অনিবার্য্য বাধ্যতা, অবশ্যতা ; নিয়তি (হিঃ কোঃ)। 2. Compulsive force of circumstances or state of things ; আবশ্যকতা। 3. (*Philos.*) The principle of universal or uniform causation,—contrasted with *chance* ; (দর্শন-শাস্ত্র) বিশ্বজনীন কারণতত্ত্ব। 4. Inevitableness ; indispensability ; অপরিহার্য্যতা ; অনিবার্য্যতা, অবশ্যকর্ত্তব্যতা, অলঙ্ঘনীয়তা, অবশ্যম্ভাবিতা। 5. Imperative need : as, *necessity* is the mother of invention ; প্রয়োজন, গরজ, আবশ্যক। 6. A necessary or indispensable thing ; আবশ্যক বা অপরিহার্য্য বিষয়। 7. (*Usu. pl.*) Indigence ; want ; দৈন্য, দারিদ্র্য, নির্ধনতা ; অভাব। **Logical necessity**—যাহার বিপরীত কল্পনা অসম্ভব তাহা বিশ্বাস করার বাধ্যতা। **Necessity has no law**—গরজ বড় বালাই, অকালে কি না খায়। **Necessity is the mother of invention**—অপরিহার্য্য প্রয়োজন হইতেই নব নব বস্তুর উদ্ভাবন হয়। **Of necessity**—Unavoidably ; অপরিহার্য্যরূপে, অলঙ্ঘনীয়রূপে, অত্যাবশ্যকরূপে। **To make a virtue of necessity**—উড়ো খই গোবিন্দায় নমঃ করা, হোঁচট খেয়ে প্রণাম করা, হোঁচট পড়ে পদ্মনাভ বলা, উড়তে না পেরে পোষ মানা। **Works of necessity**—অত্যাবশ্যক কাজ—যাহা রবিবারেও করিতে হয়।

nĕck, *n.* 1. The part of the body that connects the head with shoulders ; গ্রীবা, ঘাড়, গরদান (*colloq.*), গলা, গলদেশ। 2. The part of a garment covering, or nearest to, the neck ; পরিচ্ছদের গ্রীবাচ্ছাদক অংশ। 3. Flesh of animal's neck, as food ; জন্তুর গ্রীবার মাংস। 4. The narrow slender part of a vessel, esp. of bottle, tube, etc. or of a fruit, etc. ; বোতল প্রভৃতির গলা। 5 A pass ; an isthmus ; a channel ; also, the narrow part of a pass, channel or passage ; গিরিসঙ্কট ; ভূকন্ধরা ; প্রণালী ; বর্ত্ম, প্রণালী বা গিরিসঙ্কটের সঙ্কীর্ণ অংশ। 6. A narrow connecting part between two parts of a thing ; উভয় অংশ সংযোজক অপরিসর অংশ। 7. (*Anat.*) The constricted part of an organ ; as the *neck* of the uterus ; (শারীর-সংস্থান-বিদ্যা) কোন অঙ্গের সঙ্কুচিত অংশ। 8. (*Arch.*) The part of a column which serves to connect the capital with its body ; (স্থপতি-বিজ্ঞান) স্তম্ভের যে অংশ দ্বারা বোধিকা স্তম্ভবপুর সহিত সংযুক্ত থাকে। **Necked,** *adj.* **Neck-band**—জামার গলবেষ্টনী। **Neckcloth**—গলবস্ত্র, গলবন্ধ, কণ্ঠাবরণবস্ত্র, কণ্ঠবস্ত্র। **Neckerchief**—গলাতে জড়াইবার রুমাল। **Necklace**—কণ্ঠভূষণ, কণ্ঠহার, কণ্ঠমালা ; (of jewels) রত্নমালা, রত্নমালিকা, রত্নহার, মণিমালিকা, মণিহার ; (of beads) অক্ষমালা, জপমালা ; (of pearls) মুক্তামালা, মুক্তালতা, মুক্তাবলী, মুক্তাস্রজ, মুক্তাকলাপ (কুমারঃ), মুক্তাহার উরঃসূত্রিকা (one hanging on the breast)। (A pearl necklace of 32 or of 70 strings) গুচ্ছ (বৃঃ সং) ; (Do. of 24 strings) গুচ্ছার্দ্ধ ; (Do. of 16 or 24 strings) অর্দ্ধগুচ্ছ ; (Do. of 100 or 103 or 81 or 108 strings) দেবচ্ছন্দ (বৃঃ সং) ; (Do. of 100 strings) শতযষ্টিক ; (Do. of 4 strings) গোস্তন ; (Do. of 40 or 64 strings) অর্দ্ধহার ; (Do. of 16 strings) মাণবক (বৃং সং) ; (Do. of one string) একাবলী ; (Do. of 27 pearls) নক্ষত্রমালা, নক্ষত্রমালিকা ; *The central gem of necklace*—তরল, হারমধ্যমণি (মঃ ভাঃ) ; *A long necklace depending from the neck to the navel*—লম্বন ললন্তিকা ; *A necklace hanging down to the breast*—প্রালম্বিকা। **Necktie**—গলদেশে দোদুল্যমান রেশম প্রভৃতি বস্ত্রের খণ্ড, গলবন্ধ। **Neck-verse**—পূর্ব্বে পাণ্ডিত্যের পরীক্ষার জন্য যে শ্লোক পাঠ করান হইত। **A stiff neck**—(*Script.*) Stubbornness in sin ; পাপকার্য্যে একগুঁয়েমি। **Neck and crop**—সম্পূর্ণরূপে; সশরীরে; উদ্দামভাবে। **Neck and heels**—Same as NECK AND CROP. Securely ; as, to tie one's *neck and heels* ; আঁটসাঁট করিয়া। **Neck and neck**—Side by side ; close together (of two competitors in a race etc.) ; সমান

সমান; ঘেঁষাঘেঁষি, খুব কাছাকাছি। **Neck or nothing**—মরিয়া হইয়া; (লক্ষণায়) প্রাণপণ করিয়া। **On the neck of**—অব্যবহিত পরে, পিছু পিছু। **To break one's neck**—ঘাড়ভাঙ্গা; ঘাড় ভাঙ্গিয়া মারা। **To break the neck of a task, etc.**—কোন কাজের কঠিন ভাগ সাধন করা। **To harden the neck**—মগরা বা বিদ্রোহী হওয়া। **To lay on the neck of**—কাহারো ঘাড়ে চাপান, কাহারো ঘাড়ে ফেলা। **To risk one's neck**—নিজের জীবন পণ করা। **To save one's neck**—To escape hanging; ফাঁসীকাঠ হইতে রক্ষা পাওয়া। **To throw one's neck and crop**—অর্দ্ধচন্দ্র দিয়া বিদায় করা। **To tread on the neck**—পদদলিত করা, পদপিষ্ট করা; দলন করা।

něck, *v. t.* To stun or kill by striking on the neck; to pull the neck of, as a fowl etc.; ঘাড়ে আঘাত করিয়া স্তব্ধ বা বিনাশ করা; ঘাড় ছিঁড়িয়া ফেলা।

něck, *n.* The last sheaf of corn cut at harvest-time; শস্যচ্ছেদন কালের সকলের শেষে কাটা আঁটি।

něck'-ing, *n.* (*Arch.*) The part of a column between the shaft and the capital; (স্থপতিবিদ্যা) স্তম্ভবপু এবং বোধিকার মধ্যবর্ত্তী স্তম্ভাংশ।

něck'-lět *n.* A necklace; something worn round the neck for warmth; কণ্ঠমালিক; গলায় জড়াইবার গরম কাপড়।

něc-rŏ-bi-ō'-sis, *n.* (*Med.*) Decay in tissues of the body; (ভৈষজ্যশাস্ত্র) শরীরের বিধানতন্তুর ক্ষয়।

něc-rŏ-gěn'-ic, *adj.* Produced by contact with dead bodies; শবস্পর্শজ।

něc-rŏl'-ŏ-ġy, *n.* **1.** Death-roll, especially ecclesiastical; মৃত্যুতালিকা (বিশেষতঃ যাজকগণের)। **2.** An obituary notice; সংবাদপত্রে মৃত্যুর উল্লেখ।

něc'-rŏ-măn-cy̆, *n.* The art of revealing the future by pretended communication with the spirits of the dead; magic; enchantment; মৃত ব্যক্তির প্রেতাত্মার সহিত সংযোগস্থাপনপূর্ব্বক ভবিষ্যৎকথনের প্রণালী, পিশাচসিদ্ধি, প্রেতসিদ্ধি, শ্মশানতন্ত্র (হিঃ কোঃ), পিশাচবিদ্যা; যাদু, ইন্দ্রজাল; মায়া, কুহক। **—cer,** *n.* **—man'-tic,** *adj.*

něc-rŏph'-ă-gous (-gŭs), *adj.* Feeding on carrion; শবভোজী, গলিতপশুদেহভোজী।

něc-rŏp'-ŏ-lis, *n.* Cemetery; কবরখানা।

něc'-rŏp-sy̆, —rŏs'-cŏ-py̆, *ns.* Post-mortem examination; শবব্যবচ্ছেদ।

něc-rō'-sis, *n.* The death of circumscribed piece of tissue, esp. mortification of bones; যে রোগে বিধানতন্তু বা অস্থির অংশ মৃত বা নষ্ট হয়, অস্থিনাশ (হঃ চঃ) অস্থিপুত্ত (ডাহিঃ)। **—rot'-ic,** *adj.*

něc'-rŏ-tize, *v. i.* & *t.* To undergo, or affect with, necrosis; অস্থি ক্ষয় হওয়া, অস্থি রোগাক্রান্ত করা বা হওয়া।

něc'-târ, *n.* **1.** (*Gr. Myth.*) The drink of the gods which was imagined to contribute much towards eternal existence; (গ্রীকপুরাণ) অমৃত, সুধা, পীযূষ, অমিয় (poet), সুধারস। **2.** Any delicious drink; সুস্বাদু পানীয়। **3.** (*Bot.*) The sweet liquid or honey of flowers, esp. as collected by bees; মকরন্দ, পুষ্পরস, পুষ্পমধু, ফুলের মধু। **4.** A kind of ærated water; অঙ্গারাম্লবাষ্পসম্পূরিত পানীয়-বিশেষ। **—if'-er-ous,** *adj.* (*Bot.*) Secreting nectar; মকরন্দস্রাবী। **—ous, —ta'-re-an, —tared, —ta'-re-ous,** *adjs.*

něc'-târ-ine, *adj.* Relating to, or resembling, nectar; sweet as nectar; অমৃতসম্বন্ধীয়, সুধাসম্বন্ধীয়, অমৃতসদৃশ, অমৃততুল্য; অমৃতমধুর।

něc'-târ-ine, *n.* A kind of the common peach; একপ্রকার পীচ ফল।

něc'-tă-ry̆ *n.* (*Bot.*) A gland or organ that secretes nectar; (উদ্ভিদবিদ্যা) মকরন্দস্রাবী গ্রন্থি বা অঙ্গ।

nĕd, *n.* (*Slang*) A guinea; (ইতরভাষায়) একজাতীয় অম্লফল, সকরগুল। **To make one's ned out of**—কোন কিছু হইতে টাকা করা।

Něd'-dy (-ĭ), *n.* A donkey, (dim. of the proper name Edward); গর্দ্দভ, গাধা।

nee, (*F.*), *adj.* Born, (used in adding a woman's maiden name; as, *Mrs. Smith nee Jones*); জাত। [বিবাহিতা নারীর কুমারী-নামের পূর্ব্বে ব্যবহৃত হয়]।

need (nēd), *n.* **1.** Necessity arising from facts or circumstances; as, if *need* be; আবশ্যক, প্রয়োজনীয়তা। **2.** Imperative demand for presence or possession; আবশ্যকতা। **3.** Urgent want; emergency; জরুরি দরকার; গুরুতর প্রয়োজন। **4.** Destitution; poverty; নিঃস্বতা; দৈন্য। **5.** A thing wanted; a requirement; প্রার্থিত বিষয়; আবশ্যক বিষয়। **6.** (*Dial., pl.*) Offices of nature; as, to do one's *needs*; (উপভাষায়) মলমূত্র ক্রিয়া। **Need'-i-ness,** *n.* **Need'-y,** *adj.* **Need-fire**—ঘর্ষণ দ্বারা শুষ্ক কাষ্ঠে উৎপন্ন অগ্নি। **A friend in need is a friend indeed**—অসময়ের বন্ধুই প্রকৃত বন্ধু। **At need**—সঙ্কটে, অভাবে। **Had need**—Ought to; as, you *had need* remember; উচিত হওয়া। **In need**—অভাবগ্রস্ত। **More than needs**—আবশ্যকের অতিরিক্ত। **Needs make the old wife trot, Needs make the naked queen skin**—গরজে গয়লা ঢেলা বয়। **To have need of**—আবশ্যক হওয়া, দরকার হওয়া। **To have need to**—আবশ্যক হওয়া। **To stand in need of**—দরকার থাকা, চাওয়া।

need (nēd), *v. i.* & *t.* (*Never used with a personal nominative*) **1.** To be necessary; আবশ্যক হওয়া, আবশ্যক করা। **2.** To be in need or want; আবশ্যক হওয়া। **3.** To be under necessity or obligation *to* do something ; কোন কিছু করিতে বাধ্য হওয়া। ***Verb t.*** To require ; to want ; আবশ্যক হওয়া ; দরকার হওয়া।

need'-fûl (nēd-), *adj.* Necessary ; requisite ; আবশ্যক ; আবশ্যকানুরূপ। **—ly**, *adv.* **—ness**, *n.* **The needful**—আবশ্যক ; (ইতরভাষায়) আবশ্যক অর্থ; নগদ টাকা। **To do the needful** — (*Foot-ball*) To convert try into goal ; রাগবী ফুটবল খেলার প্রতিদ্বন্দ্বিদলের গোল লাইনের পশ্চাতে বল স্পর্শ করিলে যে সুবিধা পাওয়া হয় তাহার দরুণ বল ইপ্সিত স্থানে রাখার পর পদাঘাত করিয়া গোল করা ; আবশ্যক কার্য্য করা।

nee'-dle (nē-dl), *n., v. t.* & *i.* **1.** An instrument for interweaving thread ; সূচিকা, সূচ, সূচী, সীবনী। **2.** A piece of magnetized steel used as an indicator on dial of a compass and magnetic and electric apparatus, esp. in telegraphy ; চুম্বকশলাকা, অয়স্কান্তশলাকা, দিগ্‌দর্শন ফলকের দিঙ্‌নির্ণায়ক শলাকা। **3.** A strip of standard gold or silver used with a touchstone in testing the purity of other pieces of those metals ; চাসনির সোনা বা রূপা। **4.** A pointed instrument used in engraving or etching ; খোদাই প্রভৃতি কার্য্যে ব্যবহৃত একপ্রকার সূক্ষ্মাগ্র যন্ত্র। **5.** The sharpened end of a syringe ; পিচকারীর সূক্ষ্মাগ্র প্রান্ত। **6.** A pointed surgical instrument used in operations ; অস্ত্রোপচারকার্য্যে ব্যবহৃত সূক্ষ্মাগ্র শলাকা। **7.** A steel pin exploding the cartridge of a breechloader ; যে ইস্পাতের শঙ্কু দ্বারা বন্দুকের টোটা সশব্দে বিদীর্ণ হয়। **8.** Any slender pointed object, like a needle, as a pointed crystal, a leaf of a pine or fir ; a sharp pinnacle of rock, obelisk, etc. ; সূচ্যাগ্র বস্তু, সরল প্রভৃতি বৃক্ষের সূচিবৎ পত্র; পাষাণাদির সূক্ষ্মাগ্রস্তম্ভ, প্রভৃতি। **9.** A beam used as a temporary support for a work during und r-pinning ; খুঁটার উপর শয়ান ভাবে বিধৃত যে কাষ্ঠ প্রভৃতির ফলকের উপর প্রাচীরাদির ভিত্তিস্বরূপ প্রস্তর-শ্রেণী প্রভৃতি স্থাপন বা জীর্ণসংস্কারকালে প্রাচীর প্রভৃতি আশ্রিত থাকে, সূচীকাষ্ঠ। ***Verb t.*** **1.** To sew with a needle ; সূচদ্বারা সেলাই করা। **2.** To pierce or operate on with, or as with, a needle ; সূচদ্বারা ভেদ করা, সূচদ্বারা কাজ করা। **3.** To push (something) through, like a needle ; as, "He used to *needle* a stick between his legs" ; to thread as one's way ; সূচের মত ঢুকান ; আপন পথ চলা। **4.** To underpin with needle ; সূচিকাষ্ঠের সাহায্যে প্রাচীরাদির অবলম্বনস্বরূপ পাষাণফলকশ্রেণী প্রভৃতি স্থাপন বা সংস্কার করা। **5.** (*Slang*) To vex ; (ইতর ভাষায়) বিরক্ত করা। ***Verb i.*** **1.** To crystallize in the form of needles ; সূচের আকার দানা বাঁধা। **2.** To thread one's way ; নিজের পথে চলা। **Handled-needle**—সমুষ্টি-সূচিকা। **Needle-bath**—যে স্নানমন্দির হইতে অতি সূক্ষ্ম জলধারা নির্গত হয়। **Needle-book**—পুস্তকের আকার সূচের আধার। **Needle case**—সূচ রাখার আধার। **Needle-fish**—কাইকা মাছ, কাইকলা মাছ। **Needleful**—একবারে যতটা দৈর্ঘ্যের সূত্র সূচে ভরা যায়। **Needle-gun** — একপ্রকার বন্দুক— যাহার টোটা সূচের আকার লোহার সহিত অভিঘাতে সশব্দে বিদীর্ণ হয়, সূচীনালিকাস্ত্র। **Needle's-eye**—সূচী-রন্ধ্র। **Needle-lace**—সূচে তৈয়ারী লেইস। **Needle point**—সূচ্যগ্র ; সূচদ্বারা তৈয়ারী একপ্রকার অতি সূক্ষ্ম লেইস। **Needle-woman**—যে স্ত্রীলোক সূচীকর্ম্মদ্বারা জীবিকা নির্ব্বাহ করে। **Needle-work**—সূচীকর্ম্ম, সীবন, সূত্রকর্ম্ম ; সূচিকর্ম্মকারিণী স্ত্রীলোকের কাজ। **Straight-needle**—সরলসূচিকা। **To get the needle**—বিরক্ত হওয়া, উত্তেজিত হওয়া। **To hit the needle**—ঠিক জায়গা মত লাগান। **To look for a needle in a bottle of hay**—See under BOTTLE.

need'-lĕss (nēd-), *adj.* Unnecessary ; useless ; uncalled for ; নিষ্প্রয়োজন, নিরর্থক ; অনাবশ্যক, অনর্থক ; অকারণ। **—ly**, *adv.* **—ness**, *n.* **Needless to say**—বলা অনাবশ্যক, বলা বাহুল্য।

need'-mĕnts (nēd-), *n.* (*Pl.*), Things needed ; esp. personal necessaries carried on a journey ; আবশ্যক বস্তু, প্রয়োজনীয় বস্তু ; বিদেশে ভ্রমণকালে সঙ্গে যে মালপত্র নেওয়া হয়।

needs (nēdz), *adv.* Necessarily ; indispensably, (often with *must*) ; "It *needs must* fit"; জরুর ; অবশ্যই। **Must needs do**—Foolishly insists, or insisted, on doing ; সে করিতে চাহিবেই, ঐটা করার জন্য নির্ব্বোধের মত জেদ করিয়াছিল। **Needs must do**—না করিয়া চারা নাই, অবশ্যই করিতে হইবে। **Needs must when the Devil drives**—গরজ বড় বালাই, দায়ে পড়িলে সবই করিতে হয়।

need'-ȳ (nēd-), *adj.* Indigent ; poor ; নিঃস্ব ; দীন, দরিদ্র।

ne'er (nâr), *adv.* (*Poet.*) Never ; (কবিতায়) কখনও না। **Ne'er a**—একটীও নয়। **Ne'er-do-well, —weel**—অকর্ম্মণ্য (লোক), নচ্ছার।

nē-fâ'-ri-ous (-ŭs), *adj.* Wicked ; iniquitous ; infamous ; দুষ্ট, দুঃশীল ; দুর্বৃত্ত ; অকীর্ত্তিকর, কলঙ্কিত। **—ly**, *adv.* **—ness**, *n.*

nē-gāte', *v. t.* To deny or contradict ; to prove non-existence ; to nullify ; to be the negation of ; অস্বীকার করা, প্রতিবাদ করা ; অনস্তিত্ব প্রমাণ করা ; বাতিল করা ; প্রতিষেধস্বরূপ হওয়া।

nē-gā'-tion, *n.* **1.** Act of denying or contradicting ; প্রতিষেধ, নিষেধ, প্রত্যাখ্যান। **2.** A negative statement or doctrine ; a refusal or contradiction ; নিষেধাত্মক উক্তি, নিষেধবাচক উক্তি ; অস্বীকৃতি, প্রতিষেধ, প্রতিবাদ। **3.** (*Log.*) Description or definition by denial, exclusion or exception; (তর্ক-বিজ্ঞান) অস্বীকৃতি, অপাকরণ, অপবাদ প্রভৃতি দ্বারা বর্ণন বা সংজ্ঞা প্রদান, ব্যতিরেক। 4. Absence or opposite of something actual or positive; "Death in this case would be simply sudden *negation* of life"; কোন বাস্তব বা প্রকৃত বিষয়ের অভাব বা বিপরীতাবস্থা, অনস্তিত্ব, অভাব (হিঃ কোঃ)। 5. Scepticism or denial of reality; সংশয়বাদ, বাস্তবতা-প্রত্যাখ্যান। 6. Negative or unreal thing; অসৎ বস্তু, মায়িক বস্তু।

nē-gā'-tion-ist, *n.* One who denies accepted belief without proposing substitutes; যে ব্যক্তি প্রচলিত ধর্ম্ম প্রভৃতি অস্বীকার করে পরন্তু তৎপরিবর্ত্তে কোন নূতন মত প্রতিষ্ঠা করে না, নাস্তিবাদী।

nĕg'-ă-tive (-tĭv), *adj.* 1. Implying, or containing denial or negation; refusing assent; অস্বীকার-সূচক; নিষেধবাচক। 2. Wanting positive attributes; privative; as, a *negative* virtue (abstention from wrong-doing); অভাবাত্মক, অভাব-জ্ঞাপক; নেতিবাচক (রবীঃ), নাস্তিগর্ভ (ঐ), নিষেধাত্মক (হিঃ কোঃ), অস্বীকার-সূচক। 3. (*Math.*) A negative quantity or symbol; (গণিত-শাস্ত্র) ঋণাত্মক রাশি বা চিহ্ন। 4. (Of electricity) Produced by friction upon resin, wax, guttapercha or similar substance; containing or producing such electricity; (তাড়িত-সম্পর্কে) ধূনা, মোম, অথবা তদ্বৎ পদার্থের উপর ঘর্ষণদ্বারা জাত; উক্তরূপ তাড়িতময়, উক্তরূপ তাড়িতগর্ভ। 5. Of opposite nature to a thing regarded as positive; as, debt is *negative* capital; ঋণাত্মক। 6. (*Photog.*) Having the lights and shades and the relation of right and left of the actual or original, reversed; (আলোকচিত্র) মূলচিত্রের বাম ও দক্ষিণ এবং আলো ও ছায়া বিপর্য্যস্তভাবে স্থিত। **—ly,** *adv.* **—ness,** *n.* **—tiv'-i-ty,** *n.* **Negative electricity**—See NEGATIVE *adj.* 4. ঋণাত্মকতাড়িত, ঋণবিদ্যুৎ (হিঃ কোঃ)। **Negative instance or evidence**—কোন ব্যাপার অঘটনের দৃষ্টান্ত বা প্রমাণ। **Negative pregnant**—(আইন) যে প্রত্যাখ্যান দ্বারা সম্মতিসূচক বাক্য সূচিত হইতে পারে। **Negative proposition** — (তর্ক-বিজ্ঞান) ব্যতিরেকী প্রতিজ্ঞা। **Negative quantity**—(চলিত ভাষায়) কিছুই নয়। (গণিত-শাস্ত্র) ঋণাত্মক রাশি। **Negative sign** — বিয়োগচিহ্ন। **Negative virtue**—কুকার্য্য হইতে নিবৃত্তি। **Negative voice**—অগ্রাহ্য বা প্রতিষেধ করার অধিকার। **Negative causes of dissatisfaction**—অকরণজনিত পাপ।

nĕg'-ă-tive (-tĭv), *n.* 1. A negative reply, statement, etc.; না-বাচক উত্তর, উক্তি প্রভৃতি। 2. A refusal or withholding of assent; a right of veto; অস্বীকৃতি; অগ্রাহ্য করার অধিকার। 3. A word that denies, as *not, no*; অস্বীকৃতিবাচক শব্দ, নিষেধার্থক শব্দ। 4. A negative quality; want of something; as, his character is made up of *negatives*; অভাবাত্মক গুণ; অভাব, অসদ্ভাব। 5. (*Math.*) A negative or minus quantity; (গণিতশাস্ত্র) ঋণাত্মক সংখ্যা। 6. (*Photog.*) A photographic picture on glass in in which the lights and shades are the opposite of those in nature; (আলোকচিত্র) কাচফলকের উপর গৃহীত আলোকচিত্র — যাহাতে আলো ও ছায়ার সন্নিবেশ স্বভাবের বিপরীত হইয়া থাকে। অর্থাৎ স্বাভাবিক চিত্রের সাদা জায়গা কালো এবং কালো জায়গা সাদা হইয়া থাকে, বিপর্য্যস্তচিত্র। 7. (*Elec.*) The negative plate or metal in a voltaic battery; ভলেটেইক বিদ্যুৎ কুম্ভমালার ঋণাত্মক ধাতু বা ফলক। **In the negative**—অস্বীকৃতিসূচক বাক্যে। **The proposal was decided in the negative**—প্রস্তাব অগ্রাহ্য হইয়াছিল।

nĕg'-ă-tive (-tĭv), *v. t.* 1. To veto; to reject by vote; to refuse to accept or sanction; অগ্রাহ্য বা প্রতিষেধ করা; ভোট দ্বারা অগ্রাহ্য করা; প্রত্যাখ্যান করা, অস্বীকার করা। 2. To disprove, as a hypothesis, inference, etc.; অপ্রমাণ করা, অসত্য বলিয়া প্রমাণ করা। 3. To contradict; to deny; প্রতিবাদ করা; অস্বীকার করা। 4. To neutralize (effect); ব্যর্থ করা, অকার্য্যকর করা।

nĕg'-ă-tiv-ĭsm, *n.* The doctrines of one who holds sceptical or agnostic views, or of one who denies reality, esp. of the phenomenal universe; নাস্তিকতা, নিরীশ্বরবাদ, মায়াবাদ। **—ist,** *n.*

nĕg'-ă-tō-rў, *adj.* Expressing denial or refusal; denying; অস্বীকৃতিসূচক; প্রতিষেধাত্মক।

nĕg-lĕct', *v. t.* & *n.* 1. To slight; not to notice; তুচ্ছ করা, অবজ্ঞা করা; তাচ্ছিল্য করা, উপেক্ষা করা, অগ্রাহ্য করা। 2. To leave unattended to or uncared for; অবহেলা করা, অনাদর করা। 3. To leave undone; to omit *to* do; অসম্পন্ন রাখা; না করা। ***Noun.*** 1. Act of neglecting; state of being neglected; উপেক্ষণ; অনাদৃতাবস্থা। 2. Disregard *of* something; উপেক্ষা, অবহেলা, অনাদর। 3. Omission of proper attention; negligence; অবহেলা, ব্যতিক্রম; তাচ্ছিল্য, ত্রুটি। **—a-ble,** *adj.* (*Rare*) **—ed,** *adj.* **—ful,** *adj.* **—ful-ly,** *adv.* **—ful-ness,** *n.* **Not to be neglected**—অবহেলার বিষয় নয়, ফেলিবার নয়।

nĕg-li-ge' (-lē-zhā), *n.* An easy or unceremonious dress; বিগলিত বসন, অসম্যগবসন, স্রস্তবসন, স্খলিত-বাস।

nĕg'-lige-a-ble (-lĭj-ă-bl), *adj.* Negligible; উপেক্ষণীয়, নগণ্য।

nĕg'-lĭ-gence (-jĕns), *n.* 1. Lack of due diligence or care;

তাচ্ছিল্য, শৈথিল্য, প্রমাদ (হিঃ কোঃ), উপেক্ষণ, অবহেলা, অমনোযোগ, অসাবধানতা, শৈথিল্য, গাফিলতি (*colloq.*)। **2.** An act or instance of carelessness; অবহেলার কার্য্য। **3.** Freedom from restraint or artificiality in literature or art; সহজলীলা, অবাধগতি, সহজ-প্রবাহ। **–gent,** *adj.* Neglectful; heedless; অনবহিত; অসতর্ক, অসাবধান। **–gent-ly,** *adv.*

nĕg′-li-ġi-ble (-bl), *adj.* That may be disregarded; উপেক্ষণীয়, নগণ্য।

ne-gō′-ti-āte (-shĭ-), *v. i.* & *t.* **1.** To discuss a matter with a view to some settlement or compromise; ক্রয়, বিক্রয়, সন্ধি প্রভৃতি বিষয়ে কথা বার্ত্তা চালান, মীমাংসার জন্য কোন বিষয় আলোচনা করা। **2.** To arrange; to bring about by means of negotiation; বন্দোবস্ত করা; কথাবার্ত্তা চালাইয়া বন্দোবস্ত করা। **3.** To transfer, as a bill for consideration; to get or give value for in money; as, to *negotiate* a bill or cheque; মূল্যস্বরূপ কোন কিছু পাইয়া হুণ্ডি প্রভৃতি হস্তান্তর করা; মূল্যস্বরূপ টাকা দেওয়া বা পাওয়া। **4.** To surmount or traverse: to get over; as, the mare *negotiated* the place easily: to *negotiate* a difficulty; অতিক্রম করা; লঙ্ঘন করা। **–a-ble,** *adj.* **1.** Capable of being negotiated, as a bill, etc., ক্রয়বিক্রয়যোগ্য। **2.** That may be crossed, ascended, etc., as a road, etc.; উল্লঙ্ঘনীয়। **–ant,** *n.* **–a′tion,** *n.* **1.** A treating with another regarding sale or purchase; ক্রয়বিক্রয়-সম্বন্ধে কথাবার্ত্তা। **2.** Diplomatic bargaining; সন্ধি, বিগ্রহ প্রভৃতি আন্তর্জাতিক ব্যাপারসম্বন্ধীয় কথাবার্ত্তা। **–a-tor,** *n.* (*fem.* **–tress, –trix**) **Negotiable instruments** — পৃষ্ঠে লিখিয়া যে সমস্ত কাগজপত্র হস্তান্তর করা যায়, যথা, প্রমিসরিনোট, প্রভৃতি।

ne-gril′-lō, *n.* **1.** A small negro; ক্ষুদ্র কাফ্রী। **2.** A member of a dwarf negro race in Central and South Africa; মধ্য ও দক্ষিণ আফ্রিকা-বাসী খর্ব্বকায় নিগ্রোজাতীয় লোক।

nĕ-gri′-tō (-grē-), *n.* A member of a negroid race in Polynesia; পলিনিশিয়ার কাফ্রীজাতীয় লোক।

nē′-grō, *n.* & *adj.* **1.** One of the black-skinned woolly-haired race in Soudan and central parts of Africa; also their descendants in America; কাফ্রী, হাবসী (হিঃ কোঃ); আমেরিকার নিগ্রো। ***Adj.*** **1.** Of, or relating to, this race; black-skinned; কাফ্রীজাতি-সম্বন্ধীয়; কৃষ্ণচর্ম্মবিশিষ্ট, কৃষ্ণাঙ্গ। **2.** Connected with, or characteristic of, the negroes; কাফ্রীসংক্রান্ত, কাফ্রীপ্রকৃতিক। **3.** Black and dark; কৃষ্ণ, কালো। **–groid,** *adj.* & *n.* **1.** Characteristic of, or resembling, the negroes; কাফ্রীপ্রকৃতিক, কাফ্রীসদৃশ। **2.** Pertaining to those who resemble the negroes; কাফ্রীসদৃশজনগণসম্বন্ধীয়। (*Noun*) A member of a race perceptibly showing negro-blood; যে লোকের শরীরে কাফ্রীরক্ত আছে। **–groi′-dal,** *adj.* **–phil,** *adj.* & *n.* Friendly to the negroes; নিগ্রোজাতির প্রতি অনুরাগী। (*Noun*) Such a person; নিগ্রোজাতির প্রতি অনুরাগী ব্যক্তি। **–groph′-i-lism,** *n.* **–phō′-bi-a,** *n.* Dread of, or strong aversion to, the Negroes; কাফ্রীভীতি। **Negro ant, bat** or **monkey**—কৃষ্ণবর্ণ পিপীলিকা, বাদুড় বা বানর। **Negro coffee**—কালকাসুন্দ। **Negro-head** — একপ্রকার কাটা তামাক; নিকৃষ্ট রবার। **Negro-land**—কাফ্রীরাজ্য, আফ্রিকার যে অংশে কাফ্রীগণ বাস করে। **Negro minstrels**—গীতনৃত্যকারী কাফ্রীদল বা কাফ্রী-বেশধারী নৃত্যগীতকারীর দল।

Nē′-gŭs, *n.* The ruler of Abyssinia; আবিসিনিয়ার শাসনকর্ত্তা।

nē′-gŭs, *n.* A beverage made of wine, water, sugar, nutmeg and lemon-juice; মদ্য, জল, চিনি, জায়ফল এবং লেবুর রস দ্বারা প্রস্তুত একপ্রকার উত্তেজক পানীয়। [Francis Negus কর্ত্তৃক সর্ব্বপ্রথম প্রস্তুত হয় বলিয়া এই নাম।]

neigh (nā), *v. i., t.* & *n.* To utter the cry of a horse; to whinny; হ্রেষারব করা; চিঁহিঁ শব্দ করা। ***Verb t.*** To utter with a neigh or similar sound; চিঁহিঁ শব্দে উচ্চারণ করা। ***Noun.*** The cry of a horse; a whinny; হ্রেষারব; চিঁহিঁ শব্দ।

neigh′-bour (nā-bêr), *n., v. t.* & *i.* **1.** One who lives near, esp. in the same street, village, district, or in an adjacent country; পাড়াপড়সী, প্রতিবেশী। **2.** One who stands or sits near, or next to, another on some occasion; যে ব্যক্তি ভোজনাদি ব্যাপারে কাহারো নিকটে বা পার্শ্বে উপবেশন করে বা দণ্ডায়মান থাকে। ***Verb t.*** **1.** To adjoin; to border on or be near to; লাগালাগি হওয়া; পার্শ্ববর্ত্তী হওয়া, নিকটবর্ত্তী হওয়া। **2.** To approach; সন্নিহিত হওয়া। **3.** To bring near to something; to draw into close association; অন্য কিছুর নিকটবর্ত্তী করা; সংলগ্ন করা, মিশামিশি করা। ***Verb i.*** **1.** To dwell or be situated near; নিকটে বাস করা, নিকটে অবস্থিত থাকা। **2.** To associate on neighbourly or friendly terms; পাড়াপ্রতিবেশীর মত মিলামিশা করা। **–ing,** *adj.* **–less,** *adj.* **–li-ness,** *n.* **–ly,** *adj.* Like or becoming a neighbour; friendly; social; প্রতিবেশীতুল্য, প্রতিবেশীর উপযোগী; বন্ধুভাবাপন্ন; মিশুক, সামাজিক। **–ship,** *n.*

neigh′-boured (nā-bêrd), *adj.* **1.** Having neighbours or surroundings of a specified kind; বিশিষ্টভাবের প্রতিবেশী বা পারিপার্শ্বিক-দৃশ্যসমন্বিত। **2.** Brought or placed near (*to*); সন্নিকৃষ্ট।

neigh′-bour-hōōd (nā-bėr-), *n.* **1.** Friendly relations between neighbours ; পাড়াপড়সীর মধ্যে বন্ধুভাব। **2.** A place near ; vicinity ; nearness ; সন্নিহিত স্থান, সন্নিহিত প্রদেশ ; সামীপ্য, নৈকট্য, প্রতিবৈশিত্ব ; সান্নিধ্য। **3.** Neighbours ; প্রতিবেশিবর্গ, প্রতিবেশিমণ্ডলী। **4.** A district, esp. with reference to the characteristics of its people ; as, a squalid *neighbourhood* ; প্রদেশ। **In the neighbourhood of**—In the vicinity of ; নিকটে, কাছে। About ; nearly ; প্রায় ; কাছাকাছি।

nei′-thėr (nē- *or* nī-), *adv., conj., adj.* & *pron.* **1.** Not either ; not the one or the other ; দুয়ের একও নহে ; একটীও নয় অপরটীও নয়। **2.** (*Placed at the end to emphasize the preceding negative*) Any more than something else ; as, I don't know that *neither* ; অন্য কিছু অপেক্ষা অধিক। **3.** Not either ; as, if you do not go *neither* shall I ; ও না। **4.** (*Bibl.*) Not even ; as, but *neither* so did their witness agree ; ও না। ***Conj.*** Not either, (generally prefixed to the first of two or more co-ordinate negative propositions or clauses, the other being introduced by *nor*) ; "...I shall *neither* sell nor give, nor lose it" ; না। ***Adj.*** & ***Pron.*** **1.** Not either ; as, *neither* (*adj.*) accusation, *neither* (*pron.*) of the accusations, is true ; কোনটী না। **2.** (*Loosely*) Not any one (of more than two) ; কেহই না।

nėl′-lȳ, *n.* A large sea-bird belonging to the petrel group ; একপ্রকার বৃহৎকায় সামুদ্রিক পক্ষী।

Nē-lūm′-bō, *n.* A kind of water-lily ; একপ্রকার পদ্ম। ***Nelumbium speciosum***—পদ্ম, কমল, সরসিজ, পঙ্কজ।

nĕm-ă-tō′-cȳst′, *n.* A cell in the external layer of jelly-fishes, etc. containing a thread capable of being projected as a sting ; জেলি মাছের শরীরের কোষবিশেষ—যাহাতে এরূপ একটী সূত্র আছে যাহা হুলের মত বাহির করা যায়।

nĕm′-ă-tōde, –toid (-toyd), *adjs.* & *ns.* Of slender cylindrical shape ; নলাকার। ***Noun.*** Such a worm ; নলাকার কীট।

nem.con., *adv.* Unanimously (A contraction of the Latin *nemine contradicente*) ; সর্ব্বসম্মতিক্রমে, একবাক্যে।

nem.diss., *adv.* Without a dissentient voice (Latin *nemine dissentiente*) ; সর্ব্বসম্মতিক্রমে।

Nĕm-ē-sis, *n.* **1.** (*Gr. Myth.*) The goddess of vengeance or retribution ; (গ্রীকপুরাণ) প্রতিহিংসা দেবী, রুদ্রাণী, চণ্ডী। **2.** Retributive justice ; সমুচিত প্রতিফল।

nĕn′-ū-phâr, *n.* (*Pers. nelufar, Sans. nilotpala*) A water-lily ; কুমুদ, নীলোৎপল।

nē-ō-Căm′-bri-ăn, *adj.* (*Geol.*) Of, or relating to, the later Cambrian period ; (ভূ-বিদ্যা) নব কেম্ব্রিয়ান স্তরের।

nē′-ō-dox-ȳ, *n.* A new doctrine or view ; নব মত।

nē-ō-Hĕl′-lĕn-ĭsm, *n.* Revival of Greek ideals ; গ্রীক আদর্শের নব অভ্যুদয়।

nē-ō-lith′-ic, *adj.* Of, or pertaining to, a period in which implements of polished stones were used, the more recent of the two stone periods ; যে যুগে মসৃণীকৃত প্রস্তরের অস্ত্রশস্ত্র ব্যবহৃত হইত—তৎসম্বন্ধীয়, নবপ্রস্তরযুগসম্বন্ধীয়। **Neolithic age**—নবপ্রস্তরযুগ।

nē-ō-lō′-gi-ăn, *adj.* & *n.* Of, relating, or inclined to, theological neologism ; ধর্ম্মশাস্ত্রবিচারে যুক্তিমূলক আলোচনাসম্বন্ধীয়। ***Noun.*** A neologist ; ধর্ম্মশাস্ত্রবিচারে যুক্তিমূলক আলোচনাকারী।

nē-ŏl′-ō-gism, –gy, *ns.* **1.** Use of a new word or words ; a new-coined word ; নবশব্দব্যবহার ; নবগঠিত শব্দ। **2.** Tendency to, or adoption of, novel or rationalistic views in theology ; ধর্ম্মশাস্ত্র বিচারে নূতন বা যুক্তিমূলক মত গ্রহণে প্রবণতা, নব বা যুক্তিমূলক মত গ্রহণ। **–gist,** *n.* **–gize,** *v. t.* **1.** To use new word or phrases ; নূতন শব্দ বা শব্দাংশ ব্যবহার করা। **2.** To introduce, or accept, theological neology ; নূতন বা যুক্তিমূলক মত প্রবর্ত্তন বা গ্রহণ করা।

nē-ō-Măl-thū′-si-ăn-ism, *n.* Use of preventives, against conception ; গর্ভসঞ্চারপ্রতিষেধক যন্ত্র বা ঔষধাদি ব্যবহার। **–si-an,** *n.* & *adj.*

nē′-ŏn, *n.* (*Chem.*) An atmospheric gas discovered lately ; (রসায়নশাস্ত্র) নবাবিষ্কৃত বায়ুমণ্ডলীয় বাষ্প।

nē-ŏn-tŏl′-ō-gȳ, *n.* The scientific study of living animals and plants ; জীবিত জন্তু ও তরুগণ সম্পর্কে বৈজ্ঞানিক আলোচনা।

nē-ō-pā′-găn-ism, *n.* Modern paganism ; নবপৌত্তলিকতা।

nē′-ō-phrŏn, *n.* The white Egyptian vulture or a vulture belonging to this genus ; মিশরদেশীয় শ্বেতবর্ণ গৃধ্র।

nē′-ō-phȳte, *n.* **1.** A new convert ; a proselyte ; usually a convert among primitive Christians or Roman Catholics ; নবশিষ্য, কোন ধর্ম্মে নবদীক্ষিত ব্যক্তি ; ধর্ম্মান্তরগ্রাহী ব্যক্তি ; সাধারণতঃ আদিযুগের খৃষ্টান অথবা রোমান ক্যাথলিক সমাজ মধ্যে নবদীক্ষিত ব্যক্তি। **2.** (*R. C. Church*) A newly ordained priest ; a novice in a convent ; (রোমান ক্যাথলিক ধর্ম্মসংঘ) নবনিযুক্ত পুরোহিত ; মঠের নবীনসন্ন্যাসী, নব (বৌদ্ধ:)। **3.** A beginner ; a novice ; a tiro ; শিক্ষার্থী ; নবীনব্রতী ; নবশিষ্য।

nē-ō-plăs′-tic, *n.* Newly-formed ; নবগঠিত (বিশেষতঃ কোন ক্ষত স্থান যে বস্তুদ্বারা পূর্ণ হয় তৎসম্বন্ধে প্রযুক্ত)।

nē-ō-Plā′-tō-nism, *n.* The 3rd-century mixture of Platonic ideas with Oriental mysticism ; খৃষ্টীয় তৃতীয় শতাব্দীতে প্রাচ্যদেশের যোগতত্ত্বের সহিত প্লেটোর মতবাদের সম্মিলন।

nē-ō-têr′-ic, *adj.* & *n.* New ; recent in origin ; modern ; নব, নূতন, অভিনব ; নবজাত ; আধুনিক, অধুনাতন। ***Noun.*** A modern ; a modern writer or author ; আধুনিক কালের লোক ; আধুনিক লেখক বা গ্রন্থকার।

nē-ō-trŏp′-i-căl, *adj.* Of, relating to, or found in, a region comprising South America, tropical North America, etc. ; দক্ষিণ আমেরিকা ও উত্তর আমেরিকার উষ্ণমণ্ডল প্রভৃতি সম্পর্কীয় বা উক্ত স্থানে প্রাপ্ত।

nē-ō-zō′-ic, *adj.* (*Geol.*) Of, or relating to, the late period of the geological history ; (ভু-বিদ্যা) ভুবিদ্যার ইতিহাসের পরবর্ত্তী যুগের।

nē-pĕn′-thē, –thēs, *ns.* **1.** (*Usu. poet.*) A potion or drug causing forgetfulness of pain and sorrow ; (সচরাচর কবিতায়) দুঃখ-বেদনাবিস্মারক ঔষধ। **2.** (-THES only) A genus of plants with pitcher-shaped leaves ; the Pitcher-plant ; ঘটাকৃতি পত্রবিশিষ্ট বৃক্ষজাতি বিশেষ ; ঘটাকৃতি পত্রবিশিষ্ট বৃক্ষবিশেষ, ঘটপত্রী।

Nephelium Longana—আঁশ ফল (বোলঃ)।

neph′-ew (nĕv-ū), *n.* The son of a brother or sister ; (*loosely*) son of a borther-in-law or sister-in-law ; ভ্রাত্রীয়, ভ্রাতৃব্য, ভ্রাতুষ্পুত্র, ভাগিনেয়, স্বস্রীয়, ভগিনীসুত ; শ্যালকপুত্র, শ্যালিকা-পুত্র।

nē-phŏl′-ō-ġy̆, *n.* The study of the clouds ; মেঘবিদ্যা, বারিদবিদ্যা।

nē-phrĕc′-tō-my̆, *n.* Excision of a kidney ; মূত্রপিণ্ডচ্ছেদন।

nē-phrit′-ic, *adj.* **1.** Of, or pertaining to, or in, the kidneys ; renal ; মূত্রপিণ্ড-সম্বন্ধীয়, মূত্রাশয়-সম্বন্ধীয় ; মূত্রাশয়স্থ। **2.** (*Med.*) Affected with a disease of the kidney ; as, a *nephritic* patient ; (ভৈষজ্য-শাস্ত্র) মূত্রাশয় রোগাক্রান্ত।

nē-phrī′-tis, *n.* Inflammation of the kidneys ; মূত্রাশয়প্রদাহ।

nē-phrŏl′-ō-ġy̆, *n.* The science dealing with the kidneys, their structure, formations and diseases ; মূত্রাশয়-বিজ্ঞান।

nē-plŭs-ŭl′-tră, *n.* **1.** The highest point one has attained or can attain ; acme ; culmination ; যৎপরোনাস্তি ; পরমসীমা, চরমসীমা ; চরমোৎকর্ষ, পরাকাষ্ঠা। **2.** Prohibition of advance ; insuperable obstacle ; অগ্রসর প্রতিষেধ ; অনতিক্রমনীয় বাধা।

nĕp′-ō-tism, *n.* Undue patronage of relations ; favouritism shown to nephews and other relations ; স্বজনপ্রীতি, কুটুম্বপ্রীতি, আত্মীয়কুটুম্বের প্রতি সমধিক অনুগ্রহ ; ভ্রাতুষ্পুত্র এবং অন্যান্য কুটুম্বের প্রতি পক্ষপাত-প্রদর্শন। **–tist,** *n.*

Neptune.

Nĕp′-tūne, *n.* **1.** (*Rom. Myth.*) The son of Saturn and Ops, the god of the sea ; (রোমীয় পুরাণ) বরুণদেব। **2.** (*Rare*) The sea ; (ক্বচিদ্ব্যবহৃত) সাগর। **3.** (*Astron.*) The farthest planet of the solar system ; (জ্যোতির্বিজ্ঞান) সৌরমণ্ডলে সর্ব্বদুরবর্ত্তী গ্রহ, বরুণতারা (হিঃ কোঃ), নেপচুন (সাঃ পঃ), ইন্দ্র (সাঃ পঃ)। **A son of Neptune**—নাবিক, জাহাজের মাল্লা। **Neptune opposes Apollo**—শুষ্কতা এবং আর্দ্রতা পরস্পর বিরোধী। **Neptune's cup**—বিভিন্ন জাতীয় প্রবাল এবং শোষক (sponge)।

Nĕp-tū′-ni-ăn, *adj.* & *n.* **1.** (*Geol.*) Formed by water-action ; (ভু-বিদ্যা) জলের ক্রিয়া দ্বারা গঠিত। **2.** Maintaining aqueous origin of certain rocks, as a person ; কোন কোন পাষাণ জলের ক্রিয়া দ্বারা গঠিত—এইরূপ মতাবলম্বী। **3.** Of, or relating to, the sea-god or the sea ; সাগরদেবতাসম্বন্ধীয়, সামুদ্রিক। **4.** Of, or relating to, the planet Neptune ; বরুণগ্রহ সম্বন্ধীয়। ***Noun.*** A NEPTUNIST (see below).

Nĕp′-tūn-ist, *n.* An asserter of the Neptunian or aqueous origin of certain geological formations, (opp. to *vulcanist*); কোন কোন পাষাণের জলীয় উৎপত্তিখ্যাপক।

Nē′-rē-id, *n.* **1.** (*Class. myth.*) A sea-nymph ; সাগরপরী, জলদেবী। **2.** (*l. c., Zool.*) A long sea-worm or centipede ; (জন্তু-বিজ্ঞান) এক-প্রকার শতপদী কীট।

Nereus, *n.* The father of the fifty Nereids ; জলদেবীগণের পিতা। ইঁহার ভবিষ্যৎকথনের ক্ষমতা ছিল।

nero antico, *n.* (*It.*) A kind of black marble found in Roman ruins ; প্রাচীন রোমের ধ্বংসাবশেষের মধ্যে প্রাপ্ত একপ্রকার কৃষ্ণবর্ণ মর্ম্মর-প্রস্তর।

nĕr-ō′-li, *n.* The essential oil distilled from orange flowers used by perfumers ; কমলালেবুর পুষ্প হইতে পরিস্রুত তৈল—যাহা গন্ধ-দ্রব্যব্যবসায়িগণকর্ত্তৃক ব্যবহৃত হয়, কমলা তৈল।

Nē-rō′-ni-ăn, *adj.* Like, of, or pertaining to, Nero (Roman Emperor 54-68 A. D.) ; hence, cruel ; licentious ; tyrannical ; রোমসম্রাট নীরোর মত, নীরোসম্বন্ধীয় ; নিষ্ঠুর, ক্রূরপ্রকৃতি ; লম্পট ; অত্যাচারী। [নীরোর মত অত্যাচারী সম্রাট পৃথিবীতে অতি অল্পই জন্মগ্রহণ করিয়াছে। এই Nero উপপত্নী Poppæaএর প্রীতি-সাধনের জন্য স্বীয় জননী Agrippinaকে হত্যা করে ; পরে উক্ত Poppæaকে গর্ব্ভাবস্থায় পদাঘাতে বিনাশ করে।

খৃঃ পূঃ ৬৪ অব্দের জুলাই মাসে ভীষণ অগ্নিকাণ্ডে রোম নগরীর অধিকাংশ ভস্মসাৎ হয়। অনেকে নীরোকে এই অগ্নিকাণ্ডের কর্ত্তা বলিয়া অনুমান করেন। কথিত আছে অগ্নিকাণ্ডের সময় নীরো Capitol পর্ব্বতের উপর দাঁড়াইয়া আনন্দোচ্ছ্বসিত কণ্ঠে ট্রয় নগরীর দাহ সম্বন্ধে কবিতা আবৃত্তি করিয়াছিল।]

nêrv'-āte, *adj.* (*Bot.*, of leaves) Having nerves or veins; (উদ্ভিদ্‌বিদ্যা) শিরাল। **Ner-va'-tion,** *n.*

nerve (nêrv), *n.* & *v. t.* **1.** Sinew; tendon; (now *poet.*) (অধুনা কবিতায়) শিরা (সাঃ পঃ), বাতনাড়ী (ঐ), নাড়ী (হিঃ কোঃ), স্নায়ু; কণ্ডরা, মহাশিরা। **2.** Strength; muscular power; energy or vigour; শক্তি; পৈশিক-শক্তি; তেজঃ, বীর্য্য, ওজস্বিতা, উর্জ্জ। **3.** (*Bot.*) Rib, esp. midrib of a leaf; বৃক্ষপত্রের শিরা, বিশেষতঃ মধ্যশিরা। **4.** (*Anat.*) One of the fibres in animal bodies whose function is to convey sensation and originate motion; (শারীরসংস্থান-বিদ্যা) সর্ব্বশরীরব্যাপী সূক্ষ্ম শুভ্র সূত্রবৎ স্নায়ুজালের অন্তর্গত নাড়ী, চৈতন্যবহানাড়ী, জ্ঞানতন্তু, চৈতন্যবাহিনী। **5.** (*Pl.*) Nervousness; exaggerated sensitiveness; as, she suffered much from *nerves*; সহজ চকিতভাব; স্নায়বীয়তা; অতিরিক্ত বিচলিতভাব। **6.** Nervous fibre; স্নায়ু। **7.** Fortitude; coolness in danger; pluck; সহিষ্ণুতা, ধৈর্য্য; ধীরতা, মনঃস্থৈর্য্য; সাহস। ***Verb t.*** **1.** To give strength, vigour or courage to; as, rage *nerved* his arm; শক্তিশালী করা, শক্তিসম্পন্ন করা, সাহস সঞ্চার করা। **2.** To collect *oneself* to bear some great trouble; বিপদ্ বা ক্লেশসহনের জন্য দৃঢ়চিত্ত হওয়া। **Auditory nerve**—শব্দবহা নাড়ী (ব্রজঃ হিন্দুঃ), শব্দবাহিনী শিরা (সুশ্রুঃ)। **Efferent or motor nerves**—আজ্ঞাবহানাড়ী (ব্রজঃ হিন্দুঃ)। **Nerve cells**—ধূসরবর্ণ স্নায়ুপদার্থের মূল উপাদান, স্নায়ুকোষ (সাঃ পঃ), নাড়ীকণ (হিঃ কোঃ)। **Nerve-centre**—স্নায়ুকেন্দ্র। **Nerve energy** — বায়ু (যোঃ)। **Nerve fibre**—স্নায়ুর সূক্ষ্ম সূক্ষ্ম নির্ম্মাণতন্তু, স্নায়ুসূত্র (সাঃ পঃ)। **Nerve-knot**—স্নায়ুগ্রন্থি। **Olfactory nerve**—গন্ধবহা নাড়ী (ব্রজঃ হিন্দুঃ)। **Optical nerve**—রূপবহা নাড়ী (ব্রজঃ হিন্দুঃ)। **Sensory nerve** — সংজ্ঞানাড়ী (হিঃ কোঃ)। **Tactile nerve**—স্পর্শবহানাড়ী (ব্রজঃ হিন্দুঃ)। **A fit of nerves**—বিচলিত ভাব, সচকিত ভাব। **He dos not know what nerves are**—সে কখনও খুব বিচলিত বা অস্থির হইয়া পড়ে না। **He has iron nerves or nerves of steel**—সে সহজে ভীত বা বিচলিত হয় না। **To strain every nerve** — যথাসাধ্য চেষ্টা করা।

nerve'-lĕss (nêrv-), *adj.* **1.** Destitute of strength or courage; spiritless; weak; inert; শক্তিহীন, সাহসহীন, বলশূন্য; নিস্তেজ; দুর্ব্বল; জড়। **2.** (Of style) Flabby; diffused; (রচনাসম্পর্কে) ওজস্বিতাহীন; পল্লবিত, পুষ্পিত। **3.** (*Bot.* & *Entom.*) Having no nervures; (উদ্ভিদ-বিদ্যা বা কীটতত্ত্ব) শিরাহীন, মধ্যশলাকাহীন। **4.** (*Bot.* & *Zool.*) Having no nerves; (উদ্ভিদ্-বিদ্যা এবং জন্তুবিদ্যা) শিরাহীন। **—ly,** *adv.* **—ness,** *n.*

nêrv'-īne, *adj.* & *n.* (*Med.*) Relieving nervousness; (ভৈষজ্য-শাস্ত্র) স্নায়বিক উত্তেজনা উপশামক। ***Noun.*** (*Med.*) A nerve tonic; (ভৈষজ্যশাস্ত্র) স্নায়ুপুষ্টিকর ঔষধ।

nêrv'-ous (-ŭs), *adj.* **1.** Strong; vigorous; "*Nervous* arms"; শক্তিশালী, সবল; তেজস্বী। **2.** Full of, or abounding in, nerves, as a part of the body; স্নায়ুপূর্ণ, শিরাল। **3.** Of, or pertaining to, the nerves; শিরাসম্বন্ধীয়, স্নায়ুসম্বন্ধীয়, স্নায়বিক, স্নায়বীয়। **4.** (Of medicines) Acting upon the nerves; curative of nervous disorders; as, a *nervous* draught; (ঔষধ সম্পর্কে) স্নায়ুমণ্ডলে কার্য্যকারী, স্নায়ুরোগহর। **5.** (Of literary style) Vigorous; terse; (রচনারীতি-সম্পর্কে) ওজস্বী, অল্পাক্ষরগ্রথিত, অতিবিস্তৃতি দোষ শূন্য। **6.** Having weak or diseased nerves; easily agitated or annoyed; excitable; timid; নাড়ীকাতুরে; সহজে উত্তেজনীয়; সহজচকিত, সহজবিক্ষুব্ধ, আশুবিচলিত; ভয়তরাসে। **—ly,** *adv.* **—ness,** *n.* **1.** Strength; vigour or force; শক্তি, বল; তেজ, ওজস্বিতা। **2.** Weakness of nerves; স্নায়বিক দৌর্ব্বল্য। **Nervous-system**—স্নায়ুচক্র (প্রবাসী ১৩১৯)।

nêr'-vūre, *n.* **1.** (*Zool.*) One of the lines or ribs framing an insect's wing; (জন্তু-বিদ্যা) যে সকল অস্থিশলাকার সাহায্যে পতঙ্গের পক্ষ বিস্তারিত হয় তাহার একটী, পক্ষশলাকা, পাখার শিরা। **2.** (*Bot.*) The principal vein or nerve of a leaf; (উদ্ভিদ্‌বিদ) পাতার প্রধান শিরা।

nêrv'-ȳ, *adj.* **1.** (*Poet.*) Sinewy; strong; (কবিতায়) দৃঢ়; বলবান, সবল। **2.** (*Slang*) Cool; confident; cheeky; (ইতর-ভাষায়) অবিচলিত; কৃতনিশ্চয়; ধৃষ্ট। **3.** Nervously unsteady; jerky; as, *nervy* steps; কম্পিতপদ; নড়বড়ে।

nes'-ci-ence (nĕ-shī-ĕns), *n.* **1.** Lack of knowledge or knowableness (*of*); অবিদ্যা, অজ্ঞান, অজ্ঞেয়তা। **2.** (*Philos.*) The doctrine that God, noumenon, etc. are incapable of being known; (দর্শন-শাস্ত্র) অজ্ঞেয়তাবাদ।

nes'-ci-ĕnt (nĕ-shī-), *adj.* & *n.* **1.** Ignorant (of); অজ্ঞ। **2.** Agnostic; অজ্ঞেয়তাবাদী। ***Noun.*** An agnostic; অজ্ঞেয়তাবাদী ব্যক্তি।

nĕss, *n.* A promontory; a cape; উদগ্রভূমি; অন্তরীপ।

nĕst, *n., v. t.* & *i.* **1.** A place or bed chosen or formed by a bird for hatching her young; বাসা, কুলায়, নীড়। **2.** An animal's or insect's abode or spawning or breeding place ; কোন পশু বা কীটের বাসস্থান, বা শাবক বা ডিম্বোৎপাদনস্থলী।

Nest of American gold finch

3. A snug abode ; a secluded retreat ; a lodging ; a shelter ; a receptacle ; আরামদায়ক আবাস ; নিভৃতনিলয় ; বাসাবাটী ; আশ্রয়স্থলী ; আধার। 4. A haunt of thieves, robbers, pirates, etc. ; চোর, ডাকাত, বোম্বেটে প্রভৃতির আড্ডা। 5. A place where certain conditions such as crime, vice, etc. prevail ; as, a *nest* of vice ; পাপস্থলী, পাপপূর্ণ স্থান। 6. The occupants or frequenters of a nest collectively ; বাসার পক্ষিগণ, আড্ডায় যাতায়াতকারী দস্যু প্রভৃতি। 7. A collection or series of similar objects ; "A small *nest* of small bushes" ; সমরূপ বস্তুর সংহতি। 8. A set of small drawers ; ক্ষুদ্র দেরাজ। ***Verb t.*** 1. To place or settle in a nest ; to form a nest for ; বাসায় রাখা, কুলায়ে রাখা ; কাহারো জন্য নীড় নির্ম্মাণ করা। 2. (*Pass.*) Established in, or as in, a nest ; used for making nests in ; as, a bush *nested* in by birds ; নীড়ে স্থাপিত ; নীড় নির্ম্মাণে ব্যবহৃত। ***Verb i.*** 1. To make, or have, a nest in a specified place ; কোন নির্দ্দিষ্ট স্থানে নীড় নির্ম্মাণ করা কিম্বা বাসা থাকা। 2. To engage in nest-building ; নীড় নির্ম্মাণে নিরত হওয়া। 3. To settle as in a nest ; নীড়ে অবস্থান করা। 4. To hunt for birds' nests ; পক্ষীর বাসা খুঁজা। **Nest'-ed,** *p. p.* 1. Established in, or as in, a nest ; নীড়ে প্রতিষ্ঠিত, নীড়বৎ প্রতিষ্ঠিত। 2. Packed one inside another : একটীর ভিতর অপরটী নিবদ্ধ। **Nest-egg**—হংসী, কুক্কুটী, প্রভৃতিকে কোন স্থানে ডিম্ব প্রসব করাইবার উদ্দেশ্যে সেই স্থানে যে প্রকৃত বা কৃত্রিম ডিম্ব রাখা হইয়া থাকে ; চাঁদা সংগ্রহের পূর্ব্বে পাত্রে যে সামান্য পরিমাণ অর্থ রাখা হয়। **Nare's nest**—অশ্বডিম্ব, শশ বিষাণ। **It's an ill bird that fouls its own nest**—নিজের ঘরের অখ্যাতি করা উচিত নয়। **To feather one's nest**—See FEATHER.

nĕs'-tle (-l), *v. i.* & *t.* 1. (*Rare*) To make and occupy a nest : (কচিদ্ব্যবহৃত) নীড় নির্ম্মাণ করিয়া অধিকার করা। 2. To settle down, as in a nest or in a snug or comfortable manner ; as, she *nestled* luxuriously among cushions ; আরামে বাস করা। 3. To press oneself affectionately *to*, or *close to*, a person ; as, a child *nestles* to its mother's breast ; অনুরাগের সহিত চাপিয়া ধরা, সোহাগভরে চাপা। 4. To lie snug or half-hidden ; "The beauty of the lily *nestling* in the grass" ; আরামে শায়িত থাকা, সুখসুপ্ত থাকা, অর্দ্ধপ্রচ্ছন্ন থাকা। ***Verb t.*** 1. To provide with a nest or cozy retreat ; নীড় প্রদান করা, আরামজনক আবাসস্থান প্রদান করা। 2. To push or move, as the face, head, etc. affectionately or snugly *in* or *against* ; "...she would *nestle* her shoulder *against* mine" ; সোহাগভরে বুলান বা ঘর্ষণ করা। 3. To place in, or as in, a nest ; to set in secure place ; নীড়ে স্থাপিত করা ; নিরাপদ স্থানে রাখা। **—tled,** *adj.* 1. Settled, or placed in, or as in, a nest ; নীড়ে স্থাপিত, আরামজনক আবাসে স্থাপিত। 2. Held in embrace ; আলিঙ্গনবদ্ধ, বাহুপাশবদ্ধ।

nest'-ling (nĕs-), *n.* A young bird which has not abandoned the nest ; hence, a very young child ; ছোট পাখীর ছানা, পক্ষিশাবক ; কচি ছেলে। **Nestling place**—নিলয়।

Nĕs'-tŏr, *n.* 1. The king of Pylos in Greece, the oldest and most experienced of the chieftains who went to the siege of Troy ; গ্রীসের অন্তঃপাতী Pylos এর রাজা। ট্রয়ের যুদ্ধে যে সমস্ত রাজগণ যুদ্ধে গমন করিয়াছিলেন তিনি তাহাদের মধ্যে বয়োজ্যেষ্ঠ ও অভিজ্ঞতম ছিলেন। 2. A wise old man ; the senior of a company ; বৃদ্ধ জ্ঞানী লোক, বৃহস্পতি ; কোন কোম্পানীর বড় অংশীদার।

Nĕs-tō'-ri-ăn, *adj.* & *n.* 1. Pertaining to the doctrine of Nestorius, patriarch of Constantinople (A. D. 428) ; কনস্তান্তিনোপলের ধর্ম্মাধ্যক্ষ Nestoriusএর মতসম্বন্ধীয়। [নেষ্টরের মতে যীশুখৃষ্টের দেবদেহ এবং নরদেহ এই দুইটী স্বতন্ত্র কলেবর ছিল। কুমারী মেরী কেবলমাত্র মানবরূপী খৃষ্টের জননী ছিলেন।] 2. Of, or relating to, Nestor, the Greek warrior and counsellor ; গ্রীসদেশীয় যোদ্ধা এবং মন্ত্রণাবিশারদ Nestor সম্বন্ধীয়। ***Noun.*** An adherent of the doctrine of Nestorius ; নেষ্টরিয়ানপন্থী।

nĕt, *n.*, *v. t.* & *i.* 1. An open-work fabric, with meshes for catching fish, birds, etc. ; জাল, পাশ। 2. Anything designed or fitted to entrap or catch ; a snare ; ব্যূহ, পাশ, আনায় ; ফাঁদ। 3. A spider's web ; মাকড়সার জাল, ঊর্ণনাভ জাল। 4. A reticulation or network ; as, the *nets* of laticiferous tubes of the stem ; জালবৎ কার্য্য, জাল। 5. Anything made with interstices or meshes like a net ; as, a mosquito *net* : a tennis *net* ; জালের মত কোন কিছু। ***Verb t.*** 1. To cover, or inclose, with, or as with, a net or nets ; as, to *net* a tree ; জাল দ্বারা ঢাকা, জাল দ্বারা ঘেরা। 2. To fish (a river etc.) with a net ; to use nets n ; to catch with a net ; জাল দ্বারা মাছ ধরা ; জাল ফেলা ; জাল দ্বারা ধরা। **3.** To capture by a stratagem or wile ; জালে ফেলা। **4.** To make into a net ; as, to *net* silk ; to make, as a purse, hammock, etc. by netting ; জাল তৈয়ার করা, জাল বুনা ; জালের মত বুনিয়া টাকার থলি প্রভৃতি তৈয়ার করা। **5.** To reticulate, (*usu. in p.p.*) ; জালাঙ্কিত করা। ***Verb i.*** To make netting ; জাল তৈয়ার করা। **Net′-ful,** *n.* **Net′-ted,** *p. p.* **1.** Covered with, or as with, a net ; জালাবৃত। **2.** Made of net or network ; জালরচিত। **3.** Reticulated ; জালাঙ্কিত। **Casting-net**—ক্ষেপলাজাল। **Drag-net**—টানাজাল। **Network**—A fabric made of netted threads ; জাল। A collection or arrangement of something or things, resembling a net ; জালতুল্য বস্তুর সংহতি, জালবৎ বস্তুর বিন্যাস। A complex system, as of railways, rivers, canals, etc., (also *fig.*) ; as a *network* of falsehood ; জাল। **To dance (or march) in a net**—To do something undetected ; ধরা না পড়িয়া কোন কিছু করা।

nĕt, *adj.* & *v. t.* **1.** Free from deduction ; clear of all charges and reductions ; as, *net* profit ; নিট ; খরচাবাদ, ঝাড়া, খাঁটি, পাকা। ***Verb t.*** To produce or gain, as clear profit ; as, he *netted* thousand dollars by the operation ; নিট লাভ করা। **Net price**—(opp. to *nominal*) ; নিট মূল্য, যে মূল্য হইতে কোন বাদসাদ দেওয়া হয় না। **Net profit**—নিট লভ্য, খরচ বাদে লাভ। **Net weight**—নিট ওজন (পিপা, থলিয়া, প্রভৃতির ওজনবাদে জিনিষের ওজন)।

nĕth′-êr, *adj.* (*Archaic or facet.*) Lower ; (অপ্রচলিত বা রঙ্গচ্ছলে) নিম্নস্থ, নিম্নস্থিত, অধঃস্থ, অধস্তন, অধঃস্থিত। **Nether garments**—পাজামা। **Nether man or person**—Legs, etc. ; পা। **Nethermost hell**—নিতল। **Nether world, –regions**—The world of the dead ; hell ; (*rarely*) the earth ; অধোভুবন, অধোলোক ; নরক ; (ক্বচিদ্ব্যবহৃত) পৃথিবী।

Nĕth′-êr-lănd-êr, *n.* A native of the Netherlands ; নেদারলেণ্ডের অধিবাসী। **–ish,** *adj.* Of the Netherlands ; নেদারলেণ্ডসম্বন্ধীয়।

nĕt′-ting (-ĭng), *n.* **1.** The process of making nets ; জালরচনা প্রণালী। **2.** A piece of networks, as of cord or wire ; জালি, জালের কাজ, জালিকৰ্ম্ম। **3.** A network of ropes, formerly used for various purposes, esp. in ships ; বিভিন্ন উদ্দেশ্যে ব্যবহৃত দড়ির জালি।

nĕt′-tle (-l), *n.* & *v. t.* **1.** A weed with stinging hairs ; বিছুটিগাছ, আলকুশী, পীতপর্ণী। **2.** Any other similar plants ; বিছুটিজাতীয় গাছ। ***Verb t.*** **1.** To whip with nettles ; বিছুটিদ্বারা আঘাত করা। **2.** To get (oneself) stung with nettles ; বিছুটি লাগা। **3.** To irritate or vex ; to provoke ; বিরক্ত করা ; উত্তেজিত করা। **Nettle-rash**—বিছুটি গায়ে লাগিলে গায়ের স্থানে স্থানে যে ফোস্কা পড়ে।

neu′-răl (nū-), *adj.* Of, or relating to, the nerves, or the nervous system ; স্নায়ু বা স্নায়ুমণ্ডলসম্বন্ধীয়।

neu-răl′-gi-ă (nū-), *n.* An acute pain occurring at intervals in paroxysms in the trunk or branch of a nerve ; স্নায়ুশূল, নাড়ীব্যথা (হিঃ কোঃ)।

neu-răs-thē′-nĭ-ă (nū-), *n.* Nervous debility ; স্নায়বিক দৌর্ব্বল্য, নাড়ীদৌর্ব্বল্য (হিঃ কোঃ), ধাতুদৌর্ব্বল্য। **–then′-ic,** *adj.* & *n.*

neuration, (*F.*), *n.* The arrangement of the nervures in the wings of insects or the leaves of plants ; পতঙ্গপক্ষের শলাকাসন্নিবেশ, বৃক্ষপত্রের শিরাসন্নিবেশ।

neu-rĕc′-tŏm-ȳ (nū-), *n.* Excision of a nerve ; শিরাচ্ছেদন।

neu′-rine (nū-rĭn), *n.* A nerve tissue ; স্নায়ুবিধানতন্তু।

neu-rī′-tis (nū-), *n.* Inflammation of a nerve or nerves ; স্নায়ুপ্রদাহ, নাড়ীমুখশোথ (হিঃ কোঃ)।

neu-rŏl′-ŏ-gȳ (nū-), *n.* The science which treats of the nervous system ; স্নায়ুমণ্ডলবিজ্ঞান, মজ্জাতন্তুবর্ণন, নাড়ীশাস্ত্র (হিঃ কোঃ)। **–gist,** *n.* One versed in neurology ; স্নায়ুতত্ত্বজ্ঞ। **–ro-log′-i-cal,** *adj.*

neu-rō′-mă (nū-), *n.* (*Pathol.*) A fibrous tumour formed on the tissue of a nerve ; (নিদানশাস্ত্র) স্নায়ুর অর্ব্বুদ, স্নায়ুর বিকৃত বিবর্দ্ধন, স্নায়ুবৎ অর্ব্বুদ।

neu′-rŏn (nū-), *n.* স্নায়ুসম্ভূত অর্ব্বুদ, নাড়ীকণপুচ্ছ (হিঃ কোঃ), নাড়ীকণপাদ (ঐ)।

neu-rŏp′-ă-thȳ (nū-), *n.* (*Med.*) An affection of the nervous system, or of a nerve ; (ভৈষজ্য-শাস্ত্র) স্নায়ুমণ্ডল বা স্নায়ুর পীড়া। **Neu′-ro-path,** *n.* **1.** One liable to, or affected by, a nervous disease ; স্নায়ুরোগপ্রবণ ব্যক্তি, স্নায়ুরোগাক্রান্ত ব্যক্তি। **2.** One believing that all diseases are of nervous origin ; যে ব্যক্তি যাবতীয় রোগ স্নায়ুমূলক বলিয়া বিশ্বাস করে। **3.** Same as NEUROPATHIST. **–thist,** *n.* A specialist in neuropathy ; স্নায়ুমণ্ডলরোগের বিশেষজ্ঞ, স্নায়ুরোগে বিশেষজ্ঞ।

neu-rŏp′-têr-ă (nū-), *n.* An order of insects having four transparent finely reticulated membranous

Neuroptera.

wings ; কীটবর্গ বিশেষ—এই সকল কীটের চারিটী স্বচ্ছ সূক্ষ্ম জালাঙ্কিত ঝিল্লীবৎ পক্ষ থাকে। **–ter-ous,** *adj.*

neu-rō′-sis (nū-), *n.* **1.** A functional derangement due to the disorders of the nervous system ; a nervous disease ; স্নায়ুমণ্ডলসম্ভূত রোগ ; স্নায়ুরোগ, স্নায়বিক রোগ। 2. (*Psychol.*) Any activity of nerve-cells giving rise to mental activity or accompanying it as its physical counterpart ; (মনোবিজ্ঞান) স্নায়ুকোষের যে চাঞ্চল্যহেতু মানসিক-ক্রিয়া সঞ্জাত হয়, অথবা স্নায়ুকোষের যে বিচলন ভৌতিক প্রতিরূপস্বরূপ মানসিক ক্রিয়ার অনুসরণ করে, স্নায়ুজমনোক্রিয়া।

neu-rŏt -ic (nü-), *adj.* & *n.* 1. Acting on the nerves, as a drug ; স্নায়ুর উপর ক্রিয়াজনক। 2. Nervous, as a disease ; স্নায়বীয়। 3. (Of persons) Having disordered nerves ; of abnormal sensibility ; স্নায়ুবিকারগ্রস্ত ; অস্বাভাবিক সংবেদনসম্পন্ন। ***Noun.*** 1. A medicine for nervous affections ; স্নায়ুরোগের ঔষধ। 2. (*Pathol.*) A disease having its seat in the nerves ; (নিদান-শাস্ত্র) যে রোগের মূল স্নায়ুতে বর্ত্তমান। 3. A neurotic person ; স্নায়ুরোগাক্রান্ত ব্যক্তি, স্নায়ুবিকারগ্রস্ত ব্যক্তি।

neu-rŏt'-ō-mȳ (nü-), *n.* The cutting of a nerve to produce sensory paralysis ; শিরাচ্ছেদন।

neu'-têr (nü-), *adj.* & *n.* 1. (*Gram.*) Neither masculine nor feminine ; (ব্যাকরণ) ক্লীব। 2. (Of verb) Intransitive ; (ক্রিয়া সম্পর্কে) অকর্ম্মক। 3. Impartial ; neutral ; অপক্ষপাতী, নিরপেক্ষ, নির্লিপ্ত ; উভয়সাধারণ, উভয়সামান্য। 4. (*Bot.*) Without pistils and stamens ; asexual ; পুং বা স্ত্রী-কেশর বিহীন ; অলিঙ্গক। 5. (*Entom.*) Sexually undeveloped ; sterile ; (কীটতত্ত্ব) ক্লীব, নপুংসক ; বন্ধ্য। ***Noun.*** 1. A neuter noun, pronoun, adjective, verb or gender ; ক্লীবলিঙ্গ। 2. A person or nation that takes no part in a contest between others ; নির্লিপ্ত ব্যক্তি, নির্লিপ্তদেশ, নিরপেক্ষব্যক্তি, নিরপেক্ষদেশ। 3. A sexually undeveloped female insect, esp. bee or ant ; অস্ফুট-লিঙ্গ স্ত্রী পতঙ্গ। 4. A castrated animal, esp. a cat so treated ; ছিন্নমুষ্ক জন্তু,—বিশেষতঃ ছিন্নমুষ্ক মার্জ্জার।

neu'-tral (nü-), *adj.* & *n.* 1. Not siding with any party in a dispute or contest ; indifferent ; impartial ; নিরপেক্ষ ; উদাসীন ; পক্ষপাতশূন্য। 2. Lending no active assistance to any belligerent not involved in hostilities ; যুধ্যমান জাতিসমূহের কাহাকে সাহায্য প্রদানে বিরত, নির্লিপ্ত, সম (বুঃ সং)। 3. Of, or relating to, a neutral State ; নির্লিপ্তরাজ্যসম্বন্ধীয়। 4. Mediocre ; middling ; as, a man of *neutral* character ; মধ্যবিধ ; মধ্য, মাঝারি। 5. Not having a distinct colour, as a tint ; indefinite ; vague ; as, dissatisfied with his *neutral* life ; সুস্পষ্ট বর্ণবিহীন ; অনির্দ্দিষ্ট ; অস্পষ্ট। 6. (*Chem.*) Neither acid nor basic ; neither acid nor alkaline ; (রসায়ন-শাস্ত্র) অম্লও নয় ভস্মও নয় ; অম্লও নয় ক্ষারও নয়। 7. (*Electr.*) Neither negative nor positive ; (তাড়িত বিদ্যা) ধনাত্মকও নয় ঋণাত্মকও নয়। 8. (*Entom.* & *Bot.*) Sexually undeveloped ; asexual ; (কীটতত্ত্ব এবং উদ্ভিদবিদ্যা) অস্ফুট-লিঙ্গ ; অলিঙ্গ ***Noun.*** 1. A neutral state, party person or vessel ; নির্লিপ্তরাজ্য, পক্ষ, ব্যক্তি বা পোত। 2. A subject of a neutral state ; নির্লিপ্তরাজ্যের প্রজা **—ly,** *adv.* **—tral'-i-ty,** *n.* 1. State of being neutral ; মধ্যস্থতা, উদাসীনতা, সাম্য, মাধ্যস্থ, নিরপেক্ষতা, নির্লিপ্ততা। 2. The character of a neutral place during hostilities ; যুদ্ধকালে কোন দেশ বা স্থানের নির্লিপ্ততা। 3. Indifference in quality, specifically in chemistry ; শিথিলতা (হিঃ কোঃ)। **Neutral-tint**—ধূসরবর্ণ বা শ্লেট-পাথরের বর্ণ। **Neutral-tinted,** *adj.* (*Lit.* & *fig.*)

neu -tral-īze (nü-), *v. t.* 1. To counterbalance ; to render ineffective or void ; as, to *neutralize* an opposition ; সমতুল করা ; কোন কিছুর শক্তি বা কার্য্য ব্যর্থ করা, অকার্য্যকর করা, ক্রিয়া নষ্ট করা। 2. To make or declare, as a place or territory free from the sphere of hostilities ; কোন স্থান যুদ্ধক্ষেত্রের সীমার বহির্ভূত করা বা যুদ্ধক্ষেত্রের সীমার বহির্ভূত বলিয়া ঘোষণা করা। 3. (*Chem.*) To render neutral ; (রসায়ন-শাস্ত্র) শিথিল করা। 4. (*Electr.*) To make electrically inert ; বৈদ্যুতিক ক্রিয়া সম্পর্কে নিষ্ক্রিয় করা। **—i-za'-tion,** *n.*

neve (nā-vā), *n.* The granular snow at the head of a glacier ; তুষারনদীর উৎপত্তিস্থলে গঠিত দানাদার বরফ।

nĕv -êr, *adj.* 1. Not at any time ; at no time ; on no occasion ; কখনই না ; কখনও নয় ; কোন সময়েই না। 2 Surely not ; নিশ্চয়ই নয়। 3. Not at all, (*used in emphatic negation, often idiomatically*) ; as, *never* fear ; মোটেই না। **Never-dying**—অমর। **Never-ending**—অশেষ। **Never-fading**—অক্ষয্য। **Never-failing** — অব্যর্থ, অমোঘ। **Never-to-be-forgotten** — কখনও ভুলিবার নয়। **Never-more**—At no future time ; আর কখনও নয় **Never Never (Land)**—North Queensland ; উত্তর কুইন্সলেণ্ড। **I never did**—An exclamation of astonishment ; বিস্ময়সূচক চীৎকার। **Never a**—Not a ; not at all ; "Said *never* a word" ; কখনই একটী নয় ; মোটেই না। **Never a one**—None ; কেহই না। **It is never too late to mend**—Reformation is always possible ; সকল সময়েই সংশোধন সম্ভবপর, শোধরাইবার সময় কখনও যায় না। **Never mind**—Do not be troubled ; কোন চিন্তা নাই, গ্রাহ্য করিও না, রেখে দাও, ছেড়ে দাও। **Never say die**—নিরাশ হইও না। **Never so**—(In conditional clauses) To an unlimited extent ; ever so ;

যৎপরোনাস্তি ; যতই হউক না কেন। **Never tell me**—আমি বিশ্বাস করি না। **Never the wiser**—এখনও অজ্ঞাত। **Never tread upon a sore toe**—মরার উপর খাঁড়ার ঘা দিওনা, কাটা ঘায়ে নূণের ছিটা দিও না। **Now or never**—এখন হইলেই হইল নতুবা আর কখনো হইবে না।

nĕv-êr-t͟hĕ-lĕss′, *adv.* & *conj.* Not the less ; for all that ; notwithstanding ; in spite of ; তথাপি, পরন্ত ; অথচ, যাহাই হউক ; তথাচ, তবু, তবুও, তত্রাপি ; তৎসত্ত্বেও।

new (nü), *adj.* **1.** Lately made, or produced or discovered ; recent ; novel ; নবোৎপন্ন, নবোদ্ভাবিত ; নব, নূতন ; অভিনব, অপূর্ব্ব, নবীন, নব্য। **2.** Other than the former or old ; as, the *new* teacher ; নূতন। **3.** Strange ; unfamiliar (to one) ; "To English shopkeepers military extortion was quite *new*" ; অদ্ভুত, অপূর্ব্ব ; অপরিচিত, অনভ্যস্থ। **4.** Changed ; different from a former ; as, to lead a *new* life ; পরিবর্ত্তিত ; নূতন, নব, ভিন্নরূপ। **5.** Later ; modern ; (used with *the* to distinguish the thing spoken of from something old of the same kind) ; as, the *new* learning ; নব্য, ইদানীন্তন ; আধুনিক, অপ্রাচীন। **6.** Of recent origin, growth or manufacture ; not used before, worn or exhausted ; as, *new* potatoes : *new* furniture ; কাঁচা, তাজা ; নূতন। **7.** Fresh ; further ; additional ; "The levying of *new* regiment" ; নূতন ; আরও ; অতিরিক্ত। **8.** (Of family or person) Lately risen to distinction or notice ; নূতন। **9.** Starting afresh ; as, a *new* year ; নব, নূতন। **10** Not yet habituated *to* ; fresh *from* ; নূতন, অনভ্যস্থ ; নবাগত। **New′-ish,** *adj.* Nearly new ; প্রায় নূতন। **New′-ness,** *n.* **New comer**—নবাগত ব্যক্তি, আগন্তুক, অভ্যাগত। **New departure**—পুরাতন পথ পরিত্যাগ পূর্ব্বক নূতনপথে গমন, নব্যনীতি বা পন্থার অনুসরণ। **New England**—মার্কিণ যুক্তরাজ্যের অন্তর্গত Maine, New Hampshire, Vermont, Massachusetts, Rhode Island এবং Connecticut এই ছয় রাষ্ট্রের সম্মিলিত নাম। **New Englander**—মার্কিণ যুক্তরাজ্যের অন্তর্গত নিউইংলণ্ডের অধিবাসী। **New-fangled**—নূতনপ্রিয় (ক্বচিদ্ ব্যবহৃত) ; নবকল্পিত ; নূতন ফ্যাসনের, নব্যরীতির ; অভিনব, অপূর্ব্ব। **New-fashioned**—নূতন ফ্যাসনের। **New Jerusalem**—(See *Rev.* xxi, 2.) খৃষ্টানদিগের স্বর্গ, দেবনগরী, নিত্য জেরুজেলেম (cf. our নিত্য বৃন্দাবন)। **New land**—নূতন আবাদী-জমি। **New Learning**—Same as RENAISSANCE (which see). **New man**—খৃষ্টধর্ম্মে নবদীক্ষিত ব্যক্তি। **New Model**—১৬৪৫ খৃঃ অব্দে গঠিত সৈন্যদল বিশেষ। Cromwell এই সৈন্যদলের Lieutenant-general ছিলেন। **New moon**—অমাবস্যা ; অমাবস্যার পরবর্ত্তী প্রতিপদের চন্দ্র, সিনীবালী, মুগ্ধেন্দু (কাব্য সাঃ)। **New style**—See under STYLE. **New Testament**—See TESTAMENT. **New-year**—নববর্ষ। **New-year's day**—১লা জানুয়ারী। **New-year's eve**—৩১শে ডিসেম্বর। **New Zealander**—নিউজিলেণ্ডের আদিম অধিবাসী মেওরী জাতি ; নিউজিলেণ্ডের ইয়ুরোপিয়ান অধিবাসী। **The new diplomacy, journalism, theology, etc.**—কূটরাজনীতি, সংবাদপত্র পরিচালনা, ধর্ম্মশাস্ত্র প্রভৃতি সম্বন্ধে নব্য মত। **The new woman**—নব্যযুগের স্বাধীনতাপ্রাপ্তা মহিলা। **New brooms sweep clean**—New servants work hard ; নূতন চাকরেরা কঠোর পরিশ্রম করে। New masters keep sharp look out ; নূতন প্রভুগণ চাকরবাকরের কাজকর্ম্মের উপর খুব কড়া দৃষ্টি রাখেন। **The New World**—America ; নূতন মহাদেশ আমেরিকা। **To put on the new man**—চরিত্রের সংশোধন দ্বারা খৃষ্টধর্ম্মে দীক্ষিত হইয়াছে এরূপ—প্রদর্শন করা। **To turn over a new leaf**—See under LEAF.

new (nü), *adv.* **1.** Newly ; lately ; just ; নূতনভাবে, নবভাবে ; সম্প্রতি ; এইমাত্র। **2.** Anew ; afresh ; as, to *new*-model ; নূতনভাবে ; নবভাবে। **New-blown**—Having just come into bloom, (*lit.* & *fig.*) ; নববিকসিত, নবপ্রস্ফুটিত, নবোদ্ভিন্ন। **New-born**—নবজাত, সদ্যোজাত ; পুনর্জ্জন্মপ্রাপ্ত, নবজীবনপ্রাপ্ত। **New-built**—নবনির্ম্মিত ; পুনর্নির্ম্মিত। **New-coined**—Coined newly, (esp. of words) ; নবগঠিত। **New-come**—Lately arrived ; নবাগত। **New-front**—(*Verb*) To put a new front to ; সম্মুখভাগ নূতন করা। **New-model**—(*Verb*) To recast ; নূতন ছাঁচে গঠন করা।

new′-ĕl (nü-), *n.* **1.** (*Arch.*) The upright column in a winding staircase supporting the steps ; (স্থপতি-বিজ্ঞান) আবর্ত্তিত সোপানশ্রেণীর ধাপ সমূহের সরলোন্নত স্তম্ভ। **2.** The post at the head or foot of a stair supporting the hand-rail ; সোপানশ্রেণীর শীর্ষভাগের বা পাদদেশের স্তম্ভ। **An open** or **hollowed newel**—আবর্ত্তিত সোপানশ্রেণীর মধ্যবর্ত্তী মুক্ত স্থান।

New′-found-lănd (nü-fownd-), *n.* **1.** An island at the mouth of the St. Lawrence ; সেণ্টলরেন্সের মোহানার দ্বীপ-বিশেষ। **2.** Same as NEWFOUNDLAND DOG. **New-foundland dog**—(Also *New-foundlander*) ; একজাতীয় বৃহৎকায় সন্তরণপটু কুকুর।

New′-gāte (nü-), *n.* The name of a celebrated London prison (recently pulled down) ; লণ্ডন নগরীর সুবিখ্যাত প্রাচীন কারাগার। **Newgate-Calendar**—নিউগেট কারাগারের বন্দিগণের তালিকা—যাহাতে প্রতি বন্দীর অপরাধ প্রভৃতির বিবরণ থাকে। **New-gate fringe, frill**—মুখ কামাইলে পর

চিবুকে যে শ্মশ্রু থাকে। **Newgate knocker**—ইংলণ্ডের ফলবিক্রয়ী প্রভৃতির কর্ণাবলম্বী কুঞ্চিত কুন্তল-গুচ্ছ। **To be in Newgate**—To be a criminal; অপরাধী হওয়া।

new'-lŷ (nü-), *adv.* **1.** Lately; freshly; সম্প্রতি; নূতনভাবে, নবভাবে। **2.** In a new manner; as, a house *newly* furnished; নূতন রকমে, নূতনভাবে, নবভাবে।

New-mâr'-kĕt, (nü-), *n.* **1.** A town in England noted for horse-races; ইংলণ্ডের নগর বিশেষ—যথায় ঘোড়দৌড়ের খুব ধূম হয়। **2.** A kind of card-game; একপ্রকার তাস খেলা। **3.** Same as NEWMARKET COAT. **Newmarket coat**—পুরুষ এবং স্ত্রীলোকের এক প্রকার আঁটসাঁট কোর্ত্তা।

news (nüz), *n., pl.* **1.** (*Usu. followed by sing. verb*) Tidings; new information; a report of recent events; সমাচার, সংবাদ, বার্ত্তা, বৃত্তান্ত, সন্দেশ, খবর; নূতন সংবাদ; জনপ্রবাদ, জনশ্রুতি। **2.** (*Cap.*) Part of a newspaper title; as, Evening *News*; সংবাদপত্রের নামের অংশবিশেষ। **News'-i-ness,** *n.* **News'-less,** *adj.* **News'-y,** *adj.* (*Colloq.*) Abounding in news; সংবাদপূর্ণ। **News-agent**—A person who deals in newspapers; সংবাদপত্র বিক্রেতা। **News-boy, News-man**—যে বালক রাস্তায় রাস্তায় সংবাদপত্র ফেরি করে বা লোকের বাড়ীতে খবরের কাগজ যোগায়। **News-letter**—(ইতিহাস) সংবাদপ্রচারের জন্য লিখিত বা মুদ্রিত পত্র। **Newspaper**—সংবাদপত্র, খবরের কাগজ, সমাচারপত্র। **News-room**—সংবাদ বা সমাচার পাঠের কক্ষ, সংবাদকক্ষ। **News-sheet**—খবরের কাগজ। **News-stand**—সংবাদপত্র বিক্রয়ের জন্য বীথি। **News-vendor**—সংবাদপত্র বিক্রেতা। **Ill news fly apace, Ill news runs apace**—কুসংবাদ বাতাসের আগে ধায়। **That is no news**—এটা নূতন কথা নয়।

newt (nüt), *n.* An eft or triton; তৃণগোধিকা, তৃণগোধা, গোসাপ।

Newt.

New-tō'-ni-ăn (nü-), *adj. & n.* Of, pertaining to, or following, Sir Isaac Newton, his discoveries or doctrines; স্যর আইজাক নিউটন-সম্বন্ধীয়, তদীয় আবিষ্কার বা মত-সম্পর্কীয়। *Noun.* **1.** A follower of Newton; নিউটনের মতাবলম্বী। **2.** Newtonian telescope or reflector; একপ্রকার দূরদর্শন যন্ত্র—যাহাতে কিরণরশ্মি সমতল কাচখণ্ডের উপর প্রতিফলিত হইয়া দর্শনীয় বস্তুর চিত্র উৎপাদিত হয়। **Newtonian telescope**—See above.

nĕxt, *adj., adv., prep. & n.* Nearest in place, time, rank or degree; as, in the *next* house: the *next* week: *next* best; পরবর্ত্তী, আগামী, আসন্ন, অব্যবহিত, পার্শ্বস্থ। *Adv.* In the time, place, or order nearest or immediately succeeding; as, he is *next*: *next* we drove home; অব্যবহিত পর, অনন্তর, তারপর। *Prep.* In, or into, the next place to; on the next occasion to; in the next degree to; as, I was standing *next* him; she loves him *next* her own child; অব্যবহিত পরবর্ত্তী স্থানে; পরের বারে; পরে। *Noun.* The next person or thing; অব্যবহিত পরবর্ত্তী ব্যক্তি বা বস্তু। **Next-best**—Second-best; সর্ব্বোৎকৃষ্টটীর পরবর্ত্তী। **Next-door to**—Very close to; almost; as, it is *next door to* felony; অতিশয় সন্নিকটবর্ত্তী; প্রায় সেই রকম। **Next-door neighbour**—পার্শ্ববর্ত্তী বাটীর অধিবাসী। **Next friend**—(আইন) যে ব্যক্তি কোন অপর ব্যক্তির শৈশবে, মানসিক বিকৃতি বা বিবাহের অবস্থায় তাহার প্রতিনিধিস্বরূপ কার্য্য করে, আসন্নবন্ধু। **Her next is etc.**—তাহার পরবর্ত্তী স্বামী বা সন্তান। **Next of kin**—A person nearest of kin to some one; অতি নিকট আত্মীয়। **Next, please**—এর পর কি প্রশ্ন জিজ্ঞাসা করুন; পরবর্ত্তীলোক আসুক। **Next one's heart**—Very dear to one; কাহারো অতিশয় প্রিয়। **Next to impossible**—Almost impossible; প্রায় অসম্ভব, একরূপ অসম্ভব। **Next to none**—Almost none; প্রায় কেহই না। **Next to nothing**—Almost nothing; প্রায় কিছুই নয়, অতিসামান্য। **To live next door**—To live in the next house; পার্শ্ববর্ত্তী বাটীতে বাস করা। **What next**—এর চেয়ে অসম্ভব আরো কিছু আছে নাকি? **Will tell you in my next**—অর্থাৎ পরের পত্রে লিখিব।

nexus, (*L.*), *n.* Connection; tie; link; "The *nexus* of cause and effect"; সম্পর্ক, সম্বন্ধ; বন্ধ; শৃঙ্খলবন্ধ।

Nī-ăg'-ă-ră, *n.* (The name of a famous American waterfall) A cataract; torrent; din; জলপ্রপাত, প্রস্রবণ; নির্ঝরিণী; গর্জ্জন, রোল। **To shoot Niagara**—To run fearful risks; সাপের ফণায় হাত দেওয়া।

nib, *n. & v. t.* **1.** The point of a (quill) pen; কলমের অগ্রভাগ, কলমের মুখ, কলমাগ্র। **2.** A metal pen-point for insertion in a pen-holder; কলমের মোচ। **3.** The point of tool, etc.; যন্ত্র প্রভৃতির সূক্ষ্ম অগ্রভাগ। **4.** (*Pl.*) The particles of crushed cocoa-beans; coffee beans; কোকোচূর্ণ; কাফীর বীজ। **5.** (*Zool.*) A bill or beak; চঞ্চু। *Verb t.* To furnish with a nib; as, to *nib* a pen; to point; to mend the point of; কলমের মোচ লাগান; চোখা করা; কলম কাটা।

nib'-ble (-l), *v. t., i.* & *n.* **1.** To bite as a fish does the bait; (also *v. i.*); ঠোকরান। **2.** To eat in small bits; ঠোকরাইয়া খাওয়া। ***Verb i.*** **1.** To take little bites; to eat by small bits, (with *at*); ঠোকরাইয়া ঠোকরাইয়া খাওয়া; অল্প অল্প করিয়া খাওয়া। **2.** To carp *at*; to make petty criticism; ছিদ্রানুসন্ধান করা, খুঁত ধরা; খুঁত খুঁত করা। ***Noun.*** **1.** Act of nibbling, as of a fish at a bait; ঠোকর দেওন। **2.** A quantity, esp. of grass sufficient for nibbling at; একটু একটু করিয়া কামড়াইয়া খাইবার জন্য পর্য্যাপ্ত ঘাস প্রভৃতির আঁটি। **To nibble at**—To bite or eat gently or cautiously; ঠোকরান। (*Fig.*) To dally with temptation etc.; (লক্ষণায়) লোভ দেখান। To make petty criticism; খুঁত খুঁত করা।

nib'-lick, *n.* A kind of golf-club; একপ্রকার গোলফ্ ক্রীড়ার দণ্ড।

nīce, *adj.* **1.** Fastidious; dainty; difficult to please; of refined or critical tastes; as, some people are more *nice* than wise; খুঁত-খুঁতে; অতিরিক্ত সূক্ষ্মবিচারী; দুস্তোষ্য; সূক্ষ্মরুচি, সূক্ষ্মবিচারী। **2.** Scrupulous; punctilious; precise; as, *nice* politics do not always succeed: সূক্ষ্মাচারনিষ্ঠ; সূক্ষ্মনিয়মী; সঠিক। **3.** Demanding close discrimination, tact, care, consideration or treatment; as, *nice* experiments: *nice* problem; সূক্ষ্ম। **4.** Minute; subtle; as, a *nice* shade of meaning; অণুক; সূক্ষ্ম। **5.** Entering minutely in details; attentive; close; as, a *nice* observer; সূক্ষ্মানুসন্ধায়ী; অবহিত; সূক্ষ্ম। **6.** (Of the eye, ear, etc.) Able to distinguish or discriminate in a high degree; deft; সূক্ষ্মপ্রভেদসংবেদনশীল, সূক্ষ্মবিবেকী; নিপুণ, কুশল। **7.** (*Colloq.*) Pleasing or agreeable; delightful; well-flavoured; good; kind or considerate; satisfactory; commendable; (চলিত ভাষায়) মনোমদ, মনোরম, মজাদার (*colloq.*); প্রীতিপ্রদ, সুন্দর, রম্য, রমণীয়, ললিত, সুচারু, খাসা (*colloq.*), আচ্ছা (*collq.*), রুচির মনোজ্ঞ; সুস্বাদ, সুরস, রুচিকর; ভাল, বেশ; সদয়; সন্তোষজনক; প্রশংসার্হ, প্রশস্ত। **Nice'-ly,** *adv.* **1.** Fastidiously; দুস্তোষ্যভাবে। **2.** Exactly; সঠিকভাবে, সূক্ষ্মরূপে। **3.** Finely; becomingly; pleasantly; satisfactorily; সুন্দরভাবে, শোভনভাবে; মনোরমভাবে; সন্তোষজনকভাবে। **Nice'-ness,** *n.* **Nic'-ish,** *adj.* Rather nice; সূক্ষ্মপ্রায়। **Nice-looking**—শোভনদর্শন, সুদর্শন। **Nice and**—Satisfactorily; as, it was *nice and* high: to go *nice and* fast; সন্তোষজনকভাবে।

Ni'-cene (-sēn), *adj.* Of, or relating to, Nicaea, an ancient city of Asia Minor; এসিয়া মাইনরের অন্তঃপাতী Nicaea নামক স্থানসংক্রান্ত। [এই স্থানে ৩২৫ ও ৭৮৭ খৃঃ অব্দে খৃষ্টীয় আচার্য্যমণ্ডলীর অধিবেশন হয়]। **Nicene Creed**—Nicaea নগরীর প্রথম অধিবেশনে গৃহীত খৃষ্টীয় ধর্ম্মের মতসমূহ।

nī'-cē-ty, *n.* **1.** Delicacy of taste or feeling; fastidiousness; punctiliousness; সূক্ষ্মতা; দুস্তোষ্যতা; অতিসূক্ষ্মদৃষ্টি। **2.** Precision; accuracy; as, he depicted the scene with the greatest *nicety*; সঠিকতা; যথাযথ ভাব। **3.** Subtlety; as, matters of the utmost depth and *nicety*: সূক্ষ্মতা। **4.** Minute distinction; subtle or unimportant detail; সূক্ষ্মবৈষম্য; খুঁটিনাটি। **5.** (*Archaic*) Something elegant or dainty; (অপ্রঃ) সুশোভন বস্তু, রসনাতৃপ্তিকর বস্তু। **To a nicety**—Accurately; with extreme exactitude; সঠিকভাবে; সূক্ষ্মভাবে।

niche (nich), *n.* & *v. t.* **1.** A recess in a wall to contain a statue, vase, etc.; প্রতিমাদি রাখিবার জন্য প্রাচীর গাত্রের খোঁদল, কুলুঙ্গী, প্রতিমা-স্থান, প্রতিমাধার, মূর্ত্তিনিকেতন। **2.** (*Fig.*) A place or position suited to the merits or capacities of a person or thing; as, there is some *niche* for each man in the world's work; (লক্ষণায়) কোন ব্যক্তি বা বস্তুর শক্তি বা গুণের উপযোগী স্থান, যোগ্যস্থান। ***Verb t.*** **1.** To place as a statue etc., in a niche, (usu. in *p. p.*); কুলুঙ্গীতে স্থাপন করা, প্রতিমাস্থানে প্রতিষ্ঠিত করা। **2.** To settle (*oneself* or *in p. p.*) cozily or snugly in a corner or hollow; সুখাসীন করা, সুখোপবিষ্ট করা। **A niche in the temple of fame**—যশোমন্দিরে স্থান। [১৭৯১ খৃঃ অব্দে বিপ্লবকারিগণ St. Genevieve গির্জ্জাকে প্যারীস নগরীর Pantheon বা Temple of Fame (যশোমন্দির) নাম প্রদান করে। এই মন্দিরে ফরাসীদেশের সুপ্রসিদ্ধ ব্যক্তিগণের প্রতিমূর্ত্তি রক্ষিত হইত।]

nick, *n.* **1.** A notch; খাঁজ। **2.** One of certain throws in a game of hazard; পাশা প্রভৃতি খেলার দান। **3.** (With *the*) The precise moment required by necessity; the critical moment; ঠিকসময়; সন্ধিক্ষণ, পরমমুহূর্ত্ত। **Old nick**—শয়তান। **Nick of time**—শুভক্ষণ, উপযুক্ত সময়। **In the nick (of time)**—Just at the right moment; ঠিক সময়ে, ঠিক সময়মত।

nick, *v. t.* & *i.* **1.** To make a nick or nicks in; খাঁজ কাটা। **2.** To make an incision at the root of (a horse's tail) in order to make him carry it higher; ঘোড়ার লেজের গোড়ায় খানিক স্থান কাটা। **3.** To hit upon; to guess rightly; as, to *nick* the truth; ঠাওরান; ঠিক অনুমান করা। **4.** To catch exactly (the time, a train, etc.); ঠিক সময়ে ধরা। **5.** (*Slang*) To catch; to nab or nail, (specific. of the police); (ইতর-ভাষায়) পাকড়ান; হঠাৎ পাকড়ান। **6.** To throw, as a cast etc.; দান ফেলা। ***Verb i.*** **1.** (In hunting, racing or coursing) To cut *in* by short cut, at a corner etc.; (মৃগয়া, ঘোড়দৌড় প্রভৃতিতে) দৌড়চক্র প্রভৃতির রাস্তার ভিতরের প্রান্তের নিকট দিয়া পাশ কাটিয়া কাহাকে পশ্চাতে ফেলা। 2. (Stock breeding) To breed together and produce offspring of a good quality; একত্র সংসর্গের ফলে উৎকৃষ্ট সন্তান উৎপাদন করা।

nick'-ĕl, *n.* & *v. t.* **1.** A metal of a grayish white colour; ধূসরাভ-শ্বেত ধাতু-বিশেষ, নিকেল। **2.** (*U. S.*) A five-cent piece of coin; (মার্কিণ যুক্তরাজ্য) ৫ সেণ্ট। ***Verb t.*** To coat with nickel; নিকেলধাতুর সূক্ষ্ম পাত দ্বারা আচ্ছাদিত করা। **Nickel-silver**—নিকেল রৌপ্য [৬০ ভাগ তাম্র, ১৭½ ভাগ দস্তা এবং ২২½ ভাগ নিকেলএর মিশ্র।] **Nickel-steel**—নিকেল মিশ্রিত ইস্পাত-বিশেষ।

nick'-năck, *n.* See KNICK-KNACK.

nick'-nāme, *n.* & *v. t.* **1.** A name added in derision or familiarity; উপনাম, উপাধিনাম, নিন্দাসূচক নাম। **2.** An abbreviation or a familiar form of a Christian name; খৃষ্টীয় নামের সংক্ষেপ। ***Verb t.*** To give a nickname to; to call by a nickname; উপনাম দেওয়া; উপনামে ডাকা।

ni-cō'-ti-ăn (-shĭ-), *adj.* Of, or relating to, tobacco; তাম্রকূটসম্বন্ধীয়।

Nicotiana tabacum — তামাকু (বেলঃ)।

nic'-ŏ-tine (-tīn), *n.* (From Nicot, introducer of tobacco into France) A poisonous alkaloid base obtained from tobacco; তাম্রকূটের বিষাক্ত নির্যাস-বিশেষ, তাম্রকূট-সার, তামাকের বীর্য্য। **—tin-ism,** *n.* Morbid condition induced by excessive use of tobacco; অতিরিক্ত তাম্রকূট সেবনজনিত অসুস্থতা। **—tin-ize,** *v. t.* To drug or saturate with nicotine; তাম্রকূট সার দ্বারা অনুসিক্ত করা, তাম্রকূটসার সেবন করাইয়া অচেতন করা।

nic'-tāte, —ti-tāte, *v. t.* To close or open the eyes; to wink; চক্ষু মুদ্রিত করা, চক্ষুর পলক ফেলা; চোখ মিট মিট করা। **—ta'-tion,** *n.* The act of nictating; নেত্রস্পন্দন। **Nict(it)ating membrane**—কোন কোন জন্তুর তৃতীয় বা মধ্যবর্ত্তী অক্ষিপল্লব।

nid-ă-mĕn'-tăl, *adj.* (*Zool.*) Of, or pertaining to, a capsule or covering for an egg or a mass of eggs; as *nidamental* glands; (জন্তুবিদ্যা) ডিম্ব বা ডিম্বশ্রেণীর আবরণ সম্বন্ধীয়।

nĭd'-(d)er-ing (-ĕr-), *n.* & *adj.* A base or cowardly person; কাপুরুষ, নরাধম। ***Adj.*** Mean; cowardly; হীন; ভীরু।

nid'-dle-nod-dle (-l-nŏd-l), *adj.*, *v. i.* & *t.* Nodding; quivering; unsteady; নতিশীল; কম্পনশীল; নড়বড়ে। ***Verb i. & t.*** To nod unsteadily to and fro; নড়বড় করা।

nīde, *n.* A brood, as of pheasants; শাবকগণ।

nid'-i-fi-cāte, —fȳ, *v. i.* To build a nest or nests; নীড় নির্ম্মাণ করা, নীড়রচনা করা। **—ca'-tion,** *n.* The act of nidificating; নীড়নির্ম্মাণ, নীড়রচনা, কুলায়রচনা।

nĭd'-nŏd, *v. i.* & *t.* To nod repeatedly; বার বার নত হওয়া।

nī'-dŭs, *n.* (*Pl.* -DI, -DUSES) **1.** A place in which insects, etc. deposit eggs; কীটাদির ডিম্বসংরক্ষণস্থান। **2.** (*Bot.*) A place of development for spores, seeds, etc.; (উদ্ভিদবিদ্যা) বীজ, সূক্ষ্মবীজ, প্রভৃতির বিকাশস্থলী। **3.** A place of origin or development as of a disease, etc.; রোগ প্রভৃতির উৎপত্তি ও বিকাশ-স্থলী। **4.** A natural receptacle; নৈসর্গিক ভাণ্ড। **5.** (*Fig.*) A place where anything originates or is fostered; (লক্ষণায়) কোন বস্তুর উৎপত্তি বা পরিপুষ্টির স্থান। **6.** Collection of eggs, tubercles, etc.; ডিম্ব প্রভৃতির সমবায়, অক্ষনাড়ীগুচ্ছক (হিঃ কোঃ)।

niece (nēs), *n.* The daughter of one's brother or sister or sometimes of one's brother-in-law or sister-in-law; ভ্রাতুষ্পুত্রী, ভাগিনেয়ী, ভাইঝি, বোনঝি, শ্যালিকাকন্যা, শ্যালকপুত্রী।

ni-ĕl'-lō, *n.* (*Pl.* -LI, -LOS.) **1.** A black composition made of the alloys of sulphur, silver, copper, lead, etc. for filling engraved lines on silver or other metal; রৌপ্য বা অপর ধাতুর উপরের ক্ষোদিত রেখা পূর্ণ করার জন্য গন্ধক, রৌপ্য, তাম্র, সীসা, প্রভৃতির সহযোগে প্রস্তুত কৃষ্ণবর্ণ মিশ্রধাতু। **2.** An ornamental work executed by applying niello to an engraved design; a specimen of such work; ক্ষোদিত কারুকার্য্যে উক্ত মিশ্রধাতু প্রয়োগে রচিত শোভাসাধক কারুকার্য্য-বিশেষ; ঐরূপ শোভাসাধক কার্য্যের নমুনা। **—loed,** *adj.*

Niersteiner, (*G.*), *n.* A white hock; শ্বেতবর্ণ মদিরা-বিশেষ।

Nigella, *n.* A genus of erect annual herbs; কালাজিরা প্রভৃতির গাছ।

Nigella sativa—কালাজিরা (বেলঃ), কৃষ্ণজীরক (ঐ)।

nig'-gard (-ĕrd), *n.* & *adj.* A miser; a stingy person; one who gives something grudgingly, (with *of*); কৃপণ, ছেঁচড়া; হাতটান, কঞ্জুষ; ব্যয়কুণ্ঠ ব্যক্তি। ***Adj.*** (*Rhet.* & *Poet.*) Niggardly; stingy; (অলঙ্কারশাস্ত্র এবং কবিতায়) কৃপণ; কঞ্জুষ।

nig'-gard-lȳ (-ĕrd-), *adj.* & *adv.* Parsimonious; stingy; sparing; giving or given grudgingly or in small amount; কৃপণ; কঞ্জুষ; হাতটান, বদ্ধমুষ্টি; অনিচ্ছাসহকারে প্রদত্ত। ***Adv.*** Parsimoniously; sparingly; কৃপণের মত; পরিমিত ভাবে।

nig'-ger (-ĕr), *n.* **1.** Negro (*usu. contempt.*) (প্রায়শঃ অবজ্ঞাচ্ছলে) কাফ্রী। **2.** (Improperly or loosely) A member of any very dark-skinned race; কৃষ্ণাঙ্গ, কালাআদমী। **3.** A black turnip caterpillar;

একপ্রকার কালো শূঁয়াপোকা। **—dom,** *n.* **Nigger-head**—See NEGRO-HEAD. **Nigger melody, song, etc.**—কাফ্রীসঙ্গীত। **Nigger minstrel**—See NEGRO-MINSTREL.

nig'-gle (-l), *v. i.* To spend time; to fidget; to be over-elaborate on petty details; সময়ক্ষেপ করা, কাল কাটান; উষখুষ করা, আকুবাঁকু করা; খুঁটিনাটি করা।

nig'-gling (-lĭng), *adj.* Trifling; petty; wanting in breadth, largeness; cramped, as a handwriting; তুচ্ছ; অকিঞ্চিৎকর; ক্ষুদ্র, সংকীর্ণ; (হস্তাক্ষর সম্পর্কে) পেঁচালো।

nigh (nī), *adv., prep.* & *adj.* **1.** Near; নিকটে, কাছে, অদূরে। **2.** Almost; nearly; as, he was *nigh* dead; প্রায়; কাছাকাছি। ***Prep.*** Near to; not remote from; নিকটবর্ত্তী; অদূরবর্ত্তী। ***Adj.*** **1.** Near; not distant or remote; নিকটবর্ত্তী, সমীপবর্ত্তী; সমীপস্থ, অদূরবর্ত্তী। **2.** Closely allied; intimate; নিকটতম, নিকটসম্পর্কীয়, ঘনিষ্ঠ। **3.** (Of ways or roads) Direct; সোজা। **4.** (Of domestic animals, vehicles, etc.) On the left; near; (পালিতজন্তু, শকট, প্রভৃতি সম্পর্কে) বামদিকস্থ; বামপার্শ্ববর্ত্তী।

night (nīt), *n.* **1.** The time from sunset to sunrise; the darkness which prevails during this time; রাত্রি, রাত (*colloq.* & *Poet.*), রজনী, নিশা, বিভাবরী, যামিনী, ক্ষপা, ক্ষণদা, ত্রিযামা, নক্তং, শর্ব্বরী, যামবতী, নিশীথিনী, তমস্বিনী, [also নিরাতপা, শ্যামা, শতাক্ষী]; রজনীর অন্ধকার। **2.** (Also *nightfall*) The beginning of darkness; as, he did not come until after *night*; নিশাগম, রজনীসমাগম। **3.** Weather or experiences or occupation of a night; as, a dirty *night*; রাত্রির জলবায়ুর অবস্থা, নৈশ অভিজ্ঞতা, নৈশব্যাপার। **4.** (*Fig.*) Obscurity; concealment; "Nature and nature's law lay hid in *night*"; (লক্ষণায়) অস্পষ্টতা; প্রচ্ছন্নতা। **5.** Ignorance; intellectual darkness; as, the *night* of the middle ages; অজ্ঞতা; অজ্ঞানান্ধকার, অজ্ঞানতমিস্রা। **6.** (*Fig.*) Death; "She closed her eyes in everlasting *night*"; (লক্ষণায়) মৃত্যু বা সমাধির অন্ধকার। **7.** (*Fig.*) A state of distress; adversity; "A dreary *night* of sorrow"; (লক্ষণায়) দুঃখযামিনী, দুঃখবিভাবরী; বিপত্তি। **Night'-less,** *adj.* **Night-bird**—পেচক, বুলবুল; যে সকল অসচ্চরিত্র লোক রাত্রিকালে ঘুরিয়া বেড়ায়। **Night blind**—নিশান্ধ, রাতকাণা। **Night blindness**—নিশান্ধতা, রাতকাণারোগ। **Night-cap**—A cap worn in bed; রাত্রিতে শয্যাতে যে টুপি পরা হয়। A glass of grog taken before going to bed (supposed to promote sleep); শয়নের পূর্ব্বে পীত এক গ্লাস জলমিশ্রিত মদ্য। **Night-cellar**—ভূগর্ভস্থিত নিম্নশ্রেণীর মদ্যবিপণি। **Night-chair**—Same as NIGHT-STOOL. **Night-clothes** — রাত্রিবাস (তন্ত্রঃ), শয়নবস্ত্র, শয়নবাস (ঋতুঃ)। **Night-dress**—নৈশপরিচ্ছদ, নৈশবেশ (ঋতুঃ)। **Nightfall** — রাত্রিযোগ, নিশাসমাগম, নিশাগম, রজনীমুখ, প্রদোষ। **Night-flower**—যে পুষ্প নিশাকালে বিকশিত এবং দিবাভাগে মুদ্রিত হয়, নিশাপুষ্প (অঃ), রাত্রিপুষ্প। **Night-glass**—রাত্রিকালে ব্যবহারোপযোগী ক্ষুদ্র দূরবীণ। **Night-hag**—ডাইনী, নিশাচরী; বোবা। **Night-jar**—The goatsucker; একপ্রকার গুল্ম। **Night jasmine**—শেফালিকা, শিউলীফুল, শিঙ্গাড়া ফুল, রজনীহাস (অঃ)। **Night-light**—রোগী প্রভৃতির জন্য মৃদু আলোক প্রদানের জন্য একপ্রকার খর্ব্ব এবং পুরু মোমবাতি। **Night-line**—রাত্রিকালে মাছ ধরার জন্য টোপ বাঁধিয়া যে বড়শীর সূতা ফেলান হয়। **Night-long**—রাত্রিব্যাপী, রজনীব্যাপী। **Night-man**—যে মেথর রাত্রিতে ময়লা পরিষ্কার করে। **Nightmare**—A fiend or incubus formerly supposed to oppress people by night; বোবা। A feeling of suffocation during sleep; a horrible dream causing this; নিদ্রাবস্থায় বুকে বা পিঠে চাপ অনুভব হেতু সঙ্করণ, শ্বাসগ্রহণ ও বাক্যকথনে অসমর্থতা; যে ভয়ঙ্কর স্বপ্নদর্শনে ঐরূপ অবস্থা জাত হয়। (*Fig.*) An overwhelming or stupefying influence; বোবায় ধরার ভাব, স্তব্ধতাজনক ভাব। **Night-marish,** *adj.* **Night-piece**—A picture of a scene at night; নৈশদৃশ্যের চিত্র। A piece of literary composition descriptive of a scene by night; নৈশদৃশ্যবর্ণনাত্মক রচনা। **Night-school**—নৈশবিদ্যালয়। **Nightshade**—বিভিন্ন জাতীয় গুল্ম (see NIGHT-SHADE); darkness of night; নিশান্ধকার। **Night-soil**—পায়খানা, নর্দ্দমা প্রভৃতির ময়লা—যাহা রাত্রিতে পরিষ্কার করা হয়। **Night-stool**—A bed-room commode; শয়নগৃহস্থ মলত্যাগের কাষ্ঠাধার। **Night-suit**—এক সেট পাজামা। **Night-time**—নিশাকাল। **Night-watch**—রাত্রির পাহারা। **Night-work** — রাত্রির কাজ। **A dirty night**—দুর্য্যোগের রাত্রি, বাদলা রাত্রি, খারাপ রাত। **All night, all night long**—For the whole night; সারারাত্রি। **At night**—At nightfall; in the evening; রাত্রিযোগে, নিশাসমাগমে; প্রদোষে। **By night**—During or under cover of the night; রাত্রে। **In the night watches**—উৎকণ্ঠাপীড়িত, অবসাদজনক বা বিনিদ্র নিশায়। **Night and day**—অহোরাত্র, রাত্রিদিন, দিনরজনী, দিনযামিনী, রজনীদিন (গীতাঞ্জঃ), নক্তন্দিন। **Nightly, Night after night** — Nightly; many nights; প্রতি রজনীতে, প্রতিরাত্রিতে; বহুরজনী। **Nightmare of Europe**—নেপোলিয়ান বোনাপার্ট। **To have a good** or **bad night**—To sleep well or ill; to be comfortable or in pain; বেশ ভাল নিদ্রা যাওয়া, ভাল নিদ্রা হওয়া; সুখে বা দুঃখে থাকা। **To make a night**

of it—To spend night in festivity ; আমোদ আহ্লাদে নিশাযাপন করা।

Nightingale.

night'-in-gāle (nït-), *n.* A small migratory bird singing by night and in the day ; বুলবুল।

night'-lȳ (nït-), *adj.* 1. Of, or pertaining to, the night or every night ; নৈশ, প্রতিনৈশিক, প্রতিরাত্রির। 2. Happening, done, or used, by night or every night ; নিশাকালে সংঘটিত, প্রতিনিশায় সংঘটিত। 3. Dark as, or resembling, night ; রাত্রির মত অন্ধকারময়, নিশাসদৃশ, রাত্রিতুল্য।

night'-lȳ (nït-), *adv.* 1. Every night ; at or by night ; প্রতিরাত্রিতে ; রাত্রিকালে।

night'-shāde (nït-), *n.* A kind of plant ; কাকমাবী (বনঃ), কাইস্তাশাক (ঐ), গুরকামাই (ঐ)। **Black-nightshade** — কাকমাবী (বনঃ)। **Deadly nightshade**—বেলেডোনা। **Indian nightshade**—ব্যাকুর, কাকমাবী। **Woody nightshade** — রুবা বারিক (হিন্দিভাষায়)।

nï-grĕs'-cent (-ĕnt), *adj.* Approaching to blackness ; blackish ; কৃষ্ণপ্রায় ; কৃষ্ণাভ। **—cence,** *n.*

nig'-ri-tūde, *n.* State of being black, (*lit.* & *fig.*) ; also anything black ; কৃষ্ণতা ; কৃষ্ণবর্ণবস্তু।

nihil ad rem, (*L.*), *pred. adj.* Irrelevant ; অপ্রাসঙ্গিক।

nï'-hil-ïsm, *n.* 1. Nothingness ; শূন্যতা। 2. The total rejection of current religious beliefs or moral principles ; প্রচলিত ধর্ম্ম বা নীতিবিষয়ক মতের সম্পূর্ণ পরিহার। 3. (*Metaph.*) The denial of all existence or the knowledge of all existence ; (তত্ত্ব-বিদ্যা) শূন্যমত (শঙ্করঃ), নাস্তিতত্ত্ব, নাস্তিবাদ (হিঃ কোঃ), শূন্যবাদ (ঐ), বিনাশবাদ, ধ্বংসবাদ। 4. The doctrines of an extreme revolutionary party in Russia finding nothing to approve in the constituted order of things ; রুশিয়াদেশের উৎকট রাজনীতিক সম্প্রদায়বিশেষের মত—এই সম্প্রদায়ভুক্ত-ব্যক্তিগণ প্রচলিত শাসনপ্রণালীর ঘোরতর বিরোধী, এবং রাজা ও রাজপুরুষগণকে হত্যাপূর্ব্বক শাসনতন্ত্রের উচ্ছেদসাধন করিতে সচেষ্ট। **—ist,** *n.* 1. An advocate of nihilism ; শূন্যবাদী (শঙ্করঃ)। 2. A member of a Russian nihilistic party resorting to terrorism ; রুশিয়াদেশের উক্ত বিনাশবাদী সম্প্রদায়ের সভ্য। **—is'-tic,** *adj.*

nï-hil'-i-tȳ, *n.* 1. Nothingness ; a state of being nothing ; অসত্তা, শূন্যত্ব ; নাস্তিত্ব। 2. A nullity ; a mere trifle ; অকিঞ্চিৎকর বস্তু ; তুচ্ছ বস্তু।

Nike, *n.* The goddess of victory ; গ্রীক পুরাণোক্তা জয়দেবী।

nil, *n.* Nothing ; no number or amount, (esp. in scoring at games etc. ; as, three goals to *nil*) ; কিছুইনা ; শূন্য। ***Nil admirari***—(*L.*) The attitude of being surprised at, or admiring nothing ; nonchalance ; কোন কিছুতেই বিস্মিত না হওয়ার, বা কোন কিছুরই প্রশংসা না করার ভাব ; উদাসীন ভাব। ***Nil desperandum***—(*L.*) Never say die ; never give up in despair ; হতাশ হইওনা ; নিরাশ হইও না।

nill, *v. i.* (*Obs.*) To be unwilling, (*3rd, sing., pres., condit.*) ; (অপ্রঃ) অনিচ্ছুক হওয়া, নারাজ হওয়া, অসম্মত হওয়া। **Will he nill he**—Whether he likes it or not, (now usually *willy nilly*) ; সে ইহা পছন্দ করুক বা নাই করুক।

Nï-lŏm'-ĕ-tēr, *n.* An instrument for measuring the rise of water in the Nile during its periodical floods ; বন্যার সময়ে নীল নদীর জলের উচ্চতা মাপিবার জন্য যন্ত্র-বিশেষ।

Nï-lŏt'-ic, *adj.* & *n.* Of, or relating to, Nile or Nile region, or its inhabitants ; নীলনদীসম্বন্ধীয়, নীলনদীসন্নিহিত প্রদেশ বা তৎস্থানের অধিবাসিসম্বন্ধীয়, নৈলেয়। ***Noun.*** One of the Nilotic tribe or nation ; নীল নদী সন্নিহিত প্রদেশবাসী জাতি বা উপজাতি।

nim'-ble (-bl), *adj.* 1. Quick in motion ; swift ; agile ; as, a *nimble* foot ; চটুল, চপল, চটপটে ; ক্ষিপ্র ; লঘুগতি, চপলাঙ্গ। 2. (*Archaic*) (Of money) Circulating quickly ; as, the *nimble* ninepence ; (অপ্রঃ) (অর্থসম্বন্ধে) ক্ষিপ্রচালিত। 3. (Of the mind etc.) Versatile ; quick to apprehend ; dexterous, সর্ব্বতোমুখী প্রতিভাসম্পন্ন; ক্ষিপ্রমতি; দক্ষ, নিপুণ, কুশল। **—bly,** *adv.* **—ness,** *n.*

nim'-bŭs, *n.* (*Pl.* -BI), 1. A bright disc or halo investing a deity, person or thing ; ভামণ্ডল, ছটামুকুট, কিরণকিরীট, প্রভামণ্ডল, জ্যোতির্বলয়। 2. (*Art.*) A bright or golden disc surrounding the head, esp. of a saint ; (শিল্পকলা) খৃষ্টীয় সিদ্ধপুরুষগণের মস্তকের চতুর্দ্দিগস্থ কিরণকিরীট, ছটামুকুট। 3. (*Meteorol.*) A rain-cloud ; (আবহ-বিদ্যা) বর্ষণশীল ধূসরবর্ণ মেঘ, বর্ষপ্রদ, জলপ্রদ (হিঃ কোঃ)। **—bused,** *adj.* Furnished with a nimbus ; ছটামুকুটবিশিষ্ট।

Nimbus head.

nï-mi'-ĕ-tȳ, *n.* (*Rare*) Excess ; redundancy ; (অপ্রঃ) অতিরিক্ত বস্তু ; আধিক্য।

nim'-i-nȳ—pim'-i-nȳ, *adj.* Affected ; mincing ; lacking in force or spirit ; কৃত্রিম, কপট ; মিনমিনে ; ম্যাদামরা।

Nim'-rŏd, *n.* A son of Cush described in the Bible as a mighty hunter and ruler ; hence a great hunter or sportsman ; বাইবেলে বর্ণিত জনৈক শ্রেষ্ঠ মৃগয়াকুশল নৃপতি ; মৃগয়াকুশল ব্যক্তি ।

nin′-cŏm-poop, *n.* A fool ; a person without sense or character ; বোকা, আহাম্মক ; অল্পবুদ্ধি ব্যক্তি, চরিত্রহীন লোক ।

nīne, *adj.* & *n.* One more than eight ; as, *nine* weeks ; নব । ***Noun.*** **1.** The number nine ; a symbol indicating this ; নয় ; ৯ । **2.** A card of nine pips ; তাসের নয়লা । **Nine′-fold**, *adj.* & *adv.* Nine times repeated ; নবগুণিত । (*Adv.*) Nine times as great or as many ; নয়গুণ । **Nine holes**—A kind of game ; একপ্রকার ক্রীড়া । **Ninepins** — একপ্রকার ডাণ্ডাগুলি খেলা । **Nine-tenths**—Nearly the whole ; প্রায় সমস্ত । **A cat has nine lives**—See under CAT. **A nine days' wonder**—Something that causes great excitement for a short time and is heard of no more ; যাহা অল্প সময়ের জন্য মহা উত্তেজনার সঞ্চার করিয়া অচিরে বিস্মৃতিগর্ভে বিলীন হয় । **Dressed up to the nines**—সুসজ্জিত । **Nine points of the law**—মোকদ্দমার জয়লাভ যে নয়টী বিষয়ের উপর নির্ভর করে—(১) প্রচুর অর্থ, (২) অসীম ধৈর্য্য, (৩) ভাল উকিল, (৪) ভাল বিষয় (a good cause), (৫) ভাল সাক্ষী, (৬) ভাল কৌঁসুলি, (৭) ভাল জুরি, (৮) ভাল বিচারক, (৯) ভাল কপাল । **Nine tailors make a man**—দরজীগণ বোকা বলিয়া প্রসিদ্ধ—তাই দরজী একজন মানুষের নবমাংশ বলিয়া বিবেচিত হয় । **Nine times out of ten**—Generally ; প্রায়শঃ, সচরাচর । **Nine worthies** — নবরত্ন [আলেকজাণ্ডার, জুলিয়াস সীজার, Cannan বিজয়ী Joshua, ইজ্রায়েলরাজ David, Judas Maccabæus, শার্লেমেন, গড্‌ফ্রে, প্রায়ামের পুত্র হেক্‌টর, ব্রিটেনরাজ আর্থার] । **The Nine** — The Muses ; গ্রীকদেশীয় বাগ্‌দেবীগণ । **To the nines**—Perfectly ; elaborately ; splendidly ; সর্ব্বাঙ্গসম্পন্নরূপে ; সবিস্তারে ; আশ্চর্য্যরূপে ।

nīne′-teen (-tēn), *adj.* & *n.* Nine plus ten ; ঊনবিংশ । ***Noun.*** The number nineteen ; a symbol denoting this ; ঊনিশ ; ১৯ । **-teenth**, *adj.* & *n.* The ordinal of nineteen ; ঊনবিংশতম । (*Noun.*) A nineteenth part ; the quotient of a unit divided by nineteen ; ঊনবিংশ অংশ ; $\frac{1}{19}$ । **He is nearly nineteen**—তার প্রায় উনিশ বছর বয়স হইবে ।

nīne′-tȳ, *adj.* & *n.* Nine times ten ; নব্বই, নবতি । ***Noun.*** **1.** The product of nine times ten ; a symbol denoting this ; নবতি ; ৯০ । **Ninety-nine out of a hundred**—Nearly all ; একশতের মধ্যে নিরানব্বইটী, প্রায় সকল । **The nineties**—তাপমান যন্ত্রের ৮৯ হইতে ৯০ অংশ ; শতাব্দীর ৮৯ হইতে ১০০ বর্ষ ; ৮৯ বৎসর হইতে ১০০ বৎসর ।

Nin′-ĕ-vīte *n.* An inhabitant of Nineveh, in ancient Assyria ; প্রাচীন এসিরিয়ার অন্তঃপাতী Nineveh নগরীর অধিবাসী ।

nin′-ny (-ĭ), *n.* A fool ; a person of weak character or mind ; নির্ব্বোধ, বোকা, আহাম্মক ; ম্যাদামারা-লোক, দুর্ব্বলপ্রকৃতির লোক ।

nīnth, *adj.* & *n.* The ordinal of nine ; নবম । ***Noun.*** The quotient of a unit divided by nine ; a ninth part ; $\frac{1}{9}$; নবমাংশ । **Ninth′-ly**, *adv.* In the ninth place ; নবমতঃ । **On the ninth**—On the ninth day of a month ; মাসের ৯ তারিখ । **The ninth part of a man**—A tailor ; দরজী ।

Nī′-ō-bē, *n.* **1.** (*Gr. Myth.*) A daughter of Tantalus and Trygete ; Tantalus এর কন্যা । তিনি এক দিন গর্ব্ব করিয়া বলিয়াছিলেন যে "আমি সাত পুত্র ও সাত কন্যার মা—Letoর মাত্র দুইটী সন্তান । Apollo এবং Artemis তাঁহাদের জননীর প্রতি এরূপ কটাক্ষ করাতে ক্রুদ্ধ হইয়া Niobeর সন্তানগণকে বাণ দ্বারা নিধন করেন । Niobe পুত্রকন্যার শোকে কাঁদিতে কাঁদিতে প্রস্তরে পরিণত হইয়াছিলেন বলিয়া কথিত আছে । **2.** An inconsolable bereaved woman ; প্রিয়জন-বিয়োগবিধুরা নারী । **-be′-an**, *adj.*

nī-ō′-bĭ-ŭm, *n.* (*Chem.*) A metallic element ; (রসায়ন-শাস্ত্র) একপ্রকার ধাতব মূলপদার্থ, নবক (সাঃ পঃ) ।

nip, *v. t.*, *i.* & *n.* **1.** To compress sharply ; to pinch ; to bite ; খামচি মারা ; চিমটি কাটা ; কামড়ান । **2.** To cut or pinch *off*, as a bud, etc. ; to clip ; কাটা, ছিঁড়া, নিকৃন্তন করা ; ছাঁটিয়া ফেলা । **3.** To check the growth of, (*lit.* & *fig.*) ; as, to be *nipped* in the bud ; (শব্দানুযায়ী এবং লক্ষণায়) বৃদ্ধির ব্যাঘাত করা । **4.** (Of cold) To affect painfully or injuriously ; to blast ; আর্ত্তকরা ; কোঁকড়াইয়া দেওয়া । **5.** (*Slang* or *dial.*) To snatch ; (ইতর ভাষায় ও উপভাষায়) কাড়িয়া লওয়া । ***Verb i.*** **1.** To pinch or press tightly ; চিমটি কাটা, খামচি মারা । **2.** (*Slang*) To move briskly, quickly, or nimbly ; (ইতর ভাষায়) চটপট করিয়া চলা । ***Noun.*** **1.** Pinch ; a sharp squeeze ; a bite চিমটি ; খামচি ; কামড় । **2.** A biting remark ; sarcasm ; কাটা কাটা কথা ; বিদ্রূপ । **3.** A check to the growth of vegetation due to cold or frost ; hence, sharp cold ; শীত বা তুষারপাত হেতু বৃক্ষাদির বিকাশরোধ ; কন্‌কনে ঠাণ্ডা । **Nip′-py**, *adj.* **Nip′-ping**, *adj.* **1.** (Of language) Stinging ; sarcastic ; কাটা, খোঁচানো, খোচামারা ; বিদ্রূপাত্মক । **2.** (Of the weather, wind, etc.) Cold ; biting ; ঠাণ্ডা ; কন্‌কনে । **3.** Causing pain ; বেদনাজনক । **Nip′-ping-ly**, *adv.* **To nip a bung**—To steal a purse ; পকেট মারা, পকেট কাটিয়া চুরি করা ।

To nip in the bud—To destroy before maturity or development, (*lit.* & *fig.*) : অঙ্কুরে বিনাশ করা, কোরকে কাটা।

nĭp, *n.*, *v. i.* & *t.* A sip or small draught, esp. of some spirituous liquor ; চুমুক। ***Verb i. & t.*** To take (liquor) in sips ; esp. to tipple ; এক চুমুকে খাওয়া ; বার বার একটু একটু করিয়া মদ খাওয়া।

nĭp′-per (-ȇr) *n.* 1. One that nips ; যে ব্যক্তি চিমটি কাটে। 2. A kind of fish ; একপ্রকার মৎস্য। 3. A boy ; a lad ; esp. costermonger's assistant or a street arab ; বালক, ছোঁড়া ; ছোকরা ; বিশেষ ভাবে ফলবিক্রেতার সাহায্যকারী বালক, যে বালক রাস্তায় রাস্তায় ঘুরিয়া বেড়ায়। 4. (*Pl.*) Small pincers for holding, breaking or cutting, (often a *pair of nippers*) ; সন্দংশ, কঙ্কমুখ, মুখসন্দংশ (ব্রজঃ হিন্দুঃ), আঁকসাঁড়াশী, ডাম্বুরা। 5. (*Pl.*) Same as PINCE-NEZ (which see). 6. A foretooth of a horse ; অশ্বের কৃন্তনদন্ত। 7. A crustacean's claw ; কাঁকড়া প্রভৃতির নখর।

nĭp′-ple (-l), *n.* 1. A pap ; teat ; স্তনাগ্র, কুচাগ্র, চুচুক (or চূচুক) ; স্তনবৃন্ত, স্তনের বোঁটা, স্তনমুখ। 2. A cover for a woman's teat while the child sucks ; শিশুর স্তন্যপান কালে ব্যবহৃত স্ত্রীলোকের চুচুকত্রাণ। 3. The teat of a nursing-bottle ; শিশুদিগের স্তন্যপানের জন্য ব্যবহৃত বোতলের স্তনমুখ। 4. A nipple-like prominence on the skin ; চর্ম্মের উপর চুচুকবৎ উদ্গত অংশ। 5. A small crest on a mountain top ; a projection on metal or glass ; পর্ব্বতের ক্ষুদ্রচূড়া ; কাচ বা ধাতুর উপর বোঁটা। **Nipple-wort**—একপ্রকার পীতপুষ্পপ্রসূ গুল্ম।

nī′-sī, *conj.* (*Legal*) Unless ; যদি না। ***Nisi prius***—(*Lit.* Unless before) Hearing of civil causes by judges of the assize ; court-business of this kind ; (যদি না পূর্ব্বে) বিলাতের প্রাদেশিক দায়রার আদালতে দেওয়ানী মোকদ্দমার শুনানি ; ঐরূপ মোকদ্দমা সম্বন্ধে আদালতের কাজ। **Nisi prius court**—বিলাতের যে প্রাদেশিক দায়রার আদালতে দেওয়ানী মোকদ্দমার শুনানি হয়।

nĭt, *n.* The egg of a louse etc. ; উকুণ প্রভৃতির ডিম্ব, মৎকুণডিম্ব, লিক্ষা।

nī′-trāte, *n.* 1. A salt of nitric acid ; (the nitrates are generally soluble in water and easily decomposed by heat) ; তাম্রদ্রাবের লবণ-বিশেষ। 2. Same as POTASSIUM or SODIUM NITRATE.

nī′-trāte, *v. t.* To treat, combine, or impregnate, with nitric acid ; তামদ্রাব দ্বারা পরিপূরিত করা, তাম্রদ্রাবের সহিত মিশ্রিত করা। **—tra′-tion,** *n.* The act of nitrating ; নেত্রিক ক্রিয়া (সাঃ পঃ), যবক্ষার ক্রিয়া।

nī′-tre (-têr), *n.* Saltpetre ; সোরা, যবক্ষার, সৌবর্চ্চল (রঃ রঃ সঃ প্রঃ), সুবর্চ্চিকা (রঃ প্রঃ), গিরিমস্তক (রঃ প্রঃ), সোরক।

nī′-trĭc, *adj.* Of, or relating to, nitre ; সোরা সম্বন্ধীয়। **Nitric acid**—A compound of oxygen and nitrogen, which is of great importance in chemistry and the arts ; যবক্ষারদ্রাবক, তাম্রদ্রাব, মরুতকদ্রাব। **Nitric anhydride**—দগ্ধমরুতক (সাঃ পঃ)। **Nitric oxide**—আদগ্ধ মরুত (সাঃ পঃ)। **Nitric peroxide**—আদগ্ধ মরুতক (সাঃ পঃ)।

nī′-trĭ-fȳ, *v. t.* & *i.* To turn into nitre ; to make or become nitrous ; সোরাতে পরিণত করা ; সোরাময় করা বা হওয়া। **—fi-ca′-tion,** *n.*

nī′-trīte, *n.* A salt of nitrous acid ; মরুত দ্রাবকের লবণ।

nī-trō-bĕn′-zene (-zēn), *n.* (*Chem.*) A poisonous liquid produced by the action of nitric acid on benzene ; (রসায়ন-শাস্ত্র) বেনজিনের উপরে তাম্রদ্রাবের ক্রিয়ার ফলে উৎপন্ন বিষাক্ত তরল পদার্থ।

nī-trō-bĕn′-zōl(e), *n.* Same as NITROBENZENE above.

nī-trō-g̃ĕl′-ā-tĭn, *n.* A powerful explosive made of gun-cotton and nitroglycerine ; তাম্রদ্রাব, গন্ধকদ্রাব ও গ্লিসিরিণ অনুসিক্ত মহাশক্তিশালী বিস্ফোরক তুলা।

nī′-trō-g̃ĕn, *n.* A colourless, tasteless, scentless, permanent gas forming four-fifths of the atmosphere ; যবক্ষারজান, নেত্রজন। **—trog′-e-nous,** *adj.* **Nitrogenous food**—ছানাজাতীয় উপাদানবিশিষ্ট খাদ্য (খাঃ)।

nī-trō-glȳç′-ȇr-ĭn(e), *n.* A highly explosive oily liquid produced by the action of nitric and sulphuric acids on glycerine ; গ্লিসিরিণের উপর তাম্রদ্রাব ও গন্ধকদ্রাবকের ক্রিয়ার ফলে উৎপন্ন একপ্রকার তরল তৈলাক্ত এবং মহাশক্তিশালী বিস্ফোরক পদার্থ।

nī-trō-hȳ-drō-chlō′-rĭc, *adj.* Of, or relating to, or containing, nitric and hydrochloric acids ; তাম্রদ্রাব এবং লোহদ্রাব সম্বন্ধীয়, তাম্রদ্রাব ও লোহদ্রাবময়। **Nitro-hydrochloric acid**—সর্ব্বজারণ বিড়।

nī-trō-mū′-rĭ-āte, *n.* A substance obtained by dissolving a metal in nitro-hydrochloric acid ; সর্ব্বজারণ বিড়ে কোন ধাতু গলাইয়া প্রস্তুত পদার্থ বিশেষ।

nī-trō-sŭl-phū′-rĭc, *adj.* Formed by the mixture of nitric and sulphuric acids ; তাম্রদ্রাব ও গন্ধকদ্রাবের মিশ্রণে প্রস্তুত। **Nitro-sulphuric acid**—১ ভাগ তাম্রদ্রাবের সহিত ৮ অথবা দশ ভাগ গন্ধকদ্রাবের মিশ্র ; এই মিশ্রের সাহায্যে তাম্র হইতে স্বর্ণ পৃথক করা হয়।

nī′-trous (-trŭs), *adj.* Of, pertaining to, or impregnated with nitre ; সোরাসম্বন্ধীয়, সোরাদ্বারা পরিপূরিত। **Nitrous acid**—যে দ্রাবকে তাম্রদ্রাব অপেক্ষা অল্পতর অম্লজান থাকে, মরুতদ্রাবক (সাঃ পঃ)। **Nitrous anhydride** — দগ্ধ মরুতক (সাঃ পঃ)।

Nitrous oxide—Laughing gas ; উপদগ্ধ মরুত।

nix, *interj.* (*Slang*) A word used as a signal that some one in authority is approaching ; (ইতরভাষায়) কোন ক্ষমতাশালী ব্যক্তি অগ্রসর হইতেছেন তৎসূচনার্থ শব্দবিশেষ।

nix, *n.* (*Fem.* NIXIE) A water-elf or spirit ; জলবাসী দৈত্য।

nō, *adj.* **1.** Not any ; not a ; কেউ নয় ; একটীও নয়। **2.** Denoting complete absence of what is named ; as, a vote of *no* confidence : his faith or *no* faith ; অত্যন্তাভাবসূচক উল্লিখিত বস্তু। **3.** Denoting approximation to nullity ; as, it is *no* distance ; প্রায় কিছুই নয়। **4.** Quite other than a ; as, a service of *no* honourable kind ; সম্পূর্ণ ভিন্নরূপ। **No ball**—*n.* & *v. t.* An unlawfully deliverd ball at cricket ; an umpire's announcement of this ; ক্রীকেট ক্রীড়ায় নিয়মবিরুদ্ধ ভাবে কন্দুকক্ষেপণ ; নিয়মবিরুদ্ধ ভাবে কন্দুক ক্ষেপণ হইয়াছে—ক্রীকেট ক্রীড়ার মধ্যস্থ-কর্ত্তৃক ইহা ঘোষণা। (*Verb t., no-ball*) To pronounce the bowler to have bowled no ball ; নিয়মবিরুদ্ধ-ভাবে কন্দুক নিক্ষেপ হইয়াছে—এই কথা কন্দুকক্ষেপককে বলা। **No-being**—Non-existence ; নাস্তিত্ব। **Nobody**—No person ; কেহ নয়। A person of no importance, authority or position ; নগণ্য লোক। **No doubt**—Without any doubt ; নিঃসন্দেহে। **No end**—A great deal ; অফুরন্ত, অশেষ। **No go**—Of no use ; অকেজো। **No how**—In no way ; by no means ; কোন মতেই নয় ; কোন প্রকারেই নয়। **No joke**—ঠাট্টা নয়, তামাসা নয়। **No man's land**—অনাবাদী, অনধিকৃত বা বিরোধীয় ভূমি। **No matter**—Of no consequence or significance ; গুরুতর কিছু নয়, বিশেষ কিছু নয়। **No-meaning**—No sense ; অর্থহীন। **No song no upper**—You must sing first ; তোমাকে প্রথম গান গাহিতে হইবে। **No sweat, No sweet**—কষ্ট ছাড়া কেষ্ট মিলে না। **No thoroughfare**—See THOROUGHFARE. **Noway(s), Nowise**—In no manner ; not at all ; কোন প্রকারেই নয় ; মোটেই না। **Nowhence**—From no place ; কোন স্থান হইতে নয়। **No whit**—Not at all ; মোটেই নয়। **Nowhither**—To no place ; কোন স্থানেই নয়। **No wonder**—A matter not to be wondered at ; আশ্চর্য্যের বিষয় নয়। **To be, feel, look, etc. nohow**—শারীরিক বা মানসিক অসুস্থতা বোধ করা।

nō, *adv.* Not ; not at all ; as, *no* longer : *no* shorter : *no* more : *no* less ; না ; মোটেই না। **No less (than)**—As much or many (as) ; (চেয়ে) কম নয়। **No more,** *n., adj.* & *adv.*—Nothing further ; as, to have *no more* to say ; আর অধিক কিছু না। (*Adj.*) Not any more ; as, *no more* wine ? ; আর নয়। (*Adv.*) No longer ; as, he is *no more* ; never again ; to no greater extent ; just as little ; neither ; as, he did not come *no more* did you ; আর নয় ; পুনরায় আর কখনও নয় ; অধিক মাত্রায় নয় ; প্রায় ততটা ; দুই এর একও নয়। **He is no more**—He is dead or passed away ; সে মরিয়া গিয়াছে। **Whether or no**—In either case ; উভয়স্থলে।

nō, *n.* (*Pl.* NOES) **1.** Act of uttering no ; a refusal by use of the word *no* ; a denial ; as, two *noes* make a yes ; না শব্দ উচ্চারণ ; না শব্দে অস্বীকার ; অস্বীকার। **2.** A negative vote or decision ; (*pl.*) those who vote in the negative ; as, the *noes* have it ; অসম্মতি-জ্ঞাপক মত, না-বাচক মত বা নিষ্পত্তি ; যাহারা "না" বলিয়া মত দেয়। **The noes have it**—The negative votes are in the majority ; অসম্মতিজ্ঞাপক মতদাতৃগণের সংখ্যা অধিক। **Will not take no for a answer**—Persits in spite of refusals ; সে না কথা শুনিবে না।

Nō-ā′-chi-ăn, Nō-ăch′-ic, *adjs.* Of, or relating to, Noah or his time ; নোয়াসম্বন্ধীয়, নোয়ার সময়ের।

Nō′-ah (-ā), *n.* (*Bibl.*) A patriarch, who at God's command built an ark to save his family and a number of individuals of all living creatures in the time of the Deluge or Flood ; বাইবেলে উল্লিখিত ব্যক্তিবিশেষ—ইনি জলপ্রলয়ের কালে ঈশ্বরের আদেশে একটী পোত নির্ম্মাণ করত প্রতি জন্তুর এক একটী দম্পতীসহ তদুপরি আরোহণ পূর্ব্বক প্রাণরক্ষা করেন। **Noah's ark**—See ARK 3. A child's plaything in imitation of it ; নোয়ার জলযানের অনুকরণে তৈরী ছেলেদের খেলনা। A marine bivalve shell suggestive of an ark or ship in form ; একপ্রকার পোত বা নৌযানাকার সামুদ্রিক শম্বুক। A detached fragment of a flying cloud ; উড্ডীন মেঘের ছিন্নখণ্ড। **Noah's nightcap**—একপ্রকার গুল্ম।

nŏb, *n.* & *v. t.* **1.** (*Slang*) The head ; (ইতর ভাষায়) মুণ্ড, মুড়া। **2.** (*Cribbage*) A knave or jack of the same suit as the turn-up card, counting one to the holder ; (তাসখেলাবিশেষে) গোলাম। ***Verb t.*** (*Boxing*) To hit on the head ; (মুষ্টিযুদ্ধ) মাথায় আঘাত করা। **One for his nob**—ঐ গোলাম হাতে থাকায় জয়াঙ্ক লাভ।

nŏb, *n.* (*Slang*) A member of the aristocracy ; (ইতর ভাষায়) সম্ভ্রান্তবংশীয় লোক। **A nob of the first water**—A very high class personage ; খুব বড় মানুষ।

nŏb′-ble (-l), *v. t.* **1.** (*Slang*) To tamper with (a racehorse) to prevent its winning ; কোন ঘোড়-দৌড়ের ঘোড়া যাহাতে জয়ী হইতে না পারে তজ্জন্য গোপনে অসাধু উপায় অবলম্বন করা। **2.** To win over to one's side or interest, as by bribery ; উৎকোচ প্রভৃতি দ্বারা স্বপক্ষে আনয়ন করা। 3. To get possession of dishonestly ; to steal ; as, to *nobble* money ; অসাধু উপায়ে আত্মসাৎ করা ; চুরি করা। 4. To catch (a criminal) ; ধরা, পাকড়ান।

nŏb'-by (-ĭ), *adj.* (*Slang*) Suitable for an aristocrat ; stylish ; smart ; (ইতর ভাষায়) বড়মানুষের উপযোগী ; কেতাদুরুস্ত ; চোস্ত।

Nō-bĕl'-prī-zĕs, *n.* Five annual prizes awarded annually from the interest of money bequeathed by Alfred Bernhard Nobel, a Swedish engineer and chemist ; সুইডেনের সুবিখ্যাত রসায়নবিদ্ ও পূর্ত্তবিদ্যাবিশারদ Alfred Nobel কর্তৃক প্রদত্ত অর্থের সুদ হইতে প্রতিবৎসর ৮০০০ পাউণ্ডের (১,২০০০০ টাকার) যে পাঁচটী পুরস্কার প্রদত্ত হইয়া থাকে। এই পুরস্কার জাতি, বর্ণ এবং স্ত্রীপুরুষনির্ব্বিশেষে সকলেই পাইবার অধিকারী। প্রতি বৎসর পদার্থবিজ্ঞান, রসায়নশাস্ত্র, শারীরবিজ্ঞান কিম্বা চিকিৎসাশাস্ত্র সম্বন্ধে যে তিন ব্যক্তির কার্য্য সর্ব্বশ্রেষ্ঠ বলিয়া বিবেচিত হয়—তাঁহারা প্রত্যেকে এক একটী পুরস্কার পাইয়া থাকেন। চতুর্থ পুরস্কার সর্ব্বোত্তম ভাবপ্রধান গ্রন্থের রচয়িতাকে প্রদত্ত হয়। আন্তর্জাতিক শান্তিসংস্থাপন বিষয়ে যাঁহার কার্য্য সর্ব্বশ্রেষ্ঠ বলিয়া গণ্য হয়—তিনি পঞ্চম পুরস্কার পাইয়া থাকেন। ভারতগৌরব রবীন্দ্রনাথ ঠাকুর ১৯১৫ খৃঃ অব্দে সাহিত্যবিষয়ক নোবেল পুরস্কার লাভ করিয়াছেন। এই পুরস্কার ১৯০১ সন হইতে প্রদত্ত হইয়া আসিতেছে।

nō-bĭl'-ĭ-ā-rȳ, *adj.* Of, or relating to, the nobility ; সম্ভ্রান্তসম্প্রদায়-সম্পর্কীয়। **Nobiliary particle**—A preposition (as French *de* or German *von*, in a title of nobility) ; সম্ভ্রান্তবংশীয় ব্যক্তির উপাধিতে ব্যবহৃত অব্যয় শব্দ।

nō-bĭl'-ĭ-tȳ, *n.* **1.** Noble character, mind, birth or rank ; eminence ; কৌলীন্য, আভিজাত্য, মহাকুলতা, মহাকুলীনতা; শ্রেষ্ঠত্ব। 2. (With *the*) The body of nobles in a state or country ; কোন রাজ্য বা দেশের সম্ভ্রান্তসম্প্রদায়। 3. (With *a*) A body or class of nobles ; সম্ভ্রান্তসম্প্রদায়, সম্ভ্রান্তসমাজ, কুলীনসমাজ, অভিজাতসমাজ।

nō'-ble (-bl'), *adj.* & *n.* **1.** Illustrious by rank, title or birth ; belonging to, or forming, the nobility ; সম্ভ্রান্ত, কুলীন, অভিজাত, কুলমর্য্যাদাসম্পন্ন; উচ্চবংশীয়, উচ্চকুলজাত। 2. (Of actions) Illustrious ; great ; বিখ্যাত ; সুমহান। 3. Of lofty character or ideals ; magnanimous ; as, a *noble* heart ; উন্নতচরিত, উন্নতচেতা ; মহানুভব, মহৎ, মহোদয়। 4. Characterized by moral superiority or dignity ; "Relic of *nobler* days and noblest arts!"; উন্নত। 5. Grand, esp. in appearance ; magnificent ; impressive ; as, a *noble* edifice ; সুবিশাল; জমকালো ; প্রাণস্পর্শী। 6. Excellent ; admirable ; as a *noble* horse ; অত্যুৎকৃষ্ট ; প্রশংসনীয়। ***Noun.*** 1. One belonging to the nobility ; a nobleman ; সম্ভ্রান্তপুরুষ ; কুলীন ব্যক্তি। 2. An obsolete English coin, worth 6*s.* 8*d.* ; ইংলণ্ডের

Noble of Edward.

প্রাচীন স্বর্ণমুদ্রাবিশেষ। **–bly,** *adv.* **–ness,** *n.* State of being noble ; কৌলিন্য, মহানুভবতা, মহত্ব। **A nobleman**—A peer ; সম্ভ্রান্তপুরুষ। **Noble-minded**—*adj.* উদারমতি উদারচেতা, উন্নতমনাঃ, মহানুভব; প্রশস্তচেতা। **Noble-mindedness,** *n.* **Noble-woman**—সম্ভ্রান্ত মহিলা।

Noblesse, (*F.*), *n.* The class of nobles, (esp. of a foreign country) ; সম্ভ্রান্তসমাজ, অভিজাতবর্গ। ***Noblesse oblige*** — High rank has its obligations ; সম্ভ্রান্তপুরুষের দায়িত্ব আছে।

nŏck, *n.* & *v. t.* **1.** A notch at the ends of a bow for holding the string ; ধনুর প্রান্তে গুণ লাগাইবার জন্য খাঁজ। **2.** The notch of an arrow for receiving the bowstring ; গুণে আরোপণের জন্য বাণের প্রান্তদেশে খাঁজ, বাণের খাঁজ। ***Verb t.*** To set (an arrow) on the string ; ধনুকে গুণ যোজনা করা। **2.** To furnish, as an arrow or bow with a nock or notch ; ধনু বা বাণের প্রান্তে খাঁজ কাটা।

nŏck, *n.* The forward upper corner of some sails ; কোন কোন পাইলের সম্মুখের দিকের উপরের কোণ।

nŏck-tăm-bū-lā'-tion, *n.* SOMNAMBULISM (which see). **–lant,** *adj.*

nŏc-tĭ-flō'-rous (-rŭs), *adj.* Night-flowering ; নিশাবিকাসী।

nŏc-tĭ-lū'-că, *n.* A marine animalcule noted for its phosphorescence ; ফুক্ফুরক আলোকবিশিষ্ট সামুদ্রিক জীবাণু-বিশেষ।

nŏc-tĭv'-ă-gănt, –gous (-gŭs), *adj.* Night-wandering ; নিশাভ্রমণশীল, নিশাচর। **–ga'-tion,** *n.* (*Obs.*)

nŏc'-tūle, *n.* A large species of bat ; একপ্রকার বৃহৎকায় বাদুড়।

nŏc-tur'-năl (-têr-), *adj.* **1.** Of, or pertaining to, the night ; done, or occurring, at night ; নৈশ, রাত্রি-সম্বন্ধীয় ; রাত্রিকালীন। **2.** Moving about or active in the night ; as, *nocturnal* birds or insects ; নিশাচর, রাত্রিচর, রজনীচারী। **Nocturnal birds**—পেচক প্রভৃতি। **Nocturnal emission**—স্বপ্নদোষ।

nŏc'-turne (-têrn), *n.* **1.** A musical piece of a dreamy character ; স্বপ্নভাবাত্মক সঙ্গীত। **2.** (*Painting*) A night-scene ; (চিত্রবিদ্যা) রজনীদৃশ্য।

nŏd, *v. i., t. & n.* **1.** To incline the head with a quick motion, esp. in salutation, assent or command ; মস্তক সঞ্চালিত করা, মাথা নাড়া, শিরঃসঞ্চালন করা। **2.** To let the head fall, as in drowsiness ; to make a slip or mistake ; as, Homer sometimes *nods* ; ঢুলিয়া পড়া ; ভুলচুক করা। **3.** To incline from the vertical, as a wall, (*lit. & fig.*) ; "...Empire ...*nodding* to its fall" ; নুইয়া পড়া, হেলিয়া পড়া। **4.** (Of plumes) To dance up and down ; দোলা। ***Verb t.*** **1.** To incline or bend, as the head or top ; অবনত করা। **2.** To signify by, or say with, a nod ; as, the officer *nodded* an affirmative ; মস্তক সঞ্চালনপূর্ব্বক জ্ঞাপন করা, মাথা নাড়িয়া বলা। ***Noun.*** **1.** Nodding of the head ; শিরঃকম্পন। **2.** A sign of this kind conveying an assent or command ; শিরঃসঞ্চালনপূর্ব্বক অনুমতি বা আদেশ প্রদান। **A nodding acquaintance**—A slight acquaintance, (*with* a person or subject) ; সামান্য পরিচয়। **A nod is as good as a wink to a blind horse**—যাহারা চোখ খুলিয়া থাকিবে না বা চোখ খুলিয়া দেখিবে না তাহাদিগকে বারবার ইঙ্গিত করা বৃথা। **Homer sometimes nods** — অতি পণ্ডিত লোকেরও ভ্রম হইয়া থাকে, মুনীনাঞ্চ মতিভ্রমঃ। **Land of nod**—Sleep, (referring to a phrase in *Gen.* iv. 16) ; নিদ্রা, ঘুমের পুরী।

nŏd'-dle (-l), *n.* (*Colloq.*) The head ; pate ; (চলিত ভাষায়) মুণ্ড ; মুড়া।

nod'-dle (-l), *v. t.* To nod quickly or slightly as the head ; মাথা নাড়া।

nŏd'-dy (-ĭ), *n.* **1.** A fool ; a noodle ; বোকা ; অল্পবুদ্ধি, আহাম্মক। **2.** A tropical sea-bird ; গ্রীষ্মমণ্ডলের সাগরচর পক্ষিবিশেষ।

nōde, *n.* **1.** A knob or protuberance on a root or branch ; বৃক্ষের শাখা বা শিকড়ের স্ফীতি, আঁব। **2.** The joint of a stem at which leaves spring ; কাণ্ডের যে গ্রন্থি হইতে পত্র উদ্গত হয়, পর্ব্বসন্ধি (বিশঃ)। **3.** (*Med.*) A hard tumour, esp. on a gouty or rheumatic joint ; (ভৈষজ্য শাস্ত্র) অস্থিবেষ্ট ও অস্থির মধ্যে উৎপন্ন কঠিন অণ্ডাকার অর্ব্বুদ, অস্থিগুল্ম (ডাহিঃ)। **4** (*Astron.*) One of the two points in which the orbit of a planet cuts the ecliptic or in which two circles of the celestial sphere intersect each other ; (জ্যোতিবিজ্ঞান) গ্রহের কক্ষ এবং ক্রান্তিবৃত্ত যে বিন্দুদ্বয়ে পরস্পরকে ছেদন করে,—তাহার অন্যতর, যে বিন্দুদ্বয়ে খ মণ্ডলস্থ বৃহৎ বৃত্তদ্বয় পরস্পরকে ছেদন করে,—তাহার অন্যতর পাত (হিঃ কোঃ), পাতস্থান (সূর্য্যঃ বিঃ)। **5.** A point or line of rest in a vibrating body ; a central point in a system ; ঘূর্ণ্যমাণ বস্তুর মধ্যস্থ বিন্দু বা বিরামরেখা ; মধ্যবিন্দু। **6.** (*Geom.*) A point of intersection of one branch of a curve with another ; কোন বক্রের এক শাখা অপর শাখাকে যে বিন্দুতে ছেদন করে। **7.** A complication or difficulty as in a drama ; (নাট্যে) সঙ্কট বা জটিল রহস্য। **Nod'-al,** *adj.* **Nod'-i-cal,** *adj.* (*Astron.*) Of, or pertaining to, the nodes ; পাতসম্বন্ধীয়, পাতস্থানসম্বন্ধীয়। **Ascending node of the moon**—প্রথমসম্পাত (গোলঃ), পূর্ব্বার্দ্ধপাত (আঃ বঃ), রাহু (ঐ), উপপ্লব (সাঃ পঃ), উপরক্ত (ঐ), উপরাগ (ঐ), কৃষ্ণবর্ত্ম (ঐ), গ্রহ (ঐ), পাত (ঐ), স্বর্ভানু, সৈংহিকেয়, বিধুন্তুদ, মতঃ। **Descending node of the moon**—কেতু (সাঃ পঃ), রাহুপুচ্ছ (ঐ), সষড়ভপাত (ঐ), অকচ (ঐ), দ্বিতীয়সম্পাত (গোলঃ), পরার্দ্ধপাত (আঃ বঃ)।

nō'-dōse, *adj.* Knotty ; knobbed ; গ্রন্থিল ; অর্ব্বুদবিশিষ্ট।

nō-dŏs'-ĭ-tȳ, *n.* **1.** Knottiness ; গ্রন্থিলতা। **2.** A knot or node ; গ্রন্থি বা পর্ব্ব।

nŏd'-ūle, *n.* **1.** A small roundish lump of anything ; পিণ্ড। **2.** (*Bot.*) A tubercle or node of some plants ; (উদ্ভিদবিদ্যা) গ্রন্থি, গাঁইট। **3.** A small knotty tumour ; a ganglion ; আঁব, গুটি, স্নায়ুগণ্ড, স্নায়ুবর্তুল, স্নায়ুগুল্ম ; গ্রন্থিলস্নায়ু, বাতগ্রন্থি (সাঃ পঃ) ; **—u-lar,** *adj.* Of, or pertaining to, or in the form of, nodules or nodes ; গ্রন্থিসম্বন্ধীয়, গ্রন্থিবিশিষ্ট, গ্রন্থির আকার। **—u-lat-ed,** *adj.* **—u-la'-tion,** *n.* **—u-lose, —u-lous,** *adjs.*

nō'-dŭs, *n.* (*pl.* -DI.) A knotty point ; a difficulty or complication ; as, the *nodus* of a drama ; জটিল বিষয় ; সঙ্কট, গোলমাল।

nō-ĕt'-ic, *adj. & n.* **1.** Of, or pertaining to, the intellect or reason ; প্রজ্ঞানসম্বন্ধীয়, বুদ্ধিজ (হিঃ কোঃ), ধীসম্বন্ধীয়, জ্ঞানীয়, জ্ঞানসম্বন্ধীয়। **2.** Purely intellectual or abstract ; শুদ্ধবুদ্ধিজ, অমূর্ত্ত। **3.** Given to intellectual speculation ; "*Noetic* school" ; চিন্তাশীল। ***Noun.*** (Also *noetics*) The science of the intellect ; বুদ্ধি-বিজ্ঞান।

nŏg, *n. & v. t.* **1.** A wooden pin, peg or block of the size of a brick ; কাঠের শলাকা বা ইষ্টকাকৃতি কাষ্ঠখণ্ড। **2.** A snag or stump on a tree or branch ; বৃক্ষ বা শাখার ছিন্নমূল উদ্গত অংশ। ***Verb t.*** **1.** To secure by a nog or treenail ; কাঠের শলাকা দ্বারা আটকান। **2.** To build with timber-framing and brick ; কাঠের কাঠামের ফাঁক ইটের গাঁথুনি দ্বারা পূর্ণ করিয়া নির্ম্মাণ করা। **Nog'-ging,** *n.* Brickwork in timber-frame ; কাঠের কাঠামের ভিতর ইটের গাঁথুনি।

nŏg, *n.* A kind of strong ale formerly brewed in Norfolk ; একপ্রকার উগ্র মদিরা।

nŏg'-gin (-ĭn), *n.* **1.** A small mug or cup ; ক্ষুদ্র পেয়ালা বা চুমকী। **2.** A small measure of liquor usually ¼ pint ; অল্পপরিমাণ পানীয়, সাধারণতঃ ¼ পাইণ্ট। **To go to**

noggin staves—To go to pieces ; to fall into disorder ; চুরমার হওয়া ; বিশৃঙ্খল হওয়া।

noil (nōyl), *n.* (*Sing.* or *pl.*) The short pieces and knots of wool combed out of the long staple ; পশমের সূতা আঁচড়াইয়া যে ক্ষুদ্র পশমের টুকরা ও গ্রন্থি বাহির করা হয়।

noise (nōyz), *n.*, *v. t.* & *i.* **1.** Loud outcry ; clamour ; din or uproar of persons ; গণ্ডগোল, গোলমাল, রব ; কলরব, বিরাব ; সোরগোল, কোলাহল, শোর। **2.** Any sound, esp. a loud or harsh one ; শব্দ, ধ্বনি, স্বন, নিনাদ, নাদ। ***Verb t.*** To report ; to spread abroad by rumour ; সংবাদ দেওয়া ; জনরবদ্বারা প্রচার করা। ***Verb i.*** **1.** To talk much or loudly ; বেশী কথা বলা, উচ্চৈঃস্বরে কথা বলা। **2.** To make a noise or outcry ; চীৎকার করা, গোলমাল করা। **Noise'-less,** *adj.* Making no noise ; silent ; নীরব ; নিঃশব্দ, নিঝুম, নিস্তব্ধ। **Noise'-less-ly,** *adv.* **Noise'-less-ness,** *n.* **To make a noise**—To make a clamour or loud outcry ; কলরব করা, চীৎকার করা। To talk or complain much *about* ; কোন বিষয় লইয়া গোলযোগ করা, কোন ব্যাপার লইয়া হৈ চৈ করা। To be the object of general notice and comment ; সাধারণের লক্ষ্য বা সমালোচনার বিষয়ীভূত হওয়া। To attain notoriety (in the world) কাহারো নামে সোরগোল পড়িয়া যাওয়া। **To noise abroad**—রটনা করা।

noi-sette' (nwä-zĕt), *n.* A kind of rose, a cross between China rose and moss-rose (from the name of the grower 1817) ; এক-প্রকার গোলাব।

noisette, (*F.*), *n.* (*Usu. pl.*) Small pieces of meat cooked as a dish ; মাংসের কালিয়া।

noi'-some (nōy-sŭm), *adj.* **1.** Noxious ; insalubrious ; harmful ; বিষাক্ত ; অস্বাস্থ্যজনক, অস্বাস্থ্যকর ; অনিষ্টকর। **2.** Ill-smelling ; দুর্গন্ধ ! **3.** Disagreeable ; offensive ; অপ্রীতিজনক ; বিরক্তিকর, বিরক্তিজনক। **—ness,** *n.*

nois'-ȳ (nōyz-), *adj.* **1.** Clamorous ; boisterous ; turbulent ; as, a *noisy* crowd ; কলরবপূর্ণ ; কোলাহল-পূর্ণ, মহাশব্দকারী ; উৎপাতজনক। **2.** Full of, or characterized by, noise ; as, a *noisy* market ; কলরবপূর্ণ, কোলাহল-পূর্ণ। **3.** (Of colour, costume, literary style, etc.) Conspicuous ; glaring ; loud ; সমুজ্জ্বল ; রংচঙ্গে ; শব্দাড়ম্বরপূর্ণ। **—i-ly,** *adv.* **—i-ness,** *n.*

Nolens volens, (*L.*), *adv.* Whether one will or not ; ইচ্ছায়ই হউক বা অনিচ্ছায়ই হউক।

nŏ'-li-mĕ-tăn'-ğĕ-rĕ, *n.* (*L.*= *Touch me not*) **1.** (*Med.*) Ulcerous diseases of the skin ; (ভৈষজ্য-শাস্ত্র) গলিতকুষ্ঠ প্রভৃতি চর্ম্মরোগ। **2.** A warning against meddling or approach ; হস্তক্ষেপ না করে বা অগ্রসর না হয়—তজ্জন্য সাবধানতা। **3.** A picture of Christ as he appeared to Magdalen at the sepulchre, (*John* xx. 17) ; মেরী মেগডেলেনের সম্মুখে যীশুখৃষ্ট সমাধিপ্রাঙ্গণে যে মূর্ত্তিতে আবির্ভূত হন—তাহার চিত্র। **4.** A person or thing not to be touched or interfered with ; অনধিগম্য ব্যক্তি বা বস্তু, দুর্দ্ধর্ষ ব্যক্তি বা বস্তু।

nolle prosequi, *n.* [*L.*=*To refuse to pursue* ; আর চালাইতে না চাওয়া।] (*Legal*) A term used where a plaintiff in any action will not proceed any further ; (আইন) বাদী বিবাদীর বিরুদ্ধে মোকদ্দমা আর চালাইবে না এই বাক্য দ্বারা ইহা সূচিত হয়।

nolo episcopari, *n.* [*L.*=*I do not wish to be a bishop* ; আমি ধর্ম্মাধ্যক্ষ হইতে বাঞ্ছা করি না] Avoidance of, or objection to, responsible office ; a formula expressing this ; দায়িত্বপূর্ণ কার্য্য-পরিহার বা গ্রহণে আপত্তি ; ঐরূপ পরিহার বা আপত্তিসূচক বাক্য।

nŏm'-ăd, —ade, (*now rare*), *n.* & *adj.* (only *-ad*) One of a tribes who leads a wandering life generally for pasture ; a wanderer ; যাযাবর জাতির লোক, হাঘড়িয়া, বেদিয়া ; পর্য্যটন-শীল ব্যক্তি। ***Adj.*** Roaming from place to place in search of pasture ; wandering ; যাযাবর ; প্রব্রজন-শীল। **—ism,** *n.* **—i-za'-tion,** *n.* **—ize,** *v. t.* To roam about or live as nomads ; যাযাবরের মতন ঘুরা বা বাস করা। **No-mad'-ic,** *adj.* Relating to nomads ; wandering ; যাযাবরসম্বন্ধীয় ; প্রব্রজনশীল। **No-mad'-i-cal-ly,** *adv.*

nom de guerre, (*F.*), *n.* Pseudonym ; an assumed name under which a person fights, plays, writes, etc ; উপনাম ; কল্পিত নাম।

nom de plume, (*F.*), *n.* An author's pseudonym ; গ্রন্থকারের কল্পিত নাম।

nŏ'-mĕn-clā-tor (-têr), *n.* **1.** A giver or inventor of names, esp. in natural historical classification ; নামনির্দ্দেশক বা নামদাতা, নামস্থাপক। **2.** (In ancient Rome) A slave who attends a candidate for office to tell him the names of influential persons whom they met ; an usher assigning places at a banquet ; (প্রাচীন রোম) যে ক্রীতদাস কোন পদপ্রার্থী ব্যক্তিকে তাহারা কোন কোন প্রভাবশালী ব্যক্তির সহিত সাক্ষাৎ করিয়াছিল তাহা বলিবার জন্য ঐ পদপ্রার্থীর সঙ্গে থাকে ; যে ব্যক্তি ভোজে নিমন্ত্রিত ব্যক্তিগণে বসিবার স্থান নির্দ্দেশ করিয়া থাকে। **3.** (Modern use) One telling or announcing the names of guests or of persons generally ; যে ব্যক্তি অভ্যাগত ব্যক্তি-বর্গের নাম বলে বা ঘোষণা করে।

nŏ'-mĕn-clā-tūre, *n.* **1.** A catalogue ; a register ; (now *rare*) ;

তালিকা ; খাতা। 2. The system or set of names for things, etc. commonly employed by a person or community ; নামমালা, নামপদ্ধতি, নিঘণ্টু, নামসংগ্রহ (হিঃ কোঃ)। 3. Terminology of a science, etc. ; পরিভাষা (হিঃ কোঃ)। **–tive**, *adj.*

nŏm'-i-năl, *adj.* 1. Of, relating to, like, or as, a noun ; বিশেষ্য সম্বন্ধীয়, বিশেষ্যবৎ। 2. Pertaining to a name or term ; giving the meaning of a term ; as, a *nominal* definition ; নামসম্বন্ধীয়, পদসম্বন্ধীয়, নামীয় ; পদের অর্থ বা তাৎপর্য্যসূচক। 3. Existing in name only ; not real ; as, a *nominal* difference : a *nominal* ruler ; নামেমাত্র ; অবাস্তব। 4. Consisting of, or giving, the names ; as, a *nominal* list of officers ; নামাত্মক, নামপূর্ণ। **–ly**, *adv.* 1. By name ; নামে। 2. In name only ; নামে মাত্র। **Nominal definition**—(তর্কবিজ্ঞান) কোন পদের মূলীভূত অর্থের প্রকাশ, বিভাজকপরিভাষা (হিঃ কোঃ), নামগতলক্ষণ (ঐ)। **Nominal sum, rent, etc.**—নাম মাত্র টাকা, খাজানা, প্রভৃতি। **Nominal verb**—নামধাতু।

nŏm'-i-năl-ism, *n.* (*Philos.*) The doctrine that universals or abstract concepts are mere names ; (opp. to *realism*) ; পরাজাতি বা জাতিবাচক শব্দসমূহের কোন বাস্তবসত্তা নাই—তাহারা নামমাত্র—এই মতবাদ, শব্দার্থভেদবাদ (হিঃ কোঃ), সামান্যাসত্তাবাদ (আপ্তেঃ), নামবাদ (বিশ্বঃ)। **–ist**, *n.* An adherent of nominalism ; নামবাদী (বিশ্বঃ), শব্দার্থভেদবাদী (হিঃ কোঃ), ব্যাপিজ্ঞানবিসংবাদী (আঃ বঃ)। **–is'-tic**, *adj.*

nŏm'-i-nāte, *v. t.* 1. (*Rare*) To call by the name of ; to mention by name ; (কচিদ্ব্যবহৃত) নাম ধরিয়া ডাকা ; নাম ধরিয়া উল্লেখ করা। 2. (*Rare*) To fix or appoint as a date, place, etc. ; (কচিদ্ব্যবহৃত) স্থান, তারিখ, প্রভৃতি নির্দ্দেশ করা। 3. To name for an office or place ; to appoint ; মনোনীত করা, মনোনয়ন করা ; নিয়োগ করা। **–na-tor**, *n.* One who nominates or makes a nomination ; মনোনয়নকারী। **–nee'**, *n.* 1. The person named as the recipient of an annuity, grant, etc. ; কোন বার্ষিক বৃত্তি, দান, প্রভৃতি প্রাপ্তির জন্য মনোনীত ব্যক্তি। 2. A person nominated for some office etc. ; কোন পদের জন্য মনোনীত ব্যক্তি।

nŏm-i-nā'-tion, *n.* 1. The act or right of appointing a person to some office or duty ; মনোনয়ন, মনোনয়নের অধিকার, নিয়োজনাধিকার, নিয়োজন (হিঃ কোঃ)। 2. The fact or position of being nominated ; মনোনয়নত্ব।

nŏm'-i-nā-tive (-tĭv), *adj.* & *n.* 1. (*Gram.*) Used as, or in agreement with, the subject of a verb, as a case ; কর্ত্তৃকারকস্বরূপ ব্যবহৃত। 2. Of the nature of, or pertaining to, a nominative case ; কর্ত্তৃকারকাত্মক, কর্ত্তৃকারকসম্বন্ধীয়। 3. Of, relating to, or appointed by, nomination ; মনোনয়নসম্বন্ধীয়, মনোনয়নদ্বারা নিযুক্ত। ***Noun.*** 1. The nominative case ; a word in this case ; subject (of a verb) ; কর্ত্তৃকারক ; কর্ত্তৃকারকের পদ ; কর্ত্তা। **–ti'-val**, *adj.* Of, or relating to, the nominitive case ; কর্ত্তৃকারকসম্বন্ধীয়। **Nominative absolute**—See ABSOLUTE.

non, (*L.*), *adv.* Not ; না। ***Non assumpsit***—(He did not undertake) A plea that defendant made no promise ; প্রতিবাদী কোনরূপ প্রতিশ্রুতি করে নাই, এইরূপ আপত্তি। ***Non compos (mentis)***—(Not master of his mind) Lunatic ; mad ; উন্মাদ, বিকৃতমস্তিষ্ক, অপ্রকৃতিস্থ, ছন্নমতি ; পাগল। ***Non esse***—(Not to be) Non-existence ; নাস্তিত্ব। ***Non est inventus***—He has not been found ; তাহার সন্ধান পাওয়া যায় নাই। ***Non liquet***—(It is not clear) Jury's verdict in a doubtful case deferring the matter to another day ; কোন সন্দেহজনক ব্যাপারে কোনরূপ মীমাংসায় উপনীত হইতে না পারিয়া জুরীগণ যে বাক্য বলিয়া অন্য দিন পর্য্যন্ত মত প্রদান স্থগিত রাখেন। ***Non nobis***—(Not unto us) A formula attributing victory, etc. not to oneself but to God ; (আমাদের নয়) যে জয় প্রভৃতির কর্ত্তৃত্ব নিজের উপর না রাখিয়া ঈশ্বরের উপর আরোপ করা হয়। ***Non placet***—*n.* & *v. t.* (It does not please) A negative vote in ecclesiastical or university assemblies ; যাজকীয় বা বিশ্ববিদ্যালয়সংক্রান্ত সভায় অসম্মতিজ্ঞাপক মত। (*Verb t.*) To throw out ; ফেলিয়া দেওয়া। ***Non plus ultra***—NE PLUS ULTRA (which see). ***Non possumus***—(We cannot) A statement of inability ; refusal to act or move ; (আমরা পারি না) অসম্মতিসূচক উক্তি ; কোন কাজ করিতে অস্বীকার। ***Non sequitur***—(It does not follow) Illogical inference ; paradoxical result ; অযৌক্তিক অনুমান ; লোকসংস্কারবিরুদ্ধ পরিণাম।

nŏn–, A prefix in common use in English in the sense of *not*.

nŏn-ăb-stain'-ēr (-stān-), *n.* One who does not abstain, esp. from liquor ; অপানত্যাগী।

nŏn-ăc'-cĕss', *n.* Non-existence of opportunity for sexual intercourse ; সঙ্গমের সুযোগাভাব, অনভিগমন।

nŏn'-āge, *n.* 1. Minority ; নাবালকত্ব, বালদশা, অপ্রাপ্তবয়স্কত্ব, অপ্রাপ্তব্যবহারাবস্থা। 2. Immaturity ; early stage ; "The world's *nonage*" ; অপরিপক্কাবস্থা ; আদিম অবস্থা।

nŏn-ă-gē-nā'-ri-ăn, *adj.* & *n.* Between 89 and 100 years old ; ৮৯ বৎসর হইতে ১০০ বৎসরের মধ্যবর্ত্তী বয়স্ক। ***Noun.*** One of such ages ; নবতিবর্ষ বয়স্ক ব্যক্তি।

nŏn-ă-gĕs'-i-măl, *adj.* & *n.* (*Astron.*) A term applied to the highest point of the ecliptic above the horizon ; (জ্যোতিবিজ্ঞান) দিকচক্রবালের উর্দ্ধে ক্রান্তিবৃত্তের সর্ব্বোচ্চ বিন্দু, ত্রিভোনলগ্ন (সাঃ পঃ), বিত্রিভলগ্ন, বিত্রিভ (হিঃ কোঃ)। **Sine of altitude of nonagesimal**—দৃগ্‌গতি (সাঃ পঃ)। **Sine of zenith distance of nonagesimal**—দৃক্‌ক্ষেপ (সাঃ পঃ)।

nŏn'-ă-gŏn, *n.* (*Geom.*) A polygon having nine angles ; (জ্যামিতি) নবভুজক্ষেত্র, নবকোণক্ষেত্র (হিঃ কোঃ)।

nŏn-ăp-pear'-ance (-pēr-ăns), *n.* Absence, esp. in court, of a party of witness অনুপস্থিতি, গরহাজিরি।

nō'-nă-rȳ, *adj.* & *n.* (*Math.*) Having nine as the radix or base, (said of a system of notation) ; (গণিত) নবমূলক। ***Noun.*** A group of nine ; নবসংখ্যক ব্যক্তি বা বস্তুর সংহতি।

nŏn-ăt-tĕnd'-ance (-ăns), *n.* Failure to attend ; অনুপস্থিতি।

non avenu, (*F.*), *adj.* Not having happened ; না ঘটাতে।

nonce (nŏns), *n.* Present occasion, (only in *for the nonce*) ; বর্ত্তমান ঘটনা, বর্ত্তমান ক্ষেত্র। **Nonce-word**—বর্ত্তমান ক্ষেত্রে ব্যবহারের জন্য গঠিত নব শব্দ। **For the nonce**—For the time being ; temporarily ; আপাততঃ ; সাময়িকভাবে।

nŏn'-cha-lănt (-shă-), *adj.* Unexcited ; indifferent ; careless ; cool ; অবিক্ষুব্ধ, অনুত্তেজিত ; উদাসীন, ভাবনাহীন, অনুরাগশূন্য ; অমনোযোগী ; শান্ত, স্থির। **—lance,** *n.* Indifference ; carelessness ; coolness ; ঔদাসীন্য, উদাসীনতা ; অসতর্কতা ; স্থৈর্য্য, অবিক্ষুব্ধতা। **—ly,** *adv.*

nŏn'-claim (-klām), *n.* Failure to make claim within legal time ; বিধিনির্দ্ধারিত সময়ের মধ্যে দাবী উপস্থাপনে অকৃতকার্য্যতা।

nŏn-cŏl-lē'-gi-āte, *adj.* & *n.* Not belonging to, or connected with, a college ; (also of a university) not made up of colleges ; অ-মহাবিদ্যালয়ভুক্ত, অ মহাবিদ্যালয়সম্পৃক্ত ; (বিশ্ববিদ্যালয় সম্বন্ধে) অ-মহাবিদ্যালয়গঠিত। ***Noun.*** A non-collegiate person ; one not educated in a college ; অ-মহাবিদ্যালয়ভুক্ত ব্যক্তি ; মহাবিদ্যালয়ে শিক্ষাপ্রাপ্ত নয় এরূপ ব্যক্তি

nŏn-cŏm'-băt-ănt, *n.* (*Mil.*) Any person connected with a military or naval force whose duties do not include fighting, as a chaplain, a member of the medical or pay corps etc. or any civilian ; (সামরিক শাস্ত্র) স্থলসৈন্য বা নৌসৈন্যদলে নিযুক্ত (যাজক, চিকিৎসক, প্রভৃতি) অযুদ্ধকারী কর্ম্মচারী।

nŏn-cŏm-mis'-sioned (-mi-shŏnd), *adj.* Not having a commission ; নিম্নপদস্থ সৈনিক কর্ম্মচারী প্রভৃতি সম্পর্কে বিনা সনন্দে নিযুক্ত। **Non-comission-ed officers**—রাজার নিকট হইতে বিশেষ সনন্দ অপ্রাপ্ত সামরিক কর্ম্মচারী। [লেফ্‌টেনেন্টের নিম্নবর্ত্তী সামরিক কর্ম্মচারী, যথা—Sergeant, corporal এবং নৌবিভাগের Quarter-master এবং Gunner's mate]।

nŏn-cŏm-mit'-tal (-ăl), *n.* Avoidance of committing oneself to a definite course or either side, (also, *attrib.* ; as, a *noncommittal* answer) ; অনাবদ্ধতা।

nŏn-cŏn-dŭc'-tor (-tēr), *n.* (*Phys.*) A substance that does not conduct electricity, heat, etc., an insulator ; যে পদার্থের মধ্য দিয়া তাপ, তাড়িত, প্রভৃতি পরিচালিত হয় না ; অপরিচালক পদার্থ, অচালক (হিঃ কোঃ)।

nŏn-cŏn-fŏrm'-ist, *n.* One who does not conform to the doctrine or discipline of an established Church ; যে ব্যক্তি রাজবিধি দ্বারা প্রতিষ্ঠিত ধর্ম্মসংঘের অনুমোদিত পন্থা অনুসরণ করে না, মতাপলাপী, অননুরোধী, অননুসারী, অননুযায়ী, অননুবর্ত্তী।

nŏn-cŏn-fŏrm'-i-tȳ, *n.* 1. Refusal to conform, esp. to an established Church ; বিধিপ্রতিষ্ঠিত ধর্ম্মসংঘের অনুযায়ী চলিতে অস্বীকৃতি, অননুবর্ত্তন। 2. Nonconformists as a body ; মতাপলাপিসম্প্রদায়। 3. Principles or practice of nonconformists ; মতাপলাপীদিগের ধর্ম্মতত্ত্ব বা আচার অনুষ্ঠান। 4. Want of correspondence between things ; অসামঞ্জস্য, অনৈক্য।

nŏn'-dē-script, *adj.* & *n.* 1. Not easily described ; unclassifiable ; hybrid ; দুর্ব্বর্ণনীয় ; অশ্রেণীবিভাগযোগ্য ; সঙ্কর। 2. Strange ; odd ; অদ্ভুত ; সৃষ্টিছাড়া। ***Noun.*** A person or thing not easily described or classified, (*usually applied disparagingly*) ; দুর্ব্বর্ণনীয় বা অশ্রেণীবিভাগযোগ্য ব্যক্তি বা বস্তু।

none (nŭn), *pron.*, *adj.* & *adv.* 1. Not any (*of*) ; as, *none* of them came ; কেহই না, কোনটাই না। 2. (*Pl.*) No persons ; as, *none* but fools ever believed it ; কোন ব্যক্তিই না। ***Adj.*** No ; not any ; as, if a linguist is wanted I am *none* ; নয় ; কেহই নয়। ***Adv.*** In no way ; to no extent ; not at all ; as, I am *none* the better for it ; কোন প্রকারেই নয় ; কোন পরিমাণেই নয় ; মোটেই নয়। **None the less**—Nevertheless ; তথাপি, তবুও।

nŏn-ĕf-fĕc'-tive (-tiv), *adj.* & *n.* Not qualified for active service as a soldier or sailor ; যুদ্ধের অযোগ্য। ***Noun.*** Such a soldier or sailor ; যুদ্ধের অযোগ্য সৈন্য বা নাবিক।

nŏn-ē'-gō, *n.* (*Metaph.*) All beyond or outside of the ego or conscious thinking subject ; the object as opposed to the subject ; বিষয়ীর অতীত ও বহির্ভূত যাবতীয় বস্তু, ইদং, অনাত্মবস্তু ; বিষয়, জ্ঞেয়।

nŏn-ĕn'-ti-tȳ, *n.* 1. Non-existence ; নাস্তিত্ব, অনস্তিত্ব (হিঃ কোঃ), অবর্ত্তমানতা, অসত্তা, অত্যন্তাভাব, অসৎ (হিঃ কোঃ), অবিদ্যমানতা (ঐ)।

2. A thing not existing or existing only in imagination ; অসদ্‌বস্তু, ফেনপিণ্ড, খপুষ্প। 3. A person or thing of little or no importance ; নগণ্য লোক, অপদার্থ লোক, অসার বস্তু।

nones (nōnz), *n., pl.* 1. (*Rom. Antiq.*) The ninth day before the Ides, *i. e.* 7th of March, May, July, October and 5th of other months, in the Roman Calendar ; রোমক পঞ্জিকার মার্চ্চ, মে, জুলাই এবং অক্টোবর মাসের সপ্তম দিবস ও অপর অপর মাসের পঞ্চম দিবস। 2. (*Eccl.*) Daily office originally said at the 9th hour or 3 P. M. ; নবম ঘণ্টার সময় (অপরাহ্ণ ৩টা) অনুষ্ঠেয় রোমান-ক্যাথলিক ধর্ম্মকৃত্য-বিশেষ।

Non est, (*L.*), *n.* Departed; absconded ; প্রস্থিত ; পলাতক, ফেরার।

none'-sŭch (nŭn-), *n.* See NONSUCH.

nō-nĕt', *n.* (*Mus.*) A composition for nine instruments, or (*rarely*) for nine voices ; (সঙ্গীতশাস্ত্র) নয় যন্ত্রের জন্য অথবা (কদাচিৎ) নয় স্বরের জন্য রচিত সঙ্গীত।

nŏn-fea'-sance (-fē-zăns), *n.* (*Legal*) Omission to do what ought to have been done ; (আইন) ত্রুটি, কসুর, অকরণ।

nŏn-hū'-măn, *adj.* 1. Not of the human race ; অমানবীয়। 2. Not proper to a human being ; অমানুষিক।

nō-nĭl'-lion (-yŏn), *n.* Ninth power of million, denoted by 1 with 54 ciphers ; ১এর ডাহিনে ৫৪টী শূন্য বসাইলে যে সংখ্য হয়।

nŏn-ĭn-tĕr-fēr'-ence (-ĕns), *n.* Principle or practice, esp. in politics and international affairs of keeping aloof from other's disputes; অপরের কার্য্যে হস্তক্ষেপ না করণ।

nŏn-ĭn-tĕr-vĕn'-tion, *n.* Same as NONINTERFERENCE.

nō'-nĭ-ŭs, *n.* A device for graduating mathematical instruments of which *vernier* is an improved form ; গণিতক যন্ত্রসমূহ ক্রমচিহ্নিত করার জন্য যন্ত্রবিশেষ।

nŏn-join'-dêr (-jŏyn-), *n.* (*Legal*) The omission to join as a party to a suit ; (আইন) কোন মোকদ্দমায় পক্ষভুক্ত না করার দরুণ ত্রুটী।

nŏn-lŏg'-ĭ-căl, *adj.* Proceeding by other means than logic ; তর্কবিজ্ঞান-বিরোধী, অযৌক্তিক।

nŏn-pă-reil' (-rĕl), *adj.* & *n.* Having no equal ; peerless ; unique ; as a *nonpareil* person or thing ; অপ্রতিম, নিরুপম ; অনুপম ; অদ্বিতীয়। ***Noun.*** 1. A person or thing of unequalled excellence ; something unique ; অপ্রতিম ব্যক্তি, অদ্বিতীয় ব্যক্তি ; অতুলনীয় বস্তু। 2. (*Print.*) A size of type ; এক-প্রকার অতিক্ষুদ্র মুদ্রণের হরপ। 3. Kinds of comfit, apple, bird, moth, etc. ; বিভিন্ন জাতীয় সেওফল, পাখী, তসরে পোকা, ফলের মোরব্বা, প্রভৃতি।

nŏn-pay'-mĕnt (-pā-), *n.* Neglect or failure to pay ; অনাদায়, অপরিশোধ।

nŏn'-plŭs, *n.* & *v. t.* State of perplexity ; puzzle ; ভেবাচেকা, হতবুদ্ধিতা, কিংকর্ত্তব্যবিমূঢ়তা ; অপ্রতিভ-ভাব। ***Verb t.*** To puzzle ; to render helpless by perplexity ; as, he was *nonplussed* by the question ; হতবুদ্ধি করা ; ভেবাচেকা লাগান, কিংকর্ত্তব্যবিমূঢ় করা। **At a nonplus**—Perplexed ; হতবুদ্ধি, কিংকর্ত্তব্যবিমূঢ়।

nŏn-rĕs'-ĭ-dĕnt, *adj.* & *n.* 1. Systematically absent from one's benefice or estate ; স্বীয় যাজকীয় অধিকার অথবা জমিদারী হইতে পৃথক স্থানে বাসকারী। 2. Not resident in a particular place ; as, a *non-resident* physician ; স্থানান্তরবাসী। ***Noun.*** 1. A land-lord or a clergyman non-resident ; স্থানান্তর-বাসী ভূস্বামী বা যাজক। 2. One not residing in a particular place ; স্থানান্তরবাসী ব্যক্তি। **—dence**, *n.*

nŏn-rē-sĭst'-ance (-ăns), *n.* 1. (*Hist.*) A 17th-century principle that authority must not be resisted even if unjustly exercised ; (ইতিহাস) সপ্তদশ শতাব্দীর মতবিশেষ—মতটী এই যে বিধিসঙ্গত অধিকার অন্যায়রূপে পরিচালিত হইলেও তাহা বাধা দেওয়া কর্ত্তব্য নয়। 2. Passive or ready obedience ; অপ্রতিরোধ, অপ্রতীকার, অনিরোধ।

nŏn'-sense (-sĕns), *n.* & *interj.* 1. That which is not sense ; words which make no sense or absurd ideas ; foolish action or conduct ; অর্থহীন বিষয় ; অর্থহীন বাক্য, অসম্বদ্ধ প্রলাপ, বাজে কথা ; নির্ব্বোধোচিত কার্য্য বা আচরণ। 2. Absurdity ; অর্থশূন্যতা। 3. Trifles ; অকিঞ্চিৎকরবস্তু। ***Interj.*** You are speaking nonsense ; it surely cannot be true, etc. ; বাজে কথা ; পাগলের প্রলাপ। **—sen'-si-cal**, *adj.* Unmeaning ; absurd ; foolish ; অর্থহীন, অর্থশূন্য ; নিরর্থক ; বুদ্ধিহীন। **—sen'-si-cal-ly**, *adv.* **Nonsense-book**—যে পুস্তকে অসম্ভব ব্যাপারের বর্ণনা থাকে। **Nonsense-verses**—অর্থশূন্য কবিতা। **To speak nonsense**—আবলতাবল বকা, অর্থশূন্য প্রলাপ করা। **What nonsense**—পাগল আর কি!

nŏn'-sŭch, *n.* 1. A person or thing that is unrivalled or unique ; a paragon ; অপ্রতিম বা অদ্বিতীয় ব্যক্তি কিম্বা বস্তু; অনুপম বস্তু, নিরুপম বস্তু। 2. A knid of lucerne ; পশ্বাদির খাদ্য-গুল্মবিশেষ।

nŏn'-suit (-sūt), *n.* & *v. t.* Stoppage of a case from the default, neglect, or non-appearance of the plaintiff ; বাদীর ত্রুটি, অবহেলা বা অনুপাস্থিতির দরুণ মোকদ্দমা খারিজ। ***Verb t.*** To subject to a nonsuit ; মোকদ্দমা খারিজ করা।

nŏn-ūs'-ĕr, *n.* (*Legal*) Neglect to use a right by which it may become void ; (আইন) কোনরূপ

স্বত্ব ব্যবহারে ত্রুটি—যদ্বেতু উহা লোপ হইতে পারে।

noo′-dle, *n.* A fool or simpleton; বোকা, আহাম্মক, অল্পবুদ্ধি। **–dom,** *n.* Foolishness; an instance of this; বোকামি; বোকামির কাজ।

nŏok, *n.* An out-of-the-way corner; a secluded place; কোণ ঘাপ, ঘুঁজি; নিভৃত স্থান। **Nook and corner**—গলিঘুঁজি।

nōon, *n.* The middle of the day; twelve o'clock in the day time; দ্বিপ্রহর, দুপুর; মধ্যাহ্ন, মধ্যন্দিন, দিনযৌবন (*poet.* রঘুঃ), দিনমধ্য। **Noonday, Noontide**—Midday; (also *attributive*; as *noonday* dream, light, etc.); মধ্যাহ্ন, মধ্যাহ্নকাল, মধ্যাহ্নবেলা; মাধ্যাহ্নিক, মাধ্যন্দিন।

noose (nōōs), *n.* & *v. t.* **1.** A running knot which binds the closer the more it is drawn; ফাঁস, গলাসি। **2.** The marriage tie; বিবাহবন্ধন। **3.** A snare or bond; পাশ, বাগুরা। ***Verb t.*** **1.** To capture in a noose; to put or throw a noose round; to entrap; পাশবদ্ধ করা; পাশ ফেলা, পাশ দ্বারা জড়ান, ফাঁদে ফেলা। **2.** To make a noose on (cord); গলাসি করা। **3.** To hang; ফাঁসী দেওয়া।

nō′-păl, *n.* An American cactus, grown for breeding cochineal; লাক্ষাকীট পোষণের জন্য আমেরিকাদেশীয় একপ্রকার নাগফণা গাছ। **–ry,** *n.*

nŏr, *adv.* & *conj.* (*Archaic*) Neither; (অপ্রঃ) কোনটাই না। ***Conj.*** And not; and no more; and not either; "I neither love *nor* fear thee"; এবং না; এবং আর না; এবং কোনটাই না।

Nŏr′-dĕn-fĕlt, *n.* A kind of machine-gun, much used in the British navy, (from the name of the Swedish inventor); বৃটিশ রণপোতে ব্যবহৃত একপ্রকার কলের কামান।

Nŏr′-folk (-fŏk), *n.* A county of England; ইংলণ্ডের প্রদেশবিশেষ। **Norfolk capon**—শুষ্ক হেরীং মৎস্য। **Norfolk-dumpling, –turkey**—নরফক প্রদেশের অধিবাসী। **Norfolk Howard**—(ইতর ভাষায়) ছারপোকা। **Norfolk jacket**—শিকারীদিগের একপ্রকার ঢিলা কোর্ত্তা। **Norfolk plover**—পক্ষিবিশেষ।

nŏr′-lănd, *n.* North country; northern region; উত্তরদেশ; উত্তরাঞ্চল।

nŏrm, *n.* A rule or standard; pattern; type; নিয়ম, আদর্শ; নমুনা; প্রতিরূপ।

nŏr′-măl, *adj.* & *n.* **1.** (*Geom.*) Forming a right angle; perpendicular; (জ্যামিতি) সমকোণ গঠনকারী; লম্বস্বরূপ, অবলম্ব (হিঃ কোঃ)। **2.** Conforming to a type, standard or regular form; regular; natural; নিয়মানুরূপ, আদর্শানুরূপ; যথাবিধি, বিধিযুক্ত, নিয়মিত, যথাক্রম; স্বধর্ম্মী (হিঃ কোঃ), স্বাভাবিক, নৈসর্গিক। ***Noun.*** (*Geom.*) **1.** A normal line or plane; সমকোণকারক রেখা বা তল। **2.** (*Phys.*) Average or mean of observed quantities; (পদার্থ বিজ্ঞান) পর্য্যবেক্ষিত সংখ্যাসমূহের গড়। **3.** Usual condition, quantity, degree, level, etc.; স্বাভাবিক অবস্থা, পরিমাণ বা মাত্রা। **4.** Normal temperature of the human body (98·4°); মানবদেহের স্বাভাবিক তাপমাত্রা। **5.** Same as NORMAL SCHOOL; যে বিদ্যালয়ে শিক্ষকগণকে অধ্যাপনাকার্য্য শিক্ষা দেওয়া হয়, শিক্ষকশিক্ষানিবেশ। **–i-za′-tion,** *n.* **–ize,** *v. t.* **–ly,** *adv.* **–mal′-i-ty,** *n.*

Nŏr′-măn, *n.* & *adj.* An inhabitant or native of Normandy; a descendant of the mixed Scandinavian and Frankish race there established; নরম্যাণ্ডীর অধিবাসী; প্রাচীন নরম্যান জাতির বংশধর। ***Adj.*** Of, or relating to, the Normans or Normandy; নরম্যাণ্ডী বা তদ্দেশের অধিবাসিসম্পর্কীয়। **–esque′,** *adj.* Suggestive of, or similar to, the Norman style of architecture; নরম্যানস্থাপত্যরীতিব্যঞ্জক, নরম্যানস্থাপত্যরীতিবৎ। **–ism, –i-za′-tion,** *ns.* **–ize,** *v. t.* & *i.* To render Norman, as in character; নরম্যান প্রকৃতিক করা। (*Verb i.*) To adopt Norman speech, customs, etc.; নরম্যান ভাষা, আচার-পদ্ধতি, প্রভৃতি গ্রহণ করা। **Norman-English**—নরম্যান জাতিদ্বারা প্রভাবিত ইংরাজী। **Norman-French**—নরম্যানগণ কর্ত্তৃক কথিত বা লিখিত ফরাসী ভাষা। **Norman style**—(Also *Norman*); নরম্যান স্থাপত্যরীতি (গোলাকৃতি তোরণ এই রীতির বিশেষত্ব)।

Nŏrn, *n.* One of the female fates of the Scandinavian mythology; স্কেণ্ডেনেভিয় পুরাণে উল্লিখিত ভাগ্যদেবীবিশেষ।

Nŏr′-roy (-oy), *n.* The title of the third of the three English Kings *of Arms*, whose jurisdiction lies to the north of the Trent; ইংলণ্ডদেশের কুলাচার্য্যবিশেষ।

Norse (nŏrs), *adj.* & *n.* Of, or relating to, Norway or its language; নরওয়ে বা তদ্দেশের ভাষাসম্পর্কীয়। ***Noun.*** The language of Norway; নরওয়ে দেশের ভাষা। **Old Norse**—চতুর্দ্দশ শতাব্দী পর্য্যন্ত নরওয়ে বা ঐ দেশের উপনিবেশসমূহের ভাষা।

Nŏrsk, *adj.* & *n.* Same as NORSE.

nŏrth, *adv.*, *n.* & *adj.* Northward; in, to, or towards, the north; উত্তরে; উত্তরাভিমুখে, উত্তরদিকে। ***Noun.*** **1.** One of the cardinal points opposite to the South; উত্তরদিক, উদীচী, [in Sans. poet. কুবেরগুপ্তা, ধনদপালিতা]। **2.** A region to the north; the northern part of a country; specifically (*cap.*) the northern part of the United States in which slavery did not exist ; উত্তরদেশ ; কোন দেশের উত্তরাঞ্চল বা উত্তরভাগ ; বিশেষতঃ মার্কিণ যুক্তরাজ্যের উত্তরাংশ—যথায় দাসত্ব-প্রথা প্রচলিত ছিলনা। 3. (*Cap.*) The northern part of England (beyond Humber) or of Great Britain, Scotland, Ireland or Europe ; ইংলণ্ড, গ্রেটব্রিটেন, স্কটলণ্ড, আয়র্লণ্ড বা ইয়ুরোপের উত্তর ভাগ। 4. The north wind ; উত্তরানিল, উত্তর বায়ু। ***Adj.*** 1. Northern ; being in the north ; উদীচ্য, উদীচীন ; উত্তরদিগ্‌বর্ত্তী। 2. Facing the north, as a window ; coming from the north, as wind, light, etc. ; উদঙ্মুখ ; উত্তরদিক হইতে আগত। **North'-ward,** *adv., n. & adj.* (*Noun*) The direction or part lying to the north (of a place or thing) ; উত্তরাভিমুখ, উত্তরাঞ্চল। **North'-wards,** *adv. & n.* (*Noun*) Same as NORTHWARD. **North Country**—*n. & adj.* Northern part of England or Great Britain ; ইংলণ্ড অথবা গ্রেটব্রিটনের উত্তরাংশ। (*Adj., with hyphen*) From, or characteristic of, North Country ; ইংলণ্ড বা গ্রেটব্রিটনের উত্তরাংশ হইতে আগত বা ঐ স্থানের পক্ষে স্বাভাবিক। **North-east**—উত্তরপূর্ব্ব-কোণ, ঈশান কোণ (হিঃ কোঃ)। **North-east, North-west, passage**—ইয়ুরোপ এবং এশিয়ার পশ্চিমোপকূল এবং আমেরিকার উত্তরোপকূল দিয়া পোত চালনা—যাহা পূর্ব্বে প্রাচ্যদেশে এবং অতলান্তিক মহাসাগর হইতে প্রশান্ত-মহাসাগরে গমনের জন্ম সম্ভাবিত পথ বলিয়া মনে করা হইত। **North-easterly, —westerly, —eastward(ly), —westward(ly),** *adjs. & advs.* **Northeastward, —westward,** *adjs., advs. & ns.* **North-land** — (*Poet.*) Northern lands ; northern part of a country ; উত্তরদেশ ; কোন দেশের উত্তরাংশ। **North-light** — মেরুজ্যোতিঃ, উদীচী উষা। **North-man**—নরওয়ে অথবা স্কেণ্ডেনেভিয়ার অধিবাসী। **North-pole**—উত্তরমেরু, উত্তরধ্রুব। **North-Sea**—উত্তরসাগর। **North-star**—ধ্রুবতারা। **North of** — উত্তরে **North-north-east, —west,** *advs. ns. & adjs.* **North-west**—উত্তর পশ্চিম, বায়ুকোণ।

nŏrth'-ĕr, *n.* (*U. S.*) Strong cold north wind blowing in autumn and winter over the Texas, Florida, and the Gulf of Mexico ; (মার্কিণযুক্তরাজ্য) শরৎ ও শীত ঋতুতে Texas, Florida ও Mexico উপসাগর প্রভৃতি স্থানে প্রবাহিত অতি শীতল উত্তরানিল।

nŏrth'-ĕr-lў, *adj. & adv.* 1. Of, or pertaining to, situated in, the north (*rare*) ; towards the north, as a direction ; উত্তরদিক-সম্বন্ধীয়, উত্তরদিগ্‌বর্ত্তী (কচিদ্‌ব্যবহৃত) ; উত্তরদিকাভিমুখীন, উদীচীন। 2. (Of the wind) Blowing from the north ; উত্তর দিক হইতে প্রবাহিত। ***Adv.*** Towards the north ; as to sail *northerly* ; উত্তরাভিমুখে।

nŏrth'-ĕrn, *adj. & n.* 1. Living, situated in, or coming from, the north, esp. of England or Europe ; উত্তরদিগবাসী, উত্তরদিকে অবস্থিত, উত্তরদিক হইতে আগত (বিশেষভাবে ইংলণ্ড ও ইয়ুরোপ)। 2. (*Cap., U. S.*) Of, or relating to, the north or northern States ; (মার্কিণ যুক্তরাজ্যে) উত্তরদিক-সম্বন্ধীয়, উত্তরদিগ্‌বর্ত্তীরাষ্ট্রসমূহসম্পর্কীয়। 3. Characteristic of the north ; as, a pallid *northern* day ; উত্তর-দেশের পক্ষে স্বাভাবিক। 4. (*Rare*) Northerly, as wind ; (কচিদ্ ব্যবহৃত) উদীচ্য। ***Noun.*** A native or inhabitant of the north, of a northern country or the northern part of a contry ; উত্তর দেশের অধিবাসী, উত্তরদিগ্‌বর্ত্তী দেশের অধিবাসী, কোন দেশের উত্তরাংশের অধিবাসী। **—er,** *n.* An inhabitant of the north ; spefic. (*cap., U. S.*) a native or inhabitant of the northern States ; উত্তর দেশের অধিবাসী ; বিশেষভাবে (মার্কিণ যুক্তরাজ্যে) আমেরিকার উত্তরদিগস্থিত রাষ্ট্রসমূহের অধিবাসী। **—most,** *adj.* **Northern lights**—সুমেরুজ্যোতিঃ, উদীচী উষা।

nŏrth'-ing, *n.* Progress or deviation towards the north in sailing or travelling ; difference in latitude due to moving northwards ; জাহাজ বা পথিকের উত্তরদিকে অগ্রসর বা বিচ্যুতি ; উত্তরদিকে অগ্রসর হওয়া হেতু অক্ষাংশের বিভেদ।

Nŏrth-ŭm'-bri-ăn, *adj. & n.* Of ancient Northumbria or modern Northumberland ; প্রাচীন নরথ্যাম-ব্রিয়া বা বর্ত্তমান নরথ্যামবারল্যাণ্ড-সম্পর্কীয়। ***Noun.*** A native or dialect of this place ; ঐ স্থানের অধিবাসী বা উপভাষা।

nŏrth'-ward-lў (-wêrd-), *adj. & adv.* Having a northern direction or situation ; (of wind) blowing from the north ; উত্তরদিগবর্ত্তী ; (বায়ু সম্পর্কে) উত্তরদিক হইতে প্রবাহিত। ***Adv.*** Northwards ; উত্তরাভিমুখে।

nŏrth-wĕst'-ĕr, *n.* A wind from the north-west ; উত্তর-পশ্চিম দিক হইতে প্রবাহিত ঝঞ্ঝা, কালবৈশাখী।

Nŏr-wē'-gi-ăn, *adj. & n.* Of, or pertaining to, Norway ; নরওয়ে-সম্বন্ধীয়। ***Noun.*** A native or the language of Norway ; নরওয়ের অধিবাসী বা তথাকার ভাষা।

nŏr'-wĕst'-ĕr, *n.* 1. Same as NORTH-WESTER. 2. A glass of strong liquor, as rum ; এক গ্লাস উগ্র মদিরা। 3. An oilskin hat ; রঙ্গিন ক্যাম্বিস বা অয়েলক্লথের টুপি।

nōse, *n., v. t. & i.* 1. The organ of smell ; নাক, নাসিকা, নাসা, গন্ধবহা, ঘ্রাণেন্দ্রিয়, গন্ধেন্দ্রিয় (সুশ্রুঃ)। 2. Sense of smelling ; ঘ্রাণশক্তি। 3. Odour or perfume of hay, tea, etc. ; "It (the hay) would lack *nose* and flavour" ; শুষ্ক ঘাস,

চা, প্রভৃতির গন্ধ। 4. The snout, muzzle, or nozzle; as, the *nose* of a pipe, gun, bellows, retort, etc.; মুখ, বন্দুকাদির অগ্রভাগ। 5. A prominent or projecting part; the point or extremity of anything; উদ্গত অংশ; কোন বস্তুর প্রান্তবিন্দু। 6. The prow or stem of a ship or boat; নৌকা, জাহাজ, প্রভৃতির অগ্রভাগ। 7. (*Slang*) An informer or spy; (ইতরভাষায়) গোয়েন্দা, টিকটিকী। 8. (*Obs.* or *dial.*) An eye, as of a gooseberry, apple; টেপারী, সেওফল, প্রভৃতির চোক। *Verb t.* 1. To perceive the smell of; to discover by smell; as, you might *nose* the cheeses at a considerable distance; আঘ্রাণ করা, ঘ্রাণ লওয়া, শুঁকা; ঘ্রাণ দ্বারা বাহির করা। 2. (*Fig.*) To find ont or detect as if by means of a keen scent; (*lit.* & *fig.*) To scent or smell *out*; "Have seen a pack... *nose out* a scent"; (লক্ষণায়) সন্ধান করা; ঘ্রাণ লইয়া বাহির করা। 3. To touch or rub with the nose; to press the nose close to; "Lambs are glad, *nosing* the mother's udder"; নাসিকাদ্বারা স্পর্শ বা ঘর্ষণ করা; নাক কাছে নিয়া ঠেকান। 4. (*Rare*) To utter with a nasal sound; নাকিস্বরে বলা। 5. To be closely opposite to; to meet or encounter; প্রায় বিরুদ্ধ হওয়া; সম্মুখীন করা, সাক্ষাৎকার করা। 6. (*Obs.* or *Dial.*) To pick the noses off (gooseberries etc.); টেপারী প্রভৃতির চোক তুলিয়া ফেলা। 7. To examine with the nose; "*Nosed* all the cracks"; নাক দ্বারা পরীক্ষা করা। 8. To push, as one's way, with the nose, esp. of a ship etc.; ঠেলিয়া অগ্রসর হওয়া। *Verb i.* 1. To sniff; to smell, (with *at*, *about*); শুঁকা; ঘ্রাণ লওয়া। 2. To pry or search, (*after* or *for* something); খুঁজা, উঁকিমারা। 3. To push one's way with the nose, or front forward; "A train of cable or cars came *nosing* along"; নাক বা অগ্রভাগ দ্বারা ঠেলিয়া অগ্রসর হওয়া। 4. (Of strata or veins) To dip *in*; to run *out*; (স্তর বা পাষাণাদির মধ্যস্থ ধাতুরেখা সম্বন্ধে) ঢালু হওয়া; গড়াইয়া পড়া। **Nose′-less,** *adj.* Destitute of a nose; অনাসিক, গতনাসিক, নাসিকাহীন। **Nose-bag**—ঘোড়ার গলায় যে দানার তোড়া ঝুলাইয়া দেওয়া হয়। **Nose-band**—বল্‌গার নাসাবন্ধ। **Nose-flute**—শ্যাম, ফিজি, প্রভৃতি স্থানের নাসিকা দ্বারা বাদিত বংশিবিশেষ। **Nosegay**—ফুলের তোড়া, পুষ্পস্তবক, পুষ্পগুচ্ছ (জাতক), ফাল (বাল: রা:), প্রসূনবিততি। **Nose-monkey, —ape**—শুণ্ডবিশিষ্ট কপিবিশেষ। **Nose-piece**—অশ্ববল্‌গার নাসাবন্ধ; অনুবীক্ষণ যন্ত্রের যে অংশে দৃষ্ট বস্তু প্রতিবিম্বিত হয়। **Nose-rag**—(ইতর ভাষায়) পকেটে রাখার রুমাল। **Nose-ring**—নথ। **Nose-string**—নাস্থ। **A parson's nose**—The rump of a cooked fowl; রাঁধা মুর্গীর পাছা। **As plain as the nose in your face**—Easily seen; করামলকবৎ, নখদর্পণের মত। **Nose of wax**—মোমের পুতুল; যে ব্যক্তি সহজে প্রতারিত বা পরিচালিত হয়। **To bite or snap one's nose off**—To answer or address sharply; বেশ কড়া দু কথা শুনাইয়া দেওয়া। **To cut off one's nose to spite one's face**—নিজের নাক কেটে পরের যাত্রা ভঙ্গ করা, সতীনের বাটীতে গু গুলে খাওয়া। **To follow one's nose**—To go straightforward; to be guided by instinct; সোজা পথে চলা; সহজবুদ্ধি দ্বারা পরিচালিত হওয়া। **To keep one's nose to the grindstone**—See under GRIND (STONE). **To lead by the nose**—See under LEAD. **To make a person's nose swell**—To make him jealous; ঈর্ষাপূর্ণ করা। **To measure noses**—To meet; সম্মুখীন হওয়া। **To pay through the nose**—To pay exhorbitant prices; বেজায় দাম দেওয়া। **To put a man's nose out or out of joint**—To supplant or frustrate him; থোঁতা মুখ ভোঁতা করা। **To put, poke or thrust one's nose into another's affairs**—To pry or intrude into another's affairs; অনধিকার চর্চ্চা করা, পরের ব্যাপারে হস্তক্ষেপ করা। **To speak through the nose**—To pronounce with nasal twang; নাকিস্বরে কথা বলা। **To take pepper in the nose**—To take offence; দোষ ধরা। **To turn up one's nose at**—To express contempt for; নাসিকাকুঞ্চিত করা, নাক সিটকান। **To wipe one's nose of**—(*Obs.*) To cheat one of; (অপ্র:) ঠকাইয়া লওয়া, মাথায় হাত বুলান। **Under one's nose**—Close to one; straight before one; regardless of displeasure; খুব কাছে; কাহারো চক্ষুর উপর; কাহারো মুখের উপর। **With one's nose at the grindstone**—Hard at work; হাড়ভাঙ্গা খাটুনিতে।

nōs′-ĕr, *n.* A strong head wind, (esp. *dead nose*); জাহাজের গতির প্রতিকূলে প্রবহমাণ প্রবল বাতাস।

nōs′-ĭng, *n.* (*Arch.*) The projecting rounded edge of a moulding or step etc.; (স্থপতিবিদ্যা) দালানের কার্ণিসাদির উদ্গত ভুবা অথবা সোপান প্রভৃতির বর্ত্তুলীকৃত প্রান্ত।

nŏ-sŏg′-ră-phy, *n.* Systematic description of diseases; রোগবর্ণন।

nō-sŏl′-ŏ-ġy, *n.* 1. Classification of diseases; রোগের শ্রেণীবিভাগ। 2. The science of diseases or of their classification; রোগবিজ্ঞান, রোগনিদানশাস্ত্র, রোগবর্ণনবিদ্যা (হিঃ কোঃ)।

nŏs-tăl′-ġĭ-ă, *n.* Home-sickness esp. as a disease; গৃহপ্রত্যাগমনের

জন্য ব্যাকুলতা, গৃহবিরহকাতরতা, গৃহরোগ (হঃ চঃ)। **–gic,** *adj.*

nŏs′-tŏc, *n.* A genus of unicellular algæ ; একপ্রকার সবুজ সেওলা।

Nŏs-trā-dā′-mŭs, *n.* One who professes to be a prophet ; a seer, (From Nostradamus who made prophecies in 1555) ; ভাববাদী ; ঋষি।

nŏs′-tril, *n.* An aperture through the nose ; নাকের ছিদ্র, নাসারন্ধ্র, নাসাপুট। **–trilled,** *adj.* (*Used usually in combination*). **To stink in one's nostril**—To be offensive to him ; কাহারো নিকট বিরক্তিকর বোধ হওয়া।

nŏs′-trŭm, *n.* **1.** A quack remedy ; patent medicine ; গূঢ়ৌষধ, টোটকা ঔষধ, মুষ্টিযোগ, হাতুড়ে ঔষধ, মিথ্যৌষধ, গুপ্তৌষধ ; যে ঔষধের উপাদান গুপ্ত থাকে, প্যাটেণ্ট ঔষধ। **2.** A pet or favourite scheme for political or social reform ; a special means or device ; সামাজিক বা রাজনীতিক সংস্কারসাধনের জন্য প্রিয় উপায় ; বিশেষ উপায়, বিশেষ কৌশল।

nō′-sy̆, *adj.* **1.** Having a prominent nose ; উন্নতনাসিক। **2.** Ill-smelling (esp. of heated corn, mouldy hay, etc.) ; দুর্গন্ধ। **3.** (Of tea) Fragrant ; (চা-সম্পর্কে) সুগন্ধ। **4.** Sensitive to bad smells ; দুর্গন্ধ-সংবেদনশীল।

nŏt, n't, *adv.* A word expressing negation, denial or refusal ; না। **Not-being**—Non-existence ; নাস্তিত্ব, অনস্তিত্ব। **Not-self**—Non-ego ; নাহং। **Not a bit of it**—Not at all ; in no way ; মোটেই না ; কোন প্রকারেই না। **Not a few**—A great many ; বহুসংখ্যক। **Not a hair of one's head shall be touched**—No one shall sustain even the slightest injury ; তাহার একটী কেশও কেহ স্পর্শ করিতে পারিবে না। **Not a little**—Very much ; অল্প নয়, বিস্তর, প্রচুর। **Not at home**—আগন্তুক ব্যক্তিগণের সহিত সাক্ষাৎ করিতে অনিচ্ছুক। **Not in the least**—অণুমাত্রও নয়। **Not once or twice, Not once nor twice**—Many times ; বহুবার। **Not reluctant**—Only too glad ; খুব আহ্লাদিত। **Not sufficient** (*Usu. N. S.*)—A banker's sign on a dishonoured cheque ; অগ্রাহ্য চেকের উপর ব্যাঙ্কওয়ালার সহি। **Not to speak of**—Even when left out of consideration ; না বলিলেও, উল্লেখ না করিলেও।

nō′-tā-bē′-nē, *v. imper.* (Abbr. *N. B.*) Observe what follows ; দ্রষ্টব্য।

nō-tā-bĭl′-ĭ-ty̆, *n.* **1.** A notable thing or object (*rare*) ; আশ্চর্য্য বিষয় বা বস্তু (কচিদ্‌ব্যবহৃত)। **2.** A person of note ; বিখ্যাত লোক, খ্যাতনামা লোক, নামজাদা লোক। **3.** (*Archaic*) Skill in housewifery ; (অপ্রঃ) গৃহিণীপণায় নৈপুণ্য। **4.** Prominence ; distinction ; as, name of no historical *notability* ; প্রাধান্য ; খ্যাতি।

nō′-tā-ble (-bl), *adj.* & *n.* **1.** Worthy of note, or notice ; remarkable ; striking ; প্রসিদ্ধ, বিখ্যাত, সুবিখ্যাত, সুপ্রসিদ্ধ ; অসাধারণ ; আশ্চর্য্য। **2.** (*Chem.*) Perceptible ; (রসায়নশাস্ত্র) ইন্দ্রিয়গ্রাহ্য। **3.** (Of women) Capable ; clever or industrious in household affairs ; সুনিপুণা ; গৃহকর্ম্মে নিপুণা। ***Noun.*** A person of eminence, or distinction ; প্রখ্যাতনামা ব্যক্তি, সুবিখ্যাত ব্যক্তি। **–bly,** *adv.* **Assembly of Notables**—আকস্মিক সঙ্কট কালে অস্থায়িভাবে দেশশাসনের জন্য গঠিত সভা।

nō′-tā-ry̆, *n.* An officer authorized to attest contracts or documents, to protest bills of exchange, etc. ; চুক্তিপত্র, দলিল, প্রভৃতির সত্যতা নির্দ্দেশ এবং হুণ্ডী প্রভৃতি পরীক্ষার জন্য নিযুক্ত কর্ম্মচারী, লেখপ্রমাণক (আঃ বঃ)। **–ta′-ri-al,** *adj.* **–ta′-ri-al-ly,** *adv.* **Notary public**—যে সরকারী কর্ম্মচারী দলিল, চুক্তিপত্র, এফিডেভিট প্রভৃতির স্বাক্ষরের সত্যতা নির্দ্দেশ করেন।

nō-tā′-tion, *n.* Representing of numbers, quantities, etc., by symbols ; any set of symbols used for this, esp. in Arithmetic, Algebra and Music ; সংখ্যালেখন, অঙ্কন্যাস, অঙ্কপাতন ; সংখ্যাজ্ঞাপক সাঙ্কেতিক চিহ্নাবলী, সঙ্কেত (হিঃ কোঃ)।

notch (nŏch), *n.*, *v. t.* & *i.* **1.** A V-shaped indentation or hollow, as in a surface or edge ; খাঁজ। **2.** A run at cricket (now *rare*) ; ক্রীকেট ক্রীড়ায় "রণ" (অধুনা অপ্রঃ)। **3.** (*U. S.*) A pass or defile ; (মার্কিণযুক্তরাজ্যে) গিরিবর্ত্ম, গিরিসঙ্কট। ***Verb t.*** **1.** To make notches, in ; as, to *notch* a stick ; খাঁজ কাটা। **2.** To make *into* a saw, etc. by notching ; লোহার পাতে দাঁত কাটিয়া করাত প্রভৃতি প্রস্তুত করা। **3.** To score, mark, or record notches, (often with *up*, *down*) ; খাঁজ কাটিয়া চিহ্নিত করা, হিসাব রাখা। **4.** (*Cricket*) To score (a run etc.) ; (ক্রীকেট ক্রীড়ায়) খাঁজ কাটিয়া ক্রীকেট ক্রীড়ার জয়াঙ্ক লিপিবদ্ধ করা। **5.** To secure or insert (steps in a staircase etc.) by notches ; খাঁজ কাটিয়া (সোপানশ্রেণীর ধাপ গুলি) আটকান। **6.** (*Rare*) To cut or chop ; (কচিদ্‌ব্যবহৃত) কাটা, ছেদন করা। ***Verb i.*** To make notches ; খাঁজ কাটা। **Notched, Notch′-y,** *adjs.* **Notch-wing**—একপ্রকার তসরে পোকা।

nōte, *n.* **1.** (*Mus.*) A character or sign representing a musical sound ; (সঙ্গীত) সুর, স্বর বা ধ্বনিবোধক চিহ্ন। **2.** Key of pianofort, etc. ; পিয়ানো প্রভৃতির চাবি। **3.** A tone of definite pitch, as of a musical instrument or the human voice in singing ; মূর্চ্ছনা, মাতৃকা, স্বর, সুর,

ধ্বনি। **4.** The song or a sound or call of a bird; as, the *note* of a cuckoo or crow; বিহঙ্গ-কাকলী, পাখীর ডাক। **5.** A significant sound or way of expressing oneself; as, there is a *note* of self-complacency in his voice; ধ্বনি। **6.** A sign, mark, or token; a distinctive feature; "The welcome *notes* of fatherhood"; চিহ্ন, দাগ, লক্ষণ; বিশিষ্ট লক্ষণ। **7.** A brief writing intended to assist the memory or to serve as a basis for fuller statement, (*usu. pl.*); স্মারকলিপি। **8.** Annotation; explanatory comment; টীকা; ব্যাখ্যা। **9.** A short letter of an informal kind; ক্ষুদ্র পত্র, চিঠি। **10.** A diplomatic or official communication in writing; সরকারী পত্র। **11.** A written promise to pay a sum; as, a *note* of hand: a bank *note*; নোট, খত, কর্জ্জখত। **12.** Heed; notice; মনোযোগ, অবধান; দৃষ্টি, লক্ষ্য। **13.** Eminence; distinction; সমুন্নতি; খ্যাতি। **14.** A sign used in printing, writing, etc.; as, a *note* of interrogation; লিখন, মুদ্রণ, প্রভৃতিতে ব্যবহৃত চিহ্ন। **15.** (*Rare*) A stigma; (কচিদ্‌ব্যবহৃত) কলঙ্ক। **Note'-less,** *adj.* **1.** Not attracting notice; unnoticed; অপ্রসিদ্ধ; অলক্ষিত। **2.** Unmusical, as a bird, etc.; সুস্বরবিহীন, কাকলিবিহীন। **Note'-let,** *n.* A little or short note; ক্ষুদ্র লিপি। **Note'-worthy,** *adj.* Worthy of observation or notice; remarkable; অবধানযোগ্য, দ্রষ্টব্য, প্রণিধানযোগ্য; অসাধারণ, অপূর্ব্ব। **Currency-note**—নোট। **Note-book**—যে ক্ষুদ্র পুস্তিকাতে নানা বিষয় স্মরণার্থ লিপিবদ্ধ করা হয়। **Note-paper**—ডাক কাগজ। **A note of hand**—See NOTE, *n.* II. **A person of note**—বিখ্যাত লোক। **To change one's note**—To become suddenly more or less aggressive humble, etc.; হঠাৎ খুব দমিয়া যাওয়া বা হঠকারিতা প্রদর্শন করা। **To make** or **take a note of**—To make a brief record of; টুকিয়া লওয়া। **To note down**—টুকিয়া লওয়া। **To take note of**—To notice; লক্ষ্য করা, অবধান করা।

nōte *v. t.* **1.** To notice or observe with care; to attend to; লক্ষ্য করা; অবধান করা। **2.** To set down; to make a memorandum of; টুকিয়া নেওয়া; সংক্ষেপে লিখিয়া রাখা। **3.** To annotate; টীকা করা। **Not'-ed,** *p. adj.* Celebrated; well known *for*; বিখ্যাত, প্রসিদ্ধ; সুপরিচিত।

noth'-ing (nŭth-), *n.* & *adv.* **1.** Not anything; কিছুই না। **2.** Trifle; as, he is *nothing* without his money; (with *a* or *in the pl.*) an insignificant thing, event, remark or person; as the little *nothings* of life: he was *a nothing*; তুচ্ছ জিনিষ; অকিঞ্চিৎকর বস্তু, নগণ্য জিনিষ, নগণ্য লোক। **3.** Non-existence; that which is non-existent; "An emissary of the primeval *Nothing*"; শূন্যতা, অনস্তিত্ব, নাস্তিত্ব; যাহার কোন অস্তিত্ব নাই, অবস্তু (হিঃ কোঃ)। **4.** (*Arith.*) Cipher; (পাটীগণিত) শূন্য। ***Adv.*** Not at all; in no way; as, this differs *nothing* from that; মোটেই না; কোন প্রকারেই না। **-a'-ri-an,** *n.* One of no religious belief or political creed; কোন ধর্ম্ম বা রাজনীতিক মতশূন্য ব্যক্তি। **All to nothing**—পুরাপুরি, পুরা মাত্রায়। **Can make nothing of**—Cannot find solution of, or understand; cannot use or deal with; কিছুই বুঝিতে না পারা; ব্যবহার করিতে না পারা। **For nothing**—To no purpose; খামখা, অনর্থক, নিরর্থক, বৃথা, মিছামিছি। Gratis; as, to get a thing *for nothing*; বিনামূল্যে, অমনি। Groundlessly; অকারণ। **He has nothing in him**—He is insignificant or without individuality; সে একটা নগণ্য লোক। **Is nothing less than monstrous**—It is positively monstrous; ইহা নিশ্চয়ই একটা বিকট জিনিষ। **Learning is nothing to genius**—প্রতিভার সহিত তুলনায় বিদ্যা কিছুই নহে। **Nothing venture nothing have**—ন সংশয়মনারুহ্য নরোভদ্রাণি পশ্যতি। **Nothing venture nothing win**—যত্ন বিনা রত্ন মিলেনা। **That is nothing**—আমি যাহা বলিতে যাইতেছি—তাহার তুলনায় এটা কিছুই নয়। **That is nothing to you**—It is not your concern; ইহা তোমার কোন বিষয় নয়। **There is nothing for it but to etc.**—There is no alternative but to etc.; কোন উপায়ান্তর নাই। **There is nothing in it**—It is not true or important; ইহাতে কোন সার নাই। **To be nothing**—See NOTHING *n.* 2.; also (of religious belief) to belong to no denomination; to be an atheist or agnostic; (ধর্ম্মসম্বন্ধে) কোন শ্রেণীতে ভুক্ত না থাকা; নাস্তিক হওয়া, অজ্ঞেয়তাবাদী হওয়া। **To come to nothing**—To fail; to turn out useless; পণ্ড হওয়া; নিষ্ফল হওয়া। **To dance on nothing**—To be hanged; ফাঁসীকাঠে ঝুলা। **To fade away etc. to nothing**—To disappear gradually; ক্রমশঃ বিলীন হওয়া, ধীরে ধীরে মিলাইয়া যাওয়া। **To have nothing to do with**—Not to be concerned with; to avoid dealing with or society of; কোন সম্পর্ক না থাকা; কোন সম্পর্ক না রাখা, সঙ্গ ত্যাগ করা। **To make nothing of**—To treat as trifle; তুচ্ছ জ্ঞান করা। **To make nothing of doing**—To do without hesitation or as ordinary matter; কোনরূপ দ্বিধাবোধ না করিয়া করা, সাধারণ বিষয় মনে করিয়া করা।

noth′-ing-nĕss (nŭth-), *n.* **1.** Non-existence ; that which is non-existent ; অনস্তিত্ব, নাস্তিত্ব ; অসদ্ বস্তু । **2.** Worthlessness ; insignificance ; trifles ; অসারতা ; অকিঞ্চিৎকরত্ব ; তুচ্ছব্যাপার ।

nō′-tice (-tĭs), *n.* & *v.t.* **1.** Intimation or warning ; information ; as, a *notice* to quit a house ; বিজ্ঞাপন, বিজ্ঞাপ্তি ; সংবাদ । **2.** An intimation by one of the parties to an agreement that it is to terminate at a specified time, esp. with reference to quitting a house, lodgings or employment ; as, a week's *notice* from next Saturday ; নোটিশ, কোন নির্দ্দিষ্ট সময় কোন সর্ত্ত বাতিল হইবে এই মর্ম্মে সর্ত্তবদ্ধ এক পক্ষ হইতে অপর পক্ষের নিকট বিজ্ঞাপন । **3.** A sign or placard conveying information or directions ; বিজ্ঞাপন । **4.** Observation ; heed ; regard ; cognizance ; লক্ষ্য, দৃষ্টি ; অবেক্ষা, অবধান ; প্রণিধান ; অবগতি । **5.** A paragraph or article upon something in newspaper, esp. review of a book, play, etc. ; কোন বিষয় সম্বন্ধে সংবাদপত্রে ক্ষুদ্রপ্রবন্ধ, বিশেষতঃ পুস্তক, অভিনয়, প্রভৃতির সমালোচনা । ***Verb. t.*** **1.** To remark upon ; to refer to ; as, to *notice* a book ; মন্তব্য করা ; উল্লেখ করা । **2.** To observe ; to perceive ; to heed ; to attend to ; লক্ষ্য করা ; অনুভব করা ; অবধান করা ; গ্রাহ্য করা, মনোযোগ দেওয়া । **3.** To treat with attention and civilities ; as, to notice strangers ; শিষ্টাচার ও সমাদর প্রদর্শন করা । **4.** To give a formal notice to ; to serve a notice on, as a tenant ; নোটিশ দেওয়া ; নোটিশ জারি করা । **–a-ble,** *adj.* Capable of being noticed ; worthy of notice ; conspicuous ; অবধানযোগ্য ; লক্ষ্য ; সুস্পষ্ট । **–a-bly,** *adv.* **Notice-board**—বিজ্ঞাপনফলক । **Beneath notice**—See BENEATH. **Take notice that**—I warn you that ; তোমাকে সাবধান করিয়া দিতেছি যে । **Takes no notice of it**—Pays no heed to it ; does not observe it ; এই বিষয়ে লক্ষ্য বা ভ্রূক্ষেপ করে না ; ইহা লক্ষ্য করে না । **The baby takes notice**—It shows signs of intelligence ; শিশুটী বুদ্ধির চিহ্ন দেখাইতেছে । **To bring to one's notice** — কাহারো গোচরে আনা । **To come into notice**—To attract attention ; মনোযোগ আকর্ষণ করা । **To take notice of**—To observe or pay heed to ; লক্ষ্য করা, অবধান করা ।

nō′-ti-fī-ă-ble, *adj.* (Of diseases) That requires to be notified to the public-health authorities ; (রোগ সম্পর্কে) স্বাস্থ্যবিভাগের কর্ম্মচারিগণের নিকট বিজ্ঞাপনীয় ।

nō′-ti-fȳ, *v. t.* **1.** To make known ; to declare ; বিজ্ঞাপিত করা ; ঘোষণা করা । **2.** To give notice to ; to apprise ; বিজ্ঞাপিত করা ; গোচরে আনা । **–fi-ca′-tion,** *n.* Notifying ; an intimation ; esp. act of giving official notice ; বিজ্ঞাপন ; বিজ্ঞপ্তি ; নোটিশ জারি করণ ।

nō′-tion, *n.* **1.** A general concept ; সাধারণ ধারণা বা প্রত্যয়, সংভাবনা (হিঃ কোঃ) । **2.** Idea ; as the *notion* of my doing it is absurd ; ভাব, বিশ্বাস, সংস্কার, ধারণা, ভাবনা । **3.** A view or theory ; as, the extravagant *notions* they entertain of themselves ; মত, মতবাদ । **4.** Inclination or desire (*of*) ; as, he has no *notion of* obedience ; আসক্তি, বাসনা । **5.** (*U. S.*) Cheap, useful articles ; (মার্কিণযুক্তরাজ্যে) সস্তাদরের প্রয়োজনীয় দ্রব্য, ফটকী নাটকী জিনিষ । **The first** or **second notion**—(*Philos.*) Same as FIRST or SECOND INTENTION, which see.

nō′-tion-ăl, *adj.* **1.** (Of knowledge etc.) Involving abstract conceptions ; speculative ; অমূর্ত্ত ; ধ্যানাত্মক । **2.** (Of things, relations, etc.) Visionary ; unreal ; কাল্পনিক, কল্পনাসিদ্ধ ; অবাস্তব । **3.** (Of persons) Fanciful ; খেয়ালপরবশ । **–ist,** *n.* **–ly,** *adv.*

nō′-tō-chŏrd, *n.* The rudimentary form of the spinal column ; মেরুদণ্ডের আদি রূপ ।

Nō-tō-gae′-ă (-jē-), *n.* A zoological region comprising Australian New-Zealand, and neotropical regions ; প্রাণিরাজ্যবিশেষ, অষ্ট্রেলিয়ান নবজিল্যাণ্ড এবং নবগ্রীষ্মমণ্ডলের প্রাণিরাজ্যসমূহ ইহার অন্তর্ভুক্ত ।

Notopterous chitala—চিতল মাছ (গুপ্তঃ) ।

Notopterous kapiret—ফলী মাছ (গুপ্তঃ) ।

nō-tō′-ri-ous (-ŭs), *adj.* **1.** (Of facts) Well-known ; commonly known ; "Worship of Christ was a living and *notorious* practice" ; সুবিদিত ; সর্ব্বজনবিদিত, লোকপ্রসিদ্ধ, লোকবিশ্রুত । **2.** Unfavourably known or spoken of ; as, a *notorious* thief, act, etc. ; বিখ্যাত, নামজাদা । **–ly,** *adv.* **–ri′-e-ty,** *n.* **1.** State of being notorious ; প্রসিদ্ধি, অখ্যাতি, অপকীর্ত্তি । **2.** A notorious person ; নামজাদা লোক ।

nŏt-with-stănd′-ing, *prep., adv.* & *conj.* In spite of ; as, *nowithstanding* his resistance ; সত্ত্বেও । ***Adv.*** Nevertheless ; তথাপি, তবুও, তত্রাপি । ***Conj.*** Although ; as, I shall go *notwithstanding* you forbid me ; যদিও ।

nou′-gat (nö-gä), *n.* A sweetmeat of sugar, nuts, etc. ; বাদাম ও পেস্তার কুঁচি ভরা একপ্রকার মিঠাই ।

nought (nāt), *n.* **1.** Nothing (*Poet.* or *archaic*) ; (পদ্যে ও অপ্রঃ) কিছুই না । **2.** (*Arith.*) Zero ; also a cipher ; o ; শূন্য । **3.** A worthless person or thing ; নিষ্কর্ম্মা লোক, অপদার্থ লোক, অকেজো জিনিষ। **To bring to nought**—To ruin ; to thwart ; ধ্বংস করা ; ব্যর্থ করা, বিফল করা। **To come to nought** — To be ruined ; to fail ; ধ্বংসপ্রাপ্ত হওয়া ; ব্যর্থ হওয়া, নিষ্ফল হওয়া। **To set at nought**—To disregard ; to deride ; অগ্রাহ্য করা, উড়াইয়া দেওয়া ; বিদ্রূপ করা, উপহাস করা।

nou'-mĕ-nŏn (now-), *n.* (*pl.* -NA) (*Metaph.*) An object of rational intuition, (opp. to *phenomenon*) ; (তত্ত্ববিদ্যা) বস্তুর অজ্ঞেয় বা অজ্ঞাত স্বরূপ, প্রকৃতি (হিঃ কোঃ), সৎ (ঐ), স্বপ্রমিতিক (ঐ)। [এই শব্দটী বিখ্যাত জর্ম্মণ দার্শনিক কাণ্ট কর্ত্তৃক উদ্ভাবিত হইয়াছে। কাণ্টের মতে আমরা বস্তুর ইন্দ্রিয়গ্রাহ্য মূর্ত্তিই দেখিতে পাই—কিন্তু উহার স্বরূপ আমাদের চিরকাল অজ্ঞাত এবং অজ্ঞেয় থাকে। কাণ্টের মতে কার্য্যকরী প্রজ্ঞার (practical reason) সাহায্যে আমরা সদসৎকর্ম্মের কর্ত্তৃস্বরূপে স্বরূপলোকের আভাস পাইয়া থাকি।] **—nal,** *adj.* Not phenomenal : নিরাধার (শুক্রঃ বিনয়), সৎস্বরূপ, স্বরূপাধিষ্ঠিত, স্বরূপভূত, তত্ত্বভূত।

noun (nown), *n.* (*Gram.*) A word used as the name of, or designation of, a person or thing ; বিশেষ্য, প্রাতিপদিক, নাম, সংজ্ঞা (কেঙিঃ) **Noun'-al**—*adj.* (*Rare*). **Abstract noun**—গুণবাচক বিশেষ্য। **Collective noun**—সংঘবাচক বিশেষ্য। **Common noun**—জাতিবাচক বিশেষ্য **Material noun**—দ্রব্যবাচক বিশেষ্য। **Proper noun**—ব্যক্তিবাচক বিশেষ্য।

nour'-ish (nŭr-), *v. t.* **1.** To maintain by feeding ; (*fig.*) to encourage ; to support ; লালনপালন করা, পরিপুষ্ট করা ; (লক্ষণায়) উৎসাহিত করা ; পরিপোষণ করা। **2.** To cherish or foster in one's heart ; as, to *nourish* a hope ; পোষণ করা। **—ing,** *adj.* Helping to nourish ; nutritious ; পুষ্টিকর ; পুষ্টিজনক।

nour'-ish-mĕnt (nŭr-), *n.* **1.** That which nourishes ; nutriment ; পুষ্টিজনক দ্রব্য ; পুষ্টি। **2.** Nourishing ; state of being nourished ; পোষণ, বৃংহণ ; পরিপুষ্টি।

nous (nows), *n.* **1.** (*Gr. Philos.*) The reason ; mind ; intellect ; প্রজ্ঞা, বুদ্ধি ; মন ; মহত্তত্ত্ব (ব্রজঃ বৈষ্ণঃ), মহৎ (হিঃ কোঃ)। **2.** (*Colloq.*) Common sense ; intelligence ; (চলিত-ভাষায়) কাণ্ডজ্ঞান ; বুদ্ধি।

nŏv'-ĕl, *n.* **1.** (*Rare*) One of the tales in such a collection, as Boccaccio's *Decameron* ; (অপ্রঃ) গল্পগুচ্ছের অন্তর্গত গল্প। **2.** A fictitious prose narrative picturing real life ; উপন্যাস, উপাখ্যান। **3.** (*Rom. law*) A new decree supplementary to the Codex ; রোমীয় আইনের পরিপূর্ণক বিধান। **The novel**—ঔপন্যাসিক সাহিত্য।

nŏv'-ĕl, *adj.* Not previously known ; of a new kind or nature ; strange ; অভিনব, নূতন ; নূতন ধরণের ; অপূর্ব্ব, অপরূপ, আজব।

nŏv-ĕl-ette' (-ĕt), *n.* **1.** A short novel ; a short story of the nature a novel ; ক্ষুদ্র উপন্যাস ; গল্প। **2.** (*Mus.*) A piano piece of free form with several themes ; (সঙ্গীতবিদ্যা) বাদ্যযন্ত্রবিশেষ।

nŏv'-ĕl-ist, *n.* A novel writer ; উপন্যাসকার, উপন্যাসলেখক, ঔপন্যাসিক। **—is'-tic,** *adj.*

nŏv'-ĕl-ize, *v. t.* To put into the form of a novel ; "The desperate attempt to *novelize* history" ; উপন্যাসাকার দেওয়া। **—i-za'-tion,** *n.*

nŏv'-ĕl-tȳ, *n.* **1.** Something novel or strange ; an unusual thing or occurrence ; অপূর্ব্ব বস্তু ; অপূর্ব্ব ঘটনা, আজব জিনিষ। **2.** State of being novel ; newness ; novel character (*of*) ; অপূর্ব্বতা ; অভিনবত্ব নবীনতা।

Nō-vĕm'-bêr, *n.* The eleventh month of the year, having 30 days ; ইংরাজী বৎসরের একাদশ মাস, নভেম্বর মাস।

nō-vêr'-cal, *adj.* Stepmotherly ; বিমাতার উপযোগী।

nŏv'-ice (-ĭs), *n.* **1.** One who has entered a religious house and is on probation ; কোন আশ্রমাদিতে গৃহীত হইবার পূর্ব্বে যে ব্যক্তি কিছুকাল শিক্ষাধীন অবস্থায় থাকে, নব ছাত্র। **2.** A new convert ; নবদীক্ষিত ব্যক্তি, নব (বৌদ্ধঃ)। **3.** A beginner ; tiro ; প্রথম শিক্ষার্থী, নব ছাত্র, নূতন লোক ; নবশিক্ষার্থী ব্যক্তি।

nō-vĭ'-ti-āte (-shĭ-), **—ci—** (-shĭ-), *ns.* **1.** The state or time of being a novice ; apprenticeship ; নবছাত্রত্ব, অন্তেবাসিত্ব, নবছাত্রদশা ; শিক্ষানবীশত্ব। **2.** A novice ; নূতনশিক্ষার্থী ব্যক্তি। **3.** Quarters assigned to novices ; কোন আশ্রমে প্রবেশার্থী পরীক্ষাধীন ব্যক্তিগণের বাসের জন্য নির্দ্দিষ্ট আবাস।

now, *adv., conj.* & *n.* **1.** At the present time ; under the present circumstances ; as, *now* that I know you it is different ; এখন, ইদানীং, অধুনা ; বর্ত্তমান অবস্থায়। **2.** Immediately ; forthwith ; as, you must go *now* ; অবিলম্বে ; এখনই। **3.** Very lately, (in modern use chiefly in the phrase *Just now*) ; অতি অল্প দিন পূর্ব্বে। **4.** Then ; by that time ; next ; তখন ; সেই সময়ের মধ্যে ; পরে। **5.** Also used elliptically, esp. at the beginning of a clause ; "And *now* as to Dr. Whately I owe him a great deal" ; পদলোপ সূচনার্থেও ব্যবহৃত হয়। *Conj.* Seeing that ; *now* I am a man, I think otherwise ; যেহেতু। *Noun.* The present time or moment ; as, read the future in the *now* ; বর্ত্তমান কাল, বর্ত্তমান মুহূর্ত্ত। **Now and again**—Occasionally ; সময় সময়। **Now and then**—At intervals ; occasionally ; মাঝে মাঝে ; সময় সময়। **Now or never**—See NEVER.

Now—now—Alternately ; পরপর, পর্য্যায়ক্রমে। **Now that** — Because ; কারণ।

now'-ă-day (-dā), *adj.* & *adv.* Of the present time ; অধুনাতন। ***Adv.*** Same as NOWADAYS.

now'-ă-days (-dāz), *adv.* & *n.* At the present time ; in these days ; ইদানীং, অধুনা, বর্ত্তমানে ; ইদানীন্তন, আজকাল। ***Noun.*** The present time ; these advanced and new-fangled times ; বর্ত্তমানকাল ; নূতনযুগ।

Now'-ĕl, *interj.* A shout of joy in Christmas carols ; খৃষ্টমাসের গীতির সময় উচ্চারিত আনন্দধ্বনি।

nō'-where (-whār), *adv.* 1. Not in any place or state ; কোথাও না, কুত্রাপি নহে। 2. In no book etc. ; by no author ; as, it is *nowhere* said ; কোন গ্রন্থেই না ; কোন গ্রন্থকার দ্বারা নয়। **Nowhere near**—Not nearly ; প্রায় নয়। **To be or come in nowhere**—To fail to have a place in race or competition, (*lit.* & *fig.*) ; (শব্দানুযায়ী ও লক্ষণায়) ঘোড়দৌড় বা প্রতিযোগীতায় কোন স্থান না পাওয়া।

Nox, *n.* The goddess of night ; গ্রীকপুরাণোক্ত কৃষ্ণসেনা এবং তারাগণ-বেষ্টিতা নিশাদেবী।

nox'-ious (nŏk-shŭs), *adj.* Harmful ; pernicious ; unwholesome ; as, *noxious* air or food ; ক্ষতিজনক, অনিষ্টজনক ; অপকারক, অহিতকারক, (জন্তুসম্বন্ধে) হিংস্র ; অস্বাস্থ্যকর। **—ly,** *adv.* **—ness,** *n.*

noyade, (*F.*), *n.* Execution by drowning, esp. of many persons at once, as in France in 1794 ; জলে নিমজ্জন পূর্ব্বক নিধন, বিশেষতঃ জলে নিমজ্জনপূর্ব্বক একত্রে বহুলোক নিধন।

noyau, (*F.*), *n.* A liqueur made from brandy and flavoured with cherry or peach-kernels ; ব্রাণ্ডী হইতে প্রস্তুত এবং চেরিফল ও পিচ ফলের শাঁস দ্বারা স্বাদুকৃত মাদক পানীয়বিশেষ।

nŏz'-zle (-l), *n.* 1. A spout ; a terminal pipe or part of a pipe or tube ; চায়ের কেটলী প্রভৃতির নল ; নল প্রভৃতির অগ্রভাগ। 2. A projecting part ; a small beak or nose ; উদ্গত অংশ ; ক্ষুদ্র চঞ্চু বা নাসা।

nuance, (*F.*), *n.* A slight or delicate difference or variation in meaning, feeling, colour, opinion, tone, etc. ; সূক্ষ্ম প্রভেদ, সূক্ষ্ম বৈষম্য।

nŭb, nŭb'-ble (-l), *ns.* A small knob ; lump ; as, a *nub* of coal ; ক্ষুদ্র, গোলাকার উদ্গত অংশ ; পিণ্ড। **Nub'-bly,** *adj.*

nū'-bĭle, *adj.* Marriageable, (said of females or of age) ; বিবাহযোগ্য, বিবাহোপযুক্ত। **—bil'-i-ty,** *n.*

nū'-chăl, *adj.* Of, relating to, or about, the nape of the neck ; গ্রীবার পশ্চাদ্‌ভাগসম্বন্ধীয়।

nū-cĭf'-ĕr-ous (-ŭs), *adj.* Bearing, or producing, nuts ; গুবাকাদি-ফলপ্রসূ।

nū'-clĕ-ōle, *n.* (*Biol.*) A nucleus of, or within, a nucleus ; (জীববিজ্ঞান) অণুকোষকেন্দ্র। **—o-lar, —o-lat-ed,** *adjs.*

nū'-clē-ŭs, *n.* (*Pl.* -ES or -I) 1. (*Astron.*) The head of a comet ; (জ্যোতির্বিজ্ঞান) ধূমকেতুর শীর্ষ। 2. A kernel ; hence, a central part or point about which matter is collected or to which accretion is made ; ফলের শাঁস, বীজগর্ভ, বীজকেন্দ্র ; কেন্দ্র, হৃদ্‌বিন্দু, আকর্ষকবিন্দু (হিঃ কোঃ)। 3. (*Bot.*) The central part of an ovule, seed, plant-cell, etc. ; (উদ্ভিদবিদ্যা) বীজ, ডিম্বাণু, বৃক্ষাদির অণুকোষ প্রভৃতির কেন্দ্র, ভ্রূণস্থলী (সাঃ পঃ), ডিম্বাণুষ্ঠ (ঐ)। 4. (*Zool.*) The denser central portion of an animal cell ; a portion of medullary substance from which a nerve or a set of nerves arises ; (জন্তু-বিদ্যা) জীবের অণুকোষের ঘনতর কেন্দ্রভাগ ; অস্থিমজ্জার যে অংশে কোন শিরা বা শিরাশ্রেণী উপজাত হয়। **—al, —ar, —a-ry,** *adjs.*

nūde, *adj.* & *n.* Naked ; unclothed ; as, a *nude* room : *nude* person ; উলঙ্গ, নগ্ন ; বিবসন, বিবস্ত্র, দিগম্বর, লেংটা (*colloq.*)। ***Noun.*** 1. (*Paint.* & *sculp.*) A nude or undraped figure ; (চিত্রবিদ্যা এবং ভাস্কর্য্য) নগ্নমূর্ত্তি বা প্রতিকৃতি। 2. (With *the*) The undraped human figure or representation of it in art ; the undraped state ; নগ্নমানবমূর্ত্তি ; নগ্নতা। **Nu'-di-ty,** *n.* **Nude contract**—(আইন) কোনরূপ অর্থ, সুবিধাদি গ্রহণ বিনা চুক্তি। **Nude woman**—নগ্নিকা, বিবসনা নারী।

nudge (nŭj), *v. t., i.* & *n.* 1. To push or poke gently, as with the elbow, to draw attention ; মনোযোগ আকর্ষণের জন্য কনুই দ্বারা ধাক্কা দেওয়া। 2. (*Fig.*) To draw attention of ; (লক্ষণায়) মনোযোগ আকর্ষণ করা। ***Verb i.*** To give a nudge ; কনুই দ্বারা ধাক্কা দেওয়া। ***Noun.*** A gentle push or poke with the elbow to draw attention ; মনোযোগ আকর্ষণের জন্য কনুই দ্বারা ধাক্কা।

Nū-dĭ-bran-chĭ-ā'-tă (-brang-), *n.* An extensive division of marine gastropods, having no shell except when very young ; বৃহৎ উদরপদী সামুদ্রিক শম্বুকাদিবর্গ।

nugae, (*L.*), *n., pl.* Trifles ; silly verses ; things of little value ; তুচ্ছবস্তু ; অসার কবিতা ; নগণ্য বস্তু।

nū'-gă-tō-rў, *adj.* 1. Trifling ; worthless ; futile ; তুচ্ছ, হালকা ; অসার ; নিষ্ফল, নিরর্থক, অনর্থক। 2. Inoperative ; invalid ; "Which assignation may seem *nugatory* and void" ; অকার্য্যকর ; ব্যর্থ, বাতিল, অনর্থক, বিফল, অসিদ্ধ।

nŭg'-gar (-ăr), *n.* A large boat used on the Nile ; নীল নদীতে ব্যবহৃত বৃহৎ নৌকা।

nŭg'-get (-ĕt), *n.* A mass; esp. a native lump of gold; পিণ্ড, ঢেলা; বিশেষতঃ স্বর্ণপিণ্ড।

nui'-sance (nū-săns), *n.* **1.** (*Law*) Anything injurious or obnoxious for which legal remedy may be had; as, commit no *nuisance*; (আইন) অনিষ্টজনক কার্য্য, বিরক্তিজনক কর্ম্ম। **2.** That which is offensive or annoying; a plague or pest, (applied to persons, things or actions); বিরক্তিজনক বিষয়; উৎপাত। **Commit no nuisance**—বাহ্যপ্রস্রাব করিও না।

nŭll, *adj.* **1.** Void; of no efficacy; invalid; (usu., *null & void*); বাতিল, নাকচ; নিষ্ফল, ব্যর্থ; অসিদ্ধ। **2.** Devoid of character, significance or individuality; চরিত্রহীন, অর্থহীন, ব্যক্তিত্বহীন। **3.** (*Rare*) Nil; non-existent; (অপ্র:) শূন্য; অসত্তাবান। **Null and void**—Invalid; বাতিল, নামঞ্জুর, নাকচ।

nŭl'-li-fȳ (-ĭ-), *v. t.* **1.** To render invalid; to annul; to cancel; অসিদ্ধ করা; বাতিল করা, নাকচকরা; রদকরা। **2.** To make of no use or efficacy; to efface; ব্যর্থ করা, অকার্য্যকর করা; মুছিয়া ফেলা। **—fi-ca'-tion,** *n.*

nŭl'-li-pōre (-ĭ-), *n.* A species of marine vegetation; একপ্রকার সামুদ্রিক উদ্ভিদ্।

nŭl'-li-tȳ (-ĭ-) *n.* **1.** The state of being legally null and void; invalidity; as, *nullity* of marriage; অকার্য্যকরতা, ব্যর্থতা; অসিদ্ধতা। **2.** An act, document, etc., which is void; বাতিল কার্য্য, দলিল প্রভৃতি। **3.** Nothingness; nihility; as, it was reduced to a *nullity*; শূন্যতা, শূন্যত্ব; নাস্তিত্ব। **4.** A nothing; a nonentity; অপদার্থ লোক; নগণ্য ব্যক্তি বা বস্তু। **Nullity suit**—রদ বা বাতিল করার জন্য মোকদ্দমা।

numb (nŭm), *adj.* & *v. t.* Torpid; without feeling or power of motion; অসাড়, জড়, স্তব্ধ, অবশ, বিকল, আড়ষ্ট, নিস্তেজ; অচল, চলচ্ছক্তি-রহিত, অবসন্ন, সুপ্ত। ***Verb t.*** To make torpid; (*fig.*) to stupefy; to paralyse; জড় করা, অসাড় করা; (লক্ষণায়) স্তব্ধকরা, স্তম্ভিত করা; আড়ষ্ট করা, বিকল করা, অবশ করা। **Numb'-ly,** *adv.* **Numb'-ness,** *n.* The quality of being numb; সুপ্ততা, সুপ্তত্ব, জাড্য, স্তব্ধতা, স্তম্ভ। **Numb hand**—(*Slang*) A clumsy person; (ইতর ভাষায়) আনাড়ী লোক। **Numb-fish**—Same as TORPEDO-FISH. **Numb-skull**—Same as NUMSKULL.

nŭm'-bẽr, *n.* **1.** An aggregate or assemblage of units; as, the *number* of books was very large; রাশি, সংখ্যা, দল, গণ, সমূহ। **2.** (*Pl.*) The fourth book of the Pentateuch which contains the census of the Hebrews; বাইবেলের খণ্ড-বিশেষ। **3.** A symbol or figure or collection of these which represents graphically an arithmetical total; a numeral; as, the *number* 45; a ticket or label bearing such signs; সংখ্যা; অঙ্ক; সংখ্যা-চিহ্নিত টিকেট, লেবেল, প্রভৃতি। **4.** A single part or issue of a book or periodical; a person designated by a certain number; a part or division of an opera, oratorio, etc.; কোন পুস্তক বা সংবাদপত্রের একখণ্ড বা সংখ্যা; কোন সংখ্যাদ্বারাবিশিষ্ট ব্যক্তি; যাত্রা, প্রভৃতির খণ্ড। **5.** (*Pl.*) Numerical preponderance; as, won by force of *numbers*; সংখ্যাধিক্য। **6.** Science of abstract units; as, skill in *numbers*; সংখ্যাবিজ্ঞান। **7.** Numerical reckoning; সংখ্যাগণন। **8.** (*Gram.*) The difference of termination of a word to express unity or plurality; (ব্যাকরণ) বচন। **9.** (*Pl.*) Musical periods or groups of notes; metrical feet; verses; স্বরলহরী; কবিতার চরণ; কবিতার কলি। **10.** (*Rare*) Rhythm; (কচিদ্ব্যবহৃত) শ্রবণসুখদধ্বনিপ্রবাহ। **—less,** *adj.* **Abstract number**—নিরপেক্ষ সংখ্যা, সাধারণ সংখ্যা (হিঃ কোঃ)। **Back number**—The earlier issue of a magazine; (*fig.*) anything out of date; কোন সংবাদপত্রের পূর্ব্ববর্ত্তী সংখ্যা; (লক্ষণায়) পুরাতন জিনিষ। **Cardinal number**—এক, দুই, ইত্যাদি সংখ্যা, পরিগণিতসংখ্যা (হিঃ কোঃ)। **Concrete number**—সাপেক্ষ সংখ্যা। **In number**—When counted or estimated numerically; সংখ্যায়। **Number one**—Oneself; as, take care of *number* one; নিজ, স্বয়ং। **Ordinal number**—প্রথম, দ্বিতীয়, তৃতীয়, প্রভৃতি। **Prime number**—মৌলিক সংখ্যা, অর্থাৎ যে সংখ্যা এক ভিন্ন অন্য সংখ্যা দ্বারা বিভাজ্য। **Whole number**—পূর্ণ সংখ্যা, অভিন্ন সংখ্যা (হিঃ কোঃ)। **Looking after number one**—নিজের কোলে ঝোল টানে, সকলকেই আপনার কোলে টানে। **Science of numbers**—Arithmetic; পাটীগণিত। **To lose the number of one's mess**—To die; মরা। **To take care of number one**—নিজের কোলে ঝোল টানা। **Without number**—Innumerable; অসংখ্য।

nŭm'-bẽr, *v. t.* **1.** To count; to reckon; গণনা করা; সংখ্যা করা। **2.** (*Pass.*) To be restricted in number; as, his days are *numbered*; ফুরাইয়া আসা (তাহার দিন ফুরাইয়া আসিয়াছে)। **3.** To reckon or regard, as one of a collection or multitude; "He was *numbered* with the transgressors"; দলের একজন বলিয়া বিবেচনা করা। **4.** To mark or distinguish by a number; as, to *number* the houses; সংখ্যাদ্বারা চিহ্নিত বা স্বতন্ত্রতা নির্দ্দে

করা। 5. (*Rare*) To have lived or to live (so many years); as, he has *numbered* thirty; (অপ্রঃ) বাস করিয়া থাকা, বাস করা। 6. To amount to; as, the crew *numbered* 33; সংখ্যায় হওয়া।

nü'-mêr-ă-ble (-bl), *adj.* Capable of being numbered; সংখ্যেয়, গণনীয়, গণনার যোগ্য।

nü'-mêr-ăl, *adj.* & *n.* 1. Pertaining to number; consisting of number; সংখ্যাসম্বন্ধীয়; সংখ্যাত্মক, গণনাত্মক। 2. Expressing or representing number; as, *numeral* letters; সংখ্যাবোধক, সংখ্যাসূচক। ***Noun.*** 1. A word expressing a number; সংখ্যাবোধকশব্দ। 2. A figure or character, or group of figures, used to express a number; সংখ্যা।

nü-mêr-ā'-tion, *n.* 1. A method or process of numbering or computing; গণনাপ্রণালী। 2. Computation; calculation; assignation of numbers to things; সংখ্যান; গণন; সংখ্যানির্দ্দেশ, সংখ্যালেখন। 3. (*Arith.*) Act, or art, of reading numbers when expressed by means of numerals; সংখ্যাপঠন, সংখ্যাপঠনকৌশল। **Numeration table**—সংখ্যালিখনসারণী।

nü'-mêr-ā-tor (-têr), *n.* 1. (*Arith.*) The number above the line in vulgar fraction which shows how many parts of the unit are taken; লব (সাঃ পঃ), অংশ (ঐ), ভাগ (ঐ), বিভাগ (ঐ)। 2. One who numbers; সংখ্যাকারক, গণক, গণনাকারী।

nü-mĕr'-ic, *n.* A number; a proper, or improper fraction, or an incommensurable ratio; সংখ্যা; সমভগ্নাংশ, বিষমভগ্নাংশ।

nü-mĕr'-i-căl, *adj.* Of, relating to, in, or denoting, numbers; সংখ্যাসম্বন্ধীয়। **–ly**, *adv.* **Numerical strength**—সংখ্যাবল।

nü'-mêr-ous (-ŭs), *adj.* 1. Comprising many units; as, *numerous* family, library, army, etc.; many; as, *numerous* dangers; বহু, অনেক, বিস্তর, বহুসংখ্যক; অসংখ্য। 2. Coming from many individuals; as, a *numerous* voice; বহুকণ্ঠোচ্চারিত। 3. (*Archaic*) Crowded; thronged, as a country, a dinner, etc.; (অপ্রঃ) জনাকীর্ণ, লোকাকীর্ণ; জনসঙ্কুল। 4. (Of verse or prose) Measured; rythmic, (*rare*); (কবিতা বা গদ্য সম্বন্ধে) (ছন্দ-সম্বন্ধে) ছন্দোবদ্ধ; (অপ্রঃ) শ্রবণসুখদধ্বনিসমন্বিত। **–ly**, *adv.*

nü-mis-măt'-ic, *adj.* Of, or relating to, coins or coinage; টঙ্কসম্বন্ধীয়, মুদ্রাতত্ত্বসম্বন্ধীয়, মুদ্রাবিজ্ঞানসম্বন্ধীয়, মুদ্রানির্ম্মাণসম্বন্ধীয়। **–i-cal-ly**, *adv.* **–ics**, *n.* The science of coins or medals; মুদ্রাবিজ্ঞান, টঙ্কবিজ্ঞান, মুদ্রাতত্ত্ব, পদকবিজ্ঞান। **–ma-tol'-o-gy**, *n.* **–mis'-ma-tist**, *n.* One versed in numismatic; মুদ্রাবিজ্ঞানবিদ্, মুদ্রাবিজ্ঞানবিশারদ।

nŭm'-ma-rȳ (-ă-), **nŭm'-mu-lă-rȳ** (-ü-), *adjs.* Pertaining to, or dealing with, coins or money; মুদ্রাসম্বন্ধীয়, মুদ্রাসংক্রান্ত।

nŭm'-mu-līte (-ü-), *n.* A coin-like fossil shell of the tertiary

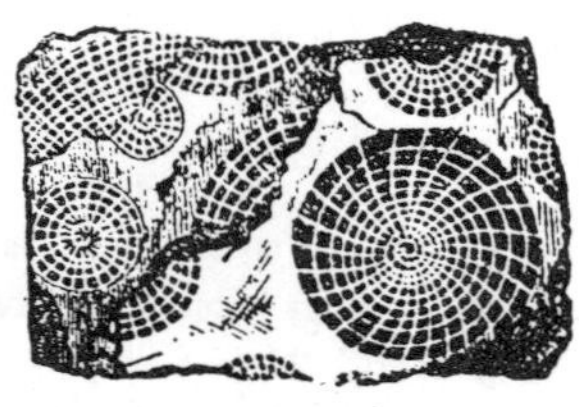

Nummulite.

strata; তৃতীয় স্তরে প্রাপ্ত মুদ্রাকৃতি শিলীভূত জন্তু।

nŭm'-nah (-nâ), *n.* A saddle-cloth; জিনপোষ।

nŭm'-skŭll, *n.* A dunce; a blockhead; also the head of such a fellow; মূর্খ; হতবুদ্ধি ব্যক্তি, জড়বুদ্ধি ব্যক্তি, হাবা, বোকা; ঐরূপ লোকের মাথা।

nŭn, *n.* 1. A woman devoted, in celibacy and seclusion, to a religious life; সন্ন্যাসিনী, তপস্বিনী, মঠবাসিনী, ভিক্ষুণী (esp. Buddhist nun), মঠনিবাসিনী। 2. A kind of bird or moth; একজাতীয় পক্ষী বা তসরে পোকা। **Nun'-hood, Nun'-ship**, *ns.* **Nun'-like, Nun'-nish**, *adjs.* **Nun'-ner-ry**, *n.* A house in which a body of nuns reside; ভিক্ষুণী-সংঘ, সন্ন্যাসিনী-সংঘ। **Nun's cloth**—একপ্রকার পাতলা পশমী কাপড়। **Nun's thread**—সেলাই করার জন্য একপ্রকার শাদা সূতা। **Nun's veiling**—পোষাকের জন্য একপ্রকার ফিনফিনে কাপড়।

nŭn'-buoy (-boy̆), *n.* A buoy tapering at each end; মৃদঙ্গাকার বয়া।

nunc dimittis, (*L.*), *n.* 1. (*Eccl.*) A hymn or canticle in the public worship of many churches, it begins with these words; খৃষ্টীয় স্তোত্র বা ভজনসঙ্গীতবিশেষ। 2. Permission to depart; departure; গমনানুমতি; যাত্রা, প্রস্থান। **To sing nunc dimittis**—To be willing to depart from life, etc.; প্রাণত্যাগ প্রভৃতিতে ইচ্ছুক হওয়া।

nŭn'-ci-ā-türe (-shī), *n.* The office of a nuncio; its tenure; পোপের প্রতিনিধির পদ; ইহার কার্য্যকাল।

nŭn'-ci-ō (-shī-), *n.* The official representative of the pope at a foreign court; বৈদেশিক রাজদরবারে পোপের প্রতিনিধি।

nŭn'-cü-pāte, *v. t.* To declare orally, as a will etc.; মৌখিক ভাবে ব্যক্ত করা। **–pa'-tion**, *n.* **–pa-tive**, *adj.* Oral; মৌখিক, বাচনিক, অলিখিত।

Nunky pays—The Government pays for everything; সরকার সমস্ত টাকা জোগায়। [Nunky শব্দ Uncle

Sam অর্থাৎ শাসনতন্ত্রের পরিবর্তে বসিয়াছে।] See UNCLE.

nŭn-nā'-tion, *n.* (*Gram.*) The addition of final *n* in declension of nouns, as in Arabic; (ব্যাকরণ) আরবী ভাষায় বিশেষ্য পদের রূপান্তর-নির্ণায়ক '*n*'এর সংযোগ।

nū'-phâr, *n.* Yellow water-lily: পীতবর্ণ কুমুদ।

nŭp'-tial (-shăl), *adj.* & *n.* Pertaining to marriage; done, or used, at a wedding; as, *nuptial* rites and ceremonies; বৈবাহিক, বিবাহসম্বন্ধীয়, ঔদ্বাহিক; বিবাহকালে কৃত বা ব্যবহৃত। ***Noun.*** (*Usu. pl.*) Wedding; বিবাহ, পরিণয়।

nurse (nêrs), *n.* **1.** A woman who suckles and takes care of an infant not her own, (usu. *wet-nurse*); also one who only takes care of children, (usu. *dry-nurse*); ধাত্রী, উপমাতা; ধাই। **2.** A country, etc. that fosters some quality etc.; as, the *nurse* of liberty; যে দেশ প্রভৃতিতে কোন বিশেষ গুণের পরিপুষ্টি সাধিত হয়, পালিনী। **3.** Nursing; শুশ্রূষা করণ। **4.** One, esp. a female, tending, or trained for tending, the sick or the infirm; শুশ্রূষাকারী, বিশেষতঃ শুশ্রূষাকারিণী, রুগ্নপরিচারিকা, রুগ্নসেবিকা। **5.** (*Forestry*) A tree planted to afford protection to other trees when young; (বনবিদ্যা) নবতরুসমূহের আশ্রয়ের জন্য রোপিত বৃক্ষ, ধাত্রীবৃক্ষ। **6.** A worker ant or bee that cares for the young; যে কর্ম্মী মক্ষিকা বা পিপীলিকা শাবকদিগকে পালন করে। **Nurse'-y,** *n.* (A pet form of *Nurse*, a child's word); ধাই মা। **Dry-nurse**—যে ধাত্রী কেবল শিশুদিগকে লালনপালন করে কিন্তু স্তন্য পান করায় না। **Nurse-child**—পালিত সন্তান। **Nurse-frog**—এক জাতীয় মণ্ডুক। **Nurse-maid**—শিশুদিগের লালনপালনকার্য্যে নিযুক্তা পরিচারিকা। **To or at nurse**—In or under the care of a nurse; ধাত্রীর অধীনে। **Wet-nurse**—যে ধাত্রী শিশুদিগকে স্তন্য পান করাইয়া থাকে, দোগ্ধ্রী-ধাত্রী (আঃ বঃ), ক্ষীরধাত্রী (বৌদ্ধঃ), দুগ্ধবতী ধাত্রী।

nurse (nêrs), *v. t.* & *i.* **1.** To suckle; to take care of in infancy; স্তন্যপান করান, স্তন্যদান করা; পালন করা, পোষণ করা। **2.** To take care of or tend, as a sick person or invalid; to attend upon; শুশ্রূষা করা; পরিচর্য্যা করা। **3.** (*Pass.*) To be brought up (in luxury, certain place, etc.); পালিত হওয়া। **4.** To promote growth or vigour in; as, to *nurse* a feeble animal or plant, (also *fig.*); as, to *nurse* the arts, etc.; পোষণ করা। **5.** To manage (estate etc.) carefully or economically; (সম্পত্তি) সুপরিচালন করা। **6.** To cherish (grievances etc.); পোষণ করা। **7.** To caress; to fondle; to dandle; আদর করা; সোহাগ করা; হাঁটু বা বাহুদ্বয়ের উপর তুলিয়া নাচান বা সোহাগ করা। **8.** To sit close to, as if taking care of; as, he found his father *nursing* a bright fire; নিকটে বসা। **9.** To keep in good humour by attentions; আদর আপ্যায়ন দ্বারা খোসমেজাজে রাখা। **10.** To keep close to (a rival omnibus to interfere with its custom, or a horse in a race to impede it); নিকটে থাকা। ***Verb i.*** **1.** To suckle, or act as a wet-nurse; (of a child) to take the breast; স্তন্যপান করান, স্তন্যধাত্রীর কার্য্য করা; মাই ধরা। **2.** To be a sick-nurse; শুশ্রূষকারিণী হওয়া। **Nursing-bottle**—শিশুদের দুগ্ধপানের জন্য রবারের নল এবং স্তনাগ্রযুক্ত বোতল, শিশুপোষণী। **Nursing father or mother**—পালক পিতা বা পালিকা মাতা। **Nursing-home**—অস্ত্রোপচারক্রিয়া বা রোগীদিগের বাসের জন্য গৃহ, রোগীবাটিকা, শুশ্রূষাগার।

nurs'-ēr-ỹ (nêrs-), *n.* **1.** A room assigned to children and their nurses; কুমারাগার (চঃ), শিশুগৃহ, লালনাগার বালগৃহ। **2.** The place where anything is fostered and developed; "Fair Padua, *nursery* of arts"; লালনস্থলী, লালননিকেতন। **3.** A plot in which young plants or trees are reared until fit for transplantation; চারাবাড়ী (প্রবোধ), তরুণতরুবাটিকা। **4.** A fish-rearing pond; যে পুকুরে মৎস্যের চাষ করা হয়। **5.** A place where young animals are reared or developed; শিশুশাবকলালনস্থলী। **Nursery governess**—যে স্ত্রীলোক দ্বারা শিশুদিগের শিক্ষা ও লালনপালন—উভয় কার্য্যই সম্পাদিত হয়। **Nursery-man**—চারাবাড়ীর মালিক বা মজুর।

nurs'-ling, nurse- (nêrs-), *ns.* A child or infant considered with reference to its nurse; দুগ্ধপোষ্য শিশু, দুধের ছেলে, কোলের ছেলে, স্তনন্ধয়। **Nurs(e)ling of**—A person or thing bred in or fostered by; পালিত।

nur'-tūre (nêr-), *n.* & *v. t.* **1.** A nourishing or nursing; tender care; training or education; পালন, পোষণ; লালনপালন; শিক্ষা। **2.** Food; as, he took *nurture* for the road; খাদ্য, আহার। ***Verb t.*** To nourish; to rear; to educate; পোষণ করা; পালন করা; শিক্ষিত করা।

nŭt, *n.* & *v. i.* **1.** A fruit containing a seed or kernel within a hard covering; কঠিন ত্বক এবং কোমল সুস্বাদু শাঁসবিশিষ্ট ফল, বাদাম, গুবাক প্রভৃতি ফল, সকবচ ফল (কেঁশুঃ)! **2.** (*Slang*) The head; (ইতরভাষায়) মুণ্ড। **3.** (*Mach.*) A small cylinder or other body with teeth or projections corresponding with the teeth or grooves of a wheel ; (যন্ত্র-বিজ্ঞান) চক্রের দন্ত বা খাঁজের অনুরূপ দন্ত বা উদ্গাত অংশবিশিষ্ট ক্ষুদ্র নল প্রভৃতি। **4.** A small block usually of metal pierced with a female screw for securing or adjusting a bolt ; বল্টু আটকাইবার জন্য ভিতরের দিকে পেঁচ-কাটা ধাতু প্রভৃতির খণ্ড, চিবরী। **5.** The contrivance at the lower end of a violin bow etc. by which the horse-hair may be relaxed or tightened ; বেহালার ছড়ের নিম্নপ্রান্তের কৌশলবিশেষ—যদ্দারা উহার তার ঢিলা করা বা আঁটা যায়। **6.** (*Pl.*) Small lumps of coal ; কয়লার ক্ষুদ্র টুকরা। ***Verb i.*** To seek or gather nuts, (*usu. in gerund*; as, went *nutting*, etc.) ; বাদামাদি ফল কুড়ান। **Nut-brown**—বাদামি রংয়ের। **Nut-butter**—বাদামবিশেষ হইতে প্রস্তুত মাখনের ন্যায় খাদ্য। **Nut-cracker**—(Usu. *pl.*) An instrument for cracking hard-shelled nuts ; যাঁতি, সরতা। The name of an insessorial bird rarely seen in Britain ; একপ্রকার পক্ষী। (*Pl., slang*) A sharp angular chin and nose ; (also *attrib.*, as, a *nut-cracker* face) ; (ইতর ভাষায়) সরু নাসা বা হনু। **Nut-gall**—মাজুফল। **Nut-hatch** — একপ্রকার

Nut-hatch.

ক্ষুদ্র পক্ষী। **Nut-hook**—আকর্ষী। **Nut-oil**—বিভিন্ন প্রকার বাদামী জাতীয় ফল হইতে প্রাপ্ত তৈল। **Nut-palm**—বাদাম জাতীয় ফলপ্রসূ অস্ট্রেলিয়াদেশীয় তালজাতীয় বৃক্ষবিশেষ। **Nutshell**—The hard external covering in which the kernel of a nut is enclosed ; বাদামের খোসা। Something small in size or scanty in amount ; "The world reduced to a *nutshell*" ; ক্ষুদ্রায়তন বস্তু। Briefest possible way of expressing ; an epitome ; as, give it in a *nutshell* ; সংক্ষেপতমভাবে প্রকাশের রীতি ; চুম্বক, সংক্ষিপ্তসার। **Nut-tree** — বাদামজাতীয় ফলপ্রসূ বৃক্ষ। **Can't shoot for nuts**—(*Slang*) Can't do a thing even tolerably well ; (ইতরভাষায়) যেমন তেমনভাবে কোন কাজ করিতে পারে না। **Hard nut to crack**—A difficult problem ; a person or thing hard to deal with or get the better of ; কঠিন সমস্যা ; শক্ত লোক, শক্ত জিনিষ। **In a nutshell**—In, or within, a small compass or limit ; in a few words ; অল্পের মধ্যে ; অল্প কথায়। **Off one's nut**—Drunk or mad ; মাতাল, বিকৃতমস্তিষ্ক। **To be (dead) nuts on**—To be fond of, or delighted with ; to be skilful at ; কোন বিষয়ে, কোন লোক বা বস্তুর প্রতি খুব অনুরাগী হওয়া ; কোন বিষয়ে নিপুণ হওয়া। **To be nuts to**—(*Slang*) To be a source of pleasure to ; (ইতরভাষায়) খুব মজার বিষয় হওয়া। **To lie in a nutshell**—To be capable of easy comprehension or solution ; সহজে বোধগম্য বা মীমাংসার যোগ্য হওয়া।

nū'-tāte, *v. i.* (*Bot.*) To nod, or droop ; (উদ্ভিদ্ বিদ্যা) নুইয়া পড়া, নত হওয়া। **—tant,** *adj.* Nodding or drooping ; নমনশীল।

nū-tā'-tion, *n.* **1.** A nodding ; (*Pathol.*) Involuntary nodding of the head ; শিরশ্চালন ; অনিচ্ছাকৃত শিরশ্চালন। **2.** (*Astron.*) A vibratory motion of the earth's axis ; (জ্যোতির্বিজ্ঞান) পৃথিবীর অক্ষের দোলন, অক্ষবিচলন (হিঃ কোঃ)। **3.** Oscillation of a top in spinning ; ঘূর্ণনকালে লাটিমের কম্পন। **4.** Curvature in the stem of a growing plant ; বৃদ্ধিশীল বৃক্ষকাণ্ডে বক্রতা।

nŭt'-mĕg, *n.* The aromatic kernel of the fruit of an East-Indian tree ; the tree itself ; জাতিকোষ, জয়ত্রী, জাতিপত্র ; জায়ফল গাছ। **Nutmeg-apple** — জায়ফল, জাতিফল, মালতিফল (ভাবঃ প্রঃ)। **Nutmeg-liver**—যকৃতের রুগ্নাবস্থা।

nū'-tri-ă, *n.* The skin or fur of an aquatic animal of South America ; দক্ষিণ আমেরিকার জলজন্তুবিশেষের লোম বা চর্ম্ম।

nū'-tri-ĕnt, *adj.* Nourishing ; nutritive ; পুষ্টিকর ; পুষ্টিজনক।

nū'-tri-mĕnt, *n.* **1.** Nourishing food ; পুষ্টিজনক খাদ্য। **2.** (*Fig.*) That which promotes growth or development ; (লক্ষণায়) পরিপুষ্টিসাধক বস্তু। **—men'-tal,** *adj.* (*Rare*).

nū-tri'-tion, *n.* **1.** Act or process of nourishing ; state of being nourished ; পরিপোষণ, পরিপাচন (হিঃ কোঃ) ; পরিপুষ্টি। **2.** Nourishment ; food ; আহার্য্য ; খাদ্য।

nū-tri'-tious (-shŭs), *adj.* Nourishing ; efficient as food ; পুষ্টিকর, পুষ্টিজনক, পুষ্টিপ্রদ ; খাদ্যরূপে কার্য্যকর। **—ly,** *adv.* **—ness,** *n.* The state of being nutritious ; পুষ্টিকরত্ব, পৌষ্টিকতা, বৃংহণত্ব।

nū'-tri-tive (-tĭv), *adj.* & *n.* **1.** Nourishing ; nutritious ; পুষ্টিজনক, পৌষ্টিক ; পরিপোষক। **2.** Pertaining to, or concerned in, nutrition ; পুষ্টিসম্পৃক্ত। ***Noun.*** A nourishing food ; পুষ্টিজনক খাদ্য।

nŭt'-ty (-ĭ), *adj.* **1.** Abounding in, or producing, nuts ; বাদাম জাতীয় ফলবহুল, বাদামজাতীয় ফল উৎপাদক। **2.** Having a taste like nuts ; বাদামাস্বাদ। **3.** (*Slang*) Amorous or enthusiastic *upon* ; (ইতর ভাষায়) কামার্ত্ত, উৎসাহী।

nŭx-vŏm'-i-că, *n.* The poisonous seed of an Asiatic tree, containing strychnine ; also the tree itself ; কুচিলার বীজ ; কুচিলা লতা।

nŭz'-zle (-l), *v. i.* & *t.* **1.** To dig, root, thrust, poke, push or snuff with the nose ; to press the nose *into* or *against* ; নাকদ্বারা খনন বা উৎপাটন করা, নাকদ্বারা খোঁচা বা ধাক্কা দেওয়া ; নাক চাপা। **2.** To lie snug ; to nestle ; আরামে শুইয়া থাকা ; আরামে বাস করা। ***Verb t.*** **1.** To touch or rub with the nose ; নাসিকাদ্বারা স্পর্শ বা ঘর্ষণ করা। **2.** To thrust in (the nose or head) ; ঠেলিয়া ঢুকান।

nÿc-tă-lō'-pi-ă, *n.* **1.** Night-blindness or recurrent loss of vision after sunset ; নিশান্ধতা, পিত্তবিদগ্ধদৃষ্টি (সাঃ পঃ)। **2.** Day-blindness ; দিবান্ধতা।

Nyctanthes Arbor-tristis—শিউলি (বেলঃ), শেফালিকা (ঐ)।

nÿc-ti-trŏp'-ic, *adj.* (*Bot.*) Turning in a certain direction at night ; (উদ্ভিদ-বিদ্যা) রাত্রে নির্দ্দিষ্ট দিকে উন্মুখ।

nÿmph, *n.* **1.** (*Class. Myth.*) One of the inferior divinities of nature, represented as beautiful maidens, dwelling in the mountains, forests, meadows, waters, etc. ; কিম্পুরুষাঙ্গনা, অপ্সরা, সুরসুন্দরী, বিদ্যাধরী। **2.** (*Poet.*) A beautiful young woman ; (পদ্যে) সুন্দরী যুবতী, ডানাকাটা পরী। **3.** (*Zool.*) A pupa ; the chrysalis of an insect ; প্রজাপতি প্রভৃতির গুটি ; প্রজাপতি প্রভৃতির পক্ষোদ্গম। **Nym-phe'-an, Nymph'-ish, Nymph'-like,** *adjs.* **Water nymph**—জলপরী, জলদেবী। **Wood nymph**—বনদেবী।

Nymphæa edulis—ছোট শুন্দী (বেলঃ)।

Nymphæa cyanea—বড় নীলপদ্ম (বেলঃ), নীলপদ্ম (ঐ)।

Nymphæa pubescens — বড় শালুক (বেলঃ)।

Nymphæa rosea—ছোট রক্তকমল (বেলঃ)।

Nymphæa rubra—রক্তকমল।

Nymphæa stellata — ছোট নীলপদ্ম (বেলঃ), শুন্দি (ঐ), নীলাম্বুজন্ম (ঐ), কহ্লার (ঐ)।

nÿm'-phō-lĕp-sÿ, *n.* A frenzy or emotion as for some unattainable object ; কোন অপ্রাপ্য বস্তু লাভের জন্য উন্মত্ততা।

nÿm'-phō-lĕpt, *n.* A person inspired by violent enthusiasm, especially for an ideal ; কোন অপ্রাপ্য বস্তু লাভের জন্য উন্মত্ত ব্যক্তি। **—lep-tic,** *adj.*

nÿm-phō-mā'-ni-ă, *n.* Morbid and unnatural sexual desire in women ; স্ত্রীলোকের শৃঙ্গারোন্মাদ, কামোন্মত্ততা, বৃষণোন্মাদ (হিঃ কোঃ)।

Nyx, *n.* See NOX.

O

O, **1.** The fifteenth letter of the English alphabet ; ইংরাজী বর্ণমালার পঞ্চদশতম অক্ষর। **2.** An O-shaped mark ; a circle ; O-আকৃতির চিহ্ন ; বৃত্ত।

O, oh (ō), *interj.* An exclamation used in earnest or solemn address ; ওমা ! মাগো ! বাপরে ! বাবারে ! বাবা ! ওরে ! ওরেরে ! অহো, আয় ! হে ! অয়ি ! **O dear me !**—হায় হায় !

ō', *prep.* **1.** Short for *of* or *on* ; as, 10 *o'*clock : cannot sleep *o'*nights ; তে, টা।

oaf (ōf), *n.* **1.** (*Pl.* OAFS, OAVES), (*Archaic*) An elf's child ; a changeling left by fairies etc. ; (পূর্ব্বে) পরীদ্বারা পরিবর্ত্তিত শিশু ; পরী বা অপদেবতা একটী সুরূপ শিশু লইয়া গিয়া তৎপরিবর্ত্তে যে কুরূপ ও বিকৃতাঙ্গ শিশু রাখিয়া যায়। **2.** A deformed or foolish child ; a simpleton ; an awkward lout ; বিকৃতাঙ্গ বা নির্ব্বোধ শিশু ; হাবা ; কদাকার চাষা লোক। **Oaf'-ish,** *adj.*

Female flowers of oak.

oak (ōk), *n.* **1.** A valuable tree of many species ; ওকবৃক্ষ, সিন্দুরবৃক্ষ (মঃ ইঃ)। **2.** The wood of the oak ; ওককাষ্ঠ। **3.** Leaves of the oak ; as, *oak* is still worn on the 29th May ; ওকবৃক্ষের পত্র। **4.** (*Poet.*) Wooden ship ; (কবিতায়) কাষ্ঠময় অর্ণবযান। **5.** A strong outer-door often made of oak ; ওককাষ্ঠনির্ম্মিত সুদৃঢ় বহির্দ্বার। **6.** The colour of young oak leaves ; তরুণ-ওকপত্রের বর্ণ, ওকগাছের কচি পাতার রং। **Oak'-en,** *adj.* **Oak'-let, Oak'-ling,** *ns.* **Oak-apple, —fig, —gall, —plum, —potato, —spangle, —wart**—ওকবৃক্ষে কীটকৃত অর্ব্বুদ। **Oak-apple day**—২য় চার্লসের পুনঃ রাজ্যপ্রাপ্তির দিবস, ২৯শে মে। ২য় চার্লস ওকবৃক্ষের উপরে লুকাইয়া তাঁহার অনুসরণকারিগণের হস্ত হইতে পরিত্রাণ লাভ করিয়াছিলেন—এই ঘটনার স্মৃতিরক্ষার্থ বালকগণ এদিবস ওকপত্রে দেহ

সজ্জিত করিয়া থাকে। **Oak-beauty, -egger, -hooktip, -lappet, -moth** — একপ্রকার কীট। **Oak-fern** — একপ্রকার পর্ণাঙ্গ। **Oak-wood** — ওকবৃক্ষের বন ; ওককাষ্ঠ। **Young oak**—তরুণ ওকবৃক্ষ। **Heart of oak**—See under HEART. **To sport one's oak**—বহির্দ্বার রুদ্ধ করা। [ইহাদ্বারা এই বুঝায় যে গৃহস্বামী বাটীর বাহিরে আছেন, কিম্বা তিনি কাহারও সহিত সাক্ষাৎ করিতে ইচ্ছুক নন।]

oa'-kŭm (ō-), *n.* Old ropes untwisted and pulled into loose fibres used for caulking ; জাহাজের জীর্ণরজ্জুর শণ—ইহাদ্বারা জাহাজের ছিদ্র রোধ করা হয়, কিৎনি, কালাপাতি।

oar (ōr), *n., v. t. & i.* **1.** An instrument to row boats ; দাঁড়, অরিত্র, ক্ষেপণী, নৌকাদণ্ড। **2.** An oarsman ; as, he is a good *oar* ; দাঁড়ী। **3.** Something like an oar in form or use, *e. g.* wing, fin, arm, used in swimming etc. ; দাঁড়ের মত কোন কিছু। ***Verb t. & i.*** To row ; দাঁড় চালান। **Oar'-age,** *n.* **Oar'-less,** *adj.* **Oar'-y,** *adj.* Having the form, or the function, of an oar; দাঁড়ের আকৃতি, দাঁড়ের মত কার্য্যকারী। **Oarsman**—One who rows with an oar ; a boatman ; যে দাঁড় টানে, দাঁড়ী ; মাল্লা, ক্ষেপণিক। **Oarsman-ship,** *n.* **A pair-oar** or **four-oar**—A boat with two or four oars ; দুই বা চার দাঁড়বিশিষ্ট নৌকা। **Chained to the oar**—Required to work hard and long (allusion to *galley-slaves*) ; হাড়ভাঙ্গা খাটুনির কার্য্যে নিযুক্ত ; **He pulls a good oar** — He is a good oarsman ; সে একজন ভাল দাঁড়ী। **To have an oar in every man's boat**—To be a meddler ; পরের ব্যাপারে হস্তক্ষেপ করা। **To lie** or **rest on one's oars**—To cease work for a while ; কিছুক্ষণের জন্য বিশ্রাম করা। **To oar one's arms** or **hands**—To move them as in swimming ; সাঁতরাইবার সময়ের মত হাত পা নাড়া। **To put in one's oar**—To interfere in other's affairs ; to break in upon a conversation uninvited ; গায়ে পড়িয়া অন্য ব্যক্তির ব্যাপারে হস্তক্ষেপ করা ; কথার উপরে কথা বলা। **To ship the oars**—To place them in row-locks ; দাঁড়গুলি যথাস্থানে রাখা। **To toss the oars**—To raise the oars vertically for the purpose of saluting ; অভিবাদনার্থ দাঁড়সকল খাড়া করা। **To unship the oars**—To take off the oars from the row-locks ; দাঁড় আটকাইবার খাঁজ হইতে দাঁড় উঠাইয়া নেওয়া।

ō-ā'-sis, *n.* (*Pl.* -SES) A fertile spot in a barren desert, (*lit. & fig.*) ; মরুমধ্যস্থ তরুগুল্মাচ্ছাদিত শ্যামল স্থান, মরূদ্যান, শাদ্বল (হিঃ কোঃ), মরুবন, মরুকান্তার, মরুদ্বীপ, অন্তর্মরুগ্রাম (সাঃ পঃ)।

oast (ōst), *n.* A kiln to dry hops or malt ; হপলতা বা (জলমিজ্জন হেতু) অঙ্কুরিত যব শুষ্ককরণার্থ পোয়ান বা চুল্লী। **Oast-house**—উক্ত কার্য্যের জন্য গৃহ।

oat (ōt), *n.* **1.** The grain or seed of a cereal grass ; also this plant ; (*commonly used collectively in the plural*) ; জই ; জইয়ের গাছ। **2.** (*Poet.*) A musical pipe made of oat stems ; (কবিতা) মেষপালকগণের জই গাছের ডাঁটার বাঁশী। **3.** (*Poet.*) A pastoral or bucolic poetry ; (কবিতায়) গোষ্ঠকবিতা, পল্লীগাথা। **Oat'-en,** *adj.* **Oatcake**—জইয়ের পিঠা। **Oatmeal**—জইয়ের ছাতু, ঐ ছাতুর মণ্ড। **Wild oats**—জইএর মত লম্বা ঘাস। **To sow one's wild oats**—To indulge in youthful dissipation and excesses ; যৌবনসুলভ অত্যাচারে নিরত হওয়া।

oath (ōth), *n.* (*Pl.* OATHS) **1.** A solemn affirmation appealing to God or divine things for its truth ; শপথ, দিব্য, উপনিবন্ধ (মঃ ভূঃ), কিরা (*colloq.*)। **2.** A statement or promise supported by such an oath ; also, the form of words containing this ; as, an *oath* of allegiance ; সত্যপাঠ ; হলফ। **3.** An expression of profane swearing ; an imprecation ; a curse ; দেবতার নাম উল্লেখপূর্ব্বক গালি ; অভিশাপ ; শাপ। **Oath of allegiance**—রাজা বা শাসনতন্ত্রের প্রতি বাধ্যতার প্রতিশ্রুতি। **Oath of office**—কোন পদের কর্ত্তব্য-কার্য্য বিশ্বস্ততার সহিত সম্পাদনের প্রতিজ্ঞা। **Oath of supremacy**—রাজ্য এবং ধর্ম্মসংঘের উপর রাজার প্রাধান্য স্বীকারসূচক প্রতিজ্ঞা। **On oath**—On solemn affirmation or declaration ; শপথপূর্ব্বক, সত্যপাঠ পূর্ব্বক।

ŏb-bli-gā'-tō (-lī-), *adj. & n.* (*Mus.*) Required ; indispensable ; (of an accompaniment or part) ; (সঙ্গীতশাস্ত্র) আবশ্যক ; অপরিহার্য্য। ***Noun.*** Such a part or accompaniment ; অপরিহার্য্য অংশ বা সুরসঙ্গত।

Obcordate leaf.

ŏb-cŏr'-date, *adj.* (*Bot.*) Shaped like a heart, with the apex downward ; (উদ্ভিদ-বিদ্যা) হরতনের আকৃতি, প্রতিতাম্বুলাকার (সাঃ পঃ)।

ŏb'-dū-rāte, *adj.* Hardened ; inflexible ; stubborn ; কঠিন, কঠোর ; অনমনীয়, অনম্র ; দৃঢ়, দুরাগ্রহী। **-ly,** *adv.* **-ra-cy,** *n.* State of being obdurate, obstinacy ; কাঠিন্য, দার্ঢ্য ; ঠেঁটামি, একগুঁয়েমি।

ō'-bē-ah (-ă), **ō'-bi,** *ns.* A kind of sorcery practised by the negroes ; কাফ্রীদিগের যাদুবিশেষ।

ō-bē'-di-ence (-ĕns), *n.* **1.** Act or practice of obeying ; submission to authority ; আজ্ঞাপালন, আদেশপালন, আজ্ঞানুবর্ত্তিতা ; বাধ্যতা, বশ্যতা, আজ্ঞানুবর্ত্তন, আজ্ঞানুসরণ। **2.** (*Eccl.*, esp. *R. C.*) State of being obeyed ; authority or its sphere ; body of persons bound to obey ; (খৃষ্টীয় যাজকসম্প্রদায়, বিশেষতঃ রোমানক্যাথলিক) মান্যতা ; আদেশ, কর্তৃত্বপ্রভাবক্ষেত্র ; আদেশপালনে বাধ্য জনসম্প্রদায়। **Passive obedience**—Unqualified submission ; নির্ব্বিচারে আদেশপালন। **In obedience to**—Actuated by, or in accordance with ; আদেশের অনুবর্ত্তী বা বশবর্ত্তী।

ō-bē'-di-ĕnt, *adj.* Submissive to authority ; willing to obey ; বাধ্য, আজ্ঞাকারী, আজ্ঞাবহ, আজ্ঞাধীন, আজ্ঞানুবর্ত্তী, বচনগ্রাহী ; বশম্বদ, বশগত, বশ্য, বশগ, বশবর্ত্তী। **—ly**, *adv.* **Your obedient servant**—আপনার অনুগত ভৃত্য—বিদায়কালে, রহস্যচ্ছলে ও সরকারী পত্রাদির শেষে নামের পূর্ব্বে ব্যবহৃত হয়।

ō-bē-di-en'-ti-ā-rȳ (-shĭ-), *n.* The holder of any office under a superior in a monastery or convent ; কোন খৃষ্টীয় মঠ বা ভিক্ষুণী-সংঘের অধ্যক্ষ বা প্রধানা সন্ন্যাসিনীর অধীন কর্ম্মচারী।

ō-bei'-sance (-bā-săns), *n.* 1. A gesture in token of respect or submission ; a bow or curtsy ; নমস্কার ; প্রণাম, প্রণিপাত। 2. Deference ; homage ; submission ; as, to pay *obeisance* ; শ্রদ্ধা ; পূজা ; বিনয়।

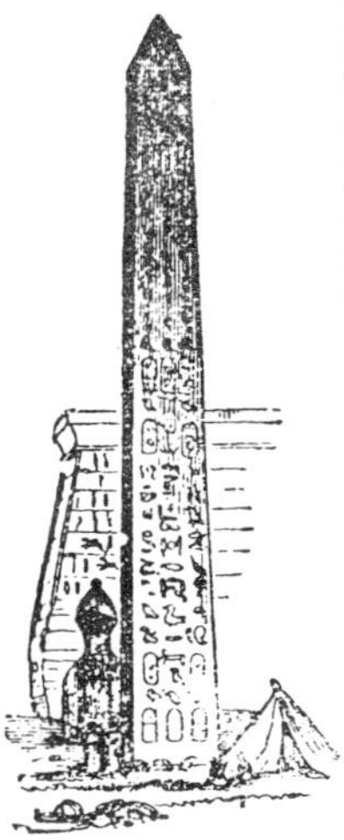

Obelisk.

ŏb'-ē-lisk, *n.* 1. An upright four-sided pillar, generally mono-lithic, tapering as it rises, and terminating in a pyramidal point ; ক্রমসূক্ষ্ম পাষাণস্তম্ভবিশেষ, চতুষ্কোণ মিনার। 2. An obelisk-shaped mountain, tree, etc. ; উক্তরূপ পাষাণস্তম্ভাকৃতি বৃক্ষ বা পর্ব্বত। 3. (Also, *obelus*) A sign (−, ÷) used in ancient manuscripts to show that a word or passage is spurious, etc. ; also a mark of reference (†) ; প্রাচীন পুঁথিতে ব্যবহৃত ইত্যাকার (−, ÷) চিহ্ন—যদ্দারা ঐ পুঁথির কোন শব্দ বা অংশ প্রক্ষিপ্ত বলিয়া প্রদর্শিত হয় ; ইত্যাকার (†) চিহ্ন। **Double obelisk**—The sign (‡) ; ইত্যাকার (‡) চিহ্ন।

ŏb'-ē-līze, *v. t.* To mark with an obelus ; to mark as spurious or doubtful ; উক্তরূপ মন্তব্যচিহ্নে চিহ্নিত করা ; কৃত্রিম বা সন্দিগ্ধ বলিয়া চিহ্নিত করা।

ŏb'-ē-lŭs, *n.* See OBELISK.

ō-bēse' (-bēs), *adj.* Corpulent ; মোটা, স্থূলাঙ্গ, মেদস্বী, স্থূলকায়, মাংসল, পীন, পীবর, পুষ্ট। **—bes'-i-ty**, *n.* Corpulence ; মেদস্বিতা, স্থূলতা, স্থৌল্য, মেদোরোগ, মেদোবৃদ্ধি।

ō-bey' (-bā), *v. t. & i.* 1. To execute the order of ; to be obedient to ; আদেশ পালন করা, আজ্ঞাপালন করা ; বাধ্য হওয়া, আজ্ঞাকারী হওয়া। 2. To be actuated by (impulse, force, etc.) ; অনুপ্রাণিত হওয়া। ***Verb i.*** To do what one is ordered or commanded ; আদেশানুরূপ কার্য্য করা।

ŏb-fŭs'-cāte, *v. t.* 1. To darken ; to obscure ; as, to *obfuscate* the mind or intellect ; অন্ধকারাচ্ছন্ন করা, অস্পষ্ট করা, ঘোরাল করা। 2. To bewilder ; to confuse ; as, to be *obfuscated* with drink ; বিভ্রান্ত করা ; হতবুদ্ধি করা। **—ca'-tion**, *n.*

obiit, (*L.*), (Abbr. *ob.*) ; He (or she) died ; সে (পুরুষ অথবা স্ত্রী) পরলোক গমন করিয়াছে।

ŏb'-i-têr, *adv.* By the way ; প্রসঙ্গক্রমে। ***Obiter dictum***, (*pl.* -DICTA)—(*Law*) An incidental opinion uttered by a judge and therefore not binding ; বিচারকের প্রাসঙ্গিকমত — যাহা অবশ্য পালনীয় নয়। An incidental remark ; প্রাসঙ্গিক মন্তব্য, উড়ো মন্তব্য।

ō-bĭt'-ū-ā-rȳ, *n. & adj.* Announcement of death or deaths, esp. in newspaper usually with a biographical sketch ; মৃত্যুসংবাদ, মৃত্যুঘোষণা, বিশেষতঃ সংবাদপত্রে কোন ব্যক্তির মৃত্যুসংবাদ প্রকাশ (সাধারণতঃ সংক্ষিপ্ত জীবনবৃত্তসম্বলিত)। ***Adj.*** Recording a death ; concerning a deceased person ; as, *obituary* poetry ; মৃত্যুসংবাদজ্ঞাপক ; মৃতব্যক্তিসম্বন্ধীয়। **—rist**, *n.* An obituary writer ; মৃত্যুসংবাদলেখক।

ŏb'-jĕct, *n.* 1. Something visible or tangible ; a concrete reality ; "The painter looking up and finding no *object* in his focus" ; পদার্থ ; দ্রব্য, বস্তু, সামগ্রী। 2. A person or thing of pitiable or ridiculous aspect ; আস্পদ, পাত্র, ভাজন। 3. That to which efforts, feelings, etc. are directed ; as, the Bible had been the *object* of his study : an *object* of wonder or fear ; আলোচনার বিষয়, ব্যাপার, বিষয়। 4. End ; aim ; as, his *object* in calling on me was etc. ; purposes ; লক্ষ্য ; উদ্দেশ্য ; অভিপ্রায়, আশয়, তাৎপর্য্য। 5. (*Metaph.*) A thing thought of, or apprehended, as correlative to the thinking mind or subject ; the non-ego ; (তত্ত্ববিদ্যা) জ্ঞেয় বস্তু, বিষয় (হিঃ কোঃ) ; জ্ঞেয়। 6. (*Gram.*) That which follows as acted upon by a transitive verb ; (ব্যাকরণ) কর্ম্ম। **—less**, *adj.* **Direct object**—মুখ্য কর্ম্ম। **Indirect object**—গৌণ কর্ম্ম। **Object-ball**—বিলিয়ার্ড প্রভৃতি খেলায় ক্রীড়ক স্বীয় কন্দুক দ্বারা যে কন্দুক আঘাত করিতে চেষ্টা করে। **Object-finder**—অণুবীক্ষণ যন্ত্রে ক্ষীণশক্তিসম্পন্ন নেত্রতাল-বিশেষ—অধিকতর শক্তিসম্পন্ন নেত্রতাল দ্বারা পরীক্ষিত হইবার পূর্ব্বে ইহার সাহায্যে কোন পদার্থ অনুসন্ধান করা হইয়া থাকে।

Object-glass or **lens**—দূরবীক্ষণ অথবা অণুবীক্ষণ যন্ত্রের যে কাচখণ্ডে দৃষ্ট বস্তুর প্রতিবিম্ব পতিত হয়, পদার্থ-কাচ (হিঃ কোঃ), প্রধান লেন্স (ঐ)। **Object lesson**—Instruction about a material object that is presented for inspection ; (*fig.*) a striking practical illustration of some principle ; বস্তু পাঠ ; (লক্ষণায়) কোন তত্ত্বের সুস্পষ্ট ব্যাবহারিক উদাহরণ। **Object-plate**—যে পাত্রের উপর কোন বস্তু আণুবীক্ষণিক পরীক্ষার জন্য রক্ষিত হয়। **Object-staff**—আমিনের ভ্রমণকারী কর্মচারিবর্গ। **Object-teaching**—বস্তু উপলক্ষে শিক্ষাপ্রদান। **Object of love**—প্রেমাস্পদ, প্রণয়াস্পদ, প্রেমপাত্র। **Object of trust**—বিশ্বাসভাজন ব্যক্তি। **Objects of knowledge**—প্রমেয় (ন্যায়সূত্র)। **With the object of**—With the purpose of ; উদ্দেশ্যে।

ŏb-jĕct′, *v. t.* & *i.* To adduce as an adverse reason ; to state as an objection, (generally followed by *to* or *against*) ; as, I have nothing to *object against* him ; বিরুদ্ধযুক্তি উপস্থাপিত করা ; আপত্তি করা। ***Verb i.*** To make opposition, (usually followed by *to*) ; as, I *object to* being treated in this way ; আপত্তি প্রকাশ করা। **–jec′-tor,** *n.*

ŏb-jĕc′-ti-fȳ, *v. t.* To render objective ; to embody ; বস্তুতন্ত্র করা ; অঙ্গীভূত করা। **–fi-ca′-tion,** *n.*

ŏb-jĕc′-tion, *n.* **1.** The act of objecting ; আপত্তি করণ। **2.** That which is, or may be, urged in opposition ; an adverse reason or argument ; as, unreasonable *objections* ; an expression or feeling of disapproval or dislike ; যাহা বিরুদ্ধযুক্তিস্বরূপ উপস্থাপিত করা যাইতে পারে ; বিরুদ্ধ যুক্তি বা তর্ক ; অপ্রীতি বা অননুমোদনসূচক বাক্য, আপত্তি। **–a-ble,** *adj.* Liable to objection ; unpleasant ; offensive ; as, *objectionable* language ; আপত্তিযোগ্য ; অপ্রীতিকর, বিরক্তিকর ; আপত্তিজনক, অসঙ্গত। **–a-bly,** *adv.*

ŏb-jĕc′-tive (-tĭv), *adj.* & *n.* **1.** (*Philos.*) Of, or pertaining to, what is external and independent to the mind ; real ; বস্তু-সম্বন্ধীয়, বিষয়াত্মক (হিঃ কোঃ), বহির্মুখ, পদার্থাশ্রিত, অনাত্ম (হিঃ কোঃ) ; বাস্তব। **2.** Dealing with external events or things ; unaffected by the thinking or feeling of the observer ; as, an *objective* art ; বস্তুতন্ত্র (শঙ্করঃ) ; বস্তুধর্ম্মী (কাব্যঃ প্রঃ)। **3.** Relating to an object, especially the material object ; বস্তুসম্বন্ধীয়। **4.** (*Gram.*) Of, or relating to, the object of a transitive verb or a preposition ; as, an *objective* case ; (ব্যাকরণ) কর্ম্মসম্বন্ধীয়। **5.** (*Med.*) Observed by another and not only felt by the patient, as symptoms ; (ভৈষজ্যশাস্ত্র) যে সকল লক্ষণ রোগী উল্লেখ না করিলেও অন্যেরা জানিতে পারেন—তৎসম্বন্ধীয়, বিষয়নিষ্ঠ (হঃ চঃ)। **6.** (*Perspective*) Of, or relating to, the object to be delineated ; as, an *objective* line (a line drawn on the geometrical plane, the representation of which is sought in the picture) ; (পরিপ্রেক্ষিত) যে বস্তু অঙ্কিত করিতে হইবে—তৎসম্বন্ধীয়। ***Noun.*** **1.** (*Gram.*) The objective case ; (ব্যাকরণ) কর্ম্মকারক। **2.** (*Mil.*) A point aimed at ; a point towards which advance of troops is directed ; (সামরিক-শাস্ত্র) লক্ষ্যীভূত বিন্দু, লক্ষ্য ; যে লক্ষ্যীভূত স্থানের অভিমুখে সৈন্যদল চালিত হয়। **3.** (*Optics*) An OBJECT-GLASS which see under OBJECT *n.* **4.** That which is external to the mind ; অনাত্মবিষয়। **–ly,** *adv.* **–ness, –tiv′-i-ty,** *ns.* The state of being objective ; বস্তুতন্ত্রতা, বস্তুতন্ত্রত্ব (শঙ্করঃ)। **–tiv-ism,** *n.* The tendency to lay stress on the objective ; a theory that the knowledge of the non-ego is prior in sequence and importance to that of the ego ; theory of objective art or literature ; বস্তুনিষ্ঠা ; দার্শনিক মতবিশেষ—এই মতানুসারে অনাত্মবস্তুর জ্ঞান অহংজ্ঞানের পূর্ব্ববর্ত্তী এবং অহংজ্ঞানাপেক্ষা শ্রেষ্ঠতর, বস্তুপ্রাধান্যবাদ ; বস্তুতন্ত্রতা। **–tiv′-ist,** *n.* **Objective case**—কর্ম্মকারক। **Objective plane**—যে বস্তু চিত্রিত করিতে হইবে বা যাহার অবস্থান নির্ণীত করিতে হইবে তাহা যে শয়ান ধরাতলের উপর অবস্থিত বলিয়া কল্পিত হয়। **Objective point**—See OBJECTIVE *n.* 2. ; (also *fig.*) the point or purpose to which anything, as a journey, argument, etc. is directed ; উদ্দিষ্টস্থান, লক্ষ্যস্থল, গন্তব্যস্থল। **Objective validity**—বস্তুগত প্রামাণ্য (অর্থাৎ দ্রষ্টার মানসক্রিয়া নিরপেক্ষ)।

ŏb-jŭ-ra′-tion *n.* (*Rare*) A bind by oath ; (কচিদ্‌ব্যবহৃত) শপথদ্বারা বন্ধকরণ।

ŏb-jur′-gāte (-jêr-) *v. t.* To reprove ; to scold ; to chide ; তিরস্কার করা ; ভৎসনা করা ; গালি দেওয়া। **–ga′-tion,** *n.* **–ga-to-ry,** *n.*

ŏb′-lāte, *adj.* & *n.* **1.** Flattened at the poles ; as, the Earth is an *oblate* spheroid ; মেরুপ্রদেশে অবনত, মেরুদ্বয়ে চাপা। **2.** (*R. C. Church*) Dedicated ; উৎসর্গীকৃত। ***Noun.*** A person dedicated to monastic life or work ; মঠের কার্য্যের জন্য উৎসর্গীকৃত ব্যক্তি। **Oblate spheroid** — কমলালেবুর ন্যায় অবনমিত গোলকাভান।

ŏb-lā′-tion, *n.* **1.** Act of offering, esp. the Eucharist elements to God ; the Eucharist ; উৎসর্গ, হোম ; খৃষ্টের অন্তিমভোজনক্রিয়ার সুরা এবং রুটিকা। **2.** A thing presented to God or a deity ; a sacrifice ; an offering ; হব্য, কব্য ; বলি ; উপহার,

দেবোপহার, অর্ঘ্য, নৈবেদ্য, উপায়ন। 3. A donation for pious uses; সৎকার্য্যে দান। **–al, Ob′-la-to-ry,** *adjs.*

ŏb′-lĭ-gate, *v. t.* **1.** To bind by a moral or legal tie; নীতি বা আইনের বন্ধনে বদ্ধ করা। **2.** (*Dial.*) To bring under some obligation; to oblige; (উপভাষায়) কোনরূপ বাধ্যতার অধীন করা; বাধিত করা।

ŏb-lĭ-gā′-tion, *n.* **1.** (*Law*) An agreement enforceable by law; a bond or contract with a condition annexed; (আইন) চুক্তি, নির্ব্বন্ধ; সর্ত্তসমন্বিত চুক্তি। **2.** The binding power of a contract, law, precept, etc.; that which constitutes a moral or legal duty; as, the *obligations* of affection; বাধ্যতা; বাধ্যবাধকতা, অবশ্যকর্ত্তব্যতা। **3.** A duty; a claim upon one; as, to forget one's *obligations*; কর্ত্তব্য; দাবী। **4.** Indebtedness for an act of kindness or favour; a favour or act of kindness; as, to put under an *obligation*: to repay an *obligation*; কৃতজ্ঞতা; অনুগ্রহ, উপকার। **5.** A promise or agreement by which one is bound; প্রতিশ্রুতি। **Obligation of duty**—কর্ত্তব্যভার। **Of obligation**—Obligatory; as, a holiday *of obligation*; বাধ্যতাজনক (অর্থাৎ যে ছুটীর দিনে সকলকে সমস্ত কাজকর্ম্ম ছাড়িয়া একান্তভাবে উপাসনাদিতে নিরত হইতে হয়।) **To lay or put a person under obligation**—To oblige a person (especially, by a favour or benefit); বাধিত করা। **Under obligation**—কৃতজ্ঞ, বাধিত, কৃতজ্ঞতাপাশবদ্ধ।

ŏb′-lĭ-gā-tō-rў, *adj.* **1.** Imposing a duty or obligation; binding in law or conscience, (generally with *on* or *upon*); as, obedience is *obligatory on* a soldier; বাধ্যতাজনক; অবশ্যপালনীয়, অবশ্যকর্ত্তব্য, অবশ্যমাননীয়, অপরিহার্য্য। **2.** Constituting an obligation; বাধ্যতাজনক।

ō-blīge′, *v. t.* & *i.* **1.** To make morally or legally bound to do or forbear something; বাধ্য করা। **2.** To bind by some favour done; to do a service to; বাধিত করা; কোন উপকারজনক কাজ করা। **3.** (*Pass. sense*) To be bound by gratitude; to be indebted; as, he is *obliged* to you for your assistance; বাধিত হওয়া; ঋণী হওয়া, উপকারবদ্ধ হওয়া। ***Verb i.*** (*Colloq.*) To do something, as a favour, esp. by way of entertainment; as, he will *oblige* with a song; (চলিত ভাষায়) বাধিত করা, অনুগৃহীত করা।

ŏb-lĭ-gee′ (-jē), *n.* **1.** (*Law*) A person to whom another is bound by a contract or to whom a bond is given, (*opp.* to *obligor*); যাহার নিকট কোন চুক্তি প্রভৃতি দ্বারা কেহ বদ্ধ হয়। **2.** One who is obliged or favoured; বাধিত বা অনুগৃহীত ব্যক্তি।

ō-blīg′-ĭng, *p. adj.* Ready to do favours; courteous; kind; "To all *obliging* yet reserv'd to all"; আজ্ঞাকারী, প্রিয়কারী; শিষ্ট, ভদ্র; সদয়, উপকারশীল, পরোপকারী। **–ly,** *adv.* **–ness,** *n.*

ŏb-lĭ-gŏr′, *n.* (*Law*) One who binds himself by a bond or gives a bond to another; চুক্তি প্রভৃতি দ্বারা বদ্ধ লোক, বাধ্য লোক।

ŏb-lique′ (-lēk), *adj.* & *v. i.* **1.** Not horizontal or perpendicular; slanting; diverging from a given straight line or course; তির্য্যক্ (হিঃ কোঃ), অনৃজু, বক্র; হেলানো; বাঁকা, টের্চ্চা। Indirect; not straightforward; perverse; "…hath in it certain *oblique* ends"; পরোক্ষ; কুটিল, অসরল, বক্র; বে-আড়া। **3.** (*Anat.*) Neither perpendicular nor parallel to the long axis of the body or limb; as, an *oblique* muscle; (শারীরসংস্থানবিদ্যা) দেহ কিম্বা হস্তপদাদির দীর্ঘ অক্ষের লম্বস্বরূপ নয় বা উহার সহিত সমান্তরাল নহে। **4.** (*Bot.*) Having unequal sides; as, an *oblique* leaf; (উদ্ভিদ্‌বিদ্যা) অসমপার্শ্বক, বক্র (সাঃ পঃ)। **5.** (*Geom.*) Inclined at some angle other than a right angle, as a line, etc.; acute or obtuse, as an angle; with the axis not perpendicular to the plane of the base, as a cone, cylinder, etc.; (জ্যামিতি) অসমকোণ উৎপাদনপূর্ব্বক তির্য্যগ্‌ভাবে স্থিত; সূক্ষ্ম বা স্থূল (কোণ); ভূমির ধরাতলের লম্বস্বরূপ অক্ষসমন্বিত নয় (সূচীক্ষেত্র প্রভৃতি)। **6.** (*Arch.* & *Engin.*) Skew; as, an *oblique* bridge; তির্য্যক। ***Verb i.*** **1.** (*Mil.*) To advance or march on a slanting direction; তির্য্যগ্‌ভাবে অগ্রসর হওয়া। **2.** To deviate from a straight line or a perpendicular; as, the path *obliques* from the river; বাঁকিয়ে যাওয়া। **–liq′-ui-ty,** *n.* **1.** Obliqueness; divergence; বক্রতা; তির্য্যগ্‌ভাব। **2.** Deviation from moral rectitude; সৎপথচ্যুতি, বিপথগমন, উন্মার্গগমন। **–ly,** *adv.* **Oblique angle**—See OBLIQUE *adj.* 5. **Oblique case**—কর্ত্তৃ এবং সম্বোধন ভিন্ন কারক। **Oblique oration, narration or speech**—(অলঙ্কার শাস্ত্র) যে বক্তৃতা, বর্ণনা বা বাক্য মূল বক্তা যে পুরুষে বলিয়াছিল — তাহা হইতে ভিন্ন পুরুষে বলা হয়। **Oblique sailing**—জাহাজ যেরূপ ভাবে চাললে উহার গতিপথ দ্রাঘিমার সহিত স্থূল বা সূক্ষ্ম কোণ গঠন করে। **Obliquity of the ecliptic**—ক্রান্তিবৃত্ত ও বিষুবমণ্ডলের ধরাতলদ্বয়ের মধ্যবর্ত্তী কোণ, রবিপরমক্রান্তি (সূর্য্যঃ বিঃ)।

ŏb-lĭt′-ĕr-āte, *v. t.* **1.** To blot out; to erase; to efface; বিলুপ্ত করা; মুছিয়া ফেলা; অপনয়ন করা। **2.** To destroy by any means; to wear out; as, to *obliterate* ideas or landmarks; ধ্বংস করা,

বিনষ্ট করা, উচ্ছেদসাধন করা; ক্ষয় করিয়া ফেলা। **—a′-tion,** *n.* The act of obliterating; বিলোপসাধন, অপহ্নব, উচ্ছেদ, অপনয়ন, বিলোপ, অবলোপন (বাসবঃ)।

ŏb-liv′-i-ŏn, *n.* **1.** The act of forgetting; forgetfulness; বিস্মরণ; বিস্মৃতি। **2.** Official overlooking or disregard of offences; a general pardon; as, an Act or Bill of *Oblivion*; শাসনতন্ত্র কর্তৃক অপরাধ উপেক্ষা; সার্বজনিক ক্ষমা, দোষবিস্মরণ। **Act or Bill of Oblivion**—যে রাজবিধি দ্বারা কোন অপরাধে অপরাধী সমস্ত ব্যক্তি ক্ষমাপ্রাপ্ত হয় এবং দণ্ড হইতে নিষ্কৃতিলাভ করে। **To be buried in oblivion**—To be forgotten; বিস্মৃতি গর্ভে নিমজ্জিত হওয়া। **To fall into oblivion**—To be forgotten or disused; বিস্মৃত বা অপ্রচলিত হওয়া।

ŏb-liv′-i-ous (-ŭs) *adj.* **1.** Forgetful; unmindful, (generally follows by *of*); বিস্মরণশীল; অনবহিত, অমনোযোগী। **2.** (*Poet.*) Causing, or inducing, forgetfulness; "Some sweet *oblivious* antidote; বিস্মৃতিজনক, স্মৃতিহর, বিস্মারক। **—ly,** *adv.* **—ness,** *n.*

ŏb′-lŏng, *adj.* & *n.* **1.** Deviating from a square or circular form; longer than broad; as, an *oblong* shield; আয়ত; জাত্যায়ত। **2.** (*Geom.*) Rectangular with adjacent sides unequal; as, an *oblong* figure; আয়ত (হিঃ কোঃ)। **3.** Rectangular; having the breadth greater than the height; as, an *oblong* picture or sheet of paper; আয়ত; উচ্চতা অপেক্ষা প্রস্থে বৃহত্তর। ***Noun.*** An oblong figure or object; আয়তক্ষেত্র, দীর্ঘচতুরস্র (শুল্বঃ)।

ŏb′-lŏ-quy̑, *n.* **1.** Abusive language; calumny; blame; গ্লানি, কুৎসা, অপবাদ; পরিবাদ, পরীবাদ; নিন্দা, নিন্দোক্তি, পরুষোক্তি। **2.** State of being spoken ill of or censured; কলঙ্কলিপ্ততা।

ŏb-mü-tĕs′-cençe (-ĕns), *n.* Obstinate silence; wilful muteness; তূষ্ণীভাব; ইচ্ছাকৃত মূকতা, গতবাকত্ব। **—cent,** *adj.*

ŏb-nox′-ous (-nŏk-shŭs), *adj.* Offensive; hateful; objectionable; unpopular; as, an *obnoxious* bill or person; ক্ষতিজনক, অনিষ্টজনক; ঘৃণাজনক; গর্হিত, আপত্তিজনক; লোকবিগর্হিত। **—ly,** *adv.* **—ness,** *n.* **Obnoxious to —** Offensive or hateful to; বিরক্তিকর, ঘৃণাজনক।

ō′-boe (-boy̆), *n.* **1.** (*Music*) Same as HAUTBOY (which see). **2.** A reed stop in an organ giving a penetrating tone; (সঙ্গীতশাস্ত্র) অর্গেন নামক বাদ্যযন্ত্রের অংশবিশেষ **-bo-ist,** *n.*

ŏ′-bŏl, ŏb′-ŏ-lŭs, *ns.* A small silver coin of ancient Greece

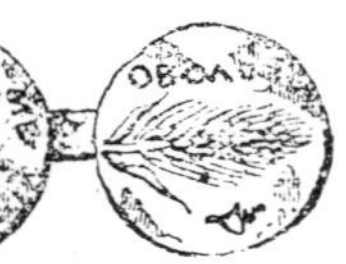

Brass obolus of Metapontum.

equal to $1\frac{1}{2}d$; প্রাচীন গ্রীসের রৌপ্যমুদ্রাবিশেষ।

Obs and sols—*Objectione et solutionis*; আপত্তি এবং সমাধান।

ŏb-scene′ (-sēn), *adj.* **1.** Impure in language or action; indecent; lewd; as, *obscene* words or pictures; অশ্লীল, অবাচ্য, অশ্রাব্য, অকথ্য; কুৎসিত; জঘন্য। **2.** (*Archaic*) Foul; repulsive; filthy; কদর্য্য; কুৎসিত; জঘন্য। **—ly,** *adv.* **—scen′-i-ty,** *n.* State of being offensive to decency or purity; impure acts or words; lewdness; অশ্লীলতা; জঘন্য কার্য্য, অশ্লীলকথা; লাম্পট্য।

ŏb-scür′-ănt, *n.* & *adj.* One who obscures; one opposing enquiry, enlightenment or reform; যে ব্যক্তি অস্পষ্টতা জন্মায়; অনুসন্ধান, আলোকদান বা সংস্কারের বিরোধী ব্যক্তি, অনালোককারী। ***Adj.*** Obscuring or darkening; relating to an obscurant; অনুজ্জ্বলকর, অন্ধকারজনক; অনালোককারিসম্পর্কীয়। **—ism,** *n.* **—ist,** *n.* & *adj.*

ŏb-scüre′, *adj.*, *n.* & *v.t.* **1.** Dark; gloomy; dim; (*Prov.* xx. 20); অন্ধকার; তমসাচ্ছন্ন; নিষ্প্রভ। **2.** Relating to darkness; hidden; secluded; as, an *obscure* corner; অন্ধকারসম্বন্ধীয়; প্রচ্ছন্ন, গুপ্ত; নিভৃত, বিজন। **3.** Indistinct; clouded; as, an *obscure* view of remote objects; অস্পষ্ট, ম্লান, অস্ফুট (হিঃ কোঃ), ঘোরাল, অপ্রকাশ, অনুজ্জ্বল; ঝাপসা। **4.** Not noted; humble; mean; অপ্রসিদ্ধ, অবিখ্যাত, অল্পপ্রসিদ্ধ, ন্যূনকীর্ত্তি, অল্পকীর্ত্তি; হীন; নীচ। **5.** Difficult to understand; not clearly expressed; abstruse; as, an *obscure* line; দুজ্ঞেয়, দুর্ব্বোধ, দুরূহ; অস্পষ্টার্থ; জটিল, অব্যক্ত, গূঢ়ার্থ, গূঢ় (হিঃ কোঃ)। ***Noun.*** Darkness; indistinctness; a shade or an obscure part, as in a picture; অন্ধকারাচ্ছন্নতা; অস্পষ্টতা; চিত্রের অনুজ্জ্বল অংশ। ***Verb t.*** **1.** To make obscure or dark; to make less intelligible; to conceal; অন্ধকার করা, অস্পষ্ট করা; অস্পষ্টার্থ করা; লুক্কায়িত করা, প্রচ্ছন্ন করা। **2.** To outshine; to dim the glory of; মলিনপ্রভ করা; মহিমাম্লান করা, গৌরবম্লান করা। **—ly,** *adv.* **—scu-ra′-tion,** *n.* Act of obscuring; আচ্ছাদন, আবরণ, অভিভব (ব্রঃ হিন্দুঃ)। **—scu′-ri-ty,** *n.* **1.** The state or quality of being obscure; gloom; dimness; state of being unintelligible; the state of inconspicuousness; অস্পষ্টতা; অন্ধকার; নিষ্প্রভতা; অস্পষ্টার্থতা, দুজ্ঞেয়তা, গহনতা, দুর্ব্বোধতা, জটিলতা; অপ্রসিদ্ধি। **2.** An obscure person, thing or place; অপ্রসিদ্ধ

ব্যক্তি, বস্তু বা স্থান। **Obscure rays**—সৌরবর্ণচ্ছত্রের অদৃশ্য রশ্মি। **Obscuration of comet**—ধূমন। **Obscuration of passage**—অস্পষ্টার্থতা, ক্লিষ্টতা (সাঃ দঃ)।

ŏb-sĕ-crā'-tion, *n.* **1.** Entreaty ; supplication ; কাকুতি, মিনতি ; অনুনয়, বিনয়। **2.** One of the prayers of the Litany beginning with *By* ; স্তোত্রবিশেষ। **3.** (*Rhet.*) A figure of speech in which the orator implores the help of God or man ; অলঙ্কারবিশেষ—যাহাতে বক্তা দেবতা বা মানবের সাহায্য প্রার্থনা করে।

ŏb'-sĕ-quies (-kwĭz), *n.* (*Pl.*) Funeral rites or ceremonies ; a funeral ; অন্ত্যেষ্টি ক্রিয়া, শবকর্ম্ম, নৈষ্ঠিক বিধি (রঃ), উত্তরক্রিয়া, অন্ত্যক্রিয়া, প্রেতকার্য্য, মৃতসংস্কার, প্রেতসংস্কার; সৎকার। **-se'-qui-al**, *adj.* **Obsequial rites**— শ্রাদ্ধ।

ŏb-sĕ'-quĭ-ous (-ŭs), *adj.* **1.** Servile ; fawning ; cringing ; as, an *obsequious* parasite ; হীনানুগত; পদলেহনকারী ; বাক্যস্থ (শুক্রঃ)। **2.** (*Archaic*) Compliant ; dutiful ; (অপ্রঃ) বশবর্ত্তী ; কর্ত্তব্যনিষ্ঠ। **-ly**, *adv.* **-ness**, *n.*

ŏb-sêrv'-ance (-ăns), *n.* **1.** Act of observing a law, custom, ritual, performance, etc. ; পালন, প্রতিপালন, সমাচরণ। **2.** A rite or ceremony ; a customary act ; practice ; as, religious *observances* ; ক্রিয়া ; অনুষ্ঠান, ব্রত, নিয়ম, আচার ; অনুষ্ঠান। **3.** A religious rule or ordinance ; ধর্ম্মবিধি, ধর্ম্মনিয়ম। **4.** (*Rare*) Act of observing or noticing ; (কচিদ্‌ব্যবহৃত) লক্ষ্যকরণ, পর্য্যবেক্ষণ, অবেক্ষণ, নিরীক্ষণ। **5.** (*Archaic*) Deference ; respect ; (অপ্রঃ) সম্ভ্রম ; শ্রদ্ধা। **-ancy**, *n.* (*Rare*)

ŏb-sêrv'-ănt, *adj.* & *n.* **1.** Noticing carefully ; attentive ; watchful ; as, an *observant* traveller or watch ; পর্য্যবেক্ষণশীল, লক্ষ্যকারী, নিরীক্ষক, প্রেক্ষক ; অবহিত ; সাবধান, সজাগ। **2.** Diligent in performing or practising ; mindful ; (with *of*) ; as, *observant of* duties ; বিশেষ মনোযোগের সহিত পালনকারী, নিষ্ঠাবান ; মনোযোগী, অভিনিবেশশীল। ***Noun.*** (*Cap.*, *R. C. Church*) A member of a branch of the Franciscan friars that strictly observes the rules of the founder ; (রোমান ক্যাথলিক ধর্ম্ম-সংঘ) নিষ্ঠাবান ফ্রানসিস্‌ক্যান সন্ন্যাসী।

ŏb-sêr-vā'-tion, *n.* **1.** Act of noticing ; state of being observed ; perception ; পরিবীক্ষণ ; পর্য্যবেক্ষণত্ব ; অনুভব। **2.** (*Mil.*) Watching of a fortress or hostile position or movement ; দুর্গ অথবা শত্রুদিগের অবস্থিতি বা গতিবিধি পর্য্যবেক্ষণ। **3.** Act of observing or taking notice of natural phenomena for scientific or practical purposes ; দর্শন (ব্রজঃ হিন্দুঃ), পর্য্যবেক্ষণ, নিরীক্ষণ, সমীক্ষা (হিঃ দঃ), প্রেক্ষা (হিঃ কোঃ)। **4.** Ascertaining of the altitude of a heavenly body to find latitude or longitude ; অক্ষাংশ বা দ্রাঘিমা গণনার জন্য কোন জ্যোতিষ্কের উচ্চতানির্ণয়, প্রত্যক্ষদর্শন (সূর্য্যঃ বিঃ)। **5.** A remark, statement or comment ; as, it's a foolish *observation* ; মন্তব্য, উক্তি। **-al**, *adj.* **-al-ly**, *adv.* **Army of observation**—পর্য্যবেক্ষণকার্য্যে নিযুক্ত সৈন্যদল। **Post of observation**—যে স্থান হইতে পর্য্যবেক্ষণ করা যায়, পর্য্যবেক্ষণস্থলী।

ŏb-sêrv'-ă-tō-rȳ, *n.* A building for making observations esp. of the heavenly bodies ; মানমন্দির, বেধালয় (সূঃ সিঃ), বেধগৃহ (ঐ), যন্ত্রালয় (ঐ), পর্য্যবেক্ষণিকা, (কেভিঃ), বেধশালা (ঐ)।

ŏb-serve' (-zêrv), *v. t.* & *i.* **1.** To perceive ; to watch ; to notice ; অনুভব করা ; পরিবীক্ষণ করা ; লক্ষ্য করা। **2.** To examine and note as phenomena ; পর্য্যবেক্ষণ করা। **3.** To utter, as a remark or comment ; মন্তব্য প্রকাশ করা। **4.** To keep or perform ; to follow ; to celebrate ; as, to *observe* a law, command, rite, etc. ; রক্ষা করা, সম্পাদন করা, পালন করা ; অনুসরণ করা ; অনুষ্ঠান করা। ***Verb i.*** **1.** To notice ; to be attentive ; লক্ষ্য করা ; অবহিত হওয়া। **2.** To remark or comment, (*on* or *upon*) ; মন্তব্য করা। **-serv'-a-ble**, *adj.* **1.** That must, or may, be kept, performed or complied with ; সম্পাদনীয়, প্রতিপালনীয়। **2.** Noticeable ; লক্ষ্য, বীক্ষণীয়। **3.** Remarkable ; notable ; মন্তব্য ; উল্লেখযোগ্য, দ্রষ্টব্য। **-serv'-er**, *n.* **1.** One who observes or notices ; পর্য্যবেক্ষক, অভিনিবেশকারী, দ্রষ্টা (ব্রজঃ হিন্দুঃ)। **2.** One who keeps, performs or complies with any law, promise, customs, etc. ; অনুষ্ঠানকারী, পালনকারী, পালক। **3.** One who makes a remark or comment ; মন্তব্যপ্রকাশকারী। **-serv'-ing-ly**, *adv.* **The observed of all observers**—সর্ব্বলোকের দৃষ্টির বিষয়ীভূত ব্যক্তি বা বস্তু, সর্ব্বলোকলোচনললামভূত ব্যক্তি বা বস্তু।

ŏb-sĕss', *v. t.* (Of an evil spirit, delusion, fixed idea) To beset ; to haunt ; to influence ; গ্রস্ত করা ; আবিষ্ট করা ; প্রভাবিত করা। **-ses'-sion**, *n.* Act of obsessing ; state of being obsessed ; আবিষ্ট করণ ; আবেশ (হিঃ কোঃ)।

ŏb-sĭd'-ĭ-ăn, *n.* A vitreous lava or volcanic rock like bottle-glass ; একপ্রকার কাচবৎ আগ্নেয়গিরিনিঃসৃত পদার্থ।

ŏb-sŏ-lĕs'-cent (-ĕnt) *adj.* **1.** Going out of use ; becoming obsolete ; অপ্রচলনোন্মুখ ; লুপ্তপ্রায়। **2.** (*Biol.*) Gradually becoming extinct ; (জীব-বিজ্ঞান) বিলোপোন্মুখ, বিলয়মান। **-cence**, *n.*

ŏb'-sŏ-lete (-lēt), *adj.* & *n.* **1.** Out of use ; antiquated ; অপ্রচলিত,

লুপ্তপ্রয়োগ, অব্যবহারিত; সাবেক, সেকেলে। 2. (*Biol.*) Rudimentary; প্রাথমিক। ***Noun.*** That which is obsolete, as a person, thing, word or phrase; সেকেলে লোক, অপ্রচলিত বস্তু, শব্দ বা বাক্যাংশ। **–let-ism, –ness,** *ns.*

ŏb'-stă-cle (-kl), *n.* A hindrance; an obstruction; an impediment; বাধা, অন্তরায়; বিঘ্ন, ব্যাঘাত; প্রতিষ্টম্ভ, প্রতিবন্ধ, প্রতিবন্ধক। **Obstacle race**—যে দৌড়ে প্রতিযোগিগণের ধাবনপথে নানাপ্রকার বাধাজনক বস্তু রাখা হয়, প্রতিবন্ধধাবন।

ŏb-stĕt'-ric, –ri-căl, *adjs.* Of, or relating to, midwifery or obstetrics; ধাত্রীবিদ্যাসম্পর্কীয়, প্রসবতত্ত্ব সম্বন্ধীয়, গর্ভমোচনবিদ্যাসম্বন্ধীয়। **–rics,** *n.* The science, or art of midwifery; the art, of assisting women in parturition; গর্ভিণী-ব্যাকরণ (সুশ্রুঃ), প্রসবতত্ত্ব; ধাত্রীবিদ্যা। **–ste-tri'-cian,** *n.* One skilled in obstetrics; প্রজননকুশল ব্যক্তি, প্রসবকর্মে নিপুণ ব্যক্তি।

ŏb'-sti-nāte, *adj.* 1. Inflexible; stubborn; refractory; অনমনীয়, অবিনেয়; একরোখা, ঠেঁটা, নাছোড়বান্দা; অবাধ্য, অদম্য, দুর্দান্ত। 2. Hard to remove or cure, as an obstruction or disease; দুরাগ্রহ, দুঃসাধ্য, দুরারোগ্য, কৃচ্ছ্রসাধ্য। **–ly,** *adv.* **–nacy,** *n.* 1. state of being obstinate; stubbornness; দৃঢ়তা, নির্বন্ধশীলতা; অবিনেয়তা, ঠেঁঠামি, গোঁ (*colloq.*), গোঁয়ার্তামি (*colloq.*)। 2. State of being difficult to remove or cure; দুঃসাধ্যতা, দুরারোগ্যতা কৃচ্ছ্রসাধ্যতা। 3. An obstinate action; একগুঁয়েমির কাজ।

ŏb-sti-pa'-tion, *n.* Costiveness; কোষ্ঠবদ্ধ (হঃ চঃ), বদ্ধকোষ্ঠ।

ŏb-strĕp'-ĕr-ous (-ŭs), *adj.* 1. Noisy; clamorous; কোলাহলপূর্ণ; কলরবপূর্ণ, মহাস্বন, ঘোরারাবপূর্ণ। 2. Noisily resisting control; কোলাহল সহকারে শাসনরোধকারী। **–ly,** *adv.* **ness,** *n.*

ŏb-strŭct', *v. t.* & *i.* 1. To block up; to place an obstacle in; as, to *obstruct* a passage; রোধ করা, অবরোধ করা; বাধা প্রদান করা। 2. To impede; to retard; as, to *obstruct* progress; বাধা দেওয়া, প্রতিবন্ধকতা জন্মান; গতিরোধ করা, প্রতিরোধ করা। 3. To cut off the sight of; দৃষ্টিরোধ করা। ***Verb i.*** To practise obstruction, esp. Parliamentary; বাধা প্রদান করা, বিশেষতঃ পার্লেমেন্টের কার্য্যে বাধা প্রদান করা।

ŏb-strŭc'-tion, *n.* 1. Act of obstructing; state of being obstructed; সংরোধন, অবরোধ, রোধন, সন্নিরোধ, সম্বাধন, সংস্তম্ভন; অবরুদ্ধতা। 2. Hindering, esp. of Parliamentary business by talking against time; বাধাপ্রদান, বিশেষতঃ পার্লেমেন্টের কার্য্যে বাধাপ্রদান। 3. An obstacle or impediment; বাধা, প্রতিবন্ধক, বিঘ্ন, ব্যাঘাত। **–ism** *n.* **–ist,** *n.* One who obstructs business in a Parliament or other legislative body; যে ব্যক্তি পার্লেমেন্টের বা অপর ব্যবস্থাপক সভার কার্য্যে বাধা জন্মায়, সভারোধক। **Obstruction guard**—লৌহবর্ত্মের পাতা রেল হইতে বাধাজনক বস্তু অপসারণের জন্য বাষ্পীয় শকটের অগ্রভাগে সংবদ্ধ দণ্ডবিশেষ।

ŏb-strŭc'-tive (-tĭv), *adj.* & *n.* Tending to obstruct; causing obstruction; বাধক, বাধাকর সংরোধী; প্রতিবন্ধক, পরিপন্থী, বিঘ্নকারী, বিঘাতী, ব্যাঘাতজনক, বিঘ্নজনক। ***Noun.*** An obstructive person or thing; পরিপন্থী ব্যক্তি, বাধাজনক বস্তু। **–ly** *adv.* **–ness,** *n.*

ŏb-tain' (-tān), *v. t.* & *i.* To acquire; to get; to gain; প্রাপ্ত হওয়া; পাওয়া; লাভ করা। ***Verb i.*** To become prevalent; to be in vogue; as, the custom *obtains* of going to the sea-shore in summer; প্রাদুর্ভাব হওয়া; প্রচলিত হওয়া। **-a-ble,** *adj.* That may be obtained or acquired; প্রাপ্য, প্রাপ্তব্য, প্রাপনীয়, উপলভ্য, অধিগম্য। **–ment,** *n.* (*Rare*).

ŏb-tĕct'-ĕd, *adj.* (*Entom.*) Covered with a hard horny case, as the pupa of certain flies; (কীটতত্ত্ব) শৃঙ্গময়খোলকাচ্ছাদিত।

ŏb-tĕst', *v. t.* & *i.* 1. (*Archaic*) To supplicate; (অপ্রঃ) অনুনয় করা, মিনতি করা। 2. To call to witness; সাক্ষিস্বরূপ আহ্বান করা। ***Verb i.*** 1. (*Rare*) To supplicate; অনুনয় করা, মিনতি করা। 2. To protest; প্রতিবাদ করা। **–tes-ta'-tion,** *n.*

ŏb-trude (-trōd), *v. t.* To thrust impertinently, (with *on* or *upon*); দুর্বিনীতভাবে প্রবেশিত করা। **–tru'-sion,** *n.* Act of obtruding; দুর্বিনীতভাবে প্রবেশন, অনাহূত প্রবেশন, অনাহূতাগমন। **–tru'-sive,** *adj.* Disposed to obtrude; forward; উপস্থাপনশীল, উপর-পড়া; ধৃষ্ট, প্রগল্ভ। **–tru'-sive-ly,** *adv.* **–tru'-sive-ness,** *n.*

ŏb-trun'-cāte (-trŭng-), *v. t.* To cut the head or top from; মস্তকচ্ছেদ করা, অগ্রভাগ ছেদন করা। **–ca'-tion,** *n.*

ŏb-tŭnd', *v. t.* (*Med.*) To blunt or deaden, as the sense or faculty; (ভৈষজ্যশাস্ত্র) সংজ্ঞাহীন করা, সংবেদনশূন্য করা।

ŏb'-tü-rāte, *v. t.* To stop or close, as an orifice in a body, the breech of a gun etc.; ছিদ্ররোধ করা। **–ra'-tion, –ra-tor,** *ns.*

ŏb-tüse', *adj.* 1. Not pointed or sharp-edged; blunt; অতীক্ষ্ণ, অধারাল; ভোঁতা। 2. Dull; stupid; not acute; as, an *obtuse* person or sense; মন্দবুদ্ধি; বুদ্ধিহীন, স্থূলবুদ্ধি, জড়বুদ্ধি; স্থূল। 3. (*Geom.*) Greater than one and less than two right angles (of an angle) ; এক সমকোণ অপেক্ষা বৃহত্তর এবং দুই সমকোণ অপেক্ষা ক্ষুদ্রতর, স্থূলকোণী, অধিককোণী। 4. Not sharp or shrill, as a sound ; অকর্কশ। **–ly,** *adv.* **–ness,** *n.*

ŏb'-verse (-vêrs), *adj.* & *n.* 1. Narrower at the base than at the top ; as an *obverse* tool or leaf ; অগ্রভাগ অপেক্ষা মূলদেশ স্বল্পতর পরিসর। 2. Being a counterpart to something else ; অন্য কিছুর প্রতিরূপ স্বরূপ। 3. Facing the observer or opponent, (opp. of *reverse*) ; সম্মুখবর্তী, মুখোমুখী। ***Noun.*** 1. The face of a coin or medal ; পদক বা মুদ্রার যে পিঠে রাজা বা রাণীর মাথা থাকে। 2. The front or principal surface of anything ; কোন বস্তুর সম্মুখভাগ বা প্রধান পৃষ্ঠ। 3. The counterpart of a fact or truth ; কোন তথ্য বা সত্যের অপর দিক। **–ly,** *adv.*

ŏb-vêrt', *v. t.* (*Log.*) To infer as a proposition by obversion ; (তর্ক-বিজ্ঞান) বিপরীত বিষয় দ্বারা কোন প্রতিপাদিত বিষয়ের সিদ্ধান্ত করা। **–ver'-sion,** *n.* Act of immediate inference by which we deny the opposite of anything affirmed ; যে অব্যবহিত অনুমানের সাহায্যে আমরা কোন প্রতিপাদিত বিষয়ের বিপরীত বিষয় অস্বীকার করি, প্রতিবর্তন (হিঃ কোঃ), ব্যাপ্যব্যাপকবিরুদ্ধপ্রতিষেধ (ঐ), ব্যবর্তন (সাঃ পঃ)।

ŏb'-vi-āte, *v. t.* To get rid of ; to remove ; as, to *obviate* a danger, difficulty, etc. ; পরিত্রাণ পাওয়া, রেহাই পাওয়া ; অপসারিত করা।

ŏb'-vi-ous (ŭs), *adj.* Clearly perceptible ; plain ; evident ; স্পষ্ট, প্রত্যক্ষ ; প্রত্যক্ষগোচর ; সুব্যক্ত, সুস্পষ্ট। **–ly,** *adv.* Evidently ; সুস্পষ্টভাবে। **–ness,** *n.*

ŏc-ă-ri'-nă, *n.* A musical instrument with an oblong terra-cotta body ; একপ্রকার বাদ্য-যন্ত্র।

ŏc-cā'-sion (-zhŭn), *n.* & *v. t.* 1. An opportunity ; as, to take *occasion* to do something ; সুবিধা, সুযোগ। 2. Reason ; justification ; incitement ; as, to give *occasion* to a burst of laughter ; হেতু, কারণ, নিমিত্ত ; সঙ্গত কারণ ; উত্তেজনা, প্ররোচনা। 3. (*Pl., Obs.*) Affairs or business ; (অপ্রঃ) কার্য, ব্যাপার, বিষয়। 4. An occurrence esp. with reference to the time of its happening ; as, on this festive *occasion* ; ঘটনা, স্থল, স্থান, ক্ষেত্র, প্রসঙ্গ, উপলক্ষ। ***Verb t.*** To bring about incidentally ; to be the cause of ; to cause ; সংঘটন করা ; কারণ হওয়া ; জন্মান। **–sioned,** *p. adj.* **On or upon occasion**—Whenever need arises ; now and then ; প্রয়োজনমত ; সময় সময়। **On the occasion of**—উপলক্ষে। **To rise to the occasion**—To show requisite energy etc. ; কালোপযোগী উৎসাহ প্রভৃতি প্রদর্শন করা। **To take occasion**—To avail oneself of an opportunity *to* do etc. ; সুযোগ গ্রহণ করা।

ŏc-cā'-sion-ăl (-zhŭn-), *adj.* 1. Occurring now and then ; casual ; incidental ; কাদাচিৎক, বিরলাগত, সাময়িক, অসচরাচারিক ; নৈমিত্তিক ; প্রাসঙ্গিক। 2. Made or designed for, or acting on, a special occasion or particular occasions ; as, an *occasional* verse or speaker ; কোন বিশেষ ঘটনা উপলক্ষে রচিত বা কল্পিত। **–al'-i-ty,** *n.* **–ly,** *adv.* At times ; now and then ; not regularly ; সময় সময় ; কখন কখন, মধ্যে মধ্যে ; সদা সর্বদা নয়। **Occasional cause**—A cause ; also, an apparent cause ; নৈমিত্তিক কারণ ; আপাতদৃষ্ট কারণ, অনিয়ত কারণ (হিঃ কোঃ)।

ŏc-cā'-sion-ăl-ism (-zhŭn-), *n.* The Cartesian theory of occasional causes which accounts for the action of the mind on the body and of the body on the mind, by assuming that a change of state in the one is the mere occasion of a change of state in the other, the efficient cause in every case being Deity ; দেকার্তের শিষ্য Guelinx কর্তৃক প্রবর্তিত অনিয়ত কারণবাদ—এই বাদ অনুসারে মনের অবস্থার পরিবর্তনে দৈহিক অবস্থার পরিবর্তন এবং দৈহিক অবস্থার পরিবর্তনে মানসিক অবস্থার অনুরূপ পরিবর্তন সংঘটিত হয়, এবং প্রতিক্ষেত্রেই ঈশ্বর দেহ ও মনের উক্তরূপ পরিবর্তন সংঘটন করেন, অনিয়তকারণবাদ (হিঃ কোঃ)। **–ist,** *n.*

Oc'-ci-dĕnt (ŏc-), *n.* (*Poet.* & *Rhet.*) The west ; Europe or Western Europe ; Europe and America or simply America ; European civilization ; (opp. to *orient*) ; পশ্চিমদিক, প্রতীচী, অপরান্ত ; ইয়ুরোপ বা পশ্চিমইয়ুরোপ, প্রতীচ্যদেশ ; ইয়ুরোপ এবং আমেরিকা, আমেরিকা ; ইয়ুরোপীয় সভ্যতা, প্রতীচ্য সভ্যতা। **–den'-tal,** *adj.* Western, (*opp.* to *oriental*) ; প্রতীচ্য। **–den'-tal-ism,** *n.* The character and spirit or culture of Europeans contrasted with Asiatics ; পাশ্চাত্যভাব, প্রতীচ্য চরিত্র। **–den'-tal-ist,** *n.* **–den'-tal-ize,** *v. t.* **–den'-tal-ly,** *adv.*

ŏc'-ci-pŭt, *n.* (*Anat.*) The back part of the head or skull ; (শারীরসংস্থানবিদ্যা) করোটীর পশ্চাদ্ভাগ, শিরঃপৃষ্ঠ, পশ্চাৎকপাল। **–cip'-i-tal,** *adj.*

ŏc-clūde', *v. t.* 1. To close or obstruct as pores or orifice ; ছিদ্র রোধ করা। 2. (*Chem.*) To absorb or retain, as gases ; (রসায়ন-শাস্ত্র) শোষণ করা, ধারণ করা। **–clu'-sion, –clu'-sor,** *ns.*

ŏc-cŭlt', *v. t.* & *i.* To conceal or hide ; (esp. *astron.*) to eclipse ; লুকায়িত করা, লুকান ; (বিশেষতঃ জ্যোতির্বিজ্ঞানে) গ্রাস করা। **–cul-ta'-tion,** *n.* 1 Concealing : state of being concealed ; প্রচ্ছাদন ;

প্রচ্ছন্নতা। 2. The concealing of one heavenly body by another ; সমাগম (সাঃ পঃ), অস্তগমন (ঐ)। **Occulting light** — (আলোকমন্দির) যে আলো নিয়ম মত কয়েক কয়েক সেকেণ্ড করিয়া অদৃশ্য থাকে।

ŏc-cŭlt′, *adj.* **1.** Concealed ; secret; গুহ্য, গুপ্ত; নিগূঢ়, নিগূঢ়ার্থ, অজ্ঞাত। **2.** Mysterious ; recondite : রহস্যপূর্ণ ; গহন, দুর্জ্ঞেয়, দুরধিগম্য। **3.** Mystical ; magical ; তান্ত্রিক ; ঐন্দ্রজালিক। **—ism,** *n.* Belief in hidden or mysterious powers and the possibility of subjecting them to human control ; occult or magical practice ; গুপ্তবিদ্যা, রহস্যবিদ্যা (হিঃ কোঃ), যুক্তি (ঐ), গুহ্যবিদ্যা (ঐ); তান্ত্রিকক্রিয়াকলাপ, ঐন্দ্রজালিকক্রিয়া। **—ist,** *n.* One who believes in, or practises, occultism ; অলৌকিকরহস্যবেত্তা, তান্ত্রিক, ঐন্দ্রজালিক, রহস্যবেত্তা (হিঃ কোঃ)। **—ly,** *adv.* **—ness,** *n.* **Occult power**—অলৌকিক শক্তি। **Occult science** — অলৌকিক রহস্যবিজ্ঞান, গুপ্তবিদ্যা।

ŏc′-cū-pănt, *n.* **1.** One in actual possession of property, esp. land ; কোন সম্পত্তির অধিকারী, বিশেষতঃ কোন ভূমির অধিকারী। **2.** One who occupies a place; কোন স্থানের বাসিন্দা। **3.** (*Law*) One who takes possession of an unowned thing and acquires a title to it by occupation ; (আইন) দখলকার। **—pancy,** *n.* Act of taking or holding possession ; (*law*) taking possession of an unowned thing, thus acquring a title thereto ; অধিকার ; (আইন) ভোগদখল। **Right of occupancy**—দখলীস্বত্ব, জোতস্বত্ব।

ŏc-cū-pā′-tion, *n.* **1.** Act of occupying ; actual possession ; tenure ; occupancy ; অধিকার ; দখল ; জোত ; জোতস্বত্ব। **2.** Business ; calling ; pursuit ; ব্যবসায়, পেশা, বৃত্তি, উপজীবিকা। **Occupation bridge, road, etc.**—কোন ভূমির দখলকারের স্বকীয় ব্যবহারের জন্য সেতু, রাস্তা, প্রভৃতি। **Occupation franchise**—প্রজাস্বরূপ মত প্রদানের অধিকার। **Army of occupation**—নিয়মিত শাসনতন্ত্র প্রতিষ্ঠিত হওয়ার পূর্ব্বে অধিকৃত ভূখণ্ড রক্ষার জন্য যে সৈন্যদল রক্ষিত হয়।

ŏc′-cū-pī-êr, *n.* One who occupies ; one who holds possession, esp. of land or house ; an occupant ; অধিকারী ; জোতদার ; দখলকার।

ŏc′-cū-pȳ, *v. t.* **1.** To take possession of by military force or settlement ; অধিকার করা। **2.** To dwell or live in ; to tenant ; বাস করা ; প্রজাস্বরূপ ভোগদখল করা। **3.** To hold, as some office ; কোন পদে স্থিত হওয়া। **4.** To take up or fill, as space, time, etc. ; পূরণ করা, জুড়িয়া থাকা, ব্যাপিয়া থাকা। **5.** To employ or engage ; to busy ; (esp. in *pass.*) ; নিযুক্ত করা ; ব্যাপৃত করা।

ŏc-cur′ (-kêr), *v. i.* **1.** To take place ; to happen ; ঘটা ; আপতিত হওয়া, সংঘটিত হওয়া। **2.** To be found or met with in some place or conditions ; কোন স্থানে বা অবস্থায় প্রাপ্ত হওয়া। **3.** To come to the mind ; as, it *occured* to me that etc. ; মনে উদয় হওয়া, মনে জাগা, মনে পড়া।

ŏc-cŭr′-rence (-rĕns), *n.* Occurring or happening ; সংঘটন। **It is of frequent occurrence**—It often occurs ; এইরূপ সচরাচর ঘটিয়া থাকে। **Place of occurrence** — ঘটনার স্থান, মাজরার স্থল, অকুস্থান।

ō′-cean (-shăn), *n.* **1.** The vast body of water covering more than three-fifths of the globe ; মহাসাগর, মহাসমুদ্র, মহার্ণব, মহোদধি (রঃ), মহাম্বুধি, অম্বুনিধি, তীর্থরাজ, সিন্ধুনাথ। **2.** Immense expanse or quantity of anything ; as, the *ocean* of eternity ; মহাবিস্তার। **—o-graph′-i-cal, —o-graph′-ic,** *adjs.* **—og′-ra-phy,** *n.* Geography dealing with the ocean and its phenomena ; মহাসমুদ্র এবং তদীয় দৃশ্যসমূহের বর্ণনামূলক ভূগোল-শাস্ত্র। **—ward(s),** *adv.* **A drop in the ocean**—সমুদ্রে পাদ্য অর্ঘ্য।

O-ce-ăn′-i-ă (ō-shē-), *n.* Islands of the Pacific and the adjacent seas ; প্রশান্ত মহাসাগর এবং তৎসন্নিহিত সাগর সমূহের দ্বীপপুঞ্জ। **—an,** *adj.* & *n.* Of, or relating to, Oceania ; ওশেনিয়া সংক্রান্ত। (*Noun*) A native of Oceania ; ওশেনিয়ার অধিবাসী।

ō-ce-ăn′-ic (-shē-), *adj.* **1.** Of, relating to, or like, the ocean ; সামুদ্র, সামুদ্রিক, সাগরিক, মহাসাগরসম্বন্ধীয়। **2.** (*Cap.*) Of, or relating to, Oceania ; ওশেনিয়াসম্বন্ধীয়।

ō-ce′-ă-nid (-shē-), *n.* (*Pl.* -NIDS, -NIDES), (*Gr. Myth.*) A nymph of the ocean ; (গ্রীকপুরাণ) সাগরপরী।

ocellus, *n.* (*Pl.* OCELLI) **1.** One of the simple eyes of insects ; একাক্ষিমুকুরবিশিষ্ট পতঙ্গের চক্ষুর্দ্বয়ের অন্তর। **2.** A facet or segment of a compound eye ; একাধিক অক্ষিমুকুরবিশিষ্ট চক্ষুর পল বা ছিন্নাংশ। **3.** A round colour-spot with a dark centre as those of the peacock ; ময়ূরের চন্দ্রক বা তৎসদৃশ কোন কিছু। **Oc′-el-late, Oc′-el-lat-ed,** *adjs.* Eye-like ; studed with little eyes ; অক্ষিবৎ ; চন্দ্রকখচিত, নেত্রকগণানুবিদ্ধ।

ō′-cĕ-lŏt, *n.* A carnivorous animal of the cat-tribe ; মার্জ্জারজাতীয় মাংসাশী জন্তুবিশেষ।

ŏch, *interj.* (*Irish*) Same as OH or AH.

ŏch-lŏc′-ră-cȳ, *n.* Government by the mob ; ভদ্রেতরজনগণদ্বারা শাসন। **—lo-crat′-ic,** *adj.* **Och′-lo-crat,** *n.*

Ochna squarrosa—কনক চাঁপা (বোঃ), কনক চম্পক।

ō′-chre (-kêr), **—chêr,** *ns.* A clay used as a pigment of a pale yellow-colour ; স্বর্ণ-গৈরিক, রক্তোৎপল, গেরু (হিঃ কোঃ)। **—ish, —ous, —chra'-ceous, —chry,** *adjs.* **Red-ochre**—গৈরিক (যোঃ)। **Yellow-ochre**—গিরিমাটী (ওয়াট)।

Ocimum adscendens—বনতুলসী (বেলঃ)।

Ocimum bacilicum—বাবুই তুলসী (বেলঃ)।

Ocimum canum—বিশ্বতুলসী (বেলঃ)।

Ocimum glabratum — গুলাল-তুলসী (বেলঃ)।

Ocimum gratissimum — রাম-তুলসী (বেলঃ)।

Ocimum sanctum — কৃষ্ণতুলসী (বেলঃ), কালাতুলসী (ঐ)।

Ocimum villosum—সফেদ তুলসী (হিন্দী—বেলঃ)।

ō-clock' (-klŏk), See under CLOCK.

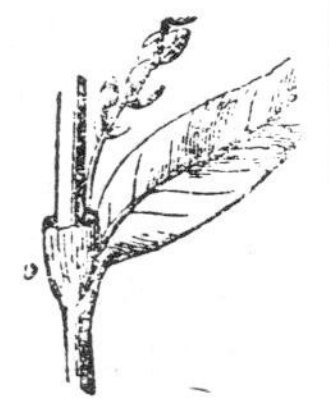

Smartweed branch ; O, ochrea.

ŏch'-rē-ă, *n.* (*Bot.*) A kind of sheath formed by two stipules united round a stem ; কাণ্ডবেষ্ট, উপপত্র (সাঃ পঃ)।

ŏc'-tă-chŏrd, *adj.* & *n.* Eight-stringed, (of a musical instrument) ; অষ্টতন্ত্রীবিশিষ্ট। ***Noun.*** **1.** An instrument of eight strings ; অষ্টতন্ত্রীবিশিষ্ট বাদ্যযন্ত্র। **2.** A series of eight notes, *e. g.* the diatonic scale ; সপ্তক।

ŏc'-tăd, *n.* **1.** (*Geom.*) Eight points of intersection of three quadric surfaces ; (জ্যামিতি) অষ্টচ্ছেদন বিন্দু, অষ্টবন্ধন (হিঃ কোঃ)। **2.** (*Chem.*) An element or radical that is octavalent ; (রসায়নশাস্ত্র) অষ্ট-পরমাণুগ্রহণশক্তিসম্পন্ন মূলপদার্থ। **3.** A group of eight ; অষ্ট-সংহতি, অষ্টক।

ŏc'-tă-gŏn, *n.* & *adj.* **1.** A plane figure of eight angles and sides ; অষ্টভুজক্ষেত্র, অষ্টাস্র (সাঃ পঃ)। **2.** An object or a building of octagonal shape ; অষ্টাস্র বস্তু, অষ্টকোণ অট্টালিকা। ***Adj.*** Octagonal ; অষ্টবাহু এবং অষ্টকোণবিশিষ্ট, অষ্টকোণ (হিঃ কোঃ)। **—tag'-o-nal,** *adj.* Having eight sides and eight angles ; অষ্টবাহু এবং অষ্টকোণবিশিষ্ট, আট-পলা, অষ্টকোণী। **—tag'-o-nal-ly,** *adv.*

ŏc-tă-hē'-drŏn, *n.* **1.** A solid formed by eight equal faces, usually eight triangles ; অষ্টত্রিভুজাবচ্ছিন্ন ঘনক্ষেত্র, অষ্টফলক (হিঃ কোঃ)। **2.** A body, esp. crystal, of regular octahedral form ; অষ্টপলা বস্তু, বিশেষতঃ আট-পলা স্ফটিক। **—dral,** *adj.* Having eight equal sides ; অষ্টসমবাহুবিশিষ্ট।

ŏc-tăn'-dri-ă, *n.* (*Bot.*) A Linnean class of plants, in which the flowers have eight stamens not united to one another or to the pistil ; (উদ্ভিদ-বিদ্যা) একজাতীয় গুল্ম—যাহাতে পুষ্পের আটটী পুংকেশর থাকে এবং ইহারা পরস্পরের সহিত বা স্ত্রী-কেশরের সহিত সংযুক্ত থাকে না।

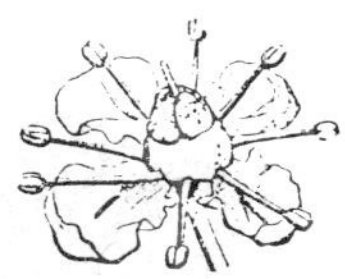

Octandria—Flower of Rue.

ŏc'-tănt, *n.* **1.** The eighth part of a circle ; an arc or angle of 45 degrees ; বৃত্তের অষ্টমাংশ ; ৪৫ অংশের বৃত্তাংশ বা কোণ। **2.** One of eight parts into which three planes intersecting (esp. at right angles) at a point divide space round it ; তিনটী তল পরস্পরকে (বিশেষতঃ সমকোণে) কোন বিন্দুতে ছেদন কালে চতুর্দিগস্থ স্থানকে যে অষ্ট অংশে বিভক্ত করে—তাহার অন্যতম। **3.** (*Astron.*) The position or aspect of a heavenly body, as the moon or a planet when halfway between conjunction (or opposition) and quadrature (that is distant from another body by 45 degrees) ; (জ্যোতির্বিজ্ঞান) এক জ্যোতিষ্ক অপর জ্যোতিষ্কের ৪৫ ডিগ্রি দূরে অবস্থান, অষ্টমাংশ (হিঃ কোঃ)। **4.** An instrument in the form of a graduated eighth of a circle for measuring angles esp. in astronomy and navigation ; কোণ-মাপক যন্ত্র।

ŏc'-târch-ȳ, *n.* An aggregate of eight petty kingdoms, (substituted by some for *Heptarchy*) ; অষ্ট-ক্ষুদ্র রাজ্যের সমবায়।

ŏc-tă-roon', **—tō—,** *ns.* The off-spring of a quadroon and a white person ; শ্বেতকায় জাতির সংসর্গে জাত সঙ্করসন্তানবিশেষ।

ŏc'-tĭ-stȳle, *adj.* & *n.* (Of a building etc.) With eight columns in front or at the end ; (অট্টালিকা প্রভৃতি সম্পর্কে) পুরোভাগে বা পশ্চাদ্‌ভাগে অষ্টস্তম্ভ-বিশিষ্ট। ***Noun.*** Such a building or portico ; ঐরূপ অষ্টস্তম্ভবিশিষ্ট অট্টালিকা বা দ্বারপ্রকোষ্ঠ।

ŏc'-tă-teuch (-tūk), *n.* A collection of eight books, esp. the first eight books of the Old Testament ; অষ্টগ্রন্থসংহতি, বিশেষতঃ বাইবেলের প্রাচীন নিয়মের প্রথম অষ্টপুস্তক।

ŏc-tāve, *n.* **1.** The eighth day after a church festival ; also the week after the festival ; কোন খৃষ্টীয় উৎসবের পরবর্ত্তী অষ্টম দিবস : কোন খৃষ্টীয় উৎসবের পরবর্ত্তী সপ্তাহ। **2.** A stanza of eight lines ; অষ্টপংক্তি-সমন্বিত শ্লোক বা কবিতা। **3.** (*Mus.*) An eighth or an interval of twelve semitones ; (সঙ্গীতশাস্ত্র) সপ্তক (ক্রেমঃ)। **4.** A group of eight ; অষ্টবস্তুর সমবায়। **5.** A fencing-position ; অসিক্রীড়ায় ভঙ্গী-বিশেষ। **6.** A cask of wine containing $13\frac{1}{2}$ gallons ; ১৩½ গ্যালনের মদের পিপা। **Higher octave**—তারা। **Lower octave** — মন্দ্র (উদারা)। **Middle octave**—মধ্য (মুদারা)।

ŏc'-tāve, *adj.* Consisting of eight ; esp. having eight lines, as a stanza ; অষ্টাত্মক, অষ্টক (হিঃ কোঃ) ; বিশেষতঃ অষ্টপংক্তিবিশিষ্ট।

ŏc-tā′-vō, *n.* A book or page given by folding sheets into eight leaves ; the size of such a book : (abbr. *8vo, oct.*) ; আটপেজী বই ; আটপেজী আকার, অষ্টাংশিত আকার, অষ্টপত্রী।

ŏc-tĕn′-ni-ăl (-ĭ-), *adj.* Lasting eight years ; happening every eighth year ; অষ্টবর্ষস্থায়ী ; প্রতি অষ্টবর্ষে সংঘটিত, অষ্টবার্ষিক।

ŏc-tet(te)′ (-tĕt), *n.* **1.** Eight singers or players performing together ; a musical composition for them ; একত্রে গীতবাদ্যকারী অষ্ট গায়ক বা বাদক ; উহাদের উপযোগী গান বা বাদ্য। **2.** A group of eight lines of verse, esp. the first eight lines of a sonnet ; কবিতার অষ্ট পংক্তি, বিশেষতঃ চতুর্দ্দশপদী কবিতার প্রথম অষ্ট পংক্তি।

ŏc-til′-lion (-yŏn), *n.* The eighth power of a million denoted by 1 followed by 48 ciphers ; ১এর ডাইনে ৪৮টী শূন্য বসাইলে যে সংখ্যা হয়। **—lionth,** *adj.* & *n.*

ŏc-tin-gĕn′-tē-na-rȳ, *n.* & *adj.* 800th anniversary ; অষ্টশতসাম্বৎসরিক উৎসব। ***Adj.*** Of, or relating to, this ; অষ্টশতসাম্বৎসরিক উৎসব-সম্বন্ধীয়।

Oc-tō′-bêr (ŏc-), *n.* **1.** The tenth month ; অক্টোবর মাস। **2.** (*Archaic*) Ale brewed in October ; (অপ্রঃ) অক্টোবরমাসের চোয়ান মদ্য।

ŏc-tō-cĕn′-tē-na-rȳ, —tĕn′-ni-ăl (-ĭ-), *ns.* & *adjs.* Same as OCTINGENTENARY.

ŏc-tō-dĕc′-i-mō, *n.* (Abbr. *18mo*) A book or page formed by dividing sheets into 18 leaves ; the size of such a book ; ১৮ পেজি বই, এক তা কাগজ আঠারো ভাঁজ করিয়া পুস্তকের যে পাতা হয় ; ঐরূপ পুস্তকের আকার।

ŏc-tō-gē-nā′-ri-ăn, *adj.* & *n.* **1.** 80 or more and less than 90 years old ; অশীতি বর্ষীয়, অশীতিপর, অশীতিক। **2.** Of, or relating to, a person of such age ; অশীতিপরবৃদ্ধসম্পর্কীয়। ***Noun.*** A person of such age ; অশীতিপর বৃদ্ধ ব্যক্তি।

ŏc′-tō-năl, *adj.* Proceeding by eights (of coinage, numeral system, etc.) ; অষ্টমিক।

ŏc-tō-nā′-ri-ăn, *adj.* & *n.* (*Pros.*) Made up of eight-feet ; (ছন্দঃ-শাস্ত্র) অষ্টচরণবিশিষ্ট। ***Noun.*** Such a line ; অষ্টচরণবিশিষ্ট কবিতা-পংক্তি।

ŏc′-tō-nă-rȳ, *adj.* & *n.* Same as OCTONAL. ***Noun.*** **1.** A group of eight ; অষ্টবস্তুর সংহতি, অষ্টক। **2.** (*Pros.*) A stanza or group of eight verses ; (ছন্দঃ-শাস্ত্র) অষ্টচরণবিশিষ্ট শ্লোক।

ŏc-tō-pŭs, *n.* (*Pl.* -PUSES) **1.** A two-gilled cuttle-fish having eight arms furnished with suckers ; অষ্টবাহু জলজন্তুবিশেষ—ইহারা বাহুসংলগ্ন শোষকের সাহায্যে শিকার ধরিয়া থাকে, অষ্টপদ। **2.** (*Fig.*) An organized power having extended ramifications, esp. destructive ; 'He was an administrative *octopus*" ; (লক্ষণায়) বহু শাখাপ্রশাখাসমন্বিত ব্যবস্থাবদ্ধ ক্ষমতা,—সাধারণতঃ অনিষ্টজনক।

Octopus.

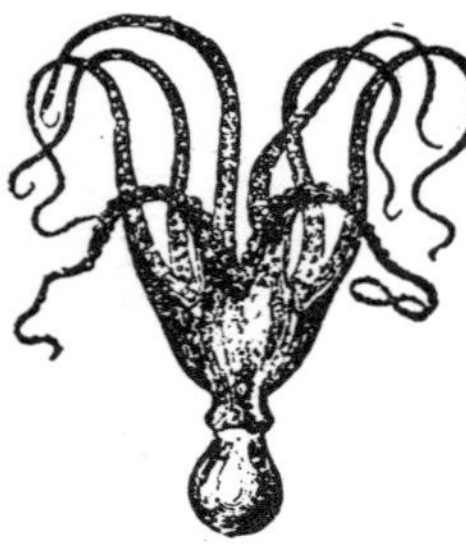

Cuttle-fish Octopus.

ŏc-tō-rōōn′, *n.* Same as OCTAROON.

ŏc-tō-sȳl-lăb′-ic, *adj.* & *n.* Made up of eight syllables ; অষ্টশব্দাংশবিশিষ্ট। ***Noun.*** Such a verse ; অষ্টশব্দাংশবিশিষ্ট কবিতা।

ŏc-tō-sȳl′-lă-ble (-bl), *n.* & *adj.* An octosyllabic verse or word ; অষ্টশব্দাংশবিশিষ্ট কবিতাপংক্তি বা শব্দ। ***Adj.*** Same as OCTOSYLLABIC.

ŏc′-troi (-trwä), *n.* **1.** (*Obs.*) A privilege, esp. commercial, granted by a sovereign ; (অপ্রঃ) রাজপ্রদত্ত বিশেষ অধিকার, বিশেষতঃ বাণিজ্য-সংক্রান্ত অধিকার। **2.** A tax levied on goods on their admission into a town, esp. in France ; কোন মাল সহরে বিক্রয়ের জন্য নিতে হইলে যে শুল্ক দিতে হয়, পুরশুল্ক। **3.** The place where it is levied ; also the officials levying it ; যে স্থানে পুরশুল্ক সংগৃহীত হয় ; পুরশুল্ক সংগ্রহকারী কর্ম্মচারিগণ।

ŏc′-tū-ple (-pl), *adj.*, *n.*, *v. t.* & *i.* Eightfold ; অষ্টগুণিত। ***Noun.*** That which is eight times something else ; যে বস্তু অপর কোন বস্তুর অষ্টগুণ। ***Verb t. & i.*** To make or become octuple ; অষ্টগুণ করা, অষ্টগুণ হওয়া।

ŏc′-ū-lar (-lêr), *adj.* & *n.* **1.** Of, or relating to, the eye or sight ; visual ; আক্ষিক ; চাক্ষুষ (হিঃ কোঃ), দর্শনেন্দ্রিয়-সংক্রান্ত। **2.** (*Entom.*) Pertaining to the compound eye of an insect ; (কীটতত্ত্ব) একাধিক অক্ষি-মুকুর-সমন্বিত কীটনেত্রসম্বন্ধীয়। **3.** Depending on, or seen by, the eye ; received by actual sight ; নেত্রাধীন, নেত্রদৃষ্ট ; চক্ষুর্গৃহীত। ***Noun.*** An eye-piece of optical instrument ; অণুবীক্ষণযন্ত্রের নেত্রতাল। **—ly,** *adv.* **Ocular demonstration**—চাক্ষুষপ্রমাণ (হিঃ কোঃ), প্রত্যক্ষ প্রমাণ।

ŏc′-ū-lar-ist (-lêr-), *n.* A maker of artificial eyes ; কৃত্রিম অক্ষি-নির্ম্মাতা, কৃত্রিম নেত্র-নির্ম্মাতা।

ŏc'-ū-list, *n.* An eye-doctor : চক্ষুরোগ চিকিৎসক, চক্ষুর্বৈদ্য, নেত্রবৈদ্য। **—lis'-tic,** *adj.*

ŏd, *n.* A presumed all-pervading force accounting for magnetism, crystallization, chemical action, mesmerism, etc., (an arbitrary term formed and used by Baron Von Reichenbach, 1788—1869) ; চৌম্বকত্ব, অর্কতাপাদন, রাসায়নিক ক্রিয়া, মৈস্মরতত্ত্বের কারণস্বরূপ বলিয়া কল্পিত সর্ব্বগতাশক্তি, ওজ (হিঃ কোঃ)।

ō'-dă-lisque, (-lĭsk), *n.* A female slave or concubine in an Eastern harem, esp. in the seraglio of the Turkish Sultan ; পাতশাহদিগের অন্তঃপুরের বাঁদী বা উপপত্নী (বিশেষতঃ তুরস্ক সুলতানের)।

ŏdd, *adj.* & *n.* **1.** Not even ; not divisible by two ; left over as a remainder when divided by two ; অযুগ্ম ; বিজোড় ; বিষম (হিঃ কোঃ)। **2.** (Of a person or thing numbered consecutively) Bearing an odd number ; wanting a match or pair ; as, an *odd* boot or glove ; অযুগ্ম সংখ্যক ; জোড়াহীন, যোটকহীন। **3.** Remaining over after a round number ; exceeding a specified number or quantity ; শূন্যান্ত সংখ্যার অতিরিক্ত ; কোন নির্দ্দিষ্ট সংখ্যা বা পরিমাণের অতিরিক্ত। **4.** Designating an inconsiderable surplus of smaller denomination ; as, forty *odd* (between 40 and 50) ; সামান্য অতিরিক্ত সংখ্যাসূচক। **5.** Additional ; casual ; unconnceted ; unoccupied ; as, *odd* jobs : at *odd* moments : *odd* volumes ; out-of-the-way, as a corner etc. ; অতিরিক্ত ; নৈমিত্তিক ; অসংলগ্ন, খাপছাড়া, বেখাপ্পা ; অব্যাপৃত ; সচরাচর লোকের গতিবিধি নাই এইরূপ। **6.** Strange ; peculiar ; queer ; remarkable ; eccentric ; অপরূপ, কিম্ভুতকিমাকার ; সৃষ্টিছাড়া ; বিদঘুটে, বিসদৃশ ; অদ্ভুত ; মাথাপাগলা, ছিটগ্রস্ত। *Noun.* Something odd or additional : esp. in golf, the handicap given to a weaker player by deducting *one*, *two*, etc., from his strokes for each hole ; অতিরিক্ত কোন কিছু ; গোলফ্ ক্রীড়ায় অপেক্ষাকৃত অল্পপটু কোন ক্রীড়ক যতবার আঘাতে কন্দুক প্রতি গর্ত্তে নিক্ষেপ করিতে পারে সেই সকল আঘাতের সংখ্যা হইতে ১, ২, ইত্যাদি বাদ দিয়া ঐ ক্রীড়ককে যে সুবিধা দেওয়া হয়। **Odd'-ish,** *adj.* Somewhat odd or peculiar ; কতকটা অদ্ভুত রকমের। **Odd'-ly,** *adv.* **Odd'-ness** *n.* **Odd-come-short** — Remnant ; (*pl.*) odds and ends ; অবশিষ্ট ; ছিট ছাঁট, টুকি টাকি। **Odd-come-shortly**—Some near day ; দুই একদিনের মধ্যে, অচিরে। **Odd fellow**—অষ্টাদশ-শতাব্দীতে প্রতিষ্ঠিত গুপ্ত সমিতি বিশেষের সভ্য। [ঐরূপ সমিতি হইতে সভ্যগণের পীড়াদির কালে অর্থসাহায্য করা হয়।] **Odd-looking**—অদ্ভুতদর্শন, বিকটাকৃতি, বিরূপ। **Odd man, lad or hand**—টুকটাক কাজ করার জন্য নিযুক্ত লোক। **Odd number**—অযুগ্ম সংখ্যা। **Odd numbers, volumes**—অসম্পূর্ণ সেটের পত্রিকা বা পুস্তকের খণ্ড। **Odd times** — অবসর কাল। **Odd and even**—জোড় বিজোড় খেলা। **One of these odd-come-shortlies**—Ere long : অচিরে, অবিলম্বে, সত্বর। **Seventy thousand odd**—সত্তর হাজার শতক দশক বা একক। **Seventy odd thousand**—৭০ এবং ৮০,০০০এর মধ্যবর্ত্তী সংখ্যা। **The odd man**—যুগ্মসংখ্যক সভ্যবিশিষ্ট সভাসমিতি প্রভৃতিতে উভয়পক্ষের মতসংখ্যা সমান হইলে—উপস্থিত বিষয় মীমাংসার জন্য যে ব্যক্তির উপর অতিরিক্ত মতপ্রদানের ভার পড়ে। **The odd trick**—প্রতিপক্ষে ছয় ছয় পিঠ পাইলে পর তেরর পিঠ।

ŏdd'-i-tў, *n.* **1.** State of being odd or strange ; queerness ; peculiarity ; a peculiar trait ; অপরূপত্ব ; সৃষ্টিছাড়াভাব, আজগবিভাব ; বিশেষত্ব ; বিশিষ্ট লক্ষণ। **2.** An odd or queer person or thing ; a strange event ; সৃষ্টিছাড়া লোক, অদ্ভুত লোক, কিম্ভুতকিমাকার বস্তু ; অদ্ভুত ঘটনা, সৃষ্টিছাড়া ব্যাপার, উদ্ভট ব্যাপার।

ŏdd'-mĕnts, *n.* (*Pl.*) Odds and ends ; টুকিটাকি, টুকরা টাকরি।

odds (ŏdz), *n.* **1.** Unequal things or conditions ; অসমান বস্তু বা সর্ত্ত সমূহ। **2.** Difference ; inequality ; advantage ; as, the *odds* are in our favour ; বৈভিন্ন, তারতম্য ; অসমতা, বৈষম্য, বিষমতা ; সুবিধা। **3.** Variance ; strife : as, they are at *odds* ; অনৈক্য ; দ্বন্দ্ব, বিবাদ, বিরোধ। **4.** The equalizing allowance to weaker competitor ; as, to give or receive *odds* ; সমতাস্থাপনের জন্য অক্ষমতর প্রতিদ্বন্দ্বীকে যে সুবিধাপ্রদান করা হয়। **5.** (In betting) The proportional excess of the amount of the bet made by one party over that of another ; একপক্ষের ডাকের উপর অপর পক্ষ যে পরিমাণ বেশী ডাকে। **6.** Chances or probability ; as, the *odds* are that he will do it ; দৈব, সম্ভাবনা। **At odds**—At variance or strife ; বিরোধী। At a disadvantage ; অসুবিধায়, প্রতিযোগীর সহিত সমান সুবিধা না পাইয়া। **By long odds**—By a great difference ; অনেকটা। **It is odds**—Most probably ; খুব সম্ভবতঃ। **No odds**—It's of no consequence ; ইহাতে বিশেষ আসিয়া-যায় না। **Odds and ends**—Remants ; ছিটছাট, টুকিটাকী, টুকরা টাকরি। **To make odds even**—To do away with inequalities ; বৈষম্য দূর করা। **What's the odds**—What does it matter ? ; এতে কি আসে যায় ?

ōde, *n.* **1.** (*Formerly*) A poem intended or adapted, to be sung ; (পূর্ব্বে) গানের সুরে বাঁধা

কবিতা। 2. (*Modern*) A rhymed lyric, often in the form of an address; (বর্ত্তমানে) গীতিকবিতা।

ō-dē′-ŭm, *n.* (*Pl.* -UMS, -A) A kind of theatre among ancient Greeks and Romans; hence, a hall or building for musical performances; প্রাচীন গ্রীক ও রোমানদিগের একপ্রকার নাট্যশালা; সঙ্গীত-শালা, গন্ধর্ব্বশালা।

ō′-dī-ous (-ŭs), *adj.* Hateful; repugnant; repulsive; ঘৃণ্য, জঘন্য; ঘৃণিত, গর্হিত; বীভৎস, কুৎসিত। **—ly**, *adv.* **—ness**, *n.*

ō′-dī-ŭm, *n.* Hatred; dislike; state of being hated; opprobrium; ঘৃণা, জুগুপ্সা; বিরাগ; বিদ্বিষ্টতা; কুৎসা। **Odium theologicum**—শাস্ত্রজ্ঞ পণ্ডিতগণের মধ্যে মতভেদ হওয়ার দরুণ অপ্রীতি।

ō-dŏm′-ē-tĕr, *n.* Same as HODOMETER (which see).

ō-dŏn-tăl′-ġī-ȧ, *n.* Tooth-ache; দন্তশূল, দন্তবেদনা।

ō-dŏn-tō-glŏs′-sum, (-ŭm), *n.* A genus of orchids; একজাতীয় অর্কিড।

ō-dŏn′-toid (-toyd), *adj.* & *n.* 1. Tooth-like; দন্তবৎ। 2. Of, or relating to, the odontoid process; দন্তবৎ বিবর্দ্ধিত অংশ সম্বন্ধীয়। ***Noun.*** Same as **Odontoid process or peg**—(জন্তুবিদ্যা এবং শারীরসংস্থান-বিদ্যা) কোন কোন পক্ষী বা স্তন্যপায়ী জন্তুর গ্রীবাদেশের কশেরুকা হইতে উদ্গত দন্তবৎ বিবর্দ্ধিত অংশ।

ō-dŏn-tŏl′-ō-ġy̆, *n.* The science treating of the structure and development of the teeth; দন্ততত্ত্ব, দন্তবিজ্ঞান, দন্তব্যাকরণশারীর (আঃ বঃ) [cf. ধমনী ব্যাকরণশারীর (সুশ্রুঃ)।]

ō-dŏn-tō-rhyn′-cous (-rĭn-cŭs), *adj.* Having toothlike serrations in the bill; দন্তরিত চঞ্চুবিশিষ্ট।

ō-dor-if′-er-ous (-dêr-ĭf-ĕr-ŭs), *adj.* Yielding an odour usually pleasant; fragrant; সুগন্ধসঞ্চারী, সুগন্ধ, সামোদ, সুগন্ধি, সুরভি, সৌরভময়, সুবাসময়। **—ly**, *adv.*

ō′-dor-ous (-dêr-ŭs), *adj.* (Chiefly *poet.*) Same as ODORIFEROUS. **—ly**, *adv.*

ō′-dour, -dor (-dêr), *ns.* **1.** Smell good or bad; বাস, গন্ধ, ঘ্রাণ। **2.** Fragrance; সৌরভ, সুবাস, আমোদ, সুগন্ধ, পরিমল। **3.** (*Archaic*) Something emitting a pleasant scent; a perfume; (usu. *pl.*); (অপ্রঃ) সুগন্ধি দ্রব্য, সুরভি দ্রব্য; গন্ধদ্রব্য। **4.** (*Fig.*) Savour; trace; "No *odour* of intolerence attaches to it"; (লক্ষণায়) নামগন্ধ, গন্ধবাস; লেশ। **5.** Repute; favour; as, to be in good or bad *odour* (*with* any one); সুখ্যাতি; দৃষ্টি। **—less**, *adj.* Free from odour; নির্গন্ধ, গন্ধহীন (হিঃ কোঃ)। **In good, bad** or **ill odour**—See ODOUR *n.* 5. **Odour of sanctity**—Reputation for holiness; পবিত্রতার সৌরভ, পুণ্যের সৌরভ। [মরণোন্মুখ বা সমাধিগর্ত্ত হইতে উৎপাতিত সিদ্ধপুরুষদিগের দেহ হইতে একরূপ সৌরভ নিঃসৃত হইত বলিয়া প্রবাদ।]

ŏd′-y̆l, *n.* Same as OD.

Od′-ys-sey (ŏd-ĭ-sē), *n.* (*Pl.* -SEYS) 1. One of the two great national epics of the ancient Greeks; হোমররচিত প্রাচীন গ্রীসের জাতীয় মহাকাব্যদ্বয়ের অন্যতর। [ট্রয় নগরীর অবরোধের পর Odysseus এর স্বদেশ-প্রত্যাগমনকালে যে সকল আশ্চর্য্য আশ্চর্য্য ঘটনা ঘটে—এই গ্রন্থে তাহা বর্ণিত আছে।] 2. (*Fig.*) A long wandering or series of travels; (লক্ষণায়) সুদীর্ঘ ভ্রমণ বা পর্য্যটনপরম্পরা।

œ′-cist (ē-), *n.* The founder of a colony, esp. of ancient Greece; উপনিবেশস্থাপক, বিশেষতঃ প্রাচীন গ্রীসের উপনিবেশস্থাপক।

œ-cŏl′-ō-ġy̆ (ē-), *n.* The branch of biology which deals with the relations of living organisms to their surroundings, their habits, modes of life, etc.; জীববিজ্ঞানের শাখাবিশেষ — যাহাতে জীবের সহিত তদীয় পারিপার্শ্বিক অবস্থা, অভ্যাস ও জীবনপ্রণালীর সম্পর্কসম্বন্ধে আলোচনা থাকে।

œ-cŭ-mĕn′-ĭ-căl (ē-), *adj.* **1.** Of, relating to, or representing, the whole Christian world, or the universal church; নিখিল খৃষ্টজাগতিক, নিখিল ধর্ম্মসংঘসম্বন্ধীয়; [বিশেষতঃ খৃষ্ট-ধর্ম্মসংক্রান্ত গুরুতর প্রশ্নসমূহ মীমাংসার জন্য ভিন্ন ভিন্ন কালে নিখিল খৃষ্ট-জগতের প্রতিনিধিগণের যে মহাসমিতির অধিবেশন হয় তৎসম্বন্ধে কথিত।] 2. Universal; world-wide; বিশ্ব-জনীন, সার্ব্বজনিক, সার্ব্বলৌকিক; নিখিল, জগদ্ব্যাপী। **—i-ci-ty**, *n.*

œ-dē′-mă (ē-), *n.* (no *pl.*) (*Path.*) Dropsy of the subcutaneous areolar tissue; রক্তাম্বুসঞ্চয়জনিত স্ফীতি, শোথ (হঃ চঃ)। **—e-dem′-a-tose, —e-dem′-a-tous, —mat′-ic,** *adjs.* **—e-dem′-a-tous-ly**, *adv.*

Ode-ĭ-pŭs (ĕd-), *n.* 1. (*Gr. Myth.*) A Theban hero who solved the riddle of the Sphinx and thereby freed the Thebans from distress; (গ্রীকপুরাণ) থীবদেশীয় বীর, ইনি Sphinxএর (Sphinx দেখ) প্রহেলিকার সমাধান করিয়া থীববাসীদিগকে বিপদ্ হইতে উদ্ধার করেন। 2. One who can solve riddles; ধাঁধা বা প্রহেলিকা সমাধানে সমর্থ ব্যক্তি।

œ-sŏph′-ă-gŭs (ē-), *ns.* (*Pl.* -GI -GUSES) The gullet or the canal from the mouth to the stomach; গলনালী, অন্ননালী (খাঃ)। **—so-phag′-e-al**, *adj.*

œ′-strŭm, —strŭs (ē-), *ns.* **1.** A gadfly; দংশমক্ষিকা, ডাঁশ। **2.** (*Fig.*) A vehement impulse or desire; a stimulus; frenzy; (লক্ষণায়) প্রবলবাসনা, প্রবল প্ররোচনা, বলবতী-স্পৃহা; উত্তেজনা; উন্মাদনা। **3.** (*Physiol.*) The sexual heat of animals; rut; (শারীর-বিজ্ঞান) কামোত্তেজনা; (পশ্বাদির) গরম।

of (ŏv), *prep.* 1. From ; as, *of* old : north *of* : upwards *of* ; হইতে। 2. Belonging to ; connected with ; বিষয়ক ; সংসৃষ্ট। 3. As a result or consequence of ; as, to die *of* cholera ; দরুণ, তে। 4. Indicating the agent, author ; as, the plays *of* Shakespere ; কর্ত্তা, গ্রন্থকার, প্রভৃতি সূচক, র। 5. Made, or composed, of ; containing ; as, a plate *of* gold : a cup *of* water ; নির্ম্মিত, রচিত ; পূর্ণ। 6. Expressing opposition, identity, etc., (used with a name or appellation) ; as, the city of Rome ; অনন্যত্ব প্রভৃতি সূচক। 7. About ; concerning ; as to ; সম্পর্কে ; বিষয়ে ; সম্বন্ধে। 8. Indicating objective relation ; as, the feeding *of* army : the drinker *of* wine ; কর্ম্মগত সম্বন্ধসূচক। 9. In respect of ; as, 40 years *of* age ; সম্পর্কে। 10. Indicating an attribute, characteristic or distinctive mark of a person or thing ; as, a man *of* valour : a time *of* drought ; কোন ব্যক্তি বা বস্তুর গুণ কিম্বা প্রকৃতি বা বিশেষত্বসূচক। 11. Out of ; from amongst ; হইতে ; মধ্য হইতে। **A fool of a man**—বেকুব, নির্ব্বোধ লোক। **Comes in of an evening**—Comes at sometime in the evenings ; বিকালে সময় সময় আসে। **Forsaken of God and man**—Forsaken by God and man ; দেবমানবপরিত্যক্ত। **He of all men**—He most or best of all ; সে সকলের উপরে বা সবার চেয়ে ভাল। **His temper is of the quickest**—সে অতি চটামেজাজের লোক। **Is one of a thousand**—হাজারের মধ্যে একজন। **Of consequence** — গুরুত্ববিশিষ্ট, প্রয়োজনীয়। **Of course**—সুতরাং, কাজেকাজেই। **Of force**—By force ; বলে, জোরে। **Of gold**—স্বর্ণনির্ম্মিত, স্বর্ণময়। **Of it**—Out of it; ইহা হইতে। **Of itself**—আপনাআপনি। **Of late**—Recently ; সম্প্রতি। **Of necessity**—বাধ্য হইয়া, কাজেকাজেই। **Of no account**—নগণ্য, ধর্ত্তব্যের মধ্যে নয়। **Of note**—বিখ্যাত। **Of one mind**—একমত। **Of old, of yore, of late years**—প্রাচীন কালের, কয়েক বৎসর পূর্ব্বের। **Of oneself**—Spontaneously ; without aid or interference ; আপনাআপনি ; স্বতঃই। **Of one's own accord** — স্বেচ্ছায়। **Of parts** — প্রতিভাশালী। **Of right**—By right ; as, it belongs to him *of right* ; অধিকার অনুসারে। **Sick of delays**—Disgusted by delays; বিলম্ব হেতু বিরক্ত। **Sick of measles** — Laid up with measles ; হামে শয্যাগত। **The worst liar of any man I know**—এমন মিথ্যাবাদী লোক আমি আর দেখি নাই। **To avail oneself of**—See under AVAIL. **To die of**—See OF 3. **To have a bad time of it**—খারাপ সময় পড়া, কষ্টে দিনপাত করা। **To smell, savour or smack of** — কোন দোষ বা গুণের লেশ থাকা। **Warned of God**—Warned by God ; ঈশ্বর দ্বারা সতর্ক। **Was sworn of the Council**—Was admitted as a member; সভ্য স্বরূপ গৃহীত হইয়াছিলেন।

ŏff, *adv., prep., adj., n.* & *v. t.* 1. At, or to, a distance ; away ; কতকটা দূরে ; দূরে, তফাতে। 2. Loose ; separate ; so as to be out of position ; as, the hat is *off* : to take *off* clothes : to shake or break *off* ; আলগা; পৃথক ; স্থানচ্যুত। 3. Discontinued ; as, the negotiation is *off* ; not attainable ; as, the gas is *off* ; স্থগিত, বন্ধ ; অপ্রাপ্য। 4. To the end ; completely ; entirely ; as, to pay, drink or work *off* ; শেষ পর্য্যন্ত ; সম্পূর্ণভাবে ; সবটা, সবটুকু। ***Prep.*** 1. From, away or distant from, so as no longer to be on ; দূরে। 2. Not up to or in ; condition for ; "I am *off* my feeding" ; কোন কিছুর জন্য উপযুক্ত অবস্থায় নয়। 3. Disengaged from ; as, to be *off* duty ; অকর্ম্মব্যাপৃত, অবকাশপ্রাপ্ত। 4. (*Naut.*) To seaward of ; as, 3 miles *off* the shore ; (নৌবিদ্যা) সমুদ্রাভিমুখে। 5. Opening out of ; as, an alley *off* main street ; কোন কিছু হইতে বহির্গত। ***Adj.*** 1. Farther ; remote ; as, the *off* side of a wall ; দূরবর্ত্তী ; দূরস্থ। 2. Removed ; gone off ; as, he is *off* to the war ; স্থানান্তরিত ; প্রস্থিত, গত। 3. Right (opp. to *near*) ; as, the *off* horse of a team : the *off* leg ; ডাহিন, দক্ষিণ। 4. (*Cricket*) Relating to, towards, in, or coming from, that part of the field which is on the right hand of the wicket-keeper, (opp. to *on*) ; (ক্রীকেট-ক্রীড়ায়) ত্রিদণ্ডরক্ষকের দক্ষিণপার্শ্বস্থ ক্রীড়াক্ষেত্রাংশ সম্বন্ধীয়, উক্ত পার্শ্বাভিমুখীন, উক্ত পার্শ্ব হইতে আগত। 5. Situated to one side ; divergent ; as, an *off* street ; (also *fig.* of an argument), as an *off* issue ; একপার্শ্বে অবস্থিত ; বিসর্পী, (লক্ষণায়, যুক্তিসম্পর্কে) অবান্তর। 6. Contingent ; improbable ; as, there is an *off* change ; অনিশ্চিত ; অসম্ভব। 7. Disengaged ; as, an *off* day, time, etc. ; প্রাপ্তাবসর, কর্ম্মশূন্য। 8. Circumstanced, esp. as to material welfare ; as, well or badly *off* ; অবস্থাপন্ন। 9. Relating to the sale of excisable liquors to be consumed away from the premises ; as, *off* licence ; যে সকল আবকারী জিনিষ দোকানের বাহিরে ব্যবহার্য্য—তৎসমূহের বিক্রয়সম্বন্ধীয়। ***Noun.*** (Cricket) The off side ; (ক্রীকেট ক্রীড়ায়) ত্রিদণ্ডরক্ষকের বামপার্শ্বের ক্রীড়াক্ষেত্রাংশ। ***Verb t.*** (*Colloq.*) To declare the intention of abandoning or annulling as an agreement, negotiation, etc.; to stop negotiation or engagement with, as a person; (চলিতভাষায়) কোন চুক্তি, কথাবার্ত্তা, প্রভৃতি বাতিল করার উদ্দেশ্য জ্ঞাপন করা; কাহারও সহিত চুক্তি অথবা কথাবার্ত্তা চালান বন্ধ করা। **Off colour**—*Adj.* & *n.* Out of sorts; অসুস্থ। (*Noun*) An inferior colour; অপকৃষ্ট বর্ণ, মলিনবর্ণ (মূল্যবান প্রস্তরসম্পর্কে ব্যবহৃত)। **Off day**—See OFF *adj.* 7. **Off drive**—*v. t.* (Cricket) To drive or hit to the off; ত্রিদণ্ডরক্ষকের দক্ষিণপার্শ্বে কন্দুকতাড়ন বা আঘাত করা। **Off duty**—See OFF *prep.* 3. **Off-hand**—*adv.* & *adj.* Extempore; without premeditation; unceremoniously; উপস্থিত মত; না ভাবিয়া চিন্তিয়া; লৌকিকতার ধার না ধারিয়া। (*Adj.*) Free and easy; without stiffness; অনায়াস; অনাড়ষ্ট, সহজ, স্বচ্ছন্দ। **Off-handed,** *adj.*, **Off-handedly,** *adv.*, **Off-handedness,** *n.* **Off-licence**—দোকানের বাহিরে পানের জন্য বীয়র মদ বিক্রয়ের লাইসেন্স। **Off-print**—উদ্ধৃত প্রবন্ধ। **Off-shoot** — কন্দশাখা, প্ররোহ। **Off shore**—A short way out to sea; সমুদ্রের দিকে অল্পদূর। **Off-shore wind** — Wind blowing seawards; সমুদ্রাভিমুখে প্রবহমাণ বায়ু। **Off side**—(*Football*) Between the ball and the goal of the opposite party; (পাদগোলক ক্রীড়ায়) কন্দুক এবং বিপক্ষদলের গোলের মধ্যবর্ত্তী স্থান। **An off-drive**—(Cricket) A drive or hit to the off; ত্রিদণ্ডরক্ষকের ডাইন পার্শ্বে কন্দুক তাড়ন বা আঘাত। **Badly, comfortably, ill** or **well off**—See OFF *adj.* 8. **(Be) off with you**—Go; দূর হও। **Far off**—বহুদূরবর্ত্তী। **Off and on**—At intervals; now and again; waveringly; মাঝে মাঝে; সময় সময়; মিট মিট করিয়া। **Off by heart**—Committed to memory; কণ্ঠস্থ। **Off one's head**—See under HEAD. **Off with his head**—Behead him; তাহার মাথা কাটিয়া ফেল। **The gilt is off**—Disillusionment has come; মোহ কাটিয়াছে, ভ্রান্তি দূর হইয়াছে। **To be off**—To depart; to refuse to come to an agreement; প্রস্থান করা; কোন বিষয়ে এক মত হইতে না চাওয়া। **To be off with the old love**—To have cut off connexion; সম্পর্ক ছিন্ন করা। **To break off**—To break so as to be separate; ভাঙ্গিয়া ফেলা। To cease to speak; কথা বলিতে বলিতে হঠাৎ থামা। **To declare off**—To refuse or rescind engagement; কোন চুক্তি অস্বীকার বা ভঙ্গ করা। **To fall off**—অপকর্ষ প্রাপ্ত হওয়া। **To get one's daughters off** — To give away one's daughters in marriage; মেয়ে বিবাহ দেওয়া। **To go off**—To deteriorate; to fall asleep; অবনতি প্রাপ্ত হওয়া; ঘুমাইয়া পড়া (see also GO)। **To leave off work**—See under LEAVE. **To make off, To take oneself off**—To depart; প্রস্থান করা। **To shake off** — ঝাড়িয়া ফেলা। **To throw off reserve** — To become open or candid; মন খুলিয়া কথা বলিতে আরম্ভ করা। **We are off now**—We have just started, are starting, or about to start; এইমাত্র রওনা হইলাম, এই রওনা হচ্চি।

ŏf′-fal, *n.* **1.** Anything thrown away as worthless; refuse; garbage; scraps; আবর্জ্জনা; উচ্ছিষ্ট; জঞ্জাল; টুকরা টাকরি। **2.** The waste parts of a butchered animal; নিহত জন্তুর অব্যবহার্য্য অংশ (রক্ত, নাড়ীভুঁড়ি, ফুসফুস, প্রভৃতি)। **3.** Carrion; গলিত মাংস। **4.** A fish of small price, (opposed to *prime*); অল্পমূল্যের মাছ। **5.** Dregs; গাদ, তলানি। **Offal milk, wheat, wood, etc.**—Inferior kinds of those materials; নিকৃষ্ট দুগ্ধ, ময়দা, কাঠ, প্রভৃতি।

ŏf-fence′ (-fĕns), *n.* **1.** (Now *rare*) An occasion of stumbling or of sin; a stumbling-block; (বর্ত্তমানে ক্বচিদ্‌ব্যবহৃত) পাপ বা পদস্খলনের উপলক্ষ; প্রতিবন্ধক। **2.** Act of attacking; aggressive action; আক্রমণ; আধর্ষণ। **3.** Displeasing or affronting; state of being offended; annoyance; অসন্তোষ উৎপাদন, মর্য্যাদাতিক্রম; মনঃক্ষুণ্ণতা; বিরক্তি। **4.** A crime; an illegal act; transgression; a misdemeanour; অপরাধ; অবৈধ কার্য্য; ত্রুটি, কসুর, প্রত্যবায়; অন্যায়াচরণ। **—less,** *adj.* **A weapon of offence**—অস্ত্র। **Do not take offence**—অপরাধ নেবেন না। **To give offence**—অসন্তুষ্ট করা, মনঃক্ষুণ্ণ করা। **To take offence**—অপরাধ নেওয়া, ত্রুটি গ্রহণ করা।

ŏf-fĕnd′, *v. i.* & *t.* **1.** To commit a crime or fault; as, to *offend against* a law, decency, person, etc.; অপরাধ করা, দোষ করা। **2.** To displease; অসন্তুষ্ট করা। ***Verb t.*** To wound the feelings of; to make angry; to affront; to outrage; মনঃক্ষুণ্ণ করা, মনে আঘাত দেওয়া, মনঃপীড়া দেওয়া; ক্রুদ্ধ করা, রুষ্ট করা; মর্য্যাদাতিক্রম করা; অত্যাচার করা। **—ed-ly,** *adv.* **—er,** *n.* One who violates any law, divine or human; a wrong-doer; দোষী, অপরাধী; অন্যায় আচরণকারী। **—ing,** *n.* Offence; transgression; অপরাধ, দোষ; প্রত্যবায়। **To offend against**—To act unjustly or injuriously toward; to violate; কাহারো প্রতি অন্যায়াচরণ করা, কাহারো ক্ষতিজনক কোন কার্য্য করা; ভঙ্গ করা, লঙ্ঘন করা।

ŏf-fĕn′-sive (-sĭv), *adj.* & *n.* **1.** Assailant; aggressive; meant for, or used, in attack; আক্রমক; পরপীড়ক, পীড়াকর; আক্রমণের জন্য

অভিপ্রেত বা ব্যবহৃত। 2. Giving offence; insulting; মনঃপীড়াদায়ক, মনঃক্ষুণ্ণকর; অপমানজনক, মর্য্যাদাহানিকর। 3. Disgusting; nauseous; obnoxious; ill-smelling; বিরক্তিকর, বিরক্তিজনক; ন্যক্কারজনক, অপ্রীতিকর, দুষ্ট; দুর্গন্ধ। *Noun.* Aggressive or attacking attitude; act of an assailing party; as, to take or abandon the *offensive*; আক্রমণাত্মকভাব; আক্রমণকারিদলের কার্য্য। **—ly.** *adv.* **—ness,** *n.* **To take or abandon the offensive**—See OFFENSIVE *n.*

ŏf'-fêr, *v. t.* & *i.* 1. To present as an act of worship, sacrifice or prayer; উপহার প্রদান করা, উপায়ন প্রদান করা, নিবেদন করা, উৎসর্গ করা, বলিদান দেওয়া। 2. To present for acceptance or refusal; to proffer; গ্রহণ বা প্রত্যাখ্যানের নিমিত্ত উপস্থাপিত করা; প্রদানের জন্য প্রস্তাব করা। 3. (*Commr.*) To show or expose for sale; (বাণিজ্য) বিক্রয়ের জন্য প্রদর্শন বা উপস্থাপিত করা। 4. To make an offer to give or pay; কোন কিছু দিবার জন্য প্রস্তাব করা। 5. To present for consideration; to propose; as, to *offer* an opinion, remarks, etc.; (*also with an infinitive object*) to show one's willingness; as, to *offer* to help one; বিবেচনার জন্য উপস্থাপিত করা; প্রস্তাব করা; ইচ্ছা প্রদর্শন করা। 6. To try to show or inflict; to give; as, to *offer* resistance, violence, insult, etc.; প্রদর্শন করিতে চেষ্টা করা; দেওয়া, প্রদান করা। 7. To give opportunity to enemy for (battle); শত্রুকে (যুদ্ধের জন্য) সুযোগপ্রদান করা। 8. To show or express readiness *to* do something if desired; "I *offered* to go to the king"; কোন কার্য্য করিতে প্রস্তুত আছে বলিয়া দেখান বা প্রকাশ করা। 9. (Of things) To present to sight or notice, etc.; as, each age *offers* its characteristic riddles; (বস্তু সম্পর্কে) দৃষ্টি পথে আনা, লক্ষ্যের বিষয়ীভূত করা। *Verb i.* 1. To make an offering or sacrifice; বলি, নৈবেদ্য বা উপহার প্রদান করা। 2. To make an offer or proposal of marriage, (usu. with *to*); বিবাহের প্রস্তাব করা। 3. To present itself; to occur; "Wherever an occasion *offered*"; উপস্থিত হওয়া, সমাগত হওয়া; ঘটা। 4. (*Rare*) To make an attempt or trial (*at*); (অপ্রঃ) চেষ্টা করা, পরীক্ষা করা। **—ing,** *n.* 1. Presenting of something in worship, prayer, etc.; নিবেদন, উপায়ন, হবন। 2. Presenting of something for acceptance or rejection or for sale; গ্রহণ, প্রত্যাখ্যান বা বিক্রয়ের জন্য উপস্থাপন। 3. A sacrifice; an oblation; উপহার; বলি, উপায়ন, নৈবেদ্য, অর্ঘ, বৈতানিক, দক্ষিণা (এতেজন), দেবোপহার, দেবোপায়ন, উৎসর্গ।

ŏf'-fêr, *n.* 1. Act of offering; a proposal, esp. of marriage; প্রদান; প্রস্তাব, বিশেষতঃ বিবাহের প্রস্তাব, বিবাহের আলাপ। 2. Expression of intention or readiness to give or do something if desired or to sell on terms; প্রস্তাব। 3. A bid; (নীলামের) ডাক। 4. (*Rare*) An attempt at doing something; an aim; কোন কাজ করার জন্য চেষ্টা; লক্ষ্য। **On offer**—For sale at a certain price; নির্দ্দিষ্ট মূল্যে বিক্রেয়।

ŏf-fêr-tō-rȳ, *n.* 1. That part of the mass at which offerings are made; the offering of these or the gifts offered; খৃষ্টের অন্তিম ভোজনানুষ্ঠানের যে অংশে নৈবেদ্যাদি প্রদান করা হয়; ঐরূপ নৈবেদ্যাদি প্রদান বা প্রদত্ত নৈবেদ্যাদি। 2. A collection of money taken at a religious service; উপাসনাকালে সংগৃহীত অর্থ।

ŏf'-fice (-fĭs), *n.* 1. Special duty; task; function; বিশিষ্ট কর্ত্তব্য; ন্যস্ত কর্ত্তব্য; কর্ম্ম, বৃত্তি, ক্রিয়া। 2. A public or private employment or business; a position of trust or authority or service; চাকুরী; পদ, অধিকার (হিঃ কোঃ)। 3. Ceremonial duty; a rite; as, to perform the last *offices* to; ক্রিয়া; অনুষ্ঠান। 4. (*Eccl.*) A formulary of devotion; a prescribed form or act of worship; any occasional service, *e. g.* for the dead; (যাজকীয়শাস্ত্র) পূজা, উপাসনা, প্রভৃতি; নির্দ্দিষ্ট উপাসনা-প্রণালী বা উপাসনা; নৈমিত্তিক উপাসনা, যথা—মৃত ব্যক্তির আত্মার কল্যাণার্থ। 5. An act, good or ill, rendered voluntarily; a service; a piece of kindness; সৎ বা অসৎ কার্য্য; উপকার; দয়ার কার্য্য। 6. A place or room for transacting business; a counting-house; কর্ম্মস্থান, কার্য্যালয়; হিসাবখানা। 7. (*Pl.*) Kitchen, outhouses, etc. of a mansion or farm; রান্নাঘর, কৃষিক্ষেত্র বা প্রাসাদবাটিকার বাহিরের গৃহ সমূহ। 8. (*Collectively*) Persons transacting business in an office; as, he has notified the *office*; আফিসের কর্ম্মচারিগণ, কার্য্যালয়ের কর্ম্মচারিগণ। 9. (*Cap.*) The quarters, staff or collective authority of a Government department; as, the Foreign *office*; the War *office*; শাসনতন্ত্রের কোন বিভাগের গৃহ, কর্ম্মচারিবর্গ বা সম্মিলিত ক্ষমতা। 10. (*Colloq.*) A privy; (চলিতভাষায়), পায়খানা। 11. (*Slang*) A hint or intimation; as, to give or take the *office*; আভাষ; ইঙ্গিত। **Holy-Office**—Same as INQUISITION. **Office-bearer**—An official or officer; কর্ম্মচারী। **It is my office to do it**—It is my function to do it; ইহা আমার কাজ। **To give or take the office**—See OFFICE 11. **To perform the last offices to**—To perform the rites to the dead ; অন্ত্যেষ্টিক্রিয়া সমাপন করা। **To say office**—(*R. C. Church*) To recite the service of the breviary ; দৈনিক উপাসনা আবৃত্তি করা।

ŏf'-fi-cêr, *n.* & *v. t.* 1. A person invested with an office ; কর্ম্মচারী। 2. An office-bearer of a society or institution ; কোন সমিতি বা প্রতিষ্ঠানের কর্ম্মচারী। 3. A bailiff ; (*rare*) a constable ; নাজিরের প্যাদা ; (কচিদ্‌-ব্যবহৃত) পুলিশ কনেষ্টবল। 4. One holding a position of authority, esp. a commission in the army or navy ; সামরিক কর্ম্মচারী, নৌবিভাগের কর্ম্মচারী। 5. One holding a position of authority in the merchantile marine ; বাণিজ্য জাহাজের উর্দ্ধতন কর্ম্মচারী। *Verb t.* (*Usu. in p. p.*) To furnish with officers ; to act as a commander of ; কর্ম্মচারিসমন্বিত করা ; অধ্যক্ষের কাজ করা। **Non-commissioned officers** — See under NON-COMMISSIONED. **Relieving officer**—See under RELIEVE.

ŏf-fi'-cial (shăl), *adj.* & *n.* 1. Of, or relating to, an office ; কার্য্যালয়-সংক্রান্ত, আধিকারিক, সরকারী। 2. Serving in a public capacity ; সরকারী কার্য্যে নিযুক্ত। 3. Derived from an officer or officers ; authorized ; authoritative ; as, from *official* source : *official* statement ; কর্ম্মচারী বা কর্ম্মচারিসমূহ হইতে জাত ; ক্ষমতাপ্রাপ্ত ; কর্ত্তৃত্বসূচক। 4. (*Med.*) According to the pharmacopœia ; (ভৈষজ্য-শাস্ত্র) সুপ্রসিদ্ধ চিকিৎসকমণ্ডলীর নির্দ্দেশানুসারে প্রস্তুত। 5. Befitting to, or characteristic of, a person in office ; as, *official* solemnity ; কর্ম্মচারিসমুচিত, কর্ম্মচারিসুলভ। *Noun.* 1. A person holding, or invested with, an office of a public nature ; কর্ম্মচারী, রাজপুরুষ, রাজকর্ম্মচারী। 2. An ecclesiastical judge ; যাজকীয় বিচারক। **—dom,** *n.* **—ism,** *n.* 1. Official system or routine ; strict adherence to office-routine ; কার্য্যালয়ের ব্যবস্থা বা দৈনন্দিন কার্য্যাবলী ; কার্য্যালয়ের দৈনন্দিন কার্য্যাবলীর উপর দৃঢ় নিষ্ঠা। 2. Officials collectively ; কর্ম্মচারিবর্গ ; রাজকর্ম্মচারিবর্গ। **—ize,** *v. t.* To make official ; to bring under official control ; সরকারী করা ; সরকারী কর্ম্মচারিগণের তত্ত্বাবধানাধীনে আনা। **—ly,** *adv.* In an official manner or capacity ; by authority ; রাজকর্ম্মচারিরূপে, সরকারী কর্ম্মচারিরূপে ; উর্দ্ধতন কর্ম্মচারী-দ্বারা।

ŏf-fi'-ci-āte (-shi-), *v. i.* 1. To conduct public worship ; পূজোপাসনাদি করা। 2. To perform official duties, esp. on a particular occasion ; কার্য্যালয়-সংক্রান্ত কাজ করা, বিশেষতঃ কোন বিশেষ সময়ে। **-ant,** *n.* An officiating priest or minister ; ক্রিয়াসম্পাদনকারী পুরোহিত বা যাজক।

ŏf-fic'-i-năl, *adj.* 1. (Of a herb, drug, etc.) Used in medicine ; ঔষধ প্রস্তুতে ব্যবহৃত। 2. (Of a medicial preparation) Kept in stock by apothecaries ; (now usu. *official*) made from the pharmacopœia recipe ; (of a scientific name) adopted by the pharmacopœia ; ঔষধ বিক্রেতৃগণ কর্ত্তৃক সর্ব্বদা বিক্রয়ার্থ রক্ষিত ; সুপ্রসিদ্ধ চিকিৎসকমণ্ডলীর ব্যবস্থানুসারে প্রস্তুত ; সুপ্রসিদ্ধ চিকিৎসকমণ্ডলী কর্ত্তৃক গৃহীত। **—ly,** *adv.*

ŏf-fi'-cious (-shŭs), *adj.* Troublesome in trying to serve ; intrusive ; meddlesome ; উপযাচক ; গায়েপড়া, ফোঁপরদালাল (*colloq.*) ; অনধিকারচর্চ্চী। 2. (*Diplomacy*) Of an informal character ; unofficial, (opp. to *official*) ; not binding ; (কূট-রাজনীতি) রীতিবহির্ভূত ; বেসরকারী ; অবশ্যপালনীয় নয়। **—ly,** *adv.* **—ness,** *n.*

ŏff'-ing, *n.* 1. The part of the sea nearer to the horizon than to the shore ; বাহির দরিয়া। 2. Position at a distance from the shore ; as, to gain or keep an *offing* ; সাগরতীর হইতে দূরবর্ত্তী স্থান।

ŏff'-ish, *adj.* (*Colloq.*) Shy ; distant or stiff in manner ; (চলিতভাষায়) মুখচোরা ; অনালাপী। **—ness,** *n.*

ŏff'-scour-ing (-skowr-), *n.* (*Pl.*) Refuse ; dregs ; (*lit* & *fig.*) ; as, the *off scouring* of society or humanity ; উচ্ছিষ্ট, জঞ্জাল ; (লক্ষণায়) আবর্জ্জনা, ময়লা।

ŏff'-sĕt, *n.* 1. (*Rare*) Act of Setting off ; outset ; (অপ্রঃ) যাত্রা ; প্রারম্ভ। 2. A young shoot from a stem or root, serving to propagate the species ; (*fig.*) an off-shoot ; a scion ; প্ররোহ ; (লক্ষণায়) অঙ্কুর ; বংশধর। 3. A mountain-spur ; শৈল-বাহু। 4. A compensation ; a sum, amount or value set off against another as an equivalent ; ক্ষতিপূরণ ; সমতুল বস্তু বা মুদ্রা, তুল্য মূল্য। 5. (*Survey*) A short distance measured perpendicularly from the main line of measurement ; প্রধান মানরেখা হইতে লম্বভাবে পরিমাপিত ক্ষুদ্র দূরত্ব। 6. A bend in a pipe made to carry it past an obstacle in its course ; নলের বক্রীকৃত অংশ—যদ্দ্বারা ইহাকে কোন বাধাজনক বস্তু অতিক্রম করাইয়া নেওয়া হয়।

ŏff'-shoot, *n.* 1. (*Bot.*) A branch or shoot of a main stem ; (উদ্ভিদ্‌বিদ্যা) প্ররোহ, অঙ্কুর। 2. (*Fig.*) That which issues from another ; a descendant ; (লক্ষণায়) উদ্ভূত বস্তু ; বংশধর। 3. A branch, as of a mountain range, street, stream, etc. ; রাস্তা, নদী, পর্ব্বতশ্রেণী প্রভৃতির শাখা। 4. A derivative ; ব্যুৎপন্ন শব্দ, কৃদন্ত শব্দ।

ŏff'-spring, *n.* 1. Progeny ; a child or children ; সন্তান ; সন্তানসন্ততি, অপত্য। 2. Result ; ফল, পরিণাম।

ŏft, *adv.* Often (*Archaic except in some combind forms*) ; as, *oft*-told : *oft*-quoted ; সদা, সৰ্ব্বদা, বারংবার। **Oft-times** — (*Archaic*) Often ; (অপ্রঃ) প্রায়শঃ। **Many a time and oft**—Often ; সৰ্ব্বদা।

ŏf'-ten (-n), *adv.* & *adj.* Many times ; frequently ; in many cases ; as, the victim *often* dies of it ; বহুবার ; সৰ্ব্বদা, সদা, প্রায়শঃ ; অনেক স্থলে। ***Adj.*** (*Archaic*) Frequent ; (অপ্রঃ) সচরাচরিক। **Often times**—(*Archaic*) Often : (অপ্রঃ) সৰ্ব্বদা।

ŏg'-dō-ăd, *n.* The number eight : a group or set of eight ; আট সংখ্যা ; অষ্ট বস্তুর মিলন বা সংহতি।

ō-gee' (-gē), *n.* & *adj.* **1.** A moulding of two members, the one concave and the other convex ; এক-প্রকার স্থাপত্য-ভূষা—উহার এক অংশ মধ্যনত ও অপর অংশ মধ্যোন্নত। **2.** A line shaped like S ; ইংরাজী S অক্ষরের আকৃতি রেখা। ***Adj.*** **1.** Showing in section a double continuous curve, convex above and concave below (of a moulding) ; দ্বিতীয় বন্ধনী সদৃশ। **2.** S-shaped ; S অক্ষরের আকৃতি। **O-geed'**, *adj.* **Ogee-arch, doorway, window**—দ্বিতীয় বন্ধনীর (bracket) আকার তোরণ, দ্বার, বাতায়ন।

Ogee Mouldings.

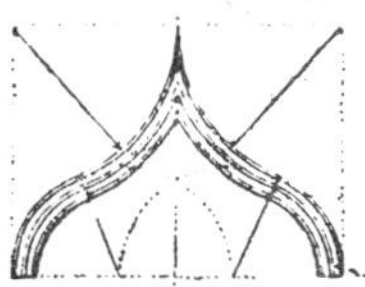
Ogee-Arch.

ŏg'-(h)ăm, *n.* **1.** An alphabet of twenty characters in use among the ancient Irish and other Celts ; one of its characters ; প্রাচীন আইরিস ও অপর কেল্ট জাতীয় লোকগণের ব্যবহৃত বিংশতি অক্ষরবিশিষ্ট বর্ণমালা ; ঐ বর্ণমালার অক্ষর। **2.** An inscription in this ; ঐরূপ অক্ষরের উৎকীর্ণ লিপি।

ō'-gīve, *n.* **1.** A diagonal groin or rib of a vault ; খিলানের কোণাকোণি শিরা। **2.** A pointed arch ; সূক্ষ্মাগ্র-তোরণ। **-gi'-val**, *adj.*

ō'-gle (-gl), *v. i.*, *t.* & *n.* To cast side glances ; to look amorously ; চোখঠারা, অপাঙ্গদৃষ্টি করা, কটাক্ষক্ষেপণ করা, আড়নয়নে চাওয়া ; কামুকের মত চাওয়া। ***Verb t.*** To view amorously with side glances ; কটাক্ষপাত করা, কটাক্ষবাণে বিদ্ধ করা। ***Noun.*** A side glance ; an amorous look ; অপাঙ্গ দর্শন, অপাঙ্গবেক্ষন, কটাক্ষ ; দৃষ্টিবিভ্রম (শকুঃ), দৃগঞ্চল (উজ্জ্বলঃ), সচিবিলোকন, লীলা-কটাক্ষ। **-gler**, *n.*

ō'-gre (-gêr), *n.* A man-eating giant ; রাক্ষস, ক্রব্যাদ। **-gress**, *n.* (*Fem.*) **-grish, -ish**, *adjs.*

O-gȳğ'-i-ăn (ō-), *adj.* **1.** Of, or relating to, Ogyges, a mythical king of ancient Attica or Bœotia ; প্রাচীন এটিকা বা বিয়োসিয়ার পৌরাণিক রাজা Ogyges সম্বন্ধীয়। **2.** Primeval ; prehistorical ; প্রাচীন ; প্রাগৈতিহাসিক, মান্ধাতার আমলের, দাদা আদমের কালের

oh (ō), *interj.* See o. **Oh God !**—ও হরি, হা ঈশ্বর।

ohm (ōm), *n.* The unit of electrical resistance ; তাড়িত প্রতিঘাতের একক, অম্‌ (হিঃ কোঃ)। **Ohm-ammeter**—তাড়িতপ্রবাহ এবং তৎপ্রতিরোধমাপক-যন্ত্র।

ohm'-mē-têr (ōm-), *n.* (*Electr.*) An instrument for indicating directly resistance in ohms ; তাড়িত-প্রবাহের প্রতিঘাত-মাপক-যন্ত্র।

ō-hō', *interj.* An exclamation of surprise or exultation ; অহো !

Oh yes — See OYEZ.

ō-ĭd'-i-ŭm, *n.* A genus of minute fungi ; একজাতীয় অতি ক্ষুদ্র ছত্রাক।

Oidium.

oil (ōyl), *n.* **1.** An unctuous liquid drawn from various animals and vegetable substances ; তৈল, তেল, স্নেহ। **2.** (Often *pl.*) Same as OIL-COLOUR ; also, a painting in oil-colour ; তৈলবর্ণ ; তৈলচিত্র। **3.** (Often. *Pl.*) Same as OIL-SKIN. **4.** Any substance of the oily consistency ; as, *oil* of vitriol ; তৈল-বৎপদার্থ। **Oil'-less**, *adj.* **Oil-bird, -nut, -palm, -seed, -tree**—যে সকল পক্ষী, বাদাম, নারিকেল, বীজ এবং গাছ হইতে তৈল পাওয়া যায়। **Oil-bush** — খাড়া টাকুর জন্য তৈলপূর্ণ কোটর। **Oilcake** — খইল, তৈল-কিট্ট, পিণ্যাক। **Oil-can**—তৈলপূর্ণ পাত্র, বিশেষতঃ কলে তৈল দেওয়ার জন্য নলাকার পাত্র। **Oil-cloth**—সফেদা মিশ্রিততৈলদ্বারা বিলেপিত ক্যাম্বিস কাপড়,—যদ্দারা গৃহতল প্রভৃতি আচ্ছাদিত করা হয়, স্নেহ-বস্ত্র, অয়েল ক্লথ, পানি-কাপড়। **Oil-coat**—জলাভেদ্য বস্ত্র দ্বারা তৈয়ারী কোর্ত্তা। **Oil-colour**—তৈলে রঞ্জকপদার্থ গুলিয়া যে রং তৈয়ার করা হয়, তৈলবর্ণ : **Oil-field**—যে প্রদেশে বা অঞ্চলে খনিজতৈল পাওয়া যায়। **Oil-gauge**—তৈলের আপেক্ষিক গুরুত্ব পরিমাপক যন্ত্রবিশেষ। **Oil-gilding, -gold** — হরিদ্রাবর্ণ রঞ্জকপদার্থে মিশ্রিত মসিনার তৈলের উপর বিন্যস্ত স্বর্ণপত্র। **Oil-gland**—তৈলস্রাবী গ্রন্থি। **Oil-hole** — যন্ত্র পিচ্ছিল করার জন্য যে রন্ধ্রপথে উহাতে তৈল ভরা হয়, তৈলরন্ধ্র। **Oil-man**—তেলী, কলু, তৈলিক, চক্রোপজীবি। **Oil-meal**—তিসির খৈলের গুঁড়া। **Oil-mill**--তৈলের কল, তৈলযন্ত্র (ভাগঃ), তৈলিক যন্ত্র। **Oil-paint**—Same as OIL-COLOUR. **Oil-painting**—তৈলচিত্র, তৈলবর্ণে চিত্রণ। **Oil-paper**—তৈল নিষেক দ্বারা জলাভেদ্য ও স্বচ্ছীকৃত কাগজ। **Oil-press**—বীজ হইতে তৈল বাহির করার জন্য পীড়ন-যন্ত্র, তৈলপীড়নযন্ত্র, কলুর ঘানি। **Oil-seed**—তিল, সর্ষপাদি। **Oil-skin**—তৈল ম্রক্ষণদ্বারা অজলাভেদ্যীকৃত বস্ত্র ; ঐরূপ কাপড়ের পোষাক।

Oil-spring—যে নির্ঝর হইতে খনিজতৈল নিঃসৃত হয়, তৈলনির্ঝর। **Oilstone**—একপ্রকার শাণপাথর—যাহাতে তৈল মাখিয়া শাণ দিতে হয়; শাণপাথর তৈয়ারের উপযোগী পাথর। **Burning oil**—জ্বালাইবার তৈল, তেজন তৈল (অর্থঃ)। **Drying oils**—যে তৈল রৌদ্রে শুকাইলে কঠিন হইয়া বার্ণিশে পরিণত হয়। **Essential** or **volatile oils**—ঔষধ ও গন্ধদ্রব্য প্রস্তুতে ব্যবহৃত তৈল। **Fatty** or **fixed oils**—জৈব বা উদ্ভিজ্জ তৈল। **Mineral oils**—See MINERAL. **Non-drying oils**—যে তৈল রৌদ্রে রাখিলে গাঁজিয়া উঠে এবং যাহা যন্ত্রাদিতে মাখিবার ও প্রদীপ জ্বালাইবার জন্য ব্যবহৃত হয়। **Oil of palms**—টাকা পয়সা। **To burn the midnight oil**—See MIDNIGHT. **To pour oil on the flame etc.**—To aggravate passion, etc.; প্রজ্বলিত অগ্নিতে ঘৃতাহুতি প্রদান করা, ক্রোধানলে ইন্ধন প্রদান করা। **To pour oil on the waters**—To smooth matters over; শান্তিবারি সেচন করা। **To pour oil on troubled waters**—উন্মত্ত বারিরাশিতে তৈলক্ষেপ করা, শান্তিস্থাপন করা। **To smell of oil**—To bear marks of study; প্রগাঢ় অধ্যয়নের চিহ্ন ধারণ করা। **To strike oil**—To discover a bed of petroleum; to make a valuable discovery; to attain prosperity or success; কেরোসিনের স্তর আবিষ্কার করা; মূল্যবান কোন কিছু আবিষ্কার করা; সমৃদ্ধি বা সিদ্ধিলাভ করা।

oil (ōyl), *v. t.* & *i.* **1.** To smear or lubricate with oil; তৈলম্রক্ষিত করা, তৈল মাখা, তৈলাক্ত করা, তৈলমর্দ্দন করা। **2.** To convert into an oily liquid; তৈলাক্ত তরলপদার্থে পরিণত করা। **3.** To impregnate or treat with oil; as, *oiled* silk; তৈলসম্পূরিত করা, তৈলম্রক্ষিত করা। ***Verb i.*** To become an oily liquid; তৈলাক্ত তরল পদার্থে পরিণত হওয়া। **Oiled silk**—তৈললিপ্ত করা হেতু জলাভেদ্য পট্টবস্ত্র। **Oil your own machine**—Mind your own affairs; নিজের চরকায় তৈল দাও। **To oil one's hand, To oil one**—To bribe him; ঘুষ দেওয়া। **To oil one's old wig**—To make the person drunk; মাতাল করা। **To oil one's tongue**—To say smooth things; to flatter; চাটু বাক্য বলা; তোষামোদ করা, তৈল দেওয়া, তৈলমর্দ্দন করা, পায় তৈল দেওয়া। **To oil the wheels**—To lubricate the wheels; (*fig.*) to make things go smoothly by courtesy, bribery, etc.; চাকায় তৈল মাখা; (লক্ষণায়) ঘুষ দিয়া, তৈলমর্দ্দন করিয়া কাজ হাঁসিল করা।

oil'-ĕr (ōyl-), *n.* One who, or that which, oils; an oil can for lubricating machinery; তৈল মর্দ্দনকারী; যন্ত্রে তৈলপ্রদানের জন্য তৈলপাত্র।

oil'-ȳ (ōyl-), *adj.* **1.** Of, relating to, or like, oil; unctuous; তৈলসম্বন্ধীয়, তৈলবৎ; তৈলময়, তেলতেলা। **2.** Covered or soaked with oil; তৈলাক্ত, তৈলময়, তৈলম্রক্ষিত। **3.** Plausible; fawning; unctuous; as, an *oily* scoundrel, word, etc.; আপাতমধুর; তোষামুদে; স্নিগ্ধ, সস্নেহ। **—i-ly**, *adv.* **—i-ness**, *n.* Oily state; স্নিগ্ধতা।

oint'-mĕnt (ōynt-), *n.* An unctuous preparation, applied to the skin for healing or beauty; unguent; মলম, অবলেপন, বিলেপন, লেপ, অক্তু; প্রলেপ, অভ্যঞ্জন, অনুলেপ, উপদেহ (চরকের টীকা), মর্দ্দনদ্রব্য।

ō-kä'-pi, *n.* A peculiar mammal closely related to the giraffe; জীরাফ জাতীয় জন্তুবিশেষ।

ōld, *adj.* & *n.* **1.** Aged; advanced in years; বৃদ্ধ; বয়োবৃদ্ধ, বয়োজ্যেষ্ঠ, বয়স্থ, স্থবির। **2.** Past the middle period of existence; as, *old* age; বৃদ্ধ। **3.** Not new or fresh; not recent; পুরাণ, পুরাতন; সাবেক, প্রাচীন, পূর্ব্বকালিক। **4.** Made long before; long established or known; ancient; বহুপূর্ব্বে প্রস্তুত; চিরন্তন, চিরপ্রতিষ্ঠিত, চিরপরিচিত; সাবেক, পুরাতন। **5.** Of age; as, three years *old*; বয়স্ক। **6.** Decayed by process of time; worn; as, *old* garment; জর্জ্জরিত; জীর্ণ। **7.** Practised; inveterate, (with *in*); as, *old in* crime, folly, diplomacy, etc.; অভিজ্ঞ; পাকা। **8.** Long past; obsolete; antiquated; bygone; former; as, the good *old* times; প্রাচীন, বহুকালিক; অপ্রচলিত; সেকেলে; অতীত; পূর্ব্ববর্ত্তী। ***Noun.*** Old time (only in *of old*); প্রাচীনকাল। **Old'-ish**, *adj.* **Old'-ness**, *n.* (*Rare*). **Old-age**—বার্দ্ধক্য, বৃদ্ধাবস্থা, জরা। **Old bachelor**—চিরকুমার। **Old Baiely**—ইংলণ্ডের সর্ব্বপ্রধান ফৌজদারী আদালত। **Old bird**—পাকা লোক—যাহাকে কোন রূপ ফাঁদে ফেলা অসম্ভব। **Old-boy**—কোন বিদ্যালয়ের প্রাচীন ছাত্র। **Old boy, chap, fellow, man**—(সাধারণতঃ সম্বোধনে ব্যবহৃত) অন্তরঙ্গ লোক। **Old clothes**—পরিত্যক্ত বস্ত্র, জীর্ণ বস্ত্র। **Old clothes-man**—পুরাতন কাপড়ের ব্যবসায়ী। **Old countries**—বহুকালযাবৎ অধ্যুষিত বা সভ্যতাপ্রাপ্ত দেশ। **Old fashions**—পুরাণ ফ্যাসন। **Old-fashioned**, *adj.* সেকেলে, প্রাচীনধরণের, সাবেক ধরণের; অপ্রচলিত। (*Old-fashionedness*, *n.*) **Old gold**—মন্দপ্রভ বা মলিনতাপ্রাপ্ত স্বর্ণের বর্ণ। **Old hand**—A practised workman; a person of experience in something or at doing something; অভিজ্ঞ কারিকর; অভিজ্ঞ ব্যক্তি, পাকা লোক। **Old London, Paris, England, etc.**—প্রাচীন লণ্ডন, প্রাচীন প্যারী; প্রাচীন লণ্ডন বা প্যারীর ভগ্নাবশেষ। **Old maid**—An old spinster; বর্ষীয়সী অনূঢ়া নারী। A precise, tidy and fidgety-man; ফিটফাট এবং চঞ্চল স্বভাবের লোক। A kind of card game; একপ্রকার তাসখেলা।

Old-maidish, *adj.* **Old school**—প্রাচীন তন্ত্র। **Old Testament**—বাইবেলের প্রাচীন নিয়ম। **Old Tom**—একপ্রকার মদ্য। **Old wine**—পুরাতন মদ, পুরাণ শীধু। **Old woman**—An aged woman; বৃদ্ধা, বুড়ী, জরতী, জরতিকা। A fussy or timid man; জটলাকারীলোক, জুজুবুড়ী। (*Old-womanish, adj. Old-womanishness, n. Old-womanliness, n. Old-womanly, adj.*) **Old-world**—*adj.* আমেরিকান নয়; প্রাচীন জগতের। **A chip of the old block**—See under CHIP. **My etc. old man**—(*Colloq.*) Husband; (চলিতভাষায়) মরদ, মিন্সে। **My etc. old woman**—(*Colloq.*) Wife; (চলিতভাষায়) স্ত্রী, গিন্নী। **Of old**—*adj.* & *adv.* Of old time; as, a man *of old*; প্রাচীন কালের। (*Adv.*) In ancient time; as, *of old* there were giants; from long age; as, I have heard it *of old*; প্রাচীনকালে; বহুদিনপূর্ব্ব হইতে। **Of old standing**—Long established; চিরপ্রতিষ্ঠিত, চিরন্তন। **Of the old school**—Old fashioned; প্রাচীন তন্ত্রের। **Old as the hills**—Very ancient; অতিপ্রাচীন। **Old/Harry, Nick, Scratch, etc.**—The devil; শয়তান। **Old head on young shoulders**—Possessing wisdom beyond one's years; জ্ঞানবৃদ্ধ (cf. বৃদ্ধত্বং জরসা বিনা।) **Old Lady of Threadneedle Street**—ইংলণ্ডের সর্ব্বশ্রেষ্ঠধনাগার, ব্যাঙ্ক অব ইংলণ্ড। **Old man of the sea**—যে লোক এমন ভাবে কাহাকে পাইয়া বসে যে তাহাকে ছাড়ানো অসম্ভব হয়, [আরব্যোপন্যাসের সিন্দবাদের ঘাড়ে যে বুড়া চাপিয়া বসিয়াছিল তাহার এই আখ্যা ছিল।] **Old man's beard**—একপ্রকার শৈবাল। **The good old times**—Customs, etc. of earlier generations; প্রাচীন কালের রীতিনীতি প্রভৃতি। **The old**—Aged people; what is not new; বৃদ্ধগণ; প্রাচীন বিষয়। **The old country, home, etc.**—ঔপনিবেশিকগণ কর্তৃক প্রাচীন বাসভূমি সম্বন্ধে কথিত হয়। **The old man**—মানবের অসংশোধিত পাপপ্রবৃত্তি। Father or guardians; পিতা বা অভিভাবক। **The old one or gentleman, The Old World**—প্রাচীন গোলার্দ্ধ (এসিয়া, ইয়ুরোপ, আফ্রিকা এবং অষ্ট্রেলিয়া)। **The old year**—পুরাতন বৎসর। **To have a fine, good, high etc. old time**—(*Slang*) To be well amused or entertained; (ইতরভাষায়) খুব আমোদ পাওয়া, খুব কৌতুক ভোগ করা। **Young and old**—Every one; আবালবৃদ্ধ-বনিতা।

öld'-en (-n), *adj.* Old; ancient; as, the *olden* time; পুরাণ, প্রাচীন; পুরাতন।

öld'-en (-n) *v. t.* & *i.* To make old or feeble with age; বৃদ্ধ করা, জরাগ্রস্ত করা। ***Verb i.*** To become old or feeble with age; বৃদ্ধ হওয়া, বার্দ্ধক্যহেতু দুর্ব্বল হওয়া।

öld'-stêr, *n.* One who is no longer a youngster; পরিণত বয়সের লোক।

ō-lē-äg'-i-nous (-nŭs), *adj.* Having the nature or qualities of oil; oily; greasy; তৈলধর্ম্মা; স্নেহাক্ত, তৈলাক্ত, তৈলময়; চর্ব্বিময়।

ō-le-ăn'-dêr, *n.* An evergreen poisonous shrub with lance-shaped leathery leaves and fine red and white flowers; করবী, করবীর [also প্রতিহাস, প্রতীহাস, হয়মার, হয়মারক, অশ্বঘ্ন, অশ্বনাশক, অশ্বমোহক, তুরঙ্গারি, কুকর, শতগ্রাস, চণ্ডাত]। **Exile and yellow oleander**—কলকাফুল (খোরী)। **Sweet-scented oleander**—করবীর।

ō-lē-ăs'-têr, *n.* 1. The wild olive; বন্য জলপাই। 2. A tree like it with yellow flowers; বন্য জলপাইয়ের মত পীতপুষ্পবান বৃক্ষ।

ō'-lē-ō-grăph, *n.* A picture painted in oils; তৈলচিত্র। **–og'-ra-phy,** *n.* Art or process of producing oleographs; তৈলচিত্রাঙ্কন, তৈলচিত্রাঙ্কনশিল্প।

ō-lē-ŏm'-ĕ-têr, *n.* An instrument for determining the density and so the purity, of oils; তৈলের ঘনতা, অতএব বিশুদ্ধতা নির্ণয়ের জন্য যন্ত্র, তৈলমাপক (হিঃ কোঃ)।

ō'-lē-ō-rĕs'-in, *n.* A natural mixture of volatile oil and resin; an artificial mixture of fixed or volatile oil and resin, etc.; উদ্বায়ী তৈল ও রজনের নৈসর্গিক মিশ্র; স্থির বা উদ্বায়ী তৈল এবং রজনের কৃত্রিম মিশ্র।

ŏl-făc'-tion, *n.* The sense of smell; act or faculty of smelling; ঘ্রাণেন্দ্রিয়; ঘ্রাণগ্রহণ। **–tive,** *adj.*

ŏl-făc'-tō-rȳ, *adj.* & *n.* Of, relating to, or concerned with, smelling; ঘ্রাণসংক্রান্ত, ঘ্রাণসম্পর্কীয়। ***Noun.*** (Usu. *pl.*) An olfactory organ; also the sense of smell; ঘ্রাণযন্ত্র; ঘ্রাণেন্দ্রিয়। **Olfactory nerves**—(See NERVE); ঘ্রাণনাড়ী (হিঃ কোঃ)। **Olfactory organ** — The nose; ঘ্রাণেন্দ্রিয়, গন্ধবহা।

ō-lĭb'-ă-nŭm, *n.* A gum-resin used as an incense; গন্ধবিরজা (বেলঃ), কুন্দুরু (বৃঃ সং), কুন্দ, কুন্দক, কুন্দু, কুন্দুরুক (সুশ্রুঃ), খোটারস, পালঙ্কী, মুকুন্দ (ভাবঃ প্রঃ), মুকুন্দু, কান্দুর (আরবী ভাষায়), লোবান (ঐ), তৈলাখ্য, শিলারস (Wilson)।

ŏl'-ĭd, *adj.* Having a rank smell; fetid; গুমসা; দুর্গন্ধ।

ŏl'-i-gärch, *n.* A member of the oligarchy; মুখ্যতান্ত্রিক।

ŏl'-i-gärch-ȳ, *n.* 1. A government by the few; a State so governed; স্বল্পসংখ্যক লোকদ্বারা পরিচালিত শাসনতন্ত্র, মুখ্যতন্ত্র (আঃ বঃ), নিয়মরহিত শিষ্টজনসভাত্মক রাজ্যপদ্ধতি; মুখ্যতন্ত্র রাজ্য। 2. Those who form the ruling few; মুখ্যতান্ত্রিক সমাজ। **–gar'-chic, –gar'-chi-cal,** *adjs.* **–gar'-chi-cal-ly,** *adv.*

ŏl-i-gō-cär'-pous (-pŭs), *adj.* Having few fruits; স্বল্পফলা।

ŏ'-li-ŏ, *n.* **1.** A dish of many ingredients ; a hotchpotch ; a stew of various meats and vegetables ; নানা উপাদানে প্রস্তুত ব্যঞ্জন ; জবা-খিচুড়ী ; বদ্ধপাত্রে একত্র সিদ্ধ বিভিন্ন প্রকার মাংস ও তরকারী। **2.** A medley ; a miscellany ; সঙ্কর, মিশ্র ; নানা দ্রব্যের সংমিশ্রণ।

ŏl-i-vā'-ceous (-shŭs), *adj.* Resembling the olive ; olive-green ; বিলাতী জলপাইয়ের মত ; বিলাতী জলপাইয়ের মত সবুজবর্ণ।

ŏl'-i-vă-rȳ, *adj.* Shaped like olive ; oval ; বিলাতি জলপাইয়ের আকার ; অণ্ডাকার।

ŏl'-ive (-ĭv), *n.* & *adj.* **1.** A plant of the genus olea ; its fruit ;

Olive.

জলপাই গাছ (Properly wild olive), জিহবৃক্ষ; জলপাই, জয়তুন (আরবী পার্সী ও হিন্দিভাষায়)। **2.** An olive branch or leaf, as an emblem of peace, (also *olive-branch*) ; শান্তির নিদর্শনস্বরূপ জলপাইগাছের শাখা বা পত্র। **3.** The wood of the olive tree ; জলপাইয়ের কাঠ। **4.** A colour of mingled violet and green, being the colour of olive ; বেগুনে ও সবুজরংয়ের মিশ্রণ-জাতবর্ণ। **5.** Kinds of gasteropod mollusc, shaped like olives ; বিলাতী জলপাইয়ের আকার উদরপদী শম্বুক। **6.** (*Cookery*, usu. *pl.*) A small slice of beef or veal rolled up and cooked ; রন্ধিত গো বা গোবৎসের মাংসের আবর্ত্তিত ক্ষুদ্র খণ্ড। **7.** An olive-shaped button for fastening a garment by insertion in a corresponding loop ; বিলাতী জলপাইয়ের আকার বোতাম। **8.** (*Colloq.*) An olive-complexioned girl or woman ; (চলিতভাষায়) যে বালিকা বা স্ত্রীলোকের বিলাতী জলপাইয়ের মত মুখের রঙ্গ। ***Adj.*** **1.** Of the colour of the green olive, (also *olive-green*) ; হরিদ্বর্ণ, বিলাতী জলপাইয়ের বর্ণের। **2.** (Of complexion) Yellowish-brown ; (মুখ-সম্বন্ধে) পীতাভবাদামি। **—i-vet, —i-vette,** *ns.* Same as OLIVE *n.* 7. **Olive-branch**—A branch of the olive as an emblem of peace ; শান্তির নিদর্শনস্বরূপ বিলাতী জলপাই গাছের শাখা। (Usu. *pl.*) A child (*Psalm* cxxviii) ; শিশু। **Olive-crown**—Garland of olive as sign of victory ; বিজয়চিহ্নস্বরূপ বিলাতী জলপাইয়ের পত্ররচিত মালিকা। **Olive-oil**—বিলাতী জলপাইয়ের তৈল। **To hold out the olive-branch**—To make overtures for reconciliation ; to show disposition for peace ; যথারীতি শান্তির প্রস্তাব করা ; শান্তি স্থাপনের জন্য ইচ্ছা প্রদর্শন করা।

ŏl'-i-vêr, *n.* A small tilt-hammer worked by the foot for shaping nails, etc. ; একপ্রকার হাতুড়ী।

Ol'-i-vêr (ŏl-), *n.* See ROLAND.

ŏl'-iv-in(e) (-ĭn), *n.* A kind of chrysoprase chiefly olive-green ; বিলাতী জলপাইয়ের মত সবুজবর্ণ মণিবিশেষ।

ŏl'-lă pō-dri'-dâ (-drē-), **ŏl'-lă,** (*Rare*) *ns.* Same as OLIO.

ŏl'-ō-ğȳ, *n.* (*Colloq.* or *humourous*) A science ; (*pl.*) the sciences ; mere theory ; (চলিতভাষায় বা রঙ্গচ্ছলে) বিজ্ঞান ; (বহুবচনে) বিজ্ঞান-সমূহ ; উপপত্তিমাত্র।

ō-lȳm'-pi-ăd, *n.* (In ancient Greece) The space of four years between one celebration of the Olympic games and another ; a system of chronology which reckons from 776 B. C. being the first year of first Olympiad ; এক অলিম্পিক ক্রীড়ার অনুষ্ঠান হইতে অপর ক্রীড়ার অনুষ্ঠান পর্য্যন্ত চারিবর্ষ কাল ; খৃঃ পূঃ ৭৭৬ অব্দ হইতে অর্থাৎ প্রথম অলিম্পিক ক্রীড়ার প্রথম বর্ষ হইতে গণিত কালগণনা পদ্ধতিবিশেষ।

O-lȳm'-pi-ăn (ŏ-), *adj.* & *n.* **1.** Of, relating to, or at, Olympia, in ancient Elis in the Peloponnesus ; অলিম্পিয়া নামক স্থানসংক্রান্ত, উক্ত স্থানে অবস্থিত। **2.** Of, or relating to, Olympus ; celestial ; গ্রীক-দেবগণের বাসভূমি অলিম্পাস গিরিসম্বন্ধীয় ; স্বর্গীয়, দিব্য। **3.** (Of manners etc.) Magnificent ; superior ; প্রতাপান্বিত ; শ্রেষ্ঠ। ***Noun.*** **1.** A native or inhabitant of Olympia ; a participator in the Olympic games ; অলিম্পিয়ার অধিবাসী ; অলিম্পীয় ক্রীড়ার ক্রীড়ক। **2.** A dweller in Olympus ; one of the greater deities of ancient Greek mythology ; অলিম্পাসপর্ব্বতের অধিবাসী ; প্রাচীন গ্রীকপুরাণে বর্ণিত শ্রেষ্ঠ দেবগণের অন্যতম। **Olympian games** — Same as OLYMPIC GAMES.

Olympian Zeus.

O-lȳm'-pic (ŏ-), *adj.* Same as OLYMPIAN *adj* 1. **Olympic games**—Games held at Olympia every four years by ancient Greeks with athletic, literary and musical competitions ; গ্রীক দেবরাজ Zeusএর পূজোপলক্ষে Olympia

নামক প্রান্তরে অনুষ্ঠিত ক্রীড়াবিশেষ—এতৎসঙ্গে কবিতা, সঙ্গীত, প্রভৃতি বিষয়ে প্রতিযোগিতা হইত। এই ক্রীড়া প্রতি চারি বৎসর অন্তে একবার অনুষ্ঠিত হইত। এই চারি বৎসর কালকে Olympiad কহে।

O-lўm'-pŭs (ŏ-), *n.* A mountain in Thessaly, being the abode of Olympian gods ; divine abode ; heaven ; গ্রীক দেবদেবীগণের বাসভূমি থেসিলির অন্তর্গত অলিম্পাস পর্ব্বত ; দেবভূমি ; স্বর্গ।

ŏm'-bre (-bêr), *n.* A popular card-game of the 17th and 18th centuries ; সপ্তদশ ও অষ্টাদশ শতাব্দীতে প্রচলিত একপ্রকার তাস খেলা।

ŏm'brŏ-grăph, *n.* (*Meteor.*) A self-registering rain-gauge ; (আবহ-বিদ্যা) একপ্রকার স্বয়ংক্রিয় বর্ষমান-যন্ত্র।

ŏm-brŏl'-ŏ-ğў, *n.* The branch of meteorology dealing with rain ; বৃষ্টিতত্ত্ব।

ŏm-brŏm'-ĕ-têr, *n.* A rain-gauge ; বর্ষমান-যন্ত্র, বৃষ্টিমান-যন্ত্র।

ō-mĕ'-gă, *n.* **1.** The last letter of the Greek alphabet ; গ্রীক-বর্ণমালার সর্ব্বশেষ অক্ষর। **2.** The last ; the end ; death ; শেষ ; অন্ত ; মৃত্যু। **Alpha and omega**—See under ALPHA.

ŏm'-ĕ-lĕt, -lette (-lĕt), *ns.* A kind of pancake or fritter ; একপ্রকার ডিমের রুটী। **Savoury omelet (te)**—ঔষধ প্রভৃতি সহযোগে প্রস্তুত ডিম্বের রুটী। **Sweet omelet(te)**—শর্করা বা মোরব্বা সহযোগে প্রস্তুত রুটী। **You cannot make an omelet (te) without breaking eggs**—End necessitates means ; কারণ বই কার্য্য হয় না।

ō'-mĕn, *n.* & *v. t.* **1.** An event or thing as a sign of something to happen ; a prognostic ; a presage ; শকুন, শাকুন ; নিমিত্ত, শুভাশুভলক্ষণ ; পূর্ব্বসূচনা। **2.** Forboding ; prognostication ; "Birds of evil *omen* fly to and fro" ; দুর্নিমিত্ত, কুলক্ষণ, অপশকুন, দুঃশকুন ; ভবিষ্যকথন। ***Verb t.*** To foreshadow ; to presage ; পূর্ব্বাভাস দেওয়া ; পূর্ব্বসূচনা করা।

ō-mĕn'-tŭm, *n.* (*Pl.*-TA) (*Anat.*) The caul ; (শারীরসংস্থান-বিদ্যা) মেদোধরা, জাল (ভাবঃ প্রঃ), বপা (সাঃ পঃ)। **-tal,** *adj.*

ŏm'-i-nous (-nŭs), *adj.* **1.** (*Rare*) Exhibiting, or being, an omen, (of good or evil) ; portentous ; অপায়া (*colloq.*), অনিষ্টসূচক ; দুর্নিমিত্তাত্মক, কুলক্ষণাক্রান্ত। **2.** Forboding evil ; inauspicious ; অমঙ্গলসূচক, অশুভসূচক, অনিষ্টসূচক ; দুর্নিমিত্তসূচক। **-ly,** *adv.*

ō-mis'-sion (-mĭ-), *n.* **1.** Act of omitting ; non-inclusion ; অকরণ ; বর্জ্জন, লোপ। **2.** The nonperformance or neglect of action or duty ; অকরণ, ত্রুটি, প্রত্যবায় (মহাঃ)। **3.** That which is omitted or left out ; বর্জ্জিত অংশ। **-sive,** *adj.* **Sins of omission and commission**—Negative and positive sins ; করণ এবং অকরণজনিত পাপ।

ō-mit, *v. t.* **1.** To leave out ; not to include ; ছাড়িয়া দেওয়া, বর্জ্জন করা, ছাড়া ; অন্তর্গত না করা। **2.** To neglect ; to leave undone ; as, to *omit* duties, doing, or to do, something ; ত্রুটি করা, অবহেলা করা, উপেক্ষা করা ; অসমাপ্ত রাখা। **-mis'-si-ble,** *adj.*

Omnia vincit amor—প্রেমে জগত বশ হয়।

ŏm'-ni-bŭs, *n.* & *adj.* **1.** A large vehicle for the conveyance of passengers at short distances ; বহুলোক বহনোপযোগী শকট, বিশ্বম্বহ (রবীঃ), গোষ্ঠীযান (মুচ্ছঃ), জনরথ (কেড়িঃ)। **2.** (Also *hotel-omnibus*) A vehicle conveying guests between a hotel and railway station ; যে বৃহৎ শকটে আগন্তুকগণ সাধারণভোজনাগার হইতে রেলওয়ে ষ্টেশনে ও ষ্টেশন হইতে সাধারণ ভোজনাগারে বাহিত হন। **3.** (Also *private* or *family omnibus*) A conveyance provided by a railway company to carry a party or luggage to, or from, a station ; রেলকোম্পানীর যে শকটে কোন পরিবারের লোক বা তাহাদের সঙ্গীয় মালপত্র ষ্টেশন হইতে বাটীতে, ও বাটী হইতে ষ্টেশনে বাহিত হয়। **4.** A man or boy assisting a waiter at an hotel, restaurant, etc. ; সাধারণ ভোজনাগারে বা জলযোগ-গৃহে যে বালক বা পুরুষ খিদমদগারকে সাহায্য করে। ***Adj.*** Pertaining to, or providing for, many things at once ; comprising many items ; বহুবস্তুসম্পর্কীয় ; বহুপ্রকরণসম্বলিত। **Omnibus bar, wire, etc.**—যে দণ্ড, তার, প্রভৃতির মধ্য দিয়া সমগ্র তাড়িতপ্রবাহ সঞ্চারিত হয়। **Omnibus box**—রঙ্গালয় প্রভৃতিতে যে বৃতিবেষ্টিত আসনশ্রেণীতে এককালে বহুলোক উপবেশন করিতে পারে। **Omnibus train**—যে গাড়ী সকল ষ্টেশনে থামিয়া থাকে।

ŏm-ni-cŏm'-pĕ-tĕnt, *adj.* Having jurisdiction in all cases ; সর্ব্ব-বিষয়ে কার্য্য করার অধিকারবান।

ŏm-ni-fā-ri'-ous (-ŭs), *adj.* Of all kinds or varieties ; সর্ব্বজাতীয়, হরেক রকমের, সকল রকমের, সর্ব্ববিধ।

ŏm-nif'-ic, *adj.* All-creating ; সর্ব্বসৃষ্টিকারী।

ŏm-niğ'-ĕ-nous (-nŭs), *adj.* Of all kinds ; সর্ব্বপ্রকারের, সকল রকমের।

ŏm-nip'-ŏ-tĕnt, *adj.* All-powerful ; সর্ব্বশক্তিমান, সর্ব্বশক্তিসমন্বিত, সর্ব্বসমর্থক, সমগ্রশক্তি, সর্ব্বশক্তিক, অপারশক্তিবিশিষ্ট, সর্ব্বকার্য্যশক্তিক। **-ly,** *adv.* **-tence,** *n.* Infinite power ; great influence ; also God ; সর্ব্ব-শক্তিমত্তা ; সর্ব্বসামর্থ্য ; পরমেশ্বর। **The Omnipotent**—সর্ব্বশক্তিমান পরমেশ্বর।

ŏm-ni-prĕs'-ence (-ĕns), *n.* State of being omnipresent ; ubiquity ; সর্ব্বগতত্ব, বিভুত্ব সর্ব্বব্যাপিত্ব, বিশ্বব্যাপকত্ব, সর্ব্বব্যাপিতা, অভিব্যাপ্তি, ত্রৈলোক্যবিস্তারত্ব, বিভুতা (হিঃ কোঃ),

বিশ্বব্যাপকতা (ঐ); সর্ব্বত্রগামিতা। **—ent,** *adj.* Ubiquitous; বিভু, সর্ব্বগামী, সর্ব্বগ, সর্ব্বগত, সর্ব্বব্যাপী (হিঃ কোঃ), বিশ্বব্যাপক।

ŏm-nĭs′-ci-ence (-nĭ-shĭ-ĕns), *n.* Infinite knowledge; wide information or the affectation of it; also, God; সর্ব্বজ্ঞতা (হিঃ কোঃ), সর্ব্বজ্ঞত্ব; অপারজ্ঞান; পরমেশ্বর। **—ent,** *adj.* One having infinite knowledge; সর্ব্ববিদ্, ত্রিকালদর্শী, সর্ব্বজ্ঞ (হিঃ কোঃ), সর্ব্ববেদী, ত্রিকালজ্ঞ, বিশ্ববেদা, সর্ব্ববেত্তা। **—ent-ly,** *adv.* **The Omniscient**—God; সর্ব্বজ্ঞ পরমেশ্বর।

ŏm′-nĭ-ŭm-găth′-ĕr-ŭm, *n.* Miscellaneous assemblage of persons or things; a confused mixture or medley; a party in which every one is invited; বিভিন্ন প্রকার ব্যক্তি বা দ্রব্যের সম্মিলন; নানাদ্রব্যের সন্নিপাত; যে প্রীতিসম্মিলনীতে সকলেই নিমন্ত্রিত হয়।

ŏm-nĭv′-ă-gănt, *adj.* Going everywhere; সর্ব্বগ, সর্ব্বত্রগ, সর্ব্বতোগামী।

ŏm-nĭv′-ŏ-rous (-rŭs), *adj.* Eating on every thing, (esp. *fig.* of reading); সর্ব্বভুক, সর্ব্বগ্রাসী, সর্ব্বখাদক, সর্ব্বাশী, সর্ব্বভোজী। **—ly,** *adv.* **—ness,** *n.* **Omnivorous reader**—যে ব্যক্তি সর্ব্বপ্রকার পুস্তকই পাঠ করে।

ō′-mŏ-plāte, *n.* The scapula; স্কন্ধাস্থি, অংসফলকাস্থি।

ŏm′-phă-lŏ-cele (-sēl), *n.* (*Med.*) Umbilical hernia; (ভৈষজ্যশাস্ত্র) নাভিবর্দ্ধন (মঃ সং)।

ŏm′-phă-lŏs, *n.* **1.** (*Anat.*) The naval; (শারীরসংস্থান-বিদ্যা) নাভি। **2.** The centre or hub; কেন্দ্র, নাভি। **3.** (*Gk. antiq.*) A boss, as of a shield; an altar of conical shape at Delphi formerly supposed to mark the centre of the earth; (গ্রীক পুরাতত্ত্ব) ঢালের উপরিস্থ টোপ; Delphi নগরীতে স্থিত মোচাকার বেদী।

m-phă-lŏt′-ŏ-mȳ, *n.* Dividing of the umbilical cord; নাভিনালচ্ছেদন, নাভিকৃন্তন, নাভিচ্ছেদন।

ŏn, *prep.* **1.** At the surface of, so as to be supported by; উপরে। **2.** With axis, pivot, basis, guarantee, confirmation, etc. consisting in; as, to work *on* a peg: based *on* fact; উপর। **3.** At or near; toward; arrived at; against; as, a hill *on* the shore: *on* the north; marched *on* Paris: to make an attack *on*; নিকটে; দিকে, অভিমুখে; আগত; বিরুদ্ধে। **4.** During; within; immediately after; as, *on* Monday: *on* arriving; as a result of; as, *on* enquiry or examination; ব্যাপিয়া; মধ্যে; অব্যবহিত পরে; ফলে। **5.** About; with respect to; concerning; as, a satire *on* society; so as to affect; as, work tells severely *on* him; বিষয়ে; সম্পর্কে; সম্বন্ধে; উপরে ক্রিয়াকারী। **6.** In addition to; as, ruin *on* ruin: loss *on* loss; উপর। **Bowling is on the wicket**—Bowling is straight; বল খুব সোজা যাইতেছে। **Gone on**—(*Slang*) Enamoured of; (ইতরভাষায়) বিমুগ্ধ। **Have you a match on you**—*i e,* about your person; তোমার কাছে কি দেয়াশলাই আছে? **Heaps on heaps**—(See ON *prep.* 6.) **On a large scale**—বিরাট রকমে। **On board a ship**—জাহাজের উপর। **On business**—কার্য্যব্যপদেশে, কার্য্যোপলক্ষে। **On duty**—কর্ত্তব্যসম্পাদনে রত। **On fire**—প্রজ্বলিত, জ্বলন্ত। **On foot**—পদব্রজে। **On guard**—প্রহরীর কার্য্যে নিযুক্ত। **On hand**—হস্তে স্থিত। **On penalty of death**—মৃত্যুদণ্ডের দায়ে। **On purpose**—Intentionally; ইচ্ছাপূর্ব্বক, উদ্দেশ্য করিয়া, মতলব আঁটিয়া। **On sale**—বিক্রয়ার্থ রক্ষিত; বিক্রেয়। **On side**—(*Foot-ball*) Not off-side; (পাদগোলক ক্রীড়ায়) কন্দুক এবং বিপক্ষদলের গোলের মধ্যবর্ত্তী স্থানের বাহির। **On the instant**—Immediately; তন্মুহূর্ত্তে, তৎক্ষণাৎ। **On the look-out**—See under LOOK. **On the move**—See under MOVE. **On the one hand**—এক পক্ষে। **On the other hand**—পক্ষান্তরে, অন্যত্র, অপরত্র। **On the wane**—ক্ষীয়মাণ। **On time, on the minute**—Punctually; ঠিক সময় মত। **On trial**—পরীক্ষাধীন। **Ruin on ruin**—See ON *prep.* 6. **To fall on knees**—হাঁটু গাড়িয়া বসা। **To go on foot**—পদব্রজে যাওয়া। **To put one on inquiring** or **inquiry**—To induce one to inquire; কাহাকেও অনুসন্ধানে প্ররোচিত করা। **To rely on**—To depend; নির্ভর করা। **To tell on**—To affect; কোনরূপ ক্রিয়া বা ফল উৎপাদন করা। **To tread on air**—To tread on one's enemies; শত্রুকে পদদলিত করা।

ŏn, *adv., adj.* & *n.* **1.** So as to be supported by something; as, to put the table cloth *on*; উপরে। **2.** In some direction; towards something; কোন দিকে; কোন কিছুর অভিমুখে। **3.** Forward; as, to move *on*; in progress; as, the game is *on*; সম্মুখে; চলিত। **4.** On the stage or platform; as, a play is *on*; রঙ্গমঞ্চে অভিনীত হইতেছে। **5.** Arranged; as, a match is *on*; স্থিরীকৃত। **6.** In continuance; as, to sleep *on*; চলিত। ***Adj.*** (*Cricket*) Designating the side of the field opposite to the *off-side*; (ক্রীকেট-ক্রীড়ায়) ত্রিদণ্ডরক্ষকের বামপার্শ্বের ক্রীড়া ক্ষেত্রাংশের সম্মুখস্থ ক্ষেত্রসূচক। ***Noun.*** (*Cricket*) The on-side; ত্রিদণ্ডরক্ষকের বামপার্শ্বের ক্রীড়া-ক্ষেত্রাংশের সম্মুখস্থ ক্ষেত্র। **Broad-side, stem, end, on**—With that part forward; ঐ সকল অংশ সম্মুখে রাখিয়া। **Gas, water is on**—*i. e.* Running or procurable by turning the tap; জল, গ্যাস প্রভৃতির কল খোলা আছে। **He is rather on**—(*Slang*) Half-drunk;

(ইতর ভাষায়) আধমাতাল। **On and off**—Same as OFF AND ON. **On and on**—Continuously; ক্রমাগত। **On drive**—*n.* (*Cricket*) A drive to the on: (ক্রীকেট ক্রীড়ায়) ত্রিদণ্ডরক্ষকের বামপার্শ্বের ক্রীড়াক্ষেত্রের সম্মুখদিকে কন্দুক তাড়ন। (*Verb t.*) (*with hyphen*) To drive to the on side; ত্রিদণ্ডরক্ষকের বামপার্শ্বস্থ ক্রীড়া-ক্ষেত্রাংশের সম্মুখদিকে কন্দুক তাড়ন করা। **On license**—A licence obtained for selling beer etc., to be drunk on the premises; ক্রেতৃগণ বীয়র প্রভৃতি দোকানে বসিয়া পান করিতে পারে—এরূপ অধিকার। **On to**—(usu. avoided in writing though common in speech) To a position on; as, to jump *on to* the stage; সম্মুখের কোন স্থানে। **On with your hat**—Put it on; টুপি পর। **To get on**—See under GET. **To speak, work or wait, on**—বলিতে থাকা, করিতে থাকা, অপেক্ষা করিতে থাকা।

ŏn'-ă-gĕr, *n.* (*pl.* -GRES, -GRI.) A wild ass; বন্য গর্দ্দভ।

ō'-năn-ism, *n.* Masterbation; [*Onan* (*Gen.* xxxviii. 9.)]; হস্ত-মৈথুন।

once (wŭns), *adv., conj.* & *n.* **1.** One time; on, or at, one occasion only; একদা, একবার; এক সময়ে। **2.** (In negative, conditional or indefinite clause, etc.) Ever; at all; as, if we *once* lose sight of him: *once* within call, we are safe; কখনও; আদৌ। **3.** At some one time in the past; formerly; as, *once* there was a king; কোন সময়ে; পূর্ব্বে। ***Conj.*** As soon as; if once; যেই মাত্র; যদি একবার। ***Noun.*** One time or occasion; as, *once* is enough for me; একবার। **At once**—Immediately; without delay; at the same time; অমনি, তৎক্ষণাৎ, সদ্য, চট্ করিয়া; অবিলম্বে; যুগপৎ। **At once stern and tender**—বজ্রাদপি কঠোরাণি মৃদুনি শিরীষাদপি। **Don't all speak at once**—এখনই না বলিলেন; কোন অনিচ্ছুক ব্যক্তির নিকট হইতে কোন বস্তুর মূল্য প্রভৃতির সম্বন্ধে কথা শুনিবার জন্য বিদ্রূপের ভঙ্গীতে বলা হয়—এখন নাইবা বলিলেন। **Once and again**—Frequently; often; প্রায়শঃ; সর্ব্বদা। **Once and away**—Same as ONCE FOR ALL, ONCE IN A WAY. **Once and for all**—Finally; definitively; আখেরের মত, জন্মের শোধ, চিরদিনের জন্য; নিশ্চিতরূপে। **Once bit twice shy**—Pain, loss, etc., teaches caution; চুণ খাইলে দধি দেখিয়াও ভয় করে, ঘরপোড়া গরু সিন্দুরে মেঘ দেখিয়া ভয় পায়। **Once in a while** or **way**—Very rarely; কচিৎ, কদাচিৎ, কালেভদ্রে। **Once more, Once again**—Another time; আবার, পুনরায়। **Once or twice, Once and again**—A few times; দুই একবার। **Once upon a time**—একদা। **This or that, once**—This or that time only; এইবার কি আর একবার।

on-cŏl'-ŏ-ğy̆ (ŏng-), *n.* (*Med.*) The study of tumours; (ভৈষজ্য-বিদ্যা) অর্ব্বুদ-তত্ত্ব। **-co-log'-i-cal,** *adj.*

on-cŏt'-ŏ-my̆ (ŏng-), *n.* (*Surg.*) The incision of an abscess or tumour; অর্ব্বুদচ্ছেদ (হঃ চঃ)।

ŏn'-com-ing (kŭm-), *n.* & *adj.* Approach; অগ্রসর। ***Adj.*** Approaching; আগামী।

on dit, (*F.*), *n.* [*Lit. They say*] A piece of hearsay; [শব্দানুযায়ী, তাহারা বলে], জনশ্রুতি, জনপ্রবাদ (cf. Sans. কিল, ইতি শ্রূয়তে)।

one (wŭn), *adj., n.* & *pron.* **1.** Single; এক। **2.** Forming a unity; (the) only; united; the same; as, *one* and undivided: the *one* way to do it: with *one* voice: remains for ever *one*; এক; একমাত্র; মিলিত; একই। **3.** A certain; as, *one* day I met him; কোন এক। **4.** Expressing a particular person or thing, etc., as contrasted with another; as, from *one* side to the other; কোন বিশেষ ব্যক্তি বা বস্তুসূচক। ***Noun.*** **1.** The number one; a unit; a symbol for it; এক; একক; ১। **2.** A single person, thing or example; as, shining *ones*; এক ব্যক্তি, এক বস্তু, এক দৃষ্টান্ত। ***Pron.*** **1.** Some person or thing, (used usu. after *any, every, some, no, such a, many a,* etc.); কোন ব্যক্তি বা বস্তু। **2.** Any person or thing whatever; as, *one* should do *one's* duty; কোনজন, কোন বস্তু। **One'-fold,** *adj.* **1.** Single; "To extract a *one-fold* lesson from his text"; একমাত্র। **2.** Simple-minded; guileless; সরল; অমায়িক। **One-eyed**—কাণা, একচক্ষুঃ, একাক্ষ। **One-hand** — Employing one hand only, as an alphabet; একমাত্র হস্ত ব্যবহারকারী। **One-handed** — Having one hand only; done, operated, or used, with one hand; একহস্ত; এক হস্ত দ্বারা সাধিত বা ব্যবহৃত। **One horse**—Drawn or worked by a single horse; (*fig.*) petty; poorly equipped; একাশ্ববাহিত, একাশ্ব-চালিত; (লক্ষণায়) সামান্য; হীনভাবে সজ্জিত। **One idea'd, -ideaed**—Possessed by a single idea; narrow-minded; একভাবান্বিত; সংকীর্ণমনাঃ। **One-legged**—Having only one leg; (*fig.*) one-sided; unequal; একপদবিশিষ্ট; (লক্ষণায়) পক্ষপাতদুষ্ট; অসম। **One-man**—Consisting of, or operated, managed, handed or performed by, one man; একজনাত্মক, এক ব্যক্তিদ্বারা পরিচালিত, ব্যবহৃত বা সম্পাদিত। **One-pair**—দ্বিতল উপরের প্রকোষ্ঠ বা প্রকোষ্ঠশ্রেণী। **Oneself**—Reflexive and emphatic apposi-tional form of *one*; নিজে, স্বয়ং।

One-sided—Having, existing, or occurring, on one side only; larger or more developed on one side; partial; prejudiced; একপার্শ্বাত্মক, একপার্শ্বস্থিত, একপার্শ্বে সংঘটিত; একপার্শ্ব বৃহৎ বা অধিকতর বিকাশপ্রাপ্ত; পক্ষপাতী, পক্ষপাতদুষ্ট; সংস্কারবদ্ধ। **One-sidedly,** *adv.* **One-sidedness,** *n.* The quality of being one; একতা, ঐক্য। **One-sided plant** — যে গাছের কাণ্ডের একপার্শ্বে পাতা বা ফুল থাকে। **One-sided street**—One with houses on one side only; যে রাজপথের কেবল একপার্শ্বে ভবনশ্রেণী বিদ্যমান থাকে। **All in one**—All combined; একেতেই সকল। **At one**—Reconciled; in agreement; পুনর্মিলিত; একমত। **Gave him one, Owe him one, That was a nasty one**—*i. e.* A blow, (*lit.* & *fig*).; এই সকল স্থলে "*one*" শব্দে আঘাত বুঝায়। **Go one better**—Bid, offer, risk, move by one point; এক বেশী ডাক। **In one word**—Briefly; to sum up; সংক্ষেপে; সংক্ষেপে বলিতে গেলে। **In the year one**—Long ago; বহুকাল পূর্ব্বে। **Is one too many for me**—Is more powerful or cunning for me; আমার চেয়ে অধিকতর চতুর বা বলবান। **It is all one to me**—It is the same thing to me; আমার পক্ষে সবই সমান। **Little ones**—Children; শিশু-সন্তানগণ। **Many a one**—Many people; বহুলোক। **Never a one**—None; কেহই না। **Number one**—Oneself, as an object of selfish care; স্বয়ং। **One and all**—Every one; সকলে, আপামর-সাধারণ, আবালবৃদ্ধবনিতা। **One and six pence**—এক শিলিং ৬ পেন্স। **One and twenty-one**—একুশ। **One and twentieth**—Twenty first; একবিংশতম। **One another**—Reciprocally; পরস্পর, অন্যোন্য, ইতরেতর। **One by one, One after another**—Singly; one at a time; successively; একে একে; এক এক জন করিয়া; পর পর। **One man in a thousand, ten thousand**—Relatively few; হাজারের মধ্যে একজন। **One man one vote**—The principle of equality in voting; প্রতি ব্যক্তির একটী মাত্র ভোট দেওয়ার ক্ষমতা। **One man's meat is another man's poison**—একের পক্ষে যাহা অমৃত অপরের পক্ষে তাহা বিষতুল্য। **One of these days**—Soon; এরই মধ্যে একদিন, শীঘ্রই, অবিলম্বেই। **One or the two people**—A few people; অল্প লোক। **One with another**—On the average; গড়ে। **Remains for ever one**—Remains always the same; চিরদিন একরূপ থাকে। **Ten to one**—High probability; as, it is *ten to one* that he will come; খুব সম্ভাবনা। **The all and the one** — Totality and unity; সামগ্র্য ও একত্ব। **The Evil one**—The devil; শয়তান। **The Holy one, One above**—God; ঈশ্বর। **To become one**—To coalesce; একীভূত হওয়া। **Were made one**—Were married; বিবাহবন্ধনে আবদ্ধ হইয়াছিল। **Will you make one** — (*Archaic*) Will you join the party?; (অপ্রঃ) তুমি কি আমাদের সহিত যোগদান করিবে?

ō-nei-rō-crit'-ic (-nī-), *n.* An interpreter of dreams; স্বপ্নবিচারী। **–i-cal.** *adj.* **–i-cism,** *n.*

ō-nei'-rō-măn-c̄y (-nī-), *n.* Divination by dreams; স্বপ্নফল বিচার।

one'-nĕss (wŭn-), *n.* **1.** State of being one; একত্ব (হিঃ কোঃ)। **2.** State of being unique; singularity; অদ্বিতীয়ত্ব; অদ্ভুতত্ব। **3.** Wholeness; union; unity; সামগ্র্য; সংযোগ; ঐক্য। **4.** Agreement; মতৈক্য। **5.** Sameness; identity; immutability; অভিন্নতা; অভিন্নতা; নিত্যতা, কৈবল্য (হিঃ কোঃ)।

on'-ĕr (wŭn-), *n.* **1.** An extraordinary or pre-eminent person or thing; also, a severe blow; অসাধারণ লোক বা বস্তু, অদ্বিতীয় ব্যক্তি; প্রচণ্ড আঘাত। **2.** (*Colloq.*) Something denoted or characterized by one; as, a *one*-run hit at cricket; (চলিতভাষায়) একদ্বারা সূচিত বস্তু। **A oner at**—An expert in; কোন বিষয়ে সিদ্ধহস্ত। **To give a oner**—To give one a severe blow; কাহাকে আচ্ছা এক ঘা লাগান।

ŏn'-êr-ous (-ŭs), *adj.* **1.** Burdensome; heavy; involving trouble; গুরুভার দুর্ব্বহ, দুর্ভর, দুঃসহ; গুরুতর; পীড়াজনক, ক্লেশজনক, কষ্টকর। **2.** Of the nature of a legal burden or obligation; বিধিসঙ্গত বাধ্যবাধকতা-সূচক। **–ly,** *adv.* **–ness,** *n.* **Onerous property**—বাধ্যবাধকতা-যুক্ত সম্পত্তি।

ŏn'-făll, *n.* Assault; আপতন, আক্রমণ।

ŏn'-flow (-flō), *n.* An onward flow; সম্মুখের দিকে প্রবাহ।

ŏn'-gō-ing, gō'-ing-ŏn, *ns.* **1.** Act of going forward; progress; অগ্রগমন; অগ্রগতি। **2.** (*Pl.*) Proceedings, usually strange or improper; অদ্ভুত বা অসঙ্গত আচরণ।

ŏn'-hăng-êr, *n.* Same as HANGER ON

on'-ion (ŭn-yŭn), *n.* & *v. t.* A plant with a bulbous root; its root much used in cooking, etc.; পেঁয়াজগাছ; পেঁয়াজ, পলাণ্ডু [also লতার্ক, তুদ্রুম, মুকন্দক, মুখগন্ধক, নীচভোজ্য, মুখদূষণ, সুকন্দ, মহাকন্দ, তীক্ষ্ণকন্দ]। ***Verb t.*** **1.** To rub as eyes with onion to make them water; জল বাহির করার জন্য চোখে পেঁয়াজ ঘর্ষণ করা। **2.** To season with onions; ব্যঞ্জনাদিতে পেঁয়াজ দেওয়া। **–y,** *adj.* Seasoned or flavoured with onions ; পলাণ্ডুমিশ্রিত, পলাণ্ডুবাসিত। **Onion-couch, –grass, –twitch**—একপ্রকার বন্য যই গাছ। **Onion-eyed**—সজল চক্ষু। **Onion-shell**—একপ্রকার শম্বুক জাতীয় প্রাণী।

ŏn'-lo͝ok-ĕr, *n.* Same as LOOKER-ON.

ōn'-lȳ, *adj.* 1. Sole ; single ; অনন্য ; একমাত্র। 2. (*Fig.*) Prominent ; chief ; "Motley's the *only* wear" ; (লক্ষণায়) প্রধান ; মুখ্য।

ōn'-lȳ, *adv.* & *conj.* 1. Solely ; merely ; exclusively ; একমাত্র ; শুদ্ধ, কেবল ; একান্তভাবে। *Conj.* 1. Except ; were it not *that* ; as, he does well, *only that* he is nervous at the start : I would do it *only that* I know not the means ; ব্যতীত ; যদি তাহা না হইত। 2. It must however be added ; but then ; as, he makes good resolutions *only* he never keeps them ; ইহা অবশ্য বলিতে হইবে ; কিন্তু, তবে। **Came only yesterday**—*i. e.* No longer ago ; সেদিন এসেছিল। **If only**—যদি কেবল। **I only thought I would do it**—I formed the design but did not execute it, or did it without external instigation ; আমি সংকল্প করিয়াছিলাম—কিন্তু কার্য্যটী সম্পাদন করি নাই, অথবা বাহিরের প্ররোচনা বিনা ইহা করিয়াছিলাম। **Not only but (also)**—শুধু তাহাই নহে। **Only not**—All but ; little else than ; প্রায় ; কেবল নয়। **Only too glad, true, etc.**—Glad, true, etc. not as might be expected ; যতটা আশা করা যাইত—ততটা সুখী বা সত্য নয়। **Only you** or **you only can guess**—*i. e.* No one else can guess ; তুমিই কেবল অনুমান করিতে পার। **You can only guess** or **guess only**—*i. e.* You can do no more ; তুমি কেবল অনুমানই করিতে পার।

ŏ-nŏm'-ă-tŏp(e), *n.* An onomatopœic word ; ধ্বন্যাত্মকশব্দ।

ŏn-ŏ-măt-ŏ-pœ'-ia (-pē-ă), *n.* 1. Formation of names or words in imitation of sounds made by, or associated with, the thing signified ; শব্দানুকৃতি, অব্যক্তানুকরণ (শকুঃ)। 2. A word so formed, (*e. g.* cuckoo) ; অনুকারশব্দ, অনুকরণ শব্দ। **–ic, –po-et'-ic,** *adjs.* Of, or relating to, onomatopœia ; imitative in origin ; echoic ; ধ্বন্যাত্মক ; অনুকরণাত্মক ; প্রতিধ্বন্যাত্মক। **–i-cal-ly,** *adv.*

ŏn'-rŭsh, *n.* A rushing onward ; ধাবন। **–ing,** *adj.* Rushing onward ; ধাবমান।

ŏn'-sĕt, *n.* 1. Attack ; assault, esp. of an army ; আক্রমণ, অবস্কন্দ ; আপতন। 2. Impetuous beginning or start ; as, at the first *onset* ; ভীষণ আক্রমণ।

ŏn'-slaught (-slät), *n.* An onset ; a furious attack ; ভীষণ আক্রমণ ; প্রচণ্ড আক্রমণ, অবপাত।

ŏn-tŏ-gĕn'-ĕ-sis, *n.* Origin and development of an individual organism ; জীবাবয়বের উৎপত্তি ও বিকাশ, ব্যক্ত্যঙ্গজাল (হিঃ কোঃ)। **–ge-net'-ic,** *adj.* **–ge-net'-i-cal-ly,** *adv.* **–tog'-e ny,** *n.* Same as ONTOGENESIS ; also embryology : ভ্রূণতত্ব, ব্যক্তিজনি (হিঃ কোঃ)।

ŏn-tŏl'-ŏ-gȳ, *n.* The science of being or reality ; that part of metaphysics relating to the essence of things or being in the abstract ; তত্ত্ব-দর্শন (বিশ্বঃ), সত্ত্ববিচার (আঃ বঃ), ভূতমাত্রবিচার, তত্ত্বমাত্র-মীমাংসা (ঐ) ; তত্ত্ব-বিদ্যা, সত্তাশাস্ত্র (হিঃ কোঃ)। **–gist,** *n.* **–to-log'-i-cal,** *adj.* **–to-log'-i-cal, –ly,** *adv.*

ō'-nŭs, *n.* A burden or responsibility ; ভার, দায়িত্ব। **Onus probandi**—Burden of proof ; প্রমাণের ভার, প্রমাণের দায়িত্ব।

ŏn'-ward (-wĕrd), *adv.* & *adj.* 1. Forward ; towards the front ; with advancing motion ; সম্মুখে ; সম্মুখের দিকে ; ক্রমশঃ বর্দ্ধিতগতিতে। 2. In front ; as, it lies farther *onward* ; সম্মুখে। *Adj.* Directed onward ; পুরোবর্ত্তী, অগ্রবর্ত্তী, সম্মুখবর্ত্তী। **–wards,** *adv.* Same as ONWARD.

ō-nȳch'-ĭ-ă, *n.* (*Med.*) An abscess round the finger-nail ; a whitlow ; (ভৈষজ্য শাস্ত্র) নখস্ফোটক ; আঙ্গুলহাড়া।

ŏn'-ȳ-mous (-mŭs), *adj.* Not anonymous ; বেনামী নয়।

ŏn'-ȳx, *n.* 1. A kind of quartz consisting of plane layers of different colours ; সুলেমানি পাথর। 2. (*Path.*) Opacity of the lower part of the cornea of the eye ; (নিদানশাস্ত্র) চক্ষুর সম্মুখভাগের স্বচ্ছাবরণের নিম্নাংশের অস্বচ্ছতা। **Onyx marble**—একপ্রকার মর্ম্মর-প্রস্তর।

ō-œ'-ci-ŭm (-ē-shĭ-), *n.* (In polyzoons) An ovicell ; ডিম্বকোষ।

o͞of, *n.* (*Slang*) Money ; cash ; (ইতরভাষায়) টাকাপয়সা ; নগদ টাকা। **Oof'-ȳ,** *adj.* **Oof-bird** — A wealthy person ; ধনী লোক, টাকার গাছ, টাকার কুমীর।

ō-ŏg'-ă-mous (-mŭs), *adj.* Reproducing by the union of male and female cells ; পুং ও স্ত্রীকোষের সংযোগে জাত।

ō-ō-gĕn'-ĕ-sis, *n* The production, or development of an ovum ; রজোডিম্বের উৎপাদন বা বিকাশ, রজোডিম্বোৎপত্তি।

ō-ō-gō-nĭ-ŭm, *n.* (*Bot.*) The female reproductive organ in the thallophytes or lower cryptogams ; (উদ্ভিদবিদ্যা) নিম্নশ্রেণীর অপুষ্পক উদ্ভিদের স্ত্রীচিহ্ন, যোষাস্থলী (সাঃ পঃ)।

ō'-ō-līte, *n.* A species of limestone ; the roestone ; একপ্রকার চূর্ণ পাথর ; মাছের ডিম্বের মত দানাদার চূর্ণ প্রস্তর, মৎস্যাণ্ড শিলা। **–lit'-ic,** *adj.*

ō-ŏl′-ŏ-ġy̆, *n.* 1. The study of birds' eggs ; পক্ষিডিম্বতত্ত্ব। 2. The practice of collecting birds' eggs ; পক্ষিডিম্বসংগ্রহ। **—gist**, *n.* **—o-log′-i-cal**, *adj.*

ōō′-păk, —păck, *ns.* A kind of black tea ; একপ্রকার কালো চা।

ō′-ŏ-phōre, ō′-ŏ-phīte, *ns.* (*Bot.*) The stage in which the sexual organs are developed ; (উদ্ভিদ্‌বিদ্যা) সঙ্গমজনন, যে অবস্থাতে জননযন্ত্রসমূহ বিকাশপ্রাপ্ত হয়।

ō′-ŏ-spêrm, *n.* 1. A fertilized egg or female cell ; পুংবীর্য্যনিষিক্ত ডিম্ব বা স্ত্রীকোষ। 2. (*Bot.*) Same as OOSPORE.

ō′-ŏ-spōre, *n.* 1. (*Bot.*) The fertilized female cell forming the germ of a future plant ; (উদ্ভিদ্‌বিদ্যা) পুংবীর্য্যনিষিক্ত স্ত্রীকোষ, যোষাঙ্কুর (সাঃ পঃ)। **—os′-po-rous**, *adj.*

ooze (ōōz), *n.* 1. Soft mud or slime, esp. in a river-bed, etc. ; কর্দ্দম, পঙ্ক, বিশেষতঃ নদী প্রভৃতির গর্ভস্থ কর্দ্দম। 2. The liquor of a tan-vat ; ভাণ্ডস্থ চর্ম্মশোধকতরলপদার্থ। 3. Act of oozing ; gentle flow ; something that oozes ; a slow stream ; অভিষ্যন্দন, পরিস্যন্দন ; স্রব ; ক্ষরণশীলবস্তু ; মৃদুস্রোতঃ।

ōō′-zy̆, *adj.* 1. Miry ; কর্দ্দমময়, সকর্দ্দম, সপঙ্ক। 2. Exuding moisture ; damp with exuded moisture ; slimy ; ক্ষরণশীল ; স্যাঁতস্যেঁতে ; পিচ্ছিল। **—zi-ly**, *adv.* **—zi-ness**, *n.* **Ooze-calf** — রঞ্জকপদার্থ প্রবিষ্ট গোবৎস-চর্ম্ম।

ooze (ōōz), *v. i.* & *t.* 1. (Of a liquid or moisture) To exude or percolate through the pores of a substance or body ; (of a substance) to exude moisture ; অভিষ্যন্দিত হওয়া, চুয়াইয়া পড়া ; রসনির্গত করা। 2. (*Fig.*) To leak *out*, or *away* ; as, the secret *oozed out* : his courage was *oozing away* ; (লক্ষণায়) প্রকাশ হইয়া পড়া, ধীরে ধীরে নিঃশেষ হওয়া, তিলে তিলে ক্ষীণ হওয়া। ***Verb t.*** To emit, as moisture, etc., also (*fig.*) ; as, to *ooze out* information, encouragement, etc. ; নিঃসৃত করা, বাহির করা। **Oo′-zing**, *n.* The act of exuding or percolating ; অভিষ্যন্দন, পরিস্যন্দন।

ō-păc′-i-ty̆, *n.* 1. State of being opaque ; non-transparency ; অপারদর্শকত্ব, প্রকাশাভেদ্যতা, প্রকাশ-প্রতিবন্ধকত্ব ; অস্বচ্ছতা। 2. Darkness ; obscurity ; অন্ধকার ; অস্পষ্টতা। 3. (*Rare*) State of not reflecting light ; (কচিৎ ব্যবহৃত) অনালোক-প্রতিবিম্বকতা, অরশ্মিপরাবর্ত্তনতা, কিরণ-রোধকত্ব, কিরণাবরোধকত্ব (হিঃ কোঃ)। 4. Imperviousness to sound, electric waves, etc. ; (ধ্বনি, তাড়িত-প্রবাহ প্রভৃতি সম্পর্কে) অপ্রবেশ্যতা। 5. Obscurity of meaning ; mental obtuseness ; dullness ; also, a dull person ; অস্পষ্টার্থতা ; স্থূলবুদ্ধিতা ; অপ্রখরতা ; স্থূলবুদ্ধি ব্যক্তি।

ō′-pah (-pă), *n.* A large sea-fish of the mackerel family ; একপ্রকার—বৃহৎ সামুদ্রিক মৎস্য।

ō′-păl, *n.* 1. A precious stone of various colours coming under the class of pellucid gems ; ইন্দ্রধনুবৎ বিচিত্রবর্ণলীলা প্রদর্শক দুগ্ধবর্ণ মূল্যবান প্রস্তর বিশেষ, উপলমণি, ক্ষীর-স্ফটিক। 2. (*Com.*) Same as OPALINE. **—es′-cence**, *n.* A play of various colours as in the opal ; milky iridescence ; উপলঝলক (হিঃ কোঃ), বিচিত্রবর্ণলীলা ; দুগ্ধবর্ণোচ্ছ্বাসপূর্ণ ইন্দ্রচাপ-বর্ণত্ব। **—es′-cent, —esque′**, *adjs.* Iridescent ; ইন্দ্রচাপবর্ণ। **Common opal**—পীত, রক্ত এবং শ্যামলপ্রভা প্রতিফলনশীল দুগ্ধশুভ্র উপলমণি বিশেষ।

ō′-păl-īne, *adj.* & *n.* Like opal in colour ; iridescent ; উপলমণিবর্ণ ; ইন্দ্রায়ুধবর্ণ। ***Noun.*** Semi-translucent white glass ; অর্দ্ধস্বচ্ছ শ্বেতকাচ। **—ize**, (*v. t.* & *i.*) To make iridescent like an opal ; উপলমণির মত ইন্দ্রায়ুধদ্যুতি করা। (*Verb i.*) To exhibit a play of colour like an opal ; উপলমণির মত ইন্দ্রায়ুধ-বর্ণ প্রদর্শন করা।

ō-paque′ (-pāk), *adj.* & *n.* 1. Not reflecting or emitting light ; not shining ; অনচ্ছ ; অনুজ্জ্বল, অপারদর্শক (হিঃ কোঃ)। 2. Not transparent ; অস্বচ্ছ। 3. Impervious to heat, electricity, etc. ; তাপ, তাড়িত প্রভৃতি দ্বারা অভেদ্য, কিরণাবরোধক (হিঃ কোঃ)। 4. Not lucid ; obscure ; অপ্রাঞ্জল ; অস্পষ্টার্থ। 5. Dull-witted ; stupid ; স্থূলবুদ্ধি ; মূর্খ। ***Noun.*** 1. Something opaque ; darkness ; (*lit.* & *fig.*) ; অস্বচ্ছ বস্তু ; অন্ধকার (শব্দানুযায়ী ও লক্ষণায়)। 2. A shade for the eyes ; নেত্রাবরক। **—ly**, *adv.* **—ness**, *n.* **The opaque**—Darkness ; অন্ধকার।

ōpe, *v. t.* & *i.* (*Poet.*) Same as OPEN.

ō′-pen (-pn), *adj.* & *n.* 1. Not shut or closed ; উন্মুক্ত, খোলা। 2. Not enclosed or confined ; uncovered ; exposed ; উদ্‌ঘাটিত, অবাধিত ; অনাবৃত ; খোলা। 3. Not secret or disguised ; public ; manifest ; as, an *open* scheme : *open* contempt ; অছদ্ম, অপ্রচ্ছন্ন ; প্রকাশ্য ; স্ফুট। 4. Sincere ; frank ; candid ; kind ; as, an *open* heart ; সরল ; অকপট ; অমায়িক ; সদয়। 5. Not folded ; expanded ; spread out ; as, with *open* arms ; স্ফুট, ফুল্ল ; প্রস্ফুট, বিকচ, বিকশিত ; বিস্তারিত। 6. With intervals ; as, *open* teeth : *open* ranks ; loose ; porous ; ফাঁক ফাঁক ; আল্গা ; সচ্ছিদ্র। 7. Free to be visited or used ; accessible ; "Courses *open* to us" ; মুক্তদ্বার, অবারিত দ্বার ; সুলভদর্শন। 8. Liable or subject *to* ; as, *open to* question or criticism ; অধীন। 9. Accessible to appeals, emotions, ideas, etc. ; amenable *to* ; "I will not name a price but I am *open* to offers" ; বশ্য ; বশ, বাধ্য। 10. (*Phonet.*, of vowels) Produced with wider opening of the mouth than those called close ; (of a syllable) ending in a vowel ; অধিকতর মুখব্যাদানপূর্ব্বক উচ্চারিত ; স্বরান্ত। 11. Not settled ; as, an *open* account or question ; অমীমাংসিত, অপরিশোধিত। 12. Generous ; liberal ; as, with *open* hand ; উদার ; মুক্ত। 13. Not frosty, as a season, weather, etc. ; অতুষারবদ্ধ। *Noun.* (With *the*) An open space or country ; open air ; public view ; মুক্তস্থান বা দেশ ; মুক্তবাতাস ; প্রকাশ্যতা। **—ness,** *n.* **Open air**—Unconfined space ; outdoors ; মুক্তস্থান, ফাঁকা জায়গা ; বাটির বাহির। (*Attrib., with hyphen*) out-door ; খোলা জায়গায়। **Open-armed** — With open arms ; hearty ; বাহুবিস্তার করিয়া ; আন্তরিক। **Open boat**—পাটাতনহীন নৌকা। **Open champion** or **scholarship**—অবাধ প্রতিযোগিতায় কৃতকার্য্য ব্যক্তি বা প্রাপ্তবৃত্তি। **Open-country** — বৃতিহীন দেশ ; নির্ব্বন প্রদেশ। **Open daylight**—স্পষ্টদিবালোক। **Open ears**—Eagerly attentive ears ; উৎকর্ণ। **Open-eared,** *adj.* **Open-eyed**—Having open or watchful eyes ; vigilant ; সতর্ক, সাবধান। **Open face**—সারল্যমাখা মুখ, মুগ্ধানন। **Open-faced,** *adj.* **Open-handed**—Having the hand open ; liberal ; munificent ; মুক্তহস্ত, উদারহস্ত ; উদার ; দানশীল। **Open-handedly,** *adv.* **Open-handedness,** *n.* **Open-heart**—Frankness ; unsuspiciousness ; kindliness ; cordiality ; খোলা মন, সরলতা ; সন্দেহশূন্যতা ; সদয়ভাব ; হৃদ্যতা। **Open-hearted,** *adj.* Frank; full of kindly feeling ; generous ; সরল ; সদয়হৃদয় ; উদারচিত্ত। **Open-heartedly,** *adv.* **Open-heartedness,** *n.* **Open ice**—Ice through which navigation is possible ; যে বরফের ভিতর দিয়া জাহাজ প্রভৃতি চালনা করা যাইতে পারে। **Open-mind**—Accessibility to new ideas ; unprejudiced or undecided state ; নবভাবগ্রহণে সমর্থ সংস্কারশূন্যমন ; সংস্কারশূন্যভাব, অনিশ্চিতাবস্থা। **Open-minded,** *adj.* **Open-mindedly,** *adv.* **Open-mindedness,** *n.* **Open-mouthed**—Having the mouth open ; rapacious ; ব্যাদিতমুখ ; লুব্ধ। Gaping with surprise, etc. ; বিস্ময়ে ব্যাদিত মুখ। Speaking freely ; vociferous ; খোলাখুলিভাবে কথিত ; উচ্চনিনাদী। **Open-mouthedness,** *n.* **Open-order**—(*Mil.* & *Nav.*) Formation with wide intervals between soldiers or ships ; খুব ফাঁক ফাঁক রণপোত বা সৈন্যসন্নিবেশ। **Open-question**—One on which differences of opinion are legitimate ; যে প্রশ্নসম্পর্কে বিভিন্ন মত পোষণ করা যাইতে পারে। **Open sea** — (*Inter. Law*) The main sea ; বাহির দরিয়া। **Open-table**—A table open to all for dinner, etc. ; সকলের ভোজনের জন্য অবারিত ভোজনদ্রব্যসজ্জিত মেজ। **Open time**—That which is not close time for fish ; মৎস্য প্রভৃতি শিকারের জন্য অনিষিদ্ধকাল। **Open verdict**—মৃত্যুর কারণ অজ্ঞাত থাকিলে, অনুসন্ধানের পর যে মত দেওয়া হয়। **Open-weather, winter**—See OPEN *adj.* 13. **Open work, open-work**—যে সূচের কাজে মাঝে মাঝে ফাঁক রাখা হয়। **An open secret**—An information though not formally declared yet known to all ; যে সংবাদ যথারীতি জনসাধারণ্যে বিজ্ঞাপিত না হইলেও সকলেরই বিদিত থাকে। **Bowels are open**—*i. e.* Not constipated ; কোষ্ঠবদ্ধ নয়। **He has an open hand**—He gives freely ; সে অকাতরে দান করে। **Open as the day**—Entirely without hypocrisy or deception ; নিষ্কপট। **The exhibition is now open**—প্রদর্শনী এখন খোলা আছে। **The open**—See OPEN *n.* **The open door**—Free admission of foreign nations to a country for trade ; কোন দেশে ব্যবসায়ের জন্য বৈদেশিক জাতিসমূহের অবাধ প্রবেশাধিকার, মুক্তদ্বার। **The river** or **harbour is open**—নদী বা পোতাশ্রয় তুষারনির্ম্মুক্ত। **To keep open doors** or **house**—To entertain all comers ; to be hospitable ; সমস্ত আগন্তুককে আতিথ্যসংকার দ্বারা আপ্যায়িত করা ; অতিথিসৎকারপরায়ণ হওয়া। **To lay open**—To lay bare as by cutting skin etc. of ; উদ্ঘাটিত করা, চর্ম্ম প্রভৃতি কাটিয়া বাহির করা। **Will be open with you**—Will speak frankly with you ; তোমার সহিত প্রাণ খুলিয়া কথা বলিব। **With open arms**—Heartily ; gladly ; বাহুবিস্তার করিয়া ; সানন্দে। **With open eyes**—Not unconsciously or under misapprehension ; also, in eager attention or surprise ; জ্ঞাতসারে, জ্ঞানপূর্ব্বক ; বিস্ময়বিস্ফারিত নেত্রে। **With open hand**—Liberally ; freely ; মুক্ত হস্তে ; অকাতরে। **With open mouth**—With mouth open to speak ; frankly ; also, gaping with wonder, etc ; কথা বলিবার জন্য মুখব্যাদানপূর্ব্বক ; সরলভাবে ; বিস্ময়ে হাঁ করিয়া।

ō'-pen (-pn), *v. t.* & *i.* **1.** To make open ; to unclose ; to clear of obstruction, as a road, etc. ; উদ্ঘাটন করা, ব্যাদান করা ; খোলা ; নির্ম্মুক্ত করা। **2.** To reveal, as one's designs ; ব্যক্ত করা, প্রকাশ করা। **3.** To enlighten ; to expand or enlarge ; as, to *open* the mind or heart ; সন্দেহ দূর করা ; প্রশস্ত করা। **4.** To make unobstructed as the bowels ; কোষ্ঠ খোলাসা করা। 5. To cut ; to make ; as, *to open* a boil or chasm ; কাটা ; করা। 6. To begin or start ; as, to *open* a discussion or an account ; আরম্ভ করা, সুরু করা। 7. To loosen, as matted cotton, etc. ; আলগা করা। 8. To declare, esp. formally, to be open to the public as a building, park, etc. ; উদ্‌ঘাটিত বলিয়া যথারীতি ঘোষণা করা। 9. (*Naut.*) To bring into view by a change of position ; as, untill we *opened* a bay ; (নৌ-বিদ্যা) অবস্থান পরিবর্তন দ্বারা দৃষ্টিগোচর করা। 10. (*Law*) To state as a case to a court, preliminary to adducing evidence; (আইন) সাক্ষ্য প্রমাণ উপস্থাপনের পূর্ব্বে মোকদ্দমার বৃত্তান্ত বিচারকের সমক্ষে বর্ণনা করা। ***Verb i.*** 1. To become open or unclosed ; উন্মুক্ত হওয়া, উদ্‌ঘাটিত হওয়া। 2. To give access ; to have an opening or outlet ; as, the door *opened* into a lawn ; প্রবেশ করিতে দেওয়া ; প্রবেশ বা নির্গম পথ থাকা। 3. (*Naut.*) To appear in view ; to come into sight ; as, the harbour light *opened* ; (নৌ-বিদ্যা) দৃষ্টিপথারূঢ় হওয়া ; দৃষ্টিগোচর হওয়া। 4. (*Hunting*) To bark on perceiving the game ; (মৃগয়া) শিকারের সন্ধান পাইয়া চীৎকার করা। 5. To begin to speak ; as, he *opened* upon the fiscal question ; বলিতে আরম্ভ করা। 6. To make a start ; as, the stock *opened* at par ; আরম্ভ হওয়া। 7. To expand or spread out ; (*fig.*) to expand in intellect or sympathy ; বিকশিত হওয়া, প্রস্ফুটিত হওয়া ; (লক্ষণায়) বুদ্ধিবৃত্তি বিকশিত হওয়া, হৃদয় প্রশস্ত হওয়া। **—a-ble,** *adj.* **—er,** *n.* **Java sugar opened active**—জাভা চিনির তৎক্ষণাৎ চাহিদা হইয়াছিল। **Not to open lips**—To remain silent ; চুপ থাকা। **Open Sesame**—সিসেম দ্বার খোল। [আরব্যোপন্যাসের আলিবাবা ও চল্লিশজন দস্যুর আখ্যায়িকায় যে মন্ত্র উচ্চারণে দস্যুগণ দ্বার খুলিত।] অব্যর্থ উপায়, মুক্তিমন্ত্র। **To open a business, shop, campaign, etc.**—To start or establish it ; দোকান খোলা, দোকান ফাঁদা (*colloq.*), কারবার খোলা। **To open a case**—See OPEN *v. t.* 10. **To open bowels**—To cause evacuation ; কোষ্ঠ পরিষ্কার করা। **To open a prospect**—(*lit.* & *fig.*) To bring it to view ; কোন স্থানের বিস্তৃত প্রাকৃতিকদৃশ্য নয়নপথবর্ত্তী করা, ভবিষ্যতের চিত্র মানসনেত্রগোচর করা। **To open fire**—গুলি ছুঁড়িতে আরম্ভ করা, গোলা বর্ষণ আরম্ভ করা। **To open ground**—লাঙ্গল প্রভৃতির সাহায্যে ভূমি কর্ষণ করা। **To open one's designs**—কাহারো সংকল্প প্রকাশ করা। **To open one's eyes**—To notice ; to look ; also, to show surprise ; লক্ষ্য করা ; দৃষ্টি করা ; বিস্ময়ে চক্ষু বিস্ফারিত করা। **To open one's shoulders** — (ক্রীকেটক্রীড়ায় — খেলোয়াড়ের পক্ষে) কন্দুক আঘাত করার জন্য বিশেষ ভঙ্গীতে অবস্থান করা। **To open the debate**—To begin it ; to be the first speaker ; বাদানুবাদ আরম্ভ করা ; সর্ব্বপ্রথম বক্তৃতা করা। **To open the door to**—To give opportunity for ; দ্বার উন্মুক্ত হওয়া, সুযোগ দেওয়া। **To open the eyes of a person**—To let him know the true state of affairs ; কাহারো চোখ ফুটাইয়া দেওয়া। **To open the mind, heart**—See OPEN *v. t.* 3. **To open out**—(*v. t.* & *i.*) To unfold ; to expand ; to develop ; to become communicative ; উদ্‌ঘাটিত হওয়া ; বিকশিত হওয়া ; বিকাশপ্রাপ্ত হওয়া ; প্রাণখুলিয়া কথা বলিতে আরম্ভ করা। **To open up**—To make accessible ; to disclose ; to bring to notice ; সুগম করা ; প্রকাশ করা ; গোচরীভূত করা।

ō'-pen-ing (-pn-), *n.* & *adj.* 1. Making open ; উদ্‌ঘাটন, উন্মোচন, ব্যাদান। 2. A breach ; a gap ; an aperture ; span ; ফাটোল ; ফাঁক ; রন্ধ্র, ছিদ্র, ফোকর, তোরণের স্তম্ভদ্বয়ের মধ্যবর্ত্তী ফাঁক। 3. Beginning ; commencement ; initial stage or part ; প্রারম্ভ ; আরম্ভ, উপক্রম ; প্রথমাবস্থা, প্রথমাংশ। 4. Preliminary statement of a case by a counsel ; কৌঁসলি কর্ত্তৃক কোন মোকদ্দমার বৃত্তান্ত সম্বন্ধে প্রাথমিক বক্তৃতা। 5. An opportunity ; as, an *opening* for business ; সুবিধা, সুযোগ। 6. (*Chess*) A recognized sequence of moves for beginning a game ; (দাবাখেলা) ক্রীড়ারম্ভের পূর্ব্বে উপর্য্যুপরি যে চাল দেওয়া হয়। ***Adj.*** 1. Making open ; aperient ; উদ্‌ঘাটনকারী, মৃদুবিরেচক। 2. Initial ; introductory ; first ; আদ্য ; প্রারম্ভক ; প্রাথমিক। 3. Unfolding ; developing ; as, an *opening* mind ; খোলা ; বিকাশী। 4. Giving tongue ; চীৎকারকারী।

ō'-pen-lȳ (-pn-), *adv.* Publicly ; frankly ; প্রকাশ্যভাবে ; সরলভাবে।

ŏp'-ĕr-ȧ, *n.* 1. A drama or dramatic performances of which music forms an essential part ; গীতিনাট্য, নাট্য। 2. A play set to music ; গীতাভিনয়। 3. A place where operas are performed ; গীতিনাট্য-মন্দির। 4. The branch of art concerned with operas and their performance ; গীতিনাট্যকলা। **Comic opera**—তরলরসিকতাপূর্ণ গীতিনাট্য। **Grand opera**—যে গীতিনাট্যে পাত্রপাত্রীদের কোন প্রকার কথোপকথন নাই। **Opera bouffe**—প্রহসনের ধরণের গীতিনাট্য। **Opera-cloak, -hood**—গীতিনাট্য বা সান্ধ্য-সম্মিলনে গমনোচিত পরিচ্ছদ। **Opera-glass-(es)**—নাট্য প্রভৃতি দর্শনকালে ব্যবহৃত ক্ষুদ্র দূরবীণ, দূরবীণ (হিঃ কোঃ)।

Opera-glass.

Opera-hat—পুরুষের মুড়িয়া রাখার যোগ্য রেশমী টুপি। **Opera-house**—গীতি-নাট্যশালা, গীতি-নাট্যগৃহ।

ŏp'-ĕr-āte, *v. i.* & *t.* **1.** To exert influence ; to act ; "The revolutionary spirit ceasing to *operate* in politics ; প্রভাব বিস্তার করা ; ক্রিয়া করা। **2.** To act ; to produce effect, as a medicine etc. ; ক্রিয়া করা, কাজ করা; ফলদায়ক হওয়া। **3.** To perform a surgical operation ; অস্ত্র করা, অস্ত্রপ্রয়োগ করা, অস্ত্রোপচার করা, অস্ত্রাবচার করা, শস্ত্রক্রিয়া করা। **4.** (*Mil.* & *nav.*) To conduct strategic movements against the enemy ; (নৌ বা সামরিক-বিদ্যা) শত্রুর বিরুদ্ধে সুকৌশলে সৈন্য বা রণপোতশ্রেণী সংস্থান করা। **5.** To perform an operation or series of operations, (with *on* or *upon*) ; "To *operate on* the ores" ; কার্য্য করা, কার্য্যপরম্পরা করা। **6.** To deal in stocks or any commodity, esp. speculatively ; কোম্পানীর কাগজ বা অন্য কোন কিছুর (বিশেষতঃ ঝুঁকিদার) ব্যবসায় করা। **7.** (*Chiefly U. S.*) To manage ; to work ; (প্রধানতঃ মার্কিণযুক্তরাজ্যে) নির্ব্বাহ করা ; কার্য্য করা। ***Verb t.*** To bring about ; to produce ; সংঘটন করা ; উৎপাদন করা। **—a-tor,** *n.* One who, or that which, operates ; কার্য্যকারক, কারক (হিঃ কোঃ), যন্ত্রচালক, অস্ত্রপ্রয়োগকারী। **Operating-room, —table**—অস্ত্রোপচারকক্ষ, অস্ত্রোপচার-পীঠিকা। **Operating theatre**—ছাত্রদিগের সমক্ষে অস্ত্রপ্রয়োগ করার জন্য কক্ষ, শস্ত্রোপচারকক্ষ।

ŏp-ĕr-ăt'-ic, *adj.* Of, relating to, or like, the opera ; গীতিনাট্যসম্বন্ধীয়, গীতিনাট্যবৎ। **—i-cal-ly,** *adv.*

ŏp-ĕr-ā'-tion, *n.* **1.** Acting ; working ; exercise of power or influence ; ক্রিয়াকরণ ; কর্ম্মকরণ ; ক্ষমতা পরিচারণ, প্রভাববিস্তার। **2.** Effect of operating ; efficacy ; ক্রিয়ার ফল ; কার্য্যকারিতা, ফল। **3.** Way of operating or working ; কার্য্য-প্রণালী, কার্য্যপদ্ধতি, প্রক্রিয়া। **4.** State of being operative ; as, to be in *operation* ; ক্রিয়াশীলতা। **5.** Activity, performance, discharge of function ; as, the *operation* of breathing and thinking ; ক্রিয়া (ব্রজঃ হিন্দুঃ), ব্যাপার, (হিঃ কোঃ), চেষ্টা। **6.** (*Commr.*) A transaction, esp. a speculative one ; (বাণিজ্য) ব্যবসায়, কারবার, বিশেষতঃ ঝুঁকিদার ব্যবসায়। **7.** (*Surg.*) A surgical proceeding to which a living body is subject ; (অস্ত্রোপচার-বিদ্যা), শস্ত্রকর্ম্ম, শস্ত্রাবচার, শস্ত্রক্রিয়া, শস্ত্রোপচার, শস্ত্রোপায়। **8.** Strategic movement of troops, ships, etc. ; রণপোত, সৈন্যদল, প্রভৃতির সুকৌশলপূর্ণ সংস্থান বা চালনা। **9.** (*Math.*) Subjection of a number of quantity to a process affecting its value or form, *e. g.* multiplication ; (গণিত-শাস্ত্র) ক্রিয়া, প্রক্রিয়া। **Must extend its operation** — Must make it valid for longer time or in wider sphere ; ইহার কার্য্যক্ষেত্র প্রসার লাভ করিবে।

ŏp'-ĕr-ā-tive (-tĭv), *adj.* & *n.* **1.** Exerting force or influence ; in operation ; কার্য্যকর, কর্ম্মকর, কর্ম্মনিপুণ, ক্রিয়াকারক ; সক্রিয়। **2.** Productive of proper effect, as a rule, penalty, etc. ; efficacious, as a medicine ; কার্য্যসাধক, কার্য্যসম্পাদক ; অভীষ্টফলপ্রদ ; ফলজনক। **3.** Not theoretical ; practical ; as, *operative* arts ; ব্যবহারিক ; কার্য্যকরী। **4.** Of, or relating to, surgical operation ; অস্ত্র-প্রয়োগসম্বন্ধীয়। **5.** Active ; occupied in productive labour ; কর্ম্মঠ ; উৎপাদনশীল কার্য্যে নিরত। ***Noun.*** A worker or artisan ; mechanic ; a factory or mill-hand ; কারিগর, শিল্পী ; যন্ত্রী ; কলের মজুর, কারখানার মজুর। **—ly,** *adv.*

ŏp'-ĕr-ā-tize, *v. t.* To turn into an opera ; গীতিনাট্যে পরিণত করা।

ō-pêr'-cū-lŭm, *n.* (*Pl.* -LA) **1.** The cover protecting the gills of fish ; মৎস্যের কানকার আবরণ। **2.** (*Conch*) The plate which closes the orifice of a shell ; (শঙ্খসম্বন্ধে) শঙ্খশম্বুকাদির রন্ধ্র আবরক ফলক। **3.** (*Bot.*) A similar lid-like structure in plants, etc. ; (উদ্ভিদ্‌বিদ্যা) ঢাকন (সাঃ পঃ), সরাব (ঐ)। **—lar, —late, —lat-ed,** *adjs.*

Shell ; o. operculum.

ŏp-ĕr-ĕt'-tă, *n.* A short light opera or drama ; ক্ষুদ্র নাট্য বা গীতিনাট্য।

ŏp'-ĕr-ōse, *adj.* Requiring or involving great labour ; laborious ; wearisome ; শ্রমসাধ্য, কষ্টসাধ্য ; শ্রমজনক ; ক্লান্তিজনক। **—ly,** *adv.* **—ness,** *n.*

Ophelia alata—চিরতা (বেলঃ)।

Ophelia angustifolia—পাহাড়ী চিরতা, (বেলঃ), চিরতা (ঐ)।

ŏph'-i-cleide (-clīd), *n.* A large brass wind-instrument of two kinds, the bass and the alto ; পিত্তলনির্ম্মিত সুষিরযন্ত্রবিশেষ।

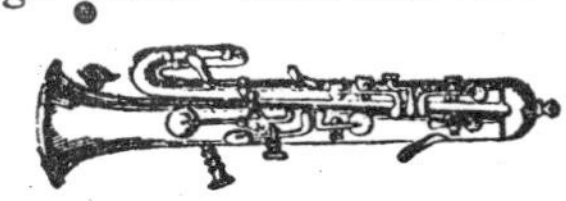

Ophicleide.

ō-phĭd'-i-ă, *n.* (*Pl.*) An order of reptiles including the snakes ; সর্পবর্গ।

ō-phĭd'-i-ăn, *adj.* & *n.* Of, or relating to, the Ophidia ; সর্প-সংক্রান্ত, সর্পবিষয়ক, সার্প। ***Noun.*** A snake ; সর্প।

Ophiocephalus gachua—চেঙ্গ

Ophiocephalus marulius—গজার (শুশ্রুঃ)।

Ophiocephalus punctatus—রক্ত চেঙ্গ (গুপ্তঃ)।

Ophiocephalus striatus—শোল (গুপ্তঃ)।

ŏ-phi-ŏl′-ă-trȳ, *n.* Serpent-worship; সর্পপূজা। **—ter,** *n.* A serpent worshipper; সর্পপূজক।

ŏ-phi-ŏl′-ŏ-ḡy, *n.* Natural history treating of ophidians; প্রাকৃতিক ইতিহাসের সর্পসম্বন্ধীয় শাখা, সর্পতত্ত্ব, সর্পশাস্ত্র।

ŏph′-i-ŏ-măn-cȳ, *n.* Divination by the observation of serpents; সর্পদর্শনে ভবিষ্যৎকথন।

Ophioxylon serpentinum—চন্দ্র (বেলঃ), চন্দ্রক (ঐ)।

ŏph′-īte, *n.* Serpentine or serpentine marble; সর্পত্বকের মত ফুট ফুট বিন্দুবিশিষ্ট মর্ম্মরপ্রস্তর। **O-phit′-ic,** *adj.*

ŏph-thăl′-mi-ă, *n.* Inflammation of the eyes, or its appendages; চক্ষুঃপ্রদাহ, চক্ষুউঠা, চক্ষুরোগ, নেত্রাময় (সুশ্রুঃ), অভিমন্থ, অধিমন্থ। **—mic,** *adj.* & *n.* **1.** Of, or relating to, the eyes; affected with ophthalmia; অক্ষিসংক্রান্ত, নেত্রসংক্রান্ত; অভিমন্থরোগাক্রান্ত। **2.** Good for diseases of the eye, as a remedy; চক্ষুরোগনাশক। (*Noun.*) An opthalmic remedy; চক্ষুরোগনাশক ঔষধ, চোখের ঔষধ। ***Ophthalmia neonatorum***—নবজাত শিশুর চক্ষুঃপ্রদাহ, ককুণক (সাঃ পঃ)। ***Ophthalmia tarsi***—চক্ষুর পক্ষ্মের মূলের প্রদাহ—ইহাতে পক্ষ্মের মূলে ক্ষুদ্র ক্ষুদ্র পূঁযপূর্ণ গুটিকা জন্মে—এবং উহা হইতে স্রাব নিঃসৃত হয়, পক্ষ্মশাত (সাঃ পঃ)।

ŏph-thăl-mī′-tis, *n.* Same as OPHTHALMIA (which see).

ŏph-thăl-mŏl′-ŏ-ḡy, *n.* The science treating of the eye and its diseases etc.; চক্ষুরোগবিজ্ঞান। **—gist,** *n.*

ŏph-thăl′-mō-scōpe *n.* An instrument for inspecting the retina; চক্ষুরোগপরীক্ষার্থ যন্ত্রবিশেষ [এই যন্ত্র দ্বারা চিত্রপত্রে (retina) আলোক প্রতিভাত হইয়া চক্ষুর অভ্যন্তরভাগ দৃষ্ট হয়], অক্ষিবীক্ষণযন্ত্র (হঃ চঃ), অক্ষিদর্শক (হিঃ কোঃ)।

ŏph-thăl-mŏt′-ŏ-mȳ, *n.* The dissection or excision of the eye; নেত্রব্যবচ্ছেদ, নেত্রচ্ছেদন।

ō′-pi-āte, *adj.* & *n.* (*Archaic*) Containing, or mixed with, opium; narcotic; soporific; (অপ্রঃ) অহিফেনমিশ্রিত; সংবেদননাশক; নিদ্রাজনক, স্বাপজনক। ***Noun.*** **1.** A medicine containing opium and inducing sleep; a narcotic; অহিফেনমিশ্রিত নিদ্রাজনক ঔষধ; নিদ্রাজনক ঔষধ। **2.** That which induces inaction, and quiets uneasiness, etc.; অবসাদক বস্তু।

ō′-pi-āte, *v. t.* **1.** To mix with opium; অহিফেনের সহিত মিশ্রিত করা। **2.** (*Fig.*) To dull the sense or sensibility of; (লক্ষণায়) সংবেদনশক্তি মন্দীভূত করা, জড়ীভূত করা।

ŏ-pīne′, *v. t.* & *i.* To express and hold an opinion; to think or suppose; মতপ্রকাশ করা, মতপোষণ করা; মনে করা, ভাবা, বোধ করা, বোধ হওয়া।

ŏ-pin′-ion (-yŭn), *n.* **1.** A provisional conviction; a view held as probable; মত; অভিমত। **2.** (Also, *public opinion*) What is generally thought about something; অভিপ্রায়, জনমত, লোকমত। **3.** A belief or conviction; "...too young to form *opinions*"; বিশ্বাস, বদ্ধমূল ধারণা। **4.** Professional advice; views of an expert; as, a legal or medical *opinion*; ডাক্তার, উকিল, প্রভৃতির পরামর্শ; বিশেষজ্ঞের অভিমত। **5.** Estimate; as, to have a high or low *opinion* of; (*with negative*) high or favourable estimation; as, to have no *opinion* of Frenchmen; ধারণা; উচ্চমত, অনুকূল মত। **A matter of opinion**—A disputable point; বিতর্কনীয় বিষয়, বিচার্য্য বিষয়, বিবদনীয় বিষয়। **In my opinion**—As it seems to me; আমার মতে। **To be of opinion that**—To believe that; এইরূপ মতাবলম্বী হওয়া যে। **To act up to one's opinions**—To act up to one's convictions; কাহারো ধারণা মত কার্য্য করা।

ŏ-pin′-ion-ā-tĕd (-yŭn-), *adj.* Stiff or obstinate in opinion; self-willed; স্বমতাভিমানী, মতাভিমানী, স্বমতবদ্ধ, দুরাগ্রহী, মতবাদী; অহম্মন্য, মতাভিমানী। **—ness,** *n.*

ŏ-pin′-ion-a-tive (-yŭn-ā-tĭv), *adj.* Same as OPINIONATED.

ŏp-i-sŏm′-ĕ-têr, *n.* An instrument for measuring curved lines as on a map; বক্ররেখামাপক।

ō′-pi-ŭm, *n.* & *v. t.* **1.** The inspissated juice of a kind of poppy; আফিং, অহিফেন, ফণিফেন, আফূক (cf. আফূকং শোষণং গ্রাহি—ভাবপ্রকাশ), খসখসরস (আপ্তে), খসফলক্ষীর [ভাবঃ প্রঃ—cf. Persian সির-ই-খস্-খস্।], অফেন (অঃ)। **2.** Something affecting like opium; অহিফেনের ন্যায় কার্য্যকারী কোন বস্তু। ***Verb t.*** To drug or treat with opium; অহিফেন সেবন করাইয়া সংজ্ঞা বিলুপ্ত করা, অহিফেনদ্বারা চিকিৎসা করা। **—ism,** *n.* The habitual use of opium; অহিফেন সেবন অভ্যাস। **—ize,** *v. t.* **Opium den**—গুলির আড্ডা, আফিংখোরের আড্ডা, মুক্তিমণ্ডপ। **Opium-eater**—আফিংখোর, অহিফেনসেবী। **Opium habit**—অহিফেনসেবনের অভ্যাস।

Oplismenus frumentaceus—শামা (বেলঃ)।

ŏp-ŏ-dĕl′-dŏc, *n.* **1.** A saponaceous camphorated liniment; একপ্রকার অর্দ্ধতরল মর্দ্দন, ঘনউপদেহ (হঃ চঃ)। [সাবান, পরিশোধিত সুরা, পরিস্রুত জল, এবং ঔষধদ্রব্য নির্দ্ধারিত পরিমাণে মিশ্রণপূর্ব্বক ইহা প্রস্তুত করা হইয়া থাকে।] **2.** (*Obs.*) A kind of plaster; (অপ্রঃ) একপ্রকার বস্ত্রলিপ্ত মলম।

ŏ-pŏp′-ă-năx, *n.* **1.** A kind of gum-resin formerly used in medicine ; পূর্ব্বে ঔষধে ব্যবহৃত বৃক্ষনির্যাস বিশেষ। **2.** A gum-resin used in perfumery ; গন্ধদ্রব্য প্রস্তুতে ব্যবহৃত বৃক্ষনির্যাস-বিশেষ।

ō-pŏs′-sŭm, *n.* **1.** A genus of marsupiale carnivorous mammals ; একপ্রকার মাংসাশী দ্বিগর্ভ জন্তু। **2.** (*Austral.*) Same as PHALANGER (which see).

Opossum.

ŏp′-pi-dăn (-ĭ-), *adj.* & *n.* Of, or relating to, a town (*rare*) ; সহরসম্বন্ধীয়, নগরীয়, নাগরিক, পৌর (ক্বচিদ্ব্যবহৃত)। ***Noun.*** **1.** (*Rare*) An inhabitant of a town ; (ক্বচিদ্ব্যবহৃত) নগরবাসী। **2.** (At Eton college) A student not on the foundation and who boards in the town—opposed to *colleger* ; (ইটনকলেজে) যে ছাত্র কলেজ হইতে কোন বৃত্তি পায় না—এবং যাহাকে সহরে আহার করিতে হয়।

ŏp′-pi-lāte, *v. t.* (*Med.*) To stop or block up ; to obstruct ; "The pipes···*oppilated* with crudities" ; (ভৈষজ্য-শাস্ত্র) থামান, অবরোধ করা ; রোধ করা। **—la′-tion** *n.*

ŏp-pō′-nĕn-cȳ, *n.* (*Rare*) Antagonism ; opposition ; (অপ্রঃ) বিরুদ্ধতা ; বিরোধ।

ŏp-pō′-nĕnt, *adj.* & *n.* Contrary ; opposed (*rare*) ; পরিপন্থী, প্রতিপক্ষ ; উত্তরবাদী, প্রতিযোগী, প্রতিরোধী, প্রতিদ্বন্দ্বী (ক্বচিদ্ব্যবহৃত)। ***Noun.*** An adversary or antagonist ; শত্রু, অরি, বৈরী।

ŏp-pŏr-tūne′, *adj.* **1.** (Of time) Fit or suitable ; proper ; উপযুক্ত, সমুচিত ; সঙ্গত। **2.** (Of an event, act, etc.) Timely ; well-timed ; সময়োচিত, কালোচিত, প্রসঙ্গোচিত ; প্রাপ্তাবসর, প্রাপ্তকাল। **—ly,** *adv.* **—ness,** *n.*

ŏp-pŏr-tū′-nĭsm, *n.* The policy of making the most of opportunities ; specifically in politics, the practice of turning circumstances to the advantages of one's party, even at the sacrifice of party principles ; putting of expediency before principle or place before power ; কোনরূপ সুযোগের পূর্ণ সুবিধা গ্রহণের নীতি ; বিশেষতঃ রাজনীতিতে মূলনীতি বর্জ্জন করিয়াও সাময়িক ঘটনাবলীর সুবিধাগ্রহণের রীতি ; অবস্থা বুঝিয়া ব্যবস্থা, সুবিধাবাদ। **—nist,** *n.*

ŏp-pŏr-tū′-nĭ-tȳ, *n.* **1.** (*Rare*) State of being opportune ; timeliness ; অবসর, অবকাশ ; কালোচিতত্ব। **2.** A favourable occasion or juncture ; a good chance ; সুযোগ ; সুবিধা। **To let slip an opportunity**—সুযোগ হারান।

ŏp-pōse′, *v. t.* & *i.* **1.** To place as an obstacle or antagonist ; to contrast ; to represent as antithetical ; as, to *oppose* patience to fury : to *oppose* Aristotle to Plato ; বাধা স্বরূপ বা বিরোধ স্বরূপ উপস্থিত করা ; পরস্পর বিরোধী রূপে উপস্থাপিত করা ; পার্থক্য প্রদর্শনার্থ তুলনা করা। **2.** To confront ; to check ; to resist ; as, to *oppose* a person, thing, resolution, etc. ; সম্মুখীন হওয়া ; বাধা দেওয়া ; প্রতিরোধ করা। **3.** (*Absol.*) To act as an antagonist or check ; as, it is the duty of an opposition to *oppose* ; প্রতিকূলাচরণ করা। **—pos-a-bil′-i-ty,** *n.* **—pos′-a-ble,** *adj.* **—posed′,** *p. adj.* **1.** Opposite ; contrary ; বিরুদ্ধ ; বিরোধী। **2.** Adverse (*to*) ; inimical ; প্রতিকূল ; পরিপন্থী।

ŏp-pōse′-lĕss, *adj.* (*Poet.*) Irresistible ; (কবিতায়) অপ্রতিরোধ্য।

ŏp′-pō-site (-zĭt), *adj.*, *n.*, *adv.* & *prep.* **1.** Standing in front ; facing ; as, the *opposite* house ; turned the other way ; contrary, as directions ; সম্মুখে অবস্থিত ; সম্মুখীন ; প্রতিমুখ ; বিপরীত। **2.** Diametrically different ; contrary ; antagonistic ; বিরোধী, বিরুদ্ধ ; উল্টা ; বিপক্ষ, প্রতিপক্ষ, প্রতিকূল। **3.** (*Bot.*) Growing in pairs, opposed at the same level, as leaves, etc. ; (উদ্ভিদবিদ্যা) পরস্পরের বিপরীতদিকে উদ্গত, অভিমুখ (সাঃ পঃ)। ***Noun.*** An opposite thing or term ; বিরুদ্ধধর্ম্মাক্রান্ত বস্তু বা বিরোধী পদ, পরস্পরবিরোধী বস্তু। ***Adv.*** In an opposite position or direction ; as, there was an explosion *opposite* ; বিপরীত দিকে। ***Prep.*** Facing on the other side ; as, a building *opposite* the Town-Hall ; সম্মুখস্থ। **—ly,** *adv.* **—ness,** *n.* **Opposite leaf**—অভিমুখপত্র। **Opposite the prompter**—(In theatre, abbr. *O. P.*) To the actor's left ; অভিনেতা বা অভিনেত্রীর বামদিকে।

ŏp-pō-sĭ′-tion, *n.* **1.** Setting opposite or over against ; state of being so set ; contrast ; antithesis ; প্রতিরোধ, বিরোধ, অবরোধন ; বিরুদ্ধতা, বিরুদ্ধভাবে স্থিতি ; বিপ্রতিপত্তি (*philos.*), বিপক্ষতা (হিঃ কোঃ) ; অর্থবৈপরীত্য, বৈপরীত্য। **2.** Opposing ; resistance ; contradiction ; নিরোধ ; বাধা ; প্রতিবাদ। **3.** (*Log.*) Difference as regards quantity, quality or both in propositions with the same subject and predicate ; (তর্ক-বিজ্ঞান) একই উদ্দেশ্য ও বিধেয়বিশিষ্ট প্রতিজ্ঞায় সংখ্যা, পরিমাণ বা উভয়গতভেদ, বিরোধ (হিঃ কোঃ), প্রতিযোগ (ঐ)। **4.** (*Astron.*) The situation of two heavenly bodies when their longitudes differ by 180° ;

(জ্যোতির্বিজ্ঞান) খগোলীয় দেশান্তরের বিভেদ ১৮০° হইলে জ্যোতিষ্কদ্বয়ের পরস্পরের সম্বন্ধে অবস্থান, ষড়ভান্তর (হিঃ কোঃ)। 5. Any party opposed to some proposal; বিরুদ্ধপক্ষ। **—al,** *adj.* (*Rare.*) **—ist,** *n.* & *adj.* (*Rare.*) **The opposition, His Majesty's opposition**—বিলাতে যে পক্ষের উপর শাসনতন্ত্র পরিচালনের ভার থাকে—তাহার বিপরীত পক্ষ। **The opposition press**—যে সকল সংবাদপত্র শাসনতন্ত্রের বিরুদ্ধপক্ষ অবলম্বন করে। **The planet is in opposition**—অর্থাৎ গ্রহটী সূর্য্যের বিপরীতদিকে অবস্থিত। **Was in opposition at the time**—Belonged to the opposition at the time; ঐ সময়ে বিরুদ্ধ পক্ষে ছিল।

ŏp'-pŏs'-i-tive (-tĭv), *adj.* (*Rare*) That may be put in opposition; opposing; (অপ্রঃ) বিরুদ্ধে স্থাপনীয়; বিরোধী।

ŏp'-prĕss, *v. t.* **1.** To overpower; to subdue; অভিভূত করা; বশীভূত করা। **2.** To lie heavy on; to weigh down; as, to *oppress* the spirits or imagination; প্রপীড়িত করা; ভারাক্রান্ত করা। **3.** To treat with unjust severity or rigour; to govern tyrannically; উৎপীড়ন করা; অত্যাচার করা। **—pressed',** *adj.* **—pres'-sion,** *n.* **1.** Cruel or unjust exercise of power; severity; tyranny; দৌরাত্ম্য, উৎপীড়ন, পীড়ন, জুলুম, প্রজাপীড়ন; কঠোরতা; অত্যাচার। **2.** Dullness of spirits; lassitude; স্ফূর্ত্তিহীনতা; অঙ্গগ্লানি। **—pres'-sive,** *adj.* **1.** Unjustly severe; অতি কঠোর, নিষ্ঠুর। **2.** Tyrannical; অত্যাচারী। **3.** Heavy or overpowering, as grief, etc.; দারুণ, নিদারুণ, ঘোর। **—pres'-sive-ly,** *adv.* **—pres'-sive-ness,** *n.* **—pres'-sor,** *n.* One who oppresses; অত্যাচারী, দৌরাত্ম্যকারী, প্রজাপীড়ক, উৎপীড়ক, উৎপীড়নকারী।

ŏp-prō'-bri-ous (-ŭs), *adj.* Abusive; scurrilous; vituperative; কুৎসাপূর্ণ; নিন্দাপূর্ণ, নিন্দাত্মক, অপবাদমূলক; তিরস্কারপূর্ণ। **—ly,** *adv.*

ŏp-prō'-bri-ŭm, *n.* Reproach with disdain; disgrace; infamy; abusive language; অখ্যাতি, গ্লানি; কলঙ্ক; কুৎসা, অপবাদ; নিন্দাত্মকবাক্য।

ŏp'-pugn' (-pūn), *v. t.* **1.** To oppose; to controvert; to call in question; বাধা দেওয়া; প্রতিরোধ করা; কোন উক্তির সত্যতা সম্বন্ধে প্রশ্ন করা। **2.** (*Rare*) To attack; to be in conflict with; (কচিদ্‌ব্যবহৃত) আক্রমণ করা; বিরোধ থাকা। **—er,** *n.* **—pug'-nan-cy,** *n.* (*Rare.*) **—pug'-nant,** *adj.* & *n.* (*Rare.*) **—pug'-na-tion,** *n.* (*Rare.*)

ŏp'-si-măth, *n.* (*Rare*) One who begins to learn late in life; (কচিদ্‌ব্যবহৃত) যে ব্যক্তি জীবনের শেষভাগে শিখিতে আরম্ভ করে। **—sim'-a-thy,** *adj.*

ŏpt, *v. t.* (*Rare*) To make a choice: (কচিদ্‌ব্যবহৃত) নির্ব্বাচন করা, বাছনি করা।

ŏp'-tă-tive (-tĭv), *adj.* & *n.* (*Gram.*) Expressing wish or desire; (ব্যাকরণ) ইচ্ছাবাচক, ইচ্ছাসূচক, ইচ্ছাবোধক, অভিলাষবোধক। ***Noun.*** The optative mood or a verbal form denoting it; ইচ্ছাবাচক ক্রিয়াপদ, সনন্ত। **—ly,** *adv.* **Optative mood**—(ব্যাকরণ) আশংসাবাচিনী ক্রিয়া (আঃ বঃ)।

ŏp'-tic, *adj.* & *n.* Of, or relating to, the eye or sense of sight; অক্ষিসম্বন্ধীয়, দৃক্‌সম্বন্ধী (হিঃ কোঃ), দর্শনেন্দ্রিয়সংক্রান্ত, দৃষ্টিবিষয়ক, চাক্ষুষ। ***Noun.*** **1.** (Usu. *facet.*) An eye; (সাধারণতঃ রহস্যচ্ছলে) চক্ষুঃ। **2.** (*Pl.* used with a single verb) The science which treats of light and the phenomena of vision; দৃষ্টিবিদ্যা, দৃষ্টিবিজ্ঞান, আলোকবিজ্ঞান, তেজোবিজ্ঞান (আঃ বঃ), প্রকাশবিজ্ঞান (ঐ), দৃক্‌শাস্ত্র (হিঃ কোঃ), দর্শনানুশাসনশাস্ত্র। **Optic angle**—কোন বস্তুর প্রান্ত হইতে চক্ষু পর্য্যন্ত প্রসারিত রেখাদ্বয়ের মধ্যবর্ত্তী কোণ, অথবা দুই চক্ষু হইতে কোন বিন্দুতে সম্মিলিত রেখাদ্বয়ের মধ্যবর্ত্তী কোণ, দৃক্‌কোণ (হিঃ কোঃ)। **Optic nerve**—See NERVE.

ŏp'-ti-căl, *adj.* **1.** Relating to the science of optics; constructed to assist sight; as, an *optical* instrument; দৃষ্টিবিজ্ঞানসংক্রান্ত, দৃক্‌শাস্ত্রবিষয়ক, দর্শনানুশাসনশাস্ত্রসম্বন্ধী; দৃষ্টিসহায়ক। **2.** Relating to vision; ocular; দৃষ্টিসম্বন্ধীয়; চাক্ষুষ (হিঃ কোঃ)। **—ly,** *adv.* **Optical illusion**—দৃষ্টিবিভ্রম, ভেল্কি।

ŏp-ti'-cian (-shăn), *n.* A maker or seller of optical instruments; দৃষ্টি-যন্ত্র নির্ম্মাতা বা বিক্রেতা, চসমা প্রভৃতি প্রস্তুত বা বিক্রয়কারী, আলোকযন্ত্রিক।

ŏp'-ti-mē, *n.* See WRANGLER.

ŏp'-ti-mĭsm, *n.* **1.** (*Metaph.*) The doctrine as propounded by Leibnitz, that the actual world is the best of all possible worlds; (তত্ত্ব-বিজ্ঞান) আমাদের বাস্তব জগৎ সম্ভাবিত সকল প্রকার জগৎ হইতে শ্রেষ্ঠ—দার্শনিক Leibnitz কর্ত্তৃক প্রবর্ত্তিত এই মতবাদ। **2.** The view supposing the ultimate predominence of good over evil in the universe; বিশ্বে চরমে অমঙ্গলের উপর মঙ্গলের প্রাধান্য বর্ত্তমান—এইরূপ মতবাদ, মঙ্গলবাদ, সর্ব্বশুভবাদ (হিঃ কোঃ), অনির্ব্বেদবাদ (ঐ), সুখবাদ। **3.** A disposition to take the most hopeful view; আশাপ্রবণতা। **—mist,** *n.* **1.** (*Metaph.*) An adherent of optimism; মঙ্গলবাদী, সুখবাদী, সর্ব্বশুভবাদী (হিঃ কোঃ)। **2.** One who takes bright or hopeful views; শুভদর্শনশীল ব্যক্তি। **—mis'-tic,** *adj.* **1.** Of, or relating to, optimism; সুখবাদসম্বন্ধীয়, সর্ব্বশুভবাদসম্বন্ধী (হিঃ কোঃ)। **2.** Hopeful; sanguine; আশাপূর্ণ; আশান্বিত। **—mis'-ti-cal-ly,** *adv.* **—mize,** *v. i.* & *t.* To take optimistic views; আশাজনকভাব গ্রহণ করা। (*Verb t.*) To treat optimistically; আশাজনক বলিয়া মনে করা।

ŏp′-tion, *n.* **1.** Act of choosing ; choice ; পছন্দ করণ ; পছন্দ, রুচি (হিঃ কোঃ)। **2.** That which is, or may be, chosen ; পছন্দ করা জিনিষ, পছন্দের যোগ্য জিনিষ। **3.** The right of choosing ; freedom of choice ; an alternative ; as, imprisonment without the *option* of a fine ; নির্ব্বাচনের অধিকার ; নির্ব্বাচনের স্বাধীনতা ; উপায়ান্তর, বিকল্প। **4.** (*Stock exchange*) The purchased right to call for, or make delivery within a specified time of specified stocks, etc. at a specified rate ; নির্দ্দিষ্ট কালের মধ্যে নির্দ্দিষ্ট মূল্যে কোম্পানীর কাগজসমূহ প্রদানের জন্য ক্রীত অধিকার। **—al,** *adj.* & *n.* Depending on one's choice ; not compulsory ; ইচ্ছাধীন ; অবশ্যকর্ত্তব্য নয়, বৈকল্পিক। (*Noun*) An optional study ; ইচ্ছাধীন পাঠ।

ŏp′-ū-lĕnt, *adj.* **1.** Rich ; wealthy ; ধনী ; ধনবান্, ধনাঢ্য, অর্থশালী, সম্পত্তিবান্, সম্পন্ন, সঙ্গতিশালী। **2.** Abundant ; profuse ; প্রচুর ; প্রভূত। **—lence,** *n.* Riches ; affluence ; as, *opulent* blossoms ; সমৃদ্ধি, ঐশ্বর্য্য, বিত্ত ; বৈভব। **—ly,** *adv.*

ō′-pŭs, *n.* (*No pl.*) **1.** (*Mus.*) A composition or set of compositions usually numbered in the order of its issue ; (সঙ্গীত-শাস্ত্র) রচিতগীত বা সংখ্যানুক্রমিক গীতাবলী। **2.** (Also *magnum opus* or *opus magnum*) A great or important literary work ; বিরাটগ্রন্থ, মহাগ্রন্থ।

ō-pŭs′-cūle, —cū-lŭm, *ns.* (*Pl.* -CULA) A small or petty musical or literary composition ; ক্ষুদ্র গীতি, ক্ষুদ্রপ্রবন্ধ।

ŏr, *n.* (*Herald.*) A gold or yellow colour denoted by dots in engraving ; (কুল-বিদ্যা) স্বর্ণবর্ণ।

ŏr, *prep.* & *conj.* (*Archaic*) Ere ; before ; (অপ্রঃ) পূর্ব্বে ; আগে। ***Conj.*** A connective that marks an alternative ; otherwise ; অথবা, কিম্বা, বা ; নতুবা। **Five or six**—A few ; গোটা কয়েক। **Or over, Or o'er**—(*Poet.*) Before ; (কবিতায়) পূর্ব্বে।

ŏr′-ăch, *n.* A genus of plants ; একজাতীয় গুল্ম।

ŏr′-ă-cle (-kl), *n.* **1.** (*Among the ancient Greeks & Romans*) The answer of a god or his priest, to an inquiry on any matter ; also, the place where such an answer was given ; (প্রাচীন গ্রীক বা রোমানদিগের মধ্যে) কোন প্রশ্নসম্বন্ধে দেবতা বা তদীয় পুরোহিতের উত্তর, দৈববাণী, প্রত্যাদেশবাণী, দেববাক্য (হিঃ কোঃ), আকাশবাণী (ঐ), দেববাণী ; যেস্থানে ঐরূপ উত্তর প্রদান করা হইত, প্রশ্নস্থান, প্রত্যাদেশস্থলী। **2.** The holy of holies of the Jewish temple ; ইহুদী মন্দিরের গর্ভগৃহ। **3.** Divine inspiration or revelation ; a medium for the communication of these ; দৈবীপ্রেরণা, প্রত্যাদেশ ; যাহার মুখ দিয়া দেবপ্রত্যাদেশ প্রচারিত হয়। **4.** A thing or person as an infalliable guide ; প্রমাণ, আপ্তপুরুষ, আপ্ত। **5.** An authoritative or wise utterance ; an oracular reply ; আপ্তোক্তি, আপ্তবাক্য, আপ্তবচন, অভিযুক্তবচন, অভিযুক্তোক্তি ; আপ্তোত্তর।

O-rac′-u-lar, *adj.* **1.** Of, or pertaining to, an oracle ; uttering oracles ; দেববাণীসম্বন্ধীয় ; দেববাণীকথক, দেবপ্রত্যাদেশকথক। **2.** Wise or authoritative ; obscure or ambiguous ; বিজ্ঞোচিত, প্রামাণিক, আপ্ত ; অস্পষ্ট, সন্দিগ্ধার্থ। **O-rac-u-lar′-i-ty,** *n.* **O-rac′-u-lar-ly,** *adv.*

ō′-răl, *adj.* **1.** Spoken ; verbal ; বাচনিক ; মৌখিক, অলিখিত। **2.** (*Anat.*) Of, or relating to, the mouth ; (শারীরসংস্থানবিদ্যা) মুখসম্বন্ধীয়। **3.** Using speech or the lips as a teacher in a deaf and dumb school ; বাক্য অথবা ওষ্ঠাধর ব্যবহারকারী। **—ly,** *adv.* Verbally ; মুখে মুখে। **Oral evidence**—শব্দপ্রমাণ।

ŏr′-ange (-ănj), *n.* & *adj.* **1.** An evergreen fruit-tree ; its fruit ; কমলা গাছ [also কির্ম্মিরত্বক্, পিচ্ছিলত্বক্, নাগরুক, রাজফণিজ্ঝক্ (তন্ত্রঃ)।] ; কমলা, কমলালেবু [also নাগরঙ্গ, নাগরঙ্গক, নারিঙ্গ (cf. Arabic *Naranj* = orange), নারঙ্গী, ভূমিজম্বুক, সুরঙ্গ (সুভাঃ), ত্বকসুগন্ধঃ (ভাব প্রঃ), ত্বকস্বাদী, (নিঘণ্টুঃ), ত্বগ্‌গন্ধ (অঃ), নাদেয়, নার্য্যঙ্গ, দন্তশঠ, কির্ম্মীর, চোলকী, নবরঙ্গ (cf. পহিল বদরীসম পুন নবরঙ্গ—বিদ্যাপতি), পিচ্ছিল। সম্ভবতঃ "কমলা" শব্দটী তেলেগু হইতে আধুনিক সংস্কৃত ও বাঙ্গালা ভাষায় প্রবেশলাভ করিয়াছে।] **2.** (Also *orange-colour*) Reddish-yellow ; কমলাবর্ণ, রক্তপীত, নারঙ্গবর্ণ, নাগরঙ্গবর্ণ। ***Adj.*** Of orange colour ; কমলাবর্ণের। **—ry,** *n.* A place for cultivating oranges ; a house for rearing orange trees ; কমলালেবু চাষের স্থান, কমলা বাগান ; কমলাতরু রোপণের জন্য গৃহ। **Mock orange**—একপ্রকার গুল্ম। **Orange-blossom**—বিবাহকালে কন্যাকর্ত্তৃক পরিহিত কমলাপুষ্প। **Orange-fin**—একপ্রকার মৎস্য। **Orange-marmalade**—See MARMALADE. **Orange-tip**—একপ্রকার প্রজাপতি। **Oranges and lemons**—শিশুদিগের ক্রীড়াবিশেষ। **Squeezed orange**—A thing from which no good can be derived ; যে বস্তু হইতে আর কোনরূপ উপকার বা সুবিধা পাওয়ার সম্ভাবনা নাই। **A sucked orange**—যে ব্যক্তির শক্তি সামর্থ্য নিঃশেষিত হইয়াছে। **To squeeze the orange**—To take all the good from anything ; কোন বস্তু হইতে সমস্তটা সার উঠাইয়া লওয়া।

Or′-ange (ŏr-ănj), *n.* & *adj.* **1.** A town on the Rhone ; রোন নদীর তীরবর্ত্তী নগরবিশেষ। ***Adj.*** Connected with the Irish ultra-protestant party, (probably from the *orangemen*) ; আয়র্লণ্ডের উৎকট প্রটেষ্ট্যান্ট দলের সহিত সংসৃষ্ট

—ism, *n.* **The orangemen**—আয়র্লণ্ডের প্রটেষ্ট্যান্ট সম্প্রদায়ের প্রাধান্য-প্রতিষ্ঠার জন্য রাজনীতিক সম্প্রদায়বিশেষ। **William of Orange**—ইংলণ্ডেশ্বর তৃতীয় উইলিয়ম।

ŏr-ange-āde (-ănj-), *n.* Orange sherbat ; কমলার সরবত।

Orang-outang.

ō-răng′-ou-tăng (-ô-), **—u-tăn** (-ô-), *ns.* One of the man-like apes ; বনমানুষ।

ō-rāte′, *v. i.* (*Joc.*) To make oration ; to harangue ; (কৌতুকচ্ছলে) বক্তৃতা করা ; গলাবাজী করা।

ō-rā′-tion, *n.* An eloquent address ; বক্তৃতা।

ŏr′-ă-tor (-têr), *n.* A public speaker ; a skilled or eloquent speaker ; বাগ্মী ; সুবক্তা, সদ্বক্তা। **—trix**, *n.* (*Fem.*) **Public Orator**—অক্সফোর্ড বিশ্ববিদ্যালয়ের কর্ম্মচারিবিশেষ।

ŏr-ă-tō′-ri-ō, *n.* A sacred semi-dramatic musical composition ; গীতিসন্দর্ভ, গীতি-নাট্যবিশেষ।

ŏr′-ă-tor-īze (-têr-), *v. i.* Same as ORATE.

ŏr′-ă-tō-rȳ, *n.* **1.** The art of public speaking ; বাগ্মিতা। **2.** Rhetorical or eloquent language ; বক্তৃতার ভাষা। **—tor′-i-cal**, *adj.* **—tor′-i-cal-ly**, *adv.*

ŏr′-ă-tō-rȳ, *n.* **1.** A smll chapel ; ক্ষুদ্র ভজনালয়, প্রার্থনাগার। 2. (*R. C. Ch.*) A religious society founded in Rome in 1564 ; ১৫৬৪ খৃঃ অব্দে রোমনগরীতে প্রতিষ্ঠিত ধর্ম্মসম্প্রদায়-বিশেষ। **—to′-ri-an**, *adj.* & *n.* (*R. C. Ch.*)

ŏrb, *n.*, *v. t.* & *i.* **1.** (*Rare*) A circular disc ; as, an *orb* of soldiers ; a circle ; a ring ; (অপ্রঃ) চক্র ; বৃত্ত ; অঙ্গুরীয়ক। **2.** A globe ; a spherical body ; মণ্ডল ; বর্ত্তুল, গোল (হিঃ কোঃ)। **3.** A heavenly body ; জ্যোতিষ্কপিণ্ড (হিঃ কোঃ)। **4.** A sphere surmounted by a cross as part of the English regalia ; ইংলণ্ডের রাজদণ্ডস্বরূপ ক্রুশাগ্রবর্ত্তুল। **5.** (*Poet.*) The eye or eyeball ; (কবিতায়) চক্ষুঃ, অক্ষিগোলক। **6.** A collective or organized whole ; as an *orb* of witnesses ; মণ্ডলী। ***Verb t.*** **1.** To enclose or encircle in ; বেষ্টিত করা, বলয়িত করা। **2.** To form into an orb or disc ; মণ্ডলীকৃত করা, বর্ত্তুলিত করা। ***Verb i.*** To form into an orb ; মণ্ডলীভূত হওয়া, বর্ত্তুলিত হওয়া, বলয়িত হওয়া। **Orb′-less**, *adj.*

ŏr-bĭc′-ū-lar (-lêr), *adj.* **1.** Circular ; ring-shaped ; গোলাকৃতি, মণ্ডলাকৃতি, বর্ত্তুলাকার ; অঙ্গুরীয়কাকৃতি। **2.** Spherical ; rounded ; বর্ত্তুল ; বিম্বাকার (সাঃ পঃ)। **3.** (*Fig.*) Forming a whole ; complete ; "An *orbicular* system of philosophy" ; (লক্ষণায়) নিখিল ; সর্ব্বাঙ্গসম্পন্ন। **—lar′-i-ty**, *n.* **—late**, *adj.* Circular or nearly circular in form as a leaf etc. ; বৃত্তাকার, বৃত্তকল্প। **—ly**, *adv.*

ŏr′-bit, *n.* **1.** (*Anat.*) The eye-socket ; (শারীর-সংস্থান বিদ্যা) অক্ষিকোটর। **2.** The border round the eye of a bird, insect, etc. ; পক্ষী, পতঙ্গ প্রভৃতির চক্ষুর প্রান্তরেখা। **3.** The path of a planet, comet, etc. ; কক্ষা, গ্রহকক্ষা (সূঃসিঃ), গ্রহপথ, গ্রহমার্গ, বিমণ্ডল (গণিতঃ), বিক্ষেপবৃত্ত (কেশিঃ)। **—al**, *adj.*

ŏrc, *n.* **1.** A kind of cetacean ; তিমিজাতীয় জীববিশেষ। **2.** A sea animal ; একপ্রকার সামুদ্রিক জীব। **3.** An ogre or monster ; রাক্ষস।

Or-cā′-di-ăn (ôr-), *adj.* & *n.* Of, or relating to, the Orkney Islands ; অর্কনি দ্বীপপুঞ্জসম্বন্ধীয়। ***Noun.*** An inhabitant of these ; ঐ দ্বীপসমূহের অধিবাসী।

ŏr′-chard (-chêrd) *n.* An enclosure of fruit-trees ; ফলের বাগান, ফলোদ্যান, বৃক্ষবাটিকা, ফলারাম, ফলবৃক্ষবাটিকা। **—ist**, *n.* **Orchardman**—যে ব্যক্তি ফলের চাষ করে, ফলারামাধিকারী।

ŏr-chĕs′-tic, *adj.* Of, or relating to, dancing ; নৃত্যসম্বন্ধীয়। **—tics**, *n.* The art of dancing ; নৃত্যকলা।

ŏr′-chĕs-tră, *n.* **1.** The semicircular part of the Greek theatre alloted to the chorus ; প্রাচীন গ্রীকনাট্যমন্দিরের যে অর্দ্ধচন্দ্রাকৃতি অংশে বৃন্দগায়কগণ উপবেশন করিত। **2.** The part of a modern theatre or concert-room assigned to the band or chorus ; আধুনিক রঙ্গালয়ে বা ঐক্যতানবাদ্যকক্ষের যে অংশে বাদিত্রবাদকগণ বা গায়কদল উপবেশন করে, বাদিত্রবাদকস্থান, বাদিত্রগায়কস্থল। **3.** A body of musicians in a theatre or concert-room ; their concerted music ; বাদিত্রবাদকদল ; ঐক্যতানবাদ্য। **—tral**, *adj.*

ŏr′-chĕs-trāte, *v. t.* & *i.* To compose or arrange (music) for an orchestra ; ঐক্যতানবাদ্যের উপযোগী করা, ঐক্যতানবাদ্যের উপযোগিভাবে রচনা বা বিন্যাস করা। **—tra′-tion**, *n.*

ŏr-chĕs-trī′-ră, *n.* A kind of barrel-organ meant to give orchestra-like effect ; একপ্রকার বাদ্যযন্ত্র।

ŏr′-chid, **—chis**, *ns.* A perennial plant with tuberous fleshy root and beautiful flowers ; ভূমি-চম্পক প্রভৃতির গাছ, অর্কিড। **—chi-da′-ceous**, *adj.* **—ist** *n.* A cultivator of orchids ; অর্কিড চাষকারী।

ŏr-chid-ŏl′-ō-gy, *n.* The branch of botany or horticulture dealing with orchids ; অর্কিডতত্ত্ব।

or-chid o-ma'-ni-a, *n.* A craze for orchids ; অর্কিডসংগ্রহের বাতিক।

or'-chil, *n.* A red or violet dye prepared from certain lichens ; কোন কোন জাতীয় শৈবাল হইতে প্রস্তুত একপ্রকার লোহিত বা নীলারুণবর্ণ রঞ্জকপদার্থ।

or-cin, *n.* (*Chem.*) A colourless crystalline substance obtained from lichens ; (রসায়নশাস্ত্র) শৈবাল-বিশেষ হইতে প্রাপ্ত একপ্রকার অবর্ণ স্ফাটিকপদার্থ।

ŏr-dain' (-dān), *v. t.* **1.** (*Eccl.*) To invest with ministerial functions ; to confer holy orders on ; যাজকীয় ক্ষমতা অর্পণ করা ; যাজকীয় পদে নিযুক্ত করা। **2.** (Of God, fate, etc.) To destine ; to appoint ; নির্দিষ্ট করা ; নিরূপিত করা। **3.** To establish authoritatively ; to decree ; as, what the laws *ordain* ; প্রতিষ্ঠিত করা, স্থাপন করা ; বিধান করা। **—ment**, *n.* (*Rare*)

ŏr'-dē-ăl, *n.* **1.** An ancient form of trial to determine guilt or innocence by fire or water or in Africa, by poison ; as, *ordeal* by fire ; দিব্য, দিব্যসাধন (শুক্রঃ বিনয়ঃ), দিব্যক্রিয়া (রাঃ তঃ), [cf. তুলাগ্ন্যাপো বিষং কোষো দিব্যানীহ বিশুদ্ধয়ে — যাজ্ঞবল্ক্যসংহিতা], পরীক্ষা (এভেলন)। **2.** A severe trial or test ; অগ্নিপরীক্ষা।

ŏr'-dêr, *n.* **1.** Rank ; class ; division of persons ; as, higher or lower *orders* ; পদবী ; শ্রেণী ; মর্য্যাদানুসারে সামাজিক বিভাগ, বর্ণ। **2.** Kind ; sort ; as, talents of a high *order* ; রকম ; ধরণ, শ্রেণী। **3.** A religious fraternity ; ধর্মমণ্ডলী। **4.** (*Eccl.*) A ministerial grade ; as, holy *orders* ; (*pl.*) the status of a clergyman ; as, to take *orders* ; যাজকীয় শ্রেণী ; যাজকের পদমর্য্যাদা। **5.** Any of the nine grades of angels (Seraphim, cherubim, thrones, dominations, principalities, powers, virtues, archangels, angels) : দেবদূতগণের নয় শ্রেণীর অন্যতম। **6.** A group or class to which persons are admitted by way of honour or reward ; as, the *order* of the Garter, the Bath, etc. ; an insignia worn by the members of this ; সম্ভ্রান্তসম্প্রদায় ; সম্ভ্রান্ত সম্প্রদায়ের চিহ্ন। **7.** (*Arch.*) A style of building, esp. one of the five classical orders, *e. g.* Tuscan, Doric, Ionic, Corinthian and Composite ; (স্থপতিবিজ্ঞান) স্থাপত্য-রীতি, স্থাপত্যধারা। **8.** (*Nat. Hist.*) A division intermediate between a class and a family ; (প্রাকৃতিক ইতিহাস) শ্রেণী এবং পরিবারের মধ্যবর্তী বিভাগ, বর্গ। **9.** Degree of complexity ; as, an equation of the first *order* ; ক্রম (হিঃ কোঃ)। **10.** Succession or sequence ; regular arrangement ; method or system : ক্রম, অনুক্রম ; পর্য্যায়, পংক্তিক্রম ; সুশৃঙ্খলা, সুব্যবস্থা (হিঃ কোঃ), ব্যবস্থা। **11.** Normal, efficient or healthy state ; as, in or out of *order* : স্বাভাবিক অবস্থা, কার্য্যক্ষম অবস্থা, সুস্থ অবস্থা। **12.** The fixed arrangement of phenomena both physical and psychical ; as, *order* of nature : moral *order* ; ঘটনাবলীর অচলপ্রতিষ্ঠ ক্রমবিন্যাস। **13.** A prescribed form of service ; as, the *order* of confirmation ; উপাসনাদির নির্দিষ্ট ধারা। **14.** Principles of decorum and rules of procedure accepted by a legislative assembly or public meeting, or enforced by its president ; কোন সভা বা ব্যবস্থাপক সভা বা ঐরূপ সভাসমিতির সভাপতি কর্ত্তৃক গৃহীত শিষ্টাচার-পদ্ধতি বা কার্য্য প্রণালীর নিয়মনিচয়। **15.** Law-abiding state ; public tranquility ; as, law and *order* ; আইনের অনুবর্ত্তিতা ; জনসাধারণের শান্তি। **16.** Command or mandate ; আজ্ঞা, আদেশ, নিদেশ, হুকুম। **17.** (*Banking etc.*) Instruction to pay money or deliver property, signed by the owner or a responsible agent ; (ব্যাঙ্ক) টাকা প্রভৃতি প্রদানের জন্য মালিক বা তদীয় দায়িত্বসম্পন্ন প্রতিনিধির আদেশ। **18.** A direction to supply goods etc. ; মালসরবরাহের জন্য আজ্ঞাপত্র, ফরমায়েস। **19.** (*Archaic*) Measures ; care ; "I take *order* for my affairs" ; (অপ্রঃ) উপায় ; মনোযোগ। **20.** A free or cheap pass for admission to a theatre etc. ; নাট্যমন্দির প্রভৃতিতে প্রবেশের জন্য বিনামূল্যে বা অল্প মূল্যে প্রাপ্ত প্রবেশ-অনুমতিপত্র। **21.** (*Mil.*) The position of a company with arms etc. ordered ; (সামরিকশাস্ত্র) বন্দুকাদির কুঁদা বা বাঁট দক্ষিণপার্শ্বে ভূমির উপর খাড়া রাখিয়া সৈন্যগণের অবস্থিতি। **22.** (*Rare*) Tier ; as, *order* on *order* of sculptured figures ; (কচিদ্ব্যবহৃত) তাক, শ্রেণী। **Order-book**—(ক) আদেশবহি, যে পুস্তকে আদেশ লিপিবদ্ধ করা হয়। (খ) (বিলাতের প্রাকৃতসভায়) যে পুস্তকে পার্লেমেণ্টে উপস্থাপনীয় প্রস্তাব-সমূহ লিপিবদ্ধ করা হইয়া থাকে। (গ) যে পুস্তকে জিনিষের ফরমায়েস লিপিবদ্ধ করা হয়। **Order cheque, Cheque to a person's order**—যে চেক ভাঙ্গাইতে হইলে উহাতে আগে প্রাপককে সহি করিতে হয়। **Order-clerk**—যে কেরাণী ক্রেতার ফরমায়েস বহিতে লিখিয়া রাখে। **Order-form**—জিনিষের ফরমায়েস দিবার ফারম। **Order-paper**—সভা প্রভৃতির লিখিত বা মুদ্রিত কার্য্য-তালিকা। **A large order**—(*Colloq.*) A difficult job ; (চলিতভাষায়) কঠিন কাজ। **By order**—According to the direction of proper authority ; আদেশক্রমে, নিদেশক্রমে। **Classical orders**—See ORDER *n.* 7. **Holy orders**—See HOLY. **In alphabetical order**—See ALPHABET.

In order of merit--গুণানুক্রমে, গুণানুসারে। **In orders**—In clerical profession or ordained ; যাজকের পদে নিযুক্ত। **In order that**—With the intention or to the end that ; যাহাতে, যেন। **In order to do etc.**—With a view to doing etc. ; করার জন্য, করার উদ্দেশ্যে। **Is in bad order**—Is not working rightly ; ইহা বিগড়াইয়া গিয়াছে। **Is in order** or **good order**—Is fit for use ; ইহা ব্যবহারের উপযুক্ত। **Is on order**—Is ordered but not yet supplied ; ফরমায়েস দেওয়া হইয়াছে—কিন্তু এখনও জোগান হয় নাই। **Made to order**—Made according to special directions to suit individual measurements etc., (opp. to *ready-made*) ; ফরমায়েস মত তৈরী। **Minor orders**—(*R. C. Church*) Those of acolyte, exorcist, reader and doorkeeper ; রোমান ক্যাথলিক ধর্ম্মসংঘের অধীন ক্ষুদ্র কর্ম্মচারী। **Natural order**—See under NATURAL. **Order of the day**—The programme or business set down for treatment in an assembly etc. ; কোন সভা প্রভৃতির কার্য্যতালিকা। The prevailing state of things ; as, industry is the *order* of the day ; প্রচলিত রীতি, চলতি, রেওয়াজ। **Order ! Order !**—সভাদিতে শিষ্টাচার-প্রভৃতির নিয়ম ভঙ্গ হইলে উচ্চারিত শব্দ। **Out of order**—Not methodically arranged ; not working rightly ; বিশৃঙ্খল ; বে-মেরামত, বিকৃত। **To keep order**—To maintain public tranquility ; সাধারণের শান্তিরক্ষা করা। **To rise to order** or **a point of order**—To interrupt a debate etc. with inquiry whether something being said or done is in, or out of, order ; কোন বিষয় আলোচনার কালে ঐ প্রসঙ্গে যাহা বলা বা করা হইতেছে তাহা শিষ্টাচারসম্মত সভার নিয়মাবলীর অনুযায়ী কি না এই বিষয়ে প্রশ্ন উত্থাপন করা। **To take orders** — (*Eccl.*) To be ordained ; যাজকের পদে নিযুক্ত হওয়া। **To take order with**—To arrange ; to dispose of ; বিন্যস্ত করা ; সজ্জিত করা। **To take things in order**—To take them one after another according to some principle ; ক্রমানুসারে গ্রহণ করা।

ŏr'-dêr, *v. t.* **1.** (*Archaic*) To arrange in order ; to regulate ; সুশৃঙ্খলভাবে সজ্জিত করা ; সুব্যবস্থা করা। **2.** (Of God, fate, etc.) To decree or ordain ; as, so we hoped, but it was otherwise *ordered* ; বিধান করা। **3.** To command ; to direct ; as, to *order* troops to advance, or a person to do something ; আদেশ করা ; নিদেশ করা, আজ্ঞা দেওয়া, হুকুম দেওয়া। **4.** (*Mil.*) To put (arms) in certain position in drill, (See ORDER ARMS below) ; কুচকাওয়াজের কালে কোন বিশেষ ভঙ্গীতে অস্ত্র স্থাপন করা। **5.** To give order for ; ফরমায়েস দেওয়া। **6.** (*Eccl., Rare*) To ordain ; (খৃষ্টীয় ধর্ম্মসংঘ—অপ্রঃ) বিধান করা। **To order about**—To send hither and thither ; to domineer over ; এখানে সেখানে প্রেরণ করা ; কর্তৃত্ব করা। **Order arms**—যে আদেশে সৈন্যগণ বন্দুকের কুঁদা ভূমিতে রাখিয়া উহা তাহাদের ডান দিকে খাড়া করিয়া ধরে। **To order dinner**—To settle what it shall consist of ; অপরাহ্ণ-ভোজনের জন্য কি কি দ্রব্য প্রস্তুত করিতে হইবে—তাহা ঠিক করা।

ŏr'dêr-lŷ, *adj.* & *n.* **1.** Systematically arranged ; regular ; সুশৃঙ্খল সুব্যবস্থিত ; যথানুক্রমিক, ক্রমশুদ্ধ। **2.** Not unruly ; well-behaved ; শান্তস্বভাব, শান্তশীল ; সুশীল। **3.** (*Mil.*) On duty ; conveying orders ; (সামরিক-শাস্ত্র) কর্ত্তব্যকার্য্যে নিযুক্ত ; আদেশবাহী। ***Noun.*** **1.** A soldier attending on a superior to carry his orders, etc. ; আর্দ্দালী। **2.** An attendant in a hospital, esp. a military one ; রুগ্নাবাসের পরিচারক—বিশেষতঃ সামরিক আরোগ্যশালার পরিচারক। **—li-ness**, *n.* **1.** Regularity ; methodicalness ; সুব্যবস্থা ; সুশৃঙ্খলা। **2.** State of being orderly in conduct, behaviour, etc. ; সুশীলতা, শান্তস্বভাবতা। **Orderly bin**—রাস্তার আবর্জ্জনা রাখার জন্য বাক্স। **Orderly book**—Same as ORDER-BOOK. **Orderly officer**—যে কর্ম্মচারী পালাক্রমে সেনাপল্টন বা সৈন্যদলের গার্হস্থ্য ব্যাপারের তত্ত্বাবধান করিয়া থাকেন। **Orderly-room** — সেনানিবাসের যে কোঠায় সেনাপল্টন, প্রভৃতির কেরাণীরা কাজ করে।

ŏr'-di-năl, *adj.* & *n.* **1.** Indicating order or succession ; as, an *ordinal* number ; পূরণবাচক, গুণবাচক। **2.** (*Nat. Hist.*) Of, or relating to, an order ; (প্রাকৃতিক-ইতিহাস) বর্গসম্বন্ধীয়। ***Noun.*** **1.** An ordinal number ; পূরণবাচক সংখ্যা। **2.** (*Eccl.*) A formula of ordination ; (খৃষ্টীয় ধর্ম্মসংঘ) যাজকপদে নিয়োগকালে উচ্চারণীয় মন্ত্রবিশেষ। **Ordinal number**—পূরণীসংখ্যা, ক্রমাঙ্ক (হিঃ কোঃ)।

ŏr'-di-nance (-năns), *n.* **1.** Authoritative decree, or direction ; a rule or law ; বিধান ; নিয়ম, বিধি। **2.** An established rite ; শাস্ত্রবিধি (হিঃ কোঃ), অনুষ্ঠান, সংস্কার।

ŏr'-di-nă-rŷ *adj.* & *n.* **1.** Conforming to order ; regular ; নিয়মানুযায়ী ; নিয়মিত। **2.** Normal ; common ; usual ; commonplace ; প্রচলিত, প্রায়িক ; সাধারণ ; ব্যবহারিক ; সচরাচর ব্যবহৃত। **3.** Having immediate and not deputed jurisdiction ; অপ্রতিনিধিত্বমূলক অধিকারবিশিষ্ট, অপরতন্ত্র অধিকারবিশিষ্ট। ***Noun.*** **1.** A judge or other officer having immediate jurisdiction ; যে বিচারক বা অন্য কর্ম্মচারীর

অপ্রতিনিধিত্বমূলক অধিকার আছে। 2. (*Eccl.*) The archbishop of a province or a bishop in a diocese; মহাধর্ম্মাধ্যক্ষ, ধর্ম্মাধ্যক্ষ। 3. A rule or book laying down an order of divine service; খৃষ্টীয় উপাসনাপদ্ধতিবিষয়ক পুস্তক। 4. A meal prepared for all comers at a tavern etc.; an eating-house; সরাই প্রভৃতিতে সকল আগন্তুকগণের জন্য প্রস্তুত খাদ্য; সাধারণ ভোজনাগার, সাধারণ ভোজনশালা। 5. (*Herald.*) A charge or bearing of the simplest kind; (কুলবিদ্যা) অতি সাদাসিধা ধরণের কুলচিহ্ন। 6. An ungeared bicycle as distinguished from a *safety* bicycle; একপ্রকার দ্বিচক্রযান। **–ri-ly,** *adv.* Generally; usually; commonly; সাধারণতঃ; প্রায়শঃ; সচরাচর। **–ri-ness,** *n.* **Ordinary seaman**–(Abbr. *O. S.*) A seaman lower than an *able* one; সাধারণ নাবিক, অর্থাৎ পোতচালনপ্রবীণ নাবিক নহে। **An ambassador in ordinary**—বৈদেশিক রাজদরবারে স্থায়িভাবে নিযুক্ত রাজদূত। **In ordinary**—By permanent appointment; not temporary, as a physician; স্থায়িভাবে নিযুক্ত; অস্থায়ী নয়।

Ship in ordinary.

(Of a ship) Laid up; (জাহাজসম্পর্কে) অকর্ম্মণ্যভাবে রক্ষিত।

ŏr'-di-nāte, *n.* (*Geom.*) A straight line in a curve terminated by its sides and bisected by the axes; any of a series of parallel chords of conic section in relation to a bisecting diameter; (জ্যামিতি) কোন বক্রের পার্শ্বদ্বয় দ্বারা সীমাবদ্ধ এবং ঐ বক্রের অক্ষযুগলদ্বারা দ্বিখণ্ডিত তন্মধ্যবর্ত্তী সরল রেখা; দ্বিখণ্ডকারী ব্যাসের সম্পর্কে শঙ্কুচ্ছিন্নের সমান্তরাল পূর্ণজ্যাসমূহের অন্যতম, কোটি (হিঃ কোঃ)।

ŏr-di-nā'-tion, *n.* 1. Arrangement in order; classification; সুবিন্যাস; শ্রেণীবিভাগ। 2. Admission to church ministry; যাজকসমাজে গ্রহণ, প্রব্রজ্যা, উপসম্পদ। 3. Act of ordaining or decreeing, esp. as a divine action; বিধান, বিধির বিধান।

ŏr-di-nee' (-nē), *n.* A deacon newly ordained; নবনিযুক্ত যাজক।

ōrd'-nance (-năns), *n.* 1. Cannon; mounted guns; কামান; স্বস্থানে আরোপিত কামান। 2. The branch of the army service having the charge of esp. military stores and materials; সৈন্যদলের যে শাখার উপর সামরিকদ্রব্যসম্ভার রক্ষার ভার থাকে। **Ordnance datum**—ইংলণ্ডের সরকারী জরীপে গৃহীত সাগরসমতল। **Ordnance survey**—গ্রেটব্রিটেন এবং আয়র্লণ্ডের সরকারী জরীপ।

ŏr'-düre *n.* 1. Excrement; বিষ্ঠা, পুরীষ, গূথ, মল, বাহ্যি, গু (*colloq.*)। 2. (*Fig.*) Anything filthy; foul language; কদর্য্য জিনিষ; কদর্য্য ভাষা।

ōre *n.* 1. A mineral substance from which metals may be extracted by smelting; আকরজ পদার্থ, খনিজবিমিশ্র-ধাতু, খনিজপদার্থ, খনিজ (আয়ুঃ রসঃ), আকরিক ধাতু (হিঃ কোঃ), অসংস্কৃত-ধাতু (ঐ)। 2. (*Poet.*) Metal, esp. gold; (কবিতায়) ধাতু, বিশেষতঃ স্বর্ণ।

ō'-rē-ăd, *n.* (*Latin & Greek Myth.*) A mountain nymph; (ল্যাটিন এবং গ্রীকপুরাণ) শৈলপরী, শৈলদেবী, গিরিদেবী, গিরিদেবতা, বনদেবী।

ō-rĕc'-tic *adj.* (*Philos. & Med.*) Of, or relating to, desires or appetites; appetitive; (দর্শন ও ভৈষজ্য-শাস্ত্র) বাসনাসম্বন্ধীয়; বাসনাত্মক।

ō'-rē-īde *n.* A kind of brass like gold in brilliance and used for imitation jewellery etc.; একপ্রকার কেমিকেল সোনা, মায়াপুরীস্বর্ণ।

O-rĕs-tēs (ŏ-), *n.* A son of Agamemnon and Clytæmnestra; এগামেমনের পুত্র। ইহার মাতা Clytæmnestraর উপপতি Aegisthus, Orestesএর পিতাকে হত্যা করে। Orestes ভগ্নীর সাহায্যে পলায়ন করিয়া Phocis এর রাজার আশ্রয়প্রাপ্ত হন; Orestes তাঁহার আজীবনবন্ধু Pylades এর সহিত শিক্ষাপ্রাপ্ত হন। তৎপর তিনি দেশে ফিরিয়া মাতার তদীয় উপপতিকে নিহত করেন।

orfe (ŏrf), *n.* A kind of fish; একপ্রকার মৎস্য।

ŏr'-găn, *n.* 1. The largest wind-instrument of music; বৃহত্তম সুষির

Church organ.

যন্ত্র, যন্ত্ররাজ। 2. A harmonium; reed-organ; হার্ম্মনিয়ম; নলবেণু। 4. A part of an animal or vegetable by which some function is carried on; অঙ্গ (হিঃ কোঃ), অবয়ব (ঐ), ইন্দ্রিয়, জ্ঞানসাধন, করণ, কর্ম্মসাধন। 5. Voice with reference to its power or quality; as, he has a magnificent *organ*; স্বর, ধ্বনি। 6. A newspaper or journal representing a party, cause, sect, etc.; কোন সম্প্রদায় বা রাজনীতিক দল প্রভৃতির মুখপত্র। 7. (*Archaic*) An instrument or means; যন্ত্র, উপায়, সাধন, করণ। **–ist,** *n.* A player on the organ; যন্ত্ররাজ-বাদক। **–less,** *adj.* **Organ blower** — যন্ত্ররাজের ভস্ত্রাপরিচালক

ব্যক্তি বা যন্ত্র। **Organ builder**—যন্ত্ররাজনির্ম্মাতা। **Organ-grinder**—যন্ত্ররাজজাতীয় বাদ্যযন্ত্রবিশেষ বাদক **Organ-loft**—যন্ত্ররাজবাদনকক্ষ। **Organ-piano**—যন্ত্ররাজের মত ধ্বনিবিশিষ্ট পিয়ানোযন্ত্র। **Organ-screen** — এক প্রকার শোভাসাধক তিরস্করণী—যাহার উপর মহাধর্ম্মমন্দির প্রভৃতিতে যন্ত্ররাজ স্থাপিত হয়। **Organ of action**—কর্ম্মেন্দ্রিয় (হস্ত, পদ, প্রভৃতি)। **Organ of excretion**—পায়ু। **Organ of generation**—উপস্থ, জননেন্দ্রিয়। **Organ of motion**—গমনেন্দ্রিয়, পদ। **Organ of prehension** — গ্রহণেন্দ্রিয় (হিঃ কোঃ), হস্ত। **Orgns of sense**—জ্ঞানেন্দ্রিয় (হিঃ কোঃ) (চক্ষুঃ, কর্ণ, নাসিকা ইত্যাদি)। **Organs of speech**—বাক্, বাণী (হিঃ কোঃ)।

ŏr′-găn-die (-dĭ), *n.* A kind of very fine thin muslin; একপ্রকার অতি ফিনফিনে মলমল কাপড়।

ŏr-găn′-ĭc, *adj.* **1.** (*Physiol*) Of, or relating to, organs; vital; (opp. to *functional*); (শারীরবিজ্ঞান) ঐন্দ্রিয়িক (হিঃ কোঃ), শরীরযন্ত্রসম্বন্ধীয়, আঙ্গিক (হিঃ কোঃ), অঙ্গসম্বন্ধীয় (ঐ); জীবনব্যাপারসম্বন্ধীয়, জীবনী। **2.** (*Pathol.*) Affecting the structure of an organ, as a disease, (opp. to *functional*); (নিদানশাস্ত্র) যান্ত্রিক, দৈহিকযন্ত্রগঠিত। **3.** Consisting of, or containing, organs; of, or relating to, animals or vegetables, (opp. to *inorganic*); সাঙ্গ (হিঃ কোঃ), অঙ্গযুত (ঐ); জৈব। **4.** (*Chem.*) Existing as a constituent of organized bodies or formed from bodies so existing, as compound substances etc.; of, or relating to, hydrocarbons or their derivatives; (রসায়নশাস্ত্র) জৈব; উদজান বাষ্প এবং অঙ্গারকের মিশ্রণে উৎপন্ন রাসায়নিক যৌগিকপদার্থ সমূহ ও তৎসম্ভূত পদার্থরাজি সম্বন্ধীয়। **5.** Constitutional; fundamental; structural: দেহগত; মৌলিক; গঠনগত, গঠনপ্রণালী-সম্বন্ধীয়। **6.** Organized; systematic; as, an *organic* whole ব্যবস্থাবদ্ধ; প্রণালীবদ্ধ, সুব্যবস্থিত। **–i-cal-ly**, *adv.* **Organic chemistry**—জৈবরসায়নশাস্ত্র। **Organic disease**—যান্ত্রিকপীড়া, যে পীড়াতে কোন শারীরিকযন্ত্র বিকারপ্রাপ্ত হয়। **Organic remains**—জন্তু বা উদ্ভিদের শিলীভূত দেহাবশেষ।

ŏr′-găn-ĭsm, *n.* **1.** A body exhibiting organization or organic life; any animal or plant; organic structure: অঙ্গী (সাঃ পঃ), দেহী; জীব বা উদ্ভিদ; জীবাবয়ব (সাঃ পঃ), ইন্দ্রিয়বিশিষ্ট রচনা (কেভিঃ), অবয়ব (হিঃ কোঃ)। **2.** A whole of interdependent parts compared to a living being; "To speak of society as an *organism*"; অঙ্গ, শরীর (হিঃ কোঃ)।

ŏr-găn-ĭ-zā′-tion, *n.* **1.** Act of organizing; দেহগঠন (সাঃ পঃ), দেহবিধান (ঐ), ব্যবস্থাপন, ব্যবহারবদ্ধ করণ, অঙ্গসম্পাদন (হিঃ কোঃ), ব্যূহন (ঐ)। **2.** State or process of being organized; মণ্ডলীবদ্ধতা, ব্যবস্থাবদ্ধতা। **3.** That which is organized; an organized body or system; ব্যবস্থাবদ্ধাবয়ব, মণ্ডলী, সম্প্রদায়, সংঘ।

ŏr′-găn-īze, *v. t. & i.* **1.** To give an organic structure to; to make into living being or tissue, (usu. in *p. p.*); অঙ্গবিশিষ্ট করা; জীব বা বিধানতন্তুতে' পরিণত করা। **2.** To form into a systematic whole (with the whole or the parts as object); as, to *organize* an army or recruits; ব্যবস্থাবদ্ধ করা, মণ্ডলীবদ্ধ করা। **3.** To systematize; to get into a working order; as, to *organize* an institution, enterprise, etc.; to arrange for; as, to *organize* a picnic or procession; শৃঙ্খলাবদ্ধ করা, সুপ্রণালীবদ্ধ করা, ব্যূহবদ্ধ করা, ব্যবস্থাবদ্ধ করা; কার্য্যোপযোগী করা; বন্দোবস্ত করা। ***Verb i.*** To become organic; জৈবপ্রকৃতিবিশিষ্ট হওয়া। **–iz-a-ble**, *adj.* **–iz-er**, *n.* One who organizes; ব্যবস্থাপক, ব্যূহকার। **–ized**, *adj.*

ŏr′-gā-nŏn, –nŭm, *ns.* A prescribed method of philosophic or scientific inquiry; as, the *organon* of Aristotle; দার্শনিক বা বৈজ্ঞানিক তত্ত্বানুসন্ধানের নির্দ্দিষ্ট ধারা।

ŏr′-găn-zine (-zĭn), *n.* A silk thread made of several singles, twisted together; রেশমের কয়েকটী সূতা একত্র পাকাইয়া যে সূতা তৈয়ার করা হয়।

ŏr′-găsm, *n.* **1.** Excitement; rage; উত্তেজনা, আবেশ; ধূম। **2.** Erethism, esp. the height of venereal excitement, as in coition; কোন অঙ্গের উত্তেজনা, কামানল, কামাগ্নি, মদনানল, মদনদহন, স্মরগরল। **–gas′-tic**, *adj.*

ŏr′-geat (-zhăt), *n.* A drink made from barley or almonds; বার্লি বা বাদাম হইতে প্রস্তুত পানীয় বিশেষ।

ŏr-gĭ-ăs′-tic, *adj.* Pertaining to, or of the nature of, orgies; তান্ত্রিকচক্রসম্বন্ধীয়।

orgue (ŏrg), *n.* **1.** A thick piece of timber pointed and shod with iron; সূক্ষ্মাগ্র ও লোহার পাতে মোড়া কাষ্ঠখণ্ড। **2.** (*Mil.*) An arrangement of gun-barrels fired simultaneously; (সামরিকশাস্ত্র) এককালে গুচ্ছিত কামানের নালিসমূহ—যাহা হইতে এককালে গুলি ছোড়া হয়।

ŏr′-gy, *n.* **1.** (*Gk. & Rom. Antiq.*, usu. *pl.*) Revels or a festival in honour of Bacchus; (গ্রীক এবং রোমীয় প্রত্নতত্ত্ব) সুরাদেবতা ব্যাকাসের সম্মানার্থ অনুষ্ঠিত মদ্যপানোৎসব [cf. our ভৈরবীচক্র]। **2.** (*Sing. & pl.*) Drunken revelry; debauchery; মদ্যপানোৎসব, ব্যসনোৎসব; লাম্পট্য, ব্যভিচার।

ō′-rĭ-ĕl, *n.* A large projecting bay or recessed window, (also, *oriel*, *window*) : একপ্রকার সুবৃহৎ উদ্গত পশ্চাদ্দিকে অপসৃত বাতায়ন।

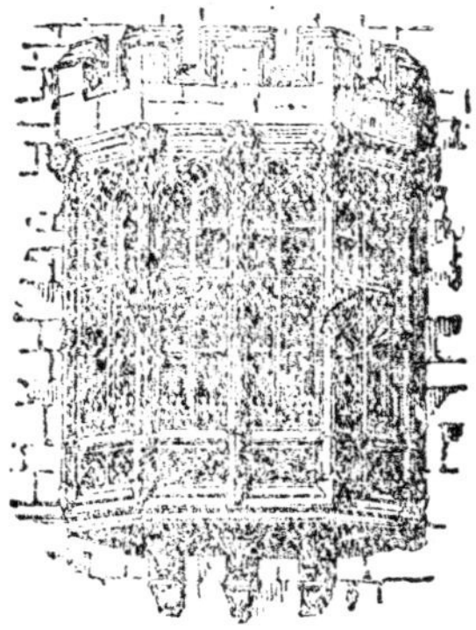

Oriel window

ō′-ri-ênt, *n.* & *adj.* **1.** (*Poet.*) The eastern part of the earth or sky ; (কবিতায়) পৃথিবী বা আকাশের পূর্ব্ব ভাগ, প্রাচী। **2.** The East ; the countries East of the Mediterranean and South Europe ; পূর্ব্বদেশ, প্রাচীদেশ, প্রাচ্যমহাদেশ ; ভূমধ্যসাগর এবং দক্ষিণ ইয়ুরোপের পূর্ব্বদিগ্‌বর্ত্তী দেশসমূহ। **3.** An orient pearl ; the lustre of a superior pearl ; উজ্জ্বল মুক্তা ; উৎকৃষ্ট মুক্তার দ্যুতি। ***Adj.*** **1.** (Of sun, daylight, etc.) Rising or appearing ; উদীয়মান, প্রকাশমান। **2.** (*Poet.*) Eastern ; (কবিতায়) প্রাচ্য, পূর্ব্বদেশীয়। **3.** Lustrous ; bright (of precious stones and esp. pearls of the best kind as coming anciently from the East) ; দ্যুতিমান, দীপ্তিমান, দীপ্যমান ; উজ্জ্বল।

ō′-ri-ĕnt, -ĕn-tāte, *v. t.* & *i.* **1.** To cause to face towards the East, as a building etc. ; to build, as a church with the chancel end due East ; পূর্ব্বাভিমুখীন করা ; খৃষ্টীয় ভজনালয়ের যে ভাগে যাজকবৃন্দ ও কীর্ত্তনসম্প্রদায় উপবেশন করে—তাহা পূর্ব্বাভিমুখীন করা। **2.** To bury with the feet eastward ; পদযুগল পূর্ব্বদিকে রাখিয়া সমাহিত করা। **3.** To set or determine the position of with reference to the points of the compass ; to ascertain the bearings of ; দিক্‌সম্পর্কে অবস্থিতি নির্ণয় করা ; দিঙ্‌নির্ণয় করা। **4.** (*Fig.*) To put, esp. oneself into a correct position or relation ; (লক্ষণায়) যথাস্থানে বা যথাযথ সম্পর্কে অবস্থিত করা। ***Verb i.*** To turn eastward or in a specified direction ; পূর্ব্বদিক অথবা কোন নির্দ্দিষ্ট দিকের অভিমুখীন হওয়া। **–en-ta′-tion**, *n.* **1.** The act or state of turning or facing towards the East ; প্রাচ্যাবর্ত্তন, পূর্ব্বমুখীকরণ, প্রাঙ্মুখকরণ, প্রাঙ্মুখত্ব, পূর্ব্বাভিমুখীনতা। **2.** Determining the East in taking bearing ; পূর্ব্বদিঙ্‌নির্ণয়। **3.** The lie of a thing ; দিক্‌সম্পর্কে কোন বস্তুর অবস্থিতি, স্থানসম্পর্ক (সাঃ পঃ)। **4.** (*Fig.*) The act of finding out one's true position ; কাহারও প্রকৃত অবস্থাননির্ণয়। **5.** The homing instinct of pigeon, etc ; কপোত প্রভৃতি যে সহজবুদ্ধির বলে অপরিচিত স্থান হইতে স্বগৃহে প্রত্যাবর্ত্তন করিতে পারে, স্বগৃহনির্ণয়শক্তি।

ō-ri-ĕn′-tăl, *adj.* & *n.* **1.** (*Archaic*) Eastern ; (অপ্রঃ) প্রাচ্য। **2.** Of, or relating to, the East, the orient or Asiatic countries ; coming from, or occurring in, the East ; characteristic of the civilization etc. of the East ; প্রাচ্য, পূর্ব্বদেশীয়, এসিয়ার অন্তর্গত দেশসমূহসম্বন্ধীয় ; পূর্ব্বদেশাগত, পূর্ব্বদেশে সংঘটিত ; প্রাচ্য-সভ্যতা প্রভৃতির বিশেষত্বদ্যোতক। **3.** (Of pearls etc.) Same as ORIENT *adj.* 3. ***Noun.*** A native of the East or an eastern country ; পূর্ব্বদেশীয় লোক, প্রাচ্যদেশবাসী। **–ism**, *n.* **1.** An eastern mode of thought or expression ; প্রাচ্যদেশসমুচিত চিন্তাপ্রণালী, প্রাচ্যদেশসমুচিত উক্তি। **2.** Erudition in oriental languages or literature ; প্রাচ্য ভাষা সমূহ বা প্রাচ্যসাহিত্যে পাণ্ডিত্য, প্রাচ্যবিদ্যায় পাণ্ডিত্য। **–ist**, *n.* **–ize**, *v. t.* & *i.* To make, or become, oriental in character, habits, etc. ; প্রাচ্যভাবাপন্ন করা, প্রাচ্যভাবাপন্ন হওয়া। **–ly**, *adv.* **Oriental stitch** — হেরীং মৎস্যের মেরুদণ্ডের অনুরূপ সেলাই বিশেষ।

ŏr′-i-fice (-fĭs), *n.* The mouth of a tube, pipe, etc. ; an aperture ; an opening ; ছিদ্র ; রন্ধ্র ; ফাঁক।

ŏr′-i-flamme (-flăm), *n.* **1.** The ancient royal standard of France, originally the banner of the abbey of St. Denis ; a standard in battle ; ফরাসীদেশের প্রাচীন রাজ-পতাকা ; রণপতাকা, যুদ্ধপতাকা। **2.** Something bright and conspicuous ; blaze of colour etc. ; "*Oriflamme* of flowers" ; সমুজ্জ্বল বস্তু ; বর্ণপ্রভৃতির দীপ্তি, দীপ্ত-রাগ।

ŏr′-i-găn, ō-rig′-ă-nŭm, *ns.* A genus of plants ; একজাতীয় বৃক্ষ।

ŏr′-i-ğin, *n.* **1.** Beginning of anything ; derivation ; আরম্ভ (হিঃ কোঃ), আদি, উৎপত্তি, উপক্রম, উদ্গম ; উদ্ভব, প্রভব (হিঃ কোঃ)। **2.** That from which anything proceeds ; source ; cause ; যোনি, উৎপত্তিস্থান, আগমস্থান ; মূল (হিঃ কোঃ), আদিকারণ (কেশ্ডিঃ) ; কারণ, হেতু (ব্রজঃ হিন্দুঃ)। **Origin of species**— See SPECIES.

ō-rig′-i-năl, *adj.* & *n.* **1.** Primitive ; innate ; initial ; as, *original* sin ; আদিম ; অন্তর্নিহিত ; প্রথম। **2.** Not derivative or dependant ; not copied ; মূলীভূত ; মৌলিক। **3.** Inventive ; thinking or acting for oneself ; novel ; উদ্ভাবনশীল ; মৌলিক চিন্তাশীল ; নূতন, নবজাত (হিঃ কোঃ), নবকল্পিত (ঐ)। ***Noun.*** **1.** (*Rare*) The origin ; descent ; source ; (অপ্রঃ) উৎপত্তি ; উদ্ভব ; মূল। **2.** Archetype ; model ; that from which anything is copied or translated ; মূল আদর্শ ; আদর্শ ; মূল। **3.** An eccentric person ; ছিটগ্রস্ত লোক, মাথাপাগলা লোক, কেমনতর

লোক। **–ly,** *adv.* Primarily ; at first ; আদিতে ; প্রথমে। **–nal′-i-ty,** *n.* State or quality of being original ; power of originating new thoughts or ideas ; আদিমতা ; মৌলিকতা। **Original research**—মৌলিক গবেষণা। **Original sin**—আদম ও ইভের পতনজনিত মানবের পাপ, আদিম পাপ, পাপাত্মতা (হিঃ কোঃ), নারকিতা (ঐ)। **In the original**—মূলগ্রন্থে, মূলে।

ŏ-rĭg′-i-nāte, *v. t.* & *i.* To give origin to ; to cause to begin ; to produce as new ; উৎপাদন করা ; প্রবর্ত্তন করা ; সৃষ্টি করা। ***Verb i.*** To have origin or beginning ; to begin to act or exist ; উৎপাদিত হওয়া, সৃষ্টি হওয়া ; প্রবর্ত্তিত হওয়া। **–na′-tion,** *n.* The act of originating ; উৎপাদন, প্রবর্ত্তন। **–na-tive,** *adj.* **–na-tor,** *n.* One who, or that which originates ; উৎপাদক, প্রবর্ত্তক, উদ্ভাবক, প্রথমোদ্ভাবক।

ŏ-rĭ-nā′-săl, *adj.* & *n.* Relating to, or uttered with, mouth and nose ; as, an *orinasal* vowel (French) ; মুখ এবং নাসিকা সম্পর্কীয়, মুখ এবং নাসিকা উভয়ের সহযোগে উচ্চারিত। ***Noun.*** An orinasal vowel ; নাসা এবং মুখ উভয়ের সাহায্যে উচ্চারিত স্বরবর্ণ।

ō′-rĭ-ōle, *n.* **1.** (Also *golden oriole*) A bird with golden

Golden oriole.

plumage ; স্বর্ণবর্ণ পালকশোভিত পক্ষি-বিশেষ। **2.** A genus of American birds of similar colour ; আমেরিকা দেশীয় স্বর্ণবর্ণ পক্ষিজাতিবিশেষ।

O-rī-ŏn (ö-), *n.* Son of Hyrieus, and a celebrated hunter ; Hyrieus এর পুত্র, ভীমকায় মৃগয়াকুশল Orion। ইনি Chios নামক স্থানে আসিলে পর তথাকার Merope নাম্নী রূপসীর প্রেমে মুগ্ধ হন। Meropeএর পিতা Orionএর নিকট কন্যা বিবাহ দিতে অযথা বিলম্ব করাতে তিনি Meropeএর সতীত্বনাশের চেষ্টা পান। এই অপরাধের জন্য সুরাদেবতা Bacchus. গভীর নিদ্রায় অভিভূত করিয়া Orionকে অন্ধীভূত করেন। Orion উদীয়মান সূর্য্যের রশ্মিতে চক্ষুর্দ্বয় স্নাত করিয়া পুনর্ব্বার দৃষ্টিশক্তি প্রাপ্ত হন। অবশেষে ইহাকে তারকাপুঞ্জের মধ্যে প্রতিষ্ঠিত করা হয়।

O-rī′-ŏn (ö-), *n.* (*Astron.*) A bright constellation of stars ; কালপুরুষ, অগ্রহায়ণী। **Orion's belt**—ইষুত্রিখণ্ড (সূর্য্যঃ বিঃ)। **Orion's hound**—মৃগব্যাধ (সাঃ পঃ)। **Stars in the head of orion**—চান্দ্রমস (সাঃ পঃ), ইন্বল (ঐ)।

O-rī′-ŏn-ĭd (ö-), *n.* A meteoric ring having its radiant point in Orion ; উল্কাবলয় বিশেষ—যাহার উজ্জ্বল-বিন্দু কালপুরুষে স্থিত আছে।

ŏr′-ĭ-sŏn, *n.* (*Archaic*) A prayer or supplication, (usu. in *pl.*); (অপ্রঃ) প্রার্থনা, স্তব, স্তোত্র, স্তুতি, মিনতি।

Or′-lē-ăns (ŏr-), *n.* (From a French city) **1.** A kind of plum ; একপ্রকার শা-আলু। **2.** A cloth of worsted and cotton ; উলসূতা ও কার্পাসের সূতায় তৈরী কাপড় বিশেষ।

ŏr′-lŏp, *n.* The lowest deck of a ship ; জাহাজের নিম্নতম পাটাতন।

ŏr′-mêr, *n.* An edible mollusc ; the Sea-ear ; একপ্রকার ভোজনোপযোগী শম্বুক ; কর্ণাকৃতি শম্বুক

ŏr-mō-lü′, *n.* **1.** Gilded bronze used in decorating furniture ; গৃহসজ্জাদি মণ্ডনে ব্যবহৃত স্বর্ণপত্রমণ্ডিত বর্ত্তলোহ। **2.** An alloy of copper, zinc and tin, having the colour of gold ; তাম্র, দস্তা ও বঙ্গের মিশ্রণে প্রস্তুত স্বর্ণবর্ণ মিশ্রধাতু। **3.** Articles made of, or decorated with, these ; ঐরূপ কৃত্রিম স্বর্ণে প্রস্তুত বা উহা দ্বারা মণ্ডিত বস্তু।

ŏr′-nă-mĕnt, *n.* **1.** (*Eccl.*, usu. *pl.*) The accessories of a church or its worship ; ভজনালয় বা তৎসংসৃষ্ট পূজোপাসনার অঙ্গ। **2.** That which adorns ; a quality or person confirming grace or honour ; as, he is an *ornament* to his country ; অলঙ্কার, গহনা, মণ্ডন, আকল্প, (cf. আকল্পসারোরূপজীবাজনঃ—দশকুঃ); ভূষণ, বিভূষণ, আভরণ। **3.** (No *pl.*) Adorning ; embellishment ; decoration ; as, by way of *ornament* ; বিভূষণ, প্রসাধন ; বিমণ্ডন ; ভূষা। **–men′-tal,** *adj.* Pertaining to ornament ; serving to ornament ; আলঙ্কারিক ; শোভাসাধক, শোভাজনক, বিভূষক, শোভাপ্রদ, শোভাদায়ক। **–men′-tal-ism,** *n.* **–men′-tal-ist,** *n.* One occupying himself with ornamental art ; শোভাসাধক শিল্পকার্য্যে নিরত ব্যক্তি। **–men′-tal-ly,** *adv.*

ŏr′-nă-mĕnt, *v. t.* To adorn ; to decorate ; অলঙ্কৃত করা ; বিমণ্ডিত করা, বিভূষিত করা। **–men-ta′-tion,** *n.* **1.** Act of ornamenting ; state of being ornamented ; অলঙ্ক্রিয়া ; কৃতালঙ্কারত্ব। **2.** Ornaments or decorations ; অলঙ্কার, ভূষা, মণ্ডন।

ŏr′-nāte′, *adj.* **1.** Richly or excessively adorned ; সমালঙ্কৃত, বিমণ্ডিত। **2.** (Of a literary style etc.) Embellished with flowers of rhetoric etc. ; (ভাষা-সম্বন্ধে) অলঙ্কারবহুল। **–ly,** *adv.* **–ness,** *n.*

ŏr′-nĭ-thoid (-thoyd), *adj.* Bird-like in structure as some reptiles ; পক্ষিবৎ গঠনবিশিষ্ট।

ŏr-nĭ-thŏl′-ŏ-ġȳ, *n.* The science treating of birds ; a treatise on this subject ; পক্ষি-বিদ্যা, পক্ষি-বর্ণনবিদ্যা, বিহঙ্গবিদ্যা ; পক্ষিবিদ্যাবিষয়ক পুস্তক। **–tho-log′-i-cal,** *adj.* Pertaining to ornithology ; পক্ষি-শাস্ত্র বিষয়ক। **–thol′-o-gist,** *n.*

ŏr′-nĭ-thō-măn-ċȳ, *n.* Divination by the observation of birds, their flight, etc. ; পক্ষী, পক্ষীর উড্ডয়ন প্রভৃতি দ্বারা ভবিষ্যৎ কথন।

ŏr-nĭ-thō-rhyn′-chŭs (-rĭng-) *n.* A duckbilled mammal ; হংসবৎচঞ্চু-বিশিষ্ট স্তন্যদায়ী জন্তু-বিশেষ।

Ornithorhynchus.

ŏr-nĭ-thŏs′-cŏ-pȳ, *n.* Augury ; শকুনবিদ্যা।

ŏ-rŏg′-ră-phȳ, –rē-ŏg′-ră-phȳ, *ns.* The branch of physical geography dealing with mountains ; শৈলতত্ত্ব। **–ro(-re-o)-graph′-ic, –ro(-re-o)-graph′-i-cal,** *adjs.*

ŏ-rŏl′-ō-ġȳ, –rē-ŏl′-ō-ġȳ, *ns.* The science of mountain ; শৈলবিজ্ঞান, গিরিবিজ্ঞান। **–ro(-re-o)-log′-i-cal,** *adjs.* **–gist,** *ns.* One versed in orology ; শৈলবিজ্ঞানবিদ্‌।

ō′-roide (-roȳd), *n.* An alloy of copper and zinc like gold in colour ; তাম্র ও দস্তার সহযোগে প্রস্তুত স্বর্ণবর্ণ মিশ্রধাতু বিশেষ, মায়াস্বর্ণ।

ō′-rō-tŭnd, *adj.* & *n.* **1.** Full, clear and musical, (of a voice or vocal delivery) ; সুশ্রাব্য ও ওজস্বী। **2.** Pompous ; magniloquent ; bombastic ; জমকালো ; বাগাড়ম্বরপূর্ণ ; শব্দাড়ম্বরপূর্ণ। ***Noun.*** The orotund voice or utterance ; উচ্চস্পষ্ট ও ওজঃপূর্ণ, স্বর বা উক্তি।

ŏr′-phăn, *n., adj.* & *v. t.* A child bereaved of father or mother or both ; পিতৃহীন বা মাতৃহীন বালক বা বালিকা, পিতৃমাতৃহীন বালক বা বালিকা, অনাথ, ছেঁওড়া (*colloq.* cf. Sans. ছেমন্ড = orphan)। ***Adj.*** Bereaved of parents or either of them ; পিতৃমাতৃহীন, পিতৃহীন, মাতৃহীন, অপিতৃক, অমাতৃক, মাতৃপিতৃবিহীন। ***Verb t.*** To deprive of a parent or parents ; পিতৃমাতৃহীন করা। **–hood,** *n.* **–ize,** *v. t.* To make orphan ; পিতৃহীন করা, মাতৃহীন করা, পিতৃমাতৃহীন করা।

ŏr′-phăn-āge, *n.* **1.** The state of an orphan ; পিতৃমাতৃহীনতা, মাতৃপিতৃবিহীনতা। **2.** An institution for the care of orphans ; অনাথ-নিবাস, অনাথাশ্রম।

Or′-pheus (ŏr-fūs), *n.* **1.** Son of the muse Calliope ; বাগ্‌দেবী Calliope এর পুত্র, গ্রীসের প্রাগ্‌ হোমরীয় যুগের সুপ্রসিদ্ধ কবি। এপলো দেব Orpheusকে একটী বীণা দান করেন। যখন তিনি এই বীণাযন্ত্র বাদন করিতেন—তখন নদী, তরু, পাষাণ প্রভৃতি পর্য্যন্ত স্বস্থানচ্যুত হইয়া তাহার ইচ্ছানুসারে চালিত হইত। Orpheus এর স্ত্রী Eurydice এর সর্পাঘাতে মৃত্যু হইলে তিনি তাহার উদ্ধারের জন্য যম-লোকে গমন করেন। অধঃলোকের অধি-পতি Pluto, Orpheusএর বীণাবাদনে বিমোহিত হইয়া Eurydiceকে এই সর্ত্তে প্রদান করেন যে Orpheus পৃথিবীতে না পৌঁছা পর্য্যন্ত স্ত্রীর দিকে ফিরিয়া চাহিতে পারিবেন না। বিধির বিড়ম্বনায় Orpheus পৃথিবীতে পদার্পণ করিতেছেন, ঠিক এমনি সময়ে একবার পশ্চাতে ফিরিয়া চাহিবামাত্র Eurydice অদৃশ্যা হইলেন। Orpheus মনের দুঃখে নির্জ্জন গিরিগুহায় গমন করেন। তৎকালে তদীয় প্রণয়লাভের জন্য আকুলিতচিত্তা থ্রেসপ্রদেশবাসিনী সুরাপানমত্তা সুন্দরীগণকে প্রত্যাখ্যান করায়—তাহারা পদদলিতা ব্যাঘ্রীর ন্যায় ক্রোধে ক্ষিপ্তা হইয়া Orpheusকে খণ্ড বিখণ্ড করেন। Orpheusএর মৃত্যুর পর বাগ্‌দেবীগণ তাঁহার দেহাবশেষ Olympus গিরির পাদদেশে সমাহিত করেন এবং দেবরাজ Zeus Orpheusএর বীণা নক্ষত্রলোকে স্থাপন করিয়াছিলেন। **2.** The mythical founder of a school of mystic theology ; থ্রীকদেশের জনৈক প্রসিদ্ধ তান্ত্রিক।

Or′-phic (ŏr), **–phē-ăn,** *adjs.* **1.** Of, or relating to, Orpheus, a Thracian poet and musician ; relating to the mysteries or doctrines associated with his name ; mysterious ; থ্রেসদেশীয় কবি এবং সঙ্গীতজ্ঞ অরফিয়াস সম্বন্ধীয় ; অরফিয়াসের নামসংসৃষ্ট তান্ত্রিকক্রিয়াকলাপ এবং উপদেশাবলী সম্বন্ধীয় ; রহস্যপূর্ণ। **2.** Like the music of Orpheus ; entrancing ; অরফিয়াসের সঙ্গীতের মত ; সম্মোহক।

ŏr′-phrey, –fray (-frā), *ns.* A band or bands of rich gold embroidery affixed to ecclesiastical vestments ; যাজকীয় পরিচ্ছদে সংবদ্ধ উজ্জ্বল স্বর্ণসূত্রের সূচীকার্য্যমণ্ডিত বেষ্টনী বা বেষ্টনীসমূহ।

ŏr′-pĭ-mĕnt, *n.* A yellow mineral consisting of sulphur and arsenic ; হরিতাল, গৌর, রক্তোপল (yellow), গোদন্ত, তাল, (সাঃ পঃ), তালক (ঐ), হরিৎ (ঐ), মনঃশিলা (red), রক্তধাতু (*ib.*), [Also পীতক, পীত-পিঞ্জর (মঃ উঃ), আল (সুশ্রুঃ), অল (অঃ), বিয়ঙ্গ (রঃ রঃ সঃ প্রঃ)]।

ŏr′-pĭn(e), *n* A succulent harbaceous plant ; একপ্রকার রসপূর্ণ গুল্ম।

Or′-ping-tŏn (ŏr-), *n.* A breed of poultry (From the name of a village in Kent) ; একজাতীয় কুক্কুট।

ŏr′-rĕr-ȳ, *n.* A contrivance to illustrate the sizes, positions and revolutions of the planets ; [after the Earl of Orrery (1700) for whom one was made] ; গ্রহের গতি, অবস্থান, ও আবর্ত্তন প্রদর্শনের জন্য কৌশলবিশেষ, গ্রহ-গতিমাপক, গ্রহগতিসূচকযন্ত্র।

ŏr′-ris (-ĭs), *n.* A sort of gold or silver lace or embroidery ; একপ্রকার জরির ফিতা বা গোটা বা স্বর্ণ বা রজতসূত্রমণ্ডিত সূচিকর্ম্ম।

ŏr′-ris (-ĭs), *n.* (*Rare*) A kind of iris (plant) ; একপ্রকার দশবাইচণ্ডী। **Orris root**—The fragrant ro of three species of iris used in perfumery and medicine;

পুষ্করমূল (গোরা), উস্তুর-উস্‌শোশন (আরবী ভাষায়), বেগ বালফ্‌শা (হিন্দী), কেওড়া কি জড় (হিন্দী বেঙ্গ:)। **Orris powder**—পুষ্করমূলচূর্ণ।

Or'-son (ŏr-sŭn), *n.* A rough valiant person. (From the tale of Valentine and Orson); সাহসী এবং রুক্ষ প্রকৃতির লোক।

ŏrt, *n.* (Usu. *pl.*) A scrap of food left, (*Archaic* or *dial.*); ভোজনাবশেষ, ভুক্তাবশিষ্ট, উচ্ছিষ্ট (অপ্রচলিত বা উপভাষায়)।

ŏr-thŏ-cē-phăl'-ic, *adj.* With the breadth of the skull from $\frac{4}{5}$ to $\frac{5}{6}$ of the length; দৈর্ঘ্যে $\frac{4}{5}$ হইতে $\frac{5}{6}$ গুণ প্রস্থ করোটীবিশিষ্ট।

ŏr-thō-chrō-măt'-ic, *adj.* (*Photog.*) Giving correct relative intensity to colours; (আলোকচিত্র) বিশুদ্ধ আপেক্ষিক বর্ণগাঢ়ত্বপ্রদ।

ŏr'-thō-clase, *n.* Potash-felspar; একপ্রকার ফেলেপাপল।

ŏr'-thŏ-dŏx, *adj.* **1.** Holding the accepted faith, belief or doctrine; not heretical; প্রচলিত ধর্ম্মানুসারী, দক্ষিণমার্গী (কেভিঃ); প্রাচীন পথাবলম্বী (হিঃ কোঃ), যথাস্থিতপন্থাগ্রাহী (ঐ); স্বধর্ম্মনিষ্ঠ। **2.** Generally accepted as right or true, esp. in theology; approved; conventional; সর্ব্বজনগৃহীত; অনুমোদিত; প্রথাসঙ্গত, যথাশাস্ত্র (কেভিঃ)। **—ly,** *adv.* **The Orthodox Church**—প্রাচ্য অথবা গ্রীক ধর্ম্মসংঘ।

ŏr'-thŏ-dŏx-ỹ, *n.* State of being orthodox; গোঁড়ামি, স্বধর্ম্মনিষ্ঠা, নৈষ্ঠিকতা, শাস্ত্রানুসারিতা, দক্ষিণাচার (কেভিঃ), যথাশাস্ত্রতা (ঐ))

ŏr'-thō-ē-pỹ, *n.* The science of correct pronunciation; শুদ্ধোচ্চারণ-বিদ্যা। **—ep'-ic,** *adj.* **—pist,** *n.*

ŏr-thŏg'-nă-thous (-thŭs), *adj.* Having the front of the face or the skull, nearly perpendicular; মুখ অথবা করোটীর সম্মুখভাগ লম্বিত।

ŏr-thŏg'-ō-năl, *adj.* Right-angled; সমকোণী।

ŏr-thŏg'-ră-phỹ, *n.* **1.** Correct spelling; mode of spelling; as, his *orthography* is shocking; বর্ণশুদ্ধি শুদ্ধাক্ষরবিন্যাস, শুদ্ধাক্ষরন্যাস; বর্ণবিন্যাসরীতি। **2.** That part of grammar treating of the nature and properties of letters and of their combination to express sounds and words; ব্যাকরণের যে অংশে বর্ণশুদ্ধি সম্বন্ধে আলোচনা থাকে, বর্ণপ্রকরণ, বর্ণন্যাস। **3.** A drawing in correct projection esp. an elevation or a vertical section; গৃহাদির উচ্চতায় ব্যবহৃত চিত্র। **—tho-graph'-ic, —tho-graph'-i-cal,** *adjs.* **—tho-graph'-i-cal-ly,** *adv.*

ŏr'-thō-pē-dỹ, *n.* The curing of deformities in the human body, esp. in children; surgery directed to this; মানবদেহের, বিশেষতঃ শিশুদেহের বিকৃতি দূরীকরণ; ঐরূপ বিকৃতিঅপসারণবিষয়ক অস্ত্রোপচার বিদ্যা। **—pe'-dic,** *adj.*

ŏr-thŏp-nē'-ă, *n.* (*Med.*) A morbid condition in which respiration can be performed only in an erect posture; (ভৈষজ্য-শাস্ত্র) অর্দ্ধ দণ্ডায়মান অবস্থা ভিন্ন অন্যপ্রকারে শ্বাসত্যাগে অসমর্থতা।

ŏr-thŏp'-tĕr-ă, *n.* An order of insects with straight narrow forewings including cockroaches,

Orthoptera.

crickets, etc.; তেলাপোকা, ঝিঁঝিঁপোকা প্রভৃতি কীটবর্গ, অসমপত্রী (সাঃ পঃ)।

ŏr-thŏp'-tĕr-ous (-ŭs), *adj.* Of, or relating to, the order of insects orthoptera; অসমপত্রি-সম্পর্কীয়।

ŏr-thŏp'-tic, *adj.* & *n.* **1.** Of, or relating to, correct vision; সঠিক দৃষ্টিসম্পর্কীয়। **2.** (Of an opaque disc) perforated with three small holes, through one of which a rifleman looks in taking aim; (অস্বচ্ছ চক্রসম্বন্ধে) রন্ধ্রত্রয়বিশিষ্ট। *Noun.* Such an opaque disc; রন্ধ্রত্রয়বিশিষ্ট অস্বচ্ছ চক্র।

ŏr'-thō-tōne, *adj.* Having an independent accent as a word; স্বতন্ত্রস্বর চিহ্নবিশিষ্ট।

ŏr'-tō-lăn, *n.* A European bird of the bunting family, esteemed as a table delicacy; ইয়ুরোপীয় পক্ষিবিশেষ—ইহার মাংস অতীব উপাদেয়।

ō'-rỹx, *n.* A large African antelope with straight horns; আফ্রিকাদেশীয় ঋজুশৃঙ্গ বৃহৎকায় কৃষ্ণসার মৃগবিশেষ।

Oryza sativa—ধান (বেঙ্গ:)।

Os'-căn (ŏs-), *adj* & *n.* Of, or relating to, a primitive people of Campania in Italy or their language; ইতালীর অন্তর্গত ক্যামপেনিয়া প্রদেশের আদিম অধিবাসীগণ বা তাহাদের ভাষাসম্বন্ধীয়। *Noun.* A member of that race of people; their language; ঐ জাতির লোক; উহাদের ভাষা।

ŏs'-cĭl-lāte, *v. i.* & *t.* **1.** To swing to and fro like a pendulum; দোদুল্যমান হওয়া, দোলা, ঝুলা, আন্দোলিত হওয়া। **2.** (*Fig.*) To vary; to fluctuate in opinion, action, condition, etc.; (লক্ষণায়) পরিবর্ত্তিত হওয়া; ইতস্ততঃ করা, সন্দেহ দোলায় দোলায়মান হওয়া। *Verb t.* (*Rare*) To swing back and forth; (অপ্রঃ) দোলান, ঝুলান। **—la'-tion,** *n.* **1.** Act or state of oscillating; vibration; আন্দোলন, দোলন; পরিস্পন্দন, পরিদোলন। **2.** Fluctuation; variation; ইতস্ততঃ বিচলন; রূপান্তর, পরিবর্ত্তন। **—la-tor,** *n.* **—la-to-ry,** *adj.*

ŏs-cĭ-tā'-tion, *n.* (*Rare*) Yawning; negligence; হাই তোলন; অসাবধানতা, অবহেলা।

ŏs'-cū-lār, *adj.* 1. Of, or relating to, the mouth or kissing; মুখসম্বন্ধীয়, চুম্বনসম্বন্ধীয়। 2. (*Geom.*) Pertaining to a higher order of contact than the first; (জ্যামিতি) স্পর্শের প্রকার বিশেষ সম্পর্কীয়।

ŏs'-cū-lāte, *v. i. & t.* 1. (*Rare*) To kiss; চুম্বন করা। 2. (*Math.*) To touch as one curve touches another when they have the same curvature at the point of contact; উভয় বক্রের বক্রতা স্পর্শবিন্দুতে সমান হইলে এক বক্র অপর বক্রকে যে ভাবে স্পর্শ করে তেমনভাবে পরস্পরকে স্পর্শ করা। 3. (*Nat. Hist.*) To have characters in common with two species or groups; (প্রাকৃতিক ইতিহাস) দুই শ্রেণী বা সম্প্রদায়ের সহিত সাধারণ প্রকৃতিবিশিষ্ট হওয়া। **—lant**, *adj.* 1. Kissing; clinging; চুম্বনকারী, চুম্বী (in comp.); আলিঙ্গনকারী। 2. (*Nat. Hist.*) Forming a connecting link between two groups or species; adhering closely; (প্রাকৃতিক ইতিহাস) দুই দল বা সম্প্রদায়ের সহিত সংযোগশৃঙ্খলস্থাপক; লাগালাগি। **—la'-tion**, *n.* **—la-to-ry**, *adj.*

ō'-sī-êr, *n.* & *adj.* Various species of willow used in basket-making; shoot of these; ঝুড়ি তৈয়ারে ব্যবহৃত বিভিন্ন প্রকার নম্রশাখতরু, শর, খাগড়া; ঐ সকল গাছের ডগা। ***Adj.*** Of, or relating to, osier; শর, খাগড়া, প্রভৃতি সম্পর্কীয়।

O-sī'-ris (ō-), *n.* The greatest god of Egypt; মিশরের সর্ব্বশ্রেষ্ঠ দেবতা। মিশর দেশে ইঁহার নাম Ausar। ইনি মানবজাতিকে সভ্য করেন এবং কৃষি, ধর্ম্ম আইন, প্রভৃতির ইনিই প্রবর্ত্তক। ইনি স্বীয় ভগিনী Isisএর পাণিগ্রহণ করেন।

Os'-man-li (ŏs-măn-lē), *adj.* & *n.* Same as **OTTOMAN.**

ŏs'-mī-ŭm, *n.* A metal of the platinum group; প্ল্যাটিনামশ্রেণীর ধাতুবিশেষ।

ŏs'-mōse ŏs-mō'-sĭs, *ns.* (*Phys.*) Percolation and intermixture of fluids separated by porous septa; tendency of fluids to such percolation and intermixture (পদার্থ বিদ্যা) সচ্ছিদ্র ব্যবধান দ্বারা পৃথকীকৃত তরলপদার্থের পরিস্রবণ, চর্ম্মান্তর্যাগ; (সাং পং); এরূপ পরিস্রবণ ও সংমিশ্রণ-প্রবণতা। **—mot'-ic**, *adj.* **—mot'-i-cal-ly**, *adv.*

ŏs'-mŭnd, *n.* 1. The Flowering Fern; পুষ্পপ্রদ পর্ণাঙ্গ। 2. Any fern of the genus Osmunda; বিলজ পর্ণাঙ্গ।

Os'-mŭn'-dá (ŏs-), *n.* (*Bot.* A genus of swamp ferns; (উদ্ভিদ্‌বিদ্যা) একজাতীয় বিলজ পর্ণাঙ্গ।

ŏs'-prey (-prā), *n.* 1. A kind of hawk or eagle feeding on fish;

Osprey.

মাছমোড়ল (যোঃ), কুরল। 2. (A milliner's name for) An egret-plume worn on a hat or bonnet; টুপি প্রভৃতির উপর পরিহিত বকজাতীয় পক্ষিবিশেষের পালক।

ŏs'-sē-ous (-ŭs), *adj.* 1. Consisting of, or resembling, bone; অস্থিময়, অস্থিবৎ। 2. Having a long skeleton; as, *osseous* fish; অস্থিপূর্ণ, কঙ্কালময়। 3. Abounding in fossil bones; শিলীভূত অস্থিপূর্ণ।

ŏs'-si-cle (-kl), *n.* (*Anat.*) A small bone; (শারীরসংস্থানবিদ্যা) ক্ষুদ্রাস্থি।

ŏs'-si-frăge, *n.* Same as **OSPREY n. 1.**

ŏs'-sĭ-fȳ, *n., v. i. & t.* 1. To turn into bone; অস্থিতে পরিণত করা। 2. To harden; as, to *ossify* the heart; কঠিন করা। **—fi-ca-tion**, *n.* **—sif-ic**, *adj.*

ŏs'-sū-ā-rȳ, *n.* 1. A receptacle for the bones of the dead; a charnel-house; মৃত ব্যক্তির অস্থি-সংরক্ষণ ভাণ্ড; শবাস্থিসংরক্ষণস্থান। 2. A cave where ancient bones are found; যে গহ্বরে প্রাচীনকালের লোকদিগের অস্থি পাওয়া যায়।

ŏs-tĕn'-sĭ-ble (-bl), *adj.* Pretended; professed; apparent and not real; কল্পিত; ব্যক্ত; আপাতদৃষ্ট, স্পষ্ট, প্রত্যক্ষ। **—bly**, *adv.* In an ostensible manner; professedly; আপাতদৃষ্টভাবে, দৃষ্টতঃ; ব্যক্তভাবে।

ŏs-tĕn'-sō-rȳ, *n.* A receptacle in which to display the Host to the congregation; যে ভাণ্ডে খৃষ্টের অন্তিমভোজনানুষ্ঠানের রুটিকা উপাসক-মণ্ডলীকে প্রদর্শিত হয়।

ŏs-tĕn-tā'-tion, *n.* Ambitious or vain display; pretentious show; an attempt to attract notice; জাঁক, জাঁকজমক; আড়ম্বর, ধুম, ধুমধাম, সমারোহ; ভড়ং, ঘটা। **—tious**, *adj.* Intended for vain display; showy; making a display from vanity; ধুমধামপূর্ণ, জাঁকাল; আড়ম্বরপূর্ণ; আড়ম্বর-প্রদর্শিত, সমারোহপূর্ণ। **—tious-ly**, *adv.*

ŏs-tē-ō-gĕn'-ē-sĭs, -gĕn-cȳ, *ns.* The formation or growth of bone; অস্থিগঠন, অস্থিবৃদ্ধি।

ŏs-tē-ŏg-rā-phȳ, *n.* Scientific description of the bones; অস্থি-বর্ণন।

ŏs'-tē-oid (-ŏyd), *adj.* Resembling bone; bony; অস্থিসদৃশ; অস্থিময়।

ŏs-tē-ŏl'-ō-gȳ, *n.* That section of anatomy dealing with bones and their structure, etc.; অস্থিবিদ্যা, অস্থিতত্ত্ব, অস্থিবর্ণন, অস্থিপ্রকরণ।

ŏs-tē-ō-mă-la'-cĭ-á (-shĭ-), *n.* Softening of bones due to the deficiency of phosphate of lime; ফস্ফেট অব লাইমের অভাব হেতু অস্থির কোমলতা।

ŏs-tī′-tis, *n.* Inflammation of bones ; অস্থিপ্রদাহ।

ost′-lêr (ŏs-), *n.* A stableman at an inn ; সরাইয়ের সহিস।

ŏs-tră′-ci-ŏn (-shē-), *n.* (*Zool.*) A genus of plectognath fishes

Ostracion or trunk-fish.

having the body covered with solid, immovable bony plates ; একজাতীয় মৎস্য।

os′-tră-cīze, *v. t.* **1.** (*Gk. antiq.*) To banish as a dangerously powerful or unpopular citizen, in Athens by popular vote inscribed on potsherd or a shell ; (গ্রীক পুরাতত্ত্ব) প্রাচীন এথেন্স নগরীতে কোন দুর্দ্দান্ত বা জনসাধারণের বিরাগভাজন ব্যক্তিকে জনগণের মত দ্বারা নির্ব্বাসিত করা। [মতদাতৃগণের মত মৃৎপাত্রখণ্ড বা শুক্তির উপর অঙ্কিত হইত।] **2.** To exclude from society ; সমাজচ্যুত করা। **—cism,** *n.* **1.** (*Gr. antiq.*) A mode of political banishment in Athens effected by public vote ; প্রাচীন এথেন্স নগরীতে জনমত দ্বারা নির্ব্বাসন-প্রথা। **2.** Expulsion from society ; সমাজচ্যুতি।

ŏs′-trē-i-cŭl-tūre, *n.* Oyster-culture ; শুক্তির চাষ।

ŏs-trē-ŏph′-ă-gous (-gŭs), *adj.* Eating oysters ; শুক্তি-খাদক।

Ostrich.

ŏs′-trich, *n.* The largest bird existing, a native of Africa, noted for its swiftness in running and most esteemed for its feathers ; উটপক্ষী, খগোষ্ট্র (আঃ বঃ)। **Ostrich-farm** — উটপক্ষী পালনের জন্য স্থান। **Ostrich-plume**— উটপক্ষীর পালকগুচ্ছ। **Ostrich policy** or **belief**—Policy or belief depending on self-delusion ; আত্মপ্রতারণামূলক নীতি বা বিশ্বাস, খগোষ্ট্রনীতি. [উটপক্ষী বালির নীচে মাথা ঢুকাইয়া মনে করে তাহাকে কেহ দেখিতে পায় না।] **Ostrich-tip**— উটপক্ষীর পালকের অগ্রভাগ।

ō-tăl′-gĭ-ă, *n.* Pain in the ear ; ear-ache ; কর্ণশূল।

oth′-êr (ŭth-), *adj., n., pron.* & *adv.* **1.** Not the same as one or more already specified ; remaining ; as, his *other* sons ; অপর, অন্য, অন্যতর, ইতর (হিঃ কোঃ) ; অবশিষ্ট। **2.** Additional ; different (*than* or *from*) ; as, a few *other* examples : gifts *other* than flowers ; অতিরিক্ত ; ভিন্ন, অন্যরূপ। ***Noun. & Pron.*** Other person, thing or specimen, etc. ; as, do good to *others* ; অপরব্যক্তি, অন্যলোক, অন্যবস্তু। ***Adv.*** Otherwise ; as, *other* than cursorily ; অন্যপ্রকারে, ভিন্নপ্রকারে, অন্যরূপে। **Otherguess**—*adj.,* (*Archaic* & *colloq.*) Of a very different kind : (অপ্রচলিত ও চলিতভাষায়) সম্পূর্ণ ভিন্ন রকমের। **Otherwhence**—From elsewhere ; অন্য স্থান হইতে। **Otherwhere(s)**—(*Poet.*) Elsewhere ; (কবিতায়) অন্যত্র। **Otherwhile(s)**— At other time ; অন্য সময়ে, অন্যকালে। **Other-world**—(*adj.*) Concerned with, or thinking of, the other world only ; পরকাল-সংসৃষ্ট, কেবল পরকালের চিন্তায় রত। **Other worldli-ness,** *n.* **Other-world-ly**—(*adv.*) **Every other**—Every second ; প্রতি দ্বিতীয়। **Every other day**—On alternate days ; একদিন অন্তর। **I can do no other**— (*Archaic*) *i. e.* nothing else ; (অপ্রঃ) আমি অন্য কিছু করিতে পারি না। **On the other hand**—পক্ষান্তরে। **One time or other**—(*adv.*) কোন না কোন সময়ে। **Some one or other**— A person unknown ; কোন একজন। **Some time or other**— (*Adv.*) কোন না কোন সময়ে। **The other day**—A few days ago ; সেদিন। **The other world**—Future life ; পরলোক।

oth′-êr-nĕss (ŭth-), *n.* **1.** (*Rare*) State of being other ; difference ; (কচিদ্‌ব্যবহৃত) অন্যতা, ভিন্নতা ; বৈভিন্ন্য। **2.** Something other than the thing mentioned or the thinking subject ; উল্লিখিত বিষয় ব্যতিরিক্ত বস্তু, জ্ঞেয়বস্তু।

oth′-êr-wīse (ŭth-), *adv.* **1.** In a different manner ; অন্যভাবে, ভিন্ন রকমে, ভিন্ন প্রকারে, ভিন্ন ভাবে। **2.** Else ; or ; as, seize the chance *otherwise* you will regret it ; না হইলে, নহিলে ; অন্যথা, নতুবা, নতু, নচেৎ। **3.** In other respects ; as, weak but *otherwise* well ; অন্যান্য সম্পর্কে, অন্যান্য বিষয়ে। **4.** In a different state ; as, how can it be *otherwise* than fatal ; অন্যরূপ, ভিন্নরূপ। **Otherwise-minded**— Having different desires or views ; averse to current opinions ; ভিন্নমতাবলম্বী ; প্রচলিত মতের বিরোধী মতাবলম্বী।

ō′-ti-ōse (-shī-), *adj.* **1.** (*Rare*) Idle ; unoccupied ; (কচিদ্‌ব্যবহৃত) অলস ; অবসর। **2.** (*Rare*) Futile ; (অপ্রঃ) ব্যর্থ, নিষ্ফল। **3.** Useless ; functionless ; ক্রিয়াশূন্য ; বৃত্তিশূন্য। **—ly,** *adv.* **—ness,** *n.*

ō-tī′-tis, *n.* Inflammation of the ear ; কর্ণপ্রদাহ, কর্ণশূল। **Otitis externa** — কর্ণপাক (সাঃ পঃ)। **Otitis media**—কর্ণপ্রতিনাহ (সাঃ পঃ)।

otium, (*L.*), *n.* Leisure ; বিরাম, অবসর। ***Otium cum dignitate,*** *n.* Dignified leisure or ease ; গৌরবজনক অবসর বা আরাম।

Otium sine dignitate, *n.* Leisure without dignity; অগৌরবজনক অবসর। ***Otium sine litteris mors est,*** *adj.* Leisure without literature is death; সাহিত্য-চর্চ্চা বিনা অবসর মৃত্যুস্বরূপ।

ō-tŏl′-ō-ġȳ, *n.* The science treating of the ear and its diseases; কর্ণ এবং কর্ণরোগসম্বন্ধীয় বিজ্ঞান; শ্রোত্রবিদ্যা (হিঃ কোঃ)।

ō-tŏr-rhœ′-ă (-rē-), *n.* A flow, esp. a purulent discharge from the ear; কর্ণস্রাব।

ō′-tō-scōpe, *n.* An instrument for examining the ear-cavity; an aural speculum; কর্ণরন্ধ্রবীক্ষণযন্ত্র; কর্ণবীক্ষণযন্ত্র।

ottava rima, (*It.*), *n.* A stanza of eight lines of heroic verse; বীররসাত্মক কবিতার অষ্টপংক্তিবিশিষ্ট শ্লোক।

ŏt′-ter (-êr), *n.* **1.** An aquatic quadruped of the weasel family;

Otter.

ভোঁদড়, জলনকুল, জলবিড়াল, জলাখু, নীরাখু, জলমার্জ্জার, উদ্বিড়াল, উদ্র। **2.** Its fur; উদ্বিড়ালের লোম। **3.** A kind of fishing-tackle; একপ্রকার বড়শীর সরঞ্জাম। **Otter-dog, —hound, —spear**—Those used in otter hunting; উদ্বিড়াল শিকারের জন্য ব্যবহৃত কুকুর, বর্শা প্রভৃতি।

ŏt′-tō, *n.* Attor; আতর।

Ot′-tō-măn(ŏt-), *adj.* & *n.* Of, or pertaining to, the Turks, (from Othman, a Sultan of Turkey 1300); তুরস্কদেশবাসিসম্পর্কীয়। ***Noun.*** **1.** A Turk; তুরস্ক দেশবাসী, তুর্কি। **2.** (*l. c.*) A stuffed seat without a back; একপ্রকার গদিআঁটা আসন।

ou′-bit (ô-), *n.* Same as WOOBUT.

ou-bli-ette′ (ô-blĭ-ĕt), *n.* A dungeon with an opening only at the top; যে ভূগর্ভস্থ কারাগারের উপরিভাগেমাত্র আলো ও বায়ুপ্রবেশের জন্য একটা ছিদ্র থাকে।

ouch (o͞wch), *n.* (*Archaic*) A clasp or brooch; a socket for setting a precious stone; (অপ্রঃ) আঁকড়া, ব্রূচ; মণি বসাইবার জন্য কোটর।

ought (ăt), *n.* (*Vulg.*) Nought (ইতর ভাষায়) কিছুই নয়।

ought (ăt), *n.* Duty or obligation, (as denoted by the verb *ought*); "The social *ought*"; কর্ত্তব্য, দায়িত্ব, বাধ্যতা।

ought (ăt), *aux. v.* **1.** To be held or bound in duty or moral obligation; কর্ত্তব্য হওয়া, উচিত হওয়া। **2.** To be necessary; to be fit or proper; আবশ্যক হওয়া; উপযুক্ত হওয়া, সঙ্গত হওয়া।

ounce (o͞wns), *n.* (Abbr. *oz.*) **1.** A weight, the twelfth part of a pound Troy and the sixteenth of a pound avoirdupois; ওজন-বিশেষ, ১ পাউণ্ড ট্রয়ের দ্বাদশভাগের একভাগ এবং ১ পাউণ্ড এভরডিউপয়জের ষোড়শভাগের এক ভাগ। **2.** (*Fig.*) A small portion or quantity; (লক্ষণায়) একরত্তি, একটুকু। **An ounce of practice is worth a pound of theory**—ঝুরি ঝুরি কল্পনা জল্পনার চেয়ে কাজের কাজ সামান্য পরিমাণও ভাল।

ounce (o͞wns), *n.* **1.** (*Poet.* etc.) A lynx or other feline beast;

Ounce.

দ্বীপী। **2.** A leopard-like animal; চিতাবাঘের মত একপ্রকার জন্তু।

our (o͞wr) *pron.* & *adj.* (*poss. of we*) Of, or relating to, us; আমাদের আমাদিগের, মোসবার (*poet.*), মোদের (*ib.*)। **Our Father** — বিশ্বপিতা, বিশ্বজনক। **Our Lady**—আমাদের দেবী কুমারী মেরী। **Our Saviour**—আমাদের পরিত্রাতা যীশুখৃষ্ট, আমাদের ত্রাণকর্ত্তা যীশুখৃষ্ট। **Given under our seal**—আমাদের (অর্থাৎ রাজা বা রাণীর) শীলমোহরযুক্ত হইল।

ours (o͞wrz) *pron.* & *pred. adj.* **1.** One or ones belonging to us; as, *ours* is a nice garden; আমাদেরটী বা গুলি। **2.** Our regiment etc.; as Jones of *ours* আমাদের পল্টন প্রভৃতি। ***Pred. adj.*** Of us; as, it became *ours* by purchase; আমাদের।

our-sĕlf′ (o͞wr-), *pron.* (*Pl.* -SELVES) **1.** (*Sing.*) Used in the regal or formal style for *myself*; রাজা, রাণী বা পত্রিকাসম্পাদক কর্ত্তৃক *myself* এর পরিবর্ত্তে ব্যবহৃত শব্দ। **2.** (Usu. *pl.*) We or us in person (*emphatically*); আমরা স্বয়ং, স্বয়ং আমাদিগকে। **3.** (*Reflex.*, usu. *pl.*, always in the *objective case*) Us as previously spoken of; as, we cannot persuade *ourself* or *ourselves,* that etc.; আমাদিগকে।

ou′-sel (ô-zel), *n.* See OUZEL.

oust (o͞wst), *v. t.* To eject; to dispossess from; to place oneself into the place of; উচ্ছেদ করা, উঠাইয়া দেওয়া; অধিকারচ্যুত করা; কাহারো স্থান অধিকার করা।

Oust′-êr (o͞wst-), *n.* (*Law*) Ejection; wrongful dispossession; (আইন) উচ্ছেদ; অন্যায়রূপে বেদখল।

out (o͞wt), *adv.*, *prep.*, *n.*, *adj.* *interj.*, *v. t.* & *i.* **1.** Away; abroad; দূরে; বাহিরে। **2.** In a state of extinction; not in the fashion etc.; as, fire is *out*: crinolines are *out*; নির্ব্বাপিত অবস্থায়; চলতি নয়। **3.** In or into a state of disclosure or publicity : in or into existence, sight clearness, etc. ; as, a book, secret, chicken, etc. are *out* : tell him right *out* ; প্রকাশিত অবস্থায় ; বর্ত্তমান, দৃষ্টিপথারূঢ়, প্রভৃতি। **4.** To a conclusion : at an end ; completely ; as, the boy has his cry *out* : tired *out* ; চরমপর্য্যন্ত, শেষপর্য্যন্ত ; সমাপ্ত ; সম্পূর্ণরূপে। **5.** In error or mistake ; as, I was *out* in my calculation ; at a loss ; ভুলে, ভ্রমে ; হতভম্ব। **6.** (*Cricket etc.*) In the state of being forced to discontinue an attempt to score ; (ক্রীকেট ক্রীড়ায়) জয়াঙ্ক লাভ হইতে বঞ্চিত অবস্থায়। ***Prep.*** Out of, (now only in *from out*) ; as, *from out* the prison came groan ; হইতে। ***Noun.*** **1.** The party out of office (usu. *pl.*) ; যে রাজনীতিক দলের হস্তে শাসনভার ন্যস্ত থাকে না। **2.** A nook or corner (usu. *fig.*) : as, the ins and *outs* of a question ; গলিঘুঁজি, অলিগলি, ঘোপঘাপ। **3.** Outside ; "Liking not the inside looked the *out*" ; বহির্ভাগ। **4.** (*Dial.*) An excursion ; (উপভাষায়) ভ্রমণ। **5.** (*Pl., In crickets* etc.) The players who are not having their innings ; (ক্রীকেট ক্রীড়ায়) যে সকল ক্রীড়ক "আউট" হইয়া গিয়াছে। ***Adj.*** **1.** External ; outer ; বহিঃ ; বাহ্য। **2.** (*In cricket* etc.) Played away from the home ground ; as, an *out* match ; not having its innings ; as, an *out* side; (ক্রীকেটক্রীড়ায় অন্যস্থানের ক্রীড়াভূমিতে ক্রীড়িত ; যাহাদের খেলার বাজী নয়। **3.** Unusual or abnormal, as a size : অস্বাভাবিক, স্বভাববহির্ভূত। **4.** (Of isles, *usu. with hyphen* Lying away from the mainland ; (দ্বীপ সম্বন্ধে) প্রধান ভূভাগ হইতে দূরবর্ত্তী। ***Interj.*** Expressing anger or desire to be rid of ; as, *out* with him ; দূর হও ! দূর কর ! ***Verb t.*** **1.** (*Rare*) To expel ; (ক্বচিদ্ব্যবহৃত) তাড়ান, বহিষ্কৃত করা। **2.** *Obs.* or *dial.* To disclose ; (অপ্রঃ বা উপভাষায় প্রকাশ করা। **3.** (*Slang*) To disable or kill as an opponent, by a blow ; (ইতরভাষায়) মুষ্ট্যাদির আঘাতে শত্রুকে বধ বা অকর্ম্মণ্য করা। ***Verb i.*** (*Ellipt.*) To come out ; as the murder will *out* ; প্রকাশ হইয়া পড়া, বাহির হইয়া পড়া। **All out**—A side's innings over; একপক্ষের খেলা শেষ হইয়াছে। **An out-of-the-way-place**—অজ্ঞাত বা অপরিচিত স্থান। **In and out**—Inside and outside ; বাহির এবং ভিতর। (*Pl.*) The details, as of a question ; খুঁটিনাটি। **Is out of drawing**—Is incorrectly drawn ; ভুল আঁকা হইয়াছে। **Out and about**—Able to leave bed or house and appear as after an illness etc. ; পীড়াদি হইতে আরোগ্যলাভের পর শয্যাত্যাগ করিতে বা বাটীর বাহিরে যাইতে সমর্থ। **Out and away**—By far ; অনেকটা, বহুপরিমাণে। **Out and out**—*Adj.* & *adv.* Thorough ; পুরা, পাকা। (*Adv.*) Thoroughly ; পুরাপুরি। **Out and outer**—*n.* A thorough-going person, thing, or specimen ; an out and out lie, scoundrel, etc. ; পাকা লোক, খাঁটিজিনিস বা ঠিক নমুনা ; পুরা মিথ্যাকথা, পাকা বদমায়েস, ইত্যাদি। **Out at elbows**—See under ELBOW. **Out at sea**—Wide of the mark ; quite in the wrong ; লক্ষ্য হইতে বহুদূরে ; সম্পূর্ণ ভ্রান্ত **Out of** From within ; from among ; beyond the range of ; owing to ; from ; by use of at a specified distance from (the town etc.) ; beyond doubt etc.) . মধ্য হইতে ; মাঝখেকে ; সীমার বাহিরে, পাল্লার বাহিরে ; বশতঃ ; হইতে ব্যবহার দ্বারা ; কোন স্থান হইতে নির্দ্দিষ্ট দূরে ; অতীত **Out of collar**—*Servants' slang*) Without a place, (চাকরদিগের ইতরভাষায়) বেকার। **Out of date**—See under DATE. **Out-of-door**—*adj.* Open-air ; খোলা ময়দানের, খোলা জায়গায়। **Out of doors**—In or into the open air ; বাহিরে, খোলা জায়গায়। **Out of doubt** — Undoubtedly ; নিঃসন্দেহে। **Out of fashion**—See under FASHION. **Out of hand**—At once ; immediately ; তৎক্ষণাৎ ; অমনি। **Out of harness**—Not in practice ; retired ; ব্যবসায় পরিচালনায় বিরত ; অবসরপ্রাপ্ত। **Out of it**—From it ; ইহা হইতে। Not includud ; forlorn ; at a loss ; mistaken ; সামিল নয় ; দুর্দ্দশাগ্রস্ত ; কিংকর্ত্তব্যবিমূঢ় ; ভ্রান্ত। **Out of one's mind** — Not in one's senses ; বিকৃতমস্তিষ্ক, উন্মাদ, বিকৃতমতি। **Out of one's time**—Having served one's apprenticeship ; শিক্ষানবিশী শেষ করিয়াছে। **Out of place**—Unsuitable ; not appropriate or proper ; অনুপযোগী ; বেখাপ্পা। **Out of pocket**—Actually paid ; as, *out of pocket*-expenses ; প্রকৃত পক্ষে প্রদত্ত। Put to expense ; আর্থিক ক্ষতিগ্রস্ত। **Out of print**—ছাপা নাই। **Out of repair**—বেমেরামত। **Out of season** — অসাময়িক, অকালোচিত, অসময়োচিত। **Out of sight, out of mind**—চোখের আড়াল হইলে মনেরও আড়াল, চোখের ভালবাসা (cf. মানুষের কুটুম এলে গেলে)। **Out of sorts**—Unwell ; অসুস্থ। In bad humour ; মেজাজ ভালনয়। **Out of temper**—In bad temper; irritated ; খারাপ মেজাজের ; ক্রুদ্ধ, রাগান্বিত। **Out of the question**—See under QUESTION. **Out of the way**—Odd ; unusual ; অপরূপ ; সৃষ্টিছাড়া। Secluded ; unfrequented ; নিভৃত, নির্জ্জন ; বিজন, জনমানববিহীন। **Out of the wood** — Out of the difficulty or danger ; বিপন্মুক্ত,

সঙ্কট হইতে মুক্ত। **Out of touch**—সম্পর্কশূন্য, সংশ্রবশূন্য। **Out of trim**—Not in good order, (esp. of ship, not well balanced for sailing); ঠিকঠাক নয়, ভালরূপে সজ্জিত নয়। **Out of tune**—Discordant; বেসুর বেতাল, শ্রুতিকটু। **Out of twist, Out of throw, Out of wind** or **winding**—Not having a wind or twist, (applied by artificers to surfaces); বক্রতা বা মোচড় বিশিষ্ট নয়। **Out of wedlock**—Without marriage; বিবাহব্যতীত। **Out to out**—From outside to outside, (applied to measurement); বহির্ভাগ হইতে বহির্ভাগ পর্য্যন্ত। **Out with him**—Turn him out; তাহাকে দূর করিয়া দেও, তাহাকে তাড়াইয়া দেও, তাহাকে বাহির করিয়া দেও। **The arm is out**—The arm is dislocated; বাহু সন্ধিচ্যুত হইয়াছে। **The girl is out**—*i.e.* Introduced to society; অর্থাৎ শিষ্টসমাজের সহিত পরিচিত হইয়াছে। **The ins and outs of a question**—The full details of a question; কোন প্রশ্নের খুঁটিনাটি বিষয়। **The milk is out**—দুধ টুকু ফুরাইয়া গিয়াছে। **The miners are out**—*i.e.* Not at work or on strike; অর্থাৎ কার্য্যে নিযুক্ত নয় বা ধর্ম্মঘট করিয়াছে। **The secret is out** — গুপ্ত কথা বাহির হইয়া পড়িয়াছে। **Times out of number** — *i.e.* Beyond counting; গণনার অতীত। **To be out**—To be in error or mistake; ভুল হওয়া, ভ্রান্ত হওয়া। To be not at home; বাড়ীতে না থাকা To be published; as, results are *out*; প্রকাশিত হওয়া **To be out of court** — To be unable to bring forward one's cause: নিজের মোকদ্দমা উপস্থাপিত করিতে না পারা। (*Fig.*) To be silenced in argument; to lose one's case hopelessly; (তর্কে পরাস্ত) নিরস্ত হওয়া; মোকদ্দমায় সম্পূর্ণরূপে হারা **To be out with anyone** To disagree with him; কাহারও সহিত অবনিবনাও হওয়া। **To have it out with any one**—To fall out with any one on a certain subject; কোন বিষয় নিয়া কাহারও সহিত ঝগড়া করা। **Tories are out**—অর্থাৎ রক্ষণশীলদলের হস্তে দেশের শাসনভার ন্যস্ত নয়।

out-bid' (ōwt-), *v. t.* **1.** To surpass in bidding at an auction; to offer a higher price than: নীলামে বেশী ডাকা; অপর অপেক্ষা বেশী দাম হাঁকা। **2.** To surpass in any quality, statement, etc.; অতিক্রম করা, ছাড়াইয়া যাওয়া।

out'-board (ōwt-bōrd), *adj.* & *adv.* (*Naut.*) On or towards or nearer than something else, to a ship's outside; (নৌ-বিদ্যা) অন্য কিছু অপেক্ষা জাহাজের বহির্ভাগের অভিমুখীন বা নিকটবর্ত্তী।

out-brave' (ōwt-), *v. t.* To defy; তুচ্ছ করা, অবজ্ঞা করা।

out'-break (ōwt-brāk), *n.* **1.** A breaking forth as of anger, hostilities, disease, etc.; eruption; উচ্ছ্বাস, প্রাদুর্ভাব; উদ্গার, সবেগনিঃসরণ; **2.** Insurrection; বিদ্রোহ। **3.** Outcrop; উদ্গম।

out'-build-ing (ōwt-), *n.* An outhouse; বাহিরের ঘর।

out'-burst (ōwt-bêrst), *n.* **1.** A breaking or bursting out, as of feeling etc. by vehement words etc.; উচ্ছ্বাস, স্ফূর্ত্তি (দমকা)। **2.** Explosion; volcanic eruption; outcrop; সংস্ফোটন, স্ফূর্জ্জ; অগ্ন্যুৎপাত; উদ্গম।

out'-cast (ōwt-), *adj.* & *n.* Exiled; homeless and friendless degraded; নির্ব্বাসিত, গৃহহীন এবং বন্ধুহারা; অধঃপাতিত। *Noun.* An exile; a homeless and friendless person; a vagabond; নির্ব্বাসিত ব্যক্তি; গৃহহীন এবং বন্ধুহীন ব্যক্তি ভবঘুরে।

out'-caste (ōwt-cāst), *adj.*, & *n.* Expelled from one's caste or society; not belonging to a caste; জাতিচ্যুত, সমাজচ্যুত, অপাংক্তেয়, পংক্তিদূষক; জাতিভ্রষ্ট। *Noun.* An out-caste person; জাতিচ্যুত ব্যক্তি, জাতিভ্রষ্ট ব্যক্তি, সমাজচ্যুত ব্যক্তি।

out-caste' (ōwt-cāst), *v. t.* To expel from caste; জাতিচ্যুত করা।

out-class' (ōwt-), *v. t.* To belong to a higher class than; উচ্চতর শ্রেণীভুক্ত হওয়া।

out'-clear-ing (ōwt-clēr-), *n.* Sending out of bills and cheques to the clearing house for settlement; হুণ্ডী, চেক, প্রভৃতি বিনিময়ের জন্য বিনিময়গৃহে প্রেরণ।

out'-col-lege (ōwt-cŏl-lĕj), *adj.* Not residing in, or belonging to, a college; মহাবিদ্যালয়বাসী নয়, মহাবিদ্যালয়ভুক্ত নয়।

out'-come (ōwt-kŭm), *n.* Issue; result; ফল; পরিণাম।

out'-crŏp (ōwt-), *n.* The coming out of a stratum at the surface; a stratum, vein, etc. coming out at the surface; ভূপৃষ্ঠে কোন স্তরের উদ্গম; উদ্গত স্তর, ধাতুশিরা, প্রভৃতি।

out'-crȳ (ōwt-), *n.* **1.** A loud cry; a cry of distress or opposition রব, কোলাহল, চীৎকার, উচ্চনাদ; সোরগোল। **2.** Clamour; uproar; কোলাহল; চীৎকার।

out-dis'-tance (ōwt-dis-tăns), *v. t.* To get far ahead of; অনেক আগে যাওয়া, অনেকটা পশ্চাতে ফেলিয়া যাওয়া।

out dô (ōwt-), *v. t.* To surpass or excel; অতিক্রম করা, ছাড়াইয়া যাওয়া, সম্পাদনে শ্রেষ্ঠ হওয়া।

out-door (ōwt-dōr), *adj.* Out of the house; open-air; বাটীর বাহিরের; খোলাজায়গায় সম্পাদিত। **Out-door games**—যে সকল খেলা খোলা জায়গায় খেলিতে হয়।

out-doors' (ōwt-dōrz), *adv.* Out of doors; abroad বাটীর বাহিরে; বাহিরে।

out'-êr (ōwt-), *adj.* & *n.* **1.** Being on the outside; external; farther from the interior; বহিঃস্থিত; বাহ্য, বহির্ভূত; ভিতরের দিক হইতে দূরবর্ত্তী। **2.** (*Philos.*) Objective; not psychical; physical; বিষয়াত্মক; অচিদাত্মক; জড়ীয়। ***Noun.*** The part of a target outside of the circle called inner; a shot striking it; শরব্যের বহির্ভাগ; ঐ স্থানে যে গুলি লাগে। **–most,** *adj.* Farthest outward; most external; নিতান্ত বহির্ব্বর্ত্তী; বাহ্যতম। **The outer man** — Personal appearance; dress; বাহিরের রূপ; পোষাক। **The outer world**—People outside one's own circle; বাহিরের লোক।

out-face' (ōwt-), *v. t.* To look (one) out of countenance; to defy; চোখ রাঙ্গাইয়া ধমক দেওয়া; তুচ্ছ করা।

out'-fall (ōwt-), *n.* The outlet of a river, drain, sewer, etc.; নদী, নর্দ্দমা, পয়ঃনালী প্রভৃতির নির্গমপথ।

out'-field (ōwt-fēld), *n.* **1.** The outlying land of a farm; the outlying field of a homestead; কৃষিক্ষেত্রবাটীকার বহির্ভাগের জমি; কোন বাটীর বহির্ভাগস্থ জমি। **2.** (*Cricket*) The part of the field farthest from the batsman; (ক্রীকেটক্রীড়ায়) ব্যাটধারী হইতে দূরতম ক্রীড়াপ্রাঙ্গণের অংশ। **3.** (*Fig.*) Outlying region of thought etc.; (লক্ষণায়) চিন্তার বহির্ব্বর্ত্তী রাজ্য।

out'-fit (ōwt-), *n.* **1.** A fitting out as for a voyage, journey, etc.; the expense for it; সাজসজ্জা; ভ্রমণব্যয়, পাথেয়। **2.** Articles forming an equipment; as, the *outfit* of a surgeon; সাজসরঞ্জাম। **3.** (*Fig.*) Mental endowments or requirements; স্বভাবদত্ত বৃত্তিসমূহ। **–ter,** *n.* A supplier of equipments; সাজসজ্জা সরবরাহকারী।

out-flank' (ōwt-flăngk), *v. t.* To manœuvre so as to attack in the flank; to get the better of; শত্রুসৈন্যের পার্শ্বভাগ আক্রমণের জন্য কৌশলসহকারে সৈন্যচালনা করা; প্রাধান্য লাভ করা।

out'-flow (ōwt-flō), *n.* A flowing out; efflux; নির্গম; নিঃস্রব।

out-gĕn'-êr-ăl (ōwt-), *v. t.* To exceed in generalship; সৈনাপত্যে অতিক্রম করা।

out'-gō (ōwt-), *n.* **1.** Outlay; expenditure, (opposite of *income*); যে টাকা কোন ব্যবসায় প্রভৃতিতে খাটানো হয়; ব্যয়। **2.** A going out; efflux; বহির্গমন; নিঃস্রব। **3.** An outlet; নির্গমপথ। **–ing,** *n.* **1.** Act of going out; বহির্গমন। **2.** (*Pl.*) Same as OUTGO. **3.** Outlet; নির্গম পথ।

out-grow' (ōwt-grō), *v. t.* **1.** To surpass in growth; অধিকতর বৃদ্ধিপ্রাপ্ত হওয়া। **2.** To grow too great or too old for anything; as, to *outgrow* clothes or childish habits or taste; কোন কিছুর জন্য অতিরিক্ত বৃহৎ বা অত্যধিক বয়সের হওয়া।

out'-growth (ōwt-grōth), *n.* An offshoot; a result or consequence; প্ররোহ; ফল, পরিণাম।

out-hĕc'-tŏr (ōwt-), *v. t.* To surpass in hectoring and blustering; to browbeat; তর্জ্জনগর্জ্জন ধুমধড়াক্কায় ছাড়াইয়া যাওয়া; চোক পাকাইয়া দাবান।

out-Hĕr'-ŏd (ōwt-), *v. t.* To surpass Herod in violence, blustering, etc.; নৃশংসতা প্রভৃতিতে হিরোডকে অতিক্রম করা [ইহুদীরাজ হিরোডের আদেশে বেথলেহেমের শিশুগণ নিহত হয়।] **To out-Herod Herod**—নৃশংসতায় কংসকে অতিক্রম করা

out'-house (ōwt-hows), *n.* A small house or building near the main one; প্রধান গৃহের নিকটবর্ত্তী ক্ষুদ্র গৃহ, উপগৃহ।

out'-ing (ōwt-), *n.* **1.** An excursion or pleasure trip; ভ্রমণ, প্রমোদভ্রমণ। **2.** A distance out at sea; বাহির দরিয়া।

out-jock'-ey (ōwt-jŏck-ĭ), *v. t.* To overreach; প্রতারণা করা, প্রবঞ্চনা করা, ঠকান।

out-lănd'-ish (ōwt-), *adj.* (From obs. out-land=foreign countries) **1.** Foreign-looking; strange; bizarre; vulgar; uncouth; পারদেশিক, বিদেশীয়, পরদেশীয়; অদ্ভুত; অপরূপ; ইতর; বিদ্‌ঘুটে। **2.** Out-of-the way; সাত সমুদ্র তের নদীর পার।

out-lăst' (ōwt-), *v. t.* To last longer than; to surpass in duration; অপেক্ষাকৃত অধিক টিঁকিয়া থাকা; অধিকতর কাল স্থায়ী হওয়া।

out'-law (ōwt-lä), *n.* & *v. t.* **1.** A person excluded from the benefit and protection of law; a banished or exiled person; আইনের আশ্রয়বহির্ভূত ব্যক্তি; নির্ব্বাসিত ব্যক্তি। **2.** A lawless person committing violence; আইনভঙ্গকারী ব্যক্তি। ***Verb t.*** To declare as an outlaw; to proscribe; আইনের আশ্রয়বহির্ভূত বলিয়া ব্যক্ত করা; আইনের আশ্রয় হইতে বঞ্চিত করা। **–ry,** *n.* Putting out of protection of law; আইনের আশ্রয়ের বহির্ভূত করণ, আইনের আশ্রয়চ্যুত করণ।

out'-lay (ōwt-lā), *n.* **1.** A laying out; বিনিয়োগ, ধনবিনিয়োগ, ধনপ্রয়োগ। **2.** Expenditure; ব্যয়, খরচ, ধনব্যয়।

out-lay' (ōwt-lā), *v. t.* **1.** To spread out; to display; বিস্তারিত করা; প্রদর্শিত করা। **2.** To lay out money; ধনপ্রয়োগ করা।

out'-lĕt (ōwt-), *n.* A passage out; an exit; নির্গমমার্গ, দ্বার; নির্গম।

out'-lī-êr (ōwt-), *n.* A detached part of something; কোন বস্তুর বিশ্লিষ্ট অংশ।

out'-līne (ōwt-), *n.* & *v. t.* **1.** (*Sing.* or *pl.*) The time by which a figure is defined; contour; সীমারেখা, প্রান্তরেখা; বাহ্যরেখা। **2.** (*Arts*) A sketch in which contours are figured without shading; (কলাশাস্ত্র) রৈখিকচিত্র,

রেখাচিত্র। 3. A general sketch in words; summary; "A bare *outline* of the contents of the passage"; মোটামুটি বর্ণনা; সার-মর্ম। 4. (*Pl.*) The main features or characteristics; general principles; স্থূল স্থূল বিষয়; সাধারণতত্ত্বসমূহ। *Verb t.* 1. To draw the outline of; প্রান্তরেখা অঙ্কন করা, রেখাপাত করা। 2. To describe in outline; মোটামুটিভাবে বর্ণনা করা, স্থূলভাবে বর্ণনা করা। 3. To mark the outline of in decorating etc.; "A line of ... gold-thread might *outline* everything"; মণ্ডনকার্যে প্রান্তরেখা চিহ্নিত করা।

out-live′ (ōwt-lĭv), *v. t.* 1. To live beyond as a century etc.; to come safely through, as an accident; to get over the effect of (disrepute etc.); অধিকতর কাল জীবিত থাকা, দীর্ঘতর কাল জীবিত থাকা; রক্ষা পাওয়া; (কলঙ্ক প্রভৃতির) পরিণাম কাটাইয়া উঠা। 2. To survive; to outlast; কাহারও মৃত্যুর পর জীবিত থাকা; অপেক্ষাকৃত অধিক কাল স্থায়ী হওয়া।

out′-lŏŏk (ōwt-), *n.* 1. A look out; "Viewed from the distant *outlook*"; অবেক্ষণ। 2. A view; a scope of vision; "A picturesque *outlook*"; দৃশ্য; দৃষ্টির প্রসর। 3. A vigilant watch; পর্য্যবেক্ষণ। 4. (*Fig.*) scope of mental vision; prospect for the future; (লক্ষণায়) কল্পনার প্রসর; ভবিষ্যতের আশা। **To be on the outlook**—*i. e.* On the lookout, or on the watch what may turn up; দৃষ্টি রাখা, চোখ রাখা।

out′-lȳ-ing (ōwt-), *adj.* Exterior; remote; detached; বাহ্য, বহির্ব্বর্ত্তী, বহিঃস্থ, বহির্দ্দেশস্থ; দূরবর্ত্তী, দূরস্থ; বিচ্ছিন্ন।

out-ma-noeu′-vre (ōwt-mă-nô-vêr), *v. t.* To surpass or get advantage of in manœuvring; কৌশলে বা কূটবুদ্ধিতে অতিক্রম করা বা কাহারও উপর সুবিধা লাভ করা।

out-mârch′ (ōwt-) *v. t.* To surpass or defeat in marching; যুদ্ধযাত্রাতে অতিক্রম বা পরাভূত করা, দ্রুততর গতিতে যুদ্ধাভিযান করা।

out-match′ (ōwt-măch), *v. t.* To prove superior to; to outdo; শ্রেষ্ঠতর বলিয়া প্রতিপন্ন হওয়া; ছাড়াইয়া যাওয়া, অতিক্রম করা।

out′-mōst (ōwt-), *adj.* Same as OUTERMOST.

out′-nĕss (ōwt-), *n.* *aph.*) Externality; objectivity, (দর্শনশাস্ত্র) বাহ্যতা, বহিরঙ্গতা; বিষয়াত্মকতা।

out-nŭm′-bêr (ōwt-), *v. t.* To exceed in number; সংখ্যায় অধিকতর হওয়া।

out-pāce′, (ōwt-), *v. t.* To exceed in speed; to outstrip in any race or rivalry; দ্রুততর গতিতে অগ্রসর হওয়া; কোন দৌড় বা প্রতিযোগিতার ক্রীড়ায় পশ্চাতে ফেলা।

out′-pa-tient (ōwt-pā-shŏnt), *n.* A patient not residing in a hospital but receiving treatment from it; যে রোগী রুগ্নাবাসের বাহিরে থাকিয়া চিকিৎসিত হয়, বাহিরের রোগী।

out′-pōst (ōwt-), *n.* A station at a distance from the main body of army; troops placed at such a station; আড্ডা, গুল্মস্থান, পল্টন, ছাউনির বাহিরের আড্ডা, ফাঁড়ি, ঘাঁটি, চৌকি, থানা; আড্ডায় স্থিত সৈন্য।

out′-pour (ōwt-pōr), *n.* Pouring out; an overflow; বর্ষণ; বন্যা, প্লাবন।

out-pour′ (ōwt-pōr), *v. t.* (*Poet.*) To pour out; (কবিতায়) ঢালা, বর্ষণ করা।

out′-pour-ing (ōwt-pōr-), *n.* 1. Act of pouring out; নিঃস্রব, উৎসেচন। 2. (*Chiefly pl.*) An effusion; an impetuous or emotional utterance; হৃদয়াবেগ; উচ্ছ্বাসপূর্ণ উক্তি, আবেগপূর্ণ উক্তি।

out′-pŭt (ōwt-), *n.* Quantity produced in a specified time by manufacture, mining, labour, etc.; নির্দ্দিষ্ট সময়ে প্রস্তুত, নির্ম্মিত, পরিশ্রমের ফলে উৎপন্ন বস্তু বা আকরোত্তোলিত খনিজপদার্থের পরিমাণ।

out′-rāge (ōwt-), *n.* & *v. t.* 1. Gross violation of others' rights, sentiments, etc.; অত্যাচার, দৌরাত্ম্য, উপমর্দ্দ। 2. A violent injury or wrong; a wanton offence; উপদ্রব; বলাৎকার। *Verb t.* 1. To do violence to; to subject to outrage; to insult; অত্যাচার করা; উপদ্রব করা, দৌরাত্ম্য করা; অপমান করা। 2. To violate or ravish, as a female; বলাৎকার করা, সতীত্ব নষ্ট করা। 3. To infringe flagrantly as a law, morality, etc.; ঘোরতররূপে ভঙ্গ করা।

out-ra′-geous (ōwt-rā-jŭs), *adj.* 1. Excessive; extravagant; ঘোর; উৎকট। 2. Furious; violent; ভীষণ; অত্যুগ্র, দারুণ, প্রবল, প্রচণ্ড। 3. Atrocious; highly offensive or abusive; অমানুষিক, পাশবিক, নৃশংস; অতিশয় গর্হিত বা কুৎসাপূর্ণ। —ly, *adv.* —ness, *n.*

out-rānge′ (ōwt-), *v. t.* To exceed in range; পাল্লায় অতিক্রম করা।

outre, (*F.*), *adj.* Out of the limits of propriety; eccentric; bizarre; লোকব্যবহারবিরুদ্ধ; ছিটগ্রস্ত, বাতিকগ্রস্ত; মাথাপাগলা।

out-reach′ (ōwt-rēch), *v. t.* To extend beyond; বাহির হওয়া, বহির্ভূত হওয়া, অতীত হওয়া।

out′-re-lief (ōwt-rē-lēf), *n.* Outdoor relief; relief given to a person not residing in a workhouse, or institution; বাহিরের লোককে যে সাহায্য দেওয়া হয়; দরিদ্রশালা বা কোন প্রতিষ্ঠানের বাহিরের লোককে যে সাহায্য দেওয়া হয়।

out-rīde′ (ōwt-), *v. t.* 1. To ride faster than; দ্রুততর বেগে অশ্ব চালনা করা। 2. (Of ships) To ride out (a storm); (জাহাজ সম্বন্ধে) দ্রুতবেগে অতিক্রম করিয়া রক্ষা পাওয়া। **Out′-rid-er**, *n.* A mounted attendant riding before, behind or with, a carriage ; শকটের অগ্রে, পশ্চাতে বা সঙ্গে যে অশ্বারোহী অনুচর চলে, অশ্বারোহী-অনুচর।

out-rigged′ (ōwt-rĭgd), *adj.* Fitted with outriggers ; পাইলের নৌকার পার্শ্ব হইতে বিলম্বিত পাইল দণ্ড প্রভৃতি দ্বারা সজ্জিত।

out′-rig-ger (ōwt-rĭg-ĕr), *n.* **1.** A spar, beam, etc., rigged out from the side of sailing boat ; পাইলের নৌকার পার্শ্ব হইতে বিলম্বিত পাইল, দণ্ড প্রভৃতি। **2.** A projecting beam etc. in a building to support hoisting-tackle etc. ; উত্তোলনরজ্জু প্রভৃতি ধারণের জন্য কোন অট্টালিকা হইতে বহির্বিলম্বিত কাষ্ঠখণ্ড প্রভৃতি। **3.** A projecting bracket in a boat with the rowlock at the extremity ; a boat with such apparatus ; নৌকা হইতে উদ্গত দণ্ডবিশেষ—যাহার প্রান্তের খাঁজে আটকাইয়া দাঁড়ী দাঁড় বাহিয়া থাকে ; ঐরূপ যন্ত্রসমন্বিত নৌকা। **5.** A projection fastened to a carriage to enable an extra horse to be driven outside the shafts ; such a horse ; অতিরিক্ত ঘোড়া জুতিবার জন্য শকটের বহির্দিগ-প্রলম্বিত দণ্ডবিশেষ ; ঐরূপ অশ্ব।

out-rig′-ging (ōwt-rĭg-ĭng), *n.* That which is rigged out or with which anything is rigged out ; outside rigging ; সজ্জিত বস্তু, পাইল এবং দড়াদড়ি দ্বারা সজ্জিত জাহজ প্রভৃতি, পাইল, দড়াদড়ি প্রভৃতি ; জাহাজের বাহিরের দড়াদড়ি।

out-right′ (ōwt-rīt), *adv.* & *adj.* **1.** Completely ; wholly ; altogether ; সম্পূর্ণরূপে ; পুরাপুরি ; সর্ব্বসাকল্যে। **2.** (*Rare*) Immediately ; (ক্বচিদ্‌ব্যবহৃত) ঝটিতি, তৎক্ষণাৎ, অবিলম্বে। **3.** Without reservation ; openly ; খোলাখুলিভাবে ; সোজাসুজি। ***Adj.*** **(out′–) 1.** Direct ; thorough ; out and out ; সোজা, বরাবর ; ডাহা, পুরা ; বিলকুল, পুরাপুরি। **2.** Complete ; পূর্ণ। **–ness,** *n.*

out-rī′-văl (ōwt-), *v. t.* To outdo as a rival ; অতিক্রম করা, ছাড়াইয়া যাওয়া।

out-rŭn′ (ōwt-), *v. t.* To exceed in running ; to outstrip or go beyond ; দৌড়ে পশ্চাতে ফেলা ; ছাড়াইয়া যাওয়া। **Out′-run-ner,** *n.* **1.** A running attendant on a carriage ; যে ব্যক্তি গাড়ীর পশ্চাৎ পশ্চাৎ দৌড়িয়া চলে। **2.** A horse in traces outside shafts ; গাড়ীর বোমের বাহিরে যে ঘোড়া জোতা হয়। **3.** A dog leading a team of sledge dogs ; বরফে-চলা গাড়ীর অগ্রগামী চালক কুকুর। **To outrun the constable**—See CONSTABLE.

out′-sĕt (ōwt-), *n.* Start ; beginning ; প্রারম্ভ, গোড়া ; আরম্ভ, আগম (কেঁড়িঃ)।

out-shīne′ (ōwt-), *v. t.* **1.** To shine brighter than ; অধিকতর দ্যুতিমান হওয়া, উজ্জ্বলতর হওয়া। **2.** (*Fig.*) To surpass in splendour or excellence ; (লক্ষণায়) শোভা বা উৎকর্ষে অতিক্রম করা।

out-sīde′ (ōwt-), *n., adj., adv.* & *prep.* **1.** The external surface ; the outer side or parts ; বহিঃপৃষ্ঠ ; বহির্ভাগ, বহিঃপার্শ্ব। **2.** All that is without ; as, impressions from the *outside* ; বহির্জগত। **3.** Outward aspect ; বাহ্যভাব। **4.** The utmost ; as, it is a mile at the *outside* ; নিতান্ত পক্ষ। **5.** (*Pl.*) The outermost sheets of a ream of paper ; (বহুবচন) কাগজের রীমের সকলের উপরের বা নীচের তা। **6.** An outside passenger in a carriage, coach, etc. ; গাড়ী প্রভৃতির বহির্দ্দেশে উপবিষ্ট যাত্রী। ***Adj.*** **(out′–) 1.** Of, or, or pertaining to, the outside ; external ; superficial ; বাহ্য ; বহির্ব্বর্ত্তী ; ভাসাভাসা, উপরি উপরি। **2.** Not belonging to some circle or institution ; as, *outside* opinion, (esp. of people outside Parliament) ; বাহিরের, বাহিরের লোকের। **3.** Utmost ; farthest ; greatest ; as, quote the *outside* prices ; নিতান্ত, চরম ; দূরতম ; অধিকতম। **4.** Situated, or done, without ; residing or working outside ; as, *outside* work : an *outside* porter ; বহিঃস্থিত, বহিঃসম্পন্ন ; বহির্বাসী, বাহিরে কার্য্যকারী ***Adv.*** **1.** On or to the outside or exterior ; without ; বাহিরে, বহির্দ্দিকে; বহির্ভাগে। ***Prep.*** On or to the outside of ; external to ; not in ; beyond the limits of ; বাহিরে ; বহির্দ্দেশে ; মধ্যে নয় ; সীমার বাহিরে। **Outside broker** — কোম্পানীর কাগজের দালাল সম্প্রদায়ের বাহিরের লোক। **Outside porter**—যে মজুর ষ্টেশন হইতে যাত্রীর মাল আনে। **Outside work**—বাহিরের কাজ। **A mile at the outside**—A mile at the utmost ; বড় জোর এক মাইল, উর্দ্ধপক্ষে এক মাইল। **Outside in**—Same as INSIDE OUT. **Outside of**—(*prep.*) Outside ; বাহিরে। **Outside of a horse**—(*Slang*) On horse-back ; (ইতরভাষায়) ঘোড়ার উপর। **To get or be outside of**—(*Slang*) To eat or drink ; (ইতরভাষায়) পান বা আহার করা।

out-sīd-′ĕr (ōwt-), *n.* **1.** One not belonging to a party, association or set ; বাহিরের লোক, বহিরঙ্গ লোক। **2.** A horse or person not known to have a chance in a race or competition ; যে অশ্ব বা ব্যক্তির কোন দৌড় বা প্রতিযোগিতার ক্রীড়ায় জয়লাভের সম্ভাবনা আছে বলিয়া জানা নাই।

out′-sight (ōwt-sīt), *n.* Perception of external things ; faculty of observation ; বহির্ব্যাপার উপলব্ধি, বহিঃদৃষ্টি ; পর্য্যবেক্ষণ-শক্তি।

out-sĭt′ (ōwt-), *v. t.* To sit or stay beyond the time of ; to sit longer than ; অতিরিক্ত সময় বসা বা অপেক্ষা করা ; অধিকতর সময় বসা।

out′-skirt (ōwt-skĕrt), *n.* (Usu. *pl.*) Edge ; border ; as, the *outskirts* of a town; উপকণ্ঠ, সীমাপ্রদেশ ; প্রান্ত।

out'-spăn (ōwt-), *v. i., t.* & *n.* (*S. Afr.*) To unyoke or unharness ; (দক্ষিণ আফ্রিকা) যুগমুক্ত করা বা হওয়া, ঘোড়ার জিন খোলা। ***Noun.*** Act or time of outspanning ; a place of outspanning ; যুগবন্ধমোচন, জিন খোলন ; যে স্থানে যুগবন্ধন মোচন করা বা জিন খোলা হয়।

out'-spo-ken (ōwt-spō-kn), *adj.* Free or bold of speech ; spoken freely or openly ; frank ; স্পষ্টভাষী, ঠোঁটকাটা (*colloq.*) ; খোলাখুলিভাবে কথিত ; উচিতবক্তা, স্পষ্টবক্তা।

out-spread' (ōwt-sprĕd), *adj., n.* & *v. t.* Spread out ; extended ; প্রসারিত ; বিস্তৃত, বিস্তারিত, বিততীকৃত। ***Noun.*** **(out'–)** Spreading out ; an expanse ; প্রসারণ ; বিস্তার। ***Verb t.*** To spread out ; প্রসারিত করা, বিস্তৃত করা।

out-stănd'-ing (ōwt-), *adj.* Projecting ; prominent ; uncollected or unpaid ; not yet settled ; বহির্বিলম্বিত, বহিঃপ্রসৃত ; স্পষ্টদৃশ্যমান, সুপ্রকট, সুপ্রকাশ ; অসংগৃহীত, অপরিশোধিত, অনাদায়ী, অনাদত্ত, অপ্রদত্ত, বাকী; অস্থিরীকৃত, এতাবৎ অপরিশোধিত। **Outstanding balance** — সাবেক বাকী, বকেয়া বাকী। **Outstanding for more than a year**—এক বৎসরের অধিক দিন যাবৎ বাকী।

out-stay' (ōwt-stā), *v. t.* To stay beyond or longer than ; অতিরিক্ত বা অধিকতর সময় অবস্থান করা।

out-stĕp' (ōwt-), *v.t.* To step outside of or beyond ; ছাড়াইয়া যাওয়া।

out-stretched' (ōwt-strĕcht), *adj.* Stretched out ; extended ; প্রসারিত, প্রসৃত ; বিস্তৃত।

out-strip' (ōwt-), *v. t.* **1.** To outrun ; to go beyond ; দৌড়িয়া অতিক্রম করা ; ছাড়াইয়া যাওয়া। **2.** To excel ; শ্রেষ্ঠ হওয়া।

out'-thrŭst (ōwt-), *n.* **1.** Thrusting forward ; সম্মুখের দিকে ধাক্কা প্রদান। **2.** Outward pressure of some part in architecture ; স্থাপত্য কার্য্যে কোন অংশের বহির্দ্দিকে চাপ।

out-val'-ue (ōwt-văl-ū), *v. t.* To exceed in value ; অধিকতর মূল্যের হওয়া।

out-vie' (ōwt-vī), *v. t.* To surpass in competition ; to vie with or excel ; প্রতিযোগিতায় জিতা ; প্রতিযোগিতায় শ্রেষ্ঠ হওয়া।

out-voice' (ōwt-voys), *v. t.* To surpass in loudness of voice ; উচ্চতর ধ্বনিবিশিষ্ট হওয়া।

out-vōte' (ōwt-), *v. t.* To defeat by a majority of votes ; মতের সংখ্যাধিক্যদ্বারা পরাভূত করা, অধিকতর সংখ্যক মত দ্বারা পরাভূত করা। **–out'-vot-er,** *n.* A non-resident Parliamentary elector qualified by holding property ; গ্রেটব্রিটেন কিম্বা আয়র্লণ্ডে সম্পত্তি থাকা হেতু ভোট প্রদানের অধিকারী ভিন্নদেশপ্রবাসী ব্যক্তি।

out'-ward (ōwt-wĕrd), *adj.,adv.* & *n.* **1.** (*Archaic*) Outer; (অপ্রঃ) বাহ্য। **2.** External ; material ; visible ; superficial ; বাহ্য, বহির্ভূত, বহির্বর্ত্তী ; ভৌতিক ; দৃশ্য ; বাহ্যস্থ। **3.** Directed towards the outside ; বহির্মুখ। ***Adv.*** Same as OUTWARDS. ***Noun.*** **1.** External appearance ; বাহ্যরূপ। **2.** (*Pl.*) Outward things ; externals ; বাহ্যবিষয়, বহিরঙ্গবিষয় ; বাহিরের জিনিষ। **–ly,** *adv.* Externally ; বাহ্যভাবে, বহির্দ্দিকে, বহির্ভাগে। **Outward bound**—Going away from home, as a ship, passenger, etc. ; বিদেশগামী। **Outward form**—Appearance ; বাহ্যাকৃতি। **Outward man**—(*Theol.*) Body (opp. to *soul*) ; also (*facet.*) clothing etc. ; (খৃষ্টীয়ধর্ম্মশাস্ত্র) শরীর ; (রঙ্গচ্ছলে) পরিচ্ছদ প্রভৃতি। **Outward things**—The world around us ; বহির্জগৎ। **The outward eye**—Physical eye, (opp. to *mind's eye*) ; স্থূলচক্ষু, চর্ম্মচক্ষু, বহিশ্চক্ষু। **The outward seeming**—Apparently ; বাহ্যতঃ, স্পষ্টতঃ, দৃষ্টতঃ।

out'-ward-nĕss (ōwt-wêrd-), *n.* **1.** Outward existence ; objectivity ; বাহ্যবিষয় ; বিষয়াত্মকতা, বাহ্যতা। **2.** Interest or belief in outward things ; বহির্মুখীনতা।

out'-wards (ōwt-wêrdz), *adv.* Towards the outside ; বহির্দ্দিকে।

out-watch' (ōwt-wŏch), *v. t.* To keep awake longer than ; to watch through and beyond (night etc.) ; অপেক্ষাকৃত অধিকতর কাল জাগিয়া থাকা ; সারারাত্রি জাগিয়া থাকা, সারারাত্রি এবং পরদিন কিছুক্ষণ জাগিয়া থাকা।

out-wear' (ōwt-wār), *v. t.* **1.** To wear out ; to spend (time) ; ক্ষয় করিয়া ফেলা ; (সময়) ব্যয় করা। **2.** To outgrow, as a habit, custom etc. ; to last longer than ; কোন অভ্যাস, রীতি প্রভৃতি কাটাইয়া উঠা ; অধিকতর কাল স্থায়ী হওয়া।

out-weigh' (ōwt-wā), *v. t.* To exceed in weight, value, importance, etc. ; অধিকতর গুরুভার হওয়া, অধিকতর মূল্যবান্ হওয়া, অধিকতর গুরুত্ববিশিষ্ট হওয়া, গুরুতর হওয়া।

out-wit' (ōwt-), *v. t.* **1.** (*Archaic*) To surpass in wit or wisdom ; (অপ্রঃ) অধিকতর বুদ্ধিমান হওয়া। **2.** To defeat by superior ingenuity or cunning ; বুদ্ধিবলে পরাস্ত করা, উপর-চালাকি করিয়া ঠকান, ভোগা দেওয়া।

out'-work (ōwt-wêrk), *n.* **1.** (*Fort.*) A work constructed beyond the main body of the place ; (দুর্গ) উপদুর্গ। **2.** Work done outside a house or shop ; কোন বাড়ী বা দোকানের বাহিরে যে কাজ করা হয়।

out-work' (ōwt-wêrk), *v. t.* To surpass in working ; to work more or faster than ; কার্য্যসম্পাদন বিষয়ে অতিক্রম করা ; অধিকতর দ্রুতভাবে কার্য্য করা।

out'-work-ĕr (ōwt-wêrk-), *n.* One working outside of the institution, shop or factory for which he works ; যে ব্যক্তি কোন প্রতিষ্ঠান, বিপণি বা কারখানার বাহিরে কাজ করে।

ou'-zel, -sel, (-ô-zl), *ns.* Various kinds of small birds ; নানাজাতীয় ক্ষুদ্র পক্ষীর সাধারণ নাম।

ō'-vă, *n., pl.* of OVUM (which see).

ō'-văl, *adj.* & *n.* Shaped like an egg ; elliptical ; অণ্ডাকৃতি, ডিম্বাকার, অণ্ডস্বরূপ ; বাদামি। ***Noun.*** 1. A figure shaped like an egg or ellipse ; উপবৃত্ত, উপমণ্ডল। 2. An object of oval shape ; অণ্ডাকৃতি বস্তু। **-ly,** *adv.* **-ness,** *n.*

ō'-vă-rў, *n.* 1. The female organ in which ova are formed ; ডিম্বাশয়, ডিম্বাধার (জাহিঃ), ডিম্বকোষ। 2. (*Bot.*) The vessel in which the seed is formed ; (উদ্ভিদ্‌বিদ্যা) বীজাগার। **-ri-ot'-o-my,** *n.* The operation of removing a tumour in the ovary ; ডিম্বাধারের স্ফোটকচ্ছেদন। **-ri'-tis,** *n.* (*Med.*) Inflammation of the ovaries ; ডিম্বাধারপ্রদাহ। **-va'-ri-an,** *adj.* Of, or relating to, the ovary ; ডিম্বাধারসম্বন্ধীয়।

ō'-vāte, *adj.* Egg-shaped ; oval ; ডিম্বাকৃতি ; অণ্ডাকার।

ō-va'-tion, *n.* 1. A lesser triumph among the ancient Romans; প্রাচীন রোমকদিগের মধ্যে রণবিজয়ী বীরগণের নগরপ্রবেশোপলক্ষে সাদরসম্বর্দ্ধনা। 2. An enthusiastic reception or tribute ; সাদর সম্বর্দ্ধনা, বিজয় সম্বর্দ্ধনা।

ov'-en (ŭv-n), *n.* 1. A place built for baking bread or other food in ; চুল্লী, আপাক। 2. A small furnace, kiln, etc. used in chemistry, metallurgy etc. ; চুল্লী, আথা (*colloq.*)। **Dutch oven**—তোরঙ্গাকৃতি ধাতুময় চুল্লী—যাহার মুক্তপার্শ্ব সাধারণতঃ অগ্নির অভিমুখীন রাখা হয়। **Oven bird**—চুল্লীর আকার নীড়নির্ম্মাণকারী পক্ষিশ্রেণীবিশেষ।

ō'-vêr, o'er (*Poet.*), *adv., n., adj.* & *prep.* 1. Outward and downward from brink or other position ; as, to lean or jump *over* : to fall *over* ; উপরে। 2. So as to cover or touch the whole surface ; as, to brush it *over* ; উপরি। 3. From one side to another so as to pass across something ; as, to climb *over* ; একদিক হইতে অপরদিকে। 4. So as to produce a fold or reverse position ; as, to bend *over* ; upside down ; as, to turn him *over* on his face ; ভাঁজ করিয়া, নোয়াইয়া ; বিপর্য্যস্তভাবে, উল্টাভাবে। 5. Across some space or distance ; as, take it *over* to the post-office ; এক স্থান হইতে অপর স্থানে। 6. Too ; in excess ; as, *over*-anxious ; more ; as, 20lb and *over* ; অতিরিক্ত ; অতিশয়, বেজায় ; আরও। 7. From beginning to end ; again ; with detailed consideration ; as, to read, talk, or think *over* ; আদ্যন্ত, আদ্যোপান্ত ; পুনরায়, পুনর্ব্বার ; সবিস্তারে। 8. At an end ; settled ; as, the quarrel was *over* ; সমাপ্ত ; মিটমাট। 9. From one to another ; as, to hand *over* a letter ; একের হাত হইতে অন্যের হাতে। ***Noun.*** (*Cricket*) An umpire's order for changing hands for bowling, etc. ; এক হাতের বল করা শেষ হইয়াছে বলিয়া মধ্যস্থের আদেশ। ***Adj.*** 1. Upper ; outer ; উপরের ; বাহিরের, বাহ্যতর। 2. Superior ; শ্রেষ্ঠ। 3. Surplus ; extra ; উদ্বৃত্ত ; অতিরিক্ত। 4. Too great ; অতি বৃহৎ। ***Prep.*** 1. Above ; upon ; উপরে ; উপরে স্থিত। 2. Throughout ; to and fro ; upon ; all through ; round about ; ব্যাপিয়া ; ইতস্ততঃ ; উপরে ; সারাসময় ; চারিদিকে। 3. Concerning ; as, to pause *over* the details ; সম্বন্ধে, বিষয়ে, সম্পর্কে। 4. More than ; as, it cost *over* Rs. 50 ; অধিকতর। 5. Above, implying superiority as to authority, power, preference, etc. ; as, to reign *over* a people : to get *over* difficulties : to give one preference *over* another ; উপর। 6. Down from ; across ; on or to the other side of ; as, to fall *over* the brink : to jump *over* a canal ; কোন কিছু হইতে নীচে ; উপর দিয়া ; অপর পার্শ্বে বা তীরে। 7. Throughout or during the time of ; to the end of ; as, payments spread *over* a series of months ; will not live *over* Wednesday ; ব্যাপিয়া, ঐ সময় ব্যাপিয়া ; কোন কিছুর শেষ পর্যান্ত। **All over**—So as to affect the whole of a surface in every part ; completely ; সর্ব্বত্র ; সর্ব্বতোভাবে। At an end ; finished ; as, it is *all over* with him ; সমাপ্ত ; সারা, শেষ। **All the world over**—In all countries ; জগৎ জুড়িয়া, পৃথিবী ব্যাপিয়া। **Ask him over**—Ask him to come as visitor from a place in the vicinity ; তাহাকে নিকটবর্ত্তী কোন স্থান হইতে আসিয়া সাক্ষাৎ করিতে বল। **Cannot live or stay over today**—আজকার বেশী বেঁচে থাকিতে পারে না, আজের দিন পার হইতে পারে না ; আজকার বেশী অপেক্ষা করিতে পারে না। **Hand over hand**—See under HAND. **It is all over with him**—He is ruined ; তাহার দফা রফা হইয়াছে। **Not over well etc.**—Rather badly etc. ; কতকটা খারাপভাবে। **Over against**—Opposite ; in front ; in contrast with ; বিপরীত ; সম্মুখস্থ ; কোন কিছুর সহিত বৈসাদৃশ্যে। **Over and above**—Besides ; এতদ্ব্যতীত, এতদতিরিক্ত। **Over and again**—Once more ; again ; আর একবার ; পুনরায়। **Over and over**—Again and again ; frequently ; পুনঃ পুনঃ ; বারংবার। Turning a complete somerset ; ডিগবাজী খাওন। **Over and over again**—বারংবার, পুনঃ পুনঃ। **Over-anxious**—See OVER *adv.* 6.

Over head and ears—Completely immersed (*lit.* & *fig.*) ; (শব্দানুযায়ী ও লক্ষণায়) একেবারে নিমগ্ন, হাবুডাবু, বিভোর। **Over our heads**—Above our heads ; beyond our comprehension ; also without consulting us ; আমাদের মাথার উপর ; আমাদের বুদ্ধির অতীত ; আমাদের সহিত পরামর্শ না করিয়া। **Over shoes over boots**—No half measures ; পূর্ণ-উদ্যমে। **Over the left**—Understand the contrary of what is said ; as, it will suit you *over the left* (*i. e.* it will not suit you অর্থাৎ ইহা তোমাকে মানাইবেনা) যাহা বলা হইয়াছে তদ্বিপরীত বুঝায়। **Over the walnuts and the wine**—At dessert ; ভোজনের শেষে ফল, মোরব্বা, মিষ্টান্নাদি ভোজনে রত। **That can stand over**—That cannot be dealt with now ; এটা এখন স্থগিত থাকিতে পারে। **The house over the way**—*i.e.* Across the way ; অর্থাৎ রাস্তার অপর পার্শ্বে। **The King over the water**—নির্বাসিত রাজা। **To hand over**—See under HAND. **To make over**—See under MAKE. **To put one over the door**—To turn him out ; কাহাকে গৃহ হইতে বহিষ্কৃত করা। **To roll over and over**—Roll so that the same point comes uppermost repeatedly ; গড়ান। **To stumble over**—To be tripped up by ; হোঁচট খাইয়া পড়া। **To talk or think the matter over**—কোন বিষয়ে ভাবা বা আলোচনা করা। **To turn over**—To turn the otherside of a (book) leaf up ; পুস্তকের পাতা উল্টান।

ō-vêr-ăct', *v. t.* & *i.* To act to excess as a part, emotion, etc. ; অতিরিক্ত মাত্রায় সম্পাদন করা, অতিমাত্রায় করা, বাড়াবাড়ি করা, অতিরিক্ত করা। ***Verb i.*** **1.** To act a part etc. to excees ; অতিরিক্ত অভিনয় করা। **2.** To act in excess of what is proper, right or lawful ; ন্যায়, বিধি বা সমীচীনতার সঙ্গতসীমা অতিক্রম করিয়া কার্য্য করা, ফাজিলচালাকি করা। **—ac'-tive,** *adj.* **—ac'-tive-ness, —ac-tiv'-i-ty,** *ns.*

ō'-vêr-all, *n.* An out-garment ; esp. (*pl.*) loose protective trousers or leggings ; বহিঃপরিচ্ছদ বিশেষ ; (বহুবচনে) ঢিলা পাজামা বা জঙ্ঘাত্রাণ।

ō-vêr-ârch', *v. t.* & *i.* To cover with an arch ; to arch over; তোরণাবৃত করা ; তোরণসমন্বিত করা বা হওয়া।

ō-vêr-awe' (-ä), *v. t.* To restrain by awe or fear ; ভয়প্রদর্শনে সংযত বা অভিভূত করা। **—awed',** *p. p.* Terrified ; সন্ত্রস্ত, ভয়াকুলিত, ভীতি-বিহ্বল।

ō-vêr-băl'-ance (-ăns), *v.i., t.* & *n.* To prevail by dint of greater weight or power ; গুরুতর ভারদ্বারা একদিকে নোয়ান, বা প্রবলতর শক্তিদ্বারা অবনমিত করা। ***Verb t.*** To outweigh, (*lit.* & *fig.*) ; গুরুতর হওয়া (শব্দানুযায়ী ও লক্ষণায়)। ***Noun.*** Excess ; amount of excess ; আধিক্য ; আধিক্যের পরিমাণ।

ō-vêr-bear' (-bār), *v. t.* **1.** To bear down ; to overcome ; দাবান ; পরাজিত করা। **2.** To domineer over ; প্রভুত্ব করা। **—ing,** *adj.* **1.** Overpowering ; অভিভবকারী। **2.** Arrogant ; domineering ; insolent ; উদ্ধত ; প্রভুত্বকারী ; ধৃষ্ট, অবিমৃশ্যকারী।

ō-vêr-blow' (-blō), *v. t.* & *i.* **1.** To blow away ; উড়াইয়া দেওয়া। **2.** To blow over the surface of ; কোন কিছুর উপর দিয়া প্রবাহিত হওয়া। ***Verb i.*** (Of a storm etc.) To abate in violence, (also *fig.*) ; (ঝটিকাদি সম্বন্ধে) বেগ মন্দীভূত হওয়া, প্রশমিত হওয়া।

ō'-vêr-blown (-blōn), *adj.* **1.** (Of flowers) Too fully open ; past prime ; অতিবিকশিত ; বিগততারুণ্য, অপগতযৌবনশ্রী। **2.** (Of storm etc.) Past ; (ঝটিকাদি সম্বন্ধে) অপগত।

ō'-vêr-board (-bōrd), *adv.* Over the side of a ship ; out of a ship ; জাহাজের পার্শ্বের উপর দিয়া ; জাহাজ হইতে। **To throw overboard**—To throw over the side of a ship ; জাহাজের পার্শ্বের উপর দিয়া ফেলিয়া দেওয়া। (*Fig.*) To abandon ; to discard ; (লক্ষণায়) পরিত্যাগ করা ; বর্জ্জন করা, পায়ে ঠেলা।

ō'-vêr-bōld, *adj.* Too bold ; impudent ; দুঃসাহসী ; ধৃষ্ট।

ō'-vêr-bridge (-brij), *n.* A bridge over a road or a railroad ; রাজপথ বা লৌহবর্ত্মের উপরিস্থ সেতু।

ō-vêr-brim', *v. t.* & *i.* To flow over the brim (of) ; উপচিয়া পড়া।

ō-vêr-build' (-bĭld), *v. t.* **1.** To build, esp. too closely over or upon (land) ; কোন জমির উপর বাড়ী তৈয়ার করা, বিশেষতঃ কোন জমির উপর খুব ঘন ঘন করিয়া বাড়ী তৈয়ার করা। **2.** To build beyond the demand ; চাহিদার অতিরিক্ত নির্ম্মাণ করা।

ō'-vêr-bur'-den (-bêr-dn), *v.t.* & *n.* To overload, (*lit.* & *fig.*) ; ভারাক্রান্ত করা, ভারপ্রপীড়িত করা (বাক্যানুযায়ী ও লক্ষণায়)। ***Noun.*** Excess of burden ; ভারাধিক্য।

ō-vêr-bus'-ȳ (-bĭz-), *adj.* Excessively busy ; officious ; অতি ব্যস্ত ; উপযাচক, গায়ে-পড়া।

ō-vêr-buy' (-bī), *v. i.* To buy more than enough to meet the demand ; আবশ্যকের অতিরিক্ত ক্রয় করা, অতিক্রয় করা।

ō-vêr-căn'-ō-pȳ, *v. t.* To form or be a canopy over ; চন্দ্রাতপ বিস্তার করা, বিতানীকৃত করা, তন্দ্রাতপবৎ বিস্তারিত হওয়া।

ō-vêr-căp'-i-tăl-īze, *v. t.* To put too high a value upon the capital of, as a company etc. ; কোন ব্যবসায়ে যে পরিমাণ মূলধন খাটান আবশ্যক তদপেক্ষা অধিক আবশ্যক হইবে বলিয়া নির্দ্ধারণ করা।

ō'-vêr-care, *n.* Too much care ; অতিসাবধানতা, অতিসতর্কতা।

ō-vêr-cāst', *v. t.* & *n.* **1.** To cover or overspread with clouds ;

to darken ; মেঘাচ্ছন্ন করা, মেঘাবৃত করা, জলদাবৃত করা ; অন্ধকার করা, তিমিরাবগুণ্ঠিত করা। 2. To throw rough stitches over (the raw edges of seam) to prevent raveling ; মুড়ি ভাঙ্গিয়া সেলাই করা। *Noun.* (*Mining*) An air-passage crossing above another passage ; (খনিজ-বিদ্যা) যে বায়ুনির্গমপথ দ্বারা অপর পথ আড়ভাবে ছেদিত হইয়া থাকে।

ŏ'-vĕr-cau'-tion (-kä-), *n.* Excessive caution; অতিসতর্কতা, অতি-সাবধানতা।

ō-vêr-charge' (-chârj), *v. t.* & *n.* **1.** To charge or burden to excess ; as, to *overcharge* a gun ; অতিরিক্ত ভার চাপান, অতিরিক্ত গুলি বারুদ ভরা। **2.** To charge too high a price for (a thing) or to a (person) ; to charge as a specified sum beyond the right price ; অতিরিক্ত মূল্য চাওয়া ; উপযুক্ত মূল্যের উপর নির্দ্দিষ্ট সংখ্যক মুদ্রা চাওয়া। **3.** To put exaggerated details into, as a description etc. ; খুঁটিনাটি বিষয় দ্বারা পূর্ণ করা। *Noun.* **(o'–)** Excessive charge both as regards load and price ; অতিরিক্ত ভার, অতিরিক্ত মূল্য।

ō-vêr-cloud' (-clowd), *v. t.* **1.** To overspread with clouds or something like cloud ; মেঘাচ্ছন্ন করা, মেঘাবৃত করা। **2.** (*Fig.*) To render gloomy ; to obscure ; (লক্ষণায়) অন্ধকার করা ; ঝাপ্সা করা, অস্পষ্ট করা।

ō-vêr-cloy', *v. t.* To cloy excessively ; to satiate ; অতিরিক্ত তৃপ্ত করা ; সন্তৃপ্ত করা।

ō'-vêr-coat (-cōt), *n.* An upper coat ; পোষাকের উপর পরিধেয় মোটা জামা।

ō-vêr-col'-our (-cŭl-ẽr), *v. t.* To colour too highly, (usu. *fig.*) ; "For *overcolouring* facts" ; অতিরঞ্জিত করা, রং চড়ান (সাধারণতঃ লক্ষণায়)।

ō-vêr-come' (-kŭm), *v. t.* & *i.* **1** To be victorious over ; to get the better of ; to subdue ; পরাজিত করা ; পরাভূত করা ; বশীভূত করা। **2.** To overpower ; to overwhelm ; অভিভূত করা ; আকুল করা। *Verb i.* To gain the superiority ; প্রাধান্য লাভ করা।

ō-vêr-cŏn'-fi-dence (-dĕns), *n.* Too great cofidence ; অতিরিক্ত বিশ্বাস। **–nent,** *adj.*

ō-vêr-crĕ-dū'-li-tў, *n.* Excessive credulity ; অতি বিশ্বাস। **–cred'-u-lous,** *adj.*

ō-vêr-crŏp', *v. t.* To exhaust the fertility of (land) by excessive cultivation ; অতিরিক্ত কর্ষণদ্বারা ভূমির উর্ব্বরতাশক্তি নষ্ট করা।

ō-vêr-crow' (-crō), *v. t.* To crow or exult over ; to overpower ; উল্লাস প্রকাশ করা ; অভিভূত করা।

ō-vêr-crowd', *v. t.* & *i.* **1.** To crowd to excess ; সঙ্কুলিত করা, ঠাসা। *Verb i.* To crowd together to excess ; সঙ্কুলিত হওয়া। **–ed,** *p. adj.*

ō-vêr-crŭst', *v. t.* To cover over with a crust or layer ; কঠিন বহিরাবরণ দ্বারা আচ্ছাদিত করা, মামড়ী দ্বারা আচ্ছাদিত করা।

ō-vêr-cŭn'-ning (-ĭng), *n.* & *adj.* Excess of cunning ; অতি চালাকি, অতিরিক্ত চতুরতা, অতি শঠতা। *Adj.* Too cunning; অতি চালাক, অতি চতুর।

ō-vêr-cū'-ri-ous (-ŭs), *adj.* Too inquisitive ; too careful or precise ; fastidious ; অতি কৌতূহলী ; অতি সতর্ক, অতি সঠিক ; উৎকটরুচি, খুঁতখুঁতে।

ō-vêr-dĕl'-i-cā-cў, *n.* Too great delicacy ; অতিসূক্ষ্মতা।

ō-vêr-dē-vĕl'-op (-ŭp), *v. t.* To develop too greatly or to excess, (esp. in *Photog.*) ; অতিরিক্ত পরিস্ফুট করা (বিশেষতঃ আলোকচিত্রণে)।

ō-vêr-dō', *v. t.* & *i.* **1.** To do too much ; to carry to excess ; অতিরিক্ত করা, অতিমাত্রায় করা ; বাড়াবাড়ি করা। **2.** To fatigue or exhaust ; পরিক্লান্ত করা, অবসন্ন করা। **3.** (*Archaic*) To excel ; (অপ্রঃ) (সন্তরণাদিতে) অতিক্রম করা। **4.** To cook too much ; as, to *overdo* meat ; অতিপক্ব করা, অতি পাক করা, অতি সিদ্ধ করা। *Verb i.* To do too much ; to go to excess ; অতিমাত্রায় করা ; বাড়াবাড়ি করা। **–done',** *p. adj.* Done too much ; অতিকৃত, অতিপক্ব, অতিসিদ্ধ।

ō'-vêr-door (-dōr), *n.* A piece of ornamental wood-work etc. placed over a door ; দ্বারোপরি স্থাপিত কারুকার্য্যখচিত কাষ্ঠখণ্ড প্রভৃতি।

ō-vêr-dōse', *v. t.* & *n.* To dose to excess ; to give too large a dose to ; অতিরিক্ত মাত্রায় প্রয়োগ করা ; মাত্রার অতিরিক্ত ঔষধ সেবন করান। *Noun.* **(o'–)** Too large a dose ; ঔষধের অতিরিক্ত মাত্রা।

ō'-vêr-drăft, –draught, (-drăft), *n.* **1.** (*Banking*) Act of overdrawing ; an amount overdrawn ; (ব্যাঙ্কিং) যত টাকা গচ্ছিত আছে তাহার অতিরিক্ত টাকা বাহির করণ ; এইরূপ ভাবে বাহির করিয়া আনা অতিরিক্ত টাকা। **2.** An excessive draft of men for military purposes ; যুদ্ধাদি কার্য্যের জন্য অতিরিক্ত সৈন্য আনয়ন। **3.** A current of air passing over a fire, kiln, etc. ; অগ্নি, পোয়ান, প্রভৃতির উপর প্রবহমাণ বায়ুস্রোতঃ।

ō-vêr-draw' (-drä) *v. t.* & *i.* **1.** (*Banking*) To draw upon for a larger sum than is standing at one's credit ; (ব্যাঙ্কিং) ব্যাঙ্কে যত টাকা গচ্ছিত আছে তাহা অপেক্ষা অতিরিক্ত টাকা বাহির করিয়া আনা। **2.** To draw too far ; to exaggerate ; অতিরঞ্জিত করা ; রং চড়ান। *Verb i.* (*Banking*) To make an overdraft ; (ব্যাঙ্কিং) গচ্ছিত টাকার অতিরিক্ত টাকা বাহির করিয়া আনা।

ō-vêr-drĕss', *v. t.* & *i.* To dress to excess or with too much display; অতিসজ্জিত করা, অতিরিক্ত বেশভূষাদ্বারা সজ্জিত করা।

ō'-vêr-drĕss, *n.* An outer dress or upper dress; বাহিরের পোষাক।

ō-vêr-drink', *v. i.* & *reflex.* To drink too much; অতিরিক্ত মদ্য পান করা।

ō-vêr-drīve', *v. t.* To drive too hard; to drive or work to exhaustion; অতি বেগে চালান; অতি বেগে চালাইয়া বা অতিশয় খাটাইয়া অবসন্ন করা।

ō'-vêr-due (-dü), *adj.* Delayed or unpaid beyond the proper time of arrival or payment; অতিরিক্ত বিলম্বিত, অতীতশোধনকাল, অতীত-গমনকাল।

ō-vêr-ea'-gêr (-ē-), *adj.* Too eager; অতিব্যস্ত, ব্যস্তবাগীশ।

ō-vêr-eat' (-ēt), *v. t.* & *reflex.* To eat to excess; to surfeit oneself with eating; অতিভোজন করা; আকণ্ঠভোজন করা।

ō-vêr-ĕs'-ti-māte, *v. t.* & *n.* To estimate too highly; to overvalue; অতি সমাদর করা; অতি মূল্যবান বলিয়া গণ্য করা। ***Noun.*** **(o'—)** Too high an estimate; অতিরিক্ত সমাদর।

ō-vêr-ĕx-pōşe', *v. t.* To expose too much, (esp. in *Photog.*); অতিরিক্ত কাল আলোকে অনাবৃত রাখা (বিশেষতঃ আলোকচিত্রণে)। **—po'-sure,** *n.*

ō'-vêr-făll, *n.* **1.** A turbulent stretch of sea etc. caused by strong currents setting over submerged ridges or shoals; জলপ্রবাহ, জলমগ্ন শৈল বা অগভীর জলে প্রবহণ হেতু সমুদ্রের যে অংশ নিত্য তরঙ্গবিক্ষুব্ধ থাকে। **2.** A place provided for the overflow of surplus water from a canal, lock, etc.; খাল, স্রোতোদ্বার প্রভৃতির অতিরিক্ত জলরাশি নির্গমের জন্য স্থান।

ō-vêr-făll', *v. t.* To fall upon or over; to attack; উপরে পতিত হওয়া, আপতিত হওয়া; আক্রমণ করা।

ō-vêr-fă-tigue' (-tēg), *v. t.* & *n.* To fatigue excessively; অতিক্লান্ত করা, পরিক্লান্ত করা। **(o'—)** ***Noun.*** Too great fatigue; অতিক্লান্তি, পরিক্লান্তি।

ō-vêr-feed' (-fēd), *v. t.* & *i.* To feed to excess; অতিরিক্ত ভোজন করান বা করা।

ō-vêr-fĭll', *v. t.* To fill to overflowing or excess; অতিপূর্ণ করা, অতিমাত্রায় পূর্ণ করা।

ō-vêr-fĭlm', *v. t.* To put a film over; উপরে পর্দা ফেলা।

ō-vêr-fĭsh', *v. t.* To fish, as a stream etc. too much; to fish to depletion; অতিরিক্ত মাত্রায় মাছ ধরা; মাছ ধরিয়া শূন্য করা।

ō-vêr-flow' (-flō), *v. t.* & *i.* **1.** To flow over; to flood; উপরে প্রবাহিত করা; বন্যাপ্লাবিত করা। **2.** (*Fig.*) To spread over like a flood; to overwhelm; পরিপ্লাবিত করা; অভিভূত করা। ***Verb i.*** **1.** To flow over the sides or brim; ছাপিয়ে পড়া, উছলিয়া পড়া, উপচিয়া পড়া। **2.** (*Fig.*, of a large crowd in a room etc.) To remove; as, the crowd *overflowed* into the street; (লক্ষণায়) স্থানান্তরিত হওয়া, সরা। **3.** To be filled to running over; to superabound; অতিমাত্রায় পূর্ণ করা; অতিবহুল পরিমাণে থাকা। **—ing,** *adj.* Flowing over; abundant; exuberant; উদ্বেল, উচ্ছল; প্রচুর; অতিবহুল।

ō'-vêr-flow (-flō), *n.* **1.** A flowing over; an innundation; পরিপ্লাবন; প্লাবন। **2.** That which flows over; superabundance; as, an *overflow* of population; যাহা প্লাবিত হয়; অতিবাহুল্য, অতিপ্রাচুর্য্য। **Overflow meeting** — লোকাধিক্য হেতু প্রধান সভাস্থলে স্থানসংকুলান না হইলে সভায় প্রবেশে অক্ষম ব্যক্তিগণের জন্য যে অতিরিক্ত সভার ব্যবস্থা করা হয়।

ō'-vêr-fōld, *n.* (*Geol.*) A fold of strata so complete that the middle part is upside down; (ভূবিদ্যা) যে স্তর বা পুটের মধ্যভাগ বিপর্য্যস্ত থাকে।

ō'-vêr-front (-frŭnt), *n.* A piece hanging over the front of a cloak, and covering the arm instead of a sleeve; ঢিলা জামার সম্মুখভাগে দোলায়মান অংশ বিশেষ—যাহা আস্তিনের কার্য্য সাধন করে।

ō'-vêr-fŭll, *adj.* Excessively full; অতিপূর্ণ।

ō-vêr-gild', *v. t.* To gild over; (*fig.*) to tinge with golden colour; স্বর্ণপত্রাচ্ছাদিত করা; (লক্ষণায়) স্বর্ণবর্ণে রঞ্জিত করা।

ō'-vêr-glăd, *adj.* Too glad; অতি-সন্তুষ্ট, অতিপ্রীত।

ō-vêr-gō', *v. t.* & *i.* **1.** (*Dial.*) To pass over; to surmount; (উপভাষায়) অতিক্রম করা; লঙ্ঘন করা। **2.** (*Fig.*) To excel; সদ্‌গুণে অতিক্রম করা, শ্রেষ্ঠতর হওয়া। **3.** To travel through; to traverse; পর্য্যটন করা, ভ্রমণ করা; বিচরণ করা। ***Verb i.*** (*Dial.*) To pass by; (উপভাষায়) নিকট দিয়া চলিয়া যাওয়া।

ō-vêr-gov'-êrn (-gŭv-), *v. t.* To subject to too much government interference; অতিশাসন করা। **—ment,** *n.*

ō'-vêr-ground (-gownd), *adj.* Situated over or above ground; ভূতলস্থ, ভূমির উপরিস্থ।

ō-vêr-grow' (-grō), *v. t.*, *i.* & *reflex.* **1.** To grow over; to cover with herbage etc. esp. rank; উপরে জন্মান; তৃণগুল্মাদিদ্বারা আচ্ছাদিত করা। **2.** To grow beyond; অতিরিক্ত বৃদ্ধি পাওয়া, অতিবর্দ্ধিত হওয়া। **3.** To grow more vigorously than; কোন কিছু অপেক্ষা অধিতর সতেজে বৃদ্ধি প্রাপ্ত হওয়া। ***Verb i.*** To grow beyond the fit or natural size; to increase unduly; অস্বাভাবিক রূপে বৃদ্ধিপ্রাপ্ত হওয়া; অসঙ্গতরূপে বৃদ্ধি প্রাপ্ত হওয়া। ***Reflex.*** To grow beyond one's strength, proper size etc. ; as, to *overgrow oneself* ; অতিরিক্ত বৃদ্ধি পাওয়া, অতিমাত্রায় বৃদ্ধি পাওয়া। **O'-ver-growth,** *n.* **1.** Exuberant or excessive growth ; অতিবৃদ্ধি। **2.** That which grows over some plant or thing ; an accretion ; যাহা অন্য কোন বৃক্ষ বা বস্তুর উপর জন্মে বা বৃদ্ধিপ্রাপ্ত হয় ; উপচয়।

ō'-vêr-hănd, *adv.* & *adj.* **1.** In an overhand manner ; with the hand over the object ; তলে তলে ; বস্তুর উপর হস্ত রাখিয়া। **2.** (*Cricket* etc.) With the hand over the shoulder ; as, to bowl *overhand* ; কাঁধের উপর হাত তুলিয়া। *Adj.* Done with the hand raised above the shoulder as bowling, pitching, etc. ; কাঁধের উপর হাত তুলিয়া কৃত। **Overhand stroke**—(In swimming) A stroke out of water ; (সন্তরণে) জলের উপর হাত তুলিয়া আঘাত।

ō-vêr-hăng', *v. t.* & *i.* **1.** To hang over ; to project over ; (*fig.*) to impend over ; ঝুলাইয়া রাখা, দোদুল্যমান করা ; প্রলম্বিত করা ; (লক্ষণায়) আসন্নবর্তী করা। **2.** To adorn with hangings ; ঝালর প্রভৃতি দ্বারা সুশোভিত করা। *Verb i.* To hang or jut over ; (*fig.*) to impend ; দোলায়মান হওয়া, উদ্গত হওয়া ; (লক্ষণায়) আসন্নবর্তী হওয়া, ঝুলা।

ō'-vêr-hăng, *n.* Projection ; the measure of the projection ; প্রলম্বন ; প্রলম্বনের পরিমাণ। **—hang'-ing,** *adj.*

ō-vêr-haul', (-häl), *v. t.* **1.** To examine thoroughly for repairs etc. ; জীর্ণসংস্কারের জন্য পুঙ্খানুপুঙ্খরূপে পরীক্ষা করা। **2.** (*Naut.*) To overtake ; (নৌ-বিদ্যা) নাগাইল ধরা। **To overhaul a rope**—(*Naut.*) To slacken it by pulling it in the opposite direction to that in which it is drawn in hoisting ; (নৌ-বিদ্যা) কোন দ্রব্য তোলার সময় যে দিকে রজ্জু টানা হয়—তদ্বিপরীতদিকে টানিয়া রজ্জু শিথিল করা। **To overhaul a ship**—To overtake a ship ; to search a ship for contraband goods ; কোন জাহাজের নাগাইল ধরা ; নিষিদ্ধ কোন পণ্যদ্রব্য আছে কিনা তাহা পরীক্ষার জন্য কোন জাহাজ খানাতল্লাস করা।

ō'-vêr-head (-hĕd), *adv.* & *adj.* **1.** Above one's head : on high ; in, or near, the zenith ; on the floor or story above ; শিরোপরি, মস্তকোপরি ; ঊর্দ্ধে ; খমধ্যে, খমধ্যাস্তিকে ; উপরের তলায়। **2.** So as to be completely submerged ; as, to plunge *overhead* into water ; সম্যগ্রূপে নিমজ্জিত করিয়া। *Adj.* **1.** Operating or situated overhead ; as, *overhead* wires ; ঊর্দ্ধেস্থিত, শিরোপরিস্থিত, শিরোপরি ক্রিয়াশীল। **2.** Average : "An *overhead* charge of so much portion" ; গড়পড়তা।

ō-vêr-hear' (-hër), *v. t.* To hear by accident or strategem ; দৈবাৎ শুনিয়া ফেলা, ঘটনাক্রমে শ্রবণ করা, অলক্ষিতে শ্রবণ করা।

ō'-vêr-house, (-hows), *adj.* Passing over or supported by the roofs of houses ; as, *overhouse* telegraphs : ছাদের উপর অবলম্বিত, ছাদের উপর দিয়া অতিক্রমী।

ō-vêr-hous'-ĕd (-hows-), *adj.* Having house-accommodation in excess of one's requirements and means ; আয় বা আবশ্যকের অতিরিক্ত বাসোপযোগী গৃহসম্পন্ন।

ō'-vêr-hŭng, *adj.* **1.** Hung or covered over ; উপরে দোলায়মান বা আবৃত। **2.** Suspended from above, as a door etc. ; দোলায়মান।

ō-vêr-in-dŭl'-gence (-gĕns), *n.* Too much indulgence ; অতি-প্রশ্রয়।

ō-vêr-is'-sue (-ĭsh-ü), *v. t.* To issue in excess ; অতিরিক্ত পরিমাণ বাহির করা।

ō'-vêr-is-sue (-ĭsh-ü), *n.* An excessive issue, esp. of coins, notes, etc. ; অতিরিক্ত পরিমাণ বাহির হওন।

ō-vêr-joy', *v. t.* To make excessively joyful ; অত্যুল্লসিত করা, আনন্দে আত্মহারা করা, প্রহৃষ্ট করা। **—joyed,** *p. adj.*

ō'-vêr-joy, *n.* Excess of joy ; অতিহর্ষ, প্রহর্ষ।

ō-vêr-jŭmp', *v. t.* **1.** To jump over ; (*fig.*) to pass over ; টপকান, ডিঙ্গাইয়া যাওয়া ; (লক্ষণায়) অতিক্রম করা। **2.** To jump too far over ; কোন কিছুর উপর দিয়া অতি দূরে লম্ফ দিয়া যাওয়া। **3.** (*Reflex.*) To jump too far for one's strength ; শক্তির অনুপাতে অতি দূরে লম্ফ দিয়া যাওয়া।

ō'-vêr-knee (-nē), *adj.* Reaching above the knee ; আজানুলম্বিত।

ō-vêr-la'-bour (-bêr), *v. t.* **1.** To overwork ; to fatigue ; অতি পরিশ্রম করান, অতিশয় খাটান ; ক্লান্ত করা। **2.** To elaborate to excess ; অতিবিস্তৃত করা।

ō'-vêr-lā-dĕn, *adj.* Laden to excess ; অতিভারাক্রান্ত।

ō'-vêr-lănd, *adv.* & *adj.* By, upon, or across, land ; স্থলপথে। *Adj.* Passing by land ; made upon or across land as journey, etc. ; স্থলপথগামী ; স্থলপথে সম্পাদিত। **An overland farm**—গৃহশূন্য কৃষিক্ষেত্র। **Overland route**—যে পথের কতকাংশ স্থলের উপর, যথা ইংলণ্ড হইতে ব্রিন্দিসি ও সুয়েজ যোজক হইয়া ভারতবর্ষে আসিবার পথ, অথবা ক্যানাডা ও যুক্তরাজ্যের উপর দিয়া ইংলণ্ড হইতে প্রশান্ত মহাসাগরে যাইবার পথ, স্থলবর্ত্ম (রঃ)।

ō-vêr-lăp', *v. t.* & *i.* **1.** To lap over ; to overlie partially ; একটীর কিনারা অপরটীর উপর রাখা বা থাকা ; আংশিক ভাবে কোন কিছুর উপর থাকা। **2.** To cover or extend beyond, (*lit.* & *fig.*) ; অতিরিক্ত আবৃত বা প্রসারিত করা (শব্দানুযায়ী এবং লক্ষণায়)। **3.** To coincide partly with ; অংশতঃ

সমস্থান অধিকার করা। *Verb i.* To lap over or coincide partly ; একটীর কিনারা অপরটীর উপর রাখা, অংশতঃ সমস্থান অধিকার করিয়া থাকা।

ō-vêr-lay′ (-lā), *v. t.* **1.** To lay over ; to cover ; পরিব্যাপ্ত করা, আস্তৃত করা ; আচ্ছাদিত করা, মোড়া, আবৃত করা, মণ্ডিত করা। **2.** To smother ; শ্বাস রোধ করা।

ō′-vêr-lay (-lā), *n.* **1.** (*Archaic*) A cravat ; গলবন্ধ। **2.** A covering esp. a temporary or removable one ; আবরণ, ঢাকনী, শরাব।

ō-vêr-leaf′ (-lēf), *adv.* On the other side of the leaf, esp. of a book ; "As said *overleaf*" ; পূর্ব্ব পৃষ্ঠায়, অপর পৃষ্ঠায়।

ō-vêr-leap′ (-lēp), *v. t.* To leap over ; to pass by leaping ; লাফাইয়া পার হওয়া ; লাফাইয়া অতিক্রম করা।

ō-vêr-lie′ (-lī), *v. t.* **1.** To lie over or upon ; উপরে থাকা বা শায়িত হওয়া। **2.** To suffocate by lying upon as an infant etc. ; উপরে শুইয়া শিশু প্রভৃতিকে শ্বাস রোধ করিয়া মারা।

ō-vêr-live′ (-līv), *v. t.* To live longer than ; to survive ; অধিকতর কাল বাঁচা ; কাহারও মৃত্যুর পর জীবিত থাকা।

ō-vêr-load′ (-lōd), *v. t.* To load excessively ; to overburden ; অতিভারাক্রান্ত করা, ভারপ্রপীড়িত করা ; অতিরিক্ত মাত্রায় বোঝাই করা।

ō′-vêr-load (-lōd), *n.* An excessive load ; অতিরিক্ত ভার।

ō-vêr-lōōk′ *v. t.* **1.** To fail to see or observe ; to disregard ; to ignore or excuse ; দেখিয়াও না দেখা ; তাচ্ছিল্য করা ; অবহেলা করা, উপেক্ষা করা। **2.** (*Rare*) To superintend or inspect ; (ক্বচিদ্‌ব্যবহৃত) পরিদর্শন করা। **3.** To view from a higher place ; to rise above ; "The brow of the hill *overlooking* the...valley" ; উচ্চতর স্থান হইতে দর্শন করা ; ঊর্দ্ধে উত্থিত হওয়া।

ō′-vêr-lôrd, *n.* A superior lord ; a lord paramount ; সর্ব্বেশ্বর ; অধিরাজ। **—ship,** *n.*

ō′-vêr-măn, *n.* **1.** An arbiter or umpire ; সালিস, মধ্যস্থ, প্রমাণপুরুষ। **2.** A foreman or overseer ; কার্য্য-পরিদর্শক। **3.** (*Philos. of Nietzsche*) A man of superior physique and powers fitted to dominate others ; (নীটসের-দর্শনশাস্ত্র) অতি-মানুষ। (See SUPERMAN.)

ō′-vêr-măn-tĕl, *n.* An ornamental cabinet work, placed over a mantelpiece ; অগ্নিসেবনকুণ্ডের উপরে স্থাপিত কারুকার্য্যখচিত কাষ্ঠখণ্ড।

ō-vêr-măn′-ȳ, *adj.* Too many ; অত্যধিক সংখ্যক।

ō-vêr-măs′-tĕd, *adj.* With too tall or heavy masts ; অতিদীর্ঘ বা গুরুভার মাস্তুল বিশিষ্ট।

ō-vêr-măs′-têr, *v. t.* To overpower ; to subdue ; পরাজিত করা ; বশীভূত করা, দমন করা।

ō-vêr-match′ (-măch), *v. t.* To be more than a match for ; to vanquish ; অধিকতর শক্তিশালী হওয়া ; পরাস্ত করা, পরাজিত করা।

ō′-vêr-match (-măch), *n.* One superior in power ; অধিকতর শক্তিশালী ব্যক্তি।

ō′-vêr-meas-üre (-mĕz-), *n.* & *v. t.* Excessive measure ; excess beyond the proper measure ; অতিমাত্রা ; উপযুক্ত পরিমাণের উপর আধিক্য। *Verb t.* **(-meas′-)** To measure or estimate in excess of the real or proper amount ; উপযুক্ত পরিমাণের উপর পরিমাপ করা বা অনুমান করা।

ō′-vêr-mŭch, *adj., adv.* & *n.* Too much ; অত্যধিক। *Adv.* In too great a degree ; নিরতিশয়। *Noun.* More than sufficient ; অতিপ্রাচুর্য্য।

ō′-vêr-nīce, *adj.* Too nice ; too scrupulous ; অতিসূক্ষ্মবিচারী, দুস্তোষ্য ; অতিশয় খুঁতখুঁতে। **—nice′-ness, —ni′-ce-ty,** *ns.*

ō-vêr-night′ (-nīt), *adv.* & *adj.* In the night before ; also, during the night ; গতনিশায়, গতযামিনীতে ; রাত্রি ব্যাপিয়া। *Adj.* **(o′—)** Of, or relating to, the preceding night ; done or lasting during the night ; পূর্ব্ব রাত্রির ; নিশায় সম্পাদিত, রাত্রিব্যাপী।

ō-vêr-păss′, *v. t.* & *i.* **1.** To pass over ; to traverse ; অতিক্রম করা ; ভ্রমণ করা। **2.** To pass through ; to get over ; as, to *overpass* a period or catastrophe ; কাটাইয়া উঠা ; অতিক্রম করা। **3.** To pass across or beyond ; পার হইয়া যাওয়া, ছাড়াইয়া যাওয়া। **4.** To surpass ; অতিক্রম করা। **5.** (*Rare*) To overlook or disregard ; to omit ; (ক্বচিদ্‌ব্যবহৃত) উপেক্ষা করা, অবহেলা করা ; বর্জ্জন করা। *Verb i.* To pass by or away, (usu. in *pl.*) ; অতিক্রম করিয়া চলা। **—passed′, —past′,** *p. adjs.*

ō-vêr-pay′ (-pā), *v. t.* To pay more than is due ; to recompense too highly ; প্রাপ্যের অতিরিক্ত দেওয়া ; অত্যধিক পুরস্কৃত করা।

ō-vêr-peo′-pled (-pē-pld), *p. adj.* Over-stocked with people ; অতিজনাকীর্ণ, অতিলোকাকীর্ণ।

ō-vêr-pêr-suade′ (-swād), *v. t.* To persuade against one's inclination or judgment ; কাহারো আসক্তি বা বিচারবুদ্ধির বিরুদ্ধে প্রোৎসাহিত করা।

ō-vêr-pitch′ (-pĭch), *v. t.* **1.** (*Cricket etc.*) To pitch (a ball) too far in bowling ; (ক্রীকেটক্রীড়ায়) কন্দুক অতিরিক্ত দূরে ক্ষেপণ করা। **2.** (*Fig.*) To exaggerate ; (লক্ষণায়) অতিরঞ্জিত করা।

ō′-vêr-plŭs, *n.* An extra quantity ; surplus ; অতিরিক্ত পরিমাণ ; উদ্বর্ত্ত।

ō-vêr-poise′ (-poyz), *v. t.* To outweigh ; অতিতুলিত করা।

ō-vĕr-pŏp′-ū-lāt-ĕd, *adj.* Excessively populated ; অতিজনাকীর্ণ।

ō′-vêr-pō-pū-lā′-tion, *n.* State of being overpopulated ; excess ;

অতিজনাকীর্ণতা, জনাধিক্য (হিঃ কোঃ) ; আধিক্য, অতিরেক।

ō-vêr-pŏt′, *v. t.* (*Hort.*) To plant in too large a pot ; (উদ্যানবিদ্যা) অতি বৃহৎ পাত্রে রোপণ করা।

ō-vêr-pow′-êr, *v. t.* 1. To be too powerful for ; to subdue ; কাহারো তুলনায় অত্যধিক শক্তিশালী হওয়া ; বশীভূত করা। 2. To overcome ; to overwhelm ; পরাভূত করা, পরাস্ত করা ; অভিভূত করা, বিহ্বল করা। **-ing**, *adj.* Irresistible ; overwhelming ; অপ্রতিরোধ্য ; অভিভাবী।

ō-vêr-praise′ (-prāz), *v. t.* & *n.* To praise too much ; অতি প্রশংসা করা। ***Noun.*** **(ō′–)** Excessive praise ; অতি প্রশংসা।

ō-vêr-preach′ (-prēch), *v. t.* (Usu. *reflex.*) To overdo or exhaust with preaching ; অতিরিক্ত প্রচার করা, অতি প্রচার দ্বারা পরিশ্রান্ত করা।

ō-vêr-pres′-sure(-prĕ-shür),*n.* Excessive pressure or urging ; overwork ; অতিরিক্ত চাপ ; অতি পরিশ্রম।

ō-vêr-print′, *v. t.* 1. (*Photog.*) To print too long so that it is too dark ; (আলোকচিত্র) দীর্ঘকাল ব্যাপিয়া মুদ্রিত করা হেতু অতিমাত্রায় কৃষ্ণবর্ণ করা। 2. To print too many copies of ; অত্যধিক সংখ্যা মুদ্রিত করা।

ō-vêr-prō-duce′ (-düs), *v. t.* & *i.* To produce in excess of the demand ; চাহিদার অতিরিক্ত উৎপাদন করা বা উৎপাদিত হওয়া। **-duc′-tion**, *n.* Excessive production ; অত্যুৎপাদন, অতিপ্রসব (হিঃ কোঃ)।

ō′-vêr-proof, *adj.* Containing more alcohol than proof spririt ; স্থাপিতমান সুরাসার অপেক্ষা অধিকতর পরিমাণ সুরাবীর্য্যসমন্বিত।

ō-vêr-rāte′, *v. t.* To rate or value at too much ; to estimate too highly ; অত্যাদর করা, অত্যধিক মূল্যবান মনে করা ; অতি বড় ভাবা।

ō-vêr-reach′ (-rēch), *v. t.* & *i.* 1. To reach or extend over or beyond ; অতি প্রসারিত হওয়া বা করা। 2. (*Dial.*) To overtake ; (উপভাষায়) নাগাইল ধরা। 3. To get the better of by cunning or artifice ; to outwit ; কৌশলে ঠকান, বুদ্ধিবলে পরাস্ত করা ; ঠকান। 4. (*Reflex.*) To carry (oneself) too far ; to strain (oneself) beyond one's strength, aim, etc. ; অত্যধিক অগ্রসর হওয়া ; অতিরিক্ত শক্তি বা চেষ্টা প্রয়োগ করা। ***Verb i.*** 1. To reach too far (*lit.* & *fig.*) ; (শব্দানুযায়ী ও লক্ষণায়) অতিমাত্রায় অগ্রসর হওয়া। 2. (Of a horse) To strike and injure the heel of the forefoot with the hind foot ; (অশ্বসম্পর্কে) পাছের পা দ্বারা আগালি পায়ের গোড়ালী আঘাত বা আহত করা।

ō-vêr-read′ (-rēd), *v. i.* To read too much ; (*reflex.*) to injure oneself by reading too much ; অত্যধিক পাঠ করা ; অত্যধিক অধ্যয়ন দ্বারা স্বাস্থ্য হানি করা।

ō-vêr-rē-fīne′ *v. i.* To make too subtle distinctions ; অতি সূক্ষ্ম বৈষম্য করা। **-ment**, *n.*

ō-vêr-rĕnt′, *v. t.* To rent (land etc.) too highly ; to charge (a tenant) too high a rent ; অত্যধিক খাজনায় পত্তন করা ; অত্যধিক খাজনা ধরা।

ō-vêr-rīde′, *v. t.* 1. To cross by riding, (*lit.* & *fig.*) ; অশ্বারোহণে লঙ্ঘন করা। 2. To trample down by riding ; অশ্বারোহণে বিমর্দ্দিত করা, অশ্বপদদলিত করা। 3. (*Fig.*) To supersede ; to annul ; to set aside ; as, one law *overrides* another ; to domineer over ; (লক্ষণায়) বাতিল করা ; রদ করা ; নাকচ করা ; প্রভুত্ব করা। 4. To exhaust as a horse by riding too much ; অতিমাত্রায় (অশ্ব) পরিক্লান্ত করা। 5. (*Surg.*, of a fractured bone) To overlap ; (অস্ত্রোপচারবিদ্যা) একটীর কিনারা অপরটীর উপর রাখা।

ō′-vêr-rīpe, *adj.* Too ripe ; অতি পক্ক।

ō-vêr-rule′ (-rōl), *v. t.* 1. To govern ; to control ; শাসন করা ; কর্তৃত্ব করা। 2. To set aside as a decision, argument, etc., by superior authority ; to annul the decision or reject the proposal of (a person), (esp. in *law*) ; রদ করা ; বাতিল করা, অগ্রাহ্য করা। 3. To overcome ; পরাস্ত করা।

ō-vêr-rŭn′, *v. t.* 1. (Of vermin, weeds, etc.) To run or spread over ; পরিব্যাপ্ত করা, সমাচ্ছন্ন করা। 2. To flood ; প্লাবিত করা। 3. To harry and spoil as an enemy's country ; ছারখার করা, লুটপাট করা, উপদ্রুত করা, উজাড় করা। 4. To exceed as a limit ; সীমা অতিক্রম করা। 5. (*Rare*) To outrun ; to surpass ; (কচিদ্-ব্যবহৃত) অতিধাবন করা ; অতিক্রম করা। 6. (*Reflex.*) To exhaust or injure oneself with running, (*lit.* & *fig.*) ; দৌড়িয়া অবসন্ন বা অনিষ্ট করা (শব্দানুযায়ী ও লক্ষণায়)। 7. (*Print.*) To carry over words or lines of type into another line or page to provide for the addition of new matter or the removal of matter already composed ; (মুদ্রণ) নূতন বিষয় সংযোগ বা পূর্ব্ববিন্যস্ত বিষয় অপসারণের জন্য বিন্যস্ত শব্দ বা পংক্তি-সমূহ অপর পংক্তি বা পৃষ্ঠায় নেওয়া। 8. (Now *dial.*) To escape by running ; to desert ; to leave undone as a duty etc. ; (বর্ত্তমানে উপভাষায়) দৌড়িয়া পালান ; পরিত্যাগ করা ; কর্ত্তব্য অসম্পন্ন রাখা। **To overrun the constable**—Same as TO OUTRUN THE CONSTABLE.

ō-vêr-sea′ (-sē), *adj.* & *adv.* Beyond the sea ; foreign ; সমুদ্রের অপর পার্শ্বস্থ ; বৈদেশিক। ***Adv.*** Across or beyond the sea ; abroad ; সমুদ্রের পরপারে ; বিদেশে। **-seas′**, *adv.* Same as OVERSEA *adv.* **Overseas edition**—সংবাদপত্র প্রভৃতির বৈদেশিক সংস্করণ।

ō-vêr-see′ (-sē), *v. t.* **1.** (*Rare*) To look at from above ; (ক্বচিদ্‌ব্যবহৃত) উপর হইতে দর্শন করা। **2.** To superintend ; to supervise ; পরিদর্শন করা ; তত্ত্বাবধান করা। **–se′-er,** *n.* One, esp. an officer supervising work or workers ; পরিদর্শক, তত্ত্বাবধায়ক, দর্শক (শুক্রঃ বিনয়)।

ō-vĕr-sĕll′, *v. i.* & *t.* To sell more of (a commodity, stock, etc.) than one can deliver ; যতটা যোগাইতে পারিবে তাহার অতিরিক্ত বিক্রয় করা।

ō-vêr-sĕt′, *v. t.* **1.** To upset ; বিপর্যস্ত করা, উল্টাইয়া ফেলা। **2.** (*Rare*) To subvert ; to cause to fail ; (ক্বচিদ্‌ ব্যবহৃত) ধ্বংস করা, উচ্ছেদ করা ; নিষ্ফল করান। **3.** To overcome mentally or physically ; পরাস্ত করা, পরাজিত করা। **4.** (*Dial.* or *obs.*) To recover from as an illness ; (উপভাষায় বা অপ্রচলিত) আরোগ্য করা।

ō′-vêr-sĕw (-sō), *v. t.* To sew over and over ; সেলাইএর উপর সেলাই করা।

ō-vêr-shă′-dow (-dō), *v. t.* **1.** To throw a shadow over ; to darken ; ছায়াবৃত করা, ছায়াচ্ছন্ন করা ; অন্ধকার করা, তমসাবৃত করা। **2.** (*Fig.*) To cover with a superior influence ; to shelter ; (লক্ষণায়) শ্রেষ্ঠতর প্রভাবের দ্বারা অধীন করা ; আশ্রয় দেওয়া। **3.** (*Fig.*) To tower over ; to be more important than ; (লক্ষণায়) সমুন্নত হওয়া ; অধিকতর গুরুত্ববিশিষ্ট হওয়া।

ō′-vêr-shoe (-shō), *n.* A shoe worn over another ; a galosh ; জুতার উপর পরিহিত জুতা ; পাদুকাত্রাণ।

ō-vêr-shoot′, *v. t.* **1.** To shoot over or beyond ; লক্ষ্য ছাড়াইয়া ছোড়া। **2.** (*Fig.*) To go or venture too far, (esp. in *To overshoot the mark*) ; (লক্ষণায়) অধিক দূর অগ্রসর হওয়া। **To overshoot the mark, To overshoot oneself**—To go too far ; to exaggerate ; to overdo something ; অধিকদূর অগ্রসর হওয়া ; অতিরঞ্জিত করা ; বাড়াবাড়ি করা।

ō-vêr-shŏt′, *adj.* Driven by water shot over from above ; উপর হইতে পতিত জলধারা দ্বারা পরিচালিত। **Overshot wheel**—উপর হইতে পতিত জলধারা দ্বারা চালিত চক্র।

ō-vêr-sīde′, *adv.* & (*o′-ver-*), *adj.* (Of loading or unloading a ship) Over the side into or out of lighters ; মালবাহী নৌকা হইতে বা জাহাজের পার্শ্বের উপর দিয়া।

ō′-vêr-sight (-sīt), *n.* **1.** Supervision ; care ; management ; পরিদর্শন ; তত্ত্বাবধান ; পরিচালন। **2.** Omission or error due to inadvertance ; ভ্রম, ভুল, চুক, ভ্রান্তি, অনবেক্ষা, দৃষ্টিদোষ (কেশিঃ)।

ō′-vêr-slaugh (-slä), *n.* (*Mil.*) Exemption from a duty because already detailed on a superior duty ; (সামরিকশাস্ত্র) কোন উচ্চতর কর্তব্যকার্যে নিযুক্ত করিয়া কোনরূপ কর্তব্য পালনের দায় হইতে নিষ্কৃতি দান।

ō-vêr-sleep′ (-slēp), *v. t.* To sleep too long or beyond (the usual hour of awaking) ; অতিমাত্রায় নিদ্রা যাওয়া।

ō′-vêr-sleeve (-slēv), *n.* An outer sleeve ; বাহিরের আস্তিন।

ō′-vêrs-măn, *n.* **1.** An overseer ; পরিদর্শক। **2.** An umpire ; সালীস, মধ্যস্থ।

ō-vêr-smōke′, *v. t. i.* & *reflex.* To cover over with smoke ; ধূমাচ্ছন্ন করা, ধূমাবৃত করা। ***Verb i.* & *reflex.*** To smoke too much ; অতিরিক্ত ধূমপান করা, অতিমাত্রায় ধূম পান করা।

ō′-vêr-soul (-sōl), *n.* The all-containing soul ; the absolute reality ; বিশ্বাত্মা (হিঃ কোঃ) ; পরমাত্মা।

ō-vêr-spĕnd′ *v. t.* & *i.* **1.** To spend too much ; to exhaust ; অতি ব্যয় করা, অমিতব্যয় করা ; অবসন্ন করা। **2.** To spend more than (a specified amount) ; (নির্দ্দিষ্ট মুদ্রার) অতিরিক্ত ব্যয় করা। ***Verb i.*** To spend beyond one's means ; অবস্থার অতিরিক্ত ব্যয় করা। **To overspend oneself**—Same as OVERSPEND, *v. i.*

ō′-vêr-spill, *n.* What overflows ; a surplus population etc. ; যাহা উপছিয়া পড়ে ; অতিরিক্ত লোক প্রভৃতি।

ō-vêr-spread′ (-sprĕd), *v. t.* & *i.* To spread over ; to extend or cover over ; পরিব্যাপ্ত করা, সমাচ্ছন্ন করা ; প্রসারিত করা, সমাবৃত করা। ***Verb i.*** To be spread or scattered over ; আস্তৃত হওয়া, আস্তীর্ণ হওয়া, আকীর্ণ হওয়া।

ō-vêr-stāte′, *v. t.* To exaggerate ; অতিরঞ্জিত করা, অত্যুক্তি করা। **–ment,** *n.* An exaggerated statement ; অত্যুক্তি।

ō-vêr-stay′ (-stā), *v. t.* To stay beyond (a certain time) ; নিরূপিত কালের অতিরিক্ত সময় অবস্থান করা।

ō-vêr-stĕp′, *v. t.* To step over or beyond ; to transgress ; নির্দ্দিষ্ট সীমার বাহিরে পদক্ষেপ করা ; অতিক্রম করা, লঙ্ঘন করা।

ō-vêr-stŏck′, *v. t.* & *n.* To supply in excess ; to fill to excess ; অতিরিক্ত পরিমাণে যোগান ; অতিপূর্ণ করা। ***Noun.*** **(o′–)** Excessive stock or supply ; অতিরিক্ত মজুত মাল, অতিরিক্ত যোগানি।

ō-vêr-strain′ (-strān), *v. t.* & *n.* **1.** To strain or stretch too much ; to damage by exertion ; অতিরিক্ত খাটান, অতিরিক্ত পরিশ্রম করা, অতি বিস্তৃত করা ; অতিপরিশ্রম দ্বারা ক্ষতি করা। **2.** To make too much of (scruples etc., usu. in *pp.*) ; অতিরিক্ত করা। ***Noun.*** **(o′–)** Act of over-straining ; state of being over-strained ; injurious effort ; অতি-পরিশ্রম, অতিপ্রযত্ন ; অতিপ্রযত্নশীলতা ; অনিষ্টজনক চেষ্টা।

ō′-vêr-strŭng, *adj.* **1.** (Of a piano) With strings in sets crossing each other obliquely ;

(পিয়ানো সম্বন্ধে) তির্য্যগ্‌ভাবে অন্যোন্য-ছেদনকারী তন্ত্রীপংক্তিসমন্বিত। 2. (Of a person, his nerves, etc.) Intensely strained or wound up; সপ্তমে-চড়া, অতি বিতত।

ö-vêr-stŭd'-ў, *v. t., i.* & *n.* To study too much; অতিরিক্ত অধ্যয়ন করা। ***Noun.*** **(ō'-)** Excessive study; অতিরিক্ত অধ্যয়ন।

ö-vêr-sŭb-scrībe', *v. t.* To subscribe more than is offered for sale; বিক্রয়ের জন্ম যত অংশ প্রদত্ত হইয়াছে তদপেক্ষা অধিক গ্রাহক হওয়া।

ō'-vêr-sŭp-plў, *n.* Excessive supply; অতিরিক্ত যোগানি।

ö-vêr-swōll'-en (-n), *adj.* Swollen to excess; অতি স্ফীত।

ō'-vêrt, *adj.* Open to view; manifest; not hidden; দৃশ্যমান; স্ফুট, প্রকট; প্রকাশিত। **—ly,** *adv.* **An overt-act**—(ফৌজদারী আইন) কোন অভিপ্রায় বা অভিসন্ধিসাধনের জন্য প্রকাশ্যে যে কার্য্য করা হয়।

ö-vêr-tāke', *v. t.* **1.** To come up with; নাগাইল ধরা, দৌড়িয়া ধরা। 2. (Of a storm, calamity, etc.) To come upon suddenly; হঠাৎ আপতিত হওয়া। 3. (*Dial.* or *obs.*) To captivate; (উপভাষায় বা অপ্রচলিত) মুগ্ধ করা, বিমোহিত করা। **Overtaken in drink**—Drunk; মাতাল।

ö-vêr-tăsk', *v. t.* To impose too heavy a task or duty upon; to be too heavy task for; কাহারো উপর গুরুতর কর্ত্তব্যভার চাপান; কাহারো পক্ষে দুর্ব্বহ কার্য্য হওয়া।

ö-vêr-tăx', *v. t.* To tax too heavily; to make too severe demands upon; অধিক কর স্থাপন করা; অতিশয় দাবী করা।

ö-vêr-throw' (-thrō), *v. t.* & *n.* **1.** To upset as a table etc.; উল্টান, বিপর্য্যস্ত করা। **2.** To defeat or vanquish; to ruin; পরাস্ত করা, পরাভূত করা; ধ্বংস করা। **3.** To subvert; to put an end to; as, to *overthrow* a government; উচ্ছেদ করা, ধ্বংস করা, উচ্ছন্ন করা; শেষ করা। ***Noun.*** **(ō'-)** Act of overthrowing; state of being overthrown; defeat; subversion; ruin; উৎপাতন; অভিভূতি; পরাজয়; বিপর্য্যয়, উচ্ছেদ, সমুচ্ছেদ; ধ্বংস।

ō'-vêr-time, *n.* Time during which one works beyond the regular hours; নিরূপিত কালের অতিরিক্ত কার্য্যের কাল, অতিরিক্ত কাল।

ō'-vêr-toil (-toil), *n.* & *v. t.* Excessive toil; অতিশ্রম। ***Verb t.*** **(-toil')** To overwork or fatigue; অতিশয় খাটান, অতিক্রান্ত করা। **—toiled,** *p. adj.*

ö-vêr-tōne', *v. t.* & *n.* **1.** (*Photog.*) To give too deep a tone to; (আলোকচিত্র) বর্ণ গাঢ় করা। 2. (*Mus.*) To drown as a tone with a stronger one; প্রবলতর ধ্বনিদ্বারা কোন ধ্বনি আচ্ছন্ন করা। ***Noun.*** **(ō'-)** (*Mus.*) Same as HARMONIC (which see); অতিস্বর (হিঃ কোঃ)।

ö-vêr-tŏp', *v. t.* **1.** To rise above the top of; to surpass in height; উপরে উঠা; উচ্চতায় অতিক্রম করা। 2. (*Fig.*) To be superior to; to excel; to surpass; (লক্ষণার) শ্রেষ্ঠতর হওয়া; অধিকতর উৎকর্ষসম্পন্ন হওয়া; অতিক্রম করা।

ö-vêr-train' (-trān), *v. t.* & *i.* To subject to, or undergo, too much athletic training with injury to condition; অত্যধিক মল্লক্রীড়া করান বা করা। **—ing,** *n.*

ö-vêr-trŭmp', *v. t.* To trump with a higher card than (an opposing player), (*lit.* & *fig.*); প্রতিপক্ষের ক্রীড়ক অপেক্ষা বড় রঙের দ্বারা তুরুপ করা (শব্দানুযায়ী ও লক্ষণায়)।

ō'-vêr-tūre, *n.* **1.** A formal proposal; an offer, (usu. *pl.*); as, to make *overtures* of peace to; প্রস্তাব; প্রসঙ্গ। **2.** (*Mus.*) A musical prologue; (সঙ্গীতশাস্ত্র) প্রস্তাবনা, পূর্ব্বরঙ্গ। 3. The beginning of a poem etc.; কোন কবিতার প্রারম্ভ। **To make overtures to**—To make a formal proposal to; রীতিমত প্রস্তাব করা।

ö-vêr-turn' (-têrn), *v. t., i.* & *n.* 1. To upset; to overset; উল্টান; বিপর্য্যস্ত করা। 2. To subvert; to destroy; উচ্ছেদ করা; ধ্বংস করা। ***Verb i.*** To upset or capsize; উল্টাইয়া যাওয়া। ***Noun.*** **(ō'-) 1.** Act of overturning; state of being overturned; উৎসাদন; বিপর্য্যাস। 2. A reversal; also, a turning over as of goods in a trade; পরিবর্ত্তন; নির্দ্দিষ্ট পরিমাণ মাল বিক্রয়।

ö-vêr ūse', *v. t.* & *n.* To use too much; অত্যধিক ব্যবহার করা। ***Noun.*** **(ō'-)** Excessive or too frequent use; অত্যধিক ব্যবহার।

ö-vêr-văl'-ue (-ū), *v. t.* To value or rate excessively; অতিরিক্ত মূল্য নির্দ্ধারণ করা।

ö-vêr-walk' (-wăk), *v. t.* **1.** To traverse by walking; কোন কিছুর উপর দিয়া ভ্রমণ করা। 2. (*Reflex.*) To walk too much; to fatigue oneself by too much walking; অত্যধিক ভ্রমণ করা; অত্যধিক ভ্রমণ দ্বারা ক্লান্ত করা। **—ing,** *n.* Walking too much; অতিভ্রমণ।

ö-vêr-watch' (-wŏch), *v. t.* **1.** To keep watch over; কাহারো উপর দৃষ্টি রাখা, নজর রাখা। **2.** To wear out with excessive watching; to exhaust by keeping awake, (usu. in *p. p.*); অত্যধিক দৃষ্টি রাখিয়া ক্লান্ত করা; জাগিয়া অবসন্ন করা। **—watched',** *p. adj.* Wearied with too much watching; অত্যবেক্ষণ-ক্লান্ত, অতিজাগরণক্লান্ত।

ō'-vêr-wear (-wār), *n.* & *v. t.* Outer clothing; বাহিরের পোষাক। ***Verb t.*** **(-wear') 1.** To exhaust as with toil etc.; অতিক্রান্ত করা। **2.** To wear out, as clothes etc.; জীর্ণ করা।

ö-vêr-ween'-ing (-wēn-), *adj.* 1. Overconfident ; conceited ; arrogant ; অতিনিশ্চিত ; দৃপ্ত, উদ্ধত। 2. (Of opinions, estimate, etc.) Conceited ; too pretentious ; exaggerated ; দৃপ্ত ; আড়ম্বরপূর্ণ ; অতিরঞ্জিত।

ö'-vêr-weight (-wāt), *n.* & *adj.* 1. Excess of weight ; extra weight ; ভারাধিক্য ; অতিরিক্ত ভার। 2. Preponderance ; আধিক্য। 3. Excessive weight ; অতিরিক্ত ভার। ***Adj.*** **(-weight')** Too heavy, (*lit.* & *fig.*) ; অতিভারী (শব্দানুযায়ী ও লক্ষণায়)।

ö-vêr-weight' (-wāt), *v. t.* To overburden ; অতিভারাক্রান্ত করা। **–ed,** *p. adj.*

ö-vêr-whĕlm', *v. t.* 1. To submerge ; নিমজ্জিত করা, প্লাবিত করা। 2. (*Fig.*) To overpower ; to crush ; (লক্ষণায়) অভিভূত করা, আকুল করা, বিহ্বল করা, পরাভূত করা ; ধ্বংস করা। **–ing,** *adj.* **–ing-ly,** *adv.*

ö-vêr-wind', *v. t.* To wind (watch etc.) beyond the proper stopping point ; অতিরিক্ত চাবী দেওয়া।

ö-vêr-wīse', *adj.* Wise to affectation ; অতিজ্ঞানী, জ্ঞানাভিমানী।

ö-vêr-work' (-wêrk), *v. t., i.* & *n.* 1. To work as a man, horse, etc. beyond strenght, capacity, etc. ; to exhaust with work ; অতিরিক্ত শ্রম করা ; অতিরিক্ত খাটাইয়া অবসন্ন করা। 2. To elaborate as a book, speech, etc. to excess ; অতি বিস্তৃত করা। 3. To stir up or excite excessively ; অতিরিক্ত উত্তেজিত করা। ***Verb i.*** To work too much or beyond one's strength ; অতিরিক্ত পরিশ্রম করা। ***Noun.*** **(o'-)** Extra work ; excessive labour ; অতিরিক্ত কার্য্য ; অতিশ্রম, গুরুতর পরিশ্রম।

ö-vêr-write' (-rīt), *v. t.* & *i.* 1. To write over or on the surface of ; কোন কিছুর উপর লিখা। 2. To write too much about (a subject) ; (কোন বিষয়ে) অতিরিক্ত লিখা। 3. (*Reflex.*) To injure or exhaust *oneself* by writing too much ; অতি লিখন দ্বারা শ্রান্ত করা। ***Verb i.*** To write too much ; অত্যধিক লিখা।

ö-vêr-wrought' (-rôt), *adj.* 1. Overworked ; অতিশ্রমক্লান্ত। 2. Too much excited ; অত্যুত্তেজিত। 3. Elaborated to excess ; অতি-বিস্তৃতিসাধিত।

ö-vêr-zeal'-ous (-zĕl-ŭs), *adj.* Over enthusiastic ; অত্যুৎসাহী, অত্যাসক্ত।

O-vid'-i-ăn (ö-), *adj.* Of, or relating to, Ovid, the Latin poet, or his poetry ; resembling his style ; রোমীয় কবি অভিড্ বা তদীয় কবিতাসম্বন্ধীয় ; তদীয় রচনারীতিসদৃশ।

ö'-vi-dŭct, *n.* A passage for the ovum or egg from the ovary, esp. in oviparous animals ; রজোডিম্বনালী।

ö'-vi-fôrm, *adj.* Egg-shaped ; অণ্ডাকৃতি, ডিম্বাকৃতি, ডিম্বাকার, অণ্ডরূপ।

ö'-vīne, *adj.* Of, relating to, or like, sheep ; মেষসম্পর্কীয়, অবিসম্পর্কীয়, আবিক।

ö-vip'-ă-rous (-rŭs), *adj.* Bringing forth eggs that hatch after exclusion from the body ; অণ্ডজ, অণ্ডজনক, অণ্ডপ্রজ, অণ্ডপ্রসূ, অণ্ডোৎপাদক, দ্বিজ (হিঃ কোঃ)।

ö-vi-pŏs'-it, *v. i.* To lay an egg or eggs—said esp. of insects ; ডিমপাড়া। **–i-tor,** *n.* A pointed organ with which insects lay eggs ; যে সূক্ষ্মাগ্র অঙ্গের সাহায্যে কীট ডিম পাড়িয়া থাকে।

ö'-void (-voyd), *adj.* & *n.* Egg-shaped ; ডিম্বাকৃতি, অণ্ডাকার। ***Noun.*** An ovoid body or surface ; ডিম্বাকৃতি বস্তু বা উপরিতল।

ö'-vö-lö, *n.* (*Arch.*) A rounded convex moulding ; (স্থপতিবিজ্ঞান) ডিম্বাকৃতি ভূষা।

ö-vŏl'-ö-ġy, *n.* The science of the formation of animals' ova ; রজোডিম্বগঠনবিদ্যা।

ö-vö-rhŏm-boi'-dăl (-rŏm-boy-), *adj.* Between rhomboid and oval ; অণ্ডাকৃতি এবং অসমকোণী চতুর্ভুজাকৃতির মধ্যবর্ত্তী।

ö-vö-vi-vip'-ă-rous (-rŭs), *adj.* Producing young by eggs hatched within the body ; দেহের মধ্যে ডিম্বে তাপ দানে শাবকোৎপাদনশীল।

ö'-vūle, *n.* 1. A small ovum ; ডিম্বাণু (সাঃ পঃ)। 2. (*Bot.*) A rudimentary or immature seed ; অপরিণত বীজ, আদিম অবস্থার বীজ। **–vu-lar,** *adj.*

ö'-vŭm, *n.* (*Pl.* -VA) A small vesicle within the ovary of a female becoming the embryo when impregnated ; রজোডিম্ব, ডিম্বাণু (সাঃ পঃ), স্ত্রীকোষ (হিঃ কোঃ)।

owe (ö), *v. t.* & *i.* To be indebted ; to be bound to pay ; ঋণী থাকা ; ধারা। 2. To be under obligation to render ; as, to *owe* one honour or gratitude ; প্রদানে বাধ্য থাকা। 3. To have or bear ; as, to *owe* grudge ; থাকা, পোষণ করা। 4. To be indebted or obliged for ; as, I *owe* the victory, to him ; ঋণী থাকা, বাধিত থাকা। ***Verb i.*** To be in debt ; as, I *owed* for all my clothes ; ধারা।

Ow'-ĕn-ĭsm (ö-), *n.* The theory or system of Robert Owen (1771-1858) who advocated the re-organization of society on a system of communistic co-operation ; ওয়েলসের অধিবাসী Robert Owen কর্ত্তৃক প্রচারিত সাম্যবাদ। [Robert Owenএর মতে মানবের স্বভাব পারিপার্শ্বিক অবস্থার ফলে গঠিত হয়। অতএব অপরাধের জন্য কাহাকেও দণ্ড দেওয়া উচিত নয়। মানব যাহাতে ধর্ম্ম-পথচ্যুত না হয় তজ্জন্য যথাসাধ্য চেষ্টা করিতে হইবে, কিন্তু তৎসত্ত্বেও যদি কেহ বিপথে গমন করে, তবে তাহাকে শাস্তি দিতে হইবে না। ইনি ১৮১৯ খৃষ্টাব্দের কারখানা আইনের প্রধান প্রস্তাবক ছিলেন।]

ow'-ing (ö-), *pred. adj.* **1.** Owed; due; as, paid all that was *owing*; দেয়; প্রাপ্য। **Owing to**—Caused by; on account of; হেতু, বশতঃ; দরুণ, কারণ, নিমিত্ত।

owl, *n.* **1.** A well-known nocturnal bird of which there are

Horned Owl.

many varieties; পেচা, পেচক, পেচকিকা, উলূক, (cf. হিন্দি উল্লু, L., *Ulu-la, A. S., ule, Germ., Eule*) [Also কাকভীরু, দিবান্ধ, ঘূক, (cf. হিন্দী *Ghuggu*) দিবাভীত (কুমারঃ), তামস, কৌশিক, নিশাট, নিশাটন, নিশাচর, নক্তঞ্চর, তিমিরারিরিপু (সুভাঃ), নক্তচারী, ধ্বাঙ্ক্ষারাতি, রজনীচর, ক্ষপাচর, বক্রনাসিক, বায়সারাতি, নক্তচারী, দিবাভীরু, কাকারি, বায়সান্তক (মঃ ভাঃ), নিশাদর্শী, নখাশী, দিবাকীর্তি, দিবসকীর্তি, দিবসান্ধ, দিবসভীরু, দিবাভীতি।] **2.** A wise-looking dullard; পণ্ডিতম্মন্য। **3.** (Also *owl-pigeon*) A fancy variety of the domestic pigeon; একপ্রকার সখের পায়রা। **Owl'-er-y**, *n.* An abode or haunt of owls; পেচকের কোটর। **2.** Owlish character; পেচকের মত স্বভাব। **Owl'-ish**, *adj.* Resembling, or characteristic of, an owl; পেচক সদৃশ, পেচকসুলভ। **Owl'-ish-ly**, *adv.* **Barn Owl**—লক্ষ্মীপেঁচা। **Owl-light**—গোধুলি, প্রদোষ, কাকজ্যোৎস্না। **Spotted owl**—কোটরিয়া পেঁচা। **Owls to Athens**—Same as COALS TO NEWCASTLE. **To fly with the owl**—রাত্রে ঘুরার অভ্যাস থাকা। **To take owl**—অপরাধ নেওয়া, দোষ দেওয়া।

owl'-ĕt, *n.* A small variety of owl; a young owl; একজাতীয় ক্ষুদ্র পেচক; পেচকশাবক।

own (ōn), *adj.* **1.** Belonging to oneself; peculiar; (*appended to possessive case or adj.*); স্ব, স্বকীয়, নিজ, আত্ম; নিজস্ব, ব্যক্তিগত। **2.** Also used absolutely indicating private property, kindred, etc.; as, may I not do what I will with my *own*: and his *own* receives him not; আত্মীয়স্বজন। **Own brother, -sister**—A brother or sister with both parents the same; আপন ভাই বা ভগিনী, সহোদর সহোদরা। **Own cousin**—First cousin; সাক্ষাৎ খুড়তুত, পিসতুত, মামাত ভাই বা ভগিনী। **My own sweetheart etc.** or **my own**—(Voc.) Expressing affection; আমার প্রাণ, আমার প্রেয়সী। **One's own**—One's private property, kindred, etc.; কাহারো নিজস্ব সম্পত্তি, কাহারো আপনজন, আত্মীয়স্বজন, নিজ জন। **On ones own**—(*Slang*) On one's own account, responsibility or resources; independently; নিজের জন্য, নিজের দায়িত্বে, নিজের সম্পত্তির উপর; স্বাধীন ভাবে। **To be one's own man**—To be independent or free; স্বাধীন হওয়া। **To hold one's own**—To maintain a position; not to be defeated or derogated; স্বস্থান রক্ষা করা, আপনার অধিকার বজায় রাখা; নিজের মান-সম্মান বজায় রাখা। **To make one's own**—To appropriate; আত্মসাৎ করা।

own (ōn), *v. t. & i.* **1.** To possess, as property; অধিকার থাকা। **2.** To acknowledge, as one's own; as, to *own* a child, book or hat; নিজের বলিয়া স্বীকার করা। **3.** To admit; as, to *own* one's drawbacks; স্বীকার করা। **4.** To submit or yield to; "...Thy creatures *own* thy sway"; বশ্যতা স্বীকার করা। ***Verb i.*** To confess (*to*); স্বীকার করা। **To own up**—(*Colloq.*) To confess frankly; (চলিতভাষায়) অকপটে স্বীকার করা, মুক্তকণ্ঠে স্বীকার করা।

own'-êr (ōn-), *n.* One who owns; a rightful possessor or proprietor; স্বামী, মালিক; স্বত্বাধীশ (কেশিঃ)। **-ship**, *n.* State of being an owner; a legal or just claim or title; স্বামিত্ব; বৈধস্বত্ব, ন্যায্য অধীকার।

ŏx, *n.* (*Pl.* OXEN) An animal of the bovine genus; a castrated male of this genus; গোজাতীয় জন্তু; বৃষ, উক্ষা, বলীবর্দ্দ, পুঙ্গব, বৃষভ। **Ox'-er**, *n.* A fence to restrain oxen; গবাদি পশুকে বাধা দেওয়ার জন্য বেড়া। **Ox'-y**, *adj.* (*Rare*) Of, or relating to, an ox; (কচিদ্ব্যবহৃত) বৃষসম্বন্ধীয়। **Ox-bird**—A kind of small bird; একপ্রকার ক্ষুদ্রকায় পক্ষী। **Ox-eye**—A large human eye; বৃহচ্চক্ষু। A kind of plant, the Corn-Marigold (Yellow Ox-eye),

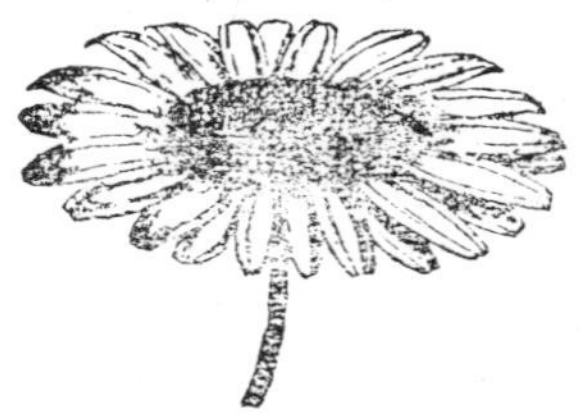

Ox-eye Daisy.

the Ox-eyed Daisy (White Ox-eye); একপ্রকার গুল্ম। **Ox'-eyed**, *adj.* Having large eyes like an ox; বৃহচ্চক্ষু। Also applied to various plants; বিভিন্ন প্রকার গুল্মাদি সম্বন্ধেও প্রযুক্ত। **Ox-fence**—Same as OXER. **Oxherd**—Cowherd; গোপাল, রাখাল। **Ox-hide**—The skin of ox; বৃষচর্ম্ম, উক্ষচর্ম্ম। **Oxlip**—A hybrid between the primrose and the cowslip; একপ্রকার গুল্ম। **Oxtail**—বৃষপুচ্ছ। **The black ox**

has trod on one's foot—সে জরা দ্বারা আক্রান্ত হইয়াছে বা দুর্দ্দশায় পতিত হইয়াছে, তাহার ঘরে পেঁচা ঢুকেছে।

ŏx'-ă-lāte, *n.* (*Chem.*) A salt of oxalic acid ; (রসায়নশাস্ত্র) চুকাপালং প্রভৃতির দ্রাবক হইতে প্রাপ্ত লবণ।

ŏx-ăl'-ic, *adj.* (*Chem.*) Pertaining to, or obtained from, the sorrel ; আমরুল সম্বন্ধীয়, আমরুল হইতে প্রাপ্ত। **Oxalic acid**—আমরুল প্রভৃতি হইতে প্রাপ্ত দ্রাবক।

Oxalis corniculata — চুক্রিক (বেলঃ), আমরুল, অম্লবেতস, চুক্র, অম্বলী (East Bengal)।

Ox'-fŏrd (-ŏx-), *n.* An English city with a university ; ইংলণ্ডের বিশ্ববিদ্যালয় সমন্বিত নগরবিশেষ। **Oxford clay** — ইংলণ্ডের মৃত্তিকাস্তর বিশেষ (ভূবিদ্যা)। **Oxford frame**—যে ছবির ফ্রেমের পার্শ্বসমূহ কোণদেশে পরস্পরকে ছেদনপূর্ব্বক প্রলম্বিত থাকে। **Oxford Indian paper**—অক্সফোর্ড বিশ্ববিদ্যালয়ের মুদ্রাযন্ত্রের ব্যবহারের জন্য প্রস্তুত একপ্রকার অতি পাতলা কাগজ। **Oxford man** — অক্সফোর্ড বিশ্ববিদ্যালয়ে শিক্ষিত ব্যক্তি। **Oxford mixture** — একপ্রকার গাঢ় ধূসরবর্ণ বস্ত্র। **Oxford movement**—(also *Tractarianism*) Movement of Catholic revival ; ইংলণ্ডীয় রাজবিধি দ্বারা প্রতিষ্ঠিত খৃষ্টীয় ধর্ম্মসংঘে আদিম খৃষ্টীয় ধর্ম্ম এবং রোমান ক্যাথলিক মত ও অনুষ্ঠান পুনরুজ্জীবনের জন্য যে ধর্ম্মান্দোলন আরম্ভ হয়। ১৮৩৩ খৃঃ অব্দে ১৪ই জুলাই তারিখে Kebb যে ধর্ম্মোপদেশ প্রদান করেন—তাহা হইতেই এই আন্দোলনের সূচনা হয়। **Oxford shirting** — একপ্রকার জামা বা পোষাকের কাপড়। **Oxford shoes**—একধরণের জুতা—যাহার উপরিভাগে ফিতা লাগান থাকে। **Oxford Tracts**—(See under TRACT).

ŏx-i-dā'-tion, *n.* Oxidizing ; state of being oxidized ; অম্লজান যোগ ; অম্লজানযুক্ততা।

ŏx'-īde, *n.* Oxygen compounded with another element or radical ; অম্লজানজারিত ধাতু। **Oxide of iron**—মৃৎলৌহ। **Oxide of lead**—মারিত সীসক। **Oxide of zinc**—মারিত যশদ।

ŏx'-i-dīze, *v. t.* & *i.* **1.** To cause to combine with oxygen ; to convert into an oxide ; অম্লজানবাষ্পের সহিত মিশ্রিত করা ; জারিত করা। **2.** To coat as a metal with oxide ; to make rusty ; অম্লজানজারিত ধাতু দ্বারা আচ্ছাদিত করা ; মরিচা ফেলান। ***Verb i.*** **1.** (*Chem.*) To become oxidized (রসায়নশাস্ত্র) জারিত হওয়া। **2.** To rust ; মরিচা পড়া। **–diz-a-ble,** *adj.* **–diz-er,** *n.* One that oxidizes ; a chemical substance used as an oxidizing agent, as nitric acid, etc. ; জারক ; যে রাসায়নিক পদার্থ দ্বারা লৌহ, প্রভৃতি জারিত করা হয়, যথা তাম্রদ্রাব প্রভৃতি। **Oxidized silver** — জারিতরৌপ্য [সিল্ভার সালফাইডের ঘনকৃষ্ণআচ্ছাদনবিশিষ্ট রৌপ্যকে ভ্রমবশতঃ এই নাম দেওয়া হইয়াছে।]

Ox-ō'-ni-ăn (ŏ-), *adj.* & *n.* Of, or relating to, Oxford or the university there ; অক্সফোর্ড বা তৎস্থানের বিশ্ববিদ্যালয়সম্বন্ধীয়। ***Noun.*** A native of Oxford ; a student or graduate of the Oxford university ; অক্সফোর্ডের অধিবাসী; অক্সফোর্ড বিশ্ববিদ্যালয়ের ছাত্র বা উপাধিধারী ব্যক্তি।

ŏx-ȳ-căr-pous (-pŭs), *adj.* (*Bot.*) Having pointed fruit ; সূক্ষ্মাগ্রফলবিশিষ্ট।

ŏx'-ȳ-gĕn, *n.* A gaseous element constituting one-fifth of the atmosphere and the supporter of animal and vegetable life ; অম্লজান, বাষ্পদাহক (সাঃ পঃ), অক্ষজন (মনীঃ), প্রাণবায়ু। **–yg'-e-nous,** *adj.*

ŏx'-ȳ-gĕ-nāte, *v. t.* **1.** To combine or treat with oxygen ; to oxidize ; অম্লজান বাষ্পের সহিত সংমিশ্রিত করা ; অম্লজানবাষ্পসম্পূরিত করা। **2.** To charge as blood with oxygen by respiration ; শ্বাসপ্রশ্বাস ক্রিয়ার ফলে অম্লজানবাষ্পদ্বারা সম্পূরিত করা। **–na'-tion,** *n.* **–yg'-e-nant,** *n.* An oxidizing agent ; অম্লজানযোজক।

ŏx'-ȳ-gĕn-īze, *v. t.* Same as OXYGENATE.

ŏx-ȳ-hȳ'-drō-gĕn, *adj.* Of, relating to, consisting of, a mixture of oxygen or hydrogen ; অম্লজানসম্বন্ধীয়, অম্লজানাত্মক।

ŏx'-ȳ-mĕl, *n.* A mixture of vinegar and honey ; সির্কামধু।

ŏx-ȳ-mō'-rŏn, *n.* (*Rhet.*) A figure of speech in which an epithet of a quite contrary signification is added to a word (*e. g.* cruel kindness) ; (অলঙ্কারশাস্ত্র) একপ্রকার অলঙ্কার যাহাতে কোন শব্দে বিপরীতার্থবোধক বিশেষণ সংযুক্ত করা হয়, বিপরীতালঙ্কার।

ŏx'-ȳ-sălt, *n.* A salt containing oxygen ; অম্লজানযুক্ত লবণ।

ŏx-ȳt-ō-cŭs, *adj.* (*Med.*) Assisting quick childbirth ; গর্ভমোচনকর (হঃ চঃ), সুপ্রসবজনক।

ŏx'-ȳ-tōne, *adj.* & *n.* (*Gk. Gram.*) With acute accent on the last syllable ; (গ্রীকপুরাণ) অন্তোদাত্ত। ***Noun.*** (*Gk. Gram.*) Such a word ; অন্তোদাত্ত শব্দ।

ō'-yêr, *n.* (*Law*) A hearing or trial of causes under the writ of oyer and terminer ; মোকদ্দমার শুনানী। **Oyer and terminer**—পর্য্যটনশীল বিচারকগণকে আদালত করার জন্য যে পরওয়ানা দেওয়া হয়।

ō'-yĕz ! ō'-yĕs ! ō'-yĕs ! *interjs.* An expression used, esp. thrice by a public crier in a court to bespeak silence or attention ; চুপ ! চুপ !, শোন ! শোন !

oys'-têr, *n.* **1.** A bivalve edible shell-fish or mollusc ; ঝিনুক, শুক্তি, শুক্তিকা [also মুক্তামাতা, পদ্মগর্ভা (সাঃ পঃ), মুক্তাস্ফোট, পটোলক, পটলিকা, পটোলী, মুক্তাগার, মুক্তাপ্রসূ

পুষ্টিকা।] 2. An oyster-shaped morsel of meat on the back of a fowl ; কুক্কুটের পৃষ্ঠদেশের শুক্তিকাকার মাংসখণ্ড। **Oyster-bank, -bed**—শুক্তিস্তর। **Oyster-bar**—যে মদ্য-বিপণিতে শুক্তি বিক্রীত হয়। **Oyster-catcher**—একপ্রকার সাগরচর বিহঙ্গ। **Oyster-farm**—সমুদ্রের যে অংশে শুক্তি পোষণ করা হয়। **Oyster-knife**—শুক্তি উন্মোচনোপযোগী ছুরিকা। **Oyster-patty**—ঝিনুকের শাঁস দ্বারা পুর দেওয়া পিষ্টক।

ō-zō-cē'-rīte, -kêr'-ĭt, *ns.* A resinous mineral like wax used for candles, insulating, etc. ; মোমের মত একপ্রকার ধুনাময় খনিজ পদার্থ।

ō'-zōne, *n.* 1. A modification of oxygen with a pungent refreshing odour ; ঝাঁঝাল এবং ক্লান্তিবারক গন্ধবিশিষ্ট অম্লজান বাষ্পের রূপান্তরবিশেষ, অম্লজান সার, ওজন (ইঃ কোঃ)। 2. (*Fig.*) An exhilarating influence ; উন্মাদনা। **-zo-nif'-er-ous, -zon'-ic-,** *adjs.* Bearnig or producing ozone ; অম্লজানসারময়, অম্লজানসার-জনক। **-zon-ize,** *v. t.* 1. To convert as oxygen into ozone ; অম্লজানসারে পরিণত করা। 2. To treat or impregnate with ozone ; অম্লজানসারসম্পূরিত করা। **-zon-iz-er,** *n.* An apparatus for producing ozone ; অম্লজানসার উৎপাদক যন্ত্র। **-zo-nom'-e-ter,** *n.* A device for ascertaining the amount of ozone in the air ; বায়ুতে অম্লজানসারের পরিমাণনির্ণায়ক যন্ত্র।

P

P, The 16th letter of the English Alphapet ; ইংরাজী বর্ণমালার ষোড়শ অক্ষর। **To mind one's P's & Q's, To be on one's P's & Q's**—To be careful in one's speech or conduct ; নিজের বক্তৃতা বা আচরণ সম্বন্ধে সতর্ক হওয়া।

pa, *n.* (*Colloq.*) Same as PAPA.

păb'-ü-lŭm, *n.* 1. Food ; খাদ্য, আহার্য্য, ভোজ্য। 2. (*Fig.*) That on which the mind or soul is nourished ; as, mental *pabulum* ; যদ্দ্বারা মন বা আত্মার পরিপুষ্টি সাধিত হয়, মানসিক খাদ্য, আত্মার আহার।

pä'-că, *n.* A small rodent of South and Central America ; মধ্য এবং দক্ষিণ-আমেরিকার দন্তুর জন্তুবিশেষ।

Paca.

pāce, *n.* 1. A step ; পদগতি, পদবিক্ষেপ, পদনিক্ষেপ, পদন্যাস। 2. The space or distance covered in one step, (about 30 inch.) ; also, the space between successive stationary positions of the same foot in walking, (about 60 inch.) ; একবার পাদবিক্ষেপে যে পরিমাণ স্থান অতিক্রম করা যায়, এক পা ; দুই পদ পরিমিত স্থান। 3. Manner of walking or running ; gait ; গমনভঙ্গী, গতিভঙ্গী, গতিভঙ্গিমা, চলনভঙ্গী ; গতি। 4. A gait of a horse, mule, etc. (*e. g.* walk, trot, canter, etc.) ; also, amble ; অশ্বাদির গতিভঙ্গী, ধারা (of horse) ; অশ্বের ধোরিত গতি। 5. Speed in walking or running ; গতিবেগ, গমনবেগ, ধাবনবেগ। 6. Mode of progress (often *fig.*) ; গতিপ্রণালী। **Paced,** *adj.* Having a certain pace,—used in composition ; as, slow-*paced* ; নির্দ্দিষ্ট গতিবিশিষ্ট। **Pace-maker**—দৌড়, ঘোড়দৌড় প্রভৃতিতে যে অশ্বারোহী, ধাবক, প্রভৃতি অপরের গতি নির্দ্দেশ করে। **To go the pace**—To go at a great speed ; (*fig.*) to indulge in dissipation ; মহাবেগে অগ্রসর হওয়া ; (লক্ষণায়) অমিতাচারে গা ঢালিয়া দেওয়া। **To keep pace with**—To go as fast as ; to progress equally with ; সমান সমান চলা ; সমগতিতে চলা। **To put a person through his paces, To try a person's paces**—To test his qualities in action etc. ; কার্য্যকালে কোন ব্যক্তির গুণ, যোগ্যতা, প্রভৃতি পরীক্ষা করা। **To try an animal's paces, To put an animal through its paces**—To find out how it goes ; অর্থাৎ জন্তুটা কিরূপ চলে তাহা দেখা।

pāce, *v. i.* & *t.* 1. To step or walk ; পদক্ষেপ করা, চলা। 2. (Of a horse) To amble ; (অশ্বসম্পর্কে) পর্য্যায়ক্রমে সম্মুখ ও পশ্চাতের পদদ্বয় তুলিয়া মৃদুগতিতে চলা, ধোরিতগতিতে চলা। ***Verb t.*** 1. To traverse by walking ; পদব্রজে অতিক্রম করা। 2. To measure as a distance by walking ; হাঁটিয়া (দূরতা) মাপা। 3. (*Racing*) To set the pace for (a rider, runner, etc.) ; (ঘোড়দৌড়ে) গতিনির্দ্দিষ্ট করা। 4. To regulate the pace of ; গতিনিয়মিত করা। **To pace the web**—(*weaving*) To wind up the cloth on the beam at regular intervals, as it is woven in a loom ; তাঁতে কাপড় বুনিতে বুনিতে নরাজে গুটান। **To pace up and down**—পায়চারী করা।

Pace, (*L.*), *Prep.* By or with the favour or leave or leave of, usually to express polite disagreement ; as, *pace tua* : *pace* Smith ; কাহারো অনুগ্রহে বা অনুমতি লইয়া।

păc'-êr, *n.* One that paces ; esp. a horse that paces ; পদক্ষেপকারী ; বিশেষতঃ যে অশ্ব সম্মুখের এবং পশ্চাতের পদদ্বয় পর্য্যায়ক্রমে তুলিয়া মৃদুগতিতে চলিয়া থাকে।

pā-cha' (-shā), *n.* See PASHA.

Pachacamac, *n.* The greatest deity of the Peruvian ; পেরুভিয়ানদিগের দেবরাজ।

păch'-ў-dêrm, *n.* (*Pl.* -DERMATA) 1. A non-ruminant animal having a thick skin, *e. g.* dog, elephant etc. ; স্থূলচর্ম্মী জন্তু। 2. (*Fig.*) One who is insensitive ; (লক্ষণায়) সংবেদনশূন্য ব্যক্তি, গন্তীরবেদী ব্যক্তি। **—der'-ma-tous,** *adj.* 1. Of, or relating to, pachyderms ; স্থূলচর্ম্মী জন্তুসম্বন্ধীয়। 2. Thick-skinned ; not sensitive to ridicule, sarcasm ; স্থূলচর্ম্মী ; গন্তীরবেদী।

pă-čif'-ic, *adj.* & *n.* 1 Tending to make peace ; of, or relating to, peace ; of a peaceful disposition ; conciliatory ; শান্তিজনক ; শান্তিসম্বন্ধীয় ; শান্তস্বভাব, শান্ত, প্রশান্ত, অনুত্তরঙ্গ ; শান্তিস্থাপনশীল। 2. (*Cap.*) Of, or relating to, the Pacific Ocean ; প্রশান্তমহাসাগরীয়। ***Noun.*** (*Cap.*) The Pacific Ocean ; প্রশান্ত মহাসাগর। **—i-cal-ly,** *adv.* **The Pacific Ocean**—See PACIFIC *n.*

păč-i-fi'-ca'-tion, *n.* 1. Act of pacifying ; reconciliation ; শমন ; শান্তিস্থাপন, প্রশমন। 2. A treaty of peace ; সন্ধি। **Pa-cif'-i-ca-to-ry,** *adj.* Conciliatory ; শান্তিস্থাপনশীল।

păč'-i-fў, *v. t.* 1. To appease ; to calm or quiet ; শান্ত করা ; ঠাণ্ডা করা, প্রসন্ন করা। 2. To establish peace or tranquility in, as a country etc. ; শান্তিসংস্থাপন করা, শান্তিপ্রতিষ্ঠা করা।

păck, *n.* 1. A bundle ; a parcel ; esp. a pedlar's bundle ; গাঠুরী ; বস্তা, গাঁইট ; মুটুরি। 2. A measure of various goods ; বিভিন্ন দ্রব্যের পরিমাণ। 3. A set of playing-cards ; একপ্রস্থ তাস। 4. (Usu. *contempt.*) A number or set (*of*), a gang ; as, a *pack* of thieves, lies, etc. ; (প্রায়শঃ অবজ্ঞাচ্ছলে) দল, পাল। 5. A number of hounds or dogs kept together for hunting ; শিকারী কুকুরের পাল। 6. A number of wild animals or birds naturally associating ; as, a *pack* of wolves or grouse ; নেকড়ে বাঘ প্রভৃতির পাল, পাখীর ঝাঁক। 7. A large area of floating pieces of ice in the polar sea ; মেরুসন্নিহিত সাগরোপরি প্লবমান হিমানীক্ষেত্র। 8. The quantity of fish, fruit, etc. packed in tins etc. in a particular season or year ; কোন বিশেষ মরসুম বা বৎসরে টীনে যে পরিমাণ ফল, মাছ, প্রভৃতি ভরা হয়। **Pack-horse** — ভারবাহী অশ্ব, ঘোরী। **Pack-saddle** — বস্তা ঝুলাইয়া রাখার উপযোগী জিন, পালান, পল্যান, পর্য্যাণ, পর্য্যয়ণ। **Pack-thread**—একপ্রকার মোটা সূতা, সুতলি, দান (আঃ বঃ), শণসূত্র। **Pack-staff**—(অপ্রঃ) ভারদণ্ড, ভারযষ্টি।

păck, *v. t.* & *i.* 1. To put together and bind fast for transport etc., (often with *up*) ; বস্তাবন্দী করা, গাইটবন্দী করা, প্যাক করা। 2. To prepare and put up in tins etc. for preservation ; as, to *pack* fruit, fish, etc. ; ফল, মাছ, প্রভৃতি টীনে প্যাক করা। 3. To crowd together closely ; as, to *pack* passengers into a car ; ঠাসা, ঠাসি করিয়া রাখা। 4. To form into a pack, as hounds etc. ; দল বাঁধা। 5. To fill with something compactly and securely ; to cram ; as, to *pack* a bag or box etc. ; ঠাসা ; গাদা। 6. To cover with something pressed lightly round ; তুলা প্রভৃতি দ্বারা মৃদুভাবে চাপিয়া রাখা বা আবৃত করা। 7. To put together as cards in a pack ; তাস প্যাক করা। 8. To load as a beast with a pack ; পশুর পৃষ্ঠে ভার চাপান। 9. (*Med.*) To envelop or wrap in wet cloth ; ভিজা কাপড় দ্বারা ঢাকা বা জড়ান। 10. To send away with baggage or belongings, (with *off*) ; পুটলীপাটলীসহ তাড়াইয়া দেওয়া। ***Verb i.*** 1. To put things together into pack for transport etc. ; প্যাক করা, বস্তাবন্দী করা, গাইট বাঁধা। 2. To assemble together ; to form into a pack ; একত্র হওয়া ; দল বাঁধা। 3. To admit of being packed in a bundle or pressed into a compact mass ; বস্তাবন্দীর যোগ্য হওয়া, ঠাসিয়া রাখার যোগ্য হওয়া। 4. To depart, esp. in haste with one's belongings ; প্রস্থান করা, বিশেষতঃ মোট মুটরী লইয়া বেগে প্রস্থান করা। **To pack a person off**—See PACK *v. t.* 10. **To pack on all sail**—(*Naut.*) To put on all sail ; (নৌবিদ্যা) সবগুলি পাইল খাটান। **To send one packing**—To dismiss him summarily ; দূর করিয়া দেওয়া, তাড়াইয়া দেওয়া।

păck'-āge, *n.* 1. A bundle or parcel ; পুটলী, মুটরী, গাঠুরী। 2. A box, case, barrel, etc. in which goods are packed ; মালের বাক্স।

păck'-êr, *n.* One who packs ; one packing meat, fruit, etc. for market ; also a machine for packing ; যে ব্যক্তি বস্তাবন্দী করে ; যে ব্যক্তি ফল, মাংস, প্রভৃতি টীনে প্যাক করিয়া থাকে ; বস্তাবন্দী করার জন্য যন্ত্র, প্যাকীং কল।

păck'-ĕt, *n.* 1. A small pack or package ; মোড়ক, পুলিন্দা, প্যাকেট। 2. (Also, *packet-boat*) A mail-boat ; ডাকের জাহাজ।

păck'-ing, *n.* 1. Putting together into a pack, as for transport, another ; অন্য ব্যক্তির সমকক্ষ ব্যক্তি। **–ly,** *adv.* **–qual′-i-ty,** *n.*

cö-erce′ (-êrs), *v. t.* **1.** To restrain by force ; বলপূর্ব্বক সংযত করা, নিরোধ করা, প্রতিরোধ করা, শাসন করা, নিগৃহীত করা। **2.** To compel or enforce ; বাধ্য করা, বলপ্রয়োগদ্বারা বাধ্য করা। **–er-ci-bil′-i-ty,** *n.* **–er′-ci-ble,** *adj.*

cö-êr′-cion (-shŭn), *n.* **1.** Controlling of voluntary agent or action by force ; compulsion ; বলপূর্ব্বক বাধ্যকরণ ; বলপ্রয়োগ, নিগ্রহ, জবরদস্তি (*Colloq.*)। **2.** Employment of force to suppress political disaffection and disorder ; government by force ; রাজনীতিক বিক্ষোভ-দমনের জন্য বলপ্রয়োগ ; বাহুবলে রাজ্যশাসন। **–a-ry,** *adv.* **–ist,** *n.*

cö-êr′-cive (-sĭv), *adj.* That has power or authority ; compulsory ; constraining ; সংযমনকর, নিয়ামক, নিরোধকারী ; বলপ্রয়োগাত্মক ; নিগ্রহাত্মক। **–ly,** *adv.* **–ness,** *n.*

cö-ĕs-sĕn′-tial (-shăl), *anj.* Having the same essence ; এক মূলক।

cö-ē-tā′-nē-ous (-ŭs), *adj.* Of the same age or duration ; contemporary ; সমবয়স্ক, সমকালস্থায়ী ; সামসময়িক।

cö-ē-têr′-năl, *adj.* Equally eternal ; সমনিত্য, সমচিরস্থায়ী, সমসনাতন। **–ly,** *adv.* **–ni-ty,** *n.*

cö-ē′-văl, *adj.* & *n.* Of the same age ; সমকালীন, সমবয়স্ক। ***Noun.*** A contemporary ; সামসময়িক ব্যক্তি।

co-ex-ec′-u-tor (kö-ĕgz-ĕk-ü-têr), (fem. **–trix**) *n.* A joint executor ; সহযোগী কর্ম্মনির্ব্বাহক।

cö-ex-ist′ (-ĕgz-), *v. i.* To exist at the same time or in the same place, etc., (*with*) ; যুগপৎ অবস্থান করা, এক স্থানে অবস্থান করা। **–ence,** *n.* Existence ; conjunction ; এককালিকত্ব, সমকালবিদ্যমানতা ; সহভাব (হিঃ কোঃ), সহাস্তিত্ব (ঐ)। **–ent,** *adj.* এককালিক ; সহবর্ত্তী।

cö-ĕx-tĕnd′, *v. t.* & *i.* To extend equally with ; সমায়ত হওয়া। ***Verb i.*** To be co-extensive ; সমস্থান ব্যাপিয়া বিস্তৃত থাকা। **–ten′-sion,** *n.* **–ten′-sive,** *adj.* Equally extensive ; সহব্যাপী (জিঃ), সমব্যাপক। **–ten′-sive-ness,** *n.*

cŏf′-fee (-fē), *n.* **1.** A drink made from the seeds of a shrub roasted and ground ; কাফি। **2.** The seeds or berries (either raw or roasted) ; also the shrub yielding this ;

Coffee Tree.

কাফির বীজ ; কাফি গুল্ম। **Coffee-cup**—কাফি পাত্র বা পেয়ালা। **Coffee-house**—কাফি এবং অন্যান্য জলযোগের সামগ্রী বিক্রয়ের দোকান। **Coffee-mill** — কাফি পেষণ যন্ত্র। **Coffee-pot**—কাফি পাত্র। **Coffee-room**—সাধারণ ভোজনাগারের কাফি পানের কক্ষ। **Coffee-tavern**—যে জলযোগের দোকানে কাফি প্রভৃতি অমাদক দ্রব্য বিক্রীত হয়।

cŏf′-fêr, *n.* **1.** A box, esp. for money or valuables ; বাক্স, তোরঙ্গ, বিশেষতঃ অর্থ বা মূল্যবান বস্তুর পেটক, রত্নাধার, মুদ্রাধার। **2.** (*Pl.*) Treasury ; funds ; "*Coffers* of the government had long been empty ;" ধনাগার ; ধনভাণ্ডার। **3.** (*Arch.*) A sunk panel in vaults and domes, etc. ; (স্থপতি-বিদ্যা) গম্বুজ, খিলানবিশিষ্ট ছাদ প্রভৃতির খোপ। **4.** (*Poet.*) A hollow trench across a dry moat ; দুর্গবেষ্টক পরিখার মধ্যস্থ খাদবিশেষ। **5.** A floating dock ; প্লবমান পোতসংস্কার-মঞ্চ। **Coffer-dam**—সেতু প্রভৃতির ভিত্তিস্থাপনকালে জলপ্রবেশের পথ রুদ্ধ করিবার উদ্দেশ্যে যে কাষ্ঠময় আধার বা কাঠাম নদীগর্ভে বসান হয়।

cŏf′-fin, *n.* & *v. t.* **1.** A chest in which a corpse is buried ; শবাধার, কাষ্ঠমল্ল (প্রঃ বাঃ)। **2.** The whole hoof of a horse below the coronet ; অশ্বের পশ্চাদ্‌ভাগস্থ সমগ্র খুর। **3.** Same as COFFINSHIP. ***Verb t.*** **1.** To inclose in a coffin ; to inclose ; শবাধারে বদ্ধ করা ; বদ্ধ করা। **2.** (*Fig.*) To store away (books, etc.) inaccessibly ; দুষ্প্রাপ্য স্থানে (পুস্তক প্রভৃতি) গুদামজাত করিয়া রাখা। **Coffin-bone** — অশ্বখুর মধ্যস্থ অস্থিবিশেষ। **Coffin-plate**—শবাধারের আবরণোপরি সম্বদ্ধ ধাতুফলকবিশেষ—ইহাতে মৃতব্যক্তির নাম ধামাদি লিখিত থাকে। **Coffin-ship**—সমুদ্রগমনের অনুপযোগী জাহাজ। **To drive** or **put a nail into one's coffin**—To hasten one's death by intemperance, etc. ; অমিতাচার, প্রভৃতি দ্বারা মৃত্যু সন্নিকট করা।

cŏf-fle, *n.* A train of men or beasts ; esp. a gang of slaves chained together ; পশুশ্রেণী, একদল মানুষ ; বিশেষতঃ শৃঙ্খলাবদ্ধ ক্রীত-দাস সমূহ।

cŏg, *n.* & *v. t.* The tooth of a wheel by which it drives another wheel or body ; চক্রদন্ত, চাকার দাঁত, প্রধি-দন্ত। ***Verb t.*** To furnish (a wheel, etc.) with cogs ; চাকা প্রভৃতিতে দাঁত লাগান। **Cogged,** *adj.* **Cog-wheel**—দন্তুর চক্র।

cŏg, *v. t.* To practise certain tricks in throwing dice ; পাশা ক্ষেপণে চাতুরী করা। **Cog′-ging,** *adj.* **To cog a die** or **the dice**—Fraudulently to control their fall ; কপট পাশা খেলা।

cō′-gĕnt, *adj.* Forcible ; convincing ; as, *cogent* reasons, argument, etc. ; প্রবল, অকাট্য, দৃঢ়,

Păd'-dy (-ĭ), *n.* An Irishman, used esp. as a nickname ; আয়র্লণ্ডবাসী।

păd'-dy (-ĭ), *n.* Rice in the husk whether in the field or gathered ; ধান, ধান্য, ব্রীহি, স্তম্বকরি (অমরঃ)। [Arab., *ruz* ; Chin., *Tau* ; Burm., *Sa-ba* ; Malay, *Padi* (rice in the straw) ; Tamil *Nellu* ; Telegu, *Uri, Bium* ; Canarese, *Bhatta, batta* (rice in the husk) ; Javanese and other Malay language, *Pari.*] [মালয় ভাষায় ধান্যের প্রাতশব্দ Padi এই শব্দ হইতে ইংরাজী paddy হইয়াছে।] **Paddy-bird**—The Java sparrow ; যবদ্বীপের চটক পক্ষী। (India) Any of various small herons; (ভারতবর্ষে) বকজাতীয় বিভিন্ন প্রকার পক্ষীর সাধারণ নাম। The Sheath bill; একপ্রকার পক্ষী। **Paddy-field**—ধান্যক্ষেত্র। **Autumnal paddy**—শালিধান্য। **Winter-paddy**—আশুধান্য।

păd'-lŏck, *n.* & *v. t.* A detachable lock hung on a staple and held by a link ; তালা, কুলুপ, তালযন্ত্র। *Verb t.* To secure with a padlock ; তালা লাগান।

padre, *n.* **1.** A Christian priest ; খৃষ্টীয়যাজক। **2.** (In India) Any Christian minister ; পাদ্রী।

padrone, *n.* **1.** The master of a trading-vessel in the Mediterranean ; ভূমধ্যসাগরবাহী বাণিজ্যপোতাধ্যক্ষ। **2.** An Italian employer of street musicians, begging-children, etc. ; ইতালীদেশবাসী যে ব্যক্তি রাজপথে গাহিবার জন্য গায়ক, ভিক্ষুক-বালকদল, প্রভৃতি নিযুক্ত করে। **3.** (In Italy) An innkeeper or landlord ; (ইতালী দেশে) সরাইওয়ালা, বাড়ীওয়ালা। ***Padronism,*** *n.* The system of bringing Italian children into a foreign country to perform street-music, etc. ; সহরের রাস্তায় রাস্তায় গান গাহিয়া ঘুরিবার জন্য ইতালীদেশীয় বালকবালিকাগণকে বিদেশে আনার প্রথা।

păd'-ū-ă-sŏy', *n.* A kind of silk fabric much used in the 18th. century ; অষ্টাদশ শতাব্দীতে বহুলপ্রচলিত একপ্রকার পট্টবস্ত্র বিশেষ।

pæ'-ăn (pē-), *n.* **1.** A song in honour of Apollo or some other God ; এপলো বা অন্য কোন দেবতার সম্মানার্থ সঙ্গীত। **2.** A song of praise or triumph ; স্তবগীতি, স্তুতিগান, জয়গীত, বিজয়গীতিকা।

pæd'-êr-ăs-tȳ (pĕd-), **pĕd'–,** *ns.* Sodomy ; পুংমৈথুন, লৌণ্ডাবাজি।

pæ-dō-băp'-tĭsm (pē-), **pē–,** *ns.* Infant baptism ; শিশুদীক্ষা। **–tist,** *n.*

pæ'-ŏn (pē-), *n.* A metrical foot of four syllables, one long and three short ; শব্দাংশচতুষ্টয়বিশিষ্ট কাবতাপংক্তি—যাহার একটী লঘু ও অপর তিনটা গুরু হইয়া থাকে। **–ic,** *adj.*

pā'-găn, *n.* & *adj.* **1.** A heathen ; অ-খৃষ্টীয়ান, অ-ইহুদী, অ-মুসলমান, প্রতিমাপূজক, মূর্ত্তিপূজক, পৌত্তলিক। **2.** An unenlightened person ; সভ্যতার আলোক অপ্রাপ্ত ব্যক্তি। ***Adj.*** Of, or relating to, pagans ; heathen ; পৌত্তলিকগণসম্বন্ধীয় ; পৌত্তলিক। **–dom,** *n.* The pagan world ; পৌত্তলিক জগৎ। **–ish,** *adj.* Like or befitting a pagan ; পৌত্তলিকগণোচিত, প্রতিমাপূজকোচিত। **–ism,** *n.* **1.** Heathenism ; পৌত্তলিকতা। **2.** Pagan character, quality or morals ; পৌত্তলিকদিগের গুণ, প্রকৃতি, বা নীতিশাস্ত্র। **–ize,** *v. t.* & *i.* To convert to heathenism ; পৌত্তলিক ধর্ম্মে দীক্ষিত করা। (*Verb i.*) To behave like a pagan ; পৌত্তলিকের মত আচরণ করা।

pāge, *n.* **1.** A boy usually in livery employed to go on errands etc. ; ছোকরা চাকর। **2.** A boy employed as an attendant on a person of distinction or rank ; সম্ভ্রান্ত ব্যক্তির বালকভৃত্য, বালভৃত্য। **3.** (*Hist.*) A youth in training for knighthood and attached to a knight's service; (ইতিহাস) কোন নাইটের অধীনে শিক্ষানিরত যুবক। **Page'-hood, Page'-ship,** *ns.* **Page of honour, page of the presence etc.**—ইংলণ্ডেশ্বরের রাজপ্রাসাদের বিভিন্ন গার্হস্থ্য-কর্ম্মচারীর উপাধি।

pāge, *n.* **1.** One side of a leaf of a book ; পুস্তকের পৃষ্ঠা। **2.** (*Fig.*) An event, episode or circumstance fit to fill a page of history etc. ; (লক্ষণায়) যে ঘটনা, প্রসঙ্গ, প্রভৃতি দ্বারা ইতিহাসের একপৃষ্ঠা পূর্ণ হইতে পারে। **The page of history**—ঐতিহাসিক ঘটনা। **The sacred page**—খৃষ্টীয় ধর্ম্মশাস্ত্র।

pāge, *v. t.* To mark or number the pages of (a book etc.) ; পত্রাঙ্ক প্রদান করা।

păg'-eant (-ĕnt), *n.* **1.** A show or spectacle ; a showy procession ; প্রদর্শনী ; সমারোহপূর্ণ শোভাযাত্রা, মিছিল। **2.** A tableau, allegorical device, etc., on a fixed stage or moving car ; স্থায়ী রঙ্গমঞ্চে বা গতিশীল যানোপরি প্রদর্শিত পৌরাণিক বা রূপকস্বরূপ মূর্ত্তি, দৃশ্য বা ঘটনাবলী, বিচিত্রদৃশ্য। **3.** (*Fig.*) An empty or unsubstantial show ; (লক্ষণায়) অসার আড়ম্বর।

păg'-eant-rȳ (-ĕnt-), *n.* Pompous or splendid display ; a specious or empty show ; সমারোহ, ধুমধাম, ঘটা, জাঁকজমক ; বৃথা আড়ম্বর।

păg'-ĭ-năl, *adj.* Pertaining to, or consisting of, a page or pages ; page for page ; পৃষ্ঠাসম্বন্ধীয়, পৃষ্ঠাত্মক ; পৃষ্ঠায় পৃষ্ঠায়। **–na-ry,** *adj.* Same as PAGINAL.

păg'-ĭ-nāte, *v. t.* To page as a book etc. ; পত্রাঙ্ক দেওয়া। **–na'-tion,** *n.* The act of paginating ; পত্রাঙ্কলিখন।

pă-gō'-dă, *n.* **1.** A Hindu or Buddhist temple ; হিন্দু বা বৌদ্ধমন্দির, সিদ্ধায়তন (আঃ বঃ)। [কাহারো কাহারো মতে Pagoda শব্দটী পারস্য ভাষার *Bhut* (idol), *Kadah* (habitation) হইতে উৎপন্ন হইয়াছে। মতান্তরে তামিল ভাষার *Pe* অথবা

Pagoda in India (Bhubaneswar).

Pei (Devil) এবং *Gudi* (Temple) এই দুই শব্দের সম্মিলনে Pagoda হইয়াছে। আবার কাহারো কাহারো মতে সংস্কৃত "ভগবৎ" শব্দ হইতে Pagoda আসিয়াছে।] 2. A South-Indian gold coin worth 8*s.* to 9*s.*; দাক্ষিণাত্যে প্রচলিত প্রাচীন স্বর্ণমুদ্রাবিশেষ। **Pagoda-tree**—Various kinds of trees in India and China; (*fig.*) a tree supposed to produce pagodas or coin; চীন অথবা ভারতবর্ষের বিভিন্ন প্রকার বৃক্ষের সাধারণ নাম; (লক্ষণায়) স্বর্ণমুদ্রাবর্ষী কল্পিত বৃক্ষবিশেষ (cf. কল্পতরু, টাকার গাছ)। **To shake the pagoda-tree**—To make rapid fortune in India; ভারতবর্ষে অতিদ্রুত অর্থার্জ্জন করা।

pă-gū'-ri-ăn, *adj.* & *n.* Of, or relating to, the hermit-crab; কর্কটজাতীয় জীববিশেষসম্বন্ধীয়। ***Noun.*** The hermit-crab; কর্কটজাতীয় জীববিশেষ।

pah (pâ), *interj.* An interjection expressing contempt or disgust; দূর! ছি!

pah (pâ), *n.* A stockaded entrenchment or fortified place in New Zealand; নবজিলণ্ডদ্বীপের সূক্ষ্মাগ্র-কাষ্ঠদণ্ডবেষ্টিত সুরক্ষিত স্থান বা পরিখা।

pail (pāl), *n.* **1.** A vessel of wood or metals for carrying liquids etc.; কেঁড়ে, দোহনপাত্র, দুগ্ধভাণ্ড, ভাঁড়। **2.** The quantity contained in this; এক ভাঁড় দুধ প্রভৃতি। **Pail'-ful**, *adj.*

pail-lasse' (păl-yăs), **păl-liasse** (-yăs), *ns.* A mattress of straw; মাদুর।

pail-lette' (păl-yĕt), *n.* Spangle; a piece of bright metal used in enamel painting; চুমকি; এনামেল চিত্রণে ব্যবহৃত ধাতুখণ্ডবিশেষ।

pain (pān), *n.* **1.** Physical or mental suffering; distress; বেদনা, পীড়া, ব্যথা, যাতনা; সন্তাপ, কষ্ট। **2.** (*Pl.*) Care or trouble; as, to take *pains*; কষ্ট। **3.** Punishment; penalty (now only in some phrases, as, on or under *pain* of death); শাস্তি; দণ্ড। **4.** (*Pl.*) Travail of childbirth; প্রসববেদনা। **Pain'-ful**, *adj.* **1.** Full of pain; distressing; grievous; দুঃখদ; পীড়াদায়ক; যন্ত্রণাদায়ক। **2.** Difficult; requiring laborious effort; কঠিন; শ্রমসাধ্য, আয়াসসাধ্য। **Pain'-ful-ly**, *adv.* **Pain'-ful-ness**, *n.* **Pain'-less**, *adj.* **Pain'-less-ly**, *adv.* **Pain-killer**—বেদনানাশক ঔষধ। **Painstaking**—Careful; industrious; সতর্ক, সাবধান; পরিশ্রমী। **No pains no gains**—কষ্ট না কল্লে কেষ্ট মিলে না। **On or under pain of death**—On penalty of death etc.; মৃত্যুদণ্ডের দায়ে। **To be at pains**—To take trouble; to be careful; কষ্ট স্বীকার করা; সতর্ক হওয়া, সাবধান হওয়া। **To be at the pains of**—To take the trouble of; কষ্ট স্বীকার করা। **To take pains**—To take troubles; কষ্ট স্বীকার করা।

pain (pān), *v. t.* To cause pain to; to afflict or distress; ব্যথা দেওয়া, যাতনা দেওয়া; কষ্ট দেওয়া; দুঃখ দেওয়া।

paint (pānt), *n.* **1.** A substance used in painting; রং, বর্ণক। **2.** A pigment *e. g.* rouge, etc. for the face, etc.; রঞ্জক বস্তু, বিশেষতঃ মুখরাগ প্রভৃতি।

paint (pānt), *v. t.* & *i.* **1.** To represent in colours; চিত্রিত করা, আলিখিত করা, আঁকা, লিখা (cf. "বিরলে বসিয়া পটেতে লিখিয়া বিশাখা দেখাল আনি")। **2.** To ornament by painting; as, a wall *painted* with Biblical scences; চিত্ররাজিদ্বারা বিমণ্ডিত করা। **3.** (*Fig.*) To describe vividly; to delineate; (লক্ষণায়) চিত্রিত করা; বর্ণিত করা। **4.** To cover with a paint; to apply a paint to; as, to *paint* a house; রঞ্জিত করা; রং দেওয়া, রং লাগান, রং ফলান। **5.** To apply rouge etc. to (the face etc.); (মুখ প্রভৃতিতে) সুগন্ধি চূর্ণ প্রভৃতি মাখা। ***Verb i.*** **1.** To paint pictures; চিত্রিত করা। **2.** To colour the face; to beautify it; মুখরঞ্জিত করা; মুখশোভিত করা। **Paint'-ed**, *p. adj.* চিত্রিত, রঞ্জিত, পটে আঁকা (cf. পটে আঁকা পদ্ম), বর্ণিত, বর্ণচিত্রিত, বর্ণময় (painted in colours)। **Paint'-ing**, *n.* **1.** Laying on, or adorning with, colours; চিত্রকর্ম্ম, চিত্রণ, রঞ্জন। **2.** Art of representing objects in colours; চিত্রকলা। **3.** A picture; চিত্র, আলেখ্য, পট। **Paint-brush**—তুলি, তুলিকা, বর্ত্তিকা (cf. বর্ত্তিকা-লেখানিপুণা—শকুন্তলা), বর্ণতুলী, বর্ণ-তুলিকা। **Painted lady**—একজাতীয় প্রজাপতি। **To paint out**—To efface with paint; রঙ্গদ্বারা বিলেপিত করা। **To Paint the town red** — (ইতরভাষায়) কোলাহলপূর্ণ আমোদপ্রমোদ প্রভৃতি করিয়া সহর তোলপাড় করা।

paint'-ĕr (pānt-), *n.* **1.** One whose occupation is to paint; রঞ্জক, রঞ্জন-শিল্পী, রঙ্গজীব, তৌলিক, চিত্র-লেখক, চিত্রকার। **2.** One who paints pictures; চিত্রশিল্পী, চিত্রকর, চিত্রলিখক, পটুয়া, পটকার। **Painter's colic**—চিত্রকরদিগের শূলরোগ।

paint′-êr (pānt-), *n.* A rope to fasten a boat ; নৌকা বাঁধার দড়ী। **To cut the painter** -(লক্ষণায়, উপনিবেশ সম্বন্ধে) বিচ্ছিন্ন করা, পৃথক করা।

paint′-ȳ (pānt-), *adj.* 1. Of, or relating to, paint ; রঙ্গসম্বন্ধীয়। 2. (Of a picture) Overcharged with paint ; (চিত্রসম্বন্ধে) বর্ণোচ্ছাসিত।

pair (pār), *n.* 1. Two things of like kind, suited or used together; a couple ; জোড়া, যুগ্ম, দ্বয়, যুগল ; মিথুন, দ্বন্দ্ব। 2. An article composed of two corresponding parts ; as, a *pair* of scissors ; অনুরূপ অংশদ্বয়বিশিষ্ট বস্তু। 3 A couple married or engaged ; দম্পতী, হৃদয়ের পরিচয়ের জন্য সম্মিলিত বাগ্‌দত্ত বর বা বাগ্‌দত্তাকন্যা। 4. A mated couple of animals or birds ; দম্পতী, মিথুন। 5. (*Parliament*) Two voters of opposite sides who agree not to vote on some special occasion or for a specified time ; (পার্লামেন্ট) বিরোধী পক্ষদ্বয়ের যে সকল মতদাতা নির্দ্দিষ্টকাল পর্য্যন্ত বা কোন বিশেষব্যাপার উপলক্ষে মতপ্রদানে বিরত থাকিবেন বলিয়া পরস্পরের সহিত প্রতিশ্রুতিবদ্ধ হন। 6. Same as PAIR OF HORSES ; as, carriage and a *pair* ; অশ্বযুগল। **Pair-horse**—(*adj.*) For a pair of horses ; as, a *pair-horse* chariot or harness ; অশ্বযুগলের জন্য। **Pair-oar**—দুই দাঁড়ের নৌকা। **A carriage and a pair**—দুই ঘোড়ার গাড়ী। **Another** or **different pair of shoes** or **boots**—A different matter ; সে আর এক কথা। **A pair of stairs, A pair of steps**—A flight of stairs ; steps ; সোপানাবলী ; সোপানশ্রেণী। **Pair of horses**—একসঙ্গে যুতা এক জোড়া ঘোড়া।

pair (pār), *v. t. & i.* 1. To arrange in a pair or couple ; জোড়ায় জোড়ায় সাজান। 2. To unite in love or marriage ; প্রেমবন্ধনে বদ্ধ করা, দাম্পত্যসূত্রে বদ্ধ করা। 3. To mate জোট বাঁধা। 4. To associate together in couples of opposite sexes as for dancing, dinner ; নৃত্য, অপরাহ্নভোজনাদির কালে স্ত্রীপুরুষযুগল একত্র হওয়া। *Verb i.* 1. To form a pair or couple ; জোড়া বাঁধা, যুগ্ম হওয়া। 2. To become united in love or marriage ; বিবাহ বা প্রেমবন্ধনে বদ্ধ হওয়া। 3. To mate ; জোট বাঁধা। 4. (*Parliament*) To agree with an opponent to abstain from voting on a given question or issue ; (পার্লেমেণ্ট) কোন বিশেষ বিষয়ে মতপ্রদানে বিরত থাকার জন্য দুই বিরোধী পক্ষের মতদাতৃগণের পরস্পরের সহিত প্রতিশ্রুতিবদ্ধ হওয়া। **To pair off**—*v. t. & i.* To separate from a company in pairs or couples ; জোড়ায় জোড়ায় পৃথক করা। (*Verb i.*) To go off in pairs ; জোড়ায় জোড়ায় চলিয়া যাওয়া। (*Parliament*) Same as PAIR *v. i.* 4. (*Colloq.*) To marry (*with*) ; (চলিত ভাষায়) বিবাহ হওয়া। **Pair′-ing**, *n.* Copulation ; মৈথুন, সঙ্গম। **Pairing-time**—শাবক উৎপাদনার্থ পশুপক্ষীর মিলনকাল, সঙ্গম-ঋতু।

păl, *n.* & *v. i.* (*Slang*) A mate ; an associate ; an accomplice ; (ইতরভাষায়) সঙ্গী ; সাথী ; সহকারী। *Verb i.* To associate (*with*) ; সঙ্গ করা।

păl′-āce, *n.* 1. The residence of an emperor, king, archbishop or bishop ; রাজপ্রাসাদ, রাজবাটী, রাজভবন, নৃপমন্দির, রাজমন্দির রাজসদ্ম, রাজবেশ্ম, নৃপতিবসতি, ধর্ম্মাধ্যক্ষ বা মহাধর্ম্মাধ্যক্ষের বাসভবন। 2. A grand mansion ; সৌধ, হর্ম্ম্য। 3. A large building used as a place of amusement, refreshment, etc. ; আমোদ প্রমোদ প্রভৃতির জন্য ব্যবহৃত প্রাসাদোপম বাটীকা। **Palace-car**—নানা বিলাসোপকরণ ও আসবাব পত্রাদি দ্বারা সজ্জিত আরামজনক বাষ্পীয় শকট।

păl′-ă-dīn, *n.* 1. Any of the Twelve Peers of the court of Charlemagne ; সার্লেমেনের রাজসভার দ্বাদশজন বীরের অন্যতম। 2. (*Fig.*) A knight-errant ; (লক্ষণায়) আর্ত্ত ও দুর্ব্বলের রক্ষার্থ ও অসমসাহসিক কার্য্যের জন্য ভ্রমণশীল বীর।

pā-læ-ō-bŏt′-ă-nȳ (-lē), **—lē**, *ns.* A science treating of fossil plants ; প্রত্নোদ্ভিদ্‌বিদ্যা (সাঃ পঃ)।

pā-læ-ō-crȳs′-tic (-lē-), **—lē—**, *adjs.* Of, or relating to, ancient ice ; প্রাচীনতুষারযুগ সম্বন্ধীয়।

pā-læ-ŏg′-ră-phȳ (-lē-), **—lē**, *ns.* Study of ancient writings and inscriptions ; প্রত্নলিপিবিদ্যা, প্রাচীন লিপিপদ্ধতি, পুরাণবর্ণলক্ষণ। **—o-graph′-ic**, *adj.* **—ra-pher**, *n.* One versed in ancient writing and inscription ; প্রত্নলিপিতত্ত্ববিদ্।

pā-læ-ō-lith′-ic (-lē-), **—lē—**, *adjs.* Marked by the use of primitive stone implements ; আদি প্রস্তরযুগসম্বন্ধীয়।

pā-læ-ŏn-tŏl′-ō-ġȳ (-lē-), **—lē—**, *ns.* The science of extinct organisms or fossil remains ; অধুনালুপ্ত জীবজন্তুবিষয়ক বিজ্ঞান, প্রত্নজীববিদ্যা (সাঃ পঃ), লুপ্তজন্তুবিদ্যা (হিঃ কোঃ)। **—gist**, *n.* **—to-log′-i-cal**, *adj.*

pā-læ-ō-phȳ-tŏl′-ō-ġȳ (-lē-), **—lē—**, *ns.* Same as PALÆOBOTANY.

pā′-læ-o-there (-lē-ō-thēr), **—thē′-ri-ŭm, —lē—**, *ns.* An extinct genus

Palæotherium restored.

of tapir-like mammals ; অধুনালুপ্ত শূকরাকৃতি জন্তু বিশেষ।

pā-læ-ō-zō′-ic (-lē-), *adj.* 1. Relating to, or containing, ancient forms of life ; আদিম অবস্থা সম্বন্ধীয়।

2. Relating to the first geological period ; মৎস্যযুগসম্বন্ধীয়। **Palæozoic period**—মৎস্যযুগ (অভিঃ)।

pă-læ-ŏ-zō-ŏl′-ŏ-ġȳ (-lē-), *n.* That branch of science dealing with fossil remains of animals ; প্রত্ন-প্রাণিবিদ্যা (সাঃ পঃ)।

pă-læs′-tră (-lĕs-), **–lĕs–,** *ns.* A gymnasium ; a school of wrestling ; ব্যায়ামাগার ; আখড়া।

păl′-ă-fitte (-fĭt), *n.* A prehistoric lake-dwelling built on piles; প্রাগৈতিহাসিক যুগের হ্রদবাটীকা।

păl-ă-mē′-dēs, *n.* One of the Greek heroes in the Trojan war ; ইনি ট্রয়ের যুদ্ধে গ্রীকদিগের পক্ষে যোগদান করেন। Oddysseus, Agamemnonএর চক্রান্তে দেশদ্রোহী বলিয়া সাব্যস্ত হওয়ায় ইনি প্রস্তরাঘাতে নিহত হন। তুলাদণ্ডের উদ্ভাবয়িতা বলিয়া Palamedes বিখ্যাত।

păl-ăn-quin′ (-kēn), **–keen′** (-kēn), *ns.* (In India, China, etc.) A covered carriage carried on the shoulders; পাল্কী, শিবিকা, নরযান (মঃ ভাঃ)।

păl′-ăt-ă-ble (-bl), *adj.* Agreeable to the palate or taste ; pleasing to the mind ; স্বাদু, উপাদেয়, রসনাতৃপ্তিকর, রসাল, সুস্বাদু, আস্বাদ্য, রোচক, মুখরোচক, রুচিকর, স্বাদনীয়, রুচির, রসনীয় (মঃ ভাঃ), মুখপ্রিয় ; মনোমদ, রুচিরোচক। **–bly,** *adv.*

păl′-ă-tăl, *adj.* & *n.* 1. Of, or relating to, the palate ; তালু-সম্বন্ধীয়। 2. (Of a sound etc.) Articulated between the tongue and the palate, esp. the hard palate তালব্য। **–ize,** *v. t.* To make palatal ; তালব্য করা।

păl′-āte, *n.* 1. The roof or upper part of the mouth ; তালু, কাকুদ্র (সাঃ পঃ)। 2. Taste ; relish ; liking ; "…Lost my *palate* for it" ; রস, তার, স্বাদ; রুচি ; অভিরুচি। **Bony** or **hard palate**—তালুর কঠিন অস্থিময় অংশ। **Cleft palate**—See under CLEAVE. **Soft palate**—উপজিহ্বা।

pă-lā′-tial (-shăl), *adj.* Like, or becoming, a palace ; magnificent ; প্রাসাদীয় ; জাঁকাল, জাঁকজমকশালী।

pă-lăt′-ĭ-nāte, *n.* The province or territory of a count palatine ; যে কাউন্ট স্বাধিকারভুক্ত স্থানের মধ্যে রাজক্ষমতা পরিচালন করিতে পারেন। **The (Rhine) Palatinate**—রাইন প্রদেশের রাজক্ষমতাধারী কাউন্টের অধিকৃত জার্ম্মাণ সাম্রাজ্যের খণ্ড।

păl′-ă-tīne, *adj.* & *n.* 1. Possessing, or exercising, royal privileges in a province ; কোন প্রদেশে রাজক্ষমতা পরিচালনের অধিকারবান, রাজক্ষমতাধারী। 2. Of, or belonging to, a Count or Earl Palatine ; রাজক্ষমতাধারী আর্ল অথবা কাউন্ট-সম্বন্ধীয়। 3. Palatial ; প্রাসাদীয়, প্রাসাদোপম। ***Noun.*** 1. One exercising royal privileges in a province ; a Count or Earl Palatine ; উপরাজ ; রাজক্ষমতাধারী আর্ল বা কাউন্ট। 2. A woman's fur tippet ; শশকাদি জন্তুর কোমলরোমরচিত স্ত্রীলোকদিগের স্কন্ধাবরণ। **Count-Palatine**—যে কাউন্ট স্বাধিকারভুক্ত স্থানে রাজক্ষমতা পরিচালন করিতে পারেন, রাজক্ষমতাধারী কাউন্ট।

păl′-ă-tīne, *adj.* & *n.* Of, or relating to, the palate ; তালুসম্বন্ধীয়, তালব্য। ***Noun.*** (*Pl.*) The two bones forming the hard palate : (also, *palate bones*) ; যে অস্থিদ্বারা মুখের উপরিভাগ বা তালু প্রস্তুত হইয়াছে, তাল্বস্থিদ্বয়।

pă-lā′-vêr, *n., v. i.* & *t.* A conference, esp. with natives of Africa, etc. ; idle talk ; cajolery ; আফ্রিকা প্রভৃতি দেশের অধিবাসীর সহিত পরামর্শ ; বাজেকথা, বাজেগল্প ; চাটূক্তি, প্রিয়বাদ, খোসামোদ। ***Verb i.*** To talk profusely ; বাজে বকা, বেজায় কথা বলা, বাচালতা করা। ***Verb t.*** To flatter ; তোষামোদ করা, খোসামোদ করা।

pāle, *n.* 1. A pointed stake ; খোঁটা, কীলক। 2. (*Archaic*) A fence ; an enclosure ; (অপ্রঃ) বেড়া ; বেষ্টিত স্থান, বৃতিবেষ্টিত স্থান। 3. A boundary, (esp. *fig.*) ; as, within or beyond the *pale* ; সীমারেখা, চতুঃসীমা। 4. (*Herald.*) A perpendicular stripe in an escutcheon ; (কুল-বিদ্যা) কুলমর্য্যাদাসূচক চিহ্নাদি অঙ্কিত চর্ম্মের উপরিস্থ লম্ব রেখা। 5. (*Cap. Hist.*) The part of Ireland under English rule, (also, *the English Pale*) ; (ইতিহাস) আয়র্লণ্ডের ইংরেজ-শাসনাধীন অংশ। **To leap the pale**—আয়ের অতিরিক্ত ব্যয় করা। **Within** or **beyond the pale of**—সীমার মধ্যে, গণ্ডীর মধ্যে, সীমার বাহিরে

pāle, *adj.* 1. Ashen ; pallid ; of whitish appearance ; as a *pale* person or complexion ; পাণ্ডু, পাণ্ডুর ; বিবর্ণ, ম্লান, মলিন ; ফেকাসিয়া, পাঙ্গাস। 2. Not bright ; faint ; dim ; মন্দপ্রভ, মন্দকান্তি ; ম্লান ; নিষ্প্রভ। **Pale′-ly,** *adv.* **Pale′-ness,** *n.* The state of being pale ; পাণ্ডুতা, বিবর্ণতা, বৈবর্ণ্য, পাণ্ডুরতা, ম্লানতা, ম্লানিমা, মলিনতা। **Pale-face**—পাণ্ডুবদন (উত্তর আমেরিকার আদিম অধিবাসিগণ শ্বেতাঙ্গদিগকে এই আখ্যা প্রদান করিয়া থাকে)।

pāle, *v. i.* & *t.* 1. To turn pale ; মলিন হওয়া, ম্লান হওয়া, বিবর্ণ হওয়া। 2. (*Fig.*) To become pale in comparison ; তুলনায় ম্লান হওয়া, বিড়ম্বিত হওয়া, লাঞ্ছিত হওয়া। ***Verb t.*** To render pale ; বিবর্ণ করা, মলিন করা।

păl′-ĕ-tot (-tō), *n.* A loose cloak ; একপ্রকার ঢিলা জামা।

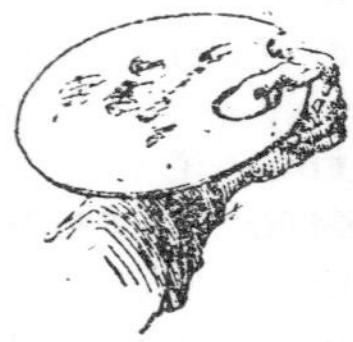

Artist's palette.

păl′-ette (-ĕt), *n.* 1. A thin oval board on which painters mix their colours ; চিত্রকরগণের ডিম্বাকৃতি বর্ণপাত্র, চিত্রকরের রঙ্গাধার,

বর্ণপাত্র, রংদানি। 2. Colours used by a particular artist, or on a particular occasion; কোন বিশিষ্ট চিত্রকর কর্তৃক বা কোন বিশেষ চিত্রে যে বর্ণসমূহ ব্যবহৃত হয়। **Palette-knife** — রঙ্গমিশ্রণের জন্য হাতলযুক্ত লোহার ফলা।

pal'-frey (-fri), *n.* (*Archaic, Poet.*) A small horse, esp. for ladies; (অপ্রঃ, কবিতায়) একপ্রকার ঘোটক, বিশেষতঃ ভদ্রমহিলাগণের জন্য ক্ষুদ্র ঘোটক।

păl'-i-kăr, *n.* A member of the band of a Greek or Albanian military chief, esp. during the War of Independence; গ্রীক অথবা আলবেনিয়ার সামরিক সর্দ্দার।

păl'-imp-sĕst, *n.* & *adj.* A parchment or manuscript from which writing has been erased to make room for other writing, the original remaining faintly visible; কোন নূতন বিষয় সংযোজনের জন্য যে চর্ম্মপট বা হস্তলিখিত কাগজ হইতে লিখিত বিষয় তুলিয়া ফেলা হইয়াছে। ***Adj.*** (Of a manuscript etc.) So treated; re-written; (হস্তলিখিত কাগজ প্রভৃতি সম্বন্ধে) পূর্ব্বের লিখা উঠাইয়া ফেলার পর নূতন লেখা সংযোজিত; পুনর্লিখিত।

păl'-in-drōme *n.* & *adj.* A word or verse that is the same when read backwards or forwards; প্রতিলোমানুলোমপদ, অনুলোমবিলোম্ শ্লোক। ***Adj.*** (Of word etc.) That reads the same backwards as forwards; প্রতিলোম ও অনুলোম পাঠে একরূপ। **—drom'-ic,** *adj.*

pāl'-ing, *n.* Pales; a fence formed with these; খোঁটা; খোঁটার বেড়া।

păl-in-gĕn'-ĕ-sis, *n.* 1. A regeneration; revival; resuscitation; (*lit.* & *fig.*); পুনরুজ্জীবন; পুনরুত্থান; সঞ্জীবন (শব্দানুযায়ী ও লক্ষণায়)। 2. (*Biol.*) The reproduction of ancestral characters without modification; (জীব-বিজ্ঞান) কোনরূপ পরিবর্ত্তন বিনা পূর্ব্বপুরুষের স্বভাবের পুনরুদ্ভব, পূর্ব্বজানুকরণ (হিঃ কোঃ)। 3. (*Entom.*) Metamorphosis; (কীটবিদ্যা) রূপান্তর। 4. The doctrine of continued rebirths; পুনর্জন্মবাদ। **—ge-net'-ic,** *adj.*

păl'-i-nōde, *n.* 1. A poem recanting something in a former one; যে কবিতাদ্বারা পূর্ব্ববর্তী কোন কবিতার বিষয় প্রত্যাহার করা হয়। 2. Recantation; প্রত্যাহার।

păl-i-sāde' *n.* & *v. t.* 1. A fence of pales or posts or of iron railings; খোঁটার বেড়া, লোহার কীলকের বেড়া, লোহার গরাদের বেড়া। 2. (*Mil.*) A strong pointed wooden stake; (সামরিকশাস্ত্র) কঠিন এবং সূক্ষ্মাগ্র কীলক। ***Verb t.*** To furnish, enclose or fortify with palisades; বৃতিবেষ্টিত করা, বৃতিদ্বারা সুরক্ষিত করা।

pāl'-ish, *adj.* Somewhat pale or wan; আপাণ্ডু, আপাণ্ডর।

pall, *n.* 1. A cloth thrown over a coffin, hearse; শবাধারাচ্ছাদন বস্ত্র, শবযানাবরণ বস্ত্র। 2. An ecclesiastical mantle; যাজকীয় প্রাবরণ। 3. An outer garment; a cloak; বহির্ব্বাস; ঢিলাজামা। **Pall-bearer**— যে ব্যক্তি অন্ত্যেষ্টিক্রিয়াকালে শবাধারাচ্ছাদন বস্ত্রের প্রান্ত ধরিয়া থাকে।

pall, *v. i.* & *t.* To become vapid or insipid, (now *fig.*); নীরস হওয়া, বিরস হওয়া, পানসা হওয়া (অধুনা লক্ষণায়)। ***Verb t.*** To satiate or cloy; পরিতৃপ্ত করা, ভোগবিতৃষ্ণ হওয়া। **To pall on (the mind, taste, etc.)**—নীরস হওয়া।

păl-lā'-di-ŭm, *n.* 1. The statue of Pallas on the preservation of which the safety of Troy was held to depend; পেলাসদেবের মূর্ত্তি—যাহার রক্ষার উপর ট্রয় নগরীর কুশল নির্ভর করিত। 2. A safeguard; আশ্রয়, শরণ।

păl-lā'-di-ŭm, *n.* A greyish metal of the platinum group; প্লাটিনামবর্গের অন্তর্ভুক্ত ধূসরবর্ণ ধাতুবিশেষ।

Păl-lăn-ti-ăs, *n.* Another name for Aurora; ঊষাদেবী।

păl'-let (-ĕt), *n.* A bed of straw; mattress; তৃণশয্যা; (খড়ের) গদি।

păl'-let (-ĕt), *n.* 1. Same as PALETTE. 2. A tool used by potters etc.; কুম্ভকার প্রভৃতি কর্তৃক ব্যবহৃত যন্ত্রবিশেষ। 3. A projection on a part of a machine serving to change the mode of motion of a wheel; কোন যন্ত্রাংশ হইতে প্রলম্বিত অংশ—যাহার সাহায্যে চক্রের গতির প্রকার পরিবর্ত্তিত হয়, চক্রগতি-পরিবর্ত্তক।

păl-liasse' (-y-ăs), *n.* See PAILLASSE.

păl'-li-āte (-ī-), *v. t.* 1. To ease as a disease without curing; উপশম করা, লাঘব করা। 2. To extenuate; to excuse; দোষ লঘু করা, দোষোপশম করা; দোষমোচনের চেষ্টা করা। **—a'-tion,** *n.*

păl'-li-a-tive (-ī-ā-tiv), *adj.* & *n.* Serving to palliate; উপশামক, উপশমকর, শান্তিপ্রদ, দোষাচ্ছাদক। ***Noun.*** Such a thing; শান্তিপ্রদ বস্তু।

păl'-lid (-ĭd), *adj.* Pale or wan; বিবর্ণ, পাণ্ডুবর্ণ, ফেকাসে, ফেকাসিয়া, পাংশুসবর্ণ। **—ly,** *adv.* **—ness,** *n.*

păl'-li-ŭm, *n.* 1. A large rectangular cloak worn, esp. by ancient Greeks; বৃহৎ সমচতুরস্রাকার প্রাবরণ, বিশেষতঃ প্রাচীন গ্রীকগণের পরিধেয় ঐরূপ প্রাবরণ। 2. Same as PALL *n.* 2. 3. The integumental fold of a mollusc; শম্বুকাদি প্রাণীর আবরক পুট। **—al,** *adj.*

pall-mall' (pĕl-mĕl), *n.* 1. A game in which a ball is driven by a mallet through an iron ring; একপ্রকার ক্রীড়া যাহাতে মুদ্গারের সাহায্যে কন্দুক লোহচক্রের ভিতর দিয়া চালিত হয়। 2. (*Cap.*) A street in London; লণ্ডন নগরীর রাজপথ-বিশেষ। 3. The War Office in this street; উক্ত রাজপথে স্থিত সামরিক-কার্য্যালয়।

păl′-lor (-ŏr), *n.* Paleness ; পাণ্ডুতা, বৈবর্ণ্য, বিবর্ণতা।

palm (pâm), *n.* 1. An Eastern plant of different varieties ; তাল, খর্জ্জুরাদি, বৃক্ষ। 2. A palm-branch as a symbol of victory ; বিজয়-চিহ্নস্বরূপ তালপত্র। 3. A branch of various trees substituted for the true palm in church observances ; খৃষ্টীয় উৎসবাদিতে ব্যবহৃত তালজাতীয় বিভিন্নপ্রকার বৃক্ষের শাখা। 4. Triumph ; supremacy ; prize ; as, to bear or yield the *palm* ; বিজয়, রণজয় ; প্রাধান্য ; পুরস্কার। **Pal-ma′-ceous,** *adj.* **Palm-house**—তাল এবং অন্যান্য উষ্ণমণ্ডল-জাত বৃক্ষোৎপাদনের জন্য কাচসমাচ্ছাদিত গৃহ, তালগৃহ। **Palm-oil**—বিভিন্ন-প্রকার তালজাতীয় বৃক্ষ হইতে নিষ্কর্ষিত তৈল। **Palm Sunday**—ইষ্টার পর্ব্বের পূর্ব্ববর্ত্তী রবিবার [এই দিবস খৃষ্টের জেরুজেলেম প্রবেশ উৎসবের অনুষ্ঠান উপলক্ষে শোভাযাত্রায় তালপত্র বাহিত হয়।] **To bear the palm**—To be pre-eminent ; শ্রেষ্ঠ হওয়া, প্রধান হওয়া। **To give** or **yield the palm to**—To acknowledge as superior ; শ্রেষ্ঠতা স্বীকার করা।

palm (pâm), *n.* 1. The inner part of the hand ; করতল, পাণিতল, হস্ততল, হাতের চেটো (*colloq.*)। 2. The part of a glove that covers this ; দস্তানার পাণিতল আবরক অংশ। 3. A lineal measure equal to the breadth (about 4 in.) or to the length (about 8 in.) of the hand ; করতলের দৈর্ঘ্য বা প্রস্থের মাপ—দৈর্ঘ্য প্রায় ৮ ইঞ্চি, প্রস্থ প্রায় ৪ ইঞ্চি, হস্তার্দ্ধ, বিঘৎ। **Palmed,** *adj.* **Palm′-ful,** *adj.* **Palm-oil**—Money (so called as it greases the palm) ; টাকা পয়সা **To grease a person's palm**—See GREASE.

palm (pâm), *v. t.* 1. To impose by fraud ; to pass *off* as a thing *on* a person ; ঠকান, মাথায় হাত বুলান, চোখে ধূলি দেওয়া ; ফাঁকি দিয়া চালাইয়া দেওয়া। 2. To conceal in the palm, as cards, dice, etc. ; করতলে লুকান। 3. To handle ; to touch with the palm ; হস্ত দ্বারা ব্যবহার করা ; করতল দ্বারা স্পর্শ করা। 4. To bribe : ঘুষ দেওয়া। **To palm off anything**—To pass anything under false pretences ; ফাঁকি দিয়া কোন জিনিস চালাইয়া দেওয়া।

Păl′-mă–Chris′-tī (-krĭs), *n.* The castor oil plant ; এরণ্ড বৃক্ষ, ভেরেণ্ডা [Also এরণ্ডক, উরুবুক, রুবুক, রবুক, রুবু, রুচক, ব্যড়ম্বক, ব্যড়ম্বন, ব্যাড়ঙ্গর, ব্যাঘ্রপুচ্ছ, চঞ্চু, পঞ্চাঙ্গুল, বর্দ্ধমান, চিত্রবীজ (red), দীর্ঘপত্রক, মণ্ড, অমণ্ড, আমণ্ড, গন্ধর্ব্বসমুষাহস্ত, গন্ধর্ব্বহস্তক, চিত্র, গন্ধর্ব্বহস্ত (from the form of the leaf resembling that of a hand. Mark resemblance of Palma Christi or Christ's palm with our গন্ধর্ব্বহস্ত)]।

păl′-mar (-mêr), *adj.* Of, relating to, the palm of the hand ; পাণিতলসম্বন্ধীয়।

păl′-mă-rȳ, *adj.* Superior ; pre-eminent ; শ্রেষ্ঠ ; সর্ব্বপ্রধান।

păl′-māte, –māt-ĕd, *adjs.* Shaped like the palm of the hand ; পাণিতলাকার।

palm′-ēr (pâm-), *n.* 1. A pilgrim returning from Holy Land so called as carrying a palm-branch or palm-leaf ; জেরুজেলেম প্রত্যাগত যাত্রী। 2. An itinerant monk under a perpetual vow of poverty ; পরিব্রাজক। 3. (Also *palmer-worm*) A kind of caterpillar ; একপ্রকার শুঁয়াপোকা। 4. (*Angling*) A hairy artificial fly ; একপ্রকার রোমশ কৃত্রিম মক্ষিকা।

păl-mĕt′-tō, *n.* A small species of palm tree ; the dwarf fan-palm ; একপ্রকার ক্ষুদ্রজাতীয় তালবৃক্ষ ; খর্ব্বতালবৃক্ষ, তালীবৃক্ষ।

păl-mi-pĕd, –pede (-pĕd), *adj.* & *n.* Web-footed ; জালপাদ। *Noun.* Such a bird ; জালপাদ-পক্ষী।

pälm′-is-trȳ, *n.* Telling fortunes by the lines on the palm of the hand ; সামুদ্রিক, সামুদ্রক, করতল-বিদ্যা, হস্তসামুদ্রিক, করসামুদ্রিক। **–ist,** *n.* One practising palmistry ; সামুদ্রিক, সামুদ্রজ্ঞ।

palm′-ȳ (pâm-), *adj.* 1. Of, or relating to, palms ; abounding in palms ; palm-like ; তালসম্বন্ধীয় ; তালবহুল ; তালবৎ। 2. Flourishing ; prosperous ; as, *palmy* days ; শ্রীমন্ত, সমৃদ্ধ ; শ্রীসম্পন্ন, সমৃদ্ধিশালী।

păl-mȳ′-ră, *n.* An East-Indian tall palm with rounded fan-shaped leaves ; তাল গাছ, [also তৃণ-নির্য্যাস, তৃণদ্রুম, তৃণ বৃক্ষ (নিঘণ্টু), দীর্ঘতরু, দীর্ঘপাদপ, দীর্ঘদ্রু, দীর্ঘপত্র, গুচ্ছপত্র, লেখ্যপত্রক, দ্রুমশ্রেষ্ঠ, দুরারোহ, দ্রুমেশ্বর।]

pălp, păl′-pŭs, *n.,* (*pl.* -PI), A jointed feeler attached to the lower jaw of insects ; কীটের নিম্ন-হনুসংলগ্ন শুঙ, স্পর্শন (প্রঃ ১৩২৩)। **–pal,** *adj.*

păl′-pă-ble (-bl), *adj.* 1. Capable of being touched or felt ; tangible ; স্পর্শজ্ঞেয়, স্পর্শগোচর, স্পর্শেন্দ্রিয়-গ্রাহ্য ; স্পষ্ট, সূচীভেদ্য (অন্ধকার), স্থূল। 2. Easily perceived by the senses or mind ; obvious ; সহজগ্রাহ্য ; জাজ্বল্যমান। **–bil′-i-ty,** *n.* **–bly,** *adv.* **Palpable darkness**—সূচীভেদ্য অন্ধকার।

păl′-pāte, *v. t.* To examine, esp. medically by touch ; স্পর্শ দ্বারা পরীক্ষা করা। **–pa′-tion,** *n.*

păl′-pĕ-brăl, *adj.* Of, or relating to, the eyelids ; অক্ষিপল্লবসম্বন্ধীয়।

păl′-pi-tāte, *v. i.* 1. To beat or throb as the heart ; ধুকধুক করা, দুরুদুরু করা, স্পন্দিত হওয়া। 2. To tremble ; কাঁপা।

păl-pi-tā′-tion, *n.* Throbbing ; an abnormal rapid beating of the heart ; স্পন্দন, প্রতিস্পন্দন, স্ফুরণ, কম্পন, বেপথু ; হৃৎকম্প।

pālš′-grāve, *n.* Same as COUNT PALATINE.

pal′-šȳ, *n.* & *v. t.* **1.** Paralysis ; পক্ষাঘাত, স্তম্ভ, অর্দ্ধাঙ্গবাত, স্বাপ, অবষ্টম্ভ। **2.** (*Fig.*) The cause or state of utter helplessness ; (লক্ষণায়) সম্পূর্ণ আশ্রয়হীনতা। ***Verb t.*** To paralyze, (usu. *fig.*) ; পক্ষাঘাতগ্রস্ত করা, আড়ষ্ট করা, অসাড় করা (প্রায়শঃ লক্ষণায়)।

pal′-têr, *v. i.* **1.** To play fast and loose ; to equivocate ; অব্যবস্থিতের মত কার্য্য করা ; দ্ব্যর্থবোধক শব্দ ব্যবহার করা। **2.** To shuffle or haggle ; দরদস্তুর করা, দর কষাকষি করা। **3.** To trifle as *with* a subject ; কোন বিষয় লইয়া ফচ্‌কেমি করা।

pal′-trȳ, *adj.* Petty ; worthless ; despicable ; ক্ষুদ্র, নীচ, তুচ্ছ ; অসার ; হেয়। **–tri-ness,** *n.*

pă-lū′-dăl, *adj.* Of, or relating to, a marsh ; malarial ; বিলসম্বন্ধীয়, জলাভূমিসম্বন্ধীয় ; ম্যালেরিয়াসম্বন্ধীয়।

pāl′-ȳ, *adj.* (*Poet.*) Palish; (কবিতায়) আপাণ্ডু, আপাণ্ডুর, ঈষৎপাণ্ডু।

păm, *n.* The knave of clubs, esp. in five-card loo ; ইস্কাবনের গোলাম।

păm′-pă, *n.* (Usu. *pl.*) A vast treeless plain in South America ; দক্ষিণ আমেরিকার সুবিশাল তরুহীন প্রান্তর, বিশালক্ষেত্র, পাম্পাস (সাঃ পঃ)।

Pampa grass.

Pampa grass—দক্ষিণ আমেরিকার একপ্রকার সুবৃহৎ তৃণ।

păm′-pêr, *v. t.* **1.** To indulge to excess ; অতিশয় প্রশ্রয় দেওয়া। **2.** (*Obs.*) To feed too much ; (অপ্রঃ) অতিমাত্রায় ভোজন করান।

păm-pē′-rō, *n.* A strong cold wind blowing from the Andes to the Atlantic; আন্দিজ পর্ব্বত হইতে অতলান্তিক মহাসাগরে প্রবহমাণ অতি শীতল বায়ু।

păm′-phlĕt, *n.* A small book, stitched but not bound ; চটী বই, ক্ষুদ্র পুস্তিকা।

păm-phlĕt-eer′ (-ēr), *n.* & *v. i.* A writer of pamphlets ; যে ব্যক্তি চটী বহি লিখে, ক্ষুদ্রপুস্তিকালেখক। ***Verb i.*** To write pamphlets ; চটী বই লিখা।

păn, *n.* **1.** A broad shallow vessel : চাটু। **2.** A vessel like pan in which substances are heated, etc. ; কড়াই, কটাহ। **3.** That part of an obsolete type of gun, holding the priming ; প্রাচীন ধরণের বন্দুকের যে অংশে রঞ্জক-ধরা থাকে। **4.** A hollow or depression in the ground ; as, salt-*pan* ; অবনমিত ভূমি। **5.** (Also, *hard-pan*) A hard substratum of the soil ; মৃত্তিকার কঠিন অন্তস্তর। **Pan′-ful,** *n.* As much as is contained in a vessel ; ভাণ্ডপূর্ণ। **Brain-pan**—করোটী। **Pancake**—লুচি, চাপাটী। **A flash in the pan**—ফাঁকা আওয়াজ। **Flat as a pan**—একেবারে চ্যাপ্টা। **To savour of the frying pan**—প্রচলিত ধর্ম্মের বিরোধী মতাবলম্বী বলিয়া সূচনা করা। **To shut one's pan**—(ইতরভাষায়) চুপ থাকা।

păn, *v. t.* & *i.* To wash as gold-bearing gravel etc. in a pan, (with *off, out*) ; ভাণ্ডের মধ্যে স্বর্ণরেণুময় কঙ্কর প্রভৃতি ধৌত করা। ***Verb i.*** **1.** (Of gravel etc.) To yield gold, (with *out*) ; স্বর্ণপ্রসূ হওয়া। **2.** (*Fig.*) To yield a result ; to succeed ; to turn out, (with *out*) ; (লক্ষণায়) ফল প্রসব করা ; কৃতকার্য্য হওয়া ; উৎপন্ন হওয়া। **To pan out**—See PAN *v. i.*

Păn, *n.* (*Greek Myth.*) A god of flocks and pastures ; গ্রীকপুরাণোক্ত নৃত্যগীতপ্রিয় বনদেবতাবিশেষ—ইঁহার শৃঙ্গ, পদ ও খুর ছাগের মত ছিল।

păn-ă-cē′-ă, *n.* A universal medicine or remedy ; সর্ব্বরোগহর, মহৌষধি, রসায়ন (হিঃ কোঃ), ত্রৈলোক্য-চিন্তামণি (কেঃভিঃ)।

pă-nache′ (-năsh), *n.* **1.** A plume or bunch of feathers on a helmet ; শিরস্ত্রাণ প্রভৃতির উপরিস্থ পালক বা পালকগুচ্ছ। **2.** (*Fig.*) Display ; swagger ; (লক্ষণায়) ধুমধড়ক্কা ; নবাবী চালচলন।

pă-nā′-dă, *n.* A bread pulp ; পাঁউরুটীর ভিতরকার কোমল অংশ।

păn-Af′-ri-căn (-ăf-), *adj.* Of, relating to, or for all, Africans ; নিখিলআফ্রিকীয়।

păn cŏs′-mišm, *n.* The doctrine that the material universe or cosmos is all that exists ; জড়জগৎ ব্যতীত অপর কোন জগতের অস্তিত্ব নাই—এইরূপ মতবাদ।

păn-crăt′-ic, *adj.* **1.** Of, or relating to, the pancratium ; ক্লোমসম্বন্ধীয়। **2.** (Of an eye-piece) Capable of adjustment to many degrees of power ; অনেক শক্তিমাত্রায় সন্নিবেশযোগ্য।

păn-crā′-ti-ŭm (-shi-), *n.* (*Gk. Antiq.*) An athletic contest combining both wrestling and boxing ; (গ্রীকপ্রত্নতত্ত্ব) একপ্রকার মল্লক্রীড়া—যাহাতে মল্লক্রীড়া ও মুষ্টিযুদ্ধ উভয়েরই সমাবেশ থাকিত। **–ast, Pan′-cra-tist,** *ns.*

păn′-crē-ăs, *n.* A gland near the stomach which secretes a fluid helpful in digestion ; ক্লোম, পক্বাশয়ের নিম্নস্থিত গ্রন্থির আকার যন্ত্রবিশেষ—ইহা হইতে রস ক্ষরিত হইয়া পরিপাক ক্রিয়ার সাহায্য করে। **–at′-tic,** *adj.* **Pancreatic juice**—ক্লোমরস।

păn'-dă, *n.* An Indian bear of the Himalayas; হিমালয় পর্ব্বত-বাসী একপ্রকার ভল্লুক।

păn-dā'-nŭs, *n.* Screw-pines; কেয়াগাছ, কেতকী, কেতক।

Pandanus odoratissimus—কেতকী (বেলঃ)।

Păn-dē'-ăn, —dæ— (-dē-), *adjs.* Of, or relating to, Pan, the Greek rural god; গ্রীক বনদেবতা-সম্বন্ধীয়। **Pand(a)ean-pipe**—Same as PAN-PIPE.

păn'-dĕct, *n.* **1.** (*Usu. pl.*) A digest of Roman civil law, made by the order of Justinian in the 6th century; জাসটিনিয়ানের আদেশানুসারে সম্পাদিত রোমীয় দেওয়ানী আইনের সারমর্ম্ম। **2.** Any complete code of laws; সংহিতা (হিঃ কোঃ)।

păn-dĕm'-ĭc, *adj.* & *n.* (Of a disease) Prevalent over a whole country or over the world; (রোগ-সম্পর্কে) বিশ্বব্যাপী, পৃথিবীব্যাপী, জগদ্ব্যাপী, সর্ব্বব্যাপক (কেঃডিঃ)।

păn-dē-mō'-nĭ-ŭm, *n.* **1.** The abode of all the demons; নিখিল-দানবনিবাস। **2.** A lawless riotous place; পিশাচসভা, হট্টগোলের স্থান। **3.** Utter confusion or tumult; লঙ্কাকাণ্ড।

păn'-dêr, *n, v. i.* & *t.* **1.** A go-between in clandestine amours; a procurer or procuress; কুট্টনী, সন্ধানকর্ত্তা, দূতী; ভেড়ুয়া (*colloq.*), রততালী, বেশ্যাচার্য্য, যোজক। **2.** A minister to evil designs etc.; দুষ্কর্ম্মে সহায়তাকারী। ***Verb i.*** To act as a pander; to minister *to* lust, evil designs, etc.; কুট্টনীর কাজ করা; লালসা, দুরভিসন্ধি, প্রভৃতির চরিতার্থতায় সহায়তা করা। ***Verb t.*** To play the pander for; to minister to (another's lust etc.); কুট্টনীর কাজ করা; লালসা প্রভৃতির চরিতার্থতায় সহায়তা করা।

păn-dō'-ră, —dore' (-dōr), *ns.* A kind of stringed instrument; একপ্রকার তন্ত্রিবিশিষ্ট বাদ্যযন্ত্র।

Păn-dō'-ră, *n.* (*Gk. Myth.*) A beautiful woman sent from heaven to earth to punish man for his audacity in thinking he could yield the fire of Jove; (গ্রীকপুরাণোক্ত) পরমরূপসী আদি মানবী। প্রমিথিয়াস নামক দানবের শাস্তিবিধানের জন্য জুপিটার ইহাকে সৃষ্টি করেন। **Pandora's box**—জুপিটার Pandoraকে নানা অশুভপূর্ণ একটী বাক্স প্রদান করেন। এই বাক্স Pandora তাহার পতিকে দিবার জন্য আদিষ্ট হয়। Prometheusএর ভ্রাতা Epimetheus Pandoraর নিকট হইতে বাক্স গ্রহণ করিয়া তাহাকে বিবাহ করে। Epimetheus, এই বাক্স খোলার পর রোগ শোক, প্রভৃতি নানা অশুভ বহির্গত হইয়া মানব জাতিকে পীড়ন করিতে আরম্ভ করে। কেবলমাত্র আশা মানবের শেষ সান্ত্বনাস্বরূপ বাক্সের নীচে রহিয়া গিয়াছিল। মতান্তরে—বাক্সের ভিতর দেবতাগণের আশীর্ব্বাদ নিহিত ছিল; বাক্স খোলার সঙ্গে সঙ্গে মানবজাতি এই আশীর্ব্বাদ হইতে বঞ্চিত হয়।

păn'-dour (-dōr), **—door** (dōr), *ns.* (*Pl.*) A military force of brutal soldiers raised by Baron Trenck in 1741 and subsequently enrolled in the Austrian army; অষ্ট্রিয়াদেশের সৈন্যশ্রেণীবিশেষ।

pāne, *n.* **1.** A plate of glass inserted in a window, door, etc.; কাচফলক, চতুরস্রকাচ। **2.** A rectangular division of a variegated pattern etc.; ছক-কাটা কাপড়ের এক একটি ছক। **3.** A panel; কপাটাদির খোপ। **4.** A flat side or face of an object having several sides; বহুপার্শ্ববিশিষ্ট বস্তুর চ্যাপ্টা পার্শ্ব। **Pane'-less,** *adj.*

pāne, *v. t.* **1.** To furnish with panes, as a window; জানালা প্রভৃতিতে কাচ লাগান। **2.** (*Chiefly in p. p.*) To make up, as a garment etc. of strips of different colours; পোষাকের কাপড় প্রভৃতিতে নানা রঙ্গের ডোরা কাটা।

păn-ē-ḡȳr'-ĭc, *n.* & *adj.* Laudatory speech; encomium; eulogy; সংস্তব, স্তুতিবাদ, গুণগ, স্তব; গুণস্তুতি, প্রশংসাবাণী; গুণবাদ, গুণকীর্ত্তন, স্তুতিপাঠ। ***Adj.*** Laudatory; প্রশংসাত্মক। **—i-cal,** *adj.*

păn'-ē-ḡȳ-rīze, *v. t.* To speak or write in praise of; to eulogize; গুণবাদ করা, স্তুতিগান করা, স্তবগান করা, প্রশংসা করা, প্রশংসাসূচক প্রবন্ধাদি লিখা; গুণকীর্ত্তন করা। **—gyr-ist,** *n.* One who panegyrizes; স্তাবক, স্তুতিবাদকারী, স্তোতা, স্তুতিপাঠক, বন্দিজন।

păn'-ĕl, *n.* **1.** A saddle-pad; a kind of saddle; জিনপোষ; একপ্রকার জিন। **2.** A slip of parchment; চর্ম্মপটখণ্ড। **3.** A list of jurymen; the jury itself; জুরির তালিকা; জুরি। **4.** (*Scot. law*) The accused; (স্কটলণ্ডের আইন) আসামী। **5.** A distinct compartment of surface, esp. wainscot, door, etc.; খুপী, ছক। **6.** A piece of stuff of different kind or colours inserted in woman's dress; স্ত্রীপরিচ্ছদে সন্নিবিষ্ট বিভিন্ন বর্ণের বস্ত্রখণ্ড। **7.** A size of photograph much longer than wide; একপ্রকার আলোকচিত্র—যাহার প্রস্থ অপেক্ষা দৈর্ঘ্য অনেক বেশী হইয়া থাকে।

păn'-ĕl, *v. t.* **1.** To put a panel on (a beast, esp. an ass); জিন লাগান। **2.** To fit with panels as a wall, door, etc.; (দরজা, প্রাচীরাদি) খোপবিশিষ্ট করা। **3.** To decorate with a panel or panels, as a dress etc.; ছক কাটা, চৌখুপী করা। **—ling,** *n.*

păn-ĕn'-thē-ĭsm, *n.* The doctrine that God includes the world as a part though not the whole, of His being; বিশ্বসংসার ঈশ্বরের

একদেশ মাত্র—এইরূপ মতবাদ, বিভুত্ববাদ (হিঃ কোঃ), 'ন ত্বহং তেষু তে ময়ি'-বাদ (ঐ), [cf. বিষ্টভ্যাহং মিদং কৃৎস্নমেকাংশেন স্থিতো জগৎ—গীতা।]

păng, *n.* **1.** Extreme or shooting pain ; agony ; বেদনা, যন্ত্রণা, ব্যথা, যাতনা ; প্রাণান্তযাতনা। **2.** A sudden, sharp mental pain ; আকস্মিক তীব্র মর্ম্মান্তিক মনোবেদনা।

Pangasius buchanani — পাঙ্গাস মাছ (গুপ্তঃ)।

păn-gĕn'-ĕ-sis, *n.* The theory that each unit of an organism reproduces itself ; কোন অঙ্গের প্রতি অবিভাজ্য অংশ পুনরুৎপাদিত হয়—এইরূপ মতবাদ, কণজনি (হিঃ কোঃ)।

păn-Gĕr'-măn, *adj.* Of, or relating to, all the Germans in political union ; নিখিলজর্ম্মণীয়।

Pangolin.

pan-gō'-lin (păng-), *n.* The scaly ant-eater ; শল্কাবৃত পিপীলিকাভুক জন্তুবিশেষ, বজ্রকীট (Indian), বজ্রকীট।

păn-hĕl'-lĕn-ĭsm, *n.* Political union of all the Greeks ; নিখিলগ্রীকজাতির রাজনৈতিক ঐক্য। **—len'-ic**, *adj.*

păn'-ic, *n.* A genus of grasses ; একজাতীয় ঘাস।

păn'-ic, *adj.* & *n.* Excessive, sudden or causeless (of terror etc.) ; অতিরিক্ত, আকস্মিক, অকারণ। ***Noun.*** A sudden extreme terror usually caused by a trifling cause ; alarm accompanied by frantic efforts to secure safety ; ত্রাস, সন্ত্রাস ; আতঙ্ক, উদ্বেগ (হিঃ কোঃ) ; **—ick-y**, *adj.* **Panic-monger**—যে ব্যক্তি আতঙ্কের সৃষ্টি করে। **Panic struck**—আতঙ্কগ্রস্ত, সন্ত্রস্ত, ভয়বিপ্লুত।

păn'-i-cle (-cl), *n.* (*Bot.*) A branching form of inflorescence as in the lilac ; (উদ্ভিদ্বিদ্যা) সরপুষ্প (সাঃ পঃ), মন্দিরাকার (ঐ)।

Panicum frumentaceum—শামা (বেলঃ)।

Panicum miliaceum—চিনা (বেলঃ), শ্যামাক (Sans.)।

păn-i-fi-cā'-tion, *n.* Bread-making ; রুটী প্রস্তুতকরণ।

păn-Is'-lăm (-Is-), *n.* Union of the Mohammedan world ; conception of such a union ; ইসলাম জগতের সম্মিলন ; ঐরূপ সম্মিলনের কল্পনা। **—lam'-ic**, *adj.* Of, or relating to, this ; নিখিলমোসলেমীয়। **—ism**, *n.* Panislamic aspirations ; নিখিল মুসলমানজগতের আশা ও আকাঙ্ক্ষা।

păn-jăn'-drŭm, *n.* **1.** The mock title of a high personage ; হোমরা চোমরা লোক। **2.** A pompous or pretentious official ; ধুমধারাক্কাকারী রাজকর্ম্মচারী। **3.** A self-important personage ; দিক্‌পাল, দিগ্‌গজ।

păn-lō-gĭsm, *n.* The doctrine that the absolute or absolute reality is of the nature of thought or reason, applied esp. to Hegel's philosophy ; সেই পরমসত্তা বা নির্ব্বিশেষ সত্তা প্রজ্ঞা বা বিচারধর্ম্মাত্মক—এইরূপ দার্শনিক মতবাদ, বুদ্ধিসর্ব্বস্ববাদ (হিঃ কোঃ), চিৎসর্ব্বস্ববাদ (ঐ), চিদ্বাদ (ঐ)।

păn-mix-ī'-ă, *n.* Fortuitous interbreeding uninfluenced by selection; প্রাকৃতিক নির্ব্বাচন দ্বারা অপ্রভাবিত আকস্মিক সঙ্কর উৎপাদন, জাত্যন্তসঙ্কর (হিঃ কোঃ)। [এই শব্দটী Weismann কর্ত্তৃক ব্যবহৃত হইয়াছে। ইহার অর্থ এই যে—যে সকল অঙ্গপ্রত্যঙ্গ অকার্য্যকর বা অল্পব্যবহৃত হইয়াছে — তৎসম্পর্কে প্রাকৃতিকনির্ব্বাচন নিবৃত্তির ফলে পূর্ব্বপুরুষের সর্ব্বপ্রকার গুণ এবং আসক্তিসমূহের প্রকীর্ণভাবে পুনরুৎপাদন।]

păn'-nage (-āj), *n.* **1.** The feeding or the right of feeding swine in a wood or forest ; the charge for it ; বনে শূকর চরাণের বা চরাইবার অধিকার ; শূকর চরাইবার জন্য দেয় কর। **2.** The beech-mast, acorns, etc. as food for swine ; শূকরের খাদ্যস্বরূপ ওক বৃক্ষের ফল প্রভৃতি।

păn'-ni-ēr (-i-), *n.* **1.** A basket for a person's or beast's back usually carried in pairs ; ঝুড়ি, চুপড়ী, বিশেষতঃ যে সব ঝুড়ি জোড়া বাঁধিয়া বলদ বা গাধার পৃষ্ঠে চাপান হয়। **2.** A covered basket holding surgical instruments, medicines, etc. for ambulance ; ঔষধ রাখার ঝাঁপি, করণ্ড। **3.** A framework of whalebone etc. used by women to distend the skirt at the hips ; স্ত্রীলোকদিগের নিতম্বদেশের নিকটবর্ত্তী প্রদেশ স্ফীত করার জন্য তিমিমৎস্যের অস্থি প্রভৃতি দ্বারা প্রস্তুত কৌশলবিশিষ্ট কাঠাম।

păn'-ni-ēr (-i-), *n.* (*Colloq.*) A robed waiter in the Inner Temple ; (চলিত ভাষায়) ইনার টেম্পলের পরিচারক।

păn'-ni-kin (-i-), *n.* A small metal drinking vessel ; ধাতুনির্ম্মিত ক্ষুদ্রপানপাত্র।

păn'-ō-plȳ, *n.* A full suit of armour, (also *fig.*) ; বর্ম্ম, সাঁজোয়া, তনুত্রাণ, সর্ব্বাঙ্গকবচ। **—plied**, *adj.*

păn-ŏp'-ti-cŏn, *n.* A prison built circularly so that the guard at a central position can see all the prisoners ; বৃত্তাকার কারাগার।

păn-ō-rā'-mă, *n.* **1.** A painting of a complete scene, viewed from a central point or made continuous on an unrolling canvas, as if the spectators were passing the particular spot consecutively ; কোন মধ্য বিন্দু হইতে দৃষ্ট চতুর্দ্দিকে কোন দৃশ্যের সম্পূর্ণ চিত্র, অথবা আবর্ত্তনশীল বৃহৎ-চোঙ্গের উপর নিবদ্ধ দৃশ্যাবলী—যাহাতে স্পষ্ট প্রতিভাত হয় যে দ্রষ্টা ক্রমান্বয়ে ঐ সমস্ত দৃশ্যের স্থান অতিক্রম করিয়া চলিয়াছে, নিখিলদৃশ্য, মহাদৃশ্য, বিশ্বপট (হিঃ কোঃ), বিশ্বদৃশ্য, সর্ব্বতোদৃশ্য, সর্ব্বদিগ্দর্শকচিত্র (কেন্তিঃ)। [চলচ্চিত্রবীক্ষণযন্ত্রের প্রবর্ত্তনের

পূর্ব্বে বিশ্বদৃশ্যের প্রচলন ছিল। বিশ্বদৃশ্যের আবিষ্কর্তা আইরিশ চিত্রশিল্পী Robert Barkar ১৭৮৮ খৃঃ অব্দে এডিনবরা নগরের দৃশ্যাবলী যে ক্যান্বিসের চোঙ্গের উপর প্রদর্শন করেন তাহার ব্যাস ২৫ ফিট ছিল।] 2. An unobstructed view of a region in every direction, (often *fig.*); কোন স্থানের চতুর্দ্দিকস্থ দৃশ্যাবলীর অবারিত দৃশ্য, মহাদৃশ্য (হিঃ কোঃ)। **–ram'-ic,** *adj.* **–ram'-i-cal-ly,** *adv.*

păn'-pīpe, *n.* A kind of wind instrument; একপ্রকার সুষির যন্ত্র।

păn'-pneu'-măt-ĭsm (-nü-), *n.* The doctrine of Evon Hartmann designed to reconcile the panlogism of Hegel and the pan-thelism of Schopenhauer—being in effect that the world or noumenal reality is both unconscious will and unconscious thought; সৎ কিম্বা অসৎ, চিৎ কিম্বা অচিৎ উভয়েই বিসংজ্ঞ বিচার ও ইচ্ছাশক্তি (unconscious thought and will)—এইরূপ মতবাদ, চিদানন্দবাদ (হিঃ কোঃ)।

păn-psy'-chĭsm (-sī-), *n.* The theory that all nature is psychical or that every particle of matter is psychical; সমস্ত বিশ্বপ্রকৃতি অথবা প্রতি অণু চিদাত্মক—এইরূপ মতবাদ, সর্ব্বচেতনত্ববাদ, (হিঃ কোঃ), সর্ব্ব-চিদাত্মকত্ববাদ, সর্ব্বচিন্ময়ত্ববাদ।

păn-slăv'-ĭsm, *n.* Movement for political union of all Slavs; রাজনীতিক ঐক্য সাধনের জন্য নিখিল স্লেভ জাতির সম্মিলন।

păn'-sy̆, *n.* A garden variety of violet; heartsease; উদ্যানরোপিত একপ্রকার বনফ্‌সা; গুল্মবিশেষ।

pănt, *v. i., t.* & *n.* 1. To gasp for breath; কষ্টে শ্বাস ফেলা, হাঁপান, হাঁস ফাঁস করা। 2. To long or desire eagerly, (*for, after*, a thing); আকুল ভাবে আকাঙ্ক্ষা করা, আই ঢাই করা। 3. To throb violently; ধুক ধুক করা, দুরু দুরু করা। *Verb t.* To utter pantingly; হাঁপাইতে হাঁপাইতে বলা। *Noun.* A gasp or throb; ধুক্ ধুক, দুরু দুরু।

păn-tă-grü'-ĕl-ĭsm, *n.* A buffoonery or coarse humour like that of Pantagruel, a character in Rabelais; ভাঁড়ামি, গ্রাম্য পরিহাস। [সুপ্রসিদ্ধ ফরাসী গ্রন্থকার Rabelais কৃত Pantagruel নামক গ্রন্থের নায়কের নাম হইতে গৃহীত।]

păn-tă-lĕts', –lettes' (lĕts), *ns.* (*Pl.*) Loose drawers or trousers, cycling knickerbockers, etc. worn by women; স্ত্রীলোকদিগের পরার উপযোগী একপ্রকার ঢিলা পাজামা বা ইজার।

păn-tă-lōōn', *n.* 1. (*Cap.*) In the Italian comedy, a character wearing pantaloons; ইতালীদেশের মিলনান্ত নাট্যের পাজামা-পরা সং। 2. In modern pantomime, a clown's butt and abettor; বর্ত্তমান কালের সংদার যাত্রায় সংএর সহায়। 3. (*Pl.*) Trousers; পাজামা।

păn-tĕch'-nĭ-cŏn, *n.* (*Orig.* a name of a bazaar) A furniture warehouse; আসবাব সামগ্রীর গুদাম। **Pantechnicon van**—আসবাবসামগ্রী বহনোপযোগী যান।

păn'-thē-ĭsm, *n.* 1. The doctrine that God is everything and everything is God; সর্ব্বেশ্বরবাদ, "সর্ব্বংখল্বিদংব্রহ্ম"বাদ, সর্ব্বেশ্বরত্ববাদ, ঈশ্বরময়ত্ববাদ (হিঃ কোঃ), বিরাট-স্বরূপমত, অদ্বৈতবাদ, অভেদবাদ। 2. The heathen worship of all the gods; সর্ব্বদেবপূজা। **–ist,** *n.* **–is'-tic, –is'-ti-cal,** *adjs.*

păn'-thē-lĭsm, *n.* The doctrine that the noumenal reality of the universe or the absolute, is will, specifically the philosophy of Schopenhauer; ইচ্ছা বা আকাঙ্ক্ষাই বিশ্বপ্রকৃতির বা নির্ব্বিশেষসত্তার পরম-তত্ত্ব—এইরূপ মতবাদ, আনন্দবাদ (হিঃ কোঃ)।

păn-thē'-ŏn, păn'–, *n.* 1. A temple dedicated to all the gods, esp. (*cap.*) one at Rome; সর্ব্বদেব মন্দির, সর্ব্বদেবালয়, বিশেষতঃ রোমনগরীর

Pantheon.

সর্ব্বদেবমন্দির, [খৃষ্টীয় ১২৩ খৃঃ অব্দে সম্রাট Hadrian কর্ত্তৃক রোমনগরীতে এই মন্দির নির্ম্মিত হয়। এই দেবালয়টী খৃঃ ৭ম শতাব্দীতে খৃষ্টীয় ভজনালয়ে পরিণত হইয়াছিল। এই মন্দিরটী প্রাচীন রোমের স্থাপত্যশিল্পের উৎকৃষ্ট নিদর্শন-স্বরূপ অদ্যাপি বিরাজমান আছে।] 2. The aggregate deities of a people; কোন জাতির দেবসমাজ, দেবসভা (হিঃ কোঃ)। 3. A building where rest the illustrious dead or their memorials; যে গৃহে কোন জাতির খ্যাতনামা লোকদিগকে সমাহিত কিম্বা তাহাদের স্মৃতিরক্ষা করা হয়। 4. A building of public entertainment in London in 1772; লণ্ডননগরীর প্রমোদভবন-বিশেষ। **The British Pantheon**—ওয়েষ্টমিনিষ্টার গির্জ্জা।

păn'-thêr, *n.* A leopard; দ্বীপি, চিতাবাঘ, পুণ্ডরীক, চিত্রব্যাঘ্র।

păn'-tīle, *n.* A tile with a cross section like the letter S.; এক-প্রকার ঢেউতোলা টালি।

păn-ti-sŏc'-ră-cy̆, *n.* A community in which all are equal and all rule; যে সমাজে সকলেই সমান বলিয়া গণ্য হয় এবং সকলেই শাসন করিয়া থাকে, সর্ব্বতন্ত্র।

păn'-tō-grăph, *n.* An instrument for copying, enlarging, plans etc. on any scale; যন্ত্রবিশেষ—ইহার সাহায্যে যে কোনরূপ মাপের চিত্র, নক্সা,

প্রভৃতি অঙ্কিত করা যাইতে পারে, সর্ব্বাঙ্কক। **–graph′-ic,** *adj.*

păn-tŏl′-ŏ-ġy̆, *n.* Universal knowledge ; a work on universal knowledge ; a systematic view of all branches of human knowledge ; বিশ্বজনীনজ্ঞান ; সর্ব্বশাস্ত্রসংগ্রহ ; সর্ব্ববিদ্যাবিচার। **–to-log′-ic** *adj.* Of, or relating to, this knowledge ; বিশ্বজনীনজ্ঞানসম্বন্ধীয়।

păn′-tŏ-mime, *n., v. t. & i.* **1.** (*Hist.*) A Roman actor in a dumb show performance; (ইতিহাস) সং, ভাঁড়। **2.** A dumb show ; মূক-অভিনয়, মূকনাট্য (কেভিঃ)। ***Verb t.*** To express as something by dumb show ; কোন প্রকার কথাবার্ত্তা না বলিয়া কেবল অঙ্গভঙ্গী প্রভৃতি দ্বারা প্রকাশ করা। ***Verb i.*** To express oneself by dumb show ; মূক অভিনয় দ্বারা ব্যক্ত করা। **–mim′-ic,** *adj.* **–mim-ist,** *n.*

păn-tŏ-mŏr′-phic, *adj.* Taking or assuming all shapes ; কামরূপী, সর্ব্বরূপগ্রাহী।

păn-tŏ-prăg-măt′-ic, *adj. & n.* Meddling in everything ; সর্ব্ব বিষয়ে হস্তক্ষেপকারী। ***Noun.*** Such a person ; যে ব্যক্তি সমস্ত ব্যাপারে হস্তক্ষেপ করে।

păn-tŏ-scŏp′-ic, *adj.* Having a wide range of view or vision ; বিশালদৃষ্টিসম্পন্ন।

păn′-try̆, *n.* A room where bread or other provisions are kept ; রুটী প্রভৃতি খাদ্যদ্রব্য রাখার প্রকোষ্ঠ, খাদ্যকোষ্ঠক, ভাণ্ডারঘর, খাদ্যশালা। **Pantry-man**—ভাণ্ডারী অথবা তাহার সাহায্যকারী।

pănts, *n.* (*Pl.*) (*Vulg.*) Trousers ; also drawers ; (ইতরভাষায়) পাজামা ; একপ্রকার আঁট সাঁট ইজার।

păp, *n.* **1.** (*Archaic*) A nipple or teat of a woman's breast ; (অপ্রঃ) চুচুক, স্তনাগ্র, কুচাগ্র, স্তনমুখ, মাইয়ের বোঁটা। **2.** The corresponding part of a man ; পুরুষের স্তনাগ্র। **3.** Something resembling a pap in form ; স্তনাগ্রাকার বস্তু। **4.** (*Pl.*) A conical hill or peak ; "The great *paps* of Jura were hidden in the mist" ; স্তনাকৃতি শৈল বা গিরিচূড়া। [cf. স্তনাবিব দিশস্তস্যাঃ শৈলৌ মলয়দর্দ্দুরৌ—রঘুবংশ।]

păp, *n.* **1.** A soft food for infant or invalids ; শিশু বা রোগীদের জন্য কোমল খাদ্য। **2.** Pulp ; মণ্ড। **Pap′-py,** *adj.*

pă-pȧ′, *n.* Father, usually a child's word ; বাবা।

pā′-pă-cy̆, *n.* **1.** The office or jurisdiction of the pope ; the tenure of his office ; রোমান-ক্যাথলিক ধর্ম্মসম্রাটের পদ বা অধিকার ; রোমান ক্যাথলিক ধর্ম্মসম্রাটের পদের স্থিতিকাল। **2.** The popes collectively ; their succession ; রোমীয়ধর্ম্ম-সম্রাট্গণ; তাহাদের উত্তরাধিকার-পদ্ধতি।

pā′-păl, *adj.* Of, or relating to, the pope or his office ; পোপ সম্বন্ধীয়, পোপের পদসম্বন্ধীয়। **–ism,** *n.* **–ist,** *n.* **–ize,** *v. t. & i.* To make or become papal ; পোপসম্বন্ধীয় করা। **–ly,** *adv.*

pă-păv′-êr-ous (-ŭs), *adj.* Relating to, allied to, or resembling, the poppy ; পোস্ত বা আফিম গাছ সম্বন্ধীয়, উক্ত বৃক্ষবৎ, উক্ত বৃক্ষের সহিত সম্বন্ধবিশিষ্ট। **–a′-ceous,** *adj.*

Papaver somniferum — পোস্ত (বেলঃ)।

pă-paw′ (-pä), *n.* **1.** Same as PAPAYA. **2.** (*U. S.*) A North-American tree with oblong edible fruits ; its fruits ; উত্তর আমেরিকার ফলতরুবিশেষ ; উক্ত বৃক্ষের ফল।

pă-pȧ′-yȧ, *n.* A tropical tree of the genus carica ; its fruit ; পেঁপে গাছ ; পেঁপে, অমৃতা (আঃ বঃ)। [(Malay) *papa, bati* (Fr.) *papayer, papaye,* (Ital.) *papajo,* (Tam.) *pappali maram,* (Burmese) *thin-baw,* (Chinese) *Muh-kwa*].

pā′-pêr, *n.* **1.** A substance formed into thin sheets used for writing, printing, etc. ; কাগজ। **2.** Negotiable documents *e.g.,* bills of exchange ; হুণ্ডী, প্রমিসরিনোট, প্রভৃতি যে সকল কাগজপত্র পৃষ্ঠে সহি-করিয়া হস্তান্তরিত করা যায়। **3.** (Also *paper money*) Bank-notes etc. ; ব্যাঙ্ক নোট প্রভৃতি। **4.** Same as NEWSPAPER ; সংবাদপত্র, খবরের কাগজ, কাগজ। **5.** An essay, article, etc. especially one read before a learned society ; প্রবন্ধ, রচনা, বিশেষতঃ বিদ্বজ্জনসমাজে পঠিত রচনা বা প্রবন্ধ। **6.** (*Pl.*) Documents establishing a person's identity, position, etc. as, the *papers* of an envoy ; কাগজপত্র। **7.** A set of questions in an examination ; প্রশ্নমালা, প্রশ্নপত্র। **8.** (*Slang*) Free passes to a theatre etc. ; (ইতরভাষায়) রঙ্গালয়ে প্রবেশের জন্য বিনামূল্যেপ্রাপ্ত অনুমতিপত্র। **9.** A paper containing a definite quantity ; as, a *paper* of pins, opium, etc. ; পুরিয়া, পুটিকা (সাঃ পঃ)। **–y,** *adj.* **Paper-hanger**—যে ব্যক্তি কাগজ দ্বারা প্রাচীর প্রভৃতি মণ্ডিত করে। **Paper-hangings, Wall-paper**—প্রাচীর প্রভৃতি মণ্ডিত করার জন্য কাগজ। **Paper-knife**—কাগজকাটার ছুরী। **Paper-mill** — কাগজের কল। **Paper money**—ধনপত্র, টঙ্ক-পত্র, নোট, হুণ্ডী, প্রভৃতি। **Paper-profit** — কাগজপত্রে লাভ। **Paper-stainer**—যে ব্যক্তি কাগজ রঞ্জিত করে; যে ব্যক্তি দেওয়াল প্রভৃতিতে লাগাইবার উপযোগী কাগজ তৈয়ার করে। **Paper warfare** — পুস্তক বা সংবাদপত্রের সাহায্যে যুদ্ধ, লিপিযুদ্ধ, মসীযুদ্ধ। **Paper-weight**—কাগজ চাপা দেওয়ার জন্য প্রস্তর প্রভৃতির খণ্ড। **Waste paper**—বাজে কাগজ, ফাস কাগজ। **A paper lord** — (স্কটলণ্ডে) লর্ড উপাধিধারী বিচারক। **On paper**—কাগজপত্র দেখিয়া বিবেচনা করিলে,

অনুমানে। **To commit to paper**—কাগজে কলমে লিখিয়া রাখা। **To put pen to paper**—লিখিতে সুরু করা। **To send in one's papers**—পদত্যাগ করা।

pā'-pêr, *v. t.* **1.** To fold or enclose in paper; কাগজে মোড়া। **2.** To furnish or decorate as a wall etc. with paper-hangings; কাগজ দ্বারা দেওয়াল প্রভৃতি মোড়া। **3.** To supply with paper; কাগজ জোগান। **4.** (*Slang*) To give out free passes for, as a theatre; (ইতর ভাষায়) রঙ্গালয় প্রভৃতিতে প্রবেশের জন্য অর্থ গ্রহণ বিনা অনুমতিপত্র প্রদান করা।

pâ-pier'-ma-che' (-pyā-mâ-shā), *n.* A paper pulp which is moulded into various articles, *e. g.* boxes, trays, etc.; কাগজের মণ্ড—যাহা দ্বারা থলিয়া, বাক্স, খেলনা, প্রভৃতি প্রস্তুত করা হয়।

pă-pil-i-ō-nā'-ceous (-shŭs), *adj.* (*Bot.*) With corolla like a butterfly; (উদ্ভিদ-বিদ্যা) প্রজাপতিবৎ অন্তর্ব্বাসবিশিষ্ট।

pă-pil'-lă, *n.* (*Pl.* -LÆ) **1.** Any small protuberance like a nipple in any part or organ of the body; as, *papillae* of the tongue (জিহ্বাকণ্টক); শরীরের নানা স্থানে চুচুকাকৃতি উদ্গাত অংশ। **2.** (*Bot.*) A small projection on any part of a plant; বৃক্ষের যে কোন স্থানের ক্ষুদ্র উদ্গাত অংশ। **Pap'-il-la-ry, Pap'-il-late, Pap'-il-lose,** *adjs.*

pā'-pist, *n.* A Roman Catholic; an adherent of the Church of Rome—used disparagingly; রোমান ক্যাথলিক; রোমান ক্যাথলিক ধর্ম্মসংঘভুক্ত ব্যক্তি। **—pis'-tic, —pis'-ti-cal,** *adjs.* **—pis'-ti-cal-ly,** *adv.* **—ry,** *n.* Same as POPERY.

pă-poose' (pōōs), *n.* (*Bot.*) A North-American-Indian young child; উত্তর আমেরিকার আদিম অধিবাসিগণের শিশু।

păp'-pus (-ŭs), *n.* A downy substance on seeds of thistles etc.;

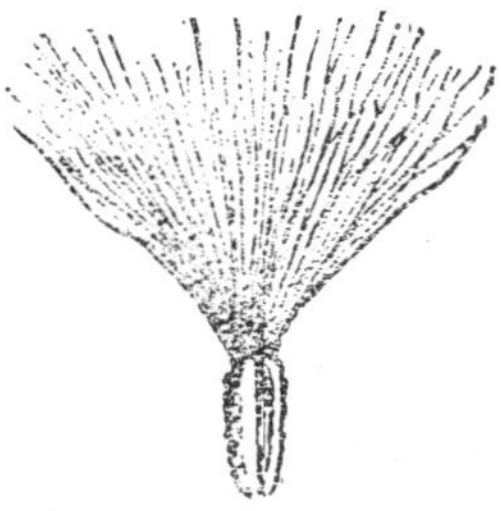

Pappus.

শিয়াল-কাঁটা প্রভৃতির বীজের উপরিস্থ তুলাবৎ পদার্থ, কোমল লোম (সাঃ পঃ), কুণ্ডলোম (ঐ)। **—pose',** *adj.*

păp'-ū-lă, —lē, *ns.* (*Pl.* -LÆ, -LES.) **1.** A pimple; ব্রণ। **2.** (*Bot.*) Same as PAPILLA. **—lar, —lose, —lous,** *adjs.*

păp-ŷ-rā'-ceous (-shŭs), *adj.* (*Nat. hist.*) Of the nature of paper; papery; thin as paper; কাগজের ধরণের; কাগজবৎ; কাগজের মত পাতলা।

pă-pȳ'-rō-grăph, *n.* A device for copying writings etc. by means of paper-stencil; হস্তলিখিত লিপি প্রভৃতির প্রতিলিপিকারকযন্ত্র। **Pap-y-rog'-ra-phy, —type,** *ns.*

pă-pȳ'-rŭs, *n.* **1.** A tall sedge; মিসর দেশীয় বিলজ তৃণ-বিশেষ। **2.** A writing material prepared by ancient Egyptians from the stems of these plants; ঐ তৃণের ডগা হইতে প্রাচীন মিসরবাসিগণ কর্ত্তৃক প্রস্তুত একপ্রকার কাগজ। **3.** A writing on this; (*pl.*) written scrolls made of papyrus; ঐ কাগজের উপর লিপি; (বহুবচনে) ঐরূপ কাগজের তাড়া।

Papyrus.

pâr, *n.* **1.** Equality; সাম্য, সমতা, তুল্যতা। **2.** An amount, condition or degree taken as an average or mean; as, on a *par*: above or below *par*; গড়, মধ্যসংখ্যা। **3.** Equality of the nominal and market values of stocks, shares, bonds, etc.; কোম্পানীর কাগজ, অংশ প্রভৃতির নামতঃ মূল্য ও বাজার মূল্যের মধ্যে সমতা। **Above par**—কোম্পানীর কাগজ প্রভৃতির লিখিত মূল্যের চেয়ে অধিকতর মূল্যে; সাধারণ মাত্রা, পরিমাণ বা অবস্থার উপরে। **At par**—লিখিত মূল্যে। **Below par**—কোম্পানীর কাগজ প্রভৃতির লিখিত মূল্য অপেক্ষা অল্প মূল্যে; সাধারণ মাত্রা, পরিমাণ বা অবস্থার নিম্নে। **On a par**—On an average; গড়ে, গড়পড়তায়। On an equality or equal footing (*with*); তুল্যাবস্থায়, তুল্য পদবীতে। **Par of exchange**—এক দেশের মুদ্রাতে অপর দেশের মুদ্রার স্বীকৃত মূল্য।

pâr, *n.* (*Colloq.*) Paragraph; (চলিত ভাষায়) প্রকরণ।

pă-răb'-ă-sis, *n.* (*Pl.* -SES.) (*In Gk. Comedy*) A part sung by the chorus, addressed to the audience in the poet's name; (গ্রীক মিলনান্ত নাটক) বৃন্দগায়কগণ কর্ত্তৃক গেয় অংশ—যাহা কবির নামে শ্রোতৃবৃন্দকে সম্বোধন করিয়া গীত হয়।

păr'-ă-ble (-bl), *n.* **1.** A fable or allegorical narrative; কথা, রূপককথা, রূপকাখ্যান, উপদেশার্থক বাক্য, দৃষ্টান্ত। **2.** An allegory; রূপক। **3.** (*Archaic*) An enigmatical saying; (অপ্রঃ) অস্পষ্টার্থ উক্তি। **To take up one's parable**—(অপ্রঃ) কোন বিষয়ে আলোচনা আরম্ভ করা।

pă-răb'-ō-lă, *n.* A conic section arising from cutting a cone by a plane parallel to its side; সমান্তরক্ষেত্র, অনুবৃত্ত, পরবলয় (হিঃ কোঃ), সমক্ষেত্র (সাঃ পঃ)।

păr-ă-bŏl′-ic, –i-căl, *adjs.* **1.** Of, relating to, or expressed in, a parable; রূপকাখ্যান সম্বন্ধীয়। **2.** Of, or relating to, or like, a parabola; পরবলয়সংক্রান্ত, পরবলয়স্বরূপ, পরবলীয় (হিঃ কোঃ)। **–i-cal-ly,** *adv.* With parable or allegory; রূপকচ্ছলে, রূপকাখ্যানচ্ছলে।

pă-răb′-ŏ-loid (-lōyd) *n.* A solid, esp. one generated by the revolution of a parabola on its axis, whose plane sections are parabolas; ঘনপরবলয়, পরবলয়াভাস (হিঃ কোঃ)।

păr-ăch′-rŏ-nĭsm, *n.* An error in chronology; কালগণনায় ভ্রম।

păr′-ă-chute (-shôt), *n.* **1.** A contrivance in the form of an umbrella for descending from a height, esp. from a balloon; আকাশ,

Parachute.

ব্যোমযান কিম্বা অন্য কোনরূপ উচ্চ স্থান হইতে অবতরণের জন্য একপ্রকার ছত্রাকার যন্ত্র, অবতরণছত্র। **2.** A natural or artificial device serving this purpose, *e.g.* the expansible fold of skin in the flying-squirrel, etc.; উচ্চ স্থান হইতে ভূমিতে অবতরণের জন্য নৈসর্গিক বা কৃত্রিম উপায়। **–chut-ism, –chut-ist,** *ns.*

păr′-ă-clete (-klēt), *n.* **1.** An advocate; সমর্থক। **2.** (*Cap.*) A consoler or comforter [a term applied to the Holy Spirit, (*John* xiv. 16,26 etc.)]; সান্ত্বনাদাতা।

pă-rāde′, *n.* **1.** Ostentatious display, আড়ম্বর, সমারোহ। **2.** A military display; সৈন্যগণের কুচকাওয়াজ, সৈন্যযাত্রা। **3.** The place for military parade; সৈন্যগণের কুচকাওয়াজের স্থান। **4.** A public walk, square or promenade; ভ্রমণবীথিকা, নগরোদ্যান, সাধারণের ভ্রমণ স্থান।

pă-rāde′ *v. t.* & *i.* **1.** To assemble as troops etc. for parade; কুচকাওয়াজের জন্য সৈন্য জড় করা। **2.** To march through (a street etc.) with display; মহাসমারোহের সহিত রাজপথ দিয়া যাত্রা করা। **3.** To show off; জাঁক দেখান, আড়ম্বর প্রদর্শন করা। **4.** To march (a person) for show or to expose him to contempt; "...*Paraded* him about the city"; অবজ্ঞাভাজন করার জন্য জনসাধারণের সমক্ষে (কোন ব্যক্তিকে) প্রদর্শন করা। *Verb i.* **1.** To assemble or march as in review; সৈন্যপ্রদর্শনীতে মিলিত হওয়া বা যাত্রা করা। **2.** To behave, talk or write, ostentatiously; জাঁক দেখান, বাগাড়ম্বরপূর্ণ ভাষায় বলা বা লিখা। **To make a parade of one's virtues**—নিজের গুণপনা জাহির করা।

păr′-ă-digm (-dĭm), *n.* **1.** An example; model; দৃষ্টান্ত; আদর্শ। **2.** (*Gram.*) A model of inflection; রূপাদর্শ (আঃ বঃ), ধাতুরূপমালিকা। **–dig-mat′-ic,** *adj.* **Paradigm of verb**—ধাতুরূপাদর্শ।

păr′-ă-dīse, *n.* **1.** (Also *earthly paradise*) The garden of Eden where Adam and Eve were placed; ইডেন উদ্যান, (cf. নন্দন কানন)। **2.** Heaven; স্বর্গ, অমরাবতী, ত্রিদিব, অমৃতলোক, সুরপুরী, সুরলোক, দেবলোক, [also আনন্দলোক, অমরলোক, অমরাবতী, সুখভুবন, সুখধাম, নাক, অপরলোক, পুণ্যলোক, ত্রিদশালয়, সুরবর্ত্ম, ত্রিপিষ্টপ, শাশ্বত, উর্দ্ধলোক, সুখাবতী (বৌদ্ধ), আনন্দভুবন, সুখলোক।] **3.** A place of supreme bliss; a state of happiness; আনন্দধাম; সুখময় অবস্থা। **4.** A pleasure garden; a park where foreign animals or birds are kept; প্রমোদকানন, প্রমোদোদ্যান; যে নগরোদ্যানে বৈদেশিক পশুপক্ষী রক্ষিত হইয়া থাকে। **–di-sa′-ic, –dis′-e-an, –dis′-i-ac, –dis′-i-al, –dis′-i-an, –di-sa′-i-cal, –di-si′-a-cal,** *adjs.* **Paradise fly-catcher** — শা-বুলবুল (যোঃ)

Golden bird of Paradise.

Bird of paradise — See under BIRD. **Fool's paradise** — See under FOOL.

păr′-ă-dŏs, *n.* An elevation of earth behind a fortification to secure it from sudden attack rearward; প্রাকারপরিখাদির পশ্চাদ্দিকস্থ উচ্চ ভূমি।

păr′-ă-dŏx, *n.* **1.** A proposition contrary to received opinion; লোকবিরুদ্ধ বাক্য। **2.** An apparently absurd statement though it may be really true; দৃষ্টতঃ অসম্ভব অথবা স্ববিরোধী উক্তি—কিন্তু যাহা বাস্তবিক পক্ষে সত্য হইতে পারে, বিরোধাভাস (হিঃ কোঃ), কূট (ঐ)। **3.** A statement actually contradictory or false; স্ববিরোধী উক্তি। **4.** A person or thing conflicting with preconceived notions of what is reasonable or possible; যাহা যুক্তিযুক্ত ও সম্ভাবনীয় বলিয়া পূর্ব্ব হইতে গৃহীত তাহার বিরোধী ব্যক্তি বা বস্তু। **–dox′-i-cal,** *adj.* **–dox′-i-cal-ly,** *adv.* **–er, –i-cal′-i-ty, –ist, –y,** *ns.*

păr-ă-dŏx′-ure (-ür), *n.* A palm-civet; একপ্রকার গন্ধগোকুলা।

păr′-af-fĭn (-ă-), *n.* & *v. t.* **1.** A fatty substance got by dry distillation from wood, coal, petroleum, etc. and used for making candles etc. ; কাঠ, পাথুরিয়াকয়লা প্রভৃতি হইতে প্রাপ্ত—বর্ণ, স্বাদ ও গন্ধবিহীন রাসায়নিক পদার্থ-বিশেষ—ইহা হইতে মোমবাতি প্রভৃতি প্রস্তুত করা হয়, পেরেফিন। 2. (Also *paraffin oil*) Oil thus obtained and used as an illuminant or lubricant ; মেটেতৈল। ***Verb t.*** To cover, impregnate or treat, with paraffin ; পেরেফিন দ্বারা মাখা। **Paraffin oil** — See PARAFFIN *n.* 2.

păr-ă-gō′-ge (-ji), *n.* The addition of a letter or syllable to the end of a word ; শব্দের অন্তে অক্ষর বা শব্দাংশ সংযোগ। **—gog′-ic,** *adj.*

păr′-ă-gŏn, *n.* & *v. t.* 1. A model or type of excellence or perfection ; দৃষ্টান্ত, আদর্শ। 2. A supremely excellent person or thing ; "A *paragon* of a wife"; "The *paragon* of easy chair"; আদর্শস্থানীয় ব্যক্তি বা বস্তু, অনুপম বস্তু, নিরুপম বস্তু। 3. A perfect diamond of 100 carats or more ; ১০০ ক্যারাট বা তদূর্দ্ধ ওজনের সর্ব্বাঙ্গসুন্দর হীরক। ***Verb t.*** 1. (*Poet.*) To compare with ; (কবিতায়) তুলনা করা। 2. (*Poet.*) To match ; (কবিতায়) অনুরূপ হওয়া। **Paragon of beauty**—রূপের ডালি, সৌন্দর্য্যের আদর্শ, সুন্দরীশিরোমণি, সুন্দরীপ্রধান, ডানাকাটা পরী, অলোকসামান্যা রূপসী নারী, লাবণ্যলক্ষ্মী (কথাঃ সঃ)।

păr′-ă-grăph, *n.* & *v. t.* 1. A distinct section of a writing etc. ; অনুচ্ছেদ। 2. The character or symbol (¶) used as a reference etc. ; এইরূপ (¶) চিহ্ন। 3. A detached item of news etc. in a newspaper with a heading ; সংবাদপত্রের ক্ষুদ্র প্রবন্ধ। ***Verb t.*** 1. To write a paragraph about ; কোন বিষয়ে ক্ষুদ্র প্রবন্ধ লিখা। 2. To divide into paragraphs ; অনুচ্ছেদে অনুচ্ছেদে বিভক্ত করা। **—er,** *n.* A writer of paragraphs, esp. in a newspaper ; সংবাদপত্রের ক্ষুদ্র প্রবন্ধলেখক। **—graph′-ic,** *adj.* **—graph′-i-cal-ly,** *adv.* **—graph-y,** *n.* Writing of newspaper paragraphs ; such paragraphs collectively ; সংবাদপত্রের ক্ষুদ্র প্রবন্ধ লিখন ; উক্তরূপ প্রবন্ধসমূহ। **—ist,** *n.*

păr′-ă-guay (-gwā), *n.* 1. (*Cap.*) A country or a river of South America ; দক্ষিণ-আমেরিকার প্রদেশ বা নদী বিশেষ। 2. The shrub called mate ; একপ্রকার গুল্ম।

păr-ă-hē-li-ŏt′-rō-pism, *n.* The tendency in plants to turn leaves in a plane parallel to the sun's rays to avoid excessive light ; অতিরিক্ত আলোকপরিহারের জন্য বৃক্ষপত্রের পক্ষে সূর্য্যরশ্মির সহিত সমান্তরাল-ধরাতলে আবর্ত্তনে উন্মুখতা, প্রাস্তন, সূর্য্যোন্মুখতা (সাঃ পঃ)।

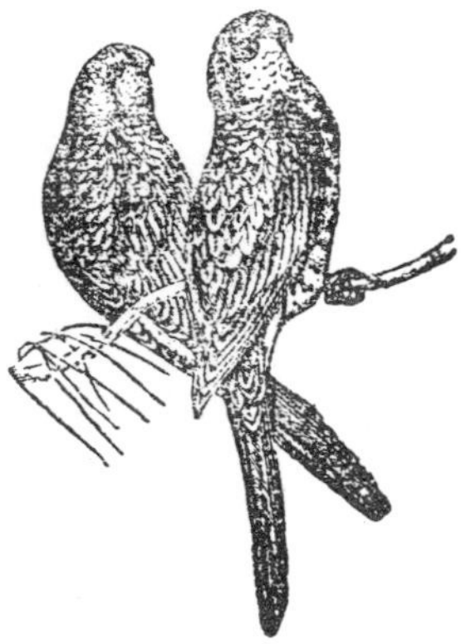

Parakeets.

păr′-ă-keet (-kēt), **—ō-quet** (-kĕt-), *ns.* A small bird of the parrot kind, esp. with a long tail ; টিয়া।

păr′-ă-kite, *n.* 1. A kite acting like a parachute ; একপ্রকার ঘুড়ী যাহার সাহায্যে উচ্চ স্থান হইতে ভূমিতে অবতরণ করা যায়। 2. A kind of tailless kite for scientific purposes ; বৈজ্ঞানিক অনুসন্ধানের জন্য একপ্রকার লাঙ্গুলহীন ঘুড়ী।

păr-ă-lip′-sis, —leip (-līp-), *ns.* (*Rhet.*) A figure in which a speaker affects to pass over what he is really calling attention to ; একপ্রকার অলঙ্কার—যাহাতে বক্তা বক্তব্য বিষয় উপেক্ষা করিয়া যাইতেছে বলিয়া ভাণ করে, আক্ষেপ (কাব্যাদর্শ Quoted by Mr. A. Barooah.)

păr′-ăl-lăx, *n.* 1. Apparent change in the position of an object due to a change in the position of the observer ; দ্রষ্টার অবস্থান পরিবর্ত্তন হেতু কোন পদার্থের স্ফুট পরিবর্ত্তন। 2. Angular amount of this apparent change : ঐরূপ স্ফুট পরিবর্ত্তনের কৌণিক পরিমাণ। 3. (*Astron.*) The difference in the position of a heavenly body as seen from the earth's surface and from the centre of the earth or the sun ; (জ্যোতির্বিজ্ঞান) ভূপৃষ্ঠ হইতে দৃষ্ট এবং পৃথিবী বা সূর্য্যের কেন্দ্র হইতে দৃষ্ট জ্যোতিষ্কের অবস্থানবিভেদ, লম্বন (সূঃ সিঃ), গমন (সূঃ সিঃ)। **—lac′-tic,** *adj.* **Annual parallax** — বার্ষিকলম্বন (হিঃ কোঃ)। **Binocular parallax**—যুগ্মদৃশ্য লম্বন (হিঃ কোঃ)। **Diurnal parallax**—ভূকেন্দ্রক লম্বন (হিঃ কোঃ)। **Geocentric parallax** — ভূকেন্দ্রক লম্বন (হিঃ কোঃ)। **Heliocentric parallax**—রবিকেন্দ্রকলম্বন (হিঃ কোঃ)। **Horizontal parallax** — পরমদৃগ্‌-লম্বন (হিঃ কোঃ)। **Optical parallax**—দৃষ্টিলম্বন (হিঃ কোঃ)। **Polar parallax**—সূর্য্যলম্বন (হিঃ কোঃ)। **Stellar parallax** — নক্ষত্রলম্বন (হিঃ কোঃ)। **Effect of the annual parallax** — স্থানীয়ান্তর কোণ বা বার্ষিক লম্বন। **Effect of the annual parallax in latitude**—বিক্ষেপের লম্বন, অবনতি, নতি। **Effect of the annual parallax in longitude**—ভুজাংশের লম্বন, লম্বন। **Parallax in altitude**—দৃঙ্‌মণ্ডল

লম্বন (সাঃ পঃ), দৃগ্‌লম্বন (ঐ)। **Parallax in latitude**—নতি (সূঃ সিঃ—টীকা), অবনতি (সাঃ পঃ)। **Parallax in longitude**—স্পর্শলম্বন (সাঃ পঃ)।

păr′-al-lĕl (-ă-), *adj.* & *n.* 1. Continuously equidistant as lines etc. ; সমান্তরাল, সমান্তর (হিঃ কোঃ)। 2. (*Fig.*) Similar in essential parts ; precisely analogous or corresponding ; as, a *parallel* case, passage, etc. ; (লক্ষণায়) প্রধান প্রধান অংশে সদৃশ; ঠিক অনুরূপ বা সদৃশ। ***Noun.*** 1. A parallel line, curve or surface ; সমান্তরাল রেখা, বক্র বা ধরাতল। 2. (Also *parallel of latitude*) Each of the circles on the earth's surface in map etc. parallel to the equator ; অক্ষবৃত্ত, সমান্তরাল। 3. A person or thing precisely analogous to another ; a counterpart ; অনুরূপ ব্যক্তি বা বস্তু ; অনুরূপ অংশ। 4. A trench in front of a fortified place, parallel to the defences ; প্রাকারাদি সুরক্ষিত স্থানের সম্মুখস্থ পরিখা। 5. Parallel position ; as, two lines in *parallel* ; সমান্তরাল অবস্থান। 6. (*Fig.*) Resemblance, analogy or correspondenc ; (লক্ষণায়) সাদৃশ্য, আনুরূপ্য, অনুরূপতা। 7. Comparison ; as, to draw a *parallel* between two things ; তুলনা। 8. A symbol composed of two parallel lines (‖) used as a reference mark ; সমান্তরাল রেখাদ্বয়-বিশিষ্ট চিহ্ন। **Parallel bars**—ব্যায়ামের জন্য খোঁটার উপর স্থাপিত সমান্তরাল দণ্ডদ্বয়। **Parallel passage**—অনুরূপ রচনা। **Parallel ruler**—সমান্তরাল রেখাকর্ষক যন্ত্র, সমরেখাকর্ষক। **Parallel of latitude**—See PARALLEL, *n.* 2. **To draw a parallel between**—To compare ; তুলনা করা।

păr′-al-lĕl (-ă-), *v. t.* 1. To compare or liken ; তুলনা করা। 2. To find or furnish something parallel or corresponding to ; "I cannot *parallel* these facts in Homer" ; অনুরূপ বা সমতুল্য কোন কিছু প্রাপ্ত হওয়া বা প্রদান করা। 3. To be equal to ; to correspond to ; সমান হওয়া ; অনুরূপ হওয়া।

păr-al-lĕl-ĕ-pĭ′-pĕd (-ă-), *n.* A solid contained by parallelograms ; দ্বাদশাস্রঘন (সাঃ পঃ), সমানান্তরখাত (হিঃ কোঃ)।

păr′-al-lĕl-ĭsm (-ă-), *n.* 1. State of being parallel, (*lit.* & *fig.*) ; (শব্দানুযায়ী ও লক্ষণায়) সমান্তরতা। 2. Comparison or correspondence of successive passages, esp. in Hebrew poetry ; পুস্তকের ক্রমিক অংশ সমূহের মধ্যে তুলনা বা সঙ্গতি, বিশেষতঃ হিব্রু কবিতায়।

păr-al-lĕl′-ŏ-grăm (-ă-), *n.* A quadrilateral whose opposite sides are parallel and equal ; যে চতুর্ভুজ ক্ষেত্রের বিপরীত পার্শ্বসমূহ সমান্তরাল, সমানান্তর চতুর্ভুজ (হিঃ কোঃ), সমান্তরিক ক্ষেত্র, আয়ত-চতুর্ভুজ (কেন্তিঃ)। **Parallelogram of forces**—যদি কোন কণিকার উপর ক্রিয়াশীল বলদ্বয় পরিমাণ এবং দিক্‌সম্পর্কে ঐ কণিকা হইতে অঙ্কিত রেখাদ্বয় দ্বারা প্রদর্শিত হয় এবং ঐ রেখাদ্বয়কে আসন্নভুজ (adjacent sides) করিয়া কোন একটী সমানান্তর চতুর্ভুজ অঙ্কিত করা হইলে ঐ বলদ্বয়ের বলজ বা যোগোদ্ভূতশক্তি (resultant) পরিমাণ এবং দিক্‌সম্পর্কে ঐ সমানান্তর চতুর্ভুজের উক্ত কণিকাভেদকারী কর্ণদ্বয় (diagonal) দ্বারা প্রদর্শিত হইয়া থাকে ; উপরিউক্ত শক্তিসূচক সমানান্তরক্ষেত্র, বলসমান্তর চতুর্ভুজ (হিঃ কোঃ)।

pă-răl′-ŏ-gĭsm, *n.* 1. A false or illogical reasoing ; মিথ্যা যুক্তি, ন্যায়বিরুদ্ধ যুক্তি, অপসিদ্ধান্ত। 2. A formal fallacy ; আভাস, হেত্বাভাস, হৈতুভ্রম (হিঃ কোঃ)। **—gize**, *v. i.* To reason or draw a conclusion falsely ; ভ্রমাত্মক যুক্তি প্রদান করা, অপসিদ্ধান্ত করা।

păr′-ă-lȳse, *v. t.* 1. To affect with paralysis ; অসাড় করা, আড়ষ্ট করা, অবশ করা। 2. (*Fig.*) To render powerless or ineffective ; (লক্ষণায়) অকার্য্যকর করা, পঙ্গু করা, বিকল করা, স্তম্ভিত করা, জড়ীভূত করা, ব্যর্থ করা। **—ly-sa′-tion**, *n.*

pă-răl′-ȳ-sis, *n.* 1. Total or partial loss of the motor or sensory function of nerves in a part of the body ; পক্ষাঘাত রোগ, অর্দ্ধাঙ্গবাত, অবশাঙ্গতা, অর্দ্ধাঙ্গ (হিঃ কোঃ), অপপ্লথন (ঐ)। 2. (*Fig.*) A condition of utter powerlessness ; (লক্ষণায়) অক্ষমতা, অসাড়তা, স্তব্ধতা, স্তম্ভ, স্তম্ভন, বিকলতা।

pă-ră-lȳt′-ic, *adj.* & *n.* Affected with paralysis, (*lit.* & *fig.*) ; (শব্দানুযায়ী ও লক্ষণায়) পক্ষাঘাতগ্রস্ত। ***Noun.*** Such a person, (*lit.* & *fig.*) ; (শব্দানুযায়ী ও লক্ষণায়) পক্ষাঘাতগ্রস্ত ব্যক্তি, অবশাঙ্গ ব্যক্তি। **—i-cal-ly**, *adv.*

păr-ă-măg-nĕt′-ic, *adj.* Capable of being attracted by the poles of a magnet ; চুম্বকের ধ্রুব দ্বারা আকর্ষণ-যোগ্য। **—mag′-net-ism**, *n.*

păr-ă-măt′-ta, *n.* A fabric of wool and cotton or silk, (form the name of a town in N. S. Wales) ; পশম এবং কার্পাস বা রেশমের সূত্র হইতে প্রস্তুত বস্ত্রবিশেষ, প্যারেম্যাটা।

pă-răm′-ĕ-têr, *n.* 1. (*Math.*) The constant quantity which enters into the equation of a curve or surface ; (গণিতশাস্ত্র) কোন বক্র বা ধরাতলের সমীকরণে যে নিত্যসংখ্যার প্রয়োজন হয়, পরমিতি (হিঃ কোঃ)। 2. (*Conics*) The focal chord at right angles to the axis in each of the three conic sections ; নাভিগতপূর্ণজ্যা।

pâ′-râ-mō, *n.* (*Pl.* -MOS.) A high bleak plateau or tract on the Andes ; আন্দিজ পর্ব্বতের তরুগুল্মহীন উচ্চ অধিত্যকা।

păr′-ă-mount (-mownt), *adj.* 1. Supreme ; pre-eminent ; as, of *paramount* importance ; প্রধান,

cat, çell, chair, chord ; go, ġem ; sin, iș ; thing, that ; citȳ, bȳ ; ph = f ; qu = kw ; sion, tion = shŭn.

একচ্ছত্র, সার্ব্বভৌম, সর্ব্বেশ্বর, সর্ব্বেশ, সর্ব্বস্বামী ; সর্ব্বশ্রেষ্ঠ, সর্ব্বপ্রধান। **2.** Superior (to) ; শ্রেষ্ঠতর। **—cy,** *n.* The state of being paramount ; একাধিপত্য, একচ্ছত্রশাসন। **—ly,** *adv.* **Paramount sovereign**—সার্ব্বভৌম সম্রাট, একচ্ছত্র অধিপতি, পরমভট্টারক (শিলালিপি)।

păr′-ă-mour (-môr), *n.* An illicit lover of a married man or woman; জার, উপপতি, পাপপতি (অঃ), রমণ, নারীতরঙ্গক, জারিণী, উপস্ত্রী, উপপত্নী।

pă′-răng, *n.* The heavy knife of the Malayas; মালয় উপদ্বীপবাসীদিগের ভোজালী।

păr-ă-noi′-ă (-noy̆-), **—nœ′-ă** (-nē-), *ns.* Mental derangement esp. when marked by delusions of grandeur etc.; বুদ্ধ্যুন্মাদ (হিঃ কোঃ), অপবুদ্ধিতা (ঐ), মানসিক বিকৃতি।

păr′-ă-pĕt, *n.* **1.** A low wall or barrier esp. one at the edge of a balcony, roof, etc. or along the sides of a bridge etc. ; অনুচ্চ বৃতি বা প্রাচীর। **2.** (*Mil.*) An elevation for covering soldiers from an enemy's shot ; (সামরিক-শাস্ত্র) শত্রু-সৈন্যের গোলাবৃষ্টি হইতে সৈন্যগণের আত্মরক্ষার্থ মৃত্তিকা বা প্রস্তররচিত প্রাকার। **—ed,** *adj.*

pă-ră-pĕt′-ăl-ous (-ŭs), *n.* (*Bot.*) Growing on each side of a petal ; (উদ্ভিদ্ বিদ্যা) দলের উভয় পার্শ্বে বর্দ্ধনশীল, দলপার্শ্বিক (সাঃ পঃ)।

păr′-ăph *n.* A flourish at the end of a signature esp. as a precaution against forgery ; নাম স্বাক্ষরের অন্তে যে টান দেওয়া হয়, বিশেষতঃ যাহাতে জাল না হয় তজ্জন্য যে টান দেওয়া হয়।

păr-ă-phêr-nā′-lĭ-ă, *n.* (*Pl.*) **1.** Apparatus ; articles of equipment ; as, the *paraphernalia* of a circus ; যন্ত্র, সামগ্রী ; উপকরণ, সাজসজ্জা। **2.** Personal belongings ; নিজের জিনিষ পত্র, লওয়াজিমা। **3** (*Law*) Articles of personal property that law allowed married women to keep and treat as her own ; বিবাহিতা নারীর ব্যক্তিগত বসনভূষণ প্রভৃতি, যৌতুক, পরিণাহ্য, স্ত্রীধন [স্মৃতিশাস্ত্রানুসারে স্ত্রীধন ছয় প্রকার—(১) অধ্যগ্নিক (*Property given to the wife at the wedding*). (২) অধ্যাবাহনিক (*That part of a wife's property which she receives when led in procession from her father's to her husband's house*). (৩) আধিবেদনিক (*Property given to first wife upon marrying a second*). (৪) প্রীতিদত্ত, also লাবণ্যার্জ্জিত (*Property given to a female by her relatives esp. by her father-in-law or mother-in-law*). (৫) শুল্ক (*Present given by the bride-groom to the bride*). (৬) অন্বাধেয় (*Property presented to the wife after marriage by her family etc.*)].

păr-ă-phĭ-mō′-sĭs, *n.* Strangulation of the glans penis by constriction of the prepuce ; যে রোগে লিঙ্গাবরক চর্ম্মদ্বারা লিঙ্গমুণ্ড আবৃত হয় না, অবপাটিকা (হঃ চঃ), উল্টামুদা (জাহিঃ)।

păr′-ă-phrāse, *n.* & *v. t.* **1.** An explanation of a text or passage in fuller and clearer terms ; expression of its sense in other words ; সংক্ষিপ্ত বাক্যান্তর ; অন্বয় মুখে ব্যাখ্যা। **2.** (*Scot. Church*) Each of the hymns contained in the paraphrases in verse of the passages of the Scripture ; (স্কটলণ্ডদেশীয় ধর্ম্মসংঘ) বাইবেলের স্তোত্র। ***Verb t.*** To give the meaning of in other words ; to express or translate freely ; মূল বাক্য বিস্তার-পূর্ব্বক ব্যাখ্যা করা, অন্বয়মুখে ব্যাখ্যা করা ; সংক্ষিপ্ত বাক্যান্তর করা, মর্ম্মানুবাদ করা। **—phras′-tic,** *adj.* **—phras′-ti-cal-ly,** *adv.*

pă-răph′-y̆-sĭs, *n.* A slender sterile filament in many cryptogamic plants ; নানাপ্রকার অপুষ্পক বৃক্ষের বন্ধ্যকেশর, বন্ধ্যতন্তু (সাঃ পঃ)।

păr-ă-plē′-gĭ-ă, **păr′-ă-plē-gy̆,** *ns.* Paralysis confined to the lower parts of the body , শরীরের নিম্নার্দ্ধের পক্ষাঘাত, উরুস্তম্ভ। **—pleg′-ic,** *adj.*

păr′-ă-săng, *n.* A Persian measure of length about $3\frac{1}{4}$ miles ; পারস্যদেশীয় দৈর্ঘ্যের পরিমাপ বিশেষ (প্রায় ৩¼ মাইল)।

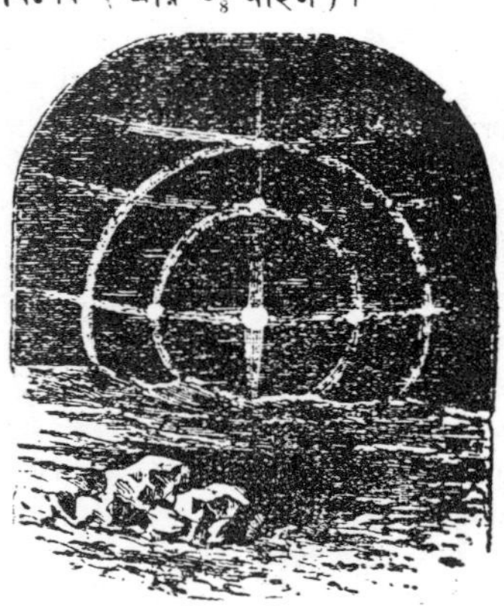

Paraselene.

păr-ă-sē-lē′-nē, *n.* A mock-moon ; মিথ্যাচন্দ্র, পরিবেষ (হিঃ কোঃ), প্রতিচন্দ্র।

păr′-ă-sīte, *n.* **1.** A hanger-on ; a sycophant ; পরজীবী, পরের গলগ্রহ ব্যক্তি, পরপিণ্ডাদ, পরসন্তোপজীবী (হিঃ কোঃ), পরভাগ্যোপজীবী, পরান্নভোজী ; মোসাহেব, চাটুকার, পীঠমর্দ্দ, খোসামুদে, তোষামোদকারী। **2.** An animal or plant living in or upon another ; পরপুষ্টজীবী, পরান্তঃপুষ্টজীব, পরাঙ্গপুষ্টজীব, পরগাছা, বৃক্ষরুহ। **3.** A plant climbing about another plant, a wall, etc. ; পরবৃক্ষজীবী, পরবৃক্ষাশ্রয়ী (সাঃ পঃ), আকাশবল্লী, বৃক্ষরুহা। **—sit′-ic, —sit′-i-cal,** *adjs.* **—sit-ism,** *n.* **—si-tol′-o-gy,** *n.* Study of parasites ; পরবৃক্ষাশ্রয়ী শাস্ত্র।

păr-ă-sĭt′-ĭ-cīde, *n.* An agent destroying parasites ; পরান্তঃপুষ্টজীবধ্বংসকারী।

păr′-ă-sit-ize, *v. t.* (*Biol.*) To infest as a parasite ; (জীববিজ্ঞান) পরান্তঃপুষ্টজীব দ্বারা পূর্ণ করা ।

păr′-ă-sŏl, *n.* A small umbrella or sunshade used usually by ladies ; স্ত্রীলোকদিগের ক্ষুদ্র আতপত্র, ছত্র, ছত্রিকা ।

păr-ă-sўn′-ĕ-sis, *n.* Corruption of words from a misunderstanding of their elements ; মৌলিক অংশ-সমূহ সম্বন্ধে ভ্রান্তজ্ঞান হেতু শব্দসমূহের বিকৃতিসাধন, শব্দবিকৃতি, (যথা আরবী ভাষার *Naranj* শব্দ ফরাসীভাষায় আদ্যক্ষর *n* লোপ হইয়া *aranj* হইল, পরে আদ্যের *a* অক্ষরের সহিত ল্যাটিন *aurum* (gold) শব্দের সহিত সম্বন্ধ আছে মনে করিয়া ভ্রমবশতঃ ঐ *a*, *o* তে পরিবর্ত্তিত হইয়া *orang* হয় । এই *orang* শব্দই পরে *orange* আকার প্রাপ্ত হয় ।)

păr-ă-sўn′-thĕ-sis, *n.* (*Philol.*) Conjoint derivation and derivation as a process of word-formation ; (ভাষা-বিজ্ঞান) উপসর্গ ও কৃদন্তাদি যোগে শব্দগঠন (যথা *de-centralize*) । **—thet′-ic,** *adj.*

păr-ă-tăx′-is, *n.* (*Gram.*) A loose arrangement of sentences or clauses ; বাক্য এবং বাক্যাংশের অসম্বদ্ধ বা অসংলগ্নভাবে সংযোগ । **—tac′-tic,** *adj.* **—tac′-ti-cal-ly,** *adv.*

pâr′-boil (-boyl), *v. t.* To boil partially ; (*fig.*) to excite anger ; to render uncomfortable by heat ; "Being squeezed and *parboiled* at nightballs"; মৃদুসিদ্ধ করা, অল্প সিদ্ধ করা ; (লক্ষণায়) রাগান্বিত করা; গরমদ্বারা অসোয়াস্তি বোধ করান, গুমট বোধ করান।

pâr′-bŭck-le (-l), *n.* & *v. t.* A device for hoisting or lowering heavy objects, by means of a rope ; রজ্জুর সাহায্যে গুরুভার দ্রব্য উঠাইবার বা নামাইবার জন্য ব্যবস্থা-বিশেষ। ***Verb t.*** To hoist or lower thus ; ঐরূপ ব্যবস্থার সাহায্যে উঠান বা নামান ।

pâr′-cĕl, *n.* & *adv.* **1.** A piece of land especially as a part of an estate ; ভূখণ্ড, বিশেষতঃ কোন সম্পত্তির অংশীভূত ভূখণ্ড । **2.** (*Archaic*) A part or portion ; as, part and *parcel* ; (অপ্রঃ) অংশ, খণ্ড । **3.** A number or quantity wrapped up in a single package ; a packet ; পুলিন্দা ; পার্শ্বেল, বাঙ্গী। **4.** (*Commr.*) A lot ; জিনিষের এক লাট । ***Adv.*** (*Archaic*) Partially ; as, *parcel* blind, drunk ; (অপ্রঃ) আংশিকভাবে । **Parcel gilt**—আংশিক ভাবে স্বর্ণপত্রমণ্ডিত, বিশেষতঃ ভিতরের দিকে স্বর্ণমণ্ডিত । **Parcel post**—ডাকঘরের যে বিভাগের উপর পুলিন্দা প্রেরণ প্রভৃতির ভার ন্যস্ত থাকে, পুলিন্দা ডাক, বাঙ্গী ডাক ।

pâr′-cĕl, *v. t.* **1.** To divide by parts or portions, (usu. with *out*, *into*) ; ভিন্ন ভিন্ন অংশে ভাগ করা । **2.** (*Naut.*) To cover or wrap with strips of canvas etc. ; (নৌবিদ্যা) ক্যাম্বিসের টুকরা দ্বারা ঢাকা বা জড়ান ।

pâr′-cĕl-ling (-ing), *n.* **1.** Act of dividing into parts ; অংশীকরণ । **2.** (*Naut.*) A strip of canvas usually tarred for binding round a rope ; (নৌবিদ্যা) রজ্জুতে জড়াইবার জন্য ক্যাম্বিস খণ্ড, বিশেষতঃ আলকাতরা মাখানো ক্যাম্বিস খণ্ড ।

pâr′-cĕ-nă-rў, *n.* Co-heirship ; সহোত্তরাধিকারিত্ব ।

pâr′-cĕ-nĕr, *n.* Co-heir; সহোত্তরাধিকারী ।

pârch, *v. t.* & *i.* **1.** To roast slightly as corn etc. ; ভাজা, (যথা খৈ ভাজা) । **2.** (Of sun, thirst, fever, etc.) To scorch ; to make hot and dry ; দগ্ধীভূত করা ; তপ্ত এবং শুষ্ক করা । **3.** To shrivel or wither with cold ; "The *parching* Air Burns fore..." ; শীতে শুকাইয়া বা মুষড়াইয়া যাওয়া । ***Verb i.*** To become hot and dry ; ভাজা হওয়া, উচ্ছোষিত হওয়া । **Parch′-ing,** *n.* ভর্জ্জন, ভাজন, উচ্ছোষণ ।

pârch′-mĕnt, *n.* **1.** The skin of sheep, goat, etc. rendered fit for writing on etc. ; লিখনোপযোগীকৃত ছাগ, মেষ, প্রভৃতির চর্ম্ম, চর্ম্মপট, চর্ম্মপত্র, লেখনচর্ম্ম, লিখনচর্ম্ম । **2.** A manuscript on this ; চর্ম্মপটোপরি লিখিত হস্তলিপি, চর্ম্মপটলিপি । **3.** A skin resembling parchment especially the husk of coffee-bean ; ফলাদির চর্ম্মপটসদৃশ ত্বক । **—y,** *adj.*

pârd, *n.* (*Archaic*) A leopard ; (অপ্রঃ) চিতাবাঘ ।

pârd *n.* (*Slang*) A partner, (chiefly *U. S.*) ; (মার্কিণ যুক্তরাজ্যের ইতরভাষায়) অংশীদার ।

pâr-don (-dn), *n.* **1.** Forgiveness ; ক্ষমা, মার্জ্জনা । **2.** (*Law*) Remission of a penalty ; (আইন) দণ্ডমুক্তি, অপরাধমোচন । **3.** (*Eccl.*) Same as INDULGENCE ; also a festival in which it is granted ; (যাজকীয়শাস্ত্র) পাপক্ষমা, অপরাধমোচন, অপরাধভঞ্জন ; যে পর্ব্বোপলক্ষে পাপক্ষমা করা হয় । **4.** Courteous forbearance ; excuse ; as, I beg your *pardon* ; মাপ; ক্ষমা । **General pardon**—সাধারণ ক্ষমা, সার্ব্বজনিক ক্ষমা, সর্ব্বাপরাধক্ষমা । **I beg your pardon**—See BEG.

pâr′-don (-dn), *v. t.* **1.** To forgive ; to forgive the penalty of ; ক্ষমা করা, মার্জ্জনা করা ; দণ্ড হইতে মুক্তি দেওয়া । **2.** To excuse ; ক্রটি না ধরা, ক্রটি উপেক্ষা করা । **—a-ble,** *adj.* That may be pardoned ; excusable ; ক্ষন্তব্য, ক্ষমার্হ, মার্জ্জনীয় ; উপেক্ষণীয়, ক্ষমণীয়, ক্ষমাযোগ্য ।

pâr′-don-ĕr (-dn-), *n.* **1.** (*Hist.*) One licensed to sell pardons or indulgences ; (ইতিহাস) পোপ কর্ত্তৃক অর্পিত "পাপ-ক্ষমা" বিক্রয় করার অধিকারপ্রাপ্ত ব্যক্তি । **2.** One who pardons ; ক্ষমাকারী ।

pâre, *v. t.* **1.** To trim by cutting irregular or superfluous parts etc. ; কাটা ছাঁটা । **2.** To cut the skin, rind, etc. of (fruit etc.) ; ফলের খোসা প্রভৃতি ছাড়ান । **3.** To shave ; to cut, (*off*, *away*) ; কামান, খেউরী করা ;

কাটা। 4. (*Fig.*) To diminish or reduce little by little, (usu. with *away, down*) ; অল্প অল্প করিয়া কমান। **Par′-er, Par′-ing,** *ns.* **To pare nails etc. to the quick**—নখ প্রভৃতি একেবারে মাংসে লাগাইয়া কাটা।

păr-ĕ-gŏr′-ic, *adj.* & *n.* Assuaging or soothing pain ; প্রশমক, শান্তিপ্রদ, উপশামক, শান্তিদ, বেদনাশামক, দুঃখশামক। ***Noun.*** A medicine soothing pain ; camphorated tincture of opium ; উপশামক ঔষধ ; কর্পূরবাসিত অহিফেনের আরক।

pă-rei′-ră (-rĭ-), *n.* A medicine got from the root of a Brazilian shrub, used in urinary disorders ; ব্রাজিলদেশীয় গুল্মবিশেষের মূল হইতে প্রাপ্ত মূত্ররোগের ঔষধ বিশেষ।

pă-rĕn′-chy̆-mă, *n.* 1. (*Anat.*) The essential substance of an organ, gland, etc. as distinguished from flesh and connective tissue ; (শারীরসংস্থানবিদ্যা) গ্রন্থি ও অন্যান্য যন্ত্রের জালবৎ নির্ম্মাণ-উপাদান, সান্তরবিধান (হঃ চঃ)। 2. (*Bot.*) One of two primary forms of vegetable tissue ; (উদ্ভিদ বিদ্যা) উদ্ভিদের আদ্যরূপদ্বয়ের অন্যতর, করণ্ড (সাঃ পঃ), কোমলকলা (ঐ), ক্লোমসফলা (ঐ)। **—chym′-a-tous, —mal,** *adjs.*

pâr′-ĕnt, *n.* 1. Father or mother ; পিতা বা মাতা, জনক কিম্বা জননী। 2. A forefather, esp. in "*Our first parents*" (Adam and Eve) ; পূর্ব্বপুরুষ। 3. An animal or plant from which another springs (*often attrib.*) ; as, a *parent* bird or tree ; যে জন্তু বা বৃক্ষ হইতে অপর জন্তু বা বৃক্ষ উৎপাদিত হয়। 4. (*Fig.*) Source or origin ; উৎপত্তি, মূল, যোনি, প্রভব। **Pa-ren′-tal,** *adj.* Of, or relating to, parents ; characteristic of parents ; পিতৃমাতৃ-সম্পর্কীয়, পৈতৃক, পিতৃমাতৃপ্রকৃতিসিদ্ধ। **Pa-ren′-tal-ly,** *adv.* **Our first parents**—আদম ও ঈভ।

pâr′-ĕnt-āge, *n.* Extraction ; lineage ; অন্বয়, বংশ ; বংশাবলী।

pă-rĕn′-thĕ-sis, *n.* (*Pl.* -SES.) 1. A clause, words, etc. inserted in a sentence by way of comment, explanation, etc. usually marked off by brackets, dashes, or commas ; নিক্ষিপ্ত বাক্য (আঃ বঃ), বন্ধনীর মধ্যস্থ অবান্তর বাক্য, অনন্বিত বাক্য। 2. (*Sing.* or *pl.*) Round brackets ( ) used for this ; নিক্ষেপবন্ধ (আঃ বঃ)। 3. (*Fig.*) An interval or interlude ; "During the *parenthesis* of bad government and national tumult" ; অবকাশ, বিরাম, মধ্যবর্ত্তী ঘটনা, আমোদজনক বিষয়, প্রভৃতি।

pă-rĕn′-thĕ-size, *v. t.* & *i.* To insert as parenthesis ; to include within parenthetical marks ; নিক্ষিপ্তবাক্য সন্নিবিষ্ট করা ; বন্ধনীর মধ্যে সন্নিবিষ্ট করা। ***Verb i.*** To say something in parenthesis ; বন্ধনীর মধ্যে কোন কিছু বলা।

păr-ĕn-thĕt′-ic, *adj.* 1. Of, relating to, parenthesis ; inserted as parenthesis ; অনন্বিতবাক্যসম্বন্ধীয় ; নিক্ষিপ্তবাক্যরূপে অন্তর্নিবিষ্ট। 2. (*Fig.*) Interposed ; "...a year...of *parenthetic* peace and happiness" ; (লক্ষণায়) অন্তর্নিবিষ্ট। **—i-cal,** *adj.* **—i-cal-ly,** *adv.*

păr′-ĕ-sis, *n.* (*Med.*) Partial paralysis affecting muscular motion but not sensation ; (ভৈষজ্য-শাস্ত্র) আংশিক পক্ষাঘাত—যেরূপ পক্ষাঘাতে পেশীর গতি সঙ্কুচিত হয়—কিন্তু কোন অঙ্গ সংবেদনশূন্য হয় না। **Pa-ret′-ic,** *adj.*

par excellence, (*F.*), *adv.* Pre-eminently ; by virtue of special excellence ; সর্ব্বোপরি ; বিশেষ উৎকর্ষ হেতু।

pâr′-gĕt, *v. t.* & *n.* To plaster over as a wall etc. ; আস্তর করা। ***Noun.*** Plaster ; আস্তর, চূণবালি।

pâr-hē′-lĭ-ŏn, *n.* A mock-sun appearing as a bright light near or opposite to the Sun ; সূর্য্যসন্নিকটস্থ বা সূর্য্যের বিপরীতদিকে দৃষ্ট

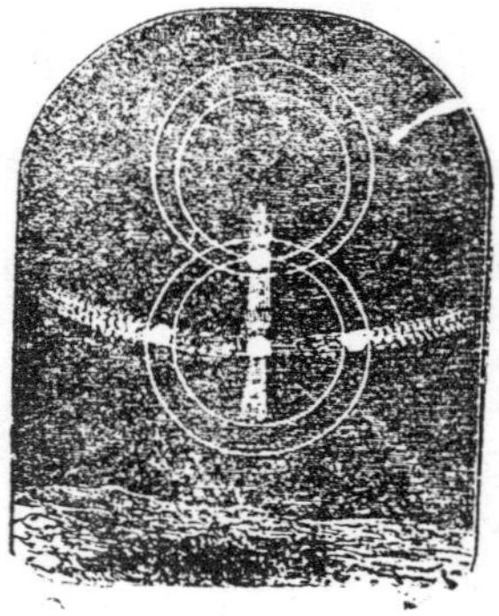

Parhelion.

জ্যোতির্বলয়, উপসূর্য্য (সাঃ পঃ), সূর্য্যাভাস, মিথ্যাসূর্য্য, প্রত্যক (বৃঃ সং)। **—li′-a-cal, —lic,** *adjs.*

pā′-rĭ-ah (-ă), *n.* 1. A member of a low caste of South India ; দাক্ষিণাত্যবাসী নীচ জাতীয় লোক। 2. One of a low or no caste ; অন্ত্যজ। 3. A person or animal of a despised class ; a social outcast ; অবজ্ঞাতজাতীয় লোক ; জাতিচ্যুত ব্যক্তি। **Pariah dog**—রাস্তার কুক্কুর।

Pā′-rĭ-ăn, *adj.* & *n.* Of, or relating to, Paros, an island famous for white marble ; শ্বেতমর্ম্মর প্রস্তরের জন্য বিখ্যাত পেরস দ্বীপসম্বন্ধীয়। ***Noun.*** A fine white kind of porcelain ; একপ্রকার ধবধবে চিনামাটী।

pă-rĭ′-ĕ-tăl, *adj.* 1. Of, or relating to, the walls of the body or of any of its cavities ; দেহপ্রাচীর সম্বন্ধীয়, দেহের কোষসম্বন্ধীয়। 2. Of, or relating to, the hollow organ or structure esp. of the ovary or of a cell ; ডিম্বাশয় বা কোষের শূন্যগর্ভ স্থানসম্বন্ধীয়। **Parietal bones**—করোটীর উর্দ্ধভাগস্থ অস্থি, করোটী প্রাচীর।

pari mutuel, (*F.*), *n.* A form of betting in which those who have staked on the winning horse divide among themselves the total of the stakes on the other horses ; একপ্রকার ঘোড়দৌড়ের বাজী—যাহাতে যাহারা জয়ী অশ্বের উপর বাজী রাখে তাহারা সেই অশ্ব এবং অপর অশ্বের বাজীর টাকা ভাগ করিয়া নেয়।

pari passu, (*L.*), *adv.* With, or at, equal pace ; simultaneously and equally ; সমগতিতে ; তুল্যভাবে, সমানভাবে, সমকালে, যুগপৎ, একসঙ্গে।

Păr′-is, *n.* Son of Priam, king of Troy ; ট্রয়রাজ Primএর পুত্র। Juno, Venus, Minerva এই দেবীত্রয়ের মধ্যে কে সমধিক রূপবতী এই বিষয়ের মীমাংসার ভার Parisএর উপর পড়িলে, তিনি Venusকেই রূপসীশ্রেষ্ঠা বলিয়া মতপ্রদান করেন। ইহাতে Venus প্রীতা হইয়া Parisকে Menelausএর পত্নী সুন্দরীপ্রধানা Helenকে পুরস্কার স্বরূপ প্রদান করেন। Paris Helenকে লইয়া Troy নগরীতে পলায়ন করেন। এই ঘটনাই ট্রয়ের মহাযুদ্ধের কারণ। এই যুদ্ধে Paris নিহত হন।

Pâr′-is, *n.* The capital of France ; ফরাসী দেশের রাজধানী প্যারী নগরী। **Paris blue** — একপ্রকার ঘনোজ্জল নীলবর্ণ। **Paris doll**—পরিচ্ছদাগারে নানাপরিচ্ছদশোভিত মানব মানবীর কৃত্রিম মূর্ত্তি। **Paris white**—পালিসের কার্য্যে ব্যবহৃত একপ্রকার অতি মনোজ্ঞ শ্বেতবর্ণ পদার্থ। **Plaster of Paris**—See under PLASTER.

păr′-ish, *n.* **1.** A division of a country with its own church and clergyman ; যাজকপল্লী। **2.** (Also, *civil parish*) A subdivision of a country constituted for administering Poor-law etc. ; পরগনা। **3.** The inhabitants of a parish collectively ; যাজকপল্লীর অধিবাসী। **Parish clerk**—যাজকপল্লীর কেরাণী। **Parish council**—পল্লীসভা। **Parish lantern**—See under LANTERN. **Parish-priest**—পল্লীপুরোহিত। **Parish-register**—যাজক পল্লীর গির্জ্জার যে খাতায় কোন ব্যক্তির দীক্ষা, বিবাহ, এবং সমাধির তারিখ প্রভৃতি লিখিত হয়।

pă-rish-ion-êr (-ŏn-), *n.* An inhabitant of a parish ; যাজকপল্লীর অধিবাসী।

Pă-ri′-si-ăn, *adj* & *n.* Of, or relating to, Paris ; প্যারীনগরীসম্বন্ধীয়। ***Noun.*** An inhabitant or native of Paris ; প্যারী নগরীর অধিবাসী।

păr-i-sȳl-lăb′-ic, *adj.* (*Of Gk.* or *L. nouns.*) Of the same number of syllables in all its inflections ; (গ্রীক ও ল্যাটিন বিশেষ্য সম্বন্ধে) সকল বিভক্তিতে বা ধাতুরূপে সমসংখ্যক শব্দাংশসম্পন্ন।

păr′-i-tȳ, *n.* **1.** Equality, esp. among members or ministers of the church ; তুল্যতা, সমতা, সাম্য, সাদৃশ্য, বিশেষতঃ খৃষ্টীয় ধর্ম্মসংঘের সভ্যগণের তুল্যতা। **2.** Close correspondence ; analogy ; as, *parity* of reasoning ; সৌসাদৃশ্য ; আনুরূপ্য। **Parity of reasoning** — See PARITY, *n.* 2.

părk, *n.* **1.** A piece of ground enclosed for recreation in or near a town ; নগরোদ্যান, প্রমোদকানন, উপবন, প্রবীথিকা, পুরোদ্যান, আক্রীড়। **2.** A tract of ground kept in its natural state for the preservation of game, for walking, riding, etc. ; ভ্রমণ, অশ্বারোহণ বা মৃগ প্রভৃতির রক্ষার জন্য নৈসর্গিক অবস্থায় রক্ষিত ভূখণ্ড, মৃগয়াবন, মৃগকানন, মৃগোদ্যান। **3.** A space occupied by artillery, stores, etc. in an encampment ; the objects themselves occupying such a place ; সেনানিবাসের কামান, সামরিক দ্রব্যসম্ভার প্রভৃতি সংরক্ষণের স্থান ; ঐ স্থানে রক্ষিত কামান, সামরিক দ্রব্যসম্ভার, প্রভৃতি। **4.** A large area of land set apart as a public property and kept in its natural state for common use ; সাধারণের ব্যবহারের জন্য রক্ষিত বিস্তৃত ভূখণ্ড। **Park′-ish,** *adj.* **Park-keeper**—নগরোদ্যানরক্ষক, উপবনরক্ষক, বনপাল। **The park**—(Formerly) St. James's Park ; (now) Hyde Park ; পূর্ব্বে সেন্ট জেমস্ পার্ক ; বর্ত্তমানে হাইড পার্ক।

pârk, *v. t.* **1.** To enclose as ground, in or as a park ; প্রাচীরবেষ্টিত করিয়া উপবনে পরিণত করা। **2.** (*Mil.*) To bring together or arrange compactly in a park as artillery etc. ; (সামরিকশাস্ত্র) একত্র সমাবেশ করা, সংহতভাবে সজ্জিত করা।

pâr′-kin, *n.* A cake of oatmeal and treacle ; যই এবং গুড়ে তৈয়ারী পিষ্টক-বিশেষ।

pâr′-lance (-lăns), *n.* Manner or way of speech ; as, in common or legal *parlance* ; কথাবার্ত্তা বলিবার রীতি বা ধারা, বাক্যরীতি, বাক্যভঙ্গী। **In common parlance**—চলিত কথায়, চল্‌তিভাষায়।

pâr′-ley (-lĭ), *n.* Mutual discourse ; a debate ; conference with an enemy in war ; কথোপকথন ; তর্কবিতর্ক, বাদানুবাদ ; যুদ্ধকালে শত্রুর সহিত মন্ত্রণা। **To beat or sound a parley**—(*Mil.*) To call for a parley by drum or trumpet ; (সামরিক শাস্ত্র) ঢক্কা বা তুরী বাজাইয়া মন্ত্রণার জন্য আহ্বান করা, ঢাক বাজাইয়া সন্ধির কথা ঘোষণা করা।

pâr′-ley (-lĭ), *v. i.* & *t.* To confer or discuss esp. with an enemy ; মন্ত্রণা করা, আলোচনা করা, বিশেষতঃ শত্রুর সহিত সন্ধি প্রভৃতির বিষয় মন্ত্রণা করা। ***Verb t.*** To speak esp. as a foreign tongue ; কোন ভাষায় কথা বলা, বিশেষতঃ বৈদেশিক ভাষায় কথা বলা।

pâr-ley-voo′ (-lĭ-), *n.* & *v. i.* **1.** (*Facet.* or *slang*) The French language ; (অবজ্ঞাচ্ছলে বা ইতরভাষায়) ফরাসী ভাষা। **2.** A Frenchman ; ফরাসীদেশীয় লোক। ***Verb i.*** To speak French ; to palaver ; ফরাসীভাষায় কথা বলা ; বাজে বকিয়া সময় কাটান।

pâr′-lia-mĕnt (-lĭ-), *n.* **1.** The deliberative legislature of the

British nation consisting of the Sovereign, the Lords and the Commons ; গ্রেটব্রিটেন এবং আয়র্লণ্ডের জাতীয় মহাসভা, পার্লেমেন্টের মহাসভা। [এই সভার দুইটী বিভাগ আছে। দেশের সম্ভ্রান্তবংশীয় এবং উচ্চ ধর্ম্মযাজকগণ প্রথম বিভাগের অন্তর্ভুক্ত এবং জনসাধারণ এবং বিশ্ববিদ্যালয়ের প্রতিনিধিগণ দ্বিতীয় বিভাগের অন্তর্ভুক্ত।] **2.** The corresponding legislative body in other countries ; অন্যান্য দেশের অনুরূপ ব্যবস্থাপক সভা। **3.** (Also *Parliament-cake*) A thin crisp cake of gingerbread ; একপ্রকার মচ্‌মচে পিঠা। **Long Parliament**—See LONG. **Short Parliament**—১৬৪০ খৃঃ অব্দের ১৩ই এপ্রিল হইতে ৫ই মে পর্য্যন্ত যে পার্লেমেন্টের অধিবেশন হয়। **To open Parliament** — (*Of King*) To declare it open ceremonially ; পার্লেমেন্ট মহাসভার উদ্বোধন করা।

păr-lia-mĕn-tā′-rĭ-ăn (-lĭ-), *n.* & *adj.* **1.** An expert debater in Parliament ; পার্লেমেন্টের বাদানুবাদকুশল সভ্য। **2.** (*Eng. Hist.*) An adherent to the Parliament in opposition to Charles I ; (ইংলণ্ডের ইতিহাস) প্রথম চার্লসের বিরোধী পার্লেমেন্টের পক্ষভুক্ত ব্যক্তি। ***Adj.*** Of, or relating to, parliament ; পার্লেমেন্ট মহাসভাসম্পর্কীয়।

păr-lia-mĕn′-tā-rŷ (-lĭ-), *adj.* **1.** Of, or relating to, parliament ; পার্লেমেন্ট মহাসভাসম্পর্কীয়। **2.** Enacted, established, or ratified by, Parliament ; পার্লেমেন্ট মহাসভাকর্ত্তৃক বিধিবদ্ধ, প্রতিষ্ঠাপিত বা দৃঢ়ীকৃত। **3.** (Of language) Admissible in Parliament ; (*colloq.*) civil ; (ভাষাসম্পর্কে) পার্লেমেন্ট মহাসভায় ব্যবহারের যোগ্য ; (চলিতভাষায়) শিষ্ট, সভ্যোচিত, ভদ্র। **Parliamentary agent**—কোন প্রস্তাবিত বা ঈপ্সিত পার্লেমেন্টের বিধি—যাহাতে কোন ব্যক্তির স্বার্থ রক্ষা হয়—তদ্বিষয়ে দৃষ্টি রাখার জন্য নিযুক্ত প্রতিনিধি। **Parliamentary borough**—পার্লেমেন্ট মহাসভায় সভ্যপ্রেরণের ক্ষমতাপ্রাপ্ত নগরী। **Parliamentary train**—যে বাষ্পীয়শকটে তৃতীয় শ্রেণীর নাবিকগণ মাইল প্রতি এক পেনির অনধিক ভাড়া দিয়া ভ্রমণ করিতে পারে।

pâr′-lour (-lĕr), *n.* **1.** A room in a private house used as a sitting room ; বৈঠকখানা, বসিবার ঘর, সংলাপপ্রকোষ্ঠ। **2.** A room in an inn for private conversation ; পান্থশালার যে প্রকোষ্ঠে গোপনীয় আলাপ করা যায়, বিশ্রম্ভালাপকক্ষ। **Parlour-boarder** — ছাত্রাবাসসমন্বিত বিদ্যালয়ের যে ছাত্র অধ্যক্ষের বাটীতে বাস করে। **Parlour-car**—(মার্কিণ যুক্তরাজ্যে) আরামজনক আসবাবপত্রাদি সুসজ্জিত বাষ্পীয় শকট। **Parlour-maid**—যে অনুচরী আহার্য্যদ্রব্য পরিবেষণ করিয়া থাকে, পরিবেষিকা।

par′-lous (-lŭs), *adj.* & *adv.* **1.** (*Archaic, facet.*) Dangerous ; risky ; (অপ্রঃ কিম্বা অবজ্ঞাচ্ছলে) বিপজ্জনক ; সঙ্কটসঙ্কুল। **2.** Dangerously or surprisingly clever ; shrewd ; অতি চালাক ; সেয়ানা। **3.** Hard to deal with ; বে-আড়া। ***Adv.*** Exceedingly ; extremely ; অতিশয়; নিরতিশয়, বেজায়।

Pâr-mē-săn′, *adj.* & *n.* Of, or relating to, Parma, in Italy ; ইতালী দেশের অন্তর্গত পার্মা নামক স্থানসম্পর্কীয়। ***Noun.*** (Also *Parmesan cheese*) A rich kind of cheese made at Parma and elsewhere ; পার্মা এবং অন্যত্র প্রস্তুত একপ্রকার সুরসাল পনীর।

Pâr-năs′-sus (-ŭs), *n.* **1.** A mountain in the central part of Greece, anciently sacred to Apollo and the Muses ; এপলো এবং বাগ্‌দেবীগণ কর্ত্তৃক নিষেবিত গ্রীকদেশের মধ্যস্থলবর্ত্তী পর্ব্বত-বিশেষ। **–si-an**, *adj.* & *n.* **1.** Of, or relating to, Parnassus ; poetic ; পার্নেসাস্ পর্ব্বতসম্পর্কীয় ; কবি বা কাব্যসম্বন্ধীয়। **2.** Designating a school of French poetry of the latter half of the 19th century ; উনবিংশ শতাব্দীর শেষ ভাগের ফরাসী কবিসম্প্রদায় সম্বন্ধীয়। (*Noun*) **1.** A poet ; কবি। **2.** A French poet of the Parnassian school ; উনবিংশ শতাব্দীর শেষভাগে ফরাসীদেশে যে এক কবিসম্প্রদায়ের প্রতিষ্ঠা হয়—তৎসম্প্রদায়ের এক কবি।

Pâr′-nĕll-ĭsm, *n.* The principles or policy of the Irish Home-Rule party led by C. S. Parnell from 1880 to 1891 ; আয়র্লণ্ডের স্বায়ত্বশাসননীতি বিশেষ। **–ite**, *n.* An adherent of C. S Parnell in his Irish Home-Rule policy ; পার্নেলপ্রবর্ত্তিত আইরিশ স্বায়ত্বশাসননীতি।

pă-rō′-chĭ-ăl, *adj.* **1.** Of, or relating to, a parish ; যাজকপল্লী-সংক্রান্ত, যাজকপল্লীসম্বন্ধীয়। **2.** Restricted or confined within narrow limits ; as, *parochial* affairs ; সংকীর্ণ, অনুদারচিত্ত, গ্রাম্য। **–al′-i-ty, –ism**, *ns.* **–ise**, *v. t.* & *i.* To form into parishes ; যাজকপল্লীতে গঠিত করা। (*Verb i.*) To do parish work ; যাজকপল্লীর কাজ করা। **–ly**, *adv.*

păr′-ō-dŷ, *n.* & *v. t.* An imitation of a poem in which the words and ideas are so far changed as to produce a ridiculous effect ; travesty ; কোন কবিতার বিদ্রূপাত্মক অনুকরণ, হাস্যোদ্দীপক অনুকরণ, ব্যঙ্গকাব্য [যথা ছুছুন্দরীবধ কাব্য সুপ্রসিদ্ধ মেঘনাদবধ কাব্যের হাস্যোদ্দীপক অনুকরণ] ; গুরুতর বিষয়ের হাস্যোদ্দীপক অনুকরণ। ***Verb t.*** To make (literary work, manner, etc.) ridiculous by imitation ; বিদ্রূপাত্মক অনুকরণ দ্বারা হাস্যজনক করা। **–dist**, *n.* One who writes a parody ; ব্যঙ্গকাব্য রচয়িতা। **Pa-rod′-ic, Pa-rod′-i-cal**, *adjs.*

pă-rōl′, *n.* & *adj.* An oral statement ; a word ; (chiefly in the legal phrase, *by parol*=by word of mouth) ; মৌখিক উক্তি ; শব্দ।

Adj. Oral (*chiefly law*); as, *parol* evidence ; (প্রধানতঃ আইনে) মৌখিক, বাচনিক। **By parol** — By word of mouth ; মুখের কথায়।

pă-role′, *n.* & *v. t.* 1. A word of honour ; a promise esp. that made by a prisoner of war that he will not try to escape if allowed to go about at liberty or will not bear arms against his captors for a certain period ; সত্যবাক্য, মুখের কথা, জবান ; প্রতিশ্রুতি, বিশেষতঃ স্বাধীনভাবে বিচরণের অনুমতি পাইলে পলয়ানের চেষ্টা করিবেনা অথবা যাহারা ধৃত করিয়াছে তাহাদের বিরুদ্ধে অস্ত্রধারণ করিবেনা, সামরিক বন্দিকর্ত্তৃক উক্তরূপ প্রতিশ্রুতি, বন্দিবাক্য। 2. (*Mil.*) The password used only by the officers or inspectors ; একমাত্র সামরিক কর্ম্মচারী বা পরিদর্শকগণ কর্ত্তৃক ব্যবহৃত সঙ্কেত বাক্য। ***Verb t.*** To liberate as a prisoner on parole ; সত্য বাক্যের উপর নির্ভর করিয়া বন্দীকে মুক্তি দান করা।

păr-ŏn-ŏ-mā′-sĭ-ă, *n.* A play upon words; pun ; শ্লেষালঙ্কার, শ্লেষোক্তি, কাঞ্চিযমক, বর্ণানুপ্রাস ; শব্দশ্লেষ। **—mas′-tic, —mas′-ti-cal**, *adjs.*

păr-ŏ-nȳ͟ch′-ĭ-ă, *n.* 1. (*Med.*) A whitlow ; প্রথম অঙ্গুলিসন্ধির প্রদাহ, আঙ্গুলহাড়া রোগ, নখম্পচ, চিপ্য (সাঃ পঃ)। 2. (*Cap.*) A genus of herbs ; একজাতীয় গুল্ম।

păr′-ŏ-nȳm, *n.* A paronymous word ; একধাতুজ শব্দ। **—ny′-mous**, *adj.* Derived from the same root ; alike in sound, but different in spelling and meaning; একধাতুজ; সমধ্বনিবিশিষ্ট কিন্তু ভিন্নার্থক এবং ভিন্ন-বর্ণবিন্যাসাত্মক। **Pa-ron′-y-my**, *n.*

păr′-ŏ-quet, păr′-rō-quet (-kĕt), *ns.* Same as PARAKEET. **Indian paroquet**—চন্দনা (যোঃ)। **Rose-ringed paroquet**—টিয়া (যোঃ)। **Slate-headed paroquet**—কাজলা (যোঃ)। **The red-breasted paroquet**—মদনা (যোঃ)।

pă-rŏt′-ĭd, *adj.* & *n.* Situated near the ear, as a gland etc. ; কর্ণাস্তিকস্থ, কর্ণমূলস্থ। ***Noun.*** Such a gland ; কর্ণনিম্নস্থ লালাস্রাবী গ্রন্থিত্রয়ের বৃহত্তমটী।

păr-ŏ-tī′-tĭs, *n.* Inflammation of the parotid glands ; কর্ণমূলপ্রদাহ (হঃ চঃ)।

păr′-ŏx-ȳsm, *n.* 1. A fit of disease ; রোগের আক্রমণ, তড়কা। 2. A convulsion or fit ; as, a *paroxysm* of rage or laughter ; আক্ষেপ, আকস্মিক প্রবল আবেগ, উচ্ছ্বাস, আবেশ। **—ys′-mal**, *adj.*

păr-ŏx′-ȳ-tōne, *adj.* & *n.* (*Gk. Gram.*) Having an accent on the last syllable but one, as a word ; (গ্রীকব্যাকরণ) উপান্ত শব্দাংশে স্বরচিহ্নবিশিষ্ট। ***Noun.*** Such a word ; ঐরূপ শব্দ।

păr′-pĕn, *n.* A stone passing from side to side through a wall acting as a binder ; প্রাচীরের উভয় পার্শ্ব ভেদকারী প্রস্তরবিশেষ।

pâr-quet′ (-kĕt), *n.* & *v. t.* 1. A part of the floor of a theatre, etc., (*chiefly U. S.*) ; (প্রধানতঃ মার্কিণ যুক্তরাজ্যের) রঙ্গালয়ের গৃহতলের অংশবিশেষ। 2. A flooring, esp. a wooden one composed of pieces of wood arranged in a pattern ; নানা নমুনায় সন্নিবিষ্ট কাষ্ঠখণ্ড সমূহরচিত গৃহতল। ***Verb t.*** To furnish with a parquetry floor ; কারুকার্য্য-খচিত কাষ্ঠখণ্ডরচিত গৃহতলসমন্বিত

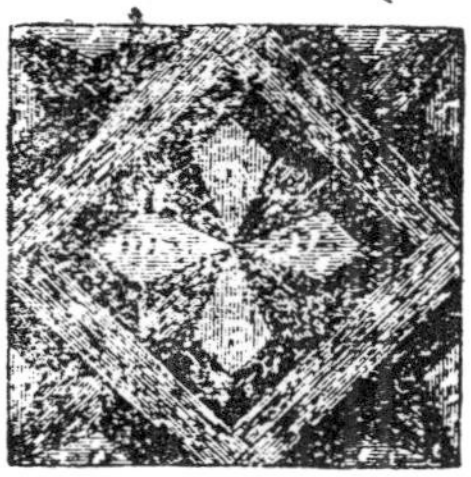

Parquetry.

করা। **Par′-quet-ry**, *n.* Wood-work inlaid with figures, for floors ; গৃহতলের জন্য নানা নমুনা-খচিত কাষ্ঠখণ্ড।

pârr, *n.* A young salmon ; স্যামন মৎস্যশাবক।

păr′-rĭ-cīde, *n.* 1. A person who murders his father, mother or a near relative ; the murder of any one to whom reverence is due ; পিতৃ বা মাতৃহন্তা, পিতৃহন্তা, পিতৃঘ্ন, পিতৃঘাতী, পিতৃঘাতক, ঘনিষ্ঠ আত্মীয় হন্তা ; পিতৃতুল্য ব্যক্তির হত্যা। 2. One guilty of treason against one's country ; স্বদেশ-দ্রোহী ব্যক্তি। 3. Any of these, crimes ; পিতৃহত্যা, পিতৃবধ, পিতৃঘাত, পিতৃতুল্য ব্যক্তির হত্যা। **—cid-al**, *adj.* Of, or pertaining to, parricide ; guilty of parricide ; পিতৃহত্যাসম্বন্ধীয় ; পিতৃহত্যাপরাধী।

păr′-rot (-ŏt), *n.*, *v. t.* & *i.* 1. A genus of birds, including parakeets, macaws etc. that can imitate the human voice ; শুক, শারী (fem.), কীর, শুকপক্ষী, তোতাপাখী, টিয়া পাখী [*Syn.* ফলাদন, ফলাশন, বক্রচঞ্চু, বক্রতুণ্ড, বক্রনক্র, রক্তপাদ, রক্ততুণ্ড, চিমি, চিরি, দাড়িমপ্রিয়, দাড়িমভক্ষণ, কুমার, কিঙ্কিরাত, মেধাবী।] 2. A repeater of the words of others ; one making unintelligent imitation of others' actions ; যে ব্যক্তি তোতার ন্যায় অন্যের কথা অনুকরণ করে ; অনুকারক ব্যক্তি। ***Verb t.*** 1. To repeat by rote ; তোতার ন্যায় মুখস্থ করা। 2. To teach, as a person ; to repeat mechanically ; তোতার ন্যায় পড়ান; তোতার মত মুখস্থ করা। ***Verb i.*** To chatter like a parrot ; to repeat words mechanically ; তোতার মত কিচির-মিচির করা ; শুকপক্ষীর মত আবৃত্তি করা। **—ry**, *n.* Servile imitation ; দাসবৎ অনুকরণ।

păr′-ry (-ĭ), *v. t.* & *n.* 1. To ward off ; to stop or turn aside, as a blow or thrust ; আটকান, বাধা দেওয়া ; সামলান, প্রতিহত করা

নিবারণ করা। 2. To avoid or evade; এড়ান, পরিহার করা। *Noun.* 1. A turning aside of a blow or a thrust; নিবারণ, আটকানি। 2. (*Fig.*) A defensive movement as a debate etc.; (লক্ষণায়) আত্মরক্ষার কৌশল।

parse (pârs), *v. t.* To describe as a word grammatically; to resolve as a sentence into its component parts and describe them; পদান্বয় করা; অন্বয়যোজনা করা। **Par′-sing,** *n.* Describing grammatical relation of a word in a sentence etc.; পদান্বয়, অন্বয়যোজনা।

Pâr′-see (-sē), **–si,** *ns.* 1. An adherent of Zoroastrianism which took refuge in India in the 7th century; a fire-worshipper; পার্শি; অগ্নিপূজক, অনলোপাসক। 2. The language of Persia under Sassanian kings; পার্শিদিগের ভাষা।

pâr′-si-mō-ny̆, *n.* Sparingness in the spending of money; niggardliness; ব্যয়কুণ্ঠতা; কার্পণ্য, কৃপণতা। **–mo′-ni-ous,** *adj.* Frugal to excess; niggardly; কৃপণ, ব্যয়কুণ্ঠ, ব্যয়শত্রু; বদ্ধমুষ্টি। **–mo′-ni-ous-ly,** *adv.* **–mo′-ni-ous-ness,** *n.*

pârs′-ley (-lī), *n.* A garden-vegetable, used for communicating an agreeable flavour to

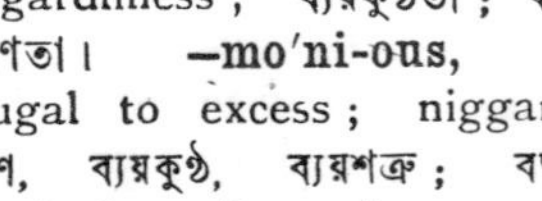

Parsley.

soups, etc.; ব্যঞ্জনাদি সুরভি করণার্থ একপ্রকার উদ্যানরোপিত শাক, অজমোদা, খোরাসানী আজোয়ান।

pârs′-nip, *n.* An edible plant with a carrot-like root, used as culinary vegetable; একপ্রকার গাজর। **Fine words butter no parsnips**—See under BUTTER.

pâr′-son (-sn), *n.* 1. The priest or incumbent of a parish; পল্লীযাজক। 2. A clergyman; a preacher; পুরোহিত; ধর্ম্মপ্রচারক। **–age,** *n.* 1. The official dwelling-house of a parson; পল্লীযাজকের বাসভবন। 2. The benefice of a parson; যাজকের বৃত্তি বা উপস্বত্ব। **–son′-ic,** *adj.*

pârt, *n.* 1. A portion of a whole; a piece; একদেশ, ভাগ, অঙ্গ, অবয়ব (বেদান্তঃ); অংশ, খণ্ড। 2. A section or division of a book etc. esp. so much as is published at one time; পুস্তকের খণ্ড। 3. Share; lot; interest; "...have neither *part* nor lot in etc."; duty; as, she has done her *part*; অংশ, হিস্যা; ভাগ; স্বার্থ; কর্ত্তব্য। 4. A side or party; পক্ষ। 5. A character taken by an actor in a play; the words of a character or actor in a play; ভূমিকা (cf. কামন্দক্যাঃ প্রথমভূমিকাং ভাব এবাধীতে— মালতীমাধব); অভিনেয়অংশ। 6. (*Math.*) An exact divisor; সম্পূর্ণ ভাজক। 7. (*Mus.*) Each of the notes making up a harmony; ঐক্যতান বাদ্যের অংশীভূত স্বর। 8. (*Pl.*) Abilities; talents; প্রতিভা, ক্ষমতা; ধীশক্তি, মনীষা। 9. A region or quarter, (usu. *pl.*); অঞ্চল, দেশ। **Part-owner**— অংশীদার। **A man of (good) parts**—*i. e.* of talents; প্রতিভাশালী ব্যক্তি। **Art and part**—See under ART. **For my part**—As far as I am concerned; আমার পক্ষে। **For the most part**—In most cases; mostly; অনেক স্থলে; প্রধানতঃ, অনেকাংশে। **I have done my part**—I have done my duty; আমার নির্দ্দিষ্ট কর্ত্তব্য কর্ম্ম সম্পাদন করিয়াছি। **In part**—Partly; আংশিকভাবে, খণ্ডশঃ, অংশতঃ। **Most part of**—Majority of; অধিকাংশ। **On the part of one, On one's part**—Proceeding from, or done by, etc., one; কাহারো পক্ষে। **Part and parcel**—Essential part; প্রধান অংশ। **Part of speech**—বাক্যের অংশ; ব্যাকরণে বিশেষ্য, বিশেষণ, প্রভৃতি। **The privy parts**—গোপনীয় অঙ্গ। **To have neither part nor lot in**—To have no concern in; কোন সম্পর্কই না থাকা। **To play a noble part**—To behave nobly; মহানুভবতা প্রদর্শন করা। **To play an unworthy part**—To behave unworthily; অযোগ্য ব্যবহারকরা। **To play a part**—To act deceitfully; কপটতা করা, অভিনয় করা। **To take as words etc. in good part**—Not to be offended at them; সদ্ভাবে গ্রহণ করা। **To take in ill part**—To take unfavourably; বিরুদ্ধভাবে গ্রহণ করা। **To take part in**—To assist in (doing, in discussion); সাহায্য করা, সহায়তা করা। **To take part of**—To support; কাহারো পক্ষাবলম্বন করা।

pârt, *v. t.* & *i.* 1. To divide into parts; অংশ করা, ভাগ করা, বিভক্ত করা। 2. (*Naut.*) To break or suffer the breaking of (a rope, anchor, chain, etc.); (নৌ-বিদ্যা) ভাঙ্গা, ভাঙ্গিয়া যাওয়া। 3. To separate as the hair with comb on each side of a dividing line; মাথায় সিঁথি কাটা। 4. To separate or stand between as combatants; to make a separation between (friends etc.); পৃথক করিয়া দেওয়া উভয়যোদ্ধার মধ্যে দণ্ডায়মান হওয়া; বন্ধুত্ব ভঙ্গ করা, সুহৃদ্ভেদ করা। 5. To separate by a process of extraction, elimination, etc.; as, to *part* gold from silver; নিষ্কর্ষণ

করা। 6. (*Archaic*) To allot or apportion ; (অপ্রঃ) বণ্টন করা, বিলি করা। ***Verb i.*** 1. To be divided into parts ; to break ; বিভিন্ন অংশে বিভক্ত হওয়া ; ভাঙ্গিয়া যাওয়া। 2. To go or come apart ; to separate ; as, here our roads *parted* ; পৃথক হইয়া থাকা ; পৃথক হওয়া। 3. To quit each other ; to take leave ; also, to die ; পরস্পরকে ছাড়িয়া যাওয়া, ছাড়াছাড়ি হওয়া ; বিদায় গ্রহণ করা ; চিরদিনের জন্য বিদায় লওয়া। 4. To give up a connection of any kind (*with*) ; as, to *part with* a friend or a property ; সম্পর্ক ছিন্ন করা। **To part company with** — To dissolve companionship with ; সঙ্গত্যাগ করা। **To part from**—To go away from ; to leave ; ছাড়িয়া যাওয়া ; পরিত্যাগ করা। **To part with**—To give up or surrender, as property etc. ; সম্পত্তি ইত্যাদি ছাড়িয়া দেওয়া।

pâr-tāke′, *v. i.* & *t.* 1. To take or have a part, (often with *of* or *in*) ; as, to *partake of* food or drink ; অংশগ্রহণ করা, ভাগ লওয়া। 2. To have something of the nature or properties ; as, his manner *partakes* of insolence ; কতকটা থাকা। ***Verb t.*** To have a part in ; to share ; as, let every one *partake* the general joy ; অংশ থাকা ; ভাগ থাকা।

pâr-terre′ (-tā.), *n.* 1. A piece of ground with flower-beds and intervening spaces of gravel or turf for walking on ; ভ্রমণের জন্য ফুলের কেয়ারী এবং মধ্যে মধ্যে কঙ্কর ভূমি ও তৃণভূমিযুক্ত ভূখণ্ড, ফুলবাগ, পুষ্পবাটিকা, মালঞ্চ। 2. The part of the floor of a theatre behind the orchestra ; বাদিত্রবাদনস্থলীর পশ্চাদ্দিকস্থ রঙ্গালয়ের অংশ।

pâr-thĕ-nō-gĕn′-ĕ-sis, *n.* (*Biol.*) Reproduction without impregnation by a male ; পুরুষসংসর্গ ব্যতীত উৎপাদন, অপুংজনন, শোণিতৈকজনি (হিঃ কোঃ)। **—ge-net′-ic**, *adj.*

Pâr′-thi-ăn, *adj.* Of, or pertaining to, ancient Parthia in Asia ; এসিয়ান্তর্গত পার্থিয়া প্রদেশসম্বন্ধীয়। **Parthian shaft** — A last or parting shot or missile ; (also see below) ; শেষ অস্ত্রক্ষেপ। **Parthian shaft, glance, etc.**—বিদায়কালীন শেষ মন্তব্য, শেষ অপাঙ্গ বিক্ষেপ। [পার্থিয়ান অশ্বারোহিগণ পলায়নকালে পশ্চাদ্দিকে অস্ত্রক্ষেপ করিতেন]।

pâr′-tial (-shăl), *adj.* 1. Belonging to, forming, or effecting, a part only ; not complete ; আংশিক ; অপূর্ণ। 2. Biassed to one party ; পক্ষপাতী, পাক্ষিক, পক্ষপাতপরায়ণ। **—ly**, *adv.* 1. Not wholly ; to some extent ; পুরাপুরি নয় ; কতক পরিমাণে। 2. With undue bias, favour or dislike ; পক্ষপাত করিয়া। **Partial eclipse**—অপূর্ণ গ্রাস, খণ্ডগ্রহণ। **Partial to**—Having a liking to a person or thing ; পক্ষপাতী।

pâr-ti-ăl′-i-tȳ (-shi-), *n.* 1. State or quality of being partial ; unfair bias ; undue favour shown ; পক্ষপাতিত্ব ; অনুচিত অনুগ্রহ ; অসমদৃষ্টি। 2. A liking or fondness, (*for, to*) ; অনুরাগ, টান।

pârt′-i-ble (-bl), *adj.* That may be parted ; divisible ; পৃথককরণীয় ; বিভাজ্য। **—bil′-i-ty**, *n.*

pâr-tĭc′-i-pāte, *v. i.* & *t.* 1. To take a part ; to partake, (*in* a thing *with* a person) ; ভাগী হওয়া ; যোগ দেওয়া, অংশী হওয়া। 2. To have something (*of*) ; as, his poems *participate of* the nature of satire ; কতকটা থাকা। ***Verb t.*** To receive a part or share of ; "Fit to *participate* all rational delight" ; অংশ বা ভাগ পাওয়া। **—pa-ble**, *adj.* Capable of being shared ; বিভাজ্য, অংশীয়, অংশয়িতব্য, বণ্টনীয়। **—pant**, *adj.* & *n.* Participating ; sharing ; অংশগ্রাহী ; অংশভাক্। (*Noun*) One that participates ; অংশভাগী। **—pa′-tion**, *n.* Participating ; sharing with others ; অংশী হওন ; বণ্টন। **—pa-tor**, *n.*

pâr′-ti-cĭ-ple (-pl), *n.* A word participating of the properties both of an adjective and of a verb ; কালবোধক কৃদন্ত। **—cip′-i-al**, *adj.* Having the nature of a participle ; formed from a participle ; কালবোধক কৃদন্তাত্মক ; কালবোধক কৃদন্ত হইতে গঠিত। **—cip′-i-al-ly**, *adv.* **First participle**—সৎ। **Second participle**—নিষ্ঠা।

pâr′-ti-cle (-kl), *n.* 1. A minute part of a matter ; a jot ; অণু, কণা, পরমাণু (হিঃ কোঃ), কণিকা, অবয়ব (ব্রজঃ হিন্দু), লব ; রতি, তিল। 2. The smallest possible amount ; as, he has not a *particle* of sense ; অণু, পরিমাণ, বিন্দুমাত্র। 3. (*Gram.*) A short indeclinable word, (*e.g.* a preposition, conjunction, etc.) ; a word not used alone, (*e.g. -ward, -ly*) ; (ব্যাকরণ) অব্যয় শব্দ ; নিপাত।

pâr′-ti(ȳ)-col-oured, (-cŭl-êrd), *adj.* Partly of one colour partly of another ; চিত্রবিচিত্র।

pâr-tic′-ū-lar (-lêr), *adj.* & *n.* 1. Relating to a single person or thing ; special ; নির্দ্দিষ্ট, বিশিষ্ট ; অব্যাপক, একদেশী। 2. Individual ; separate ; "This *particular* tax is painful ;" বিশেষ, বাপ্য (হিঃ কোঃ) ; পৃথক। 3. Noteworthy ; special ; as, he brought no *particular* news ; উল্লেখযোগ্য ; বিশেষ। 4. Minute ; precise ; as, a full and *particular* account ; fastidious (about what or as to what one eats, wears, etc.) ; পুঙ্খানুপুঙ্খ, সূক্ষ্ম ; উৎকটরুচি। ***Noun.*** A distinct part ; an item ; (*pl.*) details ; বিশিষ্ট অংশ ; দফা ; বিশেষ বিবরণ। **—i-za′-tion**, *n.* Particularizing ; বিশেষভাবে নির্দ্দেশ

বিশেষবর্ণন, বিশেষনির্দ্দেশ, অবচ্ছেদ (মঃ উঃ)। **—ize,** *v. t.* & *i.* To name specially or one by one; to specify; বিশেষভাবে নামোল্লেখ করা, একে একে নামোল্লেখ করা; বিশেষভাবে নির্দ্দিষ্ট করা। (*Verb i.*) To be attentive to details; খুঁটিনাটিরদিকে দৃষ্টি রাখা। **—lar′-i-ty,** *n.* **1.** State, or quality, of being particular; বিশেষতা (হিঃ কোঃ), ব্যাপ্যতা (ঐ), বিশেষত্ব, অব্যাপকত্ব। **2.** Minuteness of details; খুঁটিনাটি। **3.** That which is particular; বিশিষ্ট বস্তু। **—ly,** *adv.* In a particular manner; specially; বিশেষরূপে; বিশেষভাবে। **Particular Baptists**—বিশিষ্টনির্ব্বাচনবাদে বিশ্বাসী ব্যক্তিগণ। **Particular election and particular redemption**—খৃষ্টীয়শাস্ত্রানুসারে ঈশ্বরকর্ত্তৃক মানবজাতির কতকাংশমাত্র মুক্তির জন্য নির্ব্বাচন বা মোক্ষপ্রদান, বিশিষ্টনির্ব্বাচনবাদ। **Particular proposition**—(তর্কশাস্ত্রে) অব্যাপকপ্রতিজ্ঞা, ব্যাপ্যোদ্দেশ্যকবাক্য (হিঃ কোঃ), ব্যাপ্য প্রতিজ্ঞাবিশেষবাক্য (ঐ)। **Particular term**—বিশেষবাচকপদ (হিঃ কোঃ)। **In particular**—বিশেষতঃ, বিশেষভাবে।

pȧr-tic′-ū-lar-ĭsm (-lêr-), *n.* **1.** (*Theol.*) Same as the doctrine of PARTICULAR ELECTION AND PARTICULAR REDEMPTION (which see). **2.** Exclusive or special devotion to a particular cause, party, sect, etc.; কোন নির্দ্দিষ্ট বিষয়, পক্ষ বা সম্প্রদায়ের প্রতি ঐকান্তিক অনুরক্তি। **3.** The political principle of leaving each State in a federation free to promote its own interests without regard for the whole; রাজনীতিক তত্ত্ব বিশেষ—যাহাতে মিত্রতাসূত্রেবদ্ধ রাজ্যসমূহের প্রত্যেকটী সকলের স্বার্থের দিকে লক্ষ্য না রাখিয়া অবাধে স্বকীয় উন্নতি করিতে পারে। **—ist,** *n.*

pȧrt′-ing, *adj.* & *n.* **1.** Serving to part or divide; বিভাজক। **2.** Given at separation; বিদায়কালে প্রদত্ত। **3.** Departing; প্রস্থানোদ্যত, প্রস্থানোন্মুখ। ***Noun.*** **1.** Act of dividing into parts; separation; অংশীকরণ; বিরহ, বিচ্ছেদ। **2.** Leave-taking; departure; বিদায়গ্রহণ; প্রস্থান। **3.** The line where combed hair is parted; মাথার সীঁথি, সীমন্ত। **Parting salutation**—বিদায়কালীন অভিবাদন। **Parting of the ways**—The place at which a road divides into two or more; (*often fig.* of choice between courses); যে স্থানে পথ দুই বা বহু ভাগে বিভক্ত হয়; (লক্ষণায়) কঃ পন্থা।

partipris, (*F.*), *n.* A pre-conceived opinion; bias; পূর্ব্বপোষিত মত; পক্ষপাত।

pȧr′-ti-săn, —zăn, *n.* & *adj.* **1.** An adherent of a party, cause, etc.; পক্ষাবলম্বী, সপক্ষ, দলভুক্ত ব্যক্তি। **2.** (*Hist.* & *Mil.*) One of a party employed in special enterprises; কোন বিশেষ দুঃসাহসিক কার্য্যে নিযুক্ত দলের লোক। ***Adj.*** **1.** Supporting a party, esp. blindly; biassed; as, in a *partisan* spirit; পক্ষপাতী; পক্ষপাতদুষ্ট। **2.** (*Mil.*) Of, or relating to, the partisans or their operations; সপক্ষভুক্ত ব্যক্তিগণ এবং তাহাদের সৈন্যচালনাদিসংক্রান্ত। **—ship,** *n.*

pȧr′-ti-săn, —zăn, *n.* (*Hist.*) A kind of halberd or pike; (ইতিহাস) শূল, বর্শা।

pȧr′-tīte, *adj.* (*Bot.* & *Entom.*) Parted or divided; (উদ্ভিদ্‌বিদ্যা এবং কীটবিদ্যা) বিযুক্ত, বিভক্ত।

pȧr-ti′-tion, *n.* & *v. t.* **1.** Division into parts; বিভাগ, বিভাজন, বণ্টন, অংশীকরণ। **2.** A part or section; অংশ, খণ্ড। **3.** A structure separating two parts; a dividing or partition-wall; পর্দ্দা; দেওয়াল। **4.** (*Law*) Division of real joint-property between sharers; (আইন) বণ্টন, বাটোয়ারা। ***Verb t.*** **1.** To divide into parts; to divide as property into severalty; বিভাগ করা; বণ্টন করা। **2.** (Usu. with *off*) To divide or separate by a partition or partitions; প্রাচীর, পর্দ্দা, প্রভৃতি দ্বারা প্রকোষ্ঠাদি বিভক্ত করা। **—tioned** *p. adj.* Furnished or separated with partitions, such as walls etc.; প্রাচীরাদিদ্বারা বিভক্ত। **To partition off**—See PARTITION *v. t.*, 2.

pȧr′-ti-tive (-tĭv), *adj.* & *n.* **1.** Denoting a part, as a word (*e. g. some, any, etc.*); অংশসূচক, অংশবাচক। **ly,** *adv.*

Pȧrt′-lĕt, *n.* A hen; (*humorously*) a woman; মোরগী, কুক্কুটী; (কৌতুকচ্ছলে) স্ত্রীলোক। **Dame Partlet**—A hen; also applied to women; মোরগী; স্ত্রীলোকসম্পর্কেও ব্যবহৃত হয়।

pȧrt′-nêr, *n.* & *v. t.* **1.** A sharer; অংশী, হিস্যাদার (হিঃ কোঃ), অংশহর, অংশহারী, সম্ভূয়কারী, সহকারী, সমবায়ী। **2.** A joint owner of stock or capital employed in commerce, manufacture or other business; অংশীদার, বকরাদার (*colloq.*)। **3.** One who dances with another; নর্ত্তনসহযোগী, নটনসহচর। **4.** A husband or wife; পতি বা পত্নী। **5.** A player associated with another in whist, tennis, etc.; ক্রীড়ার সহযোগী। **6.** (*Naut.* usu. *pl.*) A framework of timber fitted out round an opening in a deck to strengthen it for the support of a mast, capstan or the like; (নৌবিদ্যা) জাহাজের পাটাতনের ফোকরে নিবিষ্ট কাঠের কাঠাম—যদ্দ্বারা ঐ ফোকর মাস্তুল প্রভৃতি ধারণের জন্য দৃঢ় করা হয়। ***Verb t.*** **1.** To associate or join as partners; অংশীদাররূপে যোগদান করা। **2.** To be the partner of; অংশী হওয়া। **—less,** *adj.*

—ship *n.* **1.** State of being a partner ; joint possession or interest ; অংশিত্ব ; যৌথ স্বার্থ বা অধিকার । **2.** Association of persons for the purpose of business ; সমবায় । **3.** (*Math.*) Fellowship ; সম্ভূয়সমুত্থান । **Predominant partner**—ইংলণ্ড । **Sleeping partner**—যে অংশীদার কোন কারবারে অর্থপ্রয়োগ করে কিন্তু নিজে কোন কাজ করে না ।

pâr'-tridge (-trĭj), *n.* A well-known gallinaceous game-bird

Partridges.

of the grouse family ; তিত্তিরপাখী, চিত্রভানু (নিঘণ্টু), চিত্রপক্ষ । **Black partridge**—কাল তিত্তির । **Francolin partridge, Grey partridge**—গৌরতিত্তির (যোঃ), রামতিত্তির, খয়রা, কপিঞ্জল । **Red-legged** or **Himalayan partridge**—চকোর, জীবঞ্জীব । **Snow partridge**—গোলাবী (হিউম) । **Swamp partridge**—জঙ্গলী তিত্তির । **Partridge-wood** — একপ্রকার দৃঢ় চিত্রবিচিত্র কাষ্ঠ—ইহা ব্রেজিল এবং পশ্চিম ভারতীয় দ্বীপপুঞ্জে উৎপন্ন হয় ।

pâr-tü'-ri-ĕnt, *adj.* **1.** About to bring forth young ; আসন্নপ্রসবা, উন্মুখপ্রসবা, আপন্নসত্ত্বা । **2.** (*Fig.*, of an idea, the mind etc.) About to produce discovery, etc. ; (লক্ষণায়—মনের পক্ষে) নবভাব, আবিষ্ক্রিয়া প্রভৃতি উৎপাদনোন্মুখ । **—ri'-tion,** *n.* An act of bringing forth ; childbirth, (*lit.* & *fig.*) ; প্রজনন ; (বাক্যানুযায়ী ও লক্ষণায়) সন্তান প্রসব । **—ri-tive,** *adj.*

pâr'-tȳ, *n.* **1.** A number of persons, united in a cause, opinion etc. ; দল, সম্প্রদায়, তরফ, মণ্ডলী । **2.** The system of forming sides on public questions ; কোন প্রশ্ন লইয়া দলগঠনের রীতি । **3.** A temporary company for travelling together, fishing, etc. ; ভ্রমণকারী, মৎস শিকারী, প্রভৃতির দল । **4.** A number of persons invited to a social meeting or entertainment ; also the entertainment or gathering itself ; as, a dinner *party* : to give a *party* ; প্রীতিসম্মিলনীতে নিমন্ত্রিত ব্যক্তিবর্গ ; প্রীতিসম্মিলনী । **5.** Each of the two or more persons making the two sides in legal action, contract, marriage, etc. ; মোকদ্দমার বাদী বা প্রতিবাদী, মোকদ্দমায় পক্ষ, বরপক্ষ বা কন্যাপক্ষ, চুক্তি প্রভৃতিতে পক্ষ । **6.** A participator ; an accessory ; as, a *party* to an action ; সহকারী ; সাহায্যকারী, সহায়ক । **7.** (*Vulg.* or *humorous*) A single individual spoken of ; a person ; as, he is a queer *party* ; (উপহাসচ্ছলে বা ইতরভাষায়) ব্যক্তি-বিশেষ ; লোক । **8.** (*Mil.*) A detachment of soldiers ; সৈন্য মণ্ডলী । **Parti-coated**—চিত্রবিচিত্র কোর্ত্তা-পরা, নানাবর্ণে রঞ্জিত আবরণে আবৃত । **Party-coloured**—See PARTI-COLOURED. **Party-jury**—বিভিন্ন দলের লোক দ্বারা গঠিত জুরি । **Party-politics**—সাম্প্রদায়িক রাজনীতি । **Party-spirit**—স্বপক্ষের জন্য উৎসাহ, দলাদলিরভাব, পক্ষানুরাগ । (*Party-spirited, adj.*) **Party-wall**—দুই বাটীর মধ্যবর্ত্তী প্রাচীর ।

pâr'-tȳ, *adj.* (*Herald.*) Divided into parts of different tinctures ; (কুলবিদ্যা) বিভিন্নবর্ণে রঞ্জিত খণ্ডসমূহে বিভক্ত ।

parvenu, (*F.*), *n.* Persons newly risen to eminence ; an upstart ; (sometimes used attributively) ; হঠাৎ বড় লোক, হঠাৎ নবাব ; ভুঁইফোড় ।

pâr'-vis, *n.* An enclosed area in front of a church, catherdral, etc. ; a school-room above the church-porch ; খৃষ্টীয়ধর্ম্মমন্দির, মহাধর্ম্মমন্দির প্রভৃতির সম্মুখবর্ত্তী বৃতি-বেষ্টিত স্থলী ; খৃষ্টীয়ভজনালয়ের দ্বারমণ্ডপের উপরিস্থ বিদ্যালয়কক্ষ ।

pas, (*F.*), *n.* **1.** The right of going first ; precedence ; as, to take or give the *pas* ; প্রথমগমনের অধিকার ; অগ্রগণ্যতা । **2.** A dance-step ; নটনপদক্ষেপ । ***Pas seul (serl), Pas de doux (der),***—A dance for one, two ; এক বা দুই ব্যক্তির উপযোগী নৃত্য ।

Păsch, *n.* (*Archaic*) The Jewish Passover ; the feast of Easter ; ইহুদীদিগের পর্ব্ববিশেষ ; যীশুখৃষ্টের পুনরুত্থানপর্ব্ব । **Pas'-chal,** *adj.*

pă-shâ', —cha' (-shă), *n.* A title of Turkish military commanders of high rank and governors of provinces ; তুরস্কের সেনাপতি বা প্রাদেশিক শাসনকর্ত্তার উপাধি । **—lic,** *n.* The jurisdiction of a pasha ; পাশার শাসনাধীন স্থান । **A pasha of one tail** or **of two, three tails**—তৃতীয়, দ্বিতীয় বা প্রথম শ্রেণীর পাশা [প্রথম, দ্বিতীয়, তৃতীয়শ্রেণীর পাশার পতাকায় যথাক্রমে তিন, দুই ও একটী অশ্বপুচ্ছের চিত্র থাকিত ।]

pă-sig'-ră-phȳ, *n.* A system or manner of universal writing that may be understood and used by all nations ; একপ্রকার লিপিপদ্ধতি যাহা সর্ব্বজাতি দ্বারা বোধ্য বা ব্যবহৃত হইতে পারে, একাক্ষরলিপি পদ্ধতি ।

pasque'-flow-ĕr (păsk-), *n.* A species of anemone flowering about Easter; একপ্রকার ফুল ।

păs-quin-ade', *n.* & *v. t.* A lampoon or satire ; বিদ্রূপাত্মক কবিতা, ব্যঙ্গ-কবিতা, ছড়া । ***Verb t.*** To lampoon; to satirize ; কবিতা বা ছড়া লিখিয়া বিদ্রূপ করা ; ব্যঙ্গ কবিতা লিখা ।

păss, *v. i.* & *t.* **1.** To go ; to advance ; to proceed, (*along, down, over, on,* etc.) ; গমন কর' ·

অগ্রসর হওয়া ; চলা। **2.** To be current; প্রচলিত হওয়া। **3.** To go by; as, to see a procession *pass*; to elapse; কোন লোক বা স্থানের নিকট দিয়া যাওয়া; অতীত হওয়া। **4.** To be moved or transferred from place to place; to change from one state to another; to be converted (*into*); একস্থান হইতে অন্য স্থানে যাওয়া; অবস্থান্তর প্রাপ্ত হওয়া; পরিণত হওয়া। **5.** To vanish; to disappear; অন্তর্হিত হওয়া, অদৃশ্য হওয়া, বিলীন হওয়া; তিরোহিত হওয়া। **6.** To die; মরিয়া যাওয়া। **7.** To get through; পথ করিয়া লওয়া। **8.** To be enacted; to receive the sanction of a legislative body; বিধিবদ্ধ হওয়া; ব্যবস্থাপকসভা-কর্ত্তৃক মঞ্জুর হওয়া। **9.** To come to or be at an end; as, kingdoms and nations *pass*; অবসান হওয়া। **10.** To be suffered to go on; to be received as adequate; চলিবার অনুমতি পাওয়া; যথোচিত বলিয়া গৃহীত হওয়া। **11.** To go unheeded or neglected; as, let that *pass*; উপেক্ষিত হওয়া। **12.** To be transferred from one owner; হস্তান্তরিত হওয়া। **13.** To go successfully through an examination; উত্তীর্ণ হওয়া, পাশ হওয়া। **14.** To happen; to occur; ঘটা; সংঘটিত হওয়া। **15.** (*Cards*) To decline an opportunity (*e. g.* of making trumps etc.; (also) to throw up one's hand; (তাস খেলা) সুযোগ গ্রহণে অস্বীকার করা; হাতের তাস ফেলিয়া দেওয়া। **16.** To decide or adjudicate, (with *on* or *upon*); নিষ্পত্তি করা, বিচার দ্বারা মীমাংসা বা নির্ণয় করা। **17.** (Of a judgment etc.) To be rendered or given (for plaintiff etc.); প্রদত্ত হওয়া। **18.** (*Football etc.*) To transfer the ball etc. to a player of one's own side; (পাদগোলকক্রীড়া প্রভৃতি) নিজের পক্ষের কোন ক্রীড়কের কাছে কন্দুক চালাইয়া দেওয়া। ***Verb t.*** **1.** To leave aside or behind as one goes; গমন কালে পার্শ্বে বা পশ্চাতে ফেলিয়া যাওয়া। **2.** To cross (sea, frontier, mountain-range, etc.); (সমুদ্র, সীমান্তপ্রদেশ, পর্ব্বতশ্রেণী প্রভৃতি) অতিক্রম করা। **3.** To approve as valid and just; "The Senate *passed* the law"; বিধিবদ্ধ করা। **4.** To obtain the formal sanction of, as a legislative body; as, the bill *passed* the senate; যথারীতি মঞ্জুর পাওয়া। **5.** To go successfully through, as an examination, trial, test, etc.; as, he *passed* the examination; উত্তীর্ণ হওয়া, কৃতকার্য্য হওয়া, পরীক্ষাদিতে উত্তীর্ণ হওয়া। **6.** To outstrip; to surpass; to excel; পশ্চাতে ফেলিয়া যাওয়া; অতিক্রম করা; ছাড়াইয়া উঠা। **7.** To cause to move or go; "He *passed* his hand over the forehead": *pass* your eye over the letter; চালিত করা, বুলাইয়া যাওয়া। **8.** To send or convey; to hand over or round; "The waiter *passed* biscuit and cheese"; প্রেরণ করা; হাতে হাতে দেওয়া। **9.** (*Obs.*) To go by without noticing; to disregard; (অপ্রঃ) লক্ষ্য না করিয়া চলিয়া যাওয়া; উপেক্ষা করা। **10.** To cause to go or march by; as, to *pass* troops in review; চালনা করা। **11.** To utter; to pronounce; "To *pass* a sentence"; ঘোষণা করা; উচ্চারণ করা। **12.** To pledge, as one's word, oath, etc.; শপথ করা, কথা দেওয়া। **13.** To put in circulation; "To *pass* counterfeit money"; প্রচলন করা। **14.** To spend as time etc.; কাটান, অতিবাহন করা, যাপন করা, গোঙান (*poet.*)। **15.** To cause or allow as a candidate to pass an examination; পরীক্ষায় উত্তীর্ণ করা। **16.** To cause or allow to obtain entrance, admission, etc.; as, to *pass* a person into a theatre; প্রবেশ করিতে দেওয়া। **17.** To emit from the bowels; অন্ত্র হইতে নিঃসারিত করা, মলত্যাগ করা। **18.** (*In football, hockey, etc.*) To transfer as the ball from one person to another of one's own side; (হকি প্রভৃতি ক্রীড়ায়) সপক্ষের এক ক্রীড়কের নিকট হইতে অপর ক্রীড়কের নিকট কন্দুক চালাইয়া দেওয়া। **19.** To be too great for; as, it *passes* my comprehension; (বুদ্ধির) অতীত হওয়া। **Pass'-a-ble,** *adj.* **1.** That may be passed, travelled, or navigated; উত্তরণযোগ্য, নৌচালনযোগ্য। **2.** That may be transferred from hand to hand; current; হস্তান্তরিতযোগ্য; প্রচলিত। **3.** Tolerable; admissible; pretty fair; মধ্যবিধ; একরকম; চলনসই। **Pass'-a-ble-ness,** *n.* **Pass'-a-bly,** *adv.* **To pass away**—To die; to come to an end; পরলোকে প্রয়াণ করা; সমাপ্ত হওয়া, অবসান হওয়া। **To pass by**—To omit; to disregard; to excuse; বর্জ্জন করা, উল্লেখ না করা; উপেক্ষা করা, অবহেলা করা; দোষ না ধরা, মাপ করা। **To pass by the name of**—To be currently known by the name of; কোন নামে পরিচিত হওয়া। **To pass for**—To be accepted as; গৃহীত হওয়া। **To pass muster**—See under MUSTER. **To pass off**—*v. t. & i.* To impose fraudulently, (*on* or *upon*); to secure recognition *for* or *as*; as, to *pass* oneself *as* a great man; ফাঁকি দিয়া চালান; ফাঁকি দিয়া বা চালাকি করিয়া লোকের নিকট হইতে সম্মান লাভ করা। (*Verb i.*) (Of sensations etc.) To disappear gradually; ক্রমশঃ অদৃশ্য হওয়া বিলীয়মান হওয়া। (Of proceedings) To be carried through;

গৃহীত হওয়া। **To pass on**—To proceed ; to go forward ; অগ্রসর হওয়া ; চলা। **To pass one's word**—To pledge one's word ; কথা দেওয়া, প্রতিজ্ঞা করা, সত্যবদ্ধ হওয়া, বাক্যদান করা। **To pass over**—To omit; to make no remark upon ; উল্লেখ না করা ; কোন রূপ মন্তব্য না করা, উপেক্ষা করা, গণ্য না করা, অগ্রাহ্য করা। **To pass the time of day**—To exchange any ordinary greeting of civility ; শিষ্টাচারমূলক অভিবাদনবাক্যের বিনিময় করা। **To pass through**—To experience ; ভোগ করা।

pass, *n.* **1.** Act of passing, esp. of examination ; (*univ.*) attainment of certain pecentage of marks that satisfies examiners but does not entitle to honours ; পরীক্ষায় উত্তীর্ণ হওন ; বিশ্ববিদ্যালয়ের পরীক্ষাদিতে সাধারণ পাশ। **2.** Critical situation ; juncture ; "Things came to a strange *pass*" ; সঙ্কটাপন্ন অবস্থা ; সন্ধিক্ষণ, সন্ধিবেলা। **3.** A permission, usu. a written one to pass or go into or out of a place ; a passport ; যাতায়াতের অনুমতি ; অনুমতিপত্র, ছাড়পত্র। **4.** (Usu. *A free pass*) A ticket permitting free transport, admission, etc.; as, a theatre *pass* ; প্রবেশ-অনুমতিপত্র। **5.** (*Fencing*) A thrust ; (অসি-ক্রীড়া) খোঁচা, আঘাত। **6.** Passing of hands over anything esp. in mesmerism ; যোগনিদ্রাদি উৎপাদনের জন্য হস্তচালনা। **7.** A juggler's manipulation ; a trick ; বাজিকরের হাতের চালাকী ; চাতুরী। **8.** Death (*lit.* & *fig.*) ; মৃত্যু, প্রয়াণ (বাক্যানুযায়ী ও লক্ষণায়)। **9.** (*In football, hockey, etc.*) Transference of the ball from one to another of the same side ; (পাদগোলক, হকি ইত্যাদি ক্রীড়ায়) স্বপক্ষের এক ব্যক্তির নিকট হইতে অপর ব্যক্তির নিকট পাদগোলকচালনা। **Pass-book**—ব্যাঙ্কের পাশবুক—ইহাতে যত টাকা জমা রাখা ও উঠান যায় তাহার হিসাব থাকে। **Pass-key**—ঘরে প্রবেশ করিবার চাবি ; যে চাবি দ্বারা অনেক তালা খোলা যায়। **Passman**—বিশ্ববিদ্যালয়ের (বি, এ প্রভৃতি) উপাধিধারী ব্যক্তি। **Passport**—ছাড়পত্র, মুদ্রা (মুদ্রাঃ), আদেশপট (জৈঃ সাঃ)। **Pass-word**—মিত্রভাবে শিবিরে প্রবেশার্থ সাঙ্কেতিক শব্দ, সঙ্কেতবাক্য। **To bring to pass**—To accomplish ; to carry out ; সংঘটন করা, ঘটান ; সম্পন্ন করা। **To come to a pretty pass**—To be in a critical state ; সঙ্কটজনক অবস্থায় উপনীত হওয়া। **To come to pass**—To occur or happen ; সংঘটিত হওয়া, ঘটা।

pȧss, *n.* **1.** A way through which one passes ; a narrow passage, esp. through mountains ; গমনপথ ; সরুপথ, গিরিপথ, গিরিবর্ত্ম, গিরিসঙ্কট, গিরিদ্বার (মঃ ভাঃ)। **2.** (*Mil.*) A place commanding such a passage viewed as a key to a country ; (সামরিকশাস্ত্র) কোন দেশের প্রবেশদ্বার। **3.** A passage across a river *e.g.* a ford, ferry, etc. (*rare*) ; a navigable channel ; (কচিদ্‌ব্যবহৃত) নদী পার হওয়ার রাস্তা, সুপ্রতরস্থল ; নৌতার্য্যপ্রণালী।

pȧs'-sage (-āj), *n.* **1.** Act of passing ; transit or movement : গমন ; তরণ। **2.** Transition from one state to another ; অবস্থান্তর। **3.** A journey as in a ship ; a right of transport as a passenger by sea ; জাহাজাদিতে ভ্রমণ ; স্থানান্তর গমনের অধিকার। **4.** Time occupied in passing ; ভ্রমণে যে সময় লাগে। **5.** (*Obs.*) A charge or toll levied upon passengers ; (অপ্রঃ) যাত্রীদের নিকট হইতে গৃহীত শুল্ক। **6.** A way or route ; পথ। **7.** The passing into law of a legislative measure ; বিধিবদ্ধ হওন। **8.** The right or liberty of passing through ; তরণের অধিকার। **9.** (*Obs.*) Occurrence ; (অপ্রঃ) ঘটনা। **10.** An avenue ; a corridor ; তরুবীথিকা ; দরদালান, টানা বারান্দা। **11.** A single clause or part of a book ; গ্রন্থের অংশ বা বাক্য। **12.** A modulation in music ; সঙ্গীতে স্বরবৈচিত্র্য। **13.** (Usu. *pl.*) Interchange of confidences etc. ; পরস্পরের ভাব প্রভৃতির বিনিময় বা আদান প্রদান। **Passage-money** — যাত্রীর ভাড়া, পাথেয়। **Bird of passage**—যে সকল পক্ষী ঋতুপরিবর্ত্তনের সঙ্গে সঙ্গে বাসস্থান পরিবর্ত্তন করে, দেশান্তরগামী পক্ষী। **Passage of or at, arms**—A fight ; (*fig.*) a quarrel, esp. of words ; যুদ্ধ ; (লক্ষণায়) কলহ, বাগ্‌যুদ্ধ, বাগ্‌বিতণ্ডা।

pȧs'-sage (-ȧj), *v. i.* & *t.* (Of horse or rider) To move sideways ; (ঘোড়া বা সোয়ার সম্বন্ধে) পার্শ্বের দিকে চলা। ***Verb t.*** To cause (a horse) to do this ; ঘোড়া পার্শ্বের দিকে চালান।

pȧs'-sant (-ȧnt), *adj.* (*Herald.*) Walking and looking to the dexter side, with the dexter fore-paw raised, (said of an animal represented thus) ; (কুলবিদ্যা) দক্ষিণ অগ্রপদ উত্থিত অবস্থায় দক্ষিণদিকে গমন বা দৃষ্টিশীল।

Passe, (*F.*), *adj.* (*Fem.* PASSEE) Past one's prime ; (of women) past the period of greatest beauty ; behind the times ; অতিক্রান্তযৌবন ; বিগতযৌবনা (*fem.*) ; সেকেলে।

passementerie, (*F.*), Trimmings esp. of braids, cords, beads, etc. ; পোষাকের জন্য ফিতা, মালার গুলিকা, রজ্জুবৎ ভূষা প্রভৃতি।

pȧs'-sen-gēr, (-en-), *n.* One travelling in public conveyance by land or water ; যাত্রী, আরোহী। **Foot-passenger**—Traveller on foot ; পদব্রজে ভ্রমণকারী, পাদচারী। **Passenger-pegion**—উত্তর আমেরিকার বন্যকপোতবিশেষ।

passe-partout, (*F.*), *n.* **1.** A mount for a photograph, etc.; আলোকচিত্র প্রভৃতি যে কাঠামে বাঁধাই করিয়া রাখ হয়। **2.** master-key; যে চাবি দ্বারা অনেক রকমের তালা খোলা যায়।

păss'-êr, *n.* **1.** One who passes (an examination); পরীক্ষোত্তীর্ণ ব্যক্তি। **2.** A passer-by; পথিক, পান্থ। **A passer-by**—One who passes by, esp. casually; পথিক।

Păs'-ser-ēs (-êr-), *n.* (*Zool.*) An order of birds including more than half of existing birds; একজাতীয় পক্ষী, দণ্ডবাসী।

păs'-ser-īne (-êr-), *adj.* & *n.* **1.** Of, or relating to, the order of, Passeres or Perchers; দণ্ডবাসিবর্গ-সম্পর্কীয়। **2.** Of the size of a sparrow; চটকপাখীর আকার। ***Noun.*** A bird belonging to the order of Passeres or Perchers; দণ্ডবাসিবর্গের অন্তর্ভুক্ত পক্ষী।

păs'-si-ble (-ĭ-bl), *n.* (*Theol.*) Capable of feeling or suffering; (ধর্ম্মশাস্ত্রে) কষ্টসহনক্ষম, সংবেদনক্ষম। **—bil'-i-ty**, *n.*

passim, *adv.* (Of allusions, phrase, etc.) Everywhere; here and there; as, this occurs in Milton *passim*; সর্ব্বত্র; যেখানে সেখানে।

păss'-ĭng, *adj.* & *adv.* **1.** Current; going or passing by; চলিত; প্রচলিত। **2.** Transitory; fleeting; ক্ষণস্থায়ী, অচিরস্থায়ী; ক্ষণভঙ্গুর। **3.** Cursory; incidental; উপর উপর, বাহ্য, ভাসাভাসা; আনুষঙ্গিক। ***Adv.*** Exceedingly; very; as, *passing* rich; নিরতিশয়; অত্যন্ত।

păss'-ĭng, *n.* Act of one that passes or causes to pass; তরণ, অতিক্রম। **Passing-bell**—মৃত্যুকালে বাদিত ঘণ্টা, মরণঘণ্টা। **Passing-nōte**—(*Mus.*) One not belonging to the harmony but introduced to secure smooth transition; (সঙ্গীত) অবান্তর স্বর। **In passing**—while going by; প্রসঙ্গক্রমে।

pas'-sion (pă-), *n.* **1.** Intense emotion; তীব্র আবেগ, প্রবল মানসিক উত্তেজনা। **2.** Outburst of anger; rage; ক্রোধাবেগ, ক্রোধোচ্ছ্বাস; রাগ। **3.** Strong enthusiasm or desire; অত্যুৎসাহ, সংরাগ, অনুরাগ, মনঃক্ষোভ (হিঃ কোঃ), মনোবিকার (ঐ), রাজস ভাব (ঐ)। **4.** Ardent or sexual love; কাম, কামাগ্নি, কামমোহ। **5.** (*Cap.*) Christ's sufferings on the cross; a story of this as related in the Gospels; a musical setting of it; ক্রুশবিদ্ধ যীশুখৃষ্টের যন্ত্রণা; ঐ যন্ত্রণার কাহিনী — যাহা সুসমাচারগ্রন্থে বর্ণিত হইয়াছে; উক্ত বিষয়ক গীতি। **6.** An object of ardent desire or fondness; as, his *passion* is music; তীব্রবাসনার বিষয়ীভূত বস্তু। **—less**, *adj.* Without any passion; বিরক্ত, রাগহীন, বীতস্পৃহ। **—less-ly**, *adv.* **—less-ness**, *n.* **Passion-flower**—ঝুমকা ফুল (যোঃ), ঝুমকা লতা (ঐ) [যীশুর মস্তকে যে কাঁটার মুকুট পরান হইয়াছিল তাহার কাঁটার ও তাঁহাকে যে প্রেক প্রভৃতি দ্বারা ক্রুশে নিবদ্ধ করা হইয়াছিল সেই প্রেক প্রভৃতির সহিত এই পুষ্পের কোন কোন অংশের সাদৃশ্য হেতু এই নাম।] **Passion-play** — যীশুখৃষ্টের ক্রুশ যন্ত্রণার কাহিনী অবলম্বনে রচিত যাত্রা। **Passion-Sunday**—খৃষ্টানদিগের চল্লিশদিবসব্যাপী উপবাসের পঞ্চম রবিবার। **Passion-Week** — Week before Easter; ঈষ্টার পর্ব্বের অব্যবহিত পূর্ব্ববর্ত্তী সপ্তাহ। **Passions and prejudice**—রাগ দ্বেষ (ব্যঃ মাঃ)।

păs'-sion (pă-), *v. i.* (*Poet.*) To feel or express passion; (কবিতায়) অনুরাগ বোধ করা, অনুরাগ প্রকাশ করা।

pas'-sion-ăl, (pă-), *adj.* Of, or relating to, passion; অনুরাগসম্বন্ধীয়, সংরাগসম্বন্ধীয়।

pas'-sion-ăl, (pă-), *n.* A book of the sufferings of saints and martyrs for reading on their festivals; সিদ্ধপুরুষ ও ধর্ম্মার্থে আত্মবলিদানকারী ব্যক্তিগণের যন্ত্রণা-কাহিনীপূর্ণ পুস্তক।

pas'-sion-āte (pă-), *adj.* **1.** Moved by passion; easily excited; রিপুবশীভূত, চণ্ডঃ, রাজস (হিঃ কোঃ); আশুক্রোধী। **2.** Ardent in feeling or desire; enthusiastic; intense; showing passion or strong feeling; অনুরাগী, অত্যনুরক্ত; উৎসাহী; তীব্র, গাঢ়; সরাগ, সরভস। **—ly**, *adv.*

Pas'-sion-ĭst (pă-), *n.* A member of a religious order instituted to bear witness to the spirit and import of Christ's Passion; ক্রুশবিদ্ধ যীশুর যন্ত্রণার অর্থ ও অন্তর্নিহিত তত্ত্ব সম্বন্ধে সাক্ষ্য প্রদানের জন্য সংঘটিত সম্প্রদায় বিশেষের সভ্য।

păs-sive (-ĭv), *adj.* & *n.* **1.** (*Obs.*) Suffering; (অপ্রঃ) সহনশীল, কষ্টসহিষ্ণু, ধৈর্য্যশীল। **2.** Unresisting; submissive; patient; অনিবারক, অপ্রতীকারক; অপ্রতিরোধকারী; বশ্য; কষ্টসহিষ্ণু, ধৈর্য্যশীল। **3.** Inactive; inert; নিষ্ক্রিয় (হিঃ কোঃ), ক্রিয়াশূন্য (ঐ); জড়, অপ্রবর্ত্তক। ***Noun.*** The passive voice or form of a verb; কর্ম্মবাচ্য। **—ness**, **—siv'-i-ty**, *ns.* **—ly**, *adv.* **1.** State of being passive; inactivity; inertness; নিশ্চলতা; ক্রিয়াশূন্যতা (হিঃ কোঃ); নিশ্চেষ্টতা। **2.** Patience; submission; ধৈর্য্য; বশ্যতা। **Passive debt**— বিনা সুদের ঋণ। **Passive resistance**—See UNDER RESISTANCE. **Passive verb**, or **voice**—(ব্যাকরণে) কর্ম্মবাচ্য বা তদুক্ত ক্রিয়া। **In the passive voice**—কর্ম্মণি বাচ্যে।

păss'-ō-vêr, *n.* **1.** An annual feast of the Jews to commemorate the destroying angel passing over the houses of the Israelites when he slew the first-born of the Egyptians; ধ্বংসকারী দেবদূত মিসরদেশীয় প্রথমজাত সন্তানদিগকে বিনাশ করার জন্য গমনকালে এস্রায়েলগণের গৃহ অতিক্রম করিয়া গিয়াছিলেন—তৎস্মরণার্থ ইহুদীগণকর্ত্তৃক অনুষ্ঠিত বাৎসরিক পর্ব্ববিশেষ, অতিক্রম (আঃ বঃ)। **2.** The sacrifice offered at the feast of passover; the Paschal lamb; উক্ত পর্ব্বোপলক্ষে প্রদত্ত বলি; উক্ত পর্ব্বোপলক্ষে যে মেষ বলি দেওয়া হয়। 3. (*Fig.*) Christ; (1 *Cor.* v. 7); (লক্ষণায়) যীশুখৃষ্ট।

păss'-pōrt, *n.* See under PASS.

păst, *adj.* & *n.* **1.** Gone by in time; as, "His prime is *past*"; গত, অতীত। **2.** Just elapsed; foregoing; as, "The *past* month"; গত; বিগত। **3.** (*Gram.*) Denoting past action or state; পূর্ব্ববর্ত্তী কার্য্য বা অবস্থা প্রকাশক। ***Noun.*** **1.** Past time; গতকাল। **2.** What has taken place in past time; অতীত ঘটনা। **3.** The past life or career, esp. an unknown or secret one of a person; as, a woman with a *past*; গতজীবন, পূর্ব্বজীবন। **Past-master** — One who has been master in guild, freemason's lodge, etc.; also a thorough master, (*in, of,* a subject); কোন সম্প্রদায় বা ফ্রিমেসন প্রভৃতি সমিতির অধ্যক্ষ; পাকা লোক, পুরাদরের ওস্তাদ।

păst, *prep.* & *adv.* **1.** Beyond in time; after; গত, অতীত; পরে। **2.** Beyond in place or position; as, he ran *past* the house; ছাড়াইয়া। **3.** Beyond the range or reach of; as, it is *past* endurance; অতীত। ***Adv.*** By or beyond; as, to run *past*; নিকটদিয়া, পাশদিয়া।

pāste, *n.* **1.** (*Cooking*) Moistened flour kneaded with butter, suet, etc.; কাই, কল্ক (ঠাকুরঃ), মণ্ড, পিষ্টক (সাঃ পঃ), পিষ্টিকা (ঐ), মাখা আটা, ময়দার কাই, বিলেপী (ভাবঃ প্রঃ)। **2.** A mixture of flour and water boiled, used for causing paper or other substances to adhere; ময়দার লেই। **3.** A kind of sweet confection; একপ্রকার মিঠাই। **4.** A relish made of some fish cooked, pounded and seasoned; ভাজা মৎসের চূর্ণের সহিত মসল্লাদির মিশ্রণে প্রস্তুত মুখরোচক খাদ্যবিশেষ। **5.** Any soft or plastic mixture or composition; লেই, কাই। **6.** A fine kind of glass for making artificial gems; কৃত্রিম মণি নির্ম্মাণের জন্য একপ্রকার উৎকৃষ্ট কাচ।

pāste, *v. t.* **1.** To fasten or join with paste; লেই দ্বারা জোড়া বা আঁটা। **2.** To stick up (play-bill etc.) on wall with paste; প্রাচীরগাত্রে বিজ্ঞাপনাদি লেই দ্বারা লাগান। **3.** To cover by or as by pasting, as a wall with pictures, paper, etc.; লেই দিয়া লাগাইয়া দেওয়াল প্রভৃতি মোড়া। **Paste-board**—A stiff substance made by pasting together sheets of paper; জমাটকাগজ, পুরুকাগজ, পিচবোর্ড, সংমৃষ্ট পত্র (আঃ বঃ), মলাট কাগজ। *Attrib., fig.*) Unsubstantial; flimsy; (লক্ষণায়) অসার; অন্তঃসারশূন্য। (*Slang*) A visiting-card; a playing card; railway ticket; (অপভাষায়) কাহারো সহিত দেখা করিবার স্থুল কাগজখণ্ড; খেলার তাস; রেলওয়ের টিকিট।

păs'-tĕl, *n.* **1.** Woad either the dye or the plant; নীলবর্ণ রঞ্জকপদার্থ বিশেষ, যে বৃক্ষ হইতে ঐ পদার্থ প্রাপ্ত হওয়া যায়। **2.** A dry paste made by compounding pigments with gum-water, used for crayons; চিত্রকার্য্যে ব্যবহৃত নানাবর্ণের খড়ি, চিত্রবর্ত্তিকা। **3.** A drawing in pastel; রঙ্গিন খড়িদ্বারা অঙ্কিত চিত্র। **—(l)ist,** *n.* A maker of pastel drawings; রঙ্গীন খড়ি দ্বারা চিত্রাঙ্কণকারী।

păs'-têrn, *n.* The part of a horse's foot between the fetlock and the hoof; অশ্বের গুল্ফ।

Păs-teur'-ĭsm (-têr-), *n.* A method of prevention or cure, devised by Pasteur, a French scientist, of diseases, esp. hydrophobia by successive inoculations; ক্রমাগত টীকা লইয়া জলাতঙ্কাদি রোগ নিবারণ।

Păs'-teur-īze (-têr), *v. t.* **1.** To treat by Pasteurism; ফরাসী বৈজ্ঞানিক লুই প্যাসটরের প্রণালী অনুসারে জলাতঙ্করোগের চিকিৎসা করা। **2.** To sterilize as milk, wine, etc. by the process of exposing them to high temperature, devised by Pasteur; অত্যধিক উত্তাপ দ্বারা দুগ্ধ, মদ্য, প্রভৃতির বীজাণু নষ্ট করা। **—i-za'-tion,** *n.*

păs-tic'-ci-o (-tĭch-ĭ-ö), **—tiche',** (-tĭch), *ns.* **1.** A medley; musical composition or literary production made up from various sources; মিশ্র, জবাখিচুড়ি; প্রকীর্ণ রচনা, বিবিধ-প্রবন্ধ, বিবিধসংগীত। **2.** (*Arts*) A picture in another's style or manner; অপর ব্যক্তির রীত্যনুযায়ী অঙ্কিত চিত্র।

păs'-tĭl, —tille' (-tēl), *ns.* **1.** A small roll of aromatic substances burnt for fumigation etc.; সুগন্ধি ধূপ বিশেষ। **2.** Lozenge; লজঞ্জুস।

păs'-time, *n.* **1.** That which serves to make time pass agreeably; sport; game; খেলা; আমোদ প্রমোদ, ক্রীড়াকৌতুক; লীলা, বিলাস, কেলি। **2.** Recreation; বিনোদন।

păs'-tŏr, *n.* **1.** (*Archaic*) A shepherd; (অপ্রঃ) মেষপালক। **2.** A minister of a church; a priest; a spiritual guide: যাজক; পুরোহিত; আচার্য্য, উপাধ্যায়। **3.** A kind of starling; একজাতীয় শালিখ। **—ly,** *adj.* Becoming a pastor; যাজকোচিত। **—ship,** *n.*

păs'-tŏr-ăl, *adj.* & *n.* **1.** Of, or relating to, shepherds; মেষপালক সম্বন্ধীয়। **2.** (Of land) Used for pasture; চারণের জন্য ব্যবহৃত। **3.** Portraying a rustic or country life, as a poem etc.; পল্লীবিষয়ক, গোচারণবিষয়ক। **4.** Of, or relating to, the pastor of a church; যাজকসংক্রান্ত, যাজকীয়। ***Noun.***

1. A pastoral poem, drama, picture or the like; a rural scene; মেষপালক ও তাহাদের জীবনী সম্বন্ধীয় কবিতা, গোপকাব্য, গোপগীতি, গোষ্ঠগীতি, পল্লীগীতি; পল্লীদৃশ্য। 2. A letter from a pastor, esp. bishop, to a clergy or people; যাজক বিশেষতঃ ধর্ম্মাধ্যক্ষের নিকট হইতে অপর যাজক বা লোকগণের নিকট প্রেরিত পত্র। **—al′-i-ty,** *n.* **—ism,** *n.* Pastoral or rural character; গ্রাম্য-স্বভাব। **—ly,** *adv.* **Pastoral epistles**—টিমথি এবং টিটাসের নিকট পল কর্তৃক প্রেরিত লিপি। **Pastoral staff**—ধর্ম্মযাজকগণের বক্রাগ্র দণ্ড।

păs-tō-râ′-lĕ, *n.* (*Pl.* -LI) A musical composition dealing with a pastoral subject; গোষ্ঠগীতি, গোষ্ঠগান, পল্লীগাথা।

păs′-tŏ-rāte, *n.* 1. Office, jurisdiction or tenure of office of a pastor; ধর্ম্মযাজকের পদ, এলেকা ও কার্য্যকাল। 2. A body of pastors; ধর্ম্মযাজকবর্গ।

pās′-trȳ, *n.* Eatables made of paste or mainly of paste; পিষ্টক মাংসপুরিত পিষ্টক প্রভৃতি, ফুলরী, কচুরী, বড়া। **Pastry cook**—আপুপিক, পিষ্টককার, পিষ্টকবিক্রয়ী।

pâs′-tūr-āge, *n.* 1. Act of pasturing; পশুচারণ, গোচারণ। 2. Herbage for cattle etc.; অশ্বগবাদির খাদ্য, তৃণ। 3. A grass-land for pasturing cattle; চারণভূমি, পশুচারণ-ভূমি, গোচারণভূমি।

pâs′-tūre, *n., v. t. & i.* 1. Grass for the food of cattle or other animals; অশ্বগবাদির খাদ্যার্থ ঘাস। 2. Ground covered with such grass; a grazing ground; তৃণাচ্ছাদিত ভূমি; চারণভূমি, পশুচারণ ক্ষেত্র, পশুচারণভূমি, গোচারণভূমি, ঘাস-স্থান, গোঠ, রমনা (হিঃ কোঃ), [cf. ঢাকার রমনা মাঠ], চারা (ঐ)। ***Verb t.*** 1. To feed on pasture; to graze on; চারণ করা; চরাণ। 2. To put cattle etc. on (land); মাঠে গবাদি পশু চরাণ। ***Verb i.*** To graze; চরা। **—tur-a-ble,** *adj.* Fit for pasture; পশুচারণযোগ্য, গোচারণযোগ্য।

pāst′-ȳ, *adj. & n.* 1. Of, relating, or like, paste; কল্কসম্বন্ধীয়, কল্কতুল্য। 2. Of pale complexion; পাণ্ডুবদন, পাণ্ডুরমুখ। ***Noun.*** A meat pie covered with paste; মাংসপুপ, মাংসের পুর দেওয়া পিষ্টক। **Pasty-faced** — Same as PASTY, *adj.* 2.

păt, *v. t. & i.* 1. To strike gently with the fingers or hand by way of caressing or approval; to strike lightly with a flat surface; হাতদ্বারা চাপড়ান, মৃদু মৃদু আঘাত করা, থাপড়ান; চ্যাপ্টা কোন কিছু দ্বারা মৃদুমৃদু আঘাত করা। 2. To flatten or smooth by striking gently with a flat surface; চ্যাপ্টা কোন কিছু দ্বারা মৃদুমৃদু আঘাত করিয়া মসৃণ বা চ্যাপ্টা করা। ***Verb i.*** 1. To strike or beat gently; মৃদু মৃদু আঘাত করা। 2. To walk or run with a light step emitting a sound; দপ দপ করিয়া চলা বা দৌড়ান। **Pat-a-cake**—ছেলেদের কোন এক ছড়ার প্রথম কয়েকটী কথা। **To pat a person on the back**—To express approbation of by patting on the back; কাহারো পিঠ চাপড়ান।

păt, *n.* A light, quick blow as with hand or finger as a caress or token of approval; চাপড়। 2. A small lump, esp. of butter, shaped by patting; ডেলা, বিশেষতঃ মাখনের ডেলা। 3. A sound of a pat or tap; চাপড়ের শব্দ।

păt, *adj. & adv.* 1. Fit; apt; opportune; উপযুক্ত; উপযোগী; সময়মত, সময়োচিত। 2. Ready for any occasion; as, he has the story *pat*; জিহ্বাগ্রে। ***Adv.*** Aptly; opportunely; readily; as, it came *pat* to his purpose; ঠিকমত; সময়মত, যথাসময়ে; পট করিয়া।

Păt, *n.* An Irishman; আয়র্লণ্ডের লোক।

pă-tā′-ġĭ-ŭm, *n.* (*Pl.* -GIA. *Zool.*) A wing-membrane as of a bat or similar other animal; (জন্তু-বিদ্যা) বাদুড় প্রভৃতির পক্ষপুটের ঝিল্লী।

păt-ă-vĭn′-ĭ-tȳ, *n.* 1. The dialectal peculiarities of the inhabitants of Patavium, now Padua as seen in the style of Livy, the historian; প্রাচীন Patavium (বর্ত্তমান) Paduaর ভাষার প্রাদেশিকতা। 2. Provincialism; প্রাদেশিকতা।

patch (păch), *n.* 1. A piece of cloth or metal etc. used in mending a hole or rent; পট্টি, তালি, জোড়া। 2. A small piece of silk stuck on the face for adornment or for hiding a defect; শোভা বৃদ্ধির জন্য বদনমণ্ডলে সংলগ্ন রেশমের ক্ষুদ্র খণ্ড, টিপ। 3. A small piece of ground; ক্ষুদ্র ভূখণ্ড। 4. A piece of plaster etc. applied to a wound; পলস্তারা। 5. A number of plants growing on a piece of ground; কোন ভূখণ্ডজাত বৃক্ষসমুচ্চয়। 6. A pad etc. worn over an injured eye; আহত চক্ষুর উপরে পরিহিত ক্ষুদ্র গদি প্রভৃতি। 7. A small piece; টুকরা। 8. (*Print*) A piece for use in mending; (মুদ্রণ) চিপি। **Patch′-er-ry,** *n.* Patching; clumsy or hasty repairing; a patchwork; (usu. *fig.*); তালি দেওন; জোড়াতাড়া; জোড়াতাড়া ব্যাপার। **Patch′-i-ly,** *adv.* **Patch′-i-ness,** *n.* **Patch′-y,** *adj.* Covered with patches; resembling patchwork; তালি দ্বারা আবৃত; তালি দেওয়া কাজের ন্যায়। **Patchwork** — Work formed of patches, or pieces, esp. of various colours and figures etc. sewed together; তালির কাজ, তালি দেওয়া জিনিষ। (*Fig.*) A work patched up or clumsily executed;

জোড়াতাড়া কাজ। (*Attrib.*) Made up of miscellaneous pieces or fragments ; or the nature of patchwork ; জোড়াতাড়া দিয়া তৈরী ; জোড়াতাড়া গোছের। **A patched up affair**—জোড়াতাড়া ব্যাপার। **Not a patch on**—Not comparable to ; তুলনার উপযুক্ত নহে।

patch (păch), *v. t.* **1.** To mend by means of a patch or patches ; to serve as a patch to ; তালি দেওয়া, পট্টি লাগান, সংগ্রথন করা, (cf. জীর্ণকাগুরা সংগ্রথন ব্যগ্রে—কুমারঃ) ; জোড়াতালির কাজ করা। **2.** To arrange or put together in a hasty or clumsy manner ; জোড়াতাড়া দেওয়া, জোড়াতাড়া দিয়া খাড়া করা। **3.** (*Fig.*) To set to rights, (usu. with *up*) ; as, to *patch up* a trouble, or quarrel ; (লক্ষণায়) ঠিক করা, গোলমিটান, মিটাইয়া ফেলা। **To patch up**—To repair with patches or clumsily ; জোড়াতালি দেওয়া, জোড়াতাড়া দিয়া খাড়া করা। **To patch up reconciliation** — To make a temporary truce ; কিছুকালের জন্য শান্তিস্থাপন করা।

pă-tchou'-li (-chô-), **–lў**, *ns.* An East-Indian odoriferous plant ; a perfume got from it ; পচাপাতা ; পচাপাতা হইতে প্রাপ্ত গন্ধদ্রব্যবিশেষ।

pāte, *n.* (*Now colloq.*) The crown of the head ; the head ; মাথার খুলি ; মাথা, মুণ্ড। **Pat'-ed**, *adj.*

pate, *(F.)*, *n.* A pie ; a pasty ; পিষ্টক ; মাংসপূরিত পিষ্টক।

pă-tĕl'-lă, *n.* **1.** The knee-pan or knee-cap ; হাঁটুর মালাই চাকি, ফলকাস্থি (হঃ চঃ)। **2.** (*Rom. antiq.*) A small pan ; (রোমীয় প্রত্নতত্ত্ব) ক্ষুদ্র কটাহ। **–lar, –late**, *adjs.*

păt'-ĕn, *n.* **1.** A shallow plate used for bread at eucharist ; খৃষ্টের অন্তিমভোজনপর্ব্বের রুটি রাখিবার জন্য অগভীর ভাণ্ড। **2.** A metallic circular flat dish ; চাটু।

pāt'-ĕnt, *adj.* **1.** Open, as a door etc. ; খোলা, উন্মুক্ত। **2.** (*Fig.*) Evident ; plain ; (লক্ষণায়) প্রত্যক্ষ, প্রকট, ব্যক্ত ; সর্ব্বপ্রকাশ্য, স্পষ্ট। **3.** Open to the perusal of all ; as, letters *patent* : সর্ব্বসাধারণের পাঠ্য। **4.** Secured or conferred by law or royal grant as an exclusive privilege or monopoly ; রাজসনন্দদ্বারা সংরক্ষিত। **Pa'-ten-cy**, *n.* State of being patent or evident ; স্পষ্টতা, স্পষ্টবোধ্যতা, (হিঃ কোঃ), বহির্ভাব (ঐ), ব্যক্ততা (ঐ)। **Pa'-tent-ly**, *adv.* **Letters patent**—Same as PATENT, *n.* I.

pāt'-ĕnt (*or* păt-), *n.* **1.** A writing from a sovereign etc. duly authenticated, granting a right, title or other privilege to a person or party ; সনন্দপত্র, অধিকারপত্র। **2.** A writing or government grant securing to an inventor for a term the exclusive right to make use or sell his invention ; যে পত্র দ্বারা কোন বস্তুর উদ্ভাবয়িতা নির্দ্দিষ্ট কালের জন্য কোন বস্তু প্রস্তুত, ব্যবহার বা বিক্রয়ের জন্য অনন্যসাধারণ অধিকার প্রাপ্ত হইয়া থাকে, বিশেষাধিকারপত্র। **3.** An invention or process so secured ; বিশেষাধিকারপত্রদ্বারা রক্ষিত কোনরূপ উদ্ভাবিত বস্তু বা প্রক্রিয়া। **4.** A sign or token that one is entitled to something or possesses a quality etc. ; as, a *patent* of gentility ; চিহ্ন, নিদর্শন। **Patent office**—যে কার্য্যালয় হইতে বিশেষ আধকারপত্র প্রদত্ত হয়। **Patent-roll**—গ্রেটব্রিটনে এক বৎসরে যে বিশেষ অধিকারপত্র সকল প্রদত্ত হয় তাহার তাড়া।

pāt'-ĕnt (*or* păt-), *v. t.* To obtain a patent for (an invention) ; (আবিষ্কৃত দ্রব্যের) সনন্দ লাভ করা। **–a-ble**, *adj.* Capable of being patented ; বিশেষাধিকারপত্রপ্রাপ্তিযোগ্য।

pāt-ĕnt-ee' (-ë), *n.* One who holds a patent ; বিশেষাধিকারপত্রপ্রাপ্ত ব্যক্তি।

pă'-tĕr, *n.* (*Slang*) Father ; (ইতরভাষায়) বাবা।

Patera.

păt'-ĕr-ă, *n.* (*Antiq.*) **1.** A shallow circular dish ; (প্রত্নতত্ত্ব) অগভীর গোলাকার ভাণ্ড। **2.** (*Arch.*, *Pl.*

Architectural Pateræ.

-ERÆ) Any flat round ornament, esp, in bas relief ; গোলাকৃতি সৌধভূষা বিশেষ।

pā'-tĕr-fă-mil'-ĭ-ăs, *n.* (*Rom. law*, & *facet.*) The head of a family or household ; (রোমীয় আইন ও রহস্যচ্ছলে) বাড়ীর কর্ত্তা, গৃহপতি।

pă-tĕr'-năl, *adj.* **1.** Pertaining to a father ; fatherly ; পৈত্রিক, পৈত্র, পিত্র্য ; পৈতৃক। **2.** Connected through the father ; as, *paternal* grandmother ; পিতৃসম্পর্কীয়। **–ly**, *adv.*

pă-tĕr'-nĭ-tў, *n.* **1.** State of being a father ; fatherhood ; পিতৃত্ব, জনকতা (কথাঃ সঃ), পিতৃভাব ; পৈতৃকত্ব, পিতৃধর্ম্ম। **2.** Male parentage ; পিতৃকুল। **3.** (*Fig.*) Authorship ; source ; কর্ত্তৃত্ব ; উৎপত্তি, যোনি।

pă'-tĕr-nŏs-tĕr, *n.* **1.** The Lord's Prayer, so called from the first two words of the Latin version ; প্রভু যীশুখৃষ্টের প্রার্থনা। **2.** A special bead in a rosary, usually the eleventh ; জপমালার কোন বিশেষ গুটিকা, সচরাচর একাদশতম গুটিকা। **Black, white paternoster**—যাদু মন্ত্রের শব্দ। **Paternoster-line**—একপ্রকার বড়শীর সুতা—যাহার স্থানে

স্থানে বড়শী বাঁধা থাকে। **Devil's paternoster**—বিড় বিড় করিয়া যে অভিশাপ দেওয়া হয়।

păth, *n.* **1.** (Also a *pathway*) A way trodden out by feet ; a road ; পথ, রাস্তা ; মার্গ, বর্ত্ম, পন্থা, অধ্ব। **2.** A specially constructed road for racing ; as, a cinder-*path* ; ঘোড়দৌড়ের জন্য বিশেষভাবে প্রস্তুত পথ। **3.** A line along which a person or thing moves ; course ; as, the *path* of a meteor ; গমনপথ ; গতিপথ। **Path'-less**, *adj.* **Pathway**—See PATH, *n.* I.

pă-thĕt'-ic, *adj.* & *n.* **1.** Exciting pity or sorrow ; full of pathos ; মনোদ্রাবক, হৃদয়স্পর্শী, মর্ম্মস্পর্শী, কারুণ্যোদ্দীপক ; কারুণ্যপূর্ণ, সকরুণ। **2.** Of, or relating to, emotions ; চিত্তবৃত্তিসমূহসম্বন্ধীয়। *Noun.* **1.** That which is pathetic ; (*pl.*) pathetic expression or sentiments; করুণ বিষয় ; করুণরস। **2.** (*Pl.*) The study of the emotions ; চিত্তবৃত্তিসমূহ সম্বন্ধে আলোচনা। **–i-cal**, *adj.* **–i-cal-ly**, *adv.* **Pathetic fallacy**—জড় প্রকৃতিতে মানবীয় চিত্তবৃত্তি প্রভৃতি আরোপমূলক ভ্রান্তযুক্তি। **The pathetic**—করুণ রস।

păth-ŏ-gĕn'-ĕ-sis, pă-thŏg'-ĕ-nў, *ns.* **1.** Production or development of disease ; রোগজনন, রোগোৎপাদন, রোগবিকাশ। **2.** Pathology dealing with origin and development of disease ; নিদানশাস্ত্রের যে অংশে রোগের উৎপত্তি এবং বিকাশের বিষয় আলোচিত হয়। **–ge-net'-ic, –gen'-ic, Pa-thog'-e-nous**, *adjs.*

pă-thŏg-nŏ-mŏn'-ic, *adj.* Characteristic of a disease ; রোগলক্ষণনির্দ্দেশক।

pă-thŏg'-nŏ-mў, *n.* The science or study of the emotions ; চিত্তরাগবিজ্ঞান। **Path-og-nom'-ic**, *adj.*

pă-thŏl'-ŏ-gў, *n.* The science which treats of diseases and their nature, causes, progress, etc. ; চিকিৎসাশাস্ত্রের যে অংশে রোগের প্রকৃতি, কারণ ও লক্ষণ ব্যাখ্যাত হয়, রোগনির্ণয়বিজ্ঞান, নিদানশাস্ত্র, নিদানতত্ত্ব, রোগবিজ্ঞান, রোগনিরূপণবিদ্যা। **–gist**, *n.* One versed in pathology ; নিদানশাস্ত্রবিশারদ। **Path-o-log'-ic, Path-o-log'-i-cal**, *adjs.* **Path-o-log'-i-cal-ly**, *adv.*

pā'-thŏs, *n.* That quality in a speech, writing, event, etc. which awakens tender emotions ; করুণরস।

pā'-tience (-shĕns), *n.* **1.** Uncomplaining endurance of pain or any provocation ; ধৈর্য্য, স্থৈর্য্য, সহিষ্ণুতা, সহন, তিতিক্ষা, ক্ষান্তি, দম, সহনশীলতা। **2.** Perseverance ; অধ্যবসায়। **3.** A game of cards, usually for a single person ; এক-প্রকার তাসখেলা। **Patience-dock**—নানাজাতীয় গুল্মের সাধারণ নাম। **Out of patience with**—No longer able to endure ; অসহিষ্ণু। **To have no patience with**—To be irritated by ; জ্বালাতন হওয়া।

pā'-tient (-shĕnt), *adj.* & *n.* **1.** Enduring without murmuring ; showing patience ; সহিষ্ণু ; ধীরস্বভাব। **2.** Not hasty ; not overeager : স্থির ; ধীর। **3.** Persevering ; অধ্যবসায়ী। *Noun.* (*Rare*) One who bears or suffers ; (কচিদ্ব্যবহৃত) সহনশীল ব্যক্তি, সহিষ্ণু ব্যক্তি। **2.** A person under medical treatment ; চিকিৎসাধীন ব্যক্তি, রোগী। **–ly**, *adv.* With patience ; submissively ; সহিষ্ণুতার সহিত ; নম্রভাবে। **Patient of**—Enduring patiently ; সহিষ্ণু, ধৈর্য্যশীল।

păt'-i-nă, *n.* The green rust in proof of age on bronze coins and works of art ; বর্ত্তলৌহনির্ম্মিত মুদ্রা বা শিল্পদ্রব্যের হরিদ্বর্ণ মরিচা। **–na'-tion**, *n.* **–ted, –nous**, *adjs.*

patio, (*Span.*), *n.* An open inner court in a Spănish or Spanish-American house ; স্পেনদেশীয় বা স্পেনিস আমেরিকানদিগের অন্দরমহলের উন্মুক্ত অঙ্গন।

patois, (*F.*), *n.* A vulgar or provincial dialect ; গ্রাম্যভাষা, উপভাষা, অপভাষা (সাঃ পঃ)।

patria potestas, (*L.*), *n.* A father's control over his family in ancient Rome ; প্রাচীন রোমে পরিবারের উপর গৃহস্বামীর কর্তৃত্ব।

pā'-tri-ârch, *n.* **1.** The father and ruler of a family or tribe ; কুলপতি, বংশের আদিপুরুষ, গোষ্ঠীপতি, বংশপতি, গোত্রপতি। **2.** A bishop of rank next to the Pope ; a dignitary superior to an archbishop in the Greek Church ; পোপের অব্যবহিত নিম্নপদস্থ ধর্ম্মাধ্যক্ষ ; গ্রীকধর্ম্মসংঘে মহাধর্ম্মাধ্যক্ষের অপেক্ষা শ্রেষ্ঠতর যাজক। **3.** (*Pl.*) The twelve sons of Jocob ; Abraham, Isaac, and Jacob and their forefathers ; জেকবের দ্বাদশপুত্র ; এব্রাহেম, আইজাক এবং জেকব এবং তাহাদের পুর্ব্বপুরুষগণ। **4.** The father or founder of an order, institution, science or the like ; প্রতিষ্ঠাতা। **5.** A venerable chief or old man ; সম্মানার্হ নায়ক বা বৃদ্ধ ব্যক্তি। **6.** The oldest living representative ; "I shot the *patriarch* of the herd" : the *patriarch* of trees ; প্রাচীনতম জীব বা জন্তু। **–ar'-chal**, *adj.* **–ism**, *n.*

pā'-tri-ârch-āte, *n.* The office or jurisdiction or residence of an ecclesiastical patriarch ; প্রধান ধর্ম্মাধ্যক্ষের পদ, এলাকা বা বাসস্থান।

pā'-tri-ârch-ў, *n.* A patriarchal system of society or government etc. ; বৃদ্ধতন্ত্র।

pă-tri'-cian (-shăn), *n.* & *adj.* **1.** A noble of ancient Rome ; প্রাচীন রোমের উচ্চবংশীয় ব্যক্তি, সম্ভ্রান্ত ব্যক্তি। **2.** One of an order of nobility in later Roman Empire ; পরবর্ত্তী কালের রোমসাম্রাজ্যের সম্ভ্রান্ত সমাজভুক্ত ব্যক্তি। **3.** A representative officer of the Roman Emperor in Italian and African provinces ; ইতালীয় এবং আফ্রিকার প্রদেশসমূহে রোমসম্রাটের প্রতিনিধি। 4. (*Hist.*) A noble of a mediæval Italian city republic ; মধ্যযুগের ইতালীদেশের পৌর সাধারণতন্ত্রের সম্ভ্রান্ত পুরুষ। 5. A nobleman or aristocrat ; সম্ভ্রান্ত ব্যক্তি, অভিজাত ব্যক্তি। ***Adj.*** 1. Of, or relating to, the ancient patricians of Rome or to their descendants ; প্রাচীন রোমের অভিজাতবর্গ বা তাহাদের বংশধরগণ-সম্বন্ধীয়। 2. Aristocratic ; noble ; উচ্চবংশীয় ; কুলীন, সম্ভ্রান্ত, অভিজাত।

pă-tri′-ci-āte, (-shi-), *n.* **1.** The position or dignity of a patrician ; প্রাচীন রোমের সম্ভ্রান্তপুরুষের পদ বা গৌরব। **2.** The patrician rank ; the aristocracy ; সম্ভ্রান্ত পদ ; অভিজাত সম্প্রদায়।

păt′-ri-cīde, *n.* Same as PARRICIDE (which see.) **—cid-al,** *adj.*

păt′-ri-mō-ny̆, *n.* 1. An estate inherited from one's father or from any ancestor, (*lit.* & *fig.*) ; (শব্দানুযায়ী ও লক্ষণায়) পৈতৃক সম্পত্তি, পূর্ব্বপুরুষ হইতে প্রাপ্ত সম্পত্তি, দায়। **2.** The endowment of a church etc. ; খৃষ্টীয় ধর্ম্মসংঘ প্রভৃতির ধর্ম্মোত্তর। **—mo′-ni-al,** *adj.* **The patrimony of St. Peter** — পোপের শাসনাধীন দেশসমূহ।

pā′-tri-ŏt, *n.* A person who loves his country, and zealously supports and defends it and its interests ; স্বদেশহিতৈষী, স্বদেশসেবক, স্বদেশপ্রেমিক, স্বদেশভক্ত। **—ism,** *n.* Love of one's country ; the passion for the welfare of one's country ; স্বদেশপ্রেম, স্বদেশপ্রেমিকতা, স্বাদেশিকতা, স্বদেশভক্তি স্বদেশপ্রীতি ; স্বদেশানুরাগ। **—ot′-ic,** *adj.* Like a patriot ; actuated by love of one's country ; স্বদেশভক্তসদৃশ ; স্বদেশ-প্রেমোদ্দীপ্ত। **—ot′-i-cal-ly,** *adv.* **Patriotic fund**—স্বদেশের জন্য যাঁহারা যুদ্ধে প্রাণদান করিয়াছেন — তাঁহাদের পরিবারের সাহায্যার্থ অর্থভাণ্ডার।

pă-tris′-tic, —ti-căl, *adjs.* Of, or pertaining to, the Fathers of the Christian Church ; relating to the study of their writings ; খৃষ্টীয় ধর্ম্মচার্য্যগণসংক্রান্ত ; খৃষ্টীয় ধর্ম্মাচার্য্যগণের গ্রন্থালোচনাসম্বন্ধীয়।

pă-tris′-tics, *n.* That branch of theology which treats of the doctrines of the Christian Fathers ; খৃষ্টীয় ধর্ম্মশাস্ত্রের যে অংশে প্রাচীন খৃষ্টীয়-ধর্ম্মচার্য্যগণের মতসম্বন্ধে আলোচনা থাকে।

Pă-trŏ′-clŭs, *n.* The amiable friend of Achilles ; মহাবীর একিলিসের বন্ধু। Agamemnonকে উত্ত্যক্ত করার উদ্দেশ্যে Achilles যুদ্ধ হইতে বিরত হইলে তিনি তদীয় বন্ধু Patroclusকে যুদ্ধে প্রেরণ করেন।

pă-trōl′, *n., v. i.* & *t.* **1.** The marching round of a guard in the night ; any parambulation of town etc. by police ; রাত্রিতে নগররক্ষীর পরিক্রমণ, রক্ষিনিশাপরিক্রম ; চৌকী, পাহারা। **2.** The guard or men who makes a patrol ; a policeman or policemen going round a regular beat ; নগর-রক্ষী, নগর-রক্ষিবর্গ ; প্রহরী, চৌকিদার পাহারা-ওয়ালা। **3.** A batch of troops sent out for reconnoitreing ; শত্রুসৈন্যের গতিবিধি পর্য্যবেক্ষণার্থ প্রেরিত সৈন্যদল। ***Verb i.*** To go the rounds in a camp, garrison, etc. ; to act as a patrol ; শিবিরে বা সেনানিবেশে পাহারা দেওয়া, রোঁদ ফিরা ; পাহারা-ওয়ালার কাজ করা। ***Verb t.*** **1.** To pass round as a sentry ; as, to *patrol* a frontier ; পাহারা দিবার জন্য পরিক্রমণ করা।

pā′-trŏn, *n.* **1.** One who supports or protects a person, cause, art, etc. ; an advocate ; পৃষ্ঠপোষক ; মুরুব্বী, সম্ভাবয়িতা (সম্ভাবয়িতা বুদ্ধান্), অনুপালয়িতা (আঃ বঃ), রক্ষক, পালক। **2.** A regular customer of a shop etc. ; নিয়মিত গ্রাহক বা ক্রেতা। **3.** (*Rom. antiq.*) The former owner of a manumitted slave ; the protector of a client ; (রোমীয় প্রত্ন-তত্ত্ব) মুক্তিপ্রাপ্ত ক্রীতদাসের ভূতপূর্ব্ব প্রভু ; মুরুব্বী। **4.** One having the right of presentation to an ecclesiastical benefice ; যাজকের পদ বা ধর্ম্মবৃত্তি প্রদানে অধিকারবান্ ব্যক্তি। **—ess,** *n.* (*Fem.*) **Patron deity** — ইষ্টদেব (এভেলন)। **Patron saint**—রক্ষাকারী সিদ্ধপুরুষ।

păt′-rŏn-āge, *n.* **1.** Special support or countenance given by a patron ; আনুকূল্য, পৃষ্ঠপোষকতা। **2.** The right of presentation to a benefice or office ; যাজকের পদ বা ধর্ম্মবৃত্তি প্রদানের অধিকার। **3.** The support given by a customer ; ক্রেতার সাহায্য বা পৃষ্ঠপোষকতা। **4.** Patronizing ; পৃষ্ঠপোষণ। **Patronage Secretary**—ইংলণ্ডের সরকারী ধনাগারের কর্ম্মকর্ত্তা।

păt′-rŏn-īze, *v. t.* **1.** To support, countenance or favour ; to lend aid ; to promote ; সাহায্য করা, আনুকূল্য করা, অনুগ্রহ করা; পৃষ্ঠপোষকতা করা ; শ্রীবৃদ্ধিসাধন করা। **2.** To assume the air of a patron or superior towards ; মুরুব্বিয়ানার ভাণ করা। **—i-za′-tion, —iz-er,** *ns.* **—i-zing,** *adj.* **—i-zing-ly,** *adv.*

păt′-rō-ny̆m′-ic, *adj.* & *n.* Derived from the name of a parent or ancestor ; অপত্যসূচক (যথা—মানব = মনুর পুত্র)। ***Noun.*** Such a name ; a family name ; অপত্যসূচকনাম ; পিত্র্য নাম।

pă-trōōn′, *n.* (*U. S. Hist.*) A proprietor of certain tracts of land with manorial privileges under the old Dutch Government of New York and New Jersey ; নিউইয়র্ক এবং নিউজার্সিতে প্রাচীন ওলন্দাজশাসনতন্ত্রের অধীন ভূম্যধিকারী।

păt′-ten (-ĕn), *n.* **1.** A wooden shoe or sole raised by supports upon an iron ring and worn to keep the shoes from the dirt or mud ; জুতাতে ময়লামাটী লাগিতে না পারে তজ্জন্য কাষ্ঠপাদুকা বা কাষ্ঠনির্ম্মিত তলি। 2. The base of a pillar ; স্তম্ভের পাদদেশ।

păt'-ter (-êr), *v. i., t. & n.* 1. To make or sound like that of falling drops of water or hail ; ঝুপ ঝুপিয়ে পড়া, টাপুর টাপুর করিয়া পড়া। 2. To move with short quick-sounding steps ; হট হট করিয়া চলে যাওয়া, হন হন করিয়া চলা। ***Verb t.*** To cause, as water etc. to patter ; টাপুর টাপুর করিয়া ফেলা, ঝুপ ঝুপ করিয়া ঢালা। ***Noun.*** A quick succession of small sounds or taps ; পট পট, হন হন, ঝুপ ঝুপ, টাপুর টুপুর।

păt'-ter (-êr), *v. t. & i.* To repeat in a low tone ; to mutter ; as, to *patter* prayers ; অনুচ্চস্বরে আবৃত্তি করা ; বিড়বিড় করা। ***Verb i.*** To talk glibly ; to speechify ; গলগল করিয়া বলা ; গলাবাজি করা।

păt'-ter (-êr), *n.* 1. The dialect or cant of a class or profession ; কোন শ্রেণী বা ব্যবসায়ের উপভাষা। 2. Speechifying ; chatter ; গলাবাজি ; বক বক। 3. The rapid speech introduced into a song ; the words of a comedy, song, etc. ; সঙ্গীতে অন্তর্নিবিষ্ট দ্রুত-উচ্চার্য্য বাক্য ; সঙ্গীত, মিলনান্ত নাট্য প্রভৃতির অন্তর্গত শব্দসমূহ। **Patter-song**—একপ্রকার হাসির গান, ইহাতে বহু শব্দ অতি দ্রুত গীত বা উচ্চারিত হয়। **To patter flash**—To talk in thieves' cant ; চোরের ভাষায় কথা বলা।

păt'-tern (-êrn), *n. & v. t.* 1. An excellent model or example ; অত্যুৎকৃষ্ট দৃষ্টান্ত, আদর্শ। 2. Anything designed to serve as a model ; a sample (of tailor's cloth etc.) ; আদর্শ ; নমুনা। 3. An ornamental design on carpet, wall-paper, etc. ; গালিচা, দেওয়ালের কাগজ, প্রভৃতির শোভাসাধক নমুনা। 4. The marks made by shot from a gun on target ; চাঁদমারিতে বন্দুকের গুলির চিহ্ন। ***Verb t.*** To model or fashion, as a thing *after*, or *upon* design, etc. ; to work or decorate with a pattern ; আদর্শানুযায়ী গঠন করা ; কোনরূপ নমুনা দ্বারা অলঙ্কৃত করা। **Pattern-box**—তাঁতের উভয় পার্শ্বে স্থাপিত 'মাকু' রাখিবার বাক্স। **Pattern-room, -shop**—যে স্থানে ঢালাইর কারখানা প্রভৃতির জন্য নমুনা প্রস্তুত হয়, আদর্শনির্ম্মাণাগার।

păt'-tȳ, *n.* A little pie ; a pasty ; ক্ষুদ্র পিষ্টক ; মাংস-পুপ। **Pattypan**—ক্ষুদ্র পিষ্টক বা মাংস-পুপ সেঁকিবার জন্য চাটু।

păt'-ū-lous (-lŭs), *adj.* 1. Open ; expanded ; উন্মুক্ত, প্রসারিত, ব্যাদানশীল ; মেলা, ছড়ানো। 2. Spreading, as the boughs of a tree etc. ; বিস্তারী। **-ly**, *adv.* **-ness**, *n.*

pau'-çi-tȳ (pä-), *n.* Fewness ; smallness ; স্বল্পতা, ন্যূনতা ; স্তোকতা, সংখ্যাল্পত্ব।

Paul (päl), *n.* The name of the Apostle of the Gentiles (*Act* xiii, 9) ; খৃষ্টের পার্ষদ পল। **A Paul's man**—দাম্ভিক লোক। **Paul's pigeons**—লণ্ডন নগরীস্থ St. Paul বিদ্যালয়ের ছাত্র। **Paul Pry**—An inquisitive person (a character in a comedy by J. Poole 1825) ; কৌতূহলী ব্যক্তি। **To rob Peter to pay Paul**—To take away from one to give to another ; to discharge one debt by incurring another ; একের জিনিষ লুটিয়া অপরকে দান করা, পরের গোয়ালে গোদান করা ; একজনের নিকট হইতে ঋণ করিয়া অপরের ঋণ পরিশোধ করা।

Pau-li'-cian (pä-lĭ-shăn), *n.* A member of a sect of Christian dualists originating in Armenia in the 7th century ; সপ্তম শতাব্দীতে আরমেনিয়াদেশে উদ্ভূত খৃষ্টীয় দ্বৈতবাদিসম্প্রদায়ের সভ্য।

Pau'-līne (pä-), *adj. & n.* Of, or relating to, St. Paul ; সেণ্টপল-সম্বন্ধীয়। ***Noun.*** A scholar of the St. Paul's School ; সেণ্টপল বিদ্যালয়ের ছাত্র।

pau'-lō-pōst-fü'-türe (pä-), *n.* 1. (*Gk. Gram.*) Future perfect tense ; (গ্রীক ব্যাকরণ) ক্রিয়াসমাপ্তিবাচক ভবিষ্যত কাল। 2. (*Humorous*) Immediate future ; (কৌতুকচ্ছলে) আসন্ন ভাবিকাল।

paunch (pänch), *n. & v. t.* 1. The belly ; stomach ; উদর, জঠর ; পাকস্থলী। 2. The first stomach of a ruminant ; রোমন্থনকারী জন্তুর প্রথম পাকস্থলী। 3. (*Naut.*) A strong mat ; a wooden covering on a mast to prevent chafing ; (নৌ-বিদ্যা) একপ্রকার শক্ত মাদুর ; ঘর্ষণজনিত ক্ষয় নিবারণের জন্য মাস্তুলের উপর কাষ্ঠময় আবরণবিশেষ। ***Verb t.*** To eviscerate or disembowel ; অন্ত্র নিষ্কাশিত করা।

pau'-pêr (pä-), *n.* 1. A poor person ; a beggar ; esp. one receiving poor-law relief ; দরিদ্র-ব্যক্তি, অকিঞ্চন, অনাথ, নিষ্কিঞ্চন, কাঙ্গাল, নিঃস্ব ব্যক্তি, যোত্রহীন ; ভিক্ষাজীবী, ভিখারী ; ভিক্ষাজীবী, বিশেষতঃ যাজকীয় সাহায্যপ্রাপ্ত ব্যক্তি। 2. (*Law*) One allowed to sue in *forma pauperis* ; (আইন) পাপর। **-dom**, *n.* **-ism**, *n.* State of being a pauper ; দারিদ্র্য, দরিদ্রতা, ভিক্ষোপজীবিকা। **-i-za'-tion**, *n.* **-ize**, *v. t.* To reduce to pauperism ; নিঃস্ব করা, যোত্রহীন করা, কাঙ্গাল করা।

pause (päz), *n. & v. i.* 1. A cessation or intermission, esp. from doubt or hesitation ; নিবৃত্তি, বিরাম, বিততি, অবচ্ছেদ। 2. (*Pros.*) A caesura ; (ছন্দঃশাস্ত্র) যতি। 3. A break in speaking or reading ; বিরাম। 4. (*Mus.*) A mark showing continuance of a note or rest ; (সঙ্গীতে) বিরামচিহ্ন। ***Verb i.*** **1.** To make a pause ; to wait ; বিরাম লওয়া ; থামা। **2.** To stop for a time (upon word etc.) ; "He *paused upon the word*" ; অল্পক্ষণের জন্য থামা। **To give pause to, To put to a pause**—To cause to stop or hesitate ; থামান, সংশয়দোলায় দোলায়মান করা।

păv′-āge, *n.* **1.** Act of laying a pavement ; তলপত্তনস্থাপন। **2.** A tax or toll to pay for the paving of highways ; রাস্তা পাকা করার জন্য দেয় কর বা মাশুল।

păv′-ăn, *n.* A stately dance in ceremonial or elaborate costume ; ময়ূরপুচ্ছলাঞ্ছন বিচিত্রপরিচ্ছদ পরিধানপূর্ব্বক নৃত্যবিশেষ, ময়ূর-নৃত্য।

pāve, *v. t.* **1.** To make a hard level surface on by laying with stones, earth, lime, etc. ; রাস্তা পাকা করা। **2.** To prepare; to make easy and smooth ; as, *to pave* the way to promotion ; প্রস্তুত করা ; পরিষ্কার করা, সুগম করা। **Pav′-er,** *n.*

pave, (*F.*), *n.* **1.** Same as PAVEMENT, *n.* 1 & 2. **2.** A setting of jewels in which the stones are set close together so as to cover the metal fully ; পাথর বসাইবার রীতি-বিশেষ—যাহাতে পাথরগুলি ঘন ভাবে বসানের দরুণ ধাতু সম্পূর্ণরূপে ঢাকা পড়ে।

pāve′-mĕnt, *n.* **1.** A covering of a floor, street, etc. formed of stones, tiles, etc. filled closely together ; গৃহতল, রাজপথ, প্রভৃতির টালি, পাথর, প্রভৃতি রচিত আবরণ। **2.** A paved road, or floor ; পাকারাস্তা, পাকামেঝে, তলপত্তন (উড়িষ্যা)। **3.** (*Zool.*) A level hard surface formed by close-set teeth, bony plates, etc. "Teeth are…flat forming a *pavement*" ; (জন্তুবিদ্যা) ঘনসন্নিবিষ্ট দন্ত, অস্থিময় ফলক, প্রভৃতি দ্বারা রচিত কঠিন সমতল উপরিভাগ। **Pavement artist** — পথিকগণের নিকট হইতে পয়সা আদায়ের জন্য যে ব্যক্তি পাকা রাস্তার উপর নানা প্রকার রঙ্গীন চিত্র আঁকিয়া থাকে। **To pave the way for** or **to**—(*Fig.*) To prepare the way to or for ; to remove difficulties or obstacles beforehand for accomplishing something ; (লক্ষণায়) পথ পরিষ্কার করা, পথ সুগম করা ; বাধাবিঘ্ন-দূর করা।

pă-vĭl′-ĭ-ŏn, *n.* & *v. t.* **1.** A large tent ; সুবৃহৎ পটবাস, পটমণ্ডপ, মণ্ডপ, জনাশ্রয়, বড় তাঁবু। **2.** An ornamental building, esp. one in a garden or cricket or other ground ; উদ্যান বা ক্রীকেট ক্রীড়ার অঙ্গনস্থিত কারুকার্য্যখচিত গৃহ। **3.** A projecting part of a building, usually highly decorated ; কোন অট্টালিকার বহিরুদ্গত অংশ—সচরাচর কারুকার্য্য সুশোভিত অংশ। ***Verb t.*** To furnish or cover with a pavilion or pavilions ; to shelter with a tent ; বৃহৎ পটবাস প্রদান করা, বৃহৎ পটবাস দ্বারা আচ্ছাদিত করা ; তাঁবুতে আশ্রয় দেওয়া।

Pāv′-ĭ-our (-ĕr), *n.* **1.** Same as PAVER. **2.** Stone or brick used in paving ; রাস্তা পাকা করার জন্য ইট বা পাথর। **3.** A rammer for driving paving stones ; রাস্তা, প্রভৃতিতে পাথর বসাইবার জন্য দুরমুস।

Pavis.

păv′-ĭs, *n.* A shield for the whole body, used in the middle ages ; মধ্যযুগে ব্যবহৃত সর্ব্বশরীর-রক্ষার্থ ঢাল।

pavonazzo, (*Ital.*), *adj.* & *n.* With peacock-coloured marks, as marble etc. ; ময়ূরপুচ্ছবর্ণচিহ্নবিশিষ্ট। ***Noun.*** Such a marble ; শিখিপিচ্ছবর্ণচিহ্নবিশিষ্ট মর্ম্মর।

păv′-ō-nīne, *adj.* Of, or pertaining to, the peacock ; resembling the neck or tail of a peacock ; (said of ores etc. which exhibit the brilliant hues of a peacock's tail) ; ময়ূরসম্বন্ধীয় ; ময়ূরপুচ্ছবর্ণ, শিখিপিচ্ছবর্ণ, ময়ূরকণ্ঠী।

paw (pä), *n.* **1.** The foot of animals having claws ; থাবা, পশুপদ। **2.** (*Colloq.*) The hand ; one's handwriting ; (চলিতভাষায়) হাত ; কোন ব্যক্তির হস্তাক্ষর, হস্তলিপি।

paw (pä), *v. t.* & *i.* **1.** To strike with the paws ; থাবা দ্বারা আঘাত করা। **2.** (Of a horse) To beat or strike as ground with hoofs ; খুর দ্বারা মাটী আঁচড়ান। **3.** (*Colloq.*) To handle clumsily or rudely ; (চলিত ভাষায়) রূঢ়ভাবে হস্তার্পণ করা। ***Verb i.*** **1.** To scrape with the paw ; থাবা দ্বারা আঁচড়ান। **2.** (Of a horse) To strike or scrape the ground with hoofs ; (অশ্ব সম্পর্কে) খুর দ্বারা মাটীতে আঘাত করা বা আঁচড়ান। **3.** To strike with the hand or handle clumsily or rudely ; as, to *paw over* something ; হস্তদ্বারা রূঢ়ভাবে আঘাত বা হস্তার্পণ করা। **Pawed,** *adj.* Having paws ; থাবাযুক্ত।

pawk′-ÿ (päk-), *adj.* (*Scot.*) Cunning ; sly ; (স্কচ্‌ভাষায়), ধূর্ত্ত ; চালাক, শঠ। **–i-ly,** *adv.* **–i-ness,** *n.*

pawl (päl), *n.* & *v. t.* **1.** A short bar acting as a catch to prevent the capstan or windlass of a ship from rolling back ; জাহাজের (নঙ্গর তুলিবার) চক্রযন্ত্রের আটক। **2.** A lever with a catch for the teeth of a wheel or a bar ; চাকা বা দণ্ডের দন্ত আটকাইবার জন্য আঁকড়াবিশিষ্ট দণ্ডযন্ত্র। ***Verb t.*** To stop or check as a capstan etc. by means of a pawl ; তাদৃশ আটক দিয়া জাহাজের নোঙ্গরোত্তোলক যন্ত্রের গতিরোধ করা।

pawn (pän), *n.* **1.** A person or thing given as security for the repayment of money or the performance of a promise; a pledge; (*lit.* & *fig.*); ঋণ পরিশোধ বা শপথরক্ষার প্রতিভূস্বরূপ রক্ষিত বস্তু; বন্ধকী দ্রব্য, আধি (শুক্র: বিনয়)। 2. State of being pledged; as, in or at *pawn*; বন্ধকী অবস্থা। **Pawn-broker**—যে ব্যক্তি অস্থাবর সম্পত্তি বন্ধক রাখিয়া টাকা ধার দেয়, বন্ধকী দ্রব্যের মহাজন, বন্ধকী মহাজন, অস্থাবরসম্পত্তি-বন্ধকগ্রহীতা। **Pawn-broking**—তাদৃশ মহাজনের ব্যবসায়। **Pawn-shop**—বন্ধকী ব্যবসায়ীর দোকান, বন্ধকী দোকান। **Pawn-ticket**—বন্ধকগ্রহীতা বন্ধকদাতাকে বন্ধকী জিনিষের বিবরণাদি সম্বলিত যে স্থূল কাগজখণ্ড প্রদান করে, বন্ধকী দলিল। **In or at pawn**—In or at pledge; বন্ধকদত্ত, বাঁধা-দেওয়া।

pawn (pän), *n.* A piece of smallest size and value in chess; (also, *fig.*, of persons); দাবার বড়ে, গুটি, শারি; (লক্ষণায় লোকসম্পর্কেও ব্যবহৃত হয়)।

pawn (pän), *v. t.* 1. To give in pledge; to put in pawn; বন্ধক দেওয়া বা রাখা; বাঁধা দেওয়া। 2. (*Fig.*) To pledge as one's life, honour, etc.; পণ করা।

pawn-ee′ (pän-ē), *n.* A person who takes anything in pawn; বন্ধকগ্রহীতা।

păx, *n.* 1. A small plate of gold, silver, etc., with generally the image of Christ upon the cross on it and kissed at Mass; ক্রুশোপরি আরোপিত যীশুর মূর্ত্তিসমন্বিত ক্ষুদ্র স্বর্ণ বা রজতপাত্র—যাহা Mass পর্ব্বে চুম্বন করা হইয়া থাকে। 2. (*Used interjectionally, school-slang*) Truce! peace!; (বিদ্যালয়ের ইতরভাষায়) শান্তি! শান্তি!! **Pax Romana**—রোমসাম্রাজ্যের মধ্যে শান্তি। **Pax vobis**—Peace to you; তোমার শান্তি হউক।

păx′-wăx, *n.* (*Dial.* & *colloq.*) The strong tendon in the neck of men or animals; (উপভাষায় ও চলিতভাষায়) পশু বা মানুষের গ্রীবার পশ্চাদ্দিকের শক্ত শিরা।

pay (pā), *v. t.* & *i.* 1. To give in discharge of a debt; to give (a person or money or a person money) for goods received or service rendered; পরিশোধ করা; গৃহীতদ্রব্য বা প্রাপ্তোপকারের প্রতিদান করা। 2. (*Fig.*) To compensate; to reward or punish; (*dial.* or *slang*) to beat or flog; "He had been *paying* somebody with etc."; (লক্ষণায়) ক্ষতিপূরণ করা; দণ্ড বা পুরস্কার দেওয়া; (উপভাষায় বা ইতর ভাষায়) মারা, বেতমারা। 3. To satisfy as a claim; to discharge as a debt; দাবির মীমাংসা করা; পরিশোধ করা। 4. To give an equivalent or return for (labour etc.); (of a business etc.) to yield adequate return to (a person); সমান মূল্যের জিনিষ দেওয়া; উপযুক্ত প্রতিদান পাওয়া। 5. To render or offer; as, to *pay* a visit: to *pay* attention, respect, etc. to; প্রদান করা, দান করা। ***Verb i.*** 1. To make payment; to discharge a debt; প্রতিদান দেওয়া; ঋণ পরিশোধ করা। 2. To be profitable or remunerative; as, politeness always *pays*; লাভজনক হওয়া। **Pay-ee′**, *n.* One to whom money is paid; অর্থগ্রহীতা। **Pay′-er**, *n.* **The devil to pay**—A severe penalty; গুরুতর শাস্তি। **To pay attention(s) to**—To attend to; to court; মনোযোগ দেওয়া; প্রেম যাচ্ঞা করা। **To pay away**—Same as to PAY OUT (*naut.*) **To pay court**—See under COURT. **To pay dearly for**—To suffer penalty; শাস্তিভোগ করা। **To pay down**—To deliver as money in payment; to pay at once or on the spot; পাওনা টাকা বুঝাইয়া দেওয়া; পাওনা টাকা তৎক্ষণাৎ বুঝাইয়া দেওয়া। **To pay for**—To hand over the price of; to bear the cost of; মূল্য প্রদান করা; ব্যয়ভার বহন করা। (*Fig.*) To be punished *for* (a fault etc.); as, men often *pay for* their mistakes; (লক্ষণায়) অপরাধের জন্য শাস্তি ভোগ করা। **To pay off**—To pay in full and discharge (ship's crew, workmen, bill, etc.); (জাহাজের নাবিক প্রভৃতিকে) কড়ায় গণ্ডায় পাওনা বুঝাইয়া দিয়া কাজ হইতে জবাব দেওয়া, চুকাইয়া দেওয়া। **To pay off old scores**—To pay off a debt of money or revenge; পরিশোধ করা, প্রতিশোধ লওয়া, দাদ তোলা। **To pay on**—To beat or thrash vigorously; উত্তম মধ্যম দেওয়া। **To pay one back**—To repay him; পরিশোধ করা। **To pay one in one's own coin**—To retaliate; প্রতিশোধ দেওয়া। **To pay one's way**—Not to get into debt; ঋণগ্রস্ত না হওয়া। **To pay out**—(*Naut.*) To cause to run out, as rope; (নৌবিদ্যা) রজ্জু বিস্তৃত করা। To punish as a person; শাস্তি দেওয়া। **To pay the** or **one's debt of** or **to nature**—To die; মরা। **To pay the penalty of**—To suffer the consequences of; ফল ভোগ করা। **To pay the piper**—To bear the cost, trouble or responsibility; সমস্ত ব্যয় বহন করা, সকলপ্রকার কষ্টস্বীকার করা, সমস্ত দায়িত্ব লওয়া। **To pay through the nose**—See under NOSE. **To pay up**—To pay the full amount of (arrears etc.); কড়ায় গণ্ডায় পাওনা চুকাইয়া দেওয়া। **To pay with the Roll of the Drum**—Not to pay at all (no soldier can be arrested for debt while on march); মোটেই কিছু না দেওয়া।

pay (pā), *v. t.* (*Naut.*) To smear or coat as a vessel's bottom, a seam, etc. with hot tar etc.; জাহাজের তলায়

বা তক্তার জোড়া ইত্যাদিতে গরম আলকাতরা দেওয়া।

pay (pā), *n.* **1.** Act of paying; payment: পরিশোধকরণ; পরিশোধ। **2.** Salary; wages; মাহিনা; বেতন। **Pay-bill**—কর্ম্মচারী, সৈন্যগণ প্রভৃতিকে প্রদেয় টাকার বিবরণ। **Pay-day**—বেতন দেওয়ার নির্দ্দিষ্ট দিবস; হিসাব মিটাইবার দিন। **Pay-master**—বেতনপ্রদায়ক কর্ম্মচারী। **Paymaster-general**—কোষাধ্যক্ষ। **In the pay of**—In the employment of; কাহারো অধীনে চাকুরীতে নিযুক্ত।

pay'-a-ble (pā-ă-ble), *adj.* **1.** That ought to be paid; due: প্রতিদানযোগ্য, পরিশোধনীয়; প্রদেয়। **2.** (Of mine etc.) Profitable; (খনি প্রভৃতি সম্পর্কে) লাভজনক।

pay'-mĕnt (pā-), *n.* **1.** The act of paying; discharge of a debt or obligation; প্রদান; ঋণপরিশোধ। **2.** Amount paid; recompense; প্রদত্ত অর্থের পরিমাণ; প্রতিদান।

pay'-nim (pā-), *n.* (*Archaic*) A pagan; an infidel, esp. Mohammedan; (*often attrib.*); (অপ্রঃ) বিধর্ম্মী; কাফের, বিশেষতঃ মুসলমান বিধর্ম্মী।

payn'-ize (pān-), *v. t.* To impregnate as wood with certain solutions, to preserve it; ঔষধ-জলে ভিজাইয়া কাঠ শক্ত করা, তাজা রাখা।

paysage, *n.* A landscape or landscape picture; প্রাকৃতিক দৃশ্য, নিসর্গচিত্র। ***Paysagist***, *n.* A landscape artist; নিসর্গচিত্রশিল্পী।

pea (pē-), *n.* (*Pl.* PEAS *individually*, PEASE *collectively*) A climbing annual herb of the bean family, whose seeds are nutritious; its seed; মটর গাছ; কাবুলী মটর (যোঃ), কলাইসুঁটি। **Field pea**—দেশী মটর। **Green pea**—মটরসুঁটি। **Pea-fowl**—ময়ূর বা ময়ূরী। **Peanut**—চিনা বাদামের গাছ, চিনাবাদাম, ভুচণক। **Pea-rifle**—একপ্রকার বন্দুক—যাহা হইতে মটরের মত ক্ষুদ্র ক্ষুদ্র গুলি ছোড়া যায়। **Pea-shooter**—যে নলের মধ্য হইতে শুষ্ক কলাই নিক্ষিপ্ত হয়। **Pea-soup**—মটরের যুষ। **Pea-souper**—(*Colloq.*) Thick and yellow fog; (চলিত ভাষায়) ঘন এবং পীতবর্ণ কুজ্ঝটিকা। **Pea-soupy**—Thick and yellow as fog; ঘন এবং পীতবর্ণ কুজ্ঝটিকা। **Pea-weevil**—একপ্রকার কীট। **As like as two peas**—Undistinguishable; ঠিক একরূপ।

Peanuts.

peace (pēs), *n.* **1.** A state of quiet or tranquility; freedom from disturbance or agitation; শান্তি; স্থিরাবস্থা, প্রশান্তি। **2.** Freedom from, or cessation of, war; a treaty of peace between two or more powers at war; যুদ্ধবিরাম, যুদ্ধশান্তি; সন্ধি। **3.** Friendliness; concord; বন্ধুতা; ঐক্য। **4.** Tranquility of mind; মানসিক শান্তি। **5.** (Used *interjectionally*) silence; চুপ। **Peace'-a-ble**, *adj.* **1.** Disposed, or tending, to peace; শান্তিপ্রিয়, শান্তিপ্রবণ। **2.** Not quarrelsome; peaceful; tranquil; calm; অকলহপ্রিয়; শান্তিপ্রিয়; অবিচলিত; শান্ত। **Peace'-a-ble-ness**, *n.* **Peace'-a-bly**, *adv.* **Peace'-ful**, *adj.* **1.** Full of peace; quiet; undisturbed; শান্তিময়, শান্তিপূর্ণ; শান্ত; অবিচলিত, অবিক্ষুব্ধ। **2.** Of, or relating to, a state or time of peace; as, *peaceful* occupation; শান্তিসম্বন্ধীয়, শান্তিকালসম্বন্ধীয়। **Peace'-ful-ly**, *adv.* In a peaceful manner; শান্তিতে, নিরুপদ্রবে, নির্ব্বিবাদে। **Peace establishment**—দেশের শান্তিকালে রক্ষিত সামরিক বল। **Peacemaker**—শান্তিসংস্থাপক, বিবাদভঞ্জক; (কৌতুকচ্ছলে) রিভলভার, যুদ্ধজাহাজ, প্রভৃতি। **Peace-offering**—An offering or gift to procure peace, reconciliation, etc.; satisfaction to an offended person; শান্তি বা পুনর্মিলনের জন্য প্রদত্ত উপহার; অসন্তুষ্ট ব্যক্তির তুষ্টি-বিধানের জন্য প্রদত্ত দ্রব্য। An offering presented as thanksgiving to God (Bible); ঈশ্বরের নিকট কৃতজ্ঞতা প্রকাশের জন্য প্রদত্ত দ্রব্য। **Peace-officer**—শান্তিরক্ষক রাজপুরুষ; পুলিশ কর্ম্মচারী। **Peace-party**—শান্তিস্থাপন বা শান্তিরক্ষণের জন্য শান্তিসমিতি। **Peace-pipe**—উত্তর আমেরিকার আদিম অধিবাসিগণ কর্ত্তৃক শান্তির চিহ্নস্বরূপ ব্যবহৃত ধূমপাননল। **Armed peace**—দেশের যে অবস্থায় দৃশ্যতঃ শান্তি বিরাজ করে, কিন্তু ভিতরে ভিতরে দেশবাসিগণ যুদ্ধের জন্য সম্পূর্ণ প্রস্তুত থাকে। **At peace**—In a state of peace; শান্তিতে। **Bound over to keep the peace**—শান্তিরক্ষার জন্য মুচলেকাবদ্ধ। **Peace at any price**—ব্রিটিশ পার্লেমেন্টের চরমশান্তিপন্থী সম্প্রদায়বিশেষ। এই সম্প্রদায় সর্ব্বাবস্থায়ই যুদ্ধে প্রবৃত্ত হইতে অমত প্রকাশ করে। **Peace of God**—শান্তি। **The (king's) peace**—সমগ্র রাজ্যময় শান্তি। **To be sworn of the peace**—To be made a magistrate; ম্যাজিষ্ট্রেটের পদে নিযুক্ত হওয়া। **To hold one's peace**—To keep silence; চুপ থাকা, তুষ্ণীম্ভাব অবলম্বন করা। **To keep the peace**—To abstain from causing a disturbance; to prevent strife; অন্যের শান্তি ভঙ্গ না করা; শান্তি রক্ষা করা। **To make a person's or one's peace with**—To bring oneself back into friendly relations with ; (কাহারো সহিত) পুনরায় সৌহার্দ্দ্য স্থাপন করা। **To make peace**—শান্তিসংস্থাপন করা।

peach (pēch), *v. i.* (*Slang*) To turn informer ; to give information ; গোয়েন্দা হওয়া ; সহাপরাধীর বিরুদ্ধে সংবাদ দেওয়া।

peach (pēch), *n.* **1.** A tree with a delicious, juicy fruit ; this fruit ; সুরসফলপ্রসূ বৃক্ষবিশেষ, পীচ্ গাছ ; আরু (ফার্ম্মিঃ), পীচ্ফল, সফেট আলু [কাবুল হইতে যে খুবানী আসে তাহা শুষ্কীকৃত পীচ্ফল], [Arab.—*Khookh.* Pers.—*Shaftalu, Aroo.* Fr.—*Peche.* Germ.—*Pfirsiche.* Latin—*Persica* (অর্থাৎ পারস্যদেশীয় ফল—এই *Persica* শব্দ হইতেই ইংরাজী *Peach* হইয়াছে)]। **2.** Peach colour ; মেদুররক্তিমবর্ণ, মৃদুরক্তিমবর্ণ, আরক্তিমবর্ণ, আলোহিতবর্ণ। **Peach'-i-ness,** *n.* **Peach'-y,** *adj.* **Peach-blow** — পেলবনীলারুণাভপাটলবর্ণ ; ঐ বর্ণের বর্ণক (glaze)। **Peach-brandy**—পিচফলের রস।

pea'-chick (pē-), *n.* A young pea-fowl ; ময়ূরশাবক।

pea-cŏck (pē-), *n., v. t. & i.* (*Fem.* PEA-HEN) A large and beautiful bird with splendid plumage ; ময়ূর, শিখী, কলাপী, নীলকণ্ঠ, শিখণ্ডী, বর্হী, [Syn. বর্হিণ, চিত্রবর্হী, চিত্রবর্হ, চিত্রপুচ্ছ, চিত্রমেখল, ঘনপাষণ্ড, নর্ত্তক, নর্ত্তনপ্রিয়, নৃত্যপ্রিয়, নাগান্তক, মেঘসুহৃদ, পয়ঃসুহৃদ, রাজসারস, দীপ্তাঙ্গ, দীপ্তাক্ষ, নাগরিক, ধ্বজী, নগাবাস, জীবথ, শিখাবল, শিখাধার, শ্যামকণ্ঠ, কেকী, কেকাবল, কেকিক, মেঘানন্দী, ভুজগাশন, ভুজগদারণ, ভুজগান্তক, সর্পাশন, সর্পদ্বিষ, বর্ষামদ, সর্পভুজ, সর্পারাতি, সর্পারি, অহিদ্বিষ, অহিভুজ, অহিরিপু, কুমারবাহী, কান্তপক্ষী, শাপঠিক, শাপটিক, দার্ব্বণ্ড, ভুজঙ্গভুক্, ভুজঙ্গভোজী, ভুজঙ্গহা, ফণিভুজ, শুক্লাপাঙ্গ, সিতাপাঙ্গ, শুক্রভুক্, মেঘনাদানুলাসী, মেঘনাদানুলাসক, লাসক, চন্দ্রকবান, চন্দ্রকী (শিশুঃ), অসিতগ্রীব (মঃ ভাঃ), শুক্রাঙ্গ, শুক্লাঙ্গ, পত্রাঢ্য (গেলঃ), পয়োদসুহৃদ (সাঃ দঃ), মেচকগল, চিত্রপিচ্ছ, চিত্রপত্রক (নিঘণ্টু), নাগাশন (কাব্যঃ), ঘনরুচিরকলাপ, গুহবাহন (বাল রাঃ)। *Verb t.* (*Reflex.*) To plume oneself ; to display ; জাঁকজমক প্রদর্শন করা ; জাঁক দেখান। *Verb i.* To strut about proudly or ostentatiously ; to pose ; সদর্পে পদক্ষেপ করা, গরবে পা ফেলা, সাটোপে চলা ; বিশেষভঙ্গীতে অবস্থান করা। **—er-y,** *n.* Foppery ; বাবুগিরি। **—ish, —like,** *adjs.* **Peacock-butterfly** — একপ্রকার প্রজাপতি। **Peacock-coal**—ময়ূরপুচ্ছের মত আভাবিশিষ্ট পাথুরিয়া কয়লা। **Peacock-fish**—নীল, রক্ত হরিৎ এবং শ্বেতবর্ণে বিচিত্রিত মৎস্যবিশেষ। **Peacock-flower** — কৃষ্ণচূড়াফুল। **Peacock-ore**—সস্তক (সাঃ পঃ), ময়ূরগ্রীবতুথ (ঐ)। **Peacock-tail**—কলাপ, বর্হ, পিঞ্ছ [cf. পিঞ্ছাবতংস—পদাবলী।] শিখণ্ড, ময়ূরপুচ্ছ, শিখি-পিঞ্ছ [cf. ভগবান্ শিখিপিঞ্ছমৌলী—কৃষ্ণকর্ণামৃত।]

pea'-fōwl (pē-), *n.* A peacock or peahen ; ময়ূর বা ময়ূরী।

pea-hĕn (pē-), *n.* (*Fem.* of PEACOCK) which see ; শিখিনী।

pea'-jăck-ĕt (pē-), *n.* A short overcoat of coarse woollen cloth, used by sailors ; জাহাজের মাল্লাদিগের পশমী কোর্ত্তা।

peak (pēk), *n.* **1.** A projecting front part of a cap ; টুপীর সম্মুখের দিকের বহিঃপ্রসৃত অংশ। **2.** The pointed end of something, as beard etc. ; কোন কিছুর সূক্ষ্মাগ্র। **3.** The top of a mountain etc. ; গিরিশিখর, কোটী (হিঃ কোঃ), শৃঙ্গ, কূট, চূড়া, শৈলাগ্র, অদ্রিশৃঙ্গ। **4.** (*Naut.*) The upper outer corner of sail extended by gaff or yard ; the end of this gaff or yard ; (নৌবিদ্যা) পাইলের উপরের দিকের বহিঃকোণ ; পাইলদণ্ডের প্রান্ত। **Peak'-ed,** *adj.* **1.** Pointed ; সূক্ষ্মাগ্র। **2.** Having a thin or sickly look ; রুগ্ন, পীড়িত, রোগশীর্ণ। **Peak'-y,** *adj.* **1.** Having or showing peaks ; চূড়াবিশিষ্ট। **2.** Like a peak ; pointed ; চূড়াবৎ ; সূক্ষ্মাগ্র।

peak (pēk), *v. t. & i.* **1.** (*Naut.*) To raise (a gaff or yard) perpendicularly ; to place (the oars) vertically ; (নৌবিদ্যা) খাড়াভাবে পাইলদণ্ড রাখা ; দাঁড় খাড়া করিয়া রাখা। **2.** (Of whales) To raise as tail or flukes straight up in diving vertically ; খাড়াভাবে ডুবিবার সময় লাঙ্গুল তুলা। *Verb i.* (Of whales) To raise the tail or flukes straight up in diving vertically ; খাড়াভাবে ডুবিবার কালে লাঙ্গুল তোলা।

peak (pēk), *v. i.* To look sickly or emaciated ; as, to *peak* and pine (Shakspeare) ; রোগাটে দেখান, কাহিল দেখান। **Peak'-ed,** *adj.* Thin, pinched from illness or want ; কাহিল, রোগপীড়িত, অভাবপীড়িত।

peal (pēl), *n., v. i. & t.* **1.** A loud sound as of thunder, bells, cannon, shouting ; usually a succession of loud sounds ; গর্জ্জন, রোল, নিনাদ ; নির্ঘোষ। **2.** A set of bells for change ringing ; the changes rung on such a set of bells ; ধ্বনির তারতম্যানুসারে বাদনের জন্য সজ্জিত ঘণ্টাশ্রেণী ; ঘণ্টাশ্রেণী বাজাইবার বিভিন্ন ক্রম। *Verb i.* To sound forth in a peal ; to resound ; উচ্চধ্বনি করা ; প্রতিধ্বনিত হওয়া। *Verb t.* **1.** To utter loudly and sonorously ; গর্জ্জন করা। **2.** (*Obs.*) To assail with noise ; (অপ্রঃ) উচ্চনিনাদ করত আক্রমণ করা। **Peal of laughter**—হাসির গর্‌রা। **Peal of thunder**—দেবগর্জ্জন।

pear (pār), *n.* A fleshy fruit, tapering towards the stalk ; the tree bearing this fruit ; নাসপাতী, রুচিফল ; নাসপাতীর গাছ, চীনরাজপুত্র (বৌদ্ধঃ)। **Pear-shaped**—Shaped like a pear ; নাসপাতীর আকার। **Prickly pear**—নাগফণা (ওয়াট)।

pearl (pêrl), *n.*, *v. t.* & *i.* **1.** A smooth lustrous whitish gem produced by certain molluscs ; মুক্তা, মতি, শুক্তিজ, মোতিম (প্রাঃ সাঃ), মুক্তাফল, মুকুতা (*poet.*) [*Syn.* মৌক্তিক, মৌক্ত, শুক্তিগর্ভ, শৌক্তেয়, শুক্তিবীজ, হেমবল, জলদ্রব্য, জলজদ্রব্য, স্বাতি-সম্ভব, মঙ্গলোদয়, সগর, বারিজ।] **2.** Something resembling a pearl, *e. g.* dewdrop, tear, tooth, etc. ; শিশিরবিন্দু, অশ্রু, দশন প্রভৃতি, মুক্তা-সদৃশ পদার্থ। **3.** A precious thing ; the choicest and best specimen or example ; মূল্যবান বস্তু, সর্ব্বোৎকৃষ্ট বস্তু ; রত্ন। **4.** A size of printing type ; একপ্রকার মুদ্রণের হরপ। **5.** (*Obs.* or *dial.*) A speck or film on the eye ; (অপ্রঃ বা উপভাষায়) চক্ষুর শাদা দাগ, চক্ষুর ছানি, মোতিয়া বিন্দু। **6.** A small piece or fragment as of coal or other substances ; খণ্ড বা টুকরা **7.** Same as MOTHER-OF-PEARL (which see.) **8.** The colour of a fine pearl ; উৎকৃষ্ট মুক্তার বর্ণ। ***Verb t.*** **1.** To set or adorn with pearls ; মুক্তাখচিত করা, মুক্তা বসান। **2.** To sprinkle with pearly drops ; মুক্তাফলসন্নিভ বিন্দু সমূহ দ্বারা সমালঙ্কৃত করা। **3.** To make like pearl in colour etc. ; মুক্তাধবল করা **4.** To make into small round grains ; as, to *pearl* barley ; মুক্তার মত দানা করা। ***Verb i.*** **1.** To form pearl-like drops or beads ; মুক্তাফলবিন্দু বা গুটিকা গঠন করা। **2.** To fish for pearls ; (সমুদ্রে) মুক্তান্বেষণ করা। **Pearl′-ed,** *adj.* **Pearl′-i-ness,** *n.* **Pearl′-y,** *adj.* **1.** Containing, or abounding with, pearls ; as, *pearly* shells ; মুক্তাগর্ভ, মুক্তাপূর্ণ। **2.** Resembling pearls in colour ; clear ; মুক্তাধবল ; নির্ম্মল। **Mother-of-pearl** — See under MOTHER. **Pearl-ash**—সজ্জিকাক্ষার। **Pearl-barley**—যে খোসা ছাড়ান যব ঘষিয়া মুক্তার আকার গোল করা হয়, মুক্তাযব। **Pearl-diver**—যে ব্যক্তি মুক্তাফলপ্রসূ শুক্তি তুলিবার জন্য সাগরে ডুবিয়া থাকে। **Pearl-eye**—মুক্তাফলের আকার পক্ষিচক্ষু। **Pearl-fisher** — মুক্তোতোলক। **Pearl-fishery,** *n.* মুক্তোতোলন কার্য্য ; মুক্তাপ্রাপ্তির স্থান। **Pearl-necklace**—See NECKLACE. **Pearl

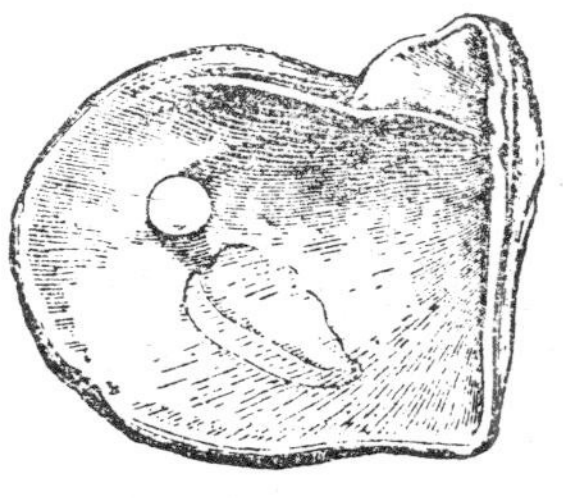

Pearl oyster.

oyster**—শুক্তি, মৌক্তিক। **Pearl-powder, —white**—ত্বক শুভ্র-করণার্থ অঙ্গরাগবিশেষ। **Pearl-shell**—শুক্তি, মুক্তামাতা, পদ্মগর্ভ। **A necklace of pearls containing 500 strings**—দেবচ্ছন্দ (বৃঃ সং)। **Casting pearls before swines**—উলু (বেণা) বনে মুক্তা ছড়ান, বানরের গলায় মুক্তার হার পরান।

pearl (pêrl), *adj.* Relating to, or made of, pearl ; like pearl or mother-of-pearl in colour etc. ; মৌক্তিক, মুক্তাময় ; মুক্তাধবল, শুক্তিবর্ণ।

pearl (pêrl), *n.* One of a row of fine loops forming a decorative ending on pillow-lace etc. ; বালিস প্রভৃতির লেইসের কিনারায় পুঁটে-ঘরাশ্রেণীর একটী।

pear′-main (pār-mān), *n.* A kind of apple ; একপ্রকার সেওফল।

peas′-ănt (pĕz-), *n.* & *adj.* A countryman ; a cultivator ; a rustic ; পাড়াগেঁয়ে লোক ; কৃষক, চাষা, কৃষাণ (হিঃ কোঃ), কৃষিজীবী, কৃষীবল (মঃ সং) ; গ্রাম্য লোক। ***Adj.*** Rural ; rustic ; গ্রাম্য ; পাড়াগেঁয়ে। **–ry,** *n.* **1.** Peasants collectively ; a body of peasants ; কৃষকসম্প্রদায় ; কৃষকের দল। **2.** Rusticity ; গ্রাম্যতা।

pease (pēz), *n.*, (*Pl.* of PEA). **Peasecod**—Pea-pod ; মটর শুঁটি।

peat (pēt), *n.* A kind of turf used as fuel ; বোদমাটী। **Peat′-y,** *adj.* **Peat-bog, —moss**—বোদমাটীময় জলাভূমি। **Peat reek**—শুষ্ক ঘাসের চাপড়ায় আগুণের ধূম ; শুষ্ক ঘাসের চাপড়ার আগুণের উপর চোলাই করা হুইস্কী বা ঐরূপ হুইস্কীবিশিষ্ট গন্ধ।

peat′-ĕr-ȳ (pēt-), *n.* A place from which peats are dug ; যে স্থান হইতে বোদমাটী খুঁড়িয়া তোলা হয়।

pĕb′-ble (-l), *n.* **1.** A small stone worn and rounded by action of water ; নুড়িপাথর, উপল, নুড়ি, শর্করা। **2.** Rock-crystal used for spectacles ; a lens of this ; চসমার পরকলা প্রস্তুতার্থ স্বচ্ছ স্ফটিক-প্রস্তর ; ঐরূপ পাথরে তৈরী চসমার পরকলা। **3.** A kind of agate ; একপ্রকার গোমেদমণি। **–bly,** *adj.*

pebrine, (*F.*), *n.* An epidemic disease of the silkworm ; গুটি-পোকার মড়ক।

pĕc′-ca-ble (-ă-bl), *adj.* Liable or prone to sin ; পাপপ্রবণ, পাপবশ, পাপাধীন, পাপক্ষম। **–bil′-i-ty,** *n.*

pĕc-ca-dil′-lo (-ă-dĭl-ō), *n.* A petty offence or fault ; সামান্য অপরাধ, অল্পাপরাধ, উপপাতক, স্খলিত।

pĕc′-cant (-ănt), *adj.* **1.** Sinning ; পাপী, সাপরাধ, অপরাধী। **2.** (*Med.*) Morbid ; unhealthy ; inducing disease ; রুগ্ন ; অসুস্থ ; রোগজনক।

Peccary.

pĕc′-ca-rȳ (-ă-), *n.* An American quadruped allied to the swine

আমেরিকাদেশীয় শূকরজাতীয় চতুষ্পদ জন্তুবিশেষ।

peccavi, (*L.*), *Sent.* & *n.* I have sinned—used colloquially to express confession or acknowledgment of an offence; as, to cry *peccavy*; আমি পাপ করিয়াছি। ***Noun.*** This confession; পাপস্বীকৃতি।

pĕck, *n.* **1.** A measure for dry goods equal to 2 gallons; the fourth part of a bushel; শুষ্কদ্রব্যাদির পরিমাণ—দুই গ্যালন; এক বুশেলের চতুর্থাংশ। **2.** A vessel used as a peck-measure; ঐ মাপের পাত্র। **3.** A large number or quantity; as, a *peck* of dirt or troubles; একরাশি। **A peck of troubles**—See PECK, *n.* 3.

pĕck, *v. t., i.* & *n.* **1.** To strike with the beak; to make (a hole etc.) by pecking; ঠোকরান; চঞ্চুদ্বারা ছিদ্র করা। **2.** (*Colloq.*) To eat (food, etc.) esp. in a nibbling manner; (চলিত ভাষায়) ঠোকরাইয়া খাওয়া। **3.** To break as ground, wall, etc. (*up, down,* etc.) with a pointed instrument; সূক্ষ্মাগ্র যন্ত্রদ্বারা (মৃত্তিকা, প্রাচীর ইত্যাদি) ভগ্ন করা। ***Verb i.*** **1.** To make strokes with the beak or a pointed instrument; ঠোকর মারা, সূক্ষ্মাগ্র যন্ত্রদ্বারা খোঁচা দেওয়া। **2.** To eat, esp. nibblingly; ঠোকরাইয়া খাওয়া। ***Noun.*** A stroke with the beak or a pointed instrument; a mark made as a result of this; ঠোকর, চঞ্চু-প্রহার; ঠোকরের দাগ। **To peck at**—To aim at something with the beak; (*fig.*) to carp at; চঞ্চুদ্বারা লক্ষ্য করা; (লক্ষণায়) খুঁত ধরা। **To peck out**—To pluck out by pecking; ঠোকরাইয়া ছিঁড়িয়া ফেলা।

pĕck'-ĕr, *n.* **1.** That which pecks, as a bird etc.; a wood-pecker; চঞ্চুদ্বারা আঘাতকারী, প্রতুদ (cf. প্রতুদা ভক্ষয়ন্ত্যেতে তুণ্ডেন প্রতুদাস্ততঃ—ভাবপ্রকাশ); কাঠঠোকরা পাখী। **2.** A kind of hoe; একপ্রকার নিড়ানী। **3.** (*Slang*) Spirits; "Keep your *pecker* up"; (ইতরভাষায়) উৎসাহ। **One's pecker**—নাক। **To put up another's pecker**—To offend or displease him; রুষ্ট করা; অসন্তুষ্ট করা।

pĕck'-ish, *adj.* (*Colloq.*) Hungry; (চলিত ভাষায়) ক্ষুধার্ত্ত।

Pĕck'-sniff, *n.* A canting hypocrite (a character in Dickens' Martin Chuzzlewit); ভণ্ড, বিড়াল-তপস্বী।

pĕc'-tĕn, *n.* **1.** (*Zool.*) A comb-like vascular membrane in animal bodies; (প্রাণিবিদ্যা) জন্তুদেহে রক্তবহানাড়ীর কঙ্কতাকার ঝিল্লীবিশেষ। **2.** A scallop; একপ্রকার ঝিনুক। **–te-na-ted, –ti-nate,** *adjs.* Comb-like, as a leaf etc.; চিরুণীর মত দন্তবিশিষ্ট, কঙ্কতাকার, কঙ্কতকর্ত্তিত (সাঃ পঃ). কাঙ্কত (ঐ)। **–ti-na'-tion,** *n.*

Pecten or Scallop.

pĕc'-tin, *n.* (*Chem.*) A neutral substance formed in fruits from pectose by ripening; (রসায়নশাস্ত্র) পক্ক ফলে প্রাপ্ত একপ্রকার শিথিল পদার্থ। **–tic,** *adj.*

pĕc'-tō-răl, *adj.* & *n.* **1.** Of, pertaining to, or for, the breast or chest; বক্ষঃস্থলসংক্রান্ত, ঔরস, বক্ষঃস্থলের জন্য। **2.** Relating to, or good for, the diseases of the chest or lungs; বক্ষঃরোগসম্বন্ধীয়, বক্ষঃরোগ উপশামক। **3.** (*Fig.*) Hearty; based on the inner feeling or consciousness; as, *pectoral* theology; (লক্ষণায়) আন্তরিক; চিদাত্মক। ***Noun.*** **1.** A breast-plate, esp. that of the Jewish High priest; উরস্ত্রাণ, বিশেষতঃ ইহুদীদিগের প্রধান পুরোহিতের উরস্ত্রাণ। **2.** A medicine for the chest; বক্ষঃপীড়া শান্তিকারক ঔষধ, কাসঘ্ন, কফনাশক। **3.** A pectoral fin; (মৎস্য প্রভৃতির বুকের ডানা।

pĕc'-tōse, *n.* (*Chem.*) A substance allied to cellulose and found with it in unripe fruits etc.; (রসায়ন-শাস্ত্র) অপক্ক ফলে প্রাপ্ত পদার্থবিশেষ।

pĕc'-ū-lāte, *v. t.* To embezzle, as, money etc.; গচ্ছিত ধন আত্মসাৎ করা, তহবিল তছরূপ করা। **–la'-tion, –la-tor,** *ns.*

pē-cū'-li-ar (-ĕr), *adj.* & *n.* **1.** One's own; individual; as, his *peculiar* character; নিজ, স্বকীয়, অনন্যস্বামিক; নিজস্ব। **2.** Belonging exclusively or solely *to*; "A timidity *peculiar* to your sex"; অনন্য-সুলভ, অনন্যসাধারণ। **3.** Special; as, a point of *peculiar* interest; বিশেষ। **4.** Odd; qeer; as, it has a *peculiar* shape; অদ্ভুত, অপূর্ব্ব, সৃষ্টিছাড়া; আজগবি, কেমনতর, নূতনরকমের। ***Noun.*** **1.** Private property, privilege, etc.; নিজস্ব সম্পত্তি, ব্যক্তিগত সম্পত্তি, ব্যক্তিগত বিশেষাধিকার। **2.** (*Hist.*) A parish or church, exempt from the jurisdiction of the diocese in which it lies; প্রধান ধর্ম্মাচার্য্যের এলাকার সীমার বহির্ভূত যাজকপল্লী বা গির্জ্জা। **3.** (*Cap.*) One of the PECULIAR PEOPLE which see. **–ize,** *v. t.* To make peculiar; স্বতন্ত্র করা, নিজস্ব করা, বিশিষ্ট করা। **–ly,** *adv.* **1.** In a peculiar manner; qeerly; বিশেষভাবে সৃষ্টিছাড়াভাবে। **2.** Individually; as, it does not effect him *peculiarly*; ব্যক্তিগতভাবে। **3.** Especially; as, *peculiarly* annoying; বিশেষভাবে, বিশিষ্টরূপে। **Peculiar people**—ইহুদীগণ। (*Cap.*) আধুনিক ধর্ম্মসম্প্রদায়বিশেষ—এই মণ্ডলীভুক্ত ব্যক্তিগণের মধ্যে গির্জ্জায় একত্র হইয়া উপাসনার প্রথা নাই। তাহাদের মতে ঈশ্বর-আরাধনাই রোগমুক্তির একমাত্র উপায়।

pē-cū-li-ăr'-i-tȳ, *n.* **1.** State of being peculiar; অসাধারণতা (হিঃ কোঃ) স্বাতন্ত্র্য, অনন্যবর্ত্তিত্ব, অনন্যসুলভত্ব। **2.** A characteristic; a singularity; an oddity ; বিশেষত্ব ; বিশেষধর্ম্ম, স্বধর্ম, বৈশিষ্ট ; নূতনত্ব, কেমনতর ভাব।

pĕ-cū'-ni-ā-rў, *adj.* 1. Relating to, or connected with, money ; consisting of money ; আর্থিক, ধনসম্বন্ধীয়, অর্থঘটিত ; ধনসম্পৃক্ত। 2. Having pecuniary penalty : as, a *pecuniary* offence ; অর্থদণ্ডযোগ্য। **–ri-ly**, *adv.*

pĕd'-ă-gogue (-gŏg), *n.* A teacher ; a schoolmaster ; a pedant, (*used in contempt*) ; বালকবালিকাগণের শিক্ষক, শিশুশিক্ষক, বালপাঠক ; পাঠশালার গুরু অধ্যাপক, গুরুমহাশয় ; (অবজ্ঞার্থে ব্যবহৃত) পণ্ডিত, বিদ্যাভিমানী পাণ্ডিত্যাভিমানী, পণ্ডিতম্মন্য। **–gog'-ic, –gog'-i-cal**, *adjs.* **–gog'-i-cal-ly**, *adv.* **–gog(u)-ism**, *n.*

pĕd'-ă-gŏ-ġў, *n.* The science or art of teaching ; শিক্ষাবিজ্ঞান, শিক্ষণশাস্ত্র (হিঃ কোঃ)। **–gog'-ics**, *n.* Same as PEDAGOGY.

pĕd'-ăl, *adj.* (*Zool.*) Of, or pertaining to, the foot or feet ; (জন্তু-বিদ্যা) পাদসম্বন্ধীয়, পাদিক।

pĕd'-ăl, *n.*, *v. i.* & *t.* 1. A lever to be pressed by the foot in various machines *e. g.* bicycle, tricycle, etc. ; দ্বিচক্রযান প্রভৃতির পাদানি। 2. A part of a musical instrument acted on by the foot, as in the piano ; পিয়ানো প্রভৃতির যে অংশ পদ দ্বারা চালিত হয়। ***Verb i.*** 1. To play on organ pedals ; অর্গেন প্রভৃতি বাদ্যযন্ত্র পা দ্বারা বাজান। 2. To work bicycle pedals ; দ্বিচক্রযান প্রভৃতির পাদানিতে পা দিয়া দ্বিচক্রযান প্রভৃতি চালনা করা। ***Verb t.*** To work the pedals of (a bicycle etc.); দ্বিচক্রযান প্রভৃতির পাদানি চালনা করা।

pĕd'-ănt, *n.* 1. One who makes a vain display of learning ; one strictly adhering to formal rules ; শিক্ষাগর্ব্বিত ব্যক্তি, বিদ্যাগর্ব্বিত ব্যক্তি, পাণ্ডিত্যাভিমানী ব্যক্তি ; কঠোর নিয়মনিষ্ঠ ব্যক্তি। 2. One possessed by a theory ; a doctrinaire ; মতবাদগ্রস্ত ব্যক্তি ; স্বমতখ্যাপক ব্যক্তি। **–an-toc'-ra-cy**, *n.* Government by a pedant ; পণ্ডিততন্ত্র। **–ize**, *v. t.* & *i.* To make a pedant of : শিক্ষাভিমানী করা, বিদ্যাগর্ব্বিত করা। (*Verb i.*) To play the pedant ; বিদ্যাভিমানকরা, বিদ্যাগর্ব্বপ্রদর্শন করা, পাণ্ডিত্য ফলান। **Pe-dan'-tic, Pe-dan'-ti-cal**, *adjs.* Of, relating to, or characteristic of, a pedant ; displaying knowledge ostentatiously ; পাণ্ডিত্যগর্ব্বসম্বন্ধীয়, পাণ্ডিত্যাভিমানী ব্যক্তিসুলভ ; পাণ্ডিত্যপ্রদর্শী। **Pe-dan'-ti-cal-ly**, *adv.* **–ry**, *n.* Acts, manners and character of a pedant ; boastful display of learning ; পাণ্ডিত্যাভিমান বিদ্যাদর্প ; পাণ্ডিত্য-প্রদর্শন।

pĕd'-āte, *adj.* (*Zool.*) 1. Having a foot or feet ; (জন্তুবিদ্যা) পদবিশিষ্ট। 2. (*Bot.*) Having divisions like toes or birds' claws, as a leaf ; (উদ্ভিদ্-বিদ্যা) পদাঙ্গুলীবৎ বা পক্ষীর নখরবৎ পর্ব্ববিশিষ্ট।

pĕd'-dle (-l), *v. i.* & *t.* 1. To travel about with a basket or bundle of goods, esp. of small wares, for sale ; ফেরি করা। 2. To be engaged in a small business ; to be busy about trifles ; সামান্য কারবার করা ; তুচ্ছ বিষয় নিয়া ব্যস্ত থাকা। ***Verb t.*** 1. To carry about and offer for sale, (*Chiefly U. S.*) ; ফেরি করা (প্রধানতঃ মার্কিণ যুক্তরাজ্যে)। 2. To deal out in small quantities ; to retail (*usu. fig.*) ; অল্প অল্প করিয়া বাঁটিয়া নেওয়া ; খুচরা বিক্রয় করা। **–dling**, *adj.* Unimportant or insignificant ; তুচ্ছ, সামান্য।

pĕd'-ĕr-ăs-tў, pead'– (pēd-), *ns.* Sodomy between males ; পুংমৈথুন, পুরুষে পুরুষে মৈথুন।

pĕd'-ĕs-tăl, *n.* & *v. t.* 1. The base or support of a column, pillar, statue, vase, etc স্তম্ভপাদ, উপপীঠ (রাঃ রাঃ), পাদপীঠ (ঐ)। 2. Each of the supports of a knee-hole writing table ; হাঁটু রাখার ছিদ্রবিশিষ্ট টেবিলের স্তম্ভদ্বয়ের অন্যতর। 3. (*Lit.* & *fig.*), Any base or foundation ; (*humorously*) the foot or leg ; (শব্দানুযায়ী ও লক্ষণায়) বেদী, পীঠ ; (কৌতুকচ্ছলে) পা। ***Verb t.*** To place or support on a pedestal ; পাদপীঠের উপর স্থাপন করা।

pĕ-dĕs'-tri-ăn, *adj.* & *n.* 1. Going on foot ; performed on foot ; পাদগামী, পাদচারী ; পদব্রজেসম্পন্ন। 2. Of, or relating to, walking ; পাদচারণ সম্বন্ধীয়। 3. Dull ; commonplace ; prosaic ; নীরস ; সাধারণ; কবিত্বহীন। ***Noun.*** One who walks or races on foot for a wager or a prize ; যে বাজি রাখিয়া হাঁটে। **–al**, *adj.* **–ism**, *n.* **–ize**, *v. t.* To walk or go on foot ; পদব্রজে ভ্রমণ করা, হাঁটা।

pĕd-i-ăt'-rics, *n.* (*Pl.*) That branch of medical science which relates to children and their special diseases ; বালচিকিৎসাশাস্ত্র।

pĕd'-i-cĕl, –cle (-kl), *ns.* (*Bot.* & *Zool.*) A small short stalk-like structure in a plant or animal, flower or fruit ; (উদ্ভিদ ও প্রাণিবিদ্যা) ফল বা পত্রের বৃন্ত, পুষ্পবৃন্ত, প্রসববন্ধন, বৃন্তিকা (সাঃ পঃ), পুষ্পবন্ধন। **Pe-dic'-u-late, –cel-late**, *adjs.* Provided with a pedicel ; বৃন্তযুক্ত, সবৃন্ত, বোঁটা সহিত।

pĕ-dic'-ū-lăr (-lĕr), **–lous** (-lŭs), *adjs.* Of, or relating to, lice ; lousy ; উকুণসম্বন্ধীয় ; উকুণপূর্ণ। **–lo'-sis**, *n.* Infestation with lice ; phthiriasis ; উকুণের উপদ্রব ; উকুণরোগ।

pĕd'-i-gree (-grē), *n.* 1. Lineage ; line of ancestors ; geneological tables ; কুল, বংশাবলী, গোত্রপট, বংশচরিত্র, বংশানুচরিত ; বংশ; কুলতালিকা কুলজী, বংশবিবরণ। 2. Ancient or notable descent ; as, boasted *pedigree* ; উচ্চবংশ, উচ্চকুল। **3.** A record of the lineage of an animal, *e. g.* horse or dog ; কোন জন্তুর বংশবিবরণ। **4.** Etymological descent or derivation, as of a word ; শব্দের উৎপত্তি-বিবরণ। **5.** (*Attrib.*) Having a pedigree or known line of descent ; as, *pedigree* cattle ; সুপরিচিত বংশানুক্রমবিশিষ্ট। **—greed,** *adj.*

pĕd′-ĭ-mĕnt, *n.* A triangular facing as a decoration over porticoes, windows, etc. ; দ্বার, বাতায়ন

P. Pediment.

বা গাড়ীবারান্দার উপরিস্থ ত্রিভুজাকৃতি সৌধভূষাবিশেষ, উদ্বহন (বুঃ সং টীকা)।

pĕd′-lar (-lĕr), **—lĕr,** *ns.* **1.** A travelling hawker ; ফেরিওয়ালা। **2.** (*Fig.*) A retailer (of a gossip, etc.) ; (লক্ষণায়) যে ব্যক্তি সংবাদ ফেরি করিয়া ঘুরে। **—y,** *n.* Hawking ; small retail business ; ফেরি ; খুচরা ব্যবসায়। **Pedlar's French**—চোরের ঠার।

pē-dŏ-băp′-tĭsm, *n.* Infant baptism ; শিশু দীক্ষা।

pē-dŏm′-ĕ-tĕr, *n.* An instrument by which paces are numbered as a person walks, and the distance thus ascertained ; টেঁক-ঘড়ীর মত যন্ত্রবিশেষ—এই যন্ত্রে কোন ব্যক্তি কত বার পদক্ষেপ করিয়াছে তাহা সূচিত হয় এবং তদ্বারা সে কি পরিমাণ স্থান অতিক্রম করিয়াছে তাহাও নির্ণয় করা যায়, পাদমানযন্ত্র, পাদন্যাসমাপক যন্ত্র।

pē-dun′-cle (-dŭng-kl), *n.* **1.** (*Bot.*) A stalk of flower, fruit or cluster ; the primary or main stalk of an inflorescence ; (উদ্ভিদবিদ্যা) বৃন্ত (সাঃ পঃ) ; পুষ্পদণ্ড (ঐ)। **2.** (*Zool.*) A stalk or stalk-like process in an animal body ; জন্তুদেহের বৃন্তাকার বিবর্দ্ধন। **—cu-lar, —cu-late, —cu-lat-ed,** *adjs.*

peek (pēk), *v. i.* To peep or pry (*in* or *out* etc.) ; উঁকি মারা। **Peek-a-boo**—(*U. S.*) Same as BO-PEEP which see.

peel (pēl), *n.* (*Hist.*) A small tower built in the 16th century in the border counties of England and Scotland ; ষোড়শ শতাব্দীতে ইংলণ্ড এবং স্কটলণ্ডের সীমান্তপ্রদেশস্থিত প্রদেশসমূহে নির্ম্মিত ক্ষুদ্র বুরুজ।

Peel tower.

peel (pēl), *n.* A shovel, esp. that used by a baker in putting loaves into and withdrawing them from the oven ; উননের ভিতরে রুটী স্থাপনের জন্য বা উনন হইতে রুটী তুলিবার জন্য রুটীওয়ালার কাঠনির্ম্মিত হাতল।

peel (pēl), *v. t., i.* & *n.* **1.** To strip the rind, bark, etc. from (orange, potato, tree, etc.) ; কমলালেবু, আলু প্রভৃতির খোসা ছাড়ান, বৃক্ষের বল্কল উন্মোচন করা। **2.** To strip, tear off, as skin, bark, etc. ; ত্বক উন্মোচন করা, ছাল তোলা। **3.** (*Obs.*) To pillage ; as, scattered and *peeled* ; (অপ্রঃ) লুঠ করা। ***Verb i.*** **1.** (Of tree, animal body etc) To lose the bark, skin, etc. ; (of bark etc.) to come off, as, the bark *peels* easily ; (বৃক্ষ বা জীবদেহ সম্পর্কে) ত্বক উঠিয়া যাওয়া, বল্কল খসিয়া পড়া ; (ছাল প্রভৃতি সম্পর্কে) উঠিয়া আসা। **2.** (*Slang*) To undress for exercise etc. ; (ইতর ভাষায়) কুস্তি প্রভৃতির জন্য পোষাক খুলিয়া ফেলা। ***Noun.*** The skin or rind of a fruit ; ফলের খোসা। **Peel′-er,** *n.* One who peels or strips a fruit etc. ; a machine for peeling ; যে ব্যক্তি ফল প্রভৃতির খোসা ছাড়ায় ; খোসা ছাড়ানের যন্ত্র। **Peel′-ing,** *n.*

peel′-ĕr (pēl-), *n.* **1.** (*Colloq.*) A policeman ; (চলিতভাষায়) পুলিশ-কর্ম্মচারী। **2.** (*Hist.*) A policeman of the Irish constabulary so called from its organizer Sir R. Peel ; স্যার রবার্ট পীল কর্ত্তৃক গঠিত আয়র্লণ্ড দেশীয় কনেষ্টবলসম্প্রদায়ভুক্ত ব্যক্তি।

Peel′-īte (pēl-), *n.* A conservative, supporting Sir Robert Peel in advocating the repeal of the Corn-laws in 1846 ; ১৮৪৬ খৃঃ অব্দের শস্যসম্বন্ধীয় আইন রদ করার আন্দোলনে রক্ষণশীল দলের যে সকল ব্যক্তি Sir Robert Peel কে সাহায্য করেন তাহাদের অন্যতম।

peep (pēp), *v. i.* & *n.* To chirp, or cry as a chicken etc. ; to squeak ; মুরগীর ছানার মত ডাকা ; চিঁ চিঁ করা। ***Noun.*** A chirp ; squeak ; চিঁ চিঁ ; কিচিরমিচির, কিচমিচ।

peep (pēp), *v. i.* **1.** To look through a narrow aperture, (*at, into,* etc.) ; ক্ষুদ্র ছিদ্রের মধ্য দিয়া দেখা। **2.** To pry ; to look slyly or cautiously ; উঁকি মারা ; সাবধানে চাওয়া, চালাকি করিয়া চাওয়া। **3.** (Of daylight, flower, distant object, etc.) To emerge partially ; to appear partly into view, (often with *out*) ; অল্প অল্প নির্গত হওয়া ;

অল্প অল্প দৃষ্ট হওয়া। **4.** (Of a quality etc.) To show itself unconsciously; অজ্ঞাতসারে ও দর্শন করা।

peep (pēp), *n.* **1.** A look through a crevice or opening; a furtive or peering glance; উঁকি; চোরাচাহনি। **2.** First appearance; as, the *peep* of dawn or of day; উদয়, আগম। **Peep'-er,** *n.* **1.** One who peeps; a spy; যে ব্যক্তি উঁকি মরিয়া দেখে; গোয়েন্দা। **2.** (*Slang*) Eye; (ইতর ভাষায়) চোক। **Peep-hole**—ক্ষুদ্র ছিদ্র — যদ্দ্বারা উঁকি দিয়া দেখা যায়। **Peep-show**—ক্ষুদ্র ছিদ্র বা বিপুল দর্শক কাচের ভিতর দিয়া দৃষ্ট ছবি প্রভৃতি। **Peeping Tom**—যে জানালায় জানালায় উঁকি মারে। **Peep-of-day boys**—১৭৮৪ খৃষ্টাব্দের আয়র্লণ্ডবাসী রাজবিদ্রোহিবর্গ। তাহারা অতি প্রত্যুষে রাজভক্ত-প্রজাগণের বাড়ীতে অস্ত্রশস্ত্রের অনুসন্ধানে গমন করিত। **Peep of day** or **of dawn**—পূর্ব্বপ্রভা, দিবসমুখ, প্রাতঃকাল, উষাগম, প্রত্যুষ, অরুণোদয়।

Pee'-pul-tree (pē-pŭl-trē), *n.* A kind of tree; অশ্বত্থ।

peer (pēr), *n.* **1.** One of the same rank, standing, qualities, etc.; an equal in any respect; as, he will not easily find his *peers*; সমপদস্থ, সমকক্ষ ব্যক্তি; দোসর। **2.** A member of one of the five degrees of the British nobility, (duke, marquis, earl, viscount; baron); ডিউক, মারকুইস্, বেরণ প্রভৃতি উপাধিধারী ব্যক্তি। **3.** A nobleman; অভিজাত ব্যক্তি। **Peer'-ess,** *n.*, (*Fem.*) **Peer'-less,** *adj.* Matchless; অতুল, অদ্বিতীয়, নিরুপম, অনুপম, অপ্রতিম। **House of Peers**—Same as the HOUSE OF LORDS (which see.) **Peers of Scotland, of Ireland**—স্কটলণ্ড ও আয়র্লণ্ড হইতে যে সকল অভিজাত বংশীয় সভ্য পার্লেমেণ্ট মহাসভার অভিজাত গৃহে সভ্য নিযুক্ত হন। [স্কটলণ্ডের ১৬জন সম্ভ্রান্ত পুরুষ প্রতি পার্লেমেণ্টে নির্ব্বাচিত হন এবং আয়র্লণ্ডের ২৮ জন অভিজাত বংশীয় ব্যক্তি আজীবন সভ্যরূপে পার্লেমেণ্টের অভিজাত সভায় বসিয়া থাকেন।] **Peers of the realm** or **United Kingdom**—পার্লেমেণ্ট মহাসভার অভিজাতগৃহে সভ্যরূপে বসিবার অধিকারী ব্যক্তিগণ। **Spiritual Peer**—বিলাতের পার্লেমেণ্ট মহাসভার অভিজাতগৃহের সভ্য হওয়ার অধিকারী ধর্ম্মাধ্যক্ষ বা মহাধর্ম্মাধ্যক্ষ।

peer (pēr), *v. t.* & *i.* **1.** To rank with; to equal; "That brave heart that knighthood might not *peer*"; সমতুল্য করা; সমকক্ষ করা। **2.** To raise to the peerage; মারকুইস্, ডিউক ইত্যাদি উপাধি প্রদান করা। ***Verb i.*** To rank on an equality; as, it cannot *peer* with that; সমান পদবী পাওয়া, সমান স্থান পাওয়া।

peer (pēr), *v. i.* **1.** To look narrowly or closely; to peep; পুঙ্খানুপুঙ্খরূপে দেখা; উঁকি দেওয়া। **2.** To appear slightly into view; to peep out; as, the sun *peeping* through the trees; অল্প দৃষ্টিগোচর হওয়া; উঁকি মারা। **3.** To show itself; to appear; "A project *peers* upon my mind"; প্রদর্শন করা; উপস্থিত হওয়া।

peer-āge (pēr-), *n.* **1.** The peers collectively; the rank or dignity of peers; কুলীন সমাজ; আভিজাত্য। **2.** Nobility; aristocracy; কৌলিন্য; অভিজাত সমাজ, সম্ভ্রান্ত সমাজ। **3.** A book containing a list of peers with geneology, etc.; সম্ভ্রান্ত ব্যক্তিবর্গের বংশাবলী। **Benefit of peerage**—সাধারণ বিচারালয়ে উপস্থিত হওয়ার দায় হইতে ইংলণ্ডের সম্ভ্রান্তপুরুষগণের অব্যাহতি।

pee'-vish (pē-), *adj.* Habitually fretful; easily annoyed; ill-tempered; কোপনস্বভাব, রাগী; খিটখিটে; বদমেজাজী। **—ly,** *adv.* **—ness,** *n.*

pee'-vit (pēe-), **—wit,** See PEWIT.

pĕg, *n.* **1.** A small pointed piece of wood or metal used in fastening things together; a pin on which to hang anything; কাঠের গজাল, খিল, গোঁজ, খোঁটা; নাগদন্ত, শঙ্কু, কীল, কীলক। **2.** A piece of wood or metal to mark a limit or a point of attainment; as, a boundary *peg*; a scribbage *peg*; সীমাশঙ্কু। **3.** (*Fig.*) A support, a reason; a pretext; as, a *peg* to hang a claim upon; (লক্ষণায়) আশ্রয়; কারণ, হেতু; ব্যপদেশ, ছল, অছিলা। **4.** One of the pins of a musical instrument on which the strings are strained; তন্ত্রীকর্ণ, (সেতারাদি) বাদ্যযন্ত্রের কাণ। **5.** A degree or step: as, to take or go down a *peg*; এক পা, এক ধাপ। **6.** A drink of soda-water with brandy, etc.; সুরা ও সোডাওয়াটার মিশ্রিত পানীয়-বিশেষ। **Peg-leg**—একপ্রকার কাষ্ঠ-নির্ম্মিত পদ; ঐরূপ পদসমন্বিত ব্যক্তি। **Peg-top**—একপ্রকার লাটিম **Peg-top trousers**—একপ্রকার পাজামা—যাহা নিতম্বদেশে চওড়া এবং গুল্ফদেশে অপ্রশস্ত। **A peg to hang a discourse, claim etc. on**—See PEG, *n.* 3. **A round peg in a square hole**—See under HOLE. **To come down a peg**—To be lowerd or humiliated; অবনত হওয়া, অপমানিত হওয়া। **To take a person down a peg or two**—To humble him; অবনত করা।

pĕg, *v. t.* & *i.* **1.** To fasten or fix with a peg or pegs; খিল দিয়া আঁটা, কীলক দ্বারা বদ্ধ করা। **2.** To keep up the market-price of (stock etc.) by selling and buying at a fixed price; নির্দ্দিষ্ট মূল্যে ক্রয়বিক্রয় করতঃ (কোম্পানীর কাগজের) বাজার দর ঠিক রাখা। **3.** (*Colloq.*) To throw as a thing at; (চলিত ভাষায়) ফেলিয়া দেওয়া। ***Verb i.*** **1.** To work with unremitting effort, (usually with *on, at* or *away*); as, to *peg away* at a task; অবিশ্রান্ত খাটা। **2.** To strike or pierce with a peg ; to aim at with a peg ; খোঁটা দ্বারা আঘাত করা, খোঁটা দ্বারা ভেদ করা ; খোঁটা দ্বারা লক্ষ্য করা। **To peg away** — To work persistently (*at*) ; অবিশ্রান্ত খাটা। **To peg down**—To restrict (to rules etc.) ; নিয়মাধীন করা।

pĕg'-ă-nŭm, (*Lat. peganon*) *n.* A genus of herbs ; সোমলতা (খোরী)।

Pĕg'-ă-sŭs, *n.* **1.** A winged horse ; পক্ষীরাজ ঘোড়া। [এই অশ্বের খুরাঘাতে বাগ্‌দেবীগণ নিষেবিত Helicon পর্ব্বতে Hippocrene নামক উৎসের উদ্ভব হয়।] **2.** (*Fig.*) Poetic genius ; (লক্ষণায়) কবিত্বশক্তি বা কবিপ্রতিভা। **3.** (*Astron.*) A northern constellation; উত্তরভাদ্রপদ (*P. γ*), পূর্ব্বভাদ্রপদ (*P. α*)। **4.** A genus of small fishes with large wing-like pectoral fins ; একজাতীয় ক্ষুদ্র মৎস্য।

peignoir, *n.* A woman's loose dressing-gown worn while hair is combed or on coming out of bath ; স্ত্রীলোকদিগের একপ্রকার ঢিলা গাউন।

peine forte et dure, (*F.*), *n.* (*lit. severe and hard punishment*) A punishment inflicted on a person charged with felony by pressing him to death on refusal to plead ; গুরুতর অপরাধে অভিযুক্ত কোন ব্যক্তি অপরাধ স্বীকারে অসম্মত হইলে তাহাকে কারাকক্ষে শায়িত করত বুকের উপর লৌহ খণ্ড চাপাইয়া বধ করার জন্য পূর্ব্বে ইংলণ্ডদেশে যে দণ্ড প্রদান করা হইত।

pē'-jō-rā-tive (-tĭv), *adj.* & *n.* Disparaging or depreciatory ; অপকর্ষসূচক। ***Noun.*** A depreciatory word ; অপকর্ষসূচক শব্দ।

pē̆k'-ăn, *n.* A species of weasel of North America, valued for fur ; উত্তর আমেরিকার নকুলজাতীয় জন্তুবিশেষ।

pē-kin', *n.* A kind of silk stuff ; একপ্রকার রেশমী কাপড়।

pĕk'-oe (-ō), *n.* (*Chinese*) A kind of scented black tea ; (চীনদেশীয় ভাষা) একজাতীয় সুগন্ধি কাল চা।

pĕl'-āge, *n.* The fur, hair, wool, etc. of a quadruped ; চতুষ্পদ জন্তুর কোমল রোম বা পশম।

Pĕ-lā'-gĭ-ăn, *adj.* & *n.* Of, or pertaining to, the monk Pelagius (4th & 5th century) who denied the doctrine of original sin; পেলাজিয়াস নামক সন্ন্যাসিসম্পর্কীয়। ***Noun.*** A follower of Pelagius ; উক্ত সন্ন্যাসীর মতাবলম্বী ব্যক্তি। **—ism,** *n.*

pĕ-lā'-gĭ-ăn, *adj.* & *n.* Of, or relating to, the ocean ; inhabiting the ocean; সামুদ্রিক; সাগরবাসী। ***Noun.*** A pelagian animal ; সামুদ্রিকজন্তু।

pĕ-lăg'-ĭc, *adj.* Of, relating to, or performed on, the ocean ; সাগরসম্পর্কীয়, সাগরে সম্পাদিত।

pĕl-âr-gō'-nĭ-ŭm, *n.* A genus of plants with showy flowers ; সমুজ্জ্বল পুষ্পপ্রসূ তরুশ্রেণীবিশেষ।

Pĕ-lăs'-gĭc, *adj.* Of, or relating to, the Pelasgians, an ancient race of South-Eastern Europe and Asia Minor ; দক্ষিণ-পূর্ব্ব ইয়ুরোপ এবং এসিয়া মাইনরের প্রাচীন জাতি-বিশেষ-সম্বন্ধীয়। **Pelasgic architecture**— গ্রীসদেশীয় প্রাচীনতম স্থাপত্য ধারা।

pĕl'-ĕr-ine (-ĭn), *n.* A lady's long cape ; স্ত্রীলোকের সুদীর্ঘ স্কন্ধাবরণ বস্ত্র।

Peleus, *n.* The king of the Myrmidons ; Peleus এবং Phocusকে হত্যাকরার দরুণ তদীয় ভ্রাতা Telamon নির্ব্বাসিত হইয়া Thessaly প্রদেশের অন্তর্গত Phthia নামক স্থানে পলায়ন করে। Phthiaর রাজা তদীয় কন্যা Antigoneকে Peleusএর সহিত বিবাহ প্রদান করেন। Peleus দৈবক্রমে মৃগয়াকালে তদীয় শ্বশুর Eurytionকে বধ করাতে Iolcusএ পলায়নে বাধ্য হন। পরে তিনি Thetis এর পাণিগ্রহণ করেন। এই Thetiএর গর্ভেই মহাবীর Achilles এর জন্ম হয়।

pĕlf, *n.* (No *pl.*) Money ; wealth ; (সাধারণতঃ অসদুপায়ে অর্জ্জিত) ধন, অর্থ ; টাকা কড়ি।

Pelias, *n.* Son of Poseidon and Tyro ; Poseidon এবং Tyroর পুত্র এবং Neleusএর যমজ ভ্রাতা। Tyro শিশু দুইটীকে বর্জ্জন করিলে, এক কৃষক উহাদিগকে বাটী নিয়া লালন পালন করে। পরে উহারা বয়ঃপ্রাপ্ত হইলে তাহাদের বৈপিত্রেয় ভ্রাতা Æson কে বিতাড়িত করিয়া Iolcusএর সিংহাসন অধিকার করে। কিছুকাল পরে Pelias তদীয় ভ্রাতা Neleusকে নির্ব্বাসিত করিল। অবশেষে Peleus বহুদিন নিষ্কণ্টকে রাজ্যভোগ করিলে পর Jason আসিয়া Iolcusএর সিংহাসন দাবী করিলে তাঁহার হস্ত হইতে উদ্ধার পাওয়ার জন্য Peleus Jasonকে স্বর্ণমেষলোম আনয়নের জন্য Colchis নামক স্থানে প্রেরণ করে।

pĕl'-ĭ-căn, *n.* A large water-fowl with a large bill and a pouch for storing fish (It is fabled to feed its young with its own blood ;

Pelicans.

গগনভেরী (বোঃ), প্লব (সাঃ পঃ)। [এইরূপ কথিত আছে যে এই পক্ষী স্বীয় রুধির দ্বারা শাবকপোষণ করিয়া থাকে, এইজন্য ইহা যীশুখৃষ্ট বা দয়াবৃত্তির চিহ্নস্বরূপ ব্যবহৃত হইয়া আসিতেছে।]

Pelion, *n.* A range of lofty mountains in Thessaly ; থেসেলি প্রদেশস্থ তুঙ্গ পর্ব্বতশ্রেণী। দৈত্যগণ স্বর্গে পৌছিবার জন্য Pelion পর্ব্বতে Ossa নামক পর্ব্বত স্থাপন করে বলিয়া কথিত আছে।

pĕ-lisse′, (-lēs), *n.* 1. An outer garment for women; স্ত্রীলোকের সরোম পশুচর্ম্মনির্ম্মিত বাহ্যচ্ছদবিশেষ। 2. A child's outer garment; শিশুদিগের একপ্রকার ঢিলা জামা।

pĕl-lag′-ră (-ā-), *n.* A disease frequent in Lombardy, marked by cracking of skin and often ending in insanity; ইতালী দেশীয় কুষ্ঠরোগ বিশেষ, রৌদ্রত্বক (হঃ চঃ)। **—rous,** *adj.*

pĕl′-let (-ĕt), *n.* & *v. t.* 1. A little ball esp. of food, medicine or the like; a small pill; ডেলা, পিণ্ড, গুলিকা; গুটিকা, বটিকা। 2. A small shot; ক্ষুদ্র গুলি, ছিটা গুলি, ছর্‌রা। 3. A small ball of wax, paper, etc. used as the charge of a pop-gun; ছেলেদের হাওয়ার বন্দুক হইতে ছুড়িবার জন্য মোম, কাগজ, প্রভৃতির দ্বারা তৈয়ারী গুলি। 4. (In coins etc.) A circular boss · টোপ। ***Verb t.*** To strike or hit with pellets, esp. paper pellets; গুলিদ্বারা আঘাত করা, বিশেষতঃ কাগজের গুলি দ্বারা আঘাত করা। **—ed,** *adj.*

pĕl′-li-cle (-î-kl), *n.* A thin skin or film; a membrane; a cuticle; সরু পর্দ্দা; ঝিল্লী; ত্বক। **—lic′-u-lar,** *adj.*

pĕl′-li-tŏ-rȳ (-î), *n.* 1. (*Pellitory of Spain*) A plant with pungent flavoured root; আকরকরা (বনঃ), আকারকরভ (ঐ)। 2. (*Pellitory of the wall*) A bushy plant growing on or at the foot of walls; দেওয়ালের উপরে বা নীচে জাত গুল্মবিশেষ।

pĕll-mĕll′, *adv., adj.* & *n.* 1. In confusion or disorder; promiscuously; এলোমেলোভাবে; বিশৃঙ্খলভাবে। 2. In furious haste; headlong; recklessly; প্রচণ্ডবেগে; উদ্দামবেগে; হিতাহিতশূন্যভাবে, দিগ্‌বিদিক জ্ঞান না করিয়া। ***Adj.*** Confused; promiscuous; tumultuous; গোলমেলে; এলোমেলো; তুমুল। ***Noun.*** 1. A confusion; a medley; a hand-to-hand fight; a melee; হুলস্থূল; বিশৃঙ্খলা; হাতাহাতি; হাঙ্গামা।

pĕl-lū′-cĭd, *adj.* 1. Transparent; clear; স্বচ্ছ; অমল, বিমল, নির্ম্মল, পরিষ্কার। 2. Clear in style, expression, etc.; প্রাঞ্জল, বিশদ প্রসাদগুণসম্পন্ন। 3. Perceiving clearly; as a *pellucid* writer or faculty; বিমল বুদ্ধি। **—cid′-i-ty,** *n.* **—ly,** *adv.*

pĕ-lō′-tă, *n.* A basque game played with a ball and a wicker racket; একপ্রকার ক্রীড়া।

pĕlt, *n.* 1. The skin of a goat, sheep, etc. with the hair on it; সরোম পশুচর্ম্ম। 2. A raw hide of sheep, goat, etc. stripped of hair; কাঁচা চামড়া। **Pelt′-ry,** *n.* Skins with fur collectively; furs; সলোম পশুচর্ম্মসমূহ; কোমল লোম।

pĕlt, *v. t., i.* & *n.* 1. To strike with something thrown; to assail with missiles; to throw (*lit.* & *fig.*); "*Pelting* me with pamphlets": ইষ্টকাদিদ্বারা আঘাত করা; বাণবর্ষণ করা, অস্ত্রবৃষ্টি করা; (শব্দানুযায়ী ও লক্ষণায়); বর্ষণ করা। ***Verb i.*** 1. To fall or beat down heavily as rain etc.; মুষলধারে বর্ষিত হওয়া, প্রচুর পরিমাণে (বৃষ্টি) পতিত হওয়া। 2. To strike with throw or missiles etc. repeatedly; অস্ত্রবৃষ্টি করা, গোলাবৃষ্টি করা। ***Noun.*** 1. Act of pelting; a blow or stroke with, or as with, missiles; বর্ষণ, ক্ষেপণ; আঘাত। 2. The beating of a storm, rain, etc.; ঝঞ্ঝাবাত, মুষলধারে বর্ষণ। **Pelt′-ing,** *adj.* & *n.* **(At) full pelt**—(At) full speed; দ্রুত গতিতে।

pĕl′-tă, *n.* 1. (*Antiq.*) A small shield; ক্ষুদ্র ঢাল। 2. (*Bot.*) A shield-like structure; (উদ্ভিদবিদ্যা) ঢালের আকার বস্তু। **—tate,** *adj.* 1. Shield-shaped; ঢালের আকৃতি। 2. (*Bot.*) Fixed to the stalk by the centre; (উদ্ভিদবিদ্যা) ছত্রবন্ধ (সাঃ পঃ)।

pĕl′-vis, *n.* 1. The bony cavity constituting a frame-work for the lower part of the abdomen; বস্তিদেশ, বাস্তকোটর, বস্তিগহ্বর, বস্তিপ্রদেশ। 2. A basin-like cavity of the kidney; মূত্রাশয়ের ঝিল্লীময় গহ্বরবিশেষ। **—vic,** *adj.*

Pĕm′-brōke, *n.* A town in Wales; ওয়েলেস্‌দেশের নগরবিশেষ। **Pembroke table, Pembroke**—এক ধরণের চারপায়ার মেজ।

pĕm′-mi-căn, *n.* 1. (Among North-American-Indians) A cake of lean venison dried and pounded mixed with melted fat; উত্তর আমেরিকার আদিম অধিবাসিগণকর্ত্তৃক প্রস্তুত একপ্রকার পিষ্টক। 2. An almost similar preparation for travellers; ভ্রমণকারিগণের জন্য উক্ত পিষ্টকের অনুরূপ পিষ্টকবিশেষ। 3. (*Fig.*) A condensed literary matter; (লক্ষণায়) স্বল্পাক্ষরগ্রথিত রচনা।

pĕm′-phi-gŭs, *n.* A skin-disease characterized by vesicular eruptions; জলবিম্বের ন্যায় একপ্রকার চর্ম্মরোগ, বিম্বিকা (হঃ চঃ)। **—goid, —gous,** *adjs.*

pĕn, *n.* & *v. t.* 1. A quill feather or a piece of metal prepared as a writing-instrument; লেখনী। [Syn. অক্ষরতুলিকা, কলম, অক্ষরজননী, বর্ণিকা, বর্ণাঙ্কা, শ্রীকরণ, মসিপথ, বর্ণবর্ত্তিকা]। 2. Writing or style of this; as, he made a living with his *pen*; লিখন, লিখনের ধরণ। ***Verb t.*** To write; to compose and commit to paper; লিখা; লিপিবদ্ধ করা। **Pen′-ful,** *n.* **Fountain pen**—See under FOUNTAIN. **Pen-and-ink**—*adj.* Written or executed with pen and ink; as, a *pen-and-ink* sketch; কালি কলমে লিখিত বা সম্পাদিত। **Pen-craft**—Penmanship; the art of composition

লিপিচাতুর্য্য ; রচনাকৌশল। **Pen-driver**—কেরাণী। **Pen-holder**—কলমের বাঁট। **Pen-knife**—কলম কাটার ছুরী, চাকু। **Pen-man**—লিপিকর; গ্রন্থকর্ত্তা, লেখক। **Pen-manship** — লিখনচাতুর্য্য ; লিপি-পদ্ধতি; লিখিবার ছাঁদ; রচনাপদ্ধতি। **Pen-name**—লেখকের কল্পিত নাম। **Pen-wiper**—ব্যবহারের পর কলম মুছিবার বস্ত্র বা চর্ম্মখণ্ড। **Pen-woman**—রচয়িত্রী, লেখিকা।

pĕn, *n.* & *v. t.* **1.** An enclosure for poultry etc. or for other purposes ; খোঁয়াড়, গোশালা (for cows), গোকুল (*ib*)। **2.** (West Indies) A farm or plantation ; (পশ্চিম-ভারতীয় দ্বীপপুঞ্জ) কৃষিক্ষেত্র, আবাদ। ***Verb t.*** **1.** To enclose ; to shut *up* or *in* ; আবদ্ধ রাখা ; নিরোধ করা। **2.** To shut up as cattle etc. in a pen ; গো, মহিষ প্রভৃতি জন্তু খোঁয়াড়ে আবদ্ধ রাখা।

pē'-năl, *adj.* **1.** Relating to punishment ; exacting or inflicting punishment, as law ; দণ্ডবিষয়ক ; দণ্ডবিধায়ক, শাস্তিপ্রদ। **2.** Incurring punishment ; as, a *penal* act or offence ; subject to a penalty ; দণ্ডযোগ্য, দণ্ডার্হ, দণ্ড্য ; দণ্ডাধীন। **3.** Inflicted as penalty or punishment ; as, *penal* servitude ; দণ্ডস্বরূপ প্রদত্ত। **4.** Used as a place of punishment ; as, a *penal* colony ; দণ্ডভোগের স্থানস্বরূপ ব্যবহৃত। **—ize,** *v. t.* **1.** To lay under penalty ; to make penal ; দণ্ডাধীন করা; দণ্ডনীয় করা। **2.** (Sports) To put a penalty or comparative disadvantage on (a competitor etc.), (*lit.* & *fig.*) ; (ক্রীড়ায়) কোন প্রতিযোগীর উপর কতকটা অসুবিধা চাপান (শব্দানুযায়ী ও লক্ষণায়)। **—ly,** *adv.* **Penal code**—দণ্ডবিধি আইন। **Penal-servitude**—অপরাধের দণ্ডস্বরূপ কারাগারে কঠোর পরিশ্রম **Penal statute**—যে বিধিদ্বারা কোন অপরাধের জন্য দণ্ডপ্রদান করা হয়।

pĕn'-ăl-tў, *n.* **1.** Punishment for breach of law, rule or contract ; a sum to be forfeited ; a fine ; দণ্ড, শাস্তি; যে টাকা বাজেয়াপ্ত করা হয় ; অর্থদণ্ড, জরিমানা। **2.** (*Fig.*) Suffering a disadvantage resulting from an act, error, quality, etc. ; "It is the *penalty* of greatness that etc." ; (লক্ষণায়) কার্য্য, ভ্রান্তি বা গুণাদিজনিত কষ্ট বা অসুবিধা। **3.** (Sport) Disadvantage imposed on competitor for breaking rule etc. ; (ক্রীড়ায়) নিয়ম-ভঙ্গ হেতু প্রতিযোগীর উপর যে অসুবিধা চাপান হয়। **On** or **under penalty of**—On pain of ; দণ্ডাধীন হইয়া। **Penalty for foolishness**—আক্কেল সেলামি।

pĕn'-ance (-ăns), *n.* & *v. t.* **1.** An ecclesiastical sacrament including contrition, confession, satisfaction and absolution ; কৃচ্ছ্র, তপস্যা, তপঃ, তপশ্চর্য্যা। **2.** An act of suffering as an expression of penitence, esp. one imposed by a priest ; প্রায়শ্চিত্ত। ***Verb t.*** To impose or inflict penance on ; to chastise ; প্রায়শ্চিত্ত চাপান ; শাস্তি দেওয়া। **To do penance**—To perform an act of self-mortification as an expression of penitence ; প্রায়শ্চিত্ত করা।

Pē-nā'-tēs, *n.* (*Pl. Rom. Myth.*) The household gods ; প্রাচীন রোমানদিগের গৃহদেবতাগণ।

pence (pĕns), *n.* Plural of PENNY.

penchant, (*F.*), *n.* Inclination ; taste ; liking ; প্রবৃত্তি, প্রবণতা ; রুচি ; পক্ষপাতিত্ব, অনুরাগ।

pĕn'-čil, *n.* **1.** (*Archaic*) A small brush used by painters ; (অপ্রঃ) চিত্রকরের তুলিকা, ঈষিকা। **2.** (*Fig.*) A painter's art or style ; (লক্ষণায়) চিত্রকৌশল, শিল্প, চিত্রপদ্ধতি। **3.** Any pointed instrument of black lead etc. for writing or drawing without ink ; সীসক-লেখনী, পেন্সিল। **4.** (*Optics*) A set of rays meeting at a point ; (আলোক বিজ্ঞান) কেন্দ্রগত রশ্মিমালা। **5.** (*Geom.*) A figure made by a set of straight lines meeting at a point ; এক বিন্দুতে মিলিত সরল রেখাসমষ্টিগঠিত ক্ষেত্র। **6.** An object shaped like a pencil ; পেন্সিলের আকার বস্তু। **Pencil case**—পেন্সিল রাখার আধার।

pĕn'-čil, *v. t.* **1.** To draw or sketch with or as with a pencil ; পেন্সিল-দ্বারা লেখা, নক্সা করা বা চিহ্নিত করা। **2.** To write, jot down or mark with a lead pencil ; পেন্সিলদ্বারা লিখা বা টুকিয়া রাখা। **3.** To enter (a horse's name) in betting book ; বাজির খাতায় ঘোড়ার নাম লিখা। **4.** To treat as a wound etc. with something applied with a fine brush ; সূক্ষ্ম ব্রুশদ্বারা মলমাদি লাগাইয়া চিকিৎসা করা। **—cilled,** *adj.* **1.** Painted, drawn, written or marked with a pencil ; তুলিদ্বারা চিত্রিত, অঙ্কিত বা চিহ্নিত। **2.** Having pencils of rays ; radiated ; রশ্মিমালাসমন্বিত ; বিকীর্ণ। **3.** Marked with thin concentric lines of colour or shading ; as, *pencilled* wings or feathers ; এককেন্দ্রিক সূক্ষ্ম রঞ্জিত ছায়াবৎ, এককেন্দ্রিক রেখাশ্রেণীচিহ্নিত। **—ling,** *n.* **1.** The work of the pencil or brush ; as, delicate *pencilling* in a picture ; পেন্সিল বা তুলিকাদ্বারা সম্পন্ন কর্ম্ম, অঙ্কনক্রিয়া। **2.** Linear markings as on feathers ; পালকাদির উপর রেখা শ্রেণীবৎ চিহ্ন।

pĕnd'-ănt, —ĕnt, *n.* **1.** Anything hanging, esp. for ornament *e. g.* an earring, locket hanging from a necklace etc. ; কুণ্ডল, কাণের ফুল, দোলক, ধুকধুকি। **2.** An apparatus hanging from a ceiling for giving light ; আলোকপ্রদানার্থ ছাদ হইতে লম্বমান যন্ত্রবিশেষ। **3.** (*Naut.*, also *pennant*) A rope hanging from the head of a mast etc. having at its free end a block or spliced thimble ; মাস্তুল'দির অগ্রভাগ হইতে বিলম্বিত রজ্জুবিশেষ। 4. A flag at the head of the principal mast of a vessel in commission ; বৃহৎ অর্ণবযানের প্রধান মাস্তুলের শীর্ষদেশস্থ পতাকা। 5. The stem or ring of a watch by which it is suspended ; ঘড়ীর আংটা। 6. A counterpart or companion ; a match ; অনুরূপ বস্তু ; সমকক্ষ বস্তু। 7. An appendix or addition, as to a book ; গ্রন্থাদির পরিশিষ্ট। 8. (*Arch.*) An ornament suspended from the roof of a building ; (স্থপতিবিদ্যা) অট্টালিকার ছাদ হইতে বিলম্বিত ভূষা-বিশেষ। **Broad pendant**—অধ্যক্ষের পোতবাহিনীর জাহাজে উড্ডীয়মান তালচঞ্চু পক্ষীর পুচ্ছাকৃতি খর্ব্ব পতাকাবিশেষ।

pĕn'-dĕnt, –dănt, *adj.* 1. Hanging ; লম্বমান, বিলম্বী। 2. (*Bot.*) Hanging downwards, as a flower or a leaf ; (উদ্ভিদবিদ্যা) নিম্নদিকে দোলায়মান। 3. Projecting as a rock ; বহির্মুখী। 4. Awaiting decision ; pending ; বিচারাধীন ; মুলতবী। 5. (*Gram.*) With construction incomplete ; অসমাপিকা। **–ly,** *adv.* **Pend'-an-cy,** *n.*

pendentelite, (*L.*), *adv.* Pending the suit ; মোকদ্দমা মুলতবী রাখিয়া।

pĕn'-dĕn-tive (-tĭv), *n.* A triangular segment of a dome inclosed

Pendentive roof. *a, a, a,* Pendentive.

by two supporting semi-circular vaults at right angles ; সমকোণ উৎপাদনপূর্ব্বক পরস্পরের উপর অবলম্বন-স্বরূপ অবস্থিত অর্দ্ধচন্দ্রাকৃতি খিলানদ্বয়ের মধ্যবর্ত্তী গুম্বজের ত্রিভুজাকৃতি ছিন্নাংশ।

pĕnd'-ing, *adj.* & *prep.* Awaiting decision ; undecided ; মুলতবী ; অমীমাংসিত, বিচারাধীন। ***Prep.*** During ; until ; as, *pending* the decision, negotiation, etc. ; ব্যাপিয়া ; যে পর্য্যন্ত নয়।

pĕn-drăg'-ŏn, *n.* A chief leader ; an ancient British or Welsh chief ; প্রধান নেতা ; প্রাচীনকালের ব্রিটিশ এবং ওয়েলস্ সর্দ্দার। **–ship,** *n.*

pĕn'-dŭ-lāte, *v. i.* 1. To swing like a pendulum ; দোলনদণ্ডের ন্যায় দুলিতে থাকা। 2. (*Fig.*) To be in suspense or undecided ; (লক্ষণায়) সন্দেহদোলায় দোলায়মান হওয়া।

pĕn'-dŭ-līne, *adj.* Hanging down as a bird's nest ; building such a nest, as a bird ; বিলম্বী ; বিলম্বী নীড়নির্ম্মাণকারী।

pĕn'-dŭ-lous (-lŭs), *adj.* 1. Hanging or suspended, as a bird's nest, flower etc. ; বিলম্বী, বিলম্বিত। 2. Oscillating ; দোলনশীল, দোলায়মান। **–ly,** *adv.*

pĕn'-dŭ-lŭm, *n.* 1. A body or rod suspended and swinging to and fro esp. one in a clock ; দোলক, দোলনদণ্ড (রবীঃ), পরিদোলক (নারায়ণ), দোলদণ্ড (আঃ বঃ), অবলম্ব (ঐ)। 2. A person or thing that oscillates, (*lit.* & *fig.*) ; (শব্দানুযায়ী ও লক্ষণায়) দোলনশীল বস্তু, সন্দেহদোলায় দোলায়মান ব্যক্তি। **The swing of the pendulum**—রাজনৈতিক দলদ্বয়ের পর্য্যায়-ক্রমে ক্ষমতার হস্তান্তর।

Pē-nĕl'-ō-pē, *n.* 1. Wife of Odyssesus ; গ্রীসদেশের অন্তঃপাতী Ithacaর অধিপতি Odysseusএর পতিব্রতা ভার্য্যার নাম। 2. (*Fig.*) A chaste wife ; (লক্ষণায়) সতীসাবিত্রী। **Penelope's web**—অন্তহীন কর্ম্ম, অফুরন্ত কাজ। [Penelopeএর পতি Odysseus ট্রয়ের যুদ্ধে গমন করিলে, বহুসংখ্যক লোক পরিণয়প্রার্থী হইয়া তাঁহাকে অহর্নিশ উত্ত্যক্ত করিতে লাগিল। Penelope তাহাদিগকে ভাঁড়াইবার উদ্দেশ্যে বলিলেন যে তিনি একখানি বস্ত্র বয়ন আরম্ভ করিয়াছেন, উহা শেষ হইলেই তিনি বিবাহ করিবেন। এদিকে Penelope দিবাভাগে যে পরিমাণ বয়ন করিতেন—রাত্রে তাহা খুলিয়া ফেলিতেন। অতএব বস্ত্র আর সমাপ্ত হইলনা।]

pĕn-ē-trā'-li-ă, *n.* (*Pl.*) The innermost parts, esp. of a palace or temple ; রাজপ্রাসাদ বা দেবমন্দিরের অন্তস্তম অংশ, গর্ভগৃহ (কাদঃ)।

pĕn'-ē-trāte, *v. t.* & *i.* 1. To enter into or pierce ; প্রবেশ করা, ভেদ করা, বিদ্ধ করা, বিদীর্ণ করা। 2. To permeate ; to imbue ; "The reader should *penetrate* himself with the atmosphere of the times" ; পরিব্যাপ্ত করা, আচ্ছন্ন করা ; ভরপুর করা। 3. To affect the mind or feelings ; to move deeply ; as, to *penetrate* one's heart with pities ; মর্ম্মে আঘাত করা ; বিচলিত করা। 4. To pierce into by the mind ; to comprehend ; মর্ম্মভেদ করা ; সম্যক উপলব্ধি করা। ***Verb i.*** 1. To pass into or through something ; কিছুর মধ্যে বা কিছুর মধ্য দিয়া ঢুকা। 2. To make way, (*into, through, to*) ; ভেদ করিয়া যাওয়া। 3. To see *into, through,* etc. ; দৃষ্টি দ্বারা ভেদ করা। **–tra-bil'-i-ty,** *n.* The quality of being penetrable ; প্রবেশ্যতা, ভেদ্যতা, অবকাশদান (ব্রজঃ হিন্দু)। **–tra-ble,** *adj.* 1. That may be penetrated, entered or pierced by another body ; প্রবেশনীয়, বিভেদ্য, ভেদ্য। 2. Capable of having impressions made upon the mind ; সংস্কার-সহ। **–trat-ing,** *adj.* 1. Sharp ; subtle ; তীক্ষ্ণ ; সূক্ষ্ম। 2. Discerning ; সূক্ষ্মদর্শী, সূক্ষ্মবুদ্ধি, মর্ম্মজ্ঞ। **–tra'-tion,** *n.* 1. Act of penetrating ; বিদারণ, বেধন, প্রবেশন,

ক্রামণ। 2. Sagacity ; discernment ; তীক্ষ্ণবুদ্ধিতা ; সূক্ষ্মবুদ্ধি, সূক্ষ্ম-দৃষ্টি, কুশাগ্রবুদ্ধি, সূক্ষ্মদর্শিতা। **—tra-tive,** *adj.* 1. Tending to penetrate ; piercing; ভেদনশীল, ভেদকারী। 2. Affecting the mind ; as, *penetrative* shame; মর্ম্মস্পর্শী, হৃদয়ভেদী। 3. Acute; discerning ; তীক্ষ্ণ; সূক্ষ্মবুদ্ধি, কুশাগ্রধী। **—tra-tive-ly,** *adv.* **—tra-tive-ness,** *n.* **—tra-tor,** *n.*

pĕn′-guin (-gwĭn), *n.* An aquatic bird in the southern hemisphere, unable to fly, but very expert in diving; নিউজিলণ্ড এবং কুমেরু অঞ্চলের অধিবাসী উড্ডয়নশক্তিহীন জলচর পক্ষিবিশেষ, পঙ্গুপক্ষী।

Penguin.

pē′-ni-ăl, *adj.* Of, or relating to, the penis ; শিশ্নসম্বন্ধীয়।

pĕn-i-cĭl′-lāte, *adj.* 1. Pencil-formed; পেন্সিলের আকার। 2. Having a small tuft or tufts of hairs etc. ; ক্ষুদ্রকেশগুচ্ছাদিবিশিষ্ট। 3. Forming a small tuft or brush ; ক্ষুদ্রগুচ্ছ রচনাকারী। 4. Streaked ; pencilled ; ডোরা-কাটা; ছায়ারেখান্বিত।

pĕn-ĭn′-sŭ-lă, *n.* A portion of land nearly surrounded by water ; উপদ্বীপ, প্রায়োদ্বীপ (প্রঃ বাঃ), দ্বীপকল্প। **—lar,** *adj.* & *n.* 1. Of, or pertaining to, a peninsula ; উপদ্বীপবিষয়ক। 2. Of, the form, or nature, of a peninsula; উপদ্বীপাকৃতি, উপদ্বীপাত্মক। 3. Of, or relating to, the Peninsula of Spain and Portugal or the war carried on there (1808-14) ; স্পেন ও পর্ত্তুগাল উপদ্বীপসম্বন্ধীয় বা উক্ত উপদ্বীপ সমূহে যে যুদ্ধ হয় তৎসম্বন্ধীয়। (*Noun*) 1. An inhabitant of a peninsula ; উপদ্বীপের অধিবাসী। 2. (*Cap.*) A soldier of the Peninsular war; ঊনবিংশ শতাব্দীর প্রথমভাগে স্পেন ও পর্ত্তুগালে যে যুদ্ধ হয় তাহাতে নিযুক্ত সৈনিক। **Peninsular war**—স্পেন ও পর্ত্তুগালে নেপোলিয়নের সহিত ইংরাজদিগের যে যুদ্ধ হয় (১৮০৮-১৮১৪)। **The Peninsula**—স্পেন ও পর্ত্তুগাল।

pĕn-ĭn′-sŭ-lāte, *v.t.* To form into a peninsula ; উপদ্বীপ গঠন করা।

pē′-nĭs, *n.* The male organ of generation ; পুরুষাঙ্গ, লিঙ্গ, শিশ্ন, মেঢ্র, জননেন্দ্রিয়, [Syn. উপস্থ, ধ্বজ (cf. ধ্বজভঙ্গ), চিহ্ন, পুংচিহ্ন, পুংলিঙ্গ, জঘন্য, মদনায়ুধ, মেহন, শেপ, শেফ (cf. শেফঃস্তম্ভ—চরক-সংহিতা), শেপস, ব্যজন (বুঃ সং), নরাঙ্গ, প্রাশি, স্মরস্তম্ভ, স্মরধ্বজ, কামাঙ্কুশ, কন্দর্প, কন্দর্পমুষল।] **Penis syringe**—মেঢ্রবস্তি (সাঃ পঃ)।

pĕn′-i-tĕnt, *adj.* & *n.* Contrite ; repentant; অনুতপ্ত, পরিতপ্ত, পশ্চাত্তাপী; জাতানুতাপ। *Noun.* 1. One who repents of sin ; one under church censure, but admitted to penance; অনুতপ্ত ব্যক্তি; খৃষ্টীয় ধর্ম্মসঙ্ঘ কর্ত্তৃক তিরস্কৃত হইয়া পাপক্ষালনার্থ প্রায়শ্চিত্তাধীন ব্যক্তি। 2. (*Pl.*) Fraternities in the Roman Catholic Church distinguished by their habits and employed in acts of charity ; রোমানক্যাথলিক ধর্ম্মসংঘভুক্ত বিভিন্ন মণ্ডলী। **—ly, —ten′-ti-al-ly,** *advs.* **—tence,** *n.* The state of being penitent ; repentance ; contrition ; অনুতপ্তাবস্থা ; অনুতাপ, পরিতাপ, অনুশোচনা ; খেদ, পশ্চাত্তাপ। **—ten′-ti-al,** *adj.* **The penitential psalms**—(vi., xxxii. xxxviii. li. cii. cxxx., cxliii) ; ধর্ম্মসংগীত।

pĕn-i-tĕn′-tia-rȳ (-shă-), *adj.* & *n.* 1. Of, or relating to, penance; প্রায়শ্চিত্তসংক্রান্ত। 2. Used for punishment and reformation of criminals ; as, a *penitentiary* house ; অপরাধিগণের দণ্ডবিধান ও সংশোধনের জন্য ব্যবহৃত। *Noun.* 1. A penitent, (*obs.*) ; (অপ্রঃ) পাপপরিতপ্ত ব্যক্তি। 2. A small building in a monastery where penitents confessed ; মঠের যে ক্ষুদ্র গৃহে পাপিগণ স্বীয় দোষ স্বীকার করিত, প্রায়শ্চিত্তশালা, পাপস্বীকারকক্ষ। 3. An office or official of the Roman Catholic Church, deciding questions of penance, dispensations, etc. ; (রোমানক্যাথলিক ধর্ম্মসংঘ) প্রায়শ্চিত্তাদিবিষয়ক প্রশ্নমীমাংসার্থ কার্য্যালয় বা কর্ম্মচারী। 4. A house of correction and punishment for offenders ; সংশোধনাগার, কারাগৃহ। 5. A place for reformation of prostitutes ; গণিকা-সংশোধনাগার। **Grand Penitentiary**—যে মহাধর্ম্মাধ্যক্ষ প্রায়শ্চিত্তাদিবিষয়ক প্রশ্ন মীমাংসা করেন।

pĕn′-nant (-ănt), *n.* 1. (*Naut.*) A pendant or short rope ; (নৌ-বিদ্যা) ক্ষুদ্র রজ্জু। 2. Same as PENNON.

pĕn′-nant (-ănt), *n.* A small flag ; a pennon ; ক্ষুদ্র পতাকা; কেতু, কেতন।

pĕn′-nate (-āte), **—nat-ĕd** (-ăt-), *adjs.* Winged ; feathered ; সপক্ষ ; পালকবিশিষ্ট।

pĕn′-ni-fŏrm (-ĭ-), *adj.* (*Nat. Hist.*) Having the form or appearance of a feather; পালকাকার, পালকাকৃতি। **—nif′-er-ous,** *adj.* Bearing feathers ; পালকপ্রসূ।

pĕn′-ni-lĕss, *adj.* Without a penny ; poor ; destitute ; কপর্দ্দকশূন্য ; দরিদ্র ; অকিঞ্চন।

pĕn′-nill (-ĭl), *n.* A kind of improvised verse, suited to harp accompaniment ; একপ্রকার উপস্থিত মত রচিত কবিতা।

pĕn′-non (-ŏn), *n.* 1. A long narrow flag, esp. as military ensign of lancer regiments ; দীর্ঘ পতাকা। 2. A long pointed flag of a ship ; জাহাজের দীর্ঘ সূক্ষ্মাগ্র পতাকা। 3. Any flag or banner ; পতাকা, ধ্বজ, কেতু, কেতন। **—noned,** *adj.* Bearing a pennon; পতাকাবাহী, পতাকাধারী, ধ্বজবাহক।

pĕn′-nȳ, *n.* (*Pl.* PENNIES AND PENCE.) 1. A bronze coin worth $\frac{1}{12}$th of a shilling; এক শিলিং এর দ্বাদশাংশ মূল্যের মুদ্রা বিশেষ। (বহুবচনে সংখ্যা বুঝাইতে *pennies* এবং মূল্য বা পরিমাণ বুঝাইতে *pence* ব্যবহৃত হয়। *Penny*র পরিবর্ত্তে সংক্ষেপে *d* লিখা হইয়া থাকে।) 2. A small sum; money; as, to turn an honest *penny*; সামান্য অর্থ; টাকা, টাকা কড়ি, টাকা পয়সা। **Penny-a-line**—*adj.* সস্তাদরের লেখা। **Penny-a-liner**—(পূর্ব্বে) পংক্তি প্রতি এক পেনি হিসাবে বা তাদৃশ সামান্য পারিশ্রমিক লাভে যাহারা সংবাদপত্রাদিতে প্রবন্ধাদি লিখে; (বর্ত্তমানে অবজ্ঞাচ্ছলে) বেতনভোগী দরিদ্র লেখক। **Penny-dog**—ব্রিটেনের দক্ষিণ উপকূলে প্রাপ্ত হাঙ্গর বিশেষ। **Penny father**—কৃপণ। **Penny-gaff**—যে স্থানে সস্তা দরে নাচ তামাসা, ভোজবাজী প্রভৃতি দেখান হয়। **Penny-in-the-slot**—See under SLOT. **Penny post**—এক আনা মাশুলের চিঠির ডাক। **Penny-rent**—আয়, রাজস্ব। **Penny-royal**—ইংলণ্ডদেশজ গুল্মবিশেষ। **Penny-wedding**—স্কটলণ্ডের বিবাহোৎসব—ইহাতে নিমন্ত্রিত ব্যক্তিবর্গ ব্যয়নির্ব্বাহার্থ অর্থ সাহায্য প্রদান করিতেন। **Pennyweight** — (Abbr. *dwt.*) ২৪ গ্রেণ ট্রয়। **Penny-wisdom**—সামান্য সামান্য বিষয়ে বিচক্ষণতা। **Penny-wise**—সামান্য বিষয়ে হিসাবী। **Pennywort** — ব্রাহ্মী (Indian—থোরী), মণ্ডুকপর্ণী (ঐ)। **Penny-worth, penn'orth**—এক পেনি মূল্যে যে পরিমাণ জিনিষ কেনা যাইতে পারে। **A good or bad penny-worth, penn'orth**—A good or bad bargain; সুলভে বা দুর্ম্মূল্যে ক্রয়। **A penny-dreadful**—হত্যা, অত্যাচার, প্রভৃতি লোমহর্ষণ ঘটনার বিবরণপূর্ণ সংবাদপত্র। **A penny for your thoughts** — (The full expression would be "I'll give you a penny if you'll tell me your thought"); বৃথা ভাবনা। **In for a penny, In for a pound**—A thing once begun must be concluded at all costs; যে কাজে একবার হাত দেওয়া হইয়াছে তাহা যে প্রকারেই হউক সম্পাদন করিতে হইবে, যাহা বাহান্ন তাহা তিপ্পান্ন। **Not a penny-worth, penn'orth**—Not the least bit or quantity; অণুমাত্রও নয়। **Penny a day is great a year**—Same as MANY A LITTLE MAKES MICKLE. **Penny wise and pound-foolish**—Careful in small but wasteful in large matters; সামান্য সামান্য বিষয়ে খুব হিসাবী কিন্তু বড় বড় ব্যাপারে ভ্রূক্ষেপশূন্য, সম্মুখ দিয়া ছুঁচ গলে না পেছন দিয়া হাতী যায়, বজ্র আঁটুনি ফসকা গেরো। **Peter's penny, — pence** — প্রাচীন কালে পোপকে প্রদত্ত করবিশেষ। **Take care of the pence, pounds will take care of themselves**—পয়সা ব্যয়ে হিসাবী হইলে টাকা, মোহর আপনা হইতেই আসে। **To think one's penny silver**—To have a good opinion of oneself; নিজের সম্বন্ধে উচ্চ মত পোষণ করা। **To turn an honest penny**—To earn money honestly; সদুপায়ে টাকাপয়সা রোজগার করা।

pē-nŏl'-ŏ-ġy̆, *n.* The science of punishment and prison management; দণ্ডবিজ্ঞান, শাস্তি-বিজ্ঞান, দণ্ডশাস্ত্র (হিঃ কোঃ)। **-gist**, *n.* **-no-log'-i-cal**, *adj.*

pĕn'-sile (-sil), *adj.* 1. Hanging; suspended; বিলম্বী; দোদুল্যমান। 2. (*Rare*) Constructing or having a hanging nest as a bird etc.; বিলম্বী নীড়নির্ম্মাণকারী, উক্তরূপ নীড়-সমন্বিত।

pĕn'-sion, *n.* & *v.t.* 1. A periodical allowance to a person in consideration of past services; অবসরবৃত্তি, পেনসন। 2. A payment or allowance to a person who is not a professed servant for good will, secret service, etc. or to artists, scientists, etc. to enable them to carry on work of public interest; বৃত্তি। 3. (*Pron. as French* পাঁ-সিয়ঁ) A boarding-house or school on the continent; ফ্রান্স্, ইটালী, জার্ম্মাণী প্রভৃতি দেশে ভোজনাগারসমন্বিত বাসাবাটী বা বিদ্যালয়। 4. A sum paid to a clergyman in place of tithes; যাজকীয় বৃত্তি। 5. An assembly of the members of Gray's Inn to consult about the affairs of the society; গ্রেজ Innএর বারিষ্টারসম্প্রদায়ের সভা। *Verb t.* To grant pension to; to discharge upon a pension, (with *off*); অবসরবৃত্তি দেওয়া, বৃত্তি প্রদান করা; অবসরবৃত্তি প্রদানে কার্য্য হইতে বিদায় দেওয়া। **-a-ble**, *adj.* Entitled, or entitling to, a pension; as a *pensionable* officer or office; অবসরবৃত্তিযোগ্য, অবসরবৃত্তি প্রাপ্তির অধিকারী। **-a-ry**, *adj.* & *n.* 1. Of, or relating to, or receiving a pension; অবসরবৃত্তিসম্বন্ধীয়, অবসরবৃত্তিভোগী। 2. Consisting of a pension, as a provision; অবসরবৃত্তিসমন্বিত। (*Noun.*) 1. A pensioner; (*contempt.*) a hireling; a creature; অবসর-বৃত্তিপ্রাপ্ত ব্যক্তি; (অবজ্ঞাচ্ছলে) বেতনগ্রাহী ভৃত্য; উপজীবি। 2. One of the chief magistrates of towns in Holland; হলণ্ডের প্রধান রাজকর্ম্মচারিবিশেষ। **-less**, *adj.* **Old-age pension**—ব্রিটিশ শাসনতন্ত্রকর্তৃক দরিদ্র, শ্রমজীবী, প্রভৃতিকে নির্দ্দিষ্ট বয়স উত্তীর্ণ হওয়ার পর যে বৃত্তি প্রদত্ত হয়। **Grand Pensionary**—হলণ্ডের এবং জীলণ্ডের প্রধান মন্ত্রী (১৬১৯—১৭৯৪)। **To pension off**—To dismiss with a pension; অবসরবৃত্তি প্রদানে কর্ম্মচ্যুত করা।

pĕn'-sion-ĕr, *n.* 1. One who receives a pension; বৃত্তিভোগী, অবসর বৃত্তিভোগী। 2. A dependant; a hireling; আশ্রিতজন, গলগ্রহ ব্যক্তি; বেতনগ্রাহী লোক। 3. A student in the Cambridge University, who pays for his board and other charges (corresponding to *Commoner* at

Oxford) ; কেম্বি জ বিশ্ববিদ্যালয়ে যে ছাত্র নিজের আহারাদির ব্যয় বহন করে।

pĕn'-sive (-sĭv), *adj.* **1.** Engaged in, or given to, serious thought or musing ; melancholy ; চিন্তাপরায়ণ, চিন্তাক্রান্ত, ধ্যানস্থ, ধ্যানশীল, চিন্তিত, চিন্তাপ্রাপ্ত, চিন্তামগ্ন ; বিষণ্ণ, বিষাদময়, বিরস। **2.** Expressing melancholy thoughtfulness ; as, *pensive* numbers ; সবিষাদ চিন্তাসূচক। **—ly,** *adv.* **—ness** *n.*

pĕn'-stŏck, *n.* Sluice or flood-gate ; স্রোতোদ্বার, কপাট-কল।

pĕn'-sŭm, *n.* An extra task given in a school by way of punishment ; বিদ্যালয়ের ছাত্রগণকে শাস্তিস্বরূপ প্রদত্ত অতিরিক্ত পাঠ।

pĕnt, *adj.* Closely shut up or confined ; আবদ্ধ, অবরুদ্ধ।

pĕn'-tă-chord, *n.* **1.** An instrument of music with five strings ; a series of five notes ; গ্রীসদেশীয় পঞ্চতন্ত্রবাদ্যযন্ত্রবিশেষ, পাঁচতারা, পঞ্চতন্ত্র বাদ্য ; পঞ্চস্বরপর্য্যায়।

pĕn'-tă-cle (-kl), *n.* Same as PENTAGRAM. **—tac'-u-lar,** *adj.*

pĕn'-tăd, *n.* **1.** A group or number of five esp. five years ; পঞ্চসংখ্যার সংহতি, পঞ্চক। **2.** (*Chem.*) An atom, radical or element with combining power of five ; (রসায়ন-শাস্ত্র) পঞ্চসংযোগ শক্তিসম্পন্ন পরমাণু বা মূলপদার্থ, পঞ্চবন্ধন।

pĕn-tă-dăc'-tȳl, —tyle (-tĭl), *adj.* & *n.* Having five toes or fingers on each limb ; পঞ্চাঙ্গুলী-বিশিষ্ট। ***Noun.*** Such a person or animal ; পঞ্চাঙ্গুলীব্যক্তি বা জন্তু। **—ic,** *adj.* **—ism,** *n.*

pĕn'-tă-glŏt, *n.* & *adj.* **1.** A work in five different tongues ; পঞ্চভাষায় লিখিত গ্রন্থ। ***Adj.*** Using five different languages ; পঞ্চভাষা ভাষী।

pĕn'-tă-gŏn, *n.* A five-sided plane figure ; পঞ্চভুজক্ষেত্র, পঞ্চকোণ, পঞ্চাস্র। **—tăg'-o-nal,** *adj.*

pĕn'-tă-grăm, *n.* A mystic figure like a five pointed star formerly used as a symbol ; (also *pentacle, pentangle, pentageron, pentalpha*) ; পঞ্চভুজক্ষেত্রের বাহু সকল উভয়দিকে বর্দ্ধিত করিয়া পরস্পরকে ছিন্ন করিলে যে পঞ্চকোণ নক্ষত্রাকার ক্ষেত্র উৎপন্ন হয়, তম্মোক্ত ক্রিয়ায় ব্যবহৃত যন্ত্রবিশেষ, পঞ্চকোণ-যন্ত্র।

pĕn-tăg'-ȳ-nous (-nŭs), *adj.* (*Bot.*) Having five pistils ; (উদ্ভিদ্ বিদ্যা) পঞ্চগর্ভকেশরবিশিষ্ট।

pĕn-tă-hē'-drŏn, *n.* A solid figure having five faces ; পঞ্চপার্শ্ব-ঘনক্ষেত্র, পঞ্চাস্রঘনক্ষেত্র। **—dral,** *adj.*

pĕn-tăm'-ĕr-ous (-ŭs), *adj.* **1.** (Also written *5-merous*) (*Bot.*) Consisting of, or divided into, five parts ; (উদ্ভিদ্‌বিদ্যা) পঞ্চাংশ-সম্পন্ন, পঞ্চঅংশে বিভক্ত, পঞ্চাংশস্তবকী (সাঃ পঃ)। **2.** (*Zool.*) Consisting of 5 joints ; (জীববিজ্ঞান) পঞ্চগ্রন্থি-বিশিষ্ট, পঞ্চপর্ব্বসমন্বিত।

pĕn-tăm'-ĕ-tĕr, *n.* & *adj.* (*Pros.*) A poetic verse of five feet, esp. the elegiac pentameter ; পঞ্চপদী-শ্লোক। ***Adj.*** Having five metrical feet ; পঞ্চপদী।

pĕn-tăn'-drous (-drŭs), *adj.* Having five stamens with distinct filaments ; পঞ্চপুংকেশরী।

pĕn'-tāne, *n.* Any of the three hydrocarbons C_5H_{12} of the paraffin series ; প্যারাফিন শ্রেণীর হাইড্রোকার্ব্বন বর্গের অন্যতম।

pĕn-tăn'-gu-lar (-tăng-gü-lêr), *adj.* Having five corners or angles ; পঞ্চকৌণিক।

pĕn-tă-pĕt'-ăl-ous (-ŭs), *adj.* Having five petals or flower leaves ; পঞ্চপত্রী, পঞ্চদল।

pĕn-tăp'-ŏ-dȳ, *n.* (*Pros.*) A measure or series of five feet ; পঞ্চপদী।

pĕn'-târch-ȳ, *n.* Government by five persons ; five joint rulers ; পঞ্চশাসকের মিলিত শাসন ; মিলিতপঞ্চ-শাসক।

pĕn'-tă-stich, *n.* A group of five lines in a verse ; পঞ্চশ্লোকী (আঃ বঃ), কোন কবিতার কলির পঞ্চপংক্তি।

pĕn'-tă-teuch (-tük), *n.* A collective term for the first five books of the Old Testament ; বাইবেলের প্রাচীন নিয়মের প্রথম পঞ্চপুস্তক। **—teu'-chal,** *adj.*

pĕn-tă-tŏm'-ic, *adj.* With five atoms of some substance in the molecule ; প্রতি অণুতে পঞ্চ পরমাণু সমন্বিত।

pĕn-tă-tŏn'-ic, *adj.* Of, or relating to, five notes ; পঞ্চস্বরসম্বন্ধীয়।

pĕn-tă-va'-lĕnt, *adj.* Having a valence or combining power of five ; পঞ্চসংযোগশক্তিসমন্বিত।

Pĕn'-tĕ-cōst, *n.* **1.** A solemn harvest festival of the Jews, so called because celebrated on the fiftieth day after the feast of the Passover ; ইহুদীদিগের শস্যসংগ্রহ কালীন উৎসব, ইহা "পাস্ অভার" ভোজের পরবর্ত্তী পঞ্চাশত্তম দিবসে সম্পাদিত হয়। **2.** (*Archaic*) Same as WHIT-SUNDAY. **—cos'-tal,** *adj.*

pĕnt'-house (-hows), **pĕn'-tice** (-tĭs), *ns.* **1.** (*Archaic*) A shed or roof sloping from the main wall or building ; প্রাচীর সংলগ্ন একচালা ঘর, চালাঘর, পরচালা। **2.** A window, awning, canopy or the like ; also, the eyebrow ; "The *penthouse* of his eye" ; বাতায়ন, বিতান, চন্দ্রাতপ ; ভ্রূলতা।

Pent roof.

pĕnt'-roof, *n.* A roof sloping on one side only ; একপার্শ্বে ঢালু ছাদ।

pĕn'-trough (-trŏf), *n.* Same as PENSTOCK.

pĕ'-nŭlt, —nŭl'-ti-māte, *adj.* & *n.* Last but one ; উপান্ত্য। ***Noun.*** The last syllable but one ; উপান্ত্য শব্দাংশ। **Penultimate letter**—উপধা।

pē-nŭm'-bră, *n.* **1.** (*Astron.*) The partial shadow on the margin of the total shadow in an eclipse; (জ্যোতির্বিজ্ঞান) গ্রহণকালীন চন্দ্রসূর্য্যের চতুঃপার্শ্ববর্ত্তী পূর্ণচ্ছায়ার প্রান্তবর্ত্তী ঈষচ্ছায়া, খণ্ডচ্ছায়া, উপচ্ছায়া (হিঃ কোঃ), অপূর্ণচ্ছায়া (কেন্ডিঃ), অবতম (সাঃ পঃ)। **2.** The lighter outer part of a sun-spot; সূর্য্যমণ্ডলস্থ বিন্দুর অপেক্ষাকৃত অগাঢ়বর্ণ বহির্ভাগ। **3.** The point of a picture where the shade blends with the light; a partial shadow; চিত্রের যে স্থানে আলো ও ছায়া মিশিয়া যায়; আংশিক ছায়া। **–bral, –brous,** *adjs.*

pē-nü'-ri-ous (-ŭs), *adj.* **1.** Needy; poor; scanty; অভাবগ্রস্ত; দীন, দরিদ্র, নিঃস্ব, গরীব; স্বল্প, সামান্য, অত্যল্প। **2.** Stingy; miserly; কৃপণ; ব্যয়কুণ্ঠ, কঞ্জুষ। **–ly,** *adv.* **–ness,** *n.*

pĕn'-ū-rȳ, *n.* **1.** Want; poverty; অভাব; দরিদ্রতা, নিঃস্বতা। **2.** Scarcity; অনটন, টানাটানি।

pē'-ŏn, *n.* **1.** (*In India*) A foot-soldier; a native constable; a foot-man; a messenger or attendant; (ভারতবর্ষে) পদাতিক সৈন্য; পিয়ন; পাদচারী; বার্ত্তাবহ, প্যাদা। **2.** (*Span Amer.*) A day-labourer; দিনমজুর, শ্রমিক। **3.** (*Mexico*) A serf; (মেক্সিকো) চিরদাস। **–age, –ism,** *ns.*

pē'-ō-nȳ, *n.* A plant with a large and beautiful flower; বৃহৎ এবং মনোহর পুষ্পপ্রসূ গুল্মবিশেষ।

peo'-ple (pē-pl), *n.* & *v. t.* **1.** Persons composing a community, race or nation, (*as sing.*); as, the English *people*; একশ্রেণী বা এক জাতিভুক্ত লোকসকল, লোকসমূহ, জনগণ। **2.** The persons of a place, persons of a class, a company etc.; কোন স্থানের অধিবাসিবর্গ, কোন শ্রেণী বা দলের লোক। **3.** The subjects of a king, monarch, etc.; the members of a society or congregation; প্রজাবর্গ; কোন মণ্ডলীর সভ্য, পল্লীযাজকের অধীন জনসমাজ। **4.** (*Colloq.*) One's parents or other relatives; as, his *people* were English; (চলিতভাষায়) পিতামাতা বা অন্যান্য স্বজনবর্গ। **5.** The commonalty; the populace; the vulgar; সাধারণ লোক; জনসমাজ; ইতর-জনসমাজ। **6.** Persons in general; সর্ব্বসাধারণ, লোকসাধারণ, জনসাধারণ। **7.** A body of retainers, servants, etc.; কর্ম্মচারিবর্গ, ভৃত্যবর্গ। **8.** The body of enfranchised citizens of a state; কোন রাজ্যের নির্ব্বাচনমত প্রদানের ক্ষমতাপ্রাপ্ত ব্যক্তি। ***Verb t.*** **1.** To stock with people or inhabitants; to fill as a place with animals, etc.; (লোকাদিদ্বারা) পূর্ণ করা; জন্তুদ্বারা পূর্ণ করা। **2.** (Of persons, animals, etc.) To inhabit, occupy, fill, esp. in *p. p.*; "A thickly *peopled* country"; অধ্যুষিত করা, অধিকৃত করা, পূর্ণ করা। **The Chosen people**—ইহুদীগণ। **The people**—ভদ্রেতর জনগণ।

pĕp-ĕr-i'-nō (-ö-), *n.* **1.** A species of volcanic rock; আগ্নেয়গিরির প্রস্তরবিশেষ। **2.** Red pepper; a plant bearing this; মরিচ; লঙ্কা গাছ। **3.** (*Fig.*) Something pungent; (লক্ষণায়) ঝাল জিনিষ।

pē'-pō, *n.* A characteristic fruit of gourd family; শশা, ফুটি, চালকুমড়া ইত্যাদির সাধারণ নাম।

Black pepper.

pĕp'-pĕr, *n.* **1.** A plant with an aromatic pungent, fruit, esp. the Black Pepper, much used in seasoning; this fruit; a condiment got from this; মরিচ গাছ, বিশেষতঃ গোলমরিচের গাছ; গোলমরিচ, কালামরিচ, শফেদমরিচ (white pepper), বহুল, (ib.) ধবলী (ib.) [সুপক্ক গোলমরিচ শুষ্ক করিয়া বা উহার খোসা ছাড়াইয়া প্রস্তুত করা হয়]। [Syn. কৃষ্ণমরিচ, ধর্ম্মপত্তন, কোল, কোলক, বেল্লজ, বেল্লন, চর্ম্মবন্ধন (নিঘণ্টু), শিরোবৃত্ত, উষণ, উষণ, বল্লীজ, শাকাঙ্গ, আপন, শ্যামবল্লী (the tree), শ্যামা, মল্লজ।] [Greek *peperi*; Latin *piper*; Arab. *filfil, aswad*; Turk. *beber*; Chinese *hu-tsiau*; Malay *lada.* ইংরাজী pepper শব্দ সংস্কৃত পিপ্পলী শব্দ হইতে আসিয়াছে।]; মরিচের গুঁড়া। **Cayenne pepper**—লালমরিচ, লঙ্কামরিচ। **Long-pepper**—পিপুল, পিপ্পলী, জটিলা, দন্তফলা, কৃষ্ণা, উপকুল্যা, বৈদেহী, মাগধী, মগধোদ্ভবা, কণা (সুশ্রুঃ), উষণা, উষণা, শৌণ্ডী, কোলা, চপলা, শ্রেয়সী, এরণ্ডা, প্রিয়ঙ্গু, কটুবীজা। **Pepper-and-salt**—একপ্রকার পশমী কাপড়। **Pepper-box**—খাদ্যদ্রব্যের উপর মরিচের চূর্ণ ছড়াইবার জন্য সচ্ছিদ্র ডালাবিশিষ্ট ক্ষুদ্র বাক্স, মরিচপাত্র। **Pepper-castor, -caster**—Same as PEPPER-BOX. **Pepper-corn** — গোলমরিচ; তুচ্ছ জিনিষ। **Pepper-corn rent**—সামান্য খাজনা। **Peppermint**—তুলস্যাদিবর্গের পুদিনাসদৃশ শাকবিশেষ (অধ্যাপক যোগেশ চন্দ্র রায়)। **Pepper-pot**—Same as PEPPER BOX; also, West-Indian dish of meat etc. stewed with red pepper etc.; লঙ্কামরিচের চূর্ণ প্রভৃতি দ্বারা রন্ধিত মাংস। **Pepper-wort**—তুম্বুরু (খোরী), নেপালী ধনিয়া (ঐ), তেজফল (ঐ)। **To take pepper in the nose**—To be irritated or excited; উত্তেজিত হওয়া, গাত্রজ্বালা হওয়া।

pĕp-pĕr, *v. t.* **1.** To sprinkle or season with pepper; (খাদ্যদ্রব্যে) মরিচ বা গোলমরিচের চূর্ণ ছড়াইয়া দেওয়া। **2.** To sprinkle like pepper; as, to *pepper* long words into a writing; গোলমরিচের

গুড়ার মত ছিটাইয়া দেওয়া। **3.** To pelt with shot or missiles (*lit.* & *fig.*); as, to *pepper* one with scolding ; (শব্দানুযায়ী ও লক্ষণায়) বর্ষণ করা, বৃষ্টি করা। **4.** To punish severely ; গুরুতর শাস্তি দেওয়া। **—y,** *adj.* **1.** Of, relating to, or abounding in, pepper ; like pepper ; মরিচের ন্যায়, মরিচপূর্ণ, মারীচ, মরিচবহুল ; মরিচবৎ। **2.** (*Fig.*) Pungent ; choleric ; hot tempered ; (লক্ষণায়) ঝাল, উগ্র, তীব্র ; বদমেজাজী ; উগ্রস্বভাব, চটামেজাজী।

pĕp′-sin, —sine (-sin), *ns.* The active principle of gastric juice ; পাচকরসের প্রধান উপাদান—এতদ্বারা পাচকরসের ভুক্তান্নপরিপাকের শক্তি বৃদ্ধিপ্রাপ্ত হয়, পাচকরসসার।

pĕp′-tic, *adj.* & *n.* **1.** Relating to, or promoting, digestion ; পরিপাকশক্তিবর্দ্ধক, সারক, অগ্নিবর্দ্ধক, অগ্নিদীপক। ***Noun.*** (*Pl., facet.*) Digestive organs ; (কৌতুকচ্ছলে) পাকযন্ত্র। **Peptic-glands**—পাচকরসস্রাবীগ্রন্থি।

pĕp′-tōne, *n.* A class of albuminoid substances into which proteids are converted by action of pepsin, etc. ; পাচকরসসার প্রভৃতির ক্রিয়াদ্বারা জীবদেহের যবক্ষারজানবিশিষ্ট উপকরণ যে অণ্ডলালাবৎ পদার্থশ্রেণীতে পরিবর্ত্তিত হয়। **—tonize,** *v. t.*

pêr, *prep.* **1.** Through ; by means of ; by ; বরাবর ; দ্বারা, দিয়া ; মারফত। **Per annum**—For each year ; yearly ; প্রতিবার্ষিক ; বৎসর বৎসর। **Per bearer**—By bearer ; লোক মারফত। **Per-capita**—By heads ; ব্যক্তি হিসাবে। **Per cent.**—By hundred ; শতকরা। **Per-contra** — *adv.* & *n.* On the contrary ; on the other side ; অন্যপক্ষে ; অপরদিকে। (*Noun*) The opposite side of an account, etc. ; হিসাব প্রভৃতির অপর দিক। **Per-diem**—Every day ; প্রতিদিন, রোজ। **Per-mensem**—Monthly ; প্রতি মাসে। **Per post, rail, steamer**—By post, rail, steamer ; ডাকে, রেলে, জাহাজে। **Per procurationem**—[abbr. *per pro(c).*, *p. p.*] By proxy ; by the action of (a person signing document) ; প্রতিনিধি দ্বারা ; দলিল স্বাক্ষরকারীর কার্য্যদ্বারা, দলিল স্বাক্ষর দ্বারা। **Per saltum**—At a single leap ; all at once ; এক লম্ফে ; একেবারে। **Per se**—By or in itself ; intrinsically ; স্বয়ং, স্বতঃ ; স্বরূপগতভাবে।

pêr-ăd-vĕn′-tūre, *adv.* & *n.* (*Archaic*) Perhaps ; সম্ভবতঃ। ***Noun.*** Chance ; uncertainty ; doubt ; as, proved beyond a *peradventure* ; দৈব ; অনিশ্চয়তা ; সংশয়। **Beyond** or **without (all) peradventure**—Beyond or without (all) doubt ; সন্দেহাতীতভাবে।

pêr-ai′ (-ī), **pe-rä′-yä,** *n.* An American fresh-water fish ; আমেরিকা দেশের একপ্রকার মিঠাজলের মাছ।

pêr-ăm′-bū-lāte, *v. t.* **1.** To walk through or over ; মধ্য বা উপর দিয়া ভ্রমণ করা। **2.** To traverse as a territory for inspection ; to survey the boundaries of (a parish etc.), by walking round them ; পরিদর্শনার্থ ভ্রমণ করা, পরিক্রম করা, প্রদক্ষিণ করা ; সীমাপরিদর্শন করা। **—la′-tion,** *n.* **1.** Act of perambulating ; a travelling survey or inspection ; পরিভ্রমণ ; পর্য্যটনপূর্ব্বক পরিদর্শন, পরিক্রম (cf. বৃন্দাবন পরিক্রম)। **2.** The district within which a person has the ritgh of inspection ; এলাকা। **—la-tors,** *n.* **1.** One who perambulates, as for fixing boundaries, (*rare*) ; (ক্বচিদ্‌ব্যবহৃত) পর্য্যটক। **2.** An instrument for measuring distances or roads, (*rare*) ; গমনদূরত্বনির্ণয়ার্থ যন্ত্রবিশেষ (ক্বচিদ্‌ব্যবহৃত)। **3.** A light carriage for a child (*collcq., abbr. pram.*) ; শিশুদিগের জন্য একপ্রকার হালকা ঠেলাগাড়ী, শিশুযান। **—la-tory,** *adj.*

pêr-cāle′ *n.* A kind of cotton cloth ; একপ্রকার কার্পাস বস্ত্র।

pêr-ceive′ (-sēv), *v. t.* To apprehend by the senses or the mind ; to observe or note ; to understand ; অনুভব করা, বোধ করা, টের পাওয়া, প্রত্যক্ষ করা, হৃদয়ঙ্গম করা ; লক্ষ্য করা ; উপলব্ধি করা। **—ceiv′-able,** *adj.* Capable of being perceived ; ইন্দ্রিয়গ্রাহ্য, প্রত্যক্ষযোগ্য, অনুভবগম্য, অনুভববেদ্য, বোধ্য, সংবেদ্য, অনুভবনীয়।

pêr-cĕnt′-āge, *n.* Rate per hundred ; (loosely), a part or proportion ; শতকরা হার ; ভাগ, অংশ।

pêr′-cĕpt, *n.* (*Philos.*) That which is perceived by means of the senses ; object of perception ; mental product of perceiving ; (দর্শনশাস্ত্র) ইন্দ্রিয় দ্বারা অনুভূত বিষয় ; অনুভূতির বিষয় ; প্রত্যক্ষ।

pêr-cĕp′-ti-ble (-bl), *adj.* Capable of being perceived by the senses or intellect ; discernible ; ইন্দ্রিয়গ্রাহ্য, অনুভবগম্য, উপলভ্য, প্রত্যক্ষযোগ্য (হিঃ কোঃ), গ্রহণীয়, গ্রাহ্য, অনুভবনীয় ; সংবেদ্য, সংবেদনীয়। **—bil′-i-ty,** *n.* Quality of being perceptible ; বোধগম্যতা, প্রত্যক্ষযোগ্যতা (হিঃ কোঃ), ইন্দ্রিয়গ্রাহ্যতা, অনুভববেদ্যতা। **—bly,** *adv.*

pêr-cĕp′-tion, *n.* **1.** Act or faculty of perceiving by the senses or the mind ; বোধ, উপলব্ধি, সংবিজ্ঞান, সংবেদন, সংবেদ, বিবোধ, প্রত্যক্ষ (ন্যায়সূত্র), প্রত্যয় (বেদান্তঃ), ইন্দ্রিয়গ্রহ (কেঙিঃ), বেদন (ঐ), প্রত্যক্ষীকরণ (হিঃ কোঃ), সবিকল্প প্রত্যক্ষ (ঐ), বিষয়ীকরণ (কেঙিঃ)। **2.** The intuitive or direct recognition of a moral or aesthetic quality *e. g.* truth, beauty, etc. ; নীতি বা রসসম্বন্ধীয় গুণসমূহের

অপরোক্ষ বা আত্মপ্রত্যয়সিদ্ধ প্রত্যভিজ্ঞান। 3. (*Philos.*) The act or process of the mind by which it refers its sensations to an external object, as their cause ; discernment : (দর্শনশাস্ত্র) যে ক্রিয়া দ্বারা মন বাহ্য বস্তুতে উহার সংবেদনসমূহ আরোপ করে, বাহ্যবিষয়ারোপ ; সংবেদন। 4. (*Law*) The receiving or collecting as of rents, profits, etc. ; (আইন) রাজস্ব, লাভ প্রভৃতি গ্রহণ বা সংগ্রহ। **—al,** *adj.* **—tive,** *adj.* Having the power of perceiving or discerning ; গ্রাহক, গ্রাহ্য, বোধক্ষম। **—tive-ness, —tiv′-i-ty,** *ns.* **—tive-ly,** *adv.*

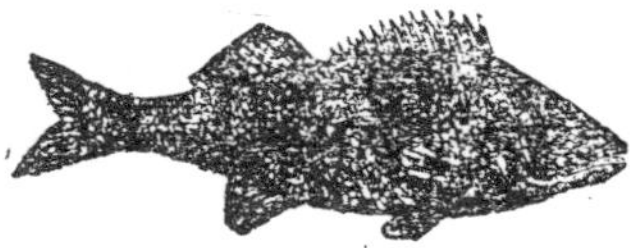

Perch.

pêrch, *n.* A European fresh-water fish ; ইয়ুরোপের একপ্রকার মিঠাজলের মাছ।

pêrch, *n.* **1.** A rod on which birds roost ; any similar things on which birds alight and rest ; পক্ষীর বসিবার দাঁড় ; বাসযষ্টি (মেঘঃ)। 2. (*Fig.*) Any high seat or position ; (লক্ষণায়) উচ্চাসন, উন্নত পদবী। 3. A measure of length = $5\frac{1}{2}$ yeards ; ৫½ গজ পরিমিত দৈর্ঘ্যের পরিমাপ। 4. The centre-pole of some four-wheeled vehicles ; কোন কোন চতুশ্চক্র যানের যুগন্ধর। **The bird takes its perch**—It alights ; ইহা নামিতেছে। **To hop the perch**—To die ; পটল তোলা। **To knock a person off his perch**—To vanquish or destroy him ; ধ্বংস করা, পরাজয় করা। **To tip over the perch**—To die ; শিঙ্গা ফুঁকা।

pêrch, *v. i.* & *t.* **1.** To sit on a perch ; to sit or rest (*on* or *upon* a bough, etc.) ; দাঁড়ে বসা ; বসা, বসিয়া বিশ্রাম করা। 2. (Of a person etc.) To settle (*upon*) ; বসা। ***Verb t.*** To place on, or as on, a perch, esp. in *p.p.* ; as, a town *perched* on a hill ; দাঁড়ে বসান, উচ্চস্থানে অধিষ্ঠিত করা।

pêr-chance′ (-chăns), *adv.* (*Archaic*) Perhaps ; (অপ্রঃ) সম্ভবতঃ, হয়তঃ, বুঝিবা।

percheron, (*F.*), *n.* A swift horse of a breed originating in Perche, a district of France ; ফরাসীদেশের Perche নামক স্থানের অশ্ববংশ হইতে জাত দ্রুতগামী ঘোটকবিশেষ।

pêr-cip′-i-ĕnt, *adj.* & *n.* Perceiving ; having the faculty of perception ; সংবিজ্ঞানশীল ; অনুভবশক্তিসম্পন্ন। ***Noun.*** 1. One who perceives or has the power of perceiving ; সংবেদনশীল ব্যক্তি, বোধক্ষম ব্যক্তি। 2. One receiving telepathic or other supersensible impressions ; অতীন্দ্রিয় প্রতীতিগ্রহণশীল ব্যক্তি, পরচিত্তজ্ঞ ব্যক্তি। **—ence,** *n.*

pêr′-cō-late, *v. t.* & *i.* To filter ; to strain ; ছাঁকা, ছাঁকিয়া পরিষ্কার করা। ***Verb i.*** To pass through small interstices or pores ; to filter (*lit.* & *fig.*) ; সূক্ষ্ম ছিদ্রের মধ্য দিয়া পড়া ; (শব্দানুযায়ী ও লক্ষণায়) চুয়াইয়া পড়া। **—la′-tion,** *n.* Act of filtering ; পরিস্রবণ, ছাঁকন। **—la-tor,** *n.* A filtering vessel ; সরু ছিদ্রবিশিষ্ট ছাঁকিবার পাত্র।

pêr-cŭss′, *v. t.* (*Med.*) To tap gently with finger or instrument for purposes of diagnosis etc. ; (ভৈষজ্যশাস্ত্র) অঙ্গুলী দ্বারা আঘাত করিয়া রোগনির্ণয় করা। **—cus′-sion,** *n.* **1.** Forcible collision ; the striking of a percussion cap, so as to set off the charge in a firearm ; সংঘট্ট, সংঘর্ষ ; বন্দুক ছুড়িবার জন্য রঞ্জকঘরায় নিবদ্ধ তামার টোপরে আঘাত। 2. (*Med.*) Act of percussing ; রোগনির্ণয়ার্থ দেহের উপর অঙ্গুলী দ্বারা মৃদুমৃদু আঘাত, অঙ্গুলীবিঘাতন (ডাহিঃ), সমাঘাত, [শরীরের উপর অঙ্গুলীর আঘাতের শব্দ দ্বারা আভ্যন্তরিক যন্ত্রাদির অবস্থা পরিজ্ঞাত হওয়া যায়।] 3. Impression of sound on the ear ; শ্রুতিতে শব্দের প্রতিঘাত। **—cus′-sion-al,** *adj.* **—cus′-sive,** *adj.* **Percussion-bullet**—বন্দুকের যে গুলি কোন কিছুর সংঘর্ষণে হঠাৎ সশব্দে বিদীর্ণ হইয়া যায়। **Percussion-cap**—See CAP. **Instrument of percussion**—(সঙ্গীতশাস্ত্র) অঙ্গুলিবিঘাতন দ্বারা বাদিত বাদ্যযন্ত্র।

pêr-cū-tā′-nē-ous (-ŭs), *adj.* (*Med. and Surg.*) Made, performed, or effected, through the skin ; (ভৈষজ্যশাস্ত্র এবং অস্ত্রোপচারবিদ্যা) চর্ম্মের ভিতর দিয়া কৃত বা সাধিত।

pêr-cū′-ti-ĕnt (-shi-), *adj.* & *n.* Striking or having power to strike ; আঘাতকারী বা ঘাতক্ষম। ***Noun.*** A striking agent or body ; আঘাতকারী বস্তু।

pêr-di′-tion, *n.* Eternal death ; utter ruin ; damnation ; অনন্ত মৃত্যু ; সর্ব্বনাশ ; অধঃপতন, অধোগমন, নরকবাস।

pêr-dū′, —due′ (-dü), *adjs.* **1.** Hidden ; in ambush ; as, to lie *perdu* ; লুক্কায়িত ; আক্রমণের উদ্দেশ্যে আড়ালে স্থিত। 2. Out of sight ; concealed ; দৃষ্টিবহির্ভূত ; গুপ্ত, প্রচ্ছন্ন। **To lie perdu(e)** — To lie ; শায়িত হওয়া।

pêr-dūr′-ā-ble (-bl), *adj.* **1.** Durable ; lasting ; permanent ; স্থায়ী ; মজবুত ; চিরস্থায়ী। 2. Eternal ; শাশ্বত, সনাতন। **—bil′-i-ty,** *n.* **—bly,** *adv.*

pere, (*F.*), *n.* Father used after French names to distinguish a father from a son ; পিতা।

pĕr′-ĕ-gri-nāte, *v. i.* & *t.* To travel or journey ; দেশপর্য্যটন করা। ***Verb t.*** To traverse ; স্থানে স্থানে পরিভ্রমণ করা। **—na′-tion,** *n.*

Travelling ; পরিভ্রমণ, দেশাটন, পর্য্যটন। **–tor,** *n.*

pĕ'-rĕ-grin(e) (-grĭn), *adj.* & *n.* **1.** (*Archaic*) Foreign ; exotic ; (অপ্রঃ) বৈদেশিক ; বিদেশীয়। **2.** (*Astrol., of a planet*) Having no essential dignity ; (ফলিতজ্যোতিষ) তুঙ্গ, মূলত্রিকোণ, স্বক্ষেত্র, কেন্দ্র, দ্রেক্কাণ, প্রভৃতিতে স্থিত নয়। ***Noun.*** A kind of falcon ; একপ্রকার বাজপক্ষী।

pĕr'-ĕmp-tŏ-rȳ, *adj.* **1.** Conclusive or decisive ; final ; অনতিক্রমণীয়, অবশ্যপালনীয়, অলঙ্ঘনীয় ; চূড়ান্ত। **2.** (Of a statement or command) Undeniable ; not to be refused ; imperative ; অস্বীকার্য্য ; অলঙ্ঘ্য ; অবশ্যপালনীয়। **3.** Positively fixed ; essential ; "It is a *peremptory* point of virtue etc." ; সুনিশ্চিত, অটল, অবধারিত, অচলপ্রতিষ্ঠ ; প্রধান, মূলীভূত। **4.** (Of persons etc.) Dogmatic ; stubborn ; dictatorial ; স্বমতপ্রধান ; দাম্ভিক ; প্রভুত্বপরায়ণ। **–ri-ly,** *adv.* **–ri-ness,** *n.*

pĕr-ĕn'-nāte, *v. i.* (*Bot.*) To live perennially ; (উদ্ভিদবিদ্যা) চিরজীবী হওয়া।

pĕr-ĕn'-ni-ăl (-i-), *adj.* & *n.* **1.** Lasting, continuing or flowing throughout the year, as a fountain, stream, etc. ; বর্ষস্থায়ী, সম্বৎসরব্যাপী। **2.** Perpetual ; lasting long or for ever ; "*Perennial* youth in her artificial flowers" ; নিত্য ; অবিনশ্বর, নিরবচ্ছিন্ন, চির, সনাতন। **3.** (*Bot.*) Lasting more than two years ; (উদ্ভিদশাস্ত্র) বহুবর্ষজীবী। ***Noun.*** A plant which lives more than two years ; যে গুল্ম দুই বৎসরের অধিক কাল বাঁচিয়া থাকে। **–al'-i-ty,** *n.* **–ly,** *adv.*

pêr'-fĕct, *adj.* & *n.* **1.** Complete ; not defective ; faultless ; সম্পূর্ণ, সম্পন্ন (হিঃ কোঃ), সর্ব্বাঙ্গসম্পন্ন, সম্পূর্ণতাপ্রাপ্ত (ধর্ম্মঃ) ; দোষস্পর্শশূন্য, অনবদ্য, সর্ব্বাঙ্গসুন্দর, চরমোৎকর্ষসম্পন্ন ; নির্দ্দোষ, অদোষ, নিখুঁত। **2.** Fully skilled, trained or accomplished ; as, *perfect* in duties etc. ; পারদর্শী, বিশারদ। **3.** Thoroughly learned, as a lesson ; সম্পূর্ণ অধীত। **4.** Exact ; as, a *perfect* circle ; নির্দ্দোষ। **5.** Utter ; downright ; as, a *perfect* stranger or nonsense ; সম্পূর্ণ ; পুরা, খাঁটি, ডাহা। **6.** (*Gram.*) Expressing an act completed ; as, the present *perfect* tense ; ক্রিয়াসমাপ্তিসূচক। **7.** (*Bot.*) Hermaphrodite ; (উদ্ভিদবিদ্যা) অব্যঙ্গ (সাঃ পঃ)। ***Noun.*** (*Gram.*) The perfect tense or a verb form denoting it ; ক্রিয়াসমাপ্তিবাচককাল, সমাপ্তিবাচক ক্রিয়া। **–ly,** *adv.* In a perfect manner ; completely ; exactly ; সর্ব্বাঙ্গসুন্দরভাবে ; সম্পূর্ণরূপে, সর্ব্বতোভাবে, সর্ব্বথা ; ঠিকভাবে, নিখুঁতভাবে। **–ness,** *n.*

pêr'-fĕct, *v. t.* **1.** To finish or complete ; সম্পূর্ণ করা, পরিসমাপ্ত করা। **2.** To make perfect or faultless ; সর্ব্বাঙ্গসম্পন্ন করা, নিখুঁত করা, সর্ব্বাঙ্গসুন্দর করা। **3.** To make fully skilled in anythig ; কোন বিষয়ে সুদক্ষ করা। **–fect'-i-ble,** *adj.* **–i-bil'-i-ty,** *n.*

pêr-fĕc'-tion, *n.* **1.** State of being perfect or complete ; full development ; maturity ; পূর্ণতা, পূর্ণত্ব, সিদ্ধাবস্থা, সংসিদ্ধি, পূর্ণাবস্থা ; সর্ব্বাঙ্গপুষ্টি ; পরিপক্বতা। **2.** Act of perfecting or making perfect ; পূর্ণতাসাধন, চরমোৎকর্ষসাধন। **3.** Faultlessness ; great excellence ; দোষহীনতা, পারমিতা (ব্রজঃ বৈষ্ণঃ) ; পরমোৎকর্ষ, চরমোৎকর্ষ। **5.** (With *pl.*) A quality, feature or accomplishment of great excellence ; অনুপম গুণ, বিশেষত্ব, প্রভৃতি। **6.** A perfect person or a thing ; চরমোৎকর্ষপ্রাপ্ত ব্যক্তি বা বস্তু। **–ism,** *n.* The doctrine that persons may and do attain to moral perfection and sinlessness in this life ; মানুষ ইহজীবনেই চরম নৈতিক উৎকর্ষ ও নিষ্পাপতা লাভ করিতে পারে—এবম্বিধ মত। **2.** The system of the American Perfectionists ; আমেরিকার ধর্ম্মসম্প্রদায়বিশেষের মত। **–ist,** *n.* **1.** One who believes that some attain to moral perfection in the present life ; ইহজীবনে কেহ কেহ নৈতিক উৎকর্ষ লাভ করিতে পারে, এই প্রকার মতাবলম্বী। **2.** (*Cap.*) One of an American sect of Christians founded on socialist principles ; John Humphrey Noyes কর্ত্তৃক ঊনবিংশ শতাব্দীর মধ্যভাগে প্রতিষ্ঠিত সম্প্রদায় বিশেষের সভ্য। [এই সম্প্রদায়ের সভ্যগণের এই চারিটী মূলমন্ত্র ছিল :—(১) ঈশ্বরের সহিত পুনর্মিলনস্থাপন। (২) পাপমুক্তি। (৩) স্ত্রী পুরুষের সৌভ্রাত্র্য। (৪) শ্রম ও শ্রমলব্ধ ফলে সকলের সমান কর্ত্তব্য ও অধিকার। এই সম্প্রদায়ের মধ্যে বিবাহপ্রথা প্রচলিত ছিলনা। স্ত্রীপুরুষগণ ইচ্ছামত পরস্পরের সহিত সম্মিলিত হইতে পারিত। এই সম্প্রদায়ের অপর নাম Bible Communists ও Free-Lovers]। **To a perfection**—Perfectly ; সর্ব্বাঙ্গসুন্দররূপে, নিখুঁতভাবে।

pêr-fêr'-vĭd, *adj.* Very fervid ; ardent ; প্রচণ্ড ; জ্বলন্ত।

pêr'-fĭ-dȳ, *n.* Violation of faith or of a trust reposed ; treachery ; বিশ্বাসঘাতকতা ; বিশ্বাসভঙ্গ। **–fid'-i-ous,** *adj.* Treacherous ; faithless ; বিশ্বাসঘাতক ; অবিশ্বাসী। **–fid'-i-ous-ly,** *adv.* **–fid'-i-ous-ness,** *n.*

pêr-fō'-lĭ-āte, *adj.* (*Bot.*) Having the stalk apparently passing through the leaf, (উদ্ভিদবিদ্যা) দৃশ্যতঃ পত্র ভেদ করিয়াছে—এইরূপ বৃত্তসমন্বিত, মধ্যচ্ছিদ্র (সাঃ পঃ)।

Perfoliate leaf.

pêr'-fō-rāte, *v. t.* & *i.* **1.** To bore or pierce through ; to make rows of small holes separating stamps, coupons, etc. in a sheet ; ছিদ্র করা, ভেদ করা, প্রবিষ্ট করান, ফোঁড়া; ডাক টিকেট প্রভৃতিকে বিভাগ করার জন্য পাতার মধ্যে ক্ষুদ্র ক্ষুদ্র রন্ধ্র-শ্রেণী করা। 2. To bore into ; গর্ত্ত করা। 3. To extend or pass through ; ভেদ করিয়া যাওয়া। ***Verb i.*** To pierce or penetrate, (*into, through*, etc.) ; ভেদ করা। **—ra'-tion,** *n.* Act of perforating ; a hole bored ; ছিদ্রকরণ ; রন্ধ্র। **—ra-tive,** *adj.* **—ra-tor,** *n.* One who bores or an instrument for boring ; ছিদ্রকারক, যন্ত্রবেধক।

pêr-force' (-förs), *adv.* & *n.* Of necessity ; বাধ্য হইয়া, কাজে কাজেই। ***Noun.*** (*Rare*) Necessity ; (কচিদ্-ব্যবহৃত) আবশ্যকতা।

pêr-fŏrm', *v. t.* & *i.* **1.** To do or accomplish ; to carry out ; পালন করা; নির্ব্বাহ করা। **2.** To act or play as on the stage ; to execute as a function, duty, etc. ; অভিনয় করা ; কর্ত্তব্য সম্পাদন করা। ***Verb i,*** 1. To do or carry out an undertaking etc. ; সম্পন্ন করা, সমাধা করা। 2. To act a part ; to play, as on a musical instrument ; to sing ; অভিনয় করা ; বাদ্যযন্ত্র বাজান, বাদন করা; গান করা। **3.** (Of trained animals etc.) To execute tricks etc. in a public show etc. ; তামাসা করা। **—a-ble,** *adj.* **—er,** *n.* **—ing,** *adj.* Exhibiting performance or tricks ; কৌশল-প্রদর্শনকারী।

pêr-fŏrm'-ance (-ăns), *n.* **1.** Execution (of command etc.) ; পালন, সমাচরণ। 2. Accomplishing ; doing ; সম্পাদন ; সাধন, সমাধান, অনুষ্ঠান, আচরণ। **3.** An achievement or notable deed ; অবদান, মহৎকর্ম্ম। **4.** Act of performing a play, part, tricks, etc. ; a public exhibition or entertainment ; as, there are two *performances* a day ; অভিনয় করণ, তামসা প্রভৃতি করণ ; নাটকাভিনয়, নাচ তামাসা, প্রভৃতি।

pêr'-fūme, *n.* **1.** Fragrant fumes from a burning substance ; দাহ্যমান পদার্থ হইতে উত্থিত সুগন্ধ ধূম, ধূপ। **2.** Sweet smell or odour ; (*fig.*) repute ; সুগন্ধ, সৌগন্ধ, সৌরভ, সুবাস, আমোদ, পরিমল, সুরভি ; (লক্ষণায়) যশঃসৌরভ। 3. A substance that emits an agreeable odour ; a fluid with essence of flowers etc. ; সুগন্ধ দ্রব্য, গন্ধদ্রব্য, আমোদদ্রব্য ; সুগন্ধি জল, সুগন্ধি তৈল, প্রভৃতি। **—less,** *adj.*

pêr-fūme', *v. t.* To fill or impregnate with a pleasant odour ; to scent (usu. in *p. p.*) ; সুবাসিত করা ; সৌরভান্বিত করা। **—fu'-ma-to-ry,** *adj.*

pêr-fūm'-êr, *n.* A maker or seller of perfumes ; সুগন্ধিদ্রব্য বিক্রয়ী বা প্রস্তুতকারী, গন্ধিক (বাৎস্যঃ), ধূপক (চঃ), গন্ধোপজীবী, গন্ধবণিক, গন্ধবিক্রয়ী। **—y,** *n.* 1. Perfumes in general ; সুগন্ধি দ্রব্য সমূহ, আতর, গোলাপ-জল প্রভৃতি। 2. The art of preparing perfumes ; সুগন্ধিদ্রব্য প্রস্তুতপ্রণালী। 3. A perfumer's place of business ; সুগন্ধি-দ্রব্যের দোকান, গন্ধবিপণি। **Perfume-set**—প্রসাধন দ্রব্য।

pêr-func'-tŏ-rȳ (-fŭngk-), *adj.* **1.** Done carelessly ; done only for the sake of getting rid of the duty ; mechanical ; superficial ; as a *perfunctory* inquirer or inspection ; অযত্নকৃত, অমাবধানেকৃত, অযত্নসম্পাদিত, অসম্যক্-সম্পাদিত; কোনরূপ দায় হইতে মুক্ত হইবার জন্য কৃত ; যন্ত্রবৎ কৃত ; অগভীর। 2. Slight ; careless ; negligent ; তুচ্ছ ; অসাবধান ; উদাসীন। **—ri-ly,** *adv.* In a careless or half-hearted manner ; অসাবধানভাবে, অনবহিতভাবে, অযত্নপূর্ব্বক, অনিচ্ছার সহিত। **—ri-ness,** *n.*

pêr-fūse', *v. t.* **1.** To besprinkle as with water ; জলসিক্ত করা, সিঞ্চন করা, ছিটান। **2.** To cover or suffuse as with light, radiance, etc. ; আবৃত করা, পরিপ্লুত করা **—fu'-sion,** *n.* **—fu'-sive,** *adj.*

pĕr-gă-mē'-nē-ous (-ŭs), *adj.* Of, relating to, or like, parchment ; চর্ম্মপটসম্বন্ধীয়, চর্ম্মপটবৎ।

pêr'-gō-lă, *n.* An arbour formed of growing plants trained over trellis-work ; a covered walk so formed ; কুঞ্জ, নিকুঞ্জ ; কুঞ্জবীথি।

pêr-hăps', (*Colloq. praps*) *adv.* It may be ; possibly ; হয়ত ; সম্ভবতঃ, বুঝিবা।

pēr'-ī, *n.* 1. (*Pers. Myth.*) Fairy ; পরী। **2.** A beautiful or graceful being ; পরীর মত সুন্দরী রমণী, ডানা-কাটা পরী।

pĕr'-ī-ănth, *n.,* (*Bot.*) A floral envelope ; (উদ্ভিদবিদ্যা) পুষ্পপরিধি (সাঃ পঃ), পরিপুষ্প (ঐ), পুট (ঐ)।

pĕr'-ī-ăpt, *n.* A charm worn as a protection from disease or mischief ; an amulet ; মাদুলী ; কবচ, তাবিজ।

pĕr-ī-ăs'-trŏn, —trŭm, *ns.* The point of nearest approach of the component of a binary star ; তারানীচ (হিঃ কোঃ)।

pĕr-ī-căr'-dī-ŭm, *n.,* (*Anat.*) A membranous sac enclosing the heart ; হৃৎপিণ্ডাবরক ঝিল্লীময় থলি, হৃদ্বেষ্ট (হঃ চঃ), হৃদ্‌বেষ্টক-কোষ, বপা (বিনয়), হৃদাশয় (সাঃ পঃ), হৃদপিণ্ডাবরক, পরিহার্দ্দিক (হিঃ কোঃ)। **—ac, —al, —an,** *adjs.* **—di'-tis,** *n.* Inflammation of the pericardium ; হৃদ্বেষ্ট-প্রদাহ, হৃদ্বেষ্ট-স্ফীতি।

pĕr'-ī-cărp, *n.,* (*Bot.*) The covering, shell, or rind of fruits ; a seed-vessel ; ফলাবরণ (সাঃ পঃ), খোসা ; বীজকোষ (সাঃ পঃ)।

pĕr-ī-chŏn'-drī-ŭm, *n.* (*Anat.*) A membrane which covers certain cartilages ; (শারীরসংস্থানবিদ্যা) কোন কোন উপাস্থির শুভ্রতন্তুময় আবরণ।

pĕr'-i-clāse, *n.* A kind of mineral found, esp. at Vesuvius ; ভিসুভিয়াস পর্ব্বতে প্রাপ্ত একপ্রকার খনিজপদার্থ।

pĕr-i-clī'-năl, *adj.* **1.** (*Bot.*) Parallel with the circumference ; (উদ্ভিদবিদ্যা) পরিধির সহিত সমান্তরাল, তলসমান্তরিত (সাঃ পঃ)। **2.** (*Geol.*) Sloping in all directions from the central point ; (ভূবিদ্যা) মধ্যবিন্দু হইতে সর্ব্বদিকে প্রবণ।

pĕ-ric'-ŏ-pĕ, *n.* **1.** An extract or passage ; উদ্ধৃত বাক্য, অধ্যায়ের অংশবিশেষ। **2.** A portion of the Bible read in the public worship ; প্রকাশ্য পূজোপাসনাকালে পঠিত বাইবেলের অংশ।

pĕr-i-crā'-ni-ŭm, *n.* **1.** The membrane that surrounds the cranium or skull ; (শারীরসংস্থানবিদ্যা) মস্তকের অস্থির আবরণঝিল্লী। **2.** (*Humourous*) The skull or brain (*rare*) ; (কৌতুকচ্ছলে) মস্তিষ্ক, করোটী। **—al,** *adj.*

pĕr'-i-dêrm, *n.* **1.** (*Bot.*) The outer layer of bark ; বল্কলের বহিঃস্তর, পরিত্বক (সাঃ পঃ)। **2.** (*Zool.*) The hard outer covering of some marine animals ; (জন্তু-বিদ্যা) কতিপয় সামুদ্রিক প্রাণীর কঠিন বহিরাবরণ।

pĕr'-i-dŏt, *n.*, (*Miner.*) Same as CHRYSOLITE.

pĕr'-i-drōme *n.* (*Arch.*) The space between the columns and the wall of a peripteral Greek or Roman temple ; সর্ব্বদিকে স্তম্ভরাজিসমন্বিত গ্রীক বা রোমকমন্দিরের প্রাচীর এবং স্তম্ভশ্রেণীর মধ্যবর্ত্তী স্থান।

pĕr-i-găs'-tric, *adj.*, (*Zool.*) Surrounding the alimentary canal ; (প্রাণিবিদ্যা) অন্ননালীপরিবেষ্টক।

pĕr'-i-gee (-jē), *n.*, (*Astron.*) The point of the moon's orbit at which it is nearest to the earth ; (জ্যোতির্ব্বিজ্ঞান) চন্দ্রকক্ষের যে অংশে উহা পৃথিবী হইতে সর্ব্বাপেক্ষা নিকটে থাকে, নীচোচ্চ (সাঃ পঃ), অনুপার্থিব (ঐ), ভূমিনীচ (হিঃ কোঃ)। **—ge'-al, —ge'-an,** *adjs.*

pĕr-i-gĕn'-ĕ-sis, *n.* (*Biol.*) The dynamic theory of reproduction propounded by Haeckel ; প্রাণপঙ্ককণার পরিস্পন্দন হইতে জীবজনন হয়—এইরূপ মতবাদ, পরিজনন।

pĕ-ri-gē'-ŭm, *n.* (*Obs.*) Same as PERIGEE.

pĕr'-i-gōne, *n.* (*Bot.*) Same as PERIANTH.

pĕ-rig'-ȳ-nous (-nŭs), *adj.* (Of stamen) Situated around pistil or ovary ; (পুংকেশর সম্পর্কে) গর্ভকেশর বা বীজাধারের চতুঃপার্শ্বে স্থিত, পরিযোষিৎ (সাঃ পঃ)।

pĕr-i-hē'-li-ŏn, *n.* That point in

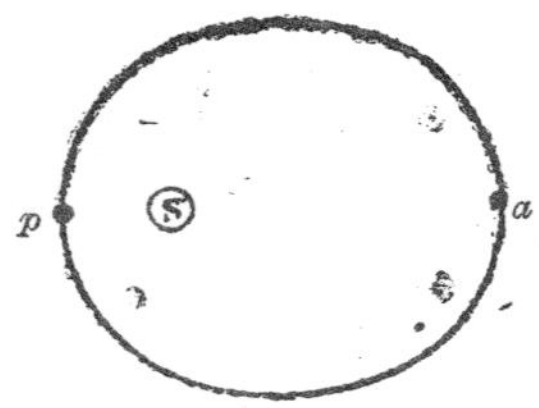

Orbit of planet.
S. Sun. *p.* Perihelion. *a.* Aphelion.

a planet's orbit at which it is nearest to the Sun (cf. *Aphelion*); গ্রহকক্ষের যে বিন্দুতে উহা সূর্য্যের নিকটতম থাকে, নীচবিন্দু (সূর্য্যঃ বিঃ), নীচোচ্চ (সাঃ পঃ), শীঘ্রোচ্চ (ঐ), রবিনীচ।

pĕr'-il, *n.* & *v. t.* Danger ; risk ; আপদ্, বিপদ্, বিপত্তি, সঙ্কট, দায় ; ঝুঁকি। *Verb t.* To expose to danger ; to risk ; বিপদাপন্ন করা, বিপদে ফেলা ; সঙ্কটাপন্ন করা। **—ous,** *adj.* Full of peril ; dangerous ; বিপৎসঙ্কুল ; সঙ্কটাপন্ন, বিপজ্জনক। **—ous-ly,** *adv.* **—ous-ness,** *n.* **At one's peril**—With risk or danger to one ; as, do it *at your peril* ; নিজের ঝুঁকিতে, নিজের দায়ে। **In peril of one's life**—In danger of losing one's life ; প্রাণ সঙ্কটাপন্ন করিয়া। **Keep off at your peril**—Take the risk if you do not keep off ; যদি অগ্রসর হও বিপদ্ ঘটিবে।

pĕr-im'-ĕ-têr, *n.* **1.** (*Geom.*) The circuit or boundary of any plane figure or the sum of all its sides ; (জ্যামিতি) কোন ক্ষেত্রের বহিঃরেখা বা ভুজসমষ্টি, পরিসীমা, পরিণাহ (সাঃ পঃ)। **2.** An instrument for measuring the field of vision ; দৃষ্টিক্ষেত্র পরিমাপক যন্ত্র। **—i-met'-ric,** *adj.* **—try,** *n.* The act of making perimetrical measurement ; পরিসীমামিতি।

pĕr-i-nē'-ŭm, *n.* (*Anat.*) The region of the body between the anus and the vagina in the female or the root of the penis in the male ; (শারীরসংস্থানবিদ্যা) স্ত্রীলোকের গুহ্য ও যোনি ও পুরুষের গুহ্য ও লিঙ্গমূলের মধ্যবর্ত্তী স্থান, মূলাধার (হঃ চঃ), বিটপ (ঐ)। **—al,** *adj.*

pē'-ri-ŏd, *n.* **1.** The time determined by some recurring phenomenon ; a division of time ; পুনঃ পুনঃ আবর্ত্তনশীল কাল, ঘটনাদ্বারা নিরূপিত কালচক্র, নিয়তকাল (হিঃ কোঃ) ; কালবিভাগ। **2.** The time of the revolution of a heavenly body ; গ্রহাদির আবর্ত্তনকাল। **3.** A certain series of years, months or the like ; as, a *period* of hundred years ; an age ; an epoch ; নির্দ্দিষ্ট বর্ষ বা মাস প্রভৃতি ; যুগ ; অব্দ। **4.** An indefinite portion of history, life, etc. ; জীবন, ইতিহাস, প্রভৃতির অনির্দ্দিষ্ট কাল। **5.** (*Archaic*) An end ; conclusion ; (অপ্রঃ) অন্ত ; সমাপ্তি। **6.** A complete sentence, esp. one of several clause ; সম্পূর্ণ বাক্য, বাক্যোচ্চয় (সাঃ পঃ)। **7.** (*Pl.*) Rhetorical or grammatical language ; আলঙ্কারিক ভাষা, ব্যাকরণসম্মত ভাষা। **8.** A fullstop (.) ; পূর্ণচ্ছেদ, দাড়ি। **9.** (*Pl.*) Menses ; ঋতু। **10.** (*Med.*) The time of the exacerbation and remission of a disease ; রোগের ভোগকাল।

11. (*Math.*) A set of figures or terms marked by points or commas placed at regular intervals, as in numeration, recurring decimals, etc. ; (গণিতশাস্ত্র) বৃহৎ রাশির মধ্যে ব্যবচ্ছিন্ন অংশ। **The period**—The present or current time ; বর্ত্তমান কাল, চলিত সময়।

pē-ri-ŏd′-ic, *adj.* **1.** Of, or pertaining to, a period ; সাময়িক, নিয়তকালিক (হিঃ কোঃ)। **2.** Of, or relating to, the revolution of a heavenly body ; গ্রহাদির আবর্ত্তনসম্বন্ধীয়। **3.** Recurring at regular intervals ; (loosely) recurring ; intermittent ; as, *periodic* epidemics ; নির্দ্দিষ্ট সময়ান্তে পুনঃ পুনঃ আগমনশীল ; পৌনঃপুনিক, পুনরাবর্ত্তনশীল ; সবিরাম। **4.** Of, relating to, or expressed in, periods or rhetorical language ; আলঙ্কারিকভাষাসম্বন্ধীয়, আলঙ্কারিক ভাষায় প্রকাশিত। **—i-cal**, *adj.* & *n.* **1.** Same as PERIODIC, *adj.* 1., 2. & 3. **2.** Published at regular intervals, *e. g.* monthly ; নির্দ্দিষ্ট সময়ে প্রকাশিত, সাময়িক। (*Noun*) A magazine, review, etc. that appears at regular intervals ; সাময়িক পত্রিকা। **—i-cal-ist**, *n.* One who publishes or writes in a periodical ; সাময়িকপত্রের লেখক। **—i-cal-ly**, *adv.* **—o-dic′-i-ty**, *n.* The state or quality of being periodical or regular ; recurrent ; নিয়তকালিকত্ব ; পুনরাবর্ত্তনশীলতা, পুনরাবর্ত্তিতা (হিঃ কোঃ)। **Periodic(al) diseases**—যে সকল রোগের লক্ষণসমূহ নির্দ্দিষ্ট কালের পরে পরে পুনঃ পুনঃ প্রকাশ পায়। **Periodic law**—(*Chem.*) A relation of elements according to their atomic weights ; (রসায়নশাস্ত্র) পারমাণবিক গুরুত্ব অনুযায়ী মূলপদার্থসমূহের সম্বন্ধ।

pĕr-i-ŏs′-tē-ŭm, *n.* A membrane enveloping the bones ; অস্থিবেষ্ট (ডাঃ)। **—al**, *adj.* **—ti′-tis**, *n.* Inflammation of the periosteum ; অস্থিবেষ্টপ্রদাহ।

pĕr-i-pă-tĕt′-ic, *adj.* & *n.* **1.** Walking about ; itinerant ; পাদচারী, পর্য্যটনশীল ; পরিব্রাজনশীল। **2.** (*Cap.*) Of, or pertaining to, Aristotle or his philosophy (so called from his custom of walking in the Lyceum at Athens while teaching) ; আরিস্তোতল বা তদীয় দার্শনিকমতসম্বন্ধীয়। [ইনি এথেন্স নগরীর Lyceum উদ্যানে পাদচারণা করিতে করিতে শিক্ষা প্রদান করিতেন।] *Noun.* **1.** (*Chiefly humorous*) An itinerant ; (প্রধানতঃ কৌতুকচ্ছলে) পরিব্রাজক, পর্য্যটক। **2.** (*Cap.*) A disciple of Aristotle ; আরিস্তোতলের শিষ্য। **—i-cal-ly**, *adv.* **—i-cism**, *n.*

pĕr-i-pĕ-tei′-ă (-ti-), **—ti′-ă**, *ns.* Sudden change of fortune in drama or in life ; নাটকে বা বাস্তব জীবনে আকস্মিক ভাগ্যবিপর্য্যয়।

pĕ-riph′-ĕr-y̆, *n.* The bounding line of a rounded surface ; the surface ; the surrounding space ; পরিধি ; উপরিভাগ ; পরিবেষ। **—al**, *adj.* **—al-ly**, *adv.*

pĕ-riph′-ră-sis, **pĕr′-i-phrāse**, *ns.* (*Pl.* -SES.) **1.** Roundabout way of speaking ; circumlocution ; বাগ্‌প্রপঞ্চ, বাগ্‌বাহুল্য ; বাগভঙ্গী। **Per′-i-phras-tic**, *adj.* **Per-i-phras′-ti-cal-ly**, *adv.*

Periploca Indica — অনন্তমূল (সাঃ পঃ)।

pĕr′-i-plŭs, *n.* A sailing round or circumnavigation ; পোতযোগে পৃথিবী পরিক্রমণ, ভূপ্রদক্ষিণ।

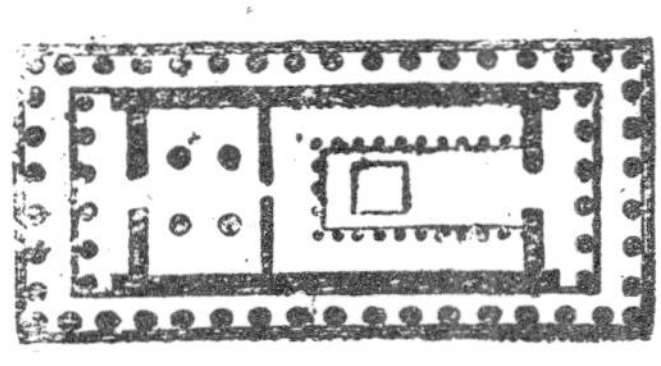

Plan of a peripteral temple.

pĕ-rip′-tĕr-ăl, *adj.* (*Arch.*) Having columns on all sides ; (স্থপতিবিদ্যা) চতুর্দ্দিকে স্তম্ভশোভিত, পরিস্তম্ভী।

pĕr′-i-scōpe *n.* **1.** An instrument used in submarine boats to see objects above water ; জলোপরিস্থ পদার্থসমূহ সন্দর্শনের জন্য মকরপোত হইতে প্রলম্বিত যন্ত্রবিশেষ, পরিদর্শক। **2.** A variety of photographic object-glass ; আলোকচিত্রগ্রাহক-যন্ত্রের কাচবিশেষ। **—scop′-ic**, *adj.* Viewing all round or on all sides ; সর্ব্বতোদর্শী।

pĕr′-ish, *v. i.* **1.** To die ; মরিয়া যাওয়া, মৃত্যুমুখে পতিত হওয়া। **2.** To be destroyed ; to decay ; to come to nothing ; ধ্বংস হওয়া ; নষ্ট হওয়া ; বিনষ্ট হওয়া। **—a-bil′-i-ty**, **—a-ble-ness**, *ns.* The quality of being liable to speedy decay or destruction ; নশ্বরতা, বিনশ্বরতা, নাশশীলতা। **—a-ble**, *adj.* & *n.* Liable to perish ; subject to decay or destruction ; নশ্বর, নাশশীল, ভঙ্গুর, অন্তবান (গীতা) ; বিধ্বংসী। (*Noun, pl.*) Things esp. food stuffs in transit, liable to speedy decay ; জাহাজাদি যোগে প্রেরিত ক্ষয়শীল বা পচনশীল দ্রব্য, বিশেষতঃ খাদ্যদ্রব্য। **—ing**, *adj.* **1.** Suffering death, decay or destruction ; নশ্বর, বিনশ্বর, ক্ষয়শীল, নাশী। **2.** (Of cold, hunger, etc.) Deadly ; মারাত্মক। **—ing-ly**, *adv.*

pĕr′-i-spĕrm, *n.* (*Bot.*) Nutritive tissue or albumen outside the embryo-sac in some seeds ; কোন কোন বীজের ভ্রূণকোষের বহিঃস্থ পুষ্টিজনক কোষস্থান বা অণ্ডলালবৎ পদার্থ, পরিভ্রূণ (সাঃ পঃ)। **—sper′-mic**, *adj.*

pĕr′-i-spōme, **—spŏm′-ē-nŏn**, *adj.* & *n.* (*Gr. Gram.*) Having circumflex accent on the last syllable ; (গ্রীসীয় ব্যাকরণ) শেষ শব্দাংশে স্বরিত চিহ্নসমন্বিত। ***Noun.*** (*Gr. Gram.*) Such a word ; (গ্রীসীয় ব্যাকরণ) ঐরূপ শব্দ।

pĕr′-i-spōre, *n.* (*Bot.*) The outer covering of a spore ; (উদ্ভিদবিদ্যা) পুষ্পবেষ্টনীর বহিরাবরণ।

pĕ-ris′-săd, *adj.* (*Chem.*) Any element whose valence is an odd number ; যে মুল পদার্থের পরমাণুগ্রহণশক্তি অযুগ্ম সংখ্যা হইয়া থাকে, অযুগ্ম (হিঃ কোঃ) ।

pĕ-ris′-tă-lith, *n.* (*Arch.*) A series of standing stones surrounding an object *e. g.* burial mound etc. ; কোন পদার্থের চতুর্দ্দিকে প্রোথিত পাষাণ শ্রেণী ।

pĕr-i-stăl′-tic, *adj.* (*Physiol.*) Designating or relating to the peculiar wormlike wave-motion of the intestines in digestion ; পরিপাক ক্রিয়াকালে অন্ত্রে যে ক্রিমিবৎ তরঙ্গ-গতি উপজাত হয়—তৎসূচক বা তৎসম্বন্ধীয়, ধমনক্রিয়াজনক (হঃ চঃ) । **–sis**, *n.* Peristaltic contraction or action ; তরঙ্গবৎ বা ক্রিমির ন্যায় গতিতে অন্ত্রসঙ্কোচন বা অন্ত্রের ক্রিয়া । **–ti-cal-ly**, *adv.*

pĕr-is-stĕr-ŏ′-nic, *adj.* Of, or relating to, pigeons ; কপোত-সম্বন্ধীয়, কাপোত ।

pĕr′-i-stōme *n.* **1.** (*Bot.*) A ring or fringe of bristles or teeth round an orifice in plants ; (উদ্ভিদ্‌বিদ্যা) বৃক্ষাদির রন্ধ্রের চতুর্দ্দিকে শূকবেষ্টনী বা দন্তবলয়, তুণ্ডবলয় (সাঃ পঃ) । **2.** (*Zool.*) The membrane surrounding the mouth of an invertebrate animal ; (জন্তুবিদ্যা) অমেরুদণ্ডী প্রাণীর মুখগহ্বরাবরক ঝিল্লী ।

pĕr′-i-stȳle, *n.* **1.** A range of columns round a building, court, square, etc. ; সৌধাদিপরিবেষ্টক স্তম্ভ-শ্রেণী । **2.** A court, or square, with columns all round ; স্তম্ভবলয়িত অঙ্গন বা চত্বর । **–sty′-lar**, *adj.*

pĕr-i-tō-nē′-ŭm, **–næ′–** (-nē-), *ns.* A serous membrane investing the internal surface of the abdomen and the viscera contained in it ; যে রক্তাম্বুপ্রকৃতিক ঝিল্লীদ্বারা নিম্নোদর এবং অন্ত্রের অভ্যন্তরভাগ আচ্ছাদিত থাকে, অন্ত্রবেষ্টনী, অন্ত্রচ্ছদ (হঃ চঃ) । **–ne′-al**, **–næ′-al**, *adjs.* **–ni′-tis**, *n.* Inflammation of the peritoneum ; অন্ত্রাবরণ প্রদাহ ।

pĕr′-i-wig, *n.* A head dress of false hair ; a wig ; পরচুলা ; উপকেশ ।

pĕr′-i-win-kle (-wĭng-kl), *n.* A creeping evergreen plant ; ফিরঙ্গী টগর (যোঃ) ।

pĕr′-i-win-kle (-wĭng-kl), *n.* A small univalve mollusc for food ; ক্ষুদ্র শম্বুকবিশেষ, গুগ্‌লি ।

pêr′-jūre, *v. t.* (*Reflex*) To swear falsely ; to forswear ; মিথ্যা শপথ করা, শপথ করিয়া মিথ্যা সাক্ষ্য দেওয়া ; শপথ ভঙ্গ করা । **–jured**—*adj. p. p.* **–jur-er**, *n.* One who perjures ; কূট সাক্ষী, মিথ্যা সাক্ষী ।

pêr′-jū-rȳ, *n.* **1.** False swearing ; violation of oath ; মিথ্যাশপথ ; শপথভঙ্গ । **2.** Giving of false evidence while on oath ; মিথ্যাসাক্ষ্য, কূটসাক্ষ্য । **–ju′-ri-ous-ly**, *adv.*

pêrk, *adj., v. i.* & *t.* (*Rare*) Same as PERKY. ***Verb i.*** To hold up the head with affected smartness ; to behave, come forward briskly or impudently ; ভঙ্গী করিয়া মাথা তোলা ; বেপরোয়াভাবে চলা, হন হন করিয়া আসা, হুট্ হাট্ করিয়া চলা । ***Verb t.*** **1.** To make smart or trim (*up*) ; পরিপাটী করা, ফিটফাট করা, তক্‌তকে ঝকঝকে করা । **2.** To hold up (the head, tail, etc.) pertly or self-assertively ; গরবে মস্তক উন্নত করা বা লাঙ্গুল তোলা । **Perk′-i-ly**, *adv.* **Perk′-i-ness**, *n.* **Perk′-y**, *adj.* Self-assertive ; jaunty ; saucy ; ধৃষ্ট ; গরবপূর্ণ ; প্রগল্‌ভ ।

pêr′-līte, *n.* A variety of obsidian with an enamel-like lustre and a gray colour ; আগ্নেয়গিরি হইতে উত্থিত চক্‌চকে ধূসরবর্ণের পদার্থবিশেষ ।

pêr′-mă-nĕnt, *adj.* Durable ; lasting indefinitely ; চিরস্থায়ী ; সনাতন, নিয়ত, শাশ্বত, ধ্রুব । **–ly**, *adv.* In a permanent manner ; চিরস্থায়িরূপে । **–nence**, **–nen-cy**, *ns.* State of being permanent ; চিরস্থায়িত্ব, অপরিবর্ত্তনীয়তা, সম্প্রতিষ্ঠা । **Permanent settlement**—চিরস্থায়ী বন্দোবস্ত । **Permanent way**—স্থায়ী লৌহবর্ত্ম ।

pêr′-mē-āte, *v. t.* & *i.* To pass through the pores or interstices of ; to pervade ; চুয়াইয়া পড়া ; আচ্ছন্ন করা, পরিব্যাপ্ত করা । ***Verb i.*** To penetrate ; to diffuse itself, (*through*, *among* etc.) ; অনুসিক্ত হওয়া ; পরিব্যাপ্ত হওয়া । **–a-bil′-i-ty**, *n.* **–a-ble**, *adj.* **1.** That may be penetrated or passed through ; ভেদ্য, অনুপ্রবেশ্য, অন্তর্গম্য । **2.** Allowing the passage of liquids ; অন্তঃপ্রবেশ্য । **–ance**, **–a′-tion**, *ns.* **–ant**, **–a-tive**, *adjs.*

Pêr′-mi-ăn, *adj.* (*Geol.*) Of, or relating to, the lower division of the new red sand-stone rocks ; [পূর্ব্ব রুশিয়ার অন্তঃপাতী Perm প্রদেশের নাম হইতে গৃহীত] (ভূবিদ্যা) নবরক্তবালুকাপ্রস্তর স্তরের নিম্নতর বিভাগ সম্বন্ধীয়, মৎস্যস্তর সম্বন্ধীয় (অভিঃ) ।

pêr-mis′-si-ble (-ĭ-bl), *adj.* Capable of being allowed ; গ্রাহ্য, অনুমন্তব্য, অনুজ্ঞেয় । **–bly**, *adv.*

pêr-mis′-sion (-mĭ-), *n.* Act of permitting ; leave ; consent ; অনুমতিপ্রদান ; অনুজ্ঞা ; অনুমতি । **–sive**, *adj.* Giving permission or liberty ; অনুমতি-প্রদায়ক । **–sive-ly**, *adv.* **–sive-ness**, *n.*

pêr-mit′, *v. t.* & *i.* To allow or suffer ; to tolerate ; অনুমতি দেওয়া ; সহা । ***Verb i.*** To admit (*of* an alteration etc.) ; পরিবর্ত্তনাদিসহ হওয়া ।

pêr-mit′, *n.* **1.** Written order giving permission esp. for landing or removal of dutiable goods etc. ; ছাড়পত্র, অনুমতিপত্র । **2.** Permission ; অনুমতি, অনুজ্ঞা, সম্মতি ।

pêr-mŭt′-ă-ble (-bl), *adj.* Exchangeable ; পরিবর্ত্তনীয়, পরিবর্ত্তনসহ । **–bil′-i-ty**, *n.* **–bly**, *adv.* **–ness**, *n.*

pêr-mü-tā′-tion, *n.* 1. (*Rare*) Alteration or change ; (কচিদ্-ব্যবহৃত) পর্য্যায় বিপর্য্যয়, পরিবর্ত্তন। 2. (*Math.*) Change or combination of any number of quantities ; any of the different ways in which a set of quantities can be arranged ; (অঙ্কশাস্ত্র) কোন নির্দ্দিষ্ট রাশির পরিবৃত্তি বা বিবিধবিন্যাস ; অঙ্কপাশ (লীলাঃ)।

pêr-müte′, *v. t.* To alter the order of ; ক্রমবিপর্য্যয় করা।

pêrn, *n.* A honey-buzzard ; এক-প্রকার পক্ষী।

pêr-nĭ′-cious (-shŭs), *adj.* 1. Ruinous or destructive ; fatal ; noxious ; mischievous ; বিনাশক, বিনাশী, ধ্বংসকারী ; মারাত্মক, সাংঘাতিক ; অত্যন্ত অনিষ্টজনক ; অহিতজনক, অপকারক, অনিষ্টকর। 2. (*Rare*) Wicked ; (কচিদ্‌ব্যবহৃত) দুষ্ট। **—ly**, *adv.*

pêr-nick′-ĕt-ȳ, *adj.* 1. (*Colloq.*) Precise in trifles ; (চলিতভাষায়) খুঁতখুঁতে। 2. Requiring precise or careful handling as things ; খুব সাবধানের সহিত ব্যবহার্য্য।

pêr-nŏc-tā′-tion, *n.* The act of passing the whole night, esp. in prayer or watching ; নিশাযাপন, নিশাজাগরণ, বিশেষতঃ ঈশ্বর আরাধনায় সমস্ত রাত্রি জাগরণ।

pĕr′-ō-rāte, *v. i.* & *t.* 1. To sum up or conclude a speech ; বক্তৃতার উপসংহার করা, বর্ণিতবিষয় সংক্ষেপে বলিয়া শেষ করা। 2. To speak at length ; to deliver an oration ; বিস্তারপূর্ব্বক বলা ; বক্তৃতা দেওয়া। ***Verb t.*** To declaim ; আলঙ্কারিক ভাষায় বক্তৃতা করা। **—ra′-tion**, *n.* The conclusion of a speech, usually the summing up the points and enforcing the argument ; বক্তৃতার উপসংহার।

pĕr-pĕnd′, *v. t.* (*Archaic*) To consider or weigh in the mind ; (অপ্রঃ) মনে মনে আন্দোলন বা তোলাপাড়া করা।

pĕr-pĕn-dĭc′-ū-lar (-lĕr), *adj.* & *n.* 1. Exactly upright or vertical ; লম্ব, অবলম্ব (লীলাঃ), তির্য্যক্ (শংকু), অধোলম্ব (বেঙ্ঃ)। 2. (*Loosely*) Steep ; erect ; খাড়া ; উন্নত। 3. (*Geom.*) At right angles to a given line or surface ; (জ্যামিতি) নির্দ্দিষ্ট রেখা বা সমতলের উপর সমকোণরচনা পূর্ব্বক দণ্ডায়মান। ***Noun.*** 1. A perpendicular line, plane or direction ; লম্বরেখা, তল বা দিক। 2. Upright position ; rectitude ; লম্বভাবে অবস্থান ; ঋজুতা, সাধুতা। 4. (*Slang*) A meal taken standing ; (ইতরভাষায়) যে ভোজনে লোকেরা দাঁড়াইয়া আহার করে। **—lar′-i-ty**, *n.* **—ly**, *adv.* **Perpendicular style**—(স্থপতিবিজ্ঞান) ইংলণ্ডদেশে প্রচলিত গথিক স্থাপত্যরীতি—চতুর্দ্দশ হইতে যোড়শ শতাব্দী পর্য্যন্ত ইহার প্রচার ছিল। সম্ভবতঃ গবাক্ষ-বিভাজকসমূহের লম্বস্বারূপ্য হইতে তাদৃশ নামাকরণ হইয়াছে।

pêr′-pē-trāte, *v. t.* 1. To perform or commit as a crime, blunder, etc. ; সাধন করা, সম্পন্ন করা। 2. To produce as a pun, caricature, etc. ; "One of the worst pun ever *perpetrated*" ; দ্ব্যর্থবোধক শব্দ, হাস্যানুকরণ, প্রভৃতি করা। **—tra′-tion**, *n.* The act of perpetrating ; a doing of something wrong ; an evil action ; সাধন ; দুষ্কর্ম্মসংসাধন ; অসৎকর্ম্ম, দুষ্ক্রিয়া। **—tra-tor**, *n.*

pêr-pĕt′-ū-ăl, *adj.* 1. Eternal ; everlasting ; permanent ; continuous ; চিরস্থায়ী ; নিত্য, শাশ্বত, সনাতন, শাশ্বতিক ; নিত্যস্থায়ী ; নিরন্তর, অবিরত, নিরবচ্ছিন্ন। 2. Applicable, valid, for ever or for indefinite time ; as, *perpetual* injunction ; চিরকাল-প্রযোজ্য। 3. Blooming continuously throughout the season ; as, a *perpetual* rose ; নিত্যবিকাশী। 4. (*Colloq.*) Frequent ; as, this *perpetual* nagging ; (চলিত ভাষায়) অবিরাম। **—ly**, *adv.* **Perpetual motion** — যে যন্ত্র বাহ্যশক্তি দ্বারা নিবারিত বা ক্ষয়প্রাপ্ত না হইলে অবিরাম চলিত—তাহার গতি, সততগতি (হিঃ কোঃ)।

pêr-pĕt′-ū-āte, *v. t.* To make perpetual or everlasting ; to preserve from extinction or oblivion ; চিরস্থায়ী করা ; চিরস্মরণীয় করা। **—a-ble**, *adj.* Capable of being perpetuated ; চিরস্মর্ত্তব্য। **—ance**, **—a′-tion**, *ns.* **—a-tor**, *n.*

pêr-pē-tū′-i-tȳ, *n.* 1. The state or quality of being perpetual ; চির-স্থায়িত্ব, নিত্যস্থায়িতা, অবিচ্ছিন্নতা, চির-স্থায়িতা, নিত্যতা, সাতত্য, নিরন্তরস্থিতি। 2. Something that is perpetual ; a perpetual possession ; নিত্যবস্তু ; চিরাধিকার। 3. The number of years in which the simple interest of any sum becomes equal to the principal ; a perpetual annuity , যে কতিপয় বৎসরে (ঋণের) টাকার সুদ আসলের সমান হয় ; চিরদিনের জন্য বার্ষিক বৃত্তি। 4. (*Law*) The quality or condition of an estate by which it becomes inalienable, either perpetually or for a very long time ; (ব্যবহারশাস্ত্র) সম্পত্তির এরূপ অবস্থা—যাহাতে ইহা চিরকাল বা বহু-কাল ব্যাপিয়া হস্তান্তর করা যাইতে পারে না। **In, to,** or **for perpetuity**—For ever ; চিরদিনের জন্য।

pêr-plĕx′, *v. t.* 1. To embarrass ; to puzzle (person, his mind) ; হতবুদ্ধি করা, গোলে ফেলা ; বিভ্রান্ত করা, আকুলিত করা, কিংকর্ত্তব্যবিমূঢ় করা। 2. To make intricate ; to confuse ; as, to *perplex* a matter ; (কোন বিষয়) জটিল করা ; দুর্ব্বোধ করা। 3. To entangle ; to intertwine ; "Street which *perplex* that portion of the city" ; জড়িত করা ; পরস্পর সংগ্রথিত করা। 4. (*Obs.*) To vex ; (অপ্রঃ) বিরক্ত করা। **—ed-ly**, *adv.* **—ed-ness**, *n.* **—ing**, *adj.* **—ing-ly**, *adv.* **—plexed′**, *p. p.* **Perplexed question**—জটিল প্রশ্ন।

pêr-plĕx′-i-tў, *n.* 1. The state of being perplexed, or at a loss; bewilderment; চিত্তবৈকল্য, মোহ; হতবুদ্ধিতা, কিংকর্ত্তব্যবিমূঢ়তা। 2. That which causes bewilderment; হতবুদ্ধিতাজনক বিষয়। 3. An entangled or confused state (of anything); জটিলতা।

pêr′-qui-site (-zit), *n.* 1. An allowance granted over and above the settled wages; নির্দ্দিষ্ট বেতনের অতিরিক্ত বৃত্তি, ভাতা। 2. (*Law*) Things got by a man's own industry or purchased with his own money; (আইন) স্বোপার্জ্জিত বা নিজের অর্থে ক্রীত বস্তু। 3. Casual profit; উপরিলাভ, অবান্তরলাভ, দস্তুরী। 4. An article that has served its primary use and to which a subordinate or servant has then a customary right; মনীব প্রভৃতির ভোগ বা ব্যবহারের পর প্রচলিত প্রথামত যে বস্তুতে ভৃত্য বা অধীনে নিযুক্ত ব্যক্তির অধিকার বর্ত্তে।

pĕr′-ron (-ŏn), *n.* An external flight of steps leading to the entrance-door of a building; কোন অট্টালিকার প্রবেশদ্বার পর্য্যন্ত গামী বাহিরের সোপানাবলী।

pĕr′-ry (-i), *n.* A drink prepared from the fermented juice of pears; নাসপাতি ফলের গাঁজলা-উঠা রস হইতে প্রস্তুত সুরাবিশেষ।

perse (pârs), *adj.* & *n.* (*Archaic*) Blue; esp. dark-blue; (অপ্রঃ) নীল; বিশেষতঃ গাঢ়নীল। ***Noun.*** This colour or a cloth of this colour; নীলবর্ণ, নীলবসন।

pêr′-sĕ-cūte, *v. t.* 1. To pursue with cruelty or injury; to harass; নির্য্যাতন করা, নিপীড়ন করা, নিগ্রহ করা, উৎপীড়ন করা; নিগৃহীত করা, অত্যাচার করা। 2. To annoy or importune as a person *with* questions etc.; পুনঃ পুনঃ প্রশ্ন করিয়া, ব্যতিব্যস্ত করা। **—cu′-tion,** *n.* Act of persecuting; state of being persecuted; নিগ্রহ, নির্য্যাতন; অত্যাচার। **—tor,** *n.* One who persecutes; অত্যাচারী, উপদ্রবকারী।

pêr-sĕ′-i-tў, *n.* Quality of being perse or self-inclusive; স্বভাবসিদ্ধতা, স্বতঃসিদ্ধতা।

Pêr′-seus (-süs), *n.* 1. প্রাচীন গ্রীক পুরাণোক্ত জনৈক মহাবীর। ইনি Medusa নাম্নী রাক্ষসীকে বিনাশ করেন এবং Andromeda নাম্নী সুন্দরীকে সামুদ্রিক দৈত্যের কবল হইতে উদ্ধার করিয়া তাহার সহিত পরিণয়পাশে বদ্ধ হন। 2. (*Astron.*) A constellation in the northern sky; (জ্যোতির্বিজ্ঞান) উত্তর গগনস্থ তারাপ্রকোষ্ঠবিশেষ।

pêr-sĕ-vĕr′-ance (-ăns), *n.* 1. Constant persistence in anything undertaken; steadiness in pursuits; অধ্যবসায়, নিয়ত চেষ্টা, দীর্ঘপ্রযত্ন; দৃঢ়প্রযত্নশীলতা। 2. (*Theol.*) Continuance in the state of grace; (খৃষ্টীয়ধর্ম্মশাস্ত্র) ঈশ্বরপ্রসাদের অবিচ্ছিন্ন প্রবাহ। **—ant,** *adj.* (*Rare*) Persevering; (কচিদ্‌ব্যবহৃত) অধ্যবসায়ী।

pêr-sĕ-vere′ (-vēr), *v. t.* To continue steadfastly in any business, or enterprise; to insist; দৃঢ়প্রযত্ন করা, নিয়তচেষ্টা করা, অধ্যবসায় করা; নির্ব্বন্ধাতিশয় করা। **—ver′-ing,** *adj.* **—ver′-ing-ly,** *adv.*

Pêr′-si-ăn (-shi-), *adj.* & *n.* Pertaining to Persia, the Persians or their language; পারসীক, পারস্য-ভাষা সংক্রান্ত। ***Noun.*** 1. A native of Persia; পারস্যদেশবাসী। 2. The language of Persia; পারস্য-ভাষা। **Persian-carpet**—পারস্যদেশীয় গালিচা। **Persian-cat** — আঙ্গোরা বিড়াল।

pĕr-si-ĕn-nĕs′, *n.* (*Pl.*) Window-blinds having movable slots; একপ্রকার জানালার পর্দ্দা বা ঝিলমিলী—যাহা ইচ্ছামত সরান যাইতে পারে।

per-si-flage′ (pār-sē-flâzh), *n.* Frivolous or bantering talk; light railery; ফচকেমি; ফষ্টিনষ্টি।

pêr-sim′-mon (-ŏn), *n.* An American date-plum; বিলাতি গাব (ফার্স্মিঃ)।

pêr-sist′, *v. i.* 1. To continue firmly, or steadily, (*in* opinion, course, doing) esp. against remonstrance; to persevere; আরব্ধ-কার্য্যে লাগিয়া থাকা, নির্ব্বন্ধাতিশয় সহকারে নিরত থাকা; অধ্যবসায়ী হওয়া। 2. To last or endure; as, leaves *persisting* from year to year; টিঁকিয়া থাকা, স্থায়ী হওয়া। **—ence, —en-cy,** *ns.* 1. The quality or state of being persistent; perseverance; obstinacy; অটলতা, দৃঢ়তা, অবিনাশ (হিঃ কোঃ), অব্যয় (ঐ), সাতত্য (ঐ), ঐকান্তিকতা, নির্ব্বন্ধাতিশয়তা, দৃঢ়ানুবন্ধতা; অধ্যবসায়; জেদ, কোট। 2. (*Phys.*) The continuance of an effect after the cause has been removed; as, *persistence* of motion; (পদার্থ-বিদ্যা) কারণের অপগমে কার্য্যের স্থিতি, অবিচলিতত্ব।

pêr-sist′-ĕnt, *adj.* 1. Persisting; pushing on, esp. against opposition; tenacious of purpose; অটল, অবিচলিত, ঐকান্তিক; বাধা-বিঘ্ন সত্ত্বেও দৃঢ়ব্রত; কৃতনিশ্চয়, দৃঢ়সংকল্প, নির্ব্বন্ধপর, অধ্যবসায়ী। 2. (*Bot.*) Remaining till or after the fruit is ripe; ফল-পকতা পর্য্যন্ত বা তদনন্তর স্থায়ী। 3. (*Biol.*) Remaining beyond the period when similar parts in other cases sometimes fall off; as, *persistent* teeth; (জীববিজ্ঞান) অন্যান্য সমরূপ অংশের অবর্ত্তমানেও স্থিতিশীল। **—ly,** *adv.*

pêr′-sŏn, *n.* 1. An individual body; a human being; ব্যক্তি; মানব। 2. Living human body; a human being indefinitely; দেহ; জন, লোক। 3. (*Theol.*) Among Trinitarians, one of the three subdivision of the Godhead (The Father, the Son, and the Holy Ghost); খৃষ্টীয় ত্রিপুরুষের মধ্যে (ঈশ্বর,

শুদ্ধাত্মা ও যীশুখৃষ্ট) অন্যতম। 4. (*Law*) A human being (natural person) or a corporation (artificial person) with recognized rights and duties; (আইন) কোন মানব (স্বাভাবিক ব্যক্তি) অথবা সংঘ বা সমবায় (কৃত্রিম ব্যক্তি)। 5. A character in a story or drama; নাটক বা উপন্যাসের চরিত্র বা পাত্র, পাত্রী। 6. (*Gram.*) A distinction in form according as the subject of the verb is the person speaking, spoken to or spoken of; (ব্যাকরণ) পুরুষ। **A person of colour** — নিগ্রো। **A person of family** — সম্ভ্রান্ত-বংশোদ্ভব বক্তি। **Artificial** or **natural person**—See PERSON, *n.* 4. **First person**—উত্তম পুরুষ। **Second person**—মধ্যম পুরুষ। **Third person**—প্রথম পুরুষ। **Young person**—যুবক বা যুবতী। **In person**—Personally; স্বয়ং, নিজে। **In the person of some one**—In some one; কোন ব্যক্তিকে।

persona, *n.* Person; ব্যক্তি। ***Persona grata***—বড় মানুষ।

pêr'-sŏn-ă-ble (-bl), *adj.* Having a well-formed body or person; handsome; সুগঠিত দেহ, দেহসৌষ্ঠব-সম্পন্ন, শোভনদেহ, রুচিরাঙ্গ; রূপবান।

pêr'-sŏn-āge, *n.* 1. The external appearance of a person; (কাহারো) বাহ্যিক আকার প্রকার। 2. Person of rank or distinction; সম্ভ্রান্ত ব্যক্তি, সম্মানার্হ ব্যক্তি, বড় লোক। 3. A person; জন, লোক, ব্যক্তি। 4. Character in play, etc.; নাটকাদির পাত্র পাত্রী।

pêr'-sŏn-ăl, *adj.* 1. Pertaining to a person; individual; private; ব্যক্তি সম্বন্ধীয়; ব্যক্তিগত; নিজস্ব, খাস। 2. Physical; দৈহিক, শারীরিক। 3. Made or done personally; as, *personal* interview; স্বয়ংকৃত। 4. Using language reflecting on the person, character, conduct, etc. of an individual; as, he is very *personal* in his remarks; ব্যক্তিগতভাবে আক্রমণকারী। 6. (*Gram.*) Denoting a person; (ব্যাকরণে) পুরুষবাচক। **–i-za'-tion** *n.* **–ize,** *v. t.* To make personal; to personify; স্বকীয় করা, নিজস্ব করা; ব্যক্তি-ধর্ম্মারোপ করা। **Personal equation**—See EQUATION. **Personal estate**—অস্থাবর সম্পত্তি। **Personal identity**—ব্যক্তিত্বের অবিচ্ছিন্ন একত্ব-বোধ, স্ববোধ (হিঃ কোঃ), স্বব্যক্তিত্ব (ঐ)। **Personal pronoun**—I, you, thou প্রভৃতি সর্ব্বনাম। **Personal rights**—ব্যক্তিগত অধিকার (যথা — ব্যক্তিগত জামিন বা ব্যক্তিগত স্বাধীনতা, ব্যক্তিগত সম্পত্তি। **Personal service**—সংবাদ বা আদেশ প্রভৃতি কাহারো হস্তে প্রদান।

pêr-sŏn-ăl'-ĭ-tȳ, *n.* 1. State of being a person or of being personal; personal existence or identity; ব্যক্তিতা; ব্যক্তিগত স্বাতন্ত্র্য। 2. Distinctive personal or individual character; individuality; ব্যক্তিগত চরিত্র, বিশিষ্ট স্বভাব; ব্যক্তিত্ব, জনত্ব, পুরুষবিধত্ব (নারায়ণ)। 3. A person; ব্যক্তি। 4. An application as of remarks usually to the conduct and character of an individual; (usu. *pl.*) such a remark or remarks; as, indulgence in *personalities*; ব্যক্তিগত আক্রমণ; কোন ব্যক্তির চরিত্র বা আচরণ সম্বন্ধে মন্তব্য। 5. (*Rare*) Personal estate; (ক্বচিদ্‌ব্যবহৃত) ব্যক্তিগত সম্পত্তি।

pêr'-sŏn-ăl-lȳ, *adv.* 1. In person; not by deputy or representative; স্বয়ং; প্রতিনিধি দ্বারা নহে। 2. As a person; as, God existing *personally*; ব্যক্তিস্বরূপ। 3. As regards oneself; ব্যক্তিগতভাবে।

pêr'-sŏn-ăl-tȳ, *n.* (*Law*) Personal property; (আইন) অস্থাবর সম্পত্তি।

pêr'-sŏn-āte, *v. t.* 1. To represent by a fictitious appearance; to pass oneself off as, for purposes of fraud; রূপ ধরা; নিজকে অন্য লোক বলিয়া চালান। 2. To act the part of (a character in a drama etc.), (*lit.* & *fig.*); অভিনয় করা (শব্দানুযায়ী ও লক্ষণায়)। **–a'-tion**, *n.* The act of personating; রূপগ্রহণ, রূপ-ধারণ। **–tor**, *n.*

pêr'-sŏn-āte, *adj.* (*Bot.*) With the opening between the lips closed by an upward projection of the lower lip, as in the snapdragon; (উদ্ভিদ্‌বিদ্যা) উপমুখ (সাঃ পঃ)।

pêr-sŏn'-ĭ-fȳ, *v. t.* 1. To represent as a person or rational being; as, to *personify* nature; মানবধর্ম্মারোপ করা, ব্যক্তিত্ব আরোপ করা, চেতন-ধর্ম্মারোপ করা, সচেতনস্বরূপে বর্ণনা করা। 2. To be the embodiment of; to impersonate; as, he *personifies* virtue; শরীরী হওয়া; মূর্ত্তিমান হওয়া। **–fi-ca'-tion**, *n.* 1. Act of personifying; embodiment; মনুষ্যধর্ম্মারোপ, ব্যক্তীকরণ (হিঃ কোঃ), ব্যক্তিত্বোৎপ্রেক্ষণ (ঐ), চেতনধর্ম্মারোপ; মূর্ত্তিমান বিগ্রহ। 2. (*Rhet.*) A metaphor representing inanimate objects as animate or rational beings; সমাসোক্তি (কাব্যঃ)। 3. A person or thing viewed as a striking example or embodiment (of a quality etc.); গুণাদির মূর্ত্তিমান বিগ্রহস্বরূপ ব্যক্তি বা বস্তু।

pêr-sŏn-nel' (-ĕl), *n.* The persons employed esp. in any public service; কোন কার্য্যে নিযুক্ত ব্যক্তিগণ।

pêr-spĕc'-tive (-tĭv), *n.* & *adj.* 1. The art of representing objects on a plane surface as they actually appear to the eye; কোন নির্দ্দিষ্ট বিন্দু হইতে দৃষ্টপদার্থ সমূহের (দূরত্ব অনুসারে) আয়তন, আপেক্ষিক অবস্থানাদি প্রদর্শনপূর্ব্বক চিত্রণ বা অঙ্কনের কলা বা কৌশল,

পরিপ্রেক্ষণের পর্য্যায়, সমন্বয় (পাঃ)। 2. A picture in perspective; তাদৃশ চিত্র, পরিপ্রেক্ষিত। 3. The apparent relation between visible objects as to position, distance etc.; দূরত্ব, অবস্থানাদি সম্পর্কে দৃশ্য পদার্থসমূহের মধ্যে আপাতদৃষ্টসম্বন্ধ, পরিপ্রেক্ষিত। 4. Same as LINEAR PERSPECTIVE which see. 5. (*Fig.*) The relation in which the parts of a subject are mentally viewed; (লক্ষণায়) মানস পরিপ্রেক্ষিত। 6. A view; a prospect, (*lit.* & *fig.*); দৃশ্য; বিস্তৃত দৃশ্য। ***Adj.*** Of, relating to, or in, perspective; পরিপ্রেক্ষিতসম্বন্ধীয়, পরিপ্রেক্ষণের পর্য্যায়ানুযায়ী। **—ly,** *adv.* **Linear perspective** — ব্যবহারিক জ্যামিতির বিভাগবিশেষ—যাহাতে কোন নির্দ্দিষ্ট বিন্দু হইতে দৃষ্ট বস্তুসমূহের আপাত-দৃশ্য দিক এবং দৈর্ঘ্য, প্রস্থ, বেধ প্রভৃতির আলোচনা থাকে। **In perspective**—পরিপ্রেক্ষিতের নিয়মানুসারে অঙ্কিত।

pêr-spĕc′-tō-grăph, *n.* An instrument for the mechanical drawing of objects in perspective; পরিপ্রেক্ষিত চিত্রক।

pêr-spi-cā′cious (-shŭs), *adj.* Having the power of discernment; of clear or acute understanding; সূক্ষ্মদর্শী, চপলদৃষ্টি, তীক্ষ্ণদর্শী; কুশাগ্রবুদ্ধি, কুশাগ্রীয়মতি। **—cac′-i-ty,** *n.* **—ly,** *adv.* **—ness,** *n.*

pêr-spi-cū′-i-ty, *n.* 1. The quality of being perspicuous; lucidity; সুস্পষ্টতা; ভাষা বা ভাবে প্রাঞ্জলতা, বিশদত্ব, প্রসাদগুণ, বৈশদ্য। 2. (*Improp.*) Sagacity; insight; তীক্ষ্ণবুদ্ধিতা; অন্তর্দৃষ্টি।

pêr-spic′-ū-ous (-ŭs), *adj.* Clear to the understanding; lucid; সুস্পষ্ট, সুজ্ঞেয়, সুব্যক্ত; বিশদ, প্রসাদগুণ-সম্পন্ন, প্রাঞ্জল, স্পষ্টার্থ। **—ly,** *adv.* **—ness,** *n.*

pêr-spīre′, *v. i.* & *t.* To sweat; ঘর্ম্মত্যাগ করা। ***Verb t.*** To emit as a liquid through pores in the form of vapour or moisture; ঘর্ম্মাক্ত হওয়া, ঘর্ম্মস্রাব করা, ঘামা। **—spir′-a-ble,** *adj.* **—spi-ra′-tion,** *n.* Sweating; sweat; স্বেদনিঃসরণ, স্বেদস্রুতি, স্বেদনির্গম, স্বেদন, স্বেদস্রাব; ঘর্ম্ম, ঘাম, স্বেদজল, শ্রমজল, ঘর্ম্মাম্বু, ক্লেদ। **—spir′-a-to-ry,** *adj.*

pêr-suade′ (-swād), *v. t.* 1. To influence successfully by argument, advice, etc.; to induce; to convince; প্ররোচিত করা; প্রবর্ত্তিত করা; প্রতীতি জন্মান। **—suad′-a-ble, —sua′-si-ble,** *adjs.* Capable of being persuaded; প্রবর্ত্তনীয়। **—suad′-ed,** *p. p.* **—sua-a-si-bil′-i-ty,** *n.*

pêr-sua′-sion (-swā-), *n.* 1. Act of persuading; প্ররোচন, প্রবর্ত্তন। 2. State of being persuaded; conviction; full belief; "Doubts were converted into *persuasion*"; প্রবর্ত্তনা, প্ররোচনা; দৃঢ়বিশ্বাস, প্রতীতি; পূর্ণবিশ্বাস। 3. Power or quality of persuading; প্ররোচনা-শক্তি। 4. A religious belief; a sect holding this; as, he is of the Roman Catholic *persuasion*; ধর্ম্মমত; কোন বিশেষ ধর্ম্মমতাবলম্বী সম্প্রদায়। 5. (*Humorous*) Sort; kind; as one of the male *persuasion*; রকম; জাতি।

pêr-sua′-sive (-swā-zĭv), *adj.* & *n.* Having the power to persuade; influencing the mind or passions; winning; প্ররোচক, প্রবর্ত্তক; উত্তেজক, উদ্দীপক; প্রবৃত্তিজনক। ***Noun.*** That which persuades; a motive; an inducement; প্রবর্ত্তনা; উদ্দেশ্য; প্ররোচনা। **—ly,** *adv.* **—ness,** *n.*

pêrt, *adj.* Saucy; forward; impertinent; ধৃষ্ট; প্রগল্‌ভ; দুর্বিনীত, বে-আদব, অবিনীত, বাচাল, ফচ্‌কে। **—ly.** *adv.* **—ness,** *n.*

pêr-tain′ (-tān), *v. i.* 1. To belong (*to*); অধিকার থাকা। 2. To be appropriate (*to*); as, weapons *pertaining to* war; প্রাসঙ্গিক হওয়া। 3. To relate (*to*); সম্পৃক্ত থাকা, অধিকারভুক্ত হওয়া, অন্তর্গত হওয়া।

pêr-ti-nā′-cious (-shŭs), *adj.* Obstinate; perversely persistent; দৃঢ়প্রতিজ্ঞ; একগুঁয়ে, নাছোড়বান্দা, অটল, দৃঢ়ব্রত। **—ly,** *adv.* **—nac′-i-ty, —ness,** *ns.*

pĕr′-ti-nĕnt, *adj.* & *n.* Being to the point; apposite; প্রাসঙ্গিক; যুক্ত, সঙ্গত (হিঃ কোঃ)। ***Noun.*** (Usu. *pl.*) An appurtenance or appurtenances; উপাঙ্গ, আনুষঙ্গিক বস্তু। **—nence, —nen-cy,** *ns.* State of being pertinent; সঙ্গতি (হিঃ কোঃ), যুক্ততা (ঐ), প্রাসঙ্গিকতা। **—nent-ly,** *adv.*

pêr-turb′ (-têrb), *v. t.* To disturb greatly (mentally or physically); to agitate; ব্যাকুল করা, উদ্বিগ্ন করা; বিক্ষুব্ধ করা। **—a-ble,** *adj.* **—tur-ba′-tion,** *n.* 1. Act of perturbing or state of being perturbed; agitation; আলোড়ন, বিক্ষোভ, উদ্বেগ; মানসিক অশান্তি, বিরক্তি, অশান্তি। 2. (*Astron.*) The disturbance produced in the simple elliptic motion of one heavenly body about another by the action of a third body; (জ্যোতির্ব্বিদ্যা) গ্রহাদির কক্ষবিবর্ত্তন, মার্গান্তর (সাঃ পঃ), মার্গান্তরগতি (ঐ), বিক্ষোভ (ঐ), কক্ষভ্রংশ (ঐ), স্থানচ্যুতি (হিঃ কোঃ)। **per′-tur-ba-tive, —turbed,** *adjs.* **Perturbating force**—স্থানচ্যুতি বল (হিঃ কোঃ)।

pĕ-rūke′, *n.* Wig; পরচুলা, উপকেশ।

pĕ-rūse′ (*or* -rōz), *v. t.* To read carefully or thoroughly; (loosely) to read; যত্নপূর্ব্বক পাঠ করা; অধ্যয়ন করা। 2. (*Fig., archaic*) To inspect or examine as a person's face etc.; (লক্ষণায় ও অপ্রঃ) পর্য্যবেক্ষণ করা, পরিদর্শন করা। **—rus′-al,** *n.* The act of perusing or reading carefully; পঠন, অধ্যয়ন। **—rus′-er,** *n.*

Pĕ-rü′-vĭ-ăn, *adj.* & *n.* Of, or pertaining to, Peru, in South America ; দক্ষিণ আমেরিকার পেরু দেশ-সম্বন্ধীয়। ***Noun.*** A native of Peru ; পেরুদেশবাসী। **Peruvian bark**—সিঙ্কোনা বৃক্ষের বল্কল—যাহা হইতে কুইনাইন প্রস্তুত হয়।

pêr-vāde′, *v. t.* To go through or penetrate ; to spread all over ; to permeate (*lit.* & *fig.*) ; অন্তঃপ্রবেশ করা ; ছাইয়া ফেলা, ব্যাপ্ত করা, পরিব্যাপ্ত করা ; আচ্ছন্ন করা (শব্দানুযায়ী ও লক্ষণায়)। **—vad′-ing,** *adj.* **—va′-sion,** *n.* **—va′-sive,** *adj.* Tending, or having power, to pervade ; বিস্তারপ্রবণ, বিসারী। **—va′-sive-ly,** *adv.* **—va′-sive-ness,** *n.*

pêr-verse′ (-vêrs), *adj.* **1.** Obstinate in error ; intractable ; ঠেঁটা ; দুর্দ্দম, অদম্য। **2.** Different from what is reasonable or required ; প্রতীপ। **3.** Wayward ; petulant ; বে-আড়া, উন্মার্গগামী, উচ্ছৃঙ্খল ; খিটখিটে। **4.** Wicked ; perverted ; একগুঁয়ে, অবাধ্য, দুষ্ট ; কুটিল, বিকৃত-স্বভাব। **5.** Against weight of evidence or direction of the judge ; as, a *perverse* verdict ; প্রমাণপ্রতিকূল, বিচারকের নির্দ্দেশের প্রতিকূল। **—ly,** *adv.* **—ness, —ver′-si-ty,** *ns.* State of being perverse ; obstinancy ; উচ্ছৃঙ্খলতা ; একগুঁয়েমি।

pêr-vêrt′, *v. t.* **1.** To turn from truth, rectitude, etc. esp. religious belief ; to lead astray ; সত্য বা ধর্ম্মভ্রষ্ট করা ; বিপথে চালিত করা, বিগড়ে দেওয়া। **2.** To misconstrue ; to misapply ; as, to *pervert* one's words etc. ; শব্দাদির অপব্যবহার করা, বিকৃত ব্যাখ্যা করা, কদর্থ করা ; অপপ্রয়োগ করা। **3.** To divert as a thing etc. from its right use ; অপব্যবহার করা। **—ver′-sion,** *n.* The act of perverting ; diversion from truth, propriety, etc. ; misapplication ; বিপথগমন, উন্মার্গগমন ; অপব্যবহার, অপলাপ, বিকার, বিকৃতি (হিঃ কোঃ) ; অপপ্রয়োগ। **—ver′-sive,** *adj.*

pêr′-vêrt, *n.* A perverted person ; an apostate ; সত্যভ্রষ্ট ব্যক্তি, ধর্ম্মভ্রষ্ট ব্যক্তি ; স্বধর্ম্মচ্যুত ব্যক্তি, স্বধর্ম্মত্যাগী ব্যক্তি।

pêr′-vĭ-ous (-ŭs), *adj.* **1.** Admitting passage (*to*) ; permeable ; অনুপ্রবেশনীয়, ভেদ্য, সচ্ছিদ্র, প্রবেশ্য, অন্তঃপ্রবেশনীয়, অরোধক ; ভেদনার্হ, ভেদ্য, ভেদশক্য। **2.** (*Fig.*) Accessible to reason etc. ; (লক্ষণায়) বোধগম্য। **—ness,** *n.*

peseta, *n.* A silver coin of Spain worth about 10d. ; প্রায় দশ পেনি মূল্যের স্পেনদেশীয় মুদ্রাবিশেষ।

Pĕ-shit′-tă, —shi′-tö, *ns.* The Syriac version of the scriptures ; বাইবেলের সীরীয় অনুবাদ।

pe′-sö (pā-), *n.* Any of several coins of South America worth about 4*s.* ; আমেরিকার রৌপ্যমুদ্রা-বিশেষ।

pĕs′-sa-rȳ (-ă-), *n.* **1.** (*Med.*) An instrument used in the vagina to prevent uterine displacement ; (ভৈষজ্য-শাস্ত্র) জরায়ুভ্রংশ ও যোনিভ্রংশ আদি রোগে যোনিতে প্রবেশনার্থ যন্ত্র বা বস্তুবিশেষ, উত্থাপক (সাঃ পঃ)। **2.** A vaginal suppository ; যোনিপ্রদেশে প্রবেশনার্থ নলাকার বা মোচাকৃতি ঔষধের খণ্ডবিশেষ।

pĕs′-si-mĭsm (-ĭ-), *n.* **1.** (*Metaph.*) Doctrine that this world is the worst possible, or that all things tend to evil ; (অধ্যাত্মবিদ্যা) দুঃখবাদ, অশুভবাদ, নৈরাশ্যবাদ, সর্ব্বাশুভবাদ, অমঙ্গলবাদ, নির্ব্বেদবাদ (হিঃ কোঃ)। **2.** A disposition to take the least hopeful view of things ; সর্ব্ববিষয়ে নৈরাশ্য। **—mist,** *n.* One who believes that everything is tending to the worst, (opp. to *optimist*) ; অশুভবাদী, দুঃখবাদী, নির্ব্বেদবাদী (হিঃ কোঃ), সর্ব্বাশুভবাদী (ঐ)। **—mis′-tic,** *adj.* **—mis′-ti-cal-ly,** *adv.*

pĕst, *n.* **1.** A troublesome or destructive person, animal or thing ; কষ্টপ্রদ, ধ্বংসকারী বা অনিষ্টকর ব্যক্তি, জন্তু বা বস্তু, উৎপাত, কণ্টক। **2.** (*Rare*) Pestilence ; plague ; (কচিদ্‌ব্যবহৃত) মহামারী ; মড়ক। **Pest-house**—A hospital for plague etc. ; প্লেগ-হাসপাতাল, মহামারী রোগগ্রস্ত ব্যক্তিগণের রুগ্নাবাস।

pĕst′-ēr, *v. t.* To trouble or disturb ; to worry ; বিরক্ত করা, উত্ত্যক্ত করা ; জ্বালাতন করা।

pĕs-tif′-êr-ous (-ŭs), *adj.* **1.** Contagious ; noxious to health ; স্পর্শসংক্রামক, মড়কাবহ, মারীজনক ; স্বাস্থ্যনাশক। **2.** Noxious to morals ; pernicious ; নীতিবিগর্হিত ; কলুষপূর্ণ।

pĕs′-ti-lence (-lĕns), *n.* Any fatal epidemic disease ; the bubonic plague ; মহামারী, মড়ক ; প্লেগ। **—len′-ti-al,** *adj.* **1.** Tending to produce pestilence or bubonic plague ; মড়কজনক। **2.** (*Fig.*) Injurious to morals etc. ; (লক্ষণায়) দুর্নীতিপূর্ণ।

pĕs′-ti-lĕnt, *adj.* **1.** Fatal ; deadly ; মারাত্মক, সাংঘাতিক ; ধ্বংসকারী, নাশকারী। **2.** (*Fig.*) Pernicious ; vicious ; (লক্ষণায়) অহিতজনক, অপকারক, অনিষ্টকারক ; পাপজনক। **3.** Annoying ; troublesome ; বিরক্তিজনক ; জ্বালাকর। **—ly** *adv.*

pĕs′-tle (-l), *n.*, *v. t.* & *i.* **1.** An instrument for pounding anything in a mortar ; মুষল, হামামদিস্তার ডাঁটি, বোঁটনা। **2.** A mechanical appliance for pounding, stamping, pressing, etc. ; মুষলযন্ত্র, মর্দ্দক (সাঃ পঃ)। ***Verb t.*** To pound with or as with a pestle ; মুষলদ্বারা চূর্ণ করা, চূর্ণবিচূর্ণ করা, ঘুঁটা। ***Verb i.*** To use a pestle ; মুষল ব্যবহার করা।

pĕt, *n.* & *v. t.* **1.** Any animal tamed and fondled ; পোষা জন্তু, **2.** A darling ; a favourite child ; প্রিয়পাত্র ; যাদুমণি, বাছাধন, দুলাল (cf. শচীর দুলাল গোরা)। ***Verb t.*** To treat as a pet ;

to fondle ; to indulge : আদর করা ; সোহাগ করা ; প্রশ্রয় দেওয়া, আসকারা দেওয়া। **Pet name**—আদরের নাম। **One's pet aversion**—কোন ব্যক্তির বিশেষ অপ্রীতির বিষয়ীভূত বস্তু

pĕt, *adj.* Indulged ; petted ; favourite ; প্রশ্রয়প্রাপ্ত ; আদরের ; সোহাগের।

pĕt, *n.* A fit of peevishness, esp. at being or feeling slighted : মান। **To take (the) pet, To be in a pet**—To be offended or sulky ; রুষ্ট হওয়া, মান করা।

pĕt'-al, *n.* (*Bot.*) A flower-leaf ; পুষ্পদল, ফুলের পাঁপড়ি, দল। **–al(l)ed**, *p. p.* **–ine, –oid, –ous, Pe-tal'-i-form,** *adjs.*

pĕt'-ă-lŏn, *n.* The plate of gold worn on the linen mitre of the Jewish high priest ; ইহুদী প্রধান পুরোহিতের ক্ষৌম উষ্ণীষোপরি পরিহিত স্বর্ণপট্ট।

pĕ-târd', *n.* **1.** A small engine of war, formerly used to blow in door etc. দুর্গদ্বারাদি (বারুদ যোগে) উড়াইয়া দিবার নিমিত্ত প্রাচীনকালীন যুদ্ধযন্ত্র বিশেষ। **2.** A kind of fire-cracker ; একপ্রকার পটকা বাজী। **Hoist with his own petard**—See under HOIST.

pĕt'-ă-sŭs, *n.* **1.** The winged cap of Mercury ; মার্কুরী দেবের সপক্ষ টুপি। **2.** A broad-brimmed low-crowned hat worn by ancient Greeks ; প্রাচীন গ্রীকদিগের একপ্রকার প্রশস্তপ্রান্ত টুপি।

pĕ-tau'-rist (-tä-), *n.* A flying phalanger ; অষ্ট্রেলিয়ার দ্বিগর্ভ জন্তুবিশেষ।

Pē'-tĕr, *n.* **1.** One of the twelve Apostles ; খৃষ্টের পার্ষদবিশেষ। **2.** Either of the two epistles of Peter ; Peter এর পত্রদ্বয়ের অন্যতর। **3.** (*l. c.*) (*thieves' cant*) A trunk or portmanteau ; (চোরের ভাষায়) ট্রাঙ্ক, পোর্টমেন্ট। **Peter-penny, Peter's-pence, –penny**—রোমের পোপের নিকট প্রেরণের জন্য ইংলণ্ডের প্রতি গৃহস্থের বাটী হইতে এক পেনি হিসাবে যে কর আদায় করা হইত। **Peter's fish**—কড্ জাতীয় সামুদ্রিক মৎস্যবিশেষ। **To rob Peter to pay Paul**—See PAUL.

pē'-tĕr, *v. i.* (*Slang*, of a stream, vein of ore, etc.) To become exhausted ; to run out, (with *out*) (*lit. & fig.*) ; (প্রবাহ, ধাতুরেখা প্রভৃতি সম্পর্কে ইতরভাষায়) নিঃশেষিত হওয়া ; ফুরাইয়া যাওয়া।

pē'-tĕr-sham, *n.* **1.** A heavy corded ribbon ; একপ্রকার দড়ীর ন্যায় ফিতা। **2.** A rough woollen cloth ; a coat made of this stuff ; একপ্রকার মোটা পশমী কাপড় ; ঐ কাপড়ের কোট।

pĕt'-i-ōle, *n.* (*Bot.*) A leaf-stalk ; (উদ্ভিদবিদ্যা) পত্রবৃন্ত, বোঁটা, বৃন্ত। **–o-lar, –o-late,** *adjs.*

petit, (*F.*), *adj.* Small ; insignificant ; ক্ষুদ্র ; তুচ্ছ, অকিঞ্চিৎকর, নগণ্য। ***Petit-maitre***—ফুলবাবু ; বকেশ্বর। ***Petit mal***—একপ্রকার মৃগীরোগ। ***Petits-chevaux***—জুয়া প্রভৃতি খেলা। ***Petit souper***—কয়েকজন অন্তরঙ্গ বন্ধুর জন্য রসনাতৃপ্তিকর নৈশভোজনের আয়োজন। ***Petits soins***—সামান্য সামান্য বিষয়ে যত্ন বা সমাদর। ***Petit verre***—A glass of liqueur ; এক গ্লাস আসব।

petitio, (*L.*), *n.* ***Petitio principii***—Begging the question ; প্রমাণীয় বিষয় প্রমাণিত বলিয়া ধরিয়া লওন, সিদ্ধসাধন (হিঃ কোঃ), সাধ্যসম (সর্ব্বঃ)। [যে প্রশ্নের বিচার চাই সেই প্রশ্নের কাছেই যদি উত্তর ভিক্ষা করা হয়, সেই প্রশ্নের দ্বারাই যদি প্রশ্নের সমাধানের চেষ্টা করা হয় তবে, সে ভ্রমের নাম *Petitio principii*—আজিত চক্রবর্ত্তী কৃত, মহর্ষি দেবেন্দ্রনাথ ঠাকুর।]

pĕ-ti-tion, *n.*, *v. t.* & *i.* **1.** Supplication ; request ; প্রার্থনা, মিনতি ; অনুরোধ, অনুনয়। **2.** A formal written request from one or more persons to a sovereign or other political superior ; দরখাস্ত, আবেদনপত্র। **3.** (*Law*) A formal written application to a court ; আবেদন। ***Verb t.*** To present a petition to ; to ask as a favour ; আবেদন করা ; অনুগ্রহ প্রার্থনা করা। ***Verb i.*** To make a petition or request ; অনুরোধ করা, আবেদন করা ; **–a-ry,** *adj.* **–er,** *n.* One who offers a petition or prayer ; দরখাস্তকারী, আবেদনকারী। **Petition of Rights**—১৬২৮ খৃঃ অব্দে ইংলণ্ডের রাজা ১ম চার্লসের নিকট হইতে পার্লেমেণ্ট মহাসভাকর্তৃক প্রজাসাধারণের স্বত্ব ও অধিকারসম্বন্ধীয় যে ঘোষণাপত্র আদায় করা হয়।

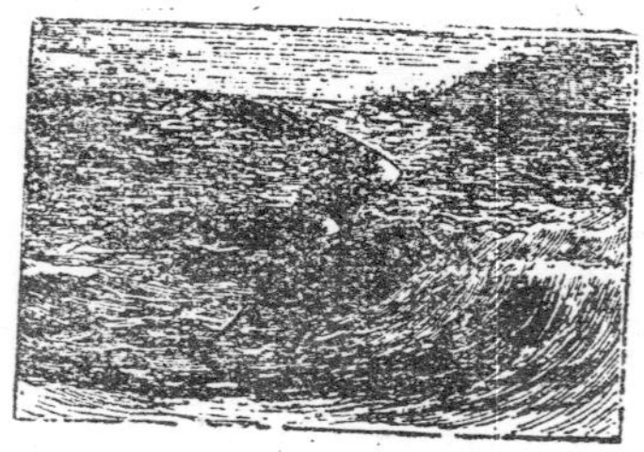

Stormy Petrel.

pĕt'-rĕl, *n.* (Also *storm-petrel*, *stormy petrel*) A webfooted sea-bird ; একপ্রকার জালপাদ পক্ষী।

pĕt'-ri-fȳ, *v. t.* & *i.* **1.** To turn into stone ; প্রস্তরীকৃত করা, পাষাণীভূত করা, শিলীভূত করা। **2.** (*Fig.*) To paralyse ; to stupefy with astonishment, terror, etc. ; to benumb or stiffen, as, heart, mind, etc. ; (লক্ষণায়) অবশ করা ; ভয়ে বা বিস্ময়ে প্রস্তর-পুত্তলিকাবৎ করা ; আড়ষ্ট করা, স্তম্ভিত করা। ***Verb i.*** To become stone or hard like stone, (*lit.* & *fig.*) ; প্রস্তরময় হওয়া বা প্রস্তরবৎ কঠিন হওয়া (শব্দানুযায়ী ও লক্ষণায়)। **–fac'-tion,** *n.* Petrifying ; প্রস্তরীকরণ, পাষাণীকরণ। **2.** State of being petrified or benumbed as with terror, astonishment, etc.; পাষাণত্ব-প্রাপ্তি, প্রস্তরপুত্তলিকাবৎ অবস্থা। 3. Petrified substance or mass; প্রস্তরীভূত বস্তু, শিলীভূত দ্রব্য।

pĕt'-rō-glȳph, *n.* A carving or inscription upon a rock; ক্ষোদিত শিলা, শিলালেখ।

pĕt'-rō-grăph, *n.* A rock-inscription; শিলালিপি, শিলালেখ।

pē-trŏg'-ră-phȳ, *n.* The study or science of rocks; শিলাবিদ্যা, শিলাবিজ্ঞান। **Pet-ro-graph'-ic, Pet-ro-graph'-i-cal,** *adjs.* **—pher,** *n.*

pĕt'-rŏl, *n.* & *v. t.* A refined petroleum as used in motor-cars etc.; হাওয়া গাড়ী প্রভৃতিতে ব্যবহৃত শোধিত কেরোসিন তৈল, শিলারস, ভূমিতৈল। ***Verb t.*** To supply as a motor with petrol; হাওয়া গাড়ী প্রভৃতিতে শোধিত কেরোসিন তৈল যোগান।

pē-trō'-lē-ŭm, *n.* Rock-oil; mineral oil; a liquid inflammable substance found in the earth, largely used for lighting and other purposes; শিলাতৈল; খনিজ তৈল, মেটে তৈল, ভূমিতৈল (কেঙিঃ); কেরোসিন তৈল।

petroleur, *n.* (*Fem.* PETROLEUSE, *pron.* PETROLERZ). An incendiary using petroleum; যে গৃহদাহকারী ব্যক্তি কেরোসিন ব্যবহার করে।

pē-trŏl'-ic, *adj.* Of, or relating to, petrol or petroleum; শোধিত কেরোসিন তৈলসম্বন্ধীয়, কেরোসিন তৈলসম্বন্ধীয়।

pĕt'-rō-lĭn, —line (-lĭn), *ns.* 1. An oil derived from petroleum; কেরোসিন তৈল হইতে প্রাপ্ত তৈলবিশেষ। 2. A paraffin got from petroleum of Rangoon; রেঙ্গুনের কেরোসিন তৈল হইতে প্রাপ্ত চর্বিজাতীয় পদার্থবিশেষ।

pē-trŏl'-ō-ġȳ, *n.* The science of the composition and classification of rocks; শিলাবিজ্ঞান, শিলাতত্ত্ব।

pĕt'-rō-nĕl, *n.* (*Hist.*) A pistol used, esp. by horse-soldiers in the 16–17th centuries; (ইতিহাস) পিস্তল, বিশেষতঃ ষোড়শ এবং সপ্তদশ শতাব্দীর অশ্বারোহী সৈন্যগণ কর্তৃক ব্যবহৃত পিস্তল।

pĕt'-rous (-rŭs), *adj.* 1. Of, relating to, or like, rock; পাষাণসম্বন্ধীয়, পাষাণবৎ। 2. (*Anat.*) Of, or relating to, the hard part of the temporal bone; (শারীরসংস্থানবিদ্যা) শঙ্খাস্থির কঠিন অংশসম্বন্ধীয়।

pĕt'-tĭ-coat (-kōt), *n.* & *adj.* 1. A skirt worn by women, girls or children covering the body below the waist; স্ত্রীলোকের বা ছেলেমেয়েদের ছোট ঘাগরা। 2. A woman or girl; (*pl.*) the female sex; স্ত্রীলোক বালিকা; স্ত্রীজাতি। ***Adj.*** Feminine স্ত্রীসংক্রান্ত, স্ত্রীঘটিত। **—ed,** *p. p.* **—less,** *adj.* **Petticoat affairs**—স্ত্রীঘটিত ব্যাপার। **Petticoat government**—স্ত্রীশাসন, স্ত্রীতন্ত্র, সীমন্তিনীর শাসন। **She is a Cromwell in petticoats**—স্ত্রীরূপী ক্রমওয়েল। **To be in petticoats**—To be still a small child; এখন কচি ছেলে বা মেয়ে। **To be of the female sex**; স্ত্রীজাতীয় হওয়া।

pĕt'-tĭ-fŏg, *v. i.* & *t.* To do a petty business as lawyer; to quibble about petty points; সামান্য উকীলের ব্যবসায় করা; আইনের কুতর্ক করা, কুতর্ক করা। ***Verb t.*** (*Colloq.*) To argue like a pettifogger; as to *pettifog* a claim; (চলিত ভাষায়) বাজে উকীলের মত তর্কবিতর্ক করা।

pĕt'-tĭ-fŏg-ger (-ĕr), *n.* 1. An inferior legal practitioner dealing in petty or mean cases: বাজে উকিল বা মোক্তার, পশার শূন্য উকিল, সামান্য উকিল, ছেঁড়া উকিল মোক্তার। 2. A petty practitioner in any department; ক্ষুদ্র ব্যবসায়ী। **—ging,** *adj.* & *n.* Acting as a pettifogger; paltry; mean; বাজে উকীলের ব্যবসায়কারী; ক্ষুদ্র; নীচ, হেয়। (*Noun.*) Pettifoggery; সামান্য ওকালতী, হীন ওকালতী। **—y,** *n.* The arts and practice of pettifoggers; legal chicanery; বাজে উকীলের ছল চাতুরী; আইনের ফন্দি, চাতুরী বা কৌশল।

pĕt'-tĭsh (-ĭsh), *adj.* Peevish; ill-tempered; fretful; খিটখিটে; বদমেজাজী; কোপনস্বভাব। **—ly,** *adv.* **—ness,** *n.*

pĕt'-tĭ-toes (-tōz), *n.* (*Pl.*) The toes or feet of a pig often used as food; শূকর ছানার পা অথবা পায়ের আঙ্গুল।

petto, *n.* The breast; বক্ষঃস্থল। **In petto** In one's own breast or private thought; hence, in secrecy; নিজের পেটের ভিতর; গোপনে।

pĕt'-tȳ, *adj.* 1. Trifling; unimportant; little-minded; "Our *petty* animosities"; ক্ষুদ্র, তুচ্ছ; নগণ্য; ক্ষুদ্রমনাঃ। 2. Inferior; subordinate; as, a *petty* prince; নীচ, হীন; অপ্রধান **—ti-ly,** *adv.* **—ti-ness,** *n.* **Petty cash**—খুচরা আদায়ী টাকা, খুচরা খরচের টাকা। **Petty officer**—নৌবিভাগের সামান্য কর্মচারী। **Petty theft**—ছিঁচকে চুরি, পাতি চুরি।

pĕt-ū-lănt, *adj.* & *n.* 1. Peevish; fretful; irritable; as, *petulant* moods; খিটখিটে; চটা; বদমেজাজী। 2. (*Rare*) Saucy; insolent; (অপ্রঃ) ধৃষ্ট; ঢুব্বিনীত। ***Noun.*** A petulant person; খিটখিটে লোক। **—lance,** *n.* State of being petulant; irritability; চটাস্বভাব; খিটখিটে মেজাজ। **—ly,** *adv.*

pe-tū'-nĭ-ă, *n.* 1. A genus of American plants with white, purple or violet flowers; a plant or flower of this genus; আমেরিকাদেশীয় একজাতীয় গুল্ম; ঐ জাতিভুক্ত গুল্ম বা তজ্জাত পুষ্প 2. (Also *attrib.*) Dark violet; purple; গাঢ় বেগুণে বর্ণ; নীলারুণ বর্ণ।

pē-tŭn′-tsē, *n.* White earth used with kaolin for making porcelain; China stone ; চীনামাটী তৈয়ারের জন্য একপ্রকার শ্বেত মৃত্তিকা; চীনা পাথর।

pew (pü), *n.* & *v. t.* An enclosed seat in a church ; a fixed bench with back in a church ; খৃষ্টীয় ভজনালয়ে গরাদেবেষ্টিত আসন, মঞ্চ ; পৃষ্ঠরক্ষণী সমন্বিত আসনবিশেষ। *Verb t.* To furnish with pews ; to place in or as in a pew; উক্তরূপ আসনসমন্বিত করা; উক্তরূপ আসনে উপবিষ্ট করা। **Pew′-age,** *n.* **Pew′-less,** *adj.* **Pew-holder**—যে ব্যক্তি ভজনালয়ে মঞ্চ ভাড়া করে। **Pew-opener**—যে পরিচারক গির্জ্জার মঞ্চ খুলিয়া দেয়।

pē′-wit, pee′- (pē-), *ns.* **1.** The lapwing ; the cry of this bird ; কোষ্টি (আঃ বঃ) ; ঐ পক্ষীর ডাক। **2.** [Also *pe(e)wit gull*] The European black-headed gull ; ইয়ুরোপীয় পক্ষিবিশেষ।

pew′-têr (pü-), *n.* **1.** An alloy mainly of tin and lead ; রূপদস্তা। **2.** Vessels made of pewter ; রূপদস্তার বাসন-পত্র। **3.** A pewter pot ; রূপদস্তার পাত্র। **4.** (*Slang*) Prize-money ; (ইতরভাষায়) ধৃত জাহাজ বা ঐরূপ জাহাজের মাল বিক্রয় দ্বারা লব্ধ অর্থ—যাহার এক অংশ ধৃতকারী জাহাজের কর্ম্মচারী ও মাল্লাদিগকে বাঁটিয়া দেওয়া হয়।

pfĕn′-nig, -ing, *ns.* A small copper coin of Germany worth $\frac{1}{10}$ of an English penny ; জর্ম্মণীদেশের ক্ষুদ্র তাম্রমুদ্রাবিশেষ।

Phae′-drȧ (fē-), *n.* See HIPPOLYTUS.

Phā′-ē-thŏn, *n.* The name of a son of Helios ; (গ্রীকপুরাণ) সূর্য্যের জনৈক পুত্র। ইঁহার কাতর প্রার্থনায় সূর্য্যদেব উঁহাকে একদিনের জন্য তদীয় রথ চালনার অনুমতি প্রদান করেন। কিন্তু অকুশল চালকের হস্তে অশ্বসকল অসংযত হইয়া পড়ায় রথ পৃথিবীর অতি নিকটে আসিয়া পৌঁছে। তাহাতে প্রায় পৃথিবী জ্বলিয়া যাইবার উপক্রম হইল। তখন দেবতা Zeus সৃষ্টিরক্ষার জন্য সূর্য্যনন্দনকে বজ্রাঘাতে নিধন করেন।

phā′-ē-tŏn, *n.* **1.** An open carriage on four wheels usually drawn by two horses ; ফিটন গাড়ী।

phăg-ē-dē′-nȧ, -dæ′- (-dē-), *ns.* A spreading obstinate ulcer ; একপ্রকার দুরারোগ্য ক্ষত। **-d(a)en′-ic,** *adj.*

phăg′-ō-cyte (-sīt), *n.* A white blood corpuscle or leucocyte that can guard the system against infection by absorbing microbes ; শ্বেতরক্তকণিকা—যাহা অণুজীবসমূহ ধ্বংস করিয়া সংক্রামক রোগের প্রভাব হইতে দেহ রক্ষা করিতে পারে, অনুজীবনাশক।

phăl′-ănge (-ănj), *n.* See PHALANX, 4.

phȧ-lăn′-gē-ȧl, *adj.* (*Anat.*) Of, or pertaining to, a phalange or phalanx ; করাঙ্গুলী ও পদাঙ্গুলীর ক্ষুদ্রাস্থিসম্বন্ধীয়। **Phalangeal-joint**—অঙ্গুলি-গ্রন্থি।

phȧ-lăn′-gêr, *n.* An Australian marsupial animal ; অষ্ট্রেলিয়া দেশীয় দ্বিগর্ভ জন্তুবিশেষ।

phăl′-ăn-stĕr-ȳ, *n.* **1.** A socialistic community organised on the plan of Fourier ; সাম্যবাদী ফুরিয়ারের আদর্শানুযায়ী গঠিত সাম্যবাদি-সম্প্রদায়। **2.** A building or buildings occupied by such a community ; উক্ত সম্প্রদায় কর্ত্তৃক অধিকৃত ভবন বা ভবনশ্রেণী। **-ste′-ri-an,** *adj.* & *n.*

phā′-lanx (-lăngks), *n.* **1.** (*Gr. Antiq.*) The heavy armed infantry drawn up in close order ; ঘন সন্নিবিষ্ট গুরুভার অস্ত্রধারী পদাতিক সৈন্য, ভেক ব্যূহ, ঘনব্যূহ (মঃ ইঃ)। **2.** A body of troops or men in close array ; নিবিড়ভাবে সন্নিবিষ্ট কোন দল বা জনগণ। **3.** A group of people united for a common purpose ; একোদ্দেশ্যে মিলিত জনগণ। **4.** (*Anat.*) One of the small bones of a finger or toe (also *phalange*) ; (শারীরসংস্থানবিদ্যা) পদাঙ্গুলি বা করাঙ্গুলির ক্ষুদ্রাস্থি, অঙ্গুল্যাস্থি (সঃ পঃ)। **5.** Same as PHALANSTERY, I.

phăl′-ȧ-rōpe, *n.* A kind of wading bird ; একপ্রকার পক্ষী।

phăl′-lŭs, *n.* **1.** An image of the penis, venerated in some religious systems as a symbol of the generative power in nature ; লিঙ্গ। **2.** (*Anat.*) The penis or clitoris ; (শারীরসংস্থানবিদ্যা) লিঙ্গ, ভগাঙ্কুর। **3.** A genus of fungi ; একজাতীয় ছত্রাক। **-lic,** *adj.* **-licism, -lism,** *ns.* The phallic worship ; লিঙ্গার্চ্চনা, লিঙ্গপূজা।

Phăn′-ar (-êr), *n.* A quarter of Constantinople ; কনস্তান্তিনোপল নগরের মহল্লাবিশেষ।

phȧ-năr′-i-ōt, *n.* One of the Greeks inhabiting the Phanar quarter of Constantinople ; one of the Greek officials of Turkey ; কনস্তান্তিনোপল নগরের ফেনার মহল্লাবাসী গ্রীক; তুরস্কদেশের গ্রীক কর্ম্মচারী।

phăn′-ĕr-ō-găm, *n.* A flowering plant ; পুষ্পপ্রসূ তরু। **-gam′-ic, -og′-a-mous,** *adjs.* Having stamens and pistils ; flowering ; সপুষ্পক (সাঃ পঃ), ব্যক্তপুষ্পক (আঃ বঃ) ; পুষ্পপ্রসূ।

phăn′-tȧ-scōpe, *n.* An instrument used in studying binocular vision ; চলচিত্র দর্শক (হিঃ কোঃ)।

phăn′-tăsm, *n.* **1.** An airy appearance ; apparition ; অপচ্ছায়া ; ছায়ামূর্ত্তি। **2.** A fancied vision ; an illusion ; মরীচিকা ; মায়া, বিভ্রম। **3.** (*Psychics*) An apparition of a person living or dead, esp. one premonitory of death or calamity ; অপচ্ছায়া, ছায়ামূর্ত্তি। **4.** An idea ; a fancy ; ধারণা ; কল্পনা। **-tas′-mal, -tas′-mic,** *adjs.* **-tas′-mal-ly,** *adv.*

phăn-tăs-mă-gō′-ri-ă, *n.* **1.** An optical effect produced by a magic lantern ; also an apparatus to produce this effect ; একপ্রকার দৃষ্টিবিভ্রম—যাহাতে কোন পর্দ্দার উপরে প্রতিফলিত প্রতিমূর্ত্তি সমূহ ক্রমশঃ দূরে অপসৃত হইতে হইতে অবশেষে বিলীন হইয়া যায়, অথবা বিরাট আকার ধারণপূর্ব্বক দর্শকের অভিমুখে প্রচণ্ডবেগে ধাবিত হয় বলিয়া প্রতিভাত হয় ; উক্তরূপ চিত্রপ্রদর্শনযন্ত্র। **2.** (*Fig.*) A medley of figures or scenes ; "This mental *phantasmagoria* ; (লক্ষণায়) বিবিধ দৃশ্যপরম্পরা। **–gor′-ic,** *adj.*

phăn′-tŏm, *n.* & *adj.* **1.** A spectre ; a ghost ; অপচ্ছায়া ; ছায়ামূর্ত্তি। **2.** An unreal form or appearance ; আভাস (হিঃ কোঃ), ছায়া (ঐ)। **3.** A fancied vision ; mental illusion ; মরীচিকা ; মায়ামোহ, মানসিক ভ্রান্তি, বিভ্রম। ***Adj.*** Of the nature of a phantom ; illusive ; অপচ্ছায়াত্মক ; ভ্রান্তিজনক, মায়াময়। **Phantom tumour**—অষ্ঠিল (সাঃ পঃ) ; বাতগুল্ম (ঐ)।

Phă′-ŏn, *n.* A ferryman of Myteline ; কুরূপ বৃদ্ধ Mytelineএর জনৈক পাটনী। ইনি রতিদেবীকে পার করিয়া দিয়া তরপণ্য না নেওয়ায় তাঁহার বরে যৌবন এবং কমনীয়কান্তি লাভ করেন। কবিশ্রেষ্ঠা Sappho উঁহার প্রেমে পতিত হন। কিন্তু তৎকর্ত্তৃক প্রত্যাখ্যাত হইয়া তিনি Leucadian পর্ব্বত হইতে ভৃগুপাতনদ্বারা আত্মহত্যা করেন।

Phā′-raoh (-rō), *n.* A title of the kings of ancient Egypt ; প্রাচীন মিশরের অধিপতিগণের উপাধি। **Pharaoh's serpent**—সর্পাকারে দ্রবণশীল রাসায়নিক ক্রীড়নক বিশেষ।

Pharbitis nil—নীলকলমী (বেলঃ)।

Phăr′-i-see (-sē), *n.* **1.** One of a sect among the Jews distinguished by a strict observance of rites and ceremonies ; অত্যধিক নিষ্ঠাবান প্রাচীন ইহুদী। **2.** A formalist ; a hypocrite ; নিষ্ঠাবান ; ভণ্ড, ধর্ম্মধ্বজী। **–sa′-ic, –sa′-i-cal,** *adjs.* **–sa′-i-cal-ly,** *adv.* **–sa-ism,** *n.* **1.** The doctrines of Pharisees as a sect ; ফেরিসি সম্প্রদায়ের মত। **2.** Hypocrisy in religion ; ভণ্ডামি, মর্কট বৈরাগ্য।

phâr-mă-ceu′-ti-căl (-sū-), *adj.* Of, or relating to, pharmacy ; relating to the use, or sale of, medicines ; ঔষধ প্রস্তুতকার্য্যসম্বন্ধীয় ; ঔষধ বিক্রয়সম্বন্ধীয়, ঔষধ ব্যবহারসম্বন্ধীয়। **–ly,** *adv.* **–tics,** *n.* The art or science of preparing medicines ; ঔষধপ্রস্তুতবিদ্যা, ঔষধপ্রস্তুত তত্ত্ব।

phâr-mă-cŏl′-ō-ğy, *n.* The science of drugs ; the art of preparing medicines ; ভৈষজ্যশাস্ত্র ; ঔষধ প্রস্তুতবিদ্যা। **–gist,** *n.*

phâr-mă-cō-poe′-ia (-pē-ă), *n.* **1.** A book containing directions for the preparation and use of medicines, usually published by authority ; ঔষধ প্রস্তুতবিষয়ক গ্রন্থ, ঔষধ প্রস্তুতপ্রণালী বিষয়ক গ্রন্থ, ভৈষজ্যতত্ত্ব, ভৈষজ্য কল্পনাবিধি (সাঃ পঃ), ঔষধক্রিয়াকল্প (কেঙিঃ)। **2.** A stock or collection of drugs ; ঔষধভাণ্ডার, ঔষধসংগ্রহ। **–ial,** *adj.*

phâr′-mă-çy, *n.* **1.** The practice of preparing, mixing and dispensing medicines ; ঔষধ সংগ্রহ, রক্ষা, প্রস্তুত, সংমিশ্রণ ও ব্যবহার, ঔষধ-কল্পনা (সাঃ পঃ), চিকিৎসকের ব্যবস্থানুযায়ী ঔষধ প্রস্তুত ও সংমিশ্রণ। **2.** A drug-store ; a dispensary ; ঔষধভাণ্ডার ; ঔষধালয়।

phā′-rŏs, *n.* A lighthouse or beacon to guide seamen ; আলোকমন্দির, সঙ্কেতপ্রদীপ, দীপস্তম্ভ প্রকাশস্তম্ভ (হিঃ কোঃ)।

phăr-ўn-ğī′-tis, *n.* (*Med.*) Inflammation of the pharynx ; গলকোষপ্রদাহ।

phă-ryn′-go-cele (-rĭng-gō-sēl), *n.* An abnormal enlargement at the base of the pharynx ; গলকোষের মূলদেশের অস্বাভাবিক বিবর্দ্ধন।

phăr-ўn-gŏt′-ō-mў, *n.* (*Surg.*) The operation of cutting into the pharynx ; গলকোষচ্ছেদন।

phăr′-ynx (-ĭngks), *n.* The dilated commencement of the gullet ; মুখগহ্বরের পশ্চাদ্‌ভাগে স্থিত আহারগ্রাহী ও বাহী পেশীময় থলী (ডাঃ হরিপ্রসাদ চক্রবর্ত্তী), গলকোষ (ঐ), শৃঙ্গাটক (সাঃ পঃ)। **Pha-ryn′-gal, Pha-ryn′-ge-al,** *adjs.* Of, or relating to, the pharynx ; গলকোষ সম্বন্ধীয়। **Pharyngeal plexus**—ষট্‌চক্রান্তর্গত পঞ্চম চক্র, বিশুদ্ধ পদ্ম (বামন)।

phāše, *n.* **1.** (*Astron.*) The appearance at a given time of the illuminated surface exhibited by the moon or a planet ; কোন নির্দ্দিষ্ট সময়ে চন্দ্র কিম্বা কোন গ্রহের যে আলোকিত অংশ দৃষ্ট হয়, কলা (হিঃ কোঃ)। **2.** One of the various aspects of an object, question or topic ; a stage ; as, the problem has many *phases* ; বিভাব, দশা, অবস্থা (হিঃ কোঃ), দর্শনপ্রকার, দর্শনভেদ ; অবস্থা, ক্রম। **Phas′-ic,** *adj.*

Phaseolus lunatus—বন বরবটী (বেলঃ)।

Phaseolus max—কালামুগ (বেলঃ), কৃষ্ণমুগ (ঐ)।

Phaseolus mungo—হালি মুগ (বেলঃ)।

Phaseolus trilobus — মুগানি (বেলঃ)।

Golden-pheasant.

pheas′-ănt (fĕz-), *n.* A gallinaceous bird abundant in Britain and reared for sport etc. ; জীবঞ্জীব। **Pheasant-eyed** — (Of a flower) জীবঞ্জীব চক্ষুবৎ।

phĕ-năc′-ĕ-tĭn, *n.* A drug used to relieve fever, insomnia, etc. ; জ্বর, অনিদ্রা, প্রভৃতির ঔষধ।

phĕn-ă-kĭs′-tŏ-scōpe, *n.* An instrument which produces the representation of actual motion ; চলচিত্রদর্শক (হিঃ কোঃ)।

phē′-nŏl, *n.* Carbolic acid ; কার্ব্বলিক এসিড।

phē′-nŏl′-ŏ-ġȳ, *n.* The branch of biology treating of animal or plant life and development as affected by climate ; জীব-বিজ্ঞানের যে শাখায় জলবায়ুর প্রভাবের তারতম্যানুসারে জীব এবং উদ্ভিদের জীবন এবং বিকাশসম্বন্ধে আলোচনা থাকে। **—no-log′-i cal,** *adj.*

phē-nŏm′-ĕ-năl, *adj.* **1.** Pertaining to, or of the nature of, a phenomenon ; perceptible : প্রপঞ্চসম্বন্ধীয়, প্রপঞ্চাত্মক, প্রতিভাসিক (দ্বিজেন্দ্র). ঔপাধিক ; পরিদৃশ্যমান, বোধগম্য, প্রত্যক্ষগোচর, ইন্দ্রিয়গ্রাহ্য। **2.** Extraordinary ; wonderful : as, a *phenomenal* memory : অসাধারণ অদ্ভুত, অপূর্ব্ব। **—ism,** *n.* The doctrine that phenomena are the only objects of knowledge ; পরিদৃশ্যমান জগৎই একমাত্র সত্য বস্তু—এইরূপ মতবাদ, গোচর-বিষয়-বিজ্ঞানবাদ (হিঃ কোঃ)। **—ist,** *n.* One advocating phenomenalism ; প্রপঞ্চবাদী। **—is′-tic,** *adj.* **—ly,** *adv.* **—nol′-o-gy,** *n.*

phē-nŏm′-ĕ-năl-īze, *v. t.* To represent or conceive as a phenomena ; প্রপঞ্চরূপ প্রদর্শন বা ধারণা করা।

phē-nŏm′-ĕ-nŏn, *n.* (*Pl.* -NA) **1.** A fact, occurrence or change as perceived by any of the senses or by the mind ; প্রপঞ্চ (জ্ঞিঃ), জগদ্‌ব্যাপার, ব্যাপার, দৃষ্টিবিষয়, ঘটনা, বিকৃতি, বিকার (হিঃ কোঃ), দৃশ্য। **2.** (*Philos.*) An immediate object of perception ; প্রত্যক্ষ অনুভূতির বিষয়, বিবর্ত্ত (হিঃ দঃ), প্রমেয় (হিঃ কোঃ)। **3.** A remarkable or unusual persor, thing or incident etc. ; as, a musical *phenomenon* ; অদ্ভুত লোক, সৃষ্টিছাড়া ব্যাপার, অপূর্ব্ব ঘটনা, অদ্ভুত বস্তু।

phē′-nȳl, *n.* A radical found in benzene, phenol, etc. ; দুর্গন্ধবারক তরল পদার্থবিশেষ।

phew (fū), *interj.* An exclamation of disgust or impatience ; ইস্!

phī′-ăl, *n.* A glass vessel or bottle especially for medicines ; শিশি, কাচকুপি।

Philadelphia lawyer—The sharpest man in existence ; শঠশিরোমণি।

phi-lăn′-dêr, *v. i.* To make love, esp. triflingly ; to dangle after women ; প্রেম করা ; স্ত্রীলোকের আঁচলে আঁচলে ঘুরা।

phil-ăn′-thrōpe, *n.* Same as PHILANTHROPIST (which see.)

phil-ăn-thrŏp′-ic, *adj.* Pertaining to philanthropy ; loving mankind ; জনহিত সম্পর্কীয় ; লোকহিতৈষী, জনহিতৈষী, জনহিতেচ্ছু, জনপ্রিয়, বিশ্বোপকারী, বিশ্বমিত্র, জনসুহৃদ্, জনবল্লভ, বিশ্বহিতৈষী।

phi-lăn′-thrŏ-pist, *n.* One who exerts himself to do good to his fellowmen ; a lover of mankind ; জনহিতৈষী ব্যক্তি, বিশ্বামিত্র ; জনসুহৃদ্, জগন্মিত্র, জগদ্বৎসল। **—pism,** *n.* Same as PHILANTHROPY.

phi-lăn-thrŏ-pīze, *v. i.* & *t.* To practise philanthropy ; জনহিতসাধন করা। ***Verb t.*** **1.** To treat philanthropically ; জনহিতৈষীর ভাবে ব্যবহার করা। **2.** To render philanthropic ; জনহিতৈষী করা।

phi-lăn′-thrŏ-pȳ, *n.* Love or benevolence towards man or mankind ; মানবপ্রেম, জনহিত, লোকোপকার, সর্ব্বজনহিতৈষিতা, ভূতানুকম্পা (বঃ), জনোপকারবুদ্ধি, জনপ্রীতি, বিশ্বপ্রীতি, মানবপ্রেমপ্রবণতা (হিঃ কোঃ), বিশ্বপ্রেম।

phi-lăt′-ĕ-lȳ, *n.* The collection of postage stamps ; ডাকটিকিট সংগ্রহ। **—list,** *n.* **Phil-a-tel′-ic,** *adj.*

phil-hâr-mŏn′-ic, *adj.* & *n.* Loving harmony or music ; গীতবাদ্য-প্রিয়, স্বরসঙ্গতিপ্রিয়। ***Noun.*** A person fond of music ; গীতবাদ্যপ্রিয় ব্যক্তি, স্বরসংগতিপ্রিয় ব্যক্তি।

phil-hĕl′-lene (-lēn), *adj.* & *n.* Loving or friendly to the Greeks ; supporting the cause of their independence ; গ্রীকানুরাগী ; গ্রীসদেশের স্বাধীনতা স্থাপনে সহায়ক। ***Noun.*** A friend of Greece ; গ্রীসদেশের বন্ধু। **—len′-ic,** *adj.* **—len-ism, —len-ist,** *ns.*

Phĭl′-ip, *n.* Father of Alexander and king of Macedon ; মসীদনের অধিপতির নাম। **To appeal from Philip drunk to Philip sober**—To ask for a reconsideration of a case on account of the first decision being improperly made ; প্রথম বার কোন বিষয়ের অন্যায়রূপে নিষ্পত্তি হইলে পুনর্বিবেচনার জন্য প্রার্থনা করা। [কথিত আছে এক স্ত্রীলোক মসীদনরাজ সুরাপানমত্ত ফিলিপের কাছে কোন বিষয়ে বিচারের প্রার্থনা করিলে তিনি তাহাকে ধমকাইয়া দেন। তখন সেই স্ত্রীলোকটী রাজাকে কহিল "আমি আপনার বিচারের বিরুদ্ধে আপিল করিব।" রাজা ক্রোধে ক্ষিপ্তপ্রায় হইয়া বজ্রগর্জনে জিজ্ঞাসা করিলেন "কার কাছে আপীল করিবি?" স্ত্রীলোকটী বিনীতভাবে উত্তর করিল "অপ্রমত্ত ফিলিপের কাছে"।]

phi-lip′-pic, *n.* **1.** (*Pl.*) Orations of Demosthenes denouncing Philip, king of Macedon ; মসীদন রাজ ফিলিপের বিরুদ্ধে এথেন্সনগরীবাসী ডিমস্থিনিস প্রদত্ত বক্তৃতা। **2.** A bitter invective ; তীব্র গঞ্জনা।

phil-ip-pī′-nă, —pīne, phil-ŏ-pœ′-nă (-pē-), *ns.* **1.** The almond or other nut with double kernel, the finding of which at dessert etc. and sharing it with another person involves the giving or receiving of a present at next meeting; the present thus claimed or given; বাদাম বা তদ্বৎ ফল—যাহা ভোজনাদির কালে কোন ব্যক্তি প্রাপ্ত হইয়া অপর ব্যক্তিকে তাহার ভাগ দিলে পরবার তাহাদের সাক্ষাৎ হইলে উপহার গ্রহণ ও প্রদান করিতে হয়; ঐরূপে প্রাপ্ত বা প্রদত্ত উপহার। 2. This custom; ঐরূপ রীতি।

Phi-lis'-tine (*or* -tin), *n.* & *adj.* 1. An inhabitant of ancient Philistia, now a part of Syria; বর্তমান সীরিয়া প্রদেশের অন্তঃপাতী প্রাচীন ফিলিষ্টিয়া নামক স্থানের অধিবাসী। 2. A person of narrow views or limited aspirations; an uncultured person; সংকীর্ণমনাঃ ব্যক্তি, অনুদারচিত্তব্যক্তি; অশিক্ষিত লোক। 3. (*Facet.*) One of a class likened to an enemy *e. g.* a bailiff, critic, etc.; (রঙ্গচ্ছলে) নাজীরের প্যাদা, সমালোচক প্রভৃতি। 4. (*German University*) An outsider; (জার্ম্মেণির বিশ্ববিদ্যালয়ে) বাহিরের লোক। *Adj.* 1. Relating to Philistines; প্রাচীন ফিলিষ্টিয়া দেশের লোকসংক্রান্ত। 2. Uncultured; prosaic; অসভ্য; গদ্যময়। **–tin-ism,** *n.* The opinions, aims and habits of modern Philistines; সংকীর্ণচিত্ততা, অনুদারতা।

phil-ŏ-bib'-lic, *adj.* Fond of books; গ্রন্থানুরাগী।

Phil-ŏc-te'-tēs, *n.* The armour-bearer of Hercules; হার্কুলিজের বর্ম্মবাহক। হার্কুলিজ ইহাকে তদীয় ধনু ও শর প্রদান করেন। Paris ইহারই হস্তে নিহত হয়।

phi-lŏg'-ў-nist, *n.* A lover or admirer of women; অঙ্গনানুরাগী, স্ত্রীপ্রিয়, স্ত্রৈণ। **–ny,** *n.* Love of women; স্ত্রৈণতা, অঙ্গনানুরাগ।

phi-lŏl'-ŏ-ġў, *n.* 1. The science of language; ভাষাতত্ত্ব, ভাষাবিজ্ঞান, নিরুক্ত, শব্দব্যুৎপত্তিশাস্ত্র (হিঃ কোঃ), ভাষাব্যুৎপত্তিশাস্ত্র (ঐ), শব্দশাসনবিদ্যা, (কেণ্ডিঃ)। 2. (*Rare*) Love of learning or literature; (কচিদ্‌-ব্যবহৃত) সাহিত্যানুরাগ, বিদ্যানুরাগ। **–ger –gist, Phil-o-lo'-gi-an,** *ns.* **–gize,** *v. i.* To study or make critical comments on, language; ভাষা অধ্যয়ন করা, ভাষার উপর সমালোচনা-মূলক মন্তব্য করা। **Phil-o-log'-i-cal,** *adj.* **Phil-o-log'-i-cal-ly,** *adv.*

phil'-ŏ-măth, *n.* A lover of learning, esp. of mathematics; বিদ্যানুরাগী বিশেষতঃ গণিতানুরাগী।

phil'-ŏ-mĕl, –mē'-lă, *ns.* (*Poet.*) The nightingale; (কবিতায়) বুলবুল পাখী।

Phil-ŏ-mē'-lă, *n.* See TEREUS.

phil-ŏ-poe'-nă (-pē-), *n.* See PHILIPPINA.

phil-ŏ-prŏ-ġĕn'-i-tive (-tiv), *adj.* Loving one's offsprieg; অপত্যানুরাগী। **–ness,** *n.* Affection towards one's offspring; অপত্যস্নেহ, অপত্যপ্রীতি।

phi-lŏs'-ŏ-phêr, *n.* 1. One versed in, or devoted to, philosophy; a lover of wisdom; দার্শনিক, দর্শনবেত্তা; তাত্ত্বিক, তত্ত্ববিচারক (হিঃ কোঃ), তত্ত্ববিদ। 2. One who conforms his life to the principles of philosophy; one who meets all vicissitudes with calmness; যে ব্যক্তি দার্শনিকতত্ত্বানুযায়ী জীবন নিয়মন করে; স্থিতপ্রজ্ঞ ব্যক্তি। **Natural** or **moral philosohher**—পদার্থশাস্ত্রবিৎ, নীতিশাস্ত্রবিৎ। **Philosophers' stone**—স্পর্শমণি, পরশমণি, দিব্যমণি, পরশপাথর, রসেন্দ্র।

phil-ŏ-sŏph'-ic, –i-căl, *adjs.* Relating to philosophy; skilled in, or devoted to, philosophy; rational; calm; wise; temperate; দর্শনসম্বন্ধীয়, তত্ত্ববিচারাত্মক; দার্শনিক, দর্শনশাস্ত্রবিৎ, দর্শনশাস্ত্রানুরাগী; যুক্তিবাদী; নির্বিকার; জ্ঞানী; মিতাচারী। **–i-cal-ly,** *adv.*

phi-lŏs'-ŏ-phism, *n.* Spurious philosophizing; sham philosophy; কৃত্রিমযুক্তিপ্রদর্শন; দর্শনাভাস। **–phist,** *n.*

phi-lŏs'-ŏ-phīze, *v. i.* & *t.* To reason like a philosopher; to form philosophical theories; to moralize; দার্শনিকের মত বিচার করা; দার্শনিক সিদ্ধান্ত করা; নৈতিক উপদেশ দেওয়া। *Verb t.* To make philosophic; দার্শনিক করা।

phi-lŏs'-ŏ-phў, *n.* 1. The love of wisdom; the science trying to account for the phenomena of the universe; a philosophical system or theory; জ্ঞানানুরাগ; দর্শনশাস্ত্র, তত্ত্ববিজ্ঞান, প্রজ্ঞানবিজ্ঞান, জ্ঞানবিজ্ঞান, তত্ত্বশাস্ত্র, অধ্যাত্মবিদ্যা (হিঃ কোঃ), তত্ত্ববিচার (ঐ); দর্শন, দার্শনিক সিদ্ধান্ত। 2. A system for conduct of life; জীবনযাত্রার পদ্ধতি বা ব্যবস্থা। 3. Calmness of temper and judgment; equanimity; as, to meet misfortune with *philosophy*; নির্বিকার ভাব, স্থিরচিত্ততা, স্থিতপ্রজ্ঞতা; ধীরতা। **Logical philosophy**—তর্কমূলক দর্শন। **Natural philosophy**—পদার্থবিদ্যা, প্রাকৃতিক দর্শন। **Moral philosophy**—নীতিবিজ্ঞান।

phil'-têr, –tre (-têr), *ns.* A charm or spell to excite love; বশীকরণের ঔষধ, বশীকরণচূর্ণ।

phiz, *n.* (*Colloq.*) The face; facial expression; (চলিতভাষায়) মুখ; মুখের ভাব।

phle-bī'-tis, *n.* Inflammation of a vein; শিরাপ্রদাহ। **–bit'-ic,** *adj.*

phleb'-ŏ-līte, –lith, *ns.* A calcareous concretion found in a vein; শিরায় প্রাপ্ত একপ্রকার চূর্ণ প্রস্তরবৎ পদার্থ। **–lit'(h)-ic,** *adj.*

phlĕ-bŏt'-ŏ-mў, *n.* Blood-letting as a medical operation; শিরাচ্ছেদ, রক্তমোক্ষণ, শিরাবেধ, শিরামোক্ষণ। **–mist,** *n.* **–mize,** *v. i.* & *t.* To let blood by opening a vein; শিরাচ্ছেদনপূর্ব্বক রক্তমোক্ষণ করা। (*Verb t.*) To let blood from; রক্তমোক্ষণ করা।

phlegm (flĕm), *n.* 1. The viscid matter secreted in the respiratory and digestive passages; কফ, শ্লেষ্মা, খেট (চঃ)। **2.** Sluggishness; indifference; coldness; as, they write with *phlegm*; জড়তা, জাড্য, আলস্য, ঢিলামি; ঔদাস্য; অনুরাগশূন্যতা। **3.** (*Formerly*) One of the four humours of which the ancients supposed the blood to be composed; (পূর্ব্বে) কফ। **Phleg-mat′-ic,** *adj.* **1.** Abounding in phlegm; as, a *phlegmatic* constitution; কফপ্রধান। **2.** Dull; sluggish; as, a *phlegmatic* person; জড়; কর্ম্মকুণ্ঠ, অলস। **Phleg-mat′-i-cal-ly,** *adv.* **Phlegm′-y,** *adj.* **1.** Of, the nature of, or characterized by, phlegm; mucous; কফাত্মক, শ্লেষ্মাত্মক; শ্লেষ্মল, শ্লৈষ্মিক। **2.** Same as PHLEGMATIC.

phlĕg′-mă-gogue (-gŏg), *adj.* A medicine expelling phlegm; কফহর (ঠাকুর)।

phlĕg-mă′-si-ă —ăl-bă-dŏ′-lĕns, *ns.* প্রসবান্তে জঙ্ঘার শ্বেতবর্ণ স্ফীতি, সূতিকাস্তম্ভ (হঃ চঃ)।

phlĕg′-mŏn, *n.* An inflammatory tumour; a boil; প্রদাহজনক অর্ব্বুদ; স্ফোটক।

phlŏ′-ĕm, *n.* (*Bot.*) Bast tissue; বল্কক (সাঃ পঃ)।

phlŏ-gis′-tic, *adj.* **1.** Relating to the phlogiston; ফ্লুজিষ্টনসম্বন্ধীয়। **2.** (*Med.*) Inflammatory; প্রদাহজনক, সন্তাপক।

phlŏ-gis′-tŏn, *n.* The hypothetical principle of inflammability formerly regarded as a chemical element; দাহ্যতার কল্পিত মূলবস্তু, ফ্লুজিষ্টন (হিঃ কোঃ)।

phlŏ-gŏ′-sis, *n.* (*Med.*) Inflammation of the external parts of the body; প্রদাহ (হঃ চঃ)।

phlŏr′-i-zin, *n.* (*Chem.*) A substance extracted from the root-bark of the apple, pear, etc.; সেওফল, নাসপাতি প্রভৃতির মূলের বল্কল হইতে নিষ্কর্ষিত পদার্থ বিশেষ।

phlŏx, *n.* A well-known garden-plant; উদ্যানরোপিত গুল্মবিশেষ।

Phoe′-bē (fē-), *n.* The Moon-god; চন্দ্রমা।

Phoe′-bŭs (fē-), *n.* The Sun-god; সূর্য্য।

phoe-ni′-ci-ăn (fē-nī-shī-), *adj.* & *n.* Of, or pertaining to, Phœnicia, an ancient country on the coast of Syria; সিরীয়ার উপকূলবর্ত্তী ফিনিসিয়া সম্বন্ধীয়। ***Noun.*** A native of Phœnicia; a Cartheginian; ফিনিসিয়ার অধিবাসী; কার্থেজের অধিবাসী।

Phœnicopterus roseus—কানঠুঁটা (বেলঃ)।

phoe′-nix (fē-), **phē-,** *ns.* **1.** (*Myth.*) A fabulous bird of Arabia said to have lived 500 years, and after burning itself on a funeral pile, to have risen from its own ashes; আরবদেশের পৌরাণিক পক্ষি-বিশেষ। এই পক্ষী পাঁচ ছয় শত বৎসর মরুভূমিতে বাস করিয়া স্বরচিত চিতানলে ভস্মীভূত হয়, পরে নবদেহ প্রাপ্ত হইয়া চিতাভস্ম হইতে পুনরুত্থিত হয়, অমরবিহগ। **2.** A paragon; অদ্বিতীয় বস্তু, অপ্রতিম বস্তু। **3.** (*Astron., cap.*) A southern constellation; (জ্যোতির্বিজ্ঞান) দক্ষিণ গগনের তারাপ্রকোষ্ঠ-বিশেষ।

phŏ′-nāte, *v. i.* To utter vocal sounds; উচ্চারণ করা। **—na′-tion,** *n.* The act of uttering vocal sounds; স্বরোচ্চারণ। **—na-to-ry,** *adj.*

phŏ-nau′-tŏ-grăph (-nä-), *n.* An instrument for automatically recording sounds; স্বয়ংবহ ধ্বনিযন্ত্র।

phōne, *n., v. i.* & *t.* (*Colloq.*) A telephone; (চলিত ভাষায়) টেলিফোঁ, দূরশ্রবণ যন্ত্র। ***Verb i. & t.*** To telephone; টেলিফোঁ করা, দূরশ্রবণ যন্ত্র সহযোগে সংবাদ প্রেরণ করা।

phōne, *n.* A simple vowel or consonant sound; অবিমিশ্র স্বর বা ব্যঞ্জন-ধ্বনি।

phŏ-nĕn′-dŏ-scōpe, *n.* A form of stethoscope for intensifying ausculatory sounds; একপ্রকার আকর্ণণযন্ত্র যাহার সাহায্যে হৃৎপিণ্ড প্রভৃতির ধ্বনি ঘনীভূত হয়, ধ্বনিবর্দ্ধক।

phŏ-nĕt′-ic, *adj.* & *n.* **1.** Of, or pertaining to, the voice; স্বরসম্বন্ধীয়। **2.** Representing vocal sounds; using always the same letter for the same sound as a system of spelling; মানবকণ্ঠোচ্চারিত ধ্বনি-প্রদর্শক; একই ধ্বনিসূচনার্থ নিত্য একই অক্ষর ব্যবহারকারী, ধ্বনিসংবাদী। ***Noun.*** **1.** (*Pl.*) The doctrine or science of sounds especially of the human voice; phonology; স্বরবিজ্ঞান; ধ্বনিবিজ্ঞান, উচ্চারণ-শাস্ত্র (হিঃ কোঃ)। **—i-cal-ly,** *adv.* **—i-cism, —i-cist,** *ns.* **—i-cize,** *v. t.* **—ne-ti′-cian,** *n.* **Phonetic law**—ভাষাতত্ত্বের নিয়ম।

phŏ′-nĕ-tist, *n.* **1.** Same as PHONETICIST. **2.** One who advocates phonetic spelling; ধ্বনি-সংবাদিনী বর্ণবিন্যাস রীতির পক্ষপাতী ব্যক্তি।

phŏn′-ic, *adj.* & *n.* **1.** Of, or pertaining to, sound; acoustic; ধ্বনিসম্বন্ধীয়; ধ্বনিবিজ্ঞানসংক্রান্ত। **2.** Of, or relating to, a vocal sound; মানবকণ্ঠোচ্চারিত ধ্বনিসম্বন্ধীয়। ***Noun.*** (*Pl.*) The science of sound; স্বরশাস্ত্র (হিঃ কোঃ), ধ্বনিশাস্ত্র (ঐ)।

phŏ′-nŏ-grăm, *n.* **1.** A character representing a speech or sound, esp. in Pitman's phonography; ধ্বনি বা শব্দসংবাদী বর্ণ—বিশেষতঃ পিটম্যান প্রবর্ত্তিত সাঙ্কেতিক লিপিবিদ্যায়। **2.** A record of sounds made by a phonograph; ধ্বনিলিখন যন্ত্রদ্বারা লিখিত ধ্বনিমালা।

phŏ′-nŏ-grăph, *n.* & *v. t.* **1.** (*Rare*) Same as PHONOGRAM. **2.** An instrument for automatically recording and reproducing sounds; মানব কণ্ঠোত্থিত বা অন্যপ্রকার ধ্বনির

স্পন্দনসমূহ অঙ্কনার্থ এবং পরে ঐ সকল অঙ্কনের সাহায্যে শব্দসমূহ পুনঃধ্বনিত করার জন্য স্বয়ংচল যন্ত্রবিশেষ, ধ্বনিযন্ত্র, শব্দযন্ত্র। ফনোগ্রাফ (হিঃ কোঃ), ধ্বনিলিখনযন্ত্র। [১৮৭৭ খৃঃ অব্দে আমেরিকার বিশ্ববিখ্যাত বৈজ্ঞানিক Edison শব্দযন্ত্র উদ্ভাবন করেন। Tainter এবং Bell কর্ত্তৃক পরবর্ত্তীকালে এই যন্ত্রের অনেক উৎকর্ষ সাধিত হয়।

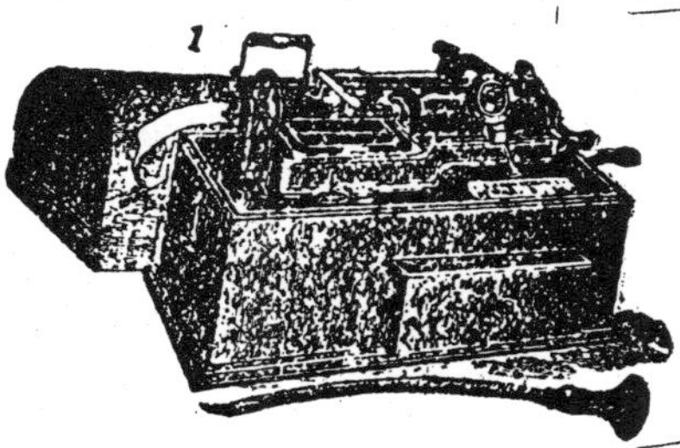

Phonograph.

মানবকণ্ঠোত্থিত বা অন্যবিধ ধ্বনির স্পন্দন মুখসংযোগ নলের ভিতর দিয়া একটী ধাতুর পাতে নীত হয়। ঐ ধাতুর পাতে একখণ্ড সূক্ষ্মাগ্র ইস্পাত (আধুনিক যন্ত্রে ইন্দ্রনীলমণিখণ্ড) সম্বদ্ধ থাকে। যন্ত্রের টীনের পাতে মোড়া-পিত্তলের চুঙ্গি (আধুনিক যন্ত্রে কঠিন মোম দ্বারা আচ্ছাদিত চুঙ্গি) ঘুরাইলে ঐ ধাতুর পাতে নীত স্পন্দনসমূহের তারতম্যানুসারে প্রাগুক্ত সূক্ষ্মাগ্র ইস্পাতখণ্ড বা ইন্দ্রনীলমণিখণ্ড দ্বারা চুঙ্গির টীন বা মোমের আবরণের উপর অল্প বা অধিক গভীর খাঁজ অঙ্কিত হয়। পরে ঐ চুঙ্গি পুনরায় ঘুরাইলে ঐ খাঁজ সকল হইতে পূর্ব্বানুরূপ স্পন্দন সমূহ ধাতুর পাতে সঞ্চারিত হইয়া পূর্ব্ব ধ্বনি পুনরুৎপাদিত হয়।] ***Verb t.*** To record by the phonograph; শব্দযন্ত্র দ্বারা লিপিবদ্ধ করা।

phō-nŏg'-rȧ-phȳ, *n.* **1.** A system of shorthand writing invented by Isaac Pitman; রেখাক্ষর বর্ণমালা, সাঙ্কেতিক লিপিবিদ্যা। **2.** Automatic recording of sounds as by the phonograph; শব্দযন্ত্র সাহায্যে স্বয়ংক্রিয়ভাবে শব্দ অঙ্কন। **—no-graph'-ic,** *adj.* **—no-graph'-i-cal-ly,** *adv.* **—pher, —phist,** *ns.* A shorthand writer; সাঙ্কেতিক লিপিলেখক।

phō'-nō-līte, *n.* Clinkstone; এক-প্রকার প্রস্তর।

phō-nŏl'-ō-ġȳ, *n.* **1.** The science of the sounds of the human voice; স্বরবিজ্ঞান, ধ্বনিবিজ্ঞান। **2.** The system of sounds, in a language; স্বর-পদ্ধতি। **—gist,** *n.* **—no-log'-ic, —no-log'-i-cal,** *adjs.* **—no-log'-i-cal-ly,** *adv.*

phō-nŏm'-ĕ-têr, *n.* An instrument for numbering the vibrations of sounds; শব্দ-স্পন্দনগণক যন্ত্র।

phō'-nō-phōre, *n.* An apparatus for transmitting telephone messages along the telegraph wire without interfering with the current transmitting telegraph messages; তাড়িত বার্ত্তাবহের বার্ত্তাবাহী-প্রবাহের কোনরূপ বাধা না জন্মাইয়া ঐ যন্ত্রের তারে দূরশ্রবণ যন্ত্রের সংবাদ প্রেরণের জন্য যন্ত্রবিশেষ, দূরতাড়িত-শ্রবণযন্ত্র।

phō'-nō-scōpe, *n.* **1.** A devise for testing the quality of musical strings; বাদ্যযন্ত্রের তন্ত্রীর গুণ পরীক্ষার জন্য যন্ত্রবিশেষ, তন্ত্রীগুণ-দর্শক। **2.** An instrument for representing sound-vibrations in a visible form; ধ্বনিস্পন্দন প্রদর্শনের জন্য যন্ত্রবিশেষ, ধ্বনিস্পন্দনদর্শক।

phō'-nō-tȳpe, *n.* A type or character, used in phonotypy; রেখাক্ষর বর্ণমালার জন্য হরফ বা অক্ষর। **—typ'-ic, —typ'-i-cal,** *adjs.* **—typ'-ist,** *n.* **—typ-y,** *n.* The art of representing sounds by distinct characters or types; বিশিষ্ট বর্ণ বা মুদ্রাক্ষর দ্বারা ধ্বনিপ্রদর্শনের কৌশল।

phō-rŏn'-ō-mȳ, *n.* The theory of motion as deducible from *a priori* conceptions—A Kantian term; গতিবিষয়ক ধারণা সহজাত জ্ঞান হইতে উপলভ্য—এইরূপ মতবাদ, গতিকল্প (হিঃ কোঃ), গতিসূত্র (ঐ)।

phŏs'-phāte, *n.* **1.** A salt of phosphoric acid; চূণ, সোডা, প্রভৃতির সহিত ফসফরিক এসিডের সংযোগে উৎপন্ন যৌগিক পদার্থ, ফুস্ফুরক দ্রাবকের লবণ। **2.** (*Commr.*) Any phosphatic material used for fertilizers; ভূমির উর্ব্বরতা বৃদ্ধির জন্য ব্যবহৃত ফুস্ফুরক জাতীয় যে কোন দ্রব্য। **—phat'-ic,** *adj.*

phŏs-phȧ-tū'-ri-ȧ, *n.* (*Med.*) Excessive discharge of phosphate in the urine; সিকতামেহ (সাঃ পঃ)।

phŏs'-phene (-fēn), *n.* The luminous image produced by pressing the eye-ball with the finger; অঙ্গুলী দ্বারা অক্ষিগোলকে চাপ দিলে যে তেজোময় প্রতিবিম্ব উপজাত হয়।

phŏs'-phīde, *n.* A combination of phosphorus with another element; ফুস্ফুরকের সহিত অপর কোন পদার্থের সংযোগে জাত দ্রব্য।

phŏs'-phīte, *n.* A salt of phosphorus acid; ফুস্ফুরদ্রাবকের লবণ।

phŏs'-phŏr-āte, *v. t.* To combine or impregnate with phosphorus; ফুস্ফুরকসম্পূরিত করা।

phŏs-phŏr-esce' (-ĕs), *v. i.* To emit a phosphoric light; ফুস্ফুরক প্রভা নির্গত করা। **—es'-cence,** *n.* **1.** The property of emitting light without sensible heat; অনুভব-উত্তাপ বিনা আলোক বিকিরণের শক্তি, ফুস্ফুরকতা, প্রস্ফুরশীলতা। **2.** A phosphoric light; ফুস্ফুরক জ্যোতিঃ, স্ফুরজ্যোতিঃ। **—es'-cent,** *adj.* Luminous without sensible heat; স্ফুরপ্রকাশিত (হিঃ কোঃ)।

phŏs'-phŏr-īte, *n.* A non-crystallized variety of phosphate of lime; একজাতীয় চূর্ণ প্রস্তর।

phŏs-phŏr-ō-ġĕn'-ic, *adj.* Generating phosphorescence; ফুস্ফুরক-জনক।

phŏs'-phŏr-ō-grăph, *n.* An evanescent picture obtained by rays acting on a phosphorescent surface; ফুস্ফুরকত্রক্ষিত বস্তুর উপর আলোকরশ্মির ক্রিয়াদ্বারা যে অচিরস্থায়ী চিত্র উপজাত হয়, ফুস্ফুরকচিত্র। **—ic,** *adj.* **—og'-ra-phy,** *n.*

phŏs'-phŏr-ō-scōpe, *n.* **1.** An instrument for measuring the duration of phosphorescence in different substances; বিভিন্ন পদার্থে ফুস্ফুরকজ্যোতির স্থায়িত্বকাল পরিমাপক যন্ত্রবিশেষ। **2.** A toy containing various phosphorescent substances glowing with different coloured light; নানাবর্ণের প্রভাভাস্বর বিভিন্ন প্রকার ফুস্ফুর পদার্থপূর্ণ ক্রীড়নকবিশেষ।

phŏs'-phŏr-ŭs, *n.* A yellowish substance like wax, inflammable and giving out light in the dark; অন্ধকারে আলোকবিকিরণশীল মধুথবৎ পীতাভ দাহ্য মূল পদার্থবিশেষ, ফুস্ফুরক, প্রস্ফুরক, স্ফুরক (সাঃ পঃ)। **—ism,** *n.* Poisoning by phosphorus; প্রস্ফুরক দ্বারা বিষক্রিয়া উৎপাদন। **—phor'-ic, —ous,** *adjs.* **Phosphoric acid**—স্ফুরকদ্রাবক (সাঃ পঃ), স্ফুরকাম্ল। **Phosphorus acid** — স্ফুরদ্রাবক (সাঃ পঃ)। **Phosphorus necrosis**—(*Colloq. phossy jaw*); ফুস্ফুরকের ধূমজনিত হনস্থির পচনরোগ। **Phosphorus oxide**—দগ্ধস্ফুরক (সাঃ পঃ)।

phŏs'-phŭ-rĕt-(t)ed (-ĕd), *adj.* Impregnated or combined with phosphorus; ফুস্ফুরকমিশ্রিত, ফুস্ফুরকসম্পূরিত।

phŏs'-sy (-ĭ), See PHOSPHORUS NECROSIS under PHOSPHORUS.

phō'-tics, *n.* The scince of light; আলোকবিজ্ঞান, প্রকাশবিজ্ঞান (হিঃ কোঃ)।

phō'-tism, *n.* A hallucinatory sensation or vision of light; মায়িক আলোকানুভব বা দর্শন।

phō'-tō, *n.* & *v. t.* Same as PHOTOGRAPH. **Photo-chemistry**—আলোকরসায়ন (হিঃ কোঃ)। **Photodrome** — প্রকাশ পরিচালক (হিঃ কোঃ)। **Photo-electric**—তড়িৎ চিত্রসম্বন্ধী (হিঃ কোঃ)। **Photo-galvanography**—তড়িৎ আলোক চিত্রণবিদ্যা (হিঃ কোঃ)। **Photo-heliograph** — রবিচিত্রক দূরদর্শক (হিঃ কোঃ)। **Photo-magnetism**—ফটোচুম্বকত্ব (ঐ)। **Photo-meter**—প্রকাশতীব্রতামাপক (ঐ)। **Photo-micrograph**—সূক্ষ্মচিত্রণ (ঐ)।

phō'-tō-chrō-mȳ, *n.* The art of reproducing colours by photograph; আলোকচিত্রের সাহায্যে স্বাভাবিক বর্ণরাজি পুনরুৎপাদনের কলা, রঞ্জিতআলোকচিত্রণ (হিঃ কোঃ)।

phō'-tō-gĕn, *n.* A kind of paraffin oil; একপ্রকার কেরোসিন তৈল।

phō-tō-gĕn'-ic, *adj.* Producing or giving out light; আলোকজনক, আলোকপ্রদ।

phō-tŏg'-lȳ-phȳ, *n.* The art of engraving by the action of light; আলোকের ক্রিয়াদ্বারা ক্ষোদনের শিল্প। **Pho'-to-glyph,** *n.* A plate engraved by this process; উক্তরূপ উপায়ে ক্ষোদিতফলক।

phō'-tō-grăph, *n.*, *v. t.* & *i.* A picture obtained by photography; আলোকলেখ্য, ছায়াচিত্র (হিঃ কোঃ), ফটোগ্রাফ (ঐ), আলোকচিত্র, জ্যোতিশ্চিত্র। ***Verb t.*** To produce a picture of by photographic means; as, to *photograph* a group; আলোকচিত্র গ্রহণ করা, আলোকচিত্র তোলা। ***Verb i.*** To take photographs; to admit of being photographed; আলোকচিত্র গ্রহণ করা; আলোকচিত্র গ্রহণসহ হওয়া। **—graph'-ic,** *adj.* **—graph'-i-cal-ly,** *adv.* **—tog'-ra-pher,** *n.* One who takes pictures by photography; আলোকলেখ্যকার, আলোকচিত্রগ্রহণকারী। **—tog'-ra-phy,** *n.* The art of producing pictures by the action of light on chemically prepared surfaces; আলোকচিত্র কলা, ছায়াচিত্রণ (হিঃ কোঃ), আলোক-চিত্রণ (ঐ)। **I always photograph badly**—ফটোগ্রাফে আমার চেহারা কোন সময়ই ভাল দেখায় না।

phō-tō-gră-vūre', *n.* & *v. t.* A process by which an engraving is produced on a metal plate by light acting on a sensitive surface; a picture produced by this process; আলোকের রাসায়নিক ক্রিয়াদ্বারা ধাতুফলকোপরি আলোকোৎকীর্ণ ফলক হইতে মুদ্রিত চিত্র উৎপাদনের প্রণালীবিশেষ, আলোকক্ষোদন; আলোকোৎকীর্ণ আলেখ্য। ***Verb t.*** To produce in this way; ঐপ্রকারে উৎপাদন করা।

phō-tŏl'-ō-ḡȳ, *n.* The science of light; আলোকশাস্ত্র (হিঃ কোঃ)।

phō-tŏm'-ē-têr, *n.* An apparatus for measuring the intensity of light; আলোকের প্রখরতা মাপনের জন্য যন্ত্রবিশেষ, প্রভামানযন্ত্র, প্রকাশতীব্রতামাপক (হিঃ কোঃ)। **—to-met'-ric,** *adj.* **—try,** *n.* The science of the measurement of the intensity of light; প্রভামিতি, জ্যোতির্মিতিশাস্ত্র (হিঃ কোঃ)।

phō-tō-phō'-bĭ-ă, *n.* (*Path.*) A morbid dread of light; (নিদানশাস্ত্র) আলোকাতঙ্ক।

phō'-tō-phōne, *n.* An instrument for communicating sounds by light; আলোকের সাহায্যে শব্দ প্রেরণের যন্ত্রবিশেষ, প্রকাশনাদকারক (হিঃ কোঃ)।

phō-tŏp'-sĭ-ă, *n.* (*Med.*) An affection of the eye presenting luminous rays; (ভৈষজ্য-শাস্ত্র) একপ্রকার চক্ষুরোগ—যাহাতে অস্বাভাবিক আলোকদর্শন হয়।

phō'-tō-scōpe, *n.* A device for observing light or luminous effects; প্রকাশপ্রদর্শক (হিঃ কোঃ)।

phō'-tō-sphere (-sfēr), *n.* A sphere of light, esp. the luminous envelope of the sun; আলোকমণ্ডল, বিশেষতঃ রবির চতুর্দিকস্থ দীপ্তিমণ্ডল, তেজোমণ্ডল (সাঃ পঃ), দীপ্তিকোষ (ঐ), প্রকাশমণ্ডল (হিঃ কোঃ)। **—spher'-ic,** *adj.*

phō′-tō-tȳpe, *n.* A plate or block with a printing surface obtained from a photograph ; a picture etc. printed from this ; আলোকচিত্র হইতে প্রাপ্ত মুদ্রণোপযোগী উপরিভাগ-সমন্বিত ক্ষোদিত ধাতু বা কাষ্ঠফলক ; ঐরূপ ফলক হইতে গৃহীত চিত্র, ছায়াচিত্রমুদ্রণ (হিঃ কোঃ) ।

phō′-tō-zin-cŏg′-ra-phȳ (-zing-), *n.* The process of photographically producing designs on a zinc plate; দস্তাফলকের উপর আলোকচিত্রের সাহায্যে চিত্রাদি উৎপাদনের প্রণালী, যশদআলোকচিত্রণ (হিঃ কোঃ)।

phrāse, *n.* & *v. t.* 1. A brief expression or part of a sentence ; as, an adverbial *phrase* ; পদসমষ্টি, বাক্যাংশ। 2. An idiom ; a short pithy expression ; রীতিসিদ্ধ প্রয়োগ, সংক্ষিপ্ত অথচ সারবান বাক্য। 3. A mode of speech ; diction ; as, in simple *phrase* ; বাক্যপদ্ধতি, বাগ্‌ধারা ; শব্দপ্রয়োগপদ্ধতি। 4. (*Pl.*) Insincere or unmeaning talk ; as, we have had enough of *phrases* ; কপট অথবা অর্থহীন আলাপ। *Verb t.* To express in words ; as, thus he *phrased* it ; শব্দদ্বারা প্রকাশ করা। **Phrase-book**—যে পুস্তকে অর্থবোধক পদসমষ্টি ও তাহাদের ব্যাখ্যা থাকে। **Phrase monger**—শ্রুতিমধুরবচনরচনা-নিপুণ ব্যক্তি ।

phra′-ŝē-ō-grăm, *n.* A written symbol representing a phrase esp. in shorthand ; অর্থবোধক পদসমষ্টিসূচক রেখাক্ষর বর্ণমালার অক্ষরসমূহ।

phra′-ŝē-ō-grăph, *n.* A phrase having a phraseogram ; যে অর্থবোধক পদসমষ্টি রেক্ষাক্ষর বর্ণমালার কতিপয় অক্ষর সংযোগে প্রদর্শিত হয়।

phra-ŝē-ŏl′-ō-ġȳ, *n.* Arrangement of words and phrases ; manner of expression ; style ; শব্দ ও পদসমষ্টির বিন্যাস ; বাগ্‌বিন্যাস-পদ্ধতি, বাক্যবন্ধ, বাক্যরচনা ; রচনারীতি। **—o-log′-i-cal**, *adj.* **—o-log′-i-cal-ly**, *adv.*

phra′-trȳ, *n.* 1. A subdivision of the phyle or tribe among the Athenians ; (গ্রীক ইতিহাস) প্রাচীন এথেন্সবাসিগণের মধ্যে গোষ্ঠিবিশেষ। 2. A tribal division among the primitive races ; প্রাচীন জাতি-সমূহের বিভাগবিশেষ।

phrĕ-nŏt′-ic, *adj.* 1. Erratic or frantic, as, an act ; উচ্ছৃঙ্খল, উন্মাদবৎ। 2. Fanatic ; উন্মত্ত।

phrĕn′-ic, *adj.* (*Anat.*) Of, or relating to, the diaphragm ; (শারীরসংস্থানবিদ্যা) বক্ষোদরব্যবধায়ক পেশীসম্বন্ধীয়।

phrĕ-nŏl′-ō-ġȳ, *n.* The science of the human mind as connected with the supposed organs of its action in the brain and as developed by the external undulations of the cranium ; যে বিদ্যাদ্বারা করোটীর বিভিন্ন অংশের উচ্চতা ও অবনতি হইতে মানবের চরিত্র, প্রবৃত্তি ও মানসিক অবস্থাসম্বন্ধে জ্ঞান লাভ করা যায় বলিয়া অনুমিত হয়, মস্তিষ্ক-বিদ্যা, কপাললক্ষণ-বিদ্যা, কপালসামুদ্রিক, মস্তিষ্ক-সামুদ্রিক (হিঃ কোঃ)। **—gist**, *n.* **—no-log′-i-cal**, *adj.* **—no-log′-i-cal-ly**, *adv.*

phrŏn′-tis-têr-ȳ, *n.* (*Facet.*) A place for thinking or study ; hence, an educational institution ; (রঙ্গচ্ছলে) শিক্ষাগার, চিন্তাগার ; শিক্ষা-প্রতিষ্ঠান।

Phrȳġ′-i-ăn, *adj.* Of, or pertaining to, Phrygia, an ancient country of Asia Minor ; এসিয়া মাইনরের অন্তঃপাতী প্রাচীন ফ্রিজিয়াদেশীয়। **Phrygian cap**—এক প্রকার মোচাকার টুপি। **Phrygian mode** — প্রাচীন গ্রীসের সামরিক বাদ্য-বিশেষ।

phthi′-sis (thī-), *n.* Pulmonary consumption ; ক্ষয়রোগ, ক্ষয়কাস, যক্ষ্মা, শোষ (সুশ্রুঃ কুঞ্জ)। **Galloping phthisis**—রাজযক্ষ্মা।

phȳ-lăc′-têr-ȳ, *n.* 1. Among the Jews, a slip of parchment inscribed with certain passages of the scriptures worn on the left arm or forehead ; প্রাচীন ইহুদীগণ কর্তৃক ব্যবহৃত তাবিজবিশেষ। 2. An amulet ; কবচ, মাদুলী। 3. A religious observance, usually an ostentatious one ; পূজানুষ্ঠান, সমারোহপূর্ণ পূজা।

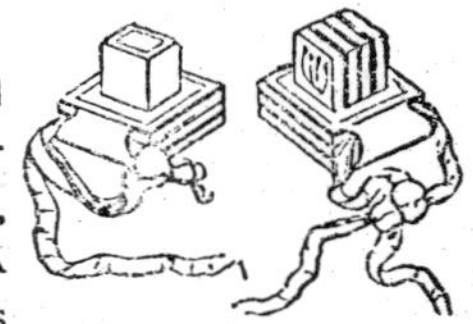

Phylacteries.

phȳ′-lē, *n.* One of the divisions into which the ancient Athenians were divided ; প্রাচীন এথেন্স বাসিগণের বিভাগ-বিশেষ।

phȳ-lĕt′-ic, *adj.* (*Biol.*) Pertaining to a phylum or race ; জাতিসম্বন্ধীয়, আবান্তর যোনিসম্বন্ধীয় (হিঃ কোঃ)।

phȳl-loph′-ă-găn(-ŏf-), *n.* An animal that feeds on leaves of trees ; পত্রভোজী জন্তু। **—gous**, *adj.* Leaf eating ; পত্রভোজী, পর্ণভোজী, পত্রাশ।

phȳl′-lō-pŏd, *adj.* & *n.* Having foliaceous feet ; পত্রপদী (সাঃ পঃ)। *Noun.* A leaf-footed crustucean ; পত্রপদী খোলকী জন্তু।

phȳl′-lo-stōme (-ŏ-), *n.* A leaf-nosed bat ; পত্রনাস বাদুড়।

phȳl-lo-tăx′-is (-ŏ-), *n.* The arrangement of leaves on the stem of a plant ; বৃক্ষকাণ্ডে পত্রবিন্যাস, পর্ণসন্নিবেশ।

phȳl-lox-ē′-ră (-ŏx-), *n.* An insect which infests the leaves and roots of the oak, vine, etc. ; ওক, আঙ্গুর, প্রভৃতি গাছের মূলে ও পত্রে প্রাপ্ত কীটবিশেষ।

phȳ-lō-ġĕn′-ē-sis, *n.* The racial evolution or history of an animal or plant type ; কোন বিশেষ জাতীয় জন্তু বা বৃক্ষের জাতিগত ক্রমবিকাশ বা ইতিহাস, জাতিজনি (হিঃ কোঃ)। **—ge-net′-ic**, *adj.* **—ge-net′-i-cal-ly**, *adv.*

phȳ-lŏġ′-ē-nȳ, *n.* Same as PHYLOGENESIS. **—lo-gen′-ic**, *adj.*

phȳ'-lŭm (*Biol, pl.* -LA) A primary division of the animal or vegetable kingdom ; প্রাণী বা উদ্ভিজ্জ জগতের প্রাথমিক বিভাগ, দেশ (সাঃ পঃ), আবান্তর যোনি (হিঃ কোঃ)।

phȳ-mō'-sis, phi-, *ns.* (*Path.*) A condition of the prepuce in which it cannot be drawn back so as to uncover the glans penis ; পুরুষাঙ্গের মুণ্ডাবরক ত্বকের রোগবিশেষ—যাহাতে উহা সঙ্কুচিত করিয়া লিঙ্গমুণ্ড অনাবৃত করিতে পারা যায় না, মুদা, পরিবর্ত্তিকা (সাঃ পঃ), নিরুদ্ধ প্রকাশ (সুশ্রুঃ কুঞ্জ)।

Physalia.

phȳ'-să'-li-ă, *n.* A genus of hydrozoa; একজাতীয় সামুদ্রিক জীব।

Physalis somnifera— অশ্বগন্ধা।

phȳs'-ic, *n.* & *v. t.* **1.** The science or art of healing ; the medical profession ; চিকিৎসাশাস্ত্র ; চিকিৎসা ব্যবসায়। **2.** (*Colloq.*) Medicine ; as, a dose of *physic* ; (চলিত ভাষায়) ঔষধ, ভেষজ। **3.** (*Pl.*) A science of the phenomena presented by bodies, treating of matter, force and motion ; পদার্থবিজ্ঞান, পদার্থশাস্ত্র, পদার্থবিদ্যা, ভৌতিক বিজ্ঞান (হিঃ কোঃ)। ***Verb t.*** To give or administer medicine to ; to cure, (*lit.* & *fig.*) ; ঔষধ প্রয়োগ করা, ঔষধ দেওয়া ; আরোগ্য করা।

phȳs'-i-căl, *adj.* **1.** Material opposed to *moral* ; ভৌতিক, পদার্থরূপ, জড় (ঐ), জড়জ (ঐ), স্থূল (হিঃ কোঃ), সাকার (ঐ)। **2.** Of, or relating to, physics ; পদার্থবিজ্ঞানসম্বন্ধীয়। **3.** Of, or relating to, natural philosoply ; প্রাকৃত দর্শনসম্বন্ধীয়। **4.** Bodily ; as, *physical* exercise ; দৈহিক, শারীরিক। **-ly,** *adv.* **1.** In a physical manner ; according to nature ; ভৌতিকভাবে ; স্বভাবানুযায়ী। **2.** Bodily ; দেহসম্পর্কে, শরীরসম্পর্কে। **Physical body**—পঞ্চভূতাত্মক দেহ, ব্রহ্মপুর (ছান্দোগ্য), অন্নময়কোষ (হিঃ কোঃ), স্থূলশরীর (ঐ), স্থূলদেহ (ঐ), আধিভৌতিক দেহ (ঐ), পিণ্ডদেহ (ঐ)। **Physical education** — শারীরিক শিক্ষা (হিঃ কোঃ), ব্যায়ামবিদ্যা (ঐ)। **Physical exercise**—ব্যায়াম, অঙ্গচালনা। **Physical eye**—চর্ম্মচক্ষুঃ, স্থূলচক্ষুঃ। **Physical geography**—প্রাকৃতিক ভূগোল। **Physical plane**—ভূলোক (হিঃ কোঃ), স্থূললোক (ঐ)। **Physical labour**—শারীরিক শ্রম। **Physical science**—পদার্থ বিজ্ঞান, ভৌতিক শাস্ত্র (হিঃ কোঃ)।

phȳ-si-cian (-shăn), *n.* **1.** A person skilled in the art of healing ; a doctor ; চিকিৎসক, বৈদ্য, ভিষক, কবিরাজ, প্রাণাচার্য্য (ভাগঃ), নরেন্দ্র (দশঃ), রোগহর (সুশ্রুঃ কুঞ্জ) ; ডাক্তার [also দোষজ্ঞ, অগদঙ্কার, জায়ু, জীবদ]। **2.** (*Fig.*) A healer of moral diseases ; as, a *physician* of the soul ; ভবরোগবৈদ্য (চৈঃ চঃ)। **Physician heal thyself**—আগে আপন সামাল কর, চাচা আপন বাঁচা।

phȳs'-i'-cist, *n.* **1.** One versed in physics ; পদার্থশাস্ত্রবিৎ। **2.** A liever in the material origin of the vital phenomena ; যে ব্যক্তি জীবনব্যাপার ভৌতিকক্রিয়া সঞ্জাত বলিয়া বিশ্বাস করে। **-cism,** *n.* A materialism in philosophy and religion ; জড়বাদ।

phȳs'-ick-ȳ *adj.* Of the nature of physic or medicine ; ঔষধপ্রকৃতিক।

phȳs'-i-ō-crăt, *n.* An upholder of physiocracy ; ভূম্যৈকবাদী। **-oc'-ra-cy,** *n.* An economical doctrine promulgated by Quesnay of France (18th century)—that society should be governed according to a natural order inherent in itself, and the soil and its products are the sole source of wealth and the only object of taxation ; ফরাসীদেশীয় অর্থনীতিশাস্ত্রবিৎ Quesnay কর্তৃক প্রবর্ত্তিত মতবিশেষ—যাহাতে অন্তর্নিহিত নৈসর্গিক ব্যবস্থাদ্বারা সমাজ শাসন করিতে হইবে এবং ভূমি ও তজ্জাত দ্রব্য জাতীয় ধনাগমের একমাত্র উপায় বলিয়া গণ্য করিতে হইবে এবং কেবলমাত্র ভূমির উপর কর বসাইতে পারা যাইবে, ভূম্যৈকবাদী।

phȳs-i-ŏg'-ō-nȳ, *n.* The development of vital activities ; জীবনীক্রিয়ার বিকাশ।

phȳs-i-ŏg'-nō-mȳ, *n.* **1.** The art of discovering a person's character from the features of his countenance ; কোন লোকের আকৃতি দর্শনে তদীয় চরিত্রানুমান করার বিদ্যা, মুখসামুদ্রিক (হিঃ কোঃ)। **2.** A particular cast, or expression of the face ; মুখের বিশিষ্ট গঠন বা ভাব। **3.** The general or characteristic aspect of anything ; as, the *physiognomy* of a plant or country ; সাধারণপ্রকৃতি, বিশিষ্টস্বভাব, বিশিষ্ট প্রকৃতি। **4.** (*Vulg.*) The face ; (ইতর ভাষায়) মুখ। **-mist,** *n.* One skilled in physiognomy ; যে ব্যক্তি লোকের আকৃতিদর্শনে চরিত্রানুমান করিতে পারে। **-nom'-ic, -nom'-i-cal,** *adjs.* **-nom'-i-cal-ly,** *adv.*

phȳs-i-ŏg'-ră-phȳ, *n.* The science of the earth's physical features and phenomena ; physical geography ; ভূবর্ণনবিদ্যা ; প্রাকৃতিক ভূগোল। **-o-graph'-ic, -o-graph'-i-cal, -ra-pher,** *n.*

phȳs-i-ŏl'-ă-trȳ, *n.* Nature worship ; নিসর্গপূজা, প্রকৃতি পূজা।

phȳs-i-ŏl'-ō-ġȳ, *n.* The science which deals with the phenomena of life in plants and animals ; শারীরবিজ্ঞান, শারীরবিধানতত্ত্ব, জীবনবিদ্যা, প্রাণতত্ত্ব, শারীরসূত্র (সাঃ পঃ), প্রাণবিদ্যা, শারীরধর্ম্মবিদ্যা (হিঃ কোঃ),

দেহধর্ম্মবিদ্যা (ঐ)। **–gist,** *n.* **–o-log′-ic, –o-log′-i-cal,** *adjs.* **–o-log′-i-cal-ly,** *adv.* **Physiological psychology**—দেহের সহিত সম্বন্ধান্বিত মনোবিজ্ঞান।

phȳ-sique′ (-zēk), *n.* Bodily structure or constitution ; শরীরের গঠন, দেহাবয়ব, শরীরের বাঁধুনি।

phȳ-tŏg′-ē-nȳ, –tō-gĕn′-ē-sis, *ns.* The doctrine of the generation of plants ; বৃক্ষজনন তত্ত্ব।

phȳ-tŏg′-rā-phȳ, *n.* Descriptive botany ; বর্ণনাত্মক উদ্ভিদ বিদ্যা।

phȳ′-tō-mêr, *n.* A plant unit ; উদ্ভিজ্জ একক।

phȳ-tŏph′-ă-gous (-gŭs), *adj.* Feeding on plants as an animal ; তরুগুল্মভোজী।

phȳ-tŏt′-ō-mȳ, *n.* The dissection of plants ; বৃক্ষব্যবচ্ছেদ।

phȳ-tō-zō′-ŏn, (*Pl.* -ZOA), A zoophite ; একজাতীয় পরম প্রাণী।

pī, *n.* The Greek letter p (π) ; গ্রীক অক্ষর P.

pī, *adj.* (*School slang*) Pious ; (স্কুলের ইতরভাষায়) সাধু।

pī-ăc′-ū-lar (-lêr), **1.** Expiatory ; প্রায়শ্চিত্তকর। **2.** Atrociously bad ; as, a *piacular* pollution ; অতি গর্হিত।

pī-affe′ (-ăf), *v. i.* To move as in a trot but move slowly, as a horse ; মৃদু কদমে চলা।

pī-ăf′-fêr, *n.* Act of piaffing ; মৃদু কদমে চলন।

pī-ā-mā-têr, *n.* A membranc investing the surface of the brain ; মস্তিষ্ক আবরক ঝিল্লীবিশেষ।

pī-ă-nette′ (-nĕt), *n.* Same as PIANINO.

pī-â-nī′-nō, *n.* A small upright piano ; ঋজু তন্ত্রী সমন্বিত ক্ষুদ্র পিয়ানো।

pianissimo, *adv.* & *n.* (*Mus.*) Very softly (a direction to execute a passage very softly) ; অতি ধীরে। ***Noun.*** (*Mus.*) A passage to be played as softly as possible ; অতিমৃদুভাবে বাদনীয় অংশ।

pī-ăn′-ist, *n.* A performer, esp. a skilled one on the piano ; পিয়ানো বাদনকুশলব্যক্তি।

piano, *adj.* & *n.* (*Mus.*) Softly ; মৃদুভাবে, কোমলভাবে। ***Noun.*** A passage to be played softly ; মৃদুভাবে বাদনীয় অংশ।

pī-ăn′-ō, *n.* A musical metal-stringed instrument in which notes are produced by hammers acting on the strings ; ধাতব তন্ত্রীবিশিষ্ট বাদ্যযন্ত্রবিশেষ, পিয়ানো। **Cottage-piano**—একপ্রকার অল্পোচ্চ পিয়ানোযন্ত্র — যাহার তন্ত্রীসমূহ বক্রভাবে উত্থিত হইয়াছে। **Grand piano**—বীণাযন্ত্রাকৃতি বৃহৎ পিয়ানো যন্ত্র। **Piano-player**—পিয়ানোবাদক ; পিয়ানো বাদনযন্ত্রবিশেষ। **Piano-school**—যে বিদ্যালয়ে পিয়ানো বাদন শিক্ষা দেওয়া হয়। **Piano stool** — পিয়ানো বাদনকালে যে উচ্চাসনে বাদক উপবেশন করে। **Upright piano**—ঋজু তন্ত্রী সম্বন্বিত পিয়নোযন্ত্র।

pī-ăn-ō-fôr′-tē, *n.* Same as PIANO.

pī-ă-nō′-lă, *n.* A kind of mechanical piano-player ; পিয়ানো বাদনের জন্য যন্ত্রবিশেষ।

pī-ăs′-têr, –tre, (-têr), *ns.* A silver coin of Spain and varions other countries ; স্পেন এবং অন্যান্য নানা দেশের রৌপ্যমুদ্রাবিশেষ।

pī-ăz′-zā, *n.* **1.** A place or square surrounded by buildings, esp. in an Italian town ; চক্, চাঁদনী, মণ্ডপপথ (কেব্ভিঃ)। **2.** (*U. S.*) A verandah ; (মার্কিণ-যুক্তরাজ্যে) বারান্দা।

pī′-brŏch, (pē-), *n.* A kind of musie usually martial for the bagpipe ; বেগপাইপযন্ত্রের সামরিক বাদ্যবিশেষ।

pī′-că, *n.* A size of type ; একপ্রকার হরফ। **Small pica**—একপ্রকার হরফ—প্রতি ইঞ্চি স্থানে যাহার ৩২ পংক্তি ধরে।

pic-ă-dôr′, *n.* A horseman with a lance for exciting the bull in a bullfight ; বৃষভযুদ্ধে বৃষগণকে উত্তেজিত করার জন্য বর্শাধারী অশ্বারোহী।

pic′-ă-mâr, *n.* An oil extracted from wood-tar ; কাষ্ঠজ আলকাতরা হইতে নিষ্কর্ষিত তৈলবিশেষ।

pic-ă-resque′ (-rĕsk), *adj.* Pertaining to rogues ; treating of rogues or robbers ; দুর্বৃত্তসম্বন্ধীয় ; দস্যু বা দুর্বৃত্তসম্বন্ধীয় বা তদ্বিষয়ক।

pic-ă-roon′, *n.* & *v. i.* **1.** A rogue ; a thief ; a pirate ; দুর্বৃত্ত ; চোর ; জলদস্যু, বোম্বেটে। **2.** A pirate ship ; জলদস্যুর জাহাজ, বোম্বেটে জাহাজ। ***Verb i.*** To act as a pirate or brigand ; দস্যুতা করা, বোম্বেটিয়াগিরি করা।

pic′-că-lil-li, *n.* A pickle of various vegetables with pungent spices ; একপ্রকার আচার।

pic′-că-nin-nȳ, pick–, *n.* & *adj.* A little child esp. a negro one ; কচিশিশু, বিশেষতঃ নিগ্রো শিশু। ***Adj.*** Very small ; young ; কচি ; অতি ছোট।

pic′-cō-lō, *n.* A small flute with notes an octave higher than the ordinary ; একপ্রকার বংশী।

pice (pīs), *n.* An East-Indian copper coin = $\frac{1}{4}$ anna ; পয়সা।

pich-i-ci-ā′-gō (-shi-), *n.* A small burrowing armadillo of South America ; দক্ষিণ আমেরিকার ক্ষুদ্র খোলকী জন্তুবিশেষ।

pick, *n.* **1.** Any sharp pointed instrument esp. for loosening and breaking up hard soil etc. ; গাঁতি। **2.** An instrument for picking ; উল্লেখনী। **3.** Same as TOOTHPICK ; দন্তোল্লেখনী।

pick, *n.* **1.** Act of picking or striking with a pointed instrument ; গাঁতিদ্বারা ভেদকরণ, উল্লেখন। **2.** Choice ; selection ; as, to have one's *pick* ; পসন্দ ; নির্ব্বাচন। **3.** The choicest or best ; as the *pick* of the flock; শ্রেষ্ঠবস্তু, বাছালোক, বাছাজিনিষ, সর্ব্বোত্তম বস্তু। **4.** (*Printing*) Foul matter collecting on printing types etc.; (মুদ্রণ) মুদ্রাক্ষরাদির উপরে সঞ্চিত কলঙ্ক। **The pick of the basket**—The best of anything; সবার সেরা জিনিষ।

pick, *v. t.* & *i.* **1.** To break the surface of (ground etc.) with or as with a pick; to make by picking as a hole; গাঁতিদ্বারা ভাঙ্গা; গাঁতি দ্বারা গর্ত্ত প্রভৃতি করা। **2.** To remove something from, as teeth etc. with a pointed instrument etc.; দাঁত প্রভৃতি খুঁটা, দন্ত প্রভৃতি উল্লেখন করা। **3.** To cleanse, of flesh etc.; as, to *pick* a bone, carcass, etc.; মাংস ছাড়ান। **4.** To pluck; to gather; as, to *pick* a flower or fruit; (*lit.* & *fig.*); তোলা; চয়ন করা, আহরণ করা, কুড়ান। **5.** To open with a pointed instrument; as, to *pick* a lock; কাঁটা দ্বারা খোলা, সূক্ষ্ম প্রযন্ত্র দ্বারা উন্মোচন করা। **6.** (Of birds) To take up with the bill as grains, food, etc.; খুঁটিয়া তোলা। **7.** To choose or select with care; as, to *pick* one's words, way or steps, etc.; সযত্নে নির্ব্বাচন করা। **8.** To steal the contents of; as, to *pick* a person's pocket; চুরি করা। **9.** (Of persons) To eat mincingly; (*colloq.*) to eat; খুঁটিয়া খুঁটিয়া খাওয়া; (চলিত ভাষায়) খাওয়া। **10.** To pull asunder; as, to *pick* oakum; আলগা করা, পেঁচ খুলা। ***Verb i.*** **1.** To eat slowly or mincingly; খুঁটিয়া খুঁটিয়া খাওয়া। **2.** To steal; to pilfer; as, *picking* and stealing; চুরি করা; ছেঁচকা চুরি করা। **3.** To select with care; সযত্নে নির্ব্বাচন করা। **Pick'-er,** *n.* **1.** One who picks or gathers; as, a *hop-picker*; সংগ্রহকারী, আহরণকারী। **2.** A pilferer; ছিঁচকেচোর, পাতিচোর। **3.** Any of various instruments for picking; উল্লেখনযন্ত্র, দন্তোল্লেখনী, কানখুস্কী, গাঁতি, প্রভৃতি। **Pick'-ing,** *n.* **1.** The act of picking; খুঁটিয়া তোলন, নির্ব্বাচন। **2.** (*Pl.*) Those which are picked or gleaned; remaining scraps; খুঁটিয়া তোলা জিনিষ; টুকিটাকি, ছিটছাট। **3.** Stealing; (*pl.*) pilferings; চুরিকরণ; ছিঁচকে চুরির জিনিষ। **Pick-lock**—An instrument for opening locks; তালা খোলার জন্য কাঁটা। A person who opens locks; যে ব্যক্তি তালা খোলে। **Pick-me-up**—উত্তেজক পানীয়। **Pickpocket** — গাঁটকাটা, পকেট কাটা, গ্রন্থিচ্ছেদক (শকু:)। **Pick-purse**—যে অন্যের টাকার থলি চুরি করে বা টাকার থলি হইতে চুরি করে। **Pick-thank**—(*Archaic*) A flatterer; a sycophant; (অপ্র:) তোষামোদকারী; চাটুকার, ধামাধরা। **Pick-up**—ক্রীকেট ক্রীড়ায় ভূমি হইতে কন্দুক উত্তোলন। **To have a bone to pick with**—See BONE. **To pick a bone with one**—(*Colloq.*) To quarrel with him; to blame him; কাহারো সহিত ঝগড়া করা; কাহারও উপর দোষারোপ করা। **To pick a hole or holes in**—To find fault in; দোষ ধরা, খুঁত ধরা, ছিদ্রান্বেষণ করা। **To pick a hole or holes in one's coat**—To find fault with one; অপরের খুঁত ধরা। **To pick a lock**—See PICK, *v. t.* 5. **To pick and choose**—To select fastidiously; খুব সাবধানে বাছা। **To pick and steal**—To pilfer; ছিঁচকে চুরি করা। **To pick a quarrel**—To find an occasion to quarrel; কোনরূপ ছল ধরিয়া ঝগড়া বাঁধান, গায়ে পড়িয়া ঝগড়া করা। **To pick at**—To find fault with continually, (now *U. S.*); সর্ব্বদা খুঁত ধরা। To try to pull; as, *to pick at* bed clothes; তুলিতে চেষ্টা করা। **To pick holes in everybody's pocket**—সকলের ছুতো ধরা। **To pick in**—To work or put in as the shadow in a painting; ছবিতে ছায়াপাত করা। **To pick oakum**—To make oakum by untwisting old ropes; পুরাতন রজ্জুর পেঁচ খুলিয়া শণ বাহির করা। **To pick off**—To pluck off; খুঁটিয়া খুঁটিয়া তুলিয়া ফেলিয়া দেওয়া। To shoot (person etc.) one by one; একজন একজন করিয়া গুলি করা। **To pick one's way**—To move carefully; সাবধানে চলা। **To pick out**—To select; to make out as a meaning; বাছিয়া লওয়া; নির্ণয় করা, বাহির করা। To mark with spots of colour etc.; রঙ্গীন ফুট ফুট বিন্দুসমূহ দ্বারা চিহ্নিত করা। **To pick to pieces**—To pull asunder; টানিয়া ছিঁড়িয়া টুকরা টুকরা কর। (*Fig.*) To criticise (persons etc.) hostilely; (লক্ষণায়) তার সমালোচনা করা। **To pick up**—To break up (ground etc.) with a pick; গাঁতিদ্বারা (মাটি প্রভৃতি) ভাঙ্গা। To take into a vehicle or into one's company; as, the train stops *to pick up* passengers; (গাড়ীতে) উঠাইয়া নেওয়া, তুলিয়া নেওয়া, (কোন দলের সঙ্গে) পথ হইতে নেওয়া। To raise oneself from a fall etc.; to recover health; উঠিয়া দাঁড়ান; স্বাস্থ্য লাভ করা। To regain (lost path etc., spirit, flesh, etc.); পুন: প্রাপ্ত হওয়া, পুনরায় লাভ করা। To acquire (livelihood, profit, tricks, information, etc.); অর্জ্জন করা, লাভ করা। To make acquaintance with; পরিচয় করা।

pick'-a-bǎck, *adv.* On the back or shoulder like a bundle; as, to take a child *pick-a-back*; পুঁটুলির মত পিঠে বা কাঁধে।

pick'-ǎx, -axe (-ǎks), *n.*, *v.t.* & *i.* A sharp pointed iron-tool used in digging, mining, etc.; একপ্রকার বড় গাঁতি, পাষাণদারণ,

পাষাণ-ভেদনী। *Verb t.* To break as ground etc., with a pickaxe ; ঐরূপ গাঁতিদ্বারা মাটী প্রভৃতি ভাঙ্গা। *Verb i.* To work with a pick-axe ; ঐরূপ গাঁতি দ্বারা কাজ করা।

pick'-êr, *n.* See under PICK, *verb.*

pick'-êr-ĕl, *n.* A small or young pike ; একপ্রকার মৎস্য।

pick'-ĕt, *n., v. t. & i.* 1. A pointed stake used in fortification ; a stake for tethering a horse etc. ; a pale ; শূল, গোঁজ, সূক্ষ্মাগ্রকীলক ; ঘোড়া প্রভৃতি বাঁধিবার খোঁটা ; খোঁটা। 2. (*Mil.*, also *piquet*) A small body of troops sent out to watch for the enemies, (called an *outlying picket*) ; such a body held ready in camp for immediate service in case of alarm, (called an *inlying picket*) ; a party of sentinels ; an outpost ; শত্রুসৈন্যের গতিবিধি পর্য্যবেক্ষণার্থ প্রেরিত সৈন্যদল ; বিপৎসংবাদ পাইবামাত্র প্রেরণ করা যাইতে পারে তজ্জন্য প্রস্তুত ঐরূপ সৈন্যদল ; রক্ষিদল ; ঘাঁটী। 3. (*Hist.*) A punishment inflicted by making a person stand on one foot on a pointed stake ; this stake ; (ইতিহাস) কোন ব্যক্তিকে শূলের উপর এক পদে দণ্ডায়মান করত পূর্ব্বে যে শাস্তি দেওয়া হইত ; ঐরূপ শূল। 4. (Usu. *pl.*) A person or persons posted by a trade-union to dissuade men from work during a strike etc. ; ধর্ম্মঘটের সময় লোকদিগকে কার্য্যে যোগদানে নিবৃত্ত করার জন্য শ্রমজীবিস্বার্থসংরক্ষণী সমিতি কর্ত্তৃক যে লোক বা লোকসকল রক্ষিত হয়। *Verb t.* 1. To fence or fortify with pointed stakes ; সূক্ষ্মাগ্রকীলক রচিত বৃতিদ্বারা বেষ্টিত বা সুরক্ষিত করা। 2. To fasten to a picket a horse ; খোঁটায় বাঁধা। 3. To place or post as a picket ; শত্রুসৈন্যের গতিবিধি পর্য্যবেক্ষণার্থ সৈন্যদল স্থাপন করা। 4. To place watchers at the approaches (to a place of employment affected by a strike) to dissuade workers from works ; যে কারখানা প্রভৃতির মজুরেরা ধর্ম্মঘট করিয়াছে তথাকার মজুরগণকে কর্ম্ম হইতে নিবৃত্ত করিবার জন্য কারখানার প্রবেশপথে পাহারা রাখা। *Verb i.* To do picket duty ; শত্রুসৈন্যের গতিবিধি পর্য্যবেক্ষণের কাজ করা। **Picket-guard**—বিপদের সময় সাহায্য করার জন্য যে রক্ষিসৈন্যগণ প্রস্তুত রাখা হয়।

pick'-ing, *n.* See under PICK, *verb.*

pick'-le (-l), *n. & v. t.* 1. Brine, vinegar, etc. for preserving flesh, vegetables, fish, etc. ; মৎস্য, মাংস, তরকারি প্রভৃতি তাজা রাখার জন্য লবণজল, সির্কা প্রভৃতি। 2. Any article of food thus preserved (usu. in *pl.*) ; আচার, চাটনি। 3. An acid solution for cleaning purposes etc. ; পরিষ্কারাদি করার জন্য দ্রাবক মিশ্রিত জল। 4. A difficult state or position (often with a qualifying word) ; as, a sad or sorry *pickle* ; সঙ্কট, লেঠা, মুস্কিল, ফ্যাসাদ, ফাঁপর। 5. (*Colloq.*) A mischievous child ; as, a little *pickle* ; (চলিত-ভাষায়) দুরন্ত ছেলে। *Verb t.* 1. To preserve in and treat with pickle ; as, to *pickle* herring ; আচার করা, চাটনি করা। 2. (*Naut.*) To rub salt or vinegar on (the back of a person) after flogging ; (নৌবিদ্যা) কাহারো পৃষ্ঠে বেত্রাঘাত করিয়া ক্ষত স্থানে লবণ অথবা সির্কা মাখান। **To have a rod in pickle for any one**—To have a punishment ready for any one ; শাস্তি প্রস্তুত রাখা।

pick'-some (-sŭm), *adj.* Fastidious ; খুঁতখুঁতে, উৎকটরুচি।

pick'-wick, *n.* A kind of cheap cigar ; একপ্রকার সস্তাদরের চুরুট।

Pick-wick'-i-ăn, *adj.* Relating to, or characteristic of, Mr. Pickwick, the hero of Dickens' Pickwick Papers ; ডিকেন্সের Pickwick Papers নামক গ্রন্থের নায়ক সম্বন্ধীয়, উক্ত Pickwickএর প্রকৃতিক। **In a Pickwickian sense**—In a technical, constructive or esoteric sense (a phrase by which the members of the Pickwick Club explained away unparliamentary language) ; পারিভাষিক অর্থে, গৌণ অর্থে, গুহ্য অর্থে

pic'-nic, *n. & v.i.* A pleasure party, the members of which carry with them provisions on an excursion into the country etc. ; বনভোজন, চড়ুইভাতি, বনবিহার। *Verb i.* To take part in this ; বনভোজন করা। **—nick-er,** *n.* One who takes part in a picnic ; বনভোজনকারী। **—nick-y,** *adj.* (*Colloq.*)

pi-cot' (-cō), *n.* One of many ornamental loops forming an edging, as on a ribbon, lace, etc. ; ফিতা প্রভৃতির কিনারায় শোভাবর্ধক গ্রন্থি।

pic-ō-tee' (-tē), *n.* A variety of carnation or clovepink ; একপ্রকার মাংসবর্ণ পুষ্প।

pic'-ric, *adj.* Designating an acid of bitter taste ; তিক্তাস্বাদ দ্রাবকবিশেষসম্বন্ধীয়। **Picric acid**—রঞ্জন কার্য্যে এবং বিস্ফোরক দ্রব্য প্রস্তুতে ব্যবহৃত পীতবর্ণ তিক্তাস্বাদ দ্রাবকবিশেষ।

Pict, *n.* One of an ancient people who inhabited North Britain ; উত্তর ব্রিটেনবাসী প্রাচীন জাতিবিশেষ। **Pict'-ish,** *adj.*

pic'-tō-grăph, *n.* A picture or hieroglyph representing an idea ; a record in such symbols ; কোনরূপ মনোভাবসূচক চিত্র ; ঐরূপ চিত্রের সাহায্যে লিখিত বিষয়, চিত্রলিপি। **—graph'-ic,** *adj.* **—tog'-ra-phy,** *n.*

pic-tō'-ri-ăl, *adj. & n.* Relating to, illustrated by, or consisting of, pictures ; picturesque ; চিত্রসম্বন্ধীয়, সচিত্র ; বিচিত্র। *Noun.* A journal of which pictures are the main feature ; সচিত্র পত্রিকা। **—ly,** *adj.*

pic'-türe, *n.* & *v. t.* **1.** A painting or drawing; a portrait; ছবি, চিত্র, আলেখ্য, চিত্রলেখা (গীতঃ); চিত্রপট, তস্বীর। **2.** An image; as, the child is the *picture* of his father; প্রতিমূর্ত্তি। **3.** A tableau; a scene; বিচিত্র চিত্র; দৃশ্য। **4.** A beautiful object; as, her hat is a *picture*; সুন্দর জিনিষ। **5.** A vivid verbal description; as, the poet has drawn an exquisite *picture* of poverty; চিত্র, বর্ণনা। *Verb t.* **1.** To paint or draw a likeness of; to represent pictorially; প্রতিকৃতি অঙ্কন বা চিত্রণ করা; অঙ্কন করা, চিত্রদ্বারা প্রদর্শন করা। **2.** To form a mental picture of; to imagine; মানসচিত্র রচনা করা; কল্পনা করা। **3.** To describe vividly; সজীব-বর্ণনা করা, চিত্রিত করা। **Picture-book**—শিশুদিগের চিত্রপুস্তক। **Picture-frame**—ছবির ফ্রেম। **Picture-gallery**—যে গৃহে প্রদর্শনার্থ নানাপ্রকার চিত্র সজ্জিত রাখা হয়, চিত্ররক্ষণ গৃহ, চিত্রশালা, জালিনী (অঃ), বীথিকা (উত্তরঃ)। **Picture hat**—স্ত্রীলোকদিগের প্রশস্তপ্রান্ত টুপি বিশেষ। **Picture-postcard**—সচিত্র পোষ্টকার্ড। **Picture writing**—চিত্রলিপি [প্রাচীন মিসরবাসিগণ অক্ষর-গ্রথিত শব্দের পরিবর্ত্তে চিত্রাবলীর সাহায্যে মনোভাব লিপিবদ্ধ করিত।]

pic-tür-esque' (-ěsk), *adj.* Like, or suited for, a picture; as, *picturesque* scene; vivid; graphic; as, *picturesque* language; চিত্রোপম, চিত্রোপযোগী, চিত্রযোগ্য; জীবন্ত, সজীব; বিচিত্র, সুরম্য (কেঃশিঃ)। **—ness,** *n.* The state of being picturesque; বিচিত্রতা।

pid'-dle (-l), *v. i.* **1.** (*Archaic*) To work in a trifling way; to trifle; (অপ্রঃ) হেলার সহিত কাজ করা; তুচ্ছব্যাপারে নিযুক্ত থাকা। **2.** To eat mincingly; খুঁটিয়া খুঁটিয়া খাওয়া। **3.** To make water (a child's word); মুতা।

pid'-dock (-ŏc), *n.* A kind of mollusc used for bait; বড়শীর টোপস্বরূপ ব্যবহৃত শম্বুকবিশেষ।

pidg'-in (pĭj-), **pi'-gě-ŏn,** *adjs.* **Pidgin** or **Pigeon English**—A jargon chiefly of English words arranged after Chinese syntax; চীনাবাজারের ইংরাজী।

pie (pī), *n.* Same as MAGPIE.

pie (pī), *n.* A paste baked with meat, fruit, etc. in or under it; as, a chicken *pie*; মাংস ফলাদি পুরিত পিষ্টক। **Bran-pie**—খ্রীষ্টমাস পর্ব্বোপলক্ষে যে তুষ-পূর্ণ ভাণ্ড হইতে ছেলেরা পুতুল বাহির করে। **Pie-crust**—মাংসাদি পুরিত পিষ্টকের বেষ্টন। **Pie-man** — পিষ্টকবিক্রয়ী। **To have a finger in every pie**—সকলের মধ্যে থাকা, সকল ব্যঞ্জনে লবণ দেওয়া। **To have a finger** or **hand in the pie**—To be (esp. officioulsy) concerned in the matter; কোন ঘটনায় সংসৃষ্ট থাকা।

pie (pī), *n.* & *v. t.* **1.** (*Print.*) A mass of types confusedly mixed; এলোমেলো হরফ, মুদ্রাক্ষর-সঙ্কর (আঃ বঃ)। **2.** (*Fig.*) Chaos or confusion; (লক্ষণায়) বিশৃঙ্খলা, গোলমাল। *Verb t.* To mix as types; অক্ষর এলোমেলো করিয়া মিশাইয়া ফেলা।

pie (pī), *n.* An Indian copper coin = $\frac{1}{12}$ of an anna; পাই।

pie'-bald (pī-), *adj.* **1.** Having spots and patches of black and white or other colours; "A *piebald* steed"; চিত্রবিচিত্র, কর্ব্বুর শবল, চিত্রাঙ্গ। **2.** (*Fig.*) Motley; mixed; "*Piebald* language"; (লক্ষণায়) সঙ্কর; মিশ্র।

piece (pēs), *n.* **1.** A part of anything; a fragment; as, to break in *pieces*; ভাগ, অংশ; খণ্ড, টুকরা। **2.** A literary or musical composition; a drama; রচনা বা সংগীত; নাটক। **3.** A gun, rifle or pistol; as, a field *piece*; কামান বন্দুক। **4.** An item; as, a *piece* of news; দফা। **5.** A coin; as, a four penny *piece*; মুদ্রা। **6.** A picture; ছবি। **7.** An individual object of a class; as, a *piece* of furniture; কোন শ্রেণীর অন্যতম বস্তু। **8.** A man in chess or draughts; বড়ে, গুটি। **9.** A cask (of wine etc.) varying in capacity; বিভিন্ন পরিমাণ মদ্য প্রভৃতির পিপা। **10.** A specimen; an example; as, a *piece* of impudence; a fine *piece* of painting; নমুনা, দৃষ্টান্ত; উদাহরণ। **Piece-goods**—কার্পাস পশম প্রভৃতির কাপড়—যাহা খুচরা বিক্রয় হয়। **Piece-work** — ফুরান কাজ। **A piece of eight**—স্পেনদেশীয় ডলার। **In pieces**—Broken; as, it is *in pieces*; ভগ্ন। **Of a piece (with)**—Consistent with; of the same sort; সঙ্গতিবিশিষ্ট; একই রকমের, একই ধরণের। **To break to pieces**—To break to fragments; খণ্ড খণ্ড করা, টুকরা টুকরা করা, চুরমার করা, খানখান করিয়া ভাঙ্গা। **To fall to pieces**—To become disorganized; ভাঙ্গিয়া পড়া, চুরমার হওয়া। To be brought to bed of a child; প্রসব করা। **To give a piece of one's mind to**—To speak plainly, bluntly or severely to (another); কাহাকেও মুখের উপর স্পষ্টাস্পষ্টি শুনাইয়া দেওয়া। **To go** or **come to pieces** — To break up; to dissolve; ভাঙ্গিয়া যাওয়া; ভঙ্গ হওয়া। **To work by the piece**—To work by the measure of quality and not by the measure of time; ফুরান কাজ করা।

piece (pēs), *v. t.* **1.** To patch; as, to *piece* a garment; to join threads together in spinning; তালি লাগান; সূতা কাটার সময় সূতায় জোড়া দেওয়া। **2.** To unite; to form into a whole; একত্র করা;

সমষ্টীভূত করা। 3. To enlarge or eke (out) by adding a piece; টুকরা যোগ করিয়া বাড়ান। **To piece in**—To unite with another by insertion; অপরটীর ভিতরে প্রবিষ্ট করিয়া জোড়া দেওয়া। **To piece on**—To join on; যোগ করা। **To piece out**—See PIECE, *v.* 3. **To piece up**—To put together; to patch up; জোড়া দেওয়া; তালি দেওয়া।

piece de resistance, (*F.*), *n.* (*Lit. & fig.*) A chief dish at a dinner; (শব্দানুযায়ী ও লক্ষণায়) অপরাহ্ণ ভোজনের সর্ব্বপ্রধান ব্যঞ্জন।

piece'-meal (pēs-mēl), *adv., adj.* & *n.* 1. In or by pieces; in fragments; as, to break *piece-meal*; খণ্ডশঃ, খণ্ডে খণ্ডে; অংশতঃ, টুকরা টুকরা করিয়া। 2. Little by little; gradually; as, to do a thing *piecemeal*; অল্পে অল্পে, একটু একটু করিয়া; ক্রমে ক্রমে। ***Adj.*** Made of pieces; done piece by piece; খণ্ডসমূহে রচিত; খণ্ডে খণ্ডে সম্পন্ন। ***Noun.*** A fragment; খণ্ড, টুকরা।

piec'-ėr (pēs-), *n.* One who pieces, esp. a boy or girl employed in a spinning mill to tie together broken threads; যে ছিন্ন সূত্র জোড়া দেয়, বিশেষতঃ কাপড়ের কলে যে বালক বা বালিকা ছিন্ন সূত্র জোড়া দেয়।

pied (pīd), *adj.* Variegated; parti-coloured; "*Pied* coats"; চিত্রবিচিত্র; রংবেরঙ্গের, বিচিত্ররঙ্গী, নানারঙ্গী।

pied a terre, (*F.*), *n.* Rest for one's foot; somewhere to stay; পদাশ্রয়; পা রাখার জায়গা।

pier (pēr), *n.* 1. The portion of a wall between the windows or doors; বাতায়ন বা দ্বারসমূহের মধ্যবর্ত্তী প্রাচীরাংশ। 2. A pillar or post on which a gate is hung; দ্বারস্তম্ভ। 3. The support of the spans of a bridge; সেতুস্তম্ভ। 4. A breakwater; a projecting wharf or other structure used as a landing place, promenade, etc.; পোস্তা, তরঙ্গের বেগ নিরোধক বাঁধ, জাঙ্গাল; জাহাজাদি হইতে অবতরণের জন্য সমুদ্রোপরি উদ্গত মঞ্চাবশেষ। 5. A buttress; উপস্তম্ভ, আশ্রয়। **Pier'-age,** *n.* Toll paid for the use of a pier; ঘাট মাশুল। **Pier-glass**—বাতায়নদ্বয়ের মধ্য স্থানে রক্ষিত বৃহৎ দর্পণ। **Pier-table** — বাতায়নদ্বয়ের মধ্যবর্ত্তী মেজ।

pierce (pērs), *v. t.* & *i.* 1. To penetrate or transfix, as with a pointed instrument; to prick as with a pin etc.; বিদ্ধ করা, ফোঁড়া, বিঁধা। 2. To make a hole or opening in, as a wall, cask, etc.; ছিদ্র করা। 3. To force a way into or through; to pass into or through; as, to *pierce* the enemy's line: the shot *pierced* the ship; ভেদ করিয়া যাওয়া; ভেদ করা। 4. (*Fig.*) To affect or move deeply; (লক্ষণায়) হৃদয় বিদীর্ণ করা। ***Verb i.*** To penetrate; ভেদ করিয়া যাওয়া।

pierc'-ing (pērs-), *adj.* 1. Penetrating; ভেদকারী। 2. Affecting or touching deeply; biting; as, *piercing* cold, remark, etc.; মর্ম্মচ্ছেদী, মর্ম্মভেদী, হৃদয়ভেদী; অরুন্তুদ **—ly,** *adv.*

Pī-ė'-ri-ăn, *adj.* Of, or pertaining to, Pieria, an ancient country in Thessaly, a place of the worship of the Muses; থেসেলির অন্তঃপাতী প্রাচীন Pieria নামক স্থান সম্বন্ধীয়।

pier-rot (pēr-ō), *n.* 1. (*In French pantomime*) A jesting character; সং। 2. (*Eng.*) A buffoon itinerant minstrel with whitened face and loose white dress, যে ভাঁড় ঢিলা সাদা পোষাক পরিয়া এবং মুখে সাদা রং মাখিয়া স্থানে স্থানে পর্য্যটন করে।

pieta, (*It.*), *n.* A picture or sculpture of the dead Christ in the lap of the Virgin Mary; কুমারী মেরীর অঙ্কে স্থিত মৃত যীশুর চিত্র।

pī'-ė-tism, *n.* 1. The principles or practice of the Pietists; ভক্তিপন্থা। 2. Strict devotion or its affectation; ভক্তি, ভক্তি-বিটলামি, ভক্তিপ্রবণতা (হিং: কোঃ)। **—tist,** *n.* One of the German religious reformers of deep devotional feeling in the 17th century; one making a show of strong religious feelings; জর্ম্মণদেশীয় ভক্তিপন্থী সাধক সম্প্রদায়-বিশেষ ভুক্ত ব্যক্তি, ভক্তিপন্থী; ভক্তিবিটল। **—tis'-tic, —tis'-ti-cal,** *adjs.*

pī'-ė-tў, *n.* 1. Reverence towards God; devotion; ধার্ম্মিষ্ঠতা, ধর্ম্মপরায়ণতা, ধার্ম্মিকতা, ধর্ম্মানুরাগ, ঈশ্বরনিষ্ঠা, পুণ্যশীলতা, ধর্ম্মশাক্ত; ভগবদ্ভক্তি, ঈশ্বরে পরানুরক্তি। 2. Dutifulness; filial reverence; কর্ত্তব্যনিষ্ঠা; পিতৃভক্তি।

pi-ė-zŏm'-ė-tėr, *n.* A kind of instrument for measuring pressure or the sensitiveness of the skin to pressure; চাপ বা ত্বকের চাপানুভূতি পরিমাপের যন্ত্রবিশেষ, চাপমান।

pif'-fle (-l), *v. i.* & *n.* (*Slang*) To talk or act triflingly or feebly; (ইতরভাষায়) বাজেকথা বলা, অনর্থক কথা বলা, তুচ্ছ কাজ করা, দুর্ব্বলের মত কাজ করা। ***Noun.*** Twaddle; বাজে কথা। **—fler,** *n.*

pig, *n., v. i.* & *t.* 1. The young of swine male or female; a hog; শূকরশাবক; শূকর, বরাহ। 2. The flesh of swine as an article of food; শূকরমাংস। 3. An oblong mass of unforged iron, lead or other metal; ঢালা লোহা, সীসা বা অন্য ধাতুর চৌপল খণ্ড। 4. (*Colloq.*) A rude, greedy, dirty, obstinate or disagreeable person; (চলিতভাষায়) শূকর প্রকৃতির লোক, রূঢ় প্রকৃতির লোক, পেটুক লোক,

নোংরালোক, একগুঁয়ে লোক, শূয়র। 5. A segment of an orange; কমলার কোয়া। *Verb i.* 1. To bring forth pigs; শূকরছানা প্রসব করা। 2. To huddle or lie together like pigs; শূকরছানার মত ঠাসাঠাসি করিয়া শুইয়া থাকা। *Verb t.* To bring forth (pigs); শূকরছানা প্রসব করা। **Pig′-gish,** *adj.* Relating to, or like, a pig; greedy; obstinate; dirty; শূকরশাবকসম্বন্ধীয়, শূকরশাবকবৎ; পেটুক; একগুঁয়ে; নোংরা। **Pig′-gish-ly,** *adv.* **Pig′-gish-ness,** *n.* **Pig′-let, Pig′-ling,** *ns.* **Pig′-like,** *adj.* **Pig-eyed** — শূয়রচোখো। **Pig-faced**—শূয়রমুখো। **Pigheaded**—একগুঁয়ে; বেকুব। (*Pigheadedly, adv. Pigheadedness, n.*) **Pig-iron**—ঢালা লোহার চৌপল। **Pig-jump** — (অশ্বের পক্ষে) চারি পা একত্র না করিয়া যে লাফ দেওয়া হয়। **Pignut**—চীনা বাদাম। **Pig-poke**—যে জিনিষ ভালরূপ না দেখিয়া শুনিয়া কেনা হয়। **Pig-sconce**—বুদ্ধিহীন ব্যক্তি, জড়মস্তিষ্ক ব্যক্তি। **Pigskin**—শূকরচর্ম্ম; জীন। **Pigsticking**—বর্শাদ্বারা বন্য বরাহশিকার; কসাই কর্তৃক শূকর মাংস কর্তন। (*Pig-sticker, n.*) **Pigsty**—শূকরগৃহ, শূকরনিবাস (আঃ মঠ), শোঁর কুড়ে। **Pig-tail**—শূকরপুচ্ছ; জড়ানো তামাক; চীনাদিগের বেণী, শিখা। **Pig-tailed,** *adj.* **Pig's wash, pigwash**—পাকশালা প্রভৃতির মলিন জল—যাহা শূকরকে পান করিতে দেওয়া যায়। **Pig's whisper**—অপরে শুনিতে পারে এরূপ কানাকানি; অত্যল্প সময়। **Pigweed**—বিভিন্নজাতীয় গুল্ম—যাহা শূকরে ভোজন করিয়া থাকে। **To bring one's pigs to a fine, a pretty, or the wrong or worse market**—To fail in a venture; কোন ব্যাপারে অকৃতকার্য্য হওয়া। To sell at a loss; লোকসান দিয়া বিক্রয় করা। **To buy a pig in a poke** — To purchase a thing without seeing it or knowing value; না দেখিয়া কোন জিনিষ কেনা, কোন জিনিষের মূল্য না জানিয়া তাহা কেনা। **To drive one's pigs to market**—To snore; নাসিকা গর্জ্জন করা, নাক ডাকান। **To go to pigs and whistles** — To be dissipated or ruined; উড়িয়া যাওয়া, উচ্ছন্ন যাওয়া, সর্ব্বনাশ হওয়া।

pi′-geon (-jŏn), *n.* & *v.t.* 1. A well-known bird of many varieties; a dove; পায়রা, কবুতর, কপোত, পারাবত [Syn. ঝল্লকণ্ঠ, ঝিল্লীকণ্ঠ, ধূম্রলোচন, ধূসর, অরুণনেত্র, রক্তলোচন, রক্তাক্ষ, চিত্রকণ্ঠ, মদনকাকুরব, পারাপত, পারবত, কলরব, গৃহনাশন, কোকদেব, গৃহোকপোত (domestic pigeon), ক্ষণরামী]; ঘুঘু। 2. (*Slang*) A simpleton; a fool; (ইতর ভাষায়) বেকুব; বোকা। *Verb t.* To swindle by tricks in gambling; to cheat; জুয়াখেলায় চালাকী করিয়া প্রতারণা করা; প্রতারণা করা। **—ry,** *n.* A pigeon-house; পায়রার টং, কপোতগৃহ, কপোতপালিকা, বিটঙ্ক। **Clay pigeon**—একপ্রকার কল হইতে নিক্ষিপ্ত মৃণ্ময় পাত্র প্রভৃতি—যাহার উপর গুলি করিয়া লক্ষ্যভেদ শিক্ষা করা হয়। **Pigeon-breast** — বিকৃতবক্ষঃ। (*Pigeon-breasted, adj.*) বিকৃতবক্ষঃ। **Pigeon-English** — See under PIDGIN. **Pigeongram** — কপোত দ্বারা বাহিত বার্ত্তা, পারাবতবার্ত্তা। **Pigeon hearted**—হরিণহৃদয়, ভীরু, ভয়াতুর। **Pigeon-hole**—A small recess for a pigeon to nest in; কপোতবিবর। A division of a case, cabinet, etc. for papers etc.; খোপ, খুপরী। (*Verb t.*) To deposit (documents etc.) in a pigeon-hole; কাগজপত্র নির্দ্দিষ্ট খোপে রাখা। To lay aside indefinitely or for future consideration; to assign (a thing) to a definite place in memory; ফেলিয়া রাখা; স্মৃতিমধ্যে নির্দ্দিষ্ট স্থান নির্দ্দেশ করা। **Pigeon-house**—টং, পায়রার ঘর, পায়রার খুপরী, পায়রাখুবী। **Pigeon-livered** — ভীরু, কাপুরুষ। **Pigeon's milk**—Partly digested food with which pigeons feed their young; যে অর্দ্ধজীর্ণ খাদ্য কপোতগণ শাবককে আহার করায়। An imaginary article for which children are sent on a fool's errand; কাল্পনিক পদার্থ—যাহার অন্বেষণে বালকদিগকে বোকা সাজাইবার উদ্দেশ্যে পাঠান হয়, বলদের দুধ। **To pluck a pigeon**—To cheat or swindle a simpleton; বোকা লোককে ঠকান।

pig′-ger-ȳ (-ĕr), *n.* 1. A place for breeding pigs; a pigsty; a dirty place; শূকরস্থলী; শূকরগৃহ; নোংরা জায়গা। 2. Piggishness; গোঁ।

pig′-gy (-ī), *n.* 1. A little pig; ক্ষুদ্র শূকর। 2. (*Nursery*) The game of tip-cat; একপ্রকার ক্রীড়া। **Piggy-wiggy**—শূকরছানা; নোংরা ছেলে।

pig′-mĕnt, *n.* 1. A colouring matter used in painting, dyeing, etc.; রঙ্গবস্তু, রঞ্জকপদার্থ, রঞ্জক (সাঃ পঃ), রঙ্গ, রাগ (সুশ্রুঃ কুঞ্জঃ), বর্ণক। 2. A colouring matter found in the tissues of animals and plants; জীব এবং উদ্ভিদের বিধান-তন্তুতে প্রাপ্ত রঞ্জক বস্তু। **—men′-tal, —men-ta-ry,** *adjs.*

pig′-mȳ, *n.* Same as PYGMY.

pig′-tail (-tāl), *n.* See under PIG.

pīke, *n.* & *v. t.* 1. A weapon with a long shaft used by foot-soldiers; বর্শা, শূল, বল্লম, শক্তি। 2. A peak; as, Langdale *pikes*; গিরিচূড়া, শৈলশৃঙ্গ। 3. (*Dial.*) A pick-axe; (উপভাষায়) টঙ্ক। 4. (*Zool.*) A large fresh-water fish; বৃহৎ মৎস্য-বিশেষ। *Verb t.* To pierce or kill with a pike; শূলাঘাতে বধ করা। **Pikeman**—যে খনির মজুর টঙ্ক ব্যবহার করে। **Pike perch**—একপ্রকার মৎস্য।

pīke, *n.* 1. A turnpike; the toll paid there; রাজপথের উপরিস্থ যে দ্বারে পূর্ব্বে মাশুল আদায় করা হইত; ঐ স্থানে প্রদত্ত মাশুল। 2. A turnpike road ; যে রাস্তায় ঐরূপ মাশুল আদায় করা হইত। **Pikeman**—পথদ্বার রক্ষক।

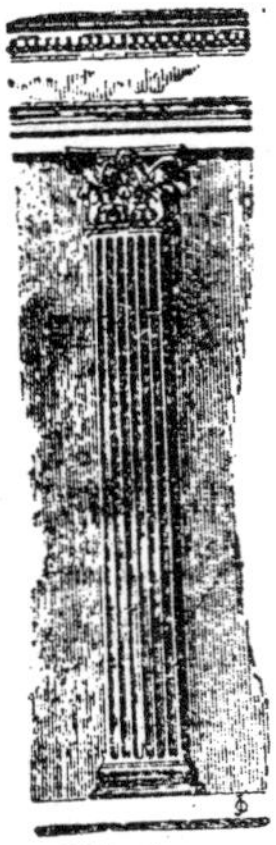

Pilaster.

pike'-stâff, *n.* The shaft of a pike; the weapon; বল্লমের বাঁট, শূলদণ্ড; বল্লম। **Plain as a pikestaff** — Quite plain; একবারে সোজা, অতিস্পষ্ট।

pi-lăs'-tẽr, *n.* A square pillar usually projecting from a pier or from a wall; চতুষ্কোণ স্তম্ভ, প্রাচীরাদির গাত্র হইতে ঈষদুদ্গাত চতুষ্কোণ স্তম্ভ, নাগ (উড়িষ্যা)।

pilch, *n.* A flannel cloth for an infant; শিশুদের গায়ে জড়াইবার জন্য একপ্রকার ফ্লানেলের কাপড়।

Pilchard.

pil'-chârd, *n.* A sea-fish like herring; একপ্রকার সামুদ্রিক মৎস্য।

pil'-côrn, *n.* A kind of oat in which husks do not adhere to grain; এক প্রকার যই।

pile, *n.* & *v. t.* **1.** A beam or timber driven into the earth to support a building or other superstructure; অট্টালিকা প্রভৃতির আশ্রয়ের জন্য ভূমিতলে প্রোথিত কাষ্ঠফলক, স্থূণা। **2.** A pointed stake or post; খোঁটা, কীলক। ***Verb t.*** To drive piles into; to strengthen with piles; অট্টালিকা প্রভৃতির আশ্রয়ের জন্য কাষ্ঠফলক প্রভৃতি ভূতলে প্রোথিত করা; খোঁটা দ্বারা দৃঢ় করা। **Pile-driver**—কাষ্ঠফলক প্রভৃতি ভূতলে নিবদ্ধ করার জন্য যন্ত্রবিশেষ।

pile, *n.* **1.** A heap; a mass of things laid together more or less regularly; as, a *pile* of stones, shot, etc.; রাশি, স্তূপ; গাদা, কাঁড়ি, পুঞ্জ। **2.** A large building or mass of buildings; "The *pile* overlooked the town"; বৃহৎ অট্টালিকা বা অট্টালিকাশ্রেণী। **3.** A funeral pyre; চিতা। **4.** (*Colloq.*) A heap of money; fortune; as, to make a *pile*; (চলিত ভাষায়) ধনরাশি; বহুধন। **5.** (*Elect.*) A number of metal plates so arranged as to produce a current; তাড়িতপ্রবাহ উৎপাদনের জন্য সজ্জিত ধাতুফলকশ্রেণী। **To make a pile**—See PILE, *n.* 4. **To make one's pile**—To make as much money as one wants; আবশ্যকানুরূপ ধন সঞ্চয় করা।

pile, *v. t.* & *i.* **1.** To lay or collect into a heap; to amass, (usu. with *up* or *on*); as, *to pile up* wood; স্তূপীকৃত করা; রাশীকৃত করা, পুঞ্জীভূত করা। **2.** To load; as, *to pile* a table with things; ভারাক্রান্ত করা। ***Verb i.*** To form a pile; to accumulate; স্তূপীকৃত হওয়া; সঞ্চিত হওয়া। **To pile arms**—কুঁদা মাটীতে রাখিয়া এবং অগ্রভাগ সমূহ একত্র সংযুক্ত করিয়া চারিটী বন্দুক তির্য্যগ্‌ভাবে খাড়া করিয়া রাখা। **To pile it on**—To exaggerate; অতিরঞ্জিত করা। **To pile up** or **on the agony**—To intensify painful description etc.; বিষাদজনক বর্ণনা তীব্রতর করা।

pile, *n.* (*Archaic*) The reverse of a coin; (অপ্রঃ) মুদ্রার উল্টা পিঠ। **Cross** or **pile**—HEADS OR TAILS (which see.)

pile, *n.* **1.** Hair, wool of sheep, the nap on a cloth, etc.; মেষলোম, মেষের পশম, কাপড় প্রভৃতির উপর ফুঁপি। **Pil'-y,** *adj.* Like pile or wool; মেষলোমবৎ।

pile, *n.*, (*Pl.*) A disease of the lower rectum; (*sing.*) one of the tumours marking this disease; অর্শ, গুদরোগ, গুদ-কীল (সুশ্রুঃ), গুদোদ্ভব (ঐ), গুদার্শ, গুদাঙ্কুর (ভাব প্রঃ), গুদজ (ঐ); বলি। **Pilewort**—এক-প্রকার গুল্ম।

pil'-fẽr, *v. t.* & *i.* To steal or gain by petty theft; ছিঁচ্‌কা চুরি করা, চক্ষুদান করা, পাতিচুরি করিয়া পাওয়া। ***Verb i.*** To practise petty theft; ছিঁচ্‌কা চুরি অভ্যাস করা। **—age,** *n.* **—er,** *n.* A petty thief; ছিঁচ্‌কা চোর, পাতিচোর, পাটচ্চর।

pil-gâr'-lic, *n.* **1.** (*Archaic*) A bald head; a man with a bald head; (অপ্রঃ) নেড়া মাথা; নেড়া। **2.** A poor creature; অভাগা লোক।

pil'-grim, *n.* & *v. i.* **1.** A wanderer; a traveller (*poet.* or *rhet.*); ভ্রমণকারী; পর্য্যটক, পরিব্রাজক। **2.** One who journeys to a sacred place as an act of religious devotion; যাত্রী, তীর্থযাত্রী। ***Verb i.*** To wander as a pilgrim; তীর্থযাত্রিরূপে পর্য্যটন করা। **—ize,** *v. i.* To go on a pilgrimage; তীর্থযাত্রা করা। **Pilgrim bottle**—গলদেশে রন্ধ্রবিশিষ্ট একপ্রকার চ্যাপ্‌টা বোতল। **Pilgrim Fathers**—যে সকল ইংরাজ ঔপনিবেশিক ১৬২০ খৃঃ অব্দে May flower নামক অর্ণবযানে আমেরিকা গমনপূর্ব্বক New England উপনিবেশ স্থাপন করেন। **Pilgrim's shell**—একপ্রকার শুক্তি—যাহা যেরুজেলেম হইতে প্রত্যাগত যাত্রিগণ চিহ্নস্বরূপ টুপির উপর পরিতেন। **Pilgrim's staff**—যেরুজেলেম যাত্রিগণের দণ্ড।

pil'-grim-âge, *n.* & *v. i.* The journey of a pilgrim; (*fig.*) mortal life viewed as a journey; তীর্থযাত্রা, তীর্থাভিগমন, তীর্থদর্শন, তীর্থপর্য্যটন, তীর্থাটন; (লক্ষণায়) ঐহিকজীবন। ***Verb i.*** To go on a pilgrimage; তীর্থযাত্রা করা। **To go on (a) pilgrimage**—To journey as a pilgrim; তীর্থগমন করা।

pi-lif'-ẽr-ous (-ŭs), *adj.* Bearing hair (esp. in *Bot.*); রোমাল।

pil′-i-fŏrm, *adj.* (*Bot.*) Hair-like in form etc.; (উদ্ভিদবিদ্যা) রোমাকৃতি।

pill, *n.* & *v. t.* **1.** A little ball of medicine; বড়ি, বটিকা, গুটিকা (সুশ্রুঃ), নিস্তনী (অঃ)। **2.** Anything disagreeable to be endured or accepted; as, a bitter *pill* to swallow; তেতো ঔষধ। **3.** (*Humorous*) A small ball *e. g.* a cannon-ball or bullet, a tennis-ball, etc.; (কৌতুকচ্ছলে) ক্ষুদ্র কন্দুক, কামানের গোলা বা গুলি, টেনিস খেলার কন্দুক **4.** (*Pl.*) Billiards: বিলিয়ার্ড খেলা **5.** (*Slang*) A tiresome person; (ইতরভাষায়) বিরক্তি উৎপাদক ব্যক্তি। ***Verb t.*** (*Slang*) To blackball: to defeat by ballot; (ইতরভাষায়) ভোট নেওয়ার বাক্সে কালো রঙ্গের গুটিকা দিয়া কাহারো বিরুদ্ধে মত দেওয়া; ঐরূপ ভাবে মত দিয়া পরাস্ত করা। **Pill-box—**A box for holding pills; বড়ির বাক্স। (*Facet.*) A small vehicle or building; (রঙ্গচ্ছলে) ক্ষুদ্র যান বা বাড়ী। **Pillwort—**বিভিন্ন জাতীয় গুল্মের সাধারণ নাম। **A bitter or hard pill to swallow—**A disagreeable thing to accept or endure; তেতো ঔষধ গিলিতে হইবে। **To gild the pill**—See under GILD

pill, *v. t.* **1.** (*Archaic*) To plunder; to rob; (অপ্রঃ) লুণ্ঠন করা; লুটপাট করা। **2.** (*Dial*) To peel or pare off as bark etc.; (উপভাষায়) তোলা, উঠান।

pil′-lage (-āj), *n.* & *v. t.* **1.** Plundering in war; robbery; লুণ্ঠন; ডাকাতি। **2.** Spoil; booty; লুণ্ঠিত দ্রব্য; লুঠের মাল। ***Verb t.*** To plunder to lay waste; as, to *pillage* the camp of an enemy; লুঠ করা, লুঠপাট করা; উজাড় করা। **—lag-er,** *n.*

pil′-lar (-êr), *n.* & *v. t.* **1.** A column; a post; a pedestal; স্তম্ভ; থাম, লাট (অথঃ); উপামত, উপপীঠ **2.** (*Fig.*) Anything like a pillar; a supporter or mainstay; as, a *pillar* of the state; (লক্ষণায়) স্তম্ভবৎ বস্তু; আশ্রয়স্তম্ভ, অবলম্বনস্তম্ভ। **3.** An upright mass of air, water, etc.; জলস্তম্ভ, বায়ুস্তম্ভ প্রভৃতি। **4.** (*Mining*) The mass of coal or ore left for the support of the ceiling of a mine; খনির ছাদের আশ্রয়-স্বরূপ কয়লা বা খনিজ বিমিশ্র ধাতুর পুঞ্জি। ***Verb t.*** To support with or as with pillars; স্তম্ভদ্বারা ধারণ করা, স্তম্ভবৎ ধারণ করা। **—et,** *n.* A little pillar; স্তম্ভক। **Pillar-box—**প্রায় পাঁচ ফিট উচ্চ শূন্যগর্ভ স্তম্ভ—যাহাতে চিঠি ফেলা যাইতে পারে। **Driven from pillar to post—**Driven to and fro; driven from one resource to another, from one state of difficulty to another; ইতস্ততঃ তাড়িত; এক বিপদ হইতে আর এক বিপদে তাড়িত। **Hexagonal pillar—**স্কন্ধ কাণ্ড (রাঃ রাঃ)। **Octangular pillar—**বিষ্ণুকাণ্ড (রাঃ রাঃ)। **Pentagonal pillar—**শিবকাণ্ড (রাঃ রাঃ)। **Pillars of Hercules—**ভূমধ্যসাগরের প্রবেশদ্বারে পরস্পরের প্রতিমুখী অন্তরীপদ্বয়। [গ্রীকপুরাণে কথিত আছে পূর্ব্বে ইহারা একত্র সংলগ্ন ছিল—হারকুলিস ইহাদিগকে বিচ্ছিন্ন করিয়া Cadiz নগরীতে প্রবেশ করেন।] **Pillars of state—**রাষ্ট্রভৃত (শুক্রঃ বিনয়ঃ)। **Sixteen sided pillar—**রুদ্রকাণ্ড (রাঃ রাঃ)। **Square pillar—**ব্রহ্মকাণ্ড (রাঃ রাঃ)।

pil-lau (-lä), *n.* A Turkish dish; পোলাও।

pil′-li-ŏn *n.* (*Hist.*) A cushion usu. for a woman behind a horseman; a light saddle for women; (ইতিহাস) অশ্বারোহীর পশ্চাতে (সাধারণতঃ) স্ত্রীলোকের জন্য গদি; স্ত্রীলোকদের জন্য হালকা জিন।

pil′-li-winks, *n.* (*Hist.*) An instrument of torture for squeezing fingers; (ইতিহাস) অঙ্গুলী নিষ্পীড়নের জন্য পীড়ন-যন্ত্র বিশেষ।

pil′-lŏ-rÿ, *n.* & *v. t.* A frame of wood set up with movable boards and holes through which were formerly put the head and hands of an offender for

Pillory.

punishment; সচ্ছিদ্র দণ্ড কাষ্ঠ—ইহার ছিদ্রের ভিতর মস্তক ও হস্তদ্বয় প্রবিষ্ট করাইয়া পূর্ব্বে অপরাধীকে শাস্তি দেওয়া হইত, স্তম্ভবন্ধ। ***Verb t.*** **1.** To punish in the pillory; স্তম্ভদণ্ডে বাঁধিয়া শাস্তি দেওয়া। **2.** (*Fig.*) To expose to public scorn or ridicule; (লক্ষণায়) সাধারণের বিদ্রূপ ও উপহাসভাজন করা।

pil′-low (-ö), *n.*, *v. t.* & *i.* **1.** A cushion of feathers etc. for resting the head on when reposing; বালিশ, উপধান (বিপুলমুপধানং ভুজলতা), উপাধান (wrongly used for উপধান), [also উপবর্হণ]। **2.** A pillow-shaped block or support; উপধানাকৃতি আশ্রয়। ***Verb t.*** To lay or rest on for support; to support; as, to *pillow* the head; অবলম্বনের জন্য ন্যস্ত করা; অবলম্বিত করা। ***Verb i.*** To rest on a pillow; বালিশে মাথা রাখা। **—y,** *adj.* Like a pillow; soft; উপধানবৎ; কোমল। **Pillow bere, —beer, —ber, —slip, —case—**(অপ্রঃ বা উপভাষায়) বালিশের ওআড়। **Pillow cup—**শয়নের পূর্ব্বে সর্ব্বশেষ যে এক পেয়ালা মদ্য পান করা হয়। **To take counsel of one's pillow—**To take a night to reflect; রাত্রি ব্যাপিয়া চিন্তা করা।

pī'-lōse, –lous (-lŭs), *adjs.* Covered with hair : রোমাবৃত, রোমময় **–los'-i-ty,** *n.*

pī'-lŏt, *n.* & *v. t.* **1.** One qualified and employed to steer a ship ; a helmsman ; কাণ্ডারী, নৌসারথি (জাতক) ; কর্ণধার, তারক (অঃ)। 2. One qualified to conduct ships in and out of a harbour, along a dangerous coast etc. ; আড়কাটি, জলনিয়ামক (জাতক), দিশারু, সমুদ্রমার্গ-প্রদর্শক (কেঙিঃ)। 3. (*Fig.*) A guide or director, esp. in a hunting field : (লক্ষণায়) পথপ্রদর্শক। ***Verb t.* 1.** To direct the course of; as, to *pilot* a ship ; to act as a pilot on (a way or piece of water) ; কাণ্ডারীর কাজ করা ; আড়কাটির কাজ করা। **2.** (*Fig.*) To guide or direct ; (লক্ষণায়) পথপ্রদর্শন করা, পথনির্দেশ করা। **–age,** *n.* **–less.** *adj.* **Pilot-boat**—দিশারুর নৌকা। **Pilot-engine**—যে অগ্রগামী বাষ্পীয়যন্ত্র পশ্চাদ্‌বর্ত্তী শকটশ্রেণীর পথ পরিষ্কার করিয়া যায়। **Pilot-fish**—একপ্রকার ক্ষুদ্র মৎস্য—ইহা হাঙ্গরের পথপ্রদর্শন করিয়া চলে বলিয়া কথিত আছে **Pilot-flag**—যে জাহাজের আড়কাটীর আবশ্যক তাহার অগ্রভাগে যে পতাকা উত্তোলিত হয়। **Pilot-house**—জাহাজের কাণ্ডারীর জন্য পাটাতনের উপরিস্থ বৃতিবেষ্টিত স্থলী। **Pilot-jacket**—Same as PEA-JACKET.

pil'-ūle, pill–, *ns.* A little pill ; a pill ; ক্ষুদ্র বটিকা ; বড়ী, বটিকা। **–u-lar, –u-lous,** *adjs.*

pīm'-ē-lōde *n.* A cat-fish ; এক প্রকার মৎস্য।

pī-mĕn'-tō, *n.* Jamaica pepper ; the tree producing it ; একপ্রকার গরম মসলা ; ঐ মসলার গাছ।

pimp, *n.* & *v. i.* Pander, or procurer ; কুটন, কুটনী (*Fem.*) ভেড়ুয়া, বিট। ***Verb i.*** To pander ; to procure lewd women ; কুটনীগিরি ; দুষ্টা স্ত্রী জোগাড় করা।

pim'-pêr-nĕl, *n.* A plant of the primrose family with reddish flowers ; একপ্রকার গাছ, শস্যক্ষেত্রে জন্মে, লাল ফুল হয়, জোঁকমারী (হিন্দী গোবী)।

Pimpinella anisum — মউরী (বেলঃ)।

pimp'-ing, *adj.* Small ; petty ; sickly ; ক্ষুদ্র ; সামান্য ; রোগা।

pim'-ple (-pl), *n.* **1.** A small elevation of the skin usu. with an inflamed base ; বয়সফোঁড়া, তনুব্রণ, পামা (সাঃ পঃ)। **2.** (*Fig.*) A small swelling ; (লক্ষণায়) ক্ষুদ্র স্ফোটক। **–pled, –ply,** *adjs.*

pin, *n.* **1.** A small piece of wire used for fastening papers etc. ; আলপিন। **2.** A piece of wood or of metal used for fastening things together ; a peg ; গুঁজি ; কীল, শঙ্কু। **3.** A more or less ornamental piece of metal, for securing the hair, dress, etc. ; as, *hairpin* ; চুলের কাঁটা, সেফটিপিন, প্রভৃতি। **4.** Anything resembling a pin ; a peg in a musical instrument ; আলপিনের মত কোন কিছু ; বাদ্যযন্ত্রের কর্ণ **5.** (*Colloq., pl.*) The legs ; as, knock one off his *pins* ; (চলিত ভাষায়) পা। **6.** A trifle ; a thing of small value ; as, do not care a *pin* for him ; তুচ্ছজিনিষ ; কাণাকড়ি। **7.** A small cask of 4½ gallons ; ৪½ গেলনের পিপা। **Pin-buttock**—সূক্ষ্মাগ্র নিতম্ব **Pin-case, –cushion**—আলপিন গুঁজিয়া রাখার জন্য ছোট গদি। **Pin-feather**—অপরিণত ক্ষুদ্র পালক। **Pin-fire cartridge**—যে বন্দুকের পশ্চাদ্ভাগে টোটা ভরিতে হয়—তাহার কার্ত্তজ। **Pin-head**—The head of a pin ; আলপিনের মাথা। (*Fig.*) A minute thing ; (লক্ষণায়) অতি ক্ষুদ্র বস্তু সূচাগ্র **Pin hold**—যে স্থানে আলপিন গুঁজিয়া রাখা হয় **Pin-hole** — আলপিনের ছিদ্র। **Pin-money**—স্বামী স্ত্রীকে হাত খরচের জন্য যে টাকা দেন **Pin-point** — সূচাগ্র ; সূক্ষ্ম বস্তু, (cf. সূচাগ্রভূমি)। **Pin-prick**—A slight thrust ; খোঁচা। (*Fig.*) A trifling irritation ; (লক্ষণায়) খোঁচা। **Pintail**—Kinds of duck and grouse with pointed tail ; বিভিন্ন প্রকার পক্ষীর নাম। **Pin wheel**—Same as CATHERINE WHEEL (which see.) **Rolling pin**—বেলন। **I don't care a pin**—I don't care at all ; আমি অণুমাত্রও গ্রাহ্য করি না। **In merry pin**—In a merry humour মনের আনন্দে, মনের স্ফূর্তিতে। **On one's pins**—On one's legs ; in good condition ; নিজের পায়ের উপর ; ভাল অবস্থায়। **On pins and needles**—Very nervous, anxious, or uneasy ; অতিশয় ভয়-তরাসে, উৎকণ্ঠিত, উদ্‌গ্রীব, উতরোল। **On the pin**—Watchfull ; সজাগ। **Pins and needles**—হাতে পায় ঝিঁঝিঁ বোধ, ঝিনঝিনি।

pin, *v. t.* **1.** To fasten with a pin or pins ; to transfix by or with a pin or lance etc. ; আলপিন দ্বারা আঁটা ; আলপিন বা বর্শাদ্বারা এপিট ওপিট করিয়া বিদ্ধ করা। **2.** To seize and hold fast (against wall etc.) ; ঠেলিয়া ধরা। **3.** To hold or keep *to* a promise or other obligation (usu. with *down*) ; as, to *pin* one *down to* a promise ; প্রতিশ্রুতিতে বদ্ধ করা, প্রতিজ্ঞাবদ্ধ করা। **4.** To enclose ; to pen ; ঘেরা ; আবদ্ধ করা। **To pin one's faith on (a person etc.)**—To depend upon him entirely ; to trust to utterly ; কাহারো উপর সম্পূর্ণ নির্ভর করা ; কাহাকে সম্পূর্ণ বিশ্বাস করা।

pin'-ā-fōre, *n.* An apron worn by children to protect the front of the dress from dirt etc. ; শিশুদিগের জামার সম্মুখ ভাগ আবরক বস্ত্রখণ্ড। **–fored** *adj.*

pī-năs′-têr, *n.* A pine of Southern Europe; দক্ষিণ ইয়ুরোপের সরলজাতীয় বৃক্ষবিশেষ।

pince-nez, (*F.*), *n.* A pair of eyeglasses with a spring to clip the nose; নাকী-চসমা।

pin′-cêrṡ, *n.* 1. An instrument for gripping anything to be held fast or drawn out, (also, *a pair of pincers*); শাঁড়াসী, সংড়শী (সাঃ পঃ), কঙ্কমুখ, চিমটা, সন্দংশ সোন্না (small)। 2. The nippers of certain crustaceans; কাঁকড়া প্রভৃতির ঠ্যাং। **Pincers for extracting tooth**—দন্তশংকু (সুশ্রুঃ কুঞ্জঃ)।

pincette, (*F.*), *n.* Small pincers; সোন্না।

pinch *n.* 1. A nip; a close compression with the ends of the fingers; খামচি; চিমটি। 2. A small quantity that can be taken up by the fingers and the thumb; a very small quantity; as, a *pinch* of snuff or salt; একচিমটি জিনিষ; অত্যল্প জিনিষ। 3. Pain; stress; as, a *pinch* of poverty; যাতনা; কৃচ্ছ্র, কষ্ট। **At a pinch**—At a critical juncture; সঙ্কট সময়ে। **At or on a pinch**—In a difficulty; সঙ্কটে।

pinch, *v. t.* & *i.* 1. To squeeze, esp. between the tips of fingers; to nip: চিমটিকাটা; খামচি দেওয়া। 2. To compress painfully; as, a shoe *pinches* the foot; আঁট হওয়ার দরুণ ব্যথা লাগা। 3. To pain; to afflict or distress; as, *pinching* cold or hunger; যাতনা দেওয়া; কষ্ট দেওয়া। 4. To extort; as, to *pinch* money *from* or *out of* a person; উৎপীড়ন করিয়া আদায় করা। 5. To straiten or stint; as, to *pinch* a person in, of, or for food etc.; কষ্টে ফেলা, সংক্ষেপ করা, সঙ্কোচ করা। 6. To urge as a horse esp. in a race; ঘোড়দৌড়ে বেগে অগ্রসর হওয়ার জন্য অশ্ব তাড়না করা। 7. (*Slang*) To steal or rob; (ইতর ভাষায়) চুরি করা, লুঠিয়া নেওয়া। 8. (*Slang*) To arrest; (ইতর ভাষায়) গ্রেপ্তার করা। 9. To sail close-hauled as a vessel; যথাসম্ভব বায়ুর প্রতিকূলে পাইল ভরে চালান। ***Verb i.*** 1. To compress painfully; to squeeze; as, the shoe *pinches*; আঁট হওয়ার দরুণ ব্যথা দেওয়া; সম্পীড়ন করা। 2. To be niggardly; কঞ্জুষ হওয়া। **That is where the shoe pinches**—That is the difficulty or trouble; এই খানেইত গোল বাঁধে বা ঠেকে। **To know where the shoe pinches**—To know where the cause of trouble or difficulty is; গোল কোথায় আছে জানা।

pinch′-bĕck, *n.* & *adj.* A yellow alloy of five parts of copper to one of zinc; একভাগ দস্তা ও পাঁচ ভাগ তাম্রের মিশ্রণে প্রস্তুত পীতবর্ণ ধাতুবিশেষ, কৃত্রিমস্বর্ণ। ***Adj.*** Sham; unreal; কৃত্রিম; অপ্রকৃত, অবাস্তব।

Pin-dā′-rī, *n.* A mounted marauder in India in the 17th and 18th centuries, পিণ্ডারী দস্যু।

Pin-dăr′-ic, *adj.* & *n.* Of, or pertaining to, Pindar, the Greek lyric poet; after the style of Pindar; as, *Pindaric* odes; প্রাচীন গ্রীক কবিতাকার Pindar সম্বন্ধীয়; পিণ্ডারের রচনারীতির অনুযায়ী। ***Noun.*** A Pindaric ode; Pindaric metre or verse; পিণ্ডারের গীতি; ছন্দঃ বা কবিতায় পিণ্ডারের মত।

Pine tree.

pīne, *n.* A cone-bearing evergreen resinous tree, furnishing valuable timber; দেবদারুবৃক্ষ, সরল বৃক্ষ, সরলদ্রুম। **Pine-barren**—সরলবৃক্ষপ্রসূ বালুকাময় সমতল স্থান। **Pine-beauty, Pine carpet**—সরলগাছের পোকা বিশেষ। **Pine chafer**—একপ্রকার গোবরে পোকা,—ইহারা সরল গাছের পাতা খায়। **Pine-clad, -crowned**—সরল দ্রুমশোভিত, সরলদ্রুমমণ্ডিত, সরলদ্রুমরাজিশোভিত শীর্ষ। **Pine-cone**—সরলগাছের ফল। **Pine-finch**—আমেরিকার পক্ষিবিশেষ। **Pine-house**—Same as PINERY below. **Pine oil**—সরল প্রভৃতি বৃক্ষের নির্যাস হইতে প্রাপ্ত তৈলবিশেষ।

pīne, *v. i.* 1. To languish; to grow weakly with pain, grief, disease, etc.; to droop; ক্ষীণ হওয়া; কৃশ হওয়া; শীর্ণ হওয়া। 2. To long intensely (followed by *for, after, to do*); as, she *pines for* her lover; আকুল ভাবে আকাঙ্ক্ষা করা, প্রবাল স্পৃহা করা।

pin′-ē-ăl, *adj.* Pertaining to, or resembling, a pine-cone; সরলগাছের ফলসম্বন্ধীয়, উক্তফলবৎ। **Pineal gland**—সহস্রার (জাহিঃ), তৃতীয় চক্ষু (হিঃ কোঃ)।

pīne′-ăp-ple (-l), *n.* A tropical plant and its fruit like pine-cone; আনারসগাছ, আনারস।

pīn′-ēr-ȳ, *n.* 1. A hothouse in which pine-apples are grown; যে কাচমন্দিরের ভিতর শীতপ্রধান দেশে আনারসের চাষ করা হয়। 2. A pine wood or forest; সরলবন।

pin′-fōld, *n.* & *v. t.* A pound or enclosure for stray cattle; খোঁয়াড়। ***Verb t.*** To confine in a pinfold; খোঁয়াড়ে আটক রাখা।

ping, *n.* & *v. i* The whistling sound made by a flying bullet; গুলির সোঁ সোঁ শব্দ। ***Verb i.*** To fly with or produce such a sound; সোঁ সোঁ শব্দে চলা বা ঐরূপ শব্দ করা।

ping′-pŏng, *n.* A kind of indoor lawn-tennis played with battledores or small racket over a net on a table; একপ্রকার আঁটা

খেলা—যাহা গৃহের ভিতর মেজের উপর খেলা হয়।

pin′-guid (ping-gwid), *adj.* (*Facet.*) Unctuous ; fat ; greasy ; (কৌতুকচ্ছলে) চট্‌চটে ; মোটা ; মেদস্বী, চর্ব্বিবিশিষ্ট।

pin′-guin (-gwin), *n.* A West-Indian plant or fruit allied to the pine-apple ; পশ্চিমভারতীয় দ্বীপপুঞ্জে জাত আনারসের ন্যায় গুল্মবিশেষ।

pin′-ion (-yŏn), *n.* **1.** A feather ; a quill of the wing ; পালক ; পাখা। **2.** A segment of the wing of a bird remotest from the body ; পক্ষীর ডানার দ্বিতীয় সন্ধি। **3.** (*Poet.*) A wing ; (কবিতায়) পাখা, পক্ষ।

pin′-ion, (-yŏn), *v. t.* **1.** To cut off or bind the pinion of to prevent flight ; উড়িতে বাধা দেওয়ার জন্য পাখা বাঁধা বা এক পাখার অগ্রভাগ কাটিয়া ফেলা। **2.** To restrain by binding the arms ; to bind (arms) ; to tie up ; বাহুযুগল বন্ধন পূর্ব্বক সংযত রাখা ; (ভুজযুগল) বন্ধন করা ; বাঁধিয়া ফেলা।

pin′-ion (-yŏn), *n.* **1.** A small toothed wheel playing into the teeth of a larger one ; ক্ষুদ্র দন্তুর চক্র—যাহা বৃহত্তর দন্তুরচক্রের উপর ঘুরিয়া থাকে। **2.** A cogged spindle engaging with the wheel ; চক্রের সহিত সংযুক্ত দন্তুর তকুটী।

pink (pingk), *n.* & *adj.* **1.** A garden plant with white pink flowers ; its flower ; শ্বেত ও পাটলবর্ণ পুষ্পপ্রসূ উদ্যানরোপিত তরুবিশেষ ; ঐ তরুর পুষ্প। **2.** A light red colour like that of this flower ; পাটল, আরক্ত। **3.** The highest type ; supreme excellence ; as, the *pink* of elegance or propriety ; চূড়ান্তসীমা, পরাকাষ্ঠা ; পরমোৎকর্ষ। **4.** A fox-hunter's coat ; a fox-hunter ; শৃগালশিকারীর কোর্ত্তা ; শৃগালশিকারী। ***Adj.*** Of a pink-colour ; as, *pink* ribbons ; পাটলবর্ণ, আরক্তবর্ণ। **Pink′-ish,** *adj.* **Pink′-ness,** *n.* **Pink′-y,** *adj.* **Pink-eye**—অশ্বের সংক্রামক জ্বররোগবিশেষ ; চোখউঠারোগ, অধিমন্থ (সুশ্রুঃ)। **A pink-coat**—ইংলণ্ডের শিকারীদিগের কোর্ত্তা। **The pink of health**—চরম স্বাস্থ্য। **The pink of perfection**—উৎকর্ষের চরমসীমা।

pink (pingk), *n.* A light red pigment ; পাটলবর্ণ রঞ্জক পদার্থ।

pink (pingk) *n.* (*Hist.*) A vessel with a very narrow stern ; প্রাচীনকালের একপ্রকার জাহাজ—যাহার পাছা গলুই অতিশয় সরু থাকিত।

pink (pingk), *v. t.* **1.** To stab ; to pierce with a sword ; ছুরিকাঘাত করা, ছুরি মারা ; অসিদ্বারা বিদ্ধ করা। **2.** To make perforations in by way of ornament, as leather etc. ; চর্ম্মাদির উপর শোভাবৃদ্ধির জন্য ছিদ্র করা। **3.** To adorn ; ভূষিত করা, মণ্ডিত করা।

pink (pingk), *n.* **1.** (*Dial.*) A minnow ; (উপভাষায়) একজাতীয় ক্ষুদ্র মৎস্য। **2.** A young salmon ; স্যামন মাছের বাচ্চা।

pinna, (*L.*), *n.* (*Pl.* PINNAE.) **1.** The upper projecting part of the ear ; কর্ণের উর্দ্ধাংশ। **2.** A primary division of a pinnate leaf ; পক্ষাকার পত্রের আদ্যবিভাগ। **3.** A fin, wing or the like ; ডানা, পাখনা, পর।

pin′-nace (-ās), *n.* **1.** A man-of-war's boat ; যুদ্ধজাহাজের ডিঙ্গী। **2.** (*Hist.*), A small vessel with oars and sails ; (ইতিহাস) পান্‌সী।

pin′-na-cle (-ă-kl), *n.* & *v. t.* **1.** A slender ornamental turret ; as, the *pinnacle* of a temple ; প্রাসাদশৃঙ্গ, মন্দিরের চূড়া, মসজিদের চূড়া। **2.** A lofty peak ; উচ্চ গিরিশৃঙ্গ, গিরিশিখর, শৃঙ্গ, শিখর। **3.** (*Fig.*) Climax ; culmination ; (লক্ষণায়) চূড়ান্ত সীমা ; পরাকাষ্ঠা। ***Verb t.*** To build or furnish with a pinnacle ; শিখরসমন্বিত করা।

pin′-nate (-āt), *adj.* (*Bot.* & *Zool.*) Shaped or branching like a feather ; as, a *pinnate* leaf ; (উপপক্ষ পত্র—সাঃ পঃ) পক্ষাকার (সাঃ পঃ)। **–ly** *adv.* **–nat-ed,** *adj.*

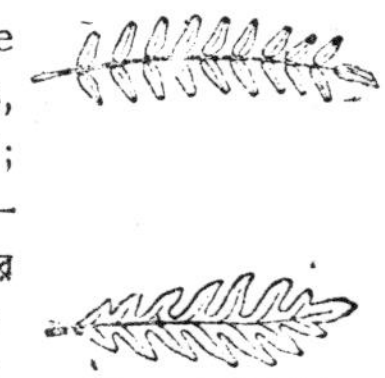

Pinnate leaf.

pin′-ner (-êr), *n.* **1.** One who, or that which, fastens as with pins ; যে ব্যক্তি শঙ্কু বা কীলক দ্বারা বদ্ধ করে। **2.** (*Hist.*) A female head-dress with two long side flaps ; উভয় পার্শ্বে শিথিল ভাবে লম্বমান বস্ত্রখণ্ডদ্বয় বিশিষ্ট স্ত্রীলোকের টুপি।

pin′-ni-grade (-i-), *adj.* & *n.* Fin-footed ; লিপ্তপাদ (অর্থাৎ অঙ্গুলীসমূহ ঝিল্লীদ্বারা সংযুক্ত)। ***Noun.*** A fin-footed animal ; লিপ্তপাদ জন্তু।

pin′-ni-pĕd (-i-), *adj.* & *n.* Same as PINIGRADE.

pin′-no-there (-ŏ-thēr), **–tere** (-tēr), *ns.* A genus of crabs ; একজাতীয় কর্কট।

pin′-nule (-ūl), *n.* **1.** (*Bot.*) The secondary division of a pinnate leaf ; (উদ্ভিদ্‌বিদ্যা) পক্ষক (সাঃ পঃ)। **2.** (*Zool.*) Small organ or part resembling a wing or fin ; পক্ষক (সাঃ পঃ)। **–nu-lar,** *adj.*

pin′-ny (-i), *n.* (*Colloq.*) Abbr. of PINAFORE.

pī′-nŏ-cle (-kl), *n.* (*U. S.*) A game at cards like bezique ; একপ্রকার তাস খেলা।

pi-nōle′, *n.* The heart of maize baked, ground and mixed with sugar ; ভুট্টাচূর্ণ চিনি প্রভৃতির সহিত মিশ্রিত করিয়া যে এক প্রকার খাদ্য প্রস্তুত করা হয়।

pint, *n.* A measure of capacity for liquids etc. equal to the eighth part of a gallon ; তরল পদার্থের পরিমাণবিশেষ (⅛ গ্যালন প্রায় দেড় পোয়া)।

pin-tā'-dō, *n.* **1.** A guinea-fowl : পক্ষিবিশেষ। **2.** A species of petrel : পক্ষিবিশেষ।

pin'-tle, (-tl), *n.* A pin or bolt esp. a pivot pin as that of a hinge or rudder ; শঙ্কু, কীল, গুঁজি।

pinx'-it (pingks-), (*L.*), *v. t.* Painted it, (a word appended to the arist's name on a painting : as, Rubens *pinxit* — Rubens painted it) ; অমকদ্বারা মুদ্রিত।

pin'-y, *adj.* Relating to, like, or abounding with, pines ; as, a *piny* wood ; সরলবৃক্ষবহুল, সরলবৃক্ষসম্বন্ধীয়, সরলবৃক্ষবৎ।

piolet, (*F.*), *n.* An Alpinist's ice-axe ; আলপ্‌স্‌ পর্ব্বতারোহিগণ কর্ত্তৃক ব্যবহৃত বরফ কাটার জন্য কুঠার

pi-ō-neer' (-nēr), *n., v. i. & t.* **1.** One of a party of soldiers who clear the road before an army sink mines etc. ; যে অগ্রগামী দল সৈন্যদলের পথ পরিষ্কার এবং পরিখাদি প্রস্তুত করিয়া অগ্রসর হয়—তাহাদের দলভুক্ত ব্যক্তি, অগ্রগামী, বেলদার। **2.** (*Fig.*) One who goes before to prepare or clear the way for others ; as, *pioneers* of reform : (লক্ষণায়) অগ্রগামী, অগ্রদূত, অগ্রনায়ক, মার্গশোধক (আপ্তেঃ)। ***Verb i.*** To act as a pioneer ; অগ্রদূতের কাজ করা, অগ্রনায়কের কাজ করা। ***Verb t.*** To open up (road etc. as a pioneer ; to act as a pioneer to or for ; অগ্রগামী হইয়া (পথ প্রভৃতি) প্রস্তুত করা ; অগ্রগামীর কাজ করা।

pi'-ous (-ŭs), *adj.* **1.** Of, or pertaining to, piety ; devout ; religious ; নিষ্ঠাসম্বন্ধীয় ; ধর্ম্মপরায়ণ, ধর্ম্মপ্রাণ, ধার্ম্মিক, ধর্ম্মনিষ্ঠ, ভক্তিমান, সাধু, ধর্ম্মাত্মা, পুণ্যাত্মা, ভক্ত (হিঃ কোঃ), ঈশ্বরপরায়ণ (কেঙিঃ), পরমার্থপরায়ণ, পরমার্থী, দেবভক্তিপ্রবণ, দেবভক্তিনিষ্ঠ, ধর্ম্মজনক, পুণ্যজনক। **2.** Prompted by mistaken piety ; as, *pious* errors ; ভ্রান্তকরুণাদ্বারা প্রেরিত **3.** (*Archaic*) Dutiful : (অপ্রঃ) কর্ত্তব্যনিষ্ঠ। **–ly,** *adv.* **Pious founder of a college etc.**—যে ব্যক্তি শ্রীভগবানের মহিমাবিস্তার অথবা লোকের উপকারের জন্য কোন মহাবিদ্যালয় প্রতিষ্ঠা করে।

pip, *n.* A disease of fowls etc. ; কুক্কুট প্রভৃতির রোগবিশেষ।

pip, *n.* **1.** A spot on playing-cards, dice, etc. ; তাস, পাসা প্রভৃতির ফোঁটা, আঁক বা চিহ্ন। **2.** One of the rhomboidal segments forming the surface of a pine-apple ; আনারসের চোখ। **3.** A single blossom of a clustered inflorescence : স্তবকান্তর্গত পুষ্প।

pip, *v. t.* (*Colloq.*) To blackball as at a club ; to defeat or hit ; ভোট লওয়ার বাক্সে কালো রঙ্গের গুটি ফেলিয়া কাহারো বিরুদ্ধে মত দেওয়া ; পরাস্ত করা, আঘাত করা।

pip, *n.* The kernel or seed of a fruit *e. g.* an orange, apple, etc. ; আতা, কমলালেবু প্রভৃতির বীজ বা বীজশস্য। **Pip'-less,** *adj.*

pīpe, *n.* **1.** A wind-instrument of music consisting of a tube

African pipes.

of wood or metal ; as, a shepherd's *pipe* : বংশী, মুরলী, বেণু, বংশনালিকা, ভেঁপু, সানাই। **2.** A long hollow body or tube for conveying water, gas, etc. ; নল, নালী, চোঙ্গা, চুঙ্গী, নালিকা (ব্রজঃ হিন্দু), নলিকা (হিঃ কোঃ)। **3.** (*Mining*) An elongated body or vein of ore ; খনিজ বিমিশ্র ধাতুর দীর্ঘ শিরা। **4.** (*Naut.*) The boatswain's whistle used to call the men to their duties, the sound of this whistle ; (নৌ-বিদ্যা) জাহাজের টাণ্ডালের সিটী ; ঐ সিটির ধ্বনি। **5.** The voice as in singing ; a call or note of a bird ; "The earliest *pipe* of half awakened birds" ; গানের ন্যায় সুর ; পক্ষীর কাকলী। **6.** (*Pl.*) The bagpipe : as, the *pipes* of Lucknow ; বাদ্যযন্ত্র বিশেষ। **7.** A tube with a bowl for smoking ; a quantity of tobacco held by this ; as, to light or smoke a *pipe* ; হুঁকা ; এক ছিলিম তামাক। **8.** A cask for wine containining 2 hogsheads ; মদের বড় পিপা [যাহাতে ১০৫ গ্যালন মদ ধরে।] **9.** The wind-pipe or one of its divisions ; শ্বাসনালী বা উহার অন্যতম বিভাগ। **10.** A tubular organ, vessel, etc. in an animal body ; জীবদেহের নলাকার যন্ত্র, বা নাড়ী। **11.** A channel of decoy for a wild fowl ; বন্য পক্ষী ধরার জন্য নলাকার ফাঁদবিশেষ। **Pipe'-ful,** *n.* **Pipe'-less, Pip'-y,** *adjs.* **Pipe-case**—চুঙ্গী রক্ষার জন্য কোমল বস্তু দ্বারা মোড়া বাক্স। **Pipe-clay**—A fine white clay used for tobacco-pipes and for cleaning white trousers etc. ; সাদা পাজামা পরিষ্কার করার নিমিত্ত এবং ধুমপান নল প্রস্তুতের জন্য একপ্রকার মিহি সাদা মাটী, শ্বেতমৃত্তিকা। (*Fig.*) Excessive attention to minutiæ of dress etc. in a regiment ; (লক্ষণায়) সেনা পল্টনে পোশাক পরিচ্ছদ প্রভৃতির দিকে অতিরিক্ত মনোযোগ। (*Verb t.*) To whiten or clean with pipe-clay ; শ্বেতমৃত্তিকা দ্বারা ধবলিত বা পরিষ্কার করা। **Pipe layer**—যে ব্যক্তি চুঙ্গী বসায়। **Pipe-laying**—চুঙ্গী বসানের কাজ, নলস্থাপন। **Pipe-light** — হুঁকা কলিকায় আগুন ধরাইবার জন্য কাগজের নল প্রভৃতি। **Pipe-rack**—হুঁকার বৈঠক। **Pipe-stone** — যে রক্তবর্ণ কঠিন মৃত্তিকায় আমেরিকার আদিম অধিবাসিগণ

ধূমপান-নল প্রস্তুত করে **Pipe-tree**—The lilac ; আনীললোহিতবর্ণ পুষ্পপ্রসূ বৃক্ষবিশেষ। **Pipe-water** — কলের জল। **Water-pipe**—জলের কল **Queen's (tobacco-) pipe**—লণ্ডননগরীর জীর্ণ পোতসংস্কারস্থলীস্থ চুল্লীবিশেষ — যাহাতে পূর্ব্বে বিজোড়া তামাক দগ্ধ করা হইত। **Put that in your pipe and smoke it**—Digest that fact etc. if you can ; যদি পার তবে তুমি নিজে এ বিষয়টা হজম কর। **To put one's pipe out**—To frustrate one's plans ; to discomfit one ; কাহারো উদ্দেশ্য ব্যর্থ করা ; কাহাকে পরাভব করা।

pipe, *v. i.* & *t.* 1. To play on a pipe or wind instrument of music ; বংশীবাদন করা, বাঁশী বাজান। 2. To whistle : "The piping shrouds" ; শিটি দেওয়া। 3. To call or summon a crew etc. with a pipe as on board ships ; শিটি দিয়া জাহাজের মাল্লাদিগকে ডাকা। ***Verb t.*** 1. To play or execute as a tune etc. on a pipe ; বাঁশীতে কোন সুর বাজান। 2. To utter in a shrill tone ; কর্কশস্বরে বলা। 3. (*Naut.*) To call or direct as a crew, by the boatswain's whistle ; শিটি দ্বারা জাহাজের মাল্লাকে ডাকা বা আদেশ দেওয়া। 4. To furnish with a pipe or pipes ; as, to *pipe* an engine ; নল বসান, চুঙ্গী বসান। 5. To trim as a dress, or ornament as a cake, with piping ; পোষাক বা পিঠা ক্ষুদ্র রজ্জুর মত ভূষা দ্বারা শোভিত করা। **As you pipe I must dance**—I must accommodate myself to your wishes ; আপনি যেমন ভাবে নাচাবেন তেমনি নাচব। **To pipe down**—To dismiss from muster, as a ship's company ; দল ভাঙ্গিয়া দেওয়া। **To pipe off**—To watch a house or person for purposes of theft ; চুরি করার উদ্দেশ্যে কোন বাটী বা ব্যক্তির উপর নজর রাখা। **To pipe one's (eyes)**—To weep ; অশ্রুমোচন করা, অশ্রুজল বর্ষণ করা। **To pipe up**—(*Both trans. and intrans.*) To begin to play as on a pipe ; to sing ; বাজাইতে আরম্ভ করা ; গান করা। (*Verb i.*) (Of a storm, wind, etc.) To increase in strength ; বলবত্তর হওয়া।

pip'-êr, *n.* 1. One who plays on a pipe, flute, or bagpipe ; বংশীবাদক, বেণুবাদক, বংশীধর। 2. A kind of fish ; একপ্রকার মৎস্য। 3. A young pigeon ; কপোতশাবক। 4. A broken-winded horse ; বায়ুকোষ ফাটিয়া যাওয়ায় কঠোর পরিশ্রমে অশক্ত ঘোড়া। 5. A decoy-dog ; যে কুকুর অন্য কুকুরকে প্রলুব্ধ করিয়া আনে। **Piper's news**—পচা খবর। **Drunk as a piper**—বদ্ধ মাতাল। **To pay the piper (and call the tune)**—To bear the expense (and have the control of a proceeding etc.) ; ব্যয় বহন করা। ***Piper cubeba***—কাবাব চিনি (বেলঃ)। ***Piper longum***—পিপুল (বেলঃ)। ***Piper nigrum***—গোলমরিচ (বেলঃ)।

pi-pette' (-pĕt), *n.* A small tube for transferring fluids as in chemical operations ; ক্ষুদ্র নল, নলিকা।

pip'-ing, *n.* 1. Playing on a pipe ; the music of a pipe ; বংশীবাদন ; বাঁশীর ধ্বনি। 2. A small cord used as trimming for dresses etc. ; ornamental cord-like lines of sugar on a cake ; যে রজ্জুবৎ ফিতাদ্বারা পোষাক প্রভৃতি সজ্জিত করা হয় ; পিষ্টকের উপর শর্করা নির্ম্মিত রজ্জুবৎ রেখা সমূহ।

pip'-ing, *adj.* Playing on a musical pipe ; বেণুবাদনশীল। **Piping hot**—Hissing hot ; ফুটন্ত গরম, গরমাগরম। **The piping time(s) of peace**—যে সময়ে বা যুগে রণবাদ্যের পরিবর্ত্তে বংশীধ্বনি হইত।

pip-is'-trĕl, -trelle' (-trĕl), *ns.* A small European bat ; ইয়ুরোপদেশীয় ক্ষুদ্র বাদুড়বিশেষ।

pip'-it, *n.* A bird like the lark ; চাতকবৎ পক্ষিবিশেষ।

pip'-kin, *n.* A small earthen pot ; ক্ষুদ্র মৃণ্ময় পাত্র।

pip'-pin (-ĭn), A kind of apple ; একপ্রকার সেওফল।

pi'-quant (pē-kănt), *adj.* 1. Stimulating to the taste ; appetizing ; sharp ; as, a *piquant* sauce ; একটু ঝাল, মিঠেকড়া ; সরস, রুচিকর, মুখরোচক ; তীক্ষ্ণ। 2. (*Fig.*) Pleasantly stimulating or disquieting to the mind ; "A *piquant* and charming maiden" ; (লক্ষণায়) রুচির, রসিকা, রসবতী (*fem.*)। 3. (*Archaic*) Piercing ; cutting to the feelings as a taunt, etc. ; (অপ্রঃ) তীক্ষ্ণ ; মর্ম্মচ্ছেদী। **—ly,** *adv.* **—quan-cy** *n.* The state of being piquant ; তীক্ষ্ণতা, সরসতা, রসিকতা।

pique (pēk), *v. t., i.* & *n.* 1. To offend by wounding the pride of ; to irritate ; "*Pique* her and sooth in turn"—*Byron* ; অভিমানে আঘাত করা ; চটান। 2. To stimulate or excite ; as, to *pique* curiosity ; উত্তেজিত করা, উদ্দীপিত করা। 3. (*Reflex.*) To plume or value on ; "Men *pique* themsevles upon their skill" ; গর্ব্ব করা, জাঁক দেখান। ***Verb i.*** To cause irritation ; জ্বালাতন করা। ***Noun.*** Irritation due to wounded pride ; মান, অভিমান।

pique, (pēk), *n., v. t.* & *i.* (*Card playing*) The scoring by one player of 30 points in piquet before the opponent scores at all; প্রতিদ্বন্দ্বী পিঠ পাইবার পূর্ব্বে ৩০ অঙ্ক লাভ। ***Verb t.*** To score a pique against ; প্রতিপক্ষের পিঠ পাইবার পূর্ব্বে নিজে ৩০ অঙ্ক লাভ করা। ***Verb i.*** To score a pique ; প্রতিপক্ষের পিঠ পাইবার আগে নিজে ৩০ অঙ্ক লাভ করা।

pique (pēk), *n.* A ribbed cotton fabric ; একপ্রকার দৃঢ় কার্পাস বস্ত্র।

pi'-quĕt (-kĕt), *n.* A game at cards played by two persons with 32 cards ; একপ্রকার তাস খেলা।

pi-râ′-gua (-gwă), **pĕr-i-âg′-ua** (-wă), *ns.* **1.** A canoe hollowed from the trunk of a single tree ; শালতী নৌকা। **2.** Two-masted sailing barge ; দ্বিমাস্তুল পাইলের জাহাজ।

pi′-rate, *n., v. t. & i.* **1.** A sea-robber ; a freebooter on the seas ; জলদস্যু, নাবিকদস্যু (চল্‌তি), বোম্বাটিয়া ; সমুদ্রদস্যু, সামুদ্রিকদস্যু। **2.** An armed ship or vessel engaged in piracy ; জলদস্যুগণের জাহাজ। **3.** A plunderer ; লুণ্ঠনকারী, লুঠেরা। **4.** An infringer of the law of copyright ; গ্রন্থস্বত্বাপহারক। **5.** An omnibus that encroaches on the route of other omnibuses or overcharges its passengers ; যে বিশ্বযান অপর বিশ্বযানের পথে অনধিকার প্রবেশ করে বা যাত্রিগণের নিকট অতিরিক্ত ভাড়া আদায় করে। *Verb t.* **1.** To publish as books etc. without permission of the author ; গ্রন্থস্বত্ব অপহরণ করা। **2.** To rob at sea ; to plunder ; সমুদ্রে দস্যুতা করা ; লুণ্ঠন করা। *Verb i.* To play the pirate ; to rob on the high seas ; বোম্বাটিয়াগিরি করা ; সমুদ্রে দস্যুতা করা। **–ra-cy,** *n.* **1.** Robbing on the high seas ; জলদস্যুতা, বোম্বাটিয়াগিরি, সমুদ্রদস্যুতা। **2.** Infringement of the law of the copyright ; গ্রন্থস্বত্বাপহরণ, লেখাচুরি। **–rat′-ic, –rat′-i-cal,** *adjs.* **–rat′-i-cal-ly,** *adv.*

pi-rogue′ (-rōg), *n.* Same as PIRAGUA.

pir-ou-ette′, (-ô-ĕt), *n. & v. i.* **1.** A whirling or turning about on the toes in dancing ; নৃত্যকালে পাদদ্বয়ের অঙ্গুলীর উপর ভর করিয়া ঘূর্ণন। **2.** The whirling about of a horse ; অশ্বের আবর্তন। *Verb i.* To execute a pirouette in dancing ; নৃত্যকালে অঙ্গুলীর উপর ভর দিয়া ঘুরা।

pis aller, (*F.*), *n.* The last resource ; শেষ উপায়।

pis′-că-ry, *n.* The right of fishing in another man's waters ; অপরের অধিকৃত বিল প্রভৃতিতে মৎস্যশিকারের অধিকার।

pis′-că-tŏ-ry, *adj.* Of, or pertaining to, fishers or fishing ; addicted to fishing ; মৎস্যশিকারসম্বন্ধীয়, ধীবরসম্বন্ধীয় ; মৎস্যশিকারে আসক্ত। **–to′-ri-al,** *adj.*

pisces, *n.* **1.** (*Astron.*) The twelfth sign of the zodiacal constellation ; মীনরাশি, মীনলগ্ন, অন্ত্যভ (বৃঃ সঃ), ঝষ। **2.** The vertebrate animals of the class fishes ; মৎস্যবর্গ।

pis′-ci-cŭl-türe (-i-), *n.* The rearing of fish by artificial methods ; মৎস্যের চাষ। **–cul′-tur-al,** *adj.* **–cul′-tur-ist,** *n.*

pis-cī′-nă, *n.* (*Pl.* -NÆ, -NÆS) **1.** A fish-pond ; among ancient Romans, a bathing pond ; মৎস্যপূর্ণপুষ্করিণী ; প্রাচীন রোমানদের স্নান করার জন্য পুষ্করিণী। **2.** A basin with a drain for carrying away water used in rinsing chalice etc. ; কোশাকুশি প্রভৃতি প্রক্ষালনের জন্য জলনিঃসরণ নালীযুক্ত ভাণ্ডবিশেষ।

pis′-cīne, *n.* A bathing pool ; স্নানকরণার্থ পুকুর।

pis′-cīne, *adj.* Pertaing to fishes ; মৎস্যসম্বন্ধীয়।

Piscium—রেবতী (হিঃ কোঃ)

pis-cĭv′-ŏ-rous (-rŭs), *adj.* (*Zool.*) Feeding on fish ; মৎস্যভোজী, মৎস্যখাদক, মৎস্যাশী, মৎস্যভুক, মৎস্যাদ।

Pise, (*F.*), *n.*, Stiff earth or clay inserted into a wall ; প্রাচীরে অন্তর্নিবিষ্ট একপ্রকার কঠিন মৃত্তিকা।

Pĭs-gah (-gâ), *n.* The mountain from which Moses viewed the Promised Land (*Deut.* iii., 27) ; যে পর্বত হইতে মুশা ঈশ্বর কর্তৃক প্রতিশ্রুত-ভূমি সন্দর্শন করিয়াছিলেন।

pish, *interj. & v. i.* An expression to denote contempt or disgust ; অরে, রে, ইস্‌, এঃ। *Verb i.* To say pish ; ইস্‌ করা, আরে বলা।

pi-shogue′ (-shŏg), *n.* Sorcery ; spell ; যাদুবিদ্যা ; যাদু, কুহক।

pi′-si-fŏrm, *adj.* Having the form of a pea ; মটরের আকার। **Pisiform bone**—মণিবন্ধের ক্ষুদ্র অস্থিবিশেষ।

pis′-mire, *n.* An ant ; পিপীলিকা।

piss, *v. i., t. & n.* (Now *vulg.*) To make water ; (অধুনা ইতরভাষায়) মুতা। *Verb t.* To discharge as blood etc. with urine ; to wet with urine ; প্রস্রাবের সহিত রক্তপাত করা ; প্রস্রাব দ্বারা ভিজান। *Noun.* Urine ; মূত্র।

pis-tā′-chi-ŏ (-shi-), *n.* **1.** The nut of a small tree cultivated for its fruits ; the tree itself ; পেস্তা ; পেস্তা গাছ। **2.** A light yellowish green colour like that of the kernel of this nut ; পেস্তার মত বর্ণ।

Pistil.
a, Style.
b, Stigma.

pis′-til, *n.* The female organ of a flower consisting of three parts—ovary, style, and stigma ; পুষ্পগর্ভতন্তু, গর্ভকেশর (সাঃ পঃ), স্ত্র্যঙ্গ, (সাঃ পঃ), পুষ্পাগ্র (ঐ), স্ত্রী-কেশর। **–la-ry, –late, –lif′-er-ous, –line,** *adjs.*

pis′-tŏl, *n. & v. t.* A small fire-arm adapted for use with one hand ; পিস্তল। *Verb t.* To shoot with a pistol ; পিস্তল দ্বারা গুলি করা। **Within** or **beyond a pistol-shot**—পিস্তলের পাল্লার ভিতরে বা বাহিরে।

pis-tōle′, *n.* An old gold coin of Spain, France, etc. worth from 16 to 18 shillings ; স্পেনদেশের প্রাচীন স্বর্ণমুদ্রাবিশেষ।

pis′-tŏl-grăph, *n.* An instantaneous photograph ; an apparatus for obtaining this ; তৎক্ষণাৎগৃহীত

আলোকচিত্র ; ঐরূপ আলোকচিত্র যে যন্ত্রদ্বারা গ্রহণ করা যায়।

pis-tŏl′-ŏ-ġy̆, *n.* Theology that deals with faith ; ভক্তিশাস্ত্র (হিঃ কোঃ), ভক্তিসূত্র (ঐ)।

pis′-tŏn, *n.* Cylindrical piece of metal or other material used in pumps, steam-engines fitting and moving up and down within a tube or hollow-cylinder ; পিচকারি প্রভৃতিতে তরলপদার্থ আকর্ষণ করার দণ্ড, চাপদণ্ড, (প্রঃ বাঃ), নলদণ্ড, সম্পীড়ন-নল, সম্পীড়নী, সম্পীড়ননালী (আঃ বঃ), ডাঁট (হিঃ কোঃ)। **Piston-rod**—সম্পীড়ন নল, নলদণ্ড, চাপদণ্ড।

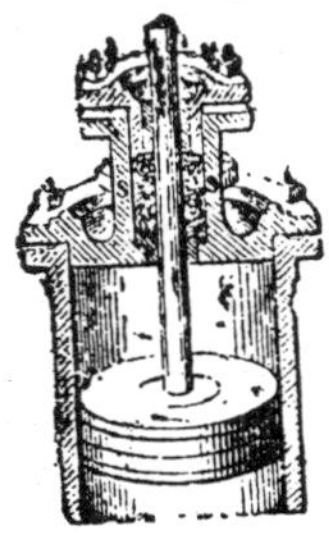
Piston and cylinder.

pit, *n.* 1. A cavity or hole in the ground either natural or artificial ; the shaft of mine ; as, a gravel *pit* ; গর্ত্ত, গহ্বর, খানা, কুণ্ড ; খনিতে প্রবেশের জন্য সুড়ঙ্গ। 2. (Also *pit of hell*) Hell ; নরক। 3. A pitfall ; a trap ; চোরাগর্ত্ত ; ফাঁদ। 4. A hollow or depression in an animal or plant body ; as, the arm *pit* ; the mark left by a pistule in small-pox ; জন্তু বা বৃক্ষগাত্রের মধ্যে ক্ষুদ্র গর্ত্ত বা কোটর ; বসন্ত প্রভৃতির দাগ। 5. The part of the auditorium of a theatre on the floor of the house ; people occupying this ; নাট্যশালার মেঝের উপর শ্রোতৃমণ্ডলীর উপবেশনের জন্য স্থান ; ঐ স্থানে উপবিষ্ট শ্রোতৃমণ্ডলী। 6. An enclosure in which cocks and dogs fight ; কুক্কুট বা কুকুরের যুদ্ধের বেষ্টিত স্থলী। 7. (*Dial.*) A grave ; (উপভাষায়) কবর। **Pit-fall**—প্রচ্ছন্ন গর্ত্ত, চোরাগর্ত্ত ; ফাঁদ। **Pit-head** — খনির গর্ত্তের মাথা। **Pitman**—(মার্কিণ যুক্তরাজ্য) কয়লার খনির মজুর ; যন্ত্রের সংযোজক দণ্ড। **The pit of the stomach**—কৃত্রিম পাঁজরের তরুণাস্থির মধ্যবর্ত্তী অবনমিত স্থান।

pit, *v. t.* 1. To lay in a pit or hole ; গর্ত্তে রাখা। 2. To mark with little hollows ; as, a face *pitted* by small-pox ; ক্ষুদ্র ক্ষুদ্র রন্ধ্র দ্বারা চিহ্নিত করা। 3. To set *against* to fight in a pit as a cock, dog, etc. ; মোরগ, কুক্কুর প্রভৃতি বেষ্টিত স্থানে রাখিয়া পরস্পরের সহিত ঝগড়া বাধাইয়া দেওয়া। 4. (*Fig.*) To match (a person) against another ; (লক্ষণায়) পরস্পরের সহিত লাগাইয়া দেওয়া।

pit′-(ă-)păt, *adv.* & *n.* With palpitation ; with a succession of quick beats ; as, his heart or feet went *pitapat* ; দুরু দুরু করিয়া ; পিট্ পিট্ করিয়া, টিপ টিপ করিয়া। *Noun.* A palpitation ; a light repeated sound ; ধুক ধুক, দুরু দুরু ; পিট পিট, টিপ টিপ, ধড় ফড়।

pitch (pĭch), *n.* & *v. t.* A thick black resinons substance obtained from tar, and used in caulking ships etc. ; আলকাতরা হইতে প্রাপ্ত একপ্রকার ঘন কৃষ্ণবর্ণ ধুনার মত পদার্থ, আলকাতরাসার। *Verb t.* 1. To cover or smear with pitch ; আলকাতরাসার দ্বারা মাখান। 2. (*Fig.*) To darken ; to obscure ; (লক্ষণায়) তমসাচ্ছন্ন করা, অন্ধকার করা ; অস্পষ্ট করা। **Pitch′-y,** *adj.* 1. Relating to, or like, pitch ; soiled with pitch ; আলকাতরা সম্বন্ধীয় ; আলকাতরা দ্বারা মলিনীকৃত। 2. Very dark ঘুটঘুটে (অন্ধকার)। **Pitch-black, -dark**—সূচীভেদ্য (অন্ধকার), ঘুটঘুটে (অন্ধকার)। **Pitch-blende**—একপ্রকার খনিজ পদার্থ—ইহা হইতে uranium ও radium পাওয়া যায়। **Pitch-cap**—আলকাতরাসার দ্বারা রক্ষিত টুপি—পূর্ব্বে ইহা পীড়নযন্ত্রস্বরূপ ব্যবহৃত হইত। **Pitch-coal** — একপ্রকার শিলাজতু-মিশ্রিত কয়লা। **Pitch-pine**—একপ্রকার সরল বৃক্ষ — যাহা হইতে আলকাতরাসার প্রাপ্ত হওয়া যায় এবং আমেরিকায় ইন্ধনস্বরূপ যাহার বহুল ব্যবহার হয়। **Pitchstone**—আগ্নেয়গিরির অগ্ন্যুৎপাতজনিত পুরাতন পাষাণ—যাহা আলকাতরার সারের মত দেখায়।

pitch (pĭch), *v. t.* & *i.* 1. To plant or thrust in the ground ; as to *pitch* a stake ; গাড়া, প্রোথিত করা, পোতা। 2. To fix and erect as a tent ; to fix in a certain position ; as, to *pitch* a beacon on a hill ; (তাঁবু) খাটান, সন্নিবেশিত করা ; স্থাপিত করা, গাড়া, পোতা। 3. (*Mus.*) To fix the pitch or tune of ; as, to *pitch* a tune ; (সঙ্গীতবিদ্যা) কোন বিশেষ গ্রামে সুর বাঁধা। 4. To throw ; to hurl (esp. with a definite aim) ; as, to *pitch* quoits : to *pitch* a ball ; নিক্ষেপ করা, ক্ষেপণ করা ; ছোড়া। 5. To expose for sale in a market etc. ; as, to *pitch* wares ; বিক্রয়ার্থ প্রদর্শন করা। 6. To pave or prepare with rubble etc. ; as, to *pitch* a road ; বাঁধা, পাকা করা, প্রস্তুত করা। 7. (*Slang*) To tell as a tale ; (ইতরভাষায়) গল্প ফাঁদা। 8. To arrange esp. for battle (now in *p. p.*) ; as, a *pitched* battle ; যুদ্ধার্থ বিন্যাস করা। *Verb i.* 1. To encamp, ; ছাউনি ফেলা। 2. To fall heavily (*on one's* head, *into*, etc.) as, he *pitched on* his head ; ধুপ করিয়া পড়া, ধপাৎ করিয়া পড়া। 3. To come to rest from flight ; উড়িতে উড়িতে ক্লান্ত হইয়া বিশ্রামের জন্য আসা। 4. (Of a ship) To rise and fall as a ship, as in a heavy sea ; উত্থান পতন হওয়া, আন্দোলিত হওয়া। 5. To fix the choice ; to decide, (with, *on* or *upon*) ; as, to *pitch on* the best course of life ; বাছিয়া লওয়া ; ঠিক করা। **Pitch-and-toss**—একপ্রকার ক্রীড়া—যাহাতে কোন চিহ্নিত স্থানে মুদ্রা নিক্ষেপ করিতে

হয় : যে ক্রীড়কের মুদ্রা চিহ্নিত স্থানের সর্ব্বাপেক্ষা নিকটে পতিত হয় সে সমস্ত মুদ্রা উৎক্ষেপের অধিকার পায়, এবং ঐ উৎক্ষিপ্ত মুদ্রাগুলি ভূতলে পতিত হইলে যেগুলির মাথাওয়ালাদিক উপরে থাকে, ঐগুলি উক্ত উৎক্ষেপকের প্রাপ্য হইয়া থাকে। **Pitched battle**—পূর্ব্ব হইতে কথাবার্ত্তা স্থির করিয়া উভয় পক্ষে যে যুদ্ধ হয়, ব্যবস্থিত যুদ্ধ। **Pitch-farthing**—See CHUCK-FARTHING. **To pitch and pay**—(*Shaks.*) To pay down at once ; to pay ready money ; তৎক্ষণাৎ দেওয়া ; রোক টাকা দেওয়া। **To pitch a yarn**—To tell a wonderful tale ; আষাঢ়ে গল্প ফাঁদা। **To pitch in**—(*Colloq.*) To set to work vigorously ; (চলিত ভাষায়) উঠিয়া পড়িয়া লাগা। **To pitch in** or **into**—To assault with blows, words, etc. ; আক্রমণ করা, কটূক্তি করা, গালি বর্ষণ করা। **To pitch it strong**—To act or speak too warmly; অতিশয় আবেগের সহিত বলা, অতিশয় উৎসাহের সহিত কাজ করা বা বলা। **To pitch upon**—To decide upon ; স্থির করা। **To play pitch-and-toss with anything**—To be careless or trust to luck about it ; কোন বিষয়ে বেপরওয়া হওয়া, কোন বিষয়ে ভাগ্যের উপর নির্ভর করা।

pitch (pĭch), *n.* **1.** A throw or cast from the hand ; a mode of pitching a cricket-ball in bowling ; ক্ষেপণ ; ক্রীকেট ক্রীড়ায় কন্দুক ক্ষেপণের প্রকারবিশেষ। **2.** Pitching as of a ship in a heavy sea ; ঝঞ্ঝাবিক্ষুব্ধ সাগরবক্ষে জাহাজের আন্দোলন। **3.** The degree of descent or slope ; as, the *pitch* of a rope ; প্রবণতার মাত্রা। **4.** The quantity of commodity pitched or exposed for sale in the market ; বাজারে বিক্রয়ের জন্য প্রদর্শিত জিনিষের পরিমাণ। **5.** (*Mus.*) The height of the key-note of a tune ; (সঙ্গীত-শাস্ত্র) গ্রাম। **6.** The height to which falcon etc. soars before swooping on the prey ; as, to fly a high *pitch* ; শিকারের উপর আপতনের পূর্ব্বে যতদূর উচ্চে বাজপক্ষী প্রভৃতি উঠিয়া থাকে। **7.** Degree ; height ; the highest reach ; as, the *pitch* of merriment ; মাত্রা ; উচ্চমাত্রা ; পরাকাষ্ঠা। **8.** A place at which one (*e. g.*) a street performer is stationed ; যে স্থানে কেহ—যথা বাজীকর প্রভৃতি অবস্থিত থাকে। **9.** (*Cricket*) That point of the ground on which the ball pitches or lights when bowled ; a place between and about wickets ; ক্রীড়াক্ষেত্রের যে স্থানে কন্দুকক্ষেপক কর্ত্তৃক নিক্ষিপ্ত কন্দুক পতিত হয় ; ত্রিদণ্ডযুগলের মধ্যবর্ত্তী বা নিকটবর্ত্তী স্থান। **10.** (*Mech.*) The distance between the threads of a screw or between the centres of two teeth in a wheel or a saw ; (যন্ত্রবিজ্ঞান) স্ক্রুপের দুই পেঁচের মধ্যবর্ত্তী বা করাতের দন্তদ্বয়ের কেন্দ্রযুগলের মধ্যবর্ত্তী স্থান। **Pitch-pipe**—ক্ষুদ্র বাঁশী প্রভৃতি—যাহার সাহায্যে গান বা সুরের গ্রাম বাঁধা হয়। **Pitch-wheel**—অপর চক্রের উপর ক্রিয়াশীল দন্তর চক্রবিশেষ।

pitch'-êr (pĭch-), *n.* **1.** A vessel usually with a spout for holding liquids ; ঘড়া, কুম্ভ, কলস, ঘট, ঘটী, গাড়ু, কমণ্ডলু, গর্গরী, গাগরী। **2.** (*Bot.*) Any of the pitcher-shaped leaves of certain plants ; (উদ্ভিদ্‌বিদ্যা) ঘটাকৃতি পত্র। **Pitcher-plant**—ঘটাকৃতি পত্রবিশিষ্ট বৃক্ষবিশেষ, ঘটপত্রী। **Little pitchers have long ears**—Children are apt to overhear ; ছেলেরাও আড়ি পাতিয়া কথা শুনিতে পারে।

Pitcher-plant.

pitch'-êr (pĭch-), *n.* **1.** One who pitches anything as quoit, ball, etc. ; ক্ষেপণকারী। **2.** Stone used for paving ; রাস্তা পাকা করার জন্য ব্যবহৃত পাথর। **3.** A street-vendor having a pitch ; যে ফেরিওয়ালার রাস্তায় ক্ষুদ্র দোকান থাকে।

pitch'-fôrk (pĭch-), *n.* & *v. t.* A fork used in pitching hay, corn, etc. ; ঘাস প্রভৃতি উঠাইবার জন্য দীর্ঘ হাতলবিশিষ্ট কাঁটাবিশেষ, উকন-ঠেঙ্গা। *Verb t.* To throw with or as with a pitchfork ; (*fig.*) to thrust (a person) forcibly (into position, office, etc.) ; উকন-ঠেঙ্গা দ্বারা উঠান ; (লক্ষণায়) জোর করিয়া ঢুকাইয়া দেওয়া।

pĭt'-ē-ous (-ŭs), *adj.* **1.** That may excite pity ; miserable ; sad ; as, a *piteous* tale ; করুণ, দীন ; আক্ষেপজনক, সকরুণ ; বিষাদময়। **2.** Compassionate ; "She was so charitable and so *piteous*" ; করুণাপূর্ণ, পরদুঃখকাতর। **—ly,** *adv.* **—ness,** *n.*

pith, *n.* & *v. t.* **1.** The soft spongy substance in the centre of plants ; any pith-like tissue ; বৃক্ষের মজ্জা বা মাইজ, মজ্জা, সার ; মাইজের ন্যায় কোন জিনিষ। **2.** The spinal cord ; মেরুদণ্ডের মজ্জা, মেরুমজ্জা। **3.** The vital or essential part ; vigour ; energy ; strength ; as, the speech lacked *pith* ; importance ; as, of great *pith* and movement (*Shakes.*) ; সারাংশ ; সত্ত্ব ; তেজঃ ; শক্তি ; সারবত্তা। *Verb t.* To kill as cattle by severing the spinal cord ; মেরুদণ্ডের মজ্জা কাটিয়া গো মহিষাদি বধ করা। **Pith'-i-ly,** *adv.* **Pith'-i-ness,** *n.* **Pith'-less,** *adj.* **Pith'-y,** *adj.* **1.** Consisting, or abounding in, pith ; মজ্জাপূর্ণ, মজ্জাবহুল। **2.** Forcible ; energetic ; terse ; as, a *pithy* speech ; ওজস্বী ; তেজঃপূর্ণ ; সারগর্ভ, সারবান। **Pith-ball**—সোলার কন্দুক।

pith-ĕ-căn'-thrōpe, *n.* Hypothetical ape-man hypothetical link between ape and man ; কল্পিত নরবানর ; নর ও বানরের মধ্যবর্ত্তী কল্পিত জীব।

pith'-ĕ-coid (-coyd), *adj.* Pertaining to apes ; ape-like ; মর্কট-সম্বন্ধীয় ; মর্কটবৎ।

pit'-i-ȧ-ble (-bl), *adj.* **1.** Deserving pity ; miserable ; lamentable ; as, *pitiable* condition ; দয়াযোগ্য, করুণাযোগ্য; দুঃখময়; শোচনীয়। **2.** Contemptible ; as, *pitiable* display of pride ; তুচ্ছ, অবজ্ঞেয়, হেয়। **—bly,** *adv.* **—ness,** *n.*

pit'-păn, *n.* A Central American canoe ; মধ্য আমেরিকার শাল্‌তি নৌকা।

pit'-tance (-ăns), *n.* **1.** (*Hist.*) A pious bequest to a religious house to provide an additional allowance of food, wine, etc. ; (ইতিহাস) অতিরিক্ত খাদ্য, মদ্য, প্রভৃতি প্রদানের জন্য মঠাদিতে যে-দান করা হয়। **2.** A small charity gift ; ক্ষুদ্র দান, সামান্য উপহার। **3.** A small allowance or remuneration ; সামান্য বেতন, সামান্য পুরস্কার। **4.** A meagre quantity or amount ; অল্প পারমাণ, সামান্য পরিমাণ।

pit'-tite (-ït), *n.* An occupier of a seat in the pit of a theatre ; যে শ্রোতা নাট্যশালার মেঝের উপর বসে।

pi-tū'-i-tȧ-rȳ, *adj.* Relating to, or secreting, mucus or phlegm ; শ্লেষ্মাসম্বন্ধীয়, শ্লেষ্মানিঃসারী, শ্লেষ্মাস্রাবী। **—tous,** *adj.*

pit'-ȳ, *n., v. t. & i.* **1.** Sympathy with distress : compassion ; as, to have *pity* on a person ; করুণা ; অনুকম্পা, দয়া, কৃপা (হিঃ কোঃ)। **2.** A ground of pity ; a thing to be regretted ; as, what a *pity* ! ; আক্ষেপের বিষয় ; শোচনীয় বিষয়। ***Verb t.*** To feel pity or grief for ; to sympathise with ; করুণা বোধ করা ; সমবেদনা প্রকাশ করা। ***Verb i.*** To be compassionate : করুণাপূর্ণ হওয়া। **—i-ful,** *adj.* **1.** Kind ; tender-hearted ; compassionate ; সদয়, করুণাময়, সকরুণ, কারুণিক, করুণাপর, করুণাশীল, করুণ; কোমলহৃদয়, দয়ার্দ্রচিত্ত ; পরদুঃখকাতর। **2.** Exciting pity ; lamentable ; as, a *pitiful* thing ; করুণোদ্রেককর ; শোচনীয়। **3.** Contemptible ; mean ; as, *pitiful* ambition ; হেয়, তুচ্ছ ; ক্ষুদ্র, নীচ। **—i-ful-ly,** *adv.* **—i-ful-ness,** *n.* **—i-less,** *adj.* Showing no pity ; cruel ; as, *pitiless* master ; নিষ্করুণ, অকরুণ ; নির্দ্দয়, নিষ্ঠুর, ক্রূর। **—i-less-ly,** *adv.* **—i-less-ness,** *n.* **—ing,** *adj.* Expressing, or feeling, pity ; as, a *pitying* glance ; করুণ, দীন, সকরুণ। **—ing-ly,** *adv.* **For pity's sake**—A form of entreaty ; দয়ার খাতিরে। **More's the pity**—So much the worse ; অধিকতর আক্ষেপের বিষয়। **To take pity on**—To feel or act compassionately towards ; করুণা করা, সকরুণ ব্যবহার করা।

piv'-ŏt, *n., v. t. & i.* **1.** A pin or pintle on which something turns or oscillates ; যে সূক্ষ্মাগ্র দণ্ডের উপর কোন বস্তু আবর্ত্তিত বা দোলায়িত হয়, যোগকীলক, বিবর্ত্তনকীলক। **2.** (*Mil.*) A soldier at the flank upon whom a company wheels ; (সামরিকশাস্ত্র) পার্শ্বভাগস্থ সৈনিক—যাহার চতুর্দ্দিকে দলের অপর সৈন্যগণ আবর্ত্তিত হয়। **3.** (*Fig.*) That on which a thing depends or turns ; a turning-point ; as, the *pivot* of an enterprise ; (লক্ষণায়) যাহার উপর অন্য বিষয় নির্ভর করে ; যে বিষয়ের উপর কোন প্রশ্নের মীমাংসা নির্ভর করে। ***Verb t.*** To place on a pivot ; to furnish with a pivot ; যোগকীলকে স্থাপন করা ; যোগকীলকসমন্বিত করা। ***Verb i.*** To turn as on a pivot, (*lit.* & *fig.*) ; যোগকীলকের উপর আবর্ত্তিত হওয়া (উপভাষায় ও লক্ষণায়)। **—al,** *adj.* **Pivot-man** — See PIVOT, *n.* 2.

pix'-ȳ, —ie (-ĭ), *ns.* A sort of English fairy ; ইংলণ্ডীয় পরীবিশেষ।

pizzicato, *adv., adj. & n.* (*It.*) By plucking the string of a violin etc. with the finger instead of using the bow ; ছড় ব্যবহার না করিয়া বেহালার তার অঙ্গুলীদ্বারা ধরিয়া। ***Adj.*** (Of a violin, note, etc.) Twitched by the finger in playing and not played with the bow ; অঙ্গুলীদ্বারা বাদিত। ***Noun.*** A passage or note played in this way ; ঐরূপে যে গৎ প্রভৃতি বাজান হয়।

piz'-zle (-l), *n.* The penis of an animal as the bull, formerly used as a whip ; বৃষভ প্রভৃতির লিঙ্গ—পূর্ব্বে যাহা চাবুক স্বরূপ ব্যবহৃত হইত।

plā'-cȧ-ble (-bl), *adj.* Easily appeased ; willing to forgive ; আশুতোষ, সুখারাধ্য, আশুপ্রসাদনীয় ; ক্ষমাপ্রবণ, ক্ষমাশীল। **—bil'-i-ty,** *n.* **—bly,** *adv.*

plăc'-ȧrd, *n. & v. t.* **1.** A written or printed paper posted up in a public place ; বৃহদ্ অক্ষরে মুদ্রিত বিজ্ঞাপন। **2.** (*Obs.*) An official proclamation ; (অপ্রঃ) সরকারী ঘোষণাপত্র। ***Verb t.*** **1.** To post placards on or within ; as, to *placard* a wall ; বৃহদক্ষরে মুদ্রিত বিজ্ঞাপন আঁটিয়া দেওয়া। **2.** To publish or notify by placards ; as, to *placard* a sale ; বৃহদক্ষরে মুদ্রিত বিজ্ঞাপন দ্বারা প্রচার বা বিজ্ঞাপিত করা।

plā'-cāte, *v. t.* To pacify ; to conciliate ; শান্ত করা, তুষ্ট করা ; প্রসন্ন করা।

plāce, **1.** A particular portion of space ; a locality ; site ; position ; as, it has changed its *place* ; স্থান ; স্থলী ; জায়গা ; অধিষ্ঠান, ঠাঁই (*poet.* or *colloq.*)। **2.** A town, village, etc. ; as one's native *place* ; নগর, গ্রাম। **3.** A residence or dwelling ; as, he has a fine *place* in the town ; আবাস-ভবন, আবাস বাটী। **4.** A fortified post ; stronghold ; সুরক্ষিতস্থান; দুর্গ। **5.** A building or a part of a building set apart for a special purpose ; as, a *place* of worship ; বিশেষ উদ্দেশ্যে রক্ষিত অট্টালিকা বা অট্টালিকার অংশ। **6.** A broadway in a city ; an area ; courtyard ; প্রশস্ত রাজবর্ত্ম ; ক্ষেত্র ; অঙ্গন, চত্বর। **7.** A seat in a theatre, on a coach etc. reserved for occupancy ; গাড়ী, রঙ্গালয় প্রভৃতিতে বিশেষভাবে রক্ষিত স্থান। **8.** Rank or position ; "Men in great *place* are thrice servants" ; পদমর্য্যাদা, পদবী, পদগৌরব। **9.** An occupation or calling, esp. a government post ; also function ; as, it is his *place* to advise ; ব্যবসায় ; পেশা, বৃত্তি। **10.** Stead ; room (with the idea of substitution) ; as, in *place* of ; স্থল ; জায়গা। **11.** A proper or suitable spot ; as, this in no *place* for boys ; উপযোগী স্থান। **12.** A particular spot on a surface ; as, sore *place* on the wrist ; a sore ; কোন কিছুর উপরিস্থিত নির্দ্দিষ্ট স্থান ; ঘা। **13.** A step in progression of argument, statement, etc. ; as, in the first or second *place* ; যুক্তি প্রভৃতির ক্রম, স্থল। **14.** A passage in a book, writing or the like ; as, in one *place* the author says etc ; পুস্তক প্রভৃতির অংশ বা স্থান। **15.** (*Racing*) Position among placed competitors ; as, to occupy the first or second *place* ; প্রতিদ্বন্দ্বিগণের মধ্যে স্থান। **16.** The position in the heavens of a heavenly body ; নভোমণ্ডলে কোন জ্যোতিষ্কের স্থান, ক্ষেত্র। **17.** (*Arith.*) The position of a figure in a series as indicating its value in decimal or similar notation ; as calculated to 50 decimal *place* ; (পাটীগণিত) স্থান। **Place-brick** — অসম্যগ্ দগ্ধ ইষ্টক। **Place-hunter**—যে ব্যক্তি ব্যগ্রভাবে সরকারী চাকুরী খুঁজিয়া বেড়ায়। **Place-man**—সরকারী কর্ম্মচারী। **Place (-kick)**—অপর ক্রীড়ক কর্তৃক পূর্ব্বে কোন স্থানে স্থাপিত কন্দুকে যে পদাঘাত প্রদান করা হয়। **In place**—In position ; suitable ; as, it is quite *in place* here ; স্থানে স্থিত ; উপযোগী, উপযুক্ত, যথাযোগ্য। **In place of**—In stead of ; স্থানে, স্থলে, জায়গায়। **It is not my place to enquire into that**—It is not the duties of my office to do so ; এবিষয়ে অনুসন্ধান করা আমার কর্ত্তব্য কাজের মধ্যে নয়। **Out of place**—Inappropriate ; unsuitable ; as, his remarks were *out of place* ; অপ্রাসঙ্গিক, অস্থানিক; অনুপযোগী, অযুক্ত। **To give place to**—To make room for ; to yield to ; স্থান করা, জায়গা করা ; বশ্যতাস্বীকার করা। **To have place**—To have existence ; বর্ত্তমান থাকা। To have a station, seat or abode ; স্থানে থাকা, বাসস্থানে থাকা। **To take place**—To happen ; ঘটা, সংঘটিত হওয়া। To take precedence ; প্রাধান্যপ্রাপ্ত হওয়া। **To take the place of**—To be substituted for ; কোন কিছুর পরিবর্ত্তে বসা।

plāce, *v. t.* **1.** To put in a particular place ; কোন স্থানে রাখা। **2.** To appoint to a post ; to find a situation for ; নিযুক্ত করা ; কাহারও জন্য চাকুরী যোগাড় করা। **3.** To put in a particular rank or station ; কোন বিশেষ স্থান বা পদবীতে প্রতিষ্ঠিত করা। **4.** To repose ; to fix ; to set ; as, to *place* cofidence in a friend ; ন্যস্ত করা ; স্থাপন করা ; নিবদ্ধ করা। **5.** To invest ; to lend ; as, to *place* money in a bank ; (টাকা) ফেলা, প্রয়োগ করা ; কর্জ্জ দেওয়া। **6.** To dispose of ; as, to *place* shares in a company ; ব্যবস্থা করা, সাধন করা। **7.** To put as an order for goods ; ফরমাইস প্রভৃতি দেওয়া। **8.** To asssign to a particular place ; কোন বিশেষ স্থানে নির্দ্দেশ করা। **9.** To announce the place of in a race ; as, he was *placed* third ; ঘোড় দৌড়ে কোন স্থান অধিকার করিয়াছে—তাহা ঘোষণা করা। **10.** To set down ; to enter in a book ; as, *place* this sum to his credit ; ; লিখিয়া রাখা ; খাতায় উঠান। **11.** (*Football*) To get (the goal) by a place-kick ; (পাদগোলক ক্রীড়ায়) অপর ব্যক্তি কর্তৃক রক্ষিত পাদগোলকে পদাঘাত পূর্ব্বক গোল করা। **To be placed**—(In race) To be among the first three winners ; (ঘোড়দৌড়ে) প্রথম তিনজন জয়ী ব্যক্তির মধ্যে হওয়া।

plă-cĕn'-tă, *n.* **1.** The organ by which the foetus is connected with the mother ; গর্ভের ফুল, গর্ভনাড়ী, ফুল, গর্ভবেষ্টন চর্ম্মপুটক (ব্রজঃ হিন্দু), জরায়ু (ঐ), পরিস্রব (সাঃ পঃ), পোত্রী (ঐ), গর্ভপোষণী। **2.** That part of the carpel to which the ovules or seeds are attached ; (উদ্ভিদ্‌বিদ্যা) কিঞ্জল্কের যে অংশে ডিম্বাণুসমূহ সংলগ্ন থাকে। **–tal**, *adj.*

plăc'-ĕr, *n.* One who places or sets ; স্থাপক, স্থাপনকর্ত্তা।

plăc'-ĕr, *n.* **1.** An alluvial or glacial deposit of sand, gravel, etc. containing valuable minerals in particles ; বালুকা, কঙ্কর প্রভৃতির পুঞ্জ—যাহাতে মূল্যবান খনিজ পদার্থের সূক্ষ্ম কণা থাকে।

placet, (*L.*), *A sentence & n.* It pleases me—A vote of assent in the governing body of a university ; ইহাতে আমি খুসী আছি—বিশ্ববিদ্যালয়ের পরিচালক-সমিতিতে সম্মতিজ্ঞাপক মত। ***Noun.*** Such a vote ; ঐরূপ মত। ***Non placet***—It pleases me not (a vote of dissent) ; ইহাতে আমি খুসী নই (অসম্মতিজ্ঞাপক মত)।

plăc'-id, *adj.* Gentle ; mild ; calm ; peaceful ; as, *placid* aspect, sleep, etc. ; স্থির, ধীর ; নম্র ; শান্ত ; শান্তিপ্রদ, সৌম্য। **—ly,** *adv.* **pla-cid'-i-ty,** *n.*

plăck'-ĕt, *n.* **1.** The opening or slit in a petticoat (called also *placket hole*) ; স্ত্রীলোকদিগের অধোবাসের দীর্ঘ ফাঁক। **2.** A pocket esp. in a woman's coat ; টেঁক, বিশেষতঃ স্ত্রীলোকের কোর্ত্তার টেঁক। **Placket-hole**—See PLACKET, *n.* I.

plăc'-oid (-ŏyd), *adj.* **1.** Like plate in shape as scales etc. ; রেকাববৎ। **2.** (Of fish) Having such scales ; রেকাববৎ শল্কবিশিষ্ট।

plafond, (*F.*), *n.* A ceiling enriched with paintings ; such paintings ; চিত্রমণ্ডিত ভিতরের ছাদ ; ঐরূপ চিত্র।

plā'-gĭ-ā-rīze, *v. t.* & *i.* To steal from the writings, ideas, etc. of another ; অপরের রচনা হইতে চুরি করা। ***Verb i.*** To commit plagiarism ; অপরের রচনা চুরি করা। **—rism,** *n.* **1.** The practice of plagiarizing ; অপরের রচনা হইতে অপহরণ, শব্দচৌর্য্য, ভাবচৌর্য্য, উচ্ছিষ্ট-ভাষণ। **2.** That which is plagiarized ; অপরের রচনা হইতে অপহৃত বিষয়। **—rist,** *n.* **—ry,** *n.* I. A plagiarist ; লিখনতস্কর, গ্রন্থতস্কর, কাব্যচোর, ভাবচোর, উক্তিচোর চন্দ্ররেণু (অঃ), কুম্ভিল (অঃ)। **2.** Literary theft ; plagiarism রচনাচৌর্য্য ; ভাবচৌর্য্য, শব্দচৌর্য্য।

plā-gĭ-ō-cĕ-phăl'-ic, *adj.* Having an oblique lateral deformity of the skull ; তির্য্যগবিকৃতকরোটীসম্পন্ন। **—y,** *n.*

plā-gĭ-ō-clăc'-tic, *adj.* (*Min.*) Having oblique cleavage ; (খনিজ বিদ্যা) তির্য্যগবিদারণসম্পন্ন। **Pla'-gi-o-clase,** *n.* (*Min.*) The triclinic feldspars in which the two principal cleavages are oblique to one another ; (খনিজ বিদ্যা) একপ্রকার দুগ্ধপাষাণ—যাহাতে মুখ্য বিদারণদ্বয় পরস্পরের সহিত তির্য্যগভাবে অবস্থিত থাকে।

plā'-gĭ-ō-stōme, *n.* A fish having its mouth placed transversely beneath the snout, as sharks etc. ; একজাতীয় মৎস্য—যাহার মুখগহ্বর লম্বিত মুখাগ্রের নীচে তির্য্যগ্‌ভাবে স্থিত থাকে।

plague (plāg), *n.* & *v. t.* **1.** An afflictive evil ; a visitation of divine anger ; উপপ্লব ; দেবতার কোপজনিত দুর্গতি। **2.** (*Colloq.*) Anything troublesome ; a nuisance ; (চলিতভাষায়) উৎপাত ; বালাই। **3.** A deadly disease or pestilence, esp. the oriental or bubonic plague ; as, the great London *plague* ; মহামারী, মড়ক। ***Verb t.*** **1.** To afflict with disease, calamity or any other evil ; মহামারীগ্রস্ত করা, দুর্দ্দশাগ্রস্ত করা। **2.** (*Fig.* & *Colloq.*) To tease ; to annoy ; "She will *plague* the man that loves her most"; (লক্ষণায় ও চলিতভাষায়) ক্ষ্যাপান ; উত্ত্যক্ত করা, উৎপাত করা। **Plague'-some**—*adj.* (*Colloq.*) Troublesome ; (চলিত ভাষায়) উৎপাতজনক। **Plague-mark**—মারী-চিহ্ন। **Plague-spot** — মহামারীর চিহ্ন ; মহামারী রোগব্যাপ্তস্থান ; কলুষকলঙ্কিত স্থলী। **Plague on (you)**—Imprecation ; কি পাপ ! **Plague take you**—মরণ আর কি ! **To be at the Plague**—To be at the trouble ; ঝঞ্চাটে পড়া, উৎপাতে পড়া।

plā'-guy (-gĭ), *adj.* & *adv.* Troublesome ; annoying ; as, a *plaguy* horse ; উৎপাতজনক ; বিরক্তিজনক। ***Adv.*** Vexatiously ; as, "He is so *plaguy* proud" ; বিরক্তজনকভাবে, বেজায়, খুব। **—gui-ly,** *adv.*

plaice (plās), *n.* A European flat fish ; ইয়ুরোপীয় মৎস্য বিশেষ।

plaid (plăd), *n.* **1.** A garment of tartan or checked woollen cloth used by both sexes in Scotland ; স্কটলণ্ডদেশের স্ত্রীপুরুষদিগের ছক-কাটা পশমী কাপড়ের পোষাক। **2.** The woollen cloth of which this is made ; যে পশমী কাপড় হইতে ঐরূপ পোষাক প্রস্তুত হয়। **Plaid'-ed,** *adj.*

plain (plān), *adj.*, *adv.* & *n.* **1.** Level ; flat ; even ; as, a *plain* surface ; সমতল ; অনুচ্চাবচ ; অবন্ধুর, মসৃণ। **2.** Not difficult ; simple ; evident ; clear ; "'Tis a *plain* case" ; সহজ ; সরল ; প্রত্যক্ষ ; স্পষ্ট, স্ফুট। **3.** Open ; as, a *plain* view ; অবারিত, মুক্ত। **4.** Unembellished ; not coloured as a drawing ; সাদামাঠা ; অরঞ্জিত। **5.** Not highly seasoned ; as, a *plain* food ; লঘুপাক। **6.** Artless ; frank ; unsophisticated ; straightforward ; "An honest mind and *plain*" ; সাদাসিধা ; সরল, অখল, সাদা ; অকপট। **7.** Of homely dress or manners ; not handsome ; ugly ; as, a *plain* woman ; সাদাসিধা পোষাকপরা ; অসুন্দর; কুৎসিত। **8.** Not extravagant ; as, *plain* living ; সাদাসিধা। **9.** Not varied by modulations ; as, a *plain* tune ; বৈচিত্র্যহীন। **10.** Not intricate, as a sewing ; অজটিল। ***Adv.*** Plainly ; clearly ; as, learn to speak *plain* ; সরলভাবে ; স্পষ্টভাবে। ***Noun.*** A piece of level land ; ময়দান মাঠ, প্রান্তর, সমভূদেশ (শুক্রঃ বিনয়), সমতলক্ষেত্র (সাঃ পঃ), সমক্ষেত্র। **Plain'-ly,** *adv.* Clearly ; openly ; স্পষ্টভাবে, স্পষ্টরূপে, বিশদরূপে ; খোলাভাবে, সোজাসুজি। **Plain'-ness,** *n.* **Plain chant**—সাদাসিধা গান। **Plain clothes** — সাদা পোষাক। **Plain cook**—যে ব্যক্তি সর্ব্বপ্রকার সাধারণ ব্যঞ্জনাদি রন্ধন করিতে পারে। **Plain dealing**—সরলতা ; অকপট ব্যবহার। **Plain-hearted**—সরলহৃদয়, সাধুচিত্ত, শুভ্রচিত্ত। **Plain-sailing**—Sailing in a plain course ; সোজা পথে পোঁত চালনা। (*Fig.*) A simple course of action ; (লক্ষণায়) সোজা-সুজি উপায়। **Plain sewing**—See PLAIN, *adj.* 10. **Plainsman**—সমতল ভূভাগবাসী ব্যক্তি। **Plain speaking**—স্পষ্টবাদিতা, স্পষ্টভাষিতা। **Plain-spoken**—স্পষ্টভাষী ; স্পষ্টবক্তা, উচিতবক্তা। **Plain tile**—চ্যাপ্টা টালি। **Plain work**—সাদাসিধা সূচের কাজ। **In plain words**—সাদা কথায়। **Plain as a pikestaff**—একেবারে সোজা, অতি স্পষ্ট।

plain (plān), *v.i.* (*Archaic & poet.*) To lament ; to complain ; to give out a plaintive sound ; (অপ্র: বা কবিতায়) শোক বা বিলাপ করা ; অভিযোগ করা ; আর্ত্তনাদ করা।

plaint (plānt), *n.* 1. (*Poet.*) Lamentation ; (কবিতায়) বিলাপ। 2. (*Law*) An accusation ; a complaint (now *rare*) ; (আইন) অভিযোগপত্র (সাঃ পঃ) ; অভিযোগ (অধুনা ক্বচিদ্‌ব্যবহৃত)।

plain'-tiff (plān-), *n.* (*Law*) One who commences a suit against another—opposed to *defendant* ; বাদী, অর্থী, ফরিয়াদী, পূর্ব্বাবেদক।

plain'-tive (plān-tiv), *adj.* 1. (*Rare*) Lamenting ; (ক্বচিদ্‌ব্যবহৃত) করুণ, আর্ত্ত, কাতর। 2. Mournful ; expressive of sorrow ; as, a *plaintive* tone ; আর্ত্ত ; শোকাবহ, শোকসূচক। **–ly**, *adv.* **–ness**, *n.*

plait (plāt), *n.* & *v.t.* 1. A doubling as of cloth upon itself ; a fold ; ঊর্ম্মি, চুনট ; কুঁচি। 2. A braid of hair, straw, etc. ; চুলের গোছা, খড়ের গোছা। *Verb t.* 1. To fold ; ভাজ করা, চুনট করা। 2. To form (hair, straw, etc.) into a plait ; বিনান।

plăn, *n.* & *v. t.* 1. A drawing or map of anything, esp. of a building, town, etc. on a flat surface ; নক্‌সা। 2. A scheme or design ; a project ; পরিকল্পনা, সংকল্প, কল্পনা ; ফন্দী। 3. A mode of procedure ; a process ; কার্য্য-পদ্ধতি ; প্রক্রিয়া। 4. (*Perspective*) Any of the imaginary planes perpendicular to the line of vision, passing through objects shown in a picture ; (পরিপ্রেক্ষিত) দৃষ্টিরেখার লম্বস্বরূপ কল্পিত যে সমস্ত তলসমূহ চিত্রে প্রদর্শিত বস্তুকে ভেদ করিয়া যায়—তাহাদের অন্যতম। *Verb t.* 1. To form a plan of ; to design ; as, to *plan* a building ; নক্সা করা ; পরিকল্পনা করা। 2. To devise ; to scheme ; as, to *plan* a campaign ; মতলব করা ; মনে মনে আঁটা, ফন্দী আঁটা। **Plan'-less**, *adj.* **Working plan**—যে বড় নক্সা হইতে কারিকরগণ কাজ করে।

plănch *n.* A slab of metal, stone, etc. ; esp. a slab of fire-clay used in an enamelling oven ; ধাতুফলক, পাষাণফলক ; অগ্নিরোধক মৃত্তিকার টালি।

plănch'-ĕt, *n.* A flat disc of metal ready for coining ; মুদ্রণের জন্য প্রস্তুত ধাতুর চ্যাপ্টা চাকতি।

plăn-chette' (-shĕt), *n.* A small usually heart-shaped piece of wood supported on castors and having a pencil attached for tracing letters etc. without conscious direction ; তাম্বূলপত্রাকার কাষ্ঠযন্ত্র—ইহার সহিত একটী পেন্সিল সংযুক্ত থাকে এবং ইহার উপর হস্ত রাখিলে স্বতই অক্ষর উৎপন্ন হয়, প্রেতলিপিযন্ত্র, প্লেন্‌সেট (হিঃ কোঃ)।

plāne, *n.* (*Bot.*) A genus of trees ; একজাতীয় বৃক্ষ। **Plane-tree**—A tree of this genus ; সরলবৃক্ষ (ওরাট)।

plāne, *n.* & *v. t.* A joiner's tool used in paring or smoothing wood ; a similar tool for

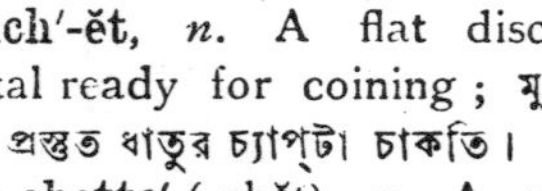

Plane.

smoothing metal ; রেঁদা ; তক্ষণী-লৌহ (হিঃ কোঃ)। *Verb t.* 1. To make smooth or even with a plane as a plank etc., (*lit.* & *fig.*) ; রেঁদা করা (শব্দানুযায়ী ও লক্ষণায়)। 2. (*Archaic*) To level ; as, to *plane* the way ; (অপ্রঃ) সমতল করা। **Moulding-plane**—একপ্রকার রেঁদা—যাহার সাহায্যে কার্ণিসের ভুষা প্রস্তুত করা হয়। **Plaining machine**—একপ্রকার রেঁদা—যদ্দ্বারা কোন বস্তু অতি উত্তমরূপে পালিস করা হয়।

plāne, *n.* 1. A perfectly smooth or level surface ; ধরাতল, সমধরাতল (হিঃ কোঃ), ক্ষেত্র (সাঃ পঃ), তল (শংকু)। 2. A flat or level material surface ; as, an inclined *plane* ; সমতল পৃষ্ঠ। 3. Any main road in a mine ; খনির প্রধান পথ। 4. Each of the natural faces of a crystal ; স্ফটিকের স্বাভাবিক পলা। 5. (*Fig.*) Level or grade as of thought, knowledge, etc. ; as, his superstition places him on the same *plane* as the savage ; (লক্ষণায়) গ্রাম, শ্রেণী, ভূমি। **Plane sailing**—জাহাজ সমতলের উপর চলিতেছে এইরূপ ধরিয়া নিয়া উহার অবস্থিতি নির্ণয়ের কৌশলবিশেষ। (*Fig.*) Now usu. PLAIN-SAILING which see. **Plane of ecliptic**—ক্রান্তিবৃত্ত ধরাতল (হিঃ কোঃ)।

plāne, *adj.* 1. Perfectly level ; even ; as, a *plane* surface ; সমতল ; চৌরস। 2. Lying wholly in a plane surface as a figure, angle, etc. ; সমতলের উপর সর্ব্বতোভাবে স্থিত। **Plane figure**—সমতল ক্ষেত্র। **Plane-geometry**—জ্যামিতি। **Plane-table**—জরীপ যন্ত্র বিশেষ। (*Verb t.*) To survey (an area) with this instrument ; ঐ যন্ত্রের সাহায্যে জরীপ করা।

plăn'-ĕt, *n.* 1. A heavenly body which revolves round the sun ; গ্রহ (সাঃ পঃ), ভ (ঐ), খল (ঐ), খেট (ঐ), খেহট, জ্যোতিষ্ক, খেচর, দ্যুচর (গোলঃ), দ্যুষদ (ঐ), খোক। 2. Among the ancients one of the seven celestial bodies esp. as supposed to influence the fate of men ; প্রাচীন জাতিদিগের মধ্যে সপ্তগ্রহের (রবি, চন্দ্র, শুক্র, বৃহস্পতি, মঙ্গলগ্রহ, বুধ, শনি, গ্রহাদির) অন্যতম। **Planet-struck, —stricken—** গ্রহোপহত, বিভ্রান্ত, বিভীষিকাগ্রস্ত, গ্রহাবিষ্ট গ্রহপীড়িত। **Auspicious planet**—শুভগ্রহ। **Exterior planet**—বহিঃগ্রহ। **Inauspicious planet**—অশুভগ্রহ, পাপগ্রহ। **Inferior planet**—লঘুগ্রহ। **Major planets**—বুধ, শুক্র, পৃথিবী, মঙ্গল, বৃহস্পতি, শনি, ইয়ুরেনাস, নেপচুন। **Minor planets**—যে সকল অবান্তর গ্রহের কক্ষসমূহ মঙ্গল ও বৃহস্পতির কক্ষের মধ্যবর্ত্তী স্থানে অবস্থিত। **Planet nebulæ**—গ্রহ, নীহারিকা। **Planet-year** — গ্রহবর্ষ (বৃঃ সং)। **Primary planets**—প্রধানগ্রহ (হিঃ কোঃ)। **Secondary planet** — উপগ্রহ। **Course of planets** — গ্রহচার (সাঃ পঃ)। **Heliocentric place of inferior planets** — শীঘ্রস্থান (সাঃ পঃ)। **Heliocentric place of superior planets** — মন্দস্ফুটস্থান (সাঃ পঃ)। **Propitiation of the plantes**—গ্রহশান্তি।

plā-nē′-ta, *n.* A chasuble ; রোমান ক্যাথলিক যাজকদিগের পরিচ্ছদবিশেষ।

plăn-ĕ-tā′-ri-ŭm, *n.* A machine which represents the motions and orbits of the planets ; গ্রহকক্ষ এবং গ্রহের গতিপ্রদর্শক যন্ত্র, গ্রহগতিদর্শক।

plăn′-ĕt-ă-rȳ, *adj.* **1.** Of, or relating to, the planets ; as, *planetary* influence ; গ্রহসম্বন্ধীয়। **2.** Consisting of planets ; as, the *planetary* system (the solar system) ; গ্রহাত্মক। **3.** Erratic ; wandering ; as, a *planetary* life ; অনির্দ্দিষ্টগতি ; ইতস্ততঃ পর্য্যটনশীল। **4.** Earthly ; mundane ; পার্থিব ; ঐহিক। **Planetary hour**—দিবামান বা রাত্রিমানের দ্বাদশাংশ। **Planetary system** — সৌরজগৎ। **Planetary division of life**—দশা।

plăn′-ĕt-oid (-oyd), *n.* An asteroid ; অবান্তর গ্রহ, ক্ষুদ্রগ্রহ (হিঃ কোঃ)।

plăn′-gĕnt, *adj.* Resounding ; noisy ; dashing ; as, *plangent* waves ; উচ্চনিনাদী ; কোলাহলপূর্ণ ; প্রচণ্ডবেগে ধাবমান। **—gen-cy,** *n.*

plā-nĭm′-ĕ-tĕr, *n.* An instrument for measuring the area of a plane figure ; সমতলের ক্ষেত্রফল মাপক যন্ত্র বিশেষ, সমতলমান।

plā-nĭm′-ĕ-trȳ, *n.* The measurement of plane surfaces ; সমতলমিতি। **—ni-met′-ric, —ni-met′-ri-cal.** *adjs.*

plan-i-pĕt′-ăl-ous (-ŭs), *adj.* Having flat petals ; সমতলদলী।

plăn′-ish, *v. t.* **1.** To make smooth as a metallic surface ; to flatten as a piece of metal etc. by light blows with a hammer or between rollers ; পালিস করা, মসৃণ করা ; হাতুড়ি দ্বারা আস্তে আস্তে পিটিয়া বা ডলনার মধ্যে চাপিয়া চ্যাপ্টা করা। **2.** To polish as a photograph with a roller etc. ; আলোকচিত্র পালিশ করা। **—er,** *n.*

plăn′-i-sphere (-sfēr), *n.* A map exhibiting the circles of a sphere ; a sphere projected on a plane ; গোলকের বৃত্তসমূহ প্রদর্শক মানচিত্র ; সমতলের উপর প্রলম্বিত গোলক। **—spher′-ic,** *adj.* **Revolving planisphere**—কোন নির্দ্দিষ্ট সময়ে নির্দ্দিষ্ট স্থান হইতে দৃষ্ট আকাশ খণ্ড প্রদর্শনের জন্য যন্ত্রবিশেষ।

plank (plăngk), *n.* **1.** A long flat piece of sawed timber thicker than a board ; কাষ্ঠফলক, তক্তা, পাট। **2.** An article or item of political or other programme ; "Another *plank* in the restriction of Chinese immigration"; রাষ্ট্রনৈতিক বা অনুরূপ ব্যাপারের প্রকরণ বা দফা। **3.** (*Fig.*) Anything serving as a support ; "The only *plank* we have to trust to" ; (লক্ষণায়) আশ্রয়স্থল। **Plank-bed**—কারাগারের কাষ্ঠফলকরচিত শয্যা। **To walk the plank**—(Said of the captives of the pirates) To be compelled to walk along a plank projecting over the ship's edge into the sea ; জাহাজের কিনারা হইতে সমুদ্র পর্য্যন্ত প্রলম্বিত কাষ্ঠফলকের উপর দিয়া চলিতে বাধ্য করা।

plank (plăngk), *v. t.* **1.** To cover or furnish with planks ; as, to *plank* a floor ; কাষ্ঠফলকাচ্ছাদিত করা, তক্তাদ্বারা ছাওয়া, পাটাতন করা। **2.** (*Slang*) To lay down as on a plank or table ; to pay, (usu. with *down*) ; as, *to plank down* money ; (ইতরভাষায়) মেজের উপর রাখা ; চুকাইয়া দেওয়া। **Plank′-ing,** *n.* Act of laying planks ; planks collectively ; work made up of planks ; কাষ্ঠফলক দ্বারা আচ্ছাদন ; কাষ্ঠফলকরাজি ; কাষ্ঠফলকরচিত বস্তু, কাষ্ঠফলকাচ্ছাদিত গৃহতল প্রভৃতি।

plank′-tŏn (plăngk-), *n.* Passively floating animal or plant organism found at various depths in the ocean, taken collectively ; সমুদ্রে প্রাপ্ত ক্ষুদ্র জীব বা উদ্ভিদ।

Plano-concave

plā′-nō-cŏn′-cāve, —vĕx, *adjs.* (Of lens etc.) Having one surface plane and the other concave or convex ; এক পৃষ্ঠ সমতল অপর পৃষ্ঠ মধ্যোন্নত (*concave*) বা মধ্যানত (*convex*), সমনতোদর (*concave*) (হিঃ কোঃ), সমোন্নতোদর (*convex*) (ঐ)।

plā-nŏm′-ĕ-tĕr, *n.* An instrument for gauging or testing a plane surface ; সমতলমান, সমতলমাপক।

plant, *n.* **1.** Any vegetable production, usu. a small one ; a sapling ; উদ্ভিদ, ক্ষুদ্র বৃক্ষ, ওষধি (ছান্দোগ্য) ; চারাগাছ, গাছগাছড়া। **2.** A crop ; growth of something planted ; ফসল ; বৃক্ষাদির বৃদ্ধি। **3.** The machinery etc. ; as, the *plant* of a foundry ; (*fig.*) machinery of intellectual work etc.; "The professors are part of the *plant*"; যন্ত্রাদি; (লক্ষণায়) বিদ্যা, জ্ঞান প্রভৃতি বিস্তারের যন্ত্র বা সাধন। 4. (*Slang*) A swindle; a plan; a trick; জুয়াচুরী; ফন্দি; চাতুরী। 5. (*Slang*) A decoy or trap for wrongdoers; a spy; (ইতরভাষায়) ফাঁদ; গোয়েন্দা। 6. Pose; "There was obstinacy in the *plant* of the figures"; ঢং, অবস্থানভঙ্গী। **Plant'-let**, *n.* **Plant house**—যে কাচাদিদ্বারা আচ্ছাদিত গৃহে শীতপ্রধান দেশে উষ্ণমণ্ডলজাত বৃক্ষাদি রোপণ করা হয়, চারাবাড়ী। **Plant-louse**—বৃক্ষকীট। **In plant**—(Of plants etc.) Growing; বৃদ্ধিশীল, বর্দ্ধিষ্ণু, বর্দ্ধমান। **To lose plant**—(Of plants etc.) To die off; মরিয়া যাওয়া। **To miss plant**—To fail to spring from the seed; অঙ্কুরিত না হওয়া।

plănt, *v. t.* 1. To put or set in the ground, as seeds, plants, etc. for growth; রোপণ করা, বপন করা, বুনা, পোতা। 2. To furnish with plants; তরুলতাদিদ্বারা সজ্জিত করা। 3. To fix; to set in position; to post or station as a policeman in the street; স্থাপন করা; স্বস্থানে স্থিত করা; দাঁড় করান। 4. To settle (a person etc.) as a colonist etc.; to colonize, as a place; উপনিবেশ স্থাপন করা; উপনিবিষ্ট করা। 5. To found or establish as a city, community, church, etc.; স্থাপিত করা, প্রতিষ্ঠিত করা। 6. To stock or provide with something; to introduce; as, *to plant* fish, oyster, etc. in a river etc.; সজ্জিত করা, সমন্বিত করা; প্রবর্ত্তিত করা। 7. To set (ideas etc.) in the mind; মনে বদ্ধমূল করা। 8. To deliver (a blow, thrust, etc.) in a specified place; বসান, মারা (কিল, ঘুষি, প্রভৃতি)। 9. (*Slang*) To place as ore, gold-dust, etc. in ground, a mine, etc. to give a false idea of the richness of the soil; (ইতরভাষায়) ভূমির মূল্য সম্বন্ধে মিথ্যা ধারণা জন্মাইবার উদ্দেশ্যে স্বর্ণরেণু, খনিজবিমিশ্র ধাতু প্রভৃতি ভূমি বা খনিতে রাখা। 10. (*Slang*) To conceal (stolen goods etc.) (ইতরভাষায়) (চোরাই মাল প্রভৃতি) লুকান। 11. To plan or devise as a fraudulent scheme etc.; ফন্দী আঁটা, মতলব আঁটা। 12. To abandon; as, there I was fairly *planted*; ত্যাগ করা, বর্জ্জন করা। **Plant'-a-ble**, *adj.* **Plant-world**—স্তব (বেদান্ত)। **To plant out**—To transfer as a plant from a pot or frame to open ground; গামলা প্রভৃতি হইতে তুলিয়া খোলা জায়গায় বৃক্ষাদি রোপণ করা। (*Archaic, landscape*) To conceal from view by plants, shrubs, etc.; (অপ্রঃ) তরুগুল্মাদি দ্বারা দৃষ্টিপথরোধ করা।

Plantago ispaghula — ইসবগুল (বেলঃ)।

Plantago major—বর্ত্তং (হিন্দি, বেলঃ)।

plăn'-tain (-tăn), *n.* Any plant of a genus of short-stemmed herbs; খর্ব্বকাণ্ড গুল্মবিশেষ।

plăn'-tain (-tăn), *n.* 1. A species of banana; its fruit; কলাগাছ, কদলীতরু; কলা, কদলী, রম্ভা [Syn. হেমফলা (tree), পিচ্ছা (*ib.*), তত্ত্ববিগ্রহা (*ib.*), তৃণসারা (*ib.*), ততপত্রী (*ib.*), গুচ্ছফলা (*ib.*), সুকুমারা (*ib.*), রাজেষ্টা (*ib.*), ঊরুস্তম্ভ (*ib.*), চর্ম্মণ্বতী (*ib.*), হস্তিবিষাণী (*ib.*), সুফলা (*ib.*), বনলক্ষ্মী (*ib.*), মোচ (both tree and fruit), অংশুমৎফলা (*ib.*), বারণবুসা (*ib.*), বারবুষা (*ib.*), বারবুষ (*ib.*), বারণবল্লভা (*ib.*), মৃত্যুফলা (*ib.*), মৃত্যুফলী (*ib.*), জালিকা (*ib.*), দ্রোণী (*ib.*), গুচ্ছদন্তিকা (*ib.*), ভানুফলা (*ib.*), [illegible]ট (fruit), রোচক (*ib.*), মোচক (*ib.*), কদল (*ib.*), [Arab. *mauz*. Jav. *gadang*. Malay *pisang*. Pers. *mauza*. Lat. *plantago*.]

plăn'-tăr, *adj.* (*Anat.*) Of, or pertaining to, the sole of the foot; (শারীরসংস্থান বিদ্যা) পদতলসম্বন্ধীয়।

plăn-tā'-tion, *n.* 1. A collection of planted growing plants or trees; a grove; বাগান; কুঞ্জ। 2. A place planted; an estate on which cotton, tobacco, etc. are cultivated; as, a cotton or coffee *plantation*; বৃক্ষরোপিত স্থান; আবাদ, বাগান, বাগিচা। 3. (*Hist.*) Original settlement in a new country; a colony; নূতন দেশে আদিম নিবাস; উপনিবেশ। **Plantation song**—আমেরিকার ইক্ষু, কাফি, প্রভৃতির বাগানে কাফ্রীরা যে গান গাহিয়া থাকে।

plănt'-ẽr, *n.* 1. A cultivator; a machine for planting or sowing; কৃষক; বপনযন্ত্র, রোপণ যন্ত্র। 2. The owner or occupier of a plantation; চা-কর, নীলকর প্রভৃতি। 3. A colonist in a new country; ঔপনিবেশিক। **—ship**, *n.*

plăn'-ti-grāde, *adj.* & *n.* Walking on the sole of the foot and not on the toes; পদতলচারী। ***Noun.*** 1. A plantigrade animal, as the polar bear; পদতলচারী জন্তু।

plăn-tŏc'-ră-çy̆, *n.* The dominant class of planters in the West Indies etc.; পশ্চিম ভারতীয় দ্বীপপুঞ্জ প্রভৃতিতে ইক্ষু, কাফি প্রভৃতি বাগানের প্রভাবশালী মালিক।

plănx'-ty̆, *n.* An Irish or Welsh melody for the harp; আয়র্লণ্ড প্রভৃতি দেশের বীণাযোগে গেয় সঙ্গীত।

plaque (plâk), *n.* 1. An ornamental tablet of China or other ware, used on a wall inserted in a furniture etc.; প্রাচীর বা গৃহ সজ্জাদিতে নিবিষ্ট চীনামাটী প্রভৃতির শোভাসাধক ফলক। 2. A small tablet as the badge of an honorary order; সম্মানচিহ্ন প্রস্তরে ব্যবহৃত ক্ষুদ্র ফলক বা পট্ট। 3. (*Med.*) A patch of eruption or the like; (ভৈষজ্যশাস্ত্র) কণ্ডু, দাদ। **Pla-quette'**, *n.* (*Dim.* of PLAQUE.)

plăsh, *n.* A small pool of standing water; puddle; ডোবা; খানা, গাড়া। **Plash'-y**, *adj.*

plăsh, *v. t., i.* & *n.* To splash or make a splashing sound in (water) ; জল ছিটকান, জলে আঘাত করা, ছলাৎ ছলাৎ শব্দ করা। ***Verb i.*** To splash ; to make a splashing noise ; জলছিটকান ; ছলাৎ ছলাৎ শব্দ করা। ***Noun.*** A splash ; a plunge ; জল-ছিটকানি, জলাস্ফালন (বঃ) ; ঝাঁপ। **Plash'-y,** *adj.*

plăsh, *v. t.* To bend down and interweave as branches, twigs, etc., to make a hedge ; to make or renew (a hedge) thus ; বৃক্ষশাখা নোয়াইয়া ও পরস্পরের সহিত সংগ্রথিত করিয়া বৃতি রচনা করা ; ঐরূপে বেড়া বাঁধা বা বেড়া মেরামত করা।

plăsm, *n.* The living matter of a cell ; same as PROTOPLASM (which see) ; কলল (হিঃ কোঃ), জীবপঙ্ক।

plăs'-mă, *n.* **1.** A green variety of quartz ; একপ্রকার সবুজবর্ণ কাচ-মণি। **2.** The fluid part of the blood in which the red corpuscles float ; রক্তের যে তরল অংশে লোহিত বর্ণ কণিকা ভাসিয়া থাকে, অরুণকণাধার। **3.** Same as PLASM. **–mat'-ic,** *adj*, Of, or relating to, plasma esp. of the blood ; অরুণকণাধার-সম্বন্ধীয়, প্রাণপঙ্কীয়। **–mic,** *adj.* Protoplasmic ; জীববীজ সম্বন্ধী।

plăs'-min, *n.* A proteid obtained from the plasma of the blood ; অরুণকণাধার হইতে প্রাপ্ত যবক্ষারজান-বিশিষ্ট পদার্থ।

plăs-mŏ'-di-ŭm, *n.* (*Biol. pl.* -DIA) **1.** A large jelly-like mass formed by an aggregation of amoebas ; আণুবীক্ষণিক প্রাণিবর্গদ্বারা গঠিত জেলির স্থায় পদার্থ। **2.** A parasitic organism found in the blood of patients with recent malaria etc. ; অচিরম্যালেরিয়াগ্রস্ত ব্যক্তিগণের রক্তে প্রাপ্ত একপ্রকার পরাঙ্গপুষ্ট জীবাবয়ব।

plăs'-mō-gĕn, *n.* (*Rare*) Essential substance of protoplasm ; (কচিদ্ ব্যবহৃত) প্রাণপঙ্কসার।

plăs'-mŏg'-ō-ny̆, –mo-gĕn-y̆, *ns.* The generation of an organism from a plasma ; অরুণকণাধার হইতে জীবাবয়বের উৎপত্তি।

plăs-mŏl'-ō-gy̆, *n.* The study of the ultimate corpuscles of living matter ; প্রাণবানবস্তুর চরমকণিকা সম্বন্ধে আলোচনা।

plăs-mŏl'-y̆-sis, *n.* The contraction of the protoplasm in living cells under the action of some reagents ; কোন কোন পরীক্ষকের (reagent) ক্রিয়াদ্বারা প্রাণিকোষের প্রাণপঙ্ক সঙ্কোচন। **–mo-lyt'-ic,** *adj.* **Plas'-mo-lyse,** *v. t.* & *i.*

plăs'-têr, *n.* **1.** A substance used in medical practice by being made to adhere to the surface of the body ; পলস্তরা, বস্ত্রলিপ্ত মলম, উপানহ, মলমপট্টি, প্রদেহ (plaster of oleagenous substance, সুশ্রুঃ কুঞ্জ)। **2.** A composition of lime, water, sand, etc. for overlaying wall etc. ; চুণবালি, পুস্ত, চুণবালির লেপ, পোঁচ (যোঃ)। **3.** Same as PLASTER OF PARIS. **–y,** *adj.* **Plaster-cast**—ছাঁচে-গড়া প্যারী প্লাষ্টারের জিনিষ। **Plaser-stone**—Same as GYPSUM (which see). **Porous plaster**—শরীরে লাগাইবার জন্য একপ্রকার সচ্ছিদ্র পলস্তারা। **Plaster of Paris**—প্যারীনগরীর নিকটবর্ত্তী স্থানসমূহে প্রাপ্ত শ্বেতবর্ণ চূর্ণ বিশেষ, প্যারী প্লাষ্টার।

plăs'-têr, *v. t.* **1.** To overlay or cover with plaster or the like, as the walls of a house ; চুণবালি লাগান, আস্তর করা। **2.** To apply a medicinal plaster to ; পলস্তারা লাগান। **3.** To smear or bedaub ; (*fig.*) to load to excess, as with praise, flattery, etc. ; লিপ্ত করা, মাখান ; (লক্ষণায়) প্রপীড়িত করা। **4.** To cover or conceal ; ঢাকা, গোপন করা, চাপা দেওয়া। **5.** (*Humorous*) To give compensation for (a blow, wound, etc.) ; "...gave the man 5 shillings to *plaster* the blow" ; (কৌতুকচ্ছলে) প্রতিশোধ দেওয়া। **6.** To stick or fix (a thing) like plaster upon the surface ; মলমের মত লাগান। **7.** To treat (wine) with plaster of Paris to neutralize acidity ; মদ্যের অম্লতা হ্রাস করার উদ্দেশ্যে উহার সহিত প্যারী প্ল্যাষ্টার মিশ্রিত করা। **–er,** *n.* **–ing,** *n.*

plăs'-tic, *adj.* **1.** Giving form or shape to clay, wax, etc ; আকারপ্রদ, রূপদ। **2.** Formative ; creative ; "*Plastic* force of nature" ; গঠনকারী ; সৃষ্টিকারী। **3.** Capable of being moulded ; (*fig.*) pliable ; as, the *plastic* mind of a child ; আকারপ্রদানক্ষম ; (লক্ষণায়) সুখনম্য, নমনীয়, সুকুমার। **4.** Of, or pertaining to, moulding or modelling ; produced by moulding ; দ্রব্যানুলিপিসম্বন্ধীয়, ভাস্কর্য্য, মৃৎশিল্প প্রভৃতি সম্বন্ধীয় ; ছাঁচে তৈরী। **5.** (*Biol.*) Capable of forming living tissues ; as, *plastic* lymph ; accompanied by this process ; as, *plastic* bronchitis ; (জীববিজ্ঞান) সজীব বিধানতন্তুনির্ম্মাণক্ষম ; সজীববিধান-তন্তু নির্ম্মাণক্রিয়া সহকৃত। **–ti-cal-ly,** *adv.* **–tic'-i-ty,** *n.* State of being plastic ; pliableness ; আকারপ্রদানক্ষমতা, প্রতিরূপতা (হিঃ কোঃ), সংস্কারগ্রহণশীলতা (ঐ) ; নমনীয়তা। **Plastic arts**—ভাস্কর্য্য, মৃৎশিল্প, প্রভৃতি। **Plastic clay**—তৃতীয়ক স্তর সমূহের সর্ব্বনিম্নস্তরের উপস্তরবিশেষ। **Plastic surgery**—অস্ত্রোপচার বিদ্যার যে শাখায় নষ্টক্ষত বা বিকৃত দেহাংশের পুনরুৎপাদন বা বিকৃতি দূরীকরণের বিষয় বিবৃত থাকে।

plăs'-ti-cine, *n.* A proprietary name for a plastic substance used esp. in schools as substitute for modelling clay ; মূর্ত্তি প্রভৃতি গঠনের উপযোগী দ্রব্য।

plăs'-trŏn, *n.* **1.** A fencer's shield of leather worn on the breast ; অসিযোদ্ধার বক্ষ উপরি পরিহিত চর্ম্ম। **2.** A trimming for the front of a woman's dress ; the starched front of a man's shirt ; স্ত্রীপরিচ্ছদের সম্মুখভাগস্থ ভূষাবিশেষ ; পুরুষদিগের জামার কলপ-লাগান বুক। 3. The ventral part of the shell of a tortoise and turtle ; also, the ventral armour of other animals ; কমঠ অথবা কচ্ছপের উদরের খোল ; অন্যান্য জন্তুর উদরের কঠিন আবরণ। 4. (*Hist.*) A steel breast-plate : (ইতিহাস) ইস্পাত নির্ম্মিত উরস্ত্রাণ।

plat, *n.* A plot or small piece of ground ; as, a grass *plat* ; ক্ষুদ্র ভূখণ্ড, এককিতা জমি।

plăt, *n.* & *v. t.* A plait or braid ; বেণী, কবরী। ***Verb t.*** To braid ; to plait ; বেণী বাঁধা ; বিনান।

plăt, *n.* A dish of food ; একথালা খাদ্য।

plăt'-ăn, *n.* The plane-tree esp. the oriental one ; সরলবৃক্ষ।

plāte, *n.* **1.** A flat piece or sheet of metal ; as, a steel *plate* ; ধাতুর চাদর, পট্ট। **2.** (*Colloq.*) Household utensils in gold and silver or other metal ; বাসনপত্র, তৈজসপত্র। **3.** A shallow, usu. round dish ; contents of this ; স্থালী, থালা, রেকাব, ভাজন ; স্থালীস্থ ব্যঞ্জনাদি। **4.** An engraved piece of metal etc. ; an impression from the engraved metal ; as, a book illustrated with *plates* ; চিত্রাদিক্ষোদিত ধাতুফলক, চিত্রফলক ; ঐরূপ ফলক হইতে গৃহীত চিত্র। **5.** A piece of metal with a name or inscription, to be attached to an object ; নামাদি ক্ষোদিত পট্ট। **6.** A page of stereotype, electrotypes, etc. to be printed from ; as, publisher's *plate* ; স্থিরাক্ষরফলক, তাড়িতাক্ষর প্রভৃতির পৃষ্ঠা—যাহা হইতে প্রতিলিপি মুদ্রিত করা হয়। **7.** Same as BOOK-PLATE. **8.** (*Photog.*) A sheet of glass, metal, etc. with a coating that is sensitive to light, (*whole-plate*, $8\frac{1}{2} \times 6\frac{1}{2}$ inches ; *half-plate* $6\frac{1}{2} \times 4\frac{3}{4}$ inches ; *quarter-plate* $4\frac{1}{4} \times 3\frac{1}{4}$ inches) ; (আলোকচিত্র) আলোকের রাসায়নিক ক্রিয়াদ্বারা বিকার্য্য প্রলেপদ্বারা আবৃত ধাতু, কাচ প্রভৃতির ফলক, আলোকচিত্রফলক। **9.** A beam on a wall or elsewhere to support other portions of a structure ; as, roof *plates* ; খুঁটা। **10.** A silver or gold cup given as prize to the winner in a contest or game ; a sporting contest esp. a horse-race for such a prize ; প্রতিদ্বন্দ্বিতামূলক ক্রীড়ায় জয়ী ব্যক্তিকে যে স্বর্ণ বা রজতনির্ম্মিত কারুকার্য্যখচিত পাত্র দেওয়া হয় ; ঐরূপ পুরস্কার প্রাপ্তির জন্য ঘোড়দৌড় প্রভৃতি। **11.** A shallow circular vessel used for collection in churches etc. ; খৃষ্টীয় ভজনালয়ে যে রেকাবীতে মুদ্রা সংগ্রহ করা হয়। **12.** (Also *plate-rail*) An old type of rail-road ; একপ্রকার সাবেকধরণের লৌহবর্ত্ম। **Book-plate**—See BOOK. **Plate-armour**—যে সুদৃঢ় লৌহপট্টদ্বারা পোত আচ্ছাদিত করা হয়। **Plate-basket**—কাঁটা, চামচ, প্রভৃতি রাখার জন্য বেতের বাক্স। **Plate-glass**—দর্পণাদির জন্য উৎকৃষ্ট পুরু কাচ। **Plate-iron**—লোহার চাদর। **Plate-layer**—যে ব্যক্তি লৌহবর্ত্মের রেল বসায়। **Plate-mark**—স্বর্ণের বা রৌপ্যের পাত্রোপরি বিশুদ্ধিসূচক বা নির্ম্মাণস্থানবোধক চিহ্ন। **Plate-powder**—রৌপ্যপাত্র পরিষ্কার করার জন্য চূর্ণবিশেষ। **Plate-printing**—ক্ষোদিত চিত্রফলক হইতে চিত্র মুদ্রণ। **Plate-rack**—বাসনপত্র রাখার জন্য তাক। **Plate-warmer**—অগ্নিকুণ্ডের নিকটস্থ তাক—যাহার উপর ব্যঞ্জনাদির স্থালী সকল রাখা হয়। **Selling plate**—যে ঘোড়দৌড়ের বিজয়ী অশ্ব নির্দ্দিষ্ট মূল্যে বিক্রয় করিতে হয়। **Plate of belt**—চাপরাস।

plāte, *v. t.* **1.** To overlay as a ship etc. with plates of metal for protection, defence, etc. ; লৌহপট্টাদি দ্বারা পোত আচ্ছাদিত করা। **2.** To cover as other metals with a coating of gold, silver or tin ; গিল্টি করা, কালাই করা, হেমপৃষ্ঠ করা (cf. হেমপৃষ্ঠ—হরিবংশ)। **3.** To adorn with metal ; as, a *plated* harness ; ধাতুখণ্ড দ্বারা মণ্ডিত করা। **4.** To make a plate of, as types for printing ; মুদ্রণের জন্য স্থিরাক্ষরফলক প্রভৃতি প্রস্তুত করা। **5.** To beat into thin plates ; পিটিয়া পাতলা পাত করা।

plâ-teau' (-tö), *n.* (*Pl.* -TEAUX, -TEAUS.) **1.** A table-land ; মালভূমি, অধিত্যকা, উচ্চসমভূমি (হিঃ কোঃ)। **2.** A large ornamental dish or salver ; also a plaque ; কারুকার্য্যখচিত বৃহৎপাত্র ; ধাতুফলক। **3.** A kind of woman's hat with a level top ; স্ত্রীলোকদিগের একপ্রকার টুপি—যাহার উপরিভাগ সমতল থাকে।

plăt'-ĕn, —ten (-ĕn), *ns.* The flat part of a printing-press by which the impression is made ; মুদ্রাযন্ত্রের যে চ্যাপ্টা অংশ দ্বারা চাপ দেওয়া হয়।

plăt'-êr, *n.* **1.** One who plates or coats articles with gold, silver, etc. ; as, a silver-*plater* ; যে ব্যক্তি গিল্টি বা কালাই করে। **2.** One who makes or applies plates in ship-building ; যে ব্যক্তি রণপোতে লৌহপট্ট সংলগ্ন করে বা রণপোতের জন্য লৌহপট্ট নির্ম্মাণ করে। **3.** An inferior race-horse ; ঘোড়দৌড়ের নিকৃষ্ট অশ্ব।

plăt'-fŏrm, *n.*, *v.t.* & *i.* **1.** A raised level surface ; a standing place ; a raised wall at a railway station ; মঞ্চ, মঞ্চক ; দাঁড়াইবার স্থান ; রেলওয়ে ষ্টেশনের প্রাঙ্গণ। **2.** A stage for speakers or performers ; (*fig.*) platform oratory, (with *the*) ; বক্তৃতা-মঞ্চ, রঙ্গমঞ্চ ; (লক্ষণায়) মঞ্চে দাঁড়াইয়া যে বক্তৃতা দেওয়া হয়। **3.** A declaration of the principles upon which a person or a party proposes to stand ; a declared policy ; as, a political *platform* ; কোন ব্যক্তি বা দলের মূলমন্ত্র ; সাধারণ্যে বিঘোষিত কার্য্যনীতি। ***Verb t.*** To place, as on a platform ; মঞ্চে স্থাপিত করা। *Verb i.* To speak on a platform; বক্তৃতামঞ্চে দাঁড়াইয়া বক্তৃতা দেওয়া।

plāt'-ing, *n.* **1.** The art or process of covering anything with a plate or plates ; গিল্টিকরণ, লৌহপট্ট দ্বারা আচ্ছাদন। **2.** A coating of gold, silver, etc., laid upon another metal ; গিল্টি, কালাই। **3.** Racing for plates or prizes ; পুরস্কারের জন্য ঘোড়দৌড়। A defensive armour of metal plates ; রণপোতের লৌহপট্টাচ্ছাদন।

plăt'-i-nīze, *v. t.* To cover or coat with platinum ; প্ল্যাটিন্যাম ধাতু দ্বারা আবৃত করা।

plăt'-i-nōde, *n.* The cathode or negative pole of a galvanic battery ; গ্যালভ্যানিক ব্যাটারীর স্ত্রীমেরু।

plăt'-i-noid (-noyd), *n.* **1.** An alloy of nickel, zinc, copper, etc. resembling platinum in some qualities ; নিকেল, দস্তা, তাম্র, প্রভৃতির মিশ্র। **2.** Any metal allied to platinum ; প্ল্যাটিনাম শ্রেণীর ধাতু।

plăt'-i-nō-tȳpe, *n.* (*Painting*) A printing process by which permanent pictures in platinum-black are produced ; a picture so produced ; একপ্রকার মুদ্রণপ্রক্রিয়া যদ্দারা প্ল্যাটিনামচূর্ণবৎ কজ্জলবর্ণে স্থায়িচিত্র মুদ্রিত হইয়া থাকে। ঐ প্রক্রিয়ায় মুদ্রিত চিত্র।

plăt'-i-nŭm, *n.* A malleable metal of a dim silvery appearance between, gold and silver in value ; ম্লানরজতবর্ণের ঘাতসহ ধাতুবিশেষ, মহারজত (আঃ বঃ), [Burm. *kum-phok* ; Chinese *Rehkin.*] [প্লাটিনামের রাসায়নিক সাঙ্কেতিক চিহ্ন Pt. আণবিকগুরুত্ব ১৯৫°। বায়ুতে এই ধাতুর কোন পরিবর্তন হয় না সর্ব্বজারক বিড়ে আস্তে আস্তে গলিয়া যায়। রাসায়নিক যন্ত্রের মুচী, বকযন্ত্র প্রভৃতি প্রস্তুতে এই ধাতু, ইহার তার ও পাতের বহুল ব্যবহার হয়। Ural পর্ব্বতে পাওয়া যায়।] **–nif'-er-ous,** *adj.* **–nous,** *adj.* **Pla-tin'-ic,** *adj.* **Platinum-black** — প্লাটিনামের কাজলের মত কাল গুঁড়া। **Platinum metals**—প্লাটিনামবৎ ধাতুসমূহ।

plat'-i-tūde, *n.* **1.** Triteness ; staleness ; নূতনত্বহীনতা ; নীরসতা। **2.** A dull remark delivered as important ; a commonplace ; নূতনত্বহীন মন্তব্য, পুরাতন উক্তি, সাধারণ উক্তি; বৈচিত্র্যশূন্য উক্তি। **–tu'-di-nize,** *v. i.* To utter truisms or platitudes ; নীরস মন্তব্য করা, বৈচিত্র্যহীন মন্তব্য করা, সাধারণকথা গুরুগম্ভীর ভাবে বলা। **–tu'-di-nous,** *adj.* **–tu'-di-nous-ly,** *adv.*

plăt'-i-tū-di-nā'-ri-ăn, *n.* & *adj.* One addicted to uttering platitudes or truisms ; যে ব্যক্তি অতি সাধারণ কথা খুব গুরুগম্ভীর ভাবে বলিতে তৎপর। *Adj.* Of the nature of platitudes ; বৈচিত্র্যহীন মন্তব্যাত্মক।

Plă-tŏn'-ic, *adj.* & *n.* **1.** Of, or relating to, Plato, the famous Greek philosopher or his doctrine ; সুপ্রসিদ্ধ প্রাচীন গ্রীক দার্শনিক প্লেতো বা তদীয় মতবাদ-সম্বন্ধীয়। **2.** (Of love, affection, etc.) Free from sensual desire ; spiritual ; কামগন্ধহীন, কামলেশহীন [cf. রজকিনী প্রেম, যেন শুদ্ধ হেম, কামগন্ধ নাহি তায়] ; সাত্ত্বিক। *Noun.* **1.** A follower of Plato ; প্লাতোর শিষ্য। **2.** A Platonic lover ; নিঃস্বার্থ প্রেমিক। **–i-cal-ly,** *adv.* **Pla'-to-nism,** *n.* The philosophical doctrines of Plato ; প্লাতোর দার্শনিক মতাবলী। **Pla'-to-nist,** *n.* **Pla'-to-nize,** *v. i.* & *t.* **Platonic love**—কামগন্ধহীন প্রেম। **Platonic year**—যে কালচক্রে সমস্ত জ্যোতিষ্ক সর্ব্বপ্রকার গতি সমাপন করিয়া পুনরায় কল্পিত পূর্ব্বস্থানে প্রত্যাবৃত্ত হয় (প্রায় ২৬০০০ বৎসর)।

plă-tōon', *n.* **1.** A small subdivision of foot-soldiers ; পদাতিক সৈন্যের ক্ষুদ্র দল। **2.** (*Rare*) A volley fired by a platoon ; (কচিদ্ব্যবহৃত) ক্ষুদ্র সৈন্যদলকর্তৃক যুগপৎ গুলিবর্ষণ। **3.** (*Fig.*) A company of people ; a coterie ; (লক্ষণায়) একদল লোক; মণ্ডলী।

plăt'-ter (-ėr), *n.* A large flat dish usu. of wood ; বারকোষ, বড় থালা।

plăt'-ȳ-pŭs, *n.* The duck-mole of Australia ; অষ্ট্রেলিয়ার জন্তুবিশেষ।

plăt-y(r) –rhine (-i-rīn), *adj.* (Of monkey) Having a broad nose ; স্থূলনাস।

plau'-dit (plā-), *n.* (Usu. in *pl.*) Applause ; emphatic expression of applause or approval ; প্রশংসাবাদ; স্তুতিবাদ।

plau'-si-ble (plā-zi-bl), *adj.* **1.** Apparently reasonable; specious; as, *plausible* arguments; আপাতযুক্তিযুক্ত, সত্যসন্নিভ, আপাতন্যায্য ; আপাতমধুর, আপাতরমণীয়। **2.** Fair-spoken ; using specious arguments or language ; as, a *plausible* man ; মিষ্টভাষী, প্রিয়ংবদ, প্রিয়ভাষী ; আপাতরম্যযুক্তিপ্রদর্শনকারী। **–bil'-i-ty,** *n.*

play (plā), *v. i.* & *t.* **1.** To sport ; to frolic ; to frisk ; খেলা করা, ক্রীড়া করা ; কেলি করা ; লাফালাফি করা, ছুটাছুটি করা। **2.** To dally ; to trifle ; to act thoughtlessly ; বিলাস করা, লীলা খেলা করা ; ছেলেমি করা ; অবিবেচকের মত কাজ করা। **3.** To perform on an instrument of music : as, to *play* on a violin ; বাদন করা, বাজান। **4.** To take part in a game ; to contend in it ; to gamble ; কোন ক্রীড়াতে যোগ দেওয়া ; কোন ক্রীড়ার প্রতিযোগিতা করা ; দ্যূতক্রীড়া করা। **5.** To act or behave in a specified manner ; as, to *play* false with any one : to *play* fair ; ব্যবহার করা, আচরণ করা। **6.** To move freely or regularly ; to move in any manner ; as, the part of a machine *plays* well ; স্বচ্ছন্দে চলা ; চলা। **7.** To move or fly to and fro ; to disport ; to strike lightly ; to change or alternate rapidly ; as, the bees *play* about flowers : tresses *play* on her neck : wind *plays* on water : his fancy *played* around the idea : smile *played* on his lips ; এদিকে ওদিকে চলা ; ক্রীড়াকৌতুক করা ; মৃদু আঘাত করা ; দ্রুত পরিবর্ত্তিত হওয়া, পর্য্যায়ক্রমে দ্রুত আগত হওয়া, খেলিয়া যাওয়া। **8.** To act upon a stage ; to personate a character ; অভিনয় করা ; কোন নাটকীয় চরিত্রের ভুমিকা গ্রহণ করা। **9.** To be fired as a gun ; আওয়াজ হওয়া। **10.** (Of light) To pass over, along, etc. ; কোন কিছুর উপর দিয়া চলিয়া যাওয়া। **11.** (*Dial.* esp. of workmen on strike) To refrain from work ; (উপভাষায়) কার্য্য হইতে বিরত হওয়া। **12.** To pretend or make believe for sport or fun ; "We *played* that we were gypsies" ; কৌতুক করিয়া ভাণ করা। ***Verb t.*** **1.** To discharge ; to put in action ; as, to *play* a cannon upon a fort ; to wield briskly or freely as a weapon etc. ; ছোড়া ; দাগা ; চালান। **2.** To execute ; to perform ; as, to *play* a trick or prank ; সাধন করা ; সম্পন্ন করা। **3.** To use as an instrument of music ; বাজান। **4.** To perform as a drama ; to act as a dramatical part ; to behave like ; as, to *play* the woman ; নাটক অভিনয় করা ; কোন ভুমিকা অভিনয় করা ; কাহারো মত আচরণ করা। **5.** To engage or contend in, as a contest for amusement or for prize ; প্রতিযোগিতামূলক ক্রীড়ায় প্রবৃত্ত হওয়া। **6.** To keep in play, as a hooked fish in order to land it ; বড়শী বিদ্ধ মাছ লইয়া খেলান। **7.** To direct (light, *on, over, along,* etc.) ; "The search-light began to *play* a dazzling ripple *along* their line" ; চালিত করা, ফেলা। **8.** To contend in a game with ; to include in a team ; ক্রীড়ায় যোগ দেওয়া ; ক্রীড়কদলভুক্ত হওয়া। **9.** To move as a piece in chess etc. ; বড়ে, গুটি প্রভৃতি চালা। **10.** To throw as a playing-card from one's hand and lay it face upwards on the table in one's turn ; তাস খেলা। **11.** (*Cricket*) To strike as in a specified esp. defensive manner ; (ক্রীকেট ক্রীড়া) কোনরূপ বিশেষভাবে আঘাত করা। **Play′-a-ble,** *adj.* **Play′-ing,** *n.* The act of one who plays ; সংক্রীড়ন। **Playing-card**—তাস। **Play-or-pay bet**—ঘোড়া না দৌড়িলেও যে বাজি বজায় থাকে। **Played out**—Tired out ; exhausted ; at the end of one's resources ; rendered obsolete ; পরিক্লান্ত ; অবসন্ন ; নিঃশেষিত ; অপ্রচলিত। **To make play**—To take the lead, as in hunting or racing ; to act effectively ; (দৌড়ে বা মৃগয়াতে) অগ্রগামী হওয়া ; কার্য্যকারিতার সহিত কর্ম্ম করা। To hurry on ; তাড়াতাড়ি করা, স্ফূর্ত্তি করা। **To play a congregation etc. in** or **out**—To play on an organ etc. as they come in or go out ; বাহির হইবার সময় বা ভিতরে প্রবেশ করার কালে অর্গেন প্রভৃতি বাজান। **To play a good knife and fork**—To eat heartily ; পরিতোষপূর্ব্বক আহার করা। **To play a good stick**—To fence well ; সুচারুরূপে অসিক্রীড়া করা। **To play a part**—To be deceitful ; কপটতা করা। **To play at**—To engage in (a game) ; (*fig.*) to engage in as fighting in a trivial or half-hearted way ; ক্রীড়ায় প্রবৃত্ত হওয়া ; (লক্ষণায়) যুদ্ধ প্রভৃতিতে অপূর্ণোদ্যমে প্রবৃত্ত হওয়া। **To play (at) chuck farthing with** — To risk or endanger carelessly or needlessly ; অকারণে বা অসাবধানে সঙ্কটাপন্ন করা। **To play at cross purposes**—To act counter to each other ; পরস্পরের প্রতিকূলাচরণ কর। **To play ducks and drakes**—See under DUCK. **To play fair**—To play fairly ; (*fig.*) to act fairly ; সাধুভাবে খেলা করা ; (লক্ষণায়) সাধু আচরণ করা। **To play fast and loose**—See under FAST. **To play fine**—(*At billiards*) To strike the object-ball near the edge (opp. to *play full*—To strike it nearer the centre than the edge) ; মধ্যস্থানের অপেক্ষা কিনারার নিকটে কন্দুকে আঘাত করা। **To play foul**—To play unfairly ; (*fig.*) to act unfairly ; অন্যায়রূপে খেলা করা ; (লক্ষণায়) অন্যায় আচরণ করা। **To play hob**—To play the part of a mischievous spirit ; নষ্টামিকরা। **To play it on, play it low on, play (low) down on**—To take mean advantage of a person ; কাহারো উপর হীনজনোচিতভাবে সুযোগ গ্রহণ করা। **To play into a person's hands**—To act or to manage matters to his advantage or benefit ; কাহারো হস্তে ক্রীড়নকের ন্যায় হওয়া, কাহারো হস্তে ক্রীড়াপুত্তলিকাবৎ হওয়া। **To play off**—To oppose (a person) against another) esp. for one's own advantage ; একের বিরুদ্ধে অপরকে লাগাইয়া দেওয়া (বিশেষতঃ নিজের সুবিধার জন্য)। To show up or expose to ridicule ; উপহাসাস্পদ করা, হাটে হাঁড়ি ভাঙ্গা। To pass (a thing) off as something else ; to display or exhibit as tricks ; ফাঁকি দিয়া চালান ; প্রদর্শন করা। (*Verb i.*) To pretend ; ছলনা করা, ভান করা। **To play on**—(ক্রীকেট ক্রীড়া) এরূপ ভাবে কন্দুক আঘাত করা, যাহাতে উহা একেবারে না থামিয়া ত্রিদণ্ডে লাগিয়া ক্রীড়ককে আউট করিয়া ফেলে। **To play on** or **upon**—To mock ; to trifle with ;

to befool ; to delude ; বিদ্রূপ করা ; তাচ্ছিল্য করা, তুচ্ছ করা ; বোকা সাজান ; প্রতারণা করা। To give a humorous or fanciful turn to ; as, *to play on* words ; রহস্যজনক ভাব প্রদান করা। **To play one false**—To deceive one; প্রতারণা করা, কপটতা করা। **To play one's cards**—To execute a scheme; কল্পনা কার্য্যে পরিণত করা। **To play one's cards well**—To make good use of opportunities ; সুযোগের সদ্ব্যবহার করা। **To play one tricks**--To deceive him; কাহাকে ঠকান। **To play out**—(*Verb i.*) To come to an end ; to be ineffective ; as, such methods soon *play out* ; শেষ হওয়া ; অকার্য্যকর হওয়া। (*Verb t.*) To perform to the end ; (*fig.*) to finish ; to render obsolete or worn out ; সম্পন্ন করা ; (লক্ষণায়) শেষ করা ; পরিক্লান্ত বা অপ্রচলিত করা। **To play the deuce, devil**—To act the deuce or devil ; শয়তানী করা, নষ্টামী করা। **To play the devil, deuce or mischief with**—To injure seriously ; লণ্ডভণ্ড করা। **To play the first** or **second fiddle**—See under FIDDLE. **To play the fool**—To act like a fool; নির্ব্বোধের মত আচরণ করা। **To play the game**—To observe the rules of the game ; (also, *fig.*) to act honourably ; খেলার নিয়ম পালন করা ; (লক্ষণায়) মর্য্যাদাবোধসম্পন্ন ব্যক্তির মত আচরণ করা। **To play the rex**—To play the master ; to domineer ; প্রভুত্ব করা ; কর্ত্তৃত্ব ফলান। **To play the role** or **part of**—To act or behave as ; কাহারো স্বরূপে কার্য্য বা আচরণ করা। **To play to the gallery** or **galleries**—To act for the applause of the multitude ; সাধারণ লোকের বাহবা পাইবার জন্য অভিনয় করা। **To play to the score**—In gaming esp. of cards to shape one's play according to the state of the score ; ক্রীড়ার জয়াঙ্ক বা পিঠের অবস্থা বুঝিয়া খেলা। **To play truant**--To stray away ; esp. to stay away from school without permission ; দল ছাড়িয়া যাওয়া ; বিশেষতঃ বিদ্যালয় হইতে পালান। **To play up**—To make a beginning of playing ; to play more vigorously ; ক্রীড়ারম্ভ করা ; অধিকতর উৎসাহের সহিত ক্রীড়া করা। **To play upon words**—To pun ; শব্দশ্লেষ করা, দ্ব্যর্থবোধক শব্দ ব্যবহার করা। **To play up to**—To act in a drama so as to support (another actor) ; (অপর অভিনেতাকে) সাহায্য করার জন্য অভিনয় করা। (*Fig.*) To back up ; to support ; to flatter ; (লক্ষণায়) পৃষ্ঠপোষণ করা ; সাহায্য করা, সমর্থন করা ; তোষামোদ করা। **To play with**—To amuse oneself with ; আমোদ করা। To trifle with ; to treat lightly ; তাচ্ছিল্য করা ; তুচ্ছ করা। **To play with edge or edged tools**—To deal with, handle or treat carelessly with dangerous things ; আগুন লইয়া খেলা। **To play with one's beard**—To trifle with ; to deceive; তাচ্ছিল্য করা; প্রতারণা করা।

play (plā), *n.* **1.** Sport ; amusement ; frolic ; ক্রীড়া ; কেলি ; ক্রীড়াকৌতুক, বিনোদ। **2.** Any exercise for amusement ; a game ; খেলা ; ক্রীড়া। **3.** Brisk handling or playing ; as, sword-*play* ; ক্রীড়া, খেলা (যথা, অসিক্রীড়া, লাঠি খেলা)। **4.** Activity ; operation ; as *play* of fancy : to come into *play* ; চটুলতা ; ক্রিয়া। **5.** Light, brisk movement ; elusive change ; as ; *play* of colours, light, etc. ; লীলা, গতিবিলাস, বিলাস, বিহার, খেলন [নয়নখেলনজনিতমনোজম্—গীতঃ] ; ভ্রান্তিজনক পরিবর্ত্তন। **6.** Gambling ; as, to lose a fortune *in play* ; জুয়াখেলা, দ্যূতক্রীড়া। **7.** Freedom of movement ; space for action or motion ; as, the *play* of a wheel ; (*fig.*) scope ; as, to give full *play* to mirth ; অবাধগতি, লীলাগতি ; ক্রিয়া বা গতির অবকাশ ; (লক্ষণায়) প্রসর, অবকাশ, স্থান। **8.** A dramatic performance ; as, he attends every *play* ; a drama ; নাট্যাভিনয়; নাটক। **9.** Fun ; jest ; as, he said it only in *play* ; কৌতুক, রহস্য, নর্ম্ম ; পরিহাস। **10.** (*Dial.*) Abstinence from work as of workmen on strike etc. ; (উপভাষায়) ধর্ম্মঘটকারী প্রভৃতির কার্য্য হইতে বিরতি। **11.** Performance on an instrument of music ; বাদন। **Play'-ful,** *adj.* Sportive ; given to play ; humorous ; jocular ; as , *playful* child : a *playful* writer ; ক্রীড়াশীল, ক্রীড়াসক্ত; লীলাপর, লীলাময়, সলীল, বিনোদী ; পরিহাসরসিক; নর্ম্মপ্রিয়। **Play'-ful-ly,** *adv.* Sportively ; jocularly ; ক্রীড়াচ্ছলে ; পরিহাসচ্ছলে। **Play'-ful-ness,** *n.* **Play-actor** — অভিনেতা, নাটুকে। **Play-bill** — অভিনয়ের বিজ্ঞাপন। **Play-club**—গোলফ্ ক্রীড়ার দণ্ডবিশেষ। **Play-day** — বিদ্যালয়ের ছুটীর দিন ; যে দিন খনির মজুর প্রভৃতি কাজ করে না। **Play-debt** — জুয়াখেলার ঋণ। **Playfellow, –mate**—খেলার সাথী, সহক্রীড়ক, ক্রীড়াসঙ্গী। **Playgoer**—যে ব্যক্তি নিত্য রঙ্গালয়ে গমন করে। **Play-ground**—ক্রীড়াঙ্গন, খেলার মাঠ। **Playhouse** — রঙ্গালয়, রঙ্গশালা, রঙ্গমণ্ডপ, নাট্যশালা, নাট্যমন্দির। **Play-mare**—খেলার ঘোড়া ; প্রাচীনকালীন নৃত্যের প্রধান অংশ। **Plaything**—ক্রীড়াসামগ্রী, খেলনা, ক্রীড়নক। **Play-time**—খেলার সময়। **Play wright, play-writer** — নাট্যকার, নাটকলেখক। **A play book**—নাট্যগ্রন্থ। **A play of colour**—বর্ণলীলা, ইন্দ্রচাপবর্ণ। **A play on or upon words**—দ্ব্যর্থবোধক শব্দ ব্যবহার ; শব্দশ্লেষ। **Fair play**—See under

FAIR. **Foul play**—See under FOUL. **Child's-play**—See under CHILD. **He said it only in play**—He said it not seriously ; তিনি ইহা ঠাট্টাচ্ছলে বলিয়াছিলেন। **In play**—(Of a ball in cricket, football, etc.) In the ordinary course of play ; ক্রীড়াতে। **Out of play**—(*Sport*) Not in play ; dead ; (ক্রীড়ায়) খেলার বাহির ; মৃত। **Play of words**—Trifling with words ; তুচ্ছভাবে শব্দব্যবহার। **To bring into play**—To bring into exercise or use ; কার্য্যে প্রয়োগ করা। **To come into play**—To come into use ; ব্যবহারে আসা। **To hold or keep in play**—To keep occupied ; to keep in exercise or practice ; কার্য্যে ব্যাপৃত রাখা ; সর্ব্বদা চালান।

play'-êr (plā-), *n.* **1.** One who plays ; ক্রীড়ক, খেলোয়াড়। **2.** A professional at cricket etc. ; ক্রীকেট প্রভৃতি ক্রীড়াব্যবসায়ী ব্যক্তি। **3.** An actor in a drama ; অভিনেতা, কুশীলব, রঙ্গাজীব, ধর্ম্মীপুত্র, ধর্ম্মক। **4.** A musician ; as a *player* on a violin ; বাদক। **5.** A gambler ; জুয়াড়ী, দ্যূতকার।

plea (plē), *n.* **1.** (*Law*) The answer of a defendant to the plaintiff's declaration ; বিবাদীর জবাব, কারণোত্তর (মিতঃ)। **2.** Pleading ; excuse ; "Necessity the tyrant's *plea*" ; অজুহাত ; ছল, ছুতা, অছিলা, ব্যপদেশ। **3.** (*Hist.*) A suit or action in law ; (ইতিহাস) মোকদ্দমা, মামলা। **4.** An entreaty ; as, a *plea* for mercy ; অনুনয়, মিনতি। **Special plea**—বিবাদীর যে জবাবে নূতন বিষয় থাকে। **On the plea of**—On the excuse of ; ব্যপদেশে, ছলে। **To set up a plea**—ছুতা দেওয়া।

pleach (plēch), *v. t.* **1.** To interweave, as the branches of trees ; বৃক্ষশাখাসকল পরস্পরের সহিত সংগ্রথিত করা।

plead (plēd), *v. i. & t.* **1.** To address the court as an advocate on behalf of or against, সওয়াল জবাব করা। **2.** To speak by way of persuasion ; to supplicate ; as, to *plead* with a father ; প্ররোচনাজনক বাক্য বলা ; প্রার্থনা করা, মিনতি করা। ***Verb t.*** **1.** To discuss or maintain by arguments or reasons presented to a tribunal ; as, to *plead* a cause before a court ; সওয়াল জবাব করা। **2.** To allege formally as a legal plea or defence ; জবাব দেওয়া। **3.** To offer or allege in excuse ; as, to *plead* inexperience ; ওজর স্বরূপ উপস্থিত করা। **Plead'-a-ble,** *adj.* **Plead'-er,** *n.* A lawyer ; ব্যবহারজীবী, উকিল। **Plead'-ing,** *n. & adj.* **1.** The act of advocating or supporting a cause by arguments ; সওয়ালজবাব করণ। **2.** The formal (usually written) statement of a party in lawsuit ; জবাব, বর্ণনা। **3.** Advocacy ; entreaty ; পক্ষসমর্থন ; অনুনয়, মিনতি। (*Adj.*) Entreating ; imploring ; as, his *pleading* tones move compassion ; অনুনয়সূচক ; মিনতিপূর্ণ। **Plead'-ing-ly,** *adv.* **Special pleading**—অন্যায় অথচ আপাতরম্য যুক্তি ; বিবাদীর যে জবাবে বাদীকর্ত্তৃক আরোপিত অভিযোগসমূহ অস্বীকার করার পরিবর্ত্তে নূতন কোন বিষয় থাকে। **To plead guilty or not guilty**—To confess or deny guilt ; অপরাধ স্বীকার করা, অপরাধ অস্বীকার করা। **To plead with**—To make earnest appeal to ; কাতরভাবে প্রার্থনা করা।

pleas'-ance (plĕz-ăns), *n.* **1.** (*Archaic*) Pleasure ; delight ; merriment ; (অপ্রঃ) সুখ ; আনন্দ ; হর্ষ। **2.** A part of a garden secluded by trees or hedges ; নিভৃত-উদ্যান, নিকুঞ্জ।

pleas'-ănt (plĕz-), *adj.* **1.** Agreeable ; pleasing ; gay ; as, *pleasant* weather, companion, etc ; মনোরম, মনোজ্ঞ, সুখাবহ ; আনন্দদায়ক, রমণীয়, রম্য, রুচির, মনোরম, প্রীতিপ্রদ ; উৎফুল্ল। **2.** (*Archaic*) Humorous ; jocular ; (অপ্রঃ) কৌতুকপূর্ণ ; রংদার। **—ly,** *adv.* **—ness** *n.* The quality of being pleasant ; মনোজ্ঞতা, রুচিরতা, রমণীয়তা, রম্যতা, কমনীয়তা, কাম্যতা, হৃদ্যতা।

pleas'-ănt-rȳ (plĕz-), *n.* **1.** Humour ; jocularity ; রসিকতা, আমোদ-প্রমোদ, প্রমোদপরিহাস ; রঙ্গরস, রঙ্গব্যঙ্গ, নর্ম্ম (দশরূঃ)। **2.** A humorous talk ; a jest ; পরিহাসবাক্য হাসিঠাট্টা, হাসিতামাসা।

please (plēz), *v. t. & i.* **1.** To afford delight to ; to be agreeable to ; তুষ্ট করা ; প্রীতিপ্রদ হওয়া। **2.** To seem good to ; "To-morrow may it *please* you" ; (*Shakes.*) ; ভাল লাগা। **3.** To think fit ; to like ; as, he may go where he *pleases* ; উপযুক্ত মনে করা ; ভাল লাগা। ***Verb i.*** To give pleasure ; to delight ; আনন্দ দেওয়া ; আনন্দিত করা। **Pleas'-ed,** *p. p. adj.* **Pleas'-ing.** *adj.* Delightful ; মনোরম, কান্ত, রম্য, মঞ্জু, মঞ্জুল, রঞ্জক, সুখাবহ। **If you please**—(A polite form of request) With your permission ; as, I will take another cup, *if you please* ; আপনি যদি রাজি হন বা অনুমতি দেন। **I shall be pleased to do etc.**—(A polite form of consent) I shall be glad to do etc. ; আমি এই কাজ করিলে খুসী হইব। **Pleased as punch**—Highly pleased ; অতীব আনন্দিত। **Please do it, Do it please**—Do it kindly ; অনুগ্রহ পূর্ব্বক করুন। **please the pigs**—If all be well ; যদি সবদিকে ভাল হয়। **Please yourself**—Do as you like ; তোমার যেরূপ খুসী কর। **To be pleased with**—To derive pleasure from ; আনন্দভোগ করা।

pleas'-ūre (plĕz-), *n.*, *v. t.* & *i.* **1.** Delight; enjoyment; সুখ, আনন্দ, উল্লাস, পরিতোষ; প্রমোদ, রঙ্গ (গীতঃ)। **2.** Amusement; sensual enjoyment; "Not sunk in carnal *pleasure*"; আমোদ প্রমোদ; ইন্দ্রিয়সুখ। **3.** Will; desire: choice; "Use your *pleasure*"; ইচ্ছা; বাসনা; পসন্দ। **4.** A source or object of pleasure; as, to converse with him is a *pleasure*; আনন্দের বিষয়। ***Verb t.*** To give pleasure to; আনন্দ প্রদান করা, সুখ প্রদান করা। ***Verb i.*** To take pleasure (*in* a thing, doing, etc.); to seek pleasure; as, to go *pleasuring*; আনন্দ পাওয়া; সুখ খুঁজা। **–ur-a-ble,** *adj.* Pleasant; gratifying; মনোরম; তৃপ্তিজনক, সুখদায়ক, আনন্দজনক, মনোজ্ঞ, রম্য, রুচির, প্রমদ। **–ur-a-ble-ness,** *n.* **–ur-a-bly,** *adv.* **Pleasure-boat**—কেলিনৌকা, কেলিতরণী, বিলাসতরী, প্রমোদতরণী। **Pleasure-garden**—বিলাসকানন, প্রমোদকানন, ক্রীড়াবন, কেলিকানন, কামারণ্য, বিলাসবন, লীলোদ্যান, রমনা (কেঙিঃ)। **Pleasure-ground** — বিহারভূমি, কেলিস্থল, প্রমোদভূমি। **Pleasure-house**—প্রমোদমন্দির; লীলামন্দির, বিলাসভবন, ক্রীড়াগৃহ, কেলিগৃহ, লীলাবেশ্ম। **A life given up to pleasure** — A profligate life; বিলাসস্রোতে নিমজ্জিত জীবন। **A man of pleasure**—A profligate man; লম্পট ব্যক্তি, ব্যসনী ব্যক্তি। **A pleasure trip**—প্রমোদভ্রমণ। **At pleasure**—At will or discretion; খুসী মত। **Do me the pleasure of dining with me**—Gratify me by dining with me; আমার সহিত অপরাহ্ণভোজন করিয়া আমাকে কৃতার্থ করুন। **It is our pleasure to etc.**—আমাদের এরূপ ইচ্ছা [রাজারাণীর লিখিত আদেশ প্রভৃতিতে ব্যবহৃত হয়।] **To take (a) pleasure in**—To like; to delight in; ভাল লাগা; আনন্দ পাওয়া।

pleat (plēt), *n.* & *v. t.* Same as PLAIT.

plĕb, *n.* (*Slang*) A plebeian; one of the lower class people; (ইতরভাষায়) হীনজাতীয় ব্যক্তি; হীনশ্রেণীর লোক, ছোটলোক।

ple'-bē'-ian (-ăn), *n.* & *adj.* **1.** One of the common people of ancient Rome (opp. to *patrician*); প্রাচীন রোমের সাধারণ শ্রেণীর লোক, প্রাকৃত লোক, সাধারণ লোক, প্রাকৃতজন। **2.** One of the lower ranks of men; সাধারণ শ্রেণীর লোক। ***Adj.*** **1.** Pertaining to the common people of ancient Rome; প্রাচীন রোমের প্রাকৃতজনসম্বন্ধীয়। **2.** Relating to a commoner; coarse; vulgar; as, *plebeian* sports; ইতরজন-সম্বন্ধীয়; অশ্লীল; গ্রাম্য, ইতর। **–ize,** *v. t.* **–ness,** *n.*

plĕb'-i-scite (-sĭt *or* -sīt), *n.* **1.** (*Rom. Hist.*) A law enacted by commonalty in *comitia tributa*; (রোমীয় ইতিহাস) সাধারণলোকগণ দ্বারা বিধিবদ্ধ আইন। **2.** A vote of a whole people or community; a public expression of a community's opinion; দেশের সমগ্র লোকের মত; গুরুতর প্রশ্নসম্পর্কে নিখিল নির্ব্বাচকগণের মত। **Ple-bis'-ci-ta-ry,** *adj.*

plĕc'-trŭm, *n.* An instrument of ivory etc. for plucking the strings

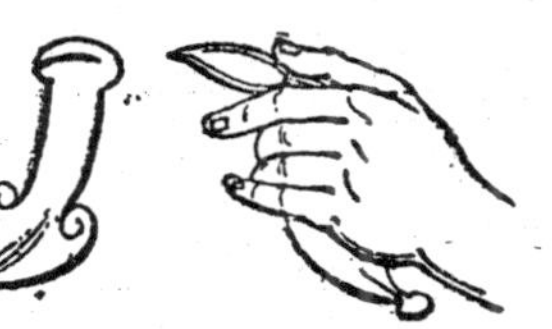

Plectrum.

of the lyre, zither, etc.; বীণাযন্ত্র প্রভৃতির তারে ঝঙ্কার দেওয়ার জন্য হস্তিদন্ত প্রভৃতিতে নির্ম্মিত যন্ত্র, মিস্রাব (মিউজিক)।

pledge (plĕj), *n.* **1.** Something given as a security; a thing pawned; বন্ধকী জিনিষ, জামিন স্বরূপ রক্ষিত জিনিষ; বন্ধক, আধি (মঃ সং) ন্যাস (ঐ), উপনিধি (ঐ)। **2.** (*Hist.*) A hostage; a surety; জামিন; প্রতিভূ। **3.** A solemn promise in writing to abstain from using intoxications; a promise; as, under *pledge* of secrecy; মাদকদ্রব্যবর্জ্জন সম্বন্ধে লিখিত প্রতিজ্ঞা; প্রতিজ্ঞা। **4.** Drinking of a health; কাহারো সম্মানার্থ স্বাস্থ্যকামনায় মদ্যপান। **5.** (*Fig.*) One's child; "Exulting over the first *pledge* of their union"; (লক্ষণায়) সন্তান। **6.** State of being pledged; as, a thing lying in *pledge*; বন্ধকী অবস্থা। **Pledge-cup**—যে পেয়ালা হইতে কাহারো সম্মানার্থ বা স্বাস্থ্যকামনায় মদ্য পান করা হয়। **To hold in pledge**—To keep as security; বন্ধকস্বরূপ রাখা, জামিনস্বরূপ রাখা। **To put in pledge**—To pawn; বন্ধক দেওয়া। **To redeem one's pledge**—বন্ধকী দ্রব্য খালাস করা। **To take, keep or sign the pledge** — See PLEDGE, *n.* 3.

pledge (plĕj), *v. t.* **1.** To give as a pledge or pawn; to pawn; as, to *pledge* one's watch; বন্ধক দেওয়া; বাঁধা দেওয়া। **2.** To plight or stake; as, to *pledge* one's word or honour; প্রতিজ্ঞাবদ্ধ হওয়া, পণ রাখা। **3.** To drink to the health of; কাহারো সম্মানার্থ বা স্বাস্থ্যকামনায় মদ্য পান করা। **Pledge'-a-ble,** *adj.* **Pledg-ee',** *n.* One to whom anything is given in pledge; বন্ধকগ্রহীতা। **Pledg'-er,** *n.* One who pledges or pawns; বন্ধকদাতা।

pledg'-ĕt (plĕj-), *n.* A small flat mass of lint laid over a wound etc.; ক্ষত স্থানের উপর নিহিত ক্ষুদ্র মৃদু বস্ত্রখণ্ড, বিবেসিক (সাঃ পঃ)।

Ple'-iad (plī-ăd), *n.* (*Pl.* -IADS -IADES) **1.** (*Gk. Myth.*) (*Pl.*) Name of the seven daughters of Atlas and Pleione; (গ্রীকপুরাণ) এটলাস

দৈত্যের সপ্ত কন্যা। **2.** A group of small stars in the neck of the constellation Taurus ; কৃত্তিকাপুঞ্জ। **3.** (*Fig.*) A brilliant group of usu. seven persons or things ; (লক্ষণায়) চাঁদের হাট, বিশেষতঃ সপ্ত শ্রেষ্ঠ ব্যক্তি বা বস্তুর সংহতি।

pleis'-to-cene (plīs-tō-sēn), *adj.* Relating to the uppermost division of the tertiary formation ; তৃতীয়ক স্তরের ঊর্দ্ধতম বিভাগ-সম্বন্ধীয়, আধুনিক (সাঃ পঃ)।

plē'-nȧ-rȳ, *adj.* Entire ; absolute ; complete ; as, *plenary* license ; অখণ্ড, সম্পূর্ণ ; অসীমাবদ্ধ ; পুরা, পূর্ণ। **—ri-ly,** *adv.* **Plenary inspiration**—পূর্ণ ভগবৎ প্রেরণা।

plĕn-i-pō-tĕn'-ti-ȧ-rȳ (-shĭ-), *adj.* & *n.* **1.** Invested with full and absolute powers as a representative or envoy of a sovereign etc. ; পূর্ণক্ষমতাপ্রদত্ত। **2.** (Of powers etc.) Absolute ; full ; অসীমাবদ্ধ, অনিয়ন্ত্রিত ; পূর্ণ, সম্পূর্ণ। ***Noun.*** A person invested with full power to act for another ; esp. an envoy or ambassador to act at discretion ; পূর্ণ ক্ষমতাপ্রাপ্ত প্রতিনিধি ; বিশেষতঃ পূর্ণ ক্ষমতাপ্রাপ্ত রাজদূত, মহাদূত।

plĕn'-i-tūde, *n.* State of being full or complete ; abundance ; as, the *plenitude* of space or power ; প্রাচুর্য্য, বাহুল্য, প্রভূততা ; পূর্ণতা, পরিপূর্ণতা, ভূমা (হিঃ কোঃ)।

plĕn'-tē-ous (-ŭs), *adj.* **1.** (*Chiefly poet.*) Plentiful ; abundant ; as, *plenteous* supply ; (প্রধানতঃ কবিতায়) প্রচুর, প্রভূত, ভূয়িষ্ঠ ; অজস্র, ভূরি, যথেষ্ট। **2.** Fruitful ; yielding plenty ; "*Plenteous* years" ; ফলশালী ; বহুপ্রদ। **—ly,** *adv.* **—ness,** *n.*

plĕn'-ti-fụl, *adj.* **1.** Copious ; ample ; abundant ; as, a *plentiful* harvest ; ভূরি, ভূয়িষ্ঠ, প্রচুর ; প্রভূত ; বিস্তর, বহুল, অজস্র, যথেষ্ট। **2.** Fruitful ; prolific ; "A more *plentiful* year" ; ফলশালী ; বহুপ্রদ। **—ly,** *adv.* Abudantly ; copiously ; প্রচুর পরিমাণে ; প্রভূত পরিমাণে, বহুল পরিমাণে। **—ness,** *n.*

plĕn'-tȳ, *n.* & *adv.* **1.** Abundance ; copiousness ; sufficiency ; প্রাচুর্য্য ; বাহুল্য ; ভূয়িষ্ঠতা। ***Adv.*** (*Colloq.*) Quite ; "*Plenty* large enough" ; পুরা। **Horn of plenty**—See HORN.

plē'-nŭm, *n.* **1.** Space considered as in every part filled with matter ; সর্ব্বাংশে জড় পরমাণু দ্বারা পরিপূর্ণ, আকাশ, শূন্যাভাব। **2.** A full assembly ; পূর্ণ সংসদ, পূর্ণ সভা।

plē'-ō-năsm, *n.* (*Gram.*) A redundancy of words ; use of more words than necessary ; (ব্যাকরণ) অধিকপদতা, অধিকপদদোষ, উক্তিদোষ, শব্দাতিশয়, শব্দবাহুল্য, শব্দপ্রকর্ষ ; প্রয়োজনাতিরিক্ত শব্দব্যবহার। **—nas'-tic,** *adj.* Redundant ; পৌনর্ব্বাচিক, অধিকপদ (কাব্যঃ)। **—nas'-ti-cal-ly,** *adv.*

plē-si-ō-sau'-rŭs (-sä-), *n.* A large extinct marine lizard, chiefly remarkable for its length of neck ; দীর্ঘগ্রীব সামুদ্রিক জন্তু-বিশেষ, লম্বগ্রীব কূর্ম্ম (অভিঃ)।

Plesiosaurus partially restored.

plĕth'-ō-rȧ, *n.* **1.** Morbid excess of blood ; রক্তাতিশয্য, অতিরক্ত (সাঃ পঃ), অস্বাস্থ্যকর রক্তাধিক্য, রক্তপিত্ত (মঃ উঃ)। **2.** Overfulness in any way ; unhealthy repletion or excess ; "A *plethora* of words" ; বাহুল্য ; ছড়াছড়ি। **Ple-thor'-ic,** *adj.* **1.** Charcterized by plethora ; রক্তপ্রধান। **2.** (*Fig.*) Full to excess ; inflated ; turgid ; "*Plethoric* volumes" ; (লক্ষণায়) অতিপূর্ণ ; স্ফীত ; শব্দাড়ম্বরপূর্ণ। **Ple-thor'-i-cal-ly,** *adv.*

pleu'-rȧ (plü-), *n.* A serous membrane covering the lungs and lining the cavity of the chest ; ফুসফুসবেষ্টক ঝিল্লী, ফুসফুসাবরণ, ফুসফুসবেষ্টক। **—ral,** *adj.*

pleu'-ri-sȳ (plü-), *n.* An inflammation of the pleura ; ফুসফুসবেষ্টপ্রদাহ, বক্ষোগ্রহ, উদরগ্রহ, পার্শ্বশূল (সুশ্রুঃ), পার্শ্বার্ত্তি (চঃ)। **—rit'-ic,** *adj.*

pleu-rō-dȳn'-i-ȧ (plü-), *n.* A painful affection of the side, simulating pleurisy, usually due to rheumatism ; পর্শুকার (পাঁজর) মধ্যবর্ত্তী পেশীর আক্ষেপিক বা আমবাতিক বেদনা, পার্শ্ববেদনা।

pleu-ro-pneu-mō'-ni-ȧ (plü-rō-nü-), *n.* A disease of cattle consisting in an inflammation of the pleura and lungs ; যুগপৎ ফুসফুসবেষ্টক ও ফুসফুসের প্রদাহ।

pleu-rō-thŏt'-ō-nŭs (plü-), **—rŏt'-ō-nŭs,** *ns.* (*Med.*) Tetanus in which the body is curved laterally ; (ভৈষজ্য-শাস্ত্র) পার্শ্ববক্রটঙ্কার রোগ।

plĕx-im'-ē-tẽr, *n.* **1.** (*Med.*) A plate of ivory etc. to examine the chest or abdomen by percussion ; অঙ্গুলীবিঘাতন দ্বারা বক্ষঃপরীক্ষার্থ গজদন্ত প্রভৃতি নির্ম্মিত ফলক বিশেষ।

plĕx'-ŏr, *n.* (*Med.*) A small hammer used with the pleximeter ; হাড়ের ক্ষুদ্র হাতুড়ী।

plĕx'-ŭs, *n.* (*Anat.*) A network of blood-vessel, nerves or fibres ; as, gastric *plexus* ; স্নায়ু বা নাড়ীর গুচ্ছ, জাল (সাঃ পঃ), গ্রন্থি (ঐ), পদ্ম (ব্রজঃ হিন্দুঃ), নাড়িগ্রন্থি, মর্ম্মগ্রন্থি (ঐ)। **2.** A network or complication ; জাল। **—i-form,** *adj.* **Cardiac plexus**—অনাহত চক্র (ব্রজঃ হিন্দু)। **Cavernous-plexus**—আজ্ঞাচক্র (বামন)। **Lumber**

plexus—মনিপুরক (ব্রজঃ হিন্দু)। **Sacral plexus**—স্বাধিষ্ঠান চক্র (ব্রজঃ হিন্দু)। **Solar plexus**—নাভিকাণ্ড (ব্রজঃ হিন্দু), ভানুভবন (ঐ), ব্রহ্মগ্রন্থি।

plī′-ă-ble (-bl), *adj.* Same as PLIANT. **—bil′-i-ty,** *n.* **—bly,** *adv.*

plī′-ănt, *adj.* **1.** Flexible; supple; as, *pliant* wax; নমনশীল, সুখনম্য; নরম, কোমল, মৃদু। **2.** (*Fig.*) Yielding; tractable; as, a *pliant* heart; (লক্ষণায়) বশ্য, নম্র, বিনয়ী; নমনশীল। **—an-cy,** *n.* State of being pliant; flexibility; (*lit.* & *fig.*) নমনশীলতা, নমনীয়তা; সুনম্যতা। **—ly,** *adv.*

plī′-că, *n.* (*Pl.* -CAE), **1.** A fold of a membrane or skin; বলি। **2.** A disease of the hair (*Plica polonica*) in which it is matted or clotted; পোলণ্ড প্রভৃতি দেশের কেশ-রোগ-বিশেষ—ইহাতে মস্তক হইতে একপ্রকার নির্য্যাসবৎ পদার্থ নিঃসৃত হইয়া কেশ ঘনীভূত ও জড়ীভূত করে।

plī-cāte, *adj.* (*Bot.* & *Zool.*) Folded; plaited; আকুঞ্চিত; কুঞ্চিত। **—cat-ed,** *adj.*

plī-cā′-tion, *n.* **1.** Folding; state of being folded; আকুঞ্চন; আকুঞ্চিত অবস্থা। **2.** A folding; a plait; ভাঁজ; কুচি।

plī′-êrs, *n.* A small pincers for bending wire etc.; জম্বুরা, পাক-সাঁড়াশী।

plight (plīt), *v. t.* & *n.* **1.** To pledge as one's word or honour; কথা দেওয়া, প্রতিজ্ঞাবদ্ধ হওয়া। **2.** To engage oneself to; to betroth, (usu. in *p. p.*); as, *plighted* lovers; বিবাহের জন্য প্রতিজ্ঞাবদ্ধ হওয়া; বাগ্দান করা। ***Noun.*** Pledge; engagement; বন্ধন; প্রতিশ্রুতি। **A plighted bride**—বাগ্দত্তাকন্যা। **To plight one's troth**—বাগ্দান করা।

plight (plīt), *n.* Condition; state; as, a sorry, evil, or hopeless *plight*; অবস্থা; দশা, গতি। **A sorry plight**—দুর্গতি, দুরবস্থা, দুর্দ্দশা।

Plim′-sŏll, *n.* The name of an agitator for the Merchant Shipping Act, 1876; ১৮৭৬ খৃঃ অব্দে বাণিজ্যপোতসম্বন্ধীয় আইনের জনৈক আন্দোলনকারী। **Plimsoll's mark, Plimsoll-line**—জলনিমজ্জন সীমা-নির্দ্দেশের নিমিত্ত সমস্ত ব্রিটিশ বাণিজ্য-পোতের পার্শ্বে অঙ্কিত চিহ্ন বিশেষ। [Plimsoll নামক জনৈক ব্যক্তির আন্দোলনের ফলে বাণিজ্যপোত অতিরিক্ত রূপে বোঝাই না হইতে পারে তজ্জন্য এক পার্লেমেণ্ট আইন বিধিবদ্ধ হয়। এই হেতু উক্ত ব্যক্তির নাম হইতে এইরূপ চিহ্নের নাম হইয়াছে।]

plinth, *n.* **1.** (*Arch.*) The square at the bottom of the base of a column; স্তম্ভমূল, উপান (রাঃ রাঃ)। **2.** The projecting part at the bottom of a wall; পীঠ (উড়িষ্যা)।

plin′-thite, *n.* (*Min.*) A sort of brick-red clay; ইষ্টকরক্তবর্ণ মৃত্তিকাবিশেষ।

plī′-ō-cene (-sēn), *adj.* (*Geol.*) Of, or pertaining to, the newest division of tertiary strata; অন্তস্তর (অভিঃ), অন্ত্যাধুনিক (সাঃ পঃ)।

plŏd, *v. i., t.* & *n.* **1.** To walk or travel laboriously; অতিকষ্টে চলা, অতি শ্রান্তভাবে চলা। **2.** To drudge; to toil; to study laboriously; কঠোর পরিশ্রম করা; অবিশ্রান্ত খাটা; কঠোর পরিশ্রমের সহিত অধ্যয়ন করা। ***Verb t.*** To make (one's way) slowly or heavily; মৃদুমন্দ গতিতে চলা, আস্তে আস্তে চলা। ***Noun.*** Laborious work or walk; কঠোর পরিশ্রম, শ্রান্তপদে ভ্রমণ। **Plod′-der,** *n.* **Plod′-ding,** *adj.* & *n.* **Plod′-ding-ly,** *adv.*

plŏp, *n., adv., v. i.* & *t.* Act of plumping into water; sound produced by this act; ঝুপ করিয়া জলে পড়ন; ঝুপ শব্দ। ***Adv.*** With a plop; ঝুপ করিয়া। ***Verb i.*** To plump into water; ঝুপ করিয়া জলে পড়া। ***Verb t.*** To cause to plump into water; জলে ঝুপ ঝুপ শব্দ করা।

plŏt, *n.* **1.** A small piece of ground; as, a garden *plot*; ভূখণ্ড, ক্ষেত্র। **2.** A conspiracy; an intrigue; as, the Ryehouse *plot*; ষড়যন্ত্র; চক্রান্ত। **3.** The plan or main story of a novel, poem, play, etc.; বস্তু, কাব্যবস্তু, আখ্যান-বস্তু। **Plot′-less,** *adj.*

plŏt, *v. t.* & *i.* **1.** To plan; to devise; as, to *plot* one's destruction; কল্পনা করা; চক্রান্ত করা। **2.** To make a plan or map of; নক্সা করা। ***Verb i.*** To make a plot; to conspire; ষড়যন্ত্র করা; চক্রান্ত করা। **Plot′-ter,** *n.*

plough (plow̄), *n.* **1.** An instrument for turning up the soil to prepare it for seed; হল, লাঙ্গল, সীর, শীর। [*Syn.* রাধরঙ্ক, কুন্তল, গোদারণ, গোকিল, গোকীল, কর্ষণী, কুন্তর।] **2.** A ploughed land; কর্ষিত ভূমি। **3.** Any of various instruments resembling a plough; as, ice-*plough*, snow-*plough* etc.; লাঙ্গলাকার যন্ত্র। **4.** A joiner's plane for making grooves; বিট তোলার রেঁদা। **5.** A bookbinder's instrument for cutting and smoothing the edges of books; কাতানী। **6.** (*Astron.*) Same as CHARLES'S WAIN. **7.** Rejection of a candidate in an examination; পরীক্ষায় অনুত্তীর্ণ করণ। **Ice-plough**—বরফখণ্ড কাটার জন্য একপ্রকার হল। **Plough-boy**—যে বালক চাষের সময় গরু, ঘোড়া, প্রভৃতি তাড়াইয়া নেয়, বালহালিক। **Plough-iron**—লাঙ্গলের ফাল। **Plough-land**—চাষের উপযোগী জমি; (ইতিহাস) ৮টী বৃষ দ্বারা বৎসরে যতটা জমি চাষ করিতে পারা যায়। **Plough-man**—কৃষাণ, কৃষক, হালিক, চাষাড়ে লোক। **Ploughshare**—ফাল, হলমুখ, জিত্যা, ফল, কুটক, কুশী, পোত্র, নিরীষ]। **Plough-shoe**—ফালরক্ষক, ফালধারক

Plough-staff—লাঙ্গলদণ্ড, ঈশা, ঈষা। **Plough-tail**—লাঙ্গলের মুষ্টি; (লক্ষণায়) কৃষিক্ষেত্রের শ্রম। **Plouh-tree**—লাঙ্গলের হাতল। **Plough-wright**—লাঙ্গল প্রস্তুতকারী, লাঙ্গল মেরামতকারী। **Snow-plough**—বরফ সরাইবার জন্য হল। **Steam-plough**—বাষ্পচালিত হল। **To look back from the plough**—To cease from work that has been seriously begun; যথার্থভাবে যে কাজে হাত দেওয়া হইয়াছে তাহা হইতে বিরত হওয়া। **To put one's hand to the plough**—To begin an undertaking; কঠিন কার্য্যে প্রবৃত্ত হওয়া।

plough (plow), *v. t. & i.* **1.** To turn up as soil with the plough; to till, as a field; চষা; চাষ করা, হলচালনা করা, কর্ষণ করা। **2.** To furrow; to produce (a furrow, line, etc.) as with a plough; (of a ship) to cleave (the surface of water, its way, etc.); নালি বা খাঁজ কাটা; লাঙ্গলরেখা কাটা; বিদারণ করা, ভেদ করা। **3.** (*Book binding*) To trim the edges of; পুস্তকের কিনারা কাটা। **4.** To produce wrinkles in (a brow etc.); কুঞ্চিত করা। **5.** (*Joinery*) To make grooves or ridges in, as a plank or board; তক্তার উপর খাঁজ কাটা। **6.** To root *out*, cast *up*, thrust *down* etc. with the plough; as, to *plough out, up, down*, roots or weeds; হল দ্বারা উন্মূলিত করা, দূর করা, নীচে ঠেলিয়া ফেলা। **7.** To proceed laboriously as *through* snow, book, etc.; পরিশ্রমের সহিত অগ্রসর হওয়া। **8.** (*Slang*) To reject as a candidate in an examination; (ইতরভাষায়) পরীক্ষার্থীকে অনুত্তীর্ণ করা। **To be ploughed**—To get plucked; অনুত্তীর্ণ হওয়া। **To plough in**—To cover by ploughing, as manure, seed, etc.; লাঙ্গলদ্বারা কর্ষণ করিয়া ঢাকা। **To plough out**—To dig out with the plough; to eradicate or cast out; লাঙ্গল দ্বারা খুঁড়িয়া বাহির করা; উৎপাটিত করা, উন্মূলিত করা। **To plough the sand** or **sands**—To labour uselessly; নিরর্থক পরিশ্রম করা, সাগরে বালির বাঁধ দেওয়া। **To plough up**—To break up as ground; to cast up or eradicate as weeds etc. by ploughing; ভূমিকর্ষণ করা; লাঙ্গল দ্বারা চষিয়া আগাছা প্রভৃতি উপড়াইয়া ফেলা।

plov'-ĕr (plŭv-), *n.* A wading bird of various species; তিত্তির (ডেওয়ার)।

plŭck, *n.* **1.** Act of plucking; a twitch; উৎপাটন; হেঁচকা টান। **2.** Courage; spirit; "Decay of manly *pluck*"; সাহস; বুকের পাটা, বুকের ছাতি। **3.** The heart, lungs, liver, etc. of an animal killed for food; নিহত জন্তুর মেটে, কলিজা। **4.** Failure in an examination; পরীক্ষায় অকৃতকার্য্যতা। **5.** (*Photog., slang*) Distinctness; boldness; স্পষ্টতা; প্রকটতা। **Plucked,** *adj.* Having courage or spirit; সাহসী। **Pluck'-i-ly,** *adv.* **Pluck'-i-ness,** *n.* **Pluck'-less,** *adj.* Timid; ভীরু, কাপুরুষ। **Pluck'-y,** *adj.* **1.** Having courage or spirit; সাহসী, নির্ভীক। **2.** (*Photog.*) Distinct or bold as a drawing; (আলোকচিত্র) স্পষ্ট, প্রকট।

plŭck, *v. t. & i.* **1.** To gather; to cull; to pull; as, *to pluck* berries, flowers, hair, etc.; আহরণ করা; তোলা, চয়ন করা, অবচিত করা; পাড়া, ছিঁড়া। **2.** To strip of feathers; as, to *pluck* a fowl; পাখা ছাড়ান। **3.** (*Archaic*) To drag; to snatch, (with *out, off, from*, etc.); (অপ্র:) টানা; কাড়িয়া নেওয়া, ছিনাইয়া নেওয়া। **4.** To jerk; to twitch; to sound as a musical string or stringed instrument by such action; হেঁচকা টানা; ঝাঁকি দেওয়া; বাদ্যযন্ত্র অঙ্গুলীদ্বারা ঝঙ্কৃত করা। **5.** To plunder; to swindle; as, to *pluck* a fool; লুণ্ঠন করা; জুয়াচুরী করা। **6.** To reject in examination; পরীক্ষায় অনুত্তীর্ণ করা। ***Verb i.*** To make a motion of pulling or twitching, (with *at*); as, to *pluck at* one's gown; হেঁচকা টান দেওয়া। **To pluck away**—To pull away; to tear away; উৎপাটন করা; ছিঁড়িয়া ফেলা। **To pluck off**—To pull or tear off; as, to *pluck off* the skin; উঠান, ছাড়ান। To descend in rank or title; পদ-গৌরবে অবনত হওয়া। **To pluck up one's heart, spirits** or **courage**—To take courage; সাহসে বুক বাঁধা। **To pluck up as a plant**—To tear up by the root; to destroy; উৎপাটন করা, উন্মূলিত করা; নষ্ট করা।

plŭg, *n.* **1.** A piece of wood etc., used to plug or stop a hole or gap; রোধনী, বর্ত্তি (সুশ্রু: কুক্ষ), ছিপি, স্থাপক (সা: প:)। **2.** A natural or morbid concretion acting thus; বলি। **3.** Tobacco pressed into a cake; তামাকের গুটি। **4.** (*Slang*) A silk hat; (ইতরভাষায়) রেশমী টুপী। **5.** (*Building*) A block of wood let into a wall, to afford a hold for nails; পেরেক বসাইবার জন্য প্রাচীরে যে কাষ্ঠখণ্ড নিবদ্ধ করা হয়। **6.** Same as FIPE-PLUG. **Fire-plug**—See under FIRE. **Plug-ugly**—গুণ্ডা।

plŭg, *v. t. & i.* **1.** To stop as a hole etc. with a plug; ছিপি দ্বারা বন্ধ করা। **2.** (*Slang*) To shoot; (ইতরভাষায়) গুলি করা। **3.** (*Slang*) To strike with the fist; (ইতরভাষায়) ঘুষি মারা। ***Verb i.*** (*Colloq.*) To plod or labour at work etc.; (চলিতভাষায়) অবিশ্রান্ত খাটা।

plŭm, *n.* **1.** A well-known stone fruit of various colours ; the tree bearing this fruit ; আলুবোখারা (ষোঃ), আরু (হিন্দী), শা-আলু (ঐ) । **2.** A dried grape or raisin ; শুষ্কীকৃত আঙ্গুর বা কিসমিস । **3.** (*Fig.*) A good thing ; the best of a collection ; the best part as of a book etc. ; "The posts...regarded as *plums* of the Indian Civil Service" ; (লক্ষণায়) ভাল জিনিষ ; সর্ব্বোৎকৃষ্ট বস্তু ; পুস্তক প্রভৃতির উৎকৃষ্ট অংশ । **4.** (*Slang*) A sum of £100,000 ; a handsome fortune (*rare*); (ইতরভাষায়) ১ লক্ষ পাউণ্ড; বিস্তর ধন (ক্বচিদ্‌ব্যবহৃত) । **Plum-cake**—কিসমিস প্রভৃতির সহযোগে প্রস্তুত পিষ্টকবিশেষ । **Plum-duff**—কিসমিস প্রভৃতি মিশ্রিত একপ্রকার ময়দার পিষ্টক—যাহা থলি বা কাপড়ের ভিতর রাখিয়া সিদ্ধ করা হয় । **Plum-porridge**—আরু, কিসমিস্ প্রভৃতি মিশ্রিত মণ্ড । **Plum-pudding**—ময়দা, কিসমিস, চর্ব্বি, প্রভৃতির সহযোগে প্রস্তুত পিষ্টকবিশেষ । **Plum-pudding stone**—নুড়ি পাথর, চকমকি পাথর, প্রভৃতি ।

plŭm'-āge, *n.* The feathers of a bird ; পালকসমূহ । **—aged,** *adj.*

plū-măs-sier' (-sēr), *n.* One who works or deals in ornamental feathers ; যে ব্যক্তি টুপি প্রভৃতিতে শোভাসাধক পালক লাগায়, পালকব্যবসায়ী ।

plumb (plŭm), *n., adj.* & *adv.* **1.** A mass of lead attached to a line and used to test the perpendicularity of a wall etc., (*lit.* & *fig.*) ; সীসার গুলি, ওলন । **2.** A sounding lead or plummet ; ওলন, ছিপের ডোর যে সীসার খণ্ডে বাঁধা থাকে । ***Adj.*** **1.** Vertical ; perpendicular, as a wall etc. ; খাড়া ; সরলোন্নত । **2.** (*Fig.*) Sheer ; downright ; as, *plumb* nonsense ; (লক্ষণায়) ডাহা ; বিলকুল । ***Adv.*** **1.** Perpendicularly ; "*Plumb* down he falls" ; খাড়াভাবে । **2.** (*Fig.*) Exactly ; as, it points *plumb* in the same direction ; (লক্ষণায়) ঠিক । **Plumb-line**—ওলন সূতা, অবলম্বনসূত্র (শংকু), সীসকসূত্র, অবলম্বসূত্র (সাঃ পঃ) । **Plumb-rule**—কোন পদার্থ ঠিক খাড়া কিনা তাহা পরীক্ষা করার জন্য অগ্রভাগে ওলন সূত্রবদ্ধ অপ্রশস্ত ফলকবিশেষ । **Out of plumb**—Not vertical ; খাড়া নয়, অসরলোন্নত ।

plumb (plŭm), *v. t.* & *i.* **1.** To make perpendicular ; as, to *plumb* a wall ; সরলোন্নত করা । **2.** To sound with a plummet as a sea, depth of water, etc. ; (*fig.*) to test ; to sound ; as, to *plumb* one's intellect ; সীসকখণ্ডবদ্ধ রজ্জুদ্বারা সমুদ্রের গভীরতা প্রভৃতি পরিমাপ করা ; (লক্ষণায়) পরীক্ষা করা ; পরিমাপ করা । ***Verb i.*** To work as a plumber ; সূত্রগ্রাহীর কাজ করা । **Plumb'-less,** *adj.*

plŭm-bā'-gō, *n.* **1.** (*Min.*) Graphite or black-lead used for pencils etc. ; কৃষ্ণসীসক । **2.** A genus of plants with blue or violet flowers ; নীল বা নীলারুণ পুষ্পপ্রসূ বৃক্ষজাতিবিশেষ । **—bag'-i-nous,** *adj.*

plŭm'-bē-ous (-ŭs), *adj.* Consisting of, or like, lead ; lead-glazed ; সীসকগর্ভ, সীসকবৎ ; সীসকস্তরাচ্ছাদিত ।

plumb'-ēr (plŭm-), *n.* **1.** An artisan who furnishes, fits, repairs pipes, cisterns, etc. ; যে ব্যক্তি নল, জলকুণ্ড, প্রভৃতি বিক্রয় সংস্থাপন বা মেরামত করে । **—y,** *n.*

plŭm'-bic, *adj.* **1.** (*Chem.*) Pertaining to, or combined with, lead ; as, *plumbic* oxide ; সীসকসম্বন্ধীয়, সীসকমিশ্রিত । **2.** (*Path.*) Caused by the presence of lead ; (নিদানশাস্ত্র) সীসকজনিত । **—bif'-er-ous,** *adj.* Producing, or containing, lead ; সীসকোৎপাদক, সীসকগর্ভ । **—bism,** *n.* Lead-poisoning ; সীসকজনিত বিষক্রিয়া ।

plūme, *n.* **1.** A feather esp. a long handsome one ; পালক, বিশেষতঃ দীর্ঘ মনোহর পালক । **2.** A feather or feathers worn as an ornament on a helmet, hat, etc. ; টুপি, শিরস্ত্রাণ, প্রভৃতির ভূষাস্বরূপ পরিহিত পালক বা পালক গুচ্ছ । **3.** A feather-like part or formation ; পালকবৎ অংশ । **4.** A token of honour ; a prize ; সম্মানচিহ্ন ; পুরস্কার । **5.** (*Bot.*) A plumule ; (উদ্ভিদবিদ্যা) পক্ষক । **Plume'-let,** *n.* **Borrowed plumes**—See BORROW. **Plume bird**—নন্দনপক্ষী । **Plume-plucked**—পালকবিরহিত ।

plūme, *v. t.* **1.** (Of a bird) **1.** To adjust or trim (feathers etc.) ; পালক ঝাড়িয়া ফেলা বা পরিষ্কার করা । **2.** To adorn or furnish with plumes ; "The *plumed* troops" ; পালকশোভিত করা, পালকভূষিত করা । **3.** To dress (oneself) with or as with plumes ; to pride ; to boast (*reflexively*) ; as, he *plumes* himself on his skill ; পালকের ভূষা দ্বারা সজ্জিত করা ; গর্ব্ব করা, বড়াই করা ; দম্ভ করা, দর্প করা । **Plumed,** *p. adj.*

plŭm'-met (-ĕt), *n.* **1.** A plumb-line ; a weight attached to it ; ওলন-সূতা ; ওলন । **2.** A sounding-lead ; সমুদ্রের গভীরতামাপক রজ্জুতে সংবদ্ধ সীসকখণ্ড । **3.** A weight attached to a fishing-line ; বড়শীর সূতায় যে সীসকপিণ্ড বাঁধা হয় । **4.** (*Fig.*) Something that weighs down or presses ; (লক্ষণায়) প্রপীড়ক বস্তু ।

plŭm'-my (-ĭ), *adj.* **1.** Of the nature of, or abounding in, plumes ; পালকাত্মক, পালকবহুল । **2.** (*Colloq.*) Desirable ; good ; (চলিত ভাষায়) বাঞ্ছনীয় ; হিতকর ।

plū-mōse', *adj.* **1.** Having feathers ; পালকবিশিষ্ট । **2.** Feathery ; feather-like ; পালকপূর্ণ ; পালকবৎ ।

plŭmp, *adj., v. t.* & *i.* (Of a person or a part of body) Fleshy ; full ; rounded ; as, a *plump* cheek ; টুকটুকে, মোটসোটা, নাদুসনুদুস, নধর, দোহারা ; পীন, পীবর, পরিপুষ্ট, পেশল ; গোলগাল। ***Verb t.*** To make plump ; to distend or flatten ; নাদুসনুদুস করা, হৃষ্টপুষ্ট করা ; স্ফীত করা। ***Verb i.*** To grow plump ; to swell *up* or *out* ; হৃষ্টপুষ্ট হওয়া ; স্ফীত হওয়া, ফুলিয়া উঠা। **Plump'-ly,** *adv.* **Plump'-ness,** *n.* **Plump'-y,** *adj.*

plŭmp, *v. i.* & *t., n., adv.* & *adj.* **1.** To drop or fall suddenly ; as, to *plump* into a chair ; ধুপ্ করিয়া পড়া, ধপ্ করিয়া পড়া। **2.** To give vote for one candidate only when one might vote for more ; একাধিক ব্যক্তির জন্য ভোট প্রদানের অধিকার থাকা স্বত্বেও কেবল এক ব্যক্তির জন্য মত প্রদান করা। ***Verb t.*** **1.** To throw or cause to fall heavily or suddenly ; ধুপ করিয়া ফেলা, ডুম্ করিয়া ফেলা। **2.** To give (a vote) as a plumper ; একাধিক ব্যক্তির জন্য ভোট প্রদানের অধিকার স্বত্বেও কেবলমাত্র একজনের জন্য ভোট দেওয়া। ***Noun.*** A sudden and heavy plunge or fall ; ডুম্ করিয়া পড়ন, ধুপ করিয়া পড়ন। ***Adv.*** Suddenly and heavily ; with a sudden fall ; as, he came *plump* into the river ; bluntly ; as, I told him *plump* ; ধুপ করিয়া, ডুম করিয়া ; ফস্ করিয়া : স্পষ্টাস্পষ্টি। ***Adj.*** Unqualified ; downright ; as, to answer with *plump* no ; বিলকুল ; ডাহা, পুরা।

plŭmp, *n.* (*Archaic*) A cluster ; a group ; a company ; (অপ্রঃ) গুচ্ছ ; সংহতি, মণ্ডলী ; দল।

plŭmp'-êr, *n.* Something *e. g.* a ball etc. carried in the mouth to fill out hollow cheeks ; শীর্ণতা হেতু যে গাল বসিয়া গিয়াছে তাহা পূর্ণ করার জন্য মুখের ভিতর যে গুলি প্রভৃতি পুরিয়া রাখা হয়।

plŭmp'-êr, *n.* **1.** Act of plumping or falling suddenly ; ধপ্ করিয়া পড়ন। **2.** One who gives a vote for one candidate only when he might vote for more ; such a vote ; যে ব্যক্তি একাধিক ব্যক্তির জন্য ভোট দেওয়ার অধিকার স্বত্বেও কেবলমাত্র একজনের জন্য ভোট প্রদান করে ; ঐ প্রকার ভোট। **3.** A downright lie ; ডাহা মিথ্যা কথা, জ্বলন্ত মিথ্যা কথা।

plü'-müle, *n.* **1.** The first bud of a seed plant ; বীজকোষোদ্গত অঙ্কুর, বীজাঙ্কুর, ভ্রূণকলি (সাঃ পঃ), পক্ষাণু (ঐ)। **2.** A down-feather ; a small feather ; কোমল পালক ; ক্ষুদ্র পালক। **—mu-la'-ceous,** *adj.* Bearing down or little feathers ; কোমলপালকধারী। **—mu-lar,** *adj.* (*Bot.*) Of, or relating to, a plumule ; বীজাঙ্কুরসম্বন্ধীয়।

plüm'-ȳ, *adj.* Covered or adorned with or like plumes ; feathery ; পালকাবৃত, পালক-ভূষিত, পালকশোভিত ; পালকময়।

plŭn'-dêr, *v. t.* & *n.* **1.** To rob ; to pillage ; as, to *plunder* a traveller or a temple ; চুরি করা ; লুণ্ঠন করা, লুটপাট করা, লুটতরাজ করা। **2.** To take by force, theft, etc. ; as, to *plunder* goods ; বলপূর্ব্বক নেওয়া ; চুরি করিয়া নেওয়া। ***Noun.*** **1.** Pillaging ; robbery ; বিলুণ্ঠন, বিলুন্ঠন ; লুঠপাট। **2.** Spoil ; লুণ্ঠিত দ্রব্য। **3.** (*Slang*) Profit ; (ইতর ভাষায়) লাভ। **—age,** *n.* Plundering ; esp. embezzling of goods on board a ship ; goods thus obtained ; লুণ্ঠন ; বিশেষতঃ জাহাজের মাল অন্যায়রূপে আত্মসাৎকরণ ; উক্ত উপায়ে প্রাপ্ত মাল। **—er,** *n.* One who plunders ; লুণ্ঠনকারী, লুঠেরা।

plunge (plŭnj), *v. t., i.* & *n.* **1.** To dip or thrust *into* water etc. ; to immerse ; ঝাঁপ দিয়া পড়া, ঝুপ করিয়া পড়া ; নিমগ্ন করা, চুবুনি দেওয়া। **2.** (*Fig.*) To thrust (a person etc. into a condition, action, etc.) ; (লক্ষণায়) ডুবান। ***Verb i.*** **1.** To cast oneself or dive into water etc. ; জলাদিতে ঝাঁপ দিয়া পড়া। **2.** (*Fig.*) To rush or fall into a condition ; (লক্ষণায়) নিমগ্ন হওয়া, ডুবা। **3.** To throw the body violently forward and the hind legs up, as a horse ; to pitch as a ship ; পশ্চাতের পদদ্বয় তুলিয়া সম্মুখের দিকে উদ্দামভাবে দেহক্ষেপ করা ; আন্দোলিত হওয়া ; **4.** To enter inpetuously or suddenly (into a room, *up* or *down* stairs etc.) ; বেগে প্রবেশ করা, সহসা প্রবেশ করা। **5.** (*Slang*) To gamble recklessly ; (ইতর ভাষায়) বেপরোয়াভাবে জুয়া খেলা। ***Noun.*** **1.** Act of plunging into water ; a dive ; মজ্জন, নিমজ্জন, অবগাহন, বিগাহন ; ডুব। **2.** (*Rare*) The breaking of a wave ; a heavy fall of rain ; তরঙ্গভঙ্গ ; ধারাবর্ষণ। **3.** Throwing oneself headlong as an unruly horse ; উদ্দামভাবে দেহক্ষেপ। **4.** (*Fig.*) A critical step ; as, to take the *plunge* ; (*dial.*) a difficulty ; "I was put to a *plunge*" ; (লক্ষণায়) অন্তিম উপায় ; (উপভাষায়) লেঠা, মুস্কিল। **5.** (*Slang*) Reckless gambling ; (ইতরভাষায়) বেপরোয়াভাবে জুয়া খেলন। **Plun'-ger,** *n.* **1.** A diver ; নিমজ্জক। **2.** A long cylinder used as a piston in a force-pump ; একপ্রকার দীর্ঘ চোঙ্গ—যাহা সম্পীড়নদণ্ডস্বরূপ ব্যবহৃত হয়। **3.** (*Slang*) A reckless gambler or speculator ; (ইতরভাষায়) যে ব্যক্তি বেপরোয়া ভাবে জুয়াখেলে বা ঝুঁকিদার ব্যবসায়ে প্রবৃত্ত হয়। **4.** (*Slang*) A cavalryman ; (ইতরভাষায়) ঘোড়সওয়ার।

plu'-pêr-fĕct (plô-), *adj.* & *n.* (Of tense) Past-perfect ; কোন অতীত ঘটনার পূর্ব্বে নিষ্পন্ন, পরোক্ষভূত,

অনদ্যতনভূত। *Noun.* The past perfect tense ; অনদ্যতনভূতকাল।

plu'-răl (plô-), *adj.* & *n.* Containing, denoting or implying more than one ; as, a *plural* word ; বহুবচনান্ত, বহুবাচক। *Noun.* (*Gram.*) The plural number (ব্যাকরণ) বহুবচন। **–ly,** *adv.* **Plural number** — Same as PLURAL, *n.*

plu'-răl-ĭsm (plô-), *n.* **1.** The state of being plural ; বহুত্ব, অনেকত্ব। **2.** (*Eccl.*) The system of holding more benefices or livings than one at a time ; (যাজকীয় শাস্ত্র) এককালে একাধিক যাজকীয় পদ অধিকারের রীতি। **3.** (*Philos.*) The system which recognises more than one ultimate principle ; (দর্শনশাস্ত্র) বহুদেববাদ, নানাত্ববাদ (হিঃ কোঃ)। **–ist,** *n.*

plu-răl'-ĭ-tў (plô-), *n.* **1.** The state of being plural ; a large number ; বহুত্ব, অনেকত্ব, নানাত্ব (হিঃ কোঃ) ; বৃহৎ সংখ্যা। **2.** (Of votes etc.) The greater number ; অধিকাংশ। **3.** (*Eccl.*) the holding of two or more benefices together ; এককালে দুই বা ততোধিক যাজকীয় পদ অধিকার। **4.** The holding by one person of two or more offices or positions at one time ; এক ব্যক্তি কর্তৃক এককালে দুই বা ততোধিক পদ অধিকার।

plu'-răl-īze (plô-), *v. t.* & *i.* To express in the plural form ; to render plural ; বহুবচনে প্রকাশ করা ; বহুবচনান্ত করা। *Verb i.* **1.** To hold two or more benefices simultaneously ; এককালে দুই বা ততোধিক যাজকীয়পদ অধিকার করা। **2.** To assume a plural form ; বহুবচনের আকার গ্রহণ করা।

plu-ri-pres'-ence (plô-rĭ-prĕz-ĕns) *n.* The presence in more places than one at the same time ; এককালে একাধিক স্থানে স্থিতি।

plŭs *prep., adj.* & *n.* With the addition of ; as, 3 plus 4 ; যোগ। *Adj.* **1** Extra ; more ; অতিরিক্ত ; অধিক। **2.** (*Math.*) positive ; (গণিতশাস্ত্র) ধন। **3.** (*Electr.*) Positively electrified ; (তাড়িতবিদ্যা) ধনতাড়িতসঞ্চারিত। *Noun.* The mark (+) ; additional or positive quantity ; যোগচিহ্ন ; যোগবাচক সংখ্যা।

plŭsh, *n.* **1.** A shaggy cloth with a velvety nap on one side ; মখমলের ন্যায় বস্ত্রবিশেষ। **2.** (*Pl.*) A footman's plush breeches ; উক্ত কাপড়ে তৈরী পাইকের জাঙ্গিয়া। **Plush'-y,** *adj.*

plu'-târ-chў (plô-), *n.* Same as PLUTOCRACY.

Plu'-tō (plô-), *n.* The God of Inferno ; গ্রীক পুরাণোক্ত যমরাজ।

plu-tŏc'-ră-çў (plô-), *n.* The rule or power of wealthy or the rich ; ধনিসম্প্রদায় কর্তৃক রাজ্য শাসন, ধনিতন্ত্র, কাঞ্চন কৌলিন্য।

plu'-tō-crăt (plô-), *n.* One who has power or influence through his wealth ; ধনতান্ত্রিক, ধনকুলীন। **–crat'-ic,** *adj.*

plu-tŏl'-ăt-rў (plô-) *n.* Worship of wealth ; ধনার্চ্চনা।

Plu-tŏn'-ic (plô-), *adj.* & *n.* **1.** Of, or pertaining to, Pluto ; subterranean ; গ্রীকপুরাণোক্ত যমরাজ-সম্বন্ধীয় ; পাতালজ, অন্তর্ভৌম। **2.** (*Geol.*) Igneous ; (ভূবিদ্যা) আগ্নেয়। **3.** Infernal ; নারকীয়। *Noun.* Igneous rock ; আগ্নেয় প্রস্তর। **–to-ni-an,** *adj.* Same as PLUTONIC. **–to-nism,** *n.* The Plutonic theory (see below). **–to-nist,** *n.* **Plutonic rock**—বারুণস্তর। **Plutonic theory**—ভূগর্ভস্থ অগ্নির ক্রিয়া দ্বারা পৃথিবীপৃষ্ঠের যাবতীয় পরিবর্তন সঞ্জাত হয়—এইরূপ মতবাদ বিশেষ।

plu-tŏn'-ŏ-mў (plô-), *n.* Political economy ; অর্থনীতিশাস্ত্র, অর্থশাস্ত্র। **–to-nom'-ic,** *adj.* **–to-nom'-ist,** *n.*

plu'-vĭ-ăl (plô-), *adj.* & *n.* **1.** Of, or pertaining to, rain ; বৃষ্টি সম্বন্ধীয়, বর্ষণ সম্বন্ধীয়। **2.** (*Geol.*) Due to rain ; বৃষ্টিজনিত। *Noun.* (*Eccl. Hist.*) A priest's cloak as a protection from rain ; যাজকদিকের বৃষ্টি নিবারক প্রাবরণ বিশেষ। **–ous,** *adj.*

plu-vĭ-ŏm'-ĕ-têr (plô-), *n.* A rain-gauge ; বর্ষমান (কোটিল্য-অর্থশাস্ত্র), বৃষ্টিমানযন্ত্র। **–o-met'-ric, –o-met'-ri-cal,** *adjs.*

plў, *n.* **1.** A fold ; a layer or thickness ; as, a three-*ply* carpet ; ভাঁজ ; পাট। **2.** A turn or twist as of a yarn, rope, etc. ; মোচড়, পাক, পেঁচ। **3.** (*Fig.*) Bent ; tendency ; turn ; as, to take *ply* ; (লক্ষণায়) প্রবণতা ; আসক্তি ; ঝোঁক। **2-ply, 3-ply**—দুই বা তিন ভাঁজ বা গুণ বিশিষ্ট।

plў, *v. t.* & *i.* **1.** To wield vigorously ; to use steadily ; as, to *ply* a weapon, implement, etc. ; to exercise as one's wit ; সতেজে চালনা করা ; চালনা করা ; পরিচালনা করা। **2.** To work at steadily ; to perform with diligence ; as, to *ply* one's task ; স্থিরভাবে কাজ করা ; সশ্রমে সম্পাদন করা। **3.** To assail vigorously ; to urge or solicit importunately ; প্রবলভাবে আক্রমণ করা ; ঝালাপালা করা। **4.** To continue to supply *with* food etc. ; সরবরাহ করিতে থাকা। *Verb i.* **1.** To work diligently and steadily ; পরিশ্রমের সহিত কাজ করা। **2.** To run between any two parts or places (of a steamer, a coach, etc.) ; দুইস্থানের মধ্যে যাতায়াত করা, চলাফেরা করা। **3.** (*Naut.*) To make way against the wind ; (নৌ বিদ্যা) বায়ুর প্রতিকূলে অগ্রসর হওয়া। **4.** (Of boatman, porter, cabman) To attend regularly for custom (*at* a place) ; (কোন নির্দ্দিষ্ট স্থানে) ভাড়ার জন্য রীতিমত উপস্থিত থাকা।

Plym'-outh (-owth), *n.* **Plymouth Brethren**—ইংলণ্ডের অন্তঃপাতী Plymouth নামক স্থানে সর্ব্বপ্রথম প্রতিষ্ঠিত ধর্ম্মসম্প্রদায় বিশেষ। **Plymouth-Rock** — একপ্রকার গৃহপালিত কুক্কুট। **–ism,** *n.* **–ist, –ite,** *ns.*

pneu'-mă (-nü), *n.* A breath; প্রাণবায়ু (হিঃ কোঃ), প্রাণ (ঐ)।

pneu-măt'-ic (nü-), *adj.* & *n.* **1.** Consisting of, or resembling, air; gaseous; বায়ুসমন্বিত, বায়ুবৎ; বাষ্পীয়, বায়ুময়। **2.** Pertaining to air, elastic fluids or to their properties; বায়বীয়, বায়ব্য। **3.** Moved or played by air or wind; বায়ুচালিত, বায়ুবাদিত। **4.** Filled with air; বায়ুপূর্ণ। **5.** Spiritual; আধ্যাত্মিক। ***Noun.*** **1.** Pneumatic tire; a cycle with such tires; রবারের শূন্যগর্ভ চক্রপ্রান্তবেষ্টনী; উক্তরূপ প্রান্তবেষ্টনীবিশিষ্ট দ্বিচক্রযান। **2.** (*Pl.*) The science which treats of air and other elastic fluids or gases; অনিলবিজ্ঞান (সাঃ পঃ), বায়ুবিজ্ঞান, বাষ্পবিজ্ঞান, বায়ুবিদ্যা (হিঃ কোঃ), বায়ুশাস্ত্র (ঐ)। **3.** (*Philos.* & *theol.*) The scientific knowledge of spiritual beings; প্রেততত্ত্ব, প্রেতবিজ্ঞান, প্রেতবিদ্যা। **–i-cal-ly,** *adv.* **–tic'-i-ty,** *n.* **Pneumatic dispatch**—সঙ্কাপিত বায়ুর সাহায্যে চুঙ্গির ভিতর দিয়া, পত্র, তাড়িতবার্ত্তা, ক্ষুদ্র ক্ষুদ্র পুলিন্দা, প্রভৃতি প্রেরণের কৌশল বিশেষ। **Pneumatic railway**—যে লৌহবর্ত্মে শকট সমূহ সঙ্কাপিত বায়ুর দ্বারা চালিত হয়। **Pneumatic tire** — See PNEUMATIC, *n.* I. **Pneumatic trough**—কাষ্ঠ বা লৌহনির্ম্মিত পাত্র—যাহার সাহায্যে নলাকার কাচভাণ্ডে বাষ্প সংগ্রহীত হয়, বাষ্পসঞ্চয়সহায়ক পাত্র।

pneu'-măt-ō-cyst (nü-), *n.* An air-sac in the body of a bird etc.; পক্ষী প্রভৃতির দেহস্থ বায়ুকোষ।

pneu-mă-tŏl'-ŏ-ġy (nü-), *n.* **1.** The science treating of spiritual beings; প্রেতবিদ্যা, প্রেততত্ত্ব, দেবযোনিবাদ (হিঃ কোঃ), দেবযোনিবিদ্যা। **2.** The doctrine of the Holy Spirit; পবিত্রাত্মার তত্ত্ব। **3.** Psychology; মনোবিজ্ঞান, মনস্তত্ত্ব। **4.** Same as PNEUMATICS. **–to-log'-i-cal,** *adj.*

pneu-mă-tŏm'-ĕ-têr, *n.* A contrivance to measure the amount of air breathed at each inspiration; নিশ্বাসবায়ুমাপক।

pneu-mō-găs'-tric (nü-) *adj.* Of, or pertaining to, the lungs and stomach; ফুসফুস এবং পাকস্থলী-সম্বন্ধীয়। **Pneumogastric nerves**—ফুসফুস-পাকাশয়িক স্নায়ু, মস্তিষ্ক হইতে প্রসৃত দশম স্নায়ুযুগ্ম।

pneu-mō'-ni-ă (nü-), *n.* Inflammation of the tissues of one (*single pneumonia*) or both (*double pneumonia*) lungs; ফুসফুস-প্রদাহ, বাতশ্লেষ্মজ জ্বর। **–mon'-ic,** *adj.* Pertaining to lungs; ফুসফুস-সম্বন্ধীয়। **–ni'-tis,** *n.* Same as PNEUMONIA.

pneu-mō-thō'-răx (nü-) *n.* (*Med.*) A state marked by the presence of air or other gas in the cavity of the chest; ফুসফুসবেষ্ট গহ্বরে বায়ু বা অন্যরূপ বাষ্প সঞ্চয়।

poach (pōch), *v. t.* To cook (eggs) by breaking and pouring them into boiling water; ডিম ভাঙ্গিয়া উহাদের ভিতরের অংশ উষ্ণ জলে ঢালিয়া পাক করা। **Poach'-er,** *n.*

poach (pōch-), *v. t.* & *i.* **1.** To thrust; as, to *poach* a stick or finger into something; ঢুকান। **2.** To tread as snow etc; to cut *up* (turfs etc.) with hoofs; বরফ প্রভৃতির উপর হাঁটিয়া চলা; খুর দিয়া কাটা। **3.** To intrude or encroach upon (land etc.) unlawfully; অনধিকার প্রবেশ করা, অন্যায়রূপে প্রবেশ করা। **4.** To capture (game, fish, etc.) illegally; to gain (an advantage, start, etc. in a race) unfairly; (মৎস্য, জন্তু প্রভৃতি) অবৈধরূপে ধরা; অন্যায়রূপে (কোনরূপ সুবিধা, দৌড়ে সুবিধাজনক অবস্থা প্রভৃতি) লাভ করা। **5.** (*Lawn-tennis*) To strike (a ball etc.) in a partner's court; (আণ্টাখেলা) সহক্রীড়কের অঙ্গনের (কন্দুক প্রভৃতিতে) আঘাত করা। ***Verb i.*** **1.** (Of land etc.) To become soft or muddy by being trampled; পা দ্বারা মাড়ান হেতু নরম বা কর্দ্দমময় হওয়া। **2.** To steal game or fish; মাছ বা শিকারের জন্য রক্ষিত জন্তু চুরি করা। **3.** To trespass or encroach as *on* a person's preserves, (often *fig.*) lands, etc.; কাহারো রক্ষিত বনে অনধিকার প্রবেশ করা। **Poach'-er,** *n.* One who poaches; শিকার অপহারক, জাঙ্গল চোর।

pŏch'-ârd, *n.* A genus of diving ducks of Europe; ইয়ুরোপের একজাতীয় জলচর পক্ষী, মুঠিয়া (হিউম) [মাথা ও গলা রক্তাভ পিঙ্গল]।

pŏck, *n.* A pustule on the skin, esp. in small pox; গুটি, বসন্তের গুটি।

pŏck'-ĕt, *n.* & *adj.* **1.** A small bag or pouch esp. one attached to a garment; টেক, জেব। **2.** (*Fig.*) Money; pecuniary resources; as, to suffer in one's *pocket*; (লক্ষণায়) টাকা; আর্থিক সম্বল। **3.** One of the bags to receive the balls in a billiard-table; বিলিয়ার্ড খেলার মেজে যে সকল থলিতে কন্দুক পতিত হয়—তাহাদের অন্যতম। **4.** (*Mining*) A cavity in the earth with grains of gold or other mineral; স্বর্ণ বা অপর খনিজ পদার্থের কণিকাপূর্ণ গর্ত্ত। **5.** (*Chiefly Geol.*) A cavity in a rock containing foreign matter; পাষাণের মধ্যে ভিন্নজাতীয় পদার্থপূর্ণ গর্ত্ত। **6.** (*Racing slang*) The position in which a competitor is hemmed in by others; (ঘোড়দৌড়ের ইতর-ভাষায়) যেরূপ অবস্থায় কোন প্রতিদ্বন্দ্বী অপর প্রতিদ্বন্দ্বিগণ দ্বারা বাধা প্রাপ্ত হয়। ***Adj.*** Suitable in size etc.

for carrying in a pocket ; as, a *pocket* edition ; ক্ষুদ্র আকারের। **—ful,** *n.* **—less,** *adj.* **—y,** *adj.* (*Mining*) Having the ore unevenly distributed ; (খনির কাজ) অসমভাবে বিভক্ত খনিজবিমিশ্র পদার্থ-সমন্বিত। **Pocket-book**—মন্তব্যপুস্তক, নোটবহি, কাগজ প্রভৃতি রাখার জন্য পুস্তকের আকার আধার। **Pocket-borough**—See BOROUGH. **Pocket-cloth** — রুমাল। **Pocket edition**—জেবে রাখার উপযোগী সংস্করণ। **Pocket expenses**—হাত খরচ, নিজ খরচের টাকা। **Pocket-glass**—ক্ষুদ্র দর্পণ। **Pocket-handkerchief**—জেব রুমাল। **Pocket-hole**—জেবের ফাঁক। **Pocket-knife** — চাকু। **Pocket-money**—হাত খরচের টাকা। **Pocket picking** — গাঁট-কাটন। **Pocket-piece**—সৌভাগ্য লাভ বা কোন বিপৎ প্রভৃতি হইতে মুক্তি লাভের জন্য জেবে যে মুদ্রা রাখা হয়। **Pocket-pistol**—একপ্রকার ক্ষুদ্র পিস্তল যাহা জেবে রাখা যায় ; (কৌতুকচ্ছলে) মদিরা রাখার জন্য জেবে রাখার উপযোগী ক্ষুদ্র ভাণ্ড। **An empty pocket**—রিক্তহস্ত। **Am 10*s.* in pocket**—আমার দশ শিলিং আছে। **Am 4*s.* in pocket or out of pocket, by the transaction**—এই ব্যাপারে আমার ৪ শিলিং লাভ বা ক্ষতি হইয়াছে। **She has him in her pocket**—She has him completely under control ; সে তাহাকে সম্পূর্ণরূপে করতল করিয়াছে। **To pick a person's pocket**—To steal from his pocket ; কাহারো পকেট কাটা, গাঁট-কাটা। **To put one's hand in one's pocket**—To spend some money ; to be charitable ; কিছু অর্থ ব্যয় করা ; দানশীল হওয়া। **To put one's pride in one's pocket**—To give up pride for a while ; কিছুকালের জন্য অহঙ্কার ছাড়া।

pŏck'-ĕt *v. t.* **1.** To put or conceal in the pocket ; জেবে রাখা, জেবে লুকান। **2.** To confine as in a pocket ; "Energy...*pocketed* in portions of matter" ; রুদ্ধ করা। **3.** To take stealthily or dishonestly ; গোপনে বা অন্যায়রূপে নেওয়া, আত্মসাৎ করা। **4.** To submit to (affront, injury, etc.) ; to suppress as a feeling ; ঘাড় পেতে নেওয়া ; রোধ করা। **5.** (*Billiards*) To strike (a ball) so that it falls into the pocket ; (বিলিয়ার্ড) যাহাতে থলির মধ্যে পড়ে—এরূপভাবে কন্দুকে আঘাত করা। **6.** To hem in as a competitor in a race ; দৌড় প্রভৃতিতে কোন প্রতিদ্বন্দ্বীকে বাধা দেওয়া। **—a-ble,** *adj.* **To pocket an insult**—To receive or submit to it without resenting ; কিল খেয়ে কিল চুরি করা, কোন অপমান ঘাড় পেতে নেওয়া। **To pocket dibs**—To receive salary or profits ; বেতন পাওয়া, লাভ পাওয়া।

pō-cō-cū-rān'-tē, *adj.* & *n.* Careless ; indifferent ; অসতর্ক ; উদাসীন। ***Noun.*** A careless man ; a trifler ; অসতর্ক লোক ; যে ব্যক্তি বাজে কাজে নিযুক্ত থাকে।

pŏd, *n.* The socket of a brace in which the end of a bit is inserted ; বর্ম্মা, তুরপুণ প্রভৃতির হাতলের কোটর—যাহাতে লৌহময় অংশের প্রান্ত প্রবিষ্ট করা হয়।

pŏd, *n., v. i.* & *t.* **1.** The seed vessel of certain plants as peas, beans, etc. ; শুঁটি, শিম্বী। **2.** The cocoon of silkworm ; গুটি। **3.** The case of a locust's eggs ; পঙ্গকীট ডিম্বের খোসা। **4.** A narrow-necked net for catching eels ; বাইন মাছ ধরার জন্য একপ্রকার জাল। ***Verb i.*** To produce pods ; শিম্বী উৎপাদন করা। ***Verb t.*** To shell (peas etc.) ; (মটর শুঁটি প্রভৃতির) খোসা ছাড়ান।

pŏd, *n.* & *v. t.* A number of seals or whales closely clustered together ; সংশ্লিষ্ট শীল বা তিমি-মৎস্যসমূহ। ***Verb t.*** To drive (seals etc.) into a pod ; শীল-মৎস্য প্রভৃতিকে তাড়না করিয়া একত্র সংশ্লিষ্ট করা।

pō-dăg'-ră, *n.* (*Med.*) Gout esp. in the feet ; (ভৈষজ্য-শাস্ত্র) পায়ের গেঁটে বাতরোগ। **Pod'-a-grous, —ric, —ral,** *adjs.*

pŏd'-ded (-ĕd), *adj.* **1.** Bearing pods ; borne in a pod as seeds ; শিম্বীধারক ; শিম্বীযুক্ত। **2.** (*Fig.*) Rich ; well-off ; "... leading ... *podded* lines" ; (লক্ষণায়) ধনী ; সঙ্গতিশালী।

podesta, *n.* **1.** (*Hist.*) A chief magistrate of the Italian republics of the middle ages ; (ইতিহাস) মধ্যযুগের ইতালীদেশের গণতন্ত্রের অধীন নগর সমূহের প্রধান ম্যাজিষ্ট্রেট। **2.** A municipal judge in some cities of Italy ; ইতালীর কোন কোন নগরে নগরবাসিগণকর্তৃক নির্ব্বাচিত বিচারক।

podge (pŏj), *n.* A short, fat man or woman ; স্থূল এবং খর্ব্বাকৃতি পুরুষ বা নারী। **Podg'-y,** *adj.*

pō'-dĭ-ŭm, *n.* (*Pl.* -DIA) **1.** A continuous pedestal on which columns rest ; the raised platform round the area of an amphitheatre ; স্তম্ভ-পীঠ ; বৃত্তাকার রঙ্গাঙ্গনের চতুঃপার্শ্ববর্ত্তী উচ্চ মঞ্চ। **2.** A continuous bench around a room ; কোন কক্ষের চতুঃপার্শ্ববর্ত্তী নিরবচ্ছিন্ন কাঠাসন। **3.** (*Zool.*) A foot ; (জন্তুবিদ্যা) পদ।

pŏd-ō-phўl'-lin (-ĭn), *n.* (*Chem.*) A resin obtained from the wild mandrake ; লক্ষণা কন্দ হইতে প্রাপ্ত রজন।

pŏd-ō-phўl'-lŭm, *n.* **1.** (*Bot.*) A genus of the May apple ; (উদ্ভিদবিদ্যা) পাপড়া শাক। **2.** (*Pharmacy*) The rhizome and rootlet of the May apples ; পাপড়া শাকের কন্দ বা মূল।

pō'-ĕ-bird (-bĕrd), *n.* The parson-bird of New Zealand ; নিউজিলেণ্ডের পক্ষিবিশেষ।

pō′-ĕm, *n.* **1.** A composition in verse ; কবিতা। **2.** An elevated composition in prose ; as, a prose *poem* ; কবিত্বপূর্ণ গদ্যরচনা। **3.** (*Fig.*) Something like, or likened to, a poem ; as, their lives are a *poem* ; (লক্ষণায়) কাব্য।

pō′-ĕ-sy̆, *n.* (*Archaic*) **1.** The art of writing poetry ; poetical skill or faculty ; (অপ্রঃ) কবিতা-রচনাকৌশল ; কবিত্ব, কবিত্বশক্তি। **2.** Poems collectively ; কবিতা-সমূহ। **3.** A motto engraved on a ring etc. ; অঙ্গুরীয়ক প্রভৃতির উপর ক্ষোদিত ক্ষুদ্র সারবান বাক্য।

pō′-ĕt, *n.* A writer of poems ; কবি, পদ্যরচক কাব্যকর্ত্তা। **—ess,** *n.* (*Fem.*) **Poet's Corner** — ওয়েষ্ট মিনিষ্টার এবির যে অংশে কতিপয় প্রসিদ্ধ কবির সমাধি এবং স্মৃতিস্তম্ভ অবস্থিত আছে ; (কৌতুকচ্ছলে), সংবাদ-পত্রের যে অংশে কবিতা প্রকাশিত হয়।

pō′-ĕt-ăs-tēr, *n.* A petty or inferior poet ; ক্ষুদ্র কবি, মন্দকবি, কুকবি, কবিকল্প। **—et′-i-cule,** *n.* Same as POETASTER.

pō-ĕt′-ic, —i-căl, *adjs.* **1.** Of, relating to, or suitable for, poetry or poets ; as, *poetic* talent, work or sentiment ; কবিতাসম্বন্ধীয়, কবিতার উপযোগী। **2.** (Usu. *-ical*) Expressed, or written, in poetry ; as, *poetical* works ; কবিত্বের সহিত প্রকাশিত। **—i-cal-ly,** *adv.* **—ics,** *n.* The principles or rules of the art of poetry ; ছন্দঃশাস্ত্র, কবিতাবিজ্ঞান (হিঃ কোঃ), কবিতা-শাস্ত্র। **Poetic justice** — কবিগণের আদর্শানুযায়ী দণ্ডপুরস্কারবিধান [যেরূপ দণ্ডপুরস্কারের কথা কেবল কাব্যেই পাঠ করা যায়—কিন্তু বাস্তবজীবনে দৃষ্ট হয় না।] **Poetic licence**—(ব্যাকরণের নিয়মাদি লঙ্ঘনে) কবির স্বাধীনতা, নিরঙ্কুশতা (cf. নিরঙ্কুশাঃ কবয়ঃ)।

pō-ĕt′-i-cīze, *v. t.* & *i.* To make poetic ; to treat poetically ; কবিত্বপূর্ণ করা ; কবিত্বপূর্ণভাবে আলোচনা করা। ***Verb i.*** To write or recite poetry ; কবিতা রচনা করা, কবিতা আবৃত্তি করা।

pō-ĕt′-īze, *v. i.* & *t.* To write as a poet ; to compose verse ; কবির মত রচনা করা ; কবিতা রচনা করা। ***Verb t.*** **1.** To make poetic ; to treat poetically ; কবিত্বময় করা ; কবিত্বপূর্ণভাবে আলোচনা করা। **2.** To celebrate in poetry ; কোন বিষয়ে কবিতা লিখা।

pō′-ĕt-ry̆, *n.* **1.** The artistic expression of thoughts in emotional and rythmical language ; কবিতা, কাব্য, পদ্য। **2.** Poems ; verse ; as, heroic *poetry* ; কবিতা ; ছন্দোবদ্ধ রচনা। **3.** Poetical quality, spirit or feeling ; "No *poetry* in railways" ; কবিত্ব। **Prose poetry**—গদ্য কাব্য।

Pogostemon patchouli — পচাপাতা (বেলঃ)।

pogrom, (*Russ.*) *n.* Organized massacre as of the Jews in Russia ; জনহত্যা, হত্যাকাণ্ড।

poign′-ănt (poyn-), *adj.* **1.** Sharp ; pungent ; stinging ; তীব্র ; উগ্র ; তীক্ষ্ণ, প্রখর। **2.** Keen ; satirical ; piquant ; as, a *poignant* sarcasm or wit ; তীক্ষ্ণ ; বিদ্রূপপূর্ণ ; ঝাঁঝাল। **3.** Bitter ; painful ; as, *poignant* hunger or regret ; দারুণ ; যন্ত্রণাপূর্ণ। **—an-cy,** *n.* **—ly,** *adv.*

poin-set′-ti-a (-poyn-sĕt-ĭ-ȧ), *n.* A Mexican shrub, (from the name of its discoverer J. R. Poinsett) ; মেক্সিকোদেশের গুল্ম বিশেষ।

point (poynt), *n.* **1.** The sharp end of an instrument, pin, needle, etc. ; tip ; অগ্র ; মুখ। **2.** An instrument with a sharp point used by engravers, etchers, etc. ; as, a stone-cutter's *point* ; সূক্ষ্মাগ্র যন্ত্র। **3.** A mark of punctuation ; বিরাম-চিহ্ন। **4.** The mark made by a sharp instrument ; a prick ; সূক্ষ্মাগ্র যন্ত্র দ্বারা কৃত চিহ্ন, বেধন চিহ্ন ; খোঁচা। **5.** A small cape ; a peak ; ক্ষুদ্র অন্তরীপ, অন্তরীপ (হিঃ কোঃ), অঙ্ক (ঐ) ; চূড়া, শৃঙ্গ। **6.** (*Geom.*) That which has position but not length, breadth or thickness ; (জ্যামিতি) যাহার অবস্থিতি আছে, কিন্তু দৈর্ঘ্য প্রস্থ বা বেধ নাই, বিন্দু। **7.** The exact moment or instant ; the verge ; "At the *point* of death" ; ঠিক মুহূর্ত্ত ; সীমা, মুখ। **8.** A salient feature, as of a story, joke, etc. ; a characteristic ; প্রধান বিশেষত্ব ; বিশেষত্ব, বিশেষগুণ বা লক্ষণ। **9.** An item ; a particular ; as, we differ on these *points* ; দফা ; প্রকরণ, বিষয়। **10.** A mark to denote degree of success ; as, he won by ten *points* ; a unit in quoting prices of stocks etc. ; কৃতকার্য্যতার পরিমাণপ্রদর্শনার্থ চিহ্ন ; কোম্পানীর কাগজ প্রভৃতির মূল্যের একক। **11.** Degree, esp. of temperature ; as, the freezing *point* ; মাত্রা, বিশেষতঃ তাপমাত্রা। **12.** (With *the*) The main thing ; as, this is just the *point* ; the precise thing for discussion ; as, come to the *point* ; প্রধান বিষয়, আসল বস্তু, মূল-বিষয় ; প্রধান আলোচ্য বিষয়। **13.** Aim ; object ; a proposition to be established ; as, to make or carry one's *point* ; লক্ষ্য ; উদ্দেশ্য, অভিপ্রায় ; যে প্রতিজ্ঞা প্রতিষ্ঠিত করিতে হইবে। **14.** (*Mus.*) A dot used to designate certain tones or time ; a dot at the right hand of a note to lengthen it by one-half ; (সঙ্গীত শাস্ত্র) কোন কোন নির্দ্দিষ্ট সুর বা লয়নির্দ্দেশক বিন্দু ; কোন ধ্বনির দক্ষিণভাগে প্রদত্ত বিন্দু বিশেষ — যাহা দ্বারা ঐ ধ্বনির অর্দ্ধেক বৃদ্ধি করা হয়। **15.** (*Naut.*) One of the points of the compass ; a short piece of cord at the lower edge of a sail to tie up a reef ; দিগ্‌দর্শনের যন্ত্রের দিক ; পাইলের কতকাংশ গুটাইয়া বাঁধার জন্য উহার নিম্নে

যে ক্ষুদ্র রজ্জু থাকে। **16.** (*Astron.*) A certain imaginary spot in the heavens; as, the equinoctial *points*; (জ্যোতির্বিজ্ঞান) নভোমণ্ডলে কল্পিত বিন্দু। **17.** Lace worked by the needle; সূচে তৈয়ারী লেইস। **18.** (*Railway, pl.*) The switches at junctions or stations; (লৌহবর্ত্ম) যে চালনযোগ্য টানা রেলের সাহায্যে বাষ্পীয় শকট বর্ত্ম হইতে বর্ত্মান্তরে নীত হয়। **19.** (*Cricket*) A fielder stationed close to, and facing, the batsman; the position of this fielder; ব্যাটধারীর নিকট তাহার দিকে মুখ ফিরাইয়া যে প্রতিপক্ষের ক্রীড়ক অবস্থান করে; ঐ ক্রীড়কের অবস্থানস্থলী। **20.** The attitude assumed by a pointer dog when he finds a game; as, the dog came to a *point*; প্রদর্শক কুকুর শিকার পাইলে যে ভঙ্গীতে অবস্থান করে। **21.** (*Fencing*) A thrust; (অসিক্রীড়া) খোঁচা। **22.** (*Mil.*) The small leading party of an advanced guard; অগ্রগামী রক্ষিসৈন্যের অন্তর্গত ক্ষুদ্র পথপ্রদর্শক দল। **23.** The tine of a deer's horn; মৃগশৃঙ্গের অগ্রভাগ। **24.** (*Hist.*) A lace for tying together certain parts of the dress; (ইতিহাস) পোষাকের কোন কোন নির্দ্দিষ্ট অংশ বাঁধিবার জন্য ব্যবহৃত একপ্রকার লেইস। **25.** (*Math.*) A dot placed before a decimal fraction; (গণিতশাস্ত্র) দশমিক-চিহ্ন। **26.** (*Print.*) A unit of measurement for type bodies; মুদ্রাক্ষরের আয়তন পরিমাপের একক। **27.** Pungency; effectiveness; as, his remarks lack *point*; ঝাঁঝ, ধার; কার্য্যকারিতা। **28.** (*Hunting*) A spot to which a straight run is made; such a run; যে স্থানের দিকে সোজাভাবে দৌড়ান যায়; ঐরূপ দৌড়। **29.** (*Herald.*) One of the several spots on a shield denoting the local position; কুলচিহ্নাঙ্কিত ঢালের উপরিস্থ চিহ্ন সমূহের অন্যতম। **30.** (*Pl.*) The extremities of a horse; as, bay with black *points*; ঘোড়ার পা। **Full point**—পূর্ণচ্ছেদ। **Point duty**—রাস্তায় গাড়ী এবং লোক চলাচলের সুব্যবস্থার জন্য নির্দ্দিষ্ট স্থানে দণ্ডায়মান পুলিশপ্রহরীর কর্ত্তব্য। **Point lace**—একপ্রকার সূচে তৈরী মিহি লেইস। **Pointsman** — যে লোক লৌহবর্ত্মদ্বয়ের সংযোগস্থলে থাকিয়া বাষ্পীয়শকট বর্ত্ম হইতে বর্ত্মান্তরে চালিত করে; যে পুলিশ প্রহরী রাজপথের নির্দ্দিষ্ট স্থানে দাঁড়াইয়া লোক এবং গাড়ী ঘোড়া চলাচল তত্ত্বাবধান করে। **Point-system** — বিভিন্নপ্রকার মুদ্রাক্ষরের আয়তনের নির্দ্দিষ্ট মান। **A case in point**—আলোচ্য বিষয়ের উদাহরণস্বরূপ ঘটনা। **A point in one's favour** — কাহারো পক্ষে অনুকূল বিষয়। **A point of honour**—যাহা না করিলে মর্য্যাদা হানি হয়, অপমান প্রভৃতির প্রতিশোধ লওয়ার দায়িত্ব (বিশেষতঃ দ্বন্দ্বযুদ্ধ দ্বারা)। **A point of law**—আইনের তর্ক। **At all points**—In every part; সর্ব্বাংশে। **At the point of**—On the verge of; মুখে। **At the point of death**—মৃত্যুমুখে। **In point**—Apposite; প্রাসঙ্গিক, প্রসঙ্গানুকূল। **In point of**—With regard to; সম্পর্কে। **In point of fact**—As a matter of fact; বাস্তবিক পক্ষে, প্রকৃতপক্ষে, বস্তুতঃ। **On or upon the point of (action, doing, etc.)**—On the very verge of; করণোদ্যত। **On the point of death**—কণ্ঠাগতপ্রাণ, মুমূর্ষু। **Point for point**—Exactly; item by item; ঠিক ভাবে; দফায় দফায়। **Point of maximum density**—মহত্তম ঘনত্ববিন্দু (হিঃ কোঃ)। **Point of order**—কোন সভায় কোনও বিষয় যথানিয়মে আলোচিত হইয়াছে কিনা তদ্বিষয়ে প্রশ্ন। **Point of view**—কোন বস্তু যেদিক হইতে দৃষ্টি করা হয়, কোন বিষয় যেদিক হইতে বিবেচনা করা হয়। **Point of support** — আধারবিন্দু (হিঃ কোঃ)। **Point of suspension**—অবলম্ব মূল (হিঃ কোঃ)। **Possession is nine points of the law**—See POSSESSION. **The point of contact**—স্পর্শবিন্দু। **The point of dispersion**—বিকিরণবিন্দু। **The point of incidence**—পাতবিন্দু। **The point of intersection**—ছেদনবিন্দু। **The points of the compass**—দিগ্দর্শন যন্ত্রের পট্টে অঙ্কিত দিকসূচক চিহ্ন, দিক্ (সাঃ পঃ)। **To carry one's point**—To secure one's object; কাহারো উদ্দেশ্য সিদ্ধ করা। **To come to the point**—See POINT, *n.* 12. **To come to points**—To fight with swords; অসিযুদ্ধ করা। **To give point to**—See POINT, *n.* 27. **To give points to**—To give odds to an opponent in a game; (*fig.*) to be superior to; ক্রীড়ায় প্রতিপক্ষ অপেক্ষা অধিকতর জয়াঙ্ক লাভ করা; (লক্ষণায়) শ্রেষ্ঠ হওয়া। **To make a point**—To establish a proposition; to prove a contention; also, to attain one's object; কোন বিষয় প্রতিষ্ঠাপিত করা; যে প্রশ্ন নিয়া তর্ক হইয়াছে—তাহার মীমাংসা করা; কাহারো উদ্দেশ্য সিদ্ধ করা। **To make a point of**—To regard, treat, as essential; to be careful about; মূল বিষয় বলিয়া গণ্য করা; সতর্ক হওয়া। **To stretch a point**—To observe a rule not so strictly; নিয়মের একটু আধটু নড়চড় বা ব্যতিক্রম করা। **To the point**—Apposite; প্রাসঙ্গিক, প্রসঙ্গানুকূল।

point (pŏynt), *v. t.* & *i.* **1.** To sharpen; to give a point to; ধারাল করা; সূক্ষ্মাগ্র করা, চোখা করা, সূচাল করা। **2.** (*Fig.*) To add to the force of; as, to *point* a moral; (লক্ষণায়) যাহাতে মনের মধ্যে গাঁথিয়া যায় সেরূপ করা, যাহাতে মর্ম্মে মর্ম্মে বিদ্ধ হয় সেরূপ ভাবে করা। **3.** To aim; to direct; as, to *point* a gun at a wolf; লক্ষ্য করা, সন্ধান করা, নির্দ্দেশ করা। **4.** To punctuate as a sentence or composition;

বিরাম-চিহ্ন প্রদান করা। **5.** To direct the eye or notice of (*to*) ; চক্ষু ফিরান, মনোযোগ আকর্ষণ করা। **6.** (Stone cutting) To cut as a surface with a pointed tool ; সূক্ষ্মাগ্র যন্ত্র-দ্বারা কাটা। **7.** (*Masonry*) To fill the joints of (a wall etc.) with cement or mortar ; (প্রাচীর প্রভৃতির) জোড়া চুণ বালি প্রভৃতি দ্বারা পূর্ণ করা। **8.** To indicate the purpose or point of ; to show, as by pointing with the finger, (with *out*) ; as, the error was *pointed out* ; উদ্দেশ্য নির্দ্দেশ করা ; অঙ্গুলী প্রভৃতি দ্বারা নির্দ্দেশ করা। **9.** (Of a hound) To indicate or discover as a game by a fixed look ; স্থির দৃষ্টি দ্বারা নির্দ্দেশ বা শিকার আবিষ্কার করা। **10.** To mark as a psalm etc. with points for chanting ; গাহিবার জন্য ধর্ম্মসংগীত প্রভৃতি চিহ্নিত করা। **11.** (*Hort.*) To dig or turn (*in* or *over*) with the point of the spade ; as, to *point over* soil ; কোদালীর অগ্রভাগ দ্বারা খনন করা বা উল্টান। ***Verb i.*** **1.** To direct the finger, eye, etc. towards an object, (with *at*) ; কোন বস্তুর দিকে অঙ্গুলী বা চক্ষু প্রভৃতি চালিত করা। **2.** (*Lit. & fig.*) To direct attention (*to, at*) ; (শব্দানুযায়ী ও লক্ষণায়) মনোযোগ আকর্ষণ করা। **3.** To aim ; to tend ; as, his action *points* towards that result ; লক্ষ্য করা, নির্দ্দেশ করা ; প্রবণ হওয়া। **4.** (*Med.*) To come to a head as an abscess etc. ; (ভৈষজ্যশাস্ত্র) ফোঁড়া প্রভৃতি মুখ তুলিয়া উঠা। **5.** (Of a hound etc.) To indicate the presence of game, by a fixed look ; স্থিরদৃষ্টি দ্বারা শিকারের অবস্থিতি নির্দ্দেশ করা। **To point a moral**—See POINT, *v. t.* 2. **To point out**—To indicate or show (a thing or fact or *that* etc.) ; নির্দ্দেশ করা, প্রদর্শন করা।

point-blank′ (pŏynt-blăngk), *adj.* & *adv.* **1.** Having a horizontal direction ; as, a *pointblank* shot ; দিকচক্রবালের সমান্তরালগামী। **2.** Direct ; plain ; explicit ; as, a *point-blank* assertion ; সোজাসুজি ; প্রত্যক্ষ ; স্পষ্ট। ***Adv.*** **1.** Horizontally ; দিকচক্রবালের সহিত সমসূত্রে। **2.** (*Fig.*) Directly ; flatly ; plainly ; (লক্ষণায়) সোজাসুজি ; স্পষ্টাক্ষরে ; প্রত্যক্ষভাবে, স্পষ্টভাবে, স্পষ্টবাক্যে। **Point-blank distance**—যে দূরত্বের মধ্যে কামান ক্ষিতিজের সহিত সমান্তরালভাবে স্থাপন করা যাইতে পারে।

point-dĕ-vĭce′ (pŏynt-), *adj.* & *adv.* (*Archaic*) Nice ; (অপ্র:) সূক্ষ্মবিচারী। ***Adv.*** To a nicety ; exactly ; সূক্ষ্মভাবে ; সঠিকভাবে।

point′-ĕd (pŏynt-), *adj.* **1.** Having a point ; তীক্ষ্ণাগ্র, সূক্ষ্মাগ্র। **2.** Epigrammatic ; terse ; cutting ; as, a *pointed* remark ; অল্পাক্ষরগ্রথিত ; স্বল্পাক্ষর ; তীব্র, মর্ম্মচ্ছেদী। **3.** Directed or aimed ; (*fig.*) marked ; emphasized ; উদ্দিষ্ট, নির্দ্দিষ্ট, সূচিত, লক্ষীকৃত ; (লক্ষণায়) বিশিষ্ট ; জোরের সহিত কথিত। **—ly,** *adv.* **—ness,** *n.* **Pointed style**—Same as GOTHIC STYLE.

point′-ĕr (pŏynt-), *n.* **1.** One who, or that which, points ; the hand of a time-piece ; নির্দ্দেশক, প্রদর্শক ; ঘড়ীর কাঁটা। **2.** A rod used for pointing towards, etc. on a black-board or map etc. ; বোর্ড বা মানচিত্রের শব্দসমূহ প্রদর্শনের জন্য যষ্টিবিশেষ, প্রদেশিনী। **3.** A dog trained to point out a

Pointer_dog.

game ; একপ্রকার শিকারী কুকুর। **4.** (*Pl.*) Two stars in the Great Bear the straight line through which points nearly to the pole-star ; সপ্তর্ষিমণ্ডলস্থ তারাদ্বয়—উক্ত তারাদ্বয় ভেদকারী সরল রেখা ধ্রুবতারা প্রায় নির্দ্দেশ করে।

point′-ĭng (pŏynt-), *n.* **1.** The act of sharpening ; সূক্ষ্মাগ্রকরণ। **2.** Punctuation ; বিরাম-চিহ্ন প্রদান। **3.** The act of filling the crevices of a wall with mortar, etc. ; চুণ, বালি প্রভৃতি দ্বারা দেওয়ালের ফোঁকর বন্ধ করণ। **4.** The act of designating anything as by *pointing* the finger ; প্রদর্শন, নির্দ্দেশ, অঙ্গুলিনির্দ্দেশ। **5.** (Of an abscess) Coming to a head ; (স্ফোটকসম্বন্ধে) মুখ তুলিয়া উঠন। **6.** Arrangements of the points on a railway ; বাষ্পীয়শকট বর্ত্মান্তরকারী টানা রেলসমূহের বিন্যাস। **Pointing-stock**—উপহাসের পাত্র, উপহাসের বিষয়ীভূত বস্তু।

point′-lĕss (pŏynt-), *adj.* **1.** Having no point ; blunt ; অতীক্ষ্ণাগ্র ; ভোঁতা। **2.** Having no effectiveness or keenness ; as, a *pointless* remark ; ঝাঁজালনয়, ধারনয়। **3.** Without force ; meaningless ; অসার ; অর্থশূন্য, নিরর্থক। **4.** Not having scored a point as a competitor or side ; অজয়াঙ্কলব্ধ। **—ly,** *adv.* **—ness,** *n.*

poise (pŏyz), *v. t., i.* & *n.* **1.** To balance ; to keep in equilibrium, (*lit. & fig.*) ; ওজন করা ; সমতুলিত অবস্থায় রাখা। **2.** To carry (one's head etc. in a specified way) ; (কোন বিশেষস্থাবে মস্তক) বহন করা। ***Verb i.*** To be balanced ; to hang in suspense ; to hover in air etc. ; তুলিত হওয়া ; দোদুল্যমান হওয়া ; পক্ষবিস্তারপূর্ব্বক শূন্যমার্গে অবস্থান করা। ***Noun.*** **1.** State of balance ; equilibrium, (*lit. & fig.*) ; সমতুলিত অবস্থা ; ভারসামঞ্জস্য, ভারসাম্য। **2.** The state of indecision or suspense ; সন্দেহ-দোলায় দোদুল্যমান অবস্থা। **3.** The bearing or carriage (of head etc.) ; বহন-ভঙ্গী।

poi'-son (pō͞y-zn), *n.* & *v. t.* **1.** Any agent capable of producing a morbid or fatal effect upon anything endowed with life ; বিষ, গরল, হলাহল, জহর, কালকূট [Syn. অমৃত (অঃ), তীক্ষ্ণ, রস, রসায়ন, জাঙ্গুল, জঙ্গুল, নিদ, ক্ষেড়, কাকোল, কলাকুল, সৌরাষ্ট্রিক, দারদ, প্রদীপন, শৌক্লিকেয় (kind of poison), শৃঙ্গিক (*ib*), শৌক্লিকেয় (*ib.*), হারিদ্র (*ib.*), নীল (*ib.*), রক্তশৃঙ্গক, রক্তশৃঙ্গী, ঘোর, ঘোরা, ব্রহ্মপুত্র, ধূলক]। **2.** (*Fig.*) That which taints or destroys moral purity ; as, the *poison* of evil example ; (লক্ষণায়) বিষময় প্রভাব। ***Verb t.*** **1.** To infect with poison ; to smear with poison ; as, to *poison* air or water : to *poison* an arrow ; বিষাক্ত করা ; বিষদিগ্ধ করা, বিষলিপ্ত করা। **2.** To injure or kill by poison ; to administer poison to ; বিষপ্রয়োগে নষ্ট করা বা বধ করা ; বিষ-প্রয়োগ করা, বিষপ্রদান করা। **3.** (*Fig.*) To corrupt ; to pervert ; to taint ; to destroy ; as, discontent *poisons* the happiness of life ; (লক্ষণায়) কলুষিত করা, দূষিত করা ; বিকৃত করা ; কলঙ্কিত করা ; নষ্ট করা। **4.** To render (land, furnace, etc.) unfit for use by noxious application etc.; অনিষ্টজনক বস্তুর উৎপাদন বা প্রয়োগ দ্বারা (ভূমি, চুল্লী প্রভৃতি) ব্যবহারের অনুপযুক্ত করা। **–er,** *n.* **–ing,** *n.* **–ous,** *adj.* Having the qualities of poison ; venomous ; বিষধর্ম্মা ; বিষাক্ত। **2.** Noxious ; দূষিত, অনিষ্টজনক, বিষময়। **–ous-ly,** *adv.* **Mild poison**—মৃদুবিষ (সাঃ পঃ)। **Mineral poison**—ধাতুবিষ (সাঃ পঃ)। **Poison fang**—বিষ দাঁত। **Poison gland**—বিষগ্রন্থি। **Poison ivy** — উত্তর আমেরিকার বিষলতা বিশেষ। **Poison-nut**—কুঁচিলা লতা। **Poison-tree**—বিষবৃক্ষ [cf. বিষবৃক্ষোঽপি সংবর্দ্ধ্য স্বয়ং ছেত্তুমসাম্প্রতম্ — কুমারসম্ভব]; বিভিন্নজাতীয় বিষাক্ত বৃক্ষের সাধারণ নাম, বিষদ্রুম (উত্তরঃ)। **Slow poison**—যে বিষ পুনঃ পুনঃ প্রয়োগ করিলে প্রাণহানিকর হইয়া থাকে। **Hate each other like poison**—একে অন্যকে বিষ নজরে দেখে [cf. তুমি আমার দুই চক্ষুর বিষ]। **To poison one's ear**—কাহারো কাণ ভারি করা, কাহারো মন ভাঙ্গান, ভাঙ্গচি দেওয়া, লাগান, ভাঙ্গান।

poissarde, *n.* **1.** One of the Parisian market-women who led riots during the first revolution ; প্রথম ফরাসীবিপ্লব কালে যে সকল নিম্নশ্রেণীর স্ত্রীলোকেরা দাঙ্গায় নেত্রীত্ব করিয়াছিল। **2.** A French fish-wife ; ফরাসীদেশীয় মেছুনী।

pōke, *n.* **1.** A bag ; a small sack ; থলি ; ক্ষুদ্র ছালা। **Poke or pock, –pudding**--(স্কটলণ্ড) স্থূলকায় ব্যক্তি, ঔদরিক ; ইংরেজ। **To buy a pig in a poke**—See PIG.

pōke, *v. t.* & *i.* **1.** To thrust or push against with something pointed ; খোঁচা দেওয়া, গুঁতা মারা। **2.** To stir up ; as, to *poke* a fire ; উস্‌কাইয়া দেওয়া। **3.** To produce as a hole etc. in a thing by poking ; খোঁচাইয়া গর্ত্ত করা। **4.** (*Colloq.*) To shut (oneself etc.) up in a poky place ; (চলিতভাষায়) সংকীর্ণ স্থানে রুদ্ধ করা। **5.** To thrust forward esp. obtrusively ; as, to *poke* one's nose into another's affairs ; ঢুকান। ***Verb i.*** **1.** To thrust or push with sticks etc. (*at* etc.) ; লাঠি প্রভৃতি দ্বারা খোঁচা বা গুঁতা মারা। **2.** To pry (*into*) ; as, to *poke into* a corner ; to feel one's way ; as, to *poke* about ; উঁকি মারা ; আঁধারে হাতড়াইয়া চলা। **Don't poke your nose into one's affairs**—See under NOSE. **Poke not fire with a sword**—জ্বলন্ত অনলে ঘৃতাহুতি বা ইন্ধনপ্রদান করিও না। **To poke fun at**—To ridicule ; to make fun of ঠাট্টা করা ; কৌতুক করা, বিদ্রূপ করা। **To poke one's head**—মস্তক নত করা।

pōke, *n.* **1.** Act of poking ; gentle thrust ; a jog ; as, a *poke* in the ribs ; খোঁচা ; ধাক্কা ; নাড়া, ঠেলা। **2.** The projecting front of a woman's hat or bonnet ; স্ত্রীলোকের টুপির প্রলম্বিত সম্মুখাংশ। **3.** A device to prevent unruly cattle from leaping fences ; অদম্য গোমহিষাদির বৃতিলঙ্ঘন নিবারণার্থ কৌশল-বিশেষ। **Poke-bonnet** — সাবেক কালে স্ত্রীলোকগণ-কর্ত্তৃক পরিহিত একপ্রকার দীর্ঘ, সরল, এবং প্রলম্বিত টুপি।

pōk'-ẽr, *n.* & *v. t.* **1.** A metal rod for poking fire ; আগুন উস্কাইবার জন্য ধাতবদণ্ড বিশেষ। **2.** (Oxford and Cambridge) A bedell who carries a silver-mace before the Vice-Chancellor ; (অক্সফোর্ড ও কেম্ব্রিজ বিশ্ববিদ্যালয়) বিশ্ববিদ্যালয়ের যে চোপদার ভাইস চেন্সেলারের অগ্রে আসা-সোটা বহন করিয়া চলে। **3.** One bearing oneself stiffly ; যে ব্যক্তির চলনে একটা সহজ লীলা বা স্বচ্ছন্দতা নাই। **4.** A kind of instrument used in poker-work ; তপ্তোল্লেখনকার্য্যে ব্যবহৃত যন্ত্র বিশেষ। ***Verb t.*** To execute (a design) in poker-work ; to decorate a thing with poker-work ; তপ্তোল্লেখন কার্য্য করা ; তপ্তোল্লেখন কার্য্য দ্বারা মণ্ডিত করা। **Old poker** — শয়তান। **Poker-work** — তপ্তোল্লেখন যন্ত্রের সাহায্যে শ্বেতকাষ্ঠের উপর নানারূপ নমুনা খোদাই ; তপ্তোল্লেখন-কার্য্য। **Red-hot poker** — একপ্রকার বৃক্ষ — যাহাতে লোহিত ও পীতবর্ণের ফুলের ছড়া হয়। **By the holy poker**—মাইরি।

pōk'-ẽr, *n.* A favourite American game at cards ; আমেরিকায় প্রচলিত একপ্রকার তাস খেলা।

pōk'-y̆, *adj.* **1.** Confined ; narrow ; cramped ; as, a *poky* corner or room ; বদ্ধ ; সংকীর্ণ ; অপ্রশস্ত।

2. Petty; poor; as, a *poky* occupation; হীন, তুচ্ছ; হেয়।

pö-läc'-ca (-ă), **—lă'-cre** (-kêr), *ns.* A vessel with three masts used in the Mediterranean; ভূমধ্যসাগরে ব্যবহৃত ত্রিমাস্তুল পোতবিশেষ।

pō'-lar (-lêr), *adj.* & *n.* **1.** Pertaining to, proceeding from, or situated near, either of the poles; as, *polar* regions, winds, etc.; মেরুসম্বন্ধীয়, মেরুজ, মেরুসন্নিহিত, মেরুসমীপস্থ। **2.** Pertaining to a magnetic pole or poles; magnetic; চৌম্বক ধ্রুব বা ধ্রুবসমূহ সম্বন্ধীয়; চৌম্বক। **3.** (*Geom.*) Having a common meeting point; as, *polar* co-ordinates; (জ্যামিতি) অভিন্নসংযোগবিন্দুসম্পন্ন। **4.** Having positive and negative electricity; ধন ও ঋণ তাড়িত সম্পন্ন। **5.** (Of molecules) Symmetrically arranged in a definite direction; (অণুসম্বন্ধে) নির্দ্দিষ্টদিকে সৌসামঞ্জস্যের সহিত বিন্যস্ত। **6.** (*Fig.*) Likened to a pole of the earth or to the pole-star as a guide; "The *polar* primary man"; (লক্ষণায়) ধ্রুববৎ, ধ্রুবীয় (হিঃ কোঃ), ধ্রুবতারাবৎ। **7.** (*Fig.*) Directly opposite in character; "Good and Evil...two *polar* elements of this creation"; (লক্ষণায়) সম্পূর্ণ বিরুদ্ধপ্রকৃতিবিশিষ্ট। ***Noun.*** Same as POLAR CURVE.

Polar bear.

—ly, *adv.* **Polar axis**—ধ্রুবাক্ষ (হিঃ কোঃ)। **Polar bear**—উত্তরমেরু অঞ্চলবাসী শ্বেতভল্লুক। **Polar circle**—ধ্রুববৃত্ত (হিঃ কোঃ)। **Polar circles**—মেরুদ্বয় হইতে ২৩°-২৮′ দূরে বিষুবরেখার সহিত সমান্তরাল বৃত্তদ্বয়, ধ্রুববৃত্ত। **Polar conic**—ধ্রুবীয় শঙ্কচ্ছিন্ন (হিঃ কোঃ)। **Polar diameter**—যাম্যোত্তর ব্যাস (সাঃ পঃ), ধ্রুবব্যাস (হিঃ কোঃ)। **Polar distance**—নিকটতর মেরু হইতে কোন গোলোকোপরিস্থ কোন নির্দ্দিষ্ট বিন্দুর কৌণিক দূরত্ব, লম্বাংশ (সাঃ পঃ), দ্যুজ্যাচাপাংশ (হিঃ কোঃ)। **Polar forces**—যে বলসমূহ যুগ্মভাবে এবং পরস্পরে বিপরীত দিকে ক্রিয়া করে, ধ্রুবীয়বল (হিঃ কোঃ)। **Polar lights**—মেরুজ্যোতিঃ, ধ্রুবীয়প্রকাশ (হিঃ কোঃ)। **Polar projection**—ধ্রুবলম্ব (হিঃ কোঃ)। **Polar star**—See POLE-STAR. **Polar circle of the eccliptic**—কদম্বভ্রমমণ্ডল, কদম্ববৃত্ত।

pō-lăr-ĭm'-ĕ-têr, *n.* An instrument for exhibiting the polarization of light; আলোকে ধ্রুবতাপত্তি প্রদর্শনের জন্য যন্ত্রবিশেষ, ধ্রুবতেজমাপক (হিঃ কোঃ)। **—i-met'-ric,** *adj.* **—try,** *n.*

Polaris—ধ্রুব (হিঃ কোঃ)।

pō-lăr'-i-scōpe, *n.* Same as POLARIMETER; ধ্রুবদর্শক (হিঃ কোঃ), পোলারিস্কোপ (ঐ)। **—scop'-ic,** *adj.*

pō-lăr'-i-tȳ, *n.* **1.** The quality or property of pointing towards the magnetic poles of the earth; as, the *polarity* of a magnetic needle; পৃথিবীর চৌম্বক ধ্রুবদ্বয়ের দিকে অভিমুখীনতা, ধ্রুবাভিসারিতা, ধ্রুবাভিমুখশীলতা, ধ্রুবাভিসরণশীলতা, মেরু-প্রবণতা, ধ্রুবাভিজিগমিষা, ধ্রুবাভিসরণ, (কেভিঃ), ধ্রুবত্ব (হিঃ কোঃ)। **2.** The tendency in a body to exhibit opposite or contrasted properties or powers in opposite or contrasted directions; the possession of two points called poles having contrary qualities or tendencies; (*lit.* & *fig.*); কোন বস্তুর বিপরীত বা বিসদৃশ দিকে বিরুদ্ধ বা বিসদৃশ ধর্ম্ম বা শক্তি প্রদর্শনের প্রবণতা, বিরুদ্ধধর্ম্মপ্রবণতা; বিরুদ্ধধর্ম্ম বা প্রবণতাবিশিষ্ট বিন্দু বা ধ্রুবদ্বয় সমন্বিতত্ব, বিরুদ্ধধর্ম্মাশ্রয়ত্ব। **3.** The electrical condition of a body as positive or negative; ধন বা ঋণতাড়িত সঞ্চারিত অবস্থা। **4.** (*Fig.*) Magnetic attraction towards an object; (লক্ষণায়) চৌম্বক আকর্ষণ।

pō'-lar-īze (-lêr-), *v. t.* & *i.* **1.** To affect the vibrations of (light, radiant heat, etc.) so that the rays exhibit different properties in different directions; (আলোক-প্রকাশ বিসর্জ্জক তাপ প্রভৃতির) কিরণসমূহ যাহাতে বিভিন্ন দিকে বিভিন্ন ধর্ম্ম প্রদর্শন করে—এরূপ ভাবে উহাদের স্পন্দনের উপর ক্রিয়া করা, বিরুদ্ধধর্ম্মাশ্রিত করা। **2.** (*Mag.* & *Elect.*) To communicate polarity to (a bar, coil, etc.); (লৌহদণ্ড, তারকুণ্ডলী প্রভৃতির) বিভিন্ন প্রান্তে বিভিন্ন ধর্ম্ম সঞ্চার করা। **3.** (*Fig.*) To give a special trend or significance; (লক্ষণায়) বিশেষ অর্থ বা ভাব প্রদান করা। **4.** (*Fig.*) To give unity of direction to; "Doing nothing to *polarize* their aim"; এক দিকে উন্মুখ করা। **—iz-a-ble,** *adj.* **—i-za'-tion,** *n.* **1.** Act of polarizing; state of being polarized; ধ্রুবতাপাদন, ধ্রুবীভবন (হিঃ কোঃ), ধ্রুবাভিসরণ। **2.** (*Optics*) A state of the rays of light including those of the infra-pred and ultra-violet parts of the spectrum resulting in their exhibiting diffe.ent properties in different directions; (দৃষ্টিবিজ্ঞান) আলোকরশ্মির অবস্থা-বিশেষ — যাহাতে উহারা বিভিন্নদিকে বিভিন্ন ধর্ম্ম প্রদর্শন করে—বর্ণচ্ছত্রের নীলারুণাতীত এবং লোহিত-নিম্নকিরণেও এই ধর্ম্ম পরিদৃষ্ট হইয়া থাকে, ধ্রুবতাপত্তি (সাঃ পঃ)। **—iz-er,** *n.*

pō-lă-touche' (-tōōsh), *n.* A flying squirrel; একপ্রকার উড্ডয়নশীল কাঠবিড়াল।

pōl'-dêr, *n.* A tract of land reclaimed from the sea, river, etc., as in Netherlands ; নদী বা সাগর হইতে যে ভূখণ্ড উদ্ধার করা হইয়াছে।

pōle, *n.* & *v. t.* **1.** A long staff or slender piece of wood ; as, a flag *pole* ; খোঁটা, দণ্ড, থাম, লগি, চোড়। **2.** A long piece of wood fitted to the fore-carriage of a vehicle separating the two horses ; ধূঃ, যুগন্ধর। **3.** A measure of length $5\frac{1}{2}$ yards ; $৫\frac{১}{২}$ গজ দৈর্ঘ্যের মাপ। ***Verb t.*** **1.** To furnish or support with poles ; খোঁটা লাগান, খোঁটা বসান। **2.** To push or impel by poles as a boat etc. ; লগি দ্বারা চালান। **3.** To stir as molten glass with a pole ; দীর্ঘযষ্টিদ্বারা গলিত কাচ নাড়া। **4.** To carry on poles ; as, to *pole* hay into a barn ; ভাঁড় করিয়া নেওয়া। **5.** To strike with a carriage-pole ; গাড়ীর যুগন্ধর দ্বারা আঘাত করা। **Pole-jumping**—খোঁটার অর্দ্ধেক হাতে ধরিয়া লম্ফপ্রদান।

pōle, *n.* **1.** One of the ends of the axis of a sphere esp. of the earth ; as, the north *pole* ; মেরু (of the earth), ধ্রুব (of the heavens), পৃষ্ঠীয় কেন্দ্র (হিঃ কোঃ)। **2.** Each of the two opposite ends of a magnetic bar where the attraction is the greatest ; চুম্বকের পরস্পর বিপরীত প্রান্তদ্বয়ের অন্যতর—যথায় আকর্ষণশক্তি অত্যন্ত বলবতী হয়, চৌম্বক ধ্রুব। **3.** Each of two terminal points (*positive* and *negative poles*) of an electric cell, battery, etc. ; বৈদ্যুতিক ঘটশ্রেণী প্রভৃতির অন্যতর প্রান্ত। **4.** (*Biol.*) An extremity of the main axis of any spherical or oval organ ; মণ্ডলাকার বা অণ্ডাকার অঙ্গের প্রধান অক্ষের প্রান্ত। **5.** (*Poet.*) The firmament ; (কবিতায়) নভোমণ্ডল। **6.** (*Fig.*) Each of the two opposite principles etc. ; "Reverting...to the very opposite *pole* of religious thought" ; পরস্পরবিরোধী মতাদির অন্যতর। **Pole′-ward,** *adj.* **Pole′-ward(s),** *adv.* **North pole** — উত্তরমেরু, ধ্রুব, মেরু, সুমেরু উত্তর ধ্রুব (হিঃ কোঃ)। **Pole-magnetic**—চুম্বকীয় ধ্রুব (হিঃ কোঃ)। **Pole-star**—A star at or near the pole of the heavens ; ধ্রুবতারা, উত্তানপাদজ (সাঃ পঃ), নক্ষত্রনেমি (ঐ), জ্যোতিরথ, জ্যোতীরথ (ঐ), দ্যুতিকর (ঐ), ঔত্তানপাদী, ধ্রুব, গ্রহাধার, গ্রহধার। (*Fig.*) That which serves as a guide or director ; a centre of attraction ; ধ্রুবতারা (cf. তোমারেই করিয়াছি জীবনেরি ধ্রুবতারা) ; সর্ব্বলোকনয়নললামভূত বস্তু। **South pole**—কুমেরু (সাঃ পঃ), বড়বা (ঐ), দক্ষিণমেরু, দক্ষিণধ্রুব (হিঃ কোঃ)। **As assunder as the pole-star** — আসমান জমি তফাৎ, আকাশ পাতাল তফাৎ। **Elevation of celestial pole** — অক্ষোন্নতি। **Pole of the ecliptic**—কদম্ব (সূঃ সিঃ)। **Poles of a battery**—সুপ্রান্ত (সাঃ পঃ), কুপ্রান্ত (ঐ), বিপাত (ঐ), নিপাত (ঐ), পুংমেরু, স্ত্রীমেরু। **Poles of a circle, of a sphere**—(জ্যামিতি) যে বিন্দুসমূহে কোন মণ্ডলের বৃত্তের তলের লম্বস্বরূপ ব্যাস ঐ মণ্ডলের পৃষ্ঠ ভেদ করিয়া থাকে। **Poles of a magnet**—উত্তরধ্রুব (সাঃ পঃ), দক্ষিণ-ধ্রুব। **Under bare poles**—With no sails spread ; পাইল বিস্তার না করিয়া।

Pōle, *n.* A native of Poland ; পোলণ্ডের অধিবাসী।

pōle′-ăx, –axe (-ăx), *ns.* **1.** A kind of axe formerly used as a weapon in the army and the navy ; যুদ্ধকুঠার, টাঙ্গী, পরশু, পরশ্বধ, স্বধিতী। **2.** An axe used in slaughtering cattle ; গবাদি জন্তু বধ করার জন্য কুঠারবিশেষ।

Boarding Pole-axes.

pōle′-căt, *n.* A kind of weasel, which emits a stink ; গন্ধমার্জ্জার, গন্ধগোকুলা, খট্টাশ [Syn. জাহক, পূতি-শারিজা, লোমশ মার্জ্জার, গন্ধোতু, মৃগচৈটক, গাত্রসঙ্কোচী, পূতিকা।]

pŏl′-ē-mârch, *n.* (*Gk. Antiq.*) The third archon ; the military commander-in-chief ; (গ্রীক প্রত্নতত্ত্ব) প্রাচীন এথেন্স নগরীর তৃতীয় শাসন-কর্ত্তা ; প্রধান সেনাপতি।

pō-lĕm′-ic, *adj.* & *n.* Pertaining to controversy ; controversial ; disputatious ; তর্কবিতর্কসম্বন্ধীয় ; তর্কাত্মক, বিবাদাত্মক ; তর্করসিক, বাদানু-বাদরসিক, বাদানুবাদাত্মক। ***Noun.*** **1.** A controversial discussion ; বাদানুবাদ, তর্কবিতর্ক, বাগ্‌বিতণ্ডা। **2.** A controversialist, or disputant ; তার্কিক, তর্করসিক। **3.** (*Pl.*) The art or practice of carrying on controversies especially in theology ; তর্কশাস্ত্র, ধর্ম্মবিষয়ক বাদানুবাদ। **–i-cal,** *adj.* **–i-cal-ly,** *adv.* **Pol′-e-mize,** *v. i.* To carry on a controversy ; তর্কবিতর্ক করা, বাদানুবাদ করা।

pō-lĕm′-ō-scōpe, *n.* An opera or field glass ; চক্ষুর ঠিক সম্মুখে নয়—এরূপ বস্তু দর্শনের একপ্রকার ক্ষুদ্র দূরবীণ, কর্ণ দূরবীণ (হিঃ কোঃ)।

polenta, (*Ital.*), *n.* A kind of pudding or porridge made of barley, chestnut-meal ; একপ্রকার পিষ্টক।

Polianthes tuberosa — রজনী গন্ধা (বেলঃ) সন্ধ্যারাগ।

Pŏl′-ĭ-ăs, *n.* Athena ; এথেনাদেবী।

pō-lice′ (-lēs), *n.* & *v. t.* **1.** A government department concerned with preservation of order and enforcement of law ; পুলিশ বিভাগ। **2.** Civil administration ; public order ; অসামরিক শাসন-ব্যবস্থা ; সাধারণের শান্তি। **3.** A body of civil officers responsible for the maintenance of public order ; পুলিশ বিভাগের কর্ম্মচারিবর্গ, পুলিশ। ***Verb t.*** **1.** To keep in order by police; as, to *police* a country; to furnish with police; পুলিশদ্বারা শান্তি রক্ষা করা; পুলিশ যোগান। 2. (*Fig.*) To administer; to control; (লক্ষণায়) শাসন করা; দমন করা। **Police commissioners**—পুলিশ বিভাগের নিয়োগ ও শাসননিয়ামক কর্ম্মচারিবর্গ। **Police constable**—পুলিশ কনেষ্টবল। **Police court**—পুলিশ আদালত। **Police force**—পুলিশ কর্ম্মচারিবর্গ। **Police magistrate**—পুলিশ আদালতের বিচারক, দণ্ডনায়ক, ফৌজদার। **Policeman**—পুলিশ। **Police office**—পুলিশের প্রধান কার্য্যালয়। **Police officer**—পুলিশ কর্ম্মচারী, দণ্ডপাশিক। **Police outpost**—ফাঁড়ি, থানা। **Police rate**—পুলিশ ট্যাক্স। **Police station**—থানা, কোতোয়ালী।

pŏl-i-clin'-ic, *n.* 1. A clinic in private houses, not in hospital; কোন ব্যক্তিবিশেষের বাটীতে রুগ্ন ব্যক্তির শয্যাপার্শ্বে রোগসম্বন্ধে ছাত্রদিগকে যে উপদেশ দেওয়া হয়। 2. A department of a hospital for the treatment of out-patients; বাহিরের রোগীদিগের চিকিৎসার জন্য আরোগ্যশালার বিভাগবিশেষ।

pŏl'-i-cy̆, *n.* 1. The course of action adopted by a government, party, etc.; a course of action adopted as expedient; নীতি (হিঃ কোঃ); অবলম্বিত কার্য্যপদ্ধতি। 2. Political sagacity; diplomacy; রাষ্ট্রনৈতিক বুদ্ধি; কূটরাজনীতি। 3. A prudent course or line of conduct; বিজ্ঞোচিত উপায় বা আচরণ, কার্য্যনীতি, সূক্ষ্মবুদ্ধিতা। 4. Line or course pursued; artfulness; craftiness; অবলম্বিত উপায়; চাতুরী; ফন্দী, কৌশল। 5. (*Scots.*) A park or pleasure-ground around a mansion; (স্কটলণ্ড) জমিদারের বাসভবনের চতুঃপার্শ্ববর্ত্তী উদ্যান বা প্রমোদ কানন। **Court of Policy**—ব্রিটিশ গিনির ব্যবস্থাপক সভা।

pŏl'-i-cy̆, *n.* A writing or document containing a contract of insurance or assurance; বীমাপত্র। **Policy holder**—বীমাকারী। **Policy of insurance** or **assurance**—Same as POLICY, *n.*

pŏl'-ish, *v. t.* & *i.* 1. To make smooth and glossy; to give a polish to; পালিশ করা, চিক্কণ করা, চক্ চকে করা; পরিকর্ম্মীকৃত করা। 2. To refine (esp. in *p. p.*); as, *polished* manners; মার্জ্জিত করা। 3. To smarten *up*; ঘসিয়া মাজিয়া দেওয়া। ***Verb i.*** To become smooth and glossy; as, steal *polishes* well; মসৃণ হওয়া, চকচকে হওয়া, পালিশ হওয়া। **–able,** *adj.* **–er,** *n.* **–ished,** *p. adj.* Highly finished; refined; polite; পরিকর্ম্মীকৃত; মার্জ্জিত; মার্জ্জিত-রুচি। **To polish off**—To finish off quickly; to get rid off summarily; শেষ করা; তাড়াতাড়ি নিকাশ করা, কুপোকাৎ করা, ঠাণ্ডা করা।

pŏl'-ish, *n.* 1. Smoothness; gloss; also, friction producing this; মসৃণতা; চমক (হিঃ কোঃ), জেল্লা, চিক্নাই; চাক্‌চিক্যজনক ঘর্ষণ। 2. A substance used to produce a gloss; as, furniture *polish*; যে জিনিষদ্বারা পালিশ করা হয়, পালিশ। 3. (*Fig.*) Refinement; elegance; "This Roman *polish*"; (লক্ষণায়) মার্জ্জিত ভাব; মার্জ্জিতত্ব।

Pōl'-ish, *adj.* Of, or pertaining to, Poland or its inhabitants; পোলাণ্ড বা তদ্দেশের অধিবাসিগণ সম্পর্কীয়।

pŏl'-i-tärch, *n.* (*Hist.*) A governor of some Oriental cities; প্রাচ্যদেশীয় নগরীর শাসনকর্ত্তা।

pō-līte', *adj.* 1. Polished in manners; courteous; well-bred; cultured; শিষ্ট, শিষ্টাচারসম্পন্ন; ভদ্র, ভদ্রোচিত; সুভব্য; সুশিক্ষিত। 2. Elegant; characterised by refinement; as, *polite* literature; মার্জ্জিতরুচি; সুকুমার। **–ly,** *adv.* **–ness,** *n.* **Polite learning**—সুকুমারবিদ্যা।

pŏl'-i-tic, *adj.* & *n.* 1. Relating to politics or the science of government; (*rare*) political; রাজনীতি-সম্বন্ধীয়; (ক্বচিদ্‌ব্যবহৃত) রাষ্ট্রনৈতিক। 2. Prudent and sagacious; judicious; as, a *politic* person; বিজ্ঞ; বিচারসম্পন্ন, নীতিকৌশলসম্পন্ন, নীতিদক্ষ। 3. Crafty; cunning; চালাক; সেয়ানা, চতুর, কৌশলী। 4. Well-devised; expedient; as, *politic* measures; সুপরিকল্পিত; উপযোগী। ***Noun.*** 1. (*Pl.*) The art or science of government; রাজনীতি, রাষ্ট্রনীতি, রাজনীতিবিদ্যা (হিঃ কোঃ)। 2. (*Pl.*) Political affairs or business; political life; রাজনৈতিক ব্যাপার, রাজনীতি (হিঃ কোঃ); রাজনৈতিক জীবন। 3. Political principles or opinions as of a man or party; as, what are his *politics*; রাজনৈতিক তত্ত্ব বা মত। 4. (*Fig.*) Conduct of private affairs; "A budget of family *politics*"; (লক্ষণায়) পারিবারিক ব্যাপার নির্ব্বাহ। **–ly,** *adv.* **Body politic**—See under BODY.

pō-lit'-i-căl, *adj.* & *n.* 1. Relating to politics or government; relating to the affairs of the State or its administration; রাষ্ট্রনৈতিক, রাজনৈতিক; রাজ্যশাসন বা রাজ্যব্যবস্থা-সম্বন্ধীয়। 2. (Of persons) Engaged in civil administration; as, a *political* officer or agent; অসামরিক বিভাগে নিযুক্ত। 3. Having, or conforming to, a polity; as, a *political* government; নির্দ্দিষ্ট শাসন-ব্যবস্থাসম্পন্ন, নির্দ্দিষ্ট শাসননীতির অনুসারী। ***Noun.*** A political agent (see below). **–ly,** *adv.* **Political agent, –resident**—দেশীয় রাজ্যে ব্রিটিশ স্বার্থ তত্ত্বাবধায়ক ইংরেজ কর্ম্মচারী। **Political economy**—অর্থনীতিশাস্ত্র, অর্থশাস্ত্র, অর্থব্যবহারশাস্ত্র, ধন-বিজ্ঞান।

Political geography—যে ভূগোলে রাষ্ট্রের সীমা, অধিকারভুক্ত স্থান, প্রভৃতি সমূহের আলোচনা থাকে, রাষ্ট্রনীতিক-ভূগোল। **Political right** — রাজনীতিক অধিকার। **Political science**—রাষ্ট্রবিজ্ঞান, রাজনীতি-শাস্ত্র (হিঃ কোঃ)। **Political verse**—আধুনিক গ্রীক কবিতা—এইরূপ কবিতার সর্ব্বশেষ শব্দাংশের অব্যবহিত পূর্ব্ব শব্দাংশে স্বরচিহ্ন থাকে।

pŏl-i-ti'-cian (-shăn), *n.* **1.** A statesman; one skilled in the art or science of government; রাজনীতিবিদ্, নীতিজ্ঞ (হিঃ কোঃ), রাজনীতিবিশারদ, রাজনীতিকুশল; নয়বিদ্, নয়বিশারদ। **2.** One interested or actively engaged in politics esp. as a profession; রাজনীতিক আন্দোলনকারী। **3.** (*U. S.*) One who lives by politics as a trade; (মার্কিণ-যুক্তরাজ্যে) রাজনীতিব্যবসায়ী।

pŏ-lit'-i-cize, *v. i.* & *t.* To act the politician; to talk politics; to take part in politics; রাজনীতিজ্ঞের মত আচরণ করা; রাজনীতি সম্বন্ধে আলাপ করা; রাজনীতিক ব্যাপারে যোগদান করা। ***Verb t.*** To give political character to; রাজনীত্যাত্মক করা।

pŏ-lit'-i-cō-rē-li'-gious (-jŭs), *adj.* Pertaining to politics as influenced by religion; ধর্ম্মভাবপ্রভাবিত রাজনীতি সম্বন্ধীয়।

pŏl'-i-ty, *n.* **1.** The form or constitution of the governmet of a state; কোন রাজ্যের শাসনপদ্ধতি বা ব্যবস্থা, শাসননীতি, শাসনব্যবস্থা, দণ্ডনীতি। **2.** The constitution or organization of any institution; কোন প্রতিষ্ঠানের ব্যবস্থা। **3.** An organized society; a state; ব্যূহবদ্ধ সম্প্রদায়; রাষ্ট্র।

pōlk, *v. i.* To dance a polka; পোলকানৃত্য করা।

pōl'-kă, *n.* **1.** A dance of Bohemian origin but now common everywhere; বোহেমিয়া দেশীয় নৃত্যবিশেষ। **2.** Music for this; উক্ত নৃত্যের উপযোগী বাদ্য। **3.** A knitted jacket worn by women; স্ত্রীলোকদিগের পরিধেয় একপ্রকার বুনা জামা।

pōll. *n.* **1.** (*Dial.* or *facet.*) The head; the back part of the head as covered by hair; as, flaxen *poll*; (উপভাষায় বা রঙ্গচ্ছলে) মস্তক; মস্তকের পশ্চাদ্ভাগ। **2.** The voting in an election; as, exclusion of women from the *poll*; নির্ব্বাচনে ভোট প্রদান। **3.** The counting or recording the names of voters in an election; কোন নির্ব্বাচনে ভোটদাতৃগণের নামগণনা বা লিপিবদ্ধ করণ। **4.** The number of votes recorded; as, a heavy or light *poll*; লিপিবদ্ধ ভোটের সংখ্যা। **5.** (*Pl.*) The place where the votes are cast or recorded; as, to go to the *polls*, (usu. *U. S.*); যে স্থানে ভোট দেওয়া বা লিপিবদ্ধ করা হয়। **6.** (*Obs.*) Same as POLL-TAX. **Poll-book**—ভোটের খাতা। **Poll clerk** — যে কেরাণী ভোট লিপিবদ্ধ করে। **Poll-tax**—প্রতি ব্যক্তির উপর নির্দ্ধারিত কর। **At the head of the poll**—নির্ব্বাচনে সর্ব্বাপেক্ষা অধিক ভোট প্রাপ্ত।

pōll, *v. t.* & *i.* **1.** To remove the head or top of; to pollard; as, to *poll* a tree; অগ্রভাগ ছেদন করা; ছিন্নাগ্র করা, নেড়ামুড়া করা। **2.** (*Archaic*) To cut off or cut short the hair of; to clip; (অপ্রঃ) চুল ছাঁটা; ছাঁটা। **3.** To cut off the horns of (cattle), (usu. in *p. p.*); (গবাদি পশুর) শৃঙ্গাগ্র ভাগ ছেদন করা। **4.** To give or to receive (a vote); (ভোট) দেওয়া বা পাওয়া। **5.** To receive the votes of; কোন ব্যক্তির ভোট পাওয়া। ***Verb i.*** To vote at an election; কোন নির্ব্বাচনে ভোট দেওয়া। **Poll'-a-ble,** *adj.*

pōll, *adj.* & *n.* Hornless; as, a *poll*-ox: (*used only in compounds*); শৃঙ্গবিহীন। ***Noun.*** A poll-beast esp. one of a species of hornless oxen; শৃঙ্গহীন পশু, বিশেষতঃ একজাতীয় শৃঙ্গহীন বৃষ।

pŏll, *n.* (*Cap.* or *l. c.*) A familiar name of parrot; তোতা পাখী।

pŏll, *n.* (Cambridge university) **1.** (*Collectively*) Those who take a pass degree or one without honours, (with *the*); (কেম্ব্রিজ বিশ্ববিদ্যালয়ের) সাধারণ উপাধিপ্রাপ্ত ব্যক্তি বা ব্যক্তিবর্গ। **2.** A poll degree; সাধারণ উপাধি। **Poll degree**—See POLL, *n.* 2. **Poll man** — সাধারণ উপাধিপ্রাপ্ত ব্যক্তি। **The Poll**—সাধারণ উপাধিধারী ব্যক্তি। **To go out in the Poll**—সাধারণ উপাধি প্রাপ্ত হওয়া।

pŏl'-lack (-ăk), **–lock** (-ŏk), *ns.* A fish akin to the cod; কড্জাতীয় মৎস্যবিশেষ।

pŏl'-lan (-ăn), *n.* An Irish species of fresh-water herring; আয়র্লণ্ড দেশীয় হেরীং মৎস্য।

pŏl'-lard (-ârd), *n.* & *v. t.* **1.** A tree that has its top cut off, so that there may be a growth of dense foliage; ছিন্নাগ্রবৃক্ষ, মুড়া গাছ, নেড়া গাছ, স্থাণু। **2.** An animal that has cast its horns; স্খলিতশৃঙ্গ পশু। **3.** An ox, sheep or goat of the hornless variety; এক জাতীয় শৃঙ্গহীন বৃষ, মেষ বা ছাগ। **4.** A coarse kind of bran obtained from flour; ময়দা হইতে প্রাপ্ত এক প্রকার মোটা রকমের ভূষি। ***Verb t.*** To make a pollard of, as a tree; নেড়মুড়া করা।

pŏl'-len (-ŏn), *n.* & *v. t.* The powdery substance contained in the anthers of flowers; the male element in flowers; রেণু, পরাগরেণু, পুষ্পরেণু, পুষ্পরজঃ, পরাগ; পুষ্পের পুং চিহ্ন। ***Verb t.*** To convey pollen to; to cover or sprinkle with pollen; পরাগ বহন করা; পরাগ দ্বারা আবৃত করা, পরাগ ছড়ান। **–less,** *adj.* **–lin'-ie,** *adj.* **–li-nif'-er-ous,** *adj.* Bearing pollen; পরাগগর্ভ।

pŏl-lĭc-i-tā′-tion, *n.* (*Civil law*) A promise not formally accepted and therefore revocable ; যথারীতি অগৃহীত প্রতিশ্রুতি — অতএব যাহা প্রত্যাহার করা যাইতে পারে।

pŏl′-li-nāte (-ĭ-), *v. t.* To besprinkle or impregnate with pollen ; as, some flowers are *pollinated* by the wind ; পরাগ ছড়ান। **—na′-tion,** *n.* Act of pollinating ; state of being pollinated ; পরাগপতন (সাঃ পঃ) ; পরাগপতনাবস্থা।

pŏl′-loi (-ōy), *n.* (*Gr. pl.* literally *the many.*) **Hoi polloi**—Most people ; the majority ; অধিকাংশ লোক ; অধিকাংশ।

pŏl-lūte′, *v. t.* **1.** To make foul or unclean ; to taint ; কলুষিত করা ; দূষিত করা। **2.** To destroy the purity or sanctity of ; to profane ; অশুদ্ধ করা ; অপবিত্র করা। **—lut′-ed,** *adj.* **—lu′-tion,** *n.*

Pollux *n.* (*Astron.*) The first-magnitude star geminorum ; পুনর্ব্বসু (সাঃ পঃ)।

pō′-lō, *n.* A game of Indian origin, played on horseback ; পোলো খেলা। **Water polo**—সন্তরণকারী ব্যক্তিগণ জলে যে হকি খেলে।

pō-lŏ-naise′ (-nāz), *n.* **1.** An article of dress for women ; স্ত্রীলোকদিগের পরিচ্ছদবিশেষ। **2.** A slow dance of Polish origin ; music for this ; একপ্রকার মৃদু নৃত্য ; ঐ নৃত্যের উপযোগী সঙ্গীত।

pŏ-lō′-nȳ, *n.* A dry sausage made of partly cookd pork ; অর্দ্ধপক্ব শূকরের মাংস হইতে প্রস্তুত পিষ্টক বিশেষ।

pōlt′-foot, *n.* & *adj.* (*Archaic*) A club-foot ; (অপ্রঃ) শ্লীপদ। ***Adj.*** Club-footed ; শ্লীপদী।

pŏl-troon′, *n.* An arrant coward ; dastard ; কাপুরুষ, ভীরু ; হীনবীর্য্য ব্যক্তি। **—er-y,** *n.* Cowardice ; কাপুরুষতা, হীনবীর্য্যতা, ভীরুতা।

pŏl-ȳ-ă-dĕl′-phous (-fŭs), *adj.* (*Bot.*) Having stamens united in three or more bundles ; বহু-গুচ্ছকপুংকেশর (সাঃ পঃ)।

pŏl-ȳ-ăn′-drist, *n.* A woman having several husbands ; বহুভর্তৃকা।

pŏl-ȳ-ăn′-drous (-drŭs), *adj.* **1.** (*Bot.*) Having many stamens ; বহুকেশর (সাঃ পঃ), বহুপুংকেশর (ঐ)। **2.** Relating to, or practising, polyandry ; বহুভর্তৃকত্বসম্বন্ধীয়, বহু-ভর্তৃগ্রহণশীল।

pŏ-lȳ-ăn′-drȳ, *n.* Plurality of husbands ; বহুভর্তৃকত্ব, বহুপতিত্ব, বহুস্বামিত্ব।

pŏ-lȳ-ăn′-thŭs, *n.* A kind of primrose ; একপ্রকার পুষ্প।

pŏl′-ȳ-âr-chȳ, *n.* Government or rule by many persons ; বহুতন্ত্র।

pŏl-ȳ-ă-tŏm′-ic, *adj.* Consisting of many atoms, esp. replaceable by hydrogen atoms ; বহুপরমাণু-সম্পন্ন, বহুপারমাণবিক, অনেকাণুসম্বন্ধীয় (হিঃ কোঃ), অনেকাণুক (ঐ), বহু-পরমাণুক (ঐ)।

pŏl-ȳ-au-tŏg′-ră-phȳ (-ä-), *n.* Same as LITHOGRAPHY.

pŏl-ȳ-băs′-ic, *adj.* (*Chem.*) Having, or combined with, several bases ; polyatomic ; (রসায়নশাস্ত্র) বহুভাস্মিক (হিঃ কোঃ) ; বহুপারমাণবিক।

pŏl-ȳ-căr′-pĕl-lă-rȳ, —pous (-pŭs), *adjs.* Having many carpels ; বহুকিঞ্জল্কী।

pŏl-ȳ-chae′-tăn (-kē-), **—tous** (-tŭs), *adjs.* Same as POLYCHAETE.

pŏl-ȳ-chae′-tē (-kē-), *adj.* & *n.* (Of a kind of worm) Having many bristles on the foot-stumps ; পদমূলে বহু-শূকবিশিষ্ট। ***Noun.*** Such a worm ; ঐরূপ কীট।

pŏl-ȳ-chrŏ′-ite, *n.* The colouring matter of saffron ; কুঙ্কুমের রঞ্জক-পদার্থ।

pŏl-ȳ-chrō-măt′-ic, *adj.* Many coloured ; বহুবর্ণ, অনেকবর্ণ।

pŏl′-ȳ-chrōme, *adj.* & *n.* Having many colours ; printed, painted, etc. in many colours ; as, *polychrome* printing ; বহুবর্ণ-বিশিষ্ট ; বহুবর্ণে মুদ্রিত, বহুবর্ণে চিত্রিত। ***Noun.*** **1.** A work of art executed in several colours ; বহুবর্ণে চিত্রিত শিল্প দ্রব্য। **2.** Variegated colouring ; বহুবর্ণ। **—chro′-mic, —chro′-mous,** *adjs.*

pŏl′-ȳ-chrō-mȳ, *n.* Decoration or execution in many colours, especially as in ancient sculpture, pottery, etc. ; বহুবর্ণে বিমণ্ডন বা সম্পাদন।

pŏl-ȳ-clĭn′-ic, *n.* A clinic treating various diseases ; a general hospital where instruction about many diseases are given ; নানারোগ সম্বন্ধে ছাত্রদিগকে উপদেশ ; সাধারণ আরোগ্যশালা—যেখানে বহুরোগ সম্বন্ধে ছাত্রদিগকে উপদেশ দেওয়া হয়।

pŏl-ȳ-cŏt-ȳ-lē′-dŏn, *n.* (*Med.*) A plant having more than two cotyledons, as pine etc. ; বহুবীজ-পত্রক (সাঃ পঃ), বহুপ্রাণপত্র (ঐ)।

pŏl-ȳ-dăc′-tȳl, *adj.* & *n.* Having more than normal number of fingers or toes ; বহুপদাঙ্গুলী-বিশিষ্ট। ***Noun.*** Such an animal ; ঐরূপ জন্তু।

pŏl-ȳ-dae′-mŏn-ĭsm (-dē-), *n.* Belief in many supernatural powers ; বহু অতিপ্রাকৃত শক্তিতে বিশ্বাস।

pŏ-lȳg′-ă-mous (-mŭs), *adj.* **1.** Pertaining to, or characterised by, polygamy ; having many wives or husbands at once ; বহুবিবাহসম্বন্ধীয়, বহুবিবাহাত্মক ; বহু-স্ত্রীসমন্বিত, বহুভার্য্য, বহুভর্তৃকা। **2.** (*Zool.*) Having more than one mate at the same time ; (প্রাণিবিদ্যা) একসময়ে একাধিক, সাথী বা সঙ্গিনী যুক্ত। **3.** (*Bot.*) Bearing both hermaphrodite and unisexual flowers on the same plant ; (উদ্ভিদবিদ্যা) একই বৃক্ষে উভলিঙ্গ ও একলিঙ্গ পুষ্পপ্রসূ।

pŏ-lўg′-ă-mў, *n.* Plurality of wives or husbands at the same-time ; বহুপত্নীকত্ব, বহুবিবাহ, বহু-ভার্য্যতা, বহুপত্নীত্ব, বহুভার্য্যাত্ব। **–mist,** *n.* **Pol-y-gam′-ic,** *adj.*

pŏl-ў-găs′-tric, *adj.* Having many stomachs ; বহুপাকস্থালীসম্পন্ন।

pŏl-ў-gĕn′-ĕ-sis, *n.* Origination of a race or species from many separate ancestors or germs ; বহু পৃথক্ পূর্ব্বপুরুষ বা জীবাঙ্কুর হইতে কোন বংশ বা জাতির উৎপত্তি। **–ge-nes′-ic, –ge-net′-ic,** *adjs.*

pŏl-ў-gĕn′-ic, *adj.* 1. (*Chem.*) Forming more than one compound with hydrogen etc. ; (রসায়নশাস্ত্র) উদজান বাষ্পের সহিত একাধিক সংযোগকারী। 2. (*Geol.*) Consisting of many kinds ; (ভূবিদ্যা) বহুজাতীয়। **–ge-nis′-tic,** *adj.* **Po-lyg′-e-nist, Po-lyg′-e-nism,** *ns.*

pŏ-lўg′-ĕ-nous (-nŭs), *adj.* 1. (*Geol.*) Containing or composed of many kinds of rock ; (ভূবিদ্যা) বহুজাতীয় পাষাণ সমন্বিত, বহুজাতীয় পাষাণ রচিত। 2. (*Chem.*) Same as POLYGENIC.

pŏ-lўg′-ĕ-nў, *n.* The doctrine that the human race consists of several species, having different origins ; মানবজাতি বিভিন্ন উপজাতিতে বিভক্ত এবং ইহারা বিভিন্ন মূল হইতে উদ্ভূত হইয়াছে—এইরূপ মতবাদ।

pŏl′-ў-glŏt, *adj.* & *n.* 1. Containing, or made up of, many languages ; as, a *polyglot* Bible ; বহুভাষায় লিখিত বা রচিত। 2. Speaking or knowing several languages ; বহুভাষাভাষী, অনেকভাষাভাষী, বহুভাষাবিদ্। ***Noun.*** 1. A person speaking or writing several languages ; যে ব্যক্তি বহুভাষায় বলিতে বা লিখিতে পারে। 2. A book (esp. a Bible) written in several languages ; বহুভাষায় লিখিত পুস্তক (বিশেষতঃ বাইবেল)। **–glot′-tal, –glot′-tic,** *adjs.* **tism,** *n.*

pŏl′-ў-gŏn, *n.* (*Geom.*) A plane figure of many esp. more than four sides and angles ; (জ্যামিতি) বহুকোণক্ষেত্র, বহুভুজক্ষেত্র, বহুভুজ (হিঃ কোঃ)। **Po-lyg′-o-nal,** *adj.* **Po-lyg′-o-nal-ly,** *adv.* **Polygon of forces**—যে বন্ধ বহুকোণ-ক্ষেত্রের বাহুসমূহ যথাক্রমে গৃহীত হইলে কোন নির্দ্দিষ্ট বিন্দুর উপর ক্রিয়াশীল সমঞ্জসীভূত বলসমূহের দিক্ এবং পরিমাণ প্রদর্শন করে।

pŏ-lўg′-ŏ-nŭm, *n.* A genus of plants ; একজাতীয় গুল্ম।

pŏl′-ў-grăm, *n.* A figure consisting of many lines ; বহুরেখক্ষেত্র।

pŏl′-ў-grăph, *n.* 1. An instrument for multiplying copies of a writing ; পত্রাদির বহুপ্রতিলিপি তোলার জন্য যন্ত্রবিশেষ। 2. A writer of many or various works ; বহুগ্রন্থ লেখক, বহুগ্রন্থরচয়িতা। **–graph′-ic,** *adj.* **Po-lyg′-ra-ply,** *n.*

pŏ-lўg′-ў-nў, *n.* The marriage by one man of several wives at the same time ; বহুবিবাহ। **–nous,** *adj.* 1. Pertaining to, or practising, polygyny ; বহুবিবাহসম্বন্ধীয়, বহুবিবাহসেবী। 2. (*Bot.*) Having many pistils, styles, etc. ; বহুকেশরসম্পন্ন, বহুকণিকাসম্পন্ন।

pŏl-ў-hē′-drŏn, *n.* A solid body bounded by many (usu. more than six) faces or planes ; বহুফলক পরিবেষ্টিত ঘনক্ষেত্র, বহুফলক (সাঃ পঃ)। **–dral, –hed′-ric,** *adjs.*

pŏl-ў-hĭs′-tor (-têr), *n.* A person of a great variety of learning ; a great scholar ; নানাবিদ্যায় পারদর্শী ব্যক্তি, বিদ্যাসাগর ; মহাপণ্ডিত ব্যক্তি।

pŏl′-ў-măth, *n.* Same as POLYHISTOR. **Po-lym′-a-thy,** *n.*

pŏl-ў-mĕr′-ic, *adj.* (Of compounds) Composed of the same elements in the same proportions but differing in molecular weight ; (যৌগিক পদার্থ সম্বন্ধে) একই মূলপদার্থসমূহ একই অনুপাতে বর্ত্তমান কিন্তু আণবিক গুরুত্বে বিভিন্ন, বহুজাতীয় (হিঃ কোঃ)। **Pol′-y-mer,** *n.* **Pol′-y-mer-ize,** *v. t.*

pŏ-lўm′-êr-ous, (-ŭs), *adj.* (*Bot.*) Composed of many parts ; বহু অংশাত্মক।

pŏl-ў-mŏr′-phic, *adj.* Same as POLYMORPHOUS.

pŏl-ў-mŏr′-phous (-fŭs), *adj.* 1. Having various forms ; বহুরূপী। 2. (*Biol.*) Having or occurring in several distinct forms ; passing through successive variations ; বহু আকারবিশিষ্ট, বহু আকারে বর্ত্তমান; পরিবর্ত্তনপরম্পরাগামী। **–phism,** *n.*

Polynemus Indicus — ছেলা (গুপ্ত)।

Polynemus paradiseus—তপসী (গুপ্তঃ)।

Pŏl-ў-nē′-sĭ-ă, *n.* Small islands in the Pacific Ocean, east of Australia ; অষ্ট্রেলিয়ার পূর্ব্বদিগ্‌বর্ত্তী প্রশান্তমহাসাগরস্থ ক্ষুদ্র দ্বীপপুঞ্জ। **–an,** *adj.*

pŏ-lўn′-ĭ-ă, *n.* An iceless space of water in a sea, river, esp. in arctic regions ; হিমানীহীন জলরাশি।

pŏl-ў-nŏ′-mĭ-ăl, *adj.* & *n.* (*Algeb.*) Same as MULTINOMIAL.

pŏl-ў-ŏn′-ў-mous (-mŭs), *adj.* Having many names or title ; বহুনামক, বহুউপাধিবিশিষ্ট।

pŏl-ў-ŏn′-ў-mў, *n.* Multiplicity of names for the same object ; একই বস্তুর বহুনামত্ব, বহুনামত্ব।

pŏl-ў-ŏ′-pĭ-ă, *n.* An affection of the eyes in which one object appears as two or more ; নেত্র-রোগবিশেষ—যাহাতে একটী বস্তু দুই বা ততোধিক বলিয়া প্রতীয়মান হয়।

pŏl′-ўp, –ype (-ĭp), *ns.* 1. Same as HYDRA, 4 (which see). 2. An individual of some compound organism ; শ্লিষ্টজীবপুঞ্জের অন্তর্গত জীব।

pŏl′-ȳ-pă-rȳ, *n.* The horny outer covering of a colony of polyps ; নদ্যাদির জলবাসী হীনস্তরের জীবপুঞ্জের শৃঙ্গবৎ বহিরাবরণ।

pŏl-ȳ-pĕt′-ăl-ous (-ŭs), *adj.* With many or separate petals as a flower ; বহুদলী (সাঃ পঃ)।

pŏ-lȳph′-ă-gous (-gŭs), *adj.* 1. (*Zool.*) Eating various kinds of food ; (প্রাণিবিদ্যা) বহুপ্রকার খাদ্যভোজী। 2. Voracious ; পেটুক, ঔদরিক, বহুভুক, অতিভোজী, মহাশন।

pŏl′-ȳ-phōne, *n.* A letter or symbol standing for different sounds (as *ea* in r*ea*d which is pronounced both as **rēd** and as **rĕd)** ; বিভিন্ন ধ্বনিসূচনার্থ ব্যবহৃত অক্ষর বা সাঙ্কেতিক চিহ্ন। **—phon′-ic,** *adj.* 1. Having, or consisting of, many sounds or voices ; বহুধ্বনিবিশিষ্ট। 2. (*Philol.*) Standing for different sounds ; বিভিন্নধ্বনিসূচক। **Po-lyph′-o-nous,** *adj.*

pŏ-lȳph′-ŏ-nȳ, *n.* 1. Multiplicity of sounds ; বহুধ্বনিত্ব। 2. (*Phon.*) Representation of different sounds by the same vocal sign or character ; একই অক্ষর দ্বারা বিভিন্ন ধ্বনিপ্রদর্শন।

pŏl-ȳ-phȳ-lĕt′-ic, *adj.* (*Biol.*) Same as POLYGENETIC.

pŏl-ȳ-phȳl′-lous (-lŭs), *adj.* (*Bot.*) Having many or separate leaves ; (উদ্ভিদ্ বিদ্যা) বহুপত্রী, অযুক্তদলী।

pŏ-lȳp′-i-dŏm, *n.* Same as POLYPARY.

pŏl′-ȳ-pite, *n.* One of the POLYPS (which see).

pŏl′-ȳ-pŏd, *adj.* & *n.* Having many feet ; বহুপদী। ***Noun.*** An animal with many feet ; বহুপদজন্তু।

pŏl-ȳ-pō′-di-ŭm, *n.* A genus of ferns ; গরুড়শাক।

pŏl′-ȳ-pŏ-dȳ, *n.* A name of various ferns ; বিভিন্নপ্রকার পর্ণাঙ্গের সাধারণ নাম।

pŏl′-ȳp-oid (-oyd), *adj.* Of, or like, a polyp ; শ্লিষ্টজীব পুঞ্জের অন্তর্গত জীবসম্বন্ধীয়। **—oi′-dal,** *adj.*

pŏl′-ȳ-pŭs, *n.* 1. (*Zool.*) A polyp (*rare*) ; শ্লিষ্টজীবপুঞ্জের অন্তর্গত জীব (কচিদ্‌ব্যবহৃত)। 2. (*Med.*) A tumour especially one growing in the nostrils or uterus ; জরায়ু, নাসিকা, স্বর যন্ত্রাদির শ্লৈষ্মিক ঝিল্লীতে উৎপন্ন একপ্রকার অর্ব্বুদ। **Polypus of the nose**—আওয়া, নাসিকার্শ (সাঃ পঃ)। **Polypus uteri**—কর্ণিনী (সাঃ পঃ)।

pŏl-ȳ-sĕp′-ăl-ous (-ŭs), *adj.* (*Bot.*) Same as POLYPHYLLOUS.

pŏl′-ȳ-stōme, *adj.* & *n.* With many mouths ; বহুমুখ। ***Noun.*** A polystome animal ; বহুমুখজন্তু। **—stom-ous,** *adj.*

pŏl-ȳ-sȳl-lăb′-ic, *adj.* Pertaining to polysyllable ; having, or characterised by, many syllables ; বহ্বক্ষর ; বহুশব্দাংশবিশিষ্ট। **—i-cal-ly,** *adv.*

pŏl′-ȳ-sȳl-lă-ble (-bl), *n.* A word of many syllables ; বহু শব্দাংশবিশিষ্ট শব্দ।

pŏl-ȳ-sȳl′-lŏ-ġism, *n.* A system of syllogisms ; ন্যায়শ্রেণী, মানশ্রেণী (হিঃ কোঃ)।

pŏl-ȳ-sȳn-thĕt′-ic, *adj.* (*Philol.*) Combining several words of a sentence (*e. g.* the verb and the object) into one ; as, a *polysynthetic* language ; (ভাষাবিজ্ঞান) কোন বাক্যের কতিপয় শব্দ সংযোগকারী, বহুশব্দসংযোগী।

pŏl-ȳ-tĕch′-nic, *adj.* & *n.* Relating to, or including, many arts and sciences ; teaching many arts or sciences ; as, a *polytechnic* school ; নানা কলা এবং বিজ্ঞান সম্বন্ধীয় ; নানা কলা ও বিজ্ঞান শিক্ষা-প্রদায়ক। ***Noun.*** A polytechnic school or instruction ; যে বিদ্যালয়ে নানাপ্রকার কলাবিদ্যা, ব্যাবহারিক বিজ্ঞান, প্রভৃতি শিক্ষা দেওয়া হয়, শিল্পবিদ্যালয়।

Polytechnic (School) — See POLYTECHNIC, *n.*

pŏl-ȳ-thăl′-ă-mous (-mŭs), *adj.* (*Nat. hist.*) Many-chambered ; বহু নালীবিশিষ্ট, বহুনাল।

pŏl′-ȳ-thē-ism, *n.* The doctrine or worship of, or belief in, a plurality of gods ; বহ্বীশ্বরবাদ, বহুদেবমত, বহুদেববাদ (হিঃ কোঃ), অনেকেশবাদ। **—ist,** *n.* A believer in the plurality of gods ; বহুদেববাদী (হিঃ কোঃ), বহুদেবমতাবলম্বী। **—is′-tic,** *adj.*

pŏl′-ȳ-tȳpe, *n.* A facsimile copy of an engraved block etc. ; a kind of stereotype to produce this ; ক্ষোদিত ফলকের প্রতিলিপি ; উক্ত প্রতিলিপি প্রস্তুতের জন্য যন্ত্রবিশেষ।

pŏl-ȳ-zō′-ă, *n.* A class of animals growing together and produced by germination from a single one ; একমাত্রজীব হইতে জাত একত্রবর্দ্ধী জীবপুঞ্জ, বহুজৈবিক (সাঃ পঃ)। **—ic,** *adj.* Pertaining to, or of the nature of, polyzoa ; বহুজৈবিক-সম্বন্ধীয়, বহুজৈবিকাত্মক।

pŏl-ȳ-zōn′-ăl, *adj.* Consisting of many ring-like segments, (esp. light-house lens) ; বহু অঙ্গুরীয়াকার পর্ব্ববিশিষ্ট।

pŏm′-āce, *n.* 1. The refuse of apples etc. after pressing in a cider-mill ; যন্ত্রে পীড়নের পর শেওফল প্রভৃতির যে ছোবড়া থাকে। 2. Any pulp ; ফলের শাঁস। 3. The refuse of fish etc. after oil has been extracted ; তৈলনিষ্কর্ষিত মৎস্যের জঞ্জাল।

pō-made′, *n.* & *v. t.* A perfumed ointment for the hair ; pomatum ; কেশে মাখিবার জন্য সুগন্ধি স্নেহদ্রব্য, কেশলেপ ; পমেটম। ***Verb t.*** To annoint with pomade ; পমেটম মাখা।

pō′-măn-dēr, *n.* 1. A perfumed ball formerly supposed to prevent infection ; সুগন্ধি কন্দুক।

2. A round case of gold or silver etc. in which pomander was carried ; যে সোণা বা রূপার ডিবায় সুগন্ধি কন্দুক নীত হইত।

pŏ-mard′ (-mâr), **pŏm-mard′** (-âr), *ns.* A red Burgundy wine ; বারগাণ্ডিতে প্রস্তুত রক্তবর্ণ মদিরা।

pō-mā′-tūm, *n.* & *v. t.* Same as POMADE.

pŏm′-bē, *n.* A kind of beer made from grain and fruit in Africa ; আফ্রিকাদেশের শস্য ও ফল হইতে প্রস্তুত একপ্রকার বীয়র মদ্য।

pōme, *n.* 1. (*Bot.*) An apple or a fruit like an apple ; সেওফল বা সেওফলের মত কোন ফল। 2. A metal ball ; specifically (R. C. Church) a ball of silver or the like, filled with hot water used by priests in the winter season ; ধাতব কন্দুক ; বিশেষতঃ উষ্ণ জল পরিপূর্ণ কন্দুক যাহা রোমান ক্যাথলিক পুরোহিতগণ শীতকালে ব্যবহার করেন। **Po-mif′-er-ous,** *adj.* Pome-bearing ; bearing fruits resembling an apple ; সেও বা তদ্বৎফলপ্রসূ ; সেওফলবৎ ফলপ্রসূ।

pome-grăn′-āte (pŏm-), *n.* **1.** A fruit of the size and shape of an orange containing numerous seeds ; the tree producing it ;

Pomegranate.

দাড়িম্ব, দাড়িম, ডালিম দালিম আনার, বেদানা ; ডালিম গাছ [Syn. কুচফল, মণিবীজ, কুট্টিম, দশনবীজ, পর্ব্বরুহ (tree), পিণ্ডপুষ্প (*ib.*), করক (*ib.*), শুকবল্লভ (*ib.*), শুকাদন (*ib.*), বক্ষফল (*ib.*), সুনীল (*ib.*), পিণ্ডীর (*ib.*), সৎফল (both tree and fruit) ফলশাড়ব (*ib.*), ফলষাড়ব (*ib.*), নীরস (*ib.*), রক্তপুষ্প (*ib.*), রক্তবীজ (*ib.*), মধুবীজ (*ib.*), সুফল (*ib.*), স্বাদ্বম্ল (*ib.*)। [It. *Granata*; Sp. *Granadas*; Fr. *Grenade* ; Arab. *Rana ruman* ; Per. *Anaar* ; Chin. *Ngan-shih-liu.*] **2.** An ornament resembling a pomegranate ; দাড়িম্ব ফলাকৃতি ভূষা।

Pŏm-ĕr-ā′-nĭ-ăn, *adj.* & *n.* Of, or relating to, Pomerania, a province in Northern Prussia ; উত্তর প্রুশিয়ার অন্তঃপাতী পমেরিনিয়া নামক প্রদেশ-সংক্রান্ত। ***Noun.*** A small dog with long silky hair, pointed muzzle and pricked ears ; একপ্রকার কুকুর।

pŏm′-frĕt, *n.* A fish generally found in Indian and Pacific Oceans ; একপ্রকার মৎস্য [তামিল ভাষায় ইহার নাম ভাওয়ালমীন]

pŏm′-frĕt-cāke, *n.* A liquorice cake, (From Pontefract, formerly called Pomfret in England where in originated) ; যষ্টিমধুর পিষ্টক।

pŏ′-mĭ-cŭl-tūre, *n.* Fruit-culture or growing ; ফলের চাষ, ফলোৎপাদন।

pom′-mĕl, (pŭm-), *n.* & *v. t.* **1.** A knob or ball ; the knob on a sword-hilt ; পিণ্ড, কন্দুক ; তরবারির হাতলের গোলাকার অংশ। **2.** The protuberant part in the front of a saddle ; ঘোড়ার জিনের সম্মুখভাগস্থ উদ্গাত অংশ, বঙ্ক। (শিশুঃ)। ***Verb t.*** **1.** To beat wlth the pommel of a sword or with something knob-like ; তরবারির মুষ্টির গোলাকার অংশদ্বারা আঘাত করা। **2.** To beat with the fists ; মুষ্ট্যাঘাত করা।

pō-mŏl′-ō-ġy̆, *n.* The science or practice of fruit-growing ; ফলোৎপাদনবিজ্ঞান, ফলোৎপাদনশাস্ত্র। **—gist,** *n.* **—mo-log′-i-cal,** *adj.*

Pō-mō′-nă, *n.* (*Rom. Myth.*) The goddess of fruits and fruit trees ; (রোমীয় পুরাণ) ফল এবং ফলতরুর অধিষ্ঠাত্রী দেবী। **Pomona green**—যে সবুজবর্ণে পীতের ভাগ অধিক থাকে।

pŏmp, *n.* **1.** Magnificence ; splendour ; আড়ম্বর, সমারোহ ; জাঁকজমক। **2.** (*Pl.*) Ostentatious display ; as, *pomps* and vanities ; ঠাট, ঘটা। **3.** (*Rare*) A splendid procession ; "All the *pomps* of a Roman triumph" ; (ক্বচিদ্‌ব্যবহৃত) মহাসমারোহপূর্ণ শোভাযাত্রা।

pŏm′-pă-nŏ, *n.* A kind of fish esteemed for food ; একজাতীয় সুখাদ্য মৎস্য।

pŏm′-pier (-pĕr), *adj.* **Pompier ladder**—অগ্নিনির্ব্বাপকের মই।

pŏm′-pŏm, *n.* **1.** An automatic quick-firing cannon, so called from its sound ; একপ্রকার দ্রুতবর্ষী কামান।

pŏm′-pŏn, *n.* **1.** An ornament of feather, ribbon, etc. for a woman's dress or bonnet ; স্ত্রীলোকদিগের পোষাক বা টুপির ভূষাস্বরূপ ফিতা, পালক, প্রভৃতি। **2.** (*Mil.*) A tuft of wool etc. worn on the front of hat, shako, etc. (সামরিকশাস্ত্র) সৈনিকদিগের টুপির সম্মুখে পরিহিত পট্টগুচ্ছ।

pom′-pous (-pŭs), *adj.* **1.** Displaying pomp ; magnificent ; splendid ; as, a *pompous* procession ; জাঁকজমকশালী ; আড়ম্বরপূর্ণ ; সমারোহপূর্ণ। **2.** Pretentious ; self-important ; boastful ; as, he is very *pompous* in his manners ; inflated ; as, a *pompous* language ; অমূলক দাবীকারী ; অহংমন্য ; গর্ব্বিত ; আড়ম্বরপূর্ণ। **—ly,** *adv.* **—ness,** *n.* **—pos′-i-ty** *n.*

ponceau, (*F.*), *n.* Bright-red ; উজ্জ্বল রক্তবর্ণ।

pŏn′-chō, *n.* **1.** A cloak worn in South America ; দক্ষিণ আমেরিকার লোকদিগের একপ্রকার ঢিলা জামা।

2. A cloak for bicycling etc. ; দ্বিচক্রযানারোহিগণের পরিধেয় এক প্রকার ঢিলা জামা।

pŏnd, *n., v. t.* & *i.* **1.** A body of water usually formed artificially ; পুকুর, পুষ্করিণী, সরসী, সরোবর, দীঘি, তড়াগ, জলাশয়, বাপী। **2.** (*Facet.*) The sea, esp. the Atlantic Ocean ; "Their reputation on either side of the big *pond*" ; (কৌতুকচ্ছলে) সাগর, বিশেষতঃ অতলান্তিক মহাসাগর। ***Verb t.*** To make into a pond ; to dam up as a stream ; পুকুরে পরিণত করা ; বাঁধ দেওয়া। ***Verb i.*** (Of water) To form a pool or pond ; পুকুর বা ডোবার আকার ধারণ করা। **Pon'-dage,** *n.* Capacity of a pond or reservoir ; storage of water ; পুকুর বা জলাধারের ধারণশক্তি ; জলসঞ্চয়। **Pond-life**—পুকুরবাসী জীব। **Pond-lily**—কুমুদ। **Pond-weed**—একপ্রকার জলজ গুল্ম।

pŏn'-dêr, *v. t.* & *i.* To weigh in the mind ; to consider carefully ; মনে তোলপাড় করা ; প্রণিধান করা। ***Verb i.*** To think ; to muse, (followed by *on* or *over*) ; ভাবা, চিন্তা করা ; অনুধ্যান করা। **—ing,** *adj.* Meditative ; thoughtful ; ধ্যানপর ; চিন্তাশীল। **—ing-ly,** *adv.*

pŏn'-dêr-ȧ-ble, (-bl), *adj.* capable of being weighed ; having sensible weight (*lit.* & *fig.*) ; তুলাযোগ্য ; (শব্দানুযায়ী ও লক্ষণায়) ভারবিশিষ্ট ভারী। **—bil'-i-ty,** *n.*

pŏn-dêr-ā'-tion, *n.* (*lit.* & *fig.*) The act of weighing ; balancing ; (শব্দানুযায়ী ও লক্ষণায়) ওজন ; তুলাযন্ত্র দ্বারা মাপন।

pŏn'-dêr-ous (-ŭs), *adj.* **1.** Very heavy ; massive ; গুরুভার ; অতিগুরু, অতিভারী। **2.** Dull ; wanting in lightness of touch ; as, a *ponderous* style ; ঢিমা ; সহজলীলা বা প্রবাহশূন্য। **—ly,** *adv.* **—ness, —os'-i-ty** *ns.*

pō'-nē, *n.* The leader or his partner in some card games ; কোন কোন তাস খেলায় নেতা বা তদীয় সহক্রীড়ক।

pōne *n.* (*U. S.*) A bread made from American Indian corn ; a fine light bread made with milk, eggs, etc. ; আমেরিকার ভুট্টা হইতে প্রস্তুত রুটি ; ডিম্ব, দুগ্ধ, প্রভৃতি হইতে প্রস্তুত একপ্রকার পাতলা রুটি।

pŏn-gee' (-jē) *n.* A kind of soft unbleached silk of China ; পঙ্গি কাপড়।

pon'-gō (pŏng-), *n.* **1.** A large African ape ; আফ্রিকাদেশীয় বৃহৎ মর্কট। **2.** The orang-outang ; বনমানুষ।

pŏn'-iard (-yârd), *n.* & *v. t.* A kind of dagger ; ছোরা, ছুরি, ছুরিকা, অসিপুত্রী। ***Verb t.*** To stab with it ; ছুরি মারা।

pons, ***n.*** (*Anat.*) Any bridge-like structure ; সেতুবৎ অঙ্গ।

Pons asinorum—Same as ASSE'S BRIDGE (which see). ***Pons (varolii)***—বৃহৎ মস্তিষ্কের উভয় গোলার্দ্ধ সংযোজক স্নায়ুগুচ্ছ।

pŏn'-ti-fĕx, *n.* (*Pl.* -FICES) **1.** (*Rom. antiq.*) A member of the highest college of priests in Rome ; রোমনগরীস্থ উচ্চতম যাজকসমাজের সভ্য। **2.** A bishop esp. the Pope ; ধর্ম্মাধ্যক্ষ, বিশেষতঃ রোমীয় ধর্ম্মসম্রাট। **Pontifex maximus**—(*Rom. antiq.*) The head of the pontifices ; (রোমীয় প্রত্নতত্ত্ব) উক্ত যাজকসভার অধ্যক্ষ।

pŏn'-tiff, *n.* **1.** A bishop ; the Pope ; ধর্ম্মেশ, প্রধান ধর্ম্মাচার্য্য, উপাধ্যায়াচার্য্য ; রোমীয় ধর্ম্মসম্রাট, পোপ। **2.** A high priest ; প্রধান পুরোহিত। **Sovereign pontiff**—রোমীয় ধর্ম্মসম্রাট।

pŏn-tif'-i-căl, *adj.* & *n.* Of, or relating to, a pontiff ; পোপসম্বন্ধীয়। ***Noun.*** **1.** A book of ecclesiastical rites and ceremonies to be performed by a bishop ; ধর্ম্মাধ্যক্ষের অনুষ্ঠেয় ক্রিয়াকাণ্ডসম্বন্ধীয় পুস্তক। **2.** (*Pl.*) The vestments and insignia of a bishop ; ধর্ম্মাধ্যক্ষের পরিচ্ছদ এবং পদমর্য্যাদাসূচক চিহ্ন। **—ly,** *adv.*

Pontificalia, (*L.*) *n.* (*Pl.*) Same as PONTIFICAL, *n.* 2.

pŏn-tif'-i-cāte, *n.* **1.** The office or dignity of a high priest, bishop or the Pope ; ধর্ম্মাধ্যক্ষ বা রোমীয় ধর্ম্মসম্রাটের পদ বা পদমর্য্যাদা। **2.** The term of that office ; ধর্ম্মাধ্যক্ষ বা রোমীয় ধর্ম্মসম্রাটের কার্য্যকাল।

pŏn-ti-fȳ, *v. i.* To play the pontiff ; রোমীয় ধর্ম্মসম্রাটের মত আচরণ করা।

pont-levis, ***n.*** (*Archaic*) Same as DRAWBRIDGE (which see).

pŏn-tō-neer' (-nēr), **—nier'** (-nēr), *ns.* One who has charge of pontoons ; one who manages the construction of pontoon-bridges ; অস্থায়ী সেতুর অবলম্বনস্বরূপ তরণীর ভারপ্রাপ্ত ব্যক্তি ; যে ব্যক্তি তরণীশ্রেণীর উপর অবলম্বিত অস্থায়ী সেতুর নির্ম্মাণ-কার্য্য পরিদর্শন করে।

pŏn-tōōn', *n.* & *v. t.* **1.** A flat vessel or boat, esp. flat-bottomed boat or other struc-

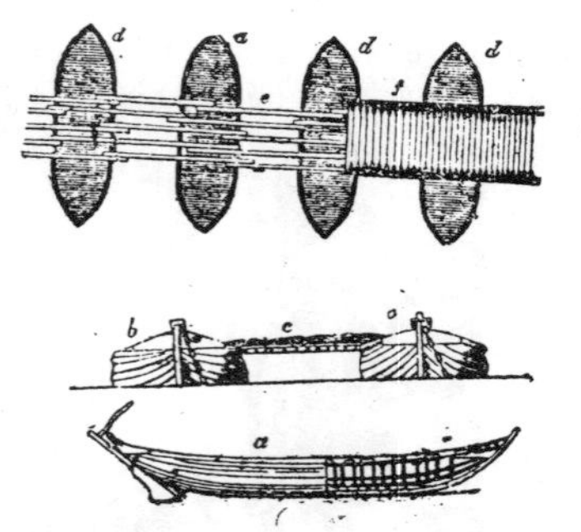

Pontoon.

a, Pontoon, external and internal structure. *bb,* End of same, supporting the roadway. *c,* Plan of bridge. *dd,* Pontoons. *e,* Rafters for supporting the roadway. *f,* Roadway complete.

ture used in making temporary bridges ; প্রশস্ততল নৌকা বা পোত,

বিশেষতঃ অস্থায়ী সেতুনির্ম্মাণে ব্যবহৃত ঐরূপ নৌকা বা পোত। **2.** Same as CAISSON, 3 & 4. ***Verb t.*** To cross as a river by means of pontoons; প্লবসেতুর উপর দিয়া নদী পার হওয়া। **Pontoon bridge**—প্লবসেতু।

pō´-nȳ, *n.* **1.** A small horse; ক্ষুদ্র ঘোটক, টাট্টু। **2.** (*Slang*) Twenty five pounds sterling; (ইতরভাষায়) ২৫ পাউণ্ড। **3.** (*Slang*) A small glass or measure of liquor; (ইতরভাষায়) ক্ষুদ্র গ্লাসপূর্ণ মদিরা, অল্প পরিমাণ মদ্য। **4.** (*Slang, U. S.*) A translation of a classical text; (মার্কিণ যুক্তরাজ্যের ইতরভাষায়) প্রাচীন গ্রীক বা ল্যাটিন পুস্তকের অনুবাদ।

pōōd, *n.* A Russian weight equal to 36 lbs. avoirdupois; রুশদেশে প্রচলিত ওজন বিশেষ।

pōō´-dle (-dl), *n.* & *v. t.* A small dog with long silky curling hair; দীর্ঘ কুঞ্চিত রেশমবৎ লোম বিশিষ্ট কুকুর বিশেষ। ***Verb t.*** To clip and shave (a dog) fantastically; উদ্ভটভাবে বা অপরূপভাবে কুকুরের লোম ছাঁটা।

pooh (pōō), *interj.* An exclamation of scorn, contempt or impatience; ফুস, দুর দুর, ইস্।

pooh´-pooh (pōō-pōō), *v. t.* To express disdain or contempt for; to make light of; as, he *pooh-poohed* the idea; তুচ্ছ করা, তাচ্ছিল্য করা; উড়াইয়া দেওয়া।

pōō´-kȧ, phoo´— (pōō-), *ns.* A malignant sprite; অপদেবতা, অনিষ্টকারী ভূত দুষ্টভূত।

pōō´-kōō, pu´-ku (pô-kô), *ns.* A red African antelope; আফ্রিকা দেশীয় লোহিতবর্ণ কৃষ্ণসার মৃগ বিশেষ।

pōōl, *n.* & *v. t.* A deep part of a stream of water; নদী প্রভৃতির গভীর অংশ, দহ (as কালিদহ)। **2.** A puddle; a piece of stagnant water; থানা, পল্বল; ডোবা। ***Verb t.*** To make (a hole) for the insertion of a wedge in quarrying; to undermine as in excavating coal; কাজল ঢুকাইবার জন্য (গর্ত্ত) করা; সুড়ঙ্গ করা।

pool (pôl), *n.* & *v. t.* **1.** The stakes played for in some games; a receptacle for these; (তাসখেলা) কোন কোন খেলায় যে সকল জিনিষ বাজি রাখা হয়; ঐ সকল জিনিষ রাখার জন্য পাত্র। **2.** A game at billiards in which the winner takes the whole stakes; একপ্রকার বিলিয়ার্ড খেলা—যাহাতে জয়ী ব্যক্তি সমস্ত বাজীর জিনিষ পাইয়া থাকে। **3.** An arrangement between competing parties by which the rates or prices are fixed and business divided to do away with competition; প্রতিদ্বন্দ্বী ব্যবসায়িগণের মধ্যে একপ্রকার বন্দোবস্ত — যদ্দারা জিনিষের মূল্যের হার স্থির করা হয় এবং প্রতিদ্বন্দ্বিতাবারণের উদ্দেশ্যে ব্যবসায় ভাগ করিয়া নেওয়া হইয়া থাকে। **4.** A combination of capitalists for united speculative operation in a stock or commodity; কোন জিনিষের ঝুঁকিদার ব্যবসায়ে মিলিতভাবে সকলের মত নিয়া কার্য্য করার জন্য মূলধনিগণের জোট। **5.** An arrangement between competing lines of railway by which the receipts of all are aggregated and then distributed *pro rata* according to agreement; প্রতিদ্বন্দ্বী রেলওয়ে কোম্পানী সমূহের মধ্যে একপ্রকার বন্দোবস্ত—যদ্দারা ঐ সকল কোম্পানীর সর্ব্বপ্রকার আয়ের টাকা এক সাধারণ ভাণ্ডারে জমা রাখা হয় এবং ঐ টাকা চুক্তির সর্ত্ত অনুসারে হারমতে বিভিন্ন কোম্পানীর মধ্যে বাঁটিয়া দেওয়া হইয়া থাকে। **6.** The collective stakes in betting etc.; বাজি সমূহ। ***Verb t.*** To put into a common fund as of competing railway companies etc.; to divide or share as profits etc.; প্রতিদ্বন্দ্বী রেলওয়ে কোম্পানী প্রভৃতির টাকা সাধারণ ধন-ভাণ্ডারে রাখা; লাভের টাকা প্রভৃতি অংশ মতে বিভাগ করা।

pōōn, *n.* A large East-Indian tree; পুন (*Malabar* — *Calophyllum elatum*), পুন্নাগ [*Calophyllum inophyllum*—যবদ্বীপ, মালাবার উপকূল, ও সিংহল দ্বীপের পশ্চিমভাগে জন্মে।] **Poon-oil** — পুন্নাগ বীজের তৈল। **Poon wood**—পুন্নাগ কাষ্ঠ।

pōō´-nah (-nȧ-) *adj.* **Poonah painting**—An artistic process in imitation of Oriental work in which pictures of flowers, birds, etc. were produced on rice or other thin paper; প্রাচ্যদেশের অনুকরণে পাতলা কাগজের উপর পুষ্প, পক্ষী, প্রভৃতির চিত্রাঙ্কণ। **Poonah-brush, Poonah-paper**—ঐরূপ চিত্রের উপযোগী তুলি; ঐরূপ চিত্রের উপযোগী কাগজ।

pōōp, *n*, & *v. t.* **1.** (*Rare*) The hinder part of a ship; (কচিদ্‌ব্যবহৃত) জাহাজের পশ্চাদ্ ভাগ। **2.** The aftermost highest part of a ship; জাহাজের সর্ব্বপশ্চাদ্বর্ত্তী পাটাতন। ***Verb t.*** To break over the stern of; (of a ship) to receive (a wave) over the stern; জাহাজের পশ্চাদ্‌ভাগে তরঙ্গাভিঘাত করা; জাহাজের পশ্চাদ্‌ভাগে তরঙ্গভঙ্গ হওয়া। **Poop´-ed,** *adj.*

pōōp, pōpe, *n.* & *v. t.* A place in the thigh on which a blow is painful or paralysing; উরুদেশের স্থানবিশেষ—যাহাতে কোন আঘাত লাগিলে তীব্র বেদনা ও অবশাঙ্গতা জন্মায়। ***Verb t.*** To take or strike the poop of; উরু দেশের উক্তস্থানে ধরা বা আঘাত করা। **To take a person's poop**—To strike it; উরুদেশের ঐ স্থানে আঘাত করা।

poor, *adj.* **1.** Indigent; needy; দরিদ্র, গরীব, কাঙ্গাল, অকিঞ্চন নিঃস্ব, নিষ্কিঞ্চন; নির্ধন, বিত্তহীন, নিঃস্বম্বল দীন, ধনহীন, নিষ্কাঞ্চন, অসম্পন্ন। **2.** Deficient; as, a *poor* language; অপ্রচুর। **3.** Lean; emaciated; as, a *poor* horse; কৃশ; কাহিল। **4.** Scanty or inadequate; as, a *poor* crop; স্বল্প

অপ্রচুর। **5.** Feeble; depressed; as, *poor* health or spirits; দুর্ব্বল; অবসাদগ্রস্ত। **6.** Mean-spirited; spiritless; as, a *poor* creature; হীনচেতা; নিস্তেজ। **7.** Barren; sterile; as, a *poor* soil; অনুর্ব্বর; ঊষর। **8.** Paltry; inferior; as, *poor* coat; নগণ্য, হেয়; অপকৃষ্ট। **9.** Wanting in beauty, fitness or merit; as, a *poor* picture or discourse; অসুন্দর, নিগুণ, অনুপযুক্ত। **10.** Unfortunate; pitiable; as, a *poor* follew; দুর্ভাগা, অভাগা, হতভাগ্য; দয়াযোগ্য। **11.** Humble; as, in my *poor* opinion; বিনীত, নম্র। **Poor-box**—দানের বাক্স। **Poor-house**—দরিদ্রশালা, অনাথনিকেতন, গরীবখানা, দরিদ্রদিগের আশ্রয়ের জন্য প্রতিষ্ঠিত ভবন, অনাথালয়। **Poor-laws**—দরিদ্রগণের ভরণপোষণের বিধায়ক বিধি। **Poor-rate**—দরিদ্রগণের ভরণ পোষণের জন্য গৃহীত কর। **Poor-Robin**—পঞ্জিকা। **Poor-spirited**—ভীরু, কাপুরুষ, ক্ষুদ্রমনাঃ, অল্পসত্ত্ব, হীনবীর্য্য, তেজোবীর্য্যহীন। **Poorwill**—আমেরিকাদেশীয় পক্ষিবিশেষ। **Poor as a church mouse**—See under CHURCH. **Poor man's herb**—একপ্রকার শাক। **Poor man's weather-glass**—Pimpernal; জোঁকমারী। **The poor**—দরিদ্রগণ।

pŏor'-lȳ, *adv.* & *pred. adj.* **1.** In a poor manner or condition; in indigence; as, to live *poorly*; (*rare*); দরিদ্রজনোচিত ভাবে; হীনাবস্থায়, অঙ্গহীনভাবে। **2.** Meanly; despicably; হীনভাবে; হেয়ভাবে। **3.** With no great success; badly; as, to do *poorly* in business; বিশেষ কৃতকার্য্যতার সহিত নয়; মন্দভাবে, খারাপভাবে। **4.** Inadequately; defectively; "*Poorly*-lighted streets"; অসম্পূর্ণভাবে, অসম্যগ্‌ভাবে; অপূর্ণভাবে। ***Pred. Adj.*** Unwell; as, he is or looks very *poorly*; অসুস্থ। **—ness**, *n.*

pŏp, *v. i.* & *t.* **1.** To make a small quick sound or report; পট পট শব্দ করা, পটাস্ শব্দ করা। **2.** To shoot (at a bird etc.); (পক্ষী প্রভৃতির উপর) গুলি করা। **3.** To move, come or go suddenly or unexpectedly, (with *in*, *out*, *upon*, *off*, etc.); to burst open with a pop when heated over a fire; as, this corn *pops* well; ফস্ করিয়া যাওয়া, ফস্ করিয়া আসা; পট্ পট্ শব্দে ফুটা। ***Verb t.*** **1.** To thrust suddenly; to bring suddenly into notice; ফস্ করিয়া ঢুকান; ফট্ করিয়া লোকের দৃষ্টি আকর্ষণ করা। **2.** To cause to pop; (*U. S.*) to parch (maize etc.) till it bursts open; পট্ পট্ শব্দ করা; (ভুট্টা প্রভৃতির) খৈ ভাজা। **3.** To fire as a gun etc.; বন্দুক প্রভৃতি আওয়াজ করা। **4.** To put as a question abruptly; ফস্ করিয়া প্রশ্ন করা। **5.** (*Slang*) To pawn; (ইতরভাষায়) বাঁধা দেওয়া। **Pop-corn**—ভুট্টা প্রভৃতির খৈ। **Pop-eyes**—উদ্গত চক্ষুঃ। **Pop-gun**—ছেলেদের খেলার বন্দুক; (অবজ্ঞাচ্ছলে) অকর্ম্মণ্য আগ্নেয়াস্ত্র। **Pop-shop**—বন্ধকী মহাজনের দোকান। **To pop off**—(*v. i.* & *t.*) To disappear suddenly; to die; ফস্ করিয়া অদৃশ্য হওয়া; মরা। (*Verb t.*) To put off promptly; as, *to pop* one *off* with a denial; ফস্ করিয়া এড়ান। **To pop off the hooks**—মরা, শিঙ্গা ফুঁকা। **To pop out**—To put out or extinguish as light etc.; বাতি প্রভৃতি নিভান। **To pop the question**—To propose marriage to a lady; কোন মহিলার নিকট বিবাহের প্রস্তাব করা।

pŏp, *n.*, *adv.* & *interj.* **1.** A small quick explosive sound; পট পট শব্দ, পটাস শব্দ। **2.** A beverage which issues from the bottle containing it with a slight explosion *e. g.* ginger-beer, champagne, etc.; যে মদ্য প্রভৃতি ফুস ফুস শব্দে ফেনাইয়া বোতল হইতে নির্গত হয়। **3.** A dot or spot especially in marking sheep etc.; বিন্দু, দাগ। **4.** (*Slang*) Act of pawning; state of being pawned; (ইতরভাষায়) বন্ধক দেওন; বন্ধকী অবস্থা। ***Adv. & Interj.*** With a pop; suddenly; পট্ করিয়া; ফট্ করিয়া। **Pop goes the weasel**—একপ্রকার পল্লী-নৃত্য।

pŏp, *n.* (*Colloq.*) A popular concert; (চলিতভাষায়) একপ্রকার জনপ্রিয় ঐক্যতান বাদ্য।

pope *n.* **1.** The Biishop of Rome being the head of the Roman Catholic Church; রোমান-ক্যাথলিক ধর্ম্মসংঘের সর্ব্বপ্রধান অধ্যক্ষ। **2.** (*Fig.*) A person who assumes or is considered to have a position or authority like that of the Pope; (লক্ষণায়) জগদ্‌গুরু। **Pope'-dom**, *n.* **Pope'-less**, *adj.* **Pope-Joan**—কাল্পনিক স্ত্রী-পোপ; **Pope's eye**—ভেড়া বা বৃষের উরুদেশের মেদবেষ্টিত গ্রন্থি। **Pope's head**—লম্বা হাতলবিশিষ্ট একপ্রকার ঝাড়ু। **Pope's-nose**—Same as PARSON'S NOSE. **To live in Rome and quarrel with the Pope**—জলে থেকে কুমীরের সঙ্গে বিবাদ বাধান।

pōpe, *n.* (*Gk. Church*) A parish priest or chaplain; (গ্রীক ধর্ম্মসংঘ) পল্লীপুরোহিত, পল্লীযাজক।

pōpe, pōop *n.* & *v. t.* See POOP.

pōp'-ĕr-ȳ, The papal system; রোমানক্যাথলিক ধর্ম্মসংঘ।

pŏp'-in-jay (-jā), *n.* **1.** (*Dial.*) The green woodpecker; (উপভাষায়) একপ্রকার সবুজবর্ণের কাঠুরিয়া পাখী। **2.** (*Archaic*) A parrot; (অপ্রঃ) শুকপাখী। **3.** (*Hist.*) A mark like a parrot, put on a pole to be shot at; (ইতিহাস) লক্ষ্যভেদ শিক্ষার জন্য দণ্ডাগ্রে স্থাপিত শুকপক্ষিবৎ চিহ্ন। **4.** A conceited person; a fop or coxcomb; গর্ব্বিত লোক; ফুলবাবু, বক্কেশর, নবকার্ত্তিক।

pŏp'-ish, *adj.* Of, or relating to, Roman Catholicism, (*used opprobriously*); রোমান ক্যাথলিক ধর্ম্মসংঘসম্বন্ধীয়। **–ly,** *adv.*

pŏp'-lâr, *n.* A tree of numerous species; একজাতীয় ঝাউ গাছ। **A trembling poplar**—বেদ-ই-মজনুন গাছ (হিন্দীভাষায়)।

pŏp'-lin, *n.* A fabric made of silk and worsted; একপ্রকার বস্ত্র—ইহার পড়েন রেশমের ও টানা পশমের হইয়া থাকে।

pŏp-lit'-ĕ-ăl, *adj.* (*Anat.*) Of, or relating to, the horn or the hollow at the back of the knee; as, *popliteal* artery; (শারীরসংস্থান-বিদ্যা) জানুর পশ্চাদ্‌ভাগসম্বন্ধীয়।

pŏp-lit'-ĕ-ŭs, *adj.* (*Anat.*) An oblique muscle placed below the knee connecting the femur and the tibia; জানুর পশ্চাৎদেশস্থ পেশী।

pŏp'-pet (-ĕt), *n.* **1.** (*Naut.*) A piece of timber for supporting a vessel while being launched, or for other purposes; (নৌবিদ্যা) জাহাজ প্রভৃতি নামাইবার কালে বা অন্য সময় ব্যবহৃত ঠেকো। **2.** (*Dial.*) A tubular case for pins, needles, etc.; (উপভাষায়) সূচ, আলপিন, প্রভৃতি রাথার জন্য কৌটা। **3.** (*Dial.*) A small person (especially a term of endearment); (উপভাষায়) ক্ষুদ্রকায় ব্যক্তি। **4.** (*Mach.*) One of the heads of a lathe; (যন্ত্র-বিজ্ঞান) কুন্দযন্ত্রের মাথা। **Poppet-head**—কুন্দযন্ত্রের মাথা।

pŏp'-ping (-îng), *n.* Act of the verb pop; পট্ করিয়া ঢুকন বা বাহির হওন। **Popping-crease**—(ক্রীকেট ক্রীড়ায়) ত্রিদণ্ডের ৪ ফিট অগ্রে উহার সহিত সমান্তরাল রেখা বিশেষ — যাহার ভিতরে ব্যাটধারীকে দাঁড়াইতে হয়।

pŏp'-ple (-l), *v. i.* & *n.* To tumble about; to ripple; উলট পালট খাওয়া; হিল্লোলিত হওয়া। ***Noun.*** Tossing; rolling; a ripple or small wave; গড়্‌গড়ি; ঘূর্ণন; তরঙ্গ, বীচি। **–ply,** *adj.*

pŏp'-pȳ, *n.* A plant having large showy flowers; আফিম গাছ। **Opium-poppy**—আফিম গাছ। **Poppy-capsule**—ঢেঁড়ী। **Poppy-head**—পোস্তের ঢেঁড়ী। **Poppy-oil**—পোস্ত তৈল। **Poppy-seed** — পোস্তদানা, খসবীজ, খসতিল, লিখ্যা।

pŏp'-sȳ, pŏp'-sȳ-wop-sȳ (-ŏp-), *ns.* An endearing term for a girl; খুকী।

pŏp'-ū-lāce, *n.* The common people; the mob; the rabble; সাধারণ লোক; প্রাকৃত জন; ইতর লোক।

pŏp'-ū-lar (-lêr), *adj.* **1.** Of, relating to, or carried on, by the people; as, *popular* meetings, election, etc.; লৌকিক। **2.** Suited to the understanding or taste of the common people; plain; as, *popular* language; সাধারণ লোকের রুচির উপযোগী বা বোধগম্য; সাদাসিধা, সরল। **3.** Adapted to the means of the common people; cheap; inferior; as, at *popular* prices; সাধারণ লোকের অবস্থার উপযোগী; সস্তা, সুলভ; অপকৃষ্ট। **4.** Liked, or highly spoken of, by the people; pleasing to the people in general; লোকবৎসল; লোকপ্রিয়, জনপ্রিয়, জনবৎসল, লোকরঞ্জক। **5.** Prevailing among the people; as, *popular* fallacies; লোকসাধারণের মধ্যে প্রচলিত, লোকসিদ্ধ, লোকপ্রসিদ্ধ। **–lar'-i-ty,** *n.* The state of being in favour with the people; জনপ্রিয়তা, লোকানুরাগ, জনরঞ্জকতা, লোকপ্রীতি, বল্লভতা, পসার (*colloq.*)। **–ly,** *adv.*

pŏp'-ū-lar-īze (-lêr-), *v. t.* **1.** To make popular; to make generally known; as, to *popularize* philosophy or physics; লোকপ্রিয় করা; লোকসাধারণের বিদিত করা। **2.** To extend to the common people; সাধারণ লোকের মধ্যে বিস্তার করা। **–i-za'-tion,** *n.*

pŏp'-ū-lāte, *v. t.* To furnish with inhabitants; to form the population of; লোকপূর্ণ করা, অধ্যুষিত করা; অধিবাসিবর্গ হওয়া। **–la'-tion,** *n.* **1.** The act of populating; লোক-পূর্ণ করণ। **2.** The total number of the inhabitants of any place; লোকসংখ্যা, অধিবাসিসংখ্যা, প্রজাসংখ্যা, দেশের জনসংখ্যা।

pŏp'-ū-list, *n.* **1.** (*U. S.*) A member of a political party formed in 1892 aiming at the public control of the railways etc.; (মার্কিণ যুক্ত-রাজ্য) লৌহবর্ত্ম প্রভৃতি লোকসাধারণের কর্তৃত্বাধীন করার জন্য প্রতিষ্ঠিত রাজনীতিক দল-বিশেষের সভ্যভুক্ত লোক। **2.** A member of the Russian political party advocating collectivism; রুশিয়ার সাম্যবাদিসম্প্রদায়বিশেষ ভুক্ত লোক। **–lism,** *n.* **–lis'-tic,** *adj.*

pŏp'-ū-lous (-lŭs), *adj.* Full of people or inhabitants; thickly populated; জনাকীর্ণ, জনপূর্ণ, জনসঙ্কুল, জনবহুল, লোকাকীর্ণ, প্রজাবহুল; ঘন-বসতিপূর্ণ। **–ness,** *n.* The state of being popular; জনাকীর্ণতা, বহুলোকতা।

pŏr'-bea-gle (-bē-gl), *n.* A kind of mackerel-shark; একপ্রকার হাঙ্গর।

pŏr'-cē-lain (-lān), *n.* & *adj.* A fine white semi-transparent earthernware; an article made of porcelain; চীনামাটি; চীনা মাটির জিনিষ। ***Adj.*** (*Fig.*) Of the nature of porcelain; delicate; "*Porcelain* opinions"; (লক্ষণায়) চীনা মাটির মত; চীনামাটীতে গড়া, হাওয়ায় গড়া। **–cel-la'-ne-ous, –cel-la'-nous, –lan'-ic, –ous,** *adjs.* **Cast or fusible porcelain**—একপ্রকার দুগ্ধাভ কাচ। [বালি, মারিতষশদ (Oxide of zinc) প্রভৃতির মিশ্রণে প্রস্তুত হয়]। **Egg shell porcelain**—একপ্রকার অতি মিহি এবং অর্দ্ধস্বচ্ছ চীনামাটি। **False porcelain**—কৃত্রিম চীনামাটি। **Porcelain-clay**—Same as KAOLIN (which see). **Porcelain shell** –কড়ি।

pŏr′-cĕ-lain-īze (-lăn-), *v. t.* To convert into porcelain or similar substance ; চীনা মাটি বা তদ্বৎ বস্তুতে পরিণত করা।

pōrch, *n.* A covered entrance to a building ; প্রাসাদের আবৃত প্রবেশদ্বার, দেউড়ী, দ্বারমণ্ডপ (হাতেঃ), মোহন (উড়িষ্যা), জগমোহন (ঐ)। **Porch′-ed, Porch′-less,** *adjs.* **The Porch**—প্রাচীন এথেন্স নগরীর যে দ্বারমণ্ডপ বা বিরাট গৃহে Stoic দার্শনিক Zeno শিষ্যদিগকে উপদেশ প্রদান করিতেন ; (লক্ষণায়) Stoic দর্শন।

pŏr′-cīne, *adj.* Pertaining to, or resembling, a swine ; বারাহ, শৌকর।

pŏr′-cū-pīne, *n.* & *adj.* **1.** A rodent quadruped covered with spines

Porcupine.

or quills ; শজারু [Syn. শল্লকী, শল্য, শল্যক (সাঃ পঃ), সেধা, শল্যকণ্ঠ, শলাকা, শ্বাবিদ্।] **2.** An apparatus with many spikes or teeth for heckling fibres etc. ; শণ বা পাট আঁচড়াইবার জন্য বহু কাঁটা বা দাঁতওয়ালা একপ্রকার যন্ত্র। ***Adj.*** Resembling porcupine in having spines etc. ; as, *porcupine* ant-eater, fish, crab, etc. ; শজারুবৎশলাকাবিশিষ্ট। **—pin-ish, —pin-y,** *adjs.*

pōre, *n.* **1.** A minute opening in the skin for perspiration etc. ; রোমকূপ, লোমকূপ, ঘর্ম্মরন্ধ্র, রোমরন্ধ্র, তনুকূপ, স্বেদদ্বার, স্বেদমার্গ। **2.** A minute hole ; an opening between the molecules of a body ; রন্ধ্র, ছিদ্র ; কোন বস্তুর অণুসমূহের মধ্যবর্ত্তী ফাঁক।

pōre, *v. i.* **1.** To study closely, (with *over*) ; গভীর অভিনিবেশের সহিত পাঠ করা, নিবিষ্ট মনে পাঠ করা। **2.** (*Archaic*) To look steadily and intently *at, on,* or *over* ; (অপ্রঃ) একদৃষ্টে তাকাইয়া থাকা। **3.** (*Fig.*) To meditate ; to ponder, (with *over*) ; (লক্ষণায়) গভীর ধ্যান করা ; অভিনিবেশ সহকারে চিন্তা করা। **To pore one's eyes out**—To tire them by close reading ; গভীর অভিনিবেশের সহিত অধ্যয়ন করিয়া চক্ষু শ্রান্ত করা। **To pore over**—See PORE, *v. i.* 1., 2. & 3.

porge (pŏrj), *v. t.* (Jewish ritual) To make ceremonially clean by removing forbidden fat, veins, etc. ; নিহত জন্তুর ভিতর হইতে নিষিদ্ধ চর্ব্বি, শিরা, প্রভৃতি অপসারণ করিয়া উহাকে শোধিত করা। **Porg′-er,** *n.*

pō-rif′-ĕr-ă, *n.* (*Pl.*) Sponges ; ছিদ্রাল দেহী।

pō′-rism, *n.* **1.** (*Math.*) A proposition affirming the possibility of finding such conditions as will render a given problem capable of innumerable solutions ; (গণিতশাস্ত্র) যে প্রতিজ্ঞা হইতে এরূপ অবস্থা পাওয়ার সম্ভাবনা—যাহাতে কোন নির্দ্দিষ্ট সম্পাদ্য অসংখ্য প্রকারে সমাধান করা যাইতে পারে। **2.** (*Gk. Geom.*) A corollary ; (গ্রীক জ্যামিতি) উপসিদ্ধান্ত। **—ris-mat′-ic, —ris′-tic,** *adjs.*

pōrk, *n.* The flesh of swine fresh or salted, used as food ; শূকর মাংস, বরাহমাংস, বরাহামিষ। **Pork′-ling,** *n.* A young or small pig ; শূকরশাবক। **Pork′-y,** *adj.* Of, relating to, or like, pork ; (*colloq.*) fat ; fleshy ; শূকরমাংস-সম্বন্ধীয়, শূকরমাংসবৎ ; (চলিত ভাষায়) মেদস্বী, মাংসল। **Pork-butcher**—যে কসাই শূকরের মাংস কাটিয়া বিক্রয় করে। **Pork-chop**—শূকরের পাঁজরের খণ্ড। **Pork-pie** — শূকরমাংসপূরিত পিষ্টক। **Pork-pie hat**—একপ্রকার টুপি—যাহার কিনারা উল্টানো থাকে।

pōrk′-ĕr, *n.* A pig fed or fattened for pork ; মাংসের জন্য পালিত শূকর। **—et,** *n.* A young hog ; শূকরশাবক।

pŏr-nŏc′-ră-cȳ, *n.* The dominant influence of courtezans, especially in the government of Rome in the 10th century ; গণিকাতন্ত্র।

pŏr-nŏg′-ră-phȳ, *n.* **1.** A description of prostitutes and their manners, etc. ; গণিকাগণের রীতি-নীতি এবং উহাদের আচার পদ্ধতির বর্ণনা, গণিকাচরিত্রচিত্রণ। **2.** Licentious or obscene writing or literature ; অশ্লীল রচনা বা সাহিত্য। **—no-graph′-ic,** *adj.* **—ra-pher,** *n.* A writer of such literature ; অশ্লীলরচনা লেখক।

pŏr′-ō plăs′-tic, *adj.* (*Surg.*) Both porous and plastic ; as, *poroplastic* felt ; সচ্ছিদ্র এবং কোমল।

pō′-rous (-rŭs), *adj.* Having, or full of, pores, (*lit.* & *fig.*) ; লোমকূপবহুল, রন্ধ্রবিশিষ্ট, রন্ধ্রবহুল, সরন্ধ্র, সচ্ছিদ্র (শব্দানুযায়ী ও লক্ষণায়)। **—ness, —ros′-i-ty,** *ns.* The state of being porous ; রন্ধ্রবহুলতা, রন্ধ্রবিশিষ্টতা।

pŏr′-phȳ-rȳ, *n.* **1.** A purple Egyptian rock like granite ; মিশরদেশে প্রাপ্ত নীলারুণবর্ণ প্রস্তরবিশেষ। **2.** (*Geol.*) An unstratified or igneous rock containing crystals of feldspar etc. ; (ভূবিদ্যা) অন্তরীভূত প্রস্তর, আগ্নেয় প্রস্তর।

Porpoise.

pŏr′-poise (-pŏys), *n.* A small cetaceous mammal ; শিশুমার, উলুপী,

ঘড়্যাল, শিশুক, শুশুক, জলকূর্ম্ম। [Syn. চুলুকী, বারিশূকর, জলশূকর, অম্বুকূর্ম্ম, সীরক, অম্বুকীশ।]

pŏr-ra′-ceous (-ā-shŭs), *adj.* Greenish like leek ; গন্ধ-পেঁয়াজের ন্যায় হরিদাভ।

por-rĕct′ (pŏ-), *v. t.* **1.** (*Nat. Hist.*) To extend or stretch out as a part of the body ; (প্রাকৃতিক ইতিহাস) বিস্তারিত করা, ছড়ান। **2.** (*Eccl. Law*) To submit as a document ; (যাজকীয় আইন) পেশ করা।

pŏr′-ridge (-ĭj), *n.* A kind of soft food made by slowly stirring oatmeal etc., in boiling water or milk; as, barley *porridge* ; যই প্রভৃতির মণ্ড, পায়স বা হালুয়া, লপসি। **To keep one's breath to cool one's porridge**—To keep one's advice etc. for one's own use ; পরোপদেশে পাণ্ডিত্য প্রকাশ না করা।

por-rī′-gō (pŏ-), *n.* (*Path.*) A skin disease ; (নিদানশাস্ত্র) খড়ের ন্যায় বর্ণ সপুষপীড়কাবিশিষ্ট চর্ম্মরোগবিশেষ, অরুংচিকা (হঃ চঃ)। **–rig′-i-nous,** *adj.*

pŏr′-rin-gĕr (-ĭn-), *n.* A porridge-dish, cup or bowl from which children eat porridge etc. ; যে পেয়ালা হইতে শিশুরা পায়স বা লপসী খায়।

pōrt, *n.* **1.** A place where ships may ride secure from storms, (*lit.* & *fig.*) ; "We are in *port*, if we have Thee" ; পোতাশ্রয়। **2.** (*Commerce*) A place frequented by vessels for the purpose of loading or discharg[illegible] cargoes ; বন্দর, পত্তন। **Close port**—নদীর উজানে স্থিত বন্দর। **Free port**—যে বন্দরে সকল জাতীয় ব্যবসায়িগণেরই মাল নামাইবার ও বোঝাই করার অধিকার আছে ; যে বন্দরে বিনা মাশুলে মাল নামান যায় ; বিনা শুল্কে আমদানী রপ্তানির অধিকার। **Port-admiral**—বন্দরের রক্ষণাবেক্ষণের ভারপ্রাপ্ত রণপোতনায়ক। **Port-charges**—বন্দর-শুল্ক। **Port of call**—যে বন্দরে জাহাজ সকল সাধারণতঃ কয়লা নেওয়ার দরুণ বা মেরামতের জন্য থামে। **Port of entry**—যে বন্দর বা অন্য স্থানে আমদানির জন্য বৈদেশিক মাল আনা যাইতে পারে।

pōrt, *n.* **1.** (*Chiefly Scot.*) A gate esp. of a walled town ; দ্বার, বিশেষতঃ প্রাচীরবেষ্টিত নগরের দ্বার। **2.** (*Naut.*) An opening in the side of a vessel for loading, entrance, etc. ; a port-hole ; also, the lid of a port-hole ; (নৌবিদ্যা) মাল বোঝাই করার নিমিত্ত বা অভ্যন্তরে প্রবেশের জন্য পোত-পার্শ্বস্থ রন্ধ্র ; আলো ও বাতাস প্রবেশের জন্য পোত-পার্শ্বস্থ রন্ধ্র ; ঐ রন্ধ্রের ঢাকনি। **3.** (*Mech.*) An opening for the inlet or outlet of steam, water, etc. ; (যন্ত্রবিজ্ঞান) বাষ্প, জল, প্রভৃতির আগম বা নির্গমের জন্য রন্ধ্র। **Port-hole**—আলো ও বাতাস প্রবেশের জন্য পোত-পার্শ্বস্থ রন্ধ্র ; (পূর্ব্বে) কামান দাগিবার জন্য পোতপার্শ্বস্থ ছিদ্র। **Port-lid**—ঝটিকাচ্ছন্ন দিনে পোতপার্শ্বস্থ রন্ধ্র বন্ধ করার জন্য ঢাকনী।

pōrt, *n.* **1.** Bearing ; demeanour ; deportment ; as, proud *port* ; আকারপ্রকার ; বাহ্যভাব ; হাবভাব। **2.** (*Fig.*) Bearing or purport as of a matter ; (লক্ষণায়) মর্ম্মার্থ, আশয়। **3.** (*Rare*) Style of living esp. a grand one (style) ; (ক্বচিদ্ব্যবহৃত) চাল।

pōrt, *v. t.* (*Mil.*) To hold, as a musket, sword, etc. in a slanting direction upward across the body ; (সামরিক শাস্ত্র) বুকের উপর তির্য্যগ্‌ভাবে বন্দুক বা তরবারী ধারণ করা।

pōrt, *n., adj., v. t.* & *i.* (*Naut.*) The larboard or left side of a ship ; as, to put the helm *to port* ; (নৌবিদ্যা) জাহাজের বামপার্শ্ব। ***Adj.*** Situated, or turned, to the left side of a ship ; জাহাজের বামপার্শ্বে অবস্থিত, জাহাজের বামভাগে ফিরানো। ***Verb t.*** To turn or put as a helm to the left side of a ship ; জাহাজের বামপার্শ্বে হাইল ঘুরান বা রাখা। ***Verb i.*** To turn to the port side as a ship ; জাহাজের বামপার্শ্বে ঘুরান।

pōrt, *n.* A dark red wine made in Portugal ; পর্ত্তুগাল দেশের একপ্রকার গাঢ় রক্তবর্ণের মদিরা।

pōrt′-ă-ble (-bl), *adj.* Capable of being carried or borne ; easy for carriage ; অনায়াসবাহ্য ; সুবহ, সহজবাহ্য। **–bil′-i-ty,** *n.*

Portable shrine.

pōr′-tāge, *n.* & *v. t.* **1.** The act of carrying or transporting ; বহন, স্থানান্তরে প্রেরণ। **2.** The cost or price of carriage ; বহনের ভাড়া বা খরচ। **3.** Carrying boats or goods overland between two lakes or rivers ; a place where this is necessary ; দুই হ্রদ বা নদীর মধ্যবর্ত্তী ভূমির উপর দিয়া নৌকা বা মাল টানিয়া নেওন ; যে স্থান দিয়া ঐরূপে নৌকা প্রভৃতি টানিয়া নেওয়া হয়। ***Verb t.*** To carry (goods, boats, etc.) overland between navigable rivers, lakes, etc. ; নদী, হ্রদ, প্রভৃতির মধ্যভূমির উপর (নৌকা, মাল প্রভৃতি) টানিয়া নেওয়া। **Mariner's portage**—কোন নাবিককে তাহার নিজের ব্যবসায়ের জন্য বা ভাড়া দেওয়ার নিমিত্ত জাহাজের মধ্যে যে স্থান নির্দ্দিষ্ট করিয়া দেওয়া হয়।

pōr′-tăl, *n.* **1.** A door, gate or entrance, especially a grand one ; ফটক, দেউড়ী, তোরণ, সিংহদ্বার।

pōr′-tăl, *adj.* (*Anat.*) Of, or pertaining to, transverse fissure of the liver ; (শারীরসংস্থান-বিদ্যা) যকৃতের তির্য্যগ্‌গামী নলীসমূহ

সম্বন্ধীয়। **Portal system**—যকৃতে প্রবিষ্ট শিরাজাল। **Portal vein**—যকৃতে প্রবিষ্ট ও ধমনীর ন্যায় বিকীর্ণ বৃহৎ শিরা-বিশেষ, যকৃৎ-শিরা (হঃ চঃ)।

portamento, (*It.*), *n.* (*Mus.*) The carrying of the sound from one note to another without a break ; অবিচ্ছিন্নভাবে কোন ধ্বনি এক সুর হইতে অন্য সুরে সঞ্চালন।

pŏr'-tă-tive (-tiv), *adj.* (*Phys.*) Serving to hold up or carry ; (পদার্থবিদ্যা) বহনকারী, বাহক, ধারক।

pŏrt-cŭl'-lis (-ĭs), *n.* **1.** (*Fort.*) A silding grating of timber or iron hung over a gateway so as to be let down to prevent entrance ; (দুর্গ) শত্রুর প্রবেশ নিরোধার্থ দুর্গতোরণোপরি লম্বিত ঝাঁপ-কপাট। **2.** An Elizabethan coin bearing the figure of a portcullis on the reverse ; রাণী এলিজাবেথের সময়ের মুদ্রা বিশেষ—এই মুদ্রার উল্টা পিঠে ঝাঁপকপাটের চিত্র অঙ্কিত থাকিত। **3.** One of the pursuivants having the figure of portcullis as a badge ; কুলাচার্য্যের অন্যতম সহচর—যাহার পদচিহ্নের উপর ঝাঁপকপাটের চিত্র অঙ্কিত থাকে।

Portcullis

Pŏrte, *n.* The Ottoman court at Constantinople ; the government of the Turkish Empire, so called from the "High gate" of the imperial palace where justice was anciently administered ; তুরস্ক সুলতানের দরবার ; তুর্কি শাসনতন্ত্র।

porte-bonheur, (*F.*), *n.* A charm carried for luck ; একপ্রকার মাদুলী—যাহা সৌভাগ্যলাভের জন্য ধারণ করা হয়।

porte-cochere, (*F.*), *n.* A gateway leading vehicles from the street into a court-yard ; শকটের প্রবেশদ্বার।

porte-crayon, *n.* A metallic handle for holding a crayon ; চিত্রবর্ত্তিকার ধাতুনির্ম্মিত হাতল।

portefeuille, *n.* Same as PORTFOLIO (which see.)

porte-monnaie, *n.* A smal pocket-book or purse ; ক্ষুদ্র মন্তব্য-পুস্তক, টাকা-পয়সার ক্ষুদ্র থলিয়া।

pŏr-tĕnd', *v. t.* To foreshow ominously ; to indicate as future events, misfortunes, etc. by previous signs ; অশুভসূচনা করা ; দুর্নিমিত্ত দ্বারা অমঙ্গলসূচনা করা।

pŏr'-tĕnt, *n.* **1.** An evil omen ; a sign ; দুর্নিমিত্ত, শাকুন, উপপ্লব, উৎপাত (cf. রাবণস্য বিনাশায়োৎপাতাদারুণাঃ সমুৎপেতুঃ—রামায়ণ), অপশাকুন, ব্যতীপাত, উপসর্গ, কুলক্ষণ ; লক্ষণ, চিহ্ন। **2.** A marvellous thing or person ; অত্যাশ্চর্য্য লোক বা বস্তু, আজব জিনিষ। **–ten'-tous**, *adj.* **1.** Ominous ; ঔৎপাতিক, দুর্নিমিত্তসূচক, উৎপাতশংসী, অশুভশংসী। **2.** Wonderful ; monstrous ; as, a thing of *portentous* size ; অপরূপ, আশ্চর্য্য ; বিকট, বিরাট, রাক্ষুসে (cf. রাক্ষুসে বেগুণ)। **–ten'-tous-ly**, *adv.*

pŏr'-têr, *n.* A man in charge of a door or gate ; a door-keeper ; দরোয়ান, দ্বারবান, দ্বারপাল, দ্বারী, দৌবারিক, প্রতিহার, দ্বারপ, দ্বারাধিপ, দ্বারনায়ক, দ্বারগোপ, দ্বারস্থ, দ্বারাধ্যক্ষ, দ্বারিক ; দ্বাররক্ষক। **Porter's lodge**—দ্বারবানের দ্বারসন্নিকটস্থ গৃহ।

pŏr'-têr, *n.* **1.** A person who carries luggage or other burdens for hire ; মুটে, বাহিক, ভারবাহক, ভারজীবী, ভারহর, ভারবাহ। **2.** A dark-brown malt liquor ; অঙ্কুরিত যব হইতে প্রস্তুত একপ্রকার গাঢ় কপিশবর্ণ মদ্য। **–age**, *n.* **1.** The business of a porter ; মুটের কাজ, ভারবাহন-কার্য্য। **2.** The money charged for carrying goods ; মুটে ভাড়া। **Porter-house**—যে গৃহে পোর্টার প্রভৃতি মদ্য বিক্রীত হয় ; চপ, কাটলেট, প্রভৃতির দোকান। **Porter-house steak**—গরুর কটিদেশ হইতে কর্ত্তিত উৎকৃষ্ট মাংস খণ্ড।

pŏrt'-fīre, *n.* A device for firing rockets, igniting explosives, in mines etc. ; হাওই, খনি, প্রভৃতির অভ্যন্তরস্থ বিস্ফোরক দ্রব্যে অগ্নিপ্রদানের জন্য একপ্রকার কল।

pŏrt-fō'-lĭ-ō, *n.* **1.** A portable case for holding loose papers, prints or drawings, etc. ; আলগা কাগজ, পত্র, ছবি, প্রভৃতি রাখার জন্য আধার। **2.** (*Fig.*) The office and duties of a minister of a state ; as, to accept the *portfolio* of war ; (লক্ষণায়) রাজমন্ত্রীর পদ এবং কার্য্য, মন্ত্রিত্ব।

pŏr'-tĭ-cō, *n.* (*Arch.*) A colonnade or covered walk esp. at the entrance of a building ; দ্বারমণ্ডপ, দ্বারপ্রকোষ্ঠ, গাড়ীবারান্দা, মণ্ডপ (রাঃ রাঃ), নিষ্কাশ [হর্ম্ম্যাদিভিত্তিবুনির্গতমস্পৃষ্টভূমিকমুপবেশনস্থানং — বীরমিত্রোদয় (Quoted by A Borooah.)]

portiere, (*F.*), *n.* A curtain hung over a doorway ; দরজার পর্দ্দা।

pŏr'-tion, *n.* & *v. t.* **1.** A division ; অংশ, খণ্ড, ভাগ, বিভাগ। **2.** A share ; অংশ, ভাগ, হিস্যা। **3.** A part or thing assigned by destiny ; one's lot ; as, his *portion* is to die ; ভাগ্য, অদৃষ্ট, নিয়তি ; কপালের লিখন, ললাটলিপি। **4.** A dowry ; যৌতুক বা স্ত্রীধন, কন্যাধন। **5.** A part of an estate that descends, or is given, to an heir or child ; সম্পত্তির যে অংশ কোন সন্তান বা উত্তরাধিকারীতে বর্ত্তে বা তাহাদিগকে দেওয়া হয়। ***Verb t.*** **1.** To divide into shares or portions ; to distribute ; to allot as a share ; ভাগ করা ; বণ্টন করা, বাঁটিয়া দেওয়া ; অংশ নির্দ্দেশ করিয়া দেওয়া। **2.** To give a portion or dowry to ; যৌতুক দেওয়া, স্ত্রীধন দেওয়া।

pōrt′-ly̆, *adj.* **1.** Having a grand appearance ; stately; মহিমাশ্রীমণ্ডিত; মহিমাব্যঞ্জক। **2.** Stout ; corpulent : হৃষ্টপুষ্ট, স্থূলকায় ; বিকটকায়, বিশালকায়। **—li-ness,** *n.*

pōrt-măn′-teau (-tō), *n.* (*Pl.* -TEAUS, -TEAUX) **1.** A bag usually of leather for carrying apparel etc. on journeys ; পোর্টমেন্ট, চর্ম্মপেটিকা। **2.** (*Fig.*) An artificial word blending the sounds and combining the meanings of two others (*e. g. slithy* = lithe & slimy) ; (লক্ষণায়) দুই শব্দের ধ্বনি ও অর্থসংযোজক কৃত্রিম শব্দ।

porto-lano, (*Ital.*), *n.* (*Hist.*) A book containing sailing directions with an account of harbours, etc. ; (ইতিহাস) পোতাশ্রয় প্রভৃতির বিবরণসম্বলিত নৌচালন-নিদর্শক পুস্তক।

pōr′-trait (-trāt), *n.* **1.** A picture of a person or animal ; প্রতিকৃতি, আলেখ্য, তস্‌বীর, জীবচিত্র (শিশুঃ). চিত্রাকৃতি। **2.** A vivid description ; as, a *portrait* in words ; সজীবচিত্র, শব্দচিত্র। **3.** An image or type ; a similitude ; "Jesus reveals a moral *portrait*" ; প্রতিরূপ ; সাদৃশ্য, তুল্যতা। **—ist,** *n.* **Composite portraits**—কোন পরিবার বা লোকবর্গের মুখাকৃতির বিশেষত্ব প্রদর্শনের জন্য চিত্রাঙ্কণপদ্ধতি বিশেষ।

pōr′-trai-tūre (-trā-), *n.* **1.** The act of making portraits ; প্রতিকৃতিরচনা, আলেখ্যাঙ্কন। **2.** A portrait or likeness ; প্রতিকৃতি। **3.** A graphic description ; জীবন্ত বর্ণনা, সজীব চিত্র।

pōr-tray′ (-trā), *v. t.* **1.** To make a picture of; to depict ; as, to *portray* a king on horseback ; চিত্রাঙ্কণ করা ; প্রতিকৃতি রচনা করা। **2.** To describe graphically ; সজীব বর্ণনা করা। **—al,** *n.* **1.** Act of portraying ; a picture ; চিত্রাঙ্কণ, প্রতিকৃতিঅঙ্কন ; প্রতিকৃতি, চিত্র। **2.** Vivid description ; সজীব বর্ণনা, জীবন্ত চিত্র।

pōrt′-reeve (-rēv), *n.* **1.** (*Hist.*) The chief magistrate of a town or borough ; (ইতিহাস) কোন নগরীর বা ভোট প্রভৃতি প্রদানের ক্ষমতাপ্রাপ্ত নগরীর শাসনকর্ত্তা। **2.** (Now) An officer inferior to the major in some towns ; পুরাধ্যক্ষের নিম্নতর কর্ম্মচারী।

pōr′-trĕss, *n.* A female porter or gate-keeper ; দ্বাররক্ষিকা, দ্বারপালিকা, প্রতিহারিণী, দ্বারপালী।

Pŏr′-tū-guese (-gēz), *adj.* & *n.* Of, or relating, to Portugal ; পর্ত্তুগাল সম্বন্ধীয়, পর্ত্তুগীয়। ***Noun.*** A native or inhabitant of Portugal ; the language of Portugal ; পর্ত্তুগালের অধিবাসী, পর্ত্তুগীজ ; পর্ত্তুগীজ ভাষা।

pōse, *v. t., i.* & *n.* **1.** To place in a certain attitude or posture ; as, to *pose* a model for a picture ; কোন বিশেষ ভঙ্গীতে বা ঢংয়ে রাখা। **2.** To put forth or assert as a claim, assertion, etc. ; উপস্থাপিত করা। ***Verb i.*** **1.** To assume an attitude ; কোনরূপ ভঙ্গীতে অবস্থান করা। **2.** To assume or affect a certain character, (often withe *as*) ; as, to *pose as* a martyr ; ভঙ্গীধারণ করা। **3.** (*Dominoes*) To place the first domino on the table ; (ডমিনো-ক্রীড়ায়) প্রথম গুটিকা মেজে স্থাপন করা। ***Noun.*** **1.** An attitude or position of the body assumed esp. for the sake of effect ; as, the *pose* of an actor ; ভঙ্গী, ঢঙ্গ, অঙ্গস্থিতি, সংস্থিতি, ললিত (উজ্জ্বল), দেহভঙ্গী, বন্ধ (কুমারঃ)। **2.** A mental attitude ; ভাব, ভঙ্গিমা। **3.** (*Dominoes*) The act of posing ; the right to pose ; প্রথম গুটিকা মেজে স্থাপন ; প্রথম গুটিকা স্থাপনের অধিকার।

pōse, *v. t.* To puzzle by a difficult question : কঠিন প্রশ্ন জিজ্ঞাসা করিয়া হতবুদ্ধি করা।

pōs′-ĕr, *n.* One who, or that which, puzzles ; a difficult question or problem ; হতবুদ্ধি কারক লোক বা বস্তু ; কঠিন প্রশ্ন, কূট প্রশ্ন, কঠিন সমস্যা, ফাঁকি।

poseur, (*F.*), *n.* One who poses mentally ; ভঙ্গিমাকারী।

pŏs′-it, *v. t.* **1.** To place in position or in relation to other objects ; "*Positing* it where it is wanted" ; ন্যস্ত করা, স্থাপন করা। **2.** To assert as a fact ; to assume as real ; as, to *posit* a principle ; খ্যাপন করা, দৃঢ়রূপে বলা ; বাস্তব বলিয়া ধরিয়া নেওয়া।

pō-si′-tion, *n.* & *v. t.* **1.** The manner of being situated ; posture or attitudes etc. ; as, an inclining *position* ; অবস্থিতি ; উপবেশন-ভঙ্গী, ভঙ্গী, ঢঙ্গ, অবস্থানভঙ্গী, অঙ্গস্থিতি। **2.** Situation ; place ; site ; অবস্থান, সংস্থান ; স্থান ; অধিষ্ঠান। **3.** Mental attitude ; way of viewing something ; মনের গতি ; ভঙ্গিমা, দর্শনপ্রকার। **4.** The laying down of a proposition or thesis ; hence, a proposition or thesis laid down ; প্রতিজ্ঞা বা নিবন্ধ উপন্যস্ত করণ ; প্রতিজ্ঞা, নিবন্ধ। **5.** A relative situation or standing ; as, it is difficult for a person in my *position* ; অবস্থা। **6.** Rank ; social status ; পদবী, পদমর্য্যাদা ; সামাজিক অবস্থা। **7.** Office ; employment ; as, to lose one's *position* ; কার্য্য ; চাকুরী। **8** (*Arith.*) A mode of solving a problem by one or two suppositions ; (পাটীগণিত) এক বা ততোধিক অনুমান দ্বারা কোন সমস্যার পদ্ধতি। ***Verb t.*** To put in position ; to determine the position of ; স্বস্থানে স্থাপিত করা ; অবস্থিতি নির্ণয় করা। **—al** *adj.* **Position angle (or angle of position)**—আয়নচলন (সাঃ পঃ)। **Strategic position** — শত্রুসৈন্যের গতিরোধ করার জন্য সৈন্যগণ কর্ত্তৃক গৃহীত স্থান। **A man of position**—পদস্থ লোক। **Gun of**

between the *aristocracy* and the working people had sprung up a middle class; অভিজাত শাসক-সম্প্রদায়; সম্ভ্রান্ত-সম্প্রদায়। **3.** The best representatives of learning, intellect, etc.; পাণ্ডিত্য, মনীষা প্রভৃতিতে শীর্ষস্থানীয় ব্যক্তিগণ। **Cold shades of aristocracy**—The unsympathetic patronage of the great; সম্ভ্রান্ত জনগণের অনুরাগশূন্য অনুগ্রহ।

ă-ris′-tŏ-crăt, *n.* One of a ruling oligarchy; a noble; hence a person of haughty and overbearing temper and manners; as, a born *aristocrat*; সম্ভ্রান্ত-বংশীয় শাসকগণের অন্যতম; সম্ভ্রান্ত পুরুষ; মানী, কুলাভিমানী। **—ism,** *n.*

ăr-is-tŏ-crăt′-ic, —i-căl, *adj.* **1.** Pertaining to, or attached to, aristocracy; আভিজাতিক। **2.** Befitting an aristocrat; grand; stylish; as, rooms more *aristocratic* than those in which she lived; সম্ভ্রান্ত জনোচিত; জাঁকোলো; বাগাড়ম্বরপ্রিয়। **—al-ly,** *adv.*

Ar-is-tŏ-lō′-chi-ă (ăr-), *n.* A genus of gynandrous plants; অর্কমূলাদি (সাঃ পঃ)। ***Aristolochia Indica***—ঈশের মূল (বেলঃ)।

Ar-is-tŏ-tē′-li-ăn (ăr-), *adj.* Pertaining to Aristotle, or to his system; প্ল্যাটোর শিষ্য সুপ্রসিদ্ধ গ্রীক্ দার্শনিক এরিষ্টোটল্ সম্বন্ধীয়।

ă-rith′-mĕ-tic, *n.* **1.** The science of numbers; the art of computation by figure; পাটীগণিত; অঙ্কবিদ্যা। **2.** A treatise of computation; পাটীগণিত পুস্তক। **Ar-ith-met′-i-cal,** *adj.* **Ar-ith-met′-i-cal-ly,** *adv.* **ti′-cian,** *n.* **Arithmetical progression**—A series of numbers increasing or decreasing by a common difference; [*e. g.* 1, 2, 3, 4, etc. 9, 7, 5, 3, etc.] ব্যক্ত শ্রেণী হিঃ কোঃ), সমান্তর শ্রেঢ়ী। **Political arithmetic**—Statistics relating to the condition of a country; কোন দেশের জনসাধারণের সংখ্যা, অবস্থা, আয়ব্যয় প্রভৃতির বিবরণ-সংগ্রহ। **Universal arithmetic**—Algebra; বীজ-গণিত।

ăr-ith-mŏm′-ĕ-têr, *n.* A calculating machine; গণনা-যন্ত্র।

Arius gagora—ঘাঘট মাছ (গুপ্ত)।

ârk, *n.* **1.** A chest; a box; as, a meal *ark*; সিন্দুক, পেটিকা; মঞ্জুষা। **2.** (*Scrip.*) The wooden coffer containing the tables of the Jewish law; (also called *Ark of the Covenant, Ark of Testimony*); ইয়ুদীদিগের ধর্ম্ম-সম্বন্ধীয় বিধি-রক্ষণার্থ কাষ্ঠময় আধার বিশেষ। **3.** The covered floating vessel in which Noah was saved at the Deluge; hence, a place of refuge; as, no safety out of the *ark* of church; বাইবেলোক্ত প্রলয় বা মহাপ্লাবন সময়ে যে আবৃত পোতোপরি আশ্রয়-গ্রহণকরত নোওয়া রক্ষা-লাভ করিয়াছিলেন; আশ্রয়-স্থল। **To touch** or **lay on the ark**—To touch irreverently what is held to be sacred; ভক্তিশূন্যভাবে পবিত্র বস্তু স্পর্শ করা।

ârm, *n.* **1.** The upper limb of the human body from the shoulder to the hand; ভুজ, বাহু। **2.** Anything resembling an arm; the forelimb of an animal; as, *arm* of apes, bears, etc; a main branch or limb of a tree; as, a huge vine with *arms* outspread; a narrower portion projecting from the main body; as, the *arm* of the sea: the *arms* of the mountain; one of the two rails at the sides of a chair, sofa etc.; ভুজাকৃতি বস্তু; জন্তুর সম্মুখের পদদ্বয়; বৃক্ষের প্রধান শাখা; সাগর, পর্ব্বত প্রভৃতির বাহু বা শাখা; কেদারা প্রভৃতির বাজু। **3.** (*Fig.*) Power; authority; as, the *arm* of the law; (লক্ষণায়) ভুজবল, বাহুবল, ক্ষমতা; কর্ত্তৃত্ব। **Arm-chair**—A chair with side-supports; হাত-কেদারা, বাজুদার কুর্শি। **Arm-holes**—The holes in a garment through which the arm is put; পরিচ্ছদে বাহু প্রবেশের ছিদ্র। **Arm in arm**—With one's arm interlocked with that of another; পরস্পরের বাহুতে বাহু জড়াইয়া। **Arm-pit**—The pit or hollow under the arm; কক্ষ, বগল। **Fore-arm**—The part of the human body from the elbow to the hand; প্রকোষ্ঠ। **Infant in arms**—Infant too young to walk; কোলের শিশু, কোলের ছেলে। **Right arm**—The arm on the right side; দক্ষিণ হস্ত, ডান হাত। (*Fig.*) Main support or assistance.

> "Sir Lancelot, my *right arm*
> The mightiest of my knights:"

(লক্ষণায়) প্রধান অবলম্বন বা সহায়, দক্ষিণহস্ত। **To keep at arm's length**—To avoid familiarity with; দূরে রাখা, অধিক ঘনিষ্ঠতা করিতে না দেওয়া। **To take the arm**—To accept one's invitation; কাহারো নিমন্ত্রণ গ্রহণ করা। **With folded arms**—বাহুতে বাহু জড়াইয়া। **With open arms**—Cordially; আন্তরিকতার সহিত।

ârm, *n.* (*Usu. pl.*) **1.** Instruments of offence used in war; weapons; as, a lesson in cleansing *arms*, armour; mail; as, to shine in brazen *arms*: অস্ত্রশস্ত্র; আয়ুধ, প্রহরণ; বর্ম্ম, কবচ; লোহময় তনুত্রাণ। **2.** Active hostilities; fighting; as, a cessation of *arms*: suspension of *arms*; যুদ্ধ-কার্য্য; যুদ্ধ। **3.** Military profession; service as a soldier; as, to take up the profession of *arms*; সৈনিকবৃত্তি, সৈনিকের কর্ম্ম। **A passage of (at) arms**—An exchange of blows by armed opponents; যুদ্ধে অস্ত্রবিনিময়। (*Fig.*) A controversial bout; (লক্ষণায়) তর্কযুদ্ধ, মসীযুদ্ধ। **Bred to arms**—Educated to the profession of a soldier; যুদ্ধবিদ্যায় শিক্ষিত। **College of Arms**—The Herald's condition (usu. specified) of control or tranquility ; স্থির রাখা, শান্ত রাখা, ধৈর্য্যাবলম্বন করা। 4. To have full power or mastery over ; as, he is *possessed* by an evil spirit, or idea ; আবিষ্ট হওয়া, ভূতাবিষ্ট হওয়া, ভর হওয়া, পাওয়া। **–sessed′**, *p. p.* 1. Held as by an owner ; অধিকৃত। 2. Seized or occupied by an evil spirit, passion or influence ; দানবগ্রস্ত, ভূতগ্রস্ত, ভূতাবিষ্ট, আবিষ্ট। **–ses′-sor,** *n.* One who possesses ; owner ; অধীকারী ; মালীক, স্বামী। **–ses′-sor-y,** *adj.* Relating to possessor or possessing ; as, a *possessory* interest ; অধিকারিসম্বন্ধীয়, অধিকারসম্বন্ধীয়, দখলীয়। **To be possessed of**—To have or own ; থাকা, অধিকারী হওয়া। **To possess oneself of**—To take, get or obtain ; অধিকার করা, পাওয়া, লাভ করা, হস্তগত করা, দখল করা। **To possess oneself, one's soul etc. in patience**—See POSSESS, 3.

pŏs-ses′-sion (-zĕ-), *n.* 1. The act of possessing ; state of being possessed ; occupancy ; ভোগ, অধিকার; অধিকৃতি ; স্বত্ব, প্রজাস্বত্ব। 2. (*Law*) Having such control over a thing as attaches usually to legal ownership ; (আইন) দখল। 3. A thing possessed ; (*pl.*) wealth ; property ; অধিকৃত বস্তু ; ধন ; সম্পত্তি। 4. A country taken by conquest ; a dominion ; অধিকৃত দেশ ; রাজ্য। 5. State of being possessed by an evil spirit, thought, idea, etc. ; আবিষ্টতা, আবেশ, ভূতাবেশ, ভর। **In possession** — (Of a person) Possessing or owing ; অধিকারী। (Of a thing) Possessed ; অধিকৃত। **Possession is nine points of the law** — বিরোধীয় সম্পত্তিতে দখল থাকিলে দখলকার বিচারকালে যথেষ্ট সুবিধা পাইয়া থাকে। **To give possession**—To put another in possession of anything ; দখল দেওয়া, অধিকার দেওয়া। **To put in possession**—To give possession to ; to furnish with ; অধিকারী করা ; প্রদান করা। To place one in charge of property recovered in ejectment ; কোন প্রজাকে উচ্ছেদ করার পর তাহার সম্পত্তির অধিকার অন্যকে দেওয়া। **To take possession**—To occupy or obtain possession ; অধিকার করা, দখল লওয়া।

pŏs-ses′-sive (-ĭv), *adj.* & *n.* 1. Of, or relating to, possession ; অধিকারসম্বন্ধীয়, অধিকারাত্মক। 2. (*Gram.*) Indicating possession ; as, a *possessive* case or pronoun ; (ব্যাকরণ) সম্বন্ধবাচক। ***Noun.*** (*Gram.*) The possessive case or a word in this case ; a possessive pronoun ; সম্বন্ধকারক, সম্বন্ধকারকের শব্দ ; সম্বন্ধবাচক সর্ব্বনাম। **–ly,** *adv.* **–ness,** *n.* **Possessive case**—সম্বন্ধকারক। **Possessive pronoun**—সম্বন্ধবাচক সর্ব্বনাম।

pŏs′-sĕt, *n.* A drink composed of hot milk curdled by wine or other liquor ; দ্রাক্ষা-সুরা, সির্কা, প্রভৃতি দ্বারা উষ্ণ দুগ্ধ জমাইয়া যে একপ্রকার পানীয় প্রস্তুত করা হয়।

pŏs-sĭb′-ĭ-lĭst, *n.* A member of a political party, (especially a Spanish republican or a French socialist) attempting those reforms only that are immediately practicable ; রাজনীতিক সম্প্রদায় বিশেষের সভ্য—ইহারা আশুসাধ্য সংস্কার-সাধনের জন্য চেষ্টা করিয়া থাকে।

pŏs-sĭ-bĭl′-ĭ-tỹ (-ĭ-), *n.* 1. The state or condition of being possible ; সম্ভাব্যতা, শক্যতা, সাধ্যতা। 2. A thing or event that may or may not happen ; a contingency ; সম্ভবপর বিষয় ; দৈব ঘটনা।

pŏs′-sĭ-ble (-ĭ-bl), *adj.* & *n.* 1. That may exist or happen ; practicable ; সম্ভাব্য, ঘটনশক্য ; সাধ্য। 2. More or less likely ; সম্ভবপর। 3. (*Rare*) Tolerable to deal with ; (কচিদ্ব্যবহৃত) সহজসাধ্য, সহজে বশ্য, সুখবোধ্য। ***Noun.*** 1. That which is possible, (with *the*) ; সম্ভবপর বিষয়। 2. The highest possible score especially in rifle-practice ; as, he scored a *possible*, at 800 yds. ; সর্ব্বোচ্চ জয়াঙ্ক। **–bly,** *adv.* In a possible manner ; perhaps ; perchance ; সম্ভবপর ভাবে ; সম্ভবতঃ ; হয়তো। **As early as possible** — As early as you can ; যত সম্ভব শীঘ্র। **If possible**—যদি সম্ভবপর হয়।

pŏs′-sŭm, *n.* (*Colloq.*) Same as OPOSSUM. **To play or act possum**—To pretend to be ill ; to dissemble, (from possum's habit of feigning death when attacked or alarmed) ; পীড়ার ভাণ করা ; ভাণ করা, কপটতা করা।

pōst, *n.* & *v. t.* 1. A piece of timber set upright generally as a support to something ; a stake or stout pole for various purposes ; খুঁটি, খাম, খাম্বা, থাম, স্তম্ভ ; স্থাণু, স্থূণা। 2. A thick compact stratum of sandstone or limestone ; বেলে পাথর বা চুণা পাথরের ঘন স্তর। 3. A pillar of coal left to support the roof in a mine ; খনির ছাদের অবলম্বনস্বরূপ কয়লার স্তম্ভ। ***Verb t.*** 1. To fix or attach to a post ; to placard ; as, to *post* a notice ; স্তম্ভে বা থামে লাগান ; বিজ্ঞাপন লাগান। 2. To publish ; to advertise ; প্রচার করা ; বিজ্ঞাপন দেওয়া। 3. (In colleges) To enter in a posted list the names of (unsuccessful candidates) ; অনুত্তীর্ণ পরিক্ষার্থিগণের নাম প্রাচীরাদিতে আঁটা তালিকায় ভুক্ত করা। 4. To announce the name of (a ship) as overdue or missing ; পঁহুছার সময় পার হইয়া গিয়াছে বা হারানো গিয়াছে—এরূপ (জাহাজের) নাম প্রকাশ করা। **Post and rails**

tea — বোঁটার সহিত মিশ্রিত চা। **Starting-post** — যে স্তম্ভ হইতে প্রতিদ্বন্দ্বিগণ দৌড় আরম্ভ করে, যাত্রাস্তম্ভ। **Winning-post**— যে স্থানে দৌড় প্রভৃতি শেষ হয়—তথায় প্রোথিত স্তম্ভ, জয়স্তম্ভ।

pōst, *n.* & *v. t.* **1.** A military station; the place at which a soldier or a body of troops is stationed; a fort; সৈন্যদিগের আড্ডা; ঘাঁটি; দুর্গ। **2.** The force stationed at a post; ঘাঁটি। **3.** (*Fig.*) A place of duty; (লক্ষণায়) যে স্থানে কোন লোক কর্ত্তব্য পালনে নিযুক্ত থাকে। **4.** An employment; an appointment; "*Post* of profit or trust"; চাকুরী; কাজ। **5.** A place occupied for carrying on trade, esp. in an uncivilized country, (also called a *trading-post*); ব্যবসায়ের জন্য অধিকৃত স্থান (বিশেষতঃ অসভ্যদেশে)। **6.** (*Naval hist.*) Position of a POST CAPTAIN (which see.) ***Verb t.*** **1.** To station; as, to *post* troops on a hill; স্থাপন করা। **2.** (*Mil., Nav.*) To commission (a person) as captain; জাহাজ প্রভৃতির অধ্যক্ষতা প্রদান করা। **First, last, post**—শয়নকালজ্ঞাপক বংশিধ্বনি। **Post captian**—২০ বা ততোধিক কামানের জাহাজের ভারপ্রাপ্ত পোতাধ্যক্ষ।

pōst, *n.* & *adv.* **1.** (*Hist.*) One of the men posted with horses at various stations along a road to carry letters etc. each from his station to the next; (ইতিহাস) ডাক হরকরা। **2.** A messenger or carrier of letters and papers; a postman; পত্রবাহক; ডাকপিয়ন। **3.** An established system of conveying letters etc.; ডাকবিভাগ। **4.** A post office; a letter-box; ডাকঘর; চিঠির বাক্স। **5.** A single or particular dispatch of letters etc.; ডাক। **6.** Letters delivered at one house on one occasion; as, the *post* has come; এক কালে এক বাটীতে যে সকল চিঠি বিলি করা হয়, ডাক। **7.** A size of writing and printing-paper measuring about 20×16 inches; ডাক কাগজ। ***Adv.*** With post horses; hence, at full speed; as, to ride *post*; ডাকের ঘোড়ায়; পূর্ণবেগে। **Morning Post**—সংবাদপত্র বিশেষের নাম। **Post-bag**—ডাকের ব্যাগ। **Post-bill**—ডাকের ব্যাগে যে চিঠি দেওয়া হয়—তাহার তালিকা। **Post-boat**—ডাকের নৌকা, গয়নার নৌকা। **Post-boy**—পত্রবাহক। Same as POSTILION. **Postcard**—পোষ্টকার্ড। **Post-chaise**—যাত্রীবাহী শকট, রাষ্ট্রযান। **Post-coach**—ডাকের গাড়ী। **Post-day**—ডাক আসা বা রওয়ানার দিন। **Post-free**—বিনা মাশুলে নীত। **Post-haste**—(*n.* & *adv.*) (*Archaic*) Haste in travelling like that of a post; (অপ্রঃ) অতি দ্রুত। (*adv.*) With all possible haste or expedition; যথাসম্ভব দ্রুত। **Post-horse**—ডাক নেওয়ার জন্য ভ্রমণকারিগণের নিমিত্ত সরাইয়ে যে ঘোড়া রাখা হয়। **Post-man** — ডাকপিয়ন। **Post-mark**—ডাকঘরের ছাপ। (*Verb t.*) To mark (an envelope etc.) with such a stamp; মোহর দেওয়া। **Postmaster**—ডাক ঘরের ভারপ্রাপ্ত কর্ম্মচারী, ডাক বাবু, পোষ্টমাষ্টার। **Post-mastership,** *n.* **Post-master general**—ডাকবিভাগের কর্ত্তা। **Post-mistress** — (*Fem.* of POSTMASTER.) **Post-office** — ডাকঘর, ডাকবিভাগ। **Post-paid**—ডাক টিকেট দেওয়া। **Post-time**—চিঠি ডাকে দিবার বা বিলি করার কাল। **Post-town**—যে সহরে ডাকঘর আছে, বিশেষতঃ যে সহরে অন্য ডাকঘরের অনধীন ডাকঘর আছে। **By post**—ডাকে। **By return of post**—(ইতিহাস) বাহকের সঙ্গে; (বর্ত্তমানে) পরবর্ত্তী ডাকে, ফেরত ডাকে। **To ride post**—To ride as a courier of dispatches from place to place; hence, to ride rapidly; এক স্থান হইতে অন্য স্থানে দ্রুতবেগে অশ্বারোহণে পত্র লইয়া যাওয়া; নক্ষত্রবেগে অশ্ব ছুটাইয়া চলা।

pōst, *v. i.* & *t.* To travel with relays of horses; (*fig.*) to travel with speed; ঘোড়ার ডাকে ভ্রমণ করা; (লক্ষণায়) অতিদ্রুত ভ্রমণ করা। ***Verb t.*** **1.** To place in the post office or in the letter-box for transmission; ডাকে দেওয়া; চিঠির বাক্সে ফেলা। **2.** (*Book-keeping*) To transfer as an account, item or entry from the journal to the ledger; to complete (a ledger) in this way, (with *up*); জাবেদা হইতে পাকা খাতায় তোলা; খতিয়ান করা। **3.** (*Fig.*) To inform fully; to make familiar with a subject, (usu. with *up*); (লক্ষণায়) সম্যক্‌রূপে বিদিত করা; কোন বিষয়ে সুপরিচিত করা। **To post oneself up in**—To get full information about; to learn thoroughly; কোন বিষয়ের সম্যক বিবরণ প্রাপ্ত হওয়া; সম্যক্‌রূপে শিক্ষা করা।

pōst'-āge, *n.* Money paid for conveyance of letters etc. by post; ডাকমাশুল। **Postage stamp**—ডাকটিকিট।

pōst'-ăl, *adj.* Of, or relating to, the post-office, or mail service; as, *postal* arrangements; ডাকঘর সম্পর্কীয়, ডাকসম্পর্কীয়। **Postal order**—এক স্থান হইতে অপর স্থানে টাকা পাঠাইবার জন্য ডাকবিভাগের বরাত চিঠি। **Postal union**—বিভিন্ন দেশে চিঠি প্রভৃতি প্রেরণের মাশুল নির্দ্ধারণের জন্য তৎ তৎ দেশের শাসনতন্ত্র সমূহের সংযোগ।

pōst-clăs'-sĭ-căl, *adj.* Occurring later than the classical period of (esp. Greek and Roman) language, literature or art; কলা বা সাহিত্যের সমৃদ্ধিযুগের পরবর্ত্তী, বিশেষতঃ প্রাচীন গ্রীক ও রোমীয় কলা বা সাহিত্যের সমৃদ্ধিযুগের পরবর্ত্তী।

pōst-cŏm-mūn'-ĭ-ŏn, *n.* The part of the eucharistic office after the act of the communion ; খৃষ্টের অন্তিমভোজন ক্রিয়ার অনুষ্ঠানবিশেষ।

pŏst-cŏs′-tăl, *adj.* Behind a rib ; (*Entom.*) behind the costal vein ; পশুকার পশ্চাদ্বর্ত্তী ; (কীট-তত্ত্ব) পঞ্জর-শিরার পশ্চাদ্বর্ত্তী।

pōst-dāte′, *v. t.* & *n.* To date after the real time ; as, to *post-date* a document ; চিঠি, দলিল প্রভৃতিতে যে দিবস সম্পাদিত বা লিখিত হইয়াছে তাহার পরবর্ত্তী তারিখ দেওয়া, পরের তারিখ দেওয়া। ***Noun.*** **(post′—)** A date on a letter etc. later than the real date on which it was written ; চিঠি দলিল প্রভৃতিতে লিখন বা সম্পাদনের পরবর্ত্তী তারিখ।

pōst-dĭ-lū′-vĭ-ăn, *adj.* & *n.* Existing, or happening, after the Flood in Noah's days ; নোয়ার সময়ের জলপ্লাবনের পরবর্ত্তী, প্রলয়োত্তরকালীন। ***Noun.*** One who lived or lives after the Flood ; যে জলপ্রলয়ের পরে বাস করিয়াছিল বা করিতেছে।

pōst′-ĕn-trȳ, *n.* A late or subsequent entry as in an account-book, for race etc. ; পরবর্ত্তী তারিখে খাতায় লিখিত বিষয়।

pōst′-ēr, *n.* **1.** A bill or placard intended to be posted in a place ; প্রকাশ্য স্থানে লাগাইবার জন্য বিজ্ঞাপন। **2.** One who posts bills, (also called a *bill-poster*) ; যে ব্যক্তি বিজ্ঞাপন লাগায়।

poste restante, (*F.*), *n.* A place in a post office where letters are kept till applied for ; ডাকঘরের যে স্থানে মালীক না চাওয়া পর্য্যন্ত চিঠি জমা রাখা হয়।

pŏs-tē′-rĭ-or (-ēr), *adj.* & *n.* **1.** Later in time ; coming after, (opp. to *prior*) ; পরবর্ত্তী, উত্তরকালীন, পশ্চাৎকালীন; পশ্চাদাগত। **2.** Hinder ; situated behind, (opp. to *anterior*); as, the *posterior* portion of the skull ; পশ্চাদ্দেশস্থ ; পশ্চাদ্বর্ত্তী। **3.** (*Anat., sing. or plu.*) The buttock ; (শারীরসংস্থানবিদ্যা) নিতম্ব, পাছা। **—ly,** *adv.* **—or′-i-ty,** *n.*

pŏs-tēr′-ĭ-tȳ, *n.* **1.** Descendants ; সন্তানসন্ততি, বংশধরগণ। **2.** All succeeding generations ; ভবিষ্যদ্-বংশধরগণ।

pŏs′-tērn, *n.* & *adj.* **1.** A back door ; a private entrance ; পশ্চাদ্দ্বার, পেছনের দরজা ; খিড়কীর দরজা। **2.** (*Fort.*) An underground passage under a rampart ; দুর্গপ্রাকারের নিম্নস্থ সুড়ঙ্গ। ***Adj.*** Situated at the back or side ; পশ্চাদ্বর্ত্তী, পেছনের।

pōst-ĕx-ĭl′-ĭ-ăn, —ic, *adjs.* Subsequent to the Babylonian exile ; ইহুদীগণের বেবিলোনিয়া নগরে নির্ব্বাসনের পরবর্ত্তী।

pōst-fĭx′, *v. t.* To add as letters etc., to the end of another word ; অন্য শব্দের অন্তে অক্ষর প্রভৃতি যোগ করা।

pōst′-fĭx, *n.* Suffix ; বিভক্তি, প্রত্যয়।

pōst-glā′-cĭ-ăl (-shĭ-), *adj.* Subsequent to the glacial epoch ; তুষারযুগোত্তর।

pōst-grăd′-ū-āte, *n.* Bolonging to study pursued after graduation ; বিশ্ববিদ্যালয়ে উপাধিপ্রাপ্তির পর অনুসৃত শিক্ষা-সম্বন্ধীয়, উপাধিলাভোত্তর।

Post hoc, ergo propter hoc— অনন্তর, অতএব এই কারণে, যদনন্তরং তৎকারণকং (হিঃ কোঃ)।

pōst′-hū-mous (-mŭs), *adj.* **1.** Born after the death of the father ; পিতৃমৃত্যুত্তর, পিত্র্যন্তরজাত পিত্রান্তরজাত, পিতৃমরণোত্তরজ। **2.** Published after the death of the author ; লেখকের মৃত্যুর পর প্রকাশিত। **3.** Occurring or continuing after one's death ; as, a *posthumous* reputation ; মৃত্যুত্তরজ, মরণপরবর্ত্তী, মরণোত্তর। **—ly,** *adv.*

pŏs′-tĭ-cous (-kŭs), *adj.* (*Bot.*) Posterior ; hinder ; (উদ্ভিদ্ বিদ্যা) পশ্চাৎকালীন, উত্তরকালীন ; পরবর্ত্তী।

pŏs′-tĭl, *n.* **1.** (*Hist.*) A note in the margin of the Bible, so called because written after the text ; hence, a marginal note ; a commentary ; (ইতিহাস) বাইবেলের পার্শ্ব-টিপ্পনী ; পার্শ্ব-টিপ্পনী ; ভাষ্য। **2.** (*R. C.*) A homily read after the Gospel ; (রোমান ক্যাথলিক ধর্ম্মসংঘ) সুসমাচার পাঠের পরে পঠিত ধর্ম্মোপদেশ।

pŏs-tĭl′-ion (-yŏn),**—lion** (-yŏn), *ns.* One who rides the near leading horse of a carriage ; one who rides the near horse when one pair only is used ; অশ্ব-শকটে দুই বা ততোধিক অশ্ব-যুগল সম্বদ্ধ থাকিলে যে ব্যক্তি পথপ্রদর্শকরূপে শকটের অব্যবহিত সম্মুখবর্ত্তী অশ্ব-যুগলের বাম পার্শ্ববর্ত্তী অশ্বে আরোহণ করে ; শকটে অশ্বযুগল সম্বদ্ধ থাকিলে যে চালক বামপার্শ্বের অশ্বে আরূঢ় থাকে।

pōst-lĭm′-ĭ-nȳ, *n.* **1.** (*Rom. Law*) The right of a banished person or captive to be restored to his original civic status on return ; (রোমান আইন) নির্ব্বাসিত ব্যক্তির স্বদেশে প্রত্যাবর্ত্তনান্তে সামাজিক পদবীতে পুনঃ প্রতিষ্ঠিত হওয়ার অধিকার। **2.** (International Law) The restoration of persons and things taken in war to their former state when they come again under the power of the nation to which they belonged ; (আন্তর্জাতিক আইন) যুদ্ধে গৃহীত ব্যক্তি বা বস্তু পুনরায় পূর্ব্বাধিকারী জাতির হস্তে আসিলে উহাদিগকে পূর্ব্বাবস্থা প্রত্যর্পণ, পুনঃ প্রদান।

pōst′-măs-tēr, *n.* **1.** A scholar of Merton College, Oxford ; অক্সফোর্ডের মার্টন কলেজের ছাত্র। 2. Same as POSTMASTER which see under POST. **—ship,** *n.*

post meridiem, (*L.*), *adv.* (*Abbr. P. M.*) After midday ; মধ্যাহ্নান্তিক, অপরাহ্লূতন।

pōst-mĭl-lĕn′-nĭ-ăl, *adj.* Of, or relating to, the period following the millennium ; বাইবেল বর্ণিত

সহস্রবর্ষব্যাপী যুগসম্বন্ধীয়। **–ism,** *n.* The doctrine that the second coming of Christ will follow the millennium ; যীশুখৃষ্ট সহস্রবর্ষ-ব্যাপী সত্যযুগের অন্তে পৃথিবীতে অবতীর্ণ হইবেন—এইরূপ মতবাদ। **–ist,** *n.*

post mortem, (*L.*), *adv.* After death ; মৃত্যুর পর, মরণোত্তর।

pōst–mŏr′-tĕm, (*L.*), *adj.* & *n.* Made after death ; as, a *post-mortem* examination ; মৃত্যুত্তর। *Noun.* A POST-MORTEM EXAMINATION (which see.) **Post-mortem examination**—মৃত্যুর পর ব্যবচ্ছেদ দ্বারা শবদেহ পরীক্ষা।

pōst-nā′-tăl, *adj.* Subsequent to birth ; জন্মপরবর্ত্তী, জন্মোত্তর।

pōst-nŭp′-tial (-shăl), *adj.* Made, or happening, after marriage ; বিবাহের পরবর্ত্তী, বিবাহোত্তর।

pōst-ō′-bit, *adj.* & *n.* That takes effect after death ; মৃত্যুর পর আমলে আসে—এরূপ। *Noun.* A bond which secures to a lender a sum on the death of some specified person from whom the borrower has expectations ; কোন ব্যক্তির মৃত্যুর পর উত্তরাধিকার বা অন্যসূত্রে কাহারো টাকা পাওয়ার আশা থাকিলে সেই টাকা দ্বারা ঋণ পরিশোধ করিবে এই করারে সে ব্যক্তি উত্তমর্ণকে যে খত দেয়।

pōst-ō′-răl, *adj.* (*Anat.*) Situated behind the mouth ; (শারীর-সংস্থান বিদ্যা) মুখপশ্চাদ্‌বর্ত্তী।

pōst-plī′-ŏ-cene (-sēn), *adj.* (*Geol.*) Of, or relating to, the formation lying just over the pliocene ; (ভূবিদ্যা) অত্যাধুনিক স্তরের উপরিস্থ স্তরসম্বন্ধীয়।

pōst-pōne′, *v. t.* & *i.* **1.** To defer to a future time ; to put off ; স্থগিত রাখা ; মুলতবী রাখা। **2.** To set in importance etc. below something else, (with *to*) ; "All other considerations should... be *postponed* to this" ; স্থগিত রাখা। *Verb i.* (*Path.*, of ague etc.) To be later in coming on or recurring ; দেরীতে আসা বা পুনরাবৃত্ত হওয়া। **–ment,** *n.*

pōst-pō-ṡi′-tion, *n.* **1.** The state of being placed after ; পশ্চাৎ-স্থিতি, পশ্চাদবস্থান। **2.** A word or particle placed after another (*e. g.* - *wards*) (distinguished from *preposition*) ; কোন শব্দের পশ্চাতে স্থাপিত অপর শব্দ বা অব্যয়। **–al,** *adj.* **–pos′-i-tive,** *adj.* Placed after another word ; as, a *post-positive* letter ; অপর শব্দের পশ্চাতে স্থাপিত।

pōst-prăn′-dĭ-ăl, *adj.* Happening, made, or done, after dinner ; as, *postprandial* oratory ; অপরাহ্ণ-ভোজনোত্তর।

pōst′-script, *n.* (*Abbr. P. S.*) A paragraph added to a letter after the signature ; an addition to a book or composition after it is finished ; পুনশ্চ (সংক্ষেপে পুঃ চঃ), অনুলেখ ; পুস্তক বা রচনার সমাপ্তির পর যে বিষয় সংযোজিত করা হয়।

pōst-tẽr′-ti-ā-rȳ (-shĭ-), *n.* (*Geol.*) More recent than the tertiary ; তৃতীয় স্তরাপেক্ষা আধুনিক।

pŏs′-tū-lănt, *n.* A candidate especially seeking admission to the religious order ; যাজক পদপ্রার্থী।

pŏs′-tū-lāte, *n.* **1.** position or supposition assumed as self-evident for reasoning ; a fundamental condition or principle ; মূলস্বীকার্য্য, স্বীকৃতপক্ষ ; মূলতত্ত্ব। **2.** (*Geom.*) The enunciation of a self-evident problem ; (জ্যামিতি) স্বীকার্য্য, গৃহীতাধার প্রতিজ্ঞা। **3.** An essential preliminary ; অত্যাবশ্যক প্রাথমিক কার্য্যাবলী।

pŏs′-tū-lāte, *v. t.* & *i.* **1.** To regard as self-evident ; to take for granted ; স্বতঃসিদ্ধ বলিয়া গণ্য করা ; মানিয়া নেওয়া, স্বীকার করিয়া নেওয়া। **2.** To demand ; দাবী করা। **3.** (*Eccl. Law*) To nominate or elect subject to superior sanction ; (যাজকীয় আইন) উর্দ্ধতন যাজকসমাজের মঞ্জুরের অপেক্ষা রাখিয়া কোন ব্যক্তিকে যাজকের পদে নিযুক্ত করা। *Verb i.* To stipulate *for* ; to make demands ; চুক্তি করা ; দাবী করা। **–la′-tion, –la-tor,** *ns.*

pŏs′-tūre, *n.*, *v. t.* & *i.* **1.** Attitude, physical or mental ; উপবেশন-ভঙ্গী, ঢং, অঙ্গবিন্যাস, সংস্থিতি, আসন (হিঃ কোঃ), গাত্রচেষ্টা, সংস্থান, অঙ্গস্থিতি শরীরস্থিতি, শরীরবিন্যাস। **2.** State or condition ; as, the *posture* of affairs ; অবস্থা, ভাব। *Verb t.* To place in a particular attitude ; বিশেষ ভঙ্গীতে স্থাপন করা। *Verb i.* **1.** To assume a posture ; কোন বিশেষ ভঙ্গীতে উপবিষ্ট হওয়া। **2.** (*Fig.*) To assume a character ; as, to *posture* as a saint ; (লক্ষণায়) কাহারো ভঙ্গী ধরা। **–tur-al,** *adj.* **–tur-er,** *n.* **Posture-maker**—An acrobat ; a contortionist ; দড়াবাজীকর ; যে বাজীকর নানা ভাবে দেহ আকুঞ্চিত করে। **Posture-master**—অঙ্গসংস্থানশিক্ষক।

pō′-ṡȳ, *n.* **1.** (*Archaic*) A verse or a motto inscribed on a ring etc. ; অঙ্গুরীয়ক প্রভৃতির উপর ক্ষোদিত কবিতা-পংক্তি বা ক্ষুদ্র সারবান বাক্য। **2.** A bunch of flowers ; a nosegay ; পুষ্পগুচ্ছ, কুসুমস্তবক ; ফুলের তোড়া। **Posy-ring**—যে অঙ্গুরীয়কের উপর নীতিবাক্যাদি ক্ষোদিত থাকে।

pŏt, *n.* **1.** A metallic or earthen vessel of rounded form for holding liquids or solids, for cooking etc. ; পাত্র, হাঁড়ি, ভাণ্ড, ঘট, কুপক (সাঃ পঃ)। **2.** A drinking vessel of pewter, etc. ; রূপদস্তা প্রভৃতির পানপাত্র। **3.** The quantity contained in a pot ; a potful ; as, a *pot* of porter or honey ; ভাণ্ডপূর্ণ জিনিষ ; একহাঁড়ী। **4.** A chimney-pot ; ধূমনির্গমনালীর ধাতব বা মৃন্ময় অগ্রভাগ। **5.** A vessel of silver etc. as a prize in athletic sports ; (*slang*) any prize in these ; মল্লক্রীড়ায় যে রজত-পাত্র পুরস্কার দেওয়া হয় ; (ইতরভাষায়) যে কোনরূপ পুরস্কার। 6. A large sum ; টাকার জালা, টাকার ঘড়া। 7. A crucible ; মূষা, ধাতু প্রভৃতি গালাইবার মুচি। 8. A wicker vessel for catching lobsters and other fishes ; চিংড়ী প্রভৃতি মাছ ধরার ঘুণি। 9. Same as CHAMBER-POT. 10. Same as FLOWER-POT. 11. (*Racing slang*) A large sum staked or betted ; (also) a favourite ; (ঘোড়দৌড়ের ইতরভাষায়) বহু টাকার বাজী ; ঘোড়দৌড়ের প্রিয় ঘোড়া। 12. A size of paper ; নির্দ্দিষ্ট আয়তনের কাগজ। 13. (*Sugar manufac.*) A perforated cask for draining sugar ; (শর্করা প্রস্তুতে) চিনি ছাঁকিবার জন্য একপ্রকার সচ্ছিদ্র পিঁপা। **Pot'-ful**, *n.* এক ভাণ্ড, এক হাঁড়ী। **Ink-pot**—See under INK. **Pot-ale** — মদের ভাঁটির আবর্জ্জনা। **Pot-bellied** — লম্বোদর, ঘটোদর (কথাঃ সঃ), তুন্দিল, পিচিণ্ডিল, ভুঁড়ে। **Pot-boiler**—বটতলার পুঁথি ; বটতলার লেখক। **Pot-bound**—(বৃক্ষ সম্বন্ধে) অনেক শিকড় ছড়াইবার দরুণ টবে প্রসারের স্থানাভাব হইয়াছে—এরূপ। **Pot-boy**—সুরাবিপণিতে মদ্যপরিবেষণে সাহায্যকারী বালক, ভাণ্ডহর, ভাণ্ডবাহ। **Pot-companion**—মদ্যপানসহচর, মদের ইয়ার, পানগোষ্ঠিসুহৃদ। **Pot-hanger** — ভাণ্ড টাঙ্গাইয়া রাখার জন্য শঙ্কু। **Pot-hat**—পুরুষদিগের একপ্রকার উঁচু টুপি। **Pot-head**—স্থূলবুদ্ধি ব্যক্তি। **Pot-herb**—শাক। **Pot-hole** — পাষাণ-স্তরে নলাকার গভীর গর্ত্ত, মণ্ডলাকার গর্ত্ত। (সাঃ পঃ)। **Pot-hook**—উষ্ণপাত্র তুলিবার জন্য অগ্নিসেবনস্থলীর উপরে ঝুলানো আঁকুশী; ঐরূপ আঁকুশীর আকার অক্ষর (যাহা ছেলেরা প্রথম লিখা শিক্ষার কালে লিখিয়া থাকে)। **Pot-house**—সুরা-বিপণি, শৌণ্ডিকালয়, পানাগার। **Pot-hunter**—যে ব্যক্তি যে কোন বস্তুর উপর গুলি করিয়া থাকে; যে ব্যক্তি কেবল পুরস্কারের জন্য মল্লযুদ্ধ প্রভৃতিতে যোগদান করে। **Pot-lead**—একপ্রকার কৃষ্ণসীসক—যাহা সাধারণতঃ বাইচের নৌকার তলায় দেওয়া হয়। **Pot lid**—ভাণ্ডের ঢাকনি। **Pot-liquor**—মাংসের একপ্রকার পাতলা যুষ। **Pot-luck**—ভাগ্যে যখন যেরূপ জোটে সেরূপ খাদ্য। **Potman**—যে ব্যক্তি পানাগারে মদ্য পরিবেষণে সাহায্য করে। **Pot-metal**—একপ্রকার রঞ্জিত কাচ—সর্ব্বাংশে রঙ্গ অনুপ্রবিষ্ট করার জন্য গলিত অবস্থায় যাহাতে রঙ্গ দেওয়া হয় ; একপ্রকার নিকৃষ্ট পিত্তল। **Pot-shop**—ক্ষুদ্র মদের দোকান, শুঁড়িখানা, তাড়িখানা। **Pot-shot**—কেবল ভোজনের উদ্দেশ্যে যে জন্তুর উপর গুলি করা হয় ; নিকটস্থ কোন জন্তু বা ব্যক্তিকে লক্ষ্য করিয়া যে গুলি করা হয় ; যদৃচ্ছাক্রমে যে গুলি করা হয় ; গুপ্ত স্থান হইতে বা বৃক্ষের আড়াল হইতে শত্রুকে যে গুলি করা হয়। **Pot-stick** — রন্ধনকালে পাত্রস্থ ব্যঞ্জনাদি নাড়িবার ক্ষুদ্র যষ্টিবিশেষ, কাটি। **Potstone**—একপ্রকার বেলে পাথর। **Pot-valiant**—মদ্যপান হেতু সাহসী। **Pot-valour**—মদ্যপানজনিত সাহস। **Potwaller, –walloper**—(১৮৩২ খৃঃ অব্দের পূর্ব্বে) গৃহস্বামিরূপে নির্ব্বাচন মতপ্রদানের ক্ষমতাবান ব্যক্তি। **Water pot** — ঘটী, ঘড়া, গাড়ু, কলসী। **A big pot**—হোমরা চোমরা লোক, জং বাহাদুর, জবড় জং। **The pot calls the kettle black**—আনারস বলে কাঁঠাল ভাই তুমি বড় খস্‌খসে, রসুন বলে কাঁচকলা ভাই তোমার বড় খোসা, চালুনি বলে ধুচুনী ভায়া তুমি বড় ফুটা, চালুনি বলেন সূচ ভাই তোমার গায়ে কেন ছেঁদা, গুয়ে বলে গোবরা দাদা তোর গায়ে বড় গন্ধ, সাতু বলেন পাঁচু ভাই তুমি বড় মরুঞ্চে। **To go to pot**—(*Vulg.*) To go to ruin or destruction ; চুলোয় যাওয়া, ধ্বংসমুখে পতিত হওয়া। **To keep the pot boiling**—To procure the necessaries of life ; হাঁড়ী চালান। To keep anything going briskly ; সতেজে চালান, পুরাদমে চালান, গরমাগরম রাখা। **To make the pot boil**—To make a living ; হাঁড়ী চালান। **To take pot-luck**—To accept an invitation to a meal where no preparation for guests has been made ; উপস্থিত মত যাহা রান্না বান্না হইয়াছে—তাহা খাওয়ার জন্য বসিয়া যাওয়া।

pŏt, *v. t.* & *i.* 1. To preserve in pots ; as, *potted* fowl and fish ; পাত্রের মধ্যে ভরিয়া তাজা রাখা। 2. To plant as a plant in a pot ; টবে রোপণ করা। 3. (*Billiards*) Same as POCKET *v. t.* 5. 4. To secure or kill as an animal by pot-shot ; যদৃচ্ছাক্রমে গুলি করিয়া কোন জন্তুকে বধ করা। 5. To seize, secure, or win ; ধরা, লাভকরা, পাওয়া। ***Verb i.*** To shoot (at an enemy, game, etc.) ; গুলি করা।

pō'-tă-ble (-bl), *adj.* & *n.* Fit, or suitable, for drinking ; পেয়। ***Noun.*** (*Pl.*) Drinkables ; পেয় দ্রব্য, পানীয় দ্রব্য।

potage, (*F.*), *n.* A soup ; সূপ।

pŏ-tăm'-ĭc, *adj.* Of, or pertaining to, rivers ; নদীসম্বন্ধীয়।

pŏt-ă-mŏl'-ŏ-ġy̆, *n.* The scientific study of rivers ; নদীতত্ত্ব, নদীবিজ্ঞান।

pŏt'-ăsh, *n.* A powerful alkali obtained from the ashes of plants ; যবক্ষার, সর্জ্জিকা, পোটাশ (হিঃ কোঃ)। **Potash water** — যবক্ষার বারি। **Nitrate of potash**—সোরা।

pō-tăss' *n.* (*Archaic*) Same as POTASH. **Potassic bromate**—অরুণকীয় পত্রক (সাঃ পঃ)। **Potassic chlorate**—হরিণকীয় পত্রক (সাঃ পঃ)। **Potassic chromate** — ক্রোমকীয় পত্রক (সাঃ পঃ)। **Potassic iodate**—নীলকীয় পত্রক (সাঃ পঃ)। **Potassic manganate** — মঙ্গলকীয় পত্রক (সাঃ পঃ)। **Potassic nitrate**—মরুতকীয় পত্রক (সাঃ পঃ)। **Potassic nitrite**—মরুতীয় পত্রক (সাঃ পঃ)। **Potassic oxide**—দগ্ধপত্রক (সাঃ পঃ)। **Potassic periodate**—পরিনীলকীয় পত্রক (সাঃ পঃ)। **Potassic permanganate** — পরিমঙ্গলকীয় পত্রক

(সাঃ পঃ)। **Potassic pyrophosphate**—অধিফ্ফুরকীয় খটিক (সাঃ পঃ)।

pō-tăs'-sĭ-ŭm, *n.* The metallic basis of potash ; a soft white metal with a slight tinge of pink ; যবক্ষারের ধাতব মূল ; ঈষৎ পাটলাভ শ্বেতবর্ণ ধাতু বিশেষ, পত্রক (সাঃ পঃ)। **—sic,** *adj.* **Potassium carbonate**—যবক্ষার। **Potassium nitrate**—সোরা।

pō-ta'-tion, *n.* **1.** The act of drinking ; a draught ; পান ; চুমুক। **2.** A drink ; পানীয়। **3.** (Usu. *pl.*) Intemperate drinking ; অতিরিক্ত মদ্য পান, পানদোষ। **Po'-ta-to-ry,** *adj.*

pō-ta'-tō, *n.* A well-known plant, the tubers of which are eaten ; its tuber ; বিলাতী আলু, গোলআলু ; বিলাতী আলুর গাছ। **Potato beetle**—একপ্রকার গোবরে পোকা—যাহা বিলাতী আলুর পাতা খাইয়া গাছের গুরুতর অনিষ্ট করে। **Potato disease**—একপ্রকার পরাশ্রয়ী ছত্রাক জনিত আলুর রোগ। **Potato-finger**—(অবজ্ঞার্থে ব্যবহৃত) মোটা আঙ্গুল। **Potato fly**—বিলাতী আলুর গাছের একপ্রকার পোকা। **Potato-ring**—পানপাত্র প্রভৃতি বসানের জন্য চক্র। **Potato-trap, —box**—(ইতরভাষায়) মুখ বিবর। **Potato rot**—ধসা (যোঃ) আলুর ধসা রোগ। **Small potatoes**—(*U. S.*) ক্ষুদ্র জিনিষ, তুচ্ছ জিনিষ। **Sweet potato** -রাঙ্গা আলু, রক্তালু (ভাবঃ প্রঃ), রক্তালুক (অঃ)। **Telinga potato** — ওল। **Quite the potato**—(*Slang*) The proper thing ; (ইতরভাষায়) ঠিক জিনিষ। **Potatoes and Point**—Potatoes to eat and bacon etc. to look at ; আলু হচ্চে খাওয়ার জন্য এবং শূয়রের মাংসাদি হচ্চে দেখার শোভা।

pŏ-teen' (-tēn), **—theen'** (-tēn), *ns.* An Irish whisky illicitly distilled ; অবৈধরূপে চোয়ান আইরিশ মদ।

pō'-tĕnt, *adj.* **1.** Having great power or influence ; mighty ; বীর্য্যবান, উর্জ্জস্বল, শক্তিমান ; প্রতাপশালী, পরাক্রমী। **2.** Efficacious : strong ; as, a *potent* drug ; ফলদায়ক ; শক্তিশালী। **3.** Cogent, as an argument ; প্রবল, অকাট্য। **4.** Having procreative power ; সৃষ্টিকারিণী শক্তিসম্পন্ন। **—ly,** *adv.* **—tence,** *n.* **—ten-cy,** *n.* **1.** Strength ; power ; বল, শক্তি, বীর্য্য, বিভব (সাঃ পঃ), প্রভব (সুশ্রু কুঞ্জঃ) ; ক্ষমতা, প্রতাপ, পরাক্রম, তেজঃ। **2.** (*Homeo.*) The increased power of a medicine as produced by attenuation ; (সদৃশচিকিৎসাবিধান) তরলতাসম্পাদন দ্বারা উৎপন্ন ঔষধের বর্দ্ধিত শক্তি।

pō'-tĕn-tāte, *n.* A monarch ; a king ; অধিপতি ; রাজা।

pō-tĕn'-tial (-shăl), *adj.* & *n.* **1.** Existing in possibility ; latent ; "Is not everyman, God be thanked a *potential* hero" ; সম্ভাবনাত্মক, উপপন্ন, ভাবিসম্ভাব্য, ভবিষ্যসম্ভাব্য ; সুপ্ত, অব্যক্ত, প্রচ্ছন্ন, প্রচ্ছন্ন-শক্তি, অব্যক্ত-শক্তি, অনুভূত (ব্রজঃ হিন্দুঃ)। **2.** (*Gram.*) Expressing possibility ; as, a *potential* mood ; সম্ভাবনাবাচক। **3.** (*Rare*) Mighty ; powerful ; (কচিদ্ ব্যবহৃত) শক্তিশালী ; ক্ষমতাশালী। ***Noun.*** **1.** A possibility ; সম্ভাবনা, সম্ভাব্যতা। **2.** Same as POTENTIAL FUNCTION. **3.** Amount of work or energy denoted by potential function ; বিভব (সাঃ পঃ)। **4.** (*Gram.*) The potential mood ; (ব্যাকরণ) বিধিলিঙ্। **—al'-i-ty,** *n.* **1.** State of being potential ; power ; প্রচ্ছন্নাবস্থা, প্রচ্ছন্নশক্তিত্ব, অনুভূতবৃত্তিত্ব, শক্তি। **2.** Possibility ; সম্ভাব্যতা, সম্ভাবনা। **3.** A capacity or possibility ; a person or animal embodying this ; "The seed is the *potentiality* of the plant" ; শক্যতা (হিঃ কোঃ) ; প্রচ্ছন্নশক্তিসম্পন্ন মানব বা জন্তু। **—ly,** *adv.* **Potential cautery, corrosive**—যে ঔষধ দ্বারা চর্ম্মের উপর উত্তপ্ত লৌহস্পর্শবৎ ক্রিয়া হয়। **Potential energy** — প্রচ্ছন্নশক্তি (রাঃ সুঃ), অব্যক্তশক্তি (সাঃ পঃ), অনুভূতশক্তি (ঐ), উপপন্নশক্তি (হিঃ কোঃ), জড়শক্তি (সাঃ পঃ), স্থিরশক্তি (ঐ), অনুভূতবৃত্তি (ব্রজঃ হিন্দুঃ), সম্ভাবনীয়শক্তি (হিঃ কোঃ), ছদ্মশক্তি। **Potenteal function**—যে সংখ্যা বা সাংকেতিক চিহ্নের বৈভিন্নীকরণ দ্বারা কোন বস্তুশ্রেণী হইতে উদ্ভূত যে কোন দেশস্থ শক্তি প্রকাশ করা যাইতে পারে। **Potential mood**—বিধিলিঙ্।

pō-tĕn'-tial-īze (-shăl-), *v. t.* & *i.* To make potential as energy etc. ; অনুভূত করা। ***Verb i.*** To become potential ; প্রচ্ছন্ন শক্তি-বিশিষ্ট হওয়া।

pō-tĕn'-ti-āte (-shĭ-), *v. t.* To give power to ; to make possible ; ক্ষমতাসম্পন্ন করা, ক্ষমতাপন্ন করা ; সম্ভবপর করা।

pŏth'-ĕr, *n.*, *v. t.* & *i.* **1.** A suffocating smoke or cloud of dust ; শ্বাসরোধক ধূমপুঞ্জ বা ধূলিপটল। **2.** Bustle ; noise ; din ; গোলমাল ; গণ্ডগোল ; রোল, কলরব। **3.** Display of sorrow or grief ; শোক প্রকাশ, দুঃখপ্রকাশ। ***Verb t.*** To trouble ; to bluster ; to worry ; to tease ; উত্যক্ত করা ; জ্বালাতন করা ; ক্ষ্যাপান ; বিরক্ত করা। ***Verb i.*** To make a stir or fuss ; গোলমাল করা, হৈ চৈ করা।

pō-ti-cho-ma'-ni-ă (-shō-), *n.* Craze for coating glass vessels on the inside with paper or linen decorations in imitation of porcelain ; চীনা মাটীর মত দেখাইবার জন্য কাচভাণ্ডের অভ্যন্তরভাগ কাগজ বা ক্ষৌমবস্ত্রের পুষ্প প্রভৃতির ভূষা দ্বারা আচ্ছাদনের বাতিক।

pō'-tion, *n.* A draught ; a dose esp. of a liquid medicine or of poison ; মাত্রা ; তরল ঔষধের মাত্রা, বিশেষতঃ বিষের মাত্রা।

pŏt-latch, —lach(e) (-lăch), *ns.* A tribal feast of North-American Indians given by an aspirant to chiefship ; উত্তর আমেরিকার আদিম অধিবাসিগণের মধ্যে সর্দার পদপ্রার্থী কর্তৃক প্রদত্ত গুষ্ঠি-ভোজ।

pot-pourri (pö-pô-rē), (*F.*) *n.* **1.** A vase of flowers and spices etc. to perfume a room ; গৃহকক্ষ সুরভিত করার জন্য পুষ্প, সুগন্ধি মসলা, প্রভৃতি দ্বারা পূর্ণ ভাণ্ডবিশেষ। **2.** A medley of musical airs ; মিশ্রসুর। **3.** A literary composition made up of unconnected parts ; অসম্বদ্ধ রচনা, পঞ্চশস্য। **4.** A dish of different kinds of meat and vegetables cooked together (*obs.*) ; বিভিন্ন প্রকার মাংস, তরিতরকারি একত্র রন্ধন করতঃ প্রস্তুত ব্যঞ্জন বিশেষ (অপ্রঃ)।

pŏt'-shērd, *n.* (*Archaic*) A piece or fragment of a broken earthen pot ; (অপ্রঃ) ভগ্নমৃৎপাত্রখণ্ড, খোলাকুঁচি।

pŏt'-tage (-āj), *n.* **1.** (*Archaic*) Soup, esp. a thick soup ; (অপ্রঃ) যুষ (ভাবঃ প্রঃ), জুষ। **2.** Same as MESS OF POTTAGE which see under MESS.

pŏt'-tər (-êr), *n.* One who makes earthen vessels ; কুমার, কুম্ভকার, ঘটীকার (কেভিঃ), কুলাল [Syn. ভরট, চক্রজীবক, চক্রজীবী, ঘটকারী, দণ্ডভৃত, দণ্ডধর, চক্রচর।] **Potter's clay**—কুমারের মাটী। **Potter's field**—বিদেশিগণের সমাধিক্ষেত্র। **Potter's lathe**—চক্রভ্রম, চক্রভ্রাম, ভ্রম। **Potter's wheel**—কুলালচক্র।

pŏt'-ter (-êr), *v. i.* & *t.* **1.** To busy oneself about trifles ; to work with little energy or effect ; তুচ্ছবিষয়ে ব্যস্ত থাকা ; ঢিমাতেতালা ভাবে কাজ করা (*colloq.*)। **2.** To walk lazily or idly ; to loiter ; অলস ভাবে ঘুরা; গড়িমসি করা। ***Verb t.*** To trifle away, as, one's time etc. ; বাজে কাজে (সময়) নষ্ট করা।

pŏt'-ter-ŷ (-êr-), *n.* **1.** The ware made by potters ; মৃদ্‌ভাণ্ড, মৃন্ময় পাত্রাদি। **2.** The place where earthen vessels are made ; কুম্ভকার-গৃহ, কুলালগৃহ। **3.** The business of a potter ; মৃৎশিল্প। **The Potteries**—মৃৎশিল্পের জন্য বিখ্যাত উত্তর ষ্টাফোর্ডসায়ারের অন্তঃপাতী জেলাবিশেষ।

pŏt'-tle (-l), *n.* **1.** (*Archaic*) A measure of 4 pints ; a pot of this capacity ; (অপ্রঃ) চারি পাইণ্ট ; ৪ পাইণ্টের পাত্র। **2.** A small basket for holding fruits ; ফলের ক্ষুদ্র ঝুড়ি, ফলকড়ণ্ডিকা।

pŏt'-tō, *n.* An animal allied to the racoons and lemur of South Africa ; একপ্রকার জন্তু।

pouch (pow̄ch), *n.* **1.** A small bag or detachable pocket esp. for carrying things ; থলি। **2.** (*Archaic*) A purse ; (অপ্রঃ) টাকার থলি। **3.** A soldier's leather bag for ammunition ; সৈনিকের গুলি বারুদ রাখার জন্য চামড়ার থলি। **4.** A mail bag ; ডাকের ব্যাগ। **5.** (*Zool.*) A natural receptacle in some animals *e.g.* marsupials ; (প্রাণিবিদ্যা) কোষ, থলি, গণ্ডকোষ (যোঃ)। **6.** (*Bot.*) A little sac or bag at the base of some petals or sepals ; (উদ্ভিদ্ বিদ্যা) কোষ। **Pouch'-y,** *adj.*

pouch (pow̄ch), *v. t.* & *i.* **1.** To put or take into a pouch ; to pocket ; থলিতে রাখা বা ভরা ; জেবে রাখা। **2.** (*Slang*) To give money to ; to tip ; (ইতর ভাষায়) টাকা দেওয়া ; বকশিশ দেওয়া। **3.** To arrange as a part of a dress so as to hang like a pouch ; পরিচ্ছদের অংশ-বিশেষ থলির মত ঝুলাইয়া রাখা। **4.** (*Rare*) To swallow ; (কচিদ্‌ব্যবহৃত) গ্রাস করা। ***Verb i.*** (Of a part of a dress) To hang like a pouch ; (পোষাকের অংশ বিশেষ) থলির মত ঝুলিয়া থাকা। **Pouched,** *adj.*

pou-drette' (pow̄-drĕt), *n.* A manure of dried night-soil mixed with charcoal etc. ; শুষ্কীকৃত পুরীষ ও কয়লা প্রভৃতির মিশ্রণে প্রস্তুত সারবিশেষ।

pouf, (*F.*), *n.* **1.** A high roll or pad of hair worn by women ; স্ত্রীলোকদিগের কবরী। **2.** (*Dress-making*) The part of a dress gathered up in a bunch ; পরিচ্ছদের গুচ্ছিত অংশ। **3.** A soft stuffed coach ; তুলাদি পূরিত ভরা নরম খট্টা।

poulp(e) (pôlp), *n.* (*Zool.*) Same as OCTOPOUS (which see).

poult (pōlt), *n.* A young chicken, partridge, grouse, etc. ; কুক্কুট, তিত্তির পক্ষী, প্রভৃতির শাবক।

poult-de-soie (*F.*), *n.* Fine corded silk ; দড়ীর মত পাকানো মিহি রেশমী সূতা।

poul'-têr-êr (pōl-), *n.* One who deals in poultry ; কুক্কুটপালক, কুক্কুট-ব্যবসায়ী, কৌক্কুটিক।

poul'-tice (pōl-tĭs), *n.* & *v. t.* A soft composition of meal, bran, etc. applied to sores or inflamed parts ; পুল্টিস, পিণ্ডি (ঠাকুরঃ), উপনাহ, উৎকারিকা (সুশ্রুঃ), লোপ্‌ত্রী (ভাবঃ প্রঃ)। ***Verb t.*** To apply a poultice to ; পুল্টিস লাগান।

poul'-trŷ (pōl-), *n.* Domestic fowls, such as cocks, hens, ducks, geese ; কুক্কুট, কুক্কুটী, হংস, হংসী, প্রভৃতি গৃহপালিত পক্ষী।

pounce (pow̄ns), *n., v. t.* & *i.* **1.** The claw or talon of a bird of prey ; শিকারী পক্ষীর নখর। **2.** Act of pouncing ; a sudden swoop ; ছোঁ ; অকস্মাৎ আপতন। ***Verb t.*** To fall on or seize with the claws and talons ; ছোঁ মারা। ***Verb i.*** **1.** To fall suddenly and seize with the claws, (with *on* or *upon*) ; ছোঁ মারিয়া ধরা। **2.** (*Fig.*) To seize eagerly or promptly (*upon*) ; as, to *pounce upon* a blunder ; (লক্ষণায়) খপ করিয়া ধরা। **3.** To spring, jump or come unexpectedly ; হঠাৎ লাফাইয়া পড়া, ঝুপ করিয়া পড়া, হঠাৎ আসা।

pounce (pow̄ns), *n.* & *v. t.* **1.** A fine powder for preparing a surface for writing to prevent ink fron spreading on paper

মসীশোষণ চূর্ণ। **2.** A powder as charcoal dust for making patterns through perforated designs; সচ্ছিদ্র নক্সার ভিতর দিয়া কোনরূপ নমুনা অপর কাগজে তোলার জন্য যে কয়লাচূর্ণ প্রভৃতি ব্যবহার হয়। ***Verb t.*** **1.** To rub smooth or finish with pounce, pumice, etc.; কয়লার চূর্ণ প্রভৃতি দ্বারা ঘষিয়া মসৃণ করা। **2.** To transfer, and trace or imprint as paper or a pattern with pounce; কয়লার চূর্ণ প্রভৃতির সাহায্যে সচ্ছিদ্র নক্সার প্রতিলিপি অপর কাগজে তোলা। **Pounce-box**—কয়লার চূর্ণ প্রভৃতি ছড়াইবার জন্য প্রকপ্রকার সচ্ছিদ্র ডালাবিশিষ্ট বাক্স।

poun'-cĕt-bŏx (pown-), *n.* (*Archaic*) A box with a perforated lid for holding perfumes; (অপ্রঃ) গন্ধদ্রব্য রাখার জন্য সচ্ছিদ্র ডালাযুক্ত বাক্স।

pound (pownd), *n.* & *v. i.* (*Abbr.* lb) **1.** A standard weight consisting of twelve ounces Troy or sixteen ounces avoirdupois; প্রায় অর্দ্ধসের ওজন, এক পাউণ্ড ওজন। **2.** A money of account consisting of twenty shillings; এক পাউণ্ড। ***Verb i.*** To test the weight of coins by weighing the number that ought to weigh a pound; যত সংখ্যক মুদ্রার ওজন এক পাউণ্ড হওয়া উচিত তাহা ওজন করিয়া ঐ মুদ্রাসমূহের ওজন পরীক্ষা করা। **Pound-cake**—যে পিষ্টকের প্রত্যেকটী প্রধান উপাদান এক পাউণ্ড ওজনের বা সমান ওজনের থাকে। **Pound-Scots**—(ইতিহাস) ১ শিলিং ৮ পেন্স। **Pound sterling** — Same as POUND, *n.* 2. **Five pound ten**—৫ পাউণ্ড ১০ শিলিং। **Penny-wise and pound-foolish**—See under PENNY. **To claim one's pound of flesh**—সাইলকের মত নিষ্ঠুরভাবে ঋণের টাকা দাবী করা। **To pay 10*s*. in the pound**—প্রতি এক পাউণ্ড ঋণের জন্য ১০ শিলিং দেওয়া।

pound (pownd), *n.* & *v. t.* **1.** An enclosure in which stray animals are confined or where distrained cattle or goods are kept until redeemed; খোঁয়াড়। **2.** (*Fig.*) A place of confinement; a trap; অবরোধস্থলী; ফাঁদ। **3.** (*Hunting*) A difficult position to get out of; (মৃগয়া) কুট-চক্র। **4.** A net-trap for fish, esp. the last compartment of a pound net; জালরচিত ফাঁদ, বিশেষতঃ ফাঁদ-জালের শেষ কোঠা। ***Verb t.*** **1.** To shut up or confine as in a pound; খোঁয়াড়ে বদ্ধ করা। **Pound net**—মাছ ধরার জন্য জালরচিত ফাঁদ, ফাঁদ-জাল। **To pound the field**—(*Hunting*) (Of a barrier) To be impassable; (of a rider) to clear a fence that others cannot; (বৃতি সম্বন্ধে) অনতিক্রমণীয় হওয়া; (অশ্বারোহীর পক্ষে) অপরে যে বৃতি লঙ্ঘন করিতে পারে নাই তাহা লঙ্ঘন করা।

pound (pownd), *v. t.* & *i.* **1.** To beat with a heavy instrument or fist; to pummel; কুট্টিত করা; নিষ্পিষ্ট করা। **2.** To bruise or break into fine particles with a pestle etc.; to pulverize; গুঁড়া করা; চূর্ণ করা। ***Verb i.*** **1.** To walk, run, ride, etc. heavily or vigorously; সতেজে দৌড়ান বা ঘোড়া চালান। **2.** To keep moving with a noise, as an engine; সশব্দে চলা। **3.** To strike heavy blows; to fire heavy shot, (with *at, on, away at*); সজোরে আঘাত করা; বৃহৎ গোলা নিক্ষেপ করা। **Pound'-er,** *n.* One who, or that which, pounds; a pestle; something for pounding in, as a mortar; কুট্টক; মুষল; খল, উদূখল। **To pound away**—To work vigorously; খুব তোড়ে কাজ করা।

pound'-āge (pownd-), *n.* **1.** A charge, commission or tax of so much per pound sterling; পাউণ্ড প্রতি কর বা শুল্ক। **2.** Payment rated by the weight of commodity; ওজন হিসাবে মূল্য, কর, প্রভৃতি নির্দ্ধারণ। **3.** The percentage of a total earnings of a business, paid as wages; কোন ব্যবসায়ের মোট আয়ের শতকরা যে অংশ বেতনস্বরূপ দেওয়া হয়।

pound'-āge (pownd-), *n.* A charge paid for the release of impounded cattle; খোঁয়াড়ের মাশুল।

pound'-ėr (pownd-), *n.* **1.** A gun as carrying so many pounds weight; as, a six-*pounder*; যে কামান হইতে পূর্ব্ববর্ত্তী সংখ্যাদ্বারা নির্দ্দিষ্ট ওজনের গোলা ছোড়া যায়। **2.** A person whose income, rent, etc. is so many pounds sterling; as, a ten-*pounder*; যে ব্যক্তির পূর্ব্ববর্ত্তী সংখ্যাদ্বারা নির্দ্দিষ্ট সংখ্যক পাউণ্ড আয়, রাজস্ব, প্রভৃতি। **3.** A bank-note, jewel, etc. worth so many pounds sterling; পূর্ব্ববর্ত্তী সংখ্যাদ্বারা নির্দ্দিষ্ট পাউণ্ডের ব্যাঙ্ক নোট, মণি, প্রভৃতি।

pour (pör), *v. t., i.* & *n.* **1.** To let flow out or in; ঢালা, প্রবাহিত করা। **2.** To send forth or out in profusion or great numbers; প্রচুর পরিমাণে নিঃসৃত করা। **3.** To utter or give forth; বর্ষণ করা। **4.** To give vent to, (a feeling etc.); প্রকাশ করা। ***Verb i.*** **1.** To flow, issue in a stream; to fall heavily; প্রবাহিত হওয়া, মুষলধারে বর্ষিত হওয়া। **2.** To come or go *in, out,* etc. abundantly; as, people or letters *pour in* from all quarters; প্রচুর পরিমাণে আসা বা নির্গত হওয়া, অজস্রভাবে নির্গত হওয়া। ***Noun.*** A heavy fall of rain; a downpour; ধারাবর্ষণ; প্রচুর বারিপাত। **Pour'-ing,** *adj.* Descending heavily; মুষলধারে পতনশীল। **It never rains but it pours**—(*Fig.*) Events, especially misfortunes always come together;

(লক্ষণায়) বিপদের পর বিপদ আসে। **To pour cold water on**—(*Fig.*) To discourage as a person, zeal, plan, etc.; (লক্ষণায়) কাহাকেও নিরুৎসাহ করা, হতোদ্যম করা। **To pour oil upon troubled waters**—(*Fig.*) To calm a disturbance with soothing words etc.; মিষ্ট কথা প্রভৃতি দ্বারা শান্তি-স্থাপন করা। **To pour out one's blood**—To give one's life; রক্ত দান করা, শোণিততর্পণ করা। **To pour out the vials of vituperations (or wrath)**—To give free vent to abusive language or angry feelings; কটূক্তি বর্ষণ করা, ঝাল ঝাড়া। **To pour water on the hands of**—To serve or minister; সেবা করা, পরিচর্য্যা করা।

pourboire, (*F.*), *n.* Drink-money; a gratuity; মদ্যপানের জন্য পয়সা; বকশিশ।

pourparler, (*F*), *n.* A conference or discussion preliminary to negotiation; পাকা কথাবার্ত্তা স্থির করার পূর্ব্বে বৈঠক বা আলোচনা, পূর্ব্বালোচনা।

pour'-point (pör-pōynt), **pŭr-** (pêr-), *ns.* (*Hist.*) A close-fitting quilted garment for males worn in the 14th century; (ইতিহাস) চতুর্দ্দশ শতাব্দীতে পুরুষদের পরিধেয় একপ্রকার তুলা-ভরা জামা।

poussette, (*F.*), *v. i.* & *n.* To swing round in couple as in a country dance; হাতে হাতে ধরিয়া পরস্পরকে প্রদক্ষিণ পূর্ব্বক নৃত্য করা, মণ্ডলনৃত্য করা। ***Noun.*** Act of poussetting; ঐরূপভাবে নর্ত্তন।

pou sto, (*Gk.*), *n.* A standing-place; a basis of operations; (from the reputed saying of Archimedes); দাঁড়াইবার স্থান; অবস্থান ভূমি।

pout (pow̄t), *v. t., i.* & *n.* **1.** To thrust out; as, to *pout* lips; ফুলান। ***Verb i.*** **1.** To thurst out lips in contempt or displeasure; hence, to look sullen; ঠোঁট ফুলান, গাল ফুলান; মুখভার দেখান। **2.** To shoot out or protrude; as, a *pouting* lip; ফুলান। ***Noun.*** A sullen protrusion of the lips; (*pl.*) a fit of sullenness; ঠোঁটফুলানি; অপ্রসন্নভাব, মুখভার। **Pout'-ing,** *adj.* **Pout'-ing-ly,** *adv.* **In the pouts**—Sulky; "Jack's *in the pouts*"; মুখভার করিয়া, ঠোঁট ফুলাইয়া, গাল ফুলাইয়া।

pout (pow̄t), *n.* (*Zool.*) A sea-fish of the cod-kind, called also *whiting-pout*, *eel-pout*, etc.; (জন্তুবিদ্যা) একপ্রকার সামুদ্রিক মৎস্য।

pout'-êr (pow̄t-), *n.* **1.** A kind of pigeon with a prominent breast; একপ্রকার কপোত—ইহারা গলদেশের থলি অতিমাত্রায় ফুলাইতে পারে। **2.** A kind of fish (also called *whiting-pout*); একপ্রকার মৎস্য।

pŏv'-êr-tȳ, *n.* **1.** State of being poor; দরিদ্রতা, দারিদ্র্য, দৈন্য, নির্ধনতা, নিঃস্বতা। **2.** Dearth; scarcity; inferiority; as, the *poverty* of ideas; অভাব; আকাল; নিকৃষ্টতা। **Poverty-stricken** — দারিদ্র্যোপহত, দারিদ্র্যগ্রস্ত, অভাবগ্রস্ত, দুঃস্থ।

pow̄'-dêr, *n.* & *v. t.* **1.** Any dry substance composed of minute particles; dust; চূর্ণ, গুড়া, ফাঁকি; ধুলি, রজঃ, রেণু, পাংশু, গুণ্ডক। **2.** Same as GUN-POWDER; বারুদ, অগ্নিচূর্ণ। **3.** A medicine in the form of powder; ঔষধচূর্ণ। **4.** A powdery cosmetic for the face, skin or hair; শরীরে, মুখে, বা চুলে মাখিবার জন্য পাউডার, মুখ, কেশ, প্রভৃতির কান্তিবর্দ্ধক সুগন্ধি চূর্ণ, পটবাস, পটবাসক, বাসযোগ। ***Verb t.*** **1.** To reduce to fine particles; to pulverize; চূর্ণ করা; গুঁড়া করা, উদ্ধূলিত করা। **2.** To sprinkle with powder; সুগন্ধিচূর্ণ ছিটান। **3.** To decorate as a surface with spots or small figures; নানারূপ দাগ বা ক্ষুদ্র চিত্র দ্বারা উপরিভাগ মণ্ডিত করা। **—i-ness,** *n.* **—y,** *adj.* Sprinkled with, or resembling, powder; চূর্ণাস্তৃত, উদ্ধূলিত, চূর্ণবৎ, চূর্ণসদৃশ। **Powder-blue** — ধোপা-খোলায় ব্যবহারের জন্য নীলকাচচূর্ণ; ঐরূপ কাচের নীলবর্ণ। **Powder box**—সুগন্ধিচূর্ণ রাখার জন্য কৌটা, পটবাসভাণ্ড। **Powder-down**—পক্ষীর শরীরের স্থানে স্থানে যে কোমল রোমগুচ্ছ থাকে। **Powder-flask, —horn**—বারুদের ভাণ্ড। **Powder-magazine**—বারুদখানা, বারুদঘর। **Powder-mill**—বারুদ প্রস্তুতের কল। **Powder-mine** — পাথরের পাহাড় প্রভৃতি ভাঙ্গিবার জন্য যে গর্ত্ত বা সুড়ঙ্গে বারুদ রাখা হয়; যুদ্ধ জাহাজে বারুদগর্ত্ত। **Powder monkey**—কামানের কাছে বারুদ নেওয়ার জন্য বালক, বারুদবাহী বালক। **Powder-puff** — পাউডার মাখিবার জন্য পক্ষীর কোমল পালকগুচ্ছ, গুচ্ছিতপালক। **Powder-room** — জাহাজের যে কামরায় বারুদ রাখা হয়, বারুদ কোঠা, অগ্নি-চূর্ণ-কক্ষ। **Food for powder**—See under FOOD. **Not worth powder and shot**—Not worth the cost or labour; পরিশ্রম এবং ব্যয়ের অনুরূপ লাভজনক নহে। **Smell of powder**—সামরিক অভিজ্ঞতা।

pow̄'-êr, *n.* **1.** Ability to act or do; physical or mental faculty; ক্ষমতা, সামর্থ্য; শক্তি। **2.** Force manifested in action; energy; vigour; বল; তেজ; পরাক্রম। **3.** Susceptibility; capacity; সংবেদনপ্রবণতা; কার্য্যক্ষমতা। **4.** Authority or influence; control; government; প্রভুত্ব; কর্তৃত্ব, প্রভাব; শাসন। **5.** Ascendency either personal, social or political; as, the party in *power*; প্রাধান্য। **6.** A person of authority or influence; an influential body or thing; as, the press has become a *power* in the State ; প্রভাবশালী ব্যক্তি ; শক্তিশালী সম্প্রদায়। **7.** A State having international influence ; আন্তর্জাতিক প্রভাববিশিষ্ট জাতি। **8.** A spirit ; a divinity ; as, celestial *powers* ; দেবযোনি ; দেবতা। **9.** (*Vulg.*) A large number or amount ; (ইতরভাষায়) বহুসংখ্যা বা বহুপরিমাণ। **10.** (*Mech.*) Capacity for exerting mechanical force ; as, an engine of twenty horse-*power* ; (যন্ত্র-বিজ্ঞান) যান্ত্রিকবল পরিচালনের শক্তি, যান্ত্রিক-শক্তি। **11.** An instrument by which mechanical energy is applied ; যে যন্ত্রের সাহায্যে যান্ত্রিক-শক্তি প্রয়োগ করা হয়। **12.** Mechanical energy as distinguished from hand-labour ; as, *power-mill* ; যান্ত্রিকশক্তি, যন্ত্রবল। **13.** (*Math.*) The result of the continued multiplication of a quantity by itself any given number of times ; as, a cube is the third *power* of a number ; (গণিত শাস্ত্র) কোন রাশি সেই রাশি-দ্বারা নির্দ্দিষ্টসংখ্যকবার গুণন করিলে যে ফল পাওয়া যায়, ঘাত (হিঃ কোঃ)। **14.** (*Optics*) The magnifying capacity of any lens or a set of lens ; (আলোক-বিজ্ঞান) কাচতাল বা কাচতালশ্রেণীর আয়তনবর্দ্ধিনী শক্তি। **15.** (*Law*) An authority, capacity, or right ; (আইন) ক্ষমতা, অধিকার। **16.** Delegated authority ; ন্যস্ত ক্ষমতা। **—ered,** *adj.* **—ful,** *adj.* Having great power or influence ; strong ; cogent ; intense ; as, a *powerful* man, mind, argument and odour, etc. ; ক্ষমতাশালী, প্রভাবশালী, শক্তিমান, শক্তিশালী, পরাক্রান্ত ; বলবান, শূর, ক্ষমতাসম্পন্ন, বলী ; প্রবল ; প্রগাঢ়। **—ful-ly,** *adv.* **—less,** *adj.* Devoid of power ; weak ; শক্তিহীন, অসমর্থ, নিষ্প্রভাব, শক্তিদরিদ্র, অক্ষম ; নির্ব্বল, বলহীন, শক্তিশূন্য, হীনশক্তি, হীনবল, দুর্ব্বল। **—less-ly,** *adv.* **—less ness,** *n.* **power-house** — যন্ত্রবলোৎপাদন গৃহ, তাড়িতশক্তি উৎপাদন গৃহ। **Power-loom**—বাষ্প, জলস্রোত, প্রভৃতির বলে চালিত তাঁত। **Great powers of Europe**—ইয়ুরোপের শক্তিপুঞ্জ [গ্রেট-ব্রিটেন, ফ্রান্স, অষ্ট্রিয়া, জর্ম্মণী, রুশিয়া ও ইতালী।] **In one's power**—Under one's control ; কাহারো কর্তৃত্বাধীনে। **Power of attorney**—আম্‌মোক্তারনামা। **The party now in power**—The party now in political ascendancy ; বর্ত্তমানে যে দলের হাতে দেশের শাসনকার্য্যের ভার ন্যস্ত আছে। **The powers that be**—The rulers or the constituted authorities for the time being ; বর্ত্তমান শাসনকর্তৃসম্প্রদায়।

pow'-wow, paw'-aw (pä-ä), *ns.* & *v. t.* **1.** A conjurer or medicine-man among the North-American-Indians ; উত্তর আমেরিকার প্রাচীন অধিবাসিগণের ভিতর ওঝা বা বাজীকর। **2.** A magic ceremony, conferences etc. of North-American Indians ; উত্তর আমেরিকার আদিম অধিবাসিগণের ঐন্দ্রজালিক ক্রিয়া বা বৈঠক। **3.** (*U. S.*) A congress or other meetings ; জাতীয় মহাসভা বা অন্য সভা।

pow-wow', *v. i.* & *t.* **1.** To practise sorcery or medicine among the Red Indians ; উত্তর আমেরিকার প্রাচীন অধিবাসীদের মধ্যে তান্ত্রিক ক্রিয়া প্রদর্শন করা। **2.** To hold the ceremony called powwow ; তান্ত্রিকক্রিয়া করা। **3.** (*U. S.*) To hold a meeting or conference ; to discuss ; to talk ; সভা আহ্বান করা ; আলোচনা করা ; কথাবার্ত্তা বলা। ***Verb t.*** To treat with magic ; তান্ত্রিক চিকিৎসা করা।

pŏx, *n.* A disease characterised by pustules or eruptions ; syphilis ; বসন্ত ; উপদংশ। **Chicken-pox**—জলবসন্ত। **Small pox**—বসন্তরোগ, শীতলা, মসূরিকা।

pozzuolana, pozzolana, (*Ital.*), *ns.* A loose rock of volcanic origin found near Pozzuoli, much used in the manufacture of hydraulic cement ; বিলাতী মাটী প্রস্তুতে ব্যবহৃত একপ্রকার আগ্নেয় প্রস্তর।

prăc'ti-că-ble (-bl), *adj.* **1.** That may be done or effected ; feasible ; as, a *practicable* method or aim ; সাধ্য, সুকর, সাধ্যায়ত্ত ; শক্য, সুখসাধ্য, সুগম, করণশক্য। **2.** Capable of being used or traversed ; as, a *practicable* road or passage ; ব্যবহার্য্য, পাদচারণযোগ্য, ভ্রমণযোগ্য। **3.** (*Theatre*) Capable of being used as real ; as, a *practicable* window or door ; (রঙ্গালয়) বাস্তববৎ ব্যবহারের উপযোগী। **—bil'-i-ty,** *n.* The state of being practical ; সাধ্যতা, সুকরতা, সুখসাধ্যতা। **—bly,** *adv.* **—ness** *n.*

prăc'-ti-căl, *adj.* **1.** Of, relating to, or manifested in, practice or action ; ব্যাবহারিক, ব্যবহারমূলক, ক্রিয়াত্মক (হিঃ কোঃ), প্রক্রিয়াত্মক (ঐ), ফলিত, ক্রিয়াসিদ্ধ। **2.** Available, or applicable, in practice ; useful ; প্রযোজ্য ; ব্যবহারজনক, ব্যবহার্য্য, ব্যবহারোচিত। **3.** Disposed to action ; engaged in practice ; as, a *practical* mind or farmer ; ব্যবহারনিষ্ঠ, ব্যবহারকুশল, কার্য্যনিষ্ঠ। **4.** Virtual ; as, *practical* control ; বাস্তবিক, প্রকৃত। **—cal'-i-ty,** *n.* **—ly,** *adv.* **1.** In a practical manner ; actually ; to all intents and purposes ; কার্য্যতঃ ; বাস্তবিকপক্ষে ; যথার্থ। **—ness,** *n.* **Practical joke**—কার্য্য দ্বারা ঠাট্টা বা পরিহাস [চাষার গদ্দি কাস্তের ঠোকর।] **Practical knowledge**—ব্যবহারিক জ্ঞান।

prăc'-tice (-tĭs), *n.* **1.** Frequent or customary action ; usage ; habit ; custom ; বৃত্তি ; জনব্যবহার, লোকব্যবহার ; অভ্যাস, রীতি, পদ্ধতি ; আচার, অনুষ্ঠান, আচরণ। **2.** (*Law*) The method of conducting and carrying on suits according to law; (আইন) আইনানুসারে মোকদ্দমা পরিচালনা। 3. Regular exercise for instruction or discipline; as, the troop called out for *practice*; অভ্যাস, শিক্ষা। 4. Professional work or business, as of a doctor, lawyer, etc.; ব্যবসায়, পসার। 5. Practical experience, skill, etc. acquired by systematic exercise; নিয়মিত অভ্যাস দ্বারা অর্জ্জিত নৈপুণ্যাদি। 6. (*Archaic*) Artful management; contrivance; artifice; (usually in a bad sense); (অপ্রঃ) সুকৌশলে পরিচালনা; কৌশল; কল। 7. (*Arith.*) A rule by which calculations are abridged; (পাটীগণিত) সাঙ্কেতিক নিয়ম। **In practice**—In action; practically; in the condition of being exercised so as to maintain skill etc.; কার্য্যতঃ; বাস্তবিকপক্ষে; অভ্যাস রাখার অবস্থায়, হাত রাখার অবস্থায়। **Out of practice**—Not in practice; অভ্যাস রাখে নাই — এরূপ অবস্থাপন্ন। **Practice makes perfect**—গাইতে গাইতে গায়ান, বাজাতে বাজাতে বায়ান, ছিঁড়ে ছিঁড়ে কাটুনী, ঝুরে ঝুরে রাঁধুনী। **To put in** or **into practice**—To carry out in practice; কার্য্যে প্রয়োগ করা।

prăc-ti′-cian (-shăn), *n.* One skilled by practice; a practitioner; যে ব্যক্তি পুনঃ পুনঃ অভ্যাস বা অনুশীলন দ্বারা পারদর্শিতা লাভ করিয়াছে; আইন অথবা চিকিৎসা ব্যবসায়ী।

prăc′-tise (-tĭs), *v. t.* & *i.* 1. To put into practice; to do habitually; কার্য্যে প্রয়োগ করা, কার্য্যে দেখান; সর্ব্বদা করা, সমাচরণ করা। 2. To exercise oneself in for improvement, instruction, etc.; অভ্যাস করা। 3. To exercise or pursue as a profession; as, to *practise* law or medicine; কোনরূপ ব্যবসায় করা। 4. To train or accustom by practice; বার বার অভ্যাস করাইয়া শিক্ষিত করা। ***Verb i.*** 1. To act or do something habitually; সর্ব্বদা করা। 2. To perform certain acts customarily for instruction, amusement, etc.; অভ্যাস করা। 3. To pursue any profession especially medicine or law; কোনরূপ ব্যবসায় করা। 4. (*Archaic*) To scheme or contrive; to use artifices; (অপ্রঃ) কৌশল করা, ফন্দি করা; কৌশল প্রয়োগ করা। **—tised,** *adj.* 1. Experienced; expert; as, a *practised* thief; অভিজ্ঞ; পাকা, সুদক্ষ। 2. Learned by practice; অভ্যস্ত। **To practise on** or **upon**—To impose upon; to take advantage of; ঠকান; সুযোগ গ্রহণ করা।

prăc-ti′-tion-ĕr, *n.* One engaged in any art or profession, especially medicine or law; কোন ব্যবসায়ে নিযুক্ত ব্যক্তি, বিশেষতঃ চিকিৎসাব্যবসায়ী, আইনব্যবসায়ী। **General practitioner**—See GENERAL.

præ co′-cial (prē-kō-shăl), *adj.* (Of birds) Whose young can feed themselves as soon as hatched; যে সকল পক্ষীর শাবক ডিম্ব হইতে ফুটিবামাত্রই নিজে আহার করিতে পারে তৎসম্বন্ধীয়।

præmunire, (*L.*), *n.* (*Eng. Law*) A writ charging the sheriff to summon a person committing the serious crime of asserting the Papal jurisdiction in England; ইংলণ্ডে পোপের প্রভাববিস্তারে সাহায্যকারী ব্যক্তিকে বিচারালয়ে আহ্বান করার জন্য নগরাধ্যক্ষকে (সেরিফকে) যে পরওয়ানা দেওয়া হয়।

prænomen, *n.* (*Rom. Antiq.*) A name prefixed to the family name; (as, *Caius* in Caius Julius Cæsar); (রোমীয় প্রত্নতত্ত্ব) পারিবারিক নামের পূর্ব্বে সংযোজিত শব্দ।

præ-pŏs′-tŏr (prē-), **pre—,** *ns.* (Public school) Same as MONITOR or PREFECT.

præ -tŏr (prē-), *n.* (*Rom. hist.*) A Roman consul or magistrate; (রোমের ইতিহাস) রোমের প্রধান সেনাপতি বা শাসনবিভাগের উচ্চ কর্ম্মচারিবিশেষ, রোমীয় দণ্ড-নায়ক। **-ship,** *n.* **—tō′-ri-al,** *adj.*

præ-tō′-ri-ăn (prē-), **prē—,** *adj.* & *n.* 1. Of, or relating to, the Roman prætor; রোমের প্রধান সেনাপতি বা শাসনবিভাগীয় উচ্চ কর্ম্মচারি-সম্বন্ধীয়। 2. Of, or pertaining to, the body-guard of a Roman general or emperor; রোমের সেনাপতি বা সম্রাটের শরীর-রক্ষি সৈন্যদল-সম্বন্ধীয়। ***Noun.*** 1. A person of prætorian rank; রোমের প্রধান সেনাপতি বা শাসনবিভাগের উচ্চকর্ম্মচারীর সমপদস্থ ব্যক্তি। 2. A soldier of the prætorian guard; রোমসম্রাট বা রোমের প্রধানসেনাপতির শরীর-রক্ষি সৈনিক। **Prætorian guard**—রোমের প্রধান সেনাপতি বা সম্রাটের শরীর-রক্ষি-সৈন্যদল।

prăg-măt′-ic, *adj.* 1. Of, or relating to, the affairs of a State; as, *pragmatic* sanction; রাষ্ট্রীয়। 2. Officious; meddlesome; উপযাচক, উপর-পড়া; অনধিকারচর্চ্চী, অনধিকারচর্চ্চক। 3. Conceited; dogmatic; গর্ব্বিত, দাম্ভিক; মতাভিমানী, স্বমতপ্রধান, আত্মমতাভিমানী। 4. Dealing with events so as to show their interconnection; "*Pragmatic* history"; ঘটনাবলীর মধ্যে সংযোগপ্রদর্শনের উদ্দেশ্যে তদালোচনা-কারী। 5. Practical; matter-of-fact; ব্যবহারিক; বাস্তব, প্রকৃত। 6. (*Philos.*) Of, or relating to, pragmatism; prescribing the means of attaining to happiness; (দর্শন-শাস্ত্র) কৃত্যসাধ্যকতাবাদ-সম্বন্ধীয়; সুখলাভের উপায়নির্দ্দেশক। **—i-cal,** *adj.* Same as PRAGMATIC, 2, 3, 5 & 6. **—i-cal -i-ty,** *n.* **—i-cal-ly,** *adv.* **Pragmatic history**—যে ইতিহাসে ঘটনা, কারণ ও পরিণাম স্পষ্টভাবে প্রদর্শিত হয়। **Pragmatic method**—কারণ, পরিণাম ও অবস্থাসম্পর্কে ঘটনা সমূহের আলোচনা।

Pragmatic sanction—Imperial decree issued as fundamental law, esp. that of Charles VI in 1724 settling Austrian succession; রাজার বিশেষ বিধান বা অনুশাসন; বিশেষতঃ জর্ম্মণ সম্রাট ৬ষ্ঠ চার্লস যে ব্যবস্থা দ্বারা (১৭২৪ খৃঃ অঃ) তদীয় কন্যা মেরিয়া থেরেসাকে অষ্ট্রিয়া, বোহেমিয়া ও হাঙ্গারী রাজ্যের সম্রাজ্ঞীপদে প্রতিষ্ঠিত করিবার ব্যবস্থা করেন।

prăg'-mă-tism, *n.* **1.** Officiousness; meddlesomeness; উপযাচকতা; অনধিকারচর্চ্চা। **2.** Matter-of-factness; practicality; বাস্তবতা; ব্যাবহারিকতা। **3.** (*Philos.*) A doctrine that estimates any assertion solely by its practical bearing upon human interests; (দর্শনশাস্ত্র) কৃত্যসাধ্যকতা বাদ (হিঃ কোঃ)। [দার্শনিক মত বিশেষ—এই মতাবলম্বিগণ তত্ত্ববিদ্যার মৌলিক তত্ত্বসমূহ গ্রহণ করিতে অস্বীকার করেন এবং যে সমস্ত সত্য স্পষ্টভাবে বাস্তবজগতের ব্যাপারের সহিত সম্পৃক্ত কেবল তৎসমূহেরই আলোচনা করিয়া থাকেন। এই মতানুসারে নানারূপ অবস্থার সংঘাতে কোন ভাবের সহিত কোন সত্য সম্বন্ধস্থাপন করে এবং ভাবসমূহ কেবল তখনই সত্য—যখন উহারা স্পষ্টরূপে দৃষ্টান্ত, প্রমাণিত, প্রতিষ্ঠাপিত, বা প্রতিপাদিত করা যাইতে পারে। See *Pragmatism* by Prof. William James.] **–tist**, *n.* **–tis'-tic**, *adj.*

prăg'-mă-tize, *v. t.* To consider or represent (something unreal) as real; to rationalize; (অবাস্তব বস্তু) বাস্তব বলিয়া গণ্য বা প্রদর্শন করা; যুক্তিমূলক ব্যাখ্যা করা।

prai'-rie (prā-rī), *n.* An extensive grassy tract of level or rolling land generally destitute of trees; বৃক্ষশূন্য বিস্তীর্ণ প্রান্তর, প্রেরী (হিঃ কোঃ), প্রেয়ারী (সাঃ পঃ)। **Prairie-chicken, –hen**—উত্তর আমেরিকার কুক্কুটজাতীয় পক্ষিবিশেষ। **Prairie-dog**—উত্তরআমেরিকার সংঘচারী দন্তুর জন্তুবিশেষ [ইহারা কুক্কুরের ন্যায় চীৎকার করিয়া থাকে বলিয়া এই নাম।]

Prairie dog.

praise (prāz), *v. t.* & *n.* **1.** To applaud; to commend; প্রশংসা করা, তারিফ করা; গুণকীর্ত্তন করা, গুণানুবাদ করা। **2.** To glorify, as in worship; as, to *praise* a god; মহিমাকীর্ত্তন করা, স্তব করা। ***Noun.*** **1.** Act of praising; state of being applauded; commendation; approbation; গুণকীর্ত্তন; স্তূয়মান অবস্থা; স্তুতি, সংস্তুতি, শ্লাঘা; স্তুতিবাদ, প্রশংসা, তারিফ, প্রশস্তি। **2.** Act of glorifying god etc.; worship especially by song; মহিমাকীর্ত্তন, গুণকীর্ত্তন; স্তবগান। **Praise'-ful**, *adj.* **Praise'-ful-ness**, *n.* **Praise'-wor-thy**, *adj.* Commendable; worthy of applause; প্রশংসনীয়, শ্লাঘ্য, স্তবনীয়, শ্লাঘনীয়; প্রশস্ত, প্রশস্য। **Praise'-wor-thi-ly**, *adv.* **Praise'-wor-thi-ness**, *n.*

pram, praam, *ns.* A flat-bottomed boat or lighter, used in Holland or in the Baltic; হলণ্ডদেশে অথবা ব্যাল্টিক সাগরে ব্যবহৃত একপ্রকার প্রশস্ত-তল নৌকা।

prăm, *n.* **1.** (*Colloq.*) Same as PERAMBULATOR, (baby carriage). **2.** A milkman's hand-cart; গোয়ালার ঠেলা-গাড়ী।

prance (prăns), *v. i., t.* & *n.* **1.** To spring or bound from the hind legs as a horse; পাছের পায়ের উপর ভর দিয়া লাফাইয়া লাফাইয়া চলা, বল্গিতগতিতে চলা। **2.** To ride on a prancing horse; to ride gaily or insolently; বল্গিতগামী অশ্ব আরোহণ করা; সোল্লাসে বা উদ্ধত ভাবে অশ্ব ছুটাইয়া চলা। **3.** (*Fig.*) To walk or move in an elated or arrogant manner; (লক্ষণায়) নাচিয়া নাচিয়া চলা, উল্লসিত হইয়া চলা, সাটোপে চলা। ***Verb t.*** To cause as a horse to prance; বল্গিতগতিতে চালান। ***Noun.*** Act of prancing; a prancing movement; বল্গিতগতিতে চলন; বল্গিত (বিনয়), সমুল্লাস (অঃ)।

prăn'-di-ăl, *adj.* (*Facet.*) Of, or relating to, dinner; (কৌতুকচ্ছলে) অপরাহ্ন-ভোজনসম্বন্ধীয়।

prank (prăngk), *n.* **1.** A wild frolic; a merry trick; a practical joke; ফষ্টিনষ্টি, রঙ্গঢঙ্গ; তামাসা, চাতুরী; কার্য্যদ্বারা ঠাট্টা। **2.** (*Fig.*) Erratic action as of a machinery etc.; (লক্ষণায়) কোন যন্ত্রের অব্যবস্থিত ক্রিয়া। **Prank'-ful, Prank'-ish**, *adjs.* **Pran'-ish-ness**, *n.* **To play pranks**—ফষ্টিনষ্টি করা, তামাসা করা।

prank (prăngk), *v. t.* & *i.* **1.** To dress or deck in a showy manner; জমকালো পোষাকে সজ্জিত করা, জমকালো ভাবে সাজান। **2.** To adorn; to spangle; ভূষিত করা, মণ্ডিত করা; চুমকি বসান। ***Verb i.*** To make a great show; to show oneself off; বেশভূষার বাহার দেখান; জাঁক বা আড়ম্বর দেখাইবার ভাবে প্রদর্শন করা।

prate, *v. i., t.* & *n.* To chatter; to be loquacious; to babble; বকা; আবলতাবল বকা; পচাল পাড়া। ***Verb t.*** To tell or say in a prating manner; বক বক করিয়া বলা। ***Noun.*** The act of prating; babble; বক বক করণ; বক বক, পচাল, আবলতাবল কথা। **Prat'-er**, *n.* **Prat'-ing**, *adj.*

prat'-in-cōle, *n.* A bird akin to the plover; তিত্তিরজাতীয় পক্ষিবিশেষ।

pratique, (*F.*), *n.* A licence granted to a ship to hold intercourse with a port after quarantine ; সংক্রামক রোগের প্রাদুর্ভাবপূর্ণ স্থান হইতে আসার দরুণ বন্দর প্রবেশে নিষিদ্ধ জাহাজকে বন্দরের সহিত যোগাযোগ রাখার জন্য যে অনুমতি দেওয়া হয়।

prăt'-tle (-l), *v. i., t.* & *n.* To talk freely and artlessly like a child ; বক বক করা, পচাল পাড়া। ***Verb t.*** To say thus ; আবল তাবল বকা। ***Noun.*** Trifling or childish talk ; babble ; ছেলেমি কথা ; বক বক, আবলতাবল। **—tler,** *n.* One who prattles esp. a child ; বকবককারী, বিশেষতঃ শিশু। **—tling,** *adj.* **Prattle box**—A prattler ; বক্‌বক্‌কারী, বাচাল।

prăv'-i-tў, *n.* **1.** (*Rare*) Depravity ; (ক্বচিদ্ ব্যবহৃত) ভ্রষ্টতা। **2.** (*Rare*) Badness or foulness (of food etc.) ; (খাদ্যপ্রভৃতির) নিকৃষ্টতা, অপকৃষ্টতা, দূষিতভাব (ক্বচিদ্‌ব্যবহৃত)।

prawn (prän), *n.* & *v. i.* A small edible crustacean like the shrimp ; চিংড়ী মাছ। [Syn. জলবৃশ্চিক, অগ্নি-মৎস্য, ইঞ্চাক (cf. ইঁচা used in Eastern districts), বৃহচ্ছল্ক, গঙ্গাটেয়, চিঙ্গট (অঃ), চিঙ্গটী (*ib.*), চিঙ্গড় (*ib.*), চিঙ্গড়ী (fem. cf. Beng. চিংড়ী)।] ***Verb i.*** To fish for prawns ; চিংড়ীমাছ ধরা। **Prawn'-ing,** *n.*

prăx'-is, *n.* **1.** Practice ; exercise of an art, science, etc. ; অভ্যাস ; অনুশীলন, চর্চ্চা। **2.** Habit ; custom ; অভ্যাস ; রীতিনীতি। **3.** (*Gram.*) An example or set of examples for practice ; (ব্যাকরণ) অনুশীলনী।

pray (prā), *v. t.* & *i.* **1.** To ask earnestly for ; to crave ; যাচ্‌ঞা করা ; প্রার্থনা করা। **2.** To beseech ; মিনতি করা। **3.** To address devoutly as God or other object of worship ; উপাসনা করা, প্রার্থনা করা, আরাধনা করা। **4.** To effect, accomplish or bring by praying ; "*Pray* them out of purgatory" ; প্রার্থনা দ্বারা সম্পাদন বা সংঘটন করা। ***Verb i.*** **1.** To beg ; to entreat ; প্রার্থনা করা ; মিনতি করা, অনুনয় করা। **2.** To offer prayer to God or a deity ; প্রার্থনা করা, দেবারাধনা করা। **Praying-machine, —mill, —wheel**—তিব্বত দেশবাসিদিগের প্রার্থনাচক্র।

prayer (prā-ĕr *or* prār), *n.* **1.** Act or practice of praying ; earnest entreaty ; supplication ; প্রার্থনা ; অনুনয় ; মিনতি। **2.** A solemn petition addressed to the Supreme Being ; প্রার্থনা, উপাসনা, বন্দনা। **3.** A form of divine service chiefly consisting of prayers ; as, family *prayers* ; প্রার্থনা। **4.** A thing prayed for ; the part of a petition to a public body, that specifies the thing desired ; প্রার্থিত বস্তু ; আবেদন পত্রের যে অংশে প্রার্থিত বিষয় উল্লেখ করা হয়। **Prayer'-ful,** *adj.* **Prayer'-ful-ly,** *adv.* **Prayer-book**—প্রার্থনাপুস্তক। **Prayer-meeting** — প্রার্থনাসভা। **Prayer-monger** — যে ব্যক্তি কলের পুতুলের মত প্রার্থনা করে। **Prayer-rug**—যে ক্ষুদ্র গালিচার উপর মুসলমানেরা নমাজের সময় জানু পাতিয়া উপবেশন করে। **Prayer-wheel**—Same as PRAYING-WHEEL (see under PRAY.)

pray'-ĕr (prā-), *n.* One who prays ; উপাসক, প্রার্থনাকারী।

preach (prēch), *v. i., t.* & *n.* **1.** To deliver a sermon or religious address ; to proclaim the Gospel ; ধর্ম্মোপদেশ প্রদান করা ; খৃষ্টের শিক্ষা বা উপদেশ প্রচার করা। **2.** To give serious moral advice, (*now usu. in an officious way*) ; as, you need not *preach* to me ; নৈতিক উপদেশ প্রদান করা, গায়ে পড়িয়া ধর্ম্ম-কথা কওয়া। ***Verb t.*** **1.** To publish in religious discourses ; to utter in a sermon ; "To *preach* the Gospel" ; প্রচার করা ; ধর্ম্মোপদেশ দেওয়া। **2.** To deliver or pronounce as a sermon ; ধর্ম্মোপদেশ প্রদান করা। **3.** To inculcate or advocate earnestly in public discourse ; "*Preach* patience to him" ; প্রচার করা। **4.** To bring or put into or out of some state by preaching ; "*Preach* me not out of my possessions" ; প্রচার করিয়া কোন অবস্থায় আনা বা কোন অবস্থা হইতে মুক্ত করা। ***Noun.*** (*Colloq.*) Preaching ; a sermon ; প্রচার ; ধর্ম্মোপদেশ। **Preach'-a-ble,** *adj.* **Preach'-er,** *n.* **1.** One who preaches or delivers a sermon ; প্রচারক, ধর্ম্মোপদেশক, ধর্ম্মোপদেষ্টা। **2.** An earnest exhorter ; উপদেষ্টা। **Preach'-er-ship,** *n.* **Preach'-i-ness,** *n.* **Preach'-ment,** *n.* A sermon (*contempt.*) ; ধর্ম্মকথা (অবজ্ঞাচ্ছলে)। **Preach'-y.** *adj.* Fond of, or given to, preaching ; characterized by a preaching-style ; প্রচারপ্রিয় ; প্রচারাত্মক। **To preach down**—To disparage or humiliate by preaching ; বিরুদ্ধে বক্তৃতা করিয়া কাহারো মর্য্যাদা হানি করা। **To preach up** — To commend ; to extol ; as, to *preach up* equality ; প্রশংসা করা ; বাড়াইয়া তোলা।

preach'-i-fў (prēch-), *v. i.* To preach tediously ; to weary with lengthy advice ; বিরক্তিজনক ভাবে প্রচার করা ; সুদীর্ঘ উপদেশ দান করিয়া বিরক্তি জন্মান।

prē-ăd'-ăm-īte, *n.* & *adj.* An inhabitant of the earth before Adam ; আদমের পূর্ব্ববর্ত্তী লোক। ***Adj.*** Existing before the time of Adam ; আদমের পূর্ব্বে বর্ত্তমান।

prē'-ăm-ble (-bl), *n.* & *v. i.* **1.** The introduction of a speech, writing, etc. ; প্রস্তাবনা, মুখবন্ধ, ভূমিকা। **2.** The introduction of a statute, deed, etc. ; আইন, দলীল, প্রভৃতির হেতুবাদ। ***Verb i.*** To make a preamble ; to preface ; ভূমিকা করা ; হেতুবাদ দেওয়া।

prē-ăr-rānge′, *v. t.* To arrange beforehand ; পূর্ব্বে বন্দোবস্ত করা। **—ment**, *n.*

prē-au′-di-ence (-ä-dĭ-ĕns), *n.* The right as of a lawyer, to be heard before another ; উকীল প্রভৃতির অন্যের পূর্ব্বে স্বীয় বক্তব্য বলিবার অধিকার।

prĕb′-ĕnd, *n.* **1.** The stipend granted to a canon of a cathedral or collegiate church out of its estate ; the land or tithe from which this stipend comes ; কোন মহাধর্ম্মমন্দিরের সম্পত্তি হইতে ঐ মন্দিরের ভারপ্রাপ্ত যাজককে যে বৃত্তি দেওয়া হয় ; যে ভূমি অথবা দশমাংশ-কর হইতে ঐ বৃত্তি দেওয়া হয়। **2.** Same as PREBENDARY.

prĕb′-ĕn-dă-rȳ, *n.* A resident clergyman enjoying a prebend ; মহাধর্ম্মমন্দিরের মুখ্যধর্ম্মাধ্যক্ষ। **Prebendary-stall**—মহাধর্ম্মমন্দিরের মুখ্যধর্ম্মাধ্যক্ষের আসন ; (লক্ষণায়) রাজকীয় পদ।

prē-cā′-ri-ous (-ŭs), *adj.* **1.** Depending upon the will of another ; uncertain ; as, *precarious* tenure, privileges, etc. ; অন্যের ইচ্ছাধীন, অন্যাধীন, পরাধীন ; অনিশ্চিত, স্থিতি-সংশয়ী, অস্থির। **2.** Unfounded ; taken for granted ; as, a *precarious* assumption ; ভিত্তিহীন, অমূলক ; বিনাপ্রমাণে স্বীকৃত। **3.** Dependent on chance ; dangerously uncertain ; as, a *precarious* state of health ; perilous ; as, the *precarious* life of a fisherman ; দৈবায়ত্ত, দৈবাধীন ; সংশয়াপন্ন, সংশয়াবহ ; বিপজ্জনক, বিপৎসঙ্কুল। **—ly**, *adv.* **—ness**, *n.*

prĕc′-ă-tō-rȳ, *adj.* (*Gram.*) Of, or denoting, entreaty ; supplicatory ; (ব্যাকরণ) মিনতিসূচক, অনুনয়সূচক, অনুরোধসূচক ; প্রার্থনাত্মক। **—tive**, *adj.* **Precatory trust**—চরমপত্রের যে অনুরোধসূচক বাক্য অবশ্যপালনীয় হইয়া থাকে। **Precatory words**—(চরমপত্রে) অনুরোধসূচক বাক্য।

prē-cau′-tion (-kä-), *n.* **1.** Previous caution or care ; prudent foresight ; সাবধানতা ; বিজ্ঞোচিত পরিণামদর্শিতা। **2.** A measure taken beforehand to prevent evil or secure good result ; as, to take *precautions* against accidents ; সাবধানতা, অনিষ্টনিবারণোপায়। **—a-ry**, *adj.*

prē-cede′ (-sēd), *v. t. & i.* **1.** To go before in importance, rank or the like ; গুরুত্ব, পদবী, প্রভৃতিতে অগ্রবর্ত্তী হওয়া। **2.** To go or come before in time or order ; অগ্রে যাওয়া বা আসা। **3.** To go in front of ; as, to be *preceded* by a guide ; সম্মুখে যাওয়া। **4.** To cause to be preceded ; to introduce ; পূর্ব্ববর্ত্তী করা, অগ্রবর্ত্তী করা ; প্রবর্ত্তিত করা। ***Verb i.*** To go or come before in time or place ; অগ্রে আসা বা যাওয়া, পূর্ব্ববর্ত্তী হওয়া।

prē-cēd′-ence (-ĕns), **—ĕn-cȳ**, (*Rare*) *ns.* **1.** The act or state of going before ; priority ; পূর্ব্ববর্ত্তিতা, পুরোগমন, অগ্রগমন, পুরোগতি ; পূর্ব্বতা। **2.** The state of being before in rank ; the right to a more honourable place in public ceremonies etc. ; superiority ; higher position ; as, to take *precedence* of (to be recognised as superior to) all others ; অগ্রগণ্যতা, অগ্রমানার্হতা ; রাজকীয় উৎসবাদিতে অধিকতর সম্মানজনক স্থান গ্রহণের অধিকার ; শ্রেষ্ঠতা ; উচ্চতর পদবী। **Order of precedence**—রাজকীয় শোভাযাত্রায় কৌলীন্য বা পদমর্য্যাদানুসারে ব্যক্তিগণ যে স্থান অধিকার করে। **To take precedence of**—To have a superior position to ; অগ্রগণ্য হওয়া, শ্রেষ্ঠতর পদবীর হওয়া।

prĕc′-ē-dĕnt, *n.* A past action which may serve as an example or rule in the future ; as, it is without a *precedent* ; নজীর, পূর্ব্বদৃষ্টান্ত। **2.** (*Law*) A decision or procedure etc. serving as a rule for future determinations in similar cases ; (আইন) নজীর।

prē-cēd′-ĕnt, *adj.* (*Now rare*) Going before in time, order or rank ; as, a condition *precedent* ; অগ্রগণ্য, অগ্রগামী, পূর্ব্বগামী, পূর্ব্ববর্ত্তী। **—ly**, *adv.*

prĕc′-ē-dĕnt-ĕd, *adj.* Having a precedent ; supported by a precedent ; নজীরবিশিষ্ট ; নজীরদ্বারা সমর্থিত।

prē-cĕnt′, *v. i. & t.* To act as a precentor ; মহামন্দিরের বৃন্দগায়কগণের নেতার কাজ করা। ***Verb t.*** To lead in singing as a psalm etc. ; বৃন্দগায়কগণের নায়কের কাজ করা।

prē-cĕn′-tor (-tēr), *n.* The leader of the choir in a cathedral ; a minor canon or chaplain ; বৃন্দগায়কশ্রেণীর মুখ্য গায়ক, অগ্রগায়ক ; সামান্য যাজক। **—ship**, **—trix**, *ns.*

prē′-cĕpt, *n.* **1.** Moral instruction ; as, example is better than *precept* ; নৈতিক উপদেশ। **2.** An injunction regarding moral conduct ; a maxim ; নৈতিক অনুশাসন ; নীতি, নীতিবাক্য। **3.** A divine command ; দেবাদেশ, ঈশ্বরাদেশ। **4.** (*Law*) An order, warrant or writ ; (আইন) হুকুমনামা, পরওয়ানা। **—cep′-tive**, *adj.* Didactic ; instructive ; as, *preceptive* parts of the Bible ; উপদেশগর্ভ ; উপদেশাত্মক।

prē-cĕp′-tor (-tēr), *n.* The head of a school ; a teacher ; instructor ; বিদ্যালয়ের প্রধান শিক্ষক ; আচার্য্য, অধ্যাপক (কেভিঃ), শিক্ষক ; উপদেষ্টা। **—ship**, **—tress**, *ns.* **—to′-ri-al**, *adj.*

prē-cĕp′-tō-rȳ, *n.* (*Hist.*) Subordinate religious house or community of the Knights Templars ; the estate or buildings belonging to this ; (ইতিহাস) জেরুজেলেমযাত্রী খৃষ্টানগণের রক্ষার্থ প্রতিষ্ঠিত খৃষ্টীয় ধর্ম্মভ্রাতৃমণ্ডলীর উপসম্প্রদায়

বা উহাদের প্রতিষ্ঠান ; উক্ত উপসম্প্রদায়ের সম্পত্তি বা গৃহ।

prē-ces′-sion (-sŏ-), *n.* The act of going before ; precedence ; অগ্রগমন; অগ্রগতি। **—al**, *adj.* **Amount of precession** — অয়নভাগ, অয়নাংশ [cf. অয়নাংশ-শোধিত লগ্নমান।] **Planetary precession** — গ্রহসম্বন্ধী অয়নাংশ (হিঃ কোঃ)। **Precession of the equinoxes**—রাশিচক্রের উপর অয়নান্ত বিন্দুদ্বয়ের পশ্চিমদিকে মৃদুগতি—যাহার ফলে প্রতি পরবর্ত্তী নাক্ষত্রিক বৎসরে পূর্ব্ব বৎসর অপেক্ষা কতকটা শীঘ্র দিবামান ও রাত্রিমাণ সমান হয়, অয়নচলন (গোলঃ), ক্রান্তিপাতগতি (তট্টীকা), অয়নগতি (সাঃ পঃ)। [হিন্দুমতে পৃথিবীর মধ্য-রেখা ও ভ-চক্রের মধ্য-রেখা সমসূত্রপাতে যে স্থানে মিলিত হইয়াছে, ঐ স্থানের নাম ক্রান্তিপাত। ঐ ক্রান্তিপাত হইতে পূর্ব্বপশ্চিমে বিস্তৃত যে রেখা কল্পিত হয়, উহার নাম বিষুব রেখা। সূর্য্য ঐ রেখার ২৭ অংশ উত্তরে ও ২৭ অংশ দক্ষিণে যে গতিতে গমন করে, উহার নাম অয়নগতি। বিষুবরেখা হইতে সূর্য্যের ২৭ অংশ একবার যাতায়াতে ৫৪ অংশ অতিক্রম করিতে হয়। এই ৫৪ অংশ অতিক্রমে সূর্য্যের ৩৬০০ বৎসর লাগে। অতএব ১ অংশ যাইতে ৬৬ বৎসর ৮ মাস লাগে (আধুনিক মতে ৭২ বৎসর)। ঐ এক এক অংশকেই অয়নাংশ কহে। এক এক অয়নাংশের পরিবর্ত্তনে বৎসরে যে দুই দিবস দিবা ও রাত্রি সমান হইয়া থাকে—তাহার এক এক দিন ব্যত্যয় হয়। যে বৎসর অয়নাংশ শূন্য সেই বৎসর ৩০শে চৈত্র ও ৩০শে আশ্বিন দিবামান ও রাত্রিমাণ সমান হইয়া থাকে; এবং অয়নাংশের এক এক অংশ বৃদ্ধির সঙ্গে দিবারাত্র এক এক দিন পূর্ব্বে সমান হয়। বর্ত্তমানে ২২শ অয়নাংশ চলিতেছে বলিয়া ৯ই চৈত্র ও ৯ই আশ্বিন দিবারাত্র সমান হইতেছে। নিম্নে অয়নাংশ আনয়ন সম্বন্ধে একটী প্রাচীন শ্লোক উদ্ধৃত হইল :—
শাকমেবাব্ধিবেদোনং দ্বিঃকৃত্বা দশভির্হরেৎ।
লব্ধং হীনঞ্চ তত্রৈব ষষ্ঠ্যাপ্তাঙ্কায়নাংশকাঃ
জাতকার্ণব। অর্থাৎ শকাব্দার অঙ্ক হইতে ৪২১ বিয়োগ করিয়া যে অঙ্ক পাওয়া যাইবে তাহা দুই স্থানে রাখিতে হইবে। তৎপর এক স্থানের সংখ্যাকে ১০ দ্বারা ভাগ করতঃ সেই ভাগলব্ধ সংখ্যাকে ২য় স্থানে স্থাপিত সংখ্যা হইতে বিয়োগ করিয়া বিয়োগ ফলকে ৬০ দ্বারা ভাগ করিলে যাহা হইবে—তাহাই সেই শকাব্দার অয়নাংশ।]

prē-Chris′-tian, *adj.* Before Christ or Christianity ; খৃষ্টপূর্ব্ববর্ত্তী, খৃষ্টধর্ম্ম-পূর্ব্ববর্ত্তী।

prē-cinct′ (-singt), *n.* **1.** The inclosure limited by walls or other boundaries of a place or building ; as, the *precincts* of a church ; (*pl.*) the environs ; চতুঃপার্শ্ব ; চতুঃপার্শ্ববর্ত্তী স্থানসমূহ। **2.** A boundary or limit ; সীমা, প্রান্ত। **3.** A minor territorial or jurisdictional division ; ক্ষুদ্র বিভাগ বা এলেকা।

prĕ′-cious (-shŭs), *adj.* & *adv.* **1.** Of great price or value ; costly ; as, a *precious* metal ; বহুমূল্য, মূল্যবান ; মহার্ঘ, মহামূল্য। **2.** Of great worth ; much esteemed ; dear ; as, *precious* recollections ; অমূল্য ; অতি আদরের ; প্রিয়, দয়িত। **3.** Fastidious ; over-refined in language, workmanship, etc. ; খুঁতখুঁতে, দুস্তোষ ; অতি-মার্জ্জিত। **4.** (*Colloq.*) Egregious ; perfect, (as *intensive*) ; as, a *precious* fool ; (চলিত ভাষায়) বিষম, পুরা ; ডাহা। ***Adv.*** (*Colloq.*) Extremely (as *intensive*) ; as, he took *precious* good care of that : (চলিত ভাষায়) অতিশয়, অতিমাত্রায়। **—ci-os′-i-ty**, *n.* **—ly**, *adv.* **—ness**, *n.* **Precious metal**—স্বর্ণ, রৌপ্য, প্ল্যাটিনাম, প্রভৃতি মূল্যবান ধাতু। **Precious stone**—মূল্যবান্ প্রস্তর, মণি, রত্ন।

prĕc′-i-pice (-pis), *n.* A headlong declivity ; a steep or overhanging cliff, mountain, etc. ; সরলোন্নত পর্ব্বতপার্শ্ব, খাড়া পাহাড়, অতট, গিরিপ্রপাত, প্রপাত।

prē-cip′-i-tate, *n.* **1.** (*Chem.*) A part of a solution, falling or causing to fall to the bottom ; (রসায়ন-শাস্ত্র) পদার্থের যে অংশ চূর্ণ অবস্থায় তলে পড়ে বা অন্য কোন অংশকে তলে ফেলে, তলছাট, অধঃপতিত (হিঃ কোঃ), অধঃপতন (ঐ), অবক্ষেপণ (ঐ)। **2.** (*Phys.*) Moisture condensed from vapour by cooling and deposited, *e. g.* rain, dew, etc. ; শৈত্য-জনিত ঘনীভূত বাষ্প, যথা—বৃষ্টি, শিশির, প্রভৃতি। **—ta-bil′-i-ty**, *n.* **—ta-ble**, *adj.* **—tant**, *n.* (*Chem.*) A substance which causes the formation of a precipitate ; (রসায়ন-শাস্ত্র) যে বস্তুর সাহায্যে তরলপদার্থের অংশ-বিশেষ চূর্ণাকারে পরিণত হইয়া তলে পতিত হয় অধক্ষেপক, অবক্ষেপক (ঐ)।

prē-cip′-i-tate, *adj.* **1.** Overhasty ; rash ; inconsiderate ; as, the king was too *precipitate* in declaring war ; অতিব্যস্ত ; হঠকারী ; অবিবেচক, অবিমৃষ্যকারী। **2.** Falling or rushing headlong ; rashly hurried ; as, *precipitate* flight ; সবেগে ধাবমান বা পতনশীল ; দিগ্‌বিদিগ্-জ্ঞানশূন্য। **—ly**, *adv.* Headlong ; with rash haste ; উদ্দামবেগে ; দিগ্‌বিদিগ্‌জ্ঞানশূন্যভাবে। **—ness**, *n.* **—tance**, **—tan-cy**, *ns.*

prē-cip′-i-tate, *v. t.* **1.** To hurl or throw headlong, (*lit.* & *fig.*) ; উদ্দামবেগে নিক্ষেপ করা (শব্দানুযায়ী ও লক্ষণায়)। **2.** To urge on with eager haste ; as, to *precipitate* a flight ; to hasten the occurrence of ; as, it served to *precipitate* his ruin ; ত্বরান্বিত করা ; দ্রুততর করা। **3.** (*Chem.*) To cause to fall to the bottom, as a substance in solution ; (রসায়ন-শাস্ত্র) তলে ফেলা, তলানি ফেলা, তলছাট ফেলা। **4.** (*Phys.*) To condense and so cause to fall as rain etc. ; as, to *precipitate* moisture ; ঘনীভূত করিয়া বৃষ্টি প্রভৃতি রূপে পাতিত করা।

—ta'-tion, *n.* The act of precipitating ; অধঃপতন (হিঃ কোঃ), অবক্ষেপ (ঐ)। —ta-tor, *n.*

prē-cip'-i-tous (-tŭs), *adj.* 1. Like a precipice ; very steep ; গিরিপ্রপাতবৎ ; খাড়া, সরলোন্নত, অবসর্পী, পাতুক। 2. (*Rare*) Same as PRECIPITATE. —ly, *adv.* —ness, *n.*

precis (prā-sē), (*F.*), *n.* An abridged statement ; summary ; abstract ; সংক্ষিপ্ত উক্তি ; সারমর্ম ; চুম্বক।

prē-cīse', *adj.* 1. Exactly stated or defined ; as, the *precise* rules of morality ; সুব্যক্ত, সুনির্দ্দিষ্ট, সুস্পষ্ট, নামনির্দ্দেশাত্মক, বস্তুনির্দ্দেশাত্মক। 2. Scrupulous in observance of rules etc. ; overnice ; punctilious ; "He was over *precise* in promise-keeping" ; কঠোর নিয়মনিষ্ঠ ; সূক্ষ্মবিচারী ; সূক্ষ্মাবধানী। 3. Minutely exact ; identical ; as, the *precise* moment of departure ; সঠিক, যথার্থ ; অভিন্ন। —ly, *adv.* 1. In a precise manner ; exactly ; সঠিকভাবে ; সূক্ষ্মভাবে। 2. (In emphatic or formal assent) Quite so ; তাইতো, ঠিক তাই। —ness, *n.*

prē-cī'-sian (-shăn), *n.* One rigidly exact in observing rules or forms ; one scrupulous in religious observance ; সূক্ষ্মভাবে নিয়ম পালনকারী ; সূক্ষ্মাচারনিষ্ঠ। —ism, *n.*

prē-cī'-sion, *n.* The state of being precise ; accuracy ; সঠিকতা ; যথার্থতা, নির্ভুলতা। —ist, *n.* **Arm of precision**—লক্ষ্যসহায়ক কৌশলাদিসমন্বিত আগ্নেয়াস্ত্র।

prē-clăs'-si-căl, *adj.* Prior to the classical age, (esp. of Gk. and Rom. literature) ; সাহিত্য বা কলায় সমৃদ্ধিযুগের পূর্ব্ববর্ত্তী (বিশেষতঃ গ্রীক ও রোমান সাহিত্যের)।

prē-clūde', *v. t.* 1. To hinder ; to prevent ; বাধা দেওয়া ; প্রতিরোধ করা। 2. To shut out or obviate by anticipation ; to render ineffectual ; as, so as to *preclude* all doubt ; পূর্ব্ব হইতে ব্যবস্থা করা, রোধ বা নিবারণ করা ; নিষ্ফল করা, অকার্য্যকর করা। —clu'-sive, *adj.*

prē-cō'-cious (-shŭs), *adj.* 1. Flowering or fruiting early ; as, a *precocious* plant ; অল্পকালের মধ্যে পুষ্প বা ফলপ্রসূ, কালপূর্ব্বপুষ্পী, কালপূর্ব্বফলী। 2. Having the mind developed very early, or too early ; forward ; as, a *precocious* child ; pertaining to, or indicative of, premature development ; as, *precocious* faculties, acts, etc. ; অকালপরিণত, অকালপক্ব, অপূর্ণকালপক্ব ; ইঁচড়ে পাকা, অকালপ্রৌঢ়, বালপ্রৌঢ়, জ্যাঠা ; অকালপরিণত সম্বন্ধীয়, অকালপরিণতিসূচক। —coc'-i-ty, *n.* The quality of being precocious ; অকালপক্বতা, পাকামি, বালপ্রৌঢ়ি। —ly, *adv.* —ness, *n.*

prē-cŏg-nī'-tion, *n.* 1. Previous knowledge ; পূর্ব্বজ্ঞান, পূর্ব্ববোধ। 2. (Scotch Law) A preliminary examination of witnesses as to whether there is ground for trial ; (স্কটলণ্ডের আইন) মোকদ্দমা করিবার যথেষ্ট হেতু আছে কিনা তাহা নির্দ্ধারণের জন্য সাক্ষীদিগের প্রাথমিক জবানবন্দী।

prē-cŏn-ceive' (-sēv), *v. t.* To form a conception of beforehand ; to anticipate in thought ; পূর্ব্বে কল্পনা করা, পূর্ব্বে চিন্তা করা ; পূর্ব্বে আশা করা। —cep'-tion, *n.*

prē-cŏn'-cĕrt, *v. t.* To arrange beforehand ; পূর্ব্বে বন্দোবস্ত করা।

prē-cŏn-dī'-tion, *n.* A previous condition ; a condition that must be fulfilled beforehand ; পূর্ব্ববর্ত্তী সর্ত্ত ; যে সর্ত্ত পূর্ব্বে পূরণ করিতে হইবে।

prē'-cō-nīze, *v. t.* 1. To proclaim publicly ; to praise publicly ; প্রকাশ্যে ঘোষণা করা ; সর্ব্বসমক্ষে প্রশংসা করা। 2. To summon publicly or by name ; প্রকাশ্যে আহ্বান করা, নাম ডাকিয়া আহ্বান করা। 3. (*R. C. Ch.*, of the Pope) To approve publicly the appointment of, as a Bishop ; (রোমান ক্যাথলিক ধর্ম্মসংঘে পোপসম্পর্কে) ধর্ম্মাধ্যক্ষ প্রভৃতির নিয়োগ প্রকাশ্যভাবে অনুমোদন করা। —ni-za'-tion, *n.*

prē-con'-quer-or (-kŏng-kêr-êr), *n.* Anterior to William the Conqueror ; রাজা উইলিয়েমের পূর্ব্ববর্ত্তী। —quest, *n.* Anterior to the Norman conquest ; নরম্যানগণকর্ত্তৃক ইংলণ্ডবিজয়ের পূর্ব্ববর্ত্তী।

prē-cŏr'-dī-ăl, *adj.* (*Anat.*) Situated in front of the heart ; (শারীরসংস্থানবিদ্যা) হৃৎপিণ্ডের সম্মুখস্থ।

prē-cŏs'-tăl, *adj.* In front of the ribs ; পশুর্কার সম্মুখস্থ।

prē-cur'-sor (-kêr-sêr), *n.* 1. A forerunner ; a harbinger ; অগ্রগামী, সংবাদবাহক ; অগ্রদূত, প্রাগ্‌গামী। 2. One who precedes in some course or office ; "Cowper was a *precursor* of Wordsworth" ; পূর্ব্বগ, প্রাগ্‌বর্ত্তী, অগ্রগ। —sive, *adj.* —so-ry, *adj.* Preceding as harbinger ; forerunning ; preliminary ; as, the *precursory* symptoms of fever ; অগ্রনায়করূপী ; অগ্রগামী ; প্রাথমিক, প্রাগ্‌ভাবী, পূর্ব্বসূচক।

prē-dā'-cious (-shŭs), *adj.* 1. Living by prey ; predatory, as animals ; হিংস্র ; শিকারজীবী। 2. Relating to such animals ; as, *predacious* instincts ; হিংস্র। —dac'-i-ty, *n.*

prē-date', *v. t.* 1. To antedate as a deed etc. ; পূর্ব্বের তারিখ দেওয়া। 2. To precede in date ; পূর্ব্ব তারিখের হওয়া।

prĕd'-ā-tō-rȳ, *adj.* 1. Of, relating to, or given to, plunder or robbery ; pillaging ; লুণ্ঠন-সম্বন্ধীয়, লুণ্ঠনাত্মক ; লুণ্ঠনপর, লুণ্ঠনকারী। 2. Living by preying on other animals ; শিকারজীবী, হিংস্রক।

prē-dē-cease' (-sēs), *v. t.* & *n.* To die before (a person) ; অগ্রে মৃত্যু হওয়া। ***Noun.*** The death of one before another ; অপর ব্যক্তির অগ্রে মৃত্যু, অগ্রমৃত্যু।

prĕd-ē-cĕs′-sor (-ĕr), *n.* **1.** One who has preceded another in any office or position ; কোন পদের পুর্ব্বাধিষ্ঠিত ব্যক্তি, পুর্ব্ববর্ত্তী ব্যক্তি। **2.** A thing that precedes another ; পুর্ব্ববর্ত্তী বস্তু, পুর্ব্বগ। **3.** A forefather; পুর্ব্বপিতামহ, পুর্ব্বপুরুষ।

prē-dĕl′-la (-ă), *n.* **1.** An altar-step ; a painting or sculpture on the face of this ; বেদীর সোপান ; বেদীর সোপানোপরি চিত্রিত বা ক্ষোদিত আলেখ্য বা মূর্ত্তি। **2.** The raised shelf at the back of an altar ; a painting or sculpture on this; বেদীর পশ্চাতে উত্থাপিত তাক ; ঐ তাকের উপর চিত্রিত বা ক্ষোদিত চিত্র বা মূর্ত্তি।

prē-dĕs′-ĭg-nāte, *v. t.* & *adj.* To preordain ; পুর্ব্বনির্দ্দিষ্ট করা। ***Adj.*** Predetermined ; পরিমিতপুর্ব্ব (হিঃ কোঃ), নিশ্চিতপুর্ব্ব (ঐ)। **—na′-tion,** ***n.***

prē-dĕs-tĭ-nā′-rĭ-ăn, *n.* & *adj.* One who holds the doctrine of predestination ; অদৃষ্টবাদী, দৈববাদী, দৈবপ্রমাণক, প্রারব্ধবাদী। ***Adj.*** Of, or relating to, predestination ; অদৃষ্টবাদসম্বন্ধীয়। **—ism,** ***n.*** The doctrine of the predestinarian ; নিয়তিবাদ (হিঃ কোঃ), দৈববাদ (ঐ)।

prē-dĕs′-tĭ-nāte, *v. t.* **1.** To determine previously ; পুর্ব্বে নিরূপণ করা, পুর্ব্বে নির্দ্দিষ্ট করা। **2.** (Of God) To preordain (a person) to salvation, any fate, etc. ; (ঈশ্বর সম্পর্কে) পুর্ব্ব হইতে মুক্তি প্রভৃতির জন্য নিরূপিত করা।

prē-dĕs′-tĭ-nāte, *adj.* Foreordained ; fated ; পুর্ব্বনিরূপিত, পুর্ব্বনির্দ্দিষ্ট ; নিয়তিনির্দ্দিষ্ট।

prē-dĕs-tĭ-nā′-tion, *n.* **1.** Act of predestinating or the state of being predestinated ; পুর্ব্বনিরূপণ, প্রাক্তন-বিধি, বিধির নির্ব্বন্ধ, পুর্ব্বনিরূপণ, অগ্রনিরূপণ। **2.** (*Theol.*) The doctrine that God has from all eternity unalterably fixed whatever is to happen, especially the eternal happiness or misery of men ; (খৃষ্টীয় ধর্ম্মশাস্ত্র) পরমেশ্বর পুর্ব্ব হইতেই মানবের নিয়তি নির্দ্দিষ্ট করিয়া রাখিয়াছেন—এইরূপ মতবাদ, বিশেষতঃ মৃত্যুর পর স্বর্গে মানবের অনন্তসুখ বা নরকে অনন্ত দুঃখ ভগবান পুর্ব্ব হইতেই নির্দ্দিষ্ট করিয়া রাখিয়াছেন—এইরূপ মতবাদ। **3.** Fate ; destiny ; নিয়তি, অদৃষ্ট ; ভাগ্য, ভবিতব্য।

prē-dĕs′-tĭne (-tĭn), *v. t.* **1.** To predetermine ; to foreordain ; to doom ; পুর্ব্বে নিরূপিত করা, পুর্ব্বে স্থির করা ; পুর্ব্বে নির্দ্দিষ্ট করা ; পুর্ব্বে বিধান করা। **2.** (*Theol.*) To foreordain by divine decree or eternal purpose ; (খৃষ্টীয় ধর্ম্মশাস্ত্র) পুর্ব্ব হইতেই মানবের অনন্ত সুখ বা দুঃখ নির্দ্দিষ্ট করিয়া রাখা।

prē-dē-tĕr′-mĭne (-mĭn), *v. t.* **1.** To determine beforehand ; পুর্ব্বে নিরূপিত করা, পুর্ব্ব হইতে নির্দ্দিষ্ট করা। **2.** (Of a motive etc.) To impel (a person etc. *to* a thing *to* do etc.) beforehand ; পুর্ব্ব হইতেই অনুপ্রাণিত করা, পুর্ব্ব হইতেই প্রেরণা দেওয়া। **—mi-nate,** *adj.* **—mi-na′-tion,** *n.* Predetermining; purpose previously formed ; পুর্ব্বনিরূপণ, পুর্ব্বনির্দ্ধারণ ; পুর্ব্বে কৃত সংকল্প।

prē′-dĭ-ăl, *adj.* & *n.* **1.** Of, or relating to, land or farms ; rural ; ভূমি বা কৃষিক্ষেত্রসম্বন্ধীয়, ক্ষেত্রিক ; গ্রাম্য। **2.** (Of slaves) Attached to the land ; (ক্রীতদাস সম্বন্ধে) ক্ষেত্রের কার্য্যে নিযুক্ত। ***Noun.*** A predial slave ; কৃষিকার্য্যে নিযুক্ত ক্রীতদাস, ক্ষেত্রদাস।

prĕd′-ĭ-că-ble (-bl), *adj.* & *n.* Capable of being predicated or affirmed ; বাচ্য, কথনীয়। ***Noun.*** **1.** A predicable thing ; an attribute ; কথনীয় বিষয় ; গুণ। **2.** (*Log.*) One of the five attributes—genus, species, difference, property and accident ; (তর্কবিজ্ঞান) পরাজাতি, অপরাজাতি, বিভেদ, গুণ এবং উপলক্ষণ ইহাদের অন্যতম, বিধেয়ক (সাঃ পঃ), বিধেয় (হিঃ কোঃ)। **—bil′-i-ty,** *n.*

prē-dĭc′-ă-mĕnt, *n.* **1.** That which is predicated ; প্রতিপাদ্য-বিষয়। **2.** (*Log.*, usu. *pl.*) A category ; (তর্কবিজ্ঞান) জ্ঞেয়বিষয়সমূহ যে সকল ব্যাপক বিভাগে শ্রেণীবদ্ধ করা যাইতে পারে, পদার্থ। **3.** An unpleasant, trying or dangerous situation ; "Piteous *predicament*" ; দায়, দুর্দ্দশা, দুরবস্থা, সঙ্কট। **—men′-tal,** *adj.* (*Log.*) Relating to predicaments ; (তর্কবিজ্ঞান) বিধেয় সম্বন্ধীয়।

prĕd′-ĭ-cănt, *adj.* & *n.* Preaching ; প্রচারকারী। ***Noun.*** A preacher ; a preaching friar ; প্রচারক ; প্রচারক সন্ন্যাসী।

prĕd′-ĭ-cāte, *n.* **1.** (*Log.*) That which is affirmed or denied of the subject by means of the copula, (*e. g. a fool,* in *he is a fool*) ; (তর্কবিজ্ঞান) উদ্দেশ্যবিধেয়সংযোজক শব্দ দ্বারা যাহা উদ্দেশ্যসম্বন্ধে কথিত বা স্বীকৃত হয়, বিধেয় (সাঃ পঃ), পদাভিধেয় (কেঃশিঃ), পদবাচ্য (ঐ)। **2.** (*Gram.*) That which is said of the subject including the copula, (*e. g. white,* in *milk is white*) ; (ব্যাকরণ) বিধেয়। **3.** An attribute ; a quality ; "... the divine *predicates*" ; ধর্ম্ম ; গুণ।

prĕd′-ĭ-cāte, *v. t.* **1.** To affirm one thing of another ; to assert ; as, to *predicate* whiteness of snow ; কোন বস্তু সম্বন্ধে কোন বিষয় নিশ্চিতরূপে বলা ; খ্যাপন করা। **2.** (*Log.*) To assert (a thing) about the subject ; উদ্দেশ্যসম্বন্ধে কোন নিশ্চিত উক্তি করা। **—ca′-tion,** *n.* The act of predicating ; বিধান। **—ca-tive,** *adj.* Expressing predication or affirmation ; asserting ; নিশ্চয়াত্মক ; বিধায়ক (হিঃ কোঃ)। **—ca-tive-ly,** *adv.* ***Predication de omni***—সার্ব্বিক-বিধান (হিঃ কোঃ)। ***Predication***

in eo quale quod—গুণবিধান (হিঃ কোঃ)। ***Predication in eo quod quid***—জাতি বিধান (হিঃ কোঃ)। ***Predicaion in quale***—গুণবিধান (হিঃ কোঃ)। ***Predication in quale quid***—ব্যাবর্ত্তক বিধান (হিঃ কোঃ)। ***Predication in quid***—জাতি-বিধান (হিঃ কোঃ)। ***Predication per causam*** — কারণত্ববিধান (হিঃ কোঃ)। ***Predication per comitantiam*** — সাহচর্য্যবিধান (হিঃ কোঃ)। ***Predication per se***—স্বতঃ (হিঃ কোঃ)। ***Predication quasi in quid***—ব্যাবর্ত্তক-বিধান (হিঃ কোঃ)।

prĕd′-i-că-tō-rȳ, *adj.* **1.** Of, or relating to, preaching; given to preaching; প্রচারসম্বন্ধীয়; প্রচারশীল। **2.** Marked by being proclaimed publicly; "*Predicatory* conversion"; প্রকাশ্যপ্রচারাত্মক।

prē-dict′, *v. t.* To foretell; to prophesy; পূর্ব্বে বলা; ভবিষ্যদ্‌-বাণী করা। **—a-bil′-i-ty,** *n.* **—a-ble,** *adj.* **—dic′-tion,** *n.* Foretelling; prophecy; ভবিষ্যকথন, ভাবিকথন; ভবিষ্যদ্‌বাণী (হিঃ কোঃ)। **—dic′-tive,** *adj.* Prophetic; predicting; ভবিষ্যৎসূচক; ভবিষ্যৎকথক। **—dic′-tive-ly,** *adv.* **—dic′-tor,** *n.*

prē-di-gĕst′, *v. t.* To render (food etc.) easily digestible before introducing into the stomach; (খাদ্য প্রভৃতি) ভোজনের পূর্ব্বে লঘুপাক করা। **—ges′-tion,** *n.* This process; লঘুপাচন ক্রিয়া।

prē-di-kănt′, *n.* A Dutch Protestant minister, especially in South Africa; প্রোটেষ্ট্যাণ্ট মতাবলম্বী ওলন্দাজ যাজক।

prē-di-lĕc′-tion, *n.* A previous liking; mental preference; partiality, (with *for*); পূর্ব্বানুরাগ; পক্ষপাত; আসক্তি।

prē-dis-pōse′, *v. t.* To render inclined beforehand; as, to *predispose* the mind to friendship; to make liable; পূর্ব্ব হইতে প্রবণ করা; অধীন করা। **—po-si′-tion,** *n.* State of being previously inclined; susceptibility; as, a *predisposition* to mirth or disease; পূর্ব্ব-প্রবণতা; পূর্ব্বসংবেদন, প্রবৃত্তি (হিঃ কোঃ), প্রবণতা (ঐ), সংস্কার (ব্রজঃ হিন্দুঃ)।

prē-dŏm′-i-nāte, *v. i.* To have surpassing power, or authority (over); to be superior; to preponderate; as, love *predominated* in her heart: he *predominated* over others; আধিপত্য থাকা; শ্রেষ্ঠতর হওয়া; প্রবল-ভাবে থাকা। **—nance,** *n.* State of being predominant; প্রবণতা, প্রভুত্বতা, আধিক্য, প্রাবল্য (হিঃ কোঃ)। **—nant,** *adj.* Predominating; ruling; controlling; prevailing; as, a *predominant* partner, colour, etc.; প্রবল; প্রভুত্বকারী; বলবৎ; প্রধান। **—nant-ly,** *adv.* **—nat-ing,** *adj.* **—nat-ing-ly** *adv.*

prē-dŏr′-săl, *adj.* Situated before the dorsal region of the spine; মেরুদণ্ডের পৃষ্ঠসন্নিহিতস্থানের অগ্রে অবস্থিত।

prē-ē-lĕc′-tion, *n.* & *adj.* Election beforehand or by anticipation; প্রাক্‌নির্ব্বাচন। ***Adj.*** Done, or given, before election; as, *pre-election* promises; নির্ব্বাচনের পূর্ব্বে কৃত বা প্রদত্ত।

prē-ĕm′-i-nĕnt, *adj.* Superior in excellence; surpassing others in some quality; অগ্রগণ্য, সর্ব্বশ্রেষ্ঠ, সর্ব্বোৎকৃষ্ট, প্রকৃষ্ট; প্রধান (হিঃ কোঃ), সর্ব্বপ্রধান। **—nence,** *n.* **1.** The state of being pre-eminent; superiority in quality, rank, etc.; as, *pre-eminence* in eloquence; সর্ব্বোৎকৃষ্টতা, উৎকর্ষ, অগ্রগণ্যতা; সর্ব্ব-শ্রেষ্ঠতা, বৈশিষ্ট্য, প্রাধান্য, মুখ্যতা, প্রকর্ষ (হিঃ কোঃ)। **2.** A quality existing pre-eminently; প্রকৃষ্ট-রূপে বর্ত্তমান গুণ। **—ly,** *adv.*

prē-empt′ (-ĕmt), *v. t.* **1.** To obtain by pre-emption; (*U. S.*) to settle upon (public land) with a right of pre-emption; অগ্র-ক্রয়াধিকার দ্বারা প্রাপ্ত হওয়া; (মার্কিণ যুক্তরাজ্য) অগ্রক্রয়ের অধিকার রাখিয়া বাস করিতে থাকা। **2.** (*Fig.*) To appropriate beforehand; (লক্ষণায়) অগ্রে অধিকার করা। **—emp′-tion,** *n.* Act or right of purchasing before others; অগ্রে ক্রয় করণ, অগ্রক্রয়াধিকার। **—emp′-tive,** *adj.*

preen (prēn), *v. t.* **1.** To trim as feathers with the beak; চঞ্চু-দ্বারা পালক পরিপাটী করা। **2.** (Of a person) To trim or dress (oneself up); ফিটফাট করা, সাজান।

prē-ĕx-il′-i-ăn, —ic, *adjs.* Before the exile, usu. the Babylonian one; নির্ব্বাসনের পূর্ব্ববর্ত্তী, বিশেষতঃ ইহুদীগণের বেবিলোনে নির্ব্বাসনের পূর্ব্ববর্ত্তী।

prĕf′-ace (-ās), *n., v. t.* & *i.* **1.** Something introductory to a discourse, book, etc.; মুখবন্ধ, বিজ্ঞাপন, উপক্রমণিকা, অবতরণিকা, গ্রন্থারম্ভ, ভূমিকা, প্রস্তাবনা। **2.** (*R. C. Ch.*) An introduction to the central part of the eucharistic service; খৃষ্টের অন্তিমভোজনানুষ্ঠানের প্রাথমিক ক্রিয়া। **3.** (*Fig.*) Something introductory or preliminary; (লক্ষণায়) ভূমিকা। ***Verb t.* 1.** To furnish with a preface; ভূমিকা দেওয়া, মুখবন্ধ করা। **2.** (Of events etc.) To precede by way of introduction; ভূমিকাস্বরূপ পূর্ব্ববর্ত্তী হওয়া। **3.** To put before or in front of; অগ্রে রাখা, অগ্রে স্থাপন করা। ***Verb i.*** To make, or write, a preface; ভূমিকা করা, ভূমিকা লেখা। **—a-to′-ri-al, —a-to-ry,** *adjs.* Pertaining to a preface; introductory; ভূমিকাসম্বন্ধীয়; প্রারম্ভক।

prē′-fĕct, *n.* **1.** (*Rom. Antiq.*) The title of various officers civil and military; (রোমীয় প্রত্নতত্ত্ব) প্রাচীন

রোমের সামরিক বা অসামরিক কতিপয় উচ্চকর্ম্মচারীর উপাধি। 2. A chief officer ; the administrative head of a modern French department ; প্রধান কর্ম্মচারী; ফরাসীশাসনতন্ত্রের অধীন বিভাগীয় শাসনকর্ত্তা। 3. A monitor in public school ; শির-পড়ো, সর্দ্দার-পড়ো। **–fec'-tor-al, –fec-to'-ri-al,** *adjs.* **Prefect of police**—প্যারী নগরীর পুলিশের বড়-কর্ত্তা, নগররক্ষিনায়ক।

prē'-fĕc-tūre, *n.* 1. The office or official residence of a prefect ; the period of this office ; প্যারীনগরীর পুলিশের বড়-কর্ত্তার পদ বা আবাসভবন ; ঐ পদের স্থিতিকাল। 2. The district governed by a prefect ; ফরাসীদেশের বিভাগ। **–fec'-tur-al,** *adj.*

prē-fêr', *v. t.* 1. To promote as a person to office etc. ; উন্নীত করা। 2. To bring forward or submit for one's acceptance, decision, etc. ; as, to *prefer* an information against an offender ; উপস্থাপিত করা, পেশ করা, দাখিল করা। 3. To choose rather ; to have a greater liking for ; as, to *prefer* a gambler *to* a hypocrite ; বরণীয় মনে করা, অপেক্ষাকৃত অধিক ভাল মনে করা ; অধিক ভাল লাগা **–ferred',** *adj.* **–ment,** *n.* 1. Advancement or promotion ; পদোন্নতি। 2. An appointment or post esp. ecclesiastical ; চাকরী, পদ, বিশেষতঃ যাজকীয় পদ। **Pref'-e-ra-ble,** *adj.* Worthy to be preferred ; more desirable ; শ্রেয়স্কর, আদরণীয় ; বরণীয়। **Pref'-er-a-bly,** *adv.* Rather ; বরং। **Preferred stock etc.** — Same as PREFERENCE STOCK ETC. **To prefer charges**—অভিযোগ করা, নালিশ করা।

prĕf'-ĕr-ence (-ĕns), *n.* 1. Act of preferring ; state of being preferred ; choice of anything before another ; বরণ ; বরত্ব, বৃতি ; অপেক্ষাকৃত অধিক রুচি বা সমাদর। 2. The object one prefers ; as, which is your *preference* ; অপেক্ষাকৃত বাঞ্ছিত বস্তু। 3. (*Law*) Priority in right to demand, esp. payment of debts ; পূর্ব্বাধিকারত্ব। 4. Favouring of one person or country before others in business relations ; ব্যবসায়সম্বন্ধে এক ব্যক্তি বা দেশকে সমধিক সুবিধা প্রদান। **Preference bond, share** or **stock**—খত, কোম্পানির কাগজ, যৌথ-কারবারের অংশ প্রভৃতি যে সকলের লভ্যাংশ সর্ব্বাগ্রে দেয়, সপক্ষভাগ (হিঃ কোঃ)।

prĕf-ĕr-ĕn'-tial (-shăl), *adj.* 1. Of, or pertaining to, preference ; giving, or having, a preference ; as, *preferential* share ; বরণসম্বন্ধীয় ; সমধিকবরণীয়, সমধিক আদরণীয়, লভ্যাংশ সর্ব্বাগ্রে দেয়। 2. (Of duties) Of, or relating to, or creating, a preference in international trade relations ; (শুল্ক-সম্বন্ধে) আন্তর্জাতিক বাণিজ্যগত সম্পর্কে কোন জাতিবিশেষকে বিশেষ সুবিধাপ্রদানসম্পর্কীয়। **–ism, –ist,** *ns.* **–ly,** *adv.*

prē-fĭg'-ūre, *v. t.* 1. To represent by antecdent types and similitudes ; to foreshadow ; পূর্ব্বরূপ সাদৃশ্য বা প্রতিরূপ দ্বারা প্রদর্শন করা ; পূর্ব্বাভাস দেওয়া। 2. To imagine beforehand ; পূর্ব্বধারণা করা। **–u-ra'-tion, –ment,** *ns.* **–ur-a-tive,** *adj.*

prē'-fĭx, *n.* 1. A letter, syllable or word put before another word to affect its meaning, (as, *pre-* in *prefix*) ; উপসর্গ। 2. A title placed before a name (*e. g. Mr.*, *Sir*, or *Dr.*, etc.) ; নামের পূর্ব্বে সংযোজিত উপাধি।

prē-fĭx', *v. t.* To put or set before or at the beginning of something ; as, to *prefix* a syllable to a word : to *prefix* an advertisement to a book ; পূর্ব্বে সংযোগ করা, উপসর্গ সংযোজন করা। **–ion, –ture,** *ns.*

prē-fŏrm', *v. t.* To form beforehand ; পূর্ব্বে গঠন করা। **–for-ma'-tion,** *n.* **The theory of preformation**—(জীব-বিজ্ঞান) পূর্ণাঙ্গদেহীর সমস্ত অঙ্গ জীবাঙ্কুরে (germ) বর্ত্তমান এবং পুনরুৎপাদনক্রিয়াদ্বারা কেবল মাত্র বিকাশপ্রাপ্ত হয়—এইরূপ মতবাদ, আকার-প্রাগ্‌ভাববাদ (হিঃ কোঃ)।

prē-fŏrm'-ă-tive (-tĭv), *adj.* & *n.* 1. Preforming ; পূর্ব্বসংগঠন। 2. (*Philol.*) Prefixed as a formative element ; as, a *preformative* syllable ; (ভাষা-বিজ্ঞান) পূর্ব্বে সংযোজিত গঠনাত্মক অংশস্বরূপ। *Noun.* (*Philol.*) A formative letter or syllable at the beginning of a word ; (ভাষা-বিজ্ঞান) কোন শব্দের পূর্ব্বে সংযোজিত গঠনাত্মক অক্ষর বা শব্দাংশ।

prē-frŏn'-tăl, *adj.* In front of the frontal bone of the skull ; in the forepart of the frontal lobe of the brain ; করোটীর সম্মুখবর্ত্তী অস্থির অগ্রস্থিত ; মস্তিষ্কের সম্মুখস্থ বিবর্দ্ধিত অংশের অগ্রভাগস্থ।

prē-glā'-ci-ăl (-shĭ-), *adj.* (*Geol.*) Prior to the glacial or drift period ; প্রাক্‌তুষারযুগীয়।

prĕg'-nă-ble (-bl), *adj.* Capable of being taken or won by force ; as, a *pregnable* fort ; বলপূর্ব্বক অধিকারযোগ্য, ভেদ্য, প্রবেশ্য।

prĕg'-nănt, *adj.* 1. Being with young ; gravid ; গর্ভবতী, গর্ভিণী, গর্ভযুতা, অন্তঃসত্ত্বা, আসন্নসত্ত্বা, অন্তর্বত্নী ; সগর্ভ, ধৃতগর্ভ। 2. Full of ideas ; inventive ; imaginative ; "...scholar poor of *pregnant* parts" ; ভাবপূর্ণ ; উদ্ভাবনীশক্তিসম্পন্ন ; কল্পনাশক্তিসম্পন্ন। 3. Full of meaning, consequence or results ; weighty ; cogent ; suggestive ; as, a *pregnant* word, argument, etc. ; অর্থপূর্ণ, গুরুত্বপূর্ণ, ফলগর্ভ ; অকাট্য ; অভিব্যঞ্জক, গূঢ়ার্থপ্রকাশক,

অর্থবৎ, নিগূঢ়ার্থ। **–ly,** *adv.* **–nan-cy,** *n.* **1.** State of being pregnant; গর্ভাবস্থা, সগর্ভতা, দৌহৃদয়, ধৃতগর্ভতা। **2.** Latent significance; suggestiveness; গূঢ়ার্থকতা; অভিব্যঞ্জকতা। **Pregnant construction** — গূঢ়ার্থপ্রকাশক বাক্য।

prē-hĕn′-sīle, *adj.* (*Zool.*, Of organs) Capable of grasping; as, the *prehensile* tail of a monkey; (জন্তু-বিদ্যা) গ্রাহী, ধারণক্ষম, ধারণোপযোগী। **–sil′-i-ty,** *n.*

prē-hĕn′-sion, *n.* **1.** Taking hold of or seizing; grasping; ধারণ; গ্রহণ (হিঃ কোঃ)। **2.** (*Psychol.*) Simple or immediate apprehension; (মনস্তত্ত্ব) ধারণা, উপলব্ধি।

prē-hĭs-tŏr′-ic, *adj.* Of, or relating to, the period before written history begins; ঐতিহাসিক কালের পূর্ব্ববর্ত্তী; প্রাগৈতিহাসিক। **–i-cal-ly,** *adv.*

prē-hĭs′-tō-rȳ, *n.* Prehistoric matters or times; প্রাগৈতিহাসিক বিষয় বা কাল।

prē-hū′-măn, *adj.* Existing before men existed; প্রাঙ্মানবীয়।

prē-judge′ (-jŭj), *v. t.* To judge before hearing the whole case; to decide or pass judgment on beforehand; সমস্ত ঘটনা না শুনিয়াই বিচার করা; বিচারের পূর্ব্বে নিষ্পত্তি করা বা রায় দেওয়া। **–judg′-ment, –ju-di-ca′-tion,** *ns.*

prĕj′-ū-dice (-dĭs), *n.* & *v. t.* **1.** Preconceived judgment or opinion; পূর্ব্বসংস্কার, পক্ষপাত, পক্ষানুরাগ। **2.** Injury; detriment; as, in or to the *prejudice* of; ক্ষতি; অনিষ্ট, হানি। ***Verb t.*** **1.** To impair the validity of (a right, claim, or statement); as to *prejudice* a good cause; বৈধতা হানি করা। **2.** To affect with prejudice; to bias the mind of; as, to *prejudice* a person against or in favour of another; পূর্ব্বসংস্কার জন্মান; পক্ষপাতযুক্ত করা।

prĕ-jü-dĭ′-cial (-shăl), *adj.* Injurious; detrimental; ক্ষতিকর, ক্ষতিজনক; অহিতকারক। **–ly,** *adv.*

prĕl′-ă-cȳ, *n.* The office or dignity of a prelate; প্রধানাচার্য্যত্ব, প্রধানাচার্য্যের পদ। **2.** Church government by prelates (usu. a hostile term for *episcopacy*); প্রধানাচার্য্যদ্বারা শাসিত ধর্ম্মসংঘ। **3.** The prelates collectively; প্রধানাচার্য্যবর্গ।

prĕl′-āte *n.* **1.** An ecclesiastic of superior rank and authority, *e. g.* archbishop, bishop, metropolitan, etc.; প্রধানাচার্য্য, আচার্য্যমুখ্য। **2.** (*Hist.*) An abbot or prior; (ইতিহাস) মঠাধ্যক্ষ। **–at-ess,** *n.* A female prelate; (*facet.*) the wife of an abbot; প্রধানা আচার্য্যানী; (কৌতুকচ্ছলে) মঠাধ্যক্ষের পত্নী। **Pre-lat′-ic, Pre-lat′-i-cal.** *adj.* **Pre-lat′-i-cal-ly,** *adv.*

prĕl′-ăt-īze, *v. t.* To bring as a church under prelatical influence or government; রোমের ধর্ম্মসংঘের প্রধানাচার্য্যের শাসনাধীনে আনা।

prĕl′-ă-türe, *n.* The office or dignity of a prelate; the order of prelates; প্রধানাচার্য্যত্ব; প্রধানাচার্য্যের সম্প্রদায়।

prē-lĕct′, *v. i.* To discourse publicly; to lecture; প্রকাশ্যভাবে কথা বলা; বক্তৃতা দেওয়া। **–lec′-tion, –lec′-tor,** *ns.*

prē-li-bā′-tion, *n.* A testing beforehand; a foretaste; (usu. *fig.*); পূর্ব্বাস্বাদগ্রহণ; পূর্ব্বাস্বাদ, পূর্ব্বভোগ, পূর্ব্বানুভব (প্রায়শঃ লক্ষণায়)।

prē-lĭm′-i-nă-rȳ, *adj.* & *n.* Introductory; prefatory; previous; as, *preliminary* measures; আনুক্রমণিক; উদ্যোগাত্মক; প্রাথমিক। ***Noun.*** Something introductory or preparatory; preliminary arrangement, (usu. in the *pl.*); as, the *preliminaries* to the treaty; প্রাথমিক বিষয়; প্রাথমিক ক্রিয়া, পূর্ব্বনির্দ্দিষ্ট বিষয়। **–ri-ly,** *adv.*

prē′-lūde, *n.* **1.** Something introductory; an introductory performance, event, act, etc.; প্রারম্ভ, মুখবন্ধ; প্রস্তাবনা, পূর্ব্বরঙ্গ, পূর্ব্বলক্ষণ, পূর্ব্বসূচক, গৌরচন্দ্রিকা। **2.** (*Mus.*) A strain or movement introducing the theme or chief subject; (সঙ্গীত) তানা-নানা, আলাপ, পূর্ব্ববাদন, পূর্ব্বরঙ্গ। **–lu′-di-al,** *adj.* **Prel′-ud-ize,** *v. i.*

prē-lüde′, *v. t.* & *i.* **1.** To precede as an introduction or prelude; to foreshadow; মুখবন্ধস্বরূপ দেওয়া, পূর্ব্বাভাস দেওয়া; পূর্ব্বসূচনা করা। **2.** To introduce with a prelude or preliminary action; মুখবন্ধ করিয়া আরম্ভ করা, ভূমিকা করিয়া আরম্ভ করা। ***Verb i.*** **1.** To serve as a prelude or introduction (*to*); to give a prelude; মুখবন্ধস্বরূপ হওয়া; আলাপ করা। **2.** (*Mus.*) To play a prelude; (সঙ্গীতশাস্ত্র) তানা নানা করা। **–lu′-sion,** *n.* **–lu′-sive,** *adj.* Introductory; indicating that something of a like kind is to follow; "*Prelusive* drops (of rain)"; প্রারম্ভক; আনুক্রমণিক; পূর্ব্বসূচক।

prē-mă-türe′, *adj.* Happening, or performed, before the proper or usual time; too early; untimely; অপূর্ণকাল, অকালপক্ব, অকালপরিণত, অকালজাত, অপূর্ণকালোৎপন্ন; আকালিক; অসাময়িক। **–ly,** *adv.* Untimely; too early; অকালে; অতি শীঘ্র। **–ness,** *n.* **–tu′-ri-ty,** *n.*

prē-mĕd′-i-tāte, *v. t.* To meditate upon beforehand; to design or contrive previously; as, to *premeditate* theft or robbery; পূর্ব্ব হইতেই মতলব আঁটা, পূর্ব্বে সংকল্প করা; পূর্ব্বে ভাবিয়া চিন্তিয়া স্থির করা। **–ta′-tion,** *n.* **–tat-ed-ly,** *adv.*

prĕ′-mĭ-ĕr, *adj.* & *n.* **1.** (*Now chiefly slang*) First in importance, position or time ; as, he secured tne *premier* place ; (প্রধানত: ইতরভাষায়) মুখ্যতম, আদি। **2.** Earliest ; most ancient ; as, a *premier* peer ; পুর্ব্বতম, আদি ; প্রাচীনতম। ***Noun.*** The prime minister as of Britain or of a British colony ; প্রধান মন্ত্রী, মুখ্যমন্ত্রী, প্রধান সচিব, মন্ত্রীশ। **—ship,** *n.*

premiere, (*F.*), *n.* The first performance of a play etc. ; কোন নাটকের প্রথম অভিনয়।

prĕm′-ise (-ĭs), **—iss,** *ns.* **1.** (*Log.*) One of the two propositions in a syllogism from which the conclusion is drawn ; as, the major or the minor *premise* ; (তর্কবিজ্ঞান) যে বাক্যের উপর নিগমন বা সিদ্ধান্ত নির্ভর করে, পুর্ব্বপক্ষ, আদ্যপক্ষ, হেত্ববয়ব (সাঃ পঃ), পুর্ব্বাবয়ব (হিঃ কোঃ)। **2.** (*Law., pl.*) Matters set forth or stated previously ; প্রাগুক্ত বিষয়াবলী। **3.** (*Pl.*) A house or building with grounds and appurtenances ; as, to be drunk in the *premises* ; বাটী। **Major premise** — মূল বাক্য, ব্যাপ্তিবাক্য, উদাহরণ। **Minor premise**—অবান্তর বাক্য, উপনয়।

prĕ-mīse′, *v. t.* & *i.* **1.** To say or write by way of introduction ; মুখবন্ধস্বরূপে বলা বা লিখা। **2.** (*Log.*) To lay down as an antecedent proposition ; (তর্ক বিজ্ঞান) পুর্ব্বপক্ষ উপন্যস্ত করা। ***Verb i.*** To set forth something as a premise ; উপন্যস্ত করা।

prē′-mĭ-ŭm, *n.* **1.** A reward or recompense ; a prize ; as, a *premium* for discoveries ; পারিতোষিক ; পুরস্কার। **2.** A bonus ; অংশীদারগণকে যে অতিরিক্ত লভ্যাংশ প্রদান করা হয়। **3.** (*Insurance*) A sum paid periodically for insurance ; (বীমা) বীমার কিস্তির টাকা। **4.** The charge for changing one currency into another of greater value ; এক দেশের মুদ্রা অপর দেশের অধিকতর মুল্যের মুদ্রায় পরিবর্ত্তন করিতে হইলে যে বাট্টা দিতে হয়। **5.** A fee paid for the privilege of being taught a trade or profession ; কোন কাজ বা ব্যবসায় শিক্ষার জন্য যে দক্ষিণা দিতে হয়। **At a premium**—At more than the nominal value, (opp. to *at a discount*) ; hence, (*fig.*) in high esteem ; প্রকৃত মুল্য অপেক্ষা অধিক মুল্যে ; (লক্ষণায়) সমাদৃত।

prē-mō-nĭ′-tion, *n.* Previous warning or notice ; as, a supernatural *premonition* of one's death ; পুর্ব্বাবগতি, প্রাগবগতি, প্রাগ্‌বিজ্ঞাপন, পুর্ব্ববোধ, পুর্ব্ববোধক, পুর্ব্বপ্রবোধ, পুর্ব্বসূচনা, প্রাক্‌শংসন (হিঃ কোঃ)। **—mon′-i-tor,** *n.* **—mon′-i-to-ri-ly,** *adv.* **—mon′-i-to-ry,** *adj.* Giving warning or notice beforehand ; as, *premonitory* symptoms ; পুর্ব্বসূচক, জ্ঞাপক, অগ্রিম। **Premonitory of a disease**—পুর্ব্বরূপ (ভাব প্রঃ)।

Prē-mŏn-stră-tĕn′-si-ăn, (-shĭ-), *adj.* & *n.* (*R. C. Ch.*) Of, or relating to, the order of regular canons founded at Premontre, in France in 1119 ; ফরাসীদেশের অন্তঃপাতী প্রেমণ্টার নামক স্থানে ১১১৯ খৃঃ অব্দে প্রতিষ্ঠিত যাজকসম্প্রদায়সম্বন্ধীয়। ***Noun.*** A member of this religious order ; উক্ত যাজকসম্প্রদায়ের সভ্য।

prē-morse′ (-mŏrs), *adj.* (*Bot.*) Ending abruptly, as if bitten off ; (উদ্ভিদবিদ্যা) ক্লিপ্ত। **Premorse root**—ক্লিপ্তমুল (সাঃ পঃ)।

prē-mō′-tion, *n.* Motion given beforehand ; especially a divine act as determining the will of the creature ; প্রাক্‌প্রেরণা ; বিশেষতঃ যে ঐশ্বরিক কার্য্যদ্বারা জীবের ইচ্ছা নিয়ন্ত্রিত হয়।

prē-nā′-tăl, *adj.* Existing, or happening, before birth ; জন্মের পুর্ব্বে বর্ত্তমান বা সংঘটিত।

prĕn′-tice (-tĭs), *n.* & *v. t.* Same as APPRENTICE. **—ship,** *n.* **Prentice hand**—শিক্ষানবীশের কাজ।

prē-ŏc-cū-pā′-tion, *n.* **1.** Occupation of a place beforehand ; পুর্ব্বাধিকার, পুর্ব্বভুক্তি। **2.** Prepossession ; prejudice ; পুর্ব্বসিদ্ধান্ত ; পুর্ব্বসংস্কার। **3.** (Of the mind) Engrossment ; নিবিষ্টতা। **4.** A business or occupation taking precedence of all others ; সর্ব্বাগ্রে করণীয় কার্য্য।

prē-ŏc′-cū-pȳ, *v. t.* **1.** To occupy or appropriate beforehand ; পুর্ব্বে অধিকার করা। **2.** To engross as mind etc., beforehand ; to prepossess ; পুর্ব্ব হইতেই অভিনিবিষ্ট করা ; পুর্ব্বসংস্কার জন্মান। **3.** To fill with something beforehand ; পুর্ব্বাহ্নে অন্য কিছু দ্বারা পুর্ণ করা। **—pied-ly,** *adv.*

prē-ŏc′-ū-lar (-lĕr), *adj.* (*Zool.*) Placed just in front of the eye ; (জন্তুবিদ্যা) চক্ষুর সম্মুখস্থ।

prē-ŏr-dain′ (-dān), *v. t.* To ordain, appoint, or determine beforehand ; পুর্ব্বে নির্দ্দিষ্ট করা, পুর্ব্বে বিধান করা, পুর্ব্বে নির্দ্ধারণ করা। **—di-na′-tion,** *n.*

prĕp, *n.* (*Abbr.*) (*School slang*) Preparation ; (বিদ্যালয়ের ইতরভাষায়) আয়োজন, উদ্যোগ।

prĕp-ă-rā′-tion, *n.* **1.** Act of preparing ; a making ready ; a previous arrangement ; সজ্জীকরণ ; প্রস্তুতকরণ ; উদ্যোগ, আয়োজন। **2.** Act of preparing lessons as a part of the routine of school work, (abbr. *prep.*) ; বিদ্যালয়ের পাঠ শিক্ষা করণ। **3.** Readiness ; fitness ; as, a nation in good *preparation* for attack or defence ; প্রস্তুতত্ব ; উপযোগিতা। **4.** (Usu. *pl.*) A preparatory act or measure, (usu. with *for*) ; প্রারম্ভক কার্য্য বা উপায়। **5.** That which is prepared, made or compounded, for a particular purpose ; কোন বিশেষ উদ্দেশ্যসাধনের জন্য প্রস্তুত বা মিশ্রিত বস্তু। **To make preparations for**—To prepare for ; কোন কিছুর জন্য আয়োজন করা।

prĕ-păr′-ă-tive (-tĭv), *adj.* & *n.* Tending, or serving, to prepare or make ready ; preparatory ; আয়োজনসাধক, প্রারম্ভক ; উদ্যোগাত্মক, উপক্রমসাধক। ***Noun.* 1.** That which prepares ; something preparatory ; উদ্যোগকারী ; প্রারম্ভক কর্ম্ম। **2.** (*Mil.* & *Naut.*) The signal on a drum, bugle, etc. as an order to make ready ; (সামরিকশাস্ত্র এবং নৌবিদ্যা) প্রস্তুত হওয়ার জন্য বংশীধ্বনি বা পটহবাদ্যদ্বারা সঙ্কেত। **—ly,** *adv.*

prĕ-păr′-ă-tō-rȳ, *adj.* **1.** Serving to prepare ; introductory ; প্রস্তুতকারী ; উদ্যোগাত্মক, প্রাথমিক, প্রারম্ভক। **—ri-ly,** *adv.* **Preparatory class** — (India) প্রবেশিকা বিদ্যালয়ের দ্বিতীয় শ্রেণী। **Preparatory school**—যে বিদ্যালয়ে ছাত্রগণ উচ্চতর বিদ্যালয়ে বা মহাবিদ্যালয়ে (College) প্রবেশের জন্য প্রস্তুত হয়। **Preparatory to**—As a preparation for ; উদ্যোগস্বরূপ।

prĕ-pāre′, *v. t.* & *i.* **1.** To make ready ; প্রস্তুত করা। **2.** To get ready by previous study ; পাঠ, বক্তৃতা, প্রভৃতি প্রস্তুত করা। **3.** To make fit by teaching or instruction ; as, to *prepare* a boy for college, examination or the army ; শিক্ষাপ্রদান দ্বারা প্রস্তুত করা। **4.** To fit mentally ; as, to *prepare* a person for illness or calamity ; মন প্রস্তুত করা। **5.** To make or compound ; as, to *prepare* food, medicine, etc. ; প্রস্তুত করা, চিকিৎসকের ব্যবস্থানুযায়ী বিভিন্ন ঔষধ মিশ্রণপূর্ব্বক প্রস্তুত করা। **6.** To get ready ; to provide ; as, to *prepare* an entertainment, welcome, etc. ; প্রস্তুত করা ; বন্দোবস্ত করা, আয়োজন করা। ***Verb i.* 1.** To make ready ; to arrange ; "...*Prepare* for dinner" ; প্রস্তুত করা ; বন্দোবস্ত করা। **2.** To get one's self ready ; as, to *prepare* for death ; প্রস্তুত হওয়া।

prĕ-pay′ (-pā), *v. t.* **1.** To pay before or in advance ; অগ্রিম মূল্য প্রদান করা। **2.** To pay the postage of, as letter etc. beforehand ; চিঠির মাশুল পূর্ব্বে দেওয়া। **—a-ble,** *adj.* **—ment,** *n.*

prĕ-pense′ (-pĕns), *adj.* Deliberate ; premeditated ; intentional (*usu. placed after the word it*) *qualifies*) ; as, malice *prepense* ; জ্ঞানকৃত ; পূর্ব্বচিন্তিত ; অভিপ্রেত। **—ly,** *adv.* **Malice prepense**—চিন্তিতপূর্ব্ব দ্বেষ—বিশেষতঃ নরহত্যা প্রভৃতি বিষয়ে পূর্ব্বাভিসন্ধি।

prĕ-pêr-cĕp′-tion, *n.* Perceiving beforehand ; প্রাক্প্রত্যক্ষ (হিঃ কোঃ)।

prĕ-pŏn′-dêr-āte, *v. i.* & *t.* **1.** To exceed in weight ; to be heavier ; ভারে অধিক হওয়া ; অপেক্ষাকৃত ভারী হওয়া। **2.** (*Fig.*) To exceed in power or influence ; to predominate ; as, self-interest is apt to *preponderate* in our deliberations ; (লক্ষণায়) অধিকতর ক্ষমতাশালী বা প্রভাববিশিষ্ট হওয়া ; আধিপত্য করা। ***Verb t.*** (*Obs.*) To outweigh ; (অপ্রঃ) অধিকতর ভারী হওয়া। **—ance,** *n.* Superiority in weight, power, influence, etc. ; ভারাধিক্য, ক্ষমতাধিক্য, প্রভাবাধিক্য। **—ant,** *adj.* **—ant-ly,** *adv.* **To preponderate over**—To exceed in number, quality, etc. ; সংখ্যা বা পরিমাণে অধিকতর হওয়া।

prĕp-ō-śĭ′-tion, *n.* (*Gram.*) A word showing the relation of one noun or pronoun to another in a sentence ; (ব্যাকরণ) সম্বন্ধবাচক অব্যয় শব্দ, শব্দযোগী অব্যয়। **—al,** *adj.* **—al-ly,** *adv.*

prĕ-pŏś′-ĭ-tive (-tĭv), *adj.* & *n.* (*Gram.*) (Of a word or particle) Proper to be placed before or prefixed ; (ব্যাকরণ) পূর্ব্বে বসাইবার উপযোগী। ***Noun.*** A prepositive word or particle ; সম্বন্ধবাচক অব্যয় শব্দ।

prĕ-pŏś′-ĭ-tor (-têr), *n.* A school monitor ; শির-পড়ো।

prē-pŏś-śĕss′, *v. t.* **1.** To occupy beforehand as land or ground ; পূর্ব্বে অধিকার করা। **2.** To preoccupy the mind or heart of ; to fill or imbue beforehand with some notion or opinion ; to prejudice favourably ; হৃদয় হরণ করা ; চিত্তরঞ্জন করা ; পূর্ব্বসংস্কার দ্বারা রঞ্জিত করা। **—ing,** *adj.* Tending to invite favour ; making a favourable impression ; চিত্তাকর্ষক ; হৃদয়হারী, চিত্তহারী, চিত্তরঞ্জক, হৃদয়গ্রাহী। **—ing-ly,** *adv.* **—ing-ness,** *n.* **—ses′-sion,** *n.* Pre-occupation ; a preconceived opinion especially favourable ; a previous favourable impression ; পূর্ব্বাধিকার ; পূর্ব্বপোষিত মত, পূর্ব্বসংস্কার ; প্রাগনুকূল-মত।

prĕ-pŏs′-têr-ous (-ŭs), *adj.* Contrary to nature or reason ; foolish ; nonsensical ; absurd ; অস্বাভাবিক, অযৌক্তিক, অযুক্ত ; মূঢ়, অর্থহীন ; অসম্ভব। **—ly,** *adv.* **—ness,** *n.*

prĕ-pō′-tĕnt, *adj.* **1.** Very powerful ; excelling others in power, influence, etc. ; অতি শক্তিশালী ; সর্ব্বাতিশায়ী। **2.** (*Biol.*) Having stronger fertilizing influence ; প্রবলতর নিষেকপ্রভাবসম্পন্ন। **—tence, —ten-cy,** *ns.* State of being prepotent ; esp. (*Biol.*) the greater capacity of the father or mother to transmit his or her own characteristics to their offsprings ;

অতিশক্তিমত্তা ; বিশেষতঃ (জীববিজ্ঞান) পিতা কিম্বা মাতার স্বকীয় বিশেষত্ব সন্তানে সঞ্চারের পরম্পরাপেক্ষা শক্তির আধিক্য।

prē-prĕf'-ĕr-ence (-ĕns), *adj.* Ranking before preference shares etc. ; যে সকল অংশের লভ্যাংশ সর্ব্বাগ্রে দেয় তদপেক্ষা অগ্রগণ্য।

prē'-puce (-pūs), *n.* The foreskin ; লিঙ্গের অগ্রত্বক, মেঢ্রত্বক, লিঙ্গাগ্রত্বক। **–pu'-tial,** *adj.*

prē-Răph'-ă-ĕl-īte, *n.* One who practises, or favours the style of art prevailing before the time of Raphael ; র‍্যাফেলের পূর্ব্ববর্ত্তী চিত্রকলাপদ্ধতির অনুসরণকারী ব্যক্তি। **–(it)ism,** *ns.* **–Raph'-a-el,** *adj.* **Pre-Raphaelite Brotherhood**—(Abbr. *P. R. B.*) Holman-Hunt, Dr. G. Rossetti, Millais প্রমুখ ইংলণ্ডীয় চিত্রকরবর্গ।

prē-req'-ui-site (-rĕk-wĭ-zĭt), *adj.* & *n.* Previously required ; necessary to something subsequent ; পূর্ব্বে প্রয়োজনীয়, পূর্ব্বাকাঙ্ক্ষিত (হিঃ কোঃ) ; পূর্ব্বাপেক্ষিত (ঐ), পূর্ব্বাবশ্যক। ***Noun.*** Something previously required ; something necessary in order to gain an end ; পূর্ব্বপ্রয়োজনীয় বিষয় ; উদ্দেশ্য-সিদ্ধির উপযোগী বিষয়।

prē-rŏg'-ă-tive (-tĭv), *n.* & *adj.* **1.** The right or privilege of a sovereign or ruler ; রাজাধিকার। **2.** A special right or privilege ; as, it is our *prerogative* to do etc. ; বিশেষ অধিকার, বিশেষ স্বত্ব, অসামান্যাধিকার, পূর্ব্বপরিগ্রহ (মঃ উঃ)। **3.** A natural or divinely-given advantage or privilege ; নৈসর্গিক অধিকার, ঈশ্বরদত্ত অধিকার। **4.** (*Pedantic*) The right to give the first vote and thus influence those that follow ; সর্ব্বপ্রথম ভোট দেওয়ার অধিকার। ***Adj.*** **1.** Having a privilege ; enjoyed by privilege ; as, a *prerogative* power ; বিশেষাধিকারবান ; বিশেষাধিকারমূলক। **2.** (*Rom. Hist.*) Privileged to vote first ; as, *prerogative* tribe ; (রোমীয় ইতিহাস) সর্ব্বপ্রথম ভোট প্রদানের অধিকারপ্রাপ্ত। **Royal prerogative**—Same as PREROGATIVE, *n.* I.

prĕs'-āge, *n.* Something which foreshows a future event ; an omen ; পূর্ব্বসূচনা, ভবিষ্যৎসূচনা, অগ্রসূচনা ; দুর্নিমিত্ত, অলক্ষণ। **2.** A foreboding ; a presentiment ; অনিষ্টসূচনা ; ভাবীঅশুভের পূর্ব্বাভাস। **3.** Predictive meaning or import ; ভবিষ্যৎসূচক অর্থ। **4.** Prescience ; foreknowledge; পূর্ব্বাবগতি ; পূর্ব্বজ্ঞান। **–ful,** *adj.*

prē-sāge', *v. t.* To have a presentiment of ; to feel beforehand ; পূর্ব্বাভাস পাওয়া ; পূর্ব্বে অনুভব করা। **2.** To prophesy ; to predict ; ভবিষ্যৎ বলা ; ভবিষ্যৎ জ্ঞাপন করা। **3.** To indicate beforehand ; to portend ; পূর্ব্বে সূচনা করা ; ভাবী অমঙ্গল সূচনা করা।

prĕs-bȳ-ō'-pi-ă, *n.* A defect of vision due to advancing age ; বার্দ্ধক্যজনিত দৃষ্টিহীনতা, দূরদৃষ্টিরোগ (হিঃ কোঃ)। **–op'-ic,** *adj.*

prĕs'-bȳ-tēr, *n.* **1.** An elder in the early Christian church ; প্রাচীন-খৃষ্টীয়ধর্ম্মসংঘের বৃদ্ধযাজক। **2.** (Episcopal church) A minister of the second order ; a priest ; (ধর্ম্মাধ্যক্ষশাসিত ধর্ম্মসংঘ) দ্বিতীয় শ্রেণীর যাজক ; পুরোহিত। **3.** (Presbyterian church) A member of a presbytery ; (বৃদ্ধযাজকসংঘ) যাজকবৃদ্ধ। **–byt'-er-al, –te'-ri-al,** *adjs.* **–byt'-er-ate,** *n.* The office or position of a presbyter ; a presbytery ; যাজকবৃদ্ধের কার্য্য বা পদ ; যাজকবৃদ্ধসংঘ। **–ship,** *n.*

Prĕs-bȳ-tē'-ri-ăn, *adj.* & *n.* Of, pertaining to, or consisting of, presbyters ; relating to the Presbyterian church ; যাজকবৃদ্ধ-সম্প্রদায় সম্বন্ধীয় ; যাজকবৃদ্ধসংঘসম্বন্ধীয়। ***Noun.*** An adherent of the Presbyterian system ; a member of the Presbyterian church ; যাজকবৃদ্ধসংঘানুরাগী ; যাজকবৃদ্ধসংঘ-ভুক্ত ব্যক্তি। **–ism,** *n.* **–ize,** *v. t.* **Presbyterian church**—যাজক বৃদ্ধগণ কর্ত্তৃক শাসিত ধর্ম্মসংঘ। **United Presbyterian church**—স্কটলণ্ডের ধর্ম্মসংঘবিশেষ। **Reformed Presbyterian church**—স্কটলণ্ডের ধর্ম্ম-সংঘ বিশেষ।

prĕs'-bȳ-tĕr-ȳ, *n.* **1.** A body of presbyters ; যাজকবৃদ্ধবর্গ। **2.** A church-court consisting of the ministers and one elder being a layman from each church within a certain district ; যাজকীয় বিচারালয় বিশেষ। **3.** The jurisdiction of a presbyter or presbytery ; যাজক-সংঘ বা যাজকীয় বিচারালয়ের এলাকা। **4.** (*R. C. Ch.*) A clergyman's house ; (রোমানক্যাথলিক ধর্ম্মসংঘ) যাজকাবাস। **5.** That part of a church reserved for the officiating priests as choir, sanctuary, etc. ; খৃষ্টীয় ধর্ম্মমন্দিরের যে অংশ যাজকদিগের উপবেশনের জন্য নির্দ্দিষ্ট থাকে।

prē'-sci-ĕnt (-shĭ-), *adj.* Having foreknowledge or foresight ; দূর-দৃষ্টিসম্পন্ন, পরিণামদর্শী, ভবিষ্যদর্শী, ভবিষ্যজ্ঞানী। **–ence,** *n.* Foreknowledge ; foresight ; পূর্ব্বজ্ঞান, ভবিষ্যদ্-জ্ঞান, ভবিষ্যজ্ঞান (হিঃ কোঃ); দূরদর্শিতা, দূরদৃষ্টি, পরিণামদর্শিতা, ভবিষ্যদর্শন। **–ly,** *adv.*

prē-sci-ĕn-tĭf'-ic (-sĭ-), *adj.* Before the rise of modern science ; আধুনিক বৈজ্ঞানিকযুগের পূর্ব্ববর্ত্তী।

prē-scind' (-sĭnd), *v. t.* & *i.* **1.** To cut off as a part from the whole prematurely ; অপরিণত অবস্থায় ছেদন করা, অকালে ছিন্ন করা। **2.** (*Metaph.*) To separate ; to abstract by a separate act of attention ; পৃথক করা ; পৃথকভাবে মনঃসংযোগ দ্বারা বিবিক্ত করা। ***Verb i.*** To withdraw the attention from ; মন নিবৃত্ত করা। **To prescind from**—To leave out of consideration ; গণনার মধ্যে না আনা।

prē-scrībe', *v. t.* & *i.* **1.** To lay down authoritatively as a rule or direction ; to dictate ; as to *prescribe* laws or rules ; বিধান করা ; ব্যবস্থা করা। **2.** (*Med.*) To advise the use of ; as, to *prescribe* a medicine *to* or *for* a patient or *for* a complaint ; (ভৈষজ্য শাস্ত্র) ব্যবস্থা করা। ***Verb i.*** **1.** To give direction ; to dictate ; ব্যবস্থা দেওয়া ; বিধান করা, নির্দ্দেশ করা। **2.** To write or give medical directions ; ঔষধ ব্যবস্থা করা। **3.** (*Law*) To assert a claim or right *to* or *for* a thing by right of prescription ; (আইন) দাবী উপস্থাপিত করা **4.** To become of no force through lapse of time ; as, certain rights *prescribe* in twenty years ; (আইন) তমাদি হওয়া।

prē-script', *adj.* (*Rare*) Ordained or prescribed ; (কচিদ্ ব্যবহৃত) বিহিত, নির্দ্দিষ্ট।

prē'-script, *n.* Something prescribed ; a rule or direction ; ব্যবস্থাপিত বিষয় ; বিধি, বিধান, ব্যবস্থা, নির্দ্দেশ, আদেশ।

prē-scrip'-tion, *n.* **1.** Prescribing or directing ; a thing prescribed ; ব্যবস্থাপ্রদান ; ব্যবস্থা। **2.** (*Med.*) A written direction for the composition and use of a medicine ; a recipe ; (ভৈষজ্যশাস্ত্র) ব্যবস্থাপত্র, প্রক্রিয়া (ভাবঃ প্রঃ), চিকিৎসালেখ (কেণ্ডিঃ) ; ঔষধবিধি। 3. (*Law*) A claim or title based on immemorial or long use or possession ; such uninterrupted use or possession, (also called *positive prescription*) ; বহুকালভোগজনিত স্বত্ব, আদ্যোপান্তের দাঁড়া (রঃ অঃ) ; আবহমান ব্যবহার, পুর্ব্বরীতি। **4.** (*Fig.*) An ancient custom esp. when viewed as authoritative ; (লক্ষণায়) প্রাচীন আচার। **Negative prescription**—যে সময়ের মধ্যে কোন দাবী বা মোকদ্দমা স্থাপন করা যাইতে পারে—তাহার সীমানির্দ্দেশ। **Positive prescription**—See PRESCRIPTION, *n.* 3.

prē-scrip'-tive (-tĭv), *adj.* **1.** Consisting in, based on, or acquired by, prescription ; ধারাবাহিক, ব্যবহারাত্মক, ব্যবহারমূলক, ধারাবাহিক ভোগজনিত, চিরকালভোগাশ্রয়ী (কেণ্ডিঃ), অনাদি পরম্পরাশ্রয়ী (ঐ), অনাদিপরম্পরায়াত (ঐ)। **2.** Prescribing or directing ; ব্যবস্থাপক। **3.** Prescribed by custom ; দেশাচারবিহিত। **–ly**, *adv.*

prĕs'-ence, (-ĕns), *n.* **1.** State of being present ; উপস্থিতি, সত্তা, বর্ত্তমানতা, প্রত্যক্ষতা। **2.** A place where a person is ; as, in one's *presence* ; সাক্ষাৎ, নিকট, গোচর, সকাশ, সন্নিধান। **3.** The person of a superior, as a sovereign ; "That *presence* fair and bright" ; a divine or spiritual being felt as present ; রাজা প্রভৃতি শ্রেষ্ঠব্যক্তি, সাক্ষাৎ (used in Hill Tippera in reference to the Maharaja) ; আবির্ভাব। **4.** Carriage ; bearing ; mien ; as, a man of noble *presence* ; দেহভঙ্গী ; আকারপ্রকার ; বাহ্যাকৃতি। **Presence-chamber** — দর্শনগৃহ, উপস্থানশালা। **In presence of**—সাক্ষাতে, গোচরে, সমক্ষে, সন্নিধানে। **In this august etc. presence**—মহিমান্বিত ব্যক্তির সাক্ষাতে। **Presence of mind**—Self-command and intelligent action in sudden emergencies ; প্রত্যুৎপন্নমতিত্ব, উপস্থিতবুদ্ধি।

prĕs'-ĕnt, *adj.* **1.** Being in a certain place ; as, he was not *present* ; উপস্থিত, হাজির, বিদ্যমান। **2.** Being now in consideration, discussion, etc. ; as, the *present* case ; বর্ত্তমান। **3.** Now existing or occurring ; as, the *present* king ; বর্ত্তমান। **4.** (*Archaic*) Ready at hand ; as, a very *present* help in trouble ; (অপ্রঃ) উপস্থিত। **Present tense**—(*Gram.*) বর্ত্তমান কাল। **The present worth of Rs. 100 in ten years**—১০০ টাকার বর্ত্তমান মূল্য (অর্থাৎ যে টাকা চক্রবৃদ্ধিহারে সুদে বর্ত্তমান কাল হইতে ১০ বৎসর পরে ১০০ টাকায় পরিণত হইবে)।

prĕs'-ĕnt, *n.* **1.** The present time ; বর্ত্তমান কাল। **2.** (*Pl., law*) A deed or document ; (আইন) দলীল। **3.** (*Gram.*) The present tense ; a verb form denoting it ; (ব্যাকরণ) বর্ত্তমানকাল ; বর্ত্তমান কালের ক্রিয়ার রূপ। **At present**—Now ; বর্ত্তমানে, সম্প্রতি, উপস্থিত। **For the present**—For the present time ; আপাততঃ।

prĕs'-ĕnt, *n.* A gift ; উপঢৌকন, উপহার, যৌতুক, সওগাদ, উপায়ন। **To make a present of**—To present (something to a person) ; উপহার দেওয়া।

prē-sĕnt', *v. t., i.* & *n.* **1.** To introduce ; to introduce formally, as to a superior ; as, to *present* a person to another or to a sovereign at court ; পরিচিত করা, পরিচয় প্রদান করা ; যথারীতি পরিচয় করা, নিবেদন করা (ভক্তিঃ)। **2.** (Of a theatre manager) To cause as an actor, to take part in a play ; (রঙ্গালয়ের অধ্যক্ষের পক্ষে) কোন অভিনেতাকে নাটকের কোন ভুমিকা গ্রহণ করান। **3.** To exhibit ; to offer to view ; to show ; প্রদর্শন করা ; দৃষ্টিপথারূঢ় করা ; দেখান। **4.** To nominate to an ecclesiastical benefice ; যাজকীয়পদে মনোনীত করা। **5.** (*Mil.*) To direct or aim as a fire-arm etc. ; (সামরিকশাস্ত্র) বন্দুক প্রভৃতি নিশানা করা। **6.** (Of an idea etc.) To offer or suggest (*itself*) ; দ্যোতিনা করা, ব্যঞ্জনা করা। **7.** To lay before or submit, as a petition, complaint, etc.

to a person in authority etc.; পেশ করা, নিবেদন করা। **8.** To give, bestow or offer as a present; উপহার প্রদান করা। **9.** To deliver as a bill etc. for acceptance; বিল দেওয়া। **10.** To give or offer as compliments, regards, etc. *to*; নমস্কারাদি প্রদান করা। ***Verb i.*** (*Med.*) To appear first at the mouth of the uterus in labour—said of parts of a fœtus; (ভৈষজ্যশাস্ত্র) প্রসবকালে জরায়ুর মুখে প্রথম দেখা দেওয়া। ***Noun.*** Act of aiming a fire-arm or other weapon; the position of a weapon when aimed; বন্দুকাদি নিশানা করণ; বন্দুকাদি নিশানা করার কালে যে ভাবে রাখা হয়। **To present a person with a thing**—To present it to him; কোন জিনিষ কাহাকেও উপহার দেওয়া। **To present arms**—To hold fire-arm etc. in a deferential position in saluting; অভিবাদনার্থ বন্দুক বিশেষভঙ্গীতে ধারণ করা। **To present oneself**—To appear, esp. as a candidate for an examination; উপস্থিত হওয়া।

prē-sĕnt′-ă-ble (-bl), *adj.* **1.** Fit to be introduced into society; fit to be shown or exhibited; শিষ্টসমাজে পরিচিত করার যোগ্য; প্রদর্শনযোগ্য, প্রদর্শনীয়। **2.** Fit or suitable for presentation as a gift etc.; উপহারপ্রদানোপযোগী। **–bil′-i-ty,** *n.* **–bly,** *adv.*

prĕs-ĕn-tā′-tion, *n.* **1.** Act of presenting; state of being presented; উপহারপ্রদান; উপহারতা, উপহারত্ব। **2.** Exhibition; representation esp. theatrical; প্রদর্শন; অভিনয়, বিশেষতঃ নাট্যাভিনয়। **3.** The formal or ceremonial introduction of a person esp. to a superior or at court; কোন লোককে যথারীতি পরিচিত করণ, নিবেদন (ভক্তিঃ)। **4.** (*Metaph.*) All the modification of consciousness directly involved in the knowing or being aware of an object in a single moment of thought; (তত্ত্ববিদ্যা) সাক্ষাৎকার প্রত্যক্ষ, অপরোক্ষানুভব (হিঃ কোঃ)। **5.** (*Med.*) The part of a fœtus which is felt presenting on examination *per vaginum*; (ভৈষজ্যশাস্ত্র) প্রসবকালে ভ্রূণের যে অংশ অপত্য-পথে প্রথম দৃষ্ট হয়। **–al,** *adj.* **Presentation copy of a book etc.**—যে পুস্তক গ্রন্থকার কর্তৃক উপহার স্বরূপ প্রদত্ত হয়।

prē-sĕnt-ā′-tion-ĭsm, *n.* (*Metaph.*) The doctrine that in perception the mind has immediate cognition of the object; (তত্ত্ববিদ্যা) অপরোক্ষভাবে মন বিষয়ের জ্ঞান লাভ করিয়া থাকে—এইরূপ মতবাদ, অপরোক্ষানুভূতিত্ব, প্রত্যক্ষবাদ (হিঃ কোঃ), বিজ্ঞানবাদ, সম্বিদ্বাদ (ঐ)। **–(al)-ist,** *n.*

prĕs-ĕn-tā′-tive (-tĭv), *adj.* **1.** (Of a benefice) To, or for which, a patron has the right of presentation; (যাজকপদসম্পর্কে) যাজকপদে নিয়োগের অধিকারবান ব্যক্তির অধীন। **2.** Having the power of presenting an idea to the mind; নিবেদনক্ষম, উপস্থাপনক্ষম। **3.** (*Metaph.*) Capable of being immediately apprehended; প্রত্যক্ষাত্মক (হিঃ কোঃ), অনুভবাত্মক (ঐ), অপরোক্ষানুভবজ (ঐ)।

prĕs-ĕn-tee′ (-tē), *n.* **1.** One presented to an ecclesiastical benefice; যাজকপদে নিযুক্ত ব্যক্তি। **2.** One recommended for any office or position; যে ব্যক্তিকে কোন চাকুরী দেওয়ার জন্য সুপারিস করা হইয়াছে। **3.** One who receives a present; উপহারপ্রাপক। **4.** A person presented, or introduced, at court; যে ব্যক্তিকে আদালতে পরিচিত করা হইয়াছে।

prē-sĕn′-ti-ĕnt (-shĭ-), *adj.* Feeling, or perceiving, beforehand; having a presentiment; অগ্রানুভবকারী; পূর্ব্বসূচনাপ্রাপ্ত।

prē-sĕn′-tĭ-mĕnt, *n.* Previous apprehension; an anticipation or foreboding as of something evil etc.; পূর্ব্বাভাস; ভাবী অশুভের সূচনা।

prē-sĕn′-tive (-tĭv), *adj.* (Of words) Presenting a conception to the mind, (opp. to *symbolic*); ভাববোধক, বস্তুবিজ্ঞাপক, ভাবাববোধক।

prĕs-ĕnt-lȳ, *adv.* **1.** Soon; shortly; শীঘ্র; অচিরে, অবিলম্বে। **2.** (*Archaic*) Directly; necessarily; as, it does not *presently* follow that etc.; (অপ্রঃ) প্রত্যক্ষভাবে; অবশ্যম্ভাবিপরিণামস্বরূপ। **3.** (*Obs.* or *dial.*) (অপ্রঃ বা উপভাষায়) At present; now; বর্ত্তমানে; এখন। **4.** (*Obs.*) Immediately; forth-with; (অপ্রঃ) তৎক্ষণাৎ; তন্মুহূর্ত্তে।

prē-sĕnt′-mĕnt, *n.* **1.** Act or manner of presenting to the mind; মনে উপস্থাপন বা উপস্থাপনের প্রণালী। **2.** (*Law*) A statement on oath by a jury of a fact known to them; জুরীকর্তৃক কোন জ্ঞাতবিষয় সম্বন্ধে শপথপূর্ব্বক উক্তি। **3.** (*Eccl.*) A formal complaint lodged by the authorities of a parish before the archdeacon or bishop; (যাজকীয় শাস্ত্র) যাজকপল্লী-ধর্ম্মাধ্যক্ষ, কর্তৃক তদুপরিস্থ যাজকের নিকট অভিযোগ। **4.** A representation esp. theatrical; anything exhibited; প্রদর্শনী, অভিনয়; প্রদর্শিত বস্তু। **5.** Delineation; a picture; বিবরণ, বিবৃতি, বর্ণনা; চিত্র-প্রতিকৃতি, আলেখ্য। **6.** Statement or description; উক্তি, বর্ণনা।

prĕs-ĕr-vā′-tion, *n.* Act of preserving; state of being preserved; সংরক্ষণ, রক্ষণ, পালন; স্থিতি।

prē-sĕrv′-ă-tive (-tĭv), *n.* & *adj.* Serving or tending to preserve; as, a *preservative* drug or measure; রক্ষণসাধক, রক্ষণক্ষম, রক্ষক। ***Noun.*** A preservative agent; রক্ষণসাধক পদার্থ। **–tize,** *v. t.*

To treat with preservative; রক্ষণসাধক পদার্থ সংযোগ করা।

prē-serve′ (-zėrv), *v. t.* **1.** To keep safe; to protect; নিরাপদ রাখা; রক্ষা করা, সংরক্ষণ করা। **2** To maintain; as, to *preserve* silence; to sustain; রক্ষা করা; অবলম্বন করা। **3.** To save from decay by some preservative substance; to prepare so as to prevent decomposition or fermentation; as, to *preserve* fruit, meat, etc.; তাজা রাখা; মোরব্বা করা। **4.** (*Hunting, fishing, etc.*) To keep up and reserve for personal or private use; as, to *preserve* game, fish, river, etc.; (মৃগয়াদিতে) ব্যক্তিগত ব্যবহারের জন্য জন্তু, প্রভৃতি রক্ষা করা। **—serv′-a-ble,** *adj.* **—serv′-er,** *n.*

prē-serve′, (-zėrv), *n.* **1.** Preserved fruit, vegetable, etc.; মোরব্বা। **2.** Ground set apart for preservation of game, (*lit.* & *fig.*); মৃগয়ার জন্য পশু প্রভৃতি রক্ষার্থ বৃতি-বেষ্টিত স্থান, অভয়বন (অর্থঃ)। **3.** A piece of water for preserving fish; মৎস্য রক্ষার জন্য পুষ্করিণী প্রভৃতি। **4.** (*Pl.*) Spectacles coloured to protect the eyes; রঙ্গীন চসমা।

prē-side′, *v. i.* **1.** To occupy the presidential chair at a meeting etc., (often with *over*); সভাপতির আসন গ্রহণ করা, সভাপতিত্ব করা। **2.** To exercise superintendence or control of; (*fig.*) to sit or reign supreme; পরিদর্শন করা, কর্তৃত্ব করা; (লক্ষণায়) প্রধান পদে অধিষ্ঠিত হওয়া, একাধিপত্য করা। **3.** To sit at the head of the table; "Will you *preside* dear lady?"; ভোজনকালে সম্মানের আসনে উপবেশন করা।

prĕs′-i-dĕn-cy, *n.* **1.** The office or function of a president; his term of office; রাষ্ট্রনায়কত্ব, সভাপতিত্ব; রাষ্ট্রনায়কের কার্য্যকাল। **2.** A province administered by a president; esp. in India one originally governed by one of the presidents of the three factories of the East India Company; রাষ্ট্রনায়ক-শাসিত প্রদেশ; বিশেষতঃ ভারতবর্ষের যে প্রদেশ পূর্ব্বে ইষ্ট ইণ্ডিয়া কোম্পানীর বাণিজ্যকুঠিত্রয়ের অন্যতম অধ্যক্ষ দ্বারা শাসিত হইত।

prĕs′-i-dĕnt, *n.* **1.** One appointed to preside over a corporation, society or assembly; সভাপতি, সভানায়ক। **2.** The chief executive officer of a republic; দেশপতি, দেশনায়ক, রাষ্ট্রনায়ক, রাষ্ট্রপতি। **3.** The head of some colleges; কোন কোন মহাবিদ্যালয়ের অধ্যক্ষ। **4.** (*U. S.*) The presiding officer of a bank or company; (মার্কিণ রাষ্ট্রমণ্ডল) কোন ধনাগার বা ব্যবসায়গোষ্ঠীর অধ্যক্ষ। **5.** (*Hist.*) The governor of a province, colony, etc.; (ইতিহাস) কোন প্রদেশ বা উপনিবেশের শাসনকর্ত্তা। **—den′-tial,** *adj.* Of, or relating to, a president or his office; সভাপতিসম্বন্ধীয়, রাষ্ট্রনায়কীয়। **—den′-tial-ly,** *adv.* **—dent-ship,** *n.* **—ess,** *n.* A female president; the wife of a president; সভাপত্নী; রাষ্ট্রনায়কপত্নী।

prē-sid′-i-ă-ry, *adj.* & *n.* Of, or having, a garrison; serving as a garrison; দুর্গরক্ষিসৈন্যদলসম্বন্ধীয়, দুর্গরক্ষিসৈন্যদলসমন্বিত; দুর্গরক্ষিসৈন্যদলরূপে কার্য্যকারী। ***Noun.*** (*Rare*) A guard; (কচিদ্ ব্যবহৃত) রক্ষী।

presidio, *n.* (In Spain & Sp. America) A garrisoned place; a fort; (স্পেন এবং স্পেনাধিকৃত আমেরিকায়) দুর্গরক্ষিসৈন্যদল সমন্বিত স্থান; দুর্গ।

prĕss, *n.* **1.** Pressing; ভিড় করণ। **2.** A crowd; throng; ভিড়; লোকসংঘট্ট। **3.** (*Obs.*) The thick or heat of battle; "Fought in the thickest *press*"; (অপ্রঃ) যুদ্ধের সঙ্কুলতা। **4.** Pressure; urgency; as, owing to *press* of work; চাপ; জরুর। **5.** An instrument for squeezing or crushing; সম্পীড়নযন্ত্র, পীড়াযন্ত্র। **6.** (Also *printing-press*) A machine for printing; a house or establishment for printing; মুদ্রাযন্ত্র; মুদ্রাযন্ত্রাগার। **7.** The art, business or process of printing; মুদ্রণকলা, মুদ্রণকার্য্য, মুদ্রণপ্রক্রিয়া। **8.** The newspapers generally; সংবাদপত্রসমূহ। **9.** A closet for the safe keeping of articles; as, a cloth *press*; জিনিষপত্র রাখার জন্য ক্ষুদ্র কক্ষ। **Press-box** — ক্রীকেটখেলার মাঠে সংবাদপত্রের সংবাদদাতৃগণের উপবেশনের জন্য স্থান। **Press-bureau**—সংবাদপত্রসংঘ। **Press-cutting**—সংবাদপত্র হইতে কর্ত্তিত প্রবন্ধাংশ প্রভৃতি। **Press-gallery**—সংবাদপত্রের সংবাদদাতৃগণের উপবেশন মঞ্চ — বিশেষতঃ বিলাতের প্রাকৃত সভার। **Pressman**—A journalist; an operator of a printing-press; সংবাদদাতা; মুদ্রাযন্ত্রচালক। **Press-mark** — গ্রন্থশালায় কোন পুস্তকের স্থাননির্দ্দেশের জন্য উহাতে যে চিহ্ন দেওয়া হয়। **A press of business**—See PRESS, *n.* 4. **Freedom of the press**—মুদ্রাযন্ত্রের স্বাধীনতা। **In the press**—In the course of being printed; যন্ত্রস্থ। **To correct the press**—To correct the errors in printing; মুদ্রণের ভুল সংশোধন করা। **To send, go** or **come to, (the) press**—*i. e.* To be printed; মুদ্রিত হওয়া।

prĕss, *v. t.* & *i.* **1.** To act upon with force or weight; পীড়ন করা। **2.** To move by pressing, (usu. with *up, down* or *against,* etc.); as, *press* it *down*; চাপ দিয়া নাড়া। **3.** To squeeze; to compress; as, to *press* cotton; to smooth by ironing as clothes; ঠাসিয়া ধরা, পীড়ন করা, চাপ দেওয়া; ইস্ত্রি করা। **4.** To squeeze; to express; as, to *press* grapes or juice out of them; সম্পীড়ন করা; চাপ দিয়া বাহির করা। **5.** To embrace closely; বুকে

চাপিয়া ধরা, গাঢ় আলিঙ্গন করা। 6. To distress or straiten; as, to be *pressed* with want; পীড়িত করা, যন্ত্রণা দেওয়া। 7. To bear heavily on, (usu. in *p. p.*); as, hard *pressed* by the enemy; প্রপীড়িত করা। 8. To weigh down or oppress as feelings, mind, spirits, etc.: প্রপীড়িত করা, ভারাক্রান্ত করা। 9. To try to persuade; to urge or entreat; as, to *press* one to do something; চাপিয়া ধরা; ধরা; পীড়াপীড়ি করা, ধর-পাকড় করা। 10. To urge or inculcate with earnestness or importunity; as, to *press* a course or opinion upon a person; চাপাইয়া দেওয়া। 11. To lay stress on; জোর দেওয়া। 12. To urge or thrust as a gift, offer, etc. *upon* a person; চাপাইয়া দেওয়া। ***Verb i.*** 1. To exert pressure; to bear with weight or force, (with *on*, *upon*, *against*, etc.); চাপপ্রয়োগ করা; চাপ দেওয়া। 2. To crowd; to throng; to urge one's way with force or effort, *on*, *forward*, etc.; ভিড় করা; লোকসংঘট্ট করা; ভিড় ঠেলিয়া অগ্রসর হওয়া। 3. To exert a strong or compelling influence; to weigh heaving *on* or *upon* (one's mind, person, etc.); as, the failure *pressed upon* his mind; প্রবল প্রভাব বিস্তার করা; মথিত করা। 4. To be urgent; জরুরী হওয়া। **Pressed,** *p. adj.* **Press'-ing** *adj.* 1. Urgent; important; as, a *pressing* need, danger, etc.; জরুরী; গুরুতর। 2. Importunate; persistent; as, a *pressing* invitation; নাছোড়বন্দা; নির্ব্বন্ধাতিশয়যুক্ত। **Press'-ing-ly,** *adv.* **Hard pressed**—প্রপীড়িত। **I am pressed for space, time, funds, etc.**—আমার স্থান, সময়, অর্থ প্রভৃতির বড় অভাব। **To press for**—To demand for; কোন কিছুর জন্য পীড়াপীড়ি করা। **To press on or upon**—To attack or pursue closely or violently; প্রবলভাবে আক্রমণ করা, ঠেলিয়া অগ্রসর হওয়া। To urge; চাপিয়া ধরা।

prĕss, *v. t.* & *n.* 1. To force into service, esp. naval or military, (also *fig.*); নৌবিভাগের বা সামরিক বিভাগের কার্য্যে জোর করিয়া নিযুক্ত করা, বেগার ধরা। 2. To take for royal or public use as horses, boats, etc.; রাজার বা সাধারণের কাজের জন্য নেওয়া। ***Noun.*** (*Hist.*) Compulsory enlistment, esp. in the navy; বলপূর্ব্বক ভর্ত্তি (বিশেষতঃ নৌবিভাগে)। **Press-gang**—বেগার-ধরা দল।

pres'-sure (prĕ-shür), *n.* 1. A pressing; force of one body acting upon another; সঙ্কোচন, চাপ; সম্পীড়ন। 2. A constraining force or influence; চাপ, ভার (হিঃ কোঃ)। 3. Affliction; distress; depression; কষ্ট, ক্ষোভ; দুঃখ, দুর্দ্দশা; মানসিক গ্লানি। 4. Embarrassment; as, financial *pressure*; ঝঞ্ঝাট। 5. Urgency as of business, etc.; পীড়াপীড়ি, জরুরৎ, তাগিদ। 6. (*Mech.*) The action of a force against some opposing force; কোন প্রতিকূল শক্তির বিরুদ্ধে কোন শক্তির ক্রিয়া। **Atmospheric pressure**—বায়ুমণ্ডলের চাপ, বায়বীয় চাপ (হিঃ কোঃ)। **High pressure**—(*Orig.*) Pressure higher than that of the atmosphere; (পূর্ব্বে) বায়ুমণ্ডলের চাপাপেক্ষা উচ্চতর চাপ, (বর্ত্তমানে) উচ্চতর চাপ। (*Fig.*) High degree of activity, speed, etc.; as, working at *high pressure*: *high-pressure* work; (লক্ষণায়) অতিদ্রুতগতি, পূর্ব্ববেগ। **Pressure gauge**—ভারপরিমাপক (হিঃ কোঃ)। **Centre of pressure**—ভারকেন্দ্র (হিঃ কোঃ)।

Prĕs'-tĕr-John (-jŏn), *n.* In the Middle ages, a supposed Christian sovereign and priest in Abyssinia or some Eastern country; মধ্যযুগে এবিসিনিয়া বা অন্য কোন দেশের কল্পিত খৃষ্টীয় নৃপতি বা পুরোহিত।

prĕs-tī-dĭg'-ĭ-tā-tor (-ĕr), *n.* A juggler; বাজীকর, ঐন্দ্রজালিক। **—ta'-tion,** *n.* Legerdemain; jugglery; হস্তকৌশল, হাতের চালাকী; ভোজের বাজী, ভোজবিদ্যা।

prĕs-tige' (-tīj), *n.* Influence or reputation etc. derived from past success, achievements, high character, etc.; প্রভাব, প্রতিপত্তি, গৌরব, ইজ্জত, সম্মান, প্রতিষ্ঠা, খাতির।

prestissimo, (*Ital.*), *adj.*, *adv.* & *n.* (*Mus.*) Very quick; অতিদ্রুত। ***Adv.*** Very quickly: অতিদ্রুত। ***Noun.*** A very quick piece or movement; ঢুন।

presto, (*Ital.*), *adj.*, *adv.* & *n.* (*Mus.*) Quick; দ্রুত। ***Adv.*** Quickly; দ্রুতভাবে। ***Noun.*** A quick piece or movement; ঢুন।

prés'-tō, *adv.* & *adj.* (In conjurer's formulæ) Quickly; দ্রুতভাবে। ***Adj.*** 1. Rapid or quick; দ্রুত, জলদি। 2. Juggling; ভোজবাজী।

prē-sūme', *v. t.* & *i.* 1. To dare; to venture; "May I *presume* to ask etc...."; সাহস করা; সাহস করিয়া বলা বা করা। 2. To assume; to take for granted; ধরিয়া নেওয়া, মানিয়া নেওয়া; স্বীকার করিয়া নেওয়া। ***Verb i.*** 1. To suppose something to be true etc.; to infer; সত্য বলিয়া অনুমান করা, আন্দাজ করা; অনুমান করা। 2. To venture beyond propriety; to take liberties, (with *on* or *upon*); as, to *presume* too much *on* one's favours; শোভনতার সীমা অতিক্রম করিয়া সাহসী হওয়া; শিষ্টাচার বা শোভনতার সীমা অতিক্রম করিয়া অন্যথা আচরণ করা। **—sum'-a-bl-,** *adj.*

–sum′-a-bly, *adv.* **–sum′-ed-ly, –sum′-ing-ly**, *advs.* **To presume on or upon**—To take advantage of; to take undue liberties of; as, to *presume upon* one's good natnre; সুবিধা-গ্রহণ করা; অনুচিত সুবিধাগ্রহণ করা।

prĕ-sump′-tion (-zŭm-), *n.* **1.** Arrogance; effrontery; প্রগল্‌ভতা, ধৃষ্টতা; বে-আদবী, ঔদ্ধত্য, উদ্ধততা। **2.** Act of taking for granted; something assumed or taken for granted; as, it is a mere *presumption*; অনুমান; অনুমিত বিষয়। **3.** A ground or reason for presuming; অনুমানের হেতু বা কারণ। **Presumption of fact**—(আইন) জ্ঞাত তথ্যসমূহ হইতে কোন তথ্যের অনুমান। **Presumption of law**—বিরুদ্ধ বিষয় প্রদর্শন না করা পর্য্যন্ত কোন বিষয় সত্য বলিয়া ধরিয়া নেওন।

prĕ-sump′-tive (-zŭm-tĭv), *adj.* Affording reasons for presumption; as, *presumptive* evidence; সম্ভাব্য, সম্ভাবনীয়, আনুমানিক, অনুমান-সিদ্ধ। **Heir presumptive**—See HEIR. **Presumptive evidence**—অনুমানসিদ্ধ প্রমাণ, অনুমানমূলক প্রমাণ, অনুভবসিদ্ধ প্রমাণ (রঃ অঃ), কোরাইন সাবুদ (ঐ)।

prĕ-sump′-tŭ-ous (-zŭm-tŭ-ŭs), *adj.* Over-confident; arrogant; insolent; forward; অতিপ্রতিভ; ধৃষ্ট; বেআদব; প্রগল্‌ভ, অবলিপ্ত। **–ly**, *adv.* **–ness**, *n.*

prĕ-sŭp-pose′ (-pōz), *v. t.* **1.** To suppose or assume beforehand; পূর্ব্বে অনুমান করা। **2.** To imply; as, effects *presuppose* causes; সূচনা করা। **–po-si′-tion**, *n.* Act of presupposing; a thing presupposed as the basis of argument, etc.; পূর্ব্বকল্পনা; যুক্তি প্রভৃতির ভিত্তিস্বরূপ পূর্ব্বকল্পিত বিষয়।

prĕ-tence′ (-tĕns), *n.* **1.** A claim; দাবী দাওয়া। **2.** False show; ostentation; as, devoid of all *pretence*; কৃত্রিম আড়ম্বর; ধুমধাম। **3.** A pretext; as, under the *pretence* of; ছল, অছিলা, বাহানা (হিঃ কোঃ), ব্যপদেশ, ব্যাজ। **Under the pretence of**—Under the pretext of; কোন কিছুর ছলে বা ব্যপদেশে।

prĕ-tĕnd′, *v. t.* & *i.* **1.** To feign; to simulate; ছল করা; ভাণ করা। **2.** To allege or declare falsely; মিথ্যা অভিযোগ আরোপ করা। **3.** To venture; to try; "Dost thou dare *pretend* to punish me ..."; সাহস করা; চেষ্টা করা। ***Verb i.*** **1.** To lay a claim (*to*); as, to *pretend to* a right, title, etc.; দাবী করা। **–ed**, *p. adj.* Feigned; ostensible; assumed; কল্পিত; আপাত-দৃষ্ট, স্পষ্ট; কৃত্রিম, ছদ্ম। **–ed-ly**, *adv.* **–ing** *adj.* **–ing-ly**, *adv.* **To pretend to**—To try to win in marriage as a person or person's hand; কাহারো পাণিগ্রহণের চেষ্টা করা। **To pretend to**—To assert or profess to possess as quality, etc.; কোনরূপ গুণ প্রভৃতি আছে বলিয়া দেখান বা ভাণ করা।

prĕ-tĕnd′-ĕr, *n.* **1.** One who makes a claim, usually a false claim, to anything; দাবীকারী, মিথ্যাদাবীকারী। **2.** One who simulates or feigns; কপটী, ছলনাকারী, ছাদ্মিক। **–ship**, *n.* **Old, Young, Pretender**—ইংলণ্ডের সিংহাসন দাবীকারী দ্বিতীয় জেম্‌সের পুত্র বা পৌত্র।

prĕ-tĕn′-sion, *n.* **1.** Pretending or making a claim to something; দাবীকরণ। **2.** A claim whether true or false; দাবী। **3.** A false show; a pretext; কৃত্রিম আড়ম্বর; ছল, অছিলা।

prĕ-tĕn′-tious (-shŭs), *adj.* Ostentatious; showy; আড়ম্বরপূর্ণ, সমারোহপূর্ণ; জমকালো। **–ly**, *adv.* **–ness**, *n.*

prĕ-tĕr-că-nine′, *adj.* More than canine; অতিকুকুরীয়।

prĕ-tĕr-hŭ′-măn, *adj.* More than human; superhuman; অতিমানুষ; অতিমর্ত্ত্য।

prĕt′-ĕr-ite (-ĭt), **–ĭt**, *adj.* & *n.* **1.** (*Gram.*) Past, applied to a tense etc.; অদ্যতন। **2.** (*Facet.*) Past; bygone; "To return to the *preterite* gala-days..."; (রঙ্গচ্ছলে) অতীত; গত। ***Noun.*** A preterite tense, word or form; অদ্যতনকালের শব্দ বা রূপ। **–ness**, *n.* **The first preterite**—লঙ্। **The second preterite**—লুঙ্। **The third preterite**—লিট্।

prĕt-ĕr-ĭ′-tion, *n.* **1.** An omission; neglect, (with *of*); অতিক্রম, অতিচার; অবহেলা। **2.** (*Theol.*) Passing over of the non-elect; (খৃষ্টীয় ধর্ম্মশাস্ত্র) মুক্তির জন্য অমনোনীত ব্যক্তিবর্গকে পরিহার।

prĕ-tĕr-mĭt′, *v. t.* **1.** To pass by; to omit to mention as a fact etc.; অতিক্রম করিয়া যাওয়া; উল্লেখ করিতে ত্রুটী করা। **2.** To leave undone; to neglect; অসম্পূর্ণ রাখা; অবহেলা করা। **3.** To leave off for a while; to cease; কিয়ৎক্ষণের জন্য বিরত হওয়া; বিরত হওয়া, ক্ষান্ত হওয়া। **–mis′-sion**, *n.*

prĕ-tĕr-năt′-ŭ-răl, *adj.* Out of the regular course of nature; supernatural; abnormal; অপ্রাকৃত, স্বভাবনিয়মবাহ্য, প্রকৃতিনিয়মবাহ্য, নিসর্গক্রমবাহ্য; অলৌকিক, নৈসর্গিক, অতিপ্রাকৃত, প্রতিপ্রকৃতিক (হিঃ কোঃ), বিপ্রকৃতিক; স্বভাববিরুদ্ধ। **–ism**, *n.* **1.** The system or doctrine of the preternatural; অলৌকিকত্ববাদ। **2.** State of being preternatural; a preternatural thing or occurrence; অলৌকিকতা, অতিপ্রাকৃতত্ব; অতিপ্রাকৃত বিষয় বা ঘটনা। **–ly**, *adv.*

prĕ′-tĕxt, *n.* An excuse; an ostensible reason or motive; ছল, ছুতা, অজুহাত, ছলছুতা, ভাণ, অছিলা, ব্যাজ, ব্যপদেশ, বাহানা; উপলক্ষ, ছুতানাতা, ফেরেব, ওজর।

prē′-tĕxt, *v. t.* To assign or allege as a pretext ; ছল করিয়া বলা বা আরোপ করা।

prē′-tone (-tŏn), *n.* The syllable or vowel preceding the stressed or accented syallable ; স্বরচিহ্নে চিহ্নিত শব্দাংশের পূর্ব্ববর্ত্তী শব্দাংশ বা স্বরবর্ণ। **–ton′-ic,** *adj.*

pret′-ti-fȳ (prĭt-), *v. t.* To make pretty ; to adorn in a pretty way ; সুন্দর করা, সুশ্রী করা ; সুচারুরূপে মণ্ডিত করা।

pret′-ti-lȳ (prĭt-), *adv.* 1. In a pretty manner ; nicely ; সুন্দররূপে ; সুচারুরূপে।

pret′-ti-nĕss (prĭt-), *n.* 1. Quality or state of being pretty ; beauty of a slight dainty or childish kind ; রমণীয়তা, সুরূপতা, মঞ্জুতা ; চারুতা। 2. A pretty act, feature, thing or ornament ; "The room was full of flowers and *prettinesses* of every kind etc." ; সুন্দর কাজ, সুন্দর আকৃতি, সুন্দর জিনিষ বা অলঙ্কার। 3. Affected or trivial beauty of style in literature or art ; (ললিতকলা বা সাহিত্য) চটক।

pret′-tȳ (prĭt-), *adj.* & *adv.* 1. Having slight or diminutive beauty as a woman, child, etc. চারু, চারুদর্শন, চটকসুন্দর (*colloq.*)। 2. Attractive to the eye, ear or aesthetic sense ; সুদর্শন, নেত্রাকর্ষক, সুভগ, সুন্দর, মঞ্জুল, লাবণ্যময়, কান্ত, কমনীয়, শোভন। 3. Good ; fine, (*often ironically*) ; as, a *pretty* trick ; *pretty* muddle ; ভাল ; সুন্দর, মজার। 4. (*Archaic*) Fine ; stout ; as, a *pretty* fellow ; (অপ্র:) সুন্দর ; হৃষ্টপুষ্ট। 5. (*Archaic*) Moderately large ; considerable ; as, a *pretty* sum ; (অপ্র:) বড় মন্দ নয় ; বেশ বড় গোছের। ***Adv.*** Moderately ; fairly ; tolerably ; almost ; as, *pretty* well ; *pretty* much the same thing ; একরূপ ; মাঝারি রকমের ; একপ্রকার ; প্রায়। **–ish,** *adj.* Somewhat pretty ; একরূপ সুন্দর। **–ism,** *n.* Affected prettiness of a style, manner, etc. ; রচনাভঙ্গী বা রীতিনীতির কৃত্রিম মনোহারিত্ব। **Pretty certain**—Almost certain ; প্রায় নিশ্চিত। **Pretty go**—A pretty state of affair ; a difficult matter ; মজার ব্যাপার ; কঠিন সমস্যা। **Pretty-pretty**—Aiming too much at prettiness ; অতিরিক্ত সৌন্দর্য্য ফলাইবার জন্য অতিরিক্ত ব্যস্ত। (*Noun Pl.*) Ornaments ; knick-knacks ; অলঙ্কার ; ফট্‌কীনাট্‌কী। **A pretty time of it**—A troublesome or unpleasant condition of affairs ; গোলমেলে ব্যাপার, গোলযোগের ব্যাপার।

pret′-zel, bret–, (*Gr.*), *ns.* A crisp biscuit shaped like a knot and flavoured with salt ; একপ্রকার নুণমাখানো মচমচে বিস্কুট।

preux chevalier, (*F.*), *n.* A gallant knight ; রমণীরঞ্জকপুরুষ।

prē-vail′ (-vāl), *v. i.* 1. To gain the victory ; to have the mastery, (with *over* or *against*) ; বিজয়ী হওয়া ; প্রভুত্ব থাকা, আধিপত্য থাকা। 2. To be in force ; to be current ; to obtain ; as, the custom *prevails* to this day ; বলবৎ থাকা ; চলিত থাকা ; প্রচলিত থাকা। 3. To have power or influence ; to predominate ; প্রভাব থাকা ; আধিপত্য করা। 4. To persuade or induce, (with *on, upon* or *with*) ; প্রবর্ত্তিত করা, প্ররোচিত করা, লওয়ান। **–ing,** *adj.* Predominant ; prevalent ; প্রধান ; প্রচলিত। **–ing-ly,** *adv.* **Prev′-a-lence,** *n.* 1. State of being prevalent ; superiority ; প্রবলতা, আধিক্য, প্রাবল্য ; শ্রেষ্ঠতা। 2. General existence, strength or influence ; wide extension ; প্রবলতা, প্রাদুর্ভাব, প্রচলতা, আধিক্য ; ব্যাপ্তি, ব্যাপকতা। **Prev′-a-lent,** *adj.* Gaining superiority ; predominant ; extensively existing ; most general ; প্রবল ; বলবৎ ; ব্যাপক ; প্রচলিত। **Prev′-a-lent-lȳ,** *adv.*

prē-văr′-i-cāte, *v. t.* To act or speak evasively ; to quibble ; to equivocate ; কথার মার পেঁচ করা, অপলাপ করা ; বাগ্‌ভঙ্গী করা ; দ্ব্যর্থবোধক বাক্য প্রয়োগ করা। **–ca′-tion,** *n.* Act of prevaricating ; quibbling ; equivocation ; কথার খেলাপ, অপলাপ ; নিহ্নব, বাক্‌ছল (হিঃ কোঃ), বক্রোক্তি ; দ্ব্যর্থবোধক বাক্য ব্যবহার। **–ca′-tor,** *n.*

prē-vēn′-i-ĕnt, *adj.* 1. Coming or going before ; previous ; পূর্ব্বগামী ; পূর্ব্ববর্ত্তী। 2. Preventive (*of*) ; প্রতিষেধক।

prē-vĕnt′, *v. t.* 1. To hinder ; to impede ; to stop ; বারণ করা, নিষেধ করা, মানা করা, নিবারণ করা ; বাধা দেওয়া, প্রতিরোধ করা, প্রতিবন্ধক জন্মান ; গতিরোধ করা। 2. (*Archaic*) To meet beforehand or anticipate ; "...to *prevent* your every wish" ; (অপ্র:) পূর্ব্বে পূর্ণ করা, পূর্ব্বাভাস পাওয়া। **–a-ble,** *adj.* That can be prevented ; নিবার্য্য, নিবারণীয়। **–i-ble,** *adj.* **–ven′-tion,** *n.* Act of preventing ; hindrance ; a measure of precaution ; বারণ, নিষেধ, প্রতিষেধ, নিরোধ ; নিবারণ ; প্রতিষেধ, প্রতিবন্ধ। **God prevents us with His grace**—শ্রীভগবান আমাদিগকে দেবানুগ্রহে পরিচালিত করিতেছেন।

prē-vĕnt′-ĕr, *n.* 1. One who, or that which, prevents ; নিষেধকারী, নিবারক। 2. (*Naut.*) An auxiliary rope, stay, bolt, etc. ; (নৌবিদ্যা) সহায়ক-রজ্জু, মাস্তল-রজ্জু, প্রভৃতি।

prē-vĕn′-tive (-tĭv), *adj.* & *n.* Tending, or serving, to prevent ; warding off ; as, *preventive* of disease ; নিবারক ; প্রতিষেধক। ***Noun.*** That which prevents ; a preventive agent, measure, drug, etc. ; নিবারক বস্তু ; প্রতিষেধক বস্তু, উপায়, ঔষধ প্রভৃতি। **–ly,** *adv.*

–vent′-a-tive, *adj.* & *n.* Same as PREVENTIVE.

prē′-vi-ous (-ŭs), *adj.* & *adv.* **1.** Coming or going before; antecedent; prior (*to*); পূর্ব্বগামী; পূর্ব্ববর্ত্তী; পূর্ব্বতন। **2.** (*Slang*) Done or acting hastily; as, you have been a little too *previous*; (ইতর ভাষায়) ব্যস্তভাবে সম্পাদিত। ***Adv.*** Previously; as, had called *previous to* writing, etc.; পূর্ব্বে, আগে। **–ly,** *adv.* Before; beforehand; পূর্ব্বে; অগ্রে। **–ness,** *n.* **Previous Examination** — Same as LITTLE-GO. **Previous question**—(পার্লেমেন্ট) প্রস্তাবিত ব্যক্তি আর অধিক বাদানুবাদ বিনা তন্মুহূর্ত্তেই নির্ব্বাচিত হইবে কি না তদ্বিষয়ে প্রশ্ন।

prē-vīse′, *v. t.* **1.** To foresee; পূর্ব্বে দর্শন করা। **2.** To inform beforehand; পূর্ব্বে বিজ্ঞাপিত করা। **–vi′-sion,** *n.* **–vi′-sion-al,** *adj.* **–vi′-sion-al-ly,** *adv.*

prey (prā), *n.* **1.** An animal hunted or killed by another to be devoured; victim; (*lit.* & *fig.*); শিকার; ভক্ষ্য, বলি, আমিষ (cf. দ্বিষামামিষতাং যযৌ)। **2.** A person, thing, etc. that falls a victim to a disease, enemy, fear, etc.; বলিস্বরূপ ব্যক্তি। **3.** (*Bible*) Spoil; লুণ্ঠিত দ্রব্য। **A beast of prey**—শিকারীপশু, হিংস্র জন্তু।

prey (prā), *v. i.* To take food by violence; শিকার করা। **To prey on** or **upon**—To seize or take as prey; to plunder or pillage; (of a disease, emotion, etc.) to exercise a baneful or wasteful influence *upon*; শিকার ধরা; লুণ্ঠিত করা, লুটপাট করা, অনিষ্টজনক বা বিষময় প্রভাব বিস্তার করা।

prī′-ă-pism, *n.* **1.** (*Med.*) A morbid and persistent erection of the penis; (ভৈষজ্যশাস্ত্র) উত্তেজনা ব্যতীত মুহুর্মুহুঃ লিঙ্গোত্থান, ধ্বজোচ্ছ্রায়, শিশ্নোচ্ছ্রায়। **2.** Licentiousness; লিঙ্গবাজি।

prīce, *n.* & *v. t.* **1.** The value a seller puts on his goods; worth; মূল্য; দাম। **2.** (*Fig.*) That which is done, given, or sacrificed, to gain something; as, we must have it at any *price*; (লক্ষণায়) মূল্য (cf. জীবনমূল্য, রক্তমূল্য)। **3.** (*Betting*) Odds; (পণক্রিয়া) একপক্ষ বাজী জিতার সম্ভাবনার অনুপাতে অপর হীনপক্ষকে যে সুবিধা দেয়। **4.** (*Archaic*) Preciousness; worth; (অপ্রঃ) মহার্ঘতা; মূল্য। ***Verb t.*** **1.** To set a price on; to ask the price of; মূল্য ধার্য্য করা; মূল্য চাওয়া। **2.** (*Fig.*) To estimate the value of; (লক্ষণায়) মূল্য নির্দ্ধারণ করা। **Price-current, –list** — জিনিষের বর্ত্তমান মূল্যের তালিকা, মূল্যতালিকা। **Above, beyond** or **without price**—Invaluable; অমূল্য, অনর্ঘ। **Every man has his price**—Eevry one can be won over by some inducement; এমন লোক নাই—যাহাকে টাকা দ্বারা বশ না করা যায়। **To set a price on one's head**—To offer a reward for his capture or death; কাহাকে ধরার জন্য বা কাহারো মাথা লওয়ার জন্য পুরস্কার নির্দ্দেশ করা।

priced (prīst), *adj.* Having a price or value set on; as, low *priced*: high *priced*; মূল্যের। **Priced catalogue**—মূল্যের তালিকা।

prīce-lĕss, *adj.* Of inestimable worth; invaluable; অমূল্য; অনর্ঘ, অনর্ঘ্য।

prick, *n.* **1.** Act of pricking; a puncture by a prick; বিঁধন; বেধনজনিত রন্ধ্র, ফুটা। **2.** (*Fig.*) Stinging pain; remorse; as, the *pricks* of conscience; (লক্ষণায়) দংশন; মনস্তাপ। **3.** A mark made by a pointed instrument; বেধনচিহ্ন, খোঁচার দাগ। **4.** A pointed instrument or weapon; সূক্ষ্মাগ্র যন্ত্র বা অস্ত্র। **5.** (*Obs.*) A goad; (অপ্রঃ) অঙ্কুশ, আজানি। **Prick-ears** — Erect pointed ears of some dogs etc.; conspicuous ears of a person esp., of the Roundheads; কুকুর প্রভৃতির খাড়া কাণ; কোন ব্যক্তির উদ্গাত কর্ণ, বিশেষতঃ ক্রমওয়েলের সময়ের পার্লেমেন্টের দলের লোকের। **Prick-eared** — খাড়া-কাণওয়ালা। **Pricks of conscience**—বিবেকের দংশন। **To kick against the pricks**—To hurt oneself by useless resistance; কণ্টকে পদাঘাত করা, বৃথা বাধা দিয়া নিজের অনিষ্ট সাধন করা।

prick, *v. t.* & *i.* **1.** To pierce slightly with a sharp instrument or the like; to make a puncture in; খোঁচা দেওয়া; বিঁধা, বিদ্ধ করা। **2.** (*Fig.*) To sting with remorse; to cause sharp pain to; মর্ম্মযাতনা প্রদান করা, মনস্তাপ দেওয়া; প্রবল মনোবেদনা সঞ্চার করা। **3.** To spur; to goad; to incite; (sometimes with *on*, *off*); খোঁচা দিয়া উত্তেজিত করা; অঙ্কুশদ্বারা তাড়না করা; উত্তেজিত করা, প্রোৎসাহিত করা। **4.** To mark or outline by pricking as a pattern etc.; সূক্ষ্মাগ্র যন্ত্রদ্বারা ক্ষুদ্র ক্ষুদ্র ছিদ্র করিয়া নমুনা প্রভৃতি অঙ্কিত করা। **5.** To mark as a name or an item in a list with a prick; to select as a sheriff in this way; সূক্ষ্মাগ্র যন্ত্রদ্বারা কোন তালিকার নাম বা দফা চিহ্নিত করা; উক্ত উপায়ে পৌরাধ্যক্ষ নির্ব্বাচিত করা। **6.** (*Rare*) To attach or hang by puncturing; to stick; as, to *prick* a paper on a wall; (কচিদ্ব্যবহৃত) ফোঁড় করিয়া লাগান; লাগান। **7.** To raise or erect as ears etc., (with *up*); কাণ প্রভৃতি খাড়া করা। ***Verb i.*** **1.** To be punctured; to feel or cause a pricking sensation; as, a forefinger *pricks*; বিদ্ধ হওয়া,

ফোঁড় হওয়া; টন্‌টনে ব্যথা করা, কণ্টকাদি বেধবৎ বেদনা ভোগ করা। 2. To make a thrust, (*at, into,* etc.), খোঁচা মারা। 3. (*Archaic*) To ride or advance on horse-back; (অপ্রঃ) অশ্বারোহণ করা, অশ্বারোহণে অগ্রসর হওয়া। 4. To rise or stand erect, (with *up*); খাড়া হওয়া, মাথা তোলা। **To prick in, out, off**—To plant as seedlings etc. in small holes pricked in the earth; মাটিতে ক্ষুদ্র ক্ষুদ্র গর্ত্ত করিয়া বীজের চারা প্রভৃতি রোপণ করা। **To prick off**—To urge on; প্রোৎসাহিত করা। To mark off; বাছিয়া নেওয়া। **To prick on**—To goad on; উৎসাহিত করা। **To prick up one's ears**—(Of dogs) To erect the ears when on the alert; (কুকুরসম্পর্কে) কাণ খাড়া করা। (*Fig.,* of persons) To listen sharply; (লক্ষণায়, ব্যক্তি সম্পর্কে) উৎকর্ণ হইয়া শুনা, কাণ খাড়া করিয়া শোনা। **To prick up oneself**—To make a display; আড়ম্বর দেখান, জাঁকজমক দেখান।

prick'-ĕr, *n.* One who, or that which, pricks; a pricking instrument; বেধন-যন্ত্র, বেধক; বেধনী, সূচিকা।

prick'-ĕt, *n.* 1. A buck in his second year; দুই বৎসর বয়স্ক মৃগশিশু। 2. A spike on which to stick a candle; মোমবাতি বসাইবার জন্য শঙ্কু। **Pricket's sister**—দুই বৎসর বয়স্কা বালহরিণী।

prick'-le (-l), *n., v. t. & i.* 1. A small sharp process growing from the bark of a plant; a small thorn; শূক; ক্ষুদ্র কাঁটা, ক্ষুদ্র কণ্টক, কণ্টক, বঙ্কিল (সাঃ পঃ)। 2. A spine as of a hedgehog, etc.; কাঁটাচুয়া প্রভৃতির কাঁটা। ***Verb t.*** To affect with a prickling sensation; কণ্টকাদিবেধবৎ বেদনা জন্মান। ***Verb i.*** To be affected with such sensation; কণ্টকাদি বেধবৎ বেদনা ভোগ করা। **—ling,** *n.* & *adj.*

prick'-le (-l), *n.* A kind of willow basket; উইলোগাছের কোমল ডালে তৈয়ারী ঝুড়ী।

prick'-lў, *adj.* 1. Full of or ornamented with prickles, etc. as an animal, plant, etc.; কণ্টকপূর্ণ, সকণ্টক, কাঁটাওয়ালা, কণ্টকশোভিত। 2. Stinging; as, a *prickly* sensation; কণ্টকবেধবৎ। **—li-ness,** *n.* **Prickly heat**—ঘামাচি, ঘর্ম্মচর্চ্চিকা। **Prickly pear**—নাগফণা (খোরী), ফণিমনসা, নাগফণার ফল।

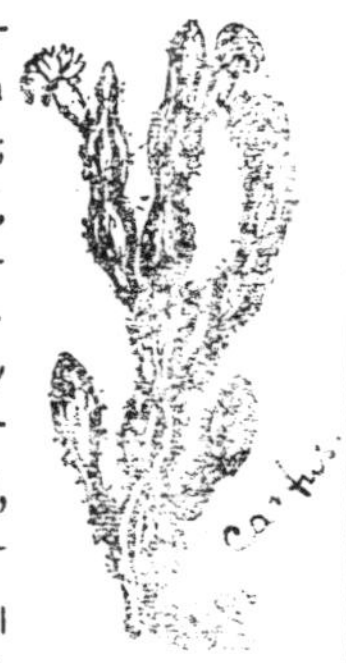

Prickly pear.

prīde, *n.* & *v. t.* Inordinate self-esteem; state or quality of being proud; অহঙ্কার, স্পর্দ্ধা, দর্প, দম্ভ, গর্ব্ব, ডেমাক (*colloq.*), গুমর (*ib.*), ঠেকার, (*ib.*), অবলেপ, অভিমান, অহমিকা, গরিমা, অহম্মতি, আত্মাভিমান; অহঙ্কৃতি, দৃপ্ততা। 2. (Also *proper pride*) Noble or lofty self-respect; আত্মগৌরব, আত্মমর্য্যাদা, স্বাভিমান। 3. Feeling of elation and delight; as, to take *pride* in the noble achievements of the ancestors; গৌরব। 4. An object of this feeling; as, he is his mother's *pride*; গৌরবের বস্তু। 5. Arrogant or haughty bearing or conduct; উদ্ধত ভাব, দৃপ্ত ভাব, দাপট (*colloq.*)। 6. The best or most flourishing state or condition; "Deer...almost in *pride* of grease"; অতি সমৃদ্ধির অবস্থা, অতি গৌরবের দিন। 7. (*Obs.*) Sexual desire or appetite esp. in a female beast; (অপ্রঃ) সঙ্গমেচ্ছা, মদ, গরম। ***Verb t.*** (*Reflex.*) To take or feel pride; to plume; as, to *pride* oneself *on* or *upon*; গর্ব্ব বোধ করা; আত্মশ্লাঘা করা। **Pride'-ful** *adj.* (*Scot.*) **Pride'-ful-ly,** *adv* **Pride'-less,** *adj.* **False pride**—Mistaken feeling or sense of self-respect; ভ্রান্ত আত্মমর্য্যাদাবোধ। **Proper pride**—See PRIDE, *n.* 2. **Peacock in his pride**—(Usu. *herald.*) (সাধারণতঃ কুলবিদ্যায়) বিস্তারিতপুচ্ছ এবং আনত-পক্ষ ময়ূর। **Pride goeth before destruction**—মরণ বা'ড় বাড়া, পিপীলিকার ডানা হয় মরিবার তরে, অত্যুত্থায় পতনায় হি লক্ষণম্‌। **Pride has a fall**—অতি বা'ড় বেড়োনা পড়ে পা যাবে, অতি দর্পে হতা লঙ্কা অতি মানে চ কৌরবাঃ। **To pride oneself on or upon**—To be proud of; গর্ব্ব করা, অহঙ্কার করা।

prie-dieu, (*F.*), *n.* 1. A kneeling desk for prayers; উপাসনার জন্য হেলানো মেজ। 2. (Also *prie-dieu chair*) A chair with a sloping back used in praying; উপাসনাকালে ব্যবহৃত একপ্রকার ক্রমপ্রবণপৃষ্ঠ কাষ্ঠাসন।

priest (prēst), *n.* & *v. t.* 1. A clergyman esp. one above a deacon and below a bishop; যাজক। 2. One who officiates at the altar or performs the rites of sacrifice; পুরোহিত, ঋত্বিক, পুরোধা। 3. (*Chiefly Irish*) A mallet used to kill fish when spent; (প্রধানতঃ আয়র্লণ্ড) মৃতপ্রায় মৎস্য বধ করার জন্য এক প্রকার হাতুড়ী। ***Verb t.*** To make one a priest; পুরোহিত করা, যাজক করা। **Priest'-ess,** *n.* (*Fem.*) A female priest; যাজিনী, যাজিকা। **Priest'-hood,** *n.* The office or character of a priest; পৌরোহিত্য, যাজকত্ব। **Priest'-less, Priest'-like, Priest'-ling,** *adjs.* **Priest-craft**—পুরোহিতগিরি, পুরোহিতের ছল বা চালাকি। **Priest's hood, Priest-in-the-pulpit**—বনকচু। **Priest-ridden**—পুরোহিতবশ, পুরোহিতায়ত্ত। **Priest-vicar**—সামান্য যাজক।

priest'-lў (prēst-), *adj.* Of, or relating to, a priest; like, or becoming, a priest ; পুরোহিত-সম্বন্ধীয়, যাজকীয় ; যাজকসমুচিত, পুরোহিতোচিত, পুরোহিততুল্য। **–li-ness,** *n.* **Priestly caste**—ব্রাহ্মণবর্ণ। **Priestly code**—বাইবেলের প্রাচীননিয়মের অন্তর্গত পুস্তকবিশেষ, যাজকসংহিতা। **Priestly writer**—যাজকসংহিতাকার।

prig, *n.* & *v. t.* **1.** A conceited narrow-minded fellow ; a conceited precisian ; গর্ব্বিত অনুদার প্রকৃতির লোক, বিজ্ঞম্মন্য ; খুঁত খুঁতে লোক, বাক্য বা আচরণে অতিরিক্ত সূক্ষ্মবিচারী গর্ব্বিত লোক, সূক্ষ্মাচারগর্ব্বিত ব্যক্তি, সূক্ষ্মরুচিসম্পন্ন গর্ব্বিত ব্যক্তি, যে ডেমাকী লোকের কিছুতেই মন উঠে না। **2.** (*Slang*) Thief ; (ইতর ভাষায়) চোর। ***Verb t.*** (*Slang*) To steal ; (ইতর ভাষায়) চুরি করা। **Prig'-ger-y,** *n.* **Prig'-gish,** *adj.* **Prig'-gish-ly,** *adv.* **Prig'-gish-ness, Prig'-gism,** *ns.*

prim, *adj., v. i.* & *t.* Formal ; affectedly nice ; demure ; as, a *prim* person, speech, etc. ; ফিটফাট, মেজাজদার ; পরিচ্ছন্ন ; কপটবিনয়ী। ***Verb i.*** To act or behave in a prim manner ; কপট বিনয় প্রদর্শন করা। ***Verb t.*** To deck or arrange with great nicety ; to form into an expression of affected preciseness, as the face, lips, etc. ; অতি খুঁটিনাটির সহিত সাজান বা গুছান ; খুঁত খুঁতে ভাব হইতে অধর, প্রভৃতি কুঞ্চিত করা। **Prim'-ly,** *adv.* **Prim'-ness,** *n.*

prima, (*Ital.*), *adj.* Chief ; first ; প্রধান ; প্রথম। ***Prima buffa***—প্রধানা হাস্যরসাত্মক সঙ্গীত গায়িকা, প্রধানা অভিনেত্রী, প্রধানা গায়িকা। ***Prima donna***—গীতিনাট্যের প্রধানা গায়িকা।

prī'-mā-cy̆, *n.* **1.** State of being prime ; excellence ; pre-eminence ; আদিমতা ; শ্রেষ্ঠতা ; প্রকৃষ্টতা। **2.** The office or rank of a primate ; মুখ্য ধর্ম্মাধ্যক্ষের পদ বা পদবী।

prī-mæ'-văl (-mē-), *n.* Same as PRIMEVAL (which see).

prima facie, *adv.* & *adj.* At first view ; on the first appearance ; "Has *prima facie* a cause of action" ; প্রথমদৃষ্টিতে ; আপাতদৃষ্টিতে। ***Adj.*** Arising at first sight ; based, or founded, on the first impression ; as, a *prima facie* reason ; আপাতদৃষ্টিমূলক ; প্রথমসংস্কারমূলক, প্রথমদৃষ্টা (হিঃ কোঃ)। **Prima facie case**—আপাতদৃষ্টিতে সত্য বলিয়া অনুমিত মোকদ্দমা। **Prima facie evidence (of a fact)**—(আইন) কোন ঘটনা সম্বন্ধে অনুমান করার পক্ষে যথেষ্ট প্রমাণ।

prī'-māge, *n.* A percentage addition to the freight paid to the owners or freighters of the vessels ; জাহাজে মাল বোঝাই করার জন্য দস্তরী।

prī'-māge, *n.* (Steam-boilers) Water carried over by priming ; (বাষ্পজনক সম্পর্কে) বাষ্পের সহিত নলের ভিতর কণাকারে যে জল নীত হয়।

prī'-māl, *adj.* **1.** Primary ; original ; primitive ; আদিম, আদ্য ; মৌলিক ; আদিম, প্রাথমিক। **2.** Chief ; first in importance ; fundamental ; "The *primal* truths" ; প্রধান ; মুখ্য ; প্রথম।

prī'-mā-ry̆, *adj.* & *n.* **1.** Primitive ; original ; প্রাথমিক, আদিম ; আদ্য। **2.** First in importance ; chief ; principal ; সর্ব্বশ্রেষ্ঠ ; প্রধান ; মুখ্য। **3.** Fundamental ; not derived ; as, *primary* vowel sounds ; মৌলিক ; অযোগজ। **4.** Lowest in order ; as, a *primary* school ; নিম্নতম। **5.** (*Geol.*) Of, or relating to, the lowest series of strata ; (ভূতত্ত্ববিদ্যা) নিম্নতম স্তরসম্বন্ধীয়। **6.** (*Biol.*) Belonging to, or directly derived from, the first stage of development ; (জীববিজ্ঞান) বিকাশের প্রথম অবস্থা হইতে অপরোক্ষভাবে উদ্ভূত। ***Noun.*** **1.** A primary meeting ; প্রাথমিক মিলন। **2.** (*Astron.*) Same as PRIMARY PLANET (which see). **3.** A large feather on the last joint of a bird's wing ; পক্ষীর পাখার শেষ সন্ধির বৃহৎ পালক। **–ri-ly,** *adv.* In a primary manner ; originally ; in the first place ; প্রধানতঃ ; মূলতঃ ; প্রথমতঃ। **–ri-ness,** *n.* **Primary amputation**—ক্ষতি আরম্ভ হওয়ার পূর্ব্বে অঙ্গচ্ছেদ। **Primary assembly, meeting, etc.**—নির্ব্বাচনী সভা। **Primary battery**—যে বৈদ্যুতিক ঘটশ্রেণীতে তাড়িতপ্রবাহ উৎপাদিত হয়। **Primary cause**—আদি কারণ, মূলকারণ। **Primary colour** — See under COLOUR. **Primary education**—প্রাথমিক শিক্ষা, নিম্নশিক্ষা। **Primary feather**—See PRIMARY, *n.* 3. **Primary laws**—মূল নিয়ম (হিঃ কোঃ)। **Primary matter** — আদিম ভূত। **Primary period**—মৎস্য যুগ (অভিঃ)। **Primary planets**—See PLANET. **Primay school** — নিম্নবিদ্যালয়। **Primary syphilis**—উপদংশ রোগের প্রাথমিক অবস্থা।

prī'-māte, *n.* A chief ecclesiastic ; an archbishop ; প্রধান যাজক ; মুখ্য ধর্ম্মাধ্যক্ষ। **–ma'-ti-al,** *adj.* **Primate of England** — ইয়র্কের প্রধান ধর্ম্মাধ্যক্ষ। **Primate of all England**—কেণ্টনগরীর প্রধান ধর্ম্মাধ্যক্ষ।

prī'-mā-tēs, *n.* (*Pl., Zool.*) The highest order of mammals consisting of man, monkeys, lemurs and bats ; (জন্তুবিদ্যা) স্তন্যপায়ী জীববর্গের সর্ব্বোচ্চ শ্রেণী, পরমপ্রাণী (সাঃ পঃ)।

prīme, *adj.* **1.** Primary ; fundamental ; প্রাথমিক ; প্রথম (হিঃ কোঃ), মৌলিক। **2.** First in importance ; chief ; as, a *prime* motive ; মুখ্য ; প্রধান। **3.** Most excellent ; of the highest quality ; as, *prime* wheat ; প্রকৃষ্ট ; উচ্চশ্রেণীর। **4.** (*Obs.*) Blooming ; (অপ্রঃ) প্রস্ফুট। **5.** (*Arith.*) Divisible by no number except itself or unity ; as, a *prime* number ; having no common divisor but one, as numbers; (পাটীগণিত) যে সংখ্যা কেবল তৎ সংখ্যা বা একদ্বারা ভাজ্য; মৌলিকসংখ্যা, দৃঢ় (হিঃ কোঃ)। **Prime'-ly,** *adv.* **Prime'-ness,** *n.* **Prime cost**—See under COST. **Prime conductor**—প্রধান চালক (হিঃ কোঃ)। **Prime factor**—দৃঢ়গুণাবয়ব (হিঃ কোঃ)। **Prime integer**—দৃঢ় অভিন্ন (ঐ) **Prime meridian**—প্রধান যাম্যোত্তর বৃত্ত। **Prime minister**—প্রধান মন্ত্রী, মুখ্য মন্ত্রী, মহামন্ত্রী, মন্ত্রীশ, মহামাত্য; গ্রেটব্রিটনের প্রধান মন্ত্রী। **Prime mover** — See under MOVER. **Prime number**—See PRIME, *adj.* 5. **Prime vertical (circle)**—খমণ্ডলে কল্পিত বৃহদ্‌বৃত্ত-বিশেষ—ইহা দিক্‌চক্রবালের (horizon) পুর্ব্ব এবং পশ্চিম বিন্দুদ্বয় ভেদ পুর্ব্বক নভোমধ্যে (zenith) যাম্যোত্তরবৃত্তকে (meridian) সমকোণ উৎপাদন পুর্ব্বক ছেদন করে, সমমণ্ডল (সুঃ সিঃ), পুর্ব্বাপর বৃত্ত (হিঃ কোঃ)।

prīme, *n.* **1.** The earliest stage; the beginning; hence, the dawn; "In the *prime* of the world; আদি অবস্থা; প্রারম্ভ, অঙ্কুর; দিনমুখ, ঊষা, অরুণোদয়। **2.** The spring of life; youth in full health, strength and beauty; "Cut off in their *prime*"; প্রথম যৌবন, নবযৌবন, তারুণ্য, যৌবনোন্মেষ, যৌবনারম্ভ; পুর্ণযৌবন, প্রৌঢ়যৌবন। **3.** The highest or most perfect state or condition; as, in the *prime* of life; প্রকৃষ্ট অবস্থা, পুর্ণাবস্থা। **4.** The best part of anything; উৎকৃষ্ট অংশ, সারাংশ। **5.** (*R. C. Ch.*) The canonical hour succeeding to lauds; (রোমান ক্যাথলিক ধর্ম্মসংঘ) ভজনকাল বিশেষ। **6.** A prime number; মৌলিক সংখ্যা। **7.** (*Archaic*) Same as GOLDEN NUMBER, which see. **8.** (*Chem.*) A single atom as unit in a combination; (রসায়নশাস্ত্র) এক পরমাণু। **In the prime of life**—তরুণ বয়সে, প্রথম যৌবনে, নবযৌবনে। **In the prime of the moon**—শুক্ল প্রতিপদে।

prīme, *v. t.* & *i.* **1.** (*Hist.*) To supply as a fire-arm with powder for communicating fire to a charge; (ইতিহাস) বন্দুকের রঞ্জক ঘরে বারুদ লাগান। **2.** To fill or furnish with information etc.; জ্ঞাতব্য বিষয়াদি যোগান, জ্ঞাতব্য বিষয় সমূহ যোগান। **3.** To fill with liquor; "A fat little man *primed* with port"; মদ্য দ্বারা পুর্ণ করা। **4.** To lay the first colour, coating, etc., upon (a surface) to prevent the paint from being absorbed; রংয়ের পোঁচ দেওয়া, আস্তর দেওয়া, পোঁচরা দেওয়া। ***Verb i.*** (Of an engine-boiler) To let water pass to the cylinder in the form of spray along with the steam; (বাষ্পীয় যন্ত্রের বাষ্পজনক সম্বন্ধে) বাষ্পের সহিত কণাকারে নলের মধ্যে জল যাইতে দেওয়া।

prim'-ẽr, *n.* **1.** An elementary book for teaching children to read; প্রথম পাঠ্য পুস্তক, প্রথম পাঠ। **2.** Any small book of elementary principles of a subject; কোন বিষয়ের প্রাথমিক গ্রন্থ, উপক্রমণিকা। **3.** (*Hist.*) A small prayer-book; (ইতিহাস) ক্ষুদ্র প্রার্থনা পুস্তক। **4.** A size-of type in printing; একপ্রকার মুদ্রাক্ষর (যথা—Great primer এবং Long primer.)

prīm'-ẽr, *n.* One that primes, esp. a contrivance such as a cap, cylinder, etc. used to ignite powder of a cartridge etc.; যদ্দ্বারা বন্দুকের রঞ্জকঘরায় বারুদ লাগান হয়, বিশেষতঃ টোঁটা প্রভৃতিতে বারুদ লাগাইবার জন্য ব্যবহৃত ক্ষুদ্র চুঙ্গী প্রভৃতি।

primero, *n.* (*Hist.*) A card-game; (ইতিহাস) একপ্রকার তাসখেলা।

primeur, *n.* A fruit before its ordinary season; first-fruits অকালের ফল; বৎসরের প্রথম উৎপন্ন ফল। **2.** An early piece of news; শীঘ্র প্রাপ্ত সংবাদ।

prī-mē'-vȧl, —maeʹ—, (-mē-), *adjs.* Of, or relating to, the first age of the world; primitive; পৃথিবীর আদিযুগসম্বন্ধীয়; আদিম, পুরাকালীন, প্রাক্‌কালীন, প্রাচীন। **—ly,** *adv.*

prīm'-ing, *n.* **1.** Act of one that primes, as in preparing a gun or charge for firing etc.; বন্দুকের রঞ্জকঘরায় বারুদ দেওন। **2.** The powder placed in the pan of a fire-arm; বন্দুকের রঞ্জকঘরায় যে বারুদ দেওয়া যায়। **3.** The first coating of colour, size or the like laid on canvas etc. in painting, পোঁচ, আস্তর। **4.** A preparation of sugar added to beer; বীয়র মদ্যে মিশ্রিত একপ্রকার শর্করাসংযুক্ত বস্তু। **5.** The hasty and imperfect imparting of knowledge; cramming; তাড়াতাড়ি অসম্পুর্ণভাবে বিদ্যা-শিক্ষাদান; মুখস্থকরণ।

prīm'-ing, *n.* Acceleration of the tides occurring from the neap to the spring tides; মন্দ জোয়ার হইতে ভরা জোয়ার পর্য্যন্ত জোয়ারের ক্রমিক বেগ-বৃদ্ধি।

prī-mip'-ȧ-rous (-rŭs), *adj.* Bearing young or child for the first time; প্রথমসন্তানপ্রসবকারী।

prim'-i-tive (-tiv), *adj.* & *n.* **1.** Ancient; প্রাচীন, আদিম, প্রাথমিক, আদ্যকালীন, আদিকালিক। **2.** Old-fashioned; সেকেলে, সাবেক ধরণের। **3.** Original; radical; not derived; as a *primitive* verb in Grammar; মৌলিক; অযৌগিক; অযোগোদ্ভুত। **4.** (*Math.* of a line, figure, etc.) From which another is derived; from which some construction begins, etc.; (গণিতশাস্ত্র—রেখা, ক্ষেত্র, প্রভৃতি, সম্পর্কে) যাহা হইতে অপর একটী উদ্ভূত হয়; যাহা হইতে কোন অঙ্কন আরব্ধ করা হয়, মৌলিক। **5.** (*Geol.*) Earliest formed ; (ভূতত্ত্ববিদ্যা) সর্ব্বপ্রথম রচিত। 6. (*Biol.*) Primordial ; (জীববিজ্ঞান) আদিম, আদ্য। 7. (Of colour) Primary ; (বর্ণ-সম্বন্ধে) মূল। ***Noun.*** 1. A primitive word (*opp.* to *derivative*) ; মৌলিক শব্দ, অব্যুৎপন্ন শব্দ। 2. (*Math.*) A primitive line, figure, etc. ; (গণিতশাস্ত্র) মূল রেখা, ক্ষেত্র, প্রভৃতি। 3. A painter of the pre-Renaissance priod ; a picture by such a painter ; ইতালিদেশীর চিত্রকলার নবযুগারম্ভের পূর্ব্ববর্ত্তী চিত্রশিল্পী ; ঐরূপ চিত্রকরগণ কর্ত্তৃক অঙ্কিত চিত্র। 4. Same as PRIMITIVE METHODIST (below) **—ly,** *adv.* **—ness,** *n.* **Primitive colours**—মূল রং (হিঃ কোঃ), মূলবর্ণ। **Primitive Methodist Connexion** — Hugh Bourne নামক জনৈক মেথডিষ্ট সম্প্রদায়ভুক্ত ব্যক্তি ১৮১০ খৃষ্টাব্দে কতিপয় মেথডিষ্টকে লইয়া যে নবসম্প্রদায় গঠন করেন—তাহার নাম। **The Primitive Church**—আদিযুগের খৃষ্টীয় ধর্ম্মসংঘ।

primo, *n.* (*Mus.*) The first or chief part in duet, etc. ; (সঙ্গীতশাস্ত্র) ব্যক্তিদ্বয় দ্বারা গেয় বা বাদনীয় সঙ্গীত কিংবা বাদ্যের প্রধান অংশ।

prī-mō-gĕn'-i-tŏr, *n.* The first or earliest ancestor ; a fore-father ; আদিপুরুষ, কুলপুরুষ ; পূর্ব্বপুরুষ।

prī-mō-gĕn'-i-tūre, *n.* 1. The state or condition of being the eldest of the children of the same parents ; অগ্রজত্ব, পূর্ব্বজত্ব, জ্যেষ্ঠত্ব, আদিজত্ব, আদিজাতত্ব, জ্যেষ্ঠতা। 2. Same as RIGHT OF PRIMOGENITURE. **—tal,** *adj.* **—ta-ry,** *adjs.* **Right of primogeniture** — প্রথমজাত সন্তানের পৈত্রিক সম্পত্তি প্রাপ্ত হওয়ার অনন্যসাধারণ অধিকার, জ্যেষ্ঠাধিকার।

prī-mŏr'-dĭ-ăl, *adj.* & *n.* 1. Existing from the beginning ; primitive ; original ; fundamental ; আদিম, আদ্য, প্রাথমিক, আদিকালীন ; প্রাক্কালিক ; মৌলিক ; মূলীভূত। 2. (*Biol.*) Earliest formed in the growth of an individual or organ ; (জীববিজ্ঞান) আদিজাত, সর্ব্বাগ্রজাত। ***Noun.*** (*Rare*) A first principle or element ; (কচিদ্ ব্যবহৃত) মূলতত্ত্ব, মূলভূত। **—al'-i-ty,** *n.* **—ly,** *adv.*

prĭm'-rōse, *n.* & *adj.* 1. A plart with pale yellow flowers ; its flowers ; মৃদুপীতাভ পুষ্পপ্রসূ তরুবিশেষ ; পীতাভ বাসন্ত কুসুম বিশেষ, বসন্ত পুষ্প, ভুসেবতী (আঃ বঃ)। 2. A pale yellow colour like that of the flower ; বসন্তপুষ্পের মত মৃদু পীত বর্ণবিশেষ। ***Adj.*** Of, or relating to, a primrose ; of the colour of a primrose ; বসন্তপুষ্পসম্বন্ধীয় ; বসন্তপুষ্পবর্ণ। **—ro-sy,** *adj.* **Primrose dame**—বসন্তকুসুম সমিতির সভ্যা, ভদ্রমহিলা। **Primrose Day**—বেনজামিন ডিজরেলির মৃত্যুর সাম্বৎসরিক দিবস। **Primrose habitation**—বসন্তকুসুম সমিতির ভবন। **Primrose knight**—বসন্তকুসুমসমিতির নাইট উপাধিধারী সভ্য। **Primrose League**—রক্ষণশীল সম্প্রদায়ের মতপ্রচারের জন্য ১৮৮৩ খৃঃ অব্দে প্রতিষ্ঠিত সমিতিবিশেষ—এই সমিতি Benjamin Disraeli (Lord Beaconsfield) এর স্মৃতিরক্ষার্থ প্রতিষ্ঠিত হয়, বসন্তকুসুম সমিতি। **Primrose peerless**—একপ্রকার নারসিসাস্ পুষ্প। **A primrose in the dunghill**—গোবরে পদ্মফুল, দৈত্যকুলে প্রহ্লাদ। **The primrose path of a dalliance** — ধ্বংসের কুসুমাস্তীর্ণ বর্ত্ম।

Primrose.

prĭm'-ū-lă, *n.* A genus of perennial herbs ; একজাতীয় বহুবর্ষজীবী গুল্ম।

Central inflorescene of primula.

Primum cognitum—প্রথমজ্ঞান (হিঃ কোঃ), প্রথমাভাস (ঐ)।

Primum mobile, *n.* 1. The first cause of motion ; গতির আদিকারণ, প্রথমকর্ত্তা। (হিঃ কোঃ) 2. (*Ancient Astron.*) The outermost of the revolving spheres of the universe ; (প্রাচীন জ্যোতির্ব্বিজ্ঞান) বিশ্বের আবর্ত্তনশীল মণ্ডল সমূহের মধ্যে অতিবহিঃস্থমণ্ডল, বহিস্তম মণ্ডল, প্রবহগোল (হিঃ কোঃ)।

prī'-mŭs, *adj.* & *n.* (In boys' school) The eldest of the name ; as, John *primus* ; (পাঠশালায়) বিদ্যালয়ের একশ্রেণীর সমনামধারী ছাত্রগণের মধ্যে সর্ব্ব জ্যেষ্ঠ বালক। ***Noun.*** The first bishop of the Scottish Episcopal Church ; স্কটলণ্ডের ধর্ম্মাধ্যক্ষশাসিত ধর্ম্মসংঘে প্রথম ধর্ম্মাধ্যক্ষ।

primus inter pares (*L.*)—The first among equals ; সমপদস্থ ব্যক্তিগণের মধ্যে প্রথম।

prince (prĭns), *n.* 1. (*Now Rhet.*) A sovereign or king ; রাজা, ভূপাল। 2. A ruler of a small State ; a chief ; ক্ষুদ্র রাজ্যের রাজা ; সর্দ্দার। 3. A son or grandson of a king or queen ; a male member of a royal family ; রাজপুত্র, রাজনন্দন, যুবরাজ, রাজকুমার, ভূপপুত্র, রাজতনয়, রাজসুত ; রাজপরিবারের পুরুষ। 4. (As a courtesy title) A duke, marquis or earl ; (শিষ্ট সম্বোধনে) ডিউক, মার্ক্‌ইস অথবা আর্ল। 5. (In some European countries) A title of nobility usually ranking next below that of duke ; (ইয়ুরোপের কোন কোন দেশে) ডিউকের নিম্নতর উপাধিবিশেষ। 6. (*Fig.*) One who is pre-eminent ; the greatest ; as, the *prince* of novelists, liars, etc. ; (লক্ষণায়) সর্ব্বশ্রেষ্ঠ ব্যক্তি ; সম্রাট, রাজা [cf. কৃষ্ণদাস কবিরাজ (now *rare*), কবি-সম্রাট রবীন্দ্রনাথ] ; সর্ব্বশ্রেষ্ঠ, রাজা। **Prince'-dom, Prince'-kin, Prince'-let,** *ns.* **Prince'-like,** *adj.* **Prince'-ling,** *n.* **Prince'-ship,** *n.* **Prince bishop**—যে ব্যক্তি একাধারে

কোন স্থানের ধর্ম্মাধ্যক্ষ এবং শাসন-কর্ত্তা। **Prince Consort**—রাজ্ঞীর পতি। রাজ্য-শাসন সংক্রান্ত ব্যাপারে ইঁহার কোনরূপ সম্বন্ধ নাই।] **Prince Regent**—যে রাজপুত্র রাজার নাবালকত্ব, অনুপস্থিতি বা অসুস্থতার কালে প্রতিনিধি-রূপে রাজ্য শাসন করে। **Prince royal**—রাজা বা রাণীর জ্যেষ্ঠ পুত্র। **Prince of darkness, the air, the world, etc.**—শয়তান। **Prince of Peace**—যীশুখৃষ্ট। **Prince of the blood**—ইংলণ্ডেশ্বরের পুত্র বা পৌত্র। **Prince of Wales**—ইংলণ্ডের যুবরাজ। **Prince Rupert's drops**—যে সকল গলিত কাচের ফোঁটা শীতলজলে পাতিত হইলে বেঙ্গাচীর আকার ধারণ করে এবং উহাদের লাঙ্গুলের অগ্রভাগ ভাঙ্গিয়া ফেলিলে যাহারা ভীম শব্দে খণ্ড-বিখণ্ড হইয়া যায়। **Prince's feather**—মুর্গা গাছ (খোরী)। **Prince's metal**—তাম্র এবং দস্তার মিশ্র।

prince'-ly (prîns-), *adj.* 1. Of, or relating to, a prince; royal; of the highest rank or authority; রাজপুত্রসম্বন্ধীয়; রাজকীয়; উচ্চপদবীর। 2. Becoming a prince; magnificent; noble; রাজপুত্রসমুচিত, রাজোপযুক্ত, নৃপোচিত; মহাপ্রতাপ; মহাকুল প্রসূত। **–li-ness**, *n.*

prin'-cĕss, *n.* 1. (*Archaic*) A queen; রাণী। 2. The consort of a prince; (অপ্রঃ) রাজপুত্র বা পত্নী, যুবরাজ্ঞী। 3. The daughter or grand-daughter of a sovereign; a female member of a royal family; রাজনন্দিনী, রাজকুমারী, রাজবালা, রাজপুত্রী, রাজপুত্রিকা, রাজসুতা; রাজপরিবারভুক্তা মহিলা। **–ship**, *n.* **Princess dress** — ভদ্রমহিলার যে পরিচ্ছদের বডিস ও গাউন একখণ্ড কাপড় হইতে কাটা হয়। **Princess Regent** — যে রাজপুত্রী বা যুবরাজপত্নী রাজার প্রতিনিধিরূপে রাজ্যশাসন করেন। **Princess royal**—ইংলণ্ডেশ্বরের জ্যেষ্ঠা কন্যা। **Princess of the blood**—রাজার পুত্রী বা পৌত্রী।

prin'-ci-păl, *adj.* & *n.* 1. Chief; highest in rank, importance, etc.; মুখ্য, প্রধান; শ্রেষ্ঠ। 2. (Of money) Constituting the primary or original sum invested or lent; ধনমূলস্বরূপ। *Noun.* 1. A leader; chief or head; নায়ক, নেতা; প্রধান, সর্দ্দার। 2. The head of some colleges; কোন কোন মহাবিদ্যালয়ের অধ্যক্ষ, অধ্যক্ষ। 3. The chief actor in a crime or an abettor present at it; হত্যাকাণ্ড প্রভৃতির প্রধান নায়ক বা ঘটনাস্থলে উপস্থিত সহায়ক। 4. One for whom another is a surety; যে ব্যক্তির জন্য অপর ব্যক্তি জামিন হইয়াছে। 5. One who employs another as agent etc.; প্রতিনিধি নিয়োক্তা। 6. A capital sum as distinguished from interest etc.; আসল, ধন (যাজ্ঞঃ), মূলধন (হিঃ কোঃ), ধনমূল (সাঃ পঃ), প্রয়োগ (গৌতমঃ), সাধক (বিষ্ণুঃ সং), মূল [cf. মূলকলান্তরে (Principal and interest) লীলাবতী।], কায় (নারদঃ), প্রযোজ্য (মঃ উঃ)। 7. A combatant in a duel; দ্বন্দ্বযুদ্ধের অন্যতর (যোদ্ধা)। 8. Same as ORGAN-STOP (which see). **–ly**, *adv.* Primarily; chiefly; mainly; মূলতঃ; প্রধানতঃ; মুখ্যতঃ। **–ship**, *n.* **Lady principal**—মহাবিদ্যালয়ের প্রধানা আচার্য্যাণী।

prin-ci-păl'-i-tÿ, *n.* 1. (*Rare*) The state of being principal; (ক্বচিদ্‌ব্যবহৃত) প্রধানতা। 2. The Government or State of a prince; যুবরাজের শাসনতন্ত্র বা রাজ্য। 3. (*Pl.*) An order of angels; একশ্রেণীর দেবদূত। **The Principality**—ওয়েল্‌স্‌।

prin'-ci-pāte, *n.* 1. A State governed by a prince; যুবরাজ-শাসিত রাজ্য। 2. (*Rom. hist.*) The rule of early emperors while some republican forms were retained; (রোমান ইতিহাস) প্রাথমিক সম্রাটদিগের শাসন—যখন গণতন্ত্রের কতকগুলি রীতিপদ্ধতি রক্ষিত হইয়াছিল।

prin-cip'-i-ă, *n.* (*Pl.*) First principles; elements; মূলতত্ত্ব; উপক্রমণিকা। **Newton's principia**—স্যর আইজাক নিউটনকৃত উচ্চাঙ্গের গণিত-বিষয়ক গ্রন্থ।

prin'-ci-ple (-pl), *n.* 1. Source; ultimate element or cause; as, water was held to be the first *principle* of things; উৎপত্তি, প্রভব; পরমকারণ, পরমতত্ত্ব, আদিকারণ, মূলকারণ, মূলভূত, বীজ, মূল (হিঃ কোঃ)। 2. A fundamental truth; মূলতত্ত্ব, মৌলিকসত্য, তত্ত্ব (ব্রজঃ বৈষ্ণঃ)। 3. A settled rule of action, opinion or belief exercising a guiding influence; a rule of conduct consistently directing one's actions; as, a man of no *principle*: the *principles* of a party; মূলসূত্র, সূত্র, নিয়ম; মূলমত বা বিশ্বাস, মূল সিদ্ধান্ত, মূলনীতি, নীতিতত্ত্ব, নীতিবুদ্ধি, নীতিজ্ঞান। 4. (*Phys.*) A general law; (পদার্থ বিদ্যা) ব্যাপক নিয়ম। 5. (*Chem.*) An element or constituent of a substance; as, an active, bitter or colouring *principle*; (রসায়নশাস্ত্র) মূল-বস্তু, বীর্য্য (হিঃ কোঃ), উপাদান। **–pled**, *adj.* **First principles**—মূলতত্ত্ব। **A man of (no) principle**—See PRINCIPLE, *n.* 3. **In principle**—আদৌ, মূলে। **On principle**—From settled moral motive and not from selfish motives, etc.; নীতিজ্ঞান দ্বারা পরিচালিত হইয়া, নীতিবুদ্ধি অনুসারে। **Principle of contradiction**—See LAW OF CONTRADICTION.

prink (pringk), *v. t.* & *i.* 1. To dress up; to deck fantastically; সাজান; অপরূপভাবে সাজান। 2. (Of birds) To trim as feathers; (পক্ষিসম্বন্ধে) পাখা ঠিক করা। *Verb i.* To dress or deck oneself up; সজ্জিত করা, সাজান।

print, *n.* 1. A mark made by pressure or impression

as, a foot*print* ; দাগ, চিহ্ন, অঙ্ক,ছাপ, ছাদ, মুদ্রা, মুদ্রিকা। **2.** A printed cotton fabric, (*often attrib.*) ; "Their *print* frocks...were gone" ; ছিটের কাপড়। **3.** Printed letters ; impression of types in general ; as, large, small or clear *print* ; মুদ্রিত অক্ষরসমূহ ; ছাপা। **4.** State of being printed ; as, the book is in *print* ; মুদ্রণাবস্থা, যন্ত্রস্থতা। **5.** A printed publication esp. a newspaper or other periodical ; মুদ্রিত পুস্তকাদি, বিশেষতঃ সংবাদপত্র বা সাময়িক পত্রিকা। **6.** A picture, design or the like printed from an engraved plate etc. ; ক্ষোদিত ফলক হইতে মুদ্রিত ছবি, পরিকল্পনা, প্রভৃতি। **7.** (*Photog.*) A copy of a picture produced from a negative ; (আলোকচিত্র) বিপর্য্যস্তচিত্র হইতে মুদ্রিত স্বভাবানুরূপ আলোকচিত্র। **Print hand, Print letters**—মুদ্রণাক্ষরের অনুরূপ হস্তলিপি। **Print-seller**—ক্ষোদিতফলক প্রভৃতি বিক্রেতা। **Print-shop**—ক্ষোদিত ফলক প্রভৃতির দোকান। **Print-works**—যে শিল্পশালায় ছিটের কাপড় মুদ্রিত করা হয়। **The book is in print**—পুস্তকখানা মুদ্রিত অবস্থায় আছে; পুস্তকখানা বিক্রীত হইতেছে। **The book is out of print**—পুস্তক আর ছাপা নাই। **To rush into print**—(Of a writer) To publish a book or to write to newspaper etc. on insufficient grounds ; অনুচিত ব্যগ্রতার সহিত পুস্তক প্রকাশ করা বা খবরের কাগজ প্রভৃতিতে লিখা।

print, *v. t.* **1.** To impress as a stamp, mark, etc., into or upon something ; ছাপ দেওয়া। **2.** To make an impression or mark upon by pressure ; মুদ্রিত করা। **3.** (*Fig.*) To impress as a thought, idea, scene, etc. on the heart, mind or memory ; (লক্ষণায়) মনোমধ্যে মুদ্রিত করা। **4.** To stamp or impress with characters, figures, patterns, etc. from plates, types or the like ; as, to *print* calico ; ছাপা করা। **5.** To impress as letters etc. on paper ; to do the type-setting, presswork, etc. of (a book, edition, etc.) ; (of an author, editor, etc.) to cause as a manuscript, book, etc. to be *printed* ; মুদ্রিত করা ; ছাপা করা ; ছাপান। **6.** To publish or express in print ; as, not bound to *print* every opinion you hold ; ছাপাইয়া প্রকাশ করা। **7.** To write in characters like those of type ; ছাপার অক্ষরে লিখা। **8.** (*Photog.*) To produce as a picture from a negative ; (আলোকচিত্র) বিপর্য্যস্ত চিত্র হইতে মুদ্রিত করা। **Print'-a-ble**, *adj.*

print'-ĕr, *n.* **1.** One who prints, esp. one printing books etc. ; মুদ্রাকর। **2.** The owner of a printing business ; মুদ্রাযন্ত্রের স্বত্বাধিকারী। **3.** An instrument for printing ; মুদ্রাযন্ত্র। **Printer's devil** — See under DEVIL. **Printer's mark**—মুদ্রাকরের ব্যবসায়-চিহ্ন। **Printer's pie**—See under PIE, *n.* & *v. t.*

print'-ing, *n.* The act, art or practice of impressing letters or figures on paper, cloth, etc. ; typography ; মুদ্রণ; মুদ্রণশিল্প, মুদ্রাঙ্কণ। **Printing-ink** — ছাপার কালি। **Printing paper**—ছাপিবার কাগজ।

Printing-press, capable of printing and folding 72,000 papers hourly.

Printing-press—মুদ্রাযন্ত্র। **Printing works, house**—ছাপাখানা।

prī'-ŏr, *adj.* & *adv.* Antecedent ; earlier ; পূর্ব্ববর্ত্তী, পূর্ব্বতন, পূর্ব্বগামী, পূর্ব্বতর (হিঃ কোঃ) ; পূর্ব্বকালিক, অগ্রবর্ত্তী, প্রাক্তন, আদ্য। ***Adv.*** Previously (to) ; পূর্ব্বে। **–or'-i-ty**, *n.* State of being prior ; পূর্ব্ববর্ত্তিতা, অগ্রবর্ত্তিতা, প্রাথম্য, পুরোবর্ত্তিতা, পূর্ব্বত্ব (হিঃ কোঃ), পূর্ব্বকালিকতা (ঐ), প্রাচীনতা (ঐ), পূর্ব্বভাব।

prī'-ŏr, *n.* **1.** The superior of a convent of monks, or one next in dignity to an abbot ; মঠাধ্যক্ষ, বিহারপাল, মহন্ত, মঠাধিপতি, মঠাধিকারী। **2.** (*Hist.*) A chief magistrate in some Italian republics ; (ইতিহাস) ইতালীদেশীয় কোন কোন গণতন্ত্রের প্রধান দণ্ডনায়ক। **–ate, –ship**, *ns.*

prī'-ō-rȳ, *n.* A convent or nunnery governed by a prior or prioress ; বিহার, মঠ, ভিক্ষুণী সংঘ। **Alien priory, priory alien**—কোন বিদেশীয় বিহারের আশ্রিত ব্যক্তি।

prism, *n.* **1.** A solid whose bases or ends are similar, equal and parallel plane figures and whose sides are parallelograms ; যে ঘনক্ষেত্রের প্রান্তদ্বয় সমরূপ, সমান এবং সমানান্তর সরলরৈখিক ক্ষেত্র এবং পার্শ্বদ্বয় সমানান্তর চতুর্ভুজ ; ফলকীয় খাত (হিঃ কোঃ), ত্রিপার্শ্ব (ঐ)। **2.** A transparent body of this form, usually triangular used in experiments in refraction, dispersion, etc. ; ত্রিপার্শ্ব কাচ, তেশিরা কাচ, ক্রকচায়ত (আঃ বঃ)। **3.** A spectrum produced by refraction through a prism ; (*pl.*) prismatic colours ; ত্রিপার্শ্ব কাচের ভিতর দিয়া আলোকরশ্মি পরিবর্ত্তিত হইলে যে বর্ণচ্ছত্র উৎপন্ন হয় ; তেশিরা কাচের ভিতর দিয়া আলোক পরবর্ত্তিত হইলে যে সপ্তবর্ণ উৎপন্ন হয়।

Pris'-mal, *adj.* **Achromatic prism**—অবর্ণ ক্রকচারত, নীরঙ্গ ত্রিপার্শ্ব (হিঃ কোঃ)। **Prune and prism**—See under PRUNE.

pris-măt'-ic, *adj.* 1. Of, relating to, or like, prism; ত্রিপার্শ্বকাচসম্বন্ধীয়, ত্রিপার্শ্বকাচবৎ। 2. (Of colours) Formed, distributed, etc. by a transparent prism; bright or brilliant; (বর্ণ সম্বন্ধে) ত্রিপার্শ্বকাচদ্বারা ঘটিত বা বিশ্লিষ্ট, ত্রিপার্শ্বকাচবিকীর্ণ; উজ্জ্বল, দীপ্তিমান। **–i-cal-ly,** *adv.* **Pris'-my,** *adj.* Of varied colours; prismatic; বিচিত্রবর্ণ; ত্রিপার্শ্বকাচাকার, ত্রিপার্শ্বকাচবিকীর্ণ। **Prismatic colours**—বেগুণে, অতিনীল, নীল, হরিৎ, পীত, জরদ এবং লোহিত এই সপ্তবর্ণ—যাহাতে ত্রিপার্শ্বকাচদ্বারা আলোকরশ্মি বিশ্লিষ্ট হয়। **Prismatic powder**—ষট্‌কোণ এবং ত্রিপার্শ্ব বারুদের কণা।

pris'-moid (-moyd), *n.* A figure that approaches the form of a prism; ত্রিপার্শ্বকল্পক্ষেত্র। **–moi-dal,** *adj.*

pris'-ŏn, *n.* & *v. t.* 1. A place of confinement; a jail; নিরোধ স্থান, বন্ধনস্থান, কারাগার, কারাগৃহ, বন্দিশালা, বন্দনাগার, বন্ধনালয়, বন্ধনস্থান, বন্দিবেশ্ম, কারাবেশ্ম; জেলখানা। 2. Custody; confinement; as, to lie or put one in *prison*; জিম্মা, হেপাজৎ; অবরোধ। *Verb t.* (*Poet.* & *Rhet.*) To imprison; (কবিতা বা অলঙ্কারশাস্ত্রে) কারারুদ্ধ করা। **Prison-bird**—Same as JAIL-BIRD. **Prison-breaking**—জেল ভাঙ্গিয়া পলায়ন। (*Prison-breaker, n.*) **Prison editor**—কোন পত্রিকার প্রকাশিত আইনানুসারে দণ্ডনীয় প্রবন্ধাদির জন্য কারাদণ্ড ভোগ করার জন্য নিযুক্ত সম্পাদক, কারাসম্পাদক। **Prison-house**—কারাগার, জেলখানা, কয়েদখানা, বন্ধনশালা, বন্ধনালয়, বন্দিশালা।

pris'-ŏn-ĕr, *n.* 1. One shut up in a prison; কয়েদী, বন্দী। 2. A captive; as, a *prisoner* of war; বন্দী। **Made her hand a prisoner**—সে তাহার হাত চাপিয়া ধরিল। **Prisoner at the bar**—বিচারালয়ে কাঠগড়ায় দণ্ডায়মান বন্দী। **Prisoner of State, State prisoner**—রাজনৈতিক বন্দী। **Prisoner of war**—সামরিক বন্দী। **Prisoners' bars, base**—ছেলেদের একপ্রকার ক্রীড়া। **To take prisoner**—To capture; বন্দী করা।

pris'-tine, *adj.* Earliest; primitive; good old; আদিম; পূর্ব্বতন; সাবেক, প্রাচীন, সেকেলে।

prith'-ee (-ঈ), *Interj.* (*Archaic*) (A corruption of *I pray thee*) Pray; (অপ্রঃ) আমার মিনতি, আমার প্রার্থনা।

prī'-vă-cy̆, *n.* 1. State of being withdrawn from society or public interest; seclusion; নির্জ্জনতা, বিজনতা, বিবিক্ততা; নিভৃতত্ব নির্জ্জনবাস, বিবিক্তবাস। 2. Absence or avoidance of publicity; as, in such matters *privacy* is impossible; গোপনীয়তা, গোপনতা।

privat-docent, -dozent, *ns.* (Gr. Univ.) A licensed private teacher or lecturer; (জর্ম্মণ বিশ্ববিদ্যালয়) সনন্দপ্রাপ্ত গৃহশিক্ষক বা অধ্যাপক।

prī'-vate (-vāt), *adj.* & *n.* 1. Not invested with public office or employment; বেসরকারী। 2. Kept from public knowledge; secret; গুপ্ত, প্রচ্ছন্ন; গূঢ়। 3. One's own; as, his *private* affair; আত্ম, খাস, স্বকীয়, নিজ, নিজস্ব। 4. Secluded; solitary; বিজন; নির্জ্জন। 5. Personal or individual; as, motives of *private* malice; ব্যক্তিগত। 6. Confidential; as, a *private* talk; গোপনীয়। 7. (*Archaic*) Sequestered from society or given to seclusion, as a person; (অপ্রঃ) বিবিক্ত। *Noun.* 1. A common soldier; সাধারণ সৈনিক। 2. (*Pl.*) The private parts; গোপনীয় অঙ্গ, অধোদেশ, গুহ্যদেশ (বাৎস্যঃ)। **–ly,** *adv.* In a private manner; not openly; secretly; নির্জ্জনে, গোপনে; রহসি, একান্তে; লুকোচুরি করিয়া। **Private affairs**—আত্মকার্য্য। **Private apartment**—খাসকামরা। **Private bill or act**—কোন ব্যক্তিবিশেষের সম্বন্ধে বা ব্যক্তিস্বরূপ কার্য্যকরার ক্ষমতাপ্রাপ্ত সমবায় সম্পর্কে বিধিবদ্ধ পার্লেমেন্টের আইন। **Private chamber**—খাস কামরা। **Private property**—ব্যক্তিগত সম্পত্তি। **Private room**—খাসকামরা। **Private school**—বেসরকারী বিদ্যালয়। **Private schoolmaster**—বেসরকারী বিদ্যালয়ের শিক্ষক। **Private soldier**—Same as PRIVATE, *n.* I. **Private tutor**—গৃহশিক্ষক। **A private member of the House of Commons**—পার্লেমেন্টের যে সভ্য মন্ত্রিসভার সদস্য নন। **In private**—Privately; in private life or company; গোপনে, রহসি; নিভৃতে, একান্তে। **This is for your private ear**—এই বিষয়টী কেবল আপনার শুনিবার জন্য।

prī-vă-teer' (-tēr), *n.* 1. A private ship of war having a commission to seize or plunder the ships of an enemy; শত্রুর জাহাজ ধৃত করণ বা লুণ্ঠনের জন্য অধিকারপ্রাপ্ত বেসরকারী যুদ্ধ জাহাজ। 2. A commander of this; (*pl.*) its crew; ঐরূপ জাহাজের অধ্যক্ষ; ঐরূপ জাহাজের মাল্লা। **–ing,** *n.* Plundering or seizing the ships of an enemy by means of privateers; বে-সরকারী যুদ্ধজাহাজ দ্বারা শত্রুপোত লুণ্ঠন বা ধৃত করণ।

prī-vā'-tion, *n.* 1. Absence; loss; as, cold is *privation* of heat; অভাব; রাহিত্য, হানি। 2. Want of what is necessary for comfort; destitution; as, he died of *privation*; অভাব, কষ্ট; নিঃস্বতা।

priv'-ă-tive (-tĭv), *adj.* 1. Marked by, or consisting in, the loss or absence of some quality, etc.; as, cold is merely *privative*; অভাবার্থক, অভাবসূচক, পর্য্যুদাসক (হিঃ কোঃ)। 2. (*Gram.*) Denoting privation or negation; (ব্যাকরণ) নঞর্থক, নাস্তিবাচক।

3. Indicating the absence of any quality or attribute, as a term ; অভাবসূচক, অভাববোধক। **—ly,** *adv.*

priv'-ĕt, *n.* A shrub much used for making hedges; বৃতিনির্ম্মাণে বহুল ব্যবহৃত গুল্ম বিশেষ, বৃতিগুল্ম। **Privet-hawk**—একপ্রকার তসরে পোকা—যাহা বৃতিগুল্মের উপর ডিম্ব পাড়িয়া থাকে।

priv'-i-lege (-lĕj), *n.* & *v. t.* **1.** A right, advantage or immunity granted to, or enjoyed by, a person, class, office, etc. ; অধিকার, সুবিধা। **2.** A special benefit or advantage ; as, to converse with him is a *privilege* ; বিশেষ সুবিধা বা উপকার। **3.** An advantage peculiar to a person, company or society, such as a monopoly, patent, etc. ; কোন ব্যক্তির বিশেষ অধিকার। ***Verb t.*** **1.** To grant some right or immunity to ; to allow as a privilege ; বিশেষ অধিকার প্রদান করা ; বিশেষ অধিকার স্বরূপ দেওয়া। **2.** To exempt (*from*) ; "Barristers are *privileged* from arrest" ; মুক্তি দেওয়া, রেহাই দেওয়া। **—leged,** *p. adj.* Invested with or enjoying a privilege ; বিশেষ অধিকারপ্রাপ্ত। **Personal privilege** — ব্যক্তিগত সুবিধা। **Privilege cab** — যে গাড়ী রেলওয়ে ষ্টেশন প্রভৃতিতে ভাড়ার জন্য অপেক্ষা করিতে পারে। **Privilege communication** — যে কথা বার্ত্তা অপরের নিকট প্রকাশ্য নহে, উকীল ও মোক্কেলের মধ্যে গোপনীয় চিঠিপত্র বা কথাবার্ত্তা—যাহা মোক্কেলের বিনা অনুমতিতে প্রকাশ্য নহে। **A bill of privilege**—লর্ড উপাধিধারী ব্যক্তি সমপদবীর ব্যক্তিগণ দ্বারা বিচারিত হইবার জন্য আবেদন। **A writ of privilege**—দেওয়ানী মোকদ্দমায় কোন বিশেষ অধিকারপ্রাপ্ত ব্যক্তি গ্রেপ্তার হইলে তাহাকে ছাড়িয়া দেওয়ার জন্য পরোয়ানা।

priv'-i-tȳ, *n.* **1.** State of being privy (to) ; joint knowledge ; জ্ঞাতসারিতা (রঃ অঃ) ; উভয় পক্ষের অবগতি। **2.** (*Law*) A connection between parties as to some particular transaction ; (আইন) যোগাযোগ, যোগ, যোগসাজস।

priv'-ȳ, *adj.* & *n.* **1.** Concealed ; secret or secluded as a thing, act or place ; private ; গুপ্ত, নিভৃত ; প্রচ্ছন্ন; গোপনীয়। **2.** Privately cognizant or aware,. (with *to*) ; as, he was *privy to* the designs ; গোপনে অবগত, জ্ঞাতসার। ***Noun.*** **1.** A latrine ; পাইখানা, মলাগার, টাট্টি (*colloq.*), শৌচখানা, অবস্কর। **2.** (*Law*) A person having an interest in any action or thing ; কোন মোকদ্দমা বা বিষয়ের স্বার্থবিশিষ্ট ব্যক্তি। **—i-ly,** *adv.* Secretly ; গোপনে, নিভৃতে, একান্তে। **Privy chamber**—রাজার খাসকামরা। **Privy Council**—মন্ত্রিসমাজ ; ইংলণ্ডের মন্ত্রিসভা। **Privy counsellor** or **councillor**—(Abbr. *P. C.*) বিলাতের মন্ত্রিসভার সভ্য। **Privy parts**—জননেন্দ্রিয়, সঙ্গমেন্দ্রিয়, উপস্থ। **Privy purse**—রাজার নিজ ব্যয়ের জন্য বৃত্তি বা ভাতা ; ঐ বৃত্তি বা ভাতার টাকা যে কর্ম্মচারীর কাছে থাকে। **Privy-seal**—সাধারণ সনন্দ প্রভৃতির উপর রাজা যে মোহর দ্বারা ছাপ দেন। **To be privy to**—To be in the secret of (a person's designs etc.) ; ভিতরের কথা জ্ঞাতসার থাকা।

prīze, *n.* & *v. t.* **1.** A reward ; পুরস্কার, পারিতোষিক। **2.** Money or money's worth won or to be won in a lottery etc. ; ভাগ্য খেলার পুরস্কার, পুরস্কার। **3.** (*Fig.*) Anything striven for or worth striving for ; as, he missed all the great *prizes* of life ; (লক্ষণায়) পুরস্কার, সারবস্তু, মূল্যবান বস্তু। **Prize'-less,** *adj.* **Prize cow, poem etc.**—প্রদর্শনী, প্রতিযোগিতা, প্রভৃতিতে পুরস্কারপ্রাপ্ত, গাভী, কবিতা, প্রভৃতি। **Prize-fellow**—কোন পরীক্ষায় বিশেষ কৃতিত্ব প্রদর্শনের জন্য কোন বিশ্ববিদ্যালয়ে ফেলোস্বরূপ নিযুক্ত ব্যক্তি। **Prize fellowship**—কোন পরীক্ষায় বিশেষ কৃতিত্বের সহিত উত্তীর্ণ হওয়ার দরুণ প্রদত্ত ফেলো-শিপ। **Prize-fight**—A boxing match for money ; মল্লযুদ্ধ। (*Prize-fighter, n.* One who fights for prizes ; মল্ল, ঝল্ল। *Prize-fighting, n.*) **Prize-man**—The winner of a prize, (often with a specific name) ; as, Smith's *prize*man (The winner of smith's prize) ; পুরস্কারপ্রাপ্ত ব্যক্তি। **Prize-ring**—An enclosed area (now usually square) for prize-fighting ; (*fig.*) the practice of prize-fighting ; মল্লযুদ্ধের জন্য বৃতিবেষ্টিত স্থান বা চত্বর, রঙ্গাঙ্গন, রঙ্গভূমি, রঙ্গক্ষেত্র মল্লভূমি ; (লক্ষণায়) মল্লযুদ্ধ শিক্ষা। **To play prizes**—To be serious or in earnest ; সত্য সত্যই কোন কথা বলা বা কোন কার্য্য করার সংকল্প করা।

prīze, *adj.* **1.** Having been awarded a prize, as a *prize* poem ; পুরস্কারপ্রাপ্ত। **2.** Awarded as a prize ; as, at *prize* fellowship ; পুরস্কারস্বরূপপ্রদত্ত।

prīze, *n.* & *v. t.* **1.** A vessel, property, etc. captured at sea in virtue of the rights of war ; যুদ্ধকালে সমুদ্রে ধৃত জাহাজ বা অন্য সম্পত্তি। **2.** (*Rare*) Anything seized or captured as in war ; (কচিদ্ ব্যবহৃত) যুদ্ধে ধৃত বস্তু। ***Verb t.*** To seize as a prize : যুদ্ধকালে জাহাজ প্রভৃতি সমুদ্রে ধৃত করা। **Prize court**—যুদ্ধকালে সমুদ্রে ধৃত জাহাজ বা অন্য সম্পত্তি সম্বন্ধে কিরূপ ব্যবস্থা হইবে—তৎ মীমাংসার্থ সামুদ্রিক সচিব সমাজের (Admiralty) বিভাগ বিশেষ। **Prize-money**—যুদ্ধকালে সমুদ্রে গৃহীত জাহাজ প্রভৃতির বিক্রয়লব্ধ অর্থ। **To become prize**—To be seized as a prize ; যুদ্ধকালে সমুদ্রে ধৃত হওয়া। **To make a prize of**—To seize as prize, as a ship, cargo, etc. ; যুদ্ধকালে সমুদ্রে জাহাজ প্রভৃতি ধৃত করা।

prīze, prīsĕ, *v. t. & n.* To force *up* or *open* with a lever ; দণ্ডযন্ত্র দ্বারা খোলা, চাড়া দিয়া খোলা। ***Noun.*** Act of prizing ; leverage ; দণ্ড-যন্ত্রদ্বারা উন্মোচন ; চাড়া দিয়া তোলন।

prō, *prep.* For ; জন্য, পক্ষে, অনুকূলে। ***Pro bono publico***—For the public welfare ; for the good of the whole company; লোকসাধারণের হিতার্থ ; সকলের উপকারের জন্য। ***Pro forma***—(*adv.* & *adj.*) For form's sake ; as a matter of form ; রীতি রক্ষার জন্য, কেবল দাঁড়ামতে (বিঃ অঃ) ; রীতিস্বরূপ। (*Adj.*) Done for form's sake ; রীতি রক্ষার জন্য সম্পাদিত। ***Pro hac vice***—For this occasion only ; কেবল এইবারের জন্য। ***Pro rata***—(*adv.* & *adj.*) Proportionately ; অনুপাতে। (*Adj.*) Proportional ; আনুপাতিক। ***Pro re nata***—(*adv.* & *adj.*) For some contingency arising unexpectedly ; কোন আকস্মিক ঘটনার জন্য। ***Pro tanto***—To such an extent ; so far ; সেই পরিমাণে ; ততদূর। ***Pro tempore***—*adv.* & *adj.* (*Abbr. pro. tem.*) Temporarily ; অস্থায়িভাবে। (*Adj.*) Temporary ; অস্থায়ী, সাময়িক।

prō, *n.* (*Pl. pros., colloq.*) Abbr. of PROFESSIONAL (which see.)

Proa.

prō'-ă, *n.* A swift-sailing canoe of the Malay Archipelago ; মালয় উপদ্বীপের একপ্রকার দ্রুতগামী শালতী নৌকা।

prō & cŏn, *adv.* & *n.* For or against (of arguments or reasons etc.); অনুকূলে এবং প্রতিকূলে, সপক্ষে ও বিপক্ষে। ***Noun.*** (*Pl.*) Arguments, reasons, etc. for and against ; প্রতিকূল বা অনুকূল যুক্তি প্রভৃতি।

prŏb-ă-bĭl'-ĭ-ō-rĭsm, *n.* (*R. C. Theol.*) The doctrine that a law is always to be obeyed unless an opinion clearly very probable is opposed to it ; (রোমান ক্যাথলিক ধর্ম্মসংঘ) অতি সম্ভবপর বিরুদ্ধ মতের অবর্ত্তমানে কোন বিধি অবশ্য-পালনীয়—এইরূপ মতবাদ। **—rist,** *n.*

prŏb'-ă-bĭ-lĭsm, *n.* **1.** The theory that certainty is impossible but that probability suffices to govern belief and action ; কোন বিষয়ে দৃঢ়প্রতীতি অসম্ভব তবে সম্ভাব্যতাই বিশ্বাস এবং কার্য্য নিয়ন্ত্রিত করার পক্ষে যথেষ্ট এইরূপ মতবাদ। **2.** (*R. C. Theol.*) The doctrine that where authorities differ any course may be followed for which a recognized doctor of the church can be cited ; (রোমান ক্যাথলিক ধর্ম্ম সংঘ) যেস্থলে প্রামাণিক ব্যক্তি বা গ্রন্থে মতভেদ দৃষ্ট হয় সে স্থলে যে ব্যবস্থা ধর্ম্মশাস্ত্রজ্ঞ কোন পণ্ডিতের অনুমোদিত তদনুসারে চলিতে হইবে—এইরূপ মত। **—list,** *n.*

prŏb-ă-bĭl'-ĭ-tȳ, *n.* **1.** State of being probable ; likelihood ; সম্ভাব্যতা ; সম্ভাবনা, সম্ভব (ন্যায়সূত্র)। **2.** That which is probable ; a probable or most probable event ; সম্ভবপর বিষয়, সম্ভাব্য বিষয় ; সম্ভাবনীয় ঘটনা। **3.** (*Math.*) The likelihood of the occurrence of an event ; (গণিতশাস্ত্র) কোন ঘটনা ঘটা সম্বন্ধে সম্ভাবনা, সম্ভাবনা।

prŏb'-ă-ble (-bl), *adj.* That is expected to take place ; likely ; সম্ভবপর, সম্ভাব্য, সম্ভাবনীয় ; সম্ভাবনার্হ, সম্ভাবী, সত্যসংকাশ। **—bly,** *adv.* In a probable manner ; likely ; সম্ভবতঃ ; হয়তঃ।

prō'-băng, *n.* (*Surg.*) A piece of whale-bone with a sponge, button, etc., at the end for removing obstructions from the throat ; (অস্ত্রোপচারবিদ্যা) গলনালী-রোধক বস্তু দূর করার জন্য শোষক, বোতাম, প্রভৃতি সংবদ্ধ তিমিমৎস্যের অস্থিখণ্ড, গলনালীশোধক।

prô'-bāte, *n.* **1.** Official proving of wills ; উইলের প্রমাণ করণ। **2.** A certified copy of a will proved ; প্রমাণীকৃত উইলের সহি-মোহরের নকল।

prō-bā'-tion, *n.* **1.** The testing or trial of a person's conduct, character, etc. ; trial or a period of trial ; as, to engage a person on *probation* ; কোন ব্যক্তির আচরণ, স্বভাব প্রভৃতি পরীক্ষণ ; পরীক্ষা বা পরীক্ষার কাল, পরীক্ষাধীন অবস্থা। **2.** The trial of a clergyman's qualifications preparatory to his settlement ; কোন যাজককে পদে প্রতিষ্ঠিত করার পূর্ব্বে তাঁহার যোগ্যতা সম্বন্ধে পরীক্ষা। **3.** Moral trial ; নৈতিক পরীক্ষা। **4.** The system of releasing young criminals, esp. first offenders on suspended sentence during good behaviour under the supervision of a person acting as a friend and adviser ; অল্পবয়স্ক বালকদিগের বিশেষতঃ প্রথম অপরাধকারিগণের দণ্ড স্থগিত রাখিয়া তাহাদিগকে বন্ধু বা পরামর্শ দাতৃরূপে কার্য্যকারী কোন ব্যক্তির তত্ত্বাবধানে মুক্তি দান। **5.** (*Rare*) Act of proving ; proof ; (কচিৎ ব্যবহৃত) প্রমাণীকরণ ; প্রমাণ। **Probation officer**—পরীক্ষাস্থলে মুক্তিপ্রদত্ত বালক অপরাধি-গণের উপদেষ্টা ও পরামর্শদাতা।

prō-bā'-tion-ă-rȳ, *adj.* Of, or relating to, probation serving for trial ; পরীক্ষাস্থলে নিয়োগসম্বন্ধীয় ; পরীক্ষাধীনে কার্য্যকারী, পরীক্ষাস্থলীয়। **—al,** *adj.*

prō-bā'-tion-êr, *n.* **1.** One who is on probation ; novice ; শিক্ষানবীশ,

উমেদার ; নবনিযুক্ত ব্যক্তি। **2.** A student in divinity licensed to preach ; ধর্ম্মপ্রচারের জন্য সনন্দপ্রাপ্ত ধর্ম্মশাস্ত্রশিক্ষার্থী। **3.** An offender or criminal under probation ; পরীক্ষা-স্থলে মুক্তিপ্রাপ্ত অপরাধী। **—ship,** *n.*

prōbe, *n.* & *v. t.* **1.** A surgeon's instrument for examining a wound etc. ; শলাকা (সুশ্রু কুঞ্জঃ), শলাকাযন্ত্র, আর (সুশ্রুঃ), এষণী (ঐ), ক্ষত শোধনী। *Verb t.* **1.** To examine as a wound etc. with a probe ; to penetrate with a sharp instrument ; শলাকাযন্ত্রদ্বারা ক্ষতের গভীরতা প্রভৃতি পরীক্ষা করা ; সূক্ষ্মাগ্র যন্ত্রদ্বারা ভেদ করা। **2.** (*Fig.*) To scrutinize or examine thoroughly ; as, to *probe* a person, motive, report, etc. ; (লক্ষণায়) পুঙ্খানুপুঙ্খরূপে পরীক্ষা করা।

prŏb′-i-tȳ, *n.* Honesty ; rectitude ; uprightness ; সাধুতা ; ন্যায়-পরায়ণতা ; আর্জ্জব।

prŏb′-lĕm, *n.* **1.** A doubtful or difficult case or question ; সমস্যা, কঠিন প্রশ্ন। **2.** Something difficult to understand ; as, his conduct is a *problem* to me ; দুর্ব্বোধ বিষয়। **3.** (*Geom.*) A proposition requiring something to be done, (opp. to *theorem*) ; (জ্যামিতি) সম্পাদ্য, সাধ্য (হিঃ কোঃ), বস্তুপপাদ্য (ঐ)। **Problem play, novel, etc.**—যে নাটক বা উপন্যাসে সামাজিক বা অন্য কোন বিষয়ক কোনরূপ প্রশ্ন বা সমস্যার আলোচনা থাকে।

prŏb-lĕm-ăt′-ic, —i-căl, *adjs.* **1.** Questionable ; disputable ; doubtful ; শঙ্কনীয় ; প্রশ্নাত্মক ; বিতর্কণীয় ; সন্দিগ্ধ, সংশয়াত্মক, অনিশ্চিত। **2.** (*Log.*) Enunciating or supporting what is possible but not necessarily true ; সবিকল্পক, সম্ভবাত্মক। **—i-cal-ly,** *adv.*

prŏb′-lĕm(-ăt)-ist, *n.* One who proposes or composes (esp. chess) problem ; যে ব্যক্তি কোন সমস্যা রচনা বা অবতারণা করে—বিশেষতঃ দাবা খেলার সমস্যা প্রস্তাব বা রচনা করে।

prō-bŏs-cĭd′-ē-ă, *n.* An order of mammals consisting of elephants and their extinct allies ; শুণ্ডধারী জন্তুবর্গ, হস্ত্যাদিবর্গ।

prō-bŏs-cĭd′-ē-ăn, —i-ăn, *adj.* & *n.* **1.** Of, relating to, or like, a proboscis ; শুণ্ডসম্বন্ধীয়, শুণ্ডবৎ। **2.** Of, or relating to, the proboscidea ; হস্ত্যাদিবর্গসম্বন্ধীয়। **3.** Having a proboscis ; শুণ্ডী, শুণ্ডাল, শুণ্ডার। *Noun.* One of the proboscidea ; হস্ত্যাদিবর্গের জন্তু।

prō-bŏs′-cis, *n.* **1.** The trunk of an elephant ; a long flexible snout in other animals ; শুঁড়, শুণ্ড, শুণ্ডা, শুণ্ডাদণ্ড ; অপর জন্তুর শুঁড়। **2.** The elongated part of the mouth of some insects ; কোন কোন পতঙ্গের মুখের দীর্ঘীভূত অংশ। **3.** A sucking organ in some worms ; কোন কোন কীটের শোষণ-যন্ত্র, শুঁড়। **4.** (*Humorous*) The human nose, esp. when very long ; (কৌতুকচ্ছলে) নাসা, বিশেষতঃ দীর্ঘনাসিকা। **—ci-dif′-er-ous, —cid′-i-form,** *adjs.* **Proboscis monkey**—দীর্ঘপ্রলম্বিত নাসাবিশিষ্ট বানর।

prō-că-thē′-drăl, *adj.* & *n.* Used as a cathedral ; মহাধর্ম্মমন্দিরস্বরূপ ব্যবহৃত। *Noun.* Such a church ; মহাধর্ম্মমন্দিরস্বরূপব্যবহৃত ভজনালয়।

prō-cē′-dūre, *n.* **1.** Act of proceeding ; ক্রিয়া, ব্যবহার। **2.** The manner of conducting a legal action or business esp. parliamentary ; কার্য্যবিধি, কার্য্যপ্রণালী, ব্যবহারমাতৃকা, বর্ত্ম (হিঃ কোঃ), প্রবর্ত্তন (ঐ), প্রবৃত্তি (ঐ), প্রসার (ঐ), সরণি (ঐ)।

prō-ceed′ (-sēd), *v. i.* **1.** To advance ; to go on ; as, to *proceed* on a journey or with an argument ; অগ্রসর হওয়া ; চলা। **2.** To adopt a course of action ; as, how will you *proceed* ; কোনরূপ কার্য্যপ্রণালী অবলম্বন করা। **3.** To issue or come forth ; to originate ; as, light *proceeds* from the sun ; নিঃসৃত হওয়া ; উদ্ভূত হওয়া। **4.** To continue to say ; as, in either case he *proceeded,* "our course is clear" ; বলিতে থাকা। **5.** (*Of a case, play, etc.*) To be carried on ; to take place ; as, the play will now *proceed* ; গৃহীত হওয়া ; ঘটা। **To proceed against**—কাহারো বিরুদ্ধে মোকদ্দমা করা। **To proceed to**—To go to ; to begin ; কোন স্থানে যাওয়া ; আরম্ভ করা। **To proceed with**—To continue ; চালান। **To proceed to the degree of M. A., To proceed M. A.**—To take M. A. degree ; এম্‌, এ উপাধি গ্রহণ করা।

prō-ceed′-ing (-sēd), *n.* **1.** Advancing ; progress ; অগ্রসর ; অগ্রগমন। **2.** A measure or course taken ; an action ; as, a high-minded *proceeding* ; কার্য্যপদ্ধতি ; কার্য্যপ্রণালী। **3.** (*Pl., Law*) The course of procedure in an action at law ; ব্যবহারপদ্ধতি, ব্যবহারমাতৃকা। **4.** (*Pl.*) The record of the transaction of a meeting, society, etc. ; কোন সমিতির কার্য্যবিবরণী, কার্য্যাবলী। **Legal proceedings**—মোকদ্দমা, মামলা।

prō′-ceeds (-sēdz), *n.* (*Pl.*) Outcome ; produce ; profit ; as, the *proceeds* of the sale will go to charity ; পরিণাম ; উৎপন্ন দ্রব্য ; লাভ।

prŏc-e-leus-măt′-ic (-lūs-), *adj.* & *n.* (*Prosody*) Of, or pertaining to, one or more proceleusmatics ; বিপ্র বা বিপ্রসমূহ-সম্বন্ধীয়। *Noun.* A foot of four short syllables ; ক্ষুদ্র শব্দাংশ চতুষ্টয়বিশিষ্ট কবিতার চরণ, বিপ্র।

prŏc-ĕl-lā′-ri-ăn, *adj.* & *n.* Of, or relating to, the genus of birds, to which the petrels belong ; সাগরবলাকা জাতীয়।

Noun. A bird of this genus ; ঐ জাতীয় পক্ষী।

prŏc′-ĕss, *n.* & *v. t.* Progress ; as, it is in the *process* of construction ; কার্য্যক্রম। 2. A line of action ; a proceeding ; কার্য্যপদ্ধতি, কার্য্যপ্রণালী ; ক্রিয়া। 3. A mode of operation ; as, a manufacturing *process* ; প্রক্রিয়া, পদ্ধতি, বিধি, রীতি, প্রণালী। 4. A series of changes as in growth, decay, etc. ; as, a *process* of decomposition ; পরিবর্তন-পরম্পরা। 5. A law suit ; formal commencement of this ; a writ, notice or summons ; মোকদ্দমা, ব্যবহার ; মোকদ্দমার আরম্ভ ; পরওয়ানা, সমন, আহ্বানপত্র, নোটিশ। 6. (*Print.*) A method other than simple engraving by hand of producing block ; a print from such a block ; (মুদ্রণ) চিত্রফলক প্রস্তুতের প্রণালীবিশেষ ; ঐরূপ চিত্রফলক হইতে মুদ্রিত চিত্র। 7. (*Anat., Zool,. Bot.*) A protuberance ; (জন্তুবিদ্যা, শারীর-সংস্থানবিদ্যা, উদ্ভিদবিদ্যা, প্রভৃতি) অস্থি প্রভৃতির উন্নত বা বিবর্দ্ধিত অংশ। *Verb t.* 1. To sue by legal process ; মোকদ্দমা করা। 2. To preserve as fruit, flesh, etc. by some process ; কোন বিশেষ উপায়ে ফল, মাংস, প্রভৃতি তাজা রাখা। 3. To reproduce as a drawing by a mechanical or photographic process ; যন্ত্র দ্বারা বা আলোকচিত্রের সাহায্যে কোন চিত্র পুনরুৎপাদন করা। **Direct Process** — অন্বয় ক্রিয়া (হিঃ কোঃ)। **Inverse process**— বিলোমক্রিয়া (হিঃ কোঃ)।

prŏ-cĕss′, *v. i.* (*Colloq.*) To walk or march in procession ; (চলিত ভাষায়) শোভাযাত্রায় গমন করা।

prŏ-ces′-sion (-sŏ-), *n., v. i.* & *t.* 1. Act of proceeding ; regular orderly progress esp. as a religious ceremony or on a festive occasion ; as, to walk or go in *procession* ; a train of persons doing this ; পুরোগমন, সংসরণ ; মিছিল, শোভাযাত্রা, যাত্রা, (cf. বরযাত্রা and বরযাত্রী) নিঃশাণ (সাঃ দঃ)। 2. (*Fig.*) An ill-contested race ; (লক্ষণায়) যে দৌড় বা কার্য্যে বিশেষ আড়াআড়ি নাই। 3. (*Theol.*) Emanation esp. of the Holy Ghost ; (খৃষ্টীয় ধর্ম্মশাস্ত্র) কায়ব্যূহ, (বিশেষতঃ পবিত্রাত্মার)। *Verb i.* To make a procession ; to go in procession ; শোভাযাত্রা করা ; শোভাযাত্রা করিয়া যাওয়া। *Verb t.* 1. To celebrate by, or carry in, a procession ; শোভাযাত্রা দ্বারা উৎসব-কার্য্য সম্পন্ন করা, শোভাযাত্রায় বহন করা। 2. To pass along (a street) in procession ; (কোন রাস্তা দিয়া) মিছিল লইয়া যাওয়া। **—a-ry,** *adj.* **Procession caterpillars, moth, etc,**—শোঁয়া পোকা, তসরে পোকা, প্রভৃতির শ্রেণী।

prŏ-ces′-sion-ăl (-sŏ-), *adj.* & *n.* 1. Of, or relating to, procession ; carried or sung in processions ; শোভাযাত্রাসম্বন্ধীয়, শোভাযাত্রায় বাহিত বা গীত। *Noun.* 1. (*R.C.Ch.*) A service-book containing processional hymns, etc. ; (রোমান ক্যাথলিক ধর্ম্মসংঘ) শোভাযাত্রায় গাহিবার উপযুক্ত স্তোত্রাবলীপূর্ণ পুস্তক। 2. A processional hymn ; শোভাযাত্রায় গীত স্তবসঙ্গীত।

prŏ-ces′-sion-ist (-sŏ-), *n.* One who takes part in a procession ; যে ব্যক্তি শোভাযাত্রায় যোগদান করে। **—ize,** *v. i.* To go in procession ; শোভাযাত্রায় গমন করা।

proces′-verbal, (*F.*), *n.* (*Pl.* -VERBAUX) 1. The minutes of the transactions of an assembly ; কোন পরিষদে পঠিত প্রবন্ধাদির আলোচনার সংক্ষিপ্তসার যে পুস্তকে থাকে। 2. (*French Law*) The written statement of facts in support of a charge ; (ফরাসীদেশের আইন) কোন অভিযোগের প্রতিপোষক বর্ণনাপত্র।

prŏ′-chrŏ-nĭsm, *n.* The antedating of an event ; কোন ঘটনাসম্বন্ধে প্রকৃত তারিখের পূর্ব্ব তারিখ প্রদান।

prŏ-claim′ (-klām), *v. t.* 1. To declare officially ; to announce publicly ; ঘোষণা করা ; খ্যাপন করা। 2. To declare as war, peace, etc. ; যুদ্ধ, শান্তি, প্রভৃতি ঘোষণা করা। 3. To place as a district etc. under legal restrictions by declaration ; রাজকীয় ঘোষণাপত্র প্রচার দ্বারা কোন জেলা প্রভৃতির লোকের কতিপয় বিষয়সম্পর্কে অধিকার সঙ্কোচ করা। **—cla-ma′-tion,** *n.* 1. Act of proclaiming ; announcement ; উদ্ঘোষণ, বিঘোষণ, প্রখ্যাপন, পরিকীর্ত্তন ; ঘোষণা (হিঃ কোঃ), কীর্ত্তন, পরিরটন। 2. That which is proclaimed ; a public notice ; বিঘোষিত বিষয় ; ঘোষণাপত্র, ইস্তাহার, জাহিরনামা। **—cla-ma′-to-ry,** *adj.*

prŏ-clit′-ic, *adj.* & *n.* (*Gk. Gram.*, of a monosyllabic word) Closely attached to a following word and having itself no accent ; (গ্রীক ব্যাকরণ) (এক মাত্রাত্মক শব্দসম্বন্ধে) স্বরচিহ্নবিহীন এবং পরবর্ত্তী শব্দের সহিত নিবিড়ভাবে সংশ্লিষ্ট। *Noun.* Such a word ; ঐরূপ শব্দ।

prŏ-cliv′-i-tȳ, *n.* Inclination ; tendency ; as, a *proclivity* to steal ; আসক্তি, প্রবণতা ; প্রাবণ্য, ঝোঁক, প্রবৃত্তি।

prŏ-cŏn′-sŭl, *n.* (*Rom. Hist.*) A Roman magistrate discharging the duties of a consul ; (রোমীয় ইতিহাস) প্রাচীন রোমের শাসনকর্ত্তৃগণের অন্যতম। 2. (*Rhet.*) The governor of a modern colony etc. ; (অলঙ্কারিক ভাষায়) আধুনিক উপনিবেশ প্রভৃতির শাসনকর্ত্তা। 3. (*Pro-consul*) A deputy consul ; প্রতিনিধি রাজদূত। **—su-lar,** *adj.* **—su-late, —sul-ship,** *ns.*

prŏ-crăs′-ti′-nāte, *v. i.* & *t.* To delay ; to be dilatory ; দেরী করা, গৌণ করা, বিলম্ব করা ; দীর্ঘসূত্রী

হওয়া। *Verb t.* (*Rare*) To put off from day to day; (কচিদ্ ব্যবহৃত) দিনের পর দিন স্থগিত রাখা। **–na′-ting,** *adj.* Delaying; দীর্ঘসূত্রী, গেঁতো (*colloq.*)। **–ra′-ting-ly,** *adv.* **–na′-tion,** *n.* Act of procrastinating; dilatoriness; বিলম্ব করণ; দীর্ঘ-সূত্রতা, চিরকারিতা। **–na-tive, –na-tor,** *n.* **–na-tive ly,** *adj.* **–na-to-ry,** *adjs.*

prō′-crē-āte, *v. t.* To generate; to beget; উৎপাদন করা; জন্ম দেওয়া। **–ant,** *adj.* Procreating; সৃষ্টিকারী। **–a-tive,** *adj.* **–a′-tion,** *n.* Generation; প্রজনন, জনন, বিজনন, উৎপাদন, সৃষ্টি।

Prō-crŭs′-tē-ăn, *adj.* **1.** Of, or pertaining to, Procrustes, a fabulous Greek robber of Attica; গ্রীকদেশের উপকথায় উক্ত এটিকাবাসী জনৈক দস্যুসম্বন্ধীয়। **2.** Producing, or tending to produce, conformity by violent method; বলপূর্ব্বক সমতাস্থাপক বা সমতাস্থাপনশীল। **Procrustean bed**—কণ্টকশয্যা। [কথিত আছে দস্যু Procrustes লোকদিগকে ধরিয়া আনিয়া তাহার এক খট্টায় শয়ন করাইত। কোন ব্যক্তি দৈর্ঘ্যে ঐ খট্টা অপেক্ষা অধিক হইলে তাহার শরীরের কতকাংশ ছেদন করিয়া ঐ খট্টার সমান করিত এবং উহা অপেক্ষা ঐ ব্যক্তির দৈর্ঘ্য অল্প হইলে শায়িত ব্যক্তিকে হাতুড়ী দ্বারা পিটিয়া তক্তপোষের সমান করিয়া দিত।]

prŏc′-tor (-têr), *n.* **1.** (*Univ.*) Each of the two officials appointed to enforce the statutes and preserve good order and discipline; বিশ্ববিদ্যালয়ের ভিতর সুশাসন ও সুব্যবস্থা প্রতিষ্ঠার জন্য ভারপ্রাপ্ত কর্ম্মচারিদ্বয়ের অন্যতর শাসক। **2.** (*Law*) A person employed to manage another's cause in a court of civil or ecclesiastical law; মোকদ্দমার তদ্বিরকারী, আম্‌মোক্তার। **–ship,** *n.* **–to′-ri-al,** *adj.* **King's or Queen's Proctor**—ইচ্ছাপত্রের সনন্দ গ্রহণ এবং বিবাহ ভঙ্গ বা বাতিলের মোকদ্দমায় উভয়পক্ষের মধ্যে যোগাযোগ থাকিলে বা কোনরূপ বৃত্তান্ত গোপন করা হইলে যে কর্ম্মচারী হস্তক্ষেপ করিতে পারেন।

prŏc′-tŏr-īze, *v. t.* To exercise proctorial authority on (an undergraduate etc.); বিশ্ববিদ্যালয়ের ছাত্রদিগের উপর শাসন ক্ষমতা পরিচালন করা। **–i za′-tion,** *n.*

prō-cŭm′-bĕnt, *adj.* **1.** Lying down; prostrate; শায়িত; পাতিত। **2.** (*Bot.*) Spread or growing over the ground; (উদ্ভিদ্‌বিদ্যা) ভূমির উপর প্রসারিত বা বর্দ্ধনশীল, লম্বমান (নাঃ পঃ)।

prŏc-ū-rā′-tion, *n.* **1.** Act of procuring; bringing about; সংগ্রহ, সংঘটন; উৎপাদন। **2.** The management of affairs for another; অপরের জন্য বৈষয়িক কার্য্য নির্ব্বাহ, আমমোক্তারি। **3.** (*Eccl.*) A customary sum paid to a bishop; ধর্ম্মাধ্যক্ষকে যে টাকা দেওয়ার প্রথা চলিত আছে। **4.** Procuring girls for illicit purposes; কোন ব্যক্তির পাপ প্রবৃত্তি চরিতার্থ করণার্থ যুবতী সংগ্রহ, কুট্টনিগিরি, দূতীগিরী। **5.** Negotiation for a loan; fee for it; ঋণের বন্দোবস্ত; ঋণের বন্দোবস্তের জন্য যে পারিশ্রমিক দেওয়া হয়। **Pro′-cu-ral, Proc′-u-rance,** *ns.* Act of procuring; obtaining; সংগ্রহ; লাভ।

prŏc′-ū-rā-tor (-tèr), *n.* **1.** (*Rom. Hist.*) An officer having the charge of the imperial revenue in a province; (রোমের ইতিহাস) কোন প্রদেশে সম্রাটের রাজস্বের ভারপ্রাপ্ত কর্ম্মচারী। **2.** An agent; one having the power of attorney; প্রতিনিধি; আমমোক্তার। **3.** (In some Italian cities) A magistrate; (ইতালী দেশের কোন কোন নগরীতে) শাসনবিভাগীয় উচ্চকর্ম্মচারী, দণ্ডনায়ক। **–ship,** *n.* **–to′-ri-al,** *adj.* **Procurator-fiscal**—স্কটলণ্ডের কোন জেলার সরকারী উকিল।

prŏc′-ū-rā-tŏ-rȳ, *n.* Authorization of a person to act for another; as, letters of *procuratory*; কোন ব্যক্তির পক্ষে মোকদ্দমা প্রভৃতি চালাইবার জন্য ক্ষমতার্পণ।

prŏc-ū-rā′-trix, *n.* The inmate who attends to the temporal concerns of a nunnery; যে নারী ভিক্ষুণীসংঘের সাংসারিক ব্যাপার নির্ব্বাহ করে।

prō-cūre′, *v. t.* & *i.* **1.** To obtain or get by any means; to acquire; সংগ্রহ করা; হস্তগত করা। **2.** To bring about; to cause; as, to *procure* a favour to be granted; ঘটান; করান। **3.** To obtain as girls for illicit purposes; অসদুদ্দেশ্যে স্ত্রীলোক সংগ্রহ করা। *Verb i.* To pimp; কোন ব্যক্তির পাপপ্রবৃত্তি চরিতার্থ করার জন্য যুবতী সংগ্রহ করা, দূতীগিরী করা, কুট্টনীগিরি করা। **–cur′-a-ble,** *adj.*

prō-cūr′-ĕr, *n.* **1.** One who procures or gains; সংগ্রহকারী, সংগ্রহকারক, প্রয়োজক। **2.** A pander; a pimp; রমণীসংগ্রাহক; বিট, ভগভক্ষক। **–ess,** *n.* (*Fem.*) A pimp; দূতী, কুটনী, কুটনী, কুট্টিনী, [also চুন্দী, ঘটদাসী, কুম্ভদাসী, মলাকা, শম্বলী।]

prŏd, *v. t.* & *n.* **1.** To prick or poke with a pointed instrument, etc.; সূক্ষ্মাগ্র যন্ত্র প্রভৃতি দ্বারা খোঁচা দেওয়া। **2.** To goad or incite as to activity; উৎসাহিত করা, উত্তেজিত করা। *Noun.* **1.** A prick; thrust or poke; খোঁচা; গুঁতা। **2.** A goad, skewer or other pointed instrument; অঙ্কুশ, প্রতোদ, শিক, প্রভৃতি।

prō-dĕl-ī′-sion, *n.* (*Prosod.*) Elision of an initial vowel; (ছন্দঃশাস্ত্র) আদ্য-স্বরলোপ।

prŏd′-ī-găl, *adj.* & *n.* Wasteful; lavish; extravagant; অতিব্যয়ী, বহুব্যয়ী; মুক্তহস্ত; অপরিমিতব্যয়ী। **Noun.** An extravagant or wasteful persons; অতিব্যয়ী ব্যক্তি, অমিতব্যয়ী ব্যক্তি, অর্থনাশক। **–gal′-i-ty,** *n.* Extravagance; waste; অমিতব্যয়; অপব্যয়, অতিব্যয়। **–ly,** *adv.* Extravagantly; lavishly; অমিতভাবে; মুক্তহস্তে।

prŏd'-ĭ-găl-īze, *v. t.* To spend as a prodigal; অমিতব্যয়ীর মত টাকা উড়ান।

prō-dĭ'-gious (-jŭs), *adj.* **1.** Marvellous; monstrous; আশ্চর্য্য, অদ্ভুত; বিরাট, অপরূপ, বিকট, অতিপ্রমাণ। **2.** Huge; enormous; প্রকাণ্ড, বিরাট, বিশাল; অতিকায়। **3.** Unnatural; abnormal; অনৈসর্গিক, অস্বাভাবিক; সৃষ্টিছাড়া। **—ly,** *adv.* **—ness,** *n.*

prŏd'-ĭ-ġy̆, *n.* **1.** Something extraordinary or marvellous; a marvel; অদ্ভুত বস্তু; আশ্চর্য্য বস্তু, অপরূপ জিনিষ, আজব জিনিষ। **2.** A wonderful example (of some quality etc.); "... a *prodigy* of beauty"; অপূর্ব্ব দৃষ্টান্ত। **3.** A person gifted with some wonderful qualities, esp. a precocious child; "The *prodigies* of the human race"; অলোকসামান্য প্রতিভা প্রভৃতি সম্পন্ন ব্যক্তি, বিশেষতঃ অকালপরিণত শিশু, অল্প বয়সে কোনরূপ শাস্ত্র বা ললিতকলায় ব্যুৎপন্ন ব্যক্তি। **4.** A portent (*rare*); (কচিদ্ব্যবহৃত) অমঙ্গল-চিহ্ন, উৎপাত। **Prodigy of learning**—বিদ্যার জাহাজ।

prō'-drōme, *n.* **1.** A preliminary or introductory book; উপক্রমণিকা, প্রথম পাঠ। **2.** (*Med.*) A premonitory symptom of a disease; (ভৈষজ্যশাস্ত্র) কোন রোগের পূর্ব্বাভাসসূচক চিহ্ন। **—drom'-ic, Prod'-ro-mal,** *adjs.*

prŏ'-dūce, *n.* **1.** That which is produced or yielded; উৎপন্ন দ্রব্য, উৎপন্ন। **2.** (Also *Raw produce*) Agricultural and natural products collectively; উৎপন্ন শস্যাদি, ফসল। **Brought to produce**—কামান, কামানের গাড়ী, প্রভৃতি অথবা নৌবিভাগের আবশ্যকীয় দ্রব্যসম্ভারের বিভিন্ন বিভিন্ন অংশসমূহ পৃথক পৃথক রক্ষিত।

prō-dūce', *v. t.* **1.** To bring forward; to bring into view or notice; as, to *produce* a witness in a court; উপস্থাপিত করা; দৃষ্টি আকর্ষণ করা। **2.** To bring before the public; as, to *produce* a play, performer, book, etc.; জনসাধারণের সমক্ষে উপস্থাপিত করা। **3.** To manufacture; to make; প্রস্তুত করা; নির্ম্মাণ করা। **4.** To cause; to bring about; as, to *produce* a sensation; উৎপাদন করা; সংঘটন করা। **5.** To bring forth as young or offspring; প্রসব করা। **6.** (Of, earth, plant, etc.) To yield; উৎপাদন করা। **7.** (*Geom.*) To extend as a line etc.; (জ্যামিতি) বর্দ্ধিত করা, প্রসারিত করা। **—du-ci-bil'-i-ty,** *n.* **—duc'-i-ble,** *adj.* That can be produced; উৎপাদ্য।

prō-dūc'-ēr, *n.* One who produces or brings forth; উৎপাদক।

prŏ'-dŭct, *n.* **1.** That which is produced by nature, as fruits, grain, metal, etc.; ফল, ফসল, উৎপন্ন (কেশিঃ), উপজ (ঐ)। **2.** A thing produced by manufacture; নির্ম্মিত জিনিষ। **3.** Outcome; result; as, the *product* of his labours; পরিণাম; ফল। **4.** (*Chem.*) A compound not previously existing in a body but formed during its decomposition; (রসায়ন শাস্ত্র) যে যৌগিক পদার্থ কোন বস্তুতে পূর্ব্বে থাকেনা—কিন্তু বিশ্লেষণকালে উৎপন্ন হয়। **5.** (*Math.*) The result obtained by multiplying quantities together; (গণিত শাস্ত্র) গুণফল, গুণনফল, ঘাত (লীলাঃ), প্রত্যুৎপন্ন (সাঃ পঃ)।

prō-dŭc'-tion, *n.* **1.** Act of producing; উৎপাদন, প্রভবন, প্রবর্দ্ধন। **2.** Something produced; a literary or artistic work; উৎপন্ন দ্রব্য, উৎপত্তি (হিঃ কোঃ), নির্ম্মিত দ্রব্য; সাহিত্য গ্রন্থ, শিল্প দ্রব্য।

prō-dŭc'-tive (-tĭv), *adj.* **1.** Producing; having power or tendency to produce; ফলপ্রদ, ফলদ, ফলদায়ী, উৎপাদক, উৎপাদনশীল; প্রজননক্ষম। **2.** Causing to exist; originative; as, an age *productive* of great men; উৎপাদক; প্রজনক, উদ্ভবকারক। **3.** Producing abundantly as a writer, soil, etc. বহুপ্রদ, বহুগ্রন্থপ্রসূ, উর্ব্বরতাপ্রদ, ফলপ্রসূ, শস্যপ্রদ। **4.** (*Pol. Econ.*) Yielding or increasing wealth or value; devoted to the production of a wealth; ধন বা মূল্যপ্রদ, ধন বা মূল্যবর্দ্ধক; ধনোৎপাদনে নিযুক্ত, দ্রব্যোৎপাদক। **—ly,** *adv.* **—ness,** *n.* **—tiv'-i-ty,** *n.* **Productive power**—উৎপাদিকাশক্তি।

prŏ'-ĕm, *n.* **1.** A preface or introduction, to a book, speech, etc.; ভূমিকা, মুখবন্ধ, অবতরণিকা। **2.** (*Fig.*) Commencement; prelude; (লক্ষণায়) প্রারম্ভ; গৌরচন্দ্রিকা। **—em'-i-ăl,** *adj.*

prō-fāne', *v. t.* To violate or treat with abuse, irreverence, disregard, contempt, etc.; লঙ্ঘন করা, কলুষিত করা, দূষিত করা। **—fa-na'-tion,** *n.* The act of profaning; দূষণ, কলুষীকরণ।

prō-fāne', *adj.* **1.** Not holy or sacred; relating to matters not sacred; secular; অপবিত্র, অপুণ্য, অমেধ্য, ব্যাবহারিক, লৌকিক; ঐহিক; বৈষয়িক। **2.** Uninitiated in certain religious rites or any esoteric knowledge; অদীক্ষিত। **3.** Irreverent; impious; blasphemous; শ্রদ্ধাহীন; অধার্ম্মিক; পাষণ্ড, দেবনিন্দক, দেবদ্বেষী, ধর্ম্মনিন্দক, ধর্ম্মদ্বেষী। **4.** (Of rites etc.) Heathen or pagan; পৌত্তলিক। **—fan'-i-ty,** *n.* **—ly,** *adv.* **—ness,** *n.*

prō-fĕss', *v. t.* & *i.* **1.** To avow; to own or admit freely; to declare freely; to declare openly; স্বীকার করা; অকপটে স্বীকার করা; স্পষ্টভাবে স্বীকার করা; প্রকাশ্যে ঘোষণা করা **2.** To lay a claim to; to pretend; as, to *profess* oneself a physician; দাবী করা; ভাণ করা। **3.** To proclaim oneself versed in; to make one's profession, as, to *profess* law, medicine, flute-playing, etc. ; কোন বিষয়ে ব্যুৎপন্ন বলিয়া প্রকাশ করা ; কাহারো বৃত্তি বা পেশা করা। **4.** To teach as a professor ; as, to *profess* a subject ; অধ্যাপকতা করা। **5.** To affirm or avow faith in or allegiance to ; as, to *profess* Christianity, God, etc. ; ধৰ্ম্ম, ঈশ্বর, প্রভৃতিতে বিশ্বাসী হওয়া। ***Verb i.*** **1.** To make a public declaration ; ঘোষণা করা। **2.** To take the vows of a religious order ; কোন যাজকশ্রেণী অথবা সন্ন্যাসী বা সন্ন্যাসিনীসমাজে ভুক্ত হওয়া। **3.** To do the duties of a professor ; অধ্যাপকের কাজ করা।

prō-fĕssĕd′, *adj.* **1.** Openly acknowledged or avowed; অকপটভাবে স্বীকৃত, স্পষ্টরূপে স্বীকৃত। **2.** Alleged ; ostensible ; আরোপিত ; ব্যক্ত, স্পষ্ট। **3.** Professing to be duly qualified ; as, a *professed* anatomist ; যথোচিত যোগ্যতাসম্পন্ন। **—fess′-ed-ly,** *adv.* Avowedly ; by profession ; প্রকাশ্যভাবে ; স্বীকৃতরূপে, স্বীকারপূর্ব্বক।

prō-fes′-sion (-fĕ-), *n.* **1.** Act of professing ; declaration ; স্বীকরণ ; ঘোষণা। **2.** Open acknowledgment or avowal as of religious faith and purpose ; Christian or religious faith openly avowed ; কোন ধৰ্ম্মমতবিশ্বাস প্রকাশ্যে স্বীকৃতি ; প্রকাশ্যে স্বীকৃত খৃষ্টীয় বা অন্যরূপ ধৰ্ম্ম। **3.** That which is professed ; a declaration or avowal ; স্বীকৃত বিষয় ; ঘোষণা। **4.** A calling or occupation such as implies a measure of learning ; as, the legal *profession* ; ব্যবশায়, পেশা, ব্যবহার, বৃত্তি, উপজীবিকা। **5.** The body of persons engaged in such a calling ; ঐরূপ ব্যবসায়ে নিযুক্ত ব্যক্তিবর্গ। **—less,** *adj.* **The three or learned professions**—যাজকত্ব আইন এবং চিকিৎসা ব্যবসায়।

prō-fes′-sion-ăl (-fĕ-), *adj.* & *n.* **1.** Of, or relating to, a profession or calling ; concerned with a profession ; ব্যবসায়সম্পর্কীয় ; ব্যবসায়-সম্পৃক্ত। **2.** Engaged in a profession ; as, a *professional* man ; কোন ব্যবসায়ে নিযুক্ত। **3.** Engaging in a profession or calling as a means of livelihood or for gain ; as, a *professional* cricketer, golfer, etc. ; পেশাদার। ***Noun.*** **1.** A professional man ; চিকিৎসা ডাক্তারী, ওকালতি, প্রভৃতি ব্যবসায়ী। **2.** (*Abbr, pro.*) A professional criketer, golfer, etc. : পেশাদার ক্রীকেট, গোলফ্ প্রভৃতি ক্রীড়ক। **—ly,** *adv.* **Professional politician, agitator, etc.** — পেশাদার রাজনীতিক আন্দোলনকারী।

prō-fes′-sion-ăl-ĭsm (-fĕ-), *n.* **1.** Professional quality or character ; ব্যবসায়সম্পর্কীয় গুণ বা প্রকৃতি। **2.** The practice or characteristics of professionals esp. in sports, athletics, etc. (opp. to *amateurism* ; পেশাদারিতা। **—ize,** *v. t.* To give a professional character to ; ব্যবসায়াত্মক করা।

prō-fĕs′-sor (-êr), *n.* **1.** One who makes a profession as of a religion ; স্বীকারকারী, স্বীকর্ত্তা। **2.** A teacher of high rank as in a university, (*abbr. prof.*) ; অধ্যাপক, আচার্য্য, উপাধ্যায়। **3.** (*Colloq.* or *humorous*) One who teaches any art, sport, etc. requiring skill ; as, a *professor* of dancing or boxing ; (চলিত ভাষায় বা কৌতুকচ্ছলে) যে ব্যক্তি কোন প্রকার ক্রীড়া, কলাবিদ্যা, প্রভৃতি শিক্ষা দেয়, আচার্য্য (cf. সঙ্গীতাচার্য্য) ওস্তাদ। **4.** (*Slang*) One who makes a profession of any art or science ; (ইতর ভাষায়) কোন বিজ্ঞান বা কলাবিদ্যা ব্যবসায়ী। **—ate,** *n.* **1.** The office, or term of office, of a professor ; অধ্যাপকের পদ বা পদের স্থিতিকাল। **2.** The professors collectively ; অধ্যাপকবর্গ **—ess,** *n.* (*Fem.*) **—so′-ri-al,** *adj.* **—so′-ri-al-ly,** *adv.* **—so′-ri-ate, —ship,** *ns.*

prŏf′-fer (-êr), *v. t.* & *n.* To offer for acceptance ; গ্রহণের জন্য প্রস্তাব করা। ***Noun.*** An offer ; প্রদানের প্রস্তাব।

prō-fĭ′-cient (-shĕnt), *adj.* & *n.* Expert or adept ; ব্যুৎপন্ন, সুদক্ষ, নিপুণ, পারদর্শী, কুশল, অভিজ্ঞ, প্রবীণ। ***Noun.*** One well-versed or skilled in any art, science or knowledge ; ব্যুৎপন্নব্যক্তি, পারদর্শী ব্যক্তি, সুনিপুণ ব্যক্তি। **—cien-cy,** *n.* State of being proficient ; expertness ; প্রাবীণ্য, কৌশল, নৈপুণ্য, বৈচক্ষণ্য, পাটব ; ব্যুৎপত্তি, পারদর্শিতা, অধিকার, দখল (*colloq.*)। **—ly,** *adv.*

prō′-fīle, *n.* & *v. t.* **1.** A head or portrait represented in a side view ; মস্তক বা প্রতিকৃতির পার্শ্বচিত্র। **2.** A side outline esp. of the

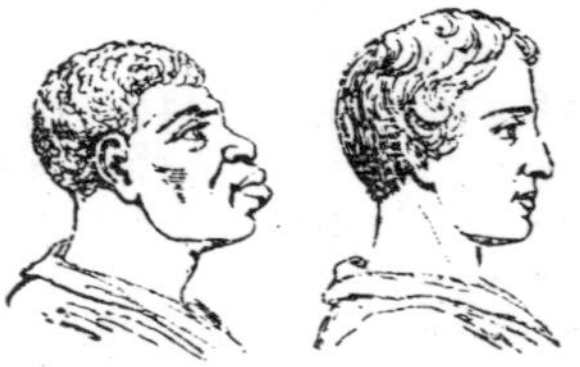

Profiles of Negro and European.

human face ; পার্শ্বচিত্র, বিশেষতঃ মুখের পার্শ্বদৃশ্য, অৰ্দ্ধাস্যচিত্র। **3.** (*Fortif.*) A section perpendicular to the principal lines of the work ; (দুর্গ) বপ্রপ্রাকারাদির সম্মুখভাগের লম্বস্বরূপ অংশ। **4.** (*Arch.*) The contour or outline of a figure, building, etc. specially in vertical section ; (স্থপতি-বিজ্ঞান) অট্টালিকা প্রভৃতির বাহ্যরেখা, বিশেষতঃ লম্বচ্ছেদে। **5.** (*Theatre*) A flat piece of a scenery on the stage cut out in outline ; রেখাকারে কর্ত্তিত সমতল দৃশ্যপট। ***Verb t.*** To draw in profile ; to give a profile of ; পার্শ্বদৃশ্য অঙ্কিত করা ;

পার্শ্বচিত্র প্রদান করা। **—fil-ist,** *n.* One who takes, or makes, profiles ; পার্শ্বচিত্রগ্রহণকারী, পার্শ্বচিত্র-অঙ্কনকারী।

prŏf′-it, *n.* **1.** Any advantage, benefit or gain ; সুবিধা, সুযোগ, হিত, উপকার, ফলোদয়। **2.** Pecuniary gain ; excess of returns over outlay (usu. *pl.*) ; লাভ ; মুনাফা। **—less,** *adj.* **—less-ly,** *adv.* **Profit-and loss**—ক্ষতিবৃদ্ধি, লাভ লোকসান। **Profit and loss account**—লাভক্ষতির হিসাব, যে হিসাবে লাভের টাকা জমার দিকে এবং ক্ষতির টাকা খরচের দিকে লিখা হয়। **Profit-sharing**—লাভ ভাগাভাগি, বিশেষতঃ মনীব এবং কর্ম্মচারীর মধ্যে লাভের টাকা বখরা।

prŏf′-it, *v. t.* & *i.* To benefit ; to be of use or advantage to ; হিত করা ; সুবিধাজনক হওয়া। ***Verb i.*** **1.** To be of use or advantage ; হিতজনক হওয়া, লাভজনক হওয়া, উপকারক হওয়া। **2.** (Of a person etc.) To gain advantage ; to be benefited ; সুবিধা পাওয়া ; লাভবান হওয়া, উপকৃত হওয়া।

prŏf′-it-ȧ-ble (-bl), *adj.* Bringing profit ; lucrative ; useful ; advantageous ; লাভকর ; লাভজনক, লাভাবহ ; হিতকর, হিতদায়ক ; হিতাবহ। **—ness,** *n.* The state of being profitable ; লাভজনকতা, সফলতা, সফলত্ব।

prŏf′-li-gȧte, *adj.* & *n.* **1.** Dissolute ; shamelessly immoral ; ভ্রষ্ট ; লোচ্চা, লম্পট, নষ্টাচার, স্খলিতচরিত্র। **2.** Recklessly prodigal ; অপরিমিতব্যয়ী, অতিব্যয়ী। ***Noun.*** A profligate person ; লম্পট ব্যক্তি। **—ga-cy,** *n.* State of being profligate ; dissoluteness ; লাম্পট্য ; ভ্রষ্টাচার। **—ly,** *adv.*

prō-found′ (-fownd), *adj.* & *n.* **1.** Very deep ; অতি গভীর, দুরবগাহ। **2.** Intellectually deep ; having or showing great knowledge or insight ; as, a *profound* scholar, treatise, etc. ; অতিগভীর ; গভীরপাণ্ডিত্যপূর্ণ। **3.** Coming from, or extending to, a great depth ; as, a *profound* sigh ; *profound* gangrene ; গভীর। **4.** Very deep ; intense ; far-reaching ; as, *profound* sleep, interest, etc. ; প্রগাঢ়, অগাধ ; বিগাঢ় (বাৎস্যঃ) ; গভীর, অতলস্পর্শ। **5.** Abstruse ; গহন, গূঢ়ার্থ, নিগূঢ়ার্থ, দুরবগাহ। **6.** Expressing deep humility, respect, etc. ; as, a *profound* bow ; গভীর ভক্তি বা বিনয়সূচক। ***Noun.*** (*Poet.*) The sea or ocean ; the vast depth as of ocean, futurity, the soul, etc. ; সাগর, মহাসাগর ; ভবিতব্যতা, আত্মা প্রভৃতির বিশাল গভীরতা। **—fun′-di-ty,** *n.* **—ly,** *adv.* Deeply ; গভীরভাবে, প্রগাঢ়ভাবে। **—ness,** *n.*

prō-fūse′, *adj.* **1.** Exceedingly liberal in spending or giving ; lavish ; মুক্তহস্ত, দানশৌণ্ড ; বহুপ্রদ। **2.** Excessively abundant or copious ; প্রচুর, প্রভূত, ভূয়িষ্ঠ, পর্য্যাপ্ত, বহুল, পুষ্কল। **—fu′-sion,** *n.* **1.** Lavishness ; extravagance ; মুক্তহস্ততা ; অপব্যয়িতা। **2.** Abundance ; copious supply ; as, *profusion* of commodities ; প্রাচুর্য্য, ভূয়িষ্ঠতা ; পুষ্কলতা। **—ly,** *adv.* Lavishly ; in profusion ; প্রচুররূপে ; পর্য্যাপ্তরূপে। **—ness,** *n.*

prŏg, *n.* (*Slang*) Victuals esp. for a journey or excursion ; (ইতরভাষায়) খাদ্যদ্রব্য, বিশেষতঃ ভ্রমণকালে সঙ্গে যে খাদ্যদ্রব্য নেওয়া হয়।

prŏg, *n.* & *v. t.* A proctor at Oxford or Cambridge ; অক্সফোর্ড বা কেম্ব্রিজ বিশ্ববিদ্যালয়ের শাসনাধ্যক্ষ। ***Verb t.*** Same as PROCTORIZE.

prō-gĕn′-i-tive (-tĭv), *adj.* Relating to, or connected with, the production of offspring ; having power to produce offspring ; সন্তানোৎপাদনসম্পর্কীয়, সন্তানোৎপাদনসংক্রান্ত ; সন্তানোৎপাদনক্ষম।

prō-gĕn′-i-tor (-tėr), *n.* **1.** An ancestor of a person, animal or plant ; পূর্ব্বপুরুষ, আদিপুরুষ, কুলপুরুষ। **2.** (*Fig.*) A predecessor ; (লক্ষণায়) পূর্ব্বাবস্থিত ব্যক্তি, পূর্ব্ববর্ত্তী ব্যক্তি। **3.** (*Fig.*) The origin ; (লক্ষণায়) মূল। **—ship,** *n.* **—to′-ri-al** *adj.* **—tress,** *n.* (*Fem.*)

prō-gĕn′-i-tūre, *n.* **1.** Begetting or generation ; উৎপাদন, প্রজনন। **2.** Offspring ; সন্তানসন্ততি।

prŏg′-ē-nȳ, *n.* **1.** Descendants ; সন্ততি, সন্তান, অপত্য, বংশধর। **2.** Offspring of a person animal or plant ; মানুষ, জন্তু বা উদ্ভিদাদির সন্ততি। **3.** (*Fig.*) Outcome ; product ; "Art is the parent, not the *progeny* of science; (লক্ষণায়) পরিণাম ; ফল।

prŏg′-gins (-ĭns), *n.* Same as PROG, *n.* in PROG, *n.* & *v. t.*

prō-glŏt′-tis, *n.* (*Pl.* -TIDES.) One of the sexually mature segments of a tapeworm ; ফিতা কৃমির যৌন-সম্পর্কে পরিণত খণ্ড।

prŏg′-nȧ-thous (-thŭs), *adj.* Having the jaws projecting beyond the upper part of the face ; (of jaws) projecting ; বর্দ্ধিত চোয়ালি (সাঃ পঃ), প্রহনু (হিঃ কোঃ) ; উদ্গতহনু (ঐ)। **—nath′-ic,** *adj.* **—thism,** *n.* প্রহনুত্ব (হিঃ কোঃ), উদ্গতহনুত্ব (ঐ)।

prŏg-nō′-sis, *n.* (*Pl.* -SES) **1.** A forecast of the course of a disease; বিশেষ বিশেষ লক্ষণ দৃষ্টে রোগের গতি ও ফলাফল নিরূপণ, সাধ্যাসাধ্য নির্দ্দেশ (হঃ চঃ), ভাবিফলতত্ত্ব (ঐ)। **2.** Prognostication ; ভবিষ্যসূচনা।

prŏg-nŏs′-tic, *n.* & *adj.* That which foreshows ; an omen ; ভাবিফলসূচক বস্তু, পূর্ব্বলক্ষণ, পূর্ব্বচিহ্ন ; শকুন, অমঙ্গলচিহ্ন। **2.** Foretelling ; prediction ; ভবিষ্যকথন ; ভবিষ্যদ্বাণী। ***Adj.*** Indicating beforehand by signs or omens ; predictive ; ভাবিফলসূচক ; ভবিষ্যসূচক, অগ্রসূচক।

prŏg-nŏs′-ti-cāte, *v. t.* **1.** To foretell or predict ; ভবিষ্যৎ বলা, ভবিষ্যৎ সূচনা করা। **2.** (Of things) To betoken ; পূর্ব্বাভাস প্রদান করা, পূর্ব্বসূচনা করা। **–ca-ble,** *adj.* **–ca′-tion,** *n.* The act of prognosticating ; ভবিষ্যসূচনা, ভাবিসূচন, পূর্ব্বসূচন। **–ca-tive, –ca-tor,** *ns.* **–ca-to-ry,** *adj.*

prō′-grăm, –gramme (-grăm), *n.* & *v. t.* **1.** An outline or sketch of the order to be pursued in any public exercise, performance or entertainment ; কার্য্যতালিকা, নাট্যপত্র, রঙ্গপত্র, অভিনয়-পত্র। **2.** A plan of future proceedings ; as, one's *program(me)* for the day ; ভাবী কার্য্যাবলীর তালিকা, পূর্ব্বলেখ। ***Verb t.*** To make a program(me) or plan of ; কার্য্যতালিকা প্রস্তুত করা। **Programme-music** — পরম্পরা অভি-ব্যঞ্জনার্থ অভিপ্রেত সঙ্গীত। **What is the program(me) for today**—(চলিতভাষায়) আজ আমাদের কি কি করিতে হইবে।

prŏg′-rĕss, *n.* **1.** A moving or going forward ; প্রয়াণ পুরোগমন, অগ্রগমন, অগ্রগতি, প্রসর্পণ। **2.** Advance ; development ; as, the *progress* of civilization ; উন্নতি, বিকাশ ; পুষ্টি, পরিণতি। **3.** (*Archaic*) A journey esp. one of state ; an official tour ; (অপ্রঃ) ভ্রমণ ; সফর।

prō-grĕss′, *v. i.* **1.** To move forward ; অগ্রসর হওয়া, অগ্রে গমন করা। **2.** To go on ; to continue ; as, the controversy still *progresses* ; চলা ; চলিতে থাকা। **3.** To advance ; to develop ; as, we *progress* in knowledge ; উন্নতি লাভ করা ; বিকাশ পাওয়া।

prō-gres′-sion (-grĕ-) *n.* **1.** Act of progressing ; moving forward ; অগ্রগমন ; অগ্রগতি, প্রগমন। **2.** (*Math.*) Regular or proportional advance in increase or decrease of numbers ; (গণিতশাস্ত্র) সংখ্যাপর্য্যায়ের আনুপাতিক বৃদ্ধি বা হ্রাস, শ্রেঢ়ীব্যবহার, শ্রেঢ়ী। **3.** (*Mus.*) Passing from one note or chord to another ; এক স্বর বা তন্ত্রী হইতে অপর স্বর বা তন্ত্রীতে সঞ্চরণ। **–al,** *adj.* **Arithmetical progression**—ব্যক্ত-শ্রেঢ়ী, সমান্তরশ্রেঢ়ী, অনুপাত (সাঃ পঃ)। [*Common difference*—চয় (আঃ বঃ)। *Common ratio*—চয়গুণ (ঐ)। *Geometrical mean*—উত্তরগুণ (লীলা)। *First term of a progression*—মুখ (আঃ বঃ), বদন (ঐ), আদি (ঐ)। *Sum of the numbers*—শ্রেঢ়ীফল (আঃ বঃ)। *Number of terms*—গুচ্ছ (আঃ বঃ)। *The last number of an arithmetical series*—অন্ত্য ধন।] **Geometrical progression**—গুণোত্তর বৃদ্ধি, সমগুণশ্রেঢ়ী (হিঃ কোঃ)। **Harmonic progression**—ধারাবাহিকশ্রেঢ়ী।

prō-gres′-sion-ist(-grĕ-),*n.* **1.** One who believes in progress *e. g.* in political and social matters ; উন্নতিবাদী। **2.** An evolutionist ; অভিব্যক্তিবাদী, ক্রমোন্নতিবাদী। **Prog′-ress-ist,** *n.* Same as PROGRESSIONIST.

prō-grĕs′-sive (-ĭv), *adj.* & *n.* **1.** Moving forward ; advancing ; অগ্রগামী, পুরোগামী ; অগ্রসর। **2.** Advancing gradually ; successive ; ক্রমোন্নতিশীল ; ক্রমিক। **3.** Improving in social condition, character, efficiency, etc. ; as, a *progressive* nation ; favouring progress, as, a party, policy, etc. ; উন্নতিশীল ; বর্দ্ধিষ্ণু, বর্দ্ধমান (হিঃ কোঃ)। **4.** Increasing unceasingly as a disease ; ক্রমবর্দ্ধমান। ***Noun.*** An advocate of progressive policy ; উন্নতিবাদী, উন্নতি-পন্থী। **–ly,** *adv.* **–ness,** *n.* **–sivism,** *n.* The principles of a progressive ; উন্নতিবাদ।

prō-hib′-it, *v. t.* To prevent ; to debar ; নিষেধ করা, প্রতিরোধ করা ; নিবারণ করা, মানা করা, বাধা দেওয়া, নিরোধ করা। **2.** To forbid by authority ; নিষেধাজ্ঞা প্রচার করা। **–i-ter, –i-tor,** *ns.*

prō-hi-bi′-tion, *n.* **1.** Act of prohibiting ; নিষেধ, প্রতিষেধ, নিবারণ, মানা। **2.** An injunction or edict forbidding some action ; নিষেধাজ্ঞা। **3.** The forbidding by law of the sale sometimes manufacture of intoxicating drinks for common consumption ; রাজবিধিপ্রচার দ্বারা সাধারণের নিকট মাদক পানীয়দ্রব্য বিক্রয় এবং স্থলবিশেষে ঐ দ্রব্য প্রস্তুত প্রতিষেধ। **–ist,** *n.* One in favour of the prohibition of the sale of intoxicating liquors ; পানীয় দ্রব্য বিক্রয়ের পক্ষপাতী ব্যক্তি।

prō-hib′-i-tive (-tĭv), *adj.* **1.** Forbidding ; implying prohibition ; নিষেধক, প্রতিষেধক ; নিরোধক। **2.** Serving to prohibit the use or abuse of a thing ; as, a *prohibitive* tax, price, etc. ; কোন বস্তুর ব্যবহার বা অপব্যবহার নিবারক। **–ly,** *adv.* **–ness,** *n.* **–to-ry,** *adj.*

prō-jĕct′, *v. t.* & *i.* **1.** To throw out or forwards ; to cast ; to shoot forth as light, shadow, etc. প্রক্ষেপ করা ; নিক্ষেপ করা ; সবেগে নির্গত করা। **2.** To scheme ; to contrive or plan ; পরিকল্পনা করা, কল্পনা করা ; উপায় স্থির করা। **3.** (*Fig.*) To cause to take shape as an idea etc. ; (লক্ষণায়) আকার প্রদান করা। **4.** (*Geom.*) To throw forward in a prescribed direction as a point, line, etc. so as to depict on a plane, cylindrical, spherical, or other given surface ; also, to depict (one figure) upon another according to any fixed correspondence between the points of the two ; (জ্যামিতি) কোন সমতল, নলাকার বা গোলকাকৃতি তলের উপর কোন কিছু অঙ্কিত করার জন্য কোন বিন্দু রেখা প্রভৃতি নির্দ্দিষ্ট দিকে

প্রস্তত করা ; ক্ষেত্রদ্বয়ের পরস্পরের বিন্দু-সমূহের মধ্যে কোনরূপ নিয়ত সামঞ্জস্যের অনুযায়ী একের উপর অপর ক্ষেত্র অঙ্কিত করা, বিক্ষেপ করা। **5.** To make a projection of (the earth, sky, etc.) ; (পৃথিবী, আকাশ প্রভৃতির) মানচিত্র সমতলের (plane) উপর অঙ্কিত করা। ***Verb i.*** To jut out ; উদ্গাত হওয়া, প্রলম্বিত হওয়া।

prŏj'-ĕct, *n.* A scheme or plan ; পরিকল্পনা, সংকল্প, প্রকল্প (হিঃ কোঃ), মতলব, অভিসন্ধি, যুক্তি, উপায়।

prŏ-jĕc'-tile (-tĭl), *adj.* & *n.* **1.** Impelling as force ; প্রণোদক, প্রেরক। **2.** That may be impelled forward by force, esp. from cannon ; ক্ষেপণীয়, প্রক্ষেপণীয়। ***Noun.*** A missile for a fire-arm ; গোলা গুলি।

prŏ-jĕc'-tion, *n.* **1.** Act of projecting or throwing ; casting ; প্রক্ষেপ, নির্গম, বহির্গমন, বহিরাগম ; নিক্ষেপ, প্রতিক্ষেপ। **2.** Scheming or planning ; পরিকল্পনা, উপায়, কল্পনা, প্রকল্পনা (হিঃ কোঃ)। **3.** Protruding ; a protruding thing or part of a thing ; বহির্বর্তন, প্রলম্বতা (হিঃ কোঃ), প্রলম্বন, প্রলম্বক, বহিরাগম ; প্রলম্বিত বস্তু। **4.** Representation on a plane of an object esp. the surface of the earth or of a celestial sphere or any part of it ; সমতলের উপর আকাশ বা নভোমণ্ডলাদি চিত্রণ, লম্বন, পরিলেখ (সূর্য্যঃ সিঃ), ছেদ্যক (ঐ)। **5.** (*Geom.*) Act of projecting on a surface ; (জ্যামিতি) কোন ধরাতলের উপর বিক্ষেপ। **6.** A mental image viewed as an objective reality ; মূর্ত্তভাব, ভাবমূর্ত্তি। **7.** (*Alchemy*) Transmutation of metals ; (কিমিয়া বিদ্যা) কিমিয়া করণ, নিকৃষ্ট ধাতুকে স্বর্ণীকরণ। **Mercator's projection**—মানচিত্র অঙ্কনের প্রণালী বিশেষ। এই প্রণালীতে দ্রাঘিমা সমূহ (meridians) পরস্পরের সহিত সমান্তরালভাবে অঙ্কিত হইয়া থাকে এবং সরল রেখাস্বরূপ শরসমানান্তর সমূহের (parallels of latitude) পরস্পর হইতে দূরত্ব বিষুবরেখা হইতে উহাদের দূরত্বের অনুপাতে বৃদ্ধি করা হয়। এই প্রণালীতে অঙ্কিত মানচিত্র নাবিকদিগের বিশেষ কাজে লাগে। **Powder of projection**—নিকৃষ্ট ধাতু স্বর্ণে পরিণত করণার্থ চূর্ণ বিশেষ। **Projection of a point**—(জ্যামিতি) মূলক্ষেত্র ও তদুৎপন্ন ক্ষেত্রস্থ বিন্দুদ্বয়সংযোজক রেখা।

prŏ-jĕc'-tive (-tĭv), *adj.* **1.** (*Geom.*) Of, relating to, or produced by, the projection of a line, figure, etc., on a surface ; (জ্যামিতি) বিক্ষেপসম্বন্ধীয়। **2.** Mentally scheming or planned ; as, *projective* imagination ; পরিকল্পনাকারী, উপায়-পরিকল্পক। **—ly,** *adv.* **Projective property (of a figure)**—(কোন ক্ষেত্রের) যে ধর্ম্ম বিক্ষেপ দ্বারা পরিবর্ত্তিত হয় না।

prŏ-jĕc'-tor, (-tẽr), *n.* **1.** One who projects a scheme or design ; পরিকল্পক, উপায়কল্পক, যোজক (কেম্ব্রিঃ)। **2.** An apparatus for projecting rays of light ; কিরণপ্রক্ষেপক।

prŏ-lapse' (-lăps), *v. i.* & *n.* (Of an organ etc.) To fall down or out from the proper position ; স্থানচ্যুত হওয়া, স্থানভ্রংশ হওয়া। ***Noun.*** Same as PROLAPSUS.

prŏ-lăp'-sŭs, *n.* (*Path.*) A falling down of an internal organ *e. g.* uterus, rectum, etc. from its proper position ; স্থানচ্যুতি, স্থানভ্রংশ, প্রপতন। **Prolapsus ano**—গুদভ্রংশ (সাঃ পঃ)। **Prolapsus uteri**—কন্দরোগ, যোন্যর্শ (সাঃ পঃ), গর্ভশিরভ্রংশ (কেম্ব্রিঃ)। **Prolapsus of the vagina**—যোনিভ্রংশ (হঃ চঃ), প্রস্রংশিনী (ঐ)।

prŏ'-lāte, *adj.* (*Geom.*) **1.** Extended or elongated in the direction of the polar axis, as a spheroid ; (জ্যামিতি) মেরুদ্বয়ের দিকে প্রলম্বিত, বাদামী। **2.** Extended or extending in width ; প্রস্থে প্রসারিত বা বৃদ্ধিশীল। **3.** (*Fig.*) Widely spread ; (লক্ষণায়) বহুদূরব্যাপ্ত। **4.** (*Gram.*) Same as PROLATIVE. **—ly,** *adv.*

prŏ-lā'-tive (-tĭv), *adj.* (*Gram.*) Having the function of extending or completing the predication ; as, "*go*" is the *prolative* infinitive in "you can *go*" ; (ব্যাকরণ) ক্রিয়াসম্পূরক।

prŏ-lĕ-gŏm'-ĕ-nŏn, *n.* (*Pl.* -NA) Prefatory remarks or discourses prefixed to a book, etc., (usu. in *pl.*) ; মুখবন্ধ, ভূমিকা। **—na-ry, —nous,** *adjs.*

prŏ-lĕp'-sis, *n.* **1.** Anticipation ; প্রত্যাশা। **2.** (*Rhet.*) A figure by which actions are anticipated and prevented ; (অলঙ্কারশাস্ত্র) অলঙ্কার-বিশেষ—যাহা দ্বারা আপত্তিসমূহ পূর্ব্বেই অবধারণ এবং বারণ করা হয়। **3.** (*Gram.*) Anticipatory use of an attribute, as the use of "*dead*" in "to strike one *dead*" ; (ব্যাকরণ) বিশেষণের পূর্ব্বাবধারণাত্মক ব্যবহার। **4.** (*Philo.*) An empirical general conception ; (দর্শনশাস্ত্র) প্রত্যক্ষা-ব্যবহিত প্রত্যয় (হিঃ কোঃ)। **5.** (*Chron.*) An error in chronology consisting in antedating an event ; কালাতিক্রম দোষ। **—tic,** *adj.* **—ti-cal-ly,** *adv.*

prŏ-lĕ-taire' (-tār), *n.* Same as PROLETARIAN, *n.*

prŏ-lĕ-tā'-ri-ăn, *adj.* & *n.* Of, or relating to, the proletariate ; প্রাকৃতজনসম্বন্ধীয়। ***Noun.*** A member of the proletariate or the poorest class ; প্রাকৃতজন, নীচ-শ্রেণীর লোক। **—ism,** *n.* **Pro'-le-ta-ry,** *adj.*

prŏ-lĕ-tā'-ri-ăt(e), *n.* **1.** The lowest class of a community ; প্রাকৃতজনসমাজ, ইতরশ্রেণী। **2.** (*Pol. Econ.*) The labouring classes ; (অর্থনীতি) শ্রমজীবী শ্রেণী।

prŏ′-li-cīde, *n.* Killing one's offspring either in the womb or after birth ; ভ্রূণহত্যা । **—ci-dal**, *adj.*

prō-lif′-ĕr-āte, *v. i* & *t.* To grow by multiplication of elementary parts ; to reproduce thus : মৌলিক অংশ সমূহের সংখ্যাবৃদ্ধি দ্বারা বৃদ্ধি পাওয়া ; উক্ত উপায়ে পুনরুৎপাদন করা। ***Verb t.*** To produce as cells etc. in this way ; ঐরূপ উপায়ে কোষ প্রভৃতি উৎপাদন করা। **—a′-tion**, *n.* **1.** The act of growing by multiplication of elementary part ; সংখ্যাবৃদ্ধি দ্বারা বর্দ্ধন, প্রোদ্ভেদ (ভিঃ কোঃ)। **2.** (*Pathol.*) The development of cells by division ; (নিদান-বিদ্যা) বিভাজন দ্বারা কোষের বিকাশ। **—a-tive**, *adj.*

prō-lif′-ĕr-ous (-ŭs), *adj.* **1.** (*Bot.*, of a flower, leaf) Producing another from within itself : (উদ্ভিদবিদ্যা) বহুপ্রজ। **2.** (*Zool.*) Multiplying by budding ; (জন্তুবিদ্যা) মৌলিক অংশ সমূহের সংখ্যাবৃদ্ধি হেতু বর্দ্ধনশীল। **3.** (*Med.*) Spreading by 'proliferation'; (ভৈষজ্য-শাস্ত্র) সংখ্যা বৃদ্ধিদ্বারা বৃদ্ধিশীল।

prō-lif′-ic, *adj.* **1.** Producing much offspring or fruits ; as, a *prolific* female or tree ; বহুপ্রজ, বহুপ্রসব, বহুফলপ্রদ, বহুফল। **2.** Serving to produce or cause esp. abundantly ; as, a controversy *prolific* of evil ; abounding *in* ; "...constellation...*prolific in* stars, etc." ; বহুপ্রসবকর, বহুসন্তানোৎপাদক ; বহুল। **—i-ca-cy**, **—i-ci-ty**, **—ness**, *ns.*

prō-lig′-ĕr-ous (-ŭs), *adj.* Producing offspring ; generative ; সন্তানপ্রসূ ; জনক।

prō′-lix, *adj.* Lengthy ; verbose or tedious, as a speech, writer, etc. ; অতিবিস্তৃত ; পুষ্পিত, অতিবিস্তৃতিদোষযুক্ত। **—lix′-i-ty**, *n.* The state of being prolix ; অতিবিস্তার, অতিপ্রসঙ্গ, বাক্‌প্রপঞ্চ, বাগবিস্তার, অতিবিস্তৃতিদোষযুক্ততা। **—ly**, *adv.*

prō-lŏc′-ū-tor (-tĕr), *n.* The chairman esp. of the lower house of a convocation in the Church of England ; (ইংলণ্ডের রাজবিধি দ্বারা প্রতিষ্ঠিত ধর্ম্মসংঘে) সভাপতি, বিশেষতঃ যাজক সভার নিম্নতর বিভাগের সভাপতি। **—ship**, *n.*

prō′-lŏg-īze, **—logu-īze** (-lŏg-) *v. i.* To write or speak a prologue ; প্রস্তাবনা লিখা, নান্দী বা পূর্ব্বরঙ্গ আবৃত্তি করা।

prō′-logue (-lŏg), *n.* & *v. t.* **1.** An introductory discourse, verse, etc. esp. in a drama ; প্রস্তাবনা, পূর্ব্বরঙ্গ, নান্দী (*benedictory prologue*), রঙ্গদ্বার। **2.** (*Fig.*) An act or event that serves as an introduction ; (লক্ষণায়) গৌরচন্দ্রিকা, প্রস্তাবনা। ***Verb t.*** To introduce or furnish with a prologue ; প্রস্তাবনা-সমন্বিত করা।

prō-lŏng′, *v. t.* **1.** To lengthen in space ; to extend the duration of ; দীর্ঘ করা, লম্বা করা, প্রবর্দ্ধিত করা ; দীর্ঘকাল স্থায়ী করা। **2.** To lengthen the pronunciation of, as a syllable, etc. ; শব্দাংশ প্রভৃতির উচ্চারণ দীর্ঘীভূত করা। **—a-ble**, *adj.* **—lon-ga′-tion**, *n.* The act of prolonging ; প্রবর্দ্ধন, দীর্ঘীকরণ।

prō-lū′-sion, *n.* A preliminary attempt ; an introductory essay ; প্রথম চেষ্টা ; প্রাথমিক রচনা। **—so-ry**, *adj.*

prŏm-ĕ-nāde′, *n.*, *v. i.* & *t.* **1.** A walk, ride, or drive for pleasure, parade or exercise ; প্রমোদভ্রমণ, বিহার, সুখবিচরণ, স্বচ্ছন্দভ্রমণ, বিলাসভ্রমণ। **2.** A place for this ; বিহারস্থান, বিচরণস্থান, বিক্রমস্থান। ***Verb i.*** To make a promenade ; বিহার করা, প্রমোদভ্রমণ করা। ***Verb t.*** **1.** To make a promenade through (a place) ; কোন স্থানের উপর দিয়া ভ্রমণ করা। **2.** To lead as a person about a place, esp. for display ; কোন লোককে (বিশেষতঃ প্রদর্শনার্থ) কোন স্থানের এদিকে সেদিকে নেওয়া। **—nad′-er**, *n.* **Promenade concert**—যে ঐক্যতান বাদ্যকালে শ্রোতৃবৃন্দ ইতস্ততঃ ভ্রমণ করিতে থাকে।

prō-mĕ-rŏps, *n.* A genus of birds of South Africa ; দক্ষিণ আফ্রিকার একজাতীয় পক্ষী।

Prō-mē′-thē-ăn, *adj.* Of, relating to, or like, Prometheus ; গ্রীক-পুরাণোক্ত প্রমিথিয়াস নামক দানব-সম্পর্কীয়।

Prō-mē′-theus (-thūs), *n.* গ্রীক-পুরাণোক্ত দানববিশেষ। এই দানব মৃত্তিকাদ্বারা মানব সৃষ্টি করে এবং স্বর্গ হইতে অগ্নি চুরি করিয়া আনিয়া মানুষকে ইহার ব্যবহার ও নানা শিল্পকার্য্য শিক্ষা দেয়। এই দানবই Pandoraকে দেবরাজ Zeusএর নিকট হইতে উপহার গ্রহণ না করার জন্য Epimetheusকে সতর্ক করে। এই সকল কারণে দেবরাজ কুপিত হইয়া প্রমিথিয়াসকে ককেসাস পর্ব্বতে শৃঙ্খলাবদ্ধ করিয়া রাখেন। দেবরাজের আদেশে একটী উৎক্রোশ পক্ষী প্রত্যহ Prometheusএর উদরবিদারণপূর্ব্বক যকৃৎ ভোজন করিত। অবশেষে মহাবীর হারকিউলেস প্রমিথিয়াসকে মুক্তি প্রদান করেন।

prŏm′-i-nĕnt, *adj.* **1.** Projecting or protruding ; উদ্গত, বহির্বিলম্বিত। **2.** Conspicuous ; সুস্পষ্ট, জ্বলজ্বল (*colloq.*)। **3.** Eminent ; distinguished ; সমুন্নত, উদগ্র ; বিখ্যাত, প্রখ্যাত। **—ly**, *adv.* **—nence**, *n.* **1.** State of being prominent ; conspicuousness ; উন্নততা ; সমুন্নতি। **2.** A protuberance ; উদ্গতি, স্ফীতি। **—nen-ces**—(Solar) সূর্য্যোন্নত-জ্বালা (হিঃ কোঃ)। **—nen-cy**, *n.*

prō-mĭs′-cū-ous (-ŭs), *adj.* **1.** Disorderly mixed ; confused ; বিশৃঙ্খল, বিমিশ্র ; এলোমেলো, প্রকীর্ণ, অবিবিক্ত। **2.** Indiscriminate ; as, *promiscuous* intercourse, murder, etc. ; নির্ব্বিশেষ। **3.** Making no distinction esp. of sex ; as, *promiscuous* bathing ; নির্ব্বিচারী। **4.** (*Colloq.*) Haphazard or casual ;

as, to take a *promiscuous* stroll ; (চলিতভাষায়) নৈমিত্তিক, দৈবিক। **—cu′-i-ty,** *n.* **—ly,** *adv.* Confusedly ; indiscriminately ; at random ; বিশৃঙ্খলভাবে ; এলোমেলোভাবে ; প্রকীর্ণভাবে, যদৃচ্ছাক্রমে। **Promiscuous-like**—(*Vulg., facet.*) Casually ; নৈমিত্তিকভাবে, দৈবাৎ।

prŏm′-ise (-ĭs), *n.* **1.** A statement binding the person who makes it ; প্রতিজ্ঞা, করার, প্রতিশ্রুতি। **2.** Something promised ; প্রতিশ্রুত বিষয়। **3.** (*Fig.*) A ground for expectation or hope of future distinction or excellence ; as, a youth of *promise* ; (লক্ষণায়) আশ্বাসের হেতু, আশার কারণ। **Breach of promise** — প্রতিজ্ঞাভঙ্গ। **Land of promise** — Same as PROMISED LAND, (which see.) **Of great promise**—See PROMISE, *n.* 3.

prŏm′-ise (-ĭs), *v. t.* & *i.* **1.** To engage to do, give or procure ; as, I *promise* you a fair hearing ; প্রতিশ্রুত হওয়া, প্রতিজ্ঞা করা। **2.** To afford reason to expect ; as, these discussions *promise* future storms ; আশ্বাস দেওয়া, আশার কারণ দেওয়া। **3.** (*Colloq.*) To assure ; as, I *promise* you it will not be so ; (চলিত ভাষায়) নিশ্চিত ভাবে বলা। ***Verb i.*** **1.** To make a promise or promises ; প্রতিশ্রুত হওয়া, প্রতিশ্রুতি দেওয়া। **2.** To afford ground for hopes or expectations ; as, the day *promises* well ; আশার কারণ হওয়া, আশ্বাস দেওয়া। **—is-er,** *n.* **Promised land**—প্যালেষ্টাইনের অন্তঃপাতী ক্যানান প্রদেশ ; স্বর্গ ; প্রত্যাশিত আনন্দ রাজ্য [ঈশ্বর এব্রাহেম, আইজাক এবং জেকবের নিকট ঐ দেশ তাহাদের সন্ততিগণকে প্রদান করিবেন বলিয়া প্রতিশ্রুত হইয়াছিলেন।] **I promise you**—I assure you ; I plainly tell you ; আমি আপনাকে নিশ্চিতরূপে বলিতেছি ; আমি আপনাকে খোলাখুলিভাবে বলিতেছি। **To promise oneself**—To resolve or to determine ; সংকল্প করা, স্থির করা। To be assured ; to entertain the (pleasing) expectation of ; কৃতনিশ্চিত হওয়া ; আশান্বিত হওয়া।

prŏm-is-ee′ (-ē), *n.* (*Law*) One to whom a promise is made ; যাহার নিকট কোন বিষয়ের প্রতিশ্রুতি করা হয়। **Prom′-i-sor,** *n.*

prŏm′-is-ing, *adj.* **1.** Making a promise ; প্রতিজ্ঞাকারী। **2.** Likely to turn out well ; affording hope or assurance ; as, a *promising* boy, sky, beginning ; আশাপ্রদ ; আশাজনক, আশ্বাসজনক। **—ly,** *adv.*

prŏm′-is-so-rȳ (-ŏ-), *adj.* **1.** Containing, or implying, a promise ; প্রতিশ্রুতিসূচক, প্রতিজ্ঞাসূচক, সপ্রতিজ্ঞ। **2.** (*Rare*) Promising ; full of promise ; (ক্বচিদ্‌ব্যবহৃত) আশাজনক ; আশাপ্রদ। **Promissory note** — ঋণপরিশোধের জন্য খত, করারী তমঃসুক।

prŏm′-ŏn-tô-rȳ, *n.* **1.** A cape or headland ; অন্তরীপ, শৈলান্তরীপ (সাঃ পঃ), অনুপর্ব্বত, ভূনাসিকা। **2.** (*Anat.*) A prominence in the body ; শরীরের মধ্যে উন্নত স্থান। **—ried,** *adj.*

prō-mōte′, *v. t.* **1.** To exalt in rank, station, etc. ; to advance ; to prefer ; as, to *promote* an officer ; উন্নীত করা ; পদোন্নতি করা ; পদবৃদ্ধি করা। **2.** To contribute to the growth or advancement of anything ; to further ; to encourage ; বৃদ্ধি বা উন্নতিসাধনে সাহায্য করা ; অগ্রসর করা ; উৎসাহবর্দ্ধন করা। **—mo′-tion,** *n.* Act of promoting ; state of being promoted ; advancement ; encouragement ; অভ্যুদয়, বর্দ্ধন ; পদোন্নতি, পদবৃদ্ধি ; উন্নতি ; উৎসাহ। **—mo′-tive,** *adj.*

prō-mōt′-êr, *n.* **1.** One who promotes ; an encourager ; উন্নতিকারক ; উৎসাহদাতা। **2.** One who takes the requisite steps for the promotion of a joint-stock company, (*often in an opprobrious sense*) ; যৌথ কারবারের প্রতিষ্ঠাতা, সমবায়স্থাপক। **—ism,** *n.* **Company promoter**—Same as PROMOTER, *n.* 2.

prompt (prŏmt), *v. t.* & *n.* **1.** To move to action ; to instigate or incite ; প্রবৃত্ত করা ; উৎসাহিত করা, উত্তেজিত করা, উদ্দীপিত করা, প্ররোচিত করা। **2.** To assist as an actor, reciter, etc. by supplying words that come next ; to assist as a hesitating speaker with suggestions ; কোন অভিনেতা বা আবৃত্তিকারককে কথিত শব্দের পরবর্ত্তী শব্দসমূহ বলিয়া সাহায্য করা ; দ্বিধাকারী বক্তাকে বক্তব্য বিষয়ের আভাস দিয়া সাহায্য করা। **3.** To suggest or inspire ; to give rise to ; as, to *prompt* a feeling, thought, etc. or an action ; ইঙ্গিত দেওয়া, অনুপ্রাণিত করা ; উদ্দীপিত করা। ***Noun.*** A thing said or suggested to help the memory esp. of an actor ; বিস্মৃত বিষয় স্মরণ করাইয়া দিবার জন্য যাহা বলা হয়, বিশেষতঃ কোন অভিনেতাকে বিস্মৃত বিষয় স্মরণ করাইয়া দিবার জন্য যাহা বলা হয়। **Prompt-book**—নাট্য পুস্তকের যে খণ্ড নাট্যোত্তরসাধক ব্যবহার করে। **Prompt-box**—নাট্যোত্তর সাধকের উপবেশনের জন্য আসন। **Prompt-side** — (*Abbr.* *P. S.*) অভিনেতার দক্ষিণভাগস্থ রঙ্গমঞ্চের পার্শ্ব।

prompt (prŏmt), *adj.* & *n.* **1.** Ready and quick to act ; acting with alacrity ; সত্বর, ক্ষিপ্র, তৎপর, চটুল, চটপটে ; ক্ষিপ্রকারী। **2.** Done, rendered or given, readily or immediately ; as, *prompt* assistance, reply, payment, etc. ; সত্বর কৃত, ক্ষিপ্রভাবে প্রদত্ত, অবিলম্বিত, আশু। **3.** (*Commr.*, of goods) For immediate delivery and payment ; as, *prompt* iron ;

(বাণিজ্য—বাণিজ্য দ্রব্য সম্পর্কে) অবিলম্বে মাল খালাস ও মূল্য প্রদানের জন্য। *Noun.* (*Commr.*) A limit of time for payment of an account for produce purchased; ক্রীত জিনিষের মূল্য পরিশোধের জন্য যে সময় দেওয়া হয়। **Promp'-ti-tude, Prompt'-ness,** *ns.* State of being prompt; alacrity; তৎপরতা; ক্ষিপ্রতা, ত্বরা, সত্বরতা, আশুকারিত্ব। **Prompt'-ly,** *adv.* Readily; তৎক্ষণাৎ, আশু, অবিলম্বে।

prompt'-ĕr (prŏmt-), *n.* One who prompts, esp. an actor; উৎসাহক, নাট্যোত্তরসাধক, রঙ্গোত্তরসাধক।

prompt'-ing (prŏmt-), *n.* Inciting to action; an instigation; as, the *promptings* of conscience; প্ররোচনা; প্রেরণা।

prō-mŭl'-gāte, *v. t.* To publish; to proclaim; প্রকাশ করা; ঘোষণা-করা, রটনা করা। **–ga'-tion,** *n.* The act of promulgating; বিঘোষণ, প্রকাশন, প্রকীর্ত্তন, প্রচারণ। **Pro'-mul-ga-tor,** *n.*

prō-mulge' (-mŭlg), *v. t.* (*Archaic*) Same as PROMULGATE.

prō-nā'-ŏs, *n.* (*Gk. Antiq.*) The area immediately in front of a temple; (গ্রীসদেশীয় প্রত্নতত্ত্ব) মন্দিরের সম্মুখস্থ অঙ্গন।

prō'-nāte, *v. t.* (*Physiol.*) To cause as the hand or the fore-limb, to assume the prone position; (জীববিজ্ঞান) হস্ত বা অগ্রপদ আনত করা। **–na'-tion,** *n.*

prō-nā'-tor (-tĕr), *n.* (*Anat.*) A muscle that serves to turn the palm of the hand downward; (শারীরসংস্থানবিদ্যা) যে পেশীর গতি-দ্বারা হাতের তালু নীচের দিকে ঘুরান যায়।

prōne, *adj.* **1.** Bending downward or forward; lying with the face or front part downwards; as, to fall *prone*; নত, প্রণত, নম্র; অধোমুখ, অবনত মুখ। **2.** Sloping; inclined; (*loosely*) steep; প্রবণ; ঢালু; গড়ানিয়া। **3.** Disposed; inclined; as, he was *prone* to do that; প্রবণ; উন্মুখ। **Prone'-ly,** *adv.* **Prone'-ness,** *n.* The state of being prone; উন্মুখতা, প্রবণতা।

proneur, (*F.*), *n.* A eulogist; স্তাবক, স্তুতিবাদকারী।

prŏng, *n.* & *v. t.* **1.** A pointed or forked instrument; a fork; শূল; কাঁটা। **2.** A spike of a fork; কাঁটার শঙ্কু। **3.** A pointed projection; as, the *prong* of an outlet, tooth, rock etc.; সূক্ষ্মাগ্র উদ্গত অংশ। ***Verb t.*** To stab or pierce with a prong or fork; শূল বা কাঁটা দ্বারা বিদ্ধ করা। **Pronged,** *adj.* **Prong-buck, –horn, –horned antelope**—উত্তর আমেরিকার হরিণজাতীয় জন্তুবিশেষ।

prō-nŏm'-i-năl, *adj.* Of, or relating to, a pronoun; of the nature of a pronoun; সর্ব্বনাম-সম্বন্ধীয়, সর্ব্বনামবিষয়ক; সর্ব্বনামাত্মক। **–ly,** *adv.*

prō'-noun (-nown), *n.* A word used instead of a noun; সর্ব্বনাম। **Demonstrative pronouns**—(This, that.) **Distributive pronouns**—Each, every, either, etc.). **Indefinite pronouns**—(Any, some, etc.). **Interrogative pronouns**—(Who, which, what). **Personal pronouns** — (I, we, thou, you, he, she, it, they); ব্যক্তিসম্পর্কীয় সর্ব্বনাম। **Possessive pronouns**—(My, our, your, his, their, etc.). **Relative pronouns**—(Who, that, which); সম্বন্ধবাচক সর্ব্বনাম।

prō-nounce' (-nowns), *v. t.* & *i.* **1.** To deliver or utter formally as a sentence, judgment, etc.; to declare or affirm; as, to *pronounce* a tale false; প্রদান করা; ব্যক্ত করা। **2.** To articulate by the organs of speech; উচ্চারণ করা। ***Verb i.*** **1.** To articulate; উচ্চারণ করা। **2.** To utter an opinion or declaration, esp. authoritatively, (with *on, upon, for, in favouor of* or *against*); কোন বিষয়ে মত ব্যক্ত করা। **–a-ble,** *adj.* **–ment,** *n.*

prō-nounced' (-nownst), *adj.* Strongly marked or defined; decided; সুনিরূপিত, সুনির্দ্দিষ্ট; অবধারিত। **–noun'-ced-ly,** *adv.*

prō-nounc-ing (-nowns-), *n.* & *adj.* Act of the verb pronouncing; উচ্চারণ। ***Adj.*** Pertaining to, indicating, or teaching, pronunciation; as, a *pronouncing* dictionary; উচ্চারণসম্বন্ধীয়, উচ্চারণ-সূচক, উচ্চারণশিক্ষাদায়ক।

prō-nûn-ĉi-ă-mĕn'-tō, *n.* A proclamation or pronouncement; ঘোষণা।

prō-nŭn-ĉi-ā'-tion, *n.* **1.** Act of pronouncing a word or words; উচ্চারণ। **2.** The mode of pronouncing a word or words; উচ্চারণপদ্ধতি।

prōōf, *n.* **1.** That which proves or establishes any truth or fact; as, this requires no *proof*; প্রমাণ; **2.** Act of proving; demonstration; প্রমাণীকরণ; প্রতিপাদন। **3.** Legal evidence either written or spoken; প্রমাণ। **4.** Act of testing; test; trial; as, to put in *proof*; পরীক্ষণ; পরীক্ষা; উপপত্তি বেদান্তঃ, (*math.*) বাসনা (গোলঃ), পরখ। **5.** (*Archaic*) Hardness; impenetrability; as, an armour of *proof*; (অপ্রঃ) কাঠিন্য; অভেদ্যতা। **6.** (*Print.*) A trial impression taken from composed type for correction; (মুদ্রণ) মুদ্রণীপত্র। **7.** (Engraving etc.) A proof impression; পরীক্ষার জন্য যে ছাপা লওয়া হয়। **8.** The standard of strength of spirit; সুরাসারের শক্তির নির্দ্দিষ্ট মান। **9.** The testing of fire-arms or explosives; a place for this; আগ্নেয়াস্ত্র বা বিস্ফোরকদ্রব্য পরীক্ষণ; ঐ সকল দ্রব্য পরীক্ষার স্থান। **10.** (*Bookbinding*) The rough uncut edges of the shorter leaves of a book, left to show that it has not been cut down; (পুস্তক-বাঁধাই) কোন পুস্তকের অকর্ত্তিত ক্ষুদ্রতর পৃষ্ঠা। 11. A test-tube; রাসায়নিক পরীক্ষায় ব্যবহৃত কাচনল, পরীক্ষক-নল। **Proof′-less**, *adj.* **Proof-plane**—ঘৃষ্ট তাড়িত সংগ্রহের জন্য অথবা ঐরূপ তাড়িৎ এক প্রবাহক হইতে অন্য প্রবাহকে সঞ্চারণের নিমিত্ত তাড়িত-বিশেষ। **Proof-reader**—মুদ্রণীপত্র সংশোধক। **Proof-reading**—মুদ্রণীপত্র সংশোধন। **Proof-sheet**—পরীক্ষাপত্র (আঃ বঃ), মুদ্রণীপত্র। **Proof-spirit** — সমান ওজনের বিশুদ্ধ সুরাসার ও জল। **Water-proof**—জলাভেদ্য। **The proof of the pudding is in the eating**—ব্যবহারে দ্রব্যের ভাল মন্দের পরিচয় পাওয়া যায়, ফলেন পরিচীয়তে। **To put to the proof**—To test; পরীক্ষা করা, পরখ করা।

proof, *adj.* & *v. t.* **1.** Firm in resisting; impenetrable; as, fire-*proof*: *proof* against the severest weather; অভেদ্য; দুর্ভেদ্য। **2.** Of tried strength as an armour; পরীক্ষিত। **3.** Of a certain standard as to strength or quality; as, *proof*-spirit; নির্দ্দিষ্ট মানের। ***Verb t.*** To render proof against something; to render as cloth, etc. impervious to water; অভেদ্য করা; বস্ত্র প্রভৃতি জলের অভেদ্য করা।

prŏp, *n.* & *v. t.* **1.** A support; a stay; আশ্রয়, শরণ, উপঘ্ন, অবলম্বন; অবষ্টম্ভ। **2.** (*Fig.*) A person or thing serving as a support, esp. one upholding an institution, etc.; (লক্ষণায়) কোন প্রতিষ্ঠানের প্রধান পৃষ্ঠপোষক, আশ্রয়স্তম্ভ। ***Verb t.*** To support as by a prop, (*lit.* & *fig.*); স্তম্ভবৎ আশ্রিত করা।

prō-pæ-deu′-tic (-pē-dū-), *adj.*&*n.* **1.** Serving as an introduction to any art or science; উপক্রমণিকা-স্বরূপ। ***Noun.*** A propædeutic subject or study; (*pl.*) introductory or preliminary learning; উপক্রমণিকা; প্রাথমিক শিক্ষা। **—ti-cal**, *adj.*

prŏp-ă-găn′-dă, *n.* **1.** (More fully *Congregation or College of the Propaganda*) A body of cardinals in charge of foreign mission; বৈদেশিক ধর্ম্মপ্রচারকার্য্যের ভারপ্রাপ্ত পোপের সভাসদসমাজ। **2.** An organization for propagating a doctrine; কোনরূপ মত প্রচারের জন্য মণ্ডলী, প্রচারকমণ্ডলী, প্রচারসমিতি। **3.** The doctrine or principles thus propagated; প্রচারিত মত বা তত্ত্ব। **4.** A scheme of propagation; মতবিস্তারের পরিকল্পনা।

prŏp-ă-găn′-dist, *n.* **1.** One devoted to the propagation of any doctrine; a proselytizer; মতবিস্তারকারী; ধর্ম্মান্তরগ্রহণকারী। **2.** A missionary or convert of the Roman Catholic propaganda; রোমানক্যাথলিক ধর্ম্মপ্রচারক, রোমান-ক্যাথলিক ধর্ম্মে দীক্ষিত ব্যক্তি। **—dism**, *n.* **—dis′-tic**, *adj.* **—dize**, *v. i.* & *t.*

prŏp′-ă-gāte, *v. t.* **1.** To multiply by generation or reproduction, esp. an animal, plant, etc.; to produce (itself); as, a plant *propagates* itself; বংশ বিস্তার করা; সংজনন করা, উৎপাদন করা। **2.** To pass on to one's descendants as a quality, etc.; সন্তান সন্ততিতে গুণ প্রভৃতি, সংক্রমিত হওয়া। **3.** To spread; to diffuse; to transmit; as, to *propagate* a belief, doctrine, etc. or sound, vibration, etc.; বিস্তার করা, ব্যাপ্ত করা, পরিব্যাপ্ত করা; সঞ্চার করা। **—ga′-tion**, *n.* The act of propagating; সংজনন। **—ga-tive**, *adj.* **—ga-tor**, *n.*

prō-păr-ŏx′-ȳ-tōne, *adj.* & *n.* (*Gk. Gram.*) Having an acute accent on the antepenult; (গ্রীক ব্যাকরণ) উপান্ত অক্ষরের পূর্ব্ববর্ত্তী মাত্রা বা শব্দাংশ উদাত্তচিহ্নে চিহ্নিত। ***Noun.*** Such a word; ঐরূপ শব্দ।

prō-pĕl′, *v. t.* To drive or push forward; to press or urge onward by force (*lit.* & *fig.*); অগ্রে ঠেলিয়া দেওয়া; ঠেলিয়া অগ্রসর করা।

prō-pĕl′-lent (-ĕnt), *adj.* & *n.* Driving forward; propelling; প্রেরক; প্রচালক। ***Noun.*** A propelling agent; an explosive for use in fire-arms; প্রচালক যন্ত্র; আগ্নেয়াস্ত্রে ব্যবহারের জন্য একপ্রকার বিস্ফোরকদ্রব্য।

prō-pĕl′-ler (-ĕr), *n.* **1.** One who, or that which, propels; প্রণোদক, প্ররোচক, প্রচালক। **2.** A revolving shaft with blades for propelling a ship; জাহাজের চালক-চক্র।

prō-pĕn′-sĭ-tȳ, *n.* Natural tendency; disposition; প্রবণতা, প্রাবণ্য, আসক্তি; স্বাভাবিক প্রবৃত্তি, ঝোঁক।

prŏ′-pĕr, *adj.* **1.** Peculiar; special; as, every animal has his *proper* instincts; নিজস্ব; বিশিষ্ট। **2.** (*Archaic*) Own; (অপ্রঃ) স্বীয়, স্বকীয়। **3.** According to usage; correct; as, a *proper* expression; প্রথানুরূপ; বিশুদ্ধ। **4.** Real; as, Greece *proper*; properly so called; প্রকৃত; খাস। **5.** Appropriate; suitable; right; as, this is the *proper* time to do it; বিধেয়, যুক্ত, সাম্প্রত (সর্ব্বঃ দঃ), সমীচীন, সমঞ্জস, বিহিত, প্রশস্ত; যথাযোগ্য, সমুচিত; প্রকৃত। **6.** (*Colloq.*) Thorough; as, there will be a *proper* row about this; পুরা। **7.** (*Archaic*) Well formed; handsome; (অপ্রঃ) সুগঠিত; সুন্দর, শোভন। **8.** Respectable; honest; decent; মান্য, মাননীয়; সাধু; শোভন। **9.** (*Herald.*) Represented in its natural colour; (কুলবিদ্যা) স্বাভাবিক বর্ণে চিত্রিত। **Proper fraction** — সম-অপূর্ণাঙ্ক। **Proper motion**—(*Astron.*) The motion of a star with relation to the other stars; (জ্যোতির্বিজ্ঞান) অপরাপর নক্ষত্রের সহিত তুলনায় কোন নক্ষত্রের গতি। **Proper name or noun**—ব্যক্তিবাচক নাম বা বিশেষ্য।

Proper psalms, lessons—কোন বিশেষ দিবসোচিত সঙ্গীত, পাঠ, প্রভৃতি।

prō-pĕr-i-spŏm'-ĕ-nŏn, *adj.* & *n.* (*Gk. Gram.*) Having the circumflex accent on the penuit ; (গ্রীক ব্যাকরণ) উপান্ত্য শব্দাংশের উপর স্বরিতচিহ্নে চিহ্নিত। ***Noun.*** Such a word ; ঐরূপ শব্দ।

prŏp'-êr-lȳ, *adv.* **1.** In a proper way ; fitly ; suitably ; rightly ; strictly ; সঙ্গতভাবে ; উপযুক্তভাবে ; যোগ্যভাবে, যথোচিতভাবে ; যথার্থতঃ ; কড়াকড়িভাবে। **2.** With good manners ; as, to behave *properly* ; শিষ্টজনোচিতভাবে, সৌজন্যের সহিত। **3.** (*Colloq.*) Completely ; perfectly ; as, puzzled him *properly* ; (চলিত ভাষায়) পুরাপুরি ; ডাহা।

prŏp'-êr-tȳ, *n.* **1.** Owning a thing ; ownership ; সম্পত্তির অধিকার ; স্বামিত্ব। **2.** A thing owned ; an estate ; অধিকৃত বস্তু ; বিত্ত, সম্পত্তি, জায়দাদ, ভূমি, বৈভব। **3.** A quality ; an essential attribute ; as, the *properties* of soda ; ধর্ম্ম, গুণ ; মৌলিক গুণ। **4.** (*Theatre*, usu. *pl.*) Articles including dresses, furniture, etc. used by actors on the stage ; (রঙ্গালয়) নাটকের সাজ। **Property-man, —master** — নাটকের সাজ যাহার তত্ত্বাবধানে থাকে। **Property qualification**—সম্পত্তির অধিকারজনিত (ভোট প্রভৃতি প্রদানের) যোগ্যতা। **Property tax**—সম্পত্তির উপর গৃহীত শুল্ক, সম্পত্তিকর (হিঃ কোঃ)। **A man of property** — One of great property ; বিভবশালী ব্যক্তি, সম্পত্তিশালী ব্যক্তি।

prŏph'-ĕ-cȳ, *n.* **1.** The action, function or faculty of a prophet ; ভাববাদিতা। **2.** A foretelling esp. an inspired one ; a prediction ; ভবিষ্যৎকথন, ভাবিকথন ; ভবিষ্যদ্বচন (হিঃ কোঃ)। **3.** The power of foretelling the future ; ভবিষ্যৎকথনশক্তি।

prŏph'-ĕ-sȳ, *v. i.* & *t.* **1.** To make predictions ; to foretell future events ; ভবিষ্যদ্ঘটনা বলা ; ভবিষ্যদ্বাণী করা। **2.** (*Archaic*) To interpret or explain the Scriptures ; (অপ্রঃ) বাইবেলের ব্যাখ্যা করা। ***Verb t.*** **1.** To foretell or predict ; ভবিষ্যদ্বাণী করা, ভবিষ্যৎ বলা। **2.** To herald or foreshow ; আগমনবার্ত্তা ঘোষণা করা, পূর্ব্বসূচনা করা।

prŏph'-ĕt, *n.* **1.** An inspired teacher or revealer of divine will ; ভাববাদী, প্রত্যাদেশপ্রাপ্ত ব্যক্তি, ভগবদ্বাণী প্রচারক, পয়গম্বর (মুসলমানশাস্ত্র)। **2.** A spokesman as of a principle, cause, etc. ; মুখপাত্র। **3.** One who predicts or foretells events ; ভবিষ্যদ্বক্তা, ভবিষ্যবাদী, ভাবিবক্তা, ভবিষ্যৎকথক, ভাবিকথক, ভবিষ্যভাষী, ভবিষ্যবাদক। **—ess,** *n.* (*Fem.*) **—hood, —ship,** *ns.* **The Prophet** — মহম্মদ ; বিশেষতঃ মরমন সম্প্রদায়ের প্রতিষ্ঠাতা জোসেফ স্মীথ। **The prophets**—বাইবেলের পুরাতন নিয়মের অন্তর্ভুক্ত গ্রন্থসমূহের লেখকগণ। **A prophet is not honoured in his country**—গেঁয়ো যুগী ভিক পায় না।

prō-phĕt'-ic, *adj.* **1.** Of, or relating to, a prophet ; ভাববাদিসম্পর্কীয়। **2.** Foretelling future events ; containing prophecies ; ভবিষ্যৎকথক, ভবিষ্যদর্শক, ভবিষ্যৎসূচক ; ভবিষ্যদ্বাণীপূর্ণ। **—i-cal,** *adj.* **—i-cal-ly,** *adv.*

prō-phȳ-lăc'-tic, *adj.* & *n.* Defending against disease ; preventive ; রোগপ্রতিষেধক ; নিবারক। ***Noun.*** Such a medicine or measure ; রোগপ্রতিষেধক ঔষধ।

prō-phȳ-lăx'-is, *n.* (*Med.*) Preventive treatment, medicine, etc. ; (ভৈষজ্যশাস্ত্র) প্রতিষেধক চিকিৎসা, ঔষধ, প্রভৃতি।

prō-pin'-qui-tȳ *n.* **1.** Proximity ; নৈকট্য, সান্নিধ্য, সন্নিকর্ষ, সামীপ্য, সমীপতা, সন্নিধান। **2.** Close kinship ; affinity ; নিকট সম্বন্ধ ; সম্বন্ধ, সম্পর্ক। **3.** Similarity ; সাদৃশ্য, সমরূপতা।

prō-pi'-ti-āte (-shī-), *v. t.* To appease ; to conciliate ; to make propitious ; প্রসন্ন করা ; তুষ্টিসাধন করা ; তুষ্ট করা। **—a'-tion,** *n.* **1.** Act of propitiating ; সন্তোষণ, সমারাধন, প্রসাদন, আরাধন (হিঃ কোঃ), অনুরঞ্জন। **2.** Atonement ; প্রায়শ্চিত্ত। **3.** (*Archaic*) A present etc. for propitiating ; as, he is the *propitiation* for our sins ; (অপ্রঃ) প্রসাদনের জন্য প্রদত্ত পুরস্কার।

prō-pi'-ti-ā-tō-rȳ (-shī-), *adj.* & *n.* Having the power or means to propitiate ; as, a *propitiatory* smile ; প্রসন্নতাসাধক, শান্তিকর, প্রসাদক। ***Noun.*** (*Jewish antiq.*) Same as MERCY-SEAT (which see). **—ri-ly,** *adv.*

prō-pi'-tious (-shŭs), *adj.* **1.** Favourable ; favourably disposed ; as, the fates were *propitious* ; সদয়, অনুকূল ; প্রসন্ন। **2.** Favourable, auspicious, as weather, occasion, omen, etc. ; শুভ, মঙ্গল, মাঙ্গলিক, শুভঙ্কর, শর্ম্মপ্রদ। **—ly,** *adv.* **—ness,** *n.* The state of being propitious ; প্রসন্নতা।

prŏp'-ō-lis, *n.* A thick waxy substance used by bees to stop the crevices of their hives ; মধুচক্রের রন্ধ্র রোধকরণার্থ মৌমাছিগণ কর্তৃক ব্যবহৃত একপ্রকার গাঢ় মধূথবৎ দ্রব্য।

prō-pōr'-tion, *n.* & *v. t.* **1.** Comparative relation ; ratio ; অনুপাত ; হার। **2.** (*Pl.*) Magnitude ; dimensions ; পরিমাণ ; আয়তন। **3.** Symmetrical arrangement or adjustment ; symmetry ; সৌসামঞ্জস্য, সমপরিমিতত্ব ; অঙ্গসৌষ্ঠব, সমপ্রমাণত্ব, সুপরিমাণ। **4.** Equal or proper share ; lot ; "...do...things in their *proportions*" ; সম অংশ, উপযুক্ত অংশ ; ভাগ, নিরূপিত অংশ। **5.** (*Math.*) Equality of ratios between two pairs of quantities ; (গণিতশাস্ত্র) সমানুপাত, যুগ্মনিষ্পত্তি (হিঃ কোঃ), অনুপাত (ঐ)। 6. (*Arith.*) Same as THE RULE OF THREE. ***Verb t.*** 1. To adjust in a suitable proportion or relation ; সমানুপাতে বিন্যস্ত করা, সামঞ্জস্য বিধান করা। 2. To make proportionate to ; as, to *proportion* the punishment to the crime ; আনুপাতিক করা। **–less,** *adj.* **–ment,** *n.* **–tioned,** *adj.* **In proportion**—According as or to ; অনুপাতে। **Out of (all) proportion to**—Too great for ; মাত্রাছাড়া।

prō-pōr′-tion-ăl, *adj.* & *n.* 1. Having due proportion ; in suitable proportion or degree ; যথানুপাতিক ; সমানুপাতিক। 2. Relating to proportions ; আনুপাতিক। ***Noun.*** (*Math.*) Any number or quantity in a proportion ; আনুপাতিক সম্বন্ধবিশিষ্ট সংখ্যা। **–a-ble,** *adj.* **–a-bly,** *adv.* **–al′-i-ty,** *n.* **–ate,** *adj.* & *v. t.* Proportional ; আনুপাতিক, যথোচিত (হিঃ কোঃ)। (*Verb t.*) To make proportional ; আনুপাতিক করা। **–ate-ly,** *adv.* With due proportion ; অনুপাতে। **–ly,** *adv.* In proportion ; সমানুপাতে, হারাহারি। **Proportional representation** — এক প্রকার নির্ব্বাচনপদ্ধতি—যাহাতে অল্পসংখ্যা শক্তির অনুপাতে নির্ব্বাচনের অধিকার পাইয়া থাকে, আনুপাতিক নির্ব্বাচন।

prō-pōr′-tion-ă-list, *n.* 1. One who plans proportions ; কোন বস্তুর আয়তন বা পরিমাণ পরিকল্পক। 2. One advocating proportional representation ; আনুপাতিক নির্ব্বাচনসমর্থক ব্যক্তি।

prō-pōṣ′-ăl, *n.* 1. Act of proposing ; প্রস্তাব করণ। 2. Something *e. g.* scheme, design, etc. proposed ; প্রস্তাব। 3. An offer of marriage ; বিবাহের প্রস্তাব, সম্বন্ধ।

prō-pose′ (-pōz), *v. t.* & *i.* 1. To bring forward or offer for consideration, discussion, acceptance, etc. ; to propound ; প্রস্তাব করা ; বিবেচনার জন্য উপস্থাপিত করা। 2. To set before oneself or others, as an aim or purpose ; as, the object I *propose* to myself ; to purpose ; to intend ; উপস্থাপিত করা ; উদ্দেশ্য করা ; অভিপ্রায় করা। 3. To nominate as a person for election to a post or office ; মনোনীত করা। 4. To offer as a toast ; as, to *propose* one's health ; স্বাস্থ্যকামনা করা। ***Verb i.*** 1. To devise a scheme or schemes ; to form or declare a purpose ; as, man *proposes* God disposes ; ফন্দী করা ; কোন উদ্দেশ্য ব্যক্ত করা। 2. To make an offer of marriage ; বিবাহের প্রস্তাব করা। **–pos′-er,** *n.* One who proposes ; প্রস্তাবকর্ত্তা, উত্থাপক। **Man proposes God disposes**—ছেলে যায় হাল নিয়ে, বিধাতা যায় তুলা নিয়ে।

prŏp-ō-ṣĭ′-tion, *n.* 1. That which is proposed ; a proposal ; a project ; প্রস্তাবিত বিষয় ; প্রস্তাব ; কল্পনা। 2. A statement ; (esp. *in Logic*) a sentence in which something is affirmed or denied ; প্রতিজ্ঞা ; সংকল্প-বাক্য (হিঃ কোঃ), প্রস্তাবপ্রমেয় (ঐ)। 3. (*Math.*) A problem or theorem formally stated ; (গণিত-শাস্ত্র) প্রতিজ্ঞা, সাধ্য (হিঃ কোঃ)। **–al,** *adj.* **Affirmative proposition**—See AFFIRMATIVE. **Categorical proposition** — See CATEGORICAL. **Conditional proposition**—সাপেক্ষ প্রতিজ্ঞা (সাঃ পঃ), সান্তর প্রতিজ্ঞা (ঐ), সাপেক্ষবাক্য (তর্কবিজ্ঞান)। **Disjunctive proposition** — বৈকল্পিক প্রতিজ্ঞা (সাঃ পঃ)। **Hypothetical proposition** — সকল্পন বাক্য (সাঃ পঃ)। **Particular proposition**—See PARTICULAR. **Universal proposition** — See UNIVERSAL.

prō-pound′ (-pound), *v. t.* 1. To propose or offer for consideration ; as, to *propound* a question, problem, matter, etc. to a person ; বিবেচনার জন্য প্রস্তাব উপস্থাপিত করা। 2. To bring forward as a will before proper authority to establish its legality ; বৈধতাপ্রতিপন্ন করার জন্য চরমপত্র প্রভৃতি উপযুক্ত আদালতে উপস্থাপিত করা। **–ed,** *adj.* **–er,** *n.* One who proposes ; প্রস্তাবক।

prō-præ′-tōr (-prē-), *n.* (*Rom. hist.*) An ex-proctor authorized to govern a province ; (রোমীয়-ইতিহাস) প্রাদেশিক শাসনকর্ত্তার পদে নিযুক্ত হওয়ার ক্ষমতাপ্রাপ্ত রোমনগরীর ভূতপূর্ব্ব দণ্ডনায়ক।

prō-prī′-ē-tă-rȳ, *adj.* & *n.* 1. Of or relating to, a proprietor ; মালীকী। 2. Privately owned, as medicines (sale of which is restricted by patent, etc.) ; ব্যক্তিবিশেষের সম্পত্তিস্বরূপ। 3. Possessing, or holding, property ; as, the *proprietary* classes ; সম্পত্তিশালী, বিত্তশালী। ***Noun.*** 1. A proprietor ; a body of proprietors collectively ; সম্পত্তিশালীব্যক্তি ; সম্পত্তিশালীব্যক্তিবর্গ। 2. Ownership or proprietorship ; as, an exclusive *proprietary* ; স্বত্ব, স্বামিত্ব।

prō-prī′-ē-tor (-tēr), *n.* An owner ; স্বত্বাধিকারী, স্বামী, মালিক, অধিকারী। **–to′-ri-al,** *adj.* **–to′-ri-al-ly,** *adv.* **–tress,** *n.* (*Fem.*) **–ship,** *n.* State, or right, of a proprietor; স্বত্বস্বামিত্ব, স্বাম্য, স্বামিত্ব, স্বামিভাব।

prō-prī′-ē-tȳ, *n.* 1. State or quality of being proper ; fitness ; appropriateness ; যুক্ততা ; যোগ্যতা ; সমুচিত্য। 2. Correctness of behaviour or morals ; as, a breach of *propriety* ; the details of correct conduct ; as, to observe the *proprieties* ; ঔচিত্য ; শোভনতা।

prŏ′-pri-ŭm, *n.* Individual or exclusive property ; ব্যাবর্ত্তক ধর্ম্ম (হিঃ কোঃ), ব্যাবর্ত্তকলক্ষণ (ঐ)।

prŏps, *n.* (*Slang*) The properties of the stage ; also, a PROPERTY-MAN ; (ইতরভাষায়) নাটকের সাজসজ্জা।

prŏp-tō′-sis, *n.* (*Med.*) Protrusion ; prolapse ; as, the *proptosis* of the eye ; (ভৈষজ্য শাস্ত্র) উদ্গতি ; চ্যুতি, ভ্রংশ। **—tosed,** *adj.*

prō-pŭl′-sion, *n.* **1.** Act of propelling or driving forward ; পুরশ্চালন। **2.** (*Fig.*) Impelling influence ; প্রণোদনা, প্ররোচনা। **3.** (*Med.*) Tendency to lean forward in walking ; (ভৈষজ্য শাস্ত্র) হাঁটিবার সময় সম্মুখেরদিকে ঝুঁকিয়া পড়ার আসক্তি। **—sive,** *adj.*

prŏp-ȳ-læ′-ŭm (-lē-), *n.* (*Pl.* -A) A vestibule of a house ; an entrance to a temple ; দ্বারমণ্ডপ ; মন্দিরতোরণ।

prŏp′-ȳ-līte, *n.* Volcanic rock found in some silver-mining regions ; রৌপ্যখনিবহুল অঞ্চলে প্রাপ্ত একপ্রকার আগ্নেয় প্রস্তর। **—lit′-ic,** *adj.*

prŏp′-ȳ-lŏn, *n.* (*Pl.* -LONS, -LONA), Same as PROPYLÆUM.

prō′-rō-gā-tor (-tẽr), *n.* (*Rare Astrol*) A planet which is in the ascendant in a nativity ; তুঙ্গগ্রহ।

prō-rogue′ (-rōg), *v. t.* & *i.* To end the session of (the British parliament etc.) ; ইংলণ্ডের পার্লেমেণ্ট প্রভৃতির অধিবেশনকালের অবসান করা। ***Verb i.*** To be prorogued as a parliament ; ইংলণ্ডের পার্লেমেণ্ট প্রভৃতির অধিবেশনকাল অবসান প্রাপ্ত হওয়া। **—ro-ga′-tion,** *n.*

prō-sā′-ic, *adj.* Resembling prose ; unpoetic ; commonplace ; dull ; গদ্যবৎ ; কবিত্বশূন্য, গদ্যময় ; সাধারণ ; নীরস। **—i-cal-ly,** *adv.* **—ness,** *n.*

prō-sā′-ist, *n.* **1.** A prose-writer ; গদ্যলেখক। **2.** A prosaic person ; কবিত্বশূন্য ব্যক্তি। **—ism,** *n.*

prō-sce′-ni-ŭm (-sē-), *n.* (*Pl.* -NIA), (*In ancient theatre*) The stage ; (প্রাচীন রঙ্গালয়) রঙ্গমঞ্চ। **2.** (*In mod. theatre*) The part of the stage in front of the curtain ; (আধুনিক রঙ্গালয়) যবনিকার সম্মুখস্থ মঞ্চাংশ।

prō-scrībe′, *v. t.* **1.** To publish or post the name of as one condemned to death or whose property is forfeited ; মৃত্যুদণ্ডে দণ্ডিত ব্যক্তিগণের বা যে সকল ব্যক্তির সম্পত্তি বাজেয়াপ্ত করা হইয়াছে—তাহাদের তালিকা প্রকাশিত করা বা প্রকাশ্য স্থানে আঁটিয়া দেওয়া। **2.** To put out of the protection of the law ; to banish ; আইনের আশ্রয় হইতে বঞ্চিত করা ; নির্ব্বাসিত করা। **3.** To denounce and condemn ; to interdict ; as, to *proscribe* a book or pamphlet ; প্রকাশ্যভাবে নিন্দা এবং ভৎর্সনা করা ; নিষেধ করা, নিবারণ করা ; বন্ধ করা। **—scrip′-tion,** *n.* **—scrip′-tive,** *adj.*

prose (prōz), *n.*, *v. i.* & *t.* **1.** Non-metrical or unrhymed composition ; গদ্য। **2.** The plain matter-of-fact quality ; as, the *prose* of existence ; গদ্যময় ভাব। **3.** A dull and tedious discourse ; নীরস একঘেয়ে কথাবার্ত্তা। ***Verb i.*** To write or talk in prose or prosily ; গদ্যে লিখা বা বলা, কবিত্বহীন ভাষায় লিখা বা বলা। ***Verb t.*** **1.** To render as a poem etc. in prose ; গদ্য করা, গদ্যে পরিবর্ত্তিত করা। **2.** To write in prose ; গদ্যে লিখা। **Pro′-ser,** *n.*

prō-sĕc′-tor (-tẽr), *n.* One who makes dissections for anatomical demonstrations ; শবব্যবচ্ছেদক।

prŏs′-ē-cūte, *v. t.* & *i.* **1.** To carry on ; to continue ; to follow up ; as, to *prosecute* studies, inquiry, a trade, etc. ; সম্পাদন করা, চালান ; পূর্ব্ববৎ চালাইয়া যাওয়া ; অনুসরণ করা। **2.** (*Law*) To sue ; কাহারো বিরুদ্ধে মোকদ্দমা রুজু করা, অভিযুক্ত করা। ***Verb i.*** To sue ; কাহারো বিরুদ্ধে মোকদ্দমা রুজু করা, অভিযুক্ত করা। **—cu′-tion,** *n.* Act of prosecuting or carrying on ; pursuit ; অনুষ্ঠান ; অনুসরণ। **2.** (*Law*) The institution and carrying on of a suit of law or of a criminal suit ; মোকদ্দমা রুজু করণ এবং পরিচালন। **3.** The prosecuting party ; বাদী পক্ষ।

prŏs′-ē-cū-tor (-tẽr), *n.* One who brings a lawsuit esp. in a criminal court ; অভিযোক্তা, বাদী, ফরিয়াদী, অর্থী। **—cu′-trix,** *n.* (*Pl.* -TRICES) A female prosecutor ; অভিযোক্ত্রী, অভিযোগকারিণী। **Public prosecutor**—যে ব্যবহারজীবী সরকার পক্ষে মোকদ্দমা পরিচালন করেন।

prŏs′-ē-lȳte, *n.*, *v. t.* & *i.* **1.** A new convert to some religion, system, opinion or party ; ধর্ম্মান্তরগ্রাহী, নবধর্ম্মগ্রাহী, অন্যধর্ম্মোৎসাহী (হিঃ কোঃ), নবধর্ম্মোৎসাহী (ঐ), পরধর্ম্মাবলম্বী, নবমতাবলম্বী। **2.** A gentile convert to Judaism ; ইহুদীধর্ম্মে নবদীক্ষিত ব্যক্তি। ***Verb t. & i.*** (*Rare*) To convert ; (কচিদ্ ব্যবহৃত) কোন ধর্ম্মে দীক্ষিত করা। **—ly-tism,** *n.* **—ly-tize,** *v. t.* & *i.* To convert ; দীক্ষিত করা। **—ly-tiz-er,** *n.*

prŏs-ĕn′-chȳ-mā, *n.* (*Bot.*) Fusiform tissue forming wood ; (উদ্ভিদ্‌বিদ্যা) সূত্রকা (সাঃ পঃ)। **—chym′-a-tous,** *adj.*

prō′-ś-i-fȳ, *v. t.* & *i.* **1.** To turn into prose ; to write prose ; গদ্যে পরিণত করা ; গদ্য লিখা। **2.** To render prosaic ; গদ্যময় করা, গদ্যবৎ করা।

prosit, (*L.*), *Interj.* May it benefit you—used in drinking healths, wishing success, etc. ; ইহা আপনার মঙ্গলের কারণ হউক।

prŏs′-ō-dȳ, *n.* The part of Grammar treating of the quantity of syllables, of accent, and of the laws of versification ; ছন্দঃপ্রকরণ, ছন্দঃশাস্ত্র, ছন্দোবিদ্যা। **–di'-a-cal**, **Pro-so'-di-al**, **Pro-sod'-ic**, *adjs.* **–dist**, *n.* One skilled in prosody ; ছন্দঃশাস্ত্র-বিশারদ, ছন্দোজ্ঞ।

prŏ-sŏ-pō-pœ'-ia (-pë-yă), *n.* (*Rhet.*) A figure by which things are represented as persons, an absent or dead person is represented as present or speaking ; (অলঙ্কারশাস্ত্র) সমাসোক্তি।

prŏs'-pĕct, *n.*, *v. i.* & *t.* **1.** View of things within the range of the eye ; a scene ; দৃষ্টি ; দৃশ্য। **2.** A mental scene ; as, opened a new *prospect* to his mind ; দৃশ্য, মানসিক দৃষ্টিপাত। **3.** Expectation or ground of expectation ; probable results ; প্রত্যাশা, আশা ; সম্ভাবিত ফল। **4.** (*Mining*) A place giving prospects of mineral deposit ; a sample of ore for testing ; the resulting yield of ore ; (খনিজ বিদ্যা) যে স্থানে স্বর্ণরৌপ্যাদি ধাতু পাওয়া যাইবে বলিয়া আশা করা যায় ; পরীক্ষার জন্য খনিজবিমিশ্র ধাতুখণ্ড ; খনিজবিমিশ্র ধাতু হইতে যে পরিমাণ খাঁটি ধাতু পাওয়া যায়। ***Verb i.*** **1.** (*Mining*) To search for mines or deposits of gold, silver, etc. ; খনির জন্য বা খনিজ স্বর্ণ রৌপ্য প্রভৃতির জন্য অনুসন্ধান করা। **2.** (Of a mine) To promise (ill or well) ; (খনি-সম্পর্কে) আশাপ্রদ বা নিরাশা-জনক হওয়া। **3.** (*Fig.*) To look out or search (*for*) ; (লক্ষণায়) অনুসন্ধান করা, খুঁজা। ***Verb t.*** **1.** To examine or explore as a region in search of gold etc. ; স্বর্ণাদি খনিজ পদার্থের জন্য কোন অঞ্চলে অনুসন্ধান করা। **2.** To work as a mine experimentally ; (of a mine) to hold out the prospect of, as a specified yield ; পরীক্ষাস্থলে কোন কোন খনির কাজ করা ; আশাজনক হওয়া। **–less**, *adj.* **–ing**, *n.* **–pec-tor**, *n.* One who explores regions for gold etc. ; যে ব্যক্তি স্বর্ণাদি খনিজ দ্রব্যের জন্য কোন অঞ্চলে অনুসন্ধান করে। **Prospecting licence**—কোন নির্দিষ্ট সীমার মধ্যে খনিজদ্রব্য অনুসন্ধানের জন্য সরকার হইতে যে অনুমতিপত্র দেওয়া হয়, অন্বেষণপত্র।

prŏ-spĕc'-tive (-tĭv), *adj.* **1.** Of, relating to, or concerned with, the future ; looking forward ; ভবিষ্যৎ-কালীয় ; আশান্বিত। **2.** Future ; expected ; as *prospective* profit, bridegroom, etc. ; ভবিষ্যৎ, ভাবী ; প্রত্যাশিত। **–ly**, *adv.* **–ness**, *n.*

prŏ-spĕc'-tŭs, *n.* (*Pl.* -TUSES) A statement of the scheme or main features of a school, business undertaking or a forthcoming book, etc. ; অনুষ্ঠানপত্র।

prŏs'-pêr, *v. i.* & *t.* To be prosperous ; to succeed ; to thrive ; সমৃদ্ধিসম্পন্ন হওয়া, সমৃদ্ধিশালী হওয়া ; কৃতকার্যতা লাভ করা ; শ্রীবৃদ্ধিপ্রাপ্ত হওয়া, উন্নতি প্রাপ্ত হওয়া। ***Verb t.*** To render successful ; কৃতকার্য্য করা।

prŏs'-pêr-ous (-ŭs), *adj.* **1.** Thriving ; flourishing ; successful ; লক্ষ্মীবান, সম্পন্ন, পয়মন্ত, শ্রীমৎ, প্রাপ্ত-যশ ; সমৃদ্ধ, সমৃদ্ধিশালী, ঐশ্বর্যশালী ; কৃতকার্য্য। **2.** Favourable ; auspicious, as wind, hour, etc. ; অনুকূল ; শুভ, মঙ্গলপ্রদ। **–ly**, *adv.* **–per'-i-ty**, *n.* State of being prosperous or flourishing ; satisfactory progress ; good fortune ; success ; সমৃদ্ধি, সম্পদ, ঐশ্বর্য্য, শ্রী, কল্যাণ অভ্যুদয়, বৈভব ; সন্তোষজনক উন্নতি ; সৌভাগ্য ; কৃতকার্য্যতা, সফলতা।

prŏs'-tāte, *adj.* & *n.* (*Anat.*) Standing before ; as, the *prostate* gland ; (শারীরসংস্থান বিদ্যা) অগ্রস্থ। ***Noun.*** Same as the PROSTRATE GLAND. **Pro-stat'-ic**, *adj.* **–ti-tis**, *n.* **Prostate-gland**—পুরুষের মূত্রাশয়ের মুখশায়ী দৃঢ় গ্রন্থিবিশেষ (হঃ চঃ)।

prŏs'-thĕ-sis, *n.* (*Gram.*) Addition of one or more letters to the beginnig of a word ; (ব্যাকরণ) কোন শব্দের প্রারম্ভে দুই বা ততোধিক অক্ষরসংযোগ। **–thet'-ic**, *adj.*

prŏs'-tĭ tūte, *n.* & *v. t.* A female given to indiscriminate lewdness ; বেশ্যা, খানকী (*colloq.*), রাঁড় (*colloq.*), কস্‌বী (*colloq.*), নটী, গণিকা, অবিদ্যা [Syn. কামরেখা, কামলেখা, স্বাধীনযৌবনা (মৃচ্ছঃ), সাধারণস্ত্রী (ঐ), প্রকাশনারী (ঐ), বারবধূ, বারবিলাসিনী, বারাঙ্গনা, বারবনিতা, বারসুন্দরী, বারস্ত্রী, বারনারী, বারকন্যকা, বারযুবতী, বাররামা, বারযোষিৎ, বারযোষা, বারবাণী, বেশনারী, বেশবনিতা, বেশবধূ (মৃচ্ছঃ), বেশযুবতী, বেশযোষিৎ, বেশস্ত্রী, বেশস্থা, পণ্যবিলাসিনী, পণ্যস্ত্রী, পণ্যযোষিৎ, পণ্যাঙ্গনা, পণ্যসুন্দরী, পণ-সুন্দরী, পণস্ত্রী, রূপাজীবা, রূপজীবনা, ভোগ্যা, সামান্যা, সামান্যনায়িকা, সামান্য-বনিতা, ভদ্রবতী (তৈত্তিঃ ব্রাঃ), সামান্যা স্ত্রী, বন্ধুরা, ত্রপারণ্ডা, গ্রামণী, নিশাচরী, দারিকা, লাঞ্জিকা, ঝর্ঝরা, রণ্ডা, ভণ্ডহাসিনী, তৎ-ক্ষণিকা, হট্টবিলাসিনী, নগরমণ্ডনা, ঋচ্ছরা (উণঃ—উজ্জ্বলদত্তের টীকা), পুরনারী (ধূর্ত্তঃ), পুংশ্চলী, রতায়নী, রম্ভা, লঙ্কা (আপ্তে), বর্চ্চটী, বন্ধুরা, বন্ধকী, কুম্ভা, স্মরবীথিকা, কুলকূণী (গেলঃ)।] ***Verb t.*** **1.** To give up (oneself) to lewdness esp. for hire ; বেশ্যাবৃত্তি করা। **2.** (*Fig.*) To devote to base or infamous purposes as one's talents etc. ; to sell as one's honours etc. for base gain ; (লক্ষণায়) কাহারো প্রতিভা প্রভৃতি কুকার্য্যে নিযুক্ত করা ; (অর্থগ্রহণে) কাহারো সম্মান, গৌরব প্রভৃতি বিক্রীত করা। **–tu'-tion**, *n.* The act or practice of prostituting ; বেশ্যাবৃত্তি, বারাঙ্গনাবৃত্তি, ভগবৃত্তি, বারসেবা।

prŏs'-trāte, *adj.* **1.** Lying at full length ; stretched out ; প্রণত ; সটান। **2.** Lying in a posture of humility or humblest adoration ; সাষ্টাঙ্গপ্রণত। **3.** Overcome ; overthrown ; as, to lay a party *prostrate* ; পর্য্যুদস্ত ; উৎপাতিত। **4.** Tired or exhausted ; অবসন্ন।

5. (*Bot.*) Trailing on the ground; (উদ্ভিদ্ বিদ্যা) লতানিয়া।

prŏs′-trāte, *v. t.* **1.** To lay flat; ভূপাতিত করা। **2.** To throw (oneself) down in humility, reverence, etc.; সাষ্টাঙ্গে প্রণত করা। **3.** (*Fig.*) To overcome; to make submissive; (লক্ষণায়) পরাভূত করা; বশীভূত করা। **4.** To deprive of strength; to reduce greatly; as, a person *prostrated* by fever; শক্তিহীন করা, কৃশ করা; কাহিল করা। **—tra′-tion** *n.* **1.** Act of prostrating; state of being prostrate; দণ্ডবৎ; সাষ্টাঙ্গপ্রণতি। **2.** (*Fig.*) Great depression; dejection, as of spirits or strength; (লক্ষণায়) অবসাদ; অবসন্নতা, গ্লানি।

prō′-stȳle, *n.* & *adj.* A portico in which the columns stand in advance of the building; যে দ্বারমণ্ডপে স্তম্ভশ্রেণী অট্টালিকার অগ্রভাগে অবস্থিত থাকে। ***Adj.*** With a prostyle; ঐরূপ দ্বারমণ্ডপবিশিষ্ট।

prōs′-ȳ, *adj.* **1.** Of, relating to, or like, prose; গদ্যসম্বন্ধীয়, গদ্যবৎ। **2.** Dull; tedious; uninteresting; as, a *prosy* talk, talker, writing, etc.; একঘেয়ে; বিরক্তিকর; নীরস। **—i-ly,** *adv.* **—i-ness,** *n.*

prō-sȳl′-lō-ġism, *n.* A syllogism of which the conclusion is the premise of another; উপকারী ন্যায় (সাঃ পঃ), সহায়কানুমান (হিঃ কোঃ), পূর্ব্বানুমানবাক্য (ঐ)।

prō-tăg′-ō-nist, *n.* **1.** The leading character or actor in a play; কোন নাটকের প্রধান অভিনেতা বা নায়ক। **2.** A leading person or character generally; প্রধান নায়ক।

prŏt′-ă-sis, *n.* (*Pl.* -SES) The antecedent clause of a conditional proposition; সাপেক্ষ প্রতিজ্ঞার পূর্ব্ববর্ত্তী বাক্যাংশ। **Pro-tat′-ic,** *adj.*

Prō′-tē-ăn, *adj.* **1.** Of, relating to, or like, Proteus; প্রটিয়াস-সম্বন্ধীয়। **2.** Exceedingly variable; changing in form or shape; বহুরূপগ্রাহী; বহুরূপধারণশীল, বহুরূপী, কামরূপী।

prō-tĕct′, *v. t.* **1.** To keep safe; to guard; নিরাপদে রাখা, বিপদ হইতে ত্রাণ করা; রক্ষা করা। **2.** (*Pol. Econ.*) To guard, as home-industry by a protective tariff; (অর্থনীতিশাস্ত্র) রক্ষাকারক শুল্ক সংস্থাপন দ্বারা স্বদেশীয় শিল্প প্রভৃতি রক্ষা করা। **3.** (*Commr.*) To provide funds to meet as a bill, draft, etc.; (বাণিজ্য) হুণ্ডী, বরাতচিঠি প্রভৃতি মিটানের জন্য টাকা দেওয়া। **4.** To provide with appliances to prevent injury from it; as, *protected* rifles; আঘাতনিবারক যন্ত্র বা কলসমন্বিত করা। **—tec-tive,** *adj.* That which protects; আবরক, রক্ষণাত্মক, রক্ষাকারক। **—tec-tive-ly,** *adv.* **—tec-tive-ness,** *n.* **Protective duties**—রক্ষণসাধকশুল্ক।

prō-tĕc′-tion, *n.* **1.** Act of protecting; state of being protected; defence; সংরক্ষণ, সংবর্দ্ধন (হিঃ কোঃ) পরিপোষণ (ঐ); গুপ্তি, আশ্রিতত্ব; পরিপালন, সমাশ্রয়। **2.** A protecting person, animal or thing; as, a man or dog is a great *protection* against burglers; রক্ষাকারী ব্যক্তি, জন্তু বা বস্তু, রক্ষক। **3.** (*Pol. Econ.*) The system of defending home-industry by imposing duties upon imported products; (অর্থনীতিশাস্ত্র) আমদানী মালের উপর শুল্কসংস্থাপন পূর্ব্বক স্বদেশজাত দ্রব্য সংরক্ষণের রীতি, সংরক্ষণনীতি। **4.** Same as SAFE-CONDUCT (which see). **—ism,** *n.* **—ist,** *n.* One who advocates protective system of tariff; সংরক্ষণবাদী।

prō-tĕc′-tor (-têr), *n.* **1.** One who protects; রক্ষক, রক্ষাকর্ত্তা, সংরক্ষক, প্রতিপালক, শরণ, ভয়ত্রাতা। **2.** A regent; প্রতিনিধি-রাজা। **3.** Something that protects; as, a breast-*protector*; রক্ষাকারক বস্তু, ত্রাণ (in compound)। **—al,** *adj.* **—ship,** *n.* **—tress,** *n.* (*Fem.*) **Lord Protector of the Common Wealth**—অলিভার ক্রমওয়েল (১৬৫৩—১৬৫৮), এবং রিচার্ড ক্রমওয়েলের (১৬৫৮—১৬৫৯) উপাধি।

prō-tĕc′-tor-āte (-têr-), *n.* **1.** Government by a protector or regent; প্রতিনিধি দ্বারা রাজ্যশাসন। **2.** The office or term of office of a protector; প্রতিনিধি-রাজার পদ বা পদের স্থিতিকাল (অলিভার ক্রমওয়েল সম্পর্কে বিশেষভাবে ব্যবহৃত হয়।) **3.** Protectorship of a weak state or territory esp. inhabited by native tribes, by a stronger one; such a weak or inferior territory; দুর্ব্বল দেশ বা রাজ্যের পরিচালক, বিশেষতঃ শক্তিশালী জাতিকর্ত্তৃক কোন দুর্ব্বল জাতির উপর পরিচালকত্ব; ঐরূপ দুর্ব্বল বা শক্তিহীন রাজ্য।

prō-tĕc′-tô-rȳ, *n.* (*Rom. Cath.*) An institution to afford protection to destitute or vicious children; (রোমানক্যাথলিক ধর্ম্মসংঘ), দুরন্ত ও নিরাশ্রয়বালকগণের আশ্রয় জন্য প্রতিষ্ঠান, অনাথনিবাস।

prō-te-ge′ (-tā-zhā), (*Fem.*, -GEE) One under the protection or care of another; আশ্রিত, পালিত।

prō′-tē-id, *n.* Same as PROTEIN, *n.* I.

prō-tē′-i-fôrm, *adj.* Very changeable in form; রূপান্তরগ্রাহী।

prō′-tē-in, *n.* **1.** (*Chem.*) Albuminoid, (now preferred to *proteid* in scientific use); অন্নসার, প্রতিদ (সাঃ পঃ)। **2.** An alkali albuminate formerly supposed to be the basis of all albuminoids; জীবদেহের যবক্ষারজানবিশিষ্ট উপাদান। **—i-na′-ceous, —te′-i-nic, —te′-i-nous,** *adjs.*

prō-têr-ăn′-drous (-drŭs), **prō-têr-ŏg′-ȳ-nous** (-nŭs), *adjs.* Having stamens (pistil) mature before pistil (stamens) ; স্ত্রীকেশরের পূর্ব্বে পরিণত পুংকেশর, এবং পুংকেশরের পূর্ব্বে পরিণত স্ত্রীকেশর বিশিষ্ট।

prŏ'-tĕst', *n.* 1. A formal declaration or statement of dissent; remonstrance ; প্রতিবাদ ; আপত্তি। 2. A solemn declaration ; দৃঢ়োক্তি।

prŏ-tĕst', *v. t.* & *i.* 1. To affirm with solemnity ; as, to *protest* one's innocence ; প্রতিবাদ করা, আপত্তি করা। ***Verb i.*** 1. To declare solemnly ; to asseverate ; দৃঢ়ভাবে বলা ; নিশ্চিত বাক্য বলা। 2. To make a solemn declaration usually a written one *against* some action, proposal, measure, etc. ; কোন ব্যক্তির বিরুদ্ধে সত্য প্রতিজ্ঞাপূর্ব্বক বলা। **—er, —tes'-tor,** *ns.* **—ing-ly,** *adv.*

prŏt'-ĕs-tănt, *n.* & *adj.* 1. (*Cap.*) One of the party who adhered to Luther at the Reformation ; লুথারপ্রবর্ত্তিত মতাবলম্বী খৃষ্টান, রোমকমতপ্রতিবাদী। 2. A member or adherent of a reformed church ; সংস্কৃতধর্ম্মসংঘভুক্ত ব্যক্তি। 3. One who makes a protest ; প্রতিবাদকারী, আপত্তিকারী। ***Adj.*** 1. (*Cap.*) Of, or relating to, Protestants or their faith and practice ; রোমক প্রতিবাদী খৃষ্টান সম্প্রদায় বা ঐ সম্প্রদায়ের ক্রিয়াকলাপসম্বন্ধীয়। 2. Making a protest ; প্রতিবাদকারী, আপত্তিকারী। **—ism,** *n.* The Protestant religion or its principles ; রোমক প্রতিবাদী খৃষ্টানগণের ধর্ম্ম বা উক্ত ধর্ম্মের তত্ত্ব। **—ize,** *v. t.* & *i.* To make protestant ; to convert to protestantism ; রোমক প্রতিবাদী করা ; রোমক প্রতিবাদী খৃষ্টানগণের ধর্ম্মে দীক্ষিত করা।

prŏt-ĕs-tā'-tion, *n.* Act of protesting ; a solemn declaration or affirmation ; a protest ; আপত্তিকরণ ; দৃঢ়োক্তি ; দৃঢ়বাক্য, নিশ্চিত বাক্য ; আপত্তি, প্রতিবাদ।

Prō'-teus (-tūs), *n.* 1. (*Class. Myth.*) A prophetic sea-god who changed his shape at will ; (গ্রীকপুরাণোক্ত) কামরূপী সাগর দেবতাবিশেষ। 2. A changeable or inconstant person or thing ; যে ব্যক্তি ঘন ঘন মত পরিবর্ত্তন করে, অব্যবস্থিত চিত্ত ব্যক্তি, বহুরূপী। 3. A kind of bacteria ; একপ্রকার রোগবীজাণু। 4. Same as AMŒBA. 5. A genus of aquatic eel-shaped amphibians ; কঁচিলার আকার উভচর জন্তুবিশেষ।

prō-thă-lā'-mi-ŭm, —ŏn, *ns.* A song in celebration of a marriage ; বিবাহগীতি, উদ্বাহ-সঙ্গীত।

prŏth'-ĕ-sis, *n.* 1. The place where the eucharistic elements are placed before being put on the altar ; the placing of these elements ; বেদীর উপর স্থাপনের পূর্ব্বে যে স্থানে খৃষ্টের অন্তিম ভোজনানুষ্ঠানের রুটি ও সুরা রক্ষিত হয় ; উক্তস্থানে ঐ সকল দ্রব্য স্থাপন। 2. (*Gram.*) Same as PROSTHESIS. **Pro-thet'-ic,** *adj.*

prō-tis-tă, *n.* (*Pl.*) Microscopic organism not distinguished as plants or animals ; একপ্রকার আণুবীক্ষণিক জীবাবয়ব, আদ্যজীবাণু (সাঃ পঃ)।

prō-tō-A'-ră-bic (-ă-), *adj.* Of, or relating to, the original Arabs ; আরবদেশীয় আদিম লোকসম্পর্কীয়।

prō'-tō-cŏl, *n.*, *v. i.* & *t.* 1. The original draft or copy of a document esp. of the terms of a treaty agreed to in conference and signed by the parties ; দলীলাদির খসড়া, সন্ধিপত্রের পাণ্ডুলিপি, আদিলেখ। 2. An account or statement of a transaction ; কোন কার্য্য-বিবরণী, কোন বিষয়ের বিবরণী। 3. Official formulas at the commencement and the end of a charter, papal edict, etc. ; সনন্দ, পোপের অনুশাসন, প্রভৃতির প্রারম্ভে লিখিত বাক্য। ***Verb i.*** To make, or write, protocols or first drafts ; দলীলাদির প্রথম খসড়া প্রস্তুত করা। ***Verb t.*** To record on a protocol ; প্রথম খসড়ায় লিখা।

prō-tō-gĕ-nĕt'-ic, —gĕn'-ic, *adjs.* Of, or relating to, the first period of growth or formation ; বৃদ্ধির প্রথম অবস্থাসম্বন্ধীয়।

prō'-tō-gīne, *n.* A kind of talcose granite ; একপ্রকার অভ্রকগর্ভ স্ফটিক প্রস্তর।

prō-tō-hip'-pŭs, *n.* An extinct quadruped allied to the horse ; অধুনালুপ্ত অশ্বজাতীয় জন্তুবিশেষ।

prō-tō-mâr'-tyr (-tėr), *n.* The first martyr in any cause, esp. applied to St. Stephen the first Christian martyr ; কোন বিষয়ে প্রথম আত্মোৎসর্গকারী ব্যক্তি।

prō-tŏn'-ō-tă-rȳ, —thŏn'—, *ns.* A chief notary or clerk in some law courts ; কোন কোন আদালতের প্রধান কেরাণী বা দলীলপত্রের সত্যপাঠগ্রহণকারী। **Protonotaries Apostolic(al)**— যে দ্বাদশ জন প্রধানাচার্য্য পোপের বিধি তালিকাভুক্ত করেন ও সাধকগণের সিদ্ধিপ্রাপ্তির বিষয় বিজ্ঞাপিত করিয়া থাকেন।

prō-tŏph'-ȳ-tă, *n.* (*Pl.*) The most simply organized plants, each consisting of a single cell ; আদ্যোদ্ভিদক (সাঃ পঃ)।

prō'-tō-phȳte, *n.* Any plant of the protophyta ; আদ্যোদ্ভিদ (সাঃ পঃ)।

prō'-tō-plăsm, *n.* A semi-transparent semi-fluid substance constituting the physical basis of life ; জীববীজ, প্রথমফেন (হিঃ কোঃ), জীবফেন (ঐ), জীবধাতু (ঐ), আদিপঙ্ক (ঐ), নারা (ঐ), প্রাণপঙ্ক (অভিঃ), জীবাদি (ঐ), জীববীজক (সাঃ পঃ), আদিরূপক (হিঃ কোঃ), ধাত্বগ্নি (সুশ্রুঃ কুঞ্জ), জীববস্তু (সাঃ পঃ), জৈবনিক (ঐ), জীবপঙ্ক (ঐ), আদিম জৈবোপদান (used in Bengali medical books.) **—plas'-mic, —plas-mat'-ic,** *adjs.*

prō'-tō-plăst, *n.* 1. The first created man ; প্রথম সৃষ্ট মানব, আদি মানব। 2. The original ; the thing first formed as a pattern to be copied ; মূল ; আদিম আদর্শ। 3. The protoplasmic cell contents considered as a vital unit ; জীবপঙ্ক কোষের অন্তর্নিহিত রস। **–plas′-tic,** *adj.*

prō-tō-thē′-rĭ-ă, *n.* The mammals of the lowest sub-class ; hypothetical ancestors of these ; নিম্নতম স্তন্যপায়িজীববর্গ ; উহাদিগের কল্পিত পূর্ব্বপুরুষ।

prō′-tō-tȳpe, *n.* An original type or model ; an archetype ; মূল আদর্শ ; মূলপ্রতিরূপ। **–typ′-al, –typ′-ic, –typ′-i-cal,** *adjs.*

prō-tō-zō′-ă, *n.* (*Pl.*) A group of animals occupying the lowest place in the animal kingdom ; নিম্নতম শ্রেণীর জীববর্গ, প্রথমজীববর্গ, প্রথমজ, আদ্যজীববর্গ। **–al,** *adj.* **–an,** *adj.* & *n.* Of, or pertaining, to the protozoa ; caused by a parasitic protozoon as a disease ; আদ্যজীব সম্বন্ধীয়, পরাঙ্গপুষ্ট-আদ্য জীবজনিত। (*Noun*) One of the protozoa ; প্রথমজ প্রাণী। **–on,** *n.* Such an animal ; নিম্নতম শ্রেণীর জীব, কণৈকজী (হিঃ কোঃ), প্রথমজীব (ঐ)।

prō-tō-zō′-ic, *adj.* **1.** Of, or relating to, the protozoa ; আদ্য-জৈবিক। **2.** (*Geol.*) Containing earliest traces of living beings, as a strata ; (ভূবিদ্যা) জীবস্থিতির পূর্ব্বতম চিহ্নবিশিষ্ট।

prō-tō-zō-ŏl′-ō-ḡȳ, *n.* The study of the protozoa ; আদ্যজীবতত্ত্ব।

prō-trăct′, *v. t.* **1.** To prolong ; as, to *protract* one's stay at a place ; দীর্ঘ করা, অধিকক্ষণ স্থায়ী করা, বিলম্ব করা। **2.** (*Survey*) To draw to a scale ; to plot ; (জরীপ) কোন রূপ মাপে অঙ্কিত করা ; নক্সা করা। **–ed-ly,** *adv.* In a protracted or prolonged manner ; চিরায়িত ভাবে, দীর্ঘীকৃতভাবে।

prō-trăc′-tile, *adj.* (*Zool.*) Capable of being extended or thrust out, as an organ, etc. ; জন্তু বিদ্যা) প্রসার্য্য।

prō-trăc′-tion, *n.* **1.** Act of protracting ; বিলম্বন। **2.** (*Survey*) A making of a plot ; নক্সা অঙ্কন। **3.** Action of a protracting muscle ; প্রসারক পেশীর ক্রিয়া।

prō-trăc′-tor (-têr), *n.* **1.** An instrument used in laying down and measuring angles on paper ; কোণাঙ্কণ যন্ত্র, কোণমাণ যন্ত্র। **2.** A muscle serving to extend a limb, etc. ; যে পেশীর সাহায্যে কোন অঙ্গপ্রত্যঙ্গ প্রসারিত করা হয়, প্রসারক-পেশী। **3.** (*Surg.*) An instrument for extracting foreign bodies from wounds ; (অস্ত্রবিদ্যা) সদ্য-ব্রণাদি হইতে শল্য উদ্ধারার্থ অস্ত্রবিশেষ।

prō-trude (-trōd), *v. t.* & *i.* **1.** To thrust forward ; to cause to project ; প্রসারিত করা ; প্রলম্বিত করা। **2.** (*Fig.*) To obtrude ; (লক্ষণায়) অনাহূতভাবে আসা, উপযাচক হইয়া আসা। ***Verb i.*** To project ; প্রলম্বিত হওয়া। **–tru′-dent, –tru′-si-ble, –tru-sive,** *adjs.* **–tru′-sion,** *n.* The act of protruding ; প্রসারণ, প্রলম্বন, বহির্ব্বর্ত্তন, বহিঃসরণ।

prō-tru′-sile (-trô-), *adj.* Capable of being protruded or thrust forth as a limb etc. ; প্রলম্বনীয়।

prō-tū′-bêr-ănt, *adj.* Swelling ; prominent ; (*lit.* & *fig.*) ; উন্নত ; প্রলম্বিত (শব্দানুযায়ী ও লক্ষণায়)। **–ance,** *n.* State of being protuberant ; that which is protuberant ; a prominence ; a bunch or knob ; প্রলম্বতা, স্ফীতি ; উদ্গত বস্তু ; স্ফোট, উপরিজ (সুশ্রুঃ) ; গুচ্ছ, আব, পিণ্ড।

prō′-tȳle, *n.* (*Chem.*) A hypothetical primordial matter supposedly differentiated into what are recognized as distinct chemical elements ; (রসায়ন শাস্ত্র) মূল পদার্থ সমূহের আদি পদার্থ, আদিভূত।

proud (prowd), *adj.* **1.** Showing too great self-esteem ; over-rating one's excellence ; arrogant ; haughty ; অহঙ্কারী, গর্ব্বপূর্ণ, গর্ব্বিত ; অহমিকাপূর্ণ ; উদ্ধত ; দৃপ্ত, সগর্ব্ব। **2.** Feeling oneself greatly honoured ; elated ; as, I am *proud* of knowing him ; গৌরবান্বিত ; উল্লসিত। **3.** Having a feeling of proper self-respect or self-esteem ; as, too *proud* to be mean ; যথোচিত আত্মমর্য্যাদাসম্পন্ন। **4.** Of which one is or may be justly proud ; as, a *proud* day for us ; গৌরবজনক, গৌরবের। **5.** (Of things) Splendid ; admirable ; চমৎকার ; প্রশংসনীয়। **6.** Manifesting pride ; daring ; presumptuous ; গর্ব্বপ্রকাশক ; সাহসী ; প্রগল্ভ। **7.** (Of waters) In flood or swollen ; (জলসম্পর্কে) বন্যাপ্লাবিত, স্ফীত, উদ্বেল। **8.** Spirited as a steed ; তেজস্বী। **–ly,** *adv.* **Proud flesh**—ক্ষতাঙ্কুরের অতিরিক্ত বৃদ্ধি। **You do me proud**—(*Colloq.*) You honour me greatly ; (চলিত ভাষায়) আপনি আমাকে অতিশয় সম্মানিত করিয়াছেন।

prôve, *v. t.* & *i.* **1.** To try or ascertain by an experiment or by a standard ; to test ; পরীক্ষা দ্বারা চেষ্টা করা, কোনরূপ স্থাপিতমানের সহিত তুলনা দ্বারা নির্ণয়ের চেষ্টা করা ; পরীক্ষা করা। **2.** To ascertain by argument or testimony ; to demonstrate ; প্রমাণ করা ; প্রতিপাদন করা। **3.** To verify as a will ; সত্যতাপ্রতিপাদন করা। **4.** (*Print.* & *lithog.*) To take a proof impression of ; পরীক্ষাস্বরূপ ছাপ নেওয়া। **5.** (*Arith.*) To test the correctness of as a calculation (পাটীগণিত) পরীক্ষা করা। ***Verb i.*** **1.** To make trial ; পরীক্ষা করা। **2.** To be found by experiment or trial ; to turn out to be ; as, it *proves* salutary ; পরীক্ষা দ্বারা প্রমাণিত বা প্রতিপন্ন হওয়া ; পরিণত হওয়া। **Prov′-a-ble,** *adj.* **Prov′-a-ble-ness,** *n.* **Prov′-a-bly,** *adv.*

prō-vĕd′-ĭ-tor (-tẽr), **prŏv′-ē-dore** (-dōr), *ns.* 1. A purveyor ; খাদ্য-দ্রব্য সরবরাহকারী। 2. (Only, *pro-veditor*) A functionary in a Venetian republic ; ভিনিসীয় গণতন্ত্রের অধীন কর্ম্মচারিবিশেষ।

prŏv′-ē-nance (-năns), *n.* Origin ; source ; a place of origin ; মূল ; উৎপত্তি ; উৎপত্তিস্থান।

Provencal, (*F.*), *adj.* & *n.* Of, or pertaining to, Provence in France ; ফরাসীদেশের অন্তর্গত প্রোভেন্স নামক স্থানসংক্রান্ত। ***Noun.*** A native of Provence ; the language of Provence ; প্রভেন্স প্রদেশবাসি ব্যক্তি ; প্রভেন্স দেশের ভাষা।

prŏv′-ĕn-dẽr, *n.* Dry food or fodder for beasts ; গবাদি জন্তুর জন্য শুষ্ক খাদ্য, বিচালি, যবস।

prō-vē′-nĭ-ence (-ĕns), *n.* Same as PROVENANCE.

prŏv′-ẽrb, *n.* 1. A short pithy sentence expressing a truth or common fact ; a maxim ; an adage ; প্রাচীনোক্তি, প্রবাদ, লোকোক্তি, লোকবাদ, জনপ্রবাদ, লোকপ্রবাদ, লৌকিকন্যায় (হিঃ কোঃ) ; নীতিবাক্য ; প্রবচন। 2. A drama usu. French, exemplifying a proverb ; কোন লোকপ্রবাদের দৃষ্টান্তস্বরূপ নাটক। 3. A byword ; an expression of contempt, hatred, etc. ; as, he is a *proverb* for inaccuracy ; প্রবাদবাক্য, সাধারণ কথা ; ঘৃণা বা অবজ্ঞাসূচক উক্তি। 4. (*Cap. Pl.*) Same as the BOOK OF PROVERBS. 5. (*Pl.*) A kind of game, as of cards, in which each plays on his account ; একপ্রকার তাসখেলা। **Book of Proverbs**—বাইবেলের প্রাচীন নিয়মের অন্তর্গত পুস্তক বিশেষ। **To a proverb**—Notoriously ; as, he is ignorant *to a proverb* ; নামজাদা রকমের।

prō-vẽr′-bĭ-ăl, *adj.* 1. Of, relating to, or like, a proverb ; mentioned or expressed in proverb ; জনপ্রবাদসম্বন্ধীয়, জনপ্রবাদবৎ ; জনপ্রবাদে উল্লিখিত বা ব্যক্ত, ন্যায়প্রসিদ্ধ। 2. Notorious ; নামজাদা। **—al′-i-ty,** *n.* **—ly,** *adv.*

prŏ′-vĭ-ănt, *n.* Supply of provision as of an army ; সৈন্যদলের খাদ্যদ্রব্যসম্ভার সরবরাহ।

prō-vīde′, *v. i.* & *t.* 1. To make preparations ; as, to *provide* for one's safety or against attack etc. ; আয়োজন করা, উদ্যোগ করা। 2. To stipulate previously ; as, the law *provides* that etc. ; পূর্ব্বেই নির্ব্বন্ধ করা। 3. To make provision, esp. to secure maintenance as for oneself, family, etc. ; পরিবার প্রভৃতির ভরণপোষণের সংস্থান করা। ***Verb t.*** 1. To supply with what is needed or necessary ; as, everyone should *provide* himself ; আবশ্যক দ্রব্যসম্ভার সরবরাহ করা। 2. To furnish or supply ; as, to *provide* one *with* a thing, *to* or *for* a person ; জোগান, সরবরাহ করা। 3. (*Hist.*) To appoint to a benefice before it is vacant ; (ইতিহাস) কোন যাজকের পদ শূন্য হওয়ার পূর্ব্বে উহাতে কাহাকেও নিযুক্ত করা।

prō-vīd′-ĕd, *adj.* & *conj.* That is equipped with necessaries ; আবশ্যক দ্রব্যসম্ভার দ্বারা সজ্জিত। ***Conj.*** On condition ; on the understanding ; সর্তে ; এই করারে, যদিস্যাৎ।

prŏv′-ĭ-dence (-dĕns), *n.* 1. Preparing for future use ; preparation ; ভবিষ্যতের ব্যবহারের জন্য প্রস্তুত করণ ; আয়োজন। 2. Foresight ; care esp. beneficent care of God or nature ; পরিণামদর্শিতা, দূরদর্শন, দূরদৃষ্টি, ভবিষ্যচিন্তন, ভবিষ্যদর্শন ; বিধাতৃশক্তি। 3. (*Cap.*) God ; বিধি (হিঃ কোঃ), দৈব (ঐ), বিধাতা। 4. An event divinely ordained ; "There is a special *providence* in the fall of the sparrow" ; বিধাতৃনির্দ্দিষ্ট ঘটনা। 5. Frugality ; thrift ; মিতব্যয় ; মিতব্যয়িতা।

prŏv′-ĭ-dĕnt, *adj.* 1. Having, or exhibiting, foresight ; পরিণামদর্শী, দীর্ঘদর্শী, ভবিষ্যদর্শী। 2. Providing for future wants ; frugal ; thrifty ; ভবিষ্যতের জন্য সংস্থানকারী ; মিতব্যয়ী ; পরিমিতব্যয়ী।

prŏv-ĭ-dĕn′-tial (-shăl), *adj.* Effected by, or referable to, divine direction ; opportune ; lucky ; as, a *providential* escape ; দৈবঘটিত ; দৈবিক ; সৌভাগ্যহেতুক। **—ly,** *adv.*

prō-vīd′-ẽr, *n.* One who provides ; সরবরাহকারী। **Universal provider**—যে ব্যবসায়ী সর্ব্বপ্রকার বা বহুপ্রকার মালের ব্যবসায় করে। **Lion's provider**—Jackal (*lit.* & *fig.*) ; শৃগাল।

prŏv′-ince (-ĭns), 1. (*Rom. Hist.*) A territory outside of Italy acquired chiefly by conquest and under Roman government ; (রোমের ইতিহাস) রোমের শাসনাধীন ইতালী-দেশের বহির্ভূত প্রদেশ। 2. A principal division of a country etc., esp. for administrative purposes ; প্রদেশ, প্রান্ত (হিঃ কোঃ)। 3. (*Eccl.*) A division of a country under an archbishop ; আর্কবিশপের অধীন প্রদেশ। 4. Sphere of action ; business, duty or function ; as, it is not my *province* or within my *province* ; কার্য্যক্ষেত্র ; অধিকার, স্বধর্ম্ম, কার্য্য, কর্ত্তব্য। 5. A department of knowledge ; a branch of learning ; শাস্ত্রের শাখা বা বিভাগ ; অঙ্গ। **The Provinces** — রাজধানীর বহির্ভূত সমগ্র প্রদেশ।

prō-vĭn′-cial (-shăl), *adj.* & *n.* 1. Of, or relating to, a province or the provinces ; প্রাদেশিক। 2. Exhibiting the ways and manners of a province ; not cosmopolitan ; rude ; narrow ; illiberal ; প্রাদেশিক ; জাতিগতসংস্কারসম্পন্ন ; রূঢ় ; সংকীর্ণচেতাঃ ; অনুদার।

Noun. 1. An inhabitant of a province or the provinces; a countrified person; প্রদেশবাসী, রাজধানীর বহির্ভূত স্থানবাসী; পাড়াগেঁয়ে। 2. (*Eccl.*) The head of a province; the head of a religious order in it; কোন প্রদেশের প্রধান যাজক; কোন প্রাদেশিক যাজক-সম্প্রদায়ের অধ্যক্ষ। **—ci-al′-ty,** *n.* **—ism,** *n.* Manner, fashion, mode thought, etc. peculiar to a province; প্রাদেশিকতা। **—ist,** *n.* 1. A provincial; also, a user of provincialism; প্রাদেশিক; প্রাদেশিক ভাষা ব্যবহারকারী। 2. A word, phrase or idiom peculiar to the natives of a province or of the provinces; কোন প্রদেশ বা রাজধানীর বহির্ভূত প্রদেশে বিশিষ্টরূপে ব্যবহৃত শব্দ, বাক্য, প্রভৃতি, দেশভাষা। 3. Attachment to the native province rather than to the country; প্রদেশানুরাগ। **—ize,** *v. t.* To make provincial; প্রাদেশিক করা। **—ly,** *adv.*

prō-vĭ′-sion (-zŭn), *n.* & *v. t.* 1. Act of providing, or making preparations (*for* or *against*); সরবরাহ করণ, আয়োজন, ব্যবস্থা। 2. (*Pl.*) A stock of food; eatables and drinkables collected and stored; as, *provisions* failed; ভোজ্যদ্রব্যসম্ভার; খাদ্য ও পানীয় ভাণ্ডার। 3. A stipulation or condition; a proviso; as, the *provisions* of a contract or statute; চুক্তি, করার; সর্ত। 4. (*Hist.*) Appointment to a benefice before it is vacant; পদশূন্য হওয়ার পূর্ব্বে যাজকের পদে নিয়োগ। *Verb t.* To supply with provisions or food; খাদ্যদ্রব্যসম্ভার সংগ্রহ করা। **—less,** *adj.* Without provisions or food; খাদ্যদ্রব্যশূন্য। **—ment,** *n.* **Provisions of Oxford** — Simon de Montfordএর নেতৃত্বাধীনে ইংলণ্ডে সম্রান্ত ভূস্বামীগণকর্ত্তৃক রাজার কুশাসন নিয়ন্ত্রিত করার জন্য ১২৫৮ খৃঃ অব্দে যে ব্যবস্থাপত্রের পাণ্ডুলিপি প্রস্তুত করা হয়।

prō-vĭ′-sion-ăl (-zŭn-), *adj.* Serving as a provision for the time being; temporary; as, a *provisional* government; সাময়িক, আপাত-নিয়োজিত; অল্পকালিক (হিঃ কোঃ)। **—al′-i-ty,** *n.* **—ly,** *adv.* For the time being; সাময়িকভাবে, আপাততঃ। **—ness,** *n.*

prō-vī′-sō, *n.* (*Pl.* -SOES) An article or clause in a statute or contract; a condition or stipulation; দলিলাদির বিশেষ চুক্তি, প্রতিপ্রসব; চুক্তি, করার।

prō-vī′-sŏr, *n.* 1. (*R. C. Ch.*) The purveyor, steward or treasurer of a religious house; (রোমান ক্যাথলিক ধর্ম্মসংঘ) মঠ প্রভৃতির খাদ্য-দ্রব্য সরবরাহকারী বা কোষাধ্যক্ষ, ভাণ্ডারী। 2. (*Hist.*) The holder of a provision or benefice; (ইতিহাস) যাজকীয় বৃত্তিভোগী। 3. Same as a STATUTE OF PROVISORS. **Statute of Provisors**—যে ব্যবস্থা-দ্বারা পোপ যাজকীয়পদ অধিকার হইতে বঞ্চিত হন।

prō-vī′-sō-rў, *adj.* 1. Of, or relating to, a proviso; conditional; সর্তসম্বন্ধীয়; আপেক্ষিক, সাপেক্ষ। 2. Making provision; provisional; সংস্থানকারী; সাময়িক। **—ri-ly,** *adv.*

prŏv-ō-cā′-tion, *n.* 1. Act of provocating; a cause of resentment; প্রকোপন; ক্রোধের হেতু। 2. Act of arousing excitement; a stimulus; as, a *provocation* to mirth; উত্তেজনা সঞ্চার; প্ররোচনা, প্রণোদনা।

prō-vŏc′-a-tive (-tĭv), *adj.* & *n.* Having a tendency to provoke; exciting or irritating; উত্তেজক; উদ্দীপক, ক্রোধোদ্রেককর। *Noun.* Something that provokes; উত্তেজনাজনক বিষয়।

prō-voke′ (-vŏk), *v. t.* 1. To arouse; to incite; as, to *provoke* one to anger, to do something, etc.; উত্তেজিত করা; উদ্রেক করা। 2. To call forth; to instigate; to excite; as, to *provoke* indignation, inquiry, etc.; উদ্দীপিত করা; প্ররোচিত করা, প্রণোদিত করা; উত্তেজিত করা। 3. To cause; as, it will *provoke* fermentation; সংঘটন করা, জন্মান, উৎপাদন করা। **—vok′-ing,** *adj.* **—vok′-ing-ly,** *adv.*

prŏv′-ŏst, *n.* 1. The head of a college at Oxford, Cambridge, etc.; অক্সফোর্ড, কেম্ব্রিজ, প্রভৃতি স্থানের মহাবিদ্যালয়ের অধ্যক্ষ। 2. The head of a municipal corporation or burgh in Scotland; স্কটলণ্ডের মিউনিসিপালিটীর অথবা স্বায়ত্তশাসনের ক্ষমতাপ্রাপ্ত নগরের অধ্যক্ষ। 3. The head of some cathedral chapters; মহাধর্ম্মমন্দিরের যাজকসভার অধ্যক্ষ। **—ship,** *n.* **Provost-marshal**—সামরিক পুলিশের অধ্যক্ষ; কোন কোন উপনিবেশের প্রধান পুলিশ কর্ম্মচারী; (ইতিহাস) ফরাসীদেশের অর্দ্ধ সামরিক কর্ম্মচারিবিশেষ। **Provost-sergeant**—সামরিক পুলিশের সার্জ্জেণ্ট।

prow, *n.* 1. The forepart of a ship or boat; (*poet.*) the vessel; নাবমুখ, নৌমুখ, পোতাগ্র (রাধা কুঃ), গলুই; (কবিতায়) নৌকা। 2. Something projecting in the forepart, like the prow of a ship; পোতাগ্রবৎ সম্মুখভাগে প্রলম্বিত বস্তু।

prow, *adj.* (*Archaic*) Valiant; brave; gallant; (অপ্রঃ) সাহসী; নির্ভীক; শূর, শৌর্য্য-সম্পন্ন।

prow′-ĕss, *n.* Valour; bravery, esp. military gallantry; শৌর্য্য, বিক্রম; পৌরুষ, পরাক্রম।

prowl, *v. i., t.* & *n.* To rove stealthily esp. for prey or plunder (also *fig.*); লুণ্ঠনের উদ্দেশ্যে পরিভ্রমণ করা, শিকারের উদ্দেশ্যে ঘুরা। *Verb t.* To rove over, through or about stealthily esp. in search of prey or booty; as, to *prowl* a place, street, etc.; লুণ্ঠন বা শিকারের উদ্দেশ্যে

ভ্রমণ করা। *Noun.* Act of prowling; as, to be on the *prowl*; শিকার বা লুণ্ঠনের উদ্দেশ্যে পরিভ্রমণ, শিকারের অন্বেষণে পর্য্যটন। **Prowl'-er,** *n.*

prŏx'-i-măl, *adj.* (*Anat.*) Nearest to the centre of a body or of a point of attachment; (শারীরসংস্থানবিদ্যা) নিকটতম। **—ly,** *adv.*

prŏx'-i-mate, *adj.* Nearest; next; immediately preceding or following; approximate; নিকটতম; পরবর্ত্তী; অব্যবহিত পূর্ব্ববর্ত্তী বা পরবর্ত্তী; প্রায় অনুরূপ, কাছাকাছি। **—ly,** *adv.*

proxime accessit, (*L.*), *Sent.* & *n.* He (or she) came very near (to winning a prize etc.); সে (পুরুষ বা স্ত্রীলোক) (পুরস্কার প্রভৃতি) প্রায় পেয়েছিল। *Noun.* Being very near (a prize etc.); as, he got a *proxime accessit*; প্রায় প্রাপ্তির অবস্থা।

prŏx-im'-i-tȳ, *n.* State of being proximate; immediate nearness; নৈকট্য, সন্নিধি, সান্নিধ্য, সন্নিকট, সামীপ্য, সমীপতা, প্রত্যাসন্নতা, অন্তিকতা; সন্নিকর্ষ, সন্নিধান, তাটস্থ্য। **Proximity of blood**—Kinship; নিকটসম্বন্ধ, রক্তগত সম্পর্ক।

prŏx'-i-mō, *adj.* (*Abbr. prox.*) In, or of, the next month; সামনের মাসের।

prŏx'-ȳ, *n.* & *adj.* **1.** The agency of another acting as a substitute; as, to vote by *proxy*; প্রতিনিধিত্ব। **2.** One deputed to act for another; প্রতিনিধি। **3.** A writing by which a person authorizes another esp. to vote for him; a vote so given; প্রতিনিধিপত্র; প্রতিনিধিদ্বারা প্রদত্ত মত *Adj.* Done, made or given, by proxy; by proxy; প্রতিনিধি দ্বারা; বরাতে।

prude (prôd), *n.* A woman of affected delicacy, reserve or modesty; woman exhibiting or affecting extreme propriety in conduct or speech; কৃত্রিম লজ্জা, সৌকুমার্য্য বা সংলাপপরাঙ্মুখতা প্রদর্শনকারিণী নারী, কপটসুশীলা, কপটিকা; বাক্য বা আচরণে অতিরিক্ত সূক্ষ্মরুচিপ্রিয়তাপ্রদর্শনকারিণী নারী, সূক্ষ্মরুচিপ্রিয়া। **Prud'-er-y,** *n.* The manners and characteristics of a prude; excessive nicety in conduct or speech; coyness; কপটিকত্ব; বাক্যে বা আচরণে অতিরিক্ত সূক্ষ্মরুচি; কৃত্রিম শালীনতা। **Prud'-ish,** *adj.* **Prud'-ish-ly,** *adv.* **Prud'-ish-ness,** *n.*

pru'-dĕnt (prô-), *adj.* **1.** Discreet; judicious; sagacious; practically wise; সদ্বিবেচক; মতিমান, বুদ্ধিমান; প্রাজ্ঞ; বিজ্ঞ। **2.** Not extravagant, as expenditure etc.; মিতাচারী। **—dence,** *n.* **1.** State or quality of being prudent; discretion; sagacity; policy; দূরদর্শিতা, প্রাজ্ঞতা; বিবেকিতা, বিমৃশ্যকারিতা, বুদ্ধিমত্তা; বিচক্ষণতা; সমীক্ষ্যকারিত্ব। **2.** Frugality; economy; পরিমিত ব্যয়; মিতব্যয়িতা। **—ly,** *adv.* Wisely; discreetly; বিজ্ঞভাবে; সদ্বিবেচকের মত।

pru-den'-tial (prô-dĕn-shăl), *adj.* & *n.* Of, or relating to, prudence; proceeding from, or dictated, or marked by, prudence; as, a *prudential* motive, policy, etc.; সদ্বিবেচনা সম্বন্ধীয়; সবিচার, সদ্বিবেচনাপ্রসূত, সদ্বিবেচনাত্মক। *Noun.* (*Pl.*) Prudential matters or considerations; সদ্বিবেচনাপ্রসূত বিষয় বা ভাব। **—ism, —ist,** *ns.* **—ly,** *adv.*

prud' homme, (*F.*), *n.* In France, a member of a council appointed to decide labour disputes; ফরাসীদেশে শ্রমজীবিগণের বিরোধনিষ্পত্তির জন্য প্রতিষ্ঠিত সভাবিশেষের সভ্য।

pru'-i-nōse (prô-), *adj.* (*Bot.* & *Zool.*) Covered with white powdery substance; (উদ্ভিদ্ বিদ্যা এবং জন্তুবিদ্যা) শ্বেতবর্ণ চূর্ণদ্বারা আচ্ছাদিত, মেদোধর (সাঃ পঃ)।

prune (prôn), *n.* **1.** A dried plum; আলুবোখারা (বোঃ), আরুক (নিঘণ্টুঃ)। **2.** Dark reddish purple, being the colour of its juice; ঐ ফলের রসের মত গাঢ় রক্তাভ ধূম্রবর্ণ।

prune (prôn), *v. t.* **1.** To trim as a tree; to cut *off*, *away*, as branches, etc.; ছাঁটা; ছেদন করা। **2.** (*Fig.*) To cut out or remove as useless parts; (লক্ষণায়) কাটিয়া ছাঁটিয়া দেওয়া। **3.** To clear *of* useless material or parts; as, to *prune* a book *of* what is superfluous; কাটিয়া ছাঁটিয়া দেওয়া। **Pruning-hook** — গাছের ডালপালা কাটার জন্য ছুরী।

prune (prôn), *v. t.* (*Rare*) Same as PREEN.

pru-nĕl'-lă (prô-) *n.* **1.** A kind of fever and of throat disorder; যে সকল রোগের শ্বাসরোধই প্রধান লক্ষণ, গলাফুলা রোগ, হৃৎশূল। **2.** A genus of plants; একজাতীয় বৃক্ষ। **Prunella salt**—গলাবেদনা ও হৃৎশূল রোগে ব্যবহৃত দ্রবীভূত সোরাসহযোগে প্রস্তুত ঔষধ বিশেষ।

pru-nĕl'-lă (prô-), **—lō,** *ns.* A smooth woollen stuff used for the uppers of ladies' shoes; মহিলাদিগের জুতার উপরিভাগের জন্য একপ্রকার মসৃণ পশমী কাপড়।

prŭnt, *n.* A piece of ornamental glass laid on to a vase etc.; an instrument for applying this; ভাণ্ড প্রভৃতির উপর যে শোভাসাধক কাচখণ্ড বসান হয়; ঐরূপ কাচখণ্ড বসাইবার জন্য একপ্রকার যন্ত্র।

Prunus Armeniaca — খুবানী (বেলঃ)।

Prunus Bokhariensis — আলুবোখারা (বেলঃ)।

Prunus domestica — শা-আলু (yellow), আরু, আলু।

pru'-ri-ĕnt (prô-), *adj.* **1.** Inclined to lascivious thoughts; lustful; কামুক; কামাতুর। **2.** (*Rare*) Having a morbid desire or curiosity; (কচিদ্ব্যবহৃত) অতি কৌতুহলী, অতিলালসাপর। **—ence, —en-cy,** *ns.* **1.** The state of being prurient; কণ্ডূতি। **2.** An itching or longing desire for something; lascivious desire; অতি স্পৃহা, কণ্ডুলভাব (নৈষধঃ); কামলালসা, কণ্ডুতি (রাঃ তঃ)। **–ly**, *adv.*

pru-rī′-gō (-prô-), *n.* (*Med.*) **1.** A skin disease attended with violent itching; অতিশয় কণ্ডুয়নশীল পীড়কাবিশিষ্ট চর্ম্মরোগ, গাত্রকণ্ডু, চুলকানি। **–rig′-i-nous**, *adj.*

pruritus, *n.* (*Med.*) Itching; কণ্ডুয়ন, কণ্ডুতি, চুলকানি।

Pruritus pudendi—ভগ কণ্ডুয়ন।

Pruritus scroti—অণ্ডকোষকণ্ডুয়ন; বৃষণকচ্ছূ (সাঃ পঃ)।

Prus′-sian (Prŭ-shăn), *adj.* & *n.* Of, or relating to, Prussia, its people or language; প্রুশিয়াদেশীয়, প্রুশিয়াদেশের লোক বা তদ্দেশের ভাষাসম্পর্কীয়। ***Noun.*** **1.** A native or inhabitant of Prussia; প্রুশিয়ার অধিবাসী। **2.** The Prussian language; প্রুশিয়াদেশের ভাষা। **–ize**, *v. t.* To make Prussian; প্রুশিয়ভাবাপন্ন করা। **Prussian blue**—A dark blue pigment; একপ্রকার গাঢ় নীলবর্ণ রঞ্জকপদার্থ, ধূপছায়া নীল। **Prussian brown**—ধূপছায়া নীল হইতে প্রাপ্ত একপ্রকার পিঙ্গল বর্ণ। **Prussian carp**—এক জাতীয় ক্ষুদ্রাকৃতি রোহিত মৎস্য। **Prussian green**—ধূপছায়া নীলজাতীয় সবুজ বর্ণ।

Prŭs′-sic, *adj.* Of, or relating to, Prussian blue; got or derived from this; ধূপছায়া নীলসম্বন্ধীয়; ঐরূপ নীল হইতে প্রাপ্ত। **Prussic acid**—অতিশয় অবসাদক ও সদ্যপ্রাণঘাতক একপ্রকার দ্রাবক, হাইড্রোসায়েনিক দ্রাবক।

prȳ, *v. i.* **1.** To look closely; to peep or peer inquisitively; অভিনিবেশপূর্ব্বক পর্য্যবেক্ষণ করা; উঁকি মারা। **2.** To inquire impertinently as *into* a person's affairs, conduct, etc.; কোন বিষয়ে বা কাহারো চরিত্র প্রভৃতি সম্বন্ধে অভদ্রভাবে অনুসন্ধান করা।

prȳ′-ing, *adj.* Inquisitive; অনুসন্ধিৎসু। **–ly**, *adv.*

prȳt-ă-nē′-ŭm, *n.* (*Gk. antiq.*) A public hall esp. one in Athens where distinguished citizens, ambassadors, generals, etc. were entertained; (গ্রীক্ প্রত্নতত্ত্ব) জনমন্দির, বিশেষতঃ প্রাচীন এথেন্স নগরীর যে জনমন্দিরে বিখ্যাত নাগরিক, রাজদূত, সেনাপতি, প্রভৃতি অভ্যর্থিত হইতেন।

psalm (sâm), *n.* A sacred song or hymn; ধর্ম্মসংগীত, স্তোত্র, স্তবসঙ্গীত, গীত, স্তুতিগীতিকা, ভজনগান, ভজনসংগীত। **Psalm-book**—স্তোত্রপুস্তক, স্তবমালা, স্তবাবলী, স্তবামৃতলহরী, ভজনগীতিকা, স্তোত্রাবলী। **The (Book of) Psalms, the Psalms of David** — বাইবেলের প্রাচীন নিয়মের অন্তর্গত স্তোত্রপুস্তক।

psalm′-ist (sâm- *or* sâlm-), *n.* A writer or composer of psalms; স্তোত্ররচক, স্তোত্রকার, স্তোত্রকবি (কেভিঃ)। **The Psalmist**—ডেভিড এবং অন্যান্য স্তোত্ররচক।

psalm′-ō-dȳ (sâm′- *or* sâlm-), *n.* **1.** Act, practice or art of singing psalms esp. in worship; স্তবগান, স্তবসংগীত বিদ্যা। **2.** Psalms orderly arranged for liturgical use; such an arrangement; উপাসনার জন্য ক্রমবিন্যস্তগীতাবলী, স্তবমালা, স্তবাবলী; উক্তরূপ বিন্যাস। **–dist**, *n.* **Psal-mod′-ic**, *adj.* **Psal′-mo-dize**, *v. i.* To practise psalmody; স্তবসঙ্গীত অভ্যাস করা।

psal′-têr (säl-), *n.* **1.** The Book of Psalms; the version of this in the book of Common Prayer; স্তোত্রসংহিতা, স্তোত্রসংগ্রহ, স্তবসংহিতা, গীতপুস্তক, গীতসংহিতা; স্তোত্রসংগীতের অনুবাদ। **2.** A book of Psalms separately printed for liturgical use; উপাসনার জন্য স্বতন্ত্রভাবে মুদ্রিত স্তোত্রপুস্তক।

psal′-têr-ȳ (säl-), *n.* A stringed instrument of music used by ancient Jews; প্রাচীন ইহুদীগণ কর্ত্তৃক ব্যবহৃত তন্ত্রীবিশিষ্ট বাদ্যযন্ত্রবিশেষ।

psē′-phism (sē-), *n.* (*Gk. antiq.*) A decree enacted by the vote of a public assembly esp. in Athens; (গ্রীকপ্রত্নতত্ত্ব) জনসংসদের মত দ্বারা বিধিবদ্ধ ব্যবস্থা।

pseu′-dĕch-is (sü-), *n.* (*Zool.*) A genus of venomous snakes; (জন্তুবিদ্যা) এক জাতীয় বিষধর সর্প। **–dech′-ic**, *adj.*

pseu′-dē-pig′-ră-phă (sü-), *n.* (*Pl.*) False or spurious writings esp. those of Jewish origin ascribed to various Biblical prophets either before or after the Christian era; কৃত্রিম বা জাল রচনা, বিশেষতঃ খ্রীষ্টাব্দের প্রারম্ভের পরবর্ত্তী ও পূর্ব্ববর্ত্তী যে সকল কৃত্রিম রচনা বাইবেল গ্রন্থোক্ত বিভিন্ন ভাববাদীর উপর আরোপ করা হয়। **–dep-i-graph′-ic, –dep-i-graph′-i-cal, –phal**, *adjs.*

pseu′-dō (sü-), *pref.* False; pretended; spurious; কৃত্রিম, কপট, ছদ্ম; কল্পিত; জাল।

pseu′-dō-âr-chā′-ic (sü-), *adj.* Artificially archaic in style, language, etc.; তথাকথিত, অপ্রচলিত। **–ism**, *n.* **–ist**, *n.*

pseu′-dō-ăx′-is (sü-), *n.* (*Bot.*) A simpodium; (উদ্ভিদ্ বিদ্যা) উপকাণ্ড (সাঃ পঃ)।

pseu′-dō-bŭlb (sü-), *n.* (*Bot.*) A stem-like bulb; (উদ্ভিদ্ বিদ্যা) উপকন্দ (সাঃ পঃ)।

pseu′-dō-cârp, *n.* (*Bot.*) A fruit that does not consist exclusively of the ripened ovary and its contents; (উদ্ভিদ্ বিদ্যা) যে ফলে কেবল মাত্র পক্ববীজাধার ও তদভ্যন্তরস্থ পদার্থ থাকেনা। **–car′-pous**, *adj.*

pseu-dō-clăs-sic (sü-), *adj.* Pretending to be classic; wrongly held to be classic; তথাকথিত পৌরাণিক; ভ্রান্তভাবে পৌরাণিক বলিয়া গৃহীত।

pseu-dō-cȳ-ē′-sis (sü-), *n.* False or spurious pregnancy; কৃত্রিমগর্ভ।

pseu-dō-Gŏth′-ic (sü-), *adj.* Falsely Gothic in style; কৃত্রিমগথিক।

pseu′-dō′-grăph (sü-) *n.* A false writing; a spurious literary work; মিথ্যা রচনা; জাল পুস্তক।

pseu-dŏl′-ō-ḡêr (sü-), *n.* (*Hum.*) A liar; (কৌতুকচ্ছলে) মিথ্যাবাদী। **–do-log′-i-cal,** *adj.* **–gist,** *n.* (*Humorous*) A liar; (কৌতুকচ্ছলে) মিথ্যাবাদী। **–gy,** *n.* (*Hum.*) Lying; falsehood; মিথ্যাকথন; মিথ্যাবাক্য।

pseu′-dō-mŏrph (sü-), *n.* **1.** A false or deceptive form; মিথ্যারূপ, ছদ্মরূপ। **2.** A mineral having the characteristic outward form of another species; যে খনিজ পদার্থের বাহ্যরূপ অপর জাতীয় পদার্থের স্বভাবগত বাহ্যরূপের অনুরূপ হইয়া থাকে। **–mor′-phic, –mor′-phous,** *adjs.* **–mor′-phism, –mor′-pho-sis,** *ns.*

pseu′-dō-nȳm (sü-), *n.* A false name esp. one assumed by another; উপনাম, কল্পিত নাম, কপট নাম, বিশেষতঃ গ্রন্থকারের কল্পিত নাম। **–don′-y-mous,** *adj.* Bearing or using a false or fictitious name as a book or an author; কল্পিতনামগ্রাহী, কল্পিতনামধারী। **–nym′-i-ty,** *n.*

pseu-dō-pă-rĕn′-c͟hȳ-mă (sü-), *n.* (*Bot.*) A tissue having filaments of distinct cells arranged in rows; (উদ্ভিদ্ বিদ্যা) উপকলা (সাঃ পঃ)।

pseu-dō-pō′-di-ă, (sü-), *n.* **1.** (*Pl.*) Organs of locomotion and prehension in the lower protozoa; উপপাদ (সাঃ পঃ), অস্থায়ীপদ (ঐ)।

pseu′-dō-scōpe (sü-), *n.* (*Optics*) An instrument exhibiting objects with their proper relief reversed; (দৃষ্টি বিজ্ঞান) যে যন্ত্রযোগে কোন বস্তুর প্রকৃত উচ্চাবচতা বিপরীতরূপে দৃষ্ট হয়। **–scop′-ic,** *adj.*

pshaw (shä), *Interj., n., v. i.* & *t.* An exclamation expressing contempt, disdain or impatience; ছিঃ, উঃ, ধিক, ইস্। ***Noun.*** This exclamation; ঐরূপ অব্যয় শব্দ। ***Verb i.*** To express contempt or impatience by uttering *pshaw*; ছি ছি করা, ধিক্ ধিক্ করা। ***Verb t.*** To show contempt or disdain for by the expression; 'ছি ছি বলিয়া অবজ্ঞা প্রকাশ করা।

psi-lăn′-thrō-pȳ (sī-), *n.* The doctrine of the merely human existence of Christ; যীশুখৃষ্টের এক মাত্র মানবীয় সত্তাই ছিল — এইরূপ মতবাদ। **–pism,** *n.* This doctrine; উক্ত মত, মানবত্ববাদ। **–pist,** *n.* **–throp′-ic,** *adj.*

psit′-ta-cine (sĭt-tă-sīn), *adj.* Of, or relating to, parrots; parrot-like; শুকপক্ষিসম্পর্কীয়; শুকপক্ষিবৎ।

psoas, *n.* Two hip muscles; কটিকশেরুকার পার্শ্বস্থিত পেশীদ্বয়, শ্রোণিপেশী। ***Psoas magnus, psoas parvus***— শ্রোণিপেশী।

pso′-ră (sō-), *n.* (*Med.*) The itch; scabies; (ভৈষজ্যশাস্ত্র) কণ্ডু; কচ্ছু।

pso-rī′-ă-sis (sō-), *n.* A skin disease marked by scaly eruption; ছুলি (যোঃ), বিচচ্চিকা।

psy′-c͟hē (sī-), *n.* **1.** (*Class. Myth., Cap.*) A lovely maiden personification of the soul, usually represented with the wings of a butterfly; প্রজাপতিপ্রতিম পক্ষধারিণী গ্রীক পুরাণোক্ত লাবণ্যবতী দেবাঙ্গনা বিশেষ — ইনি আত্মার মূর্তরূপস্বরূপ গৃহীতা হইতেন। **2.** The soul or spirit; mind; আত্মা, চিৎ জীবাত্মা; মন। **3.** A genus of day-flying moths; একজাতীয় তসরে পোকা।

psy-c͟hī′-ă-têr (sī-), *n.* A person who treats mental disease; মানসিক রোগ চিকিৎসক। **–at′-ric, –at′-ri-cal,** *adjs.* **–try,** *n.* The treatment or study of mental disease; মানসিক রোগ চিকিৎসা, মানসিক রোগতত্ত্ব।

psy′-c͟hic (-sī), **–c͟hi-căl,** *adjs.* **1.** Of, or pertaining to, the soul or mind; আধ্যাত্মিক, মানসিক, চিদাত্মক। **2.** Of, or relating to, the animal life or spirit of man; জীবাত্মবিষয়ক। **3.** Of, or relating to, the spiritualistic phenomena or conditions; আত্মিকব্যাপারসম্পর্কীয়। **–chi-cal-ly,** *adv.* **–chi-cism,** *n.* **–chi-cist,** *n.* **Psychic force**—যে অজড়ীয় শক্তিদ্বারা আত্মিক ব্যাপার সমূহ সংঘটিত হয় বলিয়া অনুমিত হইয়া থাকে। **Psychical research** — প্রেতবিজ্ঞান সম্বন্ধীয় তত্ত্বানুসন্ধান [উক্ত বিষয়ের অনুশীলনের জন্য ১৮২২ খৃঃ অব্দে Psychical Research Society নামে একটী সমিতি লণ্ডন নগরীতে প্রতিষ্ঠিত হয়।]

psy′-c͟hic (sī-), *n.* **1.** A person susceptible to psychic influence; a medium; যে ব্যক্তি সহজে আত্মিক ক্রিয়া দ্বারা অভিভূত হয়; মাধ্যমিক। **2.** (*Pl.*) Psychology; মনস্তত্ব, মনোবিজ্ঞান।

psy-c͟hō-dȳ-năm′-ic (sī-), *adj.* & *n.* Of, or relating to, psychodynamics; চিদ্বলবিজ্ঞানসম্বন্ধীয়। ***Noun.*** (*Pl.*) The science of the mental powers; চিৎশক্তিতত্ত্ব, মনোঽভিবৃদ্ধিশাস্ত্র (হিঃ কোঃ)।

psy-c͟hō-ḡĕn′-ĕ-sis (sī-), **–c͟hŏg′-ō-nȳ,** *ns.* Origin of the mind or soul or of consciousness; মনোজন্মবিদ্যা (হিঃ কোঃ), মনোজন্ম (ঐ), মনোবিকাশবিদ্যা (ঐ)। **–ge-net′-ic, –ge-net′-i-cal[1],** *adjs.* **–gon′-i-cal,** *adj.*

psy′-c͟hō-grăm (sī-), *n.* A writing supposed to come from a spirit; প্রেতলিপি।

psy′-c͟hō-grăph (sī-), *n.* An instrument for spirit-writing; প্রেতলিপি যন্ত্র। **–chog′-ra-phy,** *n.* A description of the phenomena of mind; মানসিক ব্যাপার বর্ণন।

psy-c͟hō-lŏḡ′-i-căl (sī-), *adj.* Of, or relating to, psychology; মনোবিজ্ঞানসম্বন্ধীয়। **–ly,** *adv.* **Psychological moment**— See MOMENT.

psy-c͟hŏl′-ō-ḡȳ (sī-), *n.* **1.** That branch of knowledge which deals with the mind or soul; mental science; মনোবিজ্ঞান; মনস্তত্ত্ব, চিদ্বিজ্ঞান, চিত্তবিজ্ঞান। **2.** A treatise on this; মনোবিজ্ঞানবিষয়ক গ্রন্থ। **–gist,** *n.* One who studies psychology; মনস্তত্ত্ববিদ্, মনোবিজ্ঞানবিৎ।

—gize, *v. t. & i.* **1.** To hypnotize ; সম্মোহিত করা, যোগনিদ্রাভিভূত করা। **2.** To interpret psychologically ; মনোবিজ্ঞানসম্মতরূপে ব্যাখ্যা করা। (*Verb i.*) To pursue psychological investigations ; মনস্তত্ত্বসম্বন্ধীয় গবেষণা করা।

psy′-chō-măn-çȳ (sī-), *n.* Same as NECROMANCY (which see).

psy-chŏm′-ĕ-trȳ (sī-), *n.* The art of measuring the duration of mental processes or of determining the time relations of mental phenomena ; মানসিক ক্রিয়ার স্থিতিকাল পরিমাপ এবং মানসিকব্যাপারসমূহের সময়গত সম্বন্ধ নির্ণয়ের বিদ্যা, মনোমিতি। **—cho-met′-ric, —cho-met′-rical,** *adjs.*

psy-chō-mō′-tŏr (sī-), *adj.* Inducing movement by psychic action ; মনঃপ্রেরিত, মনশ্চালিত।

psy′-chō-păth (sī-), *n.* One mentally deranged ; বিকৃতমস্তিষ্ক ব্যক্তি। **—chop′-a-thist,** *n.* One who treats mental disease ; মানসিক রোগ চিকিৎসক। **—chop′-a-thy,** *n.* (*Med.*) Mental disease ; মানসিক রোগ। **—path′-ic,** *adj.* Of, or relating to, mental disease ; মানসিকরোগসম্বন্ধীয়। **—pa-thol′-o-gy,** *n.* The science of mental disease ; মানসিকরোগবিজ্ঞান।

psy-chō-phȳs′-ics (sī-), *n.* The science of the correlation of mind and body ; মন এবং দেহের অন্যোন্যসম্বন্ধমূলক বিজ্ঞান, চিদচিৎসম্বন্ধবিদ্যা। **—i-cal,** *adj.* **—i-cist,** *n.*

psy-chō-phȳs-i-ŏl′-ō-ġȳ (sī-), *n.* The branch of psychology dealing with mental phenomena ; শারীরবিজ্ঞানের যে শাখায় মানসিক ব্যাপারসম্বন্ধে আলোচিত হইয়া থাকে, মনঃশারীরবিজ্ঞান। **—gist,** *n.* **—o-log′-ic, —o-log′-i-cal,** *adjs.*

psy-chō′-sis (sī-), *n.* (*Pl.* -SES) Mental disorder esp. one unattended with structural changes in the brain ; মানসিক রোগ, বিশেষতঃ যাহাতে মস্তিষ্কের গঠনগত কোন পরিবর্তন হয় না।

psy-chrŏm′-ĕ-têr (sī-), *n.* An instrument for measuring the tension of aqueous vapours in the atmosphere ; বায়ুমণ্ডলের জলীয় বাষ্পের আততি পরিমাপের জন্য যন্ত্রবিশেষ।

psyllidae, *n.* A family of insects ; পাতাডাঁস শ্রেণী (যোঃ)।

ptar′-mi-găn (târ-), *n.* A bird of the grouse family ; কুক্কুটজাতীয় পক্ষিবিশেষ।

pter-i-dŏl′-ō-ġȳ (-têr-), *n.* The science or study of ferns ; পর্ণাঙ্গতত্ত্ব। **—do-log′-i-cal,** *adj.* **—gist,** *n.*

Pterocarpus marsupium—বীজশাল (বেলঃ)।

Pterocarpus santalinus—রক্তচন্দন (বেলঃ)।

pter-ō-dăc′-tȳl, *n.* An extinct winged reptile ; অধুনালুপ্ত সপক্ষ কূর্ম্মবিশেষ, উৎসর্প কূর্ম্ম (অভিঃ)।

pte-rŏg′-ră-phȳ (tĕ-), *n.* (*Zool.*) The description of feathers ; (জন্তুবিদ্যা) পালকবর্ণন। **Pter-o-graph′-ic, Pter-o-graph′-i-cal,** *adjs.*

pter′-ō-pŏd (têr-), *n.* A mollusc with organs adapted either for swimming etc. ; সন্তরণাদির উপযোগী অঙ্গসমন্বিত শম্বুকাদি।

pter′-ō-pŭs (têr-), *n.* (*Pl.* -PI) Same as FLYING FOX (which see).

pter′-o-saur (ptêr-ŏ-sör), *n.* An extinct flying saurian reptile ; বৈহগ কূর্ম্ম (অভিঃ)।

Pterospermum acerifolium—কনকচাঁপা (বেলঃ)।

pter′-y-goid (têr-ĭ-goyd), *adj.* **1.** (*Anat.*) Wing-shaped ; (শারীরসংস্থানবিদ্যা) পক্ষাকৃতি। **2.** Relating to, or connected with, pterygoid processes ; পক্ষাস্থিসম্বন্ধীয়। **Pterygoid process**—করোটীর নিম্নস্থ গোঁজের (কীলক) ন্যায় অস্থির পক্ষাকৃতি বিবর্দ্ধিতঅংশদ্বয়ের অন্যতর, পক্ষাস্থি।

ptin′-i-dæ (tĭn′-ĭ-dē), *n.* A family of beetles ; ঘুণ (যোঃ)।

ptis′-ăn (tĭs-), *n.* Barley-water or other mucilaginous decoction ; বার্লির মণ্ড প্রভৃতি।

Ptol-ĕ-mā′-ic (tŏl-), *adj.* **1.** Of, or relating to, Ptolemy, the astronomer who flourished at Alexandria about 130 A. D. ; আলেকজেন্দ্রিয়া নগরবাসী সুবিখ্যাত জ্যোতির্ব্বিদ্ টলেমিসম্বন্ধীয়, টলেমীয়। **2.** Of, or relating to, the Ptolemies, the rulers of Egypt from the death of Alexander the Great to Cleopatra ; অলীকসন্দরের মৃত্যু হইতে ক্লিওপেট্রার সিংহাসনারোহণকাল পর্য্যন্ত টলেমি নামধারী যে নৃপতিবর্গ মিসর দেশ শাসন করেন তাঁহাদের সম্বন্ধীয়। **Ptolemaic system**—জ্যোতির্বিজ্ঞানের যে মতানুসারে পৃথিবীকে স্থির বলিয়া গণ্য করা হইত।

pto′-ma-ine (tö-mā-ĭn), *n.* Any of a class of organic bases or alkaloids formed by the action of putrefactive bacteria on nitrogenous matter ; a putrefactive alkaloid ; যবক্ষারজান জাতীয় পদার্থের উপর পচনকারক বীজাণুর ক্রিয়া দ্বারা উৎপন্ন জৈবক্ষার শ্রেণীর অন্যতম; পচনকারক ক্ষার।

pto′-sis (tö-), *n.* Drooping of the upper eyelid produced by the paralysis of a muscle ; পেশীর পক্ষাঘাত হেতু উপরের অক্ষিপুটের পতন, ঊর্দ্ধাক্ষিপুটপতন।

Ptychotis ajowan—যমানী।

pŭb, *n.* (*Colloq.*) A public house ; (চলিত ভাষায়) শুঁড়িখানা।

pū′-bêr-tȳ, *n.* State of being capable of procreation ; age at which persons can beget or bear children ; যৌবনোদ্ভেদ, তারুণ্য ; বয়সকাল, যৌবনাগম, বয়ঃসন্ধি, উঠ্‌তি বয়স (*colloq.*)।

pū-bĕs′-cence (-ĕns), *n.* **1.** Arrival at puberty ; যৌবনাগম। **2.** (*Zool.*)

The soft hairy down on insects, etc.; (জন্তু-বিদ্যা) কীটের শরীরের কোমল লোম। 3. (*Bot.*) The downy substance on plants; downiness; (উদ্ভিদ্ বিদ্যা) উদ্ভিদের উপর তুলার মত কোমল পদার্থ; মৃদু-রোমতা। **—cent,** *adj.*

pŭb'-lic, *adj.* & *n.* **1.** Of, relating to, or affecting, the whole people; সার্ব্বজনিক, সর্ব্বজনসংক্রান্ত। **2.** Done by, or for, or representing, the people; as, *public* prosecution, assembly, etc.; সাধারণ, সাধারণ-কর্ত্তৃক কৃত। **3.** Open to common or general use, as a road, library, etc.; সাধারণ, সরকারী। **4.** (*Univ.*) Of, or relating to, a university; for, or acting for, a university; as, a *public* orator, examination, etc.; (বিশ্ববিদ্যালয়) বিশ্ববিদ্যালয় সম্বন্ধীয়; বিশ্ববিদ্যালয়ের জন্য, বিশ্ববিদ্যালয়ের জন্য কার্য্যকারী। **5.** Of, relating to, or engaged in, the affairs of the people; as, *public* life; সাধারণ লোকসম্বন্ধীয়, সাধারণের কার্য্যে নিযুক্ত। **6.** Of, or relating to, the nations; as, he is a *public* enemy; জাতিসম্বন্ধীয়। **7.** Done, or made, in public, as a protest, utterance, etc.; প্রকাশ্যে কৃত বা সম্পাদিত। ***Noun.*** **1.** (*With sing.* or *pl. verb.*) The general body of a nation, state or community; as, the *public* is or are the best judge(s); জনসাধারণ, লোকসাধারণ, জনসমাজ। **2.** A section of the community; as, the reading *public*; সম্প্রদায়, সমাজ। **3.** Same as a PUBLIC HOUSE. **—lic'-i-ty,** *n.* State of being public; notoriety; সর্ব্বজন-রাষ্ট্রতা, প্রকাশতা; রটনা, প্রাকট্য, খ্যাতি। **—ly,** *adv.* **Public education**—বিদ্যালয়ে শিক্ষা, সাধারণের ব্যয়ে পরিচালিত বিদ্যালয়ে শিক্ষা। **Public house**—পানালয়, পানাগার, শৌণ্ডিকালয়, সুরাবিপণি। **Public school**—জনসাধারণের পরিচালনাধীন বিদ্যালয়। **Public spirit**—দেশপ্রেম, স্বদেশ হিতৈষিতা। (*Public-spirited, adj. Public-spiritedly, adv. Public-spiritedness, n.*) **Public woman**—বেশ্যা, প্রকাশনারী (মৃচ্ছঃ)। **In public**—Openly; publicly; প্রকাশ্যে; সর্ব্বজনসমক্ষে। **To make public**—জাহির করা।

pŭb'-li-căn, *n.* **1.** (*Rom. Hist.*) A farmer of public revenues; (রোমের ইতিহাস) সরকারী রাজস্বের ইজারাদার। **2.** A keeper of a public house; শুঁড়িখানার মালিক, শৌণ্ডিক।

pŭb-li-cā'-tion, *n.* **1.** Act of making public or generally known; প্রকাশন। **2.** Act of offering a book, engraving, music, etc. to the public for sale; প্রকাশ। **3.** A book etc. so published; প্রকাশিত পুস্তকাদি।

pŭb'-li-cĭst, *n.* **1.** A writer on the laws of nations or on current political events; one skilled in international law; আন্তর্জাতিক আইনসম্বন্ধীয় অথবা বর্ত্তমানকালীন রাজনীতিক ঘটনাবলীসম্বন্ধীয় গ্রন্থকর্ত্তা; আন্তর্জাতিক আইনে পারদর্শী ব্যক্তি। **—cism,** *n.* **—cis'-tic,** *adj,*

pŭb'-lish, *v. t.* **1.** To make public or generally known, esp. by means of a newspaper, circular, book, etc.; প্রকাশ করা, সাধারণ্যে প্রচার করা। **2.** To announce formally; to promulgate; as, to *publish* an edict etc.; ঘোষণা করা; প্রচার করা। **3.** To notify by posting or reading in a church; as, to *publish* banns of marriage; ধর্ম্মমন্দিরে আঁটিয়া দিয়া বা পাঠ করিয়া বিজ্ঞাপিত করা। **4.** To print, or cause to be printed and offered for sale, as a book, engraving, etc.; to put into circulation; পুস্তকাদি প্রকাশিত করা; প্রচার করা। **—a-ble,** *adj.*

pŭb'-lish-ẽr, *n.* One who publishes esp. books etc.; প্রকাশক।

pŭc-cōōn', *n.* A plant of North America yielding a red or yellow dye; লোহিত বা পীতবর্ণ রঞ্জকপদার্থপ্রদ উত্তর আমেরিকাদেশীয় বৃক্ষবিশেষ।

puce (pūs), *adj.* Of a brownish purple colour; পিঙ্গলাভ ধূমলবর্ণ, পাটকিলে।

pŭck, *n.* **1.** (*Cap.*) The goblin *Robin Goodfellow* or *Hobgoblin*; জুজু। **2.** A mischievous sprite; অনিষ্টকারী অপদেবতা। **3.** (*Fig.*) A mischievous child; দুরন্ত বালক। **Puck'-ish, Puck'-like,** *adjs.*

pŭck, *n.* **1.** The goatsucker; একপ্রার বাবুই পাখী। **2.** A disease supposed to be caused by this; একপ্রকার রোগ।

pŭck, *n.* A rubber disc used for hockey on ice in Canada; ক্যানাডাদেশে বরফের উপর হকি খেলার জন্য একপ্রকার বরফের চাকতি।

pŭck'-ẽr, *v. i., t.* & *n.* To be gathered into folds or wrinkles; কুঞ্চিত হওয়া। ***Verb t.*** To gather into folds or wrinkles; কুঞ্চিত করা, চুনট করা, কোঁচান। ***Noun.*** A fold or wrinkle; a number of folds or wrinkles; চুনট, কোঁচকা; বলি। **—y,** *adv.*

pŭd, *n.* **1.** A hand of a child; শিশুর হাত। **2.** The forefoot of some animals; কোন কোন জন্তুর আগালি পা।

pŭd'-den-ing(-n-), *n.* (*Naut.*) A pad to prevent damage to the gunwale of a boat; a bunch of soft material to prevent chafing as between spars; (নৌবিদ্যা) জাহাজের কিনারার উপরিভাগের ক্ষয় নিবারণার্থ একপ্রকার গদী; জাহাজের মাস্তুল প্রভৃতির ঘর্ষণজনিত ক্ষয়নিবারণার্থ কোমল বস্তুর গুচ্ছ।

pŭd'-ding (-ing), *n.* **1.** A food variously compounded, but generally made of flour, milk and eggs and sometimes enriched with fruits, etc. ; পিষ্টক। 2. Anything resembling a pudding in appearance, softness, etc. ; পিষ্টকবৎ বস্তু, পিষ্টিকা। 3. A kind of sausage ; একপ্রকার মাংসের কাবাব। 4. (*Naut.*) Same as PUDDENING. 5. (*Slang*) Drugged livers etc. given to dogs by burglars etc. ; (ইতর ভাষায়) সিঁধেল চোর প্রভৃতি বাটীর কুকুরকে যে নিদ্রাজনক ঔষধ মিশ্রিত যকৃৎ প্রভৃতি খাইতে দেয়। **—y,** *adj.* **Pudding face**—প্রকাণ্ড চ্যাপ্টা মুখ। **Pudding-head** — হাবা, জড়ভরত। **Pudding-heart**—ভীরু। **Pudding-pie**—মাংসাদি পুরিত পিষ্টক। **Pudding-stone**—একপ্রকার বেলে পাথর। **The proof of the pudding etc.**—See under PROOF.

pŭd'-dle (-l), *n.* 1. A small pool of dirty water ; হোড়। 2. Clay or a mixture of clay and water used as watertight covering for embankments, etc. ; বাঁধ প্রভৃতির জলনির্গম রোধ করার জন্য মৃত্তিকা বা মৃত্তিকার মিশ্র। 3. (*Colloq.*) A muddle ; mess ; (চলিত ভাষায়) গোলমাল ; জগা খিচুড়ী। **—dly,** *adj.*

pŭd'-dle (-l), *v. i.* & *t.* 1. To dabble in mud or shallow water (often with *about*) ; কাদায় বা কাদাটে জলে খেলা করা। 2. (*Fig.*) To busy oneself in a disorderly way ; (লক্ষণায়) এলোমেলো করিয়া কাজ করা। ***Verb t.*** 1. To make muddy or dirty as water, etc., (also, *fig.*) ; ঘোলা করা, পঙ্কিল করা, আবিল করা। 2. To make watertight with puddle ; to make as clay and sand into puddle ; to line as a canal etc. with puddle ; কাদা বা কাদার মিশ্র দ্বারা জলনির্গম রোধ করা ; মাটী বা বালি দ্বারা জলনির্গমরোধকর মিশ্র প্রস্তুত করা ; খালের বাঁধের গায় জলনির্গমরোধকর কাদা প্রভৃতির মিশ্র লেপন করা। 3. To convert as cast iron into wrought iron ; ঢালা লোহা প্রভৃতি পেটা লোহায় পরিণত করা। **—dler,** *n.*

pū'-dĕn-çy̆, *n.* Modesty ; লজ্জাশীলতা।

pudendum, *n.* (Usu. in *pl.*, -DA) The generative parts esp. in the female ; লিঙ্গ, যোনি। ***Pudendal,*** *adj.* ***Pudic,*** *adj.*

pudge (pŭj), *n.* (*Colloq.*) A short, thick or fat person, thing or animal ; (চলিত ভাষায়) খাটো মোটাসোটা লোক। **Pudg'-y,** *adj.*

pŭd'-sy̆, *adj.* Plump ; মোটাসোটা, গোলগাল।

pueblo, *n.* A town or village in Spain or Spanish America ; esp. a communal village or settlement of Indians ; স্পেন বা স্পেন অধিকৃত আমেরিকার অন্তঃপাতী নগর বা গ্রাম ; বিশেষতঃ আমেরিকার আদিম অধিবাসিগণের গ্রাম বা নূতন বসতি—যাহাতে সকলে এক পরিবারের ন্যায় বাস করে।

pū'-ĕr-ile, *adj.* Childish ; foolish ; trivial ; বালসুলভ, বালোচিত ; মূঢ় ; তুচ্ছ। **—il'-i-ty,** *n.* Boyishness ; childishness ; ছেলেমি, চেঙ্গড়ামি ; ছাবলামি। **—ly,** *adv.*

pū-ĕr'-pĕr-ăl, *adj.* Of, relating to, or due to, childbirth ; প্রসবসম্বন্ধীয়, প্রাসূতিক, সূতিকাসম্পর্কীয়। **Puerperal disease**—সূতিকা রোগ।

pŭff, *n.* 1. A sudden emission of breath ; a short blast of wind ; sound of these ; whiff as of air, smoke, steam, etc. ; ফুৎকার, ফুঁক ; ঝটকা বাতাসের দমক ; ঝটকা বাতাসের শব্দ ; ফুৎকৃত ধূম, বায়ু, প্রভৃতি। 2. (*Dress making*) A fold of material gathered at the edges and left loose in the centre ; পোষাকের ফুলা আস্তিন প্রভৃতি। 3. A soft loose roll of hair ; অবেণীবদ্ধ কোমল কুন্তল গুচ্ছ। 4. (Also *powder-puff*) A soft pad for applying powder to the skin or hair ; চুলে বা চর্ম্মে অঙ্গরাগচূর্ণ লাগাইবার জন্য কোমল পালক প্রভৃতির গুচ্ছ, পালকস্তবক, পালকপুষ্প। 5. An exaggerated commendation or praise esp. in a newspaper ; অতিপ্রশংসা, অতি স্তুতি, অতিশয় প্রশংসা। 6. A light pasty ; একপ্রকার হালকা মাংসপুরিত পিষ্টক। **Puff-adder**—দক্ষিণ আফ্রিকা দেশীয় একপ্রকার স্থূলাকৃতি সর্প—ক্রুদ্ধ হইলে এই সর্পের শরীর অতিশয় স্ফীত হইয়া থাকে। **Puff-ball** — একপ্রকার কন্দুকাকৃতি ছত্রাক, ভুধাল (হিন্দী—খোয়ী), কাণফুল (ঐ)। **Puff-box**—অঙ্গরাগচূর্ণ এবং পালকস্তবক রাখার জন্য ক্ষুদ্র পেটক। **Puff-paste**—ময়দার একপ্রকার হালকা তাল। **Puff-puff**—(ছেলেদের ছড়ায়) রেলগাড়ী। **Powder-puff** — See PUFF, *n.* 4.

puff, *v. i.* & *t.* 1. To emit a puff or puffs ; ফুৎকার দেওয়া, ফুঁ দেওয়া। 2. (Of air etc.) To blow in puffs or whiffs, (with *up, out,* etc.) ; দমকা বাতাস বওয়া, দমকে দমকে উঠা। 3. To breathe quick and hard ; to pant ; হাঁস ফাঁস করা ; কষ্টে শ্বাস ফেলা, হাঁপান। 4. To swell with air ; to be inflated ; (usu. with *up* or *out*) ; বায়ু দ্বারা স্ফীত হওয়া ; ফুলিয়া উঠা। 5. To bid at an auction to raise the price ; মূল্য বাড়াইবার উদ্দেশ্যে নিলামে ডাকা। ***Verb t.*** 1. To blow or drive with a puff as of air, wind, etc. (with *up, out, away,* etc.) ; as, to *puff up* dust, a light-object, etc. ; ফুৎকার দিয়া উড়ান, ফুৎকারে উড়াইয়া দেওয়া। 2. To smoke in puffs as a pipe ; দমকে দমকে ধূমপান করা। 3. To swell or inflate ; স্ফীত করা, ফুলান। 4. To put out of breath ; as, he was rather *puffed* ; হাঁপানি জন্মান, হাঁপানি তোলা। 5. To elate ; to make proud ; (with *up* and usu. in *p. p.*) ; as, *puffed up* with success ; ফুলাইয়া তোলা ; গর্ব্বস্ফীত করা,

আকাশে চড়ান। 6. To praise exaggeratedly or falsely esp. by way of advertisement; অতি প্রশংসা করা, মিথ্যা প্রশংসা করা, বাড়াইয়া তোলা। **Puf′-fer,** *n.* **Puf′-fer-y,** *n.* 1. Act of puffing or commending extravagantly; undue praise or advertisement; মিথ্যা-সংস্তব; অনুচিত প্রশংসা, অতিরিক্ত প্রশংসা, বিজ্ঞাপনের বাড়াবাড়ি। 2. Frills or frilling of puffs; পোষাকের কোঁচ, বেল। **To puff at**—To express contempt of; to defy scornfully; (*Obs.*); (অপ্র:) অবজ্ঞা করা; তুচ্ছতাচ্ছিল্য করা। **To puff out**—To utter pantingly; হাঁপাইতে হাঁপাইতে বলা। **To puff up**—See PUFF, *v. t.* 5.

pŭf′-fin, *n.* A sea-bird of the North Atlantic; উত্তর অতলান্তিক মহাসাগরচর পক্ষিবিশেষ।

pŭff′-y̆, *adj.* 1. Swollen with air or any soft matter; স্ফীত, আধ্মাত, প্রধ্মাপিত। 2. (Of a person) Corpulent; স্থূলকায়, থসথসে, মাংসল। 3. Inflated; bombastic as a style; শব্দাড়ম্বরপূর্ণ; বাগাড়ম্বরপূর্ণ। 4. Gusty as a breeze; দমকা। **–i-ness,** *n.* **Puffing and blowing**—হাঁস ফাঁস।

pŭg, *n.* 1. (Also, *pug-dog*) A dwarf variety of dog; একপ্রকার খর্ব্বাকৃতি কুক্কুর। 2. A monkey, fox, or hare (*used as a quasi proper name*); বানর, শৃগাল বা শশক। 3. (Among servants) An upper servant in a large establishment; প্রধান চাকর। 4. A small locomotive for shunting etc.; ক্ষুদ্র-রেলগাড়ী। **Pug′-gish, Pug′-gy,** *adjs.* **Pug-faced** — বাঁদর-মুখো। **Pug-nose** — খাঁদা নাক। **Pug-nosed**—খাঁদা।

pŭg, *n.* & *v. t.* 1. Tempered or pugged clay; ছানা কাদা। ***Verb t.*** 1. To prepare as clay for brick-making etc.; ইষ্টকাদি নির্ম্মাণের জন্য কাদা ছানা বা পাইট করা। 2. To fill in, or spread with, mortar for deadening sound; as, to *pug* a floor; ধ্বনি মন্দীভূত করার জন্য চুণ বালি দ্বারা আচ্ছাদিত করা। **Pug′-ging,** *n.* **Pug-mill**—কাদা পাইট করার জন্য কল।

pŭg, *n.* & *v. t.* (Angl.-Ind.) The footprint of a beast; পশুর খুরচিহ্ন। ***Verb t.*** To track by footprints; খুর চিহ্ন ধরিয়া অনুসরণ করা।

pū′-gĭl-ĭst, *n.* 1. A boxer or prizefighter; মুষ্টিযোধ, মুষ্টিযোদ্ধা। 2. (*Fig.*) A vigorous controversialist; (লক্ষণায়) তর্কযোদ্ধা। **–ism,** *n.* The art of boxing, or fighting with fists; মল্লযুদ্ধ, মুষ্টিযুদ্ধ। **–is′-tic,** *adj.* **–is′-ti-cal-ly,** *adv.*

pŭg-nā′-cious (-shŭs), *adj.* Disposed to fight; quarrelsome; যুযুৎসু; কলহপ্রিয়, বিবাদপ্রিয়, ঝগড়াটে। **–ly,** *adv.* **–nac′-i-ty,** *n.* Readiness or inclination to fight; কলহপ্রিয়তা।

puis′-nĕ (pū-), *adj.* & *n.* 1. Inferior in rank; junior; as, a *puisne* judge; নিম্নতরশ্রেণীর, অবর; কর্ম্মকনিষ্ঠ। 2. Subsequent; as, a *puisne* mortgagee: a mortgagee *puisne to* the plaintiff; পরবর্ত্তী, পশ্চাৎকালীন।

pū′-ĭs-sant (-ănt), *adj.* (*Archaic*) Powerful; mighty; (অপ্র:) পরাক্রান্ত; শক্তিশালী, বিক্রমশালী, বীর্য্যবান, ক্ষমতাশালী। **–ly,** *adv.* **–sance,** *n.* Prowess; পরাক্রম, বিক্রম।

pūke, *v. i., t.* & *n.* To vomit; বমি করা, বমন করা। ***Verb t.*** To vomit up; বমি করিয়া ফেলা, উদ্বমিত করা। ***Noun.*** Act of vomiting; that which is vomited; বমন; বমি।

pūle, *v. i.* To cry like a chicken; to whine; মুর্গীর বাচ্চার মত চীৎকার করা; নাকীসুরে কাঁদা, ঘ্যান ঘ্যান করা, প্যান প্যান করা। **Pule′-ing-ly,** *adv.*

pŭl-kah (-kă), *n.* A Laplander's

Pulkah.

travelling sledge; ল্যাপল্যাণ্ডদেশীয় বরফে-চলা গাড়ী।

pŭll, *v. t.* & *i.* 1. To draw with force towards one; to drag; to haul; সবলে টানিয়া আনা, জোরে টানা; জোরে টানিয়া নেওয়া; সবলে টানা। 2. To tear; to rend; as, to *pull* to pieces; ছিঁড়া; ছিঁড়িয়া ফেলা, বিদীর্ণ করা। 3. To pluck *up* by the root as a plant etc.; উপড়ান, উন্মূলিত করা, উৎপাটন করা, উপড়ে তোলা। 4. To set in motion as a bell by pulling or drawing; টানিয়া চালান। 5. (*Print.*) To take an impression of as a proof etc.; to print upon as a sheet; (মুদ্রণ) ছাপ লওয়া; মুদ্রিত করা। 6. To move as a boat by pulling oar; (of a boat) to be operated or rowed by (so many oars); দাঁড় টানিয়া নৌকা চালান; (নৌকা-সম্পর্কে) দাঁড়দ্বারা চালিত হওয়া। 7. (*Slang*) To make a police raid upon as a gambling-house etc.; to arrest; (ইতর ভাষায়) জুয়ার আড্ডা প্রভৃতিতে খানাতল্লাসের জন্য পুলিসের আবির্ভাব হওয়া; গ্রেপ্তার করা। 8. (*Racing*) To hold back as a horse so as to prevent from winning; (ঘোড়দৌড়) কোন ঘোড়া যাহাতে জয়লাভ না করিতে পারে তজ্জন্য উহাকে পিছনে রাখা। 9. (*Cricket*) To play or strike as a ball from the off to the leg side; also, to strike a ball bowled by (a bowler); (ক্রীকেট ক্রীড়া) ব্যাটধারীর দক্ষিণ দিক হইতে বাম

দিকে কন্দুক তাড়না করা; কন্দুক-ক্ষেপক কর্ত্তৃক নিক্ষিপ্ত কন্দুকে আঘাত করা। **10.** (*Golf*) To strike (the ball) so as to cause it to curve to the left; (গোলফ্ ক্রীড়া) (কন্দুকে) এরূপভাবে আঘাত করা যাহাতে উহা বাঁকিয়া বামদিকে যায়। ***Verb i.*** **1.** To give pull; to drag or tug; to haul; টান দেওয়া; টানা; টানিয়া নেওয়া। **2.** To row a boat; as, she *pulled* in shore; দাঁড় টানা। **3.** To tear or pluck as *at* a thing; ছেঁড়া, তোলা, পাড়া। **4.** To proceed with effort as *up* a hill etc.; কষ্টে অগ্রসর হওয়া। **5.** (Of a horse) To strain esp. habitually against the bit; (অশ্ব-সম্পর্কে) লাগামের লৌহময় অংশ ছিঁড়িবার জন্য চেষ্টা করা। **Pulled**—Reduced in health or spirits; ভগ্নস্বাস্থ্য, হতোৎসাহ। **Pull-back**—Retarding influence; check; উন্নতিরোধকপ্রভাব; বাধা, প্রতিবন্ধক। **Pulled bread**—নূতন পাঁউরুটির ভিতরের যে সকল অংশ মচমচে করিয়া সেঁকা হয়। **To pull about**—To pull from side to side; to treat roughly; টানা ছেঁড়া করা; রূঢ় ব্যবহার করা। **To pull a face**—See under FACE. **To pull a long, wry, etc. face**—To assume an expression of gloominess, melancholy, disgust, etc.; বিষণ্ণভাব ধারণ করা, অপ্রসন্নভাব ধারণ করা, বিরসবদন হওয়া। **To pull apart**—(*Verb i.*) To be separated by pulling; টানাটানিতে ছিঁড়িয়া যাওয়া। (*Verb t.*) To pull to pieces; টানিয়া টুকরা টুকরা করিয়া ছিঁড়া। **To pull a person, oneself, etc. through**—To get safely through (a danger, illness, etc.); নিরাপদে অতিক্রম করা। **To pull down**—To demolish as a building etc.; to lower in health, spirits, price, etc.; ভাঙ্গিয়া চুরিয়া ফেলা, ধ্বংস করা; স্বাস্থ্য ভঙ্গ করা, হতোৎসাহ করা, মূল্যহ্রাস করা। **To pull or draw in one's foot**—To run away (*dial.*, or *slang*); (উপভাষায় বা ইতরভাষায়) চম্পট দেওয়া। **To pull or draw in one's horns**—To restrain one's activities; to withdraw from some action or line of conduct; কর্ম্মচেষ্টা কিয়ৎপরিমাণে সংযত করা; কোন কার্য্য বা কার্য্যপ্রণালী হইতে নিবৃত্ত হওয়া। **To pull off**—To separate by pulling; to pluck; to take off as a coat, hat, etc.; টানিয়া ছিঁড়া; ছিঁড়া, তোলা; (কোট প্রভৃতি) ছাড়া। To win as a prize, contest, etc.; পুরস্কার প্রভৃতি পাওয়া, প্রতিযোগিতার ক্রীড়া প্রভৃতিতে জয়ী হওয়া। **To pull off one's hat** — To do so by way of salutation; অভিবাদনের জন্য টুপি তোলা। **To pull on**—To draw on, as one's boots, etc.; টানিয়া তোলা। **To pull one's ears, To pull him by the ear**—To do so by way of chastisement; কাহারো কাণ মলিয়া দেওয়া। **To pull oneself together**—To rally; to recover or rouse oneself; মনঃস্থির করা, বুদ্ধি স্থির করা; উদ্বুদ্ধ করা। **To pull one's leg**—To hoax or deceive one; চোখে ধূলি দেওয়া, মাথায় হাত বুলান, ঠকান। **To pull one's nose, To pull him by the nose**—To do so by way of insult; অপমান করার জন্য কাহারো নাক মলিয়া দেওয়া। **To pull one's sleeve, To pull him by the sleeve**—To do so by way of drawing attention; মনোযোগ আকর্ষণের জন্য আস্তিন ধরিয়া টানা। **To pull out**—To draw or drag out; to eradicate; উপড়ে তুলে ফেলা; উন্মূলিত করা, উৎপাটিত করা। To row out; (of a train) to move out of a station; দাঁড় টানিয়া বাহির করা; (বাষ্পীয়পোত সম্পর্কে) ছাড়া। **To pull the bell**—To pull the rope or handle to ring the bell; ঘণ্টা বাজাইবার জন্য ঘণ্টার দড়ী বা হাতল ধরিয়া টানা। **To pull the long bow**—To exaggerate; to lie boastingly; অতিরঞ্জিত করা; বড়াই করিয়া মিথ্যা কথা বলা। **To pull the strings**—To set in action secretly; অন্তরালে থাকিয়া কলকাটি নাড়া। **To pull through**—(*Verb i.*) To come safely out of a danger, illness, etc.; কোনরূপ বিপদ বা পীড়া হইতে কষ্টেসৃষ্টে রক্ষা পাওয়া। **To pull together**—To co-operate; to work in harmony; একযোগে করা; মিলিয়া মিশিয়া কাজ করা। **To pull to pieces**—To separate in parts forcibly; খণ্ডবিখণ্ড করা। (*Fig.*) To criticise as a person, thing, etc., unfavourably; (লক্ষণায়) প্রতিকূল সমালোচনা করা। **To pull up**—To cause to stop as a person, horse or carriage; (*v. i.*) to stop; থামান, ঘোড়ার লাগাম টানিয়া ধরা; থামা। To reprimand; to check oneself; to advance one's relative position in a race etc.; তিরস্কার করা, ভর্ৎসনা করা; সংযত করা; ঘোড়দৌড় প্রভৃতিতে অন্য অশ্ব হইতে আপেক্ষিক দূরত্বের মাত্রা হ্রাস করা। **To pull up stakes**—(*Colloq., U.S.*) To arrange one's affairs for removal; (মার্কিণ যুক্তরাজ্যে চলিতভাষায়) স্থানান্তরিত হওয়ার জন্য কাজ কারবারের বন্দোবস্ত করা।

pûll, *n.* **1.** Act of pulling; the force exerted in pulling; a tug; টানন, টান, সবলে আকর্ষণ; টানে যে পরিমাণ শক্তির চালনা করা হয়; টান। **2.** Pulling at the bridle to check a horse esp. in racing; অশ্ব সংযত করার জন্য লাগাম ধরিয়া টানন। **3.** (*Print.*) A rough proof; (মুদ্রণ) খসড়া মুদ্রণী পত্র। **4.** Act or exercise of rowing; দাঁড় টানন। **5.** A knob, cord, wire, handle, etc.

for pulling something; as a bell-*pull*; কোন কিছু টানিবার জন্য দড়ী, তার, হাতল, প্রভৃতি। 6. Act of drinking; a draught of liquor; পান; এক ঢোক মদ্য প্রভৃতি। 7. (In public house) A supply of beer etc. exceeding the quantity demanded; চাহিদার অতিরিক্ত বীয়র প্রভৃতি সরবরাহ। 8. (*Slang*) Influence; as, he secured the post through his *pull* with the governor; (ইতর ভাষায়) প্রভাব। **To have the pull of a person**—To have the advantage of him; কাহারো উপর সুবিধা করিয়া লওয়া।

pûll-ĕr, *n.* 1. One that pulls; আকর্ষক, উৎপাটক। 2. An instrument or device for pulling or extracting something; as, a cork or nail *puller*; কোন কিছু উৎপাটনের জন্য যন্ত্র বা কৌশলবিশেষ। 3. A horse that pulls esp. against the bit; যে ঘোড়া লাগামের অধীন ধরিয়া টানিয়া থাকে।

pŭl'-let (-ĕt), *n.* A young hen esp. one less than a year old; ক্ষুদ্র কুক্কুটী, কুক্কুটশাবক, মুরগীর ছানা।

pûl'-ley (-ĭ), *n.* & *v. t.* 1. A small wheel with a groove on a block used in raising weights; গুরুভার দ্রব্য উত্তোলনের জন্য কাষ্ঠখণ্ডে সংবদ্ধ খাঁজবিশিষ্ট ক্ষুদ্র চক্র, কপিকল, কর্ষচক্র (আঃ বঃ)। 2. A wheel or drum fixed on a shaft and turned by belt, used esp. to increase speed or powers; শক্তি বা গতিবেগবৃদ্ধির জন্য অক্ষদণ্ডের উপর সংবদ্ধ চক্র বা পিপার আকার যন্ত্রাংশ। ***Verb t.*** To raise or hoist with a pulley; to furnish or work with a pulley; কপিকলের সাহায্যে তোলা; কপিকল লাগান।

Pulley.

Pŭl'-li-cāte (-ĭ-), *n.* A coloured handkerchief originally made at Pulicat on the Madras coast; a material for this; মান্দ্রাজের উপকূলবর্ত্তী পালিকাট নামক স্থানে প্রস্তুত একপ্রকার রঙ্গীন রুমাল; যে কাপড় হইতে ঐরূপ রুমাল প্রস্তুত হয়। [মান্দ্রাজের ২০ মাইল উত্তরস্থিত পালিকেট (পালিয়া বর্কড়ু) নামক ক্ষুদ্র নগর।]

Pûll-măn, *adj.* & *n.* **Pullman (car)**—A sleeping car; ঘুমাইবার গাড়ী, শয়নশকট। [আবিষ্কর্ত্তা Pullman এর নাম হইতে গৃহীত।]

pŭl'-lū-lāte, *v. i.* 1. To germinate; to bud; অঙ্কুরোদ্গম হওয়া, অঙ্কুরিত হওয়া; মুকুলিত হওয়া। 2. (*Fig.*) To develop or spring up as a doctrine etc.; (লক্ষণায়) বিকাশ প্রাপ্ত হওয়া, উদ্ভূত হওয়া। **—la'-tion,** *n.* **—lant,** *adj.*

pŭl'-ly̆-haul (-hăl), *v. t.* & *i.* To pull or haul with all ones strength; প্রাণপণে টানা।

pŭl'-ly̆-haul'-y̆ (-hăl-), *adj.* & *n.* (*Colloq.*) Of, or relating to, pulling and hauling; (চলিত ভাষায়) টানা হেঁচড়ার। ***Noun.*** The action or work of pulling and hauling; টানা হেঁচড়া।

pŭl-mō-bran'-chi-āte (-brăng-), *adj.* Having gills modified for air breathing; শ্বাসপ্রশ্বাসের জন্য রূপান্তরিত কানকোবিশিষ্ট।

pŭl-mŏm'-ĕt-ĕr, *n.* An instrument to measure the capacity of lungs; ফুসফুসের ধারণশক্তি মাপক যন্ত্রবিশেষ। **—e-try,** *n.*

pŭl'-mō-nā-ry̆, *adj.* 1. Of, or relating to, the lungs; ফুসফুসসম্বন্ধীয়, ফুসফুসীয়, ফুসফুসবিষয়ক। 2. Having lungs or organs like lungs; ফুসফুস বা তদ্বৎ অঙ্গবিশিষ্ট। 3. Subject to, or affected with, pulmonary disease; ফুসফুসসংক্রান্ত পীড়ার অধীন বা উক্তরূপ পীড়াক্রান্ত। **—mon'-ic,** *adj.* & *n.* Same as PULMONARY *adj.* (*Noun.*) A person affected with pulmonary disease; ফুসফুসসংক্রান্ত পীড়াগ্রস্ত ব্যক্তি। **—nate,** *adj.* Having lungs; ফুসফুসবিশিষ্ট। **Pulmonary artery**—প্রধান ধমনী বা হৃৎপিণ্ড—যাহা হইতে ফুসফুসে রক্ত নীত হয়।

pŭlp, *n.*, *v. t.* & *i.* 1. The soft fleshy part of a fruit; ফলের শাঁস, সার, ফলশস্য। 2. Moist soft part of an animal body; the soft vascular and sensitive tissue filling the central cavity of teeth; মজ্জা; দন্তের অভ্যন্তর ভাগ যে সংবেদনশীল বিধানতন্তুদ্বারা পূর্ণ থাকে, দন্তমজ্জা। 3. Soft formless matter esp. that of linen, wood, etc. from which paper is made; কাঠ, কাপড়, প্রভৃতির মণ্ড—যাহা হইতে কাগজ তৈরী হয়। 4. (*Mining*) Pulverized ore mixed with water; জলের সহিত মিশ্রিত চূর্ণীকৃত খনিজবিমিশ্র ধাতু। ***Verb t.*** 1. To reduce to pulp; মণ্ডবৎ করা, লেই করা। 2. To deprive of the pulp, as coffee-beans; শাঁস ছাড়ান। ***Verb i.*** To become pulpy or pulp-like; মণ্ডবৎ হওয়া। **Pul'-per,** *n.* **Pul'-pi-fy,** *v. t.* To make pulp of, as wood fibre; মণ্ড করা। **Pulp'-less, Pulp'-ous,** *adjs.* **Pulp'-ness,** *n.* **Pulp'-y,** *adj.* Like, or consisting of, pulp; fleshy; মজ্জাবৎ, মজ্জাবহুল; মাংসল, থসথসে।

pûl'-pit, *n.* & *adj.* 1. An elevated place for a preacher; প্রচারকের বেদী, উচ্চাসন, উপদেশপীঠ, ব্যাসাসন (কেঃঅিঃ)। 2. The profession of preaching; প্রচারব্যবসায়, প্রচারকের কার্য্য। 3. Preachers generally; "It is the duty of the *pulpit* to preach politics; প্রচারকবর্গ। ***Adj.*** Of, or relating to, the pulpit; suited to the pulpit; as, a *pulpit* orator, style, etc.; প্রচারকের বেদীসম্বন্ধীয়; বেদী হইতে প্রচারের উপযোগী।

pûl-pit-eer′ (-ēr), *n.* & *v. i.* One who speaks in or delivers sermons from a pulpit ; a preacher, (*in contempt*) ; যে ব্যক্তি বেদী হইতে বক্তৃতা বা উপদেশ প্রদান করে ; প্রচারক (অবজ্ঞাচ্ছলে)। ***Verb i.*** To preach ; প্রচার করা। **—a′-ri-an,** *adj.* & *n.* Sermonical ; ধর্ম্মোপদেশ-সম্বন্ধীয়। ***Noun.*** Same as PULPITEER, *n.* **—ing,** *n.* Preaching ; প্রচার।

pûl′-que (-kā), *n.* A fermented drink made in Mexico ; মেক্সিকো প্রদেশে প্রস্তুত একপ্রকার মাদক পানীয় ; **Pulque-brandy** — একপ্রকার মাদক পানীয়।

pŭl′-sāte, *v. i.* & *t.* **1.** To throb as a pulse ; to beat as the heart, (*lit.* & *fig.*) ; স্পন্দিত হওয়া ; ধুক ধুক করা, দপ্ দপ্ করা (শব্দানুযায়ী ও লক্ষণায়) । **2.** To vibrate ; to quiver or thrill; কম্পিত হওয়া ; স্ফুরিত হওয়া। ***Verb t.*** To agitate as diamonds with a pulsator; আন্দোলকযন্ত্র দ্বারা হীরকসমূহআলোড়িত করা। **—sa′-tion,** *n.* Act of pulsating ; a beating or throbbing as of the heart or of an artery ; নাড়ীস্পন্দন ; শোণিতের গতি, নাড়ীস্ফুরণ, স্পন্দন। **—sa-tor,** *n.* A shaking machine used in separating diamonds from earth in which they are found ; মৃত্তিকাবিমিশ্র হীরকসমূহ মৃত্তিকা হইতে পৃথক করার জন্য একপ্রকার আন্দোলকযন্ত্র, আলোড়নযন্ত্র। **—sa-to-ry,** *adj.*

pŭl′-să-tile, *adj.* **1.** Capable of being struck or beaten ; played by percussion, as a musical instrument ; as drum is a *pulsatile* instrument ; তাড়নীয়; আঘাত পূর্ব্বক বাদনীয়। **2.** Pulsating ; throbbing ; স্পন্দনশীল ; কম্পমান।

pulse (pŭls), *n.*, *v. i.* & *t.* **1.** The beating of the heart or arteries ; each successive beat of arteries or the heart ; নাড়ীর গতি, ধমনীর স্পন্দন, নাড়ীর স্ফুরণ ; নাড়ীর ধুক ধুক। **2.** A stroke or beat esp. a measured or regular one *e. g.* of oars etc. ; a single beat or vibration of sound, light, etc. ; আঘাত ; ধ্বনি, আলো. প্রভৃতির প্রত্যেক স্পন্দন। **3.** (*Fig.*) The general tendency of thought or feeling, at a given time or period ; as, the *pulse* of the audience ; (লক্ষণায়) মনের গতি, মনের ভাব, নাড়ী। ***Verb i.*** To pulsate, (*lit.* & *fig.*) ; স্পন্দিত হওয়া, কম্পিত হওয়া, স্ফুরিত হওয়া, ধুক ধুক করা (শব্দানুযায়ী ও লক্ষণায়)। ***Verb t.*** To drive or send *out, in,* etc. by pulses or rhythmic beats ; স্পন্দিত করিয়া বাহির করা বা অভ্যন্তরে সঞ্চারিত করা। **Pulse′-less,** *adj.* **Pulse′-less-ness,** *n.* **To feel a person's pulse**—To do so by way of indicating his state of health by the rate and character of his pulse ; (*fig.*) to sound his intentions etc. ; কাহারও নাড়ী দেখা, কাহারও নাড়ী পরীক্ষা করিয়া দেখা, কাহারও নাড়ীর গতি পরীক্ষা করা ; (লক্ষণায়) কাহারও মনের ভাব বা গতি বুঝিবার চেষ্টা করা, কাহারও মনের ভাব পরীক্ষা করিয়া দেখা।

pulse (pŭls), *n.* **1.** Leguminous plants or their seeds *e. g.* peas, beans, lentils ; ডাইল, বৈদল (ভাব প্রঃ), দ্বিদল। **2.** Any kind of these ; কোন প্রকার ডাইল।

pŭl-sim′-ĕ-têr, *n.* An instrument for measuring the rate or force of the pulse ; নাড়ীর গতিমাপকযন্ত্র, নাড়ীস্পন্দমান, নাড়ীমান।

pŭl-sŏm′-ĕ-têr, *n.* A pump for raising water by the condensation of steam ; বাষ্পঘনীকরণ দ্বারা জল উত্তোলনের জন্য একপ্রকার দমকল।

pŭl-tā′-ceous (-shŭs), *adj.* Of, relating to, or of the nature of, a pap or poultice ; soft ; pulpy ; পুল্টিসসম্বন্ধীয় ; কোমল ; মণ্ডবৎ।

pŭl′-vêr-ize, *v. t.* & *i.* **1.** To reduce to dust or powder ; গুঁড়ান, চূর্ণ করা। **2.** To divide as a liquid into spray ; কণাকারে বিভক্ত করা। **3.** (*Fig.*) To demolish ; to smash ; (লক্ষণায়) ধ্বংস করা ; চূর্ণবিচূর্ণ করা, চুরমার করা। ***Verb i.*** To crumble or fall to dust ; চুরমার হইয়া পড়া। **—i-za-tor, —iz′-er, —i-za′-tion,** *ns* The act of pulverizing ; চূর্ণীকরণ, সংচূর্ণন।

pŭl-vĕr′-ū-lĕnt, *adj.* **1.** Dusty ; powdery ; ধূলিবৎ ; চূর্ণবৎ। **2.** Covered with dust or powder ; চূর্ণাবৃত। **3.** (Of rock etc.) Of slight cohesion ; crumbling to dust ; (প্রস্তর প্রভৃতি সম্পর্কে) স্বল্প-সংলাগশীল ; চূর্ণীভবনশীল। **—lence,** *n.* State of being pulverulent ; রেণুত্ব, চূর্ণত্ব।

pŭl′-vi-nāte, —nāt-ĕd, *adjs.* **1.** (*Bot.* & *Zool.*) Cushion-shaped ; (উদ্ভিদ্‌বিদ্যা এবং জন্তুবিদ্যা) উপধানাকৃতি **2.** (*Arch.* -NATED) Curved or swelled convexly ; বহির্বর্ত্তুলাকারে বক্রীভূত বা স্ফীত।

pū′-mă, *n.* Same as COUGAR.

pŭm′-ice (-ĭs), *n.* & *v. t.* A light and spongy stone, used for polishing etc. ; পালিশ প্রভৃতির কার্য্যে ব্যবহৃত একপ্রকার হাল্কা শোষকের ন্যায় পাথর, ঝামা পাথর। ***Verb t.*** To smooth, clean, etc. with pumice ; ঝামাপাথর দ্বারা পালিশ, পরিষ্কার, ইত্যাদি করা। **Pu-mi′-ceous,** *adj.* **Pumice stone**—Same as PUMICE. **Pumice hoof of horse** রোগহেতু শোষকবৎ (sponges) অবস্থা প্রাপ্ত অশ্ব খুর।

pŭm′-mĕl, *v. t.* To strike repeatedly esp. with the fist ; বারবার আঘাত করা, পুনঃপুনঃ মুষ্ট্যাঘাত করা।

pŭmp, *n.* **1.** A machine for raising water or extracting air etc. ; বোমাকল, দমকল। **2.** Act of pumping ; দমকলের সাহায্যে জল প্রভৃতি তোলন। **3.** (*Fig.*) The heart, insect's suckers, etc. ;

"The respiratory *pump*" ; (লক্ষণায়) হৃৎপিণ্ড, কীটের শুঁয়া, প্রভৃতি। 4. An attempt at extracting information from any one, by skilful questioning ; one who is clever at this ; চতুরভাবে প্রশ্ন করিয়া কাহারো নিকট হইতে কোন খবর বাহির করার জন্য চেষ্টা ; ঐরূপ কার্য্যে নিপুণ ব্যক্তি। **Bicycle-pump**—দ্বিচক্রযানের রবরনির্ম্মিত চক্রপ্রান্তবেষ্টনী স্ফীতকরণার্থ যন্ত্রবিশেষ। **Pump-brake** — দমকলের হাতল। **Pump-handle** — (*Noun*) The handle of a pump ; দমকলের হাতল। (*v. t. colloq.*) To shake effusively as one's hand ; (চলিতভাষায়) আবেগোচ্ছ্বসিতভাবে মস্তক আন্দোলিত করা। **Pump-room**—যে গৃহে দমকল চালান হয়, (বিশেষতঃ) উষ্ণপ্রস্রবণযুক্ত স্থানের যে জায়গায় ঔষধজল বিতরিত হয়।

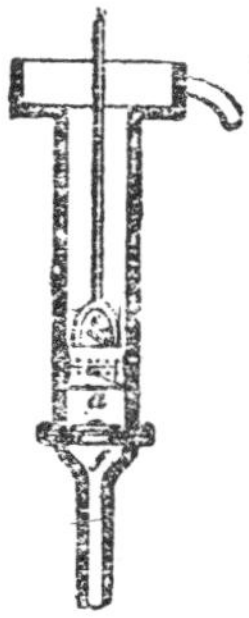

Pump.

pump, *v. i. & t.* **1.** To raise water or other liquid with a pump ; to work a pump ; দমকলের সাহায্যে জল প্রভৃতি তোলা ; দমকল চালান। **2.** (Of mercury in barometer) To rise and fall instantaneously ; (বায়ুমানযন্ত্রের পারদসম্পর্কে) চকিতে উঠা বা নামা। ***Verb t.*** **1.** To raise as water etc. with a pump ; দমকলের সাহায্যে জল উঠান। **2.** To free from water, air or the like ; as, to *pump* a ship ; জল, বায়ু, বা তদ্বৎ বস্তু শূন্য করা। **3.** To inflate as a tire etc. (with *up*) ; চক্রপ্রান্তবেষ্টনী স্ফীত করা। **4.** To draw out, pour forth, as abuse, censure, etc. *upon* somebody as by pumping ; টানিয়া বাহির করা, বর্ষণ করা। **5.** To elicit or draw out as information, etc. by artful or insistent interrogations ; চতুরতার সহিত বা পুনঃপুনঃ প্রশ্ন করিয়া ভিতরের খবর বাহির করা। **6.** To question or examine as a person artfully in order to elicit an information or secret ; কোন খবর বা গুপ্ত কথা বাহির করার জন্য চতুরতার সহিত প্রশ্ন করা। **7.** To exhaust of breath, (*esp. in the passive*) ; হাঁপাইয়া তোলা। **Pump'-er,** *n.* **Pumpship,** *v. i.* To make water ; প্রস্রাব করা (শিষ্ট প্রয়োগ নয়)।

pŭmp, *n.* A kind of light shoe for dancing ; নাচের জন্য একপ্রকার হালকা জুতা।

pŭmp'-ĕr-nick-ĕl, *n.* A kind of bread made of unbolted rye, in Germany ; জর্ম্মণ দেশে আচালা রাই হইতে প্রস্তুত একপ্রকার রুটী।

pŭmp'-kin *n.* A gourd plant and its fruit ; কুষ্মাণ্ড, লাউ, অলাবু, তুম্বী। **Melon pumpkin**—মিষ্ট কুমড়া।

pŭn, *n., v. i. & t.* A play upon words similar in sound but different in meaning ; শ্লেষালঙ্কার, শ্লেষ, শ্লেষোক্তি, শব্দশ্লেষ, কাকৈষমক। ***Verb i.*** To make puns *upon* a word, etc. ; দ্ব্যর্থবোধকভাবে ব্যবহার করা। ***Verb t.*** To pursuade by punning ; শব্দশ্লেষ দ্বারা প্ররোচিত করা। **Pun'-ning-ly,** *adv.*

pŭn, *v. t.* To consolidate by pounding or ramming as earth, rubble, etc. in setting poles etc. or for making roadway ; দুরমুষ দ্বারা আঘাত করিয়া মাটী, পাথরের টুকরা প্রভৃতি শক্ত করিয়া বসান।

pū'-nă, *n.* **1.** A table-land in Peru ; পেরুদেশের মালভূমি। **2.** A difficulty in breathing arising from a too rarefied atmosphere ; বায়ুর অভাবে শ্বাসপ্রশ্বাস ক্রিয়ায় কষ্ট।

pŭnch, *n.* **1.** An iron instrument for perforating holes, driving bolt etc. out of a hole, etc. ; a tool for driving nail heads below the surface ; ছিদ্র করণ, ছিদ্র হইতে বল্টু প্রভৃতি খুলিবার জন্য যন্ত্র, ভেনা, বেধনযন্ত্র, পঞ্চ, ফলা ; বল্টু বসাইবার জন্য যন্ত্র। **2.** An instrument for stamping a design etc. ; ছেনি। **Bell-punch**—ট্রামওয়ে চালকের ঘণ্টাসংযুক্ত টিকিট কাটা কল।

pŭnch, *v. t. & n.* **1.** To give a blow to ; to strike with a closed fist ; আঘাত করা ; মুষ্ট্যাঘাত করা। **2.** To poke or prod esp. with a stick ; খোঁচা দেওয়া, গুঁতা মারা। **3.** To perforate as paper, leather, metal, etc. with a punch or iron instrument ; বেধনযন্ত্র দ্বারা ছিদ্র করা। **4.** To drive as a nail etc. *in* or *out* with a punch ; ফলার সাহায্যে পেরেক প্রভৃতি বসান বা খোলা। ***Noun.*** A blow esp. with the fist ; আঘাত, মুষ্ট্যাঘাত। **Punch'-er,** *n.* **Punching-ball**—ঘুষি অভ্যাস করার জন্য বায়ুপুরিত কন্দুক।

pŭnch, *n.* **1.** A beverage of Indian origin consisting usually of five ingredients ; উষ্ণজলে কিম্বা মদ্যে চিনি, লেবুর রস, প্রভৃতির সংমিশ্রণে প্রস্তুত পানীয় সরবত। **2.** A bowl of punch ; a party at which punch is drunk ; সরবতের পাত্র ; যে বৈঠকে সরবত পান করা হয়। **punch-bowl** — One in which punch is mixed ; যে পাত্রে লেবুর রস, চিনি প্রভৃতি মিশ্রিত করিয়া সরবত প্রস্তুত করা হয়। A round deep hollow in a hill or hills ; পাহাড় বা পাহাড়শ্রেণীর মধ্যস্থ গভীর গোলাকার গর্ত্ত।

pŭnch, *n.* **1.** (*Dial.*) A short and thick person or thing ; (উপভাষায়) মোটা বেঁটে লোক। **2.** (Also *Suffolk-punch*) A short thick-set draft horse ; একপ্রকার খর্ব্বকায় ভারবাহী অশ্ব। **3.** (*Cap.*) A grotesque hump-backed figure in the puppet-show called *"Punch and Judy"* ; পুতুল বাজীর বিকটাকৃতি কুব্জপৃষ্ঠ মূর্ত্তি। **As pleased, as proud, as punch**—*i. e.* Very or much pleased or proud ; অতিশয় তুষ্ট বা গর্ব্বিত।

pŭnch′-eon (-ŭn), *n.* (*Hist.*) A cask for liquids, etc. containing from 72 to 120 gallons ; (ইতিহাস) তরল পদার্থ রাখার জন্য পাত্র বিশেষ—যাহাতে ৭২ হইতে ১২০ গ্যালন ধরে।

pŭnch′-eon (-ŭn), *n.* **1.** A short post esp. one for supporting a roof in a coal-mine ; খাটো খুঁটি, কয়লার খনির ছাদের অবলম্বনস্বরূপ স্তম্ভ।

Pŭn-chi-nĕl′-lō, *n.* **1.** A short fat character in Italian puppet-shows ; ইতালীদেশীয় পুতুল নাচের খর্ব্বকায় এবং হৃষ্টপুষ্ট মূর্ত্তি। **2.** A short stout person ; খর্ব্বকায় হৃষ্টপুষ্ট ব্যক্তি।

punc′-tate (pŭngk-), *adj.* (*Bot.* & *Zool.*) Dotted, or marked, with spots, points, etc. ; (উদ্ভিদ্‌বিদ্যা এবং জন্তুবিদ্যা) ফুট ফুট বিন্দুবিশিষ্ট, ফুট ফুট। **—ta′-tion**, *n.*

punc-til′-i-ō (pŭngk-), *n.* (*Pl.* -os). **1.** A nice point in conduct or in ceremony ; particularity or exactness in forms ; সূক্ষ্মবিষয় ; সূক্ষ্মদৃষ্টি, সূক্ষ্মবিধি।

punc-til′-i-ous (pŭngk-til-i-ŭs), *adj.* Attentive to punctilios ; over-precise or particular ; পিটপিটে ; সূক্ষ্মনিয়মনিষ্ঠ, সূক্ষ্মাচারনিষ্ঠ, সূক্ষ্মাচারদর্শী। **—ly**, *adv.* **—ness**, *n.*

punc′-tū-ăl (pŭngk-), *adj.* **1.** Done, made, occurring, etc. at the exact time ; not late ; যথাকাল কৃত, যথাকালসংঘটিত ; যথাকালাগত, কালানুবর্ত্তী। **2.** Particular in observing appointed time or engagements ; সময়নিষ্ঠ, নিয়মনিষ্ঠ। **3.** (*Archaic*) Punctilious ; (কচিদ্‌ ব্যবহৃত) সূক্ষ্মনিয়মনিষ্ঠ। **4.** (*Geom.*) Of, or relating to, a point ; (জ্যামিতি) বিন্দুসম্বন্ধীয়। **—al′-i-ty**, *n.* **—ly**, *adv.*

punc′-tū-āte (pŭngk-), *v. t.* **1.** To mark as a writing with points ; বিরামচিহ্নে চিহ্নিত করা। **2.** (*Fig.*) To interrupt with exclamations etc. as a speech ; (লক্ষণায়) সাধুবাদ প্রভৃতি দ্বারা বক্তৃতা প্রভৃতির ব্যাঘাত জন্মান, বিরাম চিহ্নাঙ্কিত করা। **3.** To emphasize ; as, he flung it on the ground to *punctuate* his refusal; জোর দেওয়া। **—a-tive**, *adj.* **—a-tor**, *n.*

punc-tū-ā′-tion (pŭngk-) *n.* (*Gram.*) The act or art of punctuating or inserting stops or points in a writing ; বিরামচিহ্নিবেশ, চিহ্নপ্রকরণ, বিরামচিহ্নাঙ্কন।

punc′-tŭm (pŭngk-), *n.* (*Pl.* -TA) A dot, speck or point ; a small rounded spot of colour or of elevation or depression upon a surface ; দাগ, ফোঁটা, বিন্দু ; কোন কিছুর উপরিস্থ ক্ষুদ্র রঞ্জিত এবং গোলাকার বিন্দু কিম্বা উচ্চ বা অবনত স্থান। **—tule**, *n.* A minute puncture, pit or spot ; ক্ষুদ্র ছিদ্র, গর্ত্ত বা বিন্দু। **—tu-late**, *adj.* **—tu-la′-tion**, *n.*

pŭnc′-tūre (pŭngk-), *n., v. t.* & *i.* **1.** Act of puncturing ; বেধন। **2.** Accidental pricking of a pneumatic tire, as of a bicycle etc. ; দ্বিচক্রযান প্রভৃতির বায়ুপুরিত চক্রপ্রান্ত-বেষ্টনীতে আকস্মিক কারণ বশতঃ যে ফুটা হয়। **3.** A small hole, wound, etc. made by pricking ; ফোঁড়, ক্ষুদ্রছিদ্র, বেধ। ***Verb t.*** To pierce or prick ; ভেদ করা, ছিদ্র করা, বেধ করা। ***Verb i.*** To get a puncture ; ফুটা হওয়া, ছিদ্র হওয়া। **—tured**, *adj.* **—turing**, *n.* The act of one who punctures ; ভেদ্য (সুশ্রুঃ কুঞ্জ)। **Punctured fracture**—ছিন্ন ভগ্ন (সাঃ পঃ)। **Punctured wound**—ছিন্নব্রণ (সাঃ পঃ)।

pŭn′-dit, *n.* **1.** One versed in Sanskrit etc. in India ; পণ্ডিত। **2.** (*Humour.*) A learned teacher ; (কৌতুকচ্ছলে) সুবিদ্বান অধ্যাপক।

pŭn′-gĕnt, *adj.* **1.** Affecting the organs of smell or taste or skin etc. ; ঝাল, কটু। **2.** Stinging ; biting, as a remark, satire, etc. ; তীক্ষ্ণ, উগ্র, তীব্র, প্রখর ; মর্ম্মচ্ছেদী, অরুন্তুদ, কাটা (*colloq.*) **3.** Piquant ; mentally stimulating ; "Every amusement...become more *pungent*" ; ঝাঁঝাল ; কড়া **4.** (*Bot.*) Prickly pointed ; (উদ্ভিদ্‌ বিদ্যা) সূক্ষ্মমুখ। **—gen-cy**, *n.* The quality of beng pungent ; তীব্রতা, তীক্ষ্ণতা, প্রাখর্য্য, উগ্রতা, কটুতা। **—ly**, *adv.*

Pū′-nic, *adj.* & *n.* Of, relating to, characteristic of, the Carthaginians ; কার্থেজবাসিসম্বন্ধীয়, কার্থেজবাসিসুলভ। ***Noun.*** Punic language ; কার্থেজের ভাষা। **Punic apple**—ডালিম, বেদানা। **Punic faith**—বিশ্বাসঘাতকতা। **Punic Wars**—রোম এবং কার্থেজের মধ্যে যুদ্ধ।

pûn′-ish, *v. t.* **1.** To impose punishment upon an offender ; to inflict penalty for an offence ; দণ্ডপ্রদান করা ; শাস্তি দেওয়া, সাজা দেওয়া। **2.** To chastise ; as, to *punish* a child for disobedience etc. ; প্রহার করা, শাস্তি দেওয়া। **3.** (*Cricket*) To hit freely ; as, to *punish* weak bowling or a bowler etc. ; (ক্রীকেট ক্রীড়া) অবাধে আঘাত করা। **4.** To make a considerable inroad on, as food etc. ; অধিক খরচ করা। **—a-bil′-i-ty**, *n.* **—a-ble**, *adj.* Deserving punishment ; দণ্ডযোগ্য, দণ্ড্য, দণ্ডনীয়, দণ্ডার্হ, শাসনীয়, শাস্য। **—a-bly**, *adv.* **—er**, *n.* One who punishes ; শাস্তা, দণ্ডদাতা, দণ্ডয়িতা, দণ্ডপ্রদাতা। **—ing**, *adj.* **—ment**, *n.* Act of punishing ; penalty ; দণ্ডপ্রদান ; শাস্তি, দণ্ড, সাহস (used in ancient law-books—cf. উত্তম সাহস।) **Capital punishment**—জীবান্ত দণ্ড (কেঃিঃ)। **Corporal punishment**—দেহদণ্ডন (কেঃিঃ), দেহদণ্ড (ঐ)।

pū′-ni-tive (-tiv), *adj.* Involving, or inflicting, punishment ; retributive ; দণ্ডবিধায়ক ; নিগ্রহাত্মক। **—to-ry**, *adj.* **Punitive police**—পিটুনি পুলিশ, নিগ্রহপুলিশ।

punk (pŭngk), *n.* (*Archaic*) A prostitute ; ' অপ্রঃ) বেশ্যা ।

punk (pŭngk), *n.* (*Chiefly U. S.*) Decayed or rotten wood used as tinder; an artificial tinder ; (প্রধানতঃ মার্কিণ যুক্তরাজ্যে) পচাকাঠ, জীর্ণ কাষ্ঠ ; কৃত্রিম উপায়ে প্রস্তুত আশুজ্বলনীয় দ্রব্য ।

pŭn'-ner (-ėr), *n.* **1.** One that puns or rams ; যে ব্যক্তি দুরমুষ্ দ্বারা খোঁটা প্রভৃতি মাটীতে শক্ত করিয়া বসায় । **2.** A tool used for ramming or consolidating earth as about a post etc. ; দুরমুষ ।

pŭn'-net (-ĕt), *n.* A small shallow basket for displaying fruit, flowers, etc. ; সাজি, ঝুড়ি, কড়ণ্ডিকা ।

pŭn'-stêr, *n.* One skilled or addicted to punning or in playing on words ; শব্দশ্লেষপ্রয়োগনিপুণ ব্যক্তি, শব্দশ্লেষ বক্তা (কেঙিঃ) ।

pŭnt, *n., v. t. & i.* **1.** A flat-bottomed vessel or boat ; এক-প্রকার চ্যাপ্টা-তলা নৌকা বা জাহাজ । **2.** (*Football*) Act of punting a foot ball ; such a kick ; (পাদগোলক ক্রীড়া) শূন্যে থাকা অবস্থায় কন্দুকে পদাঘাত ; ঐরূপ পদাঘাত । ***Verb t.*** **1.** To propel as a punt by pushing with a pole against the bottom of a river etc. ; চোড় বা লগি দ্বারা নৌকা চালান। **2.** To convey in a punt or boat; চ্যাপ্টা-তলা নৌকা বা জাহাজে বহন করা । **3.** (*Football*) To kick as the ball before touching the ground when let fall from the hands (*also verb i.*) ; (পাদগোলক ক্রীড়ায়) হস্ত দ্বারা নিক্ষিপ্ত কন্দুক শূন্যে থাকিতে থাকিতে তাহাতে পদাঘাত করা। ***Verb i.*** **1.** To push a punt along ; চোড় দিয়া চ্যাপ্টা-তলা নৌকা বা জাহাজ চালান । **Punt'-er,** *n.* **Punt'-ist,** *n.* **Punt-about**—অভ্যাসের জন্য পাদগোলকে পদাঘাত ; ঐরূপ কার্য্যে ব্যবহৃত কন্দুক ।

pŭnt, *v. i. & n.* **1.** To play at a gambling game against the banker ; স্ফূর্ত্তি খেলার আড্ডার মালিকের বিপক্ষে স্ফূর্ত্তি খেলা । **2.** (*Colloq.*) To bet on a horse etc. ; (চলিত ভাষায়) কোন ঘোড়ার উপর বাজী রাখা । ***Noun.*** A player or gambler who punts ; যে ব্যক্তি ক্রীড়া অভ্যাসের জন্য এদিকে ওদিকে পাদগোলক আঘাত করিয়া চালায়, যে ব্যক্তি স্ফূর্ত্তিখেলার আড্ডায় মালিকের বিপক্ষে স্ফূর্ত্তি খেলে । **Punt'-er,** *n.*

pŭn'-tȳ, pŏn'—, *ns.* (*Glass-making*) An iron rod used in manipulating hot glass ; উষ্ণ কাচ ধরার জন্য ব্যবহৃত লৌহদণ্ড ।

pū'-nȳ, *adj.* Imperfectly developed in size ; small and feeble ; petty ; অপরিণত ; ক্ষুদ্র, তুচ্ছ ; সামান্য । **—ni-ness,** *n.*

pŭp, *n., v. t. & i.* A young dog ; কুকুর ছানা, কুকুর শাবক । ***Verb t. & i.*** (Of a bitch) To bring forth as whelps or young ; শাবক প্রসব করা, বাচ্চা দেওয়া, বিয়ান । **Conceited etc. pup** — (*i. e.* boy, youngman) ; গর্ব্বিত বালক বা যুবক । **In pup**—Pregnant (of a bitch) ; (কুকুর-সম্পর্কে) গর্ভবতী । **To sell one a pup**—To swindle him esp. by selling a thing on its prospective value ; কোন লোককে ঠকান, বিশেষতঃ ভবিষ্যতে যে মূল্য হইতে পারে সেই মূল্যে তাহা বিক্রীত করিয়া তাহাকে ঠকান ।

pū'-pă, *n.* (*Pl.* -PAE) An insect in the chrysalis state ; পক্ষোদ্গমের

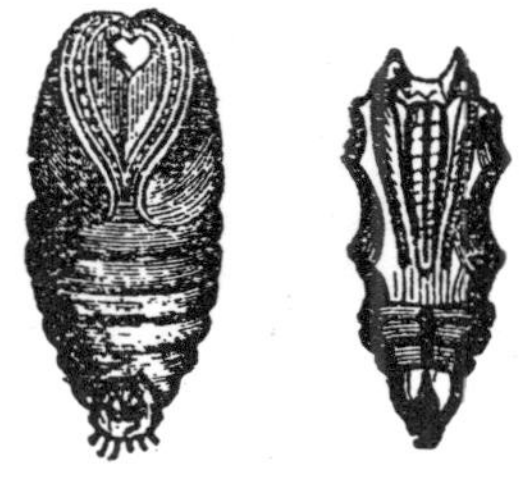

Conical pupa and angular pupa of butterfly.

পূর্ব্বাবস্থার প্রজাপতি প্রভৃতি, কোষস্থ, পুলককোষ (যোঃ) । **—pal,** *adj.*

pū'-pāte, *v.i.* To become a pupa ; পুলককোষ হওয়া । **—pa'-tion,** *n.*

pū'-pil, *n.* **1.** One under the care of a teacher or tutor ; a scholar ; ছাত্র, শিষ্য [also অন্তেবাসী] ; বিদ্যার্থী । **2.** (*Law*) A boy or girl under the age of puberty ; one under the guardianship of another ; অপ্রাপ্ত-বয়স্ক ব্যক্তি ; নাবালক । **3.** The circular opening of the iris regulating the passage of light to the retina ; চক্ষুর তারা, পুত্তলী, তারা, কনীনিকা, নয়নী (মঃ উঃ) । **—(l)ar, —(l)a-ry,** *adj.*

pū'-pil-(l)āge (-āj), *n.* **1.** State or period of being a pupil or scholar ; শিষ্যত্ব, ছাত্রত্ব, শিষ্যাবস্থা, অন্তেবাসিত্ব । **2.** Minority ; (*fig.*) early stage as of a country, language, etc. ; অপ্রাপ্তবয়স্কতা ; (লক্ষণায়) আদ্যবস্থা । **—(l)ar'-i-ty,** *n.* (*Law*) State of being below the age of puberty ; the period before puberty ; নাবালকত্ব, অপ্রাপ্তবয়স্কতা ; কৈশোর । **—ship,** *n.*

pū-pip'-ă-rous (-rŭs), *adj.* (*Entom.*) Bringing forth the young in the pupa stage (কীট-বিদ্যা) গুটিপ্রসবকারী ।

pŭp'-pet (-ĕt), *n.* **1.** A small figure in human form moved by wires etc. ; a puppet-show ; পুতুল খেলার পুতুল , পুতুল খেলা । **2.** A doll ; পুতুল, পুত্তলিকা, পুত্তলীকা । [also পঞ্চালী, পঞ্চালিকা, পুত্রিকা, কৃত্রিমপুত্রক ।] **3.** One acting as another wills ; ক্রীড়াপুত্তলী, সাক্ষীগোপাল, কাষ্ঠপুত্তলি কলেরপুতুল, কাষ্ঠপুত্তলী [কাঠের পুত্তলী যেন কুহকে নাচায়—শ্রীচৈতন্যচরিতামৃত ।] **—ry,** *n.* **1.** A puppet-show ; পুতুলনাচ, পুত্‌লোবাজী, পুত্তলিকাভিনয় । **2.** (*Fig.*) Finery ; affectation ; (লক্ষণায়) জমকালো অলঙ্কার ; কৃত্রিমতা-প্রদর্শন । **Puppet-clack, —valve**—দণ্ডাগ্রসম্বদ্ধচক্রবিশেষ — যাহা ইহার অধিষ্ঠান স্থান হইতে উঠা নামা করিয়া

থাকে। **Puppet-show, —play**—পুতলোবাজী, পুতুল নাচ।

pŭp'-pỹ, *n.* 1. A young dog; a whelp; কুকুরছানা, কুকুরশাব, কুকুরশাবক, কুকুরশিশু; সিংহ, ব্যাঘ্র, ভল্লুক, প্রভৃতির শাবক। 2. A conceited and impertinent young fellow; a coxcomb; a fop; উদ্ধত এবং গর্ব্বিত যুবক; বক্কেশ্বর; ফুলবাবু, খোসপোষাকী বাবু। **—dom, —hood,** *ns.* **—ish,** *adj.* **—ism,** *n.*

pŭr, pŭrr, *ns.* See PURR.

pŭr'-bĕck, *adj.* **Purbeck stone**—ডরসেট সায়ারের উপকূলে প্রাপ্ত একপ্রকার কঠিন চূণা পাথর। **Purbeck marble**—একপ্রকার উৎকৃষ্ট মর্ম্মর প্রস্তর।

pŭr-blind, *adj.* & *v. t.* 1. Short-sighted; having dim sight; ক্ষীণ-দৃষ্টি; অন্ধপ্রায়, মন্দদৃষ্টি। 2. (*Fig.*) Stupid; dull; (লক্ষণায়) মূর্খ; হীনবুদ্ধি, মন্দবুদ্ধি। ***Verb t.*** To make purblind; ক্ষীণদৃষ্টি সম্পন্ন করা। **—ness,** *n.*

pŭr'-chāse, *n.* 1. Buying for money or its equivalent; ক্রয়, খরিদ। 2. A thing bought; ক্রীত বস্তু, সওদা। 3. Value or worth (in yield or return); as sold at 15 years' *purchase*; মূল্য, দাম। 4. Any mechanical power or advantage in raising or moving heavy bodies, (often *fig.*); গুরুভার দ্রব্য উত্তোলন ও সঞ্চালনের জন্য কোন যান্ত্রিক শক্তি বা সুবিধা। 5. A device for gaining this mechanical advantage; (*esp. naut.*) a rope, windlass, pulley; উক্তরূপ যান্ত্রিক-সুবিধাপ্রাপ্তির জন্য কৌশল; (বিশেষতঃ নৌ-বিদ্যায়) ভারি জিনিষ তোলার চরকি-কল, কপিকল। **Purchase money**—ক্রয়মূল্য, কেনা দাম, পড়তা। **Life is not worth an hour's purchase**—যে কোন মুহূর্ত্তে মৃত্যু হইতে পারে।

pŭr'-chāse, *v. t.* 1. To buy; ক্রয় করা, খরিদ করা, কেনা। 2. To acquire; as, to *purchase* favour, freedom, release, etc. with flattery, one's blood, etc.; নিজের রক্তপাত, তোষামোদ, প্রভৃতি দ্বারা অর্জ্জন করা, লাভ করা, অধিগত করা। 3. (*Naut.*) To raise or move as an anchor etc. by means of a pulley, lever, etc.; দণ্ডযন্ত্র, চরকীকল, প্রভৃতির সাহায্যে নঙ্গর প্রভৃতি তোলা। **—chas-a-ble,** *adj.* That can be purchased; ক্রেতব্য, ক্রয়যোগ্য, ক্রয্য। **—chas-er,** *n.*

pūre, *adj.* 1. Free from any mixture; unadulterated; unpolluted; শুদ্ধ, বিমল, অনাবিল, নির্ম্মল, অকল্ক; অবিমিশ্র, খাঁটি, নির্ভাজ শুচি; পূত, মেধ্য, শুভ্র, শুক্র, পবিত্র, বিশুদ্ধ। 2. Pure-blooded; সদ্বংশজাত, বিশুদ্ধ-বংশজাত। 3. Mere; sheer; simple; as, knowledge *pure* and nonsense; শুদ্ধ; কেবল; নিছক। 4. Not morally defiled; guiltless; sincere; chaste; পবিত্রচরিত্র; শুদ্ধচিত্ত, নির্দ্দোষ, নিষ্পাপ, সাধু, সাত্ত্বিক; সরল; সতী। 5. Not corrupt; as, a *pure* taste; পবিত্র। 6. (*Bible*) Ceremonially or ritually clean; (বাইবেল) পূত, পবিত্র। 7. (*Gram.*) Of a single, simple sound, as a vowel; an unaspirated consonant etc.; (ব্যাকরণ) অমিশ্র; অল্পপ্রাণ। 8. Abstract; theoretic; as, a *pure* sceince: *pure* mathematics opposed to *applied*; অমূর্ত্ত; ঔপপত্তিক। **—ly,** *adv.* **—ness,** *n.* **Pure ego**—ক্ষেত্রজ্ঞ (ব্রজ: বৈষ্ণ:)। **Pure-hearted**—শুদ্ধচিত্ত, সিতমনাঃ। **Pure and simple**—নিছক, নির্জলা, খাঁটি, স্পষ্ট, নির্ভাজ।

puree, (*F.*), *n.* A soup made of meat, vegetables, etc. boiled into a pulp and passed through a seive; একত্র সিদ্ধ মাংস, তরকারী, প্রভৃতি মণ্ডাকারে পরিণত করার পর ছাঁকিয়া যে সুপ প্রস্তুত করা হয়।

pŭr'-fle (-fl), *n.* & *v. t.* (*Archaic*) The border of an embroidered work; (অপ্রঃ) সূচের কাজের প্রান্ত। ***Verb t.*** To decorate as a robe with a border of embroidery; to ornament; to beautify; সূচের কাজের পাড় দিয়া শোভিত করা; অলঙ্কৃত করা; শোভিত করা, মণ্ডিত করা। **—fling,** *n.*

pŭr-gā'-tion, *n.* 1. Act of purging; purification; শোধন, পাবন, শুদ্ধীকরণ, বিমলীকরণ (সর্ব্বঃ দঃ); শৌচ, শুদ্ধি। 2. Act of purging the intestines; রেচন, বিরেচন। 3. Spiritual cleansing esp. (*R. C. Ch.*) of the soul in purgatory; (রোমানক্যাথলিক ধর্ম্মসংঘ) পাপশোধন। 4. (*Hist.*) The clearing of oneself from the accusation or suspicion of crime or guilt; (ইতিহাস) কোনরূপ অভিযোগের অপবাদ হইতে মোচন। **To put one to his purgation**—To ask one to clear himself from an accusation; কোন রূপ অভিযোগের অপবাদ হইতে নিজকে মুক্ত করার জন্য কাহাকে বলা।

pŭr'-gā-tive (-tĭv), *adj.* & *n.* 1. Purging or tending to purge the intestines, as a medicine, cathartic; বিরেচন, বিরেচক, ভেদক (ঠাকুর), রেচন, সারক। 2. Cleaning from defilement, evil, guilt, etc.; শোধন, শোধক। ***Noun.*** A purgative medicine; জোলাপ, বিরেচক ঔষধ, সারকৌষধ।

pŭr'-gā-tō-rỹ, *n.* & *adj.* 1. (*Religious*) Any place or state succeeding the present life, and serving as a means of moral purification; পরলোকগত আত্মার পাপক্ষালনের স্থান বা অবস্থা, পাপ-শোধন লোক, প্রেতলোক, পাপ-শোধনাবস্থা। 2. A place or state of temporary suffering or expiation; সাময়িক দুঃখভোগ বা প্রায়শ্চিত্তের স্থান বা অবস্থা। ***Adj.*** Cleansing; expiatory; পাবন, শোধক; প্রায়শ্চিত্তসাধক। **—to'-ri-al,** *adj.*

purge (pŭrj), *v. t., i.* & *n.* 1. To cleanse or purify; শোধন করা, পরিষ্কার করা, বিশুদ্ধ করা, নির্ম্মল

করা। 2. To clear or free from moral defilement; pollution or guilt; পাপশোধন করা, দোষক্ষালন করা। 3. (*Lit.* & *fig.*) To remove by a cleansing process, (with *off, away, out*); পরিষ্কার করিয়া ফেলা। 4. To clear from accusation or suspicion of a crime; কোন অভিযোগ বা অপরাধের সন্দেহ হইতে মুক্ত করা। 5. (*Law*) To atone for or to wipe out by expiation and submission; etc.; (আইন) প্রায়শ্চিত্ত বা আত্মসমর্পণ দ্বারা ক্ষতিপূরণ বা ক্ষালন করা। 6. To operate on (bowels etc.) as a cathartic medicine; কোষ্ঠ খোলাসা করা। ***Verb i.*** (Of a drug) To act as a purgative; জোলাপের কাজ করা। ***Noun.*** 1. Act of purging; purgation; শোধন; পাবন। 2. An aperient; বিরেচক ঔষধ। **Pride's Purge**—কর্ণেল Pride কর্তৃক ১৬৪৮ খৃঃ অব্দে প্রেস্‌বিটিরিয়ান এবং রাজপক্ষীয় সভ্যগণকে লঙ্গ পার্লেমেণ্ট হইতে বিতাড়ন।

pū-ri-fi-cā'-tion, *n.* 1. Act of purifying; পাবন, শোধন, শুদ্ধি, শৌচ, বিশোধন, শুদ্ধীকরণ, বিমলীকরণ (সর্ব্ব দঃ), মলাপকর্ষণ। 2. Act or process of cleansing ceremonially esp. that of a woman after child-birth enjoined by the Jewish law; as, the *Purification* of the Virgin Mary; ধর্ম্মশাস্ত্রের ব্যবস্থানুসারে শুদ্ধীকরণ, বিশেষতঃ ইহুদীশাস্ত্রের বিধানানুসারে প্রসবান্তে স্ত্রীলোকের শুদ্ধিবিধান। **–rif'-i-ca-to-ry,** *adj.*

pū'-ri-fi-cā-tor (-têr), *n.* One that purifies; (esp. *Eccl.*) a linen cloth used to wipe the chalice after celebration of the Eucharist; শোধক, বিশোধক; খৃষ্টের অন্তিমভোজন ক্রিয়ানুষ্ঠানের পরে যে ক্ষৌমবস্ত্রখণ্ডদ্বারা পানপাত্র মুছা হয়।

pū'-ri-fȳ, *v. t.* & *i.* 1. To make pure or clear; to free from extraneous or noxious matter; পবিত্র করা, পরিষ্কার করা, বিশুদ্ধ করা; বিমল করা, নির্ম্মল করা। 2. To free from pollution ceremonially; শুদ্ধ করা, অশৌচ দূর করা। 3. To purge from guilt or moral defilement; দোষক্ষালন করা, পাপক্ষালন করা। ***Verb i.*** To grow or become pure or clear; নির্ম্মল হওয়া, বিশুদ্ধ হওয়া, পবিত্র হওয়া। **–fi-er,** *n.*

Pū'-rim, *n.* Among the Jews, a festival in commemoration of their deliverance from the machinations of Haman (*Esth.* ix); Hamanএর ষড়যন্ত্র হইতে ইহুদীদিগের মুক্তির স্মৃতিরক্ষণার্থ অনুষ্ঠিত উৎসব।

pūr'-ist, *n.* One over-solicitious about purity or nicety in language; বিশুদ্ধ ভাষা প্রয়োগের জন্য অতিরিক্ত আগ্রহশীল ব্যক্তি, বিশুদ্ধিপ্রিয়লেখক। **–ism,** *n.* **Pu-ris'-tic, Pu-ris'-ti-cal,** *adjs.*

Pū'-ri-tăn, *n.* & *adj.* 1. (*Hist.*) An early Protestant dissenter from the Church of England; যে সকল উৎকট পবিত্রতাবাদী ইংরাজ রাজ্ঞী এলিজেবেথ এবং ষ্টুয়ার্টদ্বয়ের রাজত্বকালে ইংলণ্ডের রাজবিধি প্রতিষ্ঠিত ধর্ম্মসংঘ হইতে বিচ্ছিন্ন হইয়া স্বতন্ত্র ধর্ম্মসম্প্রদায় স্থাপন করেন, পবিত্রমতাবলম্বী, পবিত্রপন্থী। 2. A member of any non-religious purist party; "By the *Puritans* of economic principle"; ধর্ম্ম-সংস্রবশূন্য পবিত্রতাবাদী সম্প্রদায়ের সভ্য। 3. One who is, or affects to be, strict or scrupulous in religion or morals; পূতস্মন্য, পবিত্রতাবাদী। ***Adj.*** Of, relating to, or characteristic of, the Puritans; scrupulous in religion or morals; পবিত্রপন্থিসম্বন্ধীয়, পবিত্রপন্থিসুলভ; উৎকটনীতিমার্গাবলম্বী, উৎকটধর্ম্মমার্গাবলম্বী, সূক্ষ্মসদাচারনিষ্ঠ। **–ism,** *n.* The doctrines, ideas or practice of Puritans; strictness esp. in matters of religion or conduct; পবিত্রপন্থা, পবিত্রতাবাদ; ধর্ম্ম বা আচরণসম্বন্ধে কঠোরনিয়মপরায়ণতা, নৈষ্ঠিকতা। **–ize,** *v. i.* & *t.* **–tan'-ic, –tan'-i-cal,** *adjs.* **–tan'-i-cal-ly,** *adv.*

pū'-ri-tȳ, *n.* 1. State or quality of being pure; cleanness; পবিত্রতা, নিষ্কলঙ্কতা, শুদ্ধি, বিমলতা, শুচিতা, প্রশুদ্ধি; পাবিত্র্য, শুদ্ধতা (হিঃ কোঃ), নির্ম্মলতা, পূততা, মেধ্যতা। 2. Innocence; chastity; নিষ্পাপত্ব; সাধুতা, নিষ্কলঙ্কতা, সতীত্ব, সাধ্বীত্ব। 3. Freedom from foreign or vicious idioms, corruptions or barbarisms; বিশুদ্ধি।

pŭrl, *n., v. t.* & *i.* 1. A gold or silver wire, formed into a spiral, used in lace work; লেইসের কাজে ব্যবহৃত পেঁচের ন্যায় জড়ানো সোনা রূপার তার। 2. A loop or a series of loops decorating the edges of a lace, ribbon, etc.; লেইস, ফিতা, প্রভৃতির কিনারার ফাঁস বা ফাঁসশ্রেণী। 3. (*Knitting*) Inversion of stitches which produces a ribbed appearance; (বুনন) ফোঁড়ের যেরূপ ক্রমবিপর্য্যয় দ্বারা মোজা প্রভৃতি শিরাল দেখায়। ***Verb t. & i.*** 1. To border with gold or silver thread or with an edging of minute twisted loops; সোনা বা রূপার তার কিম্বা ক্ষুদ্র ক্ষুদ্র জড়ানো ফাঁস দ্বারা কিনারা শোভিত করা, হাঁসিয়ার কারচুপির কাজ করা। 2. (*Knitting*) To invert the stitches; (বুনট) মোজা প্রভৃতির ফোঁড়ের ক্রমবিপর্য্যয় করা।

pŭrl, *v.i.* & *n.* 1. (Of a stream etc.) To flow or run with a gentle murmur; to run with a whirling motion; (নদীপ্রভৃতিসম্পর্কে) কুল কুল নাদে প্রবাহিত হওয়া; ঘূর্ণিত গতিতে প্রধাবিত হওয়া। ***Noun.*** Whirling motion or murmuring sound as of purling water; কুলুকুলু নাদ, ঘূর্ণিত গতি, আবর্ত্ত, পাক।

purl (pêrl), *n.* 1. (*Formerly*) Ale or beer bittered with herbs as wormwood, for tonic; (পূর্ব্বে)

বলকারক পানীয়রূপে ব্যবহৃত নাগদোনা প্রভৃতি দ্বারা তিক্তীকৃত মদ্য। **2.** (*Now*) A hot beer mixed with gin as a morning draught ; (বর্তমানে) সরাপের সহিত সংমিশ্রিত উষ্ণ বীয়র মদ্য—যাহার এক গ্লাস প্রভাতকালে পান করা হয়।

purl (pêrl), *v. t., i.* & *n.* (*Colloq., Verb t.* & *i.*) To turn upside down ; (চলিত ভাষায়) উলটপালট করা। ***Noun.*** A cropper or heavy fall ; সবেগে পতন।

purl'-êr (pêrl-), *n.* (*Colloq.*) A blow or throw hurling one head foremost ; a fall from a horse ; (চলিতভাষায়) যে আঘাত বা ধাক্কায় কেহ হুমড়ি খেয়ে পড়ে; অশ্বপৃষ্ঠ হইতে পতন।

pur'-lieu (pêr-lū), *n.* **1.** A piece of land in the border or vicinity of a forest ; বনপ্রান্তস্থ ভূখণ্ড, বনান্তিকস্থ ভূখণ্ড। **2.** (*Pl.*) Environs ; outskirts ; (*lit.* & *fig.*); চতুঃপার্শ্ববর্তী স্থানসমূহ; উপকণ্ঠ, উপান্ত। **3.** A place where one can range at large ; যে স্থানে কোন ব্যক্তি যথেচ্ছভাবে বিচরণ করিতে পারে। **4.** A squalid street or part of a town ; নগরের অপরিচ্ছন্ন রাজপথ বা অংশ।

pur'-lin (pêr-), *n.* A horizontal timber supported on a principal rafter and supporting the common rafters ; কোন প্রধান বর্গার উপর অবলম্বিত সাধারণ বর্গাসমূহের অবলম্বন-স্বরূপ শয়ান দারুখণ্ড।

pur-loin' (pêr-loyn), *v. t.* To steal or pilfer ; চুরি করা, ছিঁচকে চুরি করা। **—er,** *n.*

pur'-ple (pêr-pl), *n., adj., v. t.* & *i.* **1.** A colour produced by mixing blue and red ; আনীল লোহিত বর্ণ, ধূমলবর্ণ, ধূম্রবর্ণ। **2.** A pigment or dye which colours purple ; আনীল লোহিত বর্ণ রঞ্জক পদার্থ। **3.** Purple cloth ; রাজা, সম্রাট, প্রভৃতির ধূমলবর্ণের পরিচ্ছদ। **4.** Imperial, royal or consular rank or power ; (*colloq.*) exalted station ; great wealth ; "Born in the *purple*" ; রাজকীয়, সাম্রাজিক বা (রোমের) প্রধান দণ্ডনায়কীয় ক্ষমতা ; (চলিত ভাষায়) উচ্চপদবী ; অতুল ঐশ্বর্য্য, অতুল বৈভব। **5.** The cardinalate ; as, one raised to the *purple* ; পোপের সভাসদত্ব। **6.** (*Pl.*) Swine fever ; a disease in wheat ; স্পর্শসংক্রামক ফুসফুসের রোগ ; গোধুমের রোগ বিশেষ। ***Adj.*** **1.** Of a purple colour ; ধূমলবর্ণ। **2.** (*Poet.*) Red ; dyed as with blood ; (কবিতায়) লোহিত ; রক্তরঞ্জিত, রাগরঞ্জিত। **3.** Brilliant ; splendid ; (of sin) grave ; heinous ; দীপ্ত, উজ্জ্বল ; সমুজ্জ্বল ; (পাপসম্পর্কে) গুরুতর ; ভয়ানক, ঘোর। ***Verb t. & i.*** To make or become purple ; আনীল লোহিত বর্ণ করা, আনীল লোহিত বর্ণ ধারণ করা। **—plish, —ply,** *adjs.* **Purple emperor**—একপ্রকার প্রজাপতি। **Born in the purple**—Born as a prince, consul, etc.; রাজা বা সম্রাট রূপে জাত। **To marry into the purple**—To marry a prince or nobleman ; রাজপুত্র বা সম্ভ্রান্ত লোকের সহিত বিবাহ হওয়া, বড়ঘরে বিবাহ হওয়া।

pur'-pört (pêr-), *n.* **1.** Meaning ; sense ; import ; ভাব, অভিপ্রায়, ভাবার্থ, আশয় ; স্থূলমর্ম্ম, মর্ম্ম ; ফলিতার্থ, তাৎপর্য্য। **2.** (*Rare*) Purpose ; (ক্বচিদ্ ব্যবহৃত) উদ্দেশ্য।

pur'-pört (pêr-), *v. t.* **1.** To import ; to mean ; to convey as a meaning or import ; সূচিত করা, দ্যোতনা করা, ব্যঞ্জনা করা ; বুঝান, অর্থ প্রকাশ করা ; কোন বিশেষ অর্থ বুঝান। **2.** To profess by the tenor, (*with an infinitive*) ; কোন মর্ম্মের হওয়া, কোনরূপ ভাব প্রকাশ করা।

pur'-pose (pêr-pŭs), *n.* **1.** An object or aim ; উদ্দেশ্য, লক্ষ্য। **2.** Intention ; resolution ; as, honesty of *purpose* ; অভিপ্রায় ; সংকল্প। **—ful,** *adj.* **—ful-ly,** *adv.* **—ful-ness,** *n.* **—less,** *adj.* **—less-ly,** *adv.* **—less-ness,** *n.* **—ly,** *adv.* **A novel with a purpose, A purpose-novel**—কোনরূপ মত প্রভৃতি সমর্থন বা বিস্তারের উদ্দেশ্যে লিখিত উপন্যাস, উদ্দেশ্যমূলক উপন্যাস। **On purpose**—In order (to do that etc.); designedly ; not accidentally ; উদ্দেশ্যসহকারে ; উদ্দেশ্য-পূর্ব্বক ; ইচ্ছাপূর্ব্বক নয়। **To some, little or no purpose**—With little, some or no result or effect ; একরূপ নিষ্ফল, নিরর্থক, অকারণ, বৃথা, নিষ্ফল। **To the purpose**—Relevant ; useful for one's purpose ; প্রসঙ্গানুযায়ী, প্রসঙ্গানুকূল, প্রাসঙ্গিক ; উদ্দেশ্যানুকূল। Appositely ; প্রাসঙ্গিকভাবে।

pur'-pose (pêr-pŭs), *v.t.* & *i.* **1.** To intend or design ; to resolve ; অভিপ্রায় করা, উদ্দেশ্য করা ; সংকল্প করা। ***Verb i.*** To have a purpose ; to intend ; উদ্দেশ্য থাকা ; অভিপ্রায় করা। **Am purposed**—(*Archaic*) Intend ; (অপ্রঃ) অভিপ্রায় করি।

pur'-po-sive (pêr-pö-sĭv), *adj.* Having, or indicating, a purpose ; serving, or done with, a purpose ; উদ্দেশ্যবিশিষ্ট, উদ্দেশ্যসূচক, অভিপ্রায়সূচক ; উদ্দেশ্যসাধক, উদ্দেশ্যপূর্ব্বক কৃত।

pur'-pü-ră (pêr-), *n.* **1.** (*Med.*) A disease characterized by livid spots on the skin ; (ভৈষজ্যশাস্ত্র) বেগুণে রঙ্গের পীড়কাবিশিষ্ট একপ্রকার চর্ম্মরোগ, শীতাদ (হঃ চঃ), ধূম্ররোগ (ঐ)। **2.** A genus of molluscs secreting a purple fluid ; একজাতীয় খোলকী প্রাণী—ইহাদের দেহ হইতে একপ্রকার আনীলরক্তবর্ণের রস নিঃসৃত হয়।

pur-pü'-ric (pêr-), *adj.* (*Med.*) Of, or relating to, purpura ; (ভৈষজ্যশাস্ত্র) ধূম্ররোগ সংক্রান্ত। **Purpuric acid**—একপ্রকার কল্পিত দ্রাবক—যাহার লবণ সমূহ আনীল লোহিত বর্ণের হইয়া থাকে।

pur'-pü-rin (pêr-), *n.* A red colouring matter used in dyeing, obtained from madder ; মঞ্জিষ্ঠা হইতে প্রাপ্ত একপ্রকার রঞ্জকপদার্থ।

purr (pêr), *v. i.* To murmur as a cat ; ম্যাও ম্যাও শব্দ করা।

purr (pêr-), *n.* The murmur made by cat ; ম্যাঁও ম্যাঁও শব্দ।

pūr'-ree (-rē), *n.* A yellow colouring matter exported from India and China ; চীন এবং ভারতবর্ষ হইতে রপ্তানীকৃত পীতবর্ণ রঞ্জক পদার্থ বিশেষ [গবাদিকে জীর্ণ আম্রপত্র ভক্ষণ করাইয়া উহাদের মূত্র হইতে 'পুরী' প্রস্তুত করা হয়।]

purse (pêrs), *n.* **1.** A small bag or receptacle for money ; টাকার থলি, ধনভস্ত্রিকা, গেঁজিয়া। **2.** (*Fig.*) Money ; (লক্ষণায়) ধন, অর্থ, টাকা কড়ি। **3.** A sum of money offered as a prize or collected as a present ; as, to win the *purse* in a race ; পুরস্কারের টাকা, উপহারের জন্য সংগৃহীত অর্থ। **4.** A bag or pouch resembling a money-purse ; টাকার থলিয়ার আকার ক্ষুদ্র থলি। **Purse'-ful,** *n.* As much as a purse will contain ; থলি-ভরা, এক তোড়া। **Purse'-less,** *adj.* **Light purse** — Poverty ; নির্ধনতা। **Purse-bearer**—যে ব্যক্তির উপর কোন ব্যক্তি বা কোন সমবায়ের ধন রক্ষার ভার থাকে। **Purse-net**—সূতিজাল (গুপ্ত)। **Purse-proud**—ধনগর্ব্বিত, ধনদৃপ্ত, ধনমত্ত, ধনমদমত্ত। **Purse-seine** — একপ্রকার সূতিজাল। **Purse-strings**—টাকার থলি বাঁধিবার দড়ী। **Heavy or long purse**—Wealth ; ধনৈশ্বর্য্য। **The public purse**—জাতীয় ধনভাণ্ডার। **To hold the purse-strings**—To have the control of expenditure ; খরচের উপর কর্ত্তৃত্ব থাকা। **To loosen the purse-strings**—To be generous in spending money ; মুক্তহস্তে অর্থ ব্যয় করা। **To make up a purse**—To collect subscriptions on behalf of some individual ; to collect a sum of money ; কোন লোকের জন্য চাঁদা সংগ্রহ করা ; নির্দ্দিষ্ট পরিমাণ অর্থ সংগ্রহ করা। **To tighten the purse-strings**—To be sparing of money ; হিসাব করিয়া টাকা ব্যয় করা।

purse (pêrs), *v. t.* & *i.* **1.** To draw up or contract in wrinkles as the brow, lip, etc., (usu. with *up*) ; কুঞ্চিত করা। **2.** (*Rare*) To put into one's purse ; (ক্বচিদ্ ব্যবহৃত) কাহারো টাকার থলিতে রাখা। ***Verb i.*** To become wrinkled ; কুঞ্চিত হওয়া।

purs'-ēr (pêrs-), *n.* The officer in a ship, keeping accounts and having charge of the provisions, money, etc. ; জাহাজের যে কর্ম্মচারী হিসাব রাখে এবং যাহার উপর খাদ্যদ্রব্য, টাকা পয়সা, প্রভৃতি রক্ষার ভার থাকে।

purs'-lāne (pêrs-), *n.* A common succulent plant ; লোণিকা (খোরী), বড় লুচ্ছিয়া (ঐ)।

pur-sū'-ănce (pêr-), *n.* Act of pursuing, following, or prosecuting ; carrying out ; অনুসরণ, অনুবর্ত্তন, অনুবৃত্তি ; সম্পাদন। **In pursuance of**—In accordance with ; in fulfilment or execution of ; কোন কিছুর অনুসারে বা বশবর্ত্তী হইয়া ; কোন কিছু সাধন বা সম্পাদনের উদ্দেশ্যে।

pur-sū'-ănt (pêr-), *adj.* & *adv.* Going in pursuit ; অনুসারী, অনুবর্ত্তী, অনুযায়ী। ***Adv.*** Conformably *to* ; "...*pursuant to* an agreemet" ; অনুসারে, অনুযায়ী। **—ly,** *adv.*

pur-sue' (pêr-sü), *v. t.* & *i.* **1.** To follow with a view to capture or kill ; to chase ; অনুসরণ করা, অনুগমন করা, অনুবর্ত্তন করা ; পশ্চাৎ পশ্চাৎ ছুটা। **2.** (*Fig.*, of a disease, penalty, etc.) To follow or attend persistently ; (লক্ষণায়—রোগ, দণ্ড, প্রভৃতি সম্পর্কে) চিরসঙ্গী হওয়া, চিরসাথী হওয়া। **3.** To prosecute ; to carry on ; অনুসরণ করা ; চালান। **4.** To proceed along ; to follow ; অগ্রসর হওয়া ; অনুগমন করা। **6.** To proceed in compliance or accordance with ; অনুসরণ করা, অনুবর্ত্তন করা। ***Verb i.*** **1.** To go in pursuit ; to follow ; পশ্চাদ্ধাবিত হওয়া ; অনুসরণ করা। **2.** To continue to do or say something ; কোন কিছু বলিতে বা করিতে থাকা। **—su-a-ble,** *adj.*

pur-sū'-ēr (pêr-), *n.* **1.** One who, or that which, pursues ; অনুসরণকারী, অনুগামী। **2.** (*Eccl.* & *Scotch Law*) A prosecutor ; বাদী, ফরিয়াদী, অভিযোগকারী।

pur-suit' (pêr-süt), *n.* **1.** Act of pursuing ; অনুসরণ, অনুধাবন, অনুবর্ত্তন, অনুবৃত্তি, পশ্চাদ্ধাবন। **2.** Prosecution ; অনুসরণ। **3.** Endeavours to attain, to gain or achieve ; as, the *pursuit* of knowledge ; অনুসরণ। **4.** That which one pursues ; profession ; employment ; অনুসৃত বিষয় ; ব্যবসায় ; চাকুরী। **In pursuit of**—অন্বেষণে, অনুসরণে।

pur'-sui-vănt (pêr-swi-), *n.* **1.** An attendant on the heralds ; কুলাচার্য্যের সহচর। **2.** (*Poet.*) An attendant ; (কবিতায়) সহচর। **3.** A state messenger ; রাজদূত।

pur'-sȳ (pêr-), *adj.* Short-winded ; fat ; হাঁসফাঁসকারী, দুঃশ্বাসী ; মোটা, মেদস্বী। **—si-ness,** *n.*

pur'-sȳ (pêr-), *adj.* Puckered ; কুঞ্চিত।

pū'-rū-lĕnt, *adj.* Consisting of, or full of, pus ; of the nature of pus ; discharging pus ; সপূয, পূযময় ; পূযবৎ ; পূযস্রাবী। **—lence, —len-cy,** *ns.* The state of being purulent ; পূযত্ব, সপূযত্ব। **—ly,** *adv.*

pur-vey' (pêr-vā), *v. t.* & *i.* To furnish, provide, or supply as provisions, etc. ; সরবরাহ করা, যোগান। ***Verb i.*** To provide or supply provisions ; to act as a purveyor ; খাদ্যদ্রব্য সরবরাহ করা, খাদ্যদ্রব্য যোগান ; খাদ্যদ্রব্য সরবরাহের কার্য্য করা। **—ance,** *n.* **1.** Act of purveying esp. provisions ; খাদ্যদ্রব্য সরবরাহ। **2.** The right of the crown to provisions etc. at a fixed price and to the use of horses ; নির্দ্ধারিত মূল্যে খাদ্যদ্রব্য ক্রয়ের অথবা অশ্বব্যবহারের রাজার অধিকার ।

pur-vey′-or (pêr-vā-êr), *n.* **1.** One who provides provisions or victuals esp. for a large number ; খাদ্যদ্রব্য সরবরাহকারী । **2.** (*Hist.*) An officer making purveyance for a sovereign ; (ইতিহাস) রাজার খাদ্যদ্রব্য সরবরাহকারী কর্ম্মচারী ।

pur′-view (pêr-vü), *n.* **1.** The body of a statute ; কোন বিধির মূল অংশ । **2.** The scope or intention as of an act, document, scheme, book, occupation, etc. ; আশয়, উদ্দেশ্য । **3.** Range of vision physical or mental ; as, it never came within his *purview* ; দৃষ্টি-সীমা, চিন্তার সীমা ।

pŭs, *n.* A yellowish viscid fluid produced by suppuration ; পূয, [*Syn.* দুষ্য, মলজ, প্রসিত ।]

Pū′-sey-ĭsm (-zĭ-), *n.* (A hostile term for) TRACTARIANISM. **–ite,** *n.*

pûsh, *v. t.* & *i.* **1.** To press against with force ; to move thus ; as, to *push* something *up, down, away, back,* etc. ; ঠেলা দেওয়া, ধাক্কা দেওয়া ; ঠেলিয়া চালান । **2.** To cause to project ; to thrust *out, forth,* etc. ; as, the plant *pushes out* new roots ; উদ্গত করা ; ঠেলিয়া দেওয়া । **3.** To make as one's way forcibly or persistently ; ঠেলিয়া অগ্রসর করা । **4.** To prosecute ; to follow closely and energetically ; as, to *push* a business ; অনুসরণ করা ; উৎসাহ ও উদ্যমের সহিত চালান । **5.** To urge or impel ; প্রণোদিত করা, চালিত করা । **6.** To press the adoption, sale, use, etc. of ; "...*pushing* the sale of British goods" ; কোন বস্তু গ্রহণ, বিক্রয় বা ব্যবহারের জন্য পীড়াপীড়ি করা । **7.** To drive to a conclusion ; as, to *push* an argument to a conclusion ; কোন-রূপ সিদ্ধান্তে উপনীত করান । **8.** To press or bear hard upon ; (usu. *in pass.*) to be hard pressed or put to straits ; as, I am *pushed* for time, money, etc. ; প্রপীড়িত করা ; নিষ্পিষ্ট হওয়া, ক্লিষ্ট হওয়া । **9.** (*Bible*) To thrust against with the horns ; শিং দ্বারা গুঁতা মারা । **10.** To extend as one's conquests etc. ; বিজয় প্রভৃতি বিস্তার করা । ***Verb i.*** **1.** To make a thrust ; to press ; ধাক্কা দেওয়া ; ঠেলা দেওয়া । **2.** To press forward ; to make or force one's way ; ঠেলিয়া অগ্রসর হওয়া ; ভিড় ঠেলিয়া পথ করা । **3.** To push a business or trade ; to be energetic in business etc. ; কোন ব্যবসায় উৎসাহের সহিত চালান ; ব্যবসায় প্রভৃতি পরিচালনে উদ্যমশীল হওয়া । **4.** (*Billiards*) To make a push-stroke ; (বিলিয়ার্ড) কন্দুক ঠেলিয়া চালান । **5.** (*Bible*) To make a thrust with horns ; শিংএর গুঁতা দেওয়া । **Push′-er,** *n.* **Push′-ful, Push′-ing,** *adjs.* Enterprising or pressing in business; energetic ; ব্যবসায়ে উদ্যোগী বা উদ্যমশীল ; উৎসাহী । **Push′-ing-ly,** *adv.* **Push-pin**—ছেলেদের একপ্রকার ক্রীড়া । **I am pushed for time or money**—আমার বড় সময়ের অভাব বা টাকা পয়সার টানাটানি । **To push off**—(Of a person in a boat) To push against the bank with an oar to get the boat out into the stream etc. ; (নৌকাস্থিত লোকের পক্ষে) তটের উপর দাঁড় দ্বারা ঠেলিয়া নৌকা জলে ভাসান । To depart ; প্রস্থান করা । **To push on**—To press on or forward ; ঠেলিয়া অগ্রসর হওয়া । To hasten towards completion ; দ্রুত সিদ্ধির পথে অগ্রসর হওয়া । **To push one's fortune**—To engage actively in making one's fortune ; অতিশয় উদ্যমের সহিত অর্থোর্জ্জনে রত হওয়া । **To push out or out of**—To eject ; উচ্ছেদ করা । **To push through**—To bring to a conclusion ; সমাধা করা ।

pûsh, *n.* **1.** Act of pushing ; a thrust ; a shove ; ধাক্কাপ্রদান ; ঠেলা ; ধাক্কা । **2.** A thrust as of a weapon or animal's horn ; খোঁচা, গুঁতা । **3.** Exercise of influence to promote one's advancement ; "Whether, in this, you can give me a *push*" ; কাহারো উন্নতির জন্য প্রভাব বিস্তার, ঠেলা । **4.** An effort ; a vigorous attempt ; as, I must make a *push* to get it done ; চেষ্টা ; প্রবল চেষ্টা, উদ্যম । **5.** (*Obs.*) An attack or assault ; (অপ্রঃ) আক্রমণ, চড়াও । **6.** Emergency ; crisis ; as, to be put to the *push* ; আকস্মিক সঙ্কট ; সঙ্কট । **7.** The thrust of an arch or the like ; পিল্লা প্রভৃতির উপর তোরণাদির চাপ । **8.** Persevering energy ; enterprise ; self-assertion ; অধ্যবসায়াত্মক উৎসাহ ; উদ্যম ; আত্মম্ভরিতা । **9.** (*Slang*) A gang of thieves, convicts, etc. ; (ইতর ভাষায়) চোরের দল, কয়েদীর দল । **10.** (*Billiards*) A stroke in which a ball is pushed, not struck, (also *push-stroke*) ; (বিলিয়ার্ড) আঘাতের পরিবর্ত্তে কন্দুকে যে ঠেলা দেওয়া হয় । **11.** A part to be pushed ; যে অংশে ঠেলা বা চাপ দিতে হয় । **To be put to the push**—To be tested by difficult circumstances ; কঠিন অবস্থা দ্বারা পরীক্ষিত হওয়া । **To come to the push**—To be tried or tested seriously ; কঠিন পরীক্ষার ভিতর দিয়া অগ্রসর হওয়া ।

pŭsh′-too (or -tö), **–tû,** *ns.* The language of the Afghans ; আফগানদিগের ভাষা, পুস্তু ভাষা ।

pū-sil-lăn′-i-mous (-mŭs), *adj.* Of weak or mean spirit ; faint-hearted ; cowardly ; ক্ষুদ্রমনাঃ, হীনচেতাঃ ; দুর্ব্বলচিত্ত ; ভীরু, কাপুরুষ, হীনপরাক্রম । **–la-nim′-i-ty,** *n.*

State of being pusillanimous; want of courage; ক্ষুদ্রমনস্কতা; কাপুরুষতা। **–ly,** *adv.*

pûss, *n.* 1. A cat (a pet name); পুষি। 2. A hare or tiger; শশক, ব্যাঘ্র। 3. (*Colloq.*) A girl; as, a shy *puss*; (চলিত ভাষায়) মেয়ে। **Puss-moth**—ইয়ুরোপের একপ্রকার বৃহৎকায় তসরে পোকা।

pûss'-y (-ĭ), *n.* (Also, *pussy-cat*) 1. A pet name for a cat; পুষি। 2. An endearing name for a girl; খুকী। 3. A soft furry thing, *e. g.* hazel catkin; কোমললোমময় বস্তু, বিশেষতঃ তরুশাখাবিলম্বী, মার্জ্জার-পুচ্ছাকৃতি হরিদ্বর্ণ পুষ্পস্তবক প্রভৃতি।

pŭs'-tŭ-lāte, *v. t.* & *i.* To form into pustules or blisters; ব্রণ হওয়া, ফুসকুড়ী হওয়া। **–la'-tion,** *n.* **–tu-late,** *adj.*

pŭs'-tŭle, *n.* 1. A pimple; স্ফোট, ব্রণ, বয়সফোঁড়া, পীড়কা (সুশ্রুঃ)। 2. (*Bot.* & *Zool.*) A small wort or swelling; বটী (সাঃ পঃ)। **–tu-lar, –tu-lous,** *adjs.*

pût, *v. t.* & *i.* 1. To throw or hurl as in athletics from hands placed near the shoulder; হাত কাঁধের নিকট রাখিয়া নিক্ষেপ করা। 2. To thrust as a weapon; to send as a missile; as, to *put* a bullet through; অস্ত্রক্ষেপ করা; শরনিক্ষেপ করা, বাণ নিক্ষেপ করা। 3. To lay or set; রাখা, স্থাপন করা। 4. To bring into some specified relation, condition or the like; as, to be *put* to sale; উপস্থাপিত করা। 5. To ascribe or assign (*on* or *upon*); as, to *put* a wrong construction *on* an act or expression; আরোপ করা, নির্দ্দেশ করা। 6. To set before one for consideration, etc.; to propose; as, to *put* a question; কাহারো বিবেচনার জন্য উপস্থাপিত করা; প্রস্তাব করা। 7. To bring to a stated mental or moral condition; as, he was *put* to shame; কোনরূপ নির্দ্দিষ্ট মানসিক বা নৈতিক অবস্থায় আনা, ফেলা। 8. To express in language; to express or state in a particular way; as, to *put* into writing: "He heard a story well *put*"; to translate; ভাষায় ব্যক্ত করা; বিশিষ্টভাবে ব্যক্ত বা বর্ণনা করা; অনুবাদ করা, তর্জ্জমা করা। 9. To ask as a question; প্রশ্ন করা। 10. To force; বাধ্য করা। ***Verb i.*** (*Naut.*) To steer; to turn, (with *back, forth, to, into,* etc.); "Stepped into a fishing boat and *put to* land"; (নৌবিদ্যা) চালান; ফিরা। **Put'-ter,** *n.* **Put-off**—Evasion; postponement; এড়ানি, টালমাটাল; মুলতুবী। **Put on**—Pretended; hypocritical; ছদ্ম; কপট, কৃত্রিম। **Put-up,** *adj.* Got-up or concocted; সাজানো, কৃত্রিম। **A put-up affair**—Something that is not what it appears to be; a got-up plot; কল্পিত বিষয়; সাজানো ব্যাপার। **Cannot put American stock at present prices**—বর্ত্তমান মূল্যে আমেরিকার কোম্পানীর কাগজ দেওয়া হইতে পারে না। **Don't be put upon by him**—Do not be cheated by him; সে যেন তোমাকে না ঠকায়। **Hard put to (it)**—In great difficulty or trouble; মহাকষ্টে। **He puts the circulation at 1000**—১০০০ চলিবে বলিয়া সে অনুমান করে। **I put it to you**—I appeal to you; আমি তোমার কাছে নিবেদন করছি। I invite you to acknowledge; তোমাকে স্বীকার করার জন্য বলছি। **Put a good face on it**—See under FACE. **Put the case to him** or **to the vote**—Submit it to him or to the vote; তাহার কাছে এই বিষয়টী উপস্থাপিত কর অথবা ইহা ভোটে দেও। **Put the words into his mouth** — See under MOUTH. **Put yourself in his place**—Imagine yourself in his place; তোমাকে তাহার স্থলবর্ত্তী বলিয়া মনে কর। **Should put it at Rs. 5**—ইহার মূল্য ৫৲ টাকা ধার্য্য করা উচিত। **The land was put into or under paddy**—The land was sown with paddy; ক্ষেতে ধান দেওয়া হইয়াছে। **To be put to school**—To begin to go to school habitually; বিদ্যালয়ে যাইতে সুরু করা। **To put a bold face on or upon (anything)**—See under FACE. **To put about**—To change the course of (a sailing ship); to tack; to cause as a horse, body of men, to turn round; (of a vessel) to go about; (*chiefly Scot.*) to put to inconvenience; to trouble; (পাইলের জাহাজের) গতিপথ পরিবর্ত্তন করা; পাইলের সাহায্যে জাহাজের মুখ ফিরান; অশ্ব, লোকের দল, প্রভৃতিকে ঘুরান; (জাহাজ সম্পর্কে) এদিক ওদিক যাওয়া; অসুবিধায় ফেলা; কষ্ট দেওয়া। **To put a bullet through**—To shoot; গুলি করা। **To put a bull to a cow or a cow to a bull**—To do so for breeding; পাল দেওয়া। **To put a cheat upon**—To deceive; প্রতারণ করা, ঠকান। **To put a check or stopper**—To check; রোধ করা, বাধা দেওয়া। **To put a girdle round the earth**—To go round the earth; ভূপ্রদক্ষিণ করা। **To put a good face on or upon**—See under FACE. **To put a knife into**—To stab; ছুরি বসাইয়া দেওয়া, ছুরিকাবিদ্ধ করা। **To put an end, period, stop to it**—To stop; বন্ধ করা। **To put an end to oneself or one's life**—To destroy oneself; আত্মহত্যা করা। **To put a rod in pickle**—See PICKLE. **To put aside**—To lay aside; ফেলিয়া রাখা, রাখিয়া দেওয়া। **To put a spoke into one's wheel**—See under SPOKE. **To put (a thing) well**—To express the meanings of (anything) clearly and forcibly; কোন কিছুর অর্থ প্রাঞ্জলভাবে ও ওজস্বিনী ভাষায় ব্যক্ত করা। **To put a veto on or upon**—To prohibit authoritatively; প্রভুত্বসহকারে নিষেধ করা। **To put away**—To store or lay by, as money etc. for future use; সঞ্চিত করা, তুলিয়া রাখা। (*Slang*) To eat or consume, as food, drink, etc.; (ইতর ভাষায়) খাওয়া, পান করা, ধ্বংস করা। (*Slang*) To imprison; (ইতর ভাষায়) জেলে পুরা। (*Slang*) To pawn; (ইতর ভাষায়) বন্ধক দেওয়া। (*Archaic*) To divorce; (ক্বচিদ্ ব্যবহৃত) বিবাহভঙ্গ করা, তালাক দেওয়া (used by the Muhammadans)। To get rid of; to make away with; রেহাই পাওয়া; নিকাশ করা। **To put back**—To check the advance of; to retard; to hinder; গতিরোধ করা; বিলম্ব করান, পিছাইয়া দেওয়া; বাধা দেওয়া। To move back the hands of (a clock etc.); ঘড়ীর কাঁটা পশ্চাদ্দিকে সরাইয়া দেওয়া। To restore to the original place; স্বস্থানে পুনঃপ্রতিষ্ঠিত করা। **To put by**—To put or set aside esp. for future use; তুলিয়া রাখা, রাখিয়া দেওয়া। To thrust aside; to evade, as a question or argument; to postpone as a person with evasion; ফেলিয়া রাখা; কোন প্রশ্ন কিম্বা যুক্তি এড়ান; টালবাহানা করিয়া স্থগিত রাখা। **To put down**—To suppress by force or authority; to crush or quell; দাবাইয়া রাখা; ধ্বংস করা, শান্ত করা, দমন করা। To confute; to put to silence; খণ্ডন করা, নিরাকরণ করা; চুপ-করিয়া দেওয়া, নিরুত্তর করা। To write or set down; লিখা, লিপিবদ্ধ করা। To cease to maintain as an expensive thing; বহুব্যয়সাধ্য বলিয়া পালনে বিরত হওয়া। To reckon; to account; as, I *put* him *down* for ten years old, or as a fool etc.; গণনা করা; হিসাব করা। To attribute; as, he *puts it down* to his nervousness; আরোপ করা। **To put down into black and white**—See under BLACK. **To put forth**—To exert as strength, effort, eloquence, etc.; পরিচালনা করা, প্রয়োগ করা। To put in circulation; to publish; চালান; প্রকাশিত করা। (Of a plant) To send out as leaves, buds, etc.; (*intrans.*) to shoot; to sprout; (বৃক্ষসম্পর্কে) মুকুলাদি উদ্গত করা; (অকর্ম্মক) অঙ্কুরিত হওয়া, অঙ্কুরোদ্গম হওয়া; গজান। (*Intrans.*) To leave a port or harbour; কোন বন্দর বা পোতাশ্রয় ত্যাগ করা। (*Rare*) To stretch out or extend; (ক্বচিদ্ ব্যবহৃত) প্রসারিত করা, বাড়ান। **To put forth a feeler**—To do something to ascertain the views of others; অন্যান্যের মনোগত ভাব জানিবার জন্য কোন কার্য্য করা। **To put forward**—To push into view or prominence; to promote; অগ্রসর করিয়া দেওয়া; উন্নতি করা। To advance for consideration or acceptance; to set forth; to represent; as, *to put forward* a theory etc.; উপস্থাপিত করা; বিবৃত করা; প্রদর্শন করা। **To put heads together**—To consult; to make a plot or plan; কয়েকজনে মিলিয়া পরামর্শ করা; কোনরূপ ফন্দি আঁটা বা ষড়যন্ত্র করা। **To put in**—To install in office etc.; প্রতিষ্ঠিত করা, স্থাপিত করা। To insert, as a bud or scion; প্রবিষ্ট করা। To introduce among others; as, to *put in* a word, blow, remark, etc.; মাঝখান থেকে বলা। To present formally, as a document, evidence, claim, plea, bail, etc.; পেশ করা, উপস্থিত করা, উপস্থাপিত করা, দাখিল করা। (*Intrans.*) To make a claim as *for* election etc.; দাবী করা। To perform (a piece of work) as a part of a whole; কোন কাজের অংশ-বিশেষ সম্পাদন করা। (*Colloq.*) To pass or spend as time; (চলিতভাষায়) সময় কাটান, কাল কাটান। (*Naut.*) To conduct into harbour; (নৌ-বিদ্যা) পথপ্রদর্শন করিয়া পোতাশ্রয়ে নেওয়া। (*Med.*) To restore as a dislocated part to its place; (ভৈষজ্য শাস্ত্র) সন্ধিচ্যুত অস্থি প্রভৃতি স্বস্থানে নিবিষ্ট করা। **To put in a hole**—See under HOLE. **To put in an appearance**—To make an appearance; to be present in person; হাজির হওয়া, উপস্থিত হওয়া; স্বয়ং উপস্থিত থাকা। **To put in a word for**—(Also see under TO PUT IN.) To recommend; সুপারিশ করা। **To put in comparison**—To compare; তুলনা করা। **To put in for**—To put oneself forward, as a candidate for; উপস্থিত হওয়া। **To put in force**—To enforce; আমলে আনা, প্রয়োগ করা। **To put in mind** or **in remembrance**—To remind; স্মরণ করাইয়া দেওয়া। **To put in one's oar**—See under OAR. **To put in practice**—To apply; to make practical use of; প্রয়োগ করা; ব্যবহারে আনা। **To put in the pin**—To give over; to cease certain line esp. a bad line of conduct, পরিত্যাগ করা, ছাড়িয়া দেওয়া; কোনরূপ কার্য্যপ্রণালী পরিত্যাগ করা, বিশেষতঃ কুপথ ছাড়া। **To put into a funk**—(*Colloq.*) To frighten; (চলিত ভাষায়) ভয়ার্ত্ত করা। **To put in(to) execution**—To execute; to put in practice; সম্পাদন করা; কার্য্যে পরিণত করা। **To put into one's hand**—To give to one; কাহারো হাতে দেওয়া। **To put in** or **into one's head**—To suggest to a person; কাহারো কাছে

প্রস্তাব করা। **To put in** or **into requisition**—To require ; চাওয়া, দাবী করা। **To put into shape**—To give a shape or form to ; আকৃতি প্রদান করা, আকার প্রদান করা। **To put into the shade**—To eclipse ; নিষ্প্রভ করা, গৌরব ম্লান করা। **To put it on**—(*Colloq.*) To add to the price ; to overcharge ; (চলিতভাষায়) মূল্যের সহিত যোগ করা ; অতিরিক্ত মূল্যাদি চাওয়া। To simulate exaggerated emotion, sufferings, etc. ; কৃত্রিম আবেগ, দুঃখ, প্রভৃতির আতিশয্য দেখান। **To put it to one**—To ask one ; জিজ্ঞাসা করা, প্রশ্ন করা। **To put money on a horse**—To stake money on it ; কোন ঘোড়ার উপর টাকা বাজী রাখা। **To put new life into one**—To infuse new life into one ; নবজীবন সঞ্চার করা। **To put off**—To postpone ; to defer ; স্থগিত করা বা রাখা ; মুলতুবী রাখা। To evade as a person, demand, etc. ; টালবাহানা করিয়া এড়ান, আজ কাল করা। To lay aside or discard ; ফেলিয়া রাখা। To hinder ; to dissuade *from* ; বাধা দেওয়া ; নিবৃত্ত করা। To take off as clothes etc. ; (কাপড় প্রভৃতি) ছাড়া। To foist as a thing *upon* a person ; কোন জিনিষ ফাঁকি দিয়া চালাইয়া দেওয়া। (*Intrans.*) To depart ; esp. to leave land as a ship ; প্রস্থান করা ; বিশেষতঃ (জাহাজাদি) কূল ছাড়িয়া যাওয়া, ছাড়া। **To put on airs**—To assume airs of importance ; জাঁক দেখান, গর্ব্বিত ভাব ধারণ করা। **To put on a long face**—To look dismal and gloomy ; অপ্রসন্ন বা বিষাদ-গম্ভীর মূর্ত্তি ধারণ করা। **To put one down as**—To take one to be ; অমুক বলিয়া মনে করা। **To put one down for**—To enter one's name as willing to subscribe ; চাঁদার খাতায় কাহারো নাম লিখিয়া লওয়া বা দেওয়া। To enter one's name as qualified for some post etc. ; কোন পদের উপযুক্ত বলিয়া কাহারো নাম লিখিয়া লওয়া। **To put one in the way of**—To show one the way to ; কাহাকে পথ ধরাইয়া দেওয়া। **To put one in the wrong**—To make one appear in the wrong ; কেহ ভুল করিয়াছে বলিয়া প্রতিভাত করান। **To put one on (one's) oath**—To make him speak on (his) oath ; কাহাকে শপথপূর্ব্বক বলান। **To put one on the wrong scent**—To misguide one ; কাহাকেও ভ্রান্ত-পথে চালিত করা। **To put one out of conceit with**—To make one digusted with ; কোন বিষয়ে কাহারো বিরক্তি উৎপাদন করা। **To put one out of court**—To eclipse one ; to disqualify one from speaking with authority ; কাহারো গৌরব ম্লান করা ; প্রামাণিকভাবে বলার অযোগ্য করা। **To put one's back up**—To enrage him ; কাহাকে রাগান। **To put one's best foot foremost**—See under FOOT. **To put oneself about**—To take trouble ; কষ্টস্বীকার করা। **To put oneself out of the way**—To give oneself trouble ; নিজকে কষ্ট দেওয়া। **To put oneself upon the country**—(*Law*) To demand a trial by jury ; (আইন) জুরিদ্বারা বিচারের প্রার্থনা করা। **To put one's foot down**—See under FOOT. **To put one's foot in it**—(*Colloq.*) To spoil anything by indiscretion ; (চলিত ভাষায়) অবিবেচনার দরুণ নষ্ট করা। **To put one's foot into it**—See under FOOT. **To put one's hair up**—See under HAIR. **To put one's hand in one's pocket**—See under POCKET. **To put one's hand to**—To take hold of or seize ; মুট করিয়া ধরা, সাপটিয়া ধরা। **To put one's hand to the plough**—See under PLOUGH. **To put one's head into the lion's (or wolf's) mouth**—See under LION. **To put one's horse to or at a fence**—To invite him to jump it ; লম্ফপ্রদানে বৃতি উল্লঙ্ঘন করার জন্য অশ্বকে উৎসাহিত করা। **To put one's monkey up**—See under MONKEY. **To put one's nose out of joint**—See under NOSE. **To put one's pride in one's pocket**—(*Colloq.*) To assume an air of humility ; (চলিত ভাষায়) বিনীতভাব ধারণ করা। **To put one's shoulder to the wheel**—See under SHOULDER. **To put one through a book**—To make him read through a book ; কাহাকে কোন পুস্তক আদ্যোপান্ত পাঠ করান। **To put on** or **upon**—To dress oneself or another with, as cloths etc. ; পরিধান করা, পরা। To assume ; to take upon oneself ; as, *to put on* a character or appearance ; পরিগ্রহ করা ; ধারণ করা। To impute or ascribe to ; to charge with ; as, to *put* the blame *on* a person ; আরোপ করা ; চাপাইয়া দেওয়া। To set to work ; to put into action ; as, to *put on* workmen or steam ; কাজে লাগাইয়া দেওয়া ; চালান। To deceive ; to cheat ; ঠকান ; প্রতারণা করা, মাথায় হাত বুলান। To set as the hands of a clock to a later hour ; ঘড়ীর কাঁটা পশ্চাদ্দিকে সরাইয়া দেওয়া। To develop as flesh, weight ; "I can never take sugar, *I put on* flesh directly" ; মাংস, প্রভৃতি বৃদ্ধি পাওয়া। To add (so much) to the charge, price, runs, etc. ; মূল্য প্রভৃতির উপর যোগ করা। To stake as money *upon* a horse etc. ; ঘোড়া প্রভৃতির উপর বাজি রাখা, পণ রাখা। To impose on ; to inflict upon ; চাপান ; বিধান করা, প্রয়োগ করা।

To put on one's guard—To cause to be on one's guard ; কাহাকে সতর্ক করা, কাহাকে হুঁসিয়ার করা। **To put on** or **upon one's mettle**—To incite one to the highest pitch ; কাহাকে চরম মাত্রায় উত্তেজিত করা। **To put on one's thinking cap**—To give oneself to thinking over a matter ; কোন বিষয়ে চিন্তায় মগ্ন হওয়া। **To put out**—To hold out ; to extend ; as, *to put out* the hand ; প্রসারিত করা ; বাড়াইয়া দেওয়া। To thrust out ; to eject ; ঠেলিয়া বাহির করা ; নির্গত করা, নিঃসারিত করা। To shoot out as a bud, leaf, etc. ; উদ্গত হওয়া, অঙ্কুরিত হওয়া। To extinguish as a light or fire ; নিভান, নির্ব্বাপিত করা। To place at interest ; to invest ; as, to *put out* funds ; সুদে খাটান ; খাটান, প্রয়োগ করা। To disconcert ; to confuse ; as, to *put* one *out* in speaking ; to provoke ; to offend or annoy ; ব্যর্থ করা, পণ্ড করা ; বিভ্রান্ত করা ; উত্তেজিত করা ; রুষ্ট করা, বিরক্ত করা। To expend as money ; ব্যয় করা, খরচ করা। (*Med.*) To dislocate, as shoulder, ankle, etc. ; (ভৈষজ্যশাস্ত্র) সন্ধিচ্যুত করা। (*Cricket*) To cause as a batsman to be out ; (ক্রীকেট ক্রীড়া) "আউট" করা। To put to inconvenience ; অসুবিধায় ফেলা। To exert as strength, etc. ; শক্তি প্রভৃতি প্রয়োগ করা। To give (work) to be done off the premises ; বাটীর বাহিরে কর[illegible] জন্য (কাজ) দেওয়া। To publish as [illegible]mphlet etc. ; চটি বই প্রভৃতি প্রক[illegible] করা। To destroy the [illegible]ght [illegible]f ; দৃষ্টিশক্তি লুপ্ত করা, দৃষ্টিশক্তি নষ্ট করা। **To put out of countenance**—See under COUNTENANCE. **To put out of court**—To make as evidence of no effect or value ; to render disqualified to speak with authority ; প্রমাণ প্রভৃতি নিষ্ফল বা অকার্য্যকর করা ; প্রামাণিকভাবে বলার জন্য অযোগ্য করা। **To put out of face**—To embarrass ; to shame ; ভ্যাবাচ্যাকা লাগান ; লজ্জিত করা। **To put out of humour** or **temper**—To enrage or provoke ; চটান, রাগান, উত্তেজিত করা। **To put out of sight**—To conceal from view ; দৃষ্টিপথের অন্তরাল করা। **To put out of temper**—To enrage ; ক্রুদ্ধ করা, কুপিত করা। **To put out of the way**—To kill or destroy ; বধ করা, ধ্বংস করা। To give (one) trouble ; কষ্ট দেওয়া। **To put over**—To place in authority over ; কাহারো উপর বসাইয়া দেওয়া। To defer ; to postpone, as a cause in court ; মুলতুবী রাখা ; স্থগিত রাখা। To transfer or transport across ; as, to *put* one *over* a river ; পার করা। (*Colloq.*) To beat or defeat ; (চলিতভাষায়) হারাইয়া দেওয়া। (*Intr. naut.*) To sail over or across ; (নৌ-বিদ্যা) পাইল তুলিয়া যাওয়া বা এক পাড় হইতে অপর পাড়ে যাওয়া। **To put salt on the tail of**—To catch or capture ; ধরা। **To put (some thing) out of one's head**—To cause it to be forgotten ; কোন বিষয় মন হইতে দূর করান। **To put the cart before the horse**—See under CART. **To put the case**—To suppose the case to be ; to suppose ; বিষয়টী ঐরূপ বলিয়া অনুমান করা ; বোধ করা। **To put the hand on** or **unto**—To take hold of ; to engage in ; to begin or undertake ; ধরা ; প্রবৃত্ত হওয়া ; আরম্ভ করা। To take or seize as in theft ; ধরা, পাকড়ান। **To put the horse to (the cart)**—To harness him ; (গাড়ীতে) ঘোড়া যুতা। **To put the last** or **finishing hand** or **touch to**—To make the last corrections in ; to complete ; to perfect ; শেষ চানকান দেওয়া ; শেষ করা ; সর্ব্বাঙ্গসম্পন্ন করা। **To put the screw** or **screws on**—To use pressure upon as for extortion ; to coerce ; পীড়ন করা ; বলপ্রয়োগে বাধ্য করা। **To put this and that** (or **two and two**) **together**—To draw the proper inference from given premises or related circumstances ; প্রদত্ত হেত্ববয়ব বা অন্যোন্যসম্বন্ধবিশিষ্ট ঘটনাসমূহ হইতে সঙ্গত অনুমান করা। **To put through**—To carry out as a task ; সম্পাদন করা। To place as a person in telephonic connection wiht (to) another through one or more exchanges ; টেলিফোঁর তারযোগে কোন ব্যক্তির সহিত অপর ব্যক্তির কথাবার্ত্তা চলিতে পারে এইরূপ ব্যবস্থা করা। **To put through a course of sprouts**—To subject to hard work or discipline ; to give a thorough testing or training (*colloq.* or *dial., U. S*) ; কঠোর পরিশ্রম বা শিক্ষার অধীন করা ; পুঙ্খানুপুঙ্খরূপে পরীক্ষা করা, বিশেষ ভাবে শিক্ষা প্রদান করা। **To put to**—To attach to ; to harness to ; যুতা ; ঘোড়া প্রভৃতিতে সাজ পরান। (*Pass.*) To be reduced to straits ; কষ্টে পড়া, দুরবস্থায় পতিত হওয়া। To refer ; to expose to ; নির্দ্দেশ করা ; বাহিরে স্থাপন করা। To apply to ; প্রয়োগ করা। **To put to a stand**—To stop ; to arrest ; থামা ; গতিরোধ করা। **To put to bed**—To undress and place in bed as a child ; শিশু প্রভৃতিকে কাপড় ছাড়াইয়া বিছানায় শোয়ান। To deliver in, or make ready for, child-birth ; সন্তান প্রসব করা, সন্তান প্রসবের জন্য প্রস্তুত করা। **To put to death**—To kill ; বধ করা, হত্যা করা। **To put to flight**—To force or drive to flight ; পলায়নে বাধ্য করা। **To put**

together—To aggregate; to unite into a whole; জড় করা, একত্র করা; সংযোজিত করা। (*Cricket*) To make up or compile (a score); (ক্রীকেট ক্রীড়া) (জয়াঙ্ক) লাভ করা। **To put to it**—To distress; to press hard; to place in a state of difficulty; কষ্ট দেওয়া, পীড়া দেওয়া; পীড়ন করা। **To put to one's shifts**—To force one to resort to his shifts; কাহাকে নিজের ফিকির খাটাইতে বাধ্য করা। **To put to one's trumps, To put on one's trumps**—To force to the last expedient or to the utmost exertion; শেষ উপায় অবলম্বনে বাধ্য করা, প্রাণপণ চেষ্টা করিতে বাধ্য করা। **To put to press**—To send to the press; ছাপাইতে দেওয়া। **To put to rights**—To put in good order; সুশৃঙ্খল করা, সাজান গোছান। **To put to rout**—To put to flight in disorder; ছত্রভঙ্গ হইয়া পলায়ন করিতে বাধ্য করা। **To put to sea**—(*Intrans.*) To set sail; to leave port; নৌকা বা জাহাজ ছাড়া; বন্দর ত্যাগ করা। **To put to the blush**—See under BLUSH. **To put to the foil**—To blemish; কলঙ্কিত করা। **To put to the horn**—To declare as an outlaw or rebel for not answering to summons; সমন অমান্য করা হেতু আইনের আশ্রয় হইতে বঞ্চিত বলিয়া ঘোষণা করা। **To put to the proof** or **test**—To try or test; পরীক্ষা করা, পরখ করা। **To put to the sword**—To slay with a sword; তরবারী দ্বারা বধ করা। **To put to the vote**—To present for taking a vote upon; কোন বিষয় ভোটে দেওয়া। **To put to trial,** or **on trial**—To test; to try; পরীক্ষায় ফেলা; পরীক্ষা করা। **To put two and two together**—See TO PUT THIS AND THAT TOGETHER. **To put under the screw or screws**—To subject to pressure; to force; পীড়ন করা, নিষ্পেষণ করা; বলপ্রয়োগ করা। **To put up**—To send forth or upwards as a prayer, etc.; to present as a petition; প্রেরণ করা; পেশ করা। To expose as goods for sale; বিক্রয়ের জন্য উপস্থাপিত করা। To pack up in a parcel; to preserve; as, to *put up* pork, beef, etc.; প্যাক করা; তাজা রাখা। To cause as a game to start from a cover; ঝোঁপ হইতে তাড়ান। To employ (one) as jockey; (ঘোড়দৌড়ের) ঘোড় সওয়ার নিযুক্ত করা। To produce as a play on the stage; কোন নাটক রঙ্গমঞ্চে অভিনীত করা। To raise as price; (মূল্যাদি) বৃদ্ধি করা। To propose for elections; নির্ব্বাচনের জন্য প্রস্তাব করা। To erect or set up as a tent, etc.; তাঁবু প্রভৃতি খাটান। To lodge or entertain as travellers, etc.; পথিক প্রভৃতিকে থাকিবার স্থান দেওয়া বা পানভোজনে আপ্যায়িত করা। To publish as banns etc.; বিবাহের ঘোষণা প্রভৃতি প্রকাশিত করা। To put into its ordinary place, where a thing is kept when not in use; as, to *put up* a sword; স্বস্থানে রাখা। (*Intrans.*) To take up one's lodge (*at* an inn, etc.); বাসা নেওয়া। (*Intrans.*) To sheath the sword; অসি কোষবদ্ধ করা। To hide or conceal; লুকান, গোপন করা। **To put up a horse**—To tie it up or put it in a stable; ঘোড়া বাঁধা বা আস্তাবলে রাখা। To concoct; সাজান। **To put up a job**—(*Slang*) To arrange a plot; (ইতর ভাষায়) ষড়যন্ত্র পাকান। **To put up the back**—To arouse to resentment; ক্রোধ উদ্রিক্ত করা। **To put up to**—To incite or instigate; উত্তেজিত করা, প্ররোচিত করা। To give information respecting; to teach; as, to *put* one *up* to a trick or dodge; কোন বিষয়ে সংবাদ দেওয়া; শিক্ষা দেওয়া। **To put up to auction** or **sale**—To offer for sale at an auction sale; নিলামে দেওয়া। **To put up with**—To tolerate; to endure, as insult, etc.; সহ্য করা; অপমান প্রভৃতি সহা। **What has put him on the meddling**—What has led him to interfere; সে কেন হস্তক্ষেপ করিল?

pût, *n.* **1.** A throw as of a stone, weight, as an athletic action; প্রস্তর, গুরুভার দ্রব্য প্রভৃতি, ক্ষেপণ। **2.** A game at cards; একপ্রকার তাস খেলা। **3.** The option of delivering a fixed amount of a stock at a fixed price within a time; নির্দ্দিষ্ট সময়ের মধ্যে নিরূপিত মূল্যে নির্দ্ধারিত পরিমাণ কোম্পানীর কাগজ সমর্পণের ইচ্ছাধীনতা।

pût, pûtt, *v. i., t.* & *n.* To strike the golf-ball slightly with the club so as to get it into the hole; গর্ত্তে ফেলাইবার জন্য দণ্ড দ্বারা গোলফ খেলার কন্দুকে আঘাত করা। ***Verb t.*** To strike (the golf-ball) thus; ঐরূপ ভাবে (গোলফ্ খেলার কন্দুকে) আঘাত করা। ***Noun.*** Such a stroke; ঐরূপ আঘাত। **Put'-ter,** *n.* **Putting-green**—যে মসৃণ ভূখণ্ডের উপর দিয়া গোলফ্ খেলার কন্দুক দণ্ডদ্বারা তাড়ন পূর্ব্বক গর্ত্তে নিক্ষেপ করা হয়।

pū'-tă-tive (-tĭv), *adj.* Supposed; reputed; as, his *putative* father; কল্পিত, অনুমিত, গৃহীত, পরিগণিত, বিবেচিত; খ্যাত, লোকপ্রসিদ্ধ। **—ly,** *adv.*

pūte, *adj.* (*Archaic*) In phrases, **Pure pute, Pure and pute**—Mere; (অপ্রঃ) কেবল, শুদ্ধ।

pū'-tē-ăl, *n.* (*Rom. antiq.*) A well curb; (রোমক প্রত্নতত্ত্ব) কূয়ার মুখের ঘের, কূপ-বেষ্টনী।

pût'-lŏg, –lŏck, *ns.* A short piece of timber supporting the floor

a, putlog; *b b*, putlog-holes.

of a scaffold; মাচানএর পাটাতনের অবলম্বনস্বরূপ খাটো আড় কাঠ।

pü'-trĕ-fȳ, *v. i.* & *t.* **1.** To become putrid; to rot; পচা; গলিত হওয়া। **2.** To be gangrenous; to suppurate; পচিতে আরম্ভ করা; পুঁয হওয়া। **3.** (*Fig.*) To become morally corrupt; কলুষিত হওয়া। ***Verb t.*** **1.** To make putrid; to cause to rot, (*rare*); পচান; গলিত করা (কচিদ্‌ব্যবহৃত)। **2.** To make gangrenous; পচাইতে আরম্ভ করা। **–fac'-tion,** *n.* **1.** Act, state, or process, of putrefying; decomposition; পচন, গলিতাবস্থা, পুতি; গলন, সড়ন (সাঃ পঃ)। **2.** (*Fig.*) Moral corruption or decay; (লক্ষণায়) নীতিদুষ্টতা, নৈতিক অপকর্ষ। **–fac'-tive,** *adj.*

pü-trĕs'-cent (-ĕnt), *n.* **1.** Becoming putrid or rotten; decomposing; পচনোন্মুখ; পচনশীল। **2.** Of, or relating to, purtrefaction; পচনসম্বন্ধীয়, গলনসম্বন্ধীয়। **–cene,** *n.* **–ci-ble,** *adj.*

pü'-trid, *adj.* **1.** Decomposed; offensively rotten; গলিত, দুর্গন্ধ; পূতিগন্ধময়। **2.** Of, or pertaining to, putrefaction; foul; পচনসম্বন্ধীয়; দূষিত। **3.** (*Fig.*) Corrupt; (লক্ষণায়) দূষিত, কলুষিত। **–ly,** *adv.* **–ness, –trid'-i-ty,** *ns.* **Putrid fever**—মোহকারক সন্নিপাতজ্বর। **Putrid sore throat** — একপ্রকার রোগ — যাহাতে কণ্ঠদেশে একটী নূতন ঝিল্লী জাত হয়।

pûtt, See PUT, *v. i.*, *t.* & *n.*

pŭt'-tȳ, *n.* & *v. t.* **1.** (Also *glaziers' putty*) A kind of cement used for fixing panes of glass, filling holes, etc. compounded of whiting and linseed-oil; জানালার কাচ বসান, রন্ধ্রাদি পূর্ণ করার জন্য চাখড়ি, তিসির তৈল, প্রভৃতি সহযোগে প্রস্তুত একপ্রকার আঠা, পুটিন। **2.** (Also *jewellers' putty*) A powder of calcined tin and lead for polishing glass and metal; ধাতু এবং কাচ পালিশ করার জন্য জারিত বঙ্গের (এবং সীসক) চূর্ণ। **3.** (Also *plasterers' putty*) A fine mortar used in stopping crevices; ফোকর প্রভৃতি বন্ধ করার জন্য জলমিশ্রিত চূণা। ***Verb t.*** To fix, cement, stop, fill or *fix up* with putty; পুটিনদ্বারা লাগান, রোধ করা, জলমিশ্রিত চূণাদ্বারা পূর্ণ করা।

pŭz'-zle (-zl), *n.* **1.** Perplexity; embarrassment; হতবুদ্ধিতা; কিংকর্ত্তব্যবিমূঢ়তা, বিভ্রাট। **2.** A difficult problem or question; a toy, contrivance or problem designed to test ingenuity; ধাঁধা, সমস্যা; কূট। **Puzzle-head, –pate**—ভ্রান্তবুদ্ধি ব্যক্তি। **Puzzle-headed, –pated**—ভ্রান্তবুদ্ধি। **Puzzle-peg** — কুকুর যাহাতে ভূমির অতি নিকট নাসিকা আনত না করিতে পারে—তজ্জন্য উহার নিম্ন হনুতে যে কাষ্ঠখণ্ড সংবদ্ধ করা হয়।

pŭz'-zle (-zl), *v. t.* & *i.* **1.** To perplex; to embarrass; to confuse; হতবুদ্ধি করা; কিংকর্ত্তব্যবিমূঢ় করা; ঘুলাইয়া দেওয়া। **2.** To solve or make *out*; "The inscriptions ... not sufficiently legible to induce us to *puzzle* them *out*"; সমাধান করা, নির্ণয় করা, বাহির করা। **3.** (*Rare*) To make intricate; (কচিদ্ ব্যবহৃত) জটিল করা। **–dom,** *n.* The realm of puzzle; perplexity; ধাঁধার রাজ্য; কিংকর্ত্তব্যবিমূঢ়তা। **–ment, –zler,** *ns.* **–zling,** *adj.* **–zling-ly,** *adv.* **Monkey-puzzle**—এক প্রকার সরল বৃক্ষ।

puzzolana, *n.* See POZZOLANA.

pȳ-æ'-mĭ-ă (-ē-), *n.* Blood-poisoning due to the absorption of putrid matters into the system; রক্তে ক্ষতোৎপন্ন গলিত পদার্থের মিশ্রণ হেতু যে রক্তদুষ্টি রোগ জন্মে। **–mic,** *adj.*

pȳc'-nō-stȳle, *adj.* & *n.* With columns standing close to one another; ঘনসন্নিবিষ্ট স্তম্ভরাজিবিশিষ্ট। ***Noun.*** A pycnostyle colonnade or building; ঘনসন্নিবিষ্টস্তম্ভরাজি, ঘনসন্নিবিষ্ট স্তম্ভরাজিপরিশোভিত হর্ম্ম্য।

pȳg'-mȳ, pĭg–, *n.* & *adj.* **1.** One of a dwarfish race of men described by ancient Greek authors to have inhabited parts of Ethiopia or India; প্রাচীন গ্রীক গ্রন্থকারগণের গ্রন্থে উক্ত ভারত বা ইথিপিয়াদেশের স্থানবিশেষবাসী খর্ব্বকায় জাতির লোক, কেতুপুত্র (তাজঃ), কেতুগণ *pl.* (তাজঃ)। [হোমার, আরিস্তোতল, হীরোডোটাস প্রভৃতির গ্রন্থে এই বালখিল্য-গণের বর্ণনা দৃষ্ট হয়। হোমরের মতে ইহারা সমুদ্রের দক্ষিণোপকূলে বাস করিত। কবি হোমর এই বালখিল্যগণের সহিত ক্রৌঞ্চপক্ষীর সংগ্রাম বর্ণনা করিয়াছেন।] **2.** (*Cap.*) One of a dwarf race of equatorial Africa, (usu *pl.*, with *the*); আফ্রিকার বিষুবসন্নিহিত প্রদেশবাসী জাতিবিশেষভুক্ত খর্ব্বকায় ব্যক্তি [এই জাতীয় লোকের নাক চ্যাপ্টা, চুল কোঁকড়ানো এবং উচ্চতা প্রায় ৪½ ফিট হইয়া থাকে।] **3.** A dwarf; anything very small of its kind; বামন, খর্ব্বাকৃতি ব্যক্তি; অতি ক্ষুদ্রাকার বস্তু। **4.** (*Fig.*) A person of small importance or insignificant quality; (লক্ষণায়) খাটো লোক, (cf. আমি তোমার চেয়ে কোন অংশে খাটো)। **5.** An elf; ভূত বা অপদেবতা। ***Adj.*** Of, or relating to, the pygmies; dwarf; very small; বামনজাতিসম্বন্ধীয়; বামন; খর্ব্বাকার, হ্রস্বকায়, হ্রস্বমূর্ত্তি। **–mae'-an,** *adj.*

pȳ'-lŏn, *n.* A gateway, esp. of an Egyptian temple; তোরণ, বিশেষতঃ মিশরদেশীয় দেবমন্দিরের দ্বারমণ্ডপ।

pȳ-lö′-rŭs, *n.* (*Anat.*) The opening from the stomach into the intestine; (শারীরসংস্থানবিদ্যা) আমাশয়ের নিম্নদিগের মুখ। **—lor′-ic,** *adj.*

pȳ-ö-gĕn′-ĕ-sis, *n.* (*Physiol.*) The formation of pus; (শারীরবিজ্ঞান) পূযোৎপাদন। **Py′-oid,** *adj.*

pȳ-ŏr-rhe′-ă (-rē-), **—rhœ′—** (-rē-), *ns.* (*Med.*) A discharge of pus; (ভৈষজ্য-শাস্ত্র) পূযসঞ্চার।

pȳr′-ă-cănth, *n.* An evergreen thorny shrub; একপ্রকার কণ্টকময় চিরহরিত গুল্ম।

pȳr′-ă-mid, *n.* **1.** (*Geom.*) A solid body standing on a triangular square or polygonal base and terminating in a point at the top; (জ্যামিতি) ত্রিকোণ, চতুষ্কোণ বা পঞ্চকোণ ভূমির উপরিস্থিত ঘন, সূচি (হিঃ কোঃ)। **2.** A massive structure or monument with a polygonal (usu. square) base and with sloping sides meeting at a point, esp. in Egypt; মিসরের পিরামিড। **3.** A pyramid-shaped thing or pile of things; সূচিক্ষেত্রের আকার বস্তু বা বস্তুসমুচ্চয়। **4.** A tree grown or pruned in pyramidal shape; পিরামিডের আকারে উৎপাদিত বা ছাঁটা গাছ। **5.** (*Billiards, pl.*) A game played with 15 red balls and one white ball; (বিলিয়ার্ড খেলা) ১৫টী লোহিত ও একটী শ্বেত বর্ণের কন্দুক দ্বারা যে খেলা খেলিতে হয়। **6.** A poem in which the successive lines increase or decrease in length; একপ্রকার কবিতা—যাহার প্রতি পরবর্ত্তী পংক্তি পূর্ব্ববর্ত্তী পংক্তি অপেক্ষা দৈর্ঘ্যে অল্প বা অধিক হইয়া থাকে। **—ist,** *n.* One who studies the structure and history of the Egyptian Pyramids; যে ব্যক্তি মিসরের পিরামিডের গঠন প্রণালী ও ইতিহাস সম্বন্ধে আলোচনা করেন। **Py-ram′-i-dal,** *adj.* **Py-ram′-i-dal-ly,** *adv.*

pȳre, *n.* A funeral pile; চিতা।

pȳr′-ĕth-rŭm, *n.* A genus of plants; একজাতীয় গুল্ম।

pȳ-rĕt′-ic, *adj.* (*Med.*) Of, or relating to, fever; (ভৈষজ্যশাস্ত্র) জ্বরসম্বন্ধীয়।

pȳ-rĕx′-i-ă, *n.* Fever; জ্বর। **—al, —ic. —i-cal,** *adjs.*

pȳr-hē-li-ŏm′-ĕ-têr, *n.* An instrument for measuring the intensity of the heat of the sun's rays; রবিকিরণতাপমাপক যন্ত্র, রৌদ্রমান যন্ত্র, রবিতাপমাপক (হিঃ কোঃ)।

pȳr′-i-dīne, *n.* (*Chem.*) A nitrogenous base being a colourless liquid alkaloid; (রসায়নশাস্ত্র) অস্থি-তৈল পরিস্রবণান্তে প্রাপ্ত হাঁপানি রোগে ব্যবহৃত একপ্রকার অবর্ণ যবক্ষারজানবিশিষ্ট তরল ক্ষারপদার্থ।

pȳ-rī′-tēs, *n.* (Also *Iron-pyrites*) Either of the two sulphides of iron; মাক্ষিক (রঃ প্রঃ), মাক্ষী (ঐ), মাক্ষীক (ঐ), আবর্ত্ত (মঃ উঃ), কামারি (ঐ), বিটমক্ষিকা (ঐ), তাপীসমুদ্ভব (নিঘণ্টু), তাপীজ (মঃ উঃ), তাপ্যুত্থসংজ্ঞক, (ঐ), তাপ্য (ঐ), তাপ্যক (ঐ), মধু (ভাবঃ প্রঃ), নীলমৃত্তিকা, তণ্ডুলীয়, তণ্ডুলীয়ক। **—rit′-ic, Pyr-i-tif′-er-ous, Pyr′-i-tous,** *adjs.* **Pyr′-i-tize,** *v. t.* To convert into pyrites; মাক্ষিকে পরিণত করা। **Copper pyrites**—তাপ্য (রঃ প্রঃ সুঃ প্রঃ), বিমল (রঃ প্রঃ), মাক্ষিক (ঐ)। **Golden pyrites**—স্বর্ণমাক্ষিক (রঃ প্রঃ সুঃ প্রঃ), সুবর্ণমাক্ষিক (ধাঃ প্রঃ), তাপ্য (রঃ প্রঃ), ধাতুমাক্ষিক (রাজঃ নিঃ), মধুধাতুক (ঐ), হেমমাক্ষিক (রঃ প্রঃ)। **Silvery (radiated) pyrites**—তারামাক্ষিক (রঃ প্রঃ সাঃ প্রঃ), অমলমাক্ষিক (রঃ প্রঃ), রৌপ্যমাক্ষিক (ঐ)। **White pyrites**—তারামাক্ষিক। **Yellow pyrites**—সুবর্ণমাক্ষিক (ঠাকুর)।

pȳ′-rö. See PYROGALLIC.

pȳ-rö-ĕ-lĕc′-tric, *adj.* Becoming electrically polar under heat; উত্তাপযোগে ধ্রুবত্বপ্রাপী। **—tric′-i-ty,** *n.*

pȳ-rö-găl′-lic (-ic), *adj.* (*Chem.*) Of, relating to, or designating, a particular acid; (রসায়নশাস্ত্র) দ্রাবকবিশেষসম্পর্কীয়, দ্রাবকবিশেষসূচক। **Pyrogallic acid**—(*Abbr. pyro.*) আলোকচিত্র প্রস্তুতে ব্যবহৃত দ্রাবকবিশেষ।

pȳ-rö-gĕ-nĕt′-ic, *adj.* **1.** Producing heat esp. in the body; উত্তাপজনক, দৈহিক উত্তাপজনক। **2.** Having the property of producing fever; জ্বরোৎপাদক। **—gen′-ic,** *adj.* Same as PYROGENETIC, *adj.* 2.

pȳ-rŏg′-ĕ nous (-nŭs), *adj.* **1.** Produced by fire; igneous; অগ্নিজাত; আগ্নেয়। **2.** (*Med.*) Pyrogenic; (ভৈষজ্য-শাস্ত্র) জ্বরোৎপাদক।

pȳ-rŏg′-ră-phȳ, *n.* Same as POKER-WORK. **—pher,** *n.* **—phist,** *n.* **Py′-ro-graph,** *v. i.* **—ro-graph′-ic,** *adj.*

pȳ-rö-grā-vūre′, *n.* Same as POKER-WORK (which see).

pȳ-rŏl′-ă-trȳ, *n.* Fire-worship; অগ্নিপূজা, অনলোপাসনা।

pȳ-rö-lig′-nē-ous (-ŭs), *adj.* Derived from wood by fire or heat, as an acid; উত্তাপ বা অগ্নি-সহযোগে কাষ্ঠ হইতে জাত।

pȳ-rö-lū′-site, *n.* A native manganese dioxide; আঞ্জনী (যোঃ), আঞ্জন (ঐ)।

pȳ′-rö-măn-cȳ, *n.* Divination by means of sacrificial fire; যজ্ঞীয় অগ্নিদর্শনে ভবিষ্যকথন।

pȳ-rö-mā′-ni-ă, *n.* An insane disposition to incendiarism; গৃহদাহনোন্মাদ। **—ac,** *n.* One affected with pyromania; গৃহদাহনের বাতিকগ্রস্ত ব্যক্তি। **—a-cal,** *adj.*

pȳ-rŏm′-ĕ-têr, *n.* An instrument for measuring high degrees of heat; উচ্চতাপমান যন্ত্র, অত্যুষ্ণতাপমাপক (হিঃ কোঃ)। **—ro-met′-ric, —ro-met′-ri-cal,** *adjs.* **—ro-met′-ri-cal-ly,** *adv.* **—try,** *n.*

pȳ′-rōpe, *n.* A variety of garnet deep red in colour; একপ্রকার গাঢ় রক্তবর্ণের বৈক্রান্ত মণি।

pȳ-rŏph′-ŏ-rŭs, *adj.* A substance which ignites spontaneously on exposure to air ; একপ্রকার পদার্থ—যাহা বাতাসের সংস্পর্শে দপ্ করিয়া জ্বলিয়া উঠে। **—ro-phor′-ic, —rous,** *adjs.*

pȳ-rŏ-phŏ-tŏg′-ră-phȳ, *n.* A process in which heat is used to fix a photographic picture ; আলোকচিত্র-প্রস্তুতের পদ্ধতিবিশেষ—যাহাতে উত্তাপের সাহায্যে আলোকচিত্রের স্থাপনা করা হয়। **—pho′-to-graph,** *n.* A photographic picture burnt in on glass or porcelain ; কাচ বা চীনামাটীর উপর পোড়াইয়া যে আলোকচিত্র অঙ্কিত করা হয়। **—to-graph′-ic,** *adj.*

pȳ-rŏ-tĕch′-nic, *adj.* & *n.* **1.** Of, or relating to, fireworks ; of the nature of fireworks ; আতসবাজী-সম্বন্ধীয়, অগ্নিক্রীড়াসম্বন্ধীয়, অগ্নিক্রীড়াত্মক। **2.** (*Fig.*) Brilliant ; sensational ; "...his conversation became quite a *pyrotechnic* display" ; (লক্ষণায়) সমুজ্জ্বল, দীপ্যমান ; উত্তেজনাপূর্ণ, অগ্নি-নির্ঝর বৎ। ***Noun.*** (*Pl.*) The art of making fireworks ; the making and use of fireworks esp. for display ; (*lit.* & *fig.*) ; অগ্নিক্রীড়াকলা ; আতসবাজিতৈরী, আতসবাজি। **—ni-cal,** *adj.* **—ni-cal-ly,** *adv.* **—nist, —ny,** *ns.* Same as PYROTECHNICS.

pȳ-rŏx′-ȳ-lin, *n.* A kind of explosive; gun-cotton ; একপ্রকার বিস্ফোরক দ্রব্য ; গন্ধকদ্রাব ও তাম্রদ্রাবসিক্ত তুলা হইতে প্রস্তুত একপ্রকার মহাশক্তিশালী বিস্ফোরক দ্রব্য। **—yl′-ic,** *adj.*

Pȳr′-rhic (-ic), **pȳr—,** *n.* & *adj.* **1.** A kind of martial dance among the ancient Greeks ; প্রাচীন গ্রীকদিগের মধ্যে প্রচলিত এক-প্রকার রণতাণ্ডব। **2.** (*Pros.*) A foot consisting of two short syllables ; (ছন্দঃশাস্ত্র) ক্ষুদ্র শব্দাংশদ্বয় বিশিষ্ট কবিতার চরণ। ***Adj.*** **1.** Of, relating to, or designating, the ancient Greek martial dance ; প্রাচীন গ্রীসদেশীয় রণতাণ্ডবসম্বন্ধীয়। **2.** (*Pros.*) Of, relating to, or consisting of, Pyrrhics ; (ছন্দঃশাস্ত্র) ক্ষুদ্র শব্দাংশদ্বয়-বিশিষ্ট কবিতার চরণসম্বন্ধীয়।

Pȳr′-rhic (-ic), *adj.* Of, or relating to, Pyrrhus esp. Pyrrhus, the king of Epirus ; পিরাসসম্বন্ধীয়, বিশেষতঃ এপিরাসরাজ পিরাসসম্বন্ধীয়। **Pyrrhic-victory**—বহুসৈন্যাদি ক্ষয়ের পর যে জয়লাভ করা হয়, সর্ব্বনেশে জয়। [কথিত আছে ভীষণ লোক-ক্ষয়কর যুদ্ধে রোমানদিগকে পরাজিত করার পর যাহারা Pyrrhusকে অভিনন্দন করিতে আসেন তিনি তাহাদিগকে লক্ষ্য করিয়া বলিয়াছিলেন,—এমন আর একটী জয়, তবেই আমার দফা নিকাশ।]

Pȳr′-rhon-ĭsm (-ŏn), *n.* **1.** The doctrines of the Greek sceptic school founded by Pyrrho (300 B. C.) ; গ্রীক দার্শনিক Pyrrho কর্ত্তৃক প্রবর্ত্তিত নাস্তিকতাবাদ। **2.** Scepticism; universal doubt; নাস্তিকতা; সর্ব্ববিষয়ে সন্দেহ। **—rho-ni-an, —rhon′-ic,** *adjs.* & *ns.* **—rho-nist,** *n.*

pȳ′-rŭs, *n.* A genus of malaceous trees ; নাসপাতী, শেওফল, প্রভৃতি বৃক্ষের সাধারণ নাম।

Pȳ-thăg′-ŏ-rē-ăn, *adj.* & *n.* Of, or relating to, Pythagoras, the Greek philosopher of Samos ; গ্রীক দার্শনিক পিথাগোরাসসম্বন্ধীয়। ***Noun.*** A follower of Pythagoras ; পিথাগোরাসের মতাবলম্বী ব্যক্তি। **Pythagorean proposition**—ইউক্লিডের জ্যামিতির প্রথম খণ্ডের সপ্তচত্বারিংশৎ প্রতিজ্ঞা।

Pȳth′-ĭ-ăn, *adj.* & *n.* Of, or pertaining to, Delphi or Apollo ; relating to Apollo's oracle or priestess at Delphi ; প্রাচীন গ্রীসের অন্তঃপাতী ডেলফীনগরসম্পর্কীয়, এপলোদেব সম্পর্কীয় ; ডেলফীনগরীস্থ এপলোদেবের আদেশবাণী প্রচারস্থান সম্বন্ধীয়, উক্তস্থানের যাজিকাসম্পর্কীয়। ***Noun.*** A native of Delphi ; specifically the Delphic priestess ; also, the Delphic Apollo ; ডেলফীর অধিবাসী ; ডেলফীর দৈববাণীপ্রকাশের স্থানের যাজিকা ; ডেলফীর এপলোদেব।

pȳ′-thŏn, *n.* **1.** (*Gk. Myth.*) The huge serpent slain by Apollo near Delphi ; (গ্রীক পুরাণ) ডেলফীর নিকটে এপলোদেব কর্ত্তৃক নিহত প্রকাণ্ড ভুজঙ্গ। **2.** A genus of large snakes ; (*popularly*) any large snake ; একজাতীয় প্রকাণ্ডকায় সর্প ; বোড়া সাপ, অজগর। **—thon′-ic,** *adj.*

pȳ′-thŏn, *n.* **1.** A sooth-saying spirit ; ভবিষ্যবাদী দেবযোনি বিশেষ। **2.** One possessed by such a spirit ; ঐরূপ দেবযোনি দ্বারা আবিষ্ট ব্যক্তি। **—ess,** *n.* **—thon′-ic,** *adj.*

pȳ-ū′-rĭ-ă, *n.* (*Med.*) A morbid condition in which pus is discharged with urine ; একপ্রকার রোগ—যাহাতে মূত্রের সহিত পূয নির্গত হয়, স্বরামেহ (সাঃ পঃ)।

pȳx, *n.* & *v. i.* **1.** (*Eccl.*) The box or covered vessel in which the consecrated bread is preserved ; (যাজকীয় বিদ্যা) যে তোরঙ্গ বা আচ্ছাদিত পাত্রে পবিত্রীকৃত রুটি রক্ষিত হয়। **2.** The box in which the sample coins are placed in the English mint for trial of the weight and purity ; ইংলণ্ডের টাঁকশালায় যে তোরঙ্গে ওজন ও বিশুদ্ধি পরীক্ষার জন্য নমুনাস্বরূপ মুদ্রা রক্ষিত হয়। ***Verb t.*** To place as coins in the pyx ; to test by weight and assay as the coins in the pyx ; ওজন ও বিশুদ্ধি পরীক্ষার জন্য তোরঙ্গে নমুনা-স্বরূপ মুদ্রা রাখা ; ওজন এবং বিশুদ্ধি দ্বারা মুদ্রা পরীক্ষা করা। **Trial of the pyx** — ইংলণ্ডের স্বর্ণকারসম্প্রদায়ের সভাসদ্গণকর্ত্তৃক টাঁকশালের মুদ্রার ওজন ও বিশুদ্ধি বিষয়ে প্রতিবর্ষে যে পরীক্ষা হয়।

pȳx-ĭd′-ĭ-ŭm, *n.* (*Bot., Pl.* -A), A capsule of which the top comes off like the lid of a box ; যে বীজকোষের উপরিভাগ বাক্সের ডালার মত খুলিয়া আসে, শরাবকুট (সাঃ পঃ)।

pȳx′-ĭs, *n.* **1.** Same as PYXIDIUM. **2.** A box or casket ; বাক্স, তোরঙ্গ।

Q

Q, 1. The seventh letter of the English alphabet; ইংরাজী বর্ণমালার সপ্তদশতম অক্ষর। 2. (*Skating*) A change of edge followed by a turn; (স্কেটিং খেলা) একপ্রকার আবর্ত্তন। **Reverse Q**—(*Skating*) (স্কেটিং) একপ্রকার আবর্ত্তন। **In a merry Q (cue)**—In a merry mood or humour; আনন্দে, খোস মেজাজে। **Q in a corner**—Something not seen at first, but noticed subsequently; যাহা প্রথমে দৃষ্ট হয় না, কিন্তু পরে লক্ষ্য করা যায়। **To mind one's P's & Q's**—See under P.

quă, *conj.* In the capacity of; as being; as, he spoke *qua* a private person; কোনরূপ পদে বা কাজে; স্বরূপে।

quăck, *n., adj., v. i. & t.* A pretender to skill or knowledge, esp. medical; a charlatan; কুবৈদ্য; নাড়ী-টেপা, হাতুড়িয়া, গোবৈদ্য। *Adj.* Of, or relating to, quacks or quackery; used or prescribed by quacks; pretending to cure diseases; as, a *quack* doctor or medicine; কুবৈদ্যসম্বন্ধীয়; কুবৈদ্যগণদ্বারা ব্যবহৃত বা বিহিত; হাতুড়িয়া। *Verb i.* 1. To act the quack; হাতুড়িয়াগিরি করা। 2. To make vain pretensions; to boast; অমূলক দাবী উপস্থাপিত করা; বড়াই করা। *Verb t.* 1. To treat as a quack or charlatan; হাতুড়িয়া চিকিৎসা করা। 2. To advertize boastfully as cure etc.; বাগাড়ম্বরপূর্ণ ভাষায় ঔষধ প্রভৃতির বিজ্ঞাপন প্রচার করা। **Quack'-er-y**, *n.* Practice or boastful pretences of a quack; humbug; হাতুড়িয়াগিরি; ফাঁকি, প্রতারণা। **Quack'-ish**, *adj.*

quăck, *v. i. & n.* 1. To cry harshly as a duck; হাঁসের মত প্যাঁক প্যাঁক করা। 2. To utter a cry like that of a duck; প্যাঁক প্যাঁক করা। 3. To boast; to talk noisily and pretentiously; বড়াই করা; লম্বা চওড়া কথা বলা। *Noun.* The cry of the duck; a sound like this cry; হাঁসের ডাক; প্যাঁক প্যাঁক শব্দ। **Quack quack**—(*Nursery*) A duck; (ছেলেদের ছড়ায়) হাঁস।

quăck'-săl-vêr, *n.* (*Now rare*) A quack-doctor; a charlatan; হাতুড়িয়া; নাড়ী-টেপা।

quad (kwŏd), *n.* See QUADRANGLE, QUADRAT.

quad'-ra-ble (kwŏd-ră-bl), *adj.* (*Math.*) That may be squared; (গণিত শাস্ত্র) বর্গমূলাকর্ষণযোগ্য।

quad-ră-gē-nā'-ri-ăn (kwŏd-), *adj. & n.* Forty years old; চত্বারিংশৎবর্ষবয়স্ক। *Noun.* A person forty years old; চত্বারিংশৎ-বর্ষ বয়স্ক ব্যক্তি।

Quad-ră-gĕs'-i-mă (kwŏd-), *n.* (Also *Quadragesima Sunday*) The first Sunday in Lent; খৃষ্টানদিগের চত্বারিংশদ্দিবসব্যাপী উপবাসের প্রথম রবিবার।

quad-ră-gĕs'-i-măl (kwŏd-), *adj.* 1. Consisting of forty days (said of a fast esp. Lent); চত্বারিংশদ্দিবস-ব্যাপী। 2. Of, relating to, or used in, Lent; খৃষ্টানগণের চত্বারিংশদ্দিবসব্যাপী উৎসব সম্বন্ধীয় বা উক্ত উৎসবে ব্যবহৃত।

quad'-ran-gle (kwŏd-răng-gl), *n.* 1. (*Geom.*) A plane figure of four sides and angles; চতুরস্র, চতুর্ভুজ, চতুষ্কোণ (হিঃ কোঃ)। 2. (Also *quad*) An open square or court surrounded by buildings; অট্টালিকা-বেষ্টিত অঙ্গন, চত্বর, চতুষ্ক। **–gu-lar**, *adj.* **–gu-lar-ly**, *adv.*

quad'-rănt (kwŏd-), *n.* 1. The fourth part of a circle or its circumference; বৃত্তপাদ, বৃত্তচতুর্থ (সূর্য্যবিঃ), পাদ (হিঃ কোঃ), পদ (সুঃ সিঃ), তুরীয় (সাঃ পঃ), ত্রিজ্যা (কেজ্যিঃ)। 2. The fourth part of sphere; গোলকের চতুর্থাংশ। 3. An instrument for angular measurements and used in taking altitudes; উচ্চতা মাপের জন্য ব্যবহৃত কোণমান যন্ত্র, তুরীয় যন্ত্র। **–ran'-tal**, *adj.* **Quadrant electrometer**—পাদবিদ্যুৎমাপক (হিঃ কোঃ)। **Quadrant mural**—ভিত্তিযন্ত্র (সূর্য্য বিঃ)।

Quadrant.

quad'-răt (kwŏd-), *n.* (Also *quad*) A piece of metal used to fill the void spaces between words etc. in printing; মুদ্রণে শব্দ প্রভৃতির মধ্যস্থিত শূন্যস্থান পূরণের জন্য চতুষ্কোণ ধাতুখণ্ড।

quad'-rate (kwŏd-), *adj. & n.* Square or rectangular (esp. *zool*).

সমচতুষ্কোণ, চতুরস্রাকার, আয়ত। *Noun.* **1.** An object square or cubical in form or approximately so; সমচতুষ্কোণ বা বড়স্রাকৃতি বা তদনুরূপ বস্তু। **2.** (*Zool.*) A quadrate bone or muscle; (জন্তু-বিদ্যা) সমচতুষ্কোণাকৃতি অস্থি বা পেশী। **Quadrate bone** or **muscle**—See QUDRATE, *n.* 2.

quad-rāte′ (kwŏd-), *v. t.* & *i.* **1.** To square, as a circle etc.; বৃত্ত প্রভৃতির সমায়তন বর্গক্ষেত্র অঙ্কিত করা। **2.** To make square; সমচতুষ্কোণ করা। **3.** To conform to; অনুসারী করা, অনুযায়ী করা। *Verb i.* To square; to correspond; to suit; (followed by *with*); সঙ্গতিবিশিষ্ট হওয়া; মিলা; মানান।

quad-rāt′-ic (kwŏd-), *adj.* & *n.* **1.** (*Rare*) Square; (ক্বচিদ্ ব্যবহৃত) বর্গীয়। **2.** (*Math.*) Involving the square of an unknown quantity; as, a *quadratic* equation; (গণিতশাস্ত্র) অজ্ঞাত রাশির বর্গগঠিত, বর্গাত্মক (হিঃ কোঃ)। *Noun.* **1.** A quadratic equation; বর্গীয় সমীকরণ। **2.** (*Pl.*) The branch of Algebra, treating of quadratic equations; বীজগণিতের বর্গীয় সমীকরণ-বিষয়ক বিভাগ। **Affected quadratic**—মিশ্রিত বর্গাত্মক। **Pure quadratic**—শুদ্ধ বর্গাত্মক। **Quadratic equation**—বর্গীয় সমীকরণ।

quad′-rā-türe (kwŏd-), *n.* **1.** (*Math.*) The act of squaring; the reducing of a figure to a square; বর্গীকরণ; কোন ক্ষেত্রকে সমচতুষ্কোণক্ষেত্রে পরিণত করণ। **2.** (*Astrol.*) Position of one heavenly body in respect to another when distant from it $90°$; জ্যোতিষ্কদ্বয়ের পরস্পর হইতে ৯০° দূরে অবস্থিতি, তরবী (تربيع), পাদসংস্থান (আঃ বঃ)।

quad-ren′-ni-al (kwŏd-rĕn-ĭ-ăl), *adj.* **1.** Comprising, or consisting of, four years; occurring once in 4 years; চতুর্বার্ষিক; চতুরব্দিক।

quad′-ric (kwŏd-), *n.* (*Algeb.*) A homogeneous expression of the second degree in the variables; (বীজ-গণিত) চতুরস্রক (হিঃ কোঃ)।

quad′-ri-fid (kwŏd-), *adj.* (*Bot.*) Cleft into four divisions; চতুর্ধাবিদীর্ণ।

quad-ri′-gă (kwŏd-), *n.* (*Pl.* -GE) An ancient car drawn by four horses abreast; পার্শ্বাপার্শ্বিবদ্ধ অশ্বচতুষ্টয়বাহিত প্রাচীন যানবিশেষ।

quad-ri-lă′-tĕr-ăl (kwŏd-), *adj.* & *n.* Having four sides; চতুর্ভুজ (ক্ষেত্র)। *Noun.* A plane figure with four sides and angles; চতুর্ভুজ ক্ষেত্র। **The Quadrilateral**—উত্তর ইতালীর দুর্গচতুষ্টয় এবং তাহাদের দ্বারা অভিরক্ষিত প্রদেশ।

quad-ri-lin′-gü-ăl (kwŏd-rĭ-lĭng-), *adj.* Using, or made up of, four languages; ভাষাচতুষ্টয়-ব্যবহারকারী, ভাষাচতুষ্টয়রচিত।

quad-rille′ (kăd-rĭl), *n.* A game to be played by four persons with forty cards; একপ্রকার তাস খেলা—যাহা ৪০ খানা তাসদ্বারা চার জন লোকের খেলিতে হয়।

quad-rille′ (kăd-rĭl), *n.* **1.** A kind of square dance; একপ্রকার নৃত্য, চতুর্নৃত্য। **2.** The music composed for such a dance; ঐরূপ নৃত্যের জন্য রচিত সঙ্গীত।

quad-ril′-li-ŏn (kwŏd-), *n.* A number denoted by unity followed by 24 ciphers in English notation and by 15 ciphers in American and French notations; ইংলণ্ডীয় অঙ্কপাতনপ্রণালীতে ১ এর ডাহিনে ২৪টী শূন্য বসাইলে যে সংখ্যা হয় এবং আমেরিকা ও ফরাসীদেশের সংখ্যা-লিখন প্রণালীতে ১এর ডাহিনে ১৫টী শূন্য বসাইলে যে সংখ্যা হইয়া থাকে।

quad-ri-nŏm′-i-ăl (kwŏd-), *adj.* (*Algeb.*) Consisting of 4 terms; (বীজগণিত) পদচতুষ্টয়সমন্বিত।

quad-ri-păr′-tite (kwŏd-), *adj.* **1.** Consisting of, or divided into, 4 parts; চতুরংশক, চতুর্ধাবিভক্ত। **2.** Involving, or shared by, four parties; পক্ষচতুষ্টয়সংসৃষ্ট, পক্ষচতুষ্টয় দ্বারা অংশীকৃত।

quad′-ri-reme (kwŏd-rĭ-rēm), *n.* (*Class. Antiq.*) A galley having four rows or banks of oars; (গ্রীক ও রোমক প্রত্নতত্ত্ব) প্রাচীন কালের চারি সারি দাঁড়বিশিষ্ট পোত।

quad-ri-sȳl-lă′-bic (kwŏd-), *adj.* Of four syllables; শব্দাংশচতুষ্টয়-বিশিষ্ট, চতুরক্ষরসমন্বিত। **—syl′-la-ble,** *n.* A word of four syllables; শব্দাংশচতুষ্টয়বিশিষ্ট শব্দ।

quad′-ri-vă-lĕnt (kwŏd-), *adj.* (*Chem.*) Having a valence of four; (রসায়ন-শাস্ত্র) চতুর্ধাশক্তিক (হিঃ কোঃ) **—lence,** *n.*

quad-ri′-vi-ŭm (kwŏd-), *n.* (*Hist.*) In mediæval times, the four liberal arts—Arithmetic, Music, Geometry and Astronomy; (ইতিহাস) মধ্যযুগের চতুর্ব্বিদ্যা (পাটীগণিত, সঙ্গীত, জ্যামিতি এবং জ্যোতির্বিজ্ঞান)।

quad-roon′ (kwŏd-), *n.* **1.** The offspring of a mulatto and a white man; a person of quarter-negro blood; কাফ্রী এবং শ্বেতাঙ্গের বর্ণসঙ্কর ও শ্বেতাঙ্গের সহযোগে জাত সন্তান; যে ব্যক্তির শরীরে এক চতুর্থাংশ কাফ্রী রক্ত আছে। **2.** Any offspring either human, animal or vegetable, of an analogous cross; অনুরূপ সাঙ্কর্য্যের মাত্রাসম্পন্ন মানব, জন্তু, বা উদ্ভিদ্।

quad-ru′-mă-nă (kwŏd-rô-), *n.* (*Pl.*) Animals having four hands *e. g.* the ape, monkey, etc.; চতুর্হস্ত জন্তু, চতুর্হস্ত (সাঃ পঃ), চতুষ্করী (প্রঃ বাঃ), চতুষ্পাণিক।

quad-rum′-a-nous (kwŏd-rôm-ă-nŭs), *adj.* Of, or pertaining to, the quadrumana; four-handed; চতুষ্করিসম্বন্ধীয়; চতুর্ভুজ, চতুষ্পাণি, চতুষ্করী (প্রঃ বাঃ)।

quad-ru-pĕd′ (kwŏd-rô-), *adj.* & *n.* A four-footed animal; চতুষ্পদ

জন্তু। ***Adj.*** Having four feet; চতুষ্পদ। **—al,** *adj.*

quad′-ru-ple (kwŏd-rô-pl), *adj., n., v. t.* & *i.* **1.** Fourfold; consisting of, or involving, four parts or parties; চতুর্গুণিত, চতুর্গুণ, চারিগুণ; চতুরংশাত্মক, চতুষ্টয়, চতুর্পক্ষাত্মক, চতুর্পক্ষসংসৃষ্ট। ***Noun.*** A sum, quantity or number four times as much or as many; চতুর্গুণ। ***Verb t. & i.*** To multiply by four; চারিদ্বারা গুণ করা, চতুর্গুণিত করা। **—ply,** *adv.*

quad′-ru-plĕt (kwŏd-rô-), *n.* **1.** (*Pl.*) Four children born in the same labour; একবারে প্রসূত সন্তানচতুষ্টয়। **2.** A cycle for carrying four riders; একপ্রকার দ্বিচক্রযান—যাহাতে একসঙ্গে চারিজন আরোহী চলিতে পারে। **3.** Four things working together; একযোগে কার্য্যকারী বস্তুচতুষ্টয়।

quad-ru′-pli-cāte (kwŏd-rô-), *adj.* & *n.* Fourfold; four times repeated; চতুর্গুণ; চতুরাবৃত্ত। ***Noun.*** (*Pl.*) Four things, as copies of a document corresponding exactly in all ways; সর্ব্বাংশে অনুরূপ বস্তু-চতুষ্টয়। **In quadruplicate**—সর্ব্বাংশে অনুরূপ উদাহরণ বা অনুলিপি চতুষ্টয়ে।

quad-ru′-pli-cāte (kwŏd-rô-), *v. t.* To quadruple; to make in quadruplicate; চতুর্গুণ করা, চতুরাবৃত্ত করা; অনুরূপ চারিখানা করা। **—ca′-tion,** *n.*

quad-ru-plic′-i-tÿ (kwŏd-rô-), *n.* State of being fourfold; চতুরাবৃত্তি।

quae′-rē (kwē-), *v. t. imperative* & *n.* (*Abbr. qu.*) Inquire; প্রশ্ন কর। ***Noun.*** A question; a query; প্রশ্ন; জিজ্ঞাসা।

quaes′-tŏr (kwēs-), *n.* A public treasurer of ancient Rome; প্রাচীন রোমের সরকারী কোষাধ্যক্ষ। **—ship,** *n.* **—to′-ri-al,** *adj.*

quaff, *v. i.* & *t.* To drink deeply; to drink; অতিমাত্রায় পান করা, ঢক ঢক করিয়া গেলা; পান করা। ***Verb t.*** To drink copiously from (a cup etc.); to drink; প্রচুর পরিমাণে পান করা; পান করা।

quăg, *n.* A boggy spot; a quagmire; জলাভূমি; দলদলে জায়গা। **Quag′-gy,** *adj.*

quăg′-ga (-ă), *n.* **1.** An animal of South Africa closely allied to

Quagga.

the zebra; দক্ষিণ আফ্রিকার চিত্রগর্দ্দভ জাতীয় জন্তুবিশেষ। **2.** A zebra esp. *equus burchellii*; চিত্রগর্দ্দভ।

quăg′-mīre, *n.* A piece of marshy land that shakes or yields under the foot; a fen; a slough; (*lit.* & *fig.*); জলা জায়গা; বিলা জায়গা, দলদলে জায়গা; কর্দ্দম ভূমি।

quail (kwāl), *n.* A small bird closely allied to the partridge;

Quail

বটের (যোঃ), গঞ্জিকায়, ভারুই পক্ষী, বর্ত্তক, বর্ত্তিক, বর্ত্তিকা, লাব, বাগা, বিষ্ণুলিঙ্গী, লবা (হিন্দী), লাবক (সুশ্রুঃ), ফণিখেল, গরুদ্‌যোধী, ভারতী। **Quail′-er-y,** *n.* **Quail-call, Quail-pipe**—একপ্রকার শিটি—যাহার ধ্বনি ভারুই পক্ষীর মত।

quail (kwāl-), *v. i.* & *t.* (Of a person, his heart, courage, eyes, etc.) To lose heart; to shrink; to cower; to give way; নিরুৎসাহ হওয়া, দমিয়া যাওয়া; সঙ্কুচিত হওয়া; ভীত হওয়া, ভয়ে জড়সড় হওয়া; ভাঙ্গিয়া পড়া। ***Verb t.*** (*Rare*) To cause to quail; to daunt; (ক্বচিদ্ ব্যবহৃত) দমান; ভীত করা।

quaint (kwānt), *adj.* **1.** (*Archaic*) Finely fashioned or formed; neat; (অপ্রঃ) সুগঠিত; পরিপাটী। **2.** Strange but pleasing esp. because of being old-fashioned; daintily odd; আজব; আচানক। **Quaint′-ly,** *adv.* **Quaint′-ness,** *n.*

quake (kwāk), *n.* Trembling or shaking; a tremulous agitation esp. an earthquake; কম্পন, বেপন; কম্প, প্রকম্প, কাঁপুনি, বিশেষতঃ ভূমিকম্প, অবনীপ্রকম্পন (কুমারঃ)।

quake (kwāk), *v. i.* To shake; to tremble; কম্পিত হওয়া; থরহরি কাঁপা। **Quak′-ing,** *adj.* Quivering; trembling; কম্পমান; কম্পনশীল। **Quak′-ing-ly,** *adv.* **Quaking-grass**—একপ্রকার কম্পনশীল তৃণ। **To quake like an aspen bow**—বাঁশ-পাতার মত হী হী করে কাঁপা (রবি-রাজা)।

Quāk′-êr, *n.* **1.** One of a religious sect called the Society of Friends, founded by George Fox (1642-90); George Fox কর্ত্তৃক প্রতিষ্ঠিত ধর্ম্মসম্প্রদায় বিশেষ। **2.** (*l. c.*) One that quakes; কম্পনশীল ব্যক্তি। **3.** (*l. c.,* Also *quaker-bird, quaker-moth*) Kinds of bird and moth; বিভিন্নজাতীয় পক্ষী ও তসরে পোকা। **—dom, —ess, —ism,** *ns.* **—ish, —ly,** *adjs.* **Quaker-gun** — শত্রুগণকে প্রতারিত করার জন্য একপ্রকার কৃত্রিম কামান। **Quaker-meeting, Quaker's meeting**—ধর্ম্মভ্রাতৃমণ্ডলী বিশেষের সভা—এই সভা সভ্যের মধ্যে পবিত্র আত্মার আবেশ না হওয়া

পর্য্যন্ত সকলে মৌন থাকে, মৌন সভা ; যে মণ্ডলীতে কথাবার্ত্তা নীরস হইয়া পড়ে।
qual-i-fi-ca'-tion (kwŏl-), *n.* **1.** Act of qualifying ; state of being qualified ; গুণীকরণ ; গুণবত্তা, গুণবিশিষ্টতা, গুণবৈশিষ্ট্য, গুণসম্পন্নতা, গুণোপপন্নতা। **2.** A quality that fits a person for a post, etc. ; requisite capacity or power ; কার্য্য প্রভৃতি প্রাপ্তির উপযোগী যোগ্যতা ; উপযুক্ততা। **3.** Act of limiting ; state of being limited ; restriction ; modification ; নিয়মন ; সীমাবদ্ধতা, পরিমিতত্ব ; সীমা বিশেষ ; রূপান্তর। **4.** Attribution of a quality ; as, the *qualification* of his policy as opportunist is unfair ; গুণারোপ। **Qual'-i-fi-ca-to-ry,** *adj.*
qual'-i-fy̆ (kwŏl-), *v. t.* & *i.* **1.** To make fit for any employment, privilege, etc. ; উপযুক্ত করা, যোগ্য করা, যোগ্যতাসম্পন্ন করা, উপযুক্ত গুণসম্পন্ন করা। **2.** To modify ; to limit ; to make less absolute or sweeping ; সংযত করা, প্রশমিত করা ; সীমাবদ্ধ করা, সঙ্কোচ করা ; বিশিষ্ট করা (cf. বিশিষ্টাদ্বৈতবাদ)। **3.** To characterize by naming an attribute ; to describe *as* ; as, to *qualify* a person *as* a scoundrel ; (*Gram.*) to limit or modify the meaning of ; as, an adjective *qualifies* a noun ; কোন গুণ উল্লেখ পূর্ব্বক বর্ণনা করা ; কোন কিছু বলিয়া বর্ণনা করা ; (ব্যাকরণ) অর্থ সীমাবদ্ধ বা বিশিষ্ট করা। **4.** To mitigate ; to abate ; to assuage ; প্রশমিত করা ; উপশম করা ; লঘু করা। **5.** To modify the strength of, as a liquor, etc. ; শক্তি বা তেজঃ মন্দীভূত করা। **6.** To supply with legal power or capacity, as by administering an oath ; as, to *qualify* a jury ; আইনসঙ্গত ক্ষমতা বা অধিকার প্রদান করা। *Verb i.* To be, or become, fit or qualified, as for a post etc. ; to make oneself legally qualified as by taking oath etc. ; উপযুক্ত হওয়া, যোগ্য হওয়া ; আইনতঃ যোগ্য করা।
qual'-i-ta-tive (kwŏl-ĭ-tā-tĭv), *adj.* Pertaining to quality ; as, *qualitative* analysis ; depending in quality ; having the character of a quality ; গুণসম্বন্ধীয়, গুণসম্পর্কীয় ; গুণপরতন্ত্র, গুণায়ত্ত ; গুণাত্মক। **Qualitative analysis**—See ANALYSIS.
qual'-i-ty̆ (kwŏl-), *n.* **1.** A distinguishing property or characteristic; an attribute ; a trait ; গুণ ; ধর্ম্ম ; লক্ষণ। **2.** An acquired trait ; an accomplishment ; গুণ ; সদ্‌গুণ। **3.** Degree of excellence ; as, of good, poor, *quality* ; excellence ; as, it has *quality* ; উৎকর্ষের মাত্রা ; উৎকর্ষ, বৈশিষ্ট্য, প্রকর্ষ, প্রকৃষ্টতা। **4.** (*Archaic* or *Vulg.*) High rank ; "Persons of *quality*" ; (অপ্রঃ বা ইতরভাষায়) উচ্চ শ্রেণী। **5.** (Of sound, voice, etc.) Distinctive character ; timbre ; (ধ্বনি, স্বর, প্রভৃতি সম্পর্কে) বিশিষ্ট লক্ষণ ; কণ্ঠধ্বনি, যন্ত্রের সুর। **6.** (*Log.*) State of being affirmative or negative ; as, the *quality* of a proposition ; (তর্কবিজ্ঞান) অস্তিবাচকতা বা নাস্তিবাচকতা, গুণ (হিঃ কোঃ)। **The quality**—(*Vulg.*) The upper classes ; (ইতর ভাষায়) উচ্চশ্রেণীসমূহ। **To give a taste of one's qualities**—To show what he can do ; গুণের পরিচয় দেওয়া।
qualm (kwâm), *n.* **1.** A suddeen attack of illness, faintness, etc. esp. nausea ; হঠাৎ কোন রোগের আক্রমণ, বিশেষতঃ বমনেচ্ছা, বিবমিষা, গা বমি বমি করণ, বমনোদ্বেগ। **2.** A sudden misgiving or sinking of the heart ; আকস্মিক সংশয় বা অবসাদ। **3.** A scruple of conscience ; বিবেকের দংশন, বিবেকের তাড়না। **Qualm'-ish,** *adj.*
quan-dăr'-y̆ (kwŏn-), *n.* A state of difficulty, perplexity, hesitation, etc. ; as, I am in a *quandary* ; মুস্কিল, লেঠা, ফাঁপর, দায়, হতবুদ্ধিতা, দ্বিধা, শঙ্কা, সংশয়।
quand meme, (*F.*), *adv.* Even though ; whatever may happen ; যদিও ; যাহাই হউক না কেন।
quant (kwŏnt), *n., v. t.* & *i.* A punting pole with a disc near the end to prevent its sinking in mud ; একপ্রকার লগি—উহার প্রান্তের নিকটে একটী চাক্‌তি সংবদ্ধ থাকাতে উহা কাদাতে বসিয়া যাইতে পারেনা, সচক্র নৌচালনদণ্ড। ***Verb t. & i.*** To punt, or to be punted, with a quant ; চাক্‌তি ওয়ালা লগিদ্বারা চালান বা চালিত হওয়া।
quan'-ti-fy̆ (kwŏn-), *v. t.* **1.** (*Log.*) To determine or mark the quantity of (a proposition, term, etc.) ; (তর্কবিজ্ঞান) পরিমাণ নির্ণয় করা। **2.** To determine, fix, or express, the quantity of ; পরিমাণ স্থির করা, পরিমাণ নির্দ্ধারণ করা, পরিমাণ ব্যক্ত করা। **—fi-a-ble,** *adj.* **—fi-ca'-tion,** *n.*
quan'-ti-ta-tive (kwŏn-tĭ-tā-tĭv), *adj.* **1.** Of, or pertaining to, quantity ; finding, or expressing, quantity ; সংখ্যাসম্বন্ধীয় ; সংখ্যানির্দ্ধারক, সংখ্যাসূচক। **2.** Measured, or measurable, by quantity ; সংখ্যাদ্বারা পরিমিত বা পরিমেয়। **3.** Of, or pertaining to, quantity ; পরিমাণসংক্রান্ত। **4.** Of, relating to, or based on, the quantity of vowels ; as, *quantitative*, accent etc. ; স্বরসংখ্যাসম্বন্ধীয়, স্বরসংখ্যামূলক। **—ly,** *adv.* **Quantitative analysis**—See ANALYSIS.
quan'-ti-tive (kwŏn-tĭ-tĭv), *adj.* (*Rare*) Same as QUANTITATIVE.
quan'-ti-ty̆ (kwŏn-), *n.* **1.** That property in virtue of which anything may be measured ; পরিমাণ, মাত্রা। **2.** Amount ; number ; পরিমাণ ; সংখ্যা। **3.** A specified or

considerable number or amount of something ; (*pl.*) large amounts or numbers ; abundance ; as, it is found in *quantities* there ; নির্দ্দিষ্ট সংখ্যা, বহুসংখ্যা, নির্দ্দিষ্ট পরিমাণ ; বহু পরিমাণ; বাহুল্য, প্রাচুর্য্য। 4. (*Math.*) Anything which can be multiplied, divided or measured ; (গণিতশাস্ত্র) রাশি। 5. (*Log.*) The extent to which the predicate in a proposition is asserted of the subject ; বিধেয় যে পরিমাণে উদ্দেশ্য সম্বন্ধে নিশ্চিতরূপে কথিত হয়, গুণ (হিঃ কোঃ)। 6. (*Pros.*) Length or shortness of vowel sounds ; (ছন্দঃশাস্ত্র) স্বরবর্ণের লঘুতা বা গুরুতা, মাত্রা। **Additional quantity** — ক্ষেপক (সাঃ পঃ)। **Affirmative quantity**—ধন (সাঃ পঃ)। **3. Given quantity**—ব্যক্ত (সাঃ পঃ)। **Irrational quantity**—করণ (সাঃ পঃ)। **Negligible quantity**—One that can be neglected ; নগণ্য রাশি। (*Fig.*) A person etc. that need not be reckoned with ; নগণ্য লোক, নগণ্য বস্তু। **Quantity (assumed in Algebra)**—উদ্বর্তক। **Quantity mark**—(ছন্দঃ শাস্ত্র) লঘুতা গুরুতা-সূচক চিহ্ন। **Unknown quantity**—A quantity that is not known ; অজ্ঞাতরাশি, অব্যক্তরাশি। (*Fig.*) A person or thing whose actions cannot be foreseen ; (লক্ষণায়) যে ব্যক্তি বা বস্তুর কার্য্যকলাপ সম্বন্ধে পূর্ব্বে বুঝা যাইতে পারে না, অজ্ঞাতক্রিয় ব্যক্তি।

quan-ti′-va-lence (kwŏn-tĭ-vā-lĕns), *n.* (*Chem.*) The extent to which one of the atoms of an element can hold other atoms in combination ; (রসায়নশাস্ত্র) কোন পদার্থের কোন পরমাণু যে মাত্রায় অপর পরমাণুসমূহ সংযুক্ত অবস্থায় রাখিতে পারে, পরিমাণশক্তি (হিঃ কোঃ)।

quan′-tŭm (kwŏn-), *n.* **1.** Quality ; amount ; সংখ্যা; মাত্রা, পরিমাণ (ব্রজঃ হিন্দুঃ)। **2.** A share or portion ; অংশ ; ভাগ। **3.** An amount that is required, desired or allowed ; আবশ্যক পরিমাণ, ঈপ্সিত পরিমাণ, প্রদত্ত পরিমাণ। **Quantum hypothesis** — পরিমাণসিদ্ধান্ত (প্রতিভা)। **Quantum sufficit**—(*Abbr. quant. suff.* or *q. s.*) (ঔষধের ব্যবস্থাপত্রে) যথেষ্ট পরিমাণে ; যথেষ্ট পরিমাণ ; যথোচিত মাত্রায়। **Quantum libet** or **placet**—(*Abbr. q.l., q.p.*) (ঔষধের ব্যবস্থাপত্রে) যতটুক আবশ্যক।

quă-quă-vĕr′-săl, *adj.* (*Geol.*) Inclined towards, or facing, all directions ; (ভূবিদ্যা) সর্ব্বতঃপ্রবণ, সর্ব্বতোমুখ।

quar′-ăn-tīne (kwŏr-), *n.* & *v. t.* The period during which a ship suspected of infection, is prohibited from intercourse with a port ; such restraint of intercourse or the measures taken to enforce it ; যে কাল পর্য্যন্ত স্পর্শসংক্রামক রোগের প্রাদুর্ভাবযুক্ত স্থান হইতে আগত কোন পোত বন্দরের সহিত কোনরূপ সংসর্গ রাখিতে প্রতিষিদ্ধ হয় ; সংসর্গপ্রতিষেধ, গমনাগমন প্রতিষেধ, সংসর্গ প্রতিষেধব্যবস্থা (আঃ বঃ)। ***Verb t.*** To put in or under quarantine ; সংক্রামকরোগের প্রাদুর্ভাবপূর্ণ জাহাজের বন্দরের সহিত সংসর্গ প্রতিষেধ করা।

quar′-ĕn-dĕn (kwŏr-), **-dĕr**, *ns.* A kind of apple of Devonshire and Somerset ; ডিভনসয়ার ও সমারসেট সায়ারের একপ্রকার সেওফল।

quar-rel (kwŏr-ĕl), *n.* (*Hist.*) An arrow with a square head ;

Quarrel.

(ইতিহাস) একপ্রকার বাণ—যাহার অগ্রভাগ সমচতুষ্কোণাকৃতি থাকে।

quar′-rel (kwŏr-ĕl), *n.* **1.** Ground, or occasion of, complaint ; as, I have no *quarrel* against or with him ; অভিযোগের হেতু বা উপলক্ষ্য। **2.** A brawl ; an altercation ; a breach of friendship or concord ; disagreement ; ঝগড়া, কলহ, কোন্দল, বিবাদ, দ্বন্দ্ব ; বচসা ; সুহৃদ্ভেদ ; বিসংবাদ, বিপ্রলম্ভ, বিরোধ। **—some,** *adj.* Apt, or disposed to, quarrel ; কলহপ্রিয়, বিবাদপ্রবণ, ঝগড়াটে, বিবাদশীল। **—some-ly,** *adv.* **—some-ness,** *n.* **A good quarrel**—ন্যায্য কলহ। **To espouse one's quarrel, To fight one's quarrels for him**—To assist him in getting redress ; কোনরূপ অন্যায়ের প্রতিকারের জন্য তাহাকে সাহায্য করা। **To pick a quarrel**—To invent or eagerly avail oneself of an occasion to quarrel ; গায়ে পড়িয়া ঝগড়া করা, ঝগড়া বাঁধান, কোনরূপ ছল খুঁজিয়া ঝগড়া বাঁধান।

quar′-rel (kwŏr-ĕl), *v. i.* **1.** To find fault (*with*) ; as, to *quarrel* with one's lot ; দোষ দেওয়া, দোষ ধরা। **2.** To contend or dispute violently ; to break off friendly relations; বিবাদ করা, ঝগড়া করা, কলহ করা ; বন্ধুত্ব ছিন্ন করা। **To quarrel with one's bread and butter**—To abandon employment by which one lives ; যে চাকুরীদ্বারা গ্রাসাচ্ছাদনের ব্যবস্থা হইতেছে তাহা ত্যাগ করা।

quar′-ry, (kwŏr-ĭ), *n., v. t.* & *i.* **1.** A pit or place from which stones for buildings etc. are dug out ; যে গর্ত্ত বা স্থান হইতে অট্টালিকাদির জন্য প্রস্তরসমূহ উৎখনিত হয়, পাথরের খনি, পাষাণস্থলী, পাষাণকর্ত্তন স্থান (সাঃ পঃ)। **2.** (*Fig.*) A place from which information etc. may be gathered ; (লক্ষণায়) যে স্থান হইতে সংবাদ প্রভৃতি সংগ্রহ করা যাইতে পারে, সংবাদসংগ্রহস্থান। ***Verb t.*** **1.** To dig or take (stone) from a quarry ; পাথরের খনি হইতে (পাথর) নেওয়া বা খুঁড়িয়া বাহির করা। **2.** (*Fig.*) To extract as information, facts, etc. laboriously from books etc. ; (লক্ষণায়) গ্রন্থ প্রভৃতি হইতে গভীর পরিশ্রমের পর জ্ঞাতব্য তথ্য সমূহ উদ্ধার করা। ***Verb i.*** To labour in searching documents etc.; as, *quarrying* in the Harleian manuscripts; দলিল প্রভৃতি খোঁজার জন্য পরিশ্রম করা। **Quarryman**—পাষাণ-কর্ত্তক, পাষাণোৎখনক।

quar'-ry (kwŏr-ĭ), *n.* **1.** A game pursued by hawks, hounds or hunters; বাজপক্ষী, শিকারী কুকুর অথবা শিকারীগণ কর্ত্তৃক অনুসৃত শিকার। **2.** Any object pursued; an intended victim; prey; অনুসৃত বিষয়; অভিপ্রেত বলি; শিকার।

quart, *n.* **1.** The fourth part of a gallon; two pints; এক গ্যালনের চতুর্থাংশ (প্রায় তিনপোয়া); দুই পাইণ্ট। **2.** A pot or bottle containing this amount; প্রায় তিন পোয়া তরলপদার্থ ধরে—এরূপ ভাণ্ড বা বোতল; তিন পাইয়া বোতল। **3.** Short for a quart of beer; as, he still takes his *quart*; প্রায় তিন পোয়া বীয়র মদ্য। **Quart-pot**—See QUART, 2. **To put a quart into a pint pot**—To make less contain greater; কলসীর জল ঘটীতে ঢালা।

quart, *n., v. i. & t.* **1.** (*Fencing*) Same as CARTE. **2.** A sequence of four cards in the game of piquet etc.; (তাসখেলায়) পঞ্চাশ। ***Verb i.*** (*Fencing*) To assume position for carte; (অসিক্রীড়া) ভঙ্গিবিশেষে অবস্থান করা। ***Verb t.*** To draw back as head and shoulders in quarting; অসিক্রীড়ায় ভঙ্গিবিশেষে মস্তক ও স্কন্ধ পশ্চাদ্দিকে প্রত্যাকৃষ্ট করা। **Quart and tierce**—অসিক্রীড়া অভ্যাস।

quar'-tăn, *adj. & n.* Occurring every fourth day, reckoning inclusively, as an ague or fever; প্রতি চতুর্থদিবসে আগমনকারী, চাতুর্থক (মাঃ নিঃ)। ***Noun.*** Such an ague or fever; চাতুর্থক জ্বর (মাঃ নিঃ)।

quar-ta'-tion, *n.* The alloying of one part of gold with three parts of silver; একভাগ স্বর্ণের সহিত ৩ ভাগ রৌপ্য মিশ্রণ।

quar'-tẽr, *n.* **1.** The fourth part; চতুর্থভাগ, চতুর্থাংশ, পাদ, তুরীয়, তুর্য্য। **2.** (*Abbr. qr.*) The fourth part of a hundredweight; এক হন্দরের চতুর্থাংশ, কোয়ার্টার। **3.** Eight bushels—used esp. in measuring grain; আট বুশেল। **4.** (*Naut.*) The fourth of a fathom; (নৌ-বিদ্যা) এক ফ্যাদমের চতুর্থাংশ, একহাত। **5.** The fourth of a year; the fourth of a school or academic year; এক বৎসরের চতুর্থাংশ; ত্রিমাস। **6.** The fourth part of a mile; একমাইলের চতুর্থাংশ, সিকিমাইল। **7.** The fourth of an hour; এক ঘণ্টার চতুর্থাংশ। **8.** The fourth part into which a body or carcase is divided, including one of the limbs; নিহত-জন্তুর শরীরের চতুর্থাংশ, চৌড়, রাং। **9.** (*Astron.*) The fourth part of the moon's period; (জ্যোতির্বিজ্ঞান) চন্দ্রের ভগণের চতুর্থাংশ, চন্দ্রভগণ-চতুর্থাংশ (হিঃ কোঃ)। **10.** One of the four cardinal points; a region lying about this; district; locality; দিক্ [syn. আশা, কাষ্ঠা, ককুভ, হরিৎ, সনি, সনী, দিক্‌কন্যা (*Poet. & Rhet.*), দিগ্‌বধূ (*ib.*), দিক্‌সুন্দরী (*ib.*), দিক্‌কান্তা (*ib.*), দিক্‌কামিনী (*ib.*), দিগঙ্গনা (*ib.*)]; দিগ্‌দেশ; অঞ্চল, প্রদেশ; স্থান, জায়গা। **11.** A part of a town or city; as, the Jewish *quarter*; মহল্লা, পাড়া, টোলা। **12.** (*Pl.*) Lodgings; a residence or abode; a place where troops are lodged; as, the head-*quarters*; বাসা; নিবাস, বসতি, বাসস্থান; সেনানিবাস। **13.** (*Herald.*) One of the divisions of a shield when it is divided into four parts; a bearing or an ordinary occupying the first fourth part (dexter chief) of the field of the shield; (কুলবিদ্যা) চতুরংশিত কুলচিহ্নাঙ্কিত চর্ম্মের অন্যতম বিভাগ; কুলচিহ্নাঙ্কিত চর্ম্মের প্রথম বিভাগে স্থিত কুলচিহ্ন বা ক্রুশ প্রভৃতি সাধারণ চিহ্ন। **14.** (*Mil.*) Clemency shown to a surrendered or conquered enemy in not taking his life; (সামরিক-শাস্ত্র) পরাজিত বা পরিবেষ্টিত শত্রুর প্রাণ বধ না করিয়া যে দয়া প্রকাশ করা হয়, দয়া, অনুকম্পা, প্রাণদান, প্রাণভিক্ষা। **15.** The side of a horse's hoof between the toe and the heel; অশ্বখুরের অগ্রভাগ ও গোড়ালির মধ্যবর্ত্তী স্থান। **16.** (*Naut.*) Part of a ship's side between the aftmost end of the main-chains and the sides of the stern; জাহাজের উভয়পার্শ্বসংবদ্ধ যে লৌহপট্টদ্বয়ে প্রধান মাস্তুলের রজ্জুসমূহ সংবদ্ধ থাকে—তাহার পশ্চাৎ প্রান্ত এবং জাহাজের পশ্চাদ্ভাগের (পাছা গলুই) পার্শ্বদ্বয়ের মধ্যবর্ত্তী অংশ, চতুরংশ। **17.** A quarter-mile race or running distance; as, he has won the *quarter*; সিকি মাইলের দৌড় বা ঘোড়দৌড়। **Quarter-bell**—যে ঘণ্টা প্রতি পনের মিনিট অন্তর অন্তর বাদিত হয়। **Quarter-binding** — যে পুস্তকের পৃষ্ঠভাগ মাত্র অপ্রশস্ত চর্ম্ম দ্বারা বাঁধা হইয়া থাকে। (*Quarter-bound, adj.*) **Quarter-butt** — বিলিয়ার্ড খেলার নাতিদীর্ঘ দণ্ড। **Quarter-day**—ত্রৈমাসিক কর, রাজস্ব,প্রভৃতি প্রদানের দিন, ত্রিমাসান্ত দিবস। **Quarter-deck**—See under DECK. **Quarter-ill**—গবাদির লাক্ষণিক দাহিকা (anthrax) রোগ। **Quarter-left, –right**—(সামরিক শাস্ত্র) এক সমকোণের চতুর্থাংশ বামে বা দক্ষিণে। **Quarter-light**—আবৃতশকটের পার্শ্বগবাক্ষ। **Quarter-line** — (নৌবিদ্যা) যে পোতশ্রেণীর প্রত্যেক পশ্চাদ্বর্ত্তী পোতের অগ্রভাগ পূর্ব্ববর্ত্তী পোতের চতুরংশের সমসূত্রে অবস্থিত থাকে। **Quarter-master**—(নৌবিদ্যা) পোতচালন, দিগ্‌-দর্শনযন্ত্র, সঙ্কেতপতাকা, প্রভৃতির ভারপ্রাপ্ত ক্ষুদ্র নৌকর্ম্মচারী; (সামরিক-শাস্ত্র — সংক্ষেপে Q. M.) সেনাপল্টনের সৈন্যগণের রসদ, পোষাক, আবশ্যক দ্রব্যসম্ভার, অশ্বাদির খাদ্য, প্রভৃতির ভারপ্রাপ্ত সামরিক কর্ম্মচারী। **Quarter-master-general**—(Abbr. *Q. M. G.*) সৈন্যগণের বাসস্থান,

পোষাকপরিচ্ছদ, প্রভৃতির ব্যবস্থাকারক উচ্চ সামরিক কর্ম্মচারী। **Quarter-mile, —yard, etc.**—সিকি মাইল, সিকি গজ, ইত্যাদি। **Quarter- plate**—৩¼×৪¼ মাপের আলোক চিত্রফলক; ঐরূপ ফলক হইতে গৃহীত আলোক-চিত্র। **Quarter-sessions**—ফৌজদারী মোকদ্দমা এবং কোন কোন দেওয়ানী মোকদ্দমার বিচারের জন্য প্রতি ত্রিমাসান্তে গ্রেটব্রিটেনের প্রতি জেলার ও পার্লেমেণ্টে সভ্য প্রেরণের অধিকারপ্রাপ্ত নগরীতে যে আদালত বসে। **Quarter-staff**—একপ্রকার সুদৃঢ় যষ্টি বা লগুড়। **Quarter-tone**—(সঙ্গীতশাস্ত্র) অর্দ্ধ স্বনমাত্রা। **Quarter-wind**—জাহাজের চতুরংশে প্রবহমাণ বায়ু [এই বায়ু পাইলের জাহাজের পক্ষে নিরতিশয় অনুকূল হইয়া থাকে।] **Winter quarters**—শীতাবাস, সৈন্যগণের শীতাবাস। **Bad quarter of an hour**—অল্পকালস্থায়ী অপ্রীতিকর অভিজ্ঞতা। **It has gone the quarter**—ঘড়ীতে এক কোয়ার্টার বাজিয়াছে। **On the quarter** — (*Naut.*) Between astern and beam; (নৌবিদ্যা) জাহাজের চতুরংশিতের বিপরীত দিকে বা প্রায় বিপরীত দিকে। **To beat to quarters**—(*Naut.*) To summon crew to appointed stations as for action; (নৌবিদ্যা) যুদ্ধাদির জন্য জাহাজের মাল্লাগণকে যথাস্থানে অবস্থিত হওয়ার জন্য আহ্বান করা। **To beat up quarters of**—See under BEAT. **To give, receive** or **show quarter**—See QUARTER, *n.* 14. **To take up one's quarters** — To lodge *in, with,* etc.; বাসা নেওয়া। **What quarter is the wind in?** — (*Lit.* & *fig.*) How are things going?; কোন দিক্ থেকে বাতাস বহিতেছে, ব্যাপারটা কেমন চল্‌ছে।

quar'-têr, *v. t.* 1. To divide into four equal parts; চতুরংশিত করা। 2. To divide into parts; to dismember; as, the traitor was hanged and *quartered*; খান খান করা; খণ্ডবিখণ্ড করা। 3. To provide with quarters or lodgings; to find lodging and food for (soldiers etc.); বাসা দেওয়া; সৈন্যগণের আহার ও বাসস্থানের বন্দোবস্ত করা। 4. (Of dogs) To traverse as ground in every direction; (কুকুরসম্পর্কে) কোন স্থানের সকলদিকে সঞ্চরণ করা। 5. (*Herald.*) To add to other arms on a shield; to bear as an appendage to the hereditary arms; to divide as a shield into four parts by vertical and horizontal lines; (কুলবিদ্যা) ঢালের অন্যান্য কুলচিহ্নের সহিত সংযোগ করা; কুলচিহ্নের উপাঙ্গস্বরূপ ধারণ করা; লম্ব বা শয়ান রেখাদ্বারা চারিভাগে বিভক্ত করা।

quar'-têr-āge, *n.* A quarterly allowance or payment; a quarter's wages etc.; ত্রৈমাসিক বৃত্তি, ত্রৈমাসিক দেয়; ত্রৈমাসিক বেতন প্রভৃতি।

quar'-têr-ing, *n.* 1. Act of dividing into four equal parts; সমচতুরংশে বিভাজন, চতুর্ভাগীকরণ, চতুরংশীকরণ। 2. (*Pl.*) Coats of arms marshalled on a shield to denote alliances of a family with heiresses of others; কোন পরিবারের সহিত অপর পরিবারের উত্তরাধিকারিণীগণের সহিত সম্পর্ক আছে—ইহা সূচনার্থ প্রথমোক্ত পরিবারের ঢালে যে কুলচিহ্ন সংযুক্ত করা হয়।

quar'-têr-lŷ, *adj., n.* & *adv.* Occurring, or done, every quarter of a year; ত্রৈমাসিক। ***Noun.*** A magazine published once in every three months; ত্রৈমাসিক পত্রিকা। ***Adv.*** 1. Once in a quarter of a year; তিন মাস অন্তর একবার। 2. (*Herald.*) In quarters or quarterings; (কুলবিদ্যা) চতুরংশে। **Quarterly quartered**—(কুলবিদ্যা) ঢালের এক বা ততোধিক চতুর্থাংশ চতুর্ধাবিভক্ত।

quar'-têrn, *n.* (Also, *quartern-loaf*) A loaf of the weight of 4 lbs.; ৪ পাউণ্ড ওজনের পাঁউরুটি।

quar-tet'(te) (-tĕt), *ns.* 1. (*Mus.*) A composition in 4 parts, each performed by a single voice or instrument; (সঙ্গীতশাস্ত্র) চতুরংশে বিভক্ত সঙ্গীত—এইরূপ সঙ্গীতের প্রতি অংশ এক ব্যক্তি বা যন্ত্রদ্বারা গীত বা বাদিত হয়, চৌপদ। 2. A group consisting of four; চারিবস্তুর সমবায়, চতুষ্টয়।

quar'-tō, *n.* & *adj.* (Also written, 4 *to*, 4°) A size made by twice folding a sheet; a book consisting of sheets so folded; এক তা কাগজ দুইবার ভাঁজ করিলে যে আকার হয়; চতুরংশিত কাগজের পুস্তক। ***Adj.*** Having four leaves to the sheet; চতুরংশিত। **Quarto-paper**—চতুরংশিত কাগজ।

quartz (kwärts), *n.* A pure variety of silica, a constituent of granite and other rocks; একপ্রকার স্ফটিক-প্রস্তর, কাচমণি, কার্ত্তজোপল (আঃ বঃ)।

quash (kwŏsh), *v. t.* (*Law*) To annul; to make void; as, to *quash* an indictment; to put an end to; (আইন) বাতিল করা, নাকচ করা; অন্যথা করা, রদ করা; শেষ করা।

quash (kwŏsh), *v. t.* To suppress; as, to *quash* a rebellion; দমন করা।

Quash'-ee (kwŏsh-ē), *n.* A negro, (a national nickname); কাফ্রী।

quā'-si, *conj.* & *pref.* (*Abbr. qu.*) As if; as it were; আপাতপ্রতীয়মান; আভাসিক, কল্পিত, দেশ্য, দেশীয়। ***Pref.*** Used to denote resemblance, generally a fictitious, unreal or partial resemblance; as, a *quasi*-argument; উপ, কল্প।

quăs'-si-ă (-ĭ-), *n.* A bitter South-American plant yielding a bitter medicinal decoction; wood, bark, root, etc. of this tree; the drug derived from these; দক্ষিণ আমেরিকা-দেশজাত বৃক্ষবিশেষ—যাহার কাঠ প্রভৃতি হইতে একপ্রকার অতি তিক্ত কষায় পাওয়া যায়; ঐ বৃক্ষের কাঠ, বল্কল, শিকড়, প্রভৃতি; উক্ত কাঠ প্রভৃতি হইতে প্রাপ্ত তিক্ত ভেষজ।

quă-têr—cĕn-tē′-nă-rȳ, *n.* Four-hundredth anniversary ; চতুঃশত বার্ষিক উৎসব।

quă-têr′-nă-rȳ, *adj.* & *n.* **1.** Consisting of four parts ; চতুরংশাত্মক ; চতুরংশবান। **2.** (*Chem.*) Compounded of four elements or radicals ; (রসায়ন-শাস্ত্র) মূলপদার্থ চতুষ্টয় সমন্বিত। **3.** (*Math.*) Using, or concerned with, number four ; (গণিতশাস্ত্র) চাতুর, চতুরাত্মক। **4.** (*Geol.*) Post-tertiary ; (ভূবিদ্যা) তৃতীয়ক স্তরের পরবর্ত্তী। ***Noun.*** **1.** A group consisting of four ; the number four ; চারি বস্তুর সমবায় ; চারি। **2.** (*Geol.*) The quaternary period or system ; (ভূবিদ্যা) চতুর্থক যুগ। **The Pythagorean quaternary**—গ্রীক দার্শনিক পিথাগোরাস্ প্রবর্ত্তিত (১+২+৩+৪=১০) গূঢ়ার্থসূচক সংখ্যা।

quă-têr′-ni-ŏn, *n.* **1.** A set of four ; চতুষ্টয়। **2.** A quantity in mathematics ; রাশি। **3.** A sheet of paper folded twice ; a quire of four sheet thus folded ; চতুরংশিত কাগজ ; ঐরূপ ভাঁজ করা চার তা কাগজ। **4.** Same as PYTHAGOREAN QUATERNARY. **5.** A word of four syllables ; চতুরক্ষর শব্দ।

quă-têr′-ni-tȳ, *n.* **1.** A group of four, analogous to the theological term trinity ; চতুরীশ্বরতা। **2.** State of being four ; চতুঃসংখ্যকত্ব।

quă-tör′-zain (-zān), *n.* A poem of fourteen lines ; চতুর্দ্দশপদী কবিতা।

quat′-rain (kwŏt-rān *or* kât-rān), *n.* A stanza of four lines rhyming alternately ; পংক্তি-চতুষ্টয়বিশিষ্ট কবিতার কলি—ইহাতে প্রথম পংক্তির শেষ শব্দের সহিত তৃতীয় পংক্তির শেষ শব্দের ও দ্বিতীয় পংক্তির শেষ শব্দের সহিত চতুর্থ পংক্তির শেষ শব্দের মিল থাকে, চতুষ্পদী কবিতা।

quă′-tre (-ter), *n.* Same as CATER.

quă′-tre-foil (-têr-foyl), *n.* (*Arch.*) An ornamental figure, being an opening in tracery divided by cusps into four leaves ; (স্থপতি-বিজ্ঞান) চতুর্পত্রাত্মক ভূষাবিশেষ।

Quatrefoil

quât-tro-cĕn′-tist (-rö-), *n.* & *adj.* (*Artist etc.*) Of, or relating to, the quattrocento ; পঞ্চদশশতাব্দীর।

quât-tro-cen′-to (-rö-chĕn-tö), *n.* The fifteenth century when applied to Italian art or literature ; পঞ্চদশশতাব্দ [ইতালীদেশের সাহিত্য বা ললিতকলাসম্পর্কে ব্যবহৃত হয়।]

quā′-vêr, *v. i.* & *t.* To shake ; to tremble ; to vibrate ; esp. (*mus.*) to cause the voice or a sound to vibrate ; to trill in singing or on a musical instrument ; কাঁপা ; কম্পিত হওয়া ; স্পন্দিত হওয়া, স্ফুরিত হওয়া ; কম্পিত স্বরে গান গাওয়া, জিল টানা ; গিটকিরি দেওয়া, জমজমা বাজান। ***Verb t.*** **1.** To sing as a note, song, etc. with trills ; কম্পিত স্বরে গান গাওয়া, জিল টানা। **2.** To say or utter with quavers ; কম্পিত স্বরে বলা বা উচ্চারণ করা। **–ing-ly,** *adv.*

quā′-vêr, *n.* **1.** A shake or rapid vibration of the voice in singing ; সঙ্গীতে দ্রুত স্বর কম্পন, গিটকিরি, জমজমা। **2.** A musical note half the length of a crotchet ; একপ্রকার স্বর। **3.** Tremulousness in speech ; স্বরকম্প। **–y,** *adj.* Tremulous (of the voice in speech, etc.) ; কম্পমান।

quay (kē), *n.* A mole or wharf for loading or unloading vessels ; পোস্তা, ঘাট।

quay′-age (kē-āj), *n.* **1.** Charge for use of a quay ; পোস্তা ব্যবহারের জন্য শুল্ক। **2.** Berths on a quay for loading or discharging ships ; পোস্তার যে স্থানে জাহাজে মাল উঠান ও জাহাজ হইতে মাল নামান হয়।

quean (kwēn), *n.* **1.** A worthless impudent woman ; a hussy ; হীন-স্বভাবা, অকর্ম্মণ্যা ও প্রগল্‌ভা নারী ; বন্ধকী। **2.** (*Obs.* or *Scot.*) A girl ; (অপ্রচলিত বা স্কটলণ্ডে) ছুকরী।

quea′-șȳ (kwē-), *adj.* **1.** Tending to vomit ; বিবমিষু। **2.** (Of food and drink) Causing nausea ; বমনজনক, উদ্বামক। **3.** Ill at ease ; uncomfortable ; অসুখী ; অস্বচ্ছন্দ। **4.** Over-scrupulous ; tender or delicate ; easily disturbed ; as, a *queasy* conscience ; অতিরিক্ত সূক্ষ্মবিচারী ; সুকুমার ; আশু বিচলিত। **—si-ness,** *n.*

queen (kwēn), *n.* **1.** The wife of a king ; রাজপত্নী, রাজমহিষী, মহিষী। **2.** A female sovereign ; রাণী (cf. *Fr. Reine*), রাজ্ঞী, ঈশ্বরী (used esp. in Hill Tippera)। **3.** A female eminent in power or attractions ; as, the *queen* of beauty ; the best of her kind ; as, the *queen* of roses ; প্রভাবশালিনী নারী, নারীরত্ন ; রত্ন, রাণী। **4.** A sweetheart ; mistress or wife of a person ; হৃদয়েশ্বরী ; প্রাণেশ্বরী। **5.** A majestic woman ; মহিমান্বিতা নারী। **6.** A belle or mock-sovereign on some occasion ; as, *queen* of the May ; ক্রীড়া উৎসবাদির রাণী। **7.** A person, country, etc. regarded as reigning over some sphere ; as, the *queen* of hearts : the *queen* of the seas ; রাণী, অধীশ্বরী। **8.** Same as QUEEN-BEE, QUEEN-WASP or QUEEN-ANT. **9.** A piece in chess ; দাবা খেলার মন্ত্রী বা দাবা। **10.** (*Cards*) A card on which a queen is depicted ; (তাসের) বিবি। **Queen-dom, Queen′-hood, Queen′-ship,** *ns.* **Queen′-less, Queen′-like,** *adjs.* **Queen-ant** — পূর্ণাঙ্গী স্ত্রী পিপীলিকা। **Queen-bee**—মক্ষীরাণী

(রবীঃ), রাণীমক্ষিকা, মধুকররাজ (সর্ব্বঃ), মধুকররাজন্ (প্রশ্নঃ উপঃ)। **Queen-cake**—একপ্রকার ক্ষুদ্র (সাধারণতঃ হরতনের আকার) মিষ্ট পিষ্টক। **Queen-consort**—পাটরাণী, পট্টরাণী, পট্টমহিষী, পট্টদেবী। **Queen-dowager** — মৃত রাজার পত্নী। **Queen-metal**—কাঁসা। **Queen-mother** — রাজমাতা, রাজজননী। **Queen-post**—ধন্নার উপর অবস্থিত থাম—যাহার উপর গৃহের চালা প্রভৃতি বিধৃত থাকে। **Queen-stitch**—সূচের কাজে একপ্রকার সৌখীন ফোঁড়। **Queen-wasp**—পূর্ণাঙ্গী স্ত্রী বোলতা। **Queen's bench** — যে প্রাচীন বিচারালয়ে রাজা স্বয়ং বিচারাসনে উপবেশন করিতেন। **Queen's bishop, knight, pawn**—সতরঞ্চ ক্রীড়ার প্রারম্ভে মন্ত্রীর নিকটে স্থাপিত পিল, ঘোটক বা বড়ে। **Queen's College, Cambridge**—৬ষ্ঠ হেনরীর পত্নী মার্গারেট কর্তৃক ১৪৪৮ খৃঃ অব্দে প্রতিষ্ঠিত মহাবিদ্যালয়। **Queen's College, Oxford**—তৃতীয় এড্‌ওয়ার্ডের পত্নী ফিলিপার পুরোহিত Robert Eglesfield কর্তৃক ১৩৪০ খৃঃ অব্দে প্রতিষ্ঠিত মহাবিদ্যালয়। **Queen's colours**—সেনাপল্টনের পতাকাদ্বয়ের অন্যতর, রাজ্ঞীধ্বজ। **Queen's English**—প্রচলিত ইংরাজী। **Queen's heads**—ডাক টিকিট সমূহ। **Queen's pincushion** — একপ্রকার কন্দুকাকৃতি শ্বেতবর্ণ পুষ্প। **Queen's pipe**—সরকারে বাজেয়াপ্ত তামাক নষ্ট করার জন্য যে চুল্লী ব্যবহৃত হইত। **Queen's shilling** — See under SHILLING. **Queen's-ware** — এক প্রকার আপীত বর্ণের উৎকৃষ্ট চীনা বাসন। **Queen's weather**—রৌদ্র, সূর্য্যালোক [মহারাণী ভিক্টোরিয়ার উৎসবাদির দিবস প্রায়ই রৌদ্রকরোজ্জ্বল থাকিত বলিয়া এই নাম।] **Queen Anne is dead**—এটাতো সবাই জানে, এটাতো পুরাণ খবর। **Queen Anne's Bounty**—অপ্রচুর যাজকীয় বৃত্তির আয় বৃদ্ধির জন্য রাজ্ঞী এন কর্তৃক ১৭০৪ খৃঃ অব্দে স্থাপিত ধনভাণ্ডার। **Queen of hearts**—লাবণ্যবতী রমণী, হরতনের বিবি। **Queen of heaven**—জুনো [১ম জেমসের কন্যা এলিজেবেথকে এই আখ্যা দেওয়া হইয়া থাকে]; (রোম্যানক্যাথলিক ধর্ম্মসংঘ) কুমারী মেরী; চন্দ্রমা [Queen of the heaven — *Hera* (among the Greeks), *Juno* (among the Romans), *Anatu* (Babylonian), *Astrate* also *Ashtaroth* (Phœnicians), *Isis* (Egyptian), *Yin* (Chienese), *Shinmu* (among the Buddhists of China.)] **Queen of love**—প্রেমের রাণী, ভীনাস। **Queen of night**—Diana; the moon; গ্রীকদেবী ডায়েনা; চন্দ্রমা। **Queen of queens**—রাজরাজেশ্বরী (এভেলন)। **Queen of Scots**—স্কটলণ্ডের রাজ্ঞী মেরী। **Queen of the Adriatic**—এড্রিয়াটীকের রাণী, ভিনিস নগরী। **Queen of the Dripping-pan**—পাচক। **Queen of the Eastern Archipelago**—যবদ্বীপ। **Queen of the May**—See under MAY. **Queen of the meadows**—একপ্রকার গুল্ম। **Queen of the Northern Seas**—রাজ্ঞী এলিজেবেথ। **Queen of the seas**—সাগররাণী, গ্রেটব্রিটেন। **The White queen**—স্কটলণ্ডের রাজ্ঞী মেরী। **To turn Queen's evidence**—To turn an approver; মহারাণীর সাক্ষী হওয়া।

queen (kwēn), *v. t.* & *i.* **1.** To make a queen of; রাণী করা। **2.** (*Chess*) To make into a queen, as a pawn by advancing it to its eighth square; বড়েকে দাবা করা। ***Verb i.*** **1.** To act as a queen; রাণীর ক্ষমতা পরিচালনা করা। **2.** (*Chess*) To become a queen (of a pawn); (দাবাখেলা—বড়েরসম্বন্ধে) মন্ত্রী হওয়া।

queen'-ing (kwēn-), *n.* A kind of apple; একপ্রকার সেওফল।

queen'-ly (kwēn-), *adj.* Becoming, or suitable to, a queen; queen-like; majestic; রাজ্ঞোচিত, রাজপত্নী-সমুচিত; রাজ্ঞীতুল্য; মহিমান্বিত। **—li-ness,** *n.*

queer (kwēr), *adj.* & *v. t.* **1.** (*Slang*) Strange; odd; peculiar; as, a *queer* fellow or story; (ইতর ভাষায়) সৃষ্টিছাড়া; অপরূপ, আজগবী; একতর। **2.** Out of sorts; unwell; faint; as, to feel *queer*; অসুস্থ; কতকটা পীড়িত; দুর্ব্বল। **3.** Suspicious; questionable; as, a *queer* transaction; সন্দিগ্ধ; সন্দেহজনক। **4.** (*Slang*) Drunk; (ইতরভাষায়) মাতাল। **5.** (*Slang*) Sham; spurious (ইতর ভাষায়) কৃত্রিম; ঝুঁটা, নকল। ***Verb t.*** **1.** To spoil; নষ্ট করা। **2.** To make or feel queer or unwell; অসুস্থ বোধ করান, পীড়িত বোধ করান। **Queer'-ish,** *adj.* **Queer'-ness,** *n.* **Queer fish**—See under FISH. **Queer street**—যে কল্পিত রাস্তায় বা স্থানে সৃষ্টিছাড়া ও ছিটগ্রস্ত লোক সকল বাস করে, (বিশেষতঃ) অর্থকষ্টে পতিত বা ঋণজালে জড়িত ব্যক্তিদিগের বাসস্থান, কাঙ্গালপাড়া। **In Queer street**—(*Slang*) In a difficulty; in debt; in disrepute; (ইতর ভাষায়) মুস্কিলে, ফ্যাসাদে, লেঠায়, ঝঞ্ঝাটে; ঋণজালে জড়িত; কলঙ্কগ্রস্ত অবস্থায়। **To queer the pitch for one**—To spoil one's chance beforehand by secret dealings; তলে তলে চেষ্টা করিয়া পূর্ব্বেই কাহারো সফলতার আশা নষ্ট করা।

quĕll, *v. t.* To subdue; to put down; to crush; as, to *quell* fear, opposition, rebellion, rebels, etc.; শান্ত করা, প্রশমিত করা; দমন করা; ধ্বংস করা। **—quel'-ler,** *n.*

quĕnch, *v. t.* **1.** To put out or extinguish, as a fire, light, etc.; নির্ব্বাপিত করা, নিভান। **2.** To slake as thirst; নিবৃত্তি করা, নিবারণ করা। **3.** To suppress or extinguish, as a desire, hate, love, etc.; দমন করা, নির্ব্বাপিত করা। **4.** To cool as heat, heated things, etc. esp. with water; ঠাণ্ডা করা, শীতল করা। **5.** (*Slang*) To reduce to silence; (ইতর ভাষায়) চুপ করিয়া দেওয়া। **Quench'-a-ble,** *adj.*

That can be quenched; নির্ব্বাপণীয়, শমনীয়, উচ্ছেদ্য, দমনীয়। **Quench'-less**, *adj.* That cannot be quenched; অশাম্য, অনির্ব্বাপ্য।

quĕnch'-ĕr, *n.* One that quenches; esp. (*slang*) something to drink; as, a modest *quencher*; নির্ব্বাপক, শময়িতা, উচ্ছেদক; (ইতর ভাষায়) মদ্যাদি পানীয় দ্রব্য।

quĕ-nelle' (-nĕl), *n.* A round mass of fish or meat reduced to a paste; পিষ্টকাকারে পরিণত মাংস বা মৎস্যের পিণ্ড।

quĕr'-ist, *n.* One who asks a question; প্রশ্নকর্ত্তা, প্রশ্নকারী, প্রষ্টা, পৃচ্ছক।

quêrn, *n.* 1. A stone hand-mill for grinding corn; যাঁতা। 2. A small hand-mill for grinding spices; মসলা গুঁড়া করার জন্য ক্ষুদ্র যাঁতা। **Quern-stone** — যাঁতার পাথর।

Quern.

quĕr'-ŭ-lous (-lŭs), *adj.* 1. Habitually complaining; disposed to murmur; খুঁতখুঁতিয়া; গজগজকারী। 2. Peevish; fretful; খিটখিটে; চটা, কোপন। **—ly**, *adv.* **—ness**, *n.*

quē'-rȳ, *n., v.t.* & *i.* 1. A question; an enquiry; প্রশ্ন; জিজ্ঞাসা। 2. The mark of interrogation; প্রশ্নবোধক চিহ্ন (?)। 3. (Abbr. *qu.*) Pray; ask; as, *query* or *qu.*, was it so?; প্রশ্ন কচ্ছি; জিজ্ঞেস কচ্ছি। 4. A doubt; as, I have a *query* about his sincerity; সন্দেহ, সংশয়। ***Verb t.*** 1. To inquire into; to ask; অনুসন্ধান করা; জিজ্ঞাসা করা। 2. To question the truth or accuracy of; কোন বিষয়ের সত্যতা অথবা যাথার্থ্য সম্বন্ধে প্রশ্ন করা। ***Verb i.*** To question; to inquire; to express doubt; প্রশ্ন করা; জিজ্ঞাসা করা; সন্দেহ প্রকাশ করা।

quĕst, *n.* 1. Act of seeking; search; (in Mediæval romance) a chivalrous enterprise; অন্বেষণ; খোঁজ, তত্ত্ব; (মধ্যযুগের উপন্যাসে) ক্ষত্রজনোচিত সাহসিক কর্ম্ম। 2. An object of search or inquiry; অনুসন্ধানের বিষয়, জিজ্ঞাস্য। 3. Official inquiry or the jury etc. that makes it; [now only in (*vulg.*) *Crowner's quest* = Coroner's inquest]; সরকারী তদন্ত, যে ব্যক্তিগণ ঐরূপ তদন্ত করিয়া থাকেন। **In quest of** — In search of; seeking; অন্বেষণে; খোঁজে।

quĕst, *v.i.* & *t.* 1. (Of a dog) To go in search of game; (কুকুরসম্বন্ধে) শিকারের অন্বেষণে যাওয়া। 2. To make a search; to go in search of something; অনুসন্ধান করা, তল্লাস করা, খোঁজা; কোন কিছুর অন্বেষণে যাওয়া। ***Verb t.*** (*Poet.*) To seek; to search for; (কবিতায়) অন্বেষণ করা; খোঁজা।

quĕs'-tion (kwĕs-tyŭn), *n.* 1. Interrogation; inquiry; প্রশ্ন, জিজ্ঞাসা; পৃচ্ছা। 2. That which is asked in questioning; জিজ্ঞাসিত বিষয়। 3. Doubt; objection; as, it is true beyond *question*; সন্দেহ, সংশয়; আপত্তি। 4. A subject of dispute or enquiry; a problem; as, a difficult *question*; something depending on the condition of; as, it is a mere *question* of time; তর্কণীয় বিষয়, জিজ্ঞাসার বিষয়; প্রশ্ন, সমস্যা; যাহা কোন কিছুর উপর অপেক্ষা করে। 5. The point or matter under, or for, discussion; the point at issue; as, that is not the *question*; a thing to be voted on; আলোচ্য বিষয়, আলোচ্য প্রশ্ন; তর্কস্থলীয় বিষয়, বিচার্য্য বিষয়; যে বিষয়ে ভোট দিতে হইবে। 6. (*Archaic*) Official investigation; also, examination by torture; as, he was put to the *question*; সরকারী তদন্ত; পীড়ন বা যন্ত্রণাপূর্ব্বক পরীক্ষা। **—a-ble**, *adj.* **—less**, *adj.* Doubtless; নিঃসন্দেহ। **Leading question** — See under LEADING. **Q!** — সভাতে কোন বক্তা মূল বিষয়ে ছাড়িয়া অবান্তর বিষয় ধরিলে তাহাকে সাবধান করার জন্য যে শব্দ ব্যবহৃত হয়। **Question-stop, —mark** — প্রশ্নবোধক চিহ্ন। **A burning question** — লোক সাধারণের গভীর আন্দোলনের বিষয়ীভূত প্রশ্ন, যাহাতে বহু লোকের স্বার্থ আছে এবং যাহা লইয়া লোকে গভীর আন্দোলনে মত্ত — এরূপ প্রশ্ন। **An open question** — See under OPEN. **Beyond (all) question, Past** or **without question** — Same as OUT OF QUESTION. **In question** — Under consideration; under discussion; বিবেচনাধীন; আলোচ্য, আলোচনাধীন। **It is merely a question of time** — It will certainly happen, but may happen sooner or later; ইহা নিশ্চয়ই ঘটিবে, দুদিন আগে হউক কিম্বা দুদিন পরেই হউক। **Out of question** — Unquestionably; undoubtedly; নিশ্চিতরূপে, অবিসংবাদিতরূপে; নিঃসন্দেহ। **Out of the question** — Foreign to the question; impossible to be considered; unworthy of discussion; মূল প্রশ্নের বহির্ভূত; কথার মধ্যেই নয়, তাহারতো কথাই নাই; আলোচনার যোগ্যই নয়, উল্লেখযোগ্য নয়। **Question and answer** — প্রশ্নোত্তর; প্রশ্নোত্তরাত্মক প্রণালী। **To beg the question** — See under BEG. **That is not the question** — That is irrelevant; এটা অপ্রাসঙ্গিক বা মূল বিষয়ের বহির্ভূত। **To call in question** — To object to; to find fault with; আপত্তি করা; দোষ ধরা, খুঁত ধরা। **To come into question** — To be discussed; to become of practical importance; আলোচিত হওয়া; কার্য্যতঃ গুরুত্ববিশিষ্ট হওয়া।

ques'-tion (kwĕs-tyŭn), *v.t.* & *i.* 1. To examine by queries; to query; প্রশ্ন করা; জিজ্ঞাসা করা। 2. To call in question; to doubt; to raise objections to ; কোনও বিষয়ের সত্যতা সম্বন্ধে প্রশ্ন উত্থাপন করা ; সন্দেহ করা; আপত্তি উত্থাপন করা। *Verb i.* To ask questions ; to inquire ; প্রশ্ন জিজ্ঞাসা করা ; প্রশ্ন করা, জিজ্ঞাসা করা।

quĕt'-zăl, *n.* A handsome bird of Central America ; মধ্য আমেরিকার একপ্রকার সুন্দর পক্ষী।

queue (kū), *n., v. t. & i.* 1. The tail of a wig ; a pigtail ; পরচুলার বেণী ; শিখা। 2. A line of persons, carriages, etc. as before a ticket-window, opera house, or the like ; টিকিট ঘরের এবং গীতিনাট্যশালা প্রভৃতির সম্মুখস্থ লোক বা শকটশ্রেণী। *Verb t.* To fasten as hair in a queue ; বেণী বাঁধা। *Verb i.* To form *up* a queue ; (লোক, গাড়ী প্রভৃতি সম্পর্কে) সারি বাঁধা।

quib'-ble (-l), *n. & v. i.* 1. A play upon words ; a pun ; শব্দশ্লেষ ; বাক্‌ছল, বাগ্‌ভঙ্গী (উজ্জ্বলঃ), বক্রোক্তি, কথার মারপেঁচ। 2. An evasion ; an equivocation ; পরিহার, ছল (ন্যায়ঃ) ; দ্ব্যর্থবোধক বাক্য প্রয়োগ। *Verb i.* 1. To use quibbles ; to equivocate ; বাক্‌ছল করা ; দ্ব্যর্থবোধক বাক্য প্রয়োগ করা। **–bler,** *n.* **–bling,** *adj.*

quick, *adj., n. & adv.* 1. *(Archaic)* Alive ; living ; animate ; as, the *quick* and the dead ; সজীব ; জীবিত ; চেতন। 2. Sprightly ; active ; ready ; lively ; prompt to act, perceive, learn, think, invent, etc. ; as, a *quick* child ; প্রফুল্ল, স্ফূর্ত্তিযুক্ত ; কর্ম্মঠ ; তৎপর ; চটুল, চটপটে, চপল ; সূক্ষ্মদর্শী, শীঘ্রকর্ম্মা, প্রত্যুৎপন্নমতি। 3. Sensitive, excitable, passionate, etc. ; সহজে অভিভূত বা বিচলনীয়, আশুগ্রাহী, আশুকোপী, আশুক্রোধী, কোপন। 4. Speedy ; swift ; done or happening in a short time ; ক্ষিপ্র ; সত্বর ; শীঘ্র, শীঘ্রগ, শীঘ্র সম্পন্ন। 5. Shifting ; yielding to pressure ; as, *quick* sand ; চোরা ; চাপসহনাক্ষম। 6. Same as QUICKSET. *Noun.* 1. Same as QUICKSET. 2. The living or sensitive flesh as under the nails, skin, etc. ; the tender part of a wound, sore, etc. ; a part susceptible of keen feeling ; as, to cut a finger nail to the *quick* : the insult stung him to the *quick* ; নখ, চর্ম্ম প্রভৃতির নিম্নে তীব্র সংবেদনশীল মাংস ; ক্ষত ঘা, প্রভৃতির কোমল অংশ ; মর্ম্ম, মর্ম্মস্থান। *Adv.* Quickly ; speedily ; without delay ; সত্বর ; দ্রুত ; অবিলম্বে।

Quick'-ly, *adv.* Without delay ; swiftly ; অবিলম্বে, ত্বরা, ত্বরিৎ, দ্রুত, ঝটিতি ; ধাঁ করিয়া *(colloq.)* টপাটপ *(ib.)*, চটপট *(ib.)*, হুহু করিয়া *(ib.)*, তরস্ত *(ib)*, তূর্ণ, আশু, সহসা। **Quick**—*(Ellipt., imp.)* Make haste ; তাড়াতাড়ি কর। **Quick-change**—(Of an actor etc.) Quickly changing costume, play and the part ; (অভিনেতা প্রভৃতি সম্পর্কে) অপর ভূমিকা অভিনয়ের জন্য শীঘ্র পরিচ্ছদ প্রভৃতি পরিবর্ত্তনকারী। **Quick-eyed, –eared**—তীক্ষ্ণদর্শী, তীক্ষ্ণশ্রবণশক্তিসম্পন্ন। **Quick-firing gun, Quick-firer**—দ্রুত গোলাবর্ষী কামান। **Quicklime**—বাখারিচুণ, কলিচুণ। **Quick march**—(সামরিক) সৈন্যদিগের একপ্রকার গতি—যাহাতে মিনিটে ১১০ বার পদক্ষেপ করিতে হয়, দ্রুতগতি, দ্রুতাভিযান। **Quick-sand**—চোরা বালি। **Quickset**—*adj. & n.* (বেড়া প্রভৃতি সম্বন্ধে) ক্ষুদ্র ক্ষুদ্র সজীব বৃক্ষ দ্বারা রচিত, বিশেষতঃ বনসঞ্জলী গাছের। *(Noun.)* বেড়ার জন্য জীবিত গাছ বা গাছের ডালা, বিশেষ ভাবে বনসঞ্জলী গাছ। A hedge composed of these ; জীবিত গাছের বেড়া, বিশেষতঃ বনসঞ্জলী গাছের বেড়া। **Quick-scented**—তীব্রগন্ধী, উগ্রগন্ধ। **Quick sight**—Acute or alert sight ; তীক্ষ্ণদৃষ্টি। **Quick-sighted**—*adj.* সূক্ষ্মদর্শী, তীক্ষ্ণদৃষ্টি, প্রখরদৃষ্টি। **Quick-silver**—*n. & v. t.* Mercury ; *(fig.)* mobility of temperament or mood ; পারদ [Syn. তারাভ (নিঘণ্টু), তুঙ্গবীজ (সুঃ সিঃ) দিব্যরস, পার, পারত, অবিতাজ, রস ধাতু রসরাজ, লোহ, রেতঃ, পতঙ্গ, বীজ, লোকেশ, যশোদ। See MERCURY] ; (লক্ষণায়) চঞ্চলতা, অব্যবস্থিতচিত্ততা। *(Verb t.)* To overlay as mirror-glass with amalgam of tin ; দর্পণের কাচের পৃষ্ঠে বঙ্গমিশ্রিত পারদ মাখান। [*Calcining quick silver with sulpher* — মূর্চ্ছন (ভাবঃ প্রঃ)]। **Quick step**—দ্রুতাভিযান ; দ্রুতপাদবিক্ষেপ। **Quick-temper**—আশুকোপনস্বভাব, চটামেজাজ। **Quick-tempered**—আশুক্রোধী, আশুকোপী। **Quick time**—সৈন্যগণের গতির হারবিশেষ—যাহাতে ইংলণ্ডে প্রতি মিনিটে ১২৮ বার ও আমেরিকার যুক্তরাজ্যে মিনিটে ১২০ বার পদক্ষেপ করা হয়। **Quick-witted**—সূক্ষ্মবুদ্ধি, তীক্ষ্ণধী, শীঘ্রবুদ্ধি, তীক্ষ্ণবুদ্ধি। **A quick child**—An intelligent child ; তীক্ষ্ণবুদ্ধি বালক। **He is a Tory to the quick**—He is a Tory through and through ; সে পুরামাত্রায় রক্ষণশীল। **Quick with child**—(Orig., *with quick child*) At a stage of pregnancy when the foetus begins to move ; গর্ভের এরূপ অবস্থায় উপনীতা—যাহাতে ভ্রূণের সঞ্চরণ প্রথম অনুভূত হয়, আপন্নসত্ত্বা। **To be quick**—To make haste ; তাড়াতাড়ি করা, সত্বর হওয়া। **To have quick wits**—To be ready at grasping the situation, making repartees, etc. ; প্রত্যুৎপন্নমতিসম্পন্ন হওয়া, উপস্থিতবুদ্ধিসম্পন্ন হওয়া।

quick'-en (-n), *v. t. & i.* 1. To revive or resuscitate as from death or inanimate state ; to animate ; to stimulate ; to kindle ; to inspire ; to rouse ; সঞ্জীবিত করা, উজ্জীবিত করা ; চেতনা সঞ্চার করা ; উত্তেজিত করা, উদ্রিক্ত করা ; উদ্দীপ্ত করা, প্রদীপ্ত করা ; অনুপ্রাণিত করা ; জাগরিত করা, জাগাইয়া তোলা। 2. To make quick or rapid ; to accelarate ; দ্রুততর করা ; ত্বরান্বিত করা।

Verb i. 1. To come to life; to revive life; সঞ্জীবিত হওয়া, জীবন সঞ্চার হওয়া; পুনর্জীবিত হওয়া। 2. To show signs of life as a foetus in the womb; to reach the stage of pregnancy at which the foetus shows signs of life; গর্ভস্থ ভ্রূণের সঞ্চরণ প্রথম অনুভূত হওয়া; গর্ভের যে অবস্থায় গর্ভস্থ শিশু জীবনসঞ্চারের চিহ্ন-প্রদর্শন করে সেই অবস্থায় উপনীত হওয়া। 3. To become quicker; দ্রুততর হওয়া।

quick'-en-ing (-n-), *adj.* & *n.* Giving life; reviving; প্রাণপ্রদ; সঞ্জীবক। ***Noun.*** (*Physiol.*) The first motion of the foetus in the womb felt by the mother; (শারীরবিজ্ঞান) গর্ভিণীকর্তৃক প্রথম ভ্রূণের সঞ্চরণ অনুভব, প্রাণস্পন্দনানুভব।

quick'-nĕss, *n.* 1. Alertness; readiness; as, *quickness* of wit; hastiness, as of temper; সচকিত ভাব; প্রত্যুৎপন্নমতিত্ব; আশুকোপনত্ব। 2. Acuteness of perception or apprehension; সূক্ষ্মবুদ্ধিতা, তীক্ষ্ণবুদ্ধিতা। 3. (*Rare*) Rapidity; speed; (কচিদ্ব্যবহৃত) ক্ষিপ্রতা; দ্রুতত্ব।

quid, *n.* (*Slang*) A sovereign or pound sterling; (ইতর ভাষায়) এক সভারেণ বা এক পাউণ্ড।

quid, *n.* A piece of tobacco suitable to be chewed; দোক্তা, তামাকের কলি।

quid'-di-ty (-i-), *n.* 1. The essence of a thing; that which makes a thing what it is; সার; তত্ত্ব। 2. A quibble; a trifling nicety; a cavil; কুতর্ক; খুঁটিনাটি; তুচ্ছ আপত্তি।

quid-nunc (-nŭngk), *n.* One curious to know everything that passes; a newsmonger; a gossip; কৌতুহলী ব্যক্তি; যে ব্যক্তি স্থানে স্থানে সংবাদ প্রচার করিয়া বেড়ায়; গল্পপ্রিয় ব্যক্তি, গপ্পিয়া।

quid pro quo, (*L.*), *n.* Something given in place of another; কোন বস্তুর পরিবর্তে প্রদত্ত বস্তু; ক্ষতিপূরণ।

qui-ĕs'-cent (-ĕnt), *adj.* 1. Still or motionless; inert; নীরব, নিশ্চল, নিষ্কম্প, নিস্পন্দ; অচেষ্ট। 2. Unagitated; quiet; dormant; অবিক্ষুব্ধ; শান্ত, প্রশান্ত; প্রচ্ছন্ন, অন্তর্গূঢ়। **—cence, —cen-cy,** *ns.* **—ly,** *adv.*

quī'-ĕt, *n.* 1. A state of rest or repose; tranquillity; freedom from disturbance or agitation; peace of mind; শান্তি; স্থিরতা, নিস্তব্ধতা; অবিক্ষুব্ধতা, নিরুদ্বেগ; মানসিক শান্তি। 2. Stillness; silence; unruffled state; নীরবতা; নিস্তব্ধতা; অনুত্তরঙ্গতা। 3. Public tranquillty; সাধারণের শান্তি।

quī'-ĕt, *adj.* 1. Without stir or motion; free from noise or disturbance; still; নিশ্চল, নিস্পন্দ, স্থির; নীরব, নিস্তব্ধ, নিঝুম, অবিক্ষুব্ধ, নিরুদ্বিগ্ন; শান্ত, প্রশান্ত। 2. Gentle; of mild disposition; ধীর, নম্র; শান্তপ্রকৃতি। 3. Free from anxiety, emotion, etc.; calm; peaceful; নিরুদ্বিগ্ন, অবিক্ষুব্ধ; স্থির; শান্তিপূর্ণ। 4. Private; disguised; as, *quiet* resentment; গোপন; ছদ্ম। 5. Not showy or gaudy; as, *quiet* dress or colours; আড়ম্বরশূন্য; জমকালো নয়। 6. Enjoyed in quiet; নীরবে ভুক্ত। **—e-tude,** *n.* Rest; repose; tranquillity; বিশ্রাম; বিরাম; শান্তি। **—ly,** *adv.* In a quiet manner; নীরবে, শান্তভাবে, চুপি চুপি। **—ness,** *n.* **On the (strict) quiet** — (*Slang*, abbr. *on the q. t.*) Secretly; privately; (ইতর ভাষায়) গোপনে; চুপেচাপে, চুপুসারে, চুপিচুপি।

quī'-ĕt, *v. t.* & *i.* To reduce to rest or silence; to calm; to allay; শান্ত করা, নীরব করা; স্থির করা; প্রশমিত করা। ***Verb i.*** To become silent or calm, usu. with *down*; শান্ত হওয়া, নীরব হওয়া, নিস্তব্ধ হওয়া।

quī'-ĕt-en (-n), *v. t.* & *i.* (*Vulg.*)

quī'-ĕt-ĭsm, *n.* 1. A system of religious mysticism in which the mind is withdrawn from all worldly concerns in order to bring the soul into direct union with the Godhead; non-resistance principles; একপ্রকার ধর্ম্মমত — এই মতানুসারে জীবাত্মার সহিত পরমাত্মার মিলনসাধনের জন্য মনকে সর্ব্বপ্রকার ঐহিক বিষয় হইতে নিবৃত্ত করিতে হয়; নিশ্চেষ্টতাবাদ, শান্তিমার্গ, শান্তিবাদ, নিবৃত্তিমার্গ। [Miguel de Molinos নামক জনৈক স্পেন দেশীয় যাজক উক্ত ধর্ম্মমতের প্রবর্ত্তক; ১৬৭৫ খৃঃ অব্দে প্রকাশিত Molinos এর *Spiritual Guide* নামক গ্রন্থে এই মত বিবৃত হইয়াছে। See Denis's *Quietisme*; Heppe's *Geschichte der Quietistischen Mystik inder Kathol*; Madame Guyon's *Works* (*in 40 volumes*) including the *Autobiography*]. 2. Peace of mind; calmness; মানসিক শান্তি; শম, উপরতি। **—ist,** *n.* & *adj.* **—is'-tic,** *adj.*

quī-ē'-tŭs, *n.* 1. (*Rare*) Final discharge from debt, obligation, etc.; (কচিদ্ ব্যবহৃত) ঋণ বা বাধ্য-বাধকতা হইতে চরম মুক্তি। 2. Release from life; death; extinction; ভববন্ধনমুক্তি; মৃত্যু; নির্ব্বাণ। **To give one his quietus**—To kill one or put a check upon one's activity; কাহাকে বধ করা, কাহারো কর্ম্মচেষ্টা রোধ করা।

quill, *n.* 1. (Also, *quill-feather*) The strong feather of a bird's wing or tail; পাখা, পক্ষ। 2. A pen, fishing-float, tooth-pick, plectrum, etc. made of this; পাখার কলম, বড়শীর ফাতনা, দন্তশঙ্কু, মিস্রাব (also কোণ—কাদঃ), প্রভৃতি। 3. One of the spines of a porcupine; শজারুর কাঁটা। 4. (*Weaving*) A spindle or spool as of reed, for the thread in a shuttle; (বয়ন-শিল্প) মাকব নলী। 5. A musical pipe made of a hollow stem ; মুরলী, বংশী, বেণু। 6. A roll of dried bark ; as, a *quill* of cinnamon ; চোঙ্গার আকারে গুটানো শুষ্ক বল্কল। **Quill-coverts**—পাখার নীচের ক্ষুদ্র ক্ষুদ্র পালক। **Quill-driver**—সংবাদপত্র লেখক, গ্রন্থকার, কলমপেশা কেরাণী, মসিজীবী।

quill, *v. t.* & *i.* To form into quill-like folds ; পাখার সারির আকারে চুনট করা। ***Verb i.*** To wind thread or yarn on a quill; মাকুর নলীতে সুতা জড়ান।

quil'-let (-ĕt), *n.* A nicety or subtlety ; a quibble ; সূক্ষ্মতর্ক ; বাক্‌ছল।

Quill'-ing, *n.* A strip of lace, ribbon, etc. plaited or folded so as somewhat to resemble a row of quills ; পাখার সারির আকারে চুনট-করা ফিতা, লেইস, প্রভৃতি।

quilt, *n.* & *v. t.* A padded bed-cover ; লেপ, তোষক, গদি, বালাপোষ। ***Verb t.*** 1. To cover with padded material ; গদি দ্বারা মোড়া। 2. To join or stitch together as two pieces of cloth with a soft material between them ; লেপ, তোষক, বালাপোষ, প্রভৃতি সেলাই করা। 3. To put as letters, coin, etc. between two layers of garments, etc. and sew up ; পোষাক প্রভৃতির দুই পরতের মধ্যে পত্র, মুদ্রা, পয়সা প্রভৃতি রাখিয়া সেলাই করা। 4. To produce as a literary work out of borrowed ideas, extracts, etc. ; অপরের গ্রন্থ হইতে ভাব বা অংশ বিশেষ গ্রহণ করিয়া কোন পুস্তক উৎপাদন করা। 5. (*Slang*) To thrash ; (ইতর ভাষায়) বেদম মারা।

quilt'-ing, *n.* Act of forming a quilt ; the material used in this ; quilted work ; লেপতোষক প্রভৃতি তৈয়ার ; লেপতোষক প্রভৃতি প্রস্তুতে ব্যবহৃত কাপড় প্রভৃতি ; লেপ, তোষক, প্রভৃতি।

quin'-ăr-ў, *adj.* Of, or relating to, the number 5 ; consisting of five things ; পঞ্চসংখ্যক, পঞ্চক ; পঞ্চগর্ত্ত, পঞ্চাত্মক।

quin'-āte, *adj.* (*Bot.*) With five leaflets as a leaf ; (উদ্ভিদ্‌বিদ্যা) পঞ্চাঙ্গুল্যাকার (সাঃ পঃ)।

quince (quĭns), *n.* The fruit of a tree, allied to the pear and apple ; the tree bearing this ; নাসাপতি বা সেওফল জাতীয় ফলবিশেষ—সাফারজাল (Arab. سفرجل), বিহি (Pers. بهی, بی), আবি (Pers. آبی)। [Fr. *Semen de Coig, Quincunx* ; Germ. *Quitten Korner* ; Ital. *Melacotogna* ; Sp. *Membrillo.*] ; ঐ ফলের গাছ। **Bengal quince**—বেল, বিল্ব, শ্রীফল। **Quince-seed**—বিহিদানা (Pers.), তুকুম্-সাফারজাল (Arab.)।

quin-cĕn'-tē-na-rў, *adj.* & *n.* Same as QUINGENTENARY.

quin'-cunx (-kŭngks), *n.* 1. An arrangement of objects in a square or rectangle, one at each corner and one in the middle ; five objects so arranged ; সমচতুষ্কোণে বা আয়তক্ষেত্রে বস্তুসমূহের বিন্যাস—যাহাতে প্রতি কোণে এক একটী করিয়া ৪টী ও মধ্যস্থলে একটী স্থাপিত হয়, পঞ্চকসংস্থান ; উক্তরূপে বিন্যস্ত পঞ্চসংখ্যক বস্তু। 2. (*Astrol.*) The position of bodies distant from each other five signs or 150° ; (জ্যোতিঃশাস্ত্র) পরস্পর হইতে পাঁচ রাশি বা ১৫০° দূরে গ্রহাদির অবস্থান। **—cun'-ci-al**, *adj.* **—cun'-ci-al-ly**, *adv.* **Plantation laid out in quincunxes** — যে আবাদে বৃক্ষসমূহ (⁘ ⁘) ইত্যাকারে বিন্যস্ত করা হয়।

quin-gĕn'-tē-na-rў, *adj.* & *n.* Of, relating to, or in, the five hundredth year ; পঞ্চশতবার্ষিক। ***Noun.*** The five hundredth anniversary of an event; পঞ্চশত সাম্বৎসরিক স্মৃতি উৎসব।

quin'-i-ă, *n.* Same as QUININE.

qui-nīne', *n.* 1. An alkaloid obtained from various species of cinchona much used as a febrifuge, tonic, etc. ; কুইনাইন। 2. Sulphate of quinine ; সালফেট অব কুইনাইন। **Qui'-nism, Qui'-nin-ism**, *ns.* Cinchonism ; অতিমাত্রায় কুইনাইন সেবনজনিত বিষলক্ষণ। **Quin'-ize**, *v. t.*

quin-quă-gē-nā'-ri-ăn, *adj.* & *n.* Fifty years old ; পঞ্চাশদ্‌বর্ষীয়। ***Noun.*** A person fifty years old ; পঞ্চাশদ্‌বর্ষীয় ব্যক্তি।

quin-quă'-gē-na-rў, *adj.* & *n.* Same as QUINQUAGENARIAN. ***Noun.*** 1. Same as QUINQUAGENARIAN. 2. The fiftieth anniversary ; পঞ্চাশত্তম সাম্বৎসরিক উৎসব।

quin-quă-gĕs'-i-mă, *n.* (Also *quinquagesima Sunday*) The Sunday next before Lent ; লেণ্ট উপবাসের অব্যবহিত পূর্ব্ববর্ত্তী রবিবার।

quin-quan'-gu-lar (-quăng-gü-lêr), *adj.* Having five angles ; পঞ্চাস্র, পঞ্চকোণী।

quin-quē-cŏs'-tāte, *adj.* Five-ribbed ; পঞ্চশিরাবিশিষ্ট।

quin-quē-lat'-ĕr-ăl, *adj.* & *n.* Five-sided ; পঞ্চভুজী। ***Noun.*** Such a figure or object ; পঞ্চভুজ ক্ষেত্র, পঞ্চপার্শ্ববিশিষ্ট বস্তু।

quin-quē-lō'-bāte, *adj.* Five-lobed ; পঞ্চলতিকাবিশিষ্ট।

quin-quĕn'-ni-ăd (-ĭ-), **—ni-ŭm** (-ĭ-), *ns.* A period of five years ; পঞ্চবর্ষ কাল।

quin-quĕn'-ni-ăl (-ĭ-), *adj.* Occurring once in five years ; lasting 5 years ; five-yearly ; পঞ্চবর্ষান্তে সংঘটিত ; পঞ্চবর্ষস্থায়ী ; পঞ্চবার্ষিক, পঞ্চবর্ষীয়, পঞ্চাব্দিক। **—ly**, *adv.*

quin-quē-pâr'-tīte, *adj.* Consisting of, or divided into, five parts ; পঞ্চখণ্ডাত্মক, পঞ্চাংশিত।

quin'-quē-reme (-rēm), *n.* An ancient galley having five banks of rowers; প্রাচীন কালের নৌকা বিশেষ—যাহাতে পাঁচসারি দাঁড় থাকিত।

quin-quĕ-vălv'-ŭ-lar (-lêr), *adj.* Having five valves; পঞ্চকপাট-বিশিষ্ট।

quin'-quĭ-fĭd, *adj.* Cleft in five; পঞ্চধাবিদারিত।

quin-quĭ-vă'-lĕnt, *adj.* (*Chem.*) Same as PENTAVALENT; পঞ্চ-শক্তিক (হিঃ কোঃ)।

quin-quī'-nă, *n.* 1. Cinchona bark; সিঙ্কোনা বৃক্ষের বল্কল। 2. Quinine; কুইনাইন।

quin'-sў, *n.* (*Med.*) An inflammation of the throat esp. the tonsils; (ভৈষজ্যশাস্ত্র) তালুমুল বা গলার প্রদাহ, শ্লেষ্মজ রোহিণী (ভাবঃ প্রঃ), তুণ্ডীকেরী (সাঃ পঃ)। **–sied,** *adj.*

quint, *n.* (*Mus.*) The interval of a fifth; (সঙ্গীত-শাস্ত্র) পঞ্চম। 2. (*Piquet*) A sequence of five cards of the same suit; (তাস-খেলায়) হান্‌ড্রেড্‌। **Quint major**—(বিন্তি খেলায়) টেক্কা হইতে দশ পর্য্যন্ত পঞ্চ তাসের মধ্যে সর্ব্বোচ্চ তাস। **Quint minor**—গোলাম হইতে সাতা পর্য্যন্ত পঞ্চ তাসের মধ্যে সর্ব্বনিম্ন তাস।

quin'-tain (-tān), *n.* (*Hist.*) An object to be tilted at; a favourite English sport in the middle ages; (ইতিহাস) অশ্বারোহণপূর্ব্বক বর্শাদ্বারা যে লক্ষ্য ভেদ করিতে হয়; মধ্যযুগে ইংলণ্ডদেশে প্রচলিত ক্রীড়া বিশেষ। [এইরূপ ক্রীড়ায় সাধারণতঃ একটী থামের উপর একটী আড়-কাঠ দোলায়িত করা হইত, ঐ আড়কাঠের একপ্রান্ত হইতে একটী প্রশস্ত ফলক ও অপর প্রান্ত হইতে একটী বালির বস্তা ঝুলিত। অশ্বারোহণপূর্ব্বক বর্শা দ্বারা ফলকটী বিদ্ধকরতঃ বস্তা দ্বারা অস্পৃষ্ট হইয়া ক্রীড়ককে ঐ আড়কাঠের নীচ দিয়া যাইতে হইত।

quin'-tăl, *n.* 1. A hundredweight; 100 lb.; এক হন্দর; ১০০ পাউণ্ড। 2. 100 kilogram; ১০০ কিলোগ্রাম।

quin'-tăn, *adj.* & *n.* (Of fever, ague, etc.), Occurring every fifth day; প্রতি পঞ্চম দিবসে যে জ্বর আগত হয়। *Noun.* Such a fever; ঐরূপ জ্বর।

quinte, (*F.*), *n.* (*Fencing*) A parry a little lower than carte; (অসিক্রীড়ায়) একপ্রকার আটকানি।

quin-tĕs'-sence (-ĕns), *n.* 1. The fifth and the highest essence or power in a natural body; সারাৎসার, পরমসার। 2. The most essential part of anything; refined extract; কোন বস্তুর পরম সারাংশ; বিশোধিত সত্ত্ব। 3. A thing, person, quality or the like, in the highest and the most typical form; পরম স্বরূপ, উচ্চতম রূপ [প্রাচীন গ্রীকগণকর্ত্তৃক ক্ষিতি, মরুৎ, অপ এবং অগ্নি এই চারিটি ভুত স্বীকৃত হইত। Pythagoras এর শিষ্যগণ উক্ত চারিটী ভুতের সহিত ব্যোম নামক পঞ্চম ভুত সংযুক্ত করেন; এই ব্যোমের নামই *Quintessence*।] **–sen'-tial,** *adj.*

quin-tet'(te) (-tĕt), *ns.* 1. (*Mus.*) A composition for five voices or instruments; also, the five persons who sing or play five-part music; (সঙ্গীতশাস্ত্র) পঞ্চ ব্যক্তি বা যন্ত্রের উপযোগী সঙ্গীত; যে পঞ্চ ব্যক্তি উক্তরূপ গান করে। 2. A set of five; পঞ্চক।

quin-til'-li-ŏn, *n.* The number denoted by unit with 30 ciphers annexed; ১এর ডাহিনে ৩০টী শূন্য বসাইলে যে সংখ্যা হয়।

quin'-tŭ-ple (-pl), *adj., n., v. t.* & *i.* Fivefold; পঞ্চগুণিত। *Noun.* The number or amount five times greater than another; পঞ্চগুণ। *Verb t. & i.* To multiply by five; পঞ্চগুণিত করা, পঞ্চগুণিত হওয়া। **–plet,** *n.* 1. A collection or combination of five of a kind; পঞ্চক। 2. A cycle for five riders; পাঁচজন আরোহীর আরোহণোপযোগী দ্বিচক্রযান। 3. (*Pl.*) Five children born at a time; (বহুবচন) একত্রজাত পঞ্চ সন্তান। **–pli-cate,** *adj., n.* & *v. t.* Same as QUINTUPLE. **–pli-ca'-tion,** *n.* The act of quintuplicating; পঞ্চীকরণ। **–ply,** *adv.*

quip, *n.* 1. A sarcastic remark; a clever retort; a gibe; a smart saying; ব্যঙ্গোক্তি, বিদ্রূপ বাক্য; চটুল উত্তর; নর্ম্মোক্তি; সরস উক্তি। 2. A quibble; equivocation; বাক্‌ছল; বক্রোক্তি।

quip, *v. t.* & *i.* (*Rare*) To scoff or gibe (*at*); (ক্বচিৎ ব্যবহৃত) রহস্য করা, বিদ্রূপ করা।

quī'-pu (-pö), *n.* A contrivance used by the ancient Peruvians for arithmetical or other purposes; প্রাচীন পেরুবাসিগণকর্ত্তৃক ব্যবহৃত গণনাদি কার্য্যের জন্য যন্ত্র বিশেষ, গণনযন্ত্র।

quīre, *n.* 1. A collection of 24 sheets of unprinted paper; কাগজের দিস্তা। 2. Four sheets of paper etc. folded to form eight leaves as in mediæval manuscripts; মধ্যযুগের পুঁথির জন্য ব্যবহৃত ৮ পাতায় ভাঁজ করা ৪ তা কাগজ প্রভৃতি। 3. Any collection of leaves one within another in a manuscript or book; পত্রের ভিতর পত্র বিন্যস্ত পুঁথি বা পুস্তকের পত্র সমূহ। **In quires**—Unbound; in sheets; আবাঁধা তায় তায়।

quīre, *n., v.t.* & *i.* Same as CHOIR.

quirk (kwêrk), *n.* 1. A shift; a quibble; a quip; a clever retort; ফিকির, ফন্দী; বক্রোক্তি; ব্যঙ্গোক্তি; চটুল উত্তর। 2. A twist or flourish in writing or drawing; লিখন বা চিত্রাঙ্কণে পেঁচ বা টানটোন। 3. A knack in doing a thing; a peculiarity in behaviour; কার্য্যকৌশল; আচরণের বিশেষত্ব। 4. (*Arch.*) A small channel or groove separating a bead or other moulding from the adjoining members; (স্থপতি-বিজ্ঞান) ক্ষুদ্র নালী বা খাঁজ—যদ্দারা গুটিকাকৃতি বা অন্যরূপ ভূষা পার্শ্ববর্ত্তী গুটিকাদি হইতে পৃথক্‌কৃত করা হয়।

uit, *adj.* 1. (*Archaic*) Free ; clear ; absolved ; acquitted ; (অপ্রঃ) নির্ম্মুক্ত ; পরিষ্কার ; দোষমুক্ত ; খালাস, নিষ্কৃতিপ্রাপ্ত। **Quit claim**—*n.* & *v. t.* দাবীপরিত্যাগ, স্বত্বত্যাগ ; ফারখতী পত্র, ত্যাগপত্র। (*Verb t.*) দাবী ত্যাগ করা, স্বত্ব ত্যাগ করা ; ত্যাগ করা। **Quit-rent**—অল্প মালগুজারীর আয়মার জমা, পেশকশ (রঃ অঃ), পঞ্চক জমা।

uit, *v. t.* & *i.* 1. (*Now rare*) To relieve ; to liberate ; as, to *quit* one of fear; (বর্ত্তমানে কচিদ্ ব্যবহৃত) উদ্ধার করা ; মুক্ত করা। 2. To give up ; to let go ; as, to *quit* jesting : to *quit* hold of ; ত্যাগ করা ; ছাড়িয়া দেওয়া। 3. (*Archaic*) To conduct (*used reflexively*) ; as, *quit* yourselves like men ; (অপ্রঃ) আচরণ করা, চলা। 4. To leave ; to depart from ; to forsake ; ছাড়া ; প্রস্থান করা ; ত্যাগ করা। 5. To discharge ; to repay ; to requite ; as, to *quit* a debt or obligation : শোধ করা ; পরিশোধ করা ; প্রতিশোধ দেওয়া। ***Verb i.*** To go away from occupied premises as a tenant ; as, a notice to *quit* ; বাড়ী ছাড়িয়া দেওয়া। **To quit hold of**—To loose ; মুঠা ছাড়িয়া দেওয়া। **To quit score**—To balance account ; পাওনা দেনা শোধবোধ দেওয়া, দাবী মিটান।

—tam, *n.* (*Law*) An action on a penal statute partly at the suit of the queen and partly at that of an informer ; also, an informer ; (আইন) জরিমানা প্রভৃতির টাকা আদায়ের জন্য মোকদ্দমা—যাহাতে ঐ জরিমানার কতকাংশ সংবাদদাতা প্রাপ্ত হয় এবং অবশিষ্টাংশ সরকারী কোষভুক্ত হইয়া থাকে ; সংবাদদাতা।

itch (kwĭch), (Also, *quitch-grass*) Same as COUCH-GRASS.

e, *adv.* 1. Completely; wholly ; entirely ; altogether ; সম্পূর্ণরূপে ; পুরাপুরি ; পূর্ণভাবে ; একেবারে। 2. Positively ; absolutely ; as, he was *quite* by himself; to a great extent or degree ; very ; নিশ্চিতরূপে, শ্রেফ (*colloq.*) ; একেবারে ; অত্যন্ত ; ভারি, বেশী। **It is quite the thing**—It is the fashionable thing ; ইহাই হচ্ছে আজকালকার ফ্যাসন। **Not quite proper** — Rather improper ; কতকটা অসঙ্গত। **Quite a little**—একেবারে কম। **Quite another thing**—A very different thing ; সম্পূর্ণ ভিন্ন জিনিষ। **Quite other**—Very different ; সম্পূর্ণ ভিন্নরূপ। **Quite so** — তাইতো বটে। **Quite the kick**—Quite a dandy ; পুরা ফুলবাবু।

quits, *pred. adj.* Even or equal (with another) by having returned or repaid anything good or evil or its equivalent ; as, to be *quits* with one ; শোধবোধ। **To cry quits**—To acknowledge that things are now even ; to agree to cease struggling ; শোধবোধ হইয়াছে বলিয়া স্বীকার করা ; বিবাদ মিটাইতে স্বীকার করা।

quit'-tance (-ăns), *n.* 1. Discharge from a debt or obligation ; acquittance ; receipt ; ঋণমুক্তি, বাধ্যবাধকতা হইতে মুক্তি ; প্রাপ্তিসূচক রসিদ ; রসিদ। 2. Repayment ; requital ; reprisal ; পরিশোধ ; আদায় ; প্রতিশোধ। **Omittance is no quittance**—Debt is not annulled by not being demanded or pressed ; ঋণের টাকা আদায়ের জন্য দাবী বা পীড়াপীড়ি করা না হইলেই ঋণ পরিশোধ হয়না।

quiv'-ĕr, *n.* A case for arrows ; তূণ, তূণীর [*Syn.* শরাশ্রয়, নিষঙ্গ, ইষুধি, শরধি, উপাসঙ্গ, অপাসঙ্গ, তুলসারিণী, খোলি।] **—ful**, *n.* **A quiverful of children** — A large family, (*Psalms*, cxxvii) ; বৃহৎ পরিবার। **To have an arrow or shaft left in one's quiver**—Not to be resourceless ; একবারে নিরুপায় না হওয়া।

quiv'-ĕr, *v. i.*, *t.* & *n.* To shake with slight and tremulous motion ; to tremble ; কম্পিত হওয়া, স্ফুরিত হওয়া ; কাঁপা। ***Verb t.*** (Of, skylarks etc.) To cause as a wing to quiver ; (ভারুই পাখী প্রভৃতি সম্পর্কে) পক্ষবিধুনন করা। ***Noun.*** A quivering motion or sound ; tremor ; কম্পন, স্পন্দন, কম্পনধ্বনি ; বেপথু, কম্প, কাঁপুনি, প্রকম্প। **—ing**, *n.* & *adj.* Shaking ; স্ফুরণ, কম্পন, প্রকম্পন, প্রস্পন্দন, বিস্ফুরণ, প্রস্ফুরণ, বেপন। (*Adj.*) Quivering ; কম্পমান, বেপমান, উজ্জ্বল (কাদঃ), স্ফুরৎ, প্রস্ফুরিত, স্পন্দিত, বেপমান, সকম্প, প্রস্ফুরিত, স্পন্দমান। **—ing-ly**, *adv.*

qui-vive (kē-vēv), (*F.*) A French sentinel's challange equivalent to English "who goes there" ; কে যাচ্ছে (ফরাসী সান্ত্রীর আহ্বান)। **On the quivive**—On the alert ; watchful ; সতর্ক, সাবধান ; হুঁসিয়ার।

Quix'-ōte, *n.* One who pursues lofty but impracticable ideals ; an enthusiastic visionary ; one ready to sacrifice material interests for honour or devotion ; যে ব্যক্তি উচ্চ অথবা কাল্পনিক আদর্শের অনুসরণ করে ; কল্পনাপ্রিয় উৎসাহসম্পন্ন ব্যক্তি ; যে ব্যক্তি মর্য্যাদা বা নিষ্ঠা রক্ষার জন্য পার্থিব স্বার্থবিসর্জ্জনের জন্য সর্ব্বদা প্রস্তুত থাকে। [স্পেনদেশীয় প্রসিদ্ধ গ্রন্থকর্তা Cerventes-কৃত Don Quixote নামক জগদ্বিখ্যাত গ্রন্থের নায়কের নাম হইতে গৃহীত।] **—ot'-ic**, *adj.* Extravagantly romantic ; absurdly chivalric ; ridiculously venturesome or romantic ; উৎকট দুঃসাহসিকতা বা ঔপন্যাসিকতার ভাব প্রদর্শনকারী, উৎকট ঔপন্যাসিক ; ব্যঙ্গবীরোচিত ; হাস্যোদ্দীপক অসমসাহস ও উপন্যাসিকতার ভাব প্রদর্শনকারী। **—ot'-i-cal-ly** *adv.* **—ot'-ics**, *n.* (*Pl.*) Quixotic sentiments ; উৎকট ঔপন্যাসিক ভাব, উৎকট কল্পনা। **—ot-ism**, *n.* **—ot-ize**, *v. t.* & *i.*

quiz, *n.* & *v. t.* **1.** (*Rare*, An odd or eccentric person or thing ; সৃষ্টিছাড়া বস্তু, ছিটগ্রস্ত লোক, কেমন একতর লোক, মাথাপাগলা লোক। **2.** One who quizzes others ; যে ব্যক্তি অপরকে ধোঁকা দেয়। **3.** (*Rare*) A hoax ; a practical joke ; a jest ; (ক্বচিদ্ ব্যবহৃত) ধোঁকা ; কার্য্য দ্বারা ঠাট্টা ; পরিহাস। ***Verb t.*** **1.** To hoax ; to banter ; ধোঁকা দেওয়া ; ব্যঙ্গ করা, ফষ্টিনষ্টি করা। **2.** To peep at ; to look curiously or mockingly at ; to see through an eye-glass ; উঁকি মারিয়া দেখা ; কৌতূহলপূর্ণ বা বিদ্রূপব্যঞ্জক দৃষ্টিতে চাওয়া ; চসমার ভিতর দিয়া চাওয়া। **Quiz'-za-ble, Quiz'-zi-cal,** *adjs.* **Quiz'-zi-cal-ly, Quiz'-zing-ly,** *advs.*

quoad, *prep.* As to ; so far as ; সম্পর্কে ; এতদূর যে। ***Quoad hoc***—As regards this ; এই বিষয়ে, এই সম্বন্ধে।

quŏd, *n.* & *v. t.* (*Slang*) A prison ; (ইতর ভাষায়) জেলখানা। ***Verb t.*** (*Slang*) To put in quod or jail ; (ইতর ভাষায়) জেলে পুরা।

Quod erat demonstrandum, *L.* (Abbr. *Q. E. D.*) Which was to be demonstrated or proved ; যাহা প্রমাণ করিবার ছিল, সাধ্য-উপপন্ন।

Quod erat faciendum, *L.* (Abbr. *Q. E. F.*) Which was to be done ; যাহা করার ছিল, সাধ্য-রচনা (হিঃ কোঃ)।

Quod erat inveniendum, *L.* (Abbr. *Q. E. I.*) Which was to be found ; যাহা বাহির করার ছিল।

Quod vide, *L.* (Abbr. *Q. V.*) Which see ; তাহা দেখ (একই পুস্তকের অপর অংশ দেখার জন্য অনুরোধ)।

quoin (koyn), *n.* & *v. t.* **1.** A solid exterior angle as of a building ; a corner-stone ; অট্টালিকার বাহিরের কোণ ; কোণ-প্রস্তর। **2.** The internal angle or corner of a room ; কোন কক্ষের আভ্যন্তর কোণ। **3.** A wedge for locking printing type in a form, for raising the level of a gun or for keeping casks from rolling, etc. ; ফর্ম্মা আঁটিবার কাঠ, কামান তোলার জন্য কাজলা, পিপা প্রভৃতি যাহাতে গড়াইয়া না যায় তজ্জন্য যে কাজলা ব্যবহৃত হয়। ***Verb t.*** **1.** To wedge up, secure or raise with quoins ; কাঠ বা কাজলা দ্বারা আটক করা, আঁটা বা তোলা। **2.** To provide with quoins as a wall-corner ; কোণ প্রস্তরসমন্বিত করা। **Quoin'-ing,** *n.*

quoit (koyt), *n.* & *v. t.* **1.** A flattish ring of iron thrown at a fixed object in the game of quoits ; লৌহনির্ম্মিত ক্রীড়াচক্র, লোহার চাকতি। **2.** (*Pl.*) A game played with quoits, pitched from one fixed peg to another ; একপ্রকার খেলা—যাহাতে কোন খোঁটার নিকট হইতে অপর খোঁটাতে চাকতি নিক্ষেপ করিতে হয়। ***Verb t.*** (*Rare*) To throw like a quoit ; (ক্বচিদ্ ব্যবহৃত) চাকতির মত নিক্ষেপ করা।

quŏn'-dăm, *adj.* Sometime ; former ; as a *quondam* friend of mine ; কোন সময়ের, কোন কালের ; পূর্ব্বতন।

quō'-rŭm, *n.* The number of a body competent by law or constitution to transact business ; ন্যূন কল্পে যত জন সভ্য উপস্থিত থাকিলে সভার অধিবেশন চলিতে পারে, তাঁহাদের সংখ্যা, ন্যূন-সংখ্যা।

quō'-tă, *n.* A proportional part or share ; আনুপাতিক অংশ বা ভাগ।

quō-tā'-tion, *n.* **1.** Act of quoting or citing ; a passage quoted ; উদ্ধার, অপদেশ (অর্থঃ), উপবন্ধ ; উদ্ধৃত অংশ, উপন্যস্ত অংশ। **2.** A quadrat used for filling up blank in printing ; মুদ্রণে শূন্যস্থান পূরণের জন্য ব্যবহৃত চতুষ্কাকৃতি ধাতু খণ্ড। **3.** (*Commr.*) The current prices of stocks and commodities, published in price-currents ; a price quoted or given for a commodity ; (বাণিজ্য) কোম্পানীর কাগজ বা অপর জিনিষের চলিত বাজার দর—যাহা চলিত বাজার-দরের বিজ্ঞাপনে প্রকাশিত হয় ; কোন জিনিষের যে মূল্য দেওয়া বা উল্লেখ করা হয়। **Quotation marks** — উদ্ধার চিহ্ন (" " ' ')। **Quo'-ta-tive,** *adj.* উদ্ধার সম্বন্ধীয়।

quōte, *v. t.* & *n.* **1.** To repeat or adduce as a passage etc. from an author ; to cite ; আওড়ান ; উদ্ধৃত করা। **2.** To cite a passage from ; to cite as an author, book, etc. in confirmation of some view ; কোন গ্রন্থ হইতে কোন অংশ উদ্ধৃত করা ; কোন মত সমর্থনের জন্য কোন পুস্তক বা গ্রন্থকারের নাম উল্লেখ করা। **3.** To name the current price of ; প্রচলিত বাজারদর উল্লেখ করা। ***Noun.*** (*Colloq.*) A quotation ; (usu. *pl.*) a quotation mark or quotation marks ; উদ্ধার ; উদ্ধার চিহ্ন। **Quot'-a-ble, quote'-wor-thy,** *adjs.*

quoth, *v. t.* Said,—used in the first or third persons and always followed by the nominative ; as, *quoth* I : *quoth* he ; বলিলাম, কহিল।

quōth'-ă, *interj.* (*Archaic*) Forsooth ; সত্যসত্যই, বাস্তবিকই।

quō-tid'-i-ăn, *adj.* & *n.* **1.** Daily ; occurring every day, as a fever, ague, etc. ; প্রাত্যহিক ; ঐকাহিক। **2.** Commonplace ; সাধারণ, নীরস। ***Noun.*** A quotidian fever or ague ; অন্যেদ্যুষ্ক জ্বর, আহ্নিক জ্বর (সাঃ পঃ)। **Quotidian fever**— অন্যেদ্যুষ্ক জ্বর (মাঃ নিঃ)।

quō'-tient (-shĕnt), *n.* The number resulting from the division of one number by another, showing how often the one contains the other ; ভাগফল, আপ্ত (সাঃ পঃ), ফল (লীলাঃ) ; গুণ্য (cf. ভজনেন লব্ধো গুণ্যঃ—বীজঃ)।

quō'-tŭm, *n.* (*Rare*) A quota (ক্বচিদ্ ব্যবহৃত) অংশ, ভাগ।

THE MODERN ANGLO-BENGALI DICTIONARY

THE MODERN ANGLO BENGALI DICTIONARY

(In 6 Volumes)

(Volume-6)

CHARUCHANDRA GUHA

Publications

KALPAZ PUBLICATIONS

DELHI - 1100052

THE MODERN ANGLO- BENGALI DICTIONARY

ISBN : 81-7835 - 484 - 5 (Set)
ISBN : 81 - 7835 - 490 - X (Vol.6)

Rs. 4500 (Set)

CHARUCHANDRA GUHA

Published in 2007 in India by
Kalpaz Publications
C - 30, Satyawati Nagar,
Delhi - 110052
E-mail : kalpaz@hotmail.com

Laser Typesetting at : Tact Computer, Delhi
Printed at : Mehra Offset Press, Delhi

T

T, **1.** The twentieth letter of the English alphabet; ইংরাজী বর্ণমালার বিংশতিতম অক্ষর। **2.** As a mediaeval Roman numeral, T stands for 160, and T̄ for 160,000; ১৬০ এর সাঙ্কেতিক চিহ্ন (T), ১৬০,০০০ এর সাঙ্কেতিক চিহ্ন (T̄)। **T-bandage**—T অক্ষরের আকৃতি ক্ষত-বন্ধনী। **T-iron**—একপ্রকার লোহার বর্গা। **T-square**—একপ্রকার রেখাঙ্কন-দণ্ড—যাহার শীর্ষদেশে সমান্তরাল রেখা অঙ্কনের জন্য একটী দণ্ড অনুপ্রস্থভাবে সংবদ্ধ থাকে। **Marked with T**—দাগী (চোর)। **To a T**—Exactly; ঠিকরূপে, যথাযথভাবে। **To cross the**

T's—To be scrupulous; to emphasise a point; কোন বিষয়ে সূক্ষ্মানুসন্ধায়ী হওয়া; কোন বিষয়ে জোর দেওয়া।

tă, *n.* (*Colloq.*) Thank you; (চলিতভাষায়) আপনাকে ধন্যবাদ।

taal (tâl), *n.* A form of Dutch spoken in South Africa; দক্ষিণ আফ্রিকার প্রচলিত ওলন্দাজ ভাষা।

tăb, *n.* A small or projecting piece attached at one end to anything; a tag; জুতার ফিতা প্রভৃতির আগার ক্ষুদ্র লোহার চুঙ্গী; কোন বস্তুর প্রান্তে সংবদ্ধ ক্ষুদ্র এবং বিলম্বিত অংশ (যথা টুপীর কাণ)।

tăb'-ărd, *n.* **1.** (*Hist.*) A sort of tunic or mantle worn over the armour covering the body before and behind, and reaching below the loins, but open at the sides from the shoulders downward, and with wide sleeves or flaps; (ইতিহাস) বর্ম্মের উপর পরিধেয় প্রাচীনকালীন সামরিক প্রাবরণ। **2.** A herald's coat; কুলবিদ্যাবিশারদগণের অঙ্গত্রাণ।

tăb'-ă-rĕt, *n.* A satin-striped silk used for furniture; গদি চেয়ার, প্রভৃতি মুড়িবার জন্য একপ্রকার সাটীনের ডোরাদার রেশমী কাপড়।

tăb-ă-sheer' (-shēr), **–shir'**, *ns.* A siliceous substance found in the joints of female bamboo and used in East India as medicine; বংশপর্ব্বাশ্রিত শ্বেতবর্ণে ঔষধবিশেষ, বংশকর্পূর, বংশলোচন। [Syn. ত্বক্‌ক্ষীরা, বংশলোচনা, শুভা, তুগাক্ষীরী, বংশজা, বাংশী, তুগা, ত্বক্‌ক্ষীরী, ক্ষীরিকা, বংশক্ষীরী, শুভ্রা, বৈণবী, কর্ম্মরী, ত্বক্‌সারা, তুঙ্গা, বংশকর্পূররোচনা, রোচনিকা, পিঙ্গা, বংশশর্করা।] [বৈদ্যক শাস্ত্র মতে ইহার গুণ যথা:—রূক্ষত্বম, কষায়ত্বম, মধুরত্বম, হিমত্বম, রক্তশুদ্ধিকারীত্বম্, তাপপিত্তোদ্রেকহরত্বঞ্চ। ইতি রাজনির্ঘণ্টঃ॥ বংশজা বৃংহণী বৃষ্যা বল্যা-স্বাদ্বী চ শীতলা। তৃষ্ণাকাস জ্বরশ্বাস ক্ষয়, পিত্তাস্রকামলাঃ। হরেৎ কুষ্ঠং ব্রণংপাণ্ডুং কষায়াবাতকৃচ্ছ্রজিৎ॥ ইতি ভাবপ্রকাশঃ।] [Fr. *tabachir*; Arab. *tabashir*; Chin. *chuh-hwang, chu-kau, t'ien-chuh-hwang*; Tam. *munjil uppu*; Tel. *veduru uppu.*]

tăb'-by (-ĭ), *n., adj.* & *v. t.* **1.** A kind of rich watered silk or other stuff; একপ্রকার ঢেউতোলা জমকালো রেশমী কাপড়। **2.** A cat of a mixed or bridled colour; a female cat; একপ্রকার ডোরা-কাটা বিড়াল, চকড়াপাকড়া বিড়াল; মিনি বিড়াল। **3.** An old maid or an ill natured gossiping woman; "Why should not I pay my respects to Lady Penelope, or any other *Tabby* of quality"; অবিবাহিতা বর্ষীয়সী স্ত্রীলোক, দুঃশীলা, বহুভাষিণী স্ত্রীলোক। **4.** A mixture of lime with shells, gravel, or stones in equal proportions, with an equal proportion of water forming a mass, which, when dry, becomes as hard as rock; সমপরিমাণ চূণ, শম্বুক, কঙ্করের সহিত তুল্য পরিমাণ জলের মিশ্র—যাহা শুষ্ক হইলে প্রস্তরের মত কঠিন হয়। **5.** Kinds of moth; কয়েক প্রকার তসরে পোকার সাধারণ নাম। ***Adj.*** **1.** Having a wavy or watered appearance; ঢেউ তোলা বা ঝকঝকে। **2.** Bridled; চকড়াপাকড়া, ডোরাকাটা। ***Verb t.*** To water or cause to look wavy, by the process of calendering; নরাজ দ্বারা রেশমের কাপড়ের উপর ঢেউ তোলা।

tā-bē-făc'-tion, *n.* Emaciation due to disease; রোগজনিত কৃশতা, রোগশীর্ণতা।

tăb'-ĕr-nā-cle (-kl), *n., v. t.* & *i.* **1.** A tent or booth; তাঁবু, মেলার টাঁট বা চালা। **2.** The portable structure for religious purpose carried by the Jews during their wanderings in wilderness; মিশর দেশ হইতে প্রত্যাগমনকালে ইহুদীগণ পুজোপাসনার জন্য যে পর্দ্দা দ্বারা আবৃত কাষ্ঠমন্দির বহিয়া আনিয়াছিল। **3.** A Jewish temple or place of worship; ইহুদীদিগের উপাসনামন্দির বা দেবালয়। **4.** A temple; a place of worship; দেবমন্দির; পুজোপাসনাস্থলী, পুজার্চ্চনার স্থান। **5.** (*Fig.*) The human body; "Yea I think it meet, as long as I am in this *tabernacle*, to stir you up by putting you in remembrance; knowing that shortly, I must put off this my *tabernacle* even as our Lord Jesus Christ hath showed me"; দেহ, শরীর। **5.** (*Rom Cath.*) The place where the consecrated host is kept; যে স্থানে খৃষ্টের অন্তিমভোজনোৎসবের রুটি রক্ষিত হয়। **6.** (*Gothic building*) A canopied stall, niche or tomb; (গথিকরীত্যনুযায়ী নির্ম্মিত সৌধসমূহে) চন্দ্রাতপাচ্ছাদিত কুলুঙ্গী, কবর বা মঞ্চ। **7.** (*Naut.*) A socket for the mast of a boat; নৌকার মাস্তুলের কোঠর। ***Verb t.*** To provide with shelter; আশ্রয় স্থান প্রদান করা। ***Verb i.*** To dwell temporarily; "*Tabernacling* first in a room in Burton"; অস্থায়িভাবে বাস করা। **–nac'-u-lar**, *adj.* **Feast of Tabernacles**—ইহুদীদিগের সপ্তাহব্যাপী শারদোৎসব। **Tabernacle-work**—উক্তরূপ চন্দ্রাতপাচ্ছাদিত কুলুঙ্গীসমূহ, ঐরূপ কুলুঙ্গীর উপরের কাজ।

tăb'-ēs, *n.* (*Med.*) Progressive emaciation; ক্রমশঃ শরীরের ক্ষয়, উত্তরোত্তর দেহ ক্ষয়।

tăb-ĕt'-ic, *adj* & *n.* **1.** Pertaining to tabes; শরীরক্ষয়রোগসম্পর্কীয়। **2.** Attacked with tabes; ক্ষয়রোগাক্রান্ত। ***Noun.*** A man affected with tabes; ক্ষয়রোগাক্রান্ত ব্যক্তি। **Dorsal tabes**—কশেরুকার ক্ষয় রোগ।

tăb'-ĭ-nĕt, *n.* A more delicate kind of tabby; একপ্রকার মিহি রেশমের কাপড়।

tăb'-lă-tūre, *n.* **1.** A painting on a wall or ceiling; প্রাচীর বা ভিতরের

ছাদে অঙ্কিত চিত্র। **2.** Mental picture; "Yielding a *tablature* of benevolence and public spirit"; মানসচিত্র। **3.** A graphic description; বিচিত্র বর্ণনা। **4.** (*Anat.*) A division or parting of the skull in two tables; as, *tablature* of the cranial bones; (শারীর-সংস্থান বিদ্যা) করোটীর দ্বিধা বিভাগ। **5.** (*Mus.*) A musical notation for instrument of the lute class; (সঙ্গীতশাস্ত্র) বেহালাজাতীয় বাদ্যযন্ত্রের স্বরলিপি।

tā'-ble, (-bl), *n.* & *v. t.* **1.** An article of furniture having a flat upper surface; মেজ, টেবিল, পীঠিকা। **2.** A slab of wood, stone, etc.; "A bagnio paved with fair *tables* of marble"; ফলক, পট্ট। **3.** Something written on such slabs; ঐরূপ ফলকের উপর লিখিত বিষয়, লেখ (cf. শিলালেখ)। **4.** Food placed on a table to be partaken of; "Nothing could be in better state than his equipment and his *table*"; মেজের উপর স্থাপিত খাদ্যদ্রব্য। **5.** The person seated at table or partaking of entertainment; "To set the whole *table* on roar"; মেজের চতুর্দ্দিকে উপবিষ্ট ব্যক্তিগণ, ভোজনোপবিষ্ট ব্যক্তিগণ। **6.** A thin piece of something for writing on; a tablet; hence (*in pl.*), a memorandum book; লিপিফলক, লিখনপট্ট, লিপিপট্ট; স্মারক পুস্তক। **7.** An index or collection of heads or principal matters contained in a book; a series of many particulrs; as, *table* of houses; (লগ্নসারণী) সূচী, নির্ঘণ্ট; ফর্দ্দ। **8.** A sytem of numbers calculated to be ready for expediting operations; as, *tables* of logarithms; তালিকা, তপশীল, খণ্ডা, সারণী, নামতা। **9.** A division of the skull; করোটীর অন্যতম বিভাগ। **10.** (*Palmistry*) The palm of the hand; (করসামুদ্রিক) পাণিতল, কর (as in কররেখা)। **11.** A circular plate of crown glass; গোলাকৃতি কাচখণ্ড। **12.** (*Obs.*) A picture; a face to be drawn or painted; (অপ্রঃ), চিত্র; চিত্রফলক। **13.** (*Jewelery*) The upper or flat surface of a diamond or other precious stone of which the sides only are cut in angles; যে হীরক বা অন্য কোন মূল্যবান প্রস্তরের কেবলমাত্র পার্শ্বসমূহে ত্রিকোণাকৃতি পল কাটা হইয়াছে—তাহার উপরিভাগের সমতল অংশ। **14.** (*Archit.*) Any smooth ornament usually that of a long square; (স্থপতিবিদ্যা) মসৃণভূষা, বিশেষতঃ দীর্ঘ সমচতুর্ভুজাকৃতিভূষা। **15.** Each half of folding bacgammon table; গুটাইয়া রাখিতে পারা যায় এরূপ বেকগেমন ক্রীড়ার মেজের অন্যতর অর্দ্ধাংশ। **16.** That part of a machine-tool on which work is placed to be operated on; যন্ত্রের যে অংশে কোন বস্তু রাখিয়া উহার উপর ক্রিয়া করা হয়। ***Verb t.*** **1.** To lay on table; মেজের উপর রাখা। **2.** To tabulate; ফিরিস্তি করা, তপশীল করা। **3.** To lay on the table in business meetings; to enter upon the record; as, to *table* charges; সভার আলোচ্য কোন বিষয় মেজের উপর রাখা; লিপিবদ্ধ করা, খাতায় তোলা। **4.** To postpone the consideration or refer to a subsequent meeting; "Mr. Walpole has *tabled* a set of resolutions devised in the true conservative spirit"; কোন বিষয়ের বিবেচনা স্থগিত রাখা, অথবা পরবর্ত্তী সভায় আলোচনার জন্য মুলতবী রাখিয়া দেওয়া। **5.** To let one piece of timber into another by alternate notches and projections fitting into each other; খাঁজে খাঁজে জোড়া দেওয়া। **6.** (*Naut.*) To make broad hems in sails, in order to strengthen them; পাইল শক্ত করার জন্য উহাতে চৌড়া হাঁসিয়া লাগান। **Table-ful,** *adj.* **Tab'-ling,** *n.* **Table-book**—টেবিলের উপরে স্থাপিত সচিত্র বা কারুকার্য্যখচিত পুস্তক; নামতার পুস্তক; খণ্ডার পুস্তক। **Table-cloth**—মেজের উপর বিছাইবার চাদর। **Table-cover**—টেবিল ঢাকনি। **Table-cut**—(মণি-সম্পর্কে) উপরিভাগ সমতলভাবে কর্ত্তিত। **Table d'hôte**—(*pl., Tables d'hôte*); ভোজনাগারে যে মেজের চতুর্দ্দিকে সকলে একযোগে আহার করে। **Table d'hôte dinner**—নিরূপিত মূল্যে ভোজনাগারে নির্দ্ধারিত সময়ে যে অপরাহ্ণ ভোজন করা যায়। **Table-diamond**—যে হীরকখণ্ডের উপরিভাগ সমতলভাবে কাটা হয় এবং যাহার পার্শ্ব বা প্রান্তসমূহ টের্চ্ছাভাবে কাটা হইয়া থাকে অথবা ঐসকল স্থানে ত্রিকোণ পল কাটা হয় এবং যাহার নিম্নদেশ চ্যাপ্টা রাখা হইয়া থাকে। **Table-flap**—টেবিলের উপরিভাগে কব্জা-আঁটা প্রান্ত—যাহা আবশ্যক না হইলে নীচের দিগে গুটাইয়া রাখা হয়। **Table-knife**—ভোজনকালে পাঁউরুটি প্রভৃতি কাটার জন্য ব্যবহৃত ছুরি। **Table-land**—অধিত্যকা, মালভূমি, উচ্চ সমভূমি (হিঃ কোঃ), মালক্ষেত্র। **Table-leaf**—Same as TABLE-FLAP. **Table-lifting, Table-moving, Table-rapping, Table-tipping, Table-turning**—প্রেতাত্মাকর্ত্তৃক টেবিল উত্তোলন, টেবিলে ঠক্ ঠক্ করণ, টেবিল, সঞ্চালন, ইত্যাদি। **Table-linen**—ভোজনের টেবিলের চাদর, গামছা প্রভৃতি। **Table-money**—সরকারী কার্য্যোপলক্ষে ভোজপ্রদানাদির জন্য উচ্চ সামরিক ও নাবিক কর্ম্মচারিগণকে যে অর্থব্যয় করিতে হয়, তাহার ক্ষতিপূরণের জন্য তাঁহাদিগকে যে ভাতা দেওয়া হইয়া থাকে; ক্লাবের অপরাহ্ণভোজনকক্ষে ব্যবহারের জন্য সভ্যগণকে যে টাকা দিতে হয়। **Table-spoon**—একপ্রকার বড় চামচ। **Table-talk**—ভোজনকালে নানাবিষয়ক কথাবার্ত্তা, গল্পগুজব, গল্পসল্প, খোসগল্প। **Table-tomb**—রোমনগরীর অন্তর্ভৌম শবাগারে সিন্দুকের আকৃতি কবর। **Table-ware**—ভোজন

পীঠিকায় ব্যবহৃত বাসনপত্র। **Arithmetical table**—নামতা। **Astronomical table** — পত্তাকা (সাঃ পঃ)। **Table of mortalily** — বাৎসরিক জন্মমৃত্যুর হিসাব। **Table of Pythagoras** (See PYTHAGORAS). **Tables of weights and measures** — আর্য্যা। **The twelve tables**—৪৫১-৪৪৯ পূর্ব্ব খৃষ্টাব্দে বিধিবদ্ধ দ্বাদশ বিধি—রোমীয় ব্যবস্থাবিজ্ঞানের মূলস্বরূপ বলিয়া পরিগণিত হইয়া থাকে। **The two tables** or **the tables of the law** or **covenant** or **testimony**—ঈশ্বরের দশ আজ্ঞা। **To lay on the table**—To postpone the consideration of something for indefinite period ; কোন বিষয়ের আলোচনা অনির্দ্দিষ্ট কালের জন্য স্থগিত রাখা। **To turn the tables on**—To change the condition or fortune of contending parties; পড়তা উল্টাইয়া দেওয়া, অবস্থা বিপর্য্যয় করা, উল্টাচাপ দেওয়া।

tăb'-leau (-lö), *n.* **1.** A picture ; চিত্র। **2.** A striking or vivid representation ; জীবন্ত চিত্র, বিচিত্র চিত্র। **3.** The representation of some scene by means of persons grouped in the proper manner, placed in appropriate postures (also *tableau vivant*) ; উপযুক্ত পরিচ্ছদ পরিহিত এবং যথোচিত ভঙ্গীতে উপবিষ্ট নীরব এবং নিশ্চল নটনটীগণকর্ত্তৃক কোন দৃশ্য বা ঘটনার অভিনয়, মূক অভিনয়।

table d'hote, *n.* See under TABLE.

tăb'-lĕt, *n.* **1.** A small slab ; ক্ষুদ্র ফলক, পট্ট। **2.** A small flat piece of wood, metal, etc., for writing or drawing on ; চিত্রাঙ্কণের জন্য ফলক, লিপিফলক, লিখনপট্ট, অক্ষরভূমিকা। **3.** A slab of wood, stone, etc. or a plate of metal on which anything is painted, engraved, or the like ; an inscription plate ; শিলাফলক, ধাতুফলক, কাষ্ঠফলক ; কোন কিছু উৎকীর্ণ করার জন্য ফলক। **4.** A small flattish cake as of soap etc. ; পিষ্টিকা। **5.** A fixed weight or measure of a drug brought by or addition of gum into convenient shape ; চাপ দিয়া গঁদের সহিত মিশাইয়া ঔষধের যে ক্ষুদ্র চ্যাপ্টা খণ্ড প্রস্তুত করা হয়, ঔষধগুটিকা। **6.** (*Arch.*) A horizontal coping stone ; (স্থপতিবিজ্ঞান) ভূসমান্তরাল কপিশীর্ষ প্রস্তর।

tablier, *n.* An apron or apron-like part of a woman's dress ; স্ত্রীপরিচ্ছদের সম্মুখদেশ আবরক বস্ত্র বা ঐ পরিচ্ছদের উক্তরূপ অংশ।

tăb'-loid (-loyd), *n.* Same as TABLET 5.

tă-boo', *n., adj.* & *v. t.* **1.** The custom of, or the act of solemn setting apart of, something as consecrated or accursed among certain savage races ; কোন কোন অসভ্যজাতির মধ্যে কোন ব্যক্তি বা বস্তুকে পবিত্র বা অস্পৃশ্য জ্ঞানে পরিহার করার প্রথা, নিষিদ্ধ (সাঃ পঃ)। [যথা নবজিলণ্ডের আদিম অধিবাসী মেওরীদিগের মধ্যে কোন সর্দ্দার "নিষিদ্ধ" হওয়ার দরুণ তাহার দেহ ও তাহার কোন বস্তুও "নিষিদ্ধ" বলিয়া গণ্য হইয়া থাকে। কোন ব্যক্তি মৃতদেহ স্পর্শ করিলে সেও "নিষিদ্ধ" বলিয়া পরিগণিত হয়। এই "নিষিদ্ধ" বস্তুসম্বন্ধে নিয়মভঙ্গকারীকে সাধারণতঃ প্রাণদণ্ড ভোগ করিতে হয়। See J. A. Frazer, *The Golden Bough*] **2.** Prohibition ; নিষেধ, প্রতিষেধ। ***Adj.*** Prohibited ; নিষিদ্ধ, প্রতিষিদ্ধ। ***Verb t.*** To place under taboo ; to prohibit : "Art and poetry were *tabooed* both by my rank and my mother's sectarianism" ; to interdict intercourse ; to forbid the use of ; নিষেধের অধীন করা ; নিষিদ্ধ করা ; কোন কিছুর সহিত সংশ্রব রাখিতে নিষেধ করা ; ব্যবহার নিষেধ করা। **A tabooed subject**—যে বিষয়ের আলোচনা নিষিদ্ধ, নিষিদ্ধ বিষয়।

tā'-bŏr, *n.* A small drum ; ঢোল, মুরজ, ক্ষুদ্র ঢাক।

tăb'-ou-rĕt (-ô-), *n.* **1.** A small drum (also *tabret*) ; ক্ষুদ্র ঢক্কা। **2.** A frame for embroidery ; সূচীকার্য্যের জন্য ঠাট। **3.** A needlecase ; সূচ রাখার জন্য কৌটা। **4.** A seat without arms ; টুল। **Right of the tabouret**—পূর্ব্বকালে ফরাসীদেশে অতি সম্ভ্রান্ত পরিবারের মহিলাদিগের রাজ্ঞীর সমক্ষে কাষ্ঠাসনে উপবেশনের অধিকার।

tabula, *n.* (*Pl.* TABULAE) A tablet ; পট্ট, ফলক। ***Tabula rasa***—মসৃণীকৃত ফলক, অলিখিত ফলক, শূন্যপাত, শাদা পাত; সদ্যোজাত শিশুর মানসিক অবস্থা—যখন উহার মনে কোনরূপ ঐন্দ্রিয়িক সংবেদনের ছাপ পড়ে নাই।

tăb'-ū-lar (-lêr), *adj.* **1.** In the form of a table ; having a flat surface ; মেজের আকার, পীঠিকাকার ; সমতল। **2.** Set down in tables or formal lists ; computed by means of tables ; লতাবদ্ধ, তফসীলবদ্ধ, তালিকাবদ্ধ, ফিরিস্তিবদ্ধ ; খণ্ডার সাহায্যে গণিত। **3.** Formed in laminae or plates ; ক্ষুদ্র ক্ষুদ্র ফলকে রচিত। **—ly,** *adv.*

tăb'-ū-lāte, *v. t.* & *adj.* **1.** To make tabular ; মেজের আকৃতি করা, পীঠিকাকার করা। **2.** To reduce to tables or synopsis ; তালিকাবদ্ধ করা, ফিরিস্তিবদ্ধ করা, লতাবদ্ধ করা, তফসীলবদ্ধ করা, তফসীলবন্দী করা, নির্ঘণ্ট করা, খণ্ডা প্রস্তুত করা। ***Adj.*** Having flat surface ; সমতল। **—la'-tion,** *n.* **—la-tor,** *n.* **1.** One who tabulates ; নির্ঘণ্ট প্রস্তুতকারী, ফিরিস্তীকারী, তফসীলকারী, খণ্ডাপ্রস্তুতকারী। **2.** A Type-writer attachment for tabulating figures etc. ; সংখ্যার স্তম্ভ প্রভৃতি লিখার জন্য টাইপরাইটরে সংলগ্ন একপ্রকার কল।

tăc'-ă-mă-hăc, *n.* **1.** The balsam poplar of North America ; উত্তর আমেরিকার একপ্রকার নির্য্যাসপ্রদ বৃক্ষ। **2.** A kind of gum rasin ; এক প্রকার গঁদ।

tăc-au-tăc' (-ō-), *n.* **1.** In fencing the parry combined with riposte;

এক প্রকার আটকানি। 2. A series of rapid attacks ; দ্রুত আক্রমণ পরম্পরা।

tăc'-că, *n.* A genus of tropical plants some species of which yield a tuber used as food ; মতিমুণ্ডাদি (সাঃ পঃ)।

tace, *v. i.* Be silent ; চুপ কর।

tacet, A direction for indicating silence of a voice, instrument, etc. ; স্বর, বাদ্যযন্ত্র, প্রভৃতির নীরবতাসূচক নিদেশবাক্য।

tache, tach, *ns.* 1. A stain or blemish; দাগ, কলঙ্ক। 2. Freckles ; মেচেতা, জড়ুল, আঁচিল। 3. A fault ; দোষ, ত্রুটি।

tă-chŏm'-ĕ-têr, *n.* An instrument for measuring velocity ; বেগমানযন্ত্র, গতিবেগপরিমাপক যন্ত্র।

tă-chÿg'-ră-phÿ, *n.* Short-hand writing, esp. the form stenography as practised by the ancient Greeks and Romans ; সংকেতলিপিবিদ্যা, বিশেষতঃ প্রাচীন গ্রীক ও রোমানগণের মধ্যে প্রচলিত সংকেতলিপিবিদ্যা। **—pher,** *n.* **Tach-y-graph'-ic, Tach-y-graph'-i-cal,** *adj.*

tăch'-ÿ-lÿte, *n.* A black basaltic glass easily fused ; একপ্রকার খনিজ পদার্থ। **—lyt'-ic,** *adj.*

tă-chÿm'-ĕ-têr, *n.* A surveyor's instrument for quickly determining the distances, bearings and elevation of distant objects ; একপ্রকার জরীপের যন্ত্র—যদ্দারা অতিদ্রুত কোন বস্তুর দুরত্ব এবং দিক্‌সম্পর্কে অবস্থিতি এবং উচ্চতা নির্ণয় করা যায়।

tăc'-it, *adj.* 1. Implied but not expressed in words ; silent ; as, *tacit* consent ; স্পষ্টভাবে কথিত না হইলেও সূচিত, উপলক্ষিত, মৌনসূচিত, লক্ষিত; মৌন। 2. (*Law*) Arising without express contract or agreement ; (আইন) স্পষ্টরূপে ব্যক্ত চুক্তি ব্যতীত উপজাত। **—ly,** *adv.* **Tacit premise** — অধ্যাহার্য্যপ্রতিজ্ঞা (হিঃ কোঃ)।

tăc'-i-turn (-têrn), *adj.* Habitually silent ; not apt to talk or speak much ; মৌন, তুষ্ণীশীল ; সংযতবাক্, স্বল্পভাষী। **—tur'-ni-ty,** *n* The state or quality of being taciturn ; habitual silence ; মৌন, তুষ্ণীভাব ; বাক্‌সংযম।

tăck, *n., v. t. & i.* 1. A small, short nail, of iron, copper, etc., usually having a broad head for securing carpets etc. ; as, iron *tack* ; মাথা মোটা ক্ষুদ্র প্রেক, প্রেক। 2. (*Naut.*) A rope for securing corner of some sails ; the corner to which such sail sail is fastened ; (নৌবিদ্যা) কোন কোন পাইলের কোন বাঁধিবার জন্য দড়ী ; যে কোণে উক্তরূপ দড়ী বাঁধা হয়। 3. The part of a sail to which the tack is fastened ; পাইলের যে অংশে উক্ত রজ্জু বাঁধা হয়। 4. The course of a ship in regard to the position of her sails ; পাইল সমূহের অবস্থানসম্পর্কে জাহাজের গতির দিক্। 5. Temporary change of direction in sailing to take charge of side-wind etc. ; পার্শ্ববায়ুর সুবিধা গ্রহণের উদ্দেশ্যে কিছুকালের জন্য জাহাজের গতির দিক্ পরিবর্তন। 6. A course or method of action ; as, to change one's *tack* ; কার্য্যপ্রণালী, কার্য্যপদ্ধতি। 7. Adhesiveness ; stickiness ; সংলাগশীলতা ; অনুলগ্নশীলতা। 8. A long temporary stitch ; কাঁচা সেলাই, টাঁক। 9. A shelf for drying cheese ; পনীর শুকাইবার জন্য তাক। 10. (*Obs.*) A supplement ; (অপ্রঃ) পরিশিষ্ট। 11. Food ; as, soft *tack* : hard *tack* ; খাদ্য, ভোজ্য। ***Verb t.*** 1. To fasten by a tack or tacks ; as, to *tack* down a carpet ; প্রেক দ্বারা লাগান। 2. To attach, secure or fasten together in a slight or hasty manner ; কাঁচা সেলাই করা, টাঁকা। 3. To alter the course of a ship by means of the sails ; পাইলের সাহায্যে জাহাজের গতির দিক্ পরিবর্তন করা। 4. (*Fig.*) To change one's policy ; (লক্ষণায়) কার্য্যপ্রণালীর পরিবর্তন করা। 5. To add as a supplement ; as to *tack* a bill in its progress through parliament ; পরিশিষ্টরূপে সংযোগ করা। ***Verb i.*** To change the course of a ship by shifting the tacks and position of the sails from one side to another ; পাইলের রজ্জুর অবস্থান এক দিক হইতে অপর দিকে পরিবর্তন করতঃ জাহাজের গতির দিক্ পরিবর্তন করা। **Tack'-i-ness,** *n.* **Tack'-y,** *adj.* **Tack-hammer**—প্রেক বসাইবার জন্য একপ্রকার হালকা হাতুড়ি। **Port tack**—বামপার্শ্বে প্রবহমাণ বায়ুবিশিষ্ট। **Starboard tack**—দক্ষিণপার্শ্বে প্রবহমাণ বায়ুবিশিষ্ট। **Tack and tack**—পর্য্যায়ক্রমে বাম ও দক্ষিণ পার্শ্বে গতিশীল।

tăck'-ing, *n.* 1. Directing a vessel on to another tack ; জাহাজের গতির দিক্ পরিবর্তন। 2. (*Law*) A union of securities, given at different times, all of which must be redeemed before an intermediate purchaser can interpose his claim ; (আইন) কোন মধ্যবর্ত্তী ক্রেতা তদীয় দাবী উপস্থাপন করার পূর্ব্বে বিভিন্ন সময়ে প্রদত্ত যে সমস্ত বন্ধকের সমুদ্ধার আবশ্যক হয় তাহা। 3. (*Parliament*) Appending of an extraneous clause to a money-bill to secure its passing the House of Lords which cannot amend money-bill ; (পার্লেমেণ্ট) পার্লেমেণ্ট মহাসভায় যাহাতে মঞ্জুর হইতে পারে তজ্জন্য কোন অর্থসম্বন্ধীয় প্রস্তাবের পরিশিষ্টরূপে নূতন দফা বা প্রকরণ সংযোজন।

tăck'-le (-l), *n., v. t. & i.* 1. One or more pulleys with a rope or ropes for raising or lowering weights ; গুরুভার দ্রব্য তুলিবার বা নামাইবার জন্য রজ্জু বা রজ্জুসমূহসমন্বিত কপিকল বা কপিকলসমূহ। 2. The ropes and rigging of a ship ; জাহাজের দড়াদড়ি। **3.** Appliances ; equipments; (*formerly*) weapons ; যন্ত্রপাতি ; সাজসরঞ্জাম ; (পূর্ব্বে) অস্ত্রশস্ত্র। **4.** A seizing or grasping ; ধরণ, আঁকড়াইয়া ধরণ, পাকড়াইয়া ধরণ। ***Verb t.*** **1.** To seize ; to take hold of ; as, to *tackle* an antagonist ; ধরা ; পাকড়ান, আঁকড়াইয়া ধরা। **2.** (*American football*) To seize and stop a player running with the ball ; (আমেরিকার ফুটবল ক্রীড়ায়) পাদগোলক লইয়া সবেগে ধাবমান ক্রীড়ককে ধরিয়া থামান। **3.** To attempt ; to undertake to solve or conquer ; as, to *tackle* a problem ; to endeavour to manage or overcome ; চেষ্টা করা ; সমাধান করিতে প্রবৃত্ত হওয়া, পরাজয় করিতে প্রবৃত্ত হওয়া ; স্ববশে আনিতে চেষ্টা করা, পরাজয় করিতে চেষ্টা করা। **4.** To set vigorously to work upon ; পূর্ণোদ্যমের সহিত প্রবৃত্ত করা। **5.** To attack ; to begin to eat ; as, to *tackle* one's bread or meat ; আক্রমণ করা ; আহার করিতে আরম্ভ করা। ***Verb i.*** **1.** (*Colloq.*) To go vigorously to work ; to make a bold attack (followed by *down* or *to*) ; "We'll *tackle to* ? Very well ; so be it" ; (চলিত ভাষায়) পূর্ণ উদ্যমে কার্য্যে প্রবৃত্ত হওয়া ; সাহসের সহিত আক্রমণ করা। **2.** (*American football*) To make a tackle ; পাদগোলকসহ ধাবমান ক্রীড়ককে জাপটিয়া ধরিয়া থামান। **—ling,** *n.* **Tackle-block**—যে কপিকলের উপর রজ্জুসমূহ চালিত হয়। **Tackle-fall**—যে রজ্জুদ্বারা ভারোত্তোলন যন্ত্রের কপিকলসমূহ সংযুক্ত করা হয়।

tăct, *n.* **1.** Skill or adroitness in adapting to circumstances, words and actions ; prudent mode of action ; সময়োপযোগী কার্য্য সম্পাদনে বা বাক্যপ্রয়োগে বিচক্ষণতা ; কৌশল (হিঃ কোঃ), বৈদগ্ধ্য (ঐ), চাতুর্য্য (ঐ), কার্য্যকৌশল, বাক্‌কৌশল ; বিজ্ঞজনোচিত কার্য্যপ্রণালী। **2.** (*Mus.*) The stroke in beating time ; ঠুকা। **3.** The sense of touch ; "Sight is a very refined *tact*" ; স্পর্শ-শক্তি। **Tact'-ful,** *adj.* Full of tact ; displaying tact ; কার্য্যকৌশলী ; কার্য্যকৌশলপ্রদর্শী। **Tact'-ful-ly,** *adv.* **Tact'-ful-ness,** *n.* **Tact'-less,** *adj.*

tăc'-ti-căl, *adj.* **1.** Of, or pertaining to, tactics ; ব্যূহরচনাকৌশল-সম্পর্কীয়, বলবিন্যাসকৌশলসম্পর্কীয়। **2.** Adroitly planning or planned ; কৌশলী, সুকৌশলে পরিকল্পিত। **—ly,** *adv.* **Tactical point, Tactical unit**—যে বৃহত্তম সৈন্য সংখ্যা একজন অধিনায়কের শব্দ বা সঙ্কেত দ্বারা পরিচালিত হইতে পারে।

tăc-ti'-cian (-shăn), *n.* **1.** One skilled in tactics ; ব্যূহবিন্যাসদক্ষ-ব্যক্তি, ব্যূহরচনাকুশল ব্যক্তি। **2.** An adroit manager ; সুনিপুণ ব্যবস্থাপক, কৌশলসম্পন্ন ব্যক্তি, কার্য্যদক্ষ ব্যক্তি, নিপুণ কার্য্যনির্ব্বাহক।

tăc'-tics, *n.* **1.** The science and art of disposing military and naval forces in order for battle and performing military and naval evolutions ; ব্যূহরচনাকৌশল, বলবিন্যাসকৌশল। **2.** Skilful devices ; কৌশল, চালাকি, কলকৌশল।

tăc'-tile, *adj.* Pertaining to touch; tangible; স্পর্শসম্বন্ধীয়, স্পার্শন (হিঃ কোঃ), স্পর্শসম্বন্ধী (ঐ) ; স্পর্শযোগ্য। **—til'-i-ty,** *n.* **—tu-al,** *adj.* **—tu-al-ly,** *adv.* **Tactile-sense**—স্পর্শেন্দ্রিয়।

tăd'-pōle, *n.* The first state of a toad or frog after spawn ; বেঙ্গাচী, ব্যাঙের ছানা।

taedium vitae, *n. L.* (*Path.*) Weariness of life with tendency to suicide ; জীবনের প্রতি অবসাদের ভাব — যাহাতে আত্মহত্যার প্রবণতা জন্মে, জীবনবিরাগ, জীবনবিতৃষ্ণা।

tael (tāl), *n.* **1.** A weight of $1\frac{1}{3}$oz. ; ১⅓ আউন্স ওজন। **2.** (In China) a denomination of money worth about 3 shillings ; (চীনদেশে) ইংলণ্ডের এক শিলিংএর সমমূল্যের মুদ্রাস্বরূপ ব্যবহৃত রৌপ্য খণ্ড।

tae'-ni-ă (tē-), *n.* **1.** The tapeworm ; দীর্ঘকৃমি (সাঃ পঃ), ফিতা কৃমি। **2.** (*Anat*). The ribbon-like part esp. of brain ; ফিতার আকার দেহাংশ, বিশেষতঃ মস্তিষ্কের ফিতার আকার অংশ। **3.** (*Surg.*) A roller bandage ; (অস্ত্রোপচারবিদ্যা) দীর্ঘ ও প্রশস্ত বস্ত্র-বন্ধনী। **4.** (*Arch.*) A fillet on the top of a Doric epystyle ; (স্থপতিবিদ্যা) ডোরীয় পদ্ধতির অধঃপ্রস্তরের শীর্ষভূষাবিশেষ। **—oid,** *adj.*

tăf'-fer-ĕl (-ĕr-), *n.* Same as TAFFRAIL.

tăf'-fĕ-tă, *n.* A fine, smooth stuff of silk, having usually a remarkably wavy lustre ; একপ্রকার মিহি এবং চকচকে রেশমী কাপড়, চেলি।

tăff'-rail (-rāl), *n.* **1.** The upper flat part of a ship's stern ; জাহাজের পশ্চাদ্‌ভাগের উপরের দিকের সমতল অংশ। **2.** The rail around a ship's stern ; জাহাজের পশ্চাদ্‌ভাগের চতুর্দ্দিগস্থ বৃতি।

Tăf'-fy (-ĭ), *n.* (*Colloq*). A Welshman (from Welsh pronunciation of Davy for David) ; (চলিতভাষায়) ওয়েল্‌সের লোক।

tăf'-fy (-ĭ), *n.* Same as TOFFEE (which see).

tăf'-i-ă, *n.* A kind of rum distilled from molasses ; গুড় হইতে চুয়ানো একপ্রকার রম।

tăg, *n.* & *v. t.* **1.** A metallic tube at the end of a string, ribbon etc. ; ফিতা প্রভৃতির অগ্রভাগে সংযুক্ত ধাতুর ক্ষুদ্র চুঙ্গী। **2.** Any slight appendage as to an article of dress ; পোষাক প্রভৃতিতে সংযুক্ত ক্ষুদ্র উপাঙ্গ। **3.** Any small thing tacked or attached to another ; a card or label for attaching to a box or package ; কোন বস্তুতে সংবদ্ধ ক্ষুদ্র বস্তু ; বাক্স পুলিন্দা, প্রভৃতিতে

লাগাইবার জন্য ক্ষুদ্র চিরকুট। **4.** An unimportant addition ; কোন কিছুতে সংযোজিত সামান্য বা অসার অংশ। **5.** The tip of an animal's tail ; লাঙ্গুলাগ্র, পুচ্ছাগ্র। **6.** The end or catchword of an actor's speech ; the refrain of a song ; কোন অভিনেতার পূর্ববর্ত্তী অভিনেতৃ কর্তৃক উচ্চারিত সর্ব্বশেষ শব্দ ; গানের ধুঁয়া। **7.** A game in which a person gains, who lays, that is, touches another ; একপ্রকার ক্রীড়া—যাহাতে কোন ব্যক্তি ক্রীড়কদিগের মধ্যে কোন ব্যক্তিকে স্পর্শ করিলে জয়লাভ করিয়া থাকে। **8.** Something mean or paltry ; the rabble ; "Will you hence before the *tag* return ?"; হীন বিষয়, তুচ্ছ বিষয়, হেয় জিনিষ ; ইতর লোকের ভিড়। **9.** A young sheep of the first year (also written *teg*) ; এক বৎসরের অনধিক বয়স্ক মেষশাবক। **10.** Ragged lock of wool on sheep ; মেষের ঝাঁকড়া মাকড়া রোমের গুচ্ছ। **11.** The loose or ragged end of something ; কোন বস্তুর ছিলা বা ছিন্ন প্রান্ত। **12.** The tip of the tail of an animal ; কোন জন্তুর লাঙ্গুলাগ্র। **13.** Something appended to a writing or speech ; "A *tag* of statistics is very chilling"; the moral of a fable ; কোন রচনা বা বক্তৃতার শেষে সংযোজিত বিষয় ; কোন নৈতিক উপদেশ। ***Verb t.*** **1.** To furnish with tag ; as, to *tag* a lace : ফিতা প্রভৃতিতে চুঙ্গী লাগান। **2.** To fit one thing to another ; to append ; "His courteous host *tags* every sentence with some fawning word" ; কোন বস্তুতে অপর বস্তু লাগান, সংযুক্ত করা ; পরিশিষ্টরূপে সংযোজিত করা। **3.** To tip or touch, as in the game of tag ; ক্রীড়াবিশেষে স্পর্শ করা। **4.** To attach a card or label to ; স্থূল কাগজখণ্ড বা চিরকুট লাগান। **5.** (*Colloq.*) To dog ; পিছু পিছু চলা। **6.** To shear away ragged lock of wool from sheep ; মেষের শরীরের ঝাঁকড়ামাকড়া রোমের গুচ্ছ কাঁচিদ্বারা কাটিয়া ফেলা। **Tag-rag** — Same as RAG-TAIL. **Tag-sore**—মেষের একপ্রকার ফুস্কুড়ী। **Tagtail**—একপ্রকার কীট ; চাটুকার। **Tag-rag and bobtail** — ইতর-লোকের ভিড়।

tā-gē'-tēs, *n.* A genus of showy annuals cultivated under the names of French and American marigold with showy yellow or orange flowers ; গাঁদা গাছ। [Etruscan দিগের চিরতরুণ এবং সুন্দর দেবতা Tages এর নাম হইতে গৃহীত।] **Tagetes patula**—গাঁদা।

tăg'-ger (-ẽr), *n.* **1.** One who tags or attaches one thing to another ; সংযোজক। **2.** An appendage ; উপাঙ্গ। **3.** A pursuer ; অনুসরণকারী। **3.** (*Pl.*) A very thin sheet-metal ; অতি পাতলা ধাতুর চাদর, ধাতুর পাতলা পাত। **-y**, *n.*

Tā'-ic, *adj.* & *n.* Pertaining to the Tai, or Siamese, Shans, etc. of the Indo-Chinese peninsula ; ইণ্ডোচাইনিজ উপদ্বীপবাসী, শ্যাম, সেণ্ডস প্রভৃতি জাতীয় লোকসম্পর্কীয়। ***Noun.*** The language of the Tai ; উক্ত জাতি সমূহের ভাষা।

tail (tāl), *n.*, *v. t.* & *i.* **1.** The projecting termination of an animal behind as distinct from the trunk or the rest of the body ; লেজ, পুচ্ছ, লাঙ্গুল। **2.** The back, lower or inferior part of anything ; কোন বস্তুর নিম্ন, পশ্চাৎ বা নিকৃষ্ট ভাগ। **3.** The other side of a coin from that which bears the head ; মুদ্রার যে পিঠে রাজা বা রাণীর মাথা থাকে—তাহার বিপরীত পিঠ। **4.** (*Astron.*) A luminous train extending from the nucleus or body of a comet often to a great distance, and usnally in a direction opposite to the sun ; ধূমকেতুর পুচ্ছ। **5.** A retinue ; সহচরবৃন্দ, অনুযায়িবৃন্দ। **6.** (*Pl.*) Same as TAIL-COAT (below). **7.** (In Turkey) A horse-tail, formerly carried before a Pasha to indicate rank ; (তুরস্ক দেশে) পাশার অগ্রে বাহিত অশ্বপুচ্ছ (অশ্বপুচ্ছের সংখ্যাদ্বারা পাশার পদমর্য্যাদা সূচিত হইত)। **8.** (*Mus.*) The part of a note running downward; (সঙ্গীত) নিম্নদিকে সঞ্চারী অংশ। **9.** Anything long and hanging down like a tail as a catkin ; পুচ্ছের মত দীর্ঘ এবং বিলম্বমান বস্তু। ***Verb t.*** **1.** (*Rare*) To pull by the tail to grasp by the tail ; (কচিদ্ ব্যবহৃত) লেজ ধরিয়া টানা ; লেজ ধরা। **2.** To furnish with tail ; as, to *tail* a kite ; লেজ লাগান। **3.** To dock the tail of ; to remove the end of a fruit ; লেজ কাটা ; ফলের নিম্নভাগ অপসারণ করা। **4.** To form the tail of a procession, etc. ; শোভাযাত্রাদির সর্ব্বশেষে থাকা। **5.** To annex ; পরিশিষ্টরূপে সংযুক্ত করা। ***Verb i.*** **1.** To follow like a tail ; to hang like a tail ; পুচ্ছের মত অনুসরণ করা ; লাঙ্গুলের মত ঝুলা। **2.** To fall or flow into ; পতিত হওয়া, প্রবাহিত হওয়া। **Tail'-less,** *adj.* Without tail ; লাঙ্গুলহীন, পুচ্ছ-হীন। **Tail-bay**—কপাটকলের নিম্নতর দ্বার এবং নিম্নতর জলকুণ্ডের মধ্যবর্ত্তী অংশ। **Tail-board** — গোযানের পশ্চাদংশ—যাহা কব্জার উপর ঘুরে বা ইচ্ছামত খুলিতে পারা যায়। **Tail-coat**—Same as SWALLOW-TAILED COAT. **Tail-feather** — পুচ্ছপালক। **Tail-gate**—কপাটকলের নিম্নতর দ্বার। **Tail-light** — বাষ্পীয়শকটাদির পশ্চাভাগে নিশাকালে যে দীপ প্রজ্বালিত করা হয়। **Tail-margin**—পুস্তকের পৃষ্ঠার নীচের শাদা জায়গা। **Tail-piece**—পুস্তকের অধ্যায়ের শেষে শাদা জায়গায় কারুকার্য্য-বিশিষ্ট চিত্র ; কোন কোন বাদ্যযন্ত্রে যে ত্রিকোণ কাষ্ঠখণ্ডে তারের নিম্ন প্রান্তসমূহ বাঁধা হইয়া থাকে। **Tail-pipe**—দমকলের জলোত্তোলন নল। **Tail-race**—

যন্ত্রের চক্র ঘুরাইবার পর যে প্রণালীতে জলপ্রবাহ প্রধাবিত হয়। **Tail of a bank**—বালিয়াড়ীর যে অংশ ঢালু হইয়া গভীরতর জলে প্রবিষ্ট হয়। **Tail of a comet**—কেতুপুচ্ছ (সাঃ পঃ), ধূমকেতুর পুচ্ছ। **Tail of the eye**—নয়নকোণ, দৃগঞ্চল, নেত্রপ্রান্ত। **Tail of the trenches**—পরিখার যে অংশ আক্রমণকারিগণ প্রথম প্রস্তুত করে। **To keep the tail in the water**—To prosper; উন্নতি লাভ করা, সমৃদ্ধিলাভ করা, বর্দ্ধিষ্ণু হওয়া। **To make neither head nor tail**—See HEAD. **To tail in**—একপ্রান্ত দেওয়ালে বা কোন অবলম্বনে লাগান। **To tail off**—To taper off; ক্রমসূক্ষ্ম করা। **To tail up and down stream**—(*Naut.*) To swing up and down with the tide; (নোঙ্গরবদ্ধ জাহাজসম্পর্কে) একবার এক পার্শ্বে পুনরায় অপর পার্শ্বে আন্দোলিত হওয়া। **To turn tail**—To flee away; লেজ গুটাইয়া পালান, পৃষ্ঠপ্রদর্শন করা। **With one's tail between one's legs**—Struck with terror; ভয়ে জড়সড়, ভয়ে লেজগুটানো অবস্থায়।

tail (tāil), *n.* & *adj.* 1. (*Law*) A limitation of ownership; (আইন) স্বত্ব স্বামিত্বের সীমাবদ্ধতা। 2. (*Law*) An estate limited to a certain person and the heirs of his body; "As if The Rain-bow were in *tail* settled on him and his heirsmale"; যে সম্পত্তি কোন নির্দ্দিষ্ট ব্যক্তি এবং তদীয় অঙ্গজ উত্তরাধিকারিগণেই সীমাবদ্ধ থাকে। *Adj.* Limited to certain persons or the heirs of his body; "Estates *tail*, like estates in fee-simple, have certain incidents annexed to them, which cannot be restrained by any proviso or condition whatever"; কোন নির্দ্দিষ্ট ব্যক্তি বা তদীয় অঙ্গজাত উত্তরাধিকারীতে সীমাবদ্ধ।

tail'-ing (tāl-), *n.* 1. (*Pl.*) Chaff; তুষ। 2. The end of a projecting stone or a brick inserted into a wall; উদ্গত ইষ্টক ও প্রস্তরাদির যে অংশ প্রাচীরে নিহিত থাকে। 3. The refuse part of a crushed ore; চূর্ণীকৃত খনিজবিমিশ্র প্রস্তরের অসার অংশ। 4. A blur or other fault in calico-printing; ছিটের কাপড়ে জোবড়ানো দাগ বা অন্য কোন প্রকার চিহ্ন।

tai'-lor (tā-lėr), *n.*, *v. i.* & *t.* One whose occupation is to cut out and make man's garments; দর্জ্জী, সৌচিক, সীবনকারী। *Verb i.* 1. To follow the business of a tailor; দর্জ্জীর ব্যবসায় করা। 2. To deal with tailor or with tailors; to run up bills with tailors; দর্জ্জীর সহিত কায়কারবার করা; দর্জ্জির দোকানে হিসাব খোলা। *Verb t.* 1. (*Rare*) To make clothes for; (কচিদ্‌ব্যবহৃত) পোষাক প্রস্তুত করা। 2. To dress; as, he seemed faultlessly *tailored*; পোষাক পরান। 3. (*Slang*) To mangle badly birds etc. in shooting; (ইতরভাষায়) গুলি মারিতে পক্ষী প্রভৃতি বিশ্রীভাবে ক্ষতবিক্ষত করা। **—ess,** *n.* A woman who makes garments for men or boys; মেয়ে দর্জ্জী। **—ing,** *n.* The work of a tailor; দরজীর কায, দরজীগিরি। **Tailor-bird**—টুনটুনি পাখী, টুনি পাখী (যোঃ)। **Tailor-made**—দর্জ্জীর তৈরী; (স্ত্রীলোকের ঘাগরা প্রভৃতি সম্পর্কে) মানানসই। **Tailor's chair**—আসন করিয়া বসার জন্য দরজীদিগের একপ্রকার পীঠিকা। **Tailor's cramp**—দর্জ্জীদিগের খিলধরা রোগ। **Tailor's twist**—রেশমের একপ্রকার শক্ত সূতা।

tain (tān), *n.* 1. A thin tin plate; টীনের পাতলা পাত। 2. Tinfoil for mirrors; আয়নায় লাগাইবার জন্য টীনের তবক।

taint (tānt), *n.*, *v. t.* & *i.* Trace; stain; infection; লেশ; কলঙ্ক, দাগ; দোষ। *Verb t.* To infect; to corrupt; to poison; সংক্রামক রোগের বীজ ছড়ান; দূষিত করা, কলঙ্কিত করা, কলুষিত করা; বিষাক্ত করা। *Verb i.* 1. To be infected or corrupted; দূষিত হওয়া, কলঙ্কিত হওয়া, কলুষিত হওয়া। 2. To be affected with incipient putrefaction; পচিতে আরম্ভ করা, পচাধরা। **Taint'-ed,** *p. p.* 1. Corrupted; দূষিত। 2. Affected with incipient putrefaction; as, *tainted* meat; চিতি-ধরা, পচলা-ধরা। **Taint'-less.** *adj.* Without taint; নিষ্কলঙ্ক, অকলঙ্ক, নির্দ্দোষ, অকলুষিত, কলঙ্কহীন। **Taint'-less-ly,** *adv.*

Tā'-i-ping, Tā'-ē-, *ns.* The name given to the Chinese rebels who made their appearance in 1850 and desolated some of the best cultivated provinces of China; চীনদেশীয় যে সকল রাজদ্রোহিগণ ১৮৫০ খৃঃ অব্দে তৎকালীন রাজশক্তির বিরুদ্ধে অস্ত্রধারণপূর্ব্বক তদ্দেশের কতিপয় সমৃদ্ধিশালী প্রদেশ জনশূন্য করিয়াছিল।

tāke, *v. t.* & *i.* 1. To receive or accept, as something offered; লওয়া, গ্রহণ করা। 2. To seize; to grasp; "I *took* by the throat the circumcised dog"; ধরা; সাপটিয়া ধরা। 3. To retract; as, to *take* back one's promise; প্রত্যাহার করা, ফিরাইয়া লওয়া। 4. To hire; as, to *take* a house; ভাড়া লওয়া। 5. To marry; as, to *take* a wife; বিবাহ করা, পাণিগ্রহণ করা। 6. To catch by surprise; as, to be *taken* in a lie; to capture; সহসা ধৃত করা; ধরা। 7. To deduct; as, to *take* four from eight; বাদ দেওয়া, বিয়োগ করা। 8. To quote; as, to *take* a line from Shakespeare; উদ্ধৃত করা, উদ্ধার করা। 9. To captivate; to allure; as, his mind was *taken* by the beauty of the girl; মোহিত করা, বিমোহিত করা, মনোমুগ্ধ করা, মনোহরণ করা; প্রলুব্ধ করা। 10. To obtain possession of by force of arms; to cause to surrender or capitulate; as, to *take* a fort; অস্ত্রবলে অধিকার করা; দুর্গাদি অধিকার করা।

11. To understand in any particular sense ; to apprehend ; কোন বিশেষ অর্থে গ্রহণ করা ; বুঝা। **12.** To attack ; as, *taken* with illness ; to destory ; আক্রমণ করা ; ধ্বংস করা, নষ্ট করা। **13.** To receive and swallow food or drink ; as, to *take* medicine ; খাওয়া, পান করা, সেবন করা। **14.** To copy ; to delineate ; to draw ; as, the copy of the landscape was well *taken* ; নকল করা ; চিত্রিত করা ; অঙ্কিত করা। **15.** To convey ; to carry ; as, to *take* a sick person to the hospital ; নেওয়া ; বহিয়া নেওয়া। **16.** To feel ; as, to *take* pride in one's son ; to experience ; অনুভব করা ; উপভোগ করা। **17.** To note down ; as, *take* this down in writing ; লিখিয়া নেওয়া, টুকিয়া নেওয়া। **18.** (*Colloq.*) To make a picture, photograph, etc. ; as, to *take* a group ; চিত্র প্রস্তুত করা, আলোকচিত্র গ্রহণ করা, ফটো তোলা। **19.** To need ; as, it will *take* four days to finish this work ; আবশ্যক হওয়া, দরকার হওয়া, লাগা। **20.** To adopt ; as, to *take* necessary steps ; গ্রহণ করা। **21.** To imagine ; as, I *took* him for a thief ; to suppose ; মনে করা ; ভাবা। **19.** To have recourse to ; as, to *take* shelter ; to betake one's self to ; আশ্রয় লওয়া ; গমন করা। **20.** To accept the promise, declaration or conditions of ; as, to *take* an offer : to *take* one at one's word ; to close with ; প্রতিজ্ঞা বা সর্ত্ত স্বীকার করা ; কোন বিষয়ে সম্মত হওয়া, কোন বিষয় গ্রাহ্য করিয়া লওয়া। **21.** To place one's self in ; to occupy ; as, to *take* one's seat ; উপবিষ্ট হওয়া ; অধিকার করা, গ্রহণ করা (cf. আসন গ্রহণ করা)। **22.** To leap over ; as, to *take* a fence ; লাফ দিয়া পার হওয়া, টপকান, ডিঙ্গান। **23.** To be infected or seized with ; as, to *take* cold : to *take* fever ; (সর্দ্দি) লাগা, ধরা, আক্রান্ত হওয়া। **24.** To endure ; to tolerate ; as, he will *take* no insult ; সহ্য করা ; সহা। **25.** To make selection ; as, to *take* a side ; to choose ; নির্ব্বাচন করা ; বাছা। **26.** To ascertain ; as, to *take* the depth of a river ; নির্ণয় করা, স্থির করা **27.** To acquire as shape ; as, water *takes* the shape of the vessel in which it is placed ; গ্রহণ করা, ধারণ করা, পরিগ্রহ করা। **28.** To receive ; as, to *take* an impression ; গ্রহণ করা। ***Verb i.*** 1. To direct one's course ; পথ অনুসরণ করা। 2. To admit of being made a portrait of ; প্রতিকৃতি গ্রহণযোগ্য হওয়া। 3. To have the intended or desired effect ; ঈপ্সিত ফলপ্রদ হওয়া। 4. To meet with a favourable reception ; as, the book *takes* ; to please ; আদরের সহিত গৃহীত হওয়া ; সন্তুষ্ট করা। 5. To admit of being represented in a photograph ; to be capable of being photographed ; আলোকচিত্র গ্রহণযোগ্য হওয়া ; আলোকচিত্র গ্রহণের উপযোগী ধর্ম্মাক্রান্ত হওয়া। 6. (Of fish) To bite ; (মৎস্যসম্পর্কে) ঠোকরান। **Take-in**—জুয়াচুরি, ঠকামি। **Take-off**—ব্যঙ্গ-চিত্র ; যে স্থান হইতে কেহ লম্ফ প্রদান করে ; (ক্রোকেট ক্রীড়ায়) এরূপ আঘাত যাহাতে কোন কন্দুক অপর কন্দুককে স্থানচ্যুত না করিয়া কেবল তাহাতে ঘষড়াইয়া যায়। **Take-up**—(যন্ত্রবিজ্ঞান) মাপের ফিতা, ঢিলা সূতা প্রভৃতি আঁট করার জন্য কৌশলবিশেষ। **In a pretty take on**—Excessively enamoured ; অতিশয় বিমুগ্ধ। **I take it**—I suppose ; আমার মনে হয়। **Taken up**—Engrossed ; নিবিষ্ট, মগ্ন। **To be taken in the act**—To be caught in the very act ; হাতে নাতে ধরা পড়া। **To give and take**—To give and take in compensation or equalisation ; যাহাতে উভয় পক্ষে সমভাবে আদান প্রদানের বিনিময় হয় সেইরূপ করা। **To take aback**—To astonish ; to confound ; অবাক করা ; কিংকর্ত্তব্যবিমূঢ় করা, বিস্ময়ে বিহ্বল করা, হতভম্ব করা। **To take advantage of** — To seize or make use of any advantage offered by ; সুযোগ গ্রহণ করা, সুবিধা লওয়া। **To take after**—To imitate ; to follow the example of ; অনুকরণ করা ; দৃষ্টান্ত অনুসরণ করা। To resemble ; সদৃশ হওয়া, সাদৃশ্য থাকা। **To take again**—To resume ; পুনরায় আরম্ভ করা। **To take aim**—To aim ; লক্ষ্য করা, ঠিক করা, সন্ধান করা, তাক করা, নিশানা করা। **To take air**—To be in an open place for the sake of health ; বায়ু সেবন করা। (*Rare*) To be divulged ; (কচিদ্‌-ব্যবহৃত) প্রকাশিত হওয়া। **To take alarm**—To accept and act upon a warning of danger ; বিপদের পূর্ব্বে সংবাদ পাইয়া তদনুসারে কার্য্য করা। **To take a man at his word**—To believe in what he says ; কাহারো বাক্যে আস্থা স্থাপন করা। **To take amiss**—To take offence at ; কষ্ট হওয়া, মনে করা (cf. আপনি কিছু মনে করবেন না)। **To take anything to heart**—To be wounded by some remarks etc ; কোন কথা কাহারো প্রাণে লাগা, প্রাণে বাজা, মনে করা (*colloq.*) (cf. আপনি কিছু মনে করিবেন না)। **To take arms, To take up arms**—To rise in arms ; অস্ত্র গ্রহণ করা, অস্ত্র ধারণ করা। **To take a telling or reproof**—To accept advice or endure chiding in a calm manner ; ধীরভাবে উপদেশ গ্রহণ করা, ধীরভাবে তিরস্কার সহ্য করা। **To take a walk**—To walk on foot ; হাঁটা, পদব্রজে গমন করা। **To take away**—To remove ; অপসারিত করা। To set aside ; রহিত করা। To remove by death ; যমালয়ে প্রেরণ করা। To subtract ; বিয়োগ করা, বাদ দেওয়া। To go away ; চলিয়া যাওয়া। To clean the table after meal ; আহারের পর মেজ পরিষ্কার করা। **To take away from**—To impair the virtue or efficacy of anything ; কোন কিছুর শক্তি বা গুণ হ্রাস করা। **To take back**—To retract ; প্রত্যাহার করা। To carry back in thought to a past time ; চিন্তাদ্বারা অতীত যুগে নীত করা। **To take back seat**—To give up one's pretensions ; দীনতা অবলম্বন করা। **To take breath**—To stop ; to take rest ; থামা ; বিশ্রাম করা। **To take by storm**—To obtain possession of by a sudden violent effort ; সহসা প্রচণ্ড বেগে আক্রমণ করতঃ অধিকার করা। **To take care**—To be careful; to be vigilant ; সতর্ক থাকা, সাবধান থাকা ; সজাগ থাকা, হুঁসিয়ার থাকা। **To take care of**—To look after ; to superintend ; দৃষ্টি রাখা ; পরিদর্শন করা, তত্ত্বাবধান করা। **To take chance, To take one's chance**—To submit to hazard ; to run the risk ; বিপদাপন্ন করা ; অদৃষ্টের উপর নির্ভর করিয়া কোন কার্য্যে প্রবৃত্ত হওয়া, ঝুঁকি নেওয়া। **To take down**—To humble ; to abase ; অবনমিত করা, অবনত করা ; অপদস্থ করা। To write down from dictation; to put down in writing; শুনিয়া লিখা ; লিপিবদ্ধ করা, টুকিয়া নেওয়া। To swallow ; গলাধঃকরণ করা, উদরস্থ করা, পান করা, সেবন করা। To pull down ; to reduce to separate parts ; ভাঙ্গিয়া ফেলা ; কোন বস্তুর অংশসমূহ পৃথক করা। **To take earth**—(Of a fox) To escape into its hole ; (শৃগাল সম্বন্ধে) গর্ত্তে লুক্কায়িত হওয়া। (*Fig.*) To conceal one's self ; লুকান, লুক্কায়িত হওয়া। **To take effect**—To be efficacious ; to have the desired or natural effect ; কার্য্যকরী হওয়া, ফলপ্রদ হওয়া ; ফলদায়ক হওয়া, ফলপ্রসূ হওয়া। To come into operation ; আমলে আসা। **To take farewell**—To take leave ; বিদায় গ্রহণ করা। **To take fire** — To become ignited ; আগুণ লাগা, আগুণ ধরা। To be exceedingly excited, as with love, enthusiasm, etc. ; অতিশয় উত্তেজিত হওয়া, উদ্দীপ্ত হওয়া, উৎসাহানল প্রদীপ্ত হওয়া, ক্রোধাগ্নি প্রজ্বালিত হওয়া, কামানল উদ্দীপ্ত হওয়া। **To take flight**—To escape ; পলায়ন করা। **To take from** — To deduct ; বাদ দেওয়া, বিয়োগ করা। **To take heart**—To pluck up courage ; সাহসে বুক বাঁধা। **To take heed**—To be careful or cautious ; সতর্ক হওয়া, সাবধান হওয়া। **To take heed to**—To attend to with care ; মনোযোগ পূর্ব্বক শ্রবণ করা, মনদিয়া শোনা। **To take hold**—To seize ; জাপটিয়া ধরা, মুট করিয়া ধরা। To gain control or power over ; কাহারো উপর কর্ত্তৃত্ব লাভ করা। **To take home to one's self** — To understand fully ; সম্পূর্ণরূপে হৃদয়ঙ্গম করা, মর্ম্মে মর্ম্মে অনুভব করা। **To take horse**—To ride on horse ; অশ্বে আরোহণ করা, ঘোড়ায় উঠা। (Of a vein of ore) To divide on each side of a non-metallic rock ; অধাতব পাষাণ স্তূপের উভয় পার্শ্বে বিযুক্ত হওয়া। **To take in**—To admit into one's house, company or the like ; কোন ব্যক্তিকে অভ্যর্থনা করিয়া গৃহে লইয়া যাওয়া, সঙ্গিরূপে গ্রহণ করা। To cheat ; ঠকান, চোখে ধূলি দেওয়া, মাথায় হাত বুলান। To allow to enter ; ঢুকিতে দেওয়া। To include ; অন্তর্ভুক্ত করা। To comprehend ; to admit the truth of ; বুঝা, মর্ম্ম গ্রহণ করা, উপলব্ধি করা ; সত্য বলিয়া গ্রহণ করা, সত্যতা স্বীকার করা। To lessen ; হ্রাস করা, ক্ষুদ্রায়তন করা। To be a regular subscriber to a newspaper etc. ; নিয়মিত গ্রাহক হওয়া। **To take in good**—To receive with good will ; প্রীতির সহিত গ্রহণ করা। **To take in hand**—To undertake ; হাতে নেওয়া, কোন কার্য্যে প্রবৃত্ত হওয়া, কোন কার্য্যে হাত দেওয়া, কোন কার্য্যে হস্তক্ষেপ করা। **To take into one's confidence**—To speak something to any one in private ; কাহাকে বিশ্বাস করিয়া কোন কথা বলা। **To take in two**—To take with one's self ; সঙ্গে করিয়া নেওয়া, সাথে করিয়া নেওয়া। **To take in vain**—To utter unnecessarily ; অনর্থক উচ্চারণ করা। **To take it ill**—To take in a bad part ; মন্দভাবে গ্রহণ করা। **To take it into one's head**—To occur to him ; কাহার মাথায় ঢুকা। **To take it out**—(*Slang*) To exact satisfaction ; (ইতরভাষায়) ক্ষতিপূরণ আদায় করা। To exercise one's limbs ; অঙ্গ চালনা করা। To be compensation for ; ক্ষতিপূরণস্বরূপ হওয়া। **To take it out of**—To have revenge on ; দাদ তোলা, শোধ বোধ করা, প্রতিশোধ লওয়া। **To take it out of a person**—To exhaust his energies ; কাহাকে পরিক্লান্ত বা অবসন্ন করা। **To take kindly**—To love cordially ; to like ; অন্তরের সহিত ভালবাসা ; ভাললাগা। **To take leave**—To bid adieu ; বিদায় গ্রহণ করা। To assume or use a certain degree of liberty or licence ; to permit to one's self ; কতকটা স্বাধীনতা গ্রহণ করা ; স্বাধীনতা লওয়া। **To take notice** — To regard or observe with attention ; লক্ষ্য করা, অবধান করা। To make remark ; to mention ; উক্তি করা,

মন্তব্য প্রকাশ করা ; উল্লেখ করা। **To take oath**—To swear judicially or with authority ; হলফ লওয়া। **To take off**—To remove or lift from the surface or outside ; অপসারিত করা, খুলিয়া ফেলা, উন্মোচন করা। To remove ; স্থানান্তরিত করা। To portray ; অঙ্কিত করা। To deduct ; বাদ দেওয়া, বিয়োগ করা। To swallow ; উদরস্থ করা, গিলা। To make a copy of ; to print off ; প্রতিলিপি গ্রহণ করা, ছাপ তোলা ; মুদ্রিত করা, ছাপান। To mimic ; to ridicule ; ভেঙ্গচান, ভেঙ্গান ; বিদ্রূপ করা। To purchase ; ক্রয় করা। To accommodate ; সংস্থান করা। To kill ; বিনাশ করা, সংহার করা, নিকাশ করা, প্রাণ লওয়া। To start to jump ; লম্ফ প্রদানে উদ্যত হওয়া। To clear the table after a meal ; আহারের পর মেজ পরিষ্কার করা। To lead away summarily ; to depart ; বিনাবাক্য ব্যয়ে নেওয়া ; প্রস্থান করা। To dismiss ; পদচ্যুত করা। To withdraw a coach etc. from running ; গাড়ী প্রভৃতি উঠাইয়া নেওয়া। To drink to the lees ; নিঃশেষে পান করা। To measure off ; to mark or make out the position of ; মাপিয়া ফেলা ; অবস্থান চিহ্নিত বা নির্ণিত করা। To diminish ; হ্রাস করা। To knint off ; বুনিয়া ফেলা। To go off ; to run away ; চলিয়া যাওয়া ; ছুটিয়া চলা। To issue as a branch from a main stream ; প্রধান নদী হইতে শাখারূপে নির্গত হওয়া। **To take offence**—See OFFENCE. **To take on**—To undertake the charge or responsibility of ; ভার বা দায়িত্ব গ্রহণ করা। To be deeply agitated ; to mourn ; to fret ; অতিশয় বিক্ষুব্ধ হওয়া ; শোক করা ; খিট্ খিট্ করা। To take a person in one's services ; কাহাকে চাকুরীতে ভর্ত্তি করা। (*Colloq.*) To rave ; পাগলের মত বকা। To assume airs ; বড়লোকতা ফলান। To take service ; চাকুরী লওয়া। (*Scot.*) To buy things on credit ; (স্কটলণ্ড) ধারে জিনিষ কেনা। **To take one at one's words**—To take advantage of one's words uttered at an unguarded moment ; কেহ অসতর্কভাবে কোন কথা বলিয়া ফেলিলে তাহার সুযোগ গ্রহণে সেই ব্যক্তির অনিষ্ট করিয়া স্বকীয় স্বার্থ সাধন করা। To believe in one's word ; কাহারো কথায় আস্থা স্থাপন করা। **To take (one) for**—To regard him as some one else ; কাহাকে অন্য কেহ বলিয়া ভ্রম করা। **To take one on**—To appoint one to any post ; কাহাকে কোন আফিসে বা চাকুরীতে ঢুকান। **To take one's part**—To espouse one's cause ; to defend or support one ; কাহারো পক্ষ অবলম্বন করা ; কাহারো পক্ষ সমর্থন করা। **To take one's self off**—To go away ; চলিয়া যাওয়া, প্রস্থান করা। To commit suicide ; আত্মহত্যা করা। **To take on trust** — To accept on trust ; বিশ্বাস করিয়া লওয়া। **To take order**—See ORDER. **To take out**—To remove ; to extract ; স্থানান্তরিত করা ; নিষ্কর্ষণ করা। To remove by cleansing, erasure or the like ; উঠাইয়া ফেলা, তুলিয়া ফেলা। To put an end to ; নাশ করা, লোপ করা। To obtain or accept as equivalent ; তুল্য মূল্যের বস্তুস্বরূপ গ্রহণ করা বা প্রাপ্ত হওয়া। To ascertain by measurement or calculation ; গণনা বা পরিমাপ দ্বারা নির্ণয় করা। To obtain ; প্রাপ্ত হওয়া। To engage ব্যাপৃত করা। To espouse one's cause ; কাহারো পক্ষ গ্রহণ করা। To become clear ; নির্ম্মল হওয়া, পরিষ্কার করা। To take a copy; to extract from a book ; প্রতিলিপি গ্রহণ করা ; পুস্তকাদি হইতে উদ্ধৃত করা। To omit ; বর্জ্জন করা। **To take out of**—To withdraw ; উঠান, উঠাইয়া নেওয়া। To obtain from ; প্রাপ্ত হওয়া। To deprive ; বিরহিত করা। **To take out one's bat**—(ব্যাটধারী সম্পর্কে) ক্রীড়ার শেষ পর্য্যন্ত "আউট" না হওয়া। **To take over**:—To succeed to the management or ownership of a business, etc ; অপর কোন ব্যক্তির ব্যবসায় প্রভৃতির কর্ম্মাধ্যক্ষের কার্য্যভার গ্রহণ করা। To carry or convey across ; অপর পারে নেওয়া। **To take pains**—To undergo trouble ; কষ্ট স্বীকার করা, কষ্ট পাওয়া। To apply all one's skill, care and the like ; কাহারো চাতুর্য্য প্রভৃতি প্রয়োগ করা। **To take part**—To be united with others in some undertaking ; কোন কার্য্যে যোগদান করা। **To take one's life in one's hand**—To live in constant peril of life ; প্রাণ হাতে লইয়া থাকা। **To take part in**—To share in ; অংশী হওয়া। **To take place** — To happen ; সংঘটিত হওয়া, ঘটা। **To take root**—To strike root ; শিকড় গজান। To become firmly fixed or established ; বদ্ধমূল হওয়া। **To take stock in, of** — See STOCK. **To take the air, To take an airing**—To walk, drive or ride in open air for the sake of health ; শকটে, অশ্বপৃষ্ঠে বা পদব্রজে বায়ু সেবন করিতে যাওয়া, হাওয়া খাওয়া। **To take the cue, To take one's cue from**—See CUE. **To take the field**—To commence hostilities ; রণাঙ্গনে অবতীর্ণ হওয়া। (*Fig.*) To step into a position of activity ; (লক্ষণায়) কার্য্যক্ষেত্রে অবতীর্ণ হওয়া, প্রতিযোগিতার ক্ষেত্রে দণ্ডায়মান হওয়া। **To take thought**—To be anxious; উৎকণ্ঠিত হওয়া। To consider; ভাবিয়া দেখা। **To take time**—To undertake an work after due deliberation ; বিশেষ ভাবিয়া চিন্তিয়া কোন কার্য্যে হস্তক্ষেপ করা। To require certain amount of time ; নির্দ্দিষ্ট পরিমাণ সময় লাগা। To undertake some work; কোন কার্য্যে প্রবৃত্ত হওয়া। **To take to**—To adopt ; to resort to ; গ্রহণ করা ; আশ্রয় নেওয়া। To take in hand ; কোন কায হাতে নেওয়া। To apply one's self ; কোন কার্য্যে আত্মনিয়োগ করা। To become fond of ; অনুরাগী হওয়া। **To take together**—To consider together ; একত্রে বিবেচনা করা। **To take to heart**—To feel keenly ; প্রাণে লাগা, প্রাণে বাজা। **To take too much**—To drink excessively ; অতিমাত্রার মদ্যপান করা। **To take to one's bed**—To go to sleep ; শয্যাশায়ী হওয়া, শয্যার আশ্রয় গ্রহণ করা। **To take to one's heels**—See HEEL. **To take to task**—To upbraid ; তিরস্কার করা, ভর্ৎসনা করা। **To take turns**—To work by turns ; পালাক্রমে কাজ করা। **To take up**—To lift ; to take a person on horse-back etc ; উঠান, তোলা; ঘোড়া প্রভৃতিতে উঠাইয়া নেওয়া। To bring a horse etc. from pasture into the stable or stall ; অশ্ব প্রভৃতিকে পশুচারণ ভূমি হইতে নিয়া অশ্বশালা প্রভৃতিতে রাখা। To tighten ; শক্ত করা, আঁট করা। To tie up ; বাঁধা। To hire ; ভাড়া করা। To buy up ; কিনিয়া ফেলা। To settle upon ; বসবাস স্থাপন করা। To take land for occupation ; জমি বন্দোবস্ত লওয়া। To subscribe shares ; অংশ প্রভৃতি গ্রহণ করা। To advance money on mortgage ; বন্ধক দ্বারা টাকা কর্জ্জ দেওয়া। To apprehend ; বুঝা, উপলব্ধি করা। To accept ; গ্রহণ করা। To take into one's protection ; to patronise ; আশ্রয় দেওয়া ; পৃষ্ঠপোষকতা করা। To absorb ; to dissolve ; শুষিয়া নেওয়া ; দ্রব করা। (Of weather) To become fair ; পরিষ্কার হওয়া, নির্ম্মল হওয়া। To close spontaneously, as a small leak in a water pipe ; জলের চুঙ্গীর ক্ষুদ্র ছিদ্র আপনা আপনি বন্ধ হইয়া যাওয়া। To assume ; পরিগ্রহ করা। To preoccupy ; to engross ; ব্যাপৃত করা ; নিবিষ্ট করা। To begin where another has left ; অন্য ব্যক্তি যে স্থানে ছাড়িয়া গিয়াছে তথা হইতে আরম্ভ করা। To take on one's self ; গ্রহণ করা। To bring or gather together ; একত্র করা, জড় করা। To admit ; নেওয়া। To take into custody ; আটক করা। To pursue an enquiry etc. further ; অনুসন্ধান প্রভৃতিতে অগ্রসর হওয়া। To fasten ; বন্ধ করা, আটকান। **To take up arms**—Same as TO TAKE ARMS. **To take upon**—Same as TO TAKE ON. **To take up with**—To be intimate with ; to associate with ; কাহারো সহিত অন্তরঙ্গতা থাকা ; কাহারো সঙ্গ করা। To put up with ; সহ্য করা। To adopt ; গ্রহণ করা। **To take with**—To accept or have as companion ; সঙ্গিস্বরূপ গ্রহণ করা, সঙ্গিস্বরূপ থাকা। To please ; তুষ্ট করা।

take, *n.* **1.** Amount of fish, game etc. taken or caught ; শিকারের জন্তু, ধৃতমৎস্য, প্রভৃতির পরিমাণ। **2.** The quantity of copy taken in hand by a compositor at a time ; "The compositors are working short *takes* of half a dozen lines a piece" ; মুদ্রাযন্ত্রের অক্ষরবিন্যাসক একবারের জন্য যে পরিমাণ পাণ্ডুলিপি লইয়া থাকে। **3.** (*Obs.*) Charm ; সৌন্দর্য্য। **4.** The amount of money received from sale of ticket in theatre etc. ; "Confident of large *takes* for to-day or Sunday" ; নাট্যালয় প্রভৃতিতে টিকিট বিক্রয় হইতে প্রাপ্ত অর্থের পরিমাণ। **5.** The act of taking land ; such land ; ভূমিবন্দোবস্ত গ্রহণ ; ঐরূপ ভূমি।

tāk'-ĕr, *n.* **1.** One who takes ; গ্রহণকারী। **2.** One who takes a bet ; যে ব্যক্তি বাজি ধরে।

tāk'-ing, *n.* **1.** The act of one who takes ; গ্রহণ, ধারণ, মর্ম্মগ্রহণ। **2.** (*Pl.*) That which is taken or received ; receipts ; প্রাপ্ত বা গৃহীত বস্তু ; প্রাপ্ত অর্থ। **To be in taking**—To be agitated or distressed ; বিক্ষুব্ধ হওয়া, দুর্দ্দশাগ্রস্ত হওয়া।

tāk'-ing, *adj.* **1.** Alluring ; fascinating ; "Philis has such a *taking* way, She charms my very soul" ; লোভজনক, চিত্তাকর্ষক ; মনোমুগ্ধকর। **2.** (*Rare.*) Infectious ; "The diseases of the mind are more *taking* than the diseases of the body" ; (কচিদ্ব্যবহৃত) সংক্রামক। **–ly,** *adv.* **–ness,** *n.*

tăl-ā-poin (-pōyn), *n.* A Buddhist monk ; বৌদ্ধ সন্ন্যাসী, ফুঙ্গী।

tăl'-bō-tȳpe, *n.* A process of taking picture by the camera obscura on chemically prepared paper ; রাসায়নিক দ্রব্যলিপ্ত কাগজে আলোকচিত্র গ্রহণের প্রণালীবিশেষ। [বর্ত্তমানে আলোকচিত্রগ্রহণপদ্ধতির ইহাই মূল। আবিষ্কর্ত্তা W. A. Fox Talbot-এর নাম হইতে শব্দটী গঠিত হইয়াছে।]

tălc, *n.* & *v. t.* **1.** A magnesian mineral, unctuous to the touch ; একপ্রকার মসৃণ খনিজ পদার্থ, তালক (সাঃ পঃ), অনন্ত (মঃ উঃ)। **2.** (*Comm.*) Mica ; (বাণিজ্যে) অভ্রক (হিঃ কোঃ)। *Verb t.* To rub with talc ; তালকদ্বারা মর্দ্দিত করা। **Talc'-y, Talck'-y, Talc'-oid, Talc'-ose, Talc'-ous,** *adjs,*

tăl'-cite (-sīt), *n.* A massive variety of talc ; একপ্রকার তালক।

tāle, *n.* **1.** A short story ; a fictitious narrative ; as, a winter *tale* ; গল্প, কথা, কেচ্ছা (*colloq.*) ; আখ্যায়িকা, আখ্যান। **2.** Calumny ; কুৎসা, গ্লানি, পরিবাদ। **3.** (*Obs.*) A number ; "And every shepherd tells his *tale*, Under the hawthorn in the dale" ; (অপ্রঃ) সংখ্যা। **4.** Enumeration ; as, he keeps a just *tale* of the numbers ; গণন, সংখ্যাকরণ। **Tell-taler**—গল্প কথক ; গোপনে পরের

কুৎসাকারী। **His tale is told**—It is all over with him ; তাহার দফা রফা হইয়াছে, তাহার কায শেষ হইয়াছে। **In the same tale, In one tale**—In the same enumeration ; একই গণনায়। **It is a long tale**—সে বিস্তর কথা। **It tells his own tale**—It requires nothing external to explain itself ; It requires no comment ; এটা বুঝিতে আর অন্য কিছুর আবশ্যক হয় না ; ইহার উপর কোন সমালোচনা নিষ্প্রয়োজন। **Old wives' tales**—আষাঢ়ে গল্প। **To tell one's own tale**—To give one's own account ; নিজের বিবরণ প্রদান করা। **To tell tales**—To inform secretly ; গোপনে সংবাদ দেওয়া, কানে তোলা। **To tell tales out of school**—To divulge a secret ; গোপনীয় কথা প্রকাশ করা।

tăl'-ĕnt, *n.* 1. Natural gift or endowment ; eminent ability ; প্রতিভা, মনীষা ; প্রজ্ঞা (হিঃ কোঃ), মতি (ঐ), বুদ্ধি (ঐ), ক্ষমতা (ঐ)। 2. An ancient weight or denomination of money ; প্রাচীন এসিরিয়ান, বেবিলোনিয়ান, গ্রীক, রোমান প্রভৃতি জাতির মুদ্রা বা মুদ্রাস্বরূপ ব্যবহৃত নির্দ্দিষ্ট ওজনের স্বর্ণাদি ধাতু। [এক Attic talent—প্রায় ২৪৩ পাঃ ১৫ শিলিংএর সমান ছিল। রোমানদিগের Great talent — বর্ত্তমানকালের প্রায় ৯৯ পাঃ ৬ শিঃ ৮ পেন্সের এবং Little talent—৭৭ পাউণ্ডের সমান ছিল।] 3. A talented man ; "All the real *talents* in England" ; প্রতিভাশালী ব্যক্তি, প্রতিভাবান ব্যক্তি। 4. Special aptitude ; বিশেষ প্রবৃত্তি বা অনুরাগ। 5. (*Racing slang*) Habitual backers of horses or takers of odds, as opposed to bookmakers ; (ঘোড়দৌড়ের ইতরভাষায়) যে ব্যক্তি সর্ব্বদা ঘোড়দৌড়ে ঘোড়ার উপর বাজী রাখে। **Ministry of talents**—১৮০৬ খৃষ্টাব্দের ২৭শে জুন তারিখে প্রতিষ্ঠিত মন্ত্রি-সভা বিশেষ। Lord Grenville এই সভার সভাপতি এবং Fox তাঁহার প্রধান সহায় ছিলেন। **—ed,** *p. p.* Possessing talents ; প্রতিভাবান, প্রতিভাশালী, মনীষাসম্পন্ন, ধীশক্তিসম্পন্ন, ধীমান। **—less,** *adj.*

tā'-lēs, *n.* (*Law*) A list of persons from whom the sheriff or clerk makes selection to supply the place of absent jurors ; (আইন) আদালতের সেরিফ বা কেরাণী যে তালিকা হইতে অনুপস্থিত জুরিদিগের স্থান পূরণের জন্য লোক নিযুক্ত করিয়া থাকেন। **Talesman** — অনুপস্থিত জুরির স্থান পূরণের জন্য আদালত হইতে আহ্বানপ্রাপ্ত ব্যক্তি। **To pray a tales**—To plead that the number of jurymen be completed ; অনুপস্থিত জুরিদিগের সংখ্যা পূরণের জন্য প্রার্থনা করা।

Tăl-ĭ-ă-cō-ti-ăn (-shĭ-), *n.* **Taliacotian operation** — Formation of an artificial nose by means of flaps taken from the arm or forehead ; বাহু বা ললাট হইতে মাংস তুলিয়া লইয়া নূতন নাসিকা গঠন। [ইতালী দেশীয় অস্ত্র-চিকিৎসক Tagliacozzi্র নাম হইতে গৃহীত।]

tăl'-ĭ-ŏn, *n.* The law of retaliation or punishment of like for like ; অনুরূপ কার্য্যদ্বারা প্রতিহিংসা-সাধন। **—on'-ic,** *adj.*

tăl'-ĭ-pĕd, *adj.* & *n.* 1. Club-footed ; স্থুলপাদ। 2. (*Zool.*) Having foot twisted into unusual position ; বক্রপাদ *Noun.* 1. A club-footed person ; স্থুলপাদ ব্যক্তি। 2. An animal with foot twisted into unusual position ; বক্রপাদ জন্তু।

tăl'-ĭ-pĕs, *n.* The disease called club-foot ; স্থুলপাদরোগ।

tăl'-ĭ-pŏt, tăl'-pŭt, *ns.* (From Sanskrit তালপত্র)। A fan leafed palm ; তাল। [*Syn.* তালদ্রুম, পত্রী, দীর্ঘস্কন্ধ, ধ্বজদ্রুম, তৃণরাজ, মধুরস, মদাঢ্য, দীর্ঘপাদপ, চীরায়ুঃ, দীর্ঘপত্র, গুচ্ছপত্র, লেখ্যপত্র, মহোন্নত।]

tăl-ĭs-măn, *n.* 1. (*Astrol.*) A magical figure of an astrological nature cut or engraved under certain mystic observances to which wonderful effects are ascribed ; গ্রহদোষ শান্তির জন্য তান্ত্রিক চক্রাদি অঙ্কিত ক্ষুদ্র ধাতু বা শিলাফলক, তাবিজ। 2. An amulet ; কবচ মাদুলী, রক্ষাকবচ। **—man'-ic,** *adj.*

talk (tāk), *v. i., t.* & *n.* 1. To speak ; কথা বলা। 2. To converse familiarly ; "I will buy with you, sell with you, *talk* with you, but, I will not eat with you" ; কথাবার্ত্ত বলা, বাক্যালাপ করা। 3. To prattle ; to gossip ; "It was difficult to prevent people from *talking*" ; বকা, বেশী কথা বলা, বক্ বক্ করা, বাচালতা করা ; গল্পগুজব করা। 4. To consult ; to discuss ; "Let me *talk* with thee of thy judgment" ; পরামর্শ লওয়া ; আলোচনা করা। 5. To mention ; to communicate by writing, by signs, or by words not necessarily spoken ; "The natural histories of Switzerland *talk* much of the fall of these rocks, and the great damage done" ; উল্লেখ করা ; কোন চিহ্ন অথবা লিখন দ্বারা অথবা কোনপ্রকারে ব্যক্ত করা। 6. (*Colloq.*) To make sounds likened to speech ; as, the breeze *talks* in the ears of flowers ; কথিত বাক্যের আভাসসূচক ধ্বনি করা, *Verb t.* 1. To speak ; বলা। 2. To use as a means of conversation ; as, to *talk* English ; কথাবার্ত্তার উপায়স্বরূপ ব্যবহার করা, বলা। 3. To pass or spend in talking (with *away*) ; as, to *talk away* a morning ; কথা বলিয়া কাটান, কথাবার্ত্তায় কাটান। 4. To influence or have certain effect on by talking ; "*Talk* thy tongue weary" ; কথা বলিয়া প্রভাবিত করা, কথ বলিয়া কোন ফল বা অবস্থা প্রাপ্ত হওয়া। *Noun.* 1. Familiar conversation ; কথাবার্ত্তা, আলাপ। 2. Rumour ; report ; "I hear a *talk* up and down of raising money" ; জনরব ; গুজব, কথা (cf. সহরে একটা কথা রটেছে)। **3.** Subject of conversation ; as, it is the *talk* of the town ; আলাপের বিষয়। **Talk'-er,** *n.* **To talk a person's head off**—To prattle too much ; to tire a man by talking too much ; বেজায় বাচালতা করা ; কথা বলিতে বলিতে হয়রাণ করা। **To talk a person up to**—To flatter ; তোষামোদ করা, মিষ্টবাক্যদ্বারা পরিতুষ্ট করা। To persuade a man to do something ; কোন ব্যক্তিকে কোন কার্য্যে প্ররোচিত করা। **To talk at**—To make remarks about some person not directly addressed to him ; অসাক্ষাৎভাবে কোন লোকের উপর কোনরূপ মন্তব্য প্রকাশ করা। **To talk away**—To consume time by talking ; কথা বলিয়া সময় কাটাইয়া দেওয়া। **To talk back**—To reply in a defiant tone ; অবজ্ঞার স্বরে প্রত্যুত্তর করা। **To talk big, To talk tall**—(*Colloq.*) To talk boastfully ; (চলিতভাষায়) লম্বাচৌড়া কথা বলা, লম্বাচৌড়াই করা, লম্বা লম্বা কথা বলা। **To talk from the point, subject, etc.**—To digress ; মূল বিষয় ছাড়িয়া অবান্তর বিষয় ধরা। **To talk one down**—To silence by arguments ; যুক্তিতর্কদ্বারা কাহাকে নিরুত্তর করা। To silence one by incessant talking ; অবিশ্রান্ত কথা বলিয়া কাহাকে চুপ করাইয়া দেওয়া। **To talk one out of**—To dissuade from something ; কাহাকে কোন বিষয় হইতে নিবৃত্ত করা। **To talk out**—To delay so much in talking some subject so that there is no time to take votes ; কোন বিষয়ে বক্তৃতা করিতে করিতে এরূপ বিলম্ব করা—যাহাতে আর মত গ্রহণের সময় থাকে না। **To talk over**—To speak on certain subject : to discuss certain subject ; কোন বিষয়ে কথা বলা ; কোন বিষয়ে কথাবার্ত্তা বলা বা আলোচনা করা। To discuss at some length ; কোন বিষয়ে বিস্তৃতভাবে কথাবার্ত্তা বলা। To win over by talking ; কথা বলিয়া নিজের দলে টানিয়া আনা। **To talk sixteen to the dozen**—To talk too much ; চোখে মুখে কথা বলা, মুখে খৈ ফুটা। **To talk to**—To reprove ; তিরস্কার করা, ভৎর্সনা করা, দুর্ণাম করা। **To talk to the point subject, etc.**—To talk without digression ; আলোচ্য বিষয়ে কথা বলা, মূল বিষয়ে কথা বলা। **To talk up**—To discuss to rouse interest in a subject ; লোকের আগ্রহ উদ্রিক্ত করার জন্য, কোন বিষয়ে অলোচনা করা। **To talk round**—To discuss a subject without arriving at a conclusion ; কোনরূপ সিদ্ধান্তে উপনীত না হইয়া কোন বিষয়ে আলোচনা করা।

talk'-a-tive (täk-ā-tĭv), *adj.* Given to much talking ; loquacious ; বাচাল ; বাবদুক, বহুভাষী। **—ness,** *n.*

talk'-ee talk'-ee (täk-ē-täk-ē), *n.* **1.** Chatter ; বাচালতা, বকবক। **2.** Broken English of the Negroes; নিগ্রোদিগের ভাঙ্গা ভাঙ্গা ইংরাজী।

talk'-ing (täk-), *adj.* **1.** Having the power of speech ; as, *talking* birds ; বাক্‌শক্তিসম্পন্ন। **2.** Garrulous ; বহুভাষী, বাচাল। **3.** Expressive ; as, *talking* eyes ; ব্যঞ্জক, দ্যোতনাপূর্ণ, ব্যঞ্জনাময়, ব্যঞ্জনাপূর্ণ। **Talking-bird**—যে পক্ষী মনুষ্যের ন্যায় কথা বলিয়া থাকে, ভাষিপক্ষী, ফুটবাক্ পক্ষী। **Talking machine**—গ্রামোফোন প্রভৃতি ভাষণযন্ত্র।

tall, *adj.* **1.** (Of person) Of more than average height ; দীর্ঘ, দীর্ঘকায়, ঢেঙ্গা (*colloq.*)। **2.** High in stature ; দীর্ঘ, প্রাংশু। **3.** (*Slang*) Incredible; as, *tall* stories; boastful; as, *tall* talk; অবিশ্বাসযোগ্য ; লম্বাচৌড়া। **4.** (*Amer.*) Excellent; as, a *tall* fight; চমৎকার। **Tall'-ness,** *n.* **Tall-boy**—উচ্চ দেরাজশ্রেণী ; ধূমনির্গম নালীর উপরে লাগাইবার জন্য ধাতুফলক নির্ম্মিত চোঙ্গ। **To talk tall**—See under TALK.

tăl-lāge, —lĭ-āge, *ns.* A toll of tax levied by Norman kings ; ইংলণ্ডের নর্ম্মাণ নৃপতিগণ কর্ত্তৃক গৃহীত কর বিশেষ।

tal'-lith (-ĭth), *n.* A mantle, now a head-covering, worn by Jews at prayer ; ইহুদীগণ কর্ত্তৃক উপাসনাকালে ব্যবহৃত একপ্রকার উত্তরীয় বা শিরোবস্ত্র।

tăl'-low (-lö), *n.* & *v. t.* The fat of oxen, sheep, etc. melted and separated from the fibrous or membranous matter ; চর্ব্বি, বসা মেদ। ***Verb t.*** **1.** To grease with tallow ; as, to *tallow* candle ; চর্ব্বি মাখান। **2.** To fatten, as sheep ; মেষ প্রভৃতিকে পুষ্টাঙ্গ এবং মেদস্বী করা। **—ish, —y,** *adjs.* **Tallow-candle**—চর্ব্বির বাতি। **Tallow-chandler**—যে ব্যক্তি চর্ব্বির বাতি প্রস্তুত বা বিক্রয় করে। **Tallow drop**—হীরক প্রভৃতি কাটিবার প্রণালী, বিশেষ—যাহাতে এক পার্শ্ব বা উভয় পার্শ্ব গুম্বজাকৃতি করা হয়। **Tallow-face**—ম্লান পাণ্ডুরবদন ব্যক্তি। **Tallow-top**—যে রত্নের সম্মুখভাগ গোলাকৃতি এবং পশ্চাদ্‌ভাগ সমতল করিয়া কাটা হয়। **Tallow-tree**—বিভিন্ন প্রকার বৃক্ষ—যাহা হইতে উদ্ভিজ্জ চর্ব্বি প্রাপ্ত হওয়া যায়। **Vegetable-tallow**—উদ্ভিজ্জ চর্ব্বি।

tăl'-lȳ, *n., v. t.* & *i.* **1.** A piece of wood on which notches or scores are cut, as marks of number ; যে কাষ্ঠখণ্ডে সংখ্যাসূচক দাগ কাটা হয়, অঙ্কদণ্ড, আঁকবাড়ী। **2.** Marks made to keep a score or account ; হিসাব রাখার জন্য অঙ্কিত দাগ বা চিহ্ন। **3.** An account of goods sold esp. kept by notches or marks entered in seller's and purchaser's books ; বিক্রীত মালের হিসাববিশেষ—যাহা খাঁজ কিম্বা দাগ দ্বারা রাখা হয় এবং ক্রেতা ও বিক্রেতা উভয়ের খাতায় তোলা হয়। **4.** (*Rare*) One thing made to suit another ; (ক্বচিদ্‌ব্যবহৃত) অনুরূপ বস্তু, দোসর। **5.** A label or ticket of wood or metal used in gardens for the purpose of bearing either the name of the plant, to which it is attached or a number referring to a catalogue; as, horticultural *tally*; (ক্বচিদ্‌ব্যবহৃত) উদ্যানের বৃক্ষাদিতে সংবদ্ধ ক্ষুদ্র কাষ্ঠ বা ধাতুখণ্ড—যাহাতে বৃক্ষের নাম বা তালিকাস্থ নামসূচক সংখ্যা থাকে। 6. Short for TALLY-SHOP. ***Verb t.*** **1.** To record on a tally; দাগ কাটিয়া হিসাব রাখা। **2.** To make to correspond; to suit; অনুরূপ করা; মিলান। **3.** (*Naut.*) To pull off as the sheets or lower corners of the main or foresails; (নৌবিদ্যা) প্রধান বা অগ্রবর্ত্তী পাইলের কাপড় বা নিম্নের কোণসমূহ টানিয়া ফেলা। ***Verb i.*** To correspond; as, your ideas *tally* exactly with mine; to suit; to match; অনুরূপ হওয়া; মিলা; খাপ খাওয়া। **Tallyman**—উঠানো দোকানদার; যে ব্যক্তি কাষ্ঠখণ্ডে খাঁজ কাটিয়া হিসাব রাখে। **Tally-shop**—উঠনোর দোকান (যে দোকানে পণ্য দ্রব্য ধারে দেওয়া হয় এবং অঙ্কযষ্টির দ্বারা হিসাব রাখা হইয়া থাকে।)

tăl'-lў-hō, *n.* & *v. t.* **1.** A huntman's cry to urge on its hounds; শিকারী কুকুরকে উৎসাহিত করার জন্য শিকারী কর্তৃক উচ্চারিত ধ্বনি। **2.** A kind of vehicle for pleasure; প্রমোদশকট। ***Verb t.*** To urge on hounds with this cry; উক্তরূপ চীৎকার করিয়া কুকুরদিগকে উৎসাহিত করা।

tăl'-mă, *n.* A kind of long cloak or cape sometimes hooded; একপ্রকার প্রাবরণ বা স্কন্ধচ্ছদ।

tăl-mi'-gōld (-mē-), *n.* Brass thinly coated with gold; স্বর্ণপত্রমণ্ডিত পিত্তল।

Tăl'-mŭd, *n.* The Hebrew civil and canonical laws, traditions, etc.; ইহুদীদিগের ধর্ম্মসংহিতা। **—mud'-ic, —mud'-i-cal**, *adjs.* **Jerusalem** or **Babylonian Talmud**—ইহুদীদিগের সুবৃহৎ ধর্ম্মসংহিতাদ্বয়।

Tăl'-mŭd-ist, *n.* A compiler of Talmud; a student of Talmud; ইহুদীদিগের ধর্ম্মব্যবস্থা-সংগ্রাহক; ইহুদীদিগের ধর্ম্মসংহিতাসম্বন্ধে গবেষণাকারী। **—is'-tic**, *adj.*

tăl'-ŏn, *n.* **1.** Claw, esp. of the bird of prey; শিকারী পক্ষীর নখর। **2.** (*Arch.*) Same as OGEE. **3.** In lock, the shoulder of the bolt against which the key presses in shooting the bolt; তালার অংশ বিশেষ।

tā'-lŭs, *n.* **1.** The ankle; the ankle-bone; গুল্‌ফ; গুল্‌ফাস্থি। **2.** (*Geol.*) A sloping heap of fragments at the bottom of a rocky declivity, derived from its weathered or wasted surface; পাষাণপর্ব্বতের পাদদেশে ক্রমনিম্ন ক্ষয়প্রাপ্ত প্রস্তরখণ্ড সমূহের স্তূপ। **3.** (*Arch.*) The slope or inclination of a work; (স্থপতি-বিদ্যা) প্রাচীরাদির প্রবণতা।

tă-măn-dŭ-ă', tă-mă-noir' (-nwär), *ns.* Kinds of ant-eater of tropical America; আমেরিকার গ্রীষ্মমণ্ডলে দৃষ্ট দুইপ্রকার পিপীলিকাভুক্‌ জন্তু।

tăm'-ă-răck, *n.* The American larch; আমেরিকাদেশীয় বৃক্ষবিশেষ।

tăm-ă-ri-că'-cē-ae (-ē), *n.* A family of shrubs or trees having narrow entire leaves; ঝাবুকাদি (সাঃ পঃ)।

tăm'-ă-rin, *n.* The species of small South-American monkey of the genus midas with a fine silky hair and a tail like a squirrel; দক্ষিণ আমেরিকাদেশীয় কপিবিশেষ। [ইহাদের লোম রেশমের মত চক্‌চকে এবং পুচ্ছ কাঠবিড়ালীর মত]।

tăm'-ă-rind, *n.* **1.** A tropical leguminous tree whose fruit is acid and agreeable, and employed as medicine in fevers; তেঁতুলগাছ, তিন্তিড়ী বৃক্ষ। [Syn. চরিত্রা, চারিত্রা, মহাম্ল, যমদূতিকা, চণ্ডচুক্রিকা, চিঞ্চা, অম্লিকা, তিন্তিড়ীব, তিন্তিড়াকা, আম্লিকা, আম্লীকা, তিন্তিলী, আম্বিকা, চুক্র, চুক্রা, চুক্রিকা, অম্লা, অত্যম্ল, ভুক্তা, ভুক্তিকা, গুরুপত্রা, পিচ্ছিলা, শাকচুক্রিকা, সুচুক্রিকা, সুতিন্তিড়া, অম্লফল, চণ্ড]। [Arab. *tamar-ul-Hind*; Pers. *tamr-i-Hind*; Fr. *tamarins*; Ger. *tamarinden*; Ital. & Span. *tamarindo*; Tam. *pulie*; Teleg. *chinta-pundoo*; Turk. *demer Hindi*; Hind. *amli*; Burm. *ma-gye*; Lat. *tamarindus.*] **2.** The fruit of this tree; তেঁতুল, ফলাম্ল। **Tamarind-fish**—তেঁতুল সহযোগে রক্ষিত মৎস্য।

tăm'-ă-risk, *n.* A genus of shrub of Europe and Asia, some of them yielding manna; ঝাউ গাছ, পাঁকুড় বৃক্ষ।

tăm'-bour (-bôr), *n.*, & *v. t.* **1.** A small flat drum; একপ্রকার ময়দা চালনীর আকার ঢক্কা। **2.** A drum-like frame for working embroidery upon; যে ময়দা চালুনীর আকার ঠাটে রেশম প্রভৃতির কাপড় ছড়াইয়া উহার উপর জরীর বুটা ইত্যাদি তোলা হয়। **3.** A species of embroidery in which threads of gold and silver are worked in leaves, flowers, etc.; জরীর ফুল পাতা প্রভৃতি তোলা সূচীকর্ম্ম। **4.** (*Arch.*) A round course of stones, forming the sheet of a column; যে প্রস্তরচক্র সমূহ উপরি উপরি সন্নিবেশ দ্বারা স্তম্ভবপু রচিত হয়। **5.** (*Fort.*) A defence made of palisade; শত্রু সৈন্যের গতিরোধক কীলকরচিত বৃতি। **6.** Kinds of fish making drumming noise or drumlike in form; ঢক্কাবৎ নাদকারী বা ঢক্কাকৃতি বিভিন্নপ্রকার মৎস্য। ***Verb t.*** To embroider on a tambour; গোলাকৃতি ঠাটের উপর জরীর ফুল পাতা প্রভৃতি তোলা।

tăm-bou-rin' (-bō-rēn), *n.* **1.** A long narrow drum used in Provence; প্রভেন্স প্রদেশে ব্যবহৃত একপ্রকার ঢোল। **2.** A dance accompanied by this ; music for this ; ঐ বাদ্যযন্ত্রের সহযোগে নৃত্য ; ঐরূপ নৃত্যোপযোগী বাদ্য।

tăm-bou-rine'(-bô-rēn), *n.* **1.** A musical instrument of the drum species played on with the hand, having the hoop over which parchment is stretched attached with jingles ; খঞ্জনী। **2.** A lively French dance formerly in vogue in operas ; ফরাসীদেশীয় নৃত্যবিশেষ। **3.** A kind of African pigeon ; আফ্রিকাদেশীয় কপোত বিশেষ।

tāme, *v. t.* & *adj.* **1.** To reduce from a wild to a domestic state ; পোষ মানান। **2.** To subdue ; as, to *tame* one's passions ; বশীভূত করা, দমন করা, বশে আনা। ***Adj.*** **1.** Domesticated ; as, a *tame* animal ; পোষা, পালিত। **2.** Wanting in spirit ; subdued ; spiritless ; submissive ; as, *tame* slaves ; নিস্তেজ ; বশীভূত ; তেজোবীর্য্যহীন ; নম্র। **3.** (*Colloq.*) Cultivated ; as, *tame* land ; produced by cultivation ; as, *tame* plant ; (চলিতভাষায়) কর্ষিত, কৃষ্ট ; কর্ষণোৎপন্ন। **4.** Insipid ; as, a *tame* poem ; dull ; নীরস ; অবসাদজনক। **Tam'-able,** *adj.* **Tam'-a-ble-ness,** *n.* **Tam-a-bil'-i-ty,** *n.* **Tame'-ly,** *adv.* **Tme'-ness,** *n.*

tāme, *v. t.* (*Dial.*) To pierce or cut into ; (উপভাষায়) ছেঁদা করিয়া কাটিয়া প্রবিষ্ট করা।

Tăm'-il, *n.* **1.** A species of Dravidian spoken in Southern India ; তামিল। **2.** The Tamil-speaking people ; দক্ষিণ ভারতের তামিলভাষী লোক।

tăm'-is (-ĭ), *n.* A cloth used for straining liquids ; তরল পদার্থ ছাঁকিবার জন্য ব্যবহৃত বস্ত্রখণ্ড।

Tăm'-má-nў, *n.* A democratic organization of New York with an unsavoury reputation for corrupt influence on municipal politics ; আমেরিকার নিউইয়র্ক সহরের গণতান্ত্রিকসমিতি। [Tammany নামক আমেরিকার আদিম অধিবাসিগণের সর্দ্দার বিশেষের নাম হইতে গৃহীত। ইহাকে রহস্যচ্ছলে St. Tammany ও বলা হয়।] **–ism, –ite,** *ns.* **Tammany Hall**—এই সম্প্রদায়ের সভাগৃহ। [এই সম্প্রদায়ের সভ্যগণ রাজনীতিক ব্যাপারে নানাপ্রকার নিন্দিত উপায় অবলম্বন করিয়া থাকেন।]

tăm–ō'–shăn'-têr, *n.* A tight-fitting cap of woollen stuff ; একপ্রকার আঁটসাঁট পশমীটুপি।

tămp, *v. t.* **1.** To fill up, as hole bored in a rock for blasting especially by driving in something with frequent strokes ; বিস্ফোরক দ্রব্য দ্বারা পাথরের পাহাড় প্রভৃতি ভাঙ্গার জন্য যে ছিদ্র করা হয় তাহা মৃত্তিকা প্রভৃতি গাদিয়া বন্ধ করা। **2.** To force in by frequent light strokes ; উপর্য্যুপরি মৃদু মৃদু আঘাত করিয়া বসান।

tăm'-păn, *n.* A South-African tick remarkable for the venom of its bite ; দক্ষিণ আফ্রিকার একপ্রকার বিষাক্ত আঁটালি।

tăm'-pĕr, *v. i.* **1.** To meddle ; হস্তক্ষেপ করা, হাত দেওয়া। **2.** To make unauthorised changes in manuscript, will, etc. ; as, to *tamper* with a document ; চরমপত্র, পাণ্ডুলিপি, প্রভৃতি অসদুদ্দেশ্যে পরিবর্ত্তন করা, নাড়া চাড়া করা। **3.** To deal secretly ; to give bribe ; গোপনে কায করা, তলে তলে কায করা ; ঘুষ দেওয়া।

tăm'-pi-ŏn, *n.* **1.** The stopper for closing the mouth of a cannon ; কামানের মুখ বন্ধ করার জন্য রোধনী। **2.** A stopper ; রোধনী, ছিপি।

tăm'-pŏn, *n.* & *v. t.* **1.** A plug inserted to stop bleeding ; রক্তস্রাব বন্ধ করার জন্য ব্যবহৃত রোধনী। **2.** A pad for the hair ; চুল ফুলাইবার জন্য একপ্রকার ক্ষুদ্র গদি। ***Verb t.*** To plug tightly in order to stop bleeding ; রক্ত বন্ধ করার জন্য আঁট করিয়া গুঁজিয়া দেওয়া।

tăm-pŏn-āde', *n.* The operation of plugging a wound ; ক্ষতস্থান গুঁজি দ্বারা বন্ধ করণ। **Tam'-pon-age, Tam'-pon-ment,** *ns.*

tăm'-tăm, *n.* Kinds of drum used in East Indies and West-Africa ; ঢোল, তবলা, মৃদঙ্গ, প্রভৃতি।

tăn, *v. t., i., n.* & *adj.* **1.** To convert into leather, as animal-skins, by means of an infusion of oak or some other barks or substance ; ওক প্রভৃতি বৃক্ষের কুট্টিত বল্কল মিশ্রিত জলে ডুবাইয়া চামড়া পাকা করা, চর্ম্মশোধন করা, চর্ম্মসংস্কার করা। **2.** To apply a mixture as of oak bark etc. for hardening something ; কোন কিছু কঠিন করার জন্য বল্কল প্রভৃতির মিশ্র প্রয়োগ করা। **3.** To imbrown by exposure to the rays of the sun ; to make sunburnt ; "In war well seasoned and in labour *tanned*" ; রৌদ্রে রাখিয়া পিঙ্গলবর্ণ করা ; রৌদ্রদগ্ধ করা। **4.** (*Slang*) To thrash ; "Today you *tan* people, tomorrow they *tan* you" ; বেতান, চাবকান। ***Verb i.*** To get or become tanned ; পাকা হওয়া। **2.** To become tan-coloured or sunburnt ; as, my face *tans* quickly with the sun ; পিঙ্গলবর্ণ হওয়া, কটাবর্ণ হওয়া। ***Noun.*** **1.** The bark of oak or other trees as used for tanning ; চর্ম্মসংস্কারকার্য্যে ব্যবহৃত ওক বা অন্য কোনপ্রকার বৃক্ষের বাকল। **2.** A yellowish brown colour like that of tan ; পিঙ্গলবর্ণ, কটারঙ্গ, বাদামী রং। ***Adj.*** Of the colour of tan ; tawny ; ওক প্রভৃতির কুট্টিত বল্কলের বর্ণ ; পিঙ্গলবর্ণ, বাদামী রংয়ের। **Tan'-na-ble,** *adj.* **Tan'-nage,** *n.* **Tan'-ner,** *n.* One who tans ; চর্ম্মসংস্কারক, চর্ম্মশোধক। **Tan'-ner-y,** *n.* **1.** The place where hides are tanned ; চর্ম্মশোধনাগার,

চর্ম্মসংস্কার-শালা। 2. The act or process of tanning; চর্ম্মশোধন, চর্ম্মসংস্কার। Tan'-ning, *n*. **Tan-balls**—ইন্ধনরূপে ব্যবহৃত কষায়ণ বাহির করা কুট্টিত ওক বল্কলের পিণ্ড। **Tan-house**—যে গৃহে চর্ম্মসংস্কারের উপযোগী বল্কল রক্ষিত হয়। **Tan-liquor, Tan-pickle, Tan-ooze**—চর্ম্মসংস্কার-কার্য্যে ব্যবহৃত তরল পদার্থ। **Tan-mill**—চর্ম্মসংস্কারের উপযোগী বল্কল-কুট্টনের জন্য যন্ত্র। **Tan-pit**—যে ভূগর্ভে নির্বদ্ধ পাত্রে চর্ম্মসংস্কারের বল্কল ভিজান হয়। **Tan-yard**—চর্ম্মসংস্কার-প্রাঙ্গণ, চর্ম্মশোধনপ্রাঙ্গণ। **Spent tan**—যে ওক প্রভৃতির কুট্টিত বল্কল হইতে কষায়ণ বাহির করা হইয়াছে এবং যাহা রাস্তা প্রভৃতি আচ্ছাদনে ব্যবহৃত হয়। **The tan**—(ইতরভাষায়) সার্কাস।

tăn, *n*. Same as TANGENT (which see).

tä'-nä, tăn'-na (-ä), *ns*. Police station in India; থানা। **—dar', —na-dar'**, *ns*. The officer in charge of police-station in India; থানাদার।

tăn-ă-gêr, *n*. A name of the tropical American birds of finch family remarkable for their bright colour; আমেরিকাদেশীয় একশ্রেণীর উজ্জ্বলবর্ণ বিহঙ্গ বিশেষ।

tăn'-dĕm, *n., adj.* & *adv.* 1. A wheeled carriage drawn with two horses harnessed singly one before the other; যে শকটের অশ্বদ্বয় অগ্রে যোজিত থাকে। 2. A bicycle or tricycle for two or more persons, one behind the other; দুই বা ততোধিক ব্যক্তির জন্য অগ্রপশ্চাৎ ক্রমে যোজিত আসনবিশিষ্ট দ্বিচক্র বা ত্রিচক্রযান। ***Adj.*** 1. (Of horses) One harnessed behind the other; (অশ্বসম্বন্ধে) অগ্রপশ্চাৎ ক্রমে যোজিত। 2. (Of bicycle) With seats arranged one before the other; (দ্বিচক্রযান সম্পর্কে) অগ্রপশ্চাৎভাবে সজ্জিত আসনবিশিষ্ট। ***Adv.*** With two horses harnessed singly one before the other; অগ্রপশ্চাৎ ক্রমে যোজিত অশ্বদ্বয় দ্বারা। **To drive tandem**—To drive a carriage with horses harnessed one before the other; অগ্রপশ্চাৎ ক্রমে যোজিত অশ্বযুক্ত শকট চালনা করা।

tănd-stick'-ŏr, *n*. A Swedish wooden lucifer match; সুইডেন দেশে প্রস্তুত দীপশলাকা বিশেষ।

tăng, *n*. 1. A strong taste or flavour; উগ্রগন্ধ বা স্বাদ। 2. Characteristic property; বিশিষ্ট ধর্ম্ম বা গুণ।

tăng, *n.* & *v. t.* The part of a knife, fork, chisel, file, etc. and the like which goes into the handle; ছুরী, কাঁটা, বাটাল, উখা, প্রভৃতির যে অংশ হাতলের মধ্যে প্রবিষ্ট থাকে। ***Verb t.*** To furnish with tang; উক্তরূপ অংশ সংযোজিত করা।

tăng, *n., v. t.* & *i.* A twang; a ring; টঙ্কার; টং টং। ***Verb t.*** 1. To sound loudly; টং টং শব্দ করা (Also *Verb t.*) 2. (*Dial.*) To strike two pieces of metal together to induce a swarm of bees to settle; মৌমাছির ঝাঁককে কোন নির্দ্দিষ্ট স্থানে বসাইবার উদ্দেশ্যে দুই খণ্ড ধাতুর সাহায্যে টং টং ধ্বনি করা। ***Verb i.*** To emit a sharp ringing sound; টং টং শব্দ হওয়া।

tăng, *n*. Kinds of sea-weed; বিভিন্ন প্রকার সাগর-শৈবাল।

tăn'-gĕnt, *n.* & *adj.* A straight line which touches a circle or a curve, but which when produced does not cut it; যে সরল রেখা বৃত্তাদিকে স্পর্শ করিয়া থাকে, কিন্তু প্রবর্দ্ধিত হইলে উহাদিগকে ছেদন করে না, স্পর্শরেখা (সাঃ পঃ), স্পর্শিনী (শংকুঃ), স্পর্শক (ঐ)। ***Adj.*** Meeting a line or surface at any point but not intersecting it when produced; স্পর্শশীল। **—gen'-tial**, *adj*. **—gen'-tial-ly**, *adv*. **Tangent-balance, Tangent-scale**—একপ্রকার তুলাযন্ত্র যাহাতে ধনুরাকৃতি ক্রমাঙ্কিত দাঁড়িতে নিবদ্ধ সূচীদ্বারা গুরুত্ব প্রদর্শিত হইয়া থাকে। **Tangent-galvanometer**—একপ্রকার বিদ্যুৎশক্তিমাপক যাহাতে সূচীর বিক্ষেপ কোণের সঞ্চালিত তাড়িতপ্রবাহের আনুপাতিক হইয়া থাকে, স্পর্শবিদ্যুৎমাপক। **Tangent-screw**—অতি সূক্ষ্ম পরিমাপ বা যোজনার জন্য একপ্রকার স্ক্রু। **Tangent of an angle**—(ত্রিকোণমিতি) কোন নির্দ্দিষ্ট কোণের (সূক্ষ্মকোণ হইলে) বিপরীত দিগ্‌বর্ত্তী সমকোণী ত্রিভুজের ভুজ এবং অপর সূক্ষ্মকোণের বিপরীত দিগ্‌বর্ত্তী ভুজের অনুপাত। [স্থূল কোণের স্পর্শ (Tangent) সংখ্যাগত ভাবে উহার অনুপূরকের (supplement) সমান কিন্তু উহার চিহ্ন অনুপূরকের বিপরীত হইয়া থাকে।] **To fly off at a tangent, To go off at a tangent**—To pass suddenly from one line of action or train of thought to another, diverging widely from the first; একরূপ কার্য্যপ্রণালী ত্যাগ করিয়া অন্যরূপ কার্য্যপ্রণালী অবলম্বন করা, একরূপ চিন্তাধারা ত্যাগ করিয়া সহসা অন্যপ্রকার চিন্তাপ্রবাহের অনুবর্ত্তন করা।

Tăn'-gĕr-ine, *n.* & *adj.* 1. A native of Tangiers; ট্যাঞ্জিয়ার্স প্রদেশের অধিবাসী। 2. A small kind of orange from Tangiers; ট্যাঞ্জিয়ার্স প্রদেশে জাত একপ্রকার ক্ষুদ্রাকার কমলা। ***Adj.*** Of Tangiers; ট্যাঞ্জিয়ার্স প্রদেশসম্বন্ধীয়। **Tangerine orange**—Same as TANGERINE *n.* 2.

tăn'-ghin (-gin), *n*. A deadly poison obtained from the seeds of *tanghinia venenifera* found in Madagascar; মাদাগাস্‌কার দ্বীপের বৃক্ষবিশেষের বীজ হইতে প্রাপ্ত একপ্রকার মারাত্মক বিষ। **Trial by tanghin**—পূর্ব্বকালে মাদাগাস্‌কার দ্বীপে অভিযুক্ত ব্যক্তিকে উক্ত বৃক্ষের বীজজাত বিষচূর্ণ সেবন করান হইত। বমন প্রভৃতি দ্বারা ঐ বিষ দেহ হইতে নির্গত হইয়া সেই ব্যক্তির প্রাণ রক্ষা পাইলে সে নির্দ্দোষ বলিয়া বিবেচিত হইত।

tăn'-gĭ-ble, (-bl), *adj.* 1. Perceptible by the touch; স্পর্শযোগ্য, স্পর্শসংবেদ্য, স্পর্শনীয়, স্পৃশ্য (হিঃ কোঃ)।

2. Real; as, *tangible* security; substantial; definite; clearly intelligible; as, *tangible* evidence; বাস্তব; সারবান; সুস্পষ্ট; সুপরিজ্ঞেয়। **—bil'-i-ty**, *n*. 1. The state of being tangible; স্পর্শযোগ্যতা, স্পর্শ (হিঃ কোঃ), স্পৃশ্যতা (ঐ), স্পর্শবেদ্যতা। 2. The sensation of touch; স্পর্শশক্তি। 3. A tangible thing or matter; বাস্তব বিষয়, সুস্পষ্ট বা সুপরিজ্ঞেয় বিষয় **—bly**, *adv*. **—ness**, *n*.

tan'-gle (tăng-gl), *v. t., i.* & *n*. 1. To unite or knit together confusedly; to interweave or interlock, so as to make it difficult to unravel; পাকান, জড়ান, জড়িত করা; এলোমেলো করা, জট বাঁধা। 2. To entrap; "May never fowler's snare *Tangle* thy struggling foot"; ফাঁদে ফেলান, জালে ফেলান। 3. To confuse; to complicate; to involve; বিভ্রান্ত করা; জটিল করা; জড়িত করা। ***Verb i.*** To be entangled or united confusedly; জড়িত হওয়া, এলোমেলো হওয়া। ***Noun.*** 1. A knot of hair, threads or other things united confusedly; জট, পাক, পেঁচ, গাঁট। 2. A state of perplexity or bewilderment; as, enoromous *tangle* of facts and figures; গোল, গোলমাল, হতবুদ্ধিতা। 3. An edible sea-weed having long edible fronds (called also *tang*); একপ্রকার আহারোপযোগী সাগর-শৈবাল। 4. (*Pl.*) A contrivance which is dragged over the sea bottom to entangle and catch animals, as starfishes; তারা মাছ প্রভৃতি ধৃত করার জন্য নদী প্রভৃতির তলকর্ষণের জন্য ব্যবহৃত কৌশল বিশেষ। **—gly, —some**, *adjs*.

tăn-grăm', *n*. A Chinese toy made by cutting a square of thin wood or other suitable material into seven pieces, (these pieces are capable of being formed into a number of different figures, and are used in primary schools as a means of instruction); এক প্রকার চীনদেশীয় খেলনা। (ইহা সাত খণ্ডে কাটা পাতল কাঠের চতুষ্ক। এই সকল টুকরা বিভিন্ন রকমে সাজাইয়া নানা ছবি প্রস্তুত করা যায়। এইরূপ খেলনা শিশু বিদ্যালয়ে ব্যবহৃত হইয়া থাকে।)

tăn'-ist, *n*. The chief or holder of lands or honours, in certain Celtic races; the chief's elective successor; কোন কোন কেল্টিক্ জাতির সর্দ্দার বা ভূস্বামী; ঐরূপ সর্দ্দারের নির্ব্বাচিত উত্তরাধিকারী।

tăn'-ist-rÿ, *n*. A tenure of lands only for life, the successor being appointed from family by election; একপ্রকার জোত—যাহা কেবল ভূস্বামীর জীবিতকাল পর্য্যন্ত দেওয়া হইত এবং ভূস্বামীর পরিবার হইতে কোন ব্যক্তি উত্তরাধিকারী নির্ব্বাচিত হইতেন। (১ম জেমস্ আয়র্লণ্ড দেশে এই প্রথা রহিত করেন।)

tank (tăngk), *n*. 1. (India) A pond; পুকুর, পুষ্করিণী, দীঘি। 2. A large basin or cistern for holding any liquid; as, the gas *tank* was 10 feet in diameter; তরল পদার্থ রাখার জন্য চতুষ্কোণ আধার, কুণ্ড। 3. A tank-shaped engine of war; as, the French captured three enemy-*tanks*; জলকুণ্ডাকৃতি যুদ্ধ-যন্ত্র। **Tank drama** — যে নাটকে জলনিমজ্জিত ব্যক্তির উদ্ধারসাধন প্রভৃতি প্রদর্শনের জন্য জল ব্যবহৃত হয়। **Tank engine**— যে বাষ্পীয় যন্ত্রে জল ও ইন্ধনের জন্য স্বতন্ত্র আধার থাকে।

tank (tăngk), *v. t*. 1. To lift or measure in a tank; জলকুণ্ডে উত্তোলন বা পরিমাপ করা। 2. To store in a tank; জলকুণ্ডে সঞ্চিত করা। 3. (*Dial.*) To immerse in a tank; (উপভাষায়) পুকুরের জলে ডুবান।

tank'-āge (tăngk-), *n*. 1. Act or process of storing in tanks; জলকুণ্ডে জল সঞ্চয়ন, জলকুণ্ডে জলসঞ্চয়ের প্রণালী। 2. The contents of a tank; জলকুণ্ডের ধারণশক্তি। 3. The fees charged for storage in tanks; কুণ্ডে জলাদি রক্ষার জন্য যে মাশুল লওয়া হয়। 4. (*Agric.*) A kind of manure obtained from refuse fats; চর্ব্বি প্রভৃতির অসার অংশ হইতে প্রাপ্ত একপ্রকার সার।

tank'-ărd (tăngk-), *n*. 1. A large drinking vessel of tin with cover; বৃহৎ পানপাত্র [সাধারণতঃ রূপা বা রূপদস্তা দ্বারা নির্ম্মিত হয় এবং ঢাকনি থাকে।] 2. The contents of a tankard or the quantity held by a tankard; as, a *tankard* of ale; ঐরূপ পাত্রের ধারণশক্তি, ঐরূপ পাত্রপূর্ণ তরল পদার্থ। **Tankard-turnip**— একপ্রকার শালগম — যাহার মূলদেশ চতুষ্কোণ আকার থাকে।

tăn'-ner (-ẽr), *n*. 1. See under TAN. 2. (*Slang*) A six pence; (ইতরভাষায়) ৬ পেন্স।

tăn'-nic (-ĭc), *adj*. Of tan; ওক প্রভৃতির কুট্টিতবল্কলসম্বন্ধীয়। **—nif'-er-ous**, *adj*. **Tannic-acid**— same as TANNIN.

tăn'-nin (-ĭn), *n*. The astringent principle of oak-bark, nut-galls, and other trees used in converting raw hides into leather; ওক প্রভৃতির বল্কল প্রভৃতি হইতে প্রাপ্ত একপ্রকার কষায়রস — যদ্দারা চামড়া পাকা করা যায়, কষায়ীণ (যোঃ) কষায় রস (ঐ)।

tăn'-sÿ, *n*. A bitter aromatic plant of the genus tanacetum used in medicine and cookery; রন্ধন ও ঔষধ প্রস্তুতকার্য্যে ব্যবহৃত পীতবর্ণ পুষ্পপ্রসূ উগ্রসুগন্ধিপত্রবিশিষ্ট গুল্মবিশেষ।

tăn'-tă-lize, *v. t*. 1. To torment by presenting something desirable to the view, which cannot be attained; কোনরূপ স্পৃহণীয় বস্তু কাহারো সম্মুখে ধরিয়া সে ধরে ধরে এমন সময়ে সরাইয়া নিয়া তাহাকে জ্বালাতন করা। 2. To excite by hopes that are never realised;

"Thy vain desires, at strife within themselves, have *tantalized* thy life"; আশা বৃথা দ্বারা বিড়ম্বিত করা, আশা দিয়া নিরাশ করা। **-li-za'-tion,** *n.* **-liz-ing-ly,** *adv.*

tăn'-tă-lŭm, *n.* A rare metallic element ; একপ্রকার দুষ্প্রাপ্য ধাতব মূল পদার্থ, তন্তলক (সাঃ পঃ)।

Tăn'-tă-lŭs, *n.* **1.** (*Gk. Myth.*) A character of Greek mythology ; (গ্রীকপুরাণ) Zeusএর পুত্র Tantalus দেবতাদিগের অপ্রীতিভাজন হওয়াতে যমলোকের হ্রদবিশেষে আবদ্ধ হন। উক্ত হ্রদের বারি তৃষ্ণার্ত্ত Tantalusএর অধরপ্রান্ত পর্য্যন্ত আসিবামাত্র অন্তর্হিত হইত। অপরদিকে তাহার মস্তকের উপর সুরসাল ফলভারাবনত শাখাসকল বিলম্বিত হইত। কিন্তু যেমনি Tantalus লুব্ধ হইয়া ঐ ফল ভক্ষণ করিতে যাইত তন্মুহূর্ত্তেই ফলপূর্ণ শাখা দূরে সরিয়া যাইত। **2.** A genus of wading birds ; একজাতীয় বক পক্ষী। **Tantalus cup**—একপ্রকার বৈজ্ঞানিক ক্রীড়নক—ইহাতে একটী পানপাত্রের মধ্যে একটী পুত্তলিকা থাকে। ঐ পানপাত্রস্থ জল পুত্তলিকার চিবুকদেশে না উঠা পর্য্যন্ত পাত্রে জল ঢালা যায় ঐ স্থানে উঠিবামাত্র জল ঐ পুত্তলিকার দেহের বক্রনালী (siphon) সহযোগে ক্রমশঃ নির্গত হইতে থাকে।

tăn'-tă-mount (-mownt), *adj.* Equivalent ; "Actions were brought against persons who had defamed the Duke of York ; and damages *tantamount* to a sentence of perpetual imprisonment were demanded by the plaintiff and without difficulty obtained" ; সমান, সমতুল্য, তুল্যার্থ।

tăn'-tăr'-ă, *n.* A rapid succession of notes on trumpets or horns ; শানাই বা শিঙ্গার ক্রমনিঃসরিত ধ্বনির প্রবাহ।

tăn-tiv'-ÿ, *adv.* & *n.* (*Archaic*) Swiftly ; (অপ্রঃ) দ্রুত, ত্বরিত। ***Noun.*** Swift movement ; দ্রুতগতি।

tăn'-trŭm, *n.* A fit of ill humour ; "An author, who was always in a *tantrum* if interrupted" ; a display of temper ; বদমেজাজ ; ক্রোধপ্রকাশ।

Tao'-ĭsm (tow-), *n.* A religion of China ; চীনদেশের ধর্ম্মবিশেষ, তাওধর্ম্ম। [Lao-Tsze (জন্ম খৃঃ পূঃ ৬০৪) এই ধর্ম্মের প্রবর্ত্তক। ইনি নিষ্কামকর্ম্ম ও ভক্তিবাদ প্রচার করিয়া গিয়াছেন। তিনি দয়া, বিনয়, প্রভৃতি সদ্বৃত্তি সমূহের অনুশীলন এমন কি শত্রুর প্রতিও প্রেমপ্রদর্শন করিতে উপদেশ দিয়াছেন।]

tăp, *n., v. t.* & *i.* **1.** A hole or pipe for drawing liqour from a cask ; যে রন্ধ্র বা নলসহযোগে পিপা হইতে মদ্য বাহির করা হয়। **2.** A plug to stop hole in a cask ; পিপার গুঁজি। **3.** The liquor drawn from a cask or through a tap, esp. with regard to its quality ; পিপা হইতে নিষ্কর্ষিত মদ্য (বিশেষভাবে ঐরূপ মদ্যের গুণ সম্পর্কে ব্যবহৃত হয়)। ***Verb t.*** To pierce so as to let out a fluid, as a cask, a tree, tumour or anything containing a pent-up fluid ; অভ্যন্তরস্থ তরল পদার্থ বাহির করার জন্য ছিদ্র বা ফুটা করা। **2.** To cause to flow ; প্রবাহিত করা। **3.** To take off a telegraphic message from a telegraph or telephone wire ; "The telephone presents facilities for the dangerous practice of *tapping* the wire" ; তার হইতে তাড়িতবার্ত্তা অবৈধভাবে গ্রহণ করা। ***Verb i.*** To be, or act, as a tapster : পিপা হইতে মদ্য নিঃসারণ করা। **Tap'-ping,** *n.* (*Surg.*) The operation of removing fluid from any of the serous cavities of body in which it has collected in large quantity ; (অস্ত্রোপচারবিদ্যা) উদর বা অণ্ডকোষাদির মস্তস্রাবী গহ্বরে অধিক পরিমাণ তরল পদার্থ সঞ্চিত হইলে, ছিদ্র করিয়া বা চুঙ্গি বসাইয়া তাহা বাহির করার প্রক্রিয়া (ডাঃ হরিপ্রসাদ চক্রবর্ত্তী)। **Tap-room**—যে কক্ষে পিপা হইতে নল সহযোগে বীয়র মদ্য সরবরাহ করা হয়। **Tap-root**—মূল শিকড়, প্রধান শিকড়, প্রধান মূল (সাঃ পঃ)। **To tap the admiral**—To tap and steal liquor from cask—পিপা ফুটা করিয়া মদ্য চুরি করা [নেলসনের মৃতদেহ যে পিপাতে আনা হয়—মদ্যের পিপা মনে করিয়া চুরি করার জন্য তাহাতে ছিদ্র করা হইয়াছিল—এইরূপ প্রবাদ এই বাক্যটীর মূল।]

tap, *v. t., i.* & *n.* **1.** To strike gently ; মৃদু আঘাত করা, ঠুকা দেওয়া, ঠুকনি দেওয়া। **2.** To put a new sole or heel on, as a boot or shoe ; জুতায় নূতন গোড়ালী বা তলি লাগান, ঠোকর লাগান। ***Verb i.*** To strike a gentle blow ; ঠুকা দেওয়া, ঠুকনা দেওয়া। ***Noun.*** **1.** A gentle blow ; a tap ; ঠুকা, ঠুকনা ; চাপড়। **2.** A signal sounded with a drum to put light out ; আলোক নির্ব্বাণের জন্য ঢক্কাধ্বনি দ্বারা সঙ্কেত। **3.** A piece of leather fastened upon the bottom of a boot or shoe in repairing or renewing the sole or heel ; জুতার নূতন তলি লাগান অথবা গোড়ালী সারাইবার জন্য যে চর্ম্মখণ্ড সংযোজিত করা হয়, ঠোকর। **Tap-tap**—ঠক ঠক।

tāpe, *n.* & *v. t.* **1.** A narrow strip of woven work, used for strings and the like ; ফিতা। **2.** One of the travelling bands which hold and conduct the sheet of paper in a steam-press; যে ফিতা দ্বারা বাষ্পশক্তিচালিত মুদ্রাযন্ত্রে কাগজ যোগান হয়। **3.** A narrow band of paper on which messages are recorded by a telegraphic apparatus ; যে অপ্রশস্ত কাগজে তাড়িতবার্ত্তাযন্ত্র গৃহীত বার্ত্তা মুদ্রিত হয়। **4.** (*Slang*) Spirituous liquor ; (ইতরভাষায়) মদ্য। ***Verb t.*** **1.** To furnish or tie up with tape ; ফিতা লাগান, ফিতা দ্বারা বাঁধা। **2.** To join sections of (book) with bands of it; ফিতা দ্বারা পুস্তকের অংশ সকল সংযোগ করা। **Tape-line**—মাপফিতা। **Tape-worm**—ফিতাক্রিমি, পটক্রিমি (হঃ চঃ)।

tā'-pĕr, *n., adj., v. t.* & *i.* **1.** A small wax or other candle ; ক্ষুদ্র

মোমবাতি। 2. A tapering form ; ক্রমসূক্ষ্মায়মান বস্তু। *Adj.* Regularly narrowed to a point ; conical ; ক্রমসূক্ষ্মায়মান ; মোচাগ্র, ক্রমসূক্ষ্মাগ্র। *Verb t.* To make gradually smaller ; ক্রমশঃ সূক্ষ্ম করা। *Verb i.* To become gradually smaller ; ক্রমশঃ সূক্ষ্ম হওয়া। **–ing,** *adj.* Gradually diminished to a point ; ক্রম সূক্ষ্মাগ্র, মোচাগ্র, ক্রমসূক্ষ্ম, শুণ্ডাকার (সাঃ পঃ), গোপুচ্ছাকার (মঃ সং)। **–ing-ly,** *adv.* **To taper off**—To stop gradually ; ক্রমশঃ থামা।

tăp'-ĕs-trỹ, *n.* & *v. t.* A kind of rich woven hanging of wool and silk, with pictorial representations ; "In painting, *tapestry* is applied to a representation of a subject in wool or silk...worked on a woven ground of limp or flax" ; প্রাচীর, গৃহসজ্জা, প্রভৃতি আবরণের জন্য নানাপ্রকার চিত্রাদিসমন্বিত পর্দা বা তিরস্করিণী, চিত্রযবনিকা। *Vorb t.* To work or depict in tapestry ; "Where Elizabethan mothers and daughters had *tapestried* the love scenes of Issac Jacob" ; চিত্রযবনিকায় তোলা বা চিত্রিত করা। **–tried,** *adj.* **Bayeux tapestry**—Normandyর অন্তর্গত Bayeux নামক স্থানে রক্ষিত প্রাচীন চিত্রযবনিকা বিশেষ—যাহাতে প্রথম উইলিয়মের জীবনীর ঘটনা সমূহ চিত্রিত আছে। **Russian tapestry**—জানালার ঝিলিমিলি প্রভৃতির জন্য শণ প্রভৃতি দ্বারা প্রস্তুত স্থূলবস্ত্র।

tăp-ĭ'-ō'-că, *n.* A farinaceous substance prepared from cassava meal ; শিমুল আলুর মূল হইতে প্রাপ্ত শ্বেতসারময় খাদ্য বিশেষ।

tā'-pĭr, *n.* A hoofed animal allied to the rhinoceros, with a nose resembling a small proboscis ; গণ্ডারের মত জন্তু বিশেষ।

tapis, *n.* Table-cover ; carpet ; টেবিল ঢাকনি ; গালিচা। **On the tapis**—Under consideration ; as, the bill was *on the tapis* ; বিবেচনাধীন, আলোচ্য, আলোচনাধীন।

tapotement, *n.* (*Med.*) Percussion as used in massage ; (ভৈষজ্য-শাস্ত্র) সন্ধি রোগাদিতে হাত পা টিপিবার কালে অঙ্গুলী দ্বারা আঘাত।

tăp'-pet (-ĕt), *n.* A small projecting lever in machinery ; a small cam ; যন্ত্রের ক্ষুদ্র এবং উদ্গত দণ্ডযন্ত্র ; (যন্ত্র) প্রলম্বিত চক্রাংশ বিশেষ—ইহার সাহায্যে চক্রবৎ গতি অগ্রপশ্চাৎ বা বিষম গতিতে পরিবর্তিত হয়।

tăp'-stêr, *n.* One who taps or draws and serves ale in an alehouse ; যে ব্যক্তি পিপা হইতে মদ্য বাহির করিয়া পরিবেষণ করে।

târ, *n.* & *v. t.* **1.** A thick, dark-coloured viscid substance obtained from pine or fir, coal, shale, etc. by destructive distillation, used for coating and preserving timber, iron, etc ; আলকাতরা। 2. A sailor, so called from his tarred clothes ; "The jolly *tars* seized the horses and rode them helter skelter up hill and down dale" ; জাহাজের মাল্লা। *Verb t.* To smear with tar ; আলকাতরা দ্বারা লিপ্ত করা, আলকাতরা মাখান। **Tar'-ry,** *adj.* **Tar-board**—আলকাতরা মাখানো রজ্জু প্রভৃতি দ্বারা প্রস্তুত ফলক। **Tar-brush**—কাফ্রী রক্তের ছিটাফোঁটা (যাহা) শরীরের রঙ্গ দ্বারা অনুমান করা যায়। **Tar-water**—আলকাতরা মিশ্রিত জল। **A touch** or **lick of the tar-brush**—Admixture of negro blood ; কাফ্রীর রক্তের ছিটাফোঁটা। **To be tarred with the same brush** or **stick**—To be of the same nature ; একই প্রকৃতির হওয়া, এক স্বভাবের হওয়া।(cf. এক ক্ষুরে মাথা কামান)। **To tar and feather**—See under FEATHER.

tā'-rā, tā'-rā-fêrn, *ns.* An edible fern of New Zealand ; নবজিলণ্ড দ্বীপে জাত একপ্রকার পর্ণাঙ্গ।

tăr'-ă-dĭd-dle(-l), tăr-ra– (-ă-), *ns.* (*Colloq.*) Lie; (চলিতভাষায়) মিথ্যা কথা।

tă-răn-tăss', *n.* A four-wheeled Russian vehicle having boat-shaped body ; রুশিয়া দেশের একপ্রকার নৌকাকৃতি শকট।

tă-răn'-tĕl'-lă, –telle' (-tĕl), *ns.* **1.** A whirling Italian dance; music for the same ; ইতালীদেশীয় মণ্ডলনৃত্য বিশেষ ; ঐ নৃত্যের উপযোগী সঙ্গীত।

tăr'-ănt-ĭsm, *n.* An epidemic leaping or dancing mania ; একপ্রকার ব্যাপক তাণ্ডবরোগ।

tă-răn'-tü-lă, *n.* **1.** A kind of spider found in South Italy ; দক্ষিণ ইতালীতে প্রাপ্ত একপ্রকার দীর্ঘপাদ ঊর্ণনাভ। [ইহার দংশনে যে স্নায়ুবিকার জন্মে তাহা গীতবাদ্য শ্রবণে উপশমিত হইয়া থাকে।] **2.** Other kinds of spider ; অন্যান্য প্রকার মাকড়সা।

tăr-ă-tăn'–tă-ră, *n.* Sound of trumpet or bugle ; বংশী বা বিউগেলের ধ্বনি।

tă-răx'-ă-cŭm, *n.* Dandelion or its roots, as used medicinally ; ড্যান্ডিলিয়ন বৃক্ষ বা উহার ভেষজমূল।

târ-boosh', –bouche (-boosh), *ns.* A Turkish fez ; তুর্কি টুপি।

tardamente, *adv.* (*It.*) (*Mus.*) Slowly ; আস্তে আস্তে।

târ'-dĭ-grāde, *adj* & *n.* Slow-moving ; মৃদুগামী। *Noun.* A slow-moving animal ; মৃদুগামী জন্তু।

tardo, *adj* & *adv.* (*It.*) (*Mus.*) Slow ; (সঙ্গীতশাস্ত্র) ধীর। *Adv.* (*Mus.*) Slowly ; (সঙ্গীতশাস্ত্র) ধীরে, আস্তে আস্তে, মৃদু মৃদু।

târ'-dỹ, *adj.* **1.** Slow ; মৃদুগামী। **2.** Late ; as, he is *tardy* in his payment ; বিলম্বকারী, চিরকারী। **3.** Reluctant ; অনিচ্ছুক, নারাজ **–di-ly,** *adv.* In a tardy manner ; ধীরে ধীরে, আস্তে আস্তে, বিলম্বে। **–diness,** *n.* The state of being tardy ; ঢিলামি, দীর্ঘসূত্রতা, চিরকারিতা।

târe, *n.* A wild plant of the vetch kind ; একপ্রকার আরণ্য গুল্ম, শ্যামাঘাস।

târe, *n.* & *v. t.* **1.** An allowance made for weight of box etc. in which goods are packed ; মালের বাক্স প্রভৃতি ওজনের জন্য যে ধরাট বাদ দেওয়া হয়। 2. Weight of motor vehicle without fuel etc.; ইন্ধনাদি বাদে হাওয়া গাড়ী প্রভৃতির ওজন। 3. (*Chem.*) Weight of vessel in which a substance is weighed ; যে পাত্রে কোন বস্তু ওজন করা হয়—তাহার ওজন। ***Verb t.*** To ascertain the weight of a box etc. ; বাক্স প্রভৃতির ওজন স্থির করা। **Tare and tret**—যে পাত্রে কোন দ্রব্য ওজন করা হয় তাহার ওজন স্থির করার জন্য পাটীগণিতের প্রণালী বিশেষ।

tär′-gĕt, *n.* 1. A shield or buckler (in poetry *targe*) ; ঢাল। 2. A mark for firing at ; শরব্য, শরলক্ষ্য, চাঁদমারি। 3. An object of ridicule ; as, *target* of ridicule ; উপহাসের পাত্র, বিদ্রূপের পাত্র। 4. A circular railway signal ; গোলাকৃতি রেলওয়ের সঙ্কেত। 5. (Of lamb) A piece consisting of the neck and breast joints ; কসাইএর কাটা মেষের বুক এবং ঘাড়। **—ed,** *adj.* **—eer′,** *n.* **Target-card**—শরব্যের মত রঞ্জিত স্থূল কাগজখণ্ড—যাহাতে ধানুকীগণের নাম এবং বাণ কতবার লক্ষ্যে পতিত হইয়াছে তাহা লিখিত হইয়া থাকে। **Target-ship**—শরব্যস্বরূপ ব্যবহৃত জীর্ণ জাহাজ। **Solano target**—উপরি উপরি ক্রমে সজ্জিত কাষ্ঠফলকশ্রেণী—যাহাতে প্রকৃত যুদ্ধের অবস্থার অনুকরণেপ্রাকৃতিক দৃশ্যসমূহ চিত্রিত করা হইয়া থাকে [উদ্ভাবকের নাম E. J. Solano হইতে] **One armed with a target**—ঢালধারী যোদ্ধা, বর্ম্মধর।

Tär′-gŭm, *n.* A translation or paraphrase of the Hebrew scriptures in the Aramic or Chaldee language or dialect ; আরামিক বা চেল্ডী ভাষায় বাইবেলের অনুবাদ বা মর্ম্মানুবাদ। [ইহুদীগণ বেবিলোনে বন্দী হওয়ার পর হিব্রু ভাষা লুপ্তপ্রায় হইলে এইরূপ অনুবাদের আবশ্যক হয়।] **—ic, is′-tic,** *adjs.*

tär′-ĭff, *n.* & *v. t.* 1. A table of duties or charges ; আমদানী বা রপ্তানী মালের শুল্কতালিকা, শুল্কসূচী (হিঃ কোঃ)। 2. A list or scale of charges generally ; as, refreshment-room *tariff* ; মূল্য বা ব্যয়ের তালিকা। ***Verb t.*** 1. To make a list of duties on, as goods ; শুল্ক প্রভৃতির তালিকা করা। 2. To subject to tariff duty ; "In 1583 the best Gascony wine was *tariffed* in London......at £13 the tun" ; শুল্ক বসান। **Free tariff** — বিনা শুল্কে মাল আমদানীর ব্যবস্থা। **Preferential tariff**—একপ্রকার শুল্কব্যবস্থা—যাহাতে কোন কোন বিশেষ দেশের আমদানী মালের উপর অন্যান্য দেশ অপেক্ষা অল্প হারে শুল্ক আদায় করা হয়, বরেণ্য শুল্ক। [এই ব্যবস্থানুসারে যে শুল্ক আদায় করা যায়—তাহা Preferential duty নামে অভিহিত হয়।] **Retaliatory tariff**—কোন জাতির রপ্তানী মালের উপর বৈদেশিক কোন জাতি কর্ত্তৃক শুল্ক গৃহীত হইলে প্রথমোক্ত জাতি তজ্জন্য শেষোক্ত জাতির আমদানী মালের উপর যে শুল্ক গ্রহণ করে; প্রতিহিংসাত্মক শুল্ক। **Tariff reform**—শুল্ক সম্বন্ধে বৈষম্য প্রভৃতি দূরীকরণ।

tär′-lȧ-tăn, *n.* A thin cotton stuff resembling gauze ; একপ্রকার ফিনফিনে মলমল কাপড়।

tärn, *n.* A small mountain lake ; ক্ষুদ্র গিরিহ্রদ।

tärn, *n.* & *adj.* See TERN.

tär′-năl, tär′-nā′-tion, *ns.* (*U. S. slang*) A euphemistic substitute for damnation (used also adjectiveally and adverbially ; as, it is *tarnation* strange : a *tarnation* long word) ; (মার্কিণযুক্তরাজ্যের ইতরভাষায়) চুলোয় যাওন, অধঃপাতে যাওন।

tär′-nĭsh, *v. t., i.* & *n.* 1. To lessen or destroy the lustre of ; as, to *tarnish* a metal ; হীনপ্রভ করা, অনুজ্জ্বল করা, মলিন করা, নিষ্প্রভ করা। 2. To cast a stain upon ; to sully ; as, to *tarnish* one's reputation ; কলঙ্কিত করা ; কলুষিত করা। ***Verb i.*** To lose lustre ; to become dull ; নিষ্প্রভ হওয়া, হতপ্রভ হওয়া, অনুজ্জ্বল হওয়া ; মন্দপ্রভ হওয়া, হীনপ্রভ হওয়া। ***Noun.*** 1. A spot ; a blot ; কলঙ্ক, দাগ ; চিহ্ন। 2. (*Mineral*) A film of colour formed on exposed surface of mineral ; (খনিজবিদ্যা) ধাতু প্রভৃতির উপরে জাত পাতলা রঙ্গীন পর্দ্দা। **—a-ble,** *adj.*

tȧ′-rō, *n.* A plant of the arum order, cultivated in the South Sea Islands for its esculent roots ; একপ্রকার কচু।

tär′-ŏc, —ŏt, *ns.* A game at card played with seventy-eight cards ; একপ্রকার তাস খেলা—যাহাতে ৭৮ খানা তাসের প্রয়োজন হয়।

tär′-păn, *n.* A wild horse of Tartary ; তাতার দেশের বন্য অশ্ব।

tär-pau′-lĭn (-pä-), *n.* 1. A canvas covered with tar to render it water-proof ; আলকাতরা মাখানো কেম্বিস কাপড়, ত্রিপল, তেরপল (*colloq.*)। 2. A sailor's hat made of, or covered with, tarpauline ; "A burley fellow in a *tarpaulin* and blue jacket" ; ত্রিপলের কাপড়ে তৈরী জাহাজের মাল্লার টুপি। 3. (*Colloq.*) A sailor ; "They were but bandy-legged *tarpaulins* after all" ; (চলিতভাষায়) নাবিক, জাহাজের মাল্লা।

Tär-pē-ĭ′-ăn, *n.* **Tarpeian rock**—A cliff from which Roman criminals were hurled down in ancient times ; যে পর্ব্বতশিখর হইতে পূর্ব্বে রোমনগরীর মৃত্যুদণ্ডে দণ্ডিত ব্যক্তি ভূতল নিক্ষিপ্ত হইত।

tär′-pŏn, *n.* A large edible American sea-fish ; আমেরিকাদেশীয় আহারোপযোগী সামুদ্রিক মৎস্য বিশেষ।

tär′-ra-dĭd-dle (-ă-dĭd-l), *n.* Same as TARADIDDLE (which see.)

tär′-ra-gŏn (-ă-), *n.* A plant of the genus Artemisia ; একজাতীয় গুল্ম।

tär′-rock (-ŏk), *n.* A seafowl ; a species of gull ; একপ্রকার সাগরচর পক্ষী ; একজাতীয় সাগরবলাকা।

tăr′-ry (-ĭ), *v. t.* & *i.* To wait or stop for ; as, to *tarry* an answer ; অপেক্ষা করা, থামা। ***Verb i.*** **1.** To stay ; to wait or stop ; "*Tarry* a little Jew" ; অবস্থান করা ; থামা, অপেক্ষা করা। **2.** To delay ; "Come down to me, *tarry* not" ; বিলম্ব করা, দেরী করা, গৌণ করা।

tăr′-sĭ-ă, *n.* A kind of mosaic wood-work ; একপ্রকার কারুকার্য্য—যাহাতে প্রাচীর, গৃহতল, প্রভৃতিতে নানা বর্ণের কাষ্ঠখণ্ড দ্বারা নমুনা রচিত করা হয়।

tăr′-sĭ-ĕr, *n.* A nocturnal lemurine animal (*Tarsius spectrum*) ; একপ্রকার মর্কটজাতীয় নিশাচর জন্তু।

tăr′-sĭ–, tăr′-sō–, Combining forms of TARSUS.

tăr′-sŭs, *n.* **1.** The ankle or ankle-joint ; গোড়ালি, গুল্‌ফাস্থি। **2.** A cartilage at the edge of the eye ; নেত্রপ্রান্তের তরুণাস্থিবিশেষ, অক্ষিপুটের উপাস্থি। **3.** The shank of a bird's legs ; পক্ষীর জঙ্ঘা। **4.** The last segment of an insect's legs ; কীটের চরণের শেষ পর্ব্ব। **–sal,** *adj.*

tărt, *n.* & *adj.* **1.** A small pie containing fruit ; as, an apple *tart* ; ফলের পুর দেওয়া পিষ্টক, ফলের মিঠাই, ফুলুরী। **2.** (*Slang*) A girl or woman of loose character ; (ইতর-ভাষায়) ছেনাল। ***Adj.*** **1.** Sharp to the taste ; sour ; acid ; তীব্রাস্বাদ ; টক ; অম্ল। **2.** Severe ; as, *tart* pain ; তীব্র, গুরুতর। **3.** Sharp ; caustic ; as, a *sharp* reply ; কড়া ; তীব্র, রোখা। **Tart′-let,** *n.* **Tart′-ness,** *n.* **Jam tart**—উপরে আচার দেওয়া ফুলুরী।

tăr′-tăn, *n.* & *adj.* **1.** A checkered worsted stuff, with threads of various colours, worn in Scottish Highlands ; স্কটলণ্ডের উত্তরাঞ্চলবাসিগণ কর্ত্তৃক ব্যবহৃত নানা রংয়ের ছক-কাটা পশমী কাপড়। **2.** Other fabrics so striped ; as *silk* tartan ; ঐরূপ ছককাটা অন্যান্য প্রকার বস্ত্র। **3.** A Highlander ; the men of Highland regiment ; "The *tartan* beats us all" ; স্কটলণ্ডের অন্তঃপাতী হাইল্যাণ্ডের লোক ; লেংটাগোরা পল্টনের সৈন্য। ***Adj.*** Made of tartan ; having a checkered pattern like that of tartan ; ছককাটা পশমী কাপড়ে তৈয়ারী ; উক্ত পশমী কাপড়ের ন্যায় ছককাটা নমুনার।

tăr′-tăn, *n.* A small coasting vessel of the Mediterranean with one mast and a lateen sail ; ভূমধ্যসাগরের উপকূলগামী একপ্রকার একমাস্তুল পোত।

tăr′-tăr, *n.* **1.** A hard, redddish crust deposited by wine on the inside of the cask (also called *argol*) ; পিপার পার্শ্বে সঞ্চিত রক্ত বা পাটলবর্ণ সুরাকিট্ট। **2.** The concretion which incrusts the teeth ; দন্তমল, দন্তশর্করা, দাঁতের পাথরি। **–i-za′-tion,** *n.* **–tar′-ic, –ous,** *adjs.* **Tartar emetic**—বিরেচক, বমনকারক, প্রভৃতিরূপে ব্যবহৃত ঔষধ বিশেষ। **Tartaric acid** —শোধিত সুরাকিট্ট হইতে প্রস্তুত অম্ল বিশেষ। **Cream of Tartar**—বিশোধিত সুরাকিট্ট।

Târ′-tăr, Tâ′-tăr, *ns.* & *adjs.* **1.** A native of Tartary ; তাতার জাতীয় লোক, তাতার। **2.** An intractable or savage person ; "When provoked he proved a *Tartar*" ; বর্ব্বর, অদম্য লোক, চোয়াড়। ***Adj.*** Of, or pertaining to, Tartary or the Tartars ; তাতারদেশসম্বন্ধীয় ; তাতারগণসম্পর্কীয়। **–ta′-ri-an,** *adj.* **To catch a Tartar** — To encounter a person that proves too strong for the assailant ; অপেক্ষাকৃত অধিক বলবান প্রতিপক্ষকে আক্রমণ করিয়া নিজে বিপন্ন হওয়া, শক্ত পাল্লায় পড়া, সাপের ছুঁচো গেলা, কেঁচো ধরিতে সাপ ধরা। [কথিত আছে যে তুর্কিদিগের সহিত কোন যুদ্ধে জনৈক আইরিস সৈনিক এক ভীমকায় তুর্কীকে ধরিয়াছিল ; কিন্তু, সেই তুর্কি পাল্টা সেই আইরিস সৈনিককে এমনিভাবে ধরিয়াছিল যে, তাহার আর মুক্ত হইয়া আসার জো ছিলনা। [কম্বল ভ্রমে ভল্লুক ধরিতে গিয়া এক হিন্দুস্থানী অনুরূপ অবস্থায় তদীয় সঙ্গীকে বলিয়াছিল, ভাইয়া হাম্ কমলিকো ছোড় দিয়া লেকিন কমলি হামকো নেহি ছোড়তা হৈঁ।]

Târ′-tă-rŭs, *n.* (*Gk. Mythol.*) A void sunless waste in the depths of the earth ; the infernal region, esp. as, a place of punishment ; "The enjoyment of Elysium and the punishment of *Tartarus*" ; (গ্রীক পুরাণ) অন্ধতমোময় অধোতল ; নরক, যমলোক।

târ′-trāte, *n.* The salt of tartaric acid ; তিন্তিড়ীকাম্লের লবণ।

Târ-tufe′ (-tôf), **–tuffe′** (-tôf), *ns.* A religious hypocrite ; ভণ্ড, বিড়ালতপস্বী। [Molierএর "*Tartufe*" নামক নাট্যের প্রধান পাত্রের নাম হইতে গৃহীত।] **–tuf′-ish,** *adj.* **–tuf′-ism, –tuf′-fism,** *ns.*

tă-sĭm′-ĕ-tĕr, *n.* An instrument for determining the variations of temperature by variations of pressure ; চাপবৈষম্য দ্বারা তাপবৈষম্য নিরূপণের জন্য যন্ত্র বিশেষ, ঘনপ্রসরণ-মাপক (হিঃ কোঃ), তাপভেদমান। **Tas-i-met′-ric,** *adj.*

tăsk, *n.* & *v. t.* **1.** A piece of work imposed ; অর্পিত কার্য্য, কার্য্যভার। **2.** A lesson to be learnt ; a portion of study imposed by a teacher ; পড়া, শিক্ষণীয় বিষয়, পাঠ ; ছাত্রদিগের উপর শিক্ষক কর্ত্তৃক যে অতিরিক্ত পাঠ চাপান হয়। **3.** Labour ; শ্রম। ***Verb t.*** **1.** To impose upon ; কার্য্যভার চাপান, অতিরিক্ত পাঠ চাপান। **2.** To oppress with severe labour ; to burden ; as, to *task* one's power ; গুরুতর শ্রমদ্বারা প্রপীড়িত করা ; অতিরিক্ত ভার চাপান। **Task-master**—যে ব্যক্তি কায বিভাগ করিয়া দেয়, কার্য্যনির্দ্দেশক, কার্য্য-পরিদর্শক। **To take to task**—To reprove ; তিরস্কার করা, ভর্ৎসনা করা।

tăss, *n.* A small draught of brandy etc. ; ব্রাণ্ডি প্রভৃতির চুমুক।

tăs'-sĕl, *n.* & *v. t.* **1.** A pendant ornament attached to the corners of cushions, curtains, etc.; as, the *tassel* of an umbrella; রেশমের থোপা, থোবনা, ঝাঁপ্পা। **2.** Anything resembling a tassel, as the pendant head or flower of some plants; থোপার আকৃতি কোন কিছু। **3.** A ribbon sewn into a book to be used as a book-mark; পুস্তকের কোন্ পাতা পর্য্যন্ত পড়া হইয়াছে তাহা ঠিক রাখার জন্য উহাতে যে সরু রেশমী ফিতা লাগাইয়া দেওয়া হয়। **4.** In a tree or plant a pendant blossom, bud, etc.; বৃক্ষের ঝুলায়মান পুষ্প, কলিকা, প্রভৃতি। ***Verb t.*** **1.** To decorate with tassels; to attach tassels to; থোপনা বা ঝাপ্পা দ্বারা শোভিত করা; থোপনা লাগান। **2.** To remove tassels of Indian corn to strengthen plant; গাছ সতেজ করার জন্য জনারের ছড়া কাটিয়া ফেলা।

tāste, *v. t.* & *i.* **1.** To try by the special sense residing in the tongue; আস্বাদ করা, স্বাদ গ্রহণ করা। **2.** To try by eating; to eat; as, I did not *taste* food for six days; চাখা; খাওয়া, ভোজন করা। **3.** To partake (with *of*); as, to *taste of* the pleasures of life; গ্রহণ করা, ভোগ করা, আস্বাদন করা। ***Verb i.*** **1.** To eat or drink a little by way of trial; চাখা। **2.** To have a particular relish or savour; as, it *tastes* sweet; কোনরূপ বিশেষ স্বাদ বা আস্বাদ থাকা, লাগা। **3.** To have experience or enjoyment; অভিজ্ঞতা থাকা, আস্বাদ পরিজ্ঞাত থাকা। **Tast'-a-ble,** *adj.*

tāste, *n.* **1.** Act of tasting with the mouth; আস্বাদন, স্বাদগ্রহণ। **2.** A particular sensation excited by certain bodies, which are called *sapid*, applied to the tongue, palate etc., and moistened with saliva; স্বাদ, আস্বাদ, রস (হিঃ কোঃ)। **3.** Relish; flavour; স্বাদ, রুচি (হিঃ কোঃ); অভিরুচি (ঐ), আস্বাদ। **4.** Intellectual relish or discernment; as, he has a *taste* for music; অনুরাগ, অনুরক্তি, প্রবৃত্তি (হিঃ কোঃ), রুচি। **5.** The faculty of discerning whatever constitutes beauty or excellence, particularly in the fine arts or literature; as, he is a man of *taste*; সৌন্দর্য্যসংবেদনবৃত্তি, রসসংবেদনবৃত্তি, রুচি। **6.** Style; as, this is in bad *taste*; ধরণ, রকম, রীতি। **7.** A little piece tasted; a small portion given as speciemen; a bit; চাখনি; নমুনাস্বরূপপ্রদত্ত ক্ষুদ্র অংশ; টুকরা। **Taste'-ful,** *adj.* 1. Savoury: "*Tasteful* herbs"; স্বাদু, সুস্বাদু, সুরস। 2. Having, or exhibiting, good taste; conforming to good taste; রুচিপূর্ণ, সুরুচিসম্পন্ন, সৌন্দর্য্যবোধসম্পন্ন, রুচিরোচক, রুচির; সুরুচিসম্মত, রুচিসম্মত। **Taste'-ful-ly,** *adv.* In a tasteful manner; রুচিসম্মতভাবে, সুরুচিসম্মত ভাবে। **Taste'-ful-ness,** *n.* **Taste potential**— রসতন্মাত্র (ব্রজঃ হিন্দু)।

tāste'-lĕss, *adj.* **1.** Having no flavour; insipid; স্বাদহীন, স্বাদশূন্য; পান্‌সে, নীরস। **2.** Not possessing appreciation or enjoyment of what is good, excellent, sublime or the like; রসবোধহীন, রসসংবেদনশূন্য, রুচিজ্ঞানহীন, সৌন্দর্য্যবোধশূন্য। **—less-ly,** *adv.* **—less-ness,** *n.*

tāst'-ĕr, *n.* **1.** One that tastes; আস্বাদনকারী। **2.** One who tests tea, or liquor by tasting samples; যে ব্যক্তি আস্বাদন দ্বারা চা, মদ্য, প্রভৃতির গুণাগুণ পরীক্ষা করে, চাখনদার। **3.** (*Fig.*) A publisher's reader; (লক্ষণায়) গ্রন্থপ্রকাশকের পাঠক, গ্রন্থাস্বাদক। **4.** A small metal cup used in tasting wine; মদ্য চাখার জন্য ধাতুনির্ম্মিত ক্ষুদ্র পেয়ালা। **5.** An instrument for extracting small cylindrical samples from cheese; পনীর হইতে ক্ষুদ্র নলাকার নমুনার অংশ বাহির করার জন্য একপ্রকার যন্ত্র।

tāst'-ȳ, *adj.* **1.** (*Colloq.*) Savoury; স্বাদু, রসাল। **2.** (*Slang*) Being in good taste; conformable to good taste; (ইতর ভাষায়) রুচিসম্পন্ন; রুচিসঙ্গত।

tăt, *v.t.* & *i.* To make by tatting; বিনট করিয়া প্রস্তুত করা। ***Verb i.*** To work at tatting; বিনান ফিতা প্রস্তুত করা।

tä'-tä', *Interj.* Good bye; বিদায় হই! তবে আসি!

Tä'-tär, *n.* Same as TARTAR (which see).

tăt'-tĕr, *n.* A rag or part torn or hanging to a thing; ছিন্নবস্ত্র, ছেঁড়া কাপড়, চীর, ন্যাকড়া, কানি। **—tered, —y,** *adjs.* **Tatterdemalion**— ছেঁড়া কাপড়-পরা লোক, ছিন্নবস্ত্রপরিহিত ব্যক্তি, চিরধারী।

tăt'-ting (-ĭng), *n.* A kind of lace woven or knitted from sewing-thread, with a somewhat shuttle-shaped instrument; একপ্রকার বুনা ফিতা।

tăt'-tle (-l), *v. t., i.* & *n.* To utter in an idle prating way; বক বক করিয়া বলা। ***Verb i.*** **1.** To talk idly; to use many words with little meaning; বাজে কথা বলা; বক বক করা, পচাল পাড়া, বিড়বিড় করা। **2.** To tell tales or secrets; "When one of the gang *tattles*, confesses, and accuses the rest"; গোপনীয় কথা বলিয়া ফেলা, পেটের কথা ফাঁস করা। ***Noun.*** Idle talk; prate; অসার কথা, বাজে কথা; বক্ বক্, বিড় বিড়।

tăt'-tler (-lĕr), *n.* **1.** One that tattles; an idle talker; বক বক কারী, বিড়বিড়কারী; বাচাল, বাবদুক, বহুভাষী, জল্পক। **2.** A name applied to numerous birds of the snipe family; বিভিন্নপ্রকার কর্দ্দম-খঞ্জনা জাতীয় পক্ষীর সাধারণ নাম।

tăt-too′, *n.* A beat of drum and bugle-call at night, calling soldiers to their quarters; সৈনিক-দিগকে আবাসস্থানে আহ্বান করার জন্য রাত্রিকালীন ঢক্কানিনাদ বা বংশীধ্বনি। **To beat the devil's tattoo**—See under DEVIL.

tăt-too′, *v. t.* & *n.* To prick the skin and stain the punctured spot with colours; উল্কি পরা, উল্কি দেওয়া। ***Noun.*** An indelible mark or figure made by puncturing the body, and introducing some pigments into the punctures; উল্কি, উল্কিচিত্র (সাঃ পঃ)।

tat′-ty, (-ī), *n.* (India) A mat or screen of khuskhus grass hung at door and window and constantly kept wet to cool and perfume the air; (ভারতবর্ষে) বাতাস ঠাণ্ডা ও সুরভি করার জন্য জানালা দরজা প্রভৃতিতে যে খসখসের পর্দা সর্ব্বদা আর্দ্র অবস্থায় রাখা হয়।

tau (tä), *n.* **1.** Greek letter T; গ্রীক বর্ণমালার T অক্ষর। **2.** A cross shaped like the Greek letter T; গ্রীক T অক্ষরাকৃতি ক্রুশ। **3.** Kinds of fish etc. marked with, or suggesting, the Greek letter T; গ্রীক T অক্ষরাঙ্কিত বা উক্ত অক্ষরব্যঞ্জক মৎস্যাদি।

taught (tăt), *p. t.* & *p. p.* of TEACH (which see).

taunt (tänt), *v. t.* & *n.* To reproach with severe or sarcastic words; to upbraid; ব্যঙ্গ করা, বিদ্রূপ করা, গদ্দি করা (*colloq.*); তিরস্কার করা, ভর্ৎসনা করা। ***Noun.*** **1.** A bitter or sarcastic reproach; বিদ্রূপ, ব্যঙ্গ, শ্লেষ, গদ্দি (*colloq.*)। **2.** An object of scornful reproach; বিদ্রূপের পাত্র। **Taunt′-ing,** *adj.* & *n.* **Taunt′-ing-ly,** *adv.*

taunt (tänt), *adj.* (*Naut.*) (Of a mast) Tall; (নৌ-বিদ্যা—মাস্তুল-সম্পর্কে) দীর্ঘ।

tau′-rīne (tä-), *adj.* **1.** Relating to the genus taurus, to which the common bull, ox and the cow belong; bull-like; গোজাতিসম্পর্কীয়; বৃষভবৎ, বৃষতুল্য। **2.** Of the sign Taurus; বৃষরাশি-সম্পর্কীয়। **–ri-form,** *adj.*

tau′-rine (tä-rīn), *n.* (*Physiol.* & *Chem.*) One of the products of the decomposition of the bile ($C_2H_7NSO_7$); পিত্তজনিত পদার্থবিশেষ।

tau′-rŏm-ă-chy (tä-), *n.* A bull-fight; বৃষ-যুদ্ধ, ষাঁড়ের লড়াই।

Tau′-rŭs (tä-), *n.* **1.** The Bull, one of the twelve signs of the zodiac; বৃষরাশি, বৃষ। **2.** A constellation; তাবুরি (সাঃ পঃ)। **α Tauri**—রোহিণী (হিঃ কোঃ)। **β Tauri**—অগ্নি (জ্যোতি জ্যোঃ), হুতভুক্ (সাঃ পঃ)। **η Tauri**—কৃত্তিকা।

taut′ (tăt), *adj.* **1.** Tight; not slack; টান, শক্ত; অশিথিল। **2.** Tightly or trimly done up; neat in appearance; "The ship was clean and *taut* fore and aft"; সুসজ্জিত; ফিটফাট। **3.** Strict or severe as to duty; কঠোরব্রত, কঠোর-কর্ত্তব্যপরায়ণ। **Taut′-en,** *v. t.* & *i.* **Taut′-ly,** *adv.* **Taut′-ness,** *n.*

tau′-tŏ-băr′-ȳd (tä-), *n.* (*Math.*) The curve against which a body descending by its weight presses everywhere equally; (গণিতশাস্ত্র) নিজের গুরুত্ব দ্বারা পতিষ্যমান বস্তু যে বক্র সর্ব্বত্র সমভাবে সঞ্চাপিত করে, চাপবক্র।

tau′-tŏ-chrōne (tä-), *n.* (*Math.*) A curve line of such a property that a heavy body descending along it will always arrive at the lowest point at the same time from whatever point it may start; (গণিতশাস্ত্র) এইরূপ ধর্ম্মাক্রান্ত বক্র রেখা যাহার উপর দিয়া কোন ভারি বস্তু অবতরণ করিলে উহা যে কোন স্থান হইতে পড়িতে আরম্ভ করুক না কেন পরিণামে একই সময়ে নিম্নতম বিন্দুতে উপনীত হইবে, সমকালিক। **–toch′-ro-nism,** *n.* **–toch′-ro-nous,** *adj.*

tau-tŏg′ (tä-), *n.* A kind of fish caught on the New England coasts (called also *black-fish*); আমেরিকা দেশীয় একপ্রকার মৎস্য।

tau-tŏl′-ŏ-ġȳ (tä-), *n.* An unnecessary repetition of the same meaning in different words; পুনরুক্তি, দ্বিরুক্তি, কথিত পদ, পুনরুক্ত, (ন্যায়সূত্র) আম্রেড়ন, পুনর্ব্বাদ। **–gist,** *n.* **–gize,** *v. i.* **–gous,** *adj.* **–to-log′-i-cal,** *adj.* **Tautologous proposition**—পুনর্বাচক প্রতিজ্ঞা (হিঃ কোঃ)।

tau-tŏph′-ŏ-nȳ (tä-), *n.* Repetition of the same sound; পুনঃ পুনঃ একই শব্দ করণ।

tăv′-ẽrn, *n.* **1.** A house where liquors are sold; শুঁড়ির দোকান, ভেটারাখানা, আপানশালা, সুরাগৃহ, শৌণ্ডিকালয়, মদিরাগৃহ, মদিরাশালা, মদ্যশালা, পানগোষ্ঠিকা। **2.** An inn; সরাই, পান্থশালা, পান্থনিবাস। **Tavern-keeper**—শৌণ্ডিক, সুরাজীবী। **The sign of a tavern**—সুরাধ্বজ।

taw (tä), *v. t.* To make white leather for gloves etc. by soaking skins in alum, salt and other matters; লবণ, ফিটকিরী, প্রভৃতির জলে ভিজাইয়া দস্তানা প্রভৃতির জন্য শ্বেতচর্ম্ম প্রস্তুত করা। **Taw′-er, Taw′-er-y,** *ns.*

taw (tä), *n.* **1.** A game at marbles; মার্বেল খেলা। **2.** A marble to be played with; ক্রীড়ার জন্য মর্ম্মরগুলিকা, মারবল।

taw′-drȳ (tä-), *adj.* & *n.* Showy without taste or elegance; cheap and gaudy; as, *tawdry* dress; জমকালো অথচ রুচিসঙ্গত নয়; চটকদার, ভড়কদার, বাহারে। ***Noun.*** (*Pl.*) Showy and cheap finery; চটকদার জিনিষ। **–dri-ly,** *adv.* **–dri-ness,** *n.*

taw′-nȳ (tä-), *adj.* Of a yellowish brown colour, like things tanned and sunburnt ; কমলাবর্ণ, কপিলবর্ণ, কপিশবর্ণ, পিঙ্গলবর্ণ, কটা। **—ni-ness,** *n.*

tăx, *v. t.* **1.** To impose a tax on ; কর বসান, শুল্কসংস্থাপন করা। **2.** To accuse ; as, to *tax* a man with crime ; অভিযুক্ত করা। **3.** To task ; as, to *tax* one's power to the utmost ; প্রপীড়িত করা, চাপান, চাপ দেওয়া। **4.** *(Law)* To examine or allow or disallow the items of cost etc. ; as, the court *taxes* bills ; পরীক্ষা করিয়া মোকদ্দমার খরচের কোন দফা মঞ্জুর বা নামঞ্জুর করা। **—a-bil'-i-ty,** *n.* **—a'-tion,** *n.* **1.** The act of imposing tax ; করসংস্থাপন। **2.** Tax or assessment imposed ; কর। **Tax'-a-ble,** *adj.* **Tax'-a-ble-ness,** *n.* **Tax'-a-bly,** *adv.*

tăx, *n.* **1.** A rate or sum of money assessed on person or property for the benefit of a state, corporation or company ; কর, টেক্স, শুল্ক। **2.** Any burdensome duty ; কার্য্যভার। **3.** Strain ; as, it was a great *tax* on his mental powers ; চাপ, ভার। **Tax'-less,** *adj.* **Tax-collector**—করসংগ্রহক কর্ম্মচারী। **Tax-payer**—করদাতা।

tăx-ĭ, *n.* (Also *taxi-cab*) A motor-car ; হাওয়া গাড়ী।

tax'-ĭ-dêr-my̆, *n.* The art of stuffing animals so as to give an appearance of life and nature ; পশুর চর্ম্মের ভিতর তৃণ কেশাদি পুরিয়া উহাকে জীবিত পশুবৎ প্রতিভাত করার শিল্প, চর্ম্মসংরক্ষণবিদ্যা। **—der'-mal, —der'-mic,** *adj,* **—mist,** *n.*

tăx-ĭm'-ĕ-têr, *n.* A device for measuring distance travelled by a vehicle ; হাওয়াগাড়ী প্রভৃতিতে সংলগ্ন যন্ত্রবিশেষ—যদ্দ্বারা উহা কি পরিমাণ স্থান অতিক্রম করিয়াছে এবং তদ্দরুণ কত ভাড়া পাওনা হইয়াছে তাহা নিরূপণ করা যায়, পথমান, পণমান।

tăx-ĭn, *n.* A resinous substance from yew leaves ; ইউ বৃক্ষের পত্র হইতে প্রাপ্ত একপ্রকার রজনবৎ পদার্থ।

tăx'-ĭs, *n.* **1.** *(Gram.)* Order ; arrangement ; (ব্যাকরণ) শৃঙ্খলতা ; বিন্যাস। **2.** *(Surg.)* The art of putting parts in their natural place by means of pressure ; (অস্ত্রোপচারবিদ্যা) চাপের সাহায্যে অংশসমূহ স্বস্থানে স্থাপন। **3.** *(Gk. Antiq.)* Various divisions of troops ; (গ্রীকদেশীয় প্রত্নতত্ত্ব) সৈন্যের বিভিন্ন বিভাগ। **4.** *(Zool.)* Classification ; (জন্তুবিদ্য) শ্রেণীবিভাগ।

tăx-ŏl'-ŏ-ġy̆, *n.* The science of arrangement or classification ; শ্রেণীবিভাগবিদ্যা।

tăx-ŏn'-ŏ-my̆ *n.* **1.** The department of natural history which treats of the laws and principles of classification ; প্রাকৃতিক ইতিহাসের যে বিভাগে শ্রেণীবিভাগের নিয়ম এবং তত্ত্বসম্বন্ধে আলোচিত হইয়া থাকে, জাতিস্থাপকনিয়ম (হিঃ কোঃ)। **2.** Classification ; শ্রেণীবিভাগ। **—mist,** *n.* **—o-nom'-ic, —o-nom'-i-cal,** *adjs.*

tazza, *n.* *(It.)* A large, shallow cup or vase, esp. one with a foot (and handles) ; একপ্রকার বৃহৎ পাত্র।

tchick (chĭk), *n.* & *v. i.* The sound made in encouraging a horse ; অশ্বকে প্রোৎসাহিত করার জন্য উচ্চারিত শব্দবিশেষ। ***Verb i.*** To make this sound ; ঐরূপ শব্দ করা।

tea (tē), *n., v. i.* & *t.* **1.** The dried leaves of tea tree, produce of China, Ceylon, India, etc. ; চা। [Pers., Arab. *chai* ; Chin. *ku-tu, ku-cha, kia, sheh, cha, chuen* ; It. *te* ; Fr. *the* ; Germ. *thi* ; Jap. *tsja.*] **2.** A decoction or infusion of tea-leaves in boiling water ; তৈরী চা। **3.** An evening meal at which tea is served ; অপরাহ্ণকালীন লঘুভোজন যাহাতে চা পান করা হয়। ***Verb i.*** To take tea ; চা পান করা। ***Verb t.*** To supply with tea ; to entertain with tea ; "I breakfast, *tea* and sup my lodgers" ; চা সরবরাহ করা ; চা পান করান। **Tea-boiler**—চা সিদ্ধ করার জন্য পাত্র। **Tea-box**—চা রাখার জন্য বাক্স, চায়ের বাক্স। **Tea-bread**—চা পানকালে যে একপ্রকার হাল্কা রুটি খাওয়া হয়। **Tea-cake**—চা পান কালে যে বিভিন্ন প্রকার পিষ্টক ভোজন করা হয়। **Tea-chest**—চাএর বাক্স। **Tea-china**—চীনামাটীর চায়ের পেয়ালা, পিরিচ, প্রভৃতি। **Tea-cloth**—চার মেজের বা চার বারকোষের উপরে দিবার কাপড়। **Tea-cup**—চার পেয়ালা। **Tea-garden**—চা বাগান ; যে নগরোদ্যানে চা ও জলযোগের দ্রব্য পরিবেষণ করা হয়। **Tea-gown**—চা পান প্রভৃতির কালে বিলাতের মহিলাগণ যে গাউন পরিয়া থাকেন। **Tea-house**—যে কুটীরে চীন এবং জাপান দেশে চা পরিবেষণ করা হয়। **Tea-lead**—চায়ের বাক্সের ভিতরে যে একপ্রকার সীসার মিশ্রপাতদ্বারা আচ্ছাদন করা হয়। **Tea-party** — চা পানসম্মিলনী, চায়ের মজলিস। **Tea-pot**—চা প্রস্তুত করার পাত্র, চাএর কেটলি। **Tea-rose**—চাএর গন্ধবিশিষ্ট চীনদেশীয় গোলাপ, কাঠগোলাপ। **Tea-set, Tea-service**—চার পেয়ালা, চামচ, প্রভৃতির একপ্রস্থ। **Tea-spoon**—See under SPOON. **Tea-table**—চা পানের মেজ। **Tea-things**—চায়ের জিনিষ (চায়ের পাত্র, পেয়ালা, পিরিচ প্রভৃতি)। **Tea-tray**—চায়ের বারকোষ। **Tea-tree**—চাগাছ ; অষ্ট্রেলিয়াদেশীয় মেঁদীজাতীয় বৃক্ষ ও গুল্মশ্রেণী। **Tea-urn**—চাএর জল গরম করা বা রাখার জন্য পাত্র। **A storm or tempest in a teapot**—সামান্য বিষয় লইয়া মহা হুলস্থুল ব্যাপার। **To take tea with**—*(Slang)* To associate with ; (ইতরভাষায়) সঙ্গ করা। To encounter ; সম্মুখীন হওয়া।

teach (tēch), *v. t.* **1.** To instruct ; শিক্ষা দেওয়া, শিখান। **2.** To educate ; শিক্ষিত করা, শিক্ষা দান করা, জ্ঞানোপদেশ দেওয়া, পড়ান।

Teach'-a-ble, *adj.* **1.** Apt to learn ; শিক্ষাতৎপর। **2.** That can be taught ; শিক্ষণীয়। **3.** Docile ; "They are ... more conceited and less *teachable*" ; বশম্বদ। **Teach'-a-ble-ness,** *n.*

teach'-êr (tēch-), *n.* One who teaches ; শিক্ষক, উপদেষ্টা, অধ্যাপক, আচার্য্য, উপাধ্যায়।

teach'-ing (tēch-), *n.* **1.** The act of one who teaches ; শিক্ষাদান, অধ্যাপনা, শিক্ষা, পাঠনা **2.** That which is taught ; instruction ; doctrine ; যে বিষয় শিক্ষাদান করা হয়; উপদেশ; শিক্ষা

Teague (tēg), *n.* (*Contempt.*) Irishman; (বিদ্রূপচ্ছলে) আয়র্লণ্ডদেশের লোক

teak (tēk) *n.* **1.** A tree remarkable for its hardness and durability ; সেগুন গাছ। [*Syn.* শাকতরু, অতিপত্র, ক্রকচপত্র।] **2.** The timber of this tree ; সেগুণ কাঠ।

teal (tēl), *n.* A web-footed waterfowl, nearly allied to the common duck ; নানাপ্রকার হংসের সাধারণ নাম, বালিহাঁস। **Whistling teal**—সরালি।

team (tēm), *n.* & *v. t.* **1.** A number of animals moving together ; একত্র বিচরণশীল পশুশ্রেণী, যূথ, পাল। **2.** Two or more horses, oxen, or other beasts harnessed together for drawing, as to a coach, wagon, cart, sleigh, plough and the like ; শকট, লাঙ্গল, প্রভৃতিতে যোজিত দুই বা ততোধিক অশ্ব, বৃষভ বা অন্য কোন জন্তু। **3.** A company of players in a game ; as, a *team* of football players ; ক্রীড়ক দল। **4.** A set of persons working together ; শ্রমিক দল। ***Verb t.*** To join together in a team ; ক্রীড়কের দল প্রভৃতিতে যোগদান করা। **Team work**—শ্রমিকদলকর্ত্তৃক নিষ্পন্ন কার্য্য।

team'-stêr (tēm-), *n.* The driver of a team; শকটে যোজিত অশ্বাদির চালক।

tea'-poy (tē-), *n.* A small three-legged table or stand ; তেপায়া, টিপাই, ত্রিপদী।

tear (târ), *v. t.* & *i.* **1.** To separate the parts of by pulling ; to rend ; ছিন্নভিন্ন করা ; বিদীর্ণ করা, বিপাটিত করা। **2.** To pull, draw or drag in pieces by breaking the texture or fibre of ; as, to *tear* a paper ; ছেঁড়া, ছিঁড়িয়া ফেলা। **3.** To lacerate ; ক্ষত বিক্ষত করা। **4.** To drag by force ; as, to *tear* from one's home ; জোর করিয়া টানিয়া নেওয়া। ***Verb i.*** **1.** To part, divide or separate on being pulled or handled with more or less violence ; as, this cloth *tears* easily ; বিদীর্ণ হওয়া, বিপাটিত হওয়া, ছিন্ন হওয়া, ছিঁড়িয়া যাওয়া, ফুটিয়া যাওয়া **2.** To move or act with violence, excited haste, or the like ; as, the horse *tore* down the road ; বেগে ধাবিত হওয়া, উত্তেজিত ভাবে কার্য্য করা, উধাও হইয়া ছুটা। **Tear'-ing,** *adj.* & *n.* **1.** Rushing ; violent ; ধাবমান ; প্রচণ্ড। **2.** Hasty ; as, *tearing* hurry ; tremendous ; as, *tearing* rage ; ব্যস্ত সমস্ত ; ভীষণ। ***Noun.*** A rent ; ছিদ্র। **To tear down**—To break ; ভাঙ্গিয়া ফেলা। **To tear one's beard or hair**—To pull or pluck the hair violently as an indication of rage, grief or the like ; ক্রোধে কেশ বা শ্মশ্রু টানিয়া ছিঁড়া। **To tear one's self away**—To go off with great unwillingness ; অতিশয় অনিচ্ছার সহিত যাওয়া। **To tear up**—To rend; বিদারণ করা। To uproot ; উন্মূলিত করা, উৎপাটন করা, উপড়ান। To break into pieces ; as, to *tear up* a letter; টুকরা টুকরা করা।

tear (tēr), *n.* **1.** A drop of watery fluid appearing in the eyes ; অশ্রুবিন্দু, অশ্রুজল, অশ্রুবারি, নয়নবিন্দু নয়নসলিল বাষ্প (only in compound cf. বাষ্পাকুল নেত্র), দৃগর্ণ (গোপাল:), নেত্রোদক (ঐ), দৃশোর্জল, নয়নবারি। **2.** A tear-like thing, *e. g.* a drop of liquid, solid drop of resin, etc.; তরল পদার্থের বিন্দু, নেত্রবিন্দু, রজন প্রভৃতির বিন্দু। **Tear'-ful,** *adj.* **1.** Abounding with tears ; shedding tears ; সাশ্রু, বাষ্পাকুল, সবাষ্প, অশ্রুসঙ্কুল, অশ্রুপূর্ণ; অশ্রুবর্ষী। **2.** Sad ; বিষণ্ণ, বিষাদপূর্ণ। **Crocodile tears**—See CROCODILE. [Also cf. সাপের চোখে সাঁতার পানি]। **Flood of tear** — নয়নবারিধারা, অশ্রুবন্যা, অশ্রুজোয়ার। **Tears of joy**—আনন্দজল, আনন্দাশ্রু, আনন্দবাষ্প, হর্ষাশ্রু। **Tears of strong wine**—পোর্ট প্রভৃতি মদিরা দ্বারা আংশিকভাবে পূর্ণ গ্লাসের ভিতর যে বিন্দু রচিত হয়।

tear'-ing (târ-), *n.* & *adj.* The act of one who tears ; বিপাটন, বিদারণ। ***Adj.*** Violent ; overwhelming ; প্রবল ; অভিভবকারী।

tease (tēz), *v. t.* & *n.* **1.** To pull apart or separate the adherent fibres of ; to pick into separate fibres ; to comb or card, as wool or flax ; সংলগ্ন অংশু সমূহ পৃথক করা ; আঁশ আলগা করা ; শণ বা পশম আঁচড়ান। **2.** To scratch, as cloth with a tease to raise a nap ; ফুঁপি তুলিবার জন্য কাপড় প্রভৃতি আঁচড়ান। **3.** To vex with jests or impertinence ; "*Teasing* with obvious comment and torturing with inevitable inferences;" to annoy; ক্ষ্যাপান; জ্বালাতন করা। **4.** To importune ; জেদ করা, সনির্ব্বন্ধ অনুরোধ করা। ***Noun.*** **1** The act of teasing ; ক্ষ্যাপানি, জ্বালাতন। **2.** The man who teases another person ; যে ব্যক্তি অন্য কাহাকেও ক্ষ্যাপায়, জ্বালাতনকারী। **Teas'-ing'-ly,** *adv.*

tea'-sël (tē-), **-zël, zle** (-zl), *ns.* & *v. t.* **1.** The fuller's thistle, used to raise nap on cloths ; কাপড়ে ফুঁপি তুলিবার জন্য একপ্রকার কাঁটা গাছ। **2.** A machine substituted for teasels ; কাপড়ে ফুঁপি তোলার জন্য একপ্রকার যন্ত্র। ***Verb t.*** To raise as nap as on cloth, by teasel ; ঐ কাঁটা গাছ দ্বারা আঁচড়াইয়া কাপড়ের উপর ফুঁপি তোলা। **-er,** *n.*

teas'-êr (tēz-), *n.* 1. One who teases ; জ্বালাতনকারী। 2. (*Colloq.*) A difficult problem or task ; (চলিতভাষায়) কঠিন সমস্যা, কঠিন কার্য্য।

teat (tēt), *n.* 1. The nipple ; চুচুক, স্তনাগ্র, স্তনবৃন্ত, স্তনের বোঁটা। 2. The dug of a beast ; পশুর স্তনের বাঁট। **Teat'-ed, teat'-like,** *adjs.*

ĕc, *n.* (*Slang*) Detective (*abbreviation*) ; (ইতরভাষায়) টিক্‌টিকি, গুপ্তপুলিশ।

tĕch'-nic, *adj.* & *n.* Same as TECHNICAL. ***Noun.*** 1. (*Usu. pl.*) The doctrine of arts in general ; কলাতত্ত্ব, শিল্পতত্ত্ব বহিঃশিল্প। 2. (*Pl.*) Technical terms, methods or objects ; পারিভাষিক শব্দ, সংজ্ঞা, পরিভাষা, শিল্পপদ্ধতি, শিল্প বস্তু।

tĕch'-ni-căl, *adj.* Pertaining to the science of mechanical arts or to any particular art, science, profession, handicraft, business or the like ; যন্ত্রশিল্পসম্বন্ধীয়, শিল্পশাস্ত্রসম্বন্ধীয়, শিল্পবিজ্ঞানসম্বন্ধীয়, কোন বিশেষ ব্যবসায়সম্পর্কীয়। **–ly,** *adv.* **–ness,** *n.* **Technical education**—শিল্পশিক্ষা। **Technical school**—শিল্পবিদ্যালয়। **Technical terms**—পরিভাষা, পারিভাষিক শব্দ।

tĕch-ni-căl'-i-tŷ, *n.* That which is technical or peculiar to any science, art, calling and the like ; an idea, quality, attribute or condition peculiar to any art or science ; কোন বিশেষ শিল্পবিজ্ঞান, ব্যবসায় প্রভৃতি সম্পৃক্ত শব্দ, উক্তি বা বিষয় ; কোন শিল্প বা বিজ্ঞানসম্পৃক্ত ভাব, গুণ, অবস্থা, প্রভৃতি।

tĕch'-ni-cŏn, *n.* A gymnastic device for developing piano or organ playing ; অর্গেন অথবা পিয়ানো-যন্ত্র বাজাইবার জন্য দেহ উপযুক্ত করার নিমিত্ত একপ্রকার ব্যায়ামযন্ত্র।

tĕch'-ni-phōne, *n.* A dumb piano for exercising fingers ; অঙ্গুলি চালনা শিক্ষার জন্য একপ্রকার ধ্বনিহীন পিয়ানো।

tĕch'-nique' (-nīk-), *n.* 1. The form commonly used for method of execution in fine arts ; ললিতকলার সম্পাদনরীতি, কলাশাস্ত্রসম্মত সম্পাদন-রীতি। 2. Mechanical skill in art ; ললিতকলায় যান্ত্রিককৌশল।

tĕch-nŏl'-ŏ-ġŷ, *n.* 1. The science of industrial arts ; শ্রমশিল্প (বস্ত্রবয়নশিল্প, ধাতুশোধনবিদ্যাসম্বন্ধীয়বিজ্ঞান), শিল্পবিজ্ঞান (ব্রজঃ হিন্দুঃ) কারুকলা। 2. Terminology used in art, science, etc. ; পরিভাষা (হিঃ কোঃ), উপচার (ঐ), রূঢ়ি (ঐ), **–gist,** *n.* **–no-log'-i-cal,** *adj.*

tĕch'-ŷ, tetch'-ŷ (tĕch-), *adjs.* Peevish ; fretful ; খিটখিটে ; চটা। **–i-ly,** *adv.* **–i-ness,** *n.*

tĕc-tŏl'-ŏ-ġŷ, *n.* A division of morphology, which regards an organism as built up of individuals of different orders ; অঙ্গবিন্যাসবিদ্যার বিভাগ বিশেষ—যাহাতে কোন অঙ্গী বিভিন্ন শ্রেণীর জীব দ্বারা গঠিত বলিয়া পরিগণিত হয়, গঠনঘটিত অঙ্গবিন্যাস বিদ্যা।

Tectona grandis—সেগুণ (বেলঃ)।

tĕc-tŏn'-ic, *adj.* & *n.* 1. Of, building or construction ; গঠনসম্বন্ধীয়, নিৰ্ম্মাণসম্বন্ধীয়। 2. (*Geol*). Pertaining to, or designating, the rock structures due to the deformity of the earth's crust ; (ভূবিদ্যা) ভূপঞ্জরের বিরূপতা জানিত অঙ্গবিন্যাস-সম্বন্ধীয় বা তৎসূচক। ***Noun.*** (*Pl.*) The art of forming beautiful buildings, vessels, implements, etc. ; সুরম্য সৌধ, পাত্র, যন্ত্র, প্রভৃতি গঠনবিষয়কবিদ্যা।

tĕc-tō'-ri-ăl, *adj.* Covering ; আবরক। **Tectorial membrane**—কর্ণের ঝিল্লীবিশেষ।

tĕc-tri'-cēs, *n.* (*Orinth.*) The covering feathers of a bird's wings and tail ; পক্ষীর পক্ষ এবং পুচ্ছ-আচ্ছাদক পালকগুচ্ছ।

tĕd, *v. t.* To spread or turn new-mown grass to dry ; শুকাইবার জন্য কাঁচা ঘাস বিছান বা উল্টাইয়া দেওয়া।

Ted'-der, *n.* An implement for spreading new-mown grass ; নূতন কাটা ঘাস বিছাইবার জন্য একপ্রকার যন্ত্র।

Tĕ'-dĕs'-cō, *adj.* German ; জর্ম্মন (ইতালী বাসিগণ কর্তৃক ব্যবহৃত)।

Tē-Dē'-ŭm, *n.* 1. A famous Latin hymn named from the opening words *Te Deum Laudamus* (We praise Thee, O God) and sung at thanksgiving etc. ; সুপ্রসিদ্ধ ল্যাটিন স্তোত্র-বিশেষ। 2. A religious service in which this hymn is sung ; যে খৃষ্টীয় ধর্ম্মোপাসনারকালে এই স্তোত্র গীত হয়। 3. A music for this hymn ; এই স্তোত্রের উপযোগী বাদ্য। 4. (*Fig.*) triumph ; (লক্ষণায়) বিজয়োল্লাস।

tē'-di-ous (-ŭs), *adj.* Tiresome ; irksome ; tiresome from continuance ; ক্লান্তিজনক, ক্লান্তিকর ; বিরক্তিকর, বিরক্তিজনক; অবসাদজনক। **–ly,** *adv.* **–ness,** *n.* The state of being tedious ; ক্লান্তিজনকতা, অবসাদজনকতা।

tē'-di-ŭm, *n.* Tediousness ; wearisomeness ; অবসাদজনকতা ; ক্লান্তিজনকতা।

tee (tē), *n., v. t.* & *i.* 2. The letter T ; ইংরাজী T অক্ষর। 2. A thing shaped liked T ; ইংরাজী T অক্ষরের আকার বস্তু। 3. A T-shaped pipe ; ইংরাজী T অক্ষরাকৃতি চুঙ্গি। 4. (*In golf*) The sand or earth on which the ball is slightly raised at the beginning of play for each hole ; a smal appliance of rubber etc. for the same purpose ; (গোলফ্ ক্রীড়া) ক্রীড়ার প্রারম্ভে যে ক্ষুদ্র বালুকা বা মৃত্তিকাস্তূপের উপর কন্দুক রক্ষিত হয় ; উক্ত উদ্দেশ্য সাধনের জন্য রবার প্রভৃতি নির্ম্মিত ক্ষুদ্র যন্ত্র। 5. A mark at which missiles are aimed ; লক্ষ্য। ***Verb t.*** To place a ball on tee ; বালুকা প্রভৃতির ক্ষুদ্র স্তূপের উপর কন্দুক স্থাপন করা। ***Verb i.*** 1. To start from tee (with *off*)

(গল্‌ফ ক্রীড়ায় কন্দুক) ক্ষুদ্র বালুকা-স্তূপ হইতে অবস্থত হওয়া। 2. (*Fig.*) To begin (লক্ষণায়) আরম্ভ করা।

tee (tē), *n.* (Burmese) An umbrella-shaped metallic ornament crowning a pagoda; পেগোডার উপরে স্থাপিত ধাতুনির্মিত ছত্র।

teem (tēm), *v. t.* & *i.* (*Obs.*) To produce; to bring forth; (অপ্রঃ) উৎপাদন করা; প্রসব করা। ***Verb i.*** **1.** (*Obs.*) To bear young, as an animal; (অপ্রঃ) শাবক প্রসব করা। **2.** To be stocked to overflowing; to abound; to be prolific or abundantly fertile; বহুলপরিমাণে থাকা, পরিপূর্ণ হওয়া; প্রচুর পরিমাণে থাকা; বহুপ্রসূ হওয়া। **Teem'-ing,** *adj.* Prolific; overflowing; as, *teeming* millions; বহুপ্রসূ; অতিরিক্ত, অতিপূর্ণ, অতিবহুল।

teem (tēm),*v. t.* To pour out; ঢালা।

teen (tēn), *n.* **1.** (*Archaic*) Grief; (অপ্রঃ) বিষাদ। **2.** Injury; ক্ষতি।

teens (tēnz), *n.* (*pl.*) The years of one's age having the termination *teen*; ১৩ হইতে উনিশ পর্য্যন্ত বয়স। **In one's teens**—Between thirteen and nineteen; তের হইতে উনিশ বৎসর পর্য্যন্ত বয়সের।

tee'-nȳ (tē-), *adj.* Same as TINY (which see).

teeth (tēth), *n.* (*pl.*) See TOOTH. **To throw in one's teeth**—See TOOTH.

teethe (tēth), *v. i.* To grow or cut the teeth; দাঁত উঠা, দন্তোদ্গম হওয়া, দাঁত কাটা। **Teeth'-ing,** *n.* dentition; দন্তোদ্গম। **Teething fever**—শিশুদিগের দন্তোদ্গমকালীন জ্বর।

tee-tō'-tăl (tē-), *adj.* **1.** (*Colloq.*) Total; সম্পূর্ণ, পুরা। **2.** Pertaining to the teetotallers or teetotalism; সর্ব্বমাদকবর্জ্জনকারিগণসম্বন্ধীয়, সর্ব্বমাদকবর্জ্জনসম্বন্ধীয়। **—ly,** *adv.*

tee-to'-tal-ler (tē-tō-tăl-ẽr), *n.* A total abstainer; সর্ব্বপ্রকার মাদকত্যাগী, সর্ব্বপ্রকার পানামিষ বর্জ্জনকারী, সর্ব্বমাদকবর্জ্জক।

tee'-tō'-tŭm (tē-), *n.* A small four-sided toy of the top-kind, made to spin and used by children in a game of chance; একপ্রকার লাটিমজাতীয় চতুষ্কাকার ক্রীড়নক।

tĕg, tĕgg, *ns.* **1.** A female fallow-deer; a doe in the second year; হরিণী; দুই বৎসর বয়সের হরিণী। **2.** A young sheep; মেষশাবক।

tĕg-mĕn'-tŭm, (*Pl.*-TA), *n.* A bud-scale; মুকুলচ্ছদ (সাঃ পঃ)।

tĕg'-ū-lar (-lẽr), *adj.* **1.** Pertaining to tiles; like tiles; টালি সম্বন্ধীয়; টালিসদৃশ। **2.** Arranged like tiles; consisting of tiles; as, *tegular* pavement; টালির মত বিন্যস্ত; টালির দ্বারা রচিত। **—lat-ed,** *adj.* Composed of overlapping plates or scales; পরস্পরের প্রান্তের উপর স্থাপিত ফলক বা শল্কসমূহ সমন্বিত। **—ly,** *adv.*

tĕg'-ū-mĕnt, *n.* **1.** A cover or covering; আবরণ, আচ্ছাদন। **2.** Any natural covering as of animal; জন্তুর দেহের চর্ম্ম বা আবরণ।

tē—hee' (-hē), *n.* & *v. i.* A restrained or contemptuous laugh; চাপা হাসি, অবজ্ঞার হাসি। ***Verb i.*** To laugh in a restrained or contemptuous manner; চাপা হাসি হাসা, অবজ্ঞার হাসি হাসা।

Tē'-ian (-yăn), **Tē'-ăn,** *adj.* Pertaining to Teos in Asia Minor, where the Greek poet Anacreon was born; pertaining to Greek poet Anacreon; প্রাচীন গ্রীক কবি Anacreonএর জন্মস্থান Teos নামক স্থান সম্বন্ধীয়; গ্রীক কবি Anacreon সম্বন্ধীয়।

teil (tēl), *n.* The lime tree or linden; কাগজী লেবুর গাছ।

teind (tēnd), *n.* (*Sc.*) Same as TITHE (which see.)

tei'-nō-scōpe (tē-), *n.* An optical instrument consisting of two prisms, so combined as to correct chromatic aberration and to increase or diminish the linear dimension of objects; বস্তুসমূহের বর্ণাপচার সংশোধন এবং রৈখিক আয়তন বৃদ্ধি বা ন্যূন করার জন্য ত্রিপার্শ্বকাচফলকদ্বয়সমন্বিত বীক্ষণযন্ত্র বিশেষ, বিস্তারবীক্ষণ, ত্রিপার্শ্বদূরদর্শক (হিঃ কোঃ), তানববীক্ষণ।

tĕk-nŏn'-ȳ-mȳ, *n.* The custom of naming the parents from the child; সন্তানের নাম হইতে মাতা পিতার নাম করণ। **—mous,** *adj.*

tē'-lă, *n.* **1.** (*Anat.*) A web-like membrane; (শারীরসংস্থানবিদ্যা) জালবৎ ঝিল্লী। **2.** A tissue; বিধান তন্তু।

tĕl'-ă-mŏn, *n.* (*Arch.*) A male figure bearing pillar; (স্থপতিবিজ্ঞান) স্তম্ভধারক পুরুষমূর্ত্তি।

tĕl-au'-tō-grăph (-ä-), *n.* A telegraph that reproduces writing etc.; যে তারযন্ত্রে লিখন প্রভৃতি পুনরুৎপাদিত হয়।

tĕl'-ē-du (-dô), *n.* The stinking badger of Java and Sumatra; যব দ্বীপ এবং সুমাত্রা দ্বীপের দুর্গন্ধময় বেজী।

tē-lĕg'-ŏ-nȳ, *n.* (*Zool.*) The supposed influence of a father on offspring subsequent to his own begotten of the same mother by another father; (জন্তুবিদ্যা) পরবর্ত্তী পিতা কর্ত্তৃক পত্নীতে উৎপন্ন সন্তানের উপর পূর্ব্ব পিতার কল্পিত প্রভাব, পুংস্পর্শসংস্কার (হিঃ কোঃ)। **Tel-e-gon'-ic, —nous,** *adjs.*

tĕl'-ē-grăm, *n.* A telegraphic message; তাড়িতবার্ত্তা।

tĕl'-ē-grăph, *n.* **1.** An apparatus for transmitting message along a wire, but now wireless; তাড়িতবার্ত্তাবহযন্ত্র। **2.** A message sent by telegraph; তাড়িতবার্ত্তা, তারসঙ্কেতসমাচার (হিঃ কোঃ)। **3.** Same as SEMAPHORE. **4.** Same as TELEGRAPH-BOARD. **Electrical telegraph**—তড়িত্তার (হিঃ কোঃ)। **Electro-magnetic telegraph**—তড়িৎচুম্বকীয় তার (হিঃ কোঃ)। **Submarine telegraph**—সমুদ্রতলবর্ত্তী তার

(হিঃ কোঃ)। **Telegraph-board**—যে ফলকের উপর ঘোড়দৌড়ের ঘোড়ার সংখ্যা, ক্রীকেট ক্রীড়ার জয়াঙ্ক, প্রভৃতি লিখিত হইয়া থাকে। **Telegraph-cable**—সাগরতলগামী তাড়িতবার্ত্তাবহের ধাতবরজ্জু। **Telegraph-line**—তারের লাইন। **Telegraph-plant**—(*Desmodium gyrans*); বনচাড়াল (যোঃ)। **Telegraph-post**—টেলিগ্রাফের থাম, তারের খোঁটা। **Telegraph signal**—সাঙ্কেতিক তার (হিঃ কোঃ)। **Telegraph wire**—টেলিগ্রাফের তার।

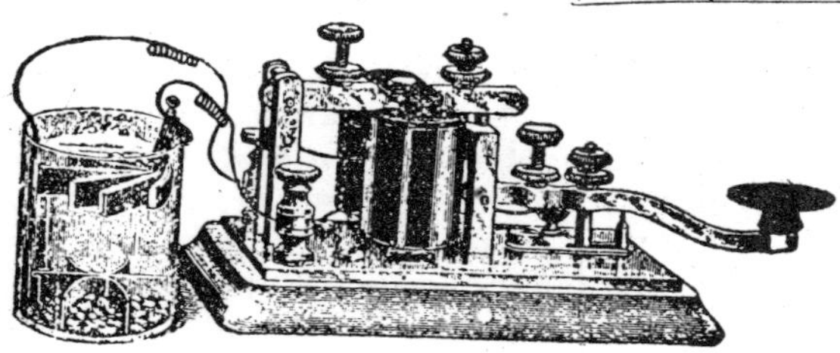

Telegraph instrument

tĕ-lĕg'-ră-phêr, —phĭst, *ns.* A person skilled, or employed in, telegraphy; তাড়িতবার্ত্তাপ্রেরক।

tĕl-ĕ-grăph'-ic, *adj.* Of, or pertaining to, a telegraph; sent or communicated by a telegraph; তাড়িতবার্ত্তাসম্বন্ধীয়; তাড়িতবার্ত্তাদ্বারা প্রেরিত। **—i-cal-ly,** *adv.* **Telegraphic address** — তাড়িতবার্ত্তায় ব্যবহারের জন্য কোম্পানী প্রভৃতির সংক্ষিপ্ত ঠিকানা।

tĕ-lĕg'-ră-phȳ, *n.* The art or practice of communicating intelligence by a telegraph; তাড়িতবার্ত্তাপ্রেরণবিদ্যা।

Tĕ-lĕm'-ă-chŭs, *n.* The son of Odysseus and Penelope; Odysseus এবং Penelopeএর পুত্র। Odysseus শিশু পুত্র Telemachusকে রাখিয়া Troy নগরীতে গমন করেন। Telemachus ২৪ বৎসর কাল পর্য্যন্ত পিতার কোনরূপ সংবাদ না পাইয়া তাঁহার অন্বেষণে অর্ণবপোতে যাত্রা করেন। তিনি নানাদেশ পর্য্যটনান্তে স্বদেশে প্রত্যাবর্ত্তন করিয়া দেখিতে পাইলেন যে, তদীয় পিতৃদেব গৃহে প্রত্যাগত হইয়াছেন।

tĕ-lĕm'-ĕ-têr, *n.* An instrumen for determining distances in surveying etc. জরীপ প্রভৃতিতে দূরত্ব নির্ণয়ের জন্য যন্ত্রবিশেষ, অন্তর মাপক (হিঃ কোঃ)। **Tel-e-met'-ric,** *adj.* **—try,** *n.*

tĕl-ĕ-ŏl'-ŏ-ġȳ, *n.* The science or doctrine of final causes; পরমকারণতত্ত্ব, হেতুবিদ্যা, মীমাংসা, পরমকারণবিদ্যা। **Teleological argument**—বুদ্ধিপূর্ব্বন্যায় (হিঃ কোঃ)।

tĕl-ĕ-ŏ-sau'-rŭs (-sä-), *n.* A genus of fossil crocodiles; একজাতীয় শিলীভূত কুম্ভীর।

tĕl'-ĕ-ŏ-stōme, *n.* (Of fishes) Characterised by well-developed mouth; পূর্ণমুখী (সাঃ পঃ)।

tĕ-lĕp'-ă-thȳ, *n.* The occult communication of facts, feelings, or impression between persons at a distance from each other; ইচ্ছাশক্তির প্রয়োগ দ্বারা দূরস্থিত ব্যক্তির মনোভাব অবগতি, পরচিত্তজ্ঞান (হিঃ কোঃ), পরচিত্তপ্রত্যক্ষ (ঐ)

tĕl'-ĕ-phōne, *n.* & *v.t.* An instrument which transmits sound beyond its natural limits of audibility; more especially an instrument for transmitting sound and words uttered by the human voice by means of electricity and telegraph wires, the vibrations of a thin plate caused by the sound being electrically transmitted and reproduced by a corresponding plate; দূরে ধ্বনি প্রেরণের জন্য যন্ত্রবিশেষ; টেলিফোঁ, তাড়িতশব্দবহ, দূরশ্রবণযন্ত্র। [Graham Bell নামক জনৈক বৈজ্ঞানিক ১৮৭৬ খৃঃ অব্দে এই যন্ত্র আবিষ্কার করেন।] *Verb t.* To communicate by telephone; দূরশ্রবণ যন্ত্রের সাহায্যে সংবাদ প্রেরণ করা, টেলিফোঁ করা। **—phon'-ic,** *adj.* **—phon'-i-cal-ly,** *adv.* **Te-leph'-o-ny,** *n.*

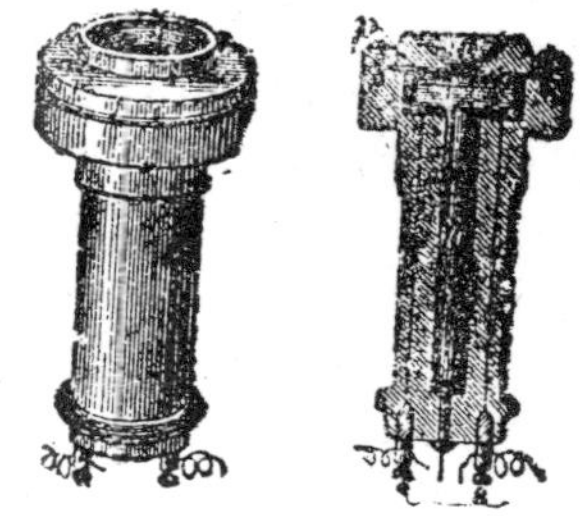

Telephone.

o, mouthpiece; *p*, thin metallic plate vibrating to the sound of the voice, connected with telegraphic wires at *ss*; *m*, bar magnet.

tĕl'-ĕ-scōpe, *n.* An optical instrument, for viewing distant objects; দূরবীক্ষণ যন্ত্র, দূরবীণ, দূরদর্শক (হিঃ কোঃ)। [Lippershey নামক জনৈক ওলন্দাজ চসমানির্ম্মাতা সর্ব্বপ্রথম এই যন্ত্র উদ্ভাবন করেন। তৎপর ইতালীর অন্তঃপাতী Pisa নগরবাসী Galileo নামক জ্যোতির্বিজ্ঞানবিৎ ১৬০৯ খৃঃ অব্দে একটী উন্নততর প্রণালীর দূরদর্শন যন্ত্র নির্ম্মাণ করিয়া প্রসিদ্ধি লাভ করেন।] **—scop'-ic, —scop'-i-cal,** *adjs.* **—scop'-i-cal-ly,** *adv.* **Te-les'-co-pist, Te-les'-co-py,** *ns.* **Achromatic telescope**—স্বচ্ছ দূরদর্শক (হিঃ কোঃ)। **Astronomical telescope**—জ্যোতিষিক দূরদর্শক (ঐ) **Dialytic telescope** — বিশ্লেষকদূরদর্শক (ঐ)। **Equatorial telescope**—দিবাদূরদর্শক (ঐ)। **Photographic telescope**—গ্রহচিত্রক (ঐ)। **Prism telescope**—ত্রিপার্শ্বদর্শক (ঐ)। **Reflecting telescope**—পরাবর্ত্তনীয় দূরদর্শক (ঐ)। **Refracting telescope**—পরাবর্ত্তক দূরবীক্ষণ।

tĕl'-ĕ-seme (-sēm), *n.* A system of electrical signalling annunciators used in hotels etc; হোটেল প্রভৃতিতে ব্যবহৃত একপ্রকার তাড়িত বিজ্ঞাপক।

tĕl-ė-thêr-mŏm′-ĕ-têr, *n.* An apparatus for indicating the temperature of a distant point ; দূরস্থতাপমাপক (হিঃ কোঃ)। **–try,** *n.*

tĕ-leu′-tō-spōre (-lü-), *n.* A spiral form of spore, usually produced in a parasitic fungi ; লগ্নরেণু।

tĕll, *v. t.* & *i.* **1.** To number, count or enumerate ; as, to *tell* money ; গণনা করা, গণা, সংখ্যা করা। **2.** To say ; as, to *tell* a lie ; বলা, কহা। **3.** To divulge ; as, to *tell* the news ; প্রকাশ করা। **4.** To order ; as, *tell* him to go ; আদেশ দেওয়া। **5.** To discern ; to distinguish ; to decide ; as, how can I *tell* what to do ?; যাহরান, ঠিক করা ; প্রভেদ করা ; স্থির করা। **6.** To inform ; জানান, জ্ঞাত করা, বিদিত করা। ***Verb i.*** **1.** To give an account ; বর্ণনা করা। **2.** (*Colloq.*) To play the informer ; (চলিতভাষায়) গোপনে বলিয়া দেওয়া। **3.** To take effect ; as, every shot *told* ; ফলপ্রদ হওয়া, কার্য্যকরী হওয়া। **Tell′-a-ble,** *adj.* **Tell′-ing,** *p. adj.* Having great effect ; বিশেষরূপে কার্য্যকর, বিশেষ ফলপ্রদ। **To tell of**—To inform against some one ; কাহারো বিরুদ্ধে খবর দেওয়া। **To tell off**—To count one by one ; এক একটী করিয়া গণা, একাদিক্রমে গণা। To detach for some special duty ; কোন বিশেষ কর্ত্তব্যকার্য্যের জন্য পৃথক করিয়া রাখা। **To tell on** or **upon**—To have effect on something ; কোন কিছুর উপর ক্রিয়া করা। **To tell one's beads**—মালা জপা। **To tell tales out of school**—See SCHOOL. **To tell up**—To count ; গণা, গণনা করা। To amount or increase so as to produce certain effect ; একুনে বা সমষ্টিতে এইরূপ হওয়া বা এইরূপ পরিমাণে বৃদ্ধি পাওয়া যাহাতে কোন নির্দ্দিষ্ট ফলোৎপাদন হইতে পারে।

tĕll′-ĕr, *n.* **1.** One who relates ; বর্ণনাকারী। **2.** One who counts ; গণনাকারী। **3.** A functionary in a bank who receives and pays out money ; ব্যাঙ্কের যে কর্ম্মচারী অর্থের আদান প্রদান করে। **4.** One appointed to count the votes given in a public assembly etc. ; যে ব্যক্তি সভা প্রভৃতিতে প্রদত্ত ভোটের সংখ্যা গণনা করিয়া থাকে। **5.** One of the four persons (two for each party) to count votes in the House of Commons ; পার্লেমেণ্টের প্রাকৃত সভায় যে ব্যক্তিচতুষ্টয় নির্ব্বাচনমত গণনা করিয়া থাকে—তাহাদিগের অন্যতম।

tĕll′-tāle, *n.* & *adj.* **1.** One who improperly discloses private concerns or makes known what he should suppress ; যে ব্যক্তি অন্য লোকের গোপনীয় কথা প্রকাশ করে, কুটনা, পরচর্চ্চাকারী। **2.** (*Fig.*) The thing or circumstances that reveals a man's thoughts ; (লক্ষণায়) যে অবস্থা বা লক্ষণ দ্বারা কোন ব্যক্তির কার্য্য, মনোভাব প্রভৃতি প্রকাশ পায়। **3.** A tattler (bird) ; একপ্রকার পক্ষী। **4.** A device to indicate or record something, esp. to keep a check on employees, drivers, etc. ; a clock to register the time of arrival and departure of work-people or of a watchman on his rounds ; কোন কিছু নির্দ্দেশের জন্য কৌশলবিশেষ, বিশেষতঃ মজুর প্রভৃতি কতটা কার্য্য করিয়াছে তাহা ঠিক করার জন্য কৌশলবিশেষ ; মজুর বা পাহারাওয়ালার আগমন ও প্রস্থান নির্দ্দেশের জন্য একপ্রকার ঘটিকাযন্ত্র। ***Adj.*** **1.** Telling tales ; blabbing ; কাহারো বিরুদ্ধে সংবাদ প্রদানকারী ; গুপ্ত কথা প্রকাশকারী। **2.** That reveals or betrays something meant to be kept secret ; as, *telltale* blushes ; গোপনবিষয়সূচক, গুপ্তভাবপ্রকটক। **Tell-tale compass** — জাহাজের গতিপথ নির্দ্দেশের জন্য পোতাধ্যক্ষের কক্ষে দোলায়িত দিগ্‌দর্শন যন্ত্র।

tĕl-lū′-rĭ-ăn, *adj.* & *n.* Pertaining to the earth or to an inhabitant of the earth ; পার্থিব, পৃথিবীবাসিসম্বন্ধীয়। ***Noun.*** An inhabitant of the earth ; পৃথিবীবাসী লোক, মর্ত্ত্যবাসী লোক। **–ral,** *adj.*

tĕl-lū′-rĭ-ŏn, *n.* An instrument for showing the succession of day and night, and the changes of the seasons ; দিবারাত্রের পর্য্যায়গমন এবং ঋতুপরিবর্ত্তন প্রদর্শনের জন্য যন্ত্রবিশেষ।

tĕl-lū′-rĭ-ŭm, *n.* A non-metallic element of a tin-white crystalline appearance resembling sulphur in its chemical relations ; একপ্রকার গন্ধকসদৃশ ভঙ্গপ্রবণ এবং শ্বেতবর্ণ মৌলিক পদার্থ, ভৌমক (সাঃ পঃ)। **Tel′-lu-rate, Tel′-lu-ret, Tel′-lu-ride,** *ns.* **Tel′-lu-ret-ted, –ric, Tel′-lu-rous,** *adjs.*

tĕl′-ō-tȳpe, *n.* **1.** An electric telegraph which prints the messages ; যে তাড়িতবার্ত্তাবহে সংবাদ মুদ্রিত হইয়া থাকে, তাড়িতমুদ্রাঙ্কক। **2.** An automatically printed telegram ; স্বয়ংমুদ্রিত তাড়িতবার্ত্তা।

tĕl′-phêr, *n.* A method by which vehicles are moved by an electric current ; বিজলীপ্রবাহ দ্বারা যান চালনার প্রণালী বিশেষ। **–age,** *n.* A system of transferring goods in a kind of elevated railway by means of electricity ; তাড়িতপ্রবাহের সাহায্যে উচ্চ লৌহবর্ত্মের উপর মাল চালিত করার প্রণালী।

tĕl′-sŏn, *n.* The last joint in the abdomen of crustacea ; খোলকী প্রাণীর নিম্নোদরের শেষ পর্ব্ব বা সন্ধি।

tĕm′-ĕ-nŏs, *n.* (*Greak Antiq.*) A sacred precinct ; (গ্রীসদেশীয় প্রত্নতত্ত্ব) মন্দিরের চতুঃপার্শ্বর্ত্তী পবিত্র স্থান।

tĕ-mĕr′-ĭ-ty, *n.* Boldness ; rashness ; দুঃসাহসিকতা, হঠকারিতা, অবিবেচকতা, গোঁয়ারতামি

temp., (Abbrev. of Latin *tempore*) In the time of ; as, *temp.* Henry I ; সময়ে।

Tĕm-pē'-ăn, *adj.* Of, or resembling, Tempe, a charming valley in Thessaly ; beautiful ; charming ; থেসালি প্রদেশের টেম্পি নামক সুন্দর উপত্যকাসম্বন্ধীয় ; অতএব, সুন্দর ; মুগ্ধকর, বিমোহন।

tĕm'-pêr, *v. t. & i.* **1.** To mix or combine in due proportion ; যথোচিত অনুপাতে মিশ্রিত করা। **2.** To qualify by the intermixture of certain elements ; to soften ; to mollify ; as, to *temper* justice with mercy ; কোমল করা ; মেদুরিত করা ; শমিত করা। **3.** To form to proper degree of hardness, as steel ; to give a certain degree of elasticity and hardness to, as steel ; ইস্পাত প্রভৃতি যথাযোগ্য দৃঢ় করা ; ইস্পাত প্রভৃতিকে নির্দ্দিষ্ট পরিমাণ দার্ঢ্য ও স্থিতিস্থাপকত্ব প্রদান করা, পাণি দেওয়া। **4.** To moisten and beat together, to proper consistency, as clay ; মাটি প্রভৃতি ছানিয়া প্রস্তুত করা, ছানা। **5.** (*Now rare*) To accommodate ; to adjust ; (বর্ত্তমানে ক্বচিদ্ ব্যবহৃত) উপযোগী করা ; ঠিকঠাক করা। **6.** To anneal glass ; কাচ যথোচিত কঠিন করা, কাচ তপ্তশীতল করা। **7.** To clarify the juice of sugarcane with lime ; চূণদ্বারা ইক্ষুরস নির্ম্মল করা। **8.** (*Mus.*) To tune or modulate ; (সঙ্গীতশাস্ত্র) সুরসংযোগ করা। ***Verb i.*** **1.** (*Obs.*) To agree ; (অপ্রঃ) মিলা, খাপ খাওয়া, সঙ্গতিবিশিষ্ট হওয়া। **2.** To have, or acquire, a proper or desired state or quality ; to become soft and pliable ; যথোচিত বা ঈপ্সিত গুণ বা অবস্থা লাভ করা ; কোমল এবং নমনীয় হওয়া। **—a-ble**, *adj.* **—a-tive**, *adj.* **—er**, *n.* **God tempers the wind to the shorn lamb**—ঈশ্বর মুণ্ডিত মেষশাবককে প্রাণরক্ষার জন্য বায়ুর শীতানুভূতি প্রশমিত করেন, অর্থাৎ তিনি দুর্ব্বলকে শক্তি এবং সহিষ্ণুতা প্রদান করিয়া তাহার বিপদ্‌ভার লঘু করিয়াছেন।

tĕm'-pêr, *n.* **1.** Mixture, esp. suitable combination of the ingredients of (mortar) ; the state of any compound substance which results from the mixture of various ingredients ; as, the *temper* of mortar ; মিশ্রণ ; বিভিন্ন উপাদানের মিশ্রণজনিত অবস্থা। **2.** Dispostion of mind ; প্রকৃতি, মেজাজ, স্বভাব, ধাত। **3.** Heat of mind or passion ; as, to show *temper* ; মানসিক উত্তেজনা, রাগ, রাগের ভাব। **4.** The state of metal, as to its hardness or elasticity ; দার্ঢ্যতা এবং স্থিতিস্থাপকতা সম্পর্কে ধাতুর অবস্থা, পাণি। **—pered**, *adj.* **In a fit of temper**—From a fit of sudden anger ; রাগের মাথায়, রাগের চোটে। **Tempering of steel**—শাস্ত্রপাঠ (সাঃ পঃ)। **To control or keep one's temper**—To restrain one's passion ; ক্রোধ সংযত করা, রাগ থামান।

tĕm'-pĕ-ră, *n.* Same as DISTEMPER.

tĕm'-pêr-ă-mĕnt, *n.* **1.** The individual peculiarity of physical organisation, by which the manner of thinking, acting and feeling of each person is permanently affected ; দেহের ধাত, ধাতু, প্রকৃতি, স্বভাব। **2.** Adjustment of opposing influences ; পরস্পরবিরুদ্ধ ভাবের সমন্বয়। **3.** (*Mus.*) The system of tuning the tones of a fixed-tone musical instrument, as the piano ; পিয়ানো প্রভৃতিতে সুরসংযোগ। **—men'-tal**, *adj.*

tĕm'-pêr-ance (-ăns), *n.* **1.** Habitual moderation in the indulgence of appetite and passions ; as, *temperance* in eating and drinking ; মিতাচার, পানভোজনাদি সম্পর্কে সংযম, সংযম (হিঃ কোঃ), নিগ্রহ (ঐ), পানসংযম, পরিমিততা। **2.** Abstinence from, or moderation in, the use of intoxicating liquors ; পানবিরতি, পানসংযম। **3.** (*Archaic*) Self-restraint ; (অপ্রঃ) আত্মসংযম। **Temperance association**—মাদকনিবারণী সভা, সংযমসমিতি। **Temperance hotel**—যে ভোজনাগারে অভ্যাগতদিগকে কোনপ্রকার মাদকদ্রব্য সরবরাহ করা হয় না, মাদকবর্জ্জিত ভোজনশালা। **Temperance movement**—মাদকবর্জ্জনের আন্দোলন। **Temperance society**—মাদকনিবারণী সভা।

tĕm'-pêr-ăte *adj.* **1.** Moderate ; পরিমিত, মিত, মিতাচারী, সংযতচিত্ত। **2.** Self-restrained ; সংযতচিত্ত, আত্মসংযমী, সংযমশীল। **3.** Not too cold or hot ; as, *temperate* climate ; নাতিশীতোষ্ণ। **—ly**, *adv.* **—ness**, *n.* **Temperate zone**—নাতিশীতোষ্ণমণ্ডল, মন্দোষ্ণবলয় (সাঃ পঃ)। **North temperate zone**—উত্তর-মন্দোষ্ণবলয় (সাঃ পঃ)। **South temperate zone**—দক্ষিণ মন্দোষ্ণবলয় (সাঃ পঃ)।

tĕm'-pêr-ă-tūre, *n.* The state of a body with regard to heat and cold, as indicated by a thermometer ; as, to take one's *temperature* ; তাপমাত্রা, তাপক্রম (হিঃ কোঃ), তাপপরিমাণ (ঐ), শীতোষ্ণ (ঐ), উষ্ণমান (ঐ), উষ্ণতা। **Absolute temperature** — পরমতাপক্রম (হিঃ কোঃ)। **Temperature curve**—যে বক্রদ্বারা তাপমাত্রার বৈষম্য প্রদর্শিত হয়। **Temperature sensation**—(মনস্তত্ত্ব) শীত বা তাপানুভূতি, শীতোষ্ণানুভূতি।

tĕm'-pĕst, *n.* **1.** A furious storm ; ঝড়, ঝটিকা, ঝঞ্ঝা, প্রভঞ্জন, চণ্ডবাত, তুফান, ঝঞ্ঝানিল, ঝঞ্ঝাবাত। **2.** (*Fig.*) Violent tumult or agitation ; "Even the king stood aghast for a moment at the violence of the *tempest*, which he had raised" ; তুমুল উত্তেজনা, তুমুল আন্দোলন, মহা হুলস্থুল ব্যাপার। **Tempest-beaten**—ঝঞ্ঝাতাড়িত। **Tempest-god**—ঝটিকার অধিষ্ঠাত্রী দেবতা। **Tempest tossed**—ঝঞ্ঝাতাড়িত, ঝটিকাবিধ্বস্ত।

tĕm-pĕs'-tū-ous (-ŭs), *adj.* **1.** Very stormy ; ঝটিকাপূর্ণ, ঝটিকাময়,

ঝটিকাসঙ্কুল, ঝটিকাবিক্ষুব্ধ। 2. Violent; turbulent; agitative; as, a *tempestuous* debate; উগ্র, প্রচণ্ড; তুমুল · বিক্ষোভজনক।

Tĕm'-plâr, *n.* **1.** One of a religious military order, first established at Jerusalem to protect pilgrims travelling to the Holy Land; জেরুজেলেমযাত্রী খৃষ্টানগণের রক্ষার্থ প্রতিষ্ঠিত সামরিক ভ্রাতৃমণ্ডলীর সভ্য। 2. (*l. c.*) A student of law (so called from having apartment in the Temple at London); লণ্ডননগরীর আইনশিক্ষার্থী ছাত্র। Free or good **Templars**—মাদক নিবারণী গুপ্তসভা বিশেষের সভ্য।

Templar.

tĕm'-plāte, *n.* Same as TEMPLET (which see)

tĕm'-ple (-pl), *n.* **1.** An edifice erected or dedicated to the service of some deity or deities; দেবমন্দির, দেবমণ্ডপ, মন্দির (হিঃ কোঃ), দেবভবন (কথাঃ সঃ), দেবালয়, দেবায়তন, দেবগৃহ, অমরাগার, দেববেশ্ম, দেবসদ্ম, দেবগেহ, দেবাগার, দেবতাগার, ঈশ্বরসদ্ম। 2. (*Cap.*) One of three successive buildings in ancient Jerusalem for the worship of Jehova; প্রাচীন জেরুজেলেম নগরীতে জিহোভার অর্চনার জন্য ক্রমান্বয়ে যে মন্দিরত্রয় বিনির্ম্মিত হইয়াছিল তাহার অন্যতম। 3. An edifice erected among Christians for worship; a church; খৃষ্টীয় ভজনালয়, খৃষ্টীয় ধর্ম্মমন্দির; গির্জ্জা। **4.** A place in which the divine presence specially resides; "Know ye not that your body is the *temple* of the Holy Ghost which is in you, which ye have of God, and ye are not your own"; দেবতার আবির্ভাবস্থান, পীঠস্থান। **5.** (*Cap.*) In London, an edifice once occupied by the Knights Templars; জেরুজেলেম যাত্রিগণের রক্ষাকারী নাইটগণের লণ্ডন নগরীস্থ বাসভবন। . 6. In London, two inns of court, (Inner Temple, Middle Temple) chiefly inhabited by lawyers, and so called because they were anciently the dwellings of the Knights Templars; লণ্ডন নগরীস্থ আইন বিদ্যালয় দ্বয়ের অন্যতর—যথায় পূর্ব্বে সামরিক ভ্রাতৃমণ্ডলীর সভ্যগণ বাস করিতেন।

tĕm'-ple (-pl), *n.* The sides of the forehead where the pulse is felt; কর্ণ এবং ললাটের মধ্যস্থিত মস্তকের উভয় পার্শ্বস্থ সমতল অংশ, রগ, শঙ্খদেশ (হঃ চঃ)।

tĕm'-ple (-pl), *n.* A device in loom for keeping cloth stretched; কাপড় টানা দিয়া রাখার জন্য তাঁতের কৌশল বিশেষ।

tĕm'-plĕt, —plate, *ns.* **1.** A board or piece of sheet-iron whose edge is shaped so that it may serve as a guide in making an article with a corresponding contour; যে ক্ষুদ্র লৌহফলক বা পট্ট দৃষ্টে উহার প্রান্তরেখার অনুরূপ বাহ্যরেখাবিশিষ্ট অন্য কোন বস্তু কাটা হইয়া থাকে। **2.** A wedge under the keel of a ship; জাহাজের প্রধান তলকাষ্ঠের নিম্নস্থ কাঁজলা। 3. (*Archit.*) A short piece or large stone placed in a wall to receive the impost of a girder, beam, etc. and distribute its weight; a beam spanning a door-way and the like and supporting joists; (স্থপতিবিজ্ঞান) প্রধান কড়িকাঠের চাপ ধারণের জন্য প্রাচীরে যে খণ্ড বা বৃহৎ প্রস্তরফলক স্থাপিত হয়; দ্বারাদির উপরে স্থাপিত কড়ি কাষ্ঠধারক দারু ফলক। 4. (Usu. *template*) Same as BEZEL.

tempo*, *n. (*Mus.*) The time or rate of movement; (সঙ্গীতশাস্ত্র) লয়।

tempo*, *n. An oval brass Japanese coin with a square hole in the middle; মধ্যদেশে চতুষ্কোণ ছিদ্রযুক্ত অণ্ডাকৃতি জাপানী পিত্তলমুদ্রা।

tĕm'-pō-răl, *adj.* & *n.* 1. Pertaining to this life or world; as, *temporal* power; secular; ঐহিক, লৌকিক (হিঃ কোঃ), পার্থিব, সাংসারিক; বৈষয়িক। 2. (*Anat.*) Of the temples of the head; (শারীরসংস্থানবিদ্যা) শঙ্খদেশসম্বন্ধীয়। ***Noun.*** **1.** Anything temporal or secular; ঐহিক বিষয়, পার্থিব ব্যাপার। 2. Same as TEMPORAL BONE below. **—ly,** *adv.* **—ness,** *n.* **Temporal augment**—আদ্যস্বরের দীর্ঘীকরণহেতু বৃদ্ধি। **Temporal bone**—শঙ্খাস্থি, মহাশঙ্খ (কর্ণ নেত্রান্তরালাস্থি মহাশঙ্খঃ প্রকীর্ত্তিতঃ—কুমারীকল্প)। **Temporal lord**—ইংলণ্ডের সম্ভ্রান্ত উপাধিধারী ব্যক্তিগণ। **Temporal power**—ঐহিক বিষয়ে যাজকগণের বিশেষতঃ পোপের ক্ষমতা।

tĕm-pō-răl'-i-tȳ, *n.* 1. Properties and revenues of an ecclesiastic proceeding from lands, tenements, tithes and like; দেবোত্তর সম্পত্তি, দেবোত্তর সম্পত্তি প্রভৃতির আয়। 2. (*Law*) Temporariness; (আইন) অচিরস্থায়িতা।

tĕm'-pō-răl-tȳ, *n.* 1. Same as TEMPORALITY I. 2. The laity; গৃহস্থবর্গ, গৃহস্থসমাজ, সাংসারিক লোকগণ।

tĕm'-pō-ră-rȳ, *adj.* Lasting for a time only; short-lived; fleeting; অস্থায়ী, সাময়িক; অশাশ্বত (হিঃ কোঃ), ক্ষণিক, ক্ষণস্থায়ী; স্বল্পকালিক, অল্পকালিক। **—ri-ly,** *adv.* **—ri-ness,** *n.* The state of being temporary; ক্ষণস্থায়িত্ব, সাময়িকতা, স্বল্পকালিকতা, ক্ষণিকতা, ক্ষণভঙ্গুরতা।

tĕm'-pŏ-rīze, *v. i.* **1.** To comply with the time or occasion; to humour or yield to the current opinion or circumstance; সাময়িকভাবে অনুবর্ত্তী হওয়া; সাময়িক মত বা ঘটনার স্রোতে গা ঢালিয়া দেওয়া। 2. To act so as to gain time; সময় লইবার উদ্দেশ্যে কোন কার্য্য করা। **—ri-za'-tion,** *n.* **—ri-zer,** *n.*

tĕm'-pŏ-ro- (In combination) = *L. tempora* temples of the head ; শঙ্খদেশ। **Temporo-facial**—মুখ এবং শঙ্খপ্রদেশ-সম্বন্ধীয়।

tempt (tĕmt), *v. t.* **1.** (*Archaic*) To put to trial ; to test ; (অপ্রঃ) পরীক্ষায় ফেলা ; পরীক্ষা করা। **2.** To incite or solicit to an evil act ; "Let not my worser spirit *tempt* me again"; to incite to something wrong by presenting inducements that are plausible and alluring ; কুপ্রবৃত্তি দেওয়া, কুকার্য্যে প্ররোচিত করা ; প্রলুব্ধ করা। **3.** To provoke ; "You shall not *tempt* the God your Lord"; উত্তেজিত করা। **—a-bil'-i-ty,** *n.* **Temp-ta'-tion,** *n.* **1.** The act of one who tempts ; প্রলোভন, বিলোভন। **2.** That which tempts, প্রলোভক, প্রলোভনজনক বস্তু, লোভনীয় বস্তু। **Tempt'-ing,** *adj.* Alluring ; প্রলোভনজনক। **Tempt'-ing-ly,** *adv.* **To tempt God**—To put to the test God's power of forbearance etc. ; to provoke ; to defy ; ঈশ্বরের সহিষ্ণুতার সীমা পরীক্ষা করা ; ঈশ্বরকে উত্তেজিত করা ; ঈশ্বরকে তুচ্ছ করা। **To tempt fortune**—To engage one's self in hazardous task ; বিপৎসঙ্কুল কার্য্যে প্রবৃত্ত হওয়া। **To tempt storm etc.**—To risk the peril of ; ঝটিকাদির বিপদ্ অগ্রাহ্য করিয়া যাত্রা করা।

tempt'-ĕr (tĕmt-), *n.* One who tempts ; প্রলোভনকারী, প্রলোভক। **—ress,** *n. fem.* **The Tempter**—শয়তান।

tĕn, *adj.* & *n.* Twice five ; দশ। ***Noun.*** **1.** The number of twice five ; দশ সংখ্যা। **2.** A playing card with ten spots ; তাসের দশ। **Ten'-fold,** *adj.* & *adv.* **Tenth,** *adj.* **Ten-pounder**—১০ পাউণ্ড রাজস্ব দেওয়ার দরুণ যে ব্যক্তি পার্লেমেণ্টের সভ্যনির্ব্বাচনে ভোট প্রদান করিতে পারে। **Tenth-meter** — দশাংশমাপক (হিঃ কোঃ)। **One of a ten thousand**—লাখজনের মধ্যে একজন। **Ten to one**—Very probable ; খুব সম্ভবপর। **The ten commandments** — (বাইবেলে উক্ত) ঈশ্বরের দশাদেশ।

tĕn'-ȧ-ble (-bl), *adj.* **1.** That may be held or maintained against an assailant or an objector ; as, a *tenable* fortress : a *tenable* argument ; সমর্থনীয়, রক্ষণীয়। **2.** That may be possessed, obtained or enjoyed ; as, a scholarship *tenable* for two years ; ভোগ্য, অধিকরণীয়, প্রাপ্য। **—bil'-i-ty, —ness,** *ns.*

tĕn'-ace (-ās), *n.* In whist the possession of the best and the third best cards by the last player, so that he wins the last trick whatever card is played against him ; তাসক্রীড়াবিশেষে শেষক্রীড়কের হস্তে, সর্ব্বশ্রেষ্ঠ এবং শ্রেষ্ঠত্বে তৃতীয় তাসের স্থিতি—যাহাতে যে কোন তাসই খেলা হউক না কেন সে ক্রীড়ক শেষ পিঠ পাইয়া থাকে। **Major tenace**—তাসক্রীড়ায় সর্ব্বশ্রেষ্ঠ এবং শ্রেষ্ঠত্বে দ্বিতীয় তাস। **Minor tenace**—তাসক্রীড়ায় শ্রেষ্ঠত্বে দ্বিতীয় এবং চতুর্থ তাস।

tĕ-nā'-cious, (-shŭs), *adj.* **1.** Holding fast ; inclined to retain what is in possession ; নাছোড়বান্দা ; দৃঢ়গ্রাহী। **2.** Retentive ; as, a *tenacious* memory ; ধারণক্ষম, দৃঢ়গ্রাহী। **3.** Adhesive ; সংলাগশীল, আঁটালো। **4.** Tough ; as, hide is *tenacious* ; চিমড়া। **—ly,** *adv.* **—ness,** *n.*

tĕ-năc'-i-tў, *n.* **1.** The quality or state of being tenacious ; দৃঢ়সংশক্তি, দৃঢ়গ্রাহিতা। **2.** Adhesiveness ; সংলাগশীলতা। **3.** (*Phys.*) The resistance of bodies to tearing or crushing ; (পদার্থবিদ্যা) দার্ঢ্য।

tĕ-năc'-ŭ-lŭm, *n.* A surgical instrument for seizing or drawing out the mouth of bleeding arteries in operations, so that they may be secured by ligaments ; বড়িশের ন্যায় সূক্ষ্ম অগ্রভাগবিশিষ্ট একপ্রকার অস্ত্র যাহা রক্তস্রাবী ধমনী বন্ধনার্থ ব্যবহৃত হয়, বড়িশাস্ত্র, বড়িশ (সাঃ পঃ), অঙ্কুশ (ঐ)।

tĕ-nail' (-nāl), **—naille'** (-nāl), *ns.* (*Fort.*) An outwork in the main ditch between two bastions ; (দুর্গ) দুর্গপ্রাকার হইতে বহিরুদ্গত পঞ্চভুজাকৃতি মৃত্তিকাস্তূপদ্বয়ের মধ্যবর্ত্তী প্রধান পরিখাস্থ উপদুর্গ।

tĕn'-ăn-cў, *n.* **1.** A holding or occupying of lands or tenements as, a tenant ; tenure ; প্রজাস্বত্ব, জোতস্বত্ব ; জোত। **2.** The period of a tenant's occupation ; জোতের কাল। **Bengal Tenancy Act**—বঙ্গীয় প্রজাস্বত্ব বিষয়ক আইন।

tĕn'-ănt, *n.* & *v. t.* **1.** One who occupies lands or other real estate under a landlord ; রায়ত, প্রজা, ভাড়াটিয়া, কেরায়াদার। **2.** A dweller ; "Sweet *tenants* of the grove" ; বাসী, নিবাসী। ***Verb t.*** **1.** To hold, occupy, or possess ; প্রজাস্বরূপ ভোগ দখল করা, জোত করা। **2.** To occupy ; to fill ; "A pair of boundless slippers that have been *tenanted* by a thousand feet" ; অধিকার করা ; পূর্ণ করা। **—less,** *adj.* Without tenants ; প্রজাশূন্য, ভাড়াটিয়াশূন্য, খালি, অনধিকৃত। **—ry,** *n.* The body of tenants ; as, the *tenantry* of a manor ; প্রজাবর্গ, রাইয়ত সকল। **Tenant-farmer**—যে ব্যক্তি অপরের কৃষিক্ষেত্রে চাষ করে। **Tenant-right** — জোতস্বত্ব। **A tenant at will**—কোর্ফা-প্রজা, ওঠবন্দী-প্রজা।

tĕn'-ănt-ȧ-ble (-bl), *adj.* Fit to be occupied by tenants ; প্রজাদ্বারা অধিকৃত হওয়ার যোগ্য, বাসযোগ্য।

tĕnch, *n.* A Europen fresh water fish of the carp family very tenacious of life ; ইয়ুরোপদেশীয় স্বাদুজলবাসী মৎস্য।

tĕnd, *v. i.* **1.** To move in a certain direction ; "Two gentlemen *tending* towards that sight"; কোনদিকে চলা। **2.** To have a tendency towards some object or objects; উন্মুখ হওয়া, প্রবণ হওয়া, ঝুঁকা।

tĕnd, *v. t.* & *i.* **1.** To take care of; to look after; তত্ত্বাবধান করা; দেখা শোনা, খবরদারী করা। **2.** To attend; পরিচর্য্যা করা। **3.** (*Naut.*) To watch so that an anchored ship may not foul during tide; নোঙ্গরবদ্ধ জাহাজের নোঙ্গর যাহাতে জোয়ারের কালে কাছির সহিত জড়াইয়া না যাইতে পারে সে বিষয়ে দৃষ্টি রাখা। ***Verb i.*** **1.** To wait (with *upon*); পরিচর্য্যা করা, খিদমদগারি করা (*colloq.*)। **2.** To heed; মনোযোগ দেওয়া, মন দেওয়া, অবধান করা।

tĕnd'-ĕn-cȳ, *n.* Bent; inclination; leaning; ঝোঁক; আসক্তি, প্রবৃত্তি; প্রবণতা।

tĕnd'-ĕr, *n.* **1.** One who attends or takes care of; পরিচর্য্যাকারী, তত্ত্বাবধায়ক। **2.** A small vessel employed to attend a larger one for supplying her with provisions and other stores; বৃহত্তর পোতের অনুগামী খাদ্যসম্ভারাদিপূর্ণ ক্ষুদ্র পোত। **3.** A carriage attached to a locomotive to supply water and fuel; বাষ্পীয়শকটের কলের সহিত সংযোজিত জল, কয়লা, প্রভৃতি পূর্ণ শকট।

tĕn'-dêr, *v. t., i.* & *n.* **1.** To offer; to present; as, to *tender* one a gift; প্রদান করা; উপস্থাপন করা। **2.** To offer in payment or satisfaction of a debt or liability; ঋণ পরিশোধের জন্য অর্পণ করা। ***Verb i.*** To make a tender or offer to do certain work or supply certain goods for a specified sum or price; কোন নির্দ্দিষ্ট কার্য্য নির্দ্দিষ্ট টাকায় সম্পাদনে বা নির্দ্দিষ্ট পরিমাণ মাল নির্দ্দিষ্ট মূল্যে সরবরাহ করার জন্য প্রস্তাব করা। ***Noun.*** **1.** Offer; প্রস্তাব। **2.** An offer, in writing to do some work or to supply some articles; কোন কার্য্য করার জন্য বা কোন জিনিষ সরবরাহের জন্য লিখিত প্রস্তাব। **3.** An offer of money or other thing in satisfaction of a debt or liability; ঋণপরিশোধের জন্য অর্থ বা অন্য কোন বস্তু। **Legal tender**—See LEGAL. **Plea of tender**—(আইন) বিবাদী সর্ব্বদাই ঋণপরিশোধে প্রস্তুত ছিল এবং বর্ত্তমানে দাবীর টাকা লইয়া আদালতে হাজির আছে—এইরূপ ওজর।

tĕn'-dêr, *adj.* **1.** Not firm, hard or tough; কোমল, নরম, সুকুমার, পেলব, মোলায়েম, মেদুর। **2.** (*Scot.*) Physically weak; delicate in health; (স্কট্‌লণ্ড) দুর্ব্বল, শক্তিহীন; ক্ষীণজীবী। **3.** Compassionate; pathetic; করুণাশীল, সানুকম্প; করুণ, বেদনশীল। **4.** Delicate; effeminate; not hardy or able to endure hardship; as, a *tender* animal; সুকুমার; স্ত্রীজনসুলভ; অপরিশ্রমসহিষ্ণু, পরিশ্রমপরাঙ্মুখ। **5.** Very susceptible to any impression, emotion, or the like, esp. to pain; as, *tender* nerve; ভাবপ্রবণ, আবেগপ্রবণ, বেদনাপ্রবণ। **6.** Immature; as, *tender* crop; কাঁচা, তরুণ। **7.** Gentle; নম্র, শান্ত। **8.** Loving; affectionate; as, a *tender* letter; প্রেমপূর্ণ; স্নেহপূর্ণ। **9.** (Of colour) Soft; as, *tender* violet (বর্ণসম্বন্ধে) কোমল, মেদুর। **10.** Careful; "Very *tender* in censuring and condemning other people"; wary; requiring careful handling; as, *tender* subject; সতর্ক; সাবধান, অবহিত; অতি সাবধানে ব্যবহার্য্য। **11.** (*Obs.*) Dear; (অপ্রঃ) মূল্যবান। **—ly,** *adv.* **—ness,** *n.* **Tender-eyed**—কোমলনেত্র। **Tenderfoot** — নূতন লোক, অনভিজ্ঞ লোক। **Tender-hearted** — কোমলচিত্ত, কোমলমতি, সুকুমারমতি। **Tender-loin**—গো বা শূকরের কটির কোমল অংশ।

tĕn'-dŏn, *n.* A hard insensible cord or bundle of fibres, by which a motion is communicated from a muscle to a bone; পেশীর প্রান্তসংলগ্ন রজ্জুবৎ কঠিন শিরা বা স্নায়ুতন্তুগুচ্ছ, অস্থিমাংসসংযোজক-শিরা, কণ্ডরা (সুশ্রুঃ), মহাশিরা (ঐ) স্নায়ুরজ্জু (সাঃ পঃ), শিরা (ঐ)। **Achilles tendon**—(*L. tendo Achillis*) গুল্‌ফ এবং পিণ্ডিকা সংযোজক কণ্ডরা, পিণ্ডলীশিরা (সাঃ পঃ)। [Achilles এর দেহের এই স্থান মাত্র অস্ত্রদ্বারা ভেদ্য ছিল।]

tĕn'-drăc, *n.* A small insectivorous mammal from Madagascar; মাদাগাস্‌কার দ্বীপের একপ্রকার ক্ষুদ্রকায় স্তন্যপায়ী কীটাদ জন্তু।

tĕn'-dril, *n.* A slender twining growth, by which a plant attaches itself to something for support; লতাতন্তু (সাঃ পঃ), লতাপ্রতান, শুঁয়া, আঁকড়ী, আকর্ষণী। **—drilled,** *p. p.*

tĕn'-ĕ-brae (-brē), *n.* (*R. C. Ch.*) Matins and lauds for Thursday, Friday, and Saturday in the Holy Week in Roman Catholic Church; (রোমানক্যাথলিক ধর্ম্মসংঘ) ইষ্টার রবিবারের পূর্ব্ববর্ত্তী সপ্তাহের বৃহস্পতি, শুক্র, এবং শনিবারের প্রথম ঘণ্টা এবং প্রাভাতিক উপাসনা।

tĕn-ĕ-brif'-ic, *adj.* Making darkness; "These are its *tenebrific* constellation from which it doth ray out darkness over the earth" তমিস্রজনক, তিমিরোৎপাদী।

tĕn'-ĕ-brous (-brŭs), *adj.* **1.** (*Archaic*) Dark; "The *tenebrous* boughs of the cypress"; (অপ্রঃ) অন্ধকার, তিমিরাচ্ছন্ন, তিমিরাবগুণ্ঠিত (Rhet.), তমসাচ্ছন্ন।

tĕn'-ĕ-mĕnt, *n.* **1.** Any species of permanent property that may be held, as land, houses, etc.; ভদ্রাসন, অট্টালিকা প্রভৃতি, জোত। **2.** A dwelling house; বসতবাটী, ভদ্রাসন। **3.** Apartments or apartment held by the family; যে কক্ষ বা কক্ষশ্রেণীতে কোন পরিবার বাস করে। **—men'-tal, —men'-tary,** *adjs.* **Tenement house**—যে

কক্ষে বহু ভাড়াটিয়া পরিবার একত্রে বসবাস করে।

tĕ-nĕs′-mŭs, *n.* A continual inclination to void the contents of one's bowels accompanied by straining without any discharge ; শূল।

tĕn′-ĕt, *n.* Any opinion, principle, dogma, or doctrine of a person ; মত, সিদ্ধান্ত (সাংখ্যঃ), মূলসূত্র (হিঃ কোঃ), মূলতত্ত্ব।

tĕn′-ner (-êr), *n.* (*Colloq.*) A ten-pound note ; (চলিত ভাষায়) দশ পাউণ্ডের নোট।

tĕn′-nis (-ĭs), *n.* A play in which a ball is kept in motion by rackets ; আণ্টাল খেলা। **Tennis-arm, Tennis-elbow**—আণ্টাল খেলার দরুণ বাহু বা কনুইয়ে যে ব্যথা হয়। **Tennis-ball**—আণ্টাল খেলার কন্দুক। **Tennis-court**—আণ্টাল খেলার প্রাঙ্গণ।

tĕn′-ŏn, *n.* & *v. t.* The specially shaped end of a piece of wood or the like to be inserted into the corresponding cavity called the mortise in order to form a secure joint ; অন্য কাঠে জোড়া দেওয়ার জন্য কোন কাঠের বিশেষভাবে গঠিত প্রান্ত। ***Verb t.*** To cut in a tenon ; to join by tenon ; ঐরূপ ভাবে কাটা ; ঐরূপ ভাবে জোড়া দেওয়া। **Tenon-saw**—See under SAW.

tĕn′-ŏr, *n.* **1.** A prevailing course or direction ; প্রচলিত ধারা, প্রচলিত গতি, ধারাবাহ। **2.** General course or drift of thought or language ; চিন্তা বা ভাষার সাধারণ গতি। **3.** General sense ; spirit ; meaning ; purport ; সাধারণ অর্থ ; মর্ম্মার্থ, অন্তর্নিহিত অর্থ ; আশয় ; মর্ম্ম, তাৎপর্য্য (হিঃ কোঃ)। **4.** (*Mus.*) The highest and most common natural pitch of a man's voice in singing ; (সঙ্গীতশাস্ত্র) পুরুষের চড়া সুর। **5.** (*Mus.*) The person who sings the tenor or the instrument which plays it ; যে ব্যক্তি উক্তরূপ চড়া সুরে গান করে, যে যন্ত্রে ঐ সুরের অনুরূপ বাদ্য উৎপন্ন হয়। **Tenor and bass drum**—পাখোয়াজ।

ten-o-ri′-no (tăn-ö-rë-nö), *n.* (*Mus.*) A falsetto tenor voice or a singer with such a voice ; (সঙ্গীতশাস্ত্র) এক প্রকার ধ্বনি, ঐরূপ ধ্বনিতে যে গান গায়।

tĕ-nŏt′-ŏ-mȳ, *n.* (*Surg.*) The operation of cutting a tendon esp. the removal of the deviation of the joints, esp. in clubfoot ; কণ্ডরা ছেদন—বিশেষতঃ শ্লীপদ রোগ আরোগ্যকরণার্থ, সন্ধিসমূহের বিকৃতি দূরকরণ।

tense (tĕns), *n.* **1.** (*Gram.*) One of the forms which a verb takes in order to express the time of action or of that which is affirmed (ব্যাকরণ) কাল। **2.** A set of such forms for various persons ; ধাতুরূপ।

tense (tĕns), *adj.* **1.** Stretched until stiff or tight ; বিতত। **2.** Strained to bitterness ; as, the feeling was *tense* ; টানটান, কষা, অশিথিল, কড়া। **Tense′-ly**, *adv.* **Tense′-ness**, *n.* **Ten′-si-ty**, *n.*

tĕn′-sĭ-ble (-bl) *adj.* **1.** Of, or pertaining to, tension ; প্রসারণসম্বন্ধীয়, বিততিসম্বন্ধীয়। **2.** Capable of being drawn out or stretched ; প্রসারণীয়, প্রসার্য্য। **–bil′-i-ty**, *n.* **–sil′-i-ty**, *n.*

tĕn′-sīle, *adj.* **1.** Tensible ; প্রসারণীয়। **2.** Pertaining ; to tension ; প্রসারণসম্বন্ধীয়।

tĕn′-sion, *n.* **1.** The act of stretching or straining ; প্রসারণ। **2.** The state of being strained or stretched to stiffness ; প্রসার্য্যতা, বিততি, টান, তনাব, আততি, আকৃষ্টতা (হিঃ কোঃ), বিস্তারভাব। **3.** Mental strain ; strong excitement of feeling ; প্রবল মানসিক পরিচালনা ; গুরুতর উত্তেজনা, প্রবল মানসিক উত্তেজনা। **4.** Strained feeling ; মন কষাকষি, টানভাব। **5.** Expansive force of gas or vapour ; গ্যাস বা বাষ্পের প্রসারণশক্তি। **6.** (*Mech.*) The strain or force by which a bar, rod or string is pulled when forming part of a system in equilibrium or motion ; (যন্ত্রবিজ্ঞান) কোন যন্ত্রাদি সমূহের অন্তর্ভুক্ত দণ্ড বা রজ্জু গতিশীল বা সামঞ্জস্যের অবস্থায় যে বল বা টান দ্বারা আকৃষ্ট হয়, প্রসারণবল। **–al**, *adj.* **Tension-bridge**—একপ্রকার সেতু—যাহাতে বিভিন্ন অংশের মধ্যে প্রসারণবলের চাপ থাকে, প্রসারণসেতু।

tĕn′-sŏn, tĕn′-zŏn, *ns.* **1.** A contest in verse between rival troubadours ; টুবাডুর কবিগণের মধ্যে কবিতাযুদ্ধ। **2.** The subdivision of a chanson composed by one of the contestants or competitors ; প্রতিদ্বন্দ্বিগণের মধ্যে কোন একজনের রচিত গীতাংশ।

tĕn′-ŏr, *n.* (*Anat.*) A muscle that extends or tightens a part to which it is fixed ; (শারীরসংস্থানবিদ্যা) যে পেশী দ্বারা শরীরের কোন অংশ বিতত বা প্রসারিত হয়, প্রসারকপেশী।

tĕnt, *n.*, *v. t.* & *i.* **1.** A portable shelter consisting of some flexible covering ; তাঁবু, বস্ত্রগৃহ, পটমণ্ডপ, পটবেশ্ম, পটশালা (হর্ষঃ), পটোটজ, দুষ্য (শিশুঃ), উপকার্য্যা (শুক্রঃ বিনয়)। **2.** (*Surg.*) A roll or lint etc. to dilate a sore ; (অস্ত্রোপচার-বিদ্যা) নালী ঘা বা শরীরের স্বাভাবিক দ্বারাদি বিস্ফারণের জন্য নেকড়া বা লিণ্টে প্রস্তুত মোচাকার পলিতা। **3.** (*Photog.*) A portable dark-room for outdoor use ; (আলোকচিত্র) বাহিরে ব্যবহারের জন্য একপ্রকার বহনযোগ্য ক্ষুদ্র কক্ষ। ***Verb t.*** **1.** To cover with tents ; বস্ত্রগৃহদ্বারা আচ্ছাদিত করা। **2.** To keep open with a tent ; মোচাকার পলিতাদ্বারা ক্ষতাদি বিস্ফারিত করা। ***Verb i.*** To encamp in a tent ; শিবিরে বাস করা। **Bell tent**—মধ্যদেশে একটী খোঁটাদ্বারা বিধৃত গোলাকার তাঁবু। **Dark-tent**—See TENT *n.* 3. **Tent-bed**—তাঁবুর আকার চন্দ্রাতপাচ্ছাদিত শয্যা। **Tent-fly**—তাঁবুর গাড়ী-বারান্দা। **Tent-pegs**—তাঁবুর খোঁটা। **Tent-pegging** — অশ্বারোহীদিগের ক্রীড়াবিশেষ—যাহাতে অশ্বারোহী পূর্ণবেগে

ধাবমান অশ্বপৃষ্ঠ হইতে বর্শাগ্রের সাহায্যে তাঁবুর প্রোথিত খোঁটা তুলিয়া নিতে চেষ্টা করে। **Tent-stitch**—সমান্তরাল এবং তির্য্যগ্‌গামী শিবিরাকৃতি সীবনপংক্তি সমূহ।

tĕnt, *n.* A kind of Spanish wine of a dark red colour ; স্পেন দেশীয় একপ্রকার গাঢ় লোহিতবর্ণের সুরা।

tĕn′-tă-cle (-kl), *n.* **1.** A filiform and movable process or organ of various animals, used for prehension or as a feeler ; পতঙ্গাদির শুঁয়া বা দাঁড়া; রেঁক। **2.** (*Bot.*) A sensitive hair or filament; (উদ্ভিদ্ বিদ্যা) শুঁয়া, শুঙ্গ। **—cled,** *p. p.* **—tac′-u-lar,** *adj.* **—tac′-u-late, —tac′-u-lat-ed,** *p. p.* **—tac′-u-li-form, —tac′-u-lif-er′-ous,** *adjs.*

tĕn′-tă-tive (-tīv), *adj.* & *n.* Done by way of trial or experiment ; experimental ; "The Baconian philosophy, which, though it allows a preliminary and *tentative* hypothesis, strongly insists upon the necessity of first collecting the facts, and then proceeding to the ideas based on trial" ; পরীক্ষার জন্য কৃত ; পরীক্ষাত্মক, পরীক্ষাসম্বন্ধীয়, পরীক্ষামূলক। ***Noun.*** **1.** An essay or trial ; পরীক্ষা, পরখ। **2.** Experimental proposal or theory ; পরীক্ষাত্মক প্রস্তাব বা মত। **—ly,** *adv.*

tĕn′-tĕr, *n.* & *v. t.* **1.** A machine for stretching cloth by means of hooks ; আঁকড়ার সাহায্যে বস্ত্র প্রসারণের জন্য যন্ত্রবিশেষ। **2.** Each of the hooks that holds the cloth ; যে সকল আঁকড়ার সাহায্যে বস্ত্র প্রসারিত হয় তাহার অন্যতম। ***Verb t.*** To hang or stretch on tenters ; ঐরূপ আঁকড়ার উপর কাপড় ছড়ান। **Tenter-hook**—Same as TENTER *n.* 2. **To be on tenter-hooks,** (or *Archaic*) **To be on the tenters**—To be in great suspense and mental pain ; কোন বিষয়ে উৎকণ্ঠাকুল হওয়া, উদ্বেগপূর্ণ হওয়া।

tĕn′-tĕr, *n.* A person in charge of something, esp. of machinery in a factory ; কোনকিছুর ভারপ্রাপ্ত ব্যক্তি, বিশেষতঃ কারখানার যন্ত্রের ভারপ্রাপ্ত ব্যক্তি, যন্ত্রাধ্যক্ষ।

tĕnth, *adj.* & *n.* The ordinal of ten ; দশম। ***Noun.*** The tenth part of anything ; দশমাংশ। **Tenth′-ly,** *adv.*

tĕn-ū-ī-rŏs′-trēs, *n.* In old classification an unnatural group of slender-billed passerine birds ; সূক্ষ্মচঞ্চু পক্ষিবর্গ। **—tral,** *adj.* Slender-billed ; সূক্ষ্মচঞ্চু।

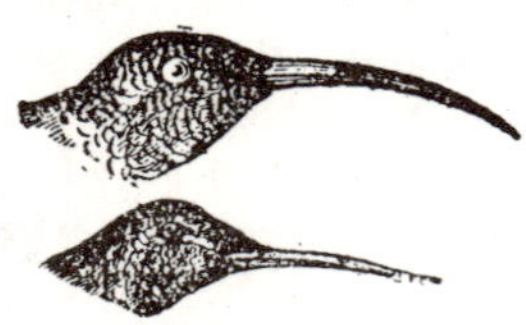

Tenuirostral beaks.
a, sun-bird ; b, humming-bird.

tĕn′-ū-ĭs, *n.* (*Greek gram.*) One of the three surd mutes ; গ্রীক-ব্যাকরণের *k, p, t* অক্ষরত্রয়ের অন্যতম।

tĕ-nū′-ĭ-tў, *n.* **1.** Slenderness ; তনুতা, তানব, কৃশতা, কার্শ্য। **2.** (Of air etc.) Thinness ; (বায়ু প্রভৃতি সম্পর্কে) বিরলতা। **3.** (Of style etc.) Plainness ; (রচনারীতি প্রভৃতি সম্পর্কে) সরলতা, আড়ম্বরশূন্যতা।

tĕn′-ū-ous (-ŭs), *adj.* **1.** (*Rare*) Thin ; small ; কৃশ ; ক্ষুদ্র। **2.** (*Rare*) subtle ; (কচিদ্ ব্যবহৃত) বিরল, সূক্ষ্ম।

tĕn′-ūre, *n.* **1.** A holding or manner of holding real estate ; জোত, জোতের প্রকার, প্রজাস্বত্বের প্রকার। **2.** The terms or conditions upon which anything is held or retained ; যে সর্ত্তে কোনকিছু ভোগ বা অধিকার করা হয়, জোতের সর্ত্ত। **3.** Period of holding or enjoying ; as, during the *tenure* of his office ; ভোগাধিকারের কাল, কার্য্যকাল।

tenuto, *adj.* (*Mus.*) A term applied to a note or series of notes having to be held or kept sounding the full time ; (সঙ্গীতশাস্ত্র) পূর্ণকাল বাদনীয় সুর সম্বন্ধে প্রযোজ্য শব্দ।

teocalli, *n.* A four sided pyramidical structure, built of earth erected for worship by the aborigines of Mexico, and surmounted by a temple ; প্রাচীন মেক্সিকোবাসিগণের একপ্রকার পিরামিডের আকার মৃণ্ময় মন্দির।

tĕp′-ĕ-fў, *v. t.* & *i.* To make tepid ; ঈষদুষ্ণ করা, মন্দোষ্ণ করা। ***Verb i.*** To become tepid ; ঈষদুষ্ণ হওয়া। **—fac′-tion,** *n.*

tĕph′-rīte, *n.* Kinds of volcanic rock ; বিভিন্ন জাতীয় আগ্নেয়গিরির প্রস্তর।

tĕp′-ĭd, *adj.* Moderately warm ; lukewarm ; ঈষদুষ্ণ ; অল্পোষ্ণ, কোষ্ণ, অনুষ্ণ, কুসুম কুসুম গরম (*colloq.*)। **—ly,** *n.*

tepidarium, *n.* (*Rom. Antiq.*) An apartment in Roman baths where tepid water was placed ; also the boiler in which the water was warmed for tepid bath ; রোমীয় স্নানাগারের যে কক্ষে উষ্ণ জল রক্ষিত হইত ; যে পাত্রে স্নানের জল উত্তপ্ত করা হইত।

ter, *adv.* (*L.*) Three times ; তিনবার।

tĕr′-ăph, *n.* (*pl. teraphim*) Among the Hebrews a household deity or image ; হিব্রুদিগের মধ্যে গৃহদেবতা বা দেবমূর্ত্তি।

tĕr′-ă-tō-, *pref.* Marvellous ; monstrous ; আশ্চর্য্যজনক ; বিকট।

tĕr-ă-tŏg′-ĕ-nў, *n.* (*Med.*) The formation of monsters ; (ভৈষজ্যশাস্ত্র) বিকটাকার মনুষ্য গঠন।

tĕr′-ăt-ō-līte, *n.* An impure variety of lithomarge ; একপ্রকার অশোধিত প্রস্তর।

tĕr-ă-tŏl′-ō-ġў, *n.* **1.** Dealing in the marvellous ; অদ্ভুত বিষয়ের আলোচনা, বিকটতত্ত্ব। **2.** (*Biol.*) Study of animal or vegetable monstrosities ; বিকট বা অসাধারণ জীবজন্তু এবং উদ্ভিদ্‌বিষয়ক বিজ্ঞান, উৎপ্রকৃতি জন্তুবিদ্যা (হিঃ কোঃ)।

terce (têrs), *n.* Same as TIERCE (which see).

tĕr′-ĉĕl, *n.* The male of the falcon ; পুং বাজপক্ষী।

têr-cĕn′-tē-nă-r̄y, *adj.* & *n.* Of three hundred years ; ত্রিশতবার্ষিক। ***Noun.*** Three hundredth anniversary ; ত্রিশতবার্ষিক উৎসব।

tĕr′-ĕ-bene (-bēn), *n.* A disinfectant derived from the oil of turpentine ; তার্পিণতৈল হইতে প্রাপ্ত একপ্রকার রোগসংক্রমণ-নিবারক বস্তু।

tĕr′-ē-binth, *n.* The turpentine-tree ; তার্পিণগাছ।

tĕr-ē-bin′-thine, *adj.* **1.** Of the turpentine-tree ; তার্পিণবৃক্ষসম্বন্ধীয়। **2.** Of turpentine ; তার্পিণসম্বন্ধীয়।

tĕr′-ē-bră, *n.* (*Pl.* -BRAE) An ovipositor of several insects adapted for boring ; ডিম্ব স্থাপনের জন্য কোন কোন পতঙ্গের ক্ষোদনোপযোগী নলাকার সূক্ষ্মাগ্র অঙ্গ। **–brate,** *adj.*

tē-rē′-dō, *n.* A worm like molluscous animal, the ship-worm

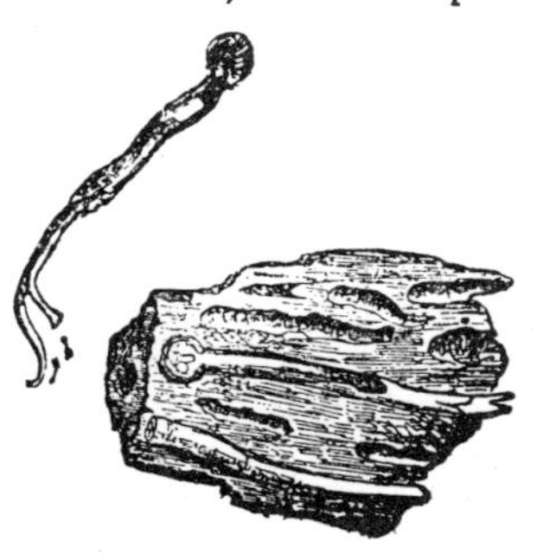

Teredo and wood perforated by it.

which perforates submerged woods ; জলনিমগ্ন কাষ্ঠে ছিদ্রকারী একপ্রকার কীটবৎ শম্বুকজাতীয় প্রাণী।

tĕr′-găl, *adj.* Of the back ; পৃষ্ঠের, পিঠের।

tēr-ḡĕm′-i-nāte, *adj.* (*Bot.*) Thrice double (applied to leaves) ; (উদ্ভিদ্ বিদ্যা—পত্রসম্বন্ধে) ত্রি-দ্বিগুণিত।

tĕr′-ḡi-vêr-sāte, *v. i.* **1.** To practise evasion ; পরিহার করা, ছল করা। **2.** To change sides or opinions ; পক্ষপরিবর্তন করা, মতপরিবর্তন করা। **–sa′-tion,** *n.* **1.** The act of tergiversating ; shift ; subterfuge ; evasion ; ফন্দি ; ছল ; এড়ানি ; পরিহার। **2.** The act of changing one's opinion ; the act of a turncoat ; স্বমতপরিবর্তন ; স্বপক্ষপরিবর্তন। **–sa′-tor,** *n.*

têrm, *n.* **1.** (*Rare*) Boundary ; সীমা। **2.** Limited period ; নির্দিষ্ট কাল, মুদ্দত। **3.** The time during which a law court holds its sittings for the trial of causes ; যে সময় ব্যাপিয়া মোকদ্দমা শুনানির জন্য আদালত খোলা থাকে। **4.** (In University and Colleges) The time during which instruction is given to the boys ; দীর্ঘবন্ধের মধ্যবর্তী যে কালে বিদ্যালয় প্রভৃতি খোলা থাকে। **5.** A day on which rent is paid ; খাজানা প্রদানের দিবস, পুণ্যাহ। **6.** A word or expression with a determinate meaning ; শব্দ, পদ, পরিভাষা। **7.** Charge ; price ; as, to quote one's *terms* ; দর ; মূল্য। **8.** (*Pl.*) Conditions or propositions offered for acceptance ; as, the *term* of a sale ; সর্ত, প্রস্তাব। **9.** (*Algeb.*) A number of a compound quantity connected with another or others by the signs of addition or subtraction ; (বীজগণিত) যোগ বা বিয়োগ চিহ্নদ্বয়ের মধ্যবর্তী কোন রাশির অংশ। **10.** (*Log.*) The subject or the predicate of a proposition ; one of the three component parts of a syllogism each one of which is used twice ; অবয়ব ; পদ। **11.** Mutual relationship ; relative position ; footing ; as, to be on good *terms* ; পরস্পরের সহিত সম্পর্ক ; পরস্পরের সম্পর্কে অবস্থান ; ভাব, সম্পর্ক। **12.** (*Pl.—Med.*) Menses ; ঋতু। **13.** Language employed ; "A fool who railed on Lady Fortune in good *terms*" ; mode of expression ; as, in the most flattering *terms* ; ব্যবহৃত ভাষা ; বলিবার ভঙ্গী। **First term**—আদি পদ। **Last term**—অন্ত্য পদ। **To bring one to terms**—To make him accept conditions ; সর্তগ্রহণে বাধ্য করা। **To come to terms**—To give way ; to conclude agreement ; ছাড়িয়া দেওয়া ; সর্ত করা।

têrm, *v. t.* To denominate ; অভিহিত করা, আখ্যা দেওয়া।

têr′-mă′-gănt, *n.* & *adj.* **1.** A brawling, turbulent woman ; উগ্রচণ্ডানারী, রণচণ্ডী, রায়বাঘিনী, (*colloq.*), জাহাঁবাজ মেয়েমানুষ, সরদারণী। ***Adj.*** Violent ; quarrelsome ; boisterous ; turbulent ; উগ্রস্বভাবা ; কোন্দলপ্রিয়া, কলহপ্রিয়া ; প্রচণ্ড ; দুর্দান্ত। **–gan-cy,** *n.* **–ly,** *adv.*

têrm′-ēr, –ŏr, *ns.* **1.** One who travels to attend a court term ; যে ব্যক্তি আদালত খোলার সময় হাজির থাকার জন্য উপস্থিত হইয়া থাকে। **2.** One who terms or names ; নামপ্রদাতা, নামদাতা। **3.** One who has estate for terms of years or life ; যে ব্যক্তি নির্দিষ্ট কয়েক বৎসর বা চিরকালের জন্য কোন সম্পত্তি গ্রহণ করে।

têr′-mēs, *n.* (*Pl.* TERMITES) A neuropterous insect ; a white ant ; একপ্রকার স্নায়ুপক্ষ কীট ; শ্বেত পিপীলিকা।

têr′-mi-nă-ble (-bl), *adj.* **1.** That may be terminated ; সমাপ্য, অবসানযোগ্য, অন্ত্য, সমাপনীয়। **2.** Coming to an end at a certain time ; নির্দিষ্ট সময়ান্তে অবসানশীল, অন্তবান।

têr′-mi-năl, *adj.* & *n.* **1.** Pertaining to the end or extremity ; terminating ; অন্তঃসম্বন্ধীয় ; অন্তঃস্বরূপ। **2.** Of, or pertaining to, the terminus of a railway ; লৌহবর্ত্মের অন্তঃসীমাসম্বন্ধীয়। **3.** (*Bot.*) Proceeding from the end ; অন্তদেশ হইতে জাত। **4.** (*Log.*) Constituted by, or relating to, a term ; (তর্কবিজ্ঞান)

পদাত্মক, পদসম্বন্ধীয়। 5. (*Bot.*) Forming an edge or extremity; প্রান্তস্বরূপ, অন্তঃস্বরূপ। ***Noun.*** 1. An extremity; অন্ত্যভাগ, প্রান্ত। 2. The clamping screw at each end of a voltaic battery; বিদ্যুদ্‌ঘটমালার উভয় প্রান্তস্থ সংযোজক পেঁচ। **–ly,** *adv.* **Terminal figure**—See TERMINUS *n.* 4. **Terminal velocity**—অন্তিম বেগ (হিঃ কোঃ)।

têr′-mi-nāte, *v. t.* & *i.* 1. To bound or limit; as, to *terminate* a surface by a line; সীমাবদ্ধ করা, সসীম করা। 2. To end; as to *terminate* a controversy; to complete; সমাপ্ত করা, শেষ করা; অবসান করা। ***Verb i.*** 1. To come to an end; অবসান প্রাপ্ত হওয়া, সাঙ্গ হওয়া, শেষ হওয়া। 2. To be limited; সীমাবদ্ধ হওয়া, সসীম হওয়া। **–na′-tion,** *n.* 1. The act of terminating; সমাপন। 2. Limit in space or extent; সসীমতা, সীমাবদ্ধতা, সমাপ্তি (হিঃ কোঃ), অন্ত (ঐ)। 3. End; conclusion; শেষ, উপসংহার। 4. (*Gram.*) The end or ending of a word; (ব্যাকরণ) শব্দের অন্ত্যভাগ বা পদান্ত। **–na′-tion-al,** *adj.* **–na-tive,** *adj.* **–na-to-ry,** *n.*

Terminalia arjuna—অর্জ্জুন বৃক্ষ [Syn. নদীসর্জ্জ, ইন্দ্রদ্রু, বীরতরু, ককুভ, শম্বর, পার্থ, ধনঞ্জয়, চিত্রযোধী, বৈরাতঙ্ক, গাণ্ডীবী, কিরীটী, শিবমল্লক, সব্যসাচী, কর্ণারী, করবীরক, ইন্দ্রসূনু, বীরদ্রু, কৃষ্ণসারথি, পৃথাজ, ফাল্গুন, ধন্বী।]

Terminalia belerica—বহেড়া [Syn. বহেড়ুক, বিভীতক, তুষ, অক্ষ, কর্ষফল, কলিদ্রুম, কলিবৃক্ষ, ভূতবাস, সংবর্ত্ত, সংবর্ত্তক, কল্পবৃক্ষ, বাসন্ত, বিষঘ্ন, হার্য্য, অনিলঘ্ন, তৈলফল, বিষঘ্ন, কাসঘ্ন।] [Arab. *beleyluj*; Pers. *bleyleh*; Tam. *tandi maram*; Teleg. *tondi, bahadha.*]

Terminalia catappa—বাদাম (বেঙ্গঃ), ইঙ্গুদী (ঐ)।

Terminalia chebula—জঙ্গি-হরীতকী (বেঙ্গঃ)। [Arab. *aleluj aswad*; Pers. *heliléh-i-kalan, helileh-i-siah*; Tel. *karaka, kadukai*; Chin. *ho-li-leh, ho-tsze*; Burm. *pang ah.*]

Terminalia citrina—হরীতকী [Syn. চেতনকী, প্রপথ্যা, জীবপ্রিয়া, জীবনিকা, ভিষগ্বরা, ভিষক্‌প্রিয়া, প্রাণদা, জীব্যা, দেবী, দিব্যা, সুধা, কায়স্থা, কন্যা, রসায়নফলা, বিজয়া। Also see CHEBULIC MYROBALAN (under MYROBALAN).] [বৈদ্যকশাস্ত্রে হরীতকীর গুণ ও শ্রেণীবিভাগ সম্বন্ধে এইরূপ লিখিত আছে:—হরীতক্যভয়া পথ্যা কায়স্থা পূতনামৃতা। হৈমবত্যব্যথাচাপি চেতকী শ্রেয়সী শিবা। বয়স্থা বিজয়া চাপি জীবন্তী রোহিণীতিচ ॥ বিজয়া রোহিণী চৈব পূতনা চামৃতাভয়া। জীবন্তী চেতকী চেতি পথ্যায়াঃ সপ্তজাতয়াঃ ॥ অলাবুবৃত্তা বিজয়া বৃত্তা সা রোহিণীস্মৃতা। পূতনাস্থিমতী সূক্ষ্মা কথিতা মাংসলাঽমৃতা ॥ পঞ্চরেখাঽভয়া প্রোক্তা জীবন্তী স্বর্ণবর্ণিনী। ত্রিরেখা চেতকী জ্ঞেয়া সপ্তানামিয়মাকৃতিঃ ॥ বিজয়া সর্ব্বরোগেষু রোহিণী ব্রণরোহিণী। প্রলেপে পূতনা যোজ্যা শোধনার্থেঽমৃতা হিতা ॥ অক্ষিরোগেঽভয়া শস্তা জীবন্তী সর্ব্বরোগহৃৎ। চূর্ণার্থং চেতকীশস্তা যথাযুক্তং প্রযোজয়েৎ ॥ চেতকীদ্বিবিধা প্রোক্তা শ্বেতা কৃষ্ণা চ বর্ণতঃ। ষড়ঙ্গুলায়তা শুক্লা কৃষ্ণা-চৈকাঙ্গুলায়তা ॥ ইতি ভাবপ্রকাশঃ।]

têr′-mi-nate, *adj.* 1. Capable of being coming to an end; সমাপ্য, সমাপনীয়, অবসানযোগ্য। 2. Limited; bounded; সীমাবদ্ধ; সসীম।

têr′-mi-nā-tor (-têr), *n.* 1. A person or thing that terminates; অবসানকারী। 2. (*Astron*). The dividing line between the illuminated and the unilluminated dark part of the moon; চন্দ্রের আলোকিত এবং অনালোকিত অংশদ্বয়ের মধ্যবর্ত্তী বিভাজক রেখা।

têr′-mi-nêr, *n.* Same as OYER (which see).

têr′-mi-nism, *n.* 1. The theological doctrine that there is a limit in the life of each man for repentance; ঈশ্বর প্রত্যেক ব্যক্তিকেই অনুতাপের জন্য নির্দ্দিষ্ট পরিমাণ সময় প্রদান করিয়া থাকেন—এইরূপ মতবাদ, সীমাবাদ। 2. Same as NOMINALISM. **–nist,** *n.*

têr-mi-nŏl′-ŏ-ġy̆, *n.* 1. The science or theory of technical terms; পরিভাষাতত্ত্ব, পরিভাষাবিজ্ঞান। 2. Terms used in science, art, etc.; বৈজ্ঞানিক পরিভাষা, সাঙ্কেতিকশব্দ (হিঃ কোঃ) সঙ্কেত, (ঐ)। **–no-log′-i-cal,** *adj.*

têr′-mi-nŭs, *n.* 1. (*Rare*) Goal; (কচিদ্‌ব্যবহৃত) চরমগম্যস্থল। 2. A station at the end of a main or branch railway; প্রধান বা শাখা লৌহবর্ত্ম যে স্থানে শেষ হইয়াছে—তথাকার বিরামস্থলী। 3. (*Rom. Antiq, Cap.*) A divinity of Rome, who was supposed to preside over boundaries; (রোমক প্রত্নতত্ত্ব) প্রাচীন রোমের সীমানির্দ্দেশক দেবতা। 4. A half statue or a bust springing from a pillar or pilaster (called also *Terminal figure*); স্তম্ভ হইতে মানবদেহের উপরার্দ্ধের মূর্ত্তি, স্তম্ভাগ্রস্থিত অর্দ্ধমূর্ত্তি। **Terminus ad quem, a quo**—(তর্ক প্রভৃতি) প্রারম্ভস্থল।

têr-mi-tā′-ri-ŭm, têr′-mi-tă-ry̆, *ns.* The residence of the white ants; শ্বেতপিপীলিকার নিবাসস্থলী।

têr′-mīte, *n.* White ant; শ্বেত পিপীলিকা, শাদা পিঁপড়া।

têrm′-ly̆, *adj.* & *adv.* Occurring every term; নির্দ্দিষ্ট সময়ান্তে সংঘটনশীল। ***Adv.*** Every term; প্রতি নির্দ্দিষ্ট সময়ের অন্তে।

têrm′-ŏr, *n.* Same as TERMER (which see).

têrn, tärn, *ns.* Kinds of sea-bird of the gull-family; বিভিন্নপ্রকার সাগরবলাকাজাতীয় পক্ষী।

têrn, *n.* & *adj.* 1. That which consists of three things or numbers together; ত্র্যাত্মক বস্তু, ত্রিসংখ্যাত্মক বস্তু। 2. A prize gained by drawing three favourable numbers in a lottery; such prize; হুণ্ডিখেলার

অনুকূল সংখ্যাত্রয় তোলার দরুণ পুরস্কার প্রাপ্তি ; উক্তরূপ পুরস্কার। ***Adj.*** Same as TERNATE.

têr′-nă-rŷ, *adj.* & *n.* **1.** Composed of three ; ত্র্যাত্মক, ত্রিক (হিঃ কোঃ), ত্রয় (ঐ), ত্রয়ো (ঐ), ত্রিতয় (ঐ), ত্রিযুত (ঐ)। **2.** (*Math.*) Having three variables ; (গণিত-শাস্ত্র) ত্রিচলবিশিষ্ট। **3.** (*Chem.*) Containing, or consisting of, three different parts, as elements, atoms, groups or radicals regarded as having different functions or relations in the molecule ; ত্রৈদেহিক (হিঃ কোঃ)। ***Noun.*** The number three ; a group of three ; তিন ; ত্রিসংখ্যক বস্তু, ত্রয়ী।

têr′-nāte, *adj.* **1.** Arranged in threes ; তিন তিনটী করিয়া বিন্যস্ত

1, Ternate leaf ; 2, biternate leaf ; 3, triternate leaf.

2. (*Bot.*) Trifoliate ; having three leaves in a whorl ; (উদ্ভিদ্-বিদ্যা) ত্রিপত্র, ত্রিপত্রিক ; এক পুষ্পবেষ্টনীতে ত্রিদলবিশিষ্ট।

terne (têrn), *n.* (Usu. *Tern-plate*), An inferior kind of tin-plate for roof and packing case ; গৃহের ছাদ বা প্যাকিং বাক্সের জন্য একপ্রকার টীনের পাত।

têrn′-ĕr-ŷ, *n,* A place where terns breed ; সাগরবলাকার পোষণস্থান।

Têrp-si-chō-rē′-ăn, *adj.* **1.** Of Terpsichore the Muse of dancing ; নৃত্যকলার অধিষ্ঠাত্রী Terpsichore নাম্নী বাগ্‌দেবী সম্বন্ধীয়। **2.** Pertaining to dancing ; নৃত্যসম্বন্ধীয়, নর্ত্তনসম্বন্ধীয়। **Terpsichorean art**—নৃত্যকলা।

tĕr′-rȧ, *n.* Earth ; পৃথিবী। **Terra alba**—একপ্রকার শ্বেতমৃত্তিকা। **Terra cariosa**—ধাতু এবং রত্নাদি পালিশ করার জন্য একপ্রকার মৃন্ময় পদার্থ। **Terra catechu**—1. Same as CATECHU. 2. Same as GAMBIER. **Terra-cotta**—মূর্ত্তি প্রভৃতি নির্ম্মাণে ব্যবহৃত কর্দ্দম, শাদা বালি, অগ্নিপ্রস্তর প্রভৃতির মিশ্রণে প্রস্তুত একপ্রকার মৃত্তিকা ; ঐরূপ মৃত্তিকায় প্রস্তুত শিল্পদ্রব্য ; বিশেষতঃ আমেরিকার সমাধিস্তম্ভসমূহে উক্ত মৃত্তিকানির্ম্মিত ক্ষুদ্র ক্ষুদ্র মূর্ত্তি। **Terrae filius**—কৃষক ; হীনবংশজ লোক। **Terra firma**—শুষ্কভূমি। **Terra incognita**—অজ্ঞাত দেশ। **Terra Japonica**—খদির। **Terra nera**—প্রাচীন চিত্রকরগণকর্ত্তৃক ব্যবহৃত একপ্রকার রঙ্গ। **Terra verde**—রঞ্জক পদার্থরূপে ব্যবহৃত একপ্রকার সবুজ মৃত্তিকা। [হরিৎ মৃত্তিকা দ্বিবিধ। ইহার একপ্রকার Verona নগরীর নিকটবর্ত্তী Mount Balodo নামক পর্ব্বতে এবং অন্যপ্রকার Cyprus দ্বীপে পাওয়া যায়।]

tĕr′-race (-ās), *n.* & *v. t.* **1.** A raised level space or platform of earth, supported on one or more sides of a wall or a bank of turf etc. ; চাতাল, পিঁড়া, বীথি। **2.** A balcony or open gallery ; অলিন্দ। **3.** The flat roof of a house ; অট্টালিকাদির সমতল ছাদ। **4.** A street having houses on one side and sloping ground on the other ; একপার্শ্ব ঢালু এবং অপর পার্শ্বে ভবনশ্রেণীসমন্বিত রাজপথ। **5.** A row of houses ; a street ; ভবনশ্রেণী ; রাজপথ। **6.** (*Geol.*) A raised level beach or level place ; উচ্চ সৈকত বা সমতলভূমি। ***Verb t.*** To form into a terrace ; to furnish with a terrace ; চাতালে পরিণত করা ; চাতালবিশিষ্ট করা।

tĕr′-race, (-ās), **—ras** (-ăs), *ns.* **1.** A defective place in marble block filled up with composition ; মর্ম্মরফলকে একপ্রকার দোষ। **2.** Same as TRASS (whish see).

tĕr-rain′, (-ān), *n.* Region ; tract of land ; অঞ্চল ; ভূখণ্ড।

tĕr-rȧ-mȧ′-rȧ, *n.* **1.** Any earthy deposit containing bones etc. capable of being used as a fertilizer ; সারস্বরূপ ব্যবহৃত অস্থি প্রভৃতি বহুল মৃত্তিকা। **2.** (*Anthrop.*) The name given to some prehistoric settlements in Northern and central Italy ; উত্তর এবং মধ্য ইতালীর প্রাগৈতিহাসিক যুগের উপনিবেশসমূহ।

tĕr-ra′-ne-ous (-ā-nē-ŭs), *adj.* (*Bot.*) Growing on land ; ভূমধ্যেজাত, ভূমিজ।

tĕr′-ra-pin (-ă-), *n.* The popular name of many species of fresh-water tortoises ; একজাতীয় স্বাদুজলবাসী কচ্ছপ।

tĕr-ra′-que-ous (-ā-kwē-ŭs), *adj.* Consisting of land and water, as the globe or earth ; (পৃথিবী সম্বন্ধে) জলস্থলাত্মক, জলস্থলসমন্বিত, জলস্থলময়।

tĕr-rene′ (-rēn), *adj.* **1.** Of earth ; earthy ; মৃৎসম্বন্ধীয় ; মৃত্তিকাবহুল। **2.** Terrestrial ; পার্থিব, ভৌম (হিঃ কোঃ), লৌকিক (ঐ)।

tĕr-rĕs′-tri-ăl, *adj.* & *n.* **1.** Pertaining to the earth ; existing on the surface of earth ; earthly ; as, *terrestrial* bodies ; পৃথিবীসম্বন্ধীয় ; পৃথিবীতে বিদ্যমান ; পার্থিব। **2.** Pertaining to the world ; mundane ; ইহজগৎসম্বন্ধীয় ; সাংসারিক। **3.** (*Zool.*) Living on the ground ; (জন্তুবিদ্যা) স্থলচর, ভূচর। ***Noun.*** An inhabitant of the earth ; পৃথিবীবাসী। **—ly,** *adv.*

tĕr′-ret, (-ĕt), **—rit** (-ĭt), *ns.* One of the two round loops or rings on a pad-tree through which the driving reins pass ; লাগামের চামড়ার ফালি জীনের যে আংটার ভিতর দিয়া চালিত করা হয়।

tĕr′-ri-ble (-bl), *adj.* **1.** Fitted to excite terror or awe ; dreadful ; ভয়ঙ্কর, বিভীষণ, উগ্রদর্শন ; করাল, রুদ্র, বিভীষিকাময়, ঘোর, দারুণ। **2.** (*Colloq.*) Excessive ; as, *terrible* heat

বেজায়, ভয়ঙ্কর, ভয়ানক। **—ness,** *n.* **—bly,** *adv.*

tĕr-ric′-ō-lous (-lŭs), *adj.* Inhabiting earth; living on the soil; পৃথিবীবাসী; ভূবাসী।

tĕr′ri-ĕr (-ĭ-), *n.* **1.** A small variety of dog that creeps into holes in the earth, after animals that burrow; একপ্রকার ক্ষুদ্রকায় খননকারী কুকুর। **2.** (*Colloq.*) A member of territorial army; স্বদেশরক্ষী সৈন্যদলভুক্ত সৈনিক। **Black-and-tan terrier, Fox-terrier, Bull-terrier**—ঐজাতীয় খর্ব্বরোমা কুকুর। **Irish terrier, Scotch terrier, Skye terrier, Yorkshire terrier**—ঐজাতীয় রূক্ষরোমা কুকুর। **Maltese terrier, Toy terrier**—ঐজাতীয় ক্ষুদ্রকায় ক্রীড়াকুকুর।

tĕr′-ri-ĕr (-ĭ-), *n.* A register or roll of landed estates; ভূসম্পত্তির তালিকা, তৌজি।

tĕr-rif′-ic, *adj.* Causing terror; terrible; ভয়জনক, ভয়াবহ, ভয়ঙ্কর; করাল, ভীম, ভৈরব, রুদ্রদর্শন, ঘোর, ভীষণ। **—al-ly,** *adv.*

tĕr′-ri-fȳ, *v. t.* To cause terror in; to frighten; ভয়সঞ্চার করা; ভয়গ্রস্ত করা, সন্ত্রস্ত করা, ভয়ার্ত্ত করা, ভয়বিপ্লুত করা।

tĕr-rig′-ĕ-nous (-nŭs), *adj.* Earthborn; মৃত্তিকাজাত, মৃত্তিকা হইতে উৎপন্ন।

terrine, *n.* An earthen vessel containing some delicacy; কোনপ্রকার রসনাতৃপ্তিকর খাদ্যপূর্ণ মৃণ্ময় পাত্র।

tĕr-ri-tō′-ri-ăl, *adj.* & *n.* **1.** Of, or pertaining to, territory or land; ভূমি বা রাজ্যসংক্রান্ত। **2.** Limited to a district; as, the right was strictly *territorial*; কোন জেলাতে সীমাবদ্ধ। **3.** Consisting of territory; রাজ্যাত্মক। **4.** Possessed of territory; as, a *territorial* magnate; বিস্তৃত ভূসম্পত্তির অধিকারী। ***Noun.*** A member of the territorial army; স্বদেশরক্ষী সৈন্যদলভুক্ত সৈনিক। **—ism,** *n.* Same as TERRITORIAL SYSTEM. **Territorial army**—প্রাচীন স্বেচ্ছাসেবক সৈন্য, নাগরিক সৈন্যদল, প্রভৃতির স্থলে সংগৃহীত স্বদেশরক্ষী সৈন্য। **Territorial jurisdiction**—(আন্তর্জাতিক আইন) কোন দেশের সীমার মধ্যে এবং ঐ দেশের সন্নিহিত সাগরাংশে এবং উহাদের অন্তবর্ত্তী জনগণ এবং সম্পত্তির উপর যে অধিকার রহিয়াছে। **Territorial system**—খৃষ্টীয় ধর্ম্মসংঘের মত বিশেষ—যদ্দ্বারা কোন জেলার প্রজাসমূহ নৃপতির যাজকীয় কর্ত্তৃত্বের অধীনতা এবং এমন কি তদীয় ধর্ম্মগ্রহণে বাধ্য থাকে।

tĕr-ri-tō′-ri-ăl-ize, *v. t.* **1.** To enlarge by extension of territory; বিস্তৃত ভূখণ্ড সংযোগপূর্ব্বক পরিবর্দ্ধিত করা। **2.** To reduce to the state of a territory; বিস্তৃত রাজ্যে বা ভূখণ্ডে পরিণত করা।

tĕr′-ri-tō-rȳ, *n.* **1.** The extent or compass of lands within the bounds or belonging to the jurisdiction of any State, city or body; দেশ, মুলুক, রাজ্য। **2.** Any large tract of land; a region; a country; বৃহৎ ভূভাগ, বিস্তৃত ভূখণ্ড; অঞ্চল; দেশ। **3.** (*U. S., Cap.*) A portion of land not yet included within any State and not yet admitted as a State in the union, but organized with a separate legislature under a territorial governor and other officers appointed by the President and the Senate; যে ভূখণ্ড অদ্যাপি কোন রাষ্ট্রের অন্তর্ভুক্ত হয় নাই এবং যাহা রাষ্ট্রপতি ও শাসন পরিষৎ কর্ত্তৃক নিযুক্ত শাসনকর্ত্তা ও অপরাপর কর্ম্মচারিকর্ত্তৃক শাসিত হইয়া থাকে।

tĕr′-rŏr, *n.* **1.** Extreme fear, alarm or dread; "Amazed and *terror* seiz'd the rebel host"; মহাভয়, বিভীষিকা, আতঙ্ক, ত্রাস। **2.** A person or thing that causes dread or extreme fear; "Her name shall be the *terror* of the earth"; মহাভয়ঙ্কর ব্যক্তি, মহাভীতিজনক বস্তু। **—ism,** *n.* A state of being terrified or a state impressing terror; a government or system of ruling by terror; "The red *terror* of the French Jacobins is insignificant by the side of the white *terror* of Ferdinand VII."; মহাভীতিজনক অবস্থা, মহাভয়গ্রস্তাবস্থা; ভয়প্রদর্শনে রাজ্যশাসন বা রাজ্যশাসন পদ্ধতি। **Terror-stricken**—ভয়ার্ত্ত, ভয়ত্রস্ত, ভয়োপহত, ভীতিবিহ্বল, ভয়গ্রস্ত। **King of terrors**—যমরাজ। **Reign of Terror, The Terror, The Red terror**—প্রথম ফরাসী বিপ্লবের (১৭৯৩-৯৪) ভয়ঙ্কর কাল—যখন নৃপতি চতুর্দ্দশ লুই, তদীয় পত্নী এবং সহস্র সহস্র ব্যক্তির শিরশ্ছেদ করা হয়।

tĕr′-rŏr-ist, *n.* **1.** One who terrorizes; one who rules by terrorism; ভীতিপ্রদর্শনকারী; যে ব্যক্তি ভয়প্রদর্শনে শাসন করে। **2.** An agent or partisan of the Revolutionary tribunal during the Reign of Terror in France; ফরাসী বিপ্লবকালে প্রতিষ্ঠিত বিচারালয়ের বিচারকর্ত্তা বা ঐ বিচারালয়ের পক্ষপাতী ব্যক্তি। **3.** A Russian nihilist; an anarchist; "Several notables believed to be more or less implicated in the actions of the *Terrorists*"; রুশিয়ার বিপ্লববাদী; বিপ্লববাদী। **4.** An alarmist; a scare-monger; "The *terrorists* of this country are extremely alarmed at the power of Bonaparte"; ত্রাসোৎপাদক; যে ব্যক্তি লোকের আতঙ্ক উৎপাদন করিয়া বেড়ায়।

tĕr′-rŏr-ize, —ise, *v. t.* To impress with terror; to force by intimidation to a certain course; 'Humiliated by the extremity of foreign despotism and *terrorized* by ecclesiastical authority"; ভয়ার্ত্ত করা; ভয় প্রদর্শনে কোন কার্য্য করিতে বাধ্য করা। **—i-za′-tion,** *n.*

tĕr′-rȳ, *n.* A textile fabric of wool or silk, woven like velvet, but with loops uncut ; একপ্রকার বস্ত্র।

terse (têrs), *adj.* Free from superfluity ; neatly or elegantly concise ; as, a *terse* style ; বাহুল্যদোষ বর্জ্জিত ; স্বল্পাক্ষরগ্রথিত, স্বল্পাক্ষর। **Terse′-ly,** *adv.* **Terse′-ness,** *n.*

têr′-ti-ăn (-shĭ-), *adj.* & *n.* Ocurring or recurring every third day ; ত্র্যহিক, তৃতীয়ক। ***Noun.*** A fever whose paroxysm returns every third day ; তৃতীয়ক জ্বর, তৃতীয় জ্বর (সাঃ পঃ), ত্রিদিবস (অগ্নিপুরাণ)। **Tertian ague**—তৃতীয়ক জ্বর (সাঃ পঃ)।

têr′-ti-ă-rȳ (-shĭ-), *adj.* & *n.* **1.** Of the third order or formation; তৃতীয়ক, তৃতীয় (হিঃ কোঃ)। **2.** (*Chem.*) Subject to the substitution of three atoms or radicals ; ত্রিপরমাণু বা মূলকত্রয় দ্বারা পরিবর্ত্তনীয়। ***Noun.*** **1.** The third geological period ; তৃতীয়ক যুগ, বরাহযুগ (অভিঃ)। **2.** An associate of a monkish fraternity under vow to observe the rules of the order but not leading a monastic life ; গৃহী-যাজকসম্প্রদায়-বিশেষ। **—al,** *adj.* & *n.* **Tertiary colours**—দুই গৌণবর্ণের মিশ্রণে প্রস্তুত রঙ্গ। **Tertiary syphilis**—উপদংশ রোগের তৃতীয় অবস্থা।

têr′-ti-āte (-shĭ-), *v. t.* **1.** To do for the third time ; তৃতীয়বার করা। **2.** To examine the thickness, and ascertain the strength of the metal of gun ; কামানের ধাতুর ঘনত্ব এবং শক্তি পরীক্ষা করা।

tertium quid, *n.* (*L.*), A third something, between two things, esp. between mind and matter ; তৃতীয় বস্তু (বিশেষতঃ জড় এবং চিৎ কিম্বা কোন পরস্পরবিরুদ্ধধর্ম্মাবলম্বী বস্তুদ্বয়ের মধ্যবর্ত্তী বস্তু)।

têr′-ti-ŭs (-shĭ-), *adj.* Third of the name ; একনামধারী তৃতীয় ব্যক্তি

terza rima, *n.* (*It.*) A form of Italian triplet in iambic decasyllables, in which the middle line of the first triplet rhymes with the first and third lines of the next triplet ; (ইতালীয় ভাষায়) ত্রিপংক্ত্যাত্মক কবিতাবিশেষ — যাহাতে প্রথম ত্রিপংক্তির মধ্যচরণের সহিত পরবর্ত্তী ত্রিপংক্তির প্রথম এবং দ্বিতীয় পংক্তির মিল থাকে।

terzetto, *n.* (*It.*) (*Mus.*) Vocal trio ; (সঙ্গীতশাস্ত্র) গায়কত্রয়ের উপযোগী সঙ্গীত।

tĕs′-sĕl-lāte, *v. t.* To form into squares, oblongs, etc. or checkers ; to lay with checkered work ; as, *tessellated* floor ; চতুষ্কোণ প্রভৃতি দ্বারা গঠিত করা ; ছক কাটা।

tĕs′-sĕl-lāt-ĕd, *adj.* **1.** Formed of little squares, oblongs, or of pieces approximating squares, as mosaic work ; নানাবর্ণের চতুষ্ক, আয়তক্ষেত্র বা সমচতুষ্কপ্রায় ক্ষেত্রাদি দ্বারা রচিত। **2.** (*Bot.* & *Zool.*) Regularly checkered ; (উদ্ভিদ্‌বিদ্যা ও জন্তুবিদ্যা) ছক-কাটা। **—lar,** *adj.* **—la′-tion,** *n.*

tĕs′-sĕr-ă, *n.* (*Pl.*-AE), **1.** A small cubical piece of marble etc. used for tessellated work ; ছককাটা গৃহতল প্রভৃতির কার্য্যে ব্যবহৃত ক্ষুদ্র মর্ম্মরফলক প্রভৃতি। **2.** (*Rom. Antiq.*) A small piece of wood, bone or metal used as a ticket of admission to the theatres, or as a token for other purposes in ancient Rome ; (রোমক প্রত্নতত্ত্ব) প্রাচীন রোমে নিদর্শন বা রঙ্গালয়ের টিকিটস্বরূপ ব্যবহৃত অস্থি, কাষ্ঠ বা ধাতুর ক্ষুদ্র খণ্ড। **—al,** *adj.*

tĕs-si-tū′-ră, *n.* **1.** (*Mus.*) The part or the total compass of a melody or voice-part in which most of its tones lie ; (সঙ্গীতশাস্ত্র) কোন তানের অংশ বা সমগ্র প্রসার—যাহার মধ্যে উহার অধিকাংশ ধ্বনিই অবস্থিত থাকে।

tĕst, *n.* & *v. t.* **1.** A vessel used in refining gold and silver ; স্বর্ণ বা রৌপ্য শোধন এবং পরীক্ষণের জন্য ব্যবহৃত পাত্র বিশেষ। **2.** Any critical trial or examination ; as, to put a man to *test* ; পরীক্ষা, অগ্নিপরীক্ষা। **3.** Means of trial ; "The issue of life and death is put upon our conduct and behaviour ; that is, made *test* we are to be tried by" ; পরীক্ষার উপায়। **4.** A criterion ; a standard ; a means of discrimination ; নিকষ ; গুণাগুণ নির্ণয়ের আদর্শ ; সূক্ষ্মভেদ নিরূপণের উপায়। **5.** (*Chem.*) A substance employed to detect the presence of any ingredient in a compound ; কোন যৌগিক পদার্থে কোনরূপ উপাদানের স্থিতি নির্ণয়ার্থ ব্যবহৃত বস্তু। ***Verb t.*** **1.** To put to the test ; as, to *test* the soundness of a principle ; পরীক্ষাধীন করা, পরখ করা, পরতাল করা। **2.** To tax ; as, to *test* one's patience ; প্রপীড়িত করা। **3.** To refine metal ; ধাতু শোধন করা। **4.** (*Chem.*) To examine or try, as by use of some reagent ; কোন দ্রব্যের সাহায্যে কোন যৌগিক পদার্থে কোনরূপ উপাদান আছে কিনা স্থির করা। **Test′-a-ble,** *adj.* Capable of being tested ; পরীক্ষণীয়, পরীক্ষাযোগ্য। **Test Act**—(১) ১৬৭৩ খৃঃ অব্দে বিধিবদ্ধ আইন বিশেষ—যদ্দ্বারা লর্ডগণ ব্যতীত প্রত্যেক পদপ্রার্থীকে রাজ্ঞী এলিজেবেথের অধীনতা স্বীকার এবং ঐহিক ব্যাপারে পোপের কর্ত্তৃত্ব অস্বীকার করিতে হইত। (২) ১৬৭২ খৃঃ অব্দে বিধিবদ্ধ আইন বিশেষ—যদ্দ্বারা প্রত্যেক বিশিষ্ট পদে অধিষ্ঠিত ব্যক্তিকে শপথ গ্রহণ করিতে হইত [এই আইন ১৮২৬ খৃষ্টাব্দে রদ হয়।] **Test-glass** — রাসায়নিক দ্রাবক রক্ষণার্থ একপ্রকার মোচাকার বা নলাকার কাচপাত্র। **Test-mixer**—একপ্রকার ঢাকনিওয়ালা দীর্ঘ কাচপাত্র। **Test-paper** — তরল পদার্থের অম্লত্ব বা ক্ষারত্ব পরীক্ষার জন্য নীল বা পীতবর্ণ কাগজ। **Test-tube** — রাসায়নিক পরীক্ষায় ব্যবহৃত কাচনল বিশেষ, পরীক্ষণ-নল (সাঃ পঃ), পরীক্ষণনলিকা

(হিঃ কোঃ)। **To put to test**—To subject to examination · পরীক্ষাধীন করা, পরখ করা।

tĕst, *n* A shell or hard covering of certain animals ; কোন কোন জন্তুর খোলস বা কঠিন দেহাবরণ।

tĕs'-tă, *n.* **1.** The shelly covering of a testaceous animal ; খোল, কঠিনত্বক। **2.** The integument of a seed ; বীজত্বক্।

tĕst'-ă-ble (-bl), *adj.* **1.** Capable of being given by a will ; চরমপত্র দ্বারা প্রদেয়। **2.** Legally qualified to bear witness ; সাক্ষ্যদানের অধিকারী।

tĕs-tā'-ceous (-shŭs), *adj.* Pertaining to shells or shell-fish ; কপর্দ্দকসম্বন্ধীয়, চিংড়ী প্রভৃতি মৎস্য সম্পর্কীয়। **—cean, -ce-ol'-o-gy,** *ns.*

tĕs'-tă-cy̆, *n.* State of being a testate ; চরমপত্রসম্পাদনকারিত্ব।

tĕs'-tă-mĕnt, *n.* **1.** Will ; ইচ্ছাপত্র, চরমপত্র, মৃত্যুলেখ (কেঃডিঃ), মৃত্যুপত্র (ঐ)। **2.** The name of either of the two general divisions of the scriptures called respectively, the Old Testament and the New Testament ; বাইবেল গ্রন্থদ্বয়ের অন্যতর। **—men'-ta-ry,** *adj.* **New Testament** — নবসংহিতা, নবনিয়ম। **Old Testament** — প্রাচীন নিয়ম, প্রাচীনসংহিতা।

tĕs-tā'-mŭr, *n.* A certificate from a university testing that the student has passed examination ; বিশ্ববিদ্যালয়ের পরীক্ষা উত্তীর্ণ হওয়ার নিদর্শনপত্র।

tĕs'-tate, *adj.* & *n.* Having made and left a will ; কৃতচরমপত্র। ***Noun.*** One who has died leaving a will ; ইচ্ছাপত্র সম্পাদনান্তে পরলোকগত ব্যক্তি, কৃতচরমপত্র ব্যক্তি।

tĕs-tā'-tŏr, *n.* **1.** On who lives a will or testament ; ইচ্ছাপত্র-সম্পাদক, চরমপত্রসম্পাদক।

tĕst'-ĕr, *n.* **1.** A canopy over a bed , শয্যার উপরে টাঙ্গানো চাঁদোয়া। **2.** A flat canopy, as over a pulpit, tomb etc. ; বেদী, সমাধিমঞ্চ প্রভৃতির উপরের চন্দ্রাতপ।

tĕs'-tĕr, *n.* **1.** A shilling of Henry VIII ; ৮ম হেনরীর সময়ের শিংলিং। **2.** (*Facet.*) A six pence ; (কৌতুকচ্ছলে) ৬ পেন্স।

tĕs'-ti-cle (-kl), *n.* One of the two glands which secrete seminal fluid in males ; অণ্ডকোষ, মুষ্ক, বৃষণ, বীচি (*colloq.*), পেল (*slang*). [*Syn.* পেলক, অণ্ডক,সীমা,ফল,ফলকোষক,বীজ পেশিকা।] **—tic'-u-lar,** *adj.* **Enlargement of testicles**—কোশ বৃদ্ধি, অণ্ড বৃদ্ধি।

tĕs-tic'-ū-lāte, *adj.* **1.** Having testicles ; shaped like testicles ; অণ্ডকোষবিশিষ্ট ; বৃষণাকৃতি। **2.** (*Bot.*) Having two tubers shaped like testicles ; (উদ্ভিদ বিদ্যা) বৃষণাকৃতি কন্দশাখাদ্বয় বিশিষ্ট।

tĕs'-ti-fy̆, *v. i.* & *t.* **1.** To make a solemn declaration, verbal or written, to establish some fact ; "Jesus ... needed not that any should *testify* of man, for he knew what was in man"; কোন বিষয়ের সত্যতা প্রতিপাদনের জন্য মৌখিক বা লিখিত ভাবে প্রতিজ্ঞাপূর্ব্বক ব্যক্ত করা। **2.** To give information ; to bear witness ; সংবাদ দেওয়া ; সাক্ষ্য দেওয়া। **3.** To serve as an evidence or indications for ; প্রমাণস্বরূপ হওয়া, সূচনা করা **4.** (*Law*) To affirm under oath ; হলফ করিয়া বলা, ধর্ম্মতঃ প্রতিজ্ঞা করিয়া বলা। ***Verb t.*** **1.** To affirm or declare solemnly for the purpose of establishing a fact ; "We speak that we do know, and *testify* that we have seen" ; ধর্ম্মতঃ প্রতিজ্ঞা করিয়া বলা। **2.** To bear witness to ; সাক্ষ্য প্রদান করা। **3.** To publish and declare freely ; মুক্তকণ্ঠে ব্যক্ত বা স্বীকার করা। **4.** To serve as an indication or evidence ; as, the voice of the cuckoo *testifies* spring ; প্রমাণস্বরূপ হওয়া, দ্যোতনা করা, সূচনা করা।

tĕs-ti-mō'-ni-ăl, *n.* **1.** A certificate of character, conduct or qualification ; প্রশংসাপত্র, প্রমাণপত্র, অভিজ্ঞানপত্র, পরিচয়পত্র। **2.** A gift in the shape of money, portrait, etc. given as mark of honour ; "The late lamented O'Connell... over whom a grateful country has raised such a magnificent *testimonial*" ; সম্মানস্বরূপ প্রদত্ত অর্থ, প্রতিকৃতি, প্রভৃতি উপহার।

tĕs-ti-mō'-ni-ăl-ize, *v. t.* **1.** To present one with a testimonial ; প্রসংশাপত্র দেওয়া, অভিজ্ঞানপত্র দেওয়া। **2.** To present with a public testimonial ; উপহারস্বরূপ অর্থ প্রভৃতি দেওয়া।

tĕs'-ti-mŏ-ny̆, *n.* **1.** A solemn verbal or written declaration or affirmation made for the purpose of establishing or proving some fact ; a statement or statements made to prove or communicate some fact ; সত্যপ্রতিজ্ঞা, ধর্ম্মপ্রতিজ্ঞা ; উক্তি। **2.** Any form of evidence or proof ; প্রমাণ, সাক্ষ্য। **3.** Any object serving as evidence ; "To this I call my friends in *testimony*" ; প্রমাণস্বরূপ বস্তু। **4.** (*Law*) A declaration made by a witness under oath or affirmation ; (আইন) শপথ গ্রহণপূর্ব্বক উক্তি। **4.** Divine revelation ; scripture ; the precepts of God ; আপ্তবাক্য ; বাইবেল ; ঈশ্বরের উপদেশ।

tĕs-tŭ-di-nā'-ri-ous (-ŭs), *adj.* Resembling a tortoise-shell in colour ; কচ্ছপের পৃষ্ঠের মত চিত্রিত।

tĕs-tū'-di-nāte, *adj.* Arched like the carapace of a tortoise ; কূর্ম্মপৃষ্ঠাকৃতি।

tĕs-tŭ-din'-ĕ-ous (-ŭs), *adj.* Like the carapace of a tortoise ; কচ্ছপপৃষ্ঠবৎ, কূর্ম্মপৃষ্ঠবৎ।

tĕs-tū'-dō, *n.* **1.** A genus of tortoise ; একজাতীয় কচ্ছপ, স্থলচর কচ্ছপ (মিউজিয়াম)। **2.** (*Rom*

Antiq.) Among the ancient Romans a cover or screen which a body of troops formed with their targets by holding them over their heads when standing close to each other; (রোমীয় প্রত্নতত্ত্ব) প্রাচীন রোমীয় সৈন্যগণ মাথার উপর পরস্পরের ঢালের কিনারায় ঢাল রাখিয়া যে আবরণ গঠন করিত। 3. An arched ceiling or vault; খিলানবিশিষ্ট ভিতরের ছাদ বা তোরণ। 4. A name applied to a species of lyre; একজাতীয় বীণা। 5. (*Med.*) A kind of flat tumour under the scalp; শিরস্তকের নিম্নে জাত একপ্রকার অর্ব্বুদ। **–di-nal**, *adj.*

tĕs′-tȳ, *n.* Fretful; "Must I stand and crouch under your *testy* humour?"; peevish; irascible; কোপণস্বভাব; চিড়চিড়ে, খিট্‌খিটে; চটা মেজাজী। **–ti-ness**, *n.*

tē-tăn′-ic, *adj.* & *n.* Pertaining to, or denoting, tetanus; ধনুষ্টঙ্কার সম্বন্ধীয়, ধনুষ্টঙ্কারসূচক। ***Noun.*** A medicine acting on the muscle through the nerves; ধনুষ্টঙ্কারের ঔষধ (যথা Strychnia).

tĕt′-ă-nŭs, *n.* A disease characterised by long continued contraction of, or spasm of, certain muscles, the muscles of the jaws and throat being first affected; ধনুষ্টঙ্কার (সাঃ পঃ), ধনুস্তম্ভ (ঐ), দাঁতকপাটী। **–ni-za′-tion**, *n.* **–nize**, *v. t.* **–noid**, *adj.*

tĕtch′-ȳ (tĕch-), *adj.* Same as TECHY.

tete′–a–tete′ (tāt-ă-tāt), *n.*, *adj.* & *adv.* 1. Private conversation, or a familiar interview between two persons; বিশ্রম্ভালাপ, রহস্যালাপ, নির্জ্জনমিলন, বিজনমিলন। 2. A sofa for two; দুই ব্যক্তির উপবেশনের জন্য আরামখট্টা। ***Adj.*** Private; confidential; as, *teteatete* dinner; গোপন, নির্জ্জন, বিজন; গোপনীয়। ***Adv.*** Face to face; in private; মুখোমুখি, সামনাসামনি; গোপনে, কাণে কাণে, রহসি নির্জ্জনে।

tĕth′-ĕr, *n.* & *v. t.* 1. A rope or chain by which a beast is confined for feeding within certain limits; গবাদিকে যে দড়ী বা শিকলে বাঁধিয়া ঘাস খাইতে দেওয়া হয়, দিগড়ী দড়ী, বন্ধনরজ্জু। 2. Scope; bounds prescribed; প্রসর; নির্দ্দিষ্টসীমা। 3. A bond or fetter; "When weary of the matrimonial *tether*"; বন্ধন; নিগড়, শৃঙ্খল। ***Verb t.*** To confine a beast with a rope or chain, for feeding within limits; গরু প্রভৃতিকে দড়ী বা শিকলদ্বারা বাঁধিয়া ঘাস খাইতে দেওয়া, দিগড়ী দেওয়া। **To the end of one's tether**—To one's farthest limit; শেষ সীমা পর্য্যন্ত।

tĕt-ră-bran′-chi-ate (-brăng-), *n.* Having four branchia; কাণকো-চতুষ্টয় বিশিষ্ট।

tĕt′-ră-chŏrd, *n.* 1. An ancient musical instrument with four strings; তন্ত্রীচতুষ্টয়সমন্বিত প্রাচীনকালীন বাদ্যযন্ত্র বিশেষ। 2. A scale series of four notes; সপ্তকের সা রে গা মা পর্য্যন্ত অংশ, অর্দ্ধসপ্তক।

tĕt-răc′-id, *adj.* (*Chem.*) Capable of combining with four molecules of a monobasic acid; (রসায়ন শাস্ত্র) চতুরম্ন।

tĕt-ră-cȳc′-lic, *adj.* Of four circles or whorles; চতুশ্চক্র বা পত্রাবর্ত্তবিশিষ্ট, চতুস্তবকী (সাঃ পঃ)।

tĕt′-răd, *n.* 1. The number four; চার, চতুঃ। 2. A collection of four things; চতুর্বস্তুর সম্মিলন, চতুষ্টয়, চতুর্ব্যূহ (ব্রজঃ হিন্দুঃ), চতুষ্ক (হিঃ কোঃ)। 3. (*Chem*). A name given to those elements which can directly unite with or replace four atoms of hydrogen, chlorine or other monatomic elements; (রসায়নশাস্ত্র) যে সকল মূল পদার্থ প্রত্যক্ষভাবে উদজানবাষ্প, হরিণ বাষ্প বা অন্য কোন এক-পরমাণুক বাষ্পের সহিত সংযুক্ত হইতে বা ঐ সকল পরমাণুর স্থান অধিকার করিতে পারে, চতুরণুক (সাঃ পঃ), চতুর্বন্ধন (হিঃ কোঃ)।

tĕt-ră-dăc′-tȳl, *adj.* & *n.* Having four toes; চতুর্পদাঙ্গুলীবিশিষ্ট। ***Noun.*** An animal having four toes; চতুর্পদাঙ্গুলীবিশিষ্ট জন্তু।

tĕt-ră-dȳn′-ă-mous (-mŭs), *adj.* (*Bot.*) Having six stamens; (উদ্ভিদ্‌বিদ্যা) ত্রিদ্বন্দ্বক (সাঃ পঃ)।

tĕt′-ră-gŏn, *n.* 1. A plane figure having four angles; চতুষ্কোণ ক্ষেত্র। 2. (*Astrol.*) An aspect of two planets with regard to the earth when they are distant from each other 90°; (ফলিত জ্যোতিষ) গ্রহগণের পরস্পর হইতে ৯০ ডিগ্রি দূরে অবস্থান। **–rag′-o-nal**, *adj.*

tĕt′-ră-grăm, *n* 1. A word of four letters; চতুরক্ষর শব্দ। 2. A figure formed by four straight lines in a plane and their six points of intersection; চতুরৈখিক ক্ষেত্র।

tĕt-ră-grăm′-mă-tŏn, *n.* Jehovah or other sacred word written in four consonants; জিহোভা বা অন্য কোনরূপ চতুর্ব্যঞ্জনবর্ণ সমন্বিত পবিত্র শব্দ।

tĕt-răg′-ȳ-nous (-nŭs), **–ră-gȳn′-i-ăn**, *adjs.* Having four pistils; চতুর্গর্ভকেশরবিশিষ্ট।

tĕt-ră-hē′-drăl, *adj.* 1. Bounded by four equal and equilateral triangles; সমান সমভুজ বিশিষ্ট। 2. (*Bot.*) Having four sides; অর্দ্ধার্দ্ধপত্রল (সাঃ পঃ)।

tĕt-ră-hē′-drŏn, *n.* A solid figure comprehended by four equilateral and equal triangles; সমান সমকোণী ত্রিভুজ চতুষ্টয়দ্বারা বেষ্টিত ঘনক্ষেত্র, চতুষ্ফলক (হিঃ কোঃ)।

tĕt-răl′-ŏ-gȳ, *n.* A group of four dramatic compositions treating of four related themes; অনুরূপবিষয়াবলম্বনে রচিত নাটক চতুষ্টয়।

tĕt-răm′-ĕr-ăl, **–ous** (-ŭs), *adjs.* Having four parts; চতুরংশবিশিষ্ট, চতুরংশক (সাঃ পঃ), চতুরংশকস্তবকী (ঐ)।

tĕt'-răm'-ĕ-tẽr, *n.* A verse of four measures ; চৌপদী।

tĕt'-ră-mŏrph, *n.* The union of the four attributes of the evangelists in a winged figure standing on winged fiery wheels, the wings covered with eyes ; খৃষ্টীয় সুসমাচারলেখক চতুষ্টয়ের চতুর্গুণ-সূচক সপক্ষ অগ্নিময় চক্রের উপর অবস্থিত অক্ষিসমাকীর্ণ পক্ষযুক্ত মূর্ত্তি।

tĕt-răn'-drĭ-ă, *n.* A class of hermaphrodite plants, having four stamens ; একপ্রকার চতুষ্পুং-কেশরযুক্ত স্ত্রীপুংধর্ম্মী ক্ষুপ।

tĕt'-răn-drous (-drŭs), *adj.* (*Bot.*) Having four stamens ; (উদ্ভিদ্‌বিদ্যা) চতুষ্পুংকেশর বিশিষ্ট।

tĕt-ră-pĕt'-ăl-ous (-ŭs), **—phỹl'-lous** (-lŭs), *adj.* Of four petals or leaves ; চতুর্পত্র, চতুর্দ্দল।

tĕt'-ră-pŏd, *adj.* & *n.* Four footed ; চতুষ্পদ। ***Noun.*** A fourfooted animal ; esp, an insect having four perfected legs ; চতুষ্পদ জন্তু ; বিশেষতঃ পূর্ণপরিণত পদচতুষ্টয়বিশিষ্ট কীট।

tĕt'-răp'-ŏ-dỹ, *n.* A set or group of four feet ; চতুশ্চরণসমবায়।

tĕ'-trârch, *n.* **1.** A Roman governor of the fourth part of a country or province ; কোন দেশ বা প্রদেশের চতুর্থাংশের রোমীয় শাসনকর্ত্তা। **2.** A subordinate commander in a Greek phalanx ; গ্রীসদেশীয় ঘন-ব্যূহের উপাধ্যক্ষ। **Tet-rar'-chi-cal,** *adj.* **Tet'-rarch-y, —ate,** *ns.*

tĕt-ră-spōre, *adj.* (*Bot.*) Having four spores ; চতুরেণু (সাঃ পঃ)।

tĕt'-ră-stĭch, *n.* A group of four lines of verse ; কবিতার পংক্তি চতুষ্টয়।

tĕt'-ră-stȳle, *adj.* & *n.* **1.** Having, or consisting of, four columns ; স্তম্ভচতুষ্টয়যুক্ত, চতুঃস্তম্ভাত্মক। 2. Having a portico consisting of four columns ; স্তম্ভচতুষ্টয়যুক্ত দ্বারপ্রকোষ্ঠ-সমন্বিত। ***Noun.*** A building or portico with four columns in front ; সম্মুখে স্তম্ভচতুষ্টয়যুক্ত অট্টালিকা বা দ্বারপ্রকোষ্ঠ।

tĕt'-ră-sȳl'-lă-ble (-bl), *n.* A word of four syllables ; চতুর্মাত্রাত্মক শব্দ। **—lab'-ic,** *adj.*

tĕt-ră-tŏm'-ĭc, *adj.* (*Chem.*) Consisting of four atoms ; চতুষ্পরমাণুক (হিঃ কোঃ)।

tĕt'-tẽr, *n.* A vague name for several skin-disease ; কতিপয় চর্ম্মরোগের নাম। **Tetter-wort**—এক-জাতীয় গাঁদা ফুল (উক্ত রোগ আরোগ্য করণে সমর্থ বলিয়া কল্পিত।)

Teu'-cẽr (tü-), *n.* **1.** The first king of Troy ; ট্রয় নগরীর প্রথম রাজা। **2.** A son of Telamon ; টীলামানের পুত্র। [এই বীর তদীয় বৈমাত্রেয় ভ্রাতা Ajaxএর মৃত্যুর প্রতি-শোধ না লইয়া ট্রয়ের যুদ্ধ হইতে প্রত্যাবৃত্ত হওয়ার দরুণ, ইঁহার পিতা ইঁহাকে গ্রহণ করেন নাই। ইনি পরে Cyprus দ্বীপের রাজা হইয়াছিলেন। ইনিই Salamis নগরীর প্রতিষ্ঠাতা।]

Teu'-crĭ-ăn (tü-), *adj* & *n.* Of, or pertaining to, Teucer, first king of Troy or to the ancient Trojans ; ট্রয় নগরীর প্রথম রাজা টিউসারএরসম্বন্ধীয়, প্রাচীন ট্রয়এর অধিবাসী-সম্বন্ধীয়। ***Noun.*** An ancient Trojan ; প্রাচীন ট্রয় নগরীর অধিবাসী।

teu'-crĭ-ŭm (tü-), *n.* Same as GERMANDER (which see).

Teu'-tŏn (tü-), *n.* One of the Teutonic race, which embraces the Germans, the Scandinavians, the Dutch, the Flemings, and the Anglo-Saxons ; টিউটন জাতি (জর্ম্মণ, স্কেণ্ডিনিভিয়্যান, ওলন্দাজ, ফ্লেমিং, প্রভৃতি জাতির লোক)।

Teu-tŏn'-ĭc (tü-), *adj.* & *n.* Pertaining to the Teutons or their language ; টিউটন জাতি সম্বন্ধীয়, টিউটন জাতির ভাষাসম্বন্ধীয়। ***Noun.*** The language of the Teutons ; টিউটন জাতির ভাষা। **—i-cism, —i-za'-tion.** *ns.* **Teu'-ton-ism,** *n.* **Teu'-ton-ize,** *v. t.*

tew (tü), Same as TAW.

tew'-ĕl (tü-), *n.* Same as TUYERE (which see).

tĕxt, *n.* **1.** That on which a note or commentary is written ; যাহার উপর টীকা করা যায়, মূলসূত্র। **2.** A verse or passage of scripture esp. one selected as the theme of a sermon or discourse ; কোনরূপ আলোচনা বা ধর্ম্মোপদেশের বিষয়স্বরূপ বাইবেলের যে বাক্য নির্ব্বাচিত করা হয়। **3.** The main body of a book, opposed to notes, pictures ; টিপ্পনী, ছবি প্রভৃতি বাদে পুস্তকের প্রধান অংশ, মূল গ্রন্থ, মূল (cf. এই কথা মূলে পাওয়া যায় না।) **4.** A large hand in writing ; অপেক্ষাকৃত বড় ছাঁদের হস্তাক্ষর। **Text-book**—পাঠ্য পুস্তক। **Text-hand**—Same as TEXT 4.

tĕx'-tĭle, *adj.* & *n.* **1.** Woven or capable of being woven ; as, *textile* materials ; formed by weaving ; বূত, বয়নযোগ্য ; বোনা। **2.** Of weaving ; বয়নসম্বন্ধীয়। ***Noun.*** That which is made by weavers ; a woven fabric ; তন্তুবায় কর্ত্তৃক প্রস্তুত বস্ত্র ; বোনা কাপড়।

tĕx'-tū-ăl, *adj.* Connected with, or contained in, text ; literal ; মূল-গ্রন্থসংক্রান্ত, মূলগ্রন্থান্তর্ভুক্ত ; আক্ষরিক। **—ly,** *adv.* **Textual criticism**—কোন গ্রন্থের মূল আদৌ কিরূপ ছিল তাহা স্থির করার জন্য ইহার বর্ত্তমান মূলের সমালোচনা (বিশেষভাবে খৃষ্টীয় বাইবেল গ্রন্থের উক্তরূপ সমালোচনা সম্পর্কে উক্ত হইয়া থাকে)।

tĕx'-tū-ăl-ĭst, *n.* **1.** One who is well versed in the Scriptures and can readily quote texts ; খৃষ্টীয় বাইবেল গ্রন্থে বিশেষ ব্যুৎপন্ন যে ব্যক্তি অতি সত্বরতার সহিত বাইবেলের বাক্য উদ্ধৃত করিতে পারে। **2.** One who adheres strictly to the words of a text ; মূলগ্রন্থের শব্দের প্রতি কঠোরভাবে আসক্ত ব্যক্তি। **—ism,** *n.*

tĕx'-tūre, *n.* **1.** The disposition or connection of threads, filaments or other slender bodies interwoven ; বুনট, জমি, জমিন । **2.** A woven fabric ; বুনা কাপড় । **3.** The disposition of the several parts of anybody in connection with each other's structure ; অঙ্গবিন্যাস, বুনট । **4.** Representation of the surface of objects in art ; (ললিত কলায়) কোন বস্তুর উপরিভাগ চিত্রণ । **5.** (*Biol.*) Tissue (*rare*) ; (জীববিজ্ঞান) বিধানগ্রন্থি (কচিদ্‌ব্যবহৃত) । **–tur-al,** *adj.*

tĕx'-türe-lĕss, *adj.* Amorphous ; অনিয়তাকার ।

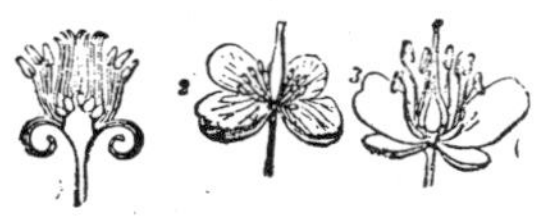

Thalamiflorae.
1, Clematis ; 2, Celandine ; 3, Geranium.

thăl-ă-mi-flō'-rae (-rē), *n.* (*Pl.*) A class of plants in which the petals are distinct and inserted with the stamens on the thalamus or receptacles ; আধারপুষ্প (সাঃ পঃ) ।

thăl-ă-mi-flō'-răl, *adj.* Hypogynous ; বিযুক্তস্তবকী (সাঃ পঃ) ।

thăl'-ă-mŭs, *n.* **1.** (*Greek Antiq.*) Woman's apartment ; (গ্রীসদেশীয় প্রত্নতত্ত্ব) অন্তঃপুর, শুদ্ধান্ত । **2.** (*Anat.*) The place where a nerve esp. the optic nerve emerges from the brain ; মস্তিষ্কের যে গ্রন্থির আকার অংশ হইতে কোন নাড়ীর বিশেষতঃ রূপবহানাড়ীর কতিপয় তন্তু উৎপন্ন হইয়া থাকে । **3.** (*Bot*). The receptacle of a flower ; (উদ্ভিদ্‌-বিদ্যা) পুষ্পধী ।

tha'-lĕr (tâ-), *n.* A German silver coin worth about 3*s.* ; জর্ম্মণদেশীয় রৌপ্যমুদ্রা বিশেষ । [বর্ত্তমান মূল্য প্রায় ৩ শিলিং ।]

Thă-lī'-ă *n.* Muse of comedy and the patroness of pastoral poetry ; মিলনান্ত নাট্য এবং পল্লী-কবিতার অধিষ্ঠাত্রী গ্রীক বাগ্‌দেবী । **–an,** *adj.*

thăl'-li-ŭm, *n.* A metallic element, bluish-white and soft—specific gravity 11. 8, atomic weight 204.2 — discovered by Crookes in 1861 (so called from the intense green line it gives in the spectrum) ; নীলাভ শ্বেতবর্ণ ধাতব মূল পদার্থ বিশেষ, স্থূলক (সাঃ পঃ) । **–lic, –lous,** *adjs.*

thăl-lō-phȳte, *n.* A plant belonging to the lowest of the four groups of vegetable kingdom including the algae, fungi and lichens ; সমাঙ্গোদ্ভিদ্‌ (সাঃ পঃ) ।

thăl'-lŭs, *n.* A plant-body without root, stem, or leaves; মূল, কাণ্ড এবং পত্র বিহীন বৃক্ষাংশ । **–loid,** *adj.* Like a thallus ; সমাঙ্গবৎ ।

Thames (tĕmz), *n.* The river on whose bank London lies ; টেমস নদী । **To set the Thames on fire**—পাহাড় টুলান (Also see under FIRE).

than, *conj.* A conjunction, denoting comparison or diversity and generally placed after a comparative adjective or adverb ; অপেক্ষা, চেয়ে, চাইতে, হইতে ।

thān'-āge, *n.* **1.** The dignity or rank of a thane ; প্রাচীন এংলো-স্যাকসন্‌দিগের মধ্যে সম্মানসূচক উপাধি-বিশেষধারীর পদগৌরব বা মর্য্যাদা । **2.** Land granted to a thane ; উক্ত উপাধিধারিগণকে প্রদত্ত ভূমি ।

thăn'-ă-toid (-toid), *adj.* Resembling death ; deadly ; মৃতবৎ, মৃতকল্প ; মারাত্মক ।

thăn-ă-tŏl'-ō-ğȳ, *n.* The description, theory, or doctrine of death ; মৃত্যুতত্ত্ব, মৃত্যুবিজ্ঞান ।

thăn-ă-tō-phĭd'-i-ă, *n.* (*pl.*) Poisonous snakes ; বিষাক্ত সর্পসমূহ ।

thă-nă-tō-phō'-bi-ă, *n.* Morbid fear of death ; মৃত্যুভীতি ।

thāne, *n.* **1.** A Saxon title of the dignity, formerly held by persons of large territorial possession ; প্রাচীন এংলোসেক্‌সন ভূম্যধিকারিগণের উপাধি । **2.** A man of a middle rank between ordinary freeman and hereditary noble ; প্রাচীন এংলোসেক্‌সন্‌দিগের মধ্যে মধ্য শ্রেণীর ভদ্রলোক । **Thane'-dom, Thane'-hood, Thane'-ship,** *ns.*

thank (thăngk), *v. t.* To express gratitude to for a favour ; ধন্যবাদ দেওয়া, ধন্যবাদ প্রদান করা । **I thank you** — আপনাকে ধন্যবাদ (এইরূপ উক্তিতে কতকটা কঠোরতার আভাস বুঝা যায়) । **I will thank you**—Will you oblige me by doing or by giving or handing me ; as, *I will thank you* to shut the door ; আপনি কি এই কার্য্যটী করিয়া বা এই জিনিষটী দিয়া আমাকে বাধিত করিবেন । **Thank you,** or **I thank you**—কোন অনুরোধ বা প্রস্তাব প্রত্যাখ্যান করিতে হইলে এই বাক্য ব্যবহৃত হয় । **To thank one's stars**—See STARS.

thank (thăngk), *n.* (*Now exclusively in pl.*) Expression of gratitude ; ধন্যবাদ । **Thank-offering**—কৃতজ্ঞতাসূচক উপহার । **Thanks**—Thank you ; তোমাকে ধন্যবাদ । **Thanks to**—As the result of ; ফলে, প্রসাদে, কল্যাণে, প্রসাদাৎ, অনুগ্রহে, দৌলতে, খাতিরে

thank'-fûl (thăngk-), *adj.* **1.** Grateful ; কৃতজ্ঞ । **2.** Expressive of thanks or gratitude ; কৃতজ্ঞতাসূচক, ধন্যবাদসূচক । **–ly,** *adv.* **–ness,** *n.*

thank'-lĕss (thăngk-), *adj.* Uuthankful ; ungrateful ; অকৃতজ্ঞ ; কৃতঘ্ন ।

thanks-giv'-ing, (thăngks-), *n.* **1.** Act of rendering thanks ; ধন্যবাদ প্রদান । **2.** A public celebration of divine goodness ; ভগবানের প্রতি কৃতজ্ঞতা প্রকাশের জন্য উৎসব । **Thanksgiving day**—(মার্কিণযুক্তরাজ্যে) ভগবানের প্রতি কৃতজ্ঞতা প্রকাশের জন্য নির্দ্দিষ্ট দিবস (সাধারণতঃ নভেম্বর মাসের শেষ বৃহস্পতিবার ।)

thăt, *adj., pron., adv.* & *conj.* A pronominal adjective pointing to a person or thing or supposed to be understood ; সেই, যে, সে, তেমন, অমন। ***Pron.*** Used as a relative pronoun, and in many cases equivalent to *who* or *which* ; যিনি, যে, যাহা। ***Adv.*** (*Vulg.*) To such a degree ; (ইতর-ভাষায়) ঐ পরিমাণে, এতদূর। ***Conj.*** Introducing subordinate clauses ; যে। **All that**—All those things : সেই সব। **In order that**—So that ; এই হেতু যে। **In that**—Since ; যেহেতু। **Now that**—Since now ; যেহেতু এখন। **So that**—যেন, যাহাতে। **That is to say**—That is ; অর্থাৎ, যেমন।

thatch (thăch), *n.* & *v. t.* A roof-covering of straw, rushes, or (in tropical countries) cocoanut and other leaves ; ঘর ছাওয়ার ছন প্রভৃতি। ***Verb t.*** To cover with straw, reeds, or some similar substance ; ঘর ছাওয়া, ছানি দেওয়া। **Thatch'-er,** *n.* One whose occupation is to thatch houses ; ঘরামি। **Thatch'-ing,** *n.*

thau'-mă-trōpe (thä-), *n.* An optical toy to illustrate the persistence of an impression upon the retina after the object is withdrawn ; দৃষ্টবস্তু অপসারণের পর অক্ষির চিত্রপটে উহার প্রতিবিম্বের পর্য্যবস্থিতি প্রদর্শনের জন্য বীক্ষণক্রীড়নক বিশেষ, প্রতিবিম্বসংস্থিতিবীক্ষণ।

thau'-ma-turge (thä-mă-tẽrj), *n.* A worker of miracles ; a conjurer ; a magician ; অলৌকিক ক্রিয়াকারী ; ঐন্দ্রজালিক ; যাদুকর। **–tur'-gic, –tur'-gi-cal,** *adjs.* **–tur'-gist,** *n.* **–tur'-gy,** *n.* The act of performing something wonderful ; magic ; অলৌকিককার্য্যসম্পাদন ; ইন্দ্রজাল, যাদুবিদ্যা।

thaw (thä), *v. i., t.* & *n.* **1.** To melt, dissolve or become fluid, as ice or snow ; গলা, দ্রব হওয়া, তরল অবস্থা প্রাপ্ত হওয়া। **2.** (Of weather) To become so warm as to melt ice and snow ; যেরূপ উষ্ণতায় বরফ গলিতে পারে সেইরূপ মাত্রায় উষ্ণ হইয়া উঠা। **3.** To become less cold, formal or reserved ; ; to become genial ; "The dreadness of my heart *thawed* and melted into peace and calm" ; অপেক্ষাকৃত অল্প অনুরাগশূন্য, লৌকিকতাযুক্ত বা অনালাপী হওয়া ; সদালাপী হওয়া, মিশুক হওয়া, প্রীতি-প্রফুল্ল হওয়া। ***Verb t.*** **1.** To melt as, ice ; snow, hail ; তুষার, বরফ, প্রভৃতি গালান। **2.** To render genial, less cold or reserved ; উৎফুল্ল করা। ***Noun.*** **1.** The melting of ice and snow ; তুষার প্রভৃতি দ্রবীকরণ। **2.** A change in the temperature that will melt ice ; বায়ুর যেরূপ উষ্ণতায় তুষার গলিতে আরম্ভ করে। **3.** (*Fig.*) State of growing less cold or reserved ; প্রীতি, অনুরাগ, প্রভৃতি সঞ্চারের অবস্থা।

thĕ, *Def. article* or *definitive adj.* & *adv.* **1.** Used before a noun in the singular to denote a species by way of distinction or a single thing representing the whole ; as, *the* cat ; একবচন বিশেষ্যের পূর্ব্বে সমগ্র-জাতি নির্দ্দেশের জন্য ব্যবহৃত হয়। **2.** Prefixed to adjectives to give them the force of abstract nouns ; as, *the* sublime and *the* beautiful ; গুণবাচক বিশেষ্যের অর্থ প্রদানার্থ বিশেষণের পূর্ব্বে ব্যবহৃত হয়। **3.** Used before nouns to denote a certain person or thing ; কোন নির্দ্দিষ্ট বস্তু বা ব্যক্তি নির্দ্দেশে ব্যবহৃত হয়। **4.** Used before proper names by way of emphatic distinction or before family names, with something of the force of a title ; as, *the* Douglas ; বিশেষ পার্থক্যসূচনার্থ কতকটা উপাধির ভাব বুঝাইবার জন্য গোত্রনামের পূর্ব্বে ব্যবহৃত হয়। **5.** Used before a noun to denote well-known object ; as, *the* Ganges ; কোন সুপরিজ্ঞাত বস্তু বুঝাইবার জন্য বিশেষ্যের পূর্ব্বে ব্যবহৃত হয়। ***Adv.*** (Used before comparatives) By that ; by so much ; as, *the* more *the* merrier ; by how much ; on that account ; তদ্দারা সেই পরিমাণে ; যত, কত ; সেইজন্য।

thē-ăn'-dric, *adj.* Indicating the co-operation of the divine and human ; partaking of both the human and the divine ; having the nature of both God and man ; দেব এবং মানব প্রকৃতির সম্মিলন-সূচক ; দেবমানবাত্মক ; দেবমানবীয়।

thē-ăn-thrŏp'-ic, –i-căl, *adjs.* Both divine and human ; দেবমানবীয়, দেবমানবাত্মক। **–an'-thro-pism,** *n.*

thē'-ăr-chy̆, *n.* **1.** Government by God ; দেবতন্ত্র। **2.** A body of divine rulers ; a class or order of gods ; দেবশাসকবর্গ ; দেববর্গ, দেবসমাজ।

thē'-ă-tre (-tẽr), *n.* **1.** A house for the exhibition of dramatic performances ; রঙ্গালয়, নাট্যাগার, রঙ্গমণ্ডপ, নাট্যমন্দির, রঙ্গশালা। **2.** A place rising by steps or gradations like the seats of a theatre ; রঙ্গালয়ের আসনশ্রেণীর মত ক্রমোচ্চস্থান। **3.** A room, hall, or other place, generally with a platform at one end, and ranks of seats rising as they recede, or otherwise arranged that a body of spectators can have an unobstructed view of the platform (Places of this description are used for public lectures, surgical operations, anatomical lectures, etc.) ; ক্রমোচ্চ আসনশ্রেণী সমন্বিত কক্ষ। **3.** Dramatic literature or art ; as, the modern *theatre* ; নাট্যসাহিত্য, নাট্যকলা। **4.** A place of action ; as, the *theatre* of war ; ক্ষেত্র, স্থান, অঙ্গন। **Theatre-goer**—যে ব্যক্তি রঙ্গালয়ে গমন করে, রঙ্গালয়যাত্রী।

thē-ăt'-ri-căl, *adj.* & *n.* **1.** Pertaining to a theatre or scenic representation ; as, *theatrical* performances ; suited to the theatre ; resembling the manner of dramatic performers ; রঙ্গালয়-সম্বন্ধীয় ; নাট্যশালাসমুচিত ; অভিনেতৃ-সদৃশ। 2. Showy ; artificial ; as, *theatrical* gestures ; জাঁকালো, জমকালো ; কৃত্রিম, লোকদেখানো। ***Noun.*** (*pl.*) Dramatic performances esp. that performed by amateurs ; নাট্যাভিনয়, বিশেষতঃ অবৈতনিক নাট্য-সম্প্রদায়ের অভিনয়। **—cal'-i-ty,** *n.* **—ly,** *adv.* **—ism,** *n.* **—ize,** *v. t.*

Thē'-bā-id, *n.* A poem concerning Thebes ; থীবস্‌নগরী সম্বন্ধীয় কবিতা। [কতিপয় কবিতা এই নামে অভিহিত হইত। বিশেষভাবে Statius কর্ত্তৃক লিখিত দ্বাদশসর্গাত্মক কবিতাগ্রন্থ—যাহা Thebaid বলিয়া উক্ত হইয়া থাকে।]

Thē'-băn, *adj.* & *n.* Of, or belonging to, Thebes ; থীবস নগরীসম্বন্ধীয়। ***Noun.*** A native of Thebes ; থীবস নগরীর অধিবাসী। **Theban year** — মিশরদেশের ৩৬৫ দিবস ও ৬ ঘণ্টাব্যাপী বৎসর।

thē'-că, *n.* A sheath or case ; কৌটা (সাঃ পঃ), কুটী (ঐ)।

thee (thē), *pron.* Objective case of THOU.

thĕft, *n.* The unlawful taking of another person's goods or movables with an intent to improvise him of them ; চৌর্য্য, তস্করতা, অপহরণ, চুরি, স্তেয়।

thē'-ic, *n.* One who drinks tea to excess ; চাখোর। **—ism,** *n.*

thē'-ine (-ĭn), *n.* Same as CAFFEINE (which see).

their (thâr), *adj.* Of, or belonging to, them ; তাহাদিগের, উহাদের, উহাদিগের।

thē'-ĭsm, *n.* The belief or acknowledgment of the existence of God, as opposed to *atheism* ; আস্তিকতা, একেশ্বরবাদ, আস্তিক্যবাদ (হিঃ কোঃ), ঈশ্বরবাদ (ঐ)। **—ist,** *n.* One who believes in God ; আস্তিক, একেশ্বরবাদী, ঈশ্বরবাদী (হিঃ কোঃ)। **—is'-tic, is'-ti-cal,** *adjs.* Pertaining to theism or to a theist ; ঈশ্বরবাদসম্বন্ধীয়, আস্তিক্য-সম্বন্ধী (হিঃ কোঃ), ঈশ্বরবাদবিষয়ক (ঐ)।

thĕm, *pron.* The objective case of THEY.

thē-măt'-ic, *adj.* 1. (*Mus.*) Pertaining to themes or subjects ; (সঙ্গীতবিদ্যা) বিষয়সম্বন্ধীয়। 2. (*Gram.*) Pertaining to the stem of a noun or verb to which inflexions are added ; ক্রিয়া বা ধাতু-বিশেষের যে মূল অংশের সহিত বিভক্তি প্রত্যয় প্রভৃতি যুক্ত হয় তৎসম্বন্ধীয়। **—i-cal-ly,** *adv.* **Thematic catalogue** — যে তালিকাতে তদন্তর্ভুক্ত প্রত্যেক গানের বিষয়ের সারমর্ম্ম দেওয়া হইয়া থাকে।

theme (thēm), *n.* 1. A proposition for discussion ; a subject ; a subject or topic on which a person writes or speaks ; আলোচ্য বিষয় ; বিষয়, প্রসঙ্গ ; বক্তৃতা বা রচনার বিষয়। 2. (*Gram.*) The part of a noun or verb which remains unchanged in declension or conjugation ; ক্রিয়া বা বিশেষ্যের যে অংশ ধাতুরূপে বা শব্দরূপে অপরিবর্ত্তিত থাকে। 3. (*Mus.*) A short melody developed with variations ; (সঙ্গীতশাস্ত্র) নানারূপ বৈচিত্র্য দ্বারা পরিস্ফুটীকৃত ক্ষুদ্র তান। 4. (*Hist.*) Any of the twenty-nine provinces of the Byzantine empire ; (ইতিহাস) বাইজেন্‌টাইন সাম্রাজ্যের উনত্রিংশ প্রদেশের অন্যতম।

Thē'-mis, *n.* 1. The Greek goddess of law and right ; বিধি এবং ন্যায়পরায়ণতার অধিষ্ঠাত্রীদেবী। 2. Law and justice personified ; ন্যায় এবং বিধির বিগ্রহ। 3. (*Astron.*) An asteroid discovered by De Gasparis at Naples, in 1853 ; (জ্যোতির্বিজ্ঞান) Naples নগরবাসী De Gasparis কর্ত্তৃক আবিষ্কৃত তারকা।

thĕm-selves' (-sĕlvz), *pron.* Plural of *himself, herself* and *itself* ; তাহাদিগকে।

thĕn, *adv., conj., adj.* & *n.* 1. At the time ; তখন, সেই সময়, তৎকালে। 2. Soon afterwards or immediately ; next ; "First be reconciled to thy brother and *then* come" ; তখনই, তন্মুহূর্ত্তে, অবিলম্বে ; তৎপর, অতঃপর। 3. At another time ; again ; "Now shaves with level wing the deep, *then* soars up to the fiery concave towering high" ; অন্যসময়ে ; পুনরায়। ***Conj.*** In that case ; therefore ; for this reason ; সেই স্থলে, সেই অবস্থায় ; তবে, তজ্জন্য ; এইহেতু, তাহা হইলে, তা'হলে, অতএব। ***Adj.*** Existing, acting or belonging to the time mentioned ; as, the *then* Governor of Bengal ; তৎকালীন। ***Noun.*** That time ; তৎকাল, সেই সময়। **But then**—But on the other-hand ; কিন্তু অপর পক্ষে। **By then**—By the time when or that ; সেই সময় লাগাইত। **Then and there**—Immediately ; on the spot ; তখনি, তখন তখন; সেইস্থানে, সেইক্ষেত্রে। **Till then**—Until that time ; সেই সময় পর্য্যন্ত।

thē'-năr, *n.* & *adj.* (*Anat.*) The palm of the hand or the sole of the foot ; the prominence of the palm at the base of the thumb ; (শারীরসংস্থানবিদ্যা) করতল, পদতল ; অঙ্গুষ্ঠের নিম্নে করতলের উন্নতস্থান। ***Adj.*** Of, or pertaining to, the thenar ; পদতল বা করতলসম্বন্ধীয়।

thence (thĕns), *adv.* 1. (*Archaic*) From that place ; (অপ্রঃ) সেই স্থান হইতে, তথা হইতে। 2. From that time ; after that ; সেই সময় হইতে, তদবধি ; তৎপর। 3. (*Rare*) For that reason ; তদ্ধেতু, সেইজন্য। **Thenceforth, Thenceforward**—তদবধি, সেই সময় হইতে।

thē-ŏc'-ră-çy̆, *n.* Government of a state by the immediate direction of God or through sacerdotal class ; the state thus governed ;

ঈশ্বর বা তৎপ্রতিনিধি যাজকসমাজকর্তৃক রাষ্ট্রশাসন, দেবতন্ত্র, ঈশ্বরতন্ত্র ; দেবতন্ত্রমূলক রাজ্য, ঈশ্বরসাম্রাজ্য (হিঃ কোঃ), দেবরাজ্য (হিঃ কোঃ), দেবরাষ্ট্র। **The Theocracy** — মূসোর সময় হইতে আরম্ভ করিয়া রাজতন্ত্রের প্রতিষ্ঠার পূর্ব্ব পর্য্যন্ত কালের ইহুদীগণতন্ত্র।

thē-ŏc′-ră-sȳ, *n.* **1.** A mixture of the worship of different gods ; বিভিন্ন দেবতার পূজার একত্র মিশ্রণ। **2.** The intimate union of soul with God in contemplation ; ঈশ্বরসাযুজ্য, সাযুজ্য (হিঃ কোঃ), নির্ব্বিকল্পসমাধি।

thē′-ō-crăt, *n.* One who lives under a theocracy ; a ruler in a theocracy ; দেবরাষ্ট্রের প্রজা ; দেবরাষ্ট্রের শাসনকর্ত্তা। **—crat′-ic,** *adj.* **—oc′-ra-tist,** *n.* A believer in the direct intervention and authority of God through revelation in government of society ; one who places revelation over human reason ; ঈশ্বর প্রত্যাদেশের সাহায্যে প্রত্যক্ষভাবে মানবসমাজের শাসনে হস্তক্ষেপ করেন—এই মতে বিশ্বাসী ব্যক্তি ; যে ব্যক্তি ঈশ্বরের প্রত্যাদেশকে মানুষের প্রজ্ঞার উপরে স্থান দিয়া থাকে।

thē-ŏd′-ī-cȳ, *n.* A vindication of the holiness and justice of God in establishing the present order of things, in which evil largely exists ; বর্ত্তমান বিশ্বব্যবস্থায় অশুভের প্রাধান্য স্বত্বেও ঈশ্বরের ন্যায়পরতা এবং অপাপবিদ্ধতার সমর্থন, ঈশ্বরনৈর্দ্দোষ্যবাদ (হিঃ কোঃ), অপাপবিদ্ধতাবাদ।

thē-ŏd′-ŏ-līte, *n.* A surveyor's instrument for measuring horizontal and vertical angles by means of a telescope ; দূরবীক্ষণ যন্ত্রের সাহায্যে শয়ান এবং উল্লম্বী কোণ পরিমাপের জন্য যন্ত্রবিশেষ, কোণমান।

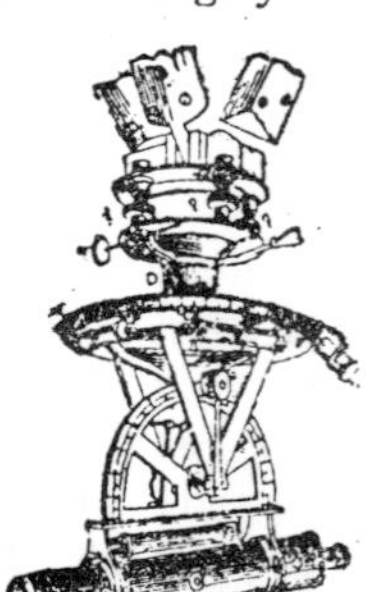

Theodolite

Thē-ō-dō′-sī-ăn, *adj.* Of the Emperor Theodosius ; রোমসম্রাট থিওডোসিয়াস্‌সম্বন্ধীয়। **Theodosian code**—রোমসম্রাট দ্বিতীয় থিওডোসিয়াসের সময়ে প্রচলিত আইন।

thē-ŏg′-ō-nȳ, *n.* **1.** The genealogy of gods ; দেবগণের বংশবিবরণ, দেবোৎপত্তি (হিঃ কোঃ), দেববংশাবলী। **2.** A book dealing with the genealogy of gods ; দেবগণের বংশবিবরণ সম্বন্ধীয় পুস্তক। **—nist,** *n.* **—o-gon′-ic,** *adj.*

thē-ō-lō′-gī-ăn, *n.* A person well-versed in theology ; a divine ; ধর্ম্মশাস্ত্রজ্ঞ ; ধর্ম্মজ্ঞ, ধর্ম্মতত্ত্ববিৎ।

thē-ŏl′-ō-gȳ, *n.* The science which treats of God and divine things in their relation to man especially exhibited in Christian religion ; পরমার্থবিদ্যা, ধর্ম্মতত্ত্ব, ঈশ্বরবিদ্যা (হিঃ কোঃ), খৃষ্টীয় ধর্ম্মবিজ্ঞান। **—gize,** *v. t. & i.* **—o-log′-i-cal,** *adj.* **—o-log′-i-cal-ly,** *adv.* **Dogmatic theology**—খৃষ্টীয় ধর্ম্মশাস্ত্র এবং ধর্ম্মসংঘের মত এবং উপদেশের উপর প্রতিষ্ঠিত ধর্ম্মশাস্ত্র। **Natural Theology**—Same as NATURAL RELIGION under NATURAL. **Pastoral theology**—ধর্ম্মশাস্ত্রের যে অংশে যাজক এবং তদধীন ব্যক্তিগণের সম্পর্ক এবং কর্ত্তব্যের বিষয় আলোচিত হইয়া থাকে। **Positive** or **revealed theology**—ঈশ্বরের প্রত্যাদেশের উপর প্রতিষ্ঠিত ধর্ম্মশাস্ত্র। **Speculative theology**—যে ধর্ম্মশাস্ত্রের অন্তর্ভূত বিষয় সমূহের আলোচনায় মানুষের চিন্তার অবসর দেওয়া হয়। **Systematic theology**—প্রণালীবদ্ধ ধর্ম্মশাস্ত্র।

thē-ŏm′-ă-chȳ, *n.* A fighting against or among the gods ; দেবতাদিগের সহিত যুদ্ধ, দেবতাদিগের মধ্যে যুদ্ধ, দেবযুদ্ধ।

thē-ō-mā′-nī-ă, *n.* An insanity in which the sufferer believes himself to be the deity ; religious insanity ; একপ্রকার উন্মাদরোগ—যাহাতে কোন ব্যক্তি আপনাকে ঈশ্বর বলিয়া মনে করে ; দিব্যোন্মাদ। **—ac,** *n.*

thē-ŏph′-ă-nȳ, *n.* Appearance of God to man ; ঈশ্বরাবির্ভাব, (হিঃ কোঃ)।

thē-ō-phī-lăn′-thrŏ-pist, *n.* One of a society formed at Paris during the French Revolution. It had for its object to establish a new religion in place of Christianity ; ফরাসীবিপ্লবকালে প্রতিষ্ঠিত ধর্ম্মসম্প্রদায়বিশেষ। ইহারা খৃষ্টধর্ম্মের পরিবর্ত্তে ঈশ্বরের সহিত মানবের প্রেমমূলক এক নবধর্ম্ম স্থাপনে প্রয়াসী ছিলেন। **—py,** *n.*

thē′-ŏp-neus-tȳ (-nüs-) *n.* Divine inspiration ; ঈশ্বরপ্রেরণা, দৈবপ্রেরণা।

thē-ŏr′-bō, *n.* A musical instrument of the lute class having two necks ; একপ্রকার দ্বিগল সেতার জাতীয় বাদ্যযন্ত্র।

thē′-ō-rĕm, *n.* **1.** (*Math.*) A proposition that has to be proved, as distinguished from a problem that has to be solved ; (গণিতশাস্ত্র) যে প্রতিজ্ঞা যুক্তিপরম্পরা দ্বারা প্রমাণিত করিতে হয়, উপপদ্য, প্রমেয়োপপাদ্য (হিঃ কোঃ)। **2.** (*Algeb.*) A rule esp. a symbolic rule or formula ; as, the binomial *theorem* ; (বীজগণিত) নিয়ম, বিশেষতঃ সাঙ্কেতিক নিয়ম বা প্রক্রিয়া। **—re-mat′-ic, —re-mat′-i-cal,** *adjs.* **—rem′-a-tist,** *n.*

thē-ō-rĕt′-ic, *adj.* & *n.* Same as THEORETICAL. ***Noun.*** (*pl.*) The speculative part of a science ; কোন বিজ্ঞানের সূত্রাত্মক অংশ।

thē-ō-rĕt′-ī-căl, *adj.* Pertaining to theory ; speculative ; ঔপপত্তিক, সূত্রাত্মক ; অনুমানাত্মক, অনুমানমূলক, কল্পনাত্মক, সিদ্ধান্তাত্মক, কাল্পনিক (হিঃ কোঃ)। **—ly,** *adv.*

thē′-ō-rīc, *adj.* (*Gk. Antiq.*) Of, or pertaining to, public spectacles ; (গ্রীসদেশীয় প্রত্নতত্ত্ব) ক্রীড়াতামাসা প্রভৃতি সম্পর্কীয়। **Theoric fund**—দরিদ্র নাগরিকগণ যাহাতে বিনা ব্যয়ে

নাট্যাভিনয় প্রভৃতি দর্শন করিতে পারে, তদুদ্দেশ্যে প্রতিষ্ঠিত ধনভাণ্ডার।

thē'-ō-rȳ, *n.* **1.** The general or abstract principle of any body of facts real or assumed ; as, the *theory* of music ; কোন বাস্তব বা কল্পিত বিষয় সমূহের সাধারণ বা বস্তুনিরেপক্ষ তত্ত্ব সমূহ, তত্ত্ব। **2.** A supposition explaining something, esp. one based on principles independent of the phenomena etc. ; as, the atomic *theory* ; উপপত্তি, সিদ্ধান্ত, সিদ্ধন (ব্রজঃ হিন্দু), যুক্তি (হিঃ কোঃ), কল্পনা (ঐ), কল্প (ঐ), সূত্র (ঐ)। **3.** (*Math.*) A systematic statement of the general principles or laws of some branch of mathematics ; as, the *theory* of equations ; a set of theorems forming a connected system ; as, *theory* of probabilities ; গণিতের কোন শাখার সাধারণ মূলসূত্র বা নিয়মসমূহের প্রণালীবদ্ধভাবে বিবৃতি ; উপপত্তিপরম্পরা। **4.** Rules of art as opposed to practice ; ললিতকলার মূলসূত্র সমূহ, সূত্রাংশ। **5.** Hypothesis ; speculation ; conjecture ; কল্পনা, অভ্যুপগম, সিদ্ধান্ত ; চিন্তা ; অনুমান। **–rist**, *n.* One who theorizes ; উপপত্তিকারী। **–ri-za'-tion**, *n.* **–rize**, *v. i.* To form a theory or theories ; to speculate ; উপপত্তি করা, কোনরূপ মতবাদ স্থাপন করা ; চিন্তা করা।

thē-ŏs'-ō-phȳ, *n.* **1.** Knowledge of divine things or of the deity obtained in some direct way, as by intuition or special illumination ; ব্রহ্মবিদ্যা, (হিঃ কোঃ), অধ্যাত্মবিদ্যা (ঐ), ঈশ্বরশাস্ত্র (ঐ), দৈববিদ্যা (ঐ), ঈশ্বরবিদ্যা, তত্ত্ববিদ্যা। **2.** A system of modern religious thought which claims to a knowledge of the divinity and his works by supernatural inspiration ; ব্রহ্মবিজ্ঞানবাদ। **—o-soph'-ic, —o-soph'-i-cal**, *adjs.* **—pher, —phist**, *ns.* **—phize**, *v. i.* **Theosophical society**—তত্ত্ববিদ্যানুশীলন সমিতি, তাত্ত্বিকসংঘ। Col. Olcot, Madame Blavatsky এবং W. R. Judge কর্ত্তৃক ১৮৭৫ খৃঃ অব্দে আমেরিকার নিউইয়র্ক নগরীতে তত্ত্ববিদ্যানুশীলন সমিতি প্রথম প্রতিষ্ঠিত হয়। এই সমিতির তিনটী মুখ্য উদ্দেশ্য এই :—(১) বিশ্বজনীন সৌভ্রাত্রের ভিত্তি গঠন। (২) আর্য্য এবং অন্যান্য প্রাচ্য সাহিত্য, ধর্ম্ম এবং বিজ্ঞানের আলোচনা। (৩) প্রকৃতির অজ্ঞাত নিয়মনিচয় এবং মানবের অন্তর্গূঢ় বৃত্তি সমূহ সম্বন্ধে অনুসন্ধান। বর্ত্তমানে শ্রীমতী Annie Besant তত্ত্ববিদ্যানুশীলন সমিতির সভাপত্নী। মান্দ্রাজনগরীর উপকণ্ঠস্থিত Adyar নামক স্থানে তত্ত্ববিদ্যানুশীলন সমিতির প্রধান কেন্দ্র। পৃথিবীর নানা স্থানে তত্ত্ববিদ্যানুশীলন সমিতির প্রায় ৮০০ শত শাখা প্রতিষ্ঠিত আছে। [See Cinnet *Occult world* ; Col. Olcott *Theosophy* ; Madame Blavatsky *Isis Unveiled, The Secret Doctrine, The Key to Theosophy* ; Annie Besant *Theosophy and New Psychology.*]

thē'-ō-tĕch-nȳ, *n.* Supernatural machinery ; অতিপ্রাকৃত যন্ত্র। **–tech'-nic**, *adj.*

thĕr-ā-peu'-tic (-pū-), *adj.* & *n.* Curative ; pertaining to the healing art ; আরোগ্যকর, আময়িক ; আরোগ্যশাস্ত্রসম্পর্কীয়। ***Noun.*** (*Pl.*) That branch of medicine which treats of remedies and their action in the cure of diseases ; ভেষজবিদ্যার যে অংশে রোগের চিকিৎসার বিষয় উল্লেখ থাকে, আরোগ্য-শাস্ত্র, চিকিৎসাবিধান, আময়িকপ্রয়োগতত্ত্ব (হঃ চঃ), ঔষধব্যবহারবিদ্যা (ঐ), চিকিৎসাস্থান (সুশ্রুঃ কুঞ্জ)। **—ti-cal**, *adj.* **—ti-cal-ly**, *adv.* **—tist**, *n.*

there (thār), *adv., interj.* & *n.* **1.** In that place ; তথায়, সেই স্থানে, সেখানে। **2.** At that point or stage ; as, he did not stop *there* ; সেই স্থানে, সেই জায়গায়। **3.** In that respect ; as, *there* you are mistaken ; সেই সম্পর্কে, সেই বিষয়ে। **4.** Often used in place of a subject before a verb when the real subject comes after it ; "Wherever *there* is sense or perception, there some idea is actually produced". ***Interj.*** An exclamation of alarm, triumph, dismay, incitement, soothing, etc. ; ঐ ঐ ! মরি মরি ! হায় হায় ! ***Noun.*** That place ; as, he lives somewhere near *there* ; সেই স্থান। **All there**—(*Slang*) Sane ; (ইতরভাষায়) মাথা ঠিক। **Thereabout, Thereabouts**—Near that place ; তাহার নিকট, তার কাছাকাছি। **Thereafter**—(*Archaic*) After that ; ইহার পর। According to that rule etc. ; সেই বিষয় প্রভৃতি অনুসারে। **Thereanent** — (*Scot.*) About that thing ; সেই বিষয়ে। (*Arch.*) **Thereat**—At that place ; সেই স্থানে। After that ; ইহার পর। For that reason; সেই জন্য, সেইহেতু। **Thereby**—By that means ; as a result of that ; তদ্দ্বারা ; তাহার ফলে। **Therefor**—(*Archaic*) For that purpose ; তজ্জন্য, তদুদ্দেশ্যে। **Therefore** — For that reason ; তজ্জন্য, তদ্ধেতু, এনিমিত্ত, সেনিমিত্ত, এইজন্য, সেইজন্য, এইকারণ, সেইকারণ, এপ্রযুক্ত, সেপ্রযুক্ত। Consequently ; সুতরাং, অতএব। **Therefrom**—(*Archaic*) From this or that ; (অপ্রঃ) ইহা হইতে, তাহা হইতে। **Therein**—In that place ; সেই স্থানে। In that respect ; তৎসম্পর্কে। **Thereinafter**—(দলিলাদিতে) ইহার পরে। **Therein-before** — In the preceding part of that (writing, docment, etc. ; (দলিলাদিতে) পূর্ব্বে। **Thereof**—Of this or that ; ইহার, তাহার। **Thereout**—Out of that or this ; তাহা হইতে, ইহা হইতে। Therefore ; in consequence of that ; অতএব ; ইহার ফলে। **Thereto**—(*Archaic*) To that or this ইহাতে, তাহাতে। **Theretofore**—Up to that time ; সেই সময় পর্য্যন্ত। **Thereunder** — Under that or this ; তন্নিম্নে, ইহার নিম্নে। **Thereunto**—To that or this ; ইহাতে, তাহাতে। **Thereupon**—Upon that or this ; immediately ; তাহার ফলে, তৎফলে, তাহার অনতিকাল বা অব্যবহিত পরে ; তৎক্ষণাৎ। **Therewith**—With that ; thereupon ; তৎসহিত ; তাহার পরে। **Therewithal** — Besides ; in addition to ; এতদ্ব্যতীত, ইহা-ছাড়া ; অধিকন্তু। **To get there**—(*Slang*) To succeed ; (ইতরভাষায়) কৃতকার্য্য হওয়া। **You have been there before**—(*Slang*) You know all about it ; তুমি সে বিষয়ে সব কথাই জান।

thē-rē-ŏl'-ō-ğȳ, *n.* Science of mammals ; স্তন্যদায়িজন্তুতত্ত্ব। **—gist**, *n.*

thē'-ri-ăc, *n.* A compound medicine used as an antidote against the bite of poisonous animals ; বিষাক্ত জন্তুর দংশনের ঔষধ বিশেষ।

thē-ri-ăn-thrŏp'-ic, *adj.* Combining human and bestial form ; pertaining to religions in which the deities worshipped are conceived as partly human and partly animal in form ; নরপশ্বাকৃতি; যে সকল ধর্ম্মে দেবতাগণের কতকাংশ মানবাকৃতি এবং কতকাংশ পশ্বাকৃতি তৎসম্বন্ধীয়। **—an'-thro-pism**, *n.*

thêrm, *n.* The amount of heat required to raise one pound of water through 1° F. (60° to 61° F.) and equals 251·9 calories ; এক পাউণ্ড জলএর তাপ ফেরেনহিট তাপমান যন্ত্রের এক অঙ্ক বৃদ্ধি করার জন্য যে পরিমাণ তাপের আবশ্যক হয়।

thêr'-mae (-mē), *n.* (*pl.*) Hot-springs ; hot-baths ; উষ্ণ প্রস্রবণ ; উষ্ণজলে স্নানের নিমিত্ত স্নানাগার, উষ্ণ-স্নানাগার।

thêr'-măl, *adj.* **1.** Of, or pertaining to, heat ; warm ; তাপসম্বন্ধীয়, তাপিক ; তপ্ত, উষ্ণ। **2.** Of thermae ; উষ্ণপ্রস্রবণসম্বন্ধীয়, উষ্ণস্নানাগার সম্বন্ধীয়। **3.** Erotic ; "*Thermal* school of poetry :" passionate ; কামানলদগ্ধ, শৃঙ্গাররসপ্রধান ; ক্রোধী। **Thermal alarm**—তাপিকবিপৎসঙ্কেত। **Thermal analysis** — তাপিক বিশ্লেষণ। **Thermal capacity**—তাপিক ধারণ-শক্তি, কোন বস্তুর তাপ এক অঙ্ক বৃদ্ধি করিতে যে পরিমাণ তাপের আবশ্যক হয়। **Thermal efficiency** — প্রদত্ত উত্তাপের অনুপাতেকোন যন্ত্র যে পরিমাণে কার্য্য করিয়া থাকে, তাপিককার্য্যক্ষমতা। **Thermal equator** — ভূপৃষ্ঠস্থ যে রেখায় সর্ব্বোচ্চ তাপ অনুভূত হয়, তাপ-রেখা। **Thermal motor**—তাপিকগতি-সঞ্চারক যন্ত্র। **Thermal springs**—উষ্ণপ্রস্রবণ। **Thermal unit**—তাপাঙ্ক (হিঃ কোঃ)। **Thermal weight**—তাপভার (হিঃ কোঃ)।

thêr-măn'-ti-dōte, *n.* An apparatus for making a current of cool air, used in India ; ভারতবর্ষের টানা পাখা।

thêr'-mic, *adj.* Pertaining, or relating, to heat ; তাপসম্বন্ধীয়, তাপিক। **Thermic balance**—তাপক্রমমান (হিঃ কোঃ)।

Thêr-mi-dŏr', *n.* The eleventh month of the year in the calendar of the first French Republic ; প্রথম ফরাসীগণতন্ত্রের পঞ্জিকার একাদশতম মাস (১৯শে জুলাই হইতে ১৭ই আগষ্ট)।

Thêr-mi-dō'-ri-ăn, *n.* One of those who took part in the *coup d'etat* by which the fall of Robespierre was effected on Thermidor 9th, 1794 ; ১৭৯৪ খৃষ্টাব্দের থার্মিডোর মাসের ৯ তারিখে Robespierreএর পতনের ব্যাপারে সংসৃষ্ট ব্যক্তি।

thêr'-mō-, (In combination) warm ; উষ্ণ।

thêr-mō-bă-rŏm'-ē-têr, *n.* **1.** Same as HYPSOMETER. **2.** A siphon barometer adapted to be used also as thermometer ; তাপবলবায়ুভারমাপক (হিঃ কোঃ)।

thêr-mō-chĕm-is-trȳ, *n.* That department of chemistry which deals with the thermal effects accompanying chemical actions, রসায়নশাস্ত্রের বিভাগবিশেষ — যাহাতে রাসায়নিক ক্রিয়ার ফলে জনিত তাপসম্বন্ধে আলোচিত হইয়া থাকে, তাপরসায়ন।

thêr-mō-dȳ-năm'-ics, *n.* The science which deals with relation between heat and work ; উত্তাপ এবং কার্য্যের সম্বন্ধমূলক বিজ্ঞান, তাপগতি-বিজ্ঞান, তাপগতিশাস্ত্র (হিঃ কোঃ)।

thêr-mō-ē-lĕc-tric'-i-tȳ, *n.* Electricity produced by difference of temperature ; তাপবৈষম্যদ্বারা উৎপন্ন তাড়িত, তাপতাড়িৎ (হিঃ কোঃ)। **—lec'-tric**, *adj.*

thêr-mō-ē-lĕc-trŏm'-ē-têr, *n.* An instrument for determining the heating power of electric currents ; তাড়িতপ্রবাহের তাপনশক্তি পরিমাপের জন্য যন্ত্রবিশেষ, তাপবিদ্যুৎ-মাপক (হিঃ কোঃ)।

thêr-mō-ğĕn'-ē-sis, *n.* Production of heat esp. in the body ; তাপজনন, দেহে তাপসঞ্চার। **—ge-net'-ic, —gen'-ic**, *adjs.*

thêr-'mō-grăm, *n.* A record made by a thermograph ; তাপাঙ্কক যন্ত্রের লিপিবদ্ধ বিষয়, তাপলিপি।

thêr'-mō-grăph, *n.* An instrument used for automatically recording the fluctuations in the temperature of the air ; বায়ুর তাপপরিমাণ লিখনের জন্য একপ্রকার স্বয়ংবহ যন্ত্র, তাপাঙ্কক, তাপমাপক (হিঃ কোঃ)।

Thermo-meter.

thêr-mŏm'-ē-têr, *n.* An instrument for measuring temperature ; তাপমানযন্ত্র, তাপমাপক (হিঃ কোঃ), তাপমান (সাঃ পঃ), উষ্ণতামান (ঐ)। **—mo-met'-ric, —mo-met'-ri-cal**, *adjs.*

thêr-mō-mō'-tŏr, *n.* An engine worked by heat ; a hot-air engine ; তাপশক্তিদ্বারা চালিত যন্ত্র, তাপযন্ত্র ; উষ্ণ বায়ুদ্বারা চালিত যন্ত্র।

thêr′-mō-pīle, *n.* A thermoelectric battery ; তাপতাড়িতবিদ্যুদ্‌ঘটমালা।

thêr′-mō-scōpe, *n.* An instrument for measuring minute differences of temperature ; তাপপরিমাণের সূক্ষ্ম বৈষম্য পরিমাপের জন্য যন্ত্রবিশেষ, তাপভেদবীক্ষণ। **—scop′-ic,** *adj.*

thêr′-mō-stăt, *n.* A self-acting apparatus for regulating temperature ; তাপপরিমাণ নিয়মনের জন্য একপ্রকার স্বয়ংবহযন্ত্র, তাপনিয়ামক। **—stat′-ic,** *adj.* **—stat′-ics,** *n.* Theory of the equilibrium of heat; তাপসামঞ্জস্যবাদ, তাপস্থিতিবিজ্ঞান।

thêr-mō-tĕn′-sīle, *adj.* **1.** Pertaining to variation of tensile strength with the temperature ; তাপপরিমাণের পরিবর্ত্তনের সঙ্গে প্রসারণ-শক্তির বৈলক্ষণ্যসম্বন্ধীয়, তাপপ্রসারণীয়।

thêr-mō-trŏp′-ic, *adj.* Turning or bending under the influence of heat ; তাপপ্রভাবে ঘূর্ণায়মান বা নমনশীল, তাপানুগামী। **—mot′-ro-pism,** *n.* The bending or growth of any organism dependent on temperature ; তাপানুগমন (সাঃ পঃ)।

thêr′-mō-tȳpe, *n.* An impression (as of a slice of wood) taken by means of wetting with dilute acid, pressing on the object, and subsequently heating the impression ; অগাঢ় দ্রাবকদ্বারা সিক্ত (কাষ্ঠ-ফলক হইতে) গৃহীত ছাপ—যাহা পরে উত্তপ্ত করিয়া বীক্ষণযোগ্য করা হয়।

thĕ′-roid (-rōyd), *adj.* Having beast-like propensities ; পাশবিক আসক্তিসম্পন্ন।

thē-sau′-rŭs (-sä-), *n.* A treasury ; a lexicon ; ভাণ্ডার ; অভিধান, শব্দভাণ্ডার।

thē′-sis, *n.* **1.** A proposition to be maintained ; a postulate ; পূর্ব্বপক্ষ (হিঃ কোঃ), সাধ্য (হিঃ কোঃ), প্রতিজ্ঞা (ঐ) ; স্বীকার্য্য। **2.** An essay or dissertation upon a specific or definite theme ; an essay presented by a candidate for a diploma or degree ; নিবন্ধ ; উপাধি প্রভৃতি লাভের জন্য পরীক্ষার্থী কর্ত্তৃক অর্পিত নিবন্ধ। **3.** (*Rhet.*) The part of a sentence preceding and corresponding to an antithesis ; (অলঙ্কার-শাস্ত্র) কোন বাক্যের বিরোধালঙ্কারের পূর্ব্ববর্ত্তী অংশ। **4.** School or college exercise ; বিদ্যালয় অথবা মহাবিদ্যালয়ের অনুশীলনী। **5.** (*Pros.*) The accented part of a foot ; (ছন্দঃশাস্ত্র) কবিতার চরণের স্বরিত অংশ।

Thĕs′-pĭ-ăn, *adj.* Of, or pertaining to, Thespis, dramatic poet of the 6th century B. C ; খৃঃ পূঃ ৬ষ্ঠ শতাব্দীর গ্রীসদেশীয় নাট্যকবি Thespis সম্বন্ধীয়। **Thespian art**—নাট্যকলা।

thē′-ur-ġȳ (-ĕr-), *adj.* The working of a divine or supernatural agency in human affairs ; the producing of effects by spiritual means ; পার্থিব ব্যাপারে দৈব বা অলৌকিক ক্রিয়া ; অলৌকিক উপায়ে কার্য্য সাধন। **—gist,** *n.* **—ur′-gic, —ur′-gi-cal,** *adjs.*

thews (thūs), *n.* (*pl.*) Sinews ; muscle ; strength ; স্নায়ু ; পেশী ; শক্তি। **Thewed, Thew′-less, Thew′-y,** *adjs.*

they (thā), *pron.* The plural form for all the genders of the third person, that is for *he, she,* or *it* ; তাহারা।

thick, *adj., n.* & *adv.* **1.** Having greater extent or depth than usual from one surface to another ; as, the board is three inches *thick* ; পুরু। **2.** Dense ; as, *thick* grass ; compact ; hence, deep ; as, *thick* darkness ; ঘন ; নিবিড়, সংহত ; গভীর, গাঢ়, সান্দ্র। **3.** Muddy ; foggy ; as, *thick* weather ; ঘোলা, কর্দ্দমাক্ত, পঙ্কিল ; কুজ্ঝটিকাচ্ছন্ন। **4.** Stupid ; dull ; as, he is too *thick* to understand this ; স্থূলবুদ্ধি ; মন্দবুদ্ধি। **5.** Indistinct ; inarticulate ; muffled ; as, a *thick* voice ; অস্পষ্ট, অস্ফুট ; অব্যক্ত ; মন্দীভূত। **6.** (*Colloq.*) Intimate ; friendly ; "Newcome and I are not very *thick* together" ; (চলিত ভাষায়) অন্তরঙ্গ ; বন্ধুভাবাপন্ন। **7.** Dull ; weak ; as, he is *thick* of hearing ; অপ্রখর ; দুর্ব্বল। **8.** Abounding ; packed with ; filled ; as, *thick* with snow ; ভূয়িষ্ঠ ; সমাচ্ছন্ন ; পরিপূর্ণ। **9.** Close set or planted ; as, the ground set *thick* with trees ; ঘনসন্নিবিষ্ট, ঘনবিন্যস্ত, ঘন ভাবে রোপিত, অবিরলবিন্যস্ত। **10.** Following each other in close succession ; অতিদ্রুত পরস্পরের অনুবর্ত্তী। **11.** Stolid ; মানাপমান-বোধশূন্য। ***Noun.*** **1.** The thickest part of anything ; the time when anything is thickest ; কোন বস্তুর নিবিড় বা ঘনতম অংশ, ভিড়, সঙ্কুল-স্থান, গভীরপ্রদেশ ; যে সময়ে কোন কিছু নিবিড়তম বা ঘনতম হয়। **2.** (*Colloq.*) A thick-headed person ; "What a *thick* I was to come" ; (চলিত ভাষায়) স্থূলবুদ্ধি ব্যক্তি। ***Adv.*** Thickly ; ঘনভাবে, নিবিড়ভাবে, গাঢ়-রূপে। **Thick′-en,** *v. i.* & *t.* **1.** To become thick or more thick ; ঘন হওয়া, নিবিড় হওয়া, সান্দ্র হওয়া, গাঢ়তর হওয়া। **2.** To be coagulated ; জমিয়া যাওয়া। ***Verb t.*** **1.** To make thick or thicker ; ঘন করা, গাঢ় করা, ঘনতর করা, নিবিড়তর করা। **2.** To inspissate ; গাঢ় করা, জমাট করা। **Thick′-en-ing,** *adj.* & *n.* **Thick′-ly,** *adv.* **Thick′-ness,** *n.* **1.** The quality or state of being thick ; ঘনতা, নিবিড়তা, গাঢ়তা, সান্দ্রতা। **2.** Depth ; গভীরতা। **3.** Closeness of the parts ; ঘন-সন্নিবিষ্টতা। **4.** Mistiness ; কুজ্ঝটিকা-চ্ছন্নতা। **5.** Dullness of wit ; মন্দবুদ্ধিতা, স্থূলবুদ্ধিতা। **Thick-and-thin,** *adj.* Ready to go whatever is in the way ; সর্ব্বাবস্থায় অনুবর্ত্তনে প্রস্তুত। **Thickhead**—স্থূল-বুদ্ধি। **Thick-knee**—একপ্রকার পক্ষী। **Thick-leaved** — ঘন পত্রাচ্ছাদিত।

Thick-lipped—নিবিড়ৌষ্ঠযুক্ত। **Thick-lips** — নিবিড় ওষ্ঠাধরযুক্ত ব্যক্তি; কাফ্রী। **Thickset** — ঘনসন্নিবিষ্ট, ঘনবিন্যস্ত; দৃঢ়সংহতদেহ। **Thick-skinned** — মানাপমানবোধশূন্য। **Thick-skulled, Thick-witted**—স্থূলবুদ্ধি, জড়বুদ্ধি। **Thick'un**—(ইতরভাষায়:) সভারেন (মুদ্রা)। **The plot thickens** — The plot is becoming more complicate; আখ্যানটী জটিলতর হইয়া উঠিতেছে। **To lay it on thick**—See under LAY. **To go through thick and thin**—See under GO.

thick'-ĕt, *n.* A wood or collection of trees and shrubs closely set; ঝোপ, কুঞ্জ, বিপিন, গহন, ঝাড়, নিকুঞ্জ।

thief (thēf), *n.* One that secretly, unlawfully, and feloniously takes the goods and personal property of another; চোর, তস্কর, অপহারক। [Syn. কুম্ভীল, স্তেন, মোষক, হৈরিক।] **Thiev'-er-y**, *n.* Theft; practice of stealing; চৌর্য্য; চৌর্য্যবৃত্তি। **Thiev'-ish**, *adj.* **Thiev'-ish-ness**, *n.* The quality of being thievish; চৌর্য্যশীলতা। **Thiev'-ish-ly**, *adv.* **Thief-catcher**—যে ব্যক্তি চোর ধরে, চৌরোদ্ধরণিক (মৃণালিনী)। **Thief-tube**—পেপা হইতে নমুনার জন্য মদ্য বাহির করার নলবিশেষ। **Thieve's vinegar** — সির্কার সহিত নানাপ্রকার পত্রাদির কাথের মিশ্রণে পূর্ব্বকালে ব্যবহৃত প্লেগের ঔষধ বিশেষ।

thieve (thēv), *v. t.* & *i.* To take by theft; চুরি করা, অপহরণ করা। ***Verb i.*** To practise stealing; to be a thief; চৌর্য্যবৃত্তি করা; চোর হওয়া।

thigh (thī), *n.* The thick part of the human leg between the knee and the hip-joint; উরু। **Thigh-bone** — উর্ব্বস্থি। **Thigh-joint**—উরু-সন্ধি। **To smite hip and thigh**—See HIP.

thill, *n.* The shaft of a cart or carriage; শকটের যুগন্ধর। **Thill-horse, Thiller**—যুগন্ধরদ্বয়ের মধ্যে সংযোজিত অশ্ব।

thim'-blie, (-bl), *n.* 1. A metal cap cover for the thumb used in sewing to protect the finger from the needle; সেলাই করার কালে অঙ্গুষ্ঠে যে ধাতুর টোপ পরা হইয়া থাকে, অঙ্গুস্তানা, অঙ্গুলীত্রাণ, অঙ্গুষ্ঠানা, অঙ্গুলিকা। 2. (*Mech.*) A thimble-shaped fixture; প্রাচীরাদিতে নিবদ্ধ অঙ্গুস্তানার আকার বস্তু। 3. An iron ring with a hollow or groove round its whole circumference, to receive the ropes, which is spliced round it; প্রান্তে খাঁজবিশিষ্ট লৌহচক্র। **Thimble-joint, Thimble-coupling**—এক-প্রকার জোড়া। **Thimbleful**—অঙ্গুষ্ঠানাপরিমাণ, অল্পপরিমাণ। **Thimble-pie** — শাস্তিস্বরূপ অঙ্গুস্তানাদ্বারা মস্তকে যে ঠুকা দেওয়া হয়। **Thimblerig**, *n.* & *v. i.* অঙ্গুস্তানার আকৃতি তিনটী পেয়ালা এবং মটর দ্বারা করকৌশল প্রদর্শনের ক্রীড়াবিশেষ। [কোন পেয়ালার নীচে মটর থাকে তাহা দর্শকগণকে বলিতে হয়। ঠিক বলিতে না পারিলে বাজি হারে।] (*Verb i.*) উক্তরূপ কৌশল প্রদর্শন করা। **Thimble-rigger**—উক্তরূপ কৌশলপ্রদর্শনকারী।

thin, *adj.*, *v. t.* & *i.* 1. Having little thickness or extent from one surface to another; as *thin* paper; পাতল। 2. Slender; fine; as, *thin* wire; সরু; সূক্ষ্ম। 3. Not thick or dense; হাল্কা, পাতল। 4. Lean; as, a *thin* body; কৃশ, কাহিল, শীর্ণ, ছিপছিপে। 5. Not dense; as a *thin* wood; not close or crowded; অনিবিড়, অঘন, বিরল; জনতাহীন, ফাঁক ফাঁক। 6. Transparent; easily seen; as, *thin* disguise; স্বচ্ছ; অনায়াসে দৃষ্ট। 7. (*Fig.*) Flimsy; slight; as, *thin* pretext; (লক্ষণায়) অকিঞ্চিৎকর, অন্তঃসারশূন্য; সামান্য। 8. Scanty; scantily provided; স্বল্প, অপ্রচুর; অপ্রচুর বস্তু প্রদত্ত। ***Verb t.*** 1. To make thin or thinner; বিরল করা, বিরলতর করা, কৃশ করা, কৃশতর করা। 2. To attenuate; হ্রাস করা। ***Verb i.*** 1. To reduce in bulk or number; আয়তন বা সংখ্যা হ্রাস করা। 2. To remove surplus plants or trees, or to take out superfluous fruits, etc. to improve the rest; অপর সকলের উন্নতির জন্য অতিরিক্ত বৃক্ষসকল বা ফলাদি অপসারিত করা। 3. To grow or become thin or thinner; to become less dense; পাতল হওয়া, কৃশ হওয়া, কৃশতর হওয়া; বিরলতর হওয়া, অঘনতর হওয়া, অনিবিড় হওয়া। **Thin'-ly**, *adv.* **Thin'-ness**, *n.* The state or quality of being thin; সূক্ষ্মত্ব, বিরলতা, তনুতা, কৃশতা, শীর্ণতা, তনিমা। **Thin'-nish**, *adj.* **Thin-skinned**—যে ব্যক্তি সহজেই চটিয়া উঠে, আশুক্রোধী ব্যক্তি, কোপন স্বভাব ব্যক্তি। **The thin end of the wedge**—See WEDGE.

thīne, See THY.

thing, *n.* 1. Whatever may be thought of, or spoken of; some thing; বস্তু, পদার্থ; কোন বস্তু। 2. An inanimate object; অচেতন পদার্থ, অচেতন বস্তু। 3. An animate object (*in contempt, pity, etc.*); as, poor *thing*; বেচারা। 4. An act; as, a foolish *thing* to do; a matter; কার্য্য; বিষয়। 5. (*Pl.*) Personal belongings; as, to pack one's *things*; apparel; as, I got my *things* soiled; জিনিষ-পত্র, লওয়াজিমা, তল্পিতল্পা; পোষাক পরিচ্ছদ, কাপড়চোপড়। 6. (*Law*) Real or personal property; স্থাবর বা অস্থাবর সম্পত্তি। 7. Type or specimen; as, latest *thing* in hat; নমুনা, ধরণ। **Thing-in-itself**—স্বরূপ, দ্রব্যমাত্র (হিঃ কোঃ), স্বরূপ বস্তু (দ্বিজেন্দ্র) [কোন বস্তুর স্বয়ংসিদ্ধরূপ — ইন্দ্রিয়সমানীত সংবেদন দ্বারা যেরূপ প্রতিভাত হয়—তাহা নয়।] **I am not feeling at all the thing**—I am not feeling well;

অসোয়াস্তি বোধ করিতেছি। **Not the thing**—Not the proper thing—সঙ্গত বিষয় নয়। **The thing**—ঠিক জিনিষ, যাহা হওয়া উচিত ঠিক তাহাই। **To do handsome things by**—To behave gracefully; মধুর ব্যবহার করা, প্রীতিজনক ব্যবহার করা। **To know a thing or two**—To be experienced; পাকা হওয়া, অভিজ্ঞ হওয়া। **To make a good thing of**—To earn a good deal of money from something; কোন কিছু দ্বারা বেশ দুপয়সা রোজগার করা।

thing'-ă-mў, thing'-ŭm-ă-jig, thing'-ŭm-bŏb, thing'-ŭm-mў, *ns.* A term used when one is at a loss for a definite name of a person or thing; what's his name; যে জিনিষ বা লোকের নাম নির্দ্দেশ করা যাইতে পারিতেছে না—তৎসম্বন্ধে ব্যবহৃত শব্দ; এটার নামটা কি? এটাকে কি বলা হয়—এইরূপ শব্দ।

think (thingk), *v. t.* & *i.* **1.** To have the mind occupied on some object; to revolve ideas in the mind; চিন্তা করা; ভাবা। **2.** To imagine; ভাবা, মনে করা। **3.** To occur to; উদয় হওয়া। ***Verb i.*** **1.** To occupy the mind on some subject; বিষয়ে চিন্তা করা। **2.** To imagine; ভাবা, মনে করা। **3.** To guess; অনুমান করা। **4.** To judge; বিচার করা। **5.** To form an opinion; কোন বিষয়ে মত করা। **Think'-a-ble,** *adj.* That can be thought of; চিন্তনীয়, চিন্ত্য। **Think'-er,** *n.* One who thinks; esp. one who thinks in a particular manner; চিন্তাকারী, চিন্তাশীল; ভাবুক। **Think'-ing,** *n.* **1.** The act of one who thinks; চিন্তা, ভাবন, চিন্তন, মনন। **2.** A thought or idea; চিন্তা, ভাব। **To think about**—To consider about; কোন বিষয়ে ভাবা। **To think aloud**—To express one's thoughts in audible language as they pass one's mind; মনের ভিতর যে সকল চিন্তা চলিতেছে তাহা উচ্চশব্দে প্রকাশ করা। **To think better of it**—To form a more favourable opinion of; কাহারো সম্বন্ধে অধিকতর অনুকূল মত পোষণ করা। To alter one's decision on a thing after reconsideration; পুনর্বিবেচনার পর কোন বিষয়ে নিজের সিদ্ধান্ত পরিবর্ত্তন করা। **To think fit** or **good**—To regard proper; উচিত মনে করা, সঙ্গত মনে করা, ঠিক মনে করা। **To think furiously**—To cogitate deeply on a complicated subject; কোন জটিল বিষয়ে গভীর চিন্তা করা। **To think highly, much, well**—To esteem greatly; অতিশয় বড় মনে করা। **To think little** or **nothing**—To regard as worthless; নগণ্য মনে করা, অকিঞ্চিৎকর বলিয়া ভাবা। **To think long**—To wait for a long time; দীর্ঘকাল প্রতীক্ষা করা; আকুলভাবে আকাঙ্ক্ষা করা। **To think no end of a person**—To have high opinion about a man's character; কোন লোকের চরিত্রসম্বন্ধে উচ্চ মত পোষণ করা। **To think of**—To consider; ভাবা। To hit upon; কোন বিষয় মনে হঠাৎ ঠেকা, হঠাৎ মনে উদিত হওয়া। To entertain the idea of; কোন ভাব পোষণ করা। **To think out**—To devise by thinking; চিন্তা করিয়া বাহির করা। To solve by a process of thought; চিন্তা দ্বারা সমাধান করা। To finish or complete by thinking; চিন্তা করিয়া সমাধা করা। **To think over**—To apply the mind steadily to decide something; কোন বিষয়ে স্থির সিদ্ধান্তে উপনীত হওয়ার জন্য ক্রমাগত চিন্তা করা। To reflect on or upon something; কোন বিষয়ে চিন্তা করা, ভাবিয়া দেখা।

third (thĕrd), *adj.* & *n.* **1.** The next after the second; তৃতীয়। **2.** Being of the three equal parts into which anything is divided; তৃতীয়াংশীভূত, তৃতীয়াংশস্বরূপ। ***Noun.*** **1.** One of the three equal parts into which a thing is divided; তৃতীয়াংশ, তৃতীয় ভাগ, ত্রিভাগ, ত্র্যংশ। **2.** The sixtieth part of a second of time or arc; একসেকেণ্ডের ষাট ভাগের একভাগ, বৃত্ত খণ্ডের ষাট ভাগের একভাগ। **3.** (*Pl.*) The third part of a husband's personal property going to the wife in certain cases; মৃত স্বামীর ব্যক্তিগত সম্পত্তির তৃতীয়াংশ—যাহা কোন কোন অবস্থায় তদীয় পত্নী প্রাপ্ত হইয়া থাকে। **Third'-ly,** *adv.* **Third day**—মঙ্গলবার। **Third estate**—ইংলণ্ডের সাধারণশ্রেণীর লোক; বিলাতের প্রাকৃত সভা। **Third man**—ক্রীকেট ক্রীড়ায় ত্রিদণ্ড হইতে কোণাকোণি পশ্চাদ্দিকে অবস্থিত ক্রীড়ক; ঐ ক্রীড়কের স্থান। **Third person**—(ব্যাকরণ) প্রথম পুরুষ। **Third-rate**—নিকৃষ্ট। **Third Republic**—১৮৭১ খৃঃ অব্দে প্রতিষ্ঠিত সাধারণতন্ত্র। **Third Founder of Rome**—কেয়্যাস্ ম্যারিয়াস।

thirst (thĕrst), *n.* & *v. i.* **1.** Dryness of mouth or throat from want of some fluid to drink; পিপাসা, তৃষ্ণা, তেষ্টা (*colloq.*), তিয়াস (*poet.*), পিয়াস (*ib.*)। **2.** An eager desire after anything (with *of, after, for*); as, *thirst for* knowlege; তৃষ্ণা, পিপাসা [cf. জ্ঞানপিপাসা, ধনাগমতৃষ্ণা)। ***Verb i.*** **1.** To feel thirst; তৃষ্ণা পাওয়া, পিপাসা বোধ করা। **2.** To have an ardent longing for something; কোন বিষয়ের জন্য প্রবল পিপাসা থাকা। **Thirst'-i-ly,** *adv.* **Thirst'-i-ness,** *n.* **Thirst'-less,** *adj.* **Thirst'-y,** *adj.* **1.** Feeling a sensation of pain or uneasiness for want of drink; পিপাসিত, তৃষ্ণার্ত্ত, তৃষ্ণাতুর, তৃষ্ণি, সতৃষ্ণ (*poet.*), তৃষ্ণাকুল, জলার্থী। **2.** (*Fig.*) Having an ardent desire for something ; (লক্ষণায়) পিপাসু। **3.** (*Colloq.*) Causing thirst ; as, a *thirsty* food ; (চলিত ভাষায়) তৃষ্ণাজনক। **4.** Dry ; parched ; as, *thirsty* fields ; শুষ্ক ; রৌদ্রদগ্ধ।

thir'-teen (thêr-tēn), *adj.* & *n.* Ten and three ; তের, ত্রয়োদশ। ***Noun.*** The number greater by three than ten ; ত্রয়োদশ বস্তু। **–teenth,** *adj.* & *n.* The third after the tenth; ত্রয়োদশতম, তেরই। ***Noun.*** One of thirteen equal parts of anything ; কোন বস্তুর ত্রয়োদশতম অংশ। **Thirteen to the dozen**—পুঁজির উপর একটী।

thir'-tў, (thêr-), *adj.* & *n.* Thrice ten or twenty and ten ; ত্রিশ, ত্রিংশৎ। ***Noun.*** The number which consists of three times ten ; ত্রিংশৎ সংখ্যা। **–ti-eth,** *adj.* & *n.* **1.** Next in order after the twenty-ninth ; ত্রিংশত্তম। **2.** Being one of the thirty equal parts of a thing ; কোন বস্তুর ত্রিংশত্তম অংশ স্বরূপ। ***Noun.*** One of the thirty equal parts of anything ; কোন বস্তুর ত্রিংশদ্ভাগের একভাগ।

t͟his, *adj.* & *pron.* **1.** Used to denote something that is present or near in place or time, or that has been just mentioned ; এই, উপস্থিত, বর্ত্তমান। **2.** *This* is used as opposed or correlative to *that* ; ইহা। ***Pron.*** Indicating a thing or person present or near ; ইহা। **This'-ness,** *n.* The state or quality of being this ; ইদংতা, বস্তুতা, ইদংত্ব, এতত্ত্বা, এততা। **This day**—অদ্য, আজি। **This day week**—আগামী সপ্তাহের এই দিবস। **This night**—অদ্য রাত্র, অদ্য রজনী।

this'-tle (-l), *n.* A prickly composite plant, the national emblem of Scotland ; একপ্রকার কাঁটা গাছ, শিয়াল কাঁটা (yellow)। [এই বৃক্ষ স্কটলণ্ড দেশের জাতীয়চিহ্নস্বরূপ ব্যবহৃত হয়।] **–tly,** *adj.* **Order of the Thistle**—স্কটলণ্ড দেশের নাইট সম্প্রদায় বিশেষ।

t͟hit͟h'-êr, *adv.* (*Archaic*) To that place ; (অপ্রঃ) তথায়, সেইস্থানে। **–ward, –wards,** *adj.* Toward that place ; সেইদিকে, সেই স্থানে।

thlip'-sis, *n.* (*Med.*) Constriction of a blood-vessel etc. by external compression; (ভৈষজ্য-শাস্ত্র) বহির্দ্দিকে সঞ্চালন হেতু রক্তবহা নাড়ী প্রভৃতির সঙ্কোচন।

t͟hō', See THOUGH.

thōle, *v. t.* & *i.* **1.** (*Archaic*) To undergo ; (অপ্রঃ) ভোগা, সহ্য করা, ভোগ করা। **2.** To permit of ; as, the style would *thole* amends ; সহ্য হওয়া। ***Verb i.*** To wait ; অপেক্ষা করা।

thōle, *n.* A pin in the gunwale of a boat to support the oar in rowing ; দাঁড় আটকাইবার গুঁজি, দাঁড়ের ঠেকো, পোলো।

Thom'-ăs (tŏm-), *n.* One of the twelves disciples of Jesus Christ ; যীশুখৃষ্টের অন্যতম শিষ্য। [ইনি কিছুকাল পর্য্যন্ত খৃষ্টের পুনরুত্থানে অবিশ্বাসী ছিলেন।] **A very Thomas**—অতিশয় অবিশ্বাসী লোক।

Tho'-mism (tŏ-), *n.* The doctrine of St. Thomas Aquinas with respect to predestination and grace, and specially the immaculate conception of the Virgin ; পূর্ব্ব-বিধানবাদ ও দেবানুগ্রহ এবং বিশেষতঃ কুমারী মেরীর অকলঙ্ক গর্ভসঞ্চার সম্বন্ধে মধ্যযুগের সিদ্ধপুরুষ Thomas Aquinasএর মত। [Thomas Aquinas পূর্ব্ববিধান এবং দেবানুগ্রহ স্বীকার করিতেন। তিনি কুমারী মেরীর অকলঙ্ক গর্ভসঞ্চার স্বীকার করিতেন না।] **–mist,** *n.* **–mis'-tic, –mis'-ti-cal,** *adjs.*

thŏng, *n.* & *v. t.* A strap of leather used for fastening anything ; a strip of leather used as whip, lash, a rein, etc. ; কোন কিছু বাঁধিবার জন্য চামড়ার দোয়ালী ; চাবুকের জন্য চর্ম্মরজ্জু, ঘোড়ার লাগামের চামড়া প্রভৃতি। ***Verb t.*** To provide with thong ; to strike with a thong ; "Mrs. Newcome *thonged* him with the lash of her indignation" ; চামড়ার দোয়ালী প্রভৃতি লাগান ; কষাঘাত করা।

Thŏr, *n.* (*In Norse Myth.*) The God of thunder, agriculture and war ; (স্কেণ্ডিনেভিয়ান পুরাণে) বজ্র, কৃষি, যুদ্ধ, প্রভৃতির দেবতা। [এই দেবতার বয়স তরুণ। কেশ ও শ্মশ্রু রক্তবর্ণ। ইনি ছাগবাহিত রথে ভ্রমণ করেন।]

thō'-răl, *adj.* Nuptial ; বৈবাহিক। **Thoral-line**—বিবাহ রেখা।

thō'-răx (*pl.* -RACES.) That part of the human body which contains lungs, heart, etc ; the chest ; গ্রীবা ও উদরের মধ্যবর্ত্তী শরীরের গহ্বর ; বক্ষঃ, বক্ষঃস্থল। **–rac'-ic,** *adj.* Of, or pertaining to, the thorax or breast ; উরস (সাঃ পঃ)। **Thoracic duct**—রসবহা নাড়ী (সাঃ পঃ)। **Thoracic leg**—বুকের পা।

thō'-ri-ă, *n.* An oxide of thorium largely used in the manufacture of gas mantles ; একপ্রকার শ্বেতবর্ণ খনিজ পদার্থ।

thō'-rīte, *n.* A black mineral found in Norway ; নরওয়ে দেশে প্রাপ্ত একপ্রকার কৃষ্ণবর্ণ খনিজ পদার্থ।

thō'-ri-ŭm, *n.* A rare metal existing as a grey powder easily inflammable ; ধূসর চূর্ণাকারে প্রাপ্ত একপ্রকার আশুদাহ্য দুষ্প্রাপ্য ধাতু, থোরক (সাঃ পঃ)।

thŏrn, *n.* **1.** A spine ; কণ্টক, কাঁটা, শল্য। **2.** A tree or shrub armed with spines or prickles ; কণ্টকবৃক্ষ, কণ্টকতরু, কাঁটা গাছ, কণ্টকগুল্ম। **3.** Anything painful, irritating or troublesome ; as, a *thorn* on one's side ; কণ্টকস্বরূপ বস্তু। **Thorn'-less,** *adj.* Without thorn; কণ্টকহীন, নিষ্কণ্টক। **Thorn'-y,** *adj.* **1.** Spiny ; full of thorns ; কণ্টকময়, কণ্টকসমাচ্ছন্ন, সকণ্টক, কণ্টকী, কণ্টকাবৃত, কণ্টকাঢ্য (বৃঃ সং)। কণ্টকবহুল। **2.** Like thorn ; vexatious ; as, a *thorny* problem ; কণ্টকবৎ ; বিরক্তিজনক। **Thorn-apple**—See STRAMONIUM. **Thorn-back** — একপ্রার চাঁদা মাছ। **Thornbill**—একপ্রকার কলকণ্ঠ পক্ষী।

Thorh-bill.

Thorntail — একপ্রকার পক্ষী। **Thorny accacia**—একপ্রকার বাবলা গাছ। **Thorny-oyster** — একপ্রকার কণ্টকময় শুক্তি। **Thorny trefoil**—দক্ষিণ ইয়ুরোপের কণ্টকগুল্মবিশেষ। **A thorn in one's sides** or **flesh**—A constant source of annoyance; কাহারো পক্ষে কণ্টকস্বরূপ, পার্শ্বকণ্টক।

thor'-ough (thŭr-ō), *adj., adv.* & *n.* Complete; out-and-out; পুরা, ডাহা, বিলকুল, সম্পূর্ণ, সম্যক্ ; পাকা, টনটনে। ***Adv.*** (*Colloq.*) Thoroughly ; সম্পূর্ণরূপে, পুরাপুরি, নিঃশেষে। ***Noun.*** The tyrannical policy of Strafford and Laud in the reign of Charles I ; ইংলণ্ডের রাজা প্রথম চার্লসের সময়ে ষ্ট্রাফর্ড এবং লডের অত্যাচারমূলক শাসননীতি। **–ly,** *adv.* Perfectly ; completey ; সম্পূর্ণরূপে ; সর্ব্বাঙ্গসম্পন্নরূপে। **–ness,** *n.* Completeness ; perfectness ; সম্পূর্ণতা ; সর্ব্বাঙ্গাসম্পন্নতা, সর্ব্বাঙ্গসুন্দরতা। **Thorough-brace** — শকটের প্রধান অংশের অবলম্বনস্বরূপ ইংরাজী C অক্ষরের অনুরূপ স্থিতিস্থাপক অংশ বিশেষ দ্বয়ের মধ্যবর্ত্তী চর্ম্মরজ্জু। **Thorough-bred**—*adj.* & *n.* (জন্তুসম্বন্ধে) সুশিক্ষিত, তেজস্বী বিশুদ্ধবংশজাত, সুজাত। (*Noun*) উৎকৃষ্ট অশ্বাদি জন্তু, তেজস্বী অশ্বাদি জন্তু। **Thoroughfare**—উভয় দিকে উন্মুক্ত রাজপথ, সরাসর রাস্তা। **Thorough-going**—আদ্যন্তগামী ; সম্পূর্ণ, সর্ব্বাঙ্গসম্পন্ন, সর্ব্বাঙ্গসুন্দর। **Thorough-paced** — ডাহা, পাকা, পুরা। **Thorough-pin**—অশ্বের পদের পশ্চাদ্‌ভাগস্থ সন্ধির কোটরের স্ফীতি। **No thoroughfare**—(মেরামত করার কালে) কোন রাজপথের উপর দিয়া শকটাদির গমনাগমন নিষিদ্ধ হইলে *No Thoroughfare* (গমনাগমন নিষিদ্ধ) এই শব্দদ্বয় অঙ্কিত কাষ্ঠফলক ঐ পথে টাঙ্গাইয়া রাখা হয়।

thorp(e) (thŏrp), *ns.* Village ; গ্রাম।

those (thōz), *Pl.* of THAT (which see)

thou (thow), *pron., v. t.* & *i.* Second person singular ; তুমি, তুই। ***Verb t.*** To address with the pronoun *thou* ; "If thou *thouest* him some thrice it shall not be amiss" ; to treat with familiarity ; তুই বা তুমি বলিয়া সম্বোধন করা, তুই তোকার করা ; পরিচিতের মত ব্যবহার করা। ***Verb i.*** To use thou and thee in discourse ; কথাবার্ত্তায় তুই তোকার ব্যবহার করা।

though (thō), **thō',** *conj.* & *adv.* 1. Granting ; allowing it to be the fact ; notwithstanding ; যদিও, যদ্যপি, যদিস্যাৎ ; তাহলেও ; তৎস্বত্বেও। 2. Yet ; as, I have no doubt he will understand, *though* you never know ; তথাপি, তবু। ***Adv.*** However ; as, a good case would do well *though* ; যাহোক, তৎস্বত্বেও, তবু।

thought (thăt) *n.* 1. The power or act of thinking ; reflection ; চিন্তাশক্তি, চিন্তন ; বিচিন্তন, বিভাবন, পর্য্যালোচন। 2. The mental faculty ; mind ; মনোবৃত্তি ; মন। 3. Intention ; design ; as, I had a *thought* of going there ; অভিপ্রায় ; উদ্দেশ্য। 4. Anxious, brooding care ; "Take no *thought* for your life" ; solicitude ; "Wed me, or else I die for *thought*" ; meditation ; দুর্ভাবনা ; চিন্তা, উদ্বেগ, উৎকণ্ঠা ; ধ্যান। 5. That which is thought ; an idea or conecpt ; চিন্তনীয় বিষয় ; ভাব, চিন্তা। 6. Sober reflection ; চিন্তা, ভাবনা। 7. A little ; somewhat ; as, to be a *thought* more considerate ; অল্প, সামান্য ; কিঞ্চিৎ।

thought'-ful, *adj.* 1. Characterized by, or devoted to, thought ; চিন্তাত্মক, চিন্তারত, চিন্তাশীল। 2. Attentive ; মনোযোগী, অবধানপর। 3. Mindful of others ; as, she is very kind and *thoughtful* of others ; considerate ; kind ; অন্যের বিষয়ে অবধানপর ; বিবেচনাশীল ; সদয়। **Thought'-ful-ly,** *adv.* **Thought'-ful-ness,** *n.* **Thought'-less,** *adj.* 1. Stupid ; নির্ব্বোধ, বুদ্ধিহীন। 2. Careless ; heedless ; as, a *thoughtless* man ; অসাবধান, অসতর্ক, অমনোযোগী ; দৃক্‌পাতশূন্য। **Thought-body**—চিন্ময়দেহ, চিন্তাত্মিক তনু, সূক্ষ্মদেহ, লিঙ্গদেহ, আতিবাহিক দেহ। **Thought-form**—ধ্যানদৃষ্টরূপ। **Thought-leader** — চিন্তানায়ক। **Thought-reader**—অন্তর্য্যামী, পরচিত্তজ্ঞানী। **Thought-reading**—অন্তর্য্যামিত্ব, পরচিত্তজ্ঞান, পরচিত্তবিবেক। **Thought-transference** — বিচারসংক্রমণ (হিঃ কোঃ), চিন্তাসংক্রমণ। Same as TELEPATHY (which see). **Thought-wave** — চিৎতরঙ্গ। **A thought**—অল্পমাত্র, ঈষৎ। **A happy thought**—সময়োচিত চিন্তা। **Quick as thought**—অতিদ্রুতগামী, মনোজব। **Second thoughts** — পুনর্ব্বিবেচনা। **Train of thoughts**—চিন্তাপরম্পরা, চিন্তাপ্রবাহ।

thou'-sand (thow-) *adj.* & *n.* Denoting the number of ten hundred ; also denoting a great number indefinitely ; সহস্র ; হাজার হাজার। ***Noun.*** 1. The number ten hundred ; সহস্র সংখ্যা। 2. A symbol representing the number of ten hundred ; সহস্র সংখ্যার সাঙ্কেতিক চিহ্ন (M.) **–fold,** *adj.* & *adv.* **–sandth,** *n.*

thrall, *n., adj.* & *v. t.* A slave ; চিরদাস, ক্রীতদাস, গোলাম্। ***Adj.***

Enslaved ; দাসভূত। *Verb t.* To enslave ; দাসত্ব শৃঙ্খলে বদ্ধ করা। **Thrall′-dom,** *n.* Slavery ; bondage ; দাসত্ব ; গোলামি।

thrăp, *v. t.* (*Naut.*) To bind on ; (নৌবিদ্যা) বাঁধা, বন্ধন করা।

thrăsh, thrĕsh, *v. t.* & *i.* **1.** (Usu. *thresh*) To beat out or separate the grain or seeds from, as by a flail or a threshing-machine ; শস্য মাড়া, শস্য মর্দ্দন করা, আছড়াইয়া ধান্য যবাদি ছাড়ান। **2.** (*thrash*) To beat soundly, esp. with a whip ; "Send them home to *thrash* the French" ; আচ্ছা করিয়া বেতান, চাবকান, বেদম প্রহার করা, মারিয়া পাটপাট করা। **3.** To conquer ; to surpass ; জয় করা ; অতিক্রম করা। *Verb i.* To drive out grain from straw ; শস্য মাড়া। **Thrash′-er, Thresh′-er,** *ns.* **1.** (*thrasher*) One who thrashes ; যে ব্যক্তি শস্য আছড়াইয়া বাহির করে। **2.** (Usu. *thresher*) A machine for thrashing grain ; শস্য মাড়াইবার কল। **3.** A kind of shark ; এক জাতীয় হাঙ্গর। **Thrash′-ing,** *n.* **Threshing-floor** — যে প্রাঙ্গণে ধান্যাদি মাড়াইয়া বাহির করা হয়, কুট্টনাগার (কৌটিল্য)। **To thrash out** — To obtain truth etc. by repeated trial or discussion ; বারংবার চেষ্টা বা আলোচনার পর সত্য প্রভৃতি আবিষ্কার করা।

thrā-sŏn′-i-căl, *adj.* Bragging ; দম্ভকারী, আস্ফালনকারী। [Terenceএর "*Eunuch*" নামক গ্রন্থের আস্ফালনকারী সৈনিক Thrasoর নাম হইতে গৃহীত।] **—ly,** *adv.*

thread, (thrĕd) *n.* **1.** A fine cord for sewing ; সূত্র, সূতা, তন্তু। **2.** A filament, as of a flower or of any fibrous substance ; পুষ্পের কেশর, অংশু, আঁশ। **3.** A fine line as of gold and silver or of mercury in a thermometer ; স্বর্ণ বা রৌপ্যের সূক্ষ্ম তার, তাপমানযন্ত্রের পারদরেখা। **4.** The central line of a stream or water-course ; মধ্য প্রবাহ। **5.** The spiral projecting rib on the shaft of a screw ; স্ক্রুপের পেঁচালো অংশ। **6.** Course ; as, the *thread* of a discourse ; গতি, ধারা। **7.** Thin seam or vein of ore ; ধাতুর ক্ষীণ শিরা। **Thread′-y,** *adj.* **1.** Like thread or filament ; সূত্রবৎ, কেশরবৎ। **2.** Containing or carrying thread ; covered with thread ; সূত্রধারী, সূত্রবাহী ; সূত্রাবৃত। **Threadbare**—(বস্ত্র সম্বন্ধে) এরূপ জীর্ণ যে সূত্র আলগা হইয়া গিয়াছে, সূত্রমাত্রাবশিষ্ট, সূত্রসার, (ব্যক্তিসম্বন্ধে) সূত্রদরিদ্র (মৃচ্ছঃ), জীর্ণবস্ত্রপরিহিত ; পুরাতন, পচা, বস্তাপচা। **thread-lace**—ক্ষৌমসূত্র হইতে প্রস্তুত লেইস। **Thread-mark**—ব্যাঙ্কে নোটের কাগজে সুরঞ্জিত পট্টসূত্র দ্বারা কৃত চিহ্ন। **Thread-needle** — শিশুদিগের ক্রীড়াবিশেষ। **Thread-paper** — সূতা জড়াইবার জন্য একপ্রকার পাতলা কাগজ। **Thread-plant**—যে সকল বৃক্ষের আঁশ হইতে সূত্র প্রস্তুত হয়। **Thread-root**—নিশমী তিতা। **Thread-soul**—সূত্রাত্মা (হিঃ কোঃ)। **Threadworm** — ক্রিমি। **Thread of life**—জীবনসূত্র, জীবনধারা। **To hang by thread**—To be impending ; to be about to fall ; বিপদ্ আসন্ন হওয়া ; পতনোন্মুখ হওয়া। **To take up the thread of**—To resume from the point where a narrative was stopped ; যে স্থানে থামা গিয়াছিল—তথা হইতে আরম্ভ করা, পুনরালোচনায় প্রবৃত্ত হওয়া।

thread, (thrĕd) *v. t.* **1.** To pass a thread through an eye or aperture; to string, as beads ; সূতা পরান ; মালা গাঁথা, গ্রন্থন করা, গুম্ফিত করা। **2.** To pass or penetrate through ; চলা, অতিক্রম করা, ভেদ করিয়া যাওয়া। **3.** To pervade ; "A haunting vision *threaded* my slumbers" ; পরিব্যাপ্ত করা, আচ্ছন্ন করা। **To thread one's way, course, etc.**—To go one's way ; পথ চলা।

threat, (thrĕt) *n.* **1.** Menace ; ভয় প্রদর্শন, ভীতিপ্রদর্শন। **2.** Any menace of such a nature and extent as to unsettle the mind of a person on whom it operates, and to take away from his acts that free voluntary action which alone constitutes consent ; ভয়সঞ্চার।

threat′-en (thrĕt-n), *v. t.* & *i.* **1.** To intimidate ; ভয় দেখান, ভয়প্রদর্শন করা, ভীতিপ্রদর্শন করা। **2.** To menace by action ; as, to *threaten* a person with a gun ; কোনরূপ কার্য্য দ্বারা ভয়প্রদর্শন করা। **3.** To give the signs of approach of something evil or unpleasant ; as, to *threaten* war ; কোনরূপ অশুভ বা অপ্রীতিকর ঘটনার সূচনা করা। *Verb i.* **1.** To use threat ; ভয় প্রদর্শন করা। **2.** To have a threatening appearance ; ভয়ঙ্কর দেখান, ভীষণদর্শন হওয়া। **—ing,** *adj.* **1.** Indicating threat or menace ; ভয়সূচক। **2.** Indicating something impending ; প্রত্যাসন্ন বিপদাদিসূচক। **—ing-ly,** *adv.* **Threatening letters**—(ক) কোনরূপ কলঙ্কজনক কথা প্রকাশ করিবার ভয় দেখাইয়া কাহারো নিকট হইতে টাকা আদায়ের জন্য যে পত্র দেওয়া হয়। (খ) কাহাকে কোনরূপ অপরাধে অভিযুক্ত করা হইবে এইরূপ ভয় দেখাইয়া টাকা আদায়ের জন্য যে পত্র দেওয়া হয়। (গ) ভয়প্রদর্শন দ্বারা টাকা আদায়ের জন্য কাহাকে যে পত্র দেওয়া হয়। (ঘ) কোন লোককে খুন করা হইবে এইরূপ ভয় দেখাইয়া তাহার নিকট হইতে টাকা আদায়ের জন্য যে পত্র দেওয়া হয়।

three, (thrē) *adj.* & *n.* One more then two ; তিন, ত্রি। *Noun.* The number which constitutes two and one ; তিনবাচক সংখ্যা। **Three colour process**—রক্ত পীত এবং নীল বর্ণের কালি দ্বারা আলোকচিত্রের সাহায্যে প্রস্তুত ফলকত্রয় হইতে

স্বাভাবিক বর্ণে প্রতিকৃতি প্রভৃতি মুদ্রণের প্রণালীবিশেষ, ত্রিবর্ণপ্রণালী। **Three-decker**—কামান দাগার জন্য পাটাতন-ত্রয়বিশিষ্ট রণপোত। **Three-fold**—ত্রিগুণিত, ত্রিপুট। **Three-handed**—ত্রিহস্ত ; তিন হাতের (খেলা)। **Three-pence**—তিন পেন্স। **Threepenny**—তিন পেন্স মুল্যের ; তুচ্ছ, নগণ্য। **Three-ply**—ত্রিগুণ (সুত্রাদিসম্পর্কে)। **Three quarters**—(চিত্রসম্পর্কে) কটি পর্য্যন্ত, দেহের ¾ অংশ প্রদর্শক। **Three-score**—তিন কুড়ি, ষাটি। **Rule of three** — See RULE. **The three F's**—আয়র্লণ্ডদেশের ভূম্যধিকারিসমিতির তিনটী দাবী যথা :—Free sale—অবাধ-বিক্রয় ; Fixity of tenure—চিরস্থায়ী বন্দোবস্ত ; Fair rent—ন্যায্য রাজস্ব। **The three R's**—See R.

three'-some (thrē-sŭm), *n.* (*Golf.*) A game for three ; (গোলফ্ ক্রীড়া) তিনজন লোকের উপযোগী ক্রীড়া।

thrĕm-mă-tŏl'-ō-ġy̆, *n.* The science of breeding animals and plants ; উদ্ভিদ্ এবং পশুপালন-বিদ্যা।

thrē'-nōde, thrĕn'-ō-dy̆, *ns.* A song of lamentation ; a dirge ; বিলাপসঙ্গীত, শোকগাথা ; মৃত্যুসঙ্গীত, মরণসঙ্গীত, শ্মশানগীতি। **–no'-di-al, –nod'-ic**, *adjs.* **Thre-net'-ic Thre-net'-i-cal**, *adjs.* **Thren'-o-dist**, *n.*

thrĕp-sŏl'-ō-ġy̆, *n.* The science of nutrition of a living organism ; a treatise thereon ; জীবদেহপোষণবিদ্যা, পোষণতত্ত্ব ; উক্ত বিদ্যাসম্বন্ধীয় পুস্তক।

thrĕsh, *v. t.* See THRASH.

thrĕsh'-ōld, *n.* **1.** The stone or piece of timber which lies under a door ; a door-sill ; দরজার নীচের পাষাণ বা কাষ্ঠফলক, গোবরাট ; দেহলী, দ্বারপিণ্ডী, গৃহাবগ্রহণী। **2.** (*Fig.*) Entrance ; outset ; "That fair new forms That float about the *threshold* of an age, Like truths of science waiting to be caught" ; প্রবেশদ্বার ; প্রারম্ভ। **To cross one's threshold** — কাহারো গৃহে পদার্পণ করা, কাহারো চৌকাঠ মাড়ান (পল্লী-সমাজ—শরৎ চট্টো)।

threw, (thrô), *p. t.* of THROW (which see).

thrīce, *adv.* Three times ; highly : as, *thrice* blessed ; তিনবার ; অতিশয়, অত্যন্ত।

thrĭd, *v. t.* (*Archaic*) Same as THREAD, *v. t.* (which see).

thrī-dā'-cĭ-ŭm, *n.* The inspissated juice of lettuce ; কাজু বা সালাদের ঘনীভূত রস।

thrift, *n.* Frugality ; economical management ; "They had been trained in *thrift* and economy" ; মিতব্যয় ; মিতব্যয়িতার সহিত সাংসারিক ব্যয়নির্ব্বাহ। **Thrift'-i-ly**, *adv.* **Thrift'-less**, *adj.* Extravagant ; অমিতব্যয়ী, অপব্যয়ী। **Thrift'-y**, *adj.* **1.** Frugal ; economical ; মিতব্যয়ী ; গুছালো। **2.** Thriving ; উন্নতিশীল।

thrill, *n.*, *v. t.* & *i.* **1.** A wave of emotion or sensation ; as, a *thrill* of joy ; a throbbing ; পুলকস্পন্দন, পুলকপ্রবাহ, পুলকশিহরণ, পুলকহিল্লোল, আনন্দরোমাঞ্চ, রোমাঞ্চ, আবেগতরঙ্গ ; স্পন্দন, বেপথু। **2.** (*Slang*) A sensational story ; a book containing sensational story ; "The sensational title of a shilling *thrill*" ; (ইতর ভাষায়) লোমাঞ্চকর কাহিনী ; লোমহর্ষণ কাহিনীপূর্ণ পুস্তক। **3.** (*Med.*) Kinds of tremor or resonance observed in auscultation ; আকর্ণন-যন্ত্রসহযোগে হৃৎপিণ্ডে যে বিভিন্নপ্রকার কম্প বা ধ্বনি অনুভূত হয়। ***Verb t.*** To affect with a pricking or tingling sensation ; রোমাঞ্চিত করা। ***Verb i.*** **1.** To pierce ; to pass, move or act causing a pricking or tingling sensation ; as, a discordant sound *thrilled* through the ear ; ভেদ করা ; রোমাঞ্চ তুলিয়া যাওয়া, পুলকহিল্লোল বহাইয়া যাওয়া। **2.** To feel a tingling or shivering sensation, as from pleasure, pain, or the like ; as, to *thrill* with delight or horror ; রোমাঞ্চিত হওয়া, পুলকশিহরণ অনুভব করা। **3.** To vibrate ; to quiver ; as, his voice *thrilled* with emotion ; স্পন্দিত হওয়া ; কম্পিত হওয়া, শিহরিয়া উঠা। **Thril'-ler**, *n*, **1.** That which causes thrill ; রোমাঞ্চকারী। **2.** (*Slang*) A sensational novel or story ; (ইতরভাষায়) লোমাঞ্চকর গল্প বা উপন্যাস। **Thrill'-ing**, *adj.* Causing a thrilling sensation ; রোমাঞ্চকর, লোমহর্ষণ। **Thrill'-ing-ly**, *adv.* **Thrill'-ing-ness**, *n.*

thrips, *n.* A genus of small insects injurious to plants, esp. cereals ; শস্যের অনিষ্টকারী কীট।

thrīve, *v. i.* **1.** To prosper ; to flourish ; উন্নতি করা, পয়মন্ত হওয়া, অভ্যুদয় হওয়া ; বর্দ্ধিষ্ণু হওয়া, সমৃদ্ধিমান হওয়া, বৃদ্ধিপ্রাপ্ত হওয়া। **2.** (Of plants or animals) To grow vigorously or luxuriantly ; (জন্তু, বৃক্ষ, প্রভৃতি সম্পর্কে) সতেজে বৃদ্ধিপ্রাপ্ত হওয়া, প্রচুর পরিমাণে জন্মা। **3.** To increase in goods and estates ; as, a farmer *thrives* by good husbandry ; ধন সম্পত্তি বৃদ্ধি প্রাপ্ত হওয়া। **Thriv'-ing**, *adj.* Flourishing ; উন্নতিশীল, অভ্যুদয়শীল, বর্দ্ধিষ্ণু, সমৃদ্ধিমান, পয়মন্ত, লক্ষ্মীবান্। **Thriv'-ing-ly** *adv.* **Thriv'-ing-ness**, *n.*

thrô', thrô, See. THROUGH

throat (thrōt), *n.* & *v. t.* **1.** The anterior part of the neck of an animal, in which are the gullet and windpipe ; কণ্ঠ, কণ্ঠদেশ। **2.** Gullet ; কণ্ঠনালী। **3.** Any throat-shaped thing ; কণ্ঠাকৃতি বস্তু। **4.** Entrance ; as, the *throat* of a valley; main passage ; প্রবেশপথ ; প্রধান পথ। **5.** (*Bot.*) The mouth of a monopetalous corolla, or the circular line at which the tube and limb unite ; (উদ্ভিদ্‌বিদ্যা) একদল পত্রাবর্ত্তের মুখ অথবা যে গোলাকৃতি রেখার নল এবং অঙ্গ একত্র থাকে। ***Verb t.*** To groove ;

থাজ কাটা, নালী কাটা। **Clergyman's sore throat**—যাজক প্রভৃতির (যাহারা প্রকাশ্যে বক্তৃতা করেন) কণ্ঠনালীর ঝিল্লীর প্রদাহ। **Sore throat**—কণ্ঠনালীর ঝিল্লীর প্রদাহ। **To cut one another's throats**—To adopt mutually destructive policy ; পরস্পরের পক্ষে সাংঘাতিক পন্থা অনুসরণ করা। **To cut one's own throat**—To adopt suicidal policy ; নিজের গলা নিজ হাতে কাটা (cf. আপন শির হাম আপন হাতে কাটিনু—চণ্ডীদাস)। **To give a person the lie in his throat**—To accuse a person of outrageous lying ; ডাহা মিথ্যা কথা কহার দরুণ কাহাকে দোষী করা। **To lie in one's throat**—To lie outrageously ; ডাহা মিথ্যা কথা বলা।

throat'-y̆, (thrōt-) *adj.* **1.** Guttural ; কণ্ঠ্য। **2.** Having prominent throat ; উদ্গাতকণ্ঠ। **—i-ness**, *n.*

thrŏb, *v. i.* & *n.* **1.** To vibrate ; স্পন্দিত হওয়া, দুর দুর করা, দুরু দুরু করা, ধড়ফড় করা। **2.** To palpitate with abnormal force or rapidity from any agitation ; কোনপ্রকার আবেগবশতঃ অতি দ্রুত বা প্রবলভাবে স্পন্দিত হওয়া। ***Noun.*** An excited palpitation ; ধুক ধুক, দুর দুরু, ধড়ফড়, স্পন্দন, পরিস্পন্দ। **Throb'-bing-ly**, *adv.*

throe (thrō), *n.* & *v. i.* **1.** Extreme pain ; violent pain ; নিদারুণ যন্ত্রণা ; প্রবল বেদনা। **2.** Anguish esp. in parturition ; প্রসব বেদনা, প্রসব যন্ত্রণা। ***Verb i.*** To be in agony ; তীব্র যাতনা ভোগ, অসহ্য বেদনা ভোগ করা, নিদারুণ যন্ত্রণা পাওয়া।

thrŏm-bō'-sis, *n.* The obstruction of a blood-vessel by the formation of a fibrinous clot ; শারীরিক যন্ত্রে সূত্রল জমাট রক্ত সঞ্চয় হেতু রক্তবহা নাড়ী প্রভৃতি অবরোধ, [সজীব রক্তবহা নাড়ীর রক্তে থম্বস অর্থাৎ বিদীর্ণ শিরা হইতে শৈরিক রক্ত সংযত হইয়া ক্ষুদ্র নীলবর্ণ অর্ব্বুদের উৎপত্তি অনন্তর নিরেট অংশের কোমলতা প্রাপ্তি এবং পূযবৎ পদার্থে পরিণতি—ডাঃ হরিপ্রসাদ চক্রবর্ত্তী।]

thrōne, *n.* & *v. t.* **1.** The seat of a king or emperor ; সিংহাসন, রাজাসন, রাজপাট, সিংহপীঠ (গোপালঃ), ভদ্রপীঠ, রাজতক্ত। **2.** The seat of a pope or bishop ; পোপ অথবা বিশপের আসন। **3.** Sovereign power and dignity ; as, he lost his *throne* ; রাজপদ, রাজক্ষমতা, রাজগৌরব। **4.** The king himself ; রাজা, নৃপতি। **5.** One of an order of angels who are usually represented with double wings supporting the throne of the Almighty in eternal space; অনন্ত আকাশে যে সপক্ষ দেবদূতগণ সর্ব্বশক্তিমান ঈশ্বরের সিংহাসন ধারণ করেন তাঁহাদের অন্যতম। ***Verb t.*** To enthrone ; সিংহাসনাধিষ্ঠিত করা, রাজপাটে বসান। **Throne'-less**, *adj.*

thrŏng, *n., v. i.* & *t.* A multitude of persons or living creatures in a close body ; a crowd ; a number of things crowded together ; লোকারণ্য, ভিড় ; জনসম্মর্দ্দ, জনতা, লোকসংঘট্ট ; সংকীর্ণ স্থানে বহু বস্তুর সমাবেশ। ***Verb i.*** To crowd together ; "I have seen the dumb men *throng* to see him" ; to come in multitudes ; to pass in multitudes ; ভিড় করা, লোকে লোকারণ্য হওয়া ; ভিড় করিয়া আসা ; ভিড় করিয়া যাওয়া। ***Verb t.*** To crowd or press ; ভিড় করা, ঘেষাঘেষি করা। **2.** To fill with a crowd ; জনতাপূর্ণ করা, লোকে লোকারণ্য করা, জনসঙ্কুল করা, জনাকীর্ণ করা।

throst'-le (thrŏs-l), *n.* **1.** The song-thrush or mavis ; একপ্রকার গায়ক-পক্ষী। **2.** A machine for spinning so called from the noise it makes (also *throstle-frame*) ; একপ্রকার সূতার কল।

throst'-ling, (thrŏs-), *n.* A disease of cattle occasioned by a swelling under the throat ; গবাদির কণ্ঠস্ফীতি রোগবিশেষ।

thrŏt'-tle (-l), *n.* & *v. t.* **1.** The windpipe or trachea ; কণ্ঠনালী, শ্বাসনালী। **2.** A valve controlling flow of steam etc. in an engine ; যন্ত্রে বাষ্প প্রভৃতির প্রবাহ নিয়মনের জন্য একপ্রকার কপাটকল। ***Verb t.*** To seize and compress the throat of so as to choke ; to strangle ; গলা টিপিয়া ধরা ; শ্বাসরোধ করা। **2.** To check or suppress, as if by choking ; as, to *throttle* sedition ; বলপূর্ব্বক রোধ করা। **3.** To stop forcibly the utterance of a person ; বলপূর্ব্বক কোন ব্যক্তির মুখ বন্ধ করা। **4.** To check or stop the flow of (a fluid in a tube etc.), esp. by means of a valve, or by compression ; to regulate the supply of steam or gas to an (engine) in this way ; চাপ প্রয়োগে বা কপাটকলের সাহায্যে (কোন নালীতে বাষ্প প্রভৃতির) প্রবাহ রোধ বা বন্ধ করা ; (যন্ত্রে) গ্যাস বা বাষ্পের সরবরাহ নিয়মন করা। **Throttle-valve**—Same as THROTTLE *n.* 2.

through (thrô), **thrô'**, **thrô**, *prep., adv.* & *adj.* **1.** From one end to another ; from one side to another ; একপ্রান্ত হইতে অপর প্রান্ত পর্য্যন্ত, এফোঁড় ওফোঁড় করিয়া ; এক পার্শ্ব হইতে অপর পার্শ্ব পর্য্যন্ত। **2.** From the beginning to the end of ; during ; as, *through* the night ; আদি হইতে শেষ পর্য্যন্ত ; ধরিয়া, ব্যাপিয়া। **3.** By way of ; as, he passed *through* the gate ; পথ দিয়া। **4.** On account of ; out of ; as, some falling merely *through* fear ; হেতু, দরুণ, জন্য ; হইতে। **5.** Over the whole extent ; as, to ride *through* the country ; জুড়িয়া, ব্যাপিয়া। **6.** In the midst ; as, the fish swims *through* the water ; মধ্যে। **7.** From one end or side to the other ; এক প্রান্ত বা পার্শ্ব হইতে অপর পার্শ্ব বা প্রান্ত পর্য্যন্ত। ***Adv.*** **1.** From the beginning to the end ; as, read the book *through* ; আদ্যন্ত, আদ্যোপান্ত আগাগোড়া (*colloq.*)। 2. To the end ; as, to carry a project *through* : শেষ পর্য্যন্ত। ***Adj.*** Going or extending with little or no interruption from one important place or centre to another ; as, a *through* train ; মধ্যে না থামিয়া বা অল্প দুই এক স্থানে থামিয়া এক স্থান হইতে অপর স্থানে গামী। **Through-bolt**—যে বল্ট্ এক পিঠ হইতে অপর পিঠ ভেদ করিয়া যায়। **Through gang**—প্রকাশ্য চলাচলের রাস্তা ; পরিশ্রম ; শক্তি। **Through ticket**—বাষ্পীয়শকট বা বাষ্পীয়পোতে সমগ্র পথ পর্য্যটনের জন্য অনুমতিপত্র ; যে প্রবেশ-অনুমতিপত্রদ্বারা বিভিন্ন কোম্পানীর বাষ্পীয় শকটে যাতায়াত করা যায়। **Through traffic**—অতি দূরবর্ত্তী স্থানদ্বয়ের মধ্যে বিভিন্ন কোম্পানীর রেলওয়ে ও জাহাজে যাত্রী ও মাল বহন। **Through train** — যে বাষ্পীয়শকটে যাত্রিগণ শকট পরিবর্ত্তন না করিয়া গন্তব্য স্থানে যাইতে পারে। **Are you through, Are you through with the job**—Have you finished the work ; তুমি কি কাযটা শেষ করিয়াছ ? **Through and through**—এফোঁড়-ওফোঁড়। Thoroughly ; একদম, পুরা, ডাহা। **Read it through and through** — Read it again and again ; বার বার ইহা পড়িও, পুনঃ পুনঃ ইহা পাঠ করিও। **Through and through coal**—একত্র মিশ্রিত ক্ষুদ্র এবং বৃহৎ কয়লার খণ্ডসমূহ (বিশেষতঃ সমপরিমাণে)। **Through fire and water**—Amidst all sorts of dangers ; সর্ব্বপ্রকার বিপদের মধ্য দিয়া। **Through good and evil report**—Regardless of praise or blame ; সুনাম দুর্নামের দিকে লক্ষ্য না করিয়া। **Through life**—আজীবন, যাবজ্জীবন। **Throughout**—সর্ব্বাংশে, সর্ব্ব বিষয়ে ; সর্ব্বতোভাবে ; সর্ব্বত্র ; আদ্যন্ত ; এক প্রান্ত হইতে অপর প্রান্ত পর্য্যন্ত; ব্যাপিয়া। **To fall through**—See FALL. **To go through**—See GO. **To look one through**—To observe searchingly ; বিশেষ করিয়া পর্য্যবেক্ষণ করা।

throw (thrō), *v. t., i. & n.* 1. To fling or cast in any manner ; to hurl ; নিক্ষেপ করা, ছোড়া ; ক্ষেপণ করা। 2. To drive or impel by violence ; as, a vessel *thrown* on a beach ; to dash ; to force ; সবলে নিক্ষিপ্ত হওয়া ; তাড়িত করা ; সবলে চালিত করা। 3. To throw in wrestling ; to cause to fall ; মল্লযুদ্ধে পাতিত করা ; ভূপাতিত করা। 4. To cast off ; "There the snake *throws* her enamell'd skin" ; ছাড়া, ত্যাগ করা, মোচন করা। 5. (Of lower animals) To produce, as young ; বাচ্চা দেওয়া, শাবক প্রসব করা। 6. To cause to take up a position by a rapid march, or by being rapidly transported ; as to *throw* troops in a town ; দ্রুত অভিযান বা চালনা দ্বারা কোন স্থানে সন্নিবেশ করা। 7. To form or shape roughly on a potter's wheel; কুলালচক্রে অমসৃণ ভাবে গঠন করা। 8. To make a cast with a dice ; পাশা ক্ষেপণ করা। 9. To twist two or more filaments of as silk, so as to form one thread ; to make by twisting ; রেশমের আঁশ পাকাইয়া সূতা প্রস্তুত করা ; পাকাইয়া প্রস্তুত করা। 10. To put on hastily ; "I have seen her *throw* her night-gown upon her" ; to spread carelessly ; তাড়াতাড়ি পরা ; অসতর্কভাবে ছড়ান। ***Verb i.*** 1. To perform the act of casting or hurling ; ছোড়া, নিক্ষেপ করা, ক্ষেপণ করা। 2. To cast dice ; পাশা ক্ষেপণ করা। ***Noun.*** 1. The act of throwing or hurling ; ক্ষেপণ, ক্ষেপ, অবপাতন। 2. A cast of dice ; পাশাক্ষেপ, দান, ঢাইল (*Dial., Slang*)। 3. Risk ; venture ; as, to stake one's fortune at a single *throw* ; ঝুঁকি ; ঝুঁকিদার ব্যবসায়। 4. The distance to which a missile is, or may be, thrown ; as, a stone's *throw* ; a slight distance ; ক্ষেপণ-দূরত্ব ; অল্পদূরত্ব। 5. (*Dial.*) A potter's wheel ; (উপভাষায়) কুমারের চাক। 6. (*Dial.*) A turner's lathe ; (উপভাষায়) কুন্দনযন্ত্র। 7. (*Geol.*) A fault or leap in a strata ; (ভূবিদ্যা) স্তরভ্রংশ, স্তরচ্যুতি। 7. Deflection from a right line ; সরল রেখা হইতে বিক্ষেপ। **Throw-crook** — খড় প্রভৃতি হইতে রজ্জু পাকাইবার জন্য একপ্রকার যন্ত্র। **Throw-off** — শিকারে অথবা দৌড়ে প্রথম গতি। **Throw-stick** — পক্ষী প্রভৃতিকে মারিবার জন্য বাটুল। **To throw across or over**—To build across or over ; কোন কিছুর উপরে বা উপর দিয়া নির্ম্মাণ করা। **To throw away**—To cast aside, as worthless ; ফেলিয়া দেওয়া। To cast or fling to a distance ; দূরে ফেলা, দূরে নিক্ষেপ করা। To lose by negligence ; অবহেলা করিয়া হারান। To sacrifice needlessly; to waste; to squander ; বৃথা নষ্ট করা, অবহেলা করিয়া হারান ; অপব্যয় করা ; উড়াইয়া দেওয়া। To reject ; to refuse ; অগ্রাহ্য করা ; প্রত্যাখ্যান করা। **To throw back**—To retort ; কাটা জবাব দেওয়া। To reject ; to refuse ; অগ্রাহ্য করা ; প্রত্যাখ্যান করা To reflect as light ; প্রতিবিম্বিত করা। To revert to some ancestral character ; পূর্ব্বপুরুষদের কোনরূপ স্বভাব প্রাপ্ত হওয়া। **To throw by**—To lay aside ; ফেলিয়া দেওয়া, ফেলিয়া রাখা। **To throw cold water on**—To dispirit ; নিরুৎসাহিত করা। **To throw dirt or mud at**—To blame ; to slander ; নিন্দা করা ; কলঙ্ক রটনা করা, কলঙ্ককালিমা লেপন করা। **To throw down**—To overthrow ; to destroy ; উৎসাদিত করা ; ধ্বংস করা, বিধ্বংস করা। **To throw dust in the eyes of**—See DUST.

To throw in—To inject ; অন্তঃপ্রবিষ্ট করা। To interpolate ; মাঝখানে বলা। 3. To put in as a supplement or addition ; পরিশিষ্টরূপে সংযোগ করা। To add gratis (also *to throw into the bargain*) ; ফাও স্বরূপ দেওয়া। (*Print.*) To distribute types ; (মুদ্রা) বিন্যস্ত অক্ষর পৃথক করিয়া বিভিন্ন বিভিন্ন কোটরে রাখা। **To throw in one's lot with**—Same as TO CAST ONE'S LOT WITH (see under CAST.) **To throw in one's teeth**—See under TEETH. **To throw into shape**—To give form to ; আকৃতি প্রদান করা, গঠন করা। **To throw into the shade**—To obscure by outshining ; স্বকীয় দীপ্তি দ্বারা পরিম্লান করা। (See under SHADE.) **To throw it up against, at, to one**—To upbraid one ; তিরস্কার করা। **To throw light on**—See LIGHT. **To throw off**—To cast off, away or aside ; ফেলিয়া দেওয়া, ফেলিয়া রাখা। To do off hurriedly ; তাড়াতাড়ি পোষাক ছাড়া। To reject ; to abandon ; to discard ; অগ্রাহ্য করা ; বর্জ্জন করা ; ত্যাগ করা, পরিত্যাগ করা। To start the hounds on the scent ; শিকারী কুকুরকে গন্ধ দ্বারা শিকারের অনুসরণে প্রেরণ করা। To expel ; তাড়ান। To produce a poem, picture, etc. or deliver a speech in off-hand manner ; উপস্থিত মত কবিতা রচনা করা, বা চিত্রাদি অঙ্কিত করা, উপস্থিত মত বক্তৃতা দেওয়া। To make a discount of ; বাদ সাদ দেওয়া। **To throw on** or **upon**—To put on hurriedly ; তাড়াতাড়ি পরা। **To throw one's self at** or **at the head of**—(Of women) To show the anxiety for marriage ; (স্ত্রীলোকের পক্ষে) বিবাহের জন্য উৎকণ্ঠা দেখান। **To throw one's self down**—To fall on the ground ; ভূপতিত হওয়া। **To throw one's self into**—To engage one's self energetically in ; কোন কার্য্যে উৎসাহের সহিত প্রবৃত্ত হওয়া, মনে প্রাণে লাগা। **To throw one's self on** or **upon**—To fall or sink upon ; গাড়িয়া বসা, পাতিয়া বসা। to resign one's self upon ; সমর্পণ করা, আত্মসমর্পণ করা। **To throw open** — To open suddenly or widely ; হঠাৎ উন্মুক্ত করা, উদ্ঘাটিত করা। To make freely accessible ; সকলকে অবাধপ্রবেশাধিকার দেওয়া, সকলের পক্ষে সুলভ এবং সুপ্রাপ্য করা। **To throw open the door to**—To make possible ; সম্ভবপর করা। **To throw out**—To cast out ; ফেলিয়া দেওয়া, ছুড়িয়া ফেলা। To suggest ; to insinuate ; আভাস দেওয়া ; ইঙ্গিত করা। To reject ; অগ্রাহ্য করা, নামঞ্জুর করা। To utter ; উচ্চারণ করা। To construct in projection ; উদ্গতভাবে বা প্রলম্বিতভাবে নির্ম্মাণ করা। To confuse ; বিভ্রান্ত করা, হতবুদ্ধি করা। To emit ; নিঃসৃত করা, বিকিরণ করা। To leave behind ; পশ্চাতে ফেলা। (*Cricket*) To put out a batsman by throwing the ball on the wicket while he is out of his ground ; ব্যাটধারী স্বস্থান হইতে বাহিরে থাকা অবস্থায় ত্রিদণ্ডে কন্দুক নিক্ষেপ করিয়া তাহাকে আউট করা। **To throw over**—To discard ; to reject ; পরিত্যাগ করা, ফেলিয়া দেওয়া ; অগ্রাহ্য করা। **To throw overboard**—See OVERBOARD. **To throw stones**—See STONE. **To throw the great cast**—To take great risk ; খুব বড় ঝুঁকি ঘাড়ে নেওয়া। **To throw the handkerchief**—See HANDKERCHIEF. **To throw upon one's hands**—To cause one to take risk ; কাহারো ঘাড়ে দায়িত্ব চাপান। **To throw up**—To construct hastily ; দ্রুত নির্ম্মাণ করা, তাড়াতাড়ি গাঁথিয়া তোলা। To eject from the stomach ; to vomit ; উদ্গিরণ করা, উদ্বমিত করা ; বমন করা। To abandon ; পরিত্যাগ করা ; বর্জ্জন করা। **To throw up one's sponge**—See SPONGE.

throw'-stẽr (thrö-), *n.* One who throws silk ; যে ব্যক্তি রেশমের আঁশ পাকাইয়া সূত্র প্রস্তুত করে, পট্টসূত্রকার।

thrŭm, *v. i., t.* & *n.* **1.** To play coarsely or listlessly on a stringed musical instrument ; আনাড়ীর মত বা অমনোযোগির সহিত কোন তন্ত্রীসমন্বিত বাদ্যযন্ত্র বাদিত করা। **2.** To make a dull and monotonous noise on anything, as with fingers ; as, to *thrum* the table ; অঙ্গুলী দ্বারা মেজ প্রভৃতির উপর তাল ঠুকা। ***Verb t.*** **1.** To play roughly with fingers ; আনাড়ীর মত বাজান। **2.** To drum ; আঙ্গুল দ্বারা তাল ঠুকা। ***Noun.*** Such playing ; the resulting sound : আনাড়ীর মত বা অমনোযোগের সহিত তন্ত্রীসমন্বিত বাদ্যযন্ত্র বাদন, তাল ঠুকন ; ঐরূপ তাল ঠুকার শব্দ। **To thrum over**—To tell over in a monotonous manner ; একঘেয়েভাবে বলিয়া যাওয়া।

thrŭm, *n.* & *v. t.* **1.** The end of a weaver's threads cut off from the web ; বুনা কাপড় কাটিয়া নেওয়ার পর তাঁতে যে সূতার প্রান্ত থাকে। **2.** Any coarse thread ; মোটা সূতা। **3.** Odds and ends ; টুকিটাকি, টুকটাক জিনিষ। ***Verb t.*** To make of thrums ; to cover with thrums ; ঐরূপ সূতার প্রান্তভাগ দ্বারা প্রস্তুত করা ; উহা দ্বারা আবৃত করা। **Thread and thrum**—All alike ; good and bad ; সকলেই ; ভাল মন্দ সকলই।

thrŭsh, *n.* A small plainly coloured singing bird, of the genus Turdidae of several species, esp. the song thrush, throstle, or mavis ; কলকণ্ঠ বিহঙ্গ বিশেষ। **Ground thrush**—দামা। [১০।১২ আঙ্গুল লম্বা মাথা ও নীচের পালক নারঙ্গ খয়রা উপরে নীলাভ পক্ষে শাদা শাদা ফোঁটা আছে—অধ্যাপক যোগেশচন্দ্র রায়।]

thrŭsh, *n.* A disease affecting the lips and mouth ; also a disease in the feet of the horse ; ক্ষুদ্র ক্ষুদ্র ক্ষতবিশিষ্ট একপ্রকার মুখরোগ, মুখোৎসঙ্গ, জাড়ী ঘা ; অশ্বের পদরোগ বিশেষ।

thrŭst, *v. t., i.* & *n.* 1. To push or drive with force ; to push with sudden impulse or force ; ঠেলিয়া দেওয়া ; গুঁতা দেওয়া। 2. To stab ; to pierce ; ছুরি বসান, ছুরি মারা, ছুরিকাদ্বারা, বিদ্ধ করা ; ভেদ করা। ***Verb i.*** 1. To make a push ; to attack with pointed weapon ; ঠেলা দেওয়া ; খোঁচা দেওয়া। 2. To enter by pushing ; ঠেলিয়া প্রবেশ করা। 3. To push forward ; ঠেলিয়া অগ্রসর হওয়া। 4. To put something forcibly into the hands of any person ; to press, force, or impose the acceptance of something ; জোর করিয়া দেওয়া ; গছাইয়া দেওয়া। ***Noun.*** 1. A violent push or drive with a pointed weapon ; খোঁচা। 2. Assault আক্রমণ। 3. (*Mech.*) A force against a resting or supporting force ; কোনরূপ স্থির বা ধারক বলের বিরুদ্ধে যুক্ত বল। 4. A horizontal outward pressure as of an arch against an abutment ; পিল্পা বা পার্শ্বাবলম্বের উপর খিলান প্রভৃতির পার্শ্বিক চাপ। **A home thrust**—আঁতে ঘা। **To thrust on**—To impel ; চালিত করা, প্ররোচিত করা, প্রণোদিত করা। **To thrust oneself** or **one's nose in**—See NOSE. **To thrust out**—To expel ; ঠেলিয়া বাহির করা। **To thrust to the wall**—To compel to yield ; আত্মসমর্পণ করিতে বাধ্য হওয়া। **To thrust upon** — To force upon ; চাপাইয়া দেওয়া, চাপান।

thŭd, *n., v. t.* & *i.* A low dull sound as of a blow on a soft thing ; ধুপ্ শব্দ, ঢিপ শব্দ, ধপাৎ শব্দ, চপাৎ শব্দ। ***Verb t. & i.*** To move or strike so as to make a dull sound ; to fall with dull sound ; ধুপধাপ করিয়া চলা, ধুবধাব করিয়া মারা ; ধপাৎ করিয়া পড়া, ঢিপ করিয়া পড়া।

thŭg, *n.* 1. One of an association of assassins formerly existing in this country, who strangled their victims ; ঠগী। 2. A cutthroat ; ruffian ; "They are called election *thugs* ;" হত্যাকারী ; গুণ্ডা।

thŭg'-gee (-gē), *n.* The practice of the thugs ; ঠগীবৃত্তি। **–ger-y, –ism,** *ns.*

Thū'-lē, *n.* The name given by the ancients to the most northern country with which they were acquainted ; প্রাচীনগণ কর্তৃক প্রদত্ত পৃথিবীর নিতান্ত উত্তরপ্রান্তবর্তী দেশ-বিশেষের নাম। **Ultima Thule**—পৃথিবীর উত্তর সীমান্ত।

thū'-līte, *n.* A mineral of a peach-blossom colour found in Norway ; নরওয়ে দেশে প্রাপ্ত পীচপুষ্পের মত বর্ণবিশিষ্ট একপ্রকার খনিজ পদার্থ।

thumb (thŭm), *n.* & *v. t.* 1. The short, thick finger of the human hand set part from and opposite to the other four ; অঙ্গুষ্ঠ, বৃদ্ধাঙ্গুলী, বৃদ্ধাঙ্গুষ্ঠ। 2. The part of a glove which covers the thumb ; দস্তানার অঙ্গুষ্ঠাবরক অংশ। 3. Influence ; as, under a person's *thumb* ; প্রভাব। ***Verb t.*** 1. To soil or wear with thumbs ; বুড়ো আঙ্গুলের দাগ লাগাইয়া পুস্তকের পাতা প্রভৃতি মলিন বা ক্ষয় করা। 2. To cover with the thumb ; বৃদ্ধাঙ্গুলীদ্বারা আচ্ছাদিত করা। 3. To handle awkwardly, as a musical instrument ; to perform clumsily ; আনাড়ীর মত বাজান ; আনাড়ীর মত কোন কায করা। **Thumb-blue** — বস্ত্রাদি ধৌত করণে ব্যবহৃত নীলের ক্ষুদ্র ক্ষুদ্র খণ্ড। **Thumb-flint**—প্রাগৈতিহাসিক যুগের একপ্রকার পাষাণ-যন্ত্র। **Thumb-impression**—বুড়ো আঙ্গুলের ছাপ, টীপসহি। **Thumb-latch**—প্রান্তে বৃদ্ধাঙ্গুলীর দ্বারা টিপ দিলে যে খিল উঠিয়া থাকে। **Thumb-mark**—পুস্তকের পৃষ্ঠায় বৃদ্ধাঙ্গুলীর ছাপ। **Thumb-print**—বুড়ো আঙ্গুলের ছাপ। **Thumb-screw**—অপরাধ স্বীকার করাইবার জন্য অঙ্গুলীনিষ্পীড়ন করতঃ যন্ত্রণা দেওয়ার জন্য একপ্রকার যন্ত্র, অঙ্গুষ্ঠপীড়ক। **Thumb-stall** — অঙ্গুষ্ঠত্রাণ। **His fingers are all thumbs** — See FINGER. **Rule of thumb**—See RULE. **To bite one's thumb at**—To show contempt for ; বৃদ্ধাঙ্গুষ্ঠ প্রদর্শন করা, কলা দেখান (*Vulg*). **To turn the thumb up**—To decide against one ; কাহারো প্রতিকূলে স্থির করা। **Under the thumb**—Completely under one's control ; কাহারো সম্পূর্ণ করতলগত।

thŭm'-mim, (-ĭm) *n.* See URIM.

thŭmp, *v. t., i.* & *n.* To strike or beat with something thick or heavy ; to bang ; দুম্ শব্দে আঘাত করা ; দুম্ করিয়া আঘাত করা। ***Verb i.*** To strike or fall as with a heavy blow ; (of the heart) to beat heavily ; দুম্ করিয়া আঘাত করা, দুম্ শব্দে পড়া ; ধপ্ ধপ্ শব্দ করা। ***Noun.*** A dull heavy blow given with anything thick ; sound made by such a blow ; দুম্ শব্দে আঘাত ; দুম্ শব্দ, ধপাস্ শব্দ।

thŭmp'-êr, *n.* 1. The person or thing that thumps ; দুম্ শব্দকারী। 2. (*Colloq.*) Anything great ; a striking lie ; "His lies are *thumpers*" ; প্রকাণ্ড বস্তু ; ডাহা মিথ্যা কথা।

thŭn'-der, *n., v. i.* & *t.* 1. The sound which follows a flash of lightning ; বজ্রধ্বনি, অশনিগর্জ্জন, বজ্রনাদ, বজ্রনির্ঘোষ, স্ফূর্জ্জথু, স্তনিত, দেবগর্জ্জন। 2. Thunder-bolt ; বজ্র, অশনি, বাজ, কুলিশ, ঠাটা (*colloq*). [Syn. হ্রাদিনী, হ্লাদিনী, (গোপালঃ) কুলিশ, ভিদুর, পবি, শতকোটি, স্বরু, শম্ব, দম্ভোলি, ভিদির, ভিদু, স্বরুস্, সম্বঃ, সংব, অশনী, বজ্রাশনি, জম্ভারি, ত্রিদশায়ুধ, ত্রিদশাঙ্কুশ, শতধার, শতার, আপোত্রম্, অব্জজ, গিরিকণ্টক, গৌ, অভ্রোত্থ, মেঘভূতি, গিরিজ্বর, গিরিধ্বজ, ইন্দ্রপ্রহরণ, পেশি, জম্হরি, ব্যাধাম, দধীচ্যস্থি, দিদ্যুৎ, নেমি, হেতি, নম, স্বক, বৃক, বধ, অর্ক, তুঞ্জ, তিগ্ম, মেনি,

স্বধিতি, সায়ক, পরশু, দম্ভ, ভিদ্র, অম্বুজ, স্তনত (ঋক্), স্তনয়িত্নু (*ib*), স্তনিত (মঃ সং), কুৎস, ছিদক, মৃদাকর, বহুধার, ষট্‌কোণ।] 3. Any noise likened to thunder ; বজ্রগর্জ্জনের সহিত তুলিত গর্জ্জন, ভীমনাদ, নির্ঘোষ, গর্জ্জন। 4. A startling threat or denunciation ; vehement eloquence ; "He directed the *thunders* of the church against heresy ; ভীষণ ভয়প্রদর্শন বা তিরস্কার ; প্রচণ্ড বাগ্মিতা। ***Verb i.*** 1. To produce the noise of thunder ; বজ্রধ্বনি হওয়া, বজ্রগর্জ্জন হওয়া। 2. To make a loud noise like thunder ; অশনিবৎ গর্জ্জন করা। 3. To utter loud denunciation ; প্রকাশ্যে তীব্র ভৎ'সনা করা। ***Verb t.*** To emit as with sound of thunder ; to denounce loudly ; বজ্র গর্জ্জনে নিঃসারিত হওয়া ; প্রকাশ্যে তীব্র ভৎ'সনা করা। **-less, -ous, -y,** *adjs.* **-ous-ly,** *adv.* **Thunder-and-lightning** — OXFORD MIXTURE. **Thunderbolt** — See THUNDER *n.* **Thunder-clap, thunder-peal**—বজ্রগর্জ্জন, অশনিগর্জ্জন। **Thunder-cloud** — বিদ্যুদ্বন্ত মেঘ, আলক (সাঃ পঃ)। **Thunder-fish**—এক প্রকার মৎস্য। **Thunder-flower**—এক প্রকার গুল্ম। **Thunder head**—Same as CUMULUS. **Thunder-storm** — বজ্রপাতসহ ঝটিকা। **To be thunder-struck**—To be struck with great awe ; বজ্রাহত হওয়া, বিস্ময়স্তম্ভিত হওয়া, অবাক্ হওয়া, মাথায় আকাশ ভাঙ্গিয়া পড়া।

thŭn'-dêr-êr, *n.* 1. One who thunders ; বজ্রনির্ঘোষকারী। 2. (*Cap.*) An epithet applied to Jupiter ; রোমকদিগের দেবরাজ। [বজ্রধারণ করিতেন বলিয়া এই নাম] । 3. (*Cap., Fact.*) An epithet applied to the Times newspaper in allusion to an article by captain Edward Sterling beginning thus—"We *thundered* forth the other day an article on the subject of social and political form" ; বিলাতের টাইমস পত্রের নাম। [উনবিংশ শতাব্দীর প্রারম্ভে উক্ত সংবাদপত্রে Captain Edward Sterling নামক জনৈক ব্যক্তির লিখিত প্রবন্ধ বিশেষকে লক্ষ্য করিয়া এই নাম প্রদত্ত হয়।] 3. A powerful orator ; a restless warrior ; an utterer of violent invective ; শক্তিশালী বাগ্মী ; অতন্দ্রিত যোদ্ধা ; তীব্রগঞ্জনাকারী।

thŭn'-dêr-ing, *n., adj. & adv.* The report or discharge of lightning ; thunder ; বজ্রগর্জ্জন ; বজ্র। ***Adj.*** 1. Producing, or characterised by, a loud or rattling noise, as that of thunder or artillery ; বজ্রনাদী। 2. Remarkable ; very great ; extraordinary ; as, a *thundering* great fish ; অত্যাশ্চর্য্য ; অতি প্রকাণ্ড ; অসাধারণ। **The Thundering legion**—খৃষ্টীয় সৈন্য দ্বারা গঠিত রোমক সৈন্যদল বিশেষ। [এই সৈন্যগণের প্রার্থনায় প্রবল ঝঞ্ঝাবাত্যা এবং বজ্রপাতে শত্রুসৈন্য বিধ্বস্ত হইয়াছিল বলিয়া কথিত আছে।]

thü'-ri-ble, (-bl) *n.* Censer ; ধূপপাত্র, ধুনাচি।

thü-rif'-êr, *n.* An acolyte who carries the censer ; রোম্যানক্যাথলিক ধর্ম্মমন্দিরের ধূপপাত্রবাহী পরিচারক।

thü'-ri-fêr-ous, (-ŭs) *adj.* Producing frankincense ; ধূপোৎপাদী, ধূপজনক।

thü'-ri-fi-cā'-tion, *n.* The act of burning incense ; ধূপপ্রজ্বালন।

Thurs'-day, (thêrz-dā) *n.* The fifth day of the week ; বৃহস্পতিবার, গুরুবার, গুরুবাসর।

thŭs, *adv.* 1. In this way ; এই প্রকারে, এইরূপে, এইভাবে, এইমত। 2. To this degree ; এই মাত্রায়। 3. Accordingly ; অতএব। **Thus'-ness,** *n.* **Thus far, Thus much**—Up to this ; এই পর্য্যন্ত, এতদুর।

thwăck, *v. t. & n.* Same as WHACK (which see).

thwaite (thwāt), *n.* A piece of ground reclaimed and converted to tillage ; কৃষিক্ষেত্রে পরিণত পতিত ভূমি, আবাদি জায়গা।

thwärt, *adv., adj. & prep.* 1. Transversely ; তির্য্যগ্‌ভাবে, টের্চ্চাভাবে। ***Adj.*** 1. Transverse ; তির্য্যগ্, টের্চ্চা। 2. Perverse ; বেআড়া। ***Prep.*** Across ; athwart ; উপর দিয়া ; আড়ভাবে।

thwärt, *v. t. & n.* To frustrate ; as, to *thwart* one's plans ; ব্যর্থ করা, বিফল করা। ***Noun.*** An oarsman's bench placed across the boat ; তির্য্যগ্‌ভাবে স্থাপিত দাঁড়ীর আসন।

thȳ, thīne, *adj. & pron.* Of, or pertaining to, thee ; তোমার, তোর। ***Pron.*** The possessive pronoun of the second person singular ; তোমার, তোর। [স্বরবর্ণের পূর্ব্বে সাধারণতঃ *thine* ব্যবহৃত হয়।]

thȳ'-lă-cīne, *n.* A carnivorous marsupial of Tasmania slightly larger than a fox and of doglike appearance ; Tasmania দ্বীপের একপ্রকার দ্বিগর্ভ কুক্কুরাকৃতি জন্তু।

thȳ'-lō'-sis, *n.* Same as TYLOSIS (which see)

thyme (tĭm), *n.* A kind of small aromatic shrub ; এক জাতীয় সুগন্ধ পত্রী গুল্ম, হাসা (খোরী)। [এই বৃক্ষের পত্র দ্বারা ব্যঞ্জনাদি সুবাসিত করা হয়।] **Thym'-y,** *adj.* **Shepherd's or wild thyme** — উক্ত জাতীয় একপ্রকার গুল্ম—যাহার পত্রের সৌরভ অপেক্ষাকৃত মৃদু হইয়া থাকে।

thy-mel-a-cea, (tĭ-mē-lā-sē-ē), *n.* An order of plants ; অগুর্ব্বাদি (সাঃ পঃ)।

thym'-ōl (tĭm-), *n.* A white crystalline substance ($C_{10}H_{13}OH$) obtained from the oil of thyme having strong antiseptic properties ; রোগজনক জীবাণুনাশক একপ্রকার শ্বেতবর্ণ দানাদার পদার্থ, থাইমল।

thȳ'-mŭs, *n.* Same as THYME. **Thymus gland**—বুকাস্থির সন্নিহিত

গ্রন্থি বিশেষ — ইহা শিশুকালে বৃহৎ থাকে, কিন্তু যৌবনকালে লুপ্ত হইয়া যায়, উন্দ্রুক গ্রন্থি (হঃ চঃ)।

thȳ'-roid (-royd), *adj.* & *n.* **1.** Pertaining to a large cartilage of the larynx, or a ductless gland of the trachea ; গলগ্রন্থিসম্বন্ধীয়। **2.** Having shield-shaped marking ; as, *thyroid* woodpecker, ফলকচিহ্নাঙ্কিত। **Thyroid cartilage**—কাকলক (সুশ্রুঃ), কাকল (হঃ চঃ)। **Thyroid gland**—গলগ্রন্থি, ফলকগ্রন্থি [এই গ্রন্থি বৃদ্ধি পাইলে গলগণ্ড রোগ জন্মে।]

thyr'-sŭs (thêr-), *n.* **1.** A staff tipped with an ornament like pine-cone, and wrapped round with ivy and vine branches ; সরল বৃক্ষের ফলকসদৃশ ভূষা দ্বারা শোভিতাগ্র এবং আইভি এবং আঙ্গুর দ্বারা সমাচ্ছাদিত যষ্টি। **2.** (*Bot.*) A form of inflorescence ; উপশৃঙ্গ (সাঃ পঃ)।

thȳ-sĕlf', *pron.* An emphasized form of the personal pronoun of the second person (used after *thou*, to express distinction with emphasis) ; তুমি স্বয়ং, স্বয়ং তোমাকে।

The papal tiara in its successive form.

tĭ-ā'-rȧ, *n.* **1.** An ornament or article of dress which the ancient Persians wore in their head ; প্রাচীন পারসীকগণের একপ্রকার শিরোভূষা। **2.** The Pope's triple crown ; (*fig.*) the papal dignity or office ; পোপের মুকুট ; (লক্ষণায়) পোপের মর্য্যাদা, পোপের পদ। **3.** An ornamental coronet ; মুকুট, কিরীট। **4.** (*Zool.*) A genus of mitre-shells ; (জন্তুবিজ্ঞান) একজাতীয় শঙ্খ। **–raed**, *adj.*

Papal tiara.

tib'-i-ȧ, *n.* **1.** A kind of ancient musical pipe ; প্রাচীনকালে ব্যবহৃত একপ্রকার বংশী। **2.** (*Anat.*) The large bone of the lower leg ; জঙ্ঘাস্থি, অনুজঙ্ঘাস্থি (সাঃ পঃ)। **–al**, *adj.*

tic, *n.* **1.** A habitual spasmodic contraction of certain muscles, esp. of the face ; পেশীর খেঁচুনি বা আক্ষেপ, বিশেষতঃ মুখের পেশীর খেঁচুনি। **2.** Same as TIC DOULOUREUX (below). **Tic douloureux**—মুখমণ্ডলের স্নায়ুশূল।

tīce, *n.* Same as YORKER.

tick, *v. i.*, *t.* & *n.* To make a slight recurring noise as a watch or clock ; টিক্‌টিক্ শব্দ করা। ***Verb t.*** To mark with a tick or dot ; to check by putting down a small mark ; ক্ষুদ্র চিহ্ন দ্বারা চিহ্নিত করা ; প্রত্যেক দফার পার্শ্বে ক্ষুদ্র ক্ষুদ্র দাগ দিয়া হিসাব পরীক্ষা করা। ***Noun.*** **1.** Slight recurring click of a watch or clock ; ঘড়ীর টিক্‌টিক্ শব্দ, টক্‌টক্ শব্দ। **2.** Any small mark to direct attention to something else, or to serve as a check ; কোন কিছুর প্রতি দৃষ্টি আকর্ষণের জন্য যে ক্ষুদ্র চিহ্ন দেওয়া হয়, পরীক্ষার কালে হিসাবের প্রত্যেক দফার পার্শ্বে যে ক্ষুদ্র চিহ্ন দেওয়া হয়। **Tick-tack**—বুকের দুরুদুরু শব্দ। **To tick off**—To mark off every item of an account with small marks; হিসাবের প্রত্যেকের দফার পার্শ্বে ক্ষুদ্র ক্ষুদ্র চিহ্ন দেওয়া।

tick, *n.* **1.** The cover or case which contains the feathers, wool, cotton or other soft materials of a bed ; গদি তোষক প্রভৃতির খোল। **2.** A striped cloth, woven linen or cotton cloth used to contain the feathers or other material of beds ; তোষক বালিশ প্রভৃতির খোলের জন্য একপ্রকার শক্ত ডোরাদার কাপড়, টিকিন্। **Tick'-ing**, *n.* Same as TICK *n.* 2.

tick, *n.* A little insect that infests dogs, sheep, etc. ; (কুকুর প্রভৃতির এঁটেলি, আঁটালি (যোঃ)।

tick, *n.* & *v. i.* Credit ; ধার, বাকী। ***Verb i.*** To give or get tick ; ধারে জিনিষ দেওয়া, ধারে জিনিষ কেনা। **To buy goods on tick**—To purchase goods on credit ; ধারে জিনিষ কেনা।

tick'-ēr, *n.* **1.** That which ticks ; টিকটিক শব্দকারী। **2.** (*Colloq.*) A watch ; (চলিত ভাষায়) টেঁকঘড়ী। **3.** A telegraphic receiver ; তাড়িত-বার্ত্তাগ্রাহক যন্ত্র।

tick'-ĕt, *n.* & *v. t.* **1.** A piece of paper or a card, which gives the holder the right to enter a place of entertainment, travel in a railway car or by other public conveyance ; প্রবেশ-অনুমতিপত্র, টিকিট। **2.** A certificate of share in a lottery etc. ; চিঠিখেলার টিকিট। **3.** (*Obs.*) A notice ; "Giving a notice of the time to his auditors in a *ticket* on the school-doors" ; (অপ্রঃ) বিজ্ঞাপন। **4.** A label stuck on, or attached to, anything to give notice of something concerning it, as to its quality, nature, price, etc. ; কোন বস্তুর মূল্য, গুণ, প্রভৃতি নির্দ্দেশের জন্য উহাতে যে ক্ষুদ্র কাগজখণ্ড বাঁধিয়া বা আঁটিয়া দেওয়া হয়। **5.** (*Obs.*) Credit ; (অপ্রঃ) ধার। **6.** (*U. S.*) A list of candidates put forward by a party for election ; কোন দলের নির্ব্বাচনপ্রার্থী ব্যক্তিগণের তালিকা ; **7.** (*Fig.*) Principles of a party ; কোন দলের মূলমন্ত্র। **8.** (*Slang*) The correct thing ; (ইতরভাষায়), ঠিক জিনিষ। **9.** A pay-warrant ; যে কাগজে কোন নাবিক বা সৈনিকের পাওনা বেতনের হিসাব লিপিবদ্ধ

থাকে, 10. Same as TICKET OF LEAVE. *Verb t.* To expose for sale ; বিক্রয়ার্থ স্থাপন করা। **Ticket-day**—(কোম্পানীর কাগজের বাজার) ক্রয় বিক্রয় ব্যাপার নিষ্পত্তির পূর্ব্ব দিবস যখন প্রকৃত ক্রেতৃগণের নাম কোম্পানীর কাগজের দালালগণকে প্রদান করা হয়। **Ticket-night**—রঙ্গালয়ের যে অভিনয়ে টিকিট বিক্রয়কারিগণের মধ্যে তাহাদের বিক্রীত টিকিটের অনুপাতে সমস্ত আমদানীর টাকা বাঁটিয়া দেওয়া হয়। **Ticket-porter**—যে সমস্ত মুটের বুকে টিকেট থাকে। **Ticket-punch**—টিকেট কাটার জন্য একপ্রকার যন্ত্র। **The ticket**—(ইতরভাষায় বা চলিতভাষায়) ঠিক জিনিষ। **Ticket of leave**—সদ্ব্যবহারের দরুণ কারাভোগের নির্দ্দিষ্ট কাল উত্তীর্ণ হইবার পূর্ব্বে বন্দীকে যে অনুমতিপত্র দ্বারা মুক্তি প্রদান করা হয়। **That's the ticket**—You have done the right thing ; বেশ করিয়াছ। **To go any ticket**—To give one's opinion in favour of something ; কোন কিছুর অনুকূলে মত প্রকাশ করা। **What is the ticket**—(*Slang*) What can be done ; কি করা যায়।

tick'-le (-l), *v. t., i.* & *n.* **1.** To touch lightly, and cause a peculiar thrilling sensation ; সুড়সুড়ি দেওয়া, কুতুকুতু দেওয়া, কুতুর কুতুর দেওয়া। **2.** To please ; to amuse ; to make merry; "That thrilled and *tickled* my heart with a feeling partly sensuous and partly spiritual" ; সন্তুষ্ট করা; আমোদিত করা ; উৎফুল্ল করা, পুলকিত করা। **3.** To touch or stir gently ; to portray lightly ; মৃদু ভাবে স্পর্শ করা, অল্প অল্প নাড়া ; মৃদুর ভাবে অঙ্কিত করা। *Verb i.* **1.** To feel titillation ; সুড়সুড়ি বোধ করা। **2.** To excite or produce the sensation of titillation ; কুতুর কুতুর দেওয়া। *Noun.* The act of tickling ; the sensation of tickling ; কুতুর কুতুর দেওন ; সুড়সুড়ি, কুতুর কুতুর। **—ling,** *n.* & *adj.*

tick'-lêr, *n.* **1.** One who tickles ; যে ব্যক্তি কুতুর কুতুর দেয়। **2.** (*Colloq.*) That which puzzles ; যাহা স্তব্ধ বা স্তম্ভিত করে। **3.** A drum of spirits ; এক পিপা মদ্য সার। **4.** A cane for whipping ; বেত, চাবুক।

tick'-lish, *adj.* **1.** Easily tickled ; as, the sole of the foot is *ticklish* ; সহজে কুতুকুতু বোধ করে এরূপ। **2.** Difficult ; delicate ; as, a *ticklish* point ; কঠিন ; দুরূহ। **3.** Unstable (said only of the things, conditions, and the like) ; as, a *ticklish* foothold ; অস্থির, চপল, চঞ্চল। **—ly,** *adv.* **—ness,** *n.*

ticpolonga, *n.* A venomous serpent of India or Ceylon ; ভারতবর্ষ এবং সিংহলদ্বীপের একপ্রকার বিষাক্ত সর্প।

tid'-ăl, *adj.* **1.** Of, or pertaining to, tides ; having tides ; caused by tides ; জোয়ারভাঁটাসম্বন্ধীয় ; জোয়ারভাঁটাবিশিষ্ট ; জোয়ার ভাঁটাজনিত। **2.** Dependent upon tide as regards arrival or departure ; as, a *tidal* steamer ; ছাড়া ও পৌঁছা-সম্পর্কে জোয়ার ভাঁটার অধীন। **Tidal air** — নিশ্বাসক্রিয়া দ্বারা ফুসফুসের উর্দ্ধাংশে যে নূতন বাতাস নীত হয়। **Tidal alarm**—জোয়ার ভাঁটা দ্বারা ক্রিয়মাণ বিপৎসূচক যন্ত্র। **Tidal basin or harbour**—যে অববাহিকায় বা পোতাশ্রয়ে জোয়ারের সময় জাহাজাদি যাইতে পারে। **Tidal dock** — যে পোতনির্ম্মাণস্থলীতে কেবল জোয়ারের কালে জাহাজ চলে। **Tidal friction**—বেলোর্ম্মির ঘর্ষণ—যদ্দারা পৃথিবীর আহ্নিক গতি বিলম্বিত হয়। **Tidal river** — যে নদীতে জোয়ার ভাঁটা খেলে। **Tidal steamer or boat**—যে জাহাজ বা নৌকা কেবল জোয়ারের সময় ছাড়া যাইতে পারে। **Tidal train**—ঐরূপ জাহাজের সঙ্গে যুক্ত রেলগাড়ী। **Tidal wave**—জোয়ারের সময়ের ঢেউ, বেলোর্ম্মি (সাঃ পঃ), ভূমিকম্পের কালে বেলাভিমুখগামী বৃহৎ কল্লোল ; মহা উন্নতির স্রোত, সর্ব্বত্র-ব্যাপী প্রবল ভাবোচ্ছ্বাস।

tid'-bit, *n.* Same as TITBIT.

tid'-dly-winks, (-li-wingks), **tid'-dle-dy-winks** (-l-di-wingks), *ns.* A kind of game ; এক প্রকার খেলা।

tide, *n.* **1.** Time ; as, even-*tide* ; season ; সময় ; কাল, বেলা। **2.** The alternate rising and falling of the waters of the ocean, and of bays, rivers, etc. connected therewith ; জোয়ার ভাঁটা। **3.** A current ; as a *tide* of blood ; স্রোত, জোয়ার। **4.** Course or tendency of causes, influences, or circumstances ; "There is a *tide* in the affairs of man, which, taken at the flood leads on to fortune" ; কারণ, প্রভাব বা অবস্থার স্রোত। **Flood-tide**—বেলোর্দ্ধসীমা (সাঃ পঃ) **High tide, Flow tide**—জোয়ার। **Low tide, Ebb-tide**—ভাঁটা। **Neap-tide** — মরা কোটাল। **Tide-gate**—যে দ্বার জোয়ারের কালে জল বা জাহাজ প্রবেশের জন্য খুলিয়া দেওয়া হয় এবং জল রাখিবার জন্য ভাঁটার সময় বন্ধ করিয়া দেওয়া হইয়া থাকে। **Tide-gauge**—বর্ত্তমানে জোয়ার ভাঁটা বা জোয়ার ভাঁটার উর্দ্ধসীমা পরিমাপের জন্য যন্ত্র বিশেষ। **Tide-lock**—জোয়ারের কালে যে পোতাশ্রয়ে জাহাজ যায় তাহার এবং তৎ পশ্চাৎস্থিত অববাহিকার মধ্যবর্ত্তী কপাটকল। **Tide-rip, –rips,** *ns.* পরস্পরের বিপরীত দিগ্‌গামী জোয়ার ভাঁটা দ্বারা বিক্ষুব্ধ জলরাশি। **Tide-waiter**—শুল্ক বিভাগের যে কর্ম্মচারী বন্দরে জাহাজ আসিলে তাহাতে আরোহণ করিয়া শুল্ক প্রভৃতি সংগ্রহ করেন। **Tide-way**—যে প্রণালীতে জোয়ার ভাঁটা খেলে ; ঐরূপ প্রণালীর জোয়ার ভাঁটা।

tide, *v. i.* & *t.* To drift with the tide ; to work in or out of a river or harbour by favour of the tide and anchoring when it becomes adverse ; জোয়ারের সহিত ভাসা ; জোয়ারের সময় চালান এবং জোয়ার বন্ধ হইলে নোঙ্গর ফেলা। *Verb t.* To drive with the tide or stream; স্রোতের জলে ভাসাইয়া দেওয়া। **To tide over**—To help a person, over a difficulty or the like; কাহাকে কোনরূপ বিপদ কাটাইতে সাহায্য করা, সারাইয়া দেওয়া। To surmount difficulties by means of a succession of favourable incidents, by prudence and skilful management, or by aid from another; বিপদ কাটাইয়া উঠা, উত্তীর্ণ হওয়া।

tī'-dings, *n.* (*pl.*) News; information; সংবাদ, খবর, বার্ত্তা; সমাচার, সন্দেশ।

tī'-dy̆, *adj.*, *n.* & *v. t.* **1.** Neat; orderly; পরিস্কার, পরিচ্ছন্ন; ফিটফাট, পরিপাটি, ঝরঝরে। **2.** (*Colloq.*) Fairly in health; (চলিত ভাষায়—শরীর সম্পর্কে) একরকম। **3.** (*Colloq.*) Considerable; pretty large or great; as, a *tidy* sum of money; (চলিত ভাষায়) অতিশয়; বড় গোছের, বেশ বড়। ***Noun.*** A more or less ornamental covering, usually of knitted or crochet work, for the back of a chair, the arms of a sofa, or the like; কেদারা প্রভৃতির পিঠে যে কারুকার্য্যখচিত আবরণ দেওয়া হয়। ***Verb t.*** To put in order; to arrange becomingly; to make neat; as, to *tidy* a room; সাজাইয়া রাখা, গুছাইয়া রাখা; পরিপাটীরূপে সজ্জিত করা; ফিটফাট করা। **–di-ly,** *adv.* **–di-ness,** *n.*

tie (tī), *v. t.* & *i.* **1.** To fasten with a cord or knot; বাঁধা, বন্ধন করা। **2.** To arrange (string, ribbon, tie, etc.) to form a knot, bow, etc.; রজ্জু, ফিতা প্রভৃতি দ্বারা গ্রন্থি, গলবন্ধনী, ইত্যাদি প্রস্তুত করা। **3.** To knit; বুনা। **4.** To unite or join firmly; to marry; "In bond of virtuous love together *tied*"; দৃঢ় বন্ধনে বন্ধন করা; বিবাহ বন্ধনে বদ্ধ করা। **5.** To restrict; "Where you were *tied* in duty"; সংযত করা, দমন করা। **6.** To make the same score as; সমসংখ্যক ক্রীড়াঙ্ক লাভ করা। **7.** To bind together two bodies by means of a piece of timber or metal; কাঠ বা ধাতুফলকদ্বারা বস্তুদ্বয় সংযোগ করা। ***Verb i.*** **1.** To make a bond or connection; সংযোগ করা। **2.** To make a tie with another or others; to be exactly equal in a contest; অন্যের সমসংখ্যক ক্রীড়াঙ্ক লাভ করা; কোনরূপ প্রতিযোগিতার ক্রীড়ায় ঠিক তুল্য হওয়া। **Tied house**—যে শৌণ্ডিকালয়ের অধিকারিণী কেবলমাত্র কোন নির্দ্দিষ্ট দোকানের সহিত কারবার করিতে পারে। **Tied to a woman's apron strings**—To be constantly in the society of women; স্ত্রীলোকের আঁচলধরা। **To tie a person's tongue**—To compel him to keep his silence; কাহারো মুখ বন্ধ করা। **To tie down**—To fasten down; বাঁধিয়া রাখা। To restrain; সংযত করা, দমন করা। **To tie to**—(*U. S.*) To rely on; (মার্কিণযুক্তরাজ্যে) নির্ভর করা। **To tie up**—To confine; to restrain; আটক করা, আবদ্ধ করা, নিরোধ করা; সংযত করা।

tie (tī), *n.* **1.** A cord or chain used for fastening; শৃঙ্খল। **2.** (*Fig.*) A bond; as, *ties* of friendship; (লক্ষণায়) বন্ধন। **3.** A piece of timber or metal for holding two bodies together; যে কাঠ বা ধাতুফলকে দুইটী বস্তু বিধৃত রাখা হয়। **4.** Any of the transverse supports to which rails are fastened; লৌহবর্ত্মের পাতারেলের অনুপ্রস্থগামী অবলম্বন। **5.** A lace for tying shoe; জুতার ফিতা। **6.** Equality of score among competitors; প্রতিদ্বন্দ্বিগণের মধ্যে ক্রীড়াঙ্কের সমতা। **7.** Match between any pairs of several competiting players; প্রতিদ্বন্দ্বী ক্রীড়কদলের মধ্যে যে কোন দুই দলের প্রতিযোগিতার ক্রীড়া। **8.** Same as NECK-TIE. **Cup-ties**—রৌপ্য পাত্রলাভের জন্য প্রতিযোগতার ক্রীড়া। **Tie-beam**—ধরা। **Tie-up**—প্রতিবন্ধকতা, স্থগিত থাকার ভাব; রেলওয়ের শ্রমিক প্রভৃতির ধর্ম্মঘট (বিশেষভাবে আমেরিকায়)। **Tie-wig**—যে পরচুলা ফিতাদ্বারা পশ্চাদ্দিকে বাঁধা হইয়া থাকে। **To play** or **shoot off a tie**—To go through a second contest, match, or the like, to decide a tie; ক্রীকেট প্রভৃতি ক্রীড়ায় উভয় পক্ষের ক্রীড়াঙ্ক সমান হইলে জয়পরাজয় নির্দ্ধারণের জন্য দ্বিতীয়বার খেলা।

tier (tīr), *n.* & *v. t.* A row (particularly when two or more rows are placed one above another); as, a *tier* of seats; থাক, শ্রেণী, সারি। ***Verb t.*** To pile, build or arrange in tiers; থাক থাক করিয়া প্রস্তুত করা, স্তরে স্তরে নির্ম্মাণ করা, সারি সারি করিয়া সজ্জিত করা, স্তরে স্তরে সজ্জিত করা। **Tiers of cable**—জাহাজের কাছির কুণ্ডলীসমূহ।

tierce (tërs), *n.* **1.** A cask whose content is one-third of a pipe or 42 gallons; একপ্রকার মাঝারি আকারের পিপা। **2.** A sequence of three cards; তাসের বিন্তি। **3.** (*Fencing*) A position in which nails and wrists are turned downwards; (অসিক্রীড়া) অবস্থান বিশেষ—যাহাতে নখ এবং মণিবন্ধ নিম্নদিকে আনত করা হয়। **4.** (*Eccles.*) The third hour of the divine office (also *terce*); প্রার্থনা বা উপাসনার তৃতীয় ঘণ্টা। **Tierce-major**—টেক্কা, বড় বিন্তি।

tier'-cĕl (tër-), *n.* Same as TERCEL.

tiers etat, *n.* (*F.*) Same as THIRD ESTATE which see.

tiff, *n.*, *v. t.* & *i.* **1.** A draught of liquor; এক চুমুক মদ্য। **2.** A fit of anger or peevishness; ঈষৎ কোপ, চিড়চিড়ি। ***Verb t.*** To sip; এক চুমুক মদ্য পান করা। ***Verb i.*** **1.** To be in a pet; চটা। **2.** (Among Anglo-Indians

To lunch; (অ্যাংলো ইণ্ডিয়্যানদিগের মধ্যে) জলযোগ করা।

tif'-fa-ny, *n.* A kind of gauze muslin; একপ্রকার সূক্ষ্ম মলমল কাপড়।

tif'-fin (-in), *n.* & *v. i.* (In India) A lunch esp. at midday; (ভারতবর্ষের ইংরাজদিগের মধ্যে) জলযোগ, বিশেষতঃ মধ্যাহ্নকালীন ফল, মিষ্ট, ব্যঞ্জনাদি আহার। ***Verb i.*** To lunch; জলযোগ করা।

tige (tēj), *n.* **1.** (*Arch.*) The shaft of a column; (স্থপতিবিদ্যা) স্তম্ভবপু। **2.** (*Bot.*) Stem or stalk; (উদ্ভিদ্‌বিদ্যা) ডগা, বৃন্ত, বোঁটা।

ti'-gêr, *n.* **1.** A fierce animal of the feline kind; ব্যাঘ্র, শার্দ্দূল, দ্বীপী। [Syn. পৃদাকু, বনস্থ, চিত্রক, পুণ্ডরীক, হিংস্রপশু, ব্যাড়, হিংস্রক, হিংসারু, শ্বাপদ, পঞ্চনখ, ব্যাল, গুহাশয়, তীক্ষ্নদংষ্ট্র, ভীরু, নখায়ুধ, বিচিত্রাঙ্গ, ভয়ানক।] **2.** A boy in livery; "His *tiger* Tim, was clean of limb...He stood in his stockings just four feet ten"; তকমাপরা বালক ভৃত্য। **3.** A person of fierce bloodthirsty disposition; দুর্দ্দান্ত এবং জিঘাংসু ব্যক্তি। **3.** An additional or more emphatic cheer or yell; as, three cheers and a *tiger*; জয়ধ্বনি, আনন্দধ্বনি বা চীৎকারের পরে প্রবলতর রবে উচ্চারিত অতিরিক্ত ধ্বনি। **4.** (*Sugar manufac.*) A tank with perforated bottom through which the molasses escape; যে সচ্ছিদ্র কুণ্ডের ভিতর দিয়া চিনি হইতে পৃথক হইয়া গুড় নীচে পতিত হয়। **–gress**, *n.* (*fem.*) The female tiger; ব্যাঘ্রী। **–ish**, *adj.* **Tiger-beetle** — শুষ্ক এবং বালুকাময় প্রদেশে বিচরণকারী একপ্রকার ইন্দ্রগোপকীট। **Tiger-cat**—বন্য মার্জ্জার। **Tiger-eye, Tiger's eye**—একপ্রকার অত্যুজ্জ্বল মণি, শার্দ্দূলাক্ষ। **Tiger-flower** — একপ্রকার ফুট ফুট দাগবিশিষ্ট পুষ্প। **Tiger-grass**—একপ্রকার অনুচ্চ তালজাতীয় বৃক্ষ, তালীবৃক্ষ। **Tiger-lily**—কৃষ্ণবর্ণের ফুট ফুট দাগবিশিষ্ট একপ্রকার কমলাবর্ণ স্থলকুমুদ। **Tiger-moth**—একপ্রকার উজ্জ্বল বর্ণের ডোরাদার পক্ষবিশিষ্ট তসরে পোকা। **Tiger-python**—একপ্রকার বৃহৎ সর্প। **Tiger-shark** — একজাতীয় বৃহদাকার হাঙ্গর। **Tiger-snake** — অষ্ট্রেলিয়া মহাদ্বীপের একপ্রকার অতি বিষাক্ত সর্প। **Tiger-wood** — ব্রিটিশ গিনি হইতে আমদানীকৃত গৃহসজ্জা নির্ম্মাণোপযোগী একপ্রকার কাষ্ঠ।

tight (tīt), *adj.*, *n.* & *adv.* **1.** Firmly held together; firm; আঁটা, দৃঢ়; শক্ত। **2.** Tensely stretched or drawn; টানটান। **3.** Not leaky; as, a *tight* ship; ছিদ্রশূন্য, অছিদ্র। **4.** Difficult; as, a *tight* work; severe; কঠিন, শক্ত; গুরুতর। **5.** Neat; as, a *tight* girl; ফিটফাট, পরিচ্ছন্ন। **6.** (*Colloq.*) Drunk; (চলিত ভাষায়) মাতাল। **7.** Fitting close to the body; as, a *tight* coat; আঁটসাট। **8.** Well-built; strong; as, *tight* body; সুগঠিত; বলবান, দৃঢ়কায়। **9.** (*Colloq.*) Niggardly; (চলিতভাষায়) কঞ্জুষ। **10.** Not easily obtainable; dear; as, a *tight* market; দুষ্প্রাপ্য; দুর্ম্মূল্যের, চড়া, কড়া, কষা। ***Noun.*** (*pl.*) A close fitting garment usually worn by acrobats, dancers, etc.; নর্ত্তক, দড়াবাজীকর, প্রভৃতির আঁটসাট পোষাক। ***Adv.*** tightly; শক্তভাবে, আঁটভাবে, দৃঢ়ভাবে। **Tight'-en**, *v. t.* & *i.* **Tight'-en-er**, *n.* **tight'-ness**, *n.* The state of being tight; আঁটুনি, কষাকষি, আঁটা আঁটি। **Tight'-ly**, *adv.* **Tight place**—কঠিন ঠাঁই (cf. সে বড় কঠিন ঠাঁই গুরু শিষ্যে ভেদ নাই।) **Tight-squeeze**—সঙ্কটের অবস্থা।

tīke, tȳke, *ns.* **1.** A cur; কুক্কুর। **2.** A low fellow; ইতর লোক। **3.** A mischievous child; দুরন্ত শিশু।

til'-bur-y (-bĕr-ĭ) *n.* (*Hist.*) A kind of gig; এক প্রকার হালকা দুই চাকার গাড়ী।

tilde, *n.* A sign placed over Spanish *n* when it is pronounced *ni* (*e.g.* Señor); ni (নি) উচ্চারণ সূচনার্থ স্পেনদেশীয় n অক্ষরের উপরে যে চিহ্ন দেওয়া হয়।

tīle, *n.* & *v. t.* **1.** A plate or small piece of slate-stone or of baked clay, used for covering the roofs of buildings, for floors, for drains, etc.; টালি, খাপরাই, খোলা, খর্পর (শুক্রঃ বিনয়)। **2.** (*Colloq.*) Silk-hat; (চলিত ভাষায়) রেশমী টুপি। ***Verb t.*** **1.** To cover with tiles; টালি দ্বারা আচ্ছাদিত করা। **2.** (In freemasonry) To guard (lodge etc.) against the entrance of the uninitiated; ফ্রিমেসনদিগের মধ্যে বহিরঙ্গ ব্যক্তিদিগের প্রবেশ নিরোধ করার জন্য পাহারা দেওয়া। **Til'-ing**, *n.* **Dutch tile** — একপ্রকার টালি — যাহাতে সচরাচর নীলবর্ণে বাইবেলের কাহিনী সমূহ চিত্রিত হইয়া থাকে। **Plain tile**—ছাদের টালি (প্রায় ১০½"×৬¼")। **Tile-fish**—একপ্রকার উজ্জ্বল বর্ণের মৎস্য। **Tile-stone**—টালি প্রস্তুতের উপযোগী প্রস্তর। **A tile loose**—Crazy; মাথার গোল।

tīl'-êr, *n.* One who makes or lays tiles; যে ব্যক্তি টালি প্রস্তুত করে, যে ব্যক্তি ছাদ প্রভৃতিতে টালি বিছায়। **2.** (Freemasonry). A door-keeper; (ফ্রিমেসন) দ্বাররক্ষক।

tilka, *n.* A sectarian mark on the forehead; তিলক।

till *v. t.* To cultivate; চাষ করা, কর্ষণ করা, চষা। **Till'-a-ble**, *adj.* That may be tilled; কর্ষণযোগ্য। **Till'-age**, *n.* The operation, practice, or art of tilling; কর্ষণ, চাষ।

till, *prep.* & *conj.* Up to; পর্য্যন্ত, অবধি, যাবৎ, তক। ***Conj.*** To the time when; to the degree that; যে পর্য্যন্ত না, যাবৎ না, যদবধি না; যে পরিমাণে না। **Till now**—বর্ত্তমান কাল পর্য্যন্ত, অদ্যাবধি। **Till then**—Up to that time; সে পর্য্যন্ত, তৎকাল পর্য্যন্ত।

till, *n.* A drawer for cash; টাকা পয়সা রাখার জন্য দেরাজ।

till, *n.* (*Geol.*) A stiff clay containing boulders, sand etc. (also called *boulder-clay*); (ভূবিদ্যা) উপল, বালুকা প্রভৃতি মিশ্রিত একপ্রকার কঠিন কৰ্দ্দম। **Till'-y**, *adj.*

till'-ĕr, *n.* One who tills; কৃষক, চাষা।

till'-ĕr, *n.* A lever fitted to the head of a rudder for steering; হাইলের কাঠি। **Tiller-chain**, **Tiller-rope**—যে শিকল বা দড়ী হাইলের অগ্রভাগের সহিত চাকাকে সংযুক্ত করে।

till'-ĕr, *n.* & *v. i.* The shoot of a plant springing from the root of the original stalk; a sucker; মূলবৃন্ত হইতে উদ্গত অঙ্কুর; মূলাধ্যজাশাখা। ***Verb i.*** To put forth shoots; ফেঁকড়ী বাহির হওয়া।

tilt, *v. i.*, *t.* & *n.* 1. To lean; কাঁত হওয়া, হেলিয়া থাকা। 2. To run or ride and thrust with a lance; দৌড়িয়া বা অশ্ব ছুটাইয়া বর্শাদ্বারা আক্রমণ করা। ***Verb t.*** 1. To set in sloping position; কাঁত করিয়া রাখা, হেলাইয়া রাখা। 2. To aim; to thrust; সন্ধান করা; প্রবিষ্ট করা। 3. To hammer or forge with a tilt hammer; বাষ্পবলে চালিত বৃহৎ হাতুড়ী দ্বারা পেটা। ***Noun.*** 1. A thrust as with a lance; বর্শাদ্বারা খোঁচা। 2. A military exercise on horseback in which the combatants attack each other with lances; অশ্বপৃষ্ঠে আরোহণ করিয়া বর্শাদ্বারা একে অন্যকে আক্রমণ, অশ্বপৃষ্ঠে বর্শাহস্তে যুদ্ধ। **Tilt'-er**, *n.* **Tilt-hammer**—বাষ্প বা স্রোতোবলে চালিত সুবৃহৎ মুদ্গর। **Tilt-yard** — বর্বাধারিযোদ্ধৃগণ যে প্রাঙ্গণে অশ্বারোহণে যুদ্ধ করে। **Full tilt**—At full speed; পূর্ণ বেগে। **On** or **upon the tilt**—In a tilted position; কাঁত।

tilt, *n.* & *v. t.* Covering of canvas etc. for cart; ক্যাম্বিস প্রভৃতি দ্বারা তৈরী গোশকটের আবরণ। ***Verb t.*** To furnish with tilt; ঐরূপ আবরণ দ্বারা আবৃত করা।

tilth, *n.* 1. Cultivation; কর্ষণ। 2. Depth of soil effected by this; কৃষ্ট ভূমির গভীরতা।

tim'-băl, **–bŭl**, **tўm'–**, *ns.* Kettle-drum; ঢোল।

timbale, *n.* (*F.*), A dish of pounded fowl or fish with white of egg etc. made in a mould; কুট্টিত কুক্কুট মাংস, মৎস্য এবং ডিম্বের শ্বেতাংশ প্রভৃতি দ্বারা ছাঁচে গড়া একপ্রকার খাদ্য।

tim'-bĕr, *n.* 1. Wood suitable for building purpose; গৃহাদি নির্ম্মাণের উপযোগী তক্তা। 2. Trees suitable for this; যে বৃক্ষের কাঠ হইতে গৃহ, আসবাব পত্র, প্রভৃতি প্রস্তুত হইয়া থাকে। 3. A rib or curving piece of wood in a ship, branching outward vertically from the keel; জাহাজের পঞ্জরকাঠ। 4. Bodily structure; "His body of small *timber*"; শারীরিক গঠন। 5. (*Fig.*) Material; "They are the fittest *timbers* to make politics of"; (লক্ষণায়) জিনিষ। **--ing**, *n.* **Timber-cart**—কাঠফলক বহনোপযোগী শকট। **Timber-head**—রজ্জু প্রভৃতি কুণ্ডলিত করিয়া রাখার জন্য জাহাজের পাটাতন হইতে উদ্গত কাষ্ঠাগ্র। **Timber-toe**, **Timber-toes**, *adjs.* কাষ্ঠনির্ম্মিতপদবিশিষ্ট লোক। **Timber-yard**--কাঠের গোলা।

tim'-bre (-br), *n.* The tone produced by each particular voice or instrument; প্রত্যেক স্বর বা যন্ত্র দ্বারা যে ধ্বনি উৎপন্ন হয়।

tim'-brĕl, *n.* Tambourine; পাখোয়াজ।

tīme, *n.* 1. The general idea of successive existence; কাল (cf. দেশকালনিমিত্ত)। 2. A particular portion or part of a duration, whether past, present or future, and conceived either as a space or as a point; moment; সময়, কাল; ক্ষণ। 3. The state of things at a particular time; as, hard *times*; সময়, দিন কাল। 4. Leisure; as, I have no *time* to see him; অবকাশ, অবসর। 5. Period; as, the *time* of Alexander; সময়, যুগ। 6. One of a number of repetition; বার। 7. The relative duration of a sound (or rest) as measured by the rhythmical proportions of the different notes; লয়। 8. (*Colloq.*) Term of imprisonment; as, he has served his *time*; কারাভোগের কাল। 9. Amount of time one has worked; কোন ব্যক্তি যে পরিমাণ সময় কায করিয়াছে। 10. One of the three dramatic unities formerly considered essential in the ancient drama; (নাটক) কাল, সময়। [প্রাচীন নাট্যে নাটকীয় ঘটনা সমূহ একদিবসে কিম্বা নাটকের অভিনয়ে যে পরিমাণ সময় লাগিত তাহাতে সীমাবদ্ধ ছিল।] 11. Hour of death; as, his *time* has come; মৃত্যুকাল, মরণসময়। **Time'-less**, *adj.* Unending; অকাল (হিঃ কোঃ), কালাতীত (ঐ), সময়াতীত। **Time'-ly**, *adj.* & *adv.* Seasonable; সময়োচিত, কালোচিত, সময়োপযোগী। ***Adv.*** In proper time; সুসময়ে, যথাসময়ে, যথাকালে, উপযুক্ত সময়ে। **Sidereal time**—নক্ষত্রকাল (হিঃ কোঃ)। **Time-ball**—(মানমন্দিরে) দণ্ডাগ্রে স্থাপিত গোলক—যাহা নির্দ্দিষ্টকালে (যথা অপরাহ্ণ ১ টায়) তাড়িতপ্রবাহের শক্তিতে পতিত হয়। **Time-bargain**—কোন নিরূপিত আগামী কালে জিনিষ প্রভৃতি বিক্রয়ের চুক্তি। **Time-card**—যে স্থূল কাগজখণ্ডে সময়তালিকা মুদ্রিত থাকে; যে স্থূল কাগজখণ্ডে কোন ব্যক্তি কত সময় কায করিয়াছে তাহা লিপিবদ্ধ থাকে, কালপট্ট। **Time-clock** — যে ঘড়ীতে শ্রমজীবিগণের উপস্থিতি ও প্রস্থানের সময় নির্দ্দেশের জন্য একটী কল সংযুক্ত থাকে, সময়-ঘটিকা। **Time-cribbing**—কারখানার শ্রমজীবিদিগকে অতিরিক্ত বেতন না দিয়া সেই বেতনে নির্দ্দিষ্ট সময়ের কয়েক মিনিট পূর্ব্বে আরম্ভ ও ছুটীর কয়েক মিনিট পর পর্য্যন্ত কার্য্য করার অনুমতি দান। **Time-decree**—কালাংশ।

Time-expired—অতিক্রান্তকাল (চুক্তিবদ্ধ মজুর বা সৈন্যসম্বন্ধে)। **Time-fuse**—বোমা প্রভৃতির যে দাহ্যদ্রব্যপূর্ণ নল বা পলিতা নির্দ্দিষ্ট কাল পর্য্যন্ত জ্বলিলে পর ঐ সকল বোমাদি বিদীর্ণ হয়। **Time-globe**—যে গোলকে কোন স্থানের স্থানীয় সময় প্রদর্শিত হয়, কাল-গোলক। **Time-honoured**—প্রাচীন, চিরপ্রচলিত, চিরাগত। **Time-immemorial**—স্মরণাতীত কাল। **Timekeeper**—ঘড়ী; যে কর্ম্মচারী কারখানার শ্রমজীবিগণ কত সময় কার্য্য করে তাহার হিসাব রাখে, সময়রক্ষক-কর্ম্মচারী। **Time-limit**—(বক্তৃতা প্রভৃতির) কালসীমা। **Time-motion**—কালগতি। **Timepiece**—ঘড়ী, কালাংশমান। **Time-server**—যে ব্যক্তি স্বীয় কার্য্য সাধনের জন্য সময় ও অবস্থার পরিবর্ত্তনের সঙ্গে সঙ্গে মত পরিবর্ত্তন করে, সময়সেবী। (*Time-serving, adj.* & *n.*) **Time-sheet**—যে কাগজে মজুরদিগের নাম ও তাহারা কত সময় কার্য্য করিয়াছে তাহা লিখা থাকে। **Time-spirit**—কালধর্ম্ম। **Time-table**—রেলওয়ের সময়তালিকা; বিচারালয়ের সময়তালিকা। **Time-work**—যে কাজের জন্য সম হিসাবে বেতন দেওয়া হয়। **Time-worn**—জীর্ণ, পুরাতন। **Against time**—With utmost speed; অতিবেগে, মহাবে[illegible]। **At the same time**—Simultaneously; সম সময়ে, যুগপৎ। **At this time of day**—At so modern a time; in the present state of civilization; এত আধুনিক কালে; সভ্যতার বর্ত্তমান অবস্থায়। **By that time**—এতক্ষণে। **For the time being**—For the present: আপাততঃ। **From time to time**—Occasionally; মাঝে মাঝে, সময় সময়, কখন কখন। **In course of time**—As time went on; কালক্রমে। **In no time**—Erelong; soon; অবিলম্বে; শীঘ্র, অচিরে। **In good time**—In due course of time; যথাকালে। Soon; শীঘ্র। **In time**—After a short time; after a few years; just in time; কিছুকাল পরে; কয়েক বৎসর পরে; ঠিক সময়। **One time with another**—On various occasions; বিভিন্ন কালে। **Out of time**—Unseasonable; অসময়োচিত। **The time of day**—সময়; (ইতরভাষায়) অবস্থা। **Time and again**—Always; সদাসর্ব্বদা। **Time hangs heavy**—সময় আর কাটে না। **Time out of mind**—Same as TIME IMMEMORIAL. **To have a good (real) time**—To enjoy happiness; সুখ ভোগ করা, সুসময়ে পড়া। **To keep good or bad time**—To record accurately or inaccurately; ঠিক সময় রাখা, ঠিক সময় না রাখা। **To keep time**—To walk or dance in time; তালে তালে পা ফেলিয়া চলা বা নাচা। **To pass the time of the day**—To exchange greetings with a person; পরস্পরকে নমস্কারাদি করা। **To take time by the forelock**—Not to make needless delay; সময় থাকিতে কার্য্য করা। **What time**—(*Poet.*) While; যখন (কবিতায়)।

tīme. *v. t.* & *i.* To adapt to the time or occasion; to bring, begin or perform at the proper season or time; সময়োপযোগী করা, কালোপযোগী করা; উপযুক্ত সময়ে আনয়ন, আরম্ভ বা সম্পাদন করা। ***Verb i.*** To keep or beat time; তাল দেওয়া।

tī-mĕn'-ō-guy (-gĭ), *n.* A rope stretched from one place to another to prevent fouling of rigging; জাহাজের দড়িদড়া যাহাতে পরস্পরের সহিত না জড়াইতে পারে তজ্জন্য যে রজ্জু এক স্থান হইতে অপর স্থানে প্রসারিত করা হয়।

tīme'-ous (-ŭs), *n.* Same as TIMOUS.

tĭm'-ĭd, *adj.* Wanting courage to meet danger; timorous; ভীরু, শঙ্কিত; সশঙ্ক। **–ly**, *adv.* **–mid'-i-ty**, *n.* Quality or state of being timid; weakness; ভীরুতা; দুর্ব্বলতা। **–ness**, *n.*

tī-mŏc'-ră-ç̆y, *n.* A form of government, in which a certain amount of property is requisite as a qualification for office; একপ্রকার শাসনতন্ত্র—যাহাতে কেবলমাত্র সম্পত্তিশালী ব্যক্তিগণ কর্ম্মচারী হইতে পারেন, বিত্ততন্ত্র। **–mo-crat'-ic**, *adj.*

tĭm'-ôr-ous (-ŭs), *adj.* Timid; indicating fear; ভীরু; ভয়সূচক।

tĭm'-ō-thy̆, –grăss, *ns.* A kind of fodder-grass; এক প্রকার গোগ্রাসোপযোগী তৃণ। [Timothy Hanson নামে এক ব্যক্তি এই ঘাস ইংলণ্ডে প্রবর্ত্তন করেন বলিয়া এই নাম।]

tĭm'-ous (-ŭs), *adj.* (*Scot.*) Timely; (স্কচভাষায়) সময়োচিত। **–ness**, *n.*

tĭm'-pă-nō, *n.* A kettle-drum; তবলা।

tĭn, *n.* & *v. t.* **1.** A white soft non-elastic metal, very malleable; রাঙ্গ, টীন। [*Syn.* বঙ্গ, রঙ্গ, ত্রপু, ত্রপুল, কুটিল, হ্রীকু, ক্ষুর, ক্ষুরক, বজ্রতারি, মিশ্রক, পুতিক, কুরূপ্য, ফলি, বক্র, চিত্ররঞ্জক, স্বর্ণজ, নাগজীবন, মৃদঙ্গ, গুরুপত্র, পিচ্চট, চক্রসংজ্ঞ, তমর, নাগজ, কস্তীর, আলীনক, সিংহল, স্ববেত, নাগ, আপুষ, তীর, তীব্র]। [Arab. *kas-din, ressas, abruz*; Pers. *urziz*; Sp. *hoja de lata*; Heb. *bedel*; Germ. *bleck, weissblech, zinn*; It. *latta, banda stagnata*; Lat. *stannum*; Fr. *etain*; Russ. *shest, blacha*; Burm. *khai ma phyn*; Chin. *yang-seih*; Tam. *tagaram*.] **2.** A thin plate of iron covered with tin; বঙ্গদ্বারা আচ্ছাদিত লৌহপট্ট, টীন। **3.** A canister or plate of tin; as, a *tin* of preserved fruit; টীনের ক্যানেস্তা, টীনের থালা। **4.** (*Slang*) Money; "She married a rich old man for his *tin*"; (ইতর ভাষায়) টাকা কড়ি। ***Verb t.*** **1.** To cover or coat with tin; টীনের পাতদ্বারা মোড়া, কালাই করা। **2.** To pack fruits etc. in tin for preservation ; টাটকা রাখার জন্য ফল প্রভৃতি টীনের পাত্রে পুরা। **Tin′-ner,** *n.* **Tin′-ny,** *adj.* **Tin-foil**—টীনের পাতলা পাত, রঙ্গপত্র (সাঃ পঃ), রঙ্গদল। **Tinman** or **Tin-smith** — টীনের কারিকর। **Tin-mouth**—আমেরিকার মিসিসিপি নদীর একপ্রকার মৎস্য। **Tinstone**—একপ্রকার প্রস্তর—যাহাতে প্রধানতঃ টীন পাওয়া যায়। **Tin-silver**—টীন হইতে প্রস্তুত একপ্রকার কৃত্রিম রৌপ্য। **A tin soldier**—তালপাতার সিপাহী। **Salt of tin, Tin-liquor** — উগ্রদ্রাবকে বিদ্রাবিত রঙ্গ—যাহা রঙ্গসংস্থাপক রূপে ব্যবহৃত হইয়া থাকে। **Tinned goods**—যে সকল পক্ব খাদ্যদ্রব্য টীনে পুরিয়া টাট্‌কা রাখা হয়।

tin′-ă-mou (-mô), *n.* A South-American bird resembling the partridge ; দক্ষিণ আমেরিকার পক্ষিবিশেষ।

tin′-căl (tĭng-), **tin′-kăl** (tĭng-), *ns.* Unrefined borax ; অশোধিত সোহাগা।

tinc-tō′-ri-ăl (tĭngk-), *adj.* Of, or pertaining to, colour or dyeing ; producing colour ; বর্ণসম্বন্ধীয়, রঞ্জন-সম্বন্ধীয় ; বর্ণপ্রদ, রঙ্গপ্রদ, বর্ণদ।

tinc′-tūre (tĭngk-), *n.* & *v. t.* **1.** A tinge or shadow ; বর্ণের আমেজ বা রঙ্গের ছায়া। **2.** A slight taste superadded to any substance ; as, a *tincture* of lemon ; কোন জিনিষে অন্য জিনিষের যে সামান্য তার সংযুক্ত করা হয়। **3.** Tinge ; as, there is a *tincture* of bitterness in his tone ; আভাস, আমেজ। **4.** The finer and more volatile parts of a substance separated by a solvent ; দ্রাবক দ্বারা পৃথকীকৃত কোন বস্তুর সূক্ষ্ম এবং অধিকতর উদ্বায়ী অংশ। **5.** Flavour, extract or solution of the active principles of a substance ; বস্তুর সারাংশ মিশ্রিত সুরাদি, অরিষ্ট (হঃ চঃ), অর্ক (সাঃ পঃ), আসব (ঠাকুর), আরক। ***Verb t.*** **1.** To impregnate or imbue with colour or a shade ; বর্ণ বা আভাদ্বারা অনুরঞ্জিত করা। **2.** To imbue ; to tinge : অনুরঞ্জিত করা ; আভাস দেওয়া, আমেজ দেওয়া।

tin′-dăl, *n.* A petty officer among lascars ; জাহাজের টিণ্ডাল।

tin′-dĕr, *n.* **1.** An inflammable substance used for obtaining fire from spark ; স্ফুলিঙ্গ হইতে অগ্নি প্রজ্বালিত করার জন্য কোনরূপ আশুদাহ্য পদার্থ। **Tinder-box**—যে ধাতুনির্ম্মিত বাক্সে সাধারণতঃ অগ্নি প্রজ্বালিত করার জন্য পাথর ও ইস্পাত খণ্ড থাকে, চকমকির বাক্স।

tīne, *n.* The tooth of a fork or harrow ; the point of a deer's horn ; কাঁটা বা বিদার দাঁত ; মৃগশৃঙ্গের অগ্রভাগ।

tĭng, *n.* & *v. i.* **1.** Tinkling sound as of a bell ; টং টং, টিং টিং। ***Verb i.*** **2.** To make a tinkling sound ; টং টং শব্দ করা।

tinge (tĭnj), *v.t.* & *n.* **1.** To imbue slightly with a colour ; to impart a taste or flavour ; ঈষৎ রঞ্জিত করা ; স্বাদ প্রদান করা। **2.** To modify the character or quality of ; প্রকৃতি বা গুণের ঈষৎ পরিবর্ত্তন করা, অনুরঞ্জিত করা। **3.** To give a taste, flavour or smack to ; আমেজ দেওয়া, আভাস দেওয়া। ***Noun.*** **1.** A slight degree of some colour ; flavour ; touch ; ঈষৎ রঙ্গ, কোন রঙ্গের ঈষৎ আভা ; স্বাদ, তার ; আভাস, আমেজ।

tin′-gle (tĭng-gl), *v. i.* & *n.* **1.** To tinkle ; রণ রণ করা, ঝন ঝন করা, রুণু ঝুনু করা, রুণু ঝুনু রবে বাজা। **2.** To feel a kind of prickling or tingling or thrilling sensation ; টন্ টন্ করা, পিট পিট করা, ঝিন ঝিনকরা, শিরশির করা। **3.** To cause a thrilling or stinging or prickly sensation ; টন টন বোধ করান, ঝিনঝিনি বোধ করান, শিরশির করান। ***Noun.*** A thrilling sansation ; শির শির, ঝিন ঝিনি।

tin′-kĕr, (tĭng-), *n., v. t.* & *i.* **1.** One who mends pots, kettles, pans or the like ; যে ব্যক্তি তাম্র পিত্তল, প্রভৃতির জিনিষ মেরামত করে, ঝালকাঁসারী। **2.** A botcher ; a bungler ; a jack of all trades ; যে ব্যক্তি জোড়াতালি দেয় ; যে ব্যক্তি আনাড়ীর মত কাজ করে ; সব-জান্তা লোক, সকল কর্ম্মের ঘট। ***Verb t.*** & ***i.*** **1.** To mend or solder, as metal wares ; ঝাইল দেওয়া, ঝালাই করা, রাং ঝাইল দেওয়া। **2.** To botch ; জোড়াতালি দেওয়া। **–ing,** *n.* Botching ; জোড়াতালি দেওন। **–ing-ly,** *adv.*

tin′-kle (tĭng-kl), *v. i., t.* & *n.* To clink ; to jingle ; ঝনঝনিয়ে উঠা, শিঞ্জিত হওয়া ; রণরণিয়ে উঠা। ***Verb t.*** To jingle ; ঝন ঝন করা, রণ রণ করা, শিঞ্জিত করা, টং টং করা। ***Noun.*** A succession of clinking sounds ; শিঞ্জা, শিঞ্জিত, রন্ রন্, রুণু রুণু, টং টং, রুণুঝুনু।

tin′-klĕr (tĭng-), *n.* **1.** One who tinkles ; ঝুনু ঝুনু ধ্বনিকারী, টং টং ধ্বনিকারী। **2.** (*Slang*) Small bell ; (ইতর-ভাষায়) ক্ষুদ্র ঘণ্টা, ঘণ্টিকা।

tĭn-nī′-tŭs, *n.* (Also *tinnitus auriun*) (*Med.*) Ringing in the ear ; (ভৈষজ্যশাস্ত্র) কর্ণে নাদ, কাণে শব্দ [এই রোগে কর্ণে একপ্রকার ভণ্ ভণ্ বা সোঁ সোঁ শব্দ অনুভূত হয়।]

Tinospora cordifolia—গুলঞ্চ (বেলঃ)। [Syn. তন্ত্রিকা, ছিন্নরুহা, জীবন্তিকা, বৎসাদনী, সোমবল্লী, বিশল্যা, মধুপর্ণী, গুড়ুচি, গুড়ুচী, কুণ্ডলী, চক্রলক্ষণা, অমৃতবল্লী, জ্বরারি, শ্যামা, বরা, সুরকৃতা, ছিন্নোদ্ভবা, মধুপর্ণিকা, অমৃতলতা, রসায়নী, ছিন্না, উৎকীর্ণ, সোমলতিকা, ভিষকপ্রিয়া, কুণ্ডলিনী, নাগকুমারিকা, বয়ঃস্থা, ছদ্মিকা, চন্দ্রহাসা, অমৃতা, অমৃতবল্লরী, চক্রলক্ষণিকা, সোমা, বয়স্থা, মণ্ডলী, দেবনির্ম্মিতা, সুধা, জীবন্তী।] [Tam. *shindi-kodi* ; Teleg. *guduchi, galuchi, manapala, tippatige* ; Punj. *gilo, gul-arich.*]

tĭn′-sĕl, *n., adj.* & *v. t.* **1.** A shining thin metallic plate ; ধাতুর

পাতলা জেল্লাদার পাত, জগজগা, ঝিলমিল। **2.** A dress-material shot or covered with tinsel ; জগজগা লাগানো কাপড়, জগজগা দ্বারা আচ্ছাদিত কাপড়। **3.** (*Fig.*) Something very shining and gaudy, or having false lustre, and more gay than valuable ; "Who can discern the *tinsel* from the gold ?" ; চটকদার জিনিষ, জিল্লাদার জিনিষ। **4.** Superficial brilliancy ; জেল্লা, চটক। ***Adj.*** Made of tinsel ; like tinsel ; gaudy ; cheaply splendid ; জগজগা দ্বারা তৈরি ; জগজগার মত ; ঝলমলে, ঝকমকে ; চটকদার, জিল্লাদার, ভড়কদার। ***Verb t.*** To adorn or cover with tinsel ; to make gaudy ; জগজগা দ্বারা শোভিত করা, জগজগা দ্বারা আচ্ছাদিত করা ; চটকদার করা, জেল্লাদার করা।

tint, *n.* & *v. t.* **1.** A pale or faint tinge of any colour ; a light variety of colour ; কোন বর্ণের ঈষৎ আমেজ বা আভা, রাগ ; পাতলা রঙ্গ। **2.** (*Loosely*) Colour ; বর্ণ, রঙ্গ। **3.** A smack ; as, there is *tinge* of sorrow in his song ; আভাস, আমেজ, লেশ। **3.** (*Engrav.*) A set of parallel lines cut to give uniform shading ; (ক্ষোদনবিদ্যা) সর্ব্বত্র সমরূপ ছায়া প্রকটনের জন্য উৎকীর্ণ সমন্তরাল রেখাশ্রেণী। **4.** (*Print.*) A light coloured surface serving as a background ; পাতলা রঙ্গে রঞ্জিত ভূমি। ***Verb t.*** To give a slight colouring ; to colour ; ঈষৎ রঞ্জিত করা ; রঞ্জিত করা। **Tint'-less,** *adj.* **Crossed tint** — যে চিত্রফলকে উৎকীর্ণ সরল রেখাশ্রেণী পরস্পরকে ছেদন করিয়া থাকে। **Ruled tint** — যে চিত্রফলকে সমান্তরাল রেখাশ্রেণী ক্ষোদিত থাকে। **Tint-block**—যে চিত্রফলকে ফিকে রঙ্গে মুদ্রিত হওয়ার উপযোগী বিষয় ক্ষোদিত থাকে। **Tint-drawing** — বিভিন্ন গাঢ়তার বর্ণের সাহায্যে অট্টালিকা প্রভৃতির চিত্র অঙ্কন। **Tint-tool** — সর্ব্বত্র একরূপ ছায়া প্রকটনের জন্য চিত্রফলকের উপর সমান্তরাল রেখাশ্রেণী কর্ত্তনের নিমিত্ত যন্ত্রবিশেষ, বর্ণযন্ত্র।

tint'-ĕr, *n.* **1.** A person who tints ; ঈষৎ রঞ্জনকারী। **2.** A plain magic-lantern slide of one colour ; যাদুপ্রদীপের একরঙ্গা চিত্রফলক।

tin-tin-năb-ü-lā'-tion, *n.* The ringing of bells ; tinkling sound of bells ; ঘণ্টার রব ; ঘণ্টার টং টং শব্দ।

tin-tin-năb'-ü-lŭm, *n.* **1.** A bell ; a small bell ; ঘণ্টা ; ঘণ্টিকা। **2.** A musical instrument of percussion, consisting of a number of bells, suspended in a frame ; কোনরূপ ঠাট বা কাঠাম হইতে দোলায়িত ঘণ্টিকাশ্রেণী— যাহা পরস্পরের সহিত ধাক্কা লাগিয়া বাজিয়া উঠে। **—la-ry, —lous,** *adj.*

tin'-tŏ, *n.* A red Maderia wine ; মেডিরিয়াতে প্রস্তুত এক প্রকার লাল মদ।

tint-ŏm'-ĕ-tĕr, *n.* An apparatus for the determination, of colours ; বর্ণনির্ণায়ক যন্ত্র, বর্ণনিরূপক যন্ত্র।

tint'-ŷ, *adj.* Abounding in tints ; having inharmonious tints ; রঞ্জনপ্রাচুর্য্যবিশিষ্ট ; সঙ্গতিশূন্যভাবে রঞ্জিত।

ti'-nŷ, teen'-ŷ (-tēn), *adjs.* (*Used in nursery*) Very small ; minute ; অতি ক্ষুদ্র ; অতি ছোট, ছোট্ট (*colloq.*)।

tip, *n., v. t.* & *i.* **1.** A tap or slight blow ; ঠুকা, ঠুকনা। **2.** Hint ; private information, esp. in regard to the chances of horses engaged for race ; আভাস, আঁচ ; গোপনীয় সংবাদ, গুপ্ত খবর, বিশেষতঃ দৌড়ের ঘোড়া সম্বন্ধে গুপ্ত সংবাদ। **3.** A small present in money ; বকশিশ। **4.** A book-binder's tool ; দপ্তরীর যন্ত্রবিশেষ। **5.** A place for depositing rubbish ; rubbish ; আবর্জ্জনা রাখার স্থান ; আবর্জ্জনার স্তূপ। ***Verb t.*** **1.** To strike slightly ; ঠুকনা দেওয়া। **2.** To lift up (a cart) for the discharge of a load ; বোঝাই মাল ফেলাইবার জন্য (শকট) একদিকে তুলিয়া কাত করা। **3.** To bestow a small gift upon ; টাকা পয়সা বকশিশ দেওয়া। **4.** To give private information to, esp. regarding a horse engaged in a race ; গোপনে সংবাদ দেওয়া, বিশেষতঃ দৌড়ের ঘোড়া সম্বন্ধে গোপনে খবর দেওয়া। ***Verb i.*** To fall on or toward one side ; to fall headlong ; to die ; কাত হওয়া, হেলিয়া পড়া ; হুমড়ি খাইয়া পড়া ; মরা। **Tip'-per,** *n.* **Tip-car, Tip-cart**—যে গাড়ীর এক প্রান্ত তুলিয়া বোঝাই মাল ফেলা হয়। **Tip-cat**—ক্রীড়াবিশেষে ব্যহৃত উভয়প্রান্ত সূক্ষ্মায়মান কাষ্ঠখণ্ড। **The straight tip**—(ইতর ভাষায়) ঝটিতিপ্রাপ্ত সঠিক সংবাদ। **To miss one's tip** — To fail in one's object ; উদ্দেশ্য ব্যর্থ হওয়া। **To tip off**—To pour out by tipping the vessel ; পাত্র কা'ত করিয়া ঢালা। **To tip one's fin** — To stretch one's hand for the purpose of handshaking ; করমর্দ্দনার্থ হস্ত প্রসারিত করা। **To tip over**—To turn over ; উলটান। **To tip the wink**—ইসারা দেওয়া, চোখে ঠার দেওয়া। **To tip up**—To raise up one end of anything, as of a cart so that the contents may pass out ; গাড়ী প্রভৃতির বোঝা ফেলিবার জন্য উহার এক প্রান্ত তোলা।

tip, *n.* & *v. t.* **1.** Extremity ; as, the *tip* of one's tongue ; প্রান্ত, অগ্র, অগ্রভাগ। **2.** A cap or small piece or part attached to the extremity of anything ; কোন বস্তুর অগ্রভাগে সংযোজিত টোপর বা ক্ষুদ্র খণ্ড। **3.** The upper part of a hat ; টুপির উপরিভাগ। **4.** A lining of the top a hat ; টুপির অগ্রভাগের আস্তর। **4.** A brush used by gilders ; গিল্টিকরগণ কর্ত্তৃক ব্যবহৃত একপ্রকার বুরুস। **5.** A sandal ; একপ্রকার পাদুকা। ***Verb t.*** **1.** To cover the tip or end of ; অগ্রভাগ মণ্ডিত করা, আগা বাঁধা। **2.** To furnish the extremity of, with caps

&c ; অগ্রভাগে টোপর প্রভৃতি লাগান । **Tipstaff**—পূর্ব্বকালে শেরিফের পেয়াদাগণের ধাতুবদ্ধ যষ্টি। **Tiptoe**—(*Adv.*) Expectantly ; eagerly ; উৎকণ্ঠিতভাবে; সচকিতভাবে। (*Verb i.*) To go or walk on tiptoe ; পদাঙ্গুলীর উপর ভর করিয়া চলা। (*Noun.*) পদাঙ্গুলীর অগ্রভাগ। **Tiptop**—*adj.* & *n.* প্রথম শ্রেণীর, উৎকৃষ্ট। (*Noun*) সর্ব্বোত্তম অংশ। **At the tip of one's finger** — Under one's full control ; সম্পূর্ণ আয়ত্ত্ব, করামলকবৎ। **Neither tip nor toe**— Not a particle or trace ; none at all ; বিন্দুমাত্রও না ; মোটেই না। **On or at the tip of one's tongue**—See TONGUE. **On the tiptoe, A tiptoe**—On the alert ; as, *on the tip toe* of expectation ; সচকিত, সজাগ।

tip'-pet (-ĕt), *n.* A cape or covering for the neck or shoulders ; বিচারক, ধর্ম্মযাজক, প্রভৃতির স্কন্ধাবরক বস্ত্র।

tip'-ple (-pl), *v. i., t.* & *n.* **1.** To drink liquors habitually ; সুরাসক্ত হওয়া, মদ্যাসক্ত হওয়া। ***Verb t.*** **1.** To drink liquor frequently or by sips ; সর্ব্বদা মদ্য পান করা, পুনঃ পুনঃ এক এক ঢোক সুরা পান করা। **2.** To cause to be affected by drink ; মদ্যপান করাইয়া অভিভূত করা। ***Noun.*** Strong drink ; উগ্রপানীয়, উগ্রসুরা, কড়া মদ। **—pler,** *n.* One who habitually indulges in the excessive use of spirituous liquors ; মদ্যপায়ী, সুরাপায়ী।

tip'-stêr, *n.* One who gives out secret information about race-horse etc.; যে ব্যক্তি দৌড়ের ঘোড়া প্রভৃতি সম্পর্কে গোপনীয় সংবাদ প্রদান করে।

tip'-sy̆, *adj.* **1.** Intoxicated ; সুরামত্ত, মাতাল। **2.** Due to tipsiness ; showing tipsiness ; মত্ততাজনিত ; মত্ততাসূচক। **—si-ly,** *adv.* **—si-ness,** *n.* **—si-fy,** *v. t.* **Tipsy-cake**—মদ্যে সিক্ত পিষ্টক বিশেষ।

tī'-rāde, *n.* **1.** A long declamatory strain of invective or abuse ; "Here he delivers a violent *tirade* against all persons who profess to know anything about angels" ; a continued burst of violent declamation ; সুদীর্ঘ তিরস্কারগর্ভ বক্তৃতা ; তিরস্কারস্রোত। **2.** (*Mus.*) The filling of an interval by the intermediate diatonic notes ; (সঙ্গীতশাস্ত্র) স্বরগ্রামের মধ্যবর্ত্তী স্বরসমূহ কোন অবকাশদ্বারা পুরণ।

tī-rail-leur' (-rāl-yêr), *n.* (*F.*) A skirmisher ; a sharp-shooter ; খণ্ডযুদ্ধকারী ; অব্যর্থলক্ষ্য ব্যক্তি।

tīre, *n.* & *v. t.* (*Archaic*) Head-dress ; (অপ্রঃ) উষ্ণীষ, পাগড়ী। ***Verb t.*** To attire ; to adorn ; পরান; প্রসাধিত করা। **Tiring house, room**—(অপ্রঃ) নাটকের সাজঘর, নেপথ্য। **Tire-woman**—(*Archaic*) কোন মহিলার বেশভূষা সম্পাদনে নিযুক্তা স্ত্রীলোক, প্রসাধিকা।

tīre, *v. t.* & *i.* **1.** To make weary ; ক্লান্ত করা, হয়রাণ করা, শ্রান্ত করা। **2.** To exhaust the patience or attention of by dulness or tediousness ; as, to *tire* one's patience ; পরিক্লান্ত করা, অবসাদগ্রস্ত করা। ***Verb i.*** To become weary or fatigued or exhausted ; ক্লান্ত হওয়া, অবসন্ন হওয়া। **To tire out**—To wear out ; to exhaust thoroughly ; ক্লান্ত করা ; অবসন্ন করা। **Tired'-ness,** *n.* **Tire'-less**—Untired ; ক্লান্তিহীন, অক্লান্ত।

tīre, *n.* & *v. t.* Same as TYRE (which see).

tīre'-some (-sŭm), *adj.* Fitted or tending to tire ; fatiguing ; tedious ; ক্লান্তিকর, শ্রমসাধ্য ; ক্লান্তিজনক, শ্রান্তিজনক, শ্রমজনক, আয়াসকর ; অবসাদজনক। **—ly,** *adv.* **—ness,** *n.*

tī'-rō, ty̆'-rō, *ns.* A beginner ; a novice ; প্রথমশিক্ষার্থী; নবশিক্ষার্থী, নবছাত্র।

tīr-ō-cĭn'-ĭ-ŭm, *n.* **1.** Apprenticeship ; শিক্ষানবিসী। **2.** The first rudiments of any art ; কোন শিল্পের মূলসূত্র।

tir'-wit (têr-), *n.* The lapwing ; একপ্রকার পক্ষী।

'tis, *n.* Contraction of *it is.*

tī'-sāne, *n.* Same as PTISAN.

tis'-sue *n.* (tĭsh-ū), **1.** A fine cloth ; a light gauzy fabric used for veils, etc. ; a cloth interwoven with gold or silver, or with figured colours ; মিহি কাপড় ; হাওয়ার কাপড় ; গুলাবতন কাপড়, ফুলপাতাতোলা কাপড়। **2.** (*Biol.*) A structure made up of cells and fibres entering into the organisation

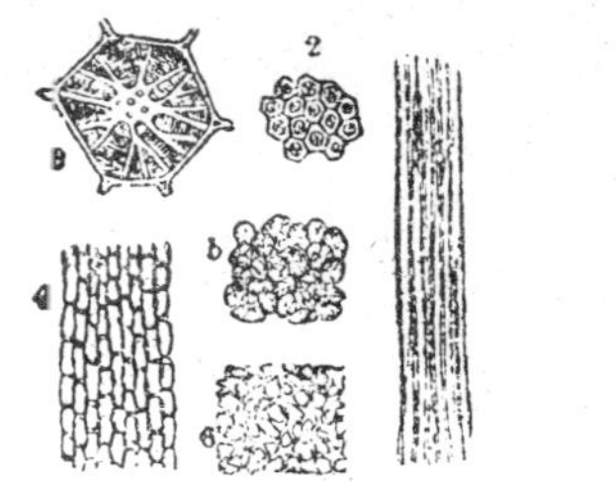

Vegetable tissue.

1, woody tissue ; 2, horizontal section ; 3, cell in section ; 4, cylindrical tissue ; 5, round or elliptical tissue ; 6, spongiform or stellate tissue.

of plants and animals ; (জীববিজ্ঞান) জীবদেহের বা উদ্ভিদের উপদানীভূত সূত্রবৎ বস্তু বা অনুকোষ সমূহ, মাংসতন্তু (হিঃ কোঃ), বিধানতন্তু, রেশা, কোষ-সংস্থান (সাঃ পঃ), কলা (ব্রজঃ বিঃ)। **3.** Interwoven series ; as, a *tissue* of lies ; set ; জাল ; শ্রেণী। **Tissue-paper**—পুস্তকের ছবি ঢাকিবার জন্য এবং কোমল জিনিষ প্রভৃতি মুড়িবার নিমিত্ত একপ্রকার অতি পাতলা কাগজ।

tit, *n.* Same as TEAT (which see).

tit, *n.* One of various small birds, titlark or titmouse ; টুনি প্রভৃতি ক্ষুদ্র পাখী।

tit, *n.* **Tit for tat**—ইটটী মারিলে পাটকেলটী খাইতে হয়, আগে জলের ছিটা পরে চোড়ের গুতা (East Bengal)।

Tī'-tăn, *n.* **1.** Fabulous giants of Greek and Roman mythology ; গ্রীক ও রোমীয় পুরাণে উক্ত মহাকায় দৈত্যগণের অন্যতম। [টাইটানগণ

Uranus (স্বর্গ) এবং Gae (পৃথিবীর) পুত্র।] **2.** The sixth of the eight satellites of Saturn ; শনৈশ্চরের অষ্ট উপগ্রহের মধ্যে ষষ্ঠসংখ্যক উপগ্রহ। **3.** The sun personified ; ' Didst thou never see *Titan* kiss a dish of butter" ; সূর্য্য। **4.** Short of TITAN-CRANE. **5.** A person of superhuman size, strength or intellect ; অতিকায় মনুষ্য, অমানুষিক শক্তিশালী ব্যক্তি, অমানুষিক ধীশক্তিসম্পন্ন ব্যক্তি। **—ess,** *n.* (*Fem.*) **Titan-crane** — সেতু প্রভৃতির স্তম্ভ, পিল্‌পা, প্রভৃতি স্থাপনের জন্য একপ্রকার বৃহদাকার ভারোত্তোলন যন্ত্র। **The weary Titan**—ব্রিটিশ বা অন্য কোন বৃহৎ সাম্রাজ্য।

Tī-tā'-nī-ă, *n.* The queen of the faires in Shakespeare's Midsummer Night's Dream ; শেক্ষপীয়রের "মধ্যনিদাঘ যামিনীর স্বপ্ন" নামক নাটকের নায়িকা, পরীরাণী।

tī-tăn'-ic, *adj.* Gigantic ; superhuman; as, *titanic* strength ; অতিকায়, মহাকায়, বিরাট ; অমানুষিক, অতিমানুষ।

tī-tăn'-ic, *adj.* Pertaining to titanium ; ত্রিতক ধাতুসম্বন্ধীয়। **Titanic acid**—ত্রিতক দ্রাবক।

tī-tăn-if'-ĕr-ous (-ŭs), *adj.* Producing titanium ; ত্রিতকগর্ভ।

tī'-tăn-īte, *n.* An ore of titanium ; খনিজবিমিশ্র ত্রিতক।

tī-tā'-nī-ŭm, *n.* A metallic element of a dark grey colour ; একপ্রকার গাঢ় ধূসরবর্ণ ধাতব মূল পদার্থ, ত্রিতক।

tit'-bit, *n.* Palatable dish ; the best part of the food ; রসনাতৃপ্তিকর খাদ্য, রসনারোচক খাদ্য ; খাদ্যদ্রব্যের উৎকৃষ্ট অংশ।

tīthe (tīth), *n.* & *v. t.* **1.** A tenth part ; any small part of anything; দশমাংশ ; ক্ষুদ্রাংশ। **2.** The tenth of the produce of land-stock and the personal industry of the inhabitants alloted for the maintenance of the clergy and other church purposes ; যাজকদিগের ভরণ-পোষণের এবং ধর্ম্মসংঘের ব্যয় নির্ব্বাহের জন্য ভূমি প্রভৃতির উৎপন্ন দ্রব্যের কিম্বা অনুরূপ আয়ের দশমাংশ, ধর্ম্মশুল্ক। ***Verb t.*** To subject to tithe ; ধর্ম্মশুল্ক বসান। **Tith'-a-ble,** *adj.* **Mixed-tithes** — ধর্ম্মশুল্কস্বরূপ গৃহীত শূকর, মেষ, প্রভৃতির দশমাংশ। **Personal tithes**—ব্যক্তিগত শ্রমলব্ধ অর্থের দশমাংশ। **Prædial tithes**—ভূমির আয়ের দশমাংশ। **Tithe-pig**—ধর্ম্মশুল্ক প্রদানের জন্য দশম শূকর।

tīth'-ing, *n.* **1.** The act of taking tithe ; ধর্ম্মশুল্কগ্রহণ। **2.** In Anglo-Saxon police arrangements, associations of ten men (in the North of England called the *tenmannetale* ; elsewhere *frithborh* or *frankpledge*) who, dwelling near each other, were sureties or free pledges to the king for each other's good behaviour ; ইংলণ্ডের ক্ষুদ্র পল্লীবাসী দশজন গৃহস্থের সমবায়—ইহারা প্রত্যেকে পরস্পরের সদাচরণের জন্য প্রতিভূ থাকিত।

tit'-il-lāte, *v. t.* **1.** To tickle; কাতুরকুতুর দেওয়া, সুড়সুড়ি দেওয়া। **2.** To excite pleasantly ; পুলক সঞ্চার করা। **—la'-tion,** *n.* **1.** The act of tickling ; the sensation of being titillated ; কাতুরকুতুর দেওন ; সুড়সুড়ি, কাতুরকুতুর। **2.** Any slight pleasure ; পুলক।

tī'-tle (-tl), *n.* **1.** An appellation ; নাম, আখ্যা। **2.** An appellation of dignity, distinction or pre-eminence given to a person ; উপাধি, খেতাব। **3.** (*Law*) Right to ownership or for property ; (আইন) স্বত্ব, অধিকার। **4.** A chapter or section of a book ; পুস্তকের অধ্যায়। **5.** The instrument or document which is evidence of a right (also *title-deed*) ; অধিকারপত্র, স্বত্বের দলীল। **6.** Fineneess of gold as expressed in carats ; ক্যারাট দ্বারা ব্যক্ত স্বর্ণের উৎকৃষ্টতা। **—less,** *adj.* **Title-deed** — অধিকারপত্র, স্বত্বের দলিল। **Title-holder** — স্বত্ববান। **Title-page**—পুস্তকের নাম, গ্রন্থকার ও প্রকাশক প্রভৃতির নামাদিসম্বলিত পৃষ্ঠা, নামপত্র। **Title-role**—নাটকের যে ভূমিকা হইতে নাটকের নাম হইয়া থাকে।

tī'-tled (-tld), *adj.* Having the title of a noble man ; সম্ভ্রান্ত উপাধিধারী।

tit'-ling, *n.* Same as TIT (in the sense of bird).

tit'-ling, *n.* The act of impressing the title of a book in gold-leaf etc. ; স্বর্ণপত্র প্রভৃতিদ্বারা পুস্তকের পৃষ্ঠে নাম প্রভৃতি মুদ্রণ।

tit'-mouse (-mows), *n.* (*pl.* -MICE), A name of several birds, small and active, with shrill, wild notes ; কয়েক প্রকার ক্ষুদ্র পক্ষীর সাধারণ নাম।

tī'-trāte, *v. t.* (*Chem.*) To ascertain the quantity of any given constituent present in a compound by observing it under the application of standard solutions ; (রসায়নশাস্ত্র) যৌগিক পদার্থের নির্দ্দিষ্ট উপাদানকে রূপান্তরিত করিতে হইলে কোন স্থাপিতমান দ্রাবক (standard solution) কি পরিমাণে আবশ্যক হয়—তাহা লক্ষ্য করতঃ ঐ যৌগিক পদার্থে উক্ত উপাদান কি মাত্রায় আছে তাহা নির্ণয় করা, দ্রবযোগ বিশ্লেষণ করা। **—tra'-tion,** *n.* The act of titrating ; দ্রবযোগবিশ্লেষণ (হিঃ কোঃ)।

tit'-tĕr, *v. i.* & *n.* To giggle, in a restrained manner ; ফিক্ ফিক্ করিয়া হাসা, খিল খিল করিয়া হাসা। ***Noun.*** A restrained laugh ; ফিক্ ফিক্ হাসি, খিল খিল হাসি। **—er,** *n.*

tit'-tle (-l), *n.* A small particle ; an iota ; কণা, কণিকা ; বিন্দু, রতি। **Not one jot or tittle**—বিন্দুবিসর্গও না।

tit'-tle-tat-tle (tit-l-tăt-l), *n.* & *v. i.* Idle trifling talk ; empty talk ; বাজে কথা ; অসার কথা, পচাল। ***Verb. i.*** To gossip ; বাজে কথা বলা, পচাল পাড়া।

tit'-tup (-ŭp), *v. i.* & *n.* To act or go in a lively or impatient manner ; তুড় তুড় করিয়া চলা। ***Noun.*** A lively or gay movement ; তুড় তুড় করিয়া চলন। **–py, –y,** *adjs.*

tit-ŭ-bā′-tion, *n.* Restlessness ; চঞ্চলতা, অস্থিরতা।

tit′-ŭ-lar (-lĕr), *adj.* & *n.* **1.** Of, or pertaining to, a title ; উপাধিসম্বন্ধীয়, ঔপাধিক। **2.** Holding a position of title or name only ; নাম বা উপাধিবলে কোন পদের অধিকারী। **3.** Nominal ; as, *titular* sovereign ; নামমাত্র। ***Noun.*** **1.** A person holding a title or office ; উপাধিধারী ব্যক্তি। **2.** A holder of benefice without corresponding functions or obligations ; যে ধর্ম্ম-বৃত্তিধারীকে কোনরূপ কাজ করিতে হয় না। **3.** The patron saint of a church ; কোন ধর্ম্মসংঘের অধিষ্ঠাতৃস্বরূপ মহাপুরুষ। **–ly,** *adv.* **Titular bishop**—(রোমানক্যাথলিক ধর্ম্মসংঘে) কোন লুপ্ত পাটের ধর্ম্মাধ্যক্ষ (অর্থাৎ মুসলমানগণের বিজয়হেতু যে স্থানের ধর্ম্মাধ্যক্ষের আসন শূন্য হইয়াছে)। **Titular saint**—Same as TITULAR, *n.* 3.

tī′-tȳ-rē-tu (-tô), *n.* A member of a gang of street-ruffians in London in the time of Charles II ; দ্বিতীয় চার্লসের সময়ে লণ্ডন নগরীর কোন বিশেষ গুণ্ডার দলের লোক।

tiz′-zȳ, *n.* (*Slang*) Sixpence ; (ইতর ভাষায়) ৬ পেন্স।

tmē′-sis, *n.* A figure by which a compound word is separated by intervention of one or more words ; একপ্রকার অলঙ্কার—যাহাতে কোন যৌগিক শব্দের মধ্যে এক বা ততোধিক শব্দ নিবিষ্ট করা হয় (*e. g. in what place sover* in place of *whatsoever place*)

to (tû), *prep.* & *adv.* **1.** Toward ; "She stretched her arms *to* heaven" ; দিকে, অভিমুখে, পানে। **2.** Indicating a point or limit reached ; "Some Americans, otherwise of quick parts, could not count *to* one thousand" ; পর্য্যন্ত, অবধি, তক। **3.** Denominating an addition, accumulation or possession ; "Wisdom he has, *to* his wisdom courage"; সহিত, সঙ্গে। **4.** Denoting comparison ; "I *to* the world am like a drop of water" ; তুলনায় **5.** Concerning ; as, *to* this ; সম্পর্কে, সম্বন্ধে। **6.** Opposition ; as, they sat face *to* face ; বিরোধ। **7.** According to ; in proportion to ; "Greeks are skilful *to* their strength" ; অনুসারে ; অনুপাতে। **8.** Belonging ; as, sister *to* the queen ; সম্বন্ধে, সম্পর্কে। **9.** Accompaniment ; as, she danced *to* the music ; তালে তালে, সঙ্গতভাবে। **10.** Effect ; as, you will learn this *to* your cost ; ফল, পরিণাম। ***Adv.*** **1.** Onward ; "*To* Achilles, *to* Ajax, *to* !" ; অগ্রে, সম্মুখে। **2.** To the normal or required position or condition ; esp. to a standstill ; as, to put *to* the door (*i. e.*, shut it) ; স্বাভাবিক অবস্থায়, ঈপ্সিত অবস্থায় ; বিশেষতঃ স্থিত অবস্থায়। **3.** Denoting motion towards a thing for the purpose of laying hold of it ; as, to fall *to* ; কোন জিনিষ ধরিবার জন্য তদভিমুখে অগ্রসর। **To-day**—অদ্য। **To-do**—Ado ; bustle ; (চলিতভাষায়) ধুমধাম, ধুমধড়াক্কা, হৈ চৈ। **To-morrow**—(*adv.* & *n.*) আগামী কল্য। **To-night** — অদ্য রাত্রি। **The door is to**—The door is almost shut ; দ্বার রুদ্ধ প্রায়। **To a certain degree**—To a certain extent; কিয়ৎপরিমাণে, অল্প পরিমাণে। **To a large extent**—Largely ; বহুল পরিমাণে। **To all appearance**—বাহ্যতঃ, আপাতদৃষ্টে। **To all intents and purposes**—Indeed ; বাস্তবিকপক্ষে, প্রকৃতপ্রস্তাবে। **To and fro**—Forward and backward; অগ্র-পশ্চাতে, এদিকে সেদিকে। **To be**—futurity ; ভবিতব্যতা। **To boot**—See BOOT. **Tomorrow comes never** — That day will never come ; সে দিন কখনও আসিবে না। **To-name**—নামের সহিত সংযোজিত। **To no purpose**—In vain , নিরর্থক, অনর্থক, মিছামিছি, বৃথা, অকারণ। **To one's cost**—To one's loss ; ঠেকিয়া। **To one's face, To his teeth**—In defiance of ; মুখের সামনে, মুখের উপর। **To one's heart's content**—To one's utmost satisfaction ; মনের সাধ মিটাইয়া, প্রাণ ভরিয়া। **To one's knowledge**—Within one's knowledge ; নিজের জ্ঞানানুসারে। **To the best of one's abilities**—As far as lies in one's power ; নিজের সাধ্যানুসারে। **To the full** — Completely ; সম্পূর্ণরূপে, পূর্ণভাবে। **To the last**—To the end ; শেষ পর্য্যন্ত। **To the letter**—Literally ; অক্ষরে অক্ষরে। **To wit**—That is ; অর্থাৎ।

toad (tōd), *n.* **1.** A reptile resembling the frog, but having a more bulky body ; সোনাবেঙ্গ (যোঃ), কোলাবেঙ্গ, (মিউজিয়াম্)। **2.** A detestable person ; ঘৃণনীয় লোক, ঘৃণ্য-ব্যক্তি। **Toad-eater**—চাটুকার, ধামাধরা, পাচাটা, খোসামুদে। **Toad-eating**—চাটুকারিতা। **Toad-fish**—আমেরিকা মহাদেশীয় একজাতীয় মৎস্য। **Toad-flax**—একপ্রকার পীত-পুষ্পপ্রসূ গুল্ম। **Toad-flower** — আফ্রিকা মহাদেশের একপ্রকার বিচিত্রবর্ণ পুষ্প। **Toad-spit**—Same as CUCKOO-SPIT **Toadstone**—সোনাব্যাঙ্গের মাথার মণি ; সোনাব্যাঙ্গের আকার একপ্রকার প্রস্তর।

Toadstool.

Toadstool—ব্যাঙ্গের ছাতা, ছত্রাক। [*Syn.* কিম্পাকু, ছত্রিকা, শিলীন্ধ্র,

গোময়ছত্রিকা, দিলীর, উর্ব্বঙ্গ, বাসারোহ, গোলাস, উচ্ছিলীন্ধ্র, বিড়্জ, বিড়জচ্ছত্র।] **Toad in a** or **in the hole**—ডিম, দুধ ও আটার লপসিতে ডুবাইয়া যে গোমাংস সেঁকা যায়।

toad'-ȳ (tōd-), *n.* & *v. t.* Same as TOAD-EATER. ***Verb t.*** To flatter obsequiously ; হীন চাটুকারিতা করা, পদলেহন করা, পা চাটা। **—ism,** *n.*

toast (tōst), *n., v. t.* & *i.* **1.** Bread scorched by fire ; a piece of toasted bread put into a beverage ; অগ্নিতে সেঁকা পাঁউরুটি ; মদ্য প্রভৃতিতে ডুবানো ভর্জ্জিত পাঁউরুটির খণ্ড। **2.** Any one or anything named in honour in drinking; "Those gentlemen whose names are down on the *toast*-list"; মদ্যপানকালে সম্মানসূচনার্থ যে বস্তু বা ব্যক্তির নাম উল্লেখ করা হয়। ***Verb t.*** **1.** To dry and scorch by the heat of fire as bread ; পাঁউরুটি প্রভৃতি ভাজা। **2.** To drink to the success or health of ; কাহারো স্বাস্থ্য বা সফলতা কামনায় মদ্য পান করা। **3.** (*Colloq.*) To warm thoroughly ; as, to *toast* one's feet at the fire ; (চলিতভাষায়) বেশ করিয়া গরম করা। **Toast'-er,** *n.* **Toast-colour** — একপ্রকার ফিকে বাদামী রং। **Toast-master**—যে ব্যক্তি ভোজে কোন ব্যক্তির সম্মানসূচনার্থ মদ্যপানের প্রস্তাব করিয়া থাকে। **Toast-rack**—ভর্জ্জিত রুটিকার খণ্ড সমূহ পৃথক পৃথক ভাবে রাখার জন্ম একপ্রকার তাক। **Toast-water** — যে জলে ঝলসানো পাঁউরুটি ডুবানো হয়। **On toast**—Served up on a slice of toast ; একটুকরা ভর্জ্জিত রুটির উপর পরিবেষিত। **Had on toast**—(*Slang*) Swindled ; জুয়াচোর দ্বারা প্রতারিত। **To drink a toast** or **toasts**—কাহারো স্বাস্থ্য বা সফলতা কামনায় মদ্য পান করা।

tō-băc'-cō, *n.* **1.** A narcotic plant of several species belonging to the potato family, a native of the warmer parts of America (also *tobacco-plant*) ; তামাক, তাম্রকূট। **2.** The prepared leaves of the plant, used for smoking and chewing or in the snuff ; মাখা তামাক, নস্য, দোক্তা। **To-bacco-cutter**—তামাক-কাটা কল। **Tobacco-heart**—Disorder of heart caused by excessive use of tobacco ; অতিরিক্ত তাম্রকূট-সেবনজনিত হৃৎপিণ্ডের বিকৃতি। **To-bacco-pouch**—অল্পপরিমাণ তাম্রকূট রাখার জন্ম থলি। **Tobacco-stopper**—তামাক সাজিবার একপ্রকার কল।

Tobacco-plant.

tō-băc'-cō-nist, *n.* A dealer in tobacco, cigar, etc. ; তাম্রকূট বিক্রয়ী, চুরুট বিক্রেতা।

tŏb'-ine (-in), *n.* A stout twilled silk ; একপ্রকার শক্ত টের্চ্চা-শির তোলা রেশমী কাপড়।

tō-bŏg'-găn, *n.* & *v. i.* A kind of sled used for going down-hill esp over snow-coverd hills or slopes ; তুষারাচ্ছাদিত পর্ব্বতের ঢালুতে চালাইবার উপযোগী একপ্রকার চক্রহীন শকট। ***Verb i.*** To go in a toboggan ; ঐরূপ শকটে চলা। **—er, —ing,** *ns.*

tō'-bȳ, *n.* A small jug in the form of an old man with three-cornered hat ; ত্রিকোণ্ টুপি পরিহিত বৃদ্ধ ব্যক্তির আকৃতি একপ্রকার ক্ষুদ্র গাড়ু।

tŏc-câ'-tâ, *n.* (*Mus.*) A composition for piano, organ, etc. originally intended to exercise the touch ; (সঙ্গীতশাস্ত্র) পিয়ানো, অর্গেন প্রভৃতির জন্ম একপ্রকার সঙ্গীত।

tŏc-câ-tĕl'-lă, —tĭ'-nă, *ns.* A short or simple toccata ; উক্ত প্রকার ক্ষুদ্র বা সরল সঙ্গীত।

tō'-cō, tō'-kō, *ns.* (*Slang*) Punishment ; pain ; (ইতর ভাষায়) শাস্তি, দণ্ড ; ব্যথা।

tŏc'-sin, *n.* **1.** A bell rung as a signal or for the purpose of giving an alarm ; সঙ্কেত-সূচক ঘণ্টা, সঙ্কেত ঘণ্টা, বিপৎসঙ্কেতসূচক ঘণ্টা। **2.** Alarm-signal; বিপৎসঙ্কেতসূচক চিহ্ন।

tŏd, *n.* **1.** A quantity of wool of 28lbs ; ২৮ পাউণ্ড ওজনের পশম। **2.** (*Archaic*) A bush or thick shrub ; a thick mass of growing foliage ; ঝোপ, ঝাড় ; ঘন পত্রপুঞ্জ।

tô-day', (-dā) **tô-day',** (-dā), *n.* & *adv.* See under TO.

tŏd'-dle (-l), *v. t.* & *n.* To walk with short to tottering steps ; শিশুর মত পড়িতে পড়িতে চলা। ***Noun.*** The act of toddling ; a stroll ; পড়িতে পড়িতে চলন ; ভ্রমণ। **—dler,** *n.*

tŏd'-dy (-ĭ), *n.* **1.** A juice drawn from the palm tree ; তালের রস, তাড়ী। **2.** A mixture of spirits and hot water, sweetened ; সুরাসার, উষ্ণ জল এবং শর্করার মিশ্রণে প্রস্তুত পানীয়।

tô-dô', *n.* See under TO.

tō'-dȳ, *n.* A small West-Indian bird ; পশ্চিম-ভারতীয় দ্বীপপুঞ্জের ক্ষুদ্র পক্ষিবিশেষ।

toe (tō), *n., v. t.* & *i.* **1.** The small members that form the extremity of the foot ; পদাঙ্গুলী। **2.** The forepart of the hoof of a horse or other hoofed animals ; অশ্ব এবং অন্যান্য ক্ষুরবিশিষ্ট জন্তুর ক্ষুরাগ্রভাগ। **3.** A projection from the end of a buttress etc. to give stability ; পোস্তা সুদৃঢ় করার জন্ম উহার প্রান্ত হইতে প্রলম্বিত অংশ, **4.** The lower end of a shaft; স্তম্ভবপুর নিম্নপ্রান্ত। ***Verb t.*** **1.** To hit or strike with the toe ; পদাঙ্গুলী দ্বারা তাড়না করা। **2.** To touch or reach with the toes ; as, to *toe* a football ; পদাঙ্গুলী দ্বারা স্পর্শ করা বা নাগাইল পাওয়া। **3.** To drive slantingly a nail or the like; প্রেক প্রভৃতি টের্চ্চা ভাবে বসান। 4. To furnish with toes; to mend the toes of a stocking etc.; আঙ্গুল লাগান; মোজা প্রভৃতির অঙ্গুলী রিপু করা। *Verb i.* To move the toe; to tap rhythmically with the toe in dancing; পদাঙ্গুলী সঞ্চালন করা; নৃত্যকালে তালে তালে পদাঙ্গুলী দ্বারা ঠুকনা দেওয়া। **Great toe** — পদের বৃদ্ধাঙ্গুষ্ঠ; পদের কনিষ্ঠাঙ্গুলি। **Toe-cap** — পদাঙ্গুলীত্রাণ। **Toe-drop**— পদাঙ্গুলীর আড়ষ্টতা। **Toe-nail**— পদনখ। **From top to toe**—From head to foot; আপাদমস্তক, সর্ব্বাঙ্গ। **To toe and heel (it)**—To dance; নৃত্য করা। **To toe the mark**—To move warily; সতর্কভাবে চলা। **To turn up one's toes**—(*Slang*) To die; মরা, চোখ উলটান।

tô'-fāll, *n.* (*Archaic, poet.*) End; অন্ত, অবসান।

tŏff, *n.* (*Slang*) Swell; (ইতরভাষার) হোমড়া চোমড়া লোক।

tŏf'-fee (-ĭ), —fy (-ĭ), *ns.* A sweet-meat made of boiled sugar with a proportion of butter; চিনির সিরা, মাখন, প্রভৃতি দ্বারা প্রস্তুত মিষ্ট দ্রব্য বিশেষ।

tŏft, *n.* (*Law*) A messuage; বসত-বাটী, ভদ্রাসন। **Toftman**—গৃহস্বামী।

tŏg, *n.* & *v. t.* (*Slang*) Garment; (ইতরভাষায়) পোষাক। *Verb t.* To dress; পোষাক পরান, পোষাক পরা। **Tog-maker**—পোষাক প্রস্তুতকারী।

tō'-gă, *n.* A garment worn by the ancient Romans, consisting of a single broad piece of cloth; প্রাচীন রোমানদিগের গাত্রবস্ত্রবিশেষ। **—gaed**, *adj.*

Roman toga.

tô-gĕth'-ĕr, *adv.* 1. Unitedly; একত্রে, একসঙ্গে, একযোগে। 2. Simultaneously; as, both *together* cried; একসঙ্গে, এক সময়ে যুগপৎ। 3. In conjunction; একত্র।

tŏg'-gle (-gl), *n.* A short wooden pin, tapered towards both ends, firmly fixed in a loop at the end of a rope; রজ্জুর প্রান্তবর্ত্তী ফাঁসে দৃঢ়রূপে সম্বদ্ধ উভয়দিকে ক্রমসূক্ষ্ম লৌহকীলকবিশেষ। **Toggle-joint**—সমকোণে চাপ দিবার জন্য একপ্রকার জোড়। **Toggle-iron**—একপ্রকার ঠেঁটা।

toil (toyl), *n.* & *v. i.* Hard labour; কঠোর পরিশ্রম, গুরুতর শ্রম। *Verb i.* 1. To labour hard; কঠোর পরিশ্রম করা। 2. To go or travel painfully or laboriously; as, he *toiled* up the hill; অতি কষ্টেসৃষ্টে বা পরিশ্রমের সহিত চলা বা ভ্রমণ করা। **Toil'-er**, *n.* **Toil'-ful**, *adj.* **Toil'-ful ly**, *adv.* **Toil'-some**, *adj.* Laborious; fatiguing; শ্রমসাধ্য; ক্লান্তিজনক, শ্রান্তিজনক, আয়াসসাধ্য, কষ্টকর। **Toil'some-ness**, *n.* **Toil-work**—শ্রমশিল্প।

toil (toyl), *n.* A net; a trap; জাল; ফাঁদ।

toile, *n.* ***Toile-ciree***—অতি মিহি পানিকাপড় (oil cloth). ***Toile-colbert***—সূচীকার্য্যের জন্য ক্যাম্বিস কাপড়। ***Toile d' Alsace, Toile de Vichy***—মহিলাদিগের গ্রীষ্মকালীন পরিচ্ছদের জন্য একপ্রকার সূক্ষ্ম ক্ষৌমবস্ত্র।

toi'-lĕt (toy-), toi-lette' (toy-lĕt), *ns.* 1. Act of dressing esp. dressing the hair; কেশবিন্যাস, কেশরচনা, প্রসাধন, শৃঙ্গার, সিঙ্গার (Poet. cf. মুকুর লেই অব করত সিঙার)। 2. Process of dressing, arranging the hair etc.; কেশবিন্যাসপদ্ধতি, কেশরচনাভঙ্গী, কেশবিন্যাসভঙ্গী, কেশবিন্যাসপ্রণালী, কেশরচনাপদ্ধতি। 3. Style or fashion of dress; as, an elaborate *toilette*; Attire; পরিচ্ছদরীতি; পরিচ্ছদ, পোষাক। 4. A bag or case for night clothes; স্ত্রীলোক বা শিশুদের রাত্রিবাসবস্ত্র রাখিবার জন্য থলিয়া। 5. A cloth put over the shoulders while shaving or hair dressing is being done; চুল দাড়ী প্রভৃতি ছাঁটিবার কালে কাঁধের উপর যে কাপড়ের টুকরা রাখা হয়। 6. Same as TOILET-TABLE. 7. A covering or cloth of silk, or tapestry spread over a table; মেজ ঢাকিবার জন্য রেশম বা কার্পাসের বস্ত্র। 8. (*Surg.*) The regular cleansing and dressing of a wound after operation; অস্ত্রোপচারের পর নিয়মমত ক্ষতস্থান ধৌত করণ ও বাঁধন। **Toilet-powder**—স্নানাদির পর ব্যবহারের জন্য একপ্রকার স্নিগ্ধতাজনক এবং রোগবীজাণু নাশক উপাদানসম্পন্ন অঙ্গরাগ, শৃঙ্গারচূর্ণ। **Toilet soap**—বেশভূষা সম্পাদনকালে ব্যবহৃত সাবান, শৃঙ্গারফেণক। **Toilet-table**—প্রসাধনের জন্য দর্পণসমন্বিত মেজ। **Toilet-water** — বেশভূষা সম্পাদনের কালে ব্যবহৃত সুগন্ধি জল। (যথা Cologne water, Florida water).

toi-li-nĕt' (toy-), toi-li-nette', (toy-lĭ-nĕt), *ns.* A cloth, the weft of which is of woollen yarn, and the warp of cotton or silk; একপ্রকার কাপড়—যাহার পড়েন পশমের এবং টানা সূতার বা রেশমের হইয়া থাকে।

Toison d'or, *n.* (*F.*), Same as GOLDEN FLEECE.

Tō-kay' (-kā), *n.* A rich highly prized wine produed at Tokay, in Northern Hungary, made from white grapes; হাঙ্গারী দেশজাত শ্বেতবর্ণ দ্রাক্ষার রস হইতে প্রস্তুত একপ্রকার উৎকৃষ্ট মদিরা।

tō'-ken (-kn), *n.* 1. A mark an indication; a sign; চিহ্ন; নিদর্শন; লক্ষণ। 2. Characteristic; বিশেষত্ব। 3. A souvenir; "This is some *token* from a newer friend"; a memorial of friendship; স্মৃতিচিহ্ন, চিহ্ন, অভিজ্ঞান; বন্ধুস্মৃতিনিদর্শন। 4. A piece of money, current by sufferance, and not coined by authority; একপ্রকার

বে-সরকারী মুদ্রা। **By token, By this token, By the same token**—(*Archaic* or *facet.*) As a proof of what I say ; আমি যাহা বলিতেছে তাহার প্রমাণস্বরূপ।

tō′-kō, *n.* Same as TOCO (which see).

tola, *n.* A unit of weight in our country ; তোলা।

Tō-lē′-dō, *n.* A fine sword-blade or sword made at Toledo in Spain ; স্পেন দেশের অন্তঃপাতী Toledo নামক স্থানে নির্ম্মিত অসি বা অসিফলক।

tŏl′-ĕr-ă-ble (-bl), *adj.* **1.** Endurable ; সহনীয়। **2.** Fairly good ; as, a *tolerable* lunch ; একরকম, মন্দনয়, চলনসই। **—bly,** *adv.* **—ness,** *n.*

tŏl′-ĕr-ance (-ăns), *n.* **1.** Patience ; সহিষ্ণুতা, সহন, উপেক্ষা (হিঃ কোঃ)। **2.** Freedom from bigotry ; গোঁড়ামী শূন্যতা। **3.** The ability of the constitution to endure dose of medicine in sickness which would injure in health ; সুস্থ অবস্থায় যে মাত্রায় ঔষধ সেবন করিলে অনিষ্ট হইতে পারে রুগ্নাবস্থায় সেই মাত্রা ঔষধের ক্রিয়া সহনের ক্ষমতা, ঔষধসহন ক্ষমতা। **—ant,** *adj.* **—ant-ly,** *adv.*

tŏl′-ĕr-āte, *v. t.* **1.** To endure ; সহ্য করা, সহা। **2.** To suffer to be or to be done without prohibition, hindrance, or support ; as, to *tolerate* all sects ; সহা, পরমত সহা। **3.** To sustain poison etc. without harm ; কোনরূপ অনিষ্ট বিনা বিষ প্রভৃতির ক্রিয়া সহ্য করিতে পারা। **—a-tor,** *n.*

tŏl-ĕr-ā′-tion, *n.* **1.** The act of tolerating ; সহন। **2.** Allowance to the opinions of others though not fully proved ; পরমতসহিষ্ণুতা। **—ist,** *n.* **Act of Toleration**—১৬৮৯ খৃঃ অব্দে বিধিবদ্ধ আইন বিশেষ। এই আইন দ্বারা Dissenters সম্প্রদায়ের উপাসনাপদ্ধতির অনুসরণের কতিপয় বাধা দূরীভূত করা হয়।

tōll, *n.* & *v. i.* **1.** A tax or duty paid for the use of market, public road, etc. ; শুল্ক, পথশুল্ক, মাশুল। **2.** A portion of grain taken by a miller as compensation for grinding corn ; শস্যপেষণের ক্ষতি-পূরণস্বরূপ পেষণযন্ত্রের মালীক শস্যের যে অংশ গ্রহণ করিয়া থাকে। **3.** (*Fig.*) Tribute ; as, the division paid its *toll* of killed and wounded ; কর, শুল্ক। ***Verb i.*** To take or pay toll ; শুল্ক আদায় করা, শুল্ক প্রদান করা। **Toll-booth**—(*Archaic, Scot.*) মাশুলঘর। **Toll-house** — মাশুল-ঘর, শুল্ক গৃহ, শুল্কস্থান (মঃ সং)। **toll′-a-ble** *adj.* Subject to toll ; শুল্কযোগ্য।

tōll, *v. t., i.* & *n.* To cause a bell to sound with strokes slowly repeated ; ঘণ্টা বাজান, ঘণ্টাধ্বনি করা, টং টং করিয়া বাজান। ***Verb i.*** To sound, or ring, as a bell, with strokes uniformly repeated at intervals ; ঘণ্টা বাজা, ঘণ্টা বাদিত হওয়া। ***Noun.*** The solemn sound of a bell slowly rung ; ঘণ্টাধ্বনি, ঘণ্টানিনাদ।

Tōl′-tĕc, *n.* One of a traditional prehistoric people of Mexico ; মেক্সিকো দেশের প্রাগৈতিহাসিক যুগের এক জাতীয় লোক। **—an,** *adj.*

tō-lū′, *n.* A resin, or oleo-resin produced by a tree of South America ; দক্ষিণ আমেরিকার বৃক্ষ-বিশেষের নির্য্যাস। ইহা ঔষধ ও সুগন্ধি দ্রব্য প্রস্তুতে ব্যবহৃত হয়।] **—ic,** *adj.*

tŏm, *n.* **1.** A male animal cat ; হুলো বিড়াল, কুনো বিড়াল। **2.** (*Cap.*) A contraction of the common Christian name Thomas ; ইংরাজী টমাস নামের সংক্ষেপ। **Long tom**—যুদ্ধ জাহাজের একপ্রকার দীর্ঘাকৃতি কামান। **Old Tom**—একপ্রকার কড়া মদ। **Tom-cat**—Same as TOM 1. **Tom-boy**—গেছো মেয়ে। **Tomfool**—বেকুব, বোকা। (*verb i.*) বেকুবি করা, হ্যাকামি করা। **Tomfoolery,** *n.* বোকামি, মস্করামি, তামাসা, ঝকমারি, হ্যাকামি। **Tom-noddy** — বোকা, বেকুব, স্থুল-বুদ্ধি, জড়বুদ্ধি। **Tomtit**—টুনি প্রভৃতি ক্ষুদ্র পাখী। **Tom and Jerry**—ডিম্বের কুসুমের সহিত মিশ্রিত রম মদ্য প্রভৃতি। **Tom, Dick and Harry**—রাম, শ্যাম, যদু।

tŏm′-ă-hawk (-hăk), *n.* & *v. t.* A light Indian war hatchet ; উত্তর-আমেরিকার প্রাচীন অধিবাসিগণের রণ-কুঠার। ***Verb t.*** **1.** To cut or kill with a tomahawk ; রণকুঠারদ্বারা

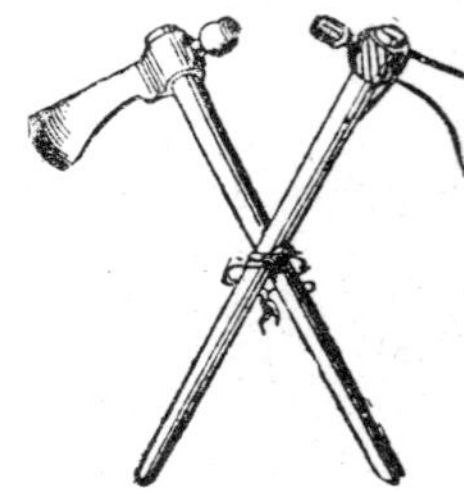

Tomahawks.

ছেদন বা নিহত করা। **2.** To criticize severely; "He afterwards goes out of his way to *tomahawks*"—*Dryden* ; তীব্র সমালোচনা করা। **To bury the tomahawk** — Same as TO BURY THE HATCHET (which see).

tŏm′-ăl-lÿ, —ley (-li), *ns.* A soft greenish substance found in lobsters ; গলদা চিংড়ীতে প্রাপ্ত একপ্রকার ঈষৎ সবুজবর্ণ কোমল পদার্থ।

toman, *n.* A Persian gold coin worth about 7*s.* 2*d.* ; পারস্যদেশের একপ্রকার স্বর্ণমুদ্রা (মূল্য ৭ শিঃ ২ পেঃ)।

tō-mā′-tō (*or* -mâ-), *n.* The pulpy edible fruit of a plant of the nightshade family ; বিলাতী বেগুণ। **Currant tomato**—একজাতীয় ক্ষুদ্রা-কৃতি বিলাতী বেগুন। **Tree tomato**—একজাতীয় বিলাতি বেগুণ—যাহার গাছ কোনরূপ অবলম্বন বিনা খাড়াভাবে বৃদ্ধি পায়।

tomb (tôm), *n.* & *v. t.* **1.** A grave ; গোর, সমাধি। **2.** A memorial erected to preserve the memory of the dead ; সমাধিস্তম্ভ, সমাধি মন্দির।

3. (*Fig.*) Death ; "Than to behold the universal *tomb*" ; (লক্ষণায়) মৃত্যু। ***Verb t.*** To place in a tomb ; to inter ; (লক্ষণায়) কবরস্থ করা ; সমাহিত করা। **Tombstone**—সমাধিপ্রস্তর, সমাধিশিলা, সমাধিফলক।

tŏm′-băc, tŏm′-băk, *ns.* An alloy of copper and zinc ; তাম্র এবং দস্তার মিশ্রবিশেষ।

tŏm′-bō-lă, *n.* A kind of lottery game played in France and the southern United States ; ফরাসীদেশে এবং মার্কিণ রাষ্ট্রমণ্ডলের দক্ষিণাঞ্চলের একপ্রকার ভাগ্যপরীক্ষার খেলা। [এই খেলাতে পুরস্কারস্বরূপ প্রত্যেক টিকিট ক্রেতাকে এক একটী সৌখীন দ্রব্য প্রদত্ত হয়।]

tōme, *n.* Volume, esp. a large one ; খণ্ড, বিশেষতঃ পুস্তকের বৃহৎ খণ্ড।

tō-mĕn-tōse, —tous (-tŭs), *adjs.* Nappy ; ঘনরোম (সাঃ পঃ)।

tō-mĕn′-tŭm, *n.* **1.** (*Bot.*) Pubescence composed of long, densely matted woolly hairs ; (উদ্ভিদ্-বিদ্যা) উদ্ভিদের উপর কোমল লোমবৎ পদার্থ। **2.** The inner surface of the pia mater which has a flocculent structure produced by numerous small vessels ; ঘন রোমাকার ক্ষুদ্র ক্ষুদ্র নাড়ীদ্বারা আচ্ছন্ন মস্তিষ্ক আবরক ঝিল্লী, লোমশ ঝিল্লি। **—tose, —tous,** *adjs.*

tō-mĭn′, *n.* Jewellers' weight of 12 grains; স্বর্ণকারগণের ১২গ্রেণ ওজন।

tŏm′-my (-ĭ), *n.* **1.** Provisions etc. as given to workmen in lieu of wages; বেতনের পরিবর্তে মজুরদিগকে যে খাদ্যবস্তু প্রভৃতি দেওয়া হয়। **2.** Same as TRUCK SYSTEM. **3.** (*Cap.*) A general name for English private soldiers ; "A group of *Tommies* in uniform" ; সাধারণ ইংরাজসৈনিক। **4.** (*Cap.*) A familiar form of Thomas; টম নামের প্রকার ভেদ। **5.** A simpleton ; বেকুব লোক। **Tommy Atkins**—Same as TOMMY 3. **Tommy-shop** — Same as TRUCK-SHOP (which see). **Soft-tommy**—কোমল পাঁউরুটি, টাটকা পাঁউরুটি।

tō-mŏr′-row (-mŏ-rō), *adv.* & *n.* See UNDER TO.

tŏm′-pĭ-ŏn, *n.* **1.** The inking-pad of lithographic printers ; লিথোগ্রাফারদিগের কালীর গদী। **2.** Same as TAMPION and TAMPON.

tŏm′-tŏm, *n.* & *v. i.* **1.** A kind of Indian drum ; ছোট ঢোল। **2.** Same as GONG (which see). ***Verb i.*** To beat a tomtom ; ঢোল বাজান।

ton (tŭn), *n.* **1.** A weight (2,240lbs.) পরিমাণবিশেষ, প্রায় ২৭।০ মণ, টন। [মার্কিণ-রাষ্ট্রমণ্ডলের কোন কোন স্থানে এক টন ওজন ২০০০ পাউণ্ডের সমান। এইরূপ টনকে *short ton* এবং ২২৪০ পাউণ্ডের টনকে *long ton* কহে।] **2.** A measure of capacity (often varying), for timber (40 ft.), stone (16 cub. ft.), salt (42 bushels), lime (40 bushels), coke (28 bushels), wheat (20 bushels), wine (252 wine gallons) ; বস্তুভেদে বিভিন্নপ্রকার পরিমাণ বিশেষ। [তক্তা (৪০ ফিট), প্রস্তর (১৬ ঘন ফিট), লবণ (৪২ বুশেল), চুণ (৪০ বুশেল), কোক কয়লা (২৮ বুশেল), ময়দা (২০ বুশেল), মদ্য (২৫২ গেলন—এই অর্থে সাধারণতঃ *tun* শব্দ ব্যবহৃত হয়।] **3.** The weight 1,000 kilograms (also called *metric ton*) ; ১,০০০ কিলোগ্রাম ওজন **4.** A unit of weight or space by which the burden of a ship is reckoned ; জাহাজের স্থানের একক বা জাহাজে যে পরিমাণ মাল বোঝাই হইতে পারে তাহার একক—যদ্দারা জাহাজের বোঝাই মালের পরিমাণ হিসাব করা হয়। **5.** A large number or amount ; as, *tons* of people ; অনেক, বহু, অসংখ্য। **Register ton**—See under TONNAGE. **Displacement ton**—৩৫ কিউবিক ফিট জল (ইহার ওজন ১ টনের সমান) ; কোন জাহাজ দ্বারা যে পরিমাণ জল স্থানান্তরিত হয়—তাহার ওজন সেই জাহাজ ও তদভ্যন্তরস্থ সমস্ত বস্তুর সমান। অতএব কোন জাহাজের displacement ton নির্ণয় করিতে হইলে ঐ জাহাজ পূর্ণ বোঝাই অবস্থায় যত কিউবিক ফিট জল স্থানচ্যুত করে তাহাকে ৩৫ (কারণ ৩৫ কিউবিক ফিটের জলের ওজন এক টনের সমান) দ্বারা ভাগ করিতে হয়। রণপোত সম্বন্ধে এইরূপ টনই সাধারণতঃ ব্যবহৃত হয়। **Shipping ton**—কোন জিনিষের এক টন ওজনে যে স্থান পূর্ণ হয়। এইরূপ টন সাধারণতঃ ৪০ ঘন ফিট ধরা হইয়া থাকে।

ton, (*F.*), *n.* The prevailing mode or fashion ; প্রচলিত রীতি, পদ্ধতি বা ধারা, ধরণ।

tōn′-ăl, *adj.* Of tone or tons ; স্বরসম্বন্ধীয়, টন সম্বন্ধীয়।

tō-năl′-ĭ-tȳ, *n.* **1.** (*Mus.*) Quality of tone ; (সঙ্গীতশাস্ত্র) স্বরত্ব। **2.** The colour scheme of a picture ; চিত্রের বর্ণ বা আলো ও ছায়া সমাবেশপদ্ধতি।

tō′-name, *n.* (*Chiefly Sc.*) Name added esp. to person's Christian name for distinction ; কোন ব্যক্তির নামের শেষে সংযোজিত উপনাম।

tŏn-dĭ′-nō, *n.* **1.** (*Arch.*) Same as ASTRAGAL (which see). **2.** A tondo with a bowl-like centre ; মধ্যদেশে বাটির আকার উদ্গত কারুকার্য্য।

tŏn′-dō, *n.* (*Carving*) A relief within a circular space ; (ক্ষোদাই) গোলাকৃতি স্থানে উদ্গত কার্য্য।

tōne, *n.* **1.** The character of a sound ; ধ্বনির প্রকৃতি। **2.** Modulation, inflection, or accent of the voice, as raised to express sentiment, emotion, or passion ; স্বর, রাগ, রাগিণী। **3.** State of mind ; temper ; mood ; as, a healthful *tone* of mind and spirits ; মানসিক অবস্থা ; প্রকৃতি ; ভাব। **4.** That state of the body in which the animal functions are healthy ; শরীরের যে অবস্থায় শারীরিক ক্রিয়াসমূহ সুস্থভাবে ও যথাযোগ্য রূপে সম্পন্ন হয়। **5.** The harmonious relation of the colours of a picture in light and shade; degree of luminosity of colour; চিত্রের বর্ণসমাবেশসঙ্গতি; বর্ণের দীপ্তির মাত্রা। 6. Prevailing character or fashion; tenor; character; spirit; as, the *tone* of his remarks was complimentary; strain; প্রচলিত ধারা; ধারা, ধরণ; প্রকৃতি; অন্তর্নিহিত ভাব; ধরণ। 7. Prevailing character of morals, sentiment, etc.; প্রচলিত নীতি,ভাব, প্রভৃতির প্রকৃতি। 8. (*Photog.*) The colour of a finished picture; আলোকচিত্রের রঙ্গ। 9. (*Gram.*) Stress on one syllable of a word; (ব্যাকরণ) কোন শব্দের কোনঅংশের উপর জোর। **Tone'-less,** *adj.* **Tone'-less-ness,** *n.* **Heart-tone**—বুকের ধুকধুকি, দুরু দুরু।

tōne, *v. t.* & *i.* **1.** To utter in an affected tone; কৃত্রিম স্বরে উচ্চারণ করা। 2. Same as TO TUNE. ***Verb i.*** To assume a tone, esp. a colour, quality or tone; কোন বিশেষ বর্ণ বা প্রকৃতি ধারণ করা। **To tone down**—To soften the colouring of a picture; চিত্রের বর্ণদীপ্তি প্রশমিত করা। To soften or subdue the colour of; বর্ণের দীপ্তি প্রশমিত করা, বর্ণদীপ্তি হ্রাস করা। To reduce or lower in tone; to soften; সুর নামান; প্রশমিত করা, হ্রাস করা, মন্দীভূত করা, মন্দপ্রভ করা। **To tone to**—To imbue with any special sentiment; কোন বিশেষ ভাবদ্বারা অনুপ্রাণিত করা। **To tone up**—To give a higher tone or character to; to heighten; to make more expressive; রঙ্গ চড়ান, সুর চড়ান; চড়ান; অধিকতর সুপ্রকট করা।

tōned, *p. p.* **1.** Having tone; স্বরবিশিষ্ট। **2.** Tense; টানটান। **Toned paper**—যে কাগজের উজ্জ্বল শ্বেতবর্ণ সরের মত আপিতবর্ণ পদার্থ বিশেষের পোছদ্বারা ঈষৎ মন্দীভূত করা হইয়াছে।

tōng-a (-gȁ),*n.* A light cart used in this country; টোঙ্গা গাড়ী, টোঙ্গা।

tōngs, *n.* (Also *a pair of tongs*) An instrument consisting of two long shafts joined at one end used for holding fire or heated metal; চিমটা, সন্দংশ, সাঁড়াসী, কঙ্কমুখ, সংড়শী, লৌহসন্দংশক, কর্কটক। **Not to touch with a pair of tongs**—Said of a repulsive person or thing; কোনরূপ ঘৃণিত বস্তু বা ব্যক্তি সম্পর্কে ব্যবহৃত হয়।

tongue (tŭng), *n.* **1.** The fleshy movable organ within the mouth, having the sense of taste, and being of great importance in eating, swallowing and uttering sounds; জিহ্বা, রসনা, জিভ, রসজ্ঞ। **2.** The tongue of an animal used as an article of food; খাদ্যস্বরূপ ব্যবহৃত গবাদি জন্তুর জিহ্বা। **3.** Faculty of speech; speech; discourse; talk; "Mince not the general *tongue*"; voice; as, a soft *tongue*; বাক্‌শক্তি; বাক্য; সংলাপ; কথাবার্ত্তা; স্বর। **4.** A language; "We must be free or die who spake the *tongue*, That Shakspeare spake"; ভাষা। **5.** Things like tongue in shape or function; জিহ্বাকৃতি বস্তু, জিহ্বার মত ক্রিয়াসাধক বস্তু। **6.** A strip of land; স্বল্পায়ত ভূখণ্ড, টেঁক। **7.** A tapering flame; অগ্নিশিখা। **8.** The clapper of a bell; ঘণ্টার নুড়নুড়ী। **9.** The pointer of a balance; তুলাদণ্ডের সূচী। **10.** A piece of leather stitched to the front of a laced shoe or boot; ফিতাওয়ালা, জুতা বা বুটের সম্মুখে সংবদ্ধ অপুরু চর্ম্মখণ্ড। **11.** A reed in a musical instrument; শানাই প্রভৃতির মুখনল। **12.** The movable rail of railroad-switch; যে নাতিদীর্ঘ সঞ্চালনীয় পাতা রেলের সাহায্যে বাষ্পীয় শকটের চক্র এক বর্ত্ম হইতে বর্ত্মান্তরে চালিত হয়। **13.** A current that rapidly runs between rocks; পাষাণ পর্ব্বত যুগলের মধ্যে দ্রুতবেগে প্রবাহিত স্রোতঃ। **14.** The projecting edge of match-board; দীপশলাকার বাক্সের উদ্গত প্রান্ত। **Tongue'-less,** *adj.* **Tongue'-let,** *n.* **Long-tongue**—বাচাল। **Mother tongue**—মাতৃভাষা। **Tongue-bit**—অশ্বের জিহ্বার রোধকফলকযুক্ত খলীন। **Tongue-doughty**—বাক্যবীর, বাক্যবাগীশ। **Tongue-fence**—বাগ্‌যুদ্ধ। **Tongue-shaped**—জিহ্বাকৃতি। **Tongue-tied**—রুদ্ধবাক্, মূক। **At the tip of one's tongues**—জিহ্বাগ্রে। **Confusion of tongues**—See BABEL. **Gift of tongues**—শক্তি সঞ্চারের পর আদিযুগের খৃষ্টধর্ম্ম প্রচারকগণের বিভিন্ন অজ্ঞাতভাষায় বক্তৃতা প্রদানের অলৌকিক শক্তিলাভ। **The tongue cleaves to the roof of one's mouth**—কথা আটকাইয়া যায়। **To give or throw tongue**—To bark out, esp. on getting scent; চীৎকার করা, শিকারের গন্ধ পাইয়া চীৎকার করা। **To give tongue**—To speak out; বলিয়া ফেলা। **To hold one's tongue**—To keep silence; চুপ করা। **Tongue and groove joint**—ক্ষুদ্র ক্ষুদ্র জিহ্বাকৃতি উদ্গত অংশসমূহের সহিত উহাদের খাপ খায় ঐরূপ খাঁজের জোড়। **Tongue and lip joint**—একপ্রকার জোড়। **Tongue of the trump**—ইহুদীদিগের বীণার ধ্বনি উৎপাদনের জন্য স্পন্দনশীল অংশ; বিষয় বা প্রধান বিশেষত্ব। **To recover one's tongue**—To regain one's power of speech; পুনরায় বাক্‌শক্তি লাভ করা। **To wag one's tongue**—To talk indiscretely or volubly; অবিবেচকের মত কথা বলা, বাচালতা করা। **With tongue in the cheek**—Mockingly; insincerely; বিদ্রূপের স্বরে; অসরলভাবে।

tongue (tŭng), *v. t.* & *i.* **1.** To speak; to utter; বলা; উচ্চারণ করা। **2.** To scold; "How might she *tongue* me"; ভর্ৎসনা করা, তিরস্কার করা। **3.** (*Mus.*) To modify, as tones or sounds with the tongue in playing, as in flute and some other wind-instruments (also *Verb i.*) ; (সঙ্গীতশাস্ত্র) বাদনকালে জিহ্বা সঞ্চালিত করিয়া বংশী প্রভৃতির ধ্বনির পরিবর্ত্তন করা। 4. To connect by means of a tongue or groove ; জিহ্বাকৃতি উদ্গত অংশ খাঁজে জোড়া দেওয়া। ***Verb i.*** 1. (*Rare* or *Colloq.*) To talk ; to prate ; as, to *tongue* incessantly ; কথা বলা; বক্ বক্ করা।

tŏn'-ĭc, *adj.* & *n.* 1. Relating to tones or sounds ; স্বরসম্বন্ধীয়, ধ্বনিসম্বন্ধীয়, রাগসম্বন্ধীয় (হিঃ কোঃ)। 2. Increasing strength or the tone of the animal-system ; বলবর্দ্ধক, পুষ্টিবর্দ্ধক, পুষ্টিকারক (হিঃ কোঃ), বলপ্রদ, অগ্নিদ, পক্বাশয় বলদ (সাঃ পঃ)। ***Noun.*** A tonic medicine ; বলকর ঔষধ, বলবর্দ্ধক ঔষধ, পোষ্টাই, বল্য। **–i-cal-ly,** *adv.* **Tonic spasm**—ক্রমাগত খেঁচুনি, নিরবচ্ছিন্ন আক্ষেপ।

tō-nĭc'-ĭ-tȳ, *n.* 1. The state of healthy elasticity of muscles etc. ; পেশী প্রভৃতির স্বাস্থ্যসূচক স্থিতিস্থাপকতা। 2. The state of being tonic ; পুষ্টিজনকতা, বলকারিতা। 3. (*Plant Physiol.*) Normal responsiveness to external stimuli ; বাহিরের উত্তেজনায় স্বাভাবিক সাড়া।

tô-night', tô-night' (-nīt), *adv.* & *n.* See under TO.

tŏn'-ĭsh, tŏn'-nish (-ĭsh), *adjs.* Stylish ; চটকদার, কেতাদুরস্ত, কায়দাদুরস্ত।

tŏn'-īte, *n.* An explosive made from pulverised gun-cotton ; চূর্ণীকৃত তুলা হইতে প্রস্তুত বিস্ফোরক দ্রব্য।

Ton'-kă-bean (tŏng-kă-bēn), *n.* The fragrant seed of a large tree of Guiana for flavouring snuff etc. ; গায়েনার এক জাতীয় বৃহৎ বৃক্ষের সুগন্ধি বীজ—যদ্দ্বারা নস্য প্রভৃতি সুবাসিত করা হয়।

ton'-nage (tŭn-āj), *n.* 1. The cubical content of a ship in tons ; যত টন মাল ধরে সেই হিসাবে জাহাজের ঘনপরিমাণ। 2. The weight of goods carried in a ship ; জাহাজে যে পরিমাণ মাল নেওয়া যায়—তাহার ওজন। 3. A duty or impost in ships, formerly estimated at so much per ton of freight, but now proportioned to the registered size of the vessels ; জাহাজের উপর গৃহীত শুল্ক [পূর্ব্বে এইরূপ শুল্ক জাহাজের প্রতি টন মাল হিসাবে ধরা হইত, বর্ত্তমানে জাহাজের আয়তনের অনুপাতে ধরা হয়।] 4. Total freightage esp. of a country's mercantile marine ; কোন দেশের সমুদয় জাহাজে বিশেষতঃ বাণিজ্যপোতে যে পরিমাণ মাল বোঝাই করা যাইতে পারে। **Tonnage-deck**—দ্বিপাটাতনবিশিষ্ট জাহাজের উপরের পাটাতন; তিন বা ততোধিক পাটাতনবিশিষ্ট জাহাজের দ্বিতীয় পাটাতন। **Tonnage-coefficient** — জাহাজের মোট মালবহনশক্তি নির্ণয়ের জন্য উহার দৈর্ঘ্য, প্রস্থ এবং গভীরতার গুণফলকে যে দশমিকদ্বারা পূরণ করিতে হয়। **Register** or **net tonnage**—কল, নাবিকদিগের বাস-কক্ষশ্রেণী প্রভৃতির স্থান বাদ দিয়া জাহাজে মাল বোঝাই করার জন্য নিট যে স্থান থাকে।

ton-neau' (tö-nö), *n.* Part of some motor-cars that contains the back seats ; এক জাতীয় হাওয়া গাড়ীর যে অংশে পশ্চাদ্ভাগের আসন সমূহ থাকে।

tō-nŏm'-ĕt-ĕr, *n.* An instrument for measuring the pitch of tones ; ধ্বনিমাপক, স্বরমাপক (হিঃ কোঃ)।

tŏn'-ō-phănt, *n.* A modification of the kaledophone for showing composition of sound vibrations ; স্বরদর্শক (হিঃ কোঃ)।

tŏn'-sĭl, *n.* One of the two oblong glands on each side of the throat which secretes a mucous humour ; তালুপার্শ্বস্থ বাদামের আকার গ্রন্থিদ্বয়ের অন্যতর, তালুপার্শ্বগ্রন্থি, নুড়নুড়ি। **–li'-tis,** *n.* An inflammation of the tonsils ; তালুগ্রন্থির প্রদাহ।

tŏn-sō'-rĭ-ăl, *adj.* Of, or pertaining to, a barber or his work ; ক্ষৌরকারসম্বন্ধীয়, ক্ষৌরকার্য্যসম্বন্ধীয়।

tŏn'-sūre, *n.* & *v. t.* 1. The act of clipping the hair or shaving the head ; কেশচ্ছেদন, কেশমুণ্ডন, চূড়াকরণ (এভেলন)। 2. The round bare place on the heads of Roman Catholic priests and monks formed by shaving or cutting the hair ; রোমানক্যাথলিক যাজকগণের মস্তকের উপর গোলাকার মুণ্ডিত অংশ। ***Verb t.*** 1. To shave the head of ; মস্তক মুণ্ডন করা, কেশচ্ছেদন করা। 2. To confer the tonsure on ; যাজকদিগের মস্তকের উপরিভাগের কিয়দংশ মুণ্ডিত করা।

tŏn'-tīne, *n.* Annuity shared by subscribers to a loan, and increased to each as the subscribers die, until at last the whole goes to the survivor ; নির্দ্দিষ্ট পরিমাণ অর্থ প্রাপ্তির পর কতিপয় ব্যক্তিকে যে বার্ষিক বৃত্তি দেওয়া হইত—ঐরূপ বৃত্তিপ্রাপ্ত কোন ব্যক্তির মৃত্যু হইলে, তাহার বৃত্তি অবশিষ্ট জীবিত বৃত্তিধারী ব্যক্তিগণের মধ্যে বিভক্ত হইত। এইরূপে এক একজন বৃত্তিধারীর মৃত্যুর পর তদীয় বৃত্তি অবশিষ্ট জীবিত বৃত্তিধারী ব্যক্তিগণের মধ্যে বিভাগ করিয়া দেওয়া হইত। অবশেষে সর্ব্বশেষ জীবিত ব্যক্তি অপর সকল মৃত বৃত্তিধারিগণের বৃত্তি প্রাপ্ত হইত। **Tontine policy of insurance**—যে বীমার লভ্যাংশ প্রভৃতি উক্ত প্রণালীতে বিভাগ করিয়া দেওয়া হয়।

tōō, *adj.* & *adv.* More than enough ; as, *too* long ; অতিশয়, অত্যন্ত, বেজায়, নিতান্ত। ***Adv.*** Also ; moreover ; as, he is a patriot *too* ; ও ; অধিকন্তু, আরো। **Too-too**—বেজায়, একশেষ, অত্যন্ত।

tōōk, *p. t.* of TAKE (which see).

tōōl, *n.* 1. A mechanical implement ; যন্ত্র, হাতিয়ার, উপস্কর (বিশ্বকর্ম্মা)। 2. A person used as an instrument by another person ; as, the king was a mere *tool* in the hands of his ministers; অন্য কাহারো হস্তে যন্ত্রস্বরূপ ব্যক্তি, যন্ত্রপুত্তলিকা, কলের পুতুল, ক্রীড়াপুত্তলিকা। 3. Same as

MACHINE-TOOL below. 4. An ornament or figure tooled on the binding of a book; যন্ত্র দ্বারা চাপ দিয়া বাঁধানো পুস্তকের মলাটের উপর যে ভুষা বা চিত্র মুদ্রিত করা হয়। **Broad tool**—Same as TOOLER. **Machine-tool**—যে বাঁট বা কাঠামাদিতে লৌহময় অংশ লাগান হয়। **Tool-chest, Tool-box**—যন্ত্রের বাক্স। **Tool-post, Tool-rest**—কুন্দন-যন্ত্রের লৌহময় অংশের ধারক বা অবলম্বন। **A poor tool**—নিকৃষ্ট কারিগর।

tool, *v. t. & i.* 1. To shape with a tool; যন্ত্র দ্বারা গঠন করা। 2. (*Slang*) To drive a vehicle etc.; (ইতর ভাষায়) শকট প্রভৃতি চালান; 3. To impress an ornament etc. on the edge of a book-cover with tooling; পুস্তকের মলাটের উপর ভুষাদি মুদ্রিত করা। ***Verb i.*** To drive; গাড়ী চালাইয়া যাওয়া।

tool'-ĕr, *n.* A broad chisel used by stone-masons; প্রস্তর-শিল্পিগণের একপ্রকার চৌড়া বাটালী।

tool'-ing, *n.* 1. Dressing a stone with a broad chisel so as to form a fluted or channelled surface; সমান্তর রেখা বা নালী ক্ষোদিবার জন্য চৌড়া বাটালি দ্বারা প্রস্তর তক্ষণ। 2. Ornamental embossing or gilding by heated tools upon the binding of books; বাঁধান পুস্তকের মলাটের উপর উত্তপ্ত যন্ত্র দ্বারা নানা প্রকার ভুষা মুদ্রণ।

toon, *n.* 1. A large Indian tree yielding a wood of reddish brown colour (*Cedrela Toona* from Tamil name *toona maram*); তুঁদগাছ, তুন্ন, তুন্নক, নন্দীবৃক্ষ। 2. The reddish brown wood of this tree (also *toon-wood*); উক্ত বৃক্ষের কপিশবর্ণ কাষ্ঠ।

toot, *v. i., t. & n.* 1. To blow or sound, as horn; শিঙ্গা প্রভৃতি ধ্বনি করা, পোঁ পোঁ করা। 2. To utter a similar sound; উক্তরূপ শব্দ করা। ***Verb t.*** To sound; as, to *toot* a horn; বাজান। ***Noun.*** A souud made by tooting; পোঁপোঁ।

tooth, *n., v. t. & i.* 1. One of the bony structures growing in the jaws used in chewing food; দন্ত, দাঁত। 2. A small narrow projecting piece, usually one of a series, as of a comb, saw, etc; a cog; করাতের দাঁত, চিরুণীর দাঁত, গাড়ীর চাকার দাঁত, প্রভৃতি; চক্রদন্ত। 3. Taste; as, he has no *tooth* for sweets; স্বাদ, রুচি। ***Verb t.*** 1. To furnish with teeth; দাঁত লাগান। 2. To jag; as, to *tooth* a saw; দন্তুরিত করা, দাঁত কাটা। 3. (Of cog-wheels) To interlock; (দন্তুর চক্র সমূহসম্পর্কে) পরস্পরের সহিত জড়াইয়া যাওয়া। ***Verb i.*** To engage by means of teeth, as cog-wheels; দন্তুরিত চক্র ইত্যাদি পরস্পরের সহিত দাঁত দ্বারা সংযুক্ত করা। **Tooth'-less,** *adj.* Without tooth; দন্তহীন, অদন্ত। **Tooth'-let,** *n.* **Toothache**—দাঁতের বেদনা, দন্তশূল। **Tooth-billed**—দন্তুরিত চঞ্চুবিশিষ্ট (পক্ষী)। **Tooth-brush**—দাঁতের বুরুশ। **Tooth-pick**—দন্তশোধনী, দাঁতন। **Tooth-powder**—দন্তমঞ্জনচূর্ণ, দাঁতের মাজন। **Armed to the teeth**—Armed completely; সম্পূর্ণভাবে অস্ত্রশস্ত্রে সুসজ্জিত। **A sweet tooth**—See SWEET. **In the teeth of**—In spite of; সত্ত্বেও। In opposition to; বিরুদ্ধে। **To cast or throw anything in one's teeth**—See THROW. **To cast a thing in a person's teeth**—To reproach him; কাহাকে তিরস্কার করা। **To cut one's eye-teeth**—To gain worldly wisdom; আক্কেল দাঁত গজান। **To escape by the skin of one's teeth**—See SKIN. **To fight or struggle tooth and nail**—To fight to one's utmost power; প্রাণপণে যুদ্ধ করা। **To set one's teeth on edge**—See SET, EDGE. **To show one's teeth**—To take a threatning tone; ভীতিজনক ভাব ধারণ করা। **To take the bit between one's teeth**—See BIT.

tooth'-ful, *n.* A small draught of spirit etc.; thimbleful; অল্পমাত্রা সুরাসার প্রভৃতি; এক ঢোক, এক চুমুক।

tooth'ing, *n.* 1. (*Bot.*) A tooth; (উদ্ভিদ্‌ বিদ্যা) দন্ত। 2. Bricks or stones left projecting at the end of a wall that they may be bounded into a continuation of it when required; প্রাচীরপ্রান্তস্থ উদ্গত ইষ্টক অথবা প্রস্তরখণ্ডসমূহ—যাহাদের সহিত অপর ইষ্টকাদি গাঁথিয়া উহা বর্দ্ধিত করা যাইতে পারে। **Toothing-plane**—কোনকিছুর উপরিভাগ কর্কশ করার জন্য ব্যবহৃত রেঁদা।

tooth'-some (-sŭm), *adj.* Palatable; "Though less *toothsome* to me, they were more wholesome for me"; মুখরোচক, রসনাতৃপ্তিকর, রসনা-সরস, মুখপ্রিয়। **—ly,** *adv.* **—ness,** *n.*

too'-tle (-tl), *v. i. & n.* To toot gently or repeatedly or continuously on a flute or other wind-instrument; জিহ্বার সাহায্যে ধ্বনি পরিবর্ত্তন করিয়া মৃদুভাবে, পুনঃ পুনঃ বা একটানা বংশী প্রভৃতি বাদন করা। ***Noun.*** 1. The noise produced by tootling; উক্তরূপ ধ্বনি। 2. (*Univ. slang*) Any weak, immature literary production; (বিশ্ববিদ্যালয়ের অবরভাষায়) কাঁচা লেখা।

tŏp, *n. & adj.* 1. Summit; highest part; as, the *top* of a tree; চূড়া, শিখর; অগ্রভাগ, শীর্ষ। 2. The upper end, edge or extremity; the upper surface; উপরি প্রান্ত; উপরের দিক (cf. the *top* of a book). 3. The highest place or rank; the chief or highest person; উচ্চতম স্থান, উচ্চতম পদবী, শীর্ষ স্থান; সর্ব্বপ্রধান লোক, শীর্ষস্থানীয় ব্যক্তি। 4. The crown; the head; as, from *top* to toe; মাথার চাঁদি; মাথা। 5. The highest degree; উচ্চতম সীমা। 6. (*Pl.*) Same as TOP-BOOTS (below.) 7. (*Naut.*) A sort of platform, surrounding the head of the lower mast and projecting on all sides; (নৌবিদ্যা) নিম্নতর মাস্তুলের অগ্রভাগের

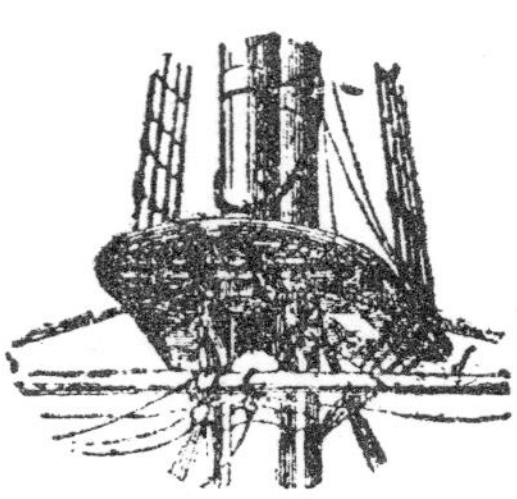

Ship's top.

চতুর্দ্দিকে উদ্গাত মঞ্চ। **8.** The part of a plant above the ground; as, turnip *tops*; গুল্মাদির ভূমির উপরের অংশ। **9.** The upper part of shoe; পাদুকার উপরিভাগ। **10.** (*Pl.*) Buttons finished as by plating only on the top or face; কেবলমাত্র উপরিভাগে গিল্টি করা বোতাম। **11.** (*Rare*) Eve; "He was on the *top* of his marriage"; প্রাক্কাল। **12.** The combed wool ready for the spinner; সূত্রকর্ত্তনকারিগণের জন্য প্রস্তুত আঁচড়ানো পশম। **13.** That portion of a cut gem which is between the extreme margin, and the table or flat surface; পল কাটা মণির শেষ সীমা এবং উপরিভাগের সমতল অংশের মধ্যবর্ত্তী স্থান। *Adj.* **1.** Highest in position or degree; উচ্চতম, উর্দ্ধতম, সর্ব্বোচ্চ, শীর্ষস্থানীয়, অগ্রভাগস্থ। **Top-bar**—মাথা কাটা। **Top-button** — উপরে সোনা বা রূপার গিল্টি করা ধাতুর বোতাম। **top-coat**— Same as OVERCOAT. **Top-boots**—অশ্বারোহণকালে ব্যবহৃত একপ্রকার উচ্চ বুট। এই প্রকার বুটের অগ্রভাগ সাধারণতঃ শাদা, ফিকে বা বাদামী চামড়ার থাকে। **Top-dress**—(*Verb t.*) জমির উপরে সার প্রয়োগ করা। **Top-dressing**—জমির উপরিভাগে সার প্রয়োগ; জমির উপরিভাগে যে সার প্রয়োগ করা হয়। **Topgallant** — জাহাজের মাস্তুলের দ্বিতীয় অংশের এবং তৎস্থানের পাইলের অব্যবহিত উপরিস্থ পাইল, দড়াদড়ী প্রভৃতি। **Top-hamper**—উপরের হাল্কা পাইল এবং দড়াদড়ী। **Top-hat**—লম্বা রেশমী টুপি। **Top-heavy**—মাথাভারি, মাথামোটা। **Top-hole**—(ইতরভাষায়) চমৎকার। **Topknot**—মেয়েরা মাথার উপর যে ফিতা বাঁধে; শিখা। **Top-lantern**—অগ্রগামী ত্রিমাস্তুল-পোতের সর্ব্বপশ্চাদ্‌বর্ত্তী মাস্তুলে টাঙ্গানো লণ্ঠন। **Top-light**—অগ্রগামী ত্রিমাস্তুলপোতের সর্ব্বপশ্চাদ্‌বর্ত্তী মাস্তুল হইতে প্রদর্শিত আলো। **Topman, Top-sawyer**—যে করাতী উপরে থাকিয়া কাষ্ঠ চিরিয়া থাকে; উচ্চপদস্থ ব্যক্তি, শীর্ষস্থানীয় ব্যক্তি। **Top-mast**—জাহাজের মাস্তুলের দ্বিতীয়াংশ। **Topmost**—সর্ব্বোচ্চ, শীর্ষস্থানীয়। **Top-rung**—মইয়ের শেষধাপ; উন্নতির শেষ সীমা। **Topsail**—মাস্তুলের দ্বিতীয়াংশে খাটানো পাইল। **Topsides**—জল-রেখার উপরে জাহাজের পার্শ্বদ্বয়। **Fighting top**—রণপোতের আকৃতি মঞ্চবিশেষ—যথায় বন্দুকধারী যোদ্ধৃগণ অবস্থান করিতে পারে। **From top to tail**—Completely; সম্পূর্ণভাবে। **From top to toe**—See TOE. **The top of the morning to you**—(*Rare*) Morning salutation; (কচিদ্ ব্যবহৃত) প্রাভাতিক অভিবাদন। **Top of the tree**—(ইতরভাষায়) কোন ব্যবসায়ের সর্ব্বোচ্চস্থান। **The top of one's bent** — The utmost that one's inclination or bias will permit; ঝোঁক বা আসক্তির সর্ব্বোচ্চ মাত্রা বা শেষ সীমা।

tŏp, *v. t.* **1.** To provide with a top or cap; ডালা লাগান, টোপর লাগান। **2.** To pass over the top of; উপর দিয়া চলা। **3.** To rise to the top of; উপরে উঠা। **4.** (*Slang*) To cover with another dye; অন্য বর্ণদ্বারা আচ্ছাদিত করা। **5.** To excel; গুণ বা উৎকর্ষে অতিক্রম করা। **6.** To perform eminently or better than before; পূর্ব্বাপেক্ষা উৎকৃষ্টতরভাবে সম্পন্ন করা। **7.** (*Thieve's slang*) To hang; ফাঁসি কাষ্ঠে ঝুলান। **8.** To crop; ছাঁটা। **9.** (*Naut.*) To rise one end of (yard etc.) above the other; পাইলদণ্ড প্রভৃতির এক প্রান্ত অপর প্রান্তের উপরে উঠান। **10.** To copulate with; পাল দেওয়া। **Top'-ping,** *adj.* **Top'-ping-ly,** *adv.* **To top off or up**—To put an end or finishing touch to; শেষ করা, শেষ চানকান দেওয়া। **To top one's boom**—To make haste; তাড়াতাড়ি করা। **To top one's part**—To surpass one's self; কাহাকে অতিক্রম করা।

tŏp, *n.* A child's toy, shaped somewhat like a pear made to whirl on its point by means of string; লাটিম, লাট্টু। **Top-shell**—লাটিমের আকৃতি খোলবিশিষ্ট বিভিন্ন প্রকার শম্বুকাদি।

tō'-păz, *n.* **1.** A mineral, one of the gems, generally yellowish, occurring in rhombic prisms, and consisting of silica, alumina, and fluoric acid; পোখরাজ, পুষ্পরাগ। [*Syn.* মঞ্জুমণি (ভাবঃ প্রঃ), বাচস্পতিবল্লভ (ঐ), পীতস্ফটিক, পীতরক্ত, পীতাশ্ম, গুরুরত্ন, পীত, পীতমণি, রত্নচমক (মলয়লম ভাষায়)।] [Germ. *topas*; Russ. *topas*; Fr. *topase*; It. *topazio*; Pers. *zabarjad*; Sp. *topacio*; Tam. Tel. *pushiaragum.*] লোহিতসাগরের Topazion দ্বীপ হইতে এই মণির নাম Topaz হইয়াছে। রাজনির্ঘণ্টে পুষ্পরাগের গুণাগুণ পরীক্ষাদি সম্বন্ধে এইরূপ লিখিত আছে:—"স্বচ্ছায়পীতগুরুগাত্রসুরঙ্গশুদ্ধং স্নিগ্ধঞ্চ নির্ম্মলমতীব সুবৃত্তশীতম। যঃ পুষ্পরাগশকলং কলয়েদমুষ্য পুষ্ণাতি কীর্ত্তিমতিশৌর্য্যসুখ্যায়ুরর্থান্।" "ঘৃষ্টো বিকাশয়েৎ পুষ্পরাগমধিকমার্দ্রিয়ম্। ন খলু পুষ্পরাগো জাত্যতয়া পরীক্ষকৈরুক্তঃ"।] **2.** A kind of humming bird; একপ্রকার গায়কপক্ষী। **False topaz**—বিভিন্নপ্রকার পীতবর্ণ স্ফটিকপ্রস্তর।

tō-păz'-ō-līte, *n.* A yellow or green kind of garnet; একপ্রকার পীত বা সবুজবর্ণ বৈক্রান্তমণি।

tōpe, *v. i.* To drink strong or spirituous liquors to excess; অতিরিক্ত মদ্যপান করা। **Top'-er,** *n.*

One who drinks to excess : a drunkard ; অতিরিক্ত মদ্যপায়ী ; নেশাখোর, মাতাল।

tōpe, *n* A Buddhistic tumulous for the preservation of relics ; "A *tope* is a shrine peculiar to the Buddhist religion" ; বৌদ্ধস্তূপ।

tōpe, *n.* (Anglo-India) Mango or other groves ; (ভারতবর্ষীয় ইংরাজদিগের মধ্যে) আম্রবণ, আম্রনিকুঞ্জ, কুঞ্জবন, নিকুঞ্জ।

tŏph, tō'-phŭs, *ns.* **1.** A species of volcanic rock of an earthy structure; এক প্রকার মৃত্তিকাবৎআগ্নেয়প্রস্তর। **2.** (*Med.*) A deposit round the teeth and at the surface of joints of gouty persons; (ভৈষজ্যশাস্ত্র) বাতরোগীদিগের দন্তে ও দেহসন্ধির উপরিভাগের চতুর্দ্দিকে সঞ্চিত পদার্থ। **To-pha'-ce-ous,** *adj.*

Tō'-phĕt, *n.* **1.** A high place in the Valley of Hinnom, near Jerusalem, where sacrifices were offered to Moloch ; জেরুজেলেম নগরীর নিকটবর্ত্তী উন্নত স্থান বিশেষ—যথায় পৌত্তলিক ইহুদীগণ Moloch দেবতার প্রীত্যর্থে শিশুদিগকে অগ্নিতে সমর্পণ করিত [পরবর্ত্তীকালে এই স্থানে জেরুজেলেমনগরীর অস্থি,মৃতদেহ,আবর্জ্জনা, প্রভৃতি দগ্ধ করা হইত,তজ্জন্য তথায় অহর্নিশ অগ্নি প্রজ্বলিত থাকিত।] **2.** Hell ; নরক।

tō'-pi-ă, *n.* A kind of mural decoration common in old Roman houses ; প্রাচীন রোমনগরবাসীদিগের গৃহের একপ্রকার প্রাচীরভূষা।

tō'-pi-ă-rȳ, *n.* The pruning of shrubs into formal or fanciful shapes ; গুল্মাদি নানা প্রকার নমুনায় ছাঁটিয়া দেওন।

tŏp'-ic, *n.* **1.** The subject of discourse ; বিষয়, প্রসঙ্গ, প্রস্তাব। **2.** (*Med.*) An external remedy ; (ভৈষজ্যশাস্ত্র) বাহ্যপ্রয়োগের ঔষধ। **3.** (*Rhet.*) A general truth or statement applicable to a great variety of individual circumstances ; a general maxim or dictum regarded as being of use in argument or oratory ; (অলঙ্কারশাস্ত্র) যে সাধারণ সত্য নানা অবস্থায় প্রযোজ্য হইতে পারে, প্রকরণ (হিঃ কোঃ) ; কোনরূপ যুক্তি বা বাগ্মিতায় যে সাধারণ প্রবচন বা নীতিবাক্য ব্যবহারযোগ্য বলিয়া বিবেচিত হয়। **A topic under discussion**—আলোচনাধীন বিষয়, প্রস্তাব।

tŏp'-i-căl, *adj.* **1.** Of topics ; প্রাকরণিক (হিঃ কোঃ), প্রাস্তাবিক (ঐ), প্রাসঙ্গিক (ঐ), প্রকরণসম্বন্ধীয়। **2.** Of, pertaining to, or dealing with, topics of the day ; as, articles on *topical* subjects ; সাময়িক ঘটনা বা বিষয় সম্পর্কীয়। **3.** (*Med.*) Local ; as, *topical* disease ; স্থানীয়, স্থানিক।

tō-pŏg'-ră-phȳ, *n.* **1.** The description of a particular place, city or town ; কোন নগর বা জেলার বিস্তৃত বর্ণনা, স্থানবর্ণন, বিশেষস্থান বর্ণন (হিঃ কোঃ)। **2.** (*Geog.*) The configuration of a surface, including its relief, the position of its streams, roads, cities, etc. ; (ভূগোল) ভূসংস্থান বর্ণন, ভূসংস্থান বিবরণ। **3.** (*Anat.*) Mapping of the surface of body with reference to the parts beneath ; (শারীরসংস্থানবিদ্যা) নিম্নবর্ত্তী অংশসমূহের সম্পর্কে দেহের উপরিভাগের নক্সা অঙ্কন। **—pher, —phist,** *ns.* One versed in topography ; ভূসংস্থানবর্ণনাকারী। **Top-o-graph'-ic, Top-o-graph'-i-cal,** *adjs.*

tō-pŏn'-ō-mȳ, *n.* The place-names of a country or district ; a register of such names ; কোন দেশের বিভিন্ন স্থানসমূহের নাম ; ঐরূপ নামের তালিকা।

tŏp'-per (-ĕr), *n.* **1.** One who tops or excels ; সর্ব্বাতিশায়ী ব্যক্তি। **2.** Same as TOP-HAT.

tŏp'-ple (-l), *v. i.* & *t.* To fall forward ; "Though castles *topple* on their warders' heads" ; to pitch or tumble down ; টলিয়া পড়া, টাকরিয়া পড়া ; হুমড়ি খাইয়া পড়া। ***Verb t.*** To cause to totter and fall ; হুমড়াইয়া ফেলান।

tŏp'-sȳ-tur'-vȳ (-tĕr-), *n., adj., adv.* & *v. t.* A state of great disorder ; উলটপালট অবস্থা, লণ্ডভণ্ড ব্যাপার। ***Adj.*** In an inverted posture ; in a state of great disorder ; উলটপালট, বিপর্য্যস্ত ; লণ্ডভণ্ড। ***Adv.*** With top or head downward ; as, to fall *topsy turvy* ; in confusion ; বিপর্য্যস্তভাবে, উল্টাইয়া ; লণ্ডভণ্ড ভাবে। **—dom,** *n.* **—vi-fi-ca'-tion,** *n.* **—vi-fy,** *v. t.* **To turn topsyturvy**—বিপর্য্যস্ত করা, উলট পালট করা, লণ্ড ভণ্ড করা।

toque (tōk), *n.* **1.** A kind of bonnet or head-dress; একপ্রকার টুপি বা উষ্ণীষ। **2.** A monkey having a a tufted head ; একজাতীয় বানর—ইহাদের গুচ্ছীকৃত কেশ টুপির মত দেখায়।

tŏr, *n.* A rocky eminence ; a rocky peak ; শৈল ; পাষাণময় চূড়া।

torah, *n.* (*Heb.*) The Mosaic law ; the Pentateuch ; (হিব্রুভাষায়) মুসার আইন ; বাইবেলের প্রাচীন নিয়মের প্রথম পঞ্চ পুস্তক।

tŏrch, *n.* A flambeau or large light to be carried in the hand, formed of resinous wood or of twisted tow dipped in some inflammable susbtance ; মশাল [*Syn.* উল্কা (cf. উল্কাহস্তৌবিচেরতুঃ—রামায়ণ), জ্বালা।] **Torch'-ing**—Same as TORCH-FISHING. **Electric torch**—একপ্রকার চোঙ্গাকার বৈদ্যুতিক প্রদীপ। **Torch-bearer**—মশালচী,মশালধারী ব্যক্তি; জ্ঞানালোকবাহী। **Torch-dance**—মশাল ধারণপূর্ব্বক নৃত্য। **Torch-fishing**—মশালের আলোতে মৎস্য ধরণ, আলো [in parts of East Bengal ; cf. তাহারা আলোতে গেছে অর্থাৎ আলোর দ্বারা মাছ ধরিতে গিয়াছে।] **Torch-light** — মশালের আলোক। **Torch-lily**—একপ্রকার গুল্ম। **To hand on the torch**—To give the light of knowledge ; জ্ঞানালোক প্রদান করা।

tŏr′-chon (-shn), *n.* (*Attrib.*) **Torchon board**—জলমিশ্রিত রঙ্গদ্বারা চিত্রণের জন্য স্থূল কাগজের ফলক। **Torchon lace**—শণ বা কার্পাসের সূতায় তৈরী একপ্রকার শক্ত লেইস। **Torchon paper**—জলমিশ্রিত রঙ্গ দ্বারা কার্য্য করার জন্য একপ্রকার শক্ত অমসৃণ কাগজ। **Torchon tree**—রঙ্গণ বৃক্ষ।

tŏr′-cū-lar (-lêr), *n.* Same as TOURNIQUET (which see).

tōre, *p. t.* of TEAR (which see).

tōre, *n.* Same as TORUS (which see).

tŏ-rē-ā-dŏr′, *n.* A bull-fighter; esp. a mounted bull-fighter; স্পেনদেশে উত্তেজিত বৃষভের সহিত যুদ্ধকারী সশস্ত্র পুরুষ; বিশেষতঃ ঐরূপ বৃষভের সহিত যুদ্ধকারী সশস্ত্র অশ্বারোহী পুরুষ।

tŏ-reu′-tic (-rü-), *adj.* & *n.* Of chasing, carving and embossing esp. metal; তক্ষণশিল্পসম্বন্ধীয়। ***Noun.*** (*Pl.*) Art of making toreutic work; ধাতু প্রভৃতি তক্ষণবিদ্যা।

tŏr-fā′-ceous (-shŭs). *adj.* Growing in bogs or marshes; বিলজ, বিলজাত।

tŏr′-gŏch, *n.* A red-bellied trout from the lakes of North Wales; উত্তর ওয়েল্সের হ্রদসমূহে প্রাপ্ত একপ্রকার লাল বুকওয়ালা মৎস্য।

tŏr′-mĕnt, *n.* 1. A torturing device; যন্ত্রণাপ্রদানের জন্য একপ্রকার যন্ত্র, একপ্রকার পীড়নযন্ত্র। 2. Extreme physical or mental pain; "The more I see pleasures about me, so much more I feel *tormĕnt* within me"; তীব্র মানসিক বা দৈহিক যন্ত্রণা, তীব্র যন্ত্রণা, তীব্র মর্ম্মবেদনা, মানসিক সন্তাপ। 3. A source of great pain; যন্ত্রণার কারণ।

tŏr-mĕnt′, *v. t.* 1. To put to extreme pain or anguish; to torture; তীব্র যন্ত্রণা প্রদান করা; পীড়ন করা, নির্যাতন করা। 2. (*Colloq.*) To harrass; উত্যক্ত করা, জ্বালাতন করা। **—ing-ly,** *adv.*

tŏr′-mĕn-til, *n.* (*Potentilla tormentilla*) A small trailing plant (order Rosaceae) with yellow flowers, common on heaths and dry banks; পীত পুষ্পপ্রসূ একপ্রকার গুল্ম। [এই গুল্মের অতি কষায়স্বাদ মূল ঔষধে ব্যবহৃত হয়।]

tŏr-mĕn′-tor (-têr), *n.* 1. A person or thing that torments; যন্ত্রণাপ্রদানকারী, উৎপীড়ক, পীড়নকারী, নির্যাতনকারী। 2. An instrument for reducing a stiff soil, resembling harrow; বিদার ন্যায় একপ্রকার কৃষিযন্ত্র। 3. A long fork for raising meat used by sea-cooks; পাকপাত্র হইতে মাংসোত্তোলনের জন্য জাহাজের পাচকগণ কর্ত্তৃক ব্যবহৃত একপ্রকার দীর্ঘ কাঁটা। **—tress,** *n.* (*fem.*)

tŏr′-mĭ-nă, *n.* Severe griping pains in the bowels; উদরবেদনা, উদরশূল।

tōrn, *p. p.* of TEAR (which see).

tŏr-nā′-dō, *n.* A violent whirling tropical wind; বাতাবর্ত্ত (সাঃ পঃ), ভ্রমি, ঝঞ্ঝানিল, প্রচণ্ডঘূর্ণিবাত্যা, ঘূর্ণিবায়ু। **—nad′-ic,** *adj.*

tō′-rous (-rŭs), **tō′-rose** (-rōs), *adjs.* 1. (*Zool.* & *Anat.*) Swelling, as a surface, into protuberances or knobs; (জন্তুবিদ্যা এবং শারীরসংস্থানবিদ্যা) টোপের মত স্ফীত, পিণ্ডীভূত। 2. (*Bot.*) Cylindrical with bulges at intervals; (উদ্ভিদ্‌বিদ্যা) মধ্যে মধ্যে ন্যুব্জ অংশসমূহবিশিষ্ট চোঙ্গাকৃতি।

tŏr-pē′-dō, *n.* & *v.t.* 1. A fish allied to the rays, noted for the power of discharging electric shocks

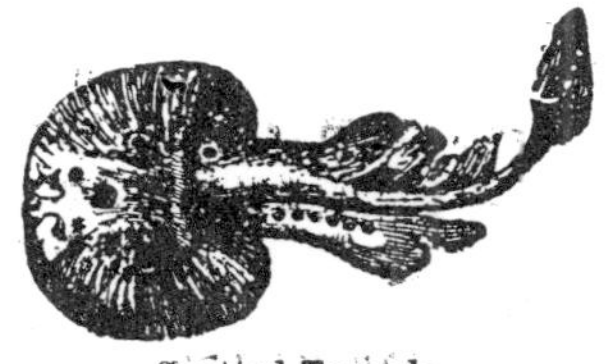

Spotted Torpedo.

when irritated; একপ্রকার মৎস্য—ইহাদের শরীরের যন্ত্র বৈদ্যুতিক শক্তিসম্পন্ন থাকার দরুণ ইহারা যখন উত্তেজিত হয় তখন, উহাদের দেহ হইতে বৈদ্যুতিকপ্রবাহ বহির্গত হইয়া অন্য মৎস্যকে নিহত বা অবসন্ন করিয়া থাকে, বৈদ্যুতিক মৎস্য, তড়িন্মীন, বৈদ্যুতক (আঃ বঃ)। 2. A cigar-shaped destructive engine propelled or concealed under water, and exploded against an enemy's ship with deadly effect; জলতলে লুক্কায়িত বা সঞ্চালিত বিস্ফোরকদ্রব্যপূর্ণ যন্ত্রবিশেষ—যাহার সহিত সংস্পৃষ্ট হইলে রণপোত প্রভৃতি ধ্বংসপ্রাপ্ত হয়, জলবজ্র। 3. Explosive cartridge for various purposes; বিভিন্ন উদ্দেশ্যে ব্যবহৃত বিদারণশীল কার্ত্তুজ। 4. A kind of detonating cartridge or shell placed on a rail and exploded by wheels of train; গাড়ীর পাতা রেলের উপর রক্ষিত কার্ত্তুজ বা গোলা—যাহা চলন্ত গাড়ীর চাকার সহিত সংঘৃষ্ট হইয়া সশব্দে বিদীর্ণ হয়। 5. A kind of fire-work or toy in the shape of a small ball, which explodes on being dashed against a hard object; একপ্রকার আতসবাজী—যাহা কোন কঠিন বস্তুতে নিক্ষিপ্ত হইলে ভীম শব্দে বিদীর্ণ হয়। ***Verb t.*** To destroy, or attack, with torpedo; জলবজ্র দ্বারা ধ্বংস বা আক্রমণ করা। **Torpedo-boat**—জলবজ্রনিক্ষেপণার্থ দ্রুতগামী তরী, জলবজ্রতরী **Torpedo-boat catcher**—জলবজ্রতরী ধৃতকরণার্থ বা জলবজ্রবহনার্থ একপ্রকার দ্রুতগামী ক্ষুদ্র তরী। **Torpedo-boat destroyer**—জলবজ্রতরী ধ্বংসকারী। **Torpedo-catcher, Torpedo-gunboat**—জলবজ্রতরীধ্বংসকরণার্থ বৃহৎ পোত। **torpedo-net**—জলবজ্রতরীর গতিরোধ করণার্থ পোত হইতে বিলম্বিত জালবিশেষ, জলবজ্রজাল।

tŏr′-pĭd, *adj.* & *n.* 1. Numb; আড়ষ্ট, অসাড়, অবশ, অবশাঙ্গ। 2. Dull stupid sluggish; inactive; "The population is comparatively *torpid* and inert"; মন্দবুদ্ধি; জড়বুদ্ধি; ঢিমা; নিশ্চেষ্ট, নিষ্ক্রিয়। ***Noun.*** 1. Lent boat-races at Oxford between second crews of colleges; অক্সফোর্ডের

নৌকাদৌড়বিশেষ। 2. A second class racing boat at Oxford; অক্সফোর্ড নগরের দ্বিতীয় শ্রেণীর দৌড়ের নৌকা। **—ly,** *adv.* **—ness,** *n.* **—pid'-i-ty,** *n.* **—pi-fy,** *v. t.*

tŏr'-pŏr, *n.* **1.** Numbness; অবশতা, জাড্য, জড়তা, আড়ষ্টতা, অবশাঙ্গতা, নিস্পন্দতা। 2. Dullness; sluggishness; inactivity; মান্দ্য; জড়বুদ্ধিতা; নিশ্চেষ্টতা, নিষ্ক্রিয়তা।

tor'-quāte, tŏr'-quāt-ĕd, *adjs.* (*Zool.*) With ring of peculiar colour or texture of hair or plumage about the neck; কণ্ঠের চতুর্দ্দিকে বিশিষ্ট রঙ্গ বা বুনটের রোম বা পালকগুচ্ছের চক্রবিশিষ্ট।

torque (tŏrk), **tŏrc,** *ns.* **1.** A collar, or similar ornament, of twisted gold or other materials worn by ancient Gauls, Britons and Germans; প্রাচীন গল, ব্রিটন এবং জার্ম্মণ কর্ত্তৃক ব্যবহৃত স্বর্ণ প্রভৃতি নির্ম্মিত রজ্জুর আকৃতি হাঁসুলি। 2. (*Mech.*, only *torque*) A twisting force; (যন্ত্রবিজ্ঞান) ব্যাবর্ত্তকশক্তি।

tŏr'-rē-fȳ, *v. t.* To dry by fire; to parch; to roast or scorch, as metallic ores; অগ্নির উত্তাপে শুষ্ক করা; বিদগ্ধ করা, ভর্জ্জিত করা; খনিজ বিমিশ্র ধাতু ভর্জ্জিত বা উত্তপ্ত করা। **—fac'-tion,** *n.*

tŏr'-rĕnt *n.* **1.** A violent rushing stream; নির্ঝরিণী, প্রপাত (সাঃ পঃ)। **2.** (*Fig.*) A violent or rapid flow; as, a *torrent* of tears; a flood; খরস্রোত, বন্যা; জোয়ার। **—ren'-ti-al,** *adj.* **—ren'-ti-al-ly,** *adv.* **Torrential rain**—ধারাবর্ষণ।

Tŏr-ri-cĕl'-li-ăn, *adj.* Of, or pertaining to, the Italian physicist Torricelli; (১৬০৮—১৬৪৮ খৃঃ) ইতালীদেশীয় বৈজ্ঞানিক টরিসেলিসম্বন্ধীয়। **Torricellian experiment** — যে পরীক্ষাদ্বারা Torricelli বায়ুমণ্ডলের গুরুত্বের সঠিক মান নির্ণয় করিয়াছিলেন। **Torricellian tube**—প্রায় এক গজ দীর্ঘ এবং ¼ ইঞ্চি আভ্যন্তরব্যাসের নল। [একপ্রান্ত সীল করার পর উহা পারদদ্বারা পূর্ণ করা হইয়া থাকে। তৎপর অপরপ্রান্ত অঙ্গুষ্ঠদ্বারা বন্ধ করিয়া চোঙ্গটী উন্টাইয়া পারদপূর্ণভাণ্ডে নিমজ্জিত করা হয়। ঐ চোঙ্গের মুক্তপ্রান্ত খাড়াভাবে ভাণ্ডে রাখার পর অঙ্গুষ্ঠ সরাইয়া আনিলে চোঙ্গের পারদ ক্রমশঃ নামিয়া (সমুদ্রের সমধরাতলে) ভাণ্ডের পারদের উপরিভাগ হইতে ৩০ ইঞ্চি উপরে আসিয়া স্থির হয়। চোঙ্গের বায়ুশূন্য অংশকে Torricellian vacuum বলা হইয়া থাকে। ভাণ্ডের পারদের উপর ভূবায়ুর চাপে ঐ পাত্রস্থিত পারদ চোঙ্গে উত্থিত হইয়া থাকে।]

tŏr'-rid (-ĭd), *adj.* **1.** Scorched; very hot; বিদগ্ধ, দগ্ধীভূত, রৌদ্রদগ্ধ; অত্যুষ্ণ, অত্যুত্তপ্ত। 2. Ardent; enthusiastic; "Tempered, 'twixt cold despair and *torrid* joy"; প্রবল, জ্বলন্ত; উৎসাহপূর্ণ। **—ness. —rid'-i-ty,** *ns.* **Torrid zone**—গ্রীষ্মমণ্ডল, উষ্ণমণ্ডল, উষ্ণবলয়, দক্ষিণায়নমণ্ডল, উষ্ণকটিবন্ধ।

tŏr'-sĕl, *n.* **1.** Anything in a twisted form; মোচড়ানো জিনিষ। **2.** A piece of stone, iron, or wood to support the end of a beam or joist; কড়ি প্রভৃতির প্রান্তের অবলম্বনস্বরূপ শিলা, লৌহ বা দারুখণ্ড।

tŏr'-sion, *n.* **1.** Act of twisting; ব্যাবর্ত্তন, মোচড়। 2. (*Bot.*) The state of being spirally twisted; (উদ্ভিদ্‌বিদ্যা) ব্যাবর্ত্তনশীলতা। **3.** (*Mech.*) The force with which a body, such as a thread, wire or slender rod, resists a twist or the force with which it tends to return to its original shape on being twisted; যে বল দ্বারা কোন বস্তু, যথা সূত্র, তার অথবা শলাকা ব্যাবর্ত্তনে বাধা প্রদান করে অথবা যে বল দ্বারা উহা ব্যাবর্ত্তিত হইলে পর পূর্ব্বাকার প্রাপ্ত হইয়া থাকে। **4.** (*Surg.*) The stopping of haemorrhage by twisting the ends of a blood-vessel after operation; অস্ত্রোপচারের পর রক্তবহানাড়ীসমূহের প্রান্ত মোচড়াইয়া রক্তস্রাব বন্ধ করণ। **—al, —less,** *adjs.* **—al-ly,** *adv.* **Torsion balance** — অতি মিহি পাকানো তারের সাহায্যে সূক্ষ্ম শক্তি পরিমাপের জন্য যন্ত্রবিশেষ।

tŏrsk, *n.* A fish of cod-family; কডজাতীয় মৎস্যবিশেষ।

tŏr'-sō, *n.* The trunk of a statue deprived of head and limbs; মূর্ত্তির মস্তক এবং হস্তপদাদিবিহীন দেহকাণ্ড।

tŏrt, *n.* Injuries done to the property or person of another, as trespass, assault, battery, defamation, or the like; ব্যক্তিগত ভাবে বা সম্পত্তিসম্পর্কে কোন ব্যক্তির যে অনিষ্ট করা হয়, ক্ষতি (যথা :—অনধিকার-প্রবেশ, মানহানি, মারপিট)।

tŏr'-ti-cŏl'-lis, *n.* Wryneck; গলদেশের আড়ষ্টতা, গলস্তম্ভ।

tŏr'-tile (-tĭl), *adj.* **1.** Twisted; curved; মোচড়ানো; ব্যাবর্ত্তিত। **2.** (*Bot.*) Coiled; কুণ্ডলিত। **—til'-i-ty,** *n.*

tortilla, *n.* A round flat cake made from maize in Mexico; মেক্সিকোদেশে ভুট্টা হইতে প্রস্তুত এক-প্রকার চাপাটি।

tŏr'-tious (-shŭs), *adj.* **1.** Injurious; ক্ষতিজনক। 2. Wrongful; অন্যায়জনক। **—ly,** *adv.*

tŏr'-toise (-tōys *or* -tĭz), *n.* **1.** A name common to an order of reptiles covered with a flattened shell, or kind of bony box, from which the head and legs protrude; কাছিম, কূর্ম্ম, চিত্রকচ্ছপ (সাঃ পঃ), কচ্ছপ। [Syn. জলবিল্ব, ধরণীধর, দৌলেয়, দদ্রু, জীবর্থ, পঞ্চনখ, গুহ, পঞ্চগুপ্ত, জীবরু, কমঠ, জলগুল্ম, গূঢ়াঙ্গ, কচ্ছেষ্ট, পল্বলাবাস, কঠিনপৃষ্ঠক, ডুলি (Fem.), ঢুলি (*ibid.*), ক্রোড়া, কুটিলগামী, অকূপার, কশ্যপ।] **2.** (*Rom. Antiq.*) Same as TESTUDO. **Tortoise-shell** — কূর্ম্মপৃষ্ঠ, কাছিমের খোল। **Tortoise-shell butterfly** — কচ্ছপের পৃষ্ঠের মত কৃষ্ণ এবং পীতবর্ণ চিহ্নযুক্ত প্রজাপতি। **Tortoise-shell cat**—উক্তপ্রকার বিড়াল।

tŏr'-tū-lous (-lŭs), *adj.* (*Bot.* & *Zool.*) Same as MONILIFORM.

tŏr'-tü-ous (-ŭs), *adj.* **1.** Twisted; winding; পাকানো; পেঁচানো, ঘূরানো, আঁকাবাঁকা। **2.** (*Fig.*) Crooked; "His master's *tortuous* policy"; deceitful; কুটিল, বক্রস্বভাব, কুটিলমতি, অসরল, কপট; প্রতারক। **–ly,** *adv.* **–os'-i-ty, –ness,** *ns.* **Tortuous curve**—কুচক্র (হিঃ কোঃ)।

tŏr'-türe, *n.* & *v. t.* **1.** Extreme pain; anguish of body or mind; তীব্রযন্ত্রণা, নিদারুণ যন্ত্রণা, অসহ্যবেদনা; যন্ত্রণা, মনঃপীড়া, মানসিক সন্তাপ, মর্ম্মবেদনা, মর্ম্মযন্ত্রণা, মনোবেদনা। **2.** Severe pain inflicted judicially either for the punishment of a crime, or for extorting confession; শাস্তিস্বরূপ বা অপরাধ স্বীকার করাইবার উদ্দেশ্যে পীড়ন বা নিদারুণ যন্ত্রণা প্রদান, পীড়ন। ***Verb t.*** **1.** To subject to torture; শাস্তিস্বরূপ বা অপরাধ স্বীকার করাইবার উদ্দেশ্যে পীড়ন করা, নির্যাতন করা, উৎপীড়ন করা। **2.** To pain extremely; as, he was *tortured* by painful emotions; নিদারুণ যন্ত্রণা প্রদান করা। **3.** (*Fig.*) To put a wrong construction on; as, a sentence might be *tortured* to bear such a meaning; অর্থ বিকৃতি করা, কদর্থ করা। **–tur-a-ble, –tur-ous,** *adjs.* **–tur-er,** *n.* **–tur-ing-ly,** *adv.* **Torture chamber**—পীড়াগৃহ, পীড়াযন্ত্রগৃহ (দিব্যাবদান)।

tŏr'-ü-lă, *n.* **1.** (*Pl.* -LAE.) A genus of fungi; এক জাতীয় ছত্রাক। **2.** A chain of spherical bacteria; জীবাণুগোলক শৃঙ্খল। **3.** (*Bot.*) A small torus; (উদ্ভিদ্-বিদ্যা) ক্ষুদ্র পুষ্পধী। **–li-form,** *adj.*

tō'-rŭs, *n.* (*Pl.* -RI) **1.** (*Arch.*) A large moulding used in the bases of columns or pilasters; স্তম্ভের পাদদেশের ভূষাবিশেষ। **2.** (*Bot.*) The part of a flower on which the carpels are seated; (উদ্ভিদ্-বিদ্যা) পুষ্পের যে অংশে কিঞ্জল্কসমূহ সংস্থিত থাকে, পুষ্পধী। **3.** (*Anat.*) A smooth rounded ridge; (শারীরসংস্থানবিদ্যা) মসৃণ এবং গোলাকৃতি অস্থি।

tō'-rȳ, *n.* & *adj.* A conservative in English politics; রক্ষণশীল সম্প্রদায়ভুক্ত ব্যক্তি। ***Adj.*** Of, or pertaining to, the tories; as, *tory* principles; রক্ষণশীলসম্প্রদায়সম্বন্ধীয়, রক্ষণশীলসম্প্রদায়ের। **–ism.** *n.* **Tory Democrat**—কিঞ্চিৎ গণতান্ত্রিক ভাবানুরাগী রক্ষণশীল সম্প্রদায়ভুক্ত ব্যক্তি।

tŏss, *v. t., i.* & *n.* **1.** To throw with the hand; to throw upward; as, to *toss* a ball; হস্তদ্বারা উৎক্ষেপ করা; উৎক্ষেপণ করা। **2.** To throw up violently or suddenly; সবলে বা সহসা উৎক্ষিপ্ত করা। **3.** To jerk; as, to *toss* one's head; আন্দোলিত করা। **4.** To heave up and down or tumble about; as, waves *tossed* by the wind; ক্রমান্বয়ে উত্থিত ও পতিত হওয়া, গড়াগড়ি করা। **5.** To agitate; সংক্ষুব্ধ করা, বিক্ষোভিত করা। ***Verb i.*** **1.** To roll and tumble; to writhe; গড়াগড়ি যাওয়া; যন্ত্রণায় ছটফট করা। **2.** To be flung or dashed about; নিক্ষিপ্ত হওয়া, প্রচণ্ড বেগে পতিত হওয়া। **3.** To move up and down; উত্থিত ও পতিত হওয়া। ***Noun.*** **1.** A throwing upwards, or with a jerk; উৎক্ষেপণ। **2.** Same as TOSS-UP. **Toss-up**—কোন বিষয় মীমাংসার জন্য মুদ্রা উৎক্ষেপণ; সন্দেহজনক বিষয়। **To toss in blanket**—See BLANKET. **To toss off**—To drink off at a draught; এক চুমুকে নিঃশেষ করা। **To toss up**—মুদ্রা উৎক্ষেপণ করিয়া কোন বিষয় স্থির করা। **To win the toss**—মুদ্রা উৎক্ষেপণ দ্বারা কোন ব্যক্তির অনুকূলে কোন বিষয় নির্দ্ধারিত হওয়া।

tŏt, *n.* **1.** Anything small esp. a small child; ছোট জিনিষ, ছোট খোকা, ছোট্টটু। **2.** (*Colloq.*) A dram of liquor; এক ড্রাম মদ্য।

tŏt, *n.* & *v. t.* (*Colloq.*) A set of figures to be added; যোগ করিবার জন্য এক সারি সংখ্যা। ***Verb t.*** **1.** (*Colloq.*) To sum up; (চলিত ভাষায়) যোগকরা, ঠিক দেওয়া। **2.** To mark with the word *tot*; as, a *totted* debt; 'tot' শব্দদ্বারা চিহ্নিত করা।

tō'-tăl, *adj., n.* & *v. t.* **1.** Whole; মোট। **2.** Complete; absolute; as, *total* failure; পূর্ণ; পুরা, সম্পূর্ণ। ***Noun.*** The whole sum or amount; মোটসংখ্যা, সমষ্টি, যোগফল, একুন। ***Verb t.*** To ascertain the sum or total of; to add; সমষ্টি করা, মোট করা; যোগ করা। **–tal'-i-ty,** *n.* Quality or state of being total or a total; সমূহ, সমষ্টি, সমাহার, সামস্ত্য (ষট্), সামগ্র্য। **Total blindness**—তিমির (সাঃ পঃ)। **Total eclipse**—পূর্ণ গ্রহণ। **Total utility**—পূর্ণ উপযুক্ততা (হিঃ কোঃ)।

tō'-tăl-īze, *v. t.* To make or reduce to completeness; সমগ্র করা, সম্পূর্ণতাসম্পাদন করা, সামগ্র্য বিধান করা, পূর্ণতা সম্পাদন করা। **–i-za-tor,** *n.* **–i-za'-tion,** *n.* **–i-zer,** *n.* An apparatus used at horse-race, which registers or indicates the number of tickets sold to betters on each horse; একপ্রকার যন্ত্র—যাহাতে ঘোড়দৌড়ে কত সংখ্যক টিকিট বিক্রীত হইয়াছে তাহা প্রদর্শিত হয়।

tō'-tĕm, *n.* A figure as of an animal, plant, etc. used as a badge of tribe or family among savage races; "A *totem* is a class of material objects which a savage regards with superstitious respect, believing that there exists between him and every member of the class an intimate and altogether special relation"; কোন কোন অসভ্য জাতিদিগের পূর্ব্বপুরুষগণের চিহ্নস্বরূপ জন্তু বা বৃক্ষাদি, জাতিবস্তু, বংশচিহ্ন, দেবক। [Trees are still worshipped as family-gods by the Marhattas of the Deccan. Marhatta families have *Devakas* or sacred symbols which appear to have been originally totems and affect marriage to the extent that a man cannot marry a woman whose *Devaka* reckoned on the male side is the same as his own. These are totems worshipped during marriage and other Ceremonies. (*Census of India* 1901., Vol. I. *Ethnographical appendices Cal.* 1904.) Among the *Devakas* of Marhatta families are Vat (Mar. *Vad*), Kadamba (Mar. *Kadum*), etc.] **—ic,** *adj.* **—i-cal-ly,** *adv.* **—ism,** *n.* A belief prevailing among primitive peoples of blood-kinship with or descent from an animal or plant ; মানবেতরজন্মবাদ (সাঃ পঃ), মানবেতরবংশানুক্রম (ঐ) [কোন কোন অসভ্য জাতির লোকদিগের মধ্যে বিশ্বাস আছে যে তাহারা ইতর জন্তু বা বৃক্ষাদি হইতে জাত হইয়াছে। সাধারণতঃ এইরূপ বিশ্বাসকে Totemism কহে। See Frazer, *Golden Bough* ; Lang, *Secret of the Totem* ; Gillen, *Northern Tribes of Central Australia* ; Gomme, *Folklore as an Historical Science* ; Seligmann, *Melanesians of British New Guinea* ; C. Hill-Tout, *British North America, Far West IX.* ; Jevon, *Introduction to the History of Religions.*]

to'th'-ĕr, toth'-ĕr (tŭth-), *adj.* & *pron.* The other ; অপর, অন্য। ***Pron.*** That other ; ঐটী।

totidem verbis, *adv.* In so many words ; এই কথা গুলিতে।

toties quoties, *adv.* Every time ; প্রত্যেকবার।

toto caelo, *adv.* ***Differ toto caelo***—By great distance ; বহুদূর।

tŏt'-ter (-ĕr), *v. i.* 1. To stand or walk unsteadily ; টলিতে টলিতে চলা বা দাঁড়ান। 2. To threaten to fall ; টলমল করা, টলা, পড় পড় হওয়া। **—er,** *n.* **—ing-ly,** *adv.* **—y,** *adj.*

tou-căn' (-tōō *or* tō̍-), *n.* A bird of tropical America of several species remarkable for the large size of its **bill** ; আমেরিকার উষ্ণমণ্ডলের কয়েকজাতীয় বৃহৎচঞ্চু পক্ষীর সাধারণ নাম।

touch (tŭch), *v. t., i.* & *n.* **1.** To perceive by putting something in contact with ; to put the hand, finger, foot, etc., against ; অন্য কোন বস্তুর সহিত সংযোগ করত অনুভব করা ; স্পর্শ করা। **2.** To be in contact esp. to be tangent with ; সংস্পর্শে আসা (বিশেষতঃ) কোন কিছুর স্পর্শরেখাস্বরূপ হওয়া। **3.** To strike gently with an instrument, stick or the like ; কোনরূপ যন্ত্র, যষ্টি বা তদ্রূপ কোন কিছু দ্বারা মৃদু আঘাত করা। **4.** To meddle or handle with ; as, I have not *touched* the book ; হস্তক্ষেপ করা। **5.** To take food or drink ; as, he did not *touch* for three days ; to taste ; পান বা আহার করা ; আস্বাদ করা। **6.** To relate to ; "The quarrel *toucheth* none but thee alone" ; সংস্রব থাকা। **7.** To play, as a musician by touch or as if by touch ; to perform, as a piece of music ; বাজান, বাদন করা ; সম্পাদন করা। **8.** To come to ; to arrive at ; to land ; to come to shore ; as, to *touch* land ; আসা ; উপনীত হওয়া, উপস্থিত হওয়া, পৌঁছা ; অবতরণ করা ; তীরে আসা। **9.** To mark or delineate slightly ; তুলিকাস্পর্শ বা তুলিকাপাত করা। **10.** To soften ; as, it *touched* her heart ; কোমল করা, দ্রবীভূত করা। **11.** To test ; পরীক্ষা করা, পরখ করা। **12.** To affect ; as, to *touch* one's mind ; মর্ম্মস্পর্শ করা, প্রাণ গলান, মন ভিজান (*collaq.*), বিগলিত করা। **13.** To infect ; সংক্রামক রোগ দ্বারা আক্রান্ত করা। **14.** To be mentally deranged in a slight degree ; "He thought, he was a little *touched* or insame" ; ঈষৎ মস্তিষ্ক বিকৃত হওয়া। **15.** To be a matter of moment to ; to affect ; as, the measure will not *touch* the poorer sections of the community ; কাহারো পক্ষে গুরুত্ববিশিষ্ট হওয়া ; প্রভাবিত করা। **16.** To compare with ; "Nothing that could *touch* this mare of mine" ; তুলিত হওয়া ; **17.** To reach ; as, to *touch* a certain price ; পৌঁছা। **18.** To test the purity of gold and silver by rubbing it on a touchstone ; সোণারূপার কষ লওয়া। **19.** To mark as gold and silver with an official stamp ; সোণারূপায় ছাপা দেওয়া। 2. To play an air ; কোনরূপ গৎ বাজান। ***Verb i.*** 1. To be in contact ; সংস্পৃষ্ট হওয়া। 2. To treat of slightly in discourse ; to mention or discuss briefly ; as, to *touch* on a subject ; প্রসঙ্গক্রমে উল্লেখ করা ; কোন বিষয়ে অল্প দুই একটী কথা বলা। **3.** To make an incidental stop at a point on shore, when on a voyage or trip by water ; as, we *touched* at many ports ; (নৌকা, জাহাজ, প্রভৃতি সম্পর্কে) সাগর নদী প্রভৃতির তীরের নির্দ্দিষ্ট নির্দ্দিষ্ট স্থানে থামা। **4.** (*Naut.*) To have the leech of a sail so struck by the wind as to cause tremulous motion ; (নৌবিদ্যা) পাইলের খাড়া বা প্রবণ পার্শ্বে এইরূপ ভাবে বায়ু দ্বারা প্রহত হওয়া যাহাতে কম্পনাত্মকগতি উৎপাদিত হয়। **5.** To verge upon ; "The time *touch* upon dinner" ; নিকটবর্ত্তী হওয়া, সন্নিহিত হওয়া। ***Noun.*** **1.** Contact ; স্পর্শ। **2.** The special feeling which resides in the nervous papillae of the skin, and forms one of the five senses ; the sense of feeling or common sensation ; স্পর্শশক্তি, স্পর্শজ্ঞান, স্পর্শবোধ, স্পর্শেন্দ্রিয়। **3.** A stroke of pen, pencil or the like ; তুলিকাপাত, তুলিকাস্পর্শ, পেন্সিল প্রভৃতির সূক্ষ্ম রেখা, কলমের আঁক। **4.** A dash ; a smack ; ছিঁটা ফোঁটা; আভাস, আমেজ, লেশ। **5.** Close relation ; accord ; harmony ; sympathy; communication ; ঘনিষ্ঠ সম্পর্ক ; মিল ; সঙ্গতি ; সুসঙ্গতি ; পত্রব্যবহার। **6.** Same as TOUCHSTONE. **7.** An official mark or stamp upon gold or silver indicating its standard of fineness ; সোণারূপার উপর মুদ্রিত সরকারী ছাপ, ছাপ। **8.** Test ; proof ; পরীক্ষা, পরখ ; প্রমাণ। **9.** A musical note; স্বর। **10.** Trait; "One *touch* of nature makes the whole world kin" ; আমেজ, স্পর্শ। **11.** A hint ; আভাস, ইসারা, আঁচ। **12.** (*Mus.*) The resistance of the keys of an instrument to the pressure of the fingers ; also the manner of touching the keys or strings of a musical instrument ; (সঙ্গীতবিদ্যা) অঙ্গুলীর চাপের বিরুদ্ধে চাবির বিরোধ ; বাদ্যযন্ত্রের চাবি বা তার স্পর্শ করার ভঙ্গী। **13.** Manner or style of workmanship in carving etc. or in writing ; ক্ষোদন প্রভৃতি রচনার রীতি বা কলাপদ্ধতি। **14.** A defect ; খুঁত, দোষ, ত্রুটি। **15.** (*Football*) That part of a field which is beyond the line of flags on either side ; (পাদগোলকক্রীড়া) ক্রীড়াপ্রাঙ্গণের পার্শ্বসীমার বহির্বর্ত্তী স্থান। **16.** (*Med.*) Exploration of organ etc. by sense of touch ; (ভৈষজ্যশাস্ত্র) স্পর্শদ্বারা কোন শারীরিক যন্ত্র পরীক্ষণ। **Touch-and-go**—একবার স্পর্শ করিয়া তৎক্ষণাৎ ছাড়িয়া দেওন ; দ্রুত বা তৎক্ষণাৎ সম্পাদিত কার্য্য ; চুলেচুলে রক্ষা ; সঙ্কটজনক অবস্থা, দায়, ঝুঁকি। (*Adj.*) তৎক্ষণাৎ সম্পাদিত ; অসাবধান ; বিপৎসঙ্কুল, ঝুঁকিদার। **Touch-body, Touch-corpuscle**—স্পর্শশীল দেহ বা রক্তকণিকা। **Touch-hole**—বন্দুকাদির রঞ্জক-ঘরা। **Touch-in-goal**—পাদগোলক ক্রীড়ায় স্পর্শরেখা দ্বারা বেষ্টিত বহির্বর্ত্তী কোণ চতুষ্টয়ের অন্যতম। **Touch-last**—ছেলেদের একপ্রকার খেলা। **Touch-line**—এক গোল রেখা হইতে অপর গোল রেখা পর্য্যন্ত বিস্তৃত ক্রীড়া প্রাঙ্গণের প্রত্তি পার্শ্বের প্রান্ত রেখা, স্পর্শরেখা। **Touch-me-not**—একপ্রকার ক্ষুপ। Same as LUPUS. যে ব্যক্তি কিম্বা বস্তুকে স্পর্শ করা নিষিদ্ধ ; নিষিদ্ধ বিষয়, নিষিদ্ধ প্রসঙ্গ (*Touch-me-notish, adj. Touch-me-notishness, n.*) **Touch-needle**—কষ্টিপাথরে সোণা পরখ করার জন্য স্বর্ণসূচী। **Touch-paper**—বারুদ প্রভৃতি জ্বালাইবার জন্য সোরাতে ডুবানো কাগজ। **Touch potential**—স্পর্শতন্মাত্র (ব্রজঃ হিন্দু)। **Touchstone**—কষ্টিপাথর, নিকষপাষাণ, নিকষোপল (গীতাঞ্জঃ), কষোপল (রসার্ণব), ব্রহ্মশিলা, কষপাষাণ, কষপট্টিকা (বিক্রমঃ), হেমল (অঃ), কক্ষপট্ট, আকষ, হৈর। (*Fig.*) Standard ; criterion ; আদর্শ ; পরীক্ষার মান (Also see STONE). **Touch-wood**—আশুদাহ্য কাষ্ঠ। **A near touch**—অল্পের জন্য বাঁচিয়া যাওন, চুলে চুলে রক্ষা। **To be in touch with**—To have close relation with something ; to have subtle perception or particular knowledge of something ; কোন বিষয়ের সহিত ঘনিষ্ঠ সম্পর্ক থাকা ; কোন বিষয়ে সূক্ষ্ম অনুভূতি বা সবিশেষ জ্ঞান থাকা। **To lose touch with, To be out of touch with**—To have no connection with ; কোন বিষয়ে সংস্রব না থাকা। **To touch at**—(Of steamers etc.) To stop at particular places ; নির্দ্দিষ্ট, নির্দ্দিষ্ট স্থানে থামা, ভিড়া, লাগা। **To touch down**—রাগবী পাদগোলক ক্রীড়ায় গোলের পশ্চাতে কন্দুকসহ ভূমি স্পর্শ করা। **To touch in**—To insert by touching with the pencil, brush ; পেন্সিল, তুলিকা প্রভৃতির সাহায্যে নিবিষ্ট করা। **To touch off**—To sketch hastily ; to finish by touches ; দ্রুত নক্সা অঙ্কিত করা ; সূক্ষ্ম তুলিকাপাত দ্বারা সম্পাদন করা। To discharge, as a cannon ; তোপ প্রভৃতি দাগা। **To touch on**—To allude to something ; কোন বিষয়ে উল্লেখ করা। To treat briefly ; কোন বিষয়ে দুই একটী কথা বলা। **To touch one on a tender point**—To allude to a subject that will deeply wound one's feeling ; যে বিষয় উল্লেখ করিলে কাহারো প্রাণে খুব বাজিবে এমন কোন কথা উল্লেখ করা। **To touch one to the quick**—See QUICK. **To touch persons off**—To be too clever for them ; কারো চেয়ে বেশী চালাক হওয়া। **To touch up**—To improve, as a picture by touches of the brush or a literary work by emendations ; তুলিকাস্পর্শ করিয়া চিত্রের উৎকর্ষ সাধন করা, স্থানে স্থানে দুই একটী শব্দ যোগ বা ঈষৎ পরিবর্ত্তন করিয়া পুস্তকের উৎকর্ষ সম্পাদন করা। To strike a horse etc. with a whip ; ঘোড়া প্রভৃতিকে চাবুক লাগান। To jog one's memory ; স্মৃতি জাগ্রত করা।

touch'-ĕr (tŭch-), *n.* **1.** One who touches ; স্পর্শকারী। **2.** A close shave ; অল্পের জন্য না লাগন। **As near as a toucher**—Almost exactly ; প্রায় সঠিকভাবে।

touch'-ing (tŭch-), *adj.* & *prep.* Affecting ; moving ; pathetic ; চিত্ত-দ্রবকর ; মর্ম্মস্পর্শী, হৃদয়স্পর্শী, হৃদয়গ্রাহী ; প্রাণস্পর্শী ; করুণ প্রাণগলানো। ***Prep.*** Concerning ; সম্পর্কে, বিষয়ে, সম্বন্ধে।

touch'-y (tŭch-), *adj.* Over-sensitive ; চিড়চিড়ে, চটা, কোপন, অতিরিক্ত উত্তেজনাপ্রবণ।

tough (tŭf), *adj.* **1.** Flexible without being brittle ; চিমড়া। **2.** Strong; as, *tough* constitution ; দৃঢ়, মজবুত। **3.** Hardy ; কষ্টসহ, পরিশ্রমী। **4.** Difficult ; কঠিন, দুরূহ। **5.** (*Colloq.*) Severe ; (চলিতভাষায়) কঠোর। **Tough'-ly,** *adv.* **Tough'-ness,** *n.*

tou-pee' (tō-pē), *n.* An artificial patch of hair worn to cover a bald spot ; মাথার টাকপড়া স্থান ঢাকার জন্য কৃত্রিম চুলের তালি।

tour (tôr), *n., v.t.* & *i.* 1. A journey in a circuit ; a ramble ; পরিভ্রমণ ; পর্য্যটন। 2. Excursion ; পরিক্রম, দেশভ্রমণ, দেশপর্য্যটন। *Verb t.* To make a tour of ; as, to *tour* France and Spain ; পরিভ্রমণ করা। *Verb i.* To make a tour ; ভ্রমণ করা, পরিভ্রমণ করা, পর্য্যটন করা, পরিক্রম করা। **The grand tour**—(ইতিহাস) শিক্ষাসমাপ্তির জন্য ফ্রান্স ইতালী প্রভৃতি দেশে পর্য্যটন **Tour de force**—চাতুর্য্য বা শারীরিক শক্তির কার্য্য।

tour-bil'lion (tôr-bĭl-yŏn), *n.* An ornamental revolving firework ; একপ্রকার আতসবাজী, চরকীবাজি।

tour'-ist (tôr-), *n.* One who makes a tour ; দেশভ্রমণকারী, দেশপর্য্যটক। **Tourist ticket**—দেশভ্রমণকারিগণকে নানাদেশ ভ্রমণের জন্য বিশেষ সুবিধাজনক সর্ত্তে যে টিকিট দেওয়া হয়।

tour'-mă-lin (tôr-), **—line** (-lĭn), *ns.* A mineral of various colours possessing strong electrical properties ; প্রবল বৈদ্যুতিক ধর্ম্মসম্পন্ন নানাবর্ণের খনিজপদার্থ, তুর্ম্মলীন (যোঃ), তুর্ণমল, তুর্ম্মলিত, তুর্ম্মোলী।

tour'-nă-mĕnt (tôr-), *n.* 1. An encounter between armed knights on horseback very popular in middle ages in which prize was given by the lady of the tournament to the knight who had displayed the greatest prowess; মধ্যযুগে অশ্বারোহী নাইটগণের একপ্রকার ক্রীড়াযুদ্ধ—এইরূপ লীলারণে সর্ব্বাপেক্ষা অধিক শক্তিপ্রদর্শনকারী নাইটকে ক্রীড়াপ্রাঙ্গণের অধিনায়িকা একটী পুরস্কার প্রদান করিতেন, ক্রীড়াসমর, লীলাযুদ্ধ, লীলারণ। [যাহাতে কোনরূপ দুর্ঘটনা না ঘটিতে পারে তজ্জন্য এইরূপ লীলাযুদ্ধে ব্যবহৃত বর্শা, তরবারি, প্রভৃতি অস্ত্রের ধার নষ্ট করিয়া দেওয়া হইত।] 2. Any contest of skill in which a number of competitors take part ; as, a chess *tournament* ; যে কোনরূপ প্রতিযোগিতার ক্রীড়ায় কতিপয় ব্যক্তি যোগদান করিয়া থাকে।

tour'-nay (tôr-nā), *n.* A printed worsted fabric for upholstery ; সোফা কেদারা প্রভৃতির গদী আচ্ছাদনের জন্য একপ্রকার পশমী ছিট।

tour'-ney (tôr-nĕ), *n.* & *v. i.* A tournament ; লীলাযুদ্ধ। *Verb i.* To take part in a tournament ; লীলাযুদ্ধে যোগদান করা।

tour'-ni-quet (tôr-nĭ-kĕt), *n.* A surgical instrument or bandage which is straitened, with a screw and used to check haemorrhage ; একপ্রকার যন্ত্র—যাহা স্ক্রুপের সাহায্যে সঙ্কাপিত করিয়া রক্তমোক্ষণ বন্ধ করা হয়।

tour-nure' (tôr-nür), *n.* 1. Contour ; figure ; shape ; বাহ্যরেখা ; আকৃতি ; গঠন। 2. A stuffed pad or cushion worn by ladies under the skirt of their dress with the intention of giving the rounded outline to hip ; নিতম্বের সুগোলত্ব বিধানের জন্য ইয়ুরোপীয় মহিলাগণ ঘাগরার নীচে যে গদী পরিয়া থাকেন।

tou'-sle (tow-zl), *v. t.* 1. (*Colloq.*) To put into disorder ; to dishevel ; to rumple ; (চলিতভাষায়) এলোমেলো করা ; আলুলায়িত করা ; কুঞ্চিত করা। 2. To ransack ; পাঁতি পাঁতি করিয়া খুঁজা।

tous-les-mois' (tô-lā-mwâ), *n.* (Fr., Lit. All the months), A granular starchy substance like arrowroot with very large, oval, flattened grain obtained from the root stocks of *canna edulis* ; এরোরুটের মত একপ্রকার শ্বেতসারবহুল চ্যাপ্টা এবং অণ্ডাকৃতি দানাদার পদার্থ।

tous'-y̆ (towz-), *adj.* Rough ; shaggy; dishevelled ; কর্কশ ; ঝাঁকড়ামাকড়া ; আলুলায়িত, এলোমেলো, আলুথালু।

tout (towt), *v. i.* & *n.* 1. To ply or seek for customers ; টর্গিগিরি করা, দালালি করা। 2. To spy out movements and condition of race horses in training ; গোপনে দৌড়ের ঘোড়ার গতিবিধি এবং অবস্থা লক্ষ্য করা। *Noun.* 1. One who secretly watches or seeks customers, as for a hotel, shop, etc. (also *touter*) ; টর্গি, দালাল। 2. One who, for a fee, watches the movements, condition, etc. of race-horses in training and supplies information ; যে ব্যক্তি গোপনে দৌড়ের ঘোড়া প্রভৃতির অবস্থা, গতিবিধি, প্রভৃতি লক্ষ্য করে। **Tout'-er**, *n.* (Same as TOUT, *n.* 1.)

tout court, *adv.* Very briefly ; অতিসংক্ষেপে।

tout ensemble, *n.* (*F.*) See ENSEMBLE.

tow (tö), *v. t.* & *n.* 1. To draw, as a boat or ship, through the water by means of a rope ; গুণ টানা। 2. To pull a person or thing along behind one ; কোন ব্যক্তি বা বস্তুকে পশ্চাতে টানিয়া নেওয়া। 3. To drag net over surface of water ; জলের উপর দিয়া জাল টানিয়া নেওয়া। 4. (*Fig.*) To take direction ; কর্ত্তৃত্বভার গ্রহণ করা। *Noun.* The act of towing, or state of being towed (with *in*) ; as, one vessel takes another *in tow* ; গুণ টানন ; কোন বস্তুর পশ্চাতে বাঁধিয়া নেওন। **Tow'-age**, *n.* **Tow-line, towing-line, tow-rope**—গুণ। **Tow-path, towing-path**—গুণের পথ।

tow (tö), *n.* The coarse part of flax or hemp ; শণ প্রভৃতির অসার অংশ, ফেঁসো।

tow'-ard (tö-ĕrd), *adj.* (*Archaic*) Compliant ; tractable ; apt ; (অপ্রঃ) বশীভূত, আজ্ঞাকারী ; সহজে দমনীয় ; উন্মুখ, প্রবণ। **—ly**, *adj.* **—ness**, *n.*

tô'-wards (-wĕrds), **tô'-ward** (-wĕrd), *prep.* 1. In the direction of ; অভিমুখে, দিকে, পানে, প্রতি। 2. For ; for the purpose of ; জন্য ; উদ্দেশ্যে। 3. Nearly ; as, *towards* five O'clock ; প্রায়।

tow'-ĕl, *n., v. t. & i.* A piece of cloth used for wiping the feet, hand, etc. usually after bath; গামছা, তোয়ালে, গাত্রমুক্ষণী, গাত্রমার্জ্জনী, পাণিতোলা (ভক্তিরত্নঃ)। *Verb t.* To wipe with towels; তোয়ালেদ্বারা মুছাইয়া দেওয়া। *Verb i.* To wipe one's self with a towel; তোয়ালেদ্বারা গা মুছা। **—ling,** *n.* **Lead towel**—(ইতর ভাষায়) গুলি। **Oaken towel**—দণ্ডাঘাত। **Roller-towel** — ঘূর্ণনশীল দণ্ডের উপর অন্তহীন গাত্রভ্রমণী। **Towel-horse**—গামছা রাখার জন্য একপ্রকার আলনা। **Wooden towels**—কাষ্ঠ,লগুড়।

tow'-ĕr, *n. & v. i.* 1. A building either square or circular of considerable elevation, and generally flat on the top; বুরুজ, গোপুর। 2. A fortress; দুর্গ, কেল্লা। 3. A place of defence; "Thou hast been a shelter for me, and a strong *tower* from the enemy"; protector; আশ্রয়স্থান; রক্ষাকর্ত্তা। 4. A lofty pile; "She had a *tower* of lace on her elevated head"; উচ্চ স্তূপ। 5. (*Astrol.*) House; (ফলিত জ্যোতিষ) গৃহ। 6. The vertical ascent of a wounded bird; আহত পক্ষীর সরলভাবে উত্থান। 7. A very high head-dress worn by women in the reigns of William III and Anne; ইংলণ্ডের নৃপতি তৃতীয় উইলিয়েম এবং রাজ্ঞী এনের রাজত্বকালে স্ত্রীলোকদিগের পরিধেয় একপ্রকার অত্যুচ্চ উষ্ণীষ। 8. The gun-turret on an ironclad; লৌহ-পট্টাচ্ছাদিত রণপোতের যে চূড়ায় কামান সংস্থাপিত থাকে। 9. Soaring; উর্দ্ধে উড্ডয়ন। 10. A tall structure used in destroying a fort in ancient time; প্রাচীনকালে দুর্গধ্বংসের জন্য ব্যবহৃত যন্ত্রবিশেষ। *Verb i.* To rise and fly high; "The pheasant does not *tower* but darts through the trees"; to soar; to be lofty; উর্দ্ধে উত্থিত হইয়া উড্ডীন হওয়া; উর্দ্ধে উত্থিত হওয়া; সমুন্নত হওয়া। **—ing,** *adj.* 1. Very high; অত্যুচ্চ, অত্যুন্নত, আকাশস্পর্শী, গগনচুম্বী, অভ্রভেদী, নভোলিহ। 2. Rising high in flight; as, *towering* birds; উর্দ্ধাকাশে উত্থিত বা উড্ডীয়মান। 3. Extreme; নিতান্ত, পরম। 4. Exalted; ambitious; উন্নত, সমুন্নত; উচ্চাভিলাষী। **Tower'-y,** *adj.* **Water-tower**—অগ্নিকাণ্ডের সময়ে জলধারা উর্দ্ধে তুলিবার জন্য একপ্রকার নল; জল সরবরাহের জন্য উর্দ্ধে স্থাপিত জলকুণ্ডের অবলম্বনস্বরূপ মঞ্চ। **The Tower** or **The Tower of London**—লণ্ডননগরীর প্রাচীন প্রাসাদ এবং দুর্গ বিশেষ, ইহা পরবর্ত্তীকালে রাজকীয় কারাগার স্বরূপ ব্যবহৃত হয়। বর্ত্তমানে এইস্থান অস্ত্রাগার এবং ঐতিহাসিক দ্রব্যের প্রদর্শনীস্বরূপ ব্যবহৃত হইয়া থাকে। **Tower of silence** — যে অত্যুচ্চ মঞ্চোপরি পারসীকগণ গৃধ্র প্রভৃতির ভোজনের জন্য মৃতদেহ রক্ষা করিয়া থাকে।

town, *n.* 1. A place enclosed or fenced in; a walled or fortified place; বৃতিবেষ্টিত স্থান; প্রাচীর-বেষ্টিত বা দুর্গাদি দ্বারা সুরক্ষিত স্থান। 2. A place larger than a village, not a city; নগর, শহর, পুর, পত্তন (esp. *port-town*)। 3. The habitants of a town or city; "The *town* talks of nothing else—I am very sorry, ma'am, the *town* has so little to do"; নগরী বা মহানগরীর অধিবাসিবৃন্দ, পুরবাসিগণ, নগরবাসিগণ, নাগরিকবৃন্দ, পৌরবৃন্দ। 4. (Without *the*) London or the chief city or the town in which or in the neighbourhood of which the speaker or writer is; লণ্ডন অথবা যে নগরীতে বক্তা বা লেখক অবস্থান করিতেছে বা তন্নিকটবর্ত্তী কোন নগরী। 5. A size of paper; নির্দ্দিষ্ট আয়তনের একপ্রকার কাগজ। **Town'-less, Town'-ward,** *adjs.* **Town'-let,** *n.* A small town; ক্ষুদ্র নগরী। **Town'-ward, Town'-wards,** *adv.* **Town adjutant**—দুর্গস্থিত সৈন্যগণের শাসনের জন্য নিযুক্ত লেফ্‌টেনেন্টের তুল্য মর্য্যাদাবিশিষ্ট কর্ম্মচারী-বিশেষ। **Town-clerk** — মিউনিসিপ্যালিটীর কেরাণী। **Town council**—স্বায়ত্ত শাসনের জন্য নাগরিকবৃন্দের প্রতিনিধিসভা, পৌরসমিতি। **Town councillor** — পৌরসমিতির সভ্য। **Town crier** — যে কর্ম্মচারী নগরীতে কোন বিষয় ঘোষণা করিয়া থাকে। **Town hall**—যে ভবনে জনপৌরসমিতির অধিবেশন প্রভৃতি হইয়া থাকে, নগরমন্দির, পৌরমণ্ডপ। **Town house** — কোন ব্যক্তির শহরের বাড়ী, পৌরগৃহ, নগরভবন। **Town land**—শহরের নিকটবর্ত্তী ভূমি। **Townsfolk**—শহরের লোক, নগরবাসী, পুরবাসী। **Township**—কোন যাজক-পল্লীর অন্তর্ভুক্ত নগর। **Townsman**—শহুরে লোক, নগরবাসী, পুরবাসী, এক-নগরের অধিবাসী। **Townspeople**—নগরবাসিগণ, পৌরবৃন্দ। **Town-talk**—শহরের আলোচনার বিষয়, সাধারণের আলাপের বিষয়। **A man about town**—শহুরে বাবু। **To paint the town red**—See PAINT. **On the town**—নাগরিক জীবনের বিলাসিতা প্রভৃতিতে নিমগ্ন; গণিকাবৃত্তি দ্বারা জীবিকার্জ্জনকারিণী।

town-ee' (-ē), *n.* (*Univ. slang*) An inhabitant of a university town who has no connection with the university; (বিশ্ববিদ্যালয়ের অবর ভাষায়) বিশ্ববিদ্যালয়সমন্বিত নগরীর যে অধিবাসীর বিশ্ববিদ্যালয়ের সহিত কোন সম্পর্ক নাই।

tŏx'-ic, —i-căl, *adjs.* Pertaining to poison; poisonous; বিষ সম্পর্কীয়; বিষাক্ত।

tŏx'-i-cănt, *n.* A poison of a stimulating, narcotic, or anaesthetic nature; উত্তেজক, নিদ্রাজনক বা সংবেদনশক্তিনাশক বিষ।

tŏx-ĭc'-i-tÿ, *n.* The quality or state of being toxic; বিষাক্ততা।

tŏx-i-cŏl'-ŏ-ġÿ, *n.* The science of poisons and their antidotes; বিষতত্ত্ব, বিষবিদ্যা, বিষবিজ্ঞান, বিষতন্ত্র, (কল্পস্থান—সুশ্রুঃ), জাঙ্গুলী (অঃ)। **—co-log'-i-cal,** *adj.* **—gist,** *n.*

tŏx-i-cō-mā'-ni-ă, *n.* **1.** An insane desire for intoxicating or poisonous drugs; বিষাক্ত, বা মাদকতাজনক ঔষধসেবনের জন্য উন্মত্ততা। **2.** Same as TOXIPHOBIA.

tŏx'-in, -ine(-în),*ns.* Any poisonous ptomaine; পচনশীল জন্তু বা উদ্ভিদে প্রাপ্ত একপ্রকার ক্ষারধর্ম্মী বিষ।

tŏx-i-phō'-bi-ă, *n.* Morbid fear of poisons or being poisoned; বিষাতঙ্ক, বিষভীতি, বিষবিভীষিকা।

tŏx-ŏph'-i-līte, *n.* & *adj.* A lover of archery; a student of archery; ধনুর্ব্বিদ্যানুরাগী; ধনুর্ব্বিদ্যাশিক্ষার্থী। ***Adj.*** Pertaining to archery; ধনুর্ব্বিদ্যাসম্বন্ধীয়। **–lit'-ic,** *adj.*

toy, *n.* & *v. i.* **1.** A plaything for children; a thing of little value; a bauble; খেলনা, ক্রীড়নক; অল্প মূল্যের জিনিষ; ফটকিনাট্‌কী। **2.** A toy dog; ক্রীড়াকুক্কুর। **3.** Sport; লীলা-খেলা, ক্রীড়াকৌতুক। **4.** A matter of no importance; তুচ্ছ বিষয়। **5.** An old story; a silly tale; প্রাচীন গল্প; অসার গল্প। ***Verb i.*** **1.** (*Obs.*) To play with; (অপ্রঃ) খেলা করা। **2.** To dally amorously; রসক্রীড়া করা, কেলি করা। **Toy'-ing-ly,** *adv.* **Toy dog**—আমোদের জন্য রক্ষিত ক্ষুদ্রকায় কুকুর। **Toyshop**—খেলনার দোকান।

trā-bē-ā'-tion, *n.* Same as ENTABLATURE (which see.) **Tra'-be-ate, Tra'-be-at-ed,** *adjs.*

tră-bĕc'-ū-lă, *n.* (*pl.* -LAE), **1.** (*Bot.*) A beam-like projection or process; (উদ্ভিদ্‌বিদ্যা) স্থূলাকৃতি প্রবর্দ্ধিত বা প্রলম্বিত অংশ। **2.** (*Anat.*) The supporting band or bar connecting tissue etc; (শারীরসংস্থানবিদ্যা) জালকোষ। **–lar, –late, –lat-ed,** *adjs.*

trace (trās), *v. t.* & *n.* **1.** To mark out; to draw or delineate with marks; চিহ্নিত করা; দাগ বুলান। **2.** To sketch; to write; নক্সা করা; লিখা। **3.** To follow by traces or marks left; to track out; চিহ্ন ধরিয়া অনুসরণ করা; পদচিহ্নাদি ধরিয়া পলায়মান জন্তু প্রভৃতির অনুসরণ করা। **4.** To follow step by step; to make out; ক্রমানুসারে অনুসরণ করা, পরম্পরাক্রমে অনুসরণ করা; নির্ণয় করা। **5.** To observe or find vestiges or signs of; চিহ্ন বা নিদর্শন বাহির করা। **6.** To walk over; "We do *trace* this alley up and down"; কোন কিছুর উপর দিয়া ভ্রমণ করা। ***Noun.*** **1.** A mark left by anything passing; as, the *trace* of a carriage; a footstep; a trail; কোন গতিশীল বস্তু পশ্চাতে যে চিহ্ন রাখিয়া যায়; পদাঙ্ক, পদচিহ্ন; পলায়িত জন্তু প্রভৃতির গন্ধ, পদচিহ্ন, প্রভৃতি। **2.** A visible evidence of something having been; "The shady empire shall retain no *trace*; Of war or blood, but in sylvan chase"; remains; vestige; token; কোন অতীত ব্যাপারের দর্শনযোগ্য চিহ্ন; অবশেষ; নিদর্শন, অভিসন্ধি; চিহ্ন। **3.** A very small quantity; "*Traces* of oxalic acid can be detected"; নামগন্ধ, লেশ, সাড়াসন্ধান, নামমাত্র, লেশমাত্র। **Trace'-a-ble,** *adj.* **Trace'-a-ble-ness,** *n.* **Trace'-a-bly,** *adv.* **Trac'-er,** *n.* **Trace'-less,** *adj.* **Trace'-less-ly,** *adv.*

trace (trās),*n.* **1.** Either of the side straps, ropes or chains by which horses draw vehicles; যে পার্শ্বরজ্জু বা চর্ম্মদ্বয়ের সাহায্যে অশ্ব শকট টানিয়া থাকে তাহার অন্যতর। **2.** (*Angling*) Line; (বড়শের) সুতা। **In the traces** — জিন আঁটা। **To kick over the traces** — To become disobedient; অবাধ্য হওয়া।

trāc'-ēr-ȳ, *n.* **1.** A series of open works often seen on the head of Gothic windows, প্রস্তরাদির উপর এক প্রকার শোভাসাধক কারুকার্য্য। **2.** Decorative pattern or natural outline suggesting this (*e.g.* in insect's wing); উক্তরূপ ভূষা, পতঙ্গ প্রভৃতির পক্ষের উক্তরূপ ভূষার অনুরূপ রেখাচিত্র। **–ied,** *adj.*

trā'-chē-ă, *n.* **1.** The wind-pipe; a cartilaginous and membranous pipe through which the air passes into and out of the lungs; কণ্ঠনালী; শ্বাসনালী, সুষুম্না (বামনঃ)। **2.** One of those vessels in insects which receive and distribute air over every part of the body; কীটের শ্বাসকোষ। **–ate, at-ed,** *adjs.* Having trachea; শ্বাসনালীবিশিষ্ট।

trā-chē-ā'-ri-ă, *n.* The tracheated Arachnida; ছিদ্রশ্বাসী।

trā-chē-ŏt'-ō-mȳ, *n.* The operation of cutting into the trachea as in cases of suffocation; কণ্ঠনালী-চ্ছেদন।

trā-chī'-tis, *n.* Inflammation of the wind-pipe; কণ্ঠনালী প্রদাহ।

tră-chō'-mă, *n.* A granular condition of the mucous lining of the eye-lids; চক্ষুর শ্লৈষ্মিক আবরণে দানাদার অবস্থা, পোথকী (সাঃ পঃ)। **–chom'-a-tous,** *adj.*

tră'-chȳte, *n.* A rough volcanic-rock containing feldspar crystals; একপ্রকার খরস্পর্শ আগ্নেয়প্রস্তর। **–chyt'-ic,** *adj.*

trāc'-ing, *n.* **1.** Act of delineating or drawing in lines; অঙ্কন। **2.** An outline; নক্সা। **3.** A copy of a design or drawing made by following its lines through a transparent medium; উপরে তৈলাদিলিপ্ত স্বচ্ছ কাগজাদি রাখিয়া কোন বস্তুর চিত্রাঙ্কণ। **Tracing paper**—চিত্র, প্রতিলিপি, প্রভৃতি অঙ্কনের জন্য তৈলাদিলিপ্ত স্বচ্ছ কাগজ।

trăck, *n.* & *v. t.* **1.** A mark left by something that has passed; as, the *track* of a wheel; কোন কিছুর পশ্চাতে যে চিহ্ন রাখিয়া যায়। **2.** A mark or impression left by the foot, either of man or beast; footprints; মানুষ, পশু প্রভৃতির পদচিহ্ন; পদাঙ্ক, পদচিহ্ন। **3.** A course or way ; as, to follow a new *track* ; a beaten path; গমনপথ, রাস্তা; সচরাচর চলাচলের রাস্তা। **4.** Trace ; vestige ; চিহ্ন ; নিদর্শন। **5.** (*Fig.*) Course of life or routine ; as, a new *track* of life ; (লক্ষণায়) জীবনগতি, চিরাচরিতকার্য্যপরম্পরা। 6. (In railways) The permanent way ; (লৌহবর্ত্মের) স্থায়ীবর্ত্ম। ***Verb t.*** **1.** To follow when guided by a track or marks of the feet ; পদচিহ্নাদি ধরিয়া অনুসরণ করা। 2. To traverse ; as, to *track* a desert ; অতিক্রম করা, বিচরণ করা। 3. To make out by vestiges, ruins, etc. ; চিহ্ন, ধ্বংসাবশেষ, প্রভৃতির সাহায্যে নির্ণয় করা। 4. To draw or tow a vessel ; গুণ টানিয়া নৌকা চালান। **Track'-less,** *adj.* Having no track or footprint ; untrodden ; পদচিহ্নহীন ; পথহীন (বঃ বিযঃ)। **Track'-less-ly,** *adv.* **Track'-less-ness,** *n.* **Double track**—পরস্পরের পার্শ্ববর্ত্তী লৌহবর্ত্মযুগল। **Single track**—এক লৌহবর্ত্ম। **Track-boat**—যে নৌকা গুণদ্বারা টানা হইয়া থাকে, গুণের নৌকা। **Track-clearer**—সম্মুখে বা পশ্চাতে পথ পরিষ্কারের জন্য বাষ্পীয় শকট ; শস্যচ্ছেদক-যন্ত্র প্রভৃতিতে সংযুক্ত কৌশলবিশেষ। **Track-road**—গুণ-টানার রাস্তা। **In one's tracks**—(*Slang*) Just where one is standing ; then and there ; যেস্থানে কোন ব্যক্তি দণ্ডায়মান রহিয়াছে তথায় ; তখন তখন। **Off the track** — Off the roadway ; derailed ; পথচ্যুত ; বর্ত্মচ্যুত। Off the subject ; মূল বিষয় হইতে চ্যুত। **To make track for**—(*Slang*) To go towards ; to go in pursuit for ; কোন কিছুর অভিমুখে অগ্রসর হওয়া ; কোনকিছুর অনুসরণ করা। **To make tracks**—(*Slang*) To proceed ; to decamp ; (ইতরভাষায়) অগ্রসর হওয়া ; চম্পট দেওয়া।

track'-āge, *n.* **1.** Towage ; গুণ টানন। **2.** Railway tracks collectivety ; লৌহবর্ত্মসমুচ্চয়। **3.** A right to use tracks of another road ; অপর লৌহবর্ত্ম ব্যবহারের অধিকার।

trăct, *n.* **1.** A region or quantity of land or water, of indefinite extent ; ভূখণ্ড, অঞ্চল, প্রদেশ, ভূভাগ। 2. Extent ; বিস্তার। 3. (*Anat.*) A system or parts of an organ serving some particular purpose ; (শারীরসংস্থানবিদ্যা) কোন বিশেষ উদ্দেশ্য-সাধক শারীরিক যন্ত্রাংশ, স্নায়ুমণ্ডল প্রভৃতি।

trăct, *n.* 1. A short treatise esp. on religious subjects ; ধর্ম্মাদি সম্বন্ধীয় ক্ষুদ্র পুস্তিকা, চটী বই। 2. (*Rom. Cath. Church*) An anthem substituted between Septuagesima and Easter-eve for the Alleluia after the gradual ; (রোমান ক্যাথলিক ধর্ম্মসংঘ) স্তোত্র বিশেষ।

trăc'-tă-ble (-bl), *adj.* That may be easily led, managed or taught ; docile ; manageable ; capable of being handled ; pliant ; বশ্য, দম্য ; বশীভূত ; শাসনীয় ; ব্যবহার-যোগ্য ; প্রণেয়, বিনেয়। **—bil'-i-ty,** *n.* **—bly,** *adv.* **—ness,** *n.*

Trăc'-tā'-ri-ăn, *adj. & n.* Pertaining to the Tractarians or their doctrines; ধর্ম্মপুস্তিকাপ্রচারকসংঘসম্বন্ধীয়, উক্ত সংঘের মতসম্বন্ধীয়। ***Noun.*** One of the promoters or adherents of Tractarianism ; ধর্ম্মপুস্তিকা প্রচারক-সংঘের মতানুবর্ত্তী বা মত প্রচারকারী।

Trăc-tā'-ri-ăn-ism, *n.* Same as OXFORD MOVEMENT (which see).

trăc'-tāte, *n.* A treatise ; পুস্তিকা।

trăc'-tile, *adj.* Ductile ; প্রসারণীয়, প্রসার্য্য, তান্তব, বিস্তার্য্য।

trăc'-tion, *n.* 1. The act of drawing or the state of being drawn ; আকর্ষণ, টান, কর্ষণ (হিঃ কোঃ)। 2. The act of drawing a solid body along a plane ; সমতল স্থানের উপর দিয়া কোন সংহত বস্তু টানিয়া আকর্ষণ। 3. Contraction ; আকুঞ্চন। **—al,** *adj.* **—tive,** *adj.* **Traction-engine**—যে বাষ্পীয় যন্ত্র রাজপথের উপর দিয়া অতি গুরুভার মাল টানিয়া লয়। **Angle of traction**—যে সমতল স্থানের উপর দিয়া কোন বস্তু টানিয়া নেওয়া হয় এবং যে রেখায় আকর্ষণের বল ক্রিয়া করে—এতদুভয়ের সংযোগে উৎপন্ন কোণ। **Line of traction**—যে রেখাতে আকর্ষণের বল ক্রিয়া করে।

trāde, *n., v. i. & t.* 1. Business pursued ; occupation ; ব্যবসায় ; পেশা। 2. The business of exchanging commodities for other commodities or for money ; commerce ; ব্যবসায়, কারবার, তেজারতি ; বাণিজ্য। 3. The persons engaged in a trade ; as, a commission of 10 p.c. is allowed to the *trade* ; esp. those engaged in the book trade ; those engaged in the liquor trade ; কোন ব্যবসায়ে নিযুক্ত ব্যক্তিবর্গ ; পুস্তক ব্যবসায়িগণ ; সুরা-ব্যবসায়িগণ। 4. (*Dial.*) Medicine ; ঔষধ। 5. Same as TRADE-WINDS. ***Verb i.*** 1. To barter or to buy and sell ; ক্রয় বিক্রয় করা। 2. To be engaged in the selling or buying of goods etc. ; to carry on commerce ; ব্যবসায়ে নিযুক্ত হওয়া ; ব্যবসায় করা, বাণিজ্য করা। 3. To be concerned with ; "She *traded* more deeply in occult sciences" ; সংসৃষ্ট থাকা। ***Verb t.*** To sell or exchange in barter ; ব্যবসায় করা। **Trade-hall**—ব্যবসায়ী-দিগের সম্মিলন-গৃহ, বাণিজ্যমন্দির। **Trade-mark**—ব্যবসায়চিহ্ন। **Trade name**—যে নামে কোন জিনিষ ব্যবসায়ী মহলে অভিহিত হয় ; যে নামে কোন কোম্পানী ব্যবসায় করিয়া থাকে। **Trade price** — পাইকারী দাম। **Tradesman**—ব্যবসায়ী, দোকানদার। **Tradespeople** — ব্যবসায়ী লোক, কারবারী লোক। **Trade-union**—শ্রমজীবিগণের সাধারণ স্বার্থ এবং সুবিধা রক্ষার্থ এবং বেতন, কার্য্যের নির্দ্ধারিত কাল, প্রভৃতি বিষয়ে সুবিধাজনক অবস্থা প্রাপ্তির জন্য সংঘ বা সম্মিলনী, শ্রমজীবিসম্প্রদায়, ব্যাপারগুষ্ঠী (হিঃ কোঃ) ; কোন ব্যবসায়ে

নিযুক্ত ব্যক্তিগণের (যথা, কলের মালিকগণের কিম্বা মনীবগণ এবং শ্রমজীবিসমূহের সম্মেলন বিশেষ)। **Trade-unionist**—শ্রমজীবিসম্প্রদায়ের পক্ষপাতী ব্যক্তি। **Trade-wind**—বাণিজ্যবায়ু [অয়নান্তবৃত্ত এবং তৎসন্নিহিত প্রদেশে প্রবাহিত বায়ু।] **Board of Trade**—শাসনতন্ত্রের বিভাগবিশেষ। [এই বিভাগ রেলওয়ে, ট্রামওয়ে, পোতাশ্রয়, ওজন, প্রভৃতির উপর কর্তৃত্ব করিয়া থাকে।] **Carrying-trade**—জলপথে এক দেশ হইতে অপর দেশে মাল প্রেরণ। **Domestic** or **Home trade**—অন্তর্বাণিজ্য। **Jack of all trades**—See JACK. **The trade**—মদ্য বিক্রয়; মদ্যবিক্রয়ে নিযুক্ত ব্যক্তিবর্গ; পুস্তক ব্যবসায়িগণ। **To trade on** or **upon** — To take advantage on a person's good nature etc.; to make use of for one's own ends; কাহারো সরল প্রকৃতি প্রভৃতির সুবিধা নেওয়া; নিজের উদ্দেশ্য সিদ্ধির জন্য প্রয়োগ করা। **Trick of the trade**—ক্রেতা জুটাইবার কৌশল; প্রতিদ্বন্দ্বীর উপর সুবিধা লাভের উপায়।

trād'-ēr, *n.* 1. One engaged in trade or commerce; a merchant; ব্যবসায়ী; সওদাগর, বণিক। 2. A vessel engaged in trade; "A *trader* for new rivers"; বাণিজ্য-পোত।

trȧd'-ĭ'-tion, *n.* 1. Oral account handed down from father to son; কিম্বদন্তী, লোকশ্রুতি, জনশ্রুতি, পরম্পরাগত প্রবাদবাক্য, পরম্পরাগত কথা (হিঃ কোঃ), ঐতিহ্য। 2. A custom which has prevailed as from generation to generation; লোকপরম্পরাগত প্রথা, প্রথাগত নিয়ম। 3. A doctrine of divine authority orally delivered; আগম (বেদান্ত)। 4. Oral teachings of Christ not recorded in writing by immediate disciples; খৃষ্টের শ্রীমুখ নিঃসৃত যে সকল উপদেশ তদীয় শিষ্যগণ লিপিবদ্ধ করেন নাই। 5. Deeds and sayings of Mohammed not in Koran; মোহম্মদের যে উপদেশ এবং কার্য্যাবলীর বিষয় কোরাণে লিপিবদ্ধ হয় নাই। 6. (*Law*) The act of handing over something in a formal legal manner; (আইন) বিধিপূর্ব্বক কোন বস্তু হস্তান্তর করণ। 7. The transmission of events, doctrines, belief, rites, opinions, etc. from father to son through successive generations; পুরুষপরম্পরাক্রমে মত, বিশ্বাস, ক্রিয়া অনুষ্ঠান, প্রভৃতির সংক্রমণ। 8. The oral laws said to be given by God to Moses in Mount Sinai; সিনাই পর্ব্বতে ঈশ্বর মুসোর নিকট যে সকল ধর্ম্মবিধি প্রকাশিত করিয়াছিলেন। **—al,** *adj.* 1. Of, or pertaining to, traditions; transmitted from age to age without writing; কিম্বদন্তীসম্বন্ধীয়, কিম্বদন্তীমূলক; পরম্পরাগত, রূঢ়। 2. (*Rare*) Conventional; (ক্বচিদ্‌ব্যবহৃত) প্রথানুযায়ী, চিরাচরিত। **—al-ism,** *n.* 1. Adherence to tradition; পরম্পরাগত মত বা বিশ্বাস প্রভৃতিতে আনুরক্তি, ঐতিহ্যনিষ্ঠা। 2. The doctrine that our faith is to be based on, or regualated by, what we are told by competent authority exclusive of the exercise of reason; আমাদের মত ধর্ম্মাচার্য্যগণের উক্তির উপর প্রতিষ্ঠিত এবং তদ্দারা নিয়ন্ত্রিত হইবে—এই মত, ঐতিহ্যবাদ। **—al-ly,** *adv.* **—a-ry,** *adj.* **Tradition of a country**—পরম্পরাগত দেশধর্ম্ম। **Tradition of a nation**—পরম্পরাগত সনাতন জাতিধর্ম্ম। **Tradition of a race**—পরম্পরাগত সনাতন যুগধর্ম্ম।

trȧd'-ĭ-tŏr, *n.* An early Christian who delivered the Scriptures or the goods of their Church to their persecutors to save their lives; যে সকল প্রাচীন খৃষ্টান প্রাণভয়ে তাহাদের নির্যাতনকারিগণকে বাইবেল কিম্বা ধর্ম্মমন্দিরের জিনিষ পত্র প্রদান করিত।

trȧ-dūce', *v. t.* To speak falsely of; to caluminate; as, to *traduce* a reputation; মিথ্যাদোষারোপ করা; নিন্দা করা, কলঙ্ক রটনা করা, কুৎসা করা, অপবাদ করা। **—duc'-er, —ment,** *ns.*

trȧ-dū'-cĭ-ăn-ĭsm, *n.* The theory that souls are propagated in a similar way to the procreation of the body; দেহের মতই মনুষ্যের আত্মাও মাতাপিতা হইতে সংক্রমিত হয়—এইরূপ মতবাদ, জীবোৎপত্তিবাদ (হিঃ কোঃ), জীবসাদিত্ববাদ (ঐ)। **—an, —ist,** *ns.*

trȧ-dŭc'-tion, *n.* (*Log.*) Reasoning in which each conclusion applies to just such an object as each of the premises applies to; (তর্কবিজ্ঞান) একতাত্মক তর্ক (হিঃ কোঃ)।

trăf'-fic (-ĭk), *v. i., t.* & *n.* 1. To trade; ব্যবসায় করা। 2. To deal; কায কারবার করা। ***Verb t.*** To exchange in traffic; to barter; পণ্যদ্রব্য ক্রয় বিক্রয় করা; বিনিময় করা। ***Noun.*** 1. Trade; ব্যবসায়, বাণিজ্য। 2. Goods or persons passing along a road, railway, etc.; লৌহবর্ত্ম, রাজপথ, প্রভৃতিতে যে সকল লোক যাতায়াত বা মালপত্র চলাচল করে। 3. Dealing; কাযকারবার। **—fick'-er,** *n.* **—less,** *adj.*

trăg'-ȧ-cănth, *n.* 1. A plant of the genus astragalus; এক জাতীয় ক্ষুপ। 2. The concrete juice or gum of several species of shurbs or herbaceous plants, usually in the form of white or yellowish semi-transparent flakes, of great toughness; এক প্রকার গঁদ।

trȧ-gē'-dĭ-ăn, *n* (*Fem. tragedienne*) A writer or an actor of tragedy; বিয়োগান্ত নাট্যলেখক, বিয়োগান্ত নাটকের অভিনেতা।

trăg'-ĕ-dȳ, *n.* 1. A dramatic poem or stage-play representing an important event or a series of events, in which the diction is elevated and the catastrophe melancholy; বিয়োগান্তনাটক, দুঃখান্ত নাট্য, (হিঃ কোঃ) শোকান্ত নাট্য। 2. Any sad or dreadful event;

serious accident ; as, a *tragedy* happened in his family ; বিষাদজনক ঘটনা, শোকাবহ ব্যাপার, শোকজনক ব্যাপার, লোমহর্ষণ ব্যাপার ; গুরুতর দুর্ঘটনা। 3. (*Cap.*) Tragedy personified, or the Muse of Tragedy ; মূর্ত্তিমান শোকান্ত নাটক, শোকান্ত নাটকের অধিষ্ঠাত্রী বাগ্‌দেবী।

trăg′-ic, –i-căl, *adjs.* 1. Of, or relating to, tragedy ; বিয়োগান্ত নাটকসম্বন্ধীয়। 2. Mournful ; lamentable ; calamitous ; as, the *tragic* event happened in the month of February ; বিষাদজনক ; দুঃখময়, শোকাবহ, শোচনীয় ; বিপজ্জনক। **–i-cal-ly,** *adv.* **–ness,** *n.*

trăg-i-cŏm′-ē-dў, *n.* A drama in which comic and tragic elements are blended ; হর্ষবিষাদাত্মক নাটক। **–com′-ic,** *adj.* **–com′-i-cal-ly,** *adv.*

trăg′-ō-păn, *n.* A beautiful crested Eastern bird, resembling a pheasant ; একপ্রকার পক্ষী।

trail (trāl), *n., v. t.* & *i.* 1. The track followed by the hunter ; পলায়িত জন্তুর পদচিহ্ন বা গন্ধ [যদ্দ্বারা শিকারীগণ শিকারের অনুসরণ করে।] 2. A long appendage in rear of something ; কোন কিছুর পশ্চাতে লম্বিত লাঙ্গুলের মত বস্তু। 3. The end of field-gun carriage that rests on the ground in firing ; ময়দানী কামানের পশ্চাদ্দিকস্থ যে অংশ কামানদাগার কালে ভূমিতে অবলম্বিত থাকে। 4. Anything drawn behind in long undulations ; পশ্চাদ্দিকে যে দীর্ঘ বস্তু টানিয়া নেওয়া হয়। 5. Beaten path ; সচরাচর চলাচলের রাস্তা। ***Verb t.*** 1. To draw along or behind one, esp. on the ground ; টানিয়া নেওয়া, মাটির উপর টানিয়া নেওয়া। 2. To hunt by the track or trail ; পলায়িত জন্তুর পদচিহ্ন বা গন্ধদ্বারা শিকার করা। 3. To tread down in a line or path, as grass ; (ঘাস) পায়ে মাড়াইয়া পথ করা। ***Verb i.*** 1. To be drawn along behind; পশ্চাদ্দিকে মাটির সহিত লুটাইয়া নেওয়া। 2. To hang loosly ; কোন কিছু হইতে দোলায়িত হওয়া। 3. To run along or climb ; লতাইয়া উঠা, লতাইয়া যাওয়া। **Trail-net**—Same as DRAG-NET. **Trailing-wheel**—শকটের পশ্চাদ্দিকের অন্যতর চক্র। **To trail arms** — হস্তে রাইফেল বন্দুক রাখিয়া ভূমির সহিত সমান্তরাল ভাবে দোলান।

trail′-ĕr (trāl-), *n.* 1. One that or that which trails ; পলায়িত জন্তুর পদচিহ্ন প্রভৃতি দ্বারা অনুসরণকারী। 2. A creeper ; লতা, ব্রততী, বল্লরী। 3. A light two-wheeled car or a wheeled-chair drawn by a bicycle, tricycle, etc. ; দ্বিচক্রযান, ত্রিচক্রযান, প্রভৃতি দ্বারা যে হালকা দুই চাকার গাড়ী বা চাকাওয়ালা কেদারা টানা হয়। 4. The tramcar which is drawn by another tramcar ; যে ট্রাম গাড়ী দ্বারা অপর ট্রাম গাড়ী টানা হয়।

train (trān), *v. t., i.* & *n.* 1. To draw along ; টানিয়া নেওয়া। 2. To bring up ; to teach ; শিক্ষিত করা ; শিক্ষা দেওয়া। 3. To break, tame and render docile ; to render able to perform certain feats ; সার করা, বশ করা ; ক্রীড়া প্রভৃতি শিক্ষা দেওয়া। 4. (*Colloq.*) To carry in a train of cars ; শকটশ্রেণীতে নেওয়া। 5. To form by growth, lopping or pruning ; as, to *train* a plant ; বৃক্ষকে কাঁটিয়া ছাঁটিয়া বা বিশেষভাবে গড়িতে দিয়া কোন নির্দ্দিষ্ট আকৃতিতে গঠন করা। 6. To aim or point at an object ; as, to *train* a cannon on the enemy ; কোন কিছুর দিকে লক্ষ্য বা নিশান করা। ***Verb i.*** 1. To travel by train ; ট্রেণে ভ্রমণ করা। 2. To drill or teach ; শিক্ষিত করা, সার করা। ***Noun.*** 1. A thing drawn along, behind or forming hinder part, esp. elongated part of a woman's skirt trailing on ground ; যে বস্তু পশ্চাতে টানিয়া নেওয়া হয়, কোন বস্তুর পশ্চাদংশ, স্ত্রীলোকের ঘাগরার যে অংশ মাটিতে লুটাইয়া যায়। 2. A retinue ; সহযায়িবর্গ, অনুযায়িবর্গ, দলবল। 3. A trail or tail, as of a meteor ; উল্কা প্রভৃতির পুচ্ছ। 4. A procession ; শোভাযাত্রা, লোকযাত্রা। 5. A continuous line of railway carriages with the engine ; বাষ্পীয়শকট, ট্রেণ। 6. A series ; শ্রেণীপরম্পরা। 7. Something used to allure and entice ; an artifice ; a device ; প্রলোভনজনক বস্তু ; চাতুরী, ফিকির, ফন্দী ; কল, কৌশল। 8. A line of combustible material to lead fire to a charge or mine ; বারুদে বা বারুদ প্রভৃতি পূর্ণ সুড়ঙ্গে অগ্নি চালিত করার জন্য দাহ্য বস্তুর পংক্তি। 9. (*Rare*) Regular method ; course ; (অপ্রঃ) সুশৃঙ্খলতা ; গতি। 9. The long tail of a bird ; পক্ষীর দীর্ঘ পুচ্ছ। 10. A set of wheels, or wheels and pinions in series, through which motion is transmitted in regular consecution ; as, the *train* of a watch ; চক্রপরম্পরা। **Train′-a-ble,** *adj.* **Train-band**—(ইংলণ্ডের ইতিহাস) লণ্ডননগরীর নাগরিক সৈন্যদলের অন্যতম বাহিনী। **Train-bearer**—যে ব্যক্তি মহিলাদিগের ঘাগরার আঁচল বহিয়া চলে। **Train-man**—Same as BRAKESMAN. **Train-mile**—এক ট্রেন কর্ত্তৃক অতিক্রান্ত এক মাইল স্থান। [রেলওয়ের হিসাবে কার্য্যের এককস্বরূপ ব্যবহৃত হয়।] **Train-oil** — তিমি মৎস্যের তৈল। **In the train**—Following someone ; পশ্চাদ্‌গামী। **To bring in its train**—To bring in company ; সঙ্গে আনা। **To train off**—To swerve ; (কামানের গোলা সম্পর্কে) গতিপথচ্যুত হওয়া।

train′-ĕr (trān-), *n.* One that trains, esp. one that prepares man for athletic exercises, or horses for the race ; শিক্ষাদাতা,

শিক্ষক, বিশেষতঃ যে ব্যক্তি লোকদিগকে মল্লক্রীড়ার জন্য এবং অশ্বদিগকে দৌড়ের নিমিত্ত শিক্ষা দেয়।

train'-ing (trān-), *n.* & *adj.* **1.** The act or one who trains; education; drill; শিক্ষাদান; শিক্ষা; কসরৎ। **2.** The art or operation of forming young trees to grow in a particular direction or shape; তরুণ বৃক্ষাদিকে কোন বিশেষ দিকে বা বিশেষ আকৃতিতে গঠন বা চালনার কলা বা প্রণালী। **3.** The act of disciplining troops; সৈন্যদিগকে শিক্ষাদান। **4.** The state of being in a fit condition for undertaking some feat requiring physical exertion; শারীরীক শক্তি-প্রয়োগের আবশ্যক এমন কোন বিশেষ কার্য্য সাধনের উপযোগী দৈহিক অবস্থা। ***Adj.*** Educating; শিক্ষাপ্রদায়ক। **Training-bit, Training-gag**—দুষ্ট অশ্বের জন্য খলীন বা মুখরোধক। **Training-school, Training-college**—শিক্ষকদিগের জন্য বিদ্যালয় বা মহাবিদ্যালয়। **Training-ship** — যে পোতে যুবকগণ পোতচালনাবিদ্যায় শিক্ষাপ্রাপ্ত হয়।

trait (trāt), *n.* **1.** A distinguishing feature or quality of mind or character; peculiarity; বিশেষ গুণ, বিশেষলক্ষণ, বিশেষ প্রকৃতি; বিশেষত্ব, বৈশিষ্ট্য,অনুভাব (হিঃ কোঃ)। **2.** Touch; আমেজ, নেশা।

trai'-tor (trā-têr), One who violates his allegiance and acts disloyally to his country, king, party or cause; দেশদ্রোহী, রাজদ্রোহী, স্বপক্ষত্যাগী, স্বজাতিদ্রোহী। **—ous,** *adj.* **—ous-ly,** *adv.* **—tress,** *n.* (*Fem.*)

trā-jĕc'-tō-rȳ *n.* **1.** The path described by a body, as a planet, projectile, etc.; গ্রহ, ধূমকেতু, গোলা, প্রভৃতির গতিপথস্বরূপ বক্ররেখা, বিক্ষেপ-মার্গ। **2.** (*Geom.*) A curve or surface which cuts all the curves or surfaces of a given system at a constan t angle; (জ্যামিতি) যে বক্র বা ধরাতল কোন নির্দ্দিষ্ট শ্রেণীর বক্র বা ধরাতল সমূহকে স্থির কোণ উৎপাদন-পূর্ব্বক ছেদন করে।

trăm, *n.*, *v. i.* & *t.* **1.** A public conveyance running on rails laid on street and moved by horses, cable traction, steam or electric power; একপ্রকার যান—যাহা রাজপথে নিহিত লৌহবর্ত্মোপোরি বাষ্পতাড়িতাদির বলে চালিত হয়, ট্রামগাড়ী। **2.** One of such rails; ট্রামের রাস্তার পাতাবেল। **3.** Line consisting of such rails (also *Tramway*); ট্রামের লাইন। **4.** A coal-wagon (in pits) running on rails; একপ্রকার কয়লার গাড়ী—যাহা পাতারেলের উপর চলিয়া থাকে। ***Verb i.*** To travel in a tram-car; ট্রামগাড়ীতে চলা। ***Verb t.*** To convey in a tram; ট্রাম গাড়ীতে বহিয়া লইয়া যাওয়া। **Tram-car**—See TRAM *n.* I. **Tram-road**—কাষ্ঠ, শিলা প্রভৃতি দ্বারা আচ্ছাদিত ট্রাম প্রভৃতির রাস্তা

trăm, *n.* A kind of silk-thread; একপ্রকার পট্টসূত্র।

trăm'-mĕl, *n.* & *v. t.* **1.** A net for birds or fishes; জাল। **2.** Shackles, esp. one used in regulating the motion of a horse; নিগড়, পদশৃঙ্খল, বিশেষতঃ অশ্বের গতি-নিয়মনের জন্য যে নিগড় ব্যবহৃত হয়। **3.** An instrument for drawing ellipse; বৃত্তাভাস অঙ্কনের জন্য যন্ত্র-বিশেষ। **4.** A beam compass; একপ্রকার কম্পাস। **5.** Obstacles; check; "They disdain the *trammels* of any sordid contract"; বাধা, বিঘ্ন, আটক; অন্তরায়। ***Verb t.*** To shackle; to hamper; শৃঙ্খলিত করা, নিগড়িত করা; বাধা দেওয়া, প্রতিবন্ধকতা জন্মান, রোধ করা। **—meled, melled,** *p. p.* **1.** Shackled; নিগড়বদ্ধ, শৃঙ্খলিত, নিগড়িত। **2.** (Of a horse) Havinng white marks on the forefoot and hind foot of one side; (অশ্ব-সম্পর্কে) একদিকের অগ্র ও পশ্চাদ্দিকের পদে শ্বেতচিহ্নবিশিষ্ট। **Cros trammelled**—(অশ্বসম্পর্কে) বিভিন্ন দিকের সম্মুখের ও পশ্চাতের পদদ্বয়ে শ্বেতচিহ্নবিশিষ্ট।

trā-mŏn-tā'-nă, *n.* **1.** North wind in the Mediterranean; ভূমধ্যসাগরের উত্তর বায়ু। **2.** A cold blighting wind in the Archipelago; ভূমধ্য-সাগরের দ্বীপপুঞ্জের একপ্রকার অতি শীতল কনকনে বাতাস।

tră-mŏn'-tāne, *adj.* Lying on the other side of the Alps; hence foreign; আল্পস্ পর্ব্বতের অপর পার্শ্ববর্ত্তী; বিদেশীয়, বৈদেশিক।

trămp, *v. i.*, *t.* & *n.* **1.** To tread heavily; ধুপ ধাপ করিয়া চলা। **2.** To travel; to wander; ভ্রমণ করা; পর্য্যটন করা। ***Verb t.*** **1.** To tread under foot; পদদলিত করা, পদপিষ্ঠ করা। **2.** To travel through on foot; কোন কিছুর উপর দিয়া পদব্রজে গমন করা। ***Noun.*** **1.** The sound of tramping; the sound of horse's step; পদধ্বনি; অশ্বখুরোথ শব্দ। **2.** A foot journey; as, to go on a *tramp*; পদব্রজে ভ্রমণ। **3.** A stroller; a vagabond; যে ব্যক্তি পদব্রজে ঘুরিয়া বেড়ায়; ভবঘুরে, টৌটো-বাজ, সঞ্চারজীবী। **4.** A vessel that takes a cargo wherever the shippers desire; যে জাহাজ যথা তথা মাল লইয়া, যাতায়াত করে। **5.** An iron sole piece to protect the foot and the shoe from injury when digging; খননকালে পদ এবং পাদুকাতে যাহাতে আঘাত না লাগে তজ্জন্য পাদুকার নীচে যে লৌহপট্ট লাগান হয়। **6.** A tool for trimming hedges; বেড়া ছাঁটিবার জন্য যন্ত্রবিশেষ। **Tramp-pick**—কঠিনমৃত্তিকা উল্টাইবার জন্য দণ্ড যন্ত্র।

trăm'-ple (-pl), *v. t.*, *i.* & *n.* **1.** To tread under foot; to crush by treading; পদদলিত করা, পদমর্দ্দিত করা; পদপিষ্ঠ করা। ***Verb i.*** **1.** To tread in contempt; পদদলিত করা, পায়ে মাড়ান। **2.** To act insultingly; অবজ্ঞতার সহিত ব্যবহার করা।

Noun. Act or sound of trampling; পদদলন, পদমর্দ্দন, পদদলনশব্দ। **—pler,** *n.*

trăn, *pref.* Same as TRANS.

trance (trăns), *n.* & *v. t.* **1.** A state in which the soul is as it were absent from the body, or is rapt in vision and insensible to outward things; সমাধি (হিঃ কোঃ), ভাবসমাধি, ভাবাবেশ। **2.** A prolonged or abnormal sleep due to hypnotism or hysteria; যোগনিদ্রা। **3.** A state of insensibility; a swoon; সংজ্ঞাহীনতা, মূর্চ্ছা, অচৈতন্য। **4.** (*Med.*) Same as CATALEPSY. ***Verb t.*** To entrance; to enchant; ভাবাবিষ্ট করা; সম্মোহিত করা, বিমুগ্ধ করা, বিমূঢ় করা, বিমোহিত করা।

trăn'-quil, *adj.* Calm; serene; not agitated; as, to *tranquil* one's mind; শান্ত; প্রশান্ত; অবিক্ষুব্ধ, বিশ্রব্ধ, স্তিমিত, স্থির, সুস্থির। **—li-za'-tion,** *n.* **—lize,** *v. t.* To make tranquil; শান্ত করা, প্রশান্ত করা, সুস্থির করা। **—liz-er,** *n.* **—liz-ing,** *adj.* **—liz-ing-ly,** *adv.* **—quil'-li-ty,** *n.* State of being tranquil; calmness; peace; শান্তভাব, প্রশান্তি; অবিক্ষুব্ধতা, স্থৈর্য্য, নিরুদ্বেগ, উদ্বেগশূন্যতা; শান্তি।

trăns—, *pref.* On the other side of; beyond; অপর পার্শ্ববর্ত্তী; অতি, অন্তর। **Trans-frontier**—সীমান্তের অপর পার্শ্ববর্ত্তী। **Trans-Gangetic**—গঙ্গানদীর অপর পার্শ্ববর্ত্তী।

trăns-ăct', *v. t.* To carry through; to perform; to manage; সম্পাদন করা; সম্পন্ন করা, নিষ্পাদন করা, নির্ব্বাহ করা; পরিচালনা করা।

trăns-ăc'-tion, *n.* **1.** Management of any affair; as, *transaction* of a business; নির্ব্বাহ, সম্পাদন, পরিচালনা। **2.** An affair; ব্যাপার, বিষয়, কার্য্য, সম্পাদিত ব্যবহার (কৌটিল্য:)। **3.** Reports of proceedings of societies; as, the *Trasactions* of the Royal Society; বৈজ্ঞানিক সমিতি বা পরিষৎ প্রভৃতির আলোচনা, বক্তৃতা বা পঠিত প্রবন্ধাদির বিবরণী। **4.** (*Law*) An adjustment of dispute between parties by mutual agreement; উভয় পক্ষের সম্মতি অনুসারে বিবাদ নিষ্পত্তি, রফা, আপোষ।

trăns-ăl'-pīne, *adj.* & *n.* On the other side of the Alps (esp. from Italy); আল্পস্ পর্ব্বতের অপর পার্শ্ববর্ত্তী (বিশেষতঃ ইতালীদেশ হইতে)। ***Noun.*** A person living in a country beyond the Alps; আল্পস্ পর্ব্বতের অপর পার্শ্ববর্ত্তী দেশবাসী লোক।

trăns-ăt-lăn'-tic, *adj.* **1.** Beyond the Atlantic Ocean; অতলান্তিক মহাসাগরের অপর পারবর্ত্তী। **2.** Crossing or across the Atlantic; as, a *transatlantic* liner: a *transatlantic* cable; অতলান্তিক মহাসাগর অতিক্রমকারী, অতলান্তিক মহাসাগরের মধ্য দিয়া নীত।

trăns-scend' (-sĕnd), *v.t.* & *i.* **1.** To pass over; to go beyond; অতিক্রম করা; অতীত হওয়া। **2.** To surpass; to excel; অতিক্রম করা, ছাড়াইয়া যাওয়া; শ্রেষ্ঠতায় বা উৎকর্ষে অতিক্রম করা। ***Verb i.*** To excel; শ্রেষ্ঠতায় অতিক্রম করা।

trăn-scend'-ĕnt (-sĕnd-), *adj.* & *n.* **1.** Superior or supreme in excellence; surpassing all others; পরমোৎকৃষ্ট, শ্রেষ্ঠতম, সর্ব্বোৎকৃষ্ট; সর্ব্বাতিশায়ী, সর্ব্বাতিক্রমী, পরমোত্তম (হিঃ কোঃ)। **2.** (*Kant*) Reaching beyond the limits of human experience; "But another road leads to the same *transcendent* question—*transcendent* because they treat the forms of human thought not merely as logically antecedent to the products of experience, but because they apply these forms, to problems where experience requires data"; (ক্যান্টের মতে) অতীন্দ্রিয় (ব্রজঃ হিন্দুঃ), ইন্দ্রিয়াতীত, অতীত (হিঃ কোঃ), সর্ব্বাতীত (ঐ), অতীতাত্মক (ঐ), অতিসর্ব্ব (ঐ), পরা। **3.** (Esp. of God) Existing apart from, not subject to, the limitations of the physical world; (ঈশ্বরসম্বন্ধে) নিগুর্ণ। **4.** An expression employed by the schoolmen to mark a term or notion which rose above and thus included the catagories of Aristotle; মধ্যযুগের খৃষ্টীয় দার্শনিকগণ কর্ত্তৃক ব্যবহৃত আরিস্তোতলের পদার্থের (see *category*) অপেক্ষা অধিকতর ব্যাপকবিষয়সূচক। ***Noun.*** **1.** Very excellent thing; পরমোত্তম বস্তু, পরমশ্রেষ্ঠ বস্তু। **2.** A transcendent thing; a transcendent concept; অতীন্দ্রিয় বিষয়; অতীন্দ্রিয় ধারণা, স্বরূপ বস্তু। **—ence, —en-cy,** *ns.* **—ly,** *adv.*

trăn-scen-dĕn'-tăl (-sĕn-), *adj.* **1.** Supereminent পরমোত্তম, পরমোৎকৃষ্ট, পরমশ্রেষ্ঠ। **2.** A term used by the schoolmen in the same sense as TRANSCENDENT, *adj.* 4. **3.** (In the Kantian Philosophy) Intuitive; a priori; সহজাত; সাক্ষাৎ, অপরোক্ষ। **4.** Transcending the ordinary range of cognition or perception; অতীন্দ্রিয়, অতীতাত্মক. পরা, নিগুর্ণ, তুরীয়, চিৎস্বরূপ, কুটস্থ। **5.** Abstrusely speculative; vague; as, a *transcendental* style of writing; জটিল; অস্পষ্ট। **6.** (*Math.*) Applied to any quantity which cannot be represented by an algebraic expression of a finite number of terms; (গণিত) কোন নির্দ্দিষ্ট সংখ্যক পদবিশিষ্ট বীজগণিতের রাশিদ্বারা অনির্দ্দেশ্য, অরূপ। **7.** Propounding the theory that matter is a product of the mind; জড় চিৎএর ক্রিয়া হইতে প্রসূত—এই মতবাদ প্রচারক, চিদৈকবাদী। **—ly,** *adv.* **Transcendental aesthetics** — Kantএর "Critique of Pure Reason" নামক গ্রন্থের প্রথম অংশ—যাহাতে কোন বস্তুর সমবধারণের

(perception) জন্ম দেশ এবং কাল একান্ত অপরিহার্য্য—এই বিষয় আলোচিত হইয়াছে, পরাবিজ্ঞান। **Transcendental analytic**—উক্তগ্রন্থের দ্বিতীয় অংশ—যাহাতে কোন বিষয়ের সমবধারণের (perception) পক্ষে পদার্থসমূহের (categories) অপরিহার্য্যতা সম্বন্ধে আলোচিত হইয়াছে। (See KANT'S CATEGORIES under CATEGORY.) **Transcendental cognition**—পরাজ্ঞান, সহজজ্ঞান, অতীন্দ্রিয়জ্ঞান। **Transcendental consciousness**—কূটস্থ-চৈতন্য (ব্রজঃ হিন্দুঃ), স্বয়ম্প্রভাসম্বিৎ (cf. নোদেতি নাস্তমেত্যেকা সম্বিৎস্বয়ম্প্রভা—পঞ্চদশী)। **Transcendental curve**—যে বক্রের সমীকরণ সমূহে অরূপফল (transcendental functions) রহিয়াছে। **Transcendental equation**—অরূপ সমীকরণ। **Transcendental functions**—যে ফল (function) কোন নির্দ্দিষ্ট সংখ্যক চলের (variable) উপর কোন নির্দ্দিষ্ট সংখ্যক বীজগণিতের প্রক্রিয়া দ্বারা ব্যক্ত করা যায় না, অরূপফল, অব্যক্তফল। **Transcendental idealism**—ক্যাণ্টের পরাতত্ত্ব। ক্যাণ্টের মতে দেশ, কাল এবং পদার্থসমূহ (categories) আমাদের মানসিক ব্যবস্থার সহিত পূর্ব্ব হইতে অনুস্যূত রহিয়াছে কোনরূপ অনুভব (experience) হইতে জাত হয় নাই, তুরীয়বিজ্ঞান। **Transcendental object**—বস্তুর ইন্দ্রিয়াতীত (অজ্ঞাত এবং অজ্ঞেয়) রূপ, পরাবস্তু, স্বরূপবস্তু। **Transcendental philosophy**—ক্যাণ্টের দর্শন্। **Transcendental reality**—প্রত্যক্ষীভূত জগদ্ব্যাপারের ইন্দ্রিয়াতীত সত্তার অবস্থা, স্বরূপাবস্থা। **Transcendental school**—আমেরিকা ও New England নামক স্থানের দার্শনিক সম্প্রদায় বিশেষ। Ralph Waldo Emerson এই সম্প্রদায়ের নেতা ছিলেন। Alcott, Thoreau, Ripley এবং Margaret Fuller এই সমিতির প্রধান ছিলেন, পরাতন্ত্র। **Transcendental unity of apperception**—বিষয়ীর আত্মবোধ (apperception) দ্বারা জ্ঞানের উপাদান সমূহের ঐক্য, [অনুভবের (experience) অঙ্গসমূহের (elements) ঐক্য বিষয়ীর (ego) সংশ্লেষণ ক্রিয়া (synthetic act) দ্বারা সম্পাদিত হইয়া থাকে] অন্তর্ব্বোধের তুরীয় ঐক্য। **Conception of transcendental object**—পরমার্থতত্ত্ব (দ্বিজেন্দ্র)।

trăn-scen-dĕn'-tăl-ĭsm (-sŏn-), *n.* **1.** The philosophy dealing with the principle going beyond the empiricism, and ascertaining the fundamental *a priori* principles that are regulative and constitutive of the form of perception and thought; প্রত্যক্ষীভূত জাগতিক ও মানসিক ব্যাপারের মূলে যে নিত্যসিদ্ধ মূলতত্ত্বসমূহ রহিয়াছে—তৎসম্বন্ধীয় দর্শন, তুরীয়দর্শন, তুরীয়তত্ত্ব। **2.** (Hegel and Schelling) The philosophical theory which asserts the absoulte identity of the subject and the object; জ্ঞাতা ও জ্ঞেয়ের পরম অভিন্নত্ব জ্ঞাপক দার্শনিক মতবাদ বিশেষ, অতীতবাদ (হিঃ কোঃ), অতীতদর্শন (ঐ)। **3.** (*Theol.*) A theological theory propounded by Emerson which asserts the idea of supersensuous religious consciousness, an intuitive perception of divine truth, as opposed to dogmatic rationalism; ইমার্সান্ কর্ত্তৃক প্রবর্ত্তিত ধর্ম্মসম্বন্ধীয় অতীন্দ্রিয় অনুভূতি এবং ঐশ্বরিক তত্ত্বসম্বন্ধে অপরোক্ষ জ্ঞানলাভমূলক ধর্ম্মমত, পরাতত্ত্ব।

trăns-cŏn-tĭ-nĕn'-tăl, *adj.* Beyond the continent (of Europe, esp. as visited by ordinary travellers or tourists); extending across a continent; as, *transcontinental* railway; মহাদেশের অপর পার্শ্ববর্ত্তী; মহাদেশেরএকপ্রান্ত হইতে অপরপ্রান্তব্যাপী।

trăn-scrībe', *v. t.* To copy; নকল করা, প্রতিলিপি প্রস্তুত করা। **—scrib'-er,** *n.* A copyist; প্রতিলিপিকারক। **—scrip'-tion,** *n.* **1.** The act of transcribing or copying; নকলকরণ। **2.** A copy; নকল, প্রতিলিপি। **—scrip'-tion-al, —scrip'-tive,** *adjs.*

trăn'-script, *n.* A written copy; নকল, প্রতিলিপি।

trăns-cŭr'-rĕnt, *adj.* Passing in cross direction; set crosswise; ব্যত্যস্তগামী; ব্যত্যস্তভাবে নিবদ্ধ।

trăn-sĕct', *v. t.* To cut across or transversely; আড়ভাবে কাটা, ব্যত্যস্তভাবে ছেদন করা। **—sec'-tion,** *n.*

trăn-sĕn'-nă, *n.* A kind of carved lattice-work or gratings of marble, silver, etc. used to shut in the shrines of the martyrs; ধর্ম্মার্থে আত্মোৎসর্গকারী ব্যক্তিগণের স্মৃতিচিহ্ন যে আধারে রক্ষিত হয়—তাহার আবরণস্বরূপ মার্ব্বেল পাথর বা রূপার জাফরি বা জালি।

trăn'-sĕpt, *n.* That portion of a church built in the form of a cross which projects externally on each side so as to form the short arm of the cross; ক্রুশ বা ঢেড়ার আকৃতি গির্জ্জার বাহুদ্বয়ের অন্যতর।

trăns-fêr', *v. t.* **1.** To convey from one place or person to another; স্থানান্তরিত করা, বদলী করা। **2.** To convey, as a right from one person to another; to sell; হস্তান্তর করা; বিক্রয় করা। **3.** To produce a facsimile of, on a prepared stone by means of a prepared paper and ink; লিথো প্রভৃতি মুদ্রিত করা। **—a-ble,** *adj.* Capable of being transferred; হস্তান্তরযোগ্য। **—ee',** *n.* The person to whom a transfer is made; যে ব্যক্তির নিকট কোন কিছু হস্তান্তরিত করা হয়, প্রাপক।

trăns'-fêr, *n.* **1.** The removal or conveyance of a person or thing from one place or person to another; স্থানান্তর, বদলী, পরিবৃত্তি (হিঃ কোঃ), সংক্রমণ (ঐ), স্থানান্তরপ্রাপ্তি (ঐ)। **2.** The conveyance of a right, title or property, either real or personal from one person to another, either by sale, gift or otherwise; হস্তান্তর। **3.** That which is transferred; স্থানান্তরিত বস্তু। **4.** A picture or design drawn or printed with a special ink on specially prepared paper, and then transferred to the surface of a stone and from which the duplicates are obtained by printing ; লিথো প্রেস হইতে মুদ্রিত ছবি, নক্সা, প্রভৃতি। 5. (*Mil.*) A soldier transferred from one troop or company to another ; (সামরিকশাস্ত্র) এক সৈন্যদল হইতে অপর সৈন্যদলে স্থানান্তরিত সৈন্য। 6. Same as TRANSFER-PICTURE. 7. A document effecting transfer ; হস্তান্তরপত্র। **Transfer-book**—সম্পত্তি, কোম্পানীর অংশ প্রভৃতির হস্তান্তরের বিষয় যে খাতায় লিখিত হয়, হস্তান্তরবহি। **Transfer-certificate** — কোন বিদ্যালয় পরিত্যাগের নিদর্শনপত্র। **Transfer-days**—ব্যাঙ্ক অব ইংলণ্ডে যে যে দিবস (শনি ও রবিবার ব্যতীত) বিনা ব্যয়ে কোম্পানীর কাগজ হস্তান্তরিত করা যায়। **Transfer-ink**—শিলাফলকে বা পরিবর্ত্তককাগজে লিখিবার উপযোগী কালি, পরিবর্ত্তককালি। **Transfer-paper**—রাসায়নিকদ্রব্য-লিপ্ত কাগজ বিশেষ—ঐ কাগজে পরিবর্ত্তক কালি দ্বারা লিখিত বিষয় অন্য কাগজে বা শিলাফলকে স্থানান্তরিত করিতে পারা যায়, পরিবর্ত্তক-কাগজ। **Transfer-picture**—জল ছবি।

trăns'-fêr-ence (-ĕns), *n.* The act of conveying from one place, person or thing to another ; স্থানান্তর, হস্তান্তর।

trăns-fig-ū-ra'-tion, *n.* 1. A change of form ; esp. the supernatural change of Christ on the mount ; রূপান্তর, রূপান্তরপরিগ্রহ ; বিশেষতঃ যীশুখৃষ্টের অলৌকিক জ্যোতির্ম্ময় দেবদেহ ধারণ, (বাইবেলের মতে তখন—"His face did shine as the sun and his raiment was as while as the light"), মহাপ্রকাশ (চৈতন্য-ভাগবত) [cf. শ্রীবাসভবনে গৌরাঙ্গের এইরূপ দেহপরিবর্ত্তনের কথা চৈতন্যভাগবতে বর্ণিত হইয়াছে। যথা—"আর সবদিনে প্রভু ভাব প্রকাশিয়া। বৈসেন বিষ্ণুর খাটে যেন না জানিয়া॥ সাত প্রহরিয়া ভাবে ছাড়ি সর্ব্বমায়া। বসিলা প্রহর সাত প্রভু ব্যক্ত হইয়া॥ যোড় হস্তে সম্মুখে সকল ভক্তগণ। রহিলেন পরম আনন্দযুক্ত মন।। কি অদ্ভুত সন্তোষের হইল প্রকাশ। সবেই বলেন যেন বৈকুণ্ঠে নিবাস॥—চৈতন্য ভাগবত। এই সম্বন্ধে গোবিন্দ দাসের একটী সুন্দর পদাবলী আছে। শ্রীবাসপণ্ডিত গেহে, রত্নাসনে শ্রীগৌর শোহে। বপু সঙ্গে জ্যোতিঃ নিকষয়ে কত। জনু উদয় ভেল ভানু শতশত"]। 2. A feast held on the 6th of August in commemoration of the above event ; উক্ত ঘটনার স্মরণভোজ বিশেষ।

trăns-fig'-ūre, *v. t.* 1. To change in form ; to assume a supernatural form ; রূপ পরিবর্ত্তন করা ; অলৌকিক রূপ পরিগ্রহ করান। 2. To change to something very elevated and glorious ; "Jesus was *transfigured* before them" ; মহিমোজ্জ্বল করা, গৌরবোজ্জ্বল করা, দিব্য-দীপ্তি বিভাসিত করা, গৌরববিমণ্ডিত করা।

trăns-fix', *v. t.* To pierce through as with a pointed weapon ; ভেদ করা, এফোঁড় ওফোঁড় করিয়া ভেদ করা।

trăns-fix'-ion (-fĭk-shŭn), *n.* 1. The act of piercing through ; এফোঁড় ওফোঁড় করিয়া ভেদ করণ, ভেদ। 2. (*Surg.*) Amputation by piercing transversely and cutting outwards ; (অস্ত্রোপচারবিদ্যা) ব্যত্যস্তভাবে ছেদন।

trăns'-flū-ĕnt, *adj.* Flowing or running across or through ; পরিস্রাবী।

trăns-fŏrm', *v. t.* 1. To change the shape, appearance or form of ; রূপ পরিবর্ত্তন করা রূপান্তরিত করা, বাহ্যাকার পরিবর্ত্তন করা, রূপান্তর করা, অন্যরূপ করা। 2. To change into another substance ; ভিন্ন বস্তুতে পরিবর্ত্তন করা। 3. (*Math.*) To change the form of ; (গণিতশাস্ত্র) রূপান্তর করা, আকার পরিবর্ত্তন করা। **—a-ble,** *adj.* **—a-tive,** *adj.*

trăns-fŏr-mā'-tion, *n.* 1. The act of transforming ; রূপান্তরীকরণ, পরিবর্ত্তন, রূপান্তর, আকারপরিবর্ত্তন, পরিণতি। 2. The new form assumed ; নববিগ্রহ, নবরূপ। 3. (*Zool.*) Metamorphosis ; (জন্তুবিদ্যা) রূপান্তর। 4. (*Alchemy*) Same as TRANSMUTATION. 5. (*Math.*) Change from one figure or expression to another equal in quality ; (গণিত-শাস্ত্র) এক অঙ্ক বা রাশি হইতে সমগুণসম্পন্ন অপর অঙ্ক বা রাশিতে পরিবর্ত্তন। 6. (*Physiol.*) The change which takes place in the blood in its passage from the arterial to the venous system ; (শারীর-বিজ্ঞান) ধমনী হইতে সঞ্চারকালে রক্তের যে পরিবর্ত্তন হয়। 7. Same as TRANSMUTATION. **Transformation-scene**—(রঙ্গমঞ্চে) যে নাটকীয় দৃশ্য দর্শকমণ্ডলীর দৃষ্টির সম্মুখে পরিবর্ত্তিত হয় ; যে দৃশ্য পরিবর্ত্তনে প্রধান সং সকল প্রধান অভিনেতৃসমূহে পরিবর্ত্তিত হয়। **Transformation-myth**—যে পৌরাণিকী কথায় মানুষের জন্তু বৃক্ষ-লতাদিতে পরিবর্ত্তনের কথা বর্ণিত হইয়া থাকে। **Transformation of energy** — পরীক্ষা দ্বারা প্রমাণিত হইয়াছে যে, যখন একজাতীয় শক্তি তিরোহিত ও ব্যয়িত হয় তখন উহার স্থলে অন্যজাতীয় শক্তি উদ্ভূত হইয়া থাকে, এবং উপযোগী অবস্থাসমূহের অধীনে কোনরূপ পরিজ্ঞাত বলের তিরোধানে অল্পাধিক পরিমাণ কোনরূপ নূতন বল উপজাত করা যাইতে পারে। যেমন ঘড়ীর দোলকের দোল মধ্যস্থলে থামিয়া গেলে পুনরায় নবসঞ্জাতশক্তির বেগে উহা অপর পার্শ্বে চালিত হয়, বলগতি-বর্ত্তন। (See ENERGY.)

trăns-fŏrm'-ĕr, trăns'-fŏr-mā-tŏr, *ns.* An apparatus for transforming an electric current of high voltage into one of low voltage and *vice versa* without changing the current energy ; প্রবাহের শক্তি পরিবর্ত্তন বিনা উচ্চ বিদ্যুৎ প্রবাহাঙ্ক সম্পন্ন তাড়িতপ্রবাহকে নিম্ন প্রবাহাঙ্কবিশিষ্ট প্রবাহে কিম্বা নিম্ন প্রবাহাঙ্কবিশিষ্ট তাড়িত প্রবাহকে উচ্চ

প্রবাহাঙ্কবিশিষ্ট প্রবাহে পরিবর্ত্তনের জন্য যন্ত্রবিশেষ, প্রবাহ বিবর্ত্তন।

trăns-fŏrm′-ĭsm, *n.* The hypothesis that all existing species are the product of the metamorphosis of other forms of living beings; সমস্ত জাতি অপর প্রাণিসমূহের রূপান্তর হইতে উপজাত এইরূপ সিদ্ধান্ত, পরিণতিবাদ, পরিবর্ত্তবাদ (হিঃ কোঃ), বিবর্ত্তনবাদ। **—for-mis′-tic,** *adj.* **—ist,** *n.*

trăns-fūse′, *v. t.* **1.** To transfer by pouring; এক পাত্র হইতে অপর পাত্রে ঢালা। **2.** (*Med.*) To transfer, as blood from veins to arteries of one animal to those of another; to inject liquid into blood-vessel to replace lost fluid; এক জন্তুর ধমনী বা শিরা হইতে অপর ব্যক্তির ধমনী বা শিরাতে রক্ত সঞ্চারিত করা; দেহ হইতে যে রক্ত পাত হইয়াছে তাহার স্থান পূরণের জন্য ধমনীতে তরল পদার্থ প্রবিষ্ট করিয়া দেওয়া। **3.** To cause to be instilled or imbibed; as, to *transfuse* a love of literature; সঞ্চার করা। **—fu′-sion,** *n.* **—fu′-sive,** *adj.*

trăns-grĕss′, *v. t.* To violate; ভঙ্গ করা, লঙ্ঘন করা। **—gres′-sion,** *n.* Infringement; an offence; ভঙ্গ, লঙ্ঘন, অতিক্রম, উল্লঙ্ঘন, ব্যতিক্রম, সমতিক্রম; অতিচার, দোষ, ত্রুটি, অপরাধ, ধর্ম্মভঙ্গ (হিঃ কোঃ), পাতক (ঐ)।

trăn-ship′, *v. t.* Same as TRANSSHIP (which see).

trăn′-sĭ-ĕnt, *adj.* **1.** Brief; short; not permanent; as, the world is *transient*; ক্ষণিক; ক্ষণস্থায়ী; ক্ষণবিধ্বংসী, ক্ষণভঙ্গুর, অচিরস্থায়ী, অনিত্য (হিঃ কোঃ), অশাশ্বত (ঐ)। **2.** (*Mus.*) (Of a chord) Serving only to connect; (সঙ্গীত-শাস্ত্র—তন্ত্রী-সম্বন্ধে) কেবল মাত্র সংযোগসাধক। **—ence,** *n.*

trăn-sĭl′-ĭ-ĕnt, *adj.* Extending across from one point of support to another; এক অবলম্বন হইতে অপর অবলম্বনে বিস্তারশীল, বর্জ (মিউজিক)। **—ence,** *n.*

trăns-ĭl-lū-mĭ-nā′-tion, *n.* The act of throwing a powerful light through an organ for medical examination; পরীক্ষার জন্য কোন দৈহিক যন্ত্রের ভিতর তীব্র আলোক প্রক্ষেপণ, অন্তর্দীপন।

trăns-ĭ′-rē, *n.* A custom-house permit to let goods be removed; মাল স্থানান্তর করার জন্য শুল্কশালার ছাড়পত্র।

trăns′-ĭt, *n.* & *v. t.* **1.** A passage; স্থানান্তরে গমন, গমন। **2.** The conveyance of goods; মাল প্রেরণ। **3.** Route; পথ, রাস্তা। **4.** (*Astron.*) The passage of a heavenly body over the meridian of a place; কোন স্থানের যাম্যোত্তরবৃত্তের উপর দিয়া কোন জ্যোতিষ্কের গমন, সংক্রমণ, ক্রান্তি, সঞ্চার, যাম্যোত্তরগমন। **5.** (*Astron.*) The passing of a planet (esp. Venus) in front of the sun's disc; রবিমণ্ডলের উপর দিয়া শুক্রাদি গ্রহের সংক্রমণ। **6.** Same as TRANSIT-CIRCLE, TRANSIT INSTRUMENT, etc. ***Verb t.*** To pass over the disc of a heavenly body; রবিমণ্ডল প্রভৃতির উপর দিয়া সংক্রমিত হওয়া। **Transit-circle**—যাম্যোত্তর বৃত্ত (হিঃ কোঃ)। **Transit-compass**—শয়ান (horizontal) কোণ পরিমাপের জন্য জরীপ যন্ত্রবিশেষ। **Transit-duty**—চালানী মাশুল। **Transit-instrument** — কোন স্থানে কোন জ্যোতিষ্কের সংক্রমণ পরিদর্শনের জন্য যন্ত্রবিশেষ, সংক্রমণদর্শক। **Transit-trade** — চালানী কারবার। **Lower transit** — অধোযাম্যোত্তর গমন (হিঃ কোঃ)। **Transit of a shadow**—যাম্যোত্তর গ্রহচ্ছায়া (হিঃ কোঃ)। **Transit of venus**—শুক্ররবি যুতি (হিঃ কোঃ)। **Upper transit** — ঊর্দ্ধ যাম্যোত্তর গমন (হিঃ কোঃ)।

trăn-sĭ′-tion, *n.* **1.** Passage from one place to another or from one state to another; change; স্থানান্তর, অবস্থান্তর; পরিবর্ত্তন। **2.** (*Mus.*) Same as MODULATION. **3.** (*Rhet.*) A passing from one subject to another; (অলঙ্কারশাস্ত্র) প্রসঙ্গ হইতে প্রসঙ্গান্তরে পরিবর্ত্তন। **4.** (*Arch.*) The period between one style and another; (স্থপতিবিজ্ঞান) স্থাপত্যধারাদ্বয়ের মধ্যবর্ত্তী কাল। **—al, —a-ry,** *adjs.* **—al-ly,** *adv.* **Transition rocks, Transition series**—অস্ফটীকীভূত এবং স্তরবিন্যস্ত নিম্নতম পাষাণ। **Transition tumour**—যে অর্ব্বুদ একবার কাটার পর পুনরায় জাত হইলে সহজে নির্ম্মূল করা যায় না।

trăn′-sĭ-tive (-tĭv), *adj.* (*Gram.*) Taking an object after it, as a verb; (ব্যাকরণ) সকর্ম্মক। **—ly,** *adv.* **Transitive state of mind**—সম্বন্ধবৃত্তি (হিঃ কোঃ)।

trăn′-sĭ-tō-rȳ, *adj.* Speedily vanishing; fleeting; evanescent; temporary; ক্ষণিক, ক্ষণভঙ্গুর, উৎপন্নবিনাশী, ক্ষণস্থায়ী; অনিত্য; অচিরস্থায়ী; অস্থায়ী। **—ri-ly,** *adv.* **—ri-ness,** *n.* The state of being transitory; ক্ষণিকতা, ক্ষণস্থায়িত্ব, অচিরস্থায়িত্ব, অনিত্যভাব, অনিত্যস্থায়িত্ব। **Transitory action**—যে মোকদ্দমা যে স্থানেই লেনাদেনা প্রভৃতি হউক না কেন যে কোন দেশে রুজু করা যাইতে পারে।

trăns-lāte′, *v. t.* **1.** To bear, carry or remove from one place to another; to transfer; "I will *translate* the kingdom from the house of Saul, and set up the throne of David"; এক স্থান হইতে অন্য স্থানে বহন বা স্থানান্তর করা; স্থানান্তরিত করা। **2.** To render into another language; অনুবাদ করা, ভাষান্তরিত করা, অনূদিত করা, তর্জ্জমা করা। **3.** To change to another condition, office, or form; অবস্থান্তর করা, রূপান্তর করা। **4.** (*Slang*) To manufacture as boots and shoes from the materials of old ones; (ইতরভাষায়) পুরাতন বুট কিম্বা জুতার চামড়া প্রভৃতি দ্বারা বুট প্রভৃতি তৈরী করা। **5.** (*Bible*)

To convey to heaven without death; (বাইবেল) সশরীরে স্বর্গারোহণ করান। 6. To transfer a bishop from one see to another; এক পাট হইতে ধর্ম্মাধ্যক্ষকে অন্য পাটে স্থানান্তরিত করা। 7. To interpret; অর্থ করা। 8. (*Teleg.*) To retransit a message; (তাড়িতবার্ত্তা) কোন স্থান হইতে প্রাপ্ত সংবাদ পুনশ্চ অন্যত্র প্রেরণ করা। 9. To express in other terms as for making more tangible, comprehensible or the like; "*Translating* into his own clear, pure and flowing language what he found in books"; অধিকতর স্পর্শযোগ্য, বোধগম্য, প্রভৃতি করার জন্য অন্য ভাবে ব্যক্ত বা প্রকটিত করা। 10. (*Mech.*) To move a body from one place to another in such a way that all its parts follow the same direction; (যন্ত্রবিজ্ঞান) কোন বস্তুকে এইরূপ ভাবে সঞ্চালিত করা—যাহাতে উহার সকল অংশ একই দিকে অনুবর্ত্তন করে। **–lat'-a-ble, –la'-tion-al,** *adjs.* **–la'-tion,** *n.* 1. The act of removing; passage from one place or state to another; change; স্থানান্তর, স্থানান্তরীকরণ; স্থানান্তরে গমন, অবস্থান্তরপ্রাপ্তি; পরিবর্ত্তন। 2. The removal of a person to heaven without subjecting him to death; সশরীরে স্বর্গে প্রেরণ। 3. The transfer of a bishop from one see to another; ধর্ম্মাধ্যক্ষকে এক পাট হইতে অন্য পাটে স্থানান্তরীকরণ। 4. The act of turning into another language; অনুবাদ, ভাষান্তর, তর্জ্জমা। 5. That which is produced by turning into another language; a version; অনুবাদিত পুস্তক, অনুবাদিত বিষয়; অনুবাদ। 6. An interpretation of something into another medium; অন্যভাবে বা উপায়ে কোন কিছুর অর্থ প্রকটন, অনুবাদ (cf. তাতে জানি তোমার পাঞাছে প্রসাদ। তাহা কিছু নহে তোমার হৃদয়ের অনুবাদ — চৈতন্যচরিতামৃত)। 7. (*Rare*) Transfer of the meaning of a word or phrase (ক্বচিদ্-ব্যবহৃত) অর্থান্তরন্যাস। 8. (*Slang*) The act of making boots or shoes from the materials of old ones; পুরাতন জুতা, বুট, প্রভৃতির উপকরণ হইতে অপর বুট প্রভৃতি প্রস্তুত করণ। 9. (*Law*) Transfer of property; সম্পত্তি হস্তান্তর। 10. (*Mech.*) Same as MOTION OF TRANSLATION (below). **–la'-tor,** *n.* 1. One who renders into another language; অনুবাদক, ভাষান্তরকারী। 2. A cobbler of low class who manufactures boots and shoes form the materials of old ones; যে চর্ম্মকার পুরাতন জুতার চর্ম্ম প্রভৃতি হইতে বুট প্রভৃতি প্রস্তুত করে। 3. (*Pl., Slang*) A pair of old boots and shoes; (ইতরভাষায়) পুরাতন বুট বা অন্যপ্রকার জুতা। **Motion of translation**—যে গতিতে গতিশীল বস্তুর প্রত্যেক বিন্দু সমান্তরাল সরল রেখায় সঞ্চালিত হইয়া থাকে, সমান্তরালগতি।

trăns-lĭt'-ĕr-āte, *v. t.* To write with the alphabet of another language; এক ভাষার শব্দ অপর ভাষার অক্ষর দ্বারা প্রকাশ করা, অক্ষরান্তর করা। **–a'-tion,** *n.* The rendering of characters of one language by equivalents in another; অক্ষরান্তরীকরণ, অক্ষরান্তর-ক্রিয়া। **–a-tor,** *n.*

trăns-lū'-cĕnt, *adj.* 1. Transmitting rays of light, but not so as to render objects distinctly visible; স্বচ্ছপ্রায়, অচ্ছপ্রায়, স্বচ্ছকল্প, অর্দ্ধস্বচ্ছ। 2. Transparent; "The uplifted frame, compact at every joint, And overlaid with clear *translucent* glass"; স্বচ্ছ। **–cence, –cen-cy,** *ns.*

trăns-lū'-cĭd, *adj.* (*Rare*) Transparent; (ক্বচিদ্ ব্যবহৃত) স্বচ্ছ।

trăns-mâr'-gĭn-ăl, *adj.* Same as SUBLIMINAL (which see).

trăns-mă-rine' (-rēn), *adj.* Situated beyond the sea; সাগরের অপর তীরবর্ত্তী, অতিসাগরিক।

trăns'-mi-grate, *v. i.* 1. (Of soul) To pass from one body to another; (জীবাত্মাসম্বন্ধে) দেহান্তরে সংক্রমিত হওয়া, পুনর্জন্ম হওয়া, জন্মান্তর পরিগ্রহ করা, দেহান্তরপরিগ্রহ করা। 2. To migrate; দেশান্তরগামী হওয়া। **–grant,** *adj.* & *n.* **–gra-tor,** *n.* **–mi'-gra-to-ry,** *adj.*

trăns-mi-grā'-tion, *n.* (Same as METEMPSYCHOSIS) জন্মান্তরপরিগ্রহ, জীবসংক্রমণ, দেহান্তরপ্রাপ্তি (হিঃ কোঃ), শরীরান্তরপ্রাপ্তি, প্রেত্যভাব (ন্যায় সূত্র), পুনর্জন্ম (হিঃ কোঃ)।

trăns-mit', *v. t.* 1. To cause to pass over or through; to hand on; to communicate; প্রেরণ করা; কাহারও হস্তে দেওয়া; সঞ্চার করা। 2. To suffer to pass through; as, glass *transmits* light; ভেদ করিয়া যাইতে দেওয়া, ভিতর দিয়া যাইতে দেওয়া। **–mis-si-bil'-i-ty, –tal,** *ns.* **–mis'-si-ble, –mis'-sive, –ta-ble,** *adjs.* **–mis'-sion,** *n.* 1. The act of transmitting or sending from one person to another; transference; প্রেরণ, সঞ্চার, সংক্রমণ (হিঃ কোঃ); হস্তান্তর। 2. The passing of a substance through any body; কোন বস্তুর ভিতর দিয়া অপর বস্তুর সঞ্চার। **–ter,** *n.*

trăns-mŏg'-ri-fȳ, *v. t.* To transform into some other person or thing, as by magic; ইন্দ্রজালাদি ক্রিয়া দ্বারা অন্য কোন ব্যক্তি বা বস্তুতে পরিবর্ত্তন করা। **–fi-ca'-tion,** *n.* The act of transmogrificating; যাদুবলে পরিবর্ত্তন।

trăns-mū-tā'-tion, *n.* 1. The change or conversion into another substance or into anything; দ্রব্যান্তরীকরণ, পদার্থান্তরে পরিবর্ত্তন, রূপান্তরীকরণ। 2. (*Alchemy*) The changing of base metal into gold etc.; (কিমিয়া বিদ্যা) নিকৃষ্ট

ধাতুকে স্বর্ণাদিতে পরিবর্ত্তন, কিমিয়াকরণ, স্বর্ণীকরণ। 3. (*Biol.*) Change of one species into another; (জীববিজ্ঞান) জাত্যন্তরপরিণমন, জাত্যন্তরপরিণাম, জাত্যন্তরীকরণ। 4. (*Geom.*) Change of a figure or body into another of same area or content; (জ্যামিতি) কোন ক্ষেত্রাদির এক ক্ষেত্রফল বিশিষ্ট অন্যপ্রকার ক্ষেত্রাদিতে পরিবর্ত্তন বা রূপান্তরীভবন। **—ist,** *n.* **Transmutation glaze**—ইন্দ্রধনুর আভাযুক্ত চীনামাটীর বর্ণক। **Transmutation of energy**—Same as TRANSFORMATION OF ENERGY.

trăns-mūte′, *v. t.* To change form one nature, substance or form to another; প্রকৃতি পরিবর্ত্তন করা, দ্রব্যান্তরে পরিবর্ত্তিত করা, আকার পরিবর্ত্তন করা, রূপান্তর করা। **—mut-a-bil′-i-ty,** *n.* **—mut′-a-ble,** *adj.* **—mut′-a-bly,** *adv.* **—mut′-a-tive,** *adj.*

trăns-nŏr′-măl, *adj.* In excess of, or beyond the normal state; নৈসর্গিক অবস্থার অতীত বা অতিরিক্ত, অতিনৈসর্গিক।

trăns-ō-ce-ăn′-ic (-shĭ-), *adj.* 1. Beyond the ocean; সাগরের তীরবর্ত্তী, অতিসাগরিক। 2. Crossing the ocean; সাগরাতিক্রমকারী।

trăn′-som (-sŭm), *n.* 1. A stregthening horizontal beam; horizontal cross-bar in window; দৃঢ়তাবিধায়ক শয়ান-কাষ্ঠ; জানালার উপর শয়ানভাবে স্থাপিত আড়কাঠ। 2. A beam or timber extended across the stern-post of a ship, to strengthen the after part and give it due form; জাহাজের পশ্চাদংশের দৃঢ়তাবিধায়ক কাষ্ঠ-ফলক। **—somed,** *adj.* **Transom-window**—সমান ভাবে স্থাপিত আড়কাঠ দ্বারা বিভক্ত জানালা, দ্বারের উপরিস্থ শয়ানকাষ্ঠের উর্দ্ধস্থ বাতায়ন।

trăns-pā-dāne′, *adj.* Lying beyond the river Po; ইতালীদেশের পো নদীর অপর তীরবর্ত্তী।

trăns-pâr′-ĕn-çy̆, —ence (-ĕns), *ns.* 1. The quality or state of being transparent; স্বচ্ছতা, বৈমল্য, (প্রপঞ্চঃ), নির্ম্মলতা, পারদর্শকতা, স্বচ্ছভাব। 2. A picture on a piece of canvas or muslin or glass, or porcelain seen by light passing through it from behind; পশ্চাদ্দিক হইতে প্রক্ষিপ্ত আলোক দ্বারা দর্শনীয় মলমল, ক্যাম্বিস, অথবা চীনামাটীর ফলকের উপর অঙ্কিত চিত্র, স্বচ্ছচিত্র। 3. A wooden framework supporting such a picture; উক্তরূপ চিত্রের অবলম্বনস্বরূপ কাঠের ঠাঁট।

trăns-pâr′-ĕnt, *adj.* 1. Having the property of transmitting rays of light so that bodies behind can be seen distinctly; স্বচ্ছ, বিমল, পারদর্শক। 2. Admitting passage of light; having interstices so that things behind may be seen; আলোক দ্বারা ভেদ্য; এরূপভাবে সচ্ছিদ্র যাহাতে পশ্চাতের বস্তু দৃষ্ট হয়। 3. (*Fig.*) Not sufficient to hide underlying feeling; as, his motive is *transparent* readily; frank; (লক্ষণায়) ভিতরের ভাব স্পষ্টরূপে বোধগম্য: সরল, অকপট। **—ly,** *adv.* **—ness,** *n.* **Transparent colours**—যে ফিকে বর্ণের ভিতর দিয়া নীচের রঙ্গ বা চিত্র দেখা যায়।

trăn-spīre′, *v. t. & i.* 1. To emit through the pores of the skin; লোমকূপদ্বারা নিঃসৃত করা। 2. To exhale water-vapour; জলীয় বাষ্প নির্গত করা। ***Verb i.*** 1. To pass off as in insensible perspiration; অজ্ঞাতসারে স্বেদরূপে নির্গত হইয়া যাওয়া। 2. To become public gradually; to come to light; ক্রমশঃ প্রকাশিত হওয়া; প্রকাশ হইয়া পড়া। 3. (*Slang*) To happen; ঘটা, সংঘটিত হওয়া। **—spir′-a-ble, —spir′-a-tor-y,** *adjs.* **—spi-ra′-tion,** *n.* The act of transpiring; প্রস্বেদ (সাঃ পঃ)।

trăns-plănt′, *v. t.* 1. To remove or plant in another place; এক স্থান হইতে তুলিয়া অপর স্থানে রোপণ করা, প্রতিরোপণ করা, পুনঃ রোপণ করা। 2. To remove or settle in another place; এক স্থান হইতে স্থানান্তরিত করিয়া অপর স্থানে স্থাপিত করা, পুনঃ রোপিত করা। 3. (*Surg.*) To transfer from one part or person to another; দেহের এক অংশ অপর অংশে বা এক ব্যক্তির দেহ হইতে অপর ব্যক্তির দেহে আরোপিত করা। **—a-ble,** *adj.* **—plan-ta′-tion,** *n.* 1. The act of transplanting; পুনঃ রোপণ, প্রতিরোপণ, পরিবপন। 2. (*Surg.*) The removal of a part of the human body to supply that has been lost; (অস্ত্রোপচারবিদ্যা) শরীরের একস্থান কোন অংশে স্থানান্তরিত করিয়া অপর স্থানে আরোপণ, অধিরোপণ।

trăns-plănt′-ēr, *n.* 1. One who transplants; প্রতিরোপক। 2. A machine for removing trees for replanting; প্রতিরোপণের বৃক্ষ উৎপাটনের জন্য যন্ত্র বিশেষ।

trăns-pŏn′-tine, *adj.* 1. Being on the other side of a bridge; সেতুর অপর পার্শ্ববর্ত্তী। 2. Designating that part of London lying on the south side of the Thames; টেমস্ নদীর দক্ষিণতীরবর্ত্তী লণ্ডননগরীর অংশসূচক। 3. Melodramatic, from the plays popular on the parts of London lying on the south side of the Thames; "Even the thorough-going *transpontine* villain seems to be guided rather by chance than by design"; উত্তেজনাপূর্ণ মিলনান্ত নাটকসম্পর্কীয় (এক সময়ে ঐরূপ নাটক টেমস্নদীর দক্ষিণতীরবর্ত্তী লণ্ডন নগরীর অংশে অতিশয় জনপ্রিয় ছিল)।

trăns-port′, *v. t.* 1. To carry or convey from one place to another; স্থানান্তরিত করা, চালান দেওয়া। 2. To carry into banishment; দ্বীপান্তরে প্রেরণ করা, দ্বীপান্তরিত করা। 3. To ravish with pleasure or any strong emotion;

আনন্দোন্মত্ত করা, হর্ষাকুল করা, আনন্দে আত্মহারা করা, সমুল্লসিত করা, ক্রোধাদি দ্বারা আত্মহারা করা। **—er,** *n.* **—ing-ly,** *adv.*

trăns'-pŏrt, *n.* **1.** Conveyance from one place to another; স্থানান্তরে প্রেরণ, চালান, বহন। **2.** A ship or vessel employed for transporting, esp. for carrying soldiers, warlike materials, etc. (also *transport ship, transport vessel*); সৈন্য, রসদ, যুদ্ধসামগ্রী প্রভৃতি বাহী পোত। **3.** Vehement emotion; passion; rapture; "The heat can never a *transport* know, That never feels a pain"; প্রচণ্ড আবেগ; ক্রোধ; পরমানন্দ, সমুল্লাস, হর্ষাবেগ, মহোল্লাস, হর্ষোচ্ছ্বাস। **4.** A transported convict; দ্বীপান্তরিত ব্যক্তি।

trăns-pŏrt'-ă-ble (-bl), *adj.* **1.** Capable of being transported or carried from place to place; স্থানান্তরবাহ্য। **2.** Liable to be punished by transportation; দ্বীপান্তরদণ্ডযোগ্য।

trăns-pŏr-tā'-tion, *n.* **1.** The act of transporting from one place to another; removal; চালান, বহন (সাঃ পঃ); স্থানান্তরী করণ। **2.** Banishment for crime; দ্বীপান্তর, দায়মল (*colloq.*), পুলিপুলাও [(*slang*) from Penang formerly used as convict settlement.)]

trăns-pōse', *v. t.* **1.** To cause (two or more things) to change places; to change the relative order of; স্থান পরিবর্তন করা, একটীর স্থানে অপরটীকে স্থাপন করা; ক্রমবিপর্যয় করা। **2.** (*Algeb.*) To bring a quantity from one member of an equation to another; (বীজগণিত) যোগের চিহ্ন বিয়োগে এবং বিয়োগের চিহ্ন যোগে পরিবর্তন করিয়া সমীকরণের এক পার্শ্বের পদ অপর পার্শ্বে আনা, স্থানবিপর্যয় করা। **3.** (*Gram.*) To change the natural order of words; (ব্যাকরণ) শব্দের স্বাভাবিক ক্রম বিপর্যয় করা। **4.** (*Mus.*) To change the key of; (সঙ্গীতশাস্ত্র) চাবির পরিবর্তন করা। **—pos'-al, —pos'-er,** *ns.*

trăns-pō-sĭ'-tion, *n.* **1.** The act of one who transposes; স্থানপরিবর্তন, স্থানবিপর্যয়, ক্রমবিপর্যয়, ব্যত্যাস (হিঃ কোঃ), সমারোপণ। **2.** (*Algeb.*) The bringing of any term of an equation from one side over to the other, without destroying the equation; যোগ বিয়োগ চিহ্ন পরিবর্তন করিয়া সমীকরণের এক পার্শ্বের পদ অপর পার্শ্বে স্থানান্তরিতকরণ, স্থানান্তরীকরণ। **3.** (*Gram.*) A change of natural order of words in a sentence; (ব্যাকরণ) কোন বাক্যে স্বাভাবিক ক্রমবিপর্যয়। **4.** (*Mus.*) A change of key into a higher or lower scale; (সঙ্গীতশাস্ত্র) বাদ্যযন্ত্রের চাবির পরিবর্তন। **—al, —pos'-i-tive,** *adjs.*

trăns-ship', *v. t.* To convey from one ship or conveyance to another; এক জাহাজ, গাড়ী, প্রভৃতি হইতে অপর জাহাজ, গাড়ী প্রভৃতিতে স্থানান্তরিত করা, স্থানপরিবর্তন করা, স্থানান্তর করা। **—ment,** *n.* The act or fact of conveying from one ship or conveyance to another; যানপরিবর্তন, যানান্তরীকরণ, যানান্তর।

trăn-sŭb-stăn'-ti-āte (-shĭ-), *v. t.* To change into another substance, esp. to change as the sacramental bread and wine, into the flesh and blood of Christ; দ্রব্যান্তরে পরিবর্তন করা, বিশেষতঃ খৃষ্টের অন্তিমভোজনের স্মৃতি অনুষ্ঠানের রুটি ও মদিরা তদীয় রুধির ও মাংসে পরিণত করা।

trăn-sŭb-stăn-ti-ā'-tion (-shĭ-), *n.* Change of substance; esp. the conversion of the bread and wine in the eucharist into the body and blood of Christ; দ্রব্যান্তরীভবন; বিশেষতঃ খৃষ্টের অন্তিম ভোজনের স্মৃতি অনুষ্ঠানের রুটি ও সুরা তদীয় রুধির ও মাংসে পরিবর্তন, দ্রব্যান্তরীকরণ।

trăn'-sūde', *v. i.* To pass through the pores or interstices of texture; ছিদ্র, লোমকূপ, প্রভৃতির ভিতর দিয়া নিঃসৃত হওয়া। **—su-da'-tion,** *n.* **—su'-da-to-ry,** *adj.*

trăns-vêr'-săl, *adj.* & *n.* Lying or running across; অনুপার্শ্বগামী, আড়ভাবে স্থিত, তির্য্যগ্‌ভাবে স্থিত, টের্চ্চা। *Noun.* **1.** A transverse line; অনুপার্শ্বগামী রেখা। **2.** (*Anat.*) A muscle etc. lying across certain parts; (শারীরসংস্থানবিদ্যা) দেহের কোন অংশের অনুপ্রস্থগামী পেশী প্রভৃতি। **—sal'-i-ty,** *n.* **—ly,** *adv.*

trăns-verse' (-vêrs), *adj.* & *n.* **1.** Lying, or being across, or in a cross direction; অনুপার্শ্বগামী, অনুপার্শ্ব (সাঃ পঃ), আড়েস্থিত, এড়ো, টের্চ্চা, তির্য্যগ্‌ভাবে স্থিত। **2.** (*Anat.*) Lying across other parts; (শারীরসংস্থানবিদ্যা) অনুপ্রস্থগামী, অনুপার্শ্বগামী। *Noun.* **1.** That which crosses, or lies in a cross direction; তির্য্যগ্‌গামী বা তির্য্যগ্‌ভাবে স্থিত রেখা প্রভৃতি। **2.** (*Anat.*) A transverse muscle; (শারীরসংস্থান-বিদ্যা) অনুপ্রস্থগামী পেশী। **—ly,** *adv.* **Transverse axis or diameter**—বৃত্তাভাস বা অতিপরবলয়ের নাভিদ্বয় সংযোজক অক্ষ। **Transverse vibration** — (*Phys.*) তির্য্যক্ কম্পন (হিঃ কোঃ)।

trăp, *n., v. t.* & *i.* **1.** A contrivance for catching unwares; ফাঁদ, বাগুড়া, কূটপাশ, কূটযন্ত্র, পঞ্জরাখেট। **2.** A strategem; a snare; as, a *trap* was laid for him; কূট উপায়, ফন্দী; ফাঁদ। **3.** A contrivance applied to drains and soil-pipes to prevent the escape of effluvia; নর্দ্দমা বা মলবাহী নলের দূষিত বাষ্পের উত্থান নিরোধক ব্যবস্থাবিশেষ, বাষ্প-নিরোধক। **4.** A machine for throwing into the air, balls, clay-pigeons, etc. to be shot at; গুলি মারিয়া লক্ষ্য ঠিক করার জন্য শূন্যে কন্দুক, মৃন্ময় কপোত প্রভৃতি প্রক্ষেপের

জন্য যন্ত্রবিশেষ, ক্ষেপণযন্ত্র। 5. (*Slang*) A sheriff's officer ; a police constable ; a police spy ; (ইতরভাষায়) নাজীরের পেয়াদা ; কনষ্টেবল ; গোয়েন্দা। 6. Kinds of wheeled vehicle ; বিভিন্ন প্রকার গাড়ী। 7. A wooden instrument shaped like a shoe which sends a ball into the air on being stricken ; কন্দুক শূন্যে প্রক্ষেপের জন্য ক্রীড়াবিশেষে ব্যবহৃত পাদুকাকৃতি কাঠময় যন্ত্রবিশেষ। ***Verb t.*** 1. To catch in a trap; বাগুড়ায় বা কূটযন্ত্রে ধরা, ঘুনিতে আটক করা। 2. To insnare ; to take by strategem ; ফাঁদে ফেলা ; কৌশলে ধরা। 3. (*Rare*) To furnish with trap-doors, as a stage ; (কচিদ্ ব্যবহৃত) রঙ্গমঞ্চে কূটদ্বার স্থাপন করা। 4. To arrest gas in a trap ; বাষ্পনিরোধকযন্ত্রে দূষিত বাষ্প আটক করা। 5. To discharge from a trap clay-pigeon etc. to be shot at ; লক্ষ্যভেদে নিপুণতা লাভের জন্য ক্ষেপণযন্ত্র হইতে মৃন্ময়-কপোত প্রভৃতি ক্ষেপণ করা। ***Verb i.*** To set traps for game ; ফাঁদ পাতা, বাগুড়া স্থাপন করা, ঘুনি পাতা। 2. (Of steam) To be impeded in pipe etc. ; (বাষ্পসম্বন্ধে) চোঙ্গ প্রভৃতিতে নিরুদ্ধ হওয়া। **Trap-ball**—পাদুকাকৃতি যন্ত্রদ্বারা একপ্রকার ক্রীড়া ; ঐরূপ ক্রীড়ায় ব্যবহৃত কন্দুক। **Trap-celler** — রঙ্গমঞ্চের নিম্নস্থ স্থান। **Trap-door**— ছাদ বা মেঝের চোরা দুয়ার, কূট-দ্বার। **Trap-door spider** — এক জাতীয় মাকড়সা। [ইহারা জালের উপরিভাগে কব্জা যুক্ত চোরা দুয়ার প্রস্তুত করিয়া থাকে।]

trăp, *n.* 1. A kind of movable ladder or straps ; একপ্রকার বহনযোগ্য মই বা অধিরোহণী। 2. A black volcanic rock of columnar structure ; একপ্রকার স্তম্ভাকৃতি কৃষ্ণবর্ণ আগ্নেয়গিরিজাত প্রস্তর, স্তম্ভপাষাণ। **Trap-rock**—Same as TRAP 2.

trăp, *v. t.* & *n.* To adorn ; to furnish with ornamental harness ; ভূষিত করা ; অশ্বকে কারুকার্য্যখচিত সাজসজ্জা পরান। ***Noun.*** luggage ; মালপত্র, লওয়াজিমা, তল্পিতল্পা।

tră'-pā, *n.* Water-caltrop (*Trapa bispinosa*), of genus trapae ; পাণিফল, সিঙ্গাড়া। [Syn. জলসূচি, সংঘটিকা, বারিকণ্টক, শৃঙ্গাট, শৃঙ্গাটক, বারিকুব্জক, ক্ষীরশুক্র, জলকণ্টক, স্বাদুকণ্টক, শৃঙ্গরুহ, জলবল্লী, জলাশয়, শৃঙ্গকন্দ, শৃঙ্গমূল, বিষাণী, কুব্জক।] [Chin. *ling* ; Tel. *parike gadda, kubjakam, sringa takamu, pandi gadda.*] **Trapa-natans** — একপ্রকার বড় আকারের পাণিফল, ইহার চারটী শির থাকে। ইহার চীনদেশীয় নাম *Fan-ling*.

trăp-ăn', *n.* Same as TREPAN (which see).

trāpes, *n.* & *v. i.* A slattern ; নোংরা স্ত্রীলোক, পেত্নী। ***Verb i.*** To gad about in a slatternly manner ; নোংরাভাবে ঘুরা।

tră-peze' (-pēz), *n.* 1. Same as TRAPEZIUM. 2. A sort of swing on which gymnastic exercises are performed consisting of one or more cross bars suspended by cords ; ব্যায়ামের জন্য দোলন-কাষ্ঠ বিশেষ। **—pe'-zi-form,** *adj.*

tră-pē'-zi-ŭm, *n.* 1. A plane figure contained by four straight lines, of which no two are parellel ; যে চতুর্ভুজের কোন দুই বাহুই সমান্তরাল নহে, বিষমচতুর্ভুজ, বিষমচতুরস্র, অতুল্যলম্বকক্ষেত্র (লীলাঃ)। 2. (*Rare*) Same as TRAPEZOID. 3. (*Anat.*) The outermost bone in the second row of carpus ; (শারীরসংস্থানবিদ্যা) মণিবন্ধাস্থির দ্বিতীয় পংক্তির বহিস্তমবর্ত্তী অস্থি।

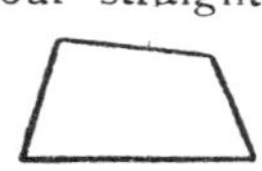

Trapezium.

trăp'-ē-zoid (-zoyd), *n.* & *adj.* 1. (*Geom.*) A plane four-sided figure having two of its sides parellel ; যে চতুর্ভুজের কেবলমাত্র দুই বাহু সমান্তরাল, সমলম্বকক্ষেত্র, সমলম্বচতুর্ভুজ (হিঃ কোঃ)। ***Adj.*** Of the form of a trapezoid ; সমলম্বকক্ষেত্রাকৃতি। **—zoi'-dal,** *adj.*

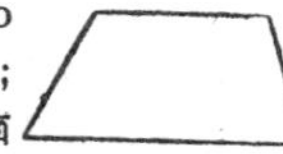

Trapezoid.

trăp'-pē-ăn, *adj.* Pertaining to, or of the nature of, trap-rock ; আগ্নেয়গিরিজাত স্তম্ভাকার কৃষ্ণবর্ণ প্রস্তরসম্বন্ধীয়। **–poid, –pous, –pose,** *adjs.*

trăp'-per (-ėr), *n.* 1. One whose business is to trap animals, esp. for furs ; যে ব্যক্তি বাগুড়াদ্বারা পশু ধৃত করে, বিশেষতঃ, যে ব্যক্তি রোমের জন্য ফাঁদ পাতিয়া পশু ধৃত করিয়া থাকে। 2. A boy who attends to the opening and closing of air-doors in a mine ; খনির বায়ুপ্রবেশদ্বার রুদ্ধ ও উন্মুক্ত করার কার্য্যে নিযুক্ত বালক।

trăp'-pings (-ĭngs), *n.* 1. Ornaments appended to the saddle ; অশ্বসজ্জা, অশ্বভূষা। 2. (*Fig.*) Ornament ; "He wore them as fine *trappings* for a show" ; মণ্ডন, ভূষা।

Trăp'-pist (-ĭst), *n.* A member of a religious body belonging to the Roman Catholic Church, of the Cistercian order, remarkable for the austere life led by the monks ; ক্যাথলিক সন্ন্যাসিসম্প্রদায়বিশেষভুক্ত ব্যক্তি।

trăp'-pist-ĭne (-ĭst-), *n.* 1. A liqueur made by the monks of La Trappe ; ফরাসীদেশের মঠ বিশেষের সন্ন্যাসিগণকর্ত্তৃক প্রস্তুত মদ্য। 2. (*Cap.*) A nun of the order of La Trappe ; খৃষ্টীয় সন্ন্যাসিনীসম্প্রদায়বিশেষভুক্তা নারী।

trap'-py (-ĭ), *adj.* Of the nature of trap-rock ; treacherous ; as, *trappy* holes ; স্তম্ভপাষাণ প্রকৃতিক ; চোরা।

trăsh, *n.* & *v. t.* 1. Loppings of trees ; broken pieces ; rubbish ; বৃক্ষের কাটা ডালপালা ; ভাঙ্গাটুকরা ; জঞ্জাল, আবর্জ্জনা, ছাইপাশ। 2. Worthless stuff ; "A haunch of venison would be *trash* to a Brahmin" ; অকিঞ্চিৎকর বস্তু, অসার জিনিষ, আগড়ম বাগড়ম (*colloq.*)। 3. Nonsensical talk ; অসার আলাপ। 4. (*Obs.*) Money ; (অপ্রঃ) টাকা, পয়সা।

Verb t. (*Archaic*) **1.** To lop ; ডালপালা ছাঁটা। **2.** To discard ; to maltreat ; অগ্রাহ্য করা ; দুর্ব্যবহার করা। **Trash'-er-y,** *n.* **Trash'-i-ly,** *adv.* **Trash'-y,** *adj.* Worthless ; অসার, বাজে, খেলো। **Cane-trash**—আখের ছোবড়া। **Trash-ice**—জলের সহিত মিশ্রিত বরফ খণ্ড সমূহ। **Poor white trash**—মার্কিণ যুক্তরাজ্যের দক্ষিণ বিভাগের নিগ্রোগণ নিঃস্ব শ্বেতাঙ্গগণকে এই নামে অভিহিত করিয়া থাকে।

trăss, *n.* Whitish or yellow earth common in volcanic districts, used as cement ; আগ্নেয়গিরিপূর্ণ প্রদেশে একপ্রকার শ্বেতাভ বা পীত মৃত্তিকা যাহা বিলাতীমাটীরূপে ব্যবহৃত হয়।

trattoria, *n.* In Italy an eating-house ; ইতালীদেশীয় ভোজনশালা।

trau'-mă (trä-), *n.* (*Pl.* -MATA) A morbid condition of body produced by wound or external violence ; ক্ষতাদিজনিত শরীরের একপ্রকার রুগ্নভাব। **–tism,** *n.*

trau'-măt-ic (trä-), *adj.* & *n.* Pertaining to, or applied to, wounds; আঘাতসম্বন্ধীয়, আভিঘাতিক, ক্ষতরোগে ব্যবহৃত। ***Noun.*** A medicine for wounds ; ক্ষতরোগের ঔষধ। **Traumatic fever**—অভিঘাত জ্বর (সাঃ পঃ), আগন্তুক জ্বর (ঐ)।

trăv'-ail (-āl), *n., v. i.* & *t.* **1.** Labour ; childbirth ; প্রসব বেদনা প্রসব যন্ত্রণা ; গর্ভযন্ত্রণা। **2.** Severe agony "He shall see the *travail* of his sons" ; নিদারুণ যন্ত্রণা, দারুণ ব্যথা। ***Verb i.*** **1.** (*Archaic*) To suffer the pangs of childbearing ; প্রসব বেদনা হওয়া, গর্ভযন্ত্রণা হওয়া। **2.** To make painful or laborious effort ; অতিশয় কষ্ট ও পরিশ্রমের সহিত চেষ্টা করা। ***Verb t.*** To harass ; to tire ; অত্যাচার করা ; হয়রাণ করা।

trăv'-ĕl, *v. t., i.* & *n.* To journey over ; to pass ; ভ্রমণ করা, পর্য্যটন করা ; অতিক্রম করা। ***Verb i.*** **1.** To pass ; to make progress ; অতিক্রম করা, চলা ; অগ্রসর হওয়া। **2.** To journey ; ভ্রমণ করা, পর্য্যটন করা। **3.** To make a journey or journeys, or to go about from place to place for the purpose of obtaining orders for goods, collecting accounts, etc. for a commercial house ; as, he has *travelled* for the firm of Bird & Co. ; জিনিষের অর্ডার সংগ্রহ প্রভৃতি কার্য্যের জন্য দেশের নানাস্থানে পর্য্যটন করা। **4.** (*Mech.*) To move in a given direction or path ; as, the piston *travels* 2ft. in each stroke ; (যন্ত্রবিজ্ঞান) নির্দ্দিষ্ট দিকে বা পথে চলা। ***Noun.*** **1.** The act of travelling or journeying ; a journeying to distant and foreign places ; ভ্রমণ, পর্য্যটন ; দেশভ্রমণ, দেশপর্য্যটন। **2.** (*Pl.*) An account of occurrence and observation made during a journey ; ভ্রমণবৃত্তান্ত, ভ্রমণকাহিনী, ভ্রমণবিবরণ। **3.** (*Mech.*) Range, rate, mode of motion of a part in machinery ; (যন্ত্রবিজ্ঞান) কোন যন্ত্রের অংশবিশেষের প্রসার, গতির হার এবং প্রকার। **–elled,** *p. p.* **1.** Having gained knowledge or experience by travelling ; as, a *travelled* man ; বহুদেশ ভ্রমণহেতু জ্ঞান এবং অভিজ্ঞতালব্ধ **2.** Experienced ; অভিজ্ঞ, পারদর্শী। **Travel-stained**—পর্য্যটনকলঙ্কিত। **To travel out of the record**—To digress ; মূল বিষয় ছাড়িয়া অবান্তর বিষয় ধরা।

trăv'-ĕl-ler (-ĕr), *n.* **1.** One who travels in any way ; a wayfarer ; পান্থ ; পথিক। **2.** One who visits foreign countries ; ভ্রমণকারী, পর্য্যটক, পরিব্রাজক (esp. religious wanderer). **3.** One who travels from place to place to solicit order for goods ; যে ব্যক্তি জিনিষের অর্ডার সংগ্রহের জন্য নানাস্থানে ভ্রমণ করে। **4.** Kinds of moving mechanism ; বিভিন্ন প্রকার চলনশীল কলের নাম। **Traveller's-joy**—একপ্রকার পুষ্পলতা। **Traveller's tale**—অলীক গল্প। **Traveller's tree**—মাদাগাস্কার দ্বীপে জাত কদলীবৎ বৃক্ষবিশেষ (এই বৃক্ষ হইতে নিঃসৃত একপ্রকার সুশীতল জলবৎ পানীয় দ্বারা শ্রান্ত পথিকদিগের পিপাসার নিবৃত্তি হয়, পান্থপাদপ। **Bona fide traveller**—যে ব্যক্তি তিন মাইল পদব্রজে চলা হেতু জলযোগের অধিকারী হইয়াছে। **He has gone to the bourne or country from which no traveller returns**—তিনি মহাযাত্রা করিয়াছেন। **To tip person the traveller**—To impose on a person by telling him lies; কাহাকেও মিথ্যা কথা বলিয়া ধোঁকা দেওয়া।

trăv-erse' (-êrs), *adj., n., v. t.* & *i.* Transverse ; ব্যত্যস্ত, তির্য্যক্, অনুপ্রস্থগামী, তির্য্যগ্‌গামী। ***Noun.*** **1.** A cross or transverse piece ; অনুপ্রস্থগামী অংশ। **2.** An impediment ; বাধা, বিঘ্ন, অন্তরায়। **3.** (*Law*) A formal denial of some matter of fact alleged by the opposite party in any stage of the pleadings ; (আইন) প্রতিপক্ষের উক্তি অস্বীকার। **4.** (*Geom.*) A transverse line ; (জ্যামিতি) তির্য্যগ্‌রেখা। **5.** The zigzag line taken by a ship owing to contrary winds or cross-currents, etc. ; প্রতিকূল বায়ু, স্রোতঃ প্রভৃতি হেতু জাহাজ যে আঁকাবাঁকা পথে চলে। **6.** Side ways movement of a part in machine ; যন্ত্রের কোন অংশের পার্শ্বিক গতি। **7.** A trench with a little parapet for protecting men on the flank ; পার্শ্ববর্ত্তী সৈন্যদিগকে রক্ষা করিবার জন্য অনুচ্চ প্রাচীর-সমন্বিত পরিখা। **8.** The turning of a gun into horizontal plane so as to point it in any direction ; যে কোন দিকে সন্ধান করার জন্য কামান শয়ানতলে আবর্ত্তন। ***Verb t.*** **1.** To lay in a cross direction ; তির্য্যক্‌ভাবে স্থাপন করা। **2.** To wander over ; to cross in travelling ; ভ্রমণ করা, পর্য্যটন করা, বিচরণ করা ; কোন দেশ অতিক্রম করা।

3. (*Law*) To deny what the opposite party has alleged; as, to *traverse* an indictment; (আইন) প্রতিপক্ষের উক্তি অস্বীকার করা। 4. To thwart; "The squadron fitted out by the court of Spain to attend over motions, and *traverse* over projects": বিফল করা, ব্যর্থ করা, পণ্ড করা। 5. To plane in a direction across the grain of the wood; as, to *traverse* a board; কাঠের আঁশের সহিত আড়ভাবে রেঁদা করা। 6. (*Gun*) To turn and point in any direction; (কামান) যে কোন দিকে ফিরান। 7. To move or turn laterally; পার্শ্বের দিকে ফিরান বা চালিত করা। 8. To examine carefully; "My purpose is to *traverse* the nature, principles and properties of this detestable vice—ingratitude"; বিশেষ মনোযোগের সহিত পরীক্ষা করা, অতিশয় মনোযোগের সহিত পরীক্ষা করা। ***Verb i.*** 1. To move across or over; to advance and retreat; (of a horse) to walk crosswise; কোন কিছুর উপর দিয়া চলা; পর্য্যায়ক্রমে অগ্রসর ওপশ্চাৎপদ হওয়া; (অশ্বসম্বন্ধে) তির্য্যগ্ ভাবে চলা। 2. To turn as on a pivot; as, the needle of the compass *traverses*; শঙ্কু প্রভৃতির উপর ঘূর্ণিত হওয়া। 3. (*Fencing*) To use the posture or motion of opposition; (অসিক্রীড়া) প্রতিরোধ-সূচক ভঙ্গীতে অবস্থান করা। **Traverse-board**—প্রতি অর্দ্ধ ঘণ্টায় জাহাজ কি পরিমাণ স্থান অতিক্রম করিয়াছে তাহা নিরূপণের জন্য গোলাকৃতি ফলক বিশেষ। **Traverse sailing**—আঁকাবাকা ভাবে পোত চালন। **Traverse-table**—বাষ্পীয় শকট প্রভৃতি বর্ত্ম হইতে বর্ত্মান্তরে স্থানান্তরিত করার জন্য মঞ্চবিশেষ। **Traversing pulley**—অবলম্বক রজ্জুর উপর চলনশীল কপিকল।

trăv'-ĕrs'-ĕr, *n.* Same as TRAVERSE-TABLE (*railway.*) Other senses as in verb.

trăv'-ĕr-tĭn, –tine (-tĭn), *ns.* A yellowish concretionary limestone formed by springs holding lime in solution; একপ্রকার কঠিন পীতাভ চূর্ণপ্রস্তর।

trăv'-ĕs-tȳ, *n.* & *v. t.* 1. A burlesque treatment or handling of a subject which had been previously treated in a serious or lofty manner; গুরুতর বিষয়ে হাস্যোদ্দীপক অনুকরণ। 2. An unintentional burlesque; as, a *travesty* of justice; a misrepresentation so gross as to be ridiculous; প্রহসন; হাস্যোদ্দীপক বিকৃতি। ***Verb t.*** To imitate so as to render ridiculous or ludicrous; হাস্যোদ্দীপক বা উপহাসজনক অনুকরণ করা। **Travesty of justice**—বিচারবিভ্রাট, বিচারপ্রহসন।

trawl (träl), *n.*, *v. t.* & *i.* 1. A long line from which short lines with baited hooks are suspended, used in sea-fishery; সমুদ্রে মৎস্য ধরার জন্য যে দীর্ঘ সূত্র হইতে টোপলাগানো বড়শী বাঁধা ক্ষুদ্র ক্ষুদ্র সূতা ঝুলিয়া পড়ে। 2. A kind of net; বেঁউতি জাল। ***Verb t. & i.*** To fish with a trawl-net; বেঁউতিজাল দ্বারা মাছ ধরা। **Trawl'-ing,** *n.* **Trawl-anchor**—দীর্ঘ বড়িশের সূত্র স্থির রাখার জন্য একপ্রকার নোঙ্গর। **Trawl-boat**—দীর্ঘ বড়িশের সূত্র স্থাপনের জন্য বা বেঁউতিজাল দ্বারা মৎস্য ধৃত করার নিমিত্ত একপ্রকার নৌকা। **Trawl-net**—বেঁউতি জাল।

trawl'-ĕr (träl-), *n.* 1. One who trawls; যে ব্যক্তি বেঁউতিজাল দ্বারা মাছ ধরে। 2. A fishing-vessel which drags a net behind it; as, 50 *trawlers* were tropedoed in the Atalantic Ocean; যে জাহাজ পশ্চাদ্দিকে সংবদ্ধ জাল টানিয়া চলে, জেলে জাহাজ।

tray (trā), *n.* 1. A shallow wooden vessel, used for various demestic and other purposes; বারকোষ, থাকা। 2. A shallow lidless box forming a compartment in a trunk; ট্রাঙ্কের কোঠা স্বরূপ ডালা বিহীন বাক্স।

treach'-er-ous (trĕch-ĕr-ŭs), *adj.* 1. Violating allegiance or plighted faith; বিশ্বাসঘাতক। 2. Illusory; deceptive; as, *treacherous* sand; ভ্রান্তিজনক; বঞ্চক, প্রতারণাশীল, ছলনাকারী, চোরা। **–ly,** *adv.* **–ness,** *n.*

treach'-ĕr-ȳ (trĕch-), *n.* Violation of allegiance or of faith and confidence; বিশ্বাসঘাতকতা, অবিশ্বাসিতা, বিশ্বাসভঙ্গ।

trea'-cle (trē-kl), *n.* 1. The spume or uncrystallised part of sugar obtained in sugar refineries; ঝোলা বা কোতরা গুড়, চিটা গুড়, মাত গুড়, রাব। 2. Same as MOLASSES. 3. A saccharine fluid; শর্করাপ্রদ রস। **–cly,** *adj.*

tread (trĕd), *v. t.*, *i.* & *n.* 1. To step on; to walk on; পদবিক্ষেপ করা, পদার্পণ করা, পদন্যাস করা, পদক্ষেপ করা; ভ্রমণ করা। 2. To trample; to subdue; পদদলিত করা, পদমর্দ্দিত করা, মাড়ান (*colloq.*); দমন করা। 3. (Of male birds) To cover; (পুংপক্ষি-সম্বন্ধে) সঙ্গম করা। ***Verb i.*** 1. To set the foot; পদক্ষেপ করা। 2. To walk; to go; পদব্রজে গমন করা; গমন করা। 3. (Of male bird) To copulate with (পুংপক্ষিসম্বন্ধে) সঙ্গম করা। ***Noun.*** 1. A step; পদক্ষেপ, পদবিক্ষেপ, পদন্যাস, চরণপাত। 2. Manner of stepping; way of walking; as, the horse has a good *tread*; sound of walking; পদক্ষেপভঙ্গী; গতিভঙ্গী, গতিভঙ্গিমা; পদশব্দ, পদধ্বনি। 3. The act of copulation in birds; পক্ষিযুগলের মৈথুন। 4. The flat horizontal part of the step of a stair; সিঁড়ির ধাপের শয়ান অংশ। 5. A track; পথ। 6. The length of a ship's keel; জাহাজের পাণিতরাসের দৈর্ঘ্য। 7. The part of the sole of a boot or shoe which touches the ground in walking ; চলিবার সময় বুট বা অন্য জুতার যে অংশ ভূমি স্পর্শ করিয়া থাকে। 8. The part of stilt on which the foot rests ; পাদযষ্টির পা-দান। 9. A piece of metal or rubber placed on a step to lessen wear or sound ; ক্ষয় নিবারণের জন্য বা পদধ্বনি মন্দীভূত করার নিমিত্ত সোপানোপরি স্থাপিত রবর বা পিত্তলফলক। 10. The distance between the pedals of a bicycle ; দ্বিচক্রযানের পাদানদ্বয়ের মধ্যবর্ত্তী স্থান। 11. The cicatrice of a bird's eggs ; পক্ষিডিম্বের পীতাংশের আবরণোপরি শ্বেতবর্ণ চিহ্নবিশেষ। 12. The part of a wheel that bears upon the rail ; চাকার যে অংশ লৌহবর্ত্মের পাতা রেলের উপর দিয়া চলে। 13. The part of a rail on which the wheels bear ; লৌহবর্ত্মের পাতারেলের যে অংশের উপর দিয়া চাকা চলে। **Treadmill**—বৃহৎ চক্রে নিবদ্ধ কাঠের ধাপ সমূহ। পূর্ব্বে কারাগারের বন্দিগণ ঐসকল ধাপের উপর পায়ের ভর দিয়া চাকা ঘুরাইত ; (লক্ষণায়) একঘেয়ে কাজ। **Tread-softly** — একপ্রকার ক্ষুপ। **Tread-wheel** — মনুষ্য বা ঘোটক প্রভৃতির পায়ের ভরে বা পায়ে ঠেলিয়া যে চাকা চালান যায়। **Fools rush in where angels fear to tread**—See FOOL. **To tread down**—To crush or destroy ; পদদলিত করা, বিমর্দ্দিত করা, পদপিষ্ঠ করা। **To tread in**—To press in or into earth by pressing with foot ; পাদদ্বারা ঠেলিয়া মাটীতে বা মাটীর ভিতরে ঢুকান। **To tread in a person's (foot)steps**—(*Fig.*) To follow his example ; কাহারো দৃষ্টান্ত অনুসরণ করা। **To tread on or upon** — To trample on ; to set the foot on in contempt ; পদদলিত করা ; অবজ্ঞার সহিত পদক্ষেপ করা। **To tread on a man's corns or toes**—To irritate ; উত্ত্যক্ত করা, জ্বালাতন করা। **To tread on or upon eggs**—See EGG. **To tread on or upon the heels of**—To follow closely ; পশ্চাৎ পশ্চাৎ যাওয়া। To happen closely ; কোন ঘটনার প্রায় অব্যবহিত পরে সংঘটিত হওয়া। **To tread on the neck of**—To oppress ; নির্যাতন করা, পদদলিত করা, দলন করা। **To tread out**—To come out after trampling with foot ; পদমর্দ্দিত করিয়া নিষ্ক্রান্ত হওয়া। To stamp out fire, etc. ; পদদলিত করিয়া অগ্নি প্রভৃতি নির্ব্বাপিত করা। To press out with feet ; পদমর্দ্দিত করা, পদদলিত করা, পদপিষ্ঠ করা। **To tread the stage or the boards**—To act as a stageplayer ; to act a part of a drama ; রঙ্গমঞ্চে অভিনয় করা ; রঙ্গালয়ে কোন ভূমিকার অভিনয় করা। **To tread the water**—To keep the body nearly upright in the water and the head above water by moving the feet regularly up and down ; নিয়মিতরূপে হস্ত এবং পদ উত্থিত ও অবনমিত করিয়া সন্তরণকালে দেহ প্রায় খাড়া এবং মাথা জলের উপরে রাখা। **To tread under**—To trample ; পদদলিত করা, পদপিষ্ঠ করা। **To tread with contempt**—অবজ্ঞার সহিত ব্যবহার করা।

trea'-dle (trĕ-dl), *n.* & *v. i.* The part of a machine worked by the foot ; যন্ত্রের যে অংশ পদদ্বারা চালিত হয়। ***Verb i.*** To operate a treadle ; যন্ত্রের পদচালনীয় অংশ চালান। **-dler**, *n.* **Treadle-machine, Treadle-press**—পদদ্বারা চালিত মুদ্রাযন্ত্র।

trea-ṡon (trē-), *n.* 1. The offence of attempting to betray the State or to subvert the government of the State to which the offender belongs ; স্বদেশের শাসনতন্ত্র উচ্ছেদের চেষ্টা বা বিশ্বাসঘাতকতাপূর্ব্বক শত্রুর নিকট দেশের স্বার্থহানিকর সংবাদপ্রদানের অপরাধ, মহাদ্রোহ। [ইংলণ্ডের আইন অনুসারে নিম্নলিখিত অপরাধসমূহ মহাদ্রোহ বলিয়া গণ্য হইয়া থাকে :—(১) রাজা, রাণী বা যুবরাজকে হত্যা বা হত্যার ষড়যন্ত্র। (২) রাণী, রাজার অবিবাহিতা জ্যেষ্ঠা কন্যা বা যুবরাজপত্নীর সতীত্বলঙ্ঘন। (৩) রাজার বিরুদ্ধে অস্ত্রধারণ। (৪) রাজার শত্রুকে সাহায্য বা আশ্রয় প্রদান। (৫) রাজার প্রধান মোহর জাল করণ। (৬) রাজনামাঙ্কিত মুদ্রা অবৈধভাবে প্রস্তুতকরণ অথবা রাজার জ্ঞাতসারে কৃত্রিম মুদ্রা প্রচলিতকরণ। (৭) চেন্সেলর, রাজকোষাধ্যক্ষ অথবা প্রধান বিচারালয়ের বিচারককে হত্যাকরণ। বর্ত্তমানে ৫, ৬, ৭এর অপরাধ মহাদ্রোহ বলিয়া গণ্য করা হয় না এতদ্ভিন্ন কোন রাজসন্তান অষ্টাদশবর্ষের নীমে সিংহাসনারোহণ করিলে যে ব্যক্তি পার্লেমেণ্ট এবং উক্ত রাজসন্তানের অভিভাবকের অনুমতি ব্যতীত তাহার বিবাহে সহায়তা করেন সে এবং যাহার সহিত বিবাহ হয় সেই ব্যক্তি মহাদ্রোহাপরাধী বলিয়া গণ্য হইয়া থাকে।] 2. Breach of faith ; বিশ্বাসঘাতকতা। **-a-ble**, *adj.* **-a-ble-ness**, *n.* **-a-bly**, *adv.* **-ous**, *adj.* **Constructive treason**—যে অপরাধ কার্য্যতঃ মহাদ্রোহের তুল্য বলিয়া পরিগণিত হইয়া থাকে। **High treason**—Same as TREASON 1. **Treason-felony** — রাজাকে সিংহাসনচ্যুত করার অথবা কোনরূপ আইনের পরিবর্তনসাধনের জন্য রাজার বিরুদ্ধে যুদ্ধ, পার্লেমেণ্টকে ভয়প্রদর্শন, দেশআক্রমণের জন্য কোন বিদেশীয় জাতিকে উত্তেজিত করার চেষ্টা।

treas'-üre (trĕz-), *n.* & *v. t.* 1. Precious metals or gems accumulated or hoarded ; ধনরত্ন, স্বর্ণরত্ন, মণিরত্ন, সঞ্চিত ধন, কোষ। 2. A store; ভাণ্ডার। 3. Something very much valued ; as, art *treasure* ; বহুমূল্য বস্তু, বহুমূল্য সামগ্রী, অতিশয় সমাদৃত বস্তু, সাতরাজার ধন (*colloq.*), সাগরছেঁচা মাণিক। 4. (*Colloq.*) A highly efficient or satisfactory person ; as, the servant is a perfect *treasure* ; (চলিতভাষায়) অতিশয় কর্ম্মক্ষম বা সন্তোষজনক ব্যক্তি, রত্ন। ***Verb t.*** 1. To hoard up ; to lay up in store ; ভাণ্ডারজাত করা ; সঞ্চিত করা। 2. To retain carefully in the mind ;

as, *treasure* this truth carefully in your mind ; সযত্নে স্মৃতিপটে অঙ্কিত রাখা । **3.** To prize ; আদর করা, সমাদর করা, মূল্যবান বলিয়া গণ্য করা । **Lost treasure** — হারানিধি । **Treasure-city**—(বাইবেল) ধন, গুলি, প্রভৃতি যে নগরে ভাণ্ডারজাত করিয়া রাখা হইত । **Treasure-house**—ভাণ্ডারগৃহ, কোষাগার, ভাণ্ডার । **Treasure trove**—ভূগর্ভেপ্রাপ্ত অস্বামিক ধন, গুপ্ত ধন, নিধি (cf. নিধিং লব্ধো নির্ধনঃ), পোঁতা টাকা ।

treas'-ür-ĕr (trĕz-), *n.* One who has the charge of a treasure or treasury ; ধনরক্ষক, কোষাধ্যক্ষ, খাজাঞ্চী, ধনাধ্যক্ষ, কোষাধীশ, তহবিলদার (*colloq.*) **—ship,** *n.* **Lord High Treasurer**—See LORD. **Treasurer of the Household**—ইংলণ্ডের রাজকর্ম্মচারিবিশেষ ।

treas'-ür-ÿ (trĕz-), *n.* **1.** A place where treasure is laid up and preserved ; ধনাগার, কোষাগার, রাজকোষ, তেরজুরি (*colloq.*, A corruption of the English word *treasury*) । **2.** A place where public revenues are deposited ; খাজানাখানা । **3.** A department of Government, having control over the management, collection, and expenditure of the public revenue ; রাজস্ববিভাগ । **4.** The officers of the treasury department ; রাজস্ববিভাগের কর্ম্মচারিবর্গ । **5.** A collection of, or book containing generally in small bulk, much valuable information or numerous striking thoughts on any subject ; নানাজ্ঞাতব্যবিষয়পূর্ণ পুস্তক, জ্ঞানভাণ্ডার । **6.** A person viewed as repository of information ; নানাশাস্ত্রজ্ঞ ব্যক্তি । **Treasury bench**—পার্লেমেণ্টের প্রাকৃতসভার সভাধ্যক্ষ (Speaker) এর দক্ষিণদিকস্থ সম্মুখের দীর্ঘ আসন—যাহাতে First Lord of the Treasury (অভিজাতবংশীয় না হইলে), Chancellor of the Exchequer এবং মন্ত্রিসভার অন্যান্য সভ্যগণ উপবেশন করিয়া থাকেন । **Treasury Board**—রাজস্বসমিতি [First Lord of the Treasury, Chancellor of Exchequer এবং ৩ জন junior lord দ্বারা গঠিত হইয়া থাকে ।] **Treasury note**—ইংলণ্ডের রাজকোষ হইতে প্রচারিত নোট—যাহা দ্বারা সরকারী প্রাপ্য প্রভৃতি প্রদান করা যাইতে পারে । **Treasury warrant**—টাকা প্রদানের জন্য ইংলণ্ডের রাজকোষের লর্ডগণ যে আদেশপত্র দিয়া থাকেন ।

treat (trēt), *v. t., i.* & *n.* **1.** To act towards ; as, how did they *treat* you? ; to behave ; আচরণ করা ; ব্যবহার করা । **2.** To handle or develop in particular manner, in writing or speaking or by any of the processes of art ; to show or bring out the nature or character of ; "Zeuxis and Polygnotus *treated* their subjects in their pictures, as Homer did in his poetry" ; কোন বিষয়ের বক্তৃতা করা, লিখা বা আলোচনা করা ; কোন কিছুর স্বভাব বা প্রকৃতি প্রকটিত করা । **3.** To entertain ; ভোজ্য পেয়াদি প্রদানে আপ্যায়িত করা । **4.** To manage in the application of remedies, as a patient or a disease ; as, to *treat* a patient ; চিকিৎসা করা । **5.** To subject to the action of ; as, to *treat* a substance with nitric acid ; কোন কিছুর ক্রিয়ার অধীন করা । ***Verb i.*** **1.** To handle a subject esp. in writing or speaking ; to make discussion ; কোন বিষয়ে লিখা বা বক্তৃতা করা ; আলোচনা করা । **2.** To negotiate ; to propose terms for accommodation ; "He was not only willing but impatient to *treat*" ; সন্ধির কথাবার্ত্তা বলা ; মিটমাটের সর্ত্তসমূহ সম্বন্ধে প্রস্তাব করা । **3.** To come to terms ; "Inform us, will the emp'ror *treat*?" ; কোন বিষয়ে উভয় পক্ষের কথাবার্ত্তা স্থির হওয়া । **4.** To give an entertainment ; ভোজ দেওয়া । ***Noun.*** **1.** A thing that gives great pleasure ; as, the concert was a great *treat* ; অতিশয় সুখদায়ক বস্তু, অতি মনোরম বস্তু । **2.** An entertainment given as an expression of regards ; প্রীতিভোজন । **Treat'-a-ble,** *adj.* **Treat'-er,** *n.* **Treat'-ing,** *n.* **To treat of**—To discuss ; আলোচনা করা । **To stand treat**—To entertain with free supply of food etc. ; প্রীতিভোজন প্রভৃতি প্রদানে আপ্যায়িত করা ।

trea'-tise (trē-têz), *n.* A written composition of some length treating of some particular subject, and in which the principles of it are discussed or explained ; কোন বিশেষ বিষয় অবলম্বনে লিখিত পুস্তক, গ্রন্থ, নিবন্ধ (হিঃ কোঃ) ।

treat'-mĕnt (trēt-), *n.* **1.** The act or manner of treating ; ব্যবহার, আচরণ । **2.** Subjecting to the action of anything ; কোন কিছুর ক্রিয়ার অধীন করণ । **3.** Manner of applying remedies to cure disease ; চিকিৎসা । **4.** (*Rare.*) Entertainment ; "Accept such *treatment* as a swain affords" ; প্রীতিভোজ ।

trea'-tÿ (trē-), *n.* **1.** A formal aggreement, league or contract between states ; সন্ধি । **2.** Agreement between persons ; চুক্তি, নিয়ম, সংবিৎ । **To be in treaty**—To be negotiating with a person for something ; কাহারো সহিত কোন কিছুর ক্রয়বিক্রয়াদি সম্বন্ধে কথাবার্ত্তা বলা ।

trĕ'-ble (-bl), *adj., n., v. t.* & *i.* **1.** Threefold ; triple ; ত্রিগুণ ; ত্রিগুণিত । **2.** (*Mus.*) Acute ; তারাগ্রামের স্বরসম্বন্ধীয় । ***Noun.*** A soprano voice ; a soprano singer ; তারাগ্রামের স্বর, জিলস্বর ; ঐ স্বরে যে গান গায় । ***Verb t.*** To multiply by three ; তিন দ্বারা গুণ করা, তিন গুণ করা । — ***Verb i.*** To be multiplied by three ; তিন দ্বারা গুণ

হওয়া, ত্রিগুণিত হওয়া। **—bly,** *adv.* **—ness,** *n.*

trĕb′-û-chet (-(shĕt), **trĕ′-bûck-ĕt,** *ns.* **1.** (*Obs.*) A kind of balance used in weighing coins etc.; (অপ্র:) মুদ্রাদি ওজনের জন্য একপ্রকার নিক্তি। **2.** A military engine used in the Middle Ages for throwing stones etc.; ইয়ুরোপে মধ্যযুগে ব্যবহৃত একপ্রকার পাষাণক্ষেপক যন্ত্র। **3.** A kind of trap; একপ্রকার ফাঁদ।

tre-cen′-tō (trā-chĕn-), *n.* The 14th century Italian art and literature; ইতালীদেশীয় সাহিত্য এবং চারুকলার ইতিহাসে চতুর্দ্দশ শতাব্দী। **—tist,** *n.*

trĕ-chom′-ĕ-tĕr, *n.* Same as HODOMETER (which see).

tree (trē), *n.* & *v. t.* **1.** A perennial plant having a woody trunk and branches; বৃক্ষ, গাছ। [*Syn.* পাদপ, তরু, দ্রুম, বিটপী, শাখী, মহীরুহ, অনোকহ, বনস্পতি (Bearing fruit without flowers), অঙ্‌ঘ্রিপ, কুট, পলাশী, দ্রু, অগম, অগচ্ছ, বিষ্টর, কুচি, স্থির, কারস্কর, নগ, অগ, কুটার, বিটপ, কুজ, অদ্রি, শিখরী, কুঠ, কুঞ্জ, ক্ষিতিরুহ, মহীজ, ধরণীরুহ, ক্ষিতিজ, শাল, ভূরুহ, ভূজ।] [Arab. *shajr*; Burm. *bin*; Guj. *j'hara*; Hind. *j'har*; Sinh. *gass, gaha*; Tam. *maram, cherri*; Tel. *chettu, manu*; Pers. *darakht.*] **2.** (*Obs.*) Cross; ক্রুশকাষ্ঠ। **3.** (*Chem.*) A tree-like aggregation of crystals; বৃক্ষাকারে সজ্জিত দানাসমূহ। **4.** (*Math.*) A graph branching like trees; (গণিতশাস্ত্র) বৃক্ষের মত শাখান্বিত গণিতচিত্র। **5,** The frame of a saddle; জিনের কাঠাম। ***Verb t.*** **1.** To compel to climb a tree; বৃক্ষারোহণে বাধ্য করা। **2.** To put in a fix; "You are *treed* and you cannot help yourself"; মুস্কিলে ফেলা, সমস্যায় ফেলা, ফাঁপরে ফেলা। **3.** To stretch a boot on boot-tree; ফর্ম্মায় বুট জুতা আঁটা। **Tree′-less,** *adj.* Without trees; বৃক্ষশূন্য, নির্বৃক্ষ, বৃক্ষহীন, তরুশূন্য। **Christmas-tree** — See CHRISTMAS. **Family** or **genealogical tree**—See GENEALOGY. **Tree-agate**—দ্রুমাঙ্কিত গোমেদমণি। **Tree calf** — পুস্তক বাঁধাইবার জন্য দ্রুমবৎ চিত্রাঙ্কিত গোবৎসের শোধিত চর্ম্ম। **Tree-climber**—কই মাছ। **Tree-coffin**—বৃক্ষকাণ্ড ক্ষোদিত করিয়া প্রস্তুত একপ্রকার শবাধার। **Tree-creeper**—একপ্রকার ক্ষুদ্র পক্ষী। **Tree-cultus**—Same as TREE-WORSHIP. **Tree-deity** — দেবতারূপে পূজিত বৃক্ষ; দেবাশ্রিত বৃক্ষ। **Tree-fern**—বৃক্ষের সমান বৃহৎ পর্ণাঙ্গ। **Tree-frog**—একপ্রকার ভেক। **Tree-goose**—উত্তরমেরুচর রাজহংসবিশেষ। **Tree-nail**—জাহাজের তক্তা সকল জুড়িবার জন্য কাঠের একপ্রকার লম্বা পেরেক। **Tree-snake** — গেছোসাপ। **Tree-sparrow**—বুনো চড়ুই (মিউজিয়্যাম)। **Tree-worship**—বৃক্ষপূজা। [প্রাচীনকালে বৃক্ষপূজার বিশেষ প্রচলন ছিল। বর্ত্তমানকালেও ভারতবর্ষে অশিক্ষিত সম্প্রদায়ের মধ্যে বৃক্ষের বা বৃক্ষবাসী দেবতার পূজা প্রচলিত আছে। প্রত্নতাত্ত্বিকগণের মতে অতি প্রাচীনকালে বৃক্ষই দেবতারূপে সম্পূজিত হইত। অতঃপর দেবতাদির আশ্রয়স্বরূপ বলিয়া বৃক্ষের পূজা হইত। আমাদের তন্ত্র পুরাণাদিতে উভয় প্রকার প্রথার নিদর্শন পাওয়া যায়। বর্ত্তমান ভারতে বিল্ব, তুলসী, প্রভৃতি বৃক্ষপূজা সেই প্রথমোক্ত প্রথার নিদর্শন বলিয়া কোন কোন পণ্ডিত অনুমান করেন। আমাদের পূজানুষ্ঠানাদি মনোযোগের সহিত আলোচনা করিলে বৃক্ষপূজার প্রমাণ প্রাপ্ত হওয়া যায়। "রম্ভা কচ্চী হরিদ্রাচ জয়ন্তী বিল্বদাড়িমৌ। অশোকমানকশ্চৈব ধান্যঞ্চ নবপত্রিকা।" দুর্গোৎসবের নবপত্রিকার এই মন্ত্র প্রত্নতত্ত্ববিৎ পণ্ডিতগণ বৃক্ষপূজার প্রমাণস্বরূপ উল্লেখ করিয়া থাকেন। এতদ্ভিন্ন দুর্গার পত্রিকা, তুলসী, শাকম্ভরী, বটেশ্বরী, প্রভৃতি নামও বৃক্ষপূজার সূচনা করে। তন্ত্রপুরাণাদি হইতে বৃক্ষপূজার বিবিধ প্রমাণ উদ্ধৃত করা যাইতে পারে। যথা পদ্মে কুলতরুং (অশোক, বিল্ব, বকুল, আম্র, নমেরু, মরুবক, কেশর, চম্পক) প্রণম্যেৎ সাধকস্তদা — তন্ত্রঃ। "আচ্ছাদয়িত্বা ত্বং বৃক্ষং গন্ধমাল্যৈর্বিভূষয়েৎ'—মৎস্যপুরাণ। অশ্বত্থং সেবতে যস্তু বিষ্ণুবুদ্ধ্যা নরোত্তমঃ। তস্য প্রসন্নো ভগবান্ দদাতি পরমং পদম্।" "শ্রী-বৃক্ষে বোধয়ামি ত্বাং পূজাং করোম্যহং (বিল্ববোধনমন্ত্র)। "অশ্বত্থং বন্দয়েন্নিত্যং পূর্ব্বাহ্ণে প্রহরদ্বয়ে। অত ঊর্দ্ধং ন বন্দেত অশ্বত্থস্তু কদাচন॥ ওঁ চক্ষুঃস্পন্দং ভুজস্পন্দং তথা দুঃস্বপ্নদর্শনম্। শত্রূণাঞ্চ সমুত্থানমশ্বত্থ শময়াশুমে॥ অশ্বত্থরূপী ভগবান্ প্রীয়তাং মে জনার্দ্দনঃ। ত্বাং দৃষ্ট্বা নশ্যতে পাপং দৃষ্ট্বা লক্ষ্মীঃ প্রবর্ত্ততে॥ প্রদক্ষিণে ভবেদায়ুঃ সদাশ্বত্থ নমোহস্তুতে॥"—ইতি অশ্বত্থ বন্দনাকালমন্ত্রাঃ। "বৈশাখে সিঞ্চয়েন্নিত্যং বিষ্ণুমশ্বত্থরূপিণম্। চতুর্ব্বর্গফলাবাপ্তিহেতবে বৈষ্ণবো জনঃ॥ গণ্ডূষমাত্রতোয়েন কুর্য্যাদ্‌যোঽশ্বত্থসেচনম্। সোঽপি যাতি পরং স্থানং বিমুক্তঃ পাপ কোটিভিঃ॥ অশ্বত্থমূলং বিপ্রর্ষে যো বধ্নাতি শিলাদিভিঃ॥ অশ্বত্থরূপী ভগবান্ কিং তস্মৈ নহি যচ্ছতি॥ অশ্বত্থদ্রুমমালোক্য প্রণামং কুরুতে তু যঃ। আয়ুর্ব্বৃদ্ধির্ভবেৎ তস্য বর্দ্ধন্তে সর্ব্বসম্পদঃ। যথাশ্বত্থতলে বিপ্র ধর্ম্মকর্ম্ম বিধীয়তে। ন্যূনাতিরিক্ততা ন স্যাৎ তস্মিন্ কর্ম্মণি জৈমিনে॥ তত্র তীর্থানি সর্ব্বাণি ত্রিস্রোতাদীনি জৈমিনে। যত্রাশ্বত্থতরুস্তিষ্ঠেৎ একোঽপি শাখিনাং বরঃ॥ অশ্বত্থপূজকো যস্তু স এব হরি-পূজকঃ॥ অশ্বত্থমূর্ত্তি ভগবান্ স্বয়মেব যতোদ্বিজঃ॥ তরুজ্ঞানাদ্দ্বিজশ্রেষ্ঠ যোঽশ্বত্থং হন্তি মূঢ়ধীঃ। সংসারে নাস্তি তৎ কর্ম্ম যৎ কৃত্বা স চ শুধ্যতি॥ অশ্বত্থো বৃক্ষরাজোঽয়ং হরিমূর্ত্তিঃ প্রকীর্ত্তিতঃ। তস্মাদশ্বত্থ হন্তৄণাং ত্রাতা কোঽপি ন বিদ্যতে॥ অশ্বত্থং পশ্যতো বিপ্র স্পৃশতঃ স্মরতস্তথা। দেহস্থং পাতকং তস্য হরেৎ প্রণমতো হরিঃ।" * * * "সাক্ষাদেব স্বয়ং বিষ্ণু রশ্বত্থোঽখিল বিশ্বরাট্॥ তদ্ভক্তিং কুর্ব্বতঃ পুংসো বিদ্যতে নাশুভং কচিৎ।" "পত্রপুষ্পফলচ্ছায়া মূলবল্কলদারুভিঃ'। পরেষামুপকুর্ব্বন্তি তারয়ন্তি পিতামহান্॥ ছেত্তারমপি সংপ্রাপ্তং ছায়া পুষ্পফলাদিতিঃ। পূজয়ন্ত্যেব তরবো মুনি বিদ্বেষবর্জ্জিতাঃ। পিতরং নোপহিংসন্তি দ্রুমা দ্রবিণলোভতঃ। তারয়ন্তি চ মে সম্যক্ সর্ব্বস্যাতিথ্য দায়কঃ॥" ইয়ুরোপেও বৃক্ষপূজার প্রচলন ছিল। Prussianগণ পবিত্র ওক বৃক্ষের পূজা

করিত। মিসেল্‌টো নামক একপ্রকার পরাশ্রয়ী বৃক্ষ প্রাচীন ব্রিটনগণ দ্বারা পূজিত হইত। See Fergusson's *Tree and Serpent Worship*; Fraser's *Golden Bough* (2nd. ed.) 1900; Tylor *Primitive Culture*.] **At the top of the tree**—Holding the highest post; সর্ব্বোচ্চপদস্থ। **Tree of knowledge of good and evil**—বাইবেলগ্রন্থে বর্ণিত জ্ঞানতরু। এই তরুর ফল ভক্ষণের জন্য আদিমানব আদম ও আদিমানবী ইভ ঈশ্বরের কোপে পতিত হইয়াছিল। **Tree of liberty**—জনসাধারণ কর্তৃক পতাকাদি শোভিত এবং স্বাধীনতার মুকুট দ্বারা মণ্ডিত বৃক্ষ। **Tree of life**—জীবনবৃক্ষ (see *Gen.* II. 9.) **Tree of porphyry**—তার্কিক তরু (হিঃ কোঃ)। **Up a tree**—Cornered; nonplussed; কোণঠাসা; হতভম্ব, কিংকর্ত্তব্যবিমূঢ়।

treen (trēn), *n.* A township in the island of Man; ম্যানদ্বীপের ক্ষুদ্র বিভাগ বিশেষ।

trĕ'-fle (-fl), *n.* **1.** Same as TREFOIL. **2.** A mine having three chambers about a common centre; ত্রিকক্ষ বিশিষ্ট খনি।

trĕ'-foil (-fo̅yl), *n.* **1.** A three-leaved plant; ত্রিপত্র বৃক্ষ। **2.** An architectural ornament containing three cusps in a circle resembling three-leaved clover; ত্রিপত্রাকার স্থাপত্য ভূষা। **3.** (*Herald.*) A three-lobed flower or leaf; ত্রিদল পুষ্প বা পত্র। **—foiled,** *adj.*

trĕ-hȧ'-lȧ, *n.* The cocoon of *Larinus* constituting a kind of manna; পারস্য ও তুরস্কদেশের কীটবিশেষ কর্তৃক গুটির আকারে নিঃসৃত একপ্রকার শিরখণ্ড।

trĕk, *v. i.* & *n.* (South Africa) To travel by ox-wagon; গোশকটে ভ্রমণ করা। ***Noun.*** The act of trekking or emigration; গোশকটে ভ্রমণ, দেশান্তরে গমন।

trĕl'-lis (-ĭs), *n.* & *v. t.* **1.** A structure or frame of cross-barred work or lattice work used for supporting plants; বৃক্ষলতাদির আশ্রয়ের জন্য একপ্রকার জাফরিকাটা বা জালির কাজ করা কাঠাম, বৃক্ষাশ্রয়। **2.** A gate or screen of lattice-work; জালির কাজ করা দরজা বা পর্দা। ***Verb t.*** To furnish or support with trellis; "Cottages *trellised* over with exotic plants"; জাফরীর কাজ করা কাঠাম সমন্বিত করা বা উক্তরূপ কাঠাম দ্বারা আশ্রিত করা।

trĕm'-ble (-bl), *v. i.* & *n.* **1.** To shake with fear, cold, weakness, etc.; কাঁপা, থরহর করিয়া কাঁপা, শিহরিয়া উঠা, শিউরে উঠা, বেপথুমান হওয়া। **2.** To move in a quivering manner; as, leaves *tremble*; স্ফুরিত হওয়া, কম্পিত হওয়া, আধুত হওয়া, কাঁপা। **3.** (*Rare*) To be uncertain; to vacillate; to be in a state of fear; as, I *tremble* for his safety; (কচিদ্‌ব্যবহৃত) সংশয়াপন্ন হওয়া; দ্বিধা করা; আশঙ্কা করা, ভয়ান্বিত হওয়া। ***Noun.*** **1.** The act or state of being trembled; কম্পন, কম্প, কাঁপুনি, বেপথু, বেপন, স্ফুরণ। **2.** (*Pl.*) The American aspen; আমেরিকার একপ্রকার কম্পনশীল-পত্রবিশিষ্ট তরু। **3.** Kinds of disease esp. of cattle marked by trembling; গোমহিষাদির একপ্রকার কম্পনাত্মক রোগ। ***Noun.*** **1.** The act or state of shaking from weakness, cold or fear; কম্পন, বেপন, স্ফুরণ, শিহরণ। **2.** An inflammatory affection of sheep caused by eating noxious grass; বিষাক্ত তৃণাদি ভোজন হেতু মেষদিগের একপ্রকার প্রদাহজনক রোগ। **—bling,** *adj.* & *n.* Shaking as with fear, cold or the like; কম্পমান, বেপথুমান, কম্পনশীল, কম্প্রমান। *Noun.* The act of one who, or that which, trembles; কম্পন, শিহরণ। **Trembling-hammer**—Same as TREMBLER 4. **Trembling poplar, Trembling-tree**—Same as ASPEN (which see). **All of a tremble**—In a state of tremble all over the body; সর্ব্বাঙ্গ ভয়ে কণ্টকিত। **Hear and tremble**—Hear and be deeply influenced by what I tell you; শোন এবং শুনিয়া হৃদয়ে ধারণ কর। **His fate or life trembles in the balance**—He is in imminent peril of his life; some very great misfortune is about to befall him; তাহার জীবন সংশয়াপন্ন; তাহার সর্ব্বনাশ হয় হয়।

trĕm'-blĕr, *n.* **1.** One who trembles; কম্পমান ব্যক্তি। **2.** One of a religious sect of the time of Elizabeth; রাজ্ঞী এলিজেবেথের সময়ের ধর্ম্মসম্প্রদায় বিশেষের লোক (উপাসনাকালে ইহাদের শরীরে সাত্ত্বিক কম্প হইত বলিয়া এই নাম।) **3.** An electric-bell; বৈদ্যুতিক ঘণ্টা। **4.** (*Electr.*) An automatic vibtrator for making and breaking electric circuit; (তাড়িত বিদ্যা) তাড়িত কুণ্ডলী গঠন ও ভঙ্গ করণার্থ একপ্রকার স্বয়ংক্রিয় স্পন্দনজনক।

trĕ-mĕl'-lȧ, *n.* A genus of fungi; এক জাতীয় শিলীন্ধ্র।

trĕm'-ĕl-lōse, *adj.* Tremulous like jelly; জেলির মত টলটলে।

trĕ-mĕn'-dous (-dŭs), *adj.* **1.** Terrible; dreadful; ভয়ঙ্কর, ভীষণ; ঘোর, লোমহর্ষণ। **2.** Very great; as, a *tremendoua* victory; মহা, বিশাল, বিপুল, বিরাট। **—ly,** *ddv.* **—ncss,** *n.*

tremolando, *adv.* (*It.*), (Mus.) Tremulously; কম্পিতভাবে।

trĕm'-ō-lănt, —ū-lănt, *ns.* An instrument for producing a rapid quivering effect; সঙ্গীতে বা বাদ্যে কম্পনাত্মক ধ্বনিপ্রবাহ উৎপাদনের জন্য যন্ত্র বিশেষ, কম্পনজনক।

trĕ'-mŏr, *n.* **1.** An involuntary trembling; কম্প, কম্পন, প্রকম্প, স্ফুরণ, বেপথু। **2.** (*Phys.*) A vibratory motion of the earth's surface inappreciable by the unaided senses; যন্ত্রাদির সাহায্য বিনা অবিজ্ঞেয়

ভূপৃষ্ঠের একপ্রকার কম্পন। **–less,** *adj.* **Intention tremor** — কোন কার্য্য করার কালে দেহের কোন অংশ সঞ্চালিত হইলে তাহাতে যে কম্পন জাত হয়। **Mercurial tremor, Mercurial palsy** — পারদের অপপ্রয়োগ জনিত পক্ষাঘাত রোগ। **Metallic tremor**— কাঁসারী প্রভৃতির একপ্রকার কম্পনাত্মক পক্ষাঘাত রোগ।

trĕm'-ū-lous (-lŭs), *adj.* **1.** Trembling; affected with tremor; shivering; কম্পনশীল, কম্পান্বিত, চঞ্চল (হিঃ কোঃ), কম্প্র; শিহরণশীল; স্ফুরৎ, বেপমান, বেপথুশীল। **2.** Affected with fear or timidity; timid; ভয়ার্ত্ত; ভীত, শঙ্কিত, সশঙ্ক। **–ly,** *adv.* **–ness,** *n.*

trĕnch, *n., v. t. & i.* **1.** A ditch; পরিখা, পগার, কুল্যা, গড়খাই, খানা, উপকুল্যা, জুলি। **2.** (*Mil.*) A deep ditch cut for defence; (সামরিকশাস্ত্র) যে গভীর পরিখার মধ্যে অবস্থান করিয়া সৈন্যগণ কামানাদির গোলা হইতে আশ্রয় প্রাপ্ত হয়, পরিখা, পগাড়। **3.** (*Agric.*) A drain or ditch cut for the purpose of preparing or improving the soil; ক্ষেতের নালা বা জুলি। ***Verb t.*** **1.** To dig a ditch; পরিখা খনন করা, গড়খাই কাটা, কুল্যা খনন করা। **2.** (*Mil.*) To fortify with trench or trenches; (সামরিকশাস্ত্র) পরিখা বা পরিখাশ্রেণী দ্বারা সুরক্ষিত করা। **3.** (*Argic.*) To cut furrow or ditches in; (কৃষিবিদ্যা কোদালী অথবা লাঙ্গল দ্বারা গভীর ভাবে নালা বা জুলি কাটা। **4.** To groove; খাঁজকাটা। ***Verb i.*** **1.** To dig a trench or trenches; পরিখা বা পরিখাশ্রেণী খনন করা। **2.** To encroach; as, to *trench* on one's rights; অনধিকার প্রবেশ করা, চড়াও করা। **Trench'-er,** *n.* **Trench-cart**–সৈন্যগণের পরিখায় ব্যবহারের জন্য একপ্রকার ক্ষুদ্র ঠেলা গাড়ী। **To mount the trenches**—To guard in the trenches; পরিখার পাহারা দেওয়া। **To open the trenches** — To begin to dig or to form the line of approach; অগ্রসর হওয়ার জন্য সম্মুখে পরিখাশ্রেণী খনন করা।

trĕnch'-ănt, *adj.* **1.** (*Rare*) Sharp; (কচিদ্ব্যবহৃত) তীক্ষ্ণ, খরধার। **2.** Severe; as, a *trenchant* style; keen; as, *trenchant* criticism; vigorous; কঠোর; তীব্র; ওজস্বী। **–an-cy,** *n.* **–ly,** *adv.*

trĕnch'-ĕr, *n.* **1.** One who cuts trenches; পরিখাখননকারী। **2.** A wooden plate to cut meat on at table; ভোজনকালে যে কাঠের বারকাষের উপর রাখিয়া মাংস কাটা হয়। **3.** (*Archaic*) The pleasures of the table; (অপ্রঃ) উৎকৃষ্ট খাদ্য এবং পানীয়। **Trencher-cap**—কলেজের ছেলেদের একপ্রকার চৌকা টুপি। **Trencher-friend**—যে ব্যক্তি সর্ব্বদা কাহারো বাটীতে ভোজনে যোগদান করে। **Trencher-knight**—পরিবেষণকারী। **Trencher-man**—ভোজনবিলাসী। **Trencher-mate**—এক সঙ্গে ভোজনকারী; মোসাহেব।

trĕnd, *v. i. & n.* To incline; to tend; উন্মুখ হওয়া; প্রবণ হওয়া। ***Noun.*** Tendency; আসক্তি, প্রবণতা, ঝোঁক, উন্মুখতা।

trĕn'-tăl, *n.* An office for the dead consisting of thirty masses rehearsed for thirty days successively after the party's death; রোমানক্যাথলিক সম্প্রদায়ের কোন ব্যক্তির মৃত্যুর পর ক্রমান্বয়ে ত্রিশ দিবস তাঁহার জন্য যে বিশেষ পুজানুষ্ঠান করা হয়।

trente-et-quarante, *n.* (*F.*), Same as ROUGE-ET-NOIR.

trē-păn', *n. & v. t.* (*Surg.*) A cylindrical saw for perforating the skull; (অস্ত্রোপচারবিদ্যা) করোটীতে ছিদ্র করার জন্য একপ্রকার বেলনাকার করাত, গোলকরপত্র। ***Verb t.*** To perforate the skull with trepan; গোলকরপত্র দ্বারা করোটীতে ছিদ্র করা। **Trep-a-na'-tion, –ning,** *ns.*

trē-păn', *n. & v. t.* A snare; a trick; ফাঁদ; চাতুরী। ***Verb t.*** To ensnare; to beguile; ফাঁদে ফেলা, কলে ফেলা; ভুলাইয়া আনা।

trē-păng', *n.* An edible sea-slug; একপ্রকার ভোজনযোগ্য সামুদ্রিক শম্বুক।

trē-phīne' (*or* -fēn), *n. & v. t.* An improved form of trepan; একপ্রকার উন্নততর গোলকরপত্র। ***Verb t.*** To perforate the skull with such instrument; উক্ত যন্ত্র দ্বারা করোটীতে ছিদ্র করা।

trĕp-i-dā'-tion, *n.* **1.** A quaking or shivering of the limb as in paralysis; পক্ষাঘাত প্রভৃতি রোগে শরীরের কম্প। **2.** A state of terror; fear; perturbation; ভয়াকুলিতভাব, ভয়বিহ্বলতা, চকিতভাব; ভয়, শঙ্কা ত্রাস; উদ্বেগ, বিক্ষেপ, মানসিকচাঞ্চল্য। **3.** (*Ancient Astron.*) A motion which the Ptolemaic system ascribes to the firmament to account for certain apparent changes in position of the ecliptic and of the stars; (প্রাচীন জ্যোতির্বিজ্ঞান) টলিমির জ্যোতিষে কল্পিত অন্তরিক্ষের গতি।

trĕs'-păss, *v. i. & n.* **1.** To enter unlawfully upon the land of another, or upon that which is the property and right of another; অনধিকার প্রবেশ করা, অবৈধভাবে অন্যের ভূমিতে প্রবেশ করা। **2.** To intrude; as to *trespass* on one's patience (কাহারও ধৈর্য্যের সীমা লঙ্ঘন করা); অনাহূতভাবে লঙ্ঘন করা। **3.** To transgress; কর্ত্তব্য লঙ্ঘন করা, অপরাধ করা, অন্যায় করা। ***Noun.*** **1.** Unlawful entry into the land or property of another; অনধিকার প্রবেশ, চড়াও, উল্লঙ্ঘন, সীমালঙ্ঘন। **2.** A violation of some law or rule laid down; নিয়মলঙ্ঘন, আইনলঙ্ঘন। **3.** A voluntary transgression of the moral law; a wrong; as, God will forgive all *trespasses*; an improper act; নীতিবহির্ভূত কার্য্য; অন্যায়; অযুক্তকার্য্য, অকরণ। **4.** Same as ACTION OF TRESPASS (অনধিকার প্রবেশের জন্য ক্ষতিপূরণের মোকদ্দমা)। **—er,** *n.* **Trespass-offering**—মূশোর বিধিলঙ্ঘনের প্রায়শ্চিত্তের জন্য যে বলি বা উপায়ন প্রদত্ত হইত।

trĕss, *n.* & *v. t.* **1.** A braid, knot or curl of hair ; কেশগুচ্ছ, অলকগুচ্ছ, কেশপাশ, চিকুরগুচ্ছ। **2.** Hair esp. of a woman ; কেশকলাপ, কুন্তলরাজি, চিকুরকলাপ, কেশরাশি, কবরী। ***Verb t.*** To furnish with, or form into, tresses ; কেশগুচ্ছ সমন্বিত করা, গুচ্ছে গুচ্ছে কেশকলাপ বিন্যাস করা। **Tress'-y,** *adj.*

trĕs'-tle (-l),*n.* **1.** A movable frame for supporting anything ; মেজ, সেতু, প্রভৃতির অবলম্বনস্বরূপ কাঠাম বা ঢাচা। **2.** (*Naut.*) Same as TRESTLE-TREE. **Trestle-bridge**—কাঠাম বা ঢাচার উপর স্থাপিত সেতু। **Trestle-tree**—মাস্তলের দ্বিতীয়াংশের অবলম্বন স্বরূপ শয়ানখণ্ড সমূহের অন্যতম।

trĕt, *n.* An allowance formerly small to purchasers for waste or refuse matter of four pounds on every 104 ; ঝড়তি প্রভৃতির জন্য পূর্ব্বে ক্রেতাকে যে ফাউ দেওয়া হইত।

trĕv'-ĕt, *n.* Same as TRIVET.

trews (trôz), *n.* Trousers, esp. those worn by Highlanders ; পাজামা, বিশেষতঃ হাইলেণ্ডারদিগের পাজামা।

troy (trā), *n.* (*Pl.*) A card or die with three spots ; তিরি, পাশার তিন পো।

tri—, *pref.* Three ; triple ; তিন ; ত্রিগুণিত।

trī'-ă-ble (-bl), *adj.* **1.** That can be tried ; পরীক্ষণীয়, পরীক্ষাসহ। **2.** That may be subjected to trial or judicial examination ; বিচার্য্য, মোকদ্দমাযোগ্য। **—ness,** *n.*

trī-ăc'-id, *adj.* (*Chem.*) Capable of combining with three molecules of a monobasic acid ; (রসায়নশাস্ত্র) একক্ষারিক অম্লের অণুত্রয়ের সহিত সংযোজনীয়, ত্র্যম্ল।

trī-ă-cŏn-tă-hē'-drăl, *adj.* Having thirty sides or surfaces ; ত্রিংশৎপার্শ্ব বা তলবিশিষ্ট।

trī'-ăd, *n.* **1.** A unit of three ; ত্রিবস্তুরসমষ্টি, ত্রিসমষ্টি, ত্রিক (হিঃ কোঃ), ত্রয় (ঐ), ত্রয়ী (ঐ), ত্রিতয় (ঐ)। **2.** (*Chem.*) An elementary substance, each atom of which will combine with three atoms of a monad ; (রসায়নশাস্ত্র) যে মৌলিক পদার্থের প্রত্যেক পরমাণু এক বন্ধনের তিন পরমাণুর সহিত সম্মিলিত হইতে পারে, ত্রি বন্ধন, ত্র্যণুক। **3.** Trinity ; ত্রীশ্বর, ত্রিদেব (যথা ব্রহ্মা, বিষ্ণু শিব)। **4.** (*Mus.*) A chord of three notes ; (সঙ্গীতবিদ্যা) ত্রিস্বরবিশিষ্ট তন্ত্রী। **5.** A Welsh composition arranged in groups of three; ওয়েলেস্ প্রদেশের গুচ্ছত্রয়ে বিন্যস্ত রচনা বিশেষ। **—ad'-ic,** *adj.* **Higher triad**—উচ্চত্রয় (হিঃ কোঃ), উচ্চতরত্রয় (ঐ), উত্তরত্রয় (ঐ)।

trī-ă-dĕl'-phous (-fŭs), *adj.* (*Bot.*) Having stamens united in three bundles ; ত্রিগুচ্ছে মিলিত পুংকেশর-মিলিত, ত্রিগুচ্ছিত।

trī'-ăge, *n.* The refuse o coffee-beans ; কাফী বীজের অসার অংশ।

trī'-ăl, *n.* **1.** Test ; পরীক্ষা, পরখ। **2.** Experiment ; বৈজ্ঞানিক পরীক্ষা। **3.** (*Law*) The examination of a cause in controversy between parties before a proper tribunal ; (আইন) বিচার। **4.** A misfortune ; affliction ; hardship ; as, the *trials* and tribulations of life ; দুর্দ্দশা ; কষ্ট, কৃচ্ছ্র ; দুর্ভাগ্য। **Trial balance**—সকরারী জমাখরচের জমা ও খরচের দিকের তুলনা। **Trial-bit** — অশ্বের মুখের বিস্তার পরিমাপের জন্য খলীন বিশেষ। **Trial-jury**—কোন মোকদ্দমার বিচারের জন্য আহুত জুরিগণ। **Trial-list** — মোকদ্দমার তালিকা। **Trial-trip** — পরীক্ষাস্থলীয় গমন; বিশেষতঃ গতি প্রভৃতি পরীক্ষার জন্য নবনির্ম্মিত পোতের প্রথম জলযাত্রা। **Under-trial**—বিচারাধীন। **Under-trial prisoner** — হাজতী আসামী। **To give one a trial**— To employ one provisionally ; পরীক্ষাস্থলে কাহাকে নিয়োগ করা। **Trial of the pyx**—See PYX.

trī-ăn'-dri -ăn, —drous, (-drŭs), *adjs.* Having three distinct and equal stamens in the same flower with a pistil or pistils; (উদ্ভিদ্-বিদ্যা) ত্রিপুংকেশরী।

trī'-an-gle (-ăng-gl), *n.* **1.** A figure bounded by three lines and consequently containing three angles; ত্রিভুজ, ত্রিকোণ, ত্র্যস্র, ত্রিপুটক। **2.** An implement etc. of triangular shape ; ত্রিকোণ যন্ত্রাদি। **3.** (*Mus.*) A steel instrument of percussion in music bent into the form of a triangle ; বাদনের জন্য ত্রিভূজাকৃতি বাদ্যযন্ত্র বিশেষ। **4.** (*Hist.*) A frame of three halberds joined at the top and stuck in the ground to which soldiers were formerly bound to be flogged ; (ইতিহাস) অগ্রভাগ একত্রসংবদ্ধ এবং ভূতলে প্রোথিত বর্শাত্রয় রচিত কাঠাম — যাহাতে বাঁধিয়া পূর্ব্বে সৈনিকদিগকে বেত্রাঘাত করা হইত। **5.** A symbol of the Holy Trinity represented by an equilateral triangle ; খৃষ্টীয় ত্রীশ্বরসূচক সমকোণী ত্রিভুজ **6.** A kind of gin for raising heavy weights ; একপ্রকার ত্রিভুজাকৃতি ভারোত্তোলন যন্ত্র। **7.** (*Astron.*) A northern constellation ; উত্তর আকাশের যোগতারা বিশেষ। **Acute angle triangle** — ন্যূনকোণ ত্রিভুজ (:হিঃ কোঃ)। **Diagonal triangle**—কর্ণত্রিভুজ (হিঃ কোঃ)। **Equilateral triangle**—সমত্রিবাহু ত্রিভুজ।

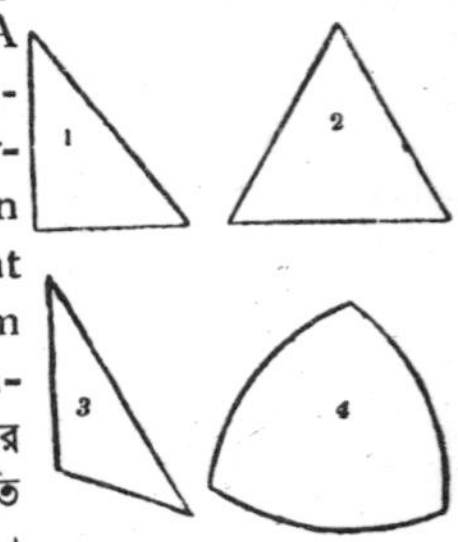

Triangles.

1. right-angled (scalene) ; 2. Equilateral ; 3. Obtuse-angled (scalene) ; 4. Spherical.

Isosceles triangle — সমদ্বিবাহু ত্রিভুজ। **Polar triangle**—ধ্রুবীয় ত্রিভুজ। **Scalene triangle**—বিষম ত্রিভুজ। **Spherical triangle**—গোলীয় ত্রিভুজ (হিঃ কোঃ), চাপীয় নক্ষত্র (*Astron.*)। **Solution of a triangle**—কোন ত্রিভুজের নির্দ্দিষ্ট ভুজ বা কোণ সমূহ প্রদত্ত হইলে অবশিষ্ট কোণ বা ভুজ সমূহ বাহির করণ। **Triangle of forces**—যদি কোন বিন্দুতে বলত্রয়ের ক্রিয়ার সামঞ্জস্য হয়—তবে উহাদিগকে দিক্‌ এবং আয়তন সম্পর্কে যথাক্রমে গৃহীত কোন রুদ্ধ ত্রিভুজের (closed triangle) ভুজসমূহ দ্বারা প্রদর্শিত করা যাইতে পারে—এই উপপাদ্য ; যে ত্রিভুজ দ্বারা উক্তরূপ বলসামঞ্জস্য প্রদর্শিত হয়। **Triangles of the neck**—ব্যবচ্ছেদের জন্য যে ত্রিকোণাকৃতি অংশ সমূহে গ্রীবা বিভক্ত করা হয়।

trī-an'-gū-lar (-ăng-gü-lêr), *adj.* **1.** Having three angles ; having the form of a triangle ; ত্রিকোণ, ত্র্যস্র; ত্রিভুজাকৃতি, ত্রিকোণাকৃতি। **—lar'-i-ty,** *n.* **—ly,** *adv.* **Triangular compass**—ত্রিপদ কম্পাস-যন্ত্র। **Triangular duel** — তিন পক্ষের মধ্যে দ্বন্দ্ব যুদ্ধ। **Triangular file**—ত্রিকোণ উখা। **Triangular numbers**—১, ২, ৩, ৪, প্রভৃতি শ্রেঢ়ীর ক্রমিক যোগফল দ্বারা ঘটিত শ্রেঢ়ী, যথা, ১, ৩, ৬, ১০, ১৫, ২১, ২৮। **Triangular prism**—যে ত্রিপার্শ্বকাচের নিম্নতল ত্রিকোণাকৃতি থাকে। **Triangular pyramid**—যে পিরামিডের পাদদেশ ত্রিকোণাকৃতি থাকে। **Triangular treaty** — তিন রাষ্ট্রের মধ্যে সন্ধি।

trī-an'-gū-lāte (-ăng-), *v. t.* **1.** To make triangular ; ত্রিকোণ করা। **2.** (*Surveying*) To divide into triangles ; (জরিপের কাজে) ত্রিভুজ সমূহে বিভক্ত করা। **3.** To survey by triangulation ; ত্রিভুজ সমূহে বিভক্ত করিয়া জরিপ করা। **—la'-tion,** *n.* **1.** The act of triangulating ; ত্রিভুজতাপাদন, ত্রিভুজমণ্ডন (হিঃ কোঃ)। **2.** The reduction of the surface of an area to triangles for the purpose of surveying ; জরীপের জন্য কোন ভুমির উপরিভাগ ত্রিকোণসমূহে বিভাজন, ত্রিকোণতাপাদন।

trī-an'-gū-lāte (-ăng-), *adj.* (*Zool.*) Marked with triangles ; (জন্তুবিদ্যা) ত্রিকোণসমূহে চিহ্নিত, ত্রিকোণাঙ্কিত। **—ly,** *adv.*

trī-ăp'-sī-dăl, *adj.* (Of a building) Having three apses ; (অট্টালিকা সম্বন্ধে) অর্দ্ধচন্দ্র বা পঞ্চভুজাকৃতি হর্ম্ম্যাংশত্রয় বিশিষ্ট।

trī'-ăs, *n.* (*Geol.*) A name sometimes given to the upper new red sandstone ; (ভুবিদ্যা) নব রক্ত-বালুকাপ্রস্তরের অপেক্ষাকৃত উর্দ্ধতর স্তর, ত্রিস্তর (অভিঃ)। **—sic,** *adj.* Pertaining to, or composed of, trias ; ত্রায়সিক।

trī-ă-tŏm'-ic, *adj.* Having three atoms ; ত্রিপরমাণুবিশিষ্ট, ত্রিপরমাণুক (হিঃ কোঃ)।

trīb'-ăl, *adj.* Pertaining to a tribe ; গুষ্টিসম্বন্ধীয়, জ্যাত্যংশসম্বন্ধীয়। **Tribal self**—জাত্যাত্মা (হিঃ কোঃ), জাত্যহংবুদ্ধি (ঐ)।

trīb'-ăl-ĭsm, *n.* The condition or state of existing or living in separate tribes ; গোষ্ঠিতা।

trī-băs'-ic, *adj.* (*Chem.*) Having three hydrogen atoms replaceable by equivalents of a base ; সমপরিমাণ ভস্ম দ্বারা অপনেয় উদজানের পরমাণুত্রয়বিশিষ্ট, ত্রিভাস্মিক।

trĭb'-ble (-l), *n.* A frame with iron threads or wires, used to dry paper ; কাগজ শুকাইবার জন্য লৌহ-তারযুক্ত এক প্রকার কাঠাম।

tribe, *n.* **1.** A nation or distinct community of savages or rude people ; অসভ্যজাতির গোষ্ঠি। **2.** A division, class or distinct portion of a people or nation ; জাত্যংশ (সাঃ পঃ), গোষ্ঠি (ঐ), উপজাতি, জাতি, (হিঃ কোঃ)। **3.** (In ancient Rome) One of the three divisions of the Roman people ; প্রাচীন রোমকগণের বিভাগত্রয়ের অন্যতম। **4.** A family, race or series of generations descending from the same progenitor, and kept distinct, as in the cases of twelve tribes of Israel ; কোন একজন পূর্ব্বপুরুষ হইতে প্রসূত ব্যক্তিগণ, কুল, বংশ। **5.** A number of plants or animals having qualities common ; সমধর্ম্মা জন্তু বা বৃক্ষবর্গ, গোষ্ঠি। **6.** (*Colloq.*) Any group of persons pursuing the same profession having common characteristics ; as, scribbling *tribe* ; একই প্রকৃতি বা স্বভাববিশিষ্টব্যক্তিগণ, একশ্রেণীর লোক। **Tribesman**—এক জাতির লোক, অসভ্য-জাতির গোষ্ঠিবিশেষের লোক।

trĭb'-lĕt, trĭb'-ŏ-lĕt, *ns.* A mandrel used in forging tubes, nuts, rings, etc. and for other purposes ; চোঙ্গা, আংটা, প্রভৃতি নির্ম্মাণে ব্যবহৃত যন্ত্রবিশেষ।

trī-bŏm'-ĕ-têr, *n.* An apparatus resembling sled used for measuring friction ; ঘর্ষণজনিত বাধার পরিমাণ মাপণার্থ যন্ত্রবিশেষ, ঘর্ষণমান।

trī'-brăch, *n.* A poetic foot of three short syllables ; লঘু অক্ষরত্রয়-বিশিষ্ট কবিতাপদ। **—brach'-ic,** *adj.*

trī-brăch'-ĭ-ăl, *n.* Three armed implements, esp. a flint implement ; ত্রিশাখযন্ত্র, বিশেষতঃ অগ্নিপ্রস্তর-নির্ম্মিত ত্রিশাখ যন্ত্রবিশেষ।

trĭb-ū-lā'-tion, *n.* A state of distress or any severe affliction ; sever suffering ; দুর্দ্দশা, দুর্গতি ; গুরুতর কষ্ট, নিদারুণ কষ্ট।

trī'-bū'-năl, *n.* **1.** The seat of a judge ; বিচারাসন। **2.** A court of justice ; বিচারালয়, বিচারমন্দির, ধর্ম্মাধিকরণ।

trĭb'-ūne, *n.* **1.** A Roman magistrate elected by the people ; জনসাধারণকর্ত্তৃক নির্ব্বাচিত প্রাচীন রোমের (প্রথমতঃ ২ জন, পরে ১০ জন) নির্দ্দিষ্টসংখ্যক কর্ম্মচারিগণের অন্যতম। এই কর্ম্মচারী রোমের প্রধান শাসনকর্ত্তা (consul), স্থবিরসভা (senate) প্রভৃতির

হস্ত হইতে প্রজাসাধারণের স্বত্ব ও অধিকার রক্ষা করিতেন। 2. (In ancient Rome) Kinds of military, fiscal or other officers; (প্রাচীন রোম্) (বিভিন্ন প্রকার) সামরিক বা রাজস্ব-বিভাগীয় কর্ম্মচারী। 3. A protector of the people; জনরক্ষক, জনবন্ধু।

trib'-üne, *n.* 1. A bench or elevated place; দীর্ঘ আসন, উচ্চস্থান। 2. A raised seat or platform; মঞ্চ, বেদী। 3. The throne of a bishop; খৃষ্টীয় ধর্ম্মাধ্যক্ষের আসন। 4. A sort of platform or rostrum where a speaker stands to address an assembly; esp. that used by speakers in French Chamber of Deputies; বক্তৃতামঞ্চ, বক্তৃতাবেদী; যে বক্তৃতামঞ্চে দণ্ডায়মান হইয়া ফরাসী দেশের জনপ্রতিনিধিগণ বক্তৃতা প্রদান করিয়া থাকেন।

trib'-ü'-tā-rȳ, *n.* & *adj.* 1. An individual, government or state that pays tribute or stated sum to a conquering power for the purpose of securing peace and protection, or as an acknowledgment of submission or the purchase of security; করদরাজ্য, করদ-রাজ, সামন্তনৃপতি। 2. An affluent; করদ নদী, সহায়ক নদী, শাখা নদী। ***Adj.*** 1. Paying tribute; as, *tributary* subjects: *tributary* nation; করদ, করপ্রদ, অধীন, পরাধীন। 2. Contributory; auxiliary; সহায়ক; সাহায্যকারী। 3. Contributing water to another river or a lake; as, a *tributary* stream; শাখা, উপ, সহায়ক।

trib'-üte, *n.* 1. An annual stated sum of money or something valuable, paid by one person or nation to another, either as an acknowledgment of submission or as the price of peace or protection or by virtue of some treaty; একরাষ্ট্র হইতে অপররাষ্ট্রে যে কর প্রদত্ত হয়, রাজ্যকর। 2. A personal contribution; কর, শুল্ক। 3. A personal contribution of any kind, as of praise, service, etc. in token of service rendered or as that which is due or deserved; anything given as a mark of respect or devotion; "The passing *tribute* of a sigh"; প্রতিদান, প্রশংসাবাদ, স্তুতিবাদ; উপহার, ভক্ত্যুপহার, প্রভৃতি। 3. The proportion of the ore or its money equivalent, given to workman for his labours; খনিজ-বিমিশ্র ধাতুর যে অংশ বা উহার মূল্য-স্বরূপ যে অর্থ শ্রমজীবিকে পারিশ্রমিকস্বরূপ প্রদত্ত হয়। **Trib'-ut-er,** *n.* One who works on tribute system; খনির যে মজুর উত্তোলিত খনিজ দ্রব্যের অংশবিশেষ বা তাহার মূল্যের পরিমিত অর্থ প্রাপ্ত হইয়া থাকে। **Tribute-work**—যে কাজের জন্ম খনির মজুর-দিগকে উত্তোলিত খনিজের অংশ বা তাহার মূল্য প্রদত্ত হইয়া থাকে।

trī-căp'-sü-lar (-lẽr), *adj.* (*Bot.* & *Zool.*) Having three capsules; (উদ্ভিদ্‌বিদ্যা এবং জন্তুবিদ্যা) ত্রি-বীজাধার-যুক্ত, ত্রিকোষবন্ধনীবিশিষ্ট।

trī-căr'-pous (-pŭs), *adj.* (*Bot.*) Having three carpels or fruits; (উদ্ভিদ্‌বিদ্যা) ত্রিকিঞ্জল্কী, ত্রিফলাণু-বিশিষ্ট, ত্রিফল।

trīce, *v. t.* (*Naut.*) To haul or tie up by means of a small rope; to hoist; (নৌ-বিদ্যা) ক্ষুদ্র রজ্জুদ্বারা টানা বা বাঁধিয়া রাখা; দড়াদড়ি দ্বারা তোলা।

trīce, *n.* A very short time; an instant; a moment; স্বল্পকাল; মুহূর্ত্ত, মুহূর্ত্তকাল; ক্ষণ। **In a trice**—In a moment; ক্ষণকালমধ্যে, চক্ষুর পলকে, চকিতে, নিমেষকালমধ্যে, ঝটপট (*colloq.*)

trī [illegible]n'-tē-nā-rȳ, *adj.* & *n.* Same as TERCENTENARY.

trī'-cēps, *adj.* & *n.* Three-headed; ত্রিশিরা। ***Noun.*** A three-headed muscle; ত্রিশিরাপেশী (বিশেষতঃ বাহুর পশ্চাদ্ভাগস্থ বৃহৎ পেশী।)

trī-cē'-rī-ŏn, *n.* (In Greek Church) A candle-stick with three brackets symbolizing Trinity; (গ্রীক ধর্ম্মসংঘে) খৃষ্টীয় ত্রি-ঈশ্বরের প্রতীকস্বরূপ ত্রিশাখ দীপবৃক্ষ।

trī-chī'-ă-sis, *n.* 1. A kidney disease in which hair-like filaments appear in the urine; মূত্রাশয়ের রোগ বিশেষ—যাহাতে মূত্রে কেশবৎ অংশু দৃষ্ট হইয়া থাকে। 2. A swelling of the breast of women in child-bed when the milk is excreted with difficulty; নবপ্রসূতার স্তনস্ফীতিরোগবিশেষ—যাহাতে দুগ্ধ অতি-কষ্টে নিঃসৃত হয়, স্তন্যকৃচ্ছ্র। 3. Introversion of the eyelashes; চক্ষুর পক্ষ্মের ভিতরের দিকে বৃদ্ধি পাইয়া অক্ষিগোলকের উপর পতিত হওন, চক্ষুর পক্ষ্মের অন্তর্মুখীনতা, পক্ষ্মকোপ, অক্ষিপক্ষ্মের বক্রতা (ডাঃ), পক্ষ্মপ্রকোপ।

trī-chī'-nă, *n.* A nematoid parasitic worm, which when immature may appear in the intestines, and when larval, in the muscles of men, pigs, etc.; মনুষ্যাদির দেহে জাত একপ্রকার কেশবৎ ক্রিমি। **Trich-i-ni'-a-sis, Trich-i-ni-za'-tion,** *ns.* **Trich'-i-nosed, Trich-i-not'-ic', Trich'-i-nous,** *adjs.*

trich'-ō-gĕm, *n.* A preparation promoting the growth of hair; কেশবর্দ্ধক তৈল প্রভৃতি।

trī-chŏg'-ĕ-nous (-nŭs), *adj.* Promoting the growth of hair; কেশবর্দ্ধক, চিকুরবর্দ্ধক।

Tricho gester chuna — খলসে (গুপ্তঃ)। [Syn. কঙ্কত্রোট, খলেশয়, খল্লিশ, খলেশ।]

Tricho gester fasciates—বড় খলসে (গুপ্ত)।

trī-chŏl'-ō-ḡȳ, *n.* The study of human hair, with a view to the prevention of baldness; কেশতত্ত্ব, চিকুরবিজ্ঞান। **—cho-log'-i-cal,** *adj.* **—gist,** *n.*

trī'-chōme, *n.* An outgrowth from the epidermis of a plant as hair or bristle or a scale; বৃক্ষের শূক, শল্ক প্রভৃতি।

trich-ō-nō'-sis, *n.* Any disease of the hair; কেশরোগ।

tri-chŏp'-ă-thy̆, *n.* **1.** Any disease of the hair; কেশরোগ। **2.** Treatment of diseases of the hair; কেশরোগ-চিকিৎসা। **Trich-o-path'-ic**, *adj.*

tri'-chŏrd, *adj.* & *n.* Three stringed; ত্রিতন্ত্রীবিশিষ্ট। ***Noun.*** An instrument with three strings; ত্রিতন্ত্রীবিশিষ্ট বাদ্যযন্ত্র।

Trichosanthes anguina — চিচিঙ্গা। [Syn. চিচিণ্ড, চিচিণ্ডা, সুদীর্ঘ, শ্বেতরাজি, গৃহকুলক।] [Tam. *pudalunkai*; Teleg. *lingapotla, pottlakaya*; Punj. *galar tori, pandol.*]

Trichosanthes cordata — ভুমিকুষ্মাণ্ড। [Syn. ভূকুষ্মাণ্ড বিদারী, ক্ষীরশুক্লা, ইক্ষুগন্ধা, ক্রোষ্ট্রী, বিদারিকা, স্বাদুকন্দা, সিতাশুক্লা, শৃগালিকা, বৃষ্যকন্দা, বিড়ালী, বৃষ্যবল্লিকা, ভূকুষ্মাণ্ডী, স্বাদুলতা, গবোষ্টা, বারিবল্লভা]

Trichosanthes cucumerina— উচ্ছে, করলা, বন পটল।

tri-chō'-sis, *n.* Same as TRICHONOSIS.

tri-chŏt'-ŏ-my̆, *n.* Division into three parts, esp. of human nature into body, soul and spirit; ত্রিধাবিভাজন, ত্রিচ্ছেদ, ত্রিধাবিভাগ (হিঃ কোঃ), বিশেষতঃ মানব প্রকৃতিকে দেহ, আত্মা ও মন এই ত্রিভাগে বিভাজন।

trī'-chrō-ĭsm, *n.* (*Phys.*) The property of some crystals of presenting different colours in three different directions; কোন কোন স্ফটিককণার তিন বিভিন্ন দিকে ত্রিবর্ণ প্রদর্শনের গুণ, ত্রিবর্ণদর্শকতা।

tri-chrō-măt'-ic, *adj.* **1.** Three-coloured; ত্রিবর্ণ। **2.** (Of the eye) Having the perception of red, green and purple; (চক্ষুসম্বন্ধে) রক্ত, হরিৎ এবং ধূম্রবর্ণগ্রাহী। **—chro'-ma-tism**, *n.*

tri'-chrōme, *adj.* Designating an apparatus printing three colours; ত্রিবর্ণমুদ্রক। **—chro'-mic**, *adj.* Same as TRICHROMATIC I.

trick, *n., v. t.* & *i.* **1.** An artifice; a stratagem; a device; চালাকী ফন্দি; ছল, চাতুরী; কৌশল, কল। **2.** A sleight of hand in performance; as, a juggler's *trick*; হাতের কৌশল, হাতের চালাকী, হস্তকৌশল। **3.** A touch; আমেজ, আভাস, লেশ। **4.** An illusicn or delusion caused to amuse; ভেল্কি। **5.** A turn or spell of duty; কাজের পালা, এক চোট কাজ। **6.** Practice; habit; mannerism; আচার; রীতি; কায়দা। **7.** (*Card-playing*) The whole number of cards played in one round and consisting of as many cards as there are players; (তাস খেলায়) পিঠ। **8.** A mischievous rougish act; দুষ্টামি, নষ্টামি, বাঁদরামি। **9.** A particular practice, habit or manner; as, he has a *trick* of drumming with his fingers; মুদ্রাদোষ। ***Verb t.*** **1.** To cheat; ঠকান, প্রবঞ্চনা করা, প্রতারণা করা, ধোঁকা দেওয়া, ফাঁকি দেওয়া। **2.** To deck; to adorn fancifully; ভূষিত করা, শোভিত করা, মণ্ডিত করা; সাজানগোজান। ***Verb i.*** **1.** (*Rare*) To practise trickrey or fraud; (ক্বচিদ্ ব্যবহৃত) চালাকি করা, ফাঁকি দেওয়া, ধোঁকা দেওয়া। **2.** To juggle; হস্তকৌশল দেখান, বাজি দেখান। **Trick'-er**, *n.* **Trick'-er-y**, *n.* Artifice; imposture; চালাকি, চাতুরী, ফন্দী, ছল, কৌশল; ফাঁকি, ধোঁকা। **Trick'-ish-ness**, *n.* **Trick'-ster**, *n.* **Trick'-y**, *adj.* **Trick-scene** — যবনিকা পতন বিনা যে দৃশ্যের অবতারণা হয়।

trick'-le (-l), *v. i., t.* & *n.* **1.** To flow in a small gentle stream; To run down in small drops; প্রবাহিত, হওয়া, বাহিয়া পড়া, দরবিগলিতধারে নির্গত হওয়া, প্রস্রুত হওয়া; বিন্দু বিন্দু করিয়া পড়া, ফোঁটা ফোঁটা করিয়া পড়া, টস টস্ করিয়া পড়া। **2.** To come out gradually; as, the secret *trickled* out; অল্পে অল্পে প্রকাশ হইয়া পড়া, অল্পে অল্পে বাহির হওয়া। ***Verb t.*** To pour, or cause to flow, in drops or in a thin stream; প্রবাহিত করা, দরবিগলিতধারে নিঃসৃত করা, দরদরধারে বিগলিত করা, বিন্দু বিন্দু করিয়া ক্ষরিত করা। ***Noun.*** A small gentle stream; a streamlet; ধারা; ক্ষুদ্র প্রবাহ। **—let**, *n.* **—ly**, *adj.*

trick'-sy̆, *adj.* **1.** Full of tricks or devices; frolicsome; কৌশলী, চাতুরীপূর্ণ; সলীল, লীলাপূর্ণ, ক্রীড়াপর, রঙ্গপ্রিয়। **2.** (*Rare*) Neat; quaint; (ক্বচিদ্ ব্যবহৃত) ফিট্‌ফাট; অপরূপ।

trick'-trăck, tick'-tăck, *ns.* An old game resembling backgammon; ক্রীড়াবিশেষ।

trī-clin'-i-ŭm, *n.* Among the Romans a dining-room or table with couches on three sides; (প্রাচীন রোমকদিগের) ত্রিপার্শ্বে বিলাসখট্টা সমন্বিত অপরাহ্নভোজনকক্ষ বা মেজ।

tri-cŏc'-cous (-ŭs), *adj.* Having three carpels; ত্রিকিঞ্জল্কী।

tri'-col-our (-kŭl-ėr), **—or** (-ėr), *adj.* & *n.* Having three colours; printed in three colours; ত্রিবর্ণ; ত্রিবর্ণে মুদ্রিত, তিন রঙ্গের। ***Noun.*** The French national standard having vertical stripes of three colours (red, white and blue); ত্রিবর্ণের (শ্বেত, রক্ত ও নীলবর্ণের) স্থুলরেখাবিশিষ্ট ফরাসীদেশের জাতীয় পতাকা।

tri'-cŏrn, *adj.* & *n.* Having three horns or horn-like pre-eminence; ত্রিশৃঙ্গ, ত্রিকুট। ***Noun.*** **1.** A three-cornered hat; ত্রিকোণ টুপি। **2.** A French gendarme's two-cornered hat; ফরাসীদেশীয় সশস্ত্র পুলিশের দ্বিকোণ টুপি।

tri-cŏr'-pō-răl, **—rāte**, *ns.* (*Herald.*) Having three bodies; (কুলবিদ্যা) ত্রিদেহী।

tricot, *n.* **1.** A sort of ribbed dress-materal; পোষাকের জন্য

একপ্রকার শিরাল কাপড়। 2. A fabric made of yarn or woollen thread woven by hand ; একপ্রকার হাতে বোনা পশমী কাপড়। **Tricot-stitch**—একপ্রকার ক্রোশের সেলাই।

trī-cŏt-ȳ-lē′-dŏ-nous (-nŭs), *adj.* (*Bot.*) Having three cotyledons ; (উদ্ভিদ্ বিদ্যা) ত্রিবীজদলবিশিষ্ট।

trī-crŏt′-ic, *adj.* (Of pulse) Having triple beats ; (নাড়ীসম্বন্ধে) ত্রিস্পন্দন-বিশিষ্ট। **Tri′-cro-tism**, *n.*

trī-cŭs′-pĭd, *adj.* **1.** Having three cusps or points ; ত্রিশিখ, ত্রিচূড়, ত্রিদণ্ড (হঃ চঃ)। **2.** (*Anat.*) Pertaining to tricuspid valve (below) ; (শারীর-সংস্থানবিদ্যা) ত্রিশিখকবাট-সম্বন্ধীয়। **Tricuspid murmur**—ত্রিশিখকবাট বিকৃত হইলে যে এক-প্রকার ধ্বনি উৎপন্ন হয়। **Tricuspid valve**—হৃৎপিণ্ডের দক্ষিণ হৃৎকোষের মুখে ত্রিকোণাকৃতি মাংসফলকত্রয় রচিত কবাট, ত্রিশিখকবাট।

trī′-cȳ-cle (-kl), *n.*, *v. t.* & *i.* A velocipede with three wheels ; ত্রিচক্রযান। ***Verb t & i.*** To ride on a three-wheeled cycle ; ত্রিচক্রযান চালাইয়া চলা। **—clist**, *n.*

trī-dăc′-tȳl, **—tȳ-lous** (**—**lŭs), *adjs.* With three fingers or toes ; ত্র্যঙ্গুলিবিশিষ্ট।

trīde, *adj.* Swift ; fleet ; দ্রুত ; সত্বর, শীঘ্র।

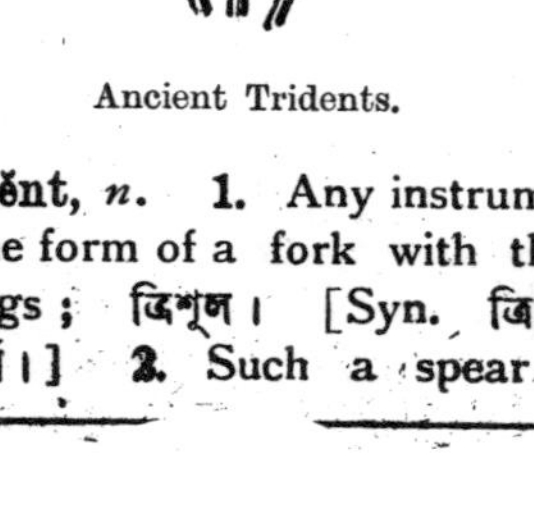

Ancient Tridents.

trī′-dĕnt, *n.* **1.** Any instrument of the form of a fork with three prongs ; ত্রিশূল। [Syn. ত্রিশিখ, ত্রিশীর্ষ।] **2.** Such a spear or sceptre as an attribute of Posidon or Neptune ; গ্রীক জল-দেবতার ত্রিশূল। **3.** A three-pronged fish spear ; মৎস্য বিদ্ধ করার জন্য একপ্রকার তিন কাটার টেঁটা।

trī-dĕn′-tāte, *adj.* With three teeth or prongs ; ত্রিদন্ত, ত্রিশঙ্কু।

Trī-dĕn′-tīne, *adj.* & *n.* Pertaining to the Council of Trent ; Trent নগরীতে (১৫৪৫—৬৩) খৃঃ অব্দে যে খৃষ্টীয়সংসদের অধিবেশন হয়—তৎসম্বন্ধীয়। ***Noun.*** A Roman Catholic ; রোমান ক্যাথলিক।

trī-dĭg′-i-tāte, *adj.* Same as TRIDACTYL.

trī-dī-mĕn′-sion-ăl, *adj.* Of three dimensions ; ত্রিপরিমাণসম্বন্ধীয়, দৈর্ঘ্য প্রস্থভেদসম্বন্ধীয়।

trīd′-ü-ō, **trīd′-ü-ŭm**, *ns.* A space of three days ; esp. as in the Roman Catholic Church, a three days' service of prayer for keeping some saint's day or as preparation for obtaining saint's intercession ; দিবসত্রয় ; (রোমান ক্যাথলিক ধর্ম্মসংঘ) কোনও খৃষ্টীয় সিদ্ধপুরুষের দিবস পালনের পূর্ব্বে বা ঐরূপ কোন মহাপুরুষের উপরোধে ভগবানের নিকট হইতে কোনপ্রকার অনুগ্রহ লাভের জন্য ত্রিদিবসব্যাপী প্রার্থনা।

trī-ĕn′-nĭ-ăl, *adj.* & *n.* **1.** Lasting for three years ; ত্রিবর্ষব্যাপী। **2.** Happening once in three years ; প্রতি তিন বর্ষ অন্তে সংঘটিত, ত্রৈবার্ষিক। ***Noun.*** **1.** A mass repeated every day for three years for the repose of the soul of a dead person ; মৃত ব্যক্তির আত্মার শান্তির জন্য তিন বৎসর পর্য্যন্ত যে উপাসনা করা হয়। **2.** Same as TRIENNIAL PLANT (below). **3.** The third anniversary of any event ; ত্রৈবার্ষিক উৎসব। **Triennial Act**—(ইংলণ্ডের ইতিহাস) ১৬৯৪ খৃঃ অব্দে বিধিবদ্ধ আইন বিশেষ—এই আইন দ্বারা পার্লেমেণ্ট সভার স্থায়িত্বকাল তিন বৎসরে সীমাবদ্ধ করা হইয়াছিল। এই আইন ১৭১৬ খৃঃ অব্দে রহিত করা হয়। **Triennial plant**—ত্রিবর্ষস্থায়ী গুল্মাদি।

trī′-ĕr, *n.* **1.** One who tries ; one who tests anything ; চেষ্টাকারী ; পরীক্ষক। **2.** One that tries judicially ; বিচারক। **3.** One who is appointed to decide whether a challenge to a juror is just ; কোন জুরীর নিয়োগের বৈধতা-সম্বন্ধে আপত্তি উত্থাপিত হইলে যে ব্যক্তি তাহার মীমাংসা করিয়া থাকেন।

trī′-ĕr-ârch, *n.* **1.** (*Gk. Antiq.*) The commander of a trireme ; (গ্রীক প্রত্নতত্ত্ব) ত্রিক্ষেপণীপংক্তি বিশিষ্ট পোতের অধ্যক্ষ। **2.** A rich man who was obliged to build such ships and furnish them at his own expenses ; যে ধনী ব্যক্তি নিজ ব্যয়ে ঐরূপ পোত নির্ম্মাণ ও সজ্জিত করিতে বাধ্য থাকিতেন, ত্রিপোত-পাল।

trī′-ĕr-ârch-ȳ, *n.* **1.** The office or duty of a trierarch ; ত্রিপোত-পালের পদ বা কর্ত্তব্য। **2.** The system in ancient Greece under which citizens furnished triremes ; প্রাচীন গ্রীসের যে ব্যবস্থা অনুসারে নাগরিকবৃন্দ ত্রিপোত জোগাইতেন।

trī-fā′-ci-ăl (-shi-), *adj.* & *n.* Pertaining to the fifth pair of cranial nerves ; মস্তিষ্কস্নায়ুর পঞ্চমযুগ্ম সম্বন্ধীয়। ***Noun.*** Same as TRIGEMINUS.

trī′-fĭd, *adj.* (*Bot.* & *Zool.*) Three cleft ; ত্রিধাবিদীর্ণ, ত্রিখণ্ডিত।

trī′-fle (-fl), *n.*, *v. t.* & *i.* **1.** Anything of little value ; তুচ্ছ জিনিষ, সামান্য জিনিষ, অকিঞ্চিৎকর বস্তু। **2.** A light kind of dish of the pudding kind ; পিষ্টক জাতীয় একপ্রকার লঘুপাক খাদ্য। **3.** A kind of pewter ; এক-প্রকার রূপদস্তা। **4.** A small amount ; as, a *trifle* of money ; অল্প পরিমাণ, সামান্য পরিমাণ। ***Verb t.*** **1.** To spend in vanity ; to waste to no good purpose ; to dissipate ; বাজেকাজে ব্যয় করা ; অনর্থক নষ্ট করা, উড়াইয়া দেওয়া। **2.** (*Rare*) To treat as trivial ; (কচিৎ ব্যবহৃত) তুচ্ছ

বলিয়া গণ্য করা। ***Verb i.*** To act or talk without seriousness ; to indulge in light amusement ; তুচ্ছ-কথা বলা, গা না দিয়া কাজ করা ; তুচ্ছ আমোদপ্রমোদে মত্ত থাকা, ছেলেমি করা। **–fler,** *n.* One who trifles or acts with levity ; তুচ্ছ আমোদ প্রমোদে নিরত ব্যক্তি, যে ব্যক্তি হেলা করিয়া কাজ করে, যে ব্যক্তি বাজে কাজে সময় নষ্ট করে। **–fling,** *n.* **–fling-ly,** *adv.* **Trifle-ring** — বাজি দেখাইবার জন্য বিভিন্নপ্রকার চক্রের গুচ্ছ। **He seems a trifle angry**—He appears to be somewhat angry ; সে যেন কিছু চটিয়াছে। **To trifle with**—To treat as of no consequence ; to make a fool of ; তুচ্ছ করা, নগণ্য বলিয়া মনে করা, তাচ্ছল্য করা, উড়াইয়া দেওয়া ; বোকা সাজান। To ridicule ; বিদ্রূপ করা। To toy with ; খেলা করা।

trī-flō′-ràl, –rous (-rŭs), *adjs,* Bearing three flowers ; ত্রিপুষ্পপ্রসূ।

trī-fō′-li-āte, –āt-ĕd, *adjs.* Three leaved ; ত্রিপত্র। **Trifoliate orange** — একপ্রকার জাপানদেশীয় কমলালেবু।

trī-fō′-li-ŭm, *n.* A genus of clovers ; একজাতীয় গুল্ম।

trī-fō′-ri-ŭm, *n.* (*pl.*-A), The arcade over the arches of a church between arches and side aisles ; গির্জ্জার তোরণসমূহ এবং পার্শ্বভাগের মধ্যবর্ত্তী তোরণসমূহের উপরিস্থ তোরণাবলি।

trī′-fôrm, –formed (-fôrmd), *adjs.* Having triple form, body or character ; ত্রিরূপ, ত্রিদেহ, ত্রিপ্রকৃতিক।

trī-fur′-cāte (-fêr-), *adj.* & *v. t.* Having three forks or branches ; ত্রিশাখ। ***Verb t.*** To divide into three parts ; ত্রিধা বিভক্ত করা।

trig, *v. t.* & *n.* To stop a wheel by placing something beneath it ; নীচে কোন বস্তু দিয়া গাড়ীর চাকার গতি রোধ করা। ***Noun.*** A skid for a wheel, etc. ; গতিরোধ করার জন্য গাড়ী প্রভৃতির চাকার নীচে যাহা দেওয়া হয়।

trig′-ă-mous (-mŭs), *adj.* **1.** Thrice-married ; তিনবার বিবাহিত, ত্রিবিবাহিত। **2.** Having three sorts of flowers male, female and hermaphrodite in the same flower head ; একই পুষ্পশীর্ষে পুং স্ত্রী এবং নপুংসক পুষ্পবিশিষ্ট। **–mist,** *n.* One who marries three wives ; ত্রি স্ত্রী বিবাহকারী। **–my,** *n.* The act or state of having three husbands or wives at the same time ; ত্রিবিবাহকরণ, ত্রিবিবাহ।

trī-gĕm′-i-năl, *adj.* & *n.* Designating the fifth cranial nerves ; পঞ্চম মস্তক-স্নায়ুসম্বন্ধীয়। ***Noun.*** A trigeminal nerve ; মস্তকের পঞ্চমস্নায়ু। **Trigeminal neuralgia**—অনন্তবাত (সাঃ পঃ)।

trī-gĕm′-i-nŭs, *n.* The trigeminal nerve ; মস্তকের পঞ্চমস্নায়ু।

trig′-ger (-êr), *n.* The catch or lever which on being pulled back, liberates the hammer of the lock of a gun or pistol ; বন্দুকের টিপকল।

trī′-glŏt, *adj.* Written in three languages ; ত্রিভাষায় লিখিত।

trī′-glȳph, *n.* A three-grooved tablet at equal distances along

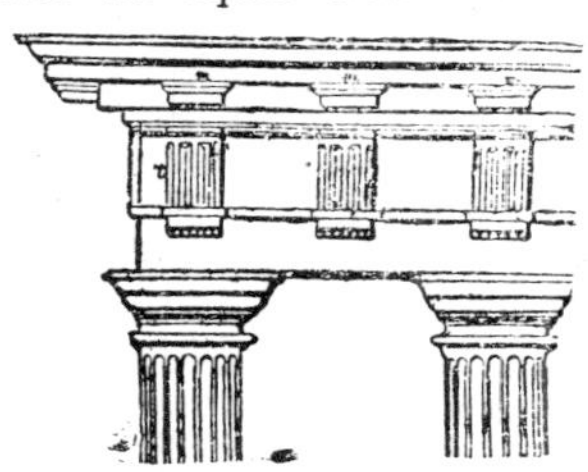

Frieze of Roman Doric order.
t, triglyphs.

the frieze in Doric architecture ; ডোরিক স্থাপত্যপদ্ধতিতে কার্ণিসের অব্যবহিত নিম্নস্থ অট্টালিকার অনুলম্বে সমদুরবর্ত্তী ত্রিখাজবিশিষ্ট ফলকসমূহের অন্যতম। **–al, –glyph′-ic, –glyph′-i-cal.** *adjs.*

trī′-gŏn, *n.* **1.** (*Astrol.*) The junction of three signs of the zodiac being divided into four groups ; তিনরাশির সংযোগ। **2.** Same as TRINE. **3.** A kind of triangular lyre or harp ; একপ্রকার ত্রিকোণ বীণা। **4.** (*Gk. Antiq.*) A game at ball for three persons ; (প্রাচীন গ্রীস) তিন ব্যক্তির জন্য একপ্রকার কন্দুকক্রীড়া। **5.** (*Math.*) A triangle ; (গণিতশাস্ত্র) ত্রিকোণ। **–gon′-ic** *adj.*

trī′-gō-năl, *adj.* (*Math.*) Triangular ; (গণিতশাস্ত্র) ত্রিকোণ। **–ly,** *adv.* **–nous,** *adj.*

trī-gō-neu′-tic (-nū-), *adj.* Having three broods in a year ; বৎসরে তিনবার সন্তান প্রসবকারী।

trig-ō-nŏm′-ĕ-têr, *n.* An instrument for solving plane right-angled triangles by inspection ; ত্রিকোণমাপক, ত্রিকোণমান।

trig-ō-nŏm′-ĕt-rȳ, *n.* The branch of mathematics which treats of the relations between sides and angles of triangles ; ত্রিকোণমিতি। **–no-met′-ric, –no-met′-ri-cal,** *adjs.* **–no-met′-ri-cal-ly,** *adv.* **Analytical trigonometry**—বৈজিক ত্রিকোণমিতি (হিঃ কোঃ)। **Plane trigonometry**—সরল ত্রিকোণমিতি (হিঃ কোঃ)। **Spherical trigonometry**—গোলীয় ত্রিকোণমিতি (হিঃ কোঃ)।

trī′-grăm, trī′-grăph, *ns.* Three letters united in pronunciation so as to have but one sound, or to form but one syllable (as *adieu*) ; একই ধ্বনি বা শব্দাংশবাচক সংযুক্ত অক্ষরত্রয়।

trī′-ḡȳ-nous (-nŭs), *adj.* Having three pistils ; স্ত্রীকেশরত্রয় বিশিষ্ট, ত্রিস্ত্রীকেশরী।

trī-hĕd′-drăl, *adj.* With three surfaces ; ত্রিপৃষ্ঠ।

trī-hē′-drŏn, *n.* A figure formed by three planes meeting at a point ; ত্রিকোণ ঘন।

trī′-jū-gāte, trī′-jū′-gous (-gŭs), *adjs.* Having three pairs of leaflets ; পত্রকযুগ্মত্রয়বিশিষ্ট।

trīke, (*Colloq.*) *n.* & *v. t.* Same as TRICYCLE.

trī'-lābe, *n.* A three-pronged instrument used in extracting foreign substances from the bladder ; মূত্রাশয় হইতে দূষিত পদার্থ নিষ্কর্ষণের জন্য যন্ত্র বিশেষ, ত্রিশঙ্কু।

trī-lā'-bi-āte, *adj.* Three-lipped ; ওষ্ঠত্রয়বিশিষ্ট।

trī-lăm'-i-nar (-nêr), *adj.* Pertaining to, or consisting of, three layers ; ত্রিস্তরীয়, ত্রিস্তরযুক্ত।

trī-lăt'-ĕr-ăl, *adj.* Pertaining to, or having, three sides ; ত্রৈপার্শ্বিক, ত্রিপার্শ্ববিশিষ্ট। **–ly,** *adv.*

trī-lĕm'-mă, *n.* A situation offering choice between three things ; ত্রিশঙ্কট, তেটানা (after দোটানা), ত্রিবিধসম্ভব (হিঃ কোঃ), ত্রিবিধবিকল্প (ঐ)।

trī-lĭn'-ĕ-ar (-êr), *adj.* Composed of, or consisting of, three lines ; ত্রিরেখ।

trī-lĭn'-guăl (-lĭng-), *adj.* Consisting of, or written in, three languages ; ত্রিভাষাত্মক, ত্রিভাষারচিত বা লিখিত।

trī-lĭt'-ĕr-ăl, *adj.* & *n.* Consisting of three letters ; ত্র্যক্ষরাত্মক। ***Noun.*** A triliteral word ; ত্র্যক্ষর শব্দ। **–al'-i-ty,** *n.* **–ism,** *n.* The character of being triliteral or consisting of three letters, as the Semitic languages ; ত্র্যক্ষরতা।

trī'-lĭth, *n.* A form of megalithic monument consisting of two upright stones supporting another lying cross-wise ; খাড়া ভাবে স্থাপিত শিলাফলক দ্বয়ের উপরে শয়ান ভাবে রক্ষিত শিলাফলক দ্বারা রচিত স্মৃতিস্তম্ভ। **–lith'-ic,** *adj.*

trĭll, *n.* & *v. t.* & *i.* **1.** A shake of the voice in singing ; স্বরকম্পন। **2.** (*Mus.*) Same as SHAKE *n.* 3. **3.** A consonant pronounced with a trilling sound e.g. *l* or *r.*; কম্পিত স্বরে উচ্চারিত স্বরবর্ণ। **4.** A warble ; কম্পিত কূজন বা কাকলী। ***Verb t.*** To sing with trill ; স্বর কাঁপাইয়া গান করা। ***Verb i.*** To sing with trill ; কম্পিত স্বরে গান করা।

trĭl'-ling (-ĭng), *n.* **1.** A composite crystal composed of three individuals ; ত্রিকোণাত্মক স্ফটিক। **2.** Any one child of a triplet ; এক সময়ে প্রসূত সন্তানত্রয়ের অন্যতম।

trĭl'-lion (-yŏn), *n.* **1.** (In England) A million million million ; (ইংলণ্ডে) একের ডাইনে ১৮টী শূন্য বসাইলে যে সংখ্যা হয়, শত পরার্দ্ধ। **2.** (In the United States and France) The number expressed by a unit with twelve zeros annexed ; ১এর ডাইনে ১২টী শূন্য বসাইলে যে সংখ্যা হয়, এক সমুদ্র।

trĭl'-li-ŭm, *n.* A plant of the liliaceous family of a species commonly called wake-robin ; একজাতীয় গুল্ম।

trī'-lō-bāte, *adj.* Three-lobed, ত্রিকর্ণ, ত্রিবল্লীক।

trī'-lō-bīte, *n.* The fossil articulated animal which existed in the paleozoic age ; প্রত্নপ্রস্তর যুগের ত্রিপর্ব্ব-বিশিষ্ট জীবের শিলীভূত দেহ, ত্রিবলি (অভিঃ)। **–bit'-ic,** *adj.*

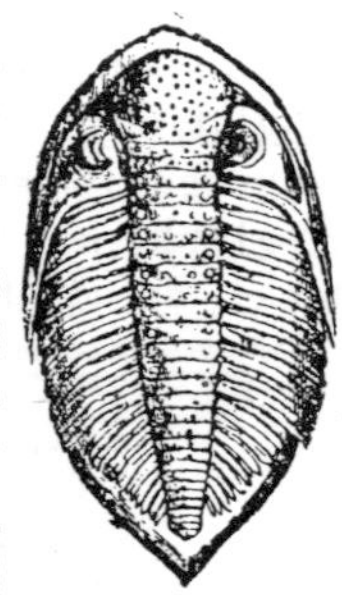

Trilobite.

trī-lŏc'-ū-lar (-lêr), *adj.* With three cells or compartments ; ত্রিকোষবিশিষ্ট, ত্রিকোষসম্বলিত, ত্রিপ্রকোষ্ঠ (সাঃ পঃ)।

trĭl'-ō-ġy, *n.* **1.** (*Gk. Antiq.*) A series of three dramas each complete in itself forming one common theme ; ক্রমান্বয়ে অভিনেয় একই বিষয় অবলম্বনে লিখিত নাটকত্রয়। **2.** Any literary production or musical composition consisting of three parts forming a connected whole ; একই বিষয় সম্বন্ধে তিন অংশে রচিত সঙ্গীত বা রচনা।

trĭm, *adj., v. t., i.* & *n.* Neat and in good order ; well-equipped ; tidy ; smart ; পরিচ্ছন্ন, পরিপাটি ; সুসজ্জিত ; ফিটফাট ; চোস্ত। ***Verb t.*** **1.** To adjust ; ঠিকঠাক করা। **2.** To dress ; পোষাক পরিচ্ছদে সজ্জিত করা। **3.** To adorn ; to embellish with or as with ribbons, laces, or other ornament ; ভূষিত করা, অলঙ্কৃত করা ; ফিতা লেইস, প্রভৃতি দ্বারা সজ্জিত করা। **4.** To clip ; as, to *trim* the hair ; to pare ; to prune ; ছাঁটা ; কাটাছাঁটা ; ছাঁটা। **5.** (*Carp.*) To make smooth ; to fit to anything ; (তক্ষণবিদ্যা) মসৃণ করা, পালিশ করা ; কোন কিছুতে লাগান। **6.** (*Colloq.*) To rebuke ; (চলিত-ভাষায়) তিরস্কার করা। **7.** To beat ; প্রহার করা। **8.** (*Naut.*) To adjust as a ship or a boat, by arranging the cargo or diposing the weight of persons or goods so equally on each side of the centre and at each end, that she shall sit well in the water and sail well ; (নৌবিদ্যা) জাহাজের মাল কিম্বা আরোহী বা জিনিষপত্র উভয় পার্শ্বে এবং প্রত্যেক প্রান্তে ঠিকঠাক করিয়া গুছাইয়া যাহাতে জাহাজ কোন দিকে না হেলিয়া সুন্দররূপে চলিতে পারে তাহার ব্যবস্থা করা [যখন জাহাজের আগা-গলুই পাছা-গলুই অপেক্ষা অধিক জল টানে তখন উহাকে *Trimmed by the head* কহে। পাছা-গলুইএর দিকে আগাগলুই অপেক্ষা অধিক জল টানিলে জাহাজকে *Trimmed by the stern* কহে] **9.** (*Naut.*) To arrange in due order for sailing ; as, to *trim* the sail of a ship ; (নৌবিদ্যা) চালাইবার জন্য (জাহাজের পাইল প্রভৃতি) ঠিকরূপে খাটান। ***Verb i.*** To maintain middle position between two parties so as to appear to favour each or to be neutral between them ; উভয় পক্ষের মধ্যে মধ্যস্থতা অবলম্বন করা।

Noun. **1.** (*Rare*) Dress ; (কচিদ্-ব্যবহৃত) পোষাক, পরিচ্ছদ, বেশভূষা। **2.** Order ; adjustment ; পারিপাট্য, শৃঙ্খলা ; ঠিকঠাক অবস্থা। **3.** The state of a ship or her cargo, ballasts, masts, etc. by which she is well prepared for sailing ; জাহাজের মাস্তুল, মাল পত্র প্রভৃতির সুসজ্জিত অবস্থা যাহাতে উহা স্বচ্ছন্দে জলযাত্রা করিতে পারে, সুসজ্জিত অবস্থা। **Trim'-ly,** *adv.* **Trim'-ness,** *n.* **To trim a person's jacket**—(*Colloq.*) To whip him ; বেত লাগান। **To trim up**—To dress up ; to make n at or trim ; সজ্জিত করা ; পরিপাটি করা, সাজান গোছান। **Trim of the masts**—জাহাজের মাস্তুলসমূহের সম্পর্কে এবং পরস্পরের সম্বন্ধে অবস্থিতি।

trī-měn'-sū-ăl, trī-měs'-trăl, trī-měs'-tri-ăl, *adjs.* Occurring every three months ; ত্রিমাসান্তে সংঘটিত, ত্রৈমাসিক।

trī'-měr-ous (-ŭs), *adj.* Having three parts or joints ; তিন অংশ বা সন্ধিত্রয়বিশিষ্ট, ত্র্যংশী, ত্র্যংশক (সাঃ পঃ)।

trim'-ĕ-těr, *n.* & *adj.* A division of verse consisting of three measures of two feet each ; ত্রৈমাত্রিক কবিতা পংক্তি। ***Adj.*** Consisting of such divisions ; ত্রৈমাত্রিক।

trim'-mer (-ěr), *n.* **1.** One who trims, fits, arranges or ornaments ; যে ব্যক্তি ঠিকঠাক করে, যে ব্যক্তি কাটাছাঁটা করে, যে ব্যক্তি সাজায় গোছায়, সজ্জাকারী। **2.** One who fluctuates between parties ; a time-server ; যে ব্যক্তি পরস্পরবিরোধী পক্ষদ্বয়ের মধ্যে মধ্যস্থ ভাব অবলম্বন করে ; সময়সেবী ব্যক্তি। **3.** One who chastizes or reprimands ; a sharp shrewdish person ; তিরস্কারকারী, গঞ্জনাকারী ; চালাক লোক। **4.** Kinds of instruments for clipping etc. ; কাটা ছাঁটার জন্য বিভিন্নপ্রকার যন্ত্র। **5.** A piece of timber inserted in a roof, floor, etc. to support the ends of any of the joists, rafters, etc. ; কড়ি, বর্গা, প্রভৃতির প্রান্ত রক্ষার জন্য ছাদ, গৃহতল, প্রভৃতিতে নিবিষ্ট কাষ্ঠখণ্ড।

trim'-ming (-ing), *n.* **1.** The act of one who trims ; কাটাছাঁটা, ফিতা জরি প্রভৃতি দ্বারা সজ্জিত করণ। **2.** Ornamental appendages such as lace, ribbon, etc. ; পোষাকের ফিতা, লেইস, ঝালর, প্রভৃতি। **3.** Behaviour of one who fluctuates between two parties ; neutrality ; উভয় পক্ষের মধ্যে মধ্যস্থ ভাব ; নির্লিপ্ততা। **4.** (*Pl.*) Any accessories, as of dish ; as, a leg of mutton and *trimmings* ; আনুষঙ্গিক বস্তু, উপস্কর, ব্যঞ্জনাদির সহিত যে চাটনী, আচার প্রভৃতি আহার করা হয়। **5.** Rebuke ; beating ; তিরস্কার ; প্রহার।

trī-mŏr'-phic, —phous (-fŭs), *adjs.* Having three distinct forms ; ত্রিরূপাত্মক।

trī-mŏr'-phism, *n.* **1.** (*Biol.*) Existence in three distinct forms ; (জীববিজ্ঞান) ত্রিরূপত্ব। **2.** The property of crystallising in three distinct forms ; বিভিন্ন আকারত্রয়ে অর্কতাপত্তি, ত্রিরূপতা।

trīne, *adj.* & *n.* **1.** Triple ; threefold ; ত্রয়াত্মক, ত্র্যাত্মক ; ত্রিগুণিত, ত্রিগুণ। **2.** (*Astrol.*) Of a trine ; in trine ; ত্রিকোণসম্বন্ধীয় ; অপর গ্রহের ত্রিকোণে অবস্থিত। ***Noun.*** (*Astrol.*) The aspect of planets distant from each other 120 degress ; (ফলিত জ্যোতিষ) রাশিচক্রের গ্রহগণের পরস্পর হইতে ১২০° দূরে অবস্থিতি, ত্রিকোণ (বৃঃ সং)। **Trī'-nal, Trī'-na-ry,** *adjs.*

trī-něrv'-āte, *adj.* Three-nerved ; ত্রিশিরাবিশিষ্ট।

trin'-gā, *n.* A genus of birds ; একপ্রকার পক্ষী।

trin'-gle (tring-gl), **1.** (*Arch.*) A little square member or ornament ; (স্থপতিবিজ্ঞান) চতুষ্কাকৃতি ক্ষুদ্র ভূষা। **2.** A curtain-rod ; খাটে মশারী টাঙ্গাইবার দণ্ড। **3.** A strip of wood at the end of a gun-platform to check recoil ; পশ্চাদ্দিকে ধাক্কা নিবারণের জন্য কামান স্থাপনের বেদীর প্রান্তে নিবদ্ধ কাষ্ঠফলক।

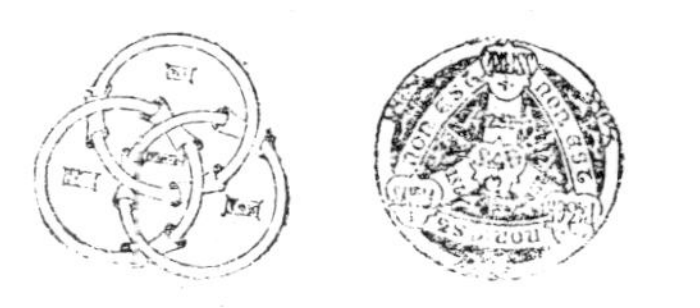

Symbols of the Holy Trinity.

trin'-i-ty̆, *n.* **1.** (*Theol., cap.*) The union of three persons in one Godhead (the Father, the Son and the Holy Ghost) ; ত্রিমূর্ত্তি, পিতা ঈশ্বর, পুত্র এবং পবিত্রাত্মা। **2.** A symbolic representation of the Trinity ; খৃষ্টীয় ত্রীশ্বরের প্রতীক (বিশেষতঃ ত্রিকোণ)। **3.** A group of three ; a triad ; ত্রিবস্তুর সম্মিলন ; ত্রিবস্তু, ত্রিমূর্ত্তি, ত্রিক (হিঃ কোঃ), ত্রিতয় (ঐ), ত্রিমুখত্ব (ঐ), ব্যক্তিত্রিতয়ত্ব (ঐ)। **4.** (*Rare*) The condition of being three ; (কচিদ্ব্যবহৃত) ত্রিত্ব, ত্রিগুণত্ব (হিঃ কোঃ)। **5.** A triple pipe-cleaner ; ত্রিমুখ ধূমনল পরিমার্জ্জক। **—ta'-ri-an,** *n.* **1.** (*Cap.*) One who believes the doctrine of the Trinity ; ত্রীশ্বরবাদী, ত্রিমূর্ত্তিবাদী। **2.** (*Cap.*) A religious order founded in Rome in 1198 to redeem Christian captives from the infidels ; মুসলমানদিগের হস্ত হইতে খৃষ্টীয় বন্দিগণের উদ্ধারসাধনের জন্য ১১৯৮ খৃঃ অব্দে রোম-নগরীতে প্রতিষ্ঠিত সমিতিবিশেষ, উদ্ধার-সমিতি। **—ta'-ri-an-ism,** *n.* (*Cap.*) The doctrine of the Trinitarians ; ত্রীশ্বরবাদ, ঈশ্বরত্রিমুখত্ববাদ (হিঃ কোঃ)। **Trinity House** — প্লবক (বয়া) আলোকমন্দির, প্রভৃতির তত্ত্বাবধানের জন্য প্রতিষ্ঠিত সমিতি বিশেষ। **Trinity-ring** — আয়র্লণ্ডে প্রাপ্ত একপ্রকার ত্রিপত্রবিশিষ্ট প্রাচীন অঙ্গুরীয়ক। **Trinity Suuday**—ইষ্টার পর্ব্বের পরবর্ত্তী অষ্টম রবিবার। **Trinity-violet**—Same as PANSY.

trin'-kĕt (trĭng-), *n.* **1.** A trifling ornament or jewel ; সামান্ত মূল্যের অলঙ্কার, ক্ষুদ্র অলঙ্কার বা অল্প মূল্যের রত্ন। **2.** A small fancy article ; ক্ষুদ্র খেলনা বা অন্য কোনরূপ সৌখীন জিনিষ, ফটকীনাটকী। **—ry,** *n.*

trī-nŏd'-ăl, *adj.* Having three joints ; ত্রিপর্ব্বক, ত্রিগ্রন্থিবিশিষ্ট।

trī-nō'-mĭ-ăl, *adj.* & *n.* Consisting of thee terms ; ত্রিপদাত্মক। ***Noun.*** **1.** (*Biol.*) Using three terms in naming objects ; কোন বস্তুর নামকরণে পদত্রয় ব্যবহার করণ। **2.** An algebraical expression consisting of three terms ; বীজগণিতের ত্রিপদাত্মক রাশি। **—ism,** *n.* (*Biol.*) The use of three terms in naming objects ; কোন বস্তুর নামকরণে পদত্রয় ব্যবহারের রীতি।

trī-nŏm'-ĭ-năl, *adj.* Same as TRINOMIAL.

trī'-ō (*or* trē-), *n.* **1.** A set of three persons etc. ; ত্রয়, ত্রয়ী। **2.** (*Mus.*) A musical composition for three voices or instruments ; তিন ব্যক্তি দ্বারা গেয় সঙ্গীত, বাদ্যযন্ত্র ত্রয়ের উপযোগী সঙ্গীত।

trī-oe'-cious (-ē-shŭs), *adj.* Having the male, female and hermaphrodites on different individuals of a plant ; বৃক্ষের বিভিন্ন অংশত্রয়ে পুং স্ত্রী এবং নপুংসক পুষ্পবিশিষ্ট।

trī'-ōle (trē-), *n.* (*Mus.*) Same as TRIPLET.

trī'-ō-lĕt, *n.* A stanza of eight lines, in which the first line is thrice repeated ; অষ্টপংক্তিবিশিষ্ট কবিতার কলি বিশেষ — যাহার প্রথম পংক্তি তিনবার উক্ত হয়।

Trī-ō'-nēs, *n.* (*Pl.*) Same as CHARLES'S WAIN.

trī'-ŏr, *n.* Same as TRIER.

trī-ŏx'-īde, *n.* An oxide containing three oxygen atoms ; অম্লজান পরমাণুত্রয়বিশিষ্ট অম্লজান জারিত ধাতু।

trip, *v. i., t.* & *n.* **1.** To walk nimbly or lightly with short steps ; ক্ষিপ্র অথচ লঘু পাদসঞ্চারে চলা। **2.** To make trip or excursion ; প্রমোদ ভ্রমণ করা। **3.** To make a false step ; to stumble ; পদস্খলন হওয়া ; হোঁচট খাওয়া, পা ফসকিয়ে পড়া। **4.** To err ; to slip ; to offend against morality ; "Till his tongue *trips*"; ভুল করা ; পদস্খলন হওয়া ; নীতিবিগর্হিত কার্য্য করা। ***Verb t.*** **1.** To perform lightly or nimbly ; মৃদু অথচ ক্ষিপ্রপদসঞ্চারে সম্পাদন করা। **2.** To cause to fall suddenly from under the person ; to cause to stumble ; পা ফসকাইয়া ফেলা ; পা ফসকান। **3.** To obstruct ; বাধা দেওয়া। **4.** To detect in a misstep ; "These her woman can *trip* me if I err" ; কোনরূপ অন্যায় কার্য্যে ধরা। **5.** (*Naut.*) To loose as an anchor from the bottom, by its cable or buoy-rope ; (নৌবিদ্যা) নোঙ্গরবদ্ধ রজ্জু বা বয়ার রজ্জুর সাহায্যে সাগরতল হইতে নোঙ্গর আল্গা করা। ***Noun.*** **1.** A light nimble step ; ক্ষিপ্র অথচ লঘুগতি, চটুলগতি। **2.** A light footfall ; মৃদুপদশব্দ। **3.** A short voyage or journey ; an excursion ; আমোদের জন্য অল্প স্থান জলপথে বা স্থলপথে পর্য্যটন ; প্রমোদভ্রমণ, বিলাসভ্রমণ, প্রমোদপর্য্যটন। **4.** A stumble ; পদস্খলন। **5.** A slight error ; ভুল, ভুলচুক, স্খলিত। **6.** The fish caught during voyage ; জলযাত্রার সময় ধৃত মৎস্য। **Trip'-ping,** *n.* **Trip-hammer**—একজাতীয় গুরুভার হাতুড়ী—যাহা চক্রের সাহায্যে উত্তোলিত করা হয়। **A round trip**—কোনস্থানে গমন এবং তথা হইতে পুনঃ পূর্ব্ব স্থানে প্রত্যাবর্ত্তন। **To trip—up**—To cause to stumble ; পা ফসকান। To detect one in blunder ; কোনরূপ ভুলচুক বা দোষ করার সময় কাহাকে ধরা। **To catch one tripping**—Same as TRIP, *v.t.* 4.

trī-pâr'-tīte (or trī-păr-tīt), *adj.* **1.** Divided into three ; ত্রি, অংশে বিভক্ত, ত্রিধাবিভক্ত, ত্রিবৃত (ছান্দোগ্য)। **2.** (Of treaty) Concluded between three parties ; (সন্ধি সম্বন্ধে) তিনপক্ষীয় লোকের মধ্যে সম্পাদিত, ত্রিপক্ষীয়। **—ly,** *adv.* **–ti'-tion,** *n.*

trīpe, *n.* **1.** The stomach of ruminant animal prepared for food ; খাদ্যস্বরূপ ব্যবহৃত রোমন্থক পশুর পাকস্থলী। **2.** (*Vulg.*) Entrails ; belly ; (ইতর ভাষায়) নাড়ীভুঁড়ি ; উদর, পেটা। **Trip'-er-y,** *n.* ***Tripe-de-roch***—কয়েক প্রকার শৈবাল হইতে প্রাপ্ত একপ্রকার তিক্ত পুষ্টিকারক পদার্থ। **Tripeman**—যে ব্যক্তি গরুর পাকস্থলীর ব্যঞ্জনাদি প্রস্তুত করিয়া বিক্রয় করে।

trī-pĕn'-nāte, *adj.* Same as TRIPINNATE.

trī-pêr-sôn-ăl'-ĭ-tȳ, *n.* The state of existing in three persons in one Godhead ; "As for the terms of trinity, triniunity, co-essentiality *tripersonality,* and the like they reject them as scholastic notions, not to be found in Scripture" ; ত্রিব্যক্তিত্ব (হিঃ কোঃ)

trī-pĕt'-ăl-ous (-ŭs), *adj.* Having three petals ; ত্রিদল।

trī-phȳ'-lous (-lŭs), *adj.* Three-leaved ; ত্রিপত্র।

trī-pĭn'-nāte, *adj.* Having a petiole which has bipinnate leaves ranged on each side of it ; ত্রিধাপক্ষাকার (সাঃ পঃ)।

trī'-plāne, *n.* A heavier-than-air flying machine having three chief supporting planes or decks ; ত্রিতল আকাশযান।

trĭ'-ple (-pl), *adj, v. t.* & *i.* Threefold ; treble ; ত্রিক (হিঃ কোঃ), ত্রিগুণিত ; ত্রয়াত্মক, তেহারা, ত্রিপুটিত। ***Verb t.*** To treble ; ত্রিগুণিত করা, ত্রিগুণ করা। ***Verb i.*** To become treble ; ত্রিগুণিত হওয়া। **Triple Alliance**—(ক) ১৬৮৮ খৃঃ অব্দে ইংলণ্ড, সুইজরলণ্ড এবং নেদারলেণ্ড এই রাষ্ট্রত্রয়ের মধ্যে চতুর্দ্দশ লুইএর সন্ধি দ্বারা যে সম্মিলন হয়। (খ) ১৮২২—২৩ খৃষ্টাব্দে রুশিয়া এবং

ফরাসীদেশের বিরুদ্ধে জর্ম্মাণি, অষ্ট্রিয়া ও ইতালি এই তিন রাজ্যের সন্ধিদ্বারা যে সম্মিলন হয়, ত্রিগুণযোগ। **Triple-crown**—পোপের মুকুট। **Triple-salt**—ত্রিধাতুক লবণ (হিঃ কোঃ)। **Triple-star**—ত্রিগুণ নক্ষত্র (হিঃ কোঃ)। **triple-turned**—(*Shaks.*) Three time sunfaithful; তিনবার অবিশ্বাসী।

trip'-lĕt, *n.* **1.** A set of three things; ত্রিবস্তুর সংহতি, ত্রয়ী। **2.** Three verses rhyming together; মিত্রাক্ষর, কবিতাপংক্তি ত্রয়। **3.** (*Mus.*) Three notes sung or played in the time of two; দুই স্বরের কালের মধ্যে গীত বা বাদিত স্বরত্রয়। **4.** (*Colloq.*) One of three children born at a birth; (চলিত ভাষায়) একবারে প্রসূত সন্তানত্রয়ের অন্যতম। **5.** (*Optics*) A combination of three lenses; (দৃষ্টিবিজ্ঞান) পরকলাত্রয়ের সম্মিলন।

trī'-plĕx, *n.* Triple time in music; ত্রিলয়।

trip'-lĭ-cāte, *adj.* & *n.* Made thrice as much; threefold; ত্রিগুণিত; ত্র্যাত্মক। ***Noun.*** A third-copy or thing corresponding to two others of the same kind; তৃতীয় প্রতিলিপি, অনুরূপ বস্তুত্রয়ের অন্যতম। **Triplicate ratio of two numbers**—দুই সংখ্যার ঘনের নিষ্পত্তি।

trip'-lĭ-cāte, *v. t.* To treble; to make triplicate; ত্রিগুণিত করা, ত্রিগুণ করা; অনুরূপ তিন খণ্ডে প্রস্তুত করা। **—ca'-tion,** *n.* **—ca-ture,** *n.*

trī-plic'-ĭ-tȳ, *n.* **1.** State of being triples; ত্রিত্ব, ত্র্যাত্মকতা। **2.** (*Astrol.*) Any of the groups of three into which the zodiac is divided; a trigon; মুষল্লহ; মুল ত্রিকোণ (বৃঃ সং)।

trī'-pŏd, *n.* **1.** A three-footed seat; তেপায়া, ত্রিপদ, টেপাই, ত্রিপাদিকা। **2.** A three-legged stand for supporting camera etc.; আলোকচিত্রের যন্ত্র প্রভৃতির অবলম্বনের জন্য ত্রিপদ। **3.** The seat over the altar on which the priestess of Apollo at Delphi sat to deliver oracles; দৈববাণী প্রকাশের জন্য বেদীর উপরিস্থিত যে ত্রিপাদিকায় ডেল্‌ফী নগরীর Apolloদেবের পূজিকা উপবেশন করিতেন। **4.** A highly ornamental tripod in imitation of the seat used by the priestess of Apollo, given as prize in the Pythian games and elsewhere; গ্রীস দেশের বিভিন্ন স্থানে অনুষ্ঠিত ক্রীড়োৎসবে বিজয়ী ব্যক্তিকে ডেল্‌ফীর পূজারিণীর ত্রিপাদিকার অনুরূপ যে কারুকার্য্যখচিত ত্রিপাদিকা পুরস্কার স্বরূপ প্রদান করা হইত।

Trip'-o-dal, *adj.*

trip'-ŏ-lĭ, *n.* Same as ROTTEN-STONE (which see).

trī'-pŏs, *n.* **1.** A tripod; ত্রিপদী, ত্রিপাদিকা। **2.** (In Cambridge university) An examination for honours at taking one's degree, the successful candidates being arranged in three classes; কেম্ব্রিজ বিশ্ববিদ্যালয়ের সসম্মান-উপাধি-পরীক্ষা বিশেষ। **3.** The list of successful candidates in such examination; উক্ত পরীক্ষায় উত্তীর্ণ ছাত্রগণের তালিকা। [Mathematical Triposএর প্রথম বিভাগে উত্তীর্ণ ছাত্রগণকে Wrangler কহে।]

trip'-thŏng (*or* trif-), *n.* A combination of three vowels forming one sound in a single syllable; একই শব্দাংশে তিন স্বরবর্ণের সংযোগ। **—al,** *adj.*

trip'-tȳch, *n.* **1.** A picture or carving in three compartments side by side; a set of three pictures so placed; পরস্পরের পার্শ্ববর্ত্তী কোঠত্রয়ে অঙ্কিত চিত্র; উক্তরূপ বিন্যস্ত আলেখ্যত্রয়। **2.** A set of tablet consisting of three leaves, each painted with a distinct subject, but joined together by hinges and capable of being folded so as to occupy a new face; বিভিন্ন বিষয় চিত্রিত ত্রিপত্র চিত্রফলক—কব্জাদ্বারা আঁটা থাকায় উহা ভিন্ন ভিন্ন প্রকারে

Triptych.

ভাঁজ করিয়া চিত্রত্রয়ের যে কোন একটী প্রদর্শিত করা যাইতে পারে।

trī-quĕ'-tră, *n.* An ornament of three interlaced arches; পরস্পরের সহিত সংগ্রথিত তোরণত্রয়ের ভূষা।

trī-quĕ'-trous (-trŭs), *adj.* **1.** Three-cornered; ত্রিকোণ। **2.** (*Bot.*) Having three acute angles; (উদ্ভিদ্‌-বিদ্যা) সূক্ষ্মকোণত্রয় বিশিষ্ট, ত্রিসূক্ষ্মাগ্র।

trī-ră'-dĭ-ăl, —āte, —āt-ĕd, *adjs.* Radiating in three directions; তিনদিকে বিকিরণশীল, ত্রিবিকিরণশীল।

trī'-reme (-rēm), *n.* (*Gk. Antiq.*) A galley or vessel with three ranks of oar on a side in ancient Greece; প্রতি পার্শ্বে তিন সারি দাঁড়বিশিষ্ট দীর্ঘ নৌকা বা পোত।

Trĭs-ăg'-ĭ-ŏn, *n.* In the Greek church, a hymn in which the word holy is repeated three times; গ্রীক ধর্ম্মসংঘের স্তোত্রবিশেষ—যাহাতে "পবিত্র" শব্দ তিনবার উচ্চারিত হয়।

trī-sĕct', *v. t.* To divide a line, angle, etc. in three esp. in three equal parts; ত্রিখণ্ডে বিভক্ত করা, ত্রিখণ্ডিত করা, ত্রিসমানাংশে বিভক্ত করা, সমত্রিখণ্ডিত করা। **—sec'-tion,** *n.*

trī-sĕp'-ăl-ous (-ŭs), *adj.* Having three sepals; বহিশ্ছদত্রয় বিশিষ্ট।

trī-sĕ'-rĭ-ăl, —āte, *adjs.* In three rows or series; শ্রেণী বা পংক্তিত্রয়ে নিবদ্ধ, ত্রিপংক্তিবদ্ধ।

tris′-mŭs, *n.* A kind of lock-jaw ; দাঁতকপাটি, দন্তলগ্ন (সাঃ পঃ), হনুগ্রহ (ঐ)।

trī-spêr′-mous (-mŭs), *adj.* Containing three seeds ; ত্রিবীজ, ত্রিবীজাত্মক।

trī-spör′-ous (-ŭs), **–ic,** *adjs.* Having three spores ; ত্রিরেণুবিশিষ্ট।

trist′-fûl, *adj.* (*Archaic*) Sad (অপ্রঃ) বিষণ্ণ।

trĭs′-tich-ous (-ŭs), *adj.* (*Bot.*) Arranged in three vertical rows ; উল্লম্বী শ্রেণীত্রয়ে বিন্যস্ত।

trī-stig-măt′-ic, *adj.* (*Bot.*) Having three stigmas ; (উদ্ভিদ্‌বিদ্যা) ত্রিচিহ্ন-বিশিষ্ট।

trī-stȳ′-lous (-lŭs), *adj.* Having three styles ; ত্রিগর্ভতন্তুবিশিষ্ট।

trī-sŭl′-cāte, *adj.* **1.** (*Bot.*) Having three grooves ; খাঁজত্রয়বিশিষ্ট। **2.** (*Zool.*) Divided into three digits or hoofs ; (জন্তুবিদ্যা) অঙ্গুলীত্রয় বা খুরত্রয়ে খণ্ডিত, ত্রিশূলাকৃতি।

trī-sȳl′-lă-ble (-bl), *n.* A word of three syllables ; ত্রিশব্দাংশবিশিষ্ট শব্দ, ত্র্যক্ষর শব্দ।

trī-tăg′-ō-nist, *n.* The third actor in the Greek drama ; গ্রীক নাট্যের তৃতীয় অভিনেতা।

trīte, *adj.* Worn out ; commonplace ; hackneyed ; পুরাতন ; সাধারণ ; পচা, বস্তাপচা। **Trite′-ly,** *adv.* **Trite′-ness,** *n.*

trī-têr′-nāte, *adj.* Having 27 leaflets ; সপ্তবিংশতিপত্রকবিশিষ্ট।

trī′-thē-ism, *n.* The doctrine of the Trinity as construed into a belief in three Gods ; ত্রীশ্বরবাদ, ত্রিত্ববাদ, ত্রিদেবত্ব (হিঃ কোঃ), ত্রিমূর্ত্তিত্ব (ঐ)। **–ist,** *n.* **–is′-tic, –is′-ti-cal,** *adjs.*

Trī′-tōn, *n.* **1.** (*Gk. Mythol.*) A sea-deity represented with his lower extremity fish-like ; (গ্রীক-পুরাণ) Posidon এবং Amphitriteএর পুত্র। ইনি জনকজননীর সহিত সাগর-তলস্থ কাঞ্চনসৌধে বাস করিতেন। এই দেবতার দেহের পূর্ব্বার্দ্ধ মনুষ্যাকৃতি—পরার্দ্ধ মৎস্যাকৃতি এবং পদদ্বয় অশ্ব-চরণাকৃতি ছিল। ইনি বরুণ দেবতার

Mythological Triton.

শঙ্খবাদকদিগের ভিতর একজন ছিলেন। **2.** A genus of mollusc with a wreathed univalve shell ; একজাতীয় শঙ্খ। **A Triton of the minnows**—বাঘ নাই বনে শেয়াল রাজা (cf. নিরস্তে পাদপে দেশে এরণ্ডোঽপি দ্রুমায়তে)।

trī′-tōne, *adj.* (*Mus.*) A musical interval of three whole tones ; (সঙ্গীতশাস্ত্র) তিন পূর্ণ ধ্বনির অবচ্ছেদ।

trī-tō′-ri-ŭm, –tū′-ri-ŭm, *ns.* A vessel for separating liquors of different densities ; বিভিন্ন গাঢ়ত্বের তরলপদার্থ সমূহ পৃথক করার জন্য পাত্র বিশেষ।

trit′-ū-rāte, *v. t.* **1.** To rub or grind to a fine powder ; পেষণ বা ঘর্ষণ দ্বারা সূক্ষ্ম চূর্ণে পরিণত করা। **2.** To masticate thoroughly ; উত্তমরূপে চর্ব্বণ করা। **–ra-ble,** *adj.* **–ra-tor,** *n.* **–ra′-tion,** *n.* **1.** The act of one who triturates ; বিচূর্ণন। **2.** A triturated powder ; সূক্ষ্মচূর্ণ।

trī′-ŭmph, *n.* & *v. i.* **1.** (In ancient Rome) A triumphal procession or exhibition ; বিজয়ী সেনাপতির সমারোহপূর্ণ শোভাযাত্রা, বিজয়োৎসব, বিজয়যাত্রা। **2.** A great victory ; মহাবিজয়। **3.** Joy for success ; "Great *triumph* and rejoicing was in heaven" ; বিজয়োল্লাস, জয়োল্লাস। ***Verb i.*** **1.** (*Rom. Antiq.*) To enjoy a triumph, as a victorious general ; (প্রাচীন রোমে) বিজয়ী সেনাপতির মহাসমারোহ-পূর্ণ শোভাযাত্রা বাহির করা। **2.** To obtain victory ; as, virtue *triumphs* in the long run ; to be successful ; to prevail ; জয় লাভ করা ; কৃতকার্য্য হওয়া ; প্রবল হওয়া। **3.** To exult upon an advantage gained ; "How will he *triumph*, leap and laugh at it" ; বিজয়োল্লাসে মত্ত হওয়া, আনন্দোল্লাসে প্রমত্ত হওয়া। **–ing-ly,** *adv.* **–um′-phal,** *adj.* **1.** Pertaining to triumph ; বিজয়যাত্রা-সম্বন্ধীয়। **2.** Used in triumph ; বিজয়যাত্রায় ব্যবহৃত। **3.** Serving to commemorate a triumph or victory ; বিজয়স্মৃতিসূচক, জয়সূচক। **Triumphal arch**—বিজয়তোরণ।

trī-ŭm′-phănt, *adj.* **1.** Victorious ; জয়ী, বিজয়ী। **2.** Exhulting ; expressive of joy for success ; বিজয়োল্লাসী ; বিজয়োল্লাসসূচক। **3.** (*Obs.*) Glorious ; "A most *triumphant* duty" ; (অপ্রঃ) বিজয়শ্রীযুক্ত। **–ly,** *adv.*

trī-ŭm′-vir (-vêr), *n.* **1.** (*Rom. Antiq.*) One of three men united in office ; একপদে প্রতিষ্ঠিত ব্যক্তিত্রয়ের অন্যতম। **2.** (*Rom. History*) Each member of the first or second triumvirate ; প্রথম ও দ্বিতীয় ত্রিশাসকসংঘভুক্ত ব্যক্তি, ত্রিশাসক। **–vi′-ral,** *adj.* **–vi-rate,** *n.* **1.** The office or term of a triumvir ; ত্রিশাসকের পদ বা পদের স্থিতিকাল। **2.** A government by three men in coalition ; একত্র সম্মিলিত ব্যক্তিত্রয় দ্বারা শাসন, ত্রিশাসকতন্ত্র। **3.** Any group, party or association of three ; ব্যক্তিত্রয় বা বস্তুত্রয়ের সমবায়, ত্রয়ী। **First triumvirate**—খৃঃ পূঃ ৬০ অব্দে Pompey, Julius Caeasar এবং Crassus ঘটিত শাসক-সংঘ। **Second triumvirate**—খৃঃ পূঃ ৪৩ অব্দে Mark Antony, Octavius এবং Lepidus দ্বারা গঠিত শাসনসংঘ।

trī′-ūne, *n.* Three in one (said of Christian God) ; একে তিন, ত্রৈক।

ni-ty, *n.* Triune God—ত্রিকৈক। (হিঃ কোঃ), ত্রৈক ঈশ্বর (ঐ)।
-vă'-lĕnt, *adj.* Having combining power of three; ত্রিসংযোগ-শক্তিসম্পন্ন, ত্রিপরমাণুগ্রাহী।

triv'-ĕt, *n.* A three-legged stool, table or other support; তেপায়া, তেপায়া মেজ, আসন, প্রভৃতি, ত্রিপাদিকা। **Trivet-table**—তেপায়া মেজ। **Right or steady as a trivet**—In good order; ঠিকঠাক। In good health or condition; সুস্থ, ভাল অবস্থায়।

triv'-ĭ-ăl, *adj.* 1. Trifling; petty; as, *trivial* objections; তুচ্ছ, সামান্য, অকিঞ্চিৎকর; ক্ষুদ্র। 2. (*Obs.*) Commonplace; (অপ্রঃ) সাধারণ, একঘেয়ে। **—al'-i-ty,** *n.* 1. The state of being trivial; তুচ্ছতা, নগণ্যতা, ক্ষুদ্রতা। 2. A trifling thing; তুচ্ছ জিনিষ। **—ism,** *n.* **—ize,** *v. t.* **—ly,** *adv.* **—ness,** *n.* **Trivial name**—(কচিদ্ব্যবহৃত) কোন উদ্ভিদ্ বা জন্তুর সাধারণ বা লৌকিক নাম (বৈজ্ঞানিক নাম নহে)।

triv'-ĭ-ŭm, *n.* In the schools of the Middle Ages, the first three liberal arts—grammar, rhetoric, and logic; মধ্যযুগের ত্রিশাস্ত্র—ন্যায়, ব্যাকরণ এবং অলঙ্কার, অলঙ্কার, তর্ক-ব্যাকৃতি-ত্রিতয় (হিঃ কোঃ), শাস্ত্রত্রয়ী (ঐ)।

trī-week'-lȳ (-wēk-), *adj.* Occurring or appearing once in three weeks; appearing thrice a week; তিন সপ্তাহে একবার সংঘটিত বা প্রকাশিত; এক সপ্তাহে তিনবার প্রকাশিত, ত্রৈসাপ্তাহিক।

troat (trōt), *v. t.* & *n.* (*Obs. or rare*) To cry as a buck in rutting time; মদাকুলিত হরিণের পক্ষে চীৎকার করা। ***Noun.*** (*Obs. or rare*) The cry of a buck in rutting time; মদাকুলিত হরিণের রব।

trō'-căr, *n.* A surgical instrument for tapping dropsical persons; জলোদরী রোগের জল বাহির করার জন্য যন্ত্র, ত্রিকূর্চ্চক (সুশ্রঃ কুঞ্জঃ), বস্ত্যাগ্র (সাঃ পঃ), ব্রীহিমুখশস্ত্র (সুশ্রঃ)।

trō-chā'-ic, *adj.* of trochees; composed of trochees; আদিগুরুদ্বিক সম্বন্ধীয়; আদিগুরুদ্বিকদ্বারা গঠিত।

trō'-chăl, *adj.* shaped like a wheel; চক্রাকৃতি।

trō-chăn'-tĕr, *n.* 1. (*Anat.* & *Zool.*) A bony process on the upper part of the thigh-bone; (শারীর-সংস্থান বিদ্যা এবং জন্তুবিদ্যা) ঊর্বস্থির উপরিভাগস্থ অস্থিবিবৃদ্ধি। 2. The second joint of an insect's wing; পতঙ্গের পক্ষের দ্বিতীয় পর্ব্ব বা সন্ধি।

trō'-chē, *n.* A circular medical tablet or lozenge; একপ্রকার ঔষধমিশ্রিত গোলাকৃতি লজঞ্জুস, ঔষধের টিকলি বা চাক্তি।

trō'-chee (-kē), *n.* A foot of two syllables, the first long and the second short or the first accented and the second unaccented; দ্বিমাত্রাত্মক চরণ বিশেষ—ইহার প্রথম মাত্রা দীর্ঘ বা গুরু, এবং দ্বিতীয়টী হ্রস্ব বা লঘু হইয়া থাকে, তাল (Wilson), আদিগুরুদ্বিক।

trō'-chĭl, trŏch'-ĭ-lŭs, *n. s.* 1. Kinds of small birds; কয়েকপ্রকার ক্ষুদ্র পক্ষীর সাধারণ নাম। 2. The crocodile bird; একপ্রকার পক্ষী। ইহারা কুম্ভীরের মুখবিবরে প্রবেশ করিয়া উহার মুখে লগ্ন জলৌকা সকল বাহির করে বলিয়া প্রবাদ আছে।

trŏch'-lē-ă, *n.* (*Anat.*) A pulley-like cartilage, through which the tendon of the trochlear muscles passes; (শারীরসংস্থানবিদ্যা) কপিকলের ন্যায় উপাস্থি বা সন্ধির উপরিভাগ। **—ar,** *adj.* Like a pulley; কপিকলের ন্যায়। **—ate,** *adj.* **Trochlear muscle**—চক্ষুর ঊর্দ্ধস্থ তির্য্যক্ পেশী। **Trochlear nerve**—অক্ষিপেশীগত স্নায়ু।

trō'-choid (-koyd), *n.* & *adj.* 1. A species of movable connexion of bones, in which one bone rotates upon another; অস্থিশ্রেণীর একপ্রকার সন্নিবেশ—যাহাতে এক অস্থি অপর অস্থির উপর ঘূর্ণিত হয়। 2. Same as ROULETTE 5. (which see) ***Adj.*** 1. Cycloid চক্রাকার। 2. Revolving like a wheel; চক্রাকারে ঘূর্ণিত। 3. (Of a conch) Topshaped; (শঙ্খসম্বন্ধে) লাটিমের আকার। **—choi'-dal,** *adj.*

trō-chŏm'-ĕ-tĕr, *n.* Same as HODOMETER.

trŏ'-cō, *n.* A kind of game played with wooden balls; একপ্রকার কন্দুক ক্রীড়া।

trŏd, trŏd'-den (-n), *pp.* of TREAD (which see).

trŏg'-lō-dȳte, *n.* 1. One dwelling in a subterranean cave; গুহাবাসী, গহ্বরবাসী, গুহায়ক। 2. A hermit; মুনি, সন্ন্যাসী। 3. An anthropoid ape; মনুষ্যাকৃতি, মর্কট। **—dyt'-i-cal,** *adj.* **—dyt-ism,** *n.*

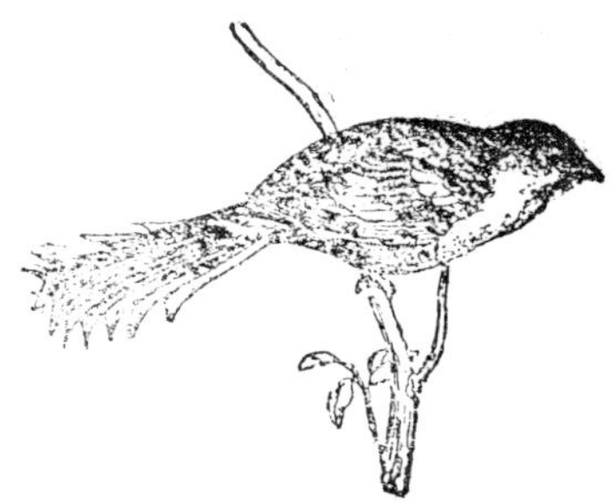

Cuban Trogon.

trō'-gŏn, *n.* Tropical nonpasserine bird of the family Trogonidae noted for the brilliant colour and lustre of the plumage; পালকের বর্ণের দীপ্তির জন্য প্রসিদ্ধ গ্রীষ্মমণ্ডলের পক্ষিবিশেষ।

troika, *n.* A Russian vehicle drawn by three horses abreast; পরস্পরের পাশাপাশি অশ্বত্রয়দ্বারা বাহিত রুশদেশীয় যান, ত্র্যশ্বযান।

Trō'-jăn, *adj.* & *n.* Of Troy; ট্রয়নগরসম্বন্ধীয়। ***Noun.*** 1. An inhabitant of Troy; ট্রয় নগরীর অধিবাসী। 2. A brave fellow; "He bore it (the amputation of his hand), of course like a *Trojan*";

শূর, বীর। **Trojan War**—ট্রয়ের যুদ্ধ। গ্রীক কবি হোমরের ইলিয়ড নামক গ্রন্থে এই যুদ্ধের জ্বলন্ত বর্ণনা প্রদত্ত হইয়াছে। **Like a Trojan**—Like a hero; বীরের মত।

trōll, *v. t., i.* & *n.* **1.** To roll; ঘূর্ণিত করা, ঘুরপাক দেওয়া, ঘুরান, গড়ান। **2.** To sing the parts of a song in succession; to sing in a full jovial voice; পর্য্যায়ক্রমে সঙ্গীতের অংশ সমূহ গান করা, মহড়া ধরা; উল্লসিত কণ্ঠে গান করা। **3.** To angle to fish in; "*Trolls* the finny deep"; মৎস্য ধৃত করার জন্য বড়শী ফেলা। **4.** To circulate; হাতে হাতে চালান। ***Verb i.*** **1.** To go round; to move or run round; ঘুরা; কোন কিছু ঘুরিয়া আসা। **2.** To wag, as the tongue; নাড়া, লক্‌লক্ করা। **3.** To fish esp. by drawing the hook along or through the water; ছিপে মাছ ধরা, বড়শী নড়কান। **4.** To allure; to entice; প্রলুব্ধ করা; ভুলান। ***Noun.*** **1.** The act of moving or going round; repetition; ঘূর্ণন, আবর্ত্তন, টহল, পরিক্রম; পুনরাবৃত্তি। **2.** (*Mus.*) A song of which the parts are sung in succession; (সঙ্গীতশাস্ত্র) যে সঙ্গীতের বিভিন্ন অংশ পর্য্যায়ক্রমে গীত হইয়া থাকে, মহড়া। **3.** (*Rare*) A reel on a fishing rod; (কচিদ্‌-ব্যবহৃত) ছিপের চরকী। **4.** A trolling-spoon; নড়কাইয়া বড়শীদ্বারা মৎস্য বিদ্ধ করার জন্য টোপস্বরূপ ব্যবহৃত চামচের আকার ক্ষুদ্র এবং উজ্জ্বল ধাতুখণ্ড।

trōll, *n.* In Scandinavian folklore a kind of evil spirit; স্কেণ্ডিন্যাভিয়ানদের উপকথায় উক্ত দেবযোনিবিশেষ।

trŏl'-ley (-ĭ), –ly (-ĭ), *ns.* **1.** A small wooden wheel not bound with iron; ক্ষুদ্র কাষ্ঠচক্র। **2.** A kind of car that can be tilted; একপ্রকার শকট—যে শকট কা'ত করিয়া ভিতরের জিনিষ ফেলান যায়। **3.** A kind of hand-cart; একপ্রকার ঠেলা-গাড়ী। **4.** A wheele carriage, running on a railway; লৌহবর্ত্মের পাতা রেলের উপর যে ক্ষুদ্র ছাদহীন শকট চালান হয়। **5.** A pulley at the end of an arm used in electric tramways to connect the car with the overhead wires; বৈদ্যুতিক ট্রামের অগ্রভাগ হইতে তির্য্যগ্‌ভাবে প্রলম্বিত দণ্ডাগ্রে নিবদ্ধ যে কপিকল উপরিস্থ তারের সহিত ঘষড়াইয়া যায়। **6.** Same as TROLLEY-LACE. **Trolley-lace** — একপ্রকার লেইস—যাহাতে মোটা সূতাদ্বারা নানা নমুনা তোলা হয়। **Trolley-pole**—বৈদ্যুতিক ট্রামের অগ্রভাগ হইতে উদ্গত যে তির্য্যগ্‌গামী দণ্ডের প্রান্তে কপিকল সংলগ্ন থাকে।

trŏl'-lop (-ŏp), *n.* **1.** A dirty, slatternly ragged woman; নোংরা স্ত্রীলোক, অপরিচ্ছন্ন স্ত্রীলোক, পেত্‌নী (*Slang*)। **2.** A prostitute; বেশ্যা, খান্‌কী, কসবী। **–ish, –y,** *adjs.*

trŏm'-bă, *n.* (*Mus.*) Same as TRUMPET (which see).

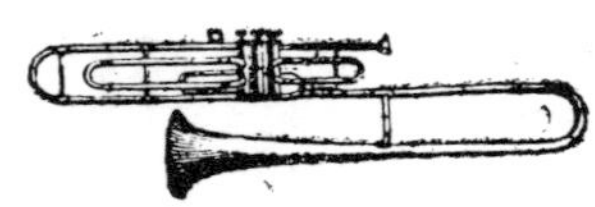

Valve Trombone.

Slide Trombone.

trŏm'-bōne, *n.* A deep-toned brass musical instrument of the trumpet kind; সানাই জাতীয় বৃহৎ বাদ্যযন্ত্রবিশেষ। **–bon'-ist,** *n.*

trŏm'-mel (-ĕl), *n.* A kind of revolving sieve for separating the richer portions of ore from the worthless; খনিজ বিমিশ্র ধাতুর উৎকৃষ্ট অংশ অপকৃষ্ট অংশ হইতে পৃথক করার জন্য একপ্রকার ঘূর্ণনশীল চালুনী।

trō-mŏm'-ē-tēr, *n.* An instrument for measuring slight earthquake shocks; ঈষৎ ভূকম্প মানের জন্য যন্ত্র-বিশেষ, ভূস্পন্দনমান।

trompe (trŏmp), *n.* The blowing machine used in a certain process of smelting iron; খনি লৌহ হইতে বিশুদ্ধ লৌহ বাহির কালে যে মাপনযন্ত্র দ্বারা চুল্লীতে প্রবাহ চালিত করা হয়।

trōōp, *n., v. i.* & *t.* **1.** A collection of people; লোক-সংঘ, লোক-দল, জন-শ্রেণী, জনতা। **2.** Soldiers collectively; সৈন্যদল, সেনাদল। **3.** A body of cavalry; অশ্বারোহী সৈন্যদল। **4.** (*Obs.*) A band or company of performers; (অপ্র:) গায়ক, নর্ত্তক, প্রভৃতির সম্প্রদায়। ***Verb i*** **1.** To move or gather together in troops; as, children *trooping* to school; দলে দলে চলা, দল বাঁধিয়া যাওয়া, দলে দলে আসিয়া মিলা। **2.** To march on; কুচ করিয়া যাওয়া। ***Verb t.*** To unite with, or form, into, a troop or troops; দলবদ্ধ করা, দলে দলে মিলিত করা। **Troop-horse** — অশ্বারোহী সৈনিকের ঘোড়া। **Troop-ship** — সৈন্যবাহী জাহাজ। **Trooping the colours**—সামরিক পর্ব্ব বিশেষ—যাহাতে সৈনিকগণ ব্যাণ্ড বাজাইয়া স্ব স্ব দলের পতাকার সম্মুখ দিয়া চলিয়া যায়। **To get or receive one's troop**—To be promoted to the captaincy or command of a troop; কোন সৈন্যদলের কাপ্তান বা অধিনায়কের পদে উন্নীত হওয়া। **To troop off, To troop away**—To walk hurriedly away; দ্রুত চলিয়া যাওয়া।

trōōp'-ēr, *n.* **1.** A private soldier in a body of cavalry; a horse-soldier; অশ্বারোহী সৈনিক; সাদী। **2.** A cavalry horse; অশ্বারোহী সৈনিকের ঘোড়া। **To swear like a trooper**—To swear very much; বেজায় গালাগালি করা।

trōpe, *n.* A figurative use of a word; a word used in a figurative sense; কোন শব্দের লাক্ষণিক প্রয়োগ; রূপক, লক্ষণাস্বরূপ ব্যবহৃত শব্দ।

trō'-phī, *n.* The part of the mouth employed in feeding; ভোজনক্রিয়ায় মুখের যে সমুদয় অংশ ব্যবহৃত হয়।

trŏph′-ic, *adj.* Pertaining to, or concerned with nutrition; as *trophic* nerve; পরিপোষণসম্বন্ধীয়, পরিপোষণসংক্রান্ত।

Trophis aspera—শেওড়া গাছ (বেল:)।

trŏ-phŏl′-ŏ-ġ̄y, *n.* The science of nutrition; পরিপোষণতত্ত্ব, পোষণ-তত্ত্ব, পুষ্টিবিজ্ঞান।

trŏph-ŏ-neu-rō′-sis (-nü-), *n.* Defective nutrition due to nervous derangement; স্নায়বিক বিকৃতি-হেতু পরিপোষণ ক্রিয়ার দুর্ব্বলতা।

trō-phō′-ni-ăn, *adj.* Pertaining to the Grecian architect Trophonius or his architecture; গ্রীসদেশীয় স্থপতি Trophonius এবং তৎপ্রবর্ত্তিত স্থাপত্যরীতিসম্বন্ধীয়।

trŏ-phŏp′-ă-thȳ, *n.* Any disorder of nutrition; পরিপোষণের বিশৃঙ্খলতা।

trŏph′-ŏ-plăsm, *n.* The nutritive or vegetative cell-substance; পরিপোষক বা উদ্ভিজ্জ পরিপোষক প্রাণকোষ বস্তু।

trō′-phȳ, *n.* **1.** A memorial of a victory, consisting of a pile of arms, erected on the field of battle; শত্রুর নিকট হইতে গৃহীত অস্ত্রশস্ত্র দ্বারা রণক্ষেত্রে যে স্মৃতি-স্তম্ভ নির্ম্মিত হয়। **2.** Anything taken from an enemy, and preserved as a memorial of victory; শত্রুর নিকট হইতে গৃহীত এবং জয়চিহ্ন স্বরূপ রক্ষিত বস্তু, বিজয়ের স্মৃতিনিদর্শন, জয়চিহ্ন, রণস্তম্ভ। **3.** Any memorial or memento; স্মৃতিনিদর্শন। **4.** Anything taken and preserved as a memorial of victory, as flags, standards, arms, and the like; শত্রুর নিকট হইতে যুদ্ধজয়ের স্মৃতিচিহ্নস্বরূপ গৃহীত পতাকা প্রভৃতি। **5.** An architectural ornament representing arms and military weapons; অস্ত্রশস্ত্রের আকৃতি স্থাপত্যভূষা।

trŏp′-ic, *n.* & *adj.* Either of the circles on the celestial sphere, each distant from the equator nearly 23½ degrees, the northern end called the tropic of Cancer, and the southern the tropic of Capricorn; নিরক্ষবৃত্তের উভয় পার্শ্ববর্ত্তী এবং উহার সহিত সমান্তরাল এবং উহা হইতে ২৩½° ডিগ্রি দূরে অবস্থিত বৃত্তদ্বয়ের অন্যতর, অয়নান্তবৃত্ত (সূর্য্যের দক্ষিণ অয়নের সীমা বলিয়া এই নাম)। ***Adj.*** Same as TROPICAL (below). **Tropic-bird**—অয়নান্তবৃত্তে দৃষ্ট নানাপ্রকার পক্ষী। **Tropic of Cancer**—উত্তরায়ণবৃত্ত, উত্তরপরমল্লক্রজ্যাবৃত্ত (সাঃ পঃ), কর্কটক্রান্তি। **Tropic of Capricorn**—দক্ষিণায়নবৃত্ত, মকরক্রান্তি, দক্ষিণপরমাল্লক্রজ্যাবৃত্ত (সাঃ পঃ)।

trŏp′-i-căl, *adj.* **1.** Pertaining to the tropic; being within the tropic; অয়নান্তবৃত্তসম্বন্ধীয়; অয়নান্তবৃত্ত-মধ্যস্থ। **2.** Characteristic of the tropic; অয়নান্তবৃত্তের পক্ষে স্বাভাবিক। **3.** (*Fig.*) Fervid; (লক্ষণায়) জ্বলন্ত। **4.** Figurative (from *trope*); "The foundation of all paralles in some analogy or similitude between the *tropical* or allusive part of the parable and the thing intended by it"; রূপকস্বরূপ, লাক্ষণিক। **—ly,** *adv.* **Tropical signs**—অয়নান্ত-লগ্নরাশি। **Tropical year**—সৌরবর্ষ।

trŏp-i-cō-pŏl′-i-tăn, *adj.* & *n.* **1.** Inhabiting all tropical countries; অয়নান্তবৃত্তবাসী। ***Noun.*** Any tropicopolitan animal; অয়নান্ত-বৃত্তবাসী জন্তু।

trō-pŏl′-ŏ-ġ̄y, *n.* **1.** A rhetorical mode of speech including tropes, or change from the original import of the word; কোন শব্দের মৌলিক অর্থ হইতে বিভিন্ন অর্থে প্রয়োগ। **2.** Figurative interpretation; রূপক ব্যাখ্যা। **Trop′-ist**, *n.* **Trop-o-log′-i-cal**, *adj.* **Trop-o-log′-i-cal-ly**, *adv.*

troppo, *adv.* (*Mus.*) Too; (সঙ্গীত শাস্ত্র) আরো বেশী।

trŏt, *v. t.*, *i.* & *n.* To cause to move, as a horse or other animal, by lifting one forefoot and the hindfoot of the opposite side at the same time; (ঘোড়া) দোলকী চালান, কদমে চালান। ***Verb i.*** **1.** To ride at a trot; কদমে চলা, দোলকী চলা। **2.** To move or walk fast; to run; দ্রুত চলা; দৌড়া। ***Noun.*** **1.** The pace of a horse, or other quadruped more rapid than a walk, when he lifts the one forefoot and the hindfoot of the opposite side at the same time; কদম, দোলকী, ধোরিতগতি। **2.** (*Rare*) A toddler; a child; (ক্বচিদ্ ব্যবহৃত) দুইএক পা হাঁটিতে শিখিয়াছে এরূপ শিশু; শিশু। **3.** Brisk movement or occupation; স্ফূর্ত্তি, চঞ্চলতা। **To trot out**—To cause a horse to show his trot; ঘোড়াকে কদমে চালাইয়া দেখান। To bring forward as for exhibition or for exciting admiration; প্রদর্শনের বা বিস্ময় উদ্রেকের জন্য উপস্থিত করা।

trŏth, *n.* **1.** (*Archaic*) Truth; সত্য। **2.** Fidelity; pledged faith; বিশ্বস্ততা, নিষ্ঠা; সত্যবাক্য। **To plight one's troth** — To pledge one's word, esp. in betrothal; বাক্য দেওয়া, বিশেষতঃ বিবাহে বাগ্‌দান করা।

trŏt′-ter (-êr), *n.* **1.** A horse etc. that trots; যে ঘোড়া কদমে বা দোলকিতে চলে। **2.** An animal-foot used as a food; (*facet.*) human foot; খাদ্যস্বরূপ ব্যবহৃত মেষ প্রভৃতির জঙ্ঘা; (কৌতুকচ্ছলে) মনুষ্যের পা।

trottoir, *n.* (*Now rare*) A sidewalk or pavement; (বর্ত্তমানে ক্বচিদ্ ব্যবহৃত) পাশ্ববর্ত্তী ভ্রমণ পথ বা তলপত্তন।

trou′-ba-dour (trô-bă-dôr), *n.* A class of poets, belonging to the south of France, who in medieval times, led a sort of minstrel life, wandering, from castle to castle and singing in courtly style the praises of chivalry and love ; (একাদশ হইতে ত্রয়োদশ শতাব্দী পর্য্যন্ত) ফরাসীদেশের Provence নামক স্থানের কবিগণ—যাঁহারা মধ্যযুগে ইয়ুরোপের স্থানে স্থানে ধনীদিগের প্রাসাদে যাইয়া প্রেম ও বীরত্বের গাথা গাহিতেন। [Troubadourগণ Provenceএর সাহিত্যে অনেক উৎকৃষ্ট কবিতা প্রদান করিয়াছেন। অনেক সময় রাজা, জমিদার, খৃষ্টীয় সন্ন্যাসী এবং যুদ্ধব্যবসায়ী নাইট প্রভৃতিও ইঁহাদের দলে যোগদান করিতেন। Aragon নৃপতি দ্বিতীয় Alfonso এবং ইংলণ্ডেশ্বর প্রথম রিচার্ড এই কবিসম্প্রদায়ে যোগদান করিয়াছিলেন। [ট্রুবাডুর কবিগণের মধ্যে Arnaut Daniel, Giraut de Bornelh, Peire Vidal, Bertrand de Born, এবং Arnaut de Merueleh, প্রভৃতির নাম বিশেষ প্রসিদ্ধ।]

trou'-ble (trŭ-bl), *v. t., i.* & *n.* **1.** To agitate ; আলোড়িত করা, সঞ্চালিত করা, নাড়া। **2.** To worry ; to disturb ; জ্বালাতন করা, উত্যক্ত করা ; বিরক্ত করা। **3.** To put to inconvenience or the like ; কষ্ট দেওয়া, অসুবিধায় ফেলা, ক্লেশ দেওয়া। ***Verb i.*** **1.** To take trouble ; কষ্ট স্বীকার করা। **2.** To worry ; to be agitated ; অস্থির হওয়া ; বিচলিত হওয়া। ***Noun.*** **1.** Annoyance ; uneasiness ; বিরক্তি ; উদ্বেগ। **2.** Labour ; pains ; শ্রম ; কষ্ট। **3.** A condition of ill-health ; as, long *trouble* ; অসুস্থতা। **2.** That which gives trouble; কষ্টজনক বিষয়, ঝঞ্ঝাটের ব্যাপার, নটখটি (*colloq.*), নটখট (*ib.*)। **3.** (*Mining*) A small fault ; (খনিজ বিদ্যা) সামান্য দোষ। **–blous,** *adj.* **–some,** *adj.* Causing trouble ; বিরক্তিকর, কষ্টজনক, ক্লেশাবহ, কষ্টকর, পীড়াজনক, পীড়াদায়ক, নটখটে, লটখটে। **To get into trouble**—To get into difficulty ; হাঙ্গামায় পড়া, সঙ্কটে পড়া। **To take the trouble**—To take pains ; কষ্ট স্বীকার করা, আয়াস স্বীকার করা।

trough (trŏf), *n.* **1.** An oblong vessel for holding water; আয়তাকার জলপাত্র, কাঠের নালা। **2.** Same as TROUGH-BATTERY. **3.** A conduit of water ; নালা। **4.** A bowl or basin usually of wood in which dough is kneeded ; ময়দা প্রভৃতি ডলার জন্য বারকোষ। **Trough-battery**—শ্রেণীতে বিভক্ত আয়তাকার-পাত্রে সজ্জিত তাড়িৎকোষাবলী। **Trough of the sea**—কল্লোলদ্বয়ের মধ্যবর্ত্তী অবনমিত স্থান।

trounce (trowns), *v. t.* To punish or to beat severely ; to castigate ; শাস্তিপ্রদান করা, গুরুতর প্রহার করা ; বেত্রাঘাত করা। **Trounc'-ing,** *n.*

troupe (trôp), *n.* A company of performers in a play or opera ; অভিনেতৃদল, বাজীকরের দল, যাত্রার দল, প্রভৃতি।

trous–de–loup, *n.* Holes or pits dug in the ground, each with a pointed stake in the middle, to serve as obstacles to the advance of an enemy ; শত্রুর অগ্রগতি রোধ করার জন্য মধ্যদেশে প্রচ্ছন্ন সূক্ষ্মাগ্র কীলকসমন্বিত গর্ত্তসমূহ।

trou'-sêr (trow-), *n.* (*Pl.*) A loose garment worn by males, extending from the waist to the knee or to the ankle, and covering the lower limbs (also *a pair of trousers*); পা-জামা, ইজের। **–ing,** *n.* **–sered,** *adj.* **Trouser-stretcher, Trousers-stretcher**—পাজামা বিস্তারের জন্য একপ্রকার কৌশল।

trousse (trôs), *n.* A case for all implements, esp. surgical instruments ; ক্ষুদ্র ক্ষুদ্র যন্ত্রাদি রাখার আধারবিশেষ, বিশেষতঃ অস্ত্র-চিকিৎসকের অস্ত্র রাখার আধার।

trous-seau' (trô-sö), *n.* The cloths and other outfit of a bride ; নববধূর বেশ, বধূসজ্জা।

trout (trowt), *n.* & *v. t.* A fresh-water fish of the salmon-kind ; স্বাদুজলের মৎস্যবিশেষ। ***Verb t.*** To fish for trout; উক্ত মৎস্য শিকার করা। **Trout'-let, Trout'-ling,** *ns.* **Trout'-y,** *adj.* **Trout-coloured**—

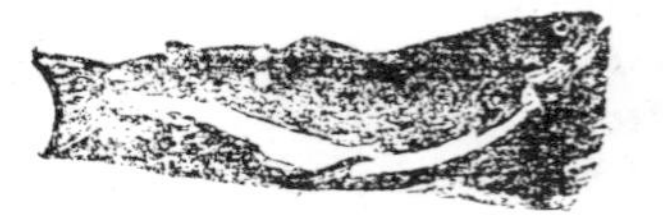

Trout.

(শ্বেত ঘোটক সম্বন্ধে) সর্ব্বাঙ্গে কৃষ্ণ বা কপিশ বর্ণের দাগবিশিষ্ট।

trou-vere' (trô-vār), *n.* A name for the ancient poets of Northern France; উত্তর ফ্রান্সের প্রাচীন কবিগণের অন্যতম।

trōve, *n.* Same as TREASURE-TROVE (which see).

trō'-vêr, *n.* **1.** (*Law*) The gaining possession of any goods, whether by finding or by other means ; (আইন) প্রাপ্তি বা অন্য কোন উপায়ে কোন জিনিষের অধিকার লাভ (ক্রয়দ্বারা নহে)। **2.** (*Law*) An action to recover damages against one that found goods, and would not deliver them to the owner on demand ; (আইন) কোন ব্যক্তি কোন জিনিষ প্রাপ্ত হইয়া উহা মালীককে প্রত্যর্পণ করিতে না চাহিলে ঐ ব্যক্তির বিরুদ্ধে যে ক্ষতিপূরণের মোকদ্দমা করা হয়।

trow (*or* trö), *v. t.* (*Archaic*) To believe ; to think ; (অপ্রঃ) বিশ্বাস করা ; মনে করা, মনে ভাবা।

trow'-ĕl, *n.* & *v. t.* **1.** A mason's tool used in spreading and dressing mortar, and breaking bricks ; রাজমিস্ত্রীর যন্ত্রবিশেষ, কর্ণিক, কুর্ণি দোস্তা (Small trowel)। **2.** A tool used by gardeners ; বাগানের মালীদের খন্তা। ***Verb t.*** **1.** To form or dress with trowel ; কর্ণিক দ্বারা গঠন করা, কুর্ণিদ্বারা ছড়ান। **2.** To flatter grossly ; অতিশয় তোষামোদ করা, তৈল মর্দ্দন করা, পা চাটা। **To lay on thick with a trowel**—See LAY.

troy, *n* (Also *troy weight*) A weight used for gold and silver, divided into 12 ounces, each of twenty penny-weights, each of 20 grains, so that the pound troy equals 5,760 grains ; ইংলণ্ডের স্বর্ণ রৌপ্য এবং রত্নাদির ওজন-প্রণালী (এই প্রণালী অনুসারে ১২ আউন্স ১ পাউণ্ডের সমান)।

tru′-ănt (trô-), *n., adj.* & *v. i.* **1.** One who shrinks from duty ; কর্ত্তব্যপালনে পরাঙ্মুখ ব্যক্তি। **2.** One who stays out of school without leave ; যে বালক ছুটি না লইয়া বিদ্যালয়ের বাহিরে ঘুরিয়া বেড়ায়, বওয়াটে ছেলে। **3.** (*Rare*) An idler ; (ক্বচিদ্ব্যবহৃত) যে ব্যক্তি আলস্যে সময়ক্ষেপ করে। ***Adj.*** Shirking duty ; idle ; as, a *truant* boy ; loitering ; কর্ত্তব্যপরাঙ্মুখ; অলস; বিদ্যালয় হইতে পলায়িত হইয়া ইতস্ততঃ বিচরণশীল। ***Verb i.*** To play truant ; বিদ্যালয় হইতে ছুটি না লইয়া ঘুরিয়া বেড়ান, বওয়াটের মত ঘুরিয়া বেড়ান। **—an-cy,** *n.* **—ly,** *adv.* **Truant-school**—যে সকল ছাত্র অভিভাবকের উপেক্ষায় অলস ভাবে রাস্তায় ঘুরিয়া সময় কাটায় তাহাদের জন্য শিল্পবিদ্যালয়।

truce (trôs), *n.* **1.** temporary cessation of hostilities ; কিছু সময়ের জন্য যুদ্ধনিবৃত্তি, অল্পকালের জন্য যুদ্ধনিবৃত্তি। **2.** Intermission of action, pain, or contest ; "There he may find *truce* to his restless thought" ; ক্ষণিক বিরাম, ক্ষণিক শান্তি, স্বল্পবিরাম। **Truce of God**—কোন কোন খৃষ্টীয় পর্ব্বকালে ব্যক্তিগত দ্বন্দ্ব, কলহ, প্রভৃতির সাময়িক নিবৃত্তি।

trŭck, *n.* & *v. t.* **1.** A small solid wheel as for a gun carriage ; ক্ষুদ্র-চাকা। **2.** A kind of hand-barow with two wheels ; একপ্রকার দুই চাকার ঠেলা-গাড়ী। **3.** A strong vehicle for heavy goods ; ভারি মালের জন্য একপ্রকার মজবুত গাড়ী। **4.** (*Railway*) An open wagon for the conveyance of goods ; (রেলওয়ে) একপ্রকার খোলা মালের গাড়ী। **5.** The cap at the end of a flag or mast-head ; পতাকা বা মাস্তলের মস্তকের অগ্রভাগে স্থাপিত গোলাকৃতি কাষ্ঠ খণ্ড। **6.** A platform running on wheels ; চক্রের উপর স্থাপিত মঞ্চ। **7.** A swiveling carriage, consisting of a frame with one or more pairs of wheels and the necessary boxes, springs, etc. to carry or guide one end of a locomotive etc. ; রেলগাড়ীর এঞ্জিন প্রভৃতির প্রান্ত চালিত বা নিয়ন্ত্রিত করার জন্য একপ্রকার স্বাধীনভাবে ঘূর্ণনশীল শকট। ***Verb t.*** To convey on truck ; খোলা গাড়ীতে নেওয়া। **Truck′-age,** *n.* **1.** Conveyance by trucks ; খোলা গাড়ীতে বহন। **2.** A charge for conveying goods by truck ; freight ; খোলা গাড়ীতে মাল প্রেরণের ভাড়া ; মাল ভাড়া। **Truck-bolster**—অনুচ্চ ঠেলা গাড়ীর প্রস্তদেশের অবলম্বন-স্বরূপ আড় কাষ্ঠ।

trŭck, *n., v. i.* & *t.* **1.** Exchange of commodities ; barter ; দ্রব্য-বিনিময় ; বিনিময়। **2.** Commodities appropriate for small trade or barter ; ক্ষুদ্র ক্ষুদ্র জিনিষ, ফটকী নাটকী। **3.** (*Colloq.*) Rubbish ; জঞ্জাল। **4.** (*Colloq.*) Nonsense ; as, he shall stand no *truck* ; মাথামুণ্ড, ছাইপাঁশ। **5.** Payment of wages in goods instead of in cash (also *truck-system*) ; নগদ টাকার পরিবর্ত্তে জিনিষ দ্বারা বেতন প্রদান। ***Verb i.*** To exchange commodities ; দ্রব্য বিনিময় করা। ***Verb t.*** **1.** To exchange ; বিনিময় করা। **2.** To hawk (wares) about ; জিনিষ ফেরি করা। **Truck Acts**—নগদ টাকার পরিবর্ত্তে জিনিষ দ্বারা বেতন প্রদানের পদ্ধতি সম্বন্ধে অনুসন্ধানের জন্য বা ঐ প্রথার উচ্ছেদের নিমিত্ত ১৮৩১ এবং ১৮৭০ খৃষ্টাব্দে বিধিবদ্ধ আইনদ্বয়। **Truck-shop**—যে দোকানের মজুরগণকে মুদ্রার পরিবর্ত্তে উৎপন্ন দ্রব্য প্রদান করা হয়। **Trunk-system** — Same as TOMMY, *n.* I.

trŭck′-le (-l), *n.* & *v. i.* **1.** Small wheel or cart ; ক্ষুদ্র চাকা। **2.** A small barrel-shaped cheese ; ক্ষুদ্র পিপার আকার পনীর। **3.** Same as TRUCKLE-BED. ***Verb i.*** To submit obsequiously ; হীনভাবে অনুগত হওয়া, নতশির হওয়া, কাহারো নিকট মাথা নীচু করা। **Truckle-bed**—চক্রযুক্ত অনুচ্চ খট্টা—যাহা ঠেলিয়া অপর খট্টার নিম্নে চালিত করিতে পারা যাইত। [পূর্ব্বকালে ইংলণ্ডের বড় লোকগণ যে শয্যায় শয়ন করিতেন—তাহার নীচে এরূপ অনুচ্চ খট্টায় ভৃত্য প্রভৃতি নিদ্রা যাইত।]

trŭc′-ŭ-lĕnt, *adj.* **1.** Fierce ; ferocious ; করাল, ভীষণ ; ভয়ঙ্কর, নিদারুণ, রুদ্র, দুর্দ্দান্ত। **2.** Cruel ; destructive ; নিষ্ঠুর, ক্রূর ; ধ্বংসকারক। **—lence,** *n.* **—ly,** *adv.*

trudge (trŭj), *v. i.* & *n.* To go on foot ; to walk along wearily or heavily ; পদব্রজে গমন করা, হাঁটিয়া চলা, পায় হাঁটা, পথ হাঁটা ; অতি কষ্টে হাঁটিয়া চলা। ***Noun.*** Such walk ; পদব্রজে গমন, অতি কষ্টে হাঁটিয়া চলন।

true (trô), *adj.* & *v. t.* **1.** Loyal ; as, a *true* friend ; একনিষ্ঠ, প্রকৃত, যথার্থ। **2.** (*Obs.*) Honest ; (অপ্রঃ) সৎ, সাধু। **3.** Not false ; সত্য। **4.** Truthful ; "Master you know that these are *true* and teachest the way of God in truth" ; সত্যবাদী। **5.** Accurate ; correct ; as, a *true* copy ; যথার্থ ; প্রকৃত। **6.** Genuine ; "A piece of *true* gold" ; খাঁটী, সাচ্চা। **7.** Legitimate ; rightful ; as, *true* heir ; ন্যায়সঙ্গত ; বিধিসঙ্গত। **8.** Certain ; as, *true* sign ; নিশ্চিত। **9.** (Of voice) In perfect tune ; (স্বরসম্বন্ধে) সুতান। ***Verb t.*** **1.** To make true exact or accurate ; সত্য করা, যথার্থ করা। **2.** To give a right form to ; to adjust nicely ; ঠিক আকার দেওয়া ; ঠিক করিয়া লাগান। **True′-ness,** *n.* **True-blue**—See BLUE. **True-born**—সুজাত। **True-bred**—সদ্বংশজাত। **True course**—প্রকৃত দ্রাঘিমার সহিত জাহাজের গতিপথের

সংযোগে যে কোণ উৎপন্ন হয়। **True-hearted**—খাঁটী; সদন্তঃকরণ। **True horizon**—See HORIZON. **True-love**—প্রণয়ী, প্রণয়িনী। **True-love knot, True-lover's knot**—প্রেম-সূচকগ্রন্থি, প্রেমগ্রন্থি। **Truepenny**—(অপ্রঃ) সাধু লোক। **True stitch**—যে শেলাই উভয় দিকে একরূপ দেখায়। **True time**—স্ফুটকাল। **As true as gospel, touch** or **steel**—Absolutely true; অতি সত্য। **A true bill**—See BILL. **True motion of the sun**—স্ফুট সূর্য্যগতি। **True place of a star** or **planet**—(জ্যোতিবিজ্ঞান) পৃথিবীর কেন্দ্র হইতে কোন গ্রহ নক্ষত্রাদি দৃষ্টি করিলে এবং ঐসকল গ্রহ নক্ষত্রাদি হইতে আগত অলোকরশ্মি তির্য্যগ্‌বর্ত্তন ক্রিয়ার অধীন না হইলে উক্ত গ্রহাদি আকাশের যে স্থানে পরিলক্ষিত হইত।

trŭf'-fle (-l), *n.* An edible fungus growing underground; ভূগর্ভে জাত একপ্রকার ভোজনযোগ্য ছত্রাক।

tru'-ism (trô-), *n.* An undoubted or self-evident truth; platitude; স্পষ্ট সত্য, স্বয়ংসিদ্ধ (হিঃ কোঃ), স্বতঃসিদ্ধ বাক্য (ঐ); নূতনত্বহীন বাক্য।

trŭll, *n.* (*Archaic*) Prostitute; (অপ্রঃ) বেশ্যা, খানকী, কসবী।

tru'-lȳ (trô-), *adv.* 1. Faithfully; as, to be *truly* attached to one; একনিষ্ঠভাবে। 2. Sincerely; অকপটভাবে, অকৃত্রিমভাবে। 3. In agreement with truth; সঙ্গতভাবে। 4. Conformably to law; "His innocent babe *truly* begotten"; বিধিসঙ্গতরূপে, বৈধভাবে। 5. Exactly; accurately; as, to state a fact *truly*; truthfully; ঠিকভাবে; অভ্রান্তরূপে; যথার্থরূপে। 6. In fact; বাস্তবিকপক্ষে, প্রকৃতপক্ষে।

trumeau, *n.* (*F.*) (*Archit.*) A pillar or any piece of wall between two openings; (মধ্যযুগের স্থাপত্যশিল্প) দ্বার প্রভৃতির ফাঁকের মধ্যবর্ত্তী স্তম্ভ বা প্রাচীরাংশ, অবকাশ-স্তম্ভ।

trŭmp, *n., v. t.* & *i.* 1. A card of the winning suit; a card turned up to determine which suit shall be trumps; তাসখেলায় রঙ্গ; যে কাটা তাস দ্বারা রঙ্গ স্থির করা হয়। 2. (*Slang*) An excellent fellow; "I wish I may die if you are not a true *trump*"; (ইতরভাষায়) খাসা লোক, চমৎকার লোক। ***Verb t.*** To take with a trump; to play a trump-card in order to win; রঙ্গ খেলিয়া লওয়া, তুরুপ করিয়া নেওয়া; রঙ্গ খেলা, তুরুপ করা। ***Verb i.*** To play a trump when another suit has been led; তুরুপ করা। **Trump-card**—যে কাটা তাসদ্বারা রঙ্গ স্থির করা হয়; রঙ্গের তাস; কোন বিষয়ে উদ্দেশ্য সিদ্ধির প্রকৃষ্টতম উপায়। **To hold the trump-card**—To be sure of victory; to be fortunate; জয়লাভ সম্বন্ধে নিশ্চিন্ত থাকা; সৌভাগ্যবান হওয়া। **To play trumps**—To use one's last means; শেষ উপায় প্রয়োগ করা, ব্রহ্মাস্ত্র নিক্ষেপ করা। **To put to one's trumps**—To reduce to the last expedient or to the utmost expedient of one's power; কোন ব্যক্তিকে এরূপ অবস্থায় আনা—যাহাতে সে তাহার সর্ব্বশেষ উপায় প্রয়োগ করিতে বাধ্য হয়। **To turn up trumps**—To prove useful; কার্য্যকরী হওয়া। To be lucky; to prove successful; ভাগ্যবান হওয়া; কৃতকার্য্য হওয়া, সিদ্ধিলাভ করা।

trŭmp, *n.* & *v. t.* (*Archaic, Poet.*) Trumpet; (অপ্রঃ কবিতায়) সানাইর মত বংশীবিশেষ। ***Verb t.*** (*Obs.*) To impose upon; to deceive; (অপ্রঃ) ঠকান, চোখে ধূলি দেওয়া; প্রতারণা করা। **To trump up**—To fabricate; মিথ্যা সাজান, জাল করা। **To trump up a charge**—To bring a false charge against some one; কোন ব্যক্তির বিরুদ্ধে মিথ্যা অভিযোগ আনয়ন করা।

trŭmp'-ĕr-ȳ, *n.* & *adj.* 1. Worthless finery; চটকদার জিনিষ, ফটকীনাটকী। 2. Rubbish; জঞ্জাল, আবর্জ্জনা। ***Adj.*** Deceptively showy; worthless; shallow; as, *trumpery* arguments; চটকদার, জিল্লাদার; অসার, মূল্যহীন; অনুদার।

trŭmp'-ĕt, *n.* & *v. t.* 1. A clear sounding instrument of music, used in military music; শানাইজাতীয়

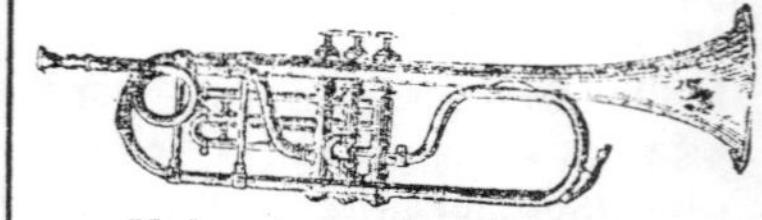

Modern trumpet with pistons.

বাদ্যযন্ত্র বিশেষ, তূরী। 2. (*Archaic*) One who praises or propagates praise; (অপ্রঃ) স্তুতি বা প্রশংসা কীর্ত্তনকারী। 3. A sound as of trumpets, esp. of elephant; ধ্বনি, বিশেষতঃ মাতঙ্গের বৃংহিত। 4. Same as REED-STOP. 5. A trumpet-shaped thing; kind of funnel; শানাইএর মত জিনিষ; একপ্রকার ফুঁদেল। 6. A trumpet-shaped instrument; শানাইএর আকার যন্ত্র। ***Verb t.*** 1. To blow a trumpet; to proclaim by a sound of trumpet; to proclaim; শানাই বাজান; শানাই বাজাইয়া ঘোষণা করা; ঘোষণা করা। 2. (Of elephant) To make trumpet-like sound; বৃংহিত ধ্বনি করা। **Trumpet-call**—শানাইর ধ্বনি দ্বারা আহ্বান; কর্ম্মক্ষেত্রে আগুয়ান হওয়ার জন্য আহ্বান। **Trumpet-conch, Trumpet-shell, Sea-trumpet**—বিভিন্নজাতীয় বুরুজাকৃতি উদরপদী শম্বুক। **Trumpet-flower**—পারুল ফুল (cf. রাজার কাননে ফুটেছে বকুল, পারুল, রজনীগন্ধা—কথা।) [Syn. পাটলা, ফলেরুহা, কৃষ্ণবৃন্তা, কালী, স্থালী অমোঘা, সুপুষ্পিকা, কুবেরাক্ষী, তাম্রপুষ্পী, কুম্ভিকা, বসন্তদূতী, স্থিরগন্ধা, অম্বুবাসী, কালবৃন্তী, কামদূতী, কুন্তী, মধুদূতী, কালাস্থলী, অলিবল্লভা, পাটলপুষ্প, কামবৃন্তা, কাচস্থালী, তোয়াধিবাসিনী, তোয়প্রষ্টা, তোপুষ্পী।] **Trumpet-leaf**—শানাইর আকার পত্রবিশিষ্ট বৃক্ষ বা গুল্ম। **Trumpet-major**—অশ্বারোহী সৈনিকদলের প্রধান তূরীবাদক, ব্যাণ্ডের দলের প্রধান তূরীবাদক। **Trumpet-swan**—উত্তর

আমেরিকার একপ্রকার বৃহৎ হংস। **Feast of trumpets**—ইহুদীদিগের নববর্ষারম্ভের উৎসব। **To blow one's own trumpet**—See under BLOW (*Verb t.*)

trŭmp'-ĕt-ẽr, *n.* **1.** One who sounds or plays a trumpet ; তুরীবাদক। **2.** One who proclaims or publishes ; ঘোষণাকারী, প্রচারকারী, কীর্ত্তনকারী। **3.** A variety of the domestic pigeon ; একজাতীয় গৃহকপোত। **4.** Same as TRUMPET-SWAN.

trun'-căl (trŭng-), *adj.* Of, or pertaining to, the trunk of a body or tree ; বৃক্ষের কাণ্ড বা দেহের কবন্ধ সম্বন্ধীয়।

trun'-cāte (trŭng-), *adj.* & *v. t.* Appearing as if cut off at the tip ; কর্ত্তিতাগ্র, ছিন্নাগ্র। ***Verb t.*** **1.** To cut off ; to lop ; কাটা ; ছেদন করা।

Truncate leaf

2. (*Min.*) To replace or cut off by a plane ; সমতল দ্বারা ছেদন বা স্থান পূরণ করা। **—ca'-tion**, *n.* **—ca'-ture**, *n.* **—ly**, *adv.*

trŭn'-cheon (-shŭn), *n.* **1.** A baton or staff of command or authority ; দণ্ড, সোটা। **2.** A short club or cudgel ; ক্ষুদ্র যষ্টি, রুল।

trŭn'-dle (-dl), *n.*, *adj.*, *v. t.* & *i.* **1.** A small wheel ; ক্ষুদ্র চাকা। **2.** A kind of low-wheeled cart or truck ; একপ্রকার অনুচ্চ শকট। **3.** A round or cylindrical body ; গোলাকৃতি বা নলাকৃতি বস্তু। **4.** Same as TRUNDLE-BED. ***Adj.*** Shaped like trundle or wheel ; round ; curled ; ক্ষুদ্র চক্রাকৃতি ; গোলাকার ; কুঞ্চিত। ***Verb t.*** To roll on little wheels ; ক্ষুদ্র ক্ষুদ্র চাকার উপর গড়াইয়া নেওয়া। ***Verb i.*** To cause to roll ; গড়াইয়া নেওয়া। **Trundle-bed** — Same as TRUCKLE-BED (which see).

trunk (trŭngk), *n.* & *v. t.* **1.** The main body of a tree ; বৃক্ষের কাণ্ড। **2.** The body without head or limbs ; মস্তক এবং হস্ত পদাদি বিহীন দেহ, কবন্ধ, ধড়। **3.** The main body of anything ; কোন কিছুর প্রধান অংশ। **4.** The proboscis of an elephant ; হাতীর শুঁড়, করিশুণ্ড, হস্তিশুণ্ড। **5.** A box or trunk ; বাক্স, তোড়ঙ্গ, মঞ্জুষা।

Trunk-hose.

6. A tank or pool for keeping fish alive ; মৎস্য জীবিত রাখার জন্য পুষ্করিণী বা নালা। **7.** An iron hoop with bag to catch crustaceans ; কর্কট প্রভৃতি ধৃত করার জন্য থলিসংযুক্ত লোহার চাকা। **8.** An open cylinder used instead of piston-rod in marine-engines ; সমুদ্রগামী পোতে ব্যবহৃত নলদণ্ডের পরিবর্তে চোঙ্গ বিশেষ। **9.** A boxed passage conveying air to and from a blast apparatus ; ধ্মাপনযন্ত্রে বায়ুচলাচলের জন্য পথ। **10.** Same as TRUNK-HOSE. ***Verb t.*** To lop off ; to curtail ; ছাঁটিয়া দেওয়া ; খর্ব্ব করা। **Trunk'-ful**, *n.* **Trunk'-less**, *adj.* **Trunk-drawers**—জানুপ্রমাণ উচ্চ দেরাজশ্রেণী। **Trunk-hose**—কটিদেশ হইতে জঙ্ঘা পর্যান্ত প্রলম্বিত একপ্রকার পাজামা (ইংলণ্ডে ষোড়শ ও সপ্তদশ শতাব্দীতে ব্যবহৃত হইত)। **Trunk-line**—লৌহবর্ত্মের প্রধান পথ। **Trunk-nail**— কারুকার্য্যশোভিত অগ্রভাগবিশিষ্ট একপ্রকার পোত। **Trunk-road**—প্রধান রাস্তা।

trŭn'-nion (-yŏn), *n.* **1.** A knob projecting on each side of a gun, mortar, etc. and serving to support it on the cheeks of the carriage ; কামানের উভয়পার্শ্বস্থ চোঙ্গাকার উদ্গত অংশ—যদ্দারা উহা শকটের উপর বিধৃত হইয়া থাকে। **2.** A hollow gudgeon on each side of an oscillatnig cylinder to support it, and through which steam is received and exhausted ; জাহাজের কলে সংলগ্ন শূন্যগর্ভ অক্ষদণ্ড বিশেষ। **Trunnion-plate** — কামানের গাড়ীর ফলক বিশেষ—যাহা কামানের শৃঙ্গদ্বয়ের নিম্নদেশ অতিক্রম করিয়া থাকে। **Trunnion-ring**—কামানের সন্ধির অব্যবহিত নিম্নস্থ বেষ্টনী।

trŭss, *n.* & *v. t.* **1.** A bundle of straw or grass ; খড় বা ঘাসের আঁটি। **2.** A combination of timbers or iron work constituting an unyielding frame, or support ; ছাদ, সেতু, প্রভৃতির অবলম্বনস্বরূপ একত্র সংবদ্ধ আড়কাঠ প্রভৃতি দ্বারা গঠিত কাঠাম। **3.** (*Surg.*) A bandage or apparatus used in cases of hernia to keep up the reduced

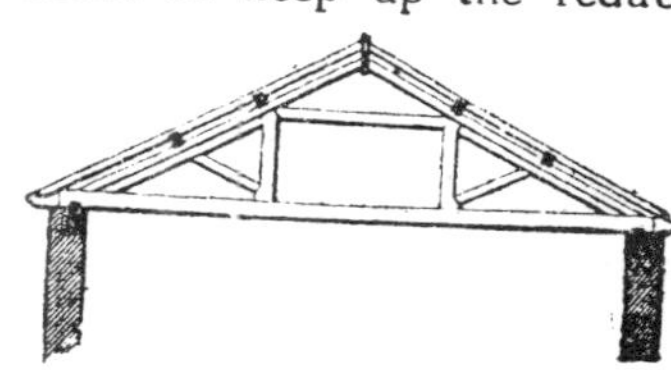

Truss.

parts and hinder further protrusion or for other purpose ; অন্ত্রবৃদ্ধি প্রভৃতি রোগে ব্যবহৃত একপ্রকার পেটি, অন্ত্রসংস্থাপক। ***Verb t.*** **1.** To put in a truss or bundle ; আঁটি বাঁধা। **2.** To fasten (wings of fowl etc.) by or as by a skewer ; "A fowl *trussed* for roasting" ; মোরগ প্রভৃতির পাখা বাঁধিয়া রাখা। **Truss-beam**—গৃহাদির আড়া প্রভৃতির জন্য লৌহ-ফলক। **Truss-bridge**—তির্য্যগ্ ফলকাদির সাহায্যে কৃত সেতু অবলম্বনসেতু। **To truss up**—To bind tightly ; আঁটিয়া বাঁধা To cause to be hanged (usu. *up*) ;

ফাঁসী কাষ্ঠে ঝুলান ; (Of a hawk) To hunt ; (বাজপক্ষিসম্বন্ধে) শিকার করা।

trŭst, *n., v. t.* & *i.* **1.** A reliance or resting of the mind on the integrity, veracity, justice, friendship, power, ptotection, or the like of another ; বিশ্বাস, প্রত্যয়, প্রতীতি। **2.** A person or thing confided in ; "O Lord God, thou art my *trust* from my youth" ; বিশ্বাসভাজন ব্যক্তি, বিশ্বাসের পাত্র। **3.** Something committed to one's care for safe keeping ; বিশ্বাসপূর্ব্বক ন্যস্ত বস্তু, ন্যাস, গচ্ছিত সম্পত্তি বা ধন। **4.** Charge ; ভার, জিম্মা। **5.** Credit given without examination, or on promise of payment ; "Most take things upon *trust*, and misemploy their assent by lazily enslaving their minds to the dictates of others" ; বিনা পরীক্ষায় বা ভবিষ্যতে পরিশোধ করিবে এই প্রতিশ্রুতিতে যে বাকী দেওয়া হয়, বাকী। **6.** Hope ; faith ; "Such *trust* have we through Christ" ; আশা, ভরসা ; বিশ্বাস। **7.** A confidence reposed by one person called the *truster*, or *celui que trust*, in conveying or bequeathing property to another (hence called the *trustee*), that the latter will apply it for the benefit of a third party (called the *cestui que trust*, or *benificiary*) or to some specified purpose or purposes ; যদি কোন ব্যক্তি অপর ব্যক্তিকে এই সর্ত্তে কোন সম্পত্তি প্রদান বা চরমপত্র দ্বারা অর্পণ করে যে ঐ ব্যক্তি উক্ত সম্পত্তি কোন তৃতীয় ব্যক্তির হিতের জন্য বা কোন বিশেষভাবে নির্দ্দিষ্ট উদ্দেশ্য বা উদ্দেশ্যসমূহ সাধনের নিমিত্ত প্রয়োগ করিবে, তবে যাহাকে উক্ত সম্পত্তি প্রদান বা অর্পণ করা হয় তাহার প্রতি যে বিশ্বাস স্থাপন করা হয়, ন্যাস। **8.** The beneficial interest created by such a transaction ; a beneficial interest or an equitable right of property unattended with the legal or possessory ownership thereof ; উক্তরূপ কার্য্য দ্বারা কোন ব্যক্তির যে হিতজনকস্বত্ব সৃষ্টি করা হয় ; কোন বিধিসঙ্গত বা প্রকৃত অধিকারজনিত স্বামিত্ব ব্যতিরেকে যে অধিকার থাকে। **9.** Property so held ; legal relation between the holder and the property so held ; উক্ত প্রকারে অধিকৃত সম্পত্তি ; উক্ত সম্পত্তি এবং উক্ত সম্পত্তির অধিকারীর মধ্যে যে বিধিসঙ্গত সম্পর্ক থাকে। **10.** (*Comm.*) A combination of companies or individual traders designed to secure monopoly of a particular market ; কোন বিশেষ বস্তুর ক্রয় বিক্রয়ে একাধিকারত্ব স্থাপনের জন্য ব্যবসায়িগণ বা ব্যবসায়ি-সম্মিলনী সমূহের সম্মেলন। ***Verb t.*** **1.** To rely upon ; নির্ভর করা, আস্থা স্থাপন করা। **2.** To believe ; বিশ্বাস করা, প্রত্যয় করা। **3.** To give credit to ; বাকী দেওয়া, ধার দেওয়া। ***Verb i.*** **1.** To have trust ; বিশ্বাস থাকা। **2.** To practise in giving credit ; ধারে জিনিষ দেওয়া। **3.** To confide or believe readily ; সহজে বিশ্বাস করা। **4.** To hope ; আশা করা।

trŭst, *adj.* Held in trust ; as, *trust* property ; ন্যাসরূপে রক্ষিত।

trŭs-tee' (-tē), *n.* **1.** A person appointed to hold property for the benefit of those entitled to it ; যে ব্যক্তির নিকট প্রকৃত উত্তরাধিকারীর অনুকূলে কোন সম্পত্তি অর্পিত করা হয়, ন্যাসরক্ষক, ন্যাসধারী। **2.** Each of a body of men, often elective, managing affairs of college, etc. ; মহাবিদ্যালয় প্রভৃতির কার্য্যনির্ব্বাহক সভ্য। **—ship,** *n.*

trŭst'-fụl, *adj.* Full of trust ; trusting ; বিশ্বাসপূর্ণ ; বিশ্বাসী।

trŭst'-wor-th̲y̆ (-wêr-), *adj.* Deserving of trust or confidence ; বিশ্বাসযোগ্য, আপ্ত, বিশ্বসনীয়, বিশ্বস্ত। **—thi-ness,** *n.*

trŭst'-y̆, *adj.* & *n.* **1.** (*Archaic*) Reliable (অপ্রঃ) বিশ্বাসযোগ্য। **2.** A trusted person ; a well-behaved convict enjoying special privileges ; বিশ্বস্ত ব্যক্তি ; যে কয়েদী সদাচরণের জন্য কোন কোন বিষয়ে বিশেষ বিশেষ সুবিধা প্রাপ্ত হইয়া থাকে। **—i-ness,** *n.*

truth (trôth), *n.* **1.** The state or quality of being true ; trueness ; সত্য, সত্যতা ; যথার্থতা, যাথার্থ্য। **2.** Veracity ; সত্যবাদিতা, সত্যপরায়ণতা, সত্যনিষ্ঠা। **3.** (*Hegel.*) The fully realised result ; "The *truth* of being is becoming *i. e.* the body is made by the soul for the soul's use" ; পূর্ণসিদ্ধফল বা পরিণাম। **4.** Fidelity ; "I will follow thee with *truth* and loyalty" ; নিষ্ঠা। **5.** True religion ; "For the law was given by Moses ; but grace and *truth* came by Jesus Christ" ; the doctrines of the gospel ; সত্য ধর্ম্ম ; খৃষ্টীয় সুসমাচারের মূলতত্ত্ব। **6.** An established fact, law or the like ; সত্য, তত্ত্ব, সিদ্ধান্ত, তত্ত্বজ্ঞান, পরমার্থ। **7.** In fine arts, the proper and correct representation of any object in nature, or of whatever subject may be under treatment ; "*Truth* is the highest quality in art" ; ললিতকলায় কোন প্রাকৃতিক বা অন্যবিধ বিষয় যথাযথ ভাবে প্রকটন। **8.** Honesty ; sincerity ; virtue ; "Even so void is your false heart of *truth*" ; সাধুতা ; সরলতা ; পুণ্য। **9.** Accuracy ; correctness ; সঠিকতা ; শুদ্ধতা। **Truth'-fụl,** *adj.* **1.** Veracious ; সত্যবাদী, সত্যপরায়ণ, সত্যসন্ধ, সত্যনিষ্ঠ। **2.** Conforming to truth ; সত্য। **Truth'-fụl-ly,** *adv.* **Truth'-fụl-ness,** *n.* **Contingent truth**—আপেক্ষিক সত্য। **Necessary, immutable** or **first truths**—মূল সত্য (যথা সংখ্যা সমূহের পরস্পরের সম্বন্ধ, গণিতের স্বতঃসিদ্ধ, প্রভৃতি)। **Phenomenal-truth** — প্রাতিভাসিক

সত্য। **Relative truth**—ব্যবহারিক সত্য। **For a truth**—In reality; বাস্তবিকপক্ষে **In truth**—Really; বাস্তবিক পক্ষে, প্রকৃতপক্ষে। **Of a truth**—In a reality; বাস্তবিক পক্ষে। **To tell the truth**—বলিতে কি, সত্য বলিতে হইলে, আসল কথা বলিলে।

truth'-lĕss (trôth-), *adj.* **1.** False; মিথ্যা, অসত্য। **2.** Faithless; অবিশ্বাসী, সত্যভঙ্গকারী, বিশ্বাসঘাতক।

trȳ, *v. t., i.* & *n.* **1.** To separate; to select; as to *try* out the bad coins from the good"; আলাহাদি করা, পৃথক করা, আল্‌গা করা; বাছনি করা। **2.** To purify; to refine; "Silver *tried* in a furnace of earth, purified seven times"; বিশুদ্ধ করা; পরিশোধিত করা, শোধন করা। **3.** To examine; to make experiment on; পরীক্ষা করা; পরখ করা। **4.** To use or apply tentatively; as, *try* this medicine; পরীক্ষাস্থলে ব্যবহার বা প্রয়োগ করা। **5.** To subject to some severe test or experience; to afflict; কঠোর পরীক্ষায় ফেলা; কষ্টে ফেলা। **6.** To examine or enquire into judicially: as, to *try* a case; to undertake; বিচার করা; কোন কার্য্যে প্রবৃত্ত হওয়া। **7.** To attempt; চেষ্টা করা। **8.** To strain; as, light *tries* one's eyes; পীড়া দেওয়া, পীড়িত করা। ***Verb i.*** **1.** To endeavour; চেষ্টা করা, প্রয়াস পাওয়া, যত্ন করা। **2.** To prove by a test; পরীক্ষাদ্বারা প্রমাণিত করা। ***Noun.*** **1.** The act of trying; trial; চেষ্টাকরণ; চেষ্টা। **2.** (*Rugby football*) The three points gained when a player manages to place the ball on or behind the opponet's goal-line; (রাগবী পাদগোলক ক্রীড়ায়) কোন ক্রীড়ক প্রতিপক্ষের গোল রেখার উপরে বা পশ্চাতে বল স্থাপন করিলে যে তিন জয়াঙ্ক লাভ করা হয়। **Try'-ing,** *adj.* Severe, afflictive; গুরুতর, নিদারুণ; কষ্টদায়ক, কষ্টজনক, ক্লেশজনক, পীড়াদায়ক, কৃচ্ছ্রসাধ্য, কষ্টকর। **Try-cock**—বাষ্পজনকের জলের ঊর্দ্ধতার সীমা পরিমাপের জন্য একপ্রকার কল। **Try-plane, Trying-plane**—সূতারদের বৃহত্তম রেঁদা। **Trysail**—অপেক্ষাকৃত অনুচ্চ মাস্তুলের উপর যে পাইল খাটান হয়। **Try-square, Trying-square** — সূতার মিস্ত্রীদের একপ্রকার মাটাম—যাহার এক অংশ কাঠের ও অপর অংশ ধাতুর হইয়া থাকে। **To try a fall with**—See FALL *n.* **To try back**—To retrace one's steps backwards to search for lost path etc.; পশ্চাদ্দিকে প্রত্যাবৃত্ত হইয়া হারাণো পথ প্রভৃতির সন্ধান করা। **To try conclusions**—To fight a decisive battle; জয়পরাজয় নিশ্চিত না হওয়া পর্য্যন্ত সংগ্রাম করা; একপক্ষ পরাজিত না হওয়া পর্য্যন্ত যুদ্ধ করা, প্রতিযোগিতা করা। **To try for**—To aim; লক্ষ্য করা। To apply for; to compete for; আবেদন করা; প্রতিযোগিতা করা। **To try on**—To fit on; to attempt; কোট প্রভৃতি গায়ে লাগে কিনা পরীক্ষা করিয়া দেখা; চেষ্টা করা। **To try one's hand at**—To try for the first time; প্রথমবার চেষ্টা করা। **To try one's nerve**—To unsettle one's mind; কাহারো চিত্ত বিচলিত করা। **To try out**—To pursue efforts till a decision is obtained; নিশ্চিন্ত ফল লাভ না করা পর্য্যন্ত চেষ্টা করা।

trȳ'-gŏn, *n.* A genus of fishes to which the sting-ray belongs; এক জাতীয় মৎস্য।

trȳ'-mȧ, *n.* (*Pl.* -TA) (*Bot.*) An inferior drupe with a two-valved separable flesh, as the walnut; অক্ষোটক (সাঃ পঃ)।

trȳst, *n.* & *v. t.* (*Archaic*) Appointed meeting; an appointed place of meeting; an appointment; as, to keep a *tryst*; সঙ্কেতমিলন; মিলনস্থলী, সঙ্কেতস্থলী, সঙ্কেতনিকেতন; মিলনসংকেত, মিলনের জন্য কথাবার্ত্তা। ***Verb t.*** To agree to meet at a certain place or time; কোন, নির্দ্দিষ্ট স্থানে বা সময়ে দেখা করার জন্য সম্মত হওয়া, সংকেতস্থানে মিলিত হইবার জন্য সম্মত হওয়া।

tsĕt'-sė, *n.* A South-African two-winged fly whose bite is often fatal to animals; দক্ষিণ আফ্রিকার

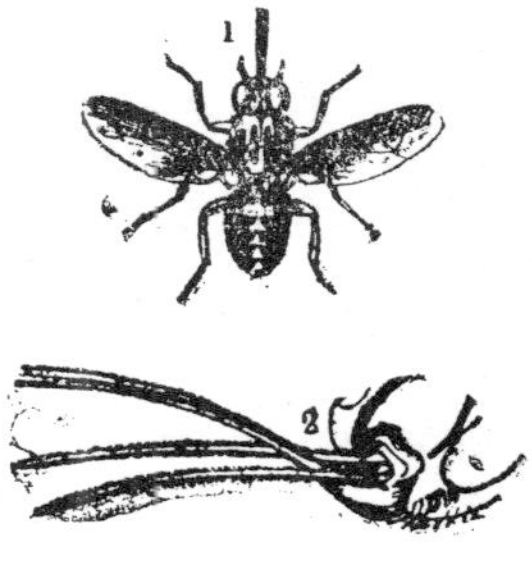

Tsetse
1, insect; 2, mouth organs (magnified)

একপ্রকার দ্বিপক্ষ পতঙ্গ (ইহাদের দংশনে অনেক সময় অশ্ব, কুকুর প্রভৃতি জন্তুর মৃত্যু ঘটিয়া থাকে)।

tŭb, *n., v. t.* & *i.* **1.** A small cask or half barrel with one bottom and open above; as, a washing *tub*; কাঠের গামলা, কেটো। **2.** The amount which a tub will hold; এক কেঠোতে যে পরিমাণ জিনিষ ধরে। **3.** A small cask or barrel for liquor; ক্ষুদ্র মদ্যের পিপা। **4.** A wooden or earthen vessel in which vegetables are planted; ফুলের টব। **5.** A kind of pulpit; একপ্রকার বেদী। **6.** (*Slang*) A clumsy boat; a slow-moving boat or vessel; (ইতরভাষায়) কদাকার নৌকা; মৃদুগামী নৌকা বা জাহাজ। **7.** Kinds of bucket or box for conveying ore, coal, etc.; কয়লা, খনিজবিমিশ্র ধাতু প্রভৃতি বহনের জন্য বিভিন্ন প্রকার পাত্র। **8.** A vessel used as a bath; bath taken in this; স্নান পাত্র; জলপূর্ণ বৃহৎ পাত্রে স্নান। **9.** A kind of rowing boat; একপ্রকার দাঁড়ের নৌকা। ***Verb t.*** **1.** To place or set in a tub; গামলায় রাখা, গামলায় রোপণ করা। **2.** To bathe in a tub or bath ; স্নানের গামলায় স্নান করান, স্নান করান। 3. To line a shaft with a casing of wood ; সুড়ঙ্গের মুখ কাঠের আস্তর দ্বারা আচ্ছাদিত করা। *Verb i.* To take bath in a tub ; জলপূর্ণ ভাণ্ডে স্নান করা। **Tub'-bing,** *n.* **1.** The act of making tubs ; কাঠের গামলা প্রস্তুত করণ। **2.** The lining or casing of the shaft of a mine of an artesian well and the like, to prevent the falling in of the sides as well as infiltration ; খনির সুড়ঙ্গ প্রভৃতির পার্শ্ব কাষ্ঠভাণ্ডপংক্তি, লৌহনলশ্রেণী প্রভৃতি দ্বারা আচ্ছাদিত করণ। **3.** The act or practice of rowing in a tub ; মৃদুগামী নৌকায় দাঁড় চালনা অভ্যাস বা দাঁড়ের সাহায্যে চলন। **4.** Act of using a tub for bathing ; জলপূর্ণ ভাণ্ডে স্নান। **Tub'-ful,** *n.* **Tub-thumper** — কোলাহলকারী। **Tub-thumping**—গলাবাজি। **Tub-wheel**—জল প্রবাহচালিত কাষ্ঠভাণ্ডাকৃতি চক্রবিশেষ ; চর্ম্ম প্রভৃতি ধৌত করার জন্য একপ্রকার ঘূর্ণনশীল চোঙ্গাকৃতি পাত্র। **Tale of a tub**—আষাঢ়ে গল্প।

tü'-bă, *n.* **1.** A brass wind-instrument, the lowest as to pitch in orchestra; শানাইর মত একপ্রকার বাদ্য যন্ত্র। **2.** Same as REED-STOP.

tŭb'-by (-ĭ), *adj.* **1.** Tub-shaped ; round bellied ; গামলার আকার ; ঘটোদর। **2.** Having a sound like that of an empty tub when struck ; শূন্য গামলা আঘাত করিলে যেরূপ ধ্বনি উৎপন্ন হয়, তদ্রূপ।

tübe, *n.* & *v. t.* **1.** A pipe ; নল, চুঙ্গী। **2.** A cylindrical receptacle for holding semi-fluid substance, as paint ; রঙ্গ প্রভৃতি অর্দ্ধদ্রব পদার্থ রাখিবার জন্য একপ্রকার চোঙ্গাকার পাত্র। **3.** A telescope ; দূরদর্শন যন্ত্র। **4.** A tunnel for tube-railway ; a tube-railway ; চোঙ্গাকার লৌহবর্ত্মের জন্য সুড়ঙ্গ ; চোঙ্গাকৃতি লৌহবর্ত্ম। **5.** A vessel of animal bodies or plants which conveys a fluid or other substance ; as, the bronchial *tube* ; নালী। *Verb t.* To furnish with tubes ; to enclose in a tube or tubes ; চুঙ্গীবিশিষ্ট করা, চুঙ্গী বসান ; চুঙ্গী বা চুঙ্গীসমূহের মধ্যে রাখা। **Crookes's tube** — গ্যাসসংক্রান্ত কতিপয় ব্যাপার প্রদর্শনার্থ একপ্রকার চুঙ্গী। **Pneumatic tube** — বায়ুপ্রবাহের সাহায্যে পত্রাদি প্রেরণের জন্য চোঙ্গা। **Test-tube** — See under TEST. **Tube-node** — নলপাত্র (হিঃ কোঃ)। **Tube-flower**—রজনীগন্ধা প্রভৃতি পুষ্প। **Tube-shell**—একপ্রকার নলাকৃতি দ্বিপুট খোলকা প্রাণী। **Tube-well**—ভূনিম্ন হইতে জল উত্তোলনের জন্য নিম্নদেশে সূক্ষ্মাগ্র এবং সরন্ধ্র চুঙ্গী। **Tube of forces**—বলনলিকা (হিঃ কোঃ)।

tü'-bêr, *n.* **1.** An underground fleshy stem or modification of the roots of plants ; কোন কোন বৃক্ষের ভূগর্ভস্থ স্ফীতকন্দ, স্থূলকন্দ (সাঃ পঃ), আলু (ঐ), কন্দশাখ (ব্রজঃ বিঃ)। **2.** A swelling part ; স্ফীত অংশ। **–i-form,** *adj.*

tü'-bêr-cle (-kl), *n.* **1.** A small aggregation of an opaque gray matter accompanying scrofula etc. ; জীবনীশক্তির ক্ষীণতাবশতঃ গণ্ডমালাদি, কোন কোন ধাতুদোষ জন্য ফুসফুস প্রভৃতিতে উপদাহনিবন্ধন ধূসর বা পীতবর্ণ একপ্রকার অর্ব্বুদ, গুটিকা (হঃ চঃ)। **2.** A small knob on leaves ; a small tuber ; পত্রের উপর জাত ক্ষুদ্র গুটিকা ; ক্ষুদ্র স্ফীত কন্দ। **3.** A small round prominence of a bone ; অস্থির ক্ষুদ্র গোলাকার উদ্গত অংশ। **–ber'-cu-lar, –ber'-cled, –ber'-cu-lat-ed, –ber'-cu-loid, –ber'-cu-lose –ber'-cu-lous,** *adjs.* **–cu-la'-tion,** *n.*

tü-bêr'-cü-līze, –lar'-īze (-ler-), *v. t.* To infect with tuberculosis ; গুটিকারোগ দ্বারা সংক্রমিত করা। **–li-za'-tion,** *n.*

tü-bêr-cü-lō'-sis, *n.* A disease due to the formation of tubercles ; গুটিকারোগ। **–losed,** *adj.* **Pulmonary tuberculosis**—ক্ষয়রোগ।

tübe'-rōse, *adj.* & *n.* **1.** Covered with tubers ; গুটিল। **2.** Consisting of tubers; bearing tubers ; resembling tubers ; স্ফীতকন্দবিশিষ্ট ; স্ফীতকন্দপ্রসূ ; স্ফীতকন্দসদৃশ। *Noun.* A fragrant plant with a tuberous root and white flowers ; রজনীগন্ধা। **Tu-ber-os'-i-ty, Tu'-ber-ous-ness,** *ns.*

tü'-bĭ-cōrn, *adj.* & *n.* Hollow-horned ; শৃঙ্গগর্ভ শৃঙ্গবিশিষ্ট। *Noun.* A hollow-horned animal ; শৃঙ্গগর্ভ শৃঙ্গবিশিষ্ট জন্তু।

tü'-bĭ-fōrm, *adj.* Having the form of a tube ; নলাকৃতি, চোঙ্গাকৃতি।

tü-bĭ-lin'-guăl (-lĭng-), *adj.* With tubular tongue ; চোঙ্গাকার জিহ্বাবিশিষ্ট, নলজিহ্ব।

tü'-bü-lar (-lêr), *adj.* **1.** Tube-shaped ; চোঙ্গাকার। **2.** (*Bot.*) Approaching a cylindrical figure and hollow ; (উদ্ভিদ্‌বিদ্যা) নলাকার, নলাকৃতি। **3.** Consisting of, or contained in, tubes ; চোঙ্গবিশিষ্ট, চোঙ্গের অভ্যন্তরে স্থিত। **4.** (Of breathing) Like sound of air passing through a tube ; (শ্বাস প্রশ্বাস সম্পর্কে) চোঙ্গের ভিতর দিয়া প্রবাহিত বায়ুর ধ্বনিবৎ। **Tubular boiler**—যে বাষ্পজনকে উত্তাপ বা উত্তপ্ত করার জন্য জল বহু চোঙ্গের দ্বারা সঞ্চালিত করা হয়। **Tubular bridge** — যে আয়তাকার চোঙ্গার ভিতর দিয়া লৌহবর্ত্ম প্রভৃতি নেওয়া হয়। **Tubular surface**—নলিকাকার পৃষ্ঠ (হিঃ কোঃ)।

tü-bü-lā'-tiōn *n.* Act of shaping or making a tube ; নলিকাকরণ, নলীকরণ (হিঃ কোঃ)।

tü'-büle, *n.* A small tube ; ক্ষুদ্র চোঙ্গ, চুঙ্গী।

tü-bü-lĭf'-ēr-ă, *n.* (*Pl.*) A group of insects in which the last segment of the abdomen forms a little tube ; এক জাতীয় কীট—যাহাতে উদরের শেষ পর্ব্ব ক্ষুদ্র চোঙ্গের মত দেখায়।

tü'-bü-lĭ-fōrm, *adj.* Having the form of a small tube ; ক্ষুদ্র চোঙ্গাকৃতি।

tŭck, *v. t., i & n.* **1.** To thrust or press together ; to gather into narrow compass ; গুটান ; গুটাইয়া রাখা, তোলা (বিছানাসম্বন্ধে)। **2.** To inclose by pushing the clothes around ; as, to *tuck* up a child ; কাপড়চোপড় দ্বারা জড়াইয়া রাখা। **3.** To shove into a snug close place ; to cram ; গুঁজিয়া দেওয়া, ঢুকাইয়া দেওয়া ; ঠাসিয়া রাখা। **4.** To make a tuck or tucks in ; পোষাক প্রভৃতিতে ভাঁজ বা কোঁচ দেওয়া। **5.** To eat ; খাওয়া। ***Verb i.*** To draw together ; গুটাইয়া রাখা। ***Noun.*** **1.** A horizontal fold in a garment to shorten it ; পোষাকের ভাঁজ। **2.** A kind of net ; একপ্রকার জাল। **3.** The after part of a ship where the ends of the bottom planks meet ; (নৌবিদ্যা) জাহাজের পশ্চাদ্ভাগের যে স্থানে নীচের তক্তা সমূহ সম্মিলিত হয়। **4.** (*Slang*) Food esp. pastry and sweet ; (ইতরভাষায়) খাদ্য, বিশেষতঃ মিষ্টদ্রব্য, মাংসপুরিত পিষ্টক প্রভৃতি। **Tuck-net, Tuck-seine**—বৃহত্তর জাল হইতে মাছ ধরিবার জন্য একপ্রকার ক্ষুদ্রজাল। **A tuck-out, A tuck-in**—A banquet ; eating of delicacies ; ভোজ ; উৎকৃষ্ট দ্রব্য ভোজন। **To tuck in**—To eat heartily ; পেট ভরিয়া খাওয়া। **To tuck up** — (*Slang*) To hang ; (ইতরভাষায়) ফাঁসীকাঠে ঝুলান। To draw tight round one ; গুটাইয়া রাখা, গুটান, শক্তকরিয়া জড়ান।

tŭck, *n.* (*Obs.*) The beat of a drum ; flourish ; (অপ্রঃ) ঢক্কানিনাদ ; বাদ্যভাণ্ড।

tŭck, *n.* (*Obs.*) A rapier ; (অপ্রঃ) তলোয়ার।

tŭck'-ă-hoe (-hō), *n.* A species of fungus or root-stock originally used by the red Indians for food ; একজাতীয় কন্দ বা ভূগর্ভজ শিলীন্ধ্র—যাহা লাল ইণ্ডিয়ানগণ ভোজন করিত।

tŭck'-ĕr, *n.* **1.** One that, or that which, tucks ; যে ব্যক্তি গুটায় বা ভাঁজ করে, যে যন্ত্রদ্বারা প্লেট বা ভাঁজ করা হয়। **2.** A small, thin piece of dress for covering the breast of women or children ; স্ত্রী বা শিশুদিগের বক্ষ আচ্ছাদক সূক্ষ্ম বস্ত্রখণ্ড। **3.** A part of sewing-machine used in making tucks ; প্লেট, ভাঁজ, প্রভৃতি করার জন্য সেলাইএর কলের অংশবিশেষ। **4.** (*Slang* or *colloq.*) Daily food ; (ইতরভাষায়) দৈনিক খাদ্য।

tŭck'-ĕt, *n.* (*Archaic*) A trumpet flourish ; (অপ্রঃ) সানাইর জমকালো বাদ্য।

tu'-cŭm (tō-), *n.* A South-American palm, valuable for its fibre ; দক্ষিণ-আমেরিকার তালজাতীয় বৃক্ষবিশেষ।

Tū'-dŏr, *adj.* **1.** Pertaining to the English dynasty from Henry VII to Elizabeth ; ৭ম হেনরী হইতে এলিজেবেথ পর্য্যন্ত ইংরেজ রাজবংশ-সম্বন্ধীয়। **2.** Pertaining to a style of architecture prevailing from Henry VII's reign to Elizabeth's ; সপ্তম হেনরীর রাজ্যকাল হইতে এলিজেবেথের রাজ্যকাল পর্য্যন্ত প্রচলিত স্থাপত্যধারাবিশেষসম্বন্ধীয়। **Tudor flower**—Tudor স্থাপত্যশিল্পে ব্যবহৃত ত্রিপত্রভূষা। **Tudor rose**—খৃঃ ১৪৮৬ অব্দে Lancaster পরিবারের সপ্তম হেনরীর সহিত York পরিবারের Elizabethএর পরিণয়ের পর Lancashireএর চিহ্ন লোহিত গোলাপ এবং Yorkshireএর চিহ্ন শ্বেত গোলাপের সম্মিলনে রচিত ইংলণ্ডের রাজচিহ্ন। **Tudor-style**—টিউডর স্থাপত্যধারা।

Tues'-day (tūz-dā), *n.* The third day of the week ; মঙ্গলবার। [*Syn.* ভৌমবার, কুজবার]।

tū'-fă, *n.* **1.** A light, porous rock of volcanic ashes cemented together ; আগ্নেয়গিরির ভস্মদ্বারা রচিত লঘু এবং ছিদ্রবহুল প্রস্তরবিশেষ। **2.** A carbonate of lime deposited by springs etc. ; নির্ঝর প্রভৃতিদ্বারা সঞ্চিত একপ্রকার চূর্ণ প্রস্তর। **-fa'-ceous,** *adj.*

tŭff, *n.* Kinds of volcanic fragmentary rock ; আগ্নেয়প্রস্তরজাত বিভিন্ন প্রকার প্রস্তরের খণ্ড।

tŭft, *n., v. t.* & *i.* **1.** A collection of small things in a bunch ; as, a *tuft* of flowers ; গুচ্ছ, স্তবক, গোছা, থোবা, ঝুঁটি। **2.** A head of flowers ; বৃন্তাগ্রস্থিত সংহত পুষ্পগুচ্ছ। **3.** Cluster ; as, a *tuft* of trees ; clump ; গুচ্ছ ; ঝোঁপ, ঝাড়। **4.** (*Slang,* In English universities) Nobleman ; a young nobleman entered as a student at a university ; "Several young *tufts,* and others of the faster men" ; (ইংলণ্ডীয় বিশ্ব-বিদ্যালয়ে) সম্ভ্রান্ত পুরুষ ; সম্ভ্রান্তবংশীয় ছাত্র। [এই সকল ছাত্রের টুপিতে একটী গুচ্ছ বা স্বর্ণের থোপনা থাকিত।] **5.** (*Anat.*) A bunch of small blood-vessels ; (শারীর-সংস্থানবিদ্যা) ক্ষুদ্র ধমনীগুচ্ছ। **6.** (*Colloq.*) A goatee; ছাগলের মত দাড়ী। ***Verb t.*** **1.** To furnish with tufts or a tuft ; গুচ্ছ বিশিষ্ট করা, স্তবকশ্রেণী সমন্বিত করা, গুচ্ছিত করা। **2.** To separate into tufts ; গুচ্ছে গুচ্ছে বিভক্ত করা। **3.** To make depressions, at regular intervals, in upholstery, mattress, etc. and attach buttons or tufts ; গদি প্রভৃতির স্থানে স্থানে সূত্রের সাহায্যে গর্ত্ত করিয়া থোপনা বসান। ***Verb i.*** To grow in tufts ; গুচ্ছে গুচ্ছে বা থোপায় থোপায় জন্মা। **Tuft'-ed,** *p. p.* Having a tuft or tufts ; গুচ্ছিত, ঝুঁটিদার। **Tuft hunter**—মোসাহেব, চাটুকার। **Tuft-hunting**—মোসাহেবি।

tŭg, *v. t., i.* & *n.* **1.** To pull with great effort ; সবলে আকর্ষণ করা, সবলে টানা, জোরে টানা। **2.** To draw by means of a steam-tug ; to tow ; ক্ষুদ্র বাষ্পীয়পোতের সাহায্যে টানিয়া নেওয়া ; টানিয়া নেওয়া। ***Verb i.*** To pull with great effort ; "We have been *tugging* a great while against the stream" ; সবলে টানা, প্রাণপণে টানা। ***Noun.*** **1.** A pull with utmost effort ; "At the *tug* he falls—Vast ruins come along" ; সবলে আকর্ষণ।

2. A steam-boat of considerable power used for towing ; কোন পোত বা পোতশ্রেণী টানার জন্য শক্তিশালী বাষ্পীয়পোত, জাহাজ-টানা জাহাজ। 3. A trace or leather-strap of harness ; any rope, chain, etc. used in pulling something along ; জিনের চর্ম্মরজ্জু; কোনকিছু টানিয়া নেওয়ার জন্য দড়ী, শিকল, প্রভৃতি। **Tugboat**—Same as TUG *n.* 2. **Tug of war**—(দুই দলের মধ্যে) দড়ী টানাটানি, রজ্জু আকর্ষণ; মহোদ্যম; কোন কার্য্যের সর্ব্বাপেক্ষা কঠিন অংশ।

Tuileries*, *n. A Royal palace in Paris, begun under Catherine de Medici in 1564 ; প্যারী নগরীস্থ রাজপ্রাসাদ বিশেষ। ১৫৬৪ খৃঃ অব্দে Catherine de Medici কর্ত্তৃক এই সৌধের নির্ম্মাণকার্য্য আরব্ধ হয়। [ফরাসীবিপ্লব কালে এই প্রাসাদে বহু ইতিহাসপ্রসিদ্ধ ঘটনা সংঘটিত হয়।]

tü'-ism, *n.* The doctrine that all thought is addressed to a second person, or to one's future self as a second person ; প্রত্যেক চিন্তাতেই কোন দ্বিতীয় ব্যক্তিকে অথবা কোন ব্যক্তির ভাবী অহংরূপ দ্বিতীয় ব্যক্তিকে সম্বোধন করা হয়, ত্বত্ত্ব।

tü-i'-tion, *n.* 1. The business of teaching ; শিক্ষা, অধ্যাপন। 2. Fee for teaching ; ছাত্রবেতন। **-al, -a-ry,** *adjs.*

tu'-lă—work (-wêrk), *n.* Same as NIELLO.

tŭl'-chăn, —chin, *ns.* A calf's skin stuffed and put beside a cow to induce the cow to give milk ; দোহনকালে মৃতবৎসাগাভীর পার্শ্বে যে বৎসচর্ম্মাচ্ছাদিত শুষ্কতৃণনির্ম্মিত বৎস রক্ষিত হইয়া থাকে। **Tulchan-bishops**—ধর্ম্মসংস্কারের (Reformation) পর যে সম্ভ্রান্ত উপাধিধারী বিশপদিগের নামে স্কটলণ্ডের বেরণগণ উক্ত বিশপগণের অধিকৃত স্থান হইতে কর আদায় করিতেন।

tü'-lip, *n.* 1. A bulbous plant producing flowers of great beauty and of a variety of colours ; নানাবর্ণের সমুজ্জ্বল ঘণ্টাকৃতি পুষ্পপ্রসূ কন্দজ গুল্মের সাধারণ নাম। 2. (*Rare*) The swell of the metal at the muzzle of an old fashioned gun ; (কচিদ্ব্যবহৃত) সাবেকধরণের কামানের

Flower of the tulip tree.

মুখের ঘণ্টাকৃতি স্ফীতি। **Tulip-tree**—উত্তর আমেরিকার বৃক্ষবিশেষ। [ইহার পুষ্পের বর্ণ হরিদাভপীত এবং মধ্যদেশ কমলারঙ্গের দাগবিশিষ্ট।] **Tulip-root**—যইগাছের একপ্রকার রোগ—যাহাতে উহার কাণ্ডের নিম্নভাগ স্ফীত হইয়া থাকে।

tü-lip-ō-mā'-ni-ă, *n.* A violent craze for the cultivation or acquisition of tulips ; টিউলিপপুষ্প উৎপাদন ও সংগ্রহের জন্য উন্মত্ততা। [হলণ্ড দেশের লোকদিগের মধ্যে ১৬৩৪ খৃঃ অব্দে এইরূপ উন্মত্ততা পরিলক্ষিত হইয়াছিল।]

tulle (tûl), *n.* A fine silk net used for veils and dresses ; অবগুণ্ঠন ও পোষাক প্রস্তুতে ব্যবহৃত একপ্রকার ফিনফিনে রেশমী কাপড়।

tŭl-wâr', *n.* A sword ; তলোয়ার, তরবারি।

Tŭm, *n.* A sun god regarded as the closer of the day ; সান্ধ্য-সূর্য্যদেবতা, সন্ধ্যাংশুমালী।

tŭm, *n.* The sound made by plucking the strings, as banjo ; টুন্ শব্দ।

tum'-ble (-bl), *v. i., t.* & *n.* 1. To roll over, or to and fro ; গড়াগড়ি যাওয়া, আছাড়ি পিছাড়ি খাওয়া, লুটোপুটি খাওয়া। 2. To fall suddenly and violently ; as to *tumble* from a height ; হুমড়ি খাইয়া পড়া, সহসা প্রবল বেগে পতিত হওয়া। 3. To move, pass or go roughly ; as, the dogs came *tumbling* at his call ; অসুষ্ঠভাবে চলা। 4. To play mountebank's or acrobat's tricks ; ডিগবাজি খাওয়া, দড়াবাজী প্রভৃতি করা। 5. (*Slang*) To comprehend ; (ইতরভাষায়) বুঝা। ***Verb t.*** 1. To turn or throw about, as for examination or search ; উল্টান পাল্টান, উল্টাইয়া পাল্টাইয়া দেখা, উলটপালট করা। 2. To disorder ; to rumple ; as, to *tumble* a bed ; এলেমেলো করা; কুঞ্চিত করা। 3. To overthrow ; to cast down ; উল্টাইয়া ফেলান; উল্টাইয়া ফেলা। ***Noun.*** 1. A fall ; পতন। 2. Performances of a tumbler ; দড়াবাজীকরদিগের উল্লম্ফন প্রভৃতি ক্রীড়া। **Tamble-down**—পতনোন্মুখ, ধ্বংসপ্রাপ্ত। Untidy or confused state ; বিশৃঙ্খল অবস্থা, এলেমেলোভাব। **To tumble home**—Said of a ship's sides when they incline inwards above the extreme breadth ; জাহাজের পার্শ্ব ভিতরের দিকে আনত হওয়া। **To tumble in**—(*Slang*) To go to bed ; (ইতরভাষায়) শুইতে যাওয়া। To fit, as a piece of timber, into other work ; কোন কিছুতে কাঠ প্রভৃতির টুকরা লাগান। Same as TO TUMBLE HOME. **To tumble to** — (*Slang*) To understand ; (ইতরভাষায়) বুঝা। **To tumble up**—To get out of bed ; to rise ; বিছানা হইতে উঠা; উঠা।

tŭm-blêr, *n.* 1. One who performs the tricks of a mountebank, such as turning somersaults, walking on the hands and the like ; যে ব্যক্তি দড়াবাজী প্রভৃতি করে, প্লবক। 2. A large drinking glass ; বৃহৎ পানপাত্র, একপ্রকার বড় গ্লাস। 3. A variety of pigeon that turns over in flight ; একজাতীয় কপোত যাহারা

উড়িবার সময় উলটপালট খাইয়া থাকে, লোটন পায়রা, লট্‌কা পায়রা। 4. A sort of dog; একজাতীয় কুকুর। 5. A sort of spring latch in a lock which detains the bolt so as to prevent its motion, until a key lifts it and sets the bolt at liberty; তালার ভিতরের ব্যবস্থাবিশেষ। 6. A piece attached to a hammer in gunlock, etc. released by trigger; বন্দুকের ঘোড়ায় সংলগ্ন অংশবিশেষ।

tŭm'-bling, *n* & *adj*. 1. The act of falling down or rolling about; উলটপালট, লুটোপুটি। 2. The performance of an acrobat etc.; দড়াবাজী প্রভৃতি। ***Adj.*** Falling; পতনশীল। **Tumbling-barrel, –box, –wheel**—একপ্রকার ঘূর্ণনশীল যন্ত্র—যাহাতে শিরীষ কাগজের সাহায্যে পিত্তলাদি পরিমার্জ্জিত করা হয়।

tŭm'-bly, *adj*. Uneven or lumpy; অসম, ডেলা-বাঁধা।

tŭm'-brĕl, –bril, *ns*. 1. A ducking stool for the punishment of scolds; দুর্ম্মুখা স্ত্রীলোকগণকে যে আসনে বসাইয়া জলে চুবুনি দেওয়া হইত। 2. A dung-cart; গোময় বহনের জন্য শকট। 3. A cart with two wheels for conveying tools, ammunition, etc.; গুলি গোলা, কার্ত্তুজ প্রভৃতি বহনের জন্য একপ্রকার শকট। 4. A vehicle for conveying condemned persons to the guillotine in the French Revolution; ফরাসীবিপ্লবকালে প্রাণদণ্ডে দণ্ডিত ব্যক্তিগণকে যে শকটে শিরশ্ছেদের জন্য গিলটিন যন্ত্রের নিকট বহন করা হইত।

tū-mē-făc'-tion, *n*. Same as TUMESCENCE. **–fa'-ci-ent,** *adj*. Same as TUMESCENT.

tū-mĕs'-cence (-ĕns), *n*. The state of being slightly tumid or swollen; ঈষৎস্ফীতি। **–scent,** *adj*. Slightly swollen; ঈষৎস্ফীত।

tū'-mid, *adj*. 1. Swollen, enlarged or distended; স্ফীত, স্ফীয়মান, বর্দ্ধিত। 2. Bombastic; "Shall gentle Coleridge pass unnoticed here, To turgid ode and *tumid* stanza dear"; শব্দাড়ম্বরপূর্ণ, বাগাড়ম্বর পূর্ণ। **–ly,** *adv*. **–mid'-i-ty, –ness,** *ns*.

tū'-mi-fȳ, *v. t.* & *i*. To cause to swell; স্ফীত করা, ফুলান। ***Verb i.*** To be swollen; ফুলা, স্ফীত হওয়া।

tŭm'-mȳ, *n*. (*Nursery*) Stomach; (ছেলেদের ছড়ায়) পেট।

tū'-mour (-mŏr), *n*. A swelling in some part of the body; অর্ব্বুদ, আঁব, রক্তার্ব্বুদ (মুশ্রুঃ কুঞ্জঃ)। **Malignant tumour**—যে অর্ব্বুদ পুনঃ পুনঃ অপসারণের পর পুনরায় জাত হয় এবং পরিণামে মৃত্যু ঘটায় (ইহার বিপরীত *benign tumour*).

tŭm'–tŭm, *n*. 1. A West-Indian dish prepared by beating the boiled plantain soft in a wooden mortar; পশ্চিম-ভারতীয় দ্বীপপুঞ্জের অধিবাসিগণকর্ত্তৃক কাঠের খলে সিদ্ধ কদলী পেষণ করিয়া প্রস্তুত খাদ্যবিশেষ। 2. (*Anglo-Indian*) A dog-cart; (ভারতবর্ষের ইংরাজদিগের মধ্যে) টম্‌টম্। 3. Same as TOM-TOM. *n*. I.

tū'-mū-lous (-lŭs), **–lōse,** *adjs*. Full of mounds or hills; গণ্ডশৈল বহুল।

tū'-mŭlt, *n*. 1. A commotion, disturbance or agitation arising from a number of persons; uproar; a great disturbance; কোলাহল; সোরগোল; হুলস্থুল ব্যাপার। 2. Agitation; high excitement; "The *tumult* of their minds having subsided, they sighed often and aloud"; বিক্ষোভ; মানসিক বিক্ষোভ। **–mul'-tu-a-ry,** *adj*. **–mul'-tu-ous,** *adj*. 1. Full of tumult; তুমুল কোলাহলপূর্ণ। 2. Conducted with, or characterised by, uproar, noise, confusion, or the like; তুমুল আরাবপূর্ণ, হুলস্থুলপূর্ণ। 3. Violent; as, a *tumultuous* battle; প্রবল, প্রচণ্ড।

tū'-mū-lŭs, *n*. A mound of earth raised as a tomb or monument সমাধি বা স্মৃতিস্তম্ভস্বরূপ মৃত্তিকা-স্তূপ **–lar, –la-ry,** *adjs*.

tŭn, *n*. & *v. t.* 1. Any large cask for liquids; মদ্যাদি রাখার জন্য বড় পিপা। 2. A measure of quantity containing 252 gallons; ২৫২ গ্যালনের পরিমাপবিশেষ। 3. A fermenting vat; মদ্য চোলাইকারিগণের অন্তরুৎসেচনপাত্র। ***Verb t.*** To put in a tun; বৃহৎ পিপায় মদ্যাদি রাখা। **Tun-bellied**—পিপার মত উদরবিশিষ্ট।

tundra, *n*. A vast swampy expanse of land with reindeer-moss, lichens, etc., in the arctic regions of Russia and Siberia, and only traversable in winter, when it is all frozen over; রুশিয়ার উত্তরাঞ্চলস্থ শৈবালপূর্ণ অনূপদেশ।

tūne, *n*., *v. t.* & *i*. 1. A sound; a tone; ধ্বনি; স্বর, তান। 2. Correct intonation in singing or playing; তাল। 3. Order; harmony; concord; "A continental parliament would but keep the common weal in *tune*, by preserving laws in their due execution and vigour"; শৃঙ্খলা; সঙ্গতি; মিল। 4. Frame of mind; mood; temper; as, to be in *tune*; মনের গতি; ভাব; প্রকৃতি, মেজাজ। 5. (*Phren.*) One of the perceptive faculties; (মস্তিষ্ক-সামুদ্রিক) বিষয়গ্রাহিণী বৃত্তি সমূহের অন্যতম। [মস্তিষ্ক সামুদ্রিকগণ ললাটের মধ্যস্থলে এই বৃত্তির স্থান নির্দ্দেশ করিয়া থাকেন।] 6. (*Phys.*) Harmony as regards vibrations other than sound; (পদার্থবিজ্ঞান) শব্দ ভিন্ন অন্য কিছুর স্পন্দন সম্পর্কে সঙ্গতি। ***Verb t.*** 1. To cause to be in tune; সুর সংযোগ করা, সুর বাঁধা। 2. To sing, play with melody or harmony; সুস্বরে গান করা, তানলয়বিশুদ্ধভাবে সঙ্গীত বা বাদ্য করা। 3. To give a special tone or character to attune; বিশিষ্ট ভাব বা প্রকৃতি প্রদান করা, সঙ্গতিবিশিষ্ট করা, ঐক্য করা। 4. To adjust or adapt something to a standard or purpose, circumstances, etc. ; কোন বিষয় কোন আদর্শ, উদ্দেশ্য বা অবস্থার অনুযায়ী বা উপযোগী করা। *Verb i.* 1. To be in tone ; তানলয়বিশুদ্ধ হওয়া। 2. To hum a tune ; অস্পষ্ট স্বরে গান করা, গুণ গুণ করিয়া গাহিয়া যাওয়া, সুর ভাঁজা। 3. To adjust instruments for playing together ; বাদ্যযন্ত্র সমূহ সঙ্গত করা। **Tun′-a-ble,** *adj.* **Tun′-a-ble-ness,** *n.* **Tun′-a-bly,** *adv.* **Tun′-er,** *n.* **Tune′-ful,** *adj.* Melodious ; musical ; তানলয় বিশিষ্ট ; সুস্বর, শ্রুতিসুখকর, সুকণ্ঠ। **Tune′-ful-ly,** *adv.* **Tune′-ful-ness,** *n.* **Tune′-less,** *adj.* Without tune ; inharmonious ; unmusical ; বিস্বর ; বেসুর ; স্বরমাধুর্য্য-বিহীন। **To change one's tune, To sing another tune**—To change from insolent to respectful tone ; সুর বদলান, উল্টা সুরে গান করা। **To the tune of**—(*Colloq.*) To the sum or amount of ; মোটে, সাকল্যে, একুনে। **To tune up**—To adjust instruments for playing together ; একত্র বাজাইবার যন্ত্র ঠিক করা, সঙ্গত করা। (In a machine) To regulate the various parts so that they work together harmoniously ; যন্ত্রের বিভিন্ন অংশ ঠিক করা—যাহাতে উহারা পরস্পরের সহিত সমঞ্জসভাবে কার্য্য করিতে পারে। To begin to sing or play ; গান বা বাদ্য আরম্ভ করা। (Of a child) to cry ; (শিশু-সম্পর্কে) কান্না জুড়া।

tŭng′-stĕn, *n.* A rare heavy metallic element of a greyish colour, nearly as hard as steel ; একপ্রকার গুরুভার ধাতব মূলপদার্থ, তুঙ্গষ্টক (সাঃ পঃ), তুঙ্গস্ত (হিঃ কোঃ)। **–state,** *n.* **–stic, –stous,** *adjs.*

tū′-nic, *n.* 1. A garment worn by the Romans of both sexes under the toga ; প্রাচীন রোমানদিগের আজানুবিলম্বিত প্রাবরণবিশেষ। 2. Any of various loose-fitting garments ; ঢিলা পোষাক। 3. A short uniform coat worn by soldiers, police constables, postal messengers ; বিলাতের সৈনিক, পুলিশ-কনেষ্টবল এবং ডাকঘরের পেয়াদাদিগের একপ্রকার খাটো কোর্ত্তা। 4. A long coat used by some clergymen in religious services ; কোন কোন যাজক উপাসনাদির কালে যে দীর্ঘ কোর্ত্তা পরিধান করিয়া থাকে। 5. A woman's loose blouse or coat gathered or belted at the waist ; স্ত্রীলোকদিগের একপ্রকার ঢিলা ব্লাউস বা কোর্ত্তা যাহা কটিদেশে পেটি দ্বারা আঁটা হয়। 6. (*Anat.*) A membrane that covers or composes some part or organ ; as, *tunics* of the eye ; (শারীরসংস্থানবিদ্যা) যে ঝিল্লী দ্বারা দেহের বা কোন দৈহিকযন্ত্রের কোন অংশ আচ্ছাদিত বা গঠিত হয়। 7. (*Bot.*) A natural covering ; (উদ্ভিদ্‌বিদ্যা) নৈসর্গিক আবরণত্বক্। **–ni-cate,** *adj.*

tū′-ni-cle (-kl), *n.* 1. A kind of robe worn by priests ; যাজকদিগের পরিধেয় আবরণবিশেষ। 2. An integument ; আবেষ্টনত্বক্।

tūn′-ing, *n.* The act of one who tunes ; সুরসংযোগ ; **Tuning-crook**—করণেটযন্ত্রের সুরবৈচিত্র সাধনের জন্য একপ্রকার বক্রাগ্র দণ্ড ; **Tuning fork**—স্বরোৎপাদনের জন্য ইস্পাতনির্ম্মিত একপ্রকার দ্বিশাখ কাঁটা। **Tuning-hammer**—কাঁটা ঘুরাইয়া পিয়ানো প্রভৃতি বাদ্যযন্ত্রের তারের টান পরিবর্ত্তনের জন্য একপ্রকার হাতুড়ীর আকার পাক-সাঁড়াশী। **Tuning-pegs, Tuning-pins**—পিয়ানো প্রভৃতি বাদ্যযন্ত্রের যে কাঁটাতে তার বাঁধা হয়।

tŭn′-nel (-ĕl), *n.*, *v. t.* & *i.* 1. A flue ; a funnel ; ধূমনির্গম নল ; ফুঁদেল। 2. A subterranean passage cut through a hill, rock, etc. (esp. in railways) ; পর্ব্বত, পাষাণস্তূপ প্রভৃতির ভিতর দিয়া কাটা রাস্তা, সুড়ঙ্গ, কুল্যা (আঃ বঃ), তলবর্ত্ম। 3. A subterranean passage cut by a burrowing animal ; খননকারী জন্তুগণকর্ত্তৃক কর্ত্তিত সুড়ঙ্গ। 4. (*Mining*)

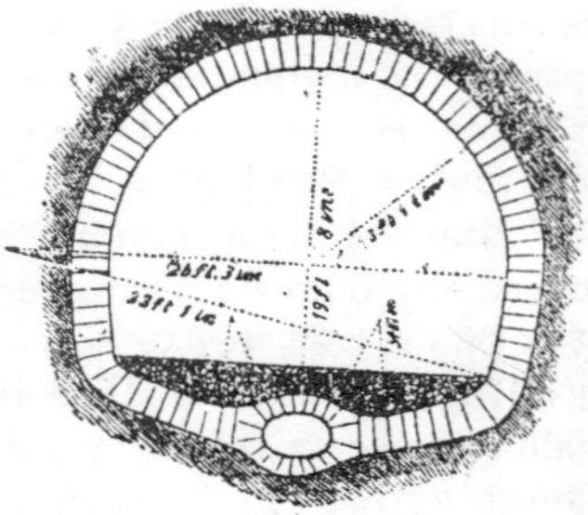

Section of a Tunnel.

A level or nearly level subterranean passage ; সমতল বা প্রায় সমতল অন্তর্ভৌমবর্ত্ম। *Verb t.* To form a tunnel through or under ; সুড়ঙ্গ খনন করা। *Verb i.* To make a tunnel ; সুড়ঙ্গ প্রস্তুত করা। **Tunnel-borer**—সুড়ঙ্গ প্রস্তুতের জন্য বিভিন্ন-প্রকার যন্ত্র। **Tunnel-net**—একপ্রকার জাল—উহার মুখ চওড়া ও অপর প্রান্ত অপ্রশস্ত থাকে, সুড়ঙ্গ জাল।

tŭn′-ny (-ĭ), *n.* A large marine fish used as food ; একপ্রকার বৃহৎ সামুদ্রিক মৎস্য।

tŭp *n.* 1. Ram ; মেষ, ভেড়া। 2. The heavy head of a steam-hammer ; বাষ্পীয় হাতুড়ীর গুরুভার অগ্রভাগ।

tuque (tük), *n.* A kind of Canadian cap ; ক্যানাডাদেশে ব্যবহৃত একপ্রকার টুপি।

tū-quō′-quē, *n.* A retort charging an adversary with being or doing the same as one's self ; তুমিও এরূপ করিয়াছ, তুমিও তাই।

Tū-rā′-nĭ-ăn, *n.* & *adj.* A term applied to Finnish, Turkish, Mongolian and certain other tongues that are neither Aryan nor Semitic ; তুরাণী ভাষা। *Adj.* Of the Turanian group of languages ; তুরাণী ভাষাপুঞ্জসম্বন্ধীয়।

tur′-băn (tėr-), *n.* 1. A head-dress worn by the orientals ; পাগড়ী,

উষ্ণীষ। 2. A head-dress worn by ladies; ইয়ুরোপীয় স্ত্রীলোকদিগের একপ্রকার উষ্ণীষ। 3. A kind of woman's or child's hat with narrow or no brim; শিশু বা স্ত্রীগণের কিনারা বা অল্প কিনারা-বিশিষ্ট টুপি। 4. The whole set of whorls in a shell; শঙ্খের আবর্ত্তপংক্তি। **–baned,** *adj.* **Turban-shell**—একপ্রকার উদরপদী শঙ্খ। **Turban-stone** — মুসলমানদিগের উষ্ণীষাকৃতি অগ্রভাগবিশিষ্ট সমাধিস্তম্ভ। **Turban-top**—একপ্রকার শিলীন্ধ্র।

tur'-bă-rў (têr-), *n.* 1. The right of digging turf on another man's land; অন্য ব্যক্তির ভূমিতে ঘাসের চাপড়া খুদিয়া তুলিবার জন্য অধিকার। 2. A place where the turf or peat is dug; যে স্থানে ঘাসের চাপড়া অথবা বোদ মাটী খুদিয়া তোলা হয়।

tur-bĕl-lā-ri-ă (-têr), *n.* The class of flat worms; চাপটাকীট (সাঃ পঃ), চাপাকীট (ঐ)।

tur'-bid (têr-), *adj.* 1. Soiled; muddy; as, *turbid* water; মলিন; পঙ্কিল, ঘোলা, আবিল। 2. (*Fig.*) Disquieted; disturbed; '*Turbid* intervals that use to attend close prisoners"; (লক্ষণায়) অশান্ত; বিক্ষুব্ধ, ক্ষুব্ধ। **–bid'-i-ty,** *n.* **–ly,** *adv.* **–ness,** *n.*

tur'-bi-nāte (têr-), *adj.* 1. Shaped like a top or inverted cone; লাটিমের আকৃতি, লাটিমাকৃতি। 2. Whirling in the manner of a top; লাটিমের মত ঘূর্ণনশীল। 3. Spiral; আবর্ত্তী। **–bin'-i-form, –noid, –nal,** *adjs.* **–na'-tion,** *n.* **Turbinal erection**—নাসাশোথ (সাঃ পঃ)।

tur-bi-nĕl'-lă (têr-), *n.* A genus of large marine rachiglossate gastropods with a pear-shaped shell; শঙ্খ, কম্বু। [*Syn.* কম্বোজ, অব্জ, জলজ, অর্ণোভব, পাবনধ্বনি, মহানাদ, অন্তঃকুটিল, শ্বেত, পূত, মুখর, বহুনাদ, দীর্ঘনাদ, হরিপ্রিয়।]

tur'-bine (têr-), *n.* A horizontal water-wheel revolved by water under the influence of pressure derived from a fall; নদী প্রবাহের জলের পতনজনিত চাপদ্বারা চালিত জলচক্র, শয়ানচক্র। **Air turbine**—চোঙ্গ হইতে নিঃসৃত বায়ুদ্বারা চালিত উক্তপ্রকার চক্র। **Steam turbine**—বাষ্পপ্রবাহ চালিত শয়ানচক্র। **Turbine boat**—শয়ানচক্রদ্বারা চালিত নৌকা।

tur'-bit (têr-), *n.* A variety of the domestic pigeon, remarkable for its short beak; একজাতীয় খর্ব্বচঞ্চু কপোত।

tur'-bŏt (têr-), *n.* A native flat-fish next in size to the halibut, but smaller, and much more circular in form; একপ্রকার বৃহৎ পায়রাচাঁদা মাছ।

tur'-bū-lĕnt (têr-), *adj.* 1. Disturbed; "'T has been a *turbulent* and stormy night"; বিক্ষুব্ধ, সংক্ষুব্ধ, উত্তেজিত, উদ্বেজিত। 2. Riotous; insubordinate; as, a *turbulent* people; হাঙ্গামাকারী, উৎপাতজনক; দুর্দ্দান্ত, বিদ্রোহী, অবাধ্য। **–lence,** *n.* The state of being turbulent; tumult; disorder; দুর্দ্দমনীয়তা, সংক্ষোভ, বিক্ষোভ; কোলাহল; বিশৃঙ্খলা। **–ly,** *adv.*

Tur'-cism (têr-), *n.* The religion, manners, character or custom of the Turks; তুরস্কবাসীদিগের ধর্ম্ম, রীতিনীতি, প্রভৃতি।

Turco, *n.* The name given by the French to the force of French Algerian infantry (techincally called *Algerian tirailleurs*); ফরাসী অধিকৃত আলজিরিয়ার পদাতিক সৈন্যদল।

Tur'-cō-phil (têr-), *n.* One that favours the Turks, or their principles or policy; তুরস্ক জাতির প্রতি পক্ষপাতিতা, তুরস্কানুরাগ, তুর্কি-প্রীতি। **–ism,** *n.*

turd (têrd), *n.* (*Vulg.*) Excrement; dung; পুরীষ; গোময়।

tur'-dine (têr-), *adj.* Thrush-like; দামা পক্ষীর মত। **–doid,** *adj.*

tū-reen' (-rēn), *n.* A large and deep dish for holding soup at table; একপ্রকার বড় বাটী, সুপপাত্র।

turf (têrf), *n.* & *v. t.* 1. The grassy layer on the surface of the ground; a piece of this layer; তৃণস্তর; ঘাসের চাপড়া। 2. (In Ireland) A peat; বোদমাটী। ***Verb t.*** To cover with turf or sod; চাপড়া-দ্বারা আচ্ছাদিত করা, চাপড়া বসান। **Turf'-i-ness,** *n.* **Turf'-ite,** *n.* **Turf'-y,** *adj.* **Turf-bound**—তৃণবদ্ধ। **Turf-drain**—ঘাসের চাপড়া-দ্বারা আচ্ছাদিত নর্দ্দমা। **Turfman**—ঘোড়দৌড়ে অনুরাগী ব্যক্তি। **On the turf**—Occupied in horse-racing; ঘোড়দৌড়ের ব্যবসায়ে নিযুক্ত। **The turf** — ঘোড়দৌড়ের মাঠ; ঘোড়-দৌড়ের ব্যবসায়।

tur'-gid (têr-), *adj.* 1. Distended beyond the natural state by some internal agent or expansive force; স্ফীত, ফুলা। 2. Bombastic; pompous; as, a *turgid* style; বাগাড়ম্বরপূর্ণ, শব্দাড়ম্বর পূর্ণ; জাঁকালো, জমকালো। **–ges'-ci-ble,** *adj.* **–ges'-cence,** *n.* **–ges'-cent,** *adj.* **–gid'-i-ty,** *n.* 1. The state of being turgid; রসস্ফীতি, স্ফীতি। 2. Pompousness; বাগাড়ম্বর, শব্দাড়ম্বর, পদাড়ম্বর। **–ly,** *adv.*

tū'-ri-ō, tū'-ri-ŏn, *ns.* (*Bot.*) A scaly shoot developed from a bud on a subterranean rootstock; (উদ্ভিদ্‌বিদ্যা) ভূগর্ভস্থ মূল হইতে জাত শল্কযুক্ত অঙ্কুর, শল্কাঙ্কুর। **–on-if'-er-ous,** *adj.*

Turk (têrk), *n.* 1. A native of Turkey; তুরস্কদেশের অধিবাসী, তুর্কি। 2. A savage fellow; বর্ব্বর, চোয়াড়। 3. Mohammedan; মুসলমান। 4. A Turkish horse; তুরস্কদেশীয় অশ্ব। **Turk's-cap** — নানাজাতীয় স্থলকুমুদ প্রভৃতির নাম। **Turk's-head**—একপ্রকার গ্রন্থি; একপ্রকার লম্বা ডাণ্ডাওয়ালা ঝাঁটা; রুটি সেঁকিবার চাটু। **To turn Turk**—To become a Mohammedan; to change for the worse; to be a renegade ; মুসলমান ধর্ম্ম অবলম্বন করা ; অবনতি হওয়া ; স্বধর্ম্মভ্রষ্ট হওয়া।

tur'-key (têr-kē), *n.* **1.** A large gallinaceous fowl, a native of North America, domesticated in Europe, so called from the erroneous notion that it was a native of Turkey ; পেরুপাখী। **2.** (*Cap.*) The country inhabited by Turks ; তুরস্ক দেশ। **Turkey-buzzard, Turkey-vulture**—আমেরিকা দেশীয় গৃধ্রবিশেষ। **Turkey carpet**—তুরস্কদেশীয় গালিচা। **Turkey-cock**—পুংপেরু পক্ষী; হাম্‌বড়া লোক। **Turkey corn**—ভুট্টা, জোয়ার। **Turkey leather**—একপ্রকার চামড়া—যাহা হইতে লোম তোলার পূর্ব্বে তৈল মাখা হয়। **Turkey-poult**—পেরু পক্ষীর ছানা। **Turkey red**—মঞ্জিষ্ঠা হইতে প্রস্তুত একপ্রকার গাঢ় লাল রং; ঐ রঙ্গে রঞ্জিত কার্পাস-বস্ত্র। **Turkey-red oil**—তুর্কি লালরঙ্গ উৎপাদনের জন্য ব্যবহৃত একপ্রকার নিকৃষ্ট জলপাইয়ের তৈল। **Turkey sponge**—ভূমধ্য এবং এড্রিয়্যাটিক সাগরে প্রাপ্ত একপ্রকার স্পঞ্জ। **Turkey-stone**—একপ্রকার শাণপাথর।

Turk'-ish (têrk-), *adj.* & *n.* Pertaining to Turkey or the Turks ; তুরস্কদেশীয়, তুরস্কজাতীয়, তুর্কি। ***Noun.*** The language of the Turks ; তুরস্কদেশীয় ভাষা, তুর্কি ভাষা। **Turkish bath**—তুরস্কদেশীয় রীতির স্নান—যাহাতে সাবান লাগান ও শরীর ডলিয়া দেওয়া হয় ; উক্ত প্রণালীর স্নানাগার, তুর্কি স্নানাগার। **Turkish music**—ঢোল, ঢাক প্রভৃতি বাদ্যযন্ত্র—যাহা অঙ্গুলীতাড়ন দ্বারা বাদন করিতে হয়। **Turkish pound**—(usu. written £ T) ১৮ পাঃ ২ শিঃ মূল্যের স্বর্ণ মুদ্রাবিশেষ। **Turkish towel**—তুর্কি তোয়ালে।

Tur'-kō-măn (têr-), *n.* One of a branch of Turkish race living mostly in Central Asia ; পারস্য, তুর্কিস্থান, আফগানিস্থান এবং রুশিয়াবাসী তুর্কি জাতীয় লোক। **Turkoman carpet**—এক প্রকার সুকোমল গালিচা।

tûr'-mă-lin, —line (-lĭn), *ns.* Same as TOURMALINE.

tur'-mĕr-ic (têr-), *n.* An East-Indian plant of the ginger family, whose rhizomes yield a condiment, a yellow die and a chemical test for alkalies ; হলুদ, হরিদ্রা। [Syn. হরিতা, হেমী, সুবর্ণবর্ণা, পীতচন্দন, ত্রিযামা, বিভাবরী, দীর্ঘরাগা, মেহঘ্নী, পীতা, বরবর্ণিনী, কাঞ্চনী, ক্রিমিঘ্নী, পীতবালুকা, যোষিৎপ্রিয়া, বর্ণবিধায়িনী, বরাঙ্গী, হেমরাগিণী, লসা, নিশা, রাত্রি, জনেষ্টা, ভদ্রা, ভঙ্গবাসা, সুন্দরী, মঙ্গলা, বর্ণবতী, বর্ণিনী, বর্ণবিলাসিনী, রঞ্জনী, যুবতী, বসা, শিফা, তমস্বিনী, গন্ধফলা, শিবা, কদম্ব, তুঙ্গী, তুঙ্গা, পীতিকা, কচ্ছুরা, শোভনা, বালা, শর্ব্বরী, কর্চ্চূর, কটংকটেরি, (সুশ্রুঃ), কুসুম্ভলা (A kind of), ক্ষণদা, হরিৎ তুঙ্গ, ক্ষপা, ধমনী, পীত (গোপালঃ), স্বর্ণবর্ণা, বর্ণদাত্রী, শ্যামা, জয়ন্তিকা, মঙ্গল্যা, মঙ্গলপ্রদা, লক্ষ্মী, কাঞ্চ (plant), স্থিররাগা, হের, মাঙ্গল্য, শোভা, দীর্ঘরঙ্গা, সুবর্ণা, কটূর, ঘর্ষণী, নিশাহ্বা, কাবেরী, উমা, গৌরী, পিঙ্গা, পিঞ্জা, হেমনাশা, ঘর্ষিণী, রজনী, বহুলা, রাত্রিনামিকা, হলদ্দী, বরা, পবিত্রা, বিষঘ্নী, সুভগাহ্বয়া, ধারা।] [Arab. *zar-sud, tumr* ; Pers. *zard-chobeh, karknm* ; Tam. *munjal* ; Teleg. *pampi, passapu* ; Chin. *keang-whang* ; Gk. *kupeiros Indicos* ; It. *turtamaglio*]. **Turmeric-paper** — কোন কিছুতে ক্ষারীয় পদার্থ আছে কিনা তাহা পরীক্ষার জন্য ব্যবহৃত হরিদ্রারঞ্জিত কাগজ।

tur'-moil (têr-moyl), *n.* & *v. t.* Disturbance ; trouble ; tumult ; গোলমাল, গণ্ডগোল ; হাঙ্গামা, কোলাহল। ***Verb t.*** To harass with commotion ; to disturb ; কোলাহল দ্বারা বিব্রত করা ; বিক্ষুব্ধ করা।

turn (têrn), *v. t., i.* & *n.* **1.** To cause to move round on a centre or axis, or as on a centre or axis ; to make to move round or revolve ; to cause to revolve ; "*Turn*, Fortune, *turn* thy wheel, and lower the proud" ; ঘূর্ণিত করা, ঘুরাণ ; পাকান ; পাক দেওয়া। **2.** To form or fashion by revolving motion ; as, to *turn* the legs of a table ; কুঁদিয়া গঠন করা, কুন্দন করা, কুঁদা। **3.** To form, fashion, or shape in any way ; "Then her shape * * * * from foot to forehead exquisitely *turned*" ; গঠন করা, গড়া, কুঁদিয়া গড়া। **4.** To apply ; "He *turned* his parts rather to books and conversation than to politics" ; প্রয়োগ করা, ব্যবহার করা, লাগান। **5.** To reverse ; to bring the inside out, as of a garment ; "A pair of old breeches thrice *turned*" ; উলটপালট করা, উল্টান ; বিপর্য্যস্ত করা। **6.** To change to another opinion or party ; as, to *turn* atheist ; দল পরিবর্ত্তন করা, মত পরিবর্ত্তন করা। **7.** To translate ; "Who *turns* a Persian tale for half-a-crown, Just writes to make his barrenness appear" ; to construe ; অনুবাদ করা ; অর্থপ্রকটন করা। **8.** To hand over ; "Our inheritance is *turnel* to strangers our houses to aliens" ; হস্তান্তরিত করা। **9.** To change ; "The empiric alchemist can *turn* or holds it possible to *turn* metals of drossest ore to perfect gold" ; পরিবর্ত্তন করা, রূপান্তরিত করা। **10.** To revolve in the mind ; "*Turn* these ideas about in your mind, and take a view of them on all sides" ; পর্য্যালোচনা করা, তোলাপাড়া করা। **11.** To adapt ; "However improper he might have been for studies of a higher nature, he was perfectly well *turned* for trade" ; উপযোগী করা। **12.** To cause to ferment ; as, acid *turns* milk ; টকাইয়া দেওয়া, জমাইয়া দেওয়া, গাঁজাইয়া তোলা। **13.** To make giddy ; মাথা ঘুরাইয়া দেওয়া। **14.** To derange ; গোলমাল করিয়া দেওয়া। ***Verb i.*** **1.** To move round ; ঘূর্ণিত হওয়া,

আবর্ত্তিত হওয়া। **2.** To depend ; "The question *turns* upon this point" ; নির্ভর করা। **3.** To shift from side to side ; পাশ ফেরা। **4.** To return ; "Ere from this war thou *turn* a conqueror" ; প্রত্যাবর্ত্তন করা, ফিরিয়া আসা। **5.** To take a new course ; অন্য দিকে যাওয়া, মোড় ফিরা। **6.** To change the posture or position of the body ; "I *turned* and tried each corner of my bed, To find if sleep were there, but sleep was lost" ; মোড় ফিরা, পাশ ফিরা। **7.** To be bent ; to have recourse to ; "I know not where to *turn*"; উন্মুখ হওয়া ; আশ্রয় নেওয়া। **8.** To be changed "Thy mirth shall *turn* to mourn"; পরিবর্ত্তিত হওয়া। **9.** To become sour or spoiled ; টকিয়া যাওয়া, ছিঁড়িয়া যাওয়া, জমিয়া যাওয়া, নষ্ট হইয়া যাওয়া। **10.** To become giddy ; মাথা ঘুরা। **11.** To become nauseated ; গা বমি বমি করা। **12.** To vacillate ; ইতস্ততঃ করা। **13.** To result ; "Is all our travail *turned* to this effect"; পরিণত হওয়া। **14.** To undergo the process of turning in a lathe ; কুন্দিত হওয়া। ***Noun.*** **1.** The act or state of turning ; আবর্ত্তন, ঘূর্ণন, পাক, আবর্ত্ত, আবৃত্তি। **2.** Change of course or direction ; দিক্ পরিবর্ত্তন, গতি পরিবর্ত্তন। **3.** A winding ; মোড়, বাঁক। **4.** Character ; disposition ; inclination ; "The very *turn* of voice the good pronunciation * * * will engage the attention" ; fashion ; প্রকৃতি স্বভাব ; ভাব, মনের গতি; আসক্তি, ঝোঁক, প্রবণতা, রীতি, ধরণ। **5.** Successive course ; পালা, পর্য্যায়। **6.** Occasion ; বার। **7.** Strolling ; as to take a *turn* in the garden ; পর্য্যটন। **8.** (*Print.*) A type upside down to take the place of the proper letter ; কোন হরফের সাময়িক অভাব ঘটিলে উহার স্থানে অপর যে হরফ উল্টাইয়া বসান হয়, উল্টা হরফ। **9.** A nervous shock ; "He gave me a *turn*, I shall not soon forget" ; চমক। **10.** A service ; as, he did me a good *turn* ; কার্য্য। **11.** An occasional act of kindness or malice ; সময়োচিত বা নৈমিত্তিক উপকার বা অনুপকার। **12.** Purpose ; as, it did serve my *turn* ; convenience ; উদ্দেশ্য ; সুবিধা। **13.** A single round of a rope or cord ; রজ্জুর এক পাক। **14.** (*Med. Pl.*) Menses ; ঋতু। **15.** (*Mining*) A pit sunk in a drift ; (খনি) খনিজ পদার্থের শিরার অনুগামী পথে যে গর্ত্ত খনন করা হয়। **16.** (*Colloq.*) A piece of work requiring little time or exertion ; a short spell ; a job ; "Not able to do a hand's *turn* for myself" ; অল্প সময় বা আয়াসসাধ্য কার্য্য ; এক চোট ; ঠিকা কাজ। **17.** A drill manoeuvre in which troops in line change direction without preserving their alignment ; একপ্রকার কাওয়াজ—যাহাতে সৈনিকগণ পংক্তি ঠিক না রাখিয়া দিক্ পরিবর্ত্তন করে। **18.** (*Nav.*) A change of course of 90° ; (নৌবিদ্যা) ৯০° ডিগ্রি পরিমাণ গতিপথ হইতে অপচার। **19.** Hanging ; ফাঁসী। **20.** (*Mus.*) The sign indicating a certain way of playing a group of notes ; (সঙ্গীতশাস্ত্র) কোন সুরপংক্তি কিপ্রকারে বাদন করিতে হইবে তৎসূচক চিহ্ন। **21.** Relapse, as of a disease ; রোগের পুনরাবৃত্তি। **Turn-bench**—বেঞ্চ বা ডেস্কের উপর স্থাপিত কুন্দনযন্ত্র। **Turn-bridge**—Same as SWING-BRIDGE. **Turn-coat** — দলত্যাগী ব্যক্তি, মতত্যাগী ব্যক্তি, স্বপক্ষত্যাগী ব্যক্তি। **Turnkey**—জেলখানার প্রহরী। **Turn-out** — প্রদর্শন ; আগমন ; ধর্ম্মঘট ; অশ্বসমেত শকট ; উৎপাদন ; উৎপন্ন বস্তুর পরিমাণ। **Turn-over**—উল্টানি ; একপ্রকার পিষ্টক ; যে শিক্ষাধীন ব্যক্তি শিক্ষাসমাপ্তির জন্য এক মনীবের নিকট হইতে অপর মনীবের নিকট স্থানান্তরিত হয় ; নির্দ্দিষ্ট কালের মধ্যে কোন ব্যবসায়ে যে পরিমাণ মূলধন নিয়োগ করা হয়। **Turnpike**—(পূর্ব্বে) রাজপথের উপরিস্থ যে দ্বারে শকট প্রভৃতির মাশুল আদায় করা হইত ; (বর্ত্তমানে) প্রধান রাস্তা। **Turn-screw**—পেঁচ বসাইবার বা উঠাইবার যন্ত্র, পেঁচ-আঁটা যন্ত্র। **Turn-sole**—A plant of the genus heliotropium ; সূর্য্যমুখী-জাতীয় ফুলের গাছ ; হস্তিশুণ্ডা (heliotropium Indicum), হস্তীশুঁড়া, (*ib.*) হস্তিনী (*ib.*), ভুরুণ্ডী (*ib*), জলেচ্ছয়া (*ib.*), নাগশুণ্ডী (*ib.*), ধূসরপত্রী (*ib.*)। **Turn-stile**—একপ্রকার ক্রুশাকৃতিদ্বার—যাহা ঘুরাইয়া কোন স্থানে প্রবেশ করিতে হয়।

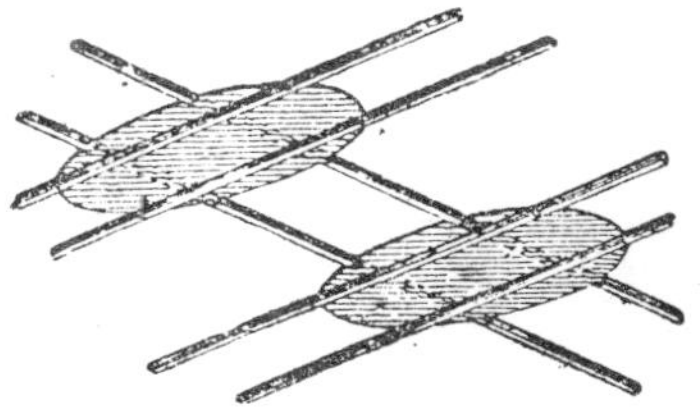

Turn-table.

Turn-table—বাষ্পীয়শকট এক বর্ত্ম-শ্রেণী হইতে অপর বর্ত্মশ্রেণীতে স্থানান্তরী-করণের জন্য ঘূর্ণনশীল গোলাকৃতি মঞ্চবিশেষ। **At every turn**—At every step ; পদে পদে। At every winding ; মোড়ে মোড়ে। **A turn of fortune's wheel** — ভাগ্যবিপর্য্যয়, অদৃষ্টচক্রের আবর্ত্তন, অদৃষ্টনেমির আবর্ত্তন। **By turns**—One by one ; alternately ; একে একে ; পর্য্যায়ক্রমে। **Done to a turn**—(Of meat) Well-cooked ; well-boiled ; সুপক্ব ; সুসিদ্ধ। **In turn, In turns**—Successively ; যথাক্রমে, যথানুক্রমে। **One good turn serves another**—উপকারীর প্রত্যুপকার করা উচিত। **To do a bad or an ill turn**—To do harm or injury ; উপকার করা, অনিষ্ট করা। **To do a good turn**—To do some work in an opportune moment ; সময়মত কোন উপকার করা। To be helpful ; উপকারে আসা। **To serve one's turns**—To serve one's purpose ; কাহারো উদ্দেশ্য পূরণ করা। To help some one ; কাহাকে সাহায্য করা। To suit some one ; কাহারো

পক্ষে উপযোগী হওয়া; **To take turns**—To come successively at the appointed time to do one's allotted work; পালামতে আসা। **To turn a barrel, organ,** or **the like**—To put into work or action; চালান। **To turn about**—To turn the face in another direction; to turn round; মুখ ফিরাণ; ঘুরা। **To turn a cold shoulder**—(See SHOULDER). **To turn a deaf ear to**—Not to listen to one's prayers etc.; কর্ণপাত না করা। **To turn adrift** — To drive out from some safe and secure position; to cast off; অকূলে ভাসাইয়া দেওয়া; পরিত্যাগ করা। **To turn again**—To return; প্রত্যাবর্ত্তন করা। **To turn against**—To direct towards or against; বিরুদ্ধে বা স্বপক্ষে প্রয়োগ করা। To render hostile or unfavourable; প্রতিকূল করা। To become hostile or unfriendly or unfavourable; প্রতিকূল হওয়া, বিপক্ষ হওয়া, বিরুদ্ধাচারী হওয়া, বিপক্ষতা করা। **To turn an enemy's flank, line, position,** or **army**—To manoeuvre so as to pass round his forces, and attack him from behind; শত্রুসৈন্যের পার্শ্বদেশ অতিক্রম করিয়া পশ্চাদ্দেশে আক্রমণ করা। **To turn an honest penny**—To earn livelihood in an honest way; সৎপথে থাকিয়া দুপয়সা উপায় বা কামাই করা। **To turn a penny**—To earn money; পয়সা কামাই করা, পয়সা উপায় করা। **To turn a penny** (or) **the penny** — To increase one's capital by trading; ব্যবসায় দ্বারা মূলধন বৃদ্ধি করা। **To turn aside**—To leave a straight course; এক দিকে সরা। To withdraw from the notice or the presence of others; সম্মুখ হইতে সরিয়া যাওয়া। **To turn a somersault** — See SOMERSAULT. **To turn a thing up**—(*Slang*) To give up; ছাড়িয়া দেওয়া, পরিত্যাগ করা। **To turn away**—To dismiss from service; কর্ম্মচ্যুত করা। To avert; নিবারণ করা। To turn the face in an opposite direction; মুখ ফিরান। To deviate; চ্যুত হওয়া, ভ্রষ্ট হওয়া। **To turn back**—To cause to retrace one's steps; to drive away; প্রত্যাবর্ত্তন করিতে বাধ্য করা; বিতাড়িত করা, তাড়াইয়া দেওয়া। **To turn down**—To fold down; গুটান। To lower, as with a stopcock or the like; নামাইয়া দেওয়া, চোঙ্গার মুখনল প্রভৃতি ঘুরাইয়া নামাইয়া দেওয়া। **To turn forth** — To expel; বিতাড়িত করা, তাড়াইয়া দেওয়া। **To turn head** — To make a stand; বাগিয়া দাঁড়ান, বাঁকিয়া দাঁড়ান। **To turn in**—To direct inwards or towards each other; প্রত্যাকর্ষণ করা, ভিতরের দিকে টানিয়া নেওয়া। To place in a particular place; কোন বিশেষ স্থানে রাখা। To bend, double or point inwards; ভিতরের দিকে নোয়ান বা ভাঁজ করিয়া রাখা। To go to bed; শয়ন করিতে যাওয়া। To enter; প্রবেশ করা। **To turn in one's grave**—See GRAVE. **To turn into**—To translate into; ভাষান্তরিত করা, অনুবাদ করা, তর্জ্জমা করা। **To turn off**—To turn aside; to deflect; এক পার্শ্বে সরা; বিচ্যুত হওয়া, বিপথে যাওয়া। To dismiss; to discard; পদচ্যুত করা; তাড়াইয়া দেওয়া। To give over; ছাড়িয়া দেওয়া, ত্যাগ করা। To complete; শেষ করা, সমাপ্ত করা, সম্পাদন করা। To shut off, as a fluid, by means of a stopcock, valve, etc.; as, to *turn off* the gas, steam, water etc.; চাবি, মুখনল, প্রভৃতি ঘুরাইয়া বন্ধ করা। (*Slang*) To marry; বিবাহ করা। (*Obs.*) To hang; (অপ্রঃ) ফাঁসী দেওয়া। To give a different meaning or effect to; ভিন্ন অর্থ বা ভাব প্রদান করা। To deviate from straight course; সরল রেখা হইতে চ্যুত হওয়া। **To turn on**—To depend upon; নির্ভর করা। To confront in a hostile manner; বাঁকিয়া দাঁড়ান। To become hostile to; বিরোধী হওয়া। To admit; or cause to flow as a fluid by means of stopcock; মুখনল প্রভৃতি ঘুরাইয়া ঢুকিতে দেওয়া বা পড়িতে দেওয়া। **To turn one round one's little finger**—See FINGER. **To turn one's back on**—To be averse to; বিমুখ হওয়া। **To turn one's coat**—See COAT. **To turn one's flank**—To attack one on a weak point; to surpass one in wit; কাহারো দুর্ব্বল স্থানে আঘাত করা; কাহাকে বুদ্ধিবলে পরাজিত করা। To fold back; গুটান, উল্টাইয়া ভাঁজ করা। To return; প্রত্যাবর্ত্তন করা। **To turn one's hand**—To devote one's self; to adapt; নিয়োগ করা, নিরত করা; উপযোগী করা। To be ready to do some work; কোন কার্য্য করিতে প্রস্তুত হওয়া। **To turn one's head** or **brains**—See HEAD and BRAIN **To turn on one's heel**—To pass along with a sneer; মুখ বাঁকাইয়া বা নাক সিঁটকাইয়া চলিয়া যাওয়া। **To turn out**—To expel; বিতাড়িত করা, তাড়াইয়া দেওয়া, বহিষ্কৃত করা, বাহির করিয়া দেওয়া। To cause to point or incline outward; বাহিরের দিকে উন্মুখ বা প্রবণ করা। To turn inside out; ভিতরের দিক উল্টাইয়া বাহিরে আনা। To bring to view; প্রকট করা। (*Colloq.*) To rise from bed; (চলিতভাষায়) ঘুম হইতে উঠা। To come or go out; to attend; আসা, যাওয়া; উপস্থিত হওয়া। To prove in the result or issue; ফলে দাঁড়ান, পরিণামে দাঁড়ান। To happen; ঘটা, সংঘটিত হওয়া। To produce as the result of labour or any process of manufacture ; পরিশ্রমফলে উৎপন্ন করা, শিল্পকার্য্য দ্বারা উৎপাদন করা। To graze ; চরান। To assemble for duty etc. ; কর্ত্তব্য কার্য্য প্রভৃতি সম্পাদনের জন্য সমবেত হওয়া। To go on strike ; ধর্ম্মঘট করা। **To turn out in the cold**—To discard ; তাড়াইয়া দেওয়া। **To turn over**—To upset ; উল্টাইয়া ফেলা। To do business to the amount of ; নির্দ্দিষ্ট পরিমাণ টাকার ব্যবসায় করা, জিনিষ পত্র ক্রয় বিক্রয়ে নির্দ্দিষ্ট পরিমাণ টাকা পাওয়া। To transfer ; হস্তান্তরিত করা। To open and turn the leaves of for examination ; পাতা উল্টাইয়া দেখা। (*Obs.*) To hang ; (অপ্রঃ) ফাঁসি দেওয়া। **To turn over a new leaf**—See LEAF. **To turn round**—To turn so that the front shall become back ; ঘুরা, পাক খাওয়া। To adopt new opinions or policy ; নূতন মত বা পন্থা অবলম্বন করা। **To turn tail**—To flee like a coward ; লেজ গুটাইয়া পালান, কাপুরুষের মত পলায়ন করা। (Also see TAIL.) **To turn the back**—See BACK. **To turn the back on** or **upon**—See BACK. **To turn the corner**—See CORNER. **To turn the head of**—To make one insane, infatuated, wild or the like ; প্রমত্ত করা, মাথা ঘুরাইয়া দেওয়া। **To turn the key**—To lock or unlock a door ; দরজায় চাবি দেওয়া, চাবিদ্বারা দরজা খোলা। **To turn the scale** or **balance of**—To change the preponderance ; আধিক্যের পরিবর্ত্তন করা। To decide or determine something doubtful ; কোন সন্দেহজনক বিষয় মীমাংসা করা। **To turn the stomach**—To cause sickness or loathing ; বিবমিষু করা, নাড়ীমোচড়ান, বিরক্তি বা বিতৃষ্ণা জন্মান। **To turn the table**—See TABLE. **To turn to**—To be directed or move towards ; উন্মুখ হওয়া, চালিত হওয়া। To bend or incline up, down, over or the like ; ঝুঁকা, আনত হওয়া। To alter ; পরিবর্ত্তন করা, বদলান। To tend or trend toward ; উন্মুখ হওয়া, প্রবণ হওয়া। To apply one's self to ; to have recourse to ; নিয়োগ করা ; আশ্রয় নেওয়া। To act vigorously ; উৎসাহের সহিত কার্য্য করা। **To turn to account** or **profit**—To make profitable or advantageous ; লাভজনক হওয়া, সুবিধাজনক হওয়া, কাজে লাগান, কোনকিছু হইতে দুপয়সা লাভ করা। **To turn turtle**—To upset ; উলটপালট করা, সম্পূর্ণরূপে বিপর্য্যস্ত করা। **To turn under**—To bend, double, or be folded downwards or under ; নীচে বা নীচের দিকে ঝুঁকিয়া পড়া। (*Colloq.*) To happen or be revealed ; (চলিতভাষায়) ঘটা, প্রকাশ পাওয়া। To put as soil, manure, etc. underneath from the surface by ploughing, digging, etc. ; খনন, কর্ষণ, প্রভৃতি দ্বারা উপরের মাটী, সার, প্রভৃতি নীচে স্থাপন করা। **To turn up**—To turn so as to bring the bottom side on top ; উল্টান। To bring from beneath the surface by ploughing, digging, etc. ; লাঙ্গল প্রভৃতি দ্বারা খুঁড়িয়া বাহির করা। To refer in a book ; কোন পুস্তকে অনুসন্ধান করা। To cause to point upwards ; উপরের দিকে উন্মুখ করা, উঁচু করা। To point upwards ; উপরের দিকে উন্মুখ হওয়া। To make one's appearance ; উপস্থিত হওয়া, দেখা দেওয়া। To happen ; ঘটা। To cause to vomit ; বমি করান। To come to light ; প্রকাশ হইয়া পড়া। **To turn upon**—To cause to operate on or against ; to retort ; কোনকিছুর উপর বা বিরুদ্ধে ক্রিয়া করা ; কাটা জবাব দেওয়া। (See also TO TURN ON.) **To turn up one's nose at**—To sneer at ; নাক সিঁটকান। **Turned out of**—Educated ; শিক্ষিত। **Turn of fortune**—কপালের ফের, অদৃষ্টের ফের। **Turn and turn about**—Alternately ; পর্য্যায়ক্রমে। **Turn of life**—স্ত্রীলোকের রজোনিবৃত্তির কাল (সাধারণতঃ ৪০ হইতে ৫০ বর্ষ পর্য্যন্ত)।

turn'-ĕr (têrn-), *n.* **1.** One who forms things with a lathe ; কুন্দনকারী। **2.** A kind of tumbler pigeon ; একপ্রকার লোটন-পায়রা। **–y,** *n.*

turn'-ing (têrn-), *n.* **1.** A place where a road diverges from another ; মোড়। **2.** Art or operation of shaping articles in a lathe ; কুন্দন। **3.** A stroll ; সামান্য ভ্রমণ। **4.** Act of bringing down the feet of the child to facilitate delivery ; সন্তানপ্রসব অনায়াসসাধ্য করার জন্য শিশুর পা বাহিরে আনয়ন। **Turning point**—যে বিষয়ের উপর কোন প্রশ্নের মীমাংসা নির্ভর করে ; যে অবস্থা হইতে পরিবর্ত্তনের সূচনা হয়।

tur'-nip (têr-), *n.* A plant of the cabbage genus, much cultivate for its bulbuous esculent root ;

Stuped Turnip-fly.
a, natural size ; b, magnified.

শালগম [*Syn.* শিখিমূল, গৃঞ্জন, যবনেষ্ট, বর্ত্তুল, গ্রন্থিমূল, শিখাকন্দ, কন্দ, ডিণ্ডীরমোদক।] **Turnip-fly, Turnip-flea**—শালগমের অনিষ্টকারী একপ্রকার মক্ষিকার ন্যায় কীট। **Turnip-top**—শালগম শাক।

tur'-pĕn-tine (têr-), *n.* & *v. t.* **1.** A resinous substance flowing from trees, as the pine, fir, etc. ; তার্পিণ। [Arab. *ratenuj rumi, butum* ; Pers. *zungbari* ; Nep. *kota.*] **2.** The oil distilled from this ; তার্পিণ তৈল। ***Verb t.*** To apply turpentine to ; তার্পিণ তৈল প্রয়োগ করা, তার্পিণ মালিস করা। **–tin'-ic,** *adj.* **Turpentine-tree**—See TEREBINTH.

tur′-pĕth (têr-), *n.* The root of plant used in India as purgative; তেউড়ী, ত্রিবৃতা। [Syn. *Ordinary species* :—সুবহা, ত্রিপুটা, ত্রিভণ্ডী, রেচনী, সবহা, সরণা, রোচনী, ত্রিপুটী, মালবিকা, মসুরী, শ্যামা, অর্দ্ধচন্দ্রা, বিদলা, সুষেণী, কালিঙ্গিক, কালী, ত্রিবেলা, কালমেষী, ত্রিবৃত্তিকা। *Black species* :—শ্যামা, পালিন্দী. সুষেণিকা, কালা, মসূরবিদলা, অর্দ্ধচন্দ্রা, কালমেষিকা, পালিন্ধী, কলমেশিকা। *White species* :—ত্রিবৃত, বৃকাক্ষী, ত্রিভণ্ডী, সুবহা, ত্রিপুটা। *Red species* :—ব্যাত্রাদনী, কুটরুণা, নিঃসৃতা, অরুণা, ত্রিবৃতা। বৈদ্যকশাস্ত্রে ত্রিবৃতার নিম্নোক্ত গুণ সমূহের উল্লেখ দৃষ্ট হয়:—সামান্য-ত্রিবৃতাগুণাঃ—কটুত্বম, উষ্ণত্বম,। কৃমি-শ্লেষ্মোদরার্ত্তিকুষ্ঠ কণ্ডূব্রণনাশিত্বম্। বিরেচনে প্রশস্তত্বঞ্চ। ইতি রাজনির্ঘণ্টঃ। অরুণবর্ণ ত্রিবৃদ্‌গুণাঃ—স্বাদুত্বম, কষায়ত্বম, মৃদুত্বম, রেচনত্বম, রূক্ষত্বম্ কটুত্বম্। দোষপাকে পিত্তকফাপহত্বঞ্চ। অশ্চাল্লান্তরগুণা বিজ্ঞেয়া ত্রিবৃতা সিতা। ইতি রাজবল্লভঃ। শ্বেতত্রিবৃদ্‌গুণাঃ — বিরেচনত্বম, স্বাদুত্বম, উষ্ণত্বম, বাযুত্বম, রূক্ষত্বম্। পিত্তজ্বরশ্লেষ্ম-পিত্তশোফোদরাপহত্বঞ্চ। কৃষ্ণ ত্রিবৃতা-গুণাঃ-শ্বেতাঙ্কীনগুণত্বম। তীব্রত্বম, বিরেচনত্বম। মূর্চ্ছাদাহমদভ্রান্তিকণ্ঠোৎকর্ষণ-কারিত্বম—ভাবপ্রকাশঃ।] **Turpeth-root**—দুধ-কলমী।

tur′-pi-tūde (têr-), *n.* Inherent baseness or vileness; shameful wickedness; moral depravity; "How wouldst thou have paid, My better service, when my *turpitude* thou thus dost crown with gold"; নীচতা; জঘন্যতা; ভ্রষ্টাচার।

tur′-quoise (têr-kōyz), *n.* A greenish-blue or blue opaque precious stone; নীল বা হরিদাভ-নীলবর্ণ মণিবিশেষ, ফিরোজা, হরিৎশ্যাম, তুরুকমণি, পেরজ, পেরোজ (cf. Pers. ফিরোজা) [It. *turchina*; Sp. *turquesa*; Germ. *Turkiss.*]

tur′-rĕt (-ĕt), *n.* 1. A little tower on a larger building, often at the angle of a wall; ক্ষুদ্র বুরুজ, শিখর। 2. A strong cylindrical structure rising from the deck of an iron-clad vessel; পাটাতন হইতে উত্থিত, রণপোতের ইস্পাতনির্ম্মিত বুরুজ—যাহা যেদিকে ইচ্ছা ঘুরাইতে পারা যায়,পোতমঞ্চ, পোতশিখর। **—ed,** *adj.* **Turret-gun**—পোতমঞ্চের উপর স্থাপিত কামান। **Turret-ship** — যে রণপোতের কামান সকল ঘূর্ণমান লৌহমঞ্চে বসানো থাকে।

tur-ric′-ū-lāte, –lāt-ĕd, *adjs.* (Of shell) Having a long spire; (শঙ্খ-সম্বন্ধে) দীর্ঘ শিখরবিশিষ্ট।

tur′-tle (têr-tl), *n.* A kind of pigeon or dove (also *turtle-dove*); একপ্রকার ঘুঘু, শ্যামঘুঘু। **Turtle-dove**—Same as TURTLE above.

tur′-tle (têr-tl), *n.* & *v. i.* 1. A tortoise; কূর্ম্ম, কমঠ, চিত্রকচ্ছপ। 2. The sea-tortoise; সামুদ্রিককচ্ছপ। 3. Green turtle; একপ্রকার সামুদ্রিক-কচ্ছপ। ইহার মাংস অতি উপাদেয় বলিয়া আদৃত হইয়া থাকে। ***Verb i.*** To hunt for turtle; চিত্রকচ্ছপ শিকার করা। **—tler,** *n.* **Turtle-shell**—কচ্ছপের খোলা, বিশেষতঃ একপ্রকার কৃষ্ণবর্ণ কচ্ছপের খোলা—যদ্দ্বারা কোন কিছু খচিত করা হয়; একপ্রকার সুন্দর কড়ি (also *turtle-cowry*). **To turn turtle**—(*Slang*) To capsize; উল্টাইয়া যাওয়া।

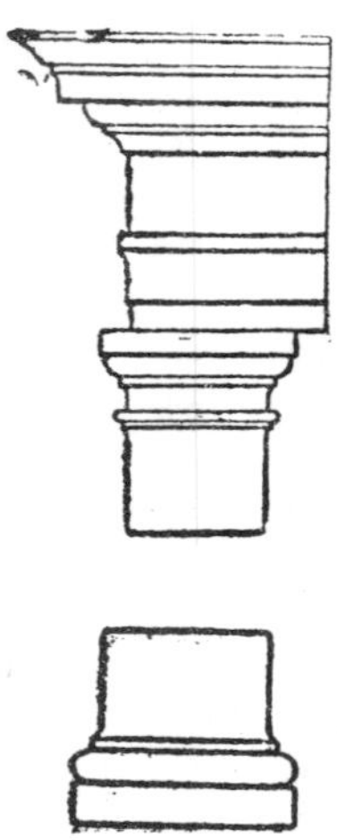

Tuscan order.

Tŭs′-căn, *adj.* & *n.* 1. Pertaining to Tuscany in Italy; ইতালী দেশের অন্তঃপাতী টাস্‌কানি প্রদেশ সম্বন্ধীয়। 2. Designating one of the five orders of architecture, which admits of no ornaments, and the columns of which are not fluted; স্থাপত্যধারাবিশেষ সম্বন্ধীয়। [এই স্থাপত্যধারায় কোনরূপ মণ্ডণ ব্যবহৃত হয় না। এই পদ্ধতির অনুসারে নির্ম্মিত স্তম্ভসমূহ নালিবিশিষ্ট করা হয় না।] ***Noun.*** 1. The language of Tuscany; টাসকানি প্রদেশের ভাষা। 2. The inhabitants of Tuscany; টাসকানি প্রদেশের অধিবাসী। **Tuscan-straw** — টুপি প্রভৃতিতে ব্যবহৃত সুন্দর পীতবর্ণ গমের খড়।

tŭsh, *int.* An exclamation indicating check, rebuke or contempt; থাম, চুপ, ফুঃ, ফুস্।

tŭsh, *n.* A long pointed tooth, esp. canine tooth of a horse; সূক্ষ্মাগ্র দীর্ঘ দন্ত, অশ্বের শ্বদন্ত।

tŭsk, *n.* & *v. t.* 1. A long prominent tooth of certain animals, as the boar, walrus, elephant, etc.; গজদন্ত, দ্বিরদরদ, শূকরদন্ত, সিন্ধুঘোটকের দন্ত। 2. A term applied to the share of a plough, a harrow-tooth, a tusk-like part in lock, etc.; লাঙ্গলের ফাল, বিদার দাঁত, তালার গজদন্তাকৃতি অংশ ইত্যাদি। ***Verb t.*** To gore, thrust, tear up, with tusk or tusks; "Nay, now you puff, *tusk,* and draw up your chin"; দন্তদ্বারা বিদ্ধ বা উৎপাটন করা, উৎপাটন করা। **Tusked,** *adj.* **Tusk′-y,** *adj.*

tŭsk′-ĕr, *n.* 1. An elephant with well-developed tusk; দ্বিরদ, দন্তী। 2. A wild boar with well-developed tusk; "A *tusker* who had, however, no idea of running away"; সুপরিস্ফুট দন্তবিশিষ্ট শূকর।

tŭs-sĕr, –sŭr, –sōre *ns.* 1. The silk spun by a common Indian silk-worm, which yields a rather coarse-looking, but very durable silk; তসর 2. Same as TUSSER SILK-WORM. **Tussur silk-worm**—তসরেপোকা।

tŭs′-sic′-ū-lar (-lĕr), *adj.* (*Med.*) Of, or pertaining to, cough; (ভৈষজ্য-শাস্ত্র) কফসম্বন্ধীয়। **—sal, –sive,** *adjs.*

tŭs-sle (-l), *n.* & *v. i.* A struggle ; a conflict ; দ্বন্দ্ব ; সংগ্রাম, হুড়াহুড়ি, ধ্বস্তাধ্বস্তি, হাতাহাতি, হুড়মুড়ি, পাছড়াপাছড়ি। ***Verb i.*** To struggle ; to scuffle ; দ্বন্দ্ব করা, সংগ্রাম করা ; হুড়াহুড়ি করা।

tŭs'-sock (-ŏk), *n.* **1.** A clump, tuft or small hillock of growing grass ; a tuft or lock of hair etc. ; তৃণগুচ্ছ, তৃণাচ্ছাদিতগিরি ; কেশগুচ্ছ, কেশকলাপ, অলকগুচ্ছ, চিকুরকলাপ। **2.** Same as TUSSOCK-MOTH. **—y,** *adj.* **Tussock-grass**—পেটাগোনিয়া প্রভৃতি স্থানের বিলাভূমিতে জাত একপ্রকার দীর্ঘতৃণ। **Tussock-moth**—বিভিন্ন প্রকার তসরে পোকার সাধারণ নাম।

tŭt, *int., n.* & *v. i.* An exclamation used for checking or rebuking ; চুপ ! থাম ! ***Noun.*** This exclamation ; চুপ শব্দ। ***Verb i.*** To exclaim *tut* ; 'চুপ' বা 'থাম' শব্দ উচ্চারণ করা।

tŭt, *n.* & *v. i.* A job ; ঠিকা কাজ। ***Verb i.*** To work by the piece ; ঠিকা কাজ করা। **Tut-work**—ঠিকা কাজ।

tutamen, *n.* (*Anat., pl.* TUTAMINA.) Protective part ; রক্ষাকারক অংশ।

tü'-ta'-ni-ă, *n.* The trade name of a variety of Britannia metal ; শুভ্রবর্ণ মিশ্রধাতু বিশেষ।

tü'-tĕ-lāge, *n.* **1.** Guardianship ; অভিভাবকতা, রক্ষণাবেক্ষণ। **2.** The period of being under a guardian ; অভিভাবকের অধীন থাকার কাল।

tü'-tĕ-lâr, tü'-tĕ-lă-rȳ, *adjs.* **1.** Guardian ; protecting ; as, *tutelary* goddess ; অধিষ্ঠাতৃস্বরূপ ; রক্ষাকারী। **2.** Pertaining to a guardian ; অভিভাবকীয়। **Tutelary-deity**—অধিদেবতা, ইষ্টদেবতা।

'tween (twēn), *adv.* & *prep.* Contraction of BETWEEN. **'Tween-decks**—পাটাতন সমূহের মধ্যবর্ত্তী (*Adj.*); পাটাতন সমূহের মধ্যবর্ত্তীস্থান (*Noun*)।

tween'-ȳ (twēn-), *n.* (*Colloq.*) A servant assisting two others *e. g.* cook and housemaid ; (চলিত ভাষায়) যে ভৃত্য অপর দুইজন ভৃত্যকে সাহায্য করে।

tweez'-ērs (twēz-), *n.* & *v. t.* A kind of small pincers ; সোন্না, ক্ষুদ্র লোম তোলা চিমটা, মোচনা, সন্দংশিকা। ***Verb t.*** To pluck out hairs, etc. with tweezers ; মোচনা দ্বারা লোম প্রভৃতি তোলা।

twĕlfth, *adj.* & *n.* **1.** The next succeeding the eleventh ; দ্বাদশতম। **2.** Being, or constituting, one of the twelve equal parts into which anything is, or may be, divided ; দ্বাদশাংশাত্মক। ***Noun.*** One of twelve equal parts ; দ্বাদশাংশ। **—ly,** *adv.* **Twelfth-cake**—খৃষ্টমাসদিবসের পরবর্ত্তী দ্বাদশতম দিবসের অপরাহ্ণ বেলার উৎসবে ব্যবহৃত পিষ্টক। **Twelfth-day**—খৃষ্টমাস দিবসের পরবর্ত্তী দ্বাদশতম দিবস। **Twelfth-night**—খৃষ্টমাসাদি দ্বাদশতম দিবসের অপরাহ্ণ বেলা। **Twelfth-tide**—Same as TWELFTH-DAY. **The twelfth**—বারই আগষ্ট—এই দিবস হইতে পল্লী গ্রামে পক্ষী শিকার আরব্ধ হয়।

twelve (twĕlv), *adj.* & *n.* The sum of ten and two ; বার, দ্বাদশ। ***Noun.*** The number which consists of two and ten ; বার। **Twelve-mo, 12mo**—Same as DUODECIMO. **Twelvemonth**—একবৎসর, বারমাস। **Twelvepence**—এক শিলিং (কেবল মাত্র দোকানে ব্যবহৃত হয়)। **Twelvepenny** — এক শিলিং। **Twelve tables** — See TABLE. **The Twelve**—দ্বাদশ জন খৃষ্টপার্ষদ। **This day twelve-month**—অদ্য হইতে এক বৎসর।

twĕn'-tȳ, *adj.* & *n.* **1.** One more than nineteen; twice ten; বিশ; বিংশ। **2.** Many; as, I have told him *twenty* times ; অনেক, বিশ [cf. সে এক কথা বিশবার বলিলেও বুঝেনা।] ***Noun.*** The number of twice ten ; score ; বিংশতি সংখ্যা ; বিশটী। **—fold,** *adj.* & *adv.* **—ti-eth,** *adj.* & *n.* Next in order after the nineteenth ; বিংশতিতম। ***Noun.*** One of twenty equal parts; বিংশতি অংশের এক অংশ। **Twentymo, Twentyfourmo (20-mo, 24 mo.)**—বিংশতি বা দ্বাবিংশতি পত্রে বিভক্ত কাগজ, ঐরূপ পত্রাত্মক পুস্তক। **Twenty-one, twenty-two**—বিংশতি, দ্বাবিংশতি, প্রভৃতি।

'twere (twâr), Contraction of *it were.*

twī'-bĭll, *n.* **1.** A double-bladed battle-axe ; একপ্রকার দ্বিধার রণকুঠার। **2.** A kind of mattock ; এক প্রকার খনিত্র।

twī'-blāde, *n.* Same as TWAY-BLADE.

twice (twīs), *adv.* **1.** Two times ; দুই গুণ, দ্বিগুণ। **2.** On two occasions ; দুই বার। **3.** Doubly ; দুইভাবে, দুইপ্রকারে। **twice-told**—দুইবার কথিত ; তুচ্ছ, পুরাতন। **He did it in twice**—(চলিত ভাষায়) সে এই কাজটার কতকটা প্রথমবার এবং অবশিষ্ট টুকু দ্বিতীয় বার করিয়াছিল।

twīc'-ēr, *n.* A printer that is both a compositor and pressman ; মুদ্রাযন্ত্রের যে অক্ষরবিন্যাসক যন্ত্রচালকের কার্য্যও করিয়া থাকে।

twid'-dle (-l), *v. t., i.* & *n.* To twirl in a light way ; as, to *twiddle* one's thumb ; to cause to rotate with rapidity, esp. with fingers ; মৃদুভাবে ঘূর্ণিত করা ; দ্রুত ঘূর্ণিত করা, অঙ্গুলী দ্বারা দ্রুত ঘুরাণ। ***Verb i.*** **1.** To trifle with ; ছেলেমি করা। **2.** To quiver or shake lightly ; দোলা, স্পন্দিত হওয়া। ***Noun.*** A slight twirl ; a twirl of the finger ; মৃদু ঘূর্ণন; অঙ্গুলীঘূর্ণন। **Twiddling-line**—কম্পাসের কাগজফলক ঘুরাইবার জন্য দড়ী।

twig, *n.* **1.** A small shoot or branch ; ডগা, প্রশাখা। **2.** (*Anat.*) A small branch of an artery ; ধমনীর ক্ষুদ্র প্রশাখা। **3.** Same as ROD *n.* II. **4.** (*Elec.*) A small distributing conductor ; বিতরণকারী ক্ষুদ্র তাড়িত-প্রবাহ চালক। **To hop the twig**—(চলিতভাষায়) মরা। **To work the**

twig – To use the divining-rod ; ভূগর্ভে ধাতু প্রভৃতি আছে কিনা তন্নির্ণয়ের জন্য যে দৈবী শক্তিসম্পন্ন দণ্ড ব্যবহার করা হয়।

tū'-tē-năg, *n.* **1.** The Indian name of zinc ; দস্তা। **2.** Chinese white copper ; চীন দেশে প্রস্তুত মিশ্র ধাতু বিশেষ। [ইহাতে ৫০ ভাগ তাম্র, ১৯ ভাগ নিকেল এবং ৩১ ভাগ দস্তা থাকে।]

tū'-tŏr, *n.* & *v. i.* **1.** One who has the charge of instructing another in various branches of learning ; a private instructor ; শিক্ষক ; গৃহশিক্ষক। **2.** A fellow of an English university directing the studies of undergraduates ; ইংলণ্ডের বিশ্ববিদ্যালয়ে যে ফেলো অনুপাধিপ্রাপ্ত ছাত্রগণের অধ্যাপনায় সাহায্য করিয়া থাকেন। **3.** (*Law*) The guardian of a minor ; (আইন) অপ্রাপ্তবয়স্ক ব্যক্তির অভিভাবক। ***Verb i.*** To act as a tutor to ; to instruct ; গৃহশিক্ষকের কার্য্য করা ; শিক্ষা দেওয়া, শিক্ষাপ্রদান করা। **–age, –ess, –ship,** *ns.* **–to'-ri-al,** *adj.* **–to'-ri-al-ly,** *adv.*

tŭt'-săn, *n.* A species of St.-John's wort ; একজাতীয় গুল্ম।

tutti, *n.* & *adv.* A direction for all the singers or players to perform together ; সকল গায়ককে একসঙ্গে গাহিবার জন্য নিদেশ। ***Adv.*** All together ; সকলে একযোগে।

tût'-ti–frût'-ti, *n.* A confection or ice-cream of mixed fruits ; ফল-মিশ্রিত মিঠাই, ফলের কুলপি।

tŭt'-tȳ, *n.* An impure protoxide of zinc, used as polishing powder ; পালিসের চূর্ণ রূপে ব্যবহৃত অবিশোধিত অম্লজান জারিত দস্তা।

tū'-ŭm, See MEUM.

tû-whit', **tû-whoo'**, *n.* & *v. i.* Cry of owl ; পেচক রব। ***Verb i.*** To make the cry of owl ; পেচকবৎ ধ্বনি করা।

tu-yère' (twi-yār *or* tû-yār), **twȳ'-ēr**, *ns.* A tube or pipe through which the blast of air enters a blast furnace ; বাত্যাগহায় চুল্লীতে যে চোঙ্গের ভিতর দিয়া বায়ুপ্রবাহ প্রবিষ্ট হয়।

twad'-dell (twŏd-l), *n.* A kind of hydrometer for liquids heavier than water ; জল অপেক্ষা গুরু তরলপদার্থ পরিমাপের জন্য একজাতীয় জলমানযন্ত্র, জলগুরুমান।

twad'-dle (tŏwd-l), *v. i.* & *n.* To indulge in empty silly talk ; অসার কথাবার্ত্তা বলা, বাজে কথা বলা, বক বক করা, বাচালতা করা। ***Noun.*** Empty simple talk ; অসার কথা, বাজে কথা, বড়বড়ানি (*colloq.*)। **–dler**, *n.* One who twaddles, "A laugh at the style of this ungrammatical *twaddler* ; যে ব্যক্তি বাজে কথা বকে। **–dly**, *adv.*

twain (twān), *adj.* & *n.* (*Obs.*, *Poet.*) Two ; (অপ্র:) যুগ্ম, যুগল। ***Noun.*** A pair ; a couple ; যুগ্ম, যুগল ; মিথুন। **Cut in twain**—দ্বিধা খণ্ডিত, দুইভাগে বিভক্ত, দ্বিধা বিভক্ত, দ্বিখণ্ডিত।

twăng, *n.*, *v. i.* & *t.* **1.** A sharp, quick sound, as of a string drawn tense and then suddenly let go ; টঙ্কার, জ্যানির্ঘোষ, টঙ্কৃত। **2.** Nasal tone ; আনুনাসিক স্বর, নাকি সুর। ***Verb i.*** **1.** To make the sound of a string which is stretched and suddenly pulled ; টঙ্কৃত হওয়া। **2.** To play on a stringed instrument ; বেহালা প্রভৃতি বাজান। ***Verb t.*** **1.** To make to sound sharply ; টঙ্কার দেওয়া। **2.** To utter with a sharp, shrill or nasal tone ; "Some whispered softly, and some *twanged* aloud" ; নাকি সুরে কথা বলা। **Twang'-ing**, *n.* **To go off twanging**—To go well or happily ; বেশ চলা, দিব্যি আরামে চলা।

twan'-gle (twăng-gl), *v. t.* & *i.* To twang lightly ; মৃদুভাবে টঙ্কার দেওয়া।

twan'-kay (twăng-kā), *n.* A kind of green tea ; একপ্রকার সবুজ চা।

'twas (twŏz), Contraction of *it was*.

tway'-blāde (twā-), *n.* A plant growing in Britain ; ব্রিটীশ দ্বীপে জাত গুল্মবিশেষ।

tweak (twēk), *v. t.* & *n.* To twitch; to pinch and pull suddenly; হেঁচকান, মোচড়ান, খামচান ; হেঁচকা টান দেওয়া। ***Noun.*** A sharp pinch or jerk ; হেঁচকা টান, খামচা।

tweed (twēd), *n.* A twilled woollen stuff; একপ্রকার টের্চ্চা-বুনা পশমী কাপড়।

twee'-dle (twē-dl), *n.* The sound of a fiddle ; বেহালার ধ্বনি। **Tweedledum and tweedledee**—যে সকল বস্তু কেবল মাত্র বা প্রধানতঃ নামতঃ বিভিন্ন হইয়া থাকে।

twig, *v. t.* **1.** To understand the meaning of ; to comprehend ; অর্থ গ্রহণ করা ; উপলব্ধি করা, বুঝা। **2.** To perceive ; to observe ; "They're *twiggin'* you, Sir, whispered Mr. Weller" ; অনুভব করা ; লক্ষ্য করিয়া দেখা।

twī'-light (-līt), *n.*, *adj.* & *v. t.* **1.** The faint light perceived before the rising and after the setting of the sun ; সূর্য্যোদয়ের পূর্ব্ববর্ত্তী (এবং সচরাচর) সূর্য্যাস্তের পরবর্ত্তী অস্পষ্ট আলোক, সন্ধ্যা, উষা, সন্ধ্যারাগ (হিঃ কোঃ), দো-আলো। (সরযুবালা দাসগুপ্ত), গোধূলি বেলা, কাকজ্যোৎস্না, ছায়ালোক, পূর্ব্বসন্ধ্যা, (*moring twilight*), প্রাতঃসন্ধ্যা (*ib.* মঃ সং)। **2.** Faint light ; "'Mid the *twilight* of the laurel grove"; ক্ষীণ আলোক, অস্পষ্টালোক, ঝাপ্সা আলো **3.** A partial revelation or disclosure ; আংশিক প্রকাশ। **4.** A state of imperfect knowledge ; জ্ঞানালোকের অপূর্ণতা। ***Adj.*** **1.** Imperfectly lighted ; অস্পষ্টালোকিত। **2.** (*Fig.*) Obscure ; "Philosophy may yield some *twilight* glimmerings thereof" ; (লক্ষণায়) অস্পষ্ট। **3.** Seen or done in twilight ; প্রদোষকালে দৃষ্ট বা কৃত। ***Verb t.*** To light obscurely ; অস্পষ্টভাবে আলোকিত করা। **Twilight arc, Twilight arch, Twilight**

curve—সন্ধ্যাকাশের উজ্জ্বলতম অংশ বেষ্টনকারী রেখা। **Twilight of the gods**—(নরওয়ে ও সুইডেনের পুরাণে)—দেবাসুরের যুদ্ধ। [এই যুদ্ধে দেব ও দানবগণ পরস্পরকে ধ্বংস করিয়াছিল।]

twill, *n.* & *v. t.* An appearance of diagonal lines or ribs produced in textile fabrics ; a fabric woven with a twill ; কাপড়ের উপর টের্চ্চা বুনন ; টের্চ্চা বুনা কাপড়। ***Verb t.*** To weave, as cloth so as to produce the appearance of diagonal lines or ribs on the surface ; টের্চ্চাভাবে বুনা, শির তুলিয়া বুনা।

'twill, Contraction of *it will.*

twin, *n., adj., v. i.* & *t.* 1. One of two born at the same birth ; যমজ, যুগ্ম। 2. One of a pair or couple ; যুগলের অন্যতর। 3. Exact counterpart of a person or thing ; কোন ব্যক্তি বা বস্তুর অবিকল প্রতিরূপ। 4. A compound crystal composed of two or more crystals or parts of crystals in reversed position with reference to each other ; পরস্পরের সম্বন্ধে বিপর্য্যস্তভাবে অবস্থিত দুই বা তদধিক দানা বা দানার অংশসমূহ দ্বারা গঠিত মিশ্র দানা। ***Adj.*** 1. Being one of two born at a birth ; যমজ। 2. Being one of a pair much resembling each other ; যুগলের অন্যতর। 3. Double ; যুগল, মিথুন, যুগ্ম। 4. (*Bot.*) Same as DIDYMOUS. ***Verb i.*** 1. To bring forth twins ; যমজ সন্তান প্রসব করা। 2. To be born at the same birth ; একসঙ্গে জাত হওয়া। 3. To be paired ; "Who *twins* (as it were) in love" ; to be like twins ; যুগল হওয়া ; যমজবৎ হওয়া। 4. To separate ; পৃথক্ হওয়া। ***Verb t.*** 1. To couple or mate ; যুগল করা, জোড় বাঁধা। 2. To separate ; পৃথক করা, বিযুক্ত করা। **Twin'-ling, Twin'-ship,** *ns.* **Twin boat** or **steamer**—যুগ্ম-নৌকা বা জাহাজ। **Twin-born**—যমজ। **Twinflower** — একপ্রকার চির হরিৎ লতা, যুগ্মপুষ্পী। **Twin-screw**—জাহাজাদি চালাইবার যুগ্ম পেঁচ যন্ত্র। **The Twins**—মিথুন রাশি।

twine, *n., v. t.* & *i.* 1. A strong thread composed of smaller threads or strands twisted together ; সুতলী, ডোর। 2. The act of winding round ; বেষ্টন। 3. (*Obs.*) A twist ; coil ; পাক, মোচড় ; কুণ্ডলী। ***Verb t.*** 1. To twist ; to form by twisting ; পাকান ; পাকাইয়া তৈয়ার করা। 2. To encircle ; to embrace ; বলয়িত করা, বেষ্টিত করা ; জড়াইয়া ধরা। ***Verb i.*** To wind ; to coil ; to bend ; পাকান ; কুণ্ডলিত হওয়া ; বাঁকিয়া যাওয়া। **Twin'-er,** *n.* One that twines ; a plant that twines ; বেষ্টনকারী ; যে ক্ষুপ লতাইয়া উঠে। **Twin'-ing-ly,** *adv.* **Twine cutter**—বস্তা বাঁধিবার কালে সুতলী কাটার জন্য একপ্রকার ছুরি। **Twinning-machine, Twinning-saw**—চিরুণীর দাঁত প্রভৃতি কাটার জন্য একপ্রকার যন্ত্র।

twinge (twinj), *v. t., i.* & *n.* To affect with a sharp sudden pain ; টন্‌টনে ব্যথা জন্মান। ***Verb i.*** To have a sharp local pain like a twitch ; টন্‌টনে ব্যথা করা, বেদনায় কট্‌কট্ করা। ***Noun.*** A sharp darting pain ; টন্‌টনে ব্যথা, কট্‌কটে ব্যথা, ফিক্‌ফিক্ বেদনা।

twin'-kle (tging-kl), *v. i., t.* & *n.* 1. To open and shut the eyes quickly ; চোখ মিটমিট করা, টিম্‌টিম্ করা, পিট্‌পিট্ করা। 2. To sparkle ; "The green blade that *twinkles* in the sun" ; ঝকমক করা, ঝলমল করা, ঝিকমিক করা, ঝিলমিল করা। ***Verb t.*** 1. To cause to twinkle ; মিটমিট করান। 2. To discharge in quick and intermittent gleams ; ঝকমক করান। ***Noun.*** 1. Twitching of eyelid ; a wink ; চক্ষুর মিটমিটানি, পিটপিটানি ; নিমেষ, পলক। 2. Glimmer ; ঝিকমিক, ঝক্‌মক্, চকমক।

twink'-ling (twing-), *n.* 1. Act of one that twinkles ; a wink ; চক্ষু মিটমিট করণ ; চক্ষুর পলক, নিমেষ। 2. A glimmer ; ঝিকমিক, ঝকমক। 3. The time occupied by a single wink ; as, in the *twinkling* of an eye ; নিমেষকাল।

twirl, (twërl) *v. t., i.* & *n.* To whirl round with great velocity ; to whirl round with finger ; to twiddle ; অতি দ্রুত ঘূর্ণিত করা, বনবন করিয়া ঘুরান, পাক দেওয়া ; অঙ্গুলী দ্বারা দ্রুত ঘূর্ণিত করা ; বৃদ্ধাঙ্গুলি ঘূর্ণিত করা। ***Verb i.*** To revolve or rotate rapidly ; দ্রুত ঘূর্ণিত হওয়া। ***Noun.*** 1. A rapid circular motion ; দ্রুত ঘূর্ণন, পাক। 2. A coil ; কুণ্ডলী। 3. A flourish or curl made with a pen ; কলমের টানটোন। 4. A device for twirling ; দ্রুত ঘূর্ণনের জন্য যন্ত্রবিশেষ।

twist, *n., v.t.* & *i.* 1. A convolution ; গ্রন্থি, পাক, পেঁচ, মোচড়। 2. A cord ; মোটা সূতা। 3. A kind of cotton yarn of many varieties ; একপ্রকার সূতা। 4. Tobacco rolled in the form of a thick cord ; রজ্জুর আকারে গুটানো তাম্রকূটপত্র। 5. A small roll of twisted dough baked ; গুটানো খমীরের ক্ষুদ্র সেঁকা টুকরা। 6. A sharp pang ; কট্‌কটে ব্যথা। 7. The spiral course of the rifling of a barrel ; বন্দুকের নালীর কুণ্ডলীবৎ কাটা খাঁজ। 8. (*Slang*) Appetite ; as, he had a tremendons *twist* ; (ইতরভাষায়) ক্ষুধা। 9. Kinds of mixed drink ; বিভিন্ন প্রকার মিশ্রপানীয়। ***Verb t.*** 1. To form as by twining or winding separate threads, filaments, etc. ; as, to *twist* cotton ; পাকান। 2. To contort ; পাকান, মোচড়ান, পেঁচান। 3. To encircle ; বলয়িত করা, বেষ্টিত করা, জড়ান। 4. To pervert the meaning of ; as, to *twist* a passage ; বিকৃত অর্থ করা, কদর্থ করা। 5. To insinuate ; ইঙ্গিত করা, আভাস দেওয়া বা আরোপ করা। 6. To cause to turn from a straight line ; as, to *twist* a ball in cricket ; সরল রেখা

হইতে বিচ্যুত করা। *Verb i.* 1. To be united by twisting; পাকাইয়া একত্র হওয়া। 2. To writhe or coil; কুণ্ডলিত হওয়া, কুণ্ডলী পাকান। 3. To have winding course; আঁকিয়া বাঁকিয়া যাওয়া। **Twist'-a-ble,** *adj.* **To twist round one's finger**—To do as another wishes; অন্যের ইচ্ছার বশবর্ত্তী হইয়া চলা।

twist'-ĕr, *n.* 1. One that twists; যাহা পাক দেয় বা মোচড়ায়। 2. A twisting ball; হাত মোচড়াইয়া যে বল করা হয়। 3. The inner part of the thigh of a rider; অশ্বারোহীর উরুর ভিতরের অংশ। 4. A reel used in twisting yarns or threads; এক-প্রকার চরকী। 5. (*Carp.*) A girder; (তক্ষণবিদ্যা) সাতীর।

twit *v. t.* To reproach as, to *twit*; an offender; to taunt; তিরস্কার করা, ভৎর্সনা করা, গঞ্জনা করা; বিদ্রূপ করা। **Twit'-ting-ly,** *adv.*

twitch (twĭch), *v. t., i. & n.* To pull with a sudden jerk; to snatch; হেঁচকাইয়া টানা; ছিনাইয়া নেওয়া, কাড়িয়া নেওয়া। *Verb i.* To be suddenly contracted, as a muscle; স্পন্দিত হওয়া। *Noun.* 1. A short sudden quick pull; হেঁচকা টান। 2. A short spasmodic contraction of the fibres of muscles; as, *twitch* of the eyes; স্পন্দন।

twitch (twĭch), *n.* Same as QUITCH.

twite, *n.* A kind of linnet; এক-প্রকার পক্ষী।

twit'-ter (-ĕr), *v. i., t. & n.* 1. To chirp; as, birds are *twittering* among the branches; কিচির মিচির করা, কলরব করা। 2. To giggle; ফিক ফিক করিয়া হাসা। 3. To have tremulous motion of the nerve; to be agitated; স্পন্দিত হওয়া; চঞ্চল হইয়া উঠা। 4. To utter in tremulous intermittent notes; কিচিরমিচির করিয়া উঠা। *Verb t.* To utter with a twitter; কিচির মিচির করা। *Noun.* 1. A series of chirping sounds; কিচিরমিচির। 2. Agitation; উত্তেজিত অবস্থা, চাঞ্চল্য। **—a'-tion,** *n.*

twit'-twăt, *n.* House-sparrow; চড়ুই, চটকপক্ষী।

twixt, *prep.* Contraction of BETWIXT.

two (tû), *adj. & n.* One more than one; দ্বি, দুই। *Noun.* 1. The number two; দুই সংখ্যা। 2. A card with two spots; তাসের দুরি। 3. A pair; জোড়া, মিথুন। 4. Short for two O'clock; দুইটা। **Two'-ness,** *n.* **Two-cleft**—প্রায় মধ্যদেশে দুই ভাগে বিভক্ত। **Two-decker**—যে রণপোতের উভয় পাটাতনে কামান স্থাপিত থাকে। **Two-edged**—দুইদিকে ধারবিশিষ্ট, যমধার, দ্বিধার। **Two-faced**—দ্বিমুখ; কপট, দ্বিজিহ্ব, অসরল। **Twofold**—দ্বিগুণ, দ্বিগুণিত, দোহারা, দুইফের। **Two-handed**—দ্বিকর; শক্ত; শক্তিশালী; উভয় হস্ত সমভাবে চালাইতে সমর্থ, সব্যসাচী; উভয় হস্ত দ্বারা ব্যবহার্য্য। **Two-line**—(মুদ্রণ) নির্দ্দিষ্ট আয়তনের হরফ অপেক্ষা দ্বিগুণ পুরু (cf. *two-line pica*). **Twopence**—(Pron. *tŭpns*) দুই পেন্স। **Twopenny**—(Pron. *tŭpeni*), *adj.* দুই পেন্স মূল্যের; অল্প মূল্যের, অকিঞ্চিৎকর। (*Noun*) যে বীয়র মদ্য প্রতি কোয়ার্ট দুই পেন্স হিসাবে বিক্রীত হয়। **Two-ply**—দুই গুণের, দুই স্তরের, দ্বিগুণ পুরু। **Two-power standard**—রাজনৈতিক মত বিশেষ (এই মতানুসারে ইংলণ্ডীয় নৌবল অপর যে কোন শক্তিদ্বয়ের সম্মিলিত নৌবল অপেক্ষা ন্যূন হইবে না।) **Two-speed**—দুইপ্রকার গতি-বিশিষ্ট। **Two-tongued**—দ্বিজিহ্ব, কপট। **Two-way**—নালীদ্বয়ের মধ্যে অন্যতর নালীতে তরল পদার্থ প্রবাহণ-কারী; (গণিত) দ্বিরূপ। **In two**—In two parts; দ্বিখণ্ডে। **In two two's**—Immediately; তৎক্ষণাৎ। **To make two bites at a cherry**—See CHERRY. **To make two bites of a cherry**—See CHERRY. **To put or lay two and two together**—To argue logically; ন্যায়শাস্ত্রের নিয়মানুগত ভাবে তর্ক করা। **To want two pence in the shilling**—To be weak in intellect; ক্ষীণবুদ্ধি হওয়া। **Two and a half**—আড়াই। **Two can play at the game**—The other man can also take revenge in like manner; অপর ব্যক্তিও এইরূপভাবে প্রতিশোধ নিতে পারে। **Two of a trade**—A rival; প্রতিদ্বন্দ্বী। **Two upon ten**—Keep an eye on him, otherwise he will flee away with something; তাহার উপর নজর রাখিও, নতুবা সে কোন জিনিষ চুরি করিয়া পালাইবে।

two'-some (tû-sŭm), *adj. & n.* For two persons; দুই ব্যক্তির জন্য। *Noun.* A game or dance for two persons; দুই ব্যক্তির উপযোগী ক্রীড়া বা নৃত্য।

'twould (twûd), Contraction of *It would.*

twȳ'-ĕr, *n.* Same as TUYERE.

Tȳ'-burn (-bĕrn), *n.* (*Hist.*) A place of execution in London; (ইতিহাস) লণ্ডন নগরীস্থ বধ্যভূমি। **Tyburn ticket**—যে টিকিট দ্বারা মৃত্যুদণ্ডের যোগ্য অপরাধকারিগণের অভিযোক্তা যাজকপল্লীর কার্য্য হইতে রেহাই প্রাপ্ত হইত। **Tyburn tippet**—ফাঁসীর রজ্জু। **Tyburn tree**—ফাঁসীকাঠ।

tȳ'-chism, *n.* A theory of evolution which considers that variations may be purely fortuitious; বিবর্ত্তনবাদের প্রকারবিশেষ—যাহাতে বৈচিত্র্য শুদ্ধ আকস্মিক বলিয়া বিবেচিত হয়, আকস্মিকত্ববাদ (হিঃ কোঃ)।

Tȳ-chŏn'-ic, *adj.* Of the Danish astronomer Tycho Brahe or his system; ডেনমার্ক দেশীয় জ্যোতির্ব্বিদ Tycho Brahe—অথবা তৎপ্রবর্ত্তিত প্রণালীসম্বন্ধীয়। [এই সুপ্রসিদ্ধ জ্যোতির্ব্বিৎ ১৫৪৬ খৃঃঅব্দে ডেনমার্ক দেশে জন্মগ্রহণ করেন। শৈশব হইতে Tycho Brahe-র জ্যোতিষশাস্ত্রের প্রতি বিশেষ অনুরাগ ছিল। কালে তিনি তদানীন্তন ইয়ুরোপের

একজন শ্রেষ্ঠ জ্যোতির্বিবিদ্‌রূপে প্রসিদ্ধি লাভ করেন। ডেনমার্কের রাজা দ্বিতীয় ফ্রেডারিক ইঁহাকে Stellberg (নক্ষত্র-নগরী) নামক একটী সুবৃহৎ মানমন্দির নির্ম্মাণ করিয়া দেন। Tycho Brahe র বাসের জন্য Hven দ্বীপে Uraniberg (অমরাপুরী) নামক এক বিশাল জ্যোতিষিক সৌধ নির্ম্মিত হয়। এই নির্জ্জন দ্বীপে Tycho Brahe একনিষ্ঠ সাধকের মত জ্যোতিঃশাস্ত্রের অনুশীলন করিতেন। ১৬০১ খৃঃঅব্দে Tycho Brahe মানবলীলা সম্বরণ করেন।]

tȳ-coon′, *n.* A title assumed by the shogun, or generalissimo of Japan, between 1854 and 1868, in order to impress the ambassador of the Western Powers with the belief that he was real ruler of the country ; জাপানের প্রধান সেনাপতির উপাধি বিশেষ।

tȳ′-ing, *n.* Same as TIE.

tȳke, *n.* Same as TIKE (which see).

tȳ-lŏp′-ō-dă, *n.* (*pl.*) A group of ruminant including the camels ; উষ্ট্রাদিবর্গ। **—dous**, *adj.*

tȳ-lō′-sis, *n.* An inflammation of the eyelids ; চক্ষুর পক্ষ্মের প্রদাহ, পক্ষ্মপ্রদাহ। 2. A callosity ; কড়। 3. (*Bot.*) A growth into a duct from a neighbouring growing cell; (উদ্ভিদ্‌বিদ্যা) নলান্তককলা (সাঃ পঃ)। **—lot′-ic**, *adj.*

tȳ′-lōte, *n.* A cylindrical sponge spicule knobbed at each end ; উভয় প্রান্তে টোপওয়ালা নলাকার শোষক-কণা।

tȳm′-băl, *n.* A kind of kettle-drum ; একপ্রকার ডঙ্কা।

tȳmp, *n.* 1. A horizontal roof-timber in a mine ; খনির ছাদের উপর বিন্যস্ত শয়ান কাষ্ঠফলক। 2. A space in the bottom of a blast-furnace, adjoining the crucible ; বাত্যাসহায় চুল্লীর নীচে মূচির সংলগ্ন স্থান।

tȳm′-păn, *n.* 1. An ancient Irish musical instrument ; আয়র্লণ্ড দেশীয় প্রাচীন বাদ্যযন্ত্রবিশেষ। 2. A stretched sheet of membrane or thin material ; প্রসারিত ঝিল্লী বা অন্য কোনরূপ পদার্থ। 3. A frame covered with parchment or cloth, on which the blank sheets are put, in order to be laid on the form to be impressed ; মুদ্রাযন্ত্রের ডালা। 4. (*Anat.*) Same as TYMPANUM. 5. (*Archit.*) Same as TYMPANUM.

tȳm-păn′-ic, *adj.* 1. Like a drunkard ; acting like a drunkard ; মাতালবৎ ; মাতালের মত কার্য্যকারী। 2. (*Anat.*) Pertaining to the tympanum ; কর্ণপটহসম্বন্ধীয়। **Tympanic membrane** — কর্ণপটহ (সাঃ পঃ)।

tȳm-pă-nī′-tēs, *n.* An elastic distension of the abdomen ; অন্ত্রে-বায়ু বা বাষ্পসঞ্চয় বশতঃ উদরে ঢাকের ন্যায় স্ফীতি, উদরাধ্মান, পেটফাঁপা, অলসক [কুক্ষিরানহ্যতেঽত্যর্থং প্রতাম্যেৎ পরিকূজতি। নিরুদ্ধো মারুতশ্চৈব কুক্ষাবুপরিধাবতি। বাতবর্চ্চোনিরোধশ্চ যস্যাত্যর্থং ভবেদপি। তস্যালসকমাচষ্টে তৃষ্ণোদ্গারৌ তু যস্য চ। তন্ত্রান্তরে—প্রযাতি নোর্দ্ধং নাধস্তাদাহারো ন চ পচ্যতে। অমাশয়েঽলসীভূতস্তেন সোঽলসকঃ স্মৃতঃ — শব্দকল্পদ্রুমঃ।] **—nit′-ic**, *adj.*

tȳm-pă-nī′-tis, *n.* An inflammation of the lining membrane of the tympanum ; কর্ণপটহের প্রদাহ, কর্ণপটহ প্রদাহ।

tȳm′-pă-nŭm, *n.* 1. (*Anat.*) A drum or frame-work covered with some tense material ; পটহ। 2. (*Anat.*) The middle or hollow portion of the ear ; মধ্যকর্ণের ঢাকের ন্যায় গহ্বর, কর্ণশষ্কুলী (ব্রজঃ বিঃ)। 3. (*Archit.*) The triangular space forming the main area of a pediment ; দ্বার, বাতায়ন প্রভৃতির উপরিস্থ ত্রিভুজাকৃতি স্থান। 4. (*Archit.*) The space between the top of a door and the arch enclosing it ; দ্বারের উপরিভাগ এবং তদূর্দ্ধস্থ তোরণের মধ্যবর্ত্তী স্থান। 5. A kind of tread-wheel ; একপ্রকার পাদচালনীয় চক্র। 6. A large wheel for lifting water from a stream ; নদী হইতে জল তুলিবার জন্য বৃহৎ চক্র।

Tȳne′-wăld, *n.* A legislative body of the Isle of Man ; ম্যানদ্বীপের ব্যবস্থাপক সভা।

tȳpe, *n.* 1. A distinguishing mark, stamp or sign ; পরিচায়ক চিহ্ন, মুদ্রা প্রভৃতির চিহ্ন, নিদর্শন, লিঙ্গ, ছাপ। 2. A symbol ; "A *type* is no longer a *type* when the thing typified comes to be actually exhibited"; মূর্ত্তি, প্রতীক। 3. Model ; আদর্শ, প্রতিরূপ। 4. A rectangular piece of metal, wood or other hard material having a raised letter, figure or character on the upper end, which when linked, is used to make impressions on paper and other smooth surfaces ; হরফ, মুদ্রাক্ষর, মুদ্রা (cf. লেখন্যা লিখিতং বিপ্রৈর্মুদ্রাভিরঙ্কিতঞ্চ যৎ শিল্পাদিনির্ম্মিতং যচ্চ পাঠ্যং ধার্য্যঞ্চ সর্ব্বদা — খড়্গমালা-তন্ত্র।) 5. A person, thing or event serving as an illustration ; উদাহরণস্বরূপ ব্যক্তি, বস্তু বা ঘটনা। 6. An example or specimen of any class which is considered as eminently possessing or exhibiting the properties or character of the class ; "*Type* necessarily resolves itself into a question of averages ; individuals possessing most of the characters peculiar to a group are said to be typical members of that group, and even this only in a relative sense" ; কোন শ্রেণীর যে দৃষ্টান্ত বা আদর্শে উক্ত শ্রেণীর গুণ বা ধর্ম্ম মুখ্যভাবে আছে বলিয়া গণ্য করা হয়, জাতিরূপ (হিঃ কোঃ), সামান্যরূপ (ঐ)। 7. (*Zool.*) A group of animals having a certain type or structure ; কোনরূপ নির্দ্দিষ্টপ্রকার

Type of the letter M.

জাতিরূপ গঠনবিশিষ্ট জন্তুবর্গ। 8. (*Chem.*) A system used for indicating the structure of compound bodies, which were regarded as derived from several inorganic bodies by the introduction of various radicals; (রসায়ন) যৌগিক পদার্থের গঠন সূচনার জন্য ব্যবহৃত পদ্ধতি। 9. The order in which the symptoms of a disease exhibit themselves and succeed each other; রোগলক্ষণ সমূহের পারম্পর্য্য। 10. The pattern or design on either side of a medal or coin; মুদ্রা বা পদকের প্রত্যেক দিকে মুদ্রিত চিত্র, নমুনা প্রভৃতি। 11. (*Fine arts*) The original object which becomes the subject of a copy; (ললিতকলা) মূল আদর্শ। **Typ′-ist**, *n.* One who uses a type-writer; মুদ্রাক্ষরলেখক। **Type-bar**—যে দণ্ডে মুদ্রাক্ষরযন্ত্রের অক্ষরমালা নিবদ্ধ থাকে। **Type-casting**—অক্ষর ঢালন। **Type foundry** — অক্ষর ঢালাইয়ের কারখানা। **Type-high**—মুদ্রণের পক্ষে উপযোগী উচ্চ (চিত্রফলক, প্রভৃতি)। **Type-metal**—মুদ্রণের হরফ প্রস্তুতের জন্য সীসকের সহিত বরনাগ (antimony), রঙ্গ, প্রভৃতির মিশ্রণে প্রস্তুত ধাতু, মুদ্রাক্ষর ধাতু। **Type-write**—মুদ্রাক্ষরযন্ত্র দ্বারা লিখা। **Type-writer**—একপ্রকার যন্ত্র—যদ্দ্বারা ছাপার মত লিখা হয়, মুদ্রাক্ষর-যন্ত্র। **Type-writing**—মুদ্রাক্ষরযন্ত্রদ্বারা লিখন।

Type-writer.

tȳpe, *v. t.* 1. To type-write; মুদ্রাক্ষর যন্ত্রদ্বারা লিখা। 2. To be a type of; আদর্শস্বরূপ হওয়া।

Typha elephantina — হোগলা (বেলঃ)।

tȳph-lī′-tis, *n.* Inflammation of the blind end of the large bowel; অন্ধান্ত্রের প্রদাহ।

Tȳph-lŏp′-ĭ-dae (-dē), *n.* (*pl.*) A widely distributed family of small burrowing snakes; দুমুখো সাপ (মিউজিয়াম)।

tȳ′-phoid (-fŏyd), *adj.* & *n.* Pertaining to enteric fever; like typhus; সান্নিপাতিক; সান্নিপাতিকজ্বরবৎ। *Noun.* Same as TYPHOID FEVER. **—al**, *adj.* **Typhoid condition**—সান্নিপাতিক জ্বরের অবস্থা। **Typhoid fever**—সান্নিপাতিক জ্বরবিকার, অতিশয় অবসন্নতা ও মস্তিষ্কের উপদ্রবাদি সহকৃত সান্নিপাতিক লক্ষণ, বিকার লক্ষণ, বাত-সন্নিপাত।

tȳ-phō-mā′-nĭ-ă, *n.* A low muttering delirium in acute cases of typhoid fever; প্রবল বাতসন্নিপাত জ্বরের অনুচ্চ প্রলাপের অবস্থা।

tȳ-phō′-nĭ-ă, *n.* A kind of sleepless stupor with or without typhomania; প্রলাপ সহকৃত বা প্রলাপাদিসহ, একপ্রকার মোহজনক অবস্থা।

tȳ-phoon′, *n.* A violent hurricane which rages on the coast of China and Japan from May to November; চীন ও জাপানের উপকূলে মে হইতে নভেম্বর পর্য্যন্ত যে প্রবল ঝঞ্ঝাবাত প্রবাহিত হয়, ঝঞ্ঝানিল (সাঃ পঃ), তুফান (ঐ)। **—phon′-ic**, *adj.*

tȳ′-phŭs, *n.* A contagious and dangerous fever caused by a peculiar bacillus, the infection being largely carried by house-flies; একপ্রকার স্পর্শসংক্রামক উৎকট অবিরাম জ্বর, মোহক সন্নিপাতজ্বর।

tȳp′-ĭ-căl, *adj.* 1. Serving as a type or characteristic example; "The Levitical priesthood was only *typical* of the Christian"; আদর্শীভূত। 2. Symbolical; figurative; সাঙ্কেতিক সূচক (হিঃ কোঃ), লাক্ষণিক (ঐ), ব্যঞ্জক (ঐ); রূপক। 3. Embodying the characteristic of a group; কোনও জন্তুশ্রেণীর বিশেষত্বসূচক, সাদৃশ্যজ্ঞাপক। **—ly**, *adv.* **—ness**, *n.*

tȳp′-ĭ-fȳ, *v. t.* To represent by an image, form, model or resemblance; to prefigure; to show in emblem; "Our Saviour was *typified* indeed by the goat that was slain"; আদর্শ দ্বারা জ্ঞাপন করা, দ্যোতনা করা, সাদৃশ্য দ্বারা জ্ঞাপন করা; পূর্ব্বে ছায়াপাত করা, পুর্ব্বাভাস দেওয়া; চিহ্ন দ্বারা প্রদর্শন করা। **—fi-ca′-tion**, *n.* **—fi-er**, *n.*

tȳ′-pō, *n.* (*Colloq.*) Same as TYPOGRAPHER.

tȳ-pō′-grăph, *n.* A type-making and type-setting machine; অক্ষর প্রস্তুত করার ও বসাইবার জন্য যন্ত্রবিশেষ।

tȳ-pŏg′-ră-phĕr, *n.* A printer; মুদ্রাকর। **—po-graph′-ic**, *adj.*

Tȳ′-pŏg′-ră-phȳ, *n.* 1. The act of printing; মুদ্রণশিল্প। 2. Style of printing; মুদ্রণরীতি।

tȳp′-ō-līte, *n.* A stone or fossil bearing the impression of a plant or animal; বৃক্ষ বা জন্তুর প্রতিকৃতি মুদ্রিত শিলা বা শিলীভূত জন্তু।

tȳ-pŏl′-ō-ḡȳ, *n.* 1. A discourse on types, esp. those of Scripture; specif. the doctrine that things in the Christian dispensation are symbolised or prefigured by things in the Old Testament; দ্যোতনতত্ত্ব; বিশেষতঃ নবনিয়মগ্রন্থোক্ত বিষয় সমূহের সূচনা বা পূর্ব্বাভাস প্রাচীন নিয়মে রহিয়াছে—এই মতবাদ। 2. A treatise on scriptural types; দ্যোতনতত্ত্ব সম্বন্ধীয় গ্রন্থ। 3. An interpretation of scriptural types; বাইবেল গ্রন্থের দ্যোতনা সমূহের ব্যাখ্যা। **—po-log′-i-cal**, *adj.*

tȳ′-pō-nȳm, *n.* (*Biol.*) A name based on a type; জাতিরূপমূলক নাম। **—pon′-y-mal**, **—nym′-ic**, *adjs.*

tȳp-tŏl′-ō-ḡȳ, *n.* The spirit-rapping; আত্মিকগণের পরলোকগত আত্মা মেজ প্রভৃতির ঠক্ ঠক্ শব্দ উৎপাদন করিয়া থাকে—এই মত। **—gist**, *n.* **—to-log′-i-cal**, *adj.*

tȳ-răn′-nic (-ĭc), **–ni-căl** (-ĭ-), **tȳr′-ăn-nous** (-ŭs), *adjs.* **1.** Despotic ; যথেচ্ছাচারী, প্রজাপীড়ক, যথেচ্ছাচারমূলক। **2.** Oppressive ; অত্যাচারী, পীড়নকারী। **–ni-cal-ly,** *adv.* **–ni-cal-ness,** *n.* **–nous-ly,** *adv.*

tȳ-răn′-ni-cīde (-ĭ-), *n.* **1.** One who kills a tyrant ; প্রজাপীড়ক হন্তা। **2.** The killing of a tyrant ; প্রজাপীড়ক হত্যা।

tȳr′-ăn-nize (-īze), *v. t.* To rule with despotic authorty or with oppressive severity ; প্রজাপীড়ন করা, যথেচ্ছাচার করা, অত্যাচার করা।

tȳr′-ăn-ny (-ĭ-), *n.* **1.** Arbitrary exercise of power ; যথেচ্ছাচার, প্রজাপীড়ন। **2.** Tyrannical act or behaviour ; অত্যাচার, পীড়ন। **3.** Severity ; inclemency ; "The *tyranny* of the open night's too rough For nature to endure" ; কঠোরতা ; নিদারুণতা। **4.** The government or authority of a tyrant ; the office or the period of rule of a tyrant ; প্রজাপীড়ন-তন্ত্র, যথেচ্ছাচার তন্ত্র ; প্রজাপীড়কের পদ বা অধিকার কাল।

tȳ′-rănt, *n.* **1.** An oppressive or cruel ruler ; অত্যাচারী শাসক। **2.** A despot ; যথেচ্ছাচারী রাজা, যথেচ্ছাচারী শাসনকর্তা। **3.** A cruel master ; নির্দ্দয় প্রভু। **4.** An oppressor ; অত্যাচারী, নির্যাতনকারী, পীড়নকারী। **5.** (In Ancient Greece) A man, who, with the help of discontented people overthrew the existing authority and possessed himself of the government ; "That *tyrant* was Miltiades" ; (প্রাচীন গ্রীসে) যে ব্যক্তি অসন্তুষ্ট লোকদিগের সাহায্যে প্রচলিত শাসনতন্ত্রের উচ্ছেদ সাধনপূর্ব্বক দেশের অধিনায়ক হইত। **Thirty-Tyrants**—যে ত্রিশ জন যথেচ্ছাচারী শাসনকর্ত্তা খৃঃ পূঃ ৪০৪—৪০৩ এথেন্স নগরী শাসন করিয়াছিলেন। **Tyrant-bird, Tyrant-fly-catcher** — আমেরিকা-দেশীয় বিভিন্ন প্রকার পক্ষীর নাম।

tȳre, *n.* A preparation of milk and rice in India ; একপ্রকার পায়সান্ন।

tȳre, *n.* See TIRE.

Tȳr′-ĭ-ăn, *adj.* **1.** Obtained at Tyre ; Tyre নগরীতে লভ্য। **2.** Being of a purple colour ; নীলারুণবর্ণ। **Tyrian alphabet**—টিরিয়ান বর্ণমালা। **Tyrian-dye**—একপ্রকার উৎকৃষ্ট নীলারুণবর্ণ রঞ্জক পদার্থ। ইহা পূর্ব্বে Tyre নগরীতে একপ্রকার শম্বুক হইতে প্রাপ্ত হওয়া যাইত।

tȳ′-rō, *n.* A beginner in learning ; a person imperfectly acquainted with a subject ; প্রথম শিক্ষার্থী, নবশিক্ষার্থী ; কোন বিষয়ে সামান্য মাত্র অভিজ্ঞ ব্যক্তি, অল্পাভিজ্ঞ ব্যক্তি।

Tȳr-ō-lese′ (-lēz *or* tĭr-), (*Pl.* same), *adj.* & *n.* Of Tyrol ; অষ্ট্রিয়ার দক্ষিণসীমান্তবর্ত্তী টাইরল প্রদেশ সম্বন্ধীয়। ***Noun.*** A native of Tyrol ; উক্ত প্রদেশের অধিবাসী।

Tyrolienne, *n.* **1.** A dance of Tyrolese peasants ; টাইরল প্রদেশের কৃষকদিগের একপ্রকার নৃত্য। **2.** A music suitable for this ; ঐ নৃত্যের উপযোগী গান।

tȳr-ō-tŏx′-ĭ-cŏn, *n.* A ptomaine in milk or cheese ; দুগ্ধ বা পনীরে প্রাপ্ত একপ্রকার বিষাক্ত পদার্থ।

Tȳr′-rhene (-ēn), **Tȳr-rhe′-ni-ăn** (-ē-), *adjs.* Same as ETRUSCAN (which see.)

tzar (tsâr), *n.* Same as CZAR.

tza-ri′-nă (tsâ-rē-), *n.* Same as CZARINA.

tzĕ′-tzĕ, *n.* Same as TSETSE (which see.)

Tzi′-gă-nȳ, *adj.* & *n.* Of the Hungarian gipsies or their music ; হাঙ্গারী প্রদেশের যাযাবর জাতি বা উক্ত জাতির গীতবাদ্যসম্বন্ধীয়। ***Noun.*** Hungarian gipsies ; হাঙ্গারী প্রদেশবাসী যাযাবর জাতি।

U

U, is the fifth vowel and the twenty-first letter of the English alphabet ; ইংরাজী বর্ণমালার একবিংশতিতম অক্ষর। **U-bolt**—ইংরেজী U অক্ষরের আকৃতি বিশিষ্ট কণ্টক। **U-tube**—ইংরাজী U অক্ষরের আকৃতি নল, ইউনলিকা (হিঃ কোঃ)।

ū′-bĕr-tȳ, *n.* Abundance ; fruitfulness ; প্রাচুর্য্য, বাহুল্য, অজস্রতা ; ফলবত্তা।

ū-bĭ-că′-tion, *n.* Same as UBIETY (below).

ū-bī′-ĕ-tȳ, *n.* (*Philos.*) The presence of one thing with reference to another ; the presence of a thing in place ; (দর্শনশাস্ত্র) এক বস্তু সম্পর্কে অপর বস্তুর অবস্থিতি, স্থাননির্দ্দেশ ; কোন বস্তুর যথাস্থানে অবস্থিতি, যথাবস্থিতি, স্বস্থানস্থিতি।

ū-biq-ui-tā′-rĭ-ăn (-bĭk-wĭ-), *adj.* & *n.* **1.** (*Theol.*) Of the omnipresence of Christ's body ; (খৃষ্টীয় ধর্ম্মশাস্ত্র) যীশুখৃষ্টের দেহের সর্ব্বব্যাপিত্ব সম্বন্ধীয়। **2.** Omnipresent ; সর্ব্বব্যাপী। ***Noun.*** A believer in the omnipresence of Christ's body ; যীশুখৃষ্টের দেহের সর্ব্বব্যাপিত্বে বিশ্বাসী ব্যক্তি। **–ism,** *n.*

ū-biq′-ui-tă-rȳ (-bĭk-wĭ-), *adj.* & *n.* **1.** Existing everywhere ; "For wealth and *ubiquitary* commerce none can excel her"; সর্ব্বত্র অবস্থিত। ***Noun.*** One who exists everywhere ; সর্ব্বত্র অবস্থানকারী, সর্ব্বগতী।

ū-biq′-ui-tous (-bĭk-wĭ-tŭs), *adj.* Existing everywhere ; বিশ্বব্যাপী, বিশ্বব্যাপক, সর্ব্বব্যাপী, সর্ব্বগত, বিশ্বাতিথি, সর্ব্বত্রবায়ী, ব্যাপক (ব্রজঃ-হিন্দু), সর্ব্বত্রগ। **—ly,** *adv.* **—ness,** *n.* **—ty,** *n.* The state of being ubiquitous ; বিশ্বব্যাপিত্ব, বিশ্বব্যাপকতা, সর্ব্বগতত্ব, সর্ব্বত্রচারিতা, ব্যাপকতা, বিভুত্ব, ত্রিলোক্যবিস্তার, সর্ব্বত্রতা (হিঃ কোঃ)।

ubi supra, *adv.* In the place of books etc. above mentioned ; উপরিলিখিত পুস্তক প্রভৃতির নির্দ্দিষ্ট স্থানে।

ū′-dăl, *n.* Same as ALLODIUM (which see).

ŭd′-der (-ėr), *n.* The glandular organ of cows etc. in which the milk is produced ; গবাদির পালান, বাঁট, উধ্ন, আপীন। **—less,** *adj.*

ū-dŏm′-ĕ-tėr, *n.* Same as RAIN-GAUGE. **—do-met′-ric,** *adj.*

ugh (ŭ), *int.* **1.** An exclamation expressive of horror, disgust, etc. ; ঘৃণা, বিরক্তি, বিভীষিকা, প্রভৃতি সূচক অব্যয়, উঃ, হিঃ, ছি।

ŭg′-lȳ, *adj.* & *n.* **1.** Unpleasing to the sight ; as, an *ugly* person ; কুৎসিত, কদাকার, কুশ্রী, কুরূপ, কদর্য্য। **2.** Hateful ; ঘৃণিত, ঘৃণ্য। **3.** Hideous ; repulsive ; "Like the toad *ugly* and venomous" ; বীভৎস ; বিকট। **4.** Ill natured ; quarrelsome; "I will not answer her when she's *ugly* to me" ; দুঃশীল; কলহপ্রিয়। **5.** Unpleasant ; as, an *ugly* customer ; অপ্রীতিকর। **6.** Threatening ; as, *ugly* weather ; unpromising ; ভয়প্রদ, ভীষণ ; অনাশাপ্রদ। ***Noun.*** A kind of shade worn by ladies about the middle of nineteenth century in front of their bonnets to protect their faces from the sun ; উনবিংশতি শতাব্দীর মধ্যভাগে রৌদ্র হইতে মুখরক্ষার জন্য মহিলাগণকর্ত্তৃক টুপির সম্মুখভাগে পরিহিত একপ্রকার আচ্ছাদনী। **—li-fy,** *v. t.* **—li-ly** *adv.* **—li-ness,** *n.* The state of being ugly ; বৈরূপ্য, কুরূপতা, কদাকারতা। **Ugly-looking —** কদাকার। **An ugly customer—**যে লোকের সহিত কাজ কারবার করা অত্যন্ত মুস্কিল। **An ugly duckling—**যে জিনিষ প্রথমতঃ কদাকার বলিয়া প্রত্যাখাত হয়, পরন্তু পরে আদরণীয় হইয়া থাকে, পোড়া কাঠ (অরক্ষণীয়া-শরৎ চট্টোঃ)। **As ugly as sin—** Very ugly ; অত্যন্ত বিশ্রী, বিদিকিচ্ছে (*colloq.*), বিদঘুটে, ছুম্‌মন।

U′-grĭ-ăn (ô-), **—grĭc,** *adjs.* Finnic ; ফিনলণ্ডের অধিবাসিসম্বন্ধীয়।

uh′-lăn (ô- *or* ū-), *n.* A light cavalry soldier or lancer of Asiatic origin, introduced first into the Polish service, and now into the Prussian and Russian ; জর্ম্মণ ও অষ্ট্রীয় সৈন্যদলের বর্শাধারী অশ্বারোহী সৈনিক, বিশেষতঃ জর্ম্মণ সৈন্যদলভুক্ত লঘু অস্ত্রধারী অশ্বারোহী সৈনিক।

ū-kase′, *n.* **1.** An edict of the late Russian Government ; ভূতপূর্ব্ব রুশশাসনতন্ত্রের আদেশবাণী। **2.** Any official degree or proclamation ; "If the French book-makers persist in refusing to bet at all until the *ukase* against them is withdrawn, victory will not be long in declaring itself on their side"; শাসনতন্ত্রের আদেশ বা ঘোষণা, শাসনবাণী, আদেশবাণী।

ŭl′-cėr, *n.* **1.** A dangerous or painful sore from which matter flows ; সপূযক্ষত, পূযস্রাবীক্ষত, নালীঘা। **2.** Moral blemish ; নৈতিক দোষ, চরিত্রহীনতা। **—cered, —ous,** *adjs.* **—ous-ly,** *adv.* **—ous-ness,** *n.*

ŭl′-cėr-ate, *v. i.* & *t.* To become ulcerous ; ক্ষতদুষ্ট হওয়া, সপূয ক্ষত হওয়া। ***Verb t.*** To affect with, or as with, an ulcer or ulcers ; ক্ষতদুষ্ট করা, ক্ষত করা। **—a-ble, —a-tive,** *adjs.* **—a′-tion,** *n.* **Ulceration of the scrotum—** বৃষণকচ্ছু। (সাঃ পঃ)।

U-lē-mâ′ (ô-), *n.* The collective name of a certain class of theological jurists in Turkey, who, as is the custom in Mohammedan countries, derive their decision from the Koran and its commentaries ; তুরস্কদেশের স্মার্ত্ত-সংঘ, উলেমা।

ū-lĭg′-ĭ-nōse, *adj.* (*Bot.*) Growing in muddy places ; (উদ্ভিদ্-বিদ্যা) কর্দ্দমাক্ত স্থানে প্রজনিষ্ণু, কর্দ্দমরুহ।

ŭl′-lage (-āj), *n.* (*Comm.*) That quantity which a cask wants of being full ; (বাণিজ্য) এক পিপাতে আর যতটুকু জিনিষ ঢালিলে উহা পূর্ণ হয়।

ŭl′-mĭn, *n.* A dark substance which exudes from the oak, elm, and some other trees ; ওক, এলম্, প্রভৃতি কতিপয় বৃক্ষ হইতে নিঃসৃত একপ্রকার কৃষ্ণবর্ণ পদার্থ। **—mic, —mous,** *adjs.*

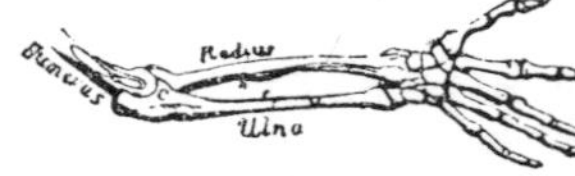

Bones of the forearm and hand.

ŭl′-nă, *n.* The larger of the two bones of the forearm, the other being the radius ; প্রকোষ্ঠের অস্থিদ্বয়ের মধ্যে বৃহত্তর অস্থি, প্রকোষ্ঠাস্থি। **-nar,** *adj.*

ū-lŏt′-rĭ-chăn, —chous (-kŭs), *adjs.* & *ns.* Woolly-haired ; লোমশ। ***Noun.*** A member of the woolly-haired division of mankind; লোমশ জাতির লোক।

ŭl′-stėr, *n.* A long overcoat made of coarse cloth, originally manufactured in Ulster ; একপ্রকার লম্বা কোর্ত্তা, অলষ্টার। [এইরূপ কোর্ত্তা যে কাপড়ে তৈরী হয়—তাহা পূর্ব্বে আয়র্লণ্ডের অন্তঃপাতী Ulster নামক স্থানে প্রস্তুত হইত বলিয়া এই নাম।]

ŭl-tē′-rĭ-ŏr, *adj.* **1.** Situated beyond or on the further side ; অপর

পার্শ্ববর্ত্তী, পরপারস্থ। 2. Remoter; succeeding; in the future or on the background; দূরতর; পরবর্ত্তী; ভবিষ্যদ্‌গর্ভনিহিত, পশ্চাদ্‌বর্ত্তী। 3. Beyond what is seen or avowed; as, some *ulterior* motive; গূঢ়, প্রচ্ছন্ন।

ultima, *adj.* & *n.* Last; most remote; সর্ব্বশেষ; দূরতম। *Noun.* The last syllable of a word; কোন শব্দের শেষ শব্দাংশ। ***Ultima ratio***—শেষ যুক্তি, চরম যুক্তি, শেষ গতি। ***Ultima ratio regum***—সামরিক অস্ত্র ব্যবহার; বল; যুদ্ধ। ***Ultima ratio populi*** — বলপূর্ব্বক বাধা। ***Ultima thule***—See THULE.

ŭl'-tĭ-mate, *adj.* Furthest; most remote; দূরতম; অতিদূরবর্ত্তী। 2. Last; final; শেষ; চরম, পরম, অন্তিম। 3. Incapable of further division or separation; as, the *ultimate* elements of a body; চরম (cf. চরম উপাদান)। 4. Fundamental; primary; as, *ultimate* truths; মৌলিক; আদিম। 5. Maximum; as, *ultimate* strain; অধিকতম। **–ly,** *adv.* **–ness,** *n.* **Ultimate truth**—পরমতত্ত্ব।

ŭl'-tĭ-mā'-tŭm, *n.* 1. A final proposition or condition offered, as the basis of treaty, the rejection of which may lead to rupture of diplomatic relation, war, etc. চরমলিপি, চরমপ্রস্তাব, বিক্রমপ্রদান (কৌটিল্য)। 2. Ultimate conclusion; চরম সিদ্ধান্ত। 3. Fundamental principle; পরমতত্ত্ব, মূলতত্ত্ব।

ultimo, *adv.* In the month preceding the present; গত মাসের।

ŭl-tĭ-mŏ-ğĕn'-ĭ-tūre, *n.* A system in which the youngest son takes inheritance (opposed to *primogeniture*); যে ব্যবস্থা অনুসারে কনিষ্ঠ পুত্র উত্তরাধিকারসূত্রে সম্পত্তি প্রাপ্ত হয়, কনিষ্ঠাধিকার।

ŭl'-trā-, *pref.* On the other side of; অতি, অতীত, পরপারবর্ত্তী। **Ultra red rays** — অদৃশ্য লোহিত আলো। **Ultra-zodiacal** — রাশিবহির্গত (হিঃ কোঃ)। **Ultra-zodiacal planet**—গ্রহবহির্গত (হিঃ কোঃ)।

ŭl'-trā *adj.* & *n.* Beyond due limit; extreme; উৎকট; নিতান্ত, চরম, পরম। *Noun.* One who advocates or holds extreme views; চরমপন্থী।

ŭl'-trā-ist, *n.* An extremist; চরমপন্থী, চরমবাদী।

ŭl'-trā-mā-rine' (-rēn), *adj.* & *n.* Beyond the sea; সাগরের পরপারবর্ত্তী, সমুদ্রের অপর পারে অবস্থিত, অতিসাগরিক *Noun.* 1. A substance of a fine blue colour originally obtained by grinding lapis lazuli; লাজবর্দ্দমণি চূর্ণ হইতে প্রস্তুত একপ্রকার মনোরম নীলবর্ণ, লাজবর্দ্দীনীল (হিঃ কোঃ), লাজবর্দ (হাবেলঃ)। 2. A dyeing substance made by heating Glauber's salt or soda with kaolin, charcoal, and sulphur, at first with exclusion of air. The dull green product is converted into the blue compound by heating with sulphur with excess of air; সূক্ষ্ম বালুকা, অঙ্গার এবং গন্ধকের সহিত সোডা বা গ্লবার্স সল্ট প্রথমতঃ বায়ু নিষ্কাশন পূর্ব্বক একত্র উত্তপ্ত করতঃ যে রঞ্জক পদার্থ প্রস্তুত করা হয়। এই রঙ্গ প্রথমতঃ অনুজ্জ্বল হরিদ্বর্ণ থাকে, পরে ইহা গন্ধক এবং প্রচুর বায়ুর সহিত উত্তপ্ত করিয়া নীলবর্ণ মিশ্র পদার্থে পরিণত করা হয়। **Ultramarine ashes**—লাজবর্দ্দী নীলবর্ণ নিষ্কর্ষণের পর মণিচূর্ণের যে অংশ অবশিষ্ট থাকে, এবং যাহা দ্বারা প্রাচীনকালের চিত্রকরগণ ধূসরবর্ণ প্রভৃতি প্রস্তুত করিতেন। **Ultramarine blue**—লাজবর্দ্দী নীল (হিঃ কোঃ)।

ŭl-trā-mŏn'-tāne, *adj.* & *n.* 1. Situated south of Alps; আলপস্‌ পর্ব্বতের দক্ষিণ দিকে অবস্থিত। 2. Italian; ইতালীয়। 3. Belonging to the extreme Popish party of the R. C. Church; রোমান ক্যাথলিক ধর্ম্মসংঘের চরম পোপপন্থী সম্বন্ধীয়। *Noun.* 1. A native of Italy; ইতালীদেশীয় লোক। 2. An adherent or advocate of extreme, or ultra-Popish views; চরমপোপপন্থী। **–ta-nism, –ta-nist,** *ns.*

ŭl-trā-mŭn'-dāne, *adj.* Beyond the world or the solar system; অতিজাগতিক, অতিসৌরজাগতিক।

ŭl'-trā-vī'-ō-lĕt, *adj.* (Of invisible light-rays of the spectrum) Lying beyond violet rays; (বর্ণচ্ছত্রের অদৃশ্য রশ্মিমালা সম্বন্ধে) বেগুনে আলোর অতীত, অতিনীলারুণ।

ultra vires, *adv.* or *pred. adj.* Beyond the legal power or authority of a court, corporation, or person; কোন আদালত, সংঘ বা ব্যক্তির বৈধ ক্ষমতার অতীত বা বহির্ভূত।

ŭl-trŏ-mō-tĭv'-ĭ-tȳ, *n.* Power of spontaneous movement; স্বতঃচলনশক্তি।

ŭl'-ū-lāte, *v. i.* To howl; to hoot; চীৎকার করা; টিট্‌কারি দেওয়া। **–la'-tion,** *n.*

ŭm'-bĕl, *n.* (*Bot.*) That mode of inflorescence which consists of a number of flower-stalks of pedicels spreading from a common centre each bearing a single flower, as, in the hemlock; (উদ্ভিদ্‌বিদ্যা) পুষ্প বৃন্তসমূহের ছত্রাকারে প্রসৃতি, ছত্রপুষ্প, উপচ্ছত্র (সাঃ পঃ)। **–lal, –lar, –late, –bel'-li-form,** *adjs.* **–let, –lule,** *ns.* A little or partial umbel; ক্ষুদ্র উপচ্ছত্র। **–lif'-er-ous,** *adj.* Furnished with an umbel; ছত্রপুষ্পী (সাঃ পঃ)।

Umbel of hemlock.

ŭm-bĕl'-lĭ-fĕr, *n.* A plant bearing an umbelliferous cluster; ছত্রপুষ্পীক্ষুপ।

ŭm-bĕl-ĭf'-ĕr-ae (-ē), *n.* The family apiaceæ; ধন্যাকাদি (সাঃ পঃ)।

ŭm'-bĕr, *n.* & *adj.* & *v. t.* A soft earthy pigment of an olive-brown colour in the natural state ; এক-প্রকার কোমল মৃদ্ধর্ম্মী রঞ্জকপদার্থ বিশেষ। ***Adj.*** Of umber colour ; dusky ; কপিশ বর্ণ ; ধূসর বর্ণ। ***Verb t.*** To colour with umber ; কপিশবর্ণে রঞ্জিত করা। **—y,** *adj.* **Burnt umber**—কপিশবর্ণ। **Raw umber**—স্বাভাবিক অবস্থায় ঐ বর্ণ। **Umber-bird**—আফ্রিকাদেশীয় সারসজাতীয় পক্ষিবিশেষ।

ŭm-bĭl′-ĭ-căl (*or* -bĭl-), *adj.* Of, or pertaining to, the navel ; navel-shaped ; নাভিসম্বন্ধীয় ; নাভির আকার। **2.** Central ; মধ্যবর্ত্তী। **3.** Connected through female line ; as, an *umbilical* ancestor ; মাতৃসম্পর্কীয়, মাতুল সম্পর্কীয়, মাতামহ সম্পর্কীয়। **Umbilical cord**—যে নাড়ীদ্বারা ফুলের সহিত গর্ভস্থ ভ্রূণ সংসৃষ্ট থাকে, নাল (বৃঃ সং), নাভিনাল, নাভিনাড়ী, গর্ভনাড়ী-প্রবন্ধ (সুশ্রুঃ)। **Umbilical region**—নাভিদেশ, নাভিচক্র, নাভিমণ্ডল।

ŭm-bĭl′-ĭ-cāte, *adj.* Shaped like a navel ; নাভ্যাকৃতি, নাভিবৎ। **—ca′-tion,** *n.*

ŭm-bĭl′-ĭ-cü-lar (-lêr), *adj.* Pertaining to the navel ; নাভিসম্বন্ধীয়। **Umbilicular contemplation**—নাভিদেশে দৃষ্টিনিবদ্ধকরতঃ ধ্যান।

ŭm′-bō, *n.* **1.** The boss or protuberant part of a shield ; ঢালের উপরের টোপ। **2.** (*Bot.* & *Zool.*) Any elevation suggestive of the boss ; (উদ্ভিদ্‌বিদ্যা, জন্তুবিদ্যা, প্রভৃতি) টোপের মত উন্নত অংশ। **—nal, —nate, —bon′-ic,** *adjs.*

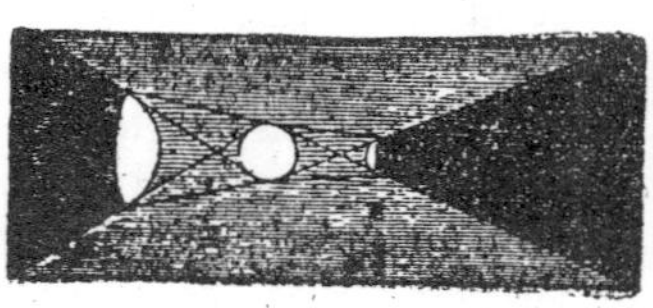

Umbra and penumbra.

ŭm′-bră, *n.* **1.** Among the Romans, one who went to a feast merely at the solicitation of one invited, so called as he followed the guest as a shadow ; প্রাচীন রোমে যে ব্যক্তি কোন নিমন্ত্রিত ব্যক্তির অনুরোধে তাহার সঙ্গে কোন ভোজে গমন করতঃ ছায়ার মত তাহার অনুবর্ত্তন করিত। **2.** The shadow of the earth or moon in total eclipse ; পৃথিবী বা চন্দ্রের যে ছায়াংশে সূর্য্য সম্পূর্ণরূপে ঢাকা পড়ে, প্রচ্ছায়া (হিঃ কোঃ)। **3.** The dark central part of sunspot ; সৌরকলঙ্কের নিবিড় কৃষ্ণবর্ণ মধ্যাংশ। **—bral,** *adj.*

ŭm-brăc′-ü-lŭm, *n.* (*Bot.*) Kinds of umbrella-shaped appendage ; বিভিন্নপ্রকার ছত্রাকার উপাঙ্গ। **—late, —lif′-er-ous, —li-form,** *adjs.*

ŭm′-brāge, *n.* **1.** Offence ; as, to take *umbrage* at one's conduct ; দোষ, ক্রটি। **2.** (*Poet.*) Shade ; (কবিতায়) ছায়া। **—bra′-geous,** *adj.* Shady ; as, *umbrageous* trees ; ছায়াবহুল, সচ্ছায়, ছায়াপূর্ণ।

ŭm-brĕl′-lă, *n.* **1.** A shade or canopy which opens and folds, carried in the hand for sheltering the person from the rays of the sun, rain or snow ; ছত্র, ছাতা, ছাতি, আতপত্র, ঘর্ম্মবারণ (কুমারঃ), বর্বত্র। **2.** The bell-shaped swimming organ of the Lucernarida ; সমুদ্র-জিহ্বা প্রভৃতি মৎস্যের ছত্রাকার সন্তরণ-যন্ত্র। **3.** A gasteropod with an umbrella-like shell (also *umbrella-shell*) ; ছত্রাকার কঞ্চুকবিশিষ্ট উদরপদী। **Umbrella-bird** — আমেরিকা দেশীয় বিভিন্ন জাতীয় পক্ষী—উহার চূড়া ছত্রাকারে প্রসৃত হইয়া থাকে। **Umbrella-shell**—Same as UMBRELLA 3. **Umbrella-stand**—একসঙ্গে বহুছত্র রাখার জন্য কাঠাম। ঐরূপ কাঠামের নীচে সাধারণতঃ ছত্র-নিঃসৃত জলবিন্দুর পতনের জন্য ক্ষুদ্র ক্ষুদ্র পাত্র থাকে। **Umbrella-tree**—যে বৃক্ষ এরূপ ভাবে কলম করা বা ছাঁটা হয়—যাহাতে উহার শাখা সমূহ ছত্রাকারে ঝুলিয়া পড়ে ; একপ্রকার ক্ষুদ্র চম্পক বৃক্ষ—উহার পত্রসমূহ ছত্রাকারে শাখার অগ্রে গুচ্ছিত থাকে।

ŭm-brette′ (-brĕt), *n.* Same as UMBER (which see.)

Um′-brĭ-ăn (ŭm-), *adj.* & *n.* Of, or pertaining to, Umbria, one of the ancient principal divisions of central Italy ; আম্ব্রিয়াদেশীয়। ***Noun*** The language of ancient Umbria ; an inhabitant of ancient Umbria ; প্রাচীন আম্ব্রিয়ার ভাষা ; প্রাচীন আম্ব্রিয়ার অধিবাসী। **Umbrian school** — চিত্রকরসংঘবিশেষ—Raphael এবং Perugino এই সংঘভুক্ত ছিলেন।

ŭm-brĭf′-êr-ous (-ŭs), *adj.* Affording shade ; ছায়াপ্রদ, সচ্ছায়, ছায়াময়।

umiak, *n.* The native name of women's large kind of Eskimo boat ; স্ত্রীলোকগণ দ্বারা চালিত একপ্রকার এস্কিমো নৌকা।

um′-laut (ôm-lowt), *n.* & *v. t.* (*Gram.*) The change of a vowel in one syllable through the influence of one of the vowels *a, i, u* immediately following ; (ভাষাবিজ্ঞান) অব্যবহিত পরবর্ত্তী a, i, u এই তিন স্বরবর্ণের অন্যতমের প্রভাবে ফলে কোন শব্দাংশের কোন স্বরবর্ণের পরিবর্ত্তন। ***Verb t.*** To modify (form, sound) by the umlaut ; উক্তরূপ পরিবর্ত্তন দ্বারা (ধ্বনি এবং রূপের) পরিবর্ত্তন করা।

ŭm′-pīre, *n., v. i.* & *t.* **1.** A person to whose sole decision a controversy or question between parties is referred ; যে ব্যক্তি উভয়পক্ষের মধ্যে বিবাদাদি মীমাংসা করে, সালীশ, মধ্যস্থ, স্থের, প্রমাণপুরুষ। **2.** (*Law*) A third person who is to decide a matter submitted to arbitrators in case of their disagreement ; সালীশদিগের মধ্যে কোন বিষয়ে অনৈক্য হইলে বিবাদ মীমাংসার ভার যে তৃতীয় ব্যক্তির উপর অর্পিত হয়। ***Verb i.*** To act or stand as an umpire ; মধ্যস্থতা করা। ***Verb t.*** **1.** To arbitrate ; সালীসী করা, মধ্যস্থতা করা। **2.** To act as arbitrator ; সালীসী কার্য্য করা, মধ্যস্থতা করা। **—ship,**

ŭn, *pron.* (*Colloq.*) One ; (চলিত ভাষায়) জন।

ŭn-, *pref.* A prefix derived from two sources with two uses, *viz.* those of negation and those of reversal or undoing, hence privation ; নাস্তি, বিপরীত এবং অভাবাচক উপসর্গ।

ŭn-ă-based (-bāst), *adj.* Not abased ; not humbled ; অনবনমিত ; অপরিভবপ্রাপ্ত, অহীন।

ŭn-ă-bashed' (-băsht), *adj.* Not abashed ; not confused with shame or by modesty ; অলজ্জিত, অলজ্জায়িত, অলজ্জান্বিত, অব্রীড়িত ; অব্রীড়াকুণ্ঠিত, অব্রীড়াসঙ্কুচিত, অহ্রীমূঢ়।

ŭn-ă-bāt'-ĕd, *adj.* Not abated ; not lessend in strength or violence ; অপ্রশমিত ; অনুপশমিত।

ŭn-ā'-ble, (-bl), *adj.* Not having sufficient means, skill, ability or the like ; impotent ; অক্ষম, অপারগ, অসমর্থ, অনিপুণ, অশক্ত। **—bil'-i-ty,** *n.*

ŭn-ă-bŏl'-ĭsh-ă-ble (-bl), *adj.* Not capable of being abolished ; অধ্বংসযোগ্য, অরদযোগ্য।

ŭn-ă-bŏl'-ished (-ĭsht), *adj.* Not abolished; not repealed; অধ্বংসীকৃত ; অরহিত।

ŭn-ăb-rād'-ĕd, *adj.* Not worn by friction ; অঘর্ষণক্ষয়িত, অলূণত্বক্।

ŭn-ă-bridged' (-brĭjd), *adj.* Not abridged ; অসংক্ষেপীকৃত, অসংক্ষিপ্ত।

ŭn-ăb'-rō-gāt-ĕd *adj.* Not annulled or repealed ; অরহিত।

ŭn-ăb-solved' (-sŏlvd), *adj.* Not acquitted or forgiven ; অক্ষমিত, অপাপমুক্ত।

ŭn-ăb-sorbed' (-sŏrbd), *adj.* Not imbibed ; অশোষিত।

ŭn-ăc-cĕl'-ĕr-āt-ĕd, *adj.* Not accelerated ; উত্তরোত্তর দ্রুতগতি অপ্রাপ্ত, অক্রমবর্দ্ধিত।

ŭn-ăc-cĕnt'-ĕd, *adj.* Having no accent ; অনুদাত্ত, অস্বরিত।

ŭn-ăc-cĕpt'-ă-ble (-bl), *adj.* 1. Not acceptable ; not such as will be received with pleasure; অপ্রতিগ্রাহ্য, অগ্রহণীয়; অনাদেয়,অস্বীকার্য্য। 2. Unpleasant ; "The marquis at that time was very *unacceptable* to his countrymen" ; অপ্রীতিকর, অপ্রিয়।

ŭn-ăc-clĭ'-māt-ĕd, *adj.* Not inured to the climate ; জলবায়ুতে অনভ্যস্ত, অশীতাতপাভ্যস্ত।

ŭn-ăc-cŏm'-mō-dāt-ĕd, *adj.* Not fitted or adopted ; অনুপযোগীকৃত।

ŭn-ăc-cŏm'-mō-dāt'-ĭng, *adj.* Not ready to oblige ; uncompliant ; অপ্রিয়কর ; অবিনেয়, অপ্রণেয়।

ŭn-ăc-com'-pa-nied (-kŭm-pă-nĭd), *adj.* Not attended ; having no attendants, companions or followers ; অসহায় ; সঙ্গীহীন, একাকী, অদ্বিতীয়।

ŭn-ăc-cŏm'-plished (-plĭsht), *adj.* 1. Not finished ; incomplete ; অসমাপ্ত, অনিষ্পন্ন, অসম্পাদিত ; অসম্পন্ন, অসম্পূর্ণ। 2. Not refined or polished by culture ; অগুণসম্পন্ন, অকৃতবিদ্য।

ŭn-ăc-cŏrd'-ănt, *adj.* 1. Not to be accounted for ; not explicable ; অনির্দ্দেশ্য, অহেতুপ্রদর্শনযোগ্য ; অব্যাখ্যেয়, অব্যাখ্যাতব্য। 2. Not responsible ; দায়িত্বশূন্য।

ŭn-ăc-crĕd'-i-tĕd, *adj.* Not accredited ; not authorised ; অবিশ্বস্ত ; অপ্রাপ্তক্ষমতা।

ŭn-ăc'-cū-rate, *adj.* Not correct or exact ; অশুদ্ধ, অযথার্থ।

ŭn-ăc-cŭs'-tomed (-tŭmd), *adj.* 1. Not habituated ; অনভ্যস্ত, অকৃতাভ্যাস, অনভ্যাসী। 2. Unfamiliar ; অপরিচিত। 3. Uncommon ; "These apparent prodigies the *unaccustomed* terror of this night" ; strange ; অসাধারণ ; আশ্চর্য্য, অদ্ভুত।

ŭn-ă-chiev'-a-ble (-chēv-ă-bl), *adj.* That cannot be accomplished ; অসমাপ্য, অসম্পাদ্য।

ŭn-āch'-ĭng, *adj.* Not aching ; not giving pain ; বেদনাহীন, বেদনাশূন্য ; অবেদনাজনক।

ŭn-ăc-knowl'-edged (-nŏl-ĕjd), *adj.* Not recognised ; not owned ; অস্বীকৃত, অননুজ্ঞাত ; অনঙ্গীকৃত।

ŭn-ăc-quaint'-ĕd (-kwānt-), *adj.* 1. Not having familiar knowledge ; অপরিচিত, অবিদিত, অজ্ঞাত, অপরিজ্ঞাত। 2. Unfamiliar ; অনভিজ্ঞ, অনভ্যস্ত। **—ance,** *n.* **—ness,** *n.*

ŭn-ăc-quired' (-kwĭrd), *adj* Not acquired ; not gained ; অনর্জ্জিত ; অলব্ধ।

ŭn-ăc-quĭt'-ted (-ĕd), *adj.* Not declared innocent ; অমুক্তিপ্রাপ্ত।

ŭn-ăct'-ĕd, *adj.* 1. Not performed ; অসম্পাদিত, অসম্পন্ন। 2. Not put on the stage ; অনভিনীত।

ŭn-ăc'-tū-āt-ĕd, *adj.* Not moved ; অননুপ্রাণিত।

ŭn-ă-dăpt'-ĕd, *adj.* Not suited ; অনুপযোগীকৃত।

ŭn-ăd-dĭct'-ĕd, *adj.* Not devoted ; অনাসক্ত, অননুরক্ত।

ŭn-ăd-judged' (-jŭjd), *adj.* Not judicially decided ; অবিচারিত।

ŭn-ăd-jŭst'-ĕd, *adj.* 1. Not settled or regulated; অমীমাংসিত, অনিয়মিত। 2. Not liquidated ; অপরিশোধিত।

ŭn-ăd-mĭn'-is-tered (-tĕrd), *adj.* Not administered ; অনির্ব্বাহিত, অপরিচালিত।

ŭn-ăd-mīred', *adj.* Not admired ; not admirable ; অপ্রশংসিত ; অপ্রশংসনীয়।

ŭn-ăd-mŏn'-ished (-ĭsht), *adj.* Not cautioned ; অসতর্কিত।

ŭn-ă-dŏpt'-ă-ble (-bl), *adj.* That cannot be adopted ; অগ্রহণীয়, অগ্রহীতব্য।

ŭn-ă-dored (-dōrd), *adj.* Not worshipped ; অপূজিত, অনর্চ্চিত।

ŭn-ă-dorned' (dŏrnd), *adj.* Not decorated ; অভূষিত, অনলঙ্কৃত, অমণ্ডিত, নিরাভরণ।

ŭn-ă-dŭl'-tĕr-āt-ĕd, *adj.* Genuine ; pure ; খাঁটি, ভেজালশূন্য ; বিশুদ্ধ (হিঃ কোঃ)।

ŭn-ă-dŭl′-têr-ous (-ŭs), *adj.* Not guilty of adultery ; অপরদারসেবী, অপরস্ত্রীগামী, অপরদারিক।

ŭn-ăd-vĕn′-tūr-ous (-ŭs), *adj.* Not bold ; অসমসাহসিকতাহীন।

ŭn-ăd-vīs′-ă-ble (bl-), *adj.* **1.** Not advisable ; অপরামর্শসিদ্ধ। **2.** Not to be recommended ; অপ্রশস্ত। **3.** Not expedient ; অযুক্ত।

ŭn-ăd-vīsed′, *adj.* **1.** Not prudent ; indiscreet ; অসমীচীন, অযৌক্তিক ; অবিবেচনাপ্রসূত। **2.** Done without due consideration ; rash ; হঠকারিতার সহিত সম্পাদিত, অবিচারিত ; হঠকারী। **—vis′-ed-ly**, *adv.* **—vis′-ed-ness**, *n.*

ŭn-ăf′-fa-ble (-ă-bl), *adj.* Not affable ; not free to converse ; reserved ; অনভিগম্য, অদাক্ষিণ্যপরবশ ; সংযতবাক্ ; অনালাপী।

ŭn-ăf-fĕct′-ĕd, *adj.* **1.** Not moved ; destitute of affection or emotion ; অবিচলিত; আবেগশূন্য, অবিকৃত, নির্ব্বিকার, অনুপহত। **2.** Natural ; not hypocriticel ; অকৃত্রিম ; সরল, স্বাভাবিক, অকপট। **—ly**, *adv.* **—ness**, *n.*

ŭn-ăf-fĕc′-tion-āte, *adj.* Wanting affection ; স্নেহহীন, স্নেহশূন্য, অস্নেহপ্রবণ।

ŭn-ăf-flīct′-ed, *adj.* Free from trouble ; অক্লিষ্ট, অনার্ত্ত, অনাতুর।

ŭn-ăf-fright′-ĕd (-frīt-), *adj.* Not frightened ; অভীত, অত্রস্ত, অশঙ্কিত।

ŭn′-ăğ-ĭ-tāt-ĕd, *adj.* Calm ; শান্ত, প্রশান্ত, অবিক্ষুব্ধ।

ŭn-ă-gree′-a-ble (-grē-ă-bl), *adj.* (*Obs.*) Not consistent ; unsuitable ; (অপ্রঃ) সঙ্গতিশূন্য ; অনুপযোগী।

ŭn-aid′-ĕd (-ād-), *adj.* Not assisted ; অসহায়ীকৃত, অসহায়, নিঃসহায়।

ŭn-aim′-ĭng (-ām-), *adj.* Having no particular aim or direction ; লক্ষ্যহীন, লক্ষ্যশূন্য।

ŭn-aired′ (-ārd), *adj.* Not aired ; অবায়ুসঞ্চালিত।

ŭn-ă-larmed′ (-lêrmd) *adj.* Not disturbed with fear ; অভীত, অভয়ত্রস্ত, অভয়াকুলিত।

ŭn-ă-lârm′-ĭng, *adj.* Not alarming ; অভয়প্রদ, অশঙ্কাজনক।

ŭn-āl′-ien-a-ble (-yŏn-ă-bl), *adj.* That cannot be alienated ; অবিশ্লেষ্য, অস্থাদেয়, নির্ব্বিঘটনীয়। **—bly**, *adv.*

ŭn-āl′-ien-āt-ĕd (-yĕn-), *adj.* Not transferred ; অনন্যহস্তসমর্পিত, অসংক্রামিত, অস্থানান্তরিত, হস্তান্তরিত নয়।

ŭn-ăl-lē′-vĭ-āt-ĕd, *adj.* Not mitigated ; অপ্রশমিত, অনুপশমিত।

ŭn-ăl-lī′-ă-ble (-bl), *adj.* That cannot be allied or connected in amity ; অনৈক্যসাধ্য, অসংযোগসাধ্য।

ŭn-ăl-lied′ (-līd), *adj.* **1.** Having no alliance or connection ; অসম্পর্কীয়, অসংযোজ্য, মিত্রত্ববন্ধনশূন্য। **2.** Having no powerful ally or relation ; শক্তিশালী মিত্র বা কুটুম্বশূন্য।

ŭn-ăl-lōw′-ă-ble (-bl), *adj.* That cannot be allowed or permitted ; অগ্রাহ্য, অননুমোদনযোগ্য।

ŭn-ăl-lowed′ (-lōwd), *adj.* Not permitted ; অননুজ্ঞাত, অননুমোদিত।

ŭn-ăl-loyed′ (-lōyd), *adj.* Not alloyed or reduced by foreign mixture ; অবিমিশ্র, নির্ভাজ।

ŭn-ăl-lūr′-ĭng, *adj.* Not tempting ; অলোভনীয়, অলোভজনক।

ŭn-ăl′-têr-ă-ble (-bl), *adj.* **1.** Unchangeable ; অপরিবর্ত্তনীয়, অবিকার্য্য, অপরিবর্ত্তনশীল (হিঃ কোঃ)। **—bil′-i-ty**, **—ness**, *ns.* The state of being unchangeable ; অপরিবর্ত্তনীয়তা, অপরিবর্ত্তনশীলতা। **—bly**, *adv.*

ŭn-ăl′-tered (-têrd), *adj.* Not altered or changed ; অপরিবর্ত্তিত।

ŭn-ă-mazed′, *adj.* Free from astonishment ; অস্তম্ভিত, অবিস্মিত।

ŭn-ăm-bĭg′-ū-ous (-ŭs), *adj.* **1.** Not of doubtful meaning ; অসন্দিগ্ধার্থক, অদ্ব্যর্থক। **2.** Plain ; clear ; স্পষ্ট ; পরিস্কার। **—ly**, *adj.* **—ness**, *n.*

ŭn-ăm-bĭ′-tious (-shŭs), *adj.* Free from ambition ; not affecting show ; উচ্চাশা রহিত, উচ্চাশাশূন্য, উচ্চাভিলাষশূন্য ; আড়ম্বরশূন্য, আড়ম্বরহীন, অনাড়ম্বর। **—ly**, *adv.* **—ness**, *n.*

ŭn-ă-mĕ′-nă-ble (-bl), *adj.* Not amenable or responsible ; অস্বসা দায়িত্বরহিত, দায়িত্বশূন্য।

ŭn-ă-mĕnd -ă-ble (-bl), *adj.* Not capable of being improved ; অসংশোধনীয়।

ŭn-ă-mĕnd′-ĕd, *adj.* Not amended ; অসংশোধিত।

ŭn-ā′-mĭ-a-ble (-ă-bl), *adj.* Not amiable ; দুর্ব্বিনীত, অবিনীত **—ness**, *n.*

ŭn-ă-mūsed′, *adj.* Not enertained ; অবিনোদিত, অসৎকৃত।

ŭn-ă-mūs′-ĭng, *adj.* Not affording amusement ; অনামোদপ্র অনামোদজনক।

ŭn-ă-mū′-sive (-sĭv), *adj.* Same as UNAMUSING.

ŭn-ăn-ă-lŏğ′-ĭ-căl, *adj.* Not analogical ; অসাদৃশ্যব্যঞ্জক, অসাদৃশ্যসূচক ;

ŭn-ă-năl′-ŏ-gous (-gŭs), *adj.* Not agreeable to ; অসমঞ্জস, সঙ্গতিহীন, সঙ্গতিশূন্য।

ŭn-ăn′-ă-lȳs-ă-ble (bl), *adj.* Incapable of analysis ; অবিশ্লেষণীয়।

ŭn-ăn′-ă-lysed (-līzd), *adj.* Not resolved into simple parts ; অবিশ্লেষিত, অবিশ্লিষ্ট।

ŭn-an′-chored (-ăng-kêrd), *adj.* Not moored ; অনোঙ্গরবদ্ধ।

ŭn-ă-neled′ (-nēld), *adj.* Not having received extreme unction ; অন্তিমতৈলমর্দ্দনানুষ্ঠানবিহীন, অমর্দ্দিতান্তিমতৈল।

ŭn-an′-gu-lar (-ăng-gū-lêr), *adj.* Having no angles ; কোণহীন, অকোণ, কোণশূন্য।

ŭn-ăn′-ĭ-măl-īsed, *adj.* Not formed into animal matter ; অজৈব পদার্থে পরিণত, অজৈবীভূত।

ŭn-ăn′-ĭ-măt-ĕd, *adj.* **1.** Not possessed of life ; অচেতন। **2.** Not enlivened ; not having spirit ; অনমুপ্রাণিত ; তেজোহীন।

ū-năn′-ĭ-mous (-mŭs), *adj.* **1.** Being of one mind ; agreeing in opinion or determination ; এক মত ;

সর্ব্বসম্মত (হিঃ কোঃ), একচিত্ত। 2. Formed by unanimity ; সর্ব্বজনসম্মত, সর্ব্বসম্মতিক্রমে গৃহীত। **–ly,** *adv.* With entire agreement of mind ; সর্ব্বসম্মতিক্রমে, সমস্বরে, একবাক্যে, সর্ব্ববাদিসম্মতিক্রমে। **–na-nim'-i-ty,** *n.* The state of being unanimous ; মতৈক্য, চিত্তৈক্য, সর্ব্বসম্মতি, ঐকমত্য, একচিত্ততা, একনিশ্চয়তা, একবাক্য। **–ness,** *n.*

ŭn-ăn-nealed' (-nēld), *adj.* Not tempered by heat ; অতপ্তশীতলীকৃত।

ŭn-ăn-nexed' (-nĕxt), *adj.* Not annexed or joined ; অসংযোজিত, অযুক্ত।

ŭn-ăn-nounced' (-nownst), *adj.* Not announced or proclaimed ; অঘোষিত, অবিঘোষিত।

ŭn-ăn-noyed' (-noyd), *adj.* Not annoyed ; অবিরক্ত।

ŭn-ă-noint'-ĕd (-noynt-), *adj.* Not anointed ; not having received extreme unction ; অতৈলাভিষিক্ত; অন্তিমতৈলমর্দ্দনহীন।

ŭn-ăn-swer-ă-bil'-i-tў (-sêr-), *n.* Same as UNANSWERABLENESS, *n.*

ŭn-ăn'-swer-a-ble (-sêr-ă-bl), *adj.* Not capable of being answered ; not capable of refutation ; অনুত্তর, দুরুত্তর, অনুত্তরসহ ; অখণ্ডনীয়। **–bly,** *adv.* **–ness,** *n.* The state of being unanswerable ; the state of being beyond refutation ; অনুত্তরসহতা ; অখণ্ডনীয়তা।

ŭn-ăn'-swered (-sêrd), *adj.* Unopposed by a reply ; not refuted ; অনুত্তরদত্ত ; অখণ্ডিত।

ŭn-ăn-tic'-i-pāt-ĕd, *adj.* Not anticipated ; অপ্রত্যাশিত।

ŭn-ăp-palled' (-päld), *adj.* Not daunted ; অভীত, অশঙ্কিত, নিঃশঙ্ক, নির্ভীক, ভয়শূন্য।

ŭn-ăp-păr'-eled (-ĕld), *adj.* Not appareled ; not clothed ; অনাচ্ছাদিত, অপ্রচ্ছাদিত; অপরিচ্ছদাবৃত,পরিচ্ছদবিহীন।

ŭn-ăp-păr'-ĕnt, *adj.* Not apparent ; obscure ; অপ্রতিভাত, অপ্রতীয়মান, অপ্রত্যক্ষ ; অস্পষ্ট।

ŭn-ăp-peal'-a-ble (-pēl-ă-ble), *adj.* Admitting no appeal ; অনাপীল-যোগ্য।

ŭn-ăp-peas'-a-ble (-pēz-ă-bl), *adj.* Not to be appeased ; অপ্রসাদনীয়।

ŭn-ăp-peased' (-pēzd), *adj.* Not appeased ; অতুষ্ট, অসন্তুষ্ট।

ŭn-ăp-plaud'-ĕd (-pläd-), *adj.* Not applauded ; অপ্রশংসিত।

ŭn-ăp-plied' (-plīd), *adj.* Not used according to the intention ; অভিপ্রায়ানুসারে অব্যবহৃত, অপ্রযুক্ত।

ŭn-ăp-prē'-ci-āt-ĕd (-shi-), *adj.* Not duly estimated or valued ; অগুণগৃহীত।

ŭn-ăp-prē-hĕnd'-ĕd, *adj.* Not apprehended ; অনুপলব্ধ।

ŭn-ăp-prē-hĕn'-si-ble (-bl), *adj.* Not capable of being understood ; অপরিজ্ঞেয়, অবিজ্ঞেয়।

ŭn-ăp-prē-hĕn'-sive (-sĭv), *adj.* 1. Not fearful or suspecting ; অশঙ্কিত, অসংশয়ী। 2. Not intelligent ; অবুদ্ধিমান। **–ness,** *n.*

ŭn-ăp-prīzed', *adj.* Not previously informed ; অপূর্ব্ববিজ্ঞাত।

ŭn-ăp-proach'-a-ble (-prōch-ă-bl), *adj.* That cannot be approached ; inaccessible ; অনধিগম্য, দুরধিগম্য, অনাগম্য ; অনুপসার্য্য, দুরাগম, অগম্য, দুর্গম, অনভিগমনীয়।

ŭn-ăp-prō'-pri-āt-ĕd, *adj.* 1. Not applied to any specific object ; কোন বিশেষ উদ্দেশ্যে অপ্রযুক্ত। 2. Not granted to any person or corporation; কোন ব্যক্তি বা সমবায়ে অপ্রদত্ত।

ŭn-ăp-proved' (-prôvd), *adj.* Not approved ; not having received approbation ; অননুমোদিত; অনভিমত, অননুমত।

ŭn-ăpt', *adj.* 1. Not apt ; not ready or inclined ; অচতুর ; অপ্রবণ, অপ্রস্তুত। 2. Unfit ; unqualified ; অনুপযুক্ত ; অযোগ্য। **–ly,** *adv.* **–ness,** *n.*

ŭn-âr'-gued (-güd), *adj.* Not debated or argued ; অতর্কিত।

ŭn-ârm', *v. t.* To disarm; নিরস্ত্র করা, নিরায়ুধ করা। **–armed',** *adj.* 1. Disarmed ; নিরস্ত্র, নিরায়ুধ, নিঃশস্ত্র, অশস্ত্র, অস্ত্রবিবর্জ্জিত। 2. Not furnished with scales or pickles ; শল্কহীন, কণ্টকশূন্য।

ŭn-ăr-rănged', *adj.* Not disposed in order ; অশ্রেণীবদ্ধ, অবিন্যস্ত।

ŭn-ar-rayed' (-ă-rād), 1. Not dressed ; অপরিচ্ছদাবৃত, নগ্ন, বিবস্ত্র। 2. Not disposed in order ; ক্রম-অবিন্যস্ত, অশ্রেণীবদ্ধ।

ŭn-ăr-rĕst'-ĕd, *adj.* Not apprehended ; অধৃত।

ŭn-ârt'-fûl, *adj.* Wanting skill ; অচতুর, অনিপুণ, অকৌশলী, অবিদগ্ধ। **–ly,** *adv.*

ŭn-âr-tic'-ū-lāt-ĕd, *adj.* Not articulated ; অব্যক্ত, অস্পষ্ট।

ŭn-âr-ti-fi'-cial (-shăl), *adj.* Not artificial ; নৈসর্গিক, স্বাভাবিক।

ŭn-âr-tis'-tic, *adj.* Not according to the rules of art অকলাশাস্ত্রসম্মত, শিল্পচাতুর্য্যহীন।

ŭn-ăs-cĕnd'-ă-ble (-bl), *adj.* That cannot be ascended ; দুরারোহ, অনারোহণীয়, অনধিরোহণীয়।

ŭn-ăs-cer-tain'-a-ble(-êr-tān-ă-bl), *adj.* That cannot be ascertained or certainly known ; অনির্ণেয়, অনির্দ্ধার্য্য, অনিশ্চেয়, অনিরূপণীয়, অনির্দ্ধারণীয়।

ŭn-ăs-cer-tained' (-êr-tānd), *adj.* Not ascertained; অনির্ণীত, অনিশ্চিত।

ŭn-ă-shamed', *adj.* Not ashamed ; অলজ্জিত, অব্রীড়িত, অত্রপিত, অলজ্জান্বিত, অত্রপান্বিত।

ŭn-asked' (-âskt), *adj.* Unsolicited; অজিজ্ঞাসিত, অযাচিত, অপ্রার্থিত।

ŭn-ăs'-pi-rāt-ĕd, *adj.* Having no aspirates ; অল্পপ্রাণ।

ŭn-ăs-pīr'-ing, *adj.* Not aspiring or ambitious ; উচ্চাভিলাষশূন্য, উচ্চাকাঙ্ক্ষারহিত, নিরাকাঙ্ক্ষ।

ŭn-ăs-sail'-a-ble (-sāl-ă-bl), *adj.* Not assailable ; incapable of being assailed ; অনাক্রমণীয়, অনাক্রম্য; দুর্দ্ধর্ষ, দুরাক্রম্য, দুষ্প্রধর্ষ।

ŭn-ăs-sayed′ (-sād), *adj.* **1.** Not attempted ; অচেষ্টিত। **2.** Not tested ; অপরিক্ষীত।

ŭn-ăs-sêrt′-ĕd, *adj.* Not affirmed or vindicated ; অদৃঢ়ীকৃত, অসমর্থিত।

ŭn-ăs-sessed′ (-ĕst), *adj.* Not sessed or rated ; অকরসংস্থাপিত।

ŭn-ăs-sign′-a-ble, (-sīn-ă-bl) *adj.* That cannot be transferred or assigned ; অপ্রকরণীয়, অনির্দ্দেষ্টব্য, অনারোপণীয়।

ŭn-ăs-sim′-i-lāt-ĕd, *adj.* **1.** Not assimilated ; not made to resemble ; অসমীকৃত ; অতুল্যীকৃত। **2.** Not converted into a fluid or solid of the body ; রক্তমাংসাদিতে অপরিণত, অসমীকৃত।

ŭn-ăs-sist′-ĕd, *adj.* Not aided or helped ; অসাহায্যপ্রাপ্ত, অসাহায্যীকৃত, অসহায়।

ŭn-ăs-sō′-ci-āt-ĕd (-shĭ-), *adj.* Not associated with a society ; অসম্প্রদায়ভুক্ত।

ŭn-ăs-sŏrt′-ĕd, *adj.* Not distributed into sorts ; কিছিম করা নয়।

ŭn-ăs-suaged′ (-swājd), *adj.* Not appeased ; অশমিত, অপ্রসাদিত।

ŭn-ăs-sūm′-ing, *adj.* Not forward or arrogant ; modest ; অপ্রগল্ভ, অনভিমানী, নিরভিমান, অধৃষ্ট ; বিনয়ী, বিনীত, বিনম্র।

ŭn-as-sured′ (-ă-shôrd), *adj.* **1.** Not assured ; not confident ; অকৃতনিশ্চয় ; অচ্ছিন্নসংশয়, অপ্রত্যয়ী। **2.** Not insured against loss ; অবীমাকৃত।

ŭn-ă-tōn′-ă-ble (-bl), *adj.* Not to be expiated ; অপ্রায়শ্চিত্তসাধ্য, অপ্রায়শ্চিত্তযোগ্য, অপ্রায়শ্চিত্তার্হ।

ŭn-ăt-tached′ (-tăcht), *adj.* **1.** Not taken on account of debt ; ক্রোক করা হয় নাই এরূপ। **2.** (Of officers) Not belonging to any one company or regiment or on half pay ; (সৈনিককর্ম্মচারিসম্পর্কে) কোন দল বা পল্টনে অভুক্ত, অর্দ্ধবেতনে অবিদায়প্রাপ্ত। **3.** Not attached ; অসংলগ্ন, অসংশ্লিষ্ট, অসংসৃষ্ট, নির্লিপ্ত।

ŭn-ăt-tăck′-ă-ble (-bl), *adj.* Not to be attacked ; অনাক্রমণীয়, দুরাক্রম্য।

ŭn-ăt-tain′-a-ble (-tān-ă-bl), *adj.* Not to be obtained; অপ্রাপ্য, অলভ্য, অগম্য, অনধিগম্য, দুষ্প্রাপ। **—ness,** *n.*

ŭn-ăt-tĕm′-pered (-pêrd), *adj.* Not tempered by mixture ; অমিশ্রণপ্রশমিত।

ŭn-ăt-tĕmpt′-ĕd, *adj.* Not tried or essayed ; অচেষ্টিত।

ŭn-ăt-tĕnd′-ĕd, *adj.* **1.** Not accompanied ; সঙ্গীহীন। **2.** Having no retinue ; অনুযায়িবর্গহীন। **3.** (*Med.*) Not attended to ; not dressed ; (চিকিৎসাশাস্ত্র) অচিকিৎসিত ; (ক্ষতাদি) অধৌত এবং পট্টি প্রভৃতি দ্বারা অনাবৃত।

ŭn-ăt-tĕnd′-ing, *adj.* Not being attentive ; অমনোযোগী।

ŭn-ăt-tĕn′-tive (-tĭv), *adj.* Inattentive ; অমনোযোগী।

ŭn-ăt-tĕn′-ū-āt-ĕd, *adj.* Not attenuated ; অতানবিত।

ŭn-ăt-tĕst′-ĕd, *adj.* Having no attestation ; অসত্যপ্রতিপাদিত।

ŭn-ăt-tired′ (-tīrd), *adj.* Not attired ; not adorned ; অপরিচ্ছদপরিহিত ; অভূষিত, অমণ্ডিত।

ŭn-ăt-trăc′-tive (-tĭv), *adj.* Not attractive ; অচিত্তাকর্ষক।

ū-nau′ (-nä), *n.* An edentate mammal ; একপ্রকার অদন্তর স্তন্যপ্রদ জন্তু।

ŭn-au′-dit-ĕd (-ä-), *adj.* Not audited or adjusted ; (হিসাব সম্বন্ধে) অপরীক্ষিত।

ŭn-au-thĕn′-tic (-ä-), *adj.* Not genuine or true ; অপ্রকৃত, অসত্য।

ŭn-au-thĕn′-ti-cāt-ĕd (-ä-), *adj.* Not authenticated ; not made certain by authority ; অসত্যপ্রতিপাদিত ; অক্ষমতাপ্রদত্ত।

ŭn-au-thor′-i-ta-tive (-ä-thŏr-ĭ-tā-tĭv), *adj.* Not authoritative ; অপ্রামাণিক।

ŭn-au′-thŏr-īsed (-ä-), *adj.* Not warranted by proper authority ; অক্ষমতাপ্রাপ্ত।

ŭn-ă-vail′-a-ble (-vāl-ă-bl), *adj.* Not effectual ; useless ; নিষ্ফল ; নিরর্থক, বৃথা, অকার্য্যকর। **—ness,** *n.*

ŭn-ă-vail′-ing (-vāl-), *adj.* Ineffectual ; useless ; vain ; নিষ্ফল ; অনর্থক ; বৃথা।

ŭn-ă-venged′ (-vĕnjd), *adj.* Not avenged ; not punished ; অপ্রতিহিংসিত ; অদণ্ডিত।

ŭn-ă-vêrt′-ĕd, *adj.* Not turned away ; অপ্রতিনিবৃত্ত।

ŭn-ă-void′-a-ble (-vōyd-ă-bl), *adj.* Not to be shunned ; inevitable ; অপরিহার্য্য ; অবশ্য প্রয়োজনীয়, অনিবার্য্য, অবশ্যম্ভাবী। **—bly,** *adv.* In an unavoidable manner ; অপরিহার্য্যরূপে, অনিবার্য্যরূপে। **—ness,** *n.* The state of being unavoidable ; অপরিহার্য্যতা, অনিবার্য্যতা, অবশ্যম্ভাবিতা।

ŭn-ă-vowed′ (-vowd), *adj.* **1.** Not acknowledged ; অস্বীকৃত।

ŭn-ă-wāk′-ened (-nd), *adj.* **1.** Not roused from sleep ; অজাগরিত। **2.** Not roused from spiritual slumber or stupidity; "*Unawakened* dream beneath the blaze of truth" ; অপ্রবুদ্ধ, অনিবোধিত, অনুদ্বুদ্ধ।

ŭn-ă-wāre′, *adj.* Not aware ; অজ্ঞাত, অপরিজ্ঞাত।

ŭn-ă-wāres′, ŭn-ă-wāre′, *adv.* Without being aware ; without premeditation ; unexpectedly ; unintentionally ; suddenly ; অজ্ঞাতসারে ; অচিন্তিতপূর্ব্বভাবে ; অপ্রত্যাশিতরূপে ; অনিচ্ছাপূর্ব্বক ; হঠাৎ, সহসা, অতর্কিতভাবে।

ŭn-awed′ (-äd), *adj.* Not restrained by fear ; অভীত।

ŭn-backed′ (-băkt), *adj.* **1.** Unbroken; অসায়েস্তা করা। **2.** Not supported or aided ; অসমর্থিত, অপৃষ্ঠপোষিত। **3.** Not moved back; অপশ্চাৎচালিত।

ŭn-băf′-fled (-fld), *adj.* Not defeated or confounded ; অপরাজিত, অপরাহত, অপ্রতিহত।

ŭn-baked′ (-bākt), *adj.* Not baked ; আসেঁকা।

ŭn-băl′-anced (-ănst), *adj.* **1.** Not poised ; অসমতুলিত। **2.** Not brought to an equality of debt nd cred it ; অসমীকৃতায়ব্যয় (হিঃ কোঃ), বৈষম্যাপন্ন। 3. Disordered ; disarranged ; as, *unbalanced* mind ; বিক্ষিপ্ত ; বিকৃত।

ŭn-băl′-lăst, *v. t.* To free from balast ; ভারসামঞ্জস্যবিধায়ক বস্তু নিক্ষেপ করা।

ŭn-băl′-lăst-ĕd, *adj.* Not furnished with ballast ; unsteady ; ভারসামঞ্জস্য-বিধায়ক বস্তু অসমন্বিত ; অস্থির।

ŭn-bănd′-āged, *adj.* Not bandaged ; অবস্ত্রবন্ধনবদ্ধ।

ŭn-bănd′-ĕd, *adj.* Stripped of a band ; having no band ; বন্ধনীশূন্য ; বন্ধনীরহিত।

ŭn-băn′-nered (-nêrd), *adj.* Having no banner ; পতাকাহীন, পতাকাশূন্য।

ŭn-băp-tīzed′, *adj.* Not baptized ; অদীক্ষিত।

ŭn-băr′, *v. t.* To remove a bar or bars from ; to unfasten ; অর্গল স্থানান্তরিত করা ; অর্গলমুক্ত করা, হুড়কা বা খিল খোলা।

ŭn-băsh′-fûl, *adj.* Not bashful ; impudent ; shameless ; লজ্জাহীন ; ধৃষ্ট ; নির্লজ্জ।

ŭn-băt′-ĕd, *adj.* **1.** Undiminished ; অপ্রশমিত। **2.** Unblunted ; অকুণ্ঠিত।

ŭn-bathed′, *adj.* Not bathed ; not wet ; অস্নাত, অকৃতস্নান ; অসিক্ত।

ŭn-băt′-tered (-têrd), *adj.* Not battered or bruised ; অচূর্ণীকৃত, অবিমথিত, অনিষ্পিষ্ট।

ŭn-bāy′ (-bā), *v. t.* To open ; to free from restraint ; মুক্ত করা, উন্মুক্ত করা ; নিগ্রহমুক্ত করা।

ŭn-bear′ (-bār), *v. t.* To remove or loose the bearing-rein off ; বলগা অপসারিত করা, বলগা শ্লথ করা।

ŭn-bear′-a-ble (-bār-ă-bl), *adj.* Intolerable ; অসহনীয়, অসহ্য, দুঃসহ, দুর্ব্বহ। **—bly,** *adv.*

ŭn-beard′-ĕd (-bērd-), *adj.* Having no beard ; beardless ; শ্মশ্রু-বিহীন ; শ্মশ্রুশূন্য।

ŭn-bear′-ĭng (-bār-), *adj.* Bearing or producing no fruit ; অফল, ফলশূন্য, অফলপ্রসূ, বন্ধ্যা।

ŭn-beat′-en (-bēt-n), *adj.* **1.** Not treated with blows ; অপ্রহৃত। **2.** Untrod ; not beaten by the feet ; অপাদন্যস্ত, অপাদস্পৃষ্ট ; অপাদাহত, অচরণমর্দ্দিত।

ŭn-beau′-te-ous (-bü-tē-ŭs), **ŭn-beau′-ti-fûl** (-bü-), *adjs.* Not beautiful ; অসুন্দর।

ŭn-beau′-ti-fied (-bü-tē-fīd), *adj.* Not beautified ; অশোভিত।

ŭn-bĕ-com′-ĭng (-cŭm-), *adj.* Not becoming ; অশোভন, অমানানসই, অভব্য। **—ly,** *adv.* **—ness,** *n.* The state of being indecorous ; অশোভনতা, অনৌচিত্য।

ŭn-bĕd′, *v. t.* To raise or rouse from bed ; শয্যোত্থিত করা, নিদ্রাভঙ্গ করা।

ŭn-bĕ-fĭt′-ting (-ĭng) *adj.* Unsuitable ; unbecoming ; অনুপযুক্ত, অনুপযোগী ; অমানানসই, অশোভন, অযুক্ত।

ŭn-bĕ-friend′-ĕd (-frĕnd-), *adj.* Not supported by friends ; অবান্ধবিত।

ŭn-bĕ-gŏt′, ŭn-bĕ-gŏt′-ten (-n), *adjs.* **1.** Not begotten or generated ; eternal ; অপ্রসূত, অজ ; অনাদি, অনন্ত। **2.** Not yet begotten ; অদ্যাপি অজাত।

ŭn-bĕ-guile′ (-gīl), *v. t.* To undeceive ; অপ্রতারিত করা, অপ্রবঞ্চিত করা।

ŭn-bĕ-gŭn′, *adj.* Not yet begun ; অনারব্ধ।

ŭn-bĕ-hĕld′, *adj.* Not beheld ; not visible ; অদৃষ্ট ; অদৃশ্য।

ŭn-bĕ-lief′ (-lēf), *n.* Incredulity ; infidelity ; scepticism ; disbelief in the truth of a gospel ; অবিশ্বাস, অপ্রত্যয় ; অবিশ্বস্ততা ; নাস্তিকতা ; খৃষ্টীয় সুসমচারের সত্যতায় অবিশ্বাস।

ŭn-bĕ-liev′-ă-bĭl-ĭ-ty (-lēv-), *n.* Incredibility ; thing unbelievable ; অবিশ্বাসিতা ; অবিশ্বাস্য বিষয়।

ŭn-bĕ-liev′-a-ble (-lēv-ă-bl), *adj.* That cannot be believed ; অবিশ্বাস্য।

ŭn-bē-lieve′ (-lēv-), *v. t.* To discredit ; অবিশ্বাস করা।

ŭn-bĕ-liev′-ẽr (-lēv-), *n.* An incredulous person ; a sceptic ; an infidel ; অবিশ্বাসী লোক ; নাস্তিক ; পাষণ্ড।

ŭn-bĕ-liev′-ĭng (-lēv-), *adj.* Incredulous ; sceptic ; অবিশ্বাসী ; নাস্তিক।

ŭn-bĕ-loved′ (-lŭvd), *adj.* Not beloved ; অপ্রিয়।

ŭn-bĕnd′, *v. t. & i.* **1.** To free from flexure ; to make straight ; অবক্র করা ; ঋজু করা, সরল করা, সোজা করা। **2.** To loosen ; ঢিলা করা, আলগা করা, শিথিল করা। **3.** To set at ease ; খাতিরজমা করা, নিরুদ্বিগ্ন করা। **4.** To unfasten, as sails from the spars or stays ; পাইল প্রভৃতি খোলা। **5.** To cast loose, as a cable ; নিক্ষেপ করা। **6.** To untie, as a rope ; গেরো খোলা। *Verb i* **1.** To cease to be bent ; ঋজু হওয়া, সরল হওয়া। **2.** To relax in severity etc. ; কঠোরতা প্রভৃতি হ্রাস পাওয়া। **—ing,** *adj.* **1.** Not suffering from flexure ; অনম্য। **2.** Unyielding ; অবশ্য, অবশীকরণযোগ্য। **—ing-ly,** *adv.* **—ing-ness,** *n.*

ŭn-bĕn′-ĕ-ficed (-fīst), *adj.* Not enjoying a benefice ; অযাজকবৃত্তিভোগী।

ŭn-bĕn′-ĕ-fĭt-ĕd, *adj* Not having received benefit ; অনুপকৃত।

ŭn-bĕ-night′-ĕd (-nīt-), *adj.* Not visited by darkness ; অনিশাপ্রাপ্ত।

ŭn-bĕ-nign′ (-nīn), *adj.* Not benign ; not benignant ; অসৌম্য ; অকারুণিক, অমঙ্গলজনক।

ŭn-bĕnt′, *adj.* **1.** Relaxed ; অশিথিলীকৃত। **2.** Unstrung ; অগুণারোপিত। **3.** Taken from the yards ; পাইল-দণ্ড হইতে উন্মোচিত।

un-bĕ-queathed′ (-kwĕthd), *adj.* Not given by legacy ; উত্তরাধিকারী-সূত্রে অদত্ত।

ŭn-bĕ-seem′-ĭng (-sēm-), *adj.* Unbecoming ; not befitting ; অশোভন ; অনুচিত। **—ly,** *adv.* **—ness,** *n.*

ŭn-bĕ-sought′ (-sät), *adj.* Not sought by petition or entreaty ; অপ্রার্থিত, অযাচিত।

ŭn-bĕ-spō′-ken (-kn), *adj.* Not bespoken or ordered beforehand ; পূর্ব্ব হইতে অনাদিষ্ট।

ŭn-bĕ-starred′ (-stârd), *adj.* Not adorned with stars ; অতারকিত, অতারকাভূষিত, অনক্ষত্রখচিত।

ŭn-bĕ-stowed′ (-stōd), *adj.* Not given ; অদত্ত, অপ্রদত্ত, অনর্পিত।

ŭn-bĕ-trayed′ (-trād), *adj.* Not betrayed ; অশত্রুকরসমর্পিত।

ŭn-bĕ-wailed′ (-wāld), *adj.* Not bewailed ; not lamented ; অশোচিত; অবিলপিত।

ŭn-bĕ-witch′ (-wĭch), *v. t.* To free from fascination ; মোহমোচন করা, অপকুহকিত করা, অমায়ামুক্ত করা।

ŭn-bī′-ăs, *v. t.* To free from bias or prejudice ; পক্ষপাতশূন্য করা, নিরপেক্ষ করা।

ŭn-bī′-ased (-ăst), **—assed** (-ăst), *adjs.* Free from prejudice or bias ; impartial ; পক্ষপাতশূন্য ; নিরপেক্ষ। **—ly,** *adv.* **—ness,** *n.*

ŭn-bĭd′, —bĭd′-den (-dn), *adjs.* **1.** Not commanded ; অনাদিষ্ট। **2.** Uninvited ; অনিমন্ত্রিত, অনাহূত।

ŭn-bĭg′-ŏt-ĕd, *adj.* Free from bigotry ; গোঁড়ামিশূন্য।

ŭn-bīnd′, *v. t.* To untie ; to unfasten ; to set free ; গ্রন্থিমোচন করা ; বন্ধন উন্মোচন করা ; মুক্ত করা।

ŭn-bĭsh′-ŏp, *v. t.* To deprive of episcopal orders ; ধর্ম্মাধ্যক্ষের পদ হইতে চ্যুত করা।

ŭn-bĭt′, *adj* Not bitten ; অদষ্ট।

ŭn-bĭt′, *v. t.* **1.** To unbridle ; রশ্মিমুক্ত করা। **2.** (*Naut.*) To remove the turns of (a rope or cable) from the bits ; (নৌবিদ্যা) রজ্জুর বা কাছির পাক খোলা।

ŭn-blām′-ă-ble (-bl), *adj.* That cannot be blamed ; অনিন্দ্য, অনিন্দনীয়, অদূষ্য, অনবদ্য। **—bly,** *adv.* **—ness,** *n.*

ŭn-blāmed′, *adj.* Free from censure ; অনিন্দিত।

ŭn-blăst′-ĕd, *adj.* Not blasted ; not made to wither ; অবিধ্বস্ত ; অশুষ্কীকৃত।

ŭn-bleached′ (-blēcht), *adj.* Not bleached ; অধৌত, কোরা।

ŭn-bleed′-ĭng (-blēd), *adj.* Not suffering from loss of blood ; অগলদ্‌রক্ত।

ŭn-blem′-ished (-ĭsht), *adj.* **1.** Spotless ; pure ; নিষ্কলঙ্ক, নিখুঁত ; বিশুদ্ধ, পবিত্র। **2.** Irreproachable ; অনিন্দ্য।

ŭn-blenched′ (-blĕncht), *adj.* Not disgraced ; not injured by stain or soil ; অকলঙ্কিত ; অমলিন।

ŭn-blĕnd′-ĕd, *adj.* Not blended ; অমিশ্রিত।

ŭn-blĕst′, *adj.* Excluded from benediction ; অধন্য।

ŭn-blight′-ĕd (-blīt-), *adj.* Not blighted ; অশুষ্কীভূত।

ŭn-blood′-ĕd (-blŭd-), *adj.* Not stained with blood ; অরক্তরঞ্জিত, অরুধিররঞ্জিত।

ŭn-blood′-ȳ (-blŭd-), *adj.* Not stained with blood ; not cruel ; অরক্তরঞ্জিত ; অক্রুর, অনিঠুর।

ŭn-blŏs′-sŏm-ĭng, *adj.* Not producing blossoms ; অপুষ্পপ্রসূ, অকুসুমপ্রসূ।

ŭn-blŏt′-ted (-ĕd), *adj.* Not blotted ; অনুপ্ত, অব্যামৃষ্ট।

ŭn-blown′ (-blōn), *adj.* Not blown ; not having the bud expanded ; not inflated with wind ; অপ্রস্ফুটিত ; অবিকশিত ; অবায়ুস্ফীত।

ŭn-blŭnt′-ĕd, *adj.* Not made obtuse or dull ; অকুণ্ঠিত।

ŭn-blŭsh′-ĭng, *adj.* Destitute of shame ; impudent ; নির্লজ্জ, বিগতলজ্জ; ধৃষ্ট, প্রগল্‌ভ : **—ly,** *adv.*

ŭn-boast′-fûl (-bōst-) *adj.* Unassuming ; modest ; অগর্ব্বিত, নিরভিমান, অভিমানশূন্য ; বিনয়ী। **ly,** *adv.* **—ness,** *n.*

ŭn-bŏd′-ied (-ĭd), *adj.* Having no material body ; "We know not where *unbodied* spirits dwell, but this we know, they are invisible" ; incorporeal ; freed from the body ; বিদেহী ; অশরীরী ; দেহমুক্ত।

ŭn-boiled′ (-boyld), *adj.* Not boiled ; অসিদ্ধ।

ŭn-bōlt′, *v. t.* To remove a bolt from ; to unfasten ; বল্টু খোলা ; বন্ধন খোলা।

ŭn-bōlt′-ĕd, *adj.* **1.** Freed from fastening by bolts ; অনর্গলবদ্ধ। **2.** Not having the bran or coarse part separated by a bolter ; as, *unbolted* meal ; আচালা।

ŭn′-bŏn′-nĕt′-ĕd, *adj.* Having no bonnet on ; টুপিহীন।

ŭn-bŏn′-nȳ, *adj.* Ugly ; unhealthy ; বিশ্রী ; অস্বাস্থ্যকর।

ŭn-booked′ (-bŏŏkt), *adj.* Not written in books ; unrecorded ; অগ্রন্থনিবদ্ধ ; অলিপিবদ্ধ।

ŭn-bŏŏk′-ĭsh, *adj.* **1.** Not addicted to books or reading ; "It is to be wondered how museless and *unbookish* they were, minding not but the feats of war" ; অগ্রন্থাসক্ত, অনধ্যয়নানুরাগী। **2.** Not cultivated by erudition ; অননুশীলিত।

ŭn-boot′, *v. t.* To take off boots from ; বুট খুলিয়া নেওয়া।

ŭn-boot′-ĕd, *adj.* Stripped of boots ; not having boots on ; বুটবিরহিত ; বুটবিহীন।

ŭn-bŏrn′, *adj.* Not born ; not yet brought into life ; future ; অজাত, অনুৎপন্ন ; অজ ; অনাগত, ভবিষ্যৎ।

ŭn-bŏr′-rowed (-rōd), *adj.* Genuine ; as, *unborrowed* gold ;

native ; of one's own ; original ; খাঁটি, সাঁচ্চা, প্রকৃত ; স্বজাতীয় ; মৌলিক, নিজস্ব ।

ŭn-bŏs'-om (-ŭm), *v. t.* To disclose ; to reveal in confidence ; as, to *unbosom* one's secret ; গুপ্তকথা প্রকাশ করা ; রহস্যউদ্‌ঘাটন করা, বিশ্বাস করিয়া বলা ।

ŭn-bŏt'-tomed (-ŏmd), *adj.* Having no bottom ; "The dark *unbottomed* infinite abyss" ; bottomless ; তলহীন ; অতল ।

ŭn-bought' (-bät), *adj.* Obtained without money ; অক্রীত ।

ŭn-bound' (-bownd), *adj.* **1.** Not bound ; বন্ধনশূন্য, অনিবদ্ধিত । **2.** Wanting a cover ; as, *unbound* books ; আবাঁধা । **3.** Not bound by obligation ; অবাধিত ।

ŭn-bound'-ĕd (-bownd-), *adj.* Having no bound or limit ; অসীম, সীমাহীন, সীমাহারা, সীমাশূন্য, সীমাতীত (*poet.*)। **—ly**, *adv.* **—ness**, *n.*

ŭn-boun'-te-ous (-bown-tē-ŭs), *adj.* Not bounteous ; not liberal ; অমুক্তহস্ত ; অবদান্য ।

ŭn-bow', *v. t.* To unbend ; ধনুকের ছিলা দেওয়া ।

ŭn-bow'-ĕl, *v. t.* To deprive of the entrails ; to eviscerate ; অন্ত্রহীন করা; অন্ত্র নিষ্কাশিত করা, নিরন্ত্রীকৃত করা।

ŭn-brace' (-brās), *v. t.* To loose ; to relax ; as, to *unbrace* the strings of a violin ; আলগা করা, শ্লথ করা ; ঢিলা করা ।

ŭn-braid' (-brād), *v. t.* To separate the strands of ; to disentangle ; রজ্জুর গুণ পৃথক করা ; জট খোলা ।

ŭn-branched' (-brăncht), *adj.* Not shooting into branches ; অশাখান্বিত ।

ŭn-brănch'-ing, *adj.* Not dividing into branches ; আশাখান্বিত ।

ŭn-breast' (-brĕst), *v. t.* To disclose or lay open ; "To whose open eye the hearts of wicked men *unbreasted* lie" ; প্রকাশ করা, উন্মুক্ত করা, উদ্‌ঘাটিত করা ।

ŭn-breath'-a-ble (-brēth-ă-bl), *adj.* Not breathable ; অপ্রশ্বাস্য ।

ŭn-brĕd', *adj.* Not well-bred ; not taught ; অসুশিক্ষিত ; অশিক্ষিত ।

ŭn-breech' (-brēch), *v. t.* To remove the breeches or the breech of ; পাজামা খোলা ।

ŭn-breeched' (-brēcht), *adj.* Having no breeches ; পাজামাবিহীন ।

ŭn-brewed' (-brōōd), *adj.* Not mixed ; pure ; "They drink the stream *Unbrewed* and ever full" ; genuine ; অমিশ্রিত ; বিশুদ্ধ ; অকৃত্রিম ।

ŭn-brībed', *adj.* Not corrupted by money ; অনুৎকোচদত্ত ।

ŭn-bridged' (-brĭjd), *adj.* Not crossed by a bridge ; অসেতুবদ্ধ ।

ŭn-brī'-dle (-dl), *v. t.* To free from the bridle ; বল্গা মুক্ত করা, রশ্মিমুক্ত করা ।

ŭn-brī'-dled (-dld), *adj.* Unrestrained ; licentious ; অসংযত ; বিলাসী, বিলাসপরায়ণ, কামাচারী, স্বৈরবৃত্তি, উচ্ছৃঙ্খল, লম্পট, ব্যভিচারী ।

ŭn-brōke', **ŭn-brō'-ken** (-kn), *adjs.* **1.** Not subdued ; "By age *unbroke*" ; not accustomed to the saddle, harness, or a yoke ; as, an *unbroken* horse ; অবশীভূত ; অসায়েস্তাকৃত । **2.** Whole ; আস্তা, গোটা, অখণ্ড ।

ŭn-broth'-ĕr-lȳ (-brŭth-), *adj.* Not becoming a brother ; unkind ; আভ্রাত্রোচিত ; নির্দয় ।

ŭn'-bruised' (-brōōzd), *adj.* Not bruised ; not crushed or hurt ; অচূর্ণীকৃত ; অধ্বংসীকৃত, অকুট্টিত ।

ŭn-buck'-le (-l), *v. t.* To loose from buckles ; as, to *unbuckle* shoe ; to unfasten ; বকলস খোলা ; গ্রন্থিমোচন করা ।

ŭn-build' (-bĭld), *v. t.* To demolish what is built ; to raze ; "To *unbuild* the city and to lay it flat" ; ধ্বংস করা ; ধূলিসাৎ করা ।

ŭn-built' (-bĭlt), *adj.* Not yet built ; অনির্মিত ।

ŭn-buoyed' (-boyd), *adj.* Not buoyed or borne up ; অনাশ্বাসিত ।

ŭn-bur'-den (-bêr-dn), *v. t.* See UNBURTHEN.

ŭn-bur'-den-some (-bêr-dn-sŭm), *adj.* Not oppressive ; অদুর্ব্বহ ।

ŭn-bur'-ied (-bĕr-ĭd), *adj.* Uninterred ; অসমাহিত, অপ্রোথিত ।

ŭn-burned' (-bêrnd) **—burnt** (-bêrnt), *adjs.* Not consumed or injured by fire ; not baked ; অদগ্ধ ; অপক্ব ।

ŭn-burn'-ing (-bêrn-), *adj.* Not consuming away by fire ; অদহনশীল, অদাহী ।

ŭn-bŭr'-row (-ō), *v. t.* To chase out of a burrow ; "He can bring down sparrows and *unburrow* rabbits" ; গর্ত্ত হইতে বাহির করা ।

ŭn-bur'-then (-bêr-thn), *v. t.* **1.** To rid of a load ; ভারমুক্ত করা । **2.** To throw off as, burden ; ভার ফেলিয়া দেওয়া । **3.** To ease as the mind or heart, by disclosing the cause of trouble, grief, etc. ; মানসিক উদ্বেগভার লঘু করা, চিত্তের ভার লঘু করা ।

ŭn-bus'-ied (-bĭz-ĭd), *adj.* Not employed ; idle ; অকর্ম্মনিরত ; অলস ।

ŭn-busi'-nĕss-like (-bĭz-), *adj.* Not businesslike ; অব্যবসায়িসমুচিত ।

ŭn-bŭt'-ton (-n), *v. t.* To loose the buttons of ; বোতাম খোলা ।

ŭn-cāge', *v. t.* To loose from a cage ; পিঞ্জরমুক্ত করা ।

ŭn-called' (-käld), *adj.* Not summoned or invited ; অনাহূত, অনিমন্ত্রিত, অযাচিত । **Uncalled for**—স্বয়ং উপস্থিত, উপরপড়া, অযাচিত ।

ŭn-calm' (-kâm), *v. t.* To disturb ; বিক্ষুব্ধ করা ।

ŭn-căn'-cĕl-lā-ble (-bl), *adj.* Not cancelled ; not erased ; অকর্ত্তিত ; অনবলুপ্ত ।

ŭn-căn'-dĭd *adj.* Not candid ; not frank or sincere ; অসরল ; কপট, কৃত্রিম ।

ŭn-căn'-nȳ, *adj.* 1. Unearthly; eerie; weird; অপার্থিব; ছমছমে; ভৌতিক। 2. Severe; গুরুতর। **—ni-ly**, *adv.* **—ni-ness**, *n.*

ŭn-că-nŏn'-i-căl, *adj.* 1. Not canonical; ধর্ম্মনিয়মবিরোধী। 2. Not acknowledged as authentic; প্রামাণিক বলিয়া অস্বীকৃত। **—ly**, *adv.* **—ness**, *n.*

ŭn-căn'-ŏn-ize, *v. t.* 1. To deprive of canonical authority; ধর্ম্মশাস্ত্র-সম্বন্ধীয় প্রামাণিকতা হইতে বিচ্যুত করা। 2. To reduce from the rank of a canonized saint; খৃষ্টীয় সিদ্ধপুরুষ-সমাজ হইতে বিচ্যুত করা।

ŭn căn'-ŏ-pied (-pîd), *adj.* Not covered by a canopy; অচন্দ্রাতপাচ্ছাদিত।

ŭn-căn'-vassed (-văst), *adj.* Not canvassed; ক্যাম্বিস্‌বস্ত্রদ্বারা অনাচ্ছাদিত।

ŭn-căp', *v. t.* To remove a cap or cover; টুপি খোলা, ঢাকনি উন্মুক্ত করা।

ŭn-cared', *adj.* Not regarded; অনবহিত।

ŭn-car-essed' (-ŏst), *adj.* Not caressed; অনাদৃত।

ŭn-că'-ri-ă, *n.* A genus of trees; একজাতীয় বৃক্ষ।

ŭn-câr'-pĕt-ĕd, *adj.* Not covered with a carpet; গালিচাবিহীন, অগালিচামণ্ডিত।

ŭn-case', *v. t.* 1. To disengage from a covering; ঢাকনী হইতে মুক্ত করা। 2. To unfurl and display, as the colours of regiment; সেনা-পল্টনের পতাকা অনাবৰ্ত্তিত করা, সেনা-পল্টনের পতাকা উড়ান।

ŭn-căt'-ĕ-c͟hised' *adj.* untaught; অনুপদিষ্ট, অনধ্যাপিত।

ŭn-caused' (-käzd), *adj.* Having no precedent cause; স্বয়ংজাত।

ŭn-ceas'-ing (-sēs-), *adj.* Not ceasing; continual; uninterrupted; সতত, অবিরত; অবিরাম, বিরাম-বিহীন, বিরামশূন্য, অবিশ্রান্ত, বিশ্রাম-শূন্য; নিরবচ্ছিন্ন।

ŭn-cēd'-ĕd, *adj.* Not ceded; not granted or transferred; অনুৎসৃষ্ট; অত্যক্ত, অভুক্ত।

ŭn-cĕl'-ĕ-brāt-ĕd, *adj.* Not celebrated or solemnized; অননুষ্ঠিত।

ŭn-cĕn'-sŭr-ă-ble (-bl), *adj.* Not worthy of censure; অনিন্দার্হ, অগর্হনীয়, অবিগর্হ্য, অনিন্দনীয়।

ŭn-cĕn-sured' (-shôrd), *adj.* Not censured; exempt from blame; অনিন্দিত; অনিন্দ্য।

ŭn-cĕn'-tri-căl, *adj.* Not central; অকেন্দ্রিক।

ŭn-cêr-ĕ-mō'-ni-ous (-us), *adj.* Without ceremony; লৌকিকতা-শূন্য। **—ly**, *adv.*

ŭn-cêr'-tain (-tān), *adj.* 1. Not certain; doubtful; not certainly known; অনিশ্চিত; সন্দেহপূর্ণ; অসম্যগ্‌জ্ঞাত। 2. Ambiguous; equivocal; সন্দিগ্ধার্থ; দ্ব্যর্থবোধক। 3. Unreliable; insecure; অবিশ্বাস-যোগ্য; অনির্ভরযোগ্য। 4. Undecided; hesitating; অনিশ্চিত; দ্বিধাকরী। 5. Not steady; অস্থির। 6. Fickle; "O women! in our hours of ease *Uncertain*, coy, and hard to please"; অস্থিরমতি, অস্থিরচিত্ত। 7. Not known; indefinite; অজ্ঞাত; অনির্দ্দিষ্ট। **—ly**, *adv.* **—ty**, *n.* 1. The quality or state of being uncertain; অনিশ্চয়তা, অনিশ্চিতত্ব, অনির্দ্দিষ্টতা, বিচিকিৎসা। 2. That which is uncertain; something unknown; অনিশ্চিত বিষয়; অজ্ঞাত বিষয়।

ŭn-chain' (-chān), *v. t.* To free from chains or slavery; শৃঙ্খলমুক্ত করা, দাসত্বনিগড় হইতে মুক্ত করা।

ŭn-chăl'-lenge-a-ble (-lĕnj-ă-bl), *adj.* That cannot be challenged; অনাহ্বানীয়। **—bly**, *adv.*

ŭn-chăl'-lenged (-lĕnjd), *adj.* Not objected to; অনাপত্তিপ্রদত্ত।

ŭn-chănc'-ȳ, *adj.* Dangerous to have to do with; বিপৎপ্রদ।

ŭn-chănge'-ă-ble (-bl), *adj.* Not capable of change; immutable; ধ্রুব, অপরিবর্ত্তনীয়, অপরিবর্ত্তনসহ, অবিক্রিয়, অবিকারী, অপরিবর্ত্ত্য, নির্ব্বিকল্প, নিত্য, স্থির; অপরিবর্ত্তনশীল। **—bly**, *adv.* **—ness**, *n.* The state of being unchangeable; অপরিবর্ত্তনীয়তা, পরিবর্ত্তনশীলতা, নিত্যতা, স্থিরতা।

ŭn-chănged', *adj.* Not altered; not alterable; অপরিবর্ত্তিত; অপরিবর্ত্তনীয়, অপরিবর্ত্তনসহ।

ŭn-chăng'-ing, *adj.* Suffering no alteration; অপরিবর্ত্তী, অবিকারী (হিঃ কোঃ), অবিক্রিয় (ঐ)। **—ly**, *adj.*

ŭn-c͟hăr-ăc-tĕr-is'-tic, *adj.* Unsuited to, or not exhibiting, the character of; অলাক্ষণিক, অবিশেষত্বসূচক।

ŭn-charged' (-chârjd), *adj.* Not charged; unloaded; as, *uncharged* gun; অসম্পূরিত; অভারাক্রান্ত।

ŭn'-chăr-i-tă-ble (-bl), *adj.* Contrary to charity; অদীনবৎসল, পরদোষদর্শী।

ŭn-chărm', *v. t.* To release from charm; কুহকবিমুক্ত করা, মোহ-মোচন করা।

ŭn-charmed' (-chârmd), *adj.* Not fascinated; অবিমোহিত, অবিমুগ্ধ।

ŭn-chărm'-ing, *adj.* Not charming; অবিমোহন।

ŭn-châr'-nĕl, *v. t.* To disentomb; কবর হইতে উৎখাতিত করা।

ŭn-châr[illegible]-ĕd, *adj.* Not delineated on a chart; নক্সার উপর অনঙ্কিত।

ŭn-châr'-tered (-têrd), *adj.* Having no charter; অপ্রাপ্তসনন্দ।

ŭn-châr'-ȳ, *adj.* Not wary; not frugal; অসতর্ক; অমিতব্যয়ী।

ŭn-chaste', *adj.* Not chaste; libidinous; lewed; লম্পট, ভ্রষ্ট; ব্যভিচারী, ব্যভিচারিণী (*fem.*), অসতী (*ib.*), অসাধ্বী (*ib.*); কুলটা, সাঙ্করিকা (বাংশুঃ)। **—chas'-ti-ty**, *n.* The state of being unchaste; অসতীত্ব, ভ্রষ্টাচার, লাম্পট্য, অব্রহ্মচর্য্য।

ŭn-chăs-tis'-ă-ble (-bl) *adj.* That cannot be chastised; অসংশোধনীয়।

ŭn-chȁs-tīsed′, *adj.* Not punished or corrected ; অদণ্ডিত ।

ŭn-chȁs′-ti-tȳ, *n.* Incontinence ; lewdness ; অসতীত্ব (of females), অব্রহ্মচর্য্য ; লাম্পট্য, ব্যভিচার ।

ŭn-checked′ (-chĕkt), *adj.* Not restrained or hindered ; অসংযত, অবাধাপ্রাপ্ত ।

ŭn-chĕck′-ered (-êrd), *adj.* Not diversified ; অবিচিত্রিত ।

ŭn-cheered′ (-chērd), *adj.* Not cheered ; অপ্রফুল্ল ।

ŭn-cheer′-fûl (-chēr-), *adj.* Not cheerful ; sad ; "*Uncheerful* in countenance"; অপ্রফুল্ল, অহৃষ্ট,অপ্রসন্ন ; বিষণ্ণ । **—ness**, *n.* The state of being uncheerful ; অপ্রফুল্লতা, অপ্রসন্নতা ।

ŭn-cheer′-ȳ (-chēr-), *adj.* Dull ; "The *uncheery* hours which perpetually overtake us" ; not enlivening; অপ্রসন্ন; অপ্রফুল্লতাজনক ।

ŭn-chewed′ (-chôd), *adj.* Not masticated ; অচর্ব্বিত ।

ŭn-chĭd′-ĕd, *adj.* Not rebuked ; অতিরস্কৃত, অভৎর্সিত ।

ŭn-chīld′, *v. t.* **1.** To bereave of children ; to make childless ; সন্তানহীন করা; নিঃসন্তান করা । **2.** To divest of the character of a child ; "They do justly *uuchild* themselves, that in main elections dispose of themselves without the consent of those who gave them being" ; শিশুসুলভ ভাব নষ্ট করা ।

ŭn-chīld′-ish, *adj.* Not childish ; not fit or proper for children ; অশিশুসুলভ ; অশৈশবোচিত ।

ŭn-chilled′ (-chīld), *adj.* Not chilled ; অশীতার্ত্ত ।

ŭn-chiv′-al-rous (-shĭv-ăl-rŭs), *adj.* Not according to chivalry ; অনারীমর্য্যাদাসম্পন্ন । **—ly**, *adv.*

ŭn-c̱hris′-tened (-nd), *adj.* Not christened ; অদীক্ষিত ।

ŭn-c̱hris′-tiăn, *v. t.* To make unchristian ; "Atheism is a sin that doth not only *unchristian* but unman, a person that is guilty of it"; অখৃষ্টীয়ভাবাপন্ন করা । **—ly**, *adv.* **—ness**, *n.*

ŭn-c̱hris′-tiăn-īze, *v. t.* To turn from the Christian faith ; to cause to degenerate from the belief and profession of Christianity ; খৃষ্টধর্ম্ম ত্যাগ করা ; খৃষ্টধর্ম্মের ভাব হইতে বিচ্যুত হওয়া ।

ŭn-c̱hrŏn′-i-cled (-kld), *adj.* Not recorded in a chronicle ; অলিখিত ।

ŭn-church′ (-chêrch), *v. t.* To expel from a church ; to deprive of the character and rights of a church ; "The Greeks......for this cause stand utterly *unchurched* by the Church of Rome" ; খৃষ্টীয় ধর্ম্মসংঘ হইতে বিতাড়িত করা ; কোন ধর্ম্মসংঘের প্রকৃতি বা অধিকার হইতে বিচ্যুত করা ।

ŭn′-ci-ăl (-shi-), *adj.* & *n.* Pertaining to, or appellative of, letters of a large size, used in ancient

Uncial letters.

Latin and Greek manuscripts ; প্রাচীন গ্রীক ও ল্যাটিন হস্তাক্ষরে ব্যবহৃত একজাতীয় বৃহৎ অক্ষর সম্বন্ধীয় বা উহার উপাধিবাচক । *Noun.* An uncial letter ; ঐ জাতীয় অক্ষর ।

ŭn′-ci-fôrm, *adj.* Hook-shaped ; বড়িশাকৃতি, বড়িশাকার ।

ŭn′-ci-nāte, *adj.* (*Bot.*) Hooked at the end ; (উদ্ভিদ্‌বিদ্যা) প্রান্তদেশে বড়িশাকৃতি ।

ŭn-cinc′-tured (-ṣingk-türd), *adj.* Without a cincture ; অমেখলাবেষ্টিত ।

ŭn-cir′-cŭm-cīsed (-sêr-), *adj.* অচ্ছিন্নত্বক্‌, অপরিকর্ত্তিত ।

ŭn-cir-cŭm-ci′-sion (-sêr-), *n.* Absence of circumcision ; অত্বক্‌ছেদন, অলিঙ্গাগ্রচর্ম্মচ্ছেদন ।

ŭn-cir-cŭm-scrībed′ (-sêr-), *adj.* Not bounded or limited; অসীমাবদ্ধ ।

ŭn-cir′-cŭm-spĕct (-sêr-), *adj.* Not circumspect ; অসতর্ক, অনবহিত । **—ly**, *adj.*

ŭn-civ′-il, *adj.* **1.** Barbarous ; বর্ব্বর । **2.** Not complaisant or courteous in manner ; as, *uncivil* behaviour ; অশিষ্ট, অভদ্র, অভব্য, অবিনীত । **—ly**, *adv.*

ŭn-civ-i-li-zā′-tion, *n.* A state of savageness ; অসভ্যতা, বর্ব্বরতা ।

ŭn-claimed′ (-klāmd), *adj.* Not claimed or demanded ; as, *unclaimed* goods ; বেওয়ারিস্‌, লাওয়ারিস্‌, অস্বামিক ।

ŭn-clăr′-i-fied (-fīd), *adj.* Not purified by a separation of feculent or foreign matter ; অশোধিত ।

ŭn-clȁsp′, *v. t.* To loose the clasp of ; to open, as something fastened with or as with a clasp ; আঁকড়া ঢিল করা ; আঁকড়াদ্বারা আঁটা কোন কিছু খোলা ।

ŭn-clȁs′-si-căl (-i-), *adj.* Not classical ; "An education totally *uuclassical*" ; অসাধু, অমার্জ্জিত ।

ŭn′-cle (ŭng-kl), *n.* **1.** The brother of one's father or mother ; কাকা, জেঠা, খুল্লতাত, পিতৃব্য, মাতুল, জ্যেষ্ঠতাত । **2.** An aunt's husband ; পিসা, মেসো । **Uncle Sam**—(কৌতুকচ্ছলে) মার্কিণ যুক্তরাজ্যের শাসনতন্ত্র বা অধিবাসিবৃন্দ । **To talk to a person like a Dutch uncle**—To talk with kindly severity ; মিঠাকড়াভাবে বলা ।

ŭn-clean′ (-clēn), *adj.* **1.** Not clean ; foul ; dirty ; অপরিষ্কার ; কলুষিত ; অপরিচ্ছন্ন ; মলিন । **2.** Ceremonially impure ; as, an *unclean* animal ; অশুচি, অশুদ্ধ, অস্পৃশ্য । **3.** Impure ; lewed ; অমেধ্য, অপবিত্রচিত্ত ; লম্পট, অসতী, ব্যভিচারপরায়ণ । **—li-ness**, *n.* The state of being uncleanly ; অপরিচ্ছন্নতা, মলিনতা, অশুদ্ধতা, অশুচিতা, অশৌচ । **—ly**, *adj.* **1.** Filthy ; অপরিস্কার, অপরিচ্ছন্ন, নোংরা । **2.** Unchaste ;

অসতী, ব্যভিচারিণী, ব্যভিচারপরায়ণ। **Unclean animals**—যে সকল জন্তুর মাংসভক্ষণ ইহুদীদিগের পক্ষে নিষিদ্ধ ছিল ; **Unclean spirit** — দুষ্টাত্মা, পাপাত্মা ; শয়তান।

ŭn-cleansed′ (-klĕnzd), *adj.* Not purified ; অবিশোধিত, অপরিষ্কৃত, অপবিত্রীকৃত।

ŭn-clĕnch′, *v. t.* Same as UNCLINCH (which see).

ŭn-clĕr′-i-căl, *adj.* Not clerical ; অযাজকীয়, অকেরাণীসম্পর্কীয়।

ŭn-clipped′ (-klipt), *adj.* Not diminished or shortened by clipping ; অলূণপক্ষ, অচ্ছিন্নাগ্র।

ŭn-cloak′ (-klōk), *v. t.* **1.** To take off a cloak ; to unmask ; প্রাবরণ উন্মোচন করা ; মুখস খোলা। **2.** To reveal ; উদ্ঘাটিত করা, অনাবৃত করা, প্রকাশিত করা, প্রকটিত করা।

ŭn-cloaked′ (-klōkt), *adj.* Not covered or disguised ; অনাবৃত, অলক্ষ্যলিঙ্গ।

ŭn-clŏg′, *v.t.* To disencumber of obstructions ; to free from anything that retards motion ; প্রতিবন্ধক হইতে মুক্ত করা ; গতিরোধক কোন কিছু হইতে মুক্ত করা।

ŭn-clois′-têr (-kloys-), *v. t.* To release from a cloister or from confinement ; খৃষ্টীয় ভিক্ষুণীসংঘের মঠ বা নির্জ্জনসাধনাশ্রম হইতে মুক্ত করা, আবদ্ধ অবস্থা হইতে মুক্ত করা।

ŭn-clōse′, *v. t.* & *i.* **1.** To open ; "Thy letter trembling I *unclose*" ; খোলা, উদ্ঘাটন করা, উন্মুক্তকরা। **2.** To disclose ; উদ্ঘাটন করা, প্রকাশ করা। ***Verb i.*** **1.** To open ; খোলা, উন্মুক্ত হওয়া। **2.** To be expanded ; বিকশিত হওয়া

ŭn-closed′ (-klōzd), *adj.* Not separated by inclosures ; open ; অবৃতিবেষ্টিত ; উন্মুক্ত। **2.** (*Rare*) Not finished ; (কদাচিদ্ব্যবহৃত) অনম্পন্ন।

ŭn-clothe′ (-klōth), *v. t.* **1.** To strip of clothes ; to make naked ; বিবস্ত্র করা ; নগ্ন করা। **2.** To divest or strip of anything ; বিরহিত করা, বিহীন করা। **–clothed′**, *adj.* Naked ; নগ্ন, বিবস্ত্র, উলঙ্গ, দিগম্বর, দিগ্বাস।

ŭn-cloud′ (-klowd), *v. t.* **1.** To clear from clouds ; মেঘমুক্ত করা। **2.** To clear from obscurity, gloom, sadness or the like ; "*Unclouded* thy covered spirits"; অস্পষ্টতা দূর করা, বিষাদমেঘ মুক্ত করা।

ŭn-cloud′-ĕd (-klowd-), *adj.* **1.** Free from clouds ; clear ; নির্মেঘ, নিরভ্র, অপমেঘ, মেঘবিমুক্ত ; স্বচ্ছ, নির্ম্মল, বিমল। **2.** Not darkened or obscured ; অস্পষ্টীকৃত, অস্পষ্টীভূত।

ŭn-cloud′-ȳ (-klowd-), *adj.* Not cloudy ; free from clouds ; অমেঘাচ্ছন্ন ; মেঘমুক্ত, মেঘবিমুক্ত।

ŭn-clutch′ (-klŭch), *v. t.* To open something closely shut ; দৃঢ়নিরুদ্ধ বস্তু উন্মুক্ত করা।

un′-cō (ŭng-), *adj.* Unknown ; strange ; (স্কটলণ্ড) অজ্ঞাত ; অপরিচিত।

ŭn-cō-ăg′-ū-lā-ble (-bl), *adj.* That cannot be coagulated ; অশ্যানীয়, অশ্যেয়, অঘনীকরণীয়।

ŭn-cō-ăg′-ū-lāt-ĕd, *adj.* Not coagulated ; অশ্যান, অঘনীভূত।

ŭn-coat′-ĕd (-kōt-), *adj.* Not covered with a coat ; অনাবৃত, অনাচ্ছাদিত।

ŭn-cŏck′, *v. t.* **1.** To let down the cock of, as of a gun or hat ; বন্দুকের ঘোড়া নামান, কিনারা উল্টানো টুপির কিনারা নামাইয়া দেওয়া। **2.** To open or spread out from a cock or heap, as hay ; বিছান।

ŭn-cŏf′-fined (-find), *adj.* Not furnished with a coffin ; not put in a coffin ; অশবাধারবিশিষ্ট ; অশবাধারন্যস্ত, অশবাধারনিহিত।

ŭn-cŏg′-i-tā-ble (-bl), *adj.* Not capable of being cogitated or thought of ; অচিন্ত্য।

ŭn-coif′ (-koyf) *v. t.* To pull the cap off ; "Two apple women scolding and just ready to *uncoif* one another" ; টুপি তুলিয়া নেওয়া।

ŭn-coil′ (-koyl), *v. t.* To unwind or open, as the turns of a rope or the line ; পাক খোলা, পেঁচ খোলা।

ŭn-coined′ (-koynd), *adj.* Not coined ; as, *uncoined* gold ; অমুদ্রিত।

ŭn-cŏl-lĕct′-ĕd, *adj.* **1.** Not collected or received ; as, *uncollected* taxes ; অসংগৃহীত। **2.** Not recovered from confusion or wandering ; "Ashamed, confused, I started from my bed, And to my soul, yet *uncollected* said" ; অপ্রকৃতিস্থ। **–ness**, *n.*

ŭn-cŏl-lĕct′-i-ble (-bl), *adj.* That cannot be collected ; অসংগৃহীতব্য, অচয়নীয়, অসঞ্চেয়।

ŭn-col′-oured (-kŭl-êrd), *adj.* **1.** Not stained or dyed ; অরঞ্জিত। **2.** Not exaggerated ; অনতিরঞ্জিত।

ŭn-combed′ (-kōmd), *adj.* Not dressed with a comb ; অকঙ্কতিকমার্জ্জিত।

ŭn-cŏm-bīn′-ă-ble (-bl), *adj.* That cannot be combined ; অমিশ্রণযোগ্য।

ŭn-cŏm-bīned′, *adj.* Not combined; simple ; অমিশ্রিত ; অমিশ্র।

ŭn-come′-lȳ (-cŭm-), *adj.* **1.** Not comely ; কুশ্রী, বিশ্রী, কুৎসিত, অসুন্দর, কুরূপ। **2.** Unbecoming ; অশোভন, অসমীচীন। **–li-ness**, *n.*

ŭn-com′-fort-a-ble (-kŭm-fêrt-ă-ble), *adj.* **1.** Affording no comfort ; unpleasant ; অসুখজনক ; অপ্রীতিকর। **2.** Feeling discomfort ; uneasy ; অসোয়াস্তিবোধকারী ; উদ্বেগপূর্ণ, অস্বচ্ছন্দ, আরামশূন্য।

ŭn-com′-fort-ĕd (-cŭm-fêrt-), *adj.* Not comforted ; অসান্ত্বনাপ্রাপ্ত, অসন্তোষিত, অনাপ্যায়িত।

ŭn-cŏm-mănd′-ĕd, *adj.* Not required by precept, order or law ; অনির্দ্দিষ্ট, অবিহিত।

ŭn-cŏm-mĕm′-ō-rāt-ĕd, *adj.* Not commemorated ; অস্মরিত, অস্মৃতিসংরক্ষিত।

ŭn-cŏm-mĕnd′-ă-ble (-bl), *adj.* Not worthy of commendation ;

অপ্রশংসার্হ, অপ্রশংসনীয়, অপ্রশস্ত, অশ্লাঘনীয়।

ŭn-cŏm-mêr′-cial (-shăl), *adj.* Not carrying on commerce; not travelling to solicit orders for goods; অবাণিজ্যকারী; জিনিষ সরবরাহের আদেশসংগ্রহে অভ্রমণনিরত।

ŭn-cŏm-mis′-ĕr-t-ĕd, *adj.* Not pitied; অকৃতানুকম্প।

ŭn-cŏm-mis′-sioned (-mĭ-shŏnd), *adj.* Not having a commission; অভারপ্রাপ্ত।

ŭn-cŏm-mit′-ted (-ĕd), *adj.* **1.** Not committed; অসমর্পিত। **2.** Not referred to a committee; আলোচনা-সমিতির মতামতের জন্য অপ্রদত্ত। **3.** Not pledged by anything said or done; কোন বাক্য বা কার্য্যদ্বারা অনাবদ্ধ।

ŭn-cŏm′-mŏn, *adj.* Unusual; rare; strange; অসাধারণ, অসামান্য, অলোকসামান্য; কচিদ্দৃষ্ট; অদ্ভুত, আশ্চর্য্য, অপূর্ব্ব। **—ly,** *adv.* **Uncommon supposition**—উৎপ্রেক্ষালঙ্কার।

ŭn-cŏm-mū′-nĭ-cāt-ĕd, *adj.* Not disclosed or imparted to others; অজ্ঞাপিত, অপ্রকাশিত।

ŭn-cŏm-mū′-nĭ-cā-tive (-tĭv), *adj.* Reserved; সংযতবাক্, অনালাপী।

ŭn-cŏm-păct′, *adj.* Not of close texture; অঘনব্যূত, অসংহত।

ŭn-cŏm-păct′-ĕd, *adj.* Not compact; not firm; অসংহত; অদৃঢ়।

ŭn-com′-pa-nied (-kŭm-pă-nĭd), *adj.* Having no companion; সঙ্গিহীন, নিঃসঙ্গ।

ŭn-cŏm-păn′-ion-a-ble (-yŏn-ă-bl), *adj.* Not sociable; অসামাজিক।

ŭn-cŏm-pas′-sion-āte (-pă-), *adj.* Having no pity; অকরুণ, নিষ্করুণ, নির্দ্দয়।

ŭn-cŏm-pas′-sioned (-pă-phŏnd), *adj.* Unpitied; অকৃতানুকম্প।

ŭn-cŏm-pĕl′-la-ble (-ă-bl), *adj.* That cannot be forced or compelled; অবশীকরণীয়।

ŭn-cŏm-pelled′ (-pĕld), *adj.* Not forced; অবলপ্রয়োগসাধিত।

ŭn-cŏm′-pĕn-sāt-ĕd, *adj.* Unrewarded; অপুরস্কৃত।

ŭn-cŏm-plain′-ĭng (-plān-), *adj.* Not disposed to murmur; অনভিযোগশীল।

ŭn-cŏm′-plai-sānt (-plā-), *adj.* Not civil or courteous; অশিষ্ট, অভদ্র। **—ly,** *adv.*

ŭn-cŏm-plete′ (-plēt), **—plĕt′-ĕd,** *adjs.* Not complete; not finished; অসমাপ্ত; অসম্পন্ন, অনিষ্পন্ন।

ŭn-cŏm′-plĭ-cāt-ĕd, *adj.* Not complicated; অসঙ্করীকৃত।

ŭn-cŏm-plĭ-mĕn′-tă-rў, *adj.* Not complimentary; অনভিনন্দনজনক।

ŭn-cŏm-plў′-ĭng, *adj.* Not yielding to request or command; "The king was compelled to take away the seal from the *uncomplying* chancellor"; unbending; অপ্রিয়ঙ্কর; অনম্য।

ŭn-cŏm-pōsed′, *adj.* Not composed; অরচিত।

ŭn-cŏm-pound′-ĕd (-pownd-), *adj.* **1.** Not mixed; simple; অমিশ্রিত; অমিশ্র। **—ness,** *n.*

ŭn-cŏm-prē-hĕn′-sive (-sĭv), *adj.* **1.** Not comprehensive; অব্যাপক। **2.** Unable to comprehend; "Narrow spirited, *uncomprehensive* zealots"; অজ্ঞানগ্রহণক্ষম, অনবধারণক্ষম।

ŭn-cŏm-pressed′ (-prĕst), *adj,* Not compressed; অসঙ্কাপিত।

ŭn-cŏm′-prō-mĭs′-ĭng, *adj.* Not yielding to compromise; unyielding; অনাপোষযোগ্য; অবশ্য।

ŭn-cŏn-cealed′ (-sēld), *adj.* Not concealed; অপ্রচ্ছন্ন, অগূঢ়।

ŭn-cŏn-ceived′ (-sēvd), *adj.* Not thought or imagined; অচিন্তিত, অকল্পিত।

ŭn-cŏn-cerned′ (-sĕrnd), *adj.* Not anxious; indifferent; "An idle person is like one that is dead, *unconcerned* in the changes and necessities of the world"; অনুৎকণ্ঠিত, অব্যগ্র; উদাসীন, নির্লিপ্ত, অসংসৃষ্ট। **—cern′-ed-ness,** *n.*

ŭn-cŏn-cĕrt′-ĕd, *adj.* Not concerted; অব্যবস্থিত।

ŭn-cŏn-cĭl′-ĭ-āt-ĕd, *adj.* Not reconciled; অপুনর্ম্মিলিত।

ŭn-cŏn-cĭl′-ĭ-ā-tō-rў, *adj.* Not tending to conciliate; অননুরঞ্জনশীল, অপ্রসাদনশীল।

ŭn-cŏn-cŏct′-ed, *adj.* Not digested; not concocted; অপাচিত, অজীর্ণ; অকল্পিত, অনুদ্ভাবিত।

ŭn-cŏn-demned (-dĕmd), *adj.* Not judged guilty; not disapproved; not pronounced criminal; অদোষিসাব্যস্ত; অননুমোদিত; অদোষীকৃত, অনপরাধিত, অনির্ণীতাপরাধ, অনির্ণিতদোষ।

ŭn-cŏn-dĕn′-să-ble (-bl), *adj.* That cannot be condensed; অঘনীকরণীয়।

ŭn-cŏn-densed′ (-dĕnst), *adj.* Not condensed; অঘনীভূত।

ŭn-cŏn-dĭ′-tion-ăl, *adj.* **1.** Absolute; unreserved; as, *unconditional* surrender; নিরুপাধিক, অনধীন, বেকরারী, অপ্রতিবন্ধ (হিঃ কোঃ), অনুপহিত (ঐ), অনবচ্ছিন্ন (ঐ), নিরবস্থ (ঐ), অবস্থাতীত (ঐ); সর্ত্তরহিত। **2.** Not limited by any condition; নির্গুণ, নিরুপাধিক, নির্ব্বিকল্প, দেশকালাতীত, পরা, তুরীয়। **—al′-i-ty,** *n.* The state of being unconditional; অন্যথাসিদ্ধিশূন্যতা (ব্রজঃ হিন্দু)।

ŭn-cŏn-dĭ′-tioned (-shŏnd), *adj.* & *n.* Having no limiting principle, and therefore, unthinkable; নির্গুণ, নির্ব্বিকল্প, নিরুপাধিক, দেশকালাতীত, অনিয়ন্ত্রিত, মুক্ত, শুদ্ধ, কেবল, অপ্রতিবদ্ধ, অপ্রতিহত, অনবচ্ছিন্ন, নিরবস্থ। ***Noun.*** That which is conditioned; দেশকালাতীত বিষয়।

ŭn-cŏn-dŭct′-ĕd, *adj.* Unled; not guided; অপরিচালিত; অপথ-প্রদর্শিত।

ŭn-cŏn-fessed′ (-fĕst), *adj.* Not acknowledged; অপাপস্বীকৃত।

ŭn-cŏn-fīn′-ă-ble (-bl), *adj.* That cannot be confined or restrained; অরোধনীয়।

ŭn-cŏn-fined′ (-fīnd), *adj.* **1.** Free from restraint or control ; অসংযমিত, অরুদ্ধ, অবদ্ধ, বাঁধনহারা (গীতাঞ্জলি)। **2.** Having no limits ; সীমাহীন, অসীম।

ŭn-cŏn-firmed′ (-fêrmd), *adj.* Not confirmed by additional testimony ; not fortified by resolution ; "In the *unconfirmed* troops much fear did breed" ; অদৃঢ়ীকৃত ; অস্থিরসংকল্পিত।

Unconformable strata.

ŭn-cŏn-fŏrm′-ă-ble, (-bl), *adj.* **1.** Not consistent; not conforming; অননুসারী; অসদৃশ, অননুরূপ। **2.** (*Geol.*) Applied to strata not parallel with those above or below ; (ভূবিদ্যা) ঊর্দ্ধ বা অধঃস্থিত স্তরনিচয়ের সহিত অসমান্তরাল স্তরসমূহসম্বন্ধে উক্ত।

ŭn-cŏn-fŏrm′-ĭ-tȳ, *n.* Incongruity ; inconsistency ; অনানুরূপ্য ; অসঙ্গতি, অসামঞ্জস্য।

ŭn-cŏn-found′-ĕd (-fownd-), *adj.* Not confounded ; অব্যাকুলিত।

ŭn-cŏn-fūsed′ *adj.* Not embarrassed ; অনাকুলিত, সপ্রতিভ, অবিভ্রান্ত। **—fus′-ed-ly,** *adv.*

ŭn-cŏn-fūt′-ă-ble (-bl), *adj.* Not to be refuted or overthrown ; as, an *unconfutable* argument ; অখণ্ডনীয়, অকাট্য।

ŭn-cŏn-geal′-a-ble (-jēl-ă-bl), *adj.* Not capable of being congealed ; অঘনীকরণীয়।

ŭn-cŏn-gealed′ (-jēld), *adj.* Not frozen or congealed ; অঘনীকৃত, অঘনীভূত।

ŭn-cŏn-ḡē′-nĭ-ăl, *adj.* Not congenial ; as, an *uncongenial* companion ; প্রকৃতির অনুপযোগী, অননুগুণ, অসমপ্রকৃতিক।

ŭn-cŏn′-jū-găl, *adj.* Not befitting a husband or wife ; অদাম্পত্যোচিত, অদম্পতীসমুচিত।

ŭn-cŏn-jŭnc′-tive (-tĭv), *adj.* That cannot be joined ; অসংযুজ্য, অসংযোজনীয়, অযোজনীয়।

ŭn-cŏn-nĕct′-ĕd, *adj.* **1.** Not united ; separate ; অসংযুক্ত, অযুক্ত ; পৃথক্। **2.** Not coherent ; as, an *unconnected* discourse ; vague ; desultory ; অসম্বদ্ধ, অসংলগ্ন ; অস্পষ্ট ; শৃঙ্খলাশূন্য, অসংসৃষ্ট।

ŭn-con′-quer-a-ble (-kŏng-kêr-ă-bl), *adj.* That cannot be overcome in contest ; as, an *unconquerable* foe ; invincible ; insuperable ; indomitable ; অজেয়, দুর্জ্জয়, অপরাজেয়, অপরাজিত ; অনতিক্রমণীয় ; অদম্য ; দুর্দ্দম। **—bly,** *adv.*

ŭn-con′-quered (-kŏng-kêrd), *adj.* Not vanquished or defeated ; unsubdued ; অপরাজিত ; অদম্য।

ŭn-cŏn-sci-en′-tious (-shē-ĕn-shŭs), *adj.* Not related or restrained by conscience ; অবিবেকসংযমিত, অবিবেকসংযত।

ŭn-cŏn′-scion-a-ble (-shŏn-a-bl), *adj.* **1.** Unreasonable ; extravagant ; as, *unconscionable* demand ; অযৌক্তিক ; অত্যধিক, অমিত। **2.** Not guided by conscience ; অবিবেকচালিত। **—bly,** *adv.* **—ness,** *n.*

ŭn-cŏn′-scious (-shŭs), *adj.* **1.** Not conscious ; অচেতন, অচেতিত (হিঃ কোঃ), চেতনাতীত (ঐ), চেতনাশূন্য, জড়। **2.** Unaware ; অবিদিত, অজ্ঞাত, অনবগত। **—ly,** *adv.* **—ness,** *n.* **Unconscious cerebration**—অজ্ঞাতসারে মস্তিষ্কের ক্রিয়া, অজ্ঞাত-মনোব্যাপার (হিঃ কোঃ), অজ্ঞাতমস্তিষ্ককার্য্য (হিঃ কোঃ)।

ŭn-cŏn′-sē-crāt-ĕd, *adj.* Not consecrated ; অনুৎসর্গীকৃত। **—ness,** *n.*

ŭn-cŏn-sĕnt′-ĭng, *adj.* Not yielding consent ; "Nor *unconsenting* hear his friends request" ; অসম্মতিপ্রদায়ী।

ŭn-cŏn-sĭd′-ered (-êrd), *adj.* Not considered or attended to ; অবিবেচিত।

ŭn-cŏn-sōled, *adj.* Not consoled or comforted ; অসান্ত্বনাপ্রাপ্ত, অনাশ্বাসিত।

ŭn-cŏn-sŏl′-ĭ-dāt′-ĕd, *adj.* Not made solid ; অকঠিনীকৃত, অসংস্তম্ভিত, অদৃঢ়ীভূত।

ŭn-cŏn-sōl′-ĭng, *adj.* Affording no comfort ; অসান্ত্বনাপ্রদ।

ŭn-cŏn-stĭ-tū-tion-ăl, *adj.* Not authorised by the constitution, or contrary to its principles ; ব্যবস্থাবিরুদ্ধ, অনিয়মতন্ত্রসম্মত। **—al′-ĭ-ty,** *n.* **—ly,** *adv.*

ŭn-cŏn-strained′ (-strānd), *adj.* Free from constraint ; voluntary; সঙ্কোচশূন্য, সঙ্কোচহীন ; ইচ্ছাপ্রসূত।

ŭn-cŏn-sŭlt′-ĕd, *adj.* Not asked or consulted ; অযাচিত, অপ্রার্থিত।

ŭn-cŏn-sŭlt′-ĭng, *adj.* **1.** Taking no advice ; অবচনগ্রাহী। **2.** Imprudent ; "*Unconsulting* love" ; অবিবেচক, মূঢ়।

ŭn-cŏn-sŭmed′, *adj.* Not consumed, wasted or dissipated ; অনষ্টীকৃত, অনিঃশেষীকৃত, অক্ষয়িত, অব্যয়িত, অনাশিত।

ŭn-cŏn-temned′ (-tĕmd), *adj.* Not despised ; অনবজ্ঞাত, অনিন্দিত।

ŭn-cŏn′-tĕm-plāt-ĕd, *adj.* Not contemplated ; "Which of the peers have *uncontemned* gone by him" ; অচিন্তিত।

ŭn-cŏn-tĕnd′-ĕd, *adj.* **1.** Not disputed for ; অবিতর্কিত, অবিচারিত।

ŭn-cŏn-tĕst′-ĕd, *adj.* Not contested ; as, an *uncontested* game ; not disputed ; অবিতর্কিত ; অবিচারিত।

ŭn-cŏn-trā-dĭct′-ă-ble (-bl), *adj.* That cannot be contradicted ; অপ্রতিবাদযোগ্য।

ŭn-cŏn-trā-dĭct′-ĕd, *adj.* Not denied ; অস্বীকৃত।

ŭn-cŏn′-trīte, *adj.* Not penitent ; অননুতপ্ত।

ŭn-cŏn-trīved′, *adj.* Not formed by design ; অকৌশলকল্পিত।

ŭn-cŏn-trīv′-ing, *adj.* Imprudent ; অপরিণামদর্শী, অদূরদর্শী।

ŭn-cŏn-trōl′-la-ble (-ă-bl), *adj.* That cannot be controlled ; as, an *uncontrollable* temper ; অশম্য, অদম্য, অনিবার্য্য, অসংযম্য, অনিয়ন্ত্রণীয়, দুর্দ্দান্ত। **—bly**, *adv.*

ŭn-cŏn-trolled′ (-tröld), *adj.* **1.** Not controlled or governed ; অশাসিত, অনিয়ন্ত্রিত। **2.** Uncontrollable ; অদম্য, অদমনীয়। **3.** (*Obs.*) Not refuted ; (অপ্রঃ) অখণ্ডিত।

ŭn-cŏn′-trō-vêrt-ĕd, *adj.* Not disputed or called into question ; "The *uncontroverted* certainty of mathematical science"; অবিতর্কিত।

ŭn-cŏn-vêrs′-ă-ble (-bl), *adj.* Not free in conversation ; unsocial ; আলাপকুণ্ঠ ; অসামাজিক।

ŭn-cŏn-vêrt′-ĕd, *adj.* **1.** Not changed in opinion ; অপরিবর্ত্তিত মত। **2.** Not turned from one faith to another ; অদীক্ষিত। **2.** Not Christianised ; খৃষ্টানধর্ম্মে অদীক্ষিত। **3.** Not renewed ; not regenerated ; অনবীভূত ; অপুনরুজ্জীবিত, অনবজীবনপ্রাপ্ত।

ŭn-cŏn-vêrt′-ĭ-ble (-bl), *adj.* That cannot be changed in form ; অরূপান্তরীয়, অরূপান্তরযোগ্য।

ŭn-cŏn-vinced′ (-vĭnst), *adj.* Not convinced ; অকৃতনিশ্চয়, অজ্ঞাতপ্রত্যয়, অচ্ছিন্নসংশয়।

ŭn-cŏn-vĭnc′-ing, *adj.* Not sufficient to convince ; অকৃতনিশ্চায়ক।

ŭn-cŏn-vulsed′ (-vŭslt), *adj.* Not convulsed ; অবিক্ষোভিত।

ŭn-cŏrd′, *v. t.* To unfasten or unbind ; বন্ধনমুক্ত করা, বন্ধনমোচন করা।

ŭn-cŏr′-dĭ-ăl, *adj.* Not cordial ; আন্তরিকতাশূন্য।

ŭn-cŏrk′, *v. t.* To draw the cork from ; কাক খোলা।

ŭn-cŏr′-ō-nĕt-ĕd, *adj.* Not honoured with a coronet ; অমুকুট-সম্মানিত।

ŭn-cor-rĕct′-ĕd (-kŏ-), *adj.* Not corrected ; অসংশোধিত।

ŭn-cŏr-rŏb′-ō-rāt-ĕd, *adj.* Not confirmed ; অদৃঢ়ীকৃত।

ŭn-cŏr-rŭpt′, *adj.* Not corrupted; not depraved ; অদূষিত, অকলুষিত ; অবিকারিত।

ŭn-cor-rŭpt′-i-ble (-kŏ-rŭpt-ĭ-bl), *adj.* That cannot be corrupted ; অদূষ্য, অদূষণক্ষম, অদূষণীয়।

ŭn-coun′-sel-la-ble, —a-ble (-kown-sĕl-ă-bl), *adjs.* Not to be advised ; not having counsel or advice; অনুপদেষ্টব্য, অনুপদেশগ্রাহী ; অপরামর্শপ্রাপ্ত অনুপদিষ্ট।

ŭn-coun′-selled (-kown-sĕld), *adj.* Not having advice ; অনুপদিষ্ট, অজ্ঞাপিত, অনিবেদিত।

ŭn-cnnt′-a-ble (-kownt-ă-bl), *adj.* That cannot be counted ; innumerable ; অগণনীয়, অগণ্য ; অসংখ্য।

ŭn-count′-ĕd (-kownt-), *adj.* Not numbered; innumerable ; অগণিত ; অসংখ্য।

ŭn-coun′-te-nanced (-kown-tĕ-nănst), *adj.* Not encouraged ; অনুৎসাহিত, অনাশ্বাসিত।

ŭn-coun′-ter-feit, (-kown-têr-fĭt), *adj.* Not spurious ; genuine ; অকৃত্রিম ; খাঁটি, সাঁচ্চা।

ŭn-cou′-ple (-kŭ-pl), *v. t.* To loose ; to disjoin ; আল্গা করা, পৃথক করা ; বিযুক্ত করা, অসংযুক্ত করা।

ŭn-cour′-te-ous (-kör-tē-ŭs), *adj.* Uncivil ; unpolite ; অশিষ্ট, অভদ্র ; অভব্য। **—ly**, *adv.* **—ness**, *n.*

ŭn-court′-lȳ (-kört-), *adj.* **1.** Unversed in the manners of a court ; রাজসভার কায়দাকানুনে অনভিজ্ঞ। **2.** Unelegant in manners ; rude ; অভব্য, অসভ্য ; রূঢ়। **—li-ness**, *n.*

ŭn-couth′ (-kôth), *adj.* **1.** (*Obs.*) Unknown ; (অপ্রঃ) অপরিচিত। **2.** Odd ; fantastic ; বিসদৃশ ; অদ্ভুত। **3.** Dreadful ; ভয়ঙ্কর, ভয়ানক। **4.** Clumsy ; কুৎসিত, কদাকার, বিশ্রী, বদ্খত (*colloq.*), বীভৎস। **5.** Foreign ; mysterious ; uncanny ; "An *uncouth* fear" ; বিদেশীয় ; রহস্যপূর্ণ ; ছমছমজনক। **—ly**, *adv.* **—ness**, *n.*

ŭn-cov-ĕ-nănt′-ĕd, (-kŭv-), *adj.* Not promised by a covenant ; not resting on a covenant or promise ; অচুক্তিবদ্ধ ; অচিহ্নিত।

ŭn-cov′-êr, (-kŭv-), *v. t.* **1.** To divest of a cover ; to remove any covering from ; অনাবৃত করা ; ঢাকনি বা আবরণ স্থানান্তরিত করা। **2.** To deprive of clothes ; to strip ; উলঙ্গ করা ; বিরহিত করা। **3.** To unroof ; ছাদবিহীন করা। **4.** To take off the hat or cap ; "None of the Eastern people use the compliment of *uncovering* their heads when they meet as we do" ; টুপি খোলা, টুপি উন্মোচন করা। **5.** To strip off a veil ; অবগুণ্ঠন উন্মোচন করা। **6.** To disclose to view ; অনাবৃত করা, উদ্ঘাটিত করা। **—ered′**, *adj.*

ŭn-cowl′, *v. t.* To deprive of a cowl ; মস্তকাবরণ উন্মোচন করা।

ŭn-cramped′ (-krămpt), *adj.* Not confined or cramped ; অনবরুদ্ধ, অসঙ্কুচিত।

ŭn-crē-āte′, *v.t.* To deprive of existence ; অসৃষ্ট করা, সত্তাবিরহিত করা।

ŭn-crē-āt′-ĕd, *adj.* **1.** Reduced to nothing ; সত্তাবিরহিত। **2.** Not produced by creation ; অসৃষ্ট্যুৎপন্ন।

ŭn-crĕd′-ĭt-ĕd, *adj.* Not believed ; অবিশ্বসিত, অপ্রতীত, অবিশ্বস্ত।

ŭn-crip′-pled (-ld), *adj.* Not crippled, lamed or maimed ; অবিকলীকৃত, অহীনাঙ্গ, অবিকলাঙ্গ।

ŭn-crĭt′-ĭ-căl, *adj.* Not critical, or according to the just rules of criticism ; অগুণদোষজ্ঞ, সমালোচনার নিয়ম বিরোধী।

ŭn-cropped′ (-krŏpt), *adj.* Not cropped or gathered ; অকর্ত্তিত, অসংগৃহীত।

ŭn-crossed′ (-krŏst), *adj.* **1.** Not crossed ; অনুত্তীর্ণ। **2.** Not thwarted ; অবিকলীকৃত।

ŭn-crowd′-ĕd, *adj.* Not crowded or compressed ; অসঙ্কুচিত, অসঙ্কাপিত।

ŭn-crown′, *v. t.* To deprive of a crown ; to dethrone ; to pull off the crown ; মুকুট বিরহিত করা ; সিংহাসনচ্যুত করা ; মুকুট উন্মোচন করা।

ŭn-crowned′, (-crownd), *adj.* Without crown ; deprived of a crown ; মুকুটবিহীন, মুকুট-বিরহিত ; সিংহাসনচ্যুত।

ŭn-crushed′ (-krŭsht), *adj.* **1.** Not crushed ; অনিষ্পেষিত, অবিমর্দ্দিত, অনিষ্পিষ্ট, অচূর্ণিত।

ŭn-crys′-tăl-line, *adj.* Not having the character of a crystal ; অস্ফটিকাত্মক, অনর্কাত্মক, অদানাদার, অস্ফাটিক।

ŭn-crys′-tăl-līz-ă-ble (-bl), *adj.* Not susceptible of crystallization ; অস্ফটিকীভবনীয়।

ŭn-crys′-tăl-līzed, *adj.* Not crystallized ; অস্ফটিকীভূত।

ŭn-cŭl′-ti-vāt-ĕd, *adj.* **1.** Not tilled ; অকর্ষিত, অকৃষ্ট। **2.** Not improved by labour, study, care, exercise or the like ; neglected ; অননুশীলিত ; অবহেলিত। **3.** Not instructed ; not civilized ; rude ; অশিক্ষিত ; অসভ্য ; রূঢ়।

ŭn-cŭm′-bered (-bĕrd), *adj.* Not burdened ; not embarrassed ; অপ্রপীড়িত ; অজড়িত।

ŭnc′-tion (ŭng-), *n.* **1.** The act of anointing ; তৈলাদি মর্দ্দন। **2.** Uuguent ; ointment ; অভ্যঙ্গ, অভ্যঞ্জন ; মলম। **3.** Religious fervour and tenderness ; "The delightful equivoque and *unction* of the passage in Farquhar" ; a factitious fervour or emotional gush ; ধর্ম্মানুরাগ, কোমলতা ; কৃত্রিম উত্তেজনা বা উচ্ছ্বাস। **4.** Divine grace ; দেবপ্রসাদ। **Extreme unction**—See EXTREME.

ŭnc-tū-os′-i-ty (ŭngk-), *n.* The state of being unctuous ; স্নৈহিকতা, স্নৈগ্ধ্য। **To lay a flattering unction to the soul**—To soothe one's self with a pleasant fancy ; সুখময় কল্পনা দ্বারা মন তৃপ্ত করা।

ŭnc′-tu-ous (ŭngk-tū-ŭs), *adj.* **1.** Oily ; greasy ; স্নৈহিক, তৈলাক্ত ; বসালিপ্ত। **2.** Bland ; suave ; fervid ; esp. nauseously suave or gushing ; as, an *unctuous* speech or address ; মধুর ; মিষ্ট ; উত্তেজনাপূর্ণ ; কৃত্রিম উচ্ছ্বাসপূর্ণ। **—ly,** *adv.* **—ness,** *n.*

ŭn-culled′ (-kŭld), *adj.* Not gathered ; not selected ; অসংগৃহীত ; অনির্ব্বাচিত।

ŭn-cŭl′-pă-ble(-bl), *adj.* Not blamable or faulty ; অদোষার্হ, অনপরাধযুক্ত।

ŭn-cŭl′-ti-vă-ble (-bl), *adj.* Not capable of being cultivated ; অকর্ষণযোগ্য।

ŭn-curbed′ (-kêrbd), *adj.* Not restrained ; licentious ; অসংযত ; লম্পট।

ŭn-curl′ (-kêrl), *v. t.* & *i.* To straighten out, anything curled ; "The lion *uncurls* his angry mane" ; অপকুঞ্চিত করা। ***Verb i.*** To become straight ; সরল হওয়া, সোজা হওয়া।

ŭn-cŭr′-rent (-ĕnt), *adj.* Not passing in common payment ; as *uncurrent* coin ; অপ্রচলিত।

ŭn-cursed′ (-kêrst), *adj.* Not execrated; "Heaven sure has kept this part of earth *uncursed*"; অনভিশপ্ত।

ŭn-cŭr-tailed′ (-tāld), *adj.* Not shortened ; অখর্ব্বীকৃত।

ŭn-cŭs′-tom-a-ble (-tŭm-ă-bl), *adj.* Not subject to custom duties ; অশুল্কযোগ্য।

ŭn-cŭs′-tom-ă-ry (-tŭm-), *adj.* Not customary ; not usual ; "A most unlawful and *uncustomary* matter" ; অপ্রথাসঙ্গত ; অপ্রাথিক।

ŭn-cŭs′-tomed (-tŭmd), *adj.* Not subject to customs or duty ; that has not paid duty ; "A bill was prepared......against the clandestine running of *uncustomed* goods" ; অশুল্কযোগ্য ; অদত্তশুল্ক।

ŭn-cŭt′, *adj.* **1.** Not cut ; অকর্ত্তিত, অচ্ছিন্ন, অখণ্ডিত। **2.** Not ground, or otherwise cut in shape ; as, an *uncut* ruby ; আকাটা, অপলকাটা।

ŭn-dăm′, *v. t.* To free from dam or obstruction ; বাঁধ ভাঙ্গা।

ŭn-dăm′-āged, *adj.* Not made worse ; অপরিক্ষত, অবিক্ষত।

ŭn-damped′ (-dămpt),*adj.* Not damped or depressed ; অক্লিন্ন, অনবসন্ন।

ŭn-dârk′-ened′ (-nd), *adj.* Not darkened or obscured ; অতমোবৃত, অতিমিরাবৃত।

ŭn′-dāt-ĕd, *adj.* Waved ; rising and falling in waves ; তরঙ্গায়িত, তরঙ্গবৎ ; তরঙ্গাকারে উত্থানপতনশীল।

ŭn-dāt′-ĕd, *adj.* Having no date ; তারিখশূন্য, তারিখবিহীন।

ŭn-daunt′-a-ble (-dänt-ă-bl), *adj.* **1.** Not to be daunted ; অভীত। **2.** Indomitable ; অদম্য, অজেয়।

ŭn-daunt′-ĕd (-dänt-), *adj.* Not subdued or depressed by fear ; "His *undaunted* hardiness of speech" ; bold ; courageous ; অভীত, ভয়শূন্য, নির্ভীক, অকুতোভয় ; সাহসী ; শূর। **—ly,** *adv.* **—ness,** *n.*

ŭn-dawn′-ing (-dän-), *adj.* Not yet growing light ; "Thou (winter) hold'st the sun A prisoner in the yet *undawning* east" ; অনাগত-প্রভাত, ঈষদসমাপ্ত প্রভাত।

ŭn-dăz′-zled (-ld), *adj.* Not confused by splendour ; অতেজোপহত।

ŭn-dē-barred′ (-bêrd), *adj.* Not debarred ; অবারিত।

ŭn-dē-based′ (-bāst), *adj.* Not adulterated ; অভেজাল।

ŭn-dē-bauched′ (-bächt), *adj.* Not corrupted; pure; অদূষিত; শুদ্ধ, পবিত্র।

ŭn-dĕc′-ă-gon, *n.* A figure of eleven angles or sides ; একাদশাস্র ক্ষেত্র, একাদশভুজ ক্ষেত্র।

ŭn-dē-cay′-ing (-cā-), *adj.* Not decaying ; not suffering diminution or decline ; অক্ষীয়মাণ ; অক্ষয়িষ্ণু।

ŭn-dē-ceit′-fûl (-sēt-), *adj.* Not deceitful ; অপ্রতারণশীল।

ŭn-dē-ceiv′-a-ble (-sēv-ă-bl), *adj.* Not subject to deception; অপ্রতারণীয়।

ŭn-dē-ceive′ (-sēv), *v. t.* To free from deception, cheat, fallacy, or mistake, whether caused by others or by yourselves ; to open one's eyes ; ভ্রমাপনোদন করা, ভ্রান্তি দূর করা, ভ্রম নিবারণ করা ; চক্ষু ফুটান (*colloq.*), চক্ষুদান করা (*slang*)।

ŭn-dē-cĕn′-nā-rŷ, *adj.* **1.** Eleventh ; একাদশতম। **2.** Occurring once in eleven years ; একাদশ বার্ষিক।

ŭn-dē-cĕp′-tive (-tĭv), *adj.* Not deceptive ; অমোহক, অভ্রান্তিজনক।

ŭn-dē-cīd′-ă-ble (-bl), *adj.* That cannot be decided ; অনিশ্চেয়।

ŭn-dē-cīd′-ĕd, *adj.* Not decided ; not determined ; অনিশ্চিত, অস্থিরীকৃত, অনির্দ্ধারিত, অমীমাংসিত ; অনিরূপিত।

ŭn-dē-cī′-phêr-ă-ble (-bl), *adj.* That cannot be deciphered ; as, *undecipherable* inscription ; অগূঢ়াক্ষরপাঠযোগ্য।

ŭn-dē-cī′-phered (-fêrd), *adj.* Not deciphered ; অরহস্যোদ্ভিন্ন।

ŭn-dē-cī′-sive (-sĭv), *adj.* Not decisive ; not conclusive ; as; *undecisive* battle ; অনিশ্চায়ক ; অনির্ণায়ক।

ŭn-dĕck′, *v. t.* To divest of ornaments ; "To *undeck* the pompous body of a king" ; ভূষণ-বিরহিত করা, অনলঙ্কৃত করা।

ŭn-decked′ (-dĕkt), *adj.* **1.** Not decked ; অনলঙ্কৃত, অভূষিত। **2.** Without a deck ; পাটাতনবিহীন।

ŭn-dē-clāred′, *adj.* Not declared ; অঘোষিত।

ŭn-dē-clīn′-ă-ble (-bl), *adj.* & *n.* **1.** (*Gram.*) Not variable in the termination ; as, an *undeclinable* noun ; (ব্যাকরণ) অব্যয়। **2.** That cannot be declined or rejected ; অপ্রত্যাখ্যেয়, অনিষিদ্ধ। *Noun* (*Pl.*) An undeclinable word ; অব্যয়শব্দ।

ŭn-dē-clined′ (-klīnd), *adj.* **1.** (*Gram.*) Not varied in termination or inflection ; (ব্যাকরণ) অব্যয়-স্বরূপ। **2.** (*Obs.*) Not deviating ; (অপ্রঃ) অব্যভিচারী।

ŭn-dē-cŏm-pōṡ′-ă-ble (-bl), *adj.* Not admitting decomposition ; অবিশ্লেষণীয়।

ŭn-dē-cŏm-pōṡed′, *adj.* Not decomposed ; অবিশ্লিষ্ট।

ŭn-dē-cŏm-pound-ĕd′ (-pownd-), *adj.* Not decompounded ; অদ্বিমিশ্রিত।

ŭn-dĕc′-ō-rāt-ĕd, *adj.* Not adorned or embellished ; অভূষিত, অনলঙ্কৃত, অমণ্ডিত।

ŭn-dĕd′-ĭ-cāt-ĕd, *adj.* Not dedicated ; অনুৎসর্গীকৃত।

ŭn-deed′-ĕd (-dēd-), *adj.* **1.** (*Rare*) Not signalized by any great action ; (কচিদ্‌ব্যবহৃত) অনবদানপ্রখ্যাত। **2.** Not transferred by deed ; as, *undeeded* land ; দলীলদ্বারা অনর্পিত।

ŭn-dē-fāce′-ă-ble (-bl), *adj.* That cannot be disfigured ; অবিকার্য্য।

ŭn-dē-faced′ (-fāst), *adj.* Not defaced ; not disfigured ; অবিকৃত ; অবিকলীকৃত।

ŭn-dē-fea′-si-ble (-fē-zĭ-bl), *adj.* Not defeasible ; অননুশয়িতব্য, অখণ্ডিতব্য।

ŭn-dē-fĕnd′-ĕd, *adj.* Not protected ; not vindicated ; অরক্ষিত ; অসমর্থিত।

ŭn-dē-fied′ (-fīd), *adj.* Not set at defiance or challenged ; অনাহূত, অস্পর্দ্ধিত, অতুচ্ছীকৃত।

ŭn-dē-fīled′ *adj.* Not defiled or polluted; অদূষিত, অকলুষিত, অমলিনীকৃত।

ŭn-dē-fīn′-ă-ble (-bl), *adj.* Not capable of being defined ; not susceptible of definition ; অসংজ্ঞাপ্রদানযোগ্য ; অসংজ্ঞাপ্রদানক্ষম।

ŭn-dē-fīned′, *adj.* Not defined ; যাহার লক্ষণ নির্দ্দেশ করা হয় নাই, অকৃতলক্ষণ, অনিরুক্ত (ছান্দোগ্য), অমূর্ত্ত (শ্রীঃ)।

ŭn-dē-formed′ (-fôrmd), *adj.* Not deformed or disfigured ; অবিকৃত, অবিরূপতাপ্রাপ্ত, অবিরূপীকৃত।

ŭn′-dē-fraud′-ĕd (-fräd-), *adj.* Not defrauded ; অপ্রতারিত।

ŭn-dē-grād′-ĕd, *adj.* Not degraded ; অনবনমিত।

ŭn-dē′-ĭ-fŷ, *v. t.* To reduce from the state of deity ; দেবভাববিরহিত করা, দেবত্বহীন করা।

ŭn-dē-layed′ (-lād), *adj.* Not delayed ; অবিলম্বিত।

ŭn-dē-lay′-ing (-lā-), *adj.* Not delaying ; অবিলম্বকারী, অচিরকারী।

ŭn-dĕl′-ē-gāt-ĕd, *adj.* Not deputed ; অনিযুক্ত, অনিয়োজিত।

ŭn-dē-lĭb′-ĕr-āte, *adj.* Not deliberate ; অচিন্তিত।

ŭn-dē-lĭb′-ĕr-āt-ĕd, *adj.* Not deliberated ; অবিবেচিত।

ŭn-dē-light′-ĕd (-līt-), *adj.* Not delighted or well pleased ; অহৃষ্ট, অনুল্লসিত।

ŭn-dē-light′-fûl (-līt-), *adj.* Not giving great pleasure ; নিরানন্দময়, নিরানন্দপূর্ণ।

ŭn-dē-lĭv′-ĕr-ă-ble (-bl), *adj.* Incapable of being delivered, released or freed ; অমোচ্য, অনুদ্ধারণীয়, অনুদ্ধার্য্য।

ŭn-dē-lĭv′-ered (-êrd), *adj.* **1.** Not delivered ; অসমর্পিত, অপ্রণিহিত। **2.** Not freed or released ; অমুক্ত, অনুদ্ধারিত।

ŭn-dē-mănd′-ĕd, *adj.* Not demanded ; not required ; অপ্রার্থিত ; অনাকাঙ্ক্ষিত।

ŭn-dē-mŏl′-ished (-ĭsht), *adj.* Not pulled down or destroyed ; অধ্বংসীকৃত।

ŭn-dē-mŏn′-stră-ble (-bl), *adj.* Not capable of being demonstrated ; as, *undemonstrable* principles ; অপ্রমাণসহ।

ŭn-dĕm-ŏn-strāt′-ĕd, *adj.* Not proved by demonstration ; অপ্রমাণিত।

ŭn-dē-mŏn′-strā-tive (-tĭv), *adj.* Not given to a display of feeling ; অপ্রমাণাত্মক।

ŭn-dē-nī′-ā-ble (-bl), *adj.* That cannot be denied ; indisputable ; as, *undeniable* evidence ; অপ্রত্যাখ্যেয়, অখণ্ডনীয়, অকাট্য ; অবিতর্ক্য।

ŭn-dē-pĕnd′-ĭng, *adj.* Not dependent ; অনধীন।

ŭn-dē-plored′ (-plōrd), *adj.* Not lamented ; অশোচিত।

ŭn-dē-pōs′-ā-ble (bl), *adj.* That cannot be deposed from office ; অপদচ্যুতকরণীয়।

ŭn-dē-prāved′, *adj.* Not corrupted ; অদূষিত, অকলুষিত।

ŭn-dĕp-rē-cāt′-ĕd, *adj.* Not deprecated ; অনবজ্ঞাত।

ŭn-dē-prē′-ci-āt-ĕd (-shĭ-), *adj.* Not depreciated ; অমূল্যাপকৃষ্ট।

ŭn-dē-prīved′, *adj.* Not divested of any possession or right ; অবঞ্চিত।

ŭn′-dêr, *prep., adv.* & *adj.* 1. In a lower place or position ; নীচে, নিম্নে, তলে। 2. Subject to ; on the condition of ; controlled by ; in accordance with ; অধীনে ; অবস্থায় ; বশবর্ত্তী হইয়া ; মতে, অনুসারে। 3. Weighed upon or oppressed by ; প্রপীড়িত। ***Adv.*** In a lower position ; in a subject or subordinate condition ; নীচে, নিম্নে ; নিম্নপদে, অধীন অবস্থায়। ***Adj.*** Subject ; subordinate ; অধীন ; নিম্নস্থ, অধস্তন। **To bring under**—To keep under subjection ; বশে আনা, বশ মানান। **To go under**—To be frustrated ; বিফল হওয়া, নিষ্ফল হওয়া। **To keep under** — To hold in subjection ; অধীন রাখা। **Under arms**—সশস্ত্র, অস্ত্রশস্ত্রে সুসজ্জিত। **Under fire**—Subject to enemy's fire ; শত্রুপক্ষের গোলাবৃষ্টির মধ্যে। **Under one's breath**—Whisperingly ; চুপি চুপি, মৃদুস্বরে। **Under one's signature**—কাহারো স্বাক্ষরে। **Under pain of death**—(See PAIN.) **Under sail**—পাইল ছড়াইয়া। **Under the guise of**—Under the pretext of ; ছলে, ব্যপদেশে। **Under the hand and seal of**—সহিমোহরযুক্ত। **Under way**—Ready to start ; গমনোন্মুখ, গমনোদ্যত। In condition to make progress ; অগ্রসর হওয়ার উপযোগী অবস্থায়। **With a good meal under his belt**—Taking delicious food ; উপাদেয় সামগ্রী দ্বারা উদর পূর্ণ করিয়া।

ŭn-dêr-ăc′-tion, *n.* Subordinate action ; action not essential to the main story ; উপকার্য্য ; প্রধান কাহিনীর সহিত গৌণভাবে অন্বিত কার্য্য, অপ্রধান কার্য্য।

ŭn-dē-rānged′, *adj.* Not deranged ; অবিক্ষিপ্ত, অনাকুলিত।

ŭn-dêr-bear′ (-bār), *v. t.* To support ; to endure ; বিধৃত করা ; সহ্য করা, সহা।

ŭn′-dêr-bear-êr (-bār-), *n.* One who sustains the corpse ; শববাহক।

ŭn-dêr-bĭd′, *v. t.* To bid or offer less than another, as in auction ; নীলামে কম ডাকা, কমদর হাঁকা।

ŭn′-dêr-brĕd, *adj.* Of inferior breeding or manners ; vulgar ; অপকৃষ্ট শিক্ষা প্রাপ্ত, অপকৃষ্ট আদবকায়দাবিশিষ্ট ; ইতর, নীচ।

ŭn′-dêr-brŭsh, *n.* Shrubs and small trees in a wood or forest, growing under large trees ; বৃহৎ বৃক্ষের নিম্নে জাত ক্ষুদ্র ক্ষুদ্র বৃক্ষ বা ঝোঁপ।

ŭn-dêr-charge′ (-chârj), *v. t.* 1. To load insufficiently ; কম বারুদ ভরা। 2. To charge less than a fair sum or price for ; প্রকৃত মূল্য অপেক্ষা অল্প মূল্য চাওয়া।

ŭn′-dêr-clay (-klā), *n.* A stratum of clay underlying coal ; কয়লার নিম্নস্থ ভূস্তর।

ŭn′-dêr-clōthes, **—clōth-ĭng**, *ns.* Clothes worn under others, or next the skin ; অন্তর্ব্বাস, অধোবস্ত্র, অধোবাস।

ŭn′-dêr-coat (-kōt), *n.* A coat worn under another ; কোর্ত্তার নিম্নে পরিধেয় একপ্রকার খাটো কোর্ত্তা।

ŭn′-dêr-crŏft, *n.* 1. A vault under the choir or chancel of a church ; খৃষ্টীয় ধর্ম্মমন্দিরের উপবেশনস্থলের নিম্নস্থ খিলান। 2. A secret walk under ground ; ভূমধ্যস্থ প্রচ্ছন্নপথ।

ŭn′-dêr-cŭr-rent (-ĕnt), *n.* & *adj.* 1. A current below the surface of water অন্তঃস্রোত, অন্তঃপ্রবাহ, অধঃস্রোত, অধঃপ্রবাহ। 2. An unseen influence ; "In the Puritan supremacy there was a strong *undercurrent* of loyalty to the banished prince" ; প্রচ্ছন্ন প্রবাহ, অদৃশ্য প্রভাব। ***Adj.*** Unseen ; অদৃশ্য, অদৃষ্ট।

ŭn-dêr-ditch′ (-dĭch), *v. t.* To form a ditch or trench to drain the surface ; ক্ষেত্রের উপরিভাগের জলসেচনের জন্য পরিখা বা পয়ঃপ্রণালী রচনা করা।

ŭn-dêr-dō′, *v. i.* & *t.* 1. To act below one's abilities ; নিজের ক্ষমতার তুলনায় অল্প কার্য্য করা। 2. To do less than is requisite ; আবশ্যক অপেক্ষা অল্প কার্য্য করা। ***Verb t.*** To do less thoroughly than is requisite ; to cook insufficiently or rarely ; অসম্যগ্রূপে করা ; অল্প সিদ্ধ করা।

ŭn′-dêr-done (-dŭn), *adj.* Done less than is requisite ; esp. cooked for a comparatively short or an insufficient time ; অসম্যগ্রূপে সম্পাদিত ; ন্যূনপক্ক, অল্পসিদ্ধ।

ŭn-dêr-dōse′, *n.* A quantity less than a dose ; একমাত্রা অপেক্ষা অল্প পরিমাণ, ন্যূনমাত্রা।

ŭn′-dêr-drain (-drān), *n.* & *v. t.* A drain or trench below the surface of ground ; ভূগর্ত্তস্থ পরিখা,

অন্তঃপরিখা, অন্তঃপ্রণালী। *Verb t.* To drain by cutting a deep channel below the surface; ভূনিম্নে গভীর পরিখা খনন করিয়া জল নিকাশের ব্যবস্থা করা।

ŭn-dêr-făc′-tion, *n.* Subordinate faction; উপকুচক্রিসমাজ।

ŭn-dêr-feed′ (-fēd), *v. t.* To feed imperfectly; অসম্যগ্‌রূপে ভোজন করান, আবশ্যক অপেক্ষা অল্প ভোজন করান।

ŭn-dêr-foot′, *adv.* Under the feet; underneath; পদতলে; নীচে, নিম্নে, তলে।

ŭn-dêr-fur′-nish (-fêr-), *v. t.* To supply with less than enough; আবশ্যক অপেক্ষা অল্প সরবরাহ করা।

ŭn-dêr-fŭr′-row (-ō-), *v. t.* & *adv.* To cover as under a furrow: নালা বা জুলির ভিতর আবৃত করা। *Adv.* Under the furrow; জুলির নীচে। **To sow under the furrow**—To plough in seed; নালার ভিতরের বীজ চষিয়া ঢাকিয়া ফেলা।

ŭn′-dêr-gâr-mĕnt, *n.* A garment to be worn under another; অন্তর্বাস, অন্তঃপরিচ্ছদ, অধরাম্বর (শিশুঃ), অধোবাস।

ŭn-dêr-gird′ (-gêrd), *v. t.* To gird round the bottom; নিম্নদিকে বেষ্টিত করা।

ŭn-dêr-gō′, *v. t.* **1.** To bear up against; to endure without fainting; to suffer; to bear; সহ্য করা; অবিচলিত ভাবে সহ্য করা; ভোগ করা; বহন করা। **2.** To be subjected to; to pass through; অধীন হওয়া; অতিক্রম করা।

ŭn-dêr-gō′-ing, *adj.* Suffering; enduring; patient; সহনশীল; সহিষ্ণু; ধৈর্য্যশীল।

ŭn-dêr-grăd′-ū-āte, *n.* A student or member of a university or college; বিশ্ববিদ্যালয়ের অনুপাধিধারী ছাত্র। **—ship,** *n.*

ŭn′-dêr-ground (-grownd), *n., adv.* & *adj.* A place or space beneath the surface; ভূমির নিম্নস্থ স্থান। *Adv.* Beneath the ground; ভূনিম্নে, মৃত্তিকার নিম্নে। *Adj.* **1.** Being below the surface of the ground; মৃত্তিকানিম্নস্থ, অধোভৌমিক, অধোভূমিক ভূনিম্নগত, অন্তর্ভৌমিক, অন্তর্ভৌম, ভূমিনিম্নগত। **2.** Secret; গুপ্ত। **Underground nut** — (*Arachis Hypogea*) চীনাবাদাম, ভূচণক। **Underground railroad** — ভূনিম্নগামী লৌহবর্ত্ম, অন্তর্ভৌম লৌহবর্ত্ম; আমেরিকার দাসত্বপ্রথা উচ্ছেদের পূর্ব্বে যে প্রণালীবদ্ধ উপায়ে পলাতক ক্রীতদাসগণকে যুক্তরাজ্য হইতে ক্যানাডা দেশে গমনে সাহায্য করা হইত।

ŭn′-dêr-growth (-grōth), *n.* That which grows under trees; shrubs or small trees growing among large one's; বৃক্ষের নিম্নে জাত উদ্ভিদাদি; বৃহৎ বৃক্ষের নিম্নে জাত ঝোঁপ বা ঝাড়।

ŭn′-dêr-hănd, *adv.* & *adj.* By secret means; by fraud; গোপনে, তলে তলে; প্রতারণাপূর্ব্বক। *Adj.* Secret; clandestine; গোপন; প্রচ্ছন্ন।

ŭn′-dêr-hăng, *adj.* Said of the lower jaw protruding beyond the upper; নিম্নহনু ঊর্দ্ধতর হনু অতিক্রম পূর্ব্বক প্রলম্বিত।

ŭn-dē-rīved′, *adj.* Not derived; অনুৎপন্ন।

ŭn-dêr-laid′ (-lād), *adj.* Having something lying or laid beneath; নিম্নবিন্যস্ত, নিম্ননিহিত।

ŭn-dêr-lay′ (-lā), *v. t.* To lay beneath; to support by something lain under; নিম্নে স্থাপন করা; নিম্নে স্থাপিত কোন বস্তু দ্বারা বিধৃত করা।

ŭn′-dêr-leaf (-lēf), *n.* (*Obs.*) A kind of apple; (অপ্রঃ) একপ্রকার সেও ফল।

ŭn′-dêr-lĕt, *v. t.* To let below the value; "All my farms were *underlet*"; to let under a lease; নির্দ্ধারিত মূল্য অপেক্ষা অল্প টাকায় ভাড়া দেওয়া; কবুলিয়ত লইয়া ভাড়া দেওয়া।

ŭn-dêr-lĕt′-ter (-ĕr), *n.* A tenant who leases; কবুলিয়তদাতা।

ŭn-dêr-lĕt′-ting (-ĭng), *n.* Practice of letting lands by leases; কবুলিয়ত প্রদানে ভূমি বন্দোবস্ত প্রদান।

ŭn-dêr-lie′ (-lī), *v. t.* **1.** To lie under or beneath; to constitute the groundwork of; নীচে থাকা, নিম্নে স্থাপিত হওয়া; ভিত্তি বা বুনিয়াদ স্বরূপ হওয়া।

ŭn-dêr-līne′, *v. t.* To mark with a line below the words; নিম্নরেখ করা, নীচে দাগ দেওয়া, অধোরেখাঙ্কিত করা।

ŭn′-dêr-lĭng, *n.* **1.** An inferior or agent; অধীন ব্যক্তি, তাঁবেদার। **2.** A mean person; নীচ ব্যক্তি, নীচ লোক, হীনলোক।

ŭn′-dêr-lŏck, *n.* A lock of wool hanging under the belly of a sheep; মেষের উদরে লম্বিত লোমগুচ্ছ।

ŭn′-dêr-măst-ĕd, *adj.* Denoting vessels with masts under the usual dimensions; অল্পমাস্তুলবিশিষ্ট।

ŭn′-dêr-meal (-mēl), *n.* A repast before dinner; অপরাহ্ণভোজনের পূর্ব্ববর্ত্তী ভোজন।

ŭn-dêr-mīne′, *v. t.* **1.** To sap; to excavate the earth beneath; to remove the foundation; অধোখনন করা; নিম্নের ভূমি খনন করা; ভিত্তি অপসারিত করা, ভিত্তি স্থানান্তরিত করা। **2.** To injure by secret means; as, to *undermine* one's influence; গোপনে অনিষ্ট সাধন করা। **3.** To be at the busis of; to support; মূলে থাকা; বিধৃত করা।

ŭn-dêr-mīn′-ĕr, *n.* One who secretly overthrows; যে ব্যক্তি গোপনে সর্ব্বনাশ সাধন করে।

ŭn′-dêr-mōst, *adj.* Lowest in place, state or degree; beneath others; নিম্নতম, সর্ব্বনিম্নবর্ত্তী; সর্ব্বনিম্নস্থ, সর্ব্বাধস্থ; অধস্তম।

ŭn-dêr-neath′ (-nēth), *adv.* Beneath; under; below; নীচে; নিম্নে; তলে।

ŭn-dē-rŏg′-ā-tō-rȳ, *adj.* Not derogatory; অহীনতাপাদক, অমর্য্যাদাহানিকর।

ŭn′-dêr-pârt, *n.* A subordinate part ; অপ্রধান অংশ।

ŭn-dêr-pay′ (-pā), *v. t.* To pay inadequately ; অসম্যগ্‌রূপে বেতন প্রদান করা।

ŭn-dêr-pĭn′, *v. t.* To pin or support beneath ; to place something under for support or foundation when a previous support is removed ; to underset ; as, (a) to support (a wall) when an excavation is made beneath, by bringing a new portion of building from the lower level (b) To support, as an overhanging bank of earth or rock by masonry or brickwork ; নিম্নদেশ হইতে বিধৃত করা ; পূর্ব্বের অবলম্বন অপসারিত করা হইলে অবলম্বন বা ভিত্তিস্বরূপ অন্য কিছু নিহিত করা; ঠেকো খোঁটা প্রভৃতি দ্বারা বিধৃত করা। **–ning,***n.*

ŭn′-dêr-plŏt, *n.* **1.** A plot subordinate to another plot, as in a play or novel ; অপ্রধান আখ্যানবস্তু। **2.** A clandestine scheme ; গুপ্ত ব্যবস্থা।

ŭn-dêr-praise′ (-prāz), *v. t.* To praise below desert ; যথাযোগ্য প্রশংসা না করা।

ŭn-dêr-prīze′, *v. t.* To undervalue ; to despise ; অল্প মূল্যবান করা ; হতাদর করা, তুচ্ছ মনে করা, হেয় জ্ঞান করা।

ŭn′-dêr-rāte, *n.* A price less than the value ; অযথোচিত মূল্য।

ŭn-dêr-rŭn′, *v. t.* (*Naut.*) To pass under for the purpose of examining ; (নৌবিদ্যা) পরীক্ষার উদ্দেশ্যে নীচ দিয়া যাওয়া। **To underrun a cable**—To pass along or under it in a boat in order to examine whether any part of it is damaged or entangled ; সাগরতলবর্ত্তী তারের কোন অংশ নষ্ট বা জড়িত হইয়া গিয়াছে কিনা তাহা পরীক্ষার জন্য উহার কিনারা দিয়া বা নীচ দিয়া নৌকায় যাওয়া। **To underrun a tackle**—To separate its parts and put them in order ; দড়াদড়ীর অংশ সমূহ আল্‌গা করিয়া পুনরায় যথাযথভাবে সন্নিবিষ্ট করা।

ŭn-dêr-săt′-ū-rāt-ĕd, *adj.* Not imbued or impregnated thoroughly ; অপূর্ণসিক্ত, অননুবিদ্ধ, অসম্পূরিত, অসংপৃক্ত (হিঃ কোঃ)।

ŭn-dêr-sĕll′, *v. t.* To sell at a lower price than another ; "The emulation betwixt these owners to *undersell* one another" ; অন্য অপেক্ষা অল্প দরে বিক্রয় করা।

ŭn-dêr-sĕt′, *v. t.* **1.** To support by a prop or stay, masonry, etc. set under ; to under-prop ; ঠেকো, খোঁটা প্রভৃতি দ্বারা বিধৃত করা ; নিম্ন হইতে অবষ্টম্ভের উপর বিধৃত করা। **2.** To underlet ; অল্প খাজানায় বা টাকায় বিক্রী করা বা ভাড়া দেওয়া।

ŭn′-dêr-sĕt, *n.* A current of water below the surface in a direction contrary to that of the wind or of the water, at the surface ; বায়ু বা উপরিস্থ জলস্রোতের বিপরীত দিকে প্রবাহী জলস্রোত, বিপরীত অন্তঃপ্রবাহ।

ŭn′-dêr-shŏt, *adj.* Moved by water passing under the wheel ; চক্রের নীচ দিয়া প্রবাহিত জল দ্বারা চালিত। **Undershot-wheel**—অধোদেশে প্রবাহিত জলস্রোত দ্বারা চালিত চক্র, অধোজলচক্র।

Undershot-wheel.

ŭn′-dêr-shrŭb, *n.* A low shurb, permanent at the base, but the ends of the branches decaying yearly ; ঝোঁপ (সাঃ পঃ), ক্ষুপ (ঐ)।

ŭn-dêr-sīgn′ (-sīn), *v. t.* To write one's name at the foot or end of ; নিম্নে স্বাক্ষর করা।

ŭn-dêr-signed′ (-sīnd), *adj.* One who undersigns ; নিম্ন স্বাক্ষরকারী। **The undersigned** — নিম্ন স্বাক্ষরকারীগণ।

ŭn′-dêr-sīzed, *adj.* Being of a size less than common ; সাধারণ অপেক্ষা ক্ষুদ্রায়তন।

ŭn′-dêr-soil (-soyl), *n.* A soil beneath the surface ; নীচের মৃত্তিকাস্তর, অধঃস্তর, নিম্নস্তর।

ŭn-dêr-stănd′, *v. t.* & *i.* **1.** To have just and adequate ideas of ; to apprehend or comprehend fully ; as, to *understand* a mathematical problem ; to grasp the idea of ; as, I do not *understand* the situation ; বুঝা ; অবধারণ করা, হৃদয়ঙ্গম করা, উপলব্ধি করা ; ধারণা করা। **2.** To be informed of ; as, I *understand* that the bill has passed ; জানা, জ্ঞাত হওয়া, অবগত হওয়া, বিদিত হওয়া। **3.** To take as meant, though not expressed ; as, in the sentence, All are mortal, we must *understand* the word men, creatures, and the like ; উহ্য থাকা। ***Verb i.*** **1.** To be an intelligent and conscious being ; "All my soul be Imparadis'd in you, in whom alone I *understand,* and grow, and see" ; to have understanding ; বোধশক্তিবিশিষ্ট হওয়া ; বুদ্ধিবৃত্তি থাকা। **2.** To be informed by another; "I came to Jerusalem, and *understood* of the evil that Eliashib did" ; বিদিত হওয়া, অবগত হওয়া। **–a-ble,** *adj.* That can be understood ; বোধগম্য, অধিগম্য, বেদ্য। **–er,** *n.* **–ing,** *adj.* & *n.* Knowing ; skilful ; জ্ঞাতসার ; নিপুণ, চতুর। ***Noun.*** **1.** The act of one who understands, comprehends or apprehends ; comprehension ; অবগতি ; বোধ। **2.** The faculty of the mind by which it apprehends the real state of thing presented to it or the representation made to it ; চিত্তবৃত্তি, বুদ্ধিবৃত্তি। 3. Intelligence ; power of abstract thought ; বুদ্ধি, বিজ্ঞান (শ্রী:) ; চিন্তাশক্তি। 4. Agreement of minds ; "The perseverance of good *understanding* between him and his people" ; an agreement of opinion ; adjustment of difference ; anything mutually understood or agreed upon ; মনের মিল ; মতৈক্য ; বিরোধসমন্বয় ; উভয়পক্ষের সম্মতিক্রমে স্থিরীকৃত বিষয়। 5. Condition ; সর্ত্ত, করার। **–ing-ly,** *adv.* **–ing-ness,** *n.* **Good understanding**—Agreement ; সদ্ভাব। **On the understanding**—On the condition ; এই বুঝিয়া, এই মনে করিয়া, এই সর্ত্তে, এই করারে। **To come to an understanding with**—To make any agreement with ; কাহারো সহিত কোন বিষয়ে সর্ত্ত করা। **To give one to understand**—To let one know ; কাহাকে জানান, অবগত করা। **To make one's self understood**—To make one's meaning intelligible to others ; নিজের বক্তব্য বুঝাইয়া বলা।

ŭn-dêr-stāte′, *v. t.* To state or represent less strongly, than may be done truthfully ; যথাযোগ্য অপেক্ষা ন্যূনভাবে বর্ণনা বা ব্যক্ত করা, অযথোচিতরূপে ব্যক্ত করা। **–ment,** *n.*

ŭn-dêr-stōōd′, *p. t.* & *p. p.* of UNDERSTAND (which see).

ŭn′-dêr-străp-per (-êr), *n.* An inferior agent ; a petty fellow ; চর ; হীন ব্যক্তি।

ŭn-dêr-tāke′, *v. t.* & *i.* To take upon one's self ; to engage in ; to attempt ; ভার লওয়া ; প্রবৃত্ত হওয়া ; চেষ্টা করা। ***Verb i.*** 1. To take up or assume any business ; কোন কার্য্যের ভার গ্রহণ করা, কোন কার্য্যে হস্তক্ষেপ করা। 2. (*Obs.*) To venture ; (অপ্র:) সাহস করা। 3. To promise ; প্রতিশ্রুত হওয়া, অঙ্গীকৃত হওয়া।

ŭn-dêr-tāk′-êr, *n.* 1. One who undertakes any business ; কোন কার্য্যে প্রবৃত্ত ব্যক্তি। 2. One whose trade or business is to manage funerals ; যে ব্যক্তি সমাধি বা প্রেতকার্য্যের বন্দোবস্ত করিয়া দেয়, সৎকারসহায়ক, সৎকারনির্ব্বাহক।

ŭn-dêr-tāk′-ing, *n.* 1. Any business or project which a person undertakes ; an enterprise ; গৃহীত কার্য্য ; উদ্যম। 2. The business of an undertaker ; সমাধিক্রিয়ার বন্দোবস্তকারীর কার্য্য। 3. A promise, engagement or obligation ; as, a written *undertaking* ; প্রতিশ্রুতি, অঙ্গীকার।

ŭn′-dêr-taxed (-tăkst), *adj.* Not taxed enough ; অসম্যক্‌শুল্ক নির্দ্ধারিত।

ŭn′-dĕr-tĕn-ănt, *n.* A tenant under a tenant ; কোর্ফা প্রজা, পেটাও প্রজা।

ŭn′-dêr-tĕn-ūre-hōld-êr, *n.* A holder of a subordinate tenure ; নিমওসক তালুকদার, দরপত্তনিদার।

ŭn′-dêr-tōne, *adj.* A tone less loud than normal ; অনুচ্চস্বর, চাপা গলা। **In an undertone**—Lowering the voice ; চাপাস্বরে, স্বর নামাইয়া।

ŭn-dêr-tōōk′, *p. p.* of UNDERTAKE (which see).

ŭn-dêr-văl-ū-ā′-tion, *n.* Act of valuing below the real worth ; উপযুক্ত মূল্য অপেক্ষা অল্প মূল্য নির্দ্ধারণ।

ŭn-dêr-văl′-ue (-ū), *v. t.* & *n.* 1. To value below the real worth ; উপযুক্ত মূল্য অপেক্ষা অল্প মূল্য নির্দ্ধারণ করা। 2. To esteem lightly ; to despise ; হতাদর করা, তুচ্ছ মনে করা ; হেয়জ্ঞান করা। ***Noun.*** A price less than the real worth ; অল্প মূল্য।

ŭn′-dêr-wear (-wār), *n.* Underclothes ; অধোবাস, নীচে পরিবার খাটো কোর্ত্তা।

ŭn-dêr-wĕnt′, *p. t.* & *p. p.* of UNDERGO (which see).

ŭn′-dêr-wōōd, *n.* Small trees that grow among large ones ; ক্ষুপ, ঝোঁপ, ঝাড়।

ŭn′-dêr-work (-wêrk), *n.* & *v. t.* Subordinate work ; petty affairs ; অপ্রধান কার্য্য ; সামান্য ব্যাপার। ***Verb t.*** 1. To work clandestinely ; গোপনে কার্য্য করা, তলে তলে কাজ করা। 2. To work at a less price than others ; অপর সকল অপেক্ষা অল্প মজুরীতে কায করা। 3. To put insufficient work or labour on ; অপ্রচুর কার্য্য বা পরিশ্রম করান।

ŭn′-dêr-world (-wêrld), *n.* 1. This world ; পৃথিবী। 2. The place of departed souls ; Hades ; প্রেতলোক ; অধোভুবন। 3. The opposite sides of the globe ; "Fresh as the first beam glittering on a sail, that brings our friends from the *underworld*" ; পৃথিবীর বিপরীত দিক। 4. The lower or inferior part of mankind ; মানব জাতির নিকৃষ্টতম অংশ।

ŭn′-dêr-wrīte′ (-rīt), *v. t.* & *i.* 1. To write under something else ; কোন কিছুর নীচে লিখা। 2. To subscribe ; esp. to subscribe or set one's name to a policy of insurance for the purpose of becoming answerable for loss or damage to a certain amount ; গ্রাহক হওয়া ; বীমাপত্রের নীচে নাম স্বাক্ষর করিয়া উক্ত বীমার লিখিত সমস্ত টাকার বা নির্দ্দিষ্ট পরিমাণ টাকার জন্য দায়িত্ব স্বীকার করা। 3. To engage to buy all stock (in company etc.), not bought by the public ; কোন কোম্পানীর জনসাধারণ কর্ত্তৃক অক্রীত সমস্ত অংশ প্রভৃতি ক্রয়ের চুক্তি করা। 4. To guarantee or subscribe to any large business enterprise ; কোন বৃহৎ যৌথকারবারের বহু অংশ গ্রহণ করা বা বহু অংশ বিক্রয়ের জন্য দায়ী থাকা। ***Verb i.*** To do the business of an underwriter ; অংশগ্রাহিকের ব্যবসায় করা, নির্দ্দিষ্ট পরিমাণ টাকার নিমিত্ত বীমাপত্রের নিম্নে নাম স্বাক্ষর করা।

ŭn′-dêr-wrīt-êr (-rīt-), *n.* One who underwrites or insures ;

যে ব্যক্তি বীমার টাকা প্রদানের জন্য দায়িত্ব স্বীকারপূর্ব্বক নাম স্বাক্ষর করে। **—writ-ing,** *n.* One who engages himself to buy all or a large number of shares, bonds, stocks, etc. of a company ; যে ব্যক্তি কোন সমবায়ের সমস্ত বা বহুসংখ্যক অংশ গ্রহণ করিবার চুক্তিতে আবদ্ধ হয়, অংশগ্রাহক।

ŭn-dē-scend'-i-ble (-sĕnd-ĭ-bl), *adj.* Not capable of being descended to heirs ; উত্তরাধিকারীতে অসংক্রমণীয়।

ŭn-dē-scrīb'-ă-ble (-bl), *adj.* That cannot be described ; অবর্ণনীয়।

ŭn-dē-scrīed' *adj.* Not descried or discovered ; অদৃষ্ট, অনাবিষ্কৃত।

ŭn-dē-served' (-zêrvd), *adj.* Not deserved ; not merited ; অযোগ্য ; অসঙ্গত, অনুচিত। **—serv'-ed-ly,** *adv.* **—serv'-ed-ness,** *n.*

ŭn-dē-ṡerv'-ing, *adj.* Not deserving ; not having merit ; অযোগ্য ; অনুপযুক্ত, অনুপযোগী। **—ly,** *adv.*

ŭn-dĕṡ'-ig-nat-ĕd, *adj.* Not designated ; অনির্দ্দিষ্ট।

ŭn-dē-signed' (-zīnd), *adj.* Not designed or intended ; অনুদ্দিষ্ট, অনভিপ্রেত। **—sign'-ed-ly,** *adv.* **—sign'-ed-ness,** *n.*

ŭn-dē-sign'-ing (-zīn-), *adj.* Sincere ; upright ; সরল ; সাধু।

ŭn-dē-ṡīr'-ă-ble (-bl), *adj.* Not to be wished ; অবাঞ্ছনীয়, অবাঞ্ছিত, অনভিলষিত, অনভিপ্রেত, অকাম্য। **—bil'-i-ty,** *n.* **—ness,** *n.*

ŭn-dē-ṡīred', *adj.* Not desired ; not solicited ; অবাঞ্ছিত ; অযাচিত।

ŭn-dē-ṡīr'-ing, *adj.* Not desiring or wishing ; অনিচ্ছুক।

ŭn-dē-ṡīr'-ous (-ŭs), *adj.* Not desiring or wishing; অনিচ্ছুক, অনভিলাষী

ŭn-dē-spair'-ing (-spâr-), *adj.* Not yielding to despair ; অনিরাশাগ্রস্ত।

un-dē-spoiled , (-spoyld), *adj.* Not despoiled ; অলুণ্ঠিত।

ŭn-dēs'-tined, (-tĭnd), *adj.* Not destined ; অনির্দ্দিষ্ট।

ŭn-dē-tached' (-tăcht), *adj.* Not separated ; অবিশ্লিষ্ট।

ŭn-dē-tect'-ĕd, *adj.* Not discovered ; অনাবিষ্কৃত।

ŭn-dē-têr'-mi-nă-ble (-bl), *adj.* That cannot be determined ; অনিশ্চেয়।

ŭn-dē-têr'-mi-nate, *adj.* Not settled or certain; অনিশ্চিত, অনির্দ্ধারিত। **Undeterminate form** — সুপ্তমান (হিঃ কোঃ)।

ŭn-dē-têr'-mined (-mĭnd), *adj.* **1.** Not determined ; not settled ; অনিশ্চিত ; অস্থিরীকৃত। **2.** Not limited ; not defined ; indeterminate ; অসীমাবদ্ধ ; অব্যবস্থাপিত ; অনির্দ্দিষ্ট।

ŭn-dē-terred' (-tërd), *adj.* Not restrained by fear ; অপ্রতিরুদ্ধ, অপ্রতিহত, অবারিত।

ŭn-dē-vĕl'-oped (-ŭpt), *adj.* Not developed ; অব্যক্ত, অপরিস্ফুট।

ŭn-dē'-vi-at-ing, *adj.* Not departing from the way, principle, rule or purpose ; as, steady, *undeviating* rectitude ; regular ; অভ্রষ্ট, অস্খলিত, অচ্যুত, অবিচলিত ; নিয়মানুগত। **—ly,** *adj.*

ŭn-dē-vout' (-vowt), *adj.* Not devout ; ভক্তিহীন।

ŭn-dĕx'-têr-ous (-ŭs), *adj.* Not dexterous ; অদক্ষ, অকুশল, অনিপুণ, অপটু।

ŭn-dī'-ă-demed' (-dĕmd), *adj.* Not adorned with a diadem ; অকিরীটভূষিত, অমুকুটশোভিত।

ŭn-di-ăph'-ă-nous (-nŭs), *adj.* Not transparent ; অস্বচ্ছ।

ŭn-dĭd', *pt.* of UNDO (which see)

ŭn-dif-fêr-ĕn'-ti-āt-ĕd (-shi-), *adj.* Not differentiated ; অব্যক্ত, নির্গুণ, নির্ব্বিশেষ, সাম্য (ব্রজঃ হিন্দু), নির্ভেদ (ভক্তিরসামৃত সিন্ধু)

ŭn-dif-fūṡed', *adj.* Not diffused ; অব্যাপ্ত, অবিস্তারিত, অপুষ্পিত।

ŭn-dĭḡ'-ĕ-nous (-nŭs), *adj.* Generated by water ; জলোৎপন্ন।

ŭn-di-ḡĕst'-ĕd, *adj.* Not digested ; অজীর্ণ, অপাচিত।

ŭn-dig'-ni-fied (-fīd), *adj.* Not dignified ; wanting in dignity ; অমার্য্যাদাসম্পন্ন ; মর্য্যাদাহীন।

ŭn-di-min'-ish-ă-ble (-bl), *adj.* That cannot be diminished ; অক্ষয্য।

ŭn-di-min'-ished (-isht), *adj.* Not diminished ; অপ্রশমিত, অখর্ব্বীকৃত, অন্যূনীভূত, অকৃতহ্রাস, অকৃ। (cf. অকৃশকীর্ত্তি)।

ŭn-dine', *n.* A water spirit of the female sex, resembling in character the sylphs or spirits of the air ; একজাতীয় জলপরী, জলদেবী।

ŭn-dint'-ĕd, *adj.* Not suppressed by a blow ; অপ্রতিহত।

ŭn-dip-lō-măt'-ic, *adj.* Not according to diplomatic rules ; কুটরাজনীতিবিরোধী।

ŭn-dipped' (-dĭpt), *adj.* Not dipped or plunged ; অনিমজ্জিত, অনিমগ্ন।

ŭn-di-rĕct'-ĕd, *adj.* **1.** Not directed ; অনির্দ্দেশিত। **2.** Not superscribed ; অশিরোনামাযুক্ত।

ŭn-dis-cerned' (-zêrnd), *adj.* Not observed ; not seen ; অলক্ষিত ; অদৃষ্ট।

ŭn-dis-cern'-i-ble (-zêrn-ĭ-bl), *adj.* That cannot be discerned or discovered ; invisible ; অলক্ষ্য ; অদৃশ্য। **—bly,** *adv.* **—ness,** *n.*

ŭn-dis-cern'-ing (-zêrn-), *adj.* Not discerning ; wanting in discernment ; অসূক্ষ্মদর্শী ; অদুরদৃষ্টিসম্পন্ন।

ŭn-dis-charged' (-chârjd), *adj.* Not discharged ; অমোচিত, অদায়মুক্ত, অনিক্ষিপ্তপ্রাপ্ত।

ŭn-dis'-ci-plined (-plĭnd), *adj.* Not disciplined ; not duly exercised, trained or taught ; raw ; অশাসিত, দুর্বিনীত ; অসম্যক্‌-পরিচালিত, অশিক্ষিত; অপরিপক্ব।

ŭn-dis-clōṡed', *adj.* Not disclosed ; not revealed ; অপ্রকাশিত ; অজ্ঞাপিত, অপ্রকটিত।

ŭn-dĭs-cour′-āğed (-kŭr-), *adj.* Not disheartened ; অনুৎসাহিত, অপ্রোৎসাহিত।

ŭn-dĭs-cov′-er-a-ble (-kŭv-ėr-ă-bl), *adj.* That cannot be discovered ; অনাবিষ্করণীয়। **—bly,** *adv.*

ŭn-dĭs-cov′-ered (-cŭv-êrd), *adj.* Not discovered ; not seen ; অনাবিষ্কৃত ; অদৃষ্ট।

ŭn-dĭs-crĭm′-ĭ-nāt-ĭng, *adj.* Not discriminating ; অবিবেকী, অসূক্ষ্ম-প্রভেদজ্ঞ।

ŭn-dĭs-cussed′ (-kŭst), *adj.* Not discussed ; অনালোচিত।

ŭn-dĭs-grăced′ *adj.* Not disgraced ; অকলঙ্কিত।

ŭn-dĭs-guis′-a-ble (-gĭz-ā-bl), *adv.* That cannot be disguised ; অসংগোপনীয়।

ŭn-dĭs-guised′ (-gĭzd), *adj.* Not disguised ; open ; frank ; plain ; অপ্রচ্ছন্ন, অগূঢ়, সুস্পষ্ট ; সুব্যক্ত, সুপ্রকট ; সরল; অকপট।

ŭn-dĭs-heart′-ened (-hêrt-nd), *adj.* Not discouraged ; অভগ্নোদ্যম।

ŭn-dĭs-hon′-oured (-ŏn-êrd), *adj.* Not dishonoured ; অনবমানিত, অকলঙ্কিত।

ŭn-dĭs-mayed′ (-mād), *adj.* Not disheartened by fear ; অসন্ত্রস্ত, অভয়াকুলিত।

ŭn-dĭs-ŏr′-dered (-dêrd), *adj.* Not disturbed ; অনুদ্বেজিত, অবিক্ষুব্ধ।

ŭn-dĭs-pensed′ (-pênst), *adj.* Not dispensed ; not freed from obligation ; অপরিত্যক্ত ; অদায়মুক্ত।

ŭn-dĭs-persed′ (-pêrst), *adj.* Not scattered ; অবিকীর্ণ, অবিক্ষিপ্ত, অনবকীর্ণ।

ŭn-dĭs-played′ (-plād), *adj.* Not displayed ; not unfurled ; অপ্রদর্শিত ; অসমুৎক্ষিপ্ত।

ŭn-dĭs-pōsed′, *adj.* **1.** Not disposed ; অনিচ্ছুক। **2.** Not bestowed ; অনর্পিত। **3.** Not set apart, appropriated or allocated (with *of*) ; অপৃথকীকৃত, অব্যবস্থিত।

ŭn-dĭs′-pū′-tā-ble (-bl), *adj.* Not disputable ; অবিতর্ক্য, অবিবদনীয়।

ŭn-dĭs-pūt′-ĕd, *adj.* Not called in question ; not contested ; as, *undisputed* sway ; নির্বিবাদ ; নির্বিরোধ।

ŭn-dĭs-quī′-ĕt-ĕd, *adj.* Not disturbed ; অনাকুলিত, অনুদ্বেজিত, অবিক্ষুব্ধ।

ŭn-dĭs-sĕm′-bled (-bld), *adj.* Undisguised ; unfeigned ; অকপট ; অকৃত্রিম।

ŭn-dĭs-sĕm′-blĭng, *adj.* Not exhibiting a false appearance ; honest ; অকপট ; সাধু।

ŭn-dĭs′-sĭ-pāt-ĕd, *adj.* Not scattered ; অবিক্ষিপ্ত, অনবকীর্ণ।

ŭn-dĭs-sŏlv′-ă-ble (-bl), *adj.* Incapable of being dissolved or melted ; indissoluble ; অদ্রাব্য, অদ্রবণীয় ; অবিলয়নীয়, অবিলয়নশীল।

ŭn-dĭs-tĕm′-pered (-pêrd), *adj.* Not diseased ; free from malady ; অপীড়িত ; রোগমুক্ত।

ŭn-dĭs-tĕnd′-ĕd, *adj.* Not enlarged ; অবিস্ফারিত, অবিতত।

ŭn-dĭs-tilled′ (-tĭld), *adj.* Not distilled ; অপরিস্রুত।

ŭn-dĭs-tĭn′-guish-a-ble (-tĭng-gwĭsh-ă-bl), *adj.* Incapable of being distinguished ; অপ্রভেদ্য। **—bly,** *adv.*

ŭn-dĭs-tĭn′-guished(-tĭng-gwĭsht), *adj.* **1.** Not so marked, as to be known from each other ; not defined or discriminated ; অবিশেষ-চিহ্নিত ; অবিশেষিত। **2.** (*Rare*) Not treated with any particular respect ; (কচিদ্ব্যবহৃত) অবিশিষ্ট-সম্মানিত। **3.** Not famous ; অবিখ্যাত, অপ্রখ্যাত, অপ্রসিদ্ধ।

ŭn-dĭs-tĭn′-guish-ĭng (-tĭng-gwĭsh-), *adj.* Making no difference ; not discriminating ; অপ্রভেদ-কারী ; অসূক্ষ্মপ্রভেদকারী।

ŭn-dĭs-tŏrt′-ĕd, *adj.* Not perverted ; অবিকৃত, অবিরূপীকৃত।

ŭn-dĭs-trăct′-ĕd, *adj.* Not perplexed by contrariety or multiplicity of thought or decrees ; অবিভ্রান্ত, অবিক্ষিপ্তচিত্ত, অবিক্ষিপ্তমতি। **—ly,** *adv.* **—ness,** *n.*

ŭn-dĭs-trĭb′-ūt-ĕd, *adj.* Not distributed ; অবিতরিত। **Undistributed middle**—অব্যাপিত মধ্যমপদ। [হেত্ববয়ব ব্যাপ্তি প্রতিজ্ঞার উদ্দেশ্য এবং নিষেধাত্মক প্রতিজ্ঞার বিধেয় হইয়া পূর্ব্বাবয়ব সমূহে অন্ততঃ একবার ব্যাপিত হইবে এই নিয়মভঙ্গ জনিত হেত্বাভাস।]

ŭn-dĭs-turbed′ (-tērbd), *adj.* Free from interruption ; not molested or hindered ; free from perturbation ; calm ; tranquil ; serene ; নিরুপদ্রব, নিষ্কণ্টক ; অনুদ্বেজিত, অনুদ্বিগ্ন ; শান্ত, অনাকুল ; প্রশান্ত ; স্থির-চিত্ত। **—turb′-ed-ly,** *adv.* **—turb′-ed-ness,** *n.*

ŭn-dĭs-turb′-ĭng (-têrb-), *adj.* Not disturbing ; অনুদ্বেগজনক, অবিরক্তিকর।

ŭn-dĭ-vêr′-sĭ-fied (-fĭd), *adj.* Not varied ; uniform ; অবৈচিত্র্যপূর্ণ, বৈচিত্র্যহীন ; একরূপ।

ŭn-dĭ-vêrt′-ĕd, *adj.* **1.** Not diverted ; not turned aside ; অবিকৃষ্ট ; মূল বিষয় হইতে অনপসৃত। **2.** Not entertained ; অনাপ্যায়িত, অমনোরঞ্জিত।

ŭn-dĭ-vĭd′-ă-ble (-bl), *adj.* That cannot be divided ; অবিভাজ্য।

ŭn-dĭ-vĭd′-ĕd, *adj.* **1.** Not divided to into parts ; অবিভক্ত, অখণ্ডিত, অবিচ্ছিন্ন। **2.** Whole ; অখণ্ড, সম্পূর্ণ। **Undivided attention**—একাগ্রতা।

ŭn-dĭ-vorced′ (-vörst), *adj.* Not divorced ; অত্যক্ত।

ŭn-dĭ-vulged′ (-vuljd), *adj.* Not divulged ; Not revealed ; অপ্রকটিত ; অপ্রকাশিত।

ŭn-dô′, *v. t.* **1.** To annul ; to bring to nought ; "To-morrow ere the setting sun, She'd all *undo* what she had done" ; রদ করা

বাতিল করা, নাকচ করা, রহিত করা। 2. To unfasten ; as, to *undo* a button ; to loose ; as, to *undo* a knot ; বন্ধন উন্মোচন করা, খোলা ; শিথিল করা, আলগা করা। 3. To solve ; সমাধান করা, পূরণ করা। 4. To ruin ; "Why, masters my good friends, my honest neighbours will you *undo* yourself" ; নষ্ট করা, নাশ করা, ধ্বংস করা। 5. (*Obs.*) To surpass ; (অপ্রঃ) অতিক্রম করা। 6. (*Obs.*) To leave undone ; (অপ্রঃ) অসম্পন্ন রাখা। **–ing,** *n.* **1.** Reversal; রদ। 2. Destruction ; নাশ, সর্ব্বনাশ।

ŭn-dŏck′, *v.t.* To take out of dock; পোতনির্ম্মাণস্থলী হইতে অপসারিত করা।

ŭn-dō′-ẽr, *n.* **1.** One who reverses what is done ; রদকারী, নাকচকারী। 2. One who ruins ; ধ্বংসকারী।

ŭn-dō′-ing, *n.* **1.** The reversal of what has been done ; বাদ, নাকচ। 2. Ruin ; ধ্বংস, নাশ।

ŭn-dō-mĕs′-tic, *adj.* Not domestic ; অগ্রাম্য, অপোষিত।

ŭn-dō-mĕs′-ti-cāt-ĕd, *adj.* **1.** Not accustomed to a family life ; অগৃহজীবনাভ্যস্ত। 2. Not tamed ; অপোষিত।

ŭn-done (-dŭn), *p.t.* & *p.p.* of UNDO (which see).

ŭn-doubt′-ĕd (-dowt-), *adj.* Not called in question ; indubitable ; অসন্দিগ্ধ ; সন্দেহাতীত।

ŭn-doubt′-fûl (-dowt-), *adj.* Not doubtful ; plain ; evident ; সন্দেহহীন ; স্ফুট ; স্পষ্টতঃপ্রতীয়মান।

ŭn-doubt′-ing (-dowt-), *adj.* Not hesitating respecting facts ; not fluctuating ; অসন্দেহাকুল, অসংশয়ী ; অদ্বিধাপর।

ŭn-drained′ (-drānd), *adj.* Not freed from water ; অজলসিক্তি।

ŭn-drā-măt′-ic, *adj.* Not according to the rules of drama ; নাট্যশাস্ত্রের নিয়মবিরোধী, অনাট্যসমুচিত।

ŭn-draped′ (-drāpt), *adj.* Not covered with drapery ; অবস্ত্রাবৃত।

ŭn-dread′-ĕd (-drĕd-), *adj.* Not dreaded ; অভীষণ।

ŭn-dreamed′ (-drēmd), **–dreamt′** (-drĕmt), *adjs.* Not thought of ; অচিন্তিত, স্বপ্নাতীত।

ŭn-drĕss′, *v. t.* & *n.* To divest of clothes ; to strip ; to disrobe ; বস্ত্রশূন্য করা ; পরিচ্ছদশূন্য করা ; বিবস্ত্রীকৃত করা। ***Noun.*** A loose negligent dress ; শ্লথপরিচ্ছদ।

ŭn-dressed′ (-drĕst), *adj.* Not dressed ; not put in order ; অপরিচ্ছদশোভিত ; অসজ্জিত।

ŭn-dried′ (-drīd), *adj.* Not dried ; অবিশুষ্ক।

ŭn-drilled′ (-drīld), *adj.* **1.** Not pierced or bored with a drill ; অছিদ্রীকৃত। 2. Untrained; অশিক্ষিত।

ŭn-drink′-a-ble (-drĭngk-ă-bl), *adj.* Not drinkable ; অপেয়।

ŭn-driv′-en (-n), *adj.* Not driven ; not impelled ; অপ্রণোদিত ; অপ্রেরিত।

ŭn-drōōp′-ing, *adj.* Not drooping; not despairing; অনত ; অনিরাশাগ্রস্ত।

ŭn-drŏs′-sȳ, *adj.* Free from dross or impurity ; অমলদূষিত, শ্যামিকাযুক্ত।

ŭn-drowned′ (-drownd), *adj.* Not drowned ; অনিমজ্জিত।

ŭn-due′ (-dū), *adj.* **1.** Not due ; অদেয়। 2. Improper ; অন্যায়, অনুচিত, অসঙ্গত। **–du′-ly,** *adv.* Improperly ; অন্যায়রূপে, অসঙ্গতভাবে, অযুক্তরূপে, অসমুচিতরূপে।

ŭn′-dū-lāte, *v. t.* & *i.* **1.** To make like a wave ; তরঙ্গায়িত করা। 2. To cause to vibrate ; স্পন্দিত করা। ***Verb i.*** To have a wavy motion ; তরঙ্গায়িত গতিবিশিষ্ট হওয়া। **–la′-tion,** *n.* **1.** The act of undulating ; তরঙ্গায়িত গতিতে চলন। 2. A wavy form ; তরঙ্গায়িত আকৃতি, লহর, তরঙ্গ। 3. (*Phys.*) Wave motion ; তরঙ্গায়িত গতি।

ŭn′-dū-lāte, –lat-ĕd, *adjs.* Wavy ; তরঙ্গায়িত, তরঙ্গিত, তরঙ্গ সদৃশ।

ŭn′-dū-lā-tō-rȳ, *adj.* **1.** Wavy ; তরঙ্গিত, তরঙ্গায়িত, ঢেউখেলানিয়া। 2. Uneven ; অসমান, নিম্নোন্নতসমন্বিত। **Undulatory motion of light**—আলোকের তরঙ্গবৎ গতি। **Undulatory theory**—তরঙ্গসিদ্ধান্ত (হিঃ কোঃ), তরঙ্গায়িত গতি মত।

ŭn-dū′-tē-ous (-us), *adj.* Not obedient ; not performing duty to parents and superiors ; কর্ত্তব্যপরাঙ্মুখ ; মাতা পিতা গুরুজনের প্রতি কর্ত্তব্য পালনে অবহেলাকারী।

ŭn-dū′-ti-fûl, *adj.* Not dutiful ; অকর্ত্তব্যনিষ্ঠ। **–ly,** *adv.* **–ness,** *n.*

ŭn-dyed′ (-dīd), *adj.* Not dyed ; অরঞ্জিত, অরক্ত (মঃ সং), অরঞ্জনীকৃত।

ŭn-dȳ′-ing, *adj.* Immortal ; "The *uudying* souls of man" ; অবিনশ্বর, অমর, অক্ষর।

ŭn-earned′ (-ẽrnd), *adj.* Not merited by labour ; অনর্জ্জিত।

ŭn-earth′ (-ẽrth), *v. t.* **1.** To drive out of the earth ; to uncover ; মাটী খুঁড়িয়া বাহির করা, উৎখাতিত করা ; অনাবৃত করা। 2. To disclose ; as, to *unearth* secret ; উদ্‌ঘাটিত করা, উদ্ভেদ্ করা, প্রকাশ করা, প্রচার করা।

ŭn-earth′-lȳ (-ẽrth-), *adj.* **1.** Not earthly or of the earth ; অপার্থিব, অলৌকিক। 2. Weird ; ভৌতিক।

ŭn-eas′-y (-ēz-), *adj.* **1.** Feeling some degree of pain, mental or physical ; restless ; উৎকণ্ঠিত, উৎকণ্ঠাকুল, উদ্বেগপূর্ণ ; ব্যাকুল, উতলা। 2. Constrained ; not graceful ; বাঁধবাঁধ, কষ্টকল্পিত ; মাধুর্য্যশূন্য। **–iness,** *n.* The state of being uneasy ; উৎকণ্ঠা, ব্যাকুলতা, উদ্বেগ, অস্বচ্ছন্দতা, উৎসুকতা।

ŭn-eat′-a-ble (-ēt-ă-bl), *adj.* Not fit to be eaten ; অভোজ্য, অখাদ্য।

ŭn-eat′-en (-ēt-n), *adj.* Not eaten ; অখাদিত।

ŭn-ē-clipsed′ (-clĭpst), *adj.* Not eclipsed ; not obscured ; অরাহুগ্রস্ত, অগ্রস্ত ; অতমোবৃত।

ŭn-ĕd′-ū-cāt-ĕd, *adj.* Not educated ; illiterate ; অশিক্ষিত ; মূর্খ।

ŭn-ĕf-faced′ (-făst), *adj.* Not obliterated ; অব্যামৃষ্ট ।
ŭn-ĕf-fĕc′-tū-ăl, *adj.* Same as INEFFECTUAL.
ŭn-ē-lăb′-ō-rāte, *adj.* Not elaborate ; finished with little labour or study ; অবহুশ্রমসিদ্ধ ; অধ্যয়ন বা পরিশ্রম দ্বারা অনুৎকর্ষসাধিত ।
ŭn-ē-lăs′-tic, *adj.* Not elastic ; having no elasticity ; অস্থিতিস্থাপক ; অস্থিতিস্থাপকগুণোপেত, স্থিতিস্থাপকতাশূন্য।
ŭn-ē-lāt′-ĕd, *adj.* Not elated ; not puffed up ; অনুল্লসিত; অগর্ব্বস্ফীত।
ŭn-ĕl′-bowed (-bōd), *adj.* Not pushed aside, as with the elbow ; অকফোণিতাড়িত ।
ŭn-ē-lĕct′-ĕd, *adj.* (*Obs.*) Not elected ; অনির্ব্বাচিত, অমনোনীত।
ŭn-ĕl′-ĭ-gĭ-ble (-bl), *adj.* Same as, INELIGIBLE.
ŭn-ē-măn′-cĭ-pāt-ĕd, *adj.* Not emancipated ; অদাসত্বমুক্ত ।
ŭn-ĕm-balmed′(-bâmd), *adj.* **1.** Not embalmed ; অসুরভিত, অসুবাসিত। **2.** Not preserved from being rotten by aromatic spice ; সুগন্ধি মসলাদি সহযোগে অবিকৃতভাবে রক্ষিত ।
ŭn-ĕm-băr′-rassed (-răst), *adj.* Not perplexed in mind ; free from pecuniary difficulties or encumbrances ; অব্যাকুলিত, অনাকুলিত ; ঝঞ্ঝাটমুক্ত, অদ্বিষ্ট ।
ŭn-ĕm-bĭt′-tered (-têrd), *adj.* Not embittered ; অনুত্যক্ত।
ŭn-ĕm-bŏd′-ied (-ĭd), *adj.* Free from corporeal body ; not embodied ; অমূর্ত্ত, অশরীরী, অবিগ্রহবান, অনঙ্গ, কায়বর্জ্জিত ; অদেহবদ্ধ ।
ŭn-ĕm-broid′-ered (-broyd-ĕrd), *adj.* Not embroidered ; সূচিকর্ম্ম দ্বারা কৃত পুষ্পপত্রাদি দ্বারা অনলঙ্কৃত।
ŭn-ē-mō′-tion-ăl, *adj.* Without emotion or feeling ; আবেগশূন্য, অনুরাগশূন্য, প্রাণহীন ।
ŭn-ĕm-phăt′-ic, *adj.* Having no emphasis ; (শব্দের উপর) জোরশূন্য । **—i-cal-ly,** *adv.*

ŭn-ĕm-ployed′ (-ployd), *adj.* **1.** Not employed ; having no work or employment ; at leisure ; অনিযুক্ত ; বেকার ; অবসর। **2.** Not being in use ; not invested ; অব্যবহৃত ; অখাটানো । **3.** Not associated or accompanied with labour and employment ; অশ্রমসহকৃত। **The unemployed**—কর্ম্মহীন জনগণ, বেকারলোকগণ। [ইহাদিগকে তিন শ্রেণীতে বিভক্ত করা যাইতে পারে। (১) যাহারা বার্দ্ধক্য বা কোনরূপ দুর্ঘটনা বশতঃ কর্ম্ম করিতে অশক্ত। (২) যাহারা কর্ম্ম করিতে ইচ্ছুক অথচ কর্ম্ম পায়না। (৩) যাহারা কোন অবস্থায়ই কর্ম্ম করিবেনা।] **Unemployed capital**—যে মূলধন ব্যবসায়ে বিনিয়োগ হয় নাই।
ŭn-ĕm-ploy′-mĕnt, *n.* The quality or state of being unemployed ; বেকার অবস্থা ।
ŭn-ĕm-pow′-ered (-êrd), *adj.* Not empowered or authorised ; অক্ষমতার্পিত ।
ŭn-ĕm′-ū-lāt′-ing, *adj.* Not striving to excel ; অবিজিগীষু।
ŭ-ĕn-chănt′-ĕd, *adj.* Not enchanted ; অমন্ত্রমুগ্ধ, অমোহিত, অবিমোহিত।
ŭn-ĕn-coun′-tered (-kown-têrd), *adj.* Not encountered ; অসম্মুখীকৃত।
ŭn-ĕn-cŭm′-bêr, *v. t.* To free from encumbrance ; ঝঞ্ঝাট মুক্ত করা, দায় মুক্ত করা।
ŭn-ĕn-cŭm′-bered (-bêrd), *adj.* Not emcumbered ; অবিঘ্নিত, অপ্রতিরুদ্ধ ।
ŭn-ĕn-deared (-dērd), *adj.* Not attended with endearment ; অস্নেহবচনসহকৃত ।
ŭn-ĕn-deav′-our-ing (-dĕv-êr-), *adj.* Making no effort ; অযত্নশীল, অচেষ্টাকারী ।
ŭn-ĕnd′-ing, *adj.* Not ending ; অনন্ত, অন্তহীন, অফুরন্ত ।
ŭn-ĕn-dowed′ (-dowd), *adj.* **1.** Not endowed ; not furnished with funds ; অসমন্বিত, অনুপেত; অবৃত্তিপ্রাপ্ত, অবৃত্তিদত্ত। **2.** Having no dower or dowry ; যৌতুকহীন যৌতুকশূন্য ।

ŭn-ĕn-dūr′-ă-ble (-bl), *adj.* Not to be endured ; intolerable ; অসহনীয় ; অসহ্য ।
ŭn-ĕn-dūr′-ing, *adj.* Temporary ; অচিরস্থায়ী, অস্থায়ী ।
ŭn-ĕn-frăn′-chīsed, *adj.* Not enfranchised ; not having the franchise or right to vote for parliament ; অমুক্ত ; পার্লেমেন্টের সভ্য-নির্ব্বাচনের মত প্রদানে ক্ষমতা অপ্রাপ্ত ।
ŭn-ē-nêr′-vāt-ĕd, *adj.* Not enervated ; অক্ষীণীকৃত, দুর্ব্বলীকৃত ।
ŭn-ĕn-fee′-bled (-fē-bld), *adj.* Not enfeebled ; অদুর্ব্বলীকৃত ।
ŭn-ĕn-gāged′, *adj.* **1.** Not bound by any covenant or promise ; অচুক্তিবদ্ধ। **2.** Free from obligation to a particular person ; কোন বিশেষ ব্যক্তির সহিত বাধ্যবাধকতাহীন। **3.** Unemployed ; at leisure ; অনিযুক্ত ; অবসর। **4.** (*Obs.*) Not appropriatd ; "*Unengaged* revenues" ; (অপ্রঃ) অবাজেয়াপ্ত ।
ŭn-ĕn-gāg′-ing, *adj.* Not attractive ; অচিত্তহারী, অমনোহারী, অচিত্তাকর্ষক, অবিনোদক ।
ŭn-eng′-lish (-ĭng-), *adj.* Not English, esp. in spirit, conduct or proceeding ; ইংরাজ চরিত্রের বিরোধী, অ-ইংরাজী, অ-ইংরেজসুলভ, অ-ইংরেজসমুচিত ।
ŭn-ĕn-joyed′ (-joyd), *adj.* Not enjoyed ; অভুক্ত ।
ŭn-ĕn-joy′-ing, *adj.* Having no fruition ; অভোগী ।
ŭn-ĕn-larged′ (-lârjd), *adj.* Not enlarged ; narrow ; "*Unenlarged* souls are disgusted with the wonders which the microscope has revealed" ; অবর্দ্ধিত ; সংকীর্ণ, অনুদার ।
ŭn-ĕn-light′-ened (-līt-ĕnd), *adj.* Not enlightened ; not illuminated ; অজ্ঞানালোকোজ্জ্বলিত ; অনালোকিত ।
ŭn-ĕn-līv′-ened (-ĕnd), *adj.* Not enlivened ; অননুপ্রাণিত ।
ŭn-ĕn-slāved′, *adj.* Not enslaved ; free ; অদাসকৃত, অদাসগত ; স্বাধীন ।

ŭn-ĕn-tăn′-gle (-tăng-gl), *v. t.* Same as DISENTANGLE (which see). **—gled,** *adj.*

ŭn-ĕn′-têr-prīṡ-ĭng, *adj.* Not enterprising ; not adventurous ; নিরুদ্যম ; অদুঃসাহসিককার্য্যপ্রবণ ।

ŭn-ĕn-têr-tain′-ĭng (-tān-), *adj.* Not entertaining or amusing ; অবিনোদক, অবিনোদজনক, অচিত্ত-বিনোদক । **—ness,** *n.*

ŭn-ĕn-thralled′, (-thrăld), *adj.* Not enslaved or reduced to thraldom : অদাস্যগত ।

ŭn-ĕn-tombed′ (-tômd), *adj.* Not buried or interred ; অসমাহিত, অনিখাত ।

ŭn-ĕn′-vĭ-ă-ble (-bl), *adj.* Not to be envied ; অঈর্ষণীয়, অলোভ্য, অলোভনীয়, অন্বেষ্য, অনাকাঙ্ক্ষণীয় ।

ŭn-ĕn′-vied (-vĭd), *adj.* Not envied ; exempt from the envy of others ; অঈর্ষিত ; ঈর্ষাশূন্য ।

ŭn-ē′-quă-ble (-bl), *adj.* Not uniform ; as, an *unequable* temper ; বিভিন্নরূপ, নিয়ত একরূপ নয়, অসম ।

ŭn-ē′-quăl, *adj.* **1.** Not equal ; not of the same size, length, quality, etc. ; অসমান ; অসম, অসমঞ্জস, বিষম । **2.** Not equable ; irregular ; নিয়ত একরূপ নয় ; অনিয়মিত । **3.** Not adequate ; as, his strength was *unequal* to the task ; অযথোচিত, অসমুচিত । **4.** (*Bot.*) Asymmetrical ; (উদ্ভিদ্‌বিদ্যা) অসমমাত্রিক ।

ŭn-ē-′qualled (-kwăld), *adj.* Unmatched ; unrivalled ; surpassing ; অতুলনীয় ; অপ্রতিম, অনুপম, নিরুপম, অদ্বিতীয় ; অতিশায়ী, সর্ব্বাতিশায়ী ।

ŭn-ē-quipped′ (-kwĭpt), *adj.* Not equipped ; অসজ্জিত ।

ŭn-ē-quĭv′-ō-căl, *adj.* Not ambiguous ; not doubtful ; clear ; অসন্দিগ্ধার্থ ; অসন্দিগ্ধ ; স্পষ্ট, পরিষ্কার, সুব্যক্ত, সুস্পষ্ট । **—ly,** *adv.* **—ness,** *n.*

ŭn-ĕrr′-ĭng, *adj.* Committing no mistake ; certain ; "Well-skilled was he to rouse and with *unerring* aim, arrest all savage kinds" ; অভ্রান্ত, নির্ভুল, ভ্রমশূন্য ; নিশ্চিন্ত, নিঃসন্দিগ্ধ, অমোঘ, অব্যর্থ । **—ly,** *adv.*

ŭn-ĕs-pied′ (-pīd), *adj.* Not seen ; অদৃষ্ট ।

ŭn-ĕs-sayed′ (-sād), *adj.* Unattempted ; অচেষ্টিত ।

ŭn-ĕs-sĕn′-tial (-shăl), *adj.* & *n.* **1.** Not absolutely necessary ; unimportant ; পরিহার্য্য ; গুরুত্বহীন, অপ্রধান । **2.** (*Rare*) Void of essence or real being ; (কচিদ্ ব্যবহৃত) সারহীন । ***Noun.*** An unessential thing ; অপ্রধান বিষয়, পরিহার্য্য বিষয় ।

ŭn-ē-văn-gĕl′-ĭ-căl, *adj.* Not according to the gospel ; অসু-সমচারানুযায়ী ।

ŭn-ē′-ven (-vn), *adj.* **1.** Not level ; rough ; অসমতল, সমবিষম, উচ্চাবচ, বন্ধুর ; আবড়োখাবড়ো । **2.** Odd ; অযুগ্ম । **3.** (*Obs.*) Full of difficulties ; (অপ্রঃ) বিপৎসঙ্কুল । **—ly,** *adv.* **—ness,** *n.*

ŭn-ē-vĕnt′-fûl, *adj.* Not eventful ; ঘটনাবৈচিত্র্যহীন, অঘটনাবহুল, অঘটনা সঙ্কুল ।

ŭn-ex-ăct′ (-ĕgz-), *adj.* Not exact ; অযথার্থ ।

ŭn-ex-act′-ĕd (-ĕgz-), *adj.* Not taken by force ; অবলগৃহীত ।

ŭn-ex-ăg′-gĕr-āt-ĕd (-ĕgz-), *adj.* Not exaggerated ; অনতিরঞ্জিত ।

ŭn-ex-am′-in-a-ble (-ĕgz-ăm-ĭn-ă-bl), *adj.* Not to be examined ; অপরীক্ষণীয় ।

ŭn-ex-am′-ined (-ĕgz-ăm-ĭnd), *adj.* **1.** Not interrogated ; অজিজ্ঞাসিত । **2.** Not enquired into or investigated ; "Untainted, *unexamined*, free, of liberty" ; অপরীক্ষিত ।

ŭn-ex-am′-pled, (-ĕgz-ăm-pld), *adj.* Having no example or similar case ; unprecedented ; peerless ; দৃষ্টান্তশূন্য ; অভূতপূর্ব্ব ; অপূর্ব্ব, অনুপম, নিরুপম ।

ŭn-ĕx-cĕp′-tion-ă-ble (-bl), *adj.* Not liable to any execption or objection ; beyond reproach ; "Man of clear and *unexceptionable* character" ; অনাপত্তিসহ ; অনিন্দ্য, অনিন্দনীয় । **—bly,** *adv.* **—ness,** *n.*

ŭn-ĕx-cīṡed′, *adj.* Not charged with the duty of excise ; আবকারীর শুল্কমুক্ত ।

ŭn-ĕx-cīt′-ĕd, *adj.* Not roused ; অনুত্তেজিত ।

ŭn-ĕx-clūd′-ĕd, *adj.* Not excluded ; অপরিবর্জ্জিত ।

ŭn-ĕx-clū′-sive (-sĭv), *adj.* Not exclusive ; অপৃথগ্‌ভূত ।

ŭn-ĕx-cŏm-mū′-nĭ-căt-ĕd, *adj.* Not excommunicated ; অসমাজ-বর্জ্জিত ।

ŭn-ĕx′-ē-cūt-ĕd, *adj.* Not performed ; অসম্পাদিত, অসম্পন্ন ।

ŭn-ex′-ĕm-plă-rȳ (-ĕgz-), *adj.* Not exemplary ; not according to example ; অদৃষ্টান্তস্বরূপ ; অদৃষ্টান্তানুসারী ।

ŭn-ex-em′-pli-fied (-ĕgz-ĕm-plĭ-fīd), *adj.* Not exemplified ; অদৃষ্টান্তদর্শিত ।

ŭn-ex-empt′ (-ĕgz-ĕmt), *adj.* Not exempt ; অনব্যাহতিপ্রাপ্ত ।

ŭn-ĕx′-ĕr-cīṡed, *adj.* Not disciplined ; অশিক্ষিত ।

ŭn-ex-haust′-ĕd (-ĕgz-häst-), *adj.* Not exhausted ; not spent ; অনিঃশেষিত ; অব্যয়িত, অশোষিত (হি কোঃ), অনপচিত (ঐ) ।

ŭn-ex-ist′-ĕnt (-ĕgz-), *adj.* Not existing ; অসত্তাবান ।

ŭn-ĕx′-ŏr-cīṡed, *adj.* Not cast out by exorcism ; অভূততাড়িত ।

ŭn-ĕx-pănd′-ĕd, *adj.* Not spread out ; অবিস্তারিত, অবিতত ।

ŭn-ĕx-pĕct′-ĕd, *adj.* Not looked for ; as, an *unexpected* event ; sudden ; as, an *unexpected* death ; অপ্রত্যাশিত ; হঠাৎ সংঘটিত । **—ly,** *adv.* **—ness,** *n.*

ŭn-ĕx-pĕnd′-ĕd, *adj.* Not expended ; not held out ; অব্যয়িত ; অবিন্যস্ত ।

ŭn-ĕx-pĕn′-sive (-sĭv), *adj.* Not costly ; অমহার্ঘ।

ŭn-ĕx-pĕ-ri-mĕn′-tăl, *adj.* Not experimental ; অপরীক্ষাত্মক।

ŭn-ĕx-pêrt′, *adj.* Not expert ; অদক্ষ, অনিপুণ, অকুশল।

ŭn-ĕx-pīred′, *adj.* Not expired ; as, an *unexpired* lease ; not ended ; অনিঃশেষিত ; অসমাপ্ত।

ŭn-ĕx-plored′ (-plōrd), *adj.* Not searched or examined ; unknown; "To regions *unexplored*"; অনিরূপিত ; অপরিচিত।

ŭn-ĕx-plō′-sive (-sĭv), *adj.* Not explosive ; অবিদারণশীল।

ŭn-ĕx-pōrt′-ĕd, *adj.* Not exported; অরপ্তানীকৃত।

ŭn-ĕx-pōsed′, *adj.* Not laid open to view ; not laid open to censure ; sheltered ; অবিবৃত, অপ্রকটীকৃত ; অবিগর্হ্য ; আশ্রিত, সমাশ্রিত।

ŭn-ĕx-pound′-ĕd (-pownd-) *adj.* Not expounded ; অব্যাখ্যাত।

ŭn-ĕx-pressed′ (-prĕst), *adj.* Not expressed ; not mentioned or named ; অপ্রকাশিত, অব্যক্ত ; অনুল্লিখিত।

ŭn-ĕx-prĕs′-sive (-ĭv), *adj.* Not having the power of expressing ; unutterable; অপ্রকাশাত্মক ; অনুচ্চার্য্য।

ŭn-ĕx-punged′ (-pŭnjd), *adj.* Not expunged ; অনুচ্ছিন্ন।

ŭn-ĕx-tĕnd′-ĕd, *adj.* 1. Not extended ; অবিস্তারিত, অপ্রসারিত। 2. Having no dimensions ; "A spiritual, that is an *unextended* substance" ; আয়তনহীন।

ŭn-ĕx-tinct′ (-tĭngkt), *adj.* Not extinct ; অনির্ব্বাণপ্রাপ্ত, অনির্ব্বাপিত।

ŭn-ĕx-tin′-guish-a-ble (-tĭng-gwĭsh-ă-bl), *adj.* That cannot be extinguished ; unquenchable ; অনির্ব্বাপ্য ; অশমনীয়, অশাম্য।

ŭn-ĕx-tin′-guished (-tĭng-gwĭsht-), *adj.* Not quenched ; not entirely suppressed ; অনির্ব্বাপিত ; অসম্যগলয়িত।

ŭn-ĕx′-tir′-păt-ĕd (-têr-), *adj.* Not rooted out ; অনুৎপাটিত।

ŭn-ĕx-tŏrt′-ĕd, *adj.* Not extorted ; অবলগৃহীত।

ŭn-ĕx-trăct′-ĕd, *adj.* Not drawn out ; অনিষ্কর্ষিত।

ŭn-făd′-ĕd, *adj.* Not faded ; unwithered ; অম্লান ; অশুষ্ক।

ŭn-făd′-ing, *adj.* Not liable to fade ; "*Unfading* rose of Eden" ; not liable to wither ; অম্লান, অপরিম্লান ; অবিশুষ্ক। **—ly,** *adv.*

ŭn-fail′-ing (-fāl-), *adj.* Not liable to fail ; as, an *unfailing* source of supply; certain ; "Thou secure of my *unfailing* word" ; অব্যর্থ, অবিচলিত, অমোঘ ; অব্যর্থ। **—ly,** *adv.* **—ness,** *n.*

ŭn-faint′-ing (-fānt-), *adj.* Not sinking ; "*Unfainting* perseverance" ; not fainting ; অনবসন্ন ; অমূর্চ্ছাপ্রাপী।

ŭn-fair′ (-fār), *adj.* 1. Not honest ; "You come like an *unfair* merchant to charge me with being in your debt" ; disengenuous ; অসাধু ; অসরল, খল, কপট। 2. Using trick or artifice ; কৌশলী, ধূর্ত্ত। **—ly,** *adv.* **—ness,** *n.* Dishonesty ; injustice ; অসাধুতা ; অন্যায়।

ŭn-faith′-fûl (-fāth-), *adj.* 1. Not observant of promise, duty or allegiance ; as, an *unfaithful* subject ; অসত্যপ্রতিজ্ঞ, অসত্যসন্ধ। 2. Treacherous ; বিশ্বাসঘাতক। **—ly,** *adv.* **—ness,** *n.*

ŭn-făl′-căt-ĕd, *adj.* Not falcated ; অবক্র।

ŭn-făll′-en (-n), *adj.* Not fallen ; অপতিত।

ŭn-făl′-lowed (-lōd), *adj.* Not fallowed ; অপতিত, আবাদী।

ŭn-fal′-têr-ing, *adj.* Unhesitating; অসন্দেহাকুল, অদ্বিধাপর, অকম্পিত, অবিচলিত, অসংশয়াকুল। **—ly,** *adv.*

ŭn-fă-mil′-iar (-yêr), *adj.* Not familiar ; অপরিচিত। **—i-ar′-i-ty,** *n.* Want of familiarity ; অপরিচয়, অঘনিষ্ঠতা।

ŭn-făsh′-ion-a-ble (-ŏn-ă-bl), *adj.* Not according to the prevailing mode ; not conforming in dress and manners to the reigning custom ; প্রচলিত রীতিবিরুদ্ধ, বেদস্তুর ; সাময়িক রীতিবিরুদ্ধ পোষাকপরিচ্ছদধারী বা রীতিনীতিপালনকারী। **—bly,** *adv.* **—ness,** *n.*

ŭn-făsh′-ioned (-ŏnd), *adj.* Not modified by art ; shapeless ; অপরিকর্ম্মীকৃত ; কদাকার।

ŭn-făst′, *adj.* Not safe or secure ; অনিরাপদ, অনির্ব্বিঘ্ন।

ŭn-făs′-ten (-n), *v. t.* 1. To loose ; to unfix ; খোলা ; উন্মোচন করা। 2. To unsettle ; as, to *unfasten* one's mind ; বিচলিত করা।

ŭd-fâ′-thered (-thêrd), *adj.* Fatherless ; পিতৃহীন, পিতৃবিহীন।

ŭn-fâ′-ther-lŷ, *adj.* Not becoming a father ; unkind ; অপিত্রোচিত ; নির্দ্দয়, অকরুণ।

ŭn-făth′-ŏm-ă-ble (-bl), *adj.* That cannot be sounded by a line ; too deep for fathoming ; অতল ; অতলস্পর্শ, অপরিসীম, দুরবগাহ।

ŭn-făth′-omed (-ŏmd), *adj.* Not sounded ; not to be sounded ; অতলস্পৃষ্ট ; দুরবগাহ্য।

ŭn-fă-tigued′ (-tēgd), *adj.* Not fatigued ; অক্লান্ত, অপরিক্লান্ত, অনবসন্ন।

ŭn-fault′-ŷ (-fălt-), *adj.* Free from fault ; নির্দ্দোষ, দোষশূন্য।

ŭn-fă-vour′-a-ble (-vêr-ă-bl), *adj.* 1. Not favourable or propitious ; not kind or obliging ; discouraging ; প্রতিকূল, অননুকূল, অশুভ, বাম ; অপ্রসন্ন, অসদয়, অপ্রিয়কর ; নিরুৎসাহজনক। 2. Contrary ; প্রতিকূল, বিপরীত।

ŭn-fă′-voured (-vêrd), *adj.* Not favoured ; not assisted ; অননুগ্রহপ্রাপ্ত ; অসাহায্যীকৃত।

ŭn-feared′ (-fērd), *adj.* Not feared or dreaded ; অভীতিপ্রাপ্ত।

ŭn-fear'-fûl (-fër-), *adj.* Not fearful ; courageous ; অভয়জনক, আশঙ্কাজনক, অত্রাসজনক ; সাহসী, সাহসসম্পন্ন।

ŭn-fear'-ing (-fër-), *adj.* Not fearing ; ভয়শূন্য, ভয়হীন, নির্ভয়।

ŭn-fea'-si-ble (-fë-zî-bl), *adj.* Impracticable ; অকার্য্যকর।

ŭn-feath'-ered (-fĕth-êrd), *adj.* Having no feathers ; unfledged ; পালকশূন্য, পালকবিহীন ; অজাতপক্ষ, অনুদ্গতপক্ষ।

ŭn-fea'-tured (-fë-türd), *adj.* Wanting regular features ; deformed ; কদাকৃতি ; কদাকার।

ŭn-fĕd', *adj.* Not fed ; not supplied with food ; অভুক্ত ; অখাদ্যদত্ত।

ŭn-feed' (-fëd), *adj.* Not retained by a fee ; অবেতনদত্ত।

ŭn-feel'-ing (-fël-), *adj.* Insensible ; void of sensibility ; callous ; অচেতন ; চেতনাশূন্য ; কঠিন। **—ly,** *adv.* **—ness,** *n.*

ŭn-feigned'(-fānd),*adj.* Not counterfeit or hypocritical; sincere ; অকপট ; সরল, অকৃত্রিম। **—ly,** *adv.*

ŭn-fĕl'-lowed (-lōd), *adj.* Not matched ; অতুলিত।

ŭn-fĕlt', *adj.* Not perceived ; অননুভূত, অনুপলব্ধ।

ŭn-fĕm'-i-nine (-nîn), *adj.* Not according to female character ; অস্ত্রীজনোচিত, অস্ত্রীজনসুলভ।

ŭn-fence' (-fĕns), *v. t.* To strip or remove a fence from ; বৃতি-বিরহিত করা।

ŭn-fenced' (-fĕnst), *adj.* Not inclosed ; defenceless ; অবৃতিবেষ্টিত ; অরক্ষিত।

ŭn-fêr-mĕnt'-ĕd, *adj.* Not having undergone the process of fermentation ; not leavened ; অসন্ধিত, অনস্তরুৎসিক্ত ; অকিণ্বমিশ্রিত।

ŭn-fêr'-tile, *adj.* Not fertile ; barren ; অনুর্ব্বর, বন্ধ্য ; বাঁজা। **—ness,** *n.*

ŭn-fĕt'-ter (-êr), *v. t.* To loose from fetters ; to unchain ; to free from restraint ; অনিগড়িত করা; শৃঙ্খল মুক্ত করা ; বন্ধন মুক্ত করা।

ŭn-fig'-ured (-ürd), *adj.* Representing no animal or vegetable figures or forms ; devoid of figures ; অমূর্ত্ত্যাত্মক ; মূর্ত্তিহীন, অমূর্ত্ত।

ŭn-fil'-i-ăl, *adj.* Undutiful ; not becoming a child ; অকর্ত্তব্যনিষ্ঠ ; অসন্তানোচিত। **—ly,** *adv.*

ŭn-filled' (-fîld), *adj.* Not filled ; not fully supplied ; অপূর্ণিত ; অপুরিত, অপরিপুরিত।

ŭn-filmed' (-fîlmd), *adj.* Not covered with a film ; পর্দ্দা দ্বারা অনাচ্ছাদিত।

ŭn-fil-tered' (-têrd), *adj.* Not filtered ; অশোধিত, অনির্ম্মলীকৃত।

ŭn-fin'-ished (-îsht), *adj.* Not complete ; imperfect ; অসমাপ্ত ; অসম্পূর্ণ, অসম্পন্ন।

ŭn-fired', *adj.* Not inflamed ; অনুদ্দীপ্ত, অনুত্তেজিত।

ŭn-firm' (-fêrm), *adj.* Weak ; feeble ; unstable ; দুর্ব্বল ; কৃশ ; অস্থির। **—ness,** *n.*

ŭn-fit', *adj.* **1.** Not fit ; improper ; unsuitable ; অনুপযুক্ত ; অসঙ্গত, অসমুচিত, অনুচিত, অনুপযোগী। **2.** Unqualified ; অযোগ্য। **—ly,** *adv.* **—ness,** *n.* **1.** The quality or state of being unfit, improper or unsuitable ; অনুপযোগিতা, অনৌচিত্য। **2.** Incompetence ; অযোগ্যতা।

ŭn-fit'-ting (-îng), *adj.* Improper ; unbecoming ; অযোগ্য, অসঙ্গত ; অনুচিত, অশোভন।

ŭn-fix', *v. t.* **1.** To loosen from a fastening ; to detach from anything ; to unhinge ; খিল খোলা, কীলকমুক্ত করা ; কোন কিছু হইতে বিশ্লিষ্ট করা ; কব্জা খোলা। **2.** To unsettle ; বিচলিত করা।

ŭn-fixed' (-fîkst), *adj.* **1.** Inconstant ; erratic ; অস্থির ; চঞ্চল। **2.** Having no settled view or object or pursuit ; অব্যবস্থিতচিত্ত, অস্থিরমতি। **—fix'-ed-ness,** *n.*

ŭn-flăg'-ging (-îng), *adj.* Not flagging ; maintaining strength or spirit ; অনবসন্ন ; অক্লান্ত, অশ্রান্ত, অখিন্ন।

ŭn-flăt'-tered (-têrd), *adj.* **1.** Not flattered ; অনারাধিত।

ŭn-flăt'-têr-ing, *adj.* **1.** Not colouring the truth to please ; অতোষামোদকারী। **2.** Not affording a favourable prospect ; as, the weather is *unflattering* ; অমনোরম। **—ly,** *adv.*

ŭn-flawed' (-flăd), *adj.* Having no flaw ; নির্দ্দোষ, নিখুঁত।

ŭn-fledged' (-flĕjd), *adj.* Not yet furnished with feathers ; young ; অজাতপক্ষ, অনুদ্গতপক্ষ ; অচিরজাত।

ŭn-fleshed' (-flĕsht), *adj.* Untrained ; অপরীক্ষিত।

ŭn-flĕsh'-lў, *adj.* Not of the flesh ; spiritual ; অশরীরী ; অমূর্ত্ত।

ŭn-flinch-ing, *adj.* Not flinching ; not shrinking ; অবিচলিত ; অদম্য। **—ly** *adv.*

ŭn-flow'-êr-ing, *adj.* Not flowering ; অপুষ্পপ্রসূ।

ŭn-foiled' (-foyld), *adj.* Not vanquished ; not defeated ; অপরাজিত, অপরাভূত ; অপরাহত।

ŭn-fōld', *v. t.* **1.** To open the folds of ; to expand ; ভাঁজ খোলা, পাট ভাঙ্গা ; বিস্তারিত করা, প্রসারিত করা। **2.** To display ; প্রকাশিত করা, প্রকটিত করা।

ŭn-fŏl'-lowed (-lōd), *adj.* Not followed ; অননুসৃত, অপশ্চাদ্ধাবিত।

ŭn-fŏr-bear'-ing (-bār-), *adj.* Not forbearing ; অসহিষ্ণু।

ŭn-fŏr-bid', —bid'-den (-n), *adj.* Not forbidden ; not prohibited ; অনিষিদ্ধ ; অনিবারিত।

ŭn-forced' (-fōrst), *adj.* **1.** Not forced ; not constrained ; অবলাৎকৃত; অযত্নসিদ্ধ, অযত্নসম্ভূত। **2.** Easy ; natural ; সহজ ; স্বাভাবিক।

ŭn-fŏr'-ci-ble (-bl), *adj.* Wanting force or strength ; অপ্রবল।

ŭn-fōrd′-ă-ble (-bl), *adj.* That cannot be forded ; অসুপ্রতর।

ŭn-fōre-bŏd′-ing, *adj.* Giving no omens ; অনিষ্টসূচক শূন্য।

ŭn-fōre-known′ (-nōn), *adj.* Not previously foreseen ; অজ্ঞাতপূর্ব্ব।

ŭn-fōre-seen′ (-sēn), *adj.* Not foreseen or foreknown ; অদৃষ্টপূর্ব্ব, অজ্ঞাতপূর্ব্ব, অচিন্তিতপূর্ব্ব।

ŭn-fōre-tōld′, *adj.* Not predicted ; অপূর্ব্বকথিত।

ŭn-fōre-warned′ (-wârnd), *adj.* Not warned before ; অপূর্ব্বসতর্কিত।

ŭn-fŏr′-feit-ĕd (-fĕt-), *adj.* Not forfeited ; অবাজেয়াপ্ত।

ŭn-fŏr-gĭv′-ă-ble (-bl), *adj.* Not to be forgiven ; অমার্জ্জনীয়, অক্ষমার্হ।

ŭn-fŏr-gĭv′-en (-n), *adj.* Not forgiven ; অক্ষমিত, অমার্জ্জিত।

ŭn-fŏr-gĭv′-ing, *adj.* Not disposed to overlook or pardon offence ; অক্ষমাশীল, অক্ষমাপর, অক্ষমাপরায়ণ, ক্ষমাবিমুখ, ক্ষমাপরাঙ্মুখ।

ŭn-fŏr-gŏt′-ten (-n), *adj.* Not lost to memory ; not neglected ; অবিস্মৃত ; অনবহেলিত।

ŭn-fŏrm′, *v. t.* To destroy ; to unmake ; ধ্বংস করা ; ভাঙ্গা, ভঙ্গ করা, নষ্ট করা।

ŭn-fŏr′-măl, *adj.* Not formal ; লৌকিকতাবিরুদ্ধ।

ŭn-formed′ (-fŏrmd), *adj.* Not formed into regular shape ; অগঠিত। **Unformed stars**—বহির্গত নক্ষত্র (হিঃ কোঃ)।

ŭn-fŏr-sak′-en (-n), *adj.* Not deserted ; not entirely neglected ; অপরিত্যক্ত ; অনবহেলিত।

ŭn-fŏr′-tĭ-fied (-fīd), *adj.* Not secured from attack ; defenceless ; দুর্গপ্রাকারাদি দ্বারা অরক্ষিত ; অরক্ষিত।

ŭn-fŏr′-tū-nāte, *adj.* **1.** Not successful or prosperous ; দুর্ভাগ্য, হতভাগ্য, মন্দভাগ্য, অভাগ্য, দৈবোপহত, দুর্দ্দশাগ্রস্ত, লক্ষ্মীছাড়া। **2.** Attended with misfortunes ; দুর্দ্দৈবপূর্ণ। **—ly,** *adv.*

ŭn-fŏs′-sĭl-īzed, *adj.* Not fossilized ; অশিলীভূত।

ŭn-fŏs′-tered (-têrd), *adj.* **1.** Not nourished ; অপোষিত, অপরিপোষিত। **2.** Not patronized ; অপৃষ্ঠপোষিত।

ŭn-fought′ (-făt), *adj.* Not fought ; অযুদ্ধীকৃত।

ŭn-found′-ĕd (-fownd-), *adj.* **1.** Not founded ; অমূলক। **2.** Having no foundation ; ভিত্তিহীন। **3.** Vain ; idle ; বৃথা ; নিষ্ফল, নিরর্থক, হেতুশূন্য, অকারণ।

ŭn-frā′-grănt, *adj.* Not fragrant ; অসুগন্ধ, অসুরভি।

ŭn-frāmed′ *adj.* **1.** Not formed ; অগঠিত।

ŭn-fră-têr′-năl, *adj.* Not brotherly ; অভ্রাত্রোচিত, অভ্রাতৃসমুচিত।

ŭn-free′ (-frē), *adj.* Not free অমুক্ত।

ŭn-frē′-quĕn-çȳ, *n.* The state of being frequent ; অসততত্য।

ŭn-frē′-quĕnt, *adj.* Not frequent ; not common ; অসতত ; অসাধারণ।

ŭn-frē-quĕnt′-ĕd, *adj.* Rarely visited ; মনুষ্যসমাগমশূন্য, জনমানবহীন।

ŭn-frī′-ă-ble (-bl), *adj.* Not easily crumbled ; অভঙ্গনীয়।

ŭn-friend′ (-frĕnd), *n.* An enemy ; শত্রু, অমিত্র।

ŭn-friend′-ĕd (-frĕnd-), *adj.* **1.** Wanting friends ; বন্ধুহীন, বন্ধুশূন্য। **2.** Not countenanced or supported ; অসমর্থিত।

ŭn-friend′-lȳ (-frĕnd-), *adj.* Not kind or benevolent ; not favourable ; অবন্ধুভাবাপন্ন ; প্রতিকূল। **—li-ness,** *n.*

ŭn-frŏck′, *v.t.* To divest of frock ; to deprive of priestly character or privileges ; আলখেল্লা বিরহিত করা ; পৌরোহিত্য হইতে বিচ্যুত করা।

ŭn-frō′-zen (-zn), *adj.* Not congealed ; অঘনীভূত, অতুষারীভূত।

ŭn-fru′-găl (-frō-), *adj.* Not saving or economical ; অমিতব্যয়ী।

ŭn-fruit′-fûl (-frōt-), *adj.* **1.** Not producing fruit ; অফলোৎপাদক, অফলপ্রসূ। **2.** Unproductive of good ; নিষ্ফল। **—ly,** *adv.* **—ness,** *n.*

ŭn-frŭs′-tră-ble (-bl), *adj.* That cannot be frustrated ; অব্যর্থ, অমোঘ।

ŭn-fûl-filled′ (-fīld), *adj.* Not accomplished ; অসমাপ্ত, অসম্পন্ন, অনিষ্পন্ন, অনিষ্পাদিত, অসিদ্ধ।

ŭn-fūmed′, *adj.* Not fumigated ; অনুদ্ধাপিত।

ŭn-fŭnd′-ĕd, *adj.* Having no permanent funds for the payment of its interest ; সুদ প্রদানের জন্য স্থায়ী তহবিল শূন্য।

ŭn-furl′ (-fêrl), *v. t.* To loose and unfold ; to expand ; ছড়ান, মেলা ; প্রসারিত করা।

ŭn-fur′-nĭsh (-fêr-), *v.t.* To divest ; to strip of furniture ; বিরহিত করা, বিহীন করা ; গৃহসজ্জা বিহীন করা। **—nished,** *adj.* Not supplied with furniture ; empty ; অসজ্জিত, সজ্জাহীন, আসবাবশূন্য ; শূন্য, খালি।

ŭn-fūsed′, *adj.* Not fused ; অবিদ্রাবিত।

ŭn-gain′-fûl (-gān-), *adj.* Unprofitable ; অলাভজনক।

ŭn-gain′-lȳ (-gān-), *adj.* Clumsy ; awkward ; uncouth ; কদাকার, কুৎসিত, বিশ্রী, বিরূপ ; বিসদৃশ ; বদখৎ (*Colloq.*) **—li-ness,** *n.*

ŭn-găl′-lănt, *adj.* Not courteous ; অশিষ্ট।

ŭn-galled′ (-găld), *adj.* Unhurt ; not galled ; অক্ষত ; অনুত্ত্যক্ত।

ŭn-gâr′-lănd-ĕd, *adj.* Not crowned with a garland ; অমাল্যভূষিত, অহারশোভিত।

ŭn-gâr′-nished (-nĭsht), *adj.* Not furnished ; unadorned ; অসজ্জিত ; অশোভিত, অমণ্ডিত, অভূষিত।

ŭn-găr′-rĭ-soned (-snd), *adj.* Not furnished with troops for defence ; দুর্গরক্ষী সৈন্যদ্বারা অরক্ষিত।

ŭn-găr′-tered (-têrd), *adj.* Without garters ; জঙ্ঘাবন্ধনীবিহীন।

ŭn-găth′-ered (-êrd), *adj.* Not gathered ; not cropped ; অসংগৃহীত ; অচ্ছিন্ন।

ŭn-gear′ (-gēr), *v. t.* To unharness ; to strip of gear ; অশ্বাদিকে সজ্জা বিহীন করা ; সজ্জাবিহীন করা ।

ŭn-gĕn′-ĕr-āt-ĕd, *adj.* **1.** Unbegotten ; অনুৎপন্ন, অজাত । **2.** Having no beginning ; অনাদি ।

ŭn-gĕn′-ĕr-a-tive (-tĭv), *adj.* Begetting nothing ; অনুৎপাদী ।

ŭn-gĕn′-êr-ous (-ŭs), *adj.* Not generous ; harsh ; mean ; অনুদার ; রূঢ়; নীচ, নীচাশয়, ক্ষুদ্রচেতাঃ । **–ly,** *adv.*

ŭn-gē′-ni-ăl, *adj.* Not favourable to nature or natural growth ; অমনোরম, অসুখকর, অরমণীয় ।

ŭn-gĕn-teel′ (-tēl), *adj.* Not consistent with polite manners ; অশিষ্ট, অভব্য, অভদ্র । **–ly,** *adv.*

ŭn-gĕn′-tle (-tl), *adj.* Rude ; harsh ; রূঢ় ; কর্কশ । **–ness,** *n.* **–tly,** *adv.*

ŭn-gĕn′-tle-măn-lў (-tl-), *adj.* Not becoming a gentleman ; অভদ্রোচিত । **–li-ness,** *n.*

ŭn-gĕn-tle′-măn-līke (-tl-), *adj.* Not becoming a gentleman ; অভদ্রজনোচিত ।

ŭn-gē-ŏm′-ĕt-ri-căl, *adj.* Not agreeable to the rules of geometry ; জ্যামিতির নিয়মনিচয়ের বিরোধী, অজ্যামিতিক ।

ŭn-gild′-ĕd, –gilt, *adjs.* Not overlaid with gold ; অস্বর্ণপত্রমণ্ডিত, অস্বর্ণপত্রমণ্ডিত ।

ŭn-gird′ (-gērd), *v.t.* To loose from girdle or band ; বেষ্টনীবিরহিত করা ।

ŭn-girt′ (-gērt), *p. p.* or *adj.* Unbound ; loosely dressed ; আবাঁধা ; শ্লথপরিচ্ছদপরিহিত ।

ŭn-giv′-en (-n), *adj.* Not given or bestowed ; অদত্ত, অনর্পিত ।

ŭn-giv′-ing, *adj.* Not bringing gifts ; অনুপহারপ্রদ ।

ŭn-glăd′-dened (-nd), *adj.* Not gladdened ; অপরিতুষ্ট, অসন্তোষিত ।

ŭn-glaze′, *v. t.* To remove the glass, as from windows ; জানালা হইতে কাচ অপসারিত করা ।

ŭn-glāzed′, *adj.* Not furnished with glass ; wanting glass-windows ; not covered with vitreous matter ; অকাচাচ্ছাদিত ; সার্সীবিহীন ; অসূক্ষ্মকাচস্তরাচ্ছাদিত ।

ŭn-glō′-ri-fied (-fīd), *adj.* Not honoured with praise or adoration ; অমহিমান্বিত, অগৌরবান্বিত ।

ŭn-glove′ (-glŭv), *v. t.* To take off the gloves ; দস্তানা খোলা ।

ŭn-gloved′ (-glŭvd), *adj.* Without glove or gloves ; দস্তানাবিহীন, দস্তানাশূন্য ।

ŭn-glue′ (-glū), *v. t.* To separate anything that is glued ; আঠা দ্বারা জোড়া-দেওয়া কোন জিনিষ খোলা ।

ŭn-goad′-ĕd (-gōd-), *adj.* Not goaded ; অনঙ্কুশতাড়িত ।

ŭn-gŏd′-lў, *adj.* Wicked ; impious ; without the fear of God ; পাপী ; অসাধু ; ঈশ্বরদ্রোহী । **–li-ness,** *n.*

ŭn-gŏred′, *adj.* Not wounded with a horn ; অশৃঙ্গবিদ্ধ ।

ŭn-gorged′ (-gŏrjd), *adj.* Not sated ; অভোগক্লান্ত ।

ŭn-gŏt′, ŭn-gŏt′-ten (-n), *adjs.* Not gained ; not begotten ; অপ্রাপ্ত ; অনুৎপন্ন ।

ŭn-gov′-ern-a-ble (-gŭv-êrn-ă-bl), *adj.* That cannot be governed ; unruly ; refractory ; licentious ; unbridled ; অশান্ত, দুর্ণিবার ; অদম্য ; দুর্দ্দান্ত ; লম্পট ; উচ্ছৃঙ্খল । **–bly,** *adv.*

ŭn-gov′-erned (-gŭv-êrnd), *adj.* Not subjected to laws or principles ; unbridled ; licentious ; অশাসিত ; উচ্ছৃঙ্খল ; লম্পট ।

ŭn-gown′, *v. t.* To strip of a gown, as a clergyman ; ধর্ম্মযাজক প্রভৃতির প্রাবরণ খুলিয়া নেওয়া ।

ŭn-graced′ (-grāst), *adj.* Not graced ; অননুগৃহীত ।

ŭn-grāce′-fûl, *adj.* **1.** Wanting ease and elegance ; মাধুর্য্যশূন্য, মাধুর্য্যবিহীন, অসুন্দর । 2. Awkward ; বিশ্রী, কুৎসিত, কদাকার, বিটকিলে (*colloq.*), বদখৎ (*ib.*) । **–ly,** *adv.* **–ness,** *n.*

ŭn-grā′-cious (-shŭs), *adj.* **1.** Not courteous ; rude ; অশিষ্ট ; রূঢ় । **2.** Odious ; hateful ; ঘৃণার্হ ; ঘৃণিত । **–ly.** *adv.*

ŭn-grăm-măt′-i-căl, *adj.* Not according to the established rules of grammar ; ব্যাকরণদুষ্ট, চ্যুত-সংস্কার (সাঃ দঃ), ব্যাকরণবিরুদ্ধ । **–ly,** *adv.*

ŭn-grănt′-ĕd, *adj.* Not bestowed ; not transferred by deed or gift ; not conceded ; অনর্পিত ; অহস্তান্তরিত ; অস্বীকৃত ।

ŭn-grāte′-fûl, *adj.* **1.** Not feeling thankful for favours ; অকৃতজ্ঞ, কৃতঘ্ন, নিমকহারাম (*colloq.*), চসমখোর (*vulg.*), বেইমান (*ib*) । **2.** Disagreeable ; harsh ; অপ্রীতিকর ; কর্কশ, কঠোর । **–ly,** *adv.* **–ness,** *n.*

ŭn-grăt′-i-fied (-fīd), *adj.* Not gratified ; not indulged ; অচরিতার্থ; অপরিতর্পিত ।

ŭn-grāve′-lў, *adj.* Without gravity ; গাম্ভীর্য্যহীন, গাম্ভীর্য্যশূন্য ।

ŭn-grē-gā′-ri-ous (-ŭs), *adj.* Not gregarious ; অযূথচারী, অসংঘচারী ।

ŭn-ground′-ĕd (-grownd-), *adj.* Having no foundation or support ; ভিত্তিহীন, অমূলক । **–ly,** *adv.* **–ness,** *n.*

ŭn-grudged′ (-grŭjd), *adj.* Not grudged ; অবিদ্বিষ্ট, অহিংসিত ।

ŭn-grudg′-ing (-grŭj-), *adj.* Freely giving ; liberal ; generous ; মুক্তহস্ত ; বদান্য ; উদার । **–ly,** *adv.* In an ungrudging manner ; cheerfully ; freely ; অম্লানচিত্তে ; সানন্দে ; মুক্তভাবে ।

ŭn-guard′-ĕd (-gârd), *adj.* **1.** Not watched or defended ; অরক্ষিত । **2.** Careless ; incautious ; negligent ; অসতর্ক, অতর্কিত ; অসাবধান ; অবহেলাপর, অনবধান, অনবহিত । **–ly,** *adv.*

un′-guent (ŭng-gwĕnt), *n.* **1.** Ointment ; অভ্যঞ্জন, অভ্যঙ্গ, অনুলেপন, বর্ণক, প্রলেপদ্রব্য, গাত্রানুলেপনী, বিলেপন । **2.** A soft composition used as a topical remedy for sores etc.; মলম

un′-guen-tă-rȳ (ŭng-gwĕn-), **un′-guen-tous** (ŭng-gwĕn-tŭs), *adjs.* Like unguent or partaking of its qualities ; অভ্যঞ্জনবৎ, বিলেপনবৎ ।

un′-guin-ous (ŭng-gwĭn-ŭs), *adj.* Oily ; unctuous ; consisting of, or resembling, fat or oil ; তৈলাক্ত ; তেলতেলে ; মেদময়, মেদাত্মক, তৈলাত্মক ।

ŭn-guessed′ (-gĕst), *adj.* Not obtained by conjecture ; অননুমিত ।

un′-gui-căl (ŭng-gwĭ-), *adj.* Pertaining to, or like, a claw ; নখরসম্বন্ধীয়, নখরবৎ ।

un-guic′-ū-lāte (ŭng-gwĭk-), **un-guic′-ū-lāt-ĕd** (ŭng-gwĭk-), *adjs.* Clawed ; having claws ; নখরবিশিষ্ট ; সনখর ।

ŭn-guid′-ĕd (-gīd-), *adj.* Not led or conducted ; not regulated ; অপরিচালিত ; অনিয়মিত, অনিয়ন্ত্রিত ।

un′-gui-fōrm (ŭng-gwĭ-), *adj.* Shaped like a claw ; নখরবৎ ।

ŭn-guilt′-ȳ (-gĭlt-), *adj.* Not stained with crime ; innocent ; নিরপরাধ ; নির্দ্দোষ । **—i-ly**, *adv.*

un′-guin-ous (ŭng-gwĭn-ŭs), *adj.* Unctuous ; consisting of fat or oil ; তৈলাক্ত ; মেদময়, তৈলময় ।

un′-gū-lă′ (ŭng-), *n.* A section or part of a cylinder, cone, etc., cut off by a plane oblique to the base ; ভূমির তির্য্যগ্‌গামী সমতল দ্বারা কর্ত্তিত নল, সূচি প্রভৃতির ছেদ বা অংশ ।

un′-gū-lāte (ŭng-), *adj.* Shaped like a hoof ; having hoofs ; ক্ষুরাকৃতি ; ক্ষুরবিশিষ্ট ।

ŭn-hă-bit′-ū-āt-ĕd, *adj.* Not accustomed ; অনভ্যস্ত ।

ŭn-hacked′ (-hăkt), *adj.* Not cut, notched or mangled ; অকর্ত্তিত, অচ্ছিন্নবিচ্ছিন, অনবচ্ছিন্ন ।

ŭn-hăck′-neyed (-nĭd), *adj.* Not worn or rendered trite, stale, flat or commonplace by constant use or repetition ; অনীরস, অবৈচিত্র্যহীন, অভিনবত্বশূন্য ।

ŭn-hăl′-low (-lō), *v. t.* To profane ; to desecrate ; অপবিত্র করা ; অপূত করা ।

ŭn-hăl′-lowed, (-lōd), *adj.* Deprived of its sacred character ; profane ; unholy ; অপবিত্রীকৃত ; অপুণ্য ; অপবিত্র, অমেধ্য ।

ŭn-hănd′, *v. t.* To loose the hands off ; to let go ; হাত ছাড়িয়া দেওয়া ; ছাড়িয়া দেওয়া ।

ŭn-hăn′-dled (-dld), *adj.* Not handled ; not touched ; not treated or managed ; অব্যবহৃত ; অস্পৃষ্ট ; অপরিচালিত, অনির্ব্বাহিত, অনাচরিত, অব্যবহৃত ।

ŭn-hănd′-some (-sŭm), *adj.* 1. Not handsome or well-shaped ; অসুন্দর, অসুগঠিত । 2. Illiberal ; uncivil ; অনুদার ; অশিষ্ট । **—ly**, *adv.* **—ness**, *n.*

ŭn-hănd′-ȳ, *adj.* Not dexterous or well-shaped ; awkward ; অদক্ষ, অসুগঠিত ; কদাকার ।

ŭn-hăng′, *v. t.* 1. To divest of hangings ; ঝালর প্রভৃতি বিহীন করা । 2. To take from the hinges ; কব্জা খুলিয়া তোলা ।

ŭn-hanged′ (-hăngd), *adj.* Not hung upon a gallows ; not punished by hanging ; অফাঁসীকাষ্ঠে ঝুলায়িত ; অদত্ত ফাঁসীদণ্ড ।

ŭn-hăp′-pȳ, *adj.* 1. Not happy ; unfortunate ; unlucky ; miserable ; অসুখী ; দুর্ভাগ্য ; হতভাগ্য, মন্দভাগ্য ; অভাগা । 2. Inauspicious ; কু, অশুভ, অমঙ্গলজনক । **—pi-ly**, *adv.* **—pi-ness**, *n.*

ŭn-hăr′-assed (-ăst), *adj.* Not harassed ; not vexed ; অক্লিষ্ট, অনুৎপীড়িত, অনির্যাতিত ; অনুত্যক্ত ।

ŭn-hăr′-bour (-bĕr), *v. t.* To drive from harbour or shelter ; পোতাশ্রয় কিম্বা অন্য কোন প্রকার আশ্রয় হইতে বিতাড়িত করা ।

ŭn-hârd′-ened (-nd), *adj.* 1. Not indurated, as metal ; অদৃঢ়ীকৃত, অকঠিনীকৃত, অকঠিনীভূত । 2. Not made obdurate ; "Our princes cousin yet *unhardened* in the crimes of nature" ; অকঠিনচিত্ত ।

ŭn-hâr′-dȳ, *adj.* 1. Not able to endure fatigue ; অপরিশ্রমসহ । 2. Without fortitude ; অসহিষ্ণু । 3. Timid ; ভীরু ।

ŭn-harmed′ (-hârmd), *adj.* Uninjured or unimpaired ; অক্ষত, অনপকৃত, অকৃতাপকার ।

ŭn-hârm′-fûl, *adj.* Not doing harm ; harmless ; অক্ষতিজনক ; অনপকারক, অনপকারী ।

ŭn-hâr-mō′-ni-ous (-ŭs), *adj.* Not having symmetry or congruity ; সঙ্গতিহীন, সামঞ্জস্যহীন ।

ŭn-hâr′-nĕss, *v. t.* 1. To strip of harness ; ঘোড়ার সাজ খোলা । 2. (*Obs.*) To divest of armour ; "They being *unharnessed* did fight with their swords" ; (অপ্রঃ) বর্ম্মবিরহিত করা । 3. To set free from work ; "An unmerciful day's work of sorrow till death *unharness* 'em" ; কাষ হইতে ছুটি দেওয়া ।

ŭn-hatched′ (-hăcht), *adj.* Not hatched ; not matured ; অতাপপ্রদত্ত ; অপরিপক্ক ।

ŭn-hăz′-ard-ĕd′ (-êrd-), *adj.* Not exposed to risk or hazard ; অসংশয়িত, অসংশয়াপন্ন ।

ŭn-hăz′-ard-ous (-êrd-ŭs), *adj.* Not hazardous ; অবিপজ্জনক ।

ŭn-head′ (-hĕd), *v. t.* (*Obs.*) To take the head off or from ; to decapitate ; (অপ্রঃ) মস্তকচ্যুত করা ; শিরশ্ছেদ করা ।

ŭn-health′-fûl (-hĕlth-), *adj.* 1. Not healthful ; injurious to health ; "The *unhealthful* east that breathes the spleen" ; অস্বাস্থ্যকর ; অস্বাস্থ্যজনক । 2. Unwell ; অসুস্থ, রুগ্ন, পীড়িত । **—ness**, *n.*

ŭn-health′-ȳ (-hĕlth-), *adj.* 1. Not healthy ; insalubrious ; অস্বাস্থ্যকর ; অস্বাস্থ্যজনক । 2. Habitually weak or indisposed ; as, an *unhealthy* child; অসুস্থ, রুগ্ন, রোগা। 3. Morally unwholesome; as, *unhealthy* influence; অশুভ, অনিষ্টজনক। **–i-ly,** *adv.* **–i-ness,** *n.*

ŭn-heard′ (-hĕrd), *adj.* 1. Not perceived by the ear; অশ্রুত। 2. Not admitted to audience; অদত্তদর্শন। 3. Not known to fame; "Yet fast they fall, *unheard,* forgot"; অবিশ্রুতনামা।

ŭn-heat′-ĕd (-hēt-), *adj.* Not made heated; অনুত্তপ্ত।

ŭn-heav′-en-lȳ (-hĕv-n-), *adj.* Not heavenly; অস্বর্গীয়, অদিব্য।

ŭn-hedged′ (-hĕjd), *adj.* Not surrounded by hedge; অবৃতিবেষ্টিত।

ŭn-heed′-ĕd (-hēd-), *adj.* Disregarded; neglected; অনাদৃত; অবহেলিত। **–ly,** *adv.*

ŭn-heed′-fûl (-hēd-), *adj.* Inattentive; অমনোযোগী, অনবহিত।

ŭn-heed′-ing (-hēd-), *adj.* Careless; negligent; অসতর্ক; অবহেলাপর, অনবহিত।

ŭn-heed′-ȳ (-hēd-),*adj.* 1. Careless; "The pride of her carnation train, Plucked up by some *unheedy* swain"; অসতর্ক। 2. Precipitate; "Wings and no eyes figure *unheedy* hasty"; হঠকারী।

ŭn-hĕlm′, *v. t.* To deprive of a helm or helmet; হাইল বিহীন করা, শিরস্ত্রাণ বিহীন করা।

ŭn-helmed′ (-hĕlmd), *adj.* Having no helmet or helm; শিরস্ত্রাণশূন্য, হাইল বিহীন।

ŭn-hĕl′-mĕt, *v. t.* To deprive of helmet; শিরস্ত্রাণবিহীন করা।

ŭn-helped′ (-hĕlpt), *adj.* Unassisted; "*Unhelped* we stand"; অসাহায্যীকৃত।

ŭn-hĕlp′-fûl, *adj.* Affording no aid; helpless; অসহায়ক, অসাহায্যপ্রদ; অসহায়।

ŭn-hē-rō′-ic, *adj.* Not heroic or brave; অবীরোচিত, অবীরজনযোগ্য, অশূরোচিত।

ŭn-hĕs′-i-tāt-ing, *adj.* Not hesitating; prompt; অদ্বিধাকারী, দ্বিধাশূন্য, সঙ্কোচশূন্য; সত্বর। **–ly,** *adv.* In an unhesitating manner; সংশয়শূন্যভাবে, দ্বিধাশূন্যভাবে।

ŭn-hewn′ (-hūn), *adj.* Not hewn; rough; অকর্ত্তিত; কর্কশ, রূঢ়।

ŭn-hin′-dered (-dêrd), *adj.* Not opposed; "With all its full effects and consequences *unhindered*"; অবাধিত, অনিষিদ্ধ, অবারিত।

ŭn-hinge′ (-hĭnj), *v. t.* To take from the hinges; as, to *unhinge* a door; to displace; to unfix; "And hills *unhinged* from their deep roots depart"; to unsettle; as, to *unhinge* one's mind; কব্জা হইতে খুলিয়া লওয়া; স্থানান্তরিত করা; বিযুক্ত করা; বিচলিত করা।

ŭn-hīred′, *adj.* Not hired; ভাড়া দ্বারা অগৃহীত।

ŭn-his-tŏr′-i-căl, *adj.* Not historical; অঐতিহাসিক।

ŭn-hīve′, *v. t.* 1. To drive from a hive; মধুচক্র হইতে তাড়িত করা। 2. To deprive of habitation; বাসস্থান হইতে চ্যুত করা।

ŭn-hoard′ (-hōrd), *v. t.* To steal from a hoard; "A thief bent to *unhoard* the cash"; to pilfer; সঞ্চিত বস্তু হইতে অপহরণ করা; ছিঁচকে চুরি করা।

ŭn-hō′-lȳ, *adj.* 1. Not holy; profane; not hallowed; অপবিত্র; অশুদ্ধ; অশুচি। 2. Impious; wicked; "To keep from a most *unholy* match"; অসাধু; দুষ্ট। **–li-ness,** *n.*

ŭn-hon′-oured (-ŏn-êrd), *adj.* Not honoured; 'And scholars, soldiers, kings, *unhonoured die*"; uncelebrated; অসম্মানিত; অননুষ্ঠিত।

ŭn-hook′, *v. t.* To loose from a hook; আকর্ষী হইতে খোলা।

ŭn-hoop′, *v. t.* To strip of hoops; পিপার হালি খোলা।

ŭn-hoped′ (-hōpt), *adj.* Not hoped for; অপ্রত্যাশিত।

ŭn-hōpe′-fûl, *adj.* Leaving no room of hope; hopeless; নিরাশাজনক; নিরাশাপূর্ণ।

ŭn-horned′ (-hŏrnd), *adj.* Having no horns; অশৃঙ্গ, শৃঙ্গশূন্য, শৃঙ্গহীন।

ŭn-horse′ (-hŏrs), *v. t.* 1. To throw from a horse; to cause to dismount; অশ্বপৃষ্ঠ হইতে পাতিত করা; অবতরণ করান। 2. To take the horse out of, as out of a vehicle; ঘোড়া খোলা।

ŭn-hŏs′-tīle, *adj.* Not hostile; not pertaining or relating to enemy; অশত্রুভাবাপন্ন; অশত্রুসম্বন্ধীয়।

ŭn-house′ (-howz), *v. t.* To drive or expel from a habitation; to dislodge; to drive out of shelter; গৃহ হইতে বিতাড়িত করা, ভিটা হইতে উচ্ছেদ করা, উদ্বাস্তু করা; বাসস্থানচ্যুত করা; আশ্রয়হীন করা। **–housed′,***adj.* Wanting a house; homeless; destitute of shelter; গৃহহীন, গৃহশূন্য; গৃহহারা; আশ্রয়হীন, আশ্রয়শূন্য।

ŭn-hurt′ (-hêrt), *adj.* Not hurt; free from hurt or injury; অক্ষত, অনাহত, নিরুপহত; অবিক্ষত, অপরিক্ষত। **I hope you are not hurt**—আপনার লাগিনেত।

ŭn-hurt′-fûl (-hêrt-), *adj.* Harmless; innoxious; ক্ষতিশূন্য; নির্দ্দোষ, অনপকারী, অনপকারক। **–ly,** *adv.*

ŭn-hŭs′-bănd-ĕd, *adj.* 1. Without or deprived of husband; পতিহীন, স্বামিহীন, স্বামিবিরহিত। 2. Unmarried; অবিবাহিত। 3. Not managed with frugality; মিতব্যয়িতার সহিত অপরিচালিত।

ŭn-husked′ (-hŭskt), *adj.* Not being stripped of husk; আঁকাড়া, নিস্তুষীকৃত।

ū-ni-ăx′-ăl, –i-ăl, *adjs.* Having but one optical axis; এককাক্ষিক।

ū-ni-căm′-êr-ăl, *adj.* Having but one chamber of legislation; ব্যবস্থাপক সভার এককোষ্ঠ সমন্বিত, এককৌষ্ঠিক।

ū-ni-căp'-sū-lar (-lêr), *adj.* (*Bot.*) Having one capsule to each flower; (উদ্ভিদ্‌বিদ্যা) একবীজাধারধারী।

ū-ni-cĕl'-lū-lar (-lêr), *adj.* Composed of but one cell; এককোষিক, এককণক (হিঃ কোঃ)। **Unicellular structure**—কলৈকরচন (ষোঃ)।

ū-ni-cŏrn, *n.* A fabulous animal said to be a native of India, resembling a horse in shape and size, and having one straight horn (the figure is used in heraldry) referred to by Greek and Latin writers; প্রাচীন গ্রীক ও ল্যাটিন লেখকগণ কর্ত্তৃক বর্ণিত একপ্রকার একশৃঙ্গী অশ্বাকৃতি কল্পিত জন্তুবিশেষ, একশৃঙ্গী।

ū-ni-fi-cā'-tion, *n.* The act of uniting with another, specially with God, so as to form but one; একীকরণ, সংযোজন (হিঃ কোঃ) সাযুজ্য।

ū-ni-fi'-lar (-lêr), *adj.* Having, or involving, the use of only one thread, wire, or fibre; একসূত্রিক, একতার। **Unifilar magnetometer**—একতারচুম্বকমাপক (হিঃ কোঃ)।

ū-ni-flō'-rous (-rŭs), *adj.* (*Bot.*) Bearing one flower only; একপুষ্পী।

ū-ni-fō'-li-āte, *adj.* (*Bot.*) Having but one leaf; (উদ্ভিদ্‌বিদ্যা) একপত্রী।

ū'-ni-fŏrm, *adj.* & *n.* **1.** Having always the same form and manner; not variable; একরূপ; অপরিবর্ত্তনীয়। **2.** Homogeneous; সমরূপ, সমাকার। **3.** Not varying in degree or rate; as, *uniform* motion; invariable; equable; as, *uniform* temperature; নিয়ত একরূপ, নিয়ত (cf. নিয়তদিগ্‌বিশিষ্ট—ব্রজঃ হিন্দু); অপরিবর্ত্তনীয়; সমভাবাপন্ন। **4.** Conforming to one rule or mode; consonant; একনিয়মানুসারী, একভাবানুসারী; অনুসারী। ***Noun.*** A dress of the same kind by which persons are assimilated that belong to the same body, whether military, naval, or any other; সামরিক, নৌবিভাগ, প্রভৃতির কর্ম্মচারিগণের একরূপ পরিচ্ছদ, সরকারী পোষাক। **—ly,** *adv.* **Uniform motion** — সমগতি (হিঃ কোঃ)। **Uniformly accelerating motion**—সমবর্দ্ধমান গতি (হিঃ কোঃ)।

ū-ni-fŏrm-i-tā'-ri-ăn-ism, *n.* The theory that all geological changes and phenomena are due to agencies working uniformly and uninterruptedly as opposed to the theory of the catastrophists who refer such changes to great occasional convulsions; একরূপবাদ (হিঃ কোঃ), প্রত্যপবাদ (ঐ), নিয়মবাদ (ঐ)।

ū-ni-fŏrm'-i-tȳ, *n.* **1.** The quality or state of being uniform or unvarying; সমরূপতা, একরূপতা, সারূপ্য (হিঃ কোঃ), সাম্য (ঐ)। **2.** Conistency; sameness; সঙ্গতি; অভিন্নতা। **Act of Uniformity**—যে রাজবিধি দ্বারা ইংলণ্ডের বিভিন্ন ধর্ম্মসংঘের উপাসনা ও ক্রিয়াকাণ্ডপদ্ধতি নিয়ন্ত্রিত হয়।

ū'-ni-fȳ, *v.t.* To make into one; to unite; to view as one; একীভূত করা, ঐক্যসাধন করা; এক বলিয়া গণ্য করা।

ū-ni-gĕn'-i-tūre, *n.* The state of being the only begotten; একজাতত্ব।

ū-nig'-ĕ-nous (-nŭs), *adj.* **1.** Of one kind; একজাতীয়। **2.** Of the same genus; একগণভুক্ত।

ū-ni-lā'-bi-āte, *adj.* (*Bot.*) Having one lip only; একৌষ্ঠিক।

ū-ni-lăt'-êr-ăl, *adj.* Being on one side; having one side; একপার্শ্ববর্ত্তী; একপার্শ্বিক।

ū-ni-lit'-êr-ăl, *adj.* Consisting of one letter; একাক্ষরাত্মক।

ŭn-il-lū'-mi-nāt-ĕd, *adj.* Not illuminated; অদীপ্ত, অনালোকিত, অদ্যোতিত।

ŭn-il-lū'-mined (-mind), *adj.* Not illumined; অদীপ্ত।

ŭn-il-lŭs'-trāt-ĕd, *adj.* Not illustrated; অচিত্রশোভিত।

ŭn-il-lŭs'-tra-tive (-tiv), *adj.* Not illustrative; অনুদাহরণপ্রদর্শী।

ū-ni-lŏc'-ū-lar (-lêr), *adj.* Having one cell only; একগর্ভ (সাঃ পঃ), এককোষ, এককণ।

ŭn-im-ăg'-i-nă-ble (-bl), *adj.* That cannot be imagined; অকল্পনীয়, অকল্পনাযোগ্য, কল্পনাতীত, ধারণাতীত। **—bly,** *adv.*

ŭn-im-ăg'-i-na-tive (-tiv), *adj.* Not imaginative; অকল্পনাপ্রবণ, অকল্পনাকুশল।

ŭn-im-ăg'-ined (-ind), *adj.* Not imagined; অকল্পিত।

ŭn-im-bit'-tered (-têrd), *adj.* Not aggravated; অগুরুত্বৰ্দ্ধিত।

ŭn-im-bued' (-būd), *adj.* Not tinctured; অরঞ্জিত।

ŭn-im'-i-tāt-ĕd, *adj.* Not imitated; অননুকৃত।

ŭn-im-pair'-a-ble (-pâr-ă-bl), *adj.* Not liable to be impaired; অক্ষয্য।

ŭn-im-paired' (-pārd), *adj.* Not impaired; অক্ষুণ্ণ, অক্ষত, অপ্রাপ্তাপকার।

ŭn-im-pas'-sion-āte (-pă-), *adj.* Not aroused the passion of; অনুত্তেজিত।

ŭn-im-pas'-sioned (-pă-shŏnd), *adj.* Not actuated or dictated by passion; calm; নির্ব্বিকার, অনুরাগশূন্য, রাগদ্বেষশূন্য, বিকাররহিত; স্থির, প্রশান্ত।

ŭn-im-peach'-a-ble (-pēch-ă-bl), *adj.* Not blamable; অনিন্দ্য, অদূষ্য, অদূষণীয়, দোষস্পর্শশূন্য।

ŭn-im-peached' (-pēcht), *adj.* **1.** Not charged or accused; অনভিযুক্ত। **2.** Not called into question; অপ্রশ্নস্পৃষ্ট।

ŭn-im-pĕd'-ĕd, *adj.* Not hindered; অবারিত, অপ্রতিহত।

ŭn-im'-pli-cāt-ĕd, *adj.* Not implicated; অজড়িত।

ŭn-im-plied' (-plid), *adj.* Not included by fair inference; অবিবক্ষিত।

ŭn-im-plored' (-plörd), *adj.* Not solicited ; অপ্রার্থিত, অযাচিত।
ŭn-im-pŏr'-tănt, *adj.* Not important ; trite ; unnecessary ; অগুরুত্ববিশিষ্ট, গুরুত্বহীন, লঘু ; অকিঞ্চিৎকর ; অনাবশ্যক, অপ্রয়োজনীয়।
ŭn-im-pŏr-tuned' (-tūnd), *adj.* Not solicited ; অপ্রার্থিত।
ŭn-im-pŏs'-ing, *adj.* Not commanding respect ; not enjoining or obligatory ; voluntary ; অশ্রদ্ধাজনক ; অনবশ্যকরণীয় ; স্বেচ্ছাকৃত।
ŭn-im-prĕs'-sive (-ĭv), *adj.* Not impressive ; অহৃদয়গ্রাহী, অহৃদয়স্পর্শী, অচিত্তহারী। **—ly,** *adv.*
ŭn-im-pris'-oned (-ŏnd), *adj.* Not imprisoned ; অকারারুদ্ধ।
ŭn-im-prō'-pri-āt-ĕd, *adj.* Not put into the hands of a layman ; অযাজকহস্তন্যস্ত।
ŭn-im-prôv'-ă-ble (-bl), *adj.* That cannot be improved ; অনুন্নেয়।
ŭn-im-proved' (-prôvd), *adj.* **1.** Not made better or wiser ; অনুন্নত। **2.** Not used ; অব্যবহৃত, অপ্রযুক্ত। **3.** Not cultivated ; অকর্ষিত, অকৃষ্ট। **4.** Not built upon ; উপরি অনির্মিত।
ŭn-im-prôv'-ing, *adj.* Not tending to advance or instruct ; অনুন্নতিদায়ক।
ū-ni-mŭs'-cū-lar (-lêr) *adj.* Having one muscle ; একমাংসপেশীবিশিষ্ট।
ŭn-in-debt'-ĕd (-det-), *adj.* Not indebted ; অঋণী।
ŭn-in-flăm'-ma-ble (-a-bl), *adj.* Not inflammable ; অদাহ্য।
ŭn-in'-flū-enced (-ĕnst), *adj.* Not influenced ; অপ্রভাবিত।
ŭn-in-flū-ĕn'-tial (-shăl), *adj.* Not influential ; অপ্রভাবসম্পন্ন।
ŭn-in-formed' (-fŏrmd), *adj.* **1.** Not instructed ; অশিক্ষিত। **2.** Unanimated ; অনুত্তেজিত।
ŭn-in-gĕn'-ū-ous (-ŭs), *adj.* Not frank or candid ; অসরল, অকপট।
ŭn-in-hăb'-it-ă-ble (-bl), *adj.* Not habitable ; বাসের অযোগ্য, অবসনীয়, অবাসোপযোগী, অবাসযোগ্য।
ŭn-in-hăb'-it-ĕd, *adj.* Not inhabited ; unfrequented ; বসতিশূন্য-বাসশূন্য, অনধ্যুষিত ; জনহীন, জনমানবহীন, জনমানববিহীন।
ŭn-in-i'-ti-āt-ĕd (-shĭ-), *adj.* Not initiated ; অদীক্ষিত।
ŭn-in'-jured (-jêrd), *adj.* Unhurt ; অক্ষত, অনপকৃত, অপ্রাপ্তাপকার।
ŭn-in-sured' (-shôrd-), *adj.* Not insured ; অবীমাকৃত।
ŭn-in-tĕl'-li-gi-ble (-bl), *adj.* Not intelligible ; বুদ্ধির অগম্য, দুর্বোধ, দুরূহ, অস্পষ্ট, অবিজ্ঞেয়, দুর্বিজ্ঞেয়, অবোধগম্য।
ŭn-in-tĕn'-tion-ăl, *adj.* Done or happening without design ; অনভিপ্রায়মূলক।
ŭn-in'-têr-ĕst-ĕd, *adj.* **1.** Not interested or personally concerned ; অসংসৃষ্ট, অসম্পর্কীয়। **2.** Not engaging the attention of ; অচিত্তগ্রাহী, অচিত্তাকর্ষক।
ŭn-in'-têr-ĕst-ing, *adj.* Not interesting ; অকৌতূহলজনক, নীরস, অচিত্তরঞ্জক।
ŭn-in-têr-mis'-sion (-mĭ-), *n.* Failure of intermission ; অবিশ্রান্তি, অবিরতি, অনিবৃত্তি।
ŭn-in-têr-mit'-ted (-ĕd), *adj.* Not interrupted ; continued ; অবিশ্রান্ত ; নিরবচ্ছিন্ন।
ŭn-in-têr-mit-ting (-ĭng), *adj.* Not ceasing for a time ; continuing ; অবিরাম, বিরামবিহীন ; অবিশ্রাম, অবিশ্রান্ত।
ŭn-in-têr-mixed' (-mĭkst), *adj.* Not mingled ; অমিশ্রিত।
ŭn-in-têr-pō-lăt'-ed, *adj.* Not inserted subsequently to the original writing ; অপ্রক্ষিপ্ত।
ŭn-in-têr'-prĕt-ĕd, *adj.* Not explained ; অব্যাখ্যাত।
ŭn-in-terred' (-têrd), *adj.* Not buried ; অসমাহিত।
ŭn-in-têr-rŭpt'-ĕd, *adj.* Not interrupted ; unceasing ; unintermitted ; অব্যাহত ; অবিরত ; অবিশ্রান্ত, অবিচ্ছিন্ন, নিরবচ্ছিন্ন।
ŭn-in-tŏx'-i-cāt-ing, *adj.* Not intoxicating ; অমাদকতাজনক।
ŭn-in-trenched' (-trĕncht), *adj.* Not defended by intrenchments ; অপরিখাবেষ্টিত।
ŭn-in-trō-duced' (-dūst), *adj.* Not introduced ; intrusive ; অপরিচয়জ্ঞাপিত ; উপযাচক, উপরপড়া (*colloq.*)।
ŭn-in-ured' (-ūrd), *adj.* Not hardened by use or practice ; অনভ্যস্ত।
ŭn-in-vĕnt'-ĕd *adj.* Not invented ; অনুদ্ভাবিত।
ŭn-in-vĕn'-tive (-tĭv), *adj.* Not invented ; অনুদ্ভাবিত।
ŭn-in-vĕst'-ĕd, *adj.* Not invested ; not converted into real property ; অপ্রযুক্ত, অবিনিযুক্ত ; স্থাবর সম্পত্তিতে অপরিণত।
ŭn-in-vĕs'-ti-gă-ble (-bl), *adj.* That cannot be investigated or searched out ; অননুসন্ধেয়, অনন্বেষণীয়।
ŭn-in-vid'-i-ous (-ŭs), *adj.* Not invidious ; অদ্বেষমূলক।
ŭn-in-vit'-ĕd, *adj.* Not invited ; অনিমন্ত্রিত, অনাহূত।
ŭn-in-vit'-ing, *adj.* Not tempting or attractive ; অপ্রলোভনজনক, অচিত্তাকর্ষক।
ŭn-in-voked' (-vōkt), *adj.* Not invoked ; অনাবাহিত।
ū'-ni-ō, *n.* A genus of fresh-water bivalves or fresh-water clams ; একজাতীয় মৎস্য।
ūn'-ion (-yŏn), *n.* **1.** The act of uniting or the state of being united ; coaliton ; মিলন, যোগ, একীভাব (হিঃ কোঃ) ; সংযোগ। **2.** Concord ; ঐক্য, মিলন। **3.** Any of various political changes effecting the political union of the different parts of the kingdom of Great Britain and Ireland ; গ্রেটব্রিটেন এবং আয়র্লণ্ডের বিভিন্ন অংশের সংযোগসাধক রাজনীতিক পরিবর্তন সমূহের অন্যতম। **4.** That which is united or made into one ; a confederation ; সংযুক্ত

বস্তু, একীভূত বস্তু; সম্মিলনী, সমিতি, গোষ্ঠী (হিঃ কোঃ)। 5. Matrimony; বিবাহ। 6. Two or more parishes consolidated into one for administration of poor laws; দরিদ্রবিধি পরিচালনার জন্য একত্র সম্মিলিত দুই বা ততোধিক যাজকপল্লী। 7. (*Obs.*) A large fine pearl; (অপ্রঃ) উৎকৃষ্ট এবং বৃহদাকার মুক্তা। 8. A mixed fabric in which cotton, flux, jute, silk, wool, etc. are united in varions combinations; একপ্রকার বস্ত্র যাহাতে বিভিন্ন পরিমাণে কার্পাস, পাট, শণ, রেশম, পশম, প্রভৃতি মিশ্রিত থাকে। 9. A tubular coupling for pipes; চোঙ্গ জোড়া দেওয়ার জন্য একপ্রকার নলাকার সংযোজনী। 10. A workhouse erected by several parishes in combination, for the reception of the pauper in each; কতিপয় যাজকপল্লীর নিঃস্ব ব্যক্তিগণের জন্য যে শ্রমশালা উক্ত পল্লীসমূহ হইতে সংগৃহীত অর্থ দ্বারা নির্মিত হয়। 11. A kind of flag either used by itself or forming the upper inner corner of an ensign; একপ্রকার পতাকা যাহা স্বতন্ত্র রূপে ব্যবহৃত হয় কিম্বা অপর ধ্বজার উর্দ্ধদিকের ভিতরের কোণস্বরূপ হইয়া থাকে। 12. A flag marked only with this device; যে পতাকার ভিতরের উর্দ্ধকোণ মাত্র প্রদর্শিত হইয়া থাকে। 13. A permanent combination among workmen engaged in the same occupation or trade; একই কার্য্য বা ব্যবসায়ে নিযুক্ত শ্রমিকজনের স্থায়ী সম্মিলনী, শ্রমিকসম্মিলনী। **Union Jack** or **flag**—St. George, St. Andrew এবং St. Patrick-এর ক্রুশত্রয়ের সম্মিলনে রচিত গ্রেটব্রিটেন এবং আয়র্লণ্ডের মিলিত জাতীয় পতাকা।

Union Jack

Union jet-burner—একপ্রকার গ্যাসের প্রদীপ যাহাতে দুইটি শিখা একত্র হইয়া এক চ্যাপ্টা দীপশিখা উৎপাদন করে। **Flag hoisted union down**—বিপর্য্যস্তভাবে উত্তোলিত বিপৎসঙ্কেতসূচক পতাকা। **Union** or **Act of Union**—যে আইনের বলে ১৭০৭ খৃঃ অব্দে ইংলণ্ড ও স্কটলণ্ডের সংযোগ সাধিত হইয়াছিল। ১৮০০ খৃষ্টাব্দে বিধিবদ্ধ যে আইন দ্বারা গ্রেটব্রিটেন এবং আয়র্লণ্ডের সংযোগ সাধিত হয়।

ūn′-ion-ĭsm (-yŏn-), *n.* The system of combination, esp. of workmen in their own interest; সম্মিলন, শ্রমজীবিসম্মিলন, শ্রমিকসমিতি।

ūn′-ion-ĭst (-yŏn-), *n.* 1. A member of a trade-union; শ্রমিকসমিতির সভ্য। 2. A person opposed to the rupture of legislative union between Great Britain and Ireland; opponent of Home rule in Ireland; ইংলণ্ডের সহিত আয়র্লণ্ডের বিচ্ছেদসাধনের বিরোধী ব্যক্তি; আয়র্লণ্ডের স্বায়ত্বশাসনের বিরোধী ব্যক্তি। 3. An adherent or supporter of federal union of the United States esp. at the time of the Civil War; আমেরিকার যুক্তরাজ্যের বিভিন্ন রাষ্ট্রসমূহের সংযোগের পক্ষপাতি ব্যক্তি।

ū-nĭp′-ă-rous (-rŭs), *adj.* 1. Producing one at a birth; একপ্রসূ। 2. Producing but one axis at each branching; একপ্রার্শ্বপ্রসূ (সাঃ পঃ)।

ū′-nĭ-pĕd, *adj.* & *n.* Having only one foot; একপদী। *Noun.* An animal having one foot; একপদী জন্তু।

ū-nĭ-pêr′-sŏn-ăl, *adj.* 1. Of only one person; একব্যক্তিক। 2. (*Gram.*) Employed only in the third person singular; কেবল প্রথম পুরুষের এক বচনে ব্যবহৃত।

ū-nĭ-pō′-lar (-lêr), *adj.* Having one pole; একমেরুক, একধ্রুবক।

ū-nique′ (-nēk), *adj.* Without like or an equal in kind or quality; অনন্যসাধারণ, অনুপম, অদ্বিতীয়, অনন্যসুলভ। **–ly,** *adv.* **–ness,** *n.*

ū-nĭ-rā′-dĭ-āt-ĕd, *adj.* Having one ray; একরশ্মিক।

ŭn-ĭr′-rĭ-tāt-ĕd, *adj.* Not fretted; not provoked or angered; অনুত্তেজিত; অনুদ্বেজিত, অক্রুদ্ধ।

ŭn-ĭr′-rĭ-tāt-ĭng, *adj.* Not provoking; অনুদ্বেজক।

ū-nĭ-sĕx′-ū-ăl, *adj.* (*Bot.*) Having one sex only; (উদ্ভিদ্‌বিদ্যা) একলিঙ্গী (সাঃ পঃ)।

ū′-nĭ-sŏn, *n.* & *adj.* 1. Harmony; concord; সঙ্গতি; ঐক্য মিল। 2. Accordance or coincidenee of sounds proceeding from an equality in the number of vibrations made in a given time by a sonorous body; স্বরসঙ্গতি, একতান। *Adj.* Agreeing in pitch; ঐক্যতান। **In unison**—In harmony; ঐক্যতান সহকারে।

ū-nĭs′-ō-nance (-năns), *n.* Accordance of sounds; স্বরসঙ্গতি, স্বরৈক্য (হিঃ কোঃ)।

ū-nĭs′-ō-nănt, –nous (-nŭs), *adjs.* Being in unison; ঐক্যতানবিশিষ্ট।

ū′-nĭt, *n.* 1. One; এক। 2. (*Math.* & *Phys.*) Any known determinate quantity by the constant repetition of which any other quantity of the same kind is measured; (গণিতশাস্ত্র এবং পদার্থবিদ্যা) একক। **Absolute unit**—নিরপেক্ষ একক। **Abstract unit**—নিরবয়ব একক। **Decimal and duodecimal units**—দশমিক একক, দ্বিদশমিক একক। **Dynamic unit**—গত্যাত্মক একক। **Electric unit**—তাড়িতৈক। **Fractional unit**—খণ্ডাত্মক একক। **Integral unit**—অখণ্ড একক। **Military unit**—সামরিক একক। **Physical unit**—প্রাকৃতিক একক (হিঃ কোঃ)। **Specific gravity unit**—আপেক্ষিক গুরুত্বৈক। **Unit character**—ধর্ম্মৈক (যোঃ), গুণৈক (ঐ)। **Unit-form**—মূল আকার (যোঃ)। **Unit-jar**—নির্দ্দিষ্ট পরিমাণ তাড়িত পরিমাপের জন্য Sir W. Snow Harris কর্ত্তৃক উদ্ভাবিত যন্ত্রবিশেষ।

Unit force—বলৈক। **Unit of account**—সিক্কাপরিমাণ (হিঃ কোঃ)। **Unit of capacity**—ধারণৈক। **Unit of current**—তাড়িত প্রবাহৈক। **Unit of electromotive force**—পরিমাণৈক। **Unit of heat (Thermal unit)**—তাপ একক (হিঃ কোঃ), তাপৈক। **Unit of illumination**—দ্যোতনাঙ্ক। **Unit of measure**—মানৈক। **Unit of quantity**—পরিমাণৈক। **Unit of resistance**—প্রতিরোধ একক (হিঃ কোঃ)। **Unit of value**—মূল্যৈক, মূল্যপরিমাণ (হিঃ কোঃ)। **Unit of work**—কার্য্যের একক (হিঃ কোঃ)। **Unit of work done**—কার্য্যৈক।

ū-ni-tā′-ri-ăn, *n.* & *adj.* **1.** (*Cap.*) One who denies the doctrine of Trinity and ascribes divinity to God the Father only ; যে ব্যক্তি খৃষ্টীয় ত্রীশ্বরের মধ্যে কেবল পিতৃরূপী ঈশ্বরের ঈশ্বরত্ব স্বীকার করে [খৃষ্টীয় একেশ্বরবাদিগণ ঈশ্বরের পিতৃত্ব ও সর্ব্বমানবের ভ্রাতৃত্বের উপর বিশেষ জোর দিয়া থাকেন।] [See J. H. Allen, *Historical Sketch of the Unitarian Movement* ; Clarke, *Unitarian Belief, Modern Unitarianism* ; See Also Writing of W. E. Channing, J. Priestley, J. Maritinean and others.] **2.** A believer in one God only ; একেশ্বরবাদী, অদ্বৈতবাদী (হিঃ কোঃ), ঈশ্বরৈক্যবাদী (ঐ)। **3.** A believer in the ultimate oneness of the subject and object in perception ; অদ্বৈতবাদী। ***Adj.*** **1.** Unitary ; ঐকিক। **2.** (*Cap.*) Pertaining to the Unitarians or their doctrines ; একেশ্বরবাদিসম্বন্ধীয়, একেশ্বরবাদীদিগের মত সম্বন্ধীয়। **3.** Holding the unity of subject and object in perception ; অদ্বৈতবাদী। **—ism**, *n.* (*Cap.*) A collective name for the views of ths Unitarians ; খৃষ্টীয় একেশ্বরবাদ, অদ্বৈতবাদ (হিঃ কোঃ), ঈশ্বরৈক্যবাদ (ঐ)। **—ize**, *v. t.* & *i.*

ū′-ni-tă-rў, *adj.* Relating to a unit ; ঐকিক। **Unitary method**—ঐকিক নিয়ম। **Unitary Theory**—(*Chem.*) একাণুকসিদ্ধান্ত (হিঃ কোঃ)।

ū-nite′, *v. t.* & *i.* **1.** To put together ; to join two or more things into one ; to connect ; to cause to adhere ; একত্র করা ; সংযুক্ত করা ; সংযোগ করা ; লাগান, জোড়া দেওয়া। **2.** To join in interest, affection, fellowship or the like ; মিলিত করা, সম্মিলিত করা। ***Verb i.*** **1.** To become one ; to be joined ; এক হওয়া ; সংযুক্ত হওয়া। **2.** To combine and to act in concert ; একযোগে কার্য্য করা।

ū-nīt′-ĕd, *adj.* Joined ; মিলিত, যুক্ত, সংযুক্ত, একত্র। **—ly**, *adv.* **United Brethren**—Same as MORAVIAN 2. **In an united manner**—সংযুক্তভাবে, একযোগে, মিলিতভাবে।

ū-nīt′-ĕr, *n.* The person or thing that unites ; সংযোজক, ঐক্যসাধক।

ū′-ni-tive (-tĭv), *adj.* Having the power of uniting ; সংযোজনক্ষম, মিলনসাধক।

ū′-ni-tў, *n.* **1.** The state or property of being one ; একত্ব, একতা, একরূপতা, অদ্বৈত, কৈবল্য। **2.** Concord ; ঐক্য, সঙ্গতি। **3.** Identity ; অভিন্নতা। **4.** (*Math.*) The abstract expression for any unit whatsoever ; এক। **5.** The principle by which an uniform tenor of story and propriety of representation is preserved in literary compositions ; conformity in a composition to these principles ; সাহিত্যিক রচনায় যে মূলতত্ত্বানুসারে সমস্ত কাহিনীর মধ্যে ঐক্যের ভাব রক্ষিত হয় ; উক্ত মূলতত্ত্বের অনুসারিতা। **6.** (*Law*) A joint possession of two rights by several titles ; কতিপয় স্বত্ববলে অধিকারদ্বয়ের সম্মিলিত অধিকার। **7.** (*Law*) Joint tenancy ; এজমালীস্বত্ব। **8.** (*Obs.*) A gold coin of the time of James I ; (অপ্রঃ) প্রথম জেমসের সময়ের একপ্রকার স্বর্ণমুদ্রা। **Aesthetic unity**—মনোমধ্যে গৃহীত কোন মূর্ত্তি বা সংবেদনের ঐকিকতা বা সঙ্গতিবিশিষ্টতা। **Formal unity**—রূপগত ঐকিকতা। **Material unity**—উপাদানগত ঐকিকতা। **Unity of time, place and action**—প্রাচীন গ্রীকনাটকের একইস্থানে একই দিবসে এবং একই ঘটনায় সীমাবদ্ধতা। **Unity of effort**—ঐকিকতা।

ū-ni-vā′-lĕnt, *adj.* Having a valency of one ; একশক্তিক।

ū′-ni-valve (-vălv), *adj.* & *n.* Having one valve only ; এককপাট। ***Noun.*** A mollusc whose shell is composed of a single piece ; এককপাট শম্বুকাদি।

ū-ni-vălv′-ū-lar (-lẽr), *adj.* Having one valve only ; এককপাট, একপুটক।

ū-ni-vẽr′-săl, *adj.* & *n.* **1.** Comprising whole ; pervading the whole ; সার্ব্বত্রিক, সামগ্রিক ; সর্ব্বব্যাপী, সর্ব্বপ্রসারী, সর্ব্বসাধারণ (হিঃ কোঃ), সর্ব্বগত (ঐ), সর্ব্বলৌকিক (ঐ), সর্ব্বজনীন, বিশ্বজনীন, সার্ব্বলৌকিক সার্ব্বভৌমিক। **2.** (*Log.*) Forming the whole of a genus ; (তর্কবিজ্ঞান) সার্ব্বিক। **3.** Whole ; সমগ্র। **4.** General ; ব্যাপক, সামান্য। **5.** (*Mech.*) Adapted or adaptable to all or various uses, shapes, sizes, etc. ; সর্ব্বপ্রকার বা নানাবিধ আকৃতি, আয়তন প্রভৃতির পক্ষে উপযোগীকৃত বা উপযোগী। ***Noun.*** **1.** (*Obs.*) The whole ; the universe ; সমগ্রটী ; বিশ্ব। **2.** (*Log.*) Same as UNIVERSAL PROPOSITION. **3.** A general notion or idea ; ব্যাপকভাব। **4.** An abstract conception which is drawn from a multitude of objects of the same class, and which embodies the features, common to all ; বিশ্বজনীন ভাব। **—ly**, *adv.* **—ness**, *n.* **Universal agent**—সর্ব্বকার্য্যসাধনের ক্ষমতার্পিত ব্যক্তি। **Universal compass**—যে

কম্পাসের কাঁটা ছড়াইয়া বৃহৎ বৃত্ত অঙ্কিত করা যায়। **Universal church**—নিখিলধর্ম্মসঙ্ঘ, সার্ব্বভৌমিক-ধর্ম্মসঙ্ঘ। **Universal coupling** — যে জোড় দ্বারা সংযুক্ত অংশসমূহ সকলদিকে চালিত করা যায়, বিশ্বসংযোগ। **Universal dial**—যে সূর্য্যঘড়ীদ্বারা পৃথিবীর যে কোন স্থানে সময় নির্ণীত হইতে পারে, বিশ্বজনীন সূর্য্যঘড়ী। **Universal Hedonism**—সমুদায় সুখোদ্দেশ্যবাদ (হিঃ কোঃ)। **Universal instrument**—জ্যোতিষ্ক সকলের উন্নতাংশ ও দিগংশকোটি পরিমাপের জন্য যন্ত্রবিশেষ, বিশ্বযন্ত্র (হিঃ কোঃ)। **Universal joint**—বস্তুদ্বয় সংযোজনের জন্য কল বিশেষ—যদ্দ্বারা উহারা সকলদিকে ঘুরিতে পারে, বিশ্বসংযোজক। **Universal language** — বিশ্বভাষা। **Universal law**—বিশ্ববিধান। **Universal legacy**—কোন ব্যক্তিকে চরম পত্রদ্বারা সমস্ত সম্পত্তি অর্পণ, বিশ্বার্পণ। **Universal legatee** — বিশ্বপ্রাপক। **Universal prime meridian**—গ্রীণ উইচের মধ্যরেখা (*Meridian*)। **Universal proposition** — সার্ব্বিকবাক্য (হিঃ কোঃ), ব্যাপ্তিপ্রতিজ্ঞা (হিঃ কোঃ), (*affirmative*) অন্বয়ব্যাপ্তিপ্রতিজ্ঞা (হিঃ কোঃ), (*Negative*) ব্যতিরেক ব্যাপ্তিপ্রতিজ্ঞা (হিঃ কোঃ)। **Universal religion** — বিশ্বধর্ম্ম। **Universal successor**—যে ব্যক্তি উত্তরাধিকারিসূত্রে কোন ব্যক্তির সমস্ত সম্পত্তি প্রাপ্ত হয়। **Universal suffrage**—সকলের ভোট প্রদানের অধিকার, বিশ্বনির্ব্বাচনাধিকারী। **Universal time**—গ্রীণ উইচের মধ্যদ্বিপ্রহর (mean-noon) হইতে গণিত সময়, এই প্রণালী মতে মধ্যরাত্র হইতে দিবস গণিত হয়। **Universal umbel**—প্রাথমিক উপচ্ছত্র, উপচ্ছত্রের প্রথম এবং বৃহত্তম বিকীর্য্যমাণ দলপংক্তি।

ū-nĭ-vêr'-săl-ĭsm, *n.* The doctrine that all men will be eventually saved; পরিণামে সকলেই মুক্তিলাভ করিবে এই মত, সর্ব্বমুক্তিবাদ, নিখিলমোক্ষবাদ। **—ist**, *n.* & *adj.* A believer in universalism; সর্ব্বমুক্তিবাদী। ***Adj.*** Pertaining to universalism; সর্ব্বমুক্তিবাদসম্বন্ধীয়।

ū-nĭ-vêr-săl'-ĭ-tў, *n.* The state of being universal or extending to the whole; সার্ব্বভৌমিকতা, সার্ব্বত্রিকত্ব (মাধুর্য্যকাদম্বিনী), সার্ব্বিকতা (হিঃ কোঃ)।

ū-nĭ-vêr'-săl-īze, *v. t.* To make universal; সার্ব্বভৌমিক করা।

ū'-nĭ-verse (-vêrs), *n.* **1.** All created things viewd as constituting one system or whole; বিশ্ব, বিশ্বসংসার, বিশ্বপৃথিবী, বিশ্বজীব, জগদ্‌ব্রহ্মাণ্ড, ব্রহ্মাণ্ড। **2.** Same as UNIVERSE OF DISCOURSE. **Universe of discourse, Soul of the universe**—জগদাত্মা, ব্রহ্ম, বিশ্বাত্মা।

ū-nĭ-vêr'-sĭ-tў, *n.* An institution or corporation, for instruction, and conferring degrees; বিশ্ববিদ্যালয়।

ū-nĭv'-ŏ-căl, *adj.* & *n.* **1.** Having one meaning only; একার্থক। **2.** Having unison of sound; স্বরসঙ্গতিবিশিষ্ট। **3.** Certain; নিশ্চিত। ***Noun.*** A word that has but one meaning; একার্থবোধক শব্দ।

ū-nĭ-vō-cā'-tion, *n.* Agreement of name and meaning; অন্বর্থতা।

ŭn-jaun'-diced (-jän-dĭst), *adj.* Impartial; পক্ষপাতশূন্য, নিরপেক্ষ।

ŭn-jeal'-ous (-jĕl-ŭs), *adj.* Not jealous; অদ্বেষ্টা।

ŭn-joined' (-jōynd), *adj.* Not joined; অসংযুক্ত।

ŭn-joint'-ĕd (-jōynt-), *adj.* Having no joints; disjointed; সন্ধিবিহীন; সন্ধিচ্যুত।

ŭn-jŏy'-ous (-ŭs), *adj.* Not joyous or cheerful; অপ্রফুল্ল, নিরানন্দ, অপ্রসন্ন।

ŭn-jŭst', *adj.* Contrary to justice and right; অন্যায়, অনুচিত, ন্যায়বিরুদ্ধ, অন্যায়পর, অন্যায্য। **—ly**, *adv.* In an unjust manner; অন্যায়রূপে, অন্যায়ভাবে।

ŭn-jŭs'-tĭ-fī-ă-ble (-bl), *adj.* That cannot be proved to be right; indefensible; অন্যায্যতাপ্রতিপাদ্য; অসমর্থনীয়। **—bly**, *adv.* **—ness**, *n.*

ŭn-jŭs'-tĭ-fied (-fīd), *adj.* Not justified; unpardoned; অন্যায্যতাপ্রতিপাদিত; অক্ষমিত, অমার্জ্জিত।

ŭn-kempt' (-kĕmt), *adj.* Uncombed; rough; অমার্জ্জিত; কর্কশ।

ŭn-kĕn'-nĕl, *v. t.* To drive from the hole; "Will *unkennel* the fox"; to rouse from secrecy or retreat; to release from a kennel; গর্ত্ত হইতে তাড়িত করা; নির্জ্জন আশ্রয়স্থান হইতে জাগ্রত করা; কুক্কুরাবাস হইতে মুক্ত করা।

ŭn-kĕpt', *adj.* **1.** Not retained or preserved; অরক্ষিত। **2.** Not observed; অপ্রতিপালিত।

ŭn-kêr'-chiefed (-chĭft), *adj.* Not having a kerchief; রুমালবিহীন।

ŭn-kêr'-nelled (-nĕld), *adj.* Destitute of kernel; ফলশস্যবিহীন, শাঁস ছাড়ানো।

ŭn-kīnd', *adj.* Not kind; cruel; নির্দ্দয়; নিষ্ঠুর, নির্ম্মম, ক্রূর। **—ness**, *n.* The quality of being unkind; নির্দ্দয়তা, নিষ্ঠুরতা।

ŭn-kīnd'-lў, *adj.* & *adv.* Unkind; unfavouable; নির্দ্দয়; অশুভ। ***Adv.*** Without kindness or affection; নির্দ্দয়ভাবে, নিষ্ঠুরভাবে। **—li-ness**, *n.* The quality of being unkind; নির্দ্দয়তা, নিষ্ঠুরতা, নৃশংসতা।

ŭn-king', *v. t.* To deprive of royalty; রাজপদ হইতে বিচ্যুত করা।

ŭn-king'-like, ŭn-king'-lў, *adjs.* Not becoming a king; অরাজোচিত, অনৃপোচিত।

ŭn-knight'-lў (-nīt-), *adj.* Not becoming a knight; অশূরোচিত।

ŭn-knit' (-nĭt-), *v. i.* To separate the threads that are knit; to open; বোনাসূতা খোলা; খোলা।

ŭn-knot' (-nŏt), *v. t.* To free from knots; to untie; গ্রন্থিমোচন করা; গেরো খোলা।

ŭn-know'-a-ble (-nō-ă-bl), *adj.* That cannot be known; অজ্ঞেয়, অপরিজ্ঞেয়। **The unknowable**—পরমেশ্বর।

ŭn-know'-ĭng (-nō-), *adj.* Not knowing; ignorant; "His hounds *unknowing* of his change, pursue the chase, and their mistaken master slew" ; অজ্ঞাত ; অজ্ঞ । **—ly,** *adv.* Without knowledge ; অজ্ঞানপূর্ব্বক, অজ্ঞানতঃ, অজ্ঞাতভাবে অজ্ঞাতসারে, না জানিয়া, অজ্ঞানাভাবে।

ŭn-known' (-nōn), *adj.* 1. Not known ; অপরিচিত, অজ্ঞাত। **2.** Incalculable ; "The planting of hemp and flax would be an *unknown* advantage to the kingdom" ; inexpressible ; immense ; অগণ্য; অনির্ব্বচনীয়, অব্যক্ত; বিশাল, বিপুল। 3. (*Obs.*) Not having had sexual intercourse ; "*Unknown* to women" ; অনভিগত। **An unknown quantity**—অজ্ঞাত রাশি। **The second unknown quantity**—কালক (বীজঃ)।

ŭn-lā-bō'-ri-ous (-ŭs), *adj.* Not difficult to be done ; অশ্রমসাধ্য, অনায়াসসাধ্য।

ŭn-lā'-boured (-bêrd), *adj.* **1.** Not produced by labour or toil ; অযত্নসম্ভূত, অনায়াসসিদ্ধ। **2.** Natural ; spontaneous ; easy ; স্বাভাবিক ; স্বতঃস্ফূর্ত্ত ; অনাড়ষ্ট।

ŭn-lāce', *v. t.* **1.** To loose from lacing ; ফিতা খোলা। **2.** To loose the dress of ; পরিচ্ছদ শ্লথ করা। **3.** (*Obs.*) To divest of ornament ; to disgrace ; (অপ্রঃ) ভূষণবিহীন করা ; কলঙ্কিত করা। **4.** To loose ; to free ; বন্ধন মুক্ত করা ; ছাড়িয়া দেওয়া।

ŭn-lāde', *v. t.* To unload ; to take out a cargo ; মাল নামান ; মাল খালাস করা। **—lad'-en,** *adj.*

ŭn-laid' (-lād), *adj.* Not placed or fixed ; "First foundations of the world being yet *unlaid*" ; অবিন্যস্ত, অনিহিত, অনিবেশিত।

ŭn-lă-mĕnt'-ĕd, *adj.* Not deplored; অশোচিত, অপরিদেবিত, অননুশোচিত, অবিলপিত।

ŭn-lăp', *v. t.* To unfold ; "Tapestry *unlapt* and laid open" ; অপুটিত করা।

ŭn-lârd'-ĕd, *adj.* **1.** Not dressed with lard ; অশূকরবসামিশ্রিত। 2. Not intermixed ; অসম্মিশ্রিত।

ŭn-latch' (-lăch), *v. t.* To open or loose by lifting the latch; খিল খোলা।

ŭn-lau'-relled (-lä-rĕld), *adj.* Not crowned with laurel ; not honoured ; অলরেলমুকুটশোভিত ; অসম্মানিত, অসম্পূজিত।

ŭn-lăv'-ish, *adj.* Not lavish or profuse ; অপ্রচুর, অবহুল।

ŭn-law'-fŭl (-lä-), *adj.* Contrary to law ; illegal ; আইনবিরুদ্ধ, বিধিবিরুদ্ধ ; বে-আইনি। **—ly,** *adv.* **—ness,** *n.*

ŭn-learn' (-lêrn), *v. t.* To forget, lose, or unschool one's self of what has been learnt ; "He (Pope) used to say that he had been seven years * * * in *unlearning* all he had been acquiring for twice that time" ; অধীত বিষয় বিস্মৃত হওয়া, শিক্ষিত বিষয় পুনরায় বিস্মৃত হওয়া, অনধীত হওয়া।

ŭn-learn'-ĕd (-lêrn-), *adj.* **1.** Not learned ; ignorant ; illiterate ; অশিক্ষিত, অপণ্ডিত, অবিদ্বান্, অকৃতবিদ্য ; অজ্ঞ ; মূর্খ। **2.** Not suitable to a learned man ; "I will prove these verses to be very *unlearned*, neither savouring of poetry, art or invention" ; শিক্ষিত লোকের অযোগ্য। **—ly,** *adv.* **—ness,** *n.*

ŭn-leav'-ened (-lĕv-nd), *adj.* Not raised by leaven or yeast ; খমীর সংযোগে অস্ফীত, অকিণ্বমিশ্রিত।

ŭn-lĕc'-tūred, *adj.* Not taught by lecture ; not lectured to ; অবক্তৃতাশিক্ষিত ; অবক্তৃতাপ্রদত্ত।

ŭn-lĕd', *adj.* Not led or conducted ; অপরিচালিত।

ŭn-lĕnt', *adj.* Not lent ; অঋণদত্ত।

ŭn-lĕss', *conj.* If it be not the case that ; if it be not that ; supposing that not ; যদি না ; যদি তাহা না হয় ; ঐরূপ না হইলে।

ŭn-lĕss'-ened (-nd), *adj.* Not diminished ; অনল্পীকৃত, অন্যূনীকৃত।

ŭn-lĕs'-soned (-nd), *adj.* (*Obs.*) Not instructed ; (অপ্রঃ) অশিক্ষাপ্রাপ্ত।

ŭn-lĕt'-tered (-êrd), *adj.* Unlearned ; untaught ; অশিক্ষিত, অজ্ঞ, নিরক্ষর, মূর্খ, অশিক্ষিত, বর্ণজ্ঞানহীন ; অশিক্ষাপ্রাপ্ত।

ŭn-lĕv'-elled (-ld), *adj.* Not levelled ; uneven ; rough ; অচোলাইকরা, অসমীকৃত ; উচ্চাবচ ; আবড়োখাবড়ো।

ŭn-lī'-censed (-sĕnst), *adj.* Not licensed ; not having permission by authority ; as, an *unlicensed* stamp-vendor ; done without license ; as, an *unlicensed* traffic ; অসনন্দপ্রাপ্ত ; অননুমতিপ্রাপ্ত, বিনাসনন্দে বা অনুমতিতে সম্পাদিত।

ŭn-licked' (-likt), *adj.* **1.** Shapeless (from the old popular notion that the she-bear licked her cubs into shape) ; "Like to a chaos or *unlicked* bear-whelp" ; আকারবিহীন, কদাকার। **2.** Rough ; rude ; কর্কশ ; রূঢ়।

ŭn-light'-ĕd (-lit-), *adj.* Not illuminated ; not kindled or set on fire ; অনালোকিত ; অপ্রজ্বালিত, অদীপ্ত।

ŭn-light'-some (-lit-sŭm), *adj.* Dark ; "First the sun, A mighty sphere, he framed, *unlightsome* first" ; wanting light ; অন্ধকার ; আলোকহীন, নিষ্প্রভ, দীপ্তিহীন।

ŭn-līke', *adj.* Not like ; dissimilar ; অতুল্য, অসম, অন্যবিধ, অসদৃশ ; বিসদৃশ। **—li-hood,** *n.* The quality or state of being unlikely ; improbability ; অসম্ভাবনীয়তা ; অসম্ভাবনা। **—ly,** *adj.* & *adv.* Not likely or probable ; দুঃসম্ভাব্য, দুর্ঘট, অসম্ভব। ***Adv.*** In an improbable manner ; অসম্ভবরূপে। **Unlike-quantities**—বিভিন্ন অক্ষর বা অক্ষর সমূহের সংযোগ দ্বারা বা বিভিন্ন ঘাত বিশিষ্ট একই অক্ষর সমূহ দ্বারা গঠিত রাশি, অসমরাশি সমূহ **Unlike-signs** + (যোগ) এবং — (বিয়োগ) চিহ্ন।

ŭn-lĭm'-bêr, *adj.* Not flexible ; not yielding ; অদমনীয় ; অদম্য।

ŭn-lĭm′-bêr, *v. t.* To take off the limbers ; কামানবাহী শকটের যে অংশে অশ্ব সংযোজিত হয়—তাহা অপসারিত করা।

ŭn-lĭm′-ĭt-ȧ-ble (-bl), *adj.* Admitting of no limits ; boundless ; অসীম ; সীমাহীন।

ŭn-lĭm′-ĭt-ĕd, *adj.* **1.** Not limited ; having no bounds ; অসীমাবদ্ধ ; অপার, নিরবধি, অপরিমিত। **2.** Undefined ; অনির্দ্দিষ্ট, অনিরুক্ত। **—ly,** *adv.* **—ness,** *n.*

ŭn-lĭn′-ē-ăl, *adj.* Not coming in the order of succession ; অননুক্রমিক।

ŭn-link′ (-lĭngk), *v. t.* To separate the links of ; to unfasten ; to untwist ; "Seeing Orlando it (the snake) *unlinked* itself" ; জোড় খোলা ; বন্ধন মুক্তকরা ; পাক খোলা, কুণ্ডলী মুক্ত করা।

ŭn-liq′-ored (-lĭk-êrd), *adj.* Not moistened ; not smeared with liquor ; not filled or drunk with liquor ; অসিক্ত ; অমদ্যলিপ্ত ; অসুরাপূরিত, অসুরামত্ত, অমদমত্ত।

ŭn-liq′-ue-fied (-lĭk-wē-fīd), *adj.* Not melted ; not dissolved ; অগলিত ; অদ্রবিত।

ŭn-liq′-ui-dāt-ĕd (-lĭk-wē-), *adj.* Not settled ; as, an *unliquidated* debt ; অপরিশোধিত।

ŭn-lĭs′-ten-ĭng (-n-), *adj.* Not hearing or regarding ; অকর্ণপাতকারী, অনবধানপর।

ŭn-līve′-lȳ, *adj.* Not lively ; dull ; অস্ফূর্ত্তিদায়ক ; নীরস। **—li-ness,** *n.*

ŭn-load (-lōd), *v. i.* To take the load from ; to disburden ; to discharge ; বোঝা নামান ; ভারমুক্ত করা ; মুক্ত করা।

ŭn-lō′-cāt-ĕd, *adj.* Not fixed in a place ; not surveyed and designated ; অনিবেশিত ; অনির্দ্দিষ্ট।

ŭn-lŏck′, *v. i.* **1.** To unfasten what is locked ; to open ; তালা খোলা ; খোলা। **2.** To disclose ; to reveal : প্রকাশ করা, প্রকট করা ; উদ্‌ঘাটন করা।

ŭn-locked′ (-lŏkt), *adj.* Not made fast with a lock ; অতালকবদ্ধ।

ŭn-looked′-fŏr, (-lookt-), *adj.* Not expected ; not foreseen ; "Nor fame I slight, nor for her favours call ; she comes *unlookd for*, if she comes at all" ; অপ্রত্যাশিত ; অপূর্ব্বচিন্তিত।

ŭn-loose′ (-lôs), *v. t.* & *i.* To loose ; শিথিল করা, শ্লথ করা। ***Verb i.*** To lose all connection or union ; "Without this virtue the public union must *unloose*" ; সংযোগ হারান।

ŭn-love′-lȳ (-lŭv-), *adj.* Not lovely ; not amiable ; not attractive ; অসুন্দর, অমাধুর্য্যময় ; অকমনীয়, অরমণীয় ; অচিত্তাকর্ষক। **—li-ness,** *n.*

ŭn-lov′-ĭng (-lŭv-), *adj.* Not loving ; not fond ; অপ্রেমিক ; অননুরক্ত। **—ly,** *adv.*

ŭn-lū′-brĭ-cāt-ĕd, *adj.* Not lubricated ; অস্নেহাক্ত, অতৈললিপ্ত, অস্নেহমার্জ্জিত।

ŭn-lŭck′-ȳ, *adj.* **1.** Unfortunate ; দুর্ভাগ্য, হতভাগ্য, ভাগ্যহীন, মন্দভাগ্য। **2.** Bringing misfortune ; দুর্ভাগ্যজনক। **3.** Inauspicious ; অশুভ, অকুশল, অপায়া (*colloq.*)।

ŭn-lŭs′-trous (-trŭs), *adj.* Wanting lustre ; not shining ; দীপ্তিহীন ; অনুজ্জ্বল।

ŭn-lŭst′-ȳ, *adj.* Not stout ; weak ; অমাংসল ; দুর্ব্বল।

ŭn-lūte′, *v. t.* To separate things cemented or luted ; মৃত্তিকাদির লেপ দ্বারা সংযোজিত বস্তুদ্বয় বিযুক্ত করা।

ŭn-māde′, *adj.* **1.** Not yet formed ; omitted to be made ; অগঠিত ; অনির্ম্মিত। **2.** Deprived of its form or qualities ; আকৃতি বা গুণ বিরহিত।

ŭn-măg-nĕt′-ĭc, *adj.* Not having magnetic qualities ; অচৌম্বকধর্ম্মাক্রান্ত, অচুম্বকধর্ম্মী।

ŭn-maid′-en-lȳ (-mād-n), *adj.* Not becoming a maiden ; অকৌমার্য্যোচিত।

ŭn-maimed′ (-māmd), *adj.* Not disabled in any limb ; sound ; entire ; অবিকলাঙ্গ, অচ্ছিন্নাঙ্গ, অহীনাঙ্গ, অন্যূনাঙ্গ ; অক্ষত ; অভগ্ন।

ŭn-māk′-ȧ-ble (-bl), *adj.* Not possible to be made ; অনির্ম্মাণযোগ্য।

ŭn-make′, *v. t.* To destroy the form and qualities of ; "God does not make or *unmake* things to try experiment" ; to deprive of being ; ভাঙ্গা, নষ্ট করা ; অস্তিত্বলুপ্ত করা, সত্তাবিরহিত করা।

ŭn-măl-lē-ȧ-bĭl′-ĭ-tȳ, *n.* The state of being unmalleable ; অনাঘাতসহতা, অতাড়নবর্দ্ধনশীলতা।

ŭn-măl′-lē-ȧ-ble (-bl), *adj.* Not malleable ; অঘাতসহ, অতাড়নবর্দ্ধী।

ŭn-măn′, *v. i.* **1.** To deprive of the qualities of a man ; মনুষ্যোচিতগুণবিরহিত করা। **2.** To emasculate ; পুরুষত্বহীন করা, নির্বীর্য্য করা, ক্লীব করা। **3.** To deprive of courage or fortitude ; to break the spirit of ; to dishearten ; ধৈর্য্য, সাহস প্রভৃতি নষ্ট করা ; উৎসাহ ভঙ্গ করা ; নিরুৎসাহ করা। **—like,** *adj.* Not becoming a man ; অপুরুষোচিত। **—li-ness,** *n.* **—ly,** *adj.* **1.** Not like a man ; অমনুষ্যোচিত, অমানবোচিত। **2.** Effiminate ; নির্বীর্য্য, কাপুরুষ, পুরুষত্বহীন।

ŭn-măn′-āge-ȧ-ble (-bl), *adj.* Not easily restrained, governed or directed ; not controllable ; দুর্দ্দম, অশাস্য, দুর্দ্দমনীয়, দুর্দ্দান্ত, দুর্দ্ধর্ষ ; অদম্য।

ŭn-măn′-āged, *adj.* **1.** Not broken in as a horse ; not trained ; অসায়েস্তা ; অশিক্ষিত। **2.** Not tutored ; অশিক্ষাপ্রাপ্ত। **3.** Unrestrained ; অসংযত।

ŭn-manned′ (-mănd), *adj.* **1.** Deprived of the qualities of a man ; effiminate ; wanting fortitude ; পুরুষোচিতগুণবিরহিত ; নির্বীর্য্য ; বীর্য্যহীন।

2. Not furnished with men; অলোকসমাযুক্ত, অলোকসমন্বিত।

ŭn-măn'-ĭ-fĕst-ĕd, *adj.* Not manifested ; অব্যক্ত।

ŭn-man'-nered (-êrd), *adj.* Uncivil ; "You have a slanderous tongue * * * *unmannered* lord"; rude ; অশিষ্ট, অভদ্র ; রূঢ়।

ŭn-măn'-ner-lȳ (-êr-) *adj.* Not mannerly ; not having good manners; rude; অশিষ্ট, অভব্য; অভদ্র; রূঢ়, দুর্বিনীত। **—li-ness,** *n.*

ŭn-măn'-tled (-tld), *adj.* Not furnished with a mantle; অপ্রাবরণমণ্ডিত।

ŭn-măn-ū-făc'-tūred, *adj.* Not wrought into proper form or use ; অনির্ম্মিত।

ŭn-mă-nūred', *adj.* **1.** Not enriched by manure ; অসারপ্রদত্ত। **2.** Uncultivated ; অকর্ষিত, অকৃষ্ট।

ŭn-marked' (-mârkt), *adj.* **1.** Having no mark ; চিহ্নশূন্য, চিহ্নবিহীন। **2.** Unobserved ; "He mixed *unmarked* among the busy throng" ; অলক্ষিত।

ŭn-mâr'-kĕt-ă-ble (-bl), *adj.* Not salable ; অবিক্রেয়।

ŭn-marred' (-mârd), *adj.* Not injured or spoiled ; অক্ষত, অনষ্ট।

ŭn-mar'-riage-a-ble (-mă-rĭj-ă-bl), *adj.* Too young to be married ; অবিবাহযোগ্য, অপরিণেয়। **—ness,** *n.*

ŭn-mar'-ried (-mă-rĭd), *adj.* Having no husband or wife ; অবিবাহিত, অনুদ্বাহিত, অপরিণীত, আইবুড়ো (*colloq.*)

ŭn-mar'-rȳ (-mă-), *v. t.* To divorce; পত্নী ত্যাগ করা, পতি ত্যাগ করা, বিবাহ না করা।

ŭn-mâr'-shalled (-shăld), *adj.* Not disposed or arranged in order ; অশ্রেণীবদ্ধ।

ŭn-măs'-cū-line, *adj.* Not manly ; effeminate ; অপুরুষোচিত ; পুরুষত্বহীন।

ŭn-mâsk', *v. t.* & *i.* To strip of any disguise ; to expose ; মুখস খোলা, স্বরূপ প্রকাশ করা ; উদ্ঘাটিত করা, অনাবৃত করা। ***Verb i.*** To put off a mask ; মুখস খোলা।

ŭn-masked' (-mâskt), *adj.* Open ; exposed to view ; অনাবৃত ; উদ্ঘাটিত।

ŭn-măs'-tered (-têrd), *adj.* Not conquered ; অপরাজিত।

ŭn-măs'-tĭ-că-ble (-bl), *adj.* Not capable of being chewed; অচর্ব্বণীয়।

ŭn-match'-a-ble (-măch-ă-bl), *adj.* That cannot be equalled ; unparalleled ; অপ্রতিম ; অদ্বিতীয়, অতুলনীয়।

ŭn-matched' (-măcht), *adj.* Matchless ; having no equal ; অতুলনীয় ; অদ্বিতীয়।

ŭn-mean'-ĭng (-mēn-), *adj.* Having no signification ; not expressive ; অর্থহীন ; দ্যোতনাশূন্য। **—ly,** *adv.* **—ness,** *n.*

ŭn-meant' (-mĕnt), *adj.* Not meant ; অনভিপ্রেত।

ŭn-meas'-ur-a-ble (-mĕz-ūr-ă-bl), *adj.* That cannot be measured ; boundless; অপ্রমেয়; অসীম। **—ly,** *adv.*

ŭn-meas'-ured (-mĕz-ūrd), *adj.* Plentiful ; beyond measure ; immense ; infinite ; as, *unmeasured* space; প্রচুর; অপরিমিত; বিপুল; অসীম।

ŭn-mĕ-chăn'-ĭ-căl, *adj.* Not according to the principles of mechanics ; যন্ত্রবিজ্ঞানের নিয়মের বিরোধী। **—ly,** *adv.*

ŭn-mĕch'-ă-nīzed, *adj.* Not formed by mechanism ; অযন্ত্রগঠিত।

ŭn-mĕd'-dling (-lĭng), *adj.* Not interfering with the concerns of others ; not officious ; পরকার্য্যে অহস্তক্ষেপকারী ; অনুপযাচক।

ŭn-mĕd'-ĭ-tāt-ĕd, *adj.* Not prepared by previous thought ; অপূর্ব্বচিন্তিত।

ŭn-meet' (-mēt), *adj.* Not suitable (In modern use followed by *for*) ; "You are all *unmeet for* a wife"; অসঙ্গত, অসমীচীন, অযুক্ত, অযোগ্য, অনুচিত।

ŭn-mĕl'-lowed (-lōd), *adj.* Not fully ripened or matured ; not toned down or softened by ripeness, length of years or the like ; "An inconstant and *unmellowed* light" ; অপরিপক্ব ; অমেদুরিত ; অপ্রশমিত।

ŭn-mĕ-lō'-dĭ-ous (-ŭs), *adj.* Not melodious ; discordant ; "The *unmelodious* noise of the braying mules" ; অসুশ্রাব্য, অশ্রুতিমধুর ; বিস্বর, শ্রুতিকটু। **—ly,** *adj.*

ŭn-mĕlt'-ĕd, *adj.* Not melted ; not dissolved ; অগলিত, অবিদ্রাবিত, অদ্রবীভূত ; অবিলীন।

ŭn-mĕn'-ticn-ă-ble (-bl), *adj.* & *n.* That may not be mentioned ; অনুল্লেখযোগ্য। ***Noun*** (*Pl.*) (*Joc.*) Trousers ; (রহস্যস্থলে) পাজামা।

ŭn-mĕn'-tioned (-shŏnd), *adj.* Not mentioned ; অনুল্লিখিত।

ŭn-mêr'-căn-tīle, *adj.* Not according to the rules of commerce ; বাণিজ্যনিয়ম বিরোধী।

ŭn-mêr'-chănt-ă-ble, (-bl), *adj.* (*Obs.*) Not fit for the market ; unsaleable ; বাজারে বিক্রয়ের অনুপযোগী ; অবিক্রেয়, অবিক্রয়োপযোগী।

ŭn-mêr'-cĭ-fŭl, *adj.* Not merciful ; cruel ; নির্দ্দয়, অকরুণ, নির্ম্মম, নিষ্করুণ ; নিষ্ঠুর। **—ly,** *adv.* **—ness,** *n.*

ŭn-mĕ'-rĭt-ĕd, *adj.* Not deserved ; unjust ; অযোগ্য ; অনুচিত।

ŭn-mĕ-tăl'-lic (-ĭk), *adj.* Not having the properties of metal ; অধাতব।

ŭn-mĭl'-ĭ-tă-rȳ, *adj.* Not according to military rules ; অসামরিক।

ŭn-milked' (-mĭlkt), *adj.* Not milked ; অকৃতদোহন।

ŭn-milled' (-mĭld), *adj.* Not milled ; not stamped in a mill ; খাঁজ কাটা নয় ; অমুদ্রিত।

ŭn-mīnd'-ĕd, *adj.* Not minded ; not heeded ; অমনোনিবিষ্ট ; অনবহিত।

ŭn-mīnd'-fŭl, *adj.* Not mindful ; heedless ; অমনোযোগী ; অসতর্ক, অসাবধান। **—ly,** *adv.*

ŭn-min′-gle (-mĭng-gl), *v. t.* To separate ; মিশ্রিত বস্তু পৃথক করা, অমিশ্রিত করা।

ŭn-mĭng′-gled (-gld), *adj.* Not mixed ; pure ; অমিশ্রিত ; অবিমিশ্র।

ŭn-min-is-tē′-ri-ăl, *adj.* Not ministerial ; অমন্ত্রিসম্পর্কীয়।

ŭn-missed′ (-mĭsts), *adj.* Not perceived to be gone or lost ; অহৃত।

ŭn-mis-tāke′-ă-ble (-bl), *adj.* That cannot be mistaken ; অভ্রান্ত।

ŭn-mis-tāk′-en (-n), *adj.* Not mistaken ; অভ্রান্ত।

ŭn-mis-trŭst′-ing, *adj.* Unsuspicious ; অসন্দেহকারী, অশঙ্কাশীল, অসংশয়ী।

ŭn-mit′-i-gă-ble (-bl), *adj.* Not capable of being softened or lessened ; অপ্রশমনীয়।

ŭn-mit′-i-gāt-ĕd, *adj.* Not softened in severity or harshness ; অপ্রশমিত, অশমিত, অনুপশান্ত।

ŭn-mixed′ (-mĭkst), *adj.* Not mingled ; unadulterated ; pure ; unalloyed ; অমিশ্রিত ; নির্ভাজ ; নির্ম্মল, বিমল ; শুদ্ধ, অবিমিশ্র। **Unmixed happiness**—অবিমিশ্র আনন্দ, বিমল আনন্দ, নির্ম্মল সুখ।

ŭn-moaned′ (-mōnd), *adj.* Not lamented ; "Our fatherless distress was left *unmoaned*"; অশোচিত, অবিলপিত।

ŭn-mŏd′-ĕrn-īzed, *adj.* Not modernized ; অনব্যরীত্যনুযায়ীকৃত।

ŭn-mŏd′-i-fī-ă-ble (-bl), *adj.* That cannot be altered in form ; অপরিবর্ত্তনীয়। **—ness,** *n.*

ŭn-mŏd′-i-fied (-fīd), *adj.* Not altered in form ; অপরিবর্ত্তিত।

ŭn-mŏd′-ish, *adj.* Not according to custom or fashion ; অরীত্যনুযায়ী, প্রথাবিরোধী।

ŭn-mŏd′-ū-lāt-ĕd, *adj.* Not modulated ; অস্বরসংক্রমিত, স্বরবিভঙ্গীকৃত।

ŭn-moist′ (-moȳst), *adj.* Not moist ; dry ; অনার্দ্র ; শুষ্ক।

ŭn-mois′-tened (-moȳs-nd), *adj.* Not made moist or humid ; অনার্দ্রীকৃত, অসিক্ত।

ŭn-mō-lĕst′-ed, *adj.* Not disturbed or molested ; free from disturbance ; "Meanwhile the swains shall *unmolested* reap what plenty sows" ; অনুদ্বেজিত, অনুত্যক্ত ; অনিরুপদ্রুত।

ŭn-mōōr′, *v. t.* **1.** To loose from that to which anything is moored ; নৌকা প্রভৃতির বাঁধ খোলা। **2.** To bring to the state of riding with a single anchor after having been moored by two or more anchors ; to loose from anchorage ; একটী ব্যতীত অপর নোঙ্গর সকল তুলিয়া দুই বা ততোধিক নোঙ্গর দ্বারা বদ্ধ জাহাজ চালাইবার উপযোগী করা ; নোঙ্গর তোলা।

ŭn-mŏr′-ăl-īzed, *adj.* Untutored by morality ; অনীতিদুষ্ট।

ŭn-mŏrt′-găged, *adj.* Not mortgaged or pleged ; অবন্ধকদত্ত।

ŭn-mŏr′-ti-fied (-fīd), *adj.* Not shamed ; not subdued by sorrow ; অলজ্জিত ; অক্ষুণ্ণ, অমর্ম্মাহত।

ŭn-moth′-ĕr-lȳ (-mŭth-), *adj.* Unbecoming a mother ; অমাতৃসমুচিত।

ŭn-mould′ (-mōld), *v. t.* To change the form of ; আকার পরিবর্ত্তন করা। **—ed,** *adj.*

ŭn-mount′-ed (-mownt-), *adj.* Not mounted ; অনারূঢ়, অনারোপিত।

ŭn-mourned′, (-mōrnd), *adj.* Not lamented ; অশোচিত, অবিলপিত।

ŭn-mŏv′-ă-ble (-bl), *adj.* That cannot be moved ; firm ; immovable ; স্থাবর ; দৃঢ়, অটল, অচঞ্চল। **—bly,** *adv.*

ŭn-mŏved′, *adj.* Not transferred from one place to another ; not changed in purpose ; unshaken ; not affected ; calm ; অস্থানান্তরিত ; অটলসংকল্প, স্থিরসংকল্প স্থিরধী, অবিচলিত ; অকম্পিত ; অচঞ্চল ; শান্ত, প্রশান্ত।

ŭn-mŏv′-ing, *adj.* **1.** Having no motion ; গতিশূন্য। **2.** Not exciting emotion ; অহৃদয়স্পর্শী, অমর্ম্মস্পর্শী, অচিত্তদ্রাবী।

ŭn-mŭf′-fle (-l), *v. t.* To take a covering from the surface ; to remove the muffling of a drum ; আচ্ছাদনবস্ত্র অপসারিত করা ; ঢাকের আবরণ অপসারিত করা।

ŭn-mur′-mured (-mêr-mêrd), *adj.* Not murmured ; অমর্ম্মরিত।

ŭn-mur′-mur-ing (-mêr-mêr), *adj.* Not complaining ; as, *unmurmuring* patience ; অমর্ম্মর শব্দকারী।

ŭn-mū′-si-căl, *adj.* Not harmonions ; harsh ; অসুখশ্রাব্য ; শ্রুতিকটু।

ŭn-mū′-ti-lāt-ĕd, *adj.* Not deprived of a member or part ; entire ; অচ্ছিন্নাঙ্গ ; অটুট, অভগ্ন।

ŭn-mŭz′-zle (-l), *v. t.* To loose from a muzzle ; মুখবন্ধনী খোলা।

ŭn-nāme′-ă-ble (-bl) *adj.* That cannot be named ; অনামোল্লেখযোগ্য। **The unnameable**—ঈশ্বর।

ŭn-nāmed′, *adj.* Not named ; not mentioned; অনামোল্লিখিত; অনুল্লেখিত।

ŭn-năt′-ū-răl, *adj.* **1.** Not natural; contrary to the laws of nature ; "*Unnatural* deeds do breed *unnatural* troubles" ; অস্বাভাবিক, অপ্রাকৃত ; স্বভাবের নিয়ম বিরুদ্ধ। **2.** Inhuman ; অমানুষোচিত। **3.** Forced ; কষ্টকল্পিত। **—ly,** *adv.* **—ness,** *n.*

ŭn-năt′-ū-răl-īze, *v. t.* To divest of natural feelings ; স্বাভাবিক প্রবৃত্তি নষ্ট করা।

ŭn-năt′-ū-răl-īzed, *adj.* Not naturalized ; not made a citizen ; অশীতাতপাভ্যস্ত ; অরাষ্ট্রীয়াধিকারপ্রাপ্ত।

ŭn-năv′-i-gă-ble (-bl), *adj.* Not navigable ; অনাব্য, অনৌতার্য্য।

ŭn-năv′-i-gāt-ĕd, *adj.* Not navigated ; অনৌতারিত।

ŭn-nĕc′-ĕs-să-rȳ, *adj.* Not necessary ; needless ; useless ; অনর্থক, অনাবশ্যক ; অকারণ, নিষ্প্রয়োজন, অহেতুক ; অপ্রয়োজনীয়। **—ri-ly,** *adv.* In an unnecessary manner ;

অকারণে, অনর্থক, খামখা (*colloq.*) নিরর্থক, নিষ্প্রয়োজন, অযথা। **–riness,** *n.*

ŭn-nĕ-cĕs'-sĭ-tāt-ĕd, *adj.* Not required by necessity ; অনাবশ্যক।

ŭn-need'-ĕd (-nēd-), *adj.* Not needed ; অনাবশ্যক।

ŭn-need'-fŭl (-nēd-), *adj.* Not needful ; not wanted ; অনাবশ্যক ; অকাঙ্ক্ষিত।

ŭn-neigh'-bour-lȳ (-nā-bêr-), *adj.* Not suitable to the duties of a neighbour ; not kind and friendly ; অপ্রতিবেশিসমুচিত ; অদয়ালু, অবন্ধুভাবাপন্ন।

ŭn-nerve' (-nêrv), *v. t.* To deprive of nerve ; to weaken ; to enfeeble ; শক্তিহীন করা ; দুর্ব্বল করা ; নির্ব্বীর্য্য করা। **–nerved',** *adj.* Weak ; feeble ; দুর্ব্বল, শক্তিহীন ; নির্বীর্য্য।

ŭn-nō'-ble (-bl), *adj.* Ignoble ; mean ; হেয় ; নীচ, হীন।

ŭn-nōt-'-ĕd, *adj.* Not observed ; not distinguished ; অলক্ষিত ; অবিখ্যাত, অপ্রসিদ্ধ।

ŭn-nō'-ticed (-tĭst), *adj.* Not taken notice of ; not hospitably entertained ; অলক্ষিত ; অসৎকৃত, অনাদৃত।

ŭn-nŭm'-bered (-bêrd), *adj.* Innumerable ; not numbered ; অসংখ্য, অগণিত ; অসংখ্যাত।

ŭn-nur'-tured (-nër-türd), *adj.* Not nurtured or educated ; অপোষিত, অশিক্ষিত।

ŭn-nū-trĭ'-tions (-shŭs), *adj.* Not affording nourishment ; অপুষ্টিজনক।

ŭn-ŏb-jĕct'-ĕd, *adj.* Not charged, as a fault ; অপর্য্যদস্ত।

ŭn-ŏb-jĕc'-tion-ă-ble (-bl), *adj.* Not liable to objection ; অনাপত্তিসহ। **–bly,** *adv.*

ŭn-ō-blīg'-ing, *adj.* Not disposed to oblige ; অপ্রিয়কারী, অপ্রিয়কর।

ŭn-ŏb-scured' (-scürd), *adj.* Not darkened ; অতিমিরীকৃত, অস্পষ্টীকৃত।

ŭn-ŏb-sêrv'-ă-ble (-bl), *adj.* Not discoverable ; অলক্ষ্য।

ŭn-ŏb-sêrv'-ance (-ăns), *n.* The quality or state of being unobservant ; Inattention ; অপর্য্যবেক্ষণশীলতা ; অমনোযোগ।

ŭn-ŏb-sêrv'-ănt, *adj.* Not attentive ; headless ; অলক্ষ্যকারী, অমনোযোগী ; অনবহিত।

ŭn-ŏb-strŭct'-ĕd, *adj.* Not filled with impediments ; not hindered ; অপ্রতিহত ; অনবরুদ্ধ, অবাধ, অবারিত, অসংবাধ।

ŭn-ŏb-strŭc'-tive (-tĭv), *adj.* Not presenting any obstacle ; "Forward run in *unobstructive* sky"; অবাধাজনক, অনিরোধকর, অপ্রতিরোধক, অপ্রতিবাধক, অবাধকর।

ŭn-ŏb-tain'-a-ble (-tān-ă-bl), *adj.* Not within reach or power ; অপ্রাপ্য।

ŭn-ŏb-tained' (-tānd), *adj.* Not obtained ; not possessed ; অপ্রাপ্ত ; অনধিগত, অনধিকৃত, অলব্ধ।

ŭn-ŏb-tru'-sive (-trô-sĭv), *adj.* Not obtrusive ; not forward ; modest ; অধৃষ্ট ; অপ্রগল্‌ভ ; বিনীত, বিনয়ী। **–ly,** *adv.* **–ness,** *n.*

ŭn-ŏb'-vĭ-ous (-us), *adj.* Not readilly occurring to the understanding ; স্পষ্টতঃ অপ্রতীয়মান, অপ্রত্যক্ষগোচর।

ŭn-ŏc'-cū-pied (-pīd), *adj.* Not possessed ; as, *unoccupied* territories ; not occupied ; not occupied in business ; অনধিকৃত ; অনিযুক্ত ; অকার্য্যরত।

ŭn-ŏf-fĕnd'-ĕd, *adj.* Not having taken offence ; অদোষগৃহীত, অরুষ্ট।

ŭn-ŏf-fĕnd'-ing, –fĕn-sive (-sĭv), *adjs.* Not giving offence ; harmless ; free from sin ; অমনঃক্ষুণ্ণকর ; অহিংসক, নিরীহ ; নির্দ্দোষ।

ŭn-ŏf-fered (-fêrd), *adj.* Not proposed for acceptance ; অপ্রদত্ত।

ŭn-ŏf-fĭ'-cial (-shăl), *adj.* Not official ; বেসরকারী।

ŭn-ŏf-fĭ'-cious (-shŭs), *adj.* (*Obs.*) Not forward or over-busy ; (অপ্রঃ) অপ্রগল্‌ভ, অনতিব্যস্ত।

ŭn-ō'-pened (-pnd), *adj.* Not opened ; "Before the yet *unopen'd* door he stay'd ; অমুক্ত, অনুদ্ঘাটিত।

ŭn-ŏp'-ĕr-ā-tive (-tĭv), *adj.* Not producing any effect ; অকার্য্যকর, অফলোৎপাদক।

ŭn-ō-pêr'-cū-lāt-ĕd, *adj.* Having no operculum ; আচ্ছাদনহীন, আবরণশূন্য।

ŭn-ŏp-pōsed' *adj.* Not resisted ; অপ্রতিরুদ্ধ, অবাধিত।

ŭn-ŏp-prĕs'-sive (-ĭv), *adj.* Not oppressive ; অপীড়াজনক।

ŭn-ŏr'-dered (-dêrd), *adj.* Not ordered ; "Those long *unordered* troops so marshalled" ; অশ্রেণীবদ্ধ, অশৃঙ্খলাবদ্ধ।

ŭn-ŏr'-dêr-lȳ, *adj.* Disorderly ; irregular ; বিশৃঙ্খল ; শৃঙ্খলারহিত।

ŭn-ŏr'-găn-īzed, *adj.* Not organized ; not having organic structure ; inorganic ; অদেহবদ্ধ ; অব্যূহবদ্ধ ; অজৈব।

ŭn-ō-rĭg'-ĭ-năl, *adj.* 1. Derived ; উৎপন্ন। 2. Ungenerated ; "*Unoriginal* night and chaos wild" ; অনাদি।

ŭn-ō-rĭg'-ĭ-nāt-ĕd, *adj.* Having no birth or creation ; অনাদি।

ŭn-ŏr-nă-mĕn'-tăl, *adj.* Plain ; undecorated ; সাদাসিধা ; অভূষিত, অনলঙ্কৃত।

ŭn-ŏr'-thō-dŏx, *adj.* Not orthodox ; অপ্রাচীনপথাবলম্বী, প্রচলিতধর্ম্মবিরোধী।

ŭn-ŏs-tĕn-tā'-tious (-shŭs), *adj.* Not showy ; as, *unostentatious* colouring ; not boastful ; modest ; আড়ম্বরহীন, অনাড়ম্বর ; অগর্ব্বিত ; বিনয়ী। **–ly,** *adv.* **–ness,** *n.*

ŭn-owed' (-ōd), *adj.* Not owed ; অঋণবদ্ধ।

ŭn-owned' (-ōnd), *adj.* 1. Not owned ; having no known owner ;

অস্বামীক ; মালীকশূন্য। 2. Not confessed ; অস্বীকৃত।

ŭn-ŏx'-ȳ-gĕn-āt-ĕd, —ized, *adjs.* Not having oxygen in combination ; অম্লজানরহিত, অজারিত।

ŭn-pă-cĭf'-ic, *adj.* Not disposed to peace ; অশান্ত।

ŭn-păc'-i-fied (-fīd), *adj.* Not appeased ; অশমিত, অপ্রসাদিত।

ŭn-păck', *v. t.* To open, as things packed ; to disburden ; "*Unpack* my heart with words" ; প্যাক খোলা ; ভার মুক্ত করা।

ŭn-packed' (-păkt), *adj.* 1. Opened, as parcels or things that have been packed ; খোলা। 2. Not collected by unlawful means ; as, an *unpacked* jury ; অবৈধ উপায়ে অসংগৃহীত।

ŭn-paid' (-pād), *adj.* 1. Not discharged, as a debt ; অপরিশোধিত। 2. Not having received what is due ; অপ্রাপ্তমূল্য, মাশুলহীন। 3. Not receiving salary ; অবৈতনিক ; **Unpaid for**—ধারে-নেওয়া।

ŭn-pained' (-pānd), *adj.* Suffering no pain ; অব্যথিত।

ŭn-pain'-fŭl (-pān-), *adj.* Giving no pain ; অযন্ত্রণাদায়ক, অব্যথাজনক।

ŭn-paint'-ĕd (-pānt-), *adj.* Not painted ; অচিত্রিত, অলিখিত।

ŭn-păl'-ăt-ă-ble (-bl), *adj.* 1. Not palatable ; disgusting to the taste ; অমুখরোচক, অরসনাতৃপ্তিকর ; বিস্বাদ। 2. Disagreeable ; as, *unpalatable* counsel ; অপ্রীতিকর।

ŭn-păn'-ŏ-plied (-plīd), *adj.* Destitute of panoply ; বর্ম্মহীন, অবর্ম্মাবৃত।

ŭn-păr'-ă-dise, *v. t.* To deprive of happiness ; সুখহীন করা।

ŭn-păr'-ă-goned (-gŏnd), *adj.* Unequalled ; unmatched ; অদ্বিতীয়, অপ্রতিম ; অতুল্য, অতুলনীয়।

ŭn-păr'-al-leled (-ă-lĕld), *adj.* Having no parallel ; unequalled ; অদ্বিতীয় ; অপ্রতিম, অতুল্য।

ŭn-pâr'-don-a-ble (-dn-ă-bl), *adj.* Not to be forgiven ; অক্ষমণীয়, অক্ষমার্হ, অক্ষন্তব্য, অক্ষমাযোগ্য, অমার্জ্জনীয়।

ŭn-pâr'-doned (-dnd), *adj.* Not forgiven ; not having received a legal pardon ; অক্ষমিত ; অক্ষমাপ্রাপ্ত, অমার্জ্জিত।

ŭn-pâr'-don-ing (-dn-), *adj.* Not disposed to pardon ; "Whom Pallas with *unpardoning* fury fired" ; অক্ষমাকারী।

ŭn-pâr-lia-mĕn'-tă-rȳ (-lĭ-), *adj.* Contrary to the rules of proceedings in parliament, or to the usages or etiquette of legislative bodies ; পার্লেমেণ্ট বা অন্য কোন ব্যবস্থাপক সভার নিয়ম বা শিষ্টাচার বিরোধী।

ŭn-pârt'-ĕd, *adj.* Not parted ; অবিযুক্ত।

ŭn-pas'-sion-ate (-pă-), *adj.* Dispassionate ; impartial ; অনুরাগশূন্য ; রাগদ্বেষহীন।

ŭn-pas'-sioned (-pă-shŏnd), *adj.* Dispassioned ; অনুরাগশূন্য।

ŭn-pás'-tŏr-ăl, *adj.* Not suitable to pastoral manners ; অপল্লীসমুচিত।

ŭn-păt'-ĕnt-ĕd, *adj.* Not granted by patent ; প্যাটেণ্টশূন্য।

ŭn-pathed' (-pâthd), *adj.* Unmarked by passage, "*Unpathed* water" ; pathless ; অপথচিহ্নিত ; পথহীন।

ŭn-pa-thĕt'-ic, *adj.* Not adapted to move the passion ; অকরুণ।

ŭn-pa-tri-ŏt'-ic, *adj.* Not patriotic ; অস্বদেশপ্রেমিক, অস্বদেশপ্রেমোদ্দীপক, অস্বদেশপ্রেমিকোচিত।

ŭn-păt'-rŏn-ized, *adj.* Not supported by men of position ; "*Unpatronized* and therefore little known" ; অপৃষ্ঠপোষিত।

ŭn-păt'-terned (-ĕrnd), *adj* Having no pattern or equal ; অতুলনীয়, অদ্বিতীয়, অপ্রতিম।

ŭn-păved', *adj.* Not covered with stone ; অপাষাণবদ্ধ, আবাঁধা, কাঁচা।

ŭn-pawned' (-pänd), *adj.* Not pledged ; অবন্ধকদত্ত।

ŭn-peace'-a-ble (-pēs-ă-bl), *adj.* Not peaceful ; as, an *unpeaceable* disorder ; অশান্তিদায়ক।

ŭn-pĕg', *v. t.* To loose from pegs ; to open ; to pull out the peg from ; খোঁটা হইতে খোলা ; খোলা ; খোঁটা তোলা।

ŭn-pĕn', *v. t.* To let out or suffer to escape ; পালাইতে দেওয়া ছাড়িয়া দেওয়া।

ŭn-pē-năl, *adj.* Not subject to penalty ; অদণ্ডার্হ।

ŭn-pĕn'-ĕ-tră-ble (-bl), *adj.* Not to be penetrated ; অভেদ্য।

ŭn-pĕn'-ĕ-trāt-ĕd, *adj.* Not entered or pierced ; অবিদ্ধ।

ŭn-pĕn'-sioned (-shŏnd), *adj.* Not rewarded by a pension ; অপেন্সনপ্রাপ্ত।

ŭn-peo'-ple (-pē-pl), *v. t.* To depopulate ; লোকশূন্য করা, জনশূন্য করা, জনহীন করা।

ŭn-pêr-ceiv'-a-ble (-sēv-ă-bl), *adj.* Not to be perceived ; অবোধ্য।

ŭn-pêr-ceived' (-sēvd), *adj.* Not perceived ; অননুভূত।

ŭn-pêr'-fŏ-rāt-ĕd, *adj.* Not penetrated by openings ; অচ্ছিদ্রীকৃত।

ŭn-pêr-formed' (-fŏrmd), *adj.* Not done ; not fulfilled ; অসম্পাদিত ; অসম্পন্ন।

ŭn-pêr'-jured (-jŭrd), *adj.* Free from the crime of perjury ; অমিথ্যাসাক্ষ্যদত্ত।

ŭn-pêr'-mă-nĕnt, *adj.* Not permanent ; অস্থায়ী।

ŭn-pêr-mĭt'-ted, (-ĕd), *adj.* Not permitted ; অননুমতিপ্রাপ্ত।

ŭn-pêr'-sĕ-cūt-ĕd, *adj.* Not persecuted ; অনির্যাতিত।

ŭn-pêr-suad'-a-ble (-swād-ă-bl), *adj.* That cannot be persuaded or influenced ; অপ্রবৃত্তিজননযোগ্য।

ŭn-pêr-turbed' (-têrbd), *adj.* Not disturbed ; "*Unperturbed* by the wrongs and sorrows of mortals" ; অবিক্ষুব্ধ, অবিচলিত।

ŭn-pē-rūsed′, *adj.* Not read; অপঠিত।

ŭn-pêr-vêrt′-ĕd, *adj.* Not wrested or turned to a wrong use; অবিকৃত।

ŭn-pĕt-rĭ-fied (-fīd), *adj.* Not converted into stone; অপাষাণীভূত, অশিলীভূত।

ŭn-phĭl-ō-sŏph′-ĭc, *adj.* Contrary to the principles or methods of philosophy; অদার্শনিক। **–i-cal-ly,** *adv.* **–i-cal-ness,** *n.*

ŭn-phĭ-lŏs′-ō-phīse, *v. t.* To degrade from the character of a philosopher; অদার্শনিক করা।

ŭn-pierce′-a-ble (-pērs-ă-bl), *adj.* That cannot be pierced; অভেদ্য।

ŭn-pierced′ (-pērst), *adj.* Not penetrated; অবিদ্ধ।

ŭn-pĭl′-lared (-ĕrd), *adj.* Deprived of pillars; অস্তম্ভসমন্বিত।

ŭn-pĭl′-lowed (-lōd), *adj.* Having no pillow; উপধানশূন্য।

ŭn-pĭn′ *v. t.* To unfasten what is held together by pins; শঙ্কু-মুক্ত করা।

ŭn-pinked′ (-pĭngkt), *adj.* Not marked with eyelet-holes; পুঁটে ঘরা বা ফাঁসের ছিদ্রবিহীন।

ŭn-pĭt′-ied (-ĭd), *adj.* Not compassionated; অনমুকম্পাপ্রাপ্ত, অসমবেদনাপ্রাপ্ত।

ŭn-pĭt′-ĭ-fŭl –ȳ-ĭng, *adj.* Having no pity; showing no compassion; অকরুণ; নিষ্করুণ, নির্মম।

ŭn-placed′ (-plāst), *adj.* **1.** Not in its proper place; অযথাস্থানে স্থিত। **2.** Having no office or employment under government; সরকারী কর্মে অনিযুক্ত।

ŭn-plagued (-plāgd), *adj.* Not harassed; "Ladies that have your feet *unplagued* with corns"; অনুপক্রত, অনুদ্বেজিত, অনুত্যক্ত।

ŭn-plant′-ĕd, *adj.* Of spontaneous growth; স্বতঃ উৎপন্ন, অরোপিত।

ŭn-plau′-sĭ-ble (-plä-zĭ-bl), *adj.* Not plausible; আপাতরম্যতাহীন।

ŭn-plead′-a-ble (-plĕd-ă-bl), *adj.* That cannot be pleaded; "Ignorance was here *unpleadable*"; অপক্ষসমর্থনীয়।

ŭn-pleas′-ănt, (-plĕz-), *adj.* Not affording pleasure; disagreeable; অমনোরম, অপ্রীতিকর; অপ্রীতিজনক। **–ly,** *adv.* **–ness,** *n.*

ŭn-pleased′ (-plēzd), *adj.* Not pleased; অসন্তুষ্ট।

ŭn-pleas′-ĭng (-plēz-), *adj.* Offensive; disgusting; অরম্য, অমনোরম; বিরক্তিকর, বিরক্তিজনক।

ŭn-pledged′ (-plĕjd), *adj.* Not mortgaged; অবন্ধকদত্ত।

ŭn-plĭ′-ă-ble (-bl), *adj.* **1.** Not easily bent; অনম্য, অনমনীয়। **2.** Stiff; not compliant; কঠিন; অনম্র, অনমনশীল।

ŭn-ploughed′ (-plowd), *adj.* Not ploughed; অকর্ষিত, অকৃষ্ট।

ŭn-plūme′ *v. t.* **1.** To strip of plumes; পালকবিহীন করা। **2.** To degrade; অবনমিত করা, অবনত করা।

ŭn-plŭn′-dered (-dêrd), *adj.* Not plundered or stripped; অলুণ্ঠিত, অবিরহিত।

ŭn-pō-ĕt′-ĭc, –ĭ-căl, *adjs.* **1.** Not poetical; কবিত্বহীন,কবিত্বশূন্য। **2.** Not becoming a poet; অকবিজনোচিত। **–i-cal-ly,** *adv.*

ŭn-point′-ĕd′ (-poynt-), *adj.* **1.** Having no point or sting; without points; অসূক্ষ্ম; সূক্ষ্মাগ্রভাগবিহীন। **2.** Not having the marks of pronunciation; বিরামচিহ্নবিহীন।

ŭn-poised′ (-poyzd), *adj.* Not balanced; অসমতুলিত।

ŭn-pō-lăr-īsed, *adj.* Not having polarity; ধ্রুবতাহীন।

ŭn-pŏl′-ĭ-cied, (-sĭd), *adj.* Not having civil polity or a regular form of government; রাষ্ট্রব্যবস্থাহীন।

ŭn-pŏl′-ished (-ĭsht), *adj.* **1.** Not made smooth or bright by rubbing; অপরিমার্জ্জিত, অপরিকর্ম্মীকৃত। **2.** Not refined in manners; uncivilized; rude; অমার্জ্জিত; অসভ্য; রূঢ়।

ŭn-pō-līte′, *adj.* Not refined in manners; not civil or courteous; অমার্জ্জিতস্বভাব; অশিষ্ট, অভদ্র। **–ly,** *adv.* **–ness,** *n.*

ŭn-pōlled′ (-pōld), *adj.* **1.** Not registered as a voter; অনির্ব্বাচক-সমাজভুক্ত। **2.** Not stripped or plundered; অলুণ্ঠিত, অবিরহিত।

ŭn-pŏl′-lu-tĕd (-ū-), *adj.* Not defiled or polluted; অকলুষিত, অকলঙ্কিত, অদূষিত।

ŭn-pŏp′-ū-lar (-lêr), *adj.* Not popular; not pleasing to the people; অজনপ্রিয়; অলোকরঞ্জক, অজনরঞ্জক। **–lar′-i-ty,** *n.* **–ly,** *adv*

ŭn-pōrt′-ă-ble (-bl), *adj.* Not capable of being carried; অবহন-যোগ্য, অবহনোপযোগী।

ŭn-pōr′-tioned (-shŏnd), *adj.* Not furnished with a portion or fortune; অযৌতুকদত্ত।

ŭn-pŏs-sessed′(-zĕst),*adj.* Not held; not occupied; অগৃহীত; অনধিকৃত।

ŭn-pŏs-sĕss′-ĭng, *adj.* Having no possession; অধিকারশূন্য।

ŭn-prăc′-tĭ-căl, *adj.* Not practical; অকৃতকর্ম্মা, অকার্য্যকর।

ŭn-prăc′-tised (-tĭst), *adj.* Not skilled; not having experience; raw; অনিপুণ; অনভ্যস্ত; কাঁচা।

ŭn-praised′-(-prāzd), *adj.* Not extolled or celebrated; অগুণকীর্ত্তিত, অপ্রশংসিত, অস্তুত।

ŭn-prē-ca′-rĭ-ous (-ŭs), *adj.* Not precarious; অদৈবায়ত্ত, অদৈবাধীন, অসংশয়াপন্ন।

ŭn-prē′-cēd′-ĕd, *adj.* Not preceded; অপুরোগত।

ŭn-prĕc′-ē-dĕnt-ĕd, *adj.* Having no precedent or example; অপূর্ব্ব, অভূতপূর্ব্ব। **–ly,** *adv.*

ŭn-prē-cīse′ *adj.* Not precise; not exact; অসঠিক; অনিশ্চিত।

ŭn-prē-dĕs′-tined′(-tĭnd),*adj.* Not previously determined; অপূর্ব্বনির্দ্দিষ্ট

ŭn-prĕj′-ū-diced (-dĭst), *adj.* Not prejudiced ; free from bias ; পক্ষপাতশূন্য, নিরপেক্ষ ; অপক্ষপাতমূলক ।

ŭn-prē-lăt′-ĭ-ăl, *adj.* Unsuitable to a prelate ; অধর্ম্মাধ্যক্ষসমুচিত ।

ŭn-prē-mĕd′-ĭ-tāt-ĕd, *adj.* Not previously prepared in the mind ; as, an *unpremeditated* verse ; not done by design ; অপূর্ব্বচিন্তিত ; অপূর্ব্বসংকল্পিত । **—ly,** *adv.*

ŭn-prē-pared′ (-pârd), *adj.* **1.** Not prepared ; অপ্রস্তুত । **2.** Not prepared for death or eternity ; "I will not kill thy *unprepared* spirit" ; মৃত্যু বা অনন্তজীবনলাভের জন্য অপ্রস্তুত ।

ŭn-prē-pŏs-sessed′ (-zĕst), *adj.* Not biassed by previous opinion ; "A competent and *unprepossessed* judge" ; অপক্ষপাতদুষ্ট, অপক্ষপাতযুক্ত ।

ŭn-prē-pŏs-sĕss′-ing, *adj.* Not having a winning appearance ; অসুন্দর, অচিত্তাপহারী, অচিত্তাকর্ষক ।

ŭn-prē-sĕrv′-ă-ble (-bl), *adj.* That cannot be preserved ; অরক্ষণযোগ্য ।

ŭn-prē-sĕnt′-ă-ble (-bl), *adj.* Not presentable; অপ্রদর্শনযোগ্য, অনিবেদ্য ।

ŭn-pressed′ (-prĕst), *adj.* **1.** Not pressed ; অসঙ্কাপিত । **2.** Not enforced ; অবলপ্রবর্ত্তিত ।

ŭn-prē-sŭm′-ing, *adj.* Not presuming; modest ; humble; অপ্রগল্ভ, অনুদ্ধত ; বিনয়ী, বিনীত ; বিনয়নম্র ।

ŭn-prē-sump′-tu-ous (-zŭm-tū-ŭs), *adj.* Not presumptuous or arrogant ; humble ; submissive ; modest ; অনুদ্ধত, অপ্রগল্ভ ; বিনীত ; বশম্বদ ; বিনয়ী, নম্রস্বভাব ।

ŭn-prē-tĕnd′-ing, *adj.* Not claiming distinction ; modest ; অগর্ব্বিত ; বিনয়ী ।

ŭn-prē-vail′-ing (-vāl-). *adj.* (*Obs.*) Unavailing ; (অপ্রঃ) নিষ্ফল, নিরর্থক ।

ŭn-prĕv′-ă-lĕnt, *adj.* Not prevalent ; অপ্রবল, অপ্রচলিত, অব্যাপক ।

ŭn-prē-vĕnt′-ă-ble (-bl), *adj.* Not preventable ; অনিবার্য্য ।

ŭn-prē-vĕnt′-ĕd, *adj.* Not prevented ; অনিবারিত, অবারিত ।

ŭn-priest′-lȳ (-prēst-), *adj.* Not becoming a priest ; অযাজকোচিত ।

ŭn-prince′ (-prĭns), *v. t.* To deprive of principality or sovereignty ; "Queen Mary......would not *unprince* herself to obey his Holiness" ; রাজপদ হইতে চ্যুত করা ।

ŭn-prince′-lȳ (-prĭns-), *adj.* Unbecoming a prince ; অরাজোচিত, অনৃপসমুচিত ।

ŭn-prĭn′-cĭ-pled (-pld), *adj.* Having no settled principles ; having no good moral principles; destitute of virtue; profligate; অব্যবস্থিতচিত্ত; নীতিজ্ঞানহীন ; ধর্ম্মহীন ; ব্যভিচারপরায়ণ ।

ŭn-print′-ĕd, *adj.* Not printed ; অমুদ্রিত ।

ŭn-prĭs′-oned (-ŏnd), *adj.* Set free from confinement ; অকারামুক্ত ।

ŭn-priv′-ĭ-leged (-lĕjd), *adj.* Not enjoying a particular privilege or immunity ; অবিশেষ অধিকারপ্রাপ্ত ।

ŭn-prīzed′, *adj.* Not valued; অনাদৃত ।

ŭn-prō-claimed′ (-klāmd), *adj.* Not notified by public declaration ; অঘোষিত ।

ŭn-prō-duc′-tive (-tĭv), *adj.* **1.** Not productive ; not producing large crops ; as, *unproductive* land ; অফলোৎপাদক ; অফলপ্রসূ । **2.** Not making profitable returns for labour ; অলাভজনক । **3.** Not efficient ; অকার্য্যকর ।

ŭn-prō-faned′ *adj.* Not profaned or violated ; অকলুষিত, অলঙ্ঘিত, অধর্ষিত ।

ŭn-prō-fes′-sion-ăl (-fĕ-), *adj.* **1.** Not pertaining to one's profession ; অব্যবসায়সম্পর্কীয় । **2.** Not belonging to a profession ; অব্যবসায়িসমাজভুক্ত । **3.** Not becoming a member of any profession ; অব্যবসায়িসমুচিত ।

ŭn-prŏf′-ĭt-ă-ble (-bl), *adj* Bringing no profit ; useless; as, an *unprofitable* servant অলাভজনক, অনর্থক ; অকার্য্যকর। **—bly,** *adv.* **—ness,** *n.*

ŭn-prŏf′-ĭt-ĕd, *adj.* Not having profit or gain ; অকৃতলাভ ।

ŭn-prō-gres′-sive (-ĭv), *adj.* Not advancing ; অনুন্নতিশীল ।

ŭn-prō-jĕct′-ĕd, *adj.* Not planned ; অকল্পিত ।

ŭn-prō-lĭf′-ĭc, *adj.* Not prolific ; barren ; not producing fruit ; অবহুপ্রজ ; বন্ধ্য ; অসন্তানোৎপাদক, নিষ্ফল ।

ŭn-prŏm′-ĭs-ing, *adj.* Not affording a favourable prospect of success ; as, an *unpromising* youth ; অনাশ্বাসজনক ।

ŭn-prompt′-ed (-prŏmt-), *adj.* Not dictated or instigated ; অপ্ররোচিত ।

ŭn-prō-nounce′-a-ble (-nowns-ă-bl), *adj.* **1.** That cannot be pronounced ; অনুচ্চার্য্য । **2.** Unfit to be pronounced ; অকথ্য, অবাচ্য ।

ŭn-prō-nounced′ (-nownst), *adj.* Not pronounced ; অনুচ্চারিত ।

ŭn-prŏp′, *v. t.* To deprive of support ; অবলম্বনবিহীন করা ।

ŭn-prō-phĕt′-ĭc, *adj.* Not foreseeing future event ; অভবিষ্যদর্শী ।

ŭn-prō-pĭ′-tious (-shŭs), *adj.* Not favourable ; inauspicious ; প্রতিকূল ; অশুভ, অপ্রসন্ন ।

ŭn-prō-pŏr′-tion-ă-ble (-bl), **—ate,** *adjs.* Wanting due proportion ; disproportionate ; unfit ; সঙ্গতিশূন্য ; অসমঞ্জস ; অযোগ্য ।

ŭn-prō-pŏr′-tioned (-shŏnd), *adj.* Not proportioned or suitable অসমঞ্জসীকৃত, অযথোচিত ।

ŭn-prō-posed′ (-pōzd), *adj.* Not proposed ; অপ্রস্তাবিত ।

ŭn-propped′ (-prŏpt), *adj.* Not supported ; অনবলম্বিত ।

ŭn-prŏs′-ē-lȳt-ĕd, *adj.* Not made a convert ; অধর্ম্মান্তরগ্রহিত ।

ŭn-prŏs′-pĕr-ous (-ŭs), *adj.* Not attended with success ; নিষ্ফল, বিফল । **—ly,** *adv.* **—ness,** *n.*

ŭn-prŏs'-ti-tūt-ĕd, *adj*. Not debased ; অকলঙ্কিত, অকলুষিত।

ŭn-prō-tĕct'-ĕd, *adj*. Not protected ; অরক্ষিত, অনভিরক্ষিত।

ŭn-prō-tĕct'-ing, *adj*. Not defending ; অরক্ষাকারী।

ŭn-prŏt'-ĕs-tănt-ize, *v. t*. To take away the protestant character; অপ্রোটেষ্টেন্টভাবাপন্ন করা।

ŭn-prō-tract'-ĕd, *adj*. Not drawn out in length ; অবিলম্বিত, অচিরায়ত।

ŭn-prôved, *adj*. Not known by trial ; not established as true ; অপ্রমাণিত ; অপ্রতিপন্ন।

ŭn-prō-vīd'-ĕd, *adj*. Not provided or furnished ; অসজ্জিত।

ŭn-prō-voked' (-vōkt), *adj*. Not incited ; not proceeding from provocation অনুত্তেজিত ; অনুত্তেজনা-প্রসূত।

ŭn-prō-vōk'-ing, *adj*. Giving no offence ; অপ্রকোপজনক, অপ্রকোপক, অক্রোধোত্তেজক।

ŭn-pruned' (-prônd), *adj*. Not pruned or lopped ; অচ্ছিন্ন, অকর্ত্তিত।

ŭn-pŭb'-lished (-lĭsht), *adj*. 1. Not made public ; secret ; অপ্রকাশিত ; গুপ্ত, গোপনীয়। 2. Not published, as a book ; (পুস্তক সম্বন্ধে) অপ্রকাশিত।

ŭn-punc'-tū-ăl (-pŭngk-), *adj*. Not exact in time; অসময়নিষ্ঠ, অসময়সেবী।

ŭn-punc'-tū-āt-ĕd (-pŭngk-), *adj*. Not pointed ; অবিরামচিহ্নিত।

ŭn-pŭn'-ish-ă-ble (-bl), *adj*. That may not be punished ; অদণ্ডার্হ, অদণ্ডনীয়।

ŭn-pur'-chas-a-ble (-pêr-chās-ă-bl), *adj*. That cannot be bought ; অক্রেয়, অক্রয়যোগ্য।

ŭn-purged' (-pêrjd), *adj*. Unpurified ; অপবিত্রীকৃত।

ŭn-pū'-ri-fied (-fīd), *adj*. Unsanctified ; অপবিত্রীকৃত, অপুণ্যীকৃত।

ŭn-pur'-posed (-pêr-pöst), *adj*. Not intended ; অনভিপ্রেত।

ŭn-pur-sued' (-pêr-süd), *adj*. Not followed ; অননুসৃত।

ŭn-pū'-trē-fied (-fīd), *adj*. Not corrupted ; অগলিত, অপূতীভূত।

ŭn-quaffed' (-kwăft), *adj*. Not quaffed ; অনিঃশেষপীত, অপান-নিঃশেষিত।

ŭn-quail'-ing (-kwāl-), *adj*. Not shaking ; firm ; অকম্পিত ; অটল।

ŭn-quāk'-ing, *adj*. Not shaking or trembling ; অকম্পিত।

ŭn-qual'-i-fied (-kwŏl-ë-fīd), *adj*. 1. Not having requisite qualities ; অযোগ্য। 2. Not modified or restricted by conditions or exceptions ; অবিমিশ্র।

ŭn-queen' (-kwēn), *v. t*. To divest of the dignity of a queen ; রাণীর মর্য্যাদা হইতে চ্যুত করা।

ŭn-quĕll'-ă-ble (-bl), *adj*. That cannot be quelled ; অপ্রশমনীয়, অশমনীয়।

ŭn-quelled' (-kwĕld), *adj*. Not quelled or subdued ; অপ্রশমিত, অদমিত, অনিবর্ত্তিত।

ŭn-quĕnch'-ă-ble (-bl), *adj*. That cannot be quenched ; inextinguishable ; অশমনীয় ; অনির্ব্বাপ্য।

ŭn-quenched' (-kwĕncht), *adj*. Not quenched ; অশমিত, অনির্ব্বাপিত।

ŭn-ques'-tion-a-ble (-kwĕs-tyŭn-ă-bl), *adj*. Not to be questioned or doubted ; as, an *unquestionable* evidence ; অবিতর্ক্য, নিঃসন্দেহ।

ŭn-ques'-tioned (-kwĕs-tyŭnd), *adj*. 1. Not called in question ; not doubted ; অতর্কিত ; অসন্দেহীকৃত। 2. Not examined ; indisputable ; অজিজ্ঞাসিত ; অবিতর্ক্য।

ŭn-ques'-tion-ing (-kwĕs-tyŭn-), *adj*. Not calling in question ; not doubting ; অপ্রশ্নকারী ; অসন্দেহকারী।

ŭn-quick'-ened (-nd), *adj*. Not matured to vitality ; অসঞ্জীবিত, অসজীবীকৃত।

ŭn-quī'-ĕt, *adj*. 1. Not calm or tranquil ; restless ; অশান্ত ; চঞ্চল, অস্থির। 2. Not quiet ; উদ্বেগপূর্ণ। **—ly**, *adv*. **—ness**, *n*.

ŭn-racked' (-răkt), *adj*. Not drawn off from the lees, as wine ; গাদ হইতে অনিষ্কর্ষিত।

ŭn-raised' (-rāzd), *adj*. Not elevated or raised ; অনুত্তোলিত।

ŭn-rānged', *adj*. Not reduced to rank or order ; অশ্রেণীবদ্ধ।

ŭn-răn'-sacked (-săkt), *adj*. Not searched ; অননুসন্ধিত, অনন্বেষিত।

ŭn-răn'-somed (-sŭmd), *adj*. Not liberated from captivity or bondage by payment ; অধনপ্রদানমুক্ত।

ŭn-răv'-āged, *adj*. Not wasted or destroyed ; অধ্বংসীকৃত, অনুৎসাদিত।

ŭn-răv'-ĕl, *v. t. & i*. 1. To disentangle or extricate ; to free from complication or difficulty ; গ্রন্থি, পাক, প্রভৃতি খোলা ; গোলযোগ ইত্যাদি হইতে মুক্ত করা। 2. To unfold ; উদ্ঘাটন করা। ***Verb i.*** To be unfolded ; to be disentangled ; উদ্ঘাটিত হওয়া ; গ্রন্থি প্রভৃতি মুক্ত হওয়া। **—ment**, *n*.

ŭn-rā'-zored (-zōrd), *adj*. Unshaven ; অক্ষৌরিত।

ŭn-reached' (-rēcht), *adj*. Not attained to ; অপ্রাপ্ত, অলব্ধ।

ŭn-read' (-rĕd), *adj*. Not perused ; untaught ; not learned in books ; "The clown *unread* or half-read gentleman" ; অপঠিত, অনধীত ; অপাঠিত ; অশিক্ষিত।

ŭn-read'-a-ble (-rēd-ă-bl), *adj*. That cannot be read ; as, an *unreadable* manuscript ; অপাঠ্য, অপাঠোদ্ধারযোগ্য।

ŭn-read'-ȳ (-rĕd-), *adj*. 1. Not prepared ; অপ্রস্তুত। 2. Not fit ; অনুপযোগী। 3. (*Obs.*) Awkward ; (অপ্রঃ) বিতিকিচ্ছি। 4. (*Obs.*) Not dressed ; (অপ্রঃ) অপরিচ্ছদপরিহিত।

ŭn-rē'-ăl, *adj*. Not real ; not substantial ; "Hence, horrible shadow ! *unreal* mockery hence" ; having appearance only ; অবাস্তব, ধার-করা (কথাটা যেন ধার করার মতন শোনাইল) ; অবাস্তবিক, অসৎ, অসার, অমূর্ত্ত ; আভাসিক। **—al'-i-ty**, *n*.

ŭn-rē-ăl-īze, *v. t.* To idealize ; অমূর্ত্ত করা।

ŭn-reaped′ (-rēpt), *adj.* Not reaped ; অকর্ত্তিত, অচ্ছিন্ন।

ŭn-rea′-son-a-ble (-rē-zn-ă-bl), *adj.* 1. Not reasonable ; অযৌক্তিক, অযুক্তিসিদ্ধ। 2. Immoderate ; অতিরিক্ত। **—bly**, *adv.* **—ness**, *n.*

ŭn-rea′-soned (-rē-znd), *adj.* Not derived from reasoning; অযুক্তিসিদ্ধ।

ŭn-rea′-son-ing, (-rē-zn-), *adj.* Not having reasoning faculties ; devoid of reasoning ; অবুদ্ধিবৃত্তিসম্পন্ন, যুক্তিহীন।

ŭn-reave′ (-rēv), *v. t.* To unwind ; to unravel; পাক খোলা; উদ্ঘাটন করা।

ŭn-rē-băt′-ĕd, *adj.* Not blunted ; "A number of fencers tried with *unrebated* swords" ; অকুণ্ঠিত।

ŭn-rē-bŭk′-ă-ble (-bl), *adj.* Not deserving rebuke ; অতিরস্করণীয়।

ŭn-rē-buked′ (-bŭkt), *adj.* Not rebuked ; অতিরস্কৃত।

ŭn-rē-cănt′-ĕd, *adj.* Not retracted ; অপ্রত্যাহৃত।

ŭn-rē-ceived′ (-sēvd), *adj.* Not received ; not come into possession ; অগৃহীত ; অনধিকারপ্রাপ্ত।

ŭn-rĕck′-oned (-nd), *adj.* Not counted ; অগণিত।

ŭn-rē-claim′-a-ble (-klām-ă-bl), *adj.* That cannot be reclaimed ; অনাবাদযোগ্য।

ŭn-rĕc′-ŏg-nīz-ă-ble (-bl), *adj.* That cannot be recognized ; অপরিচেয়।

ŭn-rĕc′-ŏg-nīsed, *adj.* Not recognised ; অপরিচিত।

ŭn-rĕc′-ŏm-pensed (-pĕnst), *adj.* Not rewarded ; অপুরস্কৃত।

ŭn-rĕc-ŏn-cīl-ă-ble (-bl), *adj.* Irreconcilable; অসমাধেয়,অপুনর্মিলনযোগ্য।

ŭn-rĕc′-ŏn-cīled, *adj.* Not reconciled ; অপুনর্মিলিত।

ŭn-rē-cŏrd′-ĕd, *adj.* 1. Not registered ; অলিপিবদ্ধ। 2. Not kept in remembrance ; অস্মৃত।

ŭn-rē-count′-ĕd, (-kownt-), *adj.* 1. Not told ; অকথিত। 2. Not related or recited ; অবর্ণিত।

ŭn-rē-cov′-er-a-ble (-kŭv-ĕr-ă-bl), *adj.* 1. That cannot be recovered ; অনুদ্ধার্য্য। 2. Past recovery ; "'T is the dead palsy, that, without almost a miracle, leaves a man *unrecoverable*" ; অচিকিৎস্য, অসাধ্য

ŭn-rē-cov′-ered (-kŭv-ĕrd), *adj.* Not recalled into possession ; অপুনরুদ্ধারিত, অপ্রত্যুপলব্ধ, অপুনঃগৃহীত।

ŭn-rĕc′-tĭ-fied (-fīd), *adj.* Not corrected ; অসংশোধিত।

ŭn-rē-deem′-a-ble(-dēm-ă-bl),*adj.* That cannot be redeemed; অনুদ্ধার্য্য, অপরিবিক্রেয়, অপরিক্রেতব্য, অপরিশোধ্য।

ŭn-rē-deemed′(-dēmd),*adj.* 1. Not ransomed ; অপরিক্রীত। 2. Not paid ; অপরিশোধ্য। 3. Without a redeeming quality ; "The *unredeemed* ugliness of a slothful people" ; গুণলেশহীন।

ŭn-rē-dressed′ (-drĕst), *adj.* Not relieved from injustice ; not reformed ; as, *unredressed* evils ; অপ্রতিকৃত ; অসংশোধিত।

ŭn-rē-duced′ (-dūst), *adj.* Not lessened in size or amount ; অন্যূনীভূত, অন্যূনীকৃত।

ŭn-rē-dŭc′-ĭ-ble (-bl), *adj.* Not capable of reduction ; অহ্রস্বীকরণীয়।

ŭn-reeled′ (-rēld), *adj.* Not reeled or wound from cocoons; অপরিবেষ্টিত।

ŭn-rē-fined′ (-fīnd), *adj.* 1. Not refined or purified ; অশোধিত, অবিশোধিত। 2. Not polished in manners ; অমার্জ্জিত, অপরিমার্জ্জিত।

ŭn-rē-fŏrm′-ă-ble (-bl), *adj.* That cannot be reformed or amended ; অসংশোধনীয়।

ŭn-rē-formed′(-fŏrmd), *adj.* 1. Not reclaimed from vice ; অসংশোধিতচরিত্র। 2. Not amended ; as, an *unreformed* calendar ; অসংশোধিত।

ŭn-rē-frăct′-ĕd, *adj.* Not refracted, as rays of light ; অপরাবর্ত্তিত।

ŭn-rē-freshed′ (-frĕsht), *adj.* Not relieved from fatigue ; অনপগতক্লান্তি, অহৃতক্লান্তি, অবিগতশ্রম।

ŭn-rē-frĕsh′-fŭl, *adj.* Not adapted to refresh : অক্লান্তিহর, অশ্রমাপহারী।

ŭn-rē-frĕsh′-ĭng, *adj.* Not invigorating ; not cooling ; অশ্রান্তিহর, অক্লান্তিনাশক ; অশৈত্যজনক।

ŭn-rē-fŭt′-ĕd, *adj.* Not proved to be false ; অখণ্ডিত।

ŭn-rē-gărd-ĕd, *adj.* Not neglected ; অনবহেলিত।

ŭn-rē-gărd′-fŭl, *adj.* Not giving attention ; heedless ; অমনোযোগী ; অনবধান, অনবহিত।

ŭn-rē-ğĕn′-ĕr-ă-ŏy̆, *n.* The state of being unregenerate ; অনবজীবনপ্রাপ্তি।

ŭn-rē-ğĕn′-ĕr-āte, *adj.* Not regenerated ; অনবজীবনপ্রাপ্ত।

ŭn-rĕğ′-ĭs-tered(-tĕrd),*adj.* 1. Not registered ; অরেজেষ্টরী। 2. Not recorded ; অলিপিবদ্ধ।

ŭn-rē-grĕt′-ted (-ĕd), *adj.* Not lamented ; অশোচিত।

ŭn-rĕg′-ū-lāt-ĕd, *adj.* Not reduced to order ; অনিয়মিত, অনিয়মবদ্ধ।

ŭn-rē-hearsed′ (-hĕrst), *adj.* Not recited or repeated ; অনাবৃত্তীকৃত।

ŭn-reined′ (-rānd), *adj.* Unrestrained ; অসংযত, উচ্ছৃঙ্খল।

ŭn-rē-joic′-ĭng (-joys-), *adj.* Unjoyous ; gloomy ; sad ; অপ্রফুল্ল ; নিরানন্দ ; বিষণ্ণ।

ŭn-rē-lăt′-ĕd, *adj.* 1. Not related by blood or affinity ; অসম্পর্কীয়, অসম্বন্ধান্বিত। 2. Having no connection ; সম্পর্কশূন্য, সম্পর্কহীন।

ŭn-rē-lĕnt′-ĭng, *adj.* Not relenting ; inflexibly rigid ; নির্দ্দয় ; কঠোর।

ŭn-rē-lī′-ă-ble (-bl), *adj.* Not reliable ; not to be relied or depended on ; অবিশ্বাসযোগ্য ; অবিশ্বাস্য, অপ্রত্যয়যোগ্য।

ŭn-rē-liev′-a-ble (-lēv-ă-bl), *adj.* Admitting of no relief ; অদুঃখপ্রশমনীয়, অশমনীয়।

ŭn-rē-lieved′ (-lēvd), *adj.* 1. Not relieved or delivered from pain; অপ্রশমিত। 2. Not succoured; অসাহায্যপ্রাপ্ত। 3. Not released from duty; অনুদ্ধারিত।

ŭn-rē-mȧrk′-ă-ble(-bl), *adj.* 1. Not worthy of particular notice; অলক্ষ্যযোগ্য। 2. Not capable of being observed; "This fleeting and *unremarkable* superficies"; অপর্যবেক্ষণীয়।

ŭn-rē-marked′ (-mȃrkt), *adj.* Unobserved; অলক্ষীকৃত।

ŭn-rē-mē′-dĭ-ă-ble (-bl), *adj.* That cannot be cured; অপ্রতীকারশক্য।

ŭn-rĕm′-ē-died (-dĭd), *adj.* Not cured; not remedied; অরোগমুক্ত: অপ্রতিকৃত।

ŭn-rē-mĕm′-bered (-bērd), *adj.* Not retained in the mind; অস্মৃত।

ŭn-rē-mĭt′-ted (-ĕd), *adj.* Not remitted; not forgiven; not relaxed; as, pain *unremitted*; অপ্রেরিত: অক্ষমিত; অশিথিলীকৃত।

ŭn-rē-mĭt′-ting (-ĭng), *adj.* Not relaxing; incessant; অবিরল; বিরামবিহীন, অবিরাম। **—ly**, *adv.*

ŭn-rē-morse′-fûl (-mörs-), *adj.* Remorseless; অনুশোচনাবিহীন।

ŭn-rē-mōve′-ă-ble (-bl), *adj.* That cannot be removed; fixed; অচালনীয়, অস্থানান্তরকরণীয়; অচল, অটল, দৃঢ়নিবদ্ধ। **—ness**, *n.*

ŭn-rē-mōved′, *adj* Not taken away; not capable of being removed: অচালিত: অস্থানান্তরচালনীয়।

ŭn-rē-newed′ (-nūd), *adj.* 1. Not made anew; অনবীকৃত, অনবীভূত। 2. Not regenerated; অনবজীবনপ্রাপ্ত।

ŭn-rē-nowned′ (-nownd), *adj.* Not renowned; অপ্রসিদ্ধ, অবিখ্যাত, অলব্ধকীর্তি, অবিশ্রুতনামা, অকীর্তিমান, অযশস্বী, অখ্যাতনামা।

ŭn-rē-paid′ (-pād), *adj.* Not compensated; অক্ষতিপূরিত।

ŭn-rē-paired′ (-pārd), *adj.* Not repaired or mended; অপুনঃসংস্কৃত।

ŭn-rē-pealed (-pēld), *adj.* Not revoked or abrogated; অখণ্ডিত, অরহিত।

ŭn-rē-pĕnt′-ănt′, **—ing**, *adjs.* Not penitent; অপশ্চাত্তাপী, অননুতপ্ত।

ŭn-rē-pĕnt′-ĕd, *adj.* Not repented of; অননুতপ্ত।

ŭn-rē-pĭn′-ing, *adj.* Not repinining or complaining; অনভিযোগকারী, অননুশোচনাকারী।

ŭn-rē-plĕn′-ished (-ĭsht), *adj.* Not filled or adequately supplied; অপূরিত।

ŭn-rē-pōrt′-ĕd, *adj.* Not reported, অজ্ঞাপিত, অগোচরীকৃত, অপ্রতিবেদিত।

ŭn-rĕp-rē-sĕnt′-ĕd *adj.* 1. Not yet represented; অপ্রদর্শিত। 2. Having no one to act in one's stead; অপ্রতিনিধিক।

ŭn-rē-pressed′ (-prĕst), *adj.* 1. Not crushed or not subdued; অদমিত, অনিগৃহীত, অনিপীড়িত।

ŭn-rē-prĕss′-ĭ-ble (-bl), *adj.* That cannot be repressed; অনিপীড়নীয়, অনিগৃহীত।

ŭn-rē-priev′-a-ble (-prēv-ă-bl), *adj.* That cannot be respited from death; অপ্রাণদণ্ডক্ষমনীয়, অবধদণ্ডমার্জ্জনীয়।

ŭn-rē-proach′-a-ble (-prōch-ă-bl), *adj.* Irreproachable; অনিন্দ্য, অনবদ্য, অকলঙ্ক।

ŭn-rē-proached′(-prōcht), *adj.* Not upbraided; অতিরস্কৃত, অভর্ৎসিত।

ŭn-rē-prôv′-ă-ble (-bl), *adj.* Not deserving reproof; অতিরস্কারযোগ্য, অভর্ৎসনীয়।

ŭn-rē-proved′ (-prôvd), *adj.* Not reproved; not liable to reproof or blame; অতিরস্কৃত; অভৎসনীয়, অনিন্দ্য।

ŭn-rē-pŭg′-nănt, *adj.* Not repugnant; অবিরোধী।

ŭn-rĕp′-ū-tă-ble (-bl), *adj.* Not reputable; অকীর্তিকর, অযশস্কর।

ŭn-rē-quĕst′-ed, *adj.* Not asked; অপ্রার্থিত, অযাচিত।

ŭn-rē-quīred′, *adj.* Not demanded; অযাচিত।

ŭn-rē-quĭt′-ă-ble (-bl), *adj.* Not to be requited; অপ্রতীকার্য, অক্ষতিপূরণযোগ্য, অপ্রতিফলপ্রদানযোগ্য।

ŭn-rĕs′-cued (-cūd), *adj.* Not delivered; অনুদ্ধারিত।

ŭn-rē-sent′-ed, *adj.* Not regarded with anger; অক্রুদ্ধ।

ŭn-rē-sent′-ing, *adj.* Not regarding with anger; অক্রোধ।

ŭn-rē-serve′ (-zērv), *n.* Absence of reserve: frankness; অরহঃশীলতা, অকপটতা; অকৃত্রিমতা।

ŭn-rē-served (zērvd), *adj.* 1. Not retained when a part is granted; not restricted: entire; অরক্ষিত, অসঙ্কুচিত; সম্পূর্ণ, নিঃশেষ, নিরবশেষ। 2. Open; frank; অকপট; সরল। **—serv′-ed-ly**, *adv.* **—serv′-ed-ness**, *n.*

ŭn-rē-signed′ (-zīnd), *adj.* 1. Not resigned; অত্যক্ত। 2. Not submissive to God's will; অনাত্মসমর্পিত।

ŭn-rē-sĭst′-ĕd, *adj.* Not opposed; resistless; অবাধিত, অনিবারিত; অপ্রতিরুদ্ধ।

ŭn-rē-sĭst′-ing, *adj.* Not making resistance; submissive; humble; অবাধাপ্রদানকারী, অনিবারক; বিনীত, বিনয়ী; নম্র।

ŭn-rē-sŏlv′-ă-ble, (-bl), *adj.* That cannot be resolved; অবিলনীয়, অদ্রবণীয়।

ŭn-rē-solved′ (-zŏlvd), *adj.* Not determined; অকৃতসংকল্প।

ŭn-rē-spĕct′-ĕd, *adj.* Not regarded with respect; অসম্মানিত, অপূজিত, অসম্পূজিত।

ŭn-rē-spīr′-ă-ble (-bl), *adj* That cannot be breathed; অশ্বাসক্রিয়াসম্পাদনীয়।

ŭn-rĕs′-pīt-ĕd, *adj.* 1. Not respited; অবিশ্রান্ত। 2. Admitting no intermission; অবিরামসহ।

ŭn-rĕst′, *n.* Disquiet, specially of minds; uneasiness; চঞ্চলতা, চাঞ্চল্য, অশান্তি; উদ্বেগ, অস্থিরতা।

ŭn-rĕst′-fûl, *adj.* Not at rest; অস্থির, চঞ্চল। **—ness**, *n.*

ŭn-rĕst'-ing, *adj.* 1. Continually in motion ; নিত্যগতিশীল, সদাগতি। 2. Never at rest ; চঞ্চল, অস্থির, অশান্ত।
ŭn-rĕ-stōred', *adj.* 1. Not restored or given back ; অপ্রত্যর্পিত। 2. Not restored to a former state or condition ; as, an *unrestored* ruin ; অপুনঃসংস্কৃত, অপুনঃপ্রতিষ্ঠিত।
ŭn-rĕ-strain'-a-ble (-strān-ă-bl), *adj.* That cannot be restrained ; অনিগৃহীতব্য, অনিবার্য্য।
ŭn-rĕ-strained' (-strānd), *adj.* Not restrained or controlled ; as, *unrestrained* power ; অনিয়মিত, অসংযত।
ŭn-rĕ-straint'(-strānt), *n.* Freedom from restraint ; অসংযম, উচ্ছৃঙ্খলতা।
ŭn-rĕ-strict'-ĕd, *adj.* Not restricted or limited ; অসঙ্কুচিত, অপরিচ্ছিন্ন।
ŭn-rĕ-trăct'-ĕd, *adj.* Not retracted or recalled ; অপ্রত্যাহৃত।
ŭn-rĕ-vealed' (-vēld), *adj.* Not revealed ; অপ্রকাশিত।
ŭn-rĕ-venged' (-vĕnjd), *adj.* Not revenged ; অপ্রতিহিংসিত, অবৈরশুদ্ধ।
ŭn-rĕ-venge'-fŭl (-vĕnj-), *adj.* Not disposed to revenge ; অপ্রতিহিংসাপ্রবণ।
ŭn-rĕ-vered' (-vērd), *adj.* Not revered ; অসম্মানিত, অপূজিত।
ŭn-rĕ-versed' (-vêrst), *adj.* Not annulled by a counter decision ; অরহিত।
ŭn-rĕ-vêrt'-ĕd, *adj.* Not reversed or turned back ; অবিপর্য্যস্ত।
ŭn-rĕ-vised' (-vīst), *adj.* Not corrected ; অসংশোধিত।
ŭn-rĕ-vived' (-vīvd), *adj.* Not recalled into life ; অসঞ্জীবিত।
ŭn-rĕ-voked' (-vōkt), *adj.* Not annulled ; অরহিত।
ŭn-rĕ-ward'-ĕd, *adj.* Not rewarded ; অপুরস্কৃত।
ŭn-rĭd'-dle (-l), *v. t.* To solve or explain ; as, to *unriddle* an enigma ; পূরণ করা, সমাধান করা।
ŭn-rī'-fled (-fld), *adj.* Not robbed or stripped ; অলুণ্ঠিত।
ŭn-rĭg', *v. t.* To strip of rigging ; দড়াদড়ী খোলা।
ŭn-rigt'-eous (-rīt-yŭs), *adj.* Not righteous ; not just ; wicked ; not honest ; অধার্ম্মিক ; অন্যায্য ; অসাধু ; অসৎ। —ly, *adv.* —ness, *n.*
ŭn-ring', *v. t.* To deprive of ring or rings ; অঙ্গুরীয় মোচন করা, কড়া খোলা।
ŭn-rĭp', *v. t.* To cut open ; বিদারণ করা।
ŭn'-rīpe', *adj.* 1. Not ripe or mature ; অপক্ক, কাঁচা। 2. Not fully prepared or mature ; as, an *unripe* scheme ; অপরিপক্ক, অপরিণত, অসময়োচিত। —ness, *n.*
ŭn-rīp'-ened (-nd), *adj.* Not-matured ; অপরিপক্ক।
ŭn-rī'-valled (-văld), *adj.* Having no rival ; having no equal ; peerless ; অপ্রতিদ্বন্দ্বী ; অপ্রতিম ; অদ্বিতীয়।
ŭn-rĭv'-ĕt, *v. t.* To loose from rivets ; to unfasten ; প্রেক খোলা ; বন্ধন খোলা।
ŭn-rōbe', *v. t.* To stripe off a robe ; বিবস্ত্র করা, পরিচ্ছদ হীন করা।
ŭn-rōll', *v. t.* 1. To open what is rolled ; গুটানো বস্তু খোলা। 2. To display ; উদ্ঘাটিত করা, প্রদর্শিত করা।
ŭn-rō-măn'-tic, *adj.* Not romantic or fanciful ; অকাল্পনিক, অকল্পলোকালোক মণ্ডিত।
ŭn-roof', *v. t.* To strip off the roof of a house ; ছাদবিহীন করা।
ŭn-root', *v. t.* & *i.* 1. To tear up by the roots ; উন্মূলিত করা, উপড়ান। 2. To extirpate ; মূলচ্ছেদ করা। *Verb i.* To be torn up by roots ; উন্মূলিত হওয়া।
ŭn-round'-ĕd (-rownd-), *adj.* Not made round ; অবর্ত্তুলীকৃত।
ŭn-rout'-ĕd (-rowt-), *adj.* Not thrown into disorder ; অছত্রভঙ্গ।
ŭn-roy'-ăl, *adj.* 1. Not royal ; অরাজকীয়। 2. Not becoming a king ; অরাজোচিত, অনৃপোচিত, অরাজসমুচিত। —ly, *adv.*
ŭn-rŭf'-fle (-l), *v. i.* To cease from being ruffled or agitated ; অচঞ্চল হওয়া, অবিক্ষুব্ধ হওয়া।
ŭn-rŭf'-fled (-ld), *adj.* Not agitated ; অচঞ্চল, অবিক্ষুব্ধ।
ŭn-ruled' (-rōld), *adj.* Not governed ; অশাসিত।
ŭn-rul'-y̆ (-rōl-), *adj.* Disregarding restraint ; ungovernable ; refractory ; উচ্ছৃঙ্খল ; অশান্ত ; দুর্দ্দান্ত। —i-ness, *n.*
ŭn-rū-mĭn-āt-ĕd, *adj.* Not ruminated ; not well digested ; অরোমন্থিত ; অসুজীর্ণ।
ŭn-rŭm'-ple (-pl), *v. t.* To free from rumple ; কুঞ্চনবিহীন করা।
ŭn-săd'-den (-n), *v. t.* To free from sadness "Music *unsaddens* melancholy" ; অবিষণ্ণ করা, বিষাদশূন্য করা, অপ্রসন্ন করা।
ŭn-săd'-dle (-l), *v. t.* To strip of a saddle ; to take the saddle from ; as, to *unsaddle* a horse ; জীন বিহীন করা ; জীন খুলিয়া নেওয়া।
ŭn-săfe', *adj.* Not free from danger ; exposed to harm ; hazardous ; অনিরাপদ, আপৎশূন্য ; বিপৎপূর্ণ ; বিপৎসঙ্কুল, সঙ্কটসঙ্কুল —ly, *adv.* —ness, *n.*
ŭn-săfe'-ty, *adj.* Unsafeness ; অনাপৎশূন্যতা, বিপৎশূন্যতা।
ŭn-said (-săd), *adj.* Not said or uttered ; অব্যক্ত অকথিত।
ŭn-sail'-a-ble (-sāl-ă-bl), *adj.* Not navigable ; অনাব্য, অনৌচালনযোগ্য।
ŭn-saint' (-sānt), *v. t.* To deprive of saintship ; খৃষ্টীয় সিদ্ধপুরুষসমাজ হইতে চ্যুত করা।
ŭn-săl'-ă-ble (-bl), *adj.* 1. That cannot be sold ; অবিক্রেয়, অবিক্রয়যোগ্য। 2. Not in demand ; চাহিদাশূন্য।
ŭn-salt'-ĕd, *adj.* 1. Not salted ; অলবণাক্ত। 2. Fresh ; তাজা, টাটকা।
ŭn-să-lūt'-ĕd, *adj.* Not saluted ; অবন্দিত।

ŭn-sanc'-ti-fied (-săngk-tĭ-fīd), *adj.* Not sanctified ; unholy ; অপবিত্র ; অমেধ্য, অপূত ।

ŭn-sanc'-tioned (-săngk-shŏnd), *adj* Not ratified or approved ; অননুমোদিত, অমঞ্জুরীকৃত ।

ŭn-săn'-i-tă-rў, *adj.* Unhealthy ; অস্বাস্থ্যকর, অস্বাস্থ্যজনক ।

ŭn-săt'-ĕd, *adj.* Not satisfied or satiated ; অতৃপ্ত, অসন্তুপ্ত, অচরিতার্থ ।

ŭn-sā'-ti-a-ble (-shĭ-ă-bl), *adj.* That cannot be satiated ; অতৃপ্ত ।

ŭn-săt'-ing, *adj.* Not sating or filling ; অতৃপ্তিকর, অতৃপ্তিজনক ।

ŭn-săt-is-făc'-tŏ-rў, *adj.* Not satisfactory ; অসন্তোষজনক । **—ri-ly,** *adv.* **—ri-ness,** *n.*

ŭn-săt'-is-fied (-fīd), *adj.* 1. Not gratified to the full ; অতৃপ্ত, অচরিতার্থ । 2. Not pleased ; অসন্তুষ্ট । 3. Not convinced or fully persuaded ; "Report me and my cause aright to the *unsatisfied*" ; অকৃতনিশ্চয়, অজাতপ্রত্যয় । 4. (*Obs.*) Not paid ; (অপ্রঃ) অপ্রদত্ত ।

ŭn-săt'-ū-rāt-ĕd, *adj.* Not supplied to the full ; অসম্পৃক্ত । **—ra'-tion,** *n.* Quality or state of being unsaturated ; অসম্পৃক্ততা (হিঃ কোঃ) ।

ŭn-sā'-vour-ў (-vĕr-), *adj.* 1. Tasteless ; বিস্বাদ, স্বাদহীন । 2. Unpleasing ; disgusting ; অপ্রীতিকর ; বিরক্তিকর । **—i-ness,** *n.*

ŭn-say' (-sā), *v. t.* To recant or recall what has been said ; কথা ফিরাইয়া লওয়া, প্রত্যাহার করা ।

ŭn-scāl'-ў, *adj.* Having no scales ; শল্কহীন, শল্কবিহীন ।

ŭn-scanned' (-skănd), *adj.* Not scanned ; not computed ; অছন্দোমাত্রাগণিত ; অগণিত ।

ŭn-scared' (-skārd), *adj.* Not frightened away ; অসন্ত্রাসিত, অবিত্রস্ত ।

ŭn-scarred' (-skārd), *adj.* Not marked with scars or wound ; অক্ষতচিহ্নিত ।

ŭn-scathed', *adj.* Uninjured; অক্ষত ।

ŭn-scăt'-tered (-tĕrd), *adj.* Not dispersed or thrown into confusion ; অবিকীর্ণ ।

ŭn-scep'-tered (-sĕp-tĕrd), *adj.* Having no sceptre or royal authority ; অরাজদণ্ডধারী, রাজক্ষমতাবিহীন ।

ŭn-schŏl'-ar-lў (-ĕr-), *adj.* Not scholarly ; অপণ্ডিতোচিত ।

ŭn-schō-lăs'-tic, *adj.* Not scholastic ; অপণ্ডিত, অপাণ্ডিত্যপূর্ণ ।

ŭn-schooled' (-skōld), *adj.* Not taught ; not educated ; অশিক্ষিত ; অশিক্ষাপ্রাপ্ত ।

ŭn-schorched' (-skŏrcht), *adj.* Not affected by fire ; অদগ্ধ, অপরিদগ্ধ ।

ŭn-sci-ĕn-tif'-ic (-sĭ-), *adj.* Not scientific ; অবৈজ্ঞানিক । **—i-cal-ly,** *adv.*

ŭn-scŏ-ri-fied (-fīd), *adj.* Not converted into dross ; অমণ্ডুরীভূত ।

ŭn-scoured' (-skowrd), *adj.* Not cleaned by rubbing ; অমার্জিত, অসম্মার্জিত ।

ŭn-scratched', (-skrăcht), *adj.* Not scratched or torn; অনুল্লিখিত, অচ্ছিন্ন ।

ŭn-screened' (-skrēnd), *adj.* 1. Not covered; অনাবৃত । 2. Not sheltered or protected ; অনাশ্রিত, অরক্ষিত ।

ŭn-screw' (-skrō), *v. t.* To loose from screws ; to unfasten ; স্ক্রু খোলা ; বাঁধন খোলা ।

ŭn-scrip'-tūr-ăl, *adj.* Not agreeable to the scriptures ; বাইবেলবিরুদ্ধ, বাইবেলবিরোধী ।

ŭn-scrū'-pū-lous (-lŭs), *adj.* Having no scruples ; দ্বিধাশূন্য, অকুণ্ঠিত, অসূক্ষ্মাচারী, অনতিসূক্ষ্মাচারী ।

ŭn-scutch'-eoned (-skŭch-ŏnd), *adj.* Deprived of, or not honoured with, a coat of arms ; কুলচিহ্নবঞ্চিত, অকুলচিহ্নসম্মানিত ।

ŭn-seal' (-sēl), *v. t.* To break or remove the seal of ; গালামোহর ভাঙ্গা ।

ŭn-sealed'(-sēld), *adj.* Not sealed ; having no seal ; অগালামোহরাঙ্কিত ; গালামোহরশূন্য ।

ŭn-seam' (-sēm), *v. t.* To cut open ; কাটিয়া খোলা ।

ŭn-search'-a-ble(-sĕrch-ă-bl), *adj.* 1. That cannot be searched or found out by searching ; অনন্বেষ্টব্য, অননুসন্ধেয় । 2. Inscrutable ; "The *unsearchable* perfections of the words of God" ; অবিতর্ক্য, অদুর্লক্ষ্য, দুষ্প্রবেশ ।

ŭn-search'-ing (-sĕrch-), *adj.* Not penetrating ; অননুসন্ধায়ী ।

ŭn-seared' (-sērd), *adj.* Not hardened ; অকঠিনীকৃত ।

ŭn-sea'-son-a-ble (-sē-zn-ă-bl), *adj.* 1. Not being at the proper season or time ; অসাময়িক । 2. Not suited to the time or occasion ; unfit ; অসময়োচিত, অকালোচিত, অসময়োপযোগী ; অযোগ্য । 3. Not agreeable to the time of the year ; as, *unseasonable* frost ; আকালিক । **—bly,** *adv.* **—ness,** *n.*

ŭn-sea'-soned (-sē-znd), *adj.* 1. Not seasoned or prepared, as wood, for use ; অশুষ্ককঠিনীকৃত । 2. Not inured ; অনভ্যস্ত । 3. Not salted or seasoned as, meat ; অলবণমিশ্রিত, অমসল্লাদার । 4. (*Obs.*) Untimely ; (অপ্রঃ) অসময়োচিত ।

ŭn-seat' (-sēt), *v. t.* 1. To throw, remove from, or deprive of, a seat ; আসনচ্যুত করা । 2. To depose from a seat in the House of Commons ; পার্লেমেন্টের কমন্স সভার সভ্যপদ হইতে বিচ্যুত করা ।

ŭn-seat'-ĕd (-sēt-), *adj.* 1. Not seated ; অনুপবিষ্ট । 2. Not settled with inhabitants ; অনধ্যুষিত, অনুপনিবিষ্ট ।

ŭn-sĕc'-ond-ĕd (-ŭnd-), *adj.* Not seconded or supported ; অসমর্থিত ।

ŭn-sē'-crĕt, *adj.* Not secret ; not trusty ; অগোপনীয় ; অবিশ্বাসী, অবিশ্বস্ত ।

ŭn-sĕc-tā'-ri-ăn, *adj.* Not sectarian ; অসাম্প্রদায়িক ।

ŭn-sĕc'-ū-lar (-lĕr), *adj.* Not secular or worldly ; অবৈষয়িক, অসাংসারিক, অপ্রাপঞ্চিক ।

ŭn-sĕc′-ū-lar-īze (-lėr-), *v. t.* To detach from secular things, or alienate from the world ; অসাংসারিক করা, অপ্রাপঞ্চিক করা।

ŭn-sē-cūre′, *adj.* Not secure ; insecure ; অনিরাপদ ; অনির্ব্বিঘ্ন।

ŭn-sĕd′-ĕn-tā-rȳ, *adj.* Not accustomed to sit much ; অদীর্ঘোপবেশনাভ্যস্ত।

ŭn-sē-duced′ (-düst), *adj.* Not seduced ; অপ্রলুব্ধ।

ŭn-seed′-ĕd (-sēd-), *adj.* Not sown ; "The *unseeded* and unfurrow'd soil!" ; অবপিত, অনুপ্ত।

ŭn-see′-ĭng (-sē-), *adj.* Wanting the power of vision ; blind ; দৃষ্টিশক্তিহীন ; অন্ধ।

ŭn-seem′-lȳ (-sēm-), *adj.* Not fit or becoming ; "Let your *unseemly* discord cease" ; indecent ; অসমীচীন, অশোভন, অনুচিত, অযোগ্য ; অশ্লীল। **—li-ness**, *n.*

ŭn-seen′ (-sēn), *adj.* 1. Not seen ; not discovered ; অদৃষ্ট, অনবলোকিত ; অনাবিষ্কৃত। 2. Invisible ; অদৃশ্য। **The unseen**—অদৃশ্যবিষয় ; প্রেতলোক ; পরকাল। **To buy a thing unseen**—To buy a thing without examining it carefully ; ভালরূপে না দেখিয়া শুনিয়া কোন জিনিষ ক্রয় করা।

ŭn-seized′ (-sēzd), *adj.* 1. Not seized ; অধৃত। 2. (*Law*) Not possessed ; অনধিগত।

ŭn-sĕlf′-ĭsh, *adj.* Not selfish ; অস্বার্থপর, স্বার্থপরতাশূন্য, নিঃস্বার্থ, স্বার্থবুদ্ধিশূন্য। **—ly**, *adv.* **—ness**, *n.*

ŭn-sĕn′-sū-ăl-īzed, *adj.* Not sensualized ; অনিন্দ্রিয়পরতন্ত্রীকৃত।

ŭn-sĕnt′, *adj.* Not sent ; অপ্রেরিত।

ŭn-sĕp′-ă-rāt-ĕd, *adj.* Not separated or parted ; অপৃথকীকৃত, অবিযুক্ত।

ŭn-sĕp-ă-ra-tive (-tĭv), *adj.* Not separative ; অব্যতিরেকী।

ŭn-sĕp′-ŭl-chered (-kėrd), *adj.* Having no grave ; unburied ; সমাধিশূন্য ; অসমাহিত।

ŭn-served′ (-sėrvd), *adj.* Not served ; বিনজারী।

ŭn-sėrv′-ice-a-ble (-ĭs-ă-bl), *adj.* Not serviceable ; useless ; অকার্য্যকর ; অব্যবহার্য্য, অকার্য্যোপযোগী। **—bly**, *adv.* **—ness**, *n.*

ŭn-sĕt′, *adj.* 1. Not placed ; অস্থাপিত, অনিবিষ্ট। 2. Not sunk below the horizon ; অনস্তমিত।

ŭn-sĕt′-tle′ (-l), *v. t.* 1. To unfix ; to unhinge ; বিচলিত করা ; গোলমাল করিয়া দেওয়া। 2. To remove ; স্থানান্তরিত করা। 3. (*Obs.*) To disorder ; (অপ্র:) বিশৃঙ্খল করা।

ŭn-sĕt′-tled (-ld), *adj.* 1. Not settled ; unsteady or wavering ; "This *unsettled* character" ; unhinged ; deranged ; "An *unsettled* fancy" ; অস্থির ; দোদুল্যমান ; বিচলিত ; বিক্ষিপ্ত। 2. Having no fixed place of abode ; নির্দ্দিষ্টবাসস্থানশূন্য। 3. Unequal ; changeable ; "*Unsettled* and unequable season" ; অসম ; পরিবর্ত্তনীয়। 4. Not having the lees or dregs deposited ; as, an *unsettled* solution ; অথিতানো। 5. Displaced from a fixed place ; স্থানচ্যুত। 6. Not liquidated ; as, an *unsettled* bill ; অপরিশোধিত। 7. Not occupied by permanent inhabitants ; লোকবসতিহীন।

ŭn-sĕt′-tle-mĕnt (-l-), *n.* Unsettled state ; অস্থিরতা।

ŭn-sĕv′-ered (-ėrd), *adj.* Not parted or divided ; অবিযুক্ত, অচ্ছিন্ন।

ŭn-sĕx′, *v. t.* 1. To make otherwise than the sex commonly is ; লিঙ্গান্তরিত করা। 2. To deprive of the qualities of women ; স্ত্রীজনসুলভ গুণসমূহ নষ্ট করা, স্ত্রীত্ব বিলোপ করা।

ŭn-shăck′-le (-l), *v. t.* To unfetter ; to set free ; নিগড় মুক্ত করা ; মুক্তিদান করা।

ŭn-shăd′-ĕd, *adj.* 1. Not having overspread with shade or darkness ; অচ্ছায়, অচ্ছায়াবৃত। 2. Not having shades or gradations of colour, as a picture ; (চিত্র সম্বন্ধে) অবর্ণক্রমবিশিষ্ট।

ŭn-shăd′-owed (-ōd), *adj.* Not darkened ; free from gloom ; অচ্ছায়াকৃত ; অবিষাদমেঘাচ্ছন্ন, অ-[illegible] মলিন, অম্লান।

ŭn-shāk′-en (-n), *adj.* 1. Not agitated ; not moved ; অবিক্ষুব্ধ ; অবিচলিত। 2. Not weakened in resolution ; firm ; দৃঢ়চিত্ত ; দৃঢ়, অকম্পিত, অটল।

ŭn-shāmed′, *adj.* Not ashamed অলজ্জিত, অব্রীড়ান্বিত।

ŭn-shāme′-faced (-fāst), *adj.* Wanting modesty ; impudent ; নির্লজ্জ, বেহায়া ; ধৃষ্ট, প্রগলভ।

ŭn-shāp′-ă-ble (-bl), *adj.* That cannot be shaped ; অগঠনীয়।

ŭn-shāpe′, *v. t.* To throw out of shape ; to deprive of shape ; কদাকার করা ; আকৃতিহীন করা।

ŭn-shāp′-en (-n), *adj.* Shapeless ; ugly ; কদাকার ; কুৎসিত।

ŭn-shāred′, *adj.* Not enjoyed in common ; অবিভক্ত।

ŭn-sheathe′ (-shēth), *v. t.* To draw from the sheath or scabbard ; কোষমুক্ত করা, নিষ্কোষিত করা।

ŭn-shĕd′, *adj.* Not shed or split ; অপতিত, অবিদারিত।

ŭn-sheet′-ĕd, (-shēt-), *adj.* Not furnished with sheets ; অপট্টাচ্ছাদিত।

ŭn-shĕl′-tered (-tėrd), *adj.* Not sheltered ; not screened ; অনাশ্রিত; অরক্ষিত।

ŭn-shĕl′-tėr-ĭng, *adj.* Not protecting ; অনাশ্রয়প্রদ।

ŭn-shield′-ĕd (-shēld-), *adj.* Not protected ; exposed ; অরক্ষিত ; অনাবৃত।

ŭn-shift′-ĭng, *adj.* Not changing place or expedients ; অপরিবর্ত্তনকারী।

ŭn-shĭp′, *v. t.* 1. To take out of ship or other water craft ; জাহাজ প্রভৃতি হইতে নামান। 2. To remove from the place where it is fixed or fitted; as, to *unship* an oar; যে স্থানে নিবদ্ধ ছিল তাহা হইতে স্থানান্তরিত করা।

ŭn-shocked′ (-shŏkt), *adj.* Not shocked or disgusted; অস্তম্ভিত, অবিরক্ত।

ŭn-shŏd′, *adj.* Having no shoes; পাদুকাবিহীন, পাদুকাশূন্য।

ŭn-shōrn′, *adj.* Not shorn, sheared or clipped; as, *unshorn* locks; অকর্ত্তিত।

ŭn-shŏt′, *adj.* & *v. t.* **1.** Not hit by a shot; অগুলিবিদ্ধ। **2.** Not discharged; অমুক্ত। ***Verb t.*** To take the shot or ball out of; গুলি বাহির করা।

ŭn-show′-ered (-ĕrd), *adj.* Not watered or sprinkled by shower; অবর্ষণসিক্ত, অবর্ষিত।

ŭn-shown′ (-shōn), **ŭn-shewn′** (-shōn), *adjs.* Not shewn or exhibited; অপ্রদর্শিত।

ŭn-shrined′ (-shrīnd), *adj.* Not deposited in a shrine; পীঠস্থানে অরক্ষিত।

ŭn-shrink′-ing (-shrĭngk-), *adj.* Not shrinking or recoiling; অকাতর।

ŭn-shrunk′ (-shrŭngk), *adj.* Not contracted; অকুঞ্চিত।

ŭn-shunned′ (-shŭnd), *adj.* Not avoided; অপরিত্যক্ত।

ŭn-shŭt′, *adj.* Not shut; open; অরুদ্ধ; মুক্ত।

ŭn-sift′-ĕd, *adj.* **1.** Not separated by a sieve; আচালা। **2.** Untried; অপরীক্ষিত।

ŭn-sight′ (-sīt), *adj.* (*Obs.*) Without sight; (অপ্র:) দৃষ্টিশক্তিহীন। **–li-ness**, *n.* **To buy a thing unsight**—See under UNSEEN.

ŭn-sight′-lȳ (-sīt-), *adj.* Disagreeable to the eye; ugly-looking; বিকটদর্শন, বিরূপদর্শন, অপ্রিয়দর্শন; কুৎসিত, কদাকার।

ŭn-sig′-năl-īzed, *adj.* Not signalized or distinguished; অবিখ্যাত, অপ্রখ্যাত।

ŭn-sil′-vered (-vĕrd), *adj.* No covered with quicksilver; অপারদস্তরাচ্ছাদিত।

ŭn-sin′-ew (-ū), *v. t.* To deprive of strength; শক্তিহীন করা।

ŭn-sin′-ewed (-ūd), *adj.* Deprived of strength or force; weak; শক্তিহীন; দুর্ব্বল।

ŭn-singed′ (-sĭnjd), *adj.* Not scorched; অপরিদগ্ধ।

ŭn-sin′-gled (-sĭng-gld), *adj.* Not singled; অপৃথকীকৃত।

ŭn-sin′-ning (-ĭng), *adj.* Committing no sin; untainted with sin; অপাপক্রিয়াসক্ত, অপাপকারী; অপাপবিদ্ধ, অপাপমলিন।

ŭn-sis′-tĕr-lȳ, *adj.* Unbecoming a sister; অভগিনীসমুচিত।

ŭn-sīz′-ă-ble (-bl), *adj.* Not being of the proper size or bulk; অযুক্তায়তন।

ŭn-sized′, *adj.* Not sized or stiffened; as, *unsized* paper; অকঠিনীকৃত।

ŭn-skil′-fŭl, *adj.* Wanting skill and dexterity; অকার্য্যকুশল, অকুশল, অনিপুণ, অদক্ষ, আনাড়ী। **–ly**, *adv.* **–ness**, *n.*

ŭn-skilled′ (-skĭld), *adj.* **1.** Wanting skill or dexterity; নৈপুণ্যবিহীন, চাতুর্য্যশূন্য। **2.** Destitute of practical knowledge; কার্য্যকরীবিদ্যাহীন। **unskilled labour**—যে কার্য্যে শিল্পনৈপুণ্যের আবশ্যক করেনা।

ŭn-slacked′ (-slăkt), *adj.* Not saturated with water; অনতিজলসিক্ত।

ŭn-slăck′-ened (-nd), *adj.* Not made more slack; অশিথিলীকৃত।

ŭn-slāked′, *adj.* **1.** Not slaked; অনির্ব্বাপিত, অতৃপ্ত। **2.** Same as UNSLACKED. **Unslaked lime**—বাথারী চুণ।

ŭn-sling′, *v. t.* (*Naut.*) To take off the slings of, as a yard, a cask, etc.; (নৌবিদ্যা) পিপা প্রভৃতি রজ্জুবন্ধনী হইতে মুক্ত করা।

ŭn-slŭm′-bĕr-ing, *adj.* Always watching or vigilant; সজাগ, সতর্ক, হুঁসিয়ার।

ŭn-smirched′ (-smĕrcht), *adj.* Not smirched; অকজ্জলিত, অমলিনীকৃত।

ŭn-smoked′ (-smōkt), *adj.* **1.** Not smoked; অধূমধূপিত। **2.** Not dried in smoke; অধূমশুষ্কীকৃত।

ŭn-smooth′, *adj.* Not smooth; rough; অমসৃণ; কর্কশ।

ŭn-soaped′ (-sōpt), *adj.* Unwashed; অধৌত।

ŭn-sō′-ci-a-ble (-shĭ-ă-bl), *adj.* Not suitable for society; unsocial; reserved; অসমাজোচিত; অসামাজিক; অনালাপী, সংযতবাক্, সঙ্গবিমুখ, রহঃশীল। **–bly**, *adv.*

ŭn-sō′-cial (-shăl), *adj.* Not social; not adapted to society; অসামাজিক; অসমাজোপযোগী।

ŭn-sŏck′-ĕt, *v. t.* To loose or take from a socket; কোটর হইতে উন্মুক্ত করা।

ŭn-soiled′ (-soyld), *adj.* Not stained; unpolluted; not tainted, as a character; অকলঙ্কিত, অমলিনীকৃত; অদূষিত; নিষ্কলঙ্ক।

ŭn-sōld′, *adj.* Not sold; অবিক্রীত।

ŭn-sŏl′-dĕr, *v. t.* To sunder what had been soldered; ঝালিদেওয়া জিনিষ বিযুক্ত করা।

ŭn-sōl′-dier-līke (-jĕr), **–lȳ**, *adjs.* Unbecoming a soldier; অসৈনিকোচিত।

ŭn-sō-lĭc′-ĭt-ĕd, *adj.* Not requested; unasked; as, *unsolicited* testimonials; অযাচিত; অপ্রার্থিত।

ŭn-sō-lĭc′-ĭ-tous (-tŭs), *adj.* Not solicitous; not anxious; আগ্রহশূন্য; উদ্বেগশূন্য।

ŭn-sŏl′-ĭd, *adj.* Not solid; fluid; not firm; not substantial; অঘন; তরল; অদৃঢ়; সারহীন, অসার।

ŭn-sŏlv′-ă-ble (-bl), *adj.* Inexplicable; অসমাধানযোগ্য, অব্যাখ্যেয়।

ŭn-solvĕd′ (-sŏlvd), *adj.* Not explained; অসমাধিত।

ŭn-sō-phĭs′-tĭ-căt-ĕd, *adj.* Not adulterated ; not corrupted ; "Feelings still native and entire *unsophisticated* by pedantry and infidelity" ; not spoiled ; pure ; অভেজাল ; অদূষিত ; অকলুষিত ; শুদ্ধ ।

ŭn-sŏr′-rowed (-ōd), *adj.* Not lamented ; not bewailed ; অশোচিত ; অবিলপিত ।

ŭn-sŏrt′-ĕd, *adj.* Not separated into sorts ; অকিসিম-করা ।

ŭn-sought′ (-sạt), *adj.* **1.** Not sought ; অনন্বেষিত । **2.** Unasked ; "Love sought is good, but given *unsought* is better" ; অযাচিত, অপ্রার্থিত ।

ŭn-souled′ (-sōld), *adj.* Without soul ; প্রাণহীন ।

ŭn-sound′ (-sownd), *adj.* **1.** Not sound ; as, an *unsound* body ; defective ; infirm ; অসুস্থ ; অপূর্ণাঙ্গ ; হীনবল । **2.** Not whole or entire ; ভগ্ন, খণ্ডিত । **3.** Not valid ; as, an *unsound* reasoning ; অযুক্তিসিদ্ধ, যুক্তিবিরুদ্ধ । **4.** Not compact ; অনিরেট । **5.** Not sincere ; not genuine or true ; "If there be anything weak and *unsound* in them [they] are willing to have it detected" ; অসরল ; কৃত্রিম, অপ্রকৃত । **6.** Erroneous ; ভ্রমসঙ্কুল ।

An unsound mind—বিকৃতচিত্ত ।

ŭn-sound′-a-ble (-sownd-ă-bl), *adj.* Not capable of being sounded or fathomed ; অগভীরতামাপনীয় ।

ŭn-sound′-ĕd (-sownd-), *adj.* Not tried with lead ; unfathomed ; অগভীরতামাপিত ; অতলস্পর্শ ।

ŭn-soured′ (-sowrd), *adj.* **1.** Not made sour ; অনম্লীকৃত । **2.** Not made morose ; "Youth *unsoured* with a sorrow" ; অবিষণ্ণ, ম্লান ।

ŭn-sown′ (-sōn), *adj.* **1.** Not furnished or planted with seed ; অবপিত । **2.** Not propagated by seed scattered ; as, *unsown* flowers ; অবীজবপনবৰ্দ্ধিত ।

ŭn-spar′-ing, *adj.* Not parsimonious ; not liberal ; not merciful or forgiving ; অমুক্তহস্ত ; অনুদার ; দয়াশূন্য, অক্ষমাশীল । **—ness,** *n.*

ŭn-speak′ (-spēk), *v.t.* To recant ; to retract what has been spoken ; প্রত্যাহার করা ; কথা ফিরাইয়া লওয়া ।

ŭn-speak′-a-ble (-spēk-ă-bl), *adj.* **1.** That cannot be uttered or expressed ; unutterable ; অবক্তব্য, অকথ্য ; অনুচ্চার্য । **2.** Indescribable ; অবর্ণনীয় । **—bly,** *adv.*

ŭn-spĕc′-i-fied (-fīd), *adj.* Not particularly mentioned ; বিশেষভাবে অনুক্ত ।

ŭn-spē′-cious (-shŭs), *adj.* Not plausible ; অনাপাতরম্য ।

ŭn-spĕc′-ū-lā-tive (-tĭv), *adj.* Not theoretical ; অচিন্তাত্মক ।

ŭn-spĕnt′, *adj.* **1.** Not used or wasted ; অব্যয়িত । **2.** Not exhausted ; অনিঃশেষিত । **3.** Not having lost its force or impluse ; অনিঃশেষিতশক্তিক ।

ŭn-sphere′ (-sfēr), *v. t.* To remove from its sphere ; ক্ষেত্রচ্যুত করা, প্রভাবক্ষেত্র, হইতে বিচ্যুত করা ।

ŭn-spied′ (-spīd), *adj.* Not explored ; not discovered ; অনন্বেষিত ; অনাবিষ্কৃত ।

ŭn′-spilt, *adj.* **1.** Not spilt ; অনিক্ষিপ্ত । **2.** Not shed ; অমোক্ষিত ।

ŭn-spir-it-ū-ăl, *adj.* Not spiritual ; worldly ; অনাধ্যাত্মিক ; সাংসারিক, ঐহিক, বৈষয়িক ।

ŭn-spir′-it-ū-ăl-ize, *v. t.* To deprive of spirituality ; আধ্যাত্মিকতাহীন করা ।

ŭn-split′, *adj.* Not split ; অবিদারিত ।

ŭn-spoiled′ (-spoyld), *adj.* **1.** Not corrupted ; অদূষিত । **2.** Not plundered ; অলুণ্ঠিত ।

ŭn-spō′-ken (-kn), *adj.* Not spoken or uttered ; অনুক্ত, অকথিত ।

ŭn-spōrts′-măn-like, *adj.* Not like a sportsman ; অমৃগয়াকারিসমুচিত ।

ŭn-spŏt′-ted (-ĕd), *adj.* **1.** Free from spot ; দাগশূন্য । **2.** Free from moral stain ; immaculate ; অকলঙ্কিতচরিত্র ; নিষ্কলঙ্ক, নিখুঁত, অনবদ্য, নিষ্কলুষিত । **3.** Unblemished ; অকলঙ্কিত, নির্দোষ ।

ŭn-squăred′, *adj.* **1.** Not made square ; অবর্গক্ষেত্রীকৃত । **2.** Not regular ; "When he speaks 'Tis like a chime a-mending with terms *unsquared*" ; অনিয়মিত ।

ŭn-squire′, *v. i.* To divest of the title or privilege of an esquire ; পল্লীবাসী ভদ্রলোকের উপাধি বা সুবিধা হইতে বঞ্চিত করা ।

ŭn-stā′-ble (-bl), *adj.* **1.** Not fixed or steady ; inconstant ; অস্থিত, অস্থায়ী ; অস্থির । **2.** Irresolute ; অস্থিতচিত্ত, অস্থিরমতি, চঞ্চলচিত্ত চঞ্চলমতি ।

ŭn-staid (-stād), *adj.* Not steady ; volatile ; fickle ; অস্থির ; অস্থিরমতি, অস্থিরচিত্ত ; চঞ্চলস্বভাব, চঞ্চলমতি । **—ness,** *n.*

ŭn-stained′ (-stānd), *adj.* **1.** Not dyed ; অরঞ্জিত । **2.** Not polluted ; অকলুষিত । **3.** Not tainted or dishonoured ; অকলঙ্কিত ।

ŭn-stamped′ (-stămpt), *adj.* Not stamped ; অমোহরাঙ্কিত ।

ŭn-stanched′ (-stânsht), *adj.* Not stanched ; অরুদ্ধ ।

ŭn-stāte′, *v. t.* To deprive of dignity ; মর্যাদা নষ্ট করা ।

ŭn-stātes′-măn-like, *adj.* Not becoming a statesman ; অরাজনীতিজ্ঞসমুচিত ।

ŭn-stăt′-ū-tă-ble (-bl), *adj.* Contrary to statute ; not warranted by statute ; অবিধিসঙ্গত ; অবিধিসম্মত ।

ŭn-stead′-fast (-stĕd-), *adj.* **1.** Not fixed ; not standing firm ; অস্থির ; চঞ্চল । **2.** Not adhering firmly to a purpose ; অস্থিরচিত্ত, অব্যবস্থিতচিত্ত । **—ness,** *n.* The state of being unsteadfast ; অস্থিরতা, চপলতা, অনবস্থিতচিত্ততা ।

ŭn-stead′-ied (-stĕd-ĭd), *adj.* Not supported ; not kept from shaking ; অনবস্থিত ; চঞ্চল ।

ŭn-stead′-ŷ (-stĕd-), *adj.* 1. Not steady ; not constant ; অস্থির ; চঞ্চল । 2. Irresolute ; অস্থিরসংকল্প, অস্থিরপ্রতিজ্ঞ । 2. Changeable ; অস্থিরচিত্ত, চপলচিত্ত, চঞ্চলমতি । **—i-ly,** *adv.* **—i-ness,** *n.* Unstableness ; inconstancy ; vacillation ; অনবস্থিতি ; অস্থিরতা ; দ্বিধা ।

ŭn-steeped′ (-stēpt), *adj.* Not steeped ; অসিক্ত ।

ŭn-stim′-ū-lat-ĕd, *adj.* Not stimulated ; not excited ; অনুত্তেজিত ; অনুদ্দীপ্ত ।

ŭn-sting′, *v. t.* To disarm of a sting ; হুল অপসারিত করা ।

ŭn-stint′-ĕd, *adj.* Not stinted ; not limited ; অকাতর ; অজস্র ।

ŭn-stirred′ (-stẽrd), *adj.* Not stirred ; not agitated ; অনালোড়িত, অনান্দোলিত ; অবিচলিত, অবিক্ষুব্ধ ।

ŭn-stitch′ (-stĭch), *v. t.* To open by picking out stitches ; সেলাই তুলিয়া খোলা ।

ŭn-stŏck′-ing, *adj.* Not wearing stocking ; অনমুপাদিনাপরিহিত ।

ŭn-stoop′-ing, *adj.* Unbending ; অনমনশীল ।

ŭn-stŏp′, *v. t.* To free from a stopple or any obstruction ; to open ; গোঁজ প্রভৃতি খোলা ; খোলা ।

ŭn-stored′ (-stōrd), *adj.* Not laid up in store ; not warehoused ; অসঞ্চিত, অভাণ্ডারজাত ; অগুদামজাত ।

ŭn-stō′-ried (-rĭd), *adj.* Not related in a story ; গল্পে অনুল্লিখিত ।

ŭn-stormed′ (-stŏrmd), *adj.* Not assaulted ; not taken by assault ; অনাক্রান্ত ; অনধিকৃত ।

ŭn-strained′ (-strānd), *adj.* Not strained ; easy ; natural ; অকষ্টকল্পিত ; সহজ ; স্বাভাবিক ।

ŭn-strait′-ened (-strāt-nd) *adj.* Not contracted ; অকুঞ্চিত ।

ŭn-străt′-i-fied (-fīd), *adj.* Not formed or being in strata ; অস্তরীভূত ।

ŭn-strĕngth′-ened (-end), *adj.* Not strengthened ; not supported ; অসবলীকৃত ; অসমর্থিত ।

ŭn-string′, *v. t.* 1. To deprive of strings ; তন্ত্রীবিহীন করা, বিতন্ত্রিত করা । 2. To loose ; to untie ; "His garland they *unstring*" ; শিথিল করা, ঢিলা করা ; অগুম্ফিত করা ।

ŭn-strŭck′, *adj.* 1. Not struck ; অনাহত । 2. Not impressed ; অনভিভূত ।

ŭn-strŭng′, *adj.* 1. Deprived of strings ; বিতন্ত্রিত, অপতন্ত্রিত । 2. Relaxed in tension ; শিথিলীকৃত ।

ŭn-stŭd′-ied (-ĭd), *adj.* 1. Not read ; অনধীত, অপঠিত । 2. Not meditated ; অপূর্ব্বচিন্তিত । 3. Not laboured ; easy ; natural ; অকৃচ্ছ্রসাধিত ; সহজ ; স্বাভাবিক । 4. Unskilled ; অনিপুণ ।

ŭn-stū′-di-ous (-ŭs), *adj.* Not diligent in study ; অপাঠবিমুখ ।

ŭn-stuffed′ (-stŭft), *adj.* Not stuffed ; অনতিপূরিত ।

ŭn-sŭb-dū′-ȧ-ble (-bl), *adj.* Not capable of being subdued ; অদমনীয়, অদম্য ।

ŭn-sŭb-dued′ (-dūd), *adj.* Not brought into subjection ; অবশীভূত ।

ŭn-sŭb-mis′-sive (-ĭv), *adj.* Not submissive ; disobedient ; অবশীভূত ; অবাধ্য । **—ly,** *adv.* **—ness,** *n.*

ŭn-sŭb-ŏr′-di-nat-ĕd, *adj.* Not subordinated ; অনধিনীকৃত ।

ŭn-sŭb-orned′ (-ŏrnd), *adj.* Not procured by secret collusion ; গোপনীয় যোগাযোগদ্বারা অপ্রাপ্ত ।

ŭn-sŭb′-si-dized, *adj.* Not engaged or supported by subsidies ; অর্থদ্বারা অনিযুক্ত বা অসাহায্যীকৃত ।

ŭn-sŭb-stăn′-tial (-shăl), *adj.* 1. Not solid ; অসার । 2. Unreal ; visionary ; অবাস্তব, অবাস্তবিক ; কাল্পনিক । 3. Flimsy ; অকিঞ্চিৎকর, তুচ্ছ, নগণ্য । 4. Not strengthening or invigorating ; অবলপ্রদ, অপুষ্টিদ ।

ŭn-sŭb-vẽrt′-ĕd, *adj.* Not overthrown ; অনুচ্ছিন্ন ।

ŭn-sŭc-cĕss′-fûl, *adj.* Not successful ; অকৃতকার্য্য, অসফলপ্রযত্ন, অকৃতকৃত্য, বিফলশ্রম । **—ly,** *adv.* **—ness,** *n.*

ŭn-sŭc-cĕs′-sive (-ĭv), *adj.* Not proceeding by regular succession ; অপরম্পরাগত, অননুক্রমণিক ।

ŭn-sucked′ (-sŭkt), *adj.* Not having the breasts drawn ; অচুষিত ।

ŭn-sŭf′-fẽr-ȧ-ble (-bl), *adj.* Insufferable ; অসহনীয়, অসহ্য ।

ŭn-sug′-ared (-shŭg-ẽrd), *adj.* Not sweetened with sugar ; অশর্করামিশ্রিত ।

ŭn-suit′-a-ble (-sūt-ȧ-bl), *adj.* Not suitable, fit or adapted ; improper ; অযোগ্য, অনুপযুক্ত, অনুপযোগী, অসঙ্গত, অনুচিত । **—bly,** *adv.* **—ness,** *n.*

ŭn-suit′-ĕd (-sūt-), *adj.* 1. Not suited or adapted ; অযোগ্য, অনুপযুক্ত । 2. (*Rare*) Not accommodated or filled ; অনুপযোগীকৃত, অপূরিত ।

ŭn-suit′-ing (-sūt-), *adj.* Not becoming ; অনুচিত, অযোগ্য, অসমুচিত ।

ŭn-sŭl′-lied (-lĭd), *adj.* Not stained or tarnished ; spotless ; pure ; অকলঙ্কিত, অকলুষিত ; অকলঙ্ক ; শুদ্ধ, বিমল ।

ŭn-sŭng′, *adj.* 1. Not sung ; অগীত । 2. Not celebrated in verse ; অকীর্ত্তিত ।

ŭn-sunned′ (-sŭnd), *adj.* Not having been exposed to the sun ; অরৌদ্রতপ্ত ।

ŭn-sŭp-plant′-ĕd, *adj.* Not overthrown by startegem ; অকূটোপায়োৎসাদিত ।

ŭn-sŭp-plī′-ȧ-ble (-bl), *adj.* Not to be supplied ; অসরবরাহযোগ্য ।

ŭn-sŭp-plied′ (-plīd), *adj.* Not furnished with things necessary ; অসরবরাহীকৃত ।

ŭn-sŭp-pōrt′-ĕd, *adj.* Not supported ; not aided ; অসমর্থিত ; অসাহায্যীকৃত ।

ŭn-sure′ (-shôr), *adj.* Not certain ; অনিশ্চিত ।

ŭn-sur-mount′-a-ble (-sêr-mownt-ă-bl), *adj.* Insuperable ; অনতিক্রমণীয়, অনতিক্রম্য ।

ŭn-sur-pass′-a-ble (-sôr-păs-ă-bl), *adj.* Not capable of being surpassed ; অনতিক্রমণীয় ।

ŭn-sur-passed′ (-sêr-păst), *adj.* Not exceeded ; অনতিশায়িত, অনতিক্রান্ত ।

ŭn-sur-ren′-dered (-sêr-rĕn-dêrd), *adj.* Not yielded up to others ; অসমর্পিত ।

ŭn-sŭs-pĭ′-cious (-shŭs), *adj.* Not suspicious ; অশঙ্কাশীল, অসংশয়ী, বিশ্বস্তচিত্ত ।

ŭn-swêrv′-ing, *adj.* Not deviating from a certain standard ; "The *unswerving* heroism of the immortal Joan" ; অটল, অবিচলিত । **–ly,** *adv.* **In an unswerving manner**—অটলভাবে, অবিচলিতভাবে ।

ŭn-sȳm-mĕt′-ri-căl, *adj.* Not symmetrical ; অসৌষ্ঠবসম্পন্ন, বেডৌল, অসমাঙ্গ, অসঙ্গত (হিঃ কোঃ) ।

ŭn-sȳm-pă-thĕt′-ic, *adj.* Not sympathetic ; সহানুভূতিশূন্য, সমবেদনাশূন্য । **–i-cal-ly,** *adv.*

ŭn-sȳs-tĕm-ăt′-ic, *adj.* Not systematic ; not having regular order, distribution or arrangement of parts ; ব্যবস্থাশূন্য ; অপ্রণালীবদ্ধ, শৃঙ্খলতাবিহীন, বেবন্দোবস্তো, অসমঞ্জ । **–i-cal-ly,** *adv.*

ŭn-taint′-ĕd (-tănt-), *adj.* **1.** Not rendered impure by admixture ; pure ; অভেজাল, নিভাঁজ ; নির্ম্মল, খাঁটি, বিশুদ্ধ । **2.** Not sullied ; unblemished ; অকলঙ্কিত ; অদূষিত ।

ŭn-taint′-ĕd (-tănt-), *adj.* Not charged with a crime; অদোষিসাব্যস্ত ।

ŭn-tam′-ă-ble (-bl), **–tāme-ă-ble** (-bl), *adjs.* Not tamable ; অবশ্য, অপোষণীয় ।

ŭn-tāme′, –tāmed, *adjs.* Not domesticated ; not brought under control ; অপোষিত, বন্য ; অদম্য ।

ŭn-târ′-nished (-nĭsht), *adj.* Spotless ; unblemished ; as, *untarnished* fame ; অমল, নির্ম্মল ; অকলঙ্ক ।

ŭn-tāst′-ĕd, *adj.* **1.** Not tasted ; অনাস্বাদিত । **2.** Not experienced or enjoyed ; অভুক্ত ।

ŭn-taught′ (-tät-), *adj.* Illiterate ; অশিক্ষিত, মূর্খ ।

ŭn-tĕn′-ă-ble (-bl), *adj.* **1.** That cannot be hold অধার্য্য । **2.** Not defensible ; অসমর্থনীয় ।

ŭn-thank′-fûl (-thăngk-), *adj.* Ungrateful ; অকৃতজ্ঞ, কৃতঘ্ন । **–ly,** *adv.*

ŭn-think′-a-ble (-thĭngk-ă-bl), *adj.* That cannot be thought ; অচিন্ত্য, অভাবনীয়, অধ্যেয়, অচিন্তনীয় ।

ŭn-think′-ing (-thĭngk-), *adj.* Thoughtless ; inconsiderate ; as, an *unthinking* youth ; বিবেচনাশূন্য, বিচারমূঢ় ; অবিমৃষ্যকারী ।

ŭn-thrĭft′-ȳ, *adj.* Prodigal ; অমিতব্যয়ী, অপব্যয়ী ।

ŭn-tĭ′-dȳ, *adj.* Slovenly ; অপরিস্কার, অপরিচ্ছন্ন, অপরিপাটী, নোংরা ।

ŭn-tie′ (-tī), *v. t.* To unfasten ; গাঁইট খোলা, গ্রন্থি মোচন করা ।

ŭn-tĭl′, *prep.* & *conj.* **1.** Till ; পর্য্যন্ত । **2.** Till the time that ; till the point or degree that ; যে পর্য্যন্ত না, যাবৎ না ; যে মাত্রা পর্য্যন্ত । ***Conj.*** As far as ; to the place or degree that ; যে পর্য্যন্ত ; যে মাত্রা বা সময় পর্য্যন্ত । **Until further orders**—দ্বিতীয় আদেশ না হওয়া পর্য্যন্ত ।

ŭn-tilled′ (-tĭld), *adj.* Not tilled ; অকর্ষিত, অকৃষ্ট ।

ŭn-tīme′-lȳ, *adj.* Inopportune ; অসময়োচিত, অকালোচিত, অসময়োপযোগী, আকালিক । **An untimely death**—অকালমৃত্যু ।

ŭn-tīr′-ing, *adj.* Indefatigable ; অক্লান্ত, অপরিশ্রান্ত, অশ্রান্ত, অনবসন্ন । **–ly,** *adv.*

ŭn′-tô, *prep.* Towards ; প্রতি, পানে, অবধি, পর্য্যন্ত । **Verily I say unto you**—তোমাকে সত্য সত্য বলিতেছি ।

ŭn-tōld′, *adj.* **1.** Not related ; not revealed ; অবর্ণিত, অকথিত ; অনুক্ত, অপ্রকাশিত । **2.** Unnumbered ; immeasurable ; অগণিত , অপরিমিত ।

ŭn-touched′ (-tŭcht), *adj.* Not touched ; অস্পৃষ্ট ।

ŭn-tō′-ward (-wêrd), *adj.* **1.** Perverse ; অবাধ্য, উচ্ছৃঙ্খল, বে-আড়া । **2.** Ungraceful ; as, an *untoward* manner ; কুৎসিত, কদর্য্য । **3.** Inconvenient ; অসুবিধাজনক, প্রতিকূল, অননুকূল । **–ly,** *adv.* **–ness,** *n.*

ŭn-trained′ (-trānd), *adj.* **1.** Not trained ; অশিক্ষিত । **2.** Ungovernable ; অদম্য ।

ŭn-tried′ (-trīd), *adj.* Not tried ; অপরীক্ষিত, অবিচারিত ।

ŭn-trimmed′ (-trĭmd), *adj.* Not pruned or dressed ; not put in order ; অকাটাছাঁটা ; অসজ্জিত ।

ŭn-trŏd′-den (-n), *adj.* **1.** Not trampled ; অপাদাহত, অপদপিষ্ট, অপদপ্রহৃত । **2.** Unfrequented ; অবিচরিত, অপদবিক্ষিপ্ত ।

ŭn-trou′-bled (-trŭ-bld), *adj.* **1.** Not disturbed by care, sorrow, or business ; not agitated ; as, an *untroubled* mind ; অনুদ্বেজিত, অবিক্ষুব্ধ । **2.** Not foul or turbid ; as, an *untroubled* stream ; অকলুষিত, অমলিন ।

ŭn-true′ (-trô), *adj.* **1.** Not true ; contrary to the fact ; অসত্য ; অনৃত । **2.** Not faithful or constant ; অনিষ্ঠ, নিষ্ঠাহীন, নিষ্ঠাশূন্য । **–tru-ly,** *adv.*

ŭn-trŭss′, *v. t.* To loose from a truss ; to let out ; অন্ত্রস্থাপক যন্ত্র হইতে মুক্ত করা ; খোলা, ছাড়িয়া দেওয়া ।

ŭn-trŭst′- wor-thȳ (-wêr-), *adj.* Not deserving of confidence ; অবিশ্বাসযোগ্য ।

ŭn-trŭst′-ȳ, *adj.* Not trusty ; not worthy of confidence ; অবিশ্বাসী ; অবিশ্বাসযোগ্য, অবিশ্বাসার্হ ।

ŭn-truth′ (-trôth), *n.* **1.** Falsehood ; মিথ্যা, অসত্য, অনৃত। **2.** A false assertion ; মিথ্যা উক্তি।

ŭn-truth′-fûl (-trôth), *adj.* Wanting in veracity ; not in accord with truth or fact; অসত্যবাদী, মিথ্যাবাদী, অনৃতবাদী ; অসত্য। **—ly,** *adv.* **—ness,** *n.* Want of veracity ; অসত্যবাদিতা, মিথ্যাবাদিতা।

ŭn-tŭck′, *v. t.* To unfold or undo a tuck ; ভাজ বা কোঁচ খোলা।

ŭn-tŭck′-ered (-ẽrd), *adj.* Having no tucker ; শেলাই যন্ত্রের যে অংশের সাহায্যে কুঁচি তোলা হয়—তদ্বিহীন।

ŭn-tŭm′-bled (-bld), *adj.* Not rolled ; not rumpled ; অনাবর্ত্তিত ; অকুঞ্চিত।

ŭn-tūn′-ă-ble (-bl), *adj.* Not musical ; not capable of making music ; not capable of being tuned ; অসুশ্রাব্য ; অবাদনশক্য ; সুরবাঁধার অযোগ্য। **—ness,** *n.*

ŭn-tūne′, *v. t.* To make incapable of harmony ; to disorder ; "*Untun'd* and jarring senses" ; স্বরসঙ্গতিহীন করা ; বিশৃঙ্খল করা।

ŭn-tur′-baned (-tẽr-bănd), *adj.* Not wearing a turban ; উষ্ণীষশূন্য, উষ্ণীষবিহীন।

ŭn-turned′ (-tẽrnd), *adj.* Not turned ; অনাবর্ত্তিত। **To leave no stone unturned** — See under STONE.

ŭn-tū′-tored (-tŏrd), *adj.* Uninstructed ; untaught ; অপাঠিত, অনধ্যাপিত ; অশিক্ষিত।

ŭn-twīne′, *v. t.* To untwist ; to disentangle ; পেঁচ খোলা ; গাঁইট খোলা, পাক খোলা।

ŭn-ŭp-hēld′, *adj.* Not sustained ; অবিধৃত, অনালম্বিত।

ŭn-urged′ (-ẽrjd), *adj.* Not pressed with solicitation ; অনির্বন্ধাতিশয় সহকারে যাচিত।

ŭn-ūsed′ *adj.* Not put to use ; not accustomed ; as, *unused* to labour ; অব্যবহৃত ; অনভ্যস্ত।

ŭn-ūse′-fûl, *adj.* Useless ; serving no good purpose ; অনর্থক, নিরর্থক ; নিষ্প্রয়োজন।

ŭn-ū′-sū-ăl, *adj.* Not usual ; uncommon ; as, person of *unusual* condition ; অসচরাচর ; অসাধারণ। **—ly,** *adv.* **—ness,** *n.*

ŭn-ŭt′-tẽr-ă-ble (-bl), *adj.* Ineffable ; inexpressible ; অনুচ্চার্য্য ; অব্যক্ত, অনির্ব্বচনীয়। **—bly,** *adv.* **—ness,** *n.*

ŭn-vā′-cāt-ĕd, *adj.* Not made vacant ; অশূন্যীকৃত।

ŭn-vail′ (-vāl), *v. t.* To remove a veil from ; to uncover ; অনবগুণ্ঠিত করা, নিরবগুণ্ঠিত করা ; অনাবৃত করা।

ŭn-văl′-ū-ă-ble (-bl), *adj.* **1.** Of great value ; অমূল্য। **2.** Of no value ; মূল্যহীন।

ŭn-văl′-ued (-ūd), *adj.* **1.** Not valued ; not prized ; অবহুমানিত ; অনাদৃত। **2.** Inestimable ; অনর্ঘ্য, অমূল্য।

ŭn-van′-quish-a-ble (-văng-kwĭsh-ă-bl), *adj.* That cannot be conquered ; অপরাজেয়।

ŭn-van′-quished (-văng-kwĭsht), *adj.* Not conquered ; অপরাজিত, অবিজিত।

ŭn-vā′-ri-ă-ble (-bl), *adj.* Not variable; অপরিবর্ত্তনীয়, অপরিবর্ত্তনসহ।

ŭn-vā′-ried (-rĭd), *adj.* Not altered or diversified ; অপরিবর্ত্তিত, অবৈচিত্র্যীকৃত।

ŭn-vā′-rie-gāt-ĕd (-rĭ-), *adj.* Not variegated ; অবিচিত্রিত।

ŭn-vär′-nished (-nĭsht), *adj.* **1.** Not overlaid with varnish ; অপরিকর্ম্মীকৃত। **2.** Not given a gloss ; অবহিরুজ্জ্বলীকৃত। **3.** Plain ; সাদাসিধা।

ŭn-vā′-rȳ-ing, *adj.* Not liable to change ; অপরিবর্ত্তনীয়, অপরিবর্ত্তনসহ।

ŭn-veil′ (-vāl), *v. t.* To divest of a veil ; to uncover ; অবগুণ্ঠনশূন্য করা ; অনাবৃত করা।

ŭn-vĕn′-ẽr-ă-ble (-bl), *adj.* Not venerable ; unworthy of veneration ; অসম্মানার্হ ; অশ্রদ্ধেয়।

ŭn-vĕn′-ti-lāt-ĕd, *adj.* Not purified by a free current of air ; অবায়ুপ্রবাহশোধিত।

ŭn-vē-rā′-cious (-shŭs), *adj.* Not veracious ; অসত্য।

ŭn-vē-răc′-i-tȳ, *n.* Want of truthfulness ; অসত্যবাদিতা।

ŭn-vẽr′-dănt, *adj.* Not green ; অশ্যামল, অসবুজ, অহরিৎ।

ŭn-versed′ (-vẽrst), *adj.* Not skilled ; unacquainted ; অনিপুণ, অপারদর্শী ; অনভিজ্ঞ।

ŭn-vexed′ (-vĕkst), *adj.* Not troubled or disturbed ; অনুদ্বেজিত, অবিক্ষুব্ধ।

ŭn-vin′-di-cāt-ĕd, *adj.* Not defended ; অসমর্থিত।

ŭn-vī′-ō-lāt-ĕd, *adj.* **1.** Not injured ; অধর্ষিত। **2.** Not violated ; অলঙ্ঘিত।

ŭn-vĭs′-it-ĕd, *adj.* Not resorted to ; অনুপাগত।

ŭn-vit′-ri-fied (-fīd), *adj.* Not converted into glass ; অকাচীভূত।

ŭn-vĭ′-ti-āt-ĕd (-shĭ-), *adj.* Not corrupted ; অদূষিত।

ŭn-vĭz′-ărd, *v. t.* To unmask ; মুখস খোলা।

ŭn-vŏl′-ă-til-īzed, *adj.* Not volatilized ; অবায়ুপরিণত।

ŭn-vouched′ (-vowcht), *adj.* Not fully tested ; অপরীক্ষিত।

ŭn-vowed′ (-vowd), *adj.* Not consecrated by promise ; অসংশিতব্রত।

ŭn-vow′-eled (-ĕld), *adj.* Having no vowels ; স্বরবর্ণশূন্য।

ŭn-voy′-āge-ă-ble (-bl), *adj.* Not to be navigated ; অনাব্য, অপোতচালনযোগ্য।

ŭn-vŭl′-nẽr-ă-ble(-bl), *adj.* Not vulnerable; অভেদ্য, অভেদনীয় অবেধনীয়।

ŭn-wā-kened′ (-kĕnd), *adj.* Not roused from sleep ; অজাগরিত, অপ্রবুদ্ধ।

ŭn-walled′ (-wäld), *adj.* Not surrounded by a wall ; অপ্রাচীরবেষ্টিত।

ŭn-wâr′-like, *adj.* Not used to war ; অরণপ্রিয়, সমরবিমুখ।

ŭn-warmed′ (-wärmd), *adj.* Not warmed or excited ; অনুত্তেজিত, অনুদ্দীপ্ত।

ŭn-warned′ (-wärnd), *adj.* Not cautioned ; অসতর্কিত।

ŭn-wârp′, *v.t.* To reduce back what is warped ; টানা-হাটান সূতা খোলা।

ŭn-warped′ (-wärpt), *adj.* **1.** Not warped ; টানা হাটানো নয়। **2.** Not biassed ; অপক্ষপাতী।

ŭn-warp′-ing, *adj.* Unyielding ; not deviating ; দৃঢ় ; নিশ্চল।

ŭn-war′-rant-a-ble (-wŏr-ănt-ă-bl), *adj.* Not justifiable ; illegal; improper ; অসমর্থনীয় ; অবৈধ; অসঙ্গত, অযুক্ত। **—bly,** *adv.* **—ness,** *n.*

ŭn-war′-rant-ĕd (-wŏr-ănt-), *adj.* **1.** Not warranted ; not authorised ; অননুজ্ঞাত ; অননুমত। **2.** Not assured or certain ; "Upon hope of an *unwarranted* conquest" ; অনিশ্চিত, অস্বীকৃত। **3.** Not guaranteed ; অপ্রতিভাব্যীকৃত।

ŭn-wa′-rŷ, *adj.* **1.** Not vigilant ; অসতর্ক। **2.** Unguarded ; অতর্কিত। **—ri-ly,** *adv.* **—ri-ness,** *n.*

ŭn-washed′ (-wŏsht), **—wash′-en** (-wŏsh-n), *adj.* Not washed ; not cleansed by water ; অধৌত ; অপ্রক্ষালিত। **The unwashed, The great unwashed**—ইতরশ্রেণীর জন সম্প্রদায়।

ŭn-wast′-ĕd, *adj.* **1.** Not wasted or lost by extravagance; অনপব্যয়িত। **2.** Not cousumed or diminished by time, violence or other measures ; অক্ষয়িত, অবিশীর্ণ, অপরিক্ষীণ।

ŭn-wast′-ing, *adj.* Not growing less ; not decaying ; অক্ষীয়মাণ, অক্ষয়িষ্ণু ; অবিশীর্যমাণ।

ŭn-watched′ (-wŏcht), *adj.* Not guarded with vigilance ; অরক্ষিত, অনভিরক্ষিত।

ŭn-watch′-fŭl (-wŏch-), *adj.* Not vigilant ; অনবহিত।

ŭn-wa′-tered (-têrd), *adj.* Not watered ; dry ; অজলসিক্তি, অজলসিক্ত ; শুষ্ক।

ŭn-wa′-vêr-ing, *adj.* Not wavering ; firm ; অবিচলিত, অটল ; দৃঢ়।

ŭn-weak′-ened (-wēk-nd), *adj.* Not enfeebled; অক্ষীণসত্ত্ব, অক্ষীণবল।

ŭn-weaned′ (-wēnd), *adj.* Not weaned ; অত্যক্তস্তন্য।

ŭn-weap′-oned (-wĕp-ŏnd), *adj.* Not furnished with weapons ; অশস্ত্রপাণি।

ŭn-wea′-ried (-wē-rĭd), *adj.* Indefatigable ; অক্লান্ত, অপরিশ্রান্ত, অক্লিষ্ট। **—ly,** *adv.* **—ness,** *n.*

ŭn-wea′-rŷ (-wē-), *adj.* Not tired ; অক্লান্ত।

ŭn-weave′ (-wēv), *v. t.* To undo what has been woven ; অবুনত করা।

ŭn-wĕd′, —wĕd′-ded (-ĕd), *adjs.* Unmarried ; অবিবাহিত, অপরিণীত।

ŭn-weighed′ (-wād), *adj.* **1.** Not having the weight ascertained ; অতুলিত। **2.** Not deliberately considered or examined ; অসুবিবেচিত।

ŭn-weigh′-ing (-wā-), *adj.* Inconsiderate ; thoughtless ; "A very superficial, ignorant, *unweighing* fellow" ; বিচারশূন্য, অবিবেচক, বিচারমূঢ় ; বিবেচনাহীন, বিবেচনাশূন্য।

ŭn-wĕl′-come (-kŭm), *adj.* Not welcome ; not well received ; as, an *unwelcome* guest ; অসৎকৃত ; অসম্বর্দ্ধিত।

ŭn-wĕll′, *adj.* Indisposed ; অসুস্থ।

ŭn-wĕpt′, *adj.* Not wept ; unmourned ; অশোচিত ; অবিলপিত।

ŭn-whipt′, *adj.* Not corrected with rod ; অদণ্ডসংকালিত।

ŭn-whis′-pered (-pêrd), *adj.* Not whispered ; অকর্ণজপিত।

ŭn-whole′-some (-hōl-sŭm), *adj.* **1.** Unfavourable to health ; অস্বাস্থ্যজনক, অস্বাস্থ্যকর। **2.** Diseased ; পীড়িত, রুগ্ন। **—ness,** *n.*

ŭn-wield′-ŷ (-wēld-), *adj.* That is wielded with difficulty; unmanageable; ponderous; হস্তদ্বারা সঞ্চালনীয়; অপরিচালনীয় ; ভারী, দুর্ব্বহ।

ŭn-willed′ (-wild), *adj.* Not produced by the will ; অসংকল্প-প্রসূত।

ŭn-will-ing, *adj.* Not willing ; averse ; reluctant ; অনিচ্ছুক ; বিমুখ; অসম্মত, নারাজ (*colloq.*), গররাজি (*vulg.*)। **—ly,** *adv.* **—ness,** *n.*

ŭn-wind′, *v. t.* & *i.* To wind off ; to loose or separate ; পাক খোলা ; আলগা করা, পৃথক করা। ***Verb i.*** To admit of being unwound ; উদ্গ্রন্থনশীল হওয়া।

ŭn-wis′-dŏm, *n.* Want of wisdom ; অজ্ঞানতা।

ŭn-wise′, *v. t.* Not wise ; defective in wisdom ; অজ্ঞানী ; অল্পজ্ঞানী। **—ly,** *adv.*

ŭn-with-draw′-ing (-drä-), *adj.* Not withdrawing ; continually liberal ; অনপনেয়ী ; সর্ব্বদা মুক্তহস্ত।

ŭn-with-ered′ (-êrd), *adj.* Not withered or faded ; অশুষ্ক, অবিশুষ্ক।

ŭn-with′-êr-ing, *adj.* Unfading ; not liable to wither ; অম্লান, অপরিম্লান।

ŭn-with-hĕld′, *adj.* Not hindered ; অপ্রতিহত।

ŭn-with-stood′, *adj.* Not opposed ; অপ্রতিহত, অপ্রতিরুদ্ধ।

ŭn-wit-nessed′ (-nĕst), *adj.* Not attested by witnesses ; অসাক্ষিপ্রমাণিত।

ŭn-wit′-ting-lŷ (-ing-), *adv.* Without knowledge or consciousness ; ignorantly ; অজ্ঞাতসারে ; অজ্ঞানতঃ।

ŭn-wit′-ty (-ĭ), *adj.* Destitute of wit ; রসিকতাশূন্য, অরসিক, বেরসিক (*colloq.*)।

ŭn-wom-ăn-lŷ (-wûm-), *adj* Unbecoming a woman ; অস্ত্রীজনোচিত, অপ্রমদাজনসমুচিত।

ŭn-wont′-ĕd (-wŭnt-), *adj.* **1.** Unaccustomed ; অনভ্যস্ত। **2.** Not common ; অসাধারণ। **—ness,** *n.*

ŭn-wood'-ĕd (-wûd-), *adj.* Destitute of trees, timber or wood ; অবনাকীর্ণ, অবৃক্ষবহুল, কাষ্ঠহীন।

ŭn-wooed' (-wōōd), *adj.* Not courted ; অপরিণয়যাচিত।

ŭn-work'-măn-like (-wêrk-), *adj.* Unskilful ; অচতুর, অকুশল, অনিপুণ।

ŭn-world'-lў (-wêrld-), *adj.* Not worldly ; অসাংসারিক। **—li-ness,** *n.* The state of being unworldly ; অসাংসারিকতা।

ŭn-wōrn', *adj.* Not worn or impaired ; অক্ষত।

ŭn-wor'-ried (-wŭr-ĭd), *adj.* 1. Not worried ; অনুত্যক্ত, অক্লিষ্ট।

ŭn-wor'-shipped (-wêr-shĭpt), *adj.* Not worshipped ; অপূজিত, অনর্চিত।

ŭn-worth' (-wêrth), *n.* 1. Want of worth ; মূল্যহীনতা।

ŭn-wor'-thy (-wêr-), *adj.* 1. Not deserving ; unbecoming ; অযুক্ত ; অযোগ্য, অপাত্র। 2. Worthless ; vile ; base ; অসার ; নিকৃষ্ট ; নীচ। **—thi-ly,** *adv.* **—thi-ness,** *n.*

ŭn-wound' (-wônd), *p. p.* of UNWIND (which see).

ŭn-wound'-ĕd (-wônd-), *adj.* Not wounded ; not injured ; অক্ষত ; অব্রণিত, অকৃতব্রণ।

ŭn-wō'-ven (-vn), *adj.* Not woven ; অব্যূত।

ŭn-wreathe' (-rēth), *v. t.* To untwist or untwine ; অমাল্যগুম্ফিত করা।

ŭn-wrenched' (-rĕncht), *adj.* Not strained or distorted ; অক্লিষ্ট, অবিকৃত।

ŭn-wrap' (-răp), *v. t.* To open what is folded ; অব্যাবর্তিত করা।

ŭn-writ'-ten (-rĭt-n), *adj.* Not reduced to writing ; blank ; অলিখিত ; শূন্য। **Unwritten law**—সাধারণ আইন—অর্থাৎ যে আইন ব্যবস্থাপক সভা প্রভৃতি দ্বারা বিধিবদ্ধ হয় নাই, অলিখিত আইন।

ŭn-wrought' (-rät), *adj.* Not manufactured ; অনির্মিত।

ŭn-yōke', *v. t.* To loose from a yoke ; to disjoin ; জোয়াল হইতে মুক্ত করা ; বিযুক্ত করা।

ŭn-yōke' *adj.* 1. Freed from the yoke ; জোয়াল হইতে মুক্ত। 2. Unrestrained ; অসংযত, অনিয়ন্ত্রিত।

ŭn-zōned' *adj.* Not bound with a girdle ; অকটিবন্ধনীবেষ্টিত।

ŭp, *prep.* & *adv.* 1. From lower to a higher place ; উপরে। 2. Out of bed ; শয্যোত্থিত। 3. From the coast towards the interior of a country ; সমুদ্রের উপকূল হইতে দেশের মধ্যভাগের অভিমুখে। 4. (*Obs.*) On ; (অপ্রঃ) উপরে। ***Adv.*** 1. To a higher place or position ; from a lower to a higher place ; উর্দ্ধে ; উপরে। 2. Aloft ; as, I see him *up* there ; on high ; উর্দ্ধে ; শূন্যে। 3. Out of bed ; শয্যোত্থিত। 4. In the saddle ; অশ্বপৃষ্ঠে। 5. Raised ; উত্তোলিত। 6. (Of streets) Under repair ; (পথসম্বন্ধে) মেরামত অবস্থায়। 7. In a state of action ; in commotion, excitement, tumult, revolt or the like ; as, his blood is *up* ; সক্রিয় ; উচ্ছল, উদ্দীপ্ত, টগবগ। 8. Above the horizon ; as, the sun is *up* ; চক্রবালের উপর। 9. At an end ; over ; as, it is all *up* ; শেষ ; অবসান। 10. In a condition of elevation or advance ; higher or advanced in rank, position, social standing, price, etc. ; উন্নত পদবী, সামাজিক পদমর্য্যা প্রভৃতি সম্পর্কে উচ্চে। 11. Wholly ; quite ; সম্পূর্ণরূপে ; একদম। 12. Aside ; একদিকে। **All up**—All over ; সব শেষ, একেবারে সর্ব্বনাশ, দফারফা। **To be up and doing**—To do any work with one's full energy ; কোন কাজে উঠিয়া পড়িয়া লাগা। **To be up to anything**—See under BE. **To come up with**—See under COME. **To go up**—See under GO. **Up and about** — Roused from bed ; শয্যোত্থিত। Dressed and moving about ; পোষাকপরিচ্ছদে শোভিত হইয়া ইতস্ততঃ বিচরণশীল। **Up and down**—Here and there ; এখানে সেখানে। **Up a tree**—See under TREE. **Up in arms**—Enraged ; ready to quarrel ; উত্তেজিত। কলহোদ্যত। **Up sticks** — Pack and go ; পুঁটুলি পাটলা লইয়া ভাগো। **Up to a thing or two**—Knowing ; expert ; নিপুণ ; দক্ষ। **Up to snuff**—(*Slang*) Cunning ; চালাক। **Up to the eyes**—See under EYE. **Up to the mark**—In excellent condition or health ; not below the average ; অত্যুৎকৃষ্ট অবস্থায়, সম্পূর্ণ সুস্থ। **What is up**—What is the matter ? ব্যাপার কি ? ব্যাপার খানা কি ?

ŭp, *n.* & *adj.* Rise ; উন্নতি, অভ্যুদয়। ***Adj.*** Moving, sloping, going, towards a hight point or to the capital ; উর্দ্ধগামী ; **Up county** — দেশের অভ্যন্তরস্থ প্রদেশ ; উক্ত প্রদেশস্থ, উক্ত প্রদেশবাসী। **Up-train** — উজান গাড়ী। **Ups and downs**—Prosperity and adversity; successive rise and fall; সম্পদ বিপদ, ভাগ্যচক্রের উত্থান পতন, উন্নতি অবনতি।

ū'-păs, *n.* 1. A tree common in the forests of Java and of the neighbouring isles, the secretions of which are poisonous, and the exhalations of which are said to be fatal to all vegetable and animal life in the neighbourhood (it has been fabulously reported that the atmosphere surrounding it is deleterious) ; যবদ্বীপের বৃক্ষবিশেষ—ইহার দুগ্ধবৎ নির্য্যাস মাখিয়া বাণাগ্র বিষাক্ত করা হয় — এবং ইহার ছায়াতে আসিবা মাত্র যে কোন প্রাণী মৃত্যুমুখে পতিত হইত এইরূপ লোকে বিশ্বাস করিত, বিষবৃক্ষ (রাঃ ভঃ), চাঁদলা। 2. The sap or juice of this tree ; উক্ত বৃক্ষের দুগ্ধবৎ বিষাক্ত রস। 3. Pernicious influence ; as, the *upas* of licentiousness ; মারাত্মক প্রভাব, সাংঘাতিক প্রভাব।

ŭp-bear' (-bār), *v. t.* **1.** To raise aloft ; উর্দ্ধে বিধৃত করা, উর্দ্ধে ধারণ করা। **2.** To sustain ; পোষণ করা, ধারণ করা।

ŭp-bīnd' *v. t.* To bind up ; উর্দ্ধে বন্ধন করা।

ŭp-braid' (-brād), *v.t.* To chide ; to reproach ; তিরস্কার করা; ভর্ৎসনা করা।

ŭp-braid'-ĭng (-brād-), *n.* A reproof or reproach ; তিরস্কার, ভর্ৎসনা, গঞ্জনা। **—ly,** *adv.*

ŭp'-brĭng-ĭng *n.* Training ; শিক্ষা।

ŭp-cȧst', *adj.* Thrown upwards; উৎক্ষিপ্ত।

ŭp-coiled' (-coyld), *adj.* Made into a coil ; কুণ্ডলিত, কুণ্ডলীকৃত।

ŭp-curl' (-kêrl), *v. i.* To curl upwards ; উর্দ্ধে কুঞ্চিত হওয়া, উৎকুঞ্চিত হওয়া।

ŭp'-hănd, *adj.* Lifted by the hand ; হস্তোত্তোলিত।

ŭp-heav'-ăl (-hĕv-), *n.* **1.** The act of heaving or lifting up ; উদ্গমন, স্ফীতি, উৎক্ষেপ। **2.** (*Geol.*) An elevation of parts of the earth's crust ; (ভূবিদ্যা) ভূপঞ্জরের উদ্গাম, উচ্ছ্বাস (সাঃ পঃ)।

Upheaval. Strata raised by Granite.

ŭp-heave' (-hēv), *v. t.* To heave or lift up ; উর্দ্ধে উত্তোলিত করা।

ŭp-hĕld', *p. t.* & *p. p.* of UPHOLD (which see).

ŭp'-hĭll, *adj.* **1.** Going up a hill ; ascending ; পর্ব্বতারোহী ; আরোহী। **2.** Difficult, like ascending a hill ; laborious ; difficult ; as an *uphill* task ; পর্ব্বতারোহণের মত কঠিন ; শ্রমসাধ্য ; কঠিন।

ŭp-hōld', *v. t.* **1.** To raise or lift on high ; তুলিয়া ধরা। **2.** To keep erect ; to keep up ; খাড়া রাখা ; ধরিয়া রাখা, বিধৃত করা। **3.** To support ; সমর্থন করা। **4.** To confirm ; to approve ; as, the conviction could not be *upheld* ; দৃঢ় করা ; অনুমোদন করা।

ŭp-hōld'-êr, *n.* A supporter ; defender ; পরিপোষক ; সমর্থক।

ŭp-hōl'-stêr, *v. t.* To deck with upholstery ; গালিচা, ঝালর, আসবাব-পত্রাদি দ্বারা সুসজ্জিত করা। **—er,** *n.*

ŭp-hōl'-stêr-y̆, *n.* **1.** Furniture, carpet, curtains, etc. supplied by an upholsterer ; গৃহসজ্জাকারী কর্তৃক প্রদত্ত পরদা, গালিচা, আসবাব, প্রভৃতি।

ŭp'-lănd, *n.* & *adj.* High land ; ground elevated about meadows and valleys ; উচ্চভূমি ; অধিত্যকা। ***Adj.*** Being on, or pertaining to, highlands ; উচ্চভূমিস্থ, উচ্চভূমি সম্বন্ধীয়।

ŭp-lift', *v.t.* To raise aloft ; to lift ; উর্দ্ধে উত্তোলিত করা ; উত্তোলিত করা।

ŭp'-līne, *n.* The line of a railway that leads up to central station ; বাষ্পীয় শকটের যে বর্ত্ম অবলম্বনে কেন্দ্রস্থানীয় ষ্টেশনে উপনীত হওয়া যায়।

ŭp'-mōst, *adj.* Highest ; topmost ; উচ্চতম ; উর্দ্ধতম।

ŭp-ŏn', *prep.* **1.** On ; resting on ; উপরি ; উপরিস্থিত। **2.** Relating to ; as, he was examined *upon* all questions ; সম্বন্ধে, বিষয়ে, সম্পর্কে। **3.** According to ; "This sheperd's passion is much *upon* my fashion" ; অনুসারে। **4.** In consequence of ; as, she died *upon* his works ; ফলে। **5.** In addition to ; উপর। **7.** By means of ; "To die *upon* the land I love so well" ; দ্বারা। **Upon God**—ঈশ্বরের শপথ করিয়া। **Upon my word**—বাস্তবিক বলিতেছি, তোমার দিব্যি। **To take upon**—To assume ; গ্রহণ করা। **Upon the anvil** — See under ANVIL.

ŭp'-per (-êr), *adj.* & *n.* Higher in place ; superior in rank or dignity ; উচ্চতর, উন্নততর ; উপরিতন, উর্দ্ধতন, উচ্চপদস্থ। ***Noun.*** **1.** The part of a boot or shoe above the sole or welt ; জুতার উপরিভাগ। **2.** Cloth gaiters ; বস্ত্রনির্মিত পাদচ্ছদ। **Upper hand** — প্রাধান্য, প্রভুত্ব। **Upper storey** — উপরের তল ; (লক্ষণায়) মস্তিষ্ক। **Upper works**—যাত্রার প্রাক্কালে যথাযথভাবে ভারসামঞ্জস্যকৃত পোতের যে ভাগ জলরেখার উর্দ্ধে থাকে। **Upper-world**—স্বর্গ (পৃথিবী সম্পর্কে), মর্ত্ত (অধোলোক সম্পর্কে)। **The Upper Bench**—(ইতিহাস) ২য় চার্লসের নির্ব্বাসন কালে কিং বেঞ্চকোর্ট। **The Upper House**—পার্লেমেণ্টের লর্ড সভা। **The upper ten, The upper ten thousand**—ইংলণ্ডের সম্ভ্রান্ত সমাজ। **To be in one's uppers**—To be indigent ; to be in difficulties ; দরিদ্র হওয়া ; কষ্টে পড়া।

ŭp'-per-mōst (-êr-), *adj.* & *adv.* **1.** Highest in place or rank ; উচ্চতমপদস্থ, উচ্চতমপদবীবিশিষ্ট। ***Adv.*** On or to the top ; as, he said whatever came *uppermost* ; সকলের উপরে, সর্ব্বাগ্রে।

ŭp'-pish (-ĭsh), *adj.* Proud ; arrogant ; গর্ব্বিত ; উদ্ধত। **—ly,** *adv.* **—ness,** *n.*

ŭp'-right (-rīt), *adj.* & *n.* **1.** Erect ; perpendicular ; খাড়া ; উল্লম্বী। **2.** Honest ; just ; as, he is an *upright* man ; সাধু ; ন্যায়পরায়ণ। ***Noun.*** **1.** Something erect or perpendicular ; উল্লম্বী বস্তু। **2.** The elevation of a building ; সৌধের উচ্চতা, খাড়াই। **—ly,** *adv.* **—ness,** *n.*

ŭp-rīse', *v. t.* **1.** To rise from a bed or seat ; গাত্রোত্থান করা। **2.** To ascend on the horizon ; উদিত হওয়া। **—ris'-ing,** *n.*

ŭp'-roar (-rōr), *n.* & *v. t.* Tumult ; violent disturbance ; clamour ; গোলমাল, গণ্ডগোল; হাঙ্গামা; কোলাহল, অট্টরোল, সোরগোল, জনকোলাহল, হৈচৈ। ***Verb t.*** To create a disturbance ; কোলাহল করা, সোরগোল করা।

ŭp-roar'-i-ous (-rōr-ĭ-ŭs), *adj.* Making or ended by great uproar ; গণ্ডগোলকারী, কোলাহলপূর্ণ। **—ly,** *adv.* **—ness,** *n.*

ŭp-root', *v. t.* To tear up by the roots ; উন্মূলিত করা, উৎপাটিত করা।

ŭp-sĕt', *v. t.* **1.** To overturn ; to overthrow ; বিপর্য্যস্ত করা ; উচ্ছেদ করা। **2.** To discompose ; স্থৈর্য্য নষ্ট করা, ধৈর্য্য চ্যুতি করা।

ŭp'-sĕt, *n.* & *adj.* An overturn ; বিপর্য্যাস। ***Adj.*** Fixed ; determined ; স্থির ; নিশ্চিত। **Upset price**—নীলামে সর্ব্বপ্রথম যে ডাক হয়, নীলামী জিনিষের সর্ব্ব নিম্ন মূল্য।

ŭp'-shŏt, *n.* Final issue ; conclusion ; end ; চরম ফল ; উপসংহার ; পরিণাম, শেষ।

ŭp'-sīde, *n.* The upper side ; উপরি ভাগ। **Upside down**—Overturned so that the side formerly the highest is now lowest ; বিপর্য্যস্ত। In complete disorder or confusion ; উলটপালট, এলোমেলো। **Up sides with a person**—On the same footing with ; কাহারো সহিত সম অবস্থায়।

ŭp'-stairs (-stārz), *adj., adv.* & *n.* In an upper storey ; উপরে। ***Adv.*** Towards, or in, an upper storey ; উপরের তালার দিকে, উপরের তালায়, উপরে। ***Noun.*** An upper storey ; উপরের তালা, উপর।

ŭp'-stärt, *n.* & *adj.* One suddenly arisen from low life to wealth, power, or honour ; "Mean *upstarts* when they come once to be preferred, forget their fathers" ; হঠাৎ বড় লোক, ভুঁইফোঁড় ব্যক্তি, আধুনিক বড় মানুষ, হঠাৎ বাবু, ঔপপাদিক (কৌটিল্য)। ***Adj.*** Suddenly raised to importance ; ভুঁইফোঁড়।

ŭp-stay' (-stā), *v. t.* To sustain ; to support ; রক্ষা করা ; ধারণ করা।

ŭp'-strōke, *n.* The upward line in writing ; লিপিকরের উপরের দিকের টান।

ŭp'-tō-date', *adj.* To the present time ; modern ; আজ পর্য্যন্ত, বর্ত্তমান কাল পর্য্যন্ত, হালনাগাদ (*colloq.*) ; আধুনিক, অধুনাতন, ইদানীন্তন, বর্ত্তমানকালীন, বর্ত্তমান, নব্য।

ŭp'-train (-trān), *n.* A train bound or making for the central station ; উজানগাড়ী।

ū'-pū-pă, *n.* The hoopoe genus of birds ; এক জাতীয় পক্ষী।

ŭp'-ward (-wẽrd), *adj.* Directed to a higher place ; উর্দ্ধাভিমুখীন, উর্দ্ধে।

ŭp'-ward (-wẽrd), **ŭp'-wards** (-wẽrdz), *adv.* **1.** Toward a higher place ; in an upward direction ; উর্দ্ধে ; উর্দ্ধাভিমুখে। **2.** Toward heaven and God ; উর্দ্ধলোকে, স্বর্গাভিমুখে। **3.** Towards the source ; উজানে। **4.** With respect to the higher parts ; উপরের দিকে। **5.** More ; as, he found *upwards* of 50 fruits ; অধিক, উপরে।

ū-rae'-mĭ-ă (-rē-), *n.* (*Med.*) A toxic condition caused by insufficient excretion of urea ; রক্তে মূত্রের অবস্থিতি ও তজ্জনিত অচৈতন্যাদি নানাপ্রকার ব্যাধি, মূত্রনাশবিকার (হঃ চঃ), মূত্রক্ষয়বিকার (ঐ)। **—mic,** *adj.*

U-ra'-ni-ă (-ū-), *n.* The Muse of Astronomy ; (গ্রীকপুরাণ) জ্যোতির্ব্বিদ্যার অধিষ্ঠাত্রী বাগ্‌দেবী।

ū-răn'-ic, *adj.* **1.** Obtained from the uranium ; বরুণক ধাতু হইতে প্রাপ্ত। **2.** Pertaining to the heavens ; স্বর্গীয়, দিব্য।

ū-rae'-ŭs (-rē-), *n.* **1.** The serpent emblem represented by the ancient Egyptians on the headdress of divinities and kings ; প্রাচীন মিশরীয় দেবতা ও রাজগণের শিরস্ত্রাণের সর্পভূষা।

U'-ral Al-tā'-ic (ū-răl-ăl-), *adj.* **1.** Pertaining to a racial and linguistic group of peoples, one of the four great branches of Mongolic stock ; ইয়ুর্যাল এবং এলটাইপর্ব্বতশ্রেণীবাসী জাতিসংঘসম্বন্ধীয়। **2.** (*Philol.*) Same as TURANIAN.

ū'-ră-nīte, *n.* A greenish ore of uranium ; খনিজবিমিশ্র বরুণক ধাতু। **—nit'-ic,** *adj.*

ū-ra'-ni-ŭm, *n.* A rare metallic element like that of nickel and never found native; একপ্রকার দুষ্প্রাপ্য শ্বেতবর্ণ ধাতু, বরুণক (সাঃ পঃ), য়ুরেনিয়ম্ (হিঃ কোঃ)। **—nic, —nous,** *adjs.*

ū-ră-nŏg'-ră-phy̆, *n.* Descriptive Astronomy; খগোল বর্ণনা। **—phist,** *n.*

ū-ră-nŏl'-ō-ġy̆, *n.* Astronomy ; জ্যোতির্ব্বিজ্ঞান।

ū-ră-nŏm'-ĕ-try̆, *n.* The measurement of the heavens ; description of the groups of constellations ; a map showing position and magnitude of stars ; খগোলমিতি ; যোগতারাপুঞ্জের বর্ণন ; তারাগণের অবস্থান এবং আয়তন প্রদর্শক মানচিত্র, তারাচিত্র।

U'-ră-nŭs (ū-), *n.* **1.** (*Gk. Myth.*) The most ancient of all the gods ; গ্রীক পুরাণোক্ত বরুণদেব। ইনি পৃথিবী (Gaea) দেবীকে বিবাহ করেন। ইনি শতভুজ Briareus, Cottus, এবং Gyges, Cyclopes, Arges, Steropes, Brontes, Titanes, Oceanus, Coeus, Saturnus, এবং দৈত্যগণের পিতা। ইহার পুত্র Saturnus ইহার অঙ্গচ্ছেদনপূর্ব্বক ইহাকে সিংহাসনচ্যুত করে। ইহার শোণিত হইতে Furies, Alecto, Trisiphone এবং Megaera জাত হয়। **2.** (*Astron.*) One of the primary planets discovered by Herschel ; জ্যোতির্ব্বিদ্ হর্শেল কর্ত্তৃক আবিষ্কৃত গ্রহবিশেষ, বরুণগ্রহ, বারুণী (হিঃ কোঃ) য়ুরেনস্ (ঐ)।

ū-rā'-ō, *n.* The natron found in dried up lakes and rivers ; শুষ্ক নদী বা হ্রদের গর্ত্তে প্রাপ্ত সর্জ্জিকাক্ষার।

ū'-rāte, *n.* A salt of uric acid ; ইয়ুরিক অম্লের লবণ।

ur'-băn (ẽr-), *adj.* Belonging to a city or town ; living or situated in a city or town ; পৌর, নাগরিক নগরীয় ; নগরবাসী, নগরস্থ।

ur-bāne' (ẽr-), *adj.* Courteous ; suave ; polite ; refined ; as, *urbane* manners ; শিষ্ট ; মাধুর্য্যসম্পন্ন;

ভদ্র, অগ্রাম্য (cf. অগ্রাম্যপরিহাস পটু—কাদম্বরী); মার্জ্জিত, সংস্কৃত। **—ban'-i-ty,** *n.* Civility or courtesy of manners ; refinement ; affability ; শিষ্টতা, ভদ্রতা ; মার্জ্জিতভাব ; মধুরতা।

ur'-băn-īze (êr-), *v. t.* To render courteous ; শিষ্টাচারসম্পন্ন করা।

ur'-cē-ō-lāte (êr-), *adj.* (*Bot.*) Shaped like a pitcher ; (উদ্ভিদ্‌বিদ্যা) কুম্ভবৎ। **Urceolate corolla**—উপকলসপুষ্পক (সাঃ পঃ)।

ur'-chin (êr-), *n.* **1.** A hedgehog ; কাঁটাচুয়া। **2.** A mischievous elf supposed to assume the form of a hedgehog ; একপ্রকার দুরন্ত ভূত—ইহারা কাঁটাচুয়ার আকৃতি ধারণ করিয়া থাকে বলিয়া কথিত আছে। **3.** A rougish or mischievous boy ; "There stood the *urchin* as you will divine" ; দুরন্ত বালক।

ū'-rē-ā, *n.* The chief organic constituent of urine ; মূত্রের প্রধান জৈব উপাদান, মূত্রীয় (সাঃ পঃ), উরীয় (ঐ)।

Urena lobata—বন ওকড়া (বেলঃ)।

ū-rē'-têr, *n.* One of the two ducts of the kidney, conveying the urine to the bladder ; মূত্রবাহী নালী, মূত্রবহ (সাঃ পঃ)।

ū-rē-têr-ī'-tis, *n.* Inflammation of the ureter ; মূত্রবাহী নালীর প্রদাহ।

ū-rē'-thrā, *n.* The canal by which the urine is discharged from the bladder ; মূত্রাশয় হইতে পুরুষাঙ্গের বা স্ত্রী অঙ্গের অভ্যন্তরস্থ যে নালীদ্বারা মূত্র পরিত্যক্ত হয়, মূত্রদ্বার (সাঃ পঃ), মূত্রপ্রবাহিণী (সাঃ পঃ), মূত্রমার্গ, মূত্রপ্রসেক, মূত্রবর্ত্ম। **—thral,** *adj.* **Stricture of urethra**—মূত্রোৎসঙ্গ (সাঃ পঃ), মূত্রমার্গনিরোধন, মূত্রবর্ত্মরোধ।

ū-rē-thrī'-tis, *n.* Inflammation of the urethra ; মূত্রদ্বারপ্রদাহ।

ū-rĕt'-ic, *adj.* & *n.* Relating to, or promoting, the flow of urine ; মূত্রসম্বন্ধীয়, মূত্রল, মূত্রবর্দ্ধক। ***Noun.*** A medicine that promotes the flow of urine ; মূত্রবর্দ্ধক ঔষধ।

urge (êrj), *v. t.* & *i.* **1.** To force or drive onward ; ঠেলিয়া দেওয়া। **2.** To press ; to present in an urgent manner ; to insist ; পীড়াপীড়ি করা ; সনির্ব্বন্ধ অনুরোধ করা, ধরিয়া পড়া ; জেদ করা। **3.** To impel ; to incite ; প্রণোদিত করা, প্ররোচিত করা ; উত্তেজিত করা। **4.** To ply hard ; to take severe measure ; জোরে চালান ; গুরুতর উপায় প্রয়োগ করা। ***Verb i.*** **1.** (*Obs.*) To press forward ; ঠেলিয়া অগ্রসর হওয়া। **2.** To press earnestly ; নির্ব্বন্ধাতিশয় সহকারে উপস্থাপিত করা।

ur'-gĕn-cȳ (êr-), *n.* **1.** Pressure of necessity ; জরুরৎ, জরুর, গরজ, তাড়া (*colloq.*) **2.** Importunity ; earnest solicitation ; নির্ব্বন্ধাতিশয় ; সনির্ব্বন্ধ অনুরোধ।

ur'-gĕnt (êr-), *adj.* **1.** Calling for instant action ; জরুরী। **2.** Importuntate ; সনির্ব্বন্ধ। **—ly,** *adv.*

ū'-ric, *adj.* Of urine ; মূত্রসম্বন্ধীয়। **Uric acid**—মূত্রমধ্যে প্রাপ্ত একপ্রকার শ্বেতবর্ণ স্বাদহীন এবং গন্ধশূন্য অম্ল মূত্রাম্ল (সাঃ পঃ), উরিকাম্ল (ঐ)।

ū'-rim, *n.* A kind of ornament or appendge belonging to the habit of the Jewish high-priest in ancient times, along with Thummim, in virtue of which he gave oracular answers to the people ; প্রাচীনকালে ইহুদীপ্রধান পুরোহিতের পরিচ্ছদে পরিধেয় বস্ত্র বিশেষ—যাহার সাহায্যে তাহারা সাধারণ লোকের নিকট দেববাণী ঘোষণা করিত।

ū'-ri-năl, *n.* **1.** A vessel for urine ; মূত্রপাত্র, মূত্রভাণ্ড। **2.** A convenience for dischargi~~ urine ; মূত্রাগার, মূত্রশালা। **3.** A glass vessel for containing urine for inspection ; পরীক্ষার জন্য মূত্ররক্ষার্থ কাচপাত্র।

ū'-ri-nā-rȳ, *adj.* & *n.* **1.** Pertaining to urine ; মূত্রসম্বন্ধীয়। ***Noun.*** A reservoir or place for reception of urine, for manure ; সারপ্রয়োগের জন্য মূত্রসংগ্রহার্থ ভাণ্ড।

ū'-ri-nāte, *v. i.* To discharge urine ; to make water ; মূত্রত্যাগ করা ; প্রস্রাব করা। **—na'-tion,** *n.* The act of passing urine ; মূত্রত্যাগ, মূত্রোৎসর্গ, মূত্রিত (মঃ উঃ)।

ū'-ri-nā-tive (-tĭv), *adj.* Provoking the flow of urine ; মূত্রবর্দ্ধক।

ū'-ri-nā-tor (-têr), *n.* A diver ; ডুবুরী।

ū'-rine (-rĭn), *n.* The fluid which is secreted or separated by the kidneys from the blood and conveyed to the bladder ; মূত্র, প্রস্রাব, মুত (*slang*)। [Syn. মেহ, বস্তিমল, গুহ্যনিস্যন্দ, মেহনৎ, স্রবণ, স্রব।] **—ri-nous,** *adj.* **Difficulty in voiding urine**—মূত্রকৃচ্ছ্র। **Discharge of urine**—মূত্রোৎসর্গ(কেঃডিঃ)। **Milky urine**—মূত্রশুক্র। **Retention of the urine**—মূত্ররোধ, মূত্রাবরোধ, মূত্রস্তম্ভ, মূত্রাঘাত, মূত্রনিরোধ, মূত্রপ্রতিগ্রহ (সুশ্রুঃ) মূত্রপ্রতিঘাত। **Scolding of urine**—মূত্রদাহ (কেঃডিঃ)।

ū-ri-nŏl'-ō-ġȳ, *n.* Study of the urine ; মূত্রতত্ত্ব।

ū-ri-nŏm'-ē-têr, *n.* An instrument for showing specific gravity of urine ; মূত্রের আপেক্ষিক গুরুত্ব নির্ণয়ের জন্য যন্ত্রবিশেষ, মূত্রমান (সাঃ পঃ)। **—no-met'-ric,** *adj.* **—try,** *n.*

ŭ-ri-nŏs'-cō-pȳ, *n.* The inspection of urine ; মূত্রপরীক্ষা। **—no-scop'-ic,** *adj.*

ur-măn' (êr-), *n.* A large forest of cone-bearing trees in Siberia esp. a swampy forest ; সাইবিরিয়ার বিশাল দেবদারু জাতীয় বৃক্ষের অনুপ ভূমির বন।

urn (êrn), *n.* & *v. t.* **1.** A kind of vase, of a roundish form, bulging in the middle ; একপ্রকার গোলাকৃতি ভাণ্ড। **2.** A vase or vessel, holding water ; a vessel ; জলপাত্র, জলভাণ্ড ; ভাণ্ড, পাত্র। **3.** A vessel in which the ashes of the dead were formerly kept ; মৃতদেহের ভস্ম রাখার জন্য পাত্র, ভস্মপাত্র। **4.** A ballot-box ;

নির্ব্বাচনমতের গুটিকা রাখার জন্য ক্ষুদ্র পেটক। *Verb t.* To inclose in or as in an urn; ভস্মপাত্রে রাখা, গোলাকৃতি ভাণ্ডে রাখা। **Urn′-al, Urn′-ful,** *adjs.* **Urn-flower**—ঘণ্টাকৃতি পুষ্প-প্রসূ একপ্রকার গুল্ম, ঘণ্টাপুষ্পী। **Urn-shaped**—ঘটাকৃতি।

ū′-rō-cȳst, *n.* The urinary bladder; মূত্রকোষ।

ū-rō-dē′-lă, *n.* (*Pl.*). A tailed amphibian; লাঙ্গুলবিশিষ্ট উভচর জন্তু। **–lan, –li-an, –lous,** *adjs.*

ū-rō-gĕn′-i-tăl, *adj.* Of, or pertaining to, the urinary and genital apparatus; মূত্র এবং জননযন্ত্র-সম্বন্ধীয়।

ū-rŏl′-ŏ-ḡy, *n.* That branch of medicine which treats of urine; মূত্রতত্ত্ব, মূত্রবিজ্ঞান।

ū-rō-pȳḡ′-i-ŭm, *n.* The rump in birds; পক্ষীর পুচ্ছের সন্নিহিত অংশ।

ū-rŏs′-cō-pȳ, *n.* The judgment of diseases by inspection of the urine; মূত্রপরীক্ষা দ্বারা রোগসম্বন্ধে বিচার, মূত্রবীক্ষণ, মূত্রপরীক্ষা (শারঙ্গধর সংহিতার একটী অধ্যায়ের নাম)।

ū′-rō-sthene (-sthĕn), *n.* An animal with a strong or highly developed tail; দৃঢ় এবং সুপরিপুষ্ট লাঙ্গুলবিশিষ্ট জন্তু।

Urostigma religiosum—অশ্বত্থ (বেলঃ)।

ur′-ry (-i), *n.* A sort of blue clay lying near a bed of coal; কয়লার স্তরের নিকট প্রাপ্ত একপ্রকার নীল কর্দ্দম।

Ursa, *n.* One of the northern constellation; উদীচ্য তারাদ্বয়ের অন্যতর। **Ursa Major**—সপ্তর্ষিমণ্ডল, সপ্তর্ষি, চিত্রশিখণ্ডী (সাঃ পঃ)। **Ursa-Minor**—লঘু সপ্তর্ষি (হিঃ কোঃ), ধ্রুব মৎস্য, শিশুমার।

ur′-si-fŏrm (êr-), *adj.* In the shape of a bear; ভল্লুকাকৃতি।

ur′-sine (êr-), *adj.* **1.** Pertaining to, or resembling, a bear; ভল্লুকসম্বন্ধীয়, ভল্লুকবৎ, ঋক্ষসদৃশ। **2.** (*Entom.*) Covered with thick bristles; (কীটতত্ত্ব) ঘনশূকাকৃতি।

Ur′-sū-line (êr-), *n.* & *adj.* One of a female teaching order; আরসালাইনসম্প্রদায়ভুক্তা সন্ন্যাসিনী। ***Adj.*** Belonging to the Ursuline order of nuns founded by St. Ursula in 1537; সেণ্ট আরসুল্যানাম্নী সন্ন্যাসিনী কর্ত্তৃক প্রতিষ্ঠিত সন্ন্যাসিসম্প্রদায়ভুক্ত।

ur′-sŭs (êr-), *n.* The bear genus of animals; ভল্লুকজাতীয় জন্তু, ঋক্ষাদিগণ। **Ursus labiatus**—ভল্লুক।

ur-ti-cā′-ri-ă (êr-), *n.* A non-contagious eruption on the skin, producing prominent patches or wheals on the skin, accompanied by great heat and itching; শরীরে বিছুটী লাগিলে চর্ম্ম যেরূপ স্থানে স্থানে ফুলিয়া উঠে ও চুলকায়—তদ্রূপ লক্ষণ-বিশিষ্ট চর্ম্মরোগ, শীতপিত্ত।

ur′-ti-cāte (êr-), *v. t.* **1.** To sting as with nettles বিছুটী লাগাইয়া যন্ত্রণা দেওয়া। **2.** To whip limbs of a paralytic with nettles to restore feeling; সংবেদনশক্তি পুনরুৎপাদনের জন্য অবশাঙ্গ ব্যক্তির দেহে বিছুটী গাছ দ্বারা আঘাত করা। **–ca′-tion,** *n.*

u-rû-bû′ (ô-), *n.* An American vulture of black colour; আমেরিকা-দেশীয় একপ্রকার কৃষ্ণবর্ণ গৃধ্র।

ū′-rŭs, *n.* **1.** A name applied by the Romans to *Bos primigenius*, an extinct wild ox; একপ্রকার অধুনালুপ্ত বন্য বৃষ। **2.** The European bison or wild ox; ইয়ুরোপদেশীয় গবয় বা বন্যবৃষ।

ŭs, *pron.* The objective case of WE; আমাদিগকে।

ūs′-āge, **1.** The mode or manner of using or treating; treatment; ব্যবহারপ্রণালী, ব্যবহারপদ্ধতি; ব্যবহার, আ[illegible]। **2.** Custom; আচার, প্রথা, রীতি, দস্তুর, দাঁড়া (*colloq.*), রেওয়াজ (*ib.*), ব্যবহার, ধারা, পদ্ধতি, জনব্যবহার, লোকব্যবহার, জনাচার লোকশাস্ত্র (শুক্রঃ বিনয়)। **3.** The customary application of a word; রূঢ়ি [cf. মুখ্যার্থবাধে তদ্যোগেরূঢ়িতোঽথ প্রয়োজনাৎ (কাব্যপ্রকাশ)]।

ūs′-ance (-āns), *n.* **1.** Treatment; ব্যবহার। **2.** Custom; রীতি, রেওয়াজ। **3.** Usury; interest paid for the use of money; কুশীদ; সুদ। **4.** (*Comm.*) The time allowed (exclusive of grace) for the payment of a foreign bill of exchange; (ব্যবসায়) বিদেশীয় হুণ্ডির টাকা পরিশোধের জন্য (অনুগ্রহদিবসের) অতিরিক্ত যে সময় দেওয়া হয়, মিয়াদ, মুদ্দত।

ūse, *n.* **1.** Employment; application; as, to put something to a good *use*; ব্যবহার; নিয়োগ, প্রয়োগ, উপযোগ (হিঃ কোঃ)। **2.** Need; necessity; as, I have no further *use* for this book; আবশ্যকতা; দরকার, প্রয়োজন। **3.** Advantage; utilty; as, what's the *use* of talking so much? সুবিধা; উপকারিতা। **4.** The right or power of using; as, he lost the *use* of his right arm; ব্যবহারের অধিকার, ব্যবহারের ক্ষমতা। **5.** Usage; প্রথা, রীতি, পদ্ধতি, আচার। **6.** (*Law*) The benefit, or profit, of lands and tenements held by another for the beneficiary; (আইন) অন্য কোন ব্যক্তির উপকারের জন্য কোন ব্যক্তির হস্তে যে ভূসম্পত্তি ন্যস্ত হয় তাহার উপস্বত্ব। **7.** A distinctive form of public worship or service peculiar to a church diocese; কোন বিশেষ ধর্ম্মসংঘ, বিশপের এলেকা, প্রভৃতিতে প্রচলিত পুজাবিধি, উপাসনাপদ্ধতি প্রভৃতি। **Of no use**—Useless; কার্য্যের অযোগ্য, অব্যবহার্য্য। **Of use**—Useful; কার্য্যকর, প্রয়োজনীয়। **To go out of use**—To be obsolete; অপ্রচলিত হওয়া। **To make use of**—To use; ব্যবহার করা। **To put to use**—To apply or employ; ব্যবহারে আনা, ব্যবহার করা, খাটান।

ūse, *v. t.* & *i.* **1.** To employ; to apply or handle for some purpose; (*rare*) to frequent; as, to *use* an alehouse; ব্যবহার করা; প্রয়োগ করা; (অপ্রঃ) সদা সর্ব্বদা যাওয়া। 2. To expend, consume or exhaust by employment; as, to *use* water for irrigation; ব্যবহার দ্বারা ব্যয় বা নিঃশেষ করা। 3. To accustom; অভ্যস্ত করা। 4. To treat; as, to *use* one well; ব্যবহার করা, আচরণ করা। ***Verb i.*** 1. To be wont or accustomed; অভ্যস্ত হওয়া। 2. (*Obs.*) To be accustomed to go; গমনে অভ্যস্ত হওয়া, সদাসর্ব্বদা যাওয়া। **Us'-a-ble,** *adj.* Fit to be used; ব্যবহার্য্য, ব্যবহারোপযোগী। **Use'-ful,** *adj.* 1. Full of use, advantage, or profit; beneficial; advantageous; profitable; কার্য্যকর, কাজের (*colloq.*), উপযোগী; হিতকর, উপকারী; সুবিধাজনক; লাভজনক। 2. (*Slang*) Highly efficient; (ইতরভাষায়) অতিশয় দক্ষ। **Use'-ful-ly,** *adv.* **Use'-ful-ness,** *n.* The quality of being useful; কার্য্যকারিতা, উপকারিতা, লাভজনকতা, সুবিধাজনকতা। **Use'-less,** *adj.* 1. Not useful, profitable or advantageous; worthless; fruitless; unavailing; অকার্য্যকর, অব্যবহার্য্য, অনুপযোগী; অসার; নিষ্ফল; নিষ্প্রয়োজন, নিরর্থক। 2. (*Slang*) Out of health or spirits; unfit for anything; অসুস্থ, স্ফূর্ত্তিহীন; কাজের বাহির, অকর্ম্মণ্য। **Use'-less-ly,** *adv.* **Use'-less-ness,** *n.* The quality or state of being useless; অকার্য্যকরতা, অলাভজনকতা, বিফলতা, নিষ্ফলতা, বৈফল্য। **To be used to** — To be accustomed to; কোন বিষয়ে অভ্যস্ত থাকা। **To use up**—To consume; শেষ করিয়া ফেলা, নিঃশেষিত করা, ফুরাইয়া ফেলা।

us'-er, *n.* One who uses; ব্যবহারকারী, ব্যবহারকর্ত্তা।

ūs'-ĕr, *n.* (*Law*) Continued use or enjoyment; (আইন) দীর্ঘকাল যাবৎ নিরবচ্ছিন্ন ভোগ বা অধিকার। **Right of user**—ব্যবহারের অধিকার; ব্যবহার হইতে জাত অনুভবসিদ্ধ ক্ষমতা।

ŭsh'-ĕr, *n.* & *v. t.* 1. An officer or servant who has the care of the door of a court, hall, chamber, or the like; an officer whose business it is to introduce strangers, or to walk before a person of rank; one who escorts persons to seats in a church, theatre, etc.; যে ভৃত্য বা কর্ম্মচারীর উপর রাজসভা, হলগৃহ, খাসকামরা প্রভৃতির দ্বার রক্ষার ভার থাকে; যে ব্যক্তি কোন পদস্থ ব্যক্তির নিকট কোন আগন্তুক ব্যক্তিকে লইয়া যায় অথবা যে ব্যক্তি কোন সম্ভ্রান্ত ব্যক্তির অগ্রে অগ্রে গমন করে; যে ব্যক্তি দর্শক, উপাসক, প্রভৃতিকে রঙ্গালয়, ধর্ম্মমন্দির প্রভৃতির আসন প্রদর্শন করিয়া থাকে। 2. A subordinate teacher in a school or academy; বিদ্যালয়ের সহকারী শিক্ষক, উপশিক্ষক। ***Verb t.*** To act as an usher to; to introduce as forerunner or harbinger; "The stars that *usher* evening rose"; to announce; কোন আগন্তুককে কোন সম্ভ্রান্ত ব্যক্তির নিকট উপস্থিত করা; অগ্রদূত স্বরূপ উপস্থিত করা; আগমন ঘোষণ করা। **—ship,** *n.* **Gentleman usher of the black rod** — See BLACK ROD (under BLACK). **Usher of the green rod**—Thistle সম্প্রদায়ভুক্ত সংঘবদ্ধ রাজা এবং নাইটগণের সভার কর্ম্মচারিবিশেষ।

ŭs'-quĕ-baugh (-bä), *n.* 1. Whisky; হুইস্কি। 2. A strong compound cordial made of brandy, or other spirits, raisins, cinnamon, cloves and other ingredients; ব্রাণ্ডি বা অন্য কোনরূপ সুরাসারের সহিত কিসমিস, দারুচিনি, লবঙ্গ প্রভৃতির মিশ্রণে প্রস্তুত উত্তেজক পানীয়।

ŭs-tū'-la-tion, *n.* 1. The act of burning or searing; দাহন। 2. The roasting or drying of moist substances, so as to prepare them for pulverising; চূর্ণ করার জন্য আর্দ্রবস্তু শুষ্কীকরণ। 3. Burning of wine; মদ্য দগ্ধীকরণ।

ū'-sū-ăl, *adj.* Customary; habitual; প্রাথিক, ব্যাবহারিক, ব্যবহারমূলক; প্রচলিতসিদ্ধ, প্রথামূলক। **—ly,** *adv.* **—ness,** *n.*

ū-sū-căp'-tion, *n.* The acquisition of title or right to property or anything by possession and enjoyment for a certain term of years; কোন নির্দ্দিষ্ট পরিমিত বৎসর ভোগ বা অধিকার করা হেতু কোন সম্পত্তিতে যে স্বত্ব বা অধিকার উপজাত হয়।

ū'-sū-frŭct, *n.* & *v. t.* The right of using and enjoying the produce, benefit, or profits of an estate or other thing belonging to another, without alienating or imparing the substance; অন্যের সম্পত্তি কোনরূপ নষ্ট না করিয়া ভোগাধিকার, ভোগস্বত্ব, ফলভোগাধিকার খাইখালাসী (*colloq.*), ভোগ (যাজ্ঞঃ), উপভোগ (অর্থঃ)। ***Verb t.*** To hold in usufruct; ফলভোগাধিকার করা।

ū-sū-frŭc'-tū-ā-ry̆, *adj.* & *n.* Of, or pertaining to, usufruct; ফলভোগাধিকারসম্বন্ধীয়, ফলভোগাধিকারগ্রস্ত। ***Noun.*** A person who has the use and enjoyment of property for a time, without having the title; ফলভোগাধিকারী, খাইখালাসি (*colloq.*), উপস্বত্বভোগী।

ū'-sū-rĕr, *n.* One who lends money at an exorbitant rate of interest; যে ব্যক্তি অত্যধিক সুদে টাকা কর্জ্জ দেয়, সুদখোর, কুসীদজীবী, বার্দ্ধুষিক।

ū-surp' (-zĕrp), *v. t.* 1. To seize and hold in possession by force or without a right; অন্যায়পূর্ব্বক অন্যের সম্পত্তি প্রভৃতি দখল করা, বলপূর্ব্বক সিংহাসনারোহণ করা। 2. To commit illegal seizure or appropriation; অবৈধভাবে অধিকার বা আত্মসাৎ করা। **—er,** *n.* One who usurps ; যে ব্যক্তি বলপূর্ব্বক সম্পত্তি প্রভৃতি অধিকার করে, যে ব্যক্তি কোন নৃপতিকে সিংহাসনচ্যুত করিয়া রাজ্যাধিকার করে। **-ing-ly**, *adv.* **-sur-pa'-tion**, *n.*

ū'-sû-rȳ, *n.* **1.** (*Obs*) Interest ; (অপ্রঃ) সুদ, কুসীদ। **2.** An excessive or exorbitant rate of interest or premium paid, or stipulated to be paid, for the loan of money ; অতিরিক্ত সুদ, অন্যায়ব্যাজ (হিঃ কোঃ)। **3.** The practice of lending money at interest ; the practice of taking exorbitant or excessive interest ; the practice of exacting interest in an exorbitant way from needy and extravagant borrower ; কুসীদবৃত্তি, কৌসীদ্য ; বৃদ্ধিজীবিকা, বার্দ্ধুষ্য ; অভাবগ্রস্ত বা অপব্যয়ী লোকদিগের নিকট হইতে অতিরিক্ত সুদ গ্রহণের রীতি। **-rer**, *n.* One who lends money at an excessive rate ; কুসীদজীবী। **-su'-ri-ous-ly**, *adv.* **-su'-rious-ness**, *n.*

ŭt, *n.* (*Mus.*) The key-note of a scale ; (সঙ্গীতশাস্ত্র) চাবি।

ut, *adv.* ***Ut supra***—পূর্ব্বে যেরূপ ব্যক্ত বা প্রদর্শিত। ***Ut infra***—পরে যেরূপ ব্যক্ত বা প্রদর্শিত।

ū-tĕn'-sil, *n.* An instrument or vessel used in a kitchen, or in a domestic and farming business ; যন্ত্রপাতি, বাসনপত্র, তৈজস, তৈজসসামগ্রী, বাসনকোষণ (*colloq.*), হাঁড়ীকুড়ী (*ib.*)।

ū'-têr-ine (-ĭn), *adj.*. **1.** Of, or pertaining to, the uterus ; as, *uterine* complaints ; জরায়ুসম্বন্ধীয়। **2.** Born of the same mother but by a different father ; বৈপিত্রেয়। **Uterine brother**—বৈপিত্রেয় ভ্রাতা। **Uterine passage** — অপত্যপথ, অপত্যবর্ত্ম।

ū-têr-ō-gĕs-tā'-tion, *n.* Gestation in the womb from conception to birth ; গর্ভাবস্থা।

ū'-têr-ŭs, *n.* The womb ; গর্ভাশয়, গর্ভকোষ, জরায়ুধর (সাঃ পঃ)।

ū-tĭl-ĭ-tā'-rĭ-ăn, *adj.* & *n.* **1.** Of, or pertaining to, utility ; কার্য্যকরী। **2.** Pertaining to utilitarianism ; হিতবাদ সম্বন্ধীয়। ***Noun.*** A holder of the doctrine of utilitarianism ; উপযোগিতাবাদী, হিতবাদী।

ū-tĭl-ĭ-tā'-rĭ-ăn-ĭsm, *n.* **1.** A word coined by John Stuart Mill to denote the doctrine that the greatest happiness of the greatest number should be the aim of all social and political institutions ; যাহাতে অধিকতম লোকের প্রভূততম সুখ হয়—তাহা সকল সামাজিক ও রাজনৈতিক প্রতিষ্ঠান সমূহের প্রধান লক্ষ্য হওয়া কর্ত্তব্য—এই মতবাদ, হিতবাদ (কৃষ্ণঃ), উপযোগিতাবাদ (হিঃ কোঃ)। [Bentham এই মতের প্রবর্ত্তক। John Stuart Mill এই মতের পরিপুষ্টি সাধন করেন। See Albee's *History of English Utilitarianism*; John Stuart Mill's *Utilitarianism* ; Leslie Stephen's *English Utilitarianism.*] **2.** The doctrine that the test of the rightness or wrongness of an action is its conductiveness to the production of well-being ; যে কোন কার্য্য দ্বারা লোকের হিত হয়—তাহাই ন্যায়-সঙ্গত—এইরূপ মতবাদ, উপযোগিতাবাদ।

ū-tĭl'-ĭ-tȳ, *n.* **1.** Usefulness ; profitableness ; কার্য্যকারিতা, উপযোগিতা, কার্য্যকরীশক্তি, উপযোগ (হিঃ কোঃ) ; উপকারিতা, হিতজনকতা। **2.** Same as UTILITARIANISM I. **3.** Same as UTILITY-MAN. **Utility-man** — নাটকের ক্ষুদ্র ক্ষুদ্র ভূমিকার অভিনেতা।

ū'-tĭ-līze, *v. t.* To make useful ; to turn to use ; to use ; ব্যবহারোপযোগী করা, কার্য্যোপযোগী করা ; ব্যবহারে আনা ; ব্যবহার করা, খাটান, প্রয়োগ করা। **-liz'-a-ble**, *adj.* **-li-za'-tion**, *n.*

uti possidetis, *n.* The principle which leaves belligerent parties in possession of what they have acquired during the war ; যে মূলতত্ত্ব অনুসারে যুধ্যমান পক্ষসমূহ যুদ্ধকালে যাহা অধিকার করে তাহা প্রাপ্ত হইয়া থাকে।

ŭt'-mōst, *adj.* & *n.* **1.** At the furthest extremity ; দূরতম, সুদূরতম। **2.** Extreme ; নিতান্ত, চরম, অধিকতম, যৎপরোনাস্তি। ***Noun.*** The mosr that can be ; the greatest power, degree or effort ; চরমসীমা, চরমক্ষমতা, চরমমাত্রা ; যথাসাধ্যচেষ্টা। **To try one's utmost**—To try one's best ; প্রাণপণ চেষ্টা করা, যথাসাধ্য চেষ্টা করা।

U-tō'-pĭ-ă (ū-), *n.* **1.** An imaginary island described in Sir Thomas More's Utopia, where everything is perfect, the laws, the morals, the politics, etc. ; Sir Thomas More কৃত Utopia নামক গ্রন্থে বর্ণিত কল্পিত দ্বীপবিশেষ — যথায় বিধিব্যবস্থা, রাজনীতি, সমাজনীতি প্রভৃতি চরম উৎকর্ষ লাভ করিয়াছিল। **2.** A place or state of ideal perfection ; আদর্শ আনন্দরাজ্য, রামরাজ্য, উত্তরকুরু (হিঃ কোঃ), সুখাবতী।

U-tō'-pĭ-ăn (ū-), *adj.* & *n.* Of, or pertaining to, Utopia ; pertaining to any state of ideal perfection ; fanciful ; chimerical ; impractical ; "The task is so difficult that I look upon it rather as an *Utopian* idea" ; ইউটোপিয়াদ্বীপ-সম্বন্ধীয় ; আদর্শ আনন্দরাজ্যসম্বন্ধীয়, কাল্পনিক উৎকর্ষতাসম্বন্ধীয় ; কাল্পনিক, অবাস্তব ; অসম্ভব, আজগুবি ; অকার্য্যকর, অমূলক, অনাস্থ। ***Noun.*** **1.** An inhabitant of Utopia ; ইউটোপিয়া নামক কল্পিত দ্বীপের অধিবাসী। **2.** An ardent but unpractical reformer ; প্রচণ্ড উৎসাহী অথচ সংসারানভিজ্ঞ সমাজ-সংসারক, কল্পলোকবিহারী। **-ism**, *n.*

ū'-trĭ-cle (-kl), *n.* **1.** A microscopic cell of an animal or plant ; জীব বা উদ্ভিজ্জের অণুকোষ, ক্ষুদ্রস্থলী (সাঃ পঃ), কুতুপ (সাঃ পঃ)। **2.** Anything shaped like a little bag ; a small cavity ; ক্ষুদ্র থলির আকার বস্তু ; ক্ষুদ্র রন্ধ্র। **-tric'-u-lar**, *adj*

Utricular vessel — স্ফীতনলিকা (সাঃ পঃ)।

ŭt'-tĕr, *adj.* **1.** Complete ; perfect ; সম্পূর্ণ ; পুরা । **2.** Unqualified ; unconditional ; অবিমিশ্র ; নির্ব্যূঢ় । **–ly,** *adv.* **–most,** *adj.* **Utter barrister**—সরকারী ব্যারিষ্টার (King's or Queen's counsel) যে গরাদবিশিষ্ট উচ্চ স্থান হইতে মোকদ্দমা পরিচালনা করেন তাহার বহির্দ্দেশে দণ্ডায়মান থাকিয়া যে নূতন ব্যারিষ্টার কার্য্য করিয়া থাকেন। **Utter darkness**—অন্ধতমিস্র (হিঃ কোঃ)।

ŭt'-tĕr, *v. t.* **1.** To pronounce ; to speak ; উচ্চারণ করা ; বলা । **2.** To put in circulation, as money ; as, to *utter* a bad coin is an offence punishable by law ; চালান । **3.** To disclose ; প্রকাশ করা ।

ŭt'-tĕr-ance (-ăns), *n.* **1.** The act of one who utters ; vocal expression ; উচ্চারণ ; বাক্যস্ফূর্ত্তি । **2.** Power of speaking ; বাকশক্তি । **3.** Speech ; বাক্য ।

ū'-vū-lă, *n.* The fleshy conical body suspended from the middle of the lower border of the soft palate ; উপজিহ্বা, আলজিহ্বা, গুড়গুড়ি, সুধাস্রবা, প্রতিজিহ্বা (সাঃ পঃ), তালুজিহ্বা, ঘণ্টিকা ।

ux-o'-ri-ous (ŭgz-ō-rĭ-ŭs), *adj.* Excessively or foolishly fond of a wife ; doting on a wife ; স্ত্রৈণ, স্ত্রীনির্জ্জিত, ভার্য্যালম্পট, মাগমুখো (*slang*) ; স্ত্রীর প্রতি অত্যধিক অনুরাগী । **–ly,** *adv.* **–ness,** *n.*

Uz'-bĕg (ŭz-), *n.* A member of a Turkish race in Central Asia ; মধ্যএশিয়ার উজবগ জাতীয় লোক ।

V

V, **1.** The twenty-second letter of the English alphabet ; ইংরাজী বর্ণমালার দ্বাবিংশতিতম অক্ষর। **2.** The Roman numeral V stands for five ; রোমক সংখ্যা ৫ । **3.** A V-shaped thing ; ইংরাজী V অক্ষরের আকৃতি বস্তু । **4.** (*U.S., colloq.*) A five-dollar bill ; (মার্কিণ যুক্তরাজ্য) পাঁচ ডলারের হুণ্ডী ।

va, (*Mus.*) Go on ; (সঙ্গীতশাস্ত্র) চালাও ।

vā'-căn-cў, *n.* **1.** The state of being vacant ; শূন্যতা, রিক্ততা । **2.** An empty space ; শূন্যস্থান । **3.** Unoccupied post ; as, there is no *vacancy* in the postal department ; শূন্যপদ, কর্ম্মখালি । **4.** Chasm ; gap ; শূন্য ; ফাঁক । **5.** Emptiness of mind ; freedom from labour ; idleness ; শূন্যচিত্ততা, উদাসভাব ; অবসর, অবকাশ ; আলস্য ।

vā'-cănt, *adj.* **1.** Empty ; unoccupied ; as, a *vacant* room ; শূন্য ; খালি । **2.** Not occupied or filled with an incumbent, possessor, or official ; as, a *vacant* throne ; শূন্য, খালি, অনধিকৃত । **3.** Unoccupied with business ; as, *vacant* hours ; empty of thought ; indicating mental vacancy ; thoughtless ; inane ; as, a *vacant* gaze : "In *vacant* or pensive mood" ; অবসর ; শূন্যচিত্ত ; উদাস ; উদাসীন ; শূন্য । **–ly,** *adv.* **To look vacantly**—To look with a thoughtless stare ; ফ্যাল ফ্যাল করিয়া তাকান, শূন্যদৃষ্টিতে নিরীক্ষণ করা ।

vă'-cāte, *v. t.* **1.** To leave empty ; to quit possession of ; as, to *vacate* the throne ; শূন্য করা, খালি করা ; ছাড়িয়া দেওয়া । **2.** To annul ; as, to *vacate* a charter ; রদ করা, রহিত করা, খণ্ডন করা, নাকচ করা ।

vă-cā'-tion, *n.* **1.** The act of vacating ; শূন্যীকরণ । **2.** The act of validating ; রদ, খণ্ডন । **3.** A fixed period of cessation from work, esp. in law-courts and schools and colleges ; as, the summer *vacation* ; ছুটী ।

văc'-ĭ-nāte, *v. t.* To inoculate with cow-pox for the purpose of securing immunity from smallpox, or of mitigating the severity of the attack ; গোবীজ দ্বারা টিকা দেওয়া । **–na'-tion,** *n.* The act of vaccinating ; গোবীজ দ্বারা টিকাপ্রদান, গোমসূর্য্যাধান । **–na'-tion-ist,** *n.* One who favours the introduction of vaccination ; গোবীজে টিকাদানের পক্ষপাতী ব্যক্তি । **–na-tor,** *n.* One who vaccinates ; যে ব্যক্তি গোবীজ দ্বারা টিকা দেয়, টীকাদার ।

văc'-cine (-sĭn), *adj.* & *n.* Pertaining to cows ; derived from cows ; গো-সম্বন্ধীয় ; গোজাত । ***Noun.*** The virus of cowpox used in process of vaccination ; গোবীজ । **–ci-nal, –ci-nic,** *adjs.* **Vaccine-farm**—যে স্থানে বলদকে টিকা দিয়া গোবসন্তের বীজ সংগ্রহ করা হয়, গোবীজসংগ্রহাগার। **Vaccine-point**—টিকা দেওয়ার জন্য সূচ্যগ্র যন্ত্রবিশেষ, টিকাসূচী । **Vaccine-therapy** — রোগের বীজাণু দ্বারা টিকা প্রদানে সংক্রামকরোগ-চিকিৎসার প্রণালীবিশেষ ।

văc-cĭn'-ĭ-ă, *n.* **1.** The cowpox ; গোবসন্ত । **2.** The disease resulting from vaccination, intended to avert the smallpox ; বসন্ত নিবারণের জন্য টিকা দিলে দেহে যে গুটিকা উৎপন্ন হয় ।

văc'-ĭl-lāte, *v. i.* **1.** To waver, এদিক ওদিক করা, টলা, দোলায়মান হওয়া । **2.** To fluctuate in mind or opinion ; ইতস্ততঃ করা, দ্বিধা করা, দোমনা হওয়া। **—lat-ing-ly,** *adv.* **—la'-tion,** *n.* **1.** The act of vacillating ; দোলন, টলন। **2.** Fluctuation of mind ; দ্বিধা, দোদুল্যমান অবস্থা। **2.** Unsteadiness of purpose ; অস্থিরচিত্ততা, চলচিত্ততা।

văc'-ū-ĭst, *n.* **1.** One who holds that there are empty spaces in nature ; প্রকৃতিতে শূন্য স্থান রহিয়াছে—এই মতাবলম্বী ব্যক্তি। **2.** One who holds that there is empty space between the molecules of matter ; জড় বস্তুর অণুদ্বয়ের মধ্যে শূন্য স্থান রহিয়াছে—এই মতাবলম্বী ব্যক্তি।

văc'-ū-ōle, *n.* (*Biol.*) A minute cell or cavity in the tissue of organisms ; (জীববিজ্ঞান) অঙ্গীর বিধানতন্তুতে অণুকোষ বা ক্ষুদ্র রন্ধ্র। **—o-lar, —o-late,** *adjs.*

văc'-ū-ous (-ŭs), *adj.* **1.** Empty ; শূন্য, খালি। **2.** Vacant ; উদাস, শূন্যচিত্ত, শূন্যমনাঃ।

văc'-ū-ŭm, *n.* A space empty or devoid of all matter or body ; শূন্যস্থান, শূন্য (হিঃ কোঃ), বায়ুশূন্য (ঐ), আবরণাভাব (সাঃ পঃ)। **Torricellian vacuum**—বায়ুচাপমানযন্ত্রের উপরিস্থ শূন্য স্থান ; যে ভাণ্ড বা স্থান হইতে বায়ুনিষ্কাশনযন্ত্রের সাহায্যে বায়ু প্রায় অপসারিত করা হইয়াছে। **Vacuum-brake** — বাষ্পীয় শকটের চক্রগতিরোধক। [এইরূপ যন্ত্র শকটশ্রেণীর প্রতি শকটে সংলগ্ন থাকে। এই যন্ত্র হইতে বায়ু নিষ্কাশিত হইলে উহা বায়ুমণ্ডলের চাপে ক্রিয়া করিয়া থাকে।] **Vacuum-cleaner**—বায়ুনিষ্কাশন দ্বারা গালিচা, গদি-মোড়া চেয়ার ইত্যাদির ধূলি অপসারণের জন্য যন্ত্রবিশেষ। **Vacuum distillation** — আকাশপাতন (আয়ুঃ রসঃ)। **Vacuum-gauge**—বায়ুশূন্যতাজনিত চাপ। **Vacuum-tube**—(তাড়িত বিদ্যা) বিদ্যুৎস্ফুলিঙ্গের সংক্রমণ পর্য্যবেক্ষণের জন্য বায়ুনিষ্কাশিত এবং বদ্ধ কাচের চোঙ্গ বিশেষ।

vā-dē-mē'-cŭm, *n.* (*Lat.* Go with me) A manual or handbook for ready reference ; নিত্যসহচর পুস্তক, অভিধান প্রভৃতি নিত্য প্রয়োজনীয় পুস্তক।

văg'-ă-bŏnd, *adj., n.* & *v. i.* Wandering from place to place without any settled habitation ; ভবঘুরে, হাঘরিয়া, টো টো বাজ, সঞ্চারজীবী। ***Noun.*** **1.** A good-for nothing fellow ; নিষ্কর্ম্মা লোক, ভবঘুরে লোক, ধর্ম্মের ষাঁড় (*slang*)। **2.** (*Colloq.*) Scamp ; rascal ; পাজী ; বিটল। ***Verb i.*** To wander about ; to play the vagabond ; টো টো করিয়া বেড়ান ; ভবঘুরেমি করা। **—age,** *n.* **—ism,** *n.* Living as a vagabond ; টো টো বাজি, ভবঘুরেমি। **—ize,** *v. t.* To wander about in idleness like a vagabond ; টো টো করিয়া ঘুরা, ভবঘুরেমি করা।

vă-gā'-rȳ, *n.* Wandering of the thoughts ; a wild freak ; a whim ; "The *vagaries* of a child" ; চিত্তবিকার, চিত্তবিক্ষেপ, বুদ্ধিবিকার, বুদ্ধিবিভ্রম ; খেয়াল ; খামখেয়াল।

vă-gī'-nă, *n.* **1.** The canal which leads from the external orifice to the uterus ; যোনিবর্ত্ম, অপত্যপথ, অধোবশা, অজ্ঞি, কন্দর্পগৃহ, রতিমন্দির, রমণমন্দির, মন্মথায়তন। **2.** (*Bot.*) The sheath formed by the convolution of a flat petiole round a stem, as in grasses ; (উদ্ভিদ্‌বিদ্যা) কাণ্ডকোষ (সাঃ পঃ)। **Vag'-i-nal, vag'-i-nate, vag'-i-nat-ed,** *adjs.* **vag'-i-ni-tis,** *n.* Inflammation of the vagina ; অপত্যবর্ত্মপ্রদাহ। **Vag-i-not'-o-my.** *n.*

văg-ĭ-nĭs'-mŭs, *n.* A painful spasmodic contraction of the vagina ; অপত্যপথের আক্ষেপ, পরিপ্লুতা (সাঃ পঃ)।

vă-gĭn'-ū-lă, *n.* (*Bot.*) One of the tubular florets in composite flowers ; (উদ্ভিদ্-বিদ্যা) পাদদোষ (সাঃ পঃ), বিমিশ্র পুষ্পের নলাকৃতি পুষ্পক সমূহের অন্যতম।

vā'-grănt, *adj.* & *n.* **1.** Wandering from place to place without any settled habitation ; হাঘরিয়া, ভবঘুরে। **2.** Wandering; ভ্রমণশীল, প্রব্রজনশীল। ***Noun.*** An idle wanderer ; a vagabond ; (*law*) idle and disorderly personages and vagabonds and incorrigible rogues ; টোটোবাজ ; ভবঘুরে ; (আইন) অলস, নিষ্কর্ম্মা এবং দুষ্ট লোকের সমবায়। **—gran-cy,** *n.* **Vagrancy Act**—১৮২৪ খৃঃ অব্দে ইংলণ্ডে বিধিবদ্ধ আইন বিশেষ। এই আইনানুসারে নিষ্কর্ম্মা লোকগণ তিন শ্রেণীতে বিভক্ত হইয়াছে। যথা—(১) অলস এবং দুর্ব্বৃত্ত ব্যক্তিগণ ; (২) দুষ্ট এবং ভবঘুরে ব্যক্তিগণ ; (৩) অসংশোধনীয় দুর্ব্বৃত্তগণ। নিম্নলিখিত শ্রেণীর ব্যক্তিগণ প্রথম শ্রেণীর সঞ্চারজীবী বলিয়া কথিত হইয়া থাকে :—(১) যাহারা নিজের সম্পত্তির বিষয় গোপন রাখিয়া অনাথনিবাসে আশ্রয়ের প্রার্থনা করে ; (২) যে সকল বারবণিতা প্রকাশ্য রাজপথ, নগরোদ্যান প্রভৃতিতে বিশদৃশ আচরণ করে ; (৩) যে ব্যক্তি কার্য্যক্ষম হওয়া স্বত্বেও স্বেচ্ছাপূর্ব্বক নিজের ও নিজ পরিবারবর্গের ভরণপোষণে অবহেলা করে, এবং তদ্দ্বারা নিজের এবং পরিজনবর্গের অন্নবস্ত্রের সংস্থানের ভার স্বীয় যাজকপল্লীবাসী লোকদিগের উপর উপন্যস্ত করে ; (৪) যে সকল ফেরিওয়ালা বিনা লাইসেন্সে জিনিষ ফেরি করে ; (৫) যে সকল ব্যক্তি কোন প্রকাশ্য স্থানে, রাজপথে, অঙ্গনে ভিক্ষার জন্য ঘুরিয়া বেড়ায়, অথবা কোন অল্প বয়স্ক বালক বা বালিকা দ্বারা ভিক্ষা করায় বা তাহাদিগকে ভিক্ষা করার জন্য উৎসাহিত করে ; (৬) যে স্ত্রীলোক তদীয় জারজ সন্তানকে সম্পূর্ণরূপে বা আংশিকভাবে ভরণপোষণে সমর্থ হইয়া উহার ভরণপোষণে অবহেলা করে ; (৭) যে ব্যক্তি কোন যাজকপল্লী হইতে আদালতের অনমত্যনুসারে বহিষ্কৃত হইয়া পুনরায় বিনানুমতিতে তথায় আগমন করে। নিম্নলিখিত শ্রেণীসমূহভুক্ত ব্যক্তিগণ দ্বিতীয় পর্য্যায়ের সঞ্চারজীবী বলিয়া গণ্য হইয়া থাকে :—(১) যে ব্যক্তি প্রথমশ্রেণীর সঞ্চারজীবিত্বের অপরাধহেতু দুইবার দণ্ডিত হইয়াছে ; (২) যাহারা প্রকাশ্য স্থানে

লোকের হাত প্রভৃতি দেখিয়া শুভাশুভ বলিয়া থাকে ; (৩) যে সকল ব্যক্তি টোঁ টোঁ করিয়া ঘুরিয়া বেড়ায় এবং গোলাবাড়ীতে বা কাহারো বাটীর অশ্বশালা প্রভৃতিতে বা কোন পরিত্যক্ত অট্টালিকায় বা মুক্তস্থানে রাত্রি যাপন করে, এবং যাহাদের দৃশ্যতঃ কোনরূপ জীবিকার সংস্থান নাই এবং নিজের সম্বন্ধে কোনরূপ সন্তোষজনক উত্তর দিতে অসমর্থ; (৪) যে সকল ব্যক্তি কোন দোকানে, রাজপথে বা প্রকাশ্যস্থানে কোনরূপ অশ্লীল পুস্তক বা ছবি প্রদর্শন করে ; (৫) যে সকল ব্যক্তি কোন প্রকাশ্যস্থলে অশ্লীল ভাবে স্বীয় দেহ প্রদর্শন করে ; (৬) যে সকল ব্যক্তি কোনরূপ ক্ষত বা দেহের বিকৃতি প্রদর্শনে বা অন্য কোনরূপ মিথ্যাছলে ভিক্ষা গ্রহণের চেষ্টা করে ; (৭) যে সকল ব্যক্তি স্ত্রী পুত্রকে অসহায় অবস্থায় পরিত্যাগ করিয়া পলায়ন করে ; (৮) যে সকল স্ত্রীলোক জারজ সন্তানের ভরণ পোষণের অবহেলা করার অপরাধে দ্বিতীয়বার দণ্ড প্রাপ্ত হইয়াছে ; (৯) যে সকল ব্যক্তি কোন প্রকাশ্যস্থলে জুয়া প্রভৃতি খেলে ; (১০) যে সকল পুরুষ বারাঙ্গনাদিগের গলগ্রহ হইয়া জীবন ধারণ করে ; (১১) যে সকল ব্যক্তি প্রকাশ্যস্থানে পুনঃ পুনঃ লোককে কুক্রিয়ার জন্য আহ্বান করে ; (১২) যে সকল ব্যক্তি নৌবিভাগ ত্যাগ সম্বন্ধে মিথ্যা স্বীকারোক্তি করে, অথবা নৌবিভাগে প্রবেশের জন্য মিথ্যা উক্তি করে ; (১৩) যে সকল লোক গুরুতর অপরাধের উদ্দেশ্যে অস্ত্র দ্বারা সজ্জিত হয় ; (১৪) যে সকল ব্যক্তি কোন অবৈধ উদ্দেশ্যে কোন বাটীতে, অশ্বশালায়, বৃতিবেষ্টিত উদ্যানে, অথবা অঙ্গনে লুক্কায়িত থাকে ; (১৫) গুরুতর অপরাধের উদ্দেশ্যে নদী, বা পথ, খাল, জাহাজ ঘাট, প্রভৃতিতে বিচরণকারী তস্কর বা সন্দেহভাজন ব্যক্তি ; (১৬) ১৯০৫ খৃঃ অব্দে বিধিবদ্ধ বৈদেশিক আইনের (Aliens Act) কোন ধারার অপরাধে অপরাধী ব্যক্তিগণ। নিম্নোক্ত শ্রেণীসমূহভুক্ত ব্যক্তিগণ তৃতীয় পর্যায়ের সকারজীবী বলিয়া গণ্য হইয়া থাকে :— (১) যে সকল ব্যক্তি দ্বিতীয় পর্য্যায়ভুক্ত সকারজীবিত্বের অপরাধে দুইবার দণ্ডিত হইয়াছে। (২) গারদ, কারাগার হইতে পলায়নকারী।

vague (văg), *adj.* 1. Indefinite ; hazy ; doubtful ; of uncertain meaning ; অনিশ্চিতার্থ ; অস্পষ্ট, ঝাপসা, ঘোয়াল (হিঃ কোঃ) ; সন্দেহজনক, সন্দিগ্ধ ; অনিশ্চিত। 2. Unauthenticated ; uncertain ; অসত্য ; অনিশ্চিত, অনির্দ্দিষ্ট। **Vague'-ly,** *adv.* **Vague'-ness,** *n.*

vail (vāl), *v. t. & i.* (*Archaic, poet.*) To lower or take off ; নামান, খুলিয়া নেওয়া। ***Verb i.*** (*Archaic & poet.*) To show respect by yielding, uncovering or otherwise ; আত্মসমর্পণ, টুপি প্রভৃতি উন্মোচন, বা অন্য কোনপ্রকারে সম্মান প্রদর্শন করা।

vail (vāl), *n.* (*Archaic, usu. pl.*) Gratuity or money, given to the servants of a household by a guest ; (ক্বচিদ্ ব্যবহৃত) কোন অভ্যাগত ব্যক্তি বাড়ীর চাকরদিগকে যে বকশিশ প্রদান করেন।

vail (vāl), *v. i.* (*Archaic* or *poet.*) To avail ; to benefit ; ফল হওয়া, ফলোদয় হওয়া ; হিত হওয়া, উপকার হওয়া।

vain (vān), *adj.* 1. Unsubstantial ; empty ; as, *vain* boast ; অসার ; শূন্যগর্ভ। 2. Fruitless ; futile ; "*Vain* is the help of man" ; নিষ্ফল ; বৃথা। 3. Trifling ; as, *vain* fancies ; তুচ্ছ, নগণ্য, অকিঞ্চিৎকর। 4. Conceited ; গর্ব্বিত, দৃপ্ত। 5. Ostentatious ; "Load some *vain* church with old theatric state" ; জমকালো, আড়ম্বরপূর্ণ, ভড়কদার (*colloq.*)। 6. Having foolish craving for admiration or applause ; প্রশংসা বা সাধুবাদের জন্য নির্ব্বোধের মত আগ্রহবান। **Vain'-ly,** *adv.* **Vain'-ness,** *n.*

vain-glō'-rȳ (vān-), *adj.* Excessive vanity ; বড়াই, গর্ব্ব, দর্প, দম্ভ, আস্ফালন। **—ri-ous,** *adj.* 1. Boastful ; গর্ব্বিত, দৃপ্ত, দাম্ভিক। 2. Characterised or proceeding from vain glory ; গর্ব্বদৃপ্ত, দম্ভপ্রসূ। **—ri-ous-ness,** *n.*

vair (vār), *n.* A kind of fur, represented by blue and white shields or bells in horizontal rows ; একপ্রকার সলোম পশু চর্ম্ম—যাহা সাধারণতঃ কুলশাস্ত্রবিদ্‌গণ কর্ত্তৃক পরম্পর সন্নিকর্ষে বিন্যস্ত নীল ও শ্বেতবর্ণ ক্ষুদ্র ঢালসমূহদ্বারা প্রদর্শিত হইয়া থাকে।

vă-keel' (-kēl). **—kil',** *ns.* 1. An ambassador ; রাজদূত। 2. A High-court pleader ; হাইকোর্টের উকীল।

văl'-ance (-ăns), **văl'-ence** (-ĕns), *ns.* & *v. t.* 1. A kind of damask used for furniture ; খাট, চেয়ার, প্রভৃতির গদি আচ্ছাদনের জন্য ফুল পাতা প্রভৃতি বুনা একপ্রকার কাপড়। 2. A hanging drapery for a bed, window, etc. ; বিছানা, জানালা, প্রভৃতির জন্য একপ্রকার পর্দ্দা। ***Verb t.*** To decorate with such ; ঐরূপ পর্দ্দা দ্বারা পরিশোভিত করা বা উক্তরূপ বস্ত্র দ্বারা আচ্ছাদিত করা। **—anced',** *pp.*

vāle, *n.* 1. (*Poet.*) Valley ; (কবিতায়) উপত্যকা। 2. A little trough or canal ; ক্ষুদ্র দ্রোণি বা পয়ঃপ্রণালী।

vă-lē-dic'-tion, *n.* 1. A farewell ; বিদায়। 2. A bidding farewell ; বিদায়গ্রহণ। **—to-ry,** *adj.* & *n.* Suitable or designed for an occasion of leave-taking ; as, a *valedictory* address ; বিদায়োচিত, বিদায়ী। ***Noun.*** 1. A valedictory address ; বিদায়কালীন বক্তৃতা। 2. A farewell oration spoken by a student of the graduating class usually the boy who stands first ; আমেরিকার বিশ্ববিদ্যালয়ে উপাধিপ্রাপক সর্ব্বোৎকৃষ্ট ছাত্রের বিদায়কালীন বক্তৃতা।

văl-ĕ-dic-tō'-ri-ăn, *n.* A graduating person of the highest rank in American university ; আমেরিকার বিশ্ববিদ্যালয়ের সর্ব্বোচ্চ শ্রেণীর উপাধিধারী ছাত্র।

vā'-lence (-lĕns), *n.* (*Chem.*) The combining power of an atom, as compared with standard hydrogen atom ; (রসায়নশাস্ত্র) পরমাণুকগ্রহণশক্তি (হিঃ কোঃ)।

Và-len-ciennes' (-lăng-sî-ŏn), *n.* **1.** A rich kind of lace made at Valenciennes ; একপ্রকার জমকালো লেইস। **2.** A kind of stuff for waistcoat ; একপ্রকার ওয়েষ্টকোটের কাপড়।

văʹ-lĕn-çȳ, *n.* **1.** (*Chem.*) Same as VALENCE. **2.** (*Chem.*) A unit of combining power ; সংযোগশক্তির একক, পরমাণুক গ্রহণশক্তিতা (হিঃ কোঃ), মিলন-সংখ্যা, সংযোগ-শক্তি [কোন নির্দ্দিষ্ট পদার্থের এক পরমাণু ঊর্দ্ধ সংখ্যার যে পরমাণু হাইড্রোজেনের সহিত যুক্ত হইতে পারে উহাকে ঐ পদার্থের মিলন-সংখ্যা বা সংযোগশক্তি কহে (অনুকূলচন্দ্র সরকার)]।

vălʹ-ĕn-tīne, *n.* **1.** Same as ST. VALENTINE'S DAY (under SAINT). **2.** A sweetheart chosen on Valentine's day ; "And I a maid at your window, to be your *Valentine*" ; সেন্ট ভেলেনটাইনের দিবসে নির্ব্বাচিত প্রণয়ী বা প্রণয়িনী। **3.** A letter containing professions of love or affection sent by one young person to another on St. Valentine's day (14th Feb.) ; ফেব্রুয়ারী মাসের ১৪ই তারিখে যুবক যুবতীদ্বয় যে প্রেমপত্রের আদান প্রদান করে।

vă-lēʹ-ri-ăn, *n.* **1.** A plant of the genus valeriana ; এক জাতীয় লতা, গন্ধমাংসী, জটাবল্লী, বিলাতী জটামাংসী। **2.** The root of this creeper used as medicine ; এই লতার মূল।

vă-lē-ri-ă-nāʹ-çē-ae (-ë), *n.* A family of herbs of the order Valerianales ; জটামাংসাদি (সাঃ পঃ)।

vă-lĕrʹ-ic, —lē-ri-ănʹ-ic, *adjs.* Pertaining to, or designating, any of four isomeric acids $C_4 H_9 CO_2H$ of the fatty acid series ; দ্রাবক শ্রেণীবিশেষ সম্বন্ধীয়।

vălʹ-ĕt, *n.* & *v. t.* **1.** A servant that attends on a gentleman's person (also *valet de chambre*) ; খানসামা। **2.** A kind of goad or stick armed with an iron point ; লৌহশঙ্কু, যষ্টি। ***Verb t*** To act as valet to ; খানসামাগিরি করা। **Valet de place**—পথপ্রদর্শক, সংবাদ-বাহক, প্রভৃতি।

văl-ē-tū-dī-nāʹ-rī-ăn, *adj.* & *n.* Pertaining to ill-health ; sickly ; weak; অস্বস্থতাসম্পর্কীয়; পীড়িত, কাতর; দুর্ব্বল। ***Noun.*** A person of a weak or sickly constitution ; a person seeking to recover health ; one who is unduly solicitous about health; রোগা লোক, চিররোগী ; আরোগ্য লাভে চেষ্টিত ব্যক্তি ; স্বাস্থ্যসম্পর্কে অতিরিক্ত আগ্রহবান ব্যক্তি। **—ism,** *n.*

Văl-hălʹ-lă, *n.* **1.** In old Norse or Scandinavian mythology, the heaven where the souls of heroes slain in battle live in repose and happiness ; (নরওয়ে এবং সুইডেনের) পুরাণে বর্ণিত স্বর্গ—যথায় যুদ্ধে নিহত বীরগণের আত্মা শান্তিতে বিরাম লাভ করে। **2.** A building at Donaustauf near Ratisbon, erected by Ludwig I Of Bavaria between 1830 and 1842 in honour of the great men of Germany ; জার্ম্মেণীর শ্রেষ্ঠ বীরপুরুষগণের সম্মানার্থ ব্যাভিরিয়া-রাজ প্রথম Ludwig কর্ত্তৃক ১৮৩০—১৮৪২ খৃঃ অব্দে Ratisbonএর নিকটবর্ত্তী Donaustauf নামক স্থানে নির্ম্মিত হর্ম্ম্য। **3.** An edifice forming the final resting place of a nation's heroes ; কোন জাতির বীরগণের স্মৃতিচিহ্ন বা প্রতিমূর্ত্তি দ্বারা সমলঙ্কৃত সৌধ।

vălʹ-i-ănt, *adj.* Brave ; heroic ; সাহসী; বীর, শূর। **—ance, —ancy, —ness,** *ns.* **—ly,** *adv.*

vălʹ-id, *adj.* **1.** (*Obs.*) Powerful ; (অপ্রঃ) শক্তিশালী। **2.** Sound ; as, a *valid* argument ; well grounded ; অখণ্ডনীয়, অকাট্য ; ন্যায্য, প্রবল। **3.** (*Law*) Having legal strength or force ; as, a *valid* deed ; executed with proper formalities ; (আইন) বৈধ, সিদ্ধ, ন্যায্য, সপ্রমাণ (হিঃ কোঃ), প্রামাণিক (ঐ) ; যথারীতি সম্পাদিত।

vă-lidʹ-i-ty, *n.* Quality or state of being valid ; strength ; প্রামাণ্য (হিঃ কোঃ) ; প্রাবল্য (ঐ), বলবত্তা (ঐ)।

vălʹ-i-dāte, *v. t.* To make valid ; to ratify ; বৈধ করা, সিদ্ধ করা ; দৃঢ় করা। **—daʹ-tion,** *n.*

vă-lise' (-lēs), *n.* A small travelling bag or portmanteau ; একপ্রকার ক্ষুদ্র তোরঙ্গ, ভ্রমণকারীর ক্ষুদ্র পেটক।

Vălʹ-kyr (-kër), **văl-kyrʹ-i-ă**(-kër-), **—ie** (-ë), *ns.* (*Norse Myth.*) One of Odin's beautiful maidens who after every battle selected which of the slain should be conducted to heaven; Odinএর সুন্দরী পরিচারিকাগণের অন্যতম— যিনি প্রতি যুদ্ধান্তে নিহত বীরগণের মধ্যে কে কে স্বর্গধামে নীত হইবে—তাহা স্থির করিতেন।

văl-lăn-çȳ, *n.* (*Obs.*) A large wig that shades the face ; (অপ্রঃ) মুখাবরক বৃহৎ পরচুলা।

văl-lĕcʹ-ū-lă, *n.* (*Anat.* & *Bot.*) (*Pl. -lae*) A groove or furrow ; খাঁজ, পদ্ধতি। **—lar,** *adj.*

vălʹ-ley (-lĭ), *n.* **1.** A hollow or low tract of ground, between hills or mountains, generally traversed by a river ; উপত্যকা। **2.** The internal angle formed by the meeting of the two inclined sides of a roof ; চাল বা ছাদের প্রবণ পার্শ্বদ্বয়ের সংযোগে উৎপন্ন আভ্যন্তর কোণ। **Valley (of a river)**—অনুনদী, (সাঃ পঃ), নিম্নভূমি (ঐ), তরাই (হিঃ কোঃ)। **Valley (of a mountain)**—উপত্যকা (হিঃ কোঃ)।

văl-lō-nī-ă, *n.* Acorn-cups of the vallonia oaks used in dyeing ; চর্ম্মরঞ্জন, চর্ম্মশোধন, প্রভৃতিতে ব্যবহৃত একজাতীয় ওকের ফল।

vălʹ-lŭm, *n.* **1.** (*In ancient Rome*) A rampart ; (প্রাচীন রোমে) বপ্র। **2.** Eye-brow ; ভ্রূ।

văl'-ŏur (-ŏr), *n.* Courage ; bravery ; prowess ; সাহস, বিক্রম ; সাহসিকতা, নির্ভীকতা ; পরাক্রম। **—ous,** *adj.* **—ous-ly,** *adv.*

văl'-ü-ă-ble (-bl), *adj.* & *n.* **1.** Having value or worth ; মূল্যবান, মহার্ঘ, মহার্হ, দামী (*colloq.*)। **2.** Esteemable ; as, *valuable* friend ; আদরণীয়, সমাদরণীয়, উপাদেয়। **3.** Capable of valuation ; as, a service not *valuable* in money ; মূল্য নির্দ্ধারণীয়, মূল্য নির্দ্ধারণযোগ্য। ***Noun.*** (*Usu.*) A thing of value ; choice articles of personal property : মূল্যবান বস্তু, দামী জিনিষ ; অলঙ্কারপত্র। **—ness,** *n.*

văl-ü-ā'-tion, *n.* **1.** The act of valuing ; মূল্যনির্দ্ধারণ, মূল্যনিরূপণ, মূল্যনির্দ্দেশ। **2.** The act of estimating ; মূল্যাবধারণ। **3.** The value set upon a thing ; "Since of your lives you set so slight a *valuation*" ; নির্দ্ধারিত মূল্য। **—tor,** *n.*

văl'-ue (-ü), *n.* & *v. t.* **1.** Worth ; utility ; importance ; মূল্য ; কার্য্যকারিতা ; গুরুত্ব, সারবত্তা। **2.** Valuation ; appreciation of worth ; মূল্যাবধারণ ; মূল্য। **3.** Price ; estimated worth ; amount obtainable in exchange for a thing ; equivalent ; মূল্য ; নির্দ্ধারিত মূল্য ; কোন জিনিষের বিনিময়ে যে পরিমাণ বস্তু পাওয়া যায় ; সমপরিমাণ জিনিষ। **4.** (*Pol. Econ.*) The quantity of labour or of the product of labour which will exchange for a given quantity of labour, or of some other product thereof, (অর্থনীতি) যে পরিমাণ শ্রম অথবা শ্রমোৎপন্ন বস্তু নির্দ্দিষ্টপরিমাণ শ্রম বা শ্রমজাত দ্রব্যের বিনিময়ে প্রাপ্ত হওয়া যায়। **5.** Import ; as, the *value* of a phrase ; তাৎপর্য্য, অভিপ্রায়। **6.** (*Mus.*) The relative length or duration of a tone or note ; (সঙ্গীতবিদ্যা) কোন সুরের আপেক্ষিক দৈর্ঘ্য বা স্থায়িত্ব। **7.** Relation of one part of a picture to others in respect of light and shade : (চিত্রবিদ্যা) আলো এবং ছায়াসম্পর্কে চিত্রের এক অংশের সহিত অপরাপর অংশের সম্পর্ক। **8.** (*Rare*) Esteem ; regard ; (কচিদ্ ব্যবহৃত) সমাদর ; শ্রদ্ধা। **9.** The precious metal contained in rock, gravel, or the like ; শিলা, কঙ্কর, প্রভৃতিতে নিহিত মূল্যবান ধাতু। **10.** (*Biol.*) Rank in classification ; (জীববিজ্ঞান) শ্রেণীবিভাগে স্থান। ***Verb t.*** **1.** To estimate the worth of ; মূল্যাবধারণ করা, মূল্য নির্দ্ধারণ করা। **2.** To prize ; to esteem ; "Which of the Dukes he *values* most" ; to attach importance to ; to pride one's self on ; মূল্যবান বলিয়া গণ্য করা ; সমাদর করা ; গুরুত্ব প্রদান করা ; কোন বিষয়ে গৌরব বোধ করা। **—less,** *adj.* Worthless ; মূল্যহীন, অসার। **—less-ness,** *n.* **Value in use**—উপযোগিতা (হিঃ কোঃ)।

valve (vălv), *n.* **1.** One of the leaves of a folding door ; পুটীকরণযোগ্য (গুটাইয়া রাখার উপযোগী) কপাটের পাট বা বাইল। **2.** A movable cover, lid or partition for a tube or orifice, opening communication in one direction but closing it in the other, to regulate the flow of water, gas, or steam ; কপাটকল। **3.** (*Anat.*) A membraneous fold resembling a valve or serving as a valve in connection with the flow of blood, lymph, or other fluid ; as, pulmonary *valves* ; (শারীরসংস্থানবিদ্যা) দেহের কোন অংশের ঝিল্লীময় অংশ—যাহার একপ্রান্তে রক্তাদি প্রবাহিত হইলে অপরপ্রান্ত বন্ধ হইয়া যায়। **4.** (*Bot.*) One of the pieces into which a pericarp naturally seperates when it bursts ; the divisons of a capsule ; (উদ্ভিদ্‌বিদ্যা) কবাট ; বীজাধারের বিভাগ। **5.** (*Zool.*) One of the separable portions of the shell of a lamellibranchiate molluscs ; ঝিনুক, শঙ্খ, প্রভৃতির খোলকের একখণ্ড। **Valv'-al, Valv'-ar, Valv'-ate** (*Anat* & *Bot.*), **Valve'-less, Val-vif'-er-ous, valv'-i-form, Val'-vu-lar,** *adjs.* **Safety-valve**—See SAFETY.

văm'-brāce, *n.* A piece of plate armour to protect the forearm ; করাগ্রভাগ রক্ষার জন্য লৌহপট্ট।

vă-mōse', *v. i.* (*Slang, U. S.*) To be off ; (মার্কিণ যুক্তরাজ্যের ইতর ভাষায়) চলিয়া যাওয়া, চম্পট দেওয়া।

vămp, *n., v. t.* & *i.* **1.** The upper leather of a boot or shoe ; জুতার উপরের চামড়া। **2.** Any piece or patch intended to give a new appearance to an old thing ; যে পুরাতন জিনিষ নূতনের মত দেখাইবার জন্য যে তালি বা টুকরা লাগান হয়। **3.** (*Mus.*) An improvised accompaniment ; (সঙ্গীতশাস্ত্র) তৎক্ষণাৎকল্পিত সুরসঙ্গত। ***Verb t.*** **1.** To put a new vamp or upper leather on ; জুতার উপরে নূতন চামড়া লাগান। **2.** To patch an old thing with a new part ; to patch ; to repair ; পুরাতন জিনিষে নূতন অংশ সংযোগ করা ; তালি দেওয়া ; মেরামত করা। **3.** To improvise an accompaniment ; কোন সুরসঙ্গত তৎক্ষণাৎ কল্পিত করা। ***Verb i.*** (*Mus.*) To play a vamp ; (সঙ্গীতশাস্ত্র) তৎক্ষণাৎকল্পিত সুরসঙ্গত বাদন করা। **Vamp'-er,** *n.*

văm'-pīre, *n.* **1.** A dead person superstitiously believed to return from the other world, and to wander about the earth by night and suck the blood of the living, as they slept ; একপ্রকার রক্তশোষক পিশাচ, বোবা (cf. বোবায় ধরা)। **2.** One that lives by preying on others ; রক্তশোষক লোক। **3.** A large species of bat found in tropical America ; আমেরিকার অয়নান্তমণ্ডলবাসী একজাতীয় বৃহৎ বাদুড়। **4.** (*Theatre*) A small spring trap of two flaps used for sudden appearance or disappearance of one person; (রঙ্গালয়) কোন অভিনেতা বা অভিনেত্রীর আকস্মিক আবির্ভাব বা তিরোভাবের জন্য যান্ত্রিকব্যবস্থাবিশেষ। **—pir'-ic,** *adj.* **Vampire-bat**—Same as VAMPIRE 3.

Vampire-bat.

văm'-pir-ĭsm, *n.* **1.** Belief in the existence of vampires; রক্তশোষক ভূতে বিশ্বাস। **2.** The practice of extortion, or preying on others; রক্তশোষণবৃত্তি, শোষণবৃত্তি।

văm'-plāte, *n.* (*Hist.*) The plate of iron carried upon the lance, the lance passing through it, serving to protect the hand; বর্শাস্থাপনকালে যে লৌহপট্ট খণ্ড দ্বারা হস্ত রক্ষিত হইত।

văn, *n.* & *v. t.* **1.** (*Archaic*) A fan or other contrivance for winnowing grain; (অপ্রঃ) শস্যাদি হইতে অসার অংশ ছাড়াইবার জন্য একপ্রকার ব্যজনী বা তদ্বৎ ব্যবস্থা। **2.** (*Archaic*) A wing; (অপ্রঃ) পক্ষ। **3.** A shovel used in lifting ore; খনিজবিমিশ্র ধাতু তুলিবার জন্য একপ্রকার বেলচা। ***Verb t.*** To test the quality of ore by washing on a shovel or by a machine; বেলচাতে ধৌত করিয়া বা কোনরূপে যন্ত্রের সাহায্যে খনিজবিমিশ্র ধাতুর উৎকর্ষাপকর্ষ পরীক্ষা করা। **Van'-ner,** *n.*

văn, *n.* **1.** The front part of an army or the foremost division of a fleet; চমুমুখ, অগ্রানীক, রণমুখ, রণমূর্দ্ধা, রণশীর্ষ, রণপোতশ্রেণীর অগ্রগামী অংশ। **2.** The front or those at the front of any movement; the leaders of a movement; as, the *van* of civilization; অগ্রযাত্রিদল; কোন আন্দোলনের নায়কবৃন্দ। **Van-guard**—অগ্রগামী সৈন্যদল; (লক্ষণায়) অগ্রযাত্রিদল।

văn, *n.* & *v. t.* **1.** A covered vehicle for conveying goods; একপ্রকার মালবাহী আবৃত শকট। **2.** A closed carriage attached to a railway train for conveying passengers' luggage or for the accommodation of the guard etc.; রেলগাড়ীতে গার্ডের গাড়ী বা যাত্রীদের সঙ্গীয় মালপত্র বহনের জন্য শকট। ***Verb t.*** To convey in van; আবৃত মালবাহী শকটে প্রেরণ করা।

vă-nā'-dĭ-ŭm, *n.* A rare metal resembling silver in appearance; রজতবৎ একপ্রকার দুষ্প্রাপ্য ধাতু। **—nad'-ic, Van'-a-dous,** *adjs.*

Văn'dăl, *n.* & *adj.* **1.** One of ancient fierce German race who sacked Rome in A. D. 455; যে টিউটন জাতীয় লোক পূর্ব্বে বল্টিক সাগরের দক্ষিণ উপকূলে বাস করিত এবং পঞ্চম শতাব্দীতে রোম নগরীর সর্ব্বপ্রকার কলাদ্রব্য ও মূল্যবান গ্রন্থাদি বিনষ্ট করিয়াছিল, বনাটক (সাঃ পঃ)। **2.** (*Also l. c.*) One who wilfully or ignorantly destroys or disfigures any work of art, literature, or the like; যে ব্যক্তি ইচ্ছাপূর্ব্বক বা অজ্ঞাতসারে কোনরূপ কলাদ্রব্য, প্রাচীন সাহিত্যগ্রন্থ, প্রভৃতি ধ্বংস করে। ***Adj.*** Pertaining to, or resembling, the Vandals; barbarous; rude; fierce; কলাদস্যুগণ সম্বন্ধীয়, কলাদস্যুবৎ; বর্ব্বর; রূঢ়; ভয়ঙ্কর, ভীষণ। **—dal'-ic,** *adj.* **—ism,** *n.* The practice or conduct of the Vandals; wilful or ignorant destruction of works or monuments of art and literature; hostility to, or irreverence for, art and literature; disregard for what is beauiful or venerable; "The removal of the stone sea-horses which disfigure the pediment will be met with a cry of *vandalism*"; কলাদস্যুবৃত্তি; কলাবস্তু, সাহিত্য বা কলাদ্রব্যের স্মৃতিস্তম্ভস্বরূপ বস্তু ধ্বংস; কলা ও সাহিত্যদ্রোহিতা, ললিতকলা ও সাহিত্যের প্রতি অশ্রদ্ধা; সুন্দর অথবা সম্মানিত বস্তুর প্রতি অশ্রদ্ধা।

văn-dȳke', *n., adj.* & *v.t.* **1.** (*Cap.*) A famous Flemish painter of the 17th century; সপ্তদশ শতাব্দীর প্রসিদ্ধ হলণ্ড দেশীয় চিত্রকর। **2.** A picture by Vandyke; ভ্যানডাইক কর্তৃক অঙ্কিত চিত্র। **3.** A pointed collar of lace or sewed work worn by both sexes during the reign of Charles I., and to be seen in the portraits painted by Vandyke (Also *Vandyke-cape*, or *Vandyke-collar*); ১ম চার্লসের রাজত্বকালে প্রচলিত ত্রিকোণশ্রেণীশোভিত লেইসের বা সূত্রের কাজের গলবেষ্টনী — যাহা স্ত্রী পুরুষ উভয়েই পরিধান করিত। **4.** Each of a series of large points forming a border to lace etc.; জরি, ফিতা, কাপড় প্রভৃতির কিনারার ত্রিকোণশ্রেণীর অন্যতম। ***Adj.*** With borders notched with points like this (M M); ইংরাজী M অক্ষরাকৃতি ত্রিকোণশ্রেণী সমন্বিতপ্রান্ত বিশিষ্ট। ***Verb t.*** To cut the edge of after the manner of a vandyke collar; উক্তরূপ গলবেষ্টনীর মত প্রান্তদেশ ত্রিকোণশ্রেণীতে কাটা।

vāne, *n.* **1.** A thin strip of metal in form of a bird, arrow, etc. placed on a spindle at the top of some elevated object to show from which direction the wind blows; প্রবহমাণ বায়ুর দিঙ্‌নির্ণয়ার্থ গির্জ্জার বুরুজ প্রভৃতির চূড়াগ্রে স্থাপিত পতাকা প্রভৃতি, বায়ুনির্ণায়ক। **2.** A similar fixture moved in or by water; জলে বা জল দ্বারা সঞ্চালিত উক্তরূপ যন্ত্র। **3.** The blade of a windmill etc.; বায়ুযন্ত্র এবং জাহাজের ইস্ক্রুপাকৃতি চাকার ফলক বা পাটা।

4. The target of a levelling staff ; one of the sights of a compass, quadrant, etc. ; সমতলের পার্থক্যমাপক ক্রমাঙ্কিত দণ্ডে নিবদ্ধ শয়ানখণ্ডবিশেষ যাহা ক্রমান্বয়ে ঊর্দ্ধে ও নিম্নে সঞ্চালিত হইয়া থাকে ; তুরীয় এবং দিগ্‌দর্শন যন্ত্রের ক্ষুদ্র ছিদ্রবিশেষ যদ্দ্বারা বস্তু দৃষ্ট এবং দিগ্ নির্ণীত হয়। **Vaned, Vane'-less,** *adjs.*

văng, *n.* A sort of brace to steady the peak of a gaff ; জাহাজের অগ্র বা পশ্চাদ্‌বর্ত্তী পাইলদণ্ডের অগ্রভাগ স্থির রাখার জন্য রজ্জু।

văn'-gee (-jē), *n.* A contrivance for working ship's pumps by barrel and crank-brakes ; জাহাজের দমকল চালাইবার জন্য যন্ত্রবিশেষ।

vá-nil'-lá, *n.* 1. A genus of plants of the orchid group with an aromatic sheath-like pod or fruit, natives of Asia and America ; আমেরিকা ও এসিয়ার একজাতীয় লতা—ইহার ফল হইতে এক প্রকার সুগন্ধি উদ্বায়ী তৈল নিষ্কষিত করা হয়। 2. Fruit of this creeper; ভ্যানিলালতার ফল। 3. The fragrant oil obtained from the vanilla bean used in medicine, confectionery and perfumery ; উক্ত লতা হইতে প্রাপ্ত একপ্রকার সুরভিতৈল, ভ্যানিলা তৈল। **—late, —lic,** *adjs.*

Vanilla-plant.

vă-nil'-lism, *n.* An eruptive disease common among workers in vanilla ; ভ্যানিলা হইতে সুগন্ধি তৈল নিষ্কর্ষণের কার্য্যে নিযুক্ত ব্যক্তিগণের একপ্রকার চর্ম্মরোগ।

văn'-ish. *v. i.* & *n.* To pass from a visible to invisible state or beyond the limit of vision ; to disappear gradually ; to pass beyond the limit of vision ; to disappear ; বিলীন হওয়া, অদৃশ্য হওয়া ; ক্রমশঃ বিলীন হওয়া ; দৃষ্টির বহির্ভূত হওয়া ; অন্তর্হিত হওয়া। 2. To become zero ; শূন্যে পরিণত হওয়া। ***Noun.*** (*Phonet.*) A sound that gradually weakens till it ceases ; a slight sound with which a principal sound ends ; যে ধ্বনি বিলুপ্ত না হওয়া পর্য্যন্ত ক্রমশঃ হ্রাস হইতে থাকে ; কোন প্রধান ধ্বনির বিরামস্বরূপ ক্রমবিলীয়মান ধ্বনি।

văn'-ish-ing, *adj.* Gradually disappearing ; passing from the sight ; ক্রমবিলীয়মান ; অন্তর্হীয়মান। **Vanishing fraction**—যে ভগ্নাংশের অন্তর্ভুক্ত কোন চল (variable) কোন বিশিষ্ট সংখ্যাগত মান প্রদান করিতে লব এবং হর উভয়েই শূন্যে পরিণত হয়, লুপ্তভিন্ন (হিঃ কোঃ)। **Vanishing line**—(পরিপ্রেক্ষিত) দিকচক্রবালের সহিত সমান্তরালভাবে অঙ্কিত এবং চক্ষুর সহিত সমতল বলিয়া কল্পিত অসীমভাবে বর্দ্ধিত রেখা—যাহাতে ক্রমবিলীয়মান বিন্দু অবস্থিত থাকে, ক্রমবিলীয়মান রেখা, লোপনরেখা (হিঃ কোঃ)। **Vanishing point**—যে বিন্দুতে একই ধরাতলে স্থিত সমান্তরাল রেখাশ্রেণী মিলনোন্মুখ হয়, ক্রমবিলীয়মান বিন্দু, লোপনবিন্দু (হিঃ কোঃ)।

văn'-i-tў, *n.* 1. Quality or state of being vain ; emptiness ; falsity ; "Here I may well show the *vanity* of what is reported in the story of Walsingham" ; futility ; অসারতা, অন্তঃসারশূন্যতা ; শূন্যতা ; অলীকতা, ব্যর্থতা, বিফলতা, নিষ্ফলতা। 2. That which is vain, empty or unsubstantial ; অসার বস্তু, অসার বিষয়। 3. Empty pride ; "*Vanity* is the food of fools" ; দম্ভ, বড়াই, দেমাক, আত্মগর্ব্ব, অহঙ্কার (হিঃ কোঃ), আত্মসম্ভাবনা (ঐ)। 4. Ostentation ; "They through *vanity*...do thereupon build many forged histories of their own antiquity" ; জাঁকজমক, ঘটা, আড়ম্বর। 5. (*Cap.*) A town in Bunyan's Pilgrim's Progress ; Bunyan কৃত Pilgrim's Progress নামক গ্রন্থে উক্ত নগরী বিশেষ। **Vanity Fair**—'ভেনিটি' সহরে সারাবৎসর ব্যাপিয়া যে মেলা বসিত ; ভবের হাট ; Thackeryএর একখানি উৎকৃষ্ট উপন্যাসের নাম।

van'-quish, (văng-), *v. t.* To conquer ; to overcome ; জয় করা ; পরাজিত করা, পরাভূত করা, পরাস্ত করা। **—a-ble,** *adj.* **—er,** *n.*

văn'-tage, *n.* Same as ADVANTAGE. **Vantage-ground**—সুবিধাজনক স্থান। **To have a vantage**—To have under one's power ; বাগে পাওয়া।

văp'-id, *adj.* Insipid ; as, *vapid* wine ; flat ; as, *vapid* talk ; বিস্বাদ, পানসে (*colloq*) ; নীরস। **Va-pid'-i-ty,** *n.* **—ly,** *adv.* **—ness,** *n.*

vā-pō-ra'-ri-ŭm, *n.* A vapour-bath ; বাষ্প-স্নান, ভাপরা, উষ্ণস্বেদ (সুশ্রুঃ)।

vā-pŏr-im'-ĕ-tĕr, *n.* An instrument for measuring the volume or the tension of vapour ; বাষ্পের আয়তন বা তনাব মাপনার্থ যন্ত্রবিশেষ, বাষ্পমান।

vā'-pŏr-ing, *adj.* & *n.* Vaunting ostentatiously or vainly ; দম্ভকারী, আস্ফালনকারী। ***Noun.*** The act of boasting ; empty ostentation or windy talk ; "Consider them with their tumid sentimental, *vapouring* about virtue, benevolence" ; দম্ভ করণ ; দম্ভপূর্ণ উক্তি।

vā'-pŏr-ize, *v. t.* & *i.* To convert into vapour ; বাষ্পে পরিণত করা, বাষ্পীভূত করা ; ***Verb i.*** To be converted into vapour ; বাষ্পে পরিণত হওয়া, বাষ্পীভূত হওয়া। **—a-bil'-i-ty,** *n.* **—i-za'-tion,** *n.* The act of converting or being converted, into vapour ; বাষ্পীকরণ, বাষ্পীভবন।

vā'-pŏr-ous (-ŭs), *adj.* 1. Being in the form of vapour ; having the nature of vapour ; বাষ্পাকার ; বাষ্পধর্ম্মা। 2. Full of vapour ;

বাষ্পময়। **3.** Unsubstantial; unreal; vain; whimsical; "Such *vaporous* speculations were inevitable for him at present"; অসার; অবাস্তব; অন্তঃসারশূন্য; খেয়ালপরবশ। **—ly,** *adv.* **—ness,** *n.*

vā'-pŏr-ȳ, —pour-ȳ (-pŏr-), *adjs.* **1.** Full of, or of the nature of, vapour; বাষ্পপূর্ণ, বাষ্পধর্ম্মা, বাষ্পীয় (হিঃ কোঃ), বাষ্পময় (ঐ)। **2.** Peevish; hypochondrial; খিটখিটে; রোগাতঙ্কিত।

vā'-pour (-pŏr), *n.* & *v. i.* **1.** The gaseous form which any solid or liquid substance assumes when sufficiently heated; বাষ্প, ধূম, ভাপ (*colloq*)। **2.** (*Rare*) Fog; (কচিদ্‌ব্যবহৃত) কুয়াসা, কুজ্‌ঝটিকা। **3.** Something unsubstantial; vain imagination; unreal fancy; transitory substance; অসার বস্তু, আকাশকুসুম; অলীক কল্পনা; ক্ষণস্থায়ী বস্তু, ক্ষণিক বস্তু। **4.** (*Pl. Archaic*) A disease of nervous debility in which a variety of strange figures float in the brain; hypochondria; depression of spirit; spleen; (অপ্রঃ) একপ্রকার স্নায়বিক দৌর্ব্বল্য—যাহাতে নানাপ্রকার অদ্ভুত মূর্ত্তি মস্তিষ্কে ভাসিতে থাকে; রোগাতঙ্ক; মানসিক গ্লানি; বদমেজাজ। **5.** Empty boasting; দম্ভ, বড়াই, দর্প, আস্ফালন। **6.** (*Med.*) Kinds of medicines to be inhaled; বিভিন্ন প্রকার ঔষধ — যাহাদ্বারা নিশ্বাস গ্রহণ করিতে হয়, শ্বসনীয়। ***Verb i.*** **1.** To emit vapour; বাষ্প নির্গত করা। **2.** To boast or vaunt; "However you *vapour,* I can what I affirm make appear"; to bully; দম্ভ করা, বড়াই করা; শাসান। **—if'-er-ous, —if'-ic,** *adjs.* **—i-form, —ish,** *adjs.* **—ish-ness,** *n.* **Aqueous vapour** — জলীয় বাষ্প (সাঃ পঃ)। **Steam vapour**—উষ্ণ বাষ্প। **Vapour-bath**—Same as VAPORARIUM. **Vapour-burner**—আলোক বা উত্তাপ উৎপাদনের জন্য উদঙ্গার (hydro carbon) বাষ্পীভূত করার যন্ত্রবিশেষ। **Vapour-engine**—বাষ্পচালিত যন্ত্র।

văp-ū-lā'-tion, *n.* (*Joc.*) Flogging (কৌতুকচ্ছলে) বেত্রাঘাত।

vaquero, *n.* (*U. S.*) Herdsman; (আমেরিকার যুক্তরাজ্য) পশুপালক।

Vā-răn'-gĭ-ăn, *n.* **1.** One of those Scandinavians who entered the service of the Byzantine Emperors and became the Imperial Guards at Constantinople; যে সকল নরওয়ে ও সুইডেনবাসিগণ রোমকসাম্রাজ্যের প্রাচ্যবিভাগে কনস্তান্তিনোপল নগরে কার্য্য গ্রহণে সম্রাটের শরীররক্ষকরূপে নিযুক্ত হইয়াছিল—তাহাদের অন্যতম। **2.** One of the Scandinavians who founded a kingdom in Russia in the 9th century; যে সকল নরওয়ে ও সুইডেনবাসিগণ নবম শতাব্দীতে রুশদেশে রাজ্য প্রতিষ্ঠা করিয়াছিল — তাহাদের অন্যতম। **Varangian Guard** — Same as VARANGIAN 1.

văr'-ĕc, *n.* The impure carbonate of soda made in Brittany; ব্রিটানি নামক স্থানে প্রস্তুত একপ্রকার সাজিমাটী।

vā'-ri-ȧ-ble (-bl), *adj.* & *n.* **1.** That may vary or alter; changeable; unsteady; fickle; পরিবর্ত্তনীয়, পরিবর্ত্তী (হিঃ কোঃ); বিকারী (ঐ), ভেদশীল (ঐ); পরিবর্ত্তনসহ; অব্যবস্থিত; অস্থিরমতি, চঞ্চলমতি, অস্থির, চঞ্চল। **2.** (*Biol*) Aberrant; ব্যভিচারী, অতিচারী, জাতিভ্রপাপচারী। **3.** (*Math.*) Subject to continual increase or decrease; (গণিতশাস্ত্র) নিরবচ্ছিন্ন ভাবে হ্রাসবৃদ্ধিশীল, চল, বিষম (হিঃ কোঃ), চর (সূর্য্যঃ বাঃ)। ***Noun.*** **1.** That which is variable; পরিবর্ত্তনশীল বস্তু, পরিবর্ত্তনসহ বস্তু। **2.** (*Math.*) A quantity subjected to continual increase or decrease; (গণিতশাস্ত্র) নিরবচ্ছিন্ন হ্রাসবৃদ্ধিশীল সংখ্যা, চলসংখ্যা, বিষমরাশি। **3.** (*Naut.*) A shifting wind; (নৌবিদ্যা) পরিবর্ত্তনশীলবায়ু। **4.** (*Pl.*) The space, region, or belt intermediate between the north-east and the south-east trade-winds. This region varies in width from 100 to 500 miles, being widest in September and narrowest in December or January, and is characterised by calms, shifting breezes, and sometimes violent squalls; উত্তর-পূর্ব্ব এবং দক্ষিণ-পূর্ব্ব বাণিজ্যবায়ুর মধ্যবর্ত্তী স্থান, অঞ্চল বা বেষ্টনী। **—bil-i-ty,** *n.* **—ness,** *n.* **Variable motion** — বিষমগতি (হিঃ কোঃ)। **Variable-stars** — যে সকল নক্ষত্রের বিভিন্ন সময়ে ঔজ্জ্বল্যের ব্যতিক্রম হয়। **Variable-toad** — ফরাসীদেশীয় একপ্রকার সোণাব্যাঙ্গ। **Variable velocity**—বিষমবেগ (হিঃ কোঃ)।

varia lecto, *n.* (*L.*) Variant reading; পাঠভেদ, পাঠান্তর।

vā'-ri-ance (-ĕns), *n.* **1.** Disagreement; difference of opinion; discord; quarrel; অনৈক্য, অমিল, ব্যতিক্রম, বৈলক্ষণ্য; মতবিরোধ; ভেদ, মনোমালিন্য; কলহ, বিসংবাদ। **2.** (*Law*) An alteration of something formerly laid in a writ, or a difference between a declaration and a writ, or the deed on which it is grounded; a departure in the oral evidence from the statement in the pleadings; কোন পরওয়ানাতে লিখিত কোন বিষয়ের পরিবর্ত্তন, অথবা কোন সত্য উক্তি বা পরওয়ানার মধ্যে অনৈক্য, কিম্বা যে দলীলের উপর সত্যপাঠ করা হইয়াছে—তাহার সহিত উক্ত উক্তির অসামঞ্জস্য; বাচিক প্রমাণের সহিত সওয়ালজবের অনৈক্য। **To be at variance with**—To be in disagreement with; অনৈক্য হওয়া। To be in a state of dissension; to be in a state of enmity; বিরোধ থাকা; শত্রুতা থাকা।

vā'-ri-ănt, *adj.* & *n.* **1.** Different; diverse; বিভিন্ন, ভিন্ন, অন্যরূপ, অন্যবিধ; নানা। **2.** Variable; পরিবর্ত্তনশীল। ***Noun.*** A different form or spelling of the same original word; a differnt reading of a sentence etc.; কোন বাক্যের অনুরূপ আকার বা বর্ণবিন্যাস, আকারভেদ; পাঠান্তর, পাঠভেদ।

vă-ri-ā'-tion, *n.* **1.** A partial change in the form, position, state, or qualities of the same thing; modification; পরিবর্তন, বৈলক্ষণ্য; বৈবিধ্যপ্রাপ্তি (হিঃ কোঃ), পরিবর্ত (ঐ), ভেদন (ঐ), বিকার (ঐ), বৈষম্য। **2.** The extent to which a thing varies; পরিবর্ত্তনের মাত্রা। **3.** (*Gram.*) Change of termination; (ব্যাকরণ) শব্দের অন্ত্যভাগের পরিবর্তন, পদান্তের পরিবর্তন। **4.** (*Astron.*) An inequality of the moon's motion depending on the angular distance of the moon from the sun; (জ্যোতির্বিজ্ঞান) চন্দ্রের গতিবৈষম্য—যাহা চন্দ্র হইতে সূর্য্যের কৌণিক দূরত্বের উপর নির্ভর করে, বলন (শংকু), বলনাংশ (ঐ)। **5.** (*Biol.*) Deviation from a given type of form or structure; (জীববিজ্ঞান) জাতিরূপাপচার, পরিবৃত্তি (অভিঃ), ব্যত্যয়, ব্যতিক্রম। **6.** (*Magnet.*) The deviation of a magnetic needle from the true north; প্রকৃত উত্তর দিক হইতে চুম্বকশলাকার ব্যত্যয়, উদীচী-ব্যতিক্রম। **Annual variation**—বার্ষিকবিকার (হিঃ কোঃ)। **Variational equation**—বিষমসমীকরণ (হিঃ কোঃ)।

vär'-i-căt-ĕd, *adj.* (*Conch*) Marked by varicose formation; (শঙ্খ) নালীবিশিষ্ট। **—ca'-tion,** *n.*

vă̆r-i-cĕl'-lă, *n.* Chicken pox; জলবসন্ত। **—lar,** *adj.* **—loid,** *adj.*

văr'-i-cōse, *adj.* **1.** Preternaturally dilated or enlarged; (শিরাদি সম্পর্কে) অস্বাভাবিকরূপে স্ফীত বা বিবর্দ্ধিত। **2.** Designed for the cure or relief of varicose veins; বিবর্দ্ধিত শিরা আরোগ্য করণে বা ঐরূপ শিরার বেদনা উপশমনে ব্যবহৃত। **—cos'-i-ty,** *n.*

vā'-ri-ĕ-gate, *v. t.* To diversify in colour; to mark with different colours in irregular patches; নানাবর্ণে রঞ্জিত করা, চিত্রবিচিত্র করা; নানাবর্ণের দাগ দ্বারা রঞ্জিত করা। **—gat-ed,** *adj.* Coloured with diverse hues or tints; চিত্রবিচিত্র, চকরাপাকরা (*colloq.*), নানাবর্ণবিচিত্র, নানাবর্ণবিচিত্রিত, নানাবর্ণরঞ্জিত, কির্ম্মীরিত। **—ga'-tion,** *n.*

vă-rī'-ĕ-tȳ, *n.* **1.** Diversity; many-sidedness; বৈচিত্র্য; বিচিত্রতা, নানাত্ব, বৈবিধ্য (হিঃ কোঃ)। **2.** Collection of different things; as, *variety* of articles; a varied assortment; kind; বিভিন্ন বস্তুর সংগ্রহ; হরেক রকমের জিনিষ; রকম, প্রকার, জাত, প্রকারভেদ। **3.** (*Biol.*) A group subordinate to a species, differing from the rest of the species in certain features, due to particular causes, but less permanent than the specific; (জীববিজ্ঞান) উপজাতি। **—tal,** *adj.* **—tal-ly,** *adv.* **Variety show**—নৃত্য গীত, দড়াবাজী, প্রভৃতি নানাপ্রকার তামাসা, বিচিত্রপ্রদর্শনী। **Variety-theatre**—যে গৃহে নৃত্য গীত, দড়াবাজী, প্রভৃতি নানাপ্রকার তামাসা হয়, বিচিত্ররঙ্গশালা, চিত্ররঙ্গশালা। **Climatic variety**—জলবায়ুর প্রভাবের ফলে উৎপন্ন প্রকারভেদ। **Geographical variety**—যে প্রকারভেদ কেবল নির্দ্দিষ্ট স্থানের মধ্যে সীমাবদ্ধ থাকে।

vā'-ri-fŏrm, *adj.* Having various forms; বহুরূপী, নানারূপী।

vă-rī'-ō-lă, *n.* Smallpox; বসন্ত। **—lar, —ol'-ic** *adjs.* **—lous,** *adj.* Pertaining to, or designating, smallpox; বসন্তসম্বন্ধীয়, বসন্তসূচক।

vā-ri-ō-lā'-tion, *n.* Inoculation with smallpox; নৃবসন্তের বীজদ্বারা টীকা প্রদান, নৃমসূর্য্যাধান।

vā'-ri-ōle, *n.* (*Zool.*) A shallow pit or pitted marking; (জন্তুবিজ্ঞান) বসন্তের দাগের মত ক্ষুদ্র ছিদ্র। **—o-late, —o-lat-ed,** *adjs.*

vā'-ri-ō-līte, *adj.* A kind of porphyritic rock, having small pustular bodies like smallpox; একপ্রকার প্রস্তর—যাহার উপরিভাগে বসন্তের মত ক্ষুদ্র ক্ষুদ্র গুটিকা দ্বার সমাচ্ছন্ন থাকে। **—lit'-ic,** *adj.*

vā'-ri-ō-loid (-loyd), *adj.* & *n.* Like smallpox; বসন্তবৎ। ***Noun.*** A mild form of smallpox occurring in persons previously inoculated; পূর্ব্বে টিকা দেওয়া হইয়াছে এইরূপ ব্যক্তির যে একপ্রকার মৃদুজাতীয় বসন্ত হইয়া থাকে।

vā-ri-ŏm'-ĕ-têr, *n.* An instrument for comparing magnetic forces; চৌম্বকবলসমূহের তুলনার জন্য একপ্রকার যন্ত্র।

vā-ri-ō'-rŭm, *adj.* Denoting an edition of work with notes by various commentators; as, the *variorum* edition of Horace; বিভিন্ন ব্যক্তিকৃত টীকাসম্বলিত (পুস্তকের সংস্করণ)।

vā'-ri-ous (-ŭs), *adj.* **1.** Different; diverse; বিভিন্ন; নানা। **2.** Several; কতিপয়, কএক। **3.** Changeable; uncertain; পরিবর্তনশীল; অনিশ্চিত। **4.** Many-sided; অনেকমুখী। **—ly,** *adv.* **—ness,** *n.*

vär'-is-cīte, *n.* A mineral very like a greenish Turquoise found in Brittany; ব্রিটানী প্রদেশে প্রাপ্ত হরিদাভ তুরষ্ক মণির মত একপ্রকার খনিজ পদার্থ।

vā'-rix, *n.* **1.** A permanent and abnormal dilation of a vein; a vein so dilated; কোন শিরার চিরস্থায়ী এবং অস্বাভাবিক স্ফীতি; উক্তরূপে বিবর্দ্ধিত শিরা। **2.** (*Zool.*) One of the ridges or spinose lines which mark the former position of the mouth in certain univalve shells; (জন্তুবিদ্যা) শঙ্খাদির যে শিরাল রেখাসমূহ দ্বারা মুখের পূর্ব্বাবস্থান সূচিত হয় তাহার অন্যতম।

vär'-lĕt, *n.* **1.** (*Hist.*) A page; (ইতিহাস) বালভৃত্য। **2.** (*Archaic*) Menial; rascal; "Thou, *varlet*, dost thou master's gain devuor; Thou milk'st his ewes and often tiwce an hour"; নীচলোক, ইতরলোক; নচ্ছার।

vâr′-mint, *n.* **1.** A troublesome or mischievous person or animal ; নষ্ট লোক, দুরন্ত লোক, খারাপ পশু। **2.** (*Slang*) Fox ; (ইতরভাষায়) শৃগাল।

vâr′-nish, *n.* & *v. t.* **1.** A thick viscid liquid laid on a work to give it a gloss ; বার্ণিশ। **2.** Outside show ; বাহিরের চটক, চাকচিক্য। **3.** Superficial polish of manner ; বাহিরের ভদ্রতা। **4.** Whitewash ; "And set double *varnish* on the fame the Frenchman gave you" ; দোষাচ্ছাদন। **5.** The glaze on pottery or porcelain ; মৃৎপাত্র বা চীনা বাসনের উপরের বর্ণক বা মসৃণোজ্জ্বল প্রলেপ। ***Verb t.*** **1.** To apply varnish to ; বার্ণিশ দেওয়া, বার্ণিশ লাগান। **2.** To give a fair appearance to ; "Beauty doth *varnish* age" ; চটকদার করা, চকচকে করা। **3.** To gloss over ; as, to *varnish* errors ; দোষ ঢাকা, দোষাচ্ছাদন করা। **Varnish-tree**—যে সকল গাছ হইতে বার্ণিশের দ্রব্য পাওয়া যায়। **Varnishing-day**—প্রদর্শনী খোলার পূর্ব্ব দিবস—যেদিন প্রদর্শকগণ প্রদর্শনী গৃহে টাঙ্গানো ছবিতে শেষ চানকান দিতে পারে।

vâr′-sal, *adj.* (*Rare* & *colloq.*) Universal ; (কচিদ্ব্যবহৃত এবং চলিত-ভাষায়) সর্ব্বকালীন, সার্ব্বভৌমিক।

vâr′-si-tў, *n.* (*Colloq.*) University ; (চলিতভাষায়) বিশ্ববিদ্যালয়।

vár-sö′-vi-enne (-ĕn), *n.* **1.** A dance imitating mazurka ; একপ্রকার নৃত্য। **2.** Music for this dance ; উক্ত প্রকার নৃত্যের উপযোগী গান।

vâr′-tá-bĕd, -bĕt, *ns.* One of an order of Armenian clergy devoted to teaching ; আর্মেনিয়ান ধর্ম্মসংঘের ধর্ম্মোপদেশক।

vā′-rŭs, *n.* **1.** A variety of club-foot ; একপ্রকার বিকৃতপাদরোগ। **2.** A knock-kneed person ; যে ব্যক্তির চলিবার সময় জানুদ্বয়ের পরস্পরের সহিত ঠুকাঠুকি লাগে।

vā′-rў, *v. t.* & *i.* **1.** To change ; to modify ; as, to *vary* a statement ; পরিবর্ত্তন করা ; রূপান্তর করা, অন্যপ্রকার করা। **2.** To make diverse or different one from another ; বিচিত্রতাসাধন করা, ভিন্নরূপ করা, প্রকারান্তর করা। **3.** To diversify ; বৈচিত্র্য সম্পাদন করা। **4.** (*Mus.*) To embellish, as a melody or theme with passing notes, cadenzas, arpeggios, etc. ; (সঙ্গীতশাস্ত্র) বিভিন্ন প্রকার গীতি ও বাদনভঙ্গী দ্বারা কোন সুর জমকালো করিয়া তোলা। ***Verb i.*** **1.** To change ; as, customs *vary* form age to age ; to alter ; to modify ; পরিবর্ত্তিত হওয়া ; প্রকারান্তর হওয়া ; রূপান্তর হওয়া। **2.** To differ ; as, the laws of different countries *vary* ; বিভিন্ন হওয়া, ভিন্নরূপ হওয়া। **3.** To swerve ; as, to *vary* from the rules of justice and reason ; (মূলবিষয় বা পন্থা হইতে) বিচ্যুত হওয়া, অপসারী হওয়া, অপচারী হওয়া, স্খলিত হওয়া। **4.** (*Math.*) To be subject to continual increase or decrease; নিরবচ্ছিন্ন হ্রাসবৃদ্ধির অধীন হওয়া। **Vary-coloured**—নানাবর্ণবিচিত্রিত।

vās, *n.* (*Anat., Pl. vasa*) vessel ; duct ; রক্তরসাদিবহানাড়ী ; নালী। **vas′-al,** *adj.*

văs′-cū-lar (-lêr), *adj.* Consisting of, or containing, animal or vegetable vessels, as arteries, veins and the like ; রক্তরসাদিবহানাড়ীসমন্বিত, বৃক্ষরসবাহী তন্তুসমন্বিত, উদ্ভিদ্রসবাহী তন্তুসমন্বিত। **-ize,** *v. t.* **-lar′-i-ty,** *n.* **-lif′-er-ous,** *adj.* **-ly,** *adv.* **Vascular bundles**—নালীগুচ্ছ (সাঃ পঃ)। **Vascular plants** — কৌষিকঝিল্লী (cellular tissue) সমন্বিত বৃক্ষাদি। **Vascular sedatives**—হৃৎপিণ্ড এবং রক্তবহানাড়ীমণ্ডলীর অবসাদক ঔষধ। **Vascular system** — রক্তবহানাড়ীমণ্ডলী। **Vascular-tissue**—Tissue composed of small vessels like the woody tissue or substance of flowering plants, and in contradistinction to cellular ; ক্ষুদ্র ক্ষুদ্র রসবহানাড়ীসমন্বিত বিধানতন্তু। **Vascular tonics**—হৃৎপিণ্ড বা রক্তবহানাড়ীমণ্ডলীর বলবিধায়ক ঔষধ।

văs′-cū-lōse, *n.* & *adj.* The name given to the substance constituting the principal part of the vessel of plants ; বৃক্ষের নালীর সারভূত অংশ, নালিকাসার (সাঃ পঃ)। ***Adj.*** Same as VASCULAR.

văs′-cū-lŭm, *n.* (*Pl. -la*) **1.** A pitcher-shaped leaf ; কলসাকার পত্র। **2.** A botanist's case for carrying specimens as he collects

Chinese, Japanese and Indians vases.

them ; নানাপ্রকার লতাপাতার নমুনা সংগ্রহের জন্য উদ্ভিদ্‌বিদ্‌গণের আধারবিশেষ। **3.** (*Anat.*) A small vessel ; penis ; (শারীরসংস্থানবিদ্যা) ক্ষুদ্র নালী ; শিশ্ন।

vāse (*or* vāz *or* vâz), *n.* **1.** An ornamental vessel, generally of an antique pattern ; কারুকার্য্যখচিত প্রাচীন ধরণের ভাণ্ড। **2.** (*Arch.*) A sculptured ornament placed on socles or pedestals, representing the vessels of the ancients, as incense-pots, flower-pots, etc ; (স্থপতিবিজ্ঞান) প্রাচীন ধরণের কারুকার্য্যখচিত ভাণ্ডের মত উপপীঠ প্রভৃতির স্থাপত্যভূষা। **Vase′-ful,** *adj.* **Coal-vase**—কারুকার্য্যখচিত আধারে স্থাপিত কয়লার পাত্র। **Vase-painting**—ভাণ্ডচিত্রণ।

văs′-ē-line (-lĭn), *n.* A substance obtained from petroleum used as ointment etc. ; খনিজ তৈল হইতে প্রাপ্ত একপ্রকার পদার্থ—যাহা মলম প্রভৃতিতে ব্যবহৃত হয়।

văs′-i-fōrm, *adj.* Shaped like a vessel or duct ; নালীসদৃশ।

văs-ō-cŏn-strĭc′-tor (-têr), *adj.* & *n.* Causing contraction of vessels ; নালীসংকোচক। ***Noun.*** A nerve or drug causing contraction of vessels ; নালীসংকোচক শিরা বা ঔষধ।

văs-ō-dī-lā′-tor (-têr), *adj.* & *n.* Causing dilatation of vessels ; নালীপ্রসারক। ***Noun.*** A nerve or drug causing dilatation of vessels : নালীপ্রসারক শিরা বা ঔষধ।

văs-ō-mō′-tor (-têr), *adj.* Controlling the size of blood-vessels ; রক্তবহানাড়ীর আয়তন-নিয়ামক। **Vaso-motor nerves** — যে সকল স্নায়ু দ্বারা ধমনী ও শিরাদির সঙ্কোচন ও প্রসারণ-কার্য্য সম্পন্ন হয়।

văs′-ō-sĕn′-sō-rȳ, *adj.* Supplying sensation to vessels ; নালীতে সংবেদনসঞ্চারক, নালীসংবেদক, নালীবেদনাজনক।

văs′-săl, *n.* 1. A tenant holding land under a lord, and bound by his tenure to feudal service ; (মধ্যযুগে) সামন্ততন্ত্রের (Feudal system) নিয়মানুসারে ভূমিগ্রহণকারী প্রজা, সামন্তপ্রজা। 2. A slave ; a dependant ; ক্রীতদাস ; অনুজীবী।

văs′-săl-āge, *n.* 1. The state of being a vassal ; সামন্তপ্রজাত্ব। 2. Servitude ; political servitude ; দাসত্ব ; অধীনতা। 3. (*Rare*) Vassals collectively ; (কচিদ্ব্যবহৃত) সামন্ত-প্রজা সম্প্রদায়।

văst, *adj.* & *n.* 1. Very spacious or large ; বিশাল, বিরাট, বিপুল, বিস্তীর্ণ, সুমহান, তেপান্তর (*colloq.* only used as an adjective of *field.*) 2. (*Colloq.*) Very great (in number, in intensity) ; as, *vast* number : *vast* army ; (চলিতভাষায়) অতিশয়, অত্যন্ত, মহা, সুমহান। ***Noun.*** 1. A boundless compass ; "With nothing but the *vast* that foamed" ; waste ; অসীম বিস্তার ; জনহীন প্রান্তর। 2. A great quantity, amount or number ; বৃহৎ সংখ্যা, বহু জিনিষ, বহু সংখ্যা। **Vast′-ly,** *adv.* **Vast′-ness,** *n.*

văs′-tŭs, *n.* **Vastus externus**—উরুর বহিস্থিত পেশীসমষ্টি। **Vastus internus**—উরুর অভ্যন্তরস্থ বৃহৎপেশীসমষ্টি।

văt, *n.* & *v. t.* A large tub, vessel, or cistern, especially one for holding liquors in an immature state, chemical preparations for dyeing, or for tanning leather and the like ; গামলা, কুণ্ড। ***Verb t.*** To place in a vat ; to treat in a vat ; গামলায়রাখা ; গামলায় রাখিয়া রঙ্গ প্রভৃতি দ্বারা ছোবান।

Vatica robusta—শালগাছ (Syn. সর্জ্জ, কার্য্য, অশ্বকর্ণক, শঙ্কুবৃক্ষ, শস্য-সংবর)। [Arab. *saj.* Tel. *guggalam chettu* ; Burm. *eing-gyin.*]

Văt′-ĭ-căn, *n.* 1. An assemblage of magnificent buildings, including one of the Pope's palaces, and adjoining the Church of St. Peter ; রোমনগরীস্থ ক্যাপিটল পর্ব্বতোপরি বিশাল প্রাসাদসমূহ। পোপের প্রাসাদ এই প্রাসাদশ্রেণীর অন্তর্ভুক্ত। 2. Papal authority ; "The resumption of these hostilities will be signalised by the despatch of a Russian diplomatic agent to *Vatican*" ; পোপের ক্ষমতা। **—ist, —ism,** *ns.* **Vatican Council**—১৮৬৯—৭০ খৃষ্টাব্দের নিখিল খৃষ্টীয়-সম্মিলনী—যাহাতে পোপের অভ্রান্ততা ঘোষিত হয়।

vā-tĭc′-ĭ-nāte, *v. t.* To prophecy ; ভবিষ্যৎ বলা, ভবিষ্যদ্বাণী উচ্চারণ করা। **—na′-tion,** *n.* The act of vaticinating ; prophecy ; ভবিষ্য-কথন ; ভবিষ্যদ্বাণী। **—na-tor,** *n.*

vaude′-ville (vōd-vēl), *n.* 1. The name given by Oliver Basselin, a French poet of the 15th century, to his convivial songs which became very popular over all France : পঞ্চদশ শতাব্দীতে ফরাসীদেশীয় কবি Oliver Basselin কর্ত্তৃক রচিত ভোজোৎ সবগীতিসমূহ—যাহা তৎকালে সমগ্র ফরাসী দেশে অতিশয় লোকপ্রিয় হইয়া উঠিয়াছিল। 2. A theatrical piece intermingled with dances and light satirical songs ; নৃত্য এবং তরল ও পরিহাসপূর্ণ সঙ্গীতসহকৃত ক্ষুদ্র নাটিকা। 3. A species of light song generally of a comic or satirical nature ; হাস্য-পরিহাসপূর্ণ তরল সঙ্গীত। **—vil-ist,** *n.*

Vau-dois′ (vō-dwâ), *adj.* & *n.* (*Pl.* same) Pertaining to Vaud in Switzerland ; সুইজরলণ্ডের অন্তঃপাতী Vaud নামক স্থানসম্বন্ধীয়। ***Noun.*** An inhabitant of Vaud ; Vaudএর অধিবাসী।

Vau-dois′ (vō-dwâ), *adj.* & *n.* (*Pl.* Same) Waldensian ; Piedmont উপত্যকাবাসী প্রোটেষ্ট্যাণ্ট সম্প্রদায়-বিশেষসম্বন্ধীয়। ***Noun.*** One holding the Waldensian doctrine ; উক্ত প্রোটেষ্ট্যাণ্ট সম্প্রদায়ভুক্ত ব্যক্তি।

vau-doo′ (vä-), *n.* & *v. t.* Same as VOODOO (which see).

vault (vält), *n.* & *v. t.* 1. An arched roof ; খিলান করা ছাদ, খিলান-বিশিষ্ট ছাদ। 2. A room or space covered by a vault ; a chamber, esp. underground with an arched roof ; subterranean place used for storing article, for a prison,

Vaulted roofs.
1, Cylindrical barrel or Wagon vault ; 2, Roman vault.

for internment, or the like ; খিলান দ্বারা আচ্ছাদিত কক্ষ বা স্থান ; খিলান-বিশিষ্ট কক্ষ, খিলানবিশিষ্ট অন্তর্ভৌমকক্ষ ; জিনিষপত্র রাখার জন্য ভূমধ্যস্থ কক্ষ, ভূগর্ভস্থ কারাকক্ষ, প্রভৃতি। 3. (*Fig.*) The canopy of heaven ; sky ; গগনচন্দ্রাতপ, গগনাঙ্গন (বাসব:) ; আকাশ, নভোমণ্ডল। 4. (*Anat.*) An arched roof of a cavity ; (শারীরসংস্থানবিদ্যা)

দেহাভ্যন্তরস্থ কোন যন্ত্রের খিলানবিশিষ্ট উপরিভাগ। ***Verb t.*** To cover with, or as with, a vault or arch ; খিলান দ্বারা আচ্ছাদিত করা, খিলানবৎ কোন কিছু দ্বারা আচ্ছাদিত করা। **Vault′-ed,** *adj.* Furnished with vault ; খিলানবিশিষ্ট, খিলানওয়ালা, খিলান করা।

vault (vält), *n., v. i. & t.* **1.** A leap or bound ; লম্ফ। **2.** The leap of a horse ; অশ্বের লম্ফ। **3.** A leap by means of a pole, or assisted by resting the hand or hands on something ; হাত বা দণ্ডের উপর ভর দিয়া লম্ফ। ***Verb i.*** **1.** To leap ; লম্ফ দেওয়া, লাফ দেওয়া। **2.** To leap by means of a pole or assisted by resting the hand or hands on something ; হস্ত বা দণ্ডের উপর ভর দিয়া লাফ দেওয়া। **3.** (*Rare*) To execute the feats of tumbling ; (ক্বচিদ্‌ব্যবহৃত) ডিগবাজী খাওয়া। ***Verb t.*** **1.** To leap over ; লাফ দিয়া পার হওয়া। **2.** To leap over by means of the hands or poles ; হস্ত বা দণ্ডের সাহায্যে লম্ফ দিয়া পার হওয়া। **Vault′-er,** *n.* **Vaulting-horse**—লম্ফশিক্ষার্থ ব্যায়ামশালায় রক্ষিত কাষ্ঠময় অশ্ব। **Vaulting-house**—(অপ্রঃ) বেশ্যালয়।

vaunt, (vänt), *v. i., t. & n.* To boast ; to talk with vain ostentation ; গর্ব্ব করা, দর্প করা, বড়াই করা, দম্ভ করা ; স্পর্দ্ধা করা, আস্ফালন করা। ***Verb t.*** To boast of, or to make a vain display of ; দম্ভ করা, আস্ফালন করা, বড়াই করা। ***Noun.*** Boast ; brag ; ostentation ; দম্ভ, দর্প ; বড়াই, আস্ফালন ; জাঁক। **Vaunt′-er,** *n.* **Vaunt′-ing-ly,** *adv.*

văv′-ă-sŏ-rȳ, *n.* **1.** The tenure of a fee, or the lands, held by a vavasour ; দ্বিতীয় শ্রেণীর ভূম্যধিকারীর জোত। **2.** Lands of a vavasour ; দ্বিতীয় শ্রেণীর ভূম্যধিকারীর ভূসম্পত্তি।

văv′-ă-sour (-sŏr), *n.* **1.** (*In feudal law*) A principal vassal not holding immediately of the sovereign but of a great lord, and having other vassals who held of him ; a vassal of the second degree or rank, inferior, but next, to the higher nobility ; (সামন্ততন্ত্রে) যে ব্যক্তি সাক্ষাৎ সম্বন্ধে রাজা হইতে ভূমি গ্রহণ করে না, পরন্তু কোন প্রধান সম্ভ্রান্ত পুরুষ হইতে ভূমি প্রাপ্ত হইয়া থাকে ; সম্ভ্রান্ত পুরুষদিগের অব্যবহিত নিম্নবর্ত্তী ভূম্যধিকারী, দ্বিতীয়শ্রেণীর ভূম্যধিকারী।

vē-ă′-dēr, *n.* The thirteenth, or intercalary month, which about the every third year is added to the Jewish year ; ইহুদিদিগের অধিমাস বিশেষ—যাহা প্রতি তিন বৎসর অন্তর ইহুদী বর্ষের সহিত যুক্ত হইয়া থাকে।

veal (vēl), *n.* The flesh of calf killed for the table ; বাছুরের মাংস, গোবৎসমাংস। **Veal′-y,** *adj.* **Veal-skin**—একপ্রকার চর্ম্মরোগ—যাহাতে মুখ ও গলদেশে মসৃণ এবং শ্বেতবর্ণ একপ্রকার অর্ব্বুদ উৎপন্ন হয়।

vĕc′-tŏr, *n.* A line conceived as having a fixed length and fixed direction, but no fixed position ; the quantity that determines the position in space of one point relatively to another ; নির্দ্দিষ্ট দৈর্ঘ্য এবং দিগ্‌বিশিষ্ট পরন্তু নির্দ্দিষ্ট অবস্থিতিশূন্য রেখা, নাভিশ্রুতি (হিঃ কোঃ) ; আকাশস্থ (in space) একবিন্দু সম্পর্কে অপর বিন্দুর অবস্থিতি যে সংখ্যাদ্বারা নিরূপিত হয়। **—to′-ri-al,** *adj.* **Radius vector**—See RADIUS. **Vector quantity**—নাভিশ্রুতিদ্বারা প্রদর্শনযোগ্য সংখ্যা।

Ve′-dä (vā- *or* vē-dă), *n.* The ancient sacred literature of the Hindus divided into four portions ; বেদ। **—dic,** *adj.*

Vē-dân′-gă, *n.* One of the six works auxiliary to the Vedas ; বেদাঙ্গ।

Vē′-dân′-tă, *n.* A system of philosophy among the Hindus ; বেদান্ত।

vē-dette′ (-dĕt), **vi—,** *ns.* A sentinel on horseback ; অশ্বারোহী সান্ত্রী।

veer (vēr), *v. i. & t.* **1.** To turn ; to change direction ; ফিরা ; দিক্ পরিবর্ত্তন করা। **2.** To change one's opinion ; মত পরিবর্ত্তন করা। ***Verb t.*** **1.** To direct to a different course ; to turn ; দিক্ পরিবর্ত্তন করা, ভিন্নদিকে চালিত করা ; ফিরান, ঘুরাণ। **2.** To let out ; to slacken ; ছাড়িয়া দেওয়া ; ঢিলা করা। **To veer and haul**—To tighten and slacken alternately ; পর্য্যায়ক্রমে কষিয়া টানা এবং ঢিল করা। (Of wind) To change alternately ; (বায়ুর গতি সম্বন্ধে) পর্য্যায়ক্রমে পরিবর্ত্তিত হওয়া। (*Fig.*) To hesitate in giving opinion ; (লক্ষণায়) মত প্রদানে ইতস্ততঃ করা। **To veer away**—To slacken and let run ; ঢিল করিয়া ছাড়িয়া দেওয়া। **To veer out**—To let out to a greater length ; অনেকটা ছাড়িয়া দেওয়া।

vega, *n.* **1.** A low flat damp tract in Cuba ; কিউবা দ্বীপের আর্দ্র এবং সমতল নিম্নভূমি। **2.** A Cubean tobacco-field ; কিউবা দ্বীপের তামাকের ক্ষেত্র।

vega, *n.* The brightest star in the constellation Lyra ; অভিজিৎ যোগতারা (সাঃ পঃ)। [জ্যোতির্ব্বিদগণের মতে এই নক্ষত্র খৃঃ পূঃ ১২০০০—১৩০০০ অব্দে ধ্রুবতারা ছিল এবং পুনরায় ইহা ১৫০০০—১৬০০০ খৃষ্টাব্দে ধ্রুবতারার স্থান অধিকার করিবে। সূর্য্য তাহার গ্রহ-পরিবার লইয়া এই Vega নক্ষত্রের দিকে প্রতি সেকেণ্ডে ১০ মাইল বেগে ধাবিত হইতেছে।]

vĕg′-ē-tă-ble (-bl), *adj. & n.* Pertaining to plants ; having the nature of plants ; consisting of, or comprising, plants ; produced from plants ; উদ্ভিদ্‌সম্বন্ধীয় ; উদ্ভিজ্জ-স্বভাব ; উদ্ভিজ্জাত্মক ; উদ্ভিজ্জ। ***Noun.*** A plant, esp. a plant used for culinary purposes ; উদ্ভিদ্, আনাজ, তরকারী, শাকসব্জী, তরিতরকারী। **—bil′-i-ty,** *n.* **Vegetable-alkali**—উদ্ভিজ্জক্ষার। **Vegetable-anatomy**—উদ্ভিদের অঙ্গবিন্যাসসম্বন্ধীয় বিদ্যা। **Vegetable-black**—দীপকজ্জল।

Vegetable-brimstone — লাইকো-পোডিয়্যামচূর্ণ। **Vegetable-butter**—উদ্ভিজ্জনবনীত (যথা নারিকেলের নবনীত)। **Vegetable-calomel** — Same as MAY-APPLE. **Vegetable casein**—Same as LEGUMIN. **Vegetable-egg**—বেগুনগাছ ; কমলালেবু প্রভৃতির মোরব্বা। **Vegetable-flannel**—জর্ম্মণীদেশে সরল গাছের আঁশ হইতে প্রস্তুত বস্ত্রবিশেষ। **Vegetable-fountain**—একপ্রকার জলজ লতা। **Vegetable-hair**—একপ্রকার ক্ষুপ। **Vegetable-horsehair**—ইয়ুরোপদেশীয় একপ্রকার তালীবৃক্ষের আঁশ—যদ্দ্বারা গদি প্রভৃতি পূর্ণ করা হয়। **Vegetable-ivory**—Same as IVORY-NUT. **Vegetable-jelly**—Same as PECTIN. **Vegetable-kingdom**—উদ্ভিজ্জ জগৎ, বনৌষধিবর্গ (অমরঃ), বনস্পতিসর্গ (হিঃ কোঃ), বৃক্ষসৃষ্টি (ঐ), বৃক্ষযোনি (ঐ)। **Vegetable-life** — উদ্ভিজ্জ জীবন। **Vegetable-marrow**—কুষ্মাণ্ড। [Syn. তিমিষ, গ্রাম্যকর্কটী, ঘৃণাবাস, কর্কারু, কুষ্মাণ্ডক, পুষ্পফল, কুষ্মাণ্ডী, কর্কোটিক, শুনী, নাগপুষ্পফলা, কুষ্ফফলা, বৃহৎফলা, সুফলা।] **Vegetable-mould** — বোদমাটী। **Vegetable-organism**—বৃক্ষ (ব্রজঃ হিন্দু)। **Vegetable-wax**—উদ্ভিজ্জ মোম।

vĕg′-ē-tăl, *adj.* & *n.* **1.** Of, or pertaining to, plants; of the nature of vegetable; উদ্ভিদ্‌সম্বন্ধীয়; উদ্ভিজ্জ প্রকৃতিক। **2.** Common to animals and plants; জীব এবং উদ্ভিদের পক্ষে সাধারণ। ***Noun.*** Plants; vegetables; উদ্ভিজ্জ; তরিতরকারী। **—tal′-i-ty**, *n.* **1.** The state of being vegetable; উদ্ভিজ্জত্ব। **2.** Vegetable life; উদ্ভিজ্জ জীবন।

vĕg′-ē-tăl-īne, *n.* A woody fibre treated with sulphuric acid so as to resemble ivory, coral, etc.; গন্ধকদ্রাবক সিক্ত করিয়া প্রবাল, গজদন্ত প্রভৃতির সদৃশ পদার্থে পরিণত একপ্রকার কাষ্ঠময় অংশু।

vĕg-ē-tā′-ri-ăn, *n.* One who abstains from the use of animal food as an article of diet; one who maintains that vegetable and farinaceous food constitute the only proper food for man; নিরামিষাশী, নিরামিষভোজী, শাকান্নভোজী; নিরামিষ ভোজনের পক্ষপাতী ব্যক্তি। [ইয়ুরোপ ও আমেরিকায় ডিম্বও নিরামিষের মধ্যে গণ্য হইয়া থাকে।] **—ism**, *n.*

vĕg′-ē-tāte, *v. i.* **1.** To grow as plants; বৃক্ষের মত বৃদ্ধি পাওয়া। **2.** To live an idle do-nothing life; "Person who...would have *vegetated* stupidly in the places where fortune had fixed them"; নিষ্কর্ম্মার মত জীবন যাপন করা, জড় এবং অলসভাবে জীবন যাপন করা।

vĕg-ē-tā′-tion, *n.* **1.** The process of growing, as plant by means of nourishment derived from earth; বৃক্ষের বর্দ্ধন, উদ্ভিজ্জজনন। **2.** Vegetables; উদ্ভিদ্। **3.** Vegetable life; উদ্ভিজ্জজীবন। **4.** Inert existence; অলসজীবন, তামসিক নিশ্চেষ্টতা, জড়তা। **5.** A morbid outgrowth esp. on heart; রোগজনক উপবৃদ্ধি, বিশেষতঃ হৃৎপিণ্ডের উপরি জাত রোগজনক উপবৃদ্ধি।

vĕg′-ē-tā-tive (-tĭv), *adj.* **1.** Growing like trees; বৃক্ষাদিবৎবৃদ্ধিশীল। **2.** Having the power to produce growth in plants; as, the *vegetative* properties of soil; বৃদ্ধিজননশীল। **3.** Inert; জড়, অলস। **4.** Pertaining to those bodily functions that are unconsciously performed; pertaining to growth or nutrition; যে সকল শারীরিক ক্রিয়া অজ্ঞাতসারে নিষ্পন্ন হয়—তৎসম্বন্ধীয়; বৃদ্ধি বা পোষণসম্বন্ধীয়। **—ly**, *adv.* **—ness**, *n.* **Vegetative organ**—বৃদ্ধিশীল ইন্দ্রিয় (সাঃ পঃ)। **Vegetative-reproduction**—ভিন্নদিক্‌উৎপত্তি (সাঃ পঃ)।

vē′-hē-mĕnt, *adj.* **1.** Acting with great force or violence; violent; as a *vehement* wind; প্রচণ্ড; প্রবল। **2.** Very ardent; জ্বলন্ত, তীব্র, উগ্র। **—mence**, *n.* The state or quality of being vehement; প্রচণ্ডতা, প্রাবল্য, তীব্রতা, উগ্রতা। **—ly**, *adv.*

vē′-hi-cle (-kl), *n.* **1.** Carriage; conveyance of any kind used on land; গাড়ী, শকট; যান। **2.** A substance in which medicine is taken; অনুপান। **3.** A medium or liquid in which pigments are dissolved for use; যে তরলপদার্থে রঙ্গ গুলা হয়। **4.** A medium; বাহন, মধ্যবর্ত্তী, আলম্বন। **—hic′-u-lar**, *adj.* **Vehicle of consciousness** — চিত্তস্থান (ব্রজঃ হিন্দু)।

vehm′-gē-richt (fām-), *n.* A tribunal in Germany in connection with a secret organisation for the execution of justice, organised at a period when the several states were too weak to uphold it; চতুর্দ্দশ এবং পঞ্চদশ শতাব্দীতে জর্ম্মণীতে প্রতিষ্ঠিত বিচারালয় বিশেষ — যাহাতে রাত্রিকালে অতি সংগোপনে গুরুতর অপরাধ সমূহের বিচার হইত।

veil (vāl), *n.* & *v. t.* **1.** A covering for the face; ঘোমটা, অবগুণ্ঠন। **2.** A covering, mask, disguise or the like; as, under the *veil* of secrecy; আবরণ, মুখস, ছদ্মবেশ। **3.** (*Bot. & Zool.*) Same as VELUM. **4.** Slight huskiness of voice; স্বরভঙ্গ। **5.** Same as CAUL. **6.** (*Eccles.*) A covering for a person or thing; কোন ব্যক্তি বা জিনিষের আচ্ছাদন। ***Verb t.*** **1.** To cover with a veil; অবগুণ্ঠনাবৃত করা, অবগুণ্ঠিত করা। **2.** To conceal; "She bow'd as if to *veil* a noble tear"; to disguise; ঢাকা, লুকান; গোপন করা। **Veiled**, *p.p.* **Veil′-less**, *adj.* Without veil; অবগুণ্ঠনশূন্য, অবগুণ্ঠনবিহীন। **Veiled plate**—(আলোকচিত্র) ঝাপ্‌সাফলক। **Veiled Prophet of Khorasan**—Thomas Mooreএর Lalla Rookh নামক গ্রন্থের অন্তর্ভুক্ত আখ্যায়িকাবিশেষের নায়ক। এই

ব্যক্তি আপনাকে দেবতা বলিয়া ঘোষণা করিত এবং তাহার মুখের তীব্রোজ্জ্বল দীপ্তিতে লোকের চক্ষু ঝলসাইয়া যাইবে, এই ছলে তাহার মুখ সর্ব্বদা আবৃত রাখিত। কিন্তু বাস্তবিকপক্ষে যুদ্ধে আঘাতপ্রাপ্ত হইয়া তাহার মুখ অতি বিকৃত অবস্থা প্রাপ্ত হইয়াছিল; ইহাই তাহার মুখ আচ্ছাদিত করিয়া রাখার প্রকৃত কারণ। **To draw aside the veil**—To uncover; ঘোমটা খোলা, অবগুণ্ঠন মোচন করা। **To draw a veil over**—To conceal; লুকান, ঢাকা, গোপন করা। **To take the veil**—To become a nun; খৃষ্টীয় সন্ন্যাসিনী হওয়া। **Within the veil**—জেরুজেলেমের ধর্ম্মমন্দিরের গর্ভগৃহের মধ্যে; স্বর্গে, পরপারে, অতীন্দ্রিয় রাজ্যে, পরলোকে।

veilleuse, *n.* *(F.)* A shaded night-lamp; দীপাবরক দ্বারা আচ্ছাদিত নিশাপ্রদীপ।

vein, (vān), *n.* & *v.t.* **1.** A blood-vessel which returns impure blood to the heart and lungs; শিরা, স্পন্দনহীন কৃষ্ণবর্ণ রক্তবহানাড়ী (ডাঃ হরিপ্রসাদ চক্রবর্ত্তী), রুধিরপ্রবাহকশিরা (হিঃ কোঃ)। **2.** A rib of a leaf; পাতার শিরা। **3.** A crack in a rock filled up by substance different from the rock; পাষাণের মধ্যস্থ ফাটোল—যাহাতে পাষাণ ব্যতিরিক্ত অন্য প্রকার পদার্থ থাকে। **4.** A streak or wave of different colour, appearing in wood, marble, and other stones; কাঠ, মার্ব্বল পাথর বা অন্য কোনরূপ পাথরের উপর ভিন্নবর্ণের শিরা, রগ বা ডোরা। **5.** A cavity or fissure; রন্ধ্র, ফাটোল। **6.** A tube or an assemblage of tubes through which the sap of plant is transmitted along leaves; যে নালী বা নালী-গুচ্ছদ্বারা বৃক্ষের রস পাতার মধ্য দিয়া সঞ্চারিত হয়। **7.** Manner of speech or action; particular style, character, disposition or cast of mind; as, he is of a humourous *vein*; বাগ্‌ভঙ্গী, কার্য্যের ধারা; বিশিষ্ট রীতি, ধারা বা প্রকৃতি। **Vein'-age,** *n.* **Vein'-less, vein'-like, vein'-y,** *adjs.* **Systematic veins**—যে শিরা দ্বারা দূষিত রক্ত শরীরের অপর অংশ সমূহ হইতে দক্ষিণ দিকে প্রত্যাবৃত্ত হয়। **To fill or cover with vein or veins**—শিরাদ্বারা পূর্ণ বা সমাবৃত করা।

velamen, (*Pl. velamina*), ***velamentum,*** (*Pl. velamenta*), *ns.* Enveloping membrane, esp. of brain; আবরক ঝিল্লী, বিশেষতঃ মস্তিষ্ক-আবরক ঝিল্লী। ***Velamen radicum***—মূলগুণ্ঠন (সাঃ পঃ)।

vē'-lar (-lêr), *adj.* A term applied to certain sound, as those represented by the letters *gw, kw, qu,* produced by the aid of the veil or soft palate; তালব্য। **Velar gutterals**—তালব্য বর্ণ (যথা (*gw, kw*).

vē-lā'-ri-ŭm, *n.* The great awning stretched over the roofless Roman theatres or amphitheatres; প্রাচীন রোমের ছাদবিহীন রঙ্গালয় অথবা রঙ্গভূমির চতুঃপার্শ্বস্থ ক্রমোচ্চ আসনশ্রেণীসমন্বিত বৃত্ত বা বৃত্তাভাসাকার অট্টালিকার উপরিভাগ যে বৃহৎ চন্দ্রাতপ দ্বারা আচ্ছাদিত করা হইত।

vē'-lăr-ȳ, *adj.* Pertaining to the sail of ship; জাহাজের পাইলসম্বন্ধীয়।

vē'-lāte, *adj.* Veiled; অবগুণ্ঠিত।

vē-lā'-tion, *n.* **1.** The act or process of veiling; secrecy; অবগুণ্ঠন; গোপনতা। **2.** The formation of a velum; ঝিল্লীময় আবরণ উৎপাদন।

velatura, *n.* Glazing of a picture by rubbing on a thin covering of colour with the hand; হস্তের সাহায্যে ঘষিয়া সূক্ষ্মবর্ণকের স্তরে চিত্র আচ্ছাদন।

veldt (vĕlt), **veld** (vĕlt), *ns.* In South Africa a grass-country; দক্ষিণ আফ্রিকার তৃণসমাচ্ছাদিত প্রদেশ।

vĕl-[illegible]ā'-tion, *n.* (*Archaic*) Slight skirmish; controversy; হাতাহাতি; বাগ্‌যুদ্ধ।

vē'-līte, *n.* (*Rom. Ant.*) A light-armed foot-soldier; (রোমক প্রত্নতত্ত্ব) লঘু অস্ত্রধারী পদাতিক সৈন্য।

vĕl-lē'-ī-tȳ, *n.* (*Archaic*) Lowest degree of desire not prompting to action; অতি সামান্যতম ইচ্ছা—যাহা হইতে কোন কার্য্যে প্রেরণা জন্মে না।

vĕl'-li-cāte, *v. t.* & *i.* To twitch; স্পন্দিত হওয়া, খিঁচা। **—ca'-tion,** *n.* **—ca-tive,** *adj.*

vĕl'-lum (-ŭm), *n.* **1.** A fine kind of parchment made from the skin of the calf, kid, etc.; গোবৎস, ছাগশিশু, প্রভৃতির চর্ম্ম হইতে প্রস্তুত একপ্রকার অতি মোলায়েম পার্চমেণ্ট বা চর্ম্ম-পট। **2.** A manuscript written on parchment; উক্ত প্রকার কাগজের উপর লিখিত লিপি। **3.** A superior kind of writing paper or a kind of cotton-cloth prepared to imitate more or less vellum in appearance; উক্তরূপ চর্ম্ম-পটের অনুরূপ একপ্রকার উৎকৃষ্ট লিখিবার কাগজ বা কার্পাসবস্ত্র। **—y,** *adj.* **Vellum-paper**—মোলায়েম পার্চমেণ্টের অনুরূপ কাগজ। **Vellum post** — একপ্রকার উৎকৃষ্টজাতীয় কাগজ।

veloce, *adv.* (*Mus.*) With great speed; অতি দ্রুত।

vĕl-ō-cīm'-ē-têr, *n.* An instrument for measuring velocity; গতিবেগমান।

vē-lŏc'-ī-pede (-pēd), *n.* A kind of cycle of old type; প্রাচীন ধরণের দ্বিচক্রযান প্রভৃতি। **—ped-ist,** *n.*

vē-lŏc'-ī-tȳ, *n.* **1.** Quickness of motion; swiftness; দ্রুতগতিত্ব, দ্রুতত্ব, ক্ষিপ্রতা, শীঘ্রতা (হিঃ কোঃ)। **2.** Speed; গতিবেগ, বেগ (হিঃ কোঃ)। **3.** Rate of motion; গতির হার। **Angular-velocity**—কোণাত্মিকা গতি (হিঃ কোঃ)।

veloute, *n.* A white sauce made by boiling down ham, veal, beef, etc.; শূকর মাংস, গোমাংস, বাছুরের মাংস, প্রভৃতি একত্র সিদ্ধ করিয়া প্রস্তুত ব্যঞ্জনবিশেষ।

veloutine, *n.* **1.** A kind of corded merino; রজ্জুবৎবুনা একপ্রকার মেরিণো কাপড়। **2.** A kind of toilet-powder; একপ্রকার অঙ্গরাগচূর্ণ।

vĕ′-lŭm, *n.* Kinds of membrane or membraneous covering, esp. the soft palate; বিভিন্ন প্রকার ঝিল্লী বা ঝিল্লীময় আবরণ, বিশেষতঃ তালু, গুণ্ঠন (সাঃ পঃ)। **Velum partiale**—অসম্পূর্ণ গুণ্ঠন (সাঃ পঃ)। **Velum universale**—চিরগুণ্ঠন (সাঃ পঃ)।

vĕl′-ūre, *n.* & *v. t.* **1.** Any fabric of, or resembling, velvet; মখমল বা তজ্জাতীয় বস্ত্র। **2.** Velvet or other pad for smoothing silk-hat; রেশমী টুপী পালিস করার জন্য মকমল প্রভৃতির ক্ষুদ্র গদি। ***Verb t.*** To smooth with velure; মকমল দ্বারা মসৃণ করা।

vĕ-lū′-ti-nous, (-nŭs), *adj.* Velvety; মকমলবৎ।

vĕl-vĕr-ĕt′, *n.* A bad kind of velvet; একপ্রকার নিকৃষ্ট মকমল।

vĕl′-vĕt, *n.* & *adj.* **1.** A soft material of silk with a short close nap; মকমল। **2.** A delicate hairy integument covering a deer's antlers in the first stages of growth; হরিণের নবোদ্গত শৃঙ্গের আবরণস্বরূপ সলোম ত্বক্‌। ***Adj.*** **1.** Pertaining to velvet; মকমল-সম্পর্কীয়, মকমলের। **2.** Soft as velvet; মকমলের মত কোমল। **—y,** *adj.* **1.** Like velvet; মকমলতুল্য। **2.** Made of velvet; মকমলে তৈরী, মকমলরচিত। **Velvet bean**—একপ্রকার গুল্ম—যাহা মার্কিণ যুক্তরাজ্যে গবাদির খাদ্যের জন্য এবং সবুজ সারস্বরূপ ব্যবহৃত হয়; ঐ গুল্মের বীজ। **Velvet bur**—একপ্রকার গুল্ম। **Velvet carpet**—একপ্রকার সুকোমল গালিচা। **Velvet cork**—একপ্রকার উৎকৃষ্ট জাতীয় কাক (cork)। **Velvet flower**—Same as LOVE-LIES-BLEEDING. **Velvet grass**—ইয়ুরোপের একপ্রকার দীর্ঘতৃণ। **Velvet guard**—(অপ্রঃ) মকমলের ঝালর; যাহারা মকমলের ঝালর পরিয়া থাকে। **Velvet-leaf**—একপ্রকার বৃক্ষ। **Velvet paw**—বিড়ালের কোমল থাবা; (লক্ষণায়) ক্ষীরের ভিতর হীরের ছুরি। **Velvet-pile**—মকমলের মত একপ্রকার কাপড়। **Velvet runner**—ইয়ুরোপ মহাদেশীয় জলচর পক্ষিবিশেষ। **Velvet-scoter**—একপ্রকার পক্ষী। **Velvet-sponge**—ফ্লোরিডা এবং পশ্চিমভারতীয়-দ্বীপপুঞ্জে প্রাপ্ত একপ্রকার মোলায়েম শোষক। **Velvet tamarind**—পশ্চিম আফ্রিকার বৃক্ষ বিশেষ; ঐ বৃক্ষের ফল। **Velvet tread**—মৃদু পাদবিক্ষেপ, মৃদু পদসঞ্চার। **Velvet-work**—মকমলের উপর সূচীকর্ম্ম। **To stand on velvet**—To have made one's bet so that one cannot lose and must in all probability win; এরূপভাবে বাজি ধরা—যাহাতে হারিবার কোনরূপ সম্ভাবনা থাকেনা, পরন্তু জয়লাভেরই সম্পূর্ণ সম্ভাবনা থাকে।

vĕl-vĕt-een′ (-ēn), *n.* Cotton velvet; সূতী মকমল।

vĕl′-vĕt-ing, *n.* Velvet goods collectively; মকমলের জিনিষ।

vē′-năl, *adj.* Pertaining to, or contained with, veins; শৈরিক, শিরাস্থিত।

vē′-năl, *adj.* & *n.* **1.** To be bought or obtained for money; mercenary; অর্থদ্বারা ক্রয়বিক্রয়যোগ্য; অর্থবশ। **2.** Ready to be bought over by lucre; as, a *venal* politician; sordid; উৎকোচ দ্বারা বশ্য; নীচ। ***Noun.*** A person who may be bought for money; যে লোককে অর্থদ্বারা বশীভূত করা যাইতে পারে। **—ly,** *adv.* **—nal′-i-ty,** *n.* **1.** The quality of being influenced by money; উৎকোচ প্রভৃতি দ্বারা বশ্যতা, অর্থবশ্যতা। **2.** Prostitution of service for reward; অর্থলোভে বিদ্যাবুদ্ধি প্রভৃতির অপব্যবহার।

vē-nā′-tion, *n.* Arrangement of veins on leaf, insects' wing etc.; পত্র, কীটের পক্ষ প্রভৃতিতে শিরাবিন্যাস, শিরাবিন্যাস (সাঃ পঃ)। **—al,** *adj.*

vĕnd, *v. t.* To sell; বিক্রয় করা, ফেরি করা। **Ven-dee′,** *n.* One who buys; ক্রেতা। **Vend-i-bil′-i-ty,** *n.* **Vend′-i-ble,** *adj.* That can be sold; বিক্রেয়, পণ্য। **Vend′-i-bly,** *adv.* **Vend′-or,** *n.* One who sells; বিক্রেতা, বিক্রয়ী।

vĕn′-dāce, *n.* A variety of white fish found in Great Britain only in Lochmaben and two or three English lakes; ইংলণ্ডদেশের Lochmaben এবং অপর দুই বা তিনটী হ্রদে প্রাপ্ত একপ্রকার শ্বেতবর্ণ মৎস্য।

Vĕn-dē′-ăn, *adj.* & *n.* **1.** Of Vendee in West France; পশ্চিম-ফ্রান্সের অন্তঃপাতী Vendee নামক স্থান সম্বন্ধীয়। **2.** Pertaining to a member of Vendee Royalist party, 1793-95; ভেণ্ডির রাজপক্ষভুক্ত দলের লোকসম্বন্ধীয়। ***Noun.*** **1.** A native of Vendee; Vendee প্রদেশের অধিবাসী। **2.** A member of Vendee Royalist party; Vendee প্রদেশের রাজপক্ষভুক্ত লোক।

Vendemiaire, *n.* The first month in French republican calendar; ফরাসী দেশের জনতান্ত্রিক-গণের পঞ্জিকার প্রথম মাস।

vĕn-dĕt′-tă, *n.* A private war excited by insult or injury; কৌলিক প্রতিহিংসা, বৈরশুদ্ধি। [কোর্শিকা, সার্ডিনিয়া, সিসিলি ও কেলেব্রিয়া প্রভৃতি স্থানে এইরূপ প্রথা প্রচলিত আছে যে, কোন ব্যক্তিকে কেহ হত্যা করিলে, নিহত ব্যক্তির নিকটতম আত্মীয়গণ তাহার মৃত্যুর প্রতিশোধ লইতে বাধ্য থাকে।]

vĕ-neer′ (-nēr), *v. t.* & *n.* **1.** To inlay the thin slices of a fine or superior wood over a coarse or inferior wood; অপকৃষ্ট কাষ্ঠ উৎকৃষ্ট কাষ্ঠের পাতল ফলক দ্বারা মণ্ডিত করা। **2.** To cover pottery etc. with the coat of same substance; মৃদ্‌ভাণ্ডাদি সূক্ষ্মমৃত্তিকার স্তর প্রভৃতি দ্বারা অচ্ছাদিত করা। **3.** (*Fig.*) To disguise with a superficial attractiveness; "As a rogue in grain *veneered* with sanctimonious theory" (লক্ষণায়) বাহ্য চাকচিক্য দ্বারা আচ্ছাদিত করা। ***Noun.*** **1.** A thin leaf of a superior wood for overlaying an inferior wood; অপকৃষ্ট কাষ্ঠ যে উৎকৃষ্ট কাষ্ঠের পাতলা ফলক দ্বারা আচ্ছাদিত করা হয়। **2.** Superficial show or gloss; বাহ্য চাকচিক্য, বাহিরের জাঁক। **Veneer-moth**—একপ্রকার তসরে পোকা—যাহার বর্ণ কতকটা নিকৃষ্ট কাষ্ঠের আচ্ছাদন স্বরূপ উৎকৃষ্ট কাষ্ঠের ফলকের মত হইয়া থাকে। **Veneer-saw**—বড় গাছ হইতে অতি পাতল কাঠের ফালি কাটিবার জন্য একপ্রকার করাত।

vĕn′-ē-nāte, *adj.* (*Med.*) Infected with poison; (ভৈষজ্যশাস্ত্র) বিষদুষ্ট।

vĕn′-êr-ă-ble (-bl), *adj.* **1.** Worthy of veneration; মাননীয়, শ্রদ্ধেয়, নমস্য, বহুমানাস্পদ, ভক্তিভাজন, শ্রদ্ধাভাজন, পূজ্যতম, পূজ্য। **2.** Rendered sacred by religious or other association; as, the *venerable* walls of a temple; সুপবিত্র, অতি প্রাচীন বলিয়া সম্মানিত **–bil′-i-ty,** *n.* **–bly,** *adv.* **–ness,** *n.* **Venerable Doctor**—বাস্তববাদের পক্ষপাতী মধ্যযুগের Guillaume de Champeaux নামক দার্শনিক। **Venerable Initiator**—ইংলণ্ডদেশবাসী মধ্যযুগের দার্শনিক William Ockham.

vĕn′-êr-āte, *v. t.* To regard with respect or reverence; ভক্তি করা, শ্রদ্ধা করা, সম্মান করা, মান্য করা। **–a-tor,** *n.*

vĕn-êr-ā′-tion, *n.* **1.** The highest degree of respect or reverence; শ্রদ্ধা, সম্মান, ভক্তি। **2.** (*Phren.*) Faculty of feeling reverence; as, the bump of *veneration*; (মস্তিষ্কসামুদ্রিক) ভক্তিসংবেদনীবৃত্তি। **3.** Worship; পূজা। **4.** An object of veneration; ভক্তির পাত্র, শ্রদ্ধার পাত্র।

vē-nē-rē′-ăl, *adj.* **1.** Of sexual intercourse; "*Venereal* signs"; সঙ্গমসম্বন্ধীয়, স্ত্রীসঙ্গমসম্বন্ধীয়, মৈথুনসম্বন্ধীয়। **2.** Arising from sexual intercourse; as, a *venereal* disease; রতিজ, মৈথুনজ। **3.** Adapted to the cure of venereal disease; as, *venereal* medicine; রতিসংক্রান্ত পীড়া আরোগ্যকর। **4.** Aphrodisiac; কামভাবোদ্দীপক, রতিবর্দ্ধক, শৃঙ্গারভাবোত্তেজক। **Venereal disease**—প্রমেহ, উপদংশ, প্রভৃতি রতিজপীড়া, রতিজরোগ, উপদংশ (সাঃ পঃ)। **Venereal remedies**—উপদংশ প্রভৃতি রোগের ঔষধ।

vĕn′-êr-ȳ, *n.* (*Archaic*) Sexual intercourse; (অপ্রঃ) রতিক্রিয়া, সঙ্গম, মৈথুন।

vĕn′-êr-ȳ, *n.* (*Archaic*) Hunting; শিকার, মৃগয়া।

vĕn-ē-sĕct′, *v. t.* & *i.* Same as, PHLEBOTOMIZE (which see). **–sec′-tion,** *n.* Phlebotomy; শিরাচ্ছেদ, শিরামোক্ষণ, শিরাভেদন (সুশ্রুঃ কুঞ্জ), রক্তমোক্ষণ (সুশ্রুঃ)।

Vē-nē′-ti-ăn (-shî-), *adj.* & *n.* Of, or pertaining to, Venice; ভিনিসনগরীয়, ভিনীসীয়। ***Noun.*** **1.** A native of Venice; ভিনীসনগরীর অধিবাসী। **2.** Same as VENETIAN BLIND. **3.** (*pl.*) A kind of tape used for holding slabs of Venetian blind; ঝিলিমিলির পাখী আটকাইবার জন্য একপ্রকার ফিতা। **4.** Same as VENETIAN CLOTH. **Venetion architecture**—গথিক স্থাপত্যধারার প্রকার ভেদ। (See Ruskin's *Stones of Venice*). **Venetian ball**—কাগজ চাপা দিবার জন্য একপ্রকার শোভাসাধক কাচকন্দুক। **Venetian blind**—ঝিলিমিলি। **Venetian carpet**—সিঁড়ি প্রভৃতি আচ্ছাদনে ব্যবহৃত একপ্রকার অল্প মূল্যের গালিচা। **Venetian cloth**—একপ্রকার অতি সূক্ষ্ম টের্চ্চাবোনা পশমী কাপড়। **Venetian-door**—যে দ্বারের উভয় পার্শ্বে দীর্ঘ স্বল্পায়ত বাতায়ন বা কাচফলক থাকে। **Venetian flat point**—একপ্রকার মিহি লেইস। **Venetian glass**—ভিনিস নগরী বা তৎসন্নিহিত স্থানে প্রস্তুত কাচভাণ্ড [উক্তরূপ কাচের পেয়ালা বিষসংস্পর্শে ভাঙ্গিয়া যায় বলিয়া কথিত আছে।] **Venetian pearl**—সংহত কাচ হইতে নির্ম্মিত একপ্রকার কৃত্রিম মুক্তা। **Venetian red**—সলফেট অব আয়রণ হইতে প্রস্তুত একপ্রকার লোহিতবর্ণ রঞ্জক পদার্থ। **Venetian School**—খৃষ্টীয় ষোড়শ শতাব্দীতে প্রাদুর্ভূত চিত্রকর সম্প্রদায়। সুপ্রসিদ্ধ চিত্রকর Titian এই সম্প্রদায়ের প্রতিষ্ঠাতা। এই সম্প্রদায়ভুক্ত অন্যান্য প্রসিদ্ধ চিত্রশিল্পিগণের নাম Giorgione, Tintoretto এবং Paul Veronese। এই সম্প্রদায়ের চিত্রকরগণ চিত্রে বর্ণ সমাবেশে বিশেষ কৃতিত্ব প্রদর্শন করিয়াছেন। **Venetian sumac**—ইয়ুরোপ মহাদেশের বৃক্ষ বিশেষ। **Venetian white**—একপ্রকার শ্বেতবর্ণ রঞ্জক পদার্থ। **Venetian window**—যে তোরণাকৃতি শীর্ষবিশিষ্ট বাতায়নের উভয়পার্শ্বে চতুষ্কাকৃতি শীর্ষসমন্বিত দুইটী দীর্ঘ এবং স্বল্পায়ত গবাক্ষ থাকে।

venge′-ance (vĕnj-ăns), *n.* Punishment inflicted in return for an injury or offence; প্রতিহিংসা, প্রতিশোধ, বৈরশুদ্ধি, বৈরনির্যাতন, বৈরসাধন, দাদ (*colloq.*), নির্যাতন (হিঃ কোঃ)। **To take (or to wreak) a vengeance on**—To take revenge; প্রতিহিংসা লওয়া, দাদ তোলা (*colloq.*), বৈরশুদ্ধি করা। **With a vengeance**—With great violence, force or the like; প্রচণ্ডবেগে, প্রচণ্ডবলে। Extremely; অত্যন্ত, অতিশয়। Without mistake; অভ্রান্তভাবে।

venge′-fûl (vĕnj-), *adj.* Vindictive; প্রতিহিংসাপরায়ণ, বৈরসাধনতৎপর, প্রতিহিংসাকামী, প্রতিজিঘাংসু। **–ly,** *adv.* **–ness,** *n.*

vē′-ni-ăl, *adj.* **1.** Pardonable; ক্ষন্তব্য, ক্ষমার্হ, মার্জ্জনীয়, ক্ষমাযোগ্য। **2.** Excusable; উপেক্ষনীয়। **–al′-i-ty,** *n.* **–ness,** *n.* **Venial sin**—(রোমান ক্যাথলিক ধর্ম্মসংঘ) যে পাপে ভগবদ্ অনুগ্রহ সঙ্কুচিত হয়, পরন্তু বিলুপ্ত হয় না।

Vĕn′-ice (-îs), *n.* A city in Italy; ভিনিসনগরী। **Venice glass**—ভিনিস নগরীতে প্রস্তুত একপ্রকার অতি বিশুদ্ধ কাচপাত্র—যাহা বিষসংস্পর্শে ভাঙ্গিয়া খণ্ড খণ্ড হইত বলিয়া কথিত হয়। **Venice treacle**—Same as THERIAC.

venire (facias), *n.* (*Law*) A writ directing the sheriff to summon jury; (আইন) জুরিদিগকে আহ্বান করার

জন্য শেরিফের উপর যে পরোয়ানা জারি করা হয়।

ven'-i-son (vĕn-zn *or* vĕn-ĭ-zn), *n.* The flesh of animals taken in hunting, esp. deer; মৃগয়ায় নিহত জন্তুর মাংস, হরিণমাংস, মৃগমাংস, হারিণ (মঃ উঃ)।

Venite, *n.* **1.** Psalm xcv; ৯৫ সংখ্যক ধর্ম্মসংগীত। **2.** A musical setting of the same; উক্ত গীতের স্বরলিপি।

vĕn'-ŏm, *n.* **1.** A matter fatal or injurious to life, esp. such as is injected from the bites and stings of serpents etc.; বিষাক্ত পদার্থ, বিষ, গরল, হলাহল, কালকূট। **2.** Spite; malice; virulence of feeling, language or conduct; বিদ্বেষ; অসূয়া, পৈশুন্য; ভাব, ভাষা, বা আচরণের প্রচণ্ডতা। **–omed,** *pp.* **–ous,** *adj.* **1.** Poisonous; বিষাক্ত, বিষধর। **2.** Spiteful; as, a *venomous* writer; বিদ্বেষপরায়ণ, অসূয়াপরবশ। **–ous-ly,** *adv.* **–ous-ness,** *n.*

vē-nŏs'-i-tȳ, *n.* **1.** Superabundance of venous blood; শৈরিক রক্তের আধিক্য। **2.** A somewhat morbid condition in which the blood appears to move more slowly than usual, all being more venous, and having a special venous blood in larger proportion than in a state of perfect health; (রক্তে) শৈরিক-রক্তের আধিক্যজনিত রক্তের মন্দগতি, শৈরিকতা।

vē'-nous (-nŭs), **–nōse,** *adjs.* **1.** Of, or pertaining to, a vein or veins; contained in the vein; শিরাসম্বন্ধীয়, শৈরিক; শিরাস্থ। **2.** Consisting of vein; শিরাত্মক। **–ly,** *adv.* **Venous blood** — শৈরিকরক্ত [এই রক্তের বর্ণ অনেকটা মেজেণ্টের মত। ধমনীর (artery) রক্ত অপেক্ষা এই রক্তে শতকরা ৮ কি ৯ ভাগ অল্প অম্লজান ও শতকরা ৬ ভাগ অধিক দ্ব্যঙ্গারাম্লজান থাকে। **Venous congestion** — কোন শারীরিকযন্ত্রে অধিক পরিমাণে শৈরিকরক্ত সঞ্চয়।

vĕnt, *n.* & *v. t.* **1.** Hole; রন্ধ্র, ছিদ্র, ফাঁক। **2.** The touch-hole of a gun; বন্দুকের রঞ্জক-ঘরা। **3.** Outlet; passage; expression; as, to give *vent* to one's passion, utterance; নির্গম; পথ; প্রকাশ, উক্তি। **4.** The openings at which excrement are discharged in birds and fishes; পক্ষী, মৎস্য এবং সরীসৃপের গুহ্যদ্বার। **5.** A hole in the top of a barrel to admit air while liquid is being drawn out; মদ্যাদি বাহির করার কালে, পিপার উপরিভাগের যে ছিদ্রপথে বাতাস প্রবেশ করে। **6.** A loophole in embattled wall; দুর্গপ্রাচীরের ছিদ্র। **7.** The odour left on the ground by which an animal's track is pursued; পলায়িত জন্তুর গন্ধ। **8.** The place where an otter comes up to breathe; উদ্বিড়াল শ্বাসপ্রশ্বাসের জন্য যে স্থানে আসিয়া থাকে। **9.** The flue or funnel of a chimney; ধূমনির্গমনালীর ফুঁদেল। ***Verb t.*** **1.** To discharge through a vent; to give outlet to; ছিদ্র দ্বারা নিঃসারিত করা; বাহির করা, বহির্নিঃসরণ করা। **2.** To utter; as, to *vent* one's feeling; to publish; উচ্চারণ করা; প্রকাশ করা, ব্যক্ত করা। **3.** To make a vent in; কোন কিছুতে ছিদ্র করা। **4.** To relieve by giving vent; প্রকাশ করিয়া উপশম করা। **Vent'-age,** *n.* **Vent'-less,** *adj.* **Vent-hole**—ছিদ্রাঙ্কুর। **To give vent to**—To give expression or utterance to; as, *to give vent to* one's anger; প্রকাশ করা, ব্যক্ত করা। **To take vent**—To come out; প্রকাশ হইয়া পড়া। **To vent one's spleen**—To give vent to one's passion; ঝাল ঝাড়া।

vĕn'-tĕr, *n.* **1.** The belly; abdomen; উদর; নিম্নোদর। **2.** The protuberant or concave part of a muscle or bone; কোন অস্থি বা মাংসপেশীর ন্যুজাকৃতি অংশ। **3.** (*Law*) Womb (of wife and mother); (আইন) গর্ভ (স্ত্রী বা মাতার)।

vĕn'-ti-dŭct, *n.* A passage for air, esp. a subterranean passage for air; বায়ুবর্ত্ম, বিশেষতঃ অন্তর্ভৌম বায়ুবর্ত্ম, কূপীবের (সাঃ পঃ)।

vĕn'-til, *n.* A valve in musical instrument; বাদ্যযন্ত্রের বায়ুনিঃসারক কবাট।

vĕn'-ti-lāte, *v. t.* **1.** To open or expose to free passage of air; as, to *ventilate* a room by opening the windows; নির্ম্মলবায়ু সঞ্চালন করা, বিশুদ্ধ বায়ু প্রবাহিত করা। **2.** To make public; to expose to public talk or consideration; "Much had been *ventilated* in private discourse"; প্রকাশ করা; জনসাধারণের আলাপ বা আলোচনার বিষয়ীভূত করা। **–la'-tion,** *n.* **1.** The act of ventilating; নির্ম্মলবায়ু সঞ্চালন, বিশুদ্ধবায়ুসঞ্চালন, বায়ুচলাচল। **2.** Free discussion; publication; প্রকাশ্য আলোচনা; প্রচার। **–la-tive,** *adj.* **–la-tor,** *n.* A contrivance for drawing off or expelling foul or stagnant air from any close place or apartment, and introducing that which is fresh and pure; বিশুদ্ধ বায়ু সঞ্চালন এবং দূষিত বায়ু নিষ্কাশনের জন্য যন্ত্রবিশেষ, বায়ুপ্রবাহক।

vĕn'-trăl, *adj.* & *n.* Of the venter; near the venter; উদর সম্পর্কীয়, উদরের, পেটের; উদরসমীপস্থ। **Ventral fin**—উদরের ডানা। **Ventral segment**—অচলস্থান (হিঃ কোঃ)।

ventre a terre, *adv.* (*F.*) At full speed; পূর্ণবেগে।

vĕn'-tri-cle (-kl), *n.* A small cavity in an animal body; a small cavity in the heart or brain; শরীরস্থ ক্ষুদ্র গহ্বর, কোটর, রক্তচালকস্থলী; হৃৎপিণ্ড বা মস্তিষ্কের ক্ষুদ্র গহ্বর। **–tric'-u-lar, –tric'-u-lous,** *adjs.*

vĕn'-tri-cōse, –cous (-kŭs), *adjs.* **1.** Bellied; উদরবিশিষ্ট। **2.** (*Bot.*)

Distended ; swelling out in the middle ; স্ফীত ; মধ্যদেশে স্ফীত।

vĕn-trĭl'-ō-quĭsm, *n.* The act, art or practice of speaking in such a manner that the voice appears to come, not from the person, but from some distant place ; বাক্যকথনের প্রণালী, কৌশল বা রীতিবিশেষ—যাহাতে সম্মুখস্থ কোন ব্যক্তি কর্তৃক উচ্চারিত বাক্য দূরস্থিত অপর কোন ব্যক্তি দ্বারা উচ্চারিত হইতেছে বলিয়া শ্রোতৃবৃন্দের নিকট প্রতিভাত হয়, গারুড়বাণী, (আঃ বঃ), উদরবাদ (ঐ), দূরাগতশব্দানুকরণবিদ্যা (হিঃ কোঃ), ঐন্দ্রজালিকবাণী (কেন্ডিঃ)। **—quise,** *v. t* **—quist,** *n.* One who ventriloquizes ; দূরাগতশব্দানুকারী।

vĕn'-trō-, in comb. for VENTER.

vĕn·trō-dŏr'-săl, *adj.* Extending from the belly to the back ; উদর হইতে পৃষ্ঠ পর্যন্ত প্রসারী।

vĕn-trŏs'-ĭ-tȳ, *n.* The state of having a pot-belly ; তুন্দিলতা।

vĕn'-tūre, *n., v. t. & i.* **1.** A hazard ; বিপদ্, শঙ্কট। **2.** An undertaking of a chance or danger ; বিপৎসঙ্কুল কার্য্য, ঝুঁকিদার কার্য্য। **3.** A commercial speculation or enterprise ; as, a mining *venture* ; ঝুঁকিদার ব্যবসায়। **4.** A stake; risk ; something sent abroad in trade ; "My *ventures* are not in one bottom trusted"; পণ ; ঝুঁকি ; বিদেশে প্রেরিত পণ্যদ্রব্য প্রভৃতি। **5.** (*Rare*) Chance ; luck ; দৈব, দৈবঘটনা ; অদৃষ্ট। ***Verb t.*** **1.** To expose to hazard ; to risk ; বিপদাপন্ন করা, সঙ্কটাপন্ন করা ; ঝুঁকিতে ফেলা। **2.** To undertake the risk of ; to dare ; ঝুঁকি নেওয়া ; সাহস করা। **3.** (*Rare*) To consider or rely on ; বিশ্বাস করা, নির্ভর করা। **4.** To put or send on a venture or commercial speculation ; "The fish *ventured* for France, they pack in staunch hogsheads, so as to keep them in their pickle" ; বাণিজ্যের জন্য প্রেরণ করা। ***Verb i.*** **1.** To dare ; সাহস করা, সাহসী হওয়া। **2.** To run into hazardous risk ; to take chances ; সঙ্কটাপন্ন হওয়া ; অদৃষ্টের উপর নির্ভর করিয়া কার্য্যে প্রবৃত্ত হওয়া। **—some,** *adj.* Venturous ; daring ; risky; বিপৎসঙ্কুল, সঙ্কটসঙ্কুল ; ঝুঁকিদার ; দুঃসাহসী। **—some-ly,** *adv.* **—some-ness,** *n.* **—tur-er,** *n.* **1.** Same as ADVENTURER. **2.** (*Obs.*) Prostitute ; (অপ্রঃ) বারাঙ্গনা। **At a venture**—At random ; যদৃচ্ছাক্রমে। **To venture at** or **to venture on** or **upon**—To dare to enter upon or engage in ; to take the risk of ; সাহস করিয়া প্রবৃত্ত হওয়া ; ঝুঁকি নেওয়া।

vĕn'-tūr-īne, *n.* A fine gold-powder strewed upon the first layer of varnishing in Japanning ; জাপানী বার্ণিশের প্রথম স্তরের উপর যে সূক্ষ্ম স্বর্ণচূর্ণ আস্তৃত করা হয়।

vĕn'-ue (-ü), *n.* **1.** A neighbourhood or near place ; the place where the alleged events from which an action arises took place ; the place from which the jury is taken ; the place where an action is laid ; নিকটবর্ত্তী স্থান ; যেস্থানে কোন মোকদ্দমার ঘটনা সংঘটিত হয় ; যে স্থান হইতে কোন মোকদ্দমার জুরী নির্ব্বাচিত করা হয় ; যে স্থানে কোন মোকদ্দমার রুজু করা হয়। **2.** The statement in indictment indicating this ; অভিযোগপত্রে ঘটনার স্থান প্রভৃতিসূচক উক্তি। **To change the venue**—To change the place to avoid riot, prejudiced jury, etc. ; হাঙ্গামা, পক্ষপাত-দুষ্ট জুরী প্রভৃতি এড়াইবার জন্য মোকদ্দমা প্রভৃতির স্থান পরিবর্ত্তন করা। **To lay the venue**—To allege or fix a place for trial ; মোকদ্দমার বিচারের স্থান স্থির বা নির্দ্দেশ করা।

vĕn'-ue (-ü), *n.* **1.** (*Obs.*) A thrust with swords ; তরবারির খোঁচা। **2.** (*Obs.*) A combat ; সংগ্রাম।

Vē'-nŭs, *n.* **1.** (*Rom. Myth.*) The Goddess of love ; (রোমক পুরাণ) রতিদেবী। [এই দেবী সাগরসম্ভবা। Cupid বা শিশুকন্দর্প ইঁহার পুত্র। ইনি হংস বা কপোতপক্ষি-বাহিত-রথে পরিভ্রমণ করিয়া থাকেন। গোলাপ-পুষ্প এবং সেওফল ইঁহার অতি প্রিয় বস্তু। ইনি Adonis নামক এক পরম মনোহর যুবকের প্রেমে পতিত হন।] **2.** (*Astron.*) One of the inferior planets whose orbit is between the earth and the Mercury ; শুক্রগ্রহ [Syn. ভৃগু, ভৃগুজ, ভার্গব, পুরোহিত, উশনা, কাব্য, দৈত্যগুরু, বারুণ, বারুণী, বেণ (Ved.—Tilak), দৈত্যাধ্যক্ষ, আস্ফুজিৎ, সিত, শতপর্ব্বেশ, ভৃগসুত, ষোড়শার্চিঃ, মঘাভূ, শ্বেত, শ্বেতরথ, ষোড়শাংশু মঘাভব, মন্ত্রী।] **3.** (*Obs.*) Sexual intercourse ; (অপ্রঃ) রতিক্রিয়া। **4.** (*Alchem.*) Copper ; (কিমিয়াবিদ্যা) তাম্র। **Canova's Venus**—অষ্টাদশ শতাব্দীতে নির্ম্মিত ভিনাস দেবীর সুপ্রসিদ্ধ শ্বেত মর্ম্মরমূর্ত্তি। **Capitoline Venus**—রোমনগরীর Capitoline চিত্রশালিকায় রক্ষিত রতিদেবীর মর্ম্মরমূর্ত্তি। **Venus Anadyomene**—সাগরগর্ভ হইতে মকর, শিশুমারাদিসহ উত্থানশীলরতিদেবীর চিত্র। Apelles নামক চিত্রকর এই বিষয়ে একখানা উৎকৃষ্ট চিত্র অঙ্কন করেন। এই চিত্র নষ্ট হইয়া গিয়াছে। Botticelli নামক সুবিখ্যাত চিত্রকর কর্তৃক অঙ্কিত উক্ত চিত্রের এক প্রতিলিপি Florence নগরীর চিত্রশালায় (Accademia della Belle Arti) রক্ষিত আছে। **Venus accroupie**—রোমনগরীস্থ ভ্যাটিক্যান প্রাসাদে রক্ষিত শ্রান্তিনিরতা রতিদেবীর নগ্নমর্ম্মরমূর্ত্তি। **Venus-berg**—রতিনগরী। [মধ্যযুগের আখ্যায়িকায় কথিত আছে যে, জর্ম্মণীর কোন গিরিগহ্বরে রতিদেবীর দরবার বসিত। রতিদেবী এইস্থানে লোককে মদিরা, সঙ্গীত, ও কামোপভোগের প্রলোভনে প্রলুব্ধ করিয়া আনিতেন। যাহারা একবার এই গহ্বরে প্রবেশ করিত তাহারা আর প্রত্যাবর্ত্তন করিতে পারিত না।] **Venus Borghese**—১৮০৫ খৃঃ অব্দে Canova নামক ভাস্কর কর্তৃক ক্ষোদিত আরামখট্টায় অর্দ্ধশায়িতা প্রথম Napoleonএর ভগ্নী Venus Pauline Borgheseএর মর্ম্মরময়ীমূর্ত্তি। **Venus**

Callipyge—(**Callipygus**) রতিদেবীর মূর্ত্তিবিশেষ। **Venus de Medici**—Florence নগরীর চিত্রশালায় রক্ষিত গ্রীক শিল্পিগণকর্ত্তৃক রচিত রতিদেবীর অলৌকিক লাবণ্যময়ী শ্বেতপ্রস্তর মূর্ত্তি। **Venus Erycine**—খৃঃ পূঃ ২১৭ অব্দে রোম নগরীতে এই দেবীর একটী মন্দির প্রতিষ্ঠিত হয়। **Venus Felix**—ভাগ্যদেবী। Sulla এই দেবীর পূজা প্রচলন করেন। **Venus Genetrix**—ইনি Aeneasএর মাতা। Caesar খৃঃ পূঃ ৪৬ অব্দে এই দেবীর উদ্দেশ্যে একটী মন্দির উৎসর্গীকৃত করেন। **Venus Kallipygos**—Same as VENUS CALLIPYGE. **Venus Pompeiana**—রোমনগরীর consul Sulla পম্পিনগরে এই দেবীর মন্দির প্রতিষ্ঠিত করেন। **Venus Verticordia**—খৃঃ পূঃ ১১৪ অব্দে তিন জন মন্দিরবাসিনী কুমারীর সতীত্বলোপের প্রায়শ্চিত্তস্বরূপ রোম নগরীতে Venus Verticordia দেবীর মূর্ত্তি প্রতিষ্ঠিত হয়। **Venus Victrix**—Goddess of victory; বিজয়া দেবী। [রোমনগরীর অধিকারভুক্ত প্রদেশসমূহে এই দেবী পূজার বহুল প্রচলন ছিল।] **Venus's basin, Venus's bath**—একপ্রকার গুল্ম। **Venus's comb**—কঙ্কতিকাকৃতি ফলপ্রসূ বর্ষজীবী ক্ষুপ বিশেষ। **Venus's flower basket**—একপ্রকার অতি সুচারু শোষক (sponge), রতিদেবীর পুষ্পকরণ্ড। **Venus's flytrap**—একপ্রকার গুল্ম—যাহার পাতার উপর কীট প্রভৃতি বসিলে উহা বুজিয়া যায়, রতিদেবীর ফাঁদ। **Venus's girdle**—ফিতার আকার একপ্রকার সামুদ্রিক জন্তু, রতিদেবীর চন্দ্রহার (মিউজিয়্যাম); (*Palm.*) শুক্রবন্ধনী। **Venus's golden apple**—মালাবার ও করোমণ্ডল উপকূলে প্রাপ্ত একপ্রার বৃক্ষ) এই বৃক্ষের ফল স্বর্ণবর্ণ এবং দেখিতে অনেকটা কাগজী লেবুর ন্যায়)। [Tam. *kat-elle-micha*; Teleg. *adivi nimma, konda nimma*; Mahr. *makhur limbo.*] **Venus's hair**—একপ্রকার কালিঝাঁপ। **Venus's looking-glass**—ঘণ্টাকৃতি পুষ্পপ্রসূ একপ্রকার বর্ষজীবী লতা, রতিদেবীর মুকুর। **Venus's navel-wort**—একপ্রকার গুল্ম, রতিদেবীর নাভি। **Venus's slipper**—একপ্রকার উদ্যানরোপিত গুল্ম। উহার পীতবর্ণ থলিয়া মহিলাদিগের চটীজুতার মত দেখায়। **Venus's sumach**—বন্য জলপাই। **Venus of Arles**—Arles নগরীর প্রাচীনরঙ্গমণ্ডপে প্রাপ্ত ভীনাসদেবীর আজানুনগ্না মর্ম্মরময়ীমূর্ত্তি। এই মূর্ত্তি ফ্রান্সের Louvre প্রাসাদে রক্ষিত আছে। **Venus of Capua**—Capua নামক স্থানের রঙ্গভূমিতে প্রাপ্ত ভীনাসদেবীর শ্বেতপ্রস্তরমূর্ত্তি। এই মূর্ত্তি Naples নগরীর জাতীয় চিত্রশালায় রক্ষিত আছে। এই মূর্ত্তিও জানুপর্য্যন্ত বিবসনা। ইহার বামপদ একটী শিরস্ত্রাণের উপর ন্যস্ত রহিয়াছে, এবং দৃষ্টি নিম্নে নিবদ্ধ। **Venus of Cnidus**—ভীনাসদেবীর নগ্নমর্ম্মরমূর্ত্তিবিশেষ। মূল মূর্ত্তি Praxiteles নামক সুবিখ্যাত ভাস্কর কর্ত্তৃক ক্ষোদিত হয়। ঐ মূর্ত্তি Cnidus নামক স্থানের মন্দিরে প্রতিষ্ঠিত ছিল। Cnidusএর মুদ্রায় ইহার প্রতিমূর্ত্তি দৃষ্ট হয়। **Venus of Milo, or Melos**—Melos নামক স্থানে প্রাপ্ত ১৮২০ খৃঃ অব্দে ভীনাসদেবীর মূর্ত্তি। ইহা বর্ত্তমানে ফ্রান্সের Lourvre প্রাসাদে রক্ষিত আছে। এই মূর্ত্তির ভুজদ্বয় নষ্ট হইয়া গিয়াছে। **Venus of the Capitol**—Same as CAPITOLINE VENUS. **Venus Urania**—সুপ্রসিদ্ধ গ্রীক ভাস্কর Phidias কর্ত্তৃক ক্ষোদিত ভীনাসদেবীর মূর্ত্তি। এই মূর্ত্তি স্বর্গীয় বা আধ্যাত্মিক প্রেমের প্রতীকস্বরূপ অর্চ্চিত হইতেন। **My Venus turns out a whelph**—Same as ALL MY SWANS ARE CHANGED INTO GEESE. See UNDER GOOSE. **Mount of Venus**—শুক্রের ক্ষেত্র (অঙ্গুষ্ঠের নিম্নবর্ত্তী স্থান)। **The Island of Venus**—Lusiad নামক গ্রন্থের নবম সর্গে বর্ণিত স্বর্গোপম দ্বীপ বিশেষ। এই দ্বীপ স্বর্গীয় এবং আধ্যাত্মিক প্রেমদ্বারা সমুদ্রগর্ভে হইতে উত্থিত হয়।

vė-rā'-cious (-shŭs), *adj.* 1. Observant of truth; habitually disposed to speak truth; সত্যবাদী, সত্যসন্ধ; সত্যনিষ্ঠ, সত্যশীল। 2. True; as, *vercious* account সত্য, প্রকৃত। **–ly,** *adv.*

vė-răc'-i-tŷ, *n.* Truthfulness habitual observance of truth; সত্যবাদিতা; সত্যশীলতা, সত্যনিষ্ঠা।

vė-răn'-dȧh (-dȧ), *n.* A kind of high open gallery or outer portico with a sloping roof; বারিন্দা, অলিন্দ।

vė-ra'-trine (-trĭn), *n.* A highly poisonous alkaloid; একপ্রকার অতি বিষাক্ত ক্ষারীয়পদার্থ। [এই পদার্থ স্নায়ুশূল, বাতরোগ, প্রভৃতিতে ঔষধস্বরূপ ব্যবহৃত হয়।] **–trate, –tric,** *adjs.* **–trize,** *v. t.*

vêrb, (*Gram.*) A word which in general tells what a person or thing does; ক্রিয়া।

vêr'-băl, *adj.* & *n.* 1. Not written; as, *verbal* contract; uttered by the mouth; অলিখিত; বাচনিক, শব্দগত, মুখোক্ত (হিঃ কোঃ), বাচিক (ঐ), শাব্দিক (ঐ)। 2. Respecting to words only; as, *verbal* difference; শব্দগত, শাব্দিক, শাব্দ। 3. Minutely exact in words, or attending to words only; "Neglect the rules each *verbal* critic lays"; শব্দসম্পর্কে সূক্ষ্মভাবে অবধানশীল, কেবল শব্দসম্বন্ধে মনোযোগী। 4. (Of translation) Literal; (অনুবাদসম্পর্কে) আক্ষরিক, অবিকল, পদানুপদিক। 5. (*Gram.*) Pertaining to a verb; of the nature of a verb; derived from a verb; ক্রিয়াসম্বন্ধীয়; ক্রিয়াত্মক, ক্রিয়াপ্রকৃতিক; ক্রিয়াজাত। ***Ncun.*** Same as VERBAL NOUN. **–ly,** *adv.* **Verbal agreement**—মৌখিক সন্ধি, অভিহিত সন্ধি (অর্থঃ)। **Verbal amnesia**—বাক্‌শক্তি লোপ। **Verbal definition**—যে সংজ্ঞাদ্বারা কেবল অল্প কথায় কোন পদের সাধারণ অর্থ ব্যক্ত হয়, বাচিক প্রমাণ। **Verbal evidence**—বাচিক প্রমাণ, শাব্দপ্রমাণ। **Verbal fallacy**—শব্দমূলক হেত্বাভাস। **Verbal inspiration**—বাইবেলের শব্দসমূহ প্রত্যাদেশসম্ভূত এই মতবাদ। **Verbal note**—(কূটরাজনীতি) কোন প্রশ্ন, অনুরোধ, প্রভৃতির উত্তর প্রাপ্ত না না হইলে, যে অস্বাক্ষরিত স্মারকলিপি

প্রেরণ করা হয়। **Verbal Noun**—ক্রিয়াবোধক বিশেষ্য।

vêr′-băl-ĭsm, *n.* **1.** Minute attention to words; শব্দের প্রতি সূক্ষ্ম অবধানশীলতা, শাব্দিকতা। **2.** Something expressed in words; শব্দ দ্বারা ব্যক্ত বিষয়। **3.** Verbal criticism; শব্দগত সমালোচনা।

vêr′-băl-ist, *n.* **1.** One that deals merely in words; শাব্দিক। **2.** A critic of mere words; শব্দ-সমালোচক।

vêr′-bal-īze, *v. t.* & *i.* To make noun into verb; বিশেষ্যপদকে ক্রিয়াপদে পরিণত করা। ***Verb i.*** To be verbose; পুষ্পিত হওয়া, পল্লবিত হওয়া, শব্দভূয়িষ্ঠ হওয়া। **—i-za′-tion**, *n.*

vêr-bā′-ri-ŭm, *n.* A game in which the players try to make as many words as possible from the letters of a given word; একপ্রকার ক্রীড়া—যাহাতে ক্রীড়ক কোন নির্দ্দিষ্ট শব্দের অক্ষর হইতে যত অধিক সংখ্যক সম্ভব শব্দ গঠন করিতে চেষ্টা করে।

vêr-bā′-tim, *adv* & *adj.* Word for word; কথায় কথায়, অক্ষরে অক্ষরে, শব্দে শব্দে, শব্দশঃ (হিঃ কোঃ), পদানুপদ (ঐ), যথোক্ত (ঐ)।

Verbena.

vêr-bē′-nă, *n.* Kinds of plant of verbain family; একজাতীয় লতা।

vêr-bē-nā′-cē-æ (-ē), *n.*, (*pl.*) A family of herbs, shrubs, and trees, the verbena family; অগ্নিমন্থাদি (সাঃ পঃ)।

vêr′-bêr-āte, *v. t.* To beat; to scourge; প্রহার করা, মারা; বেত্রাঘাত করা। **—a′-tion**, *n.*

vêr′-bi-āġe, *n.* Verbosity; "The perplexity of the abounding *verbiage*"; বাগ্‌বাহুল্য, বাক্‌প্রপঞ্চ, অতিবিস্তৃতি দোষ।

vêr′-bi-cīde, *n.* **1.** The perversion of a natural meaning of a word; কোন শব্দের স্বাভাবিক অর্থের বিকৃতি। **2.** One who perverts a word; শব্দবিকৃতিকারী।

vêr-bōse′, *adj.* Abounding in words; prolix; as, a *verbose* speaker; বাগ্‌বাহুল্যবিশিষ্ট; বাগ্‌ভূয়িষ্ঠ, বাগাড়ম্বরপূর্ণ, পুষ্পিত, পল্লবিত। **—bos′-i-ty**, *n.* **—ness**, *n.* **—ly**, *adv.*

verbum (sat) sapienti, (abbr. *verb. sap.*) *Sentence.* A word is enough to the wise; জ্ঞানী লোকের পক্ষে একটী কথাই যথেষ্ট।

vêr′-dănt, *adj.* **1.** Covered with growing plants or grass; green; fresh; শস্যশ্যামল, তৃণশ্যামল; শ্যামল, হরিত, সবুজ; নবীন। **2.** Raw; as, a *verdant* youth; কাঁচা, অনভিজ্ঞ, অপরিপক্কবুদ্ধি। **—dan-cy**, *n.* **—ly**, *adv.*

vêrd-ăn-tique′ (-tēk), *n.* **1.** A green incrustation on ancient coins, brass, or copper; প্রাচীন মুদ্রা, পিত্তল এবং তাম্রাদির উপর একপ্রকার হরিদ্বর্ণ আচ্ছাদন। **2.** A mottled green serpentine marble; একপ্রকার লম্বা ফুটফুট দাগবিশিষ্ট সবুজ মার্ব্বেল পাথর।

vêr′-dêr-êr, —ŏr, *ns.* (*Hist.*) An officer who had the charge of king's forests; (ইতিহাস্) রাজকীয় বনসমূহের ভারপ্রাপ্ত কর্ম্মচারী।

vêr′-dict, *n.* **1.** The answer of a jury given to the court concerning any matter of fact, civil or criminal, committed to their examination or determination; জুরিদিগের মত, জুরিদিগের সিদ্ধান্ত বা অভিমত। **2.** Decision; judgment; নিষ্পত্তি, মীমাংসা, সিদ্ধান্ত; রায়। **3.** Opinion pronounced; as, the *verdict* of the civilized world; মত, অভিমত। **Open verdict**—জুরিদিগের যেরূপ অভিমতে কোন অপরাধ সংঘটিত হইয়াছে বলিয়া উক্ত থাকে, কিন্তু কে অপরাধী তাহা নির্দ্দেশ করা হয় না। **Partial verdict**—অভিযোগের অংশবিশেষে মাত্র অপরাধী সাব্যস্ত করিয়া জুরিগণ যে অভিমত প্রদান করেন। **Privy** or **sealed verdict**—জুরিদিগের আলোচনার সময় আদালতের অধিবেশন স্থগিত হইলে, তাঁহারা আদালতের কেরাণীর নিকট যে লিখিত অভিমত প্রদান করেন। **Special verdict**—জুরিদিগের যেরূপ অভিমতে কেবল প্রমাণিত তথ্য সমূহ বিবৃত থাকে, এবং বিচারককে তাহা হইতে সিদ্ধান্ত করিতে হয়।

vêr′-di-gris, *n.* **1.** Green rust on copper; তাম্রের উপর হরিদ্বর্ণ কলঙ্ক, তাম্রকিট্ট, তাম্রমল। **2.** The basic acetate of copper used as a green pigment etc; তাম্রফলকের উপর ধান্যাম্লের ক্রিয়া দ্বারা প্রাপ্ত হরিদ্বর্ণ রঞ্জক পদার্থ বা ঔষধ, জাঙ্গল।

vêr′-di-têr, *n.* A blue or green pigment formed from a sulphate or nitrate of copper; সলফেট অব্ কপার বা নাইট্রেট অব্ কপার হইতে প্রাপ্ত একপ্রকার নীল বা সবুজবর্ণ রঞ্জকপদার্থ।

vêr′-di-tūre, *n.* The faintest and palest green; হরিদ্বর্ণের ঈষৎ আমেজ।

vêr′-dūre, *n.* **1.** Greenness or freshness of vegetation; green vegetation; শ্যামলতা, শ্যামলিমা, শ্যামশ্রী (*Rhet.*), শ্যামলশোভা (*ib.*), শ্যামলকান্তি (*ib.*); শ্যামল তৃণদল বা তরুগুল্মরাজি, তরুগুল্মের নবীনতা। **2.** Tapestry representing chiefly foliage, green trees etc.; পত্র হরিৎ বৃক্ষ প্রভৃতির চিত্রপ্রদর্শক চিত্রযবনিকা। **—dured, —dur-ous, —dūr-less**, *adjs.*

verein, *n.* A permanent association of persons or parties for some common purpose; সংঘ, সম্মিলনী, সম্মেলন।

verge (vêrj), *n.* **1.** Brink ; margin ; border ; limit ; ধার ; কিনারা ; প্রান্ত ; সীমা । **2.** A circumference ; a circlet or ring ; পরিধি ; ক্ষুদ্র বৃত্ত । **3.** A rod or something in the form of a rod carried as an emblem of authority or ensign of office ; "The silver *verge* with decent pride, stuck underneath his cushion side" ; আশাসোঁটা । **4.** The stick or wand with which a person is admitted as tenant, by holding it in the hand and swearing fealty to the lord ; উর্দ্ধতন ভূম্যধিকারীর প্রতি বশ্যতাসূচক যে দণ্ড হস্তে ধারণ করিয়া কোন ব্যক্তি প্রজাস্বরূপ গৃহীত হয় । **5.** (*Rare*) Compass ; space ; "Give ample room and *verge* enough" ; scope ; (ক্বচিদ্ ব্যবহৃত) প্রসার ; স্থান ; আসর । **6.** The penis ; পুংচিহ্ন । **7.** The shaft of a column or a small ornamental shaft ; স্তম্ভ ; কারুকার্য্যশোভিত ক্ষুদ্র স্তম্ভ । **8.** The edge of a tiling projecting over the gable of a roof ; গৃহের পাশকপালীর উপর উদ্গত টালির প্রান্ত । **9.** Kinds of shafts or spindles in various mechanism ; বিভিন্ন প্রকার যন্ত্রের নানারূপ দণ্ড, শঙ্কু, প্রভৃতি । **Verge-board**—ঢালু ছাদবিশিষ্ট গৃহে পাশকপালীর প্রান্তবর্ত্তী কাষ্ঠদ্বয়ের সম্মুখস্থ কারুকার্য্যশোভিত পর্দ্দা ।

verge (vêrj), *v. i.* **1.** To border ; to approach (with *on* or *upon*) ; "The hand of the clock was *verging on* the five minutes past" ; প্রান্তবর্ত্তী হওয়া ; অতি সন্নিহিত হওয়া, কাছাকাছি হওয়া । **2.** To incline ; as, the sun was *verging* toward the west ; প্রবণ হওয়া, ঢালু হওয়া ।

vêr-gee′ (-jē), *n.* A Channel-Island measure of area four-ninths of an acre ; ব্রিটিশ প্রণালীস্থ দ্বীপপুঞ্জের এক একরের $\frac{4}{9}$ ভাগ মাপ ।

vĕr′-gĕr, *n.* **1.** One who carries a verge ; আসাবরদার, চোপদার, দণ্ডধর । **2.** An official in church who shows persons to their seats ; গির্জ্জার যে কর্ম্মচারী সমাগত ব্যক্তিদিগকে আসন প্রদর্শন করে ।

vêr′-gĕn-çȳ, *n.* (*Opt.*) The reciprocal of the focal distance of a lens, a measure of divergence or convergence of pencil of rays ; (দৃষ্টিবিজ্ঞান) পরকলার নাভিগতান্তরের ব্যুৎক্রম — যাহা রশ্মিমালার কেন্দ্রাভিমুখতা বা কেন্দ্রাপসারিতার পরিমাপস্বরূপ বলিয়া গৃহীত হইয়া থাকে ।

vĕ-rid′-i-căl, *adj.* (*Facet.*) Truth-telling ; veracious ; "This *veridical* history" ; (কৌতুকচ্ছলে) সত্যবাদী ; সত্যসন্ধ ।

vĕr′-i-fȳ, *v. t.* **1.** To prove to be true ; "This is *verified* by a number of examples" ; to authenticate ; to fulfil, as a promise or prediction ; সত্য বলিয়া প্রমাণ করা ; সত্যতা প্রতিপন্ন করা, সত্যতা-প্রতিপাদন করা ; কোন প্রতিজ্ঞা বা ভবিষ্যদ্বাণী সফল করা । **2.** To bear out ; "For I have ever *verified* my friend" ; সমর্থন করা । **–fi-a-bil′-i-ty**, *n.* **–fi-a-ble**, *adj.* **–fi-er**, *n.* **–fi-ca′-tion**, *n.* The act of verifying ; the act of proving ; confirmation ; সত্যতা-প্রতিপাদন, সত্যাপন ; প্রমাণন ; প্রমাণীকরণ, দৃঢ়ীকরণ, নির্ণয় (ব্রজঃ হিন্দু) ।

vĕr′-i-lȳ, *adv.* (*Archaic*) Really ; "*Verily* I do not jest with you" ; truly ; বাস্তবিকপক্ষে ; সত্যসত্য, প্রকৃত পক্ষে ।

vĕr-i-sim′-i-lar (-lêr), *adj.* Likely ; "How *verisimilar* it looks" ; সম্ভবপর, সম্ভাব্য, সম্ভবতঃ ।

vĕr-i-si-mil′-i-tūde, *n.* **1.** Probability ; likelihood ; সম্ভাবনা ; সম্ভাব্যতা । **2.** That which is very similar ; সম্ভবপর বিষয় ।

vĕr′-i-tă-ble (-bl), *adj.* True ; agreeable to fact ; সত্য ; প্রকৃত, যথার্থ । **–bly**, *adv.*

vĕr′-i-tăs, *n.* (also *bureau veritas*) A French ship register like Lloyd's ; ফরাসীদেশের অর্ণবযান সমূহের তালিকা ।

vĕr′-i-tȳ, *n.* **1.** The quality or state of being true or real ; সত্যতা, যথার্থতা, যাথার্থ্য, বাস্তবিকতা । **2.** That which is true ; truth ; সত্য বিষয় ; সত্য ।

vêr′-juice (-jûs), *n.* **1.** The juice extracted from green or unripe fruit ; an acid liquor expressed from unripe grapes, wild apples, etc. ; অপক্ব ফল হইতে নিষ্কর্ষিত রস ; অপক্ব আঙ্গুর, জঙ্গলী সেও ফল, প্রভৃতি হইতে নিষ্কর্ষিত অম্ল রস । **2.** Sourness of disposition ; স্বভাবের কটুতা ।

vêr′-meil (-mĭl), *n.* **1.** The name given by jewellers to crimson red garnet inclining slightly to orange ; একপ্রকার কমলাবর্ণের বৈক্রান্ত মণি । **2.** A varnish used to give lustre to gilding ; গিল্টির উপর চাকচিক্য প্রদানের জন্য ব্যবহৃত একপ্রকার বার্ণিস । **3.** Gilded silver ; gilded bronze or copper ; গিল্টিকরা রূপা ; গিল্টি-করা ব্রোঞ্জ বা তাম্র । **4.** (*Poet.*) Same as VERMILION.

vêr′-mēs, *n.* Worm ; কীট, ক্রিমি ।

vêr-mi-ăn, *adj.* Of worms ; worm-like ; কীটসম্বন্ধীয় ; কীটবৎ । **–me-ol′-gy**, *n.*

vêr-mi-cel′-li (-chĕl-), *n.* Little thread or worm-like rolls of paste, being a composition of flour, eggs, sugar and saffron, used in soups and pottages ; ডিমের কুসুম, চিনি, জাফ্রান, মিশ্রিত ময়দার কাই হইতে সূত্রাকারে বা ক্রিমির আকার গুটাইয়া প্রস্তুত চাকতি ।

vêr-mi′-ceous (-shŭs), *adj.* Pertaining to worms ; কীটসম্বন্ধীয় ।

vêr′-mi-cīde, *n.* An anthelmentic ; কৃমিঘ্ন, কৃমিনাশক ঔষধ । **–cid-al**, *adj.*

vêr-mic′-ū-lar (-lêr), *adj.* **1.** Pertaining to a worm ; কীটসম্বন্ধীয় । **2.** Resembling a worm in form or movement ; কীটাকৃতি, কীটগতি । **3.** Of worm-eaten appearance ; কীটক্ষত । **4.** Covered with

;wreatned lines like the undulations of a worm ; ক্রিমির মত

Vermicular masonry.

রেখাঙ্কিত। **Vermicular motion**—ক্রিমিবৎগতি। **Vermicular** or **vermiculated work**—ক্ষুদ্র ক্ষুদ্র তরঙ্গাকৃতি রেখাবিশিষ্ট একপ্রকার স্থাপত্যভূষা ; দালানের উপর কীটক্ষতবৎ একপ্রকার স্থাপত্যভূষা।

vêr-mic′-ū-lāte, *adj.* & *v. t.* **1.** Worm-likein shape or appearance ; covered with worm-like elevation ; marked with irregular lines suggesting worm's tracks ; কীটাকৃতি ; কীটবৎ উন্নতস্থান সমাকীর্ণ ; কীটগতিসূচক অসমরেখাসমূহদ্বারা অঙ্কিত। **2.** Worm-eaten ; কীটক্ষত, কীটদষ্ট। **3.** Crawling or creeping like worm; কীটগতি। ***Verb t.*** To ornament with wavy lines ; ঢেউ খেলানো রেখাদ্বারা শোভিত করা। **–la′-tion,** *n.*

vêr-mic′-ū-līte, *n.* A mineral consisting principally of silica, aluminia and magnesia ; একপ্রকার খনিজপদার্থ। [এই পদার্থ উত্তপ্ত করিলে ইহার পত্রসমূহ কীটের আকারে বিশ্লিষ্ট হইয়া পড়ে বলিয়া—এই নাম।]

vêr-mic′-ū-lōse, –lous, (-lŭs), *adjs.* **1.** Worm-eaten ; কীটদষ্ট, কীটক্ষত। **2.** Worm-shaped ; কীটাকৃতি।

vêr′-mi-fôrm, *adj.* Worm-like in form ; ক্রিমিবৎ, কীটাকৃতি।

vêr′-mi-fūge, *n.* A drug that expels internal worms ; ক্রিমিনিঃসারক ঔষধ। **–mif′-u-gal,** *adj.*

vêr′-mi-grade, *adj.* Moving like worms ; কীটগতি।

vêr-mil′-ion (-yŏn), *n.*, *adj.* & *v. t.* **1.** A bright red sulphide of mercury, used as pigment ; সিন্দূর, হিঙ্গুল। [Syn. রক্তবালুকা, সন্ধ্যারাগ, হংসাঙ্ঘ্রি, মর্কটশীর্ষ, রক্ত, দরদ, রস, কুরুবিন্দ, হংস-পাদ, হিঙ্গুলি, রক্তপারদ, বর্ব্বর,সুরঙ্গ, সুগর, রঞ্জন, চিত্রাঙ্গ, ম্লেচ্ছ, চূর্ণপারদ, মণিরাগ, চর্ম্মারক, রসোদ্ভব, রঞ্জক, রসগর্ভ, বিত্রাস, চর্ম্মার (white), শুকতুণ্ডক (orange red), মঙ্গল্য, শৃঙ্গারভূষণ, রক্তশাসন, সৌভাগ্য, রসস্থান, সৈমন্তিক, গণেশভূষণ কপিশীর্ষক।] [Chin. *Yin-chu* ; *tsze-fen-shwang*।] **2.** A red colour like the vermilion ; সিন্দূরারুণ বর্ণ। **3.** Same as VERMEIL I. ***Adj.*** Of vermilion colonr ; সিন্দূরারুণ (cf. সিন্দূরারুণবিগ্রহাম্—তন্ত্র), সিন্দূররক্ত। ***Verb t.*** To colour with,or as with, vermilion ; সিন্দূর রঞ্জিত করা, সিন্দূরবর্ণে রঞ্জিত করা, সিন্দূররাগরঞ্জিত করা।

vêr′-min, *n.* **1.** All sorts of small animals which are destructive to grain or other produce ; শস্যাদির অনিষ্টকারী জন্তু। **2.** Noxious insect ; অনিষ্টকারীকীটসমূহ। **3.** A noxious person ; "You are my prisoner base *vermin*" ; a vile person ; অনিষ্টকারী লোক ; নরাধম, হীন লোক। **–ous,** *adj.* **–ous-ly,** *adv.*

vêr′-mi-nāte, *v. i.* To breed vermin ; to be infested with vermins; কীট জন্ম দেওয়া ; কীটাকুলিত হওয়া।

vêr-miv′-ō-rous(-rŭs), *adj.* Feeding on worms ; কীটাদিক্রিমিভুক্, কীটভুক্।

vêr′-mûth, vêr′-moth (-mûth), *ns.* A stimulating liquor, composed of white wine, absinthe, angelica, and other aromatic herbs, professedly used to excite the appetite ; নানারূপ সুগন্ধি দ্রব্য দ্বারা সুবাসিত সুরা।

vêr-năc′-ū-lar (-lêr), *adj.* & *n.* Native; belonging to one's native language ; স্বদেশীয়, দেশীয় ; দেশভাষাসম্বন্ধীয়। ***Noun.*** One's native tongue ; দেশভাষা, মাতৃভাষা, দেশীয় ভাষা। **–ism,** *n.* **–ize,** *v. t.* **–i-za′-tion,** *n.* **–ly,** *adv.* **Vernacular disease**—Same as ENDEMIC DISEASE.

vêr-năl, *adj.* **1.** Belonging to, or appearing in, spring ; as, *vernal* bloom ; বাসন্ত, বাসন্তী, বসন্তকালীন, বাসন্তিক, মাধবী। **2.** Belonging to youth ; যৌবন, যৌবনসম্বন্ধীয়, তরুণ, যৌবনকালীন। **–ly,** *adv.* **Vernal equinox**—See EQUINOX. **Vernal fever** — ম্যালেরিয়া জ্বর। **Vernal grass**—একপ্রকার সুরভি তৃণ। **Vernal migration**—বসন্তকালে পক্ষীদিগের দেশান্তরে গমন, বাসন্তপ্রয়াণ। **Vernal signs**—সায়নরাশি (হিঃ কোঃ)।

vêr-nā′-tion, *n.* (*Bot.*) Disposition of leaves in a bud ; (উদ্ভিদ্-বিদ্যা) পত্রাবস্থান (সাঃ পঃ), কিসলয়সংস্থান (ঐ)।

vêr′-ni-êr, *n.* A movable scale which subdivides the smallest divisions on a straight or circular scale; যে ক্ষুদ্র সচল মানদণ্ড সচল বা গোলাকৃতি মানদণ্ডের ক্ষুদ্রতম বিভাগসমূহকে প্রবিভক্ত করে, প্রবিভাজক, বর্ণিয়ার যন্ত্র (হিঃ কোঃ)।

vêr′-nile (-nīl), *adj.* Suiting a slave ; servile ; দাসোচিত ; নীচ, হেয়।

Vêr-ō-nese′ (-nēz), *adj.* & *n.* **1.** Pertaining to Verona in Italy ; ইতালীর অন্তঃপাতী ভেরোনানগরসম্বন্ধীয়। ***Noun.*** An inhabitant of Verona ; ভেরোনা নগরীর অধিবাসী।

vĕ-rŏn′-i-că, *n.* **1.** A genus of plants being the speedwell ; একপ্রকার গুল্ম। **2.** A portrait or representation of the face of Christ left on the handkerchief of St. Veronica, that had been given to him by her to wipe the sweat from his face ; St. Veronicaর রুমালে অলৌকিকভাবে মুদ্রিত খৃষ্টের মুখ। [ক্রুশারোহণের পূর্ব্বে যীশুখৃষ্ট St. Veronica নাম্নী জনৈকা রমণীর নিকট হইতে মুখমার্জ্জনের জন্য রুমাল চাহিয়া লন। মুখ মার্জ্জনের পর এই রুমালে অলৌকিকভাবে খৃষ্টের মুখ মুদ্রিত হয় বলিয়া কথিত আছে। রোমনগরীতে ঐ রুমাল অদ্যাপি রক্ষিত আছে।] **3.** A similar representation of Christ's face ; রুমালাদির উপর মুদ্রিত খৃষ্টের মুখ।

vêr′-ri-cūle (-i-), *n.* (*Entom.*) Thick tuft of upright hairs; (কীটতত্ত্ব) খাড়া লোমগুচ্ছ।

vêr-ru′-că (-ü-), *n.* A wart; আঁচিল।

vêr′-ru-cōse (-ü-), **—cous,** (-kŭs), *adjs.* Warty; আঁচিলযুক্ত।

vêr′-sănt, *adj.* (*Obs.*) Familiar; conversant; (অপ্রঃ) পরিচিত; সুপরিজ্ঞাত।

vêr′-sănt, *n.* The general slope of a country; কোন দেশের সাধারণ প্রবণতা।

vêr′-să-tīle, *adj.* **1.** Capable of turning; easily turned; as, *versatile* antenne; ঘূর্ণনক্ষম; সহজে ঘূর্ণিত। **2.** Capable of turning forward or backward; reversible; অগ্র বা পশ্চাতে চালনক্ষম, অগ্রপশ্চাৎ চালনীয়; বিপর্যাসযোগ্য। **3.** (*Rare*) Changeable; as, he is a man of *versatile* disposition; (কচিদ্ব্যবহৃত) পরিবর্ত্তনশীল। **4.** Manysided: as, *versatile* genius; অনেকমুখী, সর্ব্বতোমুখী। **—ly,** *adv.* **—til′-i-ty,** *n.* **Versatile authers**—ঘূর্ণমান পরাগকোষ (সাঃ পঃ)।

verse (vêrs), *n., v.t.* & *i.* **1.** A certain number (usually a line) of metrical feet; কবিতার পংক্তি। **2.** A stanza; শ্লোক, কলি। **3.** Poetry; as, the story is narrated in *verse*; metrical composition; কবিতা; ছন্দোবদ্ধ রচনা। **4.** Each of the short division of a chapter in the Bible; বাইবেলের অধ্যায় সমূহের ক্ষুদ্র বিভাগ। ***Verb t.*** To tell in verse; কবিতায় বলা, কবিতায় ব্যক্ত করা। ***Verb i.*** To make verses; কবিতা রচনা করা। **Verse′-let,** *n.* **Verse-monger**—মন্দ কবি। **Verse-mongering**—মন্দ-কবিতা বিরচন।

versed (vêrst), *adj.* **1.** Experienced; proficient; অভিজ্ঞ; বিশারদ, পারদর্শী, মর্ম্মপারগ (নৈষধ)। **2.** Reversed; বিপর্য্যস্ত। **Versed sine**—উৎক্রমজ্যা (হিঃ কোঃ)। **Table of versed sine**—উৎক্রমজ্যার্দ্ধ পিণ্ডক।

vêrs′-ĕt, *n.* (*Mus.*) A short prelude or interlude for an organ; (সঙ্গীতশাস্ত্র) অর্গেন যন্ত্রের সংক্ষিপ্ত পূর্ব্ব বা মধ্য বাদ্য।

vêr′-si-cle (-kl), *n.* **1.** A little verse; ক্ষুদ্র কবিতা। **2.** A line of poetry or short poem; কবিতা-পংক্তি, ক্ষুদ্র কবিতা। **3.** A verse recited by a priest or minister; যাজক বা পুরোহিতকর্ত্তৃক উচ্চারিত কবিতা।

vêr′-si-col-our (-kŭl-êr), **—oured** (-êrd), *adjs.* **1.** Having various colours; নানাবর্ণ, বিচিত্রবর্ণ। **2.** Changing colours; বর্ণ পরিবর্ত্তনশীল।

vêr-sic′-ū-lar (-lêr), *adj.* Pertaining to verse; কবিতাপংক্তি সম্বন্ধীয়। **Versicular division** — কবিতার পংক্তি সমূহের বিভাগ।

vêr′-si-fȳ, *v.t.* & *i.* **1.** To relate or describe in verse; কবিতায় বর্ণনা করা। **2.** To turn into verse; কবিতায় পরিণত করা। ***Verb i.*** To make verses; কবিতা রচনা করা। **—fi-ca′-tion,** *n.* **—fi-er,** *n.*

vêr′-sion, *n.* **1.** The act of translating or rendering from one language to another; ভাষান্তরীকরণ। **2.** A translation; book etc. translated from one language to another; a translation of the Bible or part of it; as Authorized *Version* of the Bibl e; ভাষান্তর, অনুবাদ; ভাষান্তরিত পুস্তক প্রভৃতি; সমগ্র বাইবেলের বা উহার অংশবিশেষের অনুবাদ। **3.** A statement or account; as, he gives a different *version* of the affair; উক্তি, বর্ণনা, বিবরণ, বৃত্তান্ত। **4.** A school exercise consisting of a translation of one language, generally one's own into another; বিদ্যালয়ের বালকগণকর্ত্তৃক এক ভাষায় লিখিত বিষয় অপর ভাষায় অনুবাদ। **6.** (*Obstetrics*) Samė as TURNING 4. **—al,** *adj.*

vêr′-sō, *n.* **1.** A left-hand page; পুস্তকের বামদিকের পৃষ্ঠা। **2.** The reverse of a coin or medal; মুদ্রা বা পদকের অপ্রধান পৃষ্ঠ।

vêrst, *n.* A Russian measure of distance, 3500 feet; রুশদেশে প্রচলিত দূরত্বের পরিমাপবিশেষ (৩৫০০ ফিট)।

versus, *n.* (*Law*) Against; as Emperor *versus* Motilal Ghosh; (আইন) বনাম [সংক্ষেপে *v.* বা *vs.* লিখিত হয়।]

vêrt, *n.* **1.** (*Law, hist.*) Everything within a forest that grows and bears a green leaf; a power to cut trees or wood; (আইন-ইতিহাস) অরণ্যের মধ্যে যাহা সবুজপত্র উৎপাদন বা ধারণ করে; সবুজ বৃক্ষ বা জঙ্গল কাটিবার অধিকার। **2.** (*Hearld.*) A green colour; সবুজবর্ণ।

vêr-tĕ-bră, *n.* (*Pl. -brae*), Each segment of the backbone; মেরুদণ্ডের পর্ব্ব, কশেরুকা (সাঃ পঃ)। **—bral,** *adj.* Pertaining to the vertebra; having a backbone; মেরুদণ্ডের পর্ব্বসম্বন্ধীয়; মেরুদণ্ডবিশিষ্ট, মেরুদণ্ডী, পৃষ্ঠবংশী (সাঃ পঃ), পঞ্জরী (ঐ)। **—bral-ly,** *adv.*

vêr′-tĕ-brāte, *adj.* & *n.* Having a backbone; মেরুদণ্ডবিশিষ্ট, মেরুদণ্ডী। ***Noun.*** A vertebrate animal; মেরুদণ্ডবিশিষ্ট প্রাণী, মেরুদণ্ডী প্রাণী। **—brat′-ed,** *adj.* **—bra′-tion,** *n.* **Vertebral column**—মেরুদণ্ড, ব্রহ্মদণ্ড (উত্তরগীতা), শিরদাঁড়া, মেরু (ব্রজঃ হিন্দু)। **The central cord in the vertebral column** — সুষুম্না, (ব্রজঃ বিঃ)।

vêr′-tĕx, *n.* **1.** Highest point; top; apex; সর্ব্বোচ্চ বিন্দু; শীর্ষ; চূড়া, শিখর (হিঃ কোঃ)। **2.** Crown of head; মাথার চাঁদি। **3.** Each of the angular points of triangle, polygon etc.; ত্রিকোণ, পঞ্চভুজ, প্রভৃতির শীর্ষবিন্দু।

vêr′-ti-căl, *adj.* & *n.* **1.** Upright; খাড়া, সরলোন্নত, উল্লম্বী, লম্বমান (সাঃ পঃ)। **2.** Exactly overhead; ঠিক মস্তকোপরিস্থিত। ***Noun.*** A vertical line, plane or circle

৬০ বৎসরের মধ্যবর্ত্তী। ***Noun.*** A person between 59 and 70; উনষাট্ট এবং সত্তর বৎসরের মধ্যবর্ত্তী বয়সের লোক।

sĕx′-ăg′-ĕ-nă-rȳ, *adj.* Pertaining to, or designating, the number sixty; ষষ্টিসংখ্যা-সম্বন্ধীয়, ষষ্টিসংখ্যাবাচক।

sĕx-ă-gĕs′-ĭ-măl, *adj.* Pertaining to, or founded on, number 60; ষষ্টিসংখ্যাসম্বন্ধীয়, ষষ্টিসংখ্যামূলক। **Sexagesimal Arithmetic**—ষষ্ট্যুত্তর গণনাপ্রণালী। **Sexagesimal fractions** or **numbers** (or **sexagesimals**) — যেসকল ভগ্নাংশের হর ৬০ বা ৬০এর কোন ঘাত (Power) হইয়া থাকে (যথা ১/৬০, ১/৩৬০০ প্রভৃতি)।

sĕx′-an-gle (-ăng-gl), *n.* A figure having six angles; ষড়স্র ক্ষেত্র। **–gu-lar,** *adj.* **–gu-lar-ly,** *adv.*

sĕx-cĕn′-tē-nă-rȳ, *adj.* & *n.* Pertaining to the number 600; ষট্‌শতসম্বন্ধীয়। ***Noun.*** 600th anniversary; ষট্‌শতবার্ষিক উৎসব।

sĕx-ĕn′-nĭ-ăl, *adj.* **1.** Lasting six years; ষড়বর্ষস্থায়ী। **2.** Happening once in six years; ষড়বর্ষান্তে সংঘটিত, ষড়বার্ষিক, ষড়াব্দক।

sĕx′-ĭ-fĭd, *adj.* (*Bot.*) Six-cleft; (উদ্ভিদ্‌বিদ্যা) ষড়ধা বিদীর্ণ।

sĕx-ĭl′-lion (-yŭn), *n.* Same as SEXTILLION.

sĕx′-ĭ-sȳl-la-ble (-ă-bl), *adj.* & *n.* Having six syllables; ছয় শব্দাংশবিশিষ্ট। ***Noun.*** A word of six syllables; ছয় শব্দাংশ-বিশিষ্ট শব্দ।

sĕx-ĭ-vā′-lĕnt, *adj.* Same as SEXVALENT.

sĕx-pâr′-tīte, *adj.* Divided into six parts; ষড়ংশিত।

sĕxt, sĕx′-te (-tĭ), *ns.* (*R. C. C.*) One of the canonical hours of prayer usually recited at noon; (রোমানক্যাথলিক ধর্ম্মসংঘ) মাধ্যাহ্নিক উপাসনার কাল।

sĕx′-tain (-tăn), *n.* A stanza of six lines; ষষ্ঠচরণাত্মক কবিতা।

sĕx′-tăn, *adj.* (Of fever) Recurring every sixth day; (জ্বর-সম্বন্ধে) ষষ্ঠাহিক।

sĕx′-tănt, *n.* **1.** The sixth part of a circle; বৃত্তের ষষ্ঠাংশ, বৃত্তষষ্ঠাংশ। **2.** An instrument having an arc equal to the 6th part of a circle

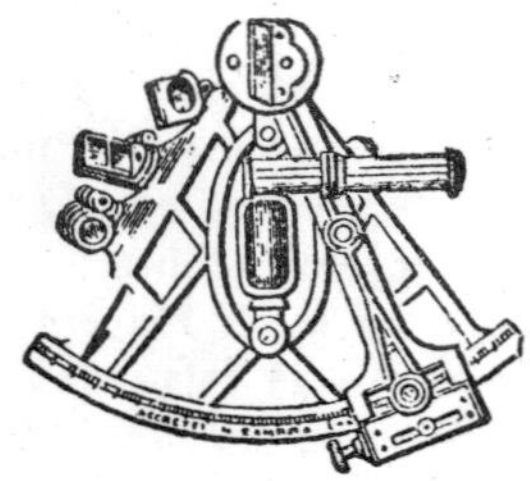

Sextant.

for measuring the angular distances of objects by reflection; কৌণিক দূরত্ব মাপের জন্য বৃত্তের ষষ্ঠাংশ পরিমিত কিরণ পরাবর্ত্তনদ্বারা চাপসমন্বিত যন্ত্রবিশেষ, ষষ্ঠাংশযন্ত্র (সাঃ পঃ), ষষ্ঠ্যংশযন্ত্র (ঐ)।

sĕx′-tīle, *n.* বৃত্তষষ্ঠ্যংশান্তর (হিঃ কোঃ), ষষ্ঠভাগান্তর (ঐ)।

sĕx-tĭl′-lĭ-ŏn, *n.* A number consisting of 1 with 36 cyphers; একের ডাহিনে ৩৬টী শূন্য বসাইলে যে সংখ্যা হয়।

sĕx′-tō, *n.* A book with the leaf folded six times; ষষ্ঠাংশিত পুস্তক।

sĕx-tō-dĕc′-ĭ-mō, *n.* The size of a book when each sheet makes sixteen leaves (usu. written 16 mo. and read *sixteenmo*); ষোড়শাংশিত পুস্তক।

sĕx′-tŏn, *n.* **1.** An under-officer of a church who has charge of the vessels, vestry, etc.; খৃষ্টীয় ধর্ম্মমন্দিরের নিম্নশ্রেণীর কর্ম্মচারিবিশেষ (ইঁহার উপর মন্দিরের বাসনপত্র প্রভৃতি রক্ষার ভার থাকে)। **Sexton-beetle**—একপ্রকার গোবরে পোকা।

sĕx′-ū-ăl, *adj.* **1.** Pertaining to sex or the sexes; স্ত্রীপুরুষসম্বন্ধীয়, যৌন, দাম্পত্য, ঔদ্বাহিক (প্রবাসী ১৩১৯), মৈথুনসম্বন্ধী। **2.** Pertaining to the genital organs; as, *sexual* disease; জননেন্দ্রিয়সম্বন্ধীয়। **3.** (*Biol.*) Having sex; (জীববিজ্ঞান) স্ত্রী বা পুংচিহ্নবিশিষ্ট। **Sexual affinity**—দাম্পত্যআকর্ষণ, যৌনআকর্ষণ। **Sexual appetite** or **desire** — রিরংসা, সঙ্গমেচ্ছা। **Sexual decoration**—যৌনসজ্জা,সঙ্গমঋতুতে পক্ষী প্রভৃতি শোভাজনক নব পালক প্রভৃতিতে ভূষিত হয়। **Sexual dimorphism**—স্ত্রীপুরুষ ভেদে ভিন্ন আকৃতি বিশিষ্টতা (মিউজিয়াম)। **Sexual enjoyment**—কামোপভোগ, সম্ভোগ। **Sexual intercourse, Sexual commerce** — সঙ্গম, সুরত [Syn. অধোপাসনা, মিথুন, ত্রিভদ্র, পশুক্রিয়া, রতিক্রিয়া, সংবেশন, রাসেরস, উপসৃষ্ট, ক্রীড়ারত্ন, মহাসুখ, ব্যবায়, গ্রাম্যধর্ম্ম, রত, নিধুবন, পঞ্চম (তন্ত্র), শৃঙ্গার, অভিমানিত, ধর্ষিত, সম্প্রয়োগ, অব্রহ্মচর্য্য, অনঙ্গপ্রসঙ্গ, মোহন, স্মরসমর (*Rhet.*), রতিরণ (*ib.*), ইন্দ্রিয়সেবা, রতিভোগ।] **Sexual organ**—জননেন্দ্রিয়। **Sexual power**—কামবল (ভাব প্রঃ)। **Sexual reproduction** — যোনিজনন, শুক্রশোণিতজনন, পিণ্ডজনন (হিঃ কোঃ)। **Sexual selection**—যে প্রাকৃতিক নির্ব্বাচনের ফলে কতিপয় বিশেষত্বের উদ্বর্ত্তন ও বিকাশ সাধিত হয়, [যথা পুংপক্ষীর সমুজ্জল বর্ণ, মোহন কণ্ঠস্বর—যদ্দ্বারা উহারা স্ত্রীপক্ষীদিগকে আকর্ষণ করে। এই ক্ষেত্রে যৌননির্ব্বাচনে দৈহিক পরিবর্ত্তন সাধিত হইয়াছে।], যৌননির্ব্বাচন, কাম্যনির্ব্বাচন (অভিঃ), লৈঙ্গিকবিচার (হিঃ কোঃ), কামিকবিচার (ঐ)। **Sexual system** or **method**—স্ত্রীপুরুষ ভেদে বৃক্ষাদির শ্রেণীবিভাগ।

sĕx′-ū-ăl-ĭst, *n.* An adherent of sexual system of botanical classification; যে ব্যক্তি স্ত্রীপুরুষভেদে বৃক্ষাদির শ্রেণীবিভাগ করিয়া থাকে, যৌনবাদী।

sĕx′-ū-ăl′-ĭ-tȳ, *n.* The state of being distinguished by the sex; স্ত্রীপুরুষভেদে পরিচয়জনকতা।

sĕx′-ū-ăl-īze, *v. t.* To attribute sex to; স্ত্রী বা পুংচিহ্ন আরোপ করা। **–i-za′-tion,** *n.*

as, to *vest* a person with authority ; অর্পণ করা, প্রদান করা। **3.** To place or put in possession formally or legally an immediate fixed right of present or future possession, occupancy or enjoyment of (with *in*) ; "Empire and dominions was *vested in* him for the good behoof of others" ; রীতিসিদ্ধ ভাবে বা বিধিসঙ্গতরূপে বর্ত্তমান বা ভাবী অধিকার, ভোগস্বত্ব, দখল, প্রভৃতি কাহাকেও অর্পণ করা। **4.** (*Rare*) Same as INVEST ; as to *vest* money in land ; (কচিদ্‌ব্যবহৃত) বিনিয়োগ করা। ***Verb i.*** To come or descend ; to devolve ; to take effect, as a title or right (with *in*) ; আসা, বর্ত্তান, স্পর্শান, সংক্রমিত হওয়া ; আমলে আসা। **Vest'-ed**, *pp.* **1.** Clothed ; পরিচ্ছদসজ্জিত। **2.** That has taken effect, as an immediate fixed right to present or future enjoyment ; ন্যস্ত, বিনিযুক্ত। **Vested interests** — বিনিযুক্ত স্বার্থ (হিঃ কোঃ), ন্যস্ত স্বার্থ। **Vested property**—যে সম্পত্তিতে বর্ত্তমান বা ভাবী ভোগের জন্য কোন ব্যক্তি অচল-প্রতিষ্ঠ স্বত্ব বা অধিকার প্রাপ্ত হইয়াছে, ন্যস্তস্বত্ব,ন্যস্তসম্পত্তি। **Vested rights**—ন্যস্ত স্বত্ব, বিনিযুক্ত অধিকার। **To vest in**—To come to ; অর্শান, বর্ত্তান।

vĕs'-tă, *n.* **1.** (*Rom. Myth., Cap.*) The goddess of the hearth and fire and hence of the preparation of food ; (রোমীয় পুরাণ) গৃহদেবী, পাকশালার অধিষ্ঠাত্রী দেবী। **2.** (*Astron., Cap.*) An asteriod ; (জ্যোতিবিজ্ঞান) গ্রহক (সাঃ পঃ)। **3.** A short match with a shank of thin wax taper ; a kind of short wooden match ; একপ্রকার দিয়াশলাই—যাহার পার্শ্বে মোম মাখানো থাকে ; একপ্রকার খর্ব্ব দীপশলাকা।

vĕs'-tăl, *adj.* **1.** Pertaining to the goddess Vesta of the Romans ; রোমানদিগের গৃহদেবীসম্বন্ধীয়। **2.** Pure; পবিত্র। **3.** Chaste ; সতী, সাধ্বী। **Vestal virgin** — গৃহদেবীর মন্দিরে উৎসর্গীকৃত কুমারীপরিচারিকা। এই সকল কুমারী দেবীর সম্মুখে নিত্য পবিত্র অগ্নি প্রজ্বালিত রাখিতেন। ইঁহারা ছয় হইতে দশ বৎসরের মধ্যে দেবীর সেবাব্রত গ্রহণ করিয়া ত্রিংশৎবৎসর কাল পর্য্যন্ত মন্দিরের কার্য্যে নিযুক্ত থাকিতেন, তৎপর তাঁহারা ইচ্ছা করিলে বিবাহবন্ধনে বদ্ধ হইতে পারিতেন। এই সকল কুমারী গণকে রোমকগণ অতিশয় ভক্তি করিতেন।

vĕs'-ti-ă-rȳ, *adj.* Pertaining to cloth or vestments ; বস্ত্রসম্বন্ধীয়, পরিচ্ছদসম্বন্ধীয়।

vĕs'-ti-büle, *n.* **1.** The port or entrance into a house ; দ্বারমণ্ডপ, দেউড়ী। **2.** A hall next the outer door of a house ; কোন অট্টালিকার বহির্দ্বার অতিক্রম করিয়া যে কক্ষে প্রবেশ করা যায়। **3.** (*Anat.*) A cavity in the labyrinth of ear ; (শারীর-সংস্থান বিদ্যা) কর্ণমধ্যস্থ গহ্বর সমূহের অন্যতম। **—tib'-u-lar**, *adj.*

vĕs'-tige (-tĭj), *n.* **1.** A foot-print ; পদাঙ্ক, পদচিহ্ন। **2.** Trace ; as, *vestiges* of ancient civilisation of India ; evidence ; চিহ্ন, সংস্কার (হিঃ কোঃ) ; প্রমাণ, নিদর্শন। **3.** Particle ; অণু, কণা। **4.** (*Biol.*) A structure in process of disappearance called a vestigal structure ; (জীববিজ্ঞান) বিলয়নশীল দেহ-যন্ত্র (যাহা কোন জন্তুর পূর্ব্বপুরুষদিগের মধ্যে পরিণত ও সুপরিস্ফুট ছিল।) **—tig'-i-al**, **—tig'-i-a-ry**, *adjs.*

vĕs'-ti-türe, *n.* The hairs, scales, etc. covering a surface ; আবরণ-স্বরূপ শল্ক, রোম, প্রভৃতি।

vĕst'-mĕnt, *n.* **1.** A covering ; আবরণ, আচ্ছাদন। **2.** A garment ; a garment for ceremony or office ; পোষাক, পরিচ্ছদ ; কোনরূপ ক্রিয়া বা পদের উপযোগী পরিচ্ছদ।

vĕs'-trȳ, *n.* **1.** A room attached to a church in which the clerical vestments and sacred utensils are kept and where parochial meetings are held ; খৃষ্টীয় ভজনালয়-সংলগ্ন কক্ষবিশেষ — যথায় যাজকীয় পরিচ্ছদ এবং পবিত্র ভাণ্ডসমূহ রক্ষিত হয়। **2.** A chapel in which religious meetings of the parish are held ; যে ক্ষুদ্র ভজনালয়ে যাজকপল্লীর ধর্ম্ম-সংক্রান্ত সভাসমূহের অধিবেশন হইয়া থাকে। **3.** An assembly of the parishoners to deal with parochial affair ; যাজকপল্লী সভা। **—dom**, *n.* The government by a vestry ; যাজক-পল্লীসভাতন্ত্র। **—tral**, *adj.* **Vestry-clerk**—যাজকপল্লীসভার কেরাণী। **Vestryman**—যাজক পল্লীসভার সভ্য।

vĕs'-türe, *n.* & *v. t.* **1.** Apparel ; পোষাক, পরিচ্ছদ। **2.** Covering ; আবরণ, আচ্ছাদন। ***Verb t.*** To clothe ; পরিচ্ছদ পরিহিত করা।

vĕs'-tür-êr, *n.* A church official in charge of vestments ; যাজকীয় পরিচ্ছদ প্রভৃতি রক্ষক কর্ম্মচারী।

Vē-sü'-vi-ăn vē—, *adjs.* & *ns.* **1.** Of, or pertaining to, Vesuvius ; ভিসুভিয়াস পর্ব্বতসম্বন্ধীয়। **2.** Volcanic ; আগ্নেয়গিরিসম্বন্ধীয়। ***Noun.*** (*l. c.*) A kind of match or fusee ; একপ্রকার দীপশলাকা। **2.** Same as VESUVIANITE.

vē-sü'-vi-ăn-īte, *n.* A mineral of green colour common at Vesuvius ; ভিসুভিয়াস পর্ব্বতে বহুল পরিমাণে প্রাপ্ত একপ্রকার খনিজ পদার্থ।

vĕt, *n.* (*Colloq.*) Same as VETERINARY and VETERINARIAN

vetch (vĕch), *n.* A common name of certain leguminous plants with herbaceous stems, used for green fodder, particularly tare ; একপ্রকার গবাদির খাদ্যোপযোগী ক্ষুপ। **Vetch'-y**, *adj.*

vetch'-ling (vĕch-), *n.* A plant allied to vetch ; উক্তজাতীয় ক্ষুপের অনুরূপ একপ্রকার ক্ষুপ।

vĕt'-ĕr-ăn, *adj.* & *n.* Experienced ; long exercised, particularly in military life; অভিজ্ঞ ; কর্ম্মপ্রবীণ, রণপ্রবীণ। ***Noun.*** One long exercised in

To set back — To oppose; প্রতিরোধ করা, বাধা দেওয়া। To put the hand of a clock to an earlier time; ঘড়ীর কাঁটা পশ্চাদ্দিকে ঘুরাইয়া দেওয়া। To flow in a reverse direction; উজান বহা. **To set before**—To hold before; সম্মুখে স্থাপিত করা, উপস্থাপিত করা। **To set books**—To prescribe books; পুস্তক নির্দ্দিষ্ট করা। **To set bounds to**—To fix a limit; সীমা নির্দ্ধারণ করা। **To set by**—To lay up for future use; তুলিয়া রাখা। (*Obs.*) To esteem; (অপ্রঃ) সমাদর করা, শ্রদ্ধা করা। **To set by the ears**—See EAR. **To set down** — To snub; to rebuke; দাবান; তিরস্কার করা। To attribute; আরোপ করা। To put upon the ground; মাটীতে বা মেঝের উপর রাখা। To put in writing; to relate; লিখিয়া রাখা; বর্ণনা করা, বিবৃত করা। To fix; নির্দ্ধারণ করা, প্রতিষ্ঠিত করা। To consider; to rank; গণ্য করা, বিবেচনা করা; এক শ্রেণীতে ফেলা। To situate; অবস্থিত হওয়া। To cause to descend from a vehicle; গাড়ী হইতে নামাইয়া দেওয়া। To be seated; বসা, উপবিষ্ট হওয়া। To begin; to undertake; আরম্ভ করা; কোন কার্য্যে প্রবৃত্ত হওয়া। To have a direction toward; কোন নির্দ্দিষ্ট দিকে উন্মুখ হওয়া। **To set down as for**—To consider to be; কোন কিছু বলিয়া গণ্য বা বিবেচনা করা। **To set down to**—To attribute to; আরোপ করা। **To set fire to**—To apply fire to; to kindle; অগ্নিসংযোগ করা; জ্বালাইয়া দেওয়া। **To set free**—To liberate; মুক্ত করা, মুক্তি দেওয়া। **To set foot on** or **in**—To place one's foot on or in; পদার্পণ করা। **To set forth**—To lay out; খাটান, (ব্যবসায়ে) টাকা ফেলা। To publish; প্রচার করা, বাহির করা, প্রকাশিত করা। To arrange; বিন্যাস করা। (*Verb t.*) To start; রওনা হওয়া, যাত্রা করা। To express in details; to narrate; সবিস্তারে বলা; বর্ণনা করা, বিবৃত করা। **To set forward**—To carry or thrust forward; অগ্রে নেওয়া, ঠেলিয়া অগ্রসর করা। To put a clock's hands onward; ঘড়ীর কাঁটা আগেরদিকে ঘুরাইয়া দেওয়া। **To set free**—To liberate; মুক্ত করা, খালাস করা, ছাড়িয়া দেওয়া, মুক্তি দেওয়া। **To set hand to, To set one's hand to**—To undertake some work; কোন কাজে হাত দেওয়া। To put one's signature; স্বাক্ষর করা। **To set in**—To begin; আরব্ধ হওয়া, সুরু হওয়া। To give a start to; to put in; আরম্ভ করা; ধরাইয়া দেওয়া, লাগাইয়া দেওয়া। To become settled in a particular state; কোন বিশেষ অবস্থাতে স্থির হওয়া। **To set in action**—To cause to act; চালাইয়া দেওয়া। To cause to move; চালান। **To set in motion**—To start; চালান। **To set in order**—To adjust or arrange; to reduce to method; ঠিকঠাক করা; শৃঙ্খলাবদ্ধ করা। **To set milk**—To expose milk in open dishes at a certain temperature in order that the cream may rise to the surface; সর ফেলার জন্য দুধ চুল্লীর উপরে উন্মুক্ত পাত্রে রাখা। To cause milk to be curdled, as by rennet; দুধ জমান, ছানা করা, দুধ বসান। **To set much** or **little by**—To esteem highly; অতিশয় সমাদর করা; অল্প আদর করা। **To set off**—To place against, as an equivalent; তুলনার জন্য তুল্য-বস্তুর বিরুদ্ধে দাঁড় করা। To adorn; অলঙ্কৃত করা, মণ্ডিত করা, ভূষিত করা। To show off to the best advantage; উৎকৃষ্টতমরূপে প্রদর্শন করা, যথাসম্ভব সুবিধাজনকরূপে প্রদর্শন করা। To form a contrast with; বৈষম্য বা বৈপরীত্য প্রদর্শন করা। To commend; প্রশংসা করা, গুণগান করা। To start; রওনা হওয়া, যাত্রা করা। To compensate; ক্ষতিপূরণ করা। To make conspicuous by contrast; বৈপরীত্যপ্রদর্শনদ্বারা সুস্পষ্ট বা সুপ্রকট করা। To assign to a particular purpose; কোন বিশেষ উদ্দেশ্য-সাধনের জন্য নির্দ্দিষ্ট করিয়া রাখা। **To set on**—To place upon; কোন কিছুর উপর রাখা, স্থাপন করা। To urge as a dog etc. to attack; লেলাইয়া দেওয়া, টোয়াইয়া দেওয়া। To incite; উত্তেজিত করা, উস্কাইয়া দেওয়া, লেলাইয়া দেওয়া। To appoint a person to do something; কোন লোককে কোন কার্য্য সম্পাদনের জন্য নিযুক্ত করা। To begin to work; কার্য্য আরম্ভ করা। (*Verb i.*) To advance; অগ্রসর হওয়া। To set a-going; চালান। **To set on edge**—To incite; উত্তেজিত করা। **To set one person against another**—To place in opposition; একজনকে অপরের বিরুদ্ধে দাঁড় করা। **To set one's cap at**—See CAP. **To set one's eyes up**—To look upon; দৃষ্টিপাত করা, দৃষ্টিনিবদ্ধ করা। **To set one's face against**—See FACE. **To set one's face** or **countenance**—To give a fixed expression to one's face; মুখে একটা স্থির ভাব প্রকটিত করা। **To set one's face like a flint**—To be determined; দৃঢ়প্রতিজ্ঞ হওয়া, স্থিরসংকল্প হওয়া। **To set one's hand to**—To undertake a work; কোন কার্য্যে হাত দেওয়া। **To set one's heart at rest**—To remove one's anxiety; কাহারো মন শান্ত করা। **To set one's heart** or **mind on**—To cause one's affections to be centred on; মনঃপ্রাণ অর্পণ করা। **To set one's house in order** — To prepare for death by making one's will; স্বীয় বিষয়সম্পত্তির শেষ বন্দোবস্ত করিয়া মৃত্যুর জন্য প্রস্তুত হওয়া। **To set one's self**

oscillate ; দোলা ; দোদুল্যমান হওয়া। 2. To quiver ; to throb ; কম্পিত হওয়া; স্পন্দিত হওয়া। 3. To hesitate; as, his mind *vibrated* between two opinions ; দ্বিধা করা, ইতস্ততঃ করা, সন্দেহদোলায় দোলায়মান হওয়া। ***Verb t.*** 1. (*Obs.*) To brandish ; ঘুরাণ। 2. To affect with vibratory motion ; to cause to quiver ; দোলনজনক গতিবিশিষ্ট করা, কম্পিত করা ; স্ফুরিত করা, স্পন্দিত করা। 3. To set in vibration ; দোলন উৎপাদন করা। 4. To measure seconds etc. by vibrating ; দোলন দ্বারা সেকেণ্ড প্রভৃতি নির্দ্ধারিত করা। **–bra-tive, –bra-to-ry,** *adjs.* Consisting of, or causing, vibration ; স্পন্দনাত্মক, কম্পনাত্মক, স্পন্দনজনক, দোলনজনক। **Vibratory-action**—স্পন্দ (হিঃ কোঃ)। **Vibratory-reaction**—স্ফুরণ (হিঃ কোঃ)।

vī'-brā-tīle, *adj.* Capable of vibrating ; দোলনক্ষম, স্পন্দনক্ষম। **–til'-i-ty,** *n.*

vī-bra'-tion, *n.* 1. The act of vibrating or oscillating ; স্পন্দন, দোলন, কম্পন, প্রকম্প পরিস্পন্দ। 2. (*Phys.*) The reciprocating motion of a body, as of a pendulum, a musical chord, elastic plate, the air, or ether ; (পদার্থবিজ্ঞান) পরিস্পন্দ, কম্পসন্তান (ব্রজঃ হিন্দু), অভীরণ (হিঃ কোঃ), স্ফুরণ (ঐ), কম্প (ঐ), ঝঙ্কার (ঐ)। **–al,** *adj.* **Potential vibration** — পরিস্পন্দ (সাঃ পঃ)। **Vibration potential** — শব্দ তন্মাত্র (সাঃ পঃ)।

vibrato, *n.* A pulsating effect in singing by variation of emphasis on some tone ; সঙ্গীতে কম্পনাত্মক ধ্বনি।

vī'-bra-tor' (-tĕr), *n.* 1. One that vibrates or causes vibration ; স্পন্দনজনক। 2. A vibrating reed used to open and close the electric current ; তাড়িতপ্রবাহ রুদ্ধ বা উন্মুক্ত করার জন্য স্পন্দনশীল ফলকবিশেষ। 3. (*Print.*) Vibrating reed used for distributing the ink ; (মুদ্রণ) কালী ছড়াইবার জন্য একপ্রকার স্পন্দনশীল ফলক, স্পন্দক, পরিস্পন্দক।

vī-bris'-sā (*Pl.*-SÆ), *n.* 1. The stiff, long, pointed bristles which grow from the upper lip and other parts of head in many mammals ; অনেক স্তন্যপায়ী জন্তুর ওষ্ঠ এবং মুখের অন্যান্য অংশ হইতে উদ্গত দীর্ঘ, শক্ত এবং সূক্ষ্মাগ্র লোম। 2. Bristle-like feather about the mouth of some birds ; কোন কোন পক্ষীর মুখের চতুঃপার্শ্ববর্ত্তী শূকবৎ পালক।

vī'-brō-scōpe, *n.* An instrument for registering vibrations ; স্পন্দনমান, দোলনমান।

vī-bur'-nŭm (-bêr-), *n.* Kinds of shrub of honeysuckle family ; একজাতীয় গুল্ম।

vic'-ar (-êr-), *n.* The clergyman of a parish, the predial tithes of which are impropriated or appropriated, that is, belong to a chapter, or to a lay-man, who receives them, and only allows the vicar the smaller tithes or a salary ; বেতনভোগী বা স্বল্পমাত্র ধর্ম্মবৃত্তিধারী পল্লীযাজক। **–ship,** *n.* **Cardinal vicar**—রোমের বিশপের পদে প্রতিষ্ঠিত পোপের প্রতিনিধি। **Clerk, lay** or **secular vicar**—খৃষ্টীয় মহাধর্ম্মমন্দিরের (cathedral) গায়ক। **Vicar apostolic**—ধর্ম্মপ্রচারক বিশপ, কেবলমাত্র উপাধিধারী বিশপ। **Vicar choral** — খৃষ্টীয় মহামন্দিরের গানে সাহায্যকারী। **Vicar forane**—নির্দ্দিষ্ট সীমাবচ্ছিন্ন স্থানের ভারপ্রাপ্ত বিশপ কর্ত্তৃক নিযুক্ত কর্ম্মচারী। **Vicar-general**—(ইংলণ্ডীয় ধর্ম্মসংঘ) যে কর্ম্মচারী বিশপ বা আর্চ্চবিশপকে যাজকীয় মোকদ্দমায় সাহায্য করে; (রোমানক্যাথলিক ধর্ম্মসংঘ) এলেকা প্রভৃতি সম্বন্ধীয় কার্য্যে বিশপের সাহায্যকারী প্রতিনিধি যাজক। **Vicar of Christ, Vicar of Jesus Christ**—পোপ।

vic'-ar-āge, (-êr-), *n.* 1. The benefice of a vicar ; বেতনভোগী যাজকের পদ। 2. The residence of a vicar ; বেতনভোগী যাজকের বাসস্থান।

vī-cā'-ri-ăl, *adj.* 1. Pertaining to a vicar ; বেতনভোগী যাজকসম্বন্ধীয়। 2. Serving as a vicar ; বেতনভোগী যাজক রূপে কার্য্যকারী।

vī-cā'-ri-ous (-ŭs), *adj.* 1. Delegated ; প্রতিনিধির হস্তে অর্পিত। 2. Acting for, or on behalf of, another ; as, the *vicarious* self-sacrifice of Christ ; প্রতিনিধিস্থলীয়, প্রতিনিধিস্থানীয়, প্রতিনিধিস্বরূপ কার্য্যকারী। **–ly,** *adv.* **–ness,** *n.* **Vicarious atonement**—প্রতিনিধি প্রায়শ্চিত্ত (হিঃ কোঃ)।

vīce, *n.* 1. Any immoral or evil habit or practice ; a moral fault or failing ; indulgence in immoral, impure or degrading appetites or passion ; পাপাচার, অধর্ম্মাচরণ ; দোষ (হিঃ কোঃ), অবগুণ (ঐ), পাপ (ঐ), অধর্ম্ম (ঐ), কল্মষ (ঐ), অধর্ম্ম ; ব্যসন। 2. Defect ; as, the *vices* of a political constitution ; খুঁত, ত্রুটি, দোষ। 3. A fault or bad trick in a horse ; অশ্বের দোষ, (ঘোড়ার) বদমায়েসী। 4. (*Cap.*) A buffoon in morality ; ইংলণ্ডের প্রাচীন নৈতিক নাটকের বিদূষক। 5. A physical defect or deformity ; খুঁত বা বিকৃতি।

vīce, *n.* & *v. t.* An iron or wooden press with a screw for holding articles fast when filed etc. ; পাকসাঁড়াশী। ***Verb t.*** To secure with vice ; পাকসাঁড়াশি দ্বারা ধরা। **Bench vice**—মিস্ত্রির বেঞ্চে বা মেজে আঁটা পাকসাঁড়াশী—যাহাতে আটক করিয়া কোন বস্তুর উপর উখা প্রভৃতি দ্বারা কাজ করা হয়।

vīce, *n.* (*Colloq.*) Same as VICE-PRESIDENT etc.

vīce, *prep.* In place of ; স্থানে, স্থলে।

vīce–, *pref.* A prefiix signifying second in rank or acting in

Seed-lobe—বৃক্ষের প্রথমোদ্গত পত্র, ভ্রূণ-পত্র। **Seed-oil** — বীজ হইতে নিষ্পীড়িত তৈল। **Seed-pearl**—বীজাকার মুক্তা, মুক্তাফল, সুবর্ত্তুল, মুক্তা, সুবৃত্ত (সর্ব্বতো বর্ত্তুলং যচ্চ সুবৃত্তং তন্নিগদ্যতে—গরুড় পুরাণ)। **Seed-plant**—বীজজাত বৃক্ষ। **Seed-plot**—বীজভূমি ; (রাজদ্রোহ প্রভৃতির) ক্ষেত্র। **Seed-pot**—বীজজাত বৃক্ষ যে গামলায় জন্মান হয়। **Seedsman**—বীজ-ব্যবসায়ী, বীজবিক্রয়ী। **Seed-time**—বীজ বপনের কাল, বপনকাল। **Seed-vessel** — বীজকোষ। **Seed-wool** — বীজযুক্ত কাঁচা কার্পাস। **The seed of the woman shall bruise the serpent's head**—যীশুখৃষ্ট শয়তানের মস্তক চূর্ণ করিবেন। **To run to seed**—See RUN.

seed'-êr (sēd-), *n.* 1. One who plants or sows seeds; বীজবপনকারী। 2. A machine for removing seeds from fruit ; a seed-drill; ফলের বীজ ছাড়াইবার জন্য একপ্রকার যন্ত্র ; যে যন্ত্রে একসঙ্গে নালা কাটা, বীজবুনা এবং বীজ ঢাকার কার্য্য সাধিত হয়। 3. A spawning fish ; ডিমওয়ালা মাছ।

seed'-ŷ (sēd-), *adj.* 1. Full of seed ; running to seed ; বীজপূর্ণ, বীচি-গজগজে ; পক্বাবস্থায় বীজধারী। 2. Shabbily dressed ; worn out ; as, a *seedy* coat ; looking miserable ; জীর্ণবস্ত্রপরিহিত ; জীর্ণ ; খিন্ন। 3. (Of brandy) Having the flavour of weeds growing among vines ; (ব্রাণ্ডি সম্পর্কে) দ্রাক্ষাক্ষেত্রে জাত আগাছার গন্ধবিশিষ্ট। **—i-ly,** *adv.* **—i-ness,** *n.*

seek (sēk), *v. t.* & *i.* 1. To search for ; তল্লাস করা, খুঁজা, অনুসন্ধান করা। 2. To ask for ; to beseech ; "Others tempting him *sought* of him a sign" ; চাওয়া ; প্রার্থনা করা। 3. To try to gain ; to try for ; as, to *seek* wealth ; পাইতে চেষ্টা করা ; কোন কিছুর জন্য চেষ্টা করা। 4. (*Obs.*) To search ; "Have I *sought* every country far and near" ; (অপ্রঃ) অনুসন্ধান করা, খোঁজা। ***Verb i.*** 1. To search ; অনুসন্ধান করা, তল্লাস করা, খুঁজা, অন্বেষণ করা। 2. To endeavour ; "They *sought* to lay hands upon him" ; চেষ্টা করা। 3. To solicit ; "*Seek* and ye shall find" ; প্রার্থনা করা। **Seek'-er,** *n.* 1. One who seeks ; অন্বেষণকারী, অন্বেষ্টা। 2. An inquirer ; অনুসন্ধানকারী। 3. An instrument for seeking ; অন্বেষণ করার জন্য যন্ত্রবিশেষ, অন্বেষক। **Sought-after**—সর্ব্বজনবাঞ্ছিত, সর্ব্বজনপ্রার্থিত। **To seek, Much to seek**—Wanting ; অভাববিশিষ্ট, বিরহিত। **To seek after**—To search ; অনুসন্ধান করা। To court ; বিবাহার্থ হৃদয় পরাজয়ের চেষ্টা করা। **To seek for**—To look for ; অনুসন্ধান করা, তল্লাস করা। **To seek to**—(*Archaic*) To resort ; to have recourse to ; (অপ্রঃ) বহুলোক এক সঙ্গে গমন করা ; আশ্রয় নেওয়া।

seel (sēl), *v. t.* 1 (*Archaic*) To close the eye of a hawk with a thread ; সূতা দ্বারা বাজ পক্ষীর চক্ষু বন্ধ করা। 2. (*fig.*) To hoodwink ; (লক্ষণায়) চোখে ঠুলি দেওয়া, চোখে ধূলি দেওয়া।

seem (sēm), *v. i.* To appear ; বোধ হওয়া, মনে হওয়া, প্রতিভাত হওয়া। প্রতীয়মান হওয়া। **It seems** — It appears ; এইরূপ প্রতিভাত হয়। **To seem well** — ভাল ঠেকা (cf. শোভাবতীর ছেলের ··· উদ্দেশ্য থাকাতে আমার ভাল ঠেকেনা—চরিত্রহীন—শরৎ চট্টো।)

seem'-ing (sēm-), *adj.* & *n.* Apparent ; আপাতপ্রতীয়মান, আপাত প্রতিভাত, আপাতদৃষ্ট, আপাতবোধ, প্রাতীতিক (cf. স প্রাতীতিক এব ন বাস্তবঃ—মাধুর্য্যকাদম্বিনী—বিশ্বনাথচক্রবর্ত্তী)। ***Noun.*** 1. Aspect ; outward look ; ভাব, বিভাব ; বাহ্যদৃশ্য, বাহ্যরূপ, মায়িকরূপ। 2. Illusion ; hypocrisy ; মায়া, বিসদৃশ প্রতীতি, প্রতিভাস (বেদান্ত), প্রতিভাসন (সাঃ দঃ), অবভাস, অনুভবাবভাস ; কপটতা।

seem'-lŷ (sēm-), *adj.* Decorous ; becoming ; শোভন, সমীচীন, ভদ্রতাসঙ্গত, সমুচিত, যোগ্য ; সঙ্গত। **—li-ness,** *n.* Decorousness ; ঔচিত্য, শোভনতা, সমীচীনতা।

seen (sēn), *p.p.* Of SEE (which see).

sē'-êr (*or* sēr), *n.* 1. One who sees ; দ্রষ্টা। 2. One gifted with special spiritual prophetic vision or insight ; দিব্যদৃষ্টিসম্পন্ন মহাপুরুষ, ঋষি, বিপশ্চিৎ (ডিউসেন), মুনি, সত্যদর্শী।

seer (sēr), *n.* A measure used in all retail dealings which varies all over India but in Bengal is equivalent to the wieght of eighty rupees ; একসের।

seer'-hănd (sēr-), *n.* A kind of muslin ; একপ্রকার মসলিন কাপড়।

seer'-paw, *n.* (From Pers. *sir*=head, *pa*=foot.) A complete set presented as a dress of honour by a sovereign or his representative ; শিরোপা, খিলাত।

seer'-sŭck-êr (sēr-), *n.* A thin linen or cotton fabric originally made in India ; শণ বা কার্পাসের সূতার একপ্রকার মিহি কাপড়।

see'-saw (sē-sä), *adj.*, *n.* & *v. i.* Moving up and down or to and fro ; পর্য্যায়ক্রমে উত্থানপতনশীল। ***Noun.*** 1. A swinging movement up and down ; পর্য্যায়ক্রমে উত্থান ও পতন। 2. A game in which children swing up and down on the two ends of a balanced piece of timber ; একপ্রকার ক্রীড়া—যাহাতে শিশুগণ দোলায়িত কাষ্ঠফলকের উভয় প্রান্তে পর্য্যায়ক্রমে উঠা নামা করিয়া থাকে। 3. A board or plank adjusted for such purpose ; উক্তরূপ তক্তা, ঢেঁকিকল। ***Verb i.*** 1. To move as in the game of see-saw ; to move up and down ; ঢেঁকি কলে উঠা-নামা করা ; পর্য্যায়ক্রমে উঠা নামা করা। 2. To vascillate ; সন্দেহদোলায় দোলায়মান হওয়া।

ইঞ্চি পর্য্যন্ত খাড়া হইয়া উঠে। ইহার পত্রের উপর একটী অল্প বয়স্ক বালক অনায়াসে দাঁড়াইয়া থাকিতে পারে। পূর্ণ বিকশিত পুষ্পের ব্যাস ৮ ইঞ্চি হইতে ১৫ ইঞ্চি পর্য্যন্ত হইয়া থাকে।]

Vic-tō′-ri-ăn, *adj.* & *n.* **1.** Relating to the reign of Queen Victoria, which began in 1837; রাণী ভিক্টোরিয়ার রাজ্যসম্বন্ধীয়। **2.** Of, or belonging to, Victoria, a division of Australia; অষ্ট্রেলিয়া মহাদ্বীপের অন্তঃপাতী ভিক্টোরিয়ানামক বিভাগসম্বন্ধীয়। ***Noun.*** A person living during the reign of Queen Victoria, esp. an author; রাণী ভিক্টোরিয়ার রাজত্বকালে বর্ত্তমান ব্যক্তি—বিশেষতঃ তৎকালীন গ্রন্থকার। **Victorian order**—রাজ্ঞী ভিক্টোরিয়া কর্ত্তৃক ১৮৯৬ খৃষ্টাব্দে প্রবর্ত্তিত সম্ভ্রান্তসম্প্রদায়।

vic-tō-rine′ (-rēn), *n.* **1.** A woman's fur tippet with long ends; স্ত্রীলোকের লোমনির্ম্মিত উত্তরীয়। **2.** A kind of peach; একজাতীয় পীচ ফল।

vic-tō′-ri-ous (-ŭs), *adj.* **1.** Conquering; as, *victorious* general; বিজয়ী, জয়ী, জয়কারী। **2.** Associated, or connected with, victory; producing victory; "Sudden these honours shall be snatched away, And cursed for ever this *victorious* day"; জয়সংক্রান্ত; বিজয়জনক। **3.** Betokening victory; "Now are our brows bound with *victorious* wreath"; জয়সূচক, বিজয়সূচক। **—ly**, *adv.* **—ness**, .

vic′-tō-rȳ, *n.* **1.** (*Cap.*) A female deity of the ancient Greeks and Romans personifying success in battle; প্রাচীন গ্রীক অথবা রোমানদিগের বিজয়াদেবী। **2.** The defeat of an enemy in battle, or of an antagonist or opponent in any contest; জয়, বিজয়।

vict′-ual (vĭt-l), *n.*, *v. t.* & *i.* Food; provisions; খাদ্য; খাদ্যসম্ভার, রসদ। ***Verb t.*** To supply with food; as, to *victual* an army; to store with provisions; as, to *victual* a ship; খাদ্যদ্রব্য সরবরাহ করা; খাদ্যসম্ভার সঞ্চিত করা। ***Verb i.*** **1.** (*Rare*) To eat; (কচিদ্ব্যবহৃত) ভোজন করা। **2.** To supply or take in provision; খাদ্যসম্ভার সরবরাহ করা, খাদ্যসম্ভার সঞ্চিত করা। **—less**, *adj.*

vict′-ual-ler (vit-l-êr), *n.* **1.** One who supplies provisions; খাদ্যদ্রব্য সরবরাহকারী। **2.** A tavern-keeper; an innkeeper; সুরাবিপণির অধিস্বামী; সরাইরক্ষক। **3.** A ship employed to carry stores for other ships; অপর জাহাজ সমূহের জন্য খাদ্যসম্ভার প্রভৃতিবাহী পোত।

vict′-ual-ling (vĭt-l-ĭng), *n.* The act of provisioning; খাদ্যসম্ভার সরবরাহ। **Victualling-bill**—যে সকল শুল্কযোগ্য বা আবগারী মাশুল প্রদানযোগ্য মাল সমুদ্রযাত্রাকালে জাহাজের যাত্রী ও নাবিকদিগের ব্যবহারের জন্য আবশ্যক হইবে তাহার যে তালিকা শুল্ক বিভাগে দেওয়া হয়। **Victualling-note**—নাবিকদিগকে খাদ্যপ্রদানের জন্য জাহাজের ভাণ্ডাররক্ষককে যে পরওয়ানা দেওয়া হয়। **Victualling-office**—নৌসৈন্যদিগের খাদ্যসম্ভার সরবরাহের জন্য কার্য্যালয়। **Victualling-ship**—Same as VICTUALLER 3. **Victualling-yard**—নৌদ্রব্যসম্ভাররক্ষণ এবং সরবরাহের জন্য প্রাঙ্গণ।

Vicugna

vi-cu′-gna (-cô-nyă), **—cu′-na** (-cô-nya), *ns.* A South-American animal of the same genus as the alpaca and llama; দক্ষিণ-আমেরিকার একপ্রকার ছাগজাতীয় জন্তু। **Vicugna wool**—উক্ত জন্তুর পশম; পশম এবং কার্পাসের মিশ্র। **Vicugna-cloth**—উক্ত জন্তুর লোম হইতে প্রাপ্ত একপ্রকার অতি মিহি পশমী কাপড়; ঐরূপ কাপড়ের অনুকরণে প্রস্তুত একপ্রকার মেরুণ কাপড়।

vide, *v. imper.* See; দেখ। ***Vide ante***—See before; পূর্ব্বে দেখ। ***Vide infra***—See below; নীচে দেখ। ***Vide post***—ইহার পরে দেখ। ***Vtde supra***—See above; উপরে দেখ। ***Quode vide***—তাহা দেখ।

videlicet, *adv.* (Abbrev. *viz.*; pronounced *namely*) That is to say; namely; অর্থাৎ; যথা, উদাহরণস্থলে।

vi-dette′ (-dĕt), *n.* Same as VEDETTE (which see).

vi′-di-mŭs, *n.* **1.** An inspection, as of account etc.; হিসাব প্রভৃতি পরিদর্শন। **2.** An abstract; চুম্বক, সারমর্ম্ম।

vie (vī), *v. i.* To strive for superiority; to compete; প্রাধান্য লাভের জন্য চেষ্টা করা, পরস্পরকে অতিক্রম করার চেষ্টা করা, টক্কর দেওয়া (*colloq.*); প্রতিযোগিতা করা।

Vi-ĕn-nese′ (-ēz), *adj.* & *n.* Pertaining to Vienna; ভিয়েনানগরীসম্বন্ধীয়। ***Noun.*** An inhabitant of Vienna; ভিয়েনানগরের অধিবাসী।

viet armis, *adv.* (*Law*) With force and arms; সবলে এবং অস্ত্রশস্ত্রের সাহায্যে।

view (vü), *n.* & *v. t.* **1.** Inspection by the eye; দর্শন, সন্দর্শন, অবলোকন, নিরীক্ষণ, পরিদর্শন। **2.** Power of seeing; range of vision; as, he stood in full *view* of the crowd; দৃষ্টিশক্তি, দর্শনশক্তি; দৃষ্টিসীমা। **3.** The act of perceiving by the mind; mental survey; as, take a *view* of the subject; অবধারণ; মানসিক দর্শন। **4.** A scene; as, a superb *view*; দৃশ্য। **5.** A picture; as, the painter has produced some fine settled tract of country ; a colony ; নব উপনিবিষ্টপ্রদেশ ; উপনিবেশ। 8. The payment of an account ; হিসাব নিষ্পত্তি। 9. Bestowal by legal act ; a deed by which prosperty is settled ; দানপত্রাদিদ্বারা বৃত্তি প্রভৃতির ব্যবস্থা ; যে পত্র বা দলিল দ্বারা সম্পত্তি প্রভৃতির বিলিব্যবস্থা করা হয়। 10. The sum secured to a person, esp. a jointure made to a woman at her marriage ; কোন লোকের জন্য বৃত্তির ব্যবস্থা, বিশেষতঃ বিবাহকালে স্বামীর মৃত্যুর পর আজীবন ভোগের জন্য স্ত্রীকে যে সম্পত্তি বিলি ব্যবস্থা করিয়া দেওয়া হয়। 11. Subsidence of wall, house, etc. ; প্রাচীর প্রভৃতি বসিয়া যাওন। 12. (*India*) The act of arranging the terms and incidence of the land revenue over specified areas between the Government and the tenants ; (ভারতবর্ষে) সরকারকর্তৃক ভূমির জরিপ এবং বন্দোবস্ত, সেটেলমেণ্ট। **Settlement day**—হিসাব পরিষ্কারের দিন; (লণ্ডন নগরীর কোম্পানীর কাগজের বাজারে) হিসাব পরিষ্কারের শেষ দিন। **Act of Settlement**—১৭০২ খৃঃ অব্দে বিধিবদ্ধ আইনবিশেষ—যদ্দ্বারা রাজ্ঞী এনের মৃত্যুর পর ১ম জেমসের পুত্রী হেনোভারের ইলেক্টরের পত্নী Sophia এবং তদীয় অঙ্গজাত Protestant মতাবলম্বী উত্তরাধিকারিগণ ইংলণ্ডের সিংহাসনে অধিরোহণ করিবে এইরূপ ব্যবস্থা করা হয়।

sĕt′-tler (-lêr), *n.* 1. One who settles in a colony ; ঔপনিবেশিক। 2. (*Colloq.*) A decisive blow, argument or the like ; "After the *settler* the man sat down" ; (চলিতভাষায়) চূড়ান্ত আঘাত, যুক্তি, প্রভৃতি, খতম ঘা। 3. A pan or vat in which something is allowed to settle ; যে পাত্রে কোন জিনিষ থিতান হয়।

sĕt′-wall, *n.* A species of valerian ; একপ্রকার লতা।

sĕv′-en (-n), *adj.* & *n.* One more than six ; সাত, সপ্ত। *Noun.* 1. The number greater than one by six ; সাত। 2. A playing card marked with seven tips ; তাসের সাতা। **–enth,** *adj.* সপ্তম। **–fold,** *adj.* সপ্তগুণ, সপ্তগুণিত। **–ti-eth,** *adj.* সপ্ততিতম। **–ty,** *adj.* & *n.* **A seven days' wonder**—যে বিষয় অল্পকাল জনসাধারণের বিস্ময় উৎপাদনের পর বিস্মৃতিগর্ভে নিমজ্জিত হয়। **Seven Bibles**—(১) খৃষ্টানদিগের বাইবেল গ্রন্থ ; (২) মুসলমানদিগের কোরাণ ; (৩) চিনাদিগের পঞ্চ কিং [পূর্ব্বে যে কাপড়ে উপর এই সমস্ত ধর্ম্মগ্রন্থ লিখিত হইত ;চীনাভাষায় তাহার নাম কিং]। (৪) বৌদ্ধদিগের ত্রিপিটক ; (৫) হিন্দুদিগের বেদ ; (৬) স্কাণ্ডিনিভিয়ানদিগের Eddas ; (৭) পারসীকদিগের জেন্দেবেস্ত (Zend-Avesta)। **Seven Bishops** — Archbishop Sancroft, এবং Bishops Ken, Lake, Lloyd, Trelawney, Turner এবং White—যাঁহারা রাজা জেমসের Declaration of Indulgenceএর বিরুদ্ধে প্রতিবাদ করিয়াছিলেন। **Seven bodies in alchemy** — ইয়ুরোপীয় তান্ত্রিকদিগের সপ্তধাতু—রবি (=স্বর্ণ), চন্দ্র (=রৌপ্য), মঙ্গল (=লৌহ), বুধ (=পারদ), শনি (=সীসক), বৃহস্পতি (=রঙ্গ), শুক্র (=তাম্র)। **Seven champions of Christendom**—ইংলণ্ড, স্কটলণ্ড, ওয়েলেস, আয়র্লণ্ড, ফ্রান্স ও ইতালীদেশের রক্ষাকারী সপ্তমহাপুরুষ St. George, St. Andrew, St. David, St. Patrick, St. Denis, St. James এবং St. Anthony. **Seven deadly sins**—অহঙ্কার, ক্রোধ, মাৎসর্য্য, কাম, লোভ, ধনতৃষ্ণা, আলস্য। **Seven-hilled**—সপ্তশৈলের উপরি অবস্থিত (রোম নগরী)। **Seven joys of Mary**—খৃষ্টজননী মেরীর সপ্ত আনন্দ—(১) দেবদূত জেব্রিয়েলকর্তৃক খৃষ্টাবতরণ-ঘোষণা (The Annunciation) ; (২) John the Baptistএর জননী এলিজেবেথকে দর্শনপ্রদান ; কুমারী মেরীর আগমন (Visitation) ; (৩) প্রাচ্যদেশাগতজ্ঞানিগণকর্তৃক খৃষ্টার্চ্চনা (Adoration of the Magi) ; (৪) খৃষ্টজন্ম ; (৫) মন্দিরে আনয়ন (Presentation to the temple) ; (৬) পণ্ডিতগণের মধ্যে খৃষ্টের দর্শন (Finding Christ among the Doctors) ; (৭) স্বর্গারোহণ (Assumption). **Seven league boats**—ছেলেদের উপকথায় উল্লিখিত বুটজুতা — যাহা পায়ে দিলে পবনবেগে বিচরণের ক্ষমতা জন্মিত। **Seven nights**—সপ্তরাত্র, একসপ্তাহ। **Seven Oceans**—উত্তর মহাসাগর, দক্ষিণ মহাসাগর, উত্তর এবং দক্ষিণ অতলান্তিক মহাসাগর, উত্তর এবং দক্ষিণ প্রশান্তমহাসাগর এবং ভারত মহাসাগর। **Seven sages** or **wise men**—প্রাচীন গ্রীসের সপ্তজ্ঞানী। (১) Athens নগরবাসী Solon (আপনাকে জান)। (২) Miletusএর Thales (জামিন হইলেই সর্ব্বনাশ)। (৩) Prieneএর Bias (বেশীর ভাগ লোকই মন্দ)। (৪) Lindusএর Cleobulus (শ্রেয়ঃ মধ্যপথ)। (৫) Spartaবাসী Chilo (অগ্রপশ্চাৎ ভাবিয়া কার্য্য করিও)। (৬) Corinthবাসী Periander (পরিশ্রমী লোকের অসাধ্য কিছুই নয়)। (৭) Myteleneবাসী Pittacus (সুযোগ বুঝিয়া কার্য করিবে)। উক্ত সপ্ত গ্রীক জ্ঞানীর নাম এবং তাঁহাদের উক্তি Delphi নগরীস্থ Appolo দেবের মন্দিরে উৎকীর্ণ ছিল। **Seven-sisters** — (অপ্রঃ) কৃত্তিকাপুঞ্জ। **Seven Sleepers**—Ephesus নগরবাসী যে সপ্তজন খৃষ্টীয় যুবক নির্যাতন হইতে রক্ষা পাওয়ার জন্য সিলিয়ন পর্ব্বতের গহ্বরে নিদ্রা যাইয়া ২৩০ বৎসর পর জাগরিত হইয়াছিল। **Seven-sisters rose, Seven-sister rose**—একজাতীয় লতা-গোলাপ — যাহাতে গুচ্ছে গুচ্ছে শ্বেত, রক্ত ও পাটলবর্ণের গোলাপ ধরিয়া থাকে। **Seven sorrows of virgin Mary** — Simeonএর ভবিষ্যদ্বাণী ; মিশরে পলায়ন ; খৃষ্টের সন্ধান অপ্রাপ্তি ; খৃষ্টের বন্ধন ; (খৃষ্টের) ক্রুশারোপণ ; ক্রুশ হইতে অবতারণ ; খৃষ্টের স্বর্গারোহণ।

vī′-king, *n.* One of the piratical Northmen, who in the 8th, 9th and 10th centuries ravaged the coasts of Western Europe ; ৮ম, ৯ম ও ১০ম শতাব্দীতে যে সকল উত্তর ইয়ুরোপবাসী জলদস্যু ইয়ুরোপের পশ্চিম উপকূলবাসী লোকদিগের ধনসম্পত্তি লুণ্ঠন করিত। **–ism** *n.*

vilayet, *n.* A province of Turkish Empire ; তুরস্ক সাম্রাজ্যের প্রদেশবিশেষ।

vīle, *adj.* **1.** Worthless ; mean ; morally impure or wicked ; অসার ; নীচ ; দুশ্চরিত্র, বদস্বভাব, দুষ্ট। **2.** (*Colloq.*) Abominably bad ; "It is a *vile* thing to lie" ; (চলিতভাষায়) ঘৃণ্য, জঘন্য। **Vile′-ly,** *adv.* **Vile′-ness,** *n.*

vĭl′-ĭ-fȳ, *v. t.* **1.** To defame ; কলঙ্ক রটনা করা, কলঙ্কিত করা, অপবাদ করা, কুৎসা রটনা করা, গ্লানি করা, সম্মান নাশ করা, দুর্নাম করা। **2.** (*Rare*) To degrade by slander ; "When themselves they *vilified* to serve ungoverned appetite" ; অবনমিত করা। **–fi-ca′-tion,** *n.* The act of one who vilifies ; নিন্দাবাদ,গ্লানি, কুৎসারটনা, কুৎসন। **–fi-er,** *n.*

vĭl′-ĭ-pĕnd, *v. t.* To depreciate : to vilify ; অনাদর করা ; অপবাদ করা।

vĭl′-lă, *n.* A country seat ; a suburban residence ; পল্লীভবন, পল্লীবাটিকা, পল্লীপ্রাসাদ ; নগরোপকণ্ঠস্থিত আবাসভবন।

vĭl′-lāge, *n.* An assemblage of houses less than a town, but larger than a hamlet ; গ্রাম, পল্লীগ্রাম, মৌজা (*colloq.*)। **Village watchman**—চৌকিদার।

vĭl′-lāg-ēr, *n.* **1.** An inhabitant of a village ; গ্রামবাসী, পল্লীবাসী, গ্রাম্য লোক।

vĭl′-lain (-lān *or* -lăn), *n.* & *adj.* **1.** A scoundrel ; a rascal ; দুর্বৃত্ত, দুর্জন, দুরাত্মা ; বদমায়েস, পাজি, দুরাচার, পাষণ্ড, নচ্ছার। **2.** (*Archaic*) A rustic ; পাড়াগেঁয়ে লোক। **3.** Feudal serf ; চাকরাণ জমিভোগী লোক। *Adj.* Of, or pertaining to, a villain ; চাকরাণ জমিভোগিসম্বন্ধীয়। **2.** Servile ; base ; দাসোচিত ; হীন, নীচ, ইতর। **–age,** *n.*

vĭl′-lain-ous (-lăn-ŭs), *adj.* **1.** Worthy of a villain ; vile ; wicked ; পাপিষ্ঠযোগ্য ; জঘন্য, নীচ ; দুষ্ট। **2.** Abominably bad ; "*Villainous* saltpetre" ; অতিশয় মন্দ। **–ly,** *adj.* **–ness,** *n.*

villanelle, *n.* A form of poem, esp. French in two rhymes ; একপ্রকার ফরাসী কবিতা।

villeggiatura, *n.* Retirement in the country ; পল্লীগ্রামে নির্জ্জন বাস।

vĭl′-lŭs, *n.* **1.** (*Anat.*) A minute projection from the surface of mucous membrane, giving the appearance of the nap of cloth ; (শারীরসংস্থানবিদ্যা) শ্লৈষ্মিক ঝিল্লীর উপরিভাগ হইতে উদ্গত বস্ত্রের ফুঁপির মত ক্ষুদ্র ক্ষুদ্র উদ্গত অংশ। **2.** (*Bot.*) Long, soft, close hair covering fruit, flowers ; etc ; (উদ্ভিদ্‌বিদ্যা) ফল অথবা ফুলের আবরক সুদীর্ঘ, ঘনসন্নিবিষ্ট এবং কোমল লোম, সুচি (সাঃ পঃ)। **–li-form,** *adj.* **–loid, –lose, –lous,** *adjs.* Covered with long soft hairs ; অতিলোমশ (সাঃ পঃ)। **–los′-i-ty,** *n.*

vĭm, *n.* (*Colloq.*) Vigour ; (চলিতভাষায়) তেজঃ, শক্তি।

vĭm′-ĭ-năl, *adj.* (*Bot.*) Pertaining to , consisting of, or producing, twigs ; (উদ্ভিদ্‌বিদ্যা) প্রশাখাসম্বন্ধীয়, প্রশাখাসমন্বিত, প্রশাখাপ্রসূ। **Vi-min′-e-ous,** *adj.*

vĭ-nā′-ceous (-shŭs), *adj.* Belonging to the wine or grapes ; of the colour of wine ; মদ্যসম্বন্ধীয়, মদীরাসম্বন্ধীয়, আঙ্গুরসম্বন্ধীয় ; মদ্যাবর্ণ।

vĭn-ai-grette′ (-ā-grĕt), *n.* A small bottle for holding aromatic vinegar ; a smelling bettle ; সুগন্ধি সির্কা প্রভৃতি রাখার জন্য শিশি ; সুরভিত নিশাদল প্রভৃতি পূর্ণ শিশি।

vĭn′-cĭ-ble (-bl), *adj.* (*Rare*) conquearble ; জেয়।

vĭn′-cū-lŭm (vĭng-), *n.* **1.** A bond or union ; বন্ধন, সংযোগ। **2.** (*Math.*) A straight mark placed over several members of a compound quantity, which are subjected to the same operation ; রাশির উপরিস্থ রেখা, বন্ধনীরেখা, শৃঙ্খলা (হিঃ কোঃ) [যথা $\overline{x+y}+z$ এখানে $(x+y)$ এই রাশির উপরিস্থ রেখার নাম বন্ধনীরেখা। **3.** (*Anat.*) Same as FRÆNUM. **4.** (*Print.*) Same as BRACE.

vin-de-fimes, *n.* (*F.*) A preparation for tinging white wine red ; সোনালী রঙ্গের মদ্যকে লোহিতবর্ণে রঞ্জিত করার জন্য একপ্রকার মিশ্রদ্রব্য।

vindemiaire, *n.* Same as VENDEMIAIRE (which see.)

vĭn′-dĭ-cāte, *v. t.* **1.** To defend with success ; to prove to be true or valid ; as, to *vindicate* a right ; to justify ; সমর্থন করা ; সত্য বা বৈধ বলিয়া প্রতিপন্ন করা ; ন্যায্যতা প্রতিপাদন করা। **2.** To maintain the cause of ; পক্ষসমর্থন করা। **3.** To clear from censure ; as, to *vindicate* one's honour ; দোষ বা অপবাদ হইতে মুক্ত করা। **4.** (*Law*) To assert one's legal right ; to recover by legal process ; আইনসঙ্গত অধিকার খ্যাপন করা ; মোকদ্দমাদি দ্বারা উদ্ধার করা। **–ca′-tion,** *n.* **1.** The act of vindicating ; সমর্থন। **2.** Defence ; support ; পক্ষ সমর্থন ; আশ্রয়। **3.** Justification against denial, censure, objection, or accusation ; দোষনিরসন, দোষক্ষালন, অপরাধখণ্ডন। **–ca-bil′-i-ty,** *n.*

vĭn′-dĭ-ca-tō-rȳ, *adj.* **1.** Tending to vindicate ; পক্ষসমর্থনশীল। **2.** (*Law, obs.*) Punitive ; (আইন, অপ্রঃ) দণ্ডাত্মক।

vĭn-dĭc′-tive (-tĭv), *adj.* Revengeful ; retaliatory ; as, *vindictive*

for—To make pretensions to the character of ; কোন কিছু বলিয়া আপনাকে দাবী করা বা চালাইতে চেষ্টা করা। **To set up for oneself**—To start on a career on one's account; স্বাধীনভাবে কোনরূপ জীবনব্যাপার আরম্ভ করা। **To set upon**—To attack ; আক্রমণ করা। **To set up one's back**—To excite one's anger ; কাহারো ক্রোধ উদ্দীপ্ত করা। **To set up one's bristles**—To be angry ; ক্রুদ্ধ হওয়া। **To set up one's comb or hair**—To be puffed up with pride ; গর্ব্বে ফুলিয়া উঠা। (*U. S.*) To treat to ; ভোজ্য, পেয়, প্রভৃতি দ্বারা আপ্যায়িত করা। To appoint ; নিযুক্ত করা। To put together the parts of a machine and cause it to stand in position ; যন্ত্রের বিভিন্ন অংশ সংযোজনপূর্ব্বক উহাকে দাঁড় করান। **Well set up**—সুগঠিত দৃঢ়কায়।

sĕt, *n.* & *adj.* **1.** The apparent descent of a heavenly body below the horizon ; অস্তগমন, অস্তপ্রয়াণ। **2.** (*Fig.*) Close ; termination; (লক্ষণায়) শেষ; অন্ত, অবসান। **3.** A collection of things of similar use ; প্রস্থ, সেট, দফা। **4.** A number of persons associated ; as, a *set* of men ; একদল লোক। **5.** A clique ; কুচক্রিদল। **6.** Attitude; build ; "Money in possession do give a *set* to the head and confidence to the voice" ; ভঙ্গী, ঢঙ্গ ; গঠন। **7.** A young plant for putting into the soil for growth ; রোপণের জন্য ক্ষুদ্র চারা। **8.** Direction or course ; as, the *set* of the tide ; দিক বা গমনপথ। **9.** (*Obs.*) A wager ; a game ; (অপ্রঃ) বাজী, পণ; খেলা। **10.** Tendency; as, the *set* of one's mind ; ঝোঁক, আসক্তি, প্রবণতা। **11.** Alternate deflection of saw-teeth ; করাতের দাঁত একটীর পর একটী করিয়া একদিকে এবং অবশিষ্ট গুলি একদিকে প্রবণ করণ। **12.** A potato or a portion of a potato used as seed ; বীজস্বরূপ ব্যবহৃত আলু বা আলুর অংশ। **13.** A square stone for paving ; রাস্তা প্রভৃতি বাঁধার জন্য সমচতুষ্কোণাকারে কর্ত্তিত প্রস্তর। **14.** A permanent change of figure caused by pressure ; চাপহেতু আকারের স্থায়ী পরিবর্ত্তন। *Adj.* **1.** Fixed ; as, a *set* countenance ; firm ; দৃঢ়সংবদ্ধ ; দৃঢ়। **2.** Etablished ; prescribed ; প্রতিষ্ঠিত; নির্দ্দিষ্ট, বিহিত। **3.** Predetermined ; পূর্ব্বনির্দ্ধারিত। **4.** Regular ; নিয়মিত। **5.** (*Colloq.*) Conceited ; (চলিতভাষায়) গর্ব্বিত, দৃপ্ত। **Dead set**—বদ্ধ অবস্থা, নিশ্চল অবস্থা; মরিয়া ভাবে আক্রমণ, বিরুদ্ধাবস্থা; পুরুষের প্রণয় লাভের জন্য স্ত্রীলোকের প্রাণান্তকর চেষ্টা। **Dinner set**—Dinner service ; অপরাহ্নভোজনের জন্য এক প্রস্থ চীনবাসন, চামচ, কাঁটা প্রভৃতি। **Set-back**—বাধা, ভাগ্যবিপর্য্যয়; পরাভব; ধাক্কা। **Set-down** — রাস্তায় চলতি গাড়ীতে উঠিয়া কিছুপথ যাওয়ার সুযোগ ; তীব্র তিরস্কার, এক চোট গাল, মুখঝামটা ; দাবানি। **Set-fair**—বায়ুমান যন্ত্রের পারদস্তম্ভের সূচীর অগ্রভাগের বিপরীতদিকে অঙ্কিত শব্দ—যদ্দারা বায়ুর অবস্থা ভালই আছে বলিয়া সূচিত হয়। **Set-in**—প্রারম্ভ। **Set-off**—যাত্রা, রওনা; পাল্টাদাবী, তুল্য মূল্য বস্তু; অলঙ্কার, ভূষা, মণ্ডন। **Set-out**—নাট্য, প্রদর্শনী, নাচ গান, তামাসা, প্রীতিসম্মিলনী; দল; গোলমাল, গণ্ডগোল, হৈচৈ; সাজসজ্জা; প্রারম্ভ ; পোষাকপরিচ্ছদ: পরিধানের ধারা, পোষাক পরার রীতি বা ধরণ ; অশ্ব এবং অশ্বসজ্জাদিসমেত শকট ; আহারের জন্য মেজের উপর সজ্জিত খাদ্যদ্রব্য; চীনাবাসন প্রভৃতির সেট, চীনাবাসন প্রভৃতি প্রদর্শন। **Set-piece, Set-scene**—কাঠামের উপর স্থাপিত দৃশ্যপট। **Set-speech**—পূর্ব্বে বাটীতে প্রস্তুত করিয়া আসিয়া সভাতে যে বক্তৃতা দেওয়া হয়, তৈরী বক্তৃতা। **Sharp-set**—ধারাল (করাত) ; ব্যগ্র, উৎকণ্ঠাকুল, উতলা ; প্রচণ্ড ক্রোধাবিষ্ট। **Set of day**—সূর্য্যাস্ত, দিনান্ত ; পশ্চিমদিক ; (লক্ষণায়) জীবনের দিনান্ত, জীবনসন্ধ্যা ; **S to**—মুষ্টিযুদ্ধ ; যুদ্ধ, সংগ্রাম ; আক্রমণ **To make a dead set at**—To make a determined attack ; মরিয়া হইয়া আক্রমণ করা। To try her utmost to win the love of a man ; পুরুষের প্রণয়-লাভের জন্য প্রাণপণে চেষ্টা করা।

sē'-tă, *n.* (*Bot.*) Bristles when short and stiff ; অনুকণ্টক (সাঃ পঃ), শূক রোম (ঐ)।

sē-tā'-ceous (-shŭs), *adj.* **1.** Bristly; সকণ্টক। **2.** (*Bot.*) Pertaining to bristle ; having the form of a bristle ; অনুকণ্টকসম্বন্ধীয় ; অনুকণ্টকাকৃতি। **–ly,** *adv.*

sē-tif'-ĕr-ous (-ŭs), *adj.* Having bristles ; কণ্টকযুক্ত।

sē'-ti-fôrm, *adj.* Having the form of a bristle ; অনুকণ্টকাকৃতি।

sē-tĭg'-ĕr-ous (-ŭs), *adj.* Same as SETIFEROUS.

sē'-tŏn, *n.* (*Surg.*) A few horse hairs, or a twist of silk or fine linen, drawn through the skin by means of large needle, by which a small opening is made, and continued for the discharge of humours ; দীর্ঘ রেশম বা কার্পাস সূত্রের গুচ্ছ—যাহা বৃহৎ সূচী দ্বারা চর্ম্মের ভিতর দিয়া নীত হওয়ায় পূযাদি নির্গমনের জন্য ক্ষুদ্র রন্ধ্র গঠিত হয়।

sē'-tōse, *adj.* Same as SETIFEROUS.

sĕtt, *n.* *Var.* of SET.

sĕt-tee' (-tē), *n.* A long seat with a back ; a kind of arm-chair or short sofa for several persons to sit on at once ; উপবেশনের জন্য একপ্রকার দীর্ঘ আসন ; কয়েকজন লোকের একসময়ে বসিবার জন্য একপ্রকার আরামকেদারা বা ক্ষুদ্র সোফা, আরামখট্টা।

sĕt-tee' (-tē), *n.* A vessel with one deck, carrying two or three masts with lateen sails, used on the Mediterranean ; ভূমধ্যসাগরের দ্বি বা ত্রিমাস্তল পোতবিশেষ।

vi'-ō-lĕnt, *adj.* **1.** Acting with physical force; impetuous; as a *violent* storm; vehement; as, a *violent* remonstrance; উগ্র; প্রচণ্ড; প্রবল। **2.** Passionate; hot-tempered; চণ্ড; রুদ্র। **3.** Outrageous; পৈশাচিক, অমানুষিক, বীভৎস। **4.** Very great; as, *violent* force; অতিশয়, অত্যন্ত। **5.** Unnatural; as, he met a *violent* death; অস্বাভাবিক, অনৈসর্গিক। **—ly,** *adv.* **Violent presumption**—নিশ্চিত প্রমাণের উপর প্রতিষ্ঠিত অনুমান। **Violent profits**—(স্কটলণ্ডের আইন) কোন প্রজাকে ভূমি ছাড়িয়া দেওয়ার নোটিস দেওয়ার পর সে অন্যায় রূপে ঐ ভূমির রাজস্ব প্রভৃতি যাহা আদায় করে।

vi'-ō-lĕt, *n.* & *adj.* **1.** A plant of many species having beautiful flowers, the flowers of the one most cultivated having a fragrant smell; একজাতীয় নীল, শ্বেত, রক্তাভনীল পুষ্পপ্রসূ বৃক্ষ, বনোসা (খোরী)। **2.** One of the primary colours; ভায়লেট রঙ্গ, ধূমল বর্ণ, বেগুনে রঙ্গ। **3.** Kinds of violet butterfly; বিভিন্নপ্রকার বেগুনে রঙ্গের প্রজাপতি। ***Adj.***

প্রকার বাদ্যতন্ত্রীবিশিষ্ট যন্ত্র — যাহা ক্ষুদ্র ছড় দ্বারা বাজাইতে হয়। **Violin-bow**—বেহালার ছড়।

vi'-ō-lin, *n.* An emetic substance contained in all parts of the common violet; ভায়লেট পুষ্পে প্রাপ্ত একপ্রকার উদ্বামক পদার্থ।

vi'-ō-lŏn-cĕl'-lō, *n.* A large four-stringed musical instrument of the violin-class, the quality of its tone even more sympathetic than that of violin; একপ্রকার বৃহৎ বেহালাজাতীয় বাদ্যযন্ত্র। **—list,** *n.*

vi'-pêr, *n.* **1.** A venomous serpent of several species; বিষধর সর্পবিশেষ, দন্দশূক। **2.** A malignant and treacherous person; "Where is the *viper*; bring the villain forth"; খল, বিশ্বাসঘাতক ব্যক্তি, বিষধর। **—i-form, —ine, —ish, —oid, —ous,** *adjs.* **To nourish a viper in one's bosom**—দুধকলা দিয়া সাপ পোষা।

vi-rā'-gō, *n.* **1.** A turbulent woman; উগ্রচণ্ডা নারী, রায়বাঘিনী, জাঁহাবাজ মেয়ে, দীপ্তজিহ্বা। **2.** (*Archaic*) A highly masculine woman;

Vir-ğil'-i-ăn (vêr-), *adj.* **1.** Of the Roman poet Virgil; রোমক কবি ভার্জ্জিলসম্বন্ধীয়। **2.** In the style of Virgil; ভার্জ্জিলের রচনারীতি অনুসারী।

vir'-ğin (vêr-), *n.* & *adj.* A maiden of inviolate chastity; কুমারী, কন্যকা (উজ্জ্বলঃ), অনন্যপূর্ব্বা (বাৎস্যঃ), অক্ষতা (বাৎস্যঃ), কন্যা। **2.** An insect producing egg without fecundation by the male; বিনা গর্ভসঞ্চারে ডিম্বপ্রসবকারী কীট। **3.** Sign Virgo; কন্যারাশি, যুবতী, পাথোন। **4.** (*Cap.*) Virgin Mary; কুমারী মেরী। ***Adj.*** **1.** Becoming a virgin; as, *virgin* modestry; কুমারীজনোচিত। **2.** Undefiled; অকলঙ্কিত, নিষ্কলঙ্ক, অকলঙ্ক, অমলিন। **3.** (Of insect) Producing eggs without impregation; গর্ভসঞ্চারবিনা ডিম্বপ্রসবকারী। **—hood, —gin'-i-ty,** *ns.* **Virginus**—চিত্রা (হিঃ কোঃ)। **Blessed Virgin**—Virgin Mary; খৃষ্টজননী কুমারী মেরী। **Virgin's-bower**—Same as TRAVELLER'S. JOY. **Virgin comb**—যে মধুচক্র হইতে কেবল মাত্র একবার মধু সংগ্রহ করা হইয়াছে।

পযোগিতা। **2.** The process of ıodifying a thing so as to suit ew condition, as the modification f a piece of music to suit a ifferent condition; the alteration of a dramatic composition to suit different audience; নূতন অবস্থার পযোগীকরণ—যথা, বিভিন্ন অবস্থার পযোগীকরণার্থ সঙ্গীতের পরিবর্ত্তন; ন্নশ্রেণীর বা ভিন্নদেশীয় শ্রোতৃবৃন্দের পযোগীকরণার্থ কোন নাটকের ভাব, ষা বা ঘটনাসমূহের পরিবর্ত্তন। **-ed-ness,** *n.* **—er,** *n.* One that dapts (in any sense); সংযোজক। **-ive,** *adj.* Given to adaptation; suitable; সংযোজনশীল; উপযোগী। **—ive-ness,** *n.*

ad captandum (vulgus), *adv.* & *adj.* Calculated to catch the fancy of the rabble; ইতর জনতার চিত্তাকর্ষণার্থ। ***Adj.*** Applied also

excitement or fury; to give a fresh incitement or provocation to; "His words *added fuel to* the already excited passion of the mob." জ্বলন্ত অনলে ঘৃতাহুতি বা ইন্ধন প্রদান করা; ক্রোধের প্রকোপ বা প্রচণ্ডতা বৃদ্ধি করা। **To add in**—To include in a sum; যোগফলের অন্তর্ভুক্ত করা। **To add to**—To augment; to increase; বর্দ্ধিতকরা; বৃদ্ধি করা। **To add up**—To find the sum of; যোগফল নির্ণয় করা, ঠিক দেওয়া।

ăd'-dăx, *n.* A species of ox-like antelope; একজাতীয় কৃষ্ণসার।

Addax.

(রোমীয় আইন) আদালতের আদেশানুসারে সমর্পণ করা; অতএব (লক্ষণায়) সমর্পণ করা। **--ed,** *p. p.* Devoted; closely attached; নিরত, রত; আসক্ত, সক্ত, অনুলগ্ন **—ed-ness,** *n.* Devotion; attachment; আসক্তি; অনুরক্তি, রতি।

ăd-dic'-tion, *n.* The state of being given to a habit or pursuit; devotion; আসক্তি; অনুরক্তি।

ăd-dit'-â-mĕnt, *n.* An addition; thing added; যোগ; যুক্ত বস্তু।

ăd-di'-tion, *n.* **1.** The act or process of adding; সংযোজন, যোজনা, সঙ্কলন-ক্রিয়া। **2.** The thing added; সংযোজিত বস্তু। **—al,** *adj.* Added; supplementary; সংযোজিত, সংযুক্ত; ন্যূনতাপূরক, অনুপূরক, অতিরিক্ত। **—al-ly,** *adv.* **In addition to**—Over and above; অধিকন্তু, অতিরিক্ত।

ăd'-dle, *adj., n., v. t.* & *i.* **1.** Putrid

হইতে আগত আলোক ; পোতপার্শ্বস্থ প্রদীপ ; গৌণভাবে প্রাপ্ত সংবাদ। **Side-line**—কোন ব্যক্তির ব্যবসায়ের অতিরিক্ত বিভাগ। **Side look, Side glance, Side-long glance**—কটাক্ষ, কুটিল-কটাক্ষ, লীলাবলোকন, দৃগঞ্চল (উজ্জ্বলঃ), দৃগ্‌ভঙ্গী (গোপালঃ), ভ্রূবিলাস (মেঘদূঃ), অপাঙ্গবিলাস (ঐ), অপাঙ্গচ্ছটা (ঐ), তেরছনয়ন, (প্রাঃ সাঃ), তেরছচাহনি (*ib.*), ভ্রূবিভ্রম, ভ্রূবিচেষ্টিত (রঃ), অপাঙ্গদর্শন, অপাঙ্গদৃষ্টি, তির্য্যক্‌প্রেক্ষণ, অপাঙ্গবীক্ষণ। **Side-niches**—কর্ণকুট। **Side-note**—পার্শ্বটীকা, পার্শ্বটিপ্পনী। **Side-piercing**—হৃদয়ভেদী। **Side-saddle**—স্ত্রীলোকের জিন। **Side-show** — অপ্রধান দৃশ্য, উপদৃশ্য। **Side-slip** — কোন যানের (বিশেষতঃ বাইসিকেল বা হাওয়াগাড়ীর চাকার) পথচ্যুতি, তির্য্যগ্‌গামী প্ররোহ ; জারজ সন্তান। **Sidesman**—খৃষ্টীয় ধর্ম্ম-মন্দিরে নিযুক্ত নিম্নশ্রেণীর কর্ম্মচারিবিশেষ ; ভজনালয়ে যে কর্ম্মচারী লোকদিগকে আসন প্রভৃতি প্রদর্শন করে। **Side-splitting**—পেটফাটা (হাসি)। **Side-stroke**—পার্শ্ব হইতে আঘাত, পার্শ্বের-দিকে আঘাত। **Side-table**—যে মেজ সাধারণতঃ প্রাচীরে ঠেস দিয়া রাখা হয়। **Side-track**—Same as SIDING. **Side-view**—এক পার্শ্ব হইতে দেখিলে যেরূপ দেখা যায়; পার্শ্বদৃশ্য। **Side-walk**—পাদযাত্রীদিগের জন্য উচ্চ পথ। **Side-wind**—পার্শ্বদেশ হইতে প্রবাহিত বায়ু; গৌণ ক্রিয়া বা প্রভাব। **Credit side**—জমার দিক। **Debit side**—খরচের দিক; **Off side**—ডাহিনদিক। **Wrong side**—উল্টাদিক। **By the side of** — Near ; নিকটে, পার্শ্বে। **From side to side**—Transversely ; অনুপার্শ্বে, আড়ে। **Side by side**—Placed near each other ; পাশাপাশি। **To choose sides**—To select parties for competition in exercise of any kind ; কোনরূপ প্রতিযোগিতার ক্রীড়ার জন্য উভয় পক্ষের লোক নির্ব্বাচন করা। **To put on side**—To treat insolently ; উদ্ধত ব্যবহার করা। **To shake one's sides**—See under SHAKE. **To take a side** — To join one party ; কোন পক্ষ অবলম্বন করা। **To take sides**—To range oneself with one or other of the contending parties ; পরস্পরবিরোধী পক্ষদ্বয়ের কোন এক পক্ষ অবলম্বন করা।

sī-dē'-rē-ăl, sĭd'-ēr-ăl, *adjs.* **1.** Pertaining to the stars ; নাক্ষত্র, নাক্ষত্রিক। **2.** Measured or marked out by the apparent motion of the stars ; নক্ষত্রের স্ফুট গতিদ্বারা পরিমিত বা চিহ্নিত। **Sidereal day**—কোন স্থানের যাম্যোত্তরবৃত্তে কোন নক্ষত্র যে মুহূর্ত্তে দৃষ্ট হওয়ার পর যে মুহূর্ত্তে উহা তথায় পুনর্দৃষ্ট হয়—এতদুভয়ের মধ্যবর্ত্তী-কাল, নাক্ষত্র অহোরাত্র (ইহার পরিমাণ প্রায় ২৩ ঘণ্টা ৫৬ মিনিট ৪·০৯ সেকেণ্ড)। **Sidereal magnetism** — জৈবচুম্বকে বিশ্বাসী ব্যক্তিগণের মতানুসারে রোগীর উপর নক্ষত্রের প্রভাব, নাক্ষত্রচুম্বক। **Sidereal system**—নক্ষত্রজগৎ [যেমন আমাদের পৃথিবী, শনি, বৃহস্পতি, প্রভৃতি এবং উহাদের উপগ্রহাদি আমাদের সৌরজগতের অন্তর্ভুক্ত তেমনি আমাদের সৌরজগৎ নাক্ষত্রজগতের অন্তর্ভুক্ত। এইরূপ এক একটী নক্ষত্রজগতে বহু সৌরজগৎ রহিয়াছে]। **Sidereal time**—নাক্ষত্র-দিবস অনুসারে গণিত সময়। **Side-real year**—যে সময়ে অচল নক্ষত্র সমূহ কোন নির্দ্দিষ্ট স্থানে একবার দৃষ্ট হইবার পর পুনরায় সেই স্থানে দৃষ্ট হয়। [এক নাক্ষত্রবর্ষ প্রায় ৩৬৬·২৫৬৩৬১২ নাক্ষত্রঅহোরাত্রের সমান।]

sĭd'-ēr-īte, *n.* The loadstone ; the native iron protocarbonate ; চুম্বক প্রস্তর ; ব্যোমায়স (সাঃ পঃ)।

sĭd-ēr-ŏg'-ră-phȳ, *n.* A process of engraving on steel ; ইস্পাত-ফলকের উপর ক্ষোদনের প্রণালীবিশেষ।

sĭd'-ēr-ō-līte, *n.* A meteoric stone of iron ; ব্যোমায়সাশ্ম (সাঃ পঃ)।

side'-ward, -wards, *adv.* & *adj.* Laterally ; এক পার্শ্বে, পার্শ্বাভিমুখে। *Adj.* Lateral ; পার্শ্বিক, পার্শ্বাভিমুখীন।

side'-ways (-wāz), *adv.* & *adj.* Same as SIDEWARD (above).

sīd'-ing, *n.* **1.** The attaching of one's self to a party ; পক্ষাবলম্বন। **2.** A short additional line of rails for shunting ; লৌহবর্ত্মের পার্শ্বস্থিত উপবর্ত্ম।

sīd-le (-l), *v. i.* To move to one side ; to go or move with one side foremost ; এক পার্শ্বে সরা ; তির্য্যগ্‌ভাবে চলা, কাতান।

Sī-dō'-nĭ-ăn, *adj.* & *n.* Of, or pertaining to, Sidon, an ancient seaport of Phoenicia ; প্রাচীন ফিনিশিয়ার সাইডন বন্দরসম্বন্ধীয়। *Noun.* An inhabitant of Sidon ; সাইডনের অধিবাসী।

siege (sēj), *n.* & *v.t.* **1.** The setting of an army around or before a fortified place, for the purpose of compelling the garrison to surrender ; অবরোধ, সৈন্যবেষ্টন (কেঃশিঃ)। **2.** Any continued attempt to persuade an unwilling person to do something ; "Love stood the *siege* and would not yield his breast" ; অনিচ্ছুক ব্যক্তিদ্বারা কোন কার্য্য করাইবার জন্য পুনঃ পুনঃ চেষ্টা, পীড়াপীড়ি। **3.** The floor of a glass-furnace ; কাঁচচুল্লীর তলদেশ। *Verb t.* (*Archaic*) To besiege ; (অপ্রঃ) অবরোধ করা। **Siege-basket**—Same as GABION (which see). **Siege-gun**—অবরুদ্ধ দুর্গ ধ্বংস করার জন্য ব্যবহৃত কামান, দুর্গধ্বংস-কারী কামান। **Siege-train**—দুর্গ অবরোধে ব্যবহৃত কামান এবং অন্যান্য যন্ত্র। **Siege-works**—দুর্গাব-রোধকারিগণের পরিখা, আশ্রয়স্থল, প্রভৃতি। **To lay siege to**—To besiege ; অবরোধ করা। **To push the siege** — To continue a siege vigorously ; প্রবল উদ্যমের সহিত অবরুদ্ধ দুর্গ অধিকারের চেষ্টা করা। **To raise the siege**—To abandon the attempt to take a fort ; দুর্গ অবরোধকার্য্য পরিত্যাগ করা।

Sieg'-fried (sēj-frēd), *n.* The hero of the first part of the Nibelungen-Lied ; Nibelungen-Lied গ্রন্থের

bitterness or malignity ; অতিবিদ্বেষদুষ্টতা, অতিকটুতা, অতিতীব্রতা ।

vir-ū-lif'-ĕr-ous (-ŭs), *adj.* (*Med.*) Containing or producing a specific virus ; (ভৈষজ্যশাস্ত্র) বিশিষ্ট বীজপূর্ণ বা উৎপাদনশীল ।

vī'-rŭs, *n.* **1.** The contagious or poisonous matter of an ulcer or pustule ; বসন্ত উপদংশাদির পূয বা বীজ । **2.** Any foul hurtful matter ; দূষিত পদার্থ, সংক্রামক বিষ । **3.** Extreme acrimony or malignity ; বিদ্বেষবিষ । **4.** Some thing that corrupts mind or soul ; as, the *virus* of licentiousness ; মন বা আত্মার পক্ষে বিষময়স্বরূপ বস্তু ।

vis, *n.* Force ; বল, শক্তি । ***Vis acceleratrix***—উত্তরোত্তর গতিবর্দ্ধক বল । ***Vis inertiae***—জড়শক্তি, জাড্য, তামসিক নিশ্চেষ্টতা । ***Vis medicatrix naturoe*** — স্বাভাবিকরোগনিবারণীশক্তি । ***Vis mortua***—যে বল হইতে কোন কার্য্য উৎপন্ন হয়না, মৃতশক্তি । ***Vis nervosa***—শিরাসমূহের ধর্ম্মসমূহ—যদ্দ্বারা উহারা পেশীতে সাড়া প্রেরণ করে, শৈরিক শক্তি । ***Vis viva***—প্রাণবল, সজীবশক্তি, জীবনবল (হিঃ কোঃ), প্রাণবল (ঐ) ; (গণিত) বর্গগতি (হিঃ কোঃ) ।

vis'-āge, *n.* **1.** The face ; মুখ । **2.** The countenance or look of a person, or of other animals ; মনুষ্য বা অন্য কোন জন্তুর মুখাকৃতি, চেহারা, মুখাবয়ব ।

vis'-ărd, *n.* Same as VISOR (which see).

vis-a-vis' (vēz-â-vē), *n.* & *adj.* **1.** One who, or that which, is face to face with another ; পরস্পরের সম্মুখে অবস্থিত ব্যক্তি বা বস্তুদ্বয়ের অন্যতর । **2.** A person facing another esp. in some dances ; পরস্পরের সম্মুখে নর্ত্তনশীল ব্যক্তিদ্বয়ের অন্যতর । **3.** A light carriage for two persons who are seated opposite each other, instead of side by side ; একপ্রকার শকট — যাহাতে দুই ব্যক্তি পরস্পরের সম্মুখে উপবেশন করিয়া থাকে ।

vis-că'-chă, viz–, *ns.* A South-American rodent of stout form about twenty inches in length ; দক্ষিণ আমেরিকার একপ্রকার দন্তুর জন্তু ।

vis'-cer-ă (-ĕr-), *n.* (*pl.*) The bowels ; অন্ত্র, নাড়ীভুঁড়ি । **–al,** *adj.*

vis'-cer-āte (-ĕr-), *v. t.* To disembowel ; নাড়ীভুঁড়ি বাহির করা, অন্ত্র নিষ্কাশিত করা ।

vis'-cid, *adj.* Sticky ; আঠালো, চটচটে, লসলসা, লসদার (হিঃ কোঃ), সান্দ্র । **–cid'-i-ty,** *n.* Quality or state of being viscid ; সান্দ্রতা ।

vis'-cin, *n.* A waxy substance, the principal constituent of birdlime, extracted from the stalk, berries and leaves of mistletoe ; মিসলটো লতার বৃন্ত, ফল, প্রভৃতি হইতে নিষ্কর্ষিত একপ্রকার মোমের মত পদার্থ ।

vis-cō-sim'-ĕ-tĕr, *n.* An instrument for measuring the degree of viscosity of liquids ; লসমাপক (হিঃ কোঃ) ।

vis-cŏs'-i-tў, *n.* The quality or state of being viscous ; stickiness ; adhesiveness ; আঠালোভাব ; সান্দ্রতা ; সংলাগশীলতা ।

vis'-count (-vī-kownt), *n.* A title of nobility immediately below an earl and above a baron ; কৌলীন্য-মর্য্যাদায় ব্যারণের নিম্নস্থ এবং আর্ল উপাধিধারীর অব্যবহিত উপরিস্থ অভিজাত ব্যক্তি । **–cy,** *n.* **–ess,** *n.* (*Fem.*) **–ship,** *n.*

Coronet of a Viscount.

vis'-cous (-kŭs), *adj.* **1.** Sticky ; আঠালো, চট্‌চটে । **2.** Having viscosity ; সংলাগশীল ।

vi-se' (vē-ză), *n.* & *v. t.* On the continent of Europe, an indorsement made on the passport of a traveller denoting that it has been examined by authorities, and that the person named in it is permitted to proceed on his journey ; বিদেশভ্রমণের সরকারী অনুমতিপত্রের পৃষ্ঠে উক্ত পত্রের লিখিত বিষয় সত্য—এই মর্ম্মে যে মন্তব্য লিখিত হয় । ***Verb t.*** To examine and indorse, as a passport ; উক্তরূপ মন্তব্য লিখা ।

vis'-i-ble (-bl), *adj.* **1.** That can be seen ; দৃশ্য, চক্ষুর্গ্রাহ্য, দর্শনযোগ্য, দর্শনীয়, বীক্ষণীয়, দৃশ্যমান, দৃষ্টিগোচর, নয়নগোচর । **2.** Apparent ; as, he has no *visible* means of support ; আপাতদৃষ্ট, প্রত্যক্ষগোচর, চাক্ষুষ, সুস্পষ্ট, আপাতপ্রতীয়মান । **–bil'-i-ty,** *n.* The quality of being visible ; চক্ষুর্গ্রাহ্যতা, দর্শনযোগ্যতা । **Visible church**—নিখিল খৃষ্টধর্ম্মাবলম্বিগণ । **Visible horizon**—See HORIZON. **Visible speech** — Alexander Melville Bell কর্ত্তৃক আবিষ্কৃত একপ্রকার বর্ণমালা — যাহাতে স্বরযন্ত্র দ্বারা সর্ব্বপ্রকার ধ্বনির প্রতিরূপ প্রদর্শিত হইয়াছে, দৃশ্যবর্ণবাণী । **Visible supply**—(বাণিজ্য) যে পরিমাণ দ্রব্য পাওয়া যাইতে পারে—তাহার সমষ্টি, দৃশ্য সরবরাহ ।

vi'-sion (-zhŏn), *n.* & *v. t.* **1.** The act of seeing ; দর্শন, দৃষ্টি, অবলোকন, নিরীক্ষণ । **2.** The power of seeing ; as, beyond our *vision* ; দর্শনশক্তি, দৃষ্টিশক্তি । **3.** Things seen in a dream or trance ; "God appeared before him in a *vision*" ; স্বপ্নদৃষ্ট বিষয়, সমাধির অবস্থায় দৃষ্ট বিষয়, অলৌকিক দর্শন । **4.** Imaginary things ; as, romantic *visions* ; কল্পলোকের বিষয় (হিঃ কোঃ) । **5.** Apparition ; অপচ্ছায়া, অপদেবতা, আভাস (হিঃ কোঃ) । ***Verb t.*** To see in a vision ; "We in the morning eyed the pleasant fields *visioned* before" ; to present in a vision ; স্বপ্নে বা সমাধির অবস্থায় দেখা ; স্বপ্নে বা সমাধির অবস্থায় প্রদর্শন করা । **Direct vision**—সাক্ষাৎ দৃশ্য (হিঃ কোঃ) । **Indirect vision**—পরোক্ষ দৃশ্য (ঐ) ।

vi'-sion-ă-rў (-zhŏn-), *adj.* & *n.* **1.** Not real ; imaginary ; অবাস্তব, অবাস্তবিক ; কাল্পনিক, স্বাপ্নিক, আভাসময় ।

2. Unpractical ; as, a *visionary* scheme or project ; অকার্য্যকর। *Noun.* A visonary person ; স্বপ্নালোকচারী, কল্পলোকবিহারী, কল্পনাপ্রিয় ব্যক্তি, স্বপ্নাবিষ্ট ব্যক্তি, যে ব্যক্তি সর্ব্বদা আকাশকুসুম চিন্তা করে। **—al,** *adj.* **—al-ly,** *adv.* **—ist,** *n.*

vĭs′-it, *v. t.* & *n.* **1.** To call upon a person ; দেখা করিতে যাওয়া, সাক্ষাৎ করিতে যাওয়া। **2.** To go for the purpose of inspection ; পরিদর্শন করিতে যাওয়া। **3.** (Of disease) To attack ; "Ere he by sickness had been *visited*" ; (রোগসম্পর্কে) আক্রমণ করা। **4.** To punish or reward ; "Now will he remember their iniquity and *visit* their sins" ; দণ্ডিত করা, শাস্তি দেওয়া, পুরস্কার দেওয়া। *Noun.* **1.** Call on a person ; সাক্ষাৎ। **2.** An official call for the purpose of inspection ; পরিদর্শন। **3.** Temporary residence at a place ; as, during *visit* to the town ; অচিরপ্রবাস। **—a-ble,** *adj.* **To pay visit to**—To visit ;

broken or penetrated ; impregnable ; বজ্র-নির্ম্মিত, হৈরিক (সাঃ পঃ), বজ্রময় ; কুলিশ-কঠিন ; দুর্ভেদ্য।

Adansonia Digitata—Baobab, monkey-bread tree or Ethiopian sour gourd ; গোরক আম্লি (হিন্দী—বেলঃ)।

ă-dăpt′, *v. t.* **1.** To fit (a person or thing *to* another) ; to make suitable (*to* or *for* a purpose) ; উপযোগী করা ; প্রয়োজনানুরূপ করা, উদ্দেশ্যোপযোগী করা। **2.** To modify so as to fit for a new use ; as, a kind of farm-house, *adapted* out of the old ruin ; নূতন কার্য্যের উপযোগী করিয়া লওয়া। **—ă-bil′-i-tȳ, —a-ble-ness,** *ns.* The state or quality of being adapted ; যোগ্যতা, সংযোজনীয়তা, যোগিতা-শক্তি (পীঃ)। **—a-ble,** Capable of being adapt- applicable ; যোগ্য, যোক্তব্য ;

এলেজিবেথের নিকট কুমারী মেরীর আবির্ভাব স্মরণার্থ পর্ব্ব বিশেষ। **5.** The act of a naval commander who visits or enters on board a vessel belonging to another state for the purpose of ascertaining her character and object, but without claiming or exercising the right of search ; তল্লাস বা তল্লাসের অধিকার খ্যাপন না করিয়া অপর কোন জাহাজে কিরূপ মাল নেওয়া হইতেছে ও উহার কি উদ্দেশ্য তাহা অবগত হওয়ার জন্য নৌসৈন্যাধ্যক্ষকর্তৃক ঐ জাহাজে আরোহণ। **Nuns of the Visitation**—See VISITANT 4.

vĭs′-it-ing, *n.* The act of making calls ; সাক্ষাৎকার। **Visiting-book**—যে খাতায় যাহারা সাক্ষাৎ করিতে আসিয়াছে কিম্বা যাহাদের সহিত সাক্ষাৎ করিতে হইবে তাহাদের নাম লিখা থাকে, সাক্ষাৎকারের খাতা। **Visiting-card**—কাহারও সহিত সাক্ষাৎ করার কালে ব্যবহৃত নামধামাদি সমন্বিত স্থূল কাগজখণ্ড, নামপট্ট, নামপত্র।

vĭs-it-ŏr, *n.* **1.** One who visits a person or place ; সাক্ষাৎকারী, দর্শক।

to meretricious attempts to catch popular favour or applause ; as, *ad captandum* (ইতরজনচিত্তাকর্ষক) oratory ; অশিক্ষিত ইতরশ্রেণীর লোকদিগের করতালি ও সাধুবাদলাভার্থ (বক্তার কৃত্রিম প্রয়াস)।

ădd, *v. t.* & *i.* **1.** To put together ; to join or unite (one thing to another) ; একত্রিত করা ; সংযুক্ত করা, সংযোগ করা, যোগ করা, যোজনা করা, সংযোজিত করা। **2.** To say or write further ; to go on to say or speak ; as, to what I have already said, let me *add* this ; আরও বলা ; বলিতে থাকা। *Verb i.* **1.** To be or serve as an addition ; to be added (*to*) ; যোগ হওয়া ; সংযুক্ত হওয়া। **2.** To perform the arithmetical operation of addition ; as, this boy can *add* very rapidly ; সঙ্কলন করা। **Add′-a-ble,** *adj.* Capable of being added or

forming the avenue ; "An interminable *vista* of tree-trunks on both sides" ; তরুবীথিকা। **3.** A long train of expected events etc. ; mental prospect or retrospect ; as, opened up new *vistas* to his ambition ; প্রত্যাশিত ঘটনা প্রবাহ ; অতীত বা অনাগত ঘটনা পরম্পরার মানসচিত্র। **—taed,** *adj.*

vĭs′-ū-ăl, *adj.* Pertaining to the sight ; serving as an instrument of seeing ; as, *visual* nerves ; দৃষ্টিশক্তিসম্পর্কীয়, দর্শনেন্দ্রিয়সম্পর্কীয় ; দৃষ্টিযন্ত্রের কার্য্যকারী। **—ize,** *v. t.* To make visible ; to materialise ; to depict in imagination ; দৃষ্টিযোগ্য করা, দর্শনযোগ্য করা ; মূর্ত্তিমান করা, বিগ্রহবান করা ; মানসপটে অঙ্কিত করা। **—i-za′-tion,** *n.* The act or power of forming visual images or mental representation of object present in the senses ; মানসদর্শন (হিঃ কোঃ), বিগ্রহবান করণ, প্রত্যক্ষগোচরীকরণ, প্রত্যক্ষীকরণ। **Visual angle**—দৃশ্যকোণ (হিঃ কোঃ)। **Visual area** — দৃষ্টিগোচর (হিঃ কোঃ),

ăd-dĕn′-dŭm, (*pl.* ADDENDA), *n.* Thing to be added ; an appendix or addition ; সংযোজনীয় বস্তু ; সংযোজিত বিষয়, পরিশিষ্ট।

ăd′-dêr, *n.* A small venomous snake ; a viper ; ক্ষুদ্র বিষধর সর্প বিশেষ ; ভুজ্যু (বেঃ সুঃ)। **Adder-bead, Adder-stone**—A stone or bead used by the Druids as an amulet ; এক প্রকার পাষাণ বা কাচনির্ম্মিত অক্ষমালা—এই মালা প্রাচীনকালে ড্রুইড্‌গণ কর্তৃক সর্প-দংশনের ঔষধস্বরূপ ব্যবহৃত হইত। **Adder-bolt, Adder-fly** or **Flying adder**—Dragon-fly ; ফড়িং (সাঃ পঃ)। **Adder's tongue**—A species of fern ; এক জাতীয় ক্রকচ-পত্র উদ্ভিদ্।

ăd-dict′, *v. t.* **1.** To devote ; to apply habitually (to a practice) ; to attach closely ; as, to *addict* one's self to intemperance ; নিরত করা, সমর্পণ করা, উৎসর্গ করা ;

matter ; অত্যাবশ্যক, অপরিহার্য্য। ***Noun.*** (*Pl.*) 'Parts, esp. lungs, heart, brain ; জীবনীশক্তির আধার (যথা মস্তিষ্ক, ফুস্ফুস্, হৃদ্‌পিণ্ড), প্রাণ, মর্ম্মস্থান। **–ly,** *adv.* **Vital-air**—অধিষ্ঠান বায়ু, প্রাণবায়ু (হিঃ কোঃ)। **Vital centre**—দেহের যে স্থানের আঘাত সাংঘাতিক হইয়া থাকে, মর্ম্মস্থান। **Vital energy**—জীবন, জীবনশক্তি (এভেলন)। **Vital fluid**—উদ্ভিদের দুগ্ধবৎ রস, জীবীয় দ্রব (হিঃ কোঃ)। **Vital force**—প্রাণশক্তি, (এভেলন)। **Vital functions**—প্রাণধারণের পক্ষে অপরিহার্য্য দৈহিক ক্রিয়াসমূহ, প্রাণক্রিয়া। **Vital parts**—মর্ম্মস্থান (সুশ্রুঃ)। **Vital principle** — জীবনীশক্তি, প্রাণবায়ু (হিঃ কোঃ), প্রাণ (ব্রজঃ হিন্দু)।

vī'-tăl-ĭsm, *n.* (*Bot.*) The theory which refers vital phenomena to a vital, as distinct from merely physical principle ; জীবন প্রাণশক্তি উদ্ভূত কোনপ্রকার জড়শক্তি হইতে উৎপন্ন নয়—এই মত, প্রাণবাদ। **–ist,** *n.* **–is'-tic,** *adj.*

vī-tăl'-ĭ-tȳ, *n.* **1.** The state of showing vital power or capacities ; প্রাণশক্তি। **2.** Animation ; সজীবত্ব, জীবনবল, জীব-শক্তি জীব (হিঃ কোঃ), জীবন (ঐ), চেতনা (ঐ), প্রাণ (ঐ)।

vī-tăl'-īze, *v. t.* To endow with life ; as, to *vitalize* the industry of a nation ; সঞ্জীবিত করা, অনুপ্রাণিত করা, উজ্জীবিত করা, জীবন সঞ্চার করা।

vī-tĕl'-lĭn, *n.* A substance consisting of casein and albumen, characteristic of the yolk of birds' eggs ; ডিম্বের পীত অংশের সারাংশ।

vī-tĕl-lus (-ŭs), *n.* **1.** Yolk of eggs ; ডিম্বের পীতাংশ। **2.** (*Bot.*) A fleshy sack interposed between the albumen and the ovule, and enveloping the latter ; (উদ্ভিদ্‌বিদ্যা) অণ্ডলাল এবং ডিম্বকোষের মধ্যবর্ত্তী এবং শেষোক্তের আবরণস্বরূপ মাংসল আধার, জীবনকোষ।

vĭ'-tĭ-āte (-shĭ-), *v. t.* **1.** To corrupt ; দূষিত করা, কলুষিত করা, বিকৃত করা। **2.** To make invalid ; as, the verdict of the jury was *vitiated* by some undue influence exerted on them ; অসিদ্ধ করা, অকার্য্যকর করা।

vī'-tĭ-cīde, *n.* An insect etc. destroying vines ; দ্রাক্ষালতা ধ্বংসকারী কীট প্রভৃতি।

vĭt'-ĭ-cŭl-tūre, *n.* Growing of grapes ; আঙ্গুরের চাষ, দ্রাক্ষার চাষ। **–tur-al,** *adj.*

Vitis vinifera—দ্রাক্ষা।

vĭt'-rē-ous (-ŭs), *adj.* Glassy ; of the nature of glass ; consisting of glass ; কাচবৎ ; কাচধর্ম্মা ; কাচময় (হিঃ কোঃ)। **Vitreous body** or **humour** — যে স্বচ্ছ জেলির মত তন্তুময় বিধান দ্বারা অক্ষিগোলক পূর্ণ থাকে, কাচপ্রভরস (সাঃ পঃ)। **Vitreous electricity**—ঘন তাড়িৎকাচময় বিদ্যুৎ (হিঃ কোঃ)। **–ness,** *n.* **–os'-i-ty,** *n.* **Vi-tres'-cence,** *n.* **Vi-tres'-cent,** *adj.*

vĭt'-rĭc, *adj.* & *n.* Pertaining to glass ; like glass ; কাচসম্বন্ধীয় ; কাচবৎ। ***Noun.*** **1.** Glass ; materials made of glass ; কাচ ; কাচ-নির্ম্মিত দ্রব্য। **2.** The study of glass manufacture ; কাচশিল্পশিক্ষা।

vĭt'-rĭ-fȳ, *v. t.* & *i.* To convert into glass ; কাচে পরিণত করা। ***Verb i.*** To be converted into glass ; কাচে পরিণত হওয়া। **–fac'-tion, –fi-a-bil'-i-ty, –fi-ca'-tion,** *ns.* **–fi-a-ble,** *adj.*

vĭt'-rĭ-ŏl, *n.* **1.** The old chemical and still the common name of sulphuric acid ; গন্ধকদ্রাবক। **2.** Caustic speech ; anything as caustic as vitriol ; (লক্ষণায়) তীব্র গালিবর্ষণ, তীব্রবাক্য, মর্ম্মচ্ছেদী বাক্য ; জ্বালাময় বস্তু। **–ol'-ic, –o-line,** *adjs.* **Blue vitriol**—তুঁতে, তুথ, হেমতার, অমৃতাসঙ্গ। **Green vitriol**—কাসীস, হীরাকস। **Oil of vitriol**—গাঢ়ীকৃত গন্ধকদ্রাবক। **Vitriol-throwing**—প্রতিহিংসা সাধনের জন্য কাহারো মুখে উগ্র গন্ধকদ্রাবক প্রক্ষেপ ; (লক্ষণায়) তীব্র গালি বর্ষণ।

vĭt'-rĭ-ŏl-īze, –ō-lāte, *v. t.* To convert into a sulphate ; গন্ধক-দ্রাবকদিগ্ধ ধাতুতে পরিণত করা। **–iz-a-ble,** *adj.* **–o-la'-tion,** *n.*

Vĭ-tru'-vĭ-ăn (-trô-), *adj.* Pertaining to Vitruvius, a Roman architect of the Augustan age ; রোমসম্রাট আগষ্টাসের সময়ে বর্ত্তমান Vitruvius নামক সৌধশিল্পিসম্বন্ধীয়। **Vitruvian-scroll**—একপ্রকার সৌধ-ভূষা।

Vitruvian scroll

vĭt'-ta (-ă), *n.* **1.** A headband, fillet or garland ; specifically, amongst ancient Greeks and Romans a ribbon or fillet used as a decoration of sacred persons ; মৌলিবন্ধনী, মাল্য ; প্রাচীন গ্রীক ও রোমক পুরোহিত-দিগের ভূষাস্বরূপ ফিতা বা কেশবন্ধনী। **2.** (*Bot.*) The receptacles of oil which are found in the fruit of umbelliferous plants ; (উদ্ভিদ্‌বিদ্যা) ছত্রপুষ্পী ক্ষুপসমূহের তৈলাধার, তৈল-নলিকা (সাঃ পঃ)। **3.** (*Zool.*) Strip of colour ; (জন্তুবিদ্যা) রঙ্গীন ডোরা। **–tate,** *adj.*

vĭt'-ū-lar (-lĕr), **–lă-rȳ,** *adjs.* **1.** Pertaining to calves ; বৎস-সম্বন্ধীয়। **2.** Calf-like ; বৎসবৎ। **–line,** *adj.* **Vitular appoplexy** or **fever**—প্রসবকালে গাভীর সন্ন্যাস বা জ্বর (রোগ)।

vī-tū'-pĕr-āte, *v. t.* **1.** To revile ; to abuse ; গালি দেওয়া, গালিগালাজ করা ; কটূক্তি করা। **2.** To find fault with ; দোষ প্রদর্শন করা। **–a'-tion,** *n.* Blame ; censure ; abuse ; দোষারোপণ ; তিরস্কার ; গালি, কটূক্তি। **–a-tive,** *adj.* **–a-tive-ly,** *adv.*

vi'-vă, *inter.* & *n.* Long live ; দীর্ঘায়ুরস্তু, বেঁচে থাক। ***Noun.*** The cry long live ; উক্ত ধ্বনি।

viva, *adj.* & *n.* See under VIVA-VOCE.

vivace, *n.* (*It. Mus.*) In lively manner ; (সঙ্গীতশাস্ত্র) সতেজে।

vi-vā'-cious (-shŭs), *adj.* **1.** Lively ; joyous ; স্ফূর্তিযুক্ত, সজীব ; প্রফুল্ল, উৎফুল্ল, উল্লাসপূর্ণ। **2.** Active ; চটুল। **3.** (*Bot.*) Tenacious (of life) ; surviving winter ; (উদ্ভিদ্‌বিদ্যা) জীবন-সংরক্ষী ; শীতকালে উদ্বর্তনশীল।

vivandiere, *n.* (*F.*) A female wine and provision seller attached to a French regiment ; ফরাসীদেশের সেনাপল্টনে সুরা ও খাদ্যদ্রব্য বিক্রেত্রী।

vi-vā'-ri-ŭm, —rȳ, *ns.* (*Pl.* *-ria*) A place for keeping living animals ; জীবন্ত পশু রক্ষার জন্য গৃহ, পশুশালা, চিড়িয়াখানা।

vivat, *inter.* & *n.* Long live ; চিরজীবী হউন, দীর্ঘজীবী হউন, দীর্ঘায়ু হউন। ***Noun.*** The cry long live ; দীর্ঘায়ু হউন এই ধ্বনি।

vi-vā-vō'-cē, *adv.*, *adj.* & *n.* By word of mouth ; orally ; মুখেমুখে ; মৌখিকভাবে। ***Adj.*** Oral ; as, a *viva voce* examination ; মৌখিক। ***Noun.*** (*colloq.* also *viva*) Oral examination ; মৌখিক পরীক্ষা।

vive, *interj.* Long live ; দীর্ঘায়ু হউন, চিরজীবী হউন।

Viverra Indica—খাটাস,গন্ধগকুলা।

Viverra zibetha — মাছ ভোঁদড়, বাগডাস।

vives, *n.* A disease of animals, particularly of horses, seated in the glands under the ear, where a tumour is formed which sometimes ends in suppuration ; অশ্বাদি জন্তুর কর্ণগ্রন্থির স্ফীতিজনক রোগবিশেষ।

viv'-id, *adj.* **1.** Lively or life like ; as, a *vivid* sketch ; জীবিতবৎ, জীবন্ত, সজীব, প্রাণবান। **2.** Strong ; as, a *vivid* recollection : *vivid* imagination ; তীব্র, প্রবল, জলন্ত, প্রগাঢ়। **3.** Bright ; as, a *vivid* flash of lightning ; fresh ; clear ; উজ্জ্বল, দীপ্ত, প্রদীপ্ত, দীপ্তিমান ; নবীন ; সুস্পষ্ট, বিশদ। **4.** Vigorous ; as, *vivid* growth ; সতেজ। **—ly,** *adv.* **—ness,** *n.*

viv'-i-fȳ, *v. t.* To give life ; to animate ; জীবন সঞ্চার করা ; উজ্জীবিত করা, সঞ্জীবিত করা, প্রাণবান করা। **—fi-ca'-tion,** *n.* The act of vivifying ; উজ্জীবন, সঞ্জীবন।

vi-vip'-ă-rous (-rŭs), *adj.* **1.** Producing young alive ; যোনিজ, জরায়ুজ, (সুশ্রুঃ কুশ্রঃ), জীবজ (হিঃ কোঃ)। **2.** (*Bot.*) Germinating from a seed while still attached to a parent plant ; (উদ্ভিদ্‌বিদ্যা) মূলবৃক্ষে সংলগ্ন বীজ হইতে অঙ্কুরিত, জরায়ুজ (সাঃ পঃ)। **—ly,** *adv.* **Viv-i-par'-i-ty, —ness,** *ns.*

viv-i-sĕct', *v. t.* To dissect an animal while living জীবিত অবস্থায় ব্যবচ্ছেদ করা। **—sec'-tion,** *n.* The act of vivisecting ; জীবিত অবস্থায় ব্যবচ্ছেদ, জীবন্তব্যবচ্ছেদ, জীবচ্ছালাক্য (হিঃ কোঃ)। **—sec'-tion-al,** *adj.* **—sec'-tor,** *n.*

vivo, *adv.* Same as VIVACE.

vix'-ĕn, *n.* **1.** A she-fox ; খেঁক-শেয়ালী। **2.** A termagant ; "She was a *vixen* when she went to school" ; উগ্রচণ্ডানারী, রায়বাঘিনী, মেয়ে-মর্দানী, জাঁহাবাজ মেয়ে। **—ish, —ly,** *adjs.*

viz. *adv.* See VIDELICET.

viz'-ărd, *n.* Same as VISOR.

viz-cā'-chă, *n.* Same as VISCACHA.

vi-zir' (-zēr) **vi'-zier** (-zēr), *ns.* A minister in Mohammedan countries ; উজীর।

Vlăch, *n.* A Wallachian ; রুমিনিয়ার অধিবাসী।

vō'-că-ble (-bl), *n.* A word ; শব্দ।

vō-căb'-ū-lă-rȳ, *n.* **1.** A list or collection of words in a language, science, etc. arranged in alphabetical order and explained ; শব্দকোষ, নিঘণ্ট, শব্দসংগ্রহ, কোশ (হিঃ কোঃ)। **2.** The collection of words of a particular book or author ; কোন নির্দিষ্ট গ্রন্থ বা গ্রন্থকারের শব্দ সংগ্রহ।

vō'-căl, *adj.* & *n.* **1.** Of, or pertaining to, the voice or speech ; uttered or delivered with the voice ; স্বরসম্বন্ধীয়, বাচিক ; স্বরের সাহায্যে উচ্চারিত। **2.** Having a voice ; endowed with, or as with, voice ; বাক্‌শক্তিবিশিষ্ট ; বাক্‌শক্তিবিশিষ্টবৎ, বাঙ্‌ময় (হিঃ কোঃ), বাক্‌শক্তিসম্পন্ন। **3.** Having a vowel character ; স্বরাত্মক, স্বরবর্ণাত্মক। ***Noun.*** **1.** A vowel ; স্বরবর্ণ। **2.** (*R. C. C.*) A person having power to vote in certain election ; (রোমানক্যাথলিক ধর্মসংঘ) কোন কোন নির্দিষ্ট নির্বাচনে মত প্রদানে অধিকারী ব্যক্তি। **—cal'-ic,** *adj.* **—cal'-i-ty,** *n.* **—ly,** *adv.* **Vocal auscultation**—আকর্ণণযন্ত্র সহযোগে হৃৎপিণ্ডের স্পন্দন-ধ্বনি শ্রবণ। **Vocal cords**—স্বরতন্ত্রী (সাঃ পঃ), ধ্বনিতার (হিঃ কোঃ)। **Vocal thrill** or **fremitus**—কথা বলিবার সময় বক্ষকপাটের স্পন্দন।

vō'-căl-ĭsm, *n.* **1.** A vowel sound ; স্বরবর্ণের ধ্বনি। **2.** The exercise of the vocal organ ; গানে ও বাক্যকথনে বাগ্‌যন্ত্রের পরিচালনা।

vō'-căl-ĭst, *n.* A singer ; গায়ক।

vō'-căl-īze, *v. t.* **1.** To form into voice ; স্বরে পরিণত করা। **2.** To utter with the voice ; ধ্বনিযুক্ত শব্দে উচ্চারণ করা, ধ্বন্যাত্মক করা। **3.** To change into, or use as, a vowel ; স্বরবর্ণে পরিবর্তিত করা, স্বরবর্ণরূপে ব্যবহৃত করা। **4.** To write with vowel points ; স্বরবর্ণসূচক বিন্দুযোজনা করিয়া লিখা। **—i-za'-tion,** *n.*

vō-cā'-tion, *n.* **1.** A summon ; a divine call ; আহ্বান, ডাক ; ভগবানের ডাক। **2.** Employment ; trade ; profession ; as, mechanical *vocation* ; বৃত্তি ; ব্যবসায় ; পেশা। **—al,** *adj.* **—al-ly,** *adv.*

vŏc'-ā-tive (-tĭv), *adj.* & *n.* (*Gram.*) Designating a case denoting that which is addressed; (ব্যাকরণ) সম্বোধনসূচক, সম্বোধনবাচক। ***Noun.*** A vocative case; সম্বোধন কারক।

vō-ŏif'-ĕr-āte, *v. t.* & *i.* To utter with a loud voice; to shout out; "*Vociferated* logic kills me quite"; উচ্চৈঃস্বরে চীৎকার করিয়া বলা; গর্জ্জন করা, চীৎকার করা। ***Verb i.*** To cry out loudly; "Through the ranks *vociferating* called his Trojans"; চীৎকার করা, গর্জ্জন করা। **—ant,** *n.* **—a'-tion,** *n.* The act of vociferating; a violent outcry; চীৎকার করণ; চীৎকার, গর্জ্জন, উচ্চরব, ভীমনাদ। **—a-tor,** *n.*

vō-ŏif'-ĕr-ous (-ŭs), *adj.* Making a loud outcry; "Thrice three *vociferous* heralds rose to check the rout"; clamorous; উচ্চনিনাদী, গর্জ্জনকারী; চীৎকারকারী, কোলাহলপূর্ণ, কোলাহলময়।

vŏd'-kă, *n.* An intoxicant spirit distilled from rye and much used in Russia; রুশদেশে ব্যবহৃত মদ্যবিশেষ।

voe (vō), *n.* A small bay; ক্ষুদ্র উপসাগর, খাঁড়ি।

vogue (vōg), *n.* **1.** The prevailing fashion; চলিত রীতি বা প্রথা, রেওয়াজ। **2.** Popular acceptation; জন সমাজে প্রচলন, চলতি, চলন। **To be in vogue**—To be in fashion; প্রচলিত হওয়া, চলতি হওয়া।

voice (vo̅ys), *n.* & *v. t.* **1.** Sound uttered by living beings esp. human beings; মনুষ্যাদির কণ্ঠস্বর, কণ্ঠধ্বনি, স্বর, বাক্ (হিঃ কোঃ) বাণী (ঐ)। **2.** The faculty of speech; utterance; as, he lost his *voice*; speech; বাক্‌শক্তি; বাক্যে প্রকাশ; বাক্, বাণী। **3.** A sound produced by an inanimate object and regarded as representing the voice of an intelligent being; sound emitted; as, the *voice* of nature: the *voice* of a trumpet; মনুষ্যের কণ্ঠস্বরের সহিত তুলনীয় কোনরূপ অচেতন পদার্থ হইতে উত্থিত ধ্বনি; কোন কিছু হইতে নির্গত ধ্বনি। **4.** Opinion; as, I have no *voice* in the matter; wish; মত; ইচ্ছা। **5.** Vote; "My *voice* is still for war"; suffrage; নির্ব্বাচনমত; নির্ব্বাচনক্ষমতা। **6.** (*Obs.*) Rumour; গুজব, জনরব। **7.** (*Gram.*) A particular mode of inflecting or conjugating verbs, according as the subject is the agent or object of the action; (ব্যাকরণ) বাচ্য। **8.** (*Phonet.*) Sonant utterance; ধ্বনিবিশিষ্ট উচ্চারণ। ***Verb t.*** **1.** To fit for producing the proper sounds; as, to *voice* the pipes of an organ; উপযুক্ত ধ্বনি উৎপাদনের উপযোগী করা, সায়ের করা। **2.** To utter; to announce: to express; as, to *voice* the sentiment of the people; উচ্চারণ করা, ভাষায় ব্যক্ত করা; ঘোষণা করা; ব্যক্ত করা, প্রকাশ করা। **Voice'-ful,** *adj.* (*Poet.*) Sonorous; (কবিতায়) মধুররাবী।

vioce'-lĕss (vo̅ys-), *adj.* **1.** Dumb; মূক, নির্ব্বাক, বাক্‌শক্তিহীন। **2.** Having no votes; as, *voiceless* multitudes; নির্ব্বাচনমত প্রদানের ক্ষমতা বিরহিত। **3.** Not sounded with voice; as, *voiceless* consonant; অব্যক্তধ্বনি। **With one voice**—Unanimously; একবাক্যে, সমস্বরে।

void (vo̅yd), *adj.*, *n.* & *v. t.* **1.** Empty; vacant; "The earth was without form and *void*"; রিক্ত, হীন, রহিত, শূন্য; খালি। **2.** Destitute; বিহীন, বিরহিত, হীন, শূন্য, রহিত। **3.** Null; বাতিল। **4.** Ineffectual; নিষ্ফল, ব্যর্থ। **5.** Unsubstantial; unreal; অসার; অবাস্তব। ***Noun.*** An empty space; শূন্য স্থান, শূন্য। ***Verb t.*** **1.** To make void or empty; to clear; to vacate; শূন্য করা; পরিষ্কার করা; খালি করিয়া দেওয়া। **2.** To nullify; বাতিল করা, রদ করা। **3.** To emit; as to *void* excrements; মলাদি নিঃসারিত করা। **Void'-ness,** *n.* **Void space**—শূন্য, অবকাশ (হিঃ কোঃ)।

void'-ance (vo̅yd-āns), *n.* **1.** The act of ejecting from a benefice; যাজকীয় অধিকার হইতে বহিষ্করণ। **2.** The act of emptying; শূন্যীকরণ। **3.** Vacancy, as of benefice; যাজকীয় বৃত্তি প্রভৃতির শূন্যতা।

void'-ĕd (vo̅yd-), *p. p.* **1.** Not occupied; অনধিকৃত **2.** Evacuated; শূন্যীকৃত। **3.** Annulled; রহিত। **4.** (*Herald.*) An epithet for any ordinary which seems to be cut in the middle, and only the outside strips left; (কুলচিহ্নসম্বন্ধে) ছিন্নমধ্যাংশ—অতএব প্রান্তরেখা মাত্রাবশিষ্ট।

void'-ĕr (vo̅yd-), *n.* **1.** One who, or that which, voids; শূন্যতাবিধায়ক, রদকারী, খণ্ডনকারী। **2.** (*Herald.*) One of the ordinaries whose figure is much like that of flanch but is not quite so circular towards the centre of the field; একপ্রকার কুল চিহ্ন।

voila, *Interj.* (*F.*) See see; দেখ! দেখ।

voile (vo̅yl), *n.* A thin dress material of cotton or woollen; পোষাক তৈরীর জন্য একপ্রকার মিহি পশমী অথবা সূতার কাপড়।

voi-tur-ette' (vo̅y-tür-ĕt), *n.* A kind of small motor-car; একপ্রকার ক্ষুদ্র হাওয়া গাড়ী।

vō'-lānt, *n.* **1.** (*Zool.*) Flying; able to fly; উড্ডয়নশীল; উড্ডয়নক্ষম। **2.** (*Herald.*) Represented as flying or having the wings spread, as, in flight; (কুলবিদ্যা) উড্ডয়নশীল, উড্ডয়নের জন্য প্রসারিতপক্ষ। **3.** Nimble; চটুল।

Vō-lā-pük, *n.* An artificial international language; একপ্রকার কৃত্রিম আন্তর্জাতিক ভাষা। [১৮৭৯ খৃঃ অব্দে J. M. Schleyer কর্তৃক এই ভাষা উদ্ভাবিত হয়।] **—ist,** *n.*

vō'-lar (-lėr), *n.* An aeroplane ; আকাশযান, খপোত।

vō'-lar (-lêr), *adj.* Of the palm or sole ; হস্ততল বা পদতল সম্বন্ধীয়।

vŏl'-ă-tile (-tĭl), *adj.* **1.** Capable of easily passing into the aereoform state, as hartshorn, musk, etc. ; উদ্বায়ী, বায়ুপরিণামশীল। **2.** Lively ; changeable ; fickle ; "As giddy and *volatile* as ever" ; উৎফুল্ল ; পরিবর্ত্তনশীল ; অস্থিরমতি, অস্থিরচিত্ত, চঞ্চল, চপল, প্রকৃতিতরল, চলচ্চিত্ত। **–til'-i-ty,** *n.* **–til-i-za'-tion,** *n.* **–til-ize,** *v. t.* To make volatile ; উদ্বায়ী করা, উবিয়ে দেওয়া।

vol-au-vent, (*F.*), *n.* A kind of cake ; একপ্রকার পিষ্টক।

vŏl-căn'-ic, *adj.* Pertaining to volcano ; like volcano ; produced by volcano ; আগ্নেয়গিরিসম্বন্ধীয় ; আগ্নেয়গিরিবৎ ; আগ্নেয়গিরিজ। **Volcanic bomb** — আগ্নেয়গিরি হইতে নিঃসৃত পদার্থের পিণ্ড, আগ্নেয়প্রস্তর, অগ্নিদগ্ধ প্রস্তর। **Volcanic glass**—Same as OBSIODIAN.

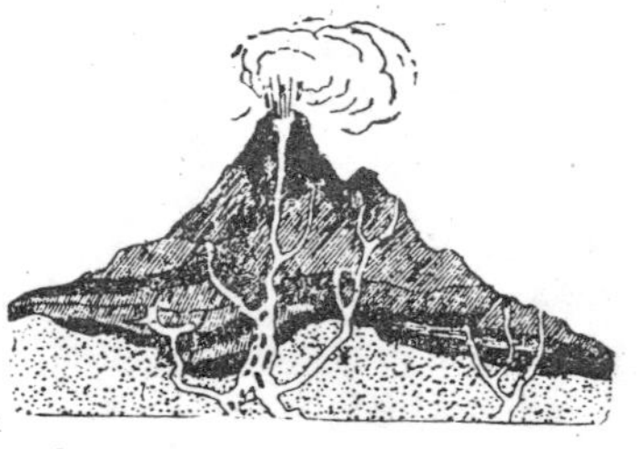

Active volcano in section.

vŏl-cā'-nō, *n.* A mountain or hill which throws up smokes, flames, stones, melted matter from its interior parts ; আগ্নেয়গিরি, অগ্নিপর্ব্বত (রামায়ণ), আগ্নেয়পর্ব্বত (সাঃ পঃ), জ্বালামুখী (হিঃ কোঃ)। **–can-o-log'-i-cal,** *adj.* **–can-ol'-o-gy,** *n.* **Vol'-can-ism,** *n.* **Vol'-can-ist,** *n.* **Submarine volcano**—যে আগ্নেয়গিরি প্রথমতঃ সাগরগর্ভ হইতে উৎপন্ন হইয়া স্তরসঞ্চয়ের ফলে ক্রমশঃ জলের উপর মাথা জাগায়। **Volcano-ship**—বিস্ফোরক দ্রব্যপূর্ণ পোত—যাহা শত্রুপোতের সংস্পর্শে আসিয়া ভীমশব্দে বিদীর্ণ হয়, আগ্নেয়পোত।

vōle, *n.* & *v. i.* A deal at cards which draws all the tricks ; তাস খেলার একরূপ বাঁট—যাহাতে যে বাঁটে সেই সব পিঠ পাইয়া থাকে। ***Verb i.*** To win all the tricks ; সব পিঠ পাওয়া।

vōle, *n.* A genus of rodents resembling rats and mice, some of which are aquatic in their habits, such as water-rats ; এক জাতীয় মূষিকবৎ দন্তর জন্তু।

vō-let' (-lā), *n.* **1.** The wing of a picture formed as a triptych ; ত্রিচিত্রের পার্শ্বচিত্র। **2.** A flowing veil worn by women in the Middle Ages ; মধ্যযুগে মহিলাগণকর্ত্তৃক পরিহিত একপ্রকার অবগুণ্ঠন।

vŏl'-i-tănt, *adj.* (*Zool.*) Same as VOLANT (which see).

vō-li'-tion, *n.* **1.** The act of willing ; the exercise of will ; মনন ; ইচ্ছাশক্তির প্রয়োগ। **2.** The power of willing ; ইচ্ছাশক্তি, সংকল্পশক্তি, সঙ্কল্প (হিঃ কোঃ), ব্যবসায় (ঐ), কৃতি (ঐ), প্রযত্ন (ব্রজঃ হিন্দুঃ)। **3.** A state of decision or choice ; নির্ব্বাচন বা নিষ্পত্তির ভার। **–al, –a-ry,** *adjs.* Relating to, or pertaining to, will ; ইচ্ছাসম্বন্ধীয়, মননসম্বন্ধীয়। **Volitional motor**—আজ্ঞাবহা (ব্রজঃ বিঃ)।

volkslied, *adj.* (*Germ.*) Folk-song ; লোকগাথা।

volksraad, *n.* The legislative assembly of former Orange Free States or Transvaal; ব্রিটিশ অধিকার প্রতিষ্ঠার পূর্ব্বে ট্রান্সভাল বা অরেঞ্জ ফ্রিষ্টেটের ব্যবস্থাপক সভা।

vŏl'-ley (-lĭ), *n., v. t.* & *i.* **1.** A flight of shot or missiles ; শরবৃষ্টি, শরবর্ষণ, গোলাবৃষ্টি। **2.** Missiles simultaneously discharged ; as, a *volley* of arrows ; যুগপৎ বর্ষিত গোলা বা শস্ত্রসমূহ। **3.** A noisy or explosive burst or emission of many things at once ; as, a *volley* of abuse ; বর্ষণ, বর্ষ। **4.** (*Football*) A kick on the ball before it rebounds ; উৎক্ষেপণের পূর্ব্বে পদদ্বারা ক্রীড়াকন্দুক তাড়ন। **5.** (*Tennis*) Return of ball in play before it touches the ground ; (টেনিস ক্রীড়ায়) ভূমি স্পর্শের পূর্ব্বে কন্দুক প্রতিক্ষেপণ। **6.** (*Cricket*) Sending of ball full to head of wicket ; (ক্রীকেট ক্রীড়ায়) ভূমি স্পর্শ না করাইয়া একবারে ত্রিদণ্ডে কন্দুক ক্ষেপণ। ***Verb t.*** **1.** To discharge missiles, etc. ; গোলা, বাক্যবাণ, প্রভৃতি বর্ষণ করা। **2.** (*Tennis*) To return the ball while on the volley ; ভূমি স্পর্শ করার পূর্ব্বে কন্দুক প্রতিক্ষেপণ করা। **3.** To bowl straight at the wicket without hitting the ground ; ভূমি স্পর্শ বিনা ত্রিদণ্ডে বল নিক্ষেপ করা। **4.** (*Football*) To kick a ball before it rebounds ; উৎক্ষেপণের পূর্ব্বে ক্রীড়াগোলকে পদাঘাত করা। ***Verb i.*** **1.** (Of missiles) To fall in a volley ; (গোলাগুলি প্রভৃতি সম্বন্ধে) বর্ষিত হওয়া, বৃষ্টিধারার মত পতিত হওয়া। **2.** (Of guns) To sound together ; "And then the *volleying* thunders pour" ; (কামানাদি সম্বন্ধে) যুগপৎ গর্জ্জন করা।

Vŏl'-plāne, *n.* The descent of an aircraft from high sky like a bird ; আকাশ হইতে পক্ষীর মত ব্যোমপোতের শনৈঃ শনৈঃ অবতরণ।

vōlt, *n.* **1.** A gait of two treads, made by a horse going sidewise round a centre ; অশ্বের চক্রগতি। **2.** (*Fenc.*) A sudden movement or leap in fencing to avoid a thrust ; অসির খোঁচা পরিহারের জন্য সহসা সঞ্চলন বা লম্ফন।

vōlt, *n.* The unit of electromotive force ; বিদ্যুৎপ্রবাহকবলের একক (অর্থাৎ তাড়িতপ্রবাহের তীব্রতা মাপের একক), তাড়িতাঙ্ক।

volta, *n.* *Mus.* (*pl. volte*). Time ; বার। ***Seconda volta***—দুইবার। ***Una volta***—একবার। 26

vŏl′-tă-ŏ-lĕc-trŏm′-ĕ-têr, *n.* An instrument to measure electric currents ; তাড়িতপ্রবাহমান।

vŏl-tă′-ic, *adj.* Of electricity produced by chemical action ; রাসায়নিকক্রিয়াদ্বারা সঞ্জাত তাড়িত সম্বন্ধীয়। **Vol′-ta-ism,** *n.* **Voltaic arc**—বোল্টীয় চাপ (হিঃ কোঃ)। **Voltaic battery**—বোল্টীয় ব্যাটারী (হিঃ কোঃ)। **Voltaic-couple** — বোল্টীয় যুগ (হিঃ কোঃ)। **Voltaic-pile**—বোল্টীর রাশি (হিঃ কোঃ)।

Vŏl-tair′-ĭsm (-tār), **—tair′-ĭ-ăn-ĭsm** (-tār), *ns.* Principles of Voltaire ; scepticism ; ফরাসী দার্শনিক ভলটেয়ারের মত ; সংশয়বাদ।

vŏl-tăm′-ĕ-têr, *n.* An instrument for measuring the quantity of electricity passed through a conductor ; প্রবাহকের মধ্য দিয়া কি পরিমাণ তাড়িত অতিক্রম করিয়াছে তাহা পরিমাপের জন্য যন্ত্রবিশেষ, তাড়িতমান, বোল্টমাপক (হিঃ কোঃ)।

volte-face, *n.* Turning round ; a change of front ; আবর্ত্তন ; মত প্রভৃতির আমূল পরিবর্ত্তন।

vŏl′-tīte, *n.* A material for insulating electric wires ; বৈদ্যুতিক তারের বিদ্যুৎবহিঃস্ফুরণ রোধনের জন্য পদার্থ বিশেষ।

vŏl′-ū-ble (-bl), *adj.* Fluent ; talkative ; glib ; বাক্‌চপল, চপলবাক্ ; বাচাল ; অনর্গলবাক্, বহুভাষী। **—bil′-i-ty,** *n.* **—ness,** *n.*

vŏl′-ume (-üm), *n.* **1.** A book ; that part of an extended work which is bound together in one cover (abbr. *vol.*); গ্রন্থ, পুস্তক ; খণ্ড। **2.** A single sheet as of parchment with a rod stretched across at each end for the convenience of rolling and unrolling in the time of reading ; a single fold or turn ; প্রাচীনকালে ব্যবহৃত আবর্ত্তিত পার্চমেণ্ট প্রভৃতিতে লিখিত পুস্তক ; কুণ্ডলী, পাক। **3.** Mass or bulk ; solid contents ; আয়তন ; ঘনফল। **4.** A quantity or strength ; পরিমাণ, শক্তি। **5.** Amount or fulness of voice ; স্বরের পরিমাণ বা পূর্ণতা। **—umed,** *adj.* **Atomic volumes**—পরমাণু আয়তন (হিঃ কোঃ)। **Molecular volume** — অণুরায়তন (হিঃ কোঃ)। **Specific volume**—বিশিষ্ট আয়তন (হিঃ কোঃ)। **To speak volume**—See SPEAK.

vŏl-ū-mĕ-nŏm′-ĕ-têr, *n.* A kind of instrument for measuring the volume of a body especially of a solid ; আয়তনমাপ, ঘনফলমাপক (হিঃ কোঃ)।

vŏ-lū′-mĕ-têr, *n.* Kinds of instrument for measuring the volume of gas ; বাষ্পের আয়তন পরিমাপের জন্য বিভিন্ন প্রকার যন্ত্র, বাষ্পায়তনমান। **—met′-ric,** *adj.* Pertaining to measurement by volume ; আয়তন দ্বারা পরিমাপসম্পর্কীয়, আয়তনমানমূলক। **—met′-ri-cal,** *adj.*

vŏ-lū′-mĕ-scōpe, *n.* (*Phys.*) An instrument with a graduated scale for reading the changes of volume of a gas ; ঘনফলদর্শক (হিঃ কোঃ)।

vŏ-lū′-mĭ-nous (-nŭs), *adj.* **1.** Consisting of many volumes ; as a *voluminous* work ; বহুখণ্ডাত্মক। **2.** Bulky ; massive ; extensive ; "I am not so *voluminous* and vast, But there are lines wherewith I might be embraced" ; large ; lengthy ; বৃহদায়তন ; বিরাট, বিশাল ; বিস্তৃত ; বৃহৎ ; সুদীর্ঘ। **3.** Copious ; as, a *voluminous* writer ; বহুগ্রন্থপ্রণয়ণকারী। **4.** Consisting of many folds or coils ; "But ended foul in many a scaly fold *voluminous* and vast" ; বহুকুণ্ডলীযুক্ত। **—ly,** *adv.* **—ness,** *n.* **—nos′-i-ty,** *n.*

vŏl′-ŭn-tă-rȳ, *adj.* & *n.* **1.** Acting from choice ; proceeding from one's will ; as, a *voluntary* action ; done without compulsion ; as, a *voluntary* gift ; ঐচ্ছিক ; স্বেচ্ছাপ্রসূত ; স্বেচ্ছাকৃত, স্বেচ্ছাদত্ত। **2.** Purposed ; intentional : as, *voluntary* manslaughter ; ইচ্ছাপূর্ব্বক (হিঃ কোঃ), ইচ্ছাকৃত ; ইচ্ছামূলক। **3.** Of, or pertaining to, the will ; subject to, or regulated by, will ; as, *voluntary* actions ; ইচ্ছাসম্বন্ধীয় ; ইচ্ছায়ত্ত, ইচ্ছাধীন, ইচ্ছানিয়ন্ত্রিত। **4.** Able to will ; free ; as, man is a *voluntary* agent ; মননক্ষম ; স্বাধীন। **5.** Spontaneous ; স্বতঃপ্রবৃত্ত, স্বয়মিচ্ছু। **6.** Of, or pertaining to, the doctrine of voluntaryism, or the doctrines of voluntaries ; ইচ্ছাবাদসম্বন্ধীয়। ***Noun.*** **1.** One who does anything of his own free will ; স্বেচ্ছামূলক কার্য্যকারী। **2.** One who advocates votuntaryism ; ইচ্ছাবাদী। **3.** (*Mus.*) A piece of music played at will ; যদৃচ্ছাক্রমে বাদিত বাদ্য। **4.** (*Mus.*) An organ solo played before, during, or after any office of the church ; খৃষ্টীয় ধর্ম্মমন্দিরের কোন ক্রিয়ার পূর্ব্বে, সময়ে বা পরে অর্গেন যন্ত্র বাদন। **—ri-ly,** *adv.* In a voluntary manner ; ইচ্ছাপূর্ব্বক, স্বেচ্ছাপূর্ব্বক, স্বতঃপ্রবৃত্তভাবে। **—ri-ness,** *n.* **Voluntary-affidavit**—আইনতঃ আবশ্যক নয় এমন ব্যাপারে সত্যপাঠ। **Voluntary-confession**—স্বেচ্ছামূলক স্বীকারোক্তি। **Voluntary-controversy**—শাসনতন্ত্র এবং ধর্ম্মসংঘ এই উভয়ের মধ্যে কি সম্বন্ধ থাকা উচিত তৎসম্পর্কে স্কটলণ্ড দেশে ১৮৩১ খৃঃ অব্দে যে আন্দোলনের সূত্রপাত হয়। **Voluntary conveyance**—কোনরূপ অর্থাদি না পাইয়া সম্পত্তি হস্তান্তর। **Voluntary-grantee**—যে ব্যক্তি কোনরূপ মূল্যস্বরূপ অর্থাদি না পাইয়া কোন সম্পত্তি হস্তান্তরিত করে। **Voluntary jurisdiction**—যে সকল মোকদ্দমার কোনরূপ আপত্তি বা প্রশ্ন উত্থিত হয় না—তৎসম্পর্কে যে অধিকার পরিচালনা করা হয়। **Voluntary-muscles**—ইচ্ছাবাহী পেশী, আজ্ঞাবাহী পেশী। **Voluntary partition**—উভয় পক্ষের

সম্মতিক্রমে সম্পত্তি বিভাগ। **Voluntary-principle**—ইচ্ছাবাদ। **Voluntary-schools** — যে সকল প্রাথমিক বিদ্যালয় স্বয়ংগঠিত সংঘ কর্ত্তৃক পরিচালিত হয় এবং ব্যয় অংশতঃ স্বেচ্ছাপ্রদত্ত চাঁদা হইতে নির্ব্বাহিত হইয়া থাকে। **Voluntary waste**—স্বেচ্ছাপূর্ব্বক জমিদারের সম্পত্তির যে ক্ষতি করা হয়।

vŏl′-ŭn-tă-rў-ĭsm, *n.* 1. The system of supporting any thing by voluntary action; ইচ্ছাবাদ, ইচ্ছামূলত্ববাদ (হিঃ কোঃ)। 2. A system of maintaining the church by voluntary offerings instead of by the aid of the state, as alone consistent with true religious liberty, involving freedom from state support, patronage or control; স্বেচ্ছাপ্রদত্ত অর্থ দ্বারা ধর্ম্মসংঘ পরিচালনা। **—ist**, *n.*

vŏl-ŭn-teer′ (-tēr), *n., v. t. & i.* 1. A person serving or offering service of his own free will; স্বেচ্ছাসেবক। 2. One who enters into the military service from choice; অবৈতনিক সৈন্য। *Verb t.* To offer or bestow voluntarily, or of one's free will and choice; স্বেচ্ছাপূর্ব্বক প্রদান করা। *Verb i.* To enter into any service of one's free will without solicitation or compulsion; স্বেচ্ছাপূর্ব্বক কোন পদ গ্রহণ করা।

vō-lŭp′-tū-ă-rў, *adj. & n.* Wholly given or devoted to sensual pleasure; voluptuous; ইন্দ্রিয়পরায়ণ, কামাতুর, রতিরসরসিক; ভোগবিলাসপরায়ণ, কামোপভোগপরায়ণ। *Noun.* A man who indulges to excess in sensual pleasure; "A good humoured but half-hearted *voluptuary*"; ইন্দ্রিয়পরায়ণ ব্যক্তি, কামাতুর ব্যক্তি।

vō-lŭp′-tū-ous (-ŭs), *adj.* 1. Pertaining to, proceeding, or arising from, sensual pleasure; ইন্দ্রিয়সুখসম্পর্কীয়, কামোপভোগসম্পর্কীয়, ইন্দ্রিয়সুখপ্রসূত, ইন্দ্রিয়সুখমূলক। 2. Indulging in sensuality; ইন্দ্রিয়সেবী, কামোপভোগপরায়ণ, ইন্দ্রিয়সুখপরতন্ত্র, ইন্দ্রিয়সুখাসক্ত, ভোগবিলাসপরায়ণ। 3. Tending to sensual gratification; ইন্দ্রিয়সুখপ্রদ, ইন্দ্রিয়ারাম (হিঃ কোঃ), ইন্দ্রিয়সুখজনক। **—ly**, *adv.* **—ness**, *n.*

vō-lūte′, *n. & adj.* The spiral scroll forming the principal element in the Ionic capital;

Volute.
1, Ionic; 2, Composite; 3. Corinthian.

আইওনিক প্রণালীর স্তম্ভাগ্রের কুণ্ডলিত-ভূষা। **—lut′-ed**, *adj.* **—lu′-tion**, *n.* **Vol′-u-toid**, *adj.*

vō-lū′-tion, *n.* 1. Spiral turn কুণ্ডলী। 2. A convolution; কুণ্ডলিতাবস্থা।

vŏm′-it, *v. i., t. & n.* 1. To eject the contents of the stomach by the mouth; বমি করা, বমন করা। *Verb t.* 1. To throw up or eject from the stomach by the mouth; বমন করা। 2. (*Fig.*) To belch out; "The volcano * * * *vomitted* up large quantities of fire and smoke"; উদ্বমিত করা, উদ্গিরণ করা, উগারিয়া ফেলা। *Noun.* 1. The matter ejected from the stomach; বমি, ছর্দ্দি, প্রচ্ছর্দ্দিকা। 2. An emetic; বমনকারক ঔষধ। **Black vomit**—পীতজ্বরের কালো বমি। **Vomit-nut** — Same as NUX-VOMICA (which see).

vŏm′-ĭ-tō-rў, *adj. & n.* An emetic; বমনজনক, উদ্বামক। *Noun.* 1. An emetic; উদ্বামক ঔষধ। 2. An opening, door or gate in an ancient theatre or amphitheatre, which gave ingress or egress to the spectators; প্রাচীনকালীন রঙ্গালয় বা রঙ্গশালার প্রবেশ ও নির্গমের দ্বার।

vŏm-ĭ-tū-rĭ′-tion, *n.* 1. An unavailing effort to relieve the stomach by vomitting; বমনের বৃথা চেষ্টা। 2. The vomitting of but little matter; vomitting with little effort; অল্পবমন; অল্প চেষ্টায় বমন।

vōō′-dōō, vau-doux (vô-dô), *n. & v.t.* 1. The name given in the southern United States to any practiser of witchcraft, secret rites, etc.; আমেরিকার দক্ষিণাংশের কাফ্রীদিগের মধ্যে ভূতের ওঝা, রোজা। 2. Belief in witchcraft etc. among the Negroes of the southern part of the United States; মার্কিণ-যুক্তরাজ্যের দক্ষিণাংশের নিগ্রোদিগের ইন্দ্রজাল, ভৌতিকক্রিয়া, প্রভৃতিতে বিশ্বাস। *Verb t.* To bewitch; মন্ত্রমুগ্ধ করা, মায়ামুগ্ধ করা। **—ism**, *n.* **—ist**, *n.* **Voodoo-doctor, Voodoo priest**—Same as VOODOO 1.

vō-rā′-cious (-shŭs), *adj.* Eating or swallowing greedily; very hungry; ঔদরিক, ভোজনবিলাসী, উদরসর্ব্বস্ব, উদরপিশাচ; অতি ক্ষুধিত। **—ly**, *adv.* **—ness**, *n.* **—rac′-i-ty**, *n.*

vŏr′-tĕx, *n.* 1. A whirling or circular motion of any fluid, forming a kind of cavity in the centre of the circle; a whirlpool; a whirlwind; তরলপদার্থের ঘূর্ণিগতি, আবর্ত্ত, পাক; জলাবর্ত্ত, ঘূর্ণিজল, জলভ্রমি; ঘূর্ণি, ঘূর্ণিবাত্যা, ঘূর্ণিবায়ু। 2. (*Phys.*) A portion of fluid whose particles have whirling motion; (পদার্থবিদ্যা) তরল পদার্থের অংশবিশেষ—যাহার কণিকাসমূহের ঘূর্ণিগতি রহিয়াছে। 3. (*Cartesian Philos.*) A collection of particles, of very subtile matetr forming a fluid or ether, endowed with a rapid rotatory motion about an axis, and filling all space, and by which Descartes accounted for the motions of the heavenly bodies; (দেকার্ত্তের দর্শন) কোন অক্ষের চতুর্দ্দিকে ঘূর্ণমান সর্ব্বব্যাপী অতি

সূক্ষ্মগতির জড়কণিকা সমূহের সম্মেলন—যাহাকে দেকার্তে জ্যোতিষ্কসমূহের কারণস্বরূপ বলিয়া নির্দ্দেশ করিতেন ; 4. Something considered as swallowing up everything that comes on its way ; as, the *vortex* of swadeshi agitation : সর্ব্বগ্রাসী আবর্ত্ত, মহাবর্ত্ত। **–ti-cal,** *adj.* **–ti-cal-ly,** *adv.* **–tic′-u-lar,** *adj.* **Vortex-atom**—জড় পরমাণুর চরমতম অংশ ; **Vortex-ring**—অক্ষের চতুর্দ্দিকে বৃত্তাকারে বিন্যস্ত ঘূর্ণনশীল সরিল পদার্থের (fluid) অঙ্গুরীয়াকৃতি সমষ্টি—যাহা বৃত্তাকারে ঘূর্ণনের ফলে চতুর্দ্দিকস্থ আধানপদার্থ (medium) হইতে পৃথক হইয়া অনেকাংশে সংহতপদার্থের ধর্ম্ম প্রাপ্ত হয়, ঘূর্ণিবলয়। **Vortex-theory** — লর্ড কেলভিন কর্ত্তৃক প্রকাশিত সিদ্ধান্ত বিশেষ—এই বাদ অনুসারে পরমাণুসমূহ অক্ষের চতুর্দ্দিকে ঘূর্ণনশীল বৃত্তাকারে বিন্যস্ত একপ্রকার সমরূপ (homogeneous), অচাপসহ এবং ঘর্ষণশূন্য অঙ্গুরিয়াকৃতি সরিলপদার্থের (fluid) সমষ্টি বলিয়া পরিগণিত হইয়া থাকে, ঘূর্ণনবাদ।

vŏr′-ti-căl, *adj.* Whirling ; ঘূর্ণনশীল।

vŏr′-ti-cĕl-lă, *n.* A bell-shaped animalculæ found in stagnant water etc. ; বদ্ধ জল প্রভৃতিতে প্রাপ্ত একপ্রকার ঘণ্টাকৃতি সূক্ষ্মপ্রাণী।

vŏr-tĭg′-i-nous (-nŭs), *adj.* Whirling ; ঘূর্ণনশীল, আবর্ত্তনশীল।

vō-tă-rȳ, *n.* 1. One devoted, consecrated, or engaged by a vow or promise ; ভক্ত, উপাসক, পূজক। 2. An ardent follower or adherent of some one or something, some cause, etc. ; as, a *votary* of liberty ; ভক্ত, উপাসক, পাণ্ডা (cf. স্ত্রীলোকের স্বাধীনতার একজন প্রধান পাণ্ডা)

vōte, *n., v. i. & t.* 1. An expression of choice or preference in regard to any measure proposed ; নির্ব্বাচন মত, মত, সম্মতি (হিঃ কোঃ)। 2. That which is given, allowed, or conveyed by the will of a majority ; a thing conferred by vote ; as, a *vote* of £100,000 ; অধিকাংশ লোকের মতানুসারে প্রদত্ত বস্তু ; ভোটদ্বারা প্রদত্ত বস্তু। 3. That by means of which will or preference is expressed in elections or in deciding propositions as a ballot, ticket, etc. ; as, a written *vote* ; যে বস্তু দ্বারা নির্ব্বাচন সময়ে ইচ্ছা বা কাহারো অনুকূলে মত প্রকাশ করা যায় বা কোন বিষয় মীমাংসিত হইয়া থাকে। 4. Votes collectively ; "Alluding to the large amount of the illiterate *votes* in Ireland"; votes given ; মোট ভোট ; প্রদত্ত ভোটসংখ্যা। ***Verb i.*** To express or signify the mind, will or preference ; মত দেওয়া, মত প্রদান করা, কাহারো অনুকূলে মত প্রদান করা। ***Verb t.*** 1. To choose by suffrage ; to elect ; ভোট দ্বারা নির্ব্বাচন করা ; নির্ব্বাচন করা। 2. To grant by vote ; ভোট দ্বারা প্রদান করা। 3. To declare by general opinion or common consent ; he was *voted* a fool ; সর্ব্বসম্মতিক্রমে ব্যক্ত করা। **Vot′-a-ble,** *adj.* **Vot′-er,** *n.* **Casting vote** — See CASTING. **Cumulative voting** — ভোট প্রদানের প্রথাবিশেষ—যাহাতে ভোটদাতা যত সংখ্যক নির্ব্বাচনপ্রার্থী আছে ততসংখ্যক ভোট প্রদান করিতে পারে এবং যে কোন নির্ব্বাচনপ্রার্থীকে তাঁহার সমস্ত ভোট কিম্বা যত ভোট ইচ্ছা দিতে পারে। **Floating vote** — কোন পক্ষের বহির্ভূত ব্যক্তির ভোট। **Voting-paper**—যে কাগজের সাহায্যে ভোটদাতৃগণ ভোট দিয়া থাকে। **To put to the vote**—To raise a question in or for the purpose of knowing the opinion of the majority ; অধিকাংশের মত জানিবার জন্য কোন প্রশ্ন উত্থাপিত করা। **To split one's votes**—To divide one's votes judiciously among several candidates so as to strengthen those one favours ; কোন বিশেষ বিশেষ প্রিয় ব্যক্তিকে সাহায্য করার জন্য সুবিবেচিত ভাবে নিজের ভোট সমূহ বিভাগ করা। **To vote down** — To defeat by voting ; ভোটদ্বারা পরাজিত করা। **To vote in**—To elect by voting ; ভোট দ্বারা নির্ব্বাচন করা, অধিকাংশের মতে নির্ব্বাচন করা।

vō′-tive (-tĭv), *adj.* Given, paid or consecrated in fulfilment of a vow ; as, *votive* offering ; মানসিক স্বরূপ প্রদত্ত, মানসিক হেতু উৎসর্গীকৃত, কোনরূপ ব্রত বা প্রতিজ্ঞা পালনের জন্য প্রদত্ত।

vouch (vowch), *v. t. & i.* 1. To attest; to maintain by affirmation; "What can you *vouch* against him signior Lucio" ; সত্য বলিয়া নির্দ্দেশ করা ; দৃঢ় করিয়া বলা। 2. To affirm ; দৃঢ় করা। 3. (*Rare*) To support ; (কচিদ্‌ব্যবহৃত) সমর্থন করা। 4. To be surety for ; to answer for ; প্রতিভূ থাকা ; দায়ী থাকা। 5. To authenticate, as a claim by vouchers ; প্রমাণপত্রের সাহায্যে সত্যতা প্রতিপাদন করা। ***Verb i.*** To bear witness ; to give testimony ; সাক্ষ্য দেওয়া ; প্রমাণ প্রদান করা।

vouch′-ĕr (vowch-), *n.* 1. One who vouches ; যে ব্যক্তি কোন কিছুর সত্যতা নির্দ্দেশ করে। 2. A written evidence of the payment of money ; টাকা প্রদানের লিখিত প্রমাণ, প্রমাণপত্র।

vouch-safe′ (vowch-), *v. t.* To condescend to grant ; as, to *vouchsafe* one no answer ; অনুগ্রহপূর্ব্বক প্রদান করা, অনুগ্রহ পুরঃসর প্রদান করা।

vous-soir′ (vôs-wâr), *n.* Those stones that immediately form the arch of a bridge, vault, etc. and which are cut more or less in the form of a wedge ; খিলানের জন্য কাঁজলার আকার প্রস্তরফলক।

vow, *n. & v. t.* 1. A solemn promise made to God ; ব্রত, মানসিক, মানত। 2. A solemn engagement to one's self to do something hereafter ; প্রতিজ্ঞা (হিঃ কোঃ). শপথ (ঐ), ধর্ম্মপ্রতিজ্ঞা। **3.** A pledge of love or affection ; as, marriage *vow* ; অবিচলিত প্রেম বা প্রীতিজ্ঞাপক প্রতিজ্ঞা। ***Verb t.*** **1.** To consecrate or set apart to God by solemn promise ; মানসিক করা, মানত করা। **2.** To declare solemnly ; ধর্ম্মতঃ প্রতিজ্ঞা করিয়া বলা। **Monastic vow** — খৃষ্টীয় সন্ন্যাসী বা সন্ন্যাসিনীগণের দারিদ্র্য, গুরুজনের প্রতি বাধ্যতা, এবং চিরজীবন অবিবাহিত থাকার প্রতিজ্ঞা। **Lover's vows** — প্রেমিক প্রেমিকার পরস্পরের প্রতি অবিচলিত নিষ্ঠা অক্ষুণ্ণ রাখার প্রতিজ্ঞা। **Baptismal vows**—দীক্ষাকালীন প্রতিজ্ঞা।

vow'-ĕl, *n.* One of the letters *a, e, i, o, u,* which represents a distinct sound, thus distinguished from the consonants which represent imperfect sounds ; স্বরবর্ণ। **—less, —ly,** *adjs.* **Vowel-gradation** — শব্দ ধাতু প্রভৃতির বিভিন্নরূপ স্বরবর্ণের প্রণালীবদ্ধ পরিবর্ত্তন। **Vowel-mutation**—Same as UMLAUT. **Vowel-point**—হিব্রু, আরবী প্রভৃতি ভাষায় স্বরবর্ণজ্ঞাপক বিন্দু বা চিহ্ন, ইরাব, হরকাত।

vow'-ĕl-ize, *v. t.* To insert the vowels in ; স্বরবর্ণসূচক চিহ্ন অন্তর্নিবিষ্ট করা (যথা হিব্রুলিপিতে)।

vox, *n.* Voice ; স্বর। ***Vox angelica***—অর্গেন নামক বাদ্যযন্ত্রের নলিকাশ্রেণীদ্বয়সমন্বিত রোধক (Stop) বিশেষ। ***Vox antecedans***—(সঙ্গীতশাস্ত্র) বিষয়। ***Vox barbara***—সঙ্কর শব্দ, অশুদ্ধভাবে গঠিত শব্দ। ***Vox caelestis***—Same as VOX ANGELICA. ***Vox clandestina***—অস্ফুটস্বর। ***Vox consequens***—(*Mus.*) উত্তর। ***Vox et praeterea nihil*** — অর্থহীন শব্দ। ***Vox faucibus haesit***—কথাগুলি গলায় আটকাইয়া গিয়াছে। ***Vox humana*** — অর্গেন যন্ত্রের রোধক (stop) বিশেষ—যদ্দারা মনুষ্যের স্বরের অনুরূপ ধ্বনি উৎপন্ন হয় বলিয়া কল্পিত হইয়া থাকে। ***Vox populi, Vox Dei***—দশের বাণী দেবের বাণী, সাধারণের বাণীই ঈশ্বরের বাণী।

voy'-ăge, *n., v. i. & t.* A passage by sea from one place to another ; জলযাত্রা, সমুদ্রযাত্রা, সমুদ্রসংযান (কৌটিল্য-অর্থশাস্ত্র)। ***Verb i. & t.*** To travel or traverse by water ; জলপথে ভ্রমণ করা, জলযাত্রা করা। **Broken voyage**—তিমিমৎস্য শিকারাদির নিষ্ফলযাত্রা। **—able,** *adj.*

vraisemblable, vraisemblance, *ns.* Appearance of truth ; plausible appearance ; সত্যাভাস ; আপাতমনোরমতা।

Vŭl'-căn, *n.* The god who presided over fire and the working of metals ; (রোমক পুরাণ) বিশ্বকর্ম্মা। **Vulcan-powder**—একপ্রকার বিস্ফোরক দ্রব্য।

Vŭl'-căn-ĭst, *n.* (*Geol.*) One who supports the Vulcanian or Plutonic theory, which ascribes the changes on the earth's surface to the agency of fire ; (ভূবিদ্যা) যে সকল ভূবিদ্যাবিদ্‌গণ পৃথিবীর বহিস্তলের পরিবর্ত্তন অগ্নির ক্রিয়াজনিত বলিয়া মনে করেন—তাঁহাদের অন্যতম, অগ্নিবাদী।

vŭl'-căn-īte, *n.* **1.** Vulcanized India rubber, combined with a large proportion of sulphur ; একপ্রকার কঠিনীকৃত রবর, বাল্কেনাইট (হিঃ কোঃ), গন্ধকধর্ম্মা রবার (ঐ), কাঁচক। **2.** A name sometimes given to volcanic garnet ; আগ্নেয় গিরিজাত বৈক্রান্ত মণি।

vŭl'-căn-īze, *v. t.* To change the properties of India rubber, by combining it with sulphur, white lead and other substances ; সফেদা, গন্ধক এবং অন্যান্য বস্তুর সংমিশ্রণে রবরের ধর্ম্ম পরিবর্ত্তন করা, কাঁচকে পরিণত করা। **—iz-a-ble,** *adj.* **—i-za'-tion,** *n.* A method of treating caoutchouc or India rubber with some form of sulphur to effect certain changes in its properties ; গন্ধকীকরণ (হিঃ কোঃ)। **—iz-er,** *n.*

vŭl'-gar (-gĕr), *adj.* **1.** Pertaining to the common people ; সাধারণ লোকসম্বন্ধীয়। **2.** Common ; generally prevalent ; national ; vernacular; as, the *vulgar* version of the Scriptures ; সাধারণতঃ প্রচলিত ; সাধারণ ; জাতীয় ; অবর। **3.** Customary ; প্রচলিত। **3.** Rude ; রূঢ়। **—gar'-i-ty,** *n.* **—ism,** *n.* **1.** The state of being vulgar ; rudeness ; গ্রাম্যতা, নীচতা, ইতরতা ; রূঢ়তা, অশিষ্টতা। **2.** An impolite act ; শিষ্টাচার বিরুদ্ধ কার্য্য। **—i-za'-tion,** *n.* **—ize,** *v. t.* **—ly,** *adv.* **Vulgar language**—অবর ভাষা, অপভ্রংশ।

vŭl-gā'-ri-ăn, *n.* A vulgar person ; ইতরপ্রকৃতি ব্যক্তি।

vŭl'-gāte, *n.* An ancient Latin version of the Scriptures, prepared by Jerome in the fourth century, and pronounced authentic by the Council of Trent ; বাইবেলের অতি প্রাচীন ল্যাটিন অনুবাদ।

vŭl'-gŭs, *n.* Greek or Latin verse-exercise in certain schools ; কোন কোন বিদ্যালয়ে গ্রীক এবং ল্যাটিন কবিতার অনুশীলনী।

vŭl'-nĕr-ă-ble (-bl), *adj.* Capable of being wounded ; susceptible of wounds or external injuries ; ভেদ্য, আহতব্য, আহননীয় ; প্রহার্য্য, আক্রমণসাধ্য। **—bil'-i-ty, —ness,** *ns.*

vŭl'-nĕr-ă-rў, *adj. & n.* Useful in healing wounds ; ক্ষতারোগ্যজনক, ক্ষতনাশক। ***Noun.*** A drug or unguent used for healing wounds ; ক্ষতের ঔষধ, ক্ষতের মলম, ক্ষতরোগের ঔষধ, ক্ষতনাশক মলম।

vŭl'-pīne, *adj.* **1.** Pertaining to fox ; শৃগালসম্বন্ধীয়, শৃগালসম্পর্কীয়। **2.** Cunning ; "*Vulpine* craft"; ধূর্ত্ত, চালাক।

vŭl'-tūre, *n.* **1.** A large voracious bird of prey with great powers of flight, feeding chiefly on carrions ; শকুনি, গৃধ্র [Syn. কামায়ু, বজ্রাঙ্কু, বজ্রতুণ্ড, গৃধিনী, দাক্ষায্য, দূরদর্শন, ভাস, দীর্ঘদর্শী, দূরদর্শী।] 2. A rapacious person, গৃধ্নু ব্যক্তি, পরপীড়ক ব্যক্তি। **–tur-ine, –tur-ish, –tur-ous,** *adjs.*

vŭl′-vă, *n.* The orifice of the external organs of generation of the female ; যোনিরন্ধ্র, জন্মবর্ত্ম, মদনাতপত্র (ভাবঃ প্রঃ), পুষ্পপথ, পুষ্পপদবী, স্মরকূপক। **–var, –vate, –vi-form,** *adjs.*

vȳ′-ing, *n.* See VIE.

W

W, is the twenty-third letter of the English alphabet ; ইংরাজী বর্ণমালার ত্রয়োবিংশতম অক্ষর।

wa′ *n.* (*or* wâ), (*Scot.*) A wall ; (স্কটলণ্ড) প্রাচীর।

wab′-ble (wŏb-l), *v. i.* & *n.* See WOBBLE.

wăck′-ē, *n.* A soft earthy variety of trap-rock of a greyish green or brownish colour resembling indurated clay, but usually containing crystals peculiar to the trap series ; একপ্রকার ধূসরাভ হরিৎ অথবা কপিলবর্ণের আগ্নেয়গিরিজাত মৃত্তিকা।

wad (wŏd), *n.* & *v. t.* **1.** A mass of loose matter thrust close together for packing etc., as hay, tow, etc. ; প্যাকিং প্রভৃতির জন্য যে শুষ্ক তৃণ, শণ প্রভৃতির অসার অংশের পিণ্ড ঠাসিয়া দেওয়া হয়। **2.** A substance made of hay or tow rolled in a ball and rammed into a gun to keep down the powder ; বন্দুকের বারুদ ঠিক রাখিবার জন্য যে শণ, শুষ্ক তৃণ, প্রভৃতির নুটী গাদিয়া দেওয়া হয়। ***Verb t.*** **1.** To form into a wad, or mass, or into wadding ; নুটি পাকান। **2.** To insert a wad into ; to stuff or line with some soft substance, or wadding, as cotton ; নুটী ভরা, তুলা প্রভৃতি ভরা।

wad′-ding (wŏd-îng), *n.* **1.** Any soft stuff of loose texture used for stuffing or padding garments, esp. prepared sheets of carded cotton ; পোষাক বা লেপতোষক প্রভৃতিতে ভরিবার জন্য পশম বা ধুনা তুলার স্তর, ধুনাতুলার আস্তরণ। **2.** The materials for making wads ; শণ, কাগজ, শুষ্ক তৃণ, প্রভৃতি—যদ্দারা প্যাকিং বাক্স প্রভৃতি ভরা হয় বা যাহার ক্ষুদ্র পিণ্ড পাকাইয়া বন্দুকাদিতে গাদা হইয়া থাকে।

wad′-dle (wŏd-l), *v. i., t.* & *n.* To sway or rock from side to side in walking like duck ; হাঁসের মতন হেলিয়া দুলিয়া চলা। ***Verb t.*** (*Rare*) To trample ; "They tread and *waddle* all the goodly grass" ; (কচিৎ ব্যবহৃত) পদদলিত করা, পায়ে মাড়ান। ***Noun.*** Waddling gait ; হংসগতি, মরালগমন।

wăd′-dȳ, *n.* A native wooden war-club in Australia ; অষ্ট্রেলিয়ার আদিম অধিবাসিগণের গদা।

wade, *v. i., t.* & *n.* **1.** To walk through any yielding substance, as water, mud, sand, etc. ; "She *waded* through the dirt to pluck him off me" ; জল, কর্দ্দম, বালুকা প্রভৃতির উপর দিয়া হাঁটিয়া চলা। **2.** To get forward with difficulty ; বহু কষ্টে অগ্রসর হওয়া। ***Verb t.*** To pass, as a river, by walking on the bottom ; as, to *wade* a stream ; নদী প্রভৃতি হাঁটিয়া পার হওয়া। ***Noun.*** A spell of wading ; জল প্রভৃতির উপর দিয়া একচোট হাঁটিয়া চলন। **Wad′-a-ble,** *adj.* **Wading bird**—একপ্রকার দীর্ঘপাদ পক্ষী—যাহারা জলের ভিতর দিয়া হাঁটিয়া চলে। **To wade through blood, slaughter** — লোক হত্যা প্রভৃতির ভিতর দিয়া অগ্রসর হওয়া, রুধির প্রবাহের ভিতর দিয়া অগ্রসর হওয়া।

wād′-ēr, *n.* **1.** Same as WADING-BIRD. **2.** High water-proof boots for wading ; জলের ভিতর দিয়া চলিবার জন্য একপ্রকার দীর্ঘ বুট জুতা।

wa′-di, –dȳ (wŏ-), *ns.* The channel of a watercourse, which is dry except in the rainy season ; পার্ব্বত্য জলপ্রণালী—যাহা বর্ষা ব্যতিরিক্ত কালে শুষ্ক অবস্থায় থাকে।

wā′-fēr, *n.* & *v. t.* **1.** A thin cake or leaf-like bread ; একপ্রকার পাতলা বিস্কুট। **2.** A sacrament bread used by the Roman Catholics in the eucharist ; রোমান ক্যাথলিকগণ কর্ত্তৃক খৃষ্টের অন্তিমভোজনস্মারক অনুষ্ঠানে ব্যবহৃত রোটিকাবিশেষ। **3.** Thin discs of dried paste, sometimes coloured, formerly used in sealing letters etc. ; পূর্ব্বে চিঠি প্রভৃতি বন্ধ করার জন্য ব্যবহৃত শুষ্কীকৃত ময়দার টিকলী। ***Verb t.*** To attach or seal with wafer ; ময়দার টিকলী দ্বারা লাগান বা বন্ধ করা। **Thin as a wafer**—Very thin ; অতিশয় পাতলা।

waf′-fle (wŏf-l), *n.* A thin cake baked hard and rolled, or a soft indented cake baked in an iron utensil on coals ; একপ্রকার পাতল এবং কঠিন রুটি, অথবা লোহার চাটুতে কয়লার উপর সেঁকা একপ্রকার কোমল এবং খাঁজকাটা রুটি। **Waffle-iron**—উক্তপ্রকার রুটি সেঁকিবার জন্য একপ্রকার চাটু।

wăft, *v. t.* & *n.* To bear through a fluid or buoyant medium ; ভাসান, অনায়াসে সঞ্চালিত

করা। *Noun.* 1. A single sweep of a bird's wing; পক্ষীর পক্ষের বিস্তার। 2. A puff; a gust; ঝটিকা; দমকা। 3. (*Obs.*) A fleeting odour or taste; (অপ্র:) দ্রুত বিলীয়মান গন্ধ বা স্বাদ। 4. fugitive sensation of joy, peace, etc.; শান্তি, আনন্দ, প্রভৃতির দ্রুত বিলীয়মান অনুভূতি।

wăg, *v. t., i.* & *n.* 1. To move one way and the other; to vibrate; নাড়া, কাঁপান; কম্পিত করা। 2. To beckon; সঙ্কেত করা। *Verb i.* 1. To move one way and the other; to vibrate; নাড়া; আন্দোলিত হওয়া, কম্পিত হওয়া। 2. To pack off; "Come neighbours we must *wag*"; প্রস্থান করা। 3. To gossip; বিড়বিড় করা, বকবক করা। *Noun.* 1. Act of wagging; নাড়ন। 2. A wit; "We wink at *wags* when they offend"; ফচ্‌কে লোক, মস্করা। **wag'-ger-y**, *n.* Mischievous merriment; pleasantry; ফক্কুড়ি, ফচকেমি, রগড়, মস্করামি; রঙ্গব্যঙ্গ রসিকতা। **Wag'-gish**, *adj.* **Wag'-gish-ly**, *adv.* **wag'-gish-ness**, *n.* **Tail wags dog**—An unimportant person controls men of weight and influence; সামান্য লোক প্রতিপত্তিশালী লোকের উপর প্রভুত্ব করিতেছে। **Wag-tail**—খঞ্জনপক্ষী। [Syn. কলাটীন, খঞ্জরীট, কাকচ্ছর্দ্দি, তাতন, মুনিপুত্রক, রত্ননিধি, ভদ্রনামা, গূঢ়নীড়, চর, খঞ্জখেট, খঞ্জনিকা, কণাটীর, কপাটীন, কনাটাঙ্ক, ভণ্ডক (water wagtail), খঞ্জখেল।] [বঙ্গীয় ও সংস্কৃত কবিগণ খঞ্জনের সহিত সুন্দরীদিগের নেত্রের তুলনা দিয়া থাকেন। (যথা:—নেত্রে খঞ্জন-গঞ্জনে—সাহিত্য-দর্পণ)।]

wāge, *n.* 1. That which is paid for stipulated services, chiefly of a mechanical character; বেতন, মজুরি, পারিশ্রমিক, মেহেনতানা, তলব (*slang*)। 2. Produce; "The niggard *wages* of the earth"; উৎপন্ন দ্রব্য। 3. Requital; "The *wages* of sin and death"; প্রতিদান। **Wage-fund, Wages-fund**—কোন সম্প্রদায়ের মূলধনের যে অংশ বেতন বাবৎ ব্যয়িত হয়, ভৃতি ভাণ্ডার।

wāge, *v. t.* To carry on war; যুদ্ধে প্রবৃত্ত হওয়া।

wā'-gêr, *n.* & *v. t.* Something deposited, laid or hazarded on the event of a contest of some useful question; বাজি, পণ। *Verb t.* To bet; বাজি রাখা, পণ রাখা। **To lay wager**—To bet; বাজিরাখা। **Wager of battle**—প্রাচীনকালীন বিচারবিশেষ—যাহা বাদী বা প্রতিবাদী বা তাহাদের সমর্থকগণের মধ্যে দ্বন্দ্বযুদ্ধ দ্বারা মীমাংসিত হইত।

wăg'-gêr-rў, *n.* See under WAG.

wăg'-gle (-l), *v. i., t.* & *n.* Same as WAG (in a more familiar sease)

wăg'-ŏn, –gŏn, *ns.* 1. A four-wheeled vehicle for carrying heavy goods; মালের জন্য চারি চাকার গাড়ী, মালবাহী শকট। 2. An open railway truck; মাল বহনের জন্য খোলা রেলের গাড়ী। 3. (*Astron.*) (*Cap.*) Charles's Wain; নক্ষত্রশকট (হিঃ কোঃ)। **To hitch one's wagon to a star**—To exercise power higher than one's own; নিজের ক্ষমতার অতিরিক্ত ক্ষমতা প্রয়োগ করা।

wăg'-ŏn-êr, –gŏn-êr, *ns.* 1. One who drives a wagon; মালবাহী গাড়ীর চালক। 2. (*Cap.*) A constellation; Charles's Wain; যোগতারাবিশেষ; সূত (হিঃ কোঃ)।

wăg'-ŏn-ette' (-ĕt), **–gŏn-ette'** (-ĕt), *ns.* A kind of open carriage seated like an omnibus for from four to eight or ten; একপ্রকার প্রমোদযান।

wagon-lit, *n.* (*F.*) A sleeping car attached to a train in the continent; ইয়ুরোপের প্রধান ভূভাগের রেলওয়ের শয়ন-যান।

wăg'-tail (-tāl), *n.* See under WAG.

Wa-hä'-bi, –bee (-bē), *ns.* A follower of Abdul Wahab, a reformer of Mohammedanism, about 1760, whose doctrines, which are of a puritanically reforming type, prevailing in larger part of Arabia; মহম্মদীয় ধর্ম্ম-সম্প্রদায়বিশেষ-ভুক্ত ব্যক্তি। [এই সম্প্রদায়ভুক্ত ব্যক্তিগণ কেবল একমাত্র ঈশ্বরের উপাসনা করিতেন। ইহা প্রেরিত পুরুষ এবং সাধু মহাজনগণের পূজা অর্চ্চনার অত্যন্ত বিরোধী ছিলেন। আরবদেশ হইতে ক্রমে ক্রমে এই সম্প্রদায়ের মত ভারতবর্ষে ব্যাপ্ত হইয়া পড়ে। ঊনবিংশ শতাব্দীর শেষভাগে পাটনানগরী Wahabiগণের এক প্রধান কেন্দ্র হইয়া উঠে। এই সম্প্রদায় কালে রাজদ্রোহিতা অবলম্বন করে। ১৮৬৩ খৃষ্টাব্দের সীমান্ত যুদ্ধে ইহারা শত্রুপক্ষকে অর্থ, লোকজন ও অস্ত্রশস্ত্রপ্রদানে সাহায্য করে।]

waif, (wăf), *n.* 1. An ownerless object or animal; অস্বামিক পশু (cf. ধর্ম্মের ষাঁড়), অস্বামিক ধন। 2. A homeless wretch; an unowned or abandoned child; গৃহছাড়া হতভাগা, ওঁছালোক (*colloq.*); পরিত্যক্ত শিশু। 3. Such goods as a thief, when pursued throws away to prevent being apprehended; ধৃত হইবার ভয়ে চোর যে সমস্ত অপহৃত দ্রব্য ইতঃস্তত ছড়াইয়া ফেলিয়া যায়। **Waifs and strays**—টুকটাক জিনিষ, টুকিটাকি; যে সকল ছেলেমেয়ের কেহ খোঁজখবর নেয় না, পরিত্যক্ত বালক-বালিকা, উপেক্ষিত বালকবালিকা।

wail (wāl), *v. i., t.* & *n.* 1. To lament; to bemoan; বিলাপ করা, শোক করা; খেদ করা। 2. To weep; to grieve over; বিলাপ করা, ক্রন্দন করা, রোদন করা; শোক করা। 3. (Of wind, forest, etc.) To make sound suggesting mournful cries of man; (বাতাস প্রভৃতি সম্পর্কে) ফুকারিয়া উঠা, হাহাকার করা। *Verb t.* To bewail; ;as he *wailed* his fate; শোক করা। *Noun.* Loud and mornful weeping; a mournful cry or song; as, the *wails* of a forest; বিলাপ, খেদ, রোদন, ক্রন্দন; হাহাকার।

Wail′-ful, *adj.* Wail′-ing, *n.* Wail′-ing-ly, *adv.*

wain (wān), *n.* **1.** Same as WAGGON. **2.** Same as CHARLES'S-WAIN. **The Wain**—সপ্তর্ষি (হিঃ কোঃ)।

wain′-scŏt (wān-), *n.* & *v. t.* **1.** The panelled timber-work lining the walls of a room; কক্ষের অন্তঃপ্রাচীরের কাষ্ঠময় আচ্ছাদন। **2.** A kind of European moth; ইয়ুরোপের এক-প্রকার তসরে কীট। ***Verb t.*** To line with wainscot; "Musick soundeth better in chambers *wainscotted*, than hanged"—*Bacon*; কক্ষের অন্তঃ-প্রাচীর কাষ্ঠফলক দ্বারা সমাচ্ছাদিত করা। **–ing,** *n.* **Wainscot-moth**—Same as WAINSCOT 2.

waist (wāst), *n.* **1.** The smaller part of the trunk of the body between the ribs and hips; কোমর, কটিদেশ, মাজা (*colloq.*), কাঁকাল (*ib.*)। [Syn. শ্রোণি, শ্রোণিফলক, বাট, ককুদ্মতী, কলত্র, কটীর, কাঞ্চীপদ, কাঞ্চীগুণস্থান (কুমারঃ)]। **2.** The middle part of various objects; বিভিন্নবস্তুর মধ্য অংশ। **3.** The part of a ship between fore-castle and quarter-deck; জাহাজের পাটাতনের মধ্যাংশ। **4.** (*Obs.*) Same as WAIST-BAND. **5.** (*Obs.*) The middle; "This was about the *waist* of the day"; (অপ্রঃ) মধ্যভাগ। **Waist-band, Waist-belt**—কোমরবন্ধ, কটিবন্ধ। **Waist-cloth** — কটিদেশ-আচ্ছাদক বস্ত্র, কটিবাস, কটিবস্ত্র। **Waist-coat**—একপ্রকার হাতকাটা খাটো জামা,মির্জ্জাই।

wait (wāt), *v. i.* & *t.* **1.** To stay or rest in expectation or patience; to stop or remain stationary or in a state of inaction, as till the arrival of some person or event, or till the proper moment or favourable opportunity for action; প্রত্যাশা করা, আশা করিয়া থাকা; অপেক্ষা করা, প্রতীক্ষা করা **2.** To lie in ambush; ওঁৎ পাতিয়া থাকা। **3.** To remain in readiness to execute the orders of a person; to be ready to serve; to perform the duties of a servant or attendant; as, to *wait on* a gentleman; to attend upon persons at table; কোন ব্যক্তির আদেশ পালনের জন্য প্রস্তুত হইয়া থাকা; পরিচর্য্যা করিতে প্রস্তুত থাকা; পরিচর্য্যা করা; ভোজনোপবিষ্ট ব্যক্তিগণের পরিচর্য্যা করা। ***Verb t.*** **1.** To stay for; অপেক্ষা করা। **2.** To postpone; to defer; as, to *wait* supper; স্থগিত করা; দেরী করা। **Wait′-ing,***n.* **Wait a-bit**—কএকপ্রকার কণ্টকগুল্মের সাধারণ নাম। **Waiting-room** — রেলওয়ে-ষ্টেশনের বিশ্রামগৃহ, প্রতীক্ষাশালা। **To wait for another's shoes**—See SHOES. **To wait on**—To attend; to visit on business; উপস্থিত হওয়া; কার্য্যোপলক্ষে পরিদর্শন করা। To be directed towards; to look to-wards; চালিত হওয়া; কোন কিছুর অভিমুখে দৃষ্টি করা। **To wait upon**—To serve as attendant; পরিচর্য্যা করা, সেবা করা। To perform; সম্পাদন করা। To accompany; অনুগমন করা। To follow as a result; ফলস্বরূপ আগত হওয়া। (*Race*) To purposely keep close behind; (দৌড়ে) ইচ্ছাপূর্ব্বক পশ্চাতে ঘেঁষিয়া থাকা। **Wait a bit**—একটু সবুর কর, বসো, খানিক অপেক্ষা কর।

wait (wāt), *n.* **1.** The act of waiting; the time during which one waits; delay; halt; অপেক্ষা করণ; অপেক্ষার কাল; দেরী; থামন। **2.** (*Obs.*) (Except in *to lie in wait*) ambush; ওঁত। **3.** One of a band of musicians in the pay of a town corporation whose duties were at first to pipe or sound the hours and guard the streets, but subsequently to act merely as town ministrels or musicians; পূর্ব্বকালে ইংলণ্ডে নগরের স্বায়ত্তশাসনসভা কর্ত্তৃক রক্ষিত বাদকবৃন্দ—যাহারা প্রথমতঃ বাদ্য বাজাইয়া সময় নির্দ্দেশ করিত ও নগরে প্রহরা দিত এবং পরে, নগরের বন্দী বা বাদ্যকরের কার্য্য করিত। **To lay wait**—To set an ambush; সুযোগ মত আক্রমণ করার জন্য প্রস্তুত রাখা। **To lie in wait**—To lie in am-bush; ওঁৎপাতিয়া থাকা।

wait′-êr (wāt-), *n.* **1.** One that waits; অপেক্ষাকারী, প্রতীক্ষাকারী। **2.** A servant in attendance; পরিচারক, পরিবেষণকারী খিদ্‌মদ্‌গার। **3.** A tray or salver; বারকোষ, থাঞ্চা। **—ress,** *n.* (*Fem.*)

waive (wāv), *v. t.* **1.** Not to insist on or claim; to relinquish; দাবী না করা, পীড়াপীড়ি না করা; ত্যাগ করা, বর্জ্জন করা। **2.** (*Law*) To relin-quish voluntarily, as a right which one may enforce if he chooses; as, to *waive* one's claim; ইচ্ছাপূর্ব্বক কোন স্বত্ব বা অধিকার ত্যাগ করা। **3.** (*Law*) To forsake; as, to *waive* a woman; to put out of the protection of law; (আইন) ত্যাগ করা, বর্জ্জন করা; আইনের আশ্রয় হইতে চ্যুত করা। **Waiv′-er,** *n.* (*Law*) The act of waiving or not insisting on some right; (আইন) দাবী পরিত্যাগ, অধিকার ত্যাগ।

wakan, wakanda, *ns.* Super-natural or divine powers; প্রাকৃত-শক্তি, দৈবশক্তি।

wāke, *v. i.* & *t.* **1.** To be, or continue, awake; জাগ্রত থাকা, জাগা থাকা, সজাগ থাকা। **2.** To awake; জাগ্রত হওয়া, জাগা। **3.** To be stirred up from a dormant, torpid, or inactive state; "Then *wake*, my soul to high desires"; উদ্বুদ্ধ হওয়া, প্রবুদ্ধ হওয়া। **4.** To un-dergo resurrection; as, to *wake* from the dead"; পুনর্জ্জীবিত হওয়া। ***Verb t.*** **1.** To rouse from sleep; জাগ্রত করা, জাগান। **2.** To arouse; উদ্বুদ্ধ করা, প্রবুদ্ধ করা। **3.** To reanimate; to revive; as, to *wake* sad memories; পুনরুজ্জীবিত করা; পুনর্জ্জীবিত করা। **4** To watch at night prior to burial as a dead body ; সমাহিত করার পূর্ব্বরাত্রে মৃত দেহের পার্শ্বে জাগিয়া থাকা। **Wake-robin**—একপ্রকার বন কচু।

wāke, *n.* **1.** The anniversary of the dedication of a church, formerly, kept by watching all night; merry-making or fair in connection with this; খৃষ্টীয় ধর্ম্মমন্দির উৎসর্গের বাৎসরিক উৎসববিশেষ—যাহাতে নিশাজাগরণ করিতে হইত ; উক্ত উৎসবসংসৃষ্ট মেলা বা আমোদপ্রমোদ। **2.** The watching of a dead body at night prior to burial by the friends and the neighbours of the deceased ; সমাহিত করার পূর্ব্বে মৃত ব্যক্তির বন্ধু ও প্রতিবেশিবৃন্দকর্ত্তৃক তদীয় মৃতদেহের পার্শ্বে জাগরণ।

wāke, *n.* **1.** The track which a ship leaves in the water, formed by the meeting of the water behind ; গতিশীল জাহাজ পশ্চাতে যে মসৃণ জলরেখা রাখিয়া যায়। **2.** (*Dial.*) A row of green damp grass ; (উপভাষায়) সবুজ এবং আর্দ্র তৃণ-পংক্তি। **3.** Track ; as, the *wake* of an army ; গমনচিহ্ন। **In the wake of**—Behind; after the example of ; পশ্চাতে ; দৃষ্টান্ত অনুসরণে, দৃষ্টান্তানুযায়ী।

wāke'-fûl, *adj.* **1.** Keeping awake after going to bed ; সজাগ, বিনিদ্র। **2.** Vigilant ; as, a *wakeful* enemy ; সজাগ, সতর্ক, অবহিত। **–ly,** *adv.* **–ness,** *n.*

wāk'-en (-n), *v. t.* & *i.* **1.** To cause to awake ; জাগ্রত করা, জাগান। ***Verb i.*** To become awake ; জাগ্রত হওয়া, জাগা।

Wal-dĕn'-sēs, *n.* A body of Presbyterian Christians, who reside in the valleys of Piedmont, Dauphine and Provence, and who arose in the 12th century, under the leadership of Peter Waldo in antagonism to the clerical corruption of the Church of Rome ; পাইডমণ্ট উপত্যকাবাসী খৃষ্টীয়সম্প্রদায়বিশেষ। উহারা বহুকাল যাবৎ রোমান ক্যাথলিক সম্প্রদায়ের সহিত বিচ্ছিন্ন হইয়া আদিযুগের খৃষ্টানদিগের সরল ধর্ম্মপদ্ধতি অনুসরণ করিত। ষোড়শ ও সপ্তদশ শতাব্দীতে ইহাদিগের উপর ভীষণ নির্যাতন হয়। **–si-an,** *adj.* & *n.*

wāle, weal (wēl), *n.* & *v. t.* **1.** A ridge raised on flesh by stroke of rod or whip ; বেতের দাগ, লাঠির আঘাতের দাগ। **2.** A ridge or streak in cloth, rising above the cloth ; a streak or stripe ; কাপড়ের উপর উদ্গত ডোরা ; ডোরা, শির। **3.** A timber bolted to a row of piles to secure them together and in position ; কাষ্ঠরাশি স্থির রাখার জন্য উহাতে যে কাষ্ঠফলক প্রেকদ্বারা নিবদ্ধ করা হয়। ***Verb t.*** To raise wales on ; বেত মারিয়া দাগ বসান, ডোরা তোলা। **Wale-knot** or **wall-knot**—রজ্জুর গুণসমূহের প্রান্ত পরস্পরের সহিত জড়াইয়া যে গ্রন্থি দেওয়া হয়।

Wā'-lēr, *n.* A horse imported from New South Wales ; any Australian horse; অষ্ট্রেলিয়া মহাদ্বীপের অন্তঃপাতী নিউ সাউথ ওয়েল্‌স হইতে সমানীত অশ্ব ; অষ্ট্রেলিয়ার অশ্ব।

Wāles, *n.* A principality inhabited by the Welsh ; ওয়েলস্ দেশ। **Prince of Wales**—ইংলণ্ডের যুবরাজ।

Wal-hăl'-lă, *n.* Same as VALHALLA.

walk (wăk), *v. i.* & *t.* **1.** To step along ; to go, move or travel on foot ; পাদচারণ করা ; চলা, ভ্রমণ করা, বেড়ান। **2.** To go or travel on foot ; as, will he be able to *walk* to the station ; পদব্রজে চলা, হাঁটা। **3.** To go or come ; as, please *walk in* ; যাওয়া, আসা। **4.** (*Colloq.*) To depart ; প্রস্থান করা। **5.** To conduct one's self ; "*Walk* humbly with thy God" ; আচরণ করা, চলা। ***Verb t.*** **1.** To pass through or upon ; as, to *walk* the streets ; ভ্রমণ করা, চলা, গমন করা। **2.** To cause to walk or step slowly ; as, to *walk* a horse ; হাঁটান, চালান, বেড়াইতে নেওয়া। **3.** To train, as a young foxhound; শিকারী কুক্কুর প্রভৃতিকে শিক্ষা দেওয়া। **4.** To frequent as a prostitue ; বেশ্যাদির পক্ষে রাস্তায় পায়চারী করা। **Walk'-a-ble,** *adj.* **Walk'-ing,** *n.* **Walking-chair**—Same as GO-CART. **Walking-delegate**—শ্রমজীবিসমাজের কর্ম্মচারিবিশেষ। [এই কর্ম্মচারী শ্রমজীবিগণ এবং তাহাদের মনীব সমাজের নিয়মনিচয় পালন করিতেছে কি না তাহা পরিদর্শন করিয়া থাকেন।] **Walking dictionary**—See DICTIONARY. **Walking-dress**—বাহিরে যাইবার জন্য পরিচ্ছদ, ভ্রমণবেশ। **Walking-fern** — উত্তর আমেরিকার পর্ণাঙ্গ বিশেষ। **Walking-fish**—শোল, চেঙ্গ, প্রভৃতি বিভিন্নপ্রকার মৎস্য—যাহারা মাটীর উপর দিয়া চলিতে পারে। **Walking gentleman, Walking lady**—যে অভিনেতা বা অভিনেত্রীর কোনরূপ রঙ্গকৌশল প্রদর্শন করিতে হয় না, কেবল বাহ্যসৌন্দর্য্য থাকিলেই চলে। **Walking-leaf**—পত্রানুকারী কীট। **Walking leg**—চলিবার পা। **Walking-papers** or **ticket**—(ইতর ভাষায়) বরখাস্ত। **Walking-stick**—বেড়াইবার ছড়ি। **Walking-sword**—পূর্ব্বকালে ভদ্রলোকগণ কর্ত্তৃক ব্যবহৃত অতি হাল্‌কা তরবারি। **Walking-tour**—পদব্রজে প্রমোদ ভ্রমণ। **Walk-out**—শ্রমজীবিগণের ধর্ম্মঘট। **Walk-tyrant**—দক্ষিণ আফ্রিকার কীটবিশেষ। **Walk-twig**—একপ্রকার কীট। **Walk-wheel**—Same as TREAD WHEEL. **Heel-and-toe walking** — যে ভ্রমণাদিতে পায়ের গোড়ালি এবং পদাঙ্গুলী উভয়ই ব্যবহৃত হয়। **The ghost walks**—It shows itself ; ভূত চক্ষুর সম্মুখে আবির্ভূত হইয়াছে। **To walk by**—To lead a righteous life ; ধর্ম্মপথে বিচরণ করা। **To walk in darkness** — To rove in ignorance ; অজ্ঞানান্ধকারে বিচরণ করা। **To walk in light**—To walk in right path ; সৎপথে চলা। **To walk into**—(*Vulg.*) To scold severely ; to punish ; (ইতর ভাষায়) তীব্র তিরস্কার করা ; সাজা দেওয়া। To devour ; উদরসাৎ করা। **To walk into food** — To eat with delight ; আনন্দের সহিত ভোজন করা। **To walk off** or **away with**—To steal ; চুরি করিয়া নেওয়া। **To walk one off one's legs**—To tire out ; ক্লান্ত করা, হয়রাণ করা। **To walk one's chalks**—To depart ; চলিয়া যাওয়া, প্রস্থান করা। **To walk out with**—To have a sweeheart ; প্রণয়ী বা প্রণয়িনী থাকা (বিশেষভাবে দাসদাসীগণে সম্পর্কে ব্যবহৃত হয়)। **To walk over**—To go over a race-course at a walking pace ; হাঁটিয়া দৌড়ের মাঠের উপর দিয়া যাওয়া। [যে দৌড়ে প্রতিযোগীদের মধ্যে কেবল একজন উপস্থিত হয়, সুতরাং কেবলমাত্র হাঁটিয়া দৌড়চক্র অতিক্রম করিলেই—সে পুরস্কার প্রাপ্ত হইয়া থাকে।] (*fig.*) To gain an easy victory ; to attain one's object without opposition ; সহজে জয় লাভ করা ; বিনা বাধায় উদ্দেশ্য সিদ্ধ হওয়া। **To walk Spanish**—(*Colloq.*) To walk on tiptoe involuntarily through another's lifting one by the seat of the trouser ; to walk cautiously ; to be forced to act or proceed ; to get discharged ; (মার্কিন যুক্তরাজ্যের চলিত ভাষায়) পাজামার নিতম্ব দেশের কাপড় টানিয়া তুলিয়া কাহাকে পা টিপিয়া হাঁটিতে বাধ্য করা ; সাবধানে পা টিপিয়া টিপিয়া চলা ; কার্য্য করিতে বা অগ্রসর হইতে বাধ্য হওয়া ; বরখাস্ত হওয়া। **To walk the chalk**—To prove one's sobriety to police by walking straight between chalked lines ; পুলিশের লোকের কাছে অপ্রমত্ততা প্রমাণ করার জন্য খড়ি দ্বারা অঙ্কিত রেখাদ্বয়ের মধ্য দিয়া সোজাসুজি যাওয়া। **To walk the chalk line**—To be careful about one's conduct ; অতিশয় সাবধানে চলা। **To walk the hospitals, To walk the wards**—To attend a hospital for instruction as a medical student ; চিকিৎসাবিদ্যাশিক্ষার্থ আরোগ্যশালায় উপস্থিত থাকা। **To walk the plank**—See PLANK. **To walk the street**—To stroll along the street ; রাস্তায় বেড়ান। To be a prostitute ; বেশ্যাবৃত্তি অবলম্বন করা, পথে দাঁড়ান। **To walk up and down**—To walk to and from ; পায়চারী করা, বেড়িয়ে বেড়ান। **To walk with God**—To fulfil God's commandments ; ঈশ্বরের দশাদেশ পালন করা। **Walk about**—(*Mil.*) This expresssion is used by military officers to a sentry that they waive salutes ; ঘুরাফিরার কালে ইংরেজ সৈনিক কর্ম্মচারিগণ এই বাক্য-দ্বারা সান্ত্রীকে জ্ঞাপন করেন যে তাঁহাকে অভিবাদন করার আবশ্যক নাই।

walk (wäk), *n.* 1. Act of walking ; ভ্রমণ। 2. Walking gait ; "And imitated best his *walk*" ; চলনভঙ্গী, গতিভঙ্গী। 3. Act of walking for recreation or exercise ; as, evening *walk* ; অঙ্গচালনাদির জন্য ভ্রমণ। 4. Excursion on foot ; পদব্রজে ভ্রমণ। 5. Conduct ; course of action ; আচরণ ; কার্য্যপ্রণালী। 6. Range ; province ; as, within the *walk* of a historian ; পাল্লা, প্রসার ; ক্ষেত্র। 7. Walking ground ; ভ্রমণস্থান, পাদচারণভূমি। 8. Pasture-land ; পশুচারণভূমি। 9. Footpath ; promenade ; পাদচারণ পথ ; বিচরণ-ভূমি। 10. The route regularly served by a vendor ; as, a fruit vendor's *walk* ; ফেরিওয়ালা সদাসর্ব্বদা যে রাস্তায় চলে। 11. An avenue set with trees or laid out in a grove or wood ; তরুবীথি, কুঞ্জ-বীথি, বনবীথি। 12. (*Dial.*) A village fair ; (অপভাষায়) গ্রাম্য মেলা। **At a walk** — Walking in ordinary way ; সাধারণ ভাবে হাঁটিয়া। **A walk over the course** or **a walk-over**—A race in which only one competitor comes forward, he gaining the prize by merely walking over the course ; victory easily won ; যে দৌড়ে কেবল-মাত্র একজন প্রতিযোগী অগ্রসর হয়, অতএব যে কেবলমাত্র দৌড়চক্র পদব্রজে অতিক্রম করিয়াই জয়লাভ করিতে পারে ; অতি সহজে যে জয়লাভ করা হইয়াছে। **Walk of life**—Calling ; profession ; ব্যবসায় ; বৃত্তি।

walk'-êr (wäk-), *n.* 1. One who walks ; ভ্রমণকারী। 2. A fuller of cloth ; রজক। 3. Same as STICK-INSECT. 4. A gressorial bird ; পাদচারী পক্ষী।

Walk'-êr (wäk-), *interj.* (*Slang*) (also *Hookey Walker*) Expression of incredulity and suspicion of being hoaxed ; (ইতর ভাষায়) ফাঁকি-বাজি, ভুঁয়াকথা।

Walk'-y-rie (wäk-ĭ-rē), *n.* Same as VALKYRIE (which see).

wall, *n.* & *v. t.* 1. A solid and permanent inclosing fence ; প্রাচির, পাঁচিল (*colloq.*)। 2. (*Pl.*) Rampart ; fortification ; বপ্র, দুর্গ, গড় ; কোট। 3. One of the upright inclosing parts of a room ; কক্ষের প্রাচীর, কক্ষপ্রাচীর, দেয়াল। ***Verb t.*** 1. To encolse with wall ; প্রাচীর দ্বারা বেষ্টিত করা, প্রাচীরবেষ্টিত করা। 2. To close or fill with a wall ; as, to *wall* an aperture ; দেওয়াল দ্বারা বন্ধ করা, দেওয়াল দ্বারা বুজাইয়া দেওয়া। **Wall'-less,** *adj.* **Foot-wall**—খনিগর্ত্তে যে নিম্নবর্ত্তী পাষাণবেষ্টনীর মধ্যে ধাতুর শিরা নিবদ্ধ থাকে। **Hanging-wall**—খনিগর্ত্তে যে উর্দ্ধস্থিত শিলাবেষ্টনীর মধ্যে ধাতুর শিরা নিবদ্ধ থাকে। **Party** or **partition wall**—কক্ষদ্বয়, গৃহদ্বয়, ক্ষেত্রদ্বয়, প্রভৃতি বিভাজক প্রাচীর। **Wall-box** — দেওয়ালে গাঁথা চিঠির বাক্স। **Wall-creeper**—কএকপ্রকার পক্ষীর সাধারণ নাম। **Wall-cress**—পাষাণসঙ্কুল স্থানে জাত কয়েকপ্রকার ক্ষুপের সাধারণ নাম। **Wallflower**—কমলা বা কপিশ বর্ণের সুগন্ধি পুষ্পগুচ্ছ প্রসূ

উদ্যানারোপিত গুল্মবিশেষ ; নর্ত্তনকালে যে রমণী সহচর প্রাপ্ত হয় না, প্রাচীর-প্রসূণ। **Wall-fruit**—প্রাচীরগাত্রসংলগ্ন বৃক্ষের ফল। **Wall-lizard** গৃহগোধিকা, টিকটিকি, জেঠী। **Wall-painting** — প্রাচীরগাত্রাঙ্কিত চিত্র। **Wall-paper**—গৃহের প্রাচীরগাত্র সজ্জিত করার জন্য নানাপ্রকার চিত্রসমন্বিত কাগজ। **Wall-pepper**—একপ্রকার প্রাচীরগাত্র-বাহিনী লতা। **Wall-plate**—প্রাচীরের উপরে নিহিত দারুফলক। **Wall-rue**—একপ্রকার ক্ষুদ্র পর্ণাঙ্গ। **Wall-shade**—দেওয়ালগিরি। **Wall-tree**—প্রেক দ্বারা প্রাচীরে নিবদ্ধ ফলবৃক্ষ। **Wall-washer**—টলটলায়মান প্রাচীর দৃঢ় করার জন্য একপ্রকার ফলক। **A blank wall**—দ্বার বাতায়ন বা প্রবেশ-দ্বারশূন্য প্রাচীর; সাদা দেওয়াল, যে প্রাচীরগাত্র কোনরূপ চিত্রাদি দ্বারা ভূষিত নহে, অচিত্রিত প্রাচীর। **The finger** or **handwriting on the wall**—আসন্ন বিপদ্। **The weakest goes to the wall**—Nobody cares for the weak ; the weak occupy the lowest place in competition ; দুর্ব্বলের প্রতি কেহই দৃক্‌পাত করে না ; প্রতিযোগিতায় দুর্ব্বলের স্থান সকলের নিম্নে। **To drive** or **thrust to the wall**—To compel to give place ; স্থান প্রদান করিতে বাধ্য করা ; কোণঠাসা করা। **To give one the wall**—To allow a man to pass by a convenient place when encountering on a narrow road, etc. ; কোন স্থান অতিক্রম করার কালে কোন ব্যক্তিকে সুবিধাজনক স্থান দিয়া যাইতে দেওয়া। **To go to the wall**—To be unsuccessful ; অকৃতকার্য্য হওয়া, নিষ্ফল হওয়া। **To hang by the wall**—To hang up neglected ; hence, not to be made use of ; অবহেলা করিয়া তুলিয়া রাখা ; ব্যবহৃত না হওয়া। **To run one's head against a wall**—To try impossibilites—অসাধ্য সাধনের চেষ্টা করা। **To see through the brickwall** — To have supersensuous sight ; অতীন্দ্রিয় দৃষ্টিসম্পন্ন হওয়া। **To take the wall**—To occupy the upper or most honourable place ; সম্মানজনক স্থান পরিগ্রহ করা। **To take the wall of**—To refuse this courtesy to ; কাহারো প্রতি শিষ্টাচার টুকু প্রদর্শনে অস্বীকার করা। **Wall of partition**—বিভাগ-রেখা। **Walls have ears**—See EAR. **With one's back to the wall** — কোণঠাসা অবস্থায় ; একা বহুলোকের সহিত যুদ্ধে নিরত।

wal'-la (wŏl-ă) **-lah** (-ă), *ns.* A person or thing concerned with something ; ওয়ালা। **Competition-walla** — সিভিলসার্ভিসের লোক। **Canalwallah** — সুয়েজ প্রণালীতে চলার উপযোগী জাহাজ।

wăl'-lă-by̆, *n.* A kind of small kangaroo ; একজাতীয় ক্ষুদ্র কেঙ্গারু। **To go on the wallaby track**—কার্য্যের অন্বেষণে ঘুরা (অষ্ট্রেলিয়ার ব্যবহৃত)।

Wăl'-lach *n.* **1.** An inhabitant of Wallachia ; ওয়ালেকিয়ার অধিবাসী, রুমেনিয়ার অধিবাসী। **2.** The language of Wallachia ; ওয়ালিকিয়ার ভাষা, রুমেনিয়ার ভাষা।

Wăl-lā'-chi-ăn, *n.* Same as WALLACH.

Wallago atta—বোয়াল (গুপ্ত)।

wăl-lă-roo', *n.* A kind of large kangaroo ; এক জাতীয় বৃহৎ কেঙ্গারু।

wal'-lĕt (wŏl-), *n.* **1.** (*Archaic*) A bag for carrying necessaries ; (অপ্র:) ঝুলি, ঝোলা। **2.** A pocket-book ; পকেটে রাখার উপযোগী ক্ষুদ্র খাতা। **3.** A tool bag ; ক্ষুদ্র ক্ষুদ্র যন্ত্রাদি রাখার জন্য ক্ষুদ্র চামড়ার ব্যাগ।

wall'-eye (-ī), *n.* **1.** (In horses) An eye in which the iris is of a very light gray or whitish colour ; (অশ্বের) ফিকে ধূসর বা সাদাটে বর্ণের চক্ষু:। **2.** (Of fish) Eye showing abnormal amount of white or large and glaring as in some fishes ; (মৎস্য সম্পর্কে) অস্বাভাবিক শ্বেতবর্ণ চক্ষু:, বৃহৎ এবং তীব্রোজ্জ্বল চক্ষু:। **—eyed**, *adj.*

wall'-knot (-nŏt), *n.* Same as WALE-KNOT under WALE.

Wâl-loon', *n.* & *adj.* **1.** One of the descendants of the old Gallic Belgae who occupy the Belgian provinces of Hainault, Liege, and Namur, Southern Brabant, Western Luxemburg and to some extent adjacent parts of France ; বেলজিয়ামের Hainault, Liege, Namur, এবং South Bravant, Luxemburg এবং কতক পরিমাণে ফরাসীদেশের তৎসংলগ্ন অঞ্চলের অধিবাসী প্রাচীন জাতি বিশেষের লোক। **2.** The language of the same territory ; উক্ত জাতি কর্তৃক অধ্যুষিত অঞ্চল সমূহে প্রচলিত ভাষা। ***Adj.*** Of the Walloons or their language ; ওয়ালুন্স জাতিসম্বন্ধীয়, উক্ত জাতির ভাষা সম্পর্কীয়।

wal'-lŏp (wŏl-), *v. t.* (*Slang*) To thrash ; to drub ; (ইতর ভাষায়) মেরে পাটপাট করা ; পিটুনি দেওয়া, মারা। **—ing**, *part. adj.* Large ; প্রকাণ্ড, মস্ত, বড়।

wal'-low (wŏl-lō), *v. i.* & *n.* **1.** To roll one's body on the earth, mire, or other substance ; লুটোপুটি খাওয়া, গড়াগড়ি দেওয়া, ধূলিতে গড়াগড়ি যাওয়া, লুটুপুটু খাওয়া। **2.** To live in filth or gross vice ; "Man *wallowing* in his native impurity" ; বিলাসপঙ্কে বা পাপপঙ্কে নিমগ্ন থাকা। ***Noun.*** A place to which buffaloes etc. resort to wallow ; কর্দ্দম, পল্বল, কর্দ্দমপূর্ণ স্থান।

wal'-nŭt (wăl-), *n.* **1.** A valuable tree, native of Persia ; আখরোট গাছ, কীরেষ্ট। **2.** The edible nut of the tree ; আখরোট, অক্ষোট। [Syn. আক্ষোড়, কর্পরাল, কন্দরাল, আক্ষোট, আক্ষোড়ক ;] [Arab. *jowz, khusif* ; Pers. *char-mughz, jouz-i-rumi, girdighan* ; Chin. *hu-t'au, kiang-t'au* ; Fr. *noix* ; Swed.

valnot ; Dan. *valnod* ; Germ. *walnuss*, *dan-walnoot.*] **3.** The timber of walnut tree ; আখরোট-গাছের কাঠ।

wal-pur'-gis-night (vâl-pûr-gis-nit), *n.* The eve of the first of May when the old pagan witch-world was supposed to hold revelry under its chief on certain high places, the Brocken, esp. in Germany ; ১লা মের পূর্ব্ব দিবস ডাইনিদিগের পানোৎসব। [জর্ম্মণীদেশে খৃষ্টধর্ম্ম প্রবর্ত্তনে সাহায্যকারিণী Walpurgis নাম্নী সিদ্ধিপ্রাপ্তা নারীর নাম হইতে গৃহীত।]

wal'-rŭs (wŏl-), *n.* A huge marine carnivorous animal inhabiting the arctic sea ; সিন্ধুঘোটক, সিন্ধুসিংহ (মিউজিয়্যাম)।

Walrus.

waltz (wälts), *n.* & *v. i.* **1.** A German national dance, originally from Bohemia, and now very fashionable in other countries, executed by two persons round a room with a whirling motion ; মণ্ডলনৃত্য। [এইরূপ নৃত্যে নর্ত্তকনর্ত্তকী-যুগল প্রায় আলিঙ্গনপাশে বদ্ধ হইয়া পরস্পরকে আবর্ত্তন পূর্ব্বক কক্ষ প্রদক্ষিণ করিতে থাকে।] **2.** Music for this dance ; মণ্ডলনৃত্যোপযোগী বাদ্য। ***Verb i.*** **1.** To dance waltz ; মণ্ডলনৃত্য করা। **2.** To dance nimbly and joyfully ; চটুল, এবং উল্লাসপূর্ণভাবে নৃত্য করা। **Waltz'-er,** *n.*

wam'-ble (wŏm-bl), *v. i.* (*Obs.* & *Dial.*) **1.** To rumble ; as, his stomach *wambles* ; (পেট) ঘড়ঘড় করা। **2.** To quiver ; কম্পিত হওয়া, কাঁপা। **3.** To tumble ; উল্টাইয়া যাওয়া। **4.** To stagger ; টলিয়া পড়া, টাউরান।

wăm-pee' (-pē), *n.* **1.** A tree of the genus cookia (*Cookia punctata*) ; একপ্রকার গাছ। **2.** Its fruit ; উক্ত গাছের ফল। [এই ফলের আয়তন কপোত ডিম্বের অনুরূপ। এই ফল চীনদেশ এবং জাভা, সুমাত্রা প্রভৃতি দ্বীপে জন্মে। ইহার বহির্ভাগ পীতবর্ণ ও ভিতরের শাঁস শুভ্রবর্ণ। এই ফল ঈষৎ অম্লাস্বাদ ও অতিশয় মুখরোচক। ইহার চীনদেশীয় নাম *Hwang-pi*, *Wham-pi*.]

wam'-pŭm (wŏm-), *n.* Small beads made of shells, by the American-Indians as money or ornaments ; কড়ি হইতে নির্ম্মিত গুটিকা—যাহা আমেরিকার আদিম অধিবাসিগণ মুদ্রা এবং অলঙ্কারস্বরূপ ব্যবহার করিয়া থাকে।

wan (wŏn) *adj.* **1.** Pale ; colourless ; bloodless ; বিবর্ণ ; পাংশু, পাঙ্গাশিয়া ; রক্তহীন। **2.** (*Obs.*) Dark ; gloomy ; as *wan* sky ; (অপ্রঃ) অন্ধকারাচ্ছন্ন ; সতিমির। **Wan'-ly,** *adj.* **Wan'-ness,** *n.*

wand (wŏnd), *n.* **1.** A rod ; দণ্ড, কাঠি। **2.** A staff of authority ; ক্ষমতাসূচক দণ্ড। **3.** A rod used by conjurers, diviners, magicians, etc. ; যাদুকরের দণ্ড, যাদুদণ্ড, মায়াদণ্ড, রসদণ্ড (পক্ষঃ)। **4.** A fishing rod ; বড়শীর কোড়া।

wan'-dêr (wŏn-), *v. i.* & *t.* **1.** To ramble here and there without any certain course or object in view ; to rove ; উদ্দেশ্যহীন ভাবে ইতস্ততঃ পর্য্যটন করা ; ঘুরা, বিচরণ করা। **2.** To go away ; চলিয়া যাওয়া। **3.** To stray off ; to go astray ; as, a writer *wanders* away from his object ; বিপথে যাওয়া, পথচ্যুত হওয়া, চ্যুত হওয়া ; বিপথগামী হওয়া। **4.** Not to be under the guidance of reason ; as, the mind *wanders* ; বিক্ষিপ্তচিত্ত হওয়া। ***Verb t.*** To traverse ; "*Wanders* a poor and thankless soil" ; বিচরণ করা, পর্য্যটন করা। **—ing,** *n.* One who wanders ; পর্য্যটনকারী, ভ্রমণকারী, বিচরণকারী। **—ing-ly,** *adv.* **Wandering abscess, kidney etc.** — যে স্ফোটক, মূত্রাশয়, প্রভৃতি স্বস্থানে স্থির থাকে না **Wandering Jew**—(১) Aristeas নামক কবি। ইনি প্রায় ৪ শতাব্দী ব্যাপিয়া আবির্ভূত ও তিরোহিত হন। ইনি পৃথিবীর সমস্ত পৌরাণিক জাতি সমূহের দেশে গমন করিয়াছিলেন বলিয়া কথিত আছে। (২) এইরূপ প্রবাদ যে Pontius Pilateএর বিচারগৃহের দ্বাররক্ষক Kartaphilos যীশুকে বিচারকের সমীপে নেওয়ার কালে "যীশু তাড়াতাড়ি চল" এই বলিয়া তাঁহাকে আঘাত করে। কথিত আছে যীশু তাহাকে তৎসময় বলেন যে "আমি যাইতেছি। কিন্তু তোমাকে আমার পুনরাগমন পর্য্যন্ত অপেক্ষা করিতে হইবে।" (৩) যীশু ক্রুশের ভারে প্রপীড়িত হইয়া Ahasuerus নামক এক চর্ম্মকারের দ্বারে বিশ্রামের জন্য দণ্ডায়মান হন তখন সেই নিষ্ঠুর চর্ম্মকার তাঁহাকে "দূর হও দূর হও বলিয়া" ঠেলিয়া তাড়াইয়া দেয়। ঐ সময়ে যীশু সেই চর্ম্মকারকে বলেন "আমি এখনই চলিয়া যাইতেছি, কিন্তু আমি পুনরায় পৃথিবীতে অবতীর্ণ না হওয়া পর্যন্ত তুমি অপেক্ষা কর।" (৪) জর্ম্মণদেশে John Buttadaeus নামক জনৈক ব্যক্তিকে Wandering Jew বলা হইয়া থাকে। কথিত আছে ইঁহাকে প্রথমবার ত্রয়োদশ, দ্বিতীয়বার চতুর্দশ এবং তৃতীয়বার পঞ্চদশ শতাব্দীতে Antwerp নগরীতে দেখা যায়। ইঁহাকে সর্ব্বশেষে ১৭৭৪ অব্দে Brussels নগরীতে দেখা গিয়াছিল। (৫) ফরাসীদেশে Issac Laquedem নামক জনৈক ইহুদী Wandering Jew বলিয়া কথিক হইয়া থাকে। [Alexander Dumas *Issac Laquedem* নামে এক উপন্যাস প্রণয়ণ করেন। Engene Sue নামে প্রসিদ্ধ ফরাসী ঔপন্যাসিক *Le Juif Errant* (Wandering Jew) নামে এক বৃহৎ উপন্যাস রচনা করিয়াছেন।] **Wandering star** — চলনক্ষত্র (হিঃ কোঃ), চর নক্ষত্র (ঐ)।

wan-dĕr-ōō', *n.* A baboon of Ceylon and Malabler ; সিংহল দ্বীপ এবং মালাবার উপকূলের একপ্রকার বানর।

wāne, *v. i.* & *n.* 1. To be diminished ; (esp. of moon) to decrease ; হ্রাস প্রাপ্ত হওয়া, ক্ষয় প্রাপ্ত হওয়া, ক্ষীণ হওয়া ; কৃষ্ণ পক্ষের চন্দ্রকলার মত ক্রমশঃ ক্ষয় প্রাপ্ত হওয়া। 2. To decline ; "I am *waning* in his favour" ; অবনতি হওয়া, পতন হওয়া। ***Noun.*** 1. The apparent decrease of the illuminated part of the moon ; চন্দ্রের ক্ষয়। 2. Decrease ; decline ; "You are cast upon an age when the church is in its *wane*" ; ক্ষয়, হ্রাস ; অবনতি, পতন। **To be on the wane**—To be on the decline ; ক্রমশঃ ক্ষয় প্রাপ্ত হওয়া, ক্ষীয়মাণ হওয়া।

want (wŏnt), *n.* 1. Lack ; অভাব, রাহিত্য, শূন্যতা। 2. Poverty ; penury ; "And *want* can quench the eye's bright grace"; অভাব, অনটন; দারিদ্র্য। 3. That which is not possessed, but is desired or necessary for use or pleasure ; "Habitual superfluities become actual *wants*" ; উপভোগ বা ব্যবহারের জন্য বাঞ্ছিত বস্তু। 4. Necessity ; আবশ্যক বস্তু। **Want of faith**—অশ্রদ্ধা (হিঃ কোঃ)।

want (wŏnt), *v. t.* & *i.* 1. To be without ; to be destitute of ; to lack ; as, to *want* intelligence ; বিরহিত হওয়া, শূন্য হওয়া ; বিহীন হওয়া ; অভাব থাকা। 2. To be deficient ; ন্যূন থাকা। 3. To need ; as, in summer we *want* cooling breeze ; আবশ্যক করা, দরকার হওয়া। 4. To wish or long for ; "If he *want* me let him come to me" ; ইচ্ছা করা, কামনা করা, চাওয়া। ***Verb i.*** 1. To lack ; অভাব থাকা। 2. To be deficient ; not to be sufficient ; ন্যূন হওয়া ; অপ্রচুর হওয়া। 3. To be in a state of destitution ; to be needy ; অর্থহীন হওয়া; অভাবগ্রস্ত হওয়া। **Want'-age,** *n.* Deficiency ; অভাব, কমতি। **Want'-ed,** *p. p.* কর্ম্মখালি। **Want'-er,** *n.* **Want'-ing,** *n.* **He is wanted**—Police are making enquiries about him ; পুলিশ তাহার খোঁজ নিতেছে।

wan'-tŏn (wŏn-), *adj.*, *n.*, *v. i.* & *t.* 1. Playful ; wandering in sport ; লীলাপর, ক্রীড়াশীল, ক্রীড়াসক্ত ; তরল, চপল, সবিভ্রম, কেলিপর। 2. Free ; wild ; luxuriant ; "What we by day...prop or bind, One night or two with *wanton* growth, derides, tending to wild" ; মুক্ত ; বন্য ; অতিবর্দ্ধনশীল। 3. Perverse ; dissolute ; "Man grown *wanton* by prosperity" ; বেআঁড়া ; লম্পট। 3. Unchaste ; lascivious ; ব্যভিচারপরায়ণ ; কামুক। 4. Reckless ; "A *wanton* injurious exercise of this prerogative" ; motiveless ; প্রমত্ত, দৃক্‌পাতশূন্য, অবিমৃষ্যকারী, অবিবেকী, বিবেচনাশূন্য ; উদ্দেশ্যহীন, উদ্দেশ্যশূন্য। ***Noun.*** 1. An unchaste woman or man ; a lewd person ; ব্যভিচারিণী ব্যক্তি, অসতী ; ব্যভিচারপরায়ণ ব্যক্তি, লম্পট ব্যক্তি। 2. A pampered pet ; "A beardless boy, a cockered silken *wanton*" ; আদুরে গোপাল, আলালের ঘরের দুলাল। ***Verb i.*** 1. To frolic ; to revel ; ক্রীড়া করা ; পানকোলাহল করা। 2. To sport lasciviously ; কেলি করা, কামক্রীড়া করা। ***Verb t.*** To pass or waste wantonly ; অবিবেকীর মত কাটান বা উড়াইয়া দেওয়া। **-ly,** *adv.* **-ness,** *n.*

wa'-pen-tāke (-pn-), *n.* A division or district, as in Yorkshire, answering to the hundred in other counties, so called because, when the overlord appeared for justice the men used to touch his spear in token of fealty ; ইয়র্কশায়ারের বিভাগ বিশেষ।

wăp'-i-ti, *n.* The North-American stag ; উত্তর আমেরিকার হরিণবিশেষ।

war, *n.*, *v. i.* & *t.* 1. A contest between nations or parties carried on by force of arms ; যুদ্ধ, সমর, আহব, রণ, সংগ্রাম, লড়াই। [*Syn.*. আয়োধন, জন্য, প্রধন, প্রবিদারণ, অনীক, কলহ, সম্প্রহার, সাম্পরায়িক, অভিসম্পাত, মৃধ, আস্কন্দ, সংখ্য, সংযৎ, সংযুগ, কলি, সংস্ফোট, অভ্যামর্দ্দ, সমাঘাত, সমিতি, আজি, সমিৎ, সংরাব, আনাহ, সম্পরায়ক, বিদার, দারণ, সংবিৎ, সম্পরায়, তীক্ষ্ম, অম্বরীষ, বলজ, আনর্ত্ত, অভিমর, সমুদয়, অভ্যাগম।] 2. Profession of arms ; as, he is a man of *war* ; যুদ্ধবৃত্তি, যুদ্ধব্যাপার। 3. Art of war ; যুদ্ধকৌশল, যুদ্ধনীতি, রণনীতি। 3. Enemity ; শত্রুতা, বিরোধ। 4. (*Poet.*) Army ; "On their embattled ranks the waves return And overwhelm their *war*" ; সৈন্যদল, বল। 5. Civil war ; অন্তর্বিগ্রহ। ***Verb i.*** 1. To make or wage war ; যুদ্ধে প্রবৃত্ত হওয়া। 2. To strive ; সংগ্রাম করা। ***Verb t.*** (*Rare*) To fight ; (কচিৎ ব্যবহৃত) যুদ্ধ করা। **War'-ring,** *adj.* 1. Competing ; প্রতিযোগী, প্রতিদ্বন্দ্বী। 2. Inconsistent ; পরস্পরবিরোধী। **War-cloud**—রণমেঘ (অর্থাৎ আন্তর্জাতিক ব্যাপার সমূহের যেরূপ অবস্থায় যুদ্ধের আশঙ্কা করা যায়)। **War-cry**—রণনাদ, সিংহনাদ, হুঙ্কার, যুদ্ধকালে ব্যবহৃত সাংকেতিক শব্দ। **War-dance**—সামরিক নৃত্য, রণনৃত্য (অসভ্য জাতীয় লোকেরা যুদ্ধের প্রাক্কালে যে নৃত্য করিয়া থাকে)। **War-god**—যুদ্ধদেবতা, রণদেবতা [কার্ত্তিকেয় is the Hindu War-god]। **War-head**—টর্পেডো প্রভৃতির বিদারণশীল অগ্রভাগ—যাহা শান্তির সময় টর্পেডো চালনা অভ্যাস করার কালে অপসারিত করা হয়। **War horse**—যুদ্ধাশ্ব, রণতুরঙ্গম। **War-Office**—সামরিক কার্য্যালয়। **War-paint**—অসভ্যজাতীয় লোকেরা যুদ্ধযাত্রা কালে দেহ যে বর্ণে রঞ্জিত করিত। **War-path** — আমেরিকার আদিম অধিবাসিগণের সামরিক অভিযান ; উক্ত অভিযানের পথ। **War-ship**—যুদ্ধজাহাজ, রণপোত, সমরপোত, রণতরী। **War-song** — সমরসঙ্গীত, রণগীতি। **War-whoop** — আমেরিকার আদিম

অধিবাসিগণের রণকোলাহল। **War-worn**—সমরক্লান্ত, রণশ্রান্ত; সমরাভিজ্ঞ। **Holy war**—See HOLY. **Man-of-war**—See under MAN. **Private war**—পারিবারিক বিগ্রহ, এক রাষ্ট্রের লোক শাসনতন্ত্রের অনুমতি বিনা অপর রাষ্ট্রের উপর যে আক্রমণ করে। **Art of war**—সমরনীতি, রণনীতি। **Laws of war**—যুদ্ধকালে পালনীয় নিয়মনিচয়, রণবিধি। **Like an old war-horse**—Of a person excited by the reminescences of past life; গতজীবনের স্মৃতিদ্বারা উত্তেজিত। **Rights of war** — যে অধিকার বলে কতিপয় কার্য্য করা যায়—যাহা শান্তির কালে অবৈধ অথচ যুদ্ধের কালে বিধিসঙ্গত বলিয়া পরিগণিত হয়। **Secretary of War**—সমরসচিব, যুদ্ধসচিব। **Sinews of war**—যুদ্ধের জন্য আবশ্যক অর্থ, কোন উদ্দেশ্য সাধনের উপযোগী অর্থ। **The army or fleet is in a war footing**—পূর্ণসংখ্যক সৈন্যাদি সমন্বিত। **The dogs of war**—যুদ্ধজনিত উৎপাত। **To be or go on the war-path**—To be engaged in hostilities; সংগ্রামে প্রবৃত্ত হওয়া। **To declare war**—To announce that hostilities will be commenced; যুদ্ধ ঘোষণা করা। **To make or wage war**—To engage in war; যুদ্ধে প্রবৃত্ত হওয়া। **To put on the war paint**—To put on ceremonial costume; উৎসবাদি সমুচিত বেশভূষায় সজ্জিত হওয়া। **To roll back tide of war**—To repel an invasion; সৈন্যস্রোতের গতি প্রতিহত করা। **Tug of war**—See under TUG. **War of the elements**—প্রাকৃতিক বিপ্লব, ভীষণ ঝঞ্ঝাবাত, ভূতসংপ্লব। **War to the knife**—Struggle to the bitter end; শেষ পর্য্যন্ত যুদ্ধ, এক জন নিহত না হওয়া পর্য্যন্ত যুদ্ধ, মৃত্যুপণ করিয়া যুদ্ধ।

wār'-ble (-bl), *v. i.* & *t.* To sing in a trilling manner; কম্পিতস্বরে গান করা। ***Verb t.*** 1. To sing with sweetly flowing trilling notes; কম্পিতস্বরে গান করা। 2. To cause to quiver or vibrate; কম্পিত করা, স্পন্দিত করা। ***Noun.*** 1. A soft, sweet flow of melodious sounds; a trilling flexible melody; কূজন; কলালাপ, কলধ্বনি, কলসঙ্গীত। 2. A quivering or modulation of voice; স্বরকম্পন। **—bling-ly,** *adv.*

wār'-ble (-bl), *n.* 1. One of those small hard tumours produced by the heat of the saddle in travelling or by the uneasiness of its situation; জিনের ঘর্ষণাদি হেতু অশ্বের পৃষ্ঠে জাত একপ্রকার আঁচিল। 2. A small tumour caused by the larva of bot-fly on the back of horses, cattle, etc.; অশ্ব গবাদির পৃষ্ঠে একপ্রকার কীড়া দ্বারা যে ক্ষুদ্র অর্ব্বুদ উৎপন্ন হয়।

wār'-blêr, *n.* A song-bird; গায়ক পক্ষী।

ward (wärd), *n.* 1. The act of guarding a place; as, to keep watch or *ward*; রক্ষণ, অভিরক্ষণ। 2. Guardianship; "I must attend his majesty's command to whom I am now in *ward*"; অভিভাবকতা, রক্ষকতা। 3. (*Obs.*) Defence; protection; (অপ্রঃ) রক্ষা; আশ্রয়। 4. custody; confinement; "He put them in *ward* in the house of the captain of the guard"; রক্ষণাবেক্ষণ, জিম্মা; আটক। 5. A minor or person under guardianship; as, you will warn your *ward* not to bother me"; অভিভাবকের অধীন ব্যক্তি। 6. A division, district or quarter of a town; as, two commissioners are elected from *ward* No. I; নগরের বিভাগ, মহল্লা। 7. One of the apartments into which a hospital is divided; as, the eye-*ward*; আরোগ্যশালার বিভাগ। 8. A separate room or division in a prison; as, the female *ward*; কারাগৃহের স্বতন্ত্র বিভাগ বা কক্ষ। 9. A curved ridge of metal inside a lock which opposes an obstacle to the passage of a key which has not a corresponding notch; also the notch or slot in the whole or bit of a key in which the above-mentioned ridge fits when the key is applied; তালার অভ্যন্তরস্থ ধাতুর বক্র আলি—যদ্দারা যে চাবিতে ঐ বক্র খাঁজের অনুরূপ খাঁজ না থাকে তাহা বাধা প্রাপ্ত হয়; চাবির যে খাঁজের সহিত উক্ত আলি খাপ খায়। **Ward-mote**—নগরীর মহল্লার সভা। **Ward-room**—রণপোতের অধিনায়কের নিম্নবর্ত্তী কমিশন-প্রাপ্ত কর্ম্মচারিগণের কক্ষ।

wärd, *v. t.* 1. To defend; রক্ষা করা। 2. To fend off; to repel; as, to *ward* a blow; আটকান; প্রতিহত করা, প্রতিক্ষেপ করা।

wärd'-ĕn, *n.* 1. (*Archaic*) A watchman; প্রহরী। 2. Guardian; governor; অভিভাবক, তত্ত্বাবধায়ক; শাসনকর্ত্তা, শাসক। **—ship,** *n.*

wärd'-ĕn, *n.* A variety of winter pear; একপ্রকার শীতকালীন নাসপাতী।

wärd'-êr, *n.* 1. (*Archaic*) A sentinel; সান্ত্রী, পাহারাওয়ালা। 2. A staff of authority; শাসনদণ্ড। 3. A keeper of prisoners; কারাপ্রহরী, কারারক্ষী, কারারক্ষক; **—ess,** *n.* (*fem.*)

wärd'-ship, *n.* The office of a ward or keeper; guardianship; care; রক্ষকত্ব; অভিভাবকতা; তত্ত্বাবধান।

wāre, *n.* 1. Articles of specified manufacture viewed collectively, esp. earthen ware; নির্ম্মিত দ্রব্যসমূহ, বিশেষতঃ মৃদ্ভাণ্ডসমূহ। 2. Merchandise; পণ্যদ্রব্য। **Glass wares**—কাচের জিনিষ, বেলোয়ারী জিনিষ। **Hardware**—লোহার জিনিষ। **Small wares**—টুকটাক জিনিষ, চুটকী চাটকী জিনিষ। **Warehouse**—গুদামঘর, মালখান, আড়ৎ। (*Verb t.*) গুদামজাত করা। **Warehouse keeper**—আড়ৎদার।

wāre, *p. p.* Aware; জ্ঞাতসার, পরিজ্ঞাত, বিদিত, অবগত।

wāre, *v. t.* **1.** (*Imperat.*) Beware ; সাবধান হও, সাবধান। **2.** Avoid ; পরিহার কর।

wār'-fāre, *n.* **1.** Hostilites ; war ; যুদ্ধবিগ্রহ; যুদ্ধ। **2.** Struggle ; সংগ্রাম।

wār'-like, *adj.* **1.** Military ; সামরিক। **2.** Belligerent ; as, *warlike* state ; যুধ্যমান। **3.** Fond of war ; as, a *warlike* nation ; রণপ্রিয়, যুদ্ধপ্রিয়, সমরপ্রিয়। **4.** Befitting war or soldiers ; as, *warlike* preparation ; সমরসমুচিত, সৈনিকসমুচিত।

wār-lŏck, *n.* A sorcerer ; a wizard ; ঐন্দ্রজালিক ; মায়াবী, যাদুকর।

warm, *adj.* **1.** Having, or containing, heat in a moderate degree ; কিঞ্চিদুষ্ণ, ঈষদুষ্ণ, মন্দোষ্ণ, কবোষ্ণ, তপ্ত, গরম। **2.** Lively ; sprightly ; "Now *warm* in youth, now withering in thy bloom, lost in a convent's solitary gloom" ; সজীব, জীবন্ত ; চটুল স্ফূর্তিযুক্ত। **3.** Enthusiastic ; উৎসাহসম্পন্ন। **4.** Furious ; violent ; animated ; "We shall have *warm* work out" ; প্রচণ্ড, তুমুল, চণ্ড ; ভয়ঙ্কর, ভীষণ প্রবল ; উত্তেজিত। **5.** Moderately rich ; "They who had *warm* fortunes were always sure of getting good husbands" ; well-off ; অর্থশালী ; সঙ্গতিসম্পন্ন। **5.** Strong ; forcible ; কড়া ; চড়া। **6.** Irritable ; as, *warm* temper ; বদমেজাজী। **7.** Sympathetic ; as, a *warm* friend; emotional ; affectionate ; as, a *warn* heart ; বেদনশীল ; আবেগপূর্ণ ; স্নেহ-প্রবণ। **8.** Passionate ; amorous ; উত্তেজনাপূর্ণ ; কামুক। **9.** (Of colour) Producing a sense of warmth ; as, *warm* red or yellow ; (বর্ণ-সম্বন্ধে) উষ্ণতাব্যঞ্জক, উত্তেজক (রক্ত, পীত ও কমলা বর্ণের সম্পর্কে কথিত হয়। নীলবর্ণ ও নীলমিশ্রিত বর্ণসম্বন্ধে Cold শব্দ প্রয়োগ করা হইয়া থাকে)। **10.** Disagreeagble ; hot ; as, the place became too *warm* for him ; অপ্রীতিকর ; উষ্ণ, অতিষ্ঠ (*colloq.*)। **11.** Fresh ; টাটকা, তাজা। **12.** Indelicate ; অশ্লীলতার আভাসযুক্ত। **13.** Arduous ; as, *warm* task ; কঠিন, শ্রমসাধ্য। **14.** Hearty ; as, he was given a *warm* reception ; আন্তরিক। **Warm'-ing,** *n.* **–ly,** *adv.* **Warm-blood**—স্তন্যপায়ী জন্তু এবং পক্ষীর শোণিত—যাহার উষ্ণতা ৯৮° হইতে ১১২° ডিগ্রী পর্য্যন্ত হইয়া থাকে ; ভাবপ্রবণতা, প্রেমশীলতা। **Warm-blooded**—উষ্ণশোণিতবিশিষ্ট ; ভাবপ্রবণ ; অনুরাগী ; কামুক। **Warm-hearted**—সমবেদনা-শীল, আবেগপ্রবণ, স্নেহপ্রবণ, করুণাপ্রবণ। **Warm with**—(ইতরভাষায়) স্পিরিট, উষ্ণজল এবং শর্করার মিশ্র। **Warm-work**—ভীষণ সংঘর্ষ। **To make it** or **things warm for one**—To create strong feelings against him ; কাহারো পক্ষে অতিষ্ঠ করিয়া তোলা।

warm, *v. t.* & *i.* **1.** To make warm ; উষ্ণ করা, উত্তপ্ত করা। **2.** To engage ; "I formerly *warmed* my head with reading controversial writing" ; to excite ; as, wine *warms* the heart ; to enliven ; to flush ; নিরত করা, রত করা ; উত্তেজিত করা, উদ্দীপ্ত করা ; উজ্জীবিত করা ; উৎফুল্ল করা, অনুরাগদীপ্ত করা। **4.** To flog ; to beat ; বেত্রাঘাত করা ; প্রহার করা। **5.** (*Colloq.*) To occupy ; as, to *warm* a chair ; অধিকার করা। ***Verb i.*** **1.** To become warm or moderately heated ; উষ্ণ হওয়া, গরম হওয়া, তপ্ত হওয়া। **2.** To be inflamed, excited or quickened ; উদ্দীপিত হওয়া, প্রজ্জ্বলিত হওয়া, উদ্দীপ্ত হওয়া। **Warm'-er,** *n.* **1.** One who, or that which, warms ; উষ্ণতা-সঞ্চারক। **2.** An apparatus for warm ing a room, etc. ; কক্ষ প্রভৃতি উষ্ণ করার জন্য যন্ত্রবিশেষ। **Warm'-ing,** *n.* **A warming-pan** — অঙ্গারধানিকা ; কোন নাবালক বয়ঃপ্রাপ্ত হওয়ার পূর্ব্ব পর্য্যন্ত যে ব্যক্তি তদীয় স্থানে অধিষ্ঠিত থাকে।

warmth, *n.* **1.** The quality or state of being warm ; moderate or gentle heat ; উষ্ণতা ; উষ্মা, তাপ। **2.** Ardour ; zeal ; earnestness ; fervour ; enthusiasm ; intensity ; as, the *warmth* of love ; উদ্দীপনা ; আন্তরিকতা ; ব্যগ্রতা ; আগ্রহ ; উৎসাহ ; প্রাবল্য, প্রবলতা। **3.** Cordiality ; আন্তরিকতা। **4.** Vigour ; strong feeling ; তেজঃ ; উষ্ণভাব। **5.** (*Paint.*) A glowing effect such as is produced by the use of warm colours ; (চিত্রণ) রক্ত, পীত কমলাবর্ণ প্রভৃতি দ্বারা যে জ্বলন্তভাব উৎপাদিত হয়।

wārn, *v. t.* **1.** To give notice of probable danger or evil that may be avoided ; to admonish ; সতর্ক করা ; সাবধান করা। **2.** To bid ; আদেশ দেওয়া। **3.** To advise ; উপদেশ দেওয়া।

wārn'-ing, *n.* **1.** The act of one who warns ; সতর্ক করণ। **2.** Previous notice "Somewhat too sudden sir, the *warning* is" ; পূর্ব্ববিজ্ঞাপন। **3.** A notice to quit given by an employer to a servant, or by a servant to an employer ; মনীব কর্ত্তৃক ভৃত্যকে বা ভৃত্য কর্ত্তৃক মনীবকে যে কার্য্যত্যাগ বা কার্য্য হইতে সরাইবার বিজ্ঞাপন দেওয়া হয়। **4.** A calling ; আহ্বান। **To take warning** — To mentally register danger ; বিপদের আভাস পাওয়া, প্রমাদ গণা।

wārp, *v. t.* & *i.* **1.** To turn or twist out of shape, or out of a straight direction by contraction ; দুমড়ান, মোচড়ান। **2.** To turn aside from the true direction ; "I have no private considerations to *warp* us in this controversy" ; to pervert ; প্রকৃত পথ হইতে বিচ্যুত করা ; বিকৃত করা। **3.** To cast the young prematurely ; অকালে প্রসব করা। **4.** (*Naut.*) To move a vessel by hauling on ropes attached to buoys, anchors, other ships, and the like ; বয়া, নোঙ্গর বা অন্য জাহাজে সংবদ্ধ কাছির সাহায্যে জাহাজ চালিত করা। **5.** (*Agric.*) To fertilize by artificial inundation ; (কৃষিবিদ্যা) কৃত্রিম উপায়ে পলি মিশ্রিত জল চালিত করিয়া উর্ব্বরতা সম্পাদন করা। 6. (*Weaving*) To arrange yarns on a warp-beam; টানা দেওয়া। ***Verb i.*** **1.** To turn, twist or to be twisted out of shape ; বাঁকিয়া যাওয়া, বক্র হওয়া, তুমড়ান। **2.** To turn from a straight or proper course ; to swerve ; সরলপথ হইতে চ্যুত হওয়া ; বিপথগামী হওয়া। **3.** To fly with a waving motion ; তরঙ্গায়িত গতিতে উড্ডীন হওয়া। **To wind upon a warp beam**—টানা হাটান।

warp, *n.* **1.** The thread extended lengthwise on the loom and crossed by the woof; টানা। **2.** The state of being warped or twisted; সরল পথ হইতে বিচ্যুতি। **3.** A premature casting of the young ; অকালে শাবক প্রসব। **4.** A rope used in hauling or moving a vessel; জাহাজ টানিবার কাছি। **5.** Alluvial deposit ; পলি। **6.** Perversion or perverse inclination in mind ; মানসিক বিকৃতি, বিকৃত আসক্তি। **Warp and woof**—টানা পড়েন।

war'-rant (wŏr-ănt), *n.* **1.** Guaranty ; security ; a voucher ; a writing that authorises a person to receive money or other things ; প্রতিভূ ; জামিন ; প্রমাণপত্র ; কোন ব্যক্তিকে টাকা বা অন্য কোনরূপ বস্তু দেওয়ার জন্য ক্ষমতাপত্র। **2.** Authorisation ; sanction ; justification ; right ; ক্ষমতার্পণ ; মঞ্জুর ; ন্যায্যতাপাদন ; ক্ষমতা। **3.** A precept authorising an officer to seize a person or property ; গ্রেপ্তার বা ক্রোকের পরওয়ানা। **4.** (*Mil. or Nav.*) A writ or authority inferior to commission; কমিশন অপেক্ষা নিম্নতর নিয়োগ-পত্র। **Distress warrant**—ক্রোকের পরওয়ানা। **Search warrant**—খানাতাল্লাসির পরওয়ানা। **Warrant-officer**—কমিশন্ প্রাপ্ত কর্ম্মচারী অপেক্ষা নিম্নতরশ্রেণীর কর্ম্মচারী। **Warrant of arrest**—গ্রেপ্তারী পরওয়ানা। **Warrant of commitment**—যে পরওয়ানা দ্বারা কোন লোককে কারাগারে দেওয়া হয়।

war'-rant (wŏr-ănt), *v. t.* **1.** To give an assurance or guarantee ; প্রতিভূ দেওয়া, জামিন দেওয়া। **2.** To support by authority or proof ; প্রমাণ বা প্রামাণ্য উক্তি দ্বারা সমর্থন করা। **3.** To furnish sufficient grounds or evidence; to justify ; "Reason *warranted* it, and we may safely receive it" ; উপযুক্ত কারণ বা প্রমাণ প্রদর্শন করা ; ন্যায্যতা প্রতিপাদন করা। **4.** To answer for genuineness ; কোন জিনিষ খাঁটি হইবে বলিয়া দায়ী থাকা। **4.** To assert as certain ; নিশ্চয় করিয়া বলা। **5.** (*Law*) To secure to a grantee, an estate granted ; (আইন) গ্রহীতাকে প্রদত্ত সম্পত্তিতে অধিকারিরূপে প্রতিষ্ঠিত করা। **—a-ble,** *adj.* **—er,** *n.*

war'-ran-tŷ (wŏr-an-), *n.* **1.** Security; জামিন। **2.** Any promise express or implied by law (according to circumstances) from a vendor to a purchaser, that the thing sold is the vendor's to sell and is good or fit for use as the purchaser intends to make of it ; বিক্রেতা বিক্রেয় জিনিষের প্রকৃত স্বত্বাধিকারী এবং ঐ জিনিষ উৎকৃষ্ট ও ক্রেতা যে কার্য্যে ব্যবহার করিতে চায় উহা তাহার উপযোগী এই মর্ম্মে বিক্রেতা ক্রেতাকে যে উক্ত করে বা তাহার সহিত যে চুক্তিতে আবদ্ধ হয়, নিশ্চিতিপত্র। **3.** (*Insurance Law*) A statement or engagement expressly or impliedly made in a policy by the party insured, that a certain fact relating to the subject of insurance or the risk exists or shall exist, or that some act relating thereto it has been done or shall be done ; (বীমা আইন) বীমা বা (বীমার) দায়সংক্রান্ত কোনও বিষয় বর্ত্তমানে আছে বা ভবিষ্যতে হইবে, এবং তৎসম্বন্ধে কোন কার্য্য করা হইয়াছে বা হইবে এই মর্ম্মে বীমাকারী বীমাপত্রে যে উক্তি লিপিবদ্ধ করে, নিয়মলিপি। **4.** A promise or covenant by deed, made by the bargainer, for himself and his heirs, to warrant or secure the bargainee and his heirs against all men in the enjoymnet of an estate or other things granted ; যে প্রতিজ্ঞাপত্র বা চুক্তিপত্র দ্বারা চুক্তিকারী এবং তদীয় উত্তরাধিকারিগণ যে ব্যক্তির অনুকূলে উক্ত প্রতিজ্ঞাপত্র ও চুক্তিপত্র সম্পাদন করা হয় তাহাকে এবং তদীয় উত্তরাধিকারিগণকে কোন সম্পত্তি বা অন্যদত্ত বস্তুর ভোগ দখলের অধিকার প্রদান করিয়া থাকে।

war'-ren (wŏr-ĕn), *n.* **1.** A place privileged by prescription or grant from the king, for keeping certain beast and fowls ; পক্ষী বা পশু রাখার জন্য রাজার নিকট হইতে প্রাপ্ত ভূমি, পশুপক্ষিরক্ষণ ভূমি। **2.** A piece of ground for the breeding and preservation of rabit ; যে ভূমিতে শশক পালন করা হয়, শশকভূমি।

war'-ri-or (wŏr-yĕr *or* wŏr-ĭ-ĕr), *n.* & *adj.* A soldier ; যোদ্ধা, যোধ, বীর, শূর। ***Adj.*** Martial ; সামরিক। **Warrior ant**—একজাতীয় পিপীলিকা — যাহারা অপর জাতীয় পিপীলিকাকে দাসে পরিণত করে।

wart, *n.* **1.** A firm hard excrescence found chiefly on the hand ; আঁচিল, উপমাংস, চর্ম্মকীল, মাষক (সাঃ পঃ), মাংসল-বৃদ্ধি (ঐ), কচ্ছপী (সুশ্রুঃ)। **2.** (*Bot.*) A hardened protuberance on the surface of plants ; (উদ্ভিদ্‌বিদ্যা) উপবৃদ্ধি। **Wart'-y,** *adj.* **Wart-grass, Wart-weed**—বিভিন্ন জাতীয় গুল্ম—যাহার রস আঁচিল সারাইবার জন্য ব্যবহৃত হইয়া থাকে। **Wart-hog**—আফ্রিকাদেশীয় একজাতীয় শূকর।

wā'-rŷ, *adj.* Cautious ; circumspect ; "It behoveth our words to be *wary* and few" ; সাবধান, হুঁসিয়ার ; চৌকস। **—ri-ly,** *adv.*

was (wŏz), *p. t.* of BE.

wash (wŏsh), *v. t.* & *i.* **1.** To cleanse by ablution ; to free from impurities or foreign matter by dipping, rubbing or passing through water ; ধৌত করা, ধোয়া ; প্রক্ষালিত করা, কাচা। **2.** To purify ; বিশুদ্ধ করা, নির্ম্মল করা। **3.** To cover with a watery or thin coat of colour ; to tint lightly and thinly ; পাতলা রঙ্গের পোছ দেওয়া ; ফিকে রঙ্গে রঞ্জিত করা। **4.** To separate, as gold, from the earthy and lighter matters, by the action of water ; জলদ্বারা ধৌত করিয়া মৃত্তিকা প্রভৃতি হইতে স্বর্ণ পৃথক করা। **5.** To perform the business of cleansing cloth in water ; কাপড় কাচা, বস্ত্র ধৌত করা। **6.** To overwhelm and sweep away or carry off as by a rush of water ; to lave ; as, a shore *washed* by waves ; জলপ্রবাহ দ্বারা ভাসাইয়া নেওয়া ; প্লাবিত করা। **7.** To overlay with a thin coat of metal ; as, *washed* with gold ; ধাতুর পাতলা পাত বা তবক দ্বারা আচ্ছাদিত করা। **8.** To moisten ; as roses *washed* with dew ; আর্দ্র করা, সিক্ত করা। ***Verb i.*** **1.** To perform the act of ablution ; হস্ত প্রক্ষালন করা। **2.** To clean anything by rubbing or dipping in water ; ধৌত করা। **3.** To bear the operation of being washed without injury ; to bear washing without loss of colour ; ধোয়ায় কোন প্রকার নষ্ট না হওয়া ; ধোয়ায় রঙ্গ না উঠা, ধোয়ায় টি কা। **4.** To be worn away by the action of water ; জলের ক্রিয়া দ্বারা ক্ষয় প্রাপ্ত হওয়া। **Wash'-a-ble,** *adj.* **Washed out**—বিবর্ণ, রক্তবর্ণ। **To wash one's dirty linen to the public**—See LINEN. **To wash one's hands**—To decline responsibility ; কোন বিষয়ে দায়িত্ব গ্রহণে অস্বীকৃত হওয়া। **To wash up**—To clean table utensils after use ; ভোজনের পর বাসনপত্র পরিষ্কার করা

wash (wŏsh), *n.* & *adj.* **1.** The act of one who washes ; as, you must get a *wash* ; ধাবন, প্রক্ষালন। **2.** The act of washing the clothes of a family ; কাপড় কাচন, চেলনির্ণেজন (মঃ সং)। **3.** quantity of cloth washed or to be washed at once ; একবারে যে পরিমাণ কাপড় ধৌত করা হয়, কাচিবার কাপড়। **4.** The shallowest part of a river or arm of the sea ; a bog ; নদী বা সাগর শাখার সংকীর্ণতম অংশ ; বিল। **5.** The visible or audible motion of agitated water ; waves caused by a passing vessel ; আন্দোলিত জলরাশির গতি বা গর্জ্জন ; চলন্ত জাহাজ কর্ত্তৃক জনিত কল্লোল। **6.** Alluvial matter ; পলি। **7.** A bog ; বিল। **8.** A cosmetic ; a lotion ; অঙ্গরাগ ; ঔষধমিশ্রিত জল। **9.** The fermented wort from which the spirit is extracted ; যে অন্তরুৎসিক্ত অঙ্কুরিত যবের ফাণ্ট হইতে সুরাসার নিষ্কর্ষিত করা হয়। **10.** The blade of an oar or the thin part that enters water ; দাঁড়ের ফলক অথবা যে পাতল অংশ জলে প্রবিষ্ট হয়। **11.** A colour spread or floated thinly over picture ; চিত্রের উপর রঙ্গের অতি পাতল পোঁচ। **12.** Kitchen water and scraps given to pigs ; শূকরদিগকে রান্নাঘরের যে ময়লা জল ও খাদ্যের টুকরা ভোজন করিতে দেওয়া হয়, রান্নাঘরের ধোয়ানি। **13.** A thin, weak or inferior liquid food ; as, this tea is mere *wash* ; পাতল, অপকৃষ্ট এবং অনুগ্র তরল খাদ্য। **14.** A thin coat of metal applied on anything for beauty or preservation ; কোন জিনিষ রক্ষার জন্য বা সুন্দর করার জন্য উহাকে যে পাতল ধাতু র পাত দ্বারা মোড়া হয়। **15.** (*Obs.*) Urine ; (অপ্রঃ) মূত্র (পূর্ব্বে ইংলণ্ডে মূত্র দ্বারা বস্ত্র ধৌত করা হইত।) ***Adj.*** Capable of being washed without injury ; washable ; as, *wash* clothes ; নষ্ট না হইয়া ধৌত হওয়ার যোগ্য, কাচিবার যোগ্য। **Wash-board**—ধোপার পাট। **Wash-boiler**—যে পাত্রে কাচিবার কাপড় সিদ্ধ করা হয়। **Wash-bottle**—তরল পদার্থের অভ্যন্তরে চালনা দ্বারা গ্যাস প্রভৃতি শোধনের জন্য যন্ত্রবিশেষ, প্রক্ষালন-বোতল (হিঃ কোঃ)। **Wash-bowl**—যে পাত্রে হস্তমুখাদি প্রক্ষালনের জল থাকে, প্রক্ষালনপাত্র। **Wash-cloth**—থালা প্রভৃতি মুছিবার জন্য কাপড়ের টুকরা, মার্জ্জনী। **Wash-hand-basin**—হস্তপ্রক্ষালনপাত্র। **Wash-hand-stand**—হস্তপ্রক্ষালনপাত্র রাখার জন্য বৈঠক, হস্তপ্রক্ষালনমঞ্চ। **Wash-house**—ধোলাইখানা, রজকালয়, রজকাগার। **Wash-leather**—সেময় চর্ম্ম বা তদনুরূপ পাতল চর্ম্ম। **Wash-tub**—যে গামলায় কাপড় প্রভৃতি কাচা হয়।

wash'-ĕr (wŏsh-), *n.* **1.** One who washes ; প্রক্ষালক। **2.** A ring of metal, leather, or other material used to relieve friction, or to secure tightness of joints ; সন্ধিস্থান দৃঢ় করার জন্য বা ঘর্ষণজনিত ক্ষয় হ্রাস করার জন্য ঐ স্থানে যে ধাতু, চর্ম্ম বা অন্য কোন কিছুর আংটা ব্যবহৃত হয়। **3.** A machine for washing ; প্রক্ষালনযন্ত্র। **Washerman**—রজক, ধোপা, চেলনির্ণেজক (মাঃ সং)। **Washer-woman**—রজকী, ধোপানী।

wash'-ing (wŏsh-), *n.* **1.** The act of one who washes ; প্রক্ষালন। **2.** The clothes or other articles washed or to be washed at one time ; একবারে কাচিবার কাপড়, একবারে যে পরিমাণ কাপড় কাচা হয়। **3.** A thin covering or coat ; পাতল আবরণ। **4.** The results or product of the washing of ores ; খনিজবিমিশ্রধাতু ধৌত করার পর যে স্বর্ণাদি ধাতু পাওয়া যায়। **A washing book**—ধোপার হিসাবের খাতা। **Washing-bottle**—অবষেক বোতল (হিঃ কোঃ)। **Washing-fluid**—অবষেক (হিঃ কোঃ)।

Wāsh-ing-tō'-ni-ȧ, *n.* A Californian genus of ornamental palms ; কালিফোর্নিয়া প্রদেশে জাত একপ্রকার শোভাসাধক তালজাতীয় বৃক্ষের "গণ" ।

wash'-ȳ (wŏsh-), *adj.* 1. (Of liquid food) Too watery ; as, *washy* soup; (তরলখাদ্যসম্বন্ধে) অতিশয় পানসে । 2. Liable to sweat profusely from slight exertion ; সামান্য পরিশ্রমেই প্রচুর ঘর্ম্মনিঃসরণশীল । 3. Lacking vigour ; ওজস্বিতাহীন, নিস্তেজ ।

wasp (wŏsp), *n.* An insect capable of stinging severely ; বোলতা, বরটা, [Syn. গন্ধোলি, বরলা, বরলী, ক্ষুদ্রা, ক্রূঢ়া, ক্ষুদ্র বর্ব্বলা কোঠাগারিক (সুশ্রুঃ), কোঠাগারী (ঐ) । **Wasp-bee, Wasp-beetle, Wasp-fly**—বিভিন্ন প্রকার বরটা জাতীয় কীট । **Wasp-waisted**—ক্ষীণকটি । **Wasp of Twickenham**—ইংরেজ কবি পোপ ।

wasp'-ish (wŏsp-), *adj.* Irritable ; petulant ; as a *waspish* and hot man ; খিটখিটে ; বদমেজাজী, কোপনস্বভাব । **—ly,** *adj.* **—ness** *n.*

wȧs'-sail (wŏs-sĕl), *n.* & *v. i.* 1. Drinking bout ; মদ্যপানোৎসব, মদের বৈঠক । 2. The liquor used on such occasions, especially about Christmas or the New year ; এইরূপ বৈঠকে যে মদ্য ব্যবহৃত হয় — বিশেষতঃ খ্রীষ্টমাসপর্ব্ব এবং নিউইয়র্সডেতে যে মদ্য ব্যবহৃত হয় । ***Verb i.*** To hold a merry drinking ; পানোৎসব করা । **—er,** *n.* **Wassail-bowl, Wassail-cup**—উক্তরূপ পানোৎসবে ব্যবহৃত মদ্যপূর্ণ পেয়ালা ।

wast (wŏst), *v. t.* See BE.

wāst'-āge, *n.* Loss by waste ; amount wasted ; ক্ষতি, অপচয় ; কম্‌তি, ঝড়তিপড়তি ।

wāste, *adj.* 1. Devastated ; ravaged ; ruined ; desolated ; উচ্ছন্ন ; লুণ্ঠিত ; ধ্বংসপ্রাপ্ত ; জনমানবহীন । 2. Uncultivated ; as, *waste* land ; অকৃষ্ট, অকর্ষিত, পতিত, অনাবাদী । 3. Monotonous ; as, the *waste* periods of history ; একঘেয়ে । 4. Dismal ; নিরানন্দ, বিষাদাচ্ছন্ন । 5. Rejected ; পরিত্যক্ত, বাজে, পয়মাল (*colloq.*), বরবাদ (*ib.*) । **Waste paper**—বাজে কাগজ, ফাস কাগজ । **Waste paper basket**—ফাস কাগজের ঝুড়ি, পরিত্যক্ত কাগজের ঝুড়ি । **Waste-land** — পতিত ভূমি, খিল, অনাবাদী ভূমি । **To lay waste**—To devastate ; ধ্বংস করা, উচ্ছন্ন করা । **To lie waste**—To lie uncultivated ; পতিত থাকা, অনাবাদী থাকা ।

wāste, *v. t.* & *i.* 1. To devastate ; ধ্বংস করা, উচ্ছন্ন করা । 2. To diminish by continued loss ; "*Waste* huge stones by little water drops" ; ক্রমশঃ ক্ষয় করা । 3. To spend vainly, foolishly or uselessly ; "I *wasted* time and now time doth *waste* me" ; অপব্যয় করা, উড়াইয়া দেওয়া । ***Verb i.*** To grow less or diminish in bulk, substance, strength, value or the like ; ক্ষয় প্রাপ্ত হওয়া, ক্ষয় পাওয়া, ক্ষয়িত হওয়া, নষ্ট হওয়া । **Waste not want not**—অপব্যয় করিও না—অভাবও হইবে না ।

wāste, *n.* 1. A desert ; waste region ; "His tall mill that *whistled* on the waste" ; dreary scenery ; মরুভূমি ; অনুর্ব্বর স্থান ; অপ্রসন্ন দৃশ্য । 2. A squandering ; অপব্যয় । 3. The refuse of a factory or shop ; কারখানা বা দোকানের আবর্জ্জনা । 4. A contrivance for allowing the escape of surplus water ; অতিরিক্ত জলনির্গমনের জন্য ব্যবস্থা বিশেষ । 5. (*Law*) Damage done to houses, lands, fences, woods, by a tenant ; প্রজাকর্ত্তৃক ভূমি, গৃহ, বৃতি, বন, প্রভৃতির যে ক্ষতি করা হয় । 6. Diminution by wear and tear ; "Beauty's *waste* hath in the world an end" ; ক্ষয় । 7. Waste material or food ; refuse ; বাজে জিনিষ, পরিত্যক্ত খাদ্য ; জঞ্জাল, আবর্জ্জনা । **Waste-book**—জাবেদা খাতা, দোকানের খসড়া খাতা । **Waste-basket**—আবর্জ্জনা রাখার জন্য ঝুড়ি, অকেজো কাগজ রাখার ঝুড়ি । **Waste-pipe** — পরীবাহ, উচ্ছিষ্ট জলনালী, অপরিষ্কার বা অতিরিক্ত জলবাহী নল । **A waste of water**—বিপুল জলরাশি । **To run to waste**—To be wasted ; নষ্ট হওয়া ।

wāst'-ĕr, *n.* 1. One who squanders ; অপব্যয়ী । 2. A devastater ; ধ্বংসকারক । 3. An imperfection in the wick of a candle causing it to waste ; মোমবাতির শলিতার একপ্রকার দোষ—যাহাতে উহা শীঘ্র ক্ষয়প্রাপ্ত হয় । 4. An article spoiled or flawed in manufacture ; নির্ম্মাণকালে নষ্টপ্রাপ্ত বা ত্রুটিত বস্তু । 5. An animal that does not thrive, or that is thin ; কৃশজন্তু যে জন্তু পুষ্টি লাভ করে না ।

wāste'-fûl, *adj.* 1. Extravagant ; অমিতব্যয়ী, অপব্যয়ী । 2. Destructive ; ruinous ; as, *wasteful* practices ; ধ্বংসকারক ; মারাত্মক ।

wāste'-lĕss, *adj.* Yielding little or no waste ; ক্ষয়াসহ, অক্ষর ।

wās'-trĕl, *n.* 1. A thing spoiled in making ; যে বস্তু নির্ম্মাণকালে নষ্টপ্রাপ্ত হয় । 2. A neglected child ; a street arab ; অনাদৃত শিশু ; যে অভিভাবকশূন্য বালকবালিকা রাস্তায় ঘুরিয়া বেড়ায় । 3. A good-for-nothing fellow ; নচ্ছার লোক, অপদার্থ লোক । 4. A squanderer ; অপব্যয়ী । 5. Same as WASTER 5.

watch (wŏch), *n.* 1. (*Rare*) Wakefulness ; জাগরণ । 2. Vigilance ; সাবহিত দৃষ্টি, নজর । 3. A sentry ; "To him that cannot so much as see, to discharge the office of *watch*" ; a body of watchmen ; সান্ত্রী, প্রহরী, রক্ষী ; প্রহরিবর্গ । 4. The time during which a guard does his duty ; a definite division of time ; পাহারার কাল ; নির্দ্দিষ্ট কালবিভাগ । 5. The place where a guard is posted ; যে স্থানে

প্রহরীগণকে স্থাপন করা হয়। 6. A small timepiece ; ক্ষুদ্রঘড়ী, টেঁক ঘড়ী, জেব ঘড়ী। 7. (*Falconry*) A flock as of nightingales ; বুল বুল প্রভৃতির দল। 8. (*Naut.*) The period of time occupied by each part of a ship's crew alternately while on duty ; (নৌবিদ্যা) জাহাজের মাল্লাগণ পর্য্যায়ক্রমে যে সময় ব্যাপিয়া প্রহরা দেয়। **Watch'-ful,** *adj.* Vigilant ; cautious ; সজাগ, হুঁসিয়ার ; সতর্ক, সাবধান, সাবহিত। **Watch'-ful-ness,** *n.* The state of being watchful ; সতর্কতা, সাবধানতা, খবরদারী (*colloq.*)। **Watch-bell**—জাহাজের বৃহৎ ঘণ্টা—যাহা প্রতি অর্দ্ধ ঘণ্টা অন্তর বাদিত করা হয়। **Watch-bill** — জাহাজের যে সকল কর্ম্মচারী ও মাল্লাগণ প্রহরীর কার্য্যে নিযুক্ত হয় তাহাদের তালিকা (এইরূপ তালিকার প্রতি ব্যক্তি কোন স্থানে থাকিয়া পাহারা দিবে তাহার উল্লেখ থাকে।) **Watch-case**—জেব ঘড়ী রাখার আধার ঘটিকাপুটক। **Watch-dog**—বাড়ীতে চোর ডাকাত প্রবেশ করিলে যে কুকুর চীৎকার করিয়া গৃহস্বামীকে জাগরিত করে, প্রহরীকুকুর, গৃহরক্ষী কুকুর। **Watch-fire** — রাত্রিকালে দুর্গাদিতে যে আলো প্রজ্বালিত রাখা হয়। **Watch-glass**—টেঁকঘড়ীর সম্মুখের কাচের ঢাকনি। **Watch-house** — প্রহরীদের গৃহ ; যে গৃহে প্রহরিগণ রাত্রের পাহারায় যাইবার পূর্ব্বে একত্র হয়। **Watch-key**—টেঁকঘড়ীর চাবি। **Watch-maker**—ঘটিকা-যন্ত্র নির্ম্মাতা, ঘটিকাযন্ত্র মেরামতকারী। **Watchman** — রক্ষী, প্রহরী, রক্ষক। **Watch-night**—বৎসরের শেষ রাত্রি। এই রাত্রে মেথডিষ্ট সম্প্রদায়ের লোকেরা নানারূপ ধর্ম্মসংগীত, উপাসনা প্রভৃতি করিয়া থাকে। **Watch-oil** — টেঁক ঘড়ীতে দেওয়ার জন্য একপ্রকার তৈল। **Watch-pocket** — টেঁকঘড়ীর জেব। **Watch spring**—টেঁক ঘড়ীর দম। **Watch-stand**—টেঁক ঘড়ী রাখার জন্য ক্ষুদ্র স্তম্ভ। **Watch-tower**—যে বুরুজ হইতে সান্ত্রীগণ পাহারা দেয়। **Watch-word** — মূলমন্ত্র ; প্রহরীর সঙ্কেতবাক্য ; কোন সম্প্রদায়বিশেষের বাক্য, সঙ্কেতবাক্য। **In the watches of the night**—While awake ; জাগ্রত অবস্থায়। **To be on the watch**—To be careful ; সতর্ক থাকা, সাবধান থাকা, হুঁসিয়ার থাকা। To wait for some event ; কোন ঘটনার জন্য প্রতীক্ষা করা। **To keep watch and ward**—To watch day and night ; দিবারাত্র পাহারা দেওয়া। **To pass as a watch in the night**—To be soon forgotten ; শীঘ্রই বিস্মৃত হওয়া। **Watch and ward**—প্রহরী পরিবর্ত্তন, পর্য্যায়ক্রমে পাহারা দেওন।

Watch (wŏch), *v. i.* & *t.* 1. To be awake ; জাগিয়া থাকা। 2. To give heed ; মনোযোগ দেওয়া, মন দেওয়া। 3. To keep watch or guard ; প্রহরা দেওয়া। 4. To be expectant ; "They that *watch* for the morning" ; প্রতীক্ষা করা। 5. (Of a buoya) To float on the surface of water ; (বয়া সম্বন্ধে) জলে ভাসা। *Verb t.* 1. To guard ; রক্ষা করা। 2. To observe the motions or actions for any purpose ; as, to *watch* a suspect ; গতিবিধি লক্ষ্য করা। 3. (*Naut.*) To divide into, or assign to watch ; (নৌবিদ্যা) প্রহরা বিভাগ করা, প্রহরা নির্দ্দেশ করিয়া দেওয়া।

watch'-êr (wŏch-), *n.* 1. One who watches ; প্রহরী। 2. One who keeps a vigil ; যে ব্যক্তি জাগিয়া থাকে। 3. A spy ; a scout ; গোয়েন্দা ; চর।

wa'-têr, *n., v. t.* & *i.* 1. The liquid which, when pure, is transparent, colourlees, and destitute of taste or smell, and which is essential to the support of vegetable and animal life ; জল, সলিল, নীর, অম্বু, বারি, উদক, জীবন, অপ, আপ, তোয়, পয়ঃ, অম্ভঃ। [*syn.* মেঘপুষ্প, ঘনরস, কমল (cf. কমলশোভিত কিবা সরসীকমল,—সদ্ভাব শতক), কীলাল, অমৃত, জীবন, ভুবন, বন, পাথ, ক্ষীর, অম্বু, সরিল, কবন্ধ, অভ্রপুষ্প, ঘৃত, কুশ, বিষ, কাণ্ড, ব্যোম, সদন, সম্বল, পুষ্কর, সর্ব্বতোমুখ, অর্ণ, পানীয়, সল, জড়, কম্, অন্ধ, কমন্ধ, উদ, দক নার, শম্বর, পীপ্পল, সবর, সর, কৃপীট, চন্দ্রোরস, কর্ব্বুর সম্ব, ইরা, বাজ, তামর, স্যন্দন, কম্বল, জলপীথ, ক্ষর, ঋত, উর্জ্জ, কোমল, সোম (The Vedic names of water :—ক্ষোদ, ক্ষদ্ম, নভঃ, অম্ভ, কবন্ধ, ঘৃত, মধু, পুরীষ, পিপ্পল, ক্ষীর, রেতঃ, কশ, জন্ম, বৃবূক, বুস, তুগ্র্যা, হুক্ষেম, ধরুণ, বর্ব্বুর, সুরা, অরবিন্দ, জামি, ধ্বস্মন্বতু, অহি, ক্ষপ, আয়ুধ, তৃপ্তি, স্রোত, অক্ষর, উদক, রহস, সহ, ভেষজ, রস, পয়ঃ, ক্ষত্র, সুপ, ওজঃ, যহ, শব, ভুত, যাদু, শুভ, আব, মহৎ, আপ, ভবিষ্যৎ, ভুবন, সর্ণীক, মহ, যশঃ, ব্যোম, গহন, সতান, স্বৃতিক, অন্ন, ঈম, গম্ভন, গভীর, যোনি, ঋত, সদন, সদ্ম, হবি, নীর, সত্য, ঋতস্যযোনি, অক্ষিত, সর্ব্ব, পূর্ণ, সৎ, রয়ি, অপঃ, সর্পি, নাম, বর্হি, হেম, ইন্দু, অমৃত, পবিত্র, বপু, অশ্ব, শম্বর, স্বর্গ, স্বঃ, কৃপীট, তূপ, তোর, অম্বু, বারি, স্বধা, তেজ, শুক্র, জলায়, জল)।] [Arab. *maa*; Pers. *ab*; Assyr. *hu*; Burm. *ya*; Chin. *yuh-yih, shwui, liu-shui* ; Germ. *eu, wasser* ; Malay. *ayar, ayar-tawar* ; Scyth. *ku* ; Tam. *tanni* ; Teleg. *neru* ; Tib. *chu* ; Anglo-Saxon *wæter* ; Icel. *vatn* ; Russ. *voda* ; Gr. *hydor* ; Lat. *unda*; Swed. *vatten* ; Dan. *vand.*] 2. The limpidity and lustre of a precious stone, esp. diamond; as, a diamond of the first *water* ; lustre of a precious stone ; হীরক প্রভৃতির পাণি ; মণির স্বচ্ছতা এবং দীপ্তি, কণ, পাণি। 3. Rain ; "By sudden floods and fall of *waters* Buckingham's army is persed and scattered" ; বৃষ্টি, জল (*colloq.*) [cf. জল এলো]। 3. A wave ; flood ; ঢেউ ; বন্যা। 4. Tears ; "Then they seemed all to be glad, but the *water* stood in their eyes" ; অশ্রুজল। 5. Urine ; as, to make *water* ; মূত্র। 6. (*Commr.*) Stock issued without any provision being made for the payment of interest thereon ; (বাণিজ্য) যে কোম্পানীর কাগজের উপর কোনরূপ সুদ প্রদানের ব্যবস্থা করা হয় নাই। 7. A distilled fluid, essence or the like ; পরিস্রুত তরলপদার্থ,পুষ্পসার বা তদ্বৎ বস্তু। 8. A wavy lustrous pattern or decoration such as is imparted to linen, silk, metals, etc.; রেশম, ধাতুফলক, প্রভৃতির উপর যে দীপ্ত ঢেউএর মত চটক দেওয়া হয়। *Verb t.* 1. To irriagate ; as, to *water* land ; to overflow with water ; জলসেচন করা ; জলপ্লাবিত করা। 2. To supply with water for drink; as, to *water* cattle ; to cause to drink ; পানীয় জল সরবরাহ করা; পান করান। 3. To dilute ; জল মিশাইয়া পাতলা করা। 4. To soak or steep in water.; জলে সিক্ত করা, জলে ডুবান। 5. To subject to calendering process, as silk, etc. in order to make it exhibit a variety of undulated reflections and plays of light ; to diversify, as with waves ; "Velvet and *watered* silk" ; রেশমী কাপড় প্রভৃতি এরূপভাবে নরাজ করা—যাহাতে উহার উপর প্রতিফলিত আলোকে নানারকমের ঢেউ খেলে এইরূপ দেখায়; ঢেউতোলা। 6. (*Commr.*) To add stock to that already issued by a company or state, without making any additional provision for the payment of interest on the same · অতিরিক্ত সুদের ব্যবস্থা না করিয়া কোন সমবায় বা রাজ্য কর্তৃক প্রচারিত কোম্পানীর কাগজ বা কোন সমবায়ের মূলধন বৃদ্ধি করা। *Verb i.* 1. To shed water or liquid matter ; as, his eyes began to *water* ; জল বা অন্য কোন তরল পদার্থ পাত করা। 2. To make water ; প্রস্রাব করা। 3. To gather saliva as a symptom of appetite ; to have a longing desire ; as, his mouth *watered* at the sight of those dainty things ; মুখে জল আসা, জিভে জল সরা ; আকুলভাবে চাওয়া। 5. To weaken anything by, or as by, addition of water ; জল মিশাইয়া পাতলা করা, জলের মত কোন কিছু মিশাইয়া পাতলা করা। 6. To get or take in water ; জল নেওয়া। 7. To drink water ; জল পান করা। **—y,** *adj.* 1. Containing too much water ; over-moist ; অতিরিক্ত জলপূর্ণ, সলিলাত্মক (হিঃ কোঃ), জলীয় (ঐ) ; অতিরিক্ত আর্দ্র। 2. Resembling water ; thin or transparent like water ; জলবৎ ; জলবৎ স্বচ্ছ এবং পাতল। 4. Tasteless ; insipid স্বাদহীন ; পানসে। 5. Tearful ; as, *watery* eyes ; অশ্রুপূর্ণ, অশ্রুজলপূর্ণ, সজল। 6. Running with any liquid secretion or humour ; লালা প্রভৃতি স্রাবী। **Blue water**—নীলাম্বুরাশি, সমুদ্র। **Cup of cold water**—বদান্যতার চিহ্ন। **Hard water**—See HARD. কড়াপানি (হিঃ কোঃ), ভারি পানি (ঐ), কঠিন জল (সাঃ পঃ)। **Holy water**—See HOLY. **Mineral water**—See MINERAL. **Red water**—রক্তের ন্যায় লাল মূত্র। **Soft water**—নরম পানি (হিঃ কোঃ), হাল্কা পানি (ঐ), কোমল জল (সাঃ পঃ)। (Also see SOFT.) **Strong water**—পরিস্রুত মদ্যাদি। **Water-anchor**—Same as DRAG-ANCHOR. **Water-bailiff**—শুল্কাগারের যে কর্ম্মচারী বন্দরের জাহাজের ভিতরে অনুসন্ধান করে ; যাহাতে কেহ নদীর মৎস্য অন্যায়রূপে না ধরে—তদ্বিষয়ে যে কর্ম্মচারী লক্ষ্য রাখেন। **Water-bath**—জলযন্ত্র। **Water-bearer**—ভিস্তি। **Water-bed**—শয্যাক্ষত দ্বারা আক্রান্ত রোগীদের জন্য রবরের খোলবিশিষ্ট জলপূর্ণ গদি ; (অপ্রঃ) জাহাজের শয্যা। **Water-boatman**—একপ্রকার জলবাসী ছারপোকা। **Water-blister** — জলীয়-পদার্থপূর্ণ ফোস্কা। **Water-brash**—অজীর্ণ রোগবিশেষ—এই রোগে পুনঃ পুনঃ লালাস্রাব ও জল বমি হইতে থাকে। **Water-carriage** — জলপথে মাল বহন। **Water-cart**—রাজপথে জল প্রদানের জন্য শকট, জলের গাড়ী। **Water-carrier** — জলবাহ, উদবহ। **Water-caltrop**—পানিফল, শৃঙ্গাটক, জলকণ্টক। **Water-chestnut**—পাণিফল, শিঙ্গাড়া। **Water-chute**—জলে অবতরণের জন্য জলপ্রবাহ দ্বারা শ্লক্ষীকৃত প্রবণভাবে স্থাপিত কাষ্ঠফলকসমূহ, অবতরণী, জলাবতরণী। **Water-closet**—একপ্রকার পাইখানা — যাহাতে জলপ্রবাহের বেগে ময়লা পরিষ্কারের ব্যবস্থা থাকে, অবস্করমন্দির। **Water-colour**—যে রঙ্গ জলের সহিত মিশ্রিত করা হইয় থাকে; উক্তরূপ রঙ্গদ্বারা চিত্রিত আলেখ্য। **Watercourse**—জলপ্রণালী, জলপ্রবাহ জলনির্গম, জলনালী। **Water-cracker**—একপ্রকার বিস্কুট। **Water-cress**—একপ্রকার জলজ শাক, সুবাসরা। **Water-cure**—Same as HYDROPATHY. **Water-deity**—জলদেবতা। **Waterfall**—জলপ্রপাত, গিরিপ্রপাত। **Water-finder**—যে ব্যক্তি জলের অবস্থিতি নির্ণয়ার্থ অনুসন্ধানদণ্ড ব্যবহার করে। **Waterfowl**—জলচর পক্ষী ; জলকুক্কুট, ডাহুক, ডাক [Syn. দাত্যূহ, কালকণ্ঠক, অত্যূহ, দাত্যোহ, কালকণ্ঠ, মাসঙ্গ, শিতিকণ্ঠ, কচাটুর, কাকমদ্গু, জলকাক।] **Water-gate**—স্রোতোদ্বার। **Water-gauge**—কোন পাত্রস্থিত জলের গভীরতা-মাপক কাচনির্ম্মিত নলবিশেষ, জলমানযন্ত্র। **Water-hyacinth** — বিলাতী পানা, কচুরী, কস্তুরী, টগই, জর্ম্মণীপানা, জর্ম্মণী। **Water-ice**—সুরভিত এবং শর্করা মিশ্রিত তুষারীকৃত জল। **Water-inch**—এক ইঞ্চি চোঙ্গ দ্বারা ২৪ ঘণ্টায় অল্পতম চাপে যে পরিমাণ জল নির্গত হয়। **Water-jacket** — যন্ত্রের যে সকল অংশ শীতল রাখিতে হয়—তাহা আবরণের জন্য যে জলপূর্ণ আধার ব্যবহৃত হয়। **Water-junket**—Same as SAND-PIPER. **Water-lens**—একপ্রার জলপূর্ণ পরকলা যাহার নিম্নভাগ পিত্তল দ্বারা সমাচ্ছাদিত থাকে। **Water-level**—জলপৃষ্ঠ, জলধরাতল। **Water-lily**—কুমুদ, কহ্লার, সাফলা, শ্বেতোৎপল, কৈরব, চন্দ্রকান্ত, গর্দ্দভ, কুমুৎ, ধবলোৎপল, শশিকান্ত, শীতলক, ইন্দুকমল, চন্দ্রিকাম্বুজ। **Water-main** — জলের কলের প্রধান

চোঙ্গ। **Waterman** — মাঝি, দাঁড়ী। **Water-mark** — কাগজের উপর যে অনুজ্জ্বল চিহ্ন, রেখা, মুদ্রণ প্রভৃতি আলোকে ধরিলে সুপ্রকট হয়, জলছাপ। (*Verb t.*) উক্তরূপ চিহ্নে চিহ্নিত করা। **Water-meadow** — যে প্রান্তর জলপ্রবাহ প্লাবিত করিয়া উর্ব্বর রাখা হয়। **Water-melon**—See MELON. [Syn. তরম্বুজ (cf. জ্যৈষ্ঠে মাসি মহেশানি পৌর্ণমাস্যাং নিশার্দ্ধকে। তৃষ্ণাতুরা মহাকালী ভ্রমন্তী পিতৃকাননে। তজ্জ্ঞাত্বা ব্রহ্মণা তস্যৈ ফলং দত্তং তরম্বুজম্। তৎফলভক্ষণাৎ তৃপ্তা বরদাসি হরপ্রিয়া। যো মে দদ্যাৎ ফলং রম্যং স চিরায়ুশ্চতুর্যুগম্—ইত্যুত্তর কামাখ্যাতন্ত্রম।), নাটাম্র, ষড়রেখা, ষড়্মুখা, চেলাল, চিত্রফল, সুখাশ, রাজতেমিষ, লতাপনস, সেদু, সুখবাস, বৃহদ্‌গোল, শীর্ণবৃন্ত, কালিন্দক (সুশ্রুঃ), কালিন্দ]। **Water-mill** — বারিঘরট্ট, জলপ্রবাহচালিতযন্ত্র, জলযন্ত্র। **Water monkey**—জল শীতল রাখিবার জন্য একপ্রকার লম্বগল কুঁজো। **Water-nymph**—জলপরী,জলদেবতা। **Water-parting**—জলবাধ (সাঃ পঃ), সীমান্ত-রেখা (ঐ)। **Water-pipe**—পয়োনালী। **Water-pitcher**—কলসী, কুম্ভ। **Water-plane**—যে সমতল জাহাজের তলরেখার উপর দিয়া চলে। **Water-pot**—জলপাত্র, ধারক। **Waterproof**—জলাভেদ্য। **Water-pump**—দমকল। **Water-power**—জলপ্রবাহজনিত শক্তি, জলশক্তি, জলীয়শক্তি। **Water-rate**—জলের কল প্রভৃতি ব্যবহারের জন্য যে শুল্ক দিতে হয়, জলকর। **Water-reservoir**—দ্রোণী, দ্রোণ। **Watershed**—বিভিন্ন নদী, সমুদ্র, প্রভৃতিতে পতিত জলপ্রবাহসমূহের বিভেদরেখা, জলসীমা, জলবিভাজকক্ষেত্র, সীমান্তরেখা (সাঃ পঃ);

Water Shrew.

Water-shrew—একপ্রকার জলবাসী কাঁটাচুয়া। **Water-side** — নদী, সাগর, হ্রদ প্রভৃতির তীর। **Water-sign**—জলরাশি (মীন, কর্কট মকর)। **Water-skin** — জলপূর্ণ চর্ম্মপুটক। **Water-snake** — জলব্যাল, জলবাসী সর্প। **Water-spout** — জলস্তম্ভ (সাঃ পঃ)। **Water-soldier** —

Water-spouts.

একপ্রকার জলজ ক্ষুপ—যাহার পুষ্প জলোপরি ফুটিয়া থাকে। **Water-supply**—নগর, গৃহ প্রভৃতিতে জল সরবরাহ, কিম্বা সরবরাহের জন্য সঞ্চিত জলরাশি, জল সরবরাহ। **Water-thermometer** — জলীয় তাপমাপক (হিঃ কোঃ)। **Water-tank**—জলকুণ্ড। **Water-tight**—জলাভেদ্য। **Water-wag tail**—হারিদ্রব। **Water-tower**—যে উচ্চ বুরুজ হইতে জলের কলের জল বেগে পতিত হয়। **Water-way**—জলস্রোতঃ, নদী প্রভৃতির যে অংশে নৌকাদি চলাচল করিতে পারে। **Water-wheel**—জলপ্রবাহচালিত চক্র, জলোত্তোলন চক্র। **Waterworks**—জল সরবরাহের কারখানা। **Between wind and water**—In great difficulty; মহাসঙ্কটে। **In deep water or waters**—In great difficulty; অগাধ সমুদ্রে, অকূল পাথারে। **Mouth waters**—মুখে জল আসে। **Of the first water**—Supremely excellent; অত্যুত্তম, অত্যুৎকৃষ্ট। **Still waters run deep**—See STILL. **To back water** — To row backwards; পশ্চাদ্দিকে দাঁড় টানা। **To be in hot water**—To be in difficulty; to be in the soceity of hot-tempered people; গোলমালে পড়া, মুস্কিলে পড়া, বিভ্রাটে পড়া; উষ্ণ প্রকৃতি লোকের সঙ্গে থাকা। **To cast one's bread upon the waters**—To do good without looking for gratitude; নিষ্কামভাবে পরোপকার করা। **To drink the waters**—To attend Spa for the sake of recruiting one's health; স্বাস্থ্যোন্নতির জন্য উষ্ণপ্রস্রবণযুক্ত স্থানে গমন করা। **To fish in troubled waters** — See FISH. **To go through fire and water**—See FIRE. **To hold water**—See HOLD. **To keep one's head above water**—See HEAD. **To make water**—To pass urine; মূত্র ত্যাগ করা। **To make one's mouth water** — To excite longing; মুখে জল আসা, মুখে জল সরা। **To pour oil over troubled water** — See OIL. **To spend money like water**—To spend extravagantly; জলের মত টাকা খরচ করা। **To throw cold water on an enterprise**—See COLD. **To take in water**—To get water; জল নেওয়া, জল লওয়া। **To water stock**—কোন কোম্পানীর কাগজের কতক অংশ অল্প মূল্যে বা বিনামূল্যে দেওয়া। **Water for feet**—পাদ্য (এভেলন)। **Water for sipping**—আচমনীয় (এভেলন)। **Water of life**—আধ্যাত্মিক জ্ঞানোদয়। **Waters of forgetfulness**—Same as LETHE. **Written in water**—Transient; অচিরস্থায়ী।

watt (wŏt), *n.* A unit of electric power; তাড়িত শক্তির একক, তাড়িতাঙ্ক। **watt′-age**, *n.*

Wat′-teau (wö-tô), *adj.* Of, or pertaining to, Antoino Watteau, the French painter; ফরাসীদেশীয় চিত্রকর Antonio Watteau সম্বন্ধীয়। **Watteau back**—স্ত্রীলোকদিগের পরিচ্ছদের গলদেশ হইতে ভূতলে পতনশীল প্রশস্ত কোঁচসমূহবিশিষ্ট পৃষ্ঠভাগ। **Watteau bodice**—গলদেশে চতুষ্কোণ ফাঁক

এবং চুনট করা খাটো আস্তিন বিশিষ্ট বডিস।

wat'-tle (wŏt-l), *n.* & *v. t.* **1.** A twig or flexible rod ; কঞ্চি। **2.** A hurdle of interlaced rods ; বুনট করা কঞ্চির বেড়া। **3.** (*Pl.*) Rods laid on a roof to support the thatch ; যে দণ্ডশ্রেণীর উপর চালের ছন স্থাপন করা হইয়া থাকে, রুয়া। **4.** An acacia which grows abundantly in Australia and New Zealand, the bark of which is used in tanning ; অষ্ট্রেলিয়া এবং নিউজিলেণ্ডে জাত একপ্রকার একেশিয়া গাছ—যাহার বল্কল চর্ম্মশোধনে ব্যবহৃত হয়। **5.** The fleshy excrescence that grows under the throat of a cock or turkey ; a barbel of a fish ; কুক্কুটের গলের নিম্নে দোদুল্যমান কোমল মাংস, গলার লতি ; মৎস্যের মুখ হইতে দোদুল্যমান একপ্রকার মাংসময় তন্তু। ***Verb t.*** To interlace with twigs or branches ; কঞ্চি প্রভৃতি দ্বারা বুনা।

waul (wäl), *v. i.* To squall ; to cry like a cat ; বিড়ালের মত শব্দ করা ; মিউ মিউ করা।

wāve, *n., v. i.* & *t.* **1.** A moving swell on the surface of the water of the sea, or a river caused by the wind ; ঢেউ, উর্ম্মি, তরঙ্গ, লহরী, বীচি, হিল্লোল, কল্লোল, [*Syn.* ভঙ্গ, জললতা, হলী, দিসি, ভৃণ্ডি।] **2.** Anything resembling a wave ; তরঙ্গাকৃতিবস্তু। **3.** An undulation ; one of a series of inequalities on a surface ; তরঙ্গবৎ আন্দোলন, তরঙ্গবৎ গতি বা ভঙ্গী ; তরঙ্গায়িত ভাব। **4.** The undulating line or streak of lustre on cloth watered and calendered ; নরাজ দেওয়া কাপড়ে যে ঢেউয়ের আভাস দেওয়া হয়। **5.** (*Phys.*) A vibration propagated through a body or elastic medium as light-waves ; (পদার্থ-বিদ্যা) কম্প, কম্পসন্তান, কোন পদার্থ বা স্থিতিস্থাপক বস্তুর মধ্য দিয়া যে কম্প বা প্রবাহ সঞ্চারিত হয়, (যথা শব্দের স্পন্দন সমূহ বায়ুর ভিতর দিয়া এবং আলোকের স্পন্দনসমূহ ইথারের মধ্য দিয়া সঞ্চারিত হয়)। **6.** (*Poet.*) Water ; a body of water ; (কবিতায়) জল ; জলরাশি। **7.** Temporary heightening of feeling etc. ; as, a *wave* of enthusiasm ; সাময়িক ভাবোচ্ছ্বাস, আবেগতরঙ্গ, ভাবোর্ম্মি। ***Verb i.*** **1.** To be moved easily one way and the other (*also v. t.*) ; দোলায়িত, হওয়া, দোদুল্যমান হওয়া। **2.** To be sinous like a wave ; তরঙ্গায়িত হওয়া। ***Verb t.*** **1.** To move to and fro ; to brandish ; আন্দোলিত করা ; চালনা করা। **2.** To give an undulating form or surface to ; তরঙ্গায়িতবৎ করা। **3.** To attract the attention of, or to direct, by a waving motion ; to signal by waving the hand or the like ; "Look with what courteous action It *waves* you to a more removed ground" ; to beckon ; হস্ত প্রভৃতি দোলায়িত করিয়া মনোযোগ আকর্ষণ করা বা নিদেশ দেওয়া ; হস্তসঞ্চালন পূর্ব্বক সঙ্কেত প্রদান করা ; ইঙ্গিত করা, সঙ্কেত করা। **Sound-wave**—শব্দসন্তান (সাঃ পঃ)। **Wave-current**—গতিসন্তান (হিঃ কোঃ)। **Wave-front**—তরঙ্গাগ্র (হিঃ কোঃ), তরঙ্গধারা (ঐ)। **Wave length**—তরঙ্গায়াম (হিঃ কোঃ), তরঙ্গান্তর (ঐ), তরঙ্গায়তি (সাঃ পঃ)। **Wave-light**—অর্চ্চি সন্তান। **Wave-surface**—তরঙ্গস্থল (হিঃ কোঃ)। **Wave theory** — তরঙ্গসিদ্ধান্ত (হিঃ কোঃ)। **Wave of light** — প্রকাশতরঙ্গ (হিঃ কোঃ), প্রকাশলহর (ঐ)। **Wave of vibration**—কম্পতরঙ্গ (হিঃ কোঃ)।

wā'-vêr, *v. i.* & *t.* **1.** To move one way and the other ; to flutter ; to quiver ; to flicker ; আন্দোলিত হওয়া ; পত পত করা ; কম্পিত হওয়া ; মিট মিট করা। **2.** To vacillate ; "Let us hold fast the profession of our faith without *wavering*" ; দ্বিধা করা, ইতস্ততঃ করা। **3.** (Of troops) To falter ; to give way ; (সেনাদলসম্বন্ধে) থতমত খাওয়া ; হটিয়া যাওয়া। ***Verb t.*** To hesitate at ; ইতস্ততঃ করা, দ্বিধা করা। **—er, —ing,** *ns.* **—ing-ly,** *adv.*

wāv'-ȳ, *adj.* Rising or swelling in waves ; abounding in waves ; ঢেউখেলানো, তরঙ্গায়িত ; তরঙ্গপূর্ণ। **—i-ly,** *adv.* **—i-ness,** *n.*

wāv'-ȳ, wāve'-ȳ, *ns.* The snow-goose ; একজাতীয় তুষারশুভ্র হংস।

wawl (wäl), *v. i.* Same as WAUL.

wăx, *n.* & *v. t.* **1.** A thick, viscid, tenacious substance, excreted by bees, and employed in the construction of their cells ; মোম [*Syn.* সিক্থ, সিক্থক, মধূচ্ছিষ্ট, মধুজ, দ্রাবক, কাল, মধূত্থিত, শিক্থ।] [Arab. *shuma* ; Pers. *mom* ; Burm. *h'pa raung* ; Chin. *peh-lah* (white), *whang-lah* (yellow) ; Fr. *cire* ; Germ. *wachs* ; Russ. *wosh, wosk* ; It. & Span. *cera* ; Tam. *mellugu* ; Teleg. *minum* ; Dan. *vox* ; Lith. *waszkas* ; Pol. *vosk.*] **2.** A substance used in sealing letters, called *sealing wax* ; গালা। **3.** A thick substance used by shoemakers for rubbing their thread ; একপ্রকার ঘন পদার্থ—যদ্দারা চর্ম্মকারগণ সূত্র ঘষিয়া থাকে। **4.** A thick tenacious substance secreted in the ear ; কাণের খইল, কর্ণমল, কর্ণগূথ। **5.** Any wax like product secreted by plants ; বৃক্ষাদি হইতে নির্গত মোমবৎ পদার্থ। ***Verb t.*** To smear, polish or encrust with wax ; মোম মাখান, মোমদ্বারা পালিশ করা, মোমদ্বারা আচ্ছাদিত করা, মোমদ্বারা উপরিভাগ মাখান। **Vegetable wax**—See VEGETABLE. **Wax-basket**—মোম দ্বারা আচ্ছাদিত তারে তৈয়ারী একপ্রকার সৌখীন করণ্ড। **Waxbill** — অর্দ্ধস্বচ্ছ চঞ্চুবিশিষ্ট পক্ষিজাতিবিশেষ। **Wax-candle**—মোমবাতি। **Wax-chandler**—মোমবাতি-বিক্রেতা। **Wax-cloth** — মোমজামা কাপড়। **Wax-cluster** — একপ্রকার

ক্ষুপ—ইহাতে ক্ষুদ্র শ্বেতবর্ণ ফল গুচ্ছে গুচ্ছে ধরিয়া থাকে Wax doll—মোমের পুতুল। Wax-end. Waxed end — চর্ম্মকারগণের মোমবৎ পদার্থ মাখানো সূতা—যাহার অগ্রভাগে একটি শঙ্কু নিবদ্ধ থাকে। Wax-flower—মোম দ্বারা নির্ম্মিত কৃত্রিম পুষ্প। Wax-insect — মধুথকীট [ইহা একপ্রকার শ্বেতবর্ণ সূক্ষ্ম কীট—ইহারা বৃক্ষের শাখায় একপ্রকার মোমের মত পদার্থ সঞ্চিত করে। এই পদার্থ হইতে একপ্রকার মোমবাতি প্রস্তুত হইয়া থাকে।] Wax-light—মোমবাতি। Wax-modelling—মোমদ্বারা পুতুল প্রভৃতি নির্ম্মাণের শিল্প, মোমশিল্প। Wax-moth—একপ্রকার প্রজাপতি—ইহার কীড়া মৌচাকের মোম আহার করিয়া থাকে। Wax-myrtle — একপ্রকার বৃক্ষ। Wax-opal—মোমের মত আভাবিশিষ্ট একপ্রকার উপলমণি। Wax-painting—Same as ENCAUSTIC. Wax-palm—একপ্রকার তালজাতীয় বৃক্ষ। ইহার কাণ্ড একপ্রকার মোমজাতীয় পদার্থে আচ্ছাদিত থাকে। Wax-paper — শাদা মোম, তার্পিণ এবং তিমিমৎস্যের মস্তকে প্রাপ্ত শ্বেতবর্ণ পদার্থের মিশ্রণ দ্বারা বিলেপিত কাগজ। Wax-pocket—মোম রক্ষণের জন্য মধুমক্ষিকার রন্ধ্রবিশেষ। Wax-red—উজ্জল রক্তবর্ণের। Wax-tree—বিভিন্ন প্রকার বৃক্ষ—যাহার কাণ্ড হইতে মোম ক্ষরিত হয় বা যাহা কীটগণ মোম দ্বারা আচ্ছাদিত করে। Waxwing—একজাতীয় পক্ষী—উহাদের কোন কোন পালকের অগ্রভাগে লাল গালার মত ক্ষুদ্র ক্ষুদ্র গুটিকা থাকে। Waxwork—মোমের পুতুল নির্ম্মাণের কার্য্য; মোমের পুতুল ইত্যাদি; পরিচ্ছদসজ্জিত মোমের প্রতিমূর্ত্তি; মোমের কাজ; মোমনির্ম্মিত দ্রব্যের প্রদর্শনী। Wax-worker — যে ব্যক্তি মোমের কাজ করে; মোম প্রস্তুতকারী মধুমক্ষিকা। Waxy degeneration of the liver—যকৃতের পীতবর্ণ মোমের মত শক্ত পদার্থে পরিণতি। এই রোগে যকৃতের ওজন ক্রমশঃ বৃদ্ধি পাইয়া ৩৪ পাউণ্ডের স্থলে ৮৷৯ পাউণ্ডে পরিণত হয়। Waxy infiltration — শরীরের কোন যন্ত্রে মোমবৎ পদার্থের অনুপ্রবেশ। To mould one like wax — To form one's character as one desires; to make one do as one wishes; ইচ্ছামত কাহারো চরিত্র গঠন করা; কাহাকে যেরূপ ইচ্ছা সেইরূপ কার্য্যে প্রবৃত্তি জন্মান।

wăx, *n.* Fit of anger; as, she is in a terrible *wax*; ক্রোধোচ্ছ্বাস।

wăx'-en (-n), *adj.* **1.** Made of wax; মোমনির্ম্মিত। **2.** Covered with wax; মোমদ্বারা আবৃত। **3.** Soft as wax; মোমের মত কোমল।

wăx'-ȳ, *adj.* **1.** Resembling wax; মোমবৎ। **2.** (*Slang*) Angry; (ইতরভাষায়) চটা। **3.** Designating, or affected with, amyloid degeneration; শ্বেতসারের মত বিকারসূচক বা উক্তরূপ বিকার দ্বারা আক্রান্ত।

way (wā), *n.* **1.** Road or track; রাস্তা, পথ, বর্ত্ম, মার্গ। **2.** Distance; as, a long *way*; দূরত্ব। **3.** Passage; গতি, গমন, চলন। **4.** Scheme; means; কার্য্যপ্রণালী, কার্য্যপদ্ধতি; উপায়। **5.** Manner; "I will one *way* or other make you amends"; method; mode; style; রীতি; পদ্ধতি; ধরণ; গতিক, রকম। **6.** (*Law*) Right of way; (আইন) কোন পথে চলার অধিকার। **7.** Direction; দিক, অভিমুখ। **8.** Occupation; as, he is in the grocery *way*; ব্যবসায়, পেশা। **9.** Condition; অবস্থা। **10.** Advance; as, my scheme has made little *way*; অগ্রসর। **11.** Feature; respect; "you wrong me every *way*"; বিশেষত্ব; বিষয়ে। **12.** Custom; manner of behaving; as, I do not understand your *ways*; personal peculiarity; রীতি; ধরণধারণ, চাল চলন; রকমসকম, ধারা, চরিত (cf. তোমার রীত বুঝিতে নারি); ব্যক্তিগত বিশেষত্ব। **13.** Unimpeded opportunity of advance; অবাধগতি। **14.** Ground over which advance is desired or would naturally take place; যে ভূমিতে অগ্রসর হওয়া যায় বা অগ্রসর বাঞ্ছিত হয়। **15.** (*Naut.*) A structure of timber etc. on which a new ship is slipped down at launch; (নৌবিদ্যা) যে কাষ্ঠরচিত ব্যবস্থার সাহায্যে নূতন জাহাজ ভাসান হয়। **16.** Progress through water; as, a vessel under *way*; জলের ভিতর দিয়া অগ্রসর। **17.** Condition of health; as, he is in a bad *way*; স্বাস্থ্য। Covered way—ছাদবিশিষ্ট পথ; (দুর্গের) পর্দ্দায় ঘেরা রাস্তা, আবৃত পথ। Milky way—See MILKY. Permanent way—স্থায়ী লৌহবর্ত্ম। Way-bill—জাহাজ প্রভৃতির আরোহী, অথবা পুলিন্দাদির তালিকা। Way-board—ঘনতর স্তরদ্বয়ব্যবধায়ক পাতল স্তর। Wayfarer—পথিক, পর্য্যটক, ভ্রমণকারী, পথচারী। Way-faring—পদব্রজে ভ্রমণ, পর্য্যটন। Wayfaring-tree—পথিপার্শ্বে জাত একপ্রকার শ্বেতপুষ্পপ্রসূ ক্ষুপ। Waylay—কাহারো সহিত সাক্ষাৎ অথবা রাহাজানি করার উদ্দেশ্যে পথিমধ্যে যাহারা অপেক্ষা করে। (*verb i.*) রাস্তায় ওঁৎ পাতিয়া থাকা। Way leave—খনির মালীক প্রভৃতি খাজানা দ্বারা কোন রাস্তায় চলার যে বিশেষ অধিকার প্রাপ্ত হয়। Way-passenger—যে যাত্রীকে ষ্টেশনদ্বয়ের মধ্যবর্ত্তী কোন স্থানে তোলা হইয়া থাকে। Way-shaft — বাষ্পীয়যন্ত্রের অংশ বিশেষ। Way-side — পথিপার্শ্ব। (*Adj.*) পথিপার্শ্বস্থ। Way-station—দুই প্রধান ষ্টেশনের মধ্যবর্ত্তী ষ্টেশন সমূহ। Way-train—যে গাড়ী সকল ষ্টেশনে থামে। Way-wise — পথজ্ঞ, যে ভালরূপ পথঘাট জানে। Way-worn—পথশ্রান্ত, পর্য্যটনক্লান্ত। By the way—See BY. By way of—With the intention of; অভিপ্রায়ে। As a substitute of or form of; পরিবর্ত্তে, ছলে, রূপে। Furthest way about is nearest way home—Short cuts are delusive; বেশী তাড়াহুড়া করিতে গেলেই দেরী হইয়া পড়ে। In a fair way of—Very probable; অতিশয় সম্ভবপর।

In a good way — Prosperous ; prosperously ; সঙ্গতিসম্পন্ন ; সঙ্গতিসম্পন্নভাবে। **In a way**—Somewhat ; কতকটা। In some sense ; কোন কোন অর্থে। Eager ; ব্যাকুল, উদ্বিগ্ন। **In the way**—পথিমধ্যে ; প্রতিবন্ধকস্বরূপ, অন্তরায়স্বরূপ; হাতের কাছে (অপ্রচলিত বা কচিদ্‌ব্যবহৃত)। **In the way of**—পাওয়া যায়, করা যায় প্রভৃতি অবস্থায় ; সম্পর্কে, বিষয়ে। **In the way of**—So as to meet, fall in with or gain ; ধরাইয়া দেওয়া। [To put one *in the way of* business কাহাকে ব্যবসায় ধরাইয়া দেওয়া।] **It is nothing out of the way**—It is nothing extraordinary ; ইহা একটা কিছু অসাধারণ নয়। **On the way**—পথিমধ্যে অগ্রসর। **Once in in a way**—Rarely ; কচিৎ। **Out of the way**—দূরবর্ত্তী, অসাধারণ; পথভ্রান্ত ; অসঙ্গত, অন্যায় ; অযথাস্থানে রক্ষিত ; হৃত ; দুরধিগম্য ; নির্জ্জন। **Parting of the ways**—A critical time ; সন্ধিক্ষণ, মহামুহূর্ত্ত। **The ship has way on, The ship is under way**—The ship moves through water ; জাহাজ জলরাশি ভেদ করিয়া চলিতেছে। **The way**—বাইবেল ; খৃষ্টধর্ম্ম। **The ways of the world**—সংসারের হাল, সংসারের গতি। **The way the wind blows**—See WIND. **To be by way of being**—To be capable of being classified ; শ্রেণী ভুক্ত হইবার উপযুক্ত হওয়া। **To be in the family way** — To be pregnant ; গর্ভবতী হওয়া, অন্তঃসত্ত্বা হওয়া। **To clear the way**—To remove obstacles ; বাধা দূর করা। To stand aside ; একপাশে দাঁড়ান। **To come all the way from**—To come travelling the whole distance ; সারাপথ অতিক্রম করিয়া আসা। **To come by way of Calcutta**—To come via Calcutta ; কলিকাতা হইয়া আসা। **To find one's way, To find the way**—To reach destination ; গন্তব্যস্থানে উপস্থিত হওয়া। **To find some way**—To find some means ; পথ বাহির করা, উপায় বাহির করা। **To gather way**—To gain speed ; দ্রুততরভাবে অগ্রসর হওয়া। **To get a thing out of the way**—To get rid of ; to settle ; কোন কিছু হইতে রেহাই পাওয়া ; মিটান, মীমাংসা করা। **To get in the way**—To be an impediment ; প্রতিবন্ধকস্বরূপ হওয়া, অন্তরায় হওয়া। **To get out of the way**—To be no longer any impediment ; বাধা বা প্রতিবন্ধক দূর হওয়া। **To give way**—To row hard ; প্রাণপণে দাঁড় চালান। To break loose ; ধৈর্য্যচ্যুত হওয়া। (Also see GIVE.) **To go a very little way with**—To have little influence ; সামান্য প্রভাব থাকা। **To go one's way** or **ways**—To depart ; প্রস্থান করা। **To go one's own way, To take one's own way**—To act independently esp. against the wishes of others ; স্বাধীনভাবে কার্য্য করা, বিশেষতঃ অন্যের ইচ্ছার বিরুদ্ধে স্বাধীনভাবে কার্য্য করা। **To go out of the way, To go out of one's way**—To show rudeness ; রূঢ়তা প্রদর্শন করা। **To go the way of all earth, of all flesh, of nature**—To die ; মৃত্যুমুখে পতিত হওয়া। **To have one's way** or **own way**—To have one's orders carried out or wishes satisfied ; কাহারো আদেশ অনুসারে অথবা ইচ্ছানুযায়ী কার্য্য হওয়া। **To lead the way**—To show the way ; পথপ্রদর্শন করা। **To look the other way**—To avoid meeting a person's eye ; কাহারো সহিত যাহাতে চোখাচোখি না হয় তজ্জন্য মুখ ফিরান। **To lose one's way, To lose the way**—To go astray ; পথ হারান, পথ ভুলা। **To lose way**—To lose speed ; পূর্ব্বাপেক্ষা অল্প বেগে চলা। **To make one's way**—To advance ; উন্নতির পথে অগ্রসর হওয়া। **To make the best of one's way** — To walk as fast as one can ; অতিদ্রুত চলা। **To make way**—To make room ; পথ করা। To advance ; অগ্রসর হওয়া। To stand aside ; কাহাকে রাস্তা দেওয়ার উদ্দেশ্যে এক পার্শ্বে সরিয়া দাঁড়ান, একপার্শ্বে সরা। **To pave the way for**—To make easier for acceptance etc. ; পথ পরিষ্কার করা। **To pay one's way**—To pass one's days without running into debt ; ধার কর্জ্জ না করিয়া সংসারযাত্রা নির্ব্বাহ করা। **To put a person out of the way**—To imprison a man or kill him secretly ; কাহাকে কারারুদ্ধ করা বা গোপনে হত্যা করা, কাহাকে সরান। **To put oneself out of the way**—To put one's self to inconvenience in order to be helpful to another ; অপরের সাহায্যের জন্য নিজের অসুবিধা করা। **To stand in the ancient ways**—To aviod new fashion ; নব্যধরণ পরিহার করা। **To stand (be) in the way of, To stand (be) in one's way, To stand (be) in the way**—To be an obstacle ; বাধাস্বরূপ হওয়া, অন্তরায় হওয়া, প্রতিবন্ধক হওয়া। **To take one's way**—To go in some direction ; কোন দিকে যাওয়া। To do as one likes ; স্বেচ্ছামত চলা। **Under way**—(জাহাজসম্বন্ধে) জলরাশি ভেদ করিয়া ; চলন্ত। **Way enough**—দাঁড় চালান বন্ধ করার জন্য নাবিকদিগকে আদেশ। **Way of** or **to St. James**—ছায়াপথ। **Ways and means** — উপায় ; কোন কার্য্য সাধনের আবশ্যক অর্থ ও তাহা প্রাপ্তির উপায় ; উপায়, প্রণালী ; রাষ্ট্রের ব্যয় নির্ব্বাহের জন্য আবশ্যক রাজস্ব সংগ্রহের জন্য উপায়সমূহ। **Ways and Means Committee**— বিলাতে কমন্স সভার সপ্তদশ সভ্য দ্বারা গঠিত সমিতিবিশেষ। এই সমিতিতে রাজস্বসংক্রান্ত সমস্ত বিষয় মীমাংসার জন্য উপস্থাপিত করা হয়, বিশেষতঃ আমদানী মালের শুল্কসংক্রান্ত

সমস্ত বিষয় এই সমিতি দ্বারা মীমাংসিত হয়। **Where there is a will there is a way** — ইচ্ছা থাকিলে উপায়ও হয়।

way'-ward (wā-wĕrd), *adj.* **1.** Perverse ; disobedient ; বে-আড়া, একগুঁয়ে ; অবাধ্য। **2.** Irregular ; as, a *wayward* course ; unsteady ; অস্থির, অনিয়মিত ; চঞ্চলমতি। **–ly,** *adv.* **–ness,** *n.*

wē, *pron.* The first person plural of *I* ; আমরা। [রাজা, গ্রন্থকার, পত্রিকাসম্পাদক, প্রভৃতি স্বীয় অভিমতাদি প্রকাশ করার কালে *I*এর পরিবর্তে *We* ব্যবহৃত করিয়া থাকেন।]

weak (wēk), *adj.* **1.** Wanting or deficient in physical strength ; দুর্ব্বল, বলহীন, অশক্ত, হীনবল, ক্ষীণবল, ক্ষীণজীবী। **2.** Brittle ; as, a *weak* vessel ; ভঙ্গপ্রবণ, ভঙ্গুর, ঠুনকা। **3.** Pliant ; as, *weak* stem of a plant ; soft ; নমনশীল ; কোমল। **4.** Inefficacious ; easily subdued or overcome ; as, a *weak* fortress ; অকার্য্যকর ; সহজবশ্য, সহজে পরাজেয়। **5.** Low ; faint ; অনুচ্চ ; ক্ষীণ। **6.** Not thoroughly impregnated with required ingredients or with stimulating substances ; as, *weak* tea ; নিস্তেজ। **7.** Vacillating ; দ্বিধাকারী, সংশয়ী। **8.** Easily led ; wanting in resolution ; আশুবিচলিত ; অস্থিরসংকল্প। **9.** Deficient in power or vigour of expression ; as, a *weak* style ; ওজস্বিতা শূন্য। **10.** A term applied to verbs the past tense and past participles of which are formed by the addition of *-ed*, or *-d* ; যে সকল ক্রিয়ার অতীত এবং অতীতকালবোধক কৃদন্তকাল *-ed* অথবা *-d*, সংযোগ গঠিত হয় তৎসম্পর্কে প্রযুক্ত। **11.** Not able to sustain or exert a great weight, pressure or strain ; as, a *weak* bridge ; অতিশয় ভার বা চাপ সহনে বা প্রদানে অক্ষম। **12.** (Of mind) Feeble ; as, *weak* intellect ; দুর্ব্বল। **13.** Foolish ; বুদ্ধিহীন, নির্ব্বোধ। **14.** Tending lower towards price ; as, wheat is *weak* ; মন্দা। **Weak'-en,** *v. t.* & *i.* **1.** To make weak or weaker ; দুর্ব্বল করা, দুর্ব্বলতর করা। **2.** To reduce in quality, strength or spirit ; পাতল করা। ***Verb i.*** To become weak ; দুর্ব্বল হওয়া। **Weak-eyed, –sighted**—ক্ষীণদৃষ্টি। **Weak-fish** — আমেরিকার একপ্রকার সামুদ্রিক মৎস্য। **Weak-headed**—অল্পবুদ্ধি, ক্ষীণমস্তিষ্ক। **Weak-hearted**—ভীরু, সাহসহীন। **Weak-kneed**—দুর্ব্বলচিত্ত, দুর্ব্বল প্রকৃতি। **Weak-minded** — দুর্ব্বলমনাঃ। **Weaker vessel**—See VESSEL. **As weak as water**—Very weak ; অতিশয় দুর্ব্বল, অতীশয় ক্ষীণ। **Weak side** or **point**—কাহারো চরিত্রের দুর্ব্বল অংশ।

weak'-ling (wēk-), *n.* A feeble person ; a sickly person ; দুর্ব্বল লোক ; রোগা লোক।

weak'-nĕss (wēk-), *n.* **1.** The state of being weak ; দুর্ব্বলতা, ক্ষীণতা। **2.** A weak point or defect ; ত্রুটি, দুর্ব্বলতা। **3.** Inability to resist a particular temptation ; "*Weakness* to resist Philistian Gold" ; প্রলোভনে বাধা প্রদানের অক্ষমতা, দুর্ব্বলতা। **4.** Lack of resolution ; অস্থিরসংকল্পতা। **5.** A fall in price ; "The trade there, in fact, has been rather inclined to harden than show *weakness*" ; বাজার দর হ্রাস।

weal (wēl), *n.* Prosperity ; good fortune ; উন্নতি, শ্রীবৃদ্ধি, সমৃদ্ধি, বৈভব, অভ্যুদয়, ক্ষেম ; সুখ, সৌভাগ্য। **Weal and woe**—শুভাশুভ, সুখদুঃখ।

weal (wēl), *n.* & *v. t.* Same as WALE (which see).

weald (wēld), *n.* **1.** A piece of open forest land ; মুক্ত অরণ্যপ্রদেশ। **2.** A valley or tract of country, including parts of the downs of Kent and Sussex ; ইংলণ্ড দেশের উপত্যকা বা ভূখণ্ডবিশেষ — কেণ্ট ও সাসেক্সের খটিকাবহুল উচ্চ ভূমির যে কোন অংশ ইহার অন্তর্ভুক্ত। **Weald-clay**—উক্ত অঞ্চলের কর্দ্দম, বালুকাপ্রস্তর, চূর্ণপ্রস্তর, লৌহ-প্রস্তর এবং শিলীভূত কঙ্কালাদিপূর্ণ ভূস্তর।

weald'-ĕn (wēld-), *adj.* & *n.* Pertaining to the weald ; কেণ্ট, সাসেক্সের অংশবিশেষের ভূমিসম্বন্ধীয়। ***Noun.*** A formation or group of rocks consisting of clay, slate sandstones, grits and limestones, constituting the lowest part of the cretaceous system ; মৃত্তিকা, শ্লেটপ্রস্তর, বালুকাপ্রস্তর, শিলাকণা, চূর্ণপ্রস্তর প্রভৃতি দ্বারা গঠিত পাষাণপংক্তি।

wealth (wĕlth), *n.* **1.** Riches ; ধন, দৌলত, অর্থ, ঐশ্বর্য্য, সম্পত্তি, বিত্ত, বিভব, সম্পৎ। **2.** Abundance ; as, a *wealth* of flowers; প্রাচুর্য্য, সম্পৎ (cf. মরুদ্দুচ্চলফ্‌টুৎপুষ্পসম্পচ্চমক দীপাবল্যা ফ্‌টুমারাত্রিকমারাত্রিকম্ — শ্রীগোপালচম্পূঃ।) **3.** (*Pol. Econ.*) Anything which has an exchange value ; বিনিময়যোগ্য মূল্যবিশিষ্ট বস্তু। **Wealth'-y,** *adj.* Rich ; ধনবান, ধনী, ধনাঢ্য, বিত্তবান, বিত্তশালী। **Wealth'-i-ly,** *adv.* **Wealth'-i-ness,** *n.* **Exchange of wealth**—সম্পত্তিবিনিময় (হিঃ কোঃ), বিত্তবিনিময়। **Distribution of wealth**—সম্পত্তিবিতরণ (হিঃ কোঃ), বিত্তবিতরণ। **Productin of wealth** — সম্পত্তিউৎপাদন (হিঃ কোঃ), বিত্তোৎপাদন।

wean (wēn), *v. t.* **1.** To accustom and reconcile, as a child or other young animal, to a want or deprivation of the breast ; মাই ছাড়ান, স্তন্যত্যাগ করান। **2.** To detach or alienate the affections of, as from some object of desire ; as, to *wean* one's soul from earthly things ; কোন অভ্যাস ছাড়ান, কোনরূপ আসক্তি দূর করা।

wean'-ling (wēn-), *n.* **1.** A newly weaned child ; যে শিশুকে অল্পদিন মাত্র মাই ছাড়ান হইয়াছে।

weap'-ŏn (wĕp-), *n.* **1.** Any instrument of offence or defence ;

অস্ত্র, শস্ত্র, আয়ুধ, প্রহরণ। 2. Any means or instrument with which one contends against another ; as tears are the only *weapon* of women ; উপায়, সাধন, অস্ত্র। 3. (*Bot.*) A thorn, prickle, sting or the like ; (উদ্ভিদ্‌বিদ্যা) শূক, কণ্টক। **-less,** *adj.*

wear (wãr), *v. i.* & *t.* 1. To be undergoing gradual impairment or diminution ; ক্রমশঃ ক্ষয়প্রাপ্ত হওয়া। 2. To be spent ; কাটা, অতীত হওয়া। 3. (*Naut.*) To go about by turning the head away from the wind ; (নৌবিদ্যা) বায়ুপ্রবাহ হইতে এক পার্শ্বে অগ্রভাগ সরাইয়া চলা। 4. To last under use ; as, a coat *wears* ill ; পরণে টিকা। 5. To move or advance slowly ; ধীরে ধীরে অগ্রসর হওয়া ; শনৈঃ শনৈঃ অগ্রসর হওয়া। ***Verb t.*** 1. To be dressed in ; পরিধান করা, পরা, পিঁধা, (*colloq.*)। 2. To carry appendent to the body, as ornamats, a sword ; পরা, ধারণ করা। 3. To allow to grow in a particular fashion ; কোনরূপ নির্দ্দিষ্ট ভাবে বৃদ্ধি পাইতে দেওয়া। 4. To have, or exhibit, an appearance of, as an aspect or manner ; as, to *wear* an aspect of melancholy ; to bear ; to show ; "He *wears* the roses of youth" ; কোনরূপ বিশেষ ভঙ্গী বা ভাব ধারণ করা ; ধারণ করা ; প্রদর্শন করা। 5. To consume by frequent or habitual use ; সর্ব্বদা ব্যবহার করিয়া ক্ষয় করা। 6. To waste or impair by rubbing or attrition ; to waste ; ঘর্ষণ দ্বারা ক্ষয় করা ; ক্ষয় করা। 7. To bring about gradually ; to affect by degrees ; to cause to think or act in a certain way or direction (often used with *in* or *into*) ; ক্রমশঃ সংঘটিত করা ; ক্রমশঃ প্রভাবিত করা ; কোন বিশেষভাবে চিন্তা করিতে অথবা কার্য্য করিতে প্রবর্ত্তিত করা। **Wear'-a-ble,** *adj.* **Wearing-apparel**—পোষাক, পরিচ্ছদ, বেষ। **Wearing-iron, Wearing-plate**—কোন কিছুর যে অংশ ঘর্ষণে ক্ষয় পাইতে পারে তাহা রক্ষার জন্য ঐ স্থানে যে ধাতুখণ্ড নিবদ্ধ করা হয়। **Never wear a brown hat in Friesland**—When at Rome do as Rome does—যস্মিন দেশে যদাচারঃ। **To be only fit to wear a steeple-crowned hat**—To be fit to be burnt as a heretic ; পাষণ্ড বলিয়া জীবন্ত দগ্ধ হওয়ার উপযোগী হওয়া। **To wear a person or principle in one's heart**—To be specially devoted to a person or principle ; কোন ব্যক্তি বা মূলতত্ত্বের বিশেষ অনুরক্ত হওয়া। **To wear away**—To impair gradually—ক্রমশঃ ক্ষয় করা। **To wear ill or well**—To last a short or long time in wear ; ব্যবহারে অল্প টেঁকসই হওয়া, ব্যবহারে বেশ টেঁকসই হওয়া। (*Colloq.*) To look well or ill for one's years ; (চলিত ভাষায়) বয়সের পক্ষে ভাল বা মন্দ দেখান। **To wear off**—To remove or diminish by attrition ; to rub off ; ঘষিয়া উঠান বা কমান ; ঘষিয়া উঠান। **To wear on**—To pass on gradually ; ধীরে ধীরে অতিবাহিত হওয়া, চলা। **To wear one's heart upon one's sleeve**—To expose one's secret intentions to general notice (cf. "When my outward action shows my secret heart, I will *wear my heart upon my sleeve,* as one does a lady's favour—*Othello.*) ; নিজের প্রাণের নিগূঢ় কথা সর্ব্বসাধারণে ব্যক্ত করা। **To wear one's years well, To wear well**—To retain one's youth ; যৌবন অক্ষুণ্ণ রাখা। **To wear out** — To wear till useless ; ব্যবহারের উপযোগী থাকা পর্য্যন্ত ব্যবহার করা। To harass ; to exhaust ; অত্যাচার করা ; অবসন্ন করা। To waste or consume the strength of ; জর্জ্জরিত করা, শক্তি ক্ষয় করা। **To wear out one's welcome**—To go too often or to stay too long as a visitor etc. ; কোথায়ও ঘন ঘন যাওয়া, কোথায়ও অতিরিক্ত কাল বাস করা। **To wear the breeches**—To have the controlling authority in a household—said chiefly of women ; গৃহের উপর প্রভুত্ব থাকা (প্রধানতঃ স্ত্রীলোক সম্পর্কে ব্যবহৃত হয়)। **To wear the crown** — To be a monarch ; মুকুটধারী রাজা হওয়া ; ধর্ম্মার্থে আত্মোৎসর্গকারী হওয়া। **To wear the gown**—To be a lawyer; আইন ব্যবসায়ী হওয়া। **To wear the sword**—To be a soldier ; সৈনিক হওয়া। **To wear the willow**—To go into mourning or grief esp. for a sweetheart ; প্রেমিক বা প্রেমিকার জন্য শোক করা কিম্বা শোকপরিচ্ছদ ধারণ করা। **To wear the wooden sword**—To keep back sales by asking too high a price ; অতিরিক্ত মূল্য চাহিয়া বিক্রয় নিরোধ করা। **To wear to one's shape**—To fit better by use ; ব্যবহার করিতে করিতে শরীরে বেশ মানানসই হওয়া।

wear, (wãr), *n.* 1. The act of wearing; the state of being worn ; পরিধান ; পরণ। 2. Diminution by friction, use, time or the like ; ঘর্ষণ, ব্যবহার, প্রভৃতিজনিত ক্ষয়। 3. The thing worn ; the style of dress ; fashion ; "Motley is the only *wear*" ; যাহা পরা হয় ; পরিচ্ছদ-রীতি ; প্রচলিত ধারা বা রীতি। 4. Capacity for resisting wear or tear ; ব্যবহারজনিত ক্ষয় নিরোধের শক্তি। **Wear and tear**—ব্যবহার-জনিত ক্ষয়, ভাঙ্গাটুটা।

wear (wĕr), *v. t.* & *i.* To cause to go about, as a vessel, by putting the helm up, instead of down as in tacking, so that the vessel's bow is turned away from, and her stern is presented to, the wind, and she is brought by the wind to a new tack ; জাহাজের হাইল

তুলিয়া উহার অগ্রভাগ বায়ু হইতে সরাইয়া নিয়া পশ্চাদ্‌ভাগ বায়ুর অভিমুখীন করা—যাহাতে বায়ু দ্বারা উহার মুখ অন্য দিকে ফিরিতে পারে। *Verb i.* To come round on the other tack ; (পোত-সম্পর্কে) অন্য দিকে অভিমুখীন হওয়া।

wear (wãr), *n.* Same as WEIR (which see).

wea'-rў (wē-), *adj., v. t. & i.* 1. Tired ; ক্লান্ত, পরিক্লান্ত, শ্রান্ত। 2. Sad ; grieved ; as, a *weary* heart ; বিষণ্ণ ; বিষাদগ্রস্ত, দুঃখভারাক্রান্ত। 3. Expressing weariness ; ক্লান্তিসূচক। 4. Causing weariness ; tedious ; as, *weary* task ; ক্লান্তিজনক ; অবসাদজনক। *Verb t.* 1. To tire ; ক্লান্ত করা। 2. To make mentally or spiritually weary; অবসন্ন করা। 3. To make impatient of continuance : অবসাদগ্রস্ত করা। *Verb i.* 1. To become weary or tired ; ক্লান্ত হওয়া, শ্রান্ত হওয়া। 2. To become impatient of continuance ; অবসাদগ্রস্ত হওয়া। **—ri-ness,** *n.* **—ri-some,** *adj.* Tiresome ; tedious ; ক্লান্তিজনক, শ্রান্তিজনক ; অবসাদজনক। **—ri-some-ly,** *adv.* **—ri-some-ness,** *n.*

wea'-sand (wē-), *n.* (*Archaic*) Wind-pipe ; (অপ্রঃ) শ্বাসনালী।

wea'-sel (wē-zl), *n.* A small carnivorous animal remarkable for its slender form ; নেউল, বেজি,

Weasel.

নকুল, বিজ্জেন (সাঃ পঃ)। [Syn. পিঙ্গল, সর্পহা, বভ্রু, সর্পারি, অঙ্গুষ, সূচিবদন।] **Weasel-faced**—ক্ষীণবদন। **To catch a weasel while asleep**—To deceive an alert person ; খুব হুঁসিয়ার লোককে ঠকান।

weath'-ẽr (wĕth-), *n. & adj.* The state of the atmosphere ; আকাশের অবস্থা, বায়ুর শৈত্য কিম্বা উষ্ণতাজনিত অবস্থা। *Adj.* Windward ; বাত্যাভিমুখীন। **April weather**—পর্য্যায়ক্রমে রৌদ্র ও বৃষ্টি; (লক্ষণায়) অশ্রু ও হাসি। **Weather-beaten**—বাতাহত, বাত্যাতাড়িত, ঝঞ্ঝাহত। **Weather-boarding, Weather-boards**—প্রাচীরাদি রক্ষার নিমিত্ত পরস্পরের প্রান্তের উপর স্থাপিত কাষ্ঠফলকসমূহরচিত আচ্ছাদন বিশেষ। **Weather-bound**—দুর্য্যোগহেতু অগ্রসর হইতে অক্ষম। **Weather-box, Weather-indicator**—স্ত্রী এবং পুরুষের মূর্ত্তিসমন্বিত যন্ত্রবিশেষ—যাহার একটী সুদিন এবং অপরটী দুর্দ্দিন সূচনার জন্য বাহির হয়। **Weather-bureau**—আবহ কার্য্যালয়। **Weather-chart**—বিস্তৃত স্থানের আকাশের অবস্থা প্রদর্শনের জন্য নক্‌সাবিশেষ, আবহচিত্র। **Weather cloth**—জাহাজের পাটাতনের কোন অংশ বাত্যাবৃষ্টি হইতে রক্ষা করার জন্য ব্যবহৃত ত্রিপল। **Weather-cock**—বায়ুপ্রবাহের দিঙ্‌নির্ণয়ের জন্য কুক্কুটাকৃতি যন্ত্রবিশেষ, বাতকুক্কুট (ভ্রান্তিবিনোদ) ; অব্যবস্থিতচিত্ত লোক, অস্থির-চিত্ত। **Weather-contact, Weather-cross**—(তাড়িত-বিদ্যা) বর্ষাকালে তাড়িতপ্রবাহরোধক বস্তু দ্বারা অসম্যগ্‌রূপে আচ্ছাদনের ফলে তাড়িতের এক তার হইতে অপর তারে অভিনির্গম। **Weather-cross**—বৃষ্টির দরুণ তারের ব্যত্যস্তভাবে সংযোগ। **Weather-forecast**—দৈনিক আকাশের অবস্থার সম্বন্ধে অনুমানসূচক মন্তব্য—যাহা পত্রিকাদিতে মুদ্রিত হয় বা আবহকার্য্যালয়ে টাঙ্গাইয়া দেওয়া হইয়া থাকে। **Weather-glass**—বায়ুমানযন্ত্র। **Weather-house**—গৃহের আকারে নির্ম্মিত একপ্রকার যন্ত্র—যাহা হইতে মূর্ত্তি বাহির হইয়া বা যাহাতে মূর্ত্তি অদৃশ্য হইয়া বাত্যাবৃষ্টির অবস্থা সূচনা করে। **Weather-map**—Same as WEATHER-CHART. **Weather-moulding**—Same as DRIP 2. **Weather-proof**—বাত্যাবৃষ্টি দ্বারা অক্ষয্য। **Weather prophet**—যে ব্যক্তি আকাশের অবস্থা সম্বন্ধে পূর্ব্বেই অনুমান করিয়া বলিতে পারে, আবহসূচক। **Weather-service**—আবহবিদসমাজ। **Weather-side**—জাহাজের যে পার্শ্বে বায়ু প্রবাহিত হয়। **Weather-stain**—বাত্যাবৃষ্টির দরুণ প্রাচীরাদিতে যে দাগ পড়ে। **Weather-station**—বাত্যাবৃষ্টির অবস্থা দর্শনের গৃহ, আবহাগার। **Weather-stone**—একপ্রকার প্রস্তর—যাহার বর্ণ বৃষ্টির প্রাক্কালে পরিবর্ত্তিত হয়, আবহপাষাণ। **Weather-strip**—বাতায়নের ফাঁক বন্ধ করার জন্য ব্যবহৃত কোন বস্তুর খণ্ড। **Weather-tiles**—যে টালি সকল পরস্পরের প্রান্তের উপর নিহিত হইয়া থাকে। **Weather vane**—Same as WEATHER-COCK. **Weather-wise**—Same as WEATHER-PROPHET. **Weather-worn**—বাত্যাবৃষ্টিক্ষত। **To keep one's weather eye open**—To be vigilant ; সতর্ক থাকা, হুঁসিয়ার থাকা। **To make fair weather**—To flatter ; তোষামোদ করা। **Under stress of weather**—Owing to storms etc. ; বাত্যাবৃষ্টিহেতু।

weath'-ẽr (wĕth-), *v.t. & i.* 1. (*Rare*) To expose to air ; (কচিদ্ ব্যবহৃত) বাতাস লাগান। 2. To sail to the windward of ; কোন কিছুর যে পার্শ্বে বাতাস প্রবাহিত হয় তদভিমুখে চালান। 3. To bear up against and come through, with difficulty ; প্রবল ঝঞ্ঝাবৃষ্টি সহ্য করিয়া আসা। 4. To come safely through danger etc. ; "You will *weather* the difficulties well" ; বিপদ্ প্রভৃতি অতিক্রম করিয়া আসা। 5. To slope as a roof so as to shed water ; জল গড়াইয়া পড়িবার জন্য ছাদ প্রভৃতি ঢালু করা। 6. (*Geol.*) To cause to alter in colour, coherence and to decay through the influence of weather ; (ভূবিদ্যা) বাত্যাবৃষ্টির প্রভাবে বর্ণ, সংশ্লিষ্টতা, প্রভৃতির পরিবর্ত্তন এবং ক্ষয় করা। *Verb i.* (*Geol.*) To undergo alteration tending to decomposition ; to decay by the action of weather ;

বাত্যাবৃষ্টির প্রভাবে ক্ষয়, বিশ্লেষ প্রভৃতি জনক পরিবর্তন হওয়া; বাত্যাবৃষ্টি হেতু ক্ষয়প্রাপ্ত হওয়া। **–ing,** *n.* **To weather point**—To gain or accomplish a point against opposition; বাধাবিঘ্ন স্বত্বেও কোন কার্য্য সাধন করা। **To weather out**—To endure; সহ্য করা। **To weather the storm**—To get out of danger; বিপদ কাটাইয়া উঠা।

weath'-ẽr-lȳ (wĕth-), *adj.* (*Naut.*) Making little headway when close-hauled; (নৌবিদ্য) বায়ুর প্রতিকূলে গমনকালে অল্পমাত্র অগ্রগমনশীল। **—li-ness,** *n.*

weave (wēv), *v. t., i.* & *n.* **1.** To form as cloth by interlacing; বয়ন করা, বুনা। **2.** To entwine; as, to *weave* a garland; গুম্ফিত করা, সংগ্রথিত করা, গাঁথা। **3.** To contrive; to fabricate, or construct with design or elaborate care; as, to *weave* a plot; সুকৌশলে গঠন করা; রচনা করা, বিরচন করা। ***Verb i.*** **1.** To make cloth etc. by interlacing yarns, threads, etc. কাপড় বুনা। **2.** To become interwoven; সংগ্রথিত হওয়া, গুম্ফিত হওয়া। ***Noun.*** Style of weaving; বুননপদ্ধতি। **Weav'-ing,** *n.* The act of one who weaves; বুনন, গুম্ফন (উজ্জ্বলঃনীলমণি)। **Wove paper, Woven paper**—তারের সূক্ষ্ম জালের ছাঁচে প্রস্তুত একপ্রকার উৎকৃষ্ট কাগজ—উহাতে কোনরূপ রেখা বা জলছাপ থাকে না, এবং উহার উপরিভাগ সর্ব্বত্র একরূপ হইয়া থাকে; কলে প্রস্তুত উক্তরূপ কাগজ।

weav'-ẽr (wēv-), *n.* **1.** One who weaves; বস্ত্রবয়নকারী, তাঁতি, তন্তুবায়, তন্ত্রবায়, কুবিন্দ। **2.** Same as WEAVER-BIRD. **Weaver-bird**—বাবুই পাখী, তাঁতবুননকারী (মিউজিয়্যাম)।

wea'-zen (wē-zn), *adj.* Same as WIZENED.

wĕb, *n.* **1.** That which is woven esp. in a loom; বুনা কাপড়। **2.** Cobweb; মাকড়সার জাল। **3.** (*Fig.*) Anything carefully contrived and artfully put together or woven; জাল। **4.** Paper in the process of manufacture in a paper-making machine; কলে প্রস্তুত হইতেছে এইরূপ কাগজ। **5.** A large roll of paper used esp. in newspaper printing; বিশেষভাবে সংবাদপত্র মুদ্রণে ব্যবহৃত আবর্ত্তিত কাগজ। **6.** A membrane filling spaces between toes esp. of swimming birds; হংস প্রভৃতির পদাঙ্গুলীসমূহ যে পর্দ্দা দ্বারা সংযুক্ত থাকে। **7.** The vane or vexillum; পালকের প্রশস্ত অংশ। **8.** A thin flat part connecting more solid parts in a machinery etc.; যন্ত্রাদির স্থূল এবং কঠিনতর অংশসংযোজক পাতল এবং চ্যাপ্টা অংশ। **Web-eye**—একপ্রকার চক্ষুরোগ—যাহাতে চক্ষে পর্দ্দা পড়ে। **Web-footed** — জালপাদ, লিপ্তপাদ, যুক্তপাদ (সাঃ পঃ)। **Web-wheel**—একপ্রকার চক্র—যাহার নাভি এবং বেষ্টনী একটি ফলক দ্বারা সংযুক্ত থাকে, লিপ্তচক্র। **Web-worm**—জাল বুননকারী কীড়া। **Web of life**—অদৃষ্টজাল।

wĕb-bing, (-ĭng), *n.* **1.** A strong fabric woven in strips; একপ্রকার শক্ত কাপড়—যাহা অল্প পরিসর করিয়া বুনন করা হয়। **2.** A stronger edging of more delicate fabric; মিহি কাপড়ের জন্য শক্ত হাঁসিয়া।

wĕd, *v. t.* & *i.* **1.** To marry; বিবাহ করা, পরিণয়সূত্রে বদ্ধ করা, পাণিগ্রহণ করা। **2.** To unite closely in affection; দৃঢ় প্রেমপাশে বদ্ধ করা। **3.** To unite for ever or inseparably to; "Thou art *wedded* to calamity"; চিরদিনের জন্য বদ্ধ করা। ***Verb i.*** To contract matrimony; বিবাহ করা, বিবাহবন্ধনে বদ্ধ হওয়া, পরিণয়সূত্রে আবদ্ধ হওয়া। **To wed over the mixen**—(*Dial.*) To marry a neighbour; (উপভাষায়) কোন প্রতিবেশীকে বিবাহ করা। **To wed over the moor**—To marry some one living in a distant place; দূরবর্ত্তী স্থানে বিবাহ করা। **To wed or marry with a rush ring**—To go through a mock form of marrying; কৃত্রিম বিবাহ করা, বিবাহের ভাণ করা।

Wedelia calendulacea—কেশুরে, কেশরাজ [Syn. ভৃঙ্গরাজ, ভৃঙ্গ, পতঙ্গ, মার্কব, নাগমার, পিতৃপ্রিয়, ভৃঙ্গমোদর কেশরঞ্জন, কেশ্য, কুন্তলবর্দ্ধন।]

wĕd'-ding (-ĭng), *n.* Marriage ceremony; বিবাহ, উদ্বাহ, পরিণয়, বিয়ে (*colloq.*), দারপরিগ্রহ (*rhet.*), পাণিপীড়ন (*ib.*), দারকর্ম্ম, করগ্রহ, পাণিগ্রহণ। **Wedding-breakfast**—বিবাহ এবং নববধূবরের প্রমোদযাত্রার পূর্ব্বে যে প্রীতিভোজন প্রদান করা হয়। **Wedding-cake** — বিবাহে উপস্থিত অভ্যাগত ব্যক্তিদিগকে যে পিষ্টক ভাঙ্গিয়া পরিবেষণ করা হয়, এবং যাহার কতকাংশ অনুপস্থিত বন্ধুবর্গের নিকট প্রেরিত হয়। **Wedding-cards**—বিবাহের নিমন্ত্রণপত্র। **Wedding clothes**—বিবাহকালে পরিহিত পরিচ্ছদ, বিবাহবেষ। **Weddingday**—বিবাহের দিবস, বিবাহের সাম্বৎসরিক উৎসব। **Wedding-favour**—বিবাহোৎসবে যে শ্বেত গোলাব বা ফিতাগুচ্ছ পরিহিত হয়। **Wedding-feast** — বিবাহের ভোজ। **Wedding-garland**—বরণমালা, বরণমালা। **Wedding-garment**—কোন বিষয়ে যোগদানের উপযোগী গুণসমূহ (See *Mat. XII. II.*)। **Wedding-ring**—পরিণয়াঙ্গুরীয়ক, যে অঙ্গুরীয় বর বধূর অঙ্গুলীতে পরাইয়া দেয় এবং যাহা পরিণীতা নারী পরিণয়ের চিহ্নস্বরূপ সর্ব্বদা ধারণ করা থাকে। **Candy-wedding**—বিবাহের তৃতীয়বার্ষিক উৎসব। **China-wedding** — বিবাহের বিংশতিবাৎসরিক উৎসব। **Coral-wedding**—বিবাহের পঞ্চত্রিংশবার্ষিক উৎসব। **Crystal wedding** — বিবাহের পঞ্চদশবার্ষিক উৎসব। **Diamond-wedding**—See DIAMOND. **Emerald-wedding** — বিবাহের চত্বারিংশদ্বার্ষিক উৎসব। **Floral-wedding**—বিবাহের সপ্তবার্ষিক উৎসব। **Golden wedding**—See GOLDEN. **Leather-wedding** — বিবাহের চতুর্থসাম্বৎসরিক

উৎসব। **Linen-wedding**—বিবাহের দ্বাদশবার্ষিক উৎসব। **Paper-wedding** — বিবাহের সাম্বৎসরিক উৎসব। **Pearl-wedding** — বিবাহের ত্রিংশৎবার্ষিক উৎসব। **Penny-wedding**—যে বিবাহোৎসব অভ্যাগত জনগণ হইতে সংগৃহীত অর্থদ্বারা সম্পাদিত হয়। **Ruby-wedding** — বিবাহের পঞ্চচত্বারিংশদ্‌বার্ষিক উৎসব। **Silver-wedding**—বিবাহের পঞ্চবিংশতিতম বর্ষে অনুষ্ঠিত উৎসব। **Tin-wedding**—বিবাহের দশসাম্বৎসরিক উৎসব। **Straw wedding** — বিবাহের দ্বিতীয়বার্ষিক উৎসব। **Wooden wedding**—বিবাহের পঞ্চবাৎসরিক উৎসব।

wedge (wĕj), *n.* & *v. t.* **1.** A piece of metal or wood, thick at one end and sloping to a thin edge at the other, used in splitting woods, rocks, etc. ; মেক, কীলক, কাজলা। **2.** Something in the form of a wedge ; কীলকাকৃতি বস্তু, ছেনি। ***Verb t.*** **1.** To drive in a wedge ; to crowd in ; to compress ; কীলক ঢুকান ; ঠাসা ; চাপ দেওয়া। **2.** To fix in the manner of a wedge ; কাজলার মত ঢুকান। **Wedge'-wise,** *adv.* **Wedge-shaped**—কীলকাকৃতি। **Wedge-tailed**—যে সকল পক্ষীর পুচ্ছের মধ্যের পালকসমূহ দীর্ঘতর থাকে তৎসম্পর্কে প্রযুক্ত। **The thin end of the wedge** — সামান্য প্রারম্ভ হইতে বিরাট কার্য্যের সূচনা। [চক্ষুপ্রবেশে মুণ্ড প্রবেশঃ।]

Wedge'-wood (wĕj-), *n.* A kind of semi-vitrified pottery ; একপ্রকার অর্দ্ধকাচীভূত ভাণ্ড। [আবিষ্কারক J. Wedgewoodএর নাম হইতে গৃহীত।]

wĕd'-lŏck, *n.* The married state ; বিবাহিত অবস্থা।

wed'-nes-day (wĕnz-dā), *n.* The fourth day of the week ; বুধবার।

wee (wē), *adj.* Very small ; as, a *wee* child ; অতি ক্ষুদ্র, ছোট্ট (*colloq.*), ছোটখাট (*ib.*), এক রত্তি (*ib.*), খুদে (*ib.*)।

weed (wēd), *n.* & *v. t.* **1.** A general name for any useless or troublesome plant ; আগাছা। **2.** (*Colloq.*) Cigar ; "Come up and have a *weed*" ; (চলিত ভাষায়) চুরুট। **3.** (*Colloq.*) Tobacco ; (চলিতভাষায়) তামাক। **4.** Something, esp. an animal, as a horse, of little value ; "There are plenty of *weeds* among their 'mobs' bred almost wild" ; অকর্ম্মণ্য জিনিষ, অকর্ম্মণ্য বস্তু, অকর্ম্মণ্য জন্তু, অকর্ম্মণ্য অশ্ব। **5.** A lanky person ; কাহিল লোক। ***Verb t.*** **1.** To clean ground of weeds ; আগাছা পরিস্কার করা, নিড়ান। **2.** To remove what is obnoxious, injurious or unseemly ; to extirpate ; as, he *weeded* the kingdom of seditious peoples ; উচ্ছেদ করা ; ধ্বংস করা। **Weed'-er,** *n.* **Weed'-i-ness,** *n.* **Weed'-less,** *adj.* **Weed'-y,** *adj.* **Weed-grown**—আগাছাপূর্ণ।

weed'-ing (wēd), *n.* The act of one who weeds ; নিড়ান, নিস্তৃণীকরণ। **A weeding-hook**—নিড়ানী।

weeds (wēds), *n.* (*Pl.*) Mourning worns by widow (usu. *widow's weed*) ; বিধবার শোকবস্ত্র।

week (wēk), *n.* The space of seven days ; সপ্তাহ, হপ্তা (*colloq.*)। **Week-day**—রবিবার ভিন্ন দিবস। **Week-end**—শনি রবি এবং সোমবারের কতক অংশ। (*Verb i.*) শনি রবি এবং সোমবারের কতক সময়ের জন্য কাহারো সহিত সাক্ষাৎ করিতে যাওয়া (Hence, *week-ender*)। **A week of sundays**—See SUNDAY. **This day week** — গত অথবা আগামী সপ্তাহের এইবার। **Feast of weeks**—ইহুদীদিগের সপ্ত সপ্তাহ ব্যাপী উৎসব।

week'-ly̆, (wēk-), *adj.*, *adv.* & *n.* **1.** Continuing, or lasting, for a week ; সপ্তাহব্যাপী, সপ্তাহস্থায়ী। **2.** Coming, happening, produced or done, once in a week ; as, *weekly* meeting ; সপ্তাহান্তে সংঘটিত, সঞ্জাত বা সম্পন্ন, সাপ্তাহিক। ***Adv.*** Every week ; প্রতি সপ্তাহে। ***Noun.*** A weekly newspaper ; সাপ্তাহিক পত্রিকা, সাপ্তাহিক।

ween (wēn), *v. t.* (*Poet.*) To be of opinion ; to consider ; "Thy father, in pity of my hard distress, levied an army, *weening* to redeem and reinstal me in the diadem" ; মতাবলম্বী হওয়া ; বিবেচনা করা।

weep (wēp), *v. i.* & *t.* **1.** To express sorrow, grief or anguish by outcry ; কাঁদা, ক্রন্দন করা, রোদন করা। **2.** To drop water ; to rain "When the sky *weep*, doth not the earth o'erflow" ; জলবিন্দু পাত হওয়া ; বৃষ্টি পড়া। **3.** To shed tears like drops of sap from a wounded branch ; ক্ষত শাখা হইতে অশ্রুবিন্দুবৎ বৃক্ষনির্য্যাসের বিন্দু ক্ষরিত হওয়া। ***Verb t.*** **1.** To weep for ; to lament ; কাঁদা, রোদন, করা ; বিলাপ করা। **2.** To shed tears ; অশ্রুপাত করা। **3.** To extinguish by shedding tears over (with *out*) ; "In compassion *weep* the fire *out*" ; অশ্রুপাত করিয়া নির্ব্বাপিত করা। **4.** To spend or consume time in weeping ; ক্রন্দনে সময় অতিবাহিত করা। **Weep'-ing,** *n.* & *adj.* **Weeping eczema**—একপ্রকার পামা যাহা হইতে পুযাদি নির্গত হয়। **Weeping pipe**—একপ্রকার চোঙ্গ যাহা হইতে বিন্দু বিন্দু জল ক্ষরিত হয়। **Weeping philosopher** — গ্রীক দার্শনিক হেরাক্লিটাস্ (Heraclitus)। **Weeping spring**—যে নির্ঝর হইতে অল্প অল্প করিয়া জল নিঃসৃত হয়। **Weeping rock**—যে সচ্ছিদ্র পাষাণ হইতে জল নির্গলিত হয়। **Weeping tree** — নতশাখ বৃক্ষ। **Weeping willow**—নতশাখ উইলো বৃক্ষ, নিম্নাবনত উইলোবৃক্ষ। **To turn by weeping cross**—কোন বিষয়ে গভীর মনস্তাপ পাওয়া, বিলাপ করা। **To weep oneself out**—To weep one's fill ; প্রাণ ভরিয়া কাঁদা। **To weep out**—To utter with tears ; সাশ্রুনয়নে বলা।

weep'-ēr (wēp-), *n.* **1.** One who weeps ; রোদনকারী। **2.** A professional mourner ; যে ব্যক্তি অর্থ

গ্রহণ করিয়া কোন মৃতব্যক্তির জন্য শোক করিয়া থাকে। **3.** A long hatband of crape worn by males at funeral অন্ত্যেষ্টি ক্রিয়াকালে পুরুষগণ যে ক্রেপ কাপড়ের দীর্ঘ টুপিবেষ্টনী পরিয়া থাকে। **4.** A widow's black crape-veil; বিধবাদিগের কৃষ্ণবর্ণ ক্রেপের অবগুণ্ঠন। **5.** A sort of white linen cuff worn by widows; বিধবাদিগের জামার সাদা রঙ্গের কফ।

Apple weevil.

weev'-ĕr (wēv-), *n.* A perch with sharp double spines; একপ্রকার মৎস্য।

wee'-vil (wē-), *n.* A small insect of the beetle-tribe with a long snout, very destructive to young plants, seeds and fruits; ঘুণ প্রভৃতি কীট।

Corn-weevil.

wĕft, *n.* **1.** The thread that crosses the warp from selvedge to selvedge; পড়েন, প্রতিতন্ত্র (যথা একেনৈব তন্তুনা ন্যানপ্রতিতন্ত্রৌ ভবতঃ—বৈশেষিকদর্শন — শঙ্করমিশ্রকৃত টীকা)। **2.** A thing woven; বুনা কাপড়।

weigh (wā), *v. t., i.* & *n.* **1.** To balance; ওজন করা, তৌল করা, মাপা, ভারনিরূপণ করা। **2.** To examine; as, to *weigh* the advantages and disadvantages of a scheme; পরীক্ষা করা। **3.** To ponder in the mind; মনে মনে বিবেচনা করা, তোলাপাড়া করা। ***Verb i.*** **1.** To weigh anchor; নোঙ্গর তোলা। **2.** To have weight; ভার থাকা। **3.** To carry weight; as, I think my arguments will *weigh* with you; গুরুত্ব বিশিষ্ট হওয়া, গুরুতর হওয়া। **4.** To press hard; "Cleanse the stuff'd bosom of that perilous stuff, which *weighs* upon the heart"; চাপা। **5.** To consider; to judge; "Could not *weigh* of worthiness weight"; to estimate; বিবেচনা করা; তোলাপাড়া করা, বিচার করা। ***Noun.*** Process of weighing; ওজনপ্রণালী। **Weigh'-age,** *n.* A rate or toll paid for weighing goods; মাল ওজনের দস্তুরি, কয়ালি। **Weigh'-er,** *n.* One who weighs; ওজনকারী, কয়াল। **Weigh-beam**—একপ্রকার বৃহৎ তুলাযন্ত্র। **Weigh-bridge** — অশ্ব এবং শকটের ওজনের জন্য একপ্রকার তুলাযন্ত্র। **Weigh-house**— সরকারী তুলা-গৃহ। **Weigh-lock**—নৌকা প্রভৃতি ওজনের ব্যবস্থাসমন্বিত খালের কপাটকল। **Weighing-machine** — তুলা-যন্ত্র। **To weigh anchor** — To raise anchor; নোঙ্গর তোলা। **To weigh down**—To sink by its own weight; নিজের ভারে নত হওয়া। **To weigh heavily upon** — To feel as a burden; ভারস্বরূপ বোধ হওয়া, চাপস্বরূপ হওয়া। To be saddening; নিরানন্দজনক হওয়া। **To weigh in** or **out**—ঘোড়সওয়ারকে দৌড়ের পরে (*in*) বা পূর্ব্বে (*out*) ওজন করা। **To weigh in with**—To produce triumphantly; বিজয়গর্ব্বের সহিত উপস্থাপিত করা। **To weigh little with**—To be inferior to some one in comparison; কাহারো সহিত তুলনায় হেয় বোধ হওয়া। **To weigh one's words**—To select such as express neither more nor less than one means; ভাবিয়া চিন্তিয়া কথা বলা, আবশ্যকের অতিরিক্ত একটীও কথা না বলা। **To weigh out**—To take definite weights of; to distribute in definite quantities, by aid of scales; নির্দ্দিষ্ট ওজনের জিনিষ নেওয়া; দাঁড়ী পাল্লার সাহায্যে নির্দ্দিষ্ট পরিমাণ বিতরণ করা। **To weigh the claim**—To compare the merits and demerits of rival candidates; প্রতিযোগীদিগের গুণাগুণ তুলনা করা। **Under weigh**—In motion; চলন্ত।

weight (wāt), *n.* **1.** The quantity of a body or its heaviness as ascertained by the balance; ভার, ওজন, তৌল। **2.** That property of bodies by which they tend toward the centre of the earth; গুরুত্ব, গুরুতা। **3.** Power; as, he is a man of *weight*; consequence; influence; "My argument carries great *weight*"; preponderance; as, the *weight* of evidence is against him; শক্তি; গুরুত্ব; প্রভাব; প্রাবল্য। **4.** A heavy body; ভারি জিনিষ, গুরুভার দ্রব্য। **5.** A piece of metal etc, for weighing articles; বাটখারা। **6.** Pressure; burden; as, pressed down under the *weight* of misfortune; চাপ; বোঝা। **7.** (*Pathol.*) A sensation of heaviness or pressure over the whole body or any portion of it; শরীরে ভার ভার বোধ। **Weight'-less,** *adj.* **A dead weight**—গুরুতর প্রতিবন্ধক। **False weight**—কূটমান। **Weight carrier** — খুব হৃষ্ট পুষ্ট এবং বলবান আরোহী বহনে সমর্থ অশ্ব। **Of great weight**— গুরুতর, গুরুত্ববিশিষ্ট। **Weight of metal**—জাহাজের কামানশ্রেণী হইতে একবারে যে ওজনের ধাতু নির্গত হইতে পারে। **Weight of observation**—নিরীক্ষণগুরুতা (হিঃ কোঃ)।

weight (wāt), *v. t.* To add or attach a weight or weights to; to load with additional weight; ভার সংযোগ করা; অতিরিক্ত জিনিষ দ্বারা বোঝাই করা।

weight'-y (wāt-), *adj.* **1.** Heavy গুরু, গুরুভার। **2.** Momentous; important; "Let me have your advice in a *weighty* affair"; গুরুতর; গুরুত্ববিশিষ্ট। **3.** Convincing; cogent; "Steeled with *weighty* argument" ; নিশ্চায়ক ; বলবৎ। 4. Burdensome ; দুর্ব্বহ, গুরুভার।

weir (wĕr), **wear** (wär), *ns.* **1.** A dam across a stream to raise the level of the water above it ; আলি, সেতুবন্ধ, জাঙ্গাল। **2.** A fence of staves in streams etc. for catching fish ; মৎস্য ধৃত করার জন্য নদ্যাদিতে যে খোঁটার বেড়া দেওয়া হয়।

weird (wērd), *n.* Fate ; অদৃষ্ট, নিয়তি।

weird (wērd), *adj.* **1.** Pertaining to fate ; নিয়তিসম্বন্ধীয়। **2.** Supernatural ; uncanny ; "Those sweet, low tones, that seemed like a *weird* incantation" ; অস্বাভাবিক, অলৌকিক, ভৌতিক, অমানুষিক ; ছমছমে। **3.** (*Colloq.*) Qeer ; odd ; incomprehensible ; (চলিত ভাবায়) অদ্ভুত ; অপরূপ, কিম্ভুতকিমাকার ; অজ্ঞেয়। **Weird'-ness,** *n.* **The weird Sisters**—Same as THE FATES (which see.)

wĕl'-come (-kŭm), *adj., interj. n.* & *v. t.* **1.** Received gladly into one's presence or companionship ; as, a *welcome* guest ; অভ্যর্থিত, সাদরে অভ্যথিত। **2.** Agreeable ; pleasing ; as, *welcome* news ; সুখদ ; আরামদায়ক, সুখপ্রদ, প্রীতিপ্রদ, আনন্দদায়ক। **3.** Free or willingly permitted ; সাদরে গৃহীত। ***Interj.*** A word used in welcoming or saluting a newcomer ; স্বাগত। ***Noun.*** A salutation to a newcomer ; অভ্যর্থনা, অভিনন্দন, সমাদর, সম্বর্দ্ধনা। ***Verb t.*** To salute, as a newcomer with a kindness ; to receive with kindness ; অভ্যর্থনা করা ; অভিনন্দন করা, সাদরসম্ভাষণ করা, স্বাগতসম্ভাষণ করা।

wĕld, *n.* A dyer's-weed, plant formerly used to dye yellow ; পীতবর্ণ রঞ্জনবস্তুপ্রদ একপ্রকার গুল্ম।

wĕld, *n., v. t.* & *i.* **1.** To unite or join together, as twe pieces by hammering or compressing them after they have been raised to a great heat ; লৌহ প্রভৃতি উত্তপ্ত করত: পিটিয়া বা চাপ দিয়া জোড়া লাগান। **2.** To unite very closely ; "Two women faster *welded* in one love" ; দৃঢ়রূপে সংলগ্ন করা। ***Verb i.*** To be, or capable of being, welded ; পিটিয়া বা চাপিয়া জোড়া লাগার যোগ্য হওয়া। ***Noun.*** A union by welding ; উত্তপ্ত অবস্থায় পিটিয়া লৌহ প্রভৃতি সংযোজন। **Weld'-a-ble,** *adj.* **–a-bil'-i-ty,** *n.*

wĕl'-fāre, *n.* Well-being ; exemption from misfortune, sickness, calamity, or evil ; মঙ্গল, কুশল ; কল্যাণ, শুভ, শ্রী, শ্রেয়ঃ।

wĕlk, *v. i.* (*Archaic*) To fade ; "When ruddy Phoebus 'gins to *welk* in the west" ; to wither ; (অপ্রঃ) ম্লান হওয়া ; শুকাইয়া যাওয়া, বিশুষ্ক হওয়া।

wĕl'-kin, *n.* & *adj.* (*Poet.*) Sky ; "When storms *welkin* rend" ; (কবিতায়) আকাশ, গগন। ***Adj.*** Sky-blue ; আসমানী।

wĕll, *n.* **1.** A spring ; নির্ঝর, ঝরণা। **2.** A pit sunk for water ; কুয়া, কূপ, পাতকুয়া। [Syn. অন্ধু, প্রহি, উদপান।] **3.** A perpendicular space in a building in which stairs are placed (Also *well-hole*) ; অট্টালিকার যে উল্লম্বী স্থানে সোপানশ্রেণী বিন্যস্ত থাকে। **4.** Source ; "Dan Chaucer, *well* of English undefiled" ; উৎপত্তিস্থল, উৎস। **5.** A receptacle for ink in inkstand ; দোয়াতদানে সংলগ্ন দোয়াত। **6.** The dark centre of a diamond cut too thick ; অতিরিক্ত গভীরভাবে পলকাটা হীরার কৃষ্ণাভ মধ্যস্থল। **7.** An enclosed space more or less resembling a well ; কূপাকৃতি বেষ্টিত স্থান। **8.** The space in a law-court immediately in front of the judge's bank, occupied by counsels etc. ; বিচারালয়ে বিচারকের আসনের সম্মুখস্থ স্থান যাহাতে কৌঁসুলী প্রভৃতি উপবেশন করে। **9.** The lower part of a furnace into which the metal falls ; চুল্লীর নিম্নতর অংশ যথায় ধাতু পতিত হয়। **10.** A compartment in the hold of a fishing vessel tight at the sides but having holes in the bottom to let in water to keep fish alive ; মৎস্য জীবিত রাখার জন্য জাহাজের খোলে কক্ষ বিশেষ। **Wel-deck**—উচ্চতর পাটাতন সমূহ এবং পাটাতনের উপরিস্থ পোতপার্শ্বদ্বারা বেষ্টিত প্রধান গোলাকার পাটাতনের অংশ। **Well-dish**—একপ্রকার থালা—যাহাতে রন্ধিত মাংসের রস জমিবার গর্ত্ত থাকে, কূপস্থালী। **Well-head**—উৎস। **Well-hole**—Same as WELL 3. **Well-room**—যে কক্ষে উষ্ণ প্রস্রবণের জল বিতরণ করা হয়, কূপগার। **Well-sinker**—কূপখননকারী। **Well-spring**—Same as WELL-HEAD. **Well-water**—কূয়ার জল, কূপজল, কূপোদক। **Truth lies at the bottom well**—It is very difficult to ascertain real truth ; প্রকৃত সত্য নির্ণয় করা অতি দুরূহ ব্যাপার।

wĕll, *v. i.* To issue forth, as water from the earth ; to flow ; "Fast from her eyes the round pearls *welled* down" ; to spring ; ভূগর্ভ হইতে উত্থিত হওয়া ; প্রবাহিত হওয়া ; উৎসারিত হওয়া।

wĕll, *adv., pred. adj.* & *n.* **1.** In good manner ; satisfactorily ; rightly ; ভালরূপে, উত্তমরূপে, সুচারুরূপে ; সন্তোষজনকভাবে ; যথোচিতভাবে, ঠিকভাবে, যথার্থরূপে। **2.** Abundantly ; fully ; প্রচুর পরিমাণে, ভূয়িষ্ঠরূপে ; সম্পূর্ণরূপে, সম্যগ্‌ভাবে, সর্ব্বতোভাবে। **3.** Properly ; "Does it take from the people more liberty than is absolutely necessary for the *well* administering of their affairs" ; সঙ্গতভাবে, সমুচিতভাবে, ন্যায্যভাবে। **4.** Not a little ; as, to be *well* advanced in life ; খুব, অত্যন্ত, বহু, অনেক। ***Adj.*** **1.** In good health ; as, I wish him *well* ; সুস্থ, নীরোগ,

2. Well-off ; সঙ্গতিশালী, সঙ্গতিসম্পন্ন। 3. Satisfactory ; advisable ; as, was it *well* to do this ? ; ভাল, বেশ, সমুচিত ; পরামর্শসিদ্ধ। 4. (*Marine Insurance*) Safe ; নিরাপদ। ***Noun.*** 1. Good things ; ভালজিনিষ। 2. What is satisfactory ; সন্তোষজনক বিষয়। **Well-advised**—সুপরামর্শপ্রাপ্ত, পরামর্শ-সিদ্ধ। **Well-aimed**—সুলক্ষ্যীকৃত। **Well-appointed** — উপযুক্ত সরঞ্জামসমন্বিত। **Well-arranged**—সুগঠিত, সুবিন্যস্ত। **Well authenticated**— সুপ্রতিপন্ন। **Well-balanced** — প্রকৃতিস্থ, বিচার-সম্পন্ন। **Well-behaved**—বিনীত, শিষ্ট, শীলবান। **Well-being**—মঙ্গল, কল্যাণ, ক্ষেম, শুভ, কুশল (হিঃ কোঃ), কুশলতা (ঐ)। **Well beloved**—প্রিয়তম, অতি প্রিয়। **Well-born**—সদ্বংশজ। **Well-bred** -- সুশিক্ষিত। **Well-chosen**---সুনির্ব্বাচিত। **Well-cleaned** — সুপরিস্কৃত, সুপরিচ্ছন্ন। **Well-conducted** — সুচরিত, সুনীত (মঃ ভাঃ)। **Well-connected**—সুসম্বন্ধ, সুসম্পৃক্ত। **Well-considered** — সুচিন্তিত, সুবিবেচিত। **Well-developed**—সুপরিণত। **Well-disposed**—অনুকূল, সদয়, অনুগ্রহশীল, সুশীল, সদাশয়। **Well-doer**—পুণ্যবান লোক ; সৎকার্য্যকারী ; উপকারী ব্যক্তি। **Well-doing** — পুণ্য, সৎকর্ম্ম। **Well done**—বেশ, সাবাস, বাহবা, বাঃ বাঃ, বেশ হইয়াছে। **Well educated**—সুশিক্ষিত। **Well-enough**—চলনসই, মন্দ নয়, কুৎসিত নয়, একরকম, একপ্রকার। **Well-equipped** — সুকল্পিত। **Well-explained** —সুব্যাখ্যাত। **Well-fashioned** — সুগঠিত,। **Well-favoured** — সুশ্রী, সুরূপ, সুদর্শন। **Well founded**—সুপ্রতিষ্ঠিত, সুপ্রতিষ্ঠ, অচলপ্রতিষ্ঠ। **Well furnished**—সুসজ্জিত। **Well-graced**—চিত্তাকর্ষক, সুগুণ, গুণসম্পন্ন। **Well-groomed**—সুবেশ, ফিটফাট। **Well grounded**—(Same as WELL-FOUNDED) প্রাথমিক জ্ঞানলব্ধ। **Well-guarded**--সুরক্ষিত, সুত্রাত, সুপরিরক্ষিত। **Well-informed**—সুবিদিত, বহুজ্ঞ। **Well-intentioned**---সদিচ্ছাবিশিষ্ট সদভিপ্রায়যুক্ত। **Well-knit**—সংহত, দৃঢ়বদ্ধ, সংহতাঙ্গ। **Well-known**—সুবিদিত, সুপরিচিত, সুপরিজ্ঞাত। **Well-judged**—বিচারবুদ্ধিসম্পন্ন। **Well-looking** --- প্রিয়দর্শন। **Well made**—সুগঠিত। **Well mannered**—শিষ্টাচারসম্পন্ন। **Well-meaning** — শুভাকাঙ্ক্ষী, শুভেচ্ছু। **Well-meant** — শুভেচ্ছাপ্রণোদিত। **Well-minded** --- সুচিত্ত, সুমানস। **Well-nigh** — প্রায়। **Well-off**—Fortunate ; prosperous ; ভাগ্যবান ; সঙ্গতিসম্পন্ন, সুব্যবস্থিত, সমৃদ্ধিসম্পন্ন। **Well-ordered**—সুশৃঙ্খল। **Well-pierced**--সুপ্রবিদ্ধ। **Well-spoken**—সুন্দররূপে কথিত; সুভাষী। **Well-proportioned** — সুগঠিত, সুরম্যাঙ্গ। **Well-read** — সুপণ্ডিত, কৃতবিদ্য, বহুশ্রুত। **Well-reputed**—সুবিখ্যাত, সুনামবিশিষ্ট। **Well-satisfied** — সুতর্পিত, সুসন্তুষ্ট। **Well-seeming**—আপাত সন্তোষজনক, আপাতচিত্তাকর্ষক। **Well-seen**—সুদৃষ্ট,বুদ্ধিসম্পন্ন। **Well-spent**—সুব্যয়িত। **Well-set**---সংহত, সুদৃঢ়। **Well-shaped**—শোভনাকৃতি সুবিভক্ত (মাঃ ভাঃ)। **Well-sifted**—সুপরীক্ষিত। **Well-timbered** — প্রচুর তরুবিশিষ্ট কাষ্ঠফলক প্রভৃতি দ্বারা দৃঢ়রূপে নির্ম্মিত। **Well-timed**—ঠিক সময়োপযোগী। **Well-to-do**—অবস্থাপন্ন অবস্থাশালী, সঙ্গতিসম্পন্ন, সঙ্গতিশালী, যোত্রশালী, সম্পন্ন। **Well-trained**—(Of horses) সুশিক্ষিত। **Well-tried** — সুপরিক্ষিত। **Well-trod, Well-trodden**—সুনিষেবিত, সুপরিসেবিত। **Well-tuned**—সুতান। **Well-weighed**—সুবিচারিত। **Well-wisher** — শুভাকাঙ্ক্ষী, হিতাকাঙ্ক্ষী। **All's well that ends well**—শেষ ভাল যার—সব ভাল তার। **As well**—Easily ; অনায়াসে, সহজে। Also ; ও, এবং। **Let well alone**—Do not meddle needlessly ; অনর্থক হস্তক্ষেপ করিওনা। **Very well**—All right; আচ্ছা, বেশ।

wĕll, *interj.* An exclamation expressing great surprise or astonishment ; আচ্ছা ! বেশ !

wĕll'-ă-day (-dā), **-ă-way** (-wā), *Interj.* Alas ; হায় ! হায় !

Wĕl-ling-tō'-ni-ă (-ing-), *n.* Kinds of sequoia ; কালিফর্ণিয়া দেশীয় বিভিন্ন প্রকার দেবদারু জাতীয় বৃক্ষ।

Wĕl'-ling-tŏns (-ing-), *n.* (*Pl.*) Boots coming up or nearly up to knees ; জানুপর্য্যন্ত বা প্রায় আজানু উচ্চ বুট জুতা।

Wĕlsh, *adj.* & *n.* 1. Pertaining to Wales or its peoples ; ওয়েল্‌স্ প্রদেশ সম্বন্ধীয়, ওয়েলস্‌বাসিসম্বন্ধীয়। ***Noun.*** 1. The language of Wales ; ওয়েলেস্ প্রদেশের ভাষা। 2. The inhabitants of Wales ; ওয়েলসের অধিবাসী। **Welsh rabbit**—ভর্জ্জিত পনীরের থালা। **Welsh-man** (*Fem. welsh-woman*) — ওয়েলেস্‌বাসী। **Welsh-mutton** — ওয়েলস্ দেশের ক্ষুদ্রকায় পার্ব্বত্য-মেষের মাংস।

wĕlsh, welch (wĕlsh), *v. t.* & *i.* To decamp without paying, esp. without paying the winner of a bet on horserace ; টাকা না দিয়া চম্পট দেওয়া, বিশেষতঃ ঘোড়দৌড়ে বিজয়ী ব্যক্তিকে বাজির টাকা না দিয়া পলায়ন করা। **Welsh'-er, Welch'-er**, *ns.*

wĕlt, *n.* & *v.t.* 1. A border or edging; কিনার, পাড়। 2. A strip of leather sewed round the upper part of a boot to which the sole is fastened ; জুতা কিম্বা বুটের কিনারার সরু চামড়া—যাহা তলির সহিত সংযুক্ত থাকে। ***Verb t.*** 1. To provide with the welt ; উক্তরূপ চামড়া লাগান। 2. To flog ; বেত্রাঘাত করা, বেত মারা।

welt, *n.* (German for) World ; জগৎ। ***Welt-schauung*** — জাগতিক স্রোতের ঘটনা, গতি এবং উদ্দেশ্যের অবধারণ। ***Welt-politik***—বিপুল বৈদেশিক রাষ্ট্রনীতি। ***Welt-schmerz*** — বর্ত্তমান এবং অনাগত জাগতিক অশুভ এবং দুর্দ্দশার জন্য দুঃখ বা বিষাদ।

wĕl′-têr, *v. i.* & *n.* **1.** To wallow in blood etc.; as, to *welter* in the blood of their enemies; রক্ত প্রভৃতিতে গড়াগড়ি দেওয়া। **2.** To toss as waves; ঢেউএর মত দোলায়িত হওয়া। ***Noun.*** General confusion; "The foul *welter* of our controversies"; গোলমাল, বিশৃঙ্খলা, হুলস্থুল।

wĕl′-têr, *n.* Heavy weight; গুরুভার।

wĕn, *n.* **1.** A harmless fatty tumour; অর্ব্বুদ, মাংসবৃদ্ধি। **2.** Goitre; গলগণ্ড। **3.** An abnormally large congested city; সুবৃহৎ জনাকীর্ণ নগরী। **The great wen**—লণ্ডননগরী।

wĕnch, *n.* & *v. i.* **1.** A young woman; তরুণী, বালা। **2.** A woman of loose character; দুশ্চরিত্রা স্ত্রীলোক। ***Verb i.*** To frequent the company of women of ill fame; দুশ্চরিত্রা স্ত্রীলোকের নিকট যাতায়াত করা।

wĕnd, *v. t.* & *i.* To go; as, to *wend* one's way; to direct; যাওয়া; পথপ্রদর্শন করা। ***Verb i.*** To go; to travel; "*Wend* my comrade and this page"; যাওয়া; বিচরণ করা।

Wĕnd, *n.* One of a powerful Slavic race now absorbed in the German race, which formerly inhabitated the North and East of Germany; বর্ত্তমানে জার্ম্মাণ জাতির সহিত একীভূত জর্ম্মাণীর উত্তর ও পূর্ব্বাঞ্চলবাসী জাতিবিশেষ।

wĕnt, *p.p.* & *p.t.* of GO (which see).

wĕn′-tle-trăp (-tl), *n.* A shell-fish with spiral shell of many whorls; একপ্রকার শঙ্খ।

wĕpt, *p. p.* & *p. t.* of WEEP (which see).

were′-wolf (wĕr-wûlf), **wĕr′-wolf** (-wûlf), *ns.* (*Myth.*) Turning of human being into wolf; মানবের নেকড়ে বাঘে রূপান্তর, বৃকদেহ প্রাপ্তি।

wĕrt, See BE.

Wĕr′-thêr-ĭsm, *n.* Morbid sentimentality; ভাবুকতা, উচ্ছ্বাসপ্রবণতা, ভাবোচ্ছ্বাস। [From Werther, a disconsolate lover in Goethe's *Sorrows of Werther.*

Wĕs′-ley-ăn (-lĭ-), *adj.* & *n.* Pertaining to John Wesley, or the religious sect established by him about 1739; জন ওয়েস্‌লী বা তৎপ্রবর্ত্তিত ধর্ম্মসম্প্রদায় সংক্রান্ত। ***Noun.*** A member of Weselyan sect; ওয়েস্‌লী সম্প্রদায়ের লোক।

wĕst, *adv., n.* & *adj.* To the western region; পশ্চিমদিকে। ***Noun.*** **1.** One of the cardinal points, being that opposite the east, and at which the sun sets at equinoxes; পশ্চিম। **2.** The region, tract, country or locality lying opposite to the east, or situated nearer the western point than another point of reckoning, as America with regard to England; প্রতীচ্যদেশ, পাশ্চাত্যদেশ। ***Adj.*** **1.** Lying toward the west; proceeding toward the west; western; পশ্চিমদিগ্‌বর্ত্তী; পশ্চিমদিগ্‌গামী; প্রতীচ্য, পাশ্চাত্য। **2.** Coming from the west; as, a *west* wind; পশ্চিমদিক হইতে আগত। **West country** — Southampton হইতে Severn নদীর মোহানা পর্য্যন্ত কল্পিত রেখার পশ্চিমদিগ্‌বর্ত্তী প্রদেশ; ইংলণ্ডের পশ্চিমাঞ্চল। **West-country**—ইংলণ্ডের পশ্চিমাঞ্চলসম্বন্ধীয়, উক্ত অঞ্চল হইতে আগত, উক্ত অঞ্চলের বিশেষত্বসূচক। **West-countryman** — ইংলণ্ডের পশ্চিমাঞ্চলের লোক। **West-End**—লণ্ডননগরীর পশ্চিমাংশ [এই অংশ নগরীর ধনী ও সম্ভ্রান্ত পুরুষগণের প্রাসাদোপম সৌধরাজি ও উৎকৃষ্ট বিপণিশ্রেণী দ্বারা সুশোভিত। **West Indies**—পশ্চিমভারতীয় দ্বীপপুঞ্জ। **West Indian**—পশ্চিমভারতীয় দ্বীপপুঞ্জের অধিবাসী।

wĕs′-têr-ĭng, *adj.* & *part.* (*Poet.*) Tending towards the west; "And, when now the *westering* sun, Touched the hills, the strife was done"; পশ্চিম অভিমুখীন।

wĕs′-têr-lȳ, *adj.* & *adv.* **1.** Being, or situated, towards the west; as, the *westerly* parts of England; পশ্চিমদিগ্‌বর্ত্তী। **2.** Coming from the west; পশ্চিমদিগাগত। ***Adv.*** Tending, moving or going, towards the west; as, *westerly* wind; পশ্চিমাভিমুখে, পশ্চিমদিকে।

wĕst′-êrn, *adj.* & *n.* **1.** Being in, or moving toward, the west; পশ্চিমদিক্‌স্থিত, পশ্চিমদিগ্‌গামী। **2.** Coming from the west; as, a *western* breeze; পশ্চিমদিগাগত। **3.** Living in the west; পশ্চিমাঞ্চলবাসী। **4.** Occidental; as, *western* learning; প্রতীচ্য, পাশ্চাত্য। ***Noun.*** Same as WESTERNER. **–er,** *n.* A native or inhabitant of the west; প্রতীচ্য দেশবাসী লোক, পাশ্চাত্য দেশবাসী লোক। **–most,** *adj.* Most western; পশ্চিমতম। **Western Empire**—রোম সম্রাট থিয়োডিশিয়াস্ কর্ত্তৃক ৩৯৫ খৃঃ অব্দে দ্বিধাবিভক্ত রোমসাম্রাজ্যের পশ্চিমতর বিভাগ—এই বিভাগের রাজধানী রোমনগরী ছিল, প্রতীচ্যসাম্রাজ্য। **Western Church** — Same as LATIN CHURCH (which see.)

wĕst′-ĭng, *n.* Departure in a western direction; (নৌবিদ্যা) ভ্রমণে বা নৌভ্রমণে পশ্চিমদিকে অপচার, পশ্চিমাপচার।

Wĕst′-mĭn-stêr, *n.* A city forming a part of London; লণ্ডননগরীর অন্তর্ভুক্ত নগর বিশেষ। **Westminster Abbey**—লণ্ডননগরী। West minster নামক স্থানে প্রাচীন খৃষ্টীয় মঠ—এই স্থানে ইংলণ্ডের নৃপতিগণের অভিষেক হয় এবং রাজা ও দেশের শ্রেষ্ঠ কবি, সাহিত্যিক, সেনাধ্যক্ষ, প্রভৃতির মৃতদেহ এই মঠের প্রাঙ্গণে সমাহিত হইয়া থাকে।

wĕt, *adj., n.* & *v. t.* **1.** Containing water; আর্দ্র, সিক্ত, সজল, ভিজা। **2.** Rainy; as, *wet* season; বাদলা, বর্ষাবহুল, প্রবার্ষিক। **3.** (*Obs.*) Drunk; "When my lost lover the tall ship ascends, with music gay, and *wet* with jovial friend"; (অপ্রঃ) মাতাল।

Noun. 1. Moisture or humidity; আর্দ্রতা, সিক্ততা। 2. Rainy or drizzling weather; rain; "The wind and the *wet*"; বাদলা দিন; বৃষ্টি। 3. (*Slang*) A drink; (ইতরভাষায়) এক গ্রাস মদ, এক ঢোক মদ। ***Verb t.*** To make wet; to dip in a liqnid; আর্দ্র করা, সিক্ত করা; কোনরূপ তরল পদার্থে ভিজান। **Wet'-tish,** *adj.* Somewhat wet; অল্প সিক্ত। **Wet bargain**—Same as DUTCH BARGAIN. **Wet blanket**—See under BLANKET. **Wet bulb thermometer** — Same as HYGROMETER. **Wet dock** — যে পোতনির্ম্মাণস্থলীতে জাহাজ ভাসিয়া থাকিতে পারে। **Wet dream**—স্বপ্নদোষ। **Wet goods** — পিপা বা বোতলে রক্ষিত তরল মাল, যথা তৈল, বিয়র, সুরাসার, প্রভৃতি। **Wet-nurse** — ধাত্রী, ক্ষীরদাত্রী (বৌদ্ধঃ)। **Wet pack**—শুষ্ক কম্বল প্রভৃতি দ্বারা আচ্ছাদিত সিক্তবস্ত্রে দেহ আবরণ। **Wet plate**—(আলোকচিত্র) যে রসায়নিক দ্রব্যাদি দ্বারা অনুলিপ্ত ফলক আর্দ্রাবস্থায় আলোকে অনাবৃত করা হয়। **Wet provisions**—মাতগুড়, সির্কা প্রভৃতি, অথবা লবণজলে নিমজ্জিত গোমাংস কিংবা শূকর মাংস। **Wet-rot**—আর্দ্রতা দ্বারা বৃক্ষাদির ক্ষয় বা বিশ্লেষ। **Wet-steam**—জলকণামিশ্রিত বাষ্প। **Wet wind**—(আবহবিদ্যা) যে বাতাসের পর সচরাচর বৃষ্টি বা তুষারপাত হয়। **To be wet to the skin**—কাপড়চোপড় ভিজিয়া যাওয়া। **To wet one's clay**—To drink; পান করা। **To wet one's whistle**—To drink; মদ্য পান করা। **With a wet finger** — Easily; সহজে, অনায়াসে।

wĕth'-ėr, *n.* A castrated ram; ছিন্নমুষ্ক মেষ, ভেড়ার খাসী।

wey (wā), *n.* A certain weight of measure (of wool 182 lbs; of wheat 5 quarters; of cheese 224 lbs); একপ্রকার ওজন (পশমের পক্ষে ১৮২ পাঃ; ময়দার পক্ষে ৫ কোয়ার্টার; পনীরের পক্ষে ২২৪ পাঃ।)

whăck, *v. t., i. & n.* 1. To thwack; লাঠি দ্বারা জোরে আঘাত করা, পেটা, ঠেঙ্গান (*colloq.*)। ***Verb i.*** To strike or continue striking anything with heavy sounding blows; দুম্‌দাম্‌ করিয়া আঘাত করা। ***Noun.*** A resounding blow; দুম্‌দাম্‌ শব্দে আঘাত, ঠেঙ্গানি।

whăck'-ėr, *n.* 1. (*Slang*) A thing or person big of its kind; (ইতর ভাষায়) বৃহত্তম বস্তু বা ব্যক্তি। 2. A great lie; মস্ত মিথ্যা কথা।

whăck'-ing, *n.* (*Slang*) Very large or big; (ইতর ভাষায়) মস্ত।

whāle, *n., v. & i.* 1. The largest of sea mammals; তিমি। 2. (*Scripture*) Any sea-monster or large fish; (বাইবেল) মহামৎস্য। ***Verb i.*** To be engaged in whale-fishing; তিমি মৎস্য শিকারে নিযুক্ত থাকা। **Bull whale**—পুং-তিমি। **Cow whale**—স্ত্রীতিমি। **Whale-boat** — তিমিমৎস্য শিকারে ব্যবহৃত নৌকা; ঐরূপ নৌকার আদর্শে নির্ম্মিত নৌকা। **Whalebone**—কোন কোন জাতীয় তিমিমৎস্যের উপরের চোয়ালের শৃঙ্গবৎ পদার্থ—যদ্দ্বারা নানাবিধ দ্রব্য প্রস্তুত হইয়া থাকে। **Whale-calf** — তিমি-

Whale.

মৎস্যের শাবক, তিমিশাবক। **Whale-fin**—তিমি মৎস্যের অস্থির বাণিজ্যিক নাম। **Whale-fishery** — তিমিমৎস্য শিকার। **Whale-head**—আফ্রিকাদেশীয় হাড়গিলাজাতীয় পক্ষিবিশেষ। **Whale-line**—তিমিমৎস্য শিকারে ব্যবহৃত ২ ইঞ্চি মোটা দড়ী। **Whale-man** — তিমি শিকারী। **Whale-oil** — তিমিমৎস্যের তৈল। **Whaling-gun**—তিমি মৎস্যের উপর টেঁটা প্রভৃতি নিক্ষেপের জন্য কামান; **Whaling-master**—তিমিমৎস্য শিকারে ব্যবহৃত জাহাজের অধ্যক্ষ।

whāl'-ėr, *n.* A person or ship employed in whale-fishery; তিমি শিকারী, তিমিমৎস্য শিকারে ব্যবহৃত জাহাজ।

whăng, *v. t., & n.* 1. To strike heavily and loudly; দুমদাম করিয়া মারা 2. (*Scot.*) To slice; টুকরা টুকরা করিয়া কাটা। ***Noun.*** 1. A whack; a whanging sound; দুমদাম করিয়া পিটন; দুমদাম শব্দ। 2. (*Scot.*) A large piece; বৃহৎ টুকরা। **Whang'-ing,** *n. & adj.*

whärf, *n. & v. t.* A perpendicular bank or mound of timber or stone or earth raised on the shore of a harbour, river, canal, etc.; জাহাজের মাল বোঝাই বা খালাস করার জন্য কাষ্ঠ কিম্বা প্রস্তররচিত মঞ্চ, ঘাট, জাহাজঘাট। ***Verb t.*** 1. To furnish with a wharf or wharves; ঘাট বা ঘাটশ্রেণীসমন্বিত করা। 2. To lodge on wharf; জাহাজ ঘাটে রাখা। 3. To moor a ship at wharf; জাহাজ ঘাটে বাঁধা। 4. To store goods on a wharf; ঘাটে মাল সঞ্চিত করা। **Wharf'-age,** *n.* 1. The duty or toll paid for the privilege of using a wharf, for loading or discharging a cargo; ঘাটমাশুল। 2. A wharf or wharves collect vety; ঘাট, ঘাটশ্রেণী।

whärf'-in-gėr, *n.* The owner of wharf; ঘাটের মালীক।

what (whŏt), *Interreg. pron. relat. pron., Indef. pron., & adv.* Used elliptically, in exclamation, or adjectively; কি। ***Relat. pron.*** That which (used adjectively); such as; whatever; যাহা, তাহা; এরূপ; যাহাই হউক। ***Indef. pron.*** Something; কোন জিনিষ। ***Adv.*** (*Obs.*) Why; in what respect; to what degree;

কেন ; কি বিষয়ে, কি পর্য্যন্ত। **Come what will or may**—In spite of anything that might happen ; যাহাই হউক না কেন, যাহাই ঘটুক না কেন। **I tell you what**—এই সম্বন্ধে তোমাকে বলিতেছি শোন। (এই বাক্য দ্বারা শ্রোতার মন কোন গুরুতর বিষয়ে আকৃষ্ট হয়।) **To know what is what**—To be able to discriminate between a good and bad things ; to be knowing ; ভাল এবং মন্দ জিনিষের পার্থক্য বুঝিতে পারা ; জ্ঞাতসার হওয়া। **What? What did you say**—কি? আপনি কি বলিলেন? **What all**—What it all might be ; যত রকমের জিনিষ হইতে পারে। **What for**—(*Colloq.*) Punishment ; whipping ; (চলিত-ভাষায়) শাস্তি ; বেত্রদণ্ড। **What if**—What would be the consequence if ; what would you say if ; যদি এরূপ হয় তবে ফলে কি দাঁড়াইবে ; যদি এরূপ হয় তুমি কি বলিবে। **What is his name? what do you call it?**—তাহার নামটা না কি? ওটাকে তোমরা কি বল? **What is what**—The correct thing ; প্রকৃত বিষয়। **What not**—Many other things of the same kind ; anything ; ঐরকমের আরো জিনিষ ; যে কোন জিনিষ। **What of**—What do you say or think of ; তুমি কি বল বা মনে কর। What follows from ; why do you mention ; what is the matter with ; what does it matter in any way ; ইহা হইতে কি বুঝায় ; উল্লেখ করিয়া কাজ কি? (তাহার) কি হইয়াছে ; ইহাতে কি আসে যায়? **What though**—What does it matter though ; তাতে কি আসে যায়। Admitting that ; তাহা স্বীকার করিলেও, সেটা মানিয়া নিলেও। **What of that**—No matter ; never mind ; তাতে কি হলো? ; তাতে কি? ; কিছু মনে করবেন না। **What of the night**—(Bible, *Isaa* XXI. 11) What part of the night ; কত রাত্রি হইয়াছে। **What Oh!**—An exclamation of calling ; ওহে শোন। **What sort of man is he**—সে কি রকম লোক, সে কি ভাবের লোক।

what-ŏv′-ĕr (-whŏt), **what′-e′er** (whŏt-ār), *prons.* & *adj.* Anything soever that ; যে কোন, যে কিছু, যাহা কিছু। ***Adj.*** Of any kind soever ; যে কোনরূপ।

what′-nŏt (whŏt-), *n.* A stand with shelves for papers, books, etc. ; কাগজ, পুস্তক প্রভৃতি রাখার জন্য থাড়া সেল্‌ফ।

what-sō-ĕv′-ĕr (whŏt-), *adj.* No matter what thing or things (a more emphatic form of *whatever*) ; যে কোনও।

whaup (whăp), *n.* Curlew ; এক-জাতীয় ক্রৌঞ্চ পক্ষী।

wheal (whēl), *n.* Pimple ; pustule ; ব্রণ ; ফুস্কুড়ী।

wheal (whēl) *n.* Mine ; esp. tin-mine ; খনি ; বিশেষতঃ টিনের খনি।

wheat (whēt), *n.* The grain from which flour is manufactured of which bread is chiefly made ; গম, গোধূম। [*Syn.* বহুদুগ্ধ, অপূপ, যবন, ম্লেচ্ছভোজন, নিস্তুষ, শীর্ষ, রসাল, সুমনা।] [Arab. *hinteh* ; Pers. *gundum* ; Chin. *lai, siau-met* ; *kia-size-ts* ; Fr. *froment, bled, ble* ; Germ. *weitzen* ; It. *grano, formento* ; Port. *trigo* ; Russ. *pscheni* ; Swed. *hvete* ; Tam. *godumbi* ; Teleg. *godumalu* ; Gk. *purvi.*] **Wheat′-en,** *adj.* **Wheat-grass**—Same as COUCH-GRASS.

wheat′-ear (whēt-ĕr), *n.* A small bird common in Europe allied to the stonechat and white-tail ; ইয়ুরোপদেশীয় একপ্রকার ক্ষুদ্র পক্ষী। **Wheat-fly**—গোধূমনাশক এক-প্রকার পীত কিম্বা কমলালেবুর বর্ণের কীট।

whee′-dle (whē-dl), *v. t.* & *i* **1.** To gain over by coaxing and flattery ; মিষ্ট কথায় বা তোষামোদ দ্বারা বশ করা। **2.** To gain or procure by flattery or coaxing ; as, to *wheedle* a rupee from a gentleman ; মিষ্ট কথা বা তোষামোদ দ্বারা প্রাপ্ত হওয়া বা লাভ করা। **3.** To cheat out of a thing by wheedling ; তোষামোদ দ্বারা বা মিষ্ট কথায় ভুলাইয়া কোন জিনিষ ঠকাইয়া নেওয়া। ***Verb i.*** To flatter ; তোষামোদ করা। **—dler,** *n.* One who wheedles ; তোষামোদ দ্বারা বশকারী। **—dling,** *n.* **—dlingly,** *adv.*

wheel (whēl), *n.* **1.** A frame of wood or iron in the form of a circle, being arranged to turn on an axis ; চক্র, চাকা। **2.** Turn ; as, the *vicissitudes* and wheel of things ; পাক, ঘূর্ণন, চক্র (cf. ভাগ্যচক্র)। **3.** A wheeled vehicle ; a chariot ; a car ; a bycycle or tricycle ; চক্রযুক্ত যান ; রথ ; যান ; দ্বিচক্রযান, ত্রিচক্রযান। **4.** (*Fig.*) The moving power or elements ; as, the *wheels* of government ; (লক্ষণায়) চক্র। **5.** An instrument of torture formerly used in France and Germany ; পূর্ব্বকালে জর্ম্মণী এবং ফরাসী দেশে ব্যবহৃত একপ্রকার পীড়নযন্ত্র। **6.** A firework of circular shape which revolves on an axis while burning ; চরকীবাজী। **Wheel′-less,** *adj.* **Eccentric wheel**—যাহার অক্ষ কেন্দ্রস্থলে স্থিত নয়—এরূপ চক্র। **Fifth wheel**—চারি চাকার গাড়ীর সম্মুখের চাকা ঘুরাইবার জন্য কল বিশেষ ; অনাবশ্যক জিনিষ। **Wheelbarrow**—একচাকার ঠেলাগাড়ী। **Wheel-barometer**—একপ্রকার বায়ুমান যন্ত্র—যাহার নল নিম্নদিকে বিপর্য্যস্ত Λ অক্ষরের মত বক্রভাবে থাকে। [এইরূপ বায়ুমান যন্ত্রে একটি প্লবক (float) থাকে—যাহা হইতে একখণ্ড রজ্জু কপিকলের উপর দিয়া যাইয়া প্রদর্শক (index) কে চালিত করে] চক্রবায়ুমান, চক্রভারমাপক (হিঃ কোঃ)। **Wheel-chair**—রুগ্ন

ব্যক্তিদিগের জন্য ক্ষুদ্র চক্রযুক্ত কেদারা। **Wheel-horse**—Same as WHEELER 3. **Wheel-house**—কর্ণধারের আশ্রয়স্থান। **Wheel-lock**—একপ্রকার প্রাচীন ধরণের বন্দুক—যাহাতে ইস্পাতের একটী চক্র কলের সাহত ঘৃষ্ট হইত ; ঐরূপ বন্দুকের কল। **Wheelman**—দ্বিচক্রযানচালক। **Wheel-ore**—একপ্রকার খনিজ পদার্থ (Bournonite). **Wheel-seat**—অক্ষদণ্ডের যে অংশ চক্রনাভিতে নিবদ্ধ থাকে। **Wheel-tread**—শকটচক্র প্রভৃতির যে অংশ ভূমির সহিত স্পৃষ্ট হয়। **Wheel-work**—(কোন যন্ত্রের) পরস্পরের সহিত সংযুক্ত চক্রপরম্পরা। **Wheel-window**—চক্রাকৃতি বাতায়ন, চক্রবাতায়ন। **Wheel-wright**—চক্রনির্মাতা। **The wheels of life**—জীবনক্রিয়া। **To break a butterfly or a fly on the wheel**—See under BREAK. **To break on the wheel**—To maim and kill in a wheel-like instrument of torture as was done in the Middle Ages ; হস্তপদাদি চক্রবৎ যন্ত্রের পেষণে ভাঙ্গিয়া অপরাধীদিগকে বধ করা (যেরূপ মধ্যযুগে করা হইত।) [অপরাধীদিগকে উক্ত চক্রাকার যন্ত্রে বাঁধিয়া উহা আবর্ত্তিত করা হইত।] **To go on wheels**—To make rapid progress ; দ্রুত উন্নতির পথে ধাবিত হওয়া। **To put a spoke in one's wheel**—See under SPOKE. **To put one's shoulder to the wheel**—See under SHOULDER. **Wheel of fortune**—ভাগ্যচক্র। **Wheel of life**—Same as ZOETROPE. **Wheels within wheels**—Intricate machinery ; indirect or secret agencies ; জটিল কলকব্জা ; গুপ্ত বা কুটিল ক্রিয়া, পাকচক্র, চক্রান্ত।

wheel (whēl), *v. t.* & *i.* **1.** To cause to turn on an axis, pivot, etc. ; চক্রবৎ ঘূর্ণিত করা, চাকার মত ঘুরাণ **2.** To convey on wheels or in a vehicle mounted on wheels ; as, to *wheel* a load of coal ; গাড়ীতে বহন করা। **3.** To provide with a wheel or wheels ; as, to *wheel* a cart ; চাকা লাগান, চক্র নিবদ্ধ করা। ***Verb i.*** **1.** To revolve ; ঘূর্ণিত হওয়া। **2.** To change direction ; as, he *wheeled* to the left ; দিক পরিবর্ত্তন করা। **3.** To go round in a circuit ; প্রদক্ষিণ করা। **4.** To ride on a bicycle or tricycle ; দ্বিচক্রযান বা ত্রিচক্রযানে আরোহণ করা। **5.** To roll forward ; গড়াইয়া চলা।

Wheel'-er, *n.* **1.** One that wheels ; যে ব্যক্তি চক্র আবর্ত্তিত করে, চক্রাবর্ত্তক। **2.** That which has wheels ; চক্রবিশিষ্ট বস্তু। **3.** A horse harnessed next to the forewheels of a vehicle ; শকট প্রভৃতির সম্মুখের চাকার অব্যবহিত পশ্চাতে যে অশ্ব যোজিত হয়। **4.** (*Obs.*) Same as WHEEL-WRIGHT.

wheeze (whēz), *v. i.* & *n.* To breathe hard and with audible sound, গোঁ গোঁ শব্দে কষ্টে নিঃশ্বাস ফেল। ***Noun.*** **1.** Sound of wheezing ; গোঁ গোঁ শব্দ। **2.** (*Theatre*) Joke, anecdote, etc. interpolated by an actor during performance ; (নাট্য) পরিহাস, ক্ষুদ্র আখ্যায়িকা, প্রভৃতি যাহা কোন অভিনেতা তদীয় ভূমিকায় অভিনয়কালে প্রক্ষিপ্ত করে। **Wheez'-i-ly,** *adv.* **Wheez'-i-nees,** *n.* **To wheeze out**—To utter with wheezing ; গোঁ গোঁ শব্দে উচ্চারণ করা।

whĕlk, *n.* A mollusc with a univalvular, spiral, and gibbous shell, and an oval aperture ending in a short canal or gutter ; একপ্রকার সামুদ্রিক শম্বু শম্বুকাদি।

whĕlk, *n.* Pimple ; ব্রণ।

whĕlm, *v. t.* **1.** To submerge ; পরিপ্লাবিত করা। **2.** To overwhelm ; অভিভূত করা। **Whelmed,** *adj.*

whĕlp, *n., v. i.* & *t.* **1.** Pup ; কুক্কুরছানা, কুক্কুরশাবক। **2.** Young lion, tiger, bear, etc ; সিংহশাবক, ভল্লুকশাবক, প্রভৃতি। **3.** A naughty child ; দুরন্ত ছেলে। **4.** (*Contempt.*) A young man ; "That awkward *whelp* with his money-bags" ; যুবক। ***Verb i.*** To bring forth young, as a female of the canine species ; (কুক্কুরীর পক্ষে) ছানা প্রসব করা। ***Verb t.*** To bring forth, as cubs or young ; (*in contempt*) to give birth to ; "Did thy foul fancy *whelp* so foul a thing" ; শাবক উৎপাদন করা, বাচ্চা দেওয়া ; প্রসব করা।

whĕn, *adv., interrog. pron, relative pron.* & *n.* **1.** At what or which time ; as, *when* shall he come ; কখন, কোন সময়। **2.** At which time ; যখন। **3.** At that time ; তখন। **4.** Which time ; then ; যখন ; তখন। **5.** While ; on the contrary ; যখন ; পরন্তু, অপর পক্ষে। **6.** While ; whereas ; although ; যখন ; যেহেতু ; যদিও। ***Interrog. Pron.*** What time ; as, tell me till *when* you can stay ; কোন সময় (প্রশ্ন জিজ্ঞাসায়)। ***Relat. Pron.*** Which time ; as, since *when* his illness have taken a better turn ; কোন সময়। ***Noun.*** Time ; occasion ; as, he told me the *when* of it ; সময় ; উপলক্ষ। **When as, when that**—(*Obs.*) When ; (অপ্র:) যখন।

whence (whĕns), *adv., interrog. pron., relat. pron.* & *n.* **1.** From what place ; কোথা হইতে, কোত্থেকে (*colloq.*) কোন স্থান হইতে। **2.** From which source, origin, cause, antecedents, principle or the like ; কোথা হইতে। ***Interrog. pron.*** What place ; as, from *whence* is he ; কোন স্থান (প্রশ্ন জিজ্ঞাসায়) ***Relat. Pron.*** Which place ; as, the stock from *whence* he sprung ; কোন স্থান। ***Noun.*** Source ; as, he knows neither her *whence* nor whether ; উৎপত্তি, আদি।

whence-sŏ-ĕv'-ĕr (whĕns-), *adv.* From what place soever ; from what cause or source whatever ; যে কোন স্থান হইতে ; যে কোন কারণ বা মূল হইতে।

whĕn-e'er (-ār), *adv.* Contracted form of WHENEVER.

whĕn-ĕv'-ẽr, *adv.* At whatever time ; "*Whenever* you have need you may be armed" ; যখনই, যে কোন সময়ে।

whĕn-sō-ĕv'-ẽr, *adv.* At what time so ever; at whatever time ; যে কোন সময়েই হউক না কেন ; যে কোন কালে।

where (whār), *adv., interrog. pron. relat. pron.* & *n.* **1.** At or in what place ; "She visited that place *where* first she was so happy" ; কোথায়, কোন স্থানে। **2.** To which place ; "*Where* runnest thou so fast" ; কোথায়, কোন জায়গায়। **3.** In what position, circumstance or the like ; "Ancient of days ! August Athena ! *where, where* are thy men of might ? Thy grand in soul ?" ; কোন অবস্থায়। ***Interrog. pron.*** What place (প্রশ্ন জিজ্ঞাসায়) কোন স্থান ? ***Relat. Pron.*** Which place ; কোন স্থান। ***Noun.*** The place ; scene of some event ; as, the *wheres* and *whens* should be known ; স্থান ; কোন ঘটনার স্থান। **Where'-ness,** *n.* Quality or state of having a place; situation ; position ; স্থানিকত্ব ; স্থান ; অবস্থান। **In what**—কিসে। **Whereabout**—কোন স্থানের নিকটে ; কোন সম্বন্ধে। (*Noun*) গতিবিধি। **Whereas**—যেহেতু ; যখন ; বাস্তবিক পক্ষে ; পরন্তু। **Whereat**—যাহাতে, যাহার ফলে, কিসে। **Whereby**—কি-দ্বারা, কিসে। (কচিদ্‌ব্যবহৃত) কি প্রকারে। **Wherefore**—কি কারণে, কিজন্য ; অতএব ; কেন। (*Noun.*) (চলিত ভাষায়) হেতু, কারণ। **Wherefrom**—কোথা হইতে, কোন স্থান হইতে। **Wherein**—কোথায়, কোনস্থানে, কি সম্পর্কে, কি বিষয়ে, কোন সময়ে। **Whereinto**—Into which ; কোথায়, কিসে। **Whereof**—যাহাদের মধ্যে, যে সকলের মধ্যে ; কিসে, কি হইতে। **Whereon**—যাহার উপর ; কিসের উপর। **Wherethrough**—কিসের দ্বারা। **Whereto**—কোথায়, কোনস্থানে। **Whereunder**—কিসের অধীনে। **Whereupon**—যাহার পর, যাহার ফলে। **Wherewith, wherewithal**—যদ্দ্বারা, যাহাতে, কিদ্বারা (প্রশ্নে)।

wher-ĕv'-ẽr (whār-), *adv.* In, or to, whatever place ; যে কোন স্থানে।

whĕr'-ry (-ĭ), *n.* A shallow light boat, built very sharp for fast rowing or sailing ; এক-প্রকার দ্রুতগামী নৌকা।

whĕt, *v. t.* & *n.* **1.** To rub for the purpose of sharpening as an edge of tools ; ধার দেওয়া, ধারাল করা, শাণ দেওয়া। **2.** To make sharp or keen ; to stimulate ; as, to *whet* one's appetite ; শাণিত করা ; উদ্দীপ্ত করা, উত্তেজিত করা। ***Noun.*** **1.** The act of sharpening by rubbing ; তেজন, শাণ দেওন। **2.** That which whets or sharpens esp. an appetite "He assisted at four hundred bowls of punch, not to mention sips, draws and *whets*" ; যদ্দ্বারা কোন কিছু উত্তেজিত হয়, যদ্দ্বারা ক্ষুধা বৃদ্ধি পায়, রুচিবৃদ্ধিকর বস্তু।

whĕth'-ẽr, *conj.* A particle used to indicate that what follows is an alternative ; কি না।

whĕth'-ẽr, *pron.* & *adj.* (*Obs.*) Which of the two ; (অপ্রঃ) উভয়ের মধ্যে কোনটী। **Whether or no**—যাহাই হউক না কেন।

whĕth'-ẽr-ing, *n.* **1.** (*Dial.*) The retention of the after-birth in cows ; (প্রাদেশিক ভাষায়) গাভীর গর্ভ পরিস্রবের (ফুল) অপতন।

whew (whū), *interj.* An exclamation expressing astonishment, scorn ; বিস্ময়, অবজ্ঞা, প্রভৃতি-সূচক অব্যয়, হিস্‌, ফুঃ।

whey (whā), *n.* The serum or watery part of milk, separated from the more thick or coagulable part, esp. in making cheese ; ছানার জল, মস্তু (সুশ্রুঃ), দধিবারি, দধিমণ্ড। **Whey-face**—মলিনবদন, পাণ্ডুবদন।

which, *adj.* & *pron.* Used as a demonstrative adjective ; as, take *which* you will ; যে কোন। ***Pron.*** (*Interrog.*) **1.** An interrogative pronoun, signifying, who, or what one, of a number ; কে, কি, কোন। **2.** (*Relative*) Serving as the neuter of *who*, and having an antecedent of the singular or plural number or of neuter gender; as, the cows *which* are grazing in the field ; যে, যা, যাহারা। **Which is which**—Which is the one, which is the other ; এদের মধ্যে কে কোন জন।

which-ĕv'-ẽr, which-sō-ĕv'-ẽr, *pron.* Whether one or other ; as, *whichever* road you take that will conduct you to the school ; যে কোন একটি, যে কোনটী।

whid'-ah-bird (-ă-bẽrd), **-finch,** *ns.* An African weaver-bird, the male having a very long tail ; আফ্রিকাদেশীয় ক্ষুদ্র পক্ষিবিশেষ।

whiff, *n., v. t.* & *i.* **1.** A sudden expulsion of the air from the mouth ; ফুৎকার। **2.** A puff of air, smoke, etc. ; "Four pipes after dinner he constantly smokes, And seasons his *whiffs* with impertinent jokes" ; ধূম, বাতাস, প্রভৃতির মৃদুল উচ্ছ্বাস। **3.** A flat fish of the turbot group ; একপ্রকার চ্যাপ্টা মৎস্য। **4.** An out rigger boat ; একপ্রকার নৌকা—যাহার পার্শ্বে দাঁড়স্থাপনের জন্য খাঁজবিশিষ্ট লৌহময় নাগদন্ত (bracket) নিবদ্ধ থাকে। **5.** Small cigar ; ক্ষুদ্র চুরুট। ***Verb t.*** **1.** To throw out in whiffs ; to exhale as tobacco smoke ; to smoke ; ফুৎকৃত করা ; ধূমাদি নিঃসৃত করা ; ধূমপান করা। **2.** To convey by whiffs ; ফুৎকৃত বায়ু প্রভৃতি দ্বারা চালিত করা। ***Verb i.*** **1.** To emit whiffs as of smoke ;

ধূমাদি ফুৎকৃত হওয়া। 2. To fish with a hand-line ; হাতে ডোর ধরিয়া বড়শী ফেলা। **Whiffs of grape-shot**—কামান হইতেউপর্য্যুপরি কয়েকবার ক্ষুদ্র ক্ষুদ্র গোলা ছোড়ন।

whig, *n.* **1.** One of a political party which had its origin in the 17th century and advocated and supported measures of a liberal character, tending to give greater power to the popular element in the government of the state (opp. to TORY) ; সপ্তদশশতাব্দীতে গঠিত রাজনীতিক দল বিশেষ—এই দলভুক্তগণ রাষ্ট্রশাসন ব্যাপারে সাধারণ প্রজাদিগের হস্তে অধিকতর ক্ষমতা প্রদানের পক্ষপাতী। **2.** A liberal in politics ; উদারনীতিক সম্প্রদায়ের লোক। **3.** A friend and supporter of the American Revolution ; আমেরিকার বিপ্লবের পক্ষপাতী এবং সমর্থক ব্যক্তি। **Whig'-ger-y,** *n.* **Whig'-gish,** *adj.* **Whig'-gish-ly,** *adv.* **Whig'-gish-ness,** *n.*

while, *n.* & *v. t.* **1.** Time ; as, all this *while* ; time occupied in doing some work ; "Pausing a *while*, thus to herself she mused", সময় ; কোন কার্য্য সাধনে যে সময় লাগে। **2.** Trouble ; as, is it worth one's *while* ? ; কষ্ট। ***Verb t.*** To pass time in a leisurely manner (with *away*) ; "Let us *while away* this life" ; অবসরবিনোদন করা, সময় কাটান। **In a little while**—Soon ; শীঘ্র। **Long while**—Long time ; অনেক দিন। **Meanwhile**—ইতঃমধ্যে। **Once in a while**—At times ; সময় সময়, কখন কখন, মাঝে মাঝে। **The while**—During that time ; in the meantime ; সেই সময়ে ; ইতঃমধ্যে। **Worth while**—troubling oneself about ; কষ্ট স্বীকার করার উপযোগী, কষ্ট স্বীকার করিয়া চেষ্টা করার উপযোগী।

while, *conj.* **1.** During the time that ; "We two, my lord, will guard your person *while* you take your rest" ; at the same time that ; for as long as ; "*While* stands the Coliseum, Rome shall stand" ; যখন ; সেই সময়ে ; যে পর্য্যন্ত, যতদিন। **2.** Although ; "*While* admitting his good points, I cannot overlook the bad points of his character" ; যদিও।

whī'-lŏm, *adv.* & *adj.* (*Obs.*) Formerly ; once ; (অপ্রঃ) পূর্ব্বে ; একদিন, একদা। ***Adj.*** Quondam ; as, his *whilom* friend ; পূর্ব্বতন, একদিনের।

whilst, *conj.* & *n.* Same as WHILE *n.* I. & *conj.*

whim, *n.* **1.** A passing fancy ; a freak ; খেয়াল ; মর্জ্জি, আঁখুটি, গোঁ। **2.** A large capstan, for raising ore etc. from mine ; খনি হইতে বিমিশ্র ধাতু প্রভৃতি উত্তোলনের জন্য জাহাজের নোঙ্গরউত্তোলক যন্ত্রের অনুরূপ একপ্রকার বৃহৎ উত্তোলনযন্ত্র।

whim'-brĕl, *n.* A bird resembling the curlew ; একপ্রকার পক্ষী, ক্রৌঞ্চজাতীয় পক্ষী।

whim'-pêr, *v. t., i.* & *n.* To utter in a low whining tone ; প্যান প্যান করিয়া বলা, ঘ্যান ঘ্যান করিয়া বলা। ***Verb i.*** To whine ; ঘ্যান ঘ্যান করা, প্যান প্যান করা। ***Noun.*** A low whining, broken cry ; ঘ্যান ঘ্যানানি, প্যান প্যানানি। **—er,** *n.* **—ing-ly,** *adv.*

whim'-sĭ-căl, *adj.* **1.** Capricious ; খেয়ালপরবশ। **1.** Odd ; fantastical ; as, a *whimsical* apperance ; কেমনতর, অপরূপ ; আজগুবি, সৃষ্টিছাড়া। **—cal'-i-ty,** *n.* **—ly,** *adv.*

whim'-sy̆, *n.* Whim ; খেয়াল, মর্জ্জি, খামখেয়ালি।

whin, *n.* Gorse ; furze ; পীতপুষ্প-প্রসূ কণ্টকাকীর্ণ গুল্মবিশেষ ; পীতপুষ্পপ্রসূ চিরহরিৎ গুল্মবিশেষ। **Whin-chat**—একপ্রকার ক্ষুদ্র পক্ষী।

whin, whin'-sill, whin'-stōne, *ns.* Kinds of basaltic rock or hard sandstone ; বিভিন্নজাতীয় কৃষ্ণবর্ণ আগ্নেয়পাষাণ অথবা কঠিন বালুকাপ্রস্তর।

whine, *v. t., i.* & *n.* To utter in a plaintive drawling tone ; to complain in a mean or unmanly way ; as, to *whine* out a tale ; ঘ্যান ঘ্যান করিয়া বলা ; প্যান প্যান করিয়া বলা। ***Verb i.*** To whimper ; ঘ্যান ঘ্যান করা, প্যান প্যান করা। ***Noun.*** A drawling, plaintive tone or voice ; a mean or affected complaint ; ঘ্যানঘ্যানানি, প্যান-প্যানানি ; ছিঁচকাঁদুনি। **Whin'-er,** *n.* **Whin'-ing-ly,** *adv.*

whing'-êr, *n.* A short sword or dirk ; ক্ষুদ্রতরবারি বা ছোরা।

whin'-ny (-ĭ), *v. t.* & *n.* To neigh gently or joyfully ; অনুচ্চস্বরে হ্রেষারব করা, আনন্দে হ্রেষারব করা। ***Noun.*** Whinnying sound ; মৃদু হ্রেষাধ্বনি, অনুচ্চ হ্রেষাধ্বনি।

whip, *v. t.* & *i.* **1.** To move suddenly and quickly ; to take or seize with a sudden motion ; to snatch ; to carry, convey or move suddenly and rapidly ; as, to *whip* a guinea into the pocket ; হঠাৎ সবেগে চলা ; খপ্ করিয়া ধরা বা নেওয়া ; কাড়িয়া নেওয়া ; হঠাৎ এবং দ্রুত বহন করা বা চালিত করা। **2.** To lash ; to beat ; বেত্রাঘাত করা, কষাঘাত করা ; প্রহার করা। **3.** To punish by whipping ; "Who for false quantities was *whipped* at school" ; শাস্তিস্বরূপ বেত্রাঘাত করা। **4.** To beat into froth, as eggs, cream, etc. ; ডিম, সর, প্রভৃতি ফেটান। **5.** To keep together, as a party ; দল প্রভৃতি একত্র রাখা। **6.** To sew lightly ; "In half-*whipped* muslin useless needles lie" ; সামান্যভাবে সেলাই করা। **7.** To fish with a fly ; মক্ষিকা গাঁথিয়া বড়শী ফেলা। **8.** To overlay a cord, rope, etc. with other cord, or the like, going round ; to wrap ; as,

"*Whipped* over with gold ; রজ্জু প্রভৃতির চতুর্দ্দিকে অপর রজ্জু জড়ান ; জড়িত করা। **9.** To wind, wreathe, or bind about something ; as, to *whip* a string about the end of a fishing-rod ; কোন কিছুর চতুর্দ্দিকে জড়ান বা বাঁধা। **10.** To make to turn or rotate with lashes ; as, to *whip* a top ; বেত্র দ্বারা আঘাত করিয়া ঘুরাণ। **11.** To treat with cutting severity, as with sarcasm, abuse or the like ; "Wilt thou *whip* thine own faults in other men" ; বিদ্রূপ, সমালোচনা প্রভৃতির কষাঘাত করা। **12.** To beat out, as grain by striking ; as, to *whip* wheat ; দণ্ড প্রভৃতি দ্বারা আঘাত করিয়া শস্য মাড়া। **13.** To overcome ; "We can *whip* all creation" ; বশীভূত করা। **14.** (*Slang*) To conquer ; (ইতর ভাষায়) জয় করা। **15.** To fish in with a rod and line with a motion employed in using a whip ; নড়কাইয়া বড়শী দ্বারা মৎস্য ধরা। **16.** To hoist coal etc. with rope passed through a pulley ; কপিকলের উপর রজ্জু চালিত করিয়া কয়লা প্রভৃতি তোলা। *Verb i.* **1.** To move nimbly ; to turn and run ; as the boy *whipped* away ; সবেগে চলা, চটুলভাবে চলা ; ঘুরিয়া দৌড়া। **2.** To fish by whipping the water ; নড়কাইয়া বড়শী দ্বারা মৎস্য ধরা। **Whip'-ping,** *n.* **Whipping-boy**—রাজপুত্রের সহিত একত্র শিক্ষাপ্রাপ্ত এবং তৎপরিবর্ত্তে বেত্রাঘাতদণ্ডভোগী বালক। (পূর্ব্বে ইংলণ্ডের রাজপুত্রের সহিত অন্য একটী বালক শিক্ষাপ্রাপ্ত হইত এবং রাজপুত্রের পরিবর্ত্তে সে দণ্ডভোগ করিত)। **Whipping-post**—যে দণ্ডে বাঁধিয়া কোন ব্যক্তিকে বেত্রাঘাত করা হয়। **Whipping-top**—একপ্রকার লাটিম—যাহা ছড়ি দ্বারা আঘাত করিয়া ঘুরাণ হয়। **To whip in**—To keep the hounds from wandering, and try to keep them to the line of scent ; শিকারী কুকুরকে বেত্রদ্বারা আঘাত করিয়া ঠিক পথে রাখা। To come last ; সর্ব্বশেষে আসা। To bring or keep the members of a party together ; কোন দলের সভ্যগণকে একত্র রাখা। **To whip off**—To drive hounds off the scents ; শিকারী কুকুরদিগকে পলায়মান জন্তুর গন্ধের পথ হইতে বিতাড়িত করা। **To whip the cat**—(*Dial.*) To practise strictest parsimony ; (উপভাষায়) অতিশয় কৃপণতা করা। (*Dial.*) To go from house to house working by the day as tailors, carpenters, etc. ; (উপভাষায়) লোকের বাড়ী বাড়ী যাইয়া দিবাভাগে দর্জ্জী, সূতার মিস্ত্রী, প্রভৃতির কার্য্য করা। **To whip the devil round** or **around the stump**—To perform by some indirect means or by subterfuge ; গৌণ উপায়ে বা কৌশলক্রমে কোন কার্য্য সাধন করা।

whip, *n.* **1.** A lash of plaited cord or such like tied to a handle ; কষা, চাবুক, বেত, বেত্র। **2.** A coachman, or driver of a carriage ; as, he is a good *whip* ; গাড়োয়ান, শকটচালক। **3.** A member of the Parliament that summons the members of his party to an important division ; the summons itself ; পার্লেমেণ্টের যে সভ্য তদীয় দলভুক্ত সভ্যগণকে কোন গুরুতর বিষয় সম্পর্কে অনুকূল বা প্রতিকূল ভাব অবলম্বনে মিলিত হইবার জন্য আহ্বান করে ; ঐরূপ আহ্বানপত্র। **4.** Same as WHIPPER-IN. **5.** A flag used for signalling ; সঙ্কেত প্রদানের জন্য ব্যবহৃত পতাকা, সঙ্কেতধ্বজ। **6.** A rope-and-pulley hoisting apparatus ; রজ্জু এবং কপিকল সমন্বিত ভার তোলনযন্ত্র বিশেষ। **7.** A dish made by whipping or beating, eggs, creams, etc. ; ফেটানো ডিম, সর, প্রভৃতি পূর্ণ পাত্র। **Whip-cord**—চাবুকের রজ্জু। **Whip-fish** — একপ্রকার মৎস্য—যাহার পিঠের পাখনার কিয়দংশ কতকটা চাবুকের রজ্জুর মত দেখায়। **Whip-gin**—যে কলকে ভারোত্তোলনরজ্জু নিবদ্ধ থাকে। **Whip-hand**—যে হস্ত দ্বারা চাবুক ধরা হয় ; প্রভুত্ব, কর্ত্তৃত্ব। **Whip-lash**—কষাগ্র। **Whip-ray**—দীর্ঘ পুচ্ছবিশিষ্ট একপ্রকার চাঁদা মাছ। **Whip-snake**—একপ্রকার সরু সাপ। **Whip-stock**—চাবুকের বাঁট। **To have the whip-hand of**—To have the authority ; কর্ত্তৃত্ব থাকা, প্রভুত্ব থাকা। **Whip-and-derry** — Same as WHIP *n.* 6. **Whip and spur**—সত্বর, দ্রুত।

whip'-per (-ẽr), *n.* **1.** One who whips ; কষাঘাতকারী। **2.** An officer who inflicts the penalty of legal whipping ; বেত্রদণ্ডপ্রদাতা। **Whipper-in**—যে ব্যক্তি শিকারী কুকুরদিগকে পলায়মান জন্তুর পথে রাখিয়া থাকে। **Whipper-snapper**—শিশু ; জ্যাঠা লোক।

whip'-pet (-ĕt), *n.* (*Obs.*) A kind of dog, a cross between a greyhound and spaniel ; (অপ্র:) একপ্রকার দোঁ-আশলা বিলাতী কুকুর।

whip'-poor-will (-poor-), *n.* An American bird allied to goatsucker ; আমেরিকাদেশীয় পক্ষিবিশেষ।

whip'-stêr, *n.* **1.** A small child ; শিশু। **2.** A little smart or nimble fellow ; "Every *whipster* gets my sword" ; চালাক ছেলে, চটপটে ছেলে (*colloq.*)।

whir, whirr (whêr), *v. i.* & *n.* To whirl round with a noise ; ভন ভন করিয়া ঘুরা, ভোঁ ভোঁ করিয়া ঘুরা, ঘর ঘর করিয়া ঘুরা। ***Noun.*** The sound from rapid whirling motion ; ভন ভন শব্দ, ভোঁ ভোঁ শব্দ, সোঁ সোঁ শব্দ।

whirl (whêrl), *v. t., i.* & *n.* **1.** To turn round rapidly ; দ্রুত ঘূর্ণিত করা। **2.** To carry off quickly with a revolving motion ; as, he was *whirled* away in his carriage ; ঘুরাইয়া তুলিয়া দ্রুত লইয়া চলা। ***Verb i.*** **1.** To revolve with great speed; দ্রুত ঘূর্ণিত হওয়া, দ্রুত পাক খাওয়া। 2. To move or go swiftly; "I'll come and be thy waggoner, And *whirl* along with thee about the globe"; দ্রুত চলা, ভূর্ণবেগে চলা। ***Noun.*** 1. A rapid turning; দ্রুত ঘূর্ণন। 2. Something that whirls; as, a *whirl* of dust; ঘূর্ণনশীল বস্তু; কুণ্ডলী। **Whirling dervish**—নর্তনশীল দরবেশসম্প্রদায় বিশেষ। **Whirlpool**—ঘূর্ণিজল, জল ভ্রম, আবর্ত্ত, জলাবর্ত্ত, উদ্ভ্রম। **Whirlwind**—ঘূর্ণিবায়ু, বাতাবর্ত্ত, চক্রবাত, পবনচক্র, ধূম্রধ্বজ, ঘূর্ণবায়ু (সাঃ পঃ), ঘূর্ণি। **To sow wind and reap whirlwind**—See sow.

whirl'-i-gig (whĕrl-), *n.* 1. A toy which children spin or whirl; লাটিম। 2. Revolving motion; পাক, ঘূর্ণন। 3. A frame, with wooden horses or seats, on which persons are whirled round for amusement's sake; বৃহৎ ছত্রাদিতে সংবদ্ধ কাষ্ঠনির্ম্মিত আসন—যাহাতে ঘূর্ণিত হইয়া লোকে মেলা প্রভৃতিতে আমোদ করিয়া থাকে। 4. A medieval instrument for punishing petty offenders, being a kind of wooden cage in which the offender was whirled round with great velocity; মধ্যযুগে অপরাধীদিগকে শাস্তিপ্রদানের জন্য একপ্রকার কাষ্ঠপিঞ্জর—যাহাতে অপরাধী ব্যক্তিকে রাখিয়া দ্রুত ঘূর্ণিত করা হইত। 4. Kinds of water-beetle that circle about on surface; জলের উপর ঘূর্ণনশীল বিভিন্ন প্রকার গোবরে পোকা।

Whirligig

whisk, *v. t. & i.* 1. To sweep or brush with a light rapid motion; as, to *whisk* the dust from a table; ঝাড়া, ঝাড়িয়া পরিষ্কার করা। 2. To beat or agitate with a light rapid motion; as, to *whisk* the yolk of an egg; ফেটান। 3. To carry off suddenly or rapidly; কস্ করিয়া লইয়া যাওয়া। ***Verb i.*** To move rapidly and nimbly; as, to *whisk* away; হন্ হন্ করিয়া চলা।

whisk'-ĕr, *n.* 1. Long hair growing on man's cheek, formerly a moustache; গালপাট্টা। 2. (*Pl.*) The stiffer hair at either side of an animal's mouth; বিড়াল প্রভৃতির গোঁফ। **Whiskered-bat**—একপ্রকার বাদুড়—ইহাদের উপরের ঠোঁটের পালক অপেক্ষাকৃত দীর্ঘতর [এইপ্রকার বাদুড় মধ্য ইয়ুরোপে এবং এসিয়ার অনেক স্থানে পাওয়া যায়], শ্মশ্রুল বাদুড়। **Whiskered-tern**—একপ্রকার পক্ষী।

whis'-ky, *n.* A spirit distilled from grain and other substance; হুইস্কি। **Whysky-liver**—হুইস্কি পান হইতে জাত যকৃতের রোগ।

whis'-ky, -key (ki-), *ns.* A light carriage for rapid motion; এক প্রকার দ্রুতগামী লঘু শকট।

whis'-pĕr, *v.i., t. & n.* 1. To speak softly or in a low tone; চুপি চুপি কথা বলা। 2. To make a rustling sound; as, the *whispering* breeze; মর্ম্মরধ্বনি করা। ***Verb t.*** 1. To speak under breath; অনুচ্চ স্বরে কথা বলা, চুপি চুপি কথা বলা। 2. To mention or speak about privately and confidentially; "He came to *whisper* Wolsey"; গোপনে উল্লেখ করা, বিশ্বাস করিয়া বলা, কাণাঘুষা করা, ফিসফাস করিয়া বলা, কাণাকাণি করা। ***Noun.*** 1. A low voice; the utterance of words without any vocal sound; অনুচ্চ স্বর; চুপি চুপি কথা বলন। 2. Words uttered by whispering; hence, something communicated stealthily or secretly; "Full well the busy *whisper* circling round conveye'd the dismal tidings when he frown'd"; কানকথা; কাণাঘুষা। 3. A low sibilant sound; as, the *whispers* of the wind; মর্ম্মর, সন্‌সন্। 4. A hint; insinuation; "Never had they breathed a *whisper* against arbitrary power"; আভাস; ইঙ্গিত। —er, *n.* —ing, *n.* —ing-ly, *adv.* **Whispering gallery**—যে গম্বুজ বা ক্রমোচ্চ আসনসমন্বিত মঞ্চ এইরূপভাবে গঠন করা হয় যাহাতে কোন কোন নির্দ্দিষ্ট অংশে উচ্চারিত অতি ক্ষীণ ধ্বনি প্রাচীর হইতে পরাবর্ত্তিত হইয়া বহুদূর পর্য্যন্ত শ্রুত হয়।

whist, whisht, *interj.* (*Rare*) An interjection enjoining silence; (ক্বচিদ্‌ব্যবহৃত) চুপ! চুপ!

whist, *adj.* (*Archaic*) Silent; "Far from the town where all is *whist* and still"; (অপ্রঃ) নীরব,নিঝুম।

whist, *n.* A game of cards, so called, it is supposed, because it imposes silence or close attention; একপ্রকার তাস খেলা। [এক এক পক্ষে এই ক্রীড়ায় চারি ব্যক্তির প্রয়োজন হয়। দুই জন করিয়া এক পক্ষে থাকে। ইহাতে ৫২ খানা তাসেরই আবশ্যক হইয়া থাকে। প্রত্যেককে ১৩ খানা তাসের এক এক খানা করিয়া বাঁটিয়া দেওয়া হয়। বণ্টনকারী প্রথম তাস গ্রহণ করে। তৎপর তদীয় বাম দিক হইতে আরম্ভ করিয়া দক্ষিণ দিকে বণ্টন শেষ করে। বণ্টনের পর সর্ব্বশেষ তাস খানা উল্টাইয়া মেজের উপর রাখা হয়। এই তাসই রঙ্গ হইয়া থাকে। এই সকল তাসের মধ্যে গোলাম, বিবি, টেক্কা, সাহেব উত্তরোত্তর শ্রেষ্ঠতর বলিয়া গণ্য হইয়া থাকে। বণ্টনকারীর বামদিগ্‌বর্ত্তী ক্রীড়ক প্রথম তাস খেলিয়া থাকে, তৎপর তাহার বামের ক্রীড়ক তাস ফেলে। তাহার নিকট জাত থাকিলে সেই জাতের তাস খেলে, আর জাত না থাকিলে তুরুপ বা ফাস দিয়া থাকে। তৎপর সেই ব্যক্তির বামের ক্রীড়ক পূর্ব্বোক্ত ভাবে তাস খেলে। ইহাদের মধ্যে যে ক্রীড়কের তাস রঙ্গ বা অঙ্ক হিসাবে সর্ব্বাপেক্ষা শ্রেষ্ঠ হয় সেই জনই পিঠ পাইয়া থাকে। অতঃপর যে ব্যক্তি পিঠ পায় তাহাকে প্রথম খেলিতে হয় এবং তৎপর তাহার বাম দিকের ক্রীড়কেরা পর পর খেলিয়া থাকে;

খেলা শেষ হইলে যে পক্ষের উভয় ক্রীড়ক একযোগে মোট ১৩ পিঠের অধিকাংশ পিঠ পাইয়া থাকে সেই পক্ষ ৬ পিঠের পর প্রত্যেক পিঠের জন্য এক ক্রীড়াঙ্ক (point) লাভ করে। রঙ্গের টেক্কা, রাজা, রাণী ও গোলামকে মানী (honours) কহে। যে পক্ষে ক্রীড়কদ্বয় এক যোগে ৩টী 'মানী' পায় সেই পক্ষ দুই ক্রীড়াঙ্ক লাভ করিয়া থাকে। যদি কোন পক্ষ ৪টী "মানী" পায় তবে সেই পক্ষ ৪ ক্রীড়াঙ্ক লাভ করে। যদি উভয় পক্ষের প্রত্যেকে দুইটী করিয়া 'মানী' পায় তবে কোন পক্ষই ক্রীড়াঙ্ক লাভ করে না। Long whist ক্রীড়াতে (এই ক্রীড়া বর্ত্তমানে বড় চলিত নাই) ১০ ক্রীড়াঙ্কে এক খেলা (game) হয়; Short whist এ পাঁচ ক্রীড়াঙ্কে এক 'খেলা' হইয়া থাকে। শেষোক্ত ক্রীড়াতে সচরাচর পিঠ দ্বারাই ক্রীড়াঙ্ক গণনা করা হইয়া থাকে। তিন "খেলা"কে রবার (rubber) কহে। যে পক্ষ ২ "খেলা" পায় সেই পক্ষেরই এক rubber হইয়া থাকে। যদি কোন পক্ষ প্রথম দুই "রবার" পায় তবে আর তৃতীয় "খেলা"র জন্য ক্রীড়ার আবশ্যক হয় না।

whis'-tle (-l), *v. i., t.* & *n.* **1.** To utter a kind of musical sound, by pressing the breath through a small orifice formed by contracting the lips; শিস্ দেওয়া। **2.** To sound a wind or steam whistle; শিটি দেওয়া, ফুঁ দেওয়া (বিশেষ ভাবে জাহাজ রেলগাড়ী প্রভৃতি সম্পর্কে)। **3.** To utter a more or less shrill or piercing sound, or series of sounds, as birds; "Sometimes the throstle *whistled* strong"; পাখীর শিস্ দেওয়া। **4.** To move or pass with a shrill sound; সোঁ সোঁ করিয়া যাওয়া। ***Verb t.*** **1.** To form, utter or modulate by whistling; as, to *whistle* a tune; শিস্ দিয়া গঠন, উচ্চারণ বা বিচিত্রতা সাধন করা। **2.** To call, signal or direct by whistling; "He cast off his friends, as a huntsman his pack, For he knew, when he pleased, he could *whistle* them"; শিস্ দিয়া ডাকা, সঙ্কেত করা, বা নির্দ্দেশ করা। ***Noun.*** **1.** A more or less pierceing sound produced by forcing the breath through a small opening formed by contracting the lips; শিস্। **2.** The shrill note of a bird; পক্ষীর শিস্। **3.** The small pipe used in signalling, by boatswains, huntsmen, policemen, etc.; শিটি। **4.** The instrument sounded by escaping steam, used for signalling on railway engines, steam-ships; জাহাজের শিটি, ইঞ্জিনের শিটি। **5.** (*Slang*) The mouth or throat; as, to wet one's *whistle*; (ইতরভাষায়) মুখ, গলা। **6.** A sound made by the wind, or by a body passing rapidly through the air; সোঁ সোঁ শব্দ। **7.** A pipe or flute; বংশী, মুরলী। **—tling** *n.* **Penny-whistle**—ছয় রন্ধ্রযুক্ত টীনের চোঙ্গা — যাহা শিশুরা বাজাইয়া থাকে। **Whistling eagle**—একপ্রকার পক্ষী। **At one's whistle**—Ready at one's call; কাহারো হুকুমের উপরে দাঁড়ানো। **To let one go whistle**—To disregard his wish; কাহারো ইচ্ছার উপেক্ষা করা। **To pay for one's whistle**—To pay high for some caprice [The allusion is to a story of Benjamin Fanklin's in which he tells how when a young boy he set his mind upon a common whistle, and bought it for four times its real value]; কোনরূপ খেয়ালের জন্য অনেক টাকা খরচ করা। **To wet one's whistle**—See WHISTLE 5. **To whistle down the wind** — To talk or argue to no purpose; বৃথা বাক্য ব্যয় করা। To abandon; পরিত্যাগ করা। **To whistle for**—To call by whistling; শিস্ দিয়া ডাকা। (*Colloq.*) To demand, but fail to get; (চলিত ভাষায়) দাবী করা, কিন্তু লাভ করিতে না পারা। **To whistle for the wind**—(*Naut.*) A superstitious practice among old seamen of whistling during a calm to obtain breeze; (নৌবিদ্যা) প্রাচীন নাবিকদের মধ্যে বাতাসের জন্য শিটি দেওয়ার একপ্রকার কুসংস্কারমূলক প্রথা। **To whistle off**—To dismiss by whistle; শিটি দিয়া তাড়ান। To abandon; to dismiss; ত্যাগ করা; তাড়ান। **Worth the whistle**—Worth calling; worth the notice; ডাকার উপযুক্ত; লক্ষ্যের যোগ্য।

whis'-tler (-lẽr), *n.* **1.** One who, or that which, whistles: যে বা যাহা শিস্ দেয়, যে শিটি দেয়, সোঁ সোঁ শব্দকারী। **2.** The name of different kinds of birds; বিভিন্নপ্রকার পক্ষীর নাম। **3.** A kind of marmot: একপ্রকার কাঠবিড়াল জাতীয় জন্তু, গিরিমূষিক।

whit, *n.* A bit; jot; টুকরা; বিন্দু, লেশ, রতি, কণা, তিল। **Every whit**—In all respects; সর্ব্বাংশে। **Not or never a whit**—Not at all; মোটেই নয়। **No whit**—In no respect; কোন হিসাবেই নয়, কোন সম্পর্কেই নয়।

Whit, Whit'-sŭn, *adj.* **Whit-Sunday**—ঈষ্টার পর্ব্বের পরবর্ত্তী সপ্তম রবিবার। **Whit-suntide** — উক্ত রবিবার এবং সেই সপ্তাহের পরবর্ত্তী দিবস সমূহ (বিশেষতঃ সোম ও মঙ্গলবার)। **Whitsun week**—Same as WHIT-WEEK. **Whit week**—উক্ত রবিবার যে সপ্তাহে আছে।

white, *adj., n. v. t.,* & *i.* **1.** Being of the colour of pure snow; শ্বেত, শুভ্র, শুক্ল, ধবল, সাদা, সিত, গৌর। [সংস্কৃত সাহিত্যে নিম্নোক্ত বস্তুসমূহ শ্বেত বলিয়া পরিগণিত হয়:—জ্যোৎস্না, উচ্চৈঃশ্রবা, শারদমেঘ, শিব, বলরাম, সৌধ, টগর, হিমালয়, সূর্য্যকান্তমণি, চন্দ্রকান্তমণি, কর্পূর, রৌপ্য, করকা, তুষার, হরি, উর্ণনাভতন্তু, মন্দাকিনী, হস্তিদন্ত, অভ্র, অনন্তনাগ, শর্করা, দুগ্ধ, দধি, গঙ্গা, মৃণাল, সিকতা, সুধা, যশঃ, জল, হংস, বক, কুমুদ, চামর, কদলীফলের

গর্ভ, পুণ্ডরীক, কেতকী, শঙ্খ, নির্ঝর, লোধ্র, সিংহ, ধ্বজ, ছত্র, চূর্ণ, শুক্তি, কড়ি, মুক্তা, নক্ষত্র, দন্ত, পুণ্য, কৈলাস, কার্পাস, কাশ, হাস ঐরাবত, নারদ, পারদ, কুন্দ, খড়ি, স্ফটিক, দধিমিশ্রিতশক্তু, শ্বেতচন্দন, সমুদ্রফেণ।] **2.** Pale; bloodless; as, to turn *white* from fear; মলিন, ম্লান, পাণ্ডুর, পাঙ্গাসবর্ণ; রক্তহীন। **3.** Free from spot or guilt; pure; clean; "Calumny the *whitest* virtue strikes"; নির্দ্দোষ, নিষ্কলঙ্ক, অকলঙ্ক; পবিত্র; অপাপবিদ্ধ। **4.** Gray; as, *white* hair; ধূসর। **5.** Lucky; favourable "The dominie reckoned this as one of the *white* days of his life"; সৌভাগ্যপূর্ণ; অনুকূল। **6.** Colourless; of a light yellow or amber colour, as certain wines; as, *white* wines; বর্ণবিহীন; মৃদু পীত বা অম্বরবর্ণ, তৈলস্ফটিকবর্ণ। **7.** Made of silver; as, *white* ware; রৌপ্য-নির্ম্মিত। **8.** Bright, said of burnished steel and iron; উজ্জ্বল। ***Noun.*** 1. A Composite colour like that of pure snow; শ্বেতবর্ণ, শুক্লবর্ণ। **2.** Something white; শ্বেতবর্ণ পদার্থ। **3.** The mark at which a missile is shot; "You hit the *white*"; বাণের লক্ষ্য (পূর্ব্বে উক্তরূপ লক্ষ্যস্থান শ্বেতবর্ণে রঞ্জিত হইত।] **4.** The albumen of an egg; ডিম্বের শ্বেতাংশ, অণ্ডলালা (সাঃ পঃ)। **5.** A white spot or thing; শ্বেতবর্ণ চিহ্ন বা বস্তু। **6.** A member of the white race of mankind; as, there are many *whites* in Assam; শ্বেতকায় জাতির লোক, শ্বেতাঙ্গ (slightly ironical) **7.** (*Dial.*) Silver; "He has both *white* and yellow (gold)"; (উপভাষায়) রৌপ্য। **8.** Kinds of white pigment; as, zinc *white*; বিভিন্নপ্রকার শ্বেতবর্ণ রঞ্জকপদার্থ। **9.** White clothes; as, he was dressed in *white*; শ্বেতবস্ত্র, শ্বেত বসন। **10.** Any of the numerous butterfly in which the colour is generally white; বিভিন্ন প্রকার (সচরাচর) শ্বেতবর্ণের প্রজাপতি। **11.** Visible part round the iris of eye; চক্ষুর শ্বেতভাগ, নেত্রশ্বেতভাগ (সাঃ পঃ), বিঞ্জমর (ঐ), শুক্রমণ্ডল। **12.** Blank space in a printed picture or design; মুদ্রিত চিত্রাদিতে শূন্যস্থান। **13.** (*Railroad*) A white light used in signalling; সঙ্কেতস্বরূপ ব্যবহৃত শ্বেত আলোক। ***Verb t.*** **1.** To make white; শ্বেতবর্ণ করা। **2.** To whitewash; চূণকাম করা। **3.** To gloss over; "*Whit'st* over all his vices"; বাহ্য চাকচিক্য সম্পাদন করা, দোষ আচ্ছাদন করা। **4.** To make blank spaces between lines; পংক্তি-সমূহের মধ্যে মধ্যে ফাঁক রাখা। ***Verb i.*** To grow or become white; সাদা হওয়া, শ্বেতবর্ণ ধারণ করা। **White'-ness,** *n.* **1.** The quality or state of being white; শুক্লতা, ধবলতা, ধাবল্য, শ্বেতিমা, সিতিমা, ধবলিমা। **2.** Paleness; "A milky *whiteness* spreads on her cheeks"; বিবর্ণতা, ম্লানিমা, পাণ্ডুরতা, পাণ্ডুতা। **3.** Purity; cleanliness পবিত্রতা, শুভ্রচিত্ততা; নির্ম্মলতা। **4.** Freedom from stain; নিষ্কলঙ্কতা। **Whit'-en,** *v. t. & i.* **White alloy**—কৃত্রিম রৌপ্য, রূপসীধাতু। **White ant**—উই, বল্মীক কীট। **White apple**—জামরুল। **White arsenic**—শঙ্খবিষ, সেঁকোবিষ, শ্বেততাল (হিঃ কোঃ)। **White-ash**—একপ্রকার বৃক্ষ। **White-bait**—একপ্রকার ক্ষুদ্রাকৃতি মৎস্য; হেরিং মৎস্যের শাবক। **Whitebeam**—একপ্রকার বৃক্ষ; একপ্রকার ক্ষুদ্রবৃক্ষ—ইহাদের পত্রের পশ্চাদ্ভাগ শ্বেতবর্ণের হইয়া থাকে। **White-bear**—মেরু প্রদেশবাসী শ্বেতভল্লুক। **Whitebeard,-bearded**—শ্বেতশ্মশ্রু-ধারী। **White bird**—মানুষের আত্মা বা ধর্ম্মবুদ্ধি। **White-blaze**—Same as WHITE FACE. **White-bordered butterfly**—ইংলণ্ড দেশের এক-প্রকার কচিদ্দৃষ্ট প্রজাপতি। **White-bottle**—একপ্রকার ক্ষুপ। **White-boy**—১৮৬২ খৃঃ অব্দে গঠিত আয়র্লণ্ডের গুপ্তসম্প্রদায় বিশেষ—যাহারা রাত্রিকালে জমিদারগণের এবং অন্যান্য বিদ্বেষভাজন ব্যক্তির ধনসম্পত্তি লুণ্ঠন করিত। এই সম্প্রদায়ের লোকগণ শ্বেতবর্ণ জামা পরিধান করিত বলিয়া এই নামে আখ্যাত হয়। **White-boyism**—উক্ত দলের মত এবং ক্রিয়াকলাপ। **White-brant**—এক জাতীয় হংস। **White-brass**—তাম্র এবং দস্তার মিশ্র বিশেষ। **White-Brethren**—ইতালীদেশীয় ধর্ম্মোন্মত্ত-ব্যক্তিগণ দ্বারা গঠিত সম্প্রদায় বিশেষ। ইহারা চতুর্দ্দশ শতাব্দীর প্রারম্ভে জেরুজেলেম প্রভৃতি উদ্ধারের জন্য তুর্কি-দিগের বিরুদ্ধে ধর্ম্মযুদ্ধ ঘোষণা করা। Viterbo নামক স্থানে পোপের সৈন্যদিগের দ্বারা পরাজিত হইয়া ইহরা ছত্রভঙ্গ হয়। সম্প্রদায়ের নেতা জনৈক পুরোহিত যে আপনাকে ভাববাদী Elias বলিয়া দাবী করিত ধৃত হইয়া রোমে প্রেরিত হয়। এই ব্যক্তি প্রচলিত ধর্ম্মদ্বেষী বলিয়া জীবন্ত দগ্ধ হইয়াছিল। **White-campion**—তৃণবৎ ক্ষুপবিশেষ। **White candlewood**—একপ্রকার বৃক্ষ—ইহার পাতা ঝাউয়ের মত এবং রস কালীর মত কৃষ্ণবর্ণ। ইহার কাষ্ঠের গন্ধ মনোরম। **White cap**—একপ্রকার গুল্ম; একপ্রকার চটক পক্ষী। **White caps**—চীনদেশের বিদ্রোহী মুসলমানের দলবিশেষ। **White-cat**—একপ্রকার মৎস্য। **White clergy**—রুশিয়ার পল্লীযাজক। **White cloud-illuminator**—কোন বস্তুকে মৃদু শুভ্রবর্ণ আলোকে দীপ্ত করার জন্য একপ্রকার প্রতিফলনযন্ত্র, শুভ্রাভ্রভাসক। **White-clover**—একপ্রকার ক্ষুপ। **White-coat**—অষ্ট্রেলিয়ার সৈনিক (শ্বেতবর্ণ কোট পরিধান করে বলিয়া এই নাম)। **White-company**—ফরাসী দস্যুদল-বিশেষ। **White-copper**—তাম্র, নিকেল, এবং দস্তার মিশ্র বিশেষ, জর্ম্মণ-সিলভার। **White corpuscles**—See CORPUSCLES. **White crime**—যে আইনভঙ্গজনিত অপরাধ দেশের লোক দ্বারা নিন্দিত হয় না। **White-crop**—গোধূম, রাইসরিষা, প্রভৃতি যে সকল শস্য পকাবস্থায় শ্বেতবর্ণ ধারণ করে—তাহাদের সাধারণ নাম। **White-cross knight**—Same as

HOSPITALLER 3. **White-crowned** — শ্বেতশীর্ষ। **White-Czar** — Muscovyর অধিপতি। **White-ear**— একপ্রকার পক্ষী। **White elephant**— See ELEPHANT. **White-eye**— কএকপ্রকার পক্ষীর সাধারণ নাম। **White-face, White-blaze**—অশ্বের ললাটে প্রায় নাসাগ্র পর্যন্ত লম্বিত শ্বেতবর্ণ চিহ্ন। **White faced**—পাণ্ডুর বদন, বিবর্ণ মুখ। **White-feather**—ভীরুতা, কাপুরুষতা। **White-film** — মেষের চক্ষুতে জাত একপ্রকার শ্বেতবর্ণের পর্দা। **White-fish**—হেরীংজাতীয় ক্ষুদ্র মৎস্য; উত্তর-আমেরিকার হ্রদসমূহে প্রাপ্ত স্যামন্-জাতীয় মৎস্যবিশেষ। **White flag**—যুদ্ধবিশ্রান্তি বা আত্মসমর্পণের জন্য উত্তোলিত শ্বেতপতাকা। **White flux**—পটাসিক কার্বোনেট এবং সোরার মিশ্র। **White-foot** — অশ্বের পদের শ্বেতবর্ণ চিহ্ন। **White-Friar**—কার্মেলাইট সম্প্রদায়ের সন্ন্যাসীবিশেষ। **White-gum**—শিশুদিগের কণ্ঠ বা বাহুতে জাত একপ্রকার উদ্ভেদ। **White-handed**—বিমলাত্ম. অকলঙ্ক চরিত্র। **Whi'e harvest**—বিলম্বিত শস্য কর্ত্তন। (অর্থাৎ যে সময়ে প্রভাতে ভূমি তুষারকণাদ্বারা সমাচ্ছাদিত থাকে)। **White Hats** — চতুর্দ্দশ শতাব্দীতে Ghent নগরীতে প্রাদুর্ভূত বিদ্রোহী দল। **White heart-cherry**—হৃৎপিণ্ডাকৃতি এবং পাণ্ডুর বর্ণ একপ্রকার চেরী ফল। **White heat**—যে উত্তাপের মাত্রায় উত্তপ্ত বস্তু শ্বেতবর্ণ ধারণ করে, শ্বেততাপ (হিঃ কোঃ); তীব্র উত্তেজনা। **White-horse**—জ্যামেক দ্বীপের একপ্রকার ক্ষুপ। **White horses**—আন্দোলনশীল ফেনচূড় কল্লোল-শ্রেণী। **White House**—আমেরিকার Washington নগরীস্থ রাষ্ট্রপতির শ্বেতবর্ণ প্রাসাদ; (চলিত ভাষায়) মার্কিণ রাষ্ট্রপতির পদ, মার্কিণ শাসনপরিষৎ। **White-iron** — কালাই করা লোহার বাসন। **White-lady** — মধ্যযুগের আখ্যায়িকায় কথিত শ্বেতবসনা নারী। ইনি কোন পরিবারে কোনরূপ গুরুতর ঘটনা সংঘটনের প্রাক্কালে দর্শন দিতেন বলিয়া প্রবাদ আছে (cf. শুক্লবসনা সুন্দরী)। **White-land**—একপ্রকার শ্বেতাভ মৃত্তিকা—এই মৃত্তিকা বৃষ্টিসিক্ত হইলে কৃষ্ণবর্ণ ধারণ করে। **White-lay** — একপ্রকার কর্দমমিশ্রিত মৃত্তিকা—যাহা শুষ্কাবস্থায় শ্বেতবর্ণ ধারণ করে এবং কঠিনতা প্রাপ্ত হয়। **White lead**—সফেদা (হিঃ কোঃ)। [Arab. *asfeidaj* ; Pers. *suffedah* ; Chin. *fen-yuen, fen-sih, kwan-fen, shwui-fen* ; Fr. *plom carbonate* ; Germ. *bleiweiss*; It. *cerussa*; Tam. *muthu vullay* ; Teleg. *sibaydu* ; Turk. *istibedsh.*] **White leprosy**—শ্বেত কুষ্ঠ, শ্বিত্র। **White lie**—See LIE. **White light**—বর্ণহীন আলোক; দিবালোক; (লক্ষণায়) নিরপেক্ষ বিচার। **White-lily**—শ্বেতবর্ণ স্থলকুমুদ। **White-lime**—চূণা। **White limed** — চূণকাম করা, সুধাধবলিত করা (*Rhet.*)। **White-livered** — ম্লানবদন; ক্ষীণ; ভীরু **White-lipped** —ভয় হেতু পাংশুবর্ণ ওষ্ঠাধর, শ্বেতৌষ্ঠ। **White magnolia**—শ্বেত-চম্পক। **White magic**—See MAGIC. **Whiteman**—শ্বেতাঙ্গ (used in slight ironcal sense), শ্বেতকায় পুরুষ। **White matter**—শ্বেতপ্রায় শৈরিক বিধানতন্তু (বিশেষতঃ মস্তিষ্ক এবং কশেরুকার)। **White meat**—মুর্গী, হাঁস, বাছুর, শশক এবং শূকরের মাংস। **White metal**—শ্বেতধাতু (হিঃ কোঃ)। **White money**—টাকা, আধুলী, ইত্যাদি। **White-mulberry**—তুঁত গাছ। **White mustard** — শ্বেত সর্ষপ [Syn. গৌর সর্ষপ, শ্বেত সর্ষপ, অনদ্য, ভূতনাশন, কটুস্নেহ, কণ্ডুঘ্ন, গ্রহঘ্ন, বালিকা ফল, রক্ষোঘ্ন, কুষ্ঠনাশন, দুরাধর্ষ, তীক্ষ্ণক, সিদ্ধপ্রয়োজন, সিদ্ধসাধন, সিতসর্ষপ।] **White night** — বিনিদ্র রজনী **White pepper**—(*piper nigrum*)—একপ্রকার গোলমরিচ—উহার কাল খোসা জলে ভিজাইয়া ছাড়ান হয়। উহার বহির্ভাগ বেশ মসৃণ ও ইহার ঝাল কালো গোল মরিচের মত তত তীব্র নহে। [Tam. *vella mellogu* ; Tel. *tella mirrialu.*] **White-poplar**—একজাতীয় বৃক্ষ। **White-poppy** — একপ্রকার আফিম গাছ—যাহাতে সাদা ফুল হয়। **White pot**—দুগ্ধ, সর, চিনি, ডিম্ব প্রভৃতির ডেলা রুটির মত সেঁকিয়া প্রস্তুত খাদ্যবিশেষ। **White pudding**—ডিম্ব, দুগ্ধ, ময়দা, মাখন দ্বারা প্রস্তুত পিষ্টকবিশেষ; স্কটলণ্ডদেশে প্রস্তুত একপ্রকার নাড়ীকাবাব—যাহাতে চর্বি প্রভৃতির পুর দেওয়া হয়। **White-precipitate**—ক্ষারিণবায়ু (ammonia) এবং রসকর্পূরের (corrosive sublimate) মিশ্র। **White-pyrites** — See PYRITES. **White race**—ককেসীয় আর্য্যজাতি। **White-rent** — Cornwal এর প্রত্যেক টিনের খনির মালীকের Duke of Cornwalকে যে কর দিতে হইত, বঙ্গশুল্ক। **White-ribbon**—ব্রহ্মচর্য্য ও মাদকবর্জ্জনের চিহ্নস্বরূপ ব্যবহৃত শ্বেতবর্ণ ফিতা। **White-rose**—শ্বেত গোলাপ, সেউতি গোলাপ, সেবন্তী: আমেরিক দেশীয় ক্ষুপবিশেষ। **White Rose**—See ROSE. **White sepulchre**—(লক্ষণায়) মাকালফল (See also under SEPULCHRE). **White-salt**—ভর্জ্জিত লবণ। **White-sheep**—তুর্কিদিগের উপজাতিবিশেষ। **White-smith**—যে ব্যক্তি টীনের কাজ করে, টিনের কারিকর। **White-squall**—উষ্ণমণ্ডলের সাগরমধ্যে সহসোত্থিত প্রবল ঝটিকা। এইরূপ ঝটিকা প্রধাবনশীল শ্বেতবর্ণ জলরেখা দ্বারা সূচিত হয়। **White-swelling** — জানুস্ফীতি রোগবিশেষ। **White-tail**—গোধূমের শীর্ষ। **White tincture** — প্রাচীন কিমিয়া বিষয়ক গ্রন্থসমূহে উক্ত একপ্রকার শ্বেতবর্ণ মিশ্র পদার্থ—যদ্দ্বারা যে কোন ধাতু রৌপ্যে পরিণত হইত বলিয়া কথিত আছে। **White-throat**—একপ্রকার শ্বেতকণ্ঠ ক্ষুদ্র গায়কপক্ষী। **White-thorn**—Same as HAWTHORN. **White vitriol**—সলফেট অব জিঙ্ক। **White wagtail**—একপ্রকার পক্ষী—যাহা গ্রীষ্মকালে ব্রিটিশদ্বীপে সমাগত হয়। **White-wash**—দালানে চূণকাম করার জন্য চূণামিশ্রিত জল। (*Verb t.*) চূণকাম করা; দোষাচ্ছাদন করা; দাউলিয়া ব্যক্তিকে ঋণের দায় হইতে উদ্ধার করা। **White-water** — মেষদিগের রোগবিশেষ। **White water-lily**—বনকুমুদ। **White water-lotus**—অষ্টাদশ

শতাব্দীতে চীনদেশে গঠিত গুপ্তসমিতি-বিশেষ, শ্বেতসরোজ সম্প্রদায়। **White wave** — ব্রিটিশদ্বীপের একপ্রকার ডসরে পোকা। **White-wax**—ধবলীকৃত মোম, শাদা মোম। **White wine**—See WHITE *adj.* 6. **White witch** — যে মায়াবিনীর অলৌকিকশক্তি লোকের মঙ্গলকার্য্যে পরিচালিত হয়, শাদা ডাইনী ; চালাক লোক। **White-wood**—আমেরিকাদেশীয় বৃক্ষবিশেষ। **White yam**—শ্বেত আলু **Spanish white**—খড়ি হইতে প্রস্তুত একপ্রকার শ্বেতবর্ণ রঞ্জক পদার্থ। **Days marked with white stone**—আনন্দের দিন, সুখের দিন। **The white lady of Ireland**—Same as BANSHEE (which see). **The white moments of life**—জীবনের শুভদিন বা মুহূর্ত্ত সকল। **To hoist, show or wave the white flag**—To show signs of cowardice or yielding; ভীরুতা বা বশ্যতার চিহ্ন প্রদর্শন করা। **To show white feather**—See FEATHER. **White softening of the brain**—See SOFTENING.

White'-chăp-ĕl-cărt, *n.* A light two-wheeled car used by shop-keepers for sending goods round ; একপ্রকার হাল্কা দুই চাকার গাড়ী—যদ্দ্বারা দোকানদারগণ ক্রেতাগণের বাটীতে বাটীতে মাল প্রেরণ করে।

white-leath'-ĕr (-leth-), *n.* Leather dressed with alum, salt, etc. remarkable for its pliability and toughness ; ফিটকিরী, লবণ, প্রভৃতি দ্বারা শোধিত চর্ম্ম।

whit'-ĕn-ing, *n.* 1. The act of one who whitens ; শুক্লীকরণ। 2. Same as WHITING below.

whites, *n.* 1. Leucorrhoea ; শ্বেতপ্রদর। 2. White dress ; শ্বেত বস্ত্র। 3. The finest flour made from white wheat ; একপ্রকার উৎকৃষ্ট ময়দা।

whith'-ĕr, *adv.* 1. To what place ; কোথায়, কোন স্থানে। 2. Whereunto ; কোথায়।

whit'-ing, *n.* Chalk prepared by drying, grinding, etc. for use in whitewashing, plate-cleaning, etc. ; চূণকাম, থালাবাসনাদি পরিষ্করণ, প্রভৃতির কার্য্যে ব্যবহৃত শুষ্কীকৃত চাখড়ি চূর্ণ।

whit'-ing, *n.* A common European food fish ; ইয়ুরোপ মহাদেশের একপ্রকার সামুদ্রিক মৎস্য। **Whiting-pout**—উক্তপ্রকার মৎস্যের সদৃশ একজাতীয় মৎস্য—যাহার মস্তকের একাংশের উপর একটী আধ্মানযোগ্য ঝিল্লী থাকে।

whit'-low (-lō), *n.* A swelling about the small bones of the fingers, generally terminating in an abscess ; আঙ্গুলহাড়া, উপনখ, অঙ্গুলিবেষ্ট (হঃ চঃ), নখশূল।

Whit'-sŭn, *adj.* See under WHIT.

whit'-tle (-l), *v. t.* & *i.* To pare or cut off the surface of something with a small knife ; ছুরী দ্বারা চাঁচা। ***Verb i.*** 1. To cut or shape a piece of wood with a knife ; ছুরী দ্বারা কোন কাষ্ঠ খণ্ড কাটা বা উহাকে বিশিষ্ট আকৃতিসম্পন্ন করা। 2. To reduce amount or effect by repeated subtraction (*usu.* with *down* or *away*) ; as, to *whittle down* the reforms ; পুনঃ পুনঃ বাদ দিয়া হ্রাস করা।

whit'-y, *adj.* Whitish ; শ্বেতাভ, শ্বেতপ্রায়, শ্বেতকল্প।

whiz, whizz, *v. i.* & *n.* To make a humming or hissing sound ; সোঁসোঁ শব্দ করা, সন্ সন্ শব্দ করা। ***Noun.*** A hissing and humming sound ; "It flew, and *whizzing* cut the air away" ; সোঁ সোঁ শব্দ, সন্ সন্ শব্দ, ভোঁ ভোঁ, বন্ বন্ শব্দ।

who (hô), *pron. pers., interrog.* & *rel.* A relative and interrogative pronoun always used substantively and with reference to person ; কে, কাহারা, যে, যিনি, যাহারা।

whō'-ă, *interj.* See WO.

who'-ĕv'-ĕr (hô-), **who'-sō** (hô-) (*archaic*), **who-sō-ĕv'-ĕr** (hô-) (*emphat.*), **who-e'er'** (hô-âr) (*poet.*), **who so-e'er'** (hô-sō-âr) (*poet.*) *prons.* Any one without exception ; any person whatsoever ; যে কেহ ; যে কোন লোক।

whole (hōl), *adj.* 1. (*Archaic*) In good health ; (অপ্রঃ) সুস্থ। 2. Intact ; "If all goes well, yet all our joints are *whole*" ; uninjured; অটুট ; অক্ষত। 3. Not broken or fractured ; as, not a plate was left *whole* ; অভগ্ন। 4. Entire ; as, can you swallow a cherry *whole* ? ; অখণ্ড, সমগ্র। [একটী কাঁঠাল যদি ভাঙ্গা না হয় তবে তাহাকে *Entire* Jack fruit কহে। যদি কাঁঠালটী ভাঙ্গা হইয়া থাকে কিন্তু তাহা হইতে কোন অংশ স্থানান্তরিত না করা হয় তবে তাহাকে *Whole* Jack fruit বলা হয়। পরন্তু যদি কাঁঠালটী বৃক্ষে পূর্ণায়তন প্রাপ্ত হয় তবে তাহাকে *Complete* Jack fruit কহে।] 5. Containing the total amount or number ; total ; complete ; as, the *whole* army ; সমগ্র ; সম্পূর্ণ, বেবাক (*colloq.*) ; সারা (*ib.*), সমস্ত। ***Noun.*** 1. The entire thing ; totality ; আস্তজিনিষ ; সামগ্র্য, সমগ্রতা, সমষ্টি। 2. A system ; "All are but parts of a stupendous *whole*, whose body Nature is, and God the soul" ; শ্রেণী, পরিবার। **Whol'-ly**, *adv.* Entirely ; সম্পূর্ণরূপ, সর্ব্বতোভাবে। **Whole-binding**—পুরা বাঁধাই। **Whole coal** — যে কয়লার স্তরে এযাবৎ খননকার্য্য আরব্ধ হয় নাই। **Whole-coloured** — একরঙ্গা। **Whole hearted**—একচিত্ত, সরল, উৎসাহপূর্ণ। **Whole-heartedly** — সর্ব্বান্তঃকরণে। **Whole-hoofed**—একশফ। **Whole-length** — পূর্ণায়তন (প্রতিকৃতি)। **Whole-milk**—যে দুগ্ধ হইতে কোন প্রকার উপাদান পৃথক করা হয় নাই। **Whole number**—অখণ্ড সংখ্যা, পূর্ণসংখ্যা। **Wholesale** — পাইকারী। **Whole-sale dealer** — পাইকারী দোকানদার, থোক বিক্রিওয়ালা (হিঃ কোঃ)। **Wholesale trade** — পাইকারী

ব্যবসায়, থোকব্যাপার (হিঃ কোঃ)। **Whole-snipe** — কাঁদাখোঁচা পাখী। **Wholesome**—স্বাস্থ্যজনক, পুষ্টিজনক, হিতজনক, কল্যাণজনক। **Whole souled**—উন্নতচিত্ত, মহাপ্রাণ। **Whole-stuff**—কাগজ প্রস্তুতের জন্য উত্তমরূপে ছানিয়া লওয়া মণ্ড। **Whole-time**—(*Noun.*) সমস্ত সময়। (*adj.*) সর্ব্বকালের, সর্ব্বকালিক, পুর্ণসাময়িক, সর্ব্বসাময়িক সব সময়কার (*colloq.*)। **A whole time officer**— যে কর্ম্মচারী সব সময় এক কার্য্যালয়ে কর্ম্ম করে, সর্ব্বকালিক বা পুর্ণসাময়িক কর্ম্মচারী। **Actual whole**—যে বস্তু অংশসমূহের অবর্ত্তমানে থাকিতে পারেনা, অর্থাৎ যে বস্তুর পক্ষে অংশসমূহ অপরিহার্য্যরূপে আবশ্যক। **Aggregate, collective** or **discrete whole**—যে বস্তু বিভিন্ন স্বতন্ত্র বস্তুসমূহদ্বারা গঠিত হয় (যথা পশুর পাল), সাংঘিক সমগ্রতা **comprehensive** or **formal whole**—কোন পদের সম্পুর্ণ অর্থ। **On the wholesale plan**—On a large scale; বিরাটভাবে, বৃহৎ পরিমাণে, বিরাট রকমে। **On** or **upon the whole**—After weighing pros and cons; মোটের উপর। **Out of the whole cloth**—Without foundation; অমূলক, ভিত্তিহীন। **To go the whole hog**—See under HOG.

whom (hôm), *pron.* The objective of WHO; কাহাকে, কাহাদিগকে।

whōop, *var.* of HOOP.

whŏp, *v. t.* **1.** (*Slang*) To thrash; (ইতর ভাষায়) বেত্রাঘাত করা। **2.** To defeat: পরাস্ত করা, পরাভূত করা। **Whop'-per**, *n.*

whore (hör), *n.* & *v. i.* **1.** Prostitute; বেশ্যা। **2.** An adulteress or fornicatress; কুলটা, ব্যভিচারিণী। ***Verb i.*** To have unlawful sexual commerce; অবৈধ সংসর্গ করা। **Whore-master**—যে ব্যক্তি অপরের জন্য কুলটা রমণী সংগ্রহ করে। Same as WHORE-MONGER. **Whore-monger**—বেশ্যাসক্ত ব্যক্তি।

whŏrl, *n.* **1.** A ring of leaves etc. of a plant all on the same plane; পত্রাবর্ত্ত। **2.** One turn of a spiral; আবৃত্তি (যোঃ)। **Whorled**, *adj.* Furnished with whorles; স্তবকীকৃত (সাঃ পঃ)।

whose (hôz), *pron.* Possessive case of WHO; কাহার, কাহাদের।

who'-sō (hô-), **who-sō-ĕv'-ĕr** (hô-), *pron.* See WHOEVER.

whȳ, *adv.* & *n.* For what cause, reason or purpose; কেন, কি উদ্দেশ্যে, কি কারণে, কি জন্য, কি হেতু, কি নিমিত্ত। ***Noun.*** Reason; as, he cannot go into the *whys* and wherefores now"; হেতু, কারণ। **Why so**—কি জন্য।

whȳ, *interj.* An interjection expressing surprise etc.; কেন।

wick, *n.* A number of threads, cotton or some similar substance, loosely twisted into a string and inserted in tallow, oil or wax, as a means of obtaining light; শলিতা, পলিতা, দীপবর্ত্তিকা, দীপবর্ত্তি।

Wick, *n.* Town, hamlet or district; as, Hampton *Wick*; নগর, গ্রাম, জেলা।

wick'-ĕd, *adj.* **1.** Evil in principle, or practice; addicted to vice; sinful; immoral; wrong; iniquitous; দুরাচার, দুর্ব্বৃত্ত; পাপাসক্ত; পাপপূর্ণ; নীতিজ্ঞানহীন; অন্যায়; অসাধু। **2.** Pernicious; as, a *wicked* winter; অনিষ্টকর, মারাত্মক, অহিতকর। **3.** (*Colloq.*) Roguish; as, a *wicked* horse; দুষ্ট, বদমায়েস, পাজি। **—ly**, *adv.* **—ness**, *n.* **Wicked bible**—Barker এবং Lucas কর্ত্তৃক ১৬৩২ খৃঃ অব্দে মুদ্রিত বাইবেল বিশেষ। এই বাইবেলে ঈশ্বরের সপ্তম আদেশে Thou shalt not commit adulteryর স্থানে "not" শব্দ বর্জ্জিত হওয়ায় Thou shalt commit adultery মুদ্রিত হইয়াছিল।

wick'-ĕr, *n.* & *adj.* **1.** A small pliable twig; কঞ্চি। **2.** Work made of such twigs; বুনট কঞ্চি দ্বারা নির্ম্মিত ঝুড়ি প্রভৃতি (also *wicker-work.*) ***Adj.*** Made of plaited twigs; বুনট করা কঞ্চি দ্বারা তৈরী বংশবেত্রাদি নির্ম্মিত।

wick'-ĕt, *n.* **1.** A small gate or door, esp. one in a larger; ক্ষুদ্রদ্বার, পক্ষদ্বার, বৃহত্তর দ্বারের অন্তর্ভুক্ত ক্ষুদ্র দ্বার। **2.** (*Cricket*) One of the three upright rods at which the bowler aims; (ক্রীকেট ক্রীড়ায়) ক্রীকেট ক্রীড়ায় ব্যবহৃত দণ্ডত্রয়, ত্রিদণ্ড। **3.** A turnstile entrance; একপ্রকার দ্বার—যাহা ঘুরাইয়া ভিতরে প্রবেশ করিতে হয়। **4.** The ground on which the wickets are set; "The play was begun with an excellent *wicket*"; যে ভূমিতে ত্রিদণ্ড প্রোথিত করা হয়। **5.** A part of an inning between the dismissal of any two consecutive batsmen; as, the 6th *wicket* added 50 runs; দুইজন ব্যাটধারীর "আউট" হওয়ার মধ্যে যে ক্রীড়াঙ্ক লাভ করা হয়। **Wicket-keeper**—(দণ্ডকন্দুক ক্রীড়ায়) ত্রিদণ্ডরক্ষক। **Three wickets down**—৩ জন আউট হইয়াছে। **To keep one's wicket up** — To succeed in not being put out; আউট না হওয়া।

wīde, *adj.*, *adv.* & *n.* **1.** Having great extent each way; চওড়া, প্রশস্ত, আয়ত। **2.** Extensive; as, the *wide* ocean; vast; বিস্তৃত; বিপুল, বিশাল। **3.** Liberal; unprejudiced; as, *wide* culture; উদার; সংস্কারবিমুক্ত। **4.** Failing to hit a mark; deviating beside the right line or aim; remote or distant from anything, as truth, propriety or the like; as, his statement is *wide* from the truth; লক্ষ্যচ্যুত; প্রকৃত পথ বা লক্ষ্য হইতে ভ্রষ্ট; দূরে স্থিত। **6.** Expanded; as, eyes *wide* with wonder; বিস্তারিত, প্রসারিত। **7.** Extending far; comprehensive; as, *wide* reading; দূরব্যাপী; বিস্তৃত, ব্যাপক। ***Adv.*** **1.** Very far; বহুদূরে, সুদূরে, অতিদূরে। **2.** Astray; মূলবিষয় হইতে চ্যুত। ***Noun.*** **1.** That which is wide; width; extent; বিস্তৃত বস্তু; প্রস্থ; বিস্তার। 2. (*Cricket*) A ball that goes wide of the wicket, and which counts one against the side that is bowling; (ক্রীকেট ক্রীড়া) যে বল ত্রিদণ্ড হইতে দূর দিয়া যাওয়ার দরুণ—যে পক্ষ দ্বারা বল নিক্ষিপ্ত হইয়াছে তাহাদের প্রতিকূলে এক ক্রীড়াঙ্ক ধরা হয়। **Wide'-ly,** *adv.* **Wid'-en,** *v. t.* & *i.* **Wide awake**—সজাগ; সতর্ক, হুঁসিয়ার। **Wide-awake** — এক প্রকার চৌড়া কিনারাওয়ালা নেমদার টুপি (felt hat)। একপ্রকার সাগরচর পক্ষী। **Wide-ball**—যে বল ব্যাটধারীর লাগাইলের বাহির দিয়া অতিক্রম করে। **Wide-spread**—সুদূর-বিস্তৃত, সুদূরব্যাপী; **The wide world**—বিপুল পৃথ্বী, বিশাল পৃথিবী। **To give wide berth to**—See BERTH.

widg'-eon (wĭj-ŏn), *n.* A migratory water-fowl of the duck group; একপ্রকার হংসজাতীয় দেশান্তরগামী পক্ষী।

wid'-ow (-ō-), *n.* & *v. t.* A woman whose husband is dead; বিধবা, স্বামীহীন, বেওয়া (*colloq.*), মৃত-পতিকা (বাৎস্যঃ), গতভর্তৃকা। *Verb t.* **1.** To reduce to the condition of a widow; to bereave of husband or mate; বিধবা করা; পতিবিরহিত করা। **2.** To strip or bereave of anything good; to bereave; "Trees of their shrivel'd fruits are *widowed*"; কোনরূপ উৎকৃষ্ট বস্তু হইতে বিরহিত করা; বিরহিত করা, বিহীন করা। **–hood,** *n.* **Widow-bird**—একপ্রকার পক্ষী—পালকের অনুজ্জ্বল কৃষ্ণবর্ণ বলিয়া ইহার এই নাম। **Widow-monkey**—দক্ষিণ-আফ্রিকার বানর বিশেষ। এই জাতীয় বানরের বর্ণ কাল, কেবল ভুজ, গলদেশ ও মুখের বর্ণ অনুজ্জ্বল শ্বেত ও মুখের চতুর্দ্দিকে শ্বেতবর্ণের একটী চক্র আছে। **Widow's chamber**—(লণ্ডনে) শয্যাগৃহের বস্ত্র ও আসবাব—যাহাতে স্বাধীন গৃহস্থের বিধবা পত্নীর অধিকার ছিল। **Widow's man**—যে কাল্পনিক নাবিকগণের বেতন বিধবাগণের সাহায্য-ভাণ্ডারে প্রেরিত হইত—তাহার অন্যতম।

wid'-ow-êr (-ō), *n.* A man bereft of his wife by death and not married again; মৃতদার, বিপত্নীক।

width, *n.* 1. Breadth; বিস্তৃতি, প্রস্থ, আয়তি। 2. Comprehensiveness; ব্যাপকতা। 3. Liberality: as, the *width* of his view; উদারতা।

wield (wēld), *v. t.* 1. To manage freely in the hands: to control; পরিচালনা করা, চালনা করা, ঘুরান; নিয়মিত করা, নিয়ন্ত্রিত করা। 2. To exercise; as, to *wield* great power; পরিচালনা করা।

wife, *n.* 1. (*Now rare*) Woman esp. a rustic or uneducated woman; as, a fish-*wife* (বর্ত্তমানে কচিদ্‌ব্যবহৃত) স্ত্রীলোক, বিশেষতঃ গ্রাম্য অশিক্ষিতা স্ত্রীলোক। 2. A married woman; স্ত্রী, ভার্য্যা, সহধর্ম্মিণী, জায়া, দার, কলত্র, গৃহিণী, বধূ, বৌ (*colloq.*), ঘরণী (*poet.*)। **Wife'-hood,** *n.* **Wife'-less, Wife'-like, Wife'-ly,** *adjs.* **Wife-ridden**—স্ত্রৈণ, স্ত্রীনির্জ্জিত। **Old wive's tales**—ঠাকুরমার গল্প। **To give or take to wife**—To give or take a woman in marriage; বিবাহ দেওয়া, বিবাহ করা।

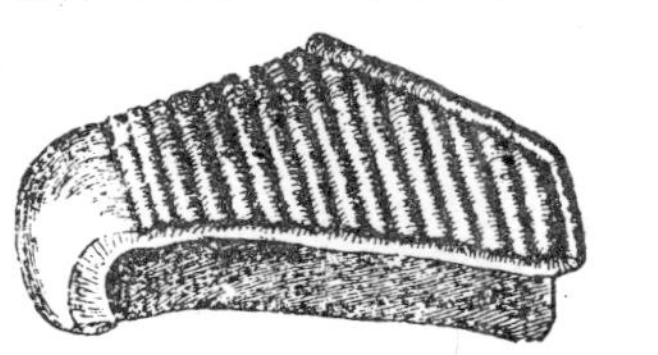

Full-bottomed wig.

wig, *n.* An artificial covering of hair for the head; পরচুলা, উপকেশ। **Wig-block** — পরচুলা লাগাইবার জন্য কাঠের ঠাঁট। **Wig-tree** — একপ্রকার বৃক্ষ। **There will be wigs on the green**—There will be free fight; দাঙ্গা হাঙ্গামা হইবে। **To get a wigging**—To be rebuked; তিরস্কৃত হওয়া, ভৎর্সিত হওয়া।

wig, *v. t.* To rebuke sharply; তীব্র তিরস্কার করা। **Wig'-ing,** *n.*

wig'-ăn, *n.* A canvas-like cotton fabric, used to stiffen parts of garments; ক্যাম্বিসের মত একপ্রকার শক্ত সুতার কাপড়।

wight (wĭt), *n.* (*Archaic*) Person; "In the whole world there scarcely was so delicate a *wight*"; লোক, ব্যক্তি।

Wigwam of North America.

wig'-wăm, *n.* North-Indian tent or hut; উত্তর আমেরিকার প্রাচীন অধিবাসিগণের তাঁবু বা কুটীর।

wild, *adj., adv.* & *n.* **1.** Not tame; as, *wild* animal; বন্য, আরণ্য। **2.** Not cultivated; as, *wild* cherry; বন্য। **3.** Not inhabited; as, a *wild* country; জনবসতিহীন। **4.** Turbulent: tempestuous; as, *wild* night; furious; as, a man of *wild* character: দুর্দ্দান্ত, প্রচণ্ড; ঝটিকা-বিক্ষুব্ধ; উদ্দাম, ভীষণ। **5.** Savage; as, *wild* tribes of Africa; অসভ্য, বন্য, বুনো (*colloq.*), বর্ব্বর। **6.** (*Colloq.*) Eager; as, boys *wild* to play; উৎকণ্ঠিত, ব্যগ্র, উতলা। **7.** Indicating, or proceeding from, strong excitement; "*Wild* seraphic fire"; উত্তেজনাসূচক, তীব্র উত্তেজনা-প্রসূত। **8.** Reckless; rash; as, *wild* adventure; দৃক্‌পাতশূন্য; হঠকারী। **9.** Bewildered; "Your looks are pale and *wild*"; mad; বিভ্রান্ত; উন্মত্ত। **10.** Deviating from an intended aim or object; অভিপ্রেত বিষয় বা লক্ষ্য হইতে চ্যুত। **11.** Wanting order or regularity ; extravagant ; eccentric . "*Wild* in their attire" : শৃঙ্খলাশূন্য, পারিপাট্যহীন ; উৎকট ; সৃষ্টিছাড়া। 12. (Of horse) Shy ; (অশ্বসম্পর্কে) সহজে চকিত। ***Adv.*** Wildly ; বন্যভাবে, দুর্দ্দান্তরূপে, তীব্র উত্তেজনার সহিত, উৎকণ্ঠিত ভাবে, ক্ষিপ্ত ভাবে। ***Noun.*** A forest or desert ; as, the *wilds* of India : বন, মরুভূমি, বিজন দেশ। **Wild'-ish,** *adj.* **Wild'-ly,** *adv.* **Wild'-ness** *n.* **Wild animal**—বন্য জন্তু। **Wild basil**—বন তুলসী। **Wild-bear**—বন্য পশু ; প্রচণ্ড আবেগ, প্রচণ্ড ক্রোধ। **Wild-bees** — বন্য মৌমাছি (অর্থাৎ পালিত মৌমাছি নয়) বনমক্ষিকা। **Wild-birds**—বন্য পক্ষী। **Wild Birds Protection Act**—ভূমির মালীক বা তৎকর্ত্তৃক ক্ষমতাপ্রাপ্ত ব্যক্তি ভিন্ন অপর লোক প্রতিবর্ষের ১লা মার্চ্চ হইতে ১লা আগষ্ট পর্য্যন্ত কোনপ্রকার বন্য পক্ষী নিহত করিতে পারিবে না এই মর্ম্মে ১৮৮০ খৃঃ অব্দে বিধিবদ্ধ আইন বিশেষ।

Wild cat.

Wildcat—বন্য মার্জ্জার ; (*Adj.*) দৃক্‌পাত শূন্য, হঠকারী। **Wild-duck**—বন্য হংস। **Wild-fire**—Same as GREEK FIRE ; বজ্রপাতহীন বিদ্যুদ্বিকাশ ; মেষের রোগ বিশেষ—যাহাতে চর্ম্মপ্রদাহ উপজাত হয় ; একপ্রকার বিসর্প রোগ। **Wild-goat** — বন্য ছাগল। **Wild-goose chase**—See GOOSE. **Wild-honey**—বন্য (অর্থাৎ পালিত নয়) মৌমাছি দ্বারা সংগৃহীত মধু। **Wild horse**—বন্য অশ্ব। **Wild-hyacinth** — Same as BLUE-BELL. **Wild land**—অকৃষ্ট ভূমি। **Wild man**—অসভ্য লোক। **Wild-scenery**—বিজনতার দৃশ্য। **Wild tribe**—বন্য জাতি। **Wild-work** — উচ্ছৃঙ্খলতা। **Woodnotes wild** — স্বতঃস্ফূর্ত্ত এবং সরল কবিতা। **A wild shot**—A random shot ; যদৃচ্ছাক্রমে যে গুলি ছোড়া হয়। **To be wild about something**—To be mad after something : কোন বিষয়ে মাতিয়া উঠা। **The report spread like wild fire**—The report spread very quickly ; সংবাদ বিদ্যুৎবেগে ছড়াইয়া পড়িল। **To grow savage** or **wild**—দুর্দ্দান্ত হওয়া, অসভ্য হওয়া। To become extravagant ; উৎকট হওয়া। **To run wild**—To escape from cultivation and let grow in a wild state ; বুনো হইয়া যাওয়া।

wil-de-beest (wēl-dā-bāst), *n.* Same as GNU (which see).

wild'-er, *v. t.* (*Poet.*) Same as BEWILDER (which see).

wil'-dêr-nêss, *n.* 1. A desert ; waste ; মরুভূমি, বসতিহীন স্থান, জনমানবহীন প্রদেশ ; বিশাল মরুপ্রান্তর। 2. The part of garden left wild ; বাগানের যে অংশে জঙ্গল হইতে দেওয়া হয়। 3. A confused or bewildering mass, heap or collection ; great number or quantity ; "*Wilderness* of things to see and do" ; বিশৃঙ্খল ভাবে স্থিত অগণ্য বস্তুর স্তূপ ; বহুসংখ্যা, রাশি, স্তূপ।

wild'-ing, *n.* A plant that is wild or grows without cultivation ; যে বৃক্ষ স্বতঃই জাত হয়।

wile, *n.* & *v. t.* A trick or stratagem ; ধূর্ত্ততা, শাঠ্য, চাতুরালি। ***Verb t.*** 1. To entice ; "That this would *wile* our folk away" ; ফুসলান, ভুলান। 2. Same as TO WHILE.

wil'-fûl, *adj.* 1. Obstinate ; refractory ; headstrong ; একগুঁয়ে, একরোখা ; স্বেচ্ছাচারী ; দুর্দ্দান্ত, মগড়া। 2. Intentional ; as, *wilful* murder ; ইচ্ছাকৃত।

will, *Aux., v. t.* & *i.* Used as auxiliary followed by infinitive without *to* and used to mean *willing to* or *desirous to* or emphatically, ইচ্ছাসূচক সহায়ক ক্রিয়া। ***Verb t.*** 1. To wish ; "Her words had issued other than she *willed*" ; ইচ্ছা করা, অভিলাষ করা, বাঞ্ছা করা। 2. To decide ; to ordain ; "Two things He [God] *willeth*, that we should be good, and that we should be happy" ; স্থির করা ; বিধান করা, নির্দ্দিষ্ট করা। 3. To bequeath ; as, to *will* one's estate to a nephew ; চরমপত্রদ্বারা দান করা। 4. To influence by one's will-power ; as, the hypnotizer *willed* her to dance, and she began to dance forthwith ; ইচ্ছাশক্তিদ্বারা প্রভাবিত করা। ***Verb i.*** 1. To determine by an act of choice ; as, he *willed* to stay ; স্থির করা। 2. To consent ; মত দেওয়া, স্বীকার করা। 3. To wish ; ইচ্ছা করা, বাঞ্ছা করা, অভিলাষ করা।

will, *n.* 1. The act of willing ; the act of deciding ; volition ; ইচ্ছাকরণ ; স্থিরীকরণ ; মনন, ইচ্ছাশক্তির প্রয়োগ। 2. That which is strongly desired or wished for ; as, he had his *will* ; ঈপ্সিত বিষয়, বাঞ্ছিত বিষয়, অভিলষিত বিষয়। 3. Desire ; ইচ্ছা, অভিলাষ। 4. Purpose ; intention ; choice ; উদ্দেশ্য ; অভিপ্রায় ; পসন্দ। 5. Discretionary pleasure ; as, one's sweet *will* ; খুসী, মর্জ্জি। 6. Request ; command ; as, thy *will* be done ; উপরোধ, অনুরোধ ; আদেশ। 7. The written instrument by which a man makes disposition of his estate to take after his death ; উইল ; চরমপত্র। 8. Power of controlling one's actions or emotions ; self-control ; as, a man of iron *will* ; ইচ্ছাশক্তি ; আত্মসংযম। 9. Arbitrary power, disposal, or authority ; absolute power to control, determine or dispose ; "Whose *will* stands but mine" ; যথেচ্ছাচারের ক্ষমতা ; একাধিপত্য। 10. (*Phil.*) The faculty of the mind by which we determine either to do, or forbear to do ; মনের যে বৃত্তি দ্বারা আমরা কোন কার্য্য করিতে বা তাহা হইতে নিবৃত্ত থাকিতে স্থির করি [জর্ম্মণ দার্শনিক শোপেনেয়ারের মতে কেবলমাত্র আমাদের জ্ঞাত অভিলাষ সমূহ ইচ্ছার অন্তর্ভুক্ত নহে কিন্তু যে অজ্ঞাতপ্রেরণা এবং যে শক্তিসমূহ জড় প্রকৃতিতে ব্যক্ত হইয়া থাকে তাহাও ইচ্ছার অঙ্গীভূত বলিয়া পরিগণিত হইয়া থাকে।] **Good-will** — See under GOOD. **Ill will**—অপ্রীতি, বিদ্বেষ। **Tenant at will**—কোর্ফা প্রজা। **Will-power**—ইচ্ছাশক্তি, সঙ্কল্প (তাঁহাদের সংকল্পকল্পিত জগদাকাশ অক্ষয় ও পূর্ণ হইয়া কিরণ প্রদান করিয়া থাকেন — যোগবাসিষ্ঠ রামায়ণ)। **Will worship**—(অপ্রঃ) নিজের ইচ্ছার সহিত সঙ্গত হয় এরূপ ধর্ম্ম, বাসনাধর্ম্ম। **At will**—At one's pleasure ; ইচ্ছামত, খুসীমত, মর্জ্জিমত। **Thy will be done**—তোমার ইচ্ছা পূর্ণ হউক। **To work one's will**—To realise one's purpose ; কাহারো উদ্দেশ্য কার্য্যে পরিণত করা। **Where there is a will there is a way**—ইচ্ছা থাকিলেই একটা উপায়ও হয়। **Will he nill he, Willy-nilly**—Whether he wishes or not—সে চাউক কিম্বা নাই চাউক।

wil'-let (-ĕt), *n.* A wading bird of America ; আমেরিকা মহাদেশীয় পক্ষিবিশেষ।

will'-ing, *adj.* 1. Desirous ; ইচ্ছুক, রাজি, সম্মত। 2. Ready to act ; prompt to do, give, or grant ; not slow, lazy or reluctant ; as, a *willing* horse ; কর্ম্মতৎপর ; তৎপর ; অনলস, অমন্থর। 3. Voluntary ; as, a *willing* sacrifice ; ইচ্ছাকৃত। **—ly**, *adv.*

will'-ō'-the-wisp', *n.* 1. Same as IGNIS FATUUS. 2. A man whose whereabouts is unknown ; যে ব্যক্তির গতিবিধি অজ্ঞাত।

wil'-low (-lō), *n.* 1. A well-known tree of numerous species of the genus salix ; দীর্ঘ এবং নমনীয় শাখাবিশিষ্ট নানাজাতীয় তরু লতা—এই সকল বৃক্ষ সাধারণতঃ নদী প্রভৃতির তটে জন্মিয়া থাকে, মজনু (Weeping willow)। 2. Cricket-bat ; as, to handle the *willow* ; ক্রিকেট ক্রীড়ার ব্যাট। **Willow beauty**—ইংলণ্ডদেশীয় একপ্রকার তসরে পোকা। **Willow-gall** — উইলোপত্রের স্ফীতিবিশেষ। **Willow herb** — একপ্রকার গুল্ম। **Willow-moth** — একপ্রকার তসরে পোকা। **Willow-pattern**—শ্বেতবর্ণ চীনা বাসনের উপর নানাপ্রকার নীলবর্ণের চিত্র। **To wear the willow**—To mourn the death or separation of one's beloved ; প্রিয়তম বা প্রিয়তমার মৃত্যু বা বিরহের জন্য শোক করা। To be forsaken ; পরিত্যক্ত হওয়া।

wil'-low (-lō), *v. t.* & *n.* To clean cotton, flax, etc. by beating, picking etc. with machinery ; যন্ত্রের সাহায্যে শণ, কার্পাস, প্রভৃতি পরিস্কার করা। ***Noun.*** A machine for cleansing cotton, wool, etc. ; পশম, কার্পাস, প্রভৃতি পরিস্কার করার জন্য যন্ত্রবিশেষ।

wil'-low-y̆ (-ō-), *adj.* 1. Abounding in willow ; উইলোবৃক্ষবহুল। 2. Pliant ; graceful ; slender ; নমনীয় ; মাধুর্য্যময় ; কৃশ।

wilt, *v. t.* The second person singular of WILL.

wilt, *v. i.* & *t.* To fade ; to wither ; ম্লান হওয়া ; শুকাইয়া যাওয়া, মুষড়াইয়া যাওয়া। ***Verb t.*** 1. To cause to wither ; বিশুষ্ক করা। 2. (*Fig.*) To depress ; "Despots have *wilted* the human races into sloth and imbecility" ; স্ফূর্ত্তিহীন করা, দমাইয়া দেওয়া, প্রফুল্লতা নষ্ট করা।

Wil'-tŏn, *n.* A carpet, like Brussels, but with a velvety surface ; একপ্রকার গালিচা—যাহার উপরিভাগ দেখিতে কতকটা মকমলের মত। **Wilton carpet**—Same as WILTON.

wil'-y̆, *adj.* Crafty ; cunning ; ধূর্ত্ত, চতুর, শঠ, ফন্দীবাজ (*colloq.*), ফেরেব্বাজ (*colloq.*) : চালাক। **—i-ly**, *adv.* **—i-ness**, *n.*

wim'-ble (-bl), *n.* 1. A gimlet ; তুরপুণ। 2. An instrument for twisting ropes or band ; রজ্জু বা ফিতা বুনট করার জন্য যন্ত্রবিশেষ। 3. A brace ; তুরপুণ প্রভৃতি ঘুরাইবার হাতল।

wim'-ple (-pl), *n.* & *v. t.* A covering, as of silk, for the neck, chin, and sides of the face, formerly worn by women, and still retained by nuns ; স্ত্রীলোকের মস্তক, চিবুক এবং গণ্ডদেশাবরক অবগুণ্ঠন বিশেষ। ***Verb t.*** To cause to appear as if plaited ; to ripple ; কুঁচ দেওয়ার মত দেখান ; তরঙ্গায়িত করা।

Wimple.

win, *v. i.*, *t.* & *n.* To gain victory ; to prevail ; জয়লাভ করা ; প্রবল হওয়া। ***Verb t.*** 1. To obtain ; to gain ; প্রাপ্ত হওয়া ; লাভ করা। 2. To gain in competition or contest ; as, to *win* the prize in a game ; প্রতিযোগিতার ক্রীড়ায় লাভ করা, জয়ী হইয়া পুরস্কার লাভ করা। 3. To persuade ; to influence ; to entice ; "She is a woman : therefore to be *won*" ; প্ররোচিত করা ; প্রভাবিত করা ; প্রলুব্ধ করা, ভুলাইয়া নেওয়া। 4. To gain to one's side or party, as by solicitation or other influence ; to procure the favour of, as for a cause which one has at heart ; as, an orator *wins* the audience ; to gain over ; অনুনয় বিনয় বা অন্য কোন উপায়ে কাহারও পক্ষে আনা ; কাহারো অনুকূল্য লাভ করা ; হাত করা। 5. To accomplish by effort ; as, to *win* one's way ; চেষ্টা দ্বারা সম্পাদন করা। 6. To earn ; as, to *win* one's livelihood ; অর্জ্জন করা, উপার্জ্জন করা। ***Noun.*** A success or victory in game ; ক্রীড়ায় কৃতকার্য্যতা ও জয়লাভ। **To win in a canter walk**—To win a race easily ; অনায়াসে দৌড়ে জয়লাভ করা। **To win on or upon**—To gain favour ; অনুগ্রহ লাভ করা। **To win one's spur**—See SPUR. **To win out**—(*Colloq.*) To be successful ; কৃতকার্য্য হওয়া। **To win the day**—To be successful ; to triumph ; কৃতকার্য্য হওয়া ; বিজয়ী হওয়া। **To win to**—To be able to go to ; যাইতে সমর্থ হওয়া। To begin to eat ; খাইতে আরম্ভ করা। To mount, as horse ; অশ্বে আরোহণ করা। To ascend a mountain ; পর্ব্বতে আরোহণ করা।

wince (wîns), *v. i.* & *n.* 1. To shrink, as from a blow, or from pain ; "Three hundred and seventeen stripes were inflicted but the sufferer never *winced*"; to flinch ; আঘাত, ব্যথা প্রভৃতি এড়াইবার জন্য কুঞ্চিত হওয়া; সরিয়া পড়া, সঙ্কুচিত হওয়া। *Noun.* A start or shrinking, as from a blow or pain ; আঘাত বা যন্ত্রণা এড়াইবার জন্য সঙ্কুচিত হওন।

win'-ning (-îng), *n.* & *adj.* 1. The act of one who wins ; অর্জ্জন, উপার্জ্জন। *Adj.* Attracting ; as, a *winning* appearance ; charming ; চিত্তাকর্ষক,হৃদয়গ্রাহী,হৃদয়হারী; মনোহারী, মনোমুগ্ধকর, বিমোহন। **–ly**, *adv.*

win'-cey (-sî), *n.* A strong, durable fabric made of wool and cotton ; পশম মিশ্রিত একপ্রকার শক্ত কার্পাসবস্ত্র।

Winch.

winch (wînsh), *n.* 1. A crank of wheel or axle ; চক্র বা অক্ষদণ্ডে নিবদ্ধ কফোনির আকৃতি যন্ত্রাংশবিশেষ। 2. A hoisting apparatus ; একপ্রকার ভারোত্তোলন যন্ত্র, চরকীকল।

wind, *n.* 1. Air naturally or artificially put in motion ; প্রবহমাণ বায়ু, বাতাস, সমীরণ, অনিল, পবন, গন্ধবহ, সমীর, মারুত, মরুৎ, হাওয়া (*colloq.*), বাত্যা, বাত [Syn. খশ্বাস, জগৎপ্রাণ, জগদ্বল, প্রধাবন, ধরাণক, শ্বসন, স্পর্শন, মাতরিশ্বা, সদাগতি, পৃষদশ্ব, পৃষতাশ্ব, প্রজীন, তান্দন, অতস, লঘটি, বিশ্বয়ু, গন্ধবাহ, আশুগ, নভস্বান, পবমান, ধূলিধ্বজ, ফণিপ্রিয়, বাতি, নভঃপ্রাণ, ভোগিকান্ত, স্বকম্পন, কম্পলক্ষ্মা, অক্ষতি, শসীনি, আবক, হরি, বাস, সুখাশ, মৃগবাহন, সার, চঞ্চল, বিহগ, প্রকম্পন, নভঃস্বর, নিশ্বাসক, স্তনূন, পৃষতাংপতি।] [Germ. *wind* ; Lat. *vent* ; Welsh. *guynt.*] 2. A direction, from which the wind may blow ; a point of the compass, esp. one of the cardinal points ; "Come from the four *winds*, O breathe, and breathe upon this plain" ; যে দিক হইতে বাতাস প্রবাহিত হয় ; দিক্। 3. The lungs or organs of breathing ; ফুসফুস, শ্বাসযন্ত্র। 4. Power of respiration ; lung-power ; "If my *wind* were but long enough to say my prayers, I would repent" ; breath ; শ্বাসপ্রশ্বাসের শক্তি ; ফুসফুসের শক্তি ; শ্বাস। 5. Gas generated in bowels ; flatulence ; উদরে সঞ্জাত দূষিত বাষ্প ; পেটফাঁপা, উদরস্ফীতি। 6. Musical wind-instruments collectively ; সুষীর বাদ্যযন্ত্রসমূহ। 7. Air impregnated with animal odour or scent ; জন্তুর গন্ধ বা সুরভি দ্বারা পরিপূরিত বায়ু। 8. (*Slang*) The part of the body near the stomach ; "To save his life he leapt into the main, But there alas ! he could not safety find, A pack of dog-fish had him in the *wind*" ; (ইতরভাষায়) পাকস্থলীর নিকটবর্ত্তী দেহাংশ। 9. A disease of sheep in which intestines are distended by air or affected by inflammation ; মেষদিগের একপ্রকার রোগ—যাহাতে অন্ত্র বাষ্প দ্বারা স্ফীত হইয়া থাকে এবং তীব্র প্রদাহ উপজাত হয়। 10. Anything light or insignificant as a wind ; idle words ; "Stop in your *wind*" ; হাল্কা বিষয় ; অসার কথা, বাজে কথা। **Wind'-y,** *adj.* Consisting of wind ; বায়বীয় (হিঃ কোঃ)। **Wind'-ward,** *adj.* & *n.* On the side toward the point from which the wind blows ; বাত্যাভিমুখী। *Noun.* The point or sides from which the wind blows ; যে দিক বা পার্শ্ব হইতে বায়ু প্রবাহিত হয়। **Windbag**—যে ব্যক্তি আড়ম্বরপূর্ণ ভাষায় বক্তৃতা প্রদান করে। **Wind-bound**—(পোতাদিসম্পর্কে) প্রতিকূল বায়ুর জন্য পোতাশ্রয় ত্যাগ করিতে অসমর্থ। **Wind-chest**—অর্গেনযন্ত্রে সঞ্চাপিত বায়ুর আধার। **Wind-colic**—উদরাধ্মানজনিত বেদনা। **Wind-cutter**—অর্গেন যন্ত্রের চোঙ্গের মুখের উপরিভাগ—যাহার সহিত যন্ত্র হইতে বায়ুপ্রবাহ অভিঘাত প্রাপ্ত হয়। **Wind-egg**—ঘোলা ডিম, বাওয়া ডিম। **Windfall**—বায়ু সঞ্চালনে পতিত ফল ; অপ্রত্যাশিতভাবে প্রাপ্ত সম্পত্তি, উত্তরাধিকারসূত্রে প্রাপ্ত সম্পত্তি। **Wind-fanner**—Same as WINDHOVER. **Wind-flower**—Same as ANEMONE. **Wind-gall**—অশ্বের পদের পশ্চাদ্দিকের খুরের অব্যবহিত উপরিস্থ সন্ধিতে জাত কোমল অর্ব্বুদ। **Wind-gauge**—বায়ুমানযন্ত্র, পবনমান ; অর্গেনবাদ্যযন্ত্রে কি পরিমাণ বায়ু আছে তৎসূচকযন্ত্র ; বন্দুকের তিলবিন্দুতে (Sight) সংবদ্ধ যন্ত্রবিশেষ—যদ্দারা বাতাসের জন্য নিশানার কিরূপ পরিবর্ত্তন করিতে হইবে তাহা সূচিত হয়। **Wind-god**—পবনদেব। **Windhover**—A species of hawk ; একপ্রকার বাজপক্ষী। **Wind-instrument**—যে সকল বাদ্যযন্ত্র সঞ্চাপিত বায়ুর সাহায্যে, বিশেষতঃ ফুৎকার দ্বারা বাজাইতে হয়,

সুষিরযন্ত্র। **Windmill** — বায়ুপ্রবাহ-চালিত যন্ত্র, পবন-চক্র (যোঃ)। **Windpipe** — শ্বাসনালী, কণ্ঠনালী, কণ্ঠ (সাঃ পঃ)। **Wind-row** — বায়ুতে শুষ্ক করার উদ্দেশ্যে রক্ষিত পুঞ্জীভূত শস্যের আঁটি প্রভৃতির পংক্তি। **Wind-sail**—যে ক্যাম্বিসের ফুঁদেল (funnel) দ্বারা পোতের নিম্নাংশসমূহে বায়ু চালিত হয়।

Wind-mill.

Wind-spout — জলস্তম্ভ, ঘূর্ণিবাত। **Wind-tight**—বায়ু প্রবেশের পথ রুদ্ধ। **Constant wind**—যে বায়ু নিয়ত একস্থান হইতে একদিকে বহিয়া থাকে, নিয়ত বায়ু। **Periodical wind** — যে বায়ু নির্দ্দিষ্ট সময়ান্তে প্রবাহিত হইয়া থাকে, সাময়িক বায়ু। **Second wind**—একবার শ্বাস-প্রশ্বাস ক্রিয়া স্থগিত থাকার পর দ্বিতীয়বার তাহার আরম্ভ। **Betwixt wind and water** — বাত্যান্দোলিত পোতের যে অংশ জলনিম্ন হইতে জলের উপর উত্থিত হয়—তথায়। **Down the wind**—In the current of wind; বায়ুস্রোতে, বায়ুপ্রবাহে। (*Obs.*) Declining; (অপ্রঃ) পতনশীল। **In the wind**—Impending; said to be possible; আসন্ন; সম্ভবপর বলিয়া কথিত। Moving; afoot; গতিশীল; আরব্ধ। **In the wind's eye, In the teeth of the wind**—Against the wind; বায়ুর প্রতিকূলে। **It is an ill wind that blows nobody good**—Nothing ill can happen which does not benefit some one in connection with it; এমন কোন দুর্ঘটনা ঘটিতে পারে না—যদ্দারা তৎসংস্পৃষ্ট কোন না কোন ব্যক্তি উপকৃত না হয়। **The four winds of heaven**—The four cardinal points; চারিদিক। **There is something in the wind** — There are indications that something is being done secretly; গোপনে কোন কিছু করা হইতেছে লক্ষণ দ্বারা ঐরূপ বুঝা যায়। **The wind of the word**—Least hint; সামান্যমাত্র আভাস। **To break the wind**—To let out wind by anus; বাতকর্ম্ম করা, অধোবায়ু মোচন করা। **To find out how the wind blows or lies**—To find out the state of public opinion; লোকমত কিরূপ তাহা বুঝা। **To fight windmills**—To fight with imaginary foe; কাল্পনিক শত্রুর সহিত যুদ্ধ করা (Referring to Don Quixote's fight with windmill). **To get the wind of**—To get information about something; কোন বিষয়ে সংবাদ পাওয়া। To get scent; to suspect; সন্ধান পাওয়া; সন্দেহ করা। **To get to the wind ward**—To get advantage over; কাহারো উপরসুবিধা লাভ করা। **To get wind**—To be rumoured; জনরব হওয়া, রব উঠা, কথা উঠা। **To go like the wind**—To go very swiftly; বায়ুবেগে চলা, পবনবেগে চলা। **To go to the winds**—To be totally ruined; সমূলে ধ্বংস প্রাপ্ত হওয়া। **To have in the wind, To have the wind of**—To be on the scent of; টের পাওয়া। **To have one's wind taken** — To be paralysed by a blow in the wind; বক্ষঃস্থলের মধ্যভাগের নিম্নস্থানে আঘাত পাওয়ার দরুণ শ্বাস বন্ধ হওয়া। **To have the wind of**—To keep strict watch on; কড়াপাহারা রাখা। **To raise the wind**—To collect necessary funds for some object; কোন উদ্দেশ্য-সাধনের জন্য আবশ্যক অর্থ সংগ্রহ করা। **To sail close to the wind**—To manage economically; মিতব্যয়িতার সহিত নির্ব্বাহ করা। To border on vulgarity or indecency in speech, conversation etc. or dishonesty in action; বক্তৃতা বা কথাবার্ত্তায় প্রায় সুচারু বা শোভনতার সীমা লঙ্ঘন করিয়া ফেলা, প্রায় অসাধু কার্য্য করা। **To sail close to or near the wind**—To sail as nearly against the wind as is consistent with using its force; এইরূপ পরিমাণে বায়ুর প্রতিকূলে অগ্রসর হওয়া যাহাতে পাইলের উপর বায়ুর শক্তি প্রয়োগে বিশেষ অন্তরায় না জন্মে। **To take wind** — To become known; প্রচারিত হওয়া, প্রকাশিত হওয়া। **To take the wind out of one's sails** — To anticipate another; to gain advantage over a competitor; কাহারও মুখের কথা কাড়িয়া লওয়া, অন্যের সংকল্পিত কোন কার্য্য পূর্ব্বভাগেই নিজে করিয়া ফেলা; প্রতিদ্বন্দ্বীর উপর কোনরূপ সুবিধা করিয়া লওয়া। **To the four winds of heaven**—Scattered in such a way as not capable of being recovered; পুনরুদ্ধারের সম্ভাবনা-শূন্য ভাবে ইতস্ততঃ বিক্ষিপ্ত।

wind, *v. t.* & *i.* **1.** To turn in this and that direction; ঘুরাণ। **2.** To twine; to twist; to form into a ball; পাকান; পেঁচান; তাল পাকান। **3.** To turn the course or direction of; to manage; to control; "He might *wind* and turn our constitution at his pleasure"; দিক্ বা গতি পরিবর্ত্তন করা; নির্ব্বাহ করা; সংযত করা। **4.** To wind up; as, to *wind* a watch; চাবি দেওয়া, দম দেওয়া। **5.** To hoist by a rope; রজ্জুর সাহায্যে তোলা। **6.** To wrap closely; জড়ান। ***Verb i.*** **1.** To turn or coil round something; as, the creeper *winds* round the tree; বেষ্টিত হওয়া, কুণ্ডলিত হওয়া, জড়ান। **2.** To meander; as, the river *winds* through a valley; আঁকিয়া বাঁকিয়া চলা। **3.** To have a circular or spiral direction; as, *winding* stair; পাকাইয়া পাকাইয়া অগ্রসর হওয়া, ঘুরিয়া ঘুরিয়া উঠা। **4.** To wrap closely; জড়ান। **5.** To work or make one's way by stealthy methods; as to *wind* into one's affections; গোপনীয় উপায়ে কোথাও উপস্থিত হওয়া বা কোন কার্য্য সাধন করা। **Wind'-ing,** *n.* & *adj.* **1.** Bend or turn; মোড়, পাক। **2.** Single turn in wind; পাক। ***Adj.*** Turning; twisting; bending; পাকানিয়া; পেঁচলিয়া; পেঁচাল, সর্পিল। **Winding-sheet** —যে বস্ত্রে শবদেহ জড়ানো হয়। **Winding up**—কারবার প্রভৃতি গুটানি। **Wind-up**—শেষ, উপসংহার। **To wind a person round one's finger**—To exercise contral over him; কাহাকে হাতের মুঠার মধ্যে রাখা, কাহাকে করতলগত করিয়া রাখা। **To wind a vessel**—জাহাজ ঘুরাণ। **To wind off**—To unwind; পাক খোলা। **To wind up**—To coil into a ball; গুটি পাকান। To bring to an end; শেষ করা, সমাপ্ত করা। To be finished; সমাপ্ত হওয়া। To make tight or tense; আঁটান, টান করা। To excite; উত্তেজিত করা। To arrange the affairs of a company and dissolve it; কারবার প্রভৃতি গুটান। To hoist by means of rope; রজ্জুর সাহায্যে তোলা।

wind, *v. t.* **1.** To sound; বাদন করা। **2.** To detect by scent; গন্ধ দ্বারা বাহির করা। **3.** To make breath quick and deep by exercise; to exhaust the wind of; to renew wind of by rest; অঙ্গ চালনা দ্বারা দ্রুত এবং গভীর শ্বাস প্রশ্বাস গ্রহণ ও মোচন করা; শ্বাসযন্ত্র অবসন্ন করা; বিশ্রাম দ্বারা শ্বাসযন্ত্র শক্তিসম্পন্ন করা।

wind'-age, *n.* **1.** The difference between the diameter of the bore of a gun or other firearms and that of a ball or shell; বন্দুক কামানাদির নলের রন্ধ্রের ব্যাস এবং গুলির ব্যাসের প্রভেদ। **2.** The influence of the wind in deflecting a ball, arrow or the like, aside from the point or object at which aimed; লক্ষ্য হইতে কোন শর, গুলি প্রভৃতির বিক্ষেপে বায়ুর প্রভাব। **3.** Allowance made for such deflection; উক্তরূপ বিক্ষেপের জন্য যে বাদসাদ দেওয়া হয়।

wind'-lass, *n.* & *v. t.* A cylinder worked with winch or lever and used for raising weight; একপ্রকার

Ship's windlass.

ভারোত্তোলন যন্ত্র। ***Verb t.*** To hoist with a windlass; উক্তরূপ যন্ত্রের সাহায্যে উত্তোলন করা।

win'-dle-straw (-dl-strä), *n.* Old stalk of different kinds of grass; বিভিন্নপ্রকার তৃণের পুরাতন বৃন্ত।

win'-dow (-dō), *n.* **1.** An opening in the wall or roof of a building for the admission of light and air when necessary; জানালা, গবাক্ষ, বাতায়ন, খিড়কী, খটক্কিকা। **2.** Blind, false or blank window; প্রাচীরাদিতে বাতায়নাকৃতি অবনমিত স্থান। **—less,** *adj.* **Window-box**—বাতায়নের দেহলীতে স্থাপিত যে বাক্সে ফুল গাছ প্রভৃতি রোপণ করা হয়। **Window-shade**—জানালার পর্দ্দা। **Window-shutter**—খড়খড়ির ঝিলিমিল।

Wind'-sor, *n.* A town in Berkshire; ইংলণ্ডের অন্তঃপাতী বার্কসায়ারের নগরবিশেষ। **Windsor-chair**—কাষ্ঠের কেদারা — এইরূপ কেদারার পিঠের দিকে খোদাইর কাজ থাকে। **Windsor uniform**—একপ্রকার নীল কোর্ত্তা—উহার গলদেশ ও আস্তীনের অগ্রভাগ লাল রঙ্গের থাকে। ইংলণ্ডের রাজপরিবারের ব্যক্তিগণ ঐরূপ কোর্ত্তা পরিয়া থাকেন, এবং রাজানুমতিপ্রাপ্ত অন্যান্য লোকেও ইহা পরিতে পারে। **Brown Windsor soap**—বাদামীরঙ্গের একপ্রকার সুগন্ধি সাবান।

wind'-y, *adj.* **1.** Wind-swept; বাত্যাতাড়িত, বাত্যাচালিত, ঝটিকাবিক্ষুব্ধ। **2.** Tempestuous; as, *windy* weather; ঝটিকাপূর্ণ, ঝটিকাময়। **3.** Generating flatulence; উদরস্ফীতিজনক, পেট ফাঁপানো, উদরাধ্মানজনক। **4.** Wordy; as, a *windy* speech; empty; বাগ্‌বহুল; অন্তঃসারশূন্য। **5.** (*Colloq.*) Proud; গর্ব্বপূর্ণ, গর্ব্বস্ফীত। **—i-ly,** *adv.* **—i-ness,** *n.*

wine, *n.* & *v. t.* **1.** The fermented juice of grapes; আঙ্গুর রসের মদ্য, দ্রাক্ষাসুরা, দ্রাক্ষামদ্য, দ্রাক্ষাসব, লালপানি (*colloq.*), মদিরা, সরাপ, কারণ (in Tantra) **2.** The juice of certain fruits prepared with sugar, spirit, etc.; as, raspbeerry *wine*; শর্করা, সুরাসার, প্রভৃতি মিশ্রিত কতিপয় ফলের রস, ফলসার। **3.** The unfermented juice of certain plants; as, palm-*wine*; তাল, খর্জ্জুর, প্রভৃতি বৃক্ষের রস। **4.** Intoxication; "Noah awoke from his *wine*"; মত্ততা। **5.** A wine-party at one of the English universities; (ইংলণ্ড বিশ্ববিদ্যালয়ে) মদ্যপানসম্মিলনী। **6.** Medicinal preparation, in some respects resembling wine; as, quinine *wine*; ঔষধমিশ্রিত মদ্য। ***Verb t.*** To treat with wine or drink wine; as, to *wine* one's friend; মদ দ্বারা আপ্যায়িত করা, মদ্য পান করা। **Wine'-less,** *adj.* **Win'-y,** *adj.* **Adam's wine**—জল। **Green-wine**—প্রথম বর্ষের মদ্য। **Winebag**—Same as WINE-SKIN. **Wine-bibber**—মাতাল, মদখোর। **Wine-biscuit**—মদ্যের সহিত পরিবেষিত হাল্‌কা বিস্কুট। **Winebowl**—মদ্যপাত্র, সুরাপাত্র; মদ্য পানের অভ্যাস। **Wine-carriage**—ভোজনোপবিষ্ট ব্যক্তিগণকে মদ্য পরিবেষণের জন্য একপ্রকার চক্রযুক্ত ভাণ্ড। **Wine-cask**—মদ্যের পিপা। **Wine cellar**—মদ্য রাখার জন্য ভূগর্ভস্থ ভাণ্ডারগৃহ। **Wine-cooler**—যে পাত্রে মদ্যের

বোতল সকল বরফ দ্বারা শীতল করা হয়। **Winecup** — মদ্যের পেয়ালা। **Winefat**—নিষ্পীড়নযন্ত্র হইতে যে পাত্রে দ্রাক্ষারস প্রবাহিত হয়। **Wine-glass** — মদের গ্লাস, মদিরাপাত্র। **Wineglassful** — ৪ টেবিল চামচে পূর্ণ। **Wine-growing**—মদ্যের জন্য আঙ্গুরের চাষ। **Wine-merchant**—মদ্য ব্যবসায়ী, শৌণ্ডিক, শুঁড়ী। **Wine-palm**—যে সকল তাল জাতীয় বৃক্ষের রস বা ফল হইতে মদ্য প্রস্তুত হয়। **Winepress**—দ্রাক্ষানিষ্পীড়ন-যন্ত্র। **Wineskin**—মদ্য রাখার জন্য ছাগ প্রভৃতির চর্ম্ম সীবনে প্রস্তুত মশক। **Wine-stone**—মদ্যের পিপার পাত্রে সঞ্চিত তিন্তিড়িকাম্ল। **Wine-vault** — ভূনিম্নস্থ যে কুঠরীতে মদ্য রক্ষিত হয়। **Good wine needs no bush**—See BUSH. **In wine**—Exhilarated or drunk with wine ; মদ্যপানোল্লসিত, সুরামত্ত। **New wine in old bottles**—যে সকল নূতন তত্ত্ব প্রাচীন রীতিনীতির ভিতর নিবদ্ধ রাখা অসম্ভব। **Spirit of wine**—সুরাসার, এলকোহল। **Wine and whey**—মদ্য এবং দধি সহযোগে প্রস্তুত আসব বিশেষ।

wing, *n.*, *v. t.* & *i.* **1.** The limb of a bird by which it flies and under which it protects young ; পক্ষ, পাখা, ডানা, পত্র। **2.** Flight ; "The crow makes *wing* to the rocky wood" ; উড্ডয়ন। **3.** Means or instrument of flight ; উড্ডয়নের উপায় বা যন্ত্র। **4.** The flank or extreme part of an army ; সৈন্য-দলের পার্শ্ব বা শেষ প্রান্ত। **5.** The side of a building ; অট্টালিকার পার্শ্ব। **6.** That which agitates the air, as a fan for winnowing grain ; যদ্দারা বায়ু সঞ্চালিত হয়, শস্য ঝাড়িবার কুলা। **7.** A membraneous expansion of plants ; উদ্ভিদের ঝিল্লীময় প্রবর্দ্ধন। **8.** Either of the parts of a double door ; কপাটের বাইল। **9.** (*Theatre*, *pl.*) Sides of a stage ; pieces of side scenes ; (রঙ্গালয়) দৃশ্যপটের পার্শ্বদ্বয় ; পার্শ্বপট। ***Verb t.*** **1.** To furnish with, or as with, wings ; to enable to fly or move swiftly ; "*Winged* the shaft that quivered in his heart" ; পক্ষসমন্বিত করা ; দ্রুত উড্ডীয়মান করা, দ্রুত সঞ্চালিত করা। **2.** To supply with side parts or divisions ; পার্শ্ববর্ত্তী অংশ বা বিভাগসমূহ সমন্বিত করা। **3.** To transport by flight "I, an old turtle, will *wing* me to some wither'd bough" ; উড়াইয়া নেওয়া। **4.** To traverse in flying ; "The crows and choughs that *wing* the midnight air" ; উড়িয়া চলা। **5.** To pass over with great rapidity ; "The ... javelin *winged* its course" ; বেগে ধাবিত হওয়া। **6.** (*Colloq.*) To cut off the wings of ; to wound in the wing ; to disable a wing or limb of ; "All right" said Snodgrass "Be steady and *wing* him" ; to wound, with a bullet without killing ; পাখা কাটিয়া ফেলা ; পাখা জখম করা ; পক্ষ বা অন্য প্রত্যঙ্গ অকর্ম্মণ্য করা ; বধ না করিয়া গুলি দ্বারা আহত করা। ***Verb i.*** **1.** To fly ; উড়া, উড্ডীন হওয়া। **2.** (Of a horse) To swing one or more of the legs ; (অশ্ব সম্পর্কে) এক বা একাধিক পা ঝুলান। **Wing'-ed**, *p. p.* **1.** Having wings ; সপক্ষ। **2.** Swift ; দ্রুত, দ্রুতগামী। **3.** (*Obs.*) Swarming with birds ; "The *winged* air dark with plumes" ; পক্ষিসমাকুল। **4.** Elevated ; sublime ; "How *winged* the sentiment that virtue is to be followed for its own sake because its essence is divine" ; উন্নত ; মহিমাময়। **Wing'-let**, *n.* **Wing'-less**, *adj.* **Wing-beat** — উড্ডয়নকালে একবার পক্ষ-সঞ্চালন। **Wing-case**—কীটদিগের পক্ষ-আবরক কঠিন আচ্ছাদন, পাখের ঢাকনি (সাঃ পঃ)। **Wing-covert**—Same as TECTRICES (which see) **Winged god**—Same as MERCURY. **Winged horse**—Same as PEGASUS (which see) ; কবিতা। **Winged stem** — সপত্র কাণ্ড (সাঃ পঃ)। **Winged Victory**—বিজয়াদেবীর পক্ষ-সমন্বিতা মূর্ত্তি। **Wing-footed**—দ্রুত-গমনক্ষম, দ্রুতগামী। **Wing-sheath**—Same as WING-CASE. **Wing-spread**—পক্ষযুগলের বিস্তার। **Wing-stroke**—Same as WING-BEAT. **On the wing**—Travelling ; in motion ; ভ্রমণশীল ; গতিশীল। **The wings of Azrael** — আসন্ন মৃত্যু। **To clip one's wing** — To lessen one's power of action ; কাহারো কার্য্যকারিতশক্তি ক্ষুণ্ণ করা। To limit one's ambition or curtail one's expense ; কাহারো উচ্চাকাঙ্ক্ষা প্রহত করা, কাহারো ব্যয় সঙ্কোচ করিয়া দেওয়া। **To come on the wings of the wind**—To come swifty ; উড়িয়া আসিয়া পড়া। **To lend wings** — To hasten ; গতিবেগ বৃদ্ধি করা, ত্বরান্বিত করা। **To take wing**—To fly off suddenly ; to depart without intimation ; হঠাৎ উড়িয়া যাওয়া ; কোনরূপ সংবাদ না দিয়া প্রস্থান করা। **To take under one's wing**—To patronize ; to protect ; পৃষ্ঠপোষকতা করা ; আশ্রয় দেওয়া।

wink (wĭngk), *v. i.*, *t.* & *n.* **1.** To close and open the eyelids quickly and involuntarily ; চোখ মিট মিট করা, চোখের পলক ফেলা। **2.** To give a significant sign by a motion of the eyelids ; "*Wink* at the footmen to leave him without a plate" ; চোখ ঠারিয়া ইসারা করা। **3.** (*Rare*) To shut the eyes ; to close the eyelids so as not to see ; চোখ বন্ধ করা ; চোখ বুঁজিয়া থাকা। **5.** To avoid seeing or noting, as if by shutting the eyes (with *at*) ; as, to *wink at* one's faults ; to connive ; চোখ বুঁজিয়া থাকা ; দেখিয়াও না দেখা, সায় দেওয়া। **6.** To twinkle ; as,

as, he *closed* with him and proved too strong ; সন্নিকটে আসা ; বাহুযুদ্ধে প্রবৃত্ত হওয়া ; আঁকড়াইয়া ধরা। 5. To come to terms or agreement, (*with, upon*) ; চুক্তি বা সর্ত্তে আবদ্ধ হওয়া। ***Noun.*** 1. Conclusion ; end ; as, to bring the matter to a *close* ; উপসংহার ; অবসান, সমাপ্তি। 2. A grappling of combatants ; encounter ; বাহুযুদ্ধ ; সম্মুখ যুদ্ধ। 3. The playground of a school ; বিদ্যালয়ের ক্রীড়াপ্রাঙ্গণ। **Close-banded**—একতাবদ্ধ। **Close-barred** — দৃঢ়-সংবদ্ধ। **Closed-fisted**—কৃপণ, হাতকষা, হাতভারী, বায়কুণ্ঠ, কঞ্জুস (*Colloq.*), বদ্ধমুষ্টি (*Colloq.*)। **Close-grained**—ঘনসংবদ্ধ ; নিরবকাশ। **Close-hauled**—যথাসম্ভব বায়ুর প্রতিকূলে পাইলভরে গমনশীল। **Close-stool**—বাক্সের ভিতরে আঁটা বাহ্যপ্রস্রাবের পাত্র। **Close-tongued**—সংযতবাক্। **A close contest**—যে দ্বন্দ্বে উভয়পক্ষ প্রায় সমবল। **At close quarters**—হাতাহাতি। **At the close of**—শেষে, অন্তে। **Close vote**—উভয় পক্ষে নির্ব্বাচন মত-সংখ্যা প্রায় তুল্য। **Draw to a close**—Be about to end ; শেষ হইয়া আসা। **Follow close upon**—Come immediately after ; অব্যবহিত পরেই বা সঙ্গে সঙ্গে আসা। **To close a bargain**—To make an agreement ; চুক্তি করা। **To close about**—To close in on all sides ; to encompass ; চারিদিকে ঘিরিয়া ফেলা ; পরিবৃত করা। To draw near to ; to come in contact *with* ; সন্নিকটে আসা, সন্নিহিত হওয়া ; সংস্পর্শে আসা। **To close in upon**—To fall upon ; আপতিত হওয়া। **To close one's days**—To die ; মরিয়া যাওয়া, জীবনলীলার অবসান হওয়া। **To close ranks or files**—To bring (soldiers) in
চিত্তাকর্ষক, বিমোহন, মুগ্ধকর ; উৎফুল্ল। —ly, *adv.* —ness, *n.*

win'-ter, *n., v. i. & t.* 1. The cold season of the year, commencing, astronomically, in the northern hemisphere, when the sun enters capricorn, or at the solstice about the 21st December, and ending at the equinox at March ; শীতকাল, শিশিরসময়, তুষারকাল (কবিতায়)। 2. A year ; as, a child of 12 *winters* ; বয়স। 3. A period marked by dreariness or activity ; "Life's autumn past, I stand on *winter's* verge" ; জড়তা, আলস্যতা, দুর্দ্দশার কাল। 4. The part of a printing-press which sustains the carriage ; মুদ্রাযন্ত্রের অংশ বিশেষ। ***Verb i.*** To hibernate ; শীতকাল যাপন করা। ***Verb t.*** To keep or feed during the winter ; শীতকালে পালন করা বা ভোজন করান। **Winter-garden**—শীতপ্রধান দেশে শীতকালে ফল-পুষ্পাদির বৃক্ষরোপণের জন্য কাচসমাচ্ছাদিত স্থান, শীতোদ্যান। **Winter-green**—একজাতীয় ক্ষুপ—যাহারা সারা শীতকাল ব্যাপিয়া সবুজবর্ণ থাকে, শীতহরিৎ। **Winter-lodge**—যে মুকুলাদি দ্বারা শীতকালে বৃক্ষের ভ্রূণ রক্ষিত হয়। **Winter quarters**—যে সেনানিবাসে সৈন্যগণ শীতকাল যাপন করে, শীতাবাস। **Winter-sleep**—Same as HIBERNATION.

win'-try, *adj.* 1. Cold ; stormy ; শীতল, ঠাণ্ডা ; ঝটিকাচ্ছন্ন। 2. Cheerless ; lacking warmth ; as, a *wintry* smile ; স্ফূর্ত্তিহীন, প্রাণশূন্য ; নিরানন্দ, অপ্রফুল্ল।

Wipe, *v. t., i. & n.* 1. To rub with something soft for clearing ; মুছা। 2. To rub off ; to obliterate ; as, to *wipe* out all traces of past affection ; মুছিয়া উঠান ; বিলুপ্ত করা, অপহৃত করা। 3. (*Slang*) To strike ; to beat ; (ইতর ভাষায়) আঘাত করা ; প্রহার করা। ***Verb i.*** (*Colloq.*) To make a motion like that of wiping something as in striking (চলিত ভাষায়) কোন কিছু মুছিবার কালে যেরূপ ভাবে হস্তসঞ্চালন করিতে হয় তেমন ভাবে হস্ত চালনা করা। ***Noun.*** 1. The act of wiping ; মুছন, মার্জ্জন, পরিমার্জ্জন। 2. (*Slang*) Handkerchief ; (ইতরভাষায়) রুমাল। 3. (*Slang*) A blow or stroke ; আঘাত। 4. (*Obs.*) Severe sarcasm ; "To touch with a satiric *wipe*" ; (অপ্রঃ) তীব্র বিদ্রূপ। 5. (*Obs.*) Brand ; (অপ্রঃ) কলঙ্ক-চিহ্ন। **To wipe one's eyes**—To dry tears ; চোখ মুছা, অশ্রু মুছিয়া ফেলা। (*Slang*) To get advantage over some one by anticipating him ; কাহারো অগ্রে কোন কাজ করিয়া তাহার উপর সুবিধা লাভ করা। **To wipe out**—To annihilate ; বিলুপ্ত করা। **To wipe the ground with**—To defeat utterly ; সম্পূর্ণরূপে পরাজিত করা। **To wipe the nose of**—(ইতর ভাষায়) মাথায় হাত বুলান, ঠকান।

wire, *n., v. t. & i.* 1. Any metallic substance drawn to an even thread ; তার। 2. A telegraph wire ; a telegram ; as, please send a *wire* to him to come here sharp ; টেলিগ্রাফের তার ; তাড়িতবার্ত্তা, তার। 3. (*Slang*) One who picks a woman's pocket ; (ইতরভাষায়) যে ব্যক্তি স্ত্রীলোকের পকেট কাটে। 4. A string of musical instrument ; a stringed musical instrument ; বাদ্যযন্ত্রের তার ; তন্ত্রীবিশিষ্ট বাদ্যযন্ত্র। 5. (*Scot.*) A knitting needle ; বুনিবার শলা। 5. A wire fencing ; তারের বেড়া। 6. The system of wires used to operate the puppetshow ; the secret influence by which a political party or movement is controlled ; as, to pull the *wires* for office ; পুতুল নাচের পুতুল যে তার-শ্রেণী দ্বারা চালিত হয় ; যে গুপ্ত প্রভাবে কোন রাজনৈতিক দল বা আন্দোলন পরিচালিত হয়। ***Verb t.*** 1. To bind with wire ; to provide with a wire ; তার দ্বারা বাঁধা ; তার লাগান। 2. To put upon wire ; তার লাগান। 3. To telegraph ; as he should be *wired* to come at once ; তার করা, তাড়িতবার্ত্তাযোগে প্রেরণ করা। 4. To snare by means of wire ; as, to *wire* a bird ; তারের ফাঁদে ফেলা। ***Verb i.*** 1. To flow in currents as thin as wire ; "Then in small streams through all isles *wiring*, sends it to every part both heat and life insuring" ; তার বা সুতার মত ক্ষীণ স্রোতে প্রবাহিত হওয়া। 2. To telegraph; তার করা। **Private wire**—কোন ব্যক্তি-বিশেষের অনন্যসাধারণ ব্যবহারের জন্য রক্ষিত তার। **Wire bed, Wire mattress**—তার দ্বারা রচিত একপ্রকার স্থিতিস্থাপক গদী বা খট্টাতল। **Wire-cloth, Wire-gauze, Wire-netting**—তারের জালি। **Wire-dancer**—যে বাজীকর তারের উপর নৃত্য করিয়া থাকে। **Wiredraw**—ছিদ্রের ভিতর দিয়া কোন ধাতুর শলাকা টানিয়া তার প্রস্তুত করা ; জোরে টানা ; অতি সূক্ষ্ম তর্ক উত্থাপন করা। **Wire entanglement**—শত্রুর আক্রমণ রোধ করার জন্য কাঁটাওয়ালা বা অন্য কোনরূপ তার দ্বারা রচিত বৃতিজাল। **Wire-gun**—একপ্রকার কামান—যাহার নালী স্থূল তার দ্বারা বেষ্টন করা হইয়া থাকে। **Wire-haired**—তারের মত শক্ত লোমবিশিষ্ট (কুক্কুরসম্বন্ধে)। **Wire-puller**—যে ব্যক্তি পুতুল নাচের পুতুল নাচায় ; যে ব্যক্তি তলে তলে কাজ করিয়া চলে ; ষড়যন্ত্রকারী। **Wire-rope**—তারের রজ্জু। **Wire-tapper**—যে ব্যক্তি টেলিগ্রাফের তারের কতকাংশ মূল তার হইতে অপসৃত করিয়া সংবাদ রোধ করে ; (ইতরভাষায়) যে ব্যক্তি স্ফূর্তি খেলার বাজি জিতিবার জন্য অসাধু উপায়ে পূর্ব্বেই তারের খবর জানিয়া লয়। **Wire-work**—তারের কাজ। **Wire-worker**—যে ব্যক্তি তার দ্বারা নানাপ্রকার দ্রব্য প্রস্তুত করে। Same as WIRE-PULLER. **Wire-worm**—একপ্রকার কৃমি কীট। **Wire-wove**—একপ্রকার উৎকৃষ্ট মসৃণ চিঠির কাগজের সম্বন্ধে প্রযুক্ত। **To pull the wires**—To control puppets by wire ; তারদ্বারা পুতুল নাচান। To manage a political party or movement by secret influence ; গুপ্ত উপায়ে কোন রাজনীতিক দল বা আন্দোলন পরিচালনা করা, তলে তলে কার্য্য করা, কল টিপা। **Wire of Lapland**—বল্গা হরিণের শিরা হইতে প্রস্তুত একপ্রকার শক্ত এবং সুদৃশ্য তার। বল্গা হরিণের শিরা জলে ভিজাইয়া পিটিবার পর উহা হইতে সুদীর্ঘ সূত্র প্রস্তুত করা হয়। অতঃপর ঐ সকল সূত্র গলিত রঙ্গে ডুবাইয়া পরে একটী শৃঙ্গের ছিদ্রের ভিতর দিয়া টানিয়া নেওয়া হয়।

wīre'-lĕss, *adj., n. & v. t.* Without wires ; তারশূন্য। ***Noun.*** Wireless telegraphy ; অতারতাড়িতবার্ত্তা, অতারবার্ত্তা। [১৮৯৭ খৃঃ অব্দে ইতালী দেশবাসী Guglielmo Marconi কর্ত্তৃক অতারতাড়িতযন্ত্র উদ্ভাবিত হয়।] ***Verb t.*** To send a message by wireless telegraph ; অতারতাড়িতবার্ত্তা যোগে সংবাদ প্রেরণ করা। **Wireless telephony**—অতারদূরশ্রবণযন্ত্র।

wīr'-ȳ, *adj.* 1. Made of wire ; তারনির্ম্মিত। 2. Tough ; sinewy ; as, a *wiry* person ; দৃঢ়কায় ; বলবান, শক্তিশালী। **–i-ly**, *adv.* **–i-ness**, *n.*

wis, *v. i.* I know well ; আমি ভালরূপে জানি।

wis'-dom (-dŭm), *n.* 1. Sound judgment and sagacity ; জ্ঞান, প্রজ্ঞা, বিজ্ঞান, মতি। 2. Knowledge ; "Moses was learned in all the *wisdom* of the Egyptians, and was mighty in words and in deeds" ; erudition ; বিদ্যা ; পাণ্ডিত্য। 3. (*Rare*) Wise sayings ; (কচিদ্ ব্যবহৃত) জ্ঞানগর্ভ উক্তি। **Wisdom literature**—প্রাচীন ইহুদীদিগের ধর্ম্ম এবং নীতিবিষয়কপ্রসঙ্গপূর্ণ পুস্তক। **Wisdom-tooth**—আক্কেল দাঁত। **To cut one's wisdom tooth**—To gain prudence ; বিজ্ঞতা লাভ করা।

wīse, *adj.* 1. Possessed of discernment, judgment and discretion ; জ্ঞানী, বিজ্ঞ, প্রাজ্ঞ, বিদগ্ধ, বিদ্বান। 2. Dictated or guided by wisdom ; judicious ; discreet ; as, a *wise* saying ; জ্ঞানগর্ভ ; বিচারবুদ্ধিসম্পন্ন ; সদ্বিবেচক। 3. Skilful ; চতুর, সুনিপুণ। 4. Knowing ; learned ; "They are *wise* to do evil, but to do good they have no knowledge" ; জ্ঞাতসার ; পণ্ডিত। 5. (*Archaic*) Having occult power ; (অপ্রঃ) অলৌকিক শক্তিসম্পন্ন। **Wise'-ly**, *adv.* **Wise-man**—ঐন্দ্রজালিক। **Wise-woman**—মায়াবিনী ; গণকী, ধাত্রী। **Wise-saw**—নীতিবাক্য। **To be wise after the event**—To be unable to foresee the result ; চোর পালালে বুদ্ধি বাড়ে।

wīse, *n.* Way ; manner ; as, in any *wise* ; প্রকার, পদ্ধতি ; রূপ।

wīse'-ā-cre (-kêr), *n.* One who makes pretension to great wisdom ; পাণ্ডম্মন্য, পাণ্ডিত্যাভিমানী।

wish, *v. i., t. & n.* To have a desire or yearning ; ইচ্ছা করা, কামনা করা, অভিলাষ করা, বাঞ্ছা করা, চাওয়া। ***Verb t.*** 1. To long for ; কামনা করা। 2. To invoke in favour of, or against, some one ; as, to *wish* one joy ; to imprecate ; ভগবানের নিকট কামনা করা ; অভিশাপ দেওয়া। ***Noun.*** 1. Desire ; ইচ্ছা, বাঞ্ছা, কামনা, বাসনা, অভিলাষ, স্পৃহা, মানসকামনা, মানস। 2. Request ; invocation ; imprecation ; "Blistered be thy tongue for such a *wish*" ; কাহারো মঙ্গল বা অমঙ্গলের জন্য ভগবানের নিকট প্রার্থনা ; কাহারো অনিষ্টের জন্য ভগবানের নিকট প্রার্থনা ; অভিশাপ। 3. An object of desire ; "Be assured···shy *wish*, exactly to thy heart's desire" ; বাঞ্ছিত বস্তু, ঈপ্সিত বস্তু, অভিলষিত বিষয়। **Wish'-ful**, *adj.* Having desire ; ইচ্ছুক, অভিলাষী। **Wish'-ing**, *n.* **Good-wishes**—মঙ্গলকামনা, শুভকামনা। **Wish-child**—পোষ্য পুত্র বা কন্যা। **Wish-maiden**—Same as VALKYR. **Wish-wife**—দেবী ; দেবতাদিগের পরিচারিকাবিশেষ ; মনুষ্যের সহিত

প্রণয়ে বদ্ধ হইয়া থাকে এরূপ দেব যোনি। **Wishing-bone** — পক্ষীর বুক এবং কণ্ঠের মধ্যস্থিত দ্বিশাখ অস্থি। এই অস্থির শাখাদ্বয় ধরিয়া দুই ব্যক্তি টানাটানি করিত। যাহার হস্তে লম্বা অংশ ভাঙ্গিয়া আসিত তাহার বিবাহ আশু হইবে কিম্বা তাহার তৎকালীন কোন কামনা পূর্ণ হইবে বলিয়া বিশ্বাস করা হইত। **Wishing-cap** — ঐন্দ্রজালিক টুপি-বিশেষ—যাহা পরিলে যে কোন কামনা করা যায় তাহা পূর্ণ হয়। **Wishing-purse**—অক্ষয় মুদ্রাধার। **Wishing-rod** — যে দণ্ডের সাহায্যে অলৌকিক উপায়ে ভূগর্ভে কোথায় স্বর্ণ বা ধনরত্ন আছে তাহা স্থির করা যায় বলিয়া কল্পিত হইয়া থাকে। **Long-wished for**—চির-বাঞ্ছিত। **To wish one joy of anything**—To wish that when the person will gain his object he may find it very troublesome; কোন জিনিষ লাভ করিয়া তাহার মজা টের পাওয়ার ইচ্ছা করা। **To wish to goodness**—To strongly desire; প্রবল ইচ্ছা হওয়া। **wish is father to the thought**—We believe a thing because we wish it to be true; কোন বিষয় সত্য হউক এরূপ আমাদের ইচ্ছা—তাই আমরা ইহাকে বিশ্বাস করি।

wish'-wash (-wŏsh), *n.* **1.** Any weak drink; (*slang*) foolish talk; নীরস পানীয়; (ইতর ভাষায়) নির্ব্বোধের মত কথাবার্ত্তা।

wish'-y̆-wash-y̆ (-wŏsh-), *adj.* & *n.* Very thin; নীরস, পান্‌সে। ***Noun.*** Any sort of thin weak or poor liquor; পান্‌সে বা নীরস মদ্য।

wisp, *n.* A small bundle or twist of straw; আঁটি, গুচ্ছ, গল্লা, গোছ।

wist, See WIT (in the sense of *To know*).

Wis-tā'-ri-ă, *n.* A genus of climbing shrubs; একজাতীয় গুল্ম।

wist'-fûl, *adj.* **1.** Longing; as, a *wistful* look; desirous; আগ্রহান্বিত, উৎসুক, ব্যগ্র; ইচ্ছুক, অভিলাষী। **2.** Meditative; as, a *wistful* face; চিন্তাশীল। **—ly,** *adv.* **—ness,** *n.*

wit, *n.* **1.** Intellect; as, you have not *wit* enough to see this; বুদ্ধি, ধী, প্রজ্ঞা। **2.** Mental faculty; as, to lose one's *wit*; মনোবৃত্তি। **3.** (*Obs.*) Ingenuity; "Passed the *wit* of mam to say what dream it was"; (অপ্রঃ) নৈপুণ্য, চাতুর্য্য, বুদ্ধিকৌশল, হেকমৎ (*colloq.*)। **4.** Faculty of associating ideas cleverly and in apt language; "True *wit* is nature to advantage dressed, what oft was thought, but never so well expressed"; রসিকতা, বাক্‌চাতুর্য্য, নর্ম্মোক্তি, বাগ্‌বৈদগ্ধ্য। [প্রকৃত বাগ্‌বৈদগ্ধ্য ভাব সমূহের সাদৃশ্যের উপর নির্ভর করে। কিন্তু কেবল ভাবসাম্য হইলেই বাগ্‌বৈদগ্ধ্য হয় না, এই ভাবসাম্য এইরূপ হওয়া আবশ্যক যাহাতে শ্রোতা বা পাঠকের মনে আনন্দের চমক খেলাইয়া যায়। বিস্ময়-জনক আনন্দের বিচ্ছুরণই বাগ্‌বৈদগ্ধ্যের প্রাণ। সাদৃশ্য অতিশয় পরিস্ফুট হইলে কোন প্রকার বিস্ময় জাত হয় না; সুতরাং এই স্থলে বাগ্‌বৈদগ্ধ্য হইল না। যথা কোন সুন্দরীর বর্ণনায়—হে কান্তে! বিধাতা তোমার নয়ন ইন্দীবর দ্বারা, মুখ পদ্মদ্বারা, দন্ত কুন্দকুসুমে এবং অঙ্গসমূহ চম্পকদলে নির্ম্মাণ করিয়াছেন—এই পর্য্যন্ত কোনরূপ বাগ্‌বৈদগ্ধ্য হইল না; কিন্তু যখন বলা হইল—তবে হে সুন্দরী তোমার মন কেন কঠিন পাষাণে নির্ম্মাণ করিলেন—এই শেষোক্ত কথায়ই বাগ্‌বৈদগ্ধ্য (wit) প্রকাশ পাইল। পরিহাসে (humour) সর্ব্বদাই হাস্যের উদ্রেক হয়। কিন্তু বাগ্‌বৈদগ্ধ্যে সচরাচর তাহা হয় না। কিন্তু বাগ্‌বৈদগ্ধ্য আনন্দের সঙ্গে মনে একটু জ্বালাও উৎপাদন করে। পরিহাস সাধারণ লোক কর্ত্তৃক আদৃত হয়। কিন্তু বাগ্‌বৈদগ্ধ্য কেবল শিক্ষিত এবং জ্ঞানী লোকের প্রীতিপ্রদ হইয়া থাকে।] **5.** Idea; thought; a trick or skilled device; ভাব, ধারণা; চিন্তা; কৌশল। **6.** Meaning; significance; অর্থ; মর্ম্মার্থ, অভিপ্রায়। **Wit'-less,** *adj.* **Wit'-less-ly,** *adv.* **Wit'-less-ness,** *n.* **Wit'-ti-ly,** *adv.* **Mother-wit**—সাধারণ বুদ্ধি। **Out of one's wits**—Mad; উন্মত্ত, বিক্ষিপ্তচিত্ত। **The fine wits**—(অপ্রঃ) ইন্দ্রিয় সমূহ; মন। **To be at one's wit's end**—To be utterly at a loss; কিংকর্ত্তব্য-বিমূঢ় হওয়া, হতবুদ্ধি হওয়া। **To have one's wits about one**—To be intelligent; বুদ্ধিসম্পন্ন হওয়া। **To live by one's wits**—To live by shifts; নানাপ্রকার ফিকিরফন্দি খাটাইয়া কোনরূপে জীবিকানির্ব্বাহ করা।

wit, *v. t.* & *i.* (*pres.* I, he, *wot*, thou *wottest*; *past* wist) (*Archaic*) To know; জানা। **I wit**—I know very will; আমি বেশ জানি। **To wit**—That is to say; namely; অর্থাৎ, যথা।

wit, *n.* **1.** (*Archaic*) Wise man; (অপ্রঃ) জ্ঞানী লোক। **2.** A witty person; সুরসিক লোক।

witch (wĭch), *n.* & *v. t.* **1.** A woman supposed to be in compact with the devil, who practises sorcery or enchantment; ডাইনী, ডাকিনী, যাদুকরী, মায়াবিনী, মায়িনী। **2.** A bewitching or fascinating woman; মোহিনী। **3.** A term of reproch for an old and ugly woman; কুরূপা বৃদ্ধানারী, ডাইনী। ***Verb t.*** **1.** To bewitch; মোহিত করা, বিমোহিত করা, বিমুগ্ধ করা। **2.** To effect by sorcery or witch-craft; যাদুবলে সম্পন্ন করা। **Witch'-er-y,** *n.* **Witch'-ing-ly,** *adv.* **Witch-alder**—See WYCH ALDER. **Witchcraft**—ডাকিনীবিদ্যা, ডাইনী-বৃত্তি, মায়া, যাদুবিদ্যা। **Witch-doctor**—ভূতের ওজা, রোজা। **Witch-elm** — Same as WYCH-ELM. **Witch-hazel**—See WYCHHAZEL. **Witch-meal**—একপ্রকার পুষ্পের রেণু। **White witch**—See WHITE. **The witch is in it**—Some miraculous power is working in it; ইহাতে কোন অলৌকিক শক্তি ক্রিয়া করিতেছে। **To**

be no witch—To be not very clever ; বেশী চালাক না হওয়া।

wit'-ĕ-nă-gĕ-mŏt, *n.* The Anglo-Saxon national council ; প্রাচীন ইংলণ্ডের জাতীয় মহাসমিতি বা পার্লেমেণ্ট সভা।

with, *prep.* **1.** Denoting competition or antagonism ; as, to fight *with* some one ; সহিত, সঙ্গে, বিরুদ্ধে। **2.** Among ; in company of ; as, I shall go *with* you; সঙ্গে; সহিত, সাথে। **3.** Denoting nearness or proximity ; "There is no living *with* thee, or without thee" ; নিকটে, কাছে। **4.** Denoting partnership or intercourse ; "*With* thee she talks, *with* thee she moans" ; সঙ্গে, সাথে। **5.** Denoting instrument or means ; "And tire the hearer *with* a book of words"; দ্বারা, কর্তৃক। **6.** Denoting an accessory ; as, to fill up a bottle *with* medicine ; দ্বারা। **7.** Denoting cause or consequence ; as, to be pale *with* fear ; কারণে, হেতু, দরুণ। **8.** Denoting concomitance, addition or accessories ; "A tongue *with* a tang"; সহভাব, সংযোগ বা, আনুষঙ্গিক বস্তু-বোধক, যুক্ত, সহিত। **9.** Denoting friendship, sympathy, partnership ; "He that is not *with* me is against me"; পক্ষে, দলে। **10.** Having, carrying, possessed of ; as, a woman *with* child ; বিশিষ্ট, যুক্ত। **11.** At the same time ; as, to rise *with* the sun ; একসঙ্গে, এককালে, সহিত। **12.** In regard to ; in the sphere of ; in the mind or view of ; as, to be patient *with* a person ; সম্বন্ধে; ক্ষেত্রে ; মনে, মতে। **13.** Notwithstanding ; "England *with* all thy faults I love thee still" ; স্বত্বেও। **Have with you**—(*Archaic*) I accept your offer; (অপ্রঃ) আমি তোমার প্রস্তাব গ্রহণ করিলাম। **I cannot do anything with him**—I cannot influence him ; আমি তাহার উপর কোনরূপ প্রভাব বিস্তার করিতে পারি না। **To begin with**—To start with ; প্রথমতঃ, প্রারম্ভে। **With that**—Thereupon ; simultaneously ; অতঃপর ; একসঙ্গে।

with'-ăl, *adv.* & *prep.* (*Archaic*) Together with ; moreover ; একসঙ্গে একযোগে ; অধিকন্তু। ***Prep.*** With (used after its object) ; "The fruit thereof shall be holy to praise the Lord *withal*" ; সহিত।

Withania somnifera—অশ্বগন্ধা।

with-draw' (-drä), *v. t.* & *i.* **1.** To draw back in an opposite direction ; to remove; as, to *withdraw* one's aid ; প্রত্যাকর্ষণ করা, প্রতিনিবৃত্ত করা ; উঠাইয়া নেওয়া। **2.** To retract ; as, to *withdraw* a statement ; প্রত্যাহার করা। ***Verb i.*** To retire from, quit, a company or place ; as, to *withdraw* from the company ; to absent one's self ; to retreat ; কোন দল বা স্থান হইতে চলিয়া যাওয়া ; অনুপস্থিত হওয়া ; হটিয়া যাওয়া। **—al,** *n.*

withe, wi'-thy̆, *n.* & *v. t.* (*Pl.*) A tough flexible twig ; শক্ত এবং নমনীয় উপশাখা। ***Verb t.*** To bind with withe ; শক্ত এবং নমনীয় উপশাখা দ্বারা বন্ধন করা।

with'-ĕr, *v. t.* & *i.* **1.** To cause to fade and become dry ; to cause to shrink, wrinkle and decay ; শুষ্ক করা ; বিশীর্ণ করা, পরিম্লান করা। **2.** To lose vigour, power, force or the like ; to languish ; "States thrive or *wither* as moons wax and wane"; তেজোহীন হওয়া, শক্তিহীন হওয়া ; শুকাইয়া যাওয়া, পরিম্লান হওয়া। **—ing,** *adj.* **—ing-ly,** *adv.* **The individual withers**—The individual ceases to be important ; তাহার আর সে প্রভাব নাই।

with'-ĕrs, *n.* A ridge between a horse's shoulder-blades ; অশ্বের স্কন্ধাস্থির মধ্যবর্তী উন্নত স্থান, স্কন্ধাস্থিদ্বয়ের সংযোগ দ্বারা গঠিত উন্নত স্থান। **My withers are unwrung**—I am untouched by his remarks etc. ; তাহার মন্তব্য প্রভৃতি আমাকে স্পর্শ করিতে পারে নাই।

with'-hōld, *v. t.* To restrain ; to keep back ; as, to *withhold* one's support ; সংযত করা, নিবৃত্ত করা, আটক করা, প্রতিরোধ করা, থামাইয়া রাখা ; না দেওয়া।

with'-in, *adv.*, *n.* & *prep.* **1.** In the inner part ; মধ্যে, ভিতরে। **2.** Inwardly ; "Ills from *within* thy reason must prevent" ; অন্তরে। **3.** Indoors ; at home ; "Who is *within* there" ; বাটীর ভিতরে ; বাটীতে। ***Noun.*** The inside ; as, he was seen from *within* ; ভিতর, মধ্যভাগ, অভ্যন্তরভাগ। ***Prep.*** **1.** Inside of ; মধ্যে, ভিতরে। **2.** Not later than ; as, *within* one hour ; সময় মধ্যে, সময়ের ভিতরে। **3.** Not exceeding ; as, to live *within* one's income ; মধ্যে, ভিতরে। **4.** Not farther in length than ; as, *within* ten miles of the city ; ভিতরে, মধ্যে। **Within a while**—Soon ; শীঘ্র।

with-out' (-ōwt), *adv.*, *n. prep.* & *conj.* Outside, to or at or on the other side ; out-of-doors ; externally ; বাহিরে ; বাটীর বাহিরে ; বাহিরে। ***Noun.*** Outside ; external sources ; বাহির ; বাহিরের বিষয়। ***Prep.*** **1.** Outside of ; বাহিরে। **2.** Out of the limits, company, range or reach of ; beyond ; সীমার বাহিরে, দলের বাহিরে ; বাহিরে। ***Conj.*** (*Archaic*) Unless ; যদি না। **It goes without saying**—It is needless to be mentioned ; ইহা না বলিলেও চলে, বলা বাহুল্য। **To do** or **go without**—To dispense with ; কোন কিছু ছাড়িয়া থাকিতে পারা, কোন কিছু ছাড়া চলা। **Without doubt**—Certainly ;

নিঃসন্দেহে নিশ্চিতই। **Without end**—Infinite ; অনন্ত, সীমাহীন, অন্তহীন।

with-stănd′, *v. t. & i.* To resist : প্রতিরোধ করা। ***Verb i.*** To make resistance ; বাধা দেওয়া, প্রতিরোধ করা।

with-ȳ, *n.* Same as WITHER.

wit′-nĕss, *n., v.t. & i.* **1.** One who gives evidence in a trial ; সাক্ষী, ইসাদী (used in legal documents), গাওয়াই (*vulg.*)। **2.** Testimony ; "This heap is a *witness* between me and thee this day"; সাক্ষ্য, প্রমাণ। **3.** One who knows or sees anything ; as, an eye-*witness* ; জ্ঞাতা, দ্রষ্টা। ***Verb t.*** **1.** To act as a witness of ; to see the execution of a legal instrument, and subscribe it ; সাক্ষী হওয়া ; দলীলাদিতে সাক্ষিস্বরূপ নাম দস্তখত করা। **2.** To give testimony to ; প্রমাণ দেওয়া। **3.** To know by reason of personal presence ; as, he did not live to *witness* his son's affluence ; দর্শন করা, প্রত্যক্ষ করা। ***Verb i.*** To bear testimony ; "The men of Belial *witnessed* against him" ; সাক্ষিস্বরূপ হওয়া। **Witness-box**—সাক্ষীর কাঠগড়া, সাক্ষ্য-মঞ্চ। **With a witness** — Effectually ; to a great degree ; কার্য্যতঃ ; অতিমাত্রায়।

wit′-ti-cĭsm, *n.* A witty remark ; jest ; সরস উক্তি, নর্ম্মোক্তি, নর্ম্মবাক্য ; রসিকতা।

wit′-ting-lȳ (-ĭng), *adv.* Knowingly ; জ্ঞাতসারে, জ্ঞাতপূর্ব্বক।

wit′-tol, (-ŏl) *n.* (*Archaic*) A man who knows his wife's infidelity and submits to it ; (অপ্রঃ) যে ব্যক্তি স্ত্রীর ব্যভিচারের বিষয় জানিয়াও চুপ করিয়া থাকে, অসতীপতি, কুলটাপতি।

wive, *v. t. & i.* (*Rare*) To provide with a wife ; (কচিদ্‌ব্যবহৃত) স্ত্রী প্রদান করা। ***Verb i.*** To take wife ; বিবাহ করা, দারপরিগ্রহ করা।

wī′-vêrn, —fêrn, *ns.* (*Herald.*) A heraldic monster, a sort of dragon, with two wings, two eagle's legs, and a tapering body ; (কুলবিদ্যা) উৎক্রোশ পক্ষীর মত পদদ্বয় এবং ক্রমসূক্ষ্মায়মান দেহবিশিষ্ট কাল্পনিক জন্তুবিশেষ।

wives, *n. pl.* of WIFE (which see).

wiz′-ard (-ẽrd), **wiš′-ard** (-êrd), (*Obs.*)*n. & adj.* **1.** A sage, "See how far, upon the eastern road, The star-led *wisards* haste with odour sweet"; জ্ঞানীলোক। **2.** A sorcerer ; a magician ; যাদুকর, মায়াবী, ভেল্‌কীওয়ালা ; ঐন্দ্রজালিক, মায়াকর, মায়াজীবী, কুহককার, কুহকজীবী। **3.** A person supposed to possess supernatural powers ; অলৌকিকশক্তিসম্পন্ন ব্যক্তি। ***Adj.*** Charming ; "The *wizard* song at distance died" ; বিমোহন, মোহকারী মনোমুগ্ধকর। **—ry**, *n.*

wiz′-en (-n), **wiz′-ened** (-nd), **weaz′-en** (wēz-n). *adjs.* Hard, dry and shrivelled ; শুষ্ক, কঠিন এবং কুঞ্চিত, বিশীর্ণ। **Wizen-faced**—বিশীর্ণবদন, শীর্ণকুঞ্চিতাস্য।

wiz′-en (-n), *v. t.* To dry up ; to shrivel ; শুষ্ক করা ; কুঞ্চিত করা।

wiz′-ier (-êr), *n.* Same as VIZIER (which see).

wō, whō′-ă, *ns.* Stop (usually to horses) ; থাম (সাধারণতঃ অশ্বসম্পর্কে ব্যবহৃত হয়)।

woad (wōd), *n.* **1.** A plant, the leaves of which yield a blue dye ; বৃক্ষবিশেষ—যাহার পত্র হইতে নীলবর্ণ রঞ্জকপদার্থবিশেষ প্রাপ্ত হওয়া যায়। **2.** The blue dye got from this plant ; উক্ত বৃক্ষ হইতে প্রাপ্ত নীলবর্ণ রঞ্জক পদার্থ।

wŏb′-ble (-l), **wăb′-ble** (-l), *v. i. & n.* **1.** To rock ; দোলা। **2.** To move in the manner of a rotating disc when the axis of rotation is inclined to that of the disc ; যে ঘূর্ণনশীল চক্রের ঘূর্ণনের অক্ষ ঐ চক্রের অক্ষের সহিত তির্য্যগ্‌ভাবে থাকে—সেইরূপ চক্রের মত সঞ্চালিত হওয়া। **3.** To vacillate ; ইতস্ততঃ করা। **4.** To go unsteadily ; টলিতে টলিতে চলা। **5.** To quiver ; কম্পিত হওয়া। ***Noun.*** **1.** Rocking movement ; দোলন। **2.** Swerve; বত্ম‌চ্যুতি। **3.** Change of policy ; কার্য্যপ্রণালীর পরিবর্ত্তন। **—bler**, *n.*

woe (wō), *n.* **1.** Grief ; sorrow ; misery ; শোক, বিষাদ ; দুঃখ, সন্তাপ ; কষ্ট, দুর্দ্দশা। **2.** Calamity ; বিপদ্‌, আপদ্‌, সঙ্কট। **woe′-ful**, *adj.* **1.** Full of woe or grief ; শোকপূর্ণ, বিষাদপূর্ণ, দুঃখময়। **2.** Expressing sorrow or grief ; as, *woeful* event ; sad ; শোকসূচক, শোকজনক ; বিষাদসূচক, বিষাদজনক। **3.** Paltry ; wretched ; "What *woeful* stuff this madrigal would be" ; তুচ্ছ ; অকিঞ্চিৎকর। **Woe′-ful-ly**, *adv.* **Woe-begone**—শোকার্ত্ত, শোকাভিভূত, বিষাদমগ্ন। **Weal and woe** — সুখ দুঃখ, সম্পদ্‌ বিপদ্‌। **Woe be to**—A curse upon ; ধ্বংস হউক, ডুবিয়া যাউক, অধঃপাতে যাউক, চুলায় যাউক, গোল্লায় যাউক। **Woe is me**—Alas ; হায় ! আমার কি দুরদৃষ্ট। **Woe worth**—Same as WOE BE TO.

wōld, *n.* A piece of uncultivated open country, down or moorland ; মুক্ত, পতিত প্রান্তর বা অনুপভূমি।

Wolf.

wolf (wûlf), *n. & v. t.* (*Pl. wolves*) **1.** A carnivorous quadruped akin to the dog, crafty and rapacious ; নেকড়ে বাঘ, বৃক, ঘোঁষ [Syn. ঈহামৃগ, কোক, বৎসাদন, বিরুক, গোবৎনাদী, ছাগভোজী, ছাগলাত্রী,

জনাশন।] [Arab. *deeb*; Ger. *vulf*; Gk. *lukos*; Heb. *zeeb*; It. *lupo, lupa*; Sp. *lobo, loba, lupia*; Swed. *ulf*; Dan. *ulv*; Russ. *volk*.] **2.** A cruel or cunning person; "Rescued is Orleans from the English *wolves*"; নিষ্ঠুর ব্যক্তি, ধূর্ত্ত ব্যক্তি। **3.** (*Obs.*) An eating ulcer; (অপ্রঃ) একপ্রকার দুষ্ট ক্ষত—যাহাতে মাংস ক্ষয় হইয়া যায়, একপ্রকার পুযস্রাবী কোমল ক্ষত। **4.** A small white worm or maggot that infests granaries; শস্যাগারের শস্যের অনিষ্টকারী একপ্রকার ক্ষুদ্র শ্বেতবর্ণ কীট। **5.** Dissonance in some chords on organs, pianos or other instruments; অর্গেন, পিয়ানো, অথবা কোন বাদ্যযন্ত্রের কোন তন্ত্রীতে স্বরবৈষম্য। ***Verb t.*** (*Colloq.*) To eat ravenously; (চলিত ভাষায়) পেটুকের মত খাওয়া। **Wolf'-ish,** *adj.* **Wolf'-ish-ly,** *adv.* **Wolf'-ish-ness,** *n.* **Wolf-fish**—একপ্রকার বৃহৎ মহাশন মৎস্য। **Wolf-hound**—একজাতীয় রুশদেশীয় কুক্কুর। **Wolf's-bane**—Same as ACONITE. **Wolf's-claws, Wolf's-foot**—একপ্রকার শৈবাল। **Wolf's-fist**—কন্দুকাকৃতি রেণুস্থলীবিশিষ্ট ছত্রাকবিশেষ। **Wolfskin**—নেকড়ের চামড়া, বৃকচর্ম্ম, বৃকচর্ম্মের আসন, প্রাবরণ, প্রভৃতি। **Wolf's-milk**—একপ্রকার ক্ষুপ—যাহা হইতে একপ্রকার অম্লস্বাদ দুগ্ধবৎ রস নির্গত হয়। **Wolf-spider**—Same as TARANTULA. **Wolf-tooth**—অশ্বের অতিরিক্ত দন্ত বিশেষ। **A wolf in sheep's clothing**—ভণ্ড, কপট। **Dark as a wolf's mouth** or **throat**—Pitch dark; ঘনান্ধকার। **To cry wolf too often**—To raise false alarms; অনর্থক বিপৎসূচক চীৎকার করা। **To have** or **hold wolf by the ears**—To be able neither to stop, retreat or advance; থামিতে, অগ্রসর হইতে বা পশ্চাতে হটিতে না পারা। **To have wolf in the stomach**—To have a ravenous appetite; বৃকোদর হওয়া, পেটে কাঁকড় ঢুকা, ক্ষুধায় ইটপাটকিল কামড়ান। **To keep the wolf from the door**—To keep out hunger or want; কোনরূপে অনশন বা দারিদ্র্য নিবারণ করা।

wolf'-răm (wŭlf-), *n.* **1.** A brownish or greyish black ore of tungsten; একপ্রকার ধাতু। **2.** (*Rare*) Same as TUNGSTEN.

wol'-ver-ene (wŭl-vêr-ēn), **–ine**. *ns.* A carnivorous animal; একপ্রকার মাংসাদ জন্তু।

wolves (wûlvs), *n. pl.* of WOLF.

wom'-ăn (wŭm-), *n.* & *v. t.* **1.** The adult female of the human race; স্ত্রীলোক, নারী, অবলা, অঙ্গনা, মহিলা, মেয়েমানুষ (*colloq.*) [Syn. সীমন্তিনী, প্রতীপদর্শিনী, প্রিয়া, যোষিতা, জোষিৎ, জোষা, জোষিতা, শর্ব্বরী, বামদৃক্, পুরন্ধ্রী, ভীরু, নিতম্বিনী মত্তকাসিনী, সুন্দরী অক্ষিতভ্রূ, ললিতা, বরা, যোষিৎ, বধূ, বামা, বনিতা, রমণী, কামিনী, প্রমদা, যোষা, রামা, জনী, বনিকা, মহেলিকা মহেলা, সিন্দূরতিলকা, শুভা, সুনয়না, ললনা, বরবর্ণিনী, সুতনু, তনু, তন্বী, তন্বঙ্গী, কুরঙ্গনয়না, ভীতা, ভামিনী, বিলাসিনী, সুনেত্রা, বাসিতা, অকিতবা, ভাবিনী, বরারোহা, নতাঙ্গী, চারুবর্দ্ধনা, ত্রিনতা, শ্যামা] হিন্দু রসশাস্ত্রে রমণীগণকে চারি শ্রেণীতে বিভক্ত করা হইয়াছে—যথা, পদ্মিনী, চিত্রিণী, শঙ্খিনী, হস্তিনী। তাহাদের লক্ষণ যথা—"ভবতি কমলনেত্রা নাসিকা ক্ষুদ্ররন্ধ্রা অবিরলকুচযুগ্মা দীর্ঘকেশী কৃশাঙ্গী। মৃদুবচনসুশীলা নৃত্যগীতানুরক্তা সকলতনুসুবেশা পদ্মিনী পদ্মগন্ধা (পদ্মিনী)। ভবতি রতিরসজ্ঞা নাতিদীর্ঘা ন খর্ব্বা, তিলকুসুমসুনাসা স্নিগ্ধদেহোৎপলাক্ষী। কঠিনঘনকুচাঢ্যা সুন্দরী সা সুশীলা সকলগুণবিচিত্রা চিত্রিণী চিত্রবক্ত্রা (চিত্রিণী)। দীর্ঘা সুদীর্ঘ নয়না বরসুন্দরী বা কামোপভোগরসিকা গুণশীলযুক্তা। রেখাত্রয়েণ চ বিভূষিতকণ্ঠদেশা সম্ভোগকেলিরসিকা কিল শঙ্খিনী সা (শঙ্খিনী)। স্থূলাধরা স্থূলনিতম্বভাগা স্থূলাঙ্গুলী স্থূলকুচা সুশীলা। কামোৎসুকগাঢ়রতিপ্রিয়া চ নিতম্বখর্ব্বা খলু হস্তিনী স্যাৎ (হস্তিনী)। রতিমঞ্জরী। বয়স ভেদে স্ত্রীদিগের বিভিন্ন অভিধাঃ—অষোড়শং ভবেদ্ বালা। তরুণী ত্রিংশতা মতা। পঞ্চ পঞ্চাশতং যাবৎ প্রৌঢ়া বৃদ্ধা ততঃ পরম্—রতিমঞ্জরী। **2.** Women collectively; স্ত্রীজন, নারীসমাজ, অবলাসমাজ, স্ত্রীজাতি। **3.** A female attendant or servant; "By her *woman* I sent your message"; পরিচারিকা, দাসী। **4.** A man with female characteristic; as, the old *women* in the cabinet; স্ত্রীস্বভাবাপন্ন পুরুষ। **5.** Womanliness; স্ত্রীজনসুলভতা। ***Verb t.*** **1.** To call one woman; স্ত্রীলোক বলিয়া সম্বোধন করা। **2.** To unite to, or accompany by, a woman; "To have him see me *woman'd*"; স্ত্রীলোকের সহিত মিলিত করা, স্ত্রীলোকের সঙ্গী করা। **3.** To behave like a woman; "The day I should have seen my daughter Silvia how she would have *woman'd* it"; স্ত্রীলোকের ন্যায় আচরণ করা। **–hood,** *n.* **1.** The state of being a woman; স্ত্রীত্ব। **2.** Womankind; স্ত্রীজাতি। **–less, –like,** *adjs.* **Single woman**—বর্ষীয়সী অনূঢ়া। **Woman-born**—স্ত্রীগর্ভজাত। **Woman-grown**—বয়ঃপ্রাপ্তা। **Woman-hater**—স্ত্রীদ্বেষী। **Womankind**—স্ত্রীজাতি। **Woman-suffrage**—স্ত্রীলোকের ভোট প্রদানের অধিকার। **A woman with a past**—A woman who was connected with some scandalous affair in the past; যে স্ত্রীলোকের গতজীবনে কোনরূপ কলঙ্কজনক ঘটনা ঘটিয়াছে। **There is a woman in it**—এই ব্যাপারের ভিতর কোন স্ত্রীলোক আছে। **To be tied to a woman's apron-strings**—See APRON. **To make an honest woman of**—See HONEST. **Woman of pleasure**—বিলাসিনী; (অপ্রঃ) বারাঙ্গনা। **Woman of the world**—সংসারাভিজ্ঞানারী, বিষয়বুদ্ধিসম্পন্না নারী। **Woman's Christian Temperance Association**—১৮৭৪ খৃষ্টাব্দে

মার্কিণযুক্তরাজ্যে প্রতিষ্ঠিত মাদকনিবারণী মহিলাসম্মিলনী। **Woman's rights, Women's rights** — স্ত্রীলোকের অধিকার (অর্থাৎ স্ত্রীলোকেরা আইনতঃ পুরুষের তুল্য অধিকারসম্পন্না—নারীগণের পক্ষে এই দাবী।)

wom'-ăn-ish (wŭm-), *adj.* **1.** Like woman ; রমণীবৎ। **2.** Effiminate ; "*Womanish* entreaties and lamentations ; মেয়েলী, স্ত্রীজনসুলভ। **—ly,** *adv.* **—ness,** *n.*

wom'-ăn-īze (wŭm-), *v. t.* & *i.* To make like a woman ; to make effiminate ; "This effiminate love of women doth *womanise* a man" ; স্ত্রীজনবৎ করা ; স্ত্রীজনসুলভ করা। ***Verb i.*** To frequent prostitutes ; বারাঙ্গনা সমাগম করা।

wom'-ăn-lȳ (wŭm-), *adj.* Befitting, or like, a woman ; as, *womanly* modesty ; feminine ; স্ত্রীজনসমুচিত, স্ত্রীজনবৎ ; স্ত্রীজনসুলভ।

womb (wôm), *n.* **1.** The uterus ; জরায়ু, গর্ভাশয়, গর্ভাধান, গর্ভস্থান, কুক্ষি। **2.** That part where the young of an animal is conceived and nourished till its birth ; জন্তুর গর্ভাশয়। **3.** Any cavity containing anything ; as, the bluebell's *womb* ; গহ্বর, গর্ভ। **Falling of the womb** — গর্ভপাত, গর্ভস্রাব। **Fruit of the womb**—সন্তানসন্ততি।

Wombat.

wŏm'-băt, *n.* An Australian mammal with a pouch ; অষ্ট্রেলিয়া দেশীয় স্তন্যদায়ী উপজঠরী জন্তু বিশেষ।

wom'-ĕn (wĭm-), *n. pl.* of WOMAN (which see).

won (wŭn', *pt.* & *pp.* of WIN (which see).

won'-dẽr (wŭn-), *n.* **1.** A cause of surprise or astonishment ; a miracle ; prodigy ; "Be you in the park about midnight and you shall see *wonders*" ; আশ্চর্য্যজনক বিষয় ; অলৌকিক ব্যাপার, অতিপ্রাকৃত ব্যাপার ; আশ্চর্য্য বস্তু, আজব জিনিষ। **2.** Astonishment ; বিস্ময়, আশ্চর্য্য। **3.** (*Phren.*) A faculty of the mind which produces the sentiment of wonder, surprise or astonishment ; (মস্তিষ্কসামুদ্রিক) মানসিক বৃত্তি বিশেষ—যদ্দ্বারা আশ্চর্য্য, বিস্ময়, প্রভৃতি ভাব উদ্ভূত হয়, বিস্ময়জননীবৃত্তি। **—ing,** *n.* & *adj.* Astonishment ; বিস্ময়। ***Adj.*** Marvelling ; আশ্চর্য্যবোধকারী। **—ing-ly,** *adv.* **—ment,** *n.* **Eighth wonder**—অত্যাশ্চর্য্যবস্তু (যথা নায়েগ্রার জলপ্রপাতের উপরিস্থ সেতু)। **Wonder-flower** — ইয়ুরোপীয় উপকথায় উক্ত একপ্রকার পুষ্প—যদ্দ্বারা গুপ্তধন আবিষ্কারে সাহায্য পাওয়া যাইত, আশ্চর্য্যপুষ্প। **Wonder-land** — পরীরাজ্য, পরীস্থান ; আশ্চর্য্য উর্ব্বর প্রদেশ প্রভৃতি। **Wonder-stone**—একপ্রকার স্বচ্ছ পীতবর্ণ দানাদার রক্তপ্রস্তর, চমকপাথর, চমকপাষাণ। **Wonder-stricken** — বিস্ময়োপহত, বিস্ময়াহত। **Wonder-struck** — বিস্ময়াভিহত। **Wonder-work** — অলৌকিকক্রিয়া। **Wonder-worker**—অলৌকিক কার্য্যসম্পাদনকারী। **Wonder-wounded**—বিস্ময়াহত। **A nine-days' wonder**—See under NINE. **Seven wonders of the world**—See under SEVEN. **Signs and wonders**—অলৌকিকক্রিয়া, অতিপ্রাকৃত ক্রিয়া। **The Eighth wonder of the world**—Toledo নগরীস্থ Escurial প্রাসাদ। এই প্রাসাদে ১৮৬০টী কক্ষ, ৬২০০ দ্বার এবং বাতায়ন, ৮০টী সোপান-শ্রেণী, ৭৩টী উৎস, ৪৮টী অন্তর্ভৌম সুরা-ভাণ্ডার, ৫১টী ঘণ্টা এবং ৮টী অর্গেন যন্ত্র ছিল। এই প্রাসাদের পরিধি প্রায় এক মাইল। **To work wonders**—To perform miracles; অলৌকিককার্য্য সম্পাদন করা।

won'-dẽr (wŭn-), *v. i.* & *t.* **1.** To be struck with astonishment ; to be amazed (followed by *at*) ; as, I *wonder at* you persistence ; বিস্ময়াভিভূত হওয়া ; আশ্চর্য্যান্বিত হওয়া। **2.** To entertain or feel some doubt or curiosity about ; to query in the mind ; to be in a state of expectation mingled with doubt and slight anxiety ; "A boy or child I *wonder*" ; কোন বিষয়ে কতকটা সন্দেহ করা বা কৌতূহল বোধ করা ; মনে মনে প্রশ্ন করা ; সংশয় এবং কিঞ্চিৎ উৎকণ্ঠা মিশ্রিত আশান্বিত অবস্থায় থাকা, আকুলভাবে অপেক্ষা করা। ***Verb t.*** (*Obs.*) To cause to feel wonder or astonisment ; আশ্চর্য্যান্বিত করা, বিস্ময়াপন্ন করা, বিস্ময়ান্বিত করা।

won'-dẽr-fûl (wŭn-), *adj.* **1.** Marvellous ; surprising ; আশ্চর্য্যজনক, বিস্ময়জনক, বিস্ময়কর ; চমকপ্রদ, আশ্চর্য্য, বিচিত্র, অলৌকিক, বিস্ময়াবহ **—ly,** *adv.* **Wonderful Doctor**—Roger Bacon.

won'-drous (wŭn-drŭs), *adj.* & *adv.* Wonderful ; আশ্চর্য্যজনক আশ্চর্য্যপূর্ণ, বিস্ময়জনক। ***Adv*** Wonderfully ; আশ্চর্য্যরূপে।

wont (wŭnt), *pred. adj.* Accustomed ; অভ্যস্ত, জাতাভ্যাস, কৃতাভ্যাস

wŏnt, *v. aux.* To be accustomed অভ্যস্ত হওয়া।

wŏnt, *n.* What is customary i general or habitual to a person "'Tis not his *wont* to be th hindmost man" ; অভ্যস্ততা, অভ্য বিষয়, অভ্যাস।

wont'-ĕd (wŭnt-), *adj.* Habitua to a person ; usual ; অভ্যাসসিদ্ধ ব্যবহারিক।

wōō, *v. t.* & *i.* **1.** To court; to solici in love ; "When she was youn you *woo'd* her" ; প্রণয়প্রার্থনা করা বিবাহার্থ উপসর্পণ করা, বিবাহার্থ উপাস করা। **2.** To solicit or entrea প্রার্থনা করা, যাচ্ঞা করা। **3.** T seek to gain or bring abou

"You......*woo* your own destruction"; আনয়নের চেষ্টা করা। ***Verb i.*** To court ; to make love ; বিবাহার্থ উপাসনা করা; প্রেম করা। **Woo'-er,*n.*** One who wooes ; one who courts or solicits in love ; বিবাহার্থ উপসর্পণ কারী ; প্রণয়প্রার্থী। **Woo'-ing,** *n.*

wood, *n.* **1.** A large and thick collection of trees growing ; বন, জঙ্গল, কানন, কান্তার, অটবী, বিপিন, গহন, দাব। **2.** A fibrous substance between pith and bark of tree, whether growing or cut for timber or fuel ; as, a chair made of *wood* ; কাষ্ঠ, কাঠ, দারু। **3.** A cask ; as, beer drawn from the *wood* ; পিপা। **4.** (*Print.*) A woodcut ; blocks etc. made of wood ; কাষ্ঠনির্ম্মিত চিত্রফলক ; মুদ্রণকার্য্যে ব্যবহৃত কাঠের গুটি প্রভৃতি। **5.** (*Mus.*) Same as WOOD-WIND. **Wood'-less,** *adj.* **Wood-agate**—একপ্রকার প্রস্তর—যাহাতে যে কাষ্ঠ হইতে উহা প্রস্তরে পরিণত হইয়াছে তাহার গঠন-বিন্যাস দৃষ্ট হয়। **Wood-anemone**—একপ্রকার লতা। **Wood-ant**—ইয়ুরোপ দেশীয় পিপীলিকা বিশেষ। **Wood-apple**—বেল, বিল্ব, শ্রীফল [Syn. শাণ্ডিল্য, শৈলূষ, মালূর, গোহরীতকী, মহাকপিথ, পূতিবাত, অতিমঙ্গল্য, মহাফল, শল্য, হৃদ্যগন্ধ, শালাটু, কর্কটাহ্ব, শৈলপত্র, শিবেষ্ট, পত্রশ্রেষ্ঠ, ত্রিপত্র, গন্ধপত্র, লক্ষ্মীফল, গন্ধফল, দুরারুহ, ত্রিশাখপত্র, ত্রিশিখ, শিবদ্রুম, সদাফল, সত্যফল, সুভূতিক, সমীরসার।] **Woodbine. Wood-bind** — একপ্রকার লতা। **Wood-block**—কাষ্ঠনির্ম্মিত চিত্রফলক। **Wood-carpet** — বস্ত্রদ্বারা আচ্ছাদিত পাতল কাষ্ঠসমূহ — যাহা গালিচাস্বরূপ ব্যবহৃত হয়। **Wood-cock**—কর্দ্দম খঞ্জনা জাতীয় বিভিন্নপ্রকার পক্ষীর সাধারণ নাম, শ্যামতিত্তির, কোকরা। **Wood-craft** — বনের কোন স্থানে মৃগয়াদিসম্পর্কে সুবিধা আছে তৎসম্বন্ধে জ্ঞান, বনবিদ্যা। **Wood-crowned**—বনমুকুটিত, কাননকিরীটিনী। **Woodcut**—কাঠের চিত্রফলক হইতে গৃহীত চিত্র ; কাঠের উপর ক্ষোদাই চিত্র ; ক্ষোদিত কাষ্ঠফলক। **Wood-cutter**—কাঠুরিয়া ; কাষ্ঠের চিত্রফলক নির্ম্মাতা। **Wood-engraver**—কাষ্ঠফলক ক্ষোদাই কার। **Wood-evil**—গো মহিষাদির একপ্রকার পাকস্থলীর রোগ। **Wood-fibre**—কাঠের আঁশ। **Wood-flour**—করাতে গুঁড়ার সূক্ষ্ম চূর্ণ—যাহা বিস্ফোরক দ্রব্য প্রস্তুত প্রভৃতি কার্য্যে ব্যবহৃত হয়। **Wood-frog** — উত্তর আমেরিকার একজাতীয় মণ্ডূক। **Wood-gas** — কাষ্ঠ হইতে প্রাপ্ত কার্ব্বারেটেড্ হাইড্রোজেন। **Wood-grass**—আমেরিকা দেশীয় একপ্রকার তৃণ। **Wood-ibis**—উত্তর আমেরিকার হাড়গিলাজাতীয় পক্ষিবিশেষ। **Wood-land**—বনভূমি, কাননভূমি, আরণ্য-প্রদেশ, বনানী, অরণ্যানী। **Wood-leopard**—একপ্রকার তসরে পোকা। **Wood-lily**—স্থলকুমুদ (Lily of the valley) ; রক্তকুমুদ ; অর্কিড (অষ্ট্রেলিয়া)। **Wood-louse**—একপ্রকার ক্ষুদ্র কীট, কাঠের উকুন (মিউজিয়াম)। **Wood-man**—বনবাসী ; কাঠুরিয়া ; অটবিক, আটবিক। **Wood-mouse**—বনপ্রদেশ বাসী মূষিক। **Wood-notes**—স্বতঃস্ফূর্ত্ত কবিতা, কাননকাকলী। **Wood-nymph**—বনদেবী ; বিভিন্নপ্রকার গুঞ্জন-কারী পক্ষী ; বিভিন্নপ্রকার তসরে পোকা। **Wood-oil**—গর্জ্জন তৈল। **Wood-opal**—সিকতায় পরিণত কাষ্ঠ। **Wood-paper**—কাষ্ঠমণ্ড হইতে প্রস্তুত কাগজ। **Wood-partridge** — যব, সুমাত্রা, প্রভৃতি দ্বীপের একপ্রকার ক্ষুদ্র চটকপক্ষী। **Wood-pavement** — রাজপথ আচ্ছাদনের জন্য কাষ্ঠফলকসমূহ। **Wood-pecker**—খুড়ুলে (মিউজিয়াম), কাঠঠোকরা পাখী। **Wood-pie**—একপ্রকার ফুটফুটদাগবিশিষ্ট কাঠঠোকরা পাখী। **Wood-pigeon** — ঘুঘু। **Wood-pulp**—কাগজ প্রস্তুতের জন্য কাঠের আঁশ হইতে যে মণ্ড প্রস্তুত হয়, কাষ্ঠমণ্ড। **Woodruff** — বিভিন্নপ্রকার ক্ষুপের সাধারণ নাম। **Wood-side**—বন-প্রান্তবর্ত্তী প্রদেশ। **Wood-snail**—ইয়ুরোপের একপ্রকার আহারোপযোগী শম্বুক। **Wood-sorrel**—বিভিন্নপ্রকার অম্লরস তরু। **Wood-tar**—কাষ্ঠ হইতে প্রাপ্ত আলকাতরা। **Wood-tortoise**—আমেরিকাদেশীয় একপ্রকার কচ্ছপ। **Wood-warbler**—বিভিন্নপ্রকার পক্ষীর সাধারণ নাম। **Wood-ward**—বন-রক্ষক কর্ম্মচারী। **Wood-wasp**—একপ্রকার বোলতা। **Wood-wind**—কাষ্ঠনির্ম্মিত সুষীর যন্ত্র। **Wood-wool**—সরল বৃক্ষের কাঠের সূক্ষ্ম চাঁচুনি—যাহা ক্ষত-স্থান প্রভৃতি বন্ধনে বা প্যাকিংএর কার্য্যে ব্যবহৃত হয়। **Woodwork**—কাঠের কাজ, কাষ্ঠকর্ম্ম (বিশ্বকর্ম্মা) ; সৌধ প্রভৃতির যে অংশ কাষ্ঠদ্বারা রচিত হয়। **Wood-worm**—একপ্রকার কাঠের পোকা। **Sweet wood-ruff**—এক জাতীয় ক্ষুপ—যাহার শুষ্ক ও মর্দ্দিত পত্র হইতে মনোরম সুরভি নিঃসৃত হয়। **Do not halloo till you are out of the wood**—See HALLOO. **The wood-land choir**—বনভূমির গায়ক বৃন্দ, পক্ষিগণ। **To be out of the wood**—To be free from danger; বিপন্মুক্ত হওয়া। **Wood-and-water joey**—জাহাজের ষ্টেশনে সর্ব্বকার্য্যে নিযুক্ত ব্যক্তি। **Wood of the Holy Cross** — Same as MISTLETOE. **Woods cannot be seen for trees** — Details hide the real matter ; প্রকৃত বিষয় তদানুষঙ্গিক বহু ক্ষুদ্র ক্ষুদ্র বিষয় দ্বারা আচ্ছন্ন হইয়া থাকে।

Wood'-bur-ȳ-tȳpe (-bêr-), *n.* **1.** A photographic printing process which involves the transfer from hard gelatine impression to a soft material ; একপ্রকার আলোক-চিত্রমুদ্রণপ্রণালী—যাহাতে কঠিন শিরিসের ফলক হইতে কোন কোমল বস্তুতে চিত্র স্থানান্তরিত করা হয়। **2.** A picture produced by this method ; উক্তরূপ প্রণালীতে উৎপাদিত চিত্র। [আবিষ্কারক Woodburyর নাম হইতে গৃহীত]

wood'-chŭck, *n.* A species of North-American marmot ; উত্তর-আমেরিকায় এক একপ্রকার কাষ্ঠবিড়াল জাতীয় জন্তু।

wood'-en (-n), *adj.* **1.** Made of wood ; কাষ্ঠময়, কাষ্ঠনির্ম্মিত, কাষ্ঠরচিত,

দারুময়, দারব। 2. Stiff; as, *wooden* grin (cf. কাষ্ঠ হাসি); without emotion; "The Government is too much *wooden*"; আড়ষ্ট; আবেগশূন্য। **–ly**, *adv.* **–ness**, *n.* **Wooden-headed**—জড়মস্তিষ্ক, স্থূলবুদ্ধি। **Wooden horse** — যে কাষ্ঠনির্ম্মিত অশ্বের সাহায্যে ট্রয় নগরী ধ্বংস করা হয়। ইউলাইসেস্ হেক্টরের মৃত্যুর পর এক প্রকাণ্ড কাষ্ঠের অশ্ব নির্ম্মাণ করিয়া এইরূপ প্রকাশ করেন যে, গ্রীসে নির্ব্বিঘ্নে প্রত্যাবর্ত্তনের জন্য উক্ত অশ্ব দেবতাদিগকে উপায়নস্বরূপ প্রদত্ত হইয়াছে। ট্রয়বাসিগণ ঐ অশ্বকে টানিয়া তাহাদের নগরে লইয়া যায়। ঐ অশ্বের উদরে অনেক সশস্ত্র গ্রীক সৈন্য লুক্কায়িত ছিল। উহারা রাত্রিকালে গোপনে ঐ দারুময় অশ্বের উদর হইতে নিষ্ক্রান্ত হইয়া নগররক্ষীদিগকে বিনাশ পূর্ব্বক ট্রয় নগরীতে অগ্নি সংযোগ করে। **Wooden spoon** — কেম্ব্রিজ বিশ্ববিদ্যালয়ে "অনার" পরীক্ষায় সর্ব্বনিম্ন স্থানপ্রাপ্ত ছাত্র। **Wooden trough**—দ্রোণি। **Wooden walls of old England**—যুদ্ধ জাহাজ সমূহ। [গ্রীকগণ পারস্য সম্রাট Xerexesএর আক্রমণ হইতে কিরূপে দেশ রক্ষা করিবে এই সম্বন্ধে Delphiনগরীস্থ Apollo দেবের মন্দিরে প্রত্যাদেশ প্রার্থনা করিলে কাষ্ঠ প্রাচীর দ্বারা Athens নগরী রক্ষা পাইবে, তাহারা এই দেবাদেশ প্রাপ্ত হয়। তদানীন্তন গ্রীকগণ প্রত্যাদেশোক্ত কাষ্ঠ প্রাচীর বলিতে কাষ্ঠনির্ম্মিত যুদ্ধ জাহাজ বুঝিয়াছিল।] **Wooden wedge**—কেম্ব্রিজের ক্লাসিকেল ট্রাইপস পরীক্ষায় যে ছাত্র সর্ব্ব নিম্ন স্থান অধিকার করে। **The wooden horse**—Provence প্রদেশবাসী Peterএর অশ্ব Babieca. **To ride the wooden horse**–To sail aboard boat, ship, etc.; নৌকা, জাহাজ, প্রভৃতিতে যাওয়া। **To wear the wooden sword**—To keep back sales by asking too high a price; অতিরিক্ত মূল্য চাহিয়া বিক্রয় স্থগিত করা।

wood'-y, *adj.* 1. Abounding with wood; as, a *woody* region; বনাকীর্ণ, অরণ্যবহুল, বনবহুল, অরণ্যসঙ্কুল, কাননসঙ্কুল। 2. Consisting of wood; as, a *woody* stern; কাষ্ঠময়। 3. (*Rare*) Found in wood; as, *woody* nightshade; (ক্বচিদ্ ব্যবহৃত) অরণ্যে প্রাপ্ত, বনজ, জঙ্গলী। **–i-ness**, *n.* **Woody tissue** — কাষ্ঠময় তন্তু (সাঃ পঃ)।

woof, *n.* Same as WEFT (which see.)

wool, *n.* 1. The soft, curly form of hair worn by some animals, useful to them in preventing loss of body heat, and adapted by men to the manufacture of textiles for clothing; পশম, উর্ণা, আবিক (sheep-wool), উল (*colloq.* cf উলসূতা)। 2. Any fibrous or fleecy substance resembling wool; পশমবৎ অংশ বা তন্তুময় বস্তু। 3. Woollen yarn; পশমের সূতা, উলসূতা উর্ণাসূত্র। 4. (*Bot.*) Same as TOMENTUM. 5. Woollen garments or cloth; as, it is healthy to wear *wool*; পশমের কাপড় বা পরিচ্ছদ। 6. The thick furry or hairy coat of some insecets; কোন কোন জাতীয় কীটের লোমপূর্ণ স্থূল আচ্ছাদন। 7. Short thick hair, esp. curled; ঘন এবং বেঁটে চুল, ঘন কোঁকড়ানো চুল। 8. A slag of iron blown by steam into fibrous form; বাষ্পের সাহায্যে অংশুগুচ্ছবৎ পদার্থে পরিণত লৌহমল। **Berlin wool**—বুনিবার জন্য একপ্রকার মিহিন রঙ্গীন পশমী সূতা। **Carding or short wool**—চারি ইঞ্চির কম দীর্ঘ আঁশওয়ালা পশম। **Combing or long wool**—চার ইঞ্চি অপেক্ষা দীর্ঘতর আঁশওয়ালা পশম। **Mineral wool**—Same as WOOL 8. **Wool-ball**—পশমের তাল; মেষ প্রভৃতির পাকস্থলীতে গঠিত পশমের গুটি **Wool-carding**—সূতা প্রস্তুতের পূর্ব্বে পশম আঁচড়ান। **Wool-dyed** — সূতা কাটা বা বুনার পূর্ব্বে রঞ্জিত (পশম)। **Wool-fat, Wool-oil** — Same as LANOLIN (which see.) **Wool-grass**—আমেরিকাদেশীয় একপ্রকার শৈবাল। **Wool-grower**—যে ব্যক্তি পশমের জন্য মেষ পালন করে। **Wool-hall** — পশম ব্যবসায়ীদের বাজার। **Wool-pack**—২৪০ পাউণ্ড পশমের বস্তা; শুভ্র পশমবৎ মেঘ, উর্ণামেঘ। **Wool-sack**—পশমের গদি মোড়া কেদারা বিশেষ — যাহাতে পার্লেমেণ্টের লর্ড সভাগৃহে Lord Chancellor উপবেশন করেন। **Wool-work**— কাপড়ের উপর উলের কাজ **Much or great cry and little wool**—Much ado about nothing; বহ্বারম্ভে লঘু ক্রিয়া, যত গর্জ্জে তত বর্ষে না। **To be wool gathering**—To be inattentive or absent-minded; অমনোযোগী হওয়া, অন্যমনস্ক হওয়া। **To draw or pull the wool over one's eye**—To cheat some one; কাহারো চোখে ধূলি দেওয়া, কাহারো মাথায় হাত বুলান। **To dye in the wool** — To dye before spinning or weaving; সূতা কাটার বা বুনিবার পূর্ব্বে পশম রঞ্জিত করা। **To reach the wool-sack**—To become Lord Chancellor; লর্ড চেন্সেলার হওয়া। **To take seat on the wool-sack**—To open proceedings in the House of Lords; লর্ড সভার কার্য্য আরম্ভ করা।

wool'-len (-ĕn), *adj.* & *n.* 1. Made of wool; as, *woollen* blanket; পশমনির্ম্মিত, উর্ণারচিত, পশমী। 2. Of, or pertaining to, wool; পশমসম্বন্ধীয়, পশমের। 3. Clad in home-spun woollen cloth, as opposed to silk, velvet, etc.; vulgar; "*Woollen* vassals"; গৃহ-প্রস্তুত পশমীবস্ত্র পরিহিত (রেশম, মকমল, প্রভৃতি মূল্যবান বস্ত্র পরিহিত নয়); গ্রাম্য, ইতর। ***Noun.*** Cloth made of wool; as, to deal in *woollens*; পশমী কাপড়, গরম কাপড়, রোমবস্ত্র। **Woollen-draper**—উর্ণাব্যবসায়ী।

wool'-ly (-ĭ), *adj.* 1. Consisting of wool; like wool; উর্ণাময়; উর্ণাবৎ, উর্ণাত্মক। 2. (*Paint.*) Lacking in luminosity; অনুজ্জ্বল। 3. (*Obs.*) Clothed or covered with wool; উর্ণাচ্ছাদিত। **Woolly aphis**—একপ্রকার সরোম কাঠের উকুণ

Woolly-bear — একপ্রকার সলোম শুঁয়া পোকা। **Woolly beard grass** — একপ্রকার তৃণ—ইহার শীষ রেশমের মত কোমল রোমে আচ্ছাদিত থাকে। **Wooly-butt** or **but**—অষ্ট্রেলিয়া দেশীয় ইউকেলিপ্টাস্ জাতীয় বৃক্ষ-বিশেষ। **Woolly-fleece** — Same as CIRRO CUMULUS CLOUD (which see under CLOUD)। **Woolly gum**—Same as WOOLLY BUT. **Woolly-monkey**—এক জাতীয় দীর্ঘ রোমা কপি। **Woolly-rhinoceros** — একজাতীয় অধুনালুপ্ত দ্বিশৃঙ্গ গণ্ডার। **Woolly soft-grass**—Same as VELVET GRASS. **Woolly voice**—ভাঙ্গা স্বর। **Woolly worm**—একজাতীয় কীটের কীড়া—ইহাদের দেহ হইতে একপ্রকার শ্বেতবর্ণ উর্ণাবৎ পদার্থ নিঃসৃত হয়।

wool′-sey (-zi), *n.* Same as LINSEY-WOOLSEY.

wŏp, *n.* Same as WHOP (which see).

word (wêrd), *n.* **1.** That which is said; a brief remark; as, I have a *word* with you on this subject; কথিত বিষয়; উক্তি, কথা। **2.** Promise; as, I shall try to keep my *word*; কথা, বাক্য, অঙ্গীকার। **3.** (*Archaic*) A saying (অপ্রঃ) প্রবাদবাক্য, উক্তি। **4.** Speech; language; a term; as, use fair *words* in a sentence; বাক্য; ভাষা; শব্দ, পদ। **5.** The smallest portion of the human language forming a grammatical part of speech; শব্দ। A watch-word; "Death's the *word*"; সঙ্কেতবাক্য। **Big words**—Boasting; লম্বা চৌড়া কথা, লম্বা চৌড়াই, বড় কথা। **Good word** — প্রশংসা। **Word-blind, Word-deaf**—মস্তিষ্কের বিকৃতিবিশেষ হেতু দৃষ্ট বা শ্রুত-শব্দের মর্ম্ম গ্রহণে অসমর্থ। **Word-book**—কোন ভাষার শব্দসম্বলিত পুস্তক, শব্দসংগ্রহপুস্তক। **Word-building**—শব্দগঠন। **Word painter**—বিচিত্র বর্ণনাশক্তিসম্পন্ন লেখক, শব্দচিত্রকর। **Word-painting**—শব্দচিত্রণ। **Word-play**—দ্ব্যর্থপূর্ণ বাক্য প্রয়োগ। **Word-spelling** — সূক্ষ্ম অর্থ ভেদ করণ। **Word-square**—এইরূপ ভাবে নির্ব্বাচিত শব্দসমূহ যাহা পরস্পরের নীচে লিপিবদ্ধ হইলে, অক্ষরগুলি ক্রমশঃ নীচ দিকে পড়িয়া গেলে সেই শব্দ সকলই হয়। [যথা bat, ace, ten] **A man of few words**—A reserved man; অল্পভাষী ব্যক্তি। **A man of word**—এক কথার মানুষ, যাহার কথার নড়চড় হয় না। **A word and a blow**—যেই বলা সেই কাজ। **By word of mouth** — Orally; মুখের কথায়। **God's Word** — Scripture; খৃষ্টীয় বাইবেল গ্রন্থ। **He has not a word to throw at a dog** - He is too proud or unsocial to speak; সে অহঙ্কারে লোকের সহিত কথা কয়না। **In a word, In one word**—Briefly; সংক্ষেপে। **In words**—Merely in speech; শুধু কথায়। **Sharp is the word** — Make hurry; সত্বর হও। **The Word, The word of God**—যীশুখৃষ্ট। **To be as good as one's word**—To fulfil one's promise; প্রতিশ্রুতি পালন করা। **To break one's word**—To fail to keep one's promise; কথা না রাখা। **To eat one's words**—See EAT. **To give a person one's good word**—To recommend for some appointment etc.; কাহারো চাকুরীর জন্য সুপারিশ করা। **To have a word with a person**--To have conversation with; কাহারো সহিত কথাবার্ত্তা হওয়া। **To have words with**—To quarrel with; কাহারো সহিত কলহ করা। **To put in words**—কথায় প্রকাশ করা। **To say a good word for some one**—To recommend for some one; কাহারো জন্য সুপারিশ করা। **To send word**—To inform; সংবাদ প্রেরণ করা, খবর পাঠান। **To suit the action to the word**—To carry out one's words at once; কোন কথা তৎক্ষণাৎ কার্য্যে পরিণত করা। **To take one at one's word**—To act assuming that one means what he says; কোন ব্যক্তি যে কথা বলিয়াছে তাহাই তাহার অভিপ্রেত বলিয়া ধরিয়া নিয়া কাজ করা। **To waste words**—To speak in vain; বৃথা বাক্য ব্যয় করা। **Upon my word** — Certainly; নিশ্চয়ই, নিশ্চিতই। **Word for word**— কথায় কথায়, আক্ষরিক। **Word of command**—আদেশবাণী (বিশেষতঃ সৈনিকদিগের উপর যে আদেশ-বাণী প্রচার করা হয়)। **Word of honour**—See HONOUR.

word (wêrd), *v. t.* **1.** To express in words; to put in words; শব্দ দ্বারা প্রকাশ করা; কথা দ্বারা ব্যক্ত করা। **2.** (*Obs.*) To flatter; (অপ্রঃ) তোষামোদ করা।

word′-y̆ (wêrd-), *adj.* Of, or pertaining to, words; consisting of words; as, a *wordy* warfare; শব্দসম্বন্ধীয়, শব্দাত্মিক; বাগ্‌বহুল, শব্দবহুল। **–i-ly,** *adv.* **–i-ness,** *n.*

wōre, *p. t.* of WEAR (which see.)

work (wêrk), *n.* **1.** Exertion of strength, energy or other faculty, physical or mental; effort or activity directed to some purpose or end; "Fie upon this life! I want *work*"; toil; labour; employment; as, he is out of *work* now; বল, শক্তি বা কোনরূপ বৃত্তির পরিচালনা; কার্য্য, কাষ; মেহনৎ (*colloq*), পরিশ্রম; শ্রম; চাকুরী, কাষ (cf. এই কাযে মাহিনা বড় কম)। **2.** That on which one spends labour; task; duty; "Now by St. Paul the *work* goes bravely on"; কার্য্যের বিষয়; নির্দ্দিষ্ট কার্য্য; কর্ত্তব্য। **3.** That which is done; action; "It is a damned and bloody *work*"; achievement; "The graceless action of heavy hand, If that be the *work* of any hand"; সম্পাদিত কার্য্য।

কার্য্য; অবদান। **4.** That which is made, manufactured, or produced; a product of nature or art; "O fairest of creation! last and best of all God's *works*"; প্রস্তুত, নির্ম্মিত বা উৎপাদিত বস্তু, নিসর্গজ দ্রব্য; শিল্পদ্রব্য। **5.** That which is produced by mental labour; a book or a piece of literary composition as, a *work* of Shakespeare; picture; song; মানসিক শ্রম-প্রসূত বস্তু; গ্রন্থ, পুস্তক; চিত্র; সঙ্গীত। **6.** Embroidery; flowers or figure wrought with needle; "This is some minx's token, and I must take out the *work*"; সূচীকর্ম্ম, সূচের কায; সূচ দ্বারা তোলা ফুল পাতা প্রভৃতি। **7.** Some extensive engineering structure, as a dock, embankment, bridge, fortifications and the like; বিশাল স্থাপত্যকর্ম্ম,—যথা, বাঁধ, সেতু, দুর্গ, পোতনির্ম্মাণস্থলী, প্রভৃতি। **8.** A place of manufacture; as, chemical *works*; a factory; নির্ম্মাণস্থলী, নির্ম্মাণশালা; শিল্পশালা, কারখানা। **9.** Performance of moral duties; righteous deeds; "Faith, if it hath not *works*, is dead"; নৈতিক কর্ত্তব্য সম্পাদন; পুণ্যকর্ম্ম। **10.** (*Phys.*) Exertion of force in overcoming resistance or producing molecular change; as, to convert heat into *work*; (পদার্থবিজ্ঞান) কোনরূপ বাধা অতিক্রমে বা আণবিক পরিবর্ত্তনসাধনে শক্তি পরিচালনা, শক্তিপ্রকাশ। **11.** The working or moving parts of a mechanism; as, the *works* of a watch; কল। **12.** Doings or experience of a specified kind; as bloody *works*; বিশিষ্ট কার্য্য, বিশিষ্ট অভিজ্ঞতা। **Work'-less,** *adj.* **Work a day**—যে সকল বারে কার্য্য করা হয়—ঐ সকল বারের উপযোগী বা ঐ সকল বারে ব্যবহৃত, বা দৃষ্ট; সাধারণ; কার্য্যকরী। **Work-bag, basket** or **box**—কার্য্যের উপযোগী যন্ত্রপাতির বাক্স, পেটরা, বা থলিয়া। **Workday**—কাজের দিন, রবিবার অথবা কোনরূপ পর্ব্বাহ ব্যতীত অন্য দিন। **Workhouse**—কোন যাজকপল্লীর নিঃস্ব ব্যক্তিগণের বাসের জন্য সরকারী আবাস, শ্রমশালা, নিঃস্ব-নিবাস, দরিদ্রশালা। **Workman**—শ্রমিক, মজুর, কারিগর, শ্রমজীবী, শ্রমী (রবীঃ), কর্ম্মিক (ঐ)। **Workmanlike**—উত্তম শিল্পিসমুচিত। **Workmanship**—কারিগরি, নৈপুণ্য। **Workpepole**—মজুর শ্রেণীর স্ত্রী বা পুরুষ। **Workshop** — কারখানা, শিল্পশালা, শিল্পগৃহ, শিল্পনিকেতন, কর্ম্মশালা। **Work-table**—সূচ সূতা প্রভৃতি রাখার জন্য দেরাজবিশিষ্ট মেজ। **Workwoman** — শ্রমজীবিনী, শ্রমিকা। **A good day's work**—একদিনের পক্ষে যথেষ্ট কায। **A work of art**—কলাদ্রব্য, উচ্চাঙ্গের শিল্পকার্য্যের নিদর্শন-স্বরূপবস্তু। **Covenant of works**—বাইবেলের প্রাচীন নিয়মের বিধান। **Internal work**—কোন বস্তুর অণুসমূহে পরিচালিত শক্তি। **In the works**—নির্ম্মাণাধীন। **Mighty works** — অলৌকিক কার্য্যসমূহ। **The works of God**—Nature; প্রকৃতি। **To make short work of**—See SHORT. **To set to work** — To begin operation; কার্য্য আরম্ভ করা। **Unit of work**—এক পাউণ্ড জিনিষ এক ফিট উচ্চে উত্তোলন; কর্ম্মের একক। **Works of mercy**—Charitable acts; পুণ্যকার্য্য। **Works of supererogation**—See SUPEREROGATION.

work (wĕrk), *v. t.* & *i.* **1.** To bestow labour, toil or exertion upon; as, to *work* a mine; to convert to use by labour or effort; as, to *work* lime; কোন কিছুর উপর পরিশ্রম বা চেষ্টা প্রয়োগ করা; চেষ্টা বা পরিশ্রম দ্বারা ব্যবহারোপযোগী করা। **2.** To make; to form; to shape; as, to *work* clay into pot; to create; তৈয়ার করা; প্রস্তুত করা; গঠন করা; সৃষ্টি করা। **3.** To stir and mix; নাড়িয়া চাড়িয়া মিশান। **4.** To embroider; "A princess *wrought* it (a handkerchief) me"; সূচিকর্ম্ম করা, সূচ দ্বারা ফুল পাতা তোলা। **5.** To cause to ferment, as liquor; গাঁজান। **6.** To solve; as, to *work* a sum; কষা। **7.** To set in action, as machinery or motive power; as, to *work* a machine; চালান। **8.** To direct the course of a ship etc.; জাহাজ প্রভৃতি চালান। **9.** To bud or graft; চোক কলম করা, কলম করা। **10.** To operate upon, as a purgative or cathartic; ক্রিয়া করা, কায করা। **11.** To bring about; to accomplish; "Our silly cross *wrought* all my loss"; সংগঠন করা; সম্পাদন করা, সম্পন্ন করা। **12.** To bring by action or motion to any state; "So the pure limpid stream, when foul with stains of rushing torrents and descending rains, *works* itself clear, and as it runs refines"; কোনরূপ ক্রিয়া বা গতির দ্বারা বিশিষ্ট অবস্থায় আনা। **13.** (*Obs.*) To influence by continued prompting, urging or the like means; to gain over; to prevail upon; to manage; to get into one's control, to induce; "What you would your *work* me to, I have some aim"; (অপ্রঃ) নিয়ত কুমন্ত্রণা দ্বারা পীড়াপীড়ি করিয়া প্রভাবিত করা; প্ররোচিত করা; লওয়ান, প্রবর্ত্তিত করা; চালিত করা; আয়ত্তাধীন করা; প্ররোচিত করা। **14.** To excite; as, to *work* one's anger; উদ্দীপ্ত করা, প্রদীপ্ত করা, উত্তেজিত করা। **15.** To knead; as, to *work* dough; ডলা। **16.** To cause to labour; as, to *work* one's horse; পরিশ্রম করান, খাটান। **17.** To attain or make by continuous or severe labour, exertion or striving; as, to *work* a passage through a crowd; নিরবচ্ছিন্ন বা কঠোর পরিশ্রমে প্রাপ্ত হওয়া বা প্রস্তুত করা। ***Verb i.*** **1.** To make exertion for some end or purpose ; to engage in, or be employed in, some task, labour or duty ; to labour ; to toil ; কোন কার্য্য সাধনে চেষ্টা করা ; কোন কার্য্যে নিযুক্ত থাকা, কোনরূপ কর্ত্তব্য পালন করা ; পরিশ্রম করা ; খাটা। **2.** To be customarily engaged or employed in any business, trade, profession, employment or the like ; to be in employment ; to be occupied as a worker ; to perform the duties of a workman, man of business, etc. ; as, he *works* in cnstom house ; কোন ব্যবসায়ে বা চাকুরীতে নিযুক্ত থাকা ; কার্য্যে থাকা ; শ্রমজীবিরূপে নিযুক্ত থাকা ; শ্রমজীবী, ব্যবসায়ী, প্রভৃতির কার্য্য করা। **3.** To operate or act, as a purgative or cathartic ; ক্রিয়া করা, কায করা। **4.** To ferment, as liquor; "Into wine or beer put some like substances, while they *work*"; গাঁজিয়া উঠা। **5.** To operate ; as, the machine *works* well ; চলা। **6.** To be effective ; to have the desired effect or influence , as, his plan will *work* well ; to act satisfactorily ; "All things *work* together for good to them that love God" ; কার্য্যকরী হওয়া ; ঈপ্সিত ফল প্রাপ্ত হওয়া, ঈপ্সিত প্রভাব বিস্তার করা ; সন্তোষজনকভাবে চলা। **7.** To be tossed or agitated ; as, the ship *works* in a rough sea ; আন্দোলিত হওয়া, বিক্ষুব্ধ হওয়া। **8.** To travel ; as, this tram *works* from Esplanade to Kalighat ; গমন করা ; যাতায়াত করা। **9.** To progress or peneterate with difficulty (with *on*, *down*, *along*, *through*) ; as, he *worked* his way *through* the crowd ; কষ্টে অগ্রসর হওয়া, কষ্টে ভেদ করিয়া যাওয়া। **Wrought iron** — পেটা লোহা। **He is in a highly wrought up state** — He is nervous, hysterical ; সে খুব নাড়ীকাতুরে, সে বড় উচ্ছ্বাসপ্রবণ। **To work and turn**—To print on both sides from the same form ; একই ফর্ম্মা কাগজের উভয় পৃষ্ঠে ছাপা। **To work at**—(*Naut.*) To be engaged in ; নিযুক্ত থাকা। **To work away** or **on**—To continue to work ; কায করিতে থাকা। **To work a thing** or **person for all it** or **he is worth**—To use in such a way as to get the utmost advantage from ; এরূপভাবে ব্যবহার করা যাহাতে কোন ব্যক্তি বা বস্তু হইতে চরম সুবিধা পাওয়া যায়। **To work double tides**—To perform the work of two days in one ; দুই দিনের কায একদিনে করা। **To work free** or **loose**—To become loose through constant use ; সর্ব্বদা ব্যবহারের দরুণ শিথিল হওয়া। **To work in**—To insert or cause to penetrate labouriously ; অতি কষ্টে ঢুকান বা প্রবিষ্ট করা। To press in ; চাপিয়া ঢুকান। To intermix ; সংমিশ্রিত করা, মিশান। **To work into**—To force into ; to insinuate into ; জোর করিয়া ঢুকা ; অলক্ষিতে প্রবেশ করা। To transform by effort or slow change ; চেষ্টা দ্বারা পরিবর্ত্তন করা বা ধীরে ধীরে পরিবর্ত্তন করা। **To work off**—To pass off ; চালাইয়া দেওয়া। To find customers etc. ; ক্রেতা প্রভৃতি প্রাপ্ত হওয়া। To remove gradually ; ক্রমশঃ দূর করা বা উঠান। To produce by work ; কার্য্য দ্বারা উৎপাদন করা। **To work on** or **upon**—To operate on ; ক্রিয়া করা। To influence on ; প্রভাবিত করা। **To work one's passage**—To work on board a ship etc. instead of paying passage money ; ভাড়া দেওয়ার পরিবর্ত্তে জাহাজে কায করা। **To work one's way**—To progress with difficulty ; কষ্টে অগ্রসর হওয়া। To succeed ; কৃতকার্য্য হওয়া। **To work one's will**—To accomplish one's purpose ; কাহারো উদ্দেশ্য সাধন করা। **To work out**—To result in practice ; কার্য্যতঃ দাঁড়ান। To accomplish ; সম্পাদন করা। To solve, as a problem ; কষা, সমাধান করা। To arrange ; to develop ; বন্দোবস্ত করা ; ক্রমশঃ পরিস্ফুট করা। To exhaust, as a mine by working ; কায করিতে করিতে খনি প্রভৃতি নিঃশেষিত করা। **To work over**—To persuade ; প্রবর্ত্তিত করা, প্ররোচিত করা। **To work to windward**—To sail against the wind ; to tack to windward ; বায়ুর প্রতিকূলে গমন করা ; বাতাসের অভিমুখে জাহাজ ফিরান। **To work up**—To influence ; প্রভাবিত করা। To agitate ; আন্দোলিত করা। To excite ; উত্তেজিত করা। To elaborate ; বহু পরিশ্রমে বিস্তারিত ভাবে বাহির করা। (*Naut.*) To keep, as a crew at work with a view to punishing ; (নৌবিদ্যা) শাস্তিদানের উদ্দেশ্যে জাহাজের মাল্লাদিগকে বাজে কাজে খাটান। To utilize in any work ; কোন কাজে লাগান। To achieve ; gradually by continued effort ; ক্রমশঃ সংঘটন বা কার্য্যে পরিণত করা, ক্রমশঃ লাভ করা। To rise ; উঠা। To convert ; to make into shape ; পরিণত করা ; কোন বিশেষ আকৃতি দেওয়া। To learn or gain knowledge by study ; অধ্যয়নের ফলে শিক্ষা করা বা বিদ্যার্জ্জন করা (*Obs.*) To wear by hard work ; (অপ্রঃ)। কঠোর পরিশ্রম দ্বারা পরিক্লান্ত করা। **To work water**—(বাষ্পীয় যন্ত্র সম্বন্ধে) চোঙ্গে বাষ্পের সহিত কুয়াসার আকারে জল প্রেরণ করা। **To work with**—To be in harmony witht ; সঙ্গতিবিশিষ্ট হওয়া। To experiment upon ; কোন বিষয়ে পরীক্ষা করা। To try to influence by appear etc. ; আবেদন প্রভৃতি দ্বারা প্রভাবিত করিতে চেষ্টা করা। To attempt to influence ; প্রভাবিত করিতে চেষ্টা করা।

work'-a-ble (wêrk-ă-ble), *adj.* Practicable; as, *workable* scheme; that can be worked ; কার্য্যোপযোগী, সম্পাদনীয়, সম্পাদ্য ; কার্য্যকর।

work'-êr (wêrk-), *n.* **1.** One who works ; কার্য্যকারী। **2.** A labourer; শ্রমজীবী। **3.** An undeveloped female of social bees, ants, etc. ; সমাজবদ্ধ মক্ষিকা, পিপীলিকা, প্রভৃতি অব্যক্তলিঙ্গ স্ত্রী-প্রাণী, কর্ম্মী। **Worker bee, Worker ant**—Same as WORKER 3.

work'-ing (wêrk-), *n.* & *adj.* **1.** The act of labouring ; শ্রম, পরিশ্রম। **2.** The way a thing works or the result of its working; "The *workings* of one's conscience" ; ক্রিয়া ; ক্রিয়ার ফল। **3.** Mine ; as, a desired *working* ; quarry ; portion of a mine or similar work where men are at work ; খনি ; প্রস্তর ; খনি বা প্রস্তরের খনির যে অংশে মজুরেরা কার্য্যে নিযুক্ত থাকে। **4.** Fermentation ; মাতন, ফাঁপন, গাঁজন। *Adj.* **1.** Engaged in, or devoted to, bodily toil ; as, *working* class ; শ্রমজনক কার্য্যে নিযুক্ত। **2.** Taking an active part in business ; as, a *working* partner ; কার্য্যকারী। **Working-capital**—কোন ব্যবসায় চালাইতে যে পরিমাণ মূলধনের আবশ্যক হয়। **Working-class**—শ্রমজীবী শ্রেণী, শ্রমীশ্রেণী। **Working-day**—কার্য্যের দিবস, কার্য্যদিন (রবিবার এবং বন্ধের দিন ব্যতিরিক্ত দিন)। **Working-drawing, working-plan**—যে নক্সা দৃষ্টে অট্টালিকা নির্ম্মাণ করা হয়। **Working-expenses**—কোন ব্যবসায় চালাইতে যে অর্থের আবশ্যক হয়, চালাইবার খরচ। **Working-man**—শ্রমজীবী শ্রমিক ; যন্ত্রশিল্পী।

world (wêrld), *n.* **1.** The whole system of created things ; the whole creation ; the universe ; external phenomena ; বিশ্বব্রহ্মাণ্ড, সৃষ্টি, বিশ্বজগৎ ; চরাচর, প্রপঞ্চ ; বিশ্ব। [Dutch *wereld* ; Icel. *verold* ; Dan. *verden* ; Swed. *verld* ; Germ. *weralt* ; Gr. *wel-*] **2.** Any celestial orb or planetary body, especially considered as peopled, and as the scene of interest kindred to those of mankind ; "Before his presence, at whose awful throne All tremble in all *worlds*, except our own" ; ব্রহ্মাণ্ড। **3.** The earth and its inhabitants, with their concerns ; the sum of human affairs and interest ; mankind ; "One touch of nature makes the whole *world* kin" ; জগৎ ; সংসার; মানবজাতি। **4.** A large portion or division of the globe as, the Old *World*; গোলার্দ্ধ, মহাদ্বীপ। **5.** The section of mankind engrossed in the concerns of this present life; the people exclusively interested in secular affairs ; the unregenerate or ungodly part of mankind ; "I pray not for the *world* but for them which thou hast given me" ; ইহসর্ব্বস্ব জনগণ ; সংসারাসক্ত লোকগণ ; অসাধু জনগণ। **6.** A course of life ; a career ; as, to begin the *world* anew ; জীবন ; জীবনযাত্রা। **7.** One of the three grand divisions or primary groups of natural objects ; as, the animal *world* ; প্রাকৃতিক পদার্থসমূহের বৃহৎ বিভাগত্রয়ের (জন্তু, উদ্ভিদ্ ও খনিজ) অন্যতম জগৎ (cf. পশুজগৎ)। **8.** A great quantity ; a large number ; as, a *world* of things ; বহুপরিমাণ ; বহুসংখ্যক, এক সংসার (*colloq.* cf. আমার হাতে এক সংসার কায পড়ে রয়েছে।) **9.** Time ; "*World* without end" ; কাল। **10.** Customs, practices and interests of man ; the present state of existence ; the secular life; "If any man loves the *world*, the love of the father is not in him"; মনুষ্যের রীতিনীতি, স্বার্থ প্রভৃতি ; ইহকাল ; সাংসারিক জীবন, সংসার (cf. তিনি একজন সংসারত্যাগী সন্ন্যাসী।) **11.** The habits, customs and usages of society ; society ; respectable and fashionable society ; সামাজিক রীতিনীতি, আচার পদ্ধতি ; সমাজ, সংসার ; সম্ভ্রান্ত সমাজ, ভদ্রসমাজ। **12.** A certain section, portion, or class of men, considered as a separate or independant whole ; a number or body of people united by a common faith, aim and object, or the like ; as the Hindu *world* ; কোন বিশিষ্ট বা স্বতন্ত্র মানবশ্রেণী ; সাধারণ লক্ষ্য, উদ্দেশ্য, প্রভৃতি দ্বারা একীভূত জনগণ, জগৎ (cf. খৃষ্টীয় জগৎ)। **World-concept** — বিশ্ববিভাবনা। **World-famous**— জগদ্বিখ্যাত, বিশ্ববিখ্যাত। **World-ground**—জগতের মূলতত্ত্ব, বিশ্বতত্ত্ব [শোপেনহেয়ারের মতে ইচ্ছা (will)ই বিশ্বের মূলতত্ত্ব।] **World-language** — বিশ্বভাষা। **World old**—সৃষ্টির আদি বা প্রারম্ভ হইতে বর্ত্তমান। **World renowned**—জগদ্‌বিখ্যাত। **World-soul**—বিশ্বাত্মা (উপযেমে স বিশ্বাত্মা শতরূপামনিন্দিতাম্—মৎস্যপুরাণম্।) **World-spirit**—জগৎপ্রাণ, ঈশ্বর। **World-tree**—স্কেণ্ডেনেভীয় পুরাণে উক্ত বৃক্ষ বিশেষ—যদ্দারা স্বর্গ, নরক এবং পৃথিবী সংযুক্ত করিয়াছে বলিয়া কথিত আছে। **World-wide**—জগৎজোড়া, বিশ্বজোড়া, পৃথিবীব্যাপী, বিশ্বব্যাপী, জগৎশুদ্ধ, বিশ্বশুদ্ধ। **All the world**—The whole world ; সমগ্র জগৎ। **All the world over**—পৃথিবীশুদ্ধ, দুনিয়াশুদ্ধ। **A woman of the world**—(অপ্রঃ) বিবাহিতা স্ত্রীলোক। **A world of water**—সাগরের তরল বিস্তার, জলজগৎ। **A world to see**—Something wonderful to see; চমকপ্রদ বস্তু। **Citizen of the world** — বিশ্বনাগরিক, বিশ্বপুরবাসী। **For all the world like**—Precisely similar ; ঠিক একরূপ। **Man of the world**—A worldly man ; সাংসারিক লোক, সাংসারিক ব্যক্তি, পাকা বিষয়ী লোক। **Prince of this world**—শয়তান। **Rose of the world**—একপ্রকার ক্ষুপ। **The lower**

world — অধোলোক, নরক। The New World—আমেরিকা,নূতন মহাদ্বীপ। The Old World—এসিয়া, আফ্রিকা ও ইয়ুরোপ, পুরাতন মহাদ্বীপ। The snare of the world—মায়াজাল। The world—ইহলোক। The world and his wife—Everybody; esp. everyone belonging to cultured society; প্রত্যেকে, সকলেই; বিশেষতঃ ভদ্র সমাজের সকলেই। The world of dreams—স্বপ্নলোক, স্বপ্নজগৎ। The world, the flesh and the devil—আমোদ উপভোগ, ইন্দ্রিয়চরিতার্থতা, পাপপ্রবৃত্তি চরিতার্থতার বাসনা। The world to come, The next world, The other world—Next world; পরকাল,পরলোক। This world, The world—নশ্বর জীবন। To begin the world—To begin the worldly life; সংসারে প্রবেশ করা। To carry the world before one—To have speedy and complete success; অতি দ্রুত এবং সর্ব্বতোভাবে কৃতকার্য্য হওয়া। To come into the world—To be born; জন্মগ্রহণ করা, ভূমিষ্ঠ হওয়া। To go to the world—To get married; (অপ্রঃ) বিবাহিত হওয়া। To go to the world's end — To go to the utmost limit; শেষসীমা পর্য্যন্ত যাওয়া। To know or see the world—To gain worldly experience; সাংসারিক অভিজ্ঞতা লাভ করা। To let the world slide—To let the world go in its usual course; পৃথিবী যেমন চলিতেছে তেমনভাবে চলিতে দেওয়া, লৌকিকতা, লোকমত প্রভৃতি উপেক্ষা করা। To live out of the world—To live in seclusion; সংসার হইতে দূরে বাস করা। To make a noise in the world—To be the subject of talk all ovr the world—সমগ্রজগতের আলোচনার বিষয়ীভূত হওয়া। To make the best of both worlds—To reconcile secular and spiritual lives; ঐহিক এবং আধ্যাত্মিক জীবনের মধ্যে সমন্বয় সাধন করা। World's end—প্রলয় World without end—For ever; চিরকাল, অনন্তকাল।

world'-ly (wĕrld-), *adj.* 1. Temporal; earthly; "Thou thy *worldly* task hast done"; সাংসারিক, ঐহিক; বৈষয়িক, পার্থিব। 2. Devoted to, interested in, or connected with, the present world, its cares, advantages or pleasures, to the exclusion of those of a future life; sordid; vile; বিষয়রত, ইহকালসর্ব্বস্ব; নীচ; জঘন্য। **—li-ness,** *n.* **Worldly-minded**—ঐহিকবিষয়ে লিপ্ত, বিষয়ানুরক্ত, সংসারানুরক্ত, ঐহিকদর্শী। **Worldly wisdom**—সাংসারিকজ্ঞান, বিষয়বুদ্ধি। **Worldly wise**—সাংসারিক জ্ঞানসম্পন্ন, বৈষয়িকজ্ঞানসম্পন্ন, বিষয়বুদ্ধিসম্পন্ন।

worm (wĕrm), *n.* 1. Any long, small, creeping animal entirely without feet, or with very short ones; কীট, পতঙ্গ, পোকা, ক্রিমি। 2. A poor, grovelling, debased, despised creature; "Poor *worm,* thou art infected"; নগণ্য লোক, হীন ব্যক্তি। 3. The thread of a screw; স্ক্রুপের পেঁচ। 4. A spiral pipe of still in which vapour is cooled and condensed; বকযন্ত্রের যে পেঁচালো নলে বাষ্প শীতলীকৃত ও ঘনীভূত হয়। 5. A spiral cartridge-extractor; কার্ত্তুজ বাহির করার জন্য একপ্রকার পেঁচ। 6. Remorse; "The *worm* of conscience still begnaw the soul"; পশ্চাত্তাপ, মনস্তাপ। 7. One who silently, slowly and persistently works and studies; as, a book-*worm*; যে ব্যক্তি নীরবে ধীরে ধীরে এবং ক্রমাগত কোন কার্য্য করে, গভীর অধ্যয়নরত ব্যক্তি, কীট (cf. গ্রন্থ-কীট)। 8. A ligament under a dog's tongue; কুকুরের জিহ্বার নীচের সন্ধি বিশেষ। **Worm'-i-ness,** *n.* **Worm'-y,** *adj.* **Worm-cast**—কেঁচোর উদর হইতে নির্গত নলাকার কর্দ্দম। **Worm-eaten**—কীটক্ষত, কীটদষ্ট; সেকেলে। **Worm-fishing**—পোকার টোপ বড়শীতে গাঁথিয়া মৎস্যধরণ। **Worm-gear**—ঘূর্ণায়মান পেঁচালো দণ্ড দ্বারা সঞ্চালিত দন্তুরচক্র-পরম্পরা। **Worm-hole**—কীটরন্ধ্র। **Worm-holed**—কীটক্ষত। **Worm-seed**—একপ্রকার ক্রিমিনিঃসারক বীজ; Levantএর বৃক্ষ বিশেষ—যাহা হইতে উক্ত বীজ প্রাপ্ত হওয়া যায়।

worm (wĕrm), *v. i.* & *t.* To advance by wriggling; কেঁচোর মত কিলবিল করিয়া চলা। ***Verb t.*** 1. To free of worm; as, to *worm* a garden; কীটশূন্য করা। 2. To cut the vermicular ligament, called a worm, from under the tongue of dogs; কুকুরের জিহ্বার নীচের সন্ধিবন্ধনী ছেদনকরা। 3. To remove the charge etc. of a gun by means of worm (see WORM *n.* 5.); পেঁচ দ্বারা কার্ত্তুজ প্রভৃতি বাহির করা। 5. To insinuate oneself into; as, to *worm* into one's favour; অলক্ষিতে প্রাপ্ত হওয়া বা লাভ করা। 6. To make one's way with crawling motion; হামাগুড়ি দিয়া চলা। 7. To draw out slyly; as, to *worm* a secret out of a person; চালাকি করিয়া বাহির করা।

wŏr'-mŭl, *n.* Same as WARBLE *n.* 2.

wŏrm'-wood (-wŭd), *n.* 1. A plant of a bitter nauseous taste, the artemisia absinthi or any other species of artemisia (The worm-wood of the Old Testament is the Artemisia abrotanum); দোনা, নাগদোনা [Syn. দমন, দমনক, দান্ত, গন্ধোৎকটা, মুনি, জটিলা, দণ্ডী, পাণ্ডুরাগ, ব্রহ্মজটা, পুণ্ডরীক, তাপসপত্রী, পত্রী, পবিত্রক, দেবশেখর, কুলপত্র, বিনীত, তপস্বিপত্র, মুনিপুত্র তপোধন, ব্রহ্মজটী, কুলপুত্রক, বৃন্দা, জম্বূ, জম্বুবতী, রক্তপুষ্পা, জাম্ববী, মধুর।

Worm-wood.

দুঃসহা] [Syn. Arab. *afsuntin*; Pers. *buranjasif-kohi*; Tam. *mashipattiri*; Chin. *yin-ch'in-hau.*] **2.** Anything very bitter or grievous; as, gall and *wormwood*; bitterness; অতিশয় তিক্ত এবং দুঃখজনক ব্যাপার; তিক্ততা।

wōrn, See WEAR.

wor'-rit (wŭr-ĭt), *v. t., i.* & *n.* (*Vulg.*) Same as, WORRY.

wor'-ry (wŭr-ĭ), *v.t.,i.* & *n.* **1.** To seize by the throat with the teeth; to tear with the teeth, as dogs when fighting; to kill by repeated fighting; গলায় কামড়াইয়া ধরা; ঝগড়াকারী কুকুরের মত দাঁত দ্বারা কামড়াইয়া ছিঁড়া; পুনঃ পুনঃ আক্রমণ করিয়া বধ করা। **2.** To tease: to trouble: to harass; "Witness when I was *worried* with thy peals"; to vex; ক্ষ্যাপান, উৎপাত করা, অত্যাচার করা; পীড়ন করা; বিরক্ত করা, উত্ত্যক্ত করা; জ্বালাতন করা। ***Verb i.*** **1.** To be engaged in mangling something by tearing it with teeth; দংশন দ্বারা ক্ষতবিক্ষত বা ছিন্নভিন্ন করা। **2.** To be unduly anxious or troubled; to make one's self anxious or harassed; বিরক্ত হওয়া, নিঃগৃহীত হওয়া; জ্বালাতন হওয়া। **3.** To feel or express great care or anxiety; উৎকণ্ঠা বা উদ্বেগ বোধ করা বা প্রকাশ করা, ক্ষুব্ধ হওয়া। ***Noun.*** **1.** The act of worrying or mangling by the teeth; দংশন দ্বারা ক্ষতবিক্ষত করণ। **2.** Turmoil; as, the *worry* of politics; vexation; anxiety; গোলমাল, ঝঞ্ঝাট; জ্বালা, জ্বালাতন, বিরক্তি; উৎকণ্ঠা, উদ্বেগ। **–ing,** *n.* **–ri-less,** *adj.* **–ri-ment,** *n.* **To worry along**—To avance in the face of obstacles; বাধাবিঘ্ন স্বত্বেও অগ্রসর হওয়া। **To worry a problem out**—To try to solve it again and again till it is solved; কোন সমস্যা সমাধান না হওয়া পর্য্যন্ত পুনঃ পুনঃ তাহা সমাধানের জন্য চেষ্টা করা। **To worry down**—To swallow down with difficulty; কষ্টে গ্রাস করা। **To worry one's self**—To take needless trouble; বৃথা কষ্ট পাওয়া। **To worry the sword**—To try to frustrate an adversary by quick balking motions; পুনঃ পুনঃ অতি দ্রুত সঞ্চালিত হইয়া প্রতিরোধের চেষ্টা ব্যর্থ করা।

worse (wêrs), *adj., adv.* & *n.* **1.** More bad or badly; মন্দতর। **2.** More unwell; more sick; অপেক্ষাকৃত খারাপ; আরো পীড়িত, আরো কাতর। ***Adv.*** In a manner more evil or bad; মন্দতরভাবে। ***Noun.*** Worse thing or things; as, I have *worse* to tell; মন্দতর বিষয়, আরো খারাপ সংবাদ। **Wors'-en,** *v. t.* & *i.* To put to disadvantage; to defeat; অসুবিধাজনক অবস্থায় ফেলা; পরাভূত করা। ***Verb i.*** To become worse; to deteriorate; আরো খারাপ হওয়া, মন্দতর হওয়া; অপকর্ষ প্রাপ্ত হওয়া। **A change for the worse**—মন্দের দিকে পরিবর্ত্তন। **The worse half**—স্বামী (কৌতুকচ্ছলে cf. *better-half*)। **To put to the worse**—To be defeated; পরাভূত হওয়া, পরাস্ত হওয়া। **To think the worse of a person**—To consider a man more bad for some cause; কোন কারণে কোন লোককে আরো খারাপ ভাবা। **Worse and worse**—ক্রমশঃ আরো খারাপ, ক্রমশঃ মন্দতর।

wor'-ship (wêr-), *n., v. t.* & *i.* **1.** Courtesy or reverence paid to merit or worth; "Kings are like stars—they rise and set—they have the *worship* of the world, but no repose"; সম্মান, শ্রদ্ধা। **2.** A title of honour used in addresses to those of high station esp. to magistrates and judges; as I invite your *worship's* notice to this statement of the witness; ধর্ম্মাবতার, হুজুর। **3.** A religious reverence and homage; পূজা, অর্চ্চনা, আরাধনা, উপাসনা, তপশ্চর্য্যা। **4.** Extravagant admiration; adoration; "Loyalty disciplines all that was ever meant by hero-*worship*, lies perennially in human bosom"; পূজা; অর্চ্চনা। **5.** An object of worship; "At once the artist's *worship* and despair"; পূজার পাত্র। ***Verb t.*** **1.** To venerate with religious rites; "Our fathers *worshipped* in this mountain"; পূজা করা, অর্চ্চনা করা, উপাসনা করা। **2.** To adore; to idolize; "With bended knees I daily *worship* her"; অতিশয় সম্মান করা, দেববৎ পূজা করা; প্রাণের দেবতার মত ভালবাসা। ***Verb i.*** To perform acts of worship or adoration; to perform religious services; অর্চ্চনা করা; পূজা করা। **–er, –per,** *ns.* **–ful, –ful-ly,** *adjs.* **Men of worship**—পূজার্হ ব্যক্তিগণ। **Place of worship**—ধর্ম্ম-মন্দির।

worst (wêrst), *adj.* (*sup.*), *adv., n.* & *v. t.* Most; অতিশয় মন্দ, নিকৃষ্টতম, মন্দতম, হীনতম, দুষ্টতম, জঘন্যতম। ***Adv.*** To the extreme degree of badness or inferiority; in a manner most bad or the like; নিকৃষ্টভাবে, মন্দতমভাবে; অতিশয় মন্দভাবে, অত্যন্ত মন্দভাবে। ***Noun.*** That which is most bad or evil; the most severe, calamitous, or wicked state or degree; নিকৃষ্টতম অবস্থা, হীনতম অবস্থা, সর্ব্বাপেক্ষা খারাপ অবস্থা; চরমবিপৎ। ***Verb t.*** To gain advantage over in contest; to outdo; to defeat; as, to *worst* one's enemies; যুদ্ধে সুবিধা লাভ করা; পরাজিত করা, পরাভূত করা; পরাস্ত করা। **At the worst**—খারাপের পক্ষে, বড় জোর। **If the worst comes to the worst**—If the utmost evil happen; চরম

দুর্ব্বিপাক উপস্থিত হইলে। **Let him do his worst**—Let him harm me as much as he can ; তাহার যতদূর সাধ্য কুলায় আমার অনিষ্ট করুক। **The worst ways**—(*Colloq.*) As much as can be; যতদূর হইতে পারে। **To have the worst of it** — To be defeated ; পরাভূত হওয়া, পরাস্ত হওয়া, পরাহত হওয়া।

wor'-stĕd (wŭr-), *n.* & *adj.* A well-twisted yarn spun of long-staple wool ; উলসূতা। ***Adj.*** made of worsted ; as, *worsted* cloth ; consisting of worsted ; উলসূতার তৈরী ; ঊর্ণাতন্তুময়।

wort (wêrt), *n.* **1.** A plant or herb ; ক্ষুপ, ওষধি। **2.** (*Obs.*) Cabbage ; (অপ্রঃ) কপি। **3.** Infusion of malt before is it fermented into beer ; অঙ্কুরিত যবের নির্য্যাস—যাহা হইতে বীয়র প্রস্তুত হয়।

worth (wêrth), *pred. adj.* & *n.* **1.** Deserving ; as, it is *worth* keeping in memory ; উপযোগী, উপযুক্ত, যোগ্য, অর্হ (in combination)। **2.** Equal in price to ; as, the book is *worth* 10s. ; মূল্যের, দামের। **3.** Having wealth to the value of ; as, he is *worth* 10 lacks of rupees ; নির্দ্দিষ্টমূল্যের সম্পত্তিবিশিষ্ট। ***Noun.*** **1.** Value ; price ; মূল্য ; দাম। **2.** Virtue ; merit ; importance; excellence; "And in a word, for far behind his *worth* comes all the praises that I now bestow, He is complete in feature and in mind" ; ধর্ম্ম ; গুণ, সারবত্তা ; গুরুত্ব ; উৎকর্ষ। **3.** Wealth ; property ; "They are but beggars that can count their *worth*"; ধন ; বিত্ত, সম্পত্তি। **Worth'-less,** *adj.* Having no worth ; অসার, মূল্যহীন, নগণ্য, সারশূন্য, ছার (*colloq.*), কাষের বার (*colloq.*)। **Worth'-less-ly,** *adv.* **Worth'-less-ness,** *n.* **Worth-seeing**—দর্শনযোগ্য। **For all one is worth**—With one's utmost effort ; প্রাণপণ চেষ্টায়। **Not worth a cent, a curse, a rap, a hair**—Of little or no value ; এক কাণাকড়ি দামেরও নয়। **Not worth one's salt**—See SALT. **Worth powder and shot**—See POWDER. **Worth one's while**—See WHILE.

wor'-thy, (wêrth-), *adj.* & *n.* **1.** Valuable , noble ; estimable ; মূল্যবান ; সম্ভ্রান্ত ; আদরণীয়, শ্রদ্ধেয়। **2.** Deserving ; as, he is *worthy* of great praise ; উপযুক্ত, উপযোগী, যোগ্য, অনুরূপ। **3.** Qualified ; as, he is a *worthy* man ; গুণবান, উপযুক্ত-গুণসম্পন্ন। ***Noun.*** A person of eminent worth ; a local celebrity ; অতিশয় গুণবান ব্যক্তি ; কোন স্থানের প্রসিদ্ধ বা সুবিখ্যাত ব্যক্তি। **—i-ly,** *adv.* **—i-ness,** *n.* **The nine worthies of the World** — ট্রয় নগরবাসী হেক্টর (Hector), অলীকসন্দর (Alexander the Great), জুলিয়াস সীজর (Julius Caesar), জসুয়া (Joshua), ডেভিড (David), জুডাস মেকেবাস (Judas Maceabaeous), রাজা আর্থার (King Arthur), সার্লেমেন (Charlemagne) এবং বুইলনের গডফ্রে (Godfrey of Bouillon)।

wŏt, *v. t.* & *i.* See WIT *v. t.* & *i.*

would (wûd), See WILL. **Would-be**—ভাবী, হবু (*Slang*, cf. হবু স্কুলের কল্পনাদিনের স্মাত — জ্যোতিঃহারা)। **Would rather**—বরং। **Would to God**—ঈশ্বর করুণ।

wound (wônd), *n., v. t.* & *i.* **1.** A cut or stab etc. ; injury ; জখম, ঘা, ক্ষত, অস্ত্রাঘাত, ক্ষতচিহ্ন, ত্বক্‌কণ্ডুরা (সাঃ পঃ), সদ্যোব্রণ ; আঘাত, চোট। **2.** A hurt or pain to the feelings ; আঘাত (cf. তোমার কথায় আমার মনে বড় আঘাত লেগেছে), মর্ম্মব্যথা। **3.** Damage ; অনিষ্ট, ক্ষতি। ***Verb t.*** **1.** To inflict wound ; আঘাত করা। **2.** (*Fig.*) To cause pain to one's feelings ; (লজ্জায়) কাহারো মনে আঘাত দেওয়া। ***Verb i.*** To inflict a wound or wounds on ; আঘাত করা, জখম করা। **Wound'-less,** *adj.* **Wound-Wort** — এক-জাতীয় ক্ষুপের সাধারণ নাম। **Willing to wound**—বিদ্বেষপরায়ণ, ঈর্ষা-পরায়ণ।

wound (wônd), *pt.* & *pp.* of WIND (which see.)

wou-ră'-li (wô-), *n.* Same as CURARI.

wōve, wōv'-en, (n), See WEAVE.

wrack (răk), *n.* A sea-weed, thrown ashore ; সাগরতটে নিক্ষিপ্ত শৈবাল [ইহাদ্বারা জমিতে সার দেওয় হয়।]

wraith (rāth), *n.* An apparition of a person about to die or newly dead ; মুমূর্ষু ব্যক্তির বা সদ্যোমৃত ব্যক্তির প্রেতাত্মা বা ছায়ামূর্ত্তি।

wran'-gle (răng-gl), *v. i.* & *n.* To dispute angrily ; to quarrel peevishly and angrily ; তর্কবিতর্ক করা, বাদানুবাদ করা, বচসা করা; কোন্দল করা, কলহ করা, ঝগড়া করা। ***Noun.*** An angry and noisy dispute or quarrel ; an altercation ; কলহ ; বাদানুবাদ, বচসা।

wran'-glêr (răng-), *n.* **1.** One who wrangles , বাদবিতণ্ডাকারী, বচসা-কারী। **2.** (In Cambridge University) One who attains a certain rank in the examination for honours in mathematics ; কেম্ব্রিজ বিশ্ববিদ্যালয়ে যে ছাত্র গণিত-শাস্ত্রের অনার পরীক্ষায় প্রথমবিভাগে উত্তীর্ণ হয়, রেংলার। **—ship,** *n.* **Senior wrangler**—রেংলারশিপ পরীক্ষায় প্রথমস্থান প্রাপ্ত ব্যক্তি।

wrap (răp), *v. t., i.* & *n.* **1.** To fold or roll ; পাট করা, তহ করা, ভাঁজ করা, পাকান। **2.** To enevelop completely ; as, *wrap* that thing in paper ; জড়ান, আবৃত করা, আচ্ছাদন করা, মোড়া। **3.** To conceal ; "Lamentably *wrapped* in twofold night" ; ঢাকা, লুকায়িত করা, প্রচ্ছন্ন করা। ***Verb i.*** To overlap ; একটীর কিনারা অপরটীর উপর থাকা। ***Noun.*** **1.** An outer article of dress, as shawls etc. ; শাল, আলোয়ান, প্রভৃতি গাত্রবস্ত্র। 2. That which wraps and envelopes ; যদ্দ্বারা কোনকিছু আবৃত করা হয় বা জড়ান যায়। **Wrap'-ping, Wrap'-page,** *ns.* **To be wrapped up in**—To be covered or enveloped with ; আবৃত হওয়া, জড়িত হওয়া। To be devoted to ; অনুরক্ত থাকা। To be engrossed in ; জড়িত থাকা, নিবিষ্ট থাকা। To be included ; অন্তর্ভুক্ত হওয়া।

wrap'-per (răp-êr), *n.* 1. One that wraps ; আচ্ছাদক। 2 That in which anything is wrapped or enclosed ; যাহাতে কোন জিনিষ জড়ানো যায়, মোড়ক। 3. The detachable paper cover put on a book to protect the binding ; পুস্তকের বাঁধাই যাহাতে নষ্ট না হইতে পারে তজ্জন্য মলাটের উপরে যে পাতলা কাগজের আবরণ দেওয়া হয়। 4. A loose upper garment ; আলোয়ান, শাল, প্রভৃতি, র‍্যাপার।

wrapt (răpt), *p. p.* & *adj.* Same as RAPT.

wrasse (răs), *n.* A prickly spined and hard-boned fish, with a long single dorsal fin and thick-lipped protrusive mouth, several species of them inhabiting the rocky parts of the English coast ; ইয়ুরোপ-দেশের একজাতীয় মৎস্য। [ইহাদের শিরদাঁড়া কণ্টকপূর্ণ, অস্থি কঠিন, ঠোঁট পুরু, মুখ প্রলম্বিত এবং মাত্র একটী লম্বা পাখনা থাকে।]

wrath (râth *or* räth), *n.* Anger ; indignation ; রাগ, ক্রোধ, রোষ ; কোপ, মন্যু। **Wrath'-ful,** *adj.* **Wrath'-ful-ly,** *adv.* **Slow to wrath**—অক্রোধ (cf. অক্রোধ পরমানন্দ নিত্যানন্দ রায়—চৈতন্যভাগবৎ), অক্রোধপ্রবণ। **Vessels** or **children of wrath**—ভগবানের দণ্ডের পাত্র।

wreak (rēk), *v. t.* 1. (*Archaic*) To revenge ; to avenge ; (অপ্র:) প্রতিহিংসা লওয়া ; প্রতিশোধ লওয়া। 2. To execute ; to inflict ; as, to *wreak* vengeance ; to hurl ; চরিতার্থ করা ; লওয়া ; নিক্ষেপ করা

wreath (rēth) *n.* 1. A garland ; a chaplet : মাল্য, মালা, মালিকা পুষ্প-মালা, পুষ্পস্রজ, দাম ; মৌলিমাল্য। 2. A twisted garland of cloth ; বস্ত্রখণ্ড রজ্জুর মত পাকাইয়া যে মাল্য বা শিরো-বেষ্টনী রচিত হয়। 3. A drift as of snow or sand ; বায়ুদ্বারা স্তূপীকৃত তুষার বা বালুকারাশি। 4. A curl of smoke ; a circular or curved band of cloud ; ধূমকুণ্ডলী ; মেঘমালা। **Wreath-shell**—একজাতীয় শঙ্খ।

wreathe (rēth), *v. t.* & *i.* 1. To form into a wreath ; to twist into a wreath ; মাল্যরচনা করা, মাল্যপ্রস্তুত করা ; রজ্জুর মত পাকাইয়া শিরোবেষ্টনী প্রভৃতি প্রস্তুত করা। 2. To entwine ; to wind or twine together ; to surround ; সংগ্রথিত করা, মাল্যাকারে বেষ্টিত করা ; পাকান ; বেষ্টিত করা, বলয়িত করা। 3. To twist ; as, his face was *wreathed* in smiles ; কুঞ্চিত করা। 4. To cover or overlay by drifting ; বায়ুদ্বারা স্তূপীকৃত তুষার কিংবা বালুকারাশি দ্বারা আচ্ছাদিত করা। ***Verb i.*** 1. To interlace ; "A bower of *wrething* trees" ; সংগ্রথিত হওয়া, পরস্পরের সহিত জড়িত হওয়া। 2. To move in the shape of wreathes ; মাল্যাকারে চালিত হওয়া।

wreck (rĕk), *n.*, *v. t.* & *i.* 1. Ruin ; ধ্বংস, নাশ। 2. The destruction of a vessel, by being driven ashore, dashed against rocks, etc.; পোতভঙ্গ, জাহাজডুবি, পোতব্যসন। 3. The ruins of a wrecked or stranded ship ; as, the *wrecks* of a steamer ; ভগ্ন বা চড়ায় আবদ্ধ জাহাজের ধ্বংসাবশেষ। 4. A greatly damaged building ; a person worn out by disease or dissipation ; "The *wreck* of what I was, fatigued I come" ; অট্টালিকার ধ্বংসাবশেষ ; ভগ্নস্বাস্থ্য ব্যক্তি 5. Goods etc., which, after a shipwreck, are cast upon the land by the sea ; ভগ্ন জাহাজের যে মাল প্রভৃতি সমুদ্রের তরঙ্গদ্বারা তীরে নিক্ষিপ্ত হয়। ***Verb t.*** 1. To cause to become a wreck ; পোত ধ্বংস করা, চড়ায় ঠেকিয়া জাহাজ মারা যাওয়া। 2. To ruin ; as, to *wreck* one's health ; ধ্বংস করা, নষ্ট করা। 3. To involve in shipwreck ; as, a *wrecked* sailor ; পোতধ্বংসে পতিত হওয়া। ***Verb i.*** To suffer wreck or ruin ; to be shipwrecked ; ধ্বংসপ্রাপ্ত হওয়া ; পোত ধ্বংস হওয়ায় অসহায় অবস্থায় পড়া। **Wreck-chart**—পোতভঙ্গের দিবস ও স্থান-নির্দ্দেশক নক্সা। **Wreck-fish**—একপ্রকার মৎস্য—ইহারা সচরাচর ভগ্ন পোতের কাষ্ঠের সহিত আসিয়া থাকে। **Wreck-master**—ভগ্নপোতের জিনিষ-পত্রের ভারগ্রহণের জন্য নিযুক্ত কর্ম্মচারী। **Wreck-wood**—ভগ্ন পোতের কাষ্ঠ।

wreck'-age (rĕk-), *n.* 1. Act of wrecking ; পোত ধ্বংস 2. Remains of ship or cargo that has been wrecked ; ভগ্নপোতাদির ধ্বংসাবশেষ বা অবশিষ্ট মালপত্র।

wreck'-er (rĕk-), *n.* 1. One who wrecks ; ধ্বংসকারী। 2. One who plunders the wrecks ; যে ব্যক্তি ভগ্ন জাহাজের মাল লুণ্ঠন করে। 3. One who is employed in recovering a wrecked ship or its cargo from a wreck ; ভগ্ন জাহাজ বা তৎস্থিত মাল প্রভৃতি উদ্ধারের জন্য নিযুক্ত ব্যক্তি। 4. One that causes wrecks, যে ব্যক্তি ভগ্ন জাহাজের কাষ্ঠ, মাল প্রভৃতি দ্বারা লাভবান হওয়ার উদ্দেশ্যে পোতভঙ্গ সংঘটিত করে।

wren (rĕn), *n.* 1. A name of various small song birds ; বিভিন্ন প্রকার ক্ষুদ্র গায়কপক্ষীর সাধারণ নাম। **Wren-boy**—খৃষ্টমাস দিবসে যে বালকের দল উক্ত পক্ষীর শিকারে যাইয়া থাকে—তাহাদের একজন।

wrench (rĕnch), *n.* & *v. t.* 1. A violent twist ; মোচড়, মচকানি 2. (*Fig.*) Pain caused by parting ; (লক্ষণায়) বিদায়কালীন কষ্ট

3. An instrument for exerting a twisting strain ; পাক সাঁড়াশী। ***Verb t.*** **1.** To twist or force by violence ; মোচড়ান। **2.** To

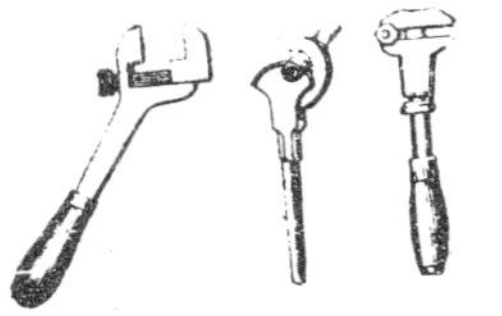

Wrenches.
1, angle-wrench ; 2, tub-wrench ; 3, monkey-wrench.

sprain ; মটকান, মচকান। **3.** To distort ; as, to *wrench* the meaning of a passage ; to pervert ; অর্থ বিকৃত করা ; বিকৃত করা। **4.** To drag or extort by violence ; টানিয়া বাহির করা, পীড়ন করিয়া আদায় করা।

wrest (rĕst), *v. t.* & *n.* **1.** To turn ; to twist ; ঘুরান ; মোচড়ান। **2.** To force or wrench away from a person's grasp ; কোন ব্যক্তির মুষ্টি হইতে জোর করিয়া বাহির করা, ছিনাইয়া লওয়া। **3.** To distort the meaning of ; as, to *wrest* the meaning of a word ; অর্থ বিকৃত করা। **4.** To tune with a wrest, or key ; কুঁজির সাহায্যে স্বরসংযোগ করা। ***Noun.*** **1.** A violent pulling or twisting ; মোচড়। **2.** A wrench ; পাক সাঁড়াশী। **3.** (*Mus.*) A key used in tuning a musical instrument ; (সঙ্গীতশাস্ত্র) বাদ্যযন্ত্রে স্বরসংযোগ করার জন্য ব্যবহৃত একপ্রকার চাবি, কুঁজি। **Wrest-block**—পিয়ানোর যে অংশে তন্ত্রীসমূহ বন্ধন করা হয়।

wres'-tle (rĕs-l), *v. i., t.* & *n.* **1.** To contend by grappling or trying to throw down ; মল্ল যুদ্ধ করা, কুস্তি করা। **2.** To struggle ; as, to *wrestle* with one's difficulties ; সংগ্রাম করা, ধ্বস্তাধ্বস্তি করা। ***Verb t.*** To contend with, as in wrestling ; ধ্বস্তাধ্বস্তি করা। ***Noun.*** **1.** A wrestling match ; মল্লযুদ্ধ, কুস্তি, মল্লক্রীড়া, মল্লরণ। **2.** A hard struggle ; কঠোর সংগ্রাম। **–tler,** *n.* One who wrestles ; মল্ল, কুস্তিগীর, পালোয়ান। **Wrestling-ground**—মল্লভূমি, অক্ষক্ষেত্র, অক্ষবাট। **To wrestle with God or in prayer**—to pray fervently ; আকুলভাবে প্রার্থনা করা।

wretch (rĕch), *n.* A miserable person ; a mean, base or vile creature ; হতভাগ্য লোক ; পামর, নরাধম, নচ্ছার, অধম [অনেক সময় রহস্যচ্ছলে গালি দেওয়ার কালেও ব্যবহৃত হয়]

wretch'-ĕd (rĕch-), *adj.* **1.** Miserable ; unhappy ; sunk in deep affliction, distress, or woe, as from want, anxiety or grief দুঃখী, হতভাগ্য ; দুর্ভাগ্য, মন্দভাগ্য ; দুর্দ্দশাগ্রস্ত। **2.** Woeful ; as, he is living a *wretched* life ; grievous ; calamitous ; দুঃখপূর্ণ ; কষ্টজনক ; বিপজ্জনক। **3.** Hateful ; contemptible ; as, a *wretched* house ; হেয়, জঘন্য ; ঘৃণ্য। **4.** Great ; severe ; as, *wretched* stupidity ; অত্যন্ত ; গুরুতর। **–ly,** *adv.*

wrick, rick (rĭk), *v. t.* & *n.* To slightly sprain or strain ; ঈষৎ মোচড়ান বা মচকান। ***Noun.*** A sprain or strain ; মোচড়, মচকানি।

wrig'-gle (rĭg-l), *v. i., t.* & *n.* **1.** To move with writhing contortions or twists of the body ; শরীর আঁকিয়া বাঁকিয়া চলা, মোচড়াইয়া চলা, কিলবিল করিয়া চলা। **2.** To proceed by crooked ways or shifts ; to gain one's ends by poltroonery; as, to *wriggle* out of a difficulty, বক্র পথে চলা ; হীনজনোচিত চাতুরী দ্বারা কিংবা কুট উপায়ে কোন কার্য্য সাধন করা। ***Verb t.*** To put into a wriggling motion ; to move by twisting and shifting ; আঁকিয়া বাঁকিয়া চলিতে বাধ্য করা ; আঁকিয়া বাঁকিয়া চলা, কিলবিল করিয়া চলা। ***Noun.*** Wriggling movement ; বক্রগতি, আঁকিয়া বাঁকিয়া চলন।

wright (rīt), *n.* A workman ; maker ; as, wheel-*wright* ; শ্রমজীবী ; প্রস্তুতকারী, নির্ম্মাতা।

wring (rĭng), *v. t, i.* & *n.* **1.** To twist and compress ; to turn and strain with violence ; as, to *wring* one's hands in pain ; চাপিয়া মোচড়ান ; মোচড়ান। **2.** To bend or strain out of its position ; as, to *wring* a mast ; নোয়াইয়া বা জোর করিয়া স্থানচ্যুত করা। **3.** To pain as by twisting, squeezing or racking ; to distress ; to torment ; as, let me *wring* your heart ; মোচড়াইয়া যন্ত্রণা দেওয়া ; কষ্ট দেওয়া ; নির্যাতন করা, পীড়ন করা। **4.** To distort the meaning of ; অর্থ বিকৃত করা। **5.** To squeeze or press out as moisture from wet cloth ; to draw forth by violence ; নিংড়ান ; নিংড়াইয়া বাহির করা। ***Verb i.*** **1.** To perform the action of wringing ; নিংড়ান। **2.** To cause pain as by twisting or compression ; মোচড়াইয়া যন্ত্রণা দেওয়া। ***Noun.*** Squeeze; চাপ, নিংড়ানি, মর্দ্দন। **Wring'-ing,** *pr. adj.* **Wringing-wet**—এরূপ ভিজা যে নিংড়াইলে জল পড়ে। **To wring a person's hand**—আবেগ বশে কাহারো হস্ত মর্দ্দন করা। **To wring neck of**—To kill chickens etc. by the wringing of neck ; গলা মোচড়াইয়া কুক্কুট শাবক প্রভৃতিকে বধ করা।

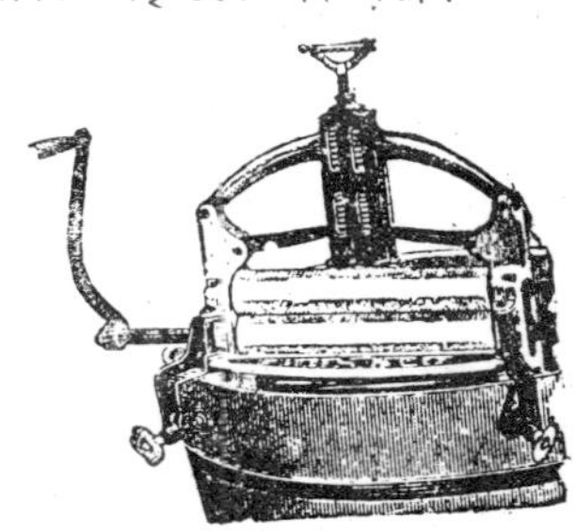

Wringer.

wring'-ĕr (rĭng-), *n.* **1.** One that wrings ; যে বা যাহা মোচড়ায়। **2.** A machine or device for pressing water out of anything, as from clothes after they have been washed ; ভিজা কাপড় নিংড়াইবার জন্য যন্ত্র বিশেষ।

wrin'-kle (rĭng-kl), *n., v. t.* & *i.* A small ridge, prominence or furrow formed by shrinking or contraction esp. of the skin produced by age; "A million *wrinkles* carved his skin"; কোঁচ, বলি, চর্ম্মরেখা, চর্ম্মতরঙ্গ, চর্ম্মভঙ্গ (cf. বলিপলিত), বার্দ্ধক্যের রেখা, চিন্তারেখা। ***Verb t.*** **1.** To contract into furrows and prominence; as, to *wrinkle* one's skin; to make rough and uneven; বলিপলিত করা, কুঞ্চিত করা; আবড়োথাবড়ো করা। **2.** To make or form by wrinkling; কুঞ্চিত করিয়া গঠন করা। ***Verb i.*** To form or become contracted into wrinkles; বলিপলিত হওয়া, কুঞ্চিত হওয়া। **-kly,** *adj.*

wrin'-kle (rĭng-kl), *n.* **1.** A hint; a notion; "It is one of the incidents out of which many folk may get a *wrinkle*"; আভাস, ইঙ্গিত, ইসারা, আঁচ; ধারণা। **2.** A bit of information; a tip; সংবাদ; গুপ্ত খবর। **3.** A dodge; চালাকি। **A wrinkle on one's horn**—কোন ব্যাপারে বিশেষ সুবিধালাভের সঙ্কেত।

wrist (rĭst), *n.* **1.** The joint by which the hand is united to arm কব্জা, মণিবন্ধ, করগ্রন্থি করগ্রন্থিক। **2.** The stud or pin projecting from a wheel to which a connecting rod is attached; সংযোজকদণ্ড সংলগ্ন করার জন্য চক্র হইতে উদ্গত শঙ্কুবিশেষ। **Wrist-band**—জামার আস্তিনের যে অংশদ্বারা কব্জা আবৃত হয়, কব্জিবন্ধ; জামার কপ্। **Wrist-drop**—করাগ্রের পেশীসমূহের শুস্ক বা জাড্য। **Wrist-pin**—Same as WRIST 2.

wrist'-let (rĭst-), *n.* **1.** An elastic band worn by ladies about the wrist to confine the upper of the glove; যে স্থিতিস্থাপক বেষ্টনীদ্বারা মহিলাগণ কব্জার সহিত দস্তানা বাঁধিয়া থাকেন, দস্তানাবন্ধ। **2.** Bracelet; বলয়, কঙ্কণ, বালা। **3.** (*Slang*) Hand-cuff; (ইতর ভাষায়) হাতকড়ি, হাতকড়া।

writ (rĭt), *n.* **1.** That which is written; লিখিত বিষয়। **2.** A legal document commanding a person to do something; as, a *writ* of attachment; পরোয়ানা। **3.** Scriptures; বাইবেল। **Holy** or **Sacred writ**—Same as WRIT 3. **To serve a writ on one**—To deliver a writ on one; পরোয়ানা জারি করা।

write rīt), *v. i.* & *t.* **1.** To form characters representing sounds or ideas; লেখা। **2.** To compose, as an author; as, to *write* a poem; লেখা, রচনা করা। **3.** To conduct correspondence; as, *write* to him; পত্রলিখা, পত্রব্যবহার করা। **4.** To act as a clerk or amanuensis; as, he *writes* in the local Sub-Registrary office; কেরাণীর কার্য করা, লিপিকরের কার্য্য করা। ***Verb t.*** **1.** To form or trace, as with a pen, pencil, or the like, on a paper or other material or by an engraver on wood; as, to *write* something on a piece of paper লেখা। **2.** To compose or publish as an author; গ্রন্থাদি রচনা করা, লেখা। **3.** To conduct epistolary correspondence; পত্র লিখা, পত্র ব্যবহার করা, লিখা (cf. আমি তাহাকে এই বিষয় লিখিতেছি)। **4.** To cover with character or letters traced by pen etc.; as, to *write* a sheet of paper; লিখিয়া পূর্ণ করা। **5.** To impress durably; "Whose memory is *written* on the earth with yet appearing blood"; মুদ্রিত করা। **6.** To make known, express, announce, indicate, disclose by means of characters formed by pen, etc.; "I chose to *write* the thing I dare not speak"; লিখিয়া জানান, ব্যক্ত করা, ঘোষণা করা বা সূচনা করা। **7.** To designate by writing; "By his *writing* he styled himself an ass"; to style in writing; to entitle; to record; to declare; "O that he were here to *write* me down an ass"; লিখিয়া নির্দ্দেশ করা; লিখিয়া অভিহিত করা; অভিহিত করা; লিপিবদ্ধ করা; ব্যক্ত করা। **To have one's name written in the book of life**—পরিত্রাণ প্রাপ্ত ব্যক্তিগণের তালিকায় নাম লিপিবদ্ধ হওয়া। **To write anything up**—To praise anything in paper; পত্রিকাদিতে কোন কিছুর প্রশংসা করা। **To write down**—To note down; to record; লিখিয়া রাখা; লিপিবদ্ধ করা। To disparage in writing; কোন কিছু লিখিয়া কাহাকে অপদস্থ করা। **To write off**—To cancel; হিসাব হইতে কাটিয়া দেওয়া; খরচের খাতায় লিখা, হিসাবের খাতায় খরচের দিকে লিখা। To compose with facility; অনায়াসে লিখা। **To write out**—To write down; লিখিয়া রাখা। To make a full record or statement of in writing; পূর্ণভাবে লিপিবদ্ধ করা। To exhaust literary ability or resources by writing too much; অতিরিক্ত লিখিয়া সাহিত্যিক ক্ষমতা বা সম্পদ নিঃশেষিত করা। **To write out fair**—To make a fair copy of; পরিচ্ছন্নভাবে নকল করা। **To write to**—To write a letter to some one; কাহারো নিকট চিঠি লিখা। **Writ large**—Aggravated; গুরুতর।

writ'-ĕr (rīt-), *n.* **1.** One who writes; লিপিকর, লিখক, লিখিয়ে (*colloq.*)। **2.** An author; as, he is a *writer* of great repute; লেখক, গ্রন্থকার। **3.** (*Scot.*) Law-agents, solicitors, attorneys or the like, sometimes their principal clerks; (স্কটলণ্ড) ব্যবহারজীবী, এটর্ণি, প্রভৃতি বা তাহাদের প্রধান কেরাণী। **4.** (*Obs.*) A clerk under the East-India Company, being the lowest in rank among company's servants; (অপ্রঃ) ইষ্টইণ্ডিয়া কোম্পানীর কেরাণী। **5.** A manual teaching how to write specified language : হস্তলিপি পুস্তক, লিপি-শিক্ষা। **—ship,** *n.* **Writer's cramp or palsy**—লেখকদিগের হস্তের পেশী-সমূহের একপ্রকার আড়ষ্টতা রোগ।

writhe (rīth), *v. i., t. & n.* **1.** To twist or roll the body about as in pain ; as, to *writhe* with agony ; to be distorted : to be stunned or mentally annoyed : as, to *writhe* under insult : যন্ত্রণায় গা মোচড়ান, যন্ত্রণায় গড়াগড়ি দেওয়া, আইঢাই করা, ধড়ফড় করা ; বিকৃত হওয়া ; মর্ম্মাহত হওয়া ; মনস্তাপ পাওয়া। ***Verb t.*** **1.** To twist or distort, as the body or limbs ; "Then Satan first knew pain, And *writhed* him to and fro" শরীর বা হাত পা মোচড়াইয়া দেওয়া। **2.** (*Rare*) To extort ; as, to *writhe* money out of a person ; (ক্বচিৎ ব্যবহৃত) পীড়ন করিয়া নেওয়া। **3.** To turn as in pain or distress ; "And *writhe*d his look towards the royal walls" ; কষ্ট বা যাতনার সহিত ফিরান। ***Noun.*** The act of writhing ; অঙ্গাকুঞ্চন, অঙ্গাকর্ষ, যন্ত্রণায় শরীর মোচড়ানি, যন্ত্রণায় গড়াগড়ি।

writ'-ing (rĭt-), *n.* **1.** The act of one who writes ; লিখন, লিপিবদ্ধকরণ, অক্ষরবিন্যাস। **2.** A written document ; দলীল। **3.** Handwriting : হস্তলিপি, হস্তাক্ষর। **4.** Any literary composition, books, pamhlets, etc.; as, the *writings* of Tennyson রচনা, গ্রন্থাবলী। **5.** An inscription ; "And Pilate wrote a title, and put on the cross, And the *writing* was, Jesus of Nazareth the King of the Jews"; ক্ষোদিত লিপি, ক্ষোদিতাক্ষর। **6.** A letter; পত্র, চিঠি। **7.** Manner or style of writing ; লিপিপদ্ধতি। **Writing-case**—মসী, লেখনী প্রভৃতি রাখার জন্য আধার। **Writing-desk**—সুবিধামত লিখার জন্য ঢালু মেজ। **Writing-paper**—লিখিবার কাগজ। **To put a thing in writing**—To note it down ; লিখিয়া রাখা।

writ'-ten (rĭt-n), See WRITE.

wrong (rŏng), *adj., adv., v. t. & n.* **1.** Improper : অনুচিত, অসঙ্গত, অযোগ্য, অনুপযোগী, অন্যায়। **2.** Incorrect ; অশুদ্ধ। **3.** Unjust or illegitimate : "If his cause be *wrong*" ; অন্যায়, ন্যায়বিরুদ্ধ, অবৈধ। **4.** Holding erroneous notion or view in matters of doctrine, opinion, or fact ; mistaken as, a *wrong* notion ; ভ্রান্ত মতাবলম্বী ; ভ্রান্ত, ভ্রমসঙ্কুল, ভ্রমাত্মক। **5.** In a bad condition ; out of order : as, this clock has gone *wrong* ; মন্দাবস্থ ; বিশৃঙ্খল। ***Adv.*** Wrongly ; unjustly : ভ্রান্তভাবে ; অন্যায়রূপে। ***Verb t.*** **1.** To treat unjustly ; to do wrong to : as, you have *wronged* me in this matter" : অন্যায় ব্যবহার করা ; কাহারো উপর অন্যায় করা। **2.** To impute evil unjustly to : "To *wrong* the dead, to *wrong* myself, and you" : অন্যায় দোষারোপ করা। **3.** To take a wrong view of ; ভ্রান্ত ধারণা পোষণ করা। ***Noun.*** **1.** Wrong action ; অন্যায় কার্য্য, অন্যায় কর্ম্ম, অন্যায়। **2.** Error : as, to be in the *wrong* ; ভ্রান্তি, ভুল। **3.** An insult or disgrace ; "'Tis he foul creature, that hath done thee *wrong*" ; অপমান, অবমাননা, কলঙ্ক। **5.** Any injury ; mischief ; "Each had suffered some exceeding *wrong*" ; ক্ষতি ; অনিষ্ট। **Wrong'-ly,** *adv.* **Wrong-doer**—অন্যায়কারী কুকর্ম্মকারী। (*Wrong-doing, n.*) **Wrong fount,** (*abbrev. wf*)—কোন অক্ষর বা শব্দ ঠিক হরফে কম্পোজ হয় নাই—ইহা নির্দ্দেশ করিতে এই সাঙ্কেতিক শব্দ ব্যবহৃত হয়। **Wrong-headed**—ভ্রান্ত এবং একগুঁয়ে। **He has hold of the wrong end of the stick**—He is pursuing a contrary course ; সে উল্টা পথ ধরিয়াছে। **He is on the wrong side of 50**—তিনি পঞ্চাশ বৎসর অপেক্ষা অধিকবয়স্ক।

In the wrong box—See under BOX. **King can do no wrong**—রাজা কোনরূপ অন্যায় কার্য্য করিতে পারেন না (ইংলণ্ডের রাজনৈতিক সূত্রবিশেষ। এই সূত্রানুসারে রাজার কার্য্যের জন্য মন্ত্রিগণই দায়ী রাজার স্বয়ং কোন দায়িত্ব নাই।) **Wrong side of the blanket**—See UNDER BLANKET.

wrote (rōt), *pt.* of WRITE (which see).

wroth (räth), *adj.* (*Poet. or rhet.*) Angry : (কবিতায় বা আলঙ্কারিক ভাষায়) ক্রুদ্ধ, কোপাবিষ্ট, রোষাবিষ্ট, খাপ্পা (*colloq.*)।

wrought, (rät), *pp.* & *pt.* of WORK (which see).

wrung, (rŭng), *pt.* & *pp.* of WRING (which see).

wry (rī), *adj.* Distorted ; bent ; skew : বিকৃত ; বাঁকা ; টেড়া, টের্চ্চা। **Wry'-ness,** *n.* The state of being wry ; বিরূপতা, বৈরূপ্য। **Wry-bill**—একপ্রকার তিত্তির পক্ষী। **Wrymouth**—বিভিন্ন প্রকার মৎস্য। **Wry-mouthed**—পরিহাসমিশ্র তোষামোদকারী। **Wryneck**—গ্রীবাস্তম্ভ

Wryneck.

(সাঃ পঃ) ; কাঠঠোকরা জাতীয় পক্ষি বিশেষ। **Wry-necked**—গ্রীবাস্তম্ভ রোগগ্রস্ত। **To make a wry face**—See FACE.

wȳ-ăn-dŏt, —dotte (-dŏt), *ns.* An American breed of fowl ; আমেরিকা দেশীয় একজাতীয় কুক্কুট।

wȳch-, wich-, witch- (wĭch), *pref.* Added in names of trees (as *wych-alder, wych-elm, wych-hazel*).

wye (wī) *n.* **1.** The letter Y ; Y অক্ষর। **2.** A Y-shaped thing ; Y অক্ষরের আকৃতি বস্তু।

Wȳke'-ham-ist (-ăm-), *n.* & *adj.* Of Winchester College; উইনচেষ্টার কলেজসম্বন্ধীয়। *Noun.* A student of the Win chester College (from the name of its founder William of Wikeham) ; উইনচেষ্টার কলেজের ছাত্র।

wȳnd, *n.* An alley in Scotch town ; স্কটলণ্ডের নগরীর উদ্যানবীথিকা।

wȳ'-vêrn, *n.* Same as WIVERN (which see).

X

X, **1.** The twenty-fourth letter of the English alphabet ; ইংরাজী বর্ণমালার চতুর্বিংশতিতম অক্ষর। **2.** The Roman numeral 10 ; রোমীয় সংখ্যা দশ। **3.** (*Algeb.*) The first unknown quantity ; প্রথম অজ্ঞাত রাশি (এই অর্থে ছোট হাতের *x* অক্ষর ব্যবহৃত হয়।) **4.** (*cap.*) Mysterious factor or influence ; অজ্ঞাত অঙ্গ বা প্রভাব। **5.** (*Chem, cap.*) Used as a symbol of Xenon ; জিনন নামক মূলপদার্থের সাঙ্কেতিক চিহ্ন। **5.** (*Cap.*) Christ, Christian ; খৃষ্ট ; খৃষ্ট-ধর্ম্মাবলম্বী। **XX** or **double-X, XXX** or **triple-X** — নির্দ্দিষ্ট শক্তিসম্পন্ন যবসুরা। **Xmas** —বড়দিন। **X-rays**—

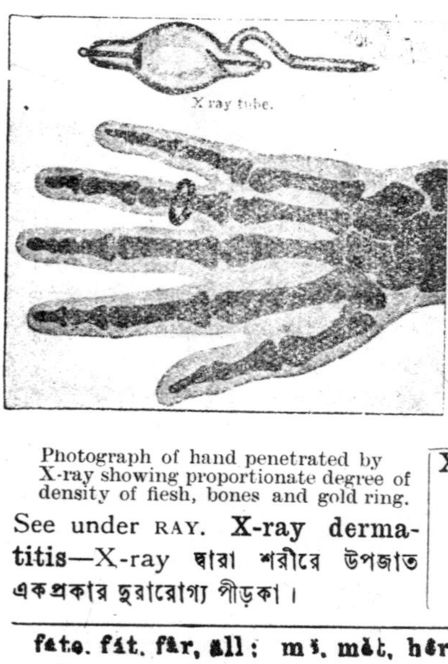

Photograph of hand penetrated by X-ray showing proportionate degree of density of flesh, bones and gold ring.

See under RAY. **X-ray dermatitis**—X-ray দ্বারা শরীরে উপজাত একপ্রকার দুরারোগ্য পীড়কা।

Xang'-ti (zăng-), *n.* The supreme being of the Chinese mythology ; চীনদিগের দেবরাজ।

xan'-thāte, (zăn-), *n.* A salt of xanthic acid ; xanthic অম্লের লবণ।

Xan'-thĭ-ăn (zăn-), *adj.* Pertaining to, or brought from, Xanthus ; as, the *Xanthian* marbles ; Xanthus নামক স্থানসম্বন্ধীয়, Xanthus হইতে সমানীত।

xan'-thic (zăn-), *adj.* Yellowish ; পীতাভ, বাসন্তী। **Xanthic acid**—একপ্রকার দ্রাবক। **Xanthic flowers**—একজাতীয় পীতবর্ণ পুষ্প—ইহারা কখনও নীলবর্ণে পরিণত হইতে পারে না, কেবল লোহিত ও শ্বেতবর্ণে পরিণত হইতে পারে।

xan'-thin (zăn-), **xan'-thine** (zăn-thīn), *ns.* **1.** The yellow colouring matter in flower which is insoluble in water; পুষ্পের পীতবর্ণ রঞ্জক-পদার্থ—যাহা জলে দ্রবণীয় নহে। **2.** The yellow dyeing matter contained in madder ; ম্যাডার লতার শিকড়ে প্রাপ্ত পীতবর্ণ রঞ্জকপদার্থ। **3.** A substance related to uric acid occurring in blood, urine, liver, etc. ; রক্ত, মূত্র, যকৃত, প্রভৃতিতে প্রাপ্ত ইয়ুরিক অম্লজাতীয় একপ্রকার পদার্থ।

Xan-thip'-pē (zăn-thĭ-*or*-tĭ-), *n.* A shrewish wife ; দুঃশীলা ভার্য্যা, কুঁদুলে স্ত্রী। [সক্রেটিসের পত্নী Xanthippeএর নাম হইতে গৃহীত।]

xan'-thīte (zăn-), *n.* A minealr of a yellowish colour ; একপ্রকার পীতবর্ণ খনিজ পদার্থ।

xan'-thĭ-ŭm (zăn-), *n.* A composite plant that bears yellow flowers ; পীতপুষ্পপ্রসূ একপ্রকার মিশ্র ক্ষুপ। *Xanthium orientate* — বন ওকড়া (বেলঃ)।

xan-tho-car'-pous (zăn-thŏ-câr-pŭs), *adj.* (*Bot.*) Having yellow fruits ; (উদ্ভিদ্‌বিদ্যা) পীত-ফলপ্রসূ, পীতফলা।

Xan'-thŏch'-rŏ-ī (zăn-), *n. pl.* (*Ethnol.*) The fair, white race, including the Teutons, Scandinavians, Celts and Slavs ; টিউটন, স্কেনডিনেভিয়, কেল্ট এবং শ্লেভ প্রভৃতি শ্বেতকায় (জাতি), শ্বেতকায় (সাঃ পঃ)। **—tho-chro'-ic,** *adj.*

xan-tho-mel'-a-nous (zăn-thŏ-mĕl-ă-nŭs), *adj.* Denoting a type of man with black hair, and yellow, brown or olive skin : কৃষ্ণকেশ এবং পীত, কপিশ, এবং শ্যামকায় মানবজাতিসমূহ সম্পর্কীয়।

xan'-thŏ-phȳll (zăn-), *n.* The yellow colouring-matter of autumn leaves ; শরৎকালীন পত্রের পীতবর্ণ রঞ্জকপদার্থ, পর্ণপীত (সাঃ পঃ)।

xan-tho-sper'-mous (zăn-thŏ-spêr-mŭs), *adj.* Having yellow seeds ; পীতবীজ।

xan'-thous (zăn-thŭs), *adj.* Denoting the yellow tribes of mankind ; পীতজাতিসমূহ সম্পর্কীয়।

xe′-bĕc (zē-), *n.* A small threemasted vessel with lateen and square sails ; একপ্রকার ক্ষুদ্র ত্রিমাস্তুল পোত।

Xebec.

xen′-ĕ-lā′-sĭ-ă (zĕn-), *n.* A Spartan law forbidding the unauthorised residence in Sparta of aliens ; প্রাচীন স্পার্টা নগরীতে প্রচলিত আইন বিশেষ—যাহার বলে বিদেশীয়গণ অনুমতি বিনা নগরে বাস করিতে পারিত না।

xe′-nĭ-ăl (zē-), *adj.* Pertaining to hospitality ; অতিথিসৎকারসম্বন্ধীয়, আতিথ্যসম্বন্ধীয়।

xe′-nĭ-ŭm (zē-), *pl. xenia n.* A present given to an ambassador, a guest or stranger ; রাজদূত, বিদেশী এবং অতিথিদিগকে প্রদত্ত উপহার।

Xe-noc-ra-te′-ăn (zē-nŏc-rā-shĭ-), **Xen-ŏ-crăt′-ĭc** (zĕn-), *adj.* Pertaining to the Greek philosopher Xenocrates ; গ্রীক দার্শনিক Xenocrates ; সম্বন্ধীয়।

xen-ŏ-dō-chē′-ŭm (zĕn-), **-chī′-ŭm,** *ns.* (*pl. xenodochea, xenenodochia*). **1.** (*Antiq.*) A building for the reception of stranger ; (প্রত্নতত্ত্ব) অতিথিশালা। **2.** (Middle Ages) A room in a monastery for the reception and entertainment of strangers and for the relief of paupers ; মধ্যযুগে খৃষ্টীয় মঠের যে কক্ষ অতিথিশালা বা অনাথ-নিবাসরূপে ব্যবহৃত হইত।

xe-nŏg′-ă-my̆ (zĕ-), *n.* (*Bot.*) Same as CROSS FERTILIZATION. **-mous,** *adj.*

xen-ŏ-gĕn′-ĕ-sĭs (zĕn-), *n.* **1.** (*Biol.*) Same as HETEROGENESIS (which see). **2.** The fancied production of an organism altogether and permanently unlike the parents ; জনক বা জননীর সহিত সম্পূর্ণরূপে এবং স্থায়ীভাবে বিসদৃশ অঙ্গীর কল্পিত উৎপাদন।

xen′-ŏn (zĕn-), *n.* A gas somewhat like argon and helium, found in very minute quantities in the air (Symbol, X ; atom. wt., 130·7) ; একপ্রকার বাষ্প—যাহা বায়ুতে ঈষৎ পরিমাণে পাওয়া যায়, অজ্ঞাতিক।

xe-răn′-thĕ-mŭm (zē-), *n.* Kinds of annual with composite flowers. এক জাতীয় ক্ষুপ।

xe-rā′-sĭ-ă (zē-), *n.* A disease in the hair, in which it becomes dry and ceases to grow ; একপ্রকার কেশরোগ—যাহাতে কেশ শুষ্ক হয় এবং বৃদ্ধি পায় না, কেশশোষ।

xe-rō-dêr′-mă (zē-), *n.* A general dryness of the surface of the skin, occasioned by abnormal diminution of the secretion of the sebiparous organs ; একপ্রকার চর্ম্মরোগ—যাহাতে চর্ম্ম শুষ্ক ও খসখসে হয়, বিশেষতঃ যাহাতে চর্ম্ম হইতে একপ্রকার দূষিত তরল পদার্থ নিঃসৃত হইয়া থাকে।

xe-roph′-ĭ-lous (zē-rŏf-ĭ-lŭs), *adj.* Adapted to hot and dry chimate ; উষ্ণ এবং শুষ্ক আবহাওয়ার উপযোগী।

xe-rŏph-thăl′-mĭ-ă (zē-), *n.* An abnormal dryness of the eyeball ; অক্ষিগোলকের অস্বাভাবিক শুষ্কতা রোগ।

xe′-rō-tēs (zē-), *n.* A dry habit or disposition : শুষ্কপ্রকৃতি।

xiph′-oid (zĭf-ŏyd), *adj.* Sword-shaped ; অস্যাকৃতি **Xiphoid appendge, cartilage** or **process**—বুকাস্থির (sternum) তলোয়ারের আকৃতি উপাঙ্গ বা উপবৃদ্ধি।

xiph-ō-stêr′-nŭm (zĭf-), *n.* Same as XIPHOID APPENDAGE.

xo′-ă-nŏn (zŏ-), *n.* (*Pl. xoana*) A primitive usu. wooden image of deity, supposed to have fallen from heaven ; আকাশ হইতে পতিত বলিয়া কল্পিত প্রাচীন মূর্ত্তি, বিশেষতঃ দারুমূর্ত্তি।

xy′-lĕm (zĭ-) *n.* (*Bot.*) Woody tissue ; (উদ্ভিদ্ বিদ্যা) কাষ্ঠময় বিতান-তন্তু, দারুক (সাঃ পঃ)।

xy′-lene (zĭ-lēn), *n.* (*Chem.*) A volatile inflammable liquid ; একপ্রকার উদ্বায়ী এবং দাহ্য তরল পদার্থ [$C_2 H_4 (CH_3)_2$].

xy′-līte (zĭ-), *n.* A kind of asbestos ; একপ্রকার শঙ্খপলিতা।

xy-lō-băl′-să-mŭm (zĭ-), *n.* **1.** The wood of the balsam-tree একপ্রকার নির্য্যাসপ্রদ বৃক্ষের কাষ্ঠ। **2.** A decoction of the dry twigs of this tree ; উক্ত বৃক্ষের শুষ্ক প্রশাখা সমূহ হইতে প্রস্তুত ক্বাথ।

xy′-lō-cărp (zĭ-), *n.* **1.** Hard woody fruit ; কঠিন কাষ্ঠবৎ ফল। **2.** A tree bearing such fruit ; উক্তরূপ ফলপ্রসূ বৃক্ষ, দারুফলা। **-car′-pous,** *adj.*

xy′-lō-grăph (zĭ-), *n.* **1.** Wood-engraving ; কাষ্ঠের উপর খোদাই। **2.** A mechanical copy of the grain of wood used for surface decoration ; কোন কিছুর উপরিভাগে মুদ্রিত করার জন্য কাষ্ঠের অংশু বিন্যাসের ছাপ। **-log′-ra-pher,** *n.* **-log′-raph-y,** *n.*

xy-lŏm′-ĕ-têr (zĭ-), *n.* An instrument for determining the specific gravity of wood ; কাষ্ঠের আপেক্ষিক গুরুত্ব নির্ণয়ের জন্য একপ্রকার যন্ত্র, দারুমান।

xy′-lŏn-ĭte (zĭ-), *n.* Same as CELLULOID, *n.*

xy-loph′-a-gous (zĭ-lŏf-ă-gŭs), *adj.* Feeding on wood ; as, *xylophagous* insects ; কাষ্ঠভোজী, দারুভোজী, কাষ্ঠভুক্।

xy′-lō-phōne (zĭ-), *n.* **1.** A musical instrument consisting of wooden bars, sounded by hammers or rubbing ; একপ্রকার বাদ্যযন্ত্র। **2.** An instrument to determine the vibrative properties of different kinds of wood ; বিভিন্ন প্রকার কাষ্ঠের

স্পন্দনশক্তি নির্ণয়ের জন্য যন্ত্রবিশেষ, স্পন্দনমান।

xy-lŏs′-tĕ-ĭn (zī-), *n.* A poisonous principle obtained from the seeds of a species of honeysuckle; বৃক্ষবিশেষের বীজ হইতে প্রাপ্ত একপ্রকার বিষাক্ত দ্রব্য।

xys′-têr (zĭs-), *n.* A surgeon's instrument for scraping bones; হাড় চাঁচিবার জন্য অস্ত্রচিকিৎসকদিগের একপ্রকার যন্ত্র, অস্থিউল্লেখন যন্ত্র, অস্থিপ্রলেখন যন্ত্র।

xys′-tŭs (zĭs-), *n.* A covered portico or open court for athletic exercises; মল্লক্রীড়ার জন্য আবৃতদ্বারপ্রকোষ্ঠ বা প্রাঙ্গণ।

Y

Y, **1.** The twenty-fifth letter of the English alphabet; ইংরাজী বর্ণমালার পঞ্চবিংশতিতম অক্ষর। **2.** (*Algeb., l.c.*) The second unknown quantity; (বীজগণিত) দ্বিতীয় অব্যক্ত রাশি। **3.** (*Cap. chem.*) Symbol used to denote Yttrium; ইত্রিবক ধাতুর সাঙ্কেতিক চিহ্ন। **4.** As a medieval Roman numeral, Y stands for 150, and $\bar{Y}$ for 150,000; মধ্যযুগে Y ১৫০ এবং $\bar{Y}$ ১৫০,০০০ এই সংখ্যাদ্বয়ের সাঙ্কেতিক চিহ্ন। **Y-cartilage**—Y-অক্ষরাকৃতি তরুণাস্থি। **Y-cross**—Y-অক্ষরাকৃতি ক্রুশ। **Y-joint**—Y-অক্ষরাকৃতি সন্ধি। **Y-level**—ইঞ্জিনীয়রগণের স্থরাসূত্র (See SPIRIT-LEVEL under LEVEL). **Y-ligament**—Y-অক্ষরাকৃতি সন্ধিবন্ধ। **Y-moth**—একপ্রকার তসরে পোকা। **Y-track**—যে লৌহবর্ত্মের প্রথম পথে Y-অক্ষরের আকারে দুইটী শাখাপথ মিলিত হইয়াছে।

yăc′-ca (-ă), *n.* The wood of a West-Indian evergreen tree suitable for cabinet work; পশ্চিম ভারতীয় দ্বীপপুঞ্জের চিরহরিৎ বৃক্ষবিশেষ।

yacht (yŏt), *n.* & *v. i.* A light, elegantly-furnished vessel, used for pleasure trips or for racing; a state-vessel; একপ্রকার সুসজ্জিত প্রমোদতরণী, প্রমোদপোত, কেলিতরণী, কেলিপোত; রাজকীয় প্রমোদতরী। ***Verb i.*** To race or cruise in yacht; প্রমোদতরণীতে বিচরণ বা যাত্রা করা, প্রমোদতরণীদ্বারা বাইচ খেলা, প্রমোদতরণী চালনা করা। **Yacht′-er, Yacht-ing,** *ns.* **Yacht-built**—প্রমোদতরণীবৎ নির্ম্মিত। **Yacht-club** — প্রমোদতরণীর অধিকারীদিগের সম্মিলনী। **Yachtsman** — One that owns or sails a yacht; প্রমোদতরণীর অধিকারী, প্রমোদতরণীর চালক।

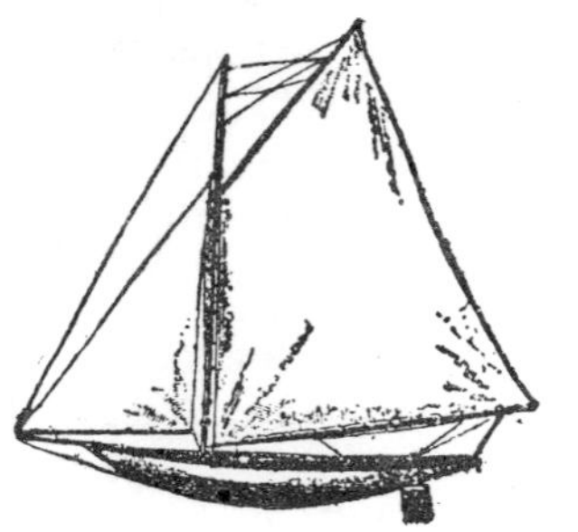

Yacht.

yä′-gêr, *n.* One belonging to a body of German light infantry armed with rifles; জর্ম্মণদেশীয় লঘু অস্ত্রধারী সৈন্যদল বিশেষের লোক।

yah (yă), *Interj.* An interjection indicating derision; ছি ছি!, রাম রাম!

yă′-hōō, *n.* **1.** A brute in human shape; নরাকৃতি পশু (Swift কৃত Gulliver's Travels নামক গ্রন্থোক্ত ব্যক্তি বিশেষ)। **2.** A rough boorish person; ইতর প্রকৃতির লোক, বর্ব্বর, নরপশু।

Yah′-veh (yâ-vă), **Yah′-vist** (yâ-), *ns.* Same as JEEHOVAH, JEEHOVIST. **—vis′-tic,** *adj.*

yăk, *n.* A wild ox with long silky hair found in Tibet; চমরী গাই, চমরী। [Syn. দীর্ঘবালা, গিরিপ্রিয়া।]

Yak.

yăm, *n.* A climbing plant, cultivated in tropical climates for its large roots; চুবড়ী আলু, সুথকন্দ, কাম আলু (Dioscorea alata), খুম আলু (*ib.*) [Tel. *Perin-valli-kelenga* (Dioscorea sativa), Tam. *yams-colung* (*ib.*)]

yăm′-bōō, *n.* A plant which produces fruit like plum: একপ্রকার ফল।

yamen, yamun, *ns.* A Chinese mandarin's official residence: চীনদেশীয় রাজকর্ম্মচারিগণের সরকারী বাসভবন।

Yan′-kee (yăng-kē), *n.* & *adj.* **1.** The popular name of the American citizens of New England, but applied indiscriminately to the inhabitants of the United States; মার্কিণ মুলুকের লোক। **2.** An inhabitant of New England; New Englandএর অধিবাসী। ***Adj.***

Pertaining to the inhabitants of America ; আমেরিকার অধিবাসিগণ-সম্পর্কীয়। **–dom, –ism,** *ns.* **Yankee Doodle**—আমেরিকার স্বর ও তান। **Yankee shilling** — নিউ-ইংলণ্ডের শিলিং (= ১৬⅔ সেণ্ট)।

yăp, *v. t.* & *n.* To bark ; ঘেউ ঘেউ করা। ***Noun.*** Cry of dog ; ঘেউ ঘেউ।

yăpp, *n.* A style of binding, used esp. on Bible, in which a limp cover projects over the edges on both sides, so that the flaps protect them ; এক ধরণের পুস্তক বাঁধাই—যাহাতে কোমল স্থিতিস্থাপক চর্ম্ম উভয় পার্শ্বে প্রান্তের উপর প্রলম্বিত থাকে।

yärd, *n.* **1.** A standard measure of three feet ; গজ। **2.** A yard-length of material ; এক গজ জিনিষ। **3.** A long beam slung crosswise to a mast and supporting a sail ; মাস্তুল-সংলগ্ন পাইলদণ্ড। **4.** (*Obs.*) Penis ; (অপ্রঃ) লিঙ্গ। **Lateen yard**—টেরছাভাবে স্থাপিত পাইলদণ্ড। **Square yard**—শয়ানভাবে স্থাপিত পাইলদণ্ড। **Yard-arm**—পাইলদণ্ডের অন্যতম প্রান্ত। **Yard-measure**—গজের মাপের জন্য দণ্ড ফিতা, প্রভৃতি। **Yard-stick, Yard-wand**—গজকাঠি, মাপকাঠি। **Man the yards**—পাইলদণ্ডের সহিত এক লাইনে লোক রাখ বা দাঁড়াও (অভিবাদনের জন্য)।

yärd, *n.* & *v. t.* **1.** A piece of enclosed ground ; as, timber *yard* ; বৃতিবেষ্টিত অঙ্গন, চত্বর। ***Verb t.*** To put cattle in stock-yard ; খোঁয়াড়ে গোমহিষাদি রাখা। **Yard'-age,** *n.* **Cab-yard**—গাড়ীর আড্ডা। **Railway-yard** — রেলওয়ে ষ্টেশনের নিকটবর্ত্তী যে স্থানে রেলগাড়ী প্রভৃতি রক্ষিত হয়। **Stock-yard**—গোমহিষাদির খোঁয়াড়। **Tan-yard**—যে প্রাঙ্গণে চর্ম্মসংস্কার করা হয়। **Yard-man** — রেলওয়ের কারখানার মিস্ত্রী, রেলওয়ের কারখানার অধ্যক্ষ।

yāre, *n.* (*Obs.*) Ready ; dexterous ; prompt ; (অপ্রঃ) প্রস্তুত ; দক্ষ ; সত্বর।

yärn, *n.* & *v. i.* **1.** Woollen thread ; material spun and prepared for weaving, knitting, etc. ; পশমীসূতা, উর্ণাসূত্র ; সূত্র, সূতা। **2.** Any of the threads forming a strand of rope ; রজ্জুর গুণ। **3.** A story ; an anecdote ; as, to spin a *yarn* ; গল্প, কেচ্ছা (*colloq.*) ; উপকথা। ***Verb i.*** To tell a yarn ; গল্প বলা। **To spin yarns**—গল্প ফাঁদা।

yăr'-row (-ō), *n.* A plant having a strong odour and pungent taste ; একপ্রকার তীব্রাস্বাদবিশিষ্ট উগ্রগন্ধ ক্ষুপ।

yăsh-măk', *n.* A veil worn by Moslem women in public ; এক-প্রকার অবগুণ্ঠন—যাহা মুসলমান রমণীগণ প্রকাশ্য রাস্তায় বাহির হইবার সময় পরিধান করিয়া থাকেন।

yăt'-ă-ghan, (-găn), *n.* A long Turkish dagger ; তুরস্কদেশীয় দীর্ঘ ছোরা।

yaw (yä), *v. i.* & *n.* To steer wild or from a straight course, as a ship ; জাহাজ বিপথে চালান, প্রকৃত পথ হইতে বিচ্যুত ভাবে পোত চালনা করা। ***Noun.*** Deviation of a ship from the direct line of her course ; পথ হইতে জাহাজের বিচ্যুতি।

yawl (yäl), *v. i.* & *n.* To howl ; চীৎকার করা। ***Noun.*** Yell ; চীৎকার।

yawl(yäl), *n.* A small ship's boat ; a small-decked fishing boat ; জালিবোট, ডিঙ্গি নৌকা ; জেলে ডিঙ্গি।

yawn (yän), *v. i., t.* & *n.* **1.** To be wide open ; as, the hell *yawns* for him ; ফাঁক হওয়া। **2.** To to have the mouth open involuntarily while a deep breath is taken ; to gape ; জৃম্ভন করা, হাঁইতোলা ; হাঁ করা। **3.** To desire to swallow anything ; to express desire by yawning ; to be eager ; to long ; "The chiefest thing at which lay reformers *yawn* is, that the clergy may, through conformity in condition, be poor, as the apostles were" ; কোন কিছু গ্রাস করার ইচ্ছা করা ; মুখ ব্যাদান করিয়া ইচ্ছা প্রকাশ করা ; ব্যগ্র হওয়া ; কামনা করা, স্পৃহা করা। **3.** To open the mouth in wonder ; বিস্ময়ে মুখ ব্যাদান করা। ***Verb t.*** To utter with a yawn ; as, he *yawned* good night ; হাঁই দিয়া উচ্চারণ করা বা বলা। ***Noun.*** The act of yawning ; হাঁইতোলন, জৃম্ভন, জৃম্ভা। **Yawn'-ing-ly,** *adv.*

yaws (yäz), *n.* Same as FRAMBOESIA.

y-clĕpt' (ĭ-), *adj.* (*Archaic*) Called ; কথিত।

yē', *n.* The nominative plural of the second person, of which *thou* is the singular, now superseded by *you*, except in the solemn style ; তোমরা (সাধারণতঃ কবিতায় ব্যবহৃত হয়)।

yea (yā), *Particle* & *n.* (*Archaic, pl. yeas*) Yes ; হাঁ, তাই বটে। ***Noun.*** **1.** Consistency ; harmony ; সঙ্গতি ; সামঞ্জস্য। **2.** An affirmative vote ; নির্ব্বাচনে সম্মতি-সূচক মত। **Yeas and nays**—(অপ্রঃ) সম্মতিসূচক বা অসম্মতিসূচক শব্দ।

yean (yēn), *v. t.* & *i.* To bring forth young, as a sheep or lamb ; বাচ্চা দেওয়া। **Yean'-ling,** *n.* A young lamb or a kid ; ছাগলছানা, ভেড়ার ছানা, মেষ শাবক, ছাগল শাবক, অজশিশু।

year (yēr), *n.* **1.** The period of time during which any planet makes one revolution in its orbit ; as, the *year* of Jupiter ; যে কালে কোন গ্রহ স্বীয় কক্ষের চতুর্দ্দিকে ভ্রমণ করে, বর্ষ। **2.** Twelve months ; বৎসর, বর্ষ, বছর (*colloq.*)। **3.** (*Pl.*) Old age ; as, a man in *years* ; বার্দ্ধক্য। **Calendar year** — যে কোন ক্রমিক দ্বাদশ মাস। **Civil or legal year**—১লা জানুয়ারী হইতে ৩১শে ডিসেম্বর পর্য্যন্ত কাল, সাবনবর্ষ। **Leap-year**—পরিবৎসর (See also LEAP)। **Lunar year**—চান্দ্রবর্ষ। **Platonic, Great**

or **Perfect year**—২৬,০০০ বর্ষ পরিমিত কাল। **Sidereal year** —সৌরবর্ষ। **Year-book**—বর্ষে বর্ষে প্রকাশিত যে পুস্তকে বর্ত্তমান বর্ষ পর্য্যন্ত নানা বিষয়ের জ্ঞাতব্য বিবরণ প্রদত্ত হইয়া থাকে, বর্ষ-পুস্তক। **Year-long**—Lasting a year; বর্ষস্থায়ী। **All the year round**—The wole year; সারাবৎসর। **From year to year, Year by year**—As years go by; বর্ষে বর্ষে, প্রতি বৎসর। **In the year**—Long time ago; মান্ধাতার আমলে। **In years**—বৃদ্ধ। **The school year**—বিদ্যালয়ের বর্ষ। **Year in year out**—Throughout the year; সারাবৎসর ধরিয়া। **Years of discretion** — যে বয়সে বালকের হিতাহিত জ্ঞান জন্মে। **Year of Grace**—খৃষ্টাব্দ।

year′-ling (yĕr-), *n.* & *adj.* **1.** A beast one year old; এক বৎসর বয়স্ক পশুশাবক। **2.** (*Racing*) A colt a year old dating from first January of the year of foaling; যে বৎসর প্রসূত হইয়াছে তাহার ১লা জানুয়ারী হইতে ধরিয়া এক বৎসর বয়স্ক অশ্বশাবক। ***Adj.*** Being a year old; as, a *yearling* heifer; of a year's duration; একবৎসর বয়স্ক; বর্ষস্থায়ী।

year′-ly (yĕr-), *adj.* & *adv.* **1.** Annual; বার্ষিক। **2.** Lasting a year; as, a *yearly* plant; বর্ষস্থায়ী। ***Adv.*** Annually; once a year; বর্ষে, বর্ষে, প্রতি বৎসর; বৎসরে একবার।

yearn (yĕrn), *v. i.* **1.** To feel an earnest desire; to desire wistfully; to be rendered uneasy with eager longing for or want of a thing; "Your mother's heart *yearns* towards you"; আকুলভাবে আকাঙ্ক্ষা করা, ব্যাকুলতা বোধ করা; লালসা করা, স্পৃহা করা; আকুল হইয়া উঠা, উতলা হইয়া উঠা। **2.** (*Rare*) To grieve; "Falstaff is dead, and we must *yearn* therefore"; (কচিদ্ ব্যবহৃত) শোক করা, দুঃখ করা। **Yearn′-ing,** *adj.* & *n.* Longing; আকুল, সতৃষ্ণ। ***Noun.*** A longing desire; a strong feeling of tenderness; স্পৃহা; আকুলতা, ব্যাকুলতা, সকরুণভাব। **Yearn′-ing-ly,** *adv.*

yeast (yēst), *n.* Barm or ferment, appearing in the foam, froth or flower of beer or other liquor in fermentation; সুরামণ্ড, মণ্ডোদক, কিণ্ব, গাঁজলা, কাদম্বরীবীজ, সুরাবীজ। **2.** Ferment; agitation; "The crudities and *yeast* of youth"; উত্তেজনা; বিক্ষোভ। **3.** Foam; ফেন। **Yeast-plant**—দারুকাণু (সাঃ পঃ)। **Yeast-powder**—রুটি প্রস্তুতে সুরামণ্ডের পরিবর্ত্তে যে চূর্ণ ব্যবহৃত হয়, কিণ্ব চূর্ণ, সুরাবীজ চূর্ণ।

yeast′-y (yēst-), *adj.* **1.** Pertaining to, containing, or resembling, yeast; frothy; spumy; সুরাবীজ-সম্বন্ধীয়, সুরাবীজাত্মক, সুরাবীজবৎ; ফেনিল, ফেনাযুক্ত; গাঁজলাদার। **2.** Superficial; as, *yeasty* profession; wordy; ভাসা ভাসা; শব্দবহুল। **—i-ness,** *n.*

yělk, *n.* Same as YOLK (which see).

yěll, *v. i., t.* & *n.* **1.** To cry out with a hideous noise; to cry or scream with agony or horror; "Poor Puck doth *yell*, poor Puck doth roar"; বিকট চীৎকার করা; ভয় বা বিভীষিকায় ভীষণ চীৎকার করা। **2.** To indulge in a violent fit of laughter; বিকট অট্টহাস্য করা। ***Verb t.*** To utter with a yell or shrill tone; to scream out; বিকট চীৎকার করিয়া বলা; বিকট চীৎকার করিয়া উঠা। ***Noun.*** **1.** A loud hideous cry; a shriek or scream as of horror or agony; an uncontrollable burst of laughter; বিকট চীৎকার; বিকট আর্ত্তনাদ; বিকট অট্টহাস্য। **2.** (*U. S. Univ.*) A shout or cheer used esp. by college-students; (মার্কিণযুক্তরাজ্যে) বিশ্ববিদ্যালয়ে বালকগণের চীৎকার বা উৎসাহসূচক ধ্বনি।

yěl′-low (-ō), *n., adj., v. t.* & *i.* **1.** A colour like that of gold; পীতবর্ণ, হরিদ্রাবর্ণ, স্বর্ণবর্ণ, হলুদে রঙ্গ সোণালী রঙ্গ। [কতিপয় পীতবস্তুর নাম:—স্বর্ণ, মণ্ডুক, কুঞ্জের বস্ত্র, বানর, চক্রবাক শালি, কর্ণিকার, হরিতাল, মনঃশিলা, শারিকামুখ, কিঞ্জল্ক, বল্কল, গৌরী, দ্বাপর, ব্রহ্মা, গোমূত্র মধু, পিত্তল, গন্ধক, দীপ, হরিদ্রা, গোরোচনা, পুষ্পরাগ, শণ, অতসী, গাঁদা, চম্পক, কাঞ্চনপুষ্প, পাকা লেবু।] **2.** (*Archaic*) Jaundice; jealousy; (অপ্রঃ) কামলারোগ; ঈর্ষা, অসূয়া। **3.** Any pigment or dye which colours yellow; পীতবর্ণ রঞ্জকপদার্থ। **4.** The name of various kinds of moth or butterfly; নানাপ্রকার তসরে পোকা ও প্রজাপতির নাম। **5.** A very destructive disease of the peach; পীচগাছের একপ্রকার সাংঘাতিক রোগ। ***Adj.*** **1.** Of the colour yellow; পীত, পীতবর্ণ, স্বর্ণবর্ণ, হরিদ্রাবর্ণ। **2.** Jaundiced; hence, envious; suspicious; melancholy; "With a green and *yellow* melancholy"; কামলারোগগ্রস্ত হিংসুক; সন্দিগ্ধচিত্ত, ঈর্ষাপরায়ণ, অসূয়া, পরবশ; বিষাদময়। **3.** Sensational; as, a *yellow* paper; উত্তেজনাপূর্ণ। **4.** (*Slang*) Cowardly; mean; (ইতরভাষায়) কাপুরুষোচিত; হীন, নীচ। ***Verb t.*** To render yellow (also *v. i.*) পীতবর্ণে পরিণত করা হরিদ্রাবর্ণ করা। ***Verb i.*** To grow or become yellow; "The *yellowing* plains"; পীতবর্ণে পরিণত হওয়া, পীতবর্ণ ধারণ করা। **—ing,** *n.* A process in the manufacture of pins; আলপিন প্রস্তুতের প্রক্রিয়া-বিশেষ। ইহাতে রাঙ্গ লাগাইবার পূর্ব্বে দ্রাবকরক্ষিত আলপিন জলে সিদ্ধ করিতে হয়। **—ish,** *adj.* Slightly yellow; পীতাভ, ঈষৎ পীতবর্ণ, হরিদ্রাভ, স্বর্ণাভ। **—ness,** *n.* The quality of being yellow; পীতিমা, হরিদ্রত্ব। **Yellow-archangel** — একপ্রকার ক্ষুপ। **Yellowback**—পূর্ব্বে মলাটরূপে ব্যবহৃত পীতবর্ণ কাগজ হইতে প্রস্তুত সস্তা উপন্যাস। **Yellow-balsam**—একপ্রকার গন্ধবিরজার গাছ।

Yellow-bark—সিন্‌কোনা বৃক্ষের পীত বা কমলাবর্ণ জরঘ্ন ত্বক্। **Yellow-barred-brindle**—একপ্রকার পীতবর্ণ তসরে পোকা। **Yellow-bellies**—ভেক-সকল; মেক্‌সিকো দেশের লোক. **Yellow-belly**—একপ্রকার পীতবর্ণ তসরে পোকা। **Yellow-berries**—Levantএর এক-প্রকার ক্ষুপের শুষ্ক ফল—যাহা হইতে একপ্রকার পীতবর্ণ রঞ্জকপদার্থ প্রাপ্ত হওয়া যায়। **Yellow-billed wood-pecker**—একপ্রকার পীতচঞ্চু কাঠঠোকরা পক্ষী। **Yellow-bird**—আমেরিকা-দেশীয় একপ্রকার সুবর্ণ পক্ষী। **Yellow-blossomed**—পীতপুষ্পী। **Yellow-Book, Yellow-paper**—ফরাসী শাসন-তন্ত্রের কার্য্যবিবরণী। **Yellow-boy**—(ইতর-ভাষায়) স্বর্ণমুদ্রা। **Yellow-browed warbler**—পশ্চিম এসিয়ার একপ্রকার পীতবর্ণ পক্ষী। **Yellow-bugle**—একপ্রকার ক্ষুপ। **Yellow caps**—চীন সম্রাট Han-ling-tee এর সময়ের প্রজাবিদ্রোহ (বিদ্রোহিগণ এই বিদ্রোহে পীতবর্ণ টুপি পরিধান করিয়াছিল।) **Yellow-cartilage**—একপ্রকার তরুণাস্থি—যাহার অংশসমূহ স্থিতিস্থাপক বিধানগ্রন্থির (tissue) সদৃশ হইয়া থাকে। **Yellow-centaury**—Same as YELLOW-WORT. **Yellow-chestnut**—একপ্রকার বৃক্ষ। **Yellow-copperas**—একপ্রকার অর্দ্ধস্বচ্ছ পীতবর্ণ খনিজ পদার্থ। **Yellow-coralline**—গন্ধকদ্রাবক, কার্ব্বলিক এসিড এবং অক্‌সালিক এসিড হইতে প্রস্তুত একপ্রকার কমলাবর্ণ রঞ্জক পদার্থ। **Yellow-covered**—পীতমলাটযুক্ত। **Yellow-covered literature**—সস্তা-দামের উত্তেজনাপূর্ণ উপন্যাস প্রভৃতি। **Yellow-earth**—গৈরিক, গিরিমাটী। **Yellow-eye**—কটাচক্ষু, পিঙ্গলনেত্র। **Yellow-fever**—পীতজ্বর (এই জ্বরাক্রান্ত রোগী-দিগের দেহের চর্ম্ম পীতবর্ণ ধারণ করে)। **Yellow-fish**—পীতপুচ্ছী মৎস্য। **Yellow-flag**—একপ্রকার ক্ষুপ। কুষ্ঠাশ্রম এবং নৌবিভাগীয় আরোগ্যশালা হইতে এবং সংক্রামক রোগের প্রাদুর্ভাবকালে জাহাজ হইতে প্রদর্শিত পীতপতাকা। **Yellow-gum**—শিশুদিগের কামলারোগ। **Yellow-gum tree**—কয়েক প্রকার Eucalyptus গাছের নাম। **Yellow-hammer, Yellow-ammer**—এক-প্রকার পক্ষী। ইহাদের মাথা ও গলা পীতবর্ণের থাকে। এই পক্ষীর ডিম্ব ফুট ফুট লাল দাগ বিশিষ্ট। প্রবাদ এইরূপ যে, ঐ পক্ষী যীশুখৃষ্টের ক্রুশের চতুর্দ্দিকে উড়িয়াছিল। এই সময়ে খৃষ্টের দেহোৎসারিত রক্ত দ্বারা ইহার পালক রঞ্জিত হয়। **Yellow-Hercules**—একপ্রকার ক্ষুপ। **Yellow-jack**—Same as YELLOW FLAG. The yellow fever; পীতজ্বর। **Yellow jacket**—চীন দেশের রাজপরিবারভুক্ত এবং রাজসম্মানিত ব্যক্তিগণের পীতবর্ণ পট্টপরিচ্ছদ। **Yellow jasmine**—পীতমল্লিকা। **Yellow-legs**—এক প্রকার পক্ষী। **Yellow-legged clear-wing**—একপ্রকার তসরে পোকা। **Yellow-metal**—২ ভাগ তাম্র ও একভাগ দস্তার সংমিশ্রণে প্রস্তুত মিশ্রধাতুবিশেষ। **Yellow-nuphar**—একপ্রকার পীতবর্ণ কুমুদ। **Yellow-ochre**—See OCHRE. **Yellow-orpiment**—See ORPIMENT. **Yellow-oxeye**—এক প্রকার ক্ষুপ। **Yellow-peril**—চীন প্রভৃতি মঙ্গোলিয় জাতি জাগ্রত হইয়া সমগ্র পৃথিবীর উপর প্রাধান্য লাভ করিবে এই আতঙ্ক, পীতাতঙ্ক, পীতভীতি। **Yellow press, Yellow-literature**—যে সকল সংবাদপত্র এবং পুস্তকাদি জন-সাধারণের মনে উত্তেজনা ও বিভীষিকার সৃষ্টি করে, পীতপত্রিকা, পীতসাহিত্য। **Yellow-race**—চীন, জাপান ও মঙ্গো-লিয়ার অধিবাসিগণ, পীত জাতি। **Yellow-ringed carpet**—একপ্রকার তসরে পোকা। **Yellow-root**—এক-প্রকার ক্ষুপ—উহার দীর্ঘ শিকড়, পত্র এবং বল্কল উজ্জ্বল পীতবর্ণ। **Yellow-sea**—পীতসাগর, পীতসমুদ্র (উত্তর প্রশান্ত মহাসাগরের উপসাগর বিশেষ)। **Yellow-shanked sand piper, Yellow-shanks**—আমেরিকার একপ্রকার পক্ষী। **Yellow-shell**—একপ্রকার তসরে পোকা। **Yellow-snake**—জ্যামেকা দ্বীপের একপ্রকার পীতবর্ণ সর্প। **Yellow sponge**—সাধারণ স্পঞ্জ। **Yellow spot**—চক্ষুর চিত্রপত্রস্থ (retina) পীতবর্ণ বিন্দুবিশেষ—এই বিন্দুতে দৃষ্টিশক্তি তীব্রতম হইয়া থাকে; আমেরিকাদেশীয় একপ্রকার পীতবর্ণের ক্ষুদ্র প্রজাপতি। **Yellow-sultan**—একপ্রকার ক্ষুপ। **Yellow-throated**—পীতকণ্ঠ। **Yellow-tissue**—স্থিতিস্থাপক বিধান তন্তু। **Yellow-top**—একপ্রকার শালগম। **Yellow-wood**—একপ্রকার বৃহৎ বৃক্ষ **Yellow-wood tree**—একপ্রকার বৃক্ষ। **Yellow-woven**—একপ্রকার পীতবর্ণ উৎকৃষ্ট কাগজ।

yĕlp, *v. i.* & *n.* To bark with quick sharp sounds, as a dog; ঘেউ ঘেউ করা, খেঁক করিয়া উঠা, খেউ খেউ করা। ***Noun.*** A quick sharp bark; ঘেউ ঘেউ, খেউ খেউ।

yĕn, *n.* A Japanese coin (both gold and silver) worth about *2s.* $1\frac{1}{2}$*d.*; জাপানের স্বর্ণ বা রৌপ্য মুদ্রা বিশেষ (মূল্য প্রায় ২ শিলিং ১½ পেন্স)।

yeo'-măn (yō-), **1.** In early English history, a common menial attendant, but after the fifteenth century, one of a class of small free-holders, forming the next grade below a gentleman; ইংলণ্ডের মধ্যবিত্তশ্রেণীর কৃষিজীবী প্রজা। **2.** A small landowner, farmer person of middle class engaged in agriculture; জোতদার, গৃহস্থ। **3.** Same as YEOMANRY 2. **To do yeoman's duty** or **service**—To do excellent work; প্রকৃষ্টরূপে সাহায্য করা, প্রকৃষ্ট কার্য্য করা।

yeo'-măn-rȳ (yō-), *n.* **1.** Same as YEOMAN. **2.** A volunteer cavalry force raised from farmers etc.; কৃষিজীবি, ভূম্যধিকারী প্রভৃতি হইতে গঠিত স্বেচ্ছাসেবী সাদী সৈন্য।

yer'-cŭm, *n.* Same as MUDAR.

yĕs, *adv.* & *n.* An expression of affirmation or consent; হাঁ, বটে, তাইতো, আচ্ছা, তাই। ***Noun.*** An affirmative reply; হাঁ-সূচক উত্তর, সম্মতিসূচক উত্তর। **To say yes**—To consent; সম্মতি দেওয়া।

yĕs'-têr-day (-dā), *n.* The day next before the present ; গতকল্য ।

yĕs'-têr-eve (-ēv), **—ning**, *n.* The evening of day before ; পূর্ব্ব দিনের সায়াহ্ন, গতকল্য অপরাহ্ণ, পূর্ব্ব সায়াহ্ন।

yĕs'-têr-mŏrn-ing, *n.* The morning of the day before ; গতকল্য প্রভাত।

yĕs'-têr-night (-nīt), *n.* The night before the present ; গতরাত্র, গতরজনী, গতযামিনী।

yĕt, *adv.* & *conj.* **1.** In addition; "This furnishes us with *yet* one more reason" ; অধিকন্তু, আরো। **2.** Although such is the case ; at least ; তথাপি, তবু; অন্ততঃ। **3.** At or before some future time ; কোন ভাবী কালে বা তাহার পূর্ব্বে। **4.** Eventually ; "He'll be hanged *yet*" ; in time ; পরিণামে ; সময়ে। **5.** Still ; "Are you *yet* living" ; অদ্য পর্য্যন্ত, এখন পর্য্যন্ত। ***Conj.*** Nevertheless ; notwithstanding ; "A rough yet *ready* helper" ; তথাপি ; তবুও।

yew (yū), *n.* An ever-green tree of the genus taxus allied to the pines, valued for its wood, which has been used from an early date, for making bows ; এক-প্রকার বৃহৎ চির-হরিৎ বৃক্ষ (পূর্ব্বে ইহার কাষ্ঠ হইতে ধনুক প্রস্তুত হইত। **Himalayan yew**—তালীশপত্র, বর্ম্মি, সুগন্ধা, নাহ্‌রী (ভুটান), :ধুনু (জিলাম), ধুঙ্গ (কাশ্মীর)।

Yew twig.

Yĕz'-dĕ-gir'-di-ăn (-gêr-), **Yĕz'-dĕ-gêr'-di-ăn**, *adj.* Of, or pertaining to, Yezdegird III, a monarch of Persia ; পারস্যরাজ Yezdigird সম্বন্ধীয়।

Yĕz'-i-dee (-dē), *n.* One of a sect of reputed devil-worshippers of Armenia and Caucasus ; আর্ম্মেনিয়া এবং ককেশাস পর্ব্বতবাসী সুপ্রসিদ্ধ শয়তানপূজক সম্প্রদায়ের লোক।

ŷg (g)'-dră-sil, *n.* (*Scand. Myth.*) A tree whose root and branches bind together heaven and earth ; স্ক্যাণ্ডিনিভিয় পুরাণোক্ত বৃক্ষ বিশেষ—যাহার মূল এবং শাখা দ্বারা স্বর্গমর্ত্ত্য সংযুক্ত হইয়াছে।

Yid'-dish, *n.* A kind of modern slang Hebrew containing many words of German orgin spoken by Jews from Central Europe ; মধ্য ইয়ুরোপের ইহুদীদিগের বিকৃত জর্ম্মণ-শব্দবহুল হিব্রুভাষা।

yield (yēld), *v. t., i.* & *n.* **1.** To produce or give or bring as fruit or result ; as, to *yield* a good harvest ; উৎপাদন করা। **2.** To afford ; to give ; as, vine *yields* nectar ; প্রদান করা ; দান করা, দেওয়া। **3.** To concede ; as, to *yield* the point ; স্বীকার করিয়া লওয়, মানিয়া লওয়া। **4.** To surrender as, to *yield* a fortress ; to resign ; সমর্পণ করা ; ত্যাগ করা। ***Verb i.*** **1.** To produce ; to bear ; as, the tree *yields* fruit ; উৎপাদন করা ; ধারণ করা। **2.** To give way ; as, the door *yielded* ; to submit ; to surrender ; to comply ; to assent ; not to oppose ; "You shall not say, I *yield*, being silent" ; ভাঙ্গিয়া যাওয়া ; বশ্যতা স্বীকার করা; সমর্পণ করা ; পূরণ করা ; স্বীকার করা; বাধা না দেওয়া। ***Noun.*** Amount yielded ; "A good *yield* of fruits" ; outturn ; উৎপন্ন দ্রব্যাদি ; উৎপন্ন দ্রব্যাদির পরিমাণ, উৎপন্ন। **Yield'-ing**, *adj.* **Yield-ing-ly**, *adv.* **To yield the palm**—To be surpassed ; অন্যের নিকট পরাভব মানা। **To yield up the ghost**—To die ; দেহ ত্যাগ করা।

ŷ'-lăng-ŷ'-lăng, *n.* **1.** A tree of the Philippines etc. bearing very fragrant greenish yellow flowers ; ফিলিপাইন দ্বীপপুঞ্জের বৃক্ষ-বিশেষ। এই বৃক্ষের পুষ্প অতি সুগন্ধি এবং হরিদ্রাবর্ণ, ইলাং ইলাং। **2.** An essence of the above ; উক্ত পুষ্পের সার।

y'-mir (ē-mêr), **y'-mêr** (ē-), *ns.* (*Scand. Myth.*) The primeval giant from whose body the gods created the world ; (স্কেণ্ডেনিভিয় পুরাণ) যে আদিদানবের দেহ হইতে দেবতাগণ জগৎ সৃষ্টি করিয়াছিলেন। কথিত আছে যে Odin, Vili এবং Ve ইহাকে বধ করেন। ইহার রুধির হইতে সমুদ্র, মাংস হইতে মেদিনী, অস্থি হইতে পর্ব্বতসমূহ এবং ললাট হইতে আকাশ নির্ম্মিত হইয়াছিল।

yō'-del (-dl), **—dle** (-dl), *v. t., i.* & *n.* To sing, changing frequently from the ordinary voice to falsetto and back again after the manner of the mountaineers of Tyrol ; টাইরলের কৃষকদিগের মত সাধারণ স্বর পুনঃ পুনঃ জিলহ্বরে পরিবর্ত্তন করিয়া গান গাওয়া। ***Noun.*** A song or refrain sung by yodeling ; উক্তরূপ গান বা ধুয়া।

yō'-gă, *n.* Self concentration, abstract meditation and mental abstraction, its chief aim is the final union of the finite self with the infinite Brahma ; যোগ (cf. যোগশ্চিত্তবৃত্তিনিরোধঃ)।

yōg-i, *n.* One who practises yoga ; যোগী।

yō-heave-hō' (-hēv-), **yō-hō'**, *interjs.* Used by sailors in heaving together ; নোঙ্গর তোলার সময় জাহাজের মাল্লাগণ সমস্বরে যে একপ্রকার ধ্বনি করে, ইয়োহো।

yō-ick, *v. t.* To urge on by the cry of yoicks ; ইয়ক্ শব্দে চীৎকার করিয়া উৎসাহিত করা।

yō'-icks, A cry of encouragement to foxhounds ; শিকারী কুকুর-দিগকে উৎসাহিত করার জন্য ধ্বনিবিশেষ

yōke, *n., v. t. & i.* **1.** The frame of wood binding two oxen together for drawing ; যুগ্ম, যোয়াল। **2.** A similar frame for carrying two pails ; as, a milkman's *yoke* ; বাঁক। **3.** A mark of servitude ; slavery ; chain ; as, the *yoke* of bondage ; subjection ; দাসত্বের চিহ্ন ; দাসত্ব ; বন্ধন ; শৃঙ্খল। (প্রাচীনকালে রোমানগণ পরাজিত শত্রুকে প্রোথিত বর্শাদ্বয়ের উপর শয়ানভাবে স্থাপিত বর্শার নীচ দিয়া বশ্যতার চিহ্নস্বরূপ গমনে বাধ্য করিত)। **4.** A crossbar or curved piece from which a bell is suspended for ringing it ; যে আড়কাঠ বা বক্র কাষ্ঠখণ্ড হইতে ঘণ্টা ঝুলান হয়। **5.** Bond of union, esp. marriage tie ; বন্ধন, বিবাহবন্ধন। **6.** A pair or couple, esp. a pair of oxen ; "I have bought five *yoke* of oxen" ; যুগ্ম, যুগল, এক জোড়া ষাঁড়। **7.** (*Dial*) A chain of hills (উপভাষায়) গিরিমালা। **8.** A part of a shirt, a lady's-dress, etc., across the shoulders, back and front ; জামার বা স্ত্রীলোকের ব্লাউজ প্রভৃতির স্কন্ধাবরক অংশ—যাহা পৃথকভাবে কাটা হয়। **9.** A cross-bar of rudder to which ropes are attached ; জাহাজের হাইলের যে কাঠিতে রজ্জু বাঁধা হয়। **10.** (*Mech.*) Kinds of coupling or controlling piece in machinery ; (যন্ত্রবিজ্ঞান) যন্ত্রের বিভিন্নপ্রকার নিয়ামক অংশ, জোড়া। ***Verb t.*** **1.** To put yoke upon ; কাঁধে জোয়াল দেওয়া। **2.** To couple or unite ; to couple or unite in marriage ; সংযোগ করা, মিলিত করা ; বিবাহবন্ধনে বদ্ধ করা। **3.** To attach a horse or horses or other draft animals to ; যোতা, যুগবদ্ধ করা। ***Verb i.*** To join ; to be coupled : সংযুক্ত হওয়া ; মিলিত হওয়া। **Yoke-bone** — গণ্ডফলক। **Yoke-fellow, Yokemate**—সঙ্গী, সহকর্মী, সহচর, জীবনের সঙ্গিনী। **Yoke-lines, Yoke-ropes**—যে রজ্জু দ্বারা হাইলের কাঠি চালিত হয়। **Yoke-toed**—সম্মুখ ও পশ্চাৎ উভয়দিকে পদাঙ্গুলীদ্বয়বিশিষ্ট। **To throw off the yoke**—To sever the bond of subjection ; অধীনতাপাশ ছিন্ন করা। **Yoke of the sky**—রাশিচক্র।

yō'-kel (-kl), *n.* A rustic ; পাড়াগেঁয়ে লোক, চাষাড়ে লোক।

yolk (yōk), *n.* **1.** The yellow part of an egg ; ডিম্বের শ্বেতাংশ, ডিমের কুসুম, অণ্ডকুসুম। **2.** The unctuous secretion from the skin of sheep which renders the pile soft and pliable ; মেষের চর্ম্ম হইতে নিঃসৃত একপ্রকার তৈলাক্ত পদার্থ। **Yolk-bag, yolk-sac**—ডিম্বের শ্বেতাংশ যে পর্দ্দাদ্বারা আচ্ছাদিত থাকে। **Yolk'-y,** *adj.*

yŏn, *adv., adj. & pron.* At, or in that place ; ঐ, অদূরে, ঐখানে। ***Adj.*** Situated there : অদূরবর্ত্তী, ঐ। ***Pron.*** (*Archaic*) Yon person or thing ; ঐ লোক, ঐ জিনিষ।

yŏn'-dêr, *adj.* Being at a distance ; within view ; অদূরবর্ত্তী ; দৃষ্টিসীমার ভিতর। ***Adv.*** At a distance but within view ; ঐ, অদূরে।

yōre, *n.* Old times ; as, in times of *yore* ; প্রাচীনকাল, সাবেককাল, পুরাকাল, পুরা। **Of yore** — পূর্ব্বে, প্রাচীনকালে।

Yŏrk, *n.* **York and Lancaster**—Wars of Roses এর প্রতিদ্বন্দ্বী দলের অন্যতর (House of York)।

yŏrk, *v. t.* To bowl with yorker ; কন্দুক অভিনিক্ষিপ্ত করা।

yŏrk'-ėr, *n.* A ball pitched just under the batsman's bat ; ক্রিকেট ক্রীড়ায় যে কন্দুক ব্যাটধারীর ব্যাটের অব্যবহিত নিম্নে নিক্ষিপ্ত হয়।

Yŏrk'-ĭst, *adj. & n.* Of, or pertaining to, the dukes or Royal House of York ; ইয়র্কের ডিউকগণ সম্বন্ধীয়, ইয়র্কের রাজপরিবার সম্পর্কীয়। ***Noun.*** A member or supporter of the Royal House of York ; ইয়র্ক পরিবারের লোক, ইয়র্ক রাজপরিবারভুক্ত ব্যক্তি।

Yŏrk'-shīre, *n.* A county of England ; ইংলণ্ডের প্রদেশবিশেষ। **Yorkshire flannel** — অরঞ্জিত ফ্লানেল। **Yorkshire grit** — মার্ব্বেলপ্রস্তর পরিষ্কার করার জন্য ব্যবহৃত একপ্রকার শিলা। **Yorkshire pie**—মাংসের পুর দেওয়া একপ্রকার পিষ্টক। **Yorkshire pudding** — ডিম, দুধ, আটার লেই প্রভৃতি মাংসের নীচে সেঁকিয়া যে একপ্রকার পিষ্টক প্রস্তুত করা হয়। **Yorkshire stone** — অট্টালিকাদি নির্ম্মাণে ব্যবহৃত প্রস্তরবিশেষ। **Yorkshire terrier** — একপ্রকার ঘনলোমশ ক্ষুদ্র কুকুর। **To come Yorkshire over a man**—To cheat a man ; কাহাকে প্রতারিত করা।

you (yō), *pron. pl.* as well as *sing.* The pronoun of the second person in the nominative or objective case ; তুমি, তোমরা, আপনারা, তোরা, তোমাদিগকে, তোরে, তোকে।

young (yŭng), *adj. & n.* **1.** Not long born ; not having arrived at maturity or full age ; not old ; as a *young* man ; অচিরজাত, নবজাত ; অল্পবয়স্ক, অপ্রাপ্তবয়স্ক, তরুণবয়স্ক ; যুবক। **2.** Being in the first or early stage of growth ; as, a *young* tree ; তরুণ। **3.** Pertaining to youth or early life ; as, *young* days ; যৌবনসম্বন্ধীয়, যৌবনের। **4.** Immature ; youthful ; inexperienced ; "Come, come elder brother, you are too *young* in this" ; কাঁচা ; তরুণ ; অনভিজ্ঞ, অপরিপক্ব। **5.** Youthful in appearance or feeling ; "Whom the gods love, live *young* for ever" ; vigorous ; fresh ; তরুণ ; সতেজ ; নবীন। **6.** (*Colloq.*) Junior ; as, the *younger* Pitt ; কনিষ্ঠ। **7.** (*Dial.*) Unmarried ; (উপভাষায়) অবিবাহিত। **8.** Not yet far advanced, of long duration, or of full development ; recent ; as, *young* ice ; তরুণ, অচিরগত, অসম্যগবিকশিত নূতন। **9.** Indicating names of political parties claiming to represent the rising generation; নবপন্থী, নব্য (cf. Young Turkey নব্যতুর্কী সম্প্রদায়)। 10. Characteristic of youth; যৌবনসুলভ। *Noun*. The offspring of an animal; as, the *young* of a dog; বাচ্চা, শাবক। **Young'-ish,** *adj.* **Young'-ling,** *n.* **Young-Adventurer**—Same as YOUNG PRETENDER. **Young-America** — আমেরিকার যুবকসম্প্রদায়। **Young-blood**—তরুণ যুবক। **Young Chevalier**—Same as YOUNG PRETENDER. **Young England** — ১৮৪৩ খৃষ্টাব্দে কতিপয় রক্ষণশীল ব্যক্তি দ্বারা গঠিত সম্প্রদায়বিশেষ। এই সম্প্রদায় শস্য আইনের রদ এবং অন্যান্য সংস্কারের বিরুদ্ধে তীব্র আন্দোলনে প্রবৃত্ত হয়। **Younger son** — কোন পরিবারের জ্যেষ্ঠেতর সন্তান। ইংলণ্ডে জ্যেষ্ঠ সন্তান পৈত্রিক সম্পত্তির উত্তরাধিকারী হন বলিয়া জ্যেষ্ঠেতর সন্তানগণ অপেক্ষাকৃত দরিদ্র হইয়া থাকেন। **Young Europe**—সমগ্র ইয়ুরোপে সাম্য, মৈত্রী, স্বাধীনতার ভাব বিস্তারের জন্য নব্যইতালী, নব্যজর্ম্মণী, নব্যপোলাণ্ডএর প্রতিনিধিগণ দ্বারা ম্যাটিসিনীর নেতৃত্বাধীনে ১৮৩৪ খৃষ্টাব্দের এপ্রিল মাসে সুইজরলণ্ড দেশে প্রতিষ্ঠিত সমিতি বিশেষ, নব্যইয়ুরোপ। **Young-flood**—জোয়ারের প্রারম্ভাবস্থা। **Young fustic** — ইয়ুরোপদেশীয় বৃক্ষবিশেষ—যাহা হইতে একপ্রকার কমলাবর্ণ রঞ্জকপদার্থ প্রাপ্ত হওয়া যায়। **Young-Germany**—জর্ম্মণীর গ্রন্থকারসংঘবিশেষ। ইঁহারা গণতন্ত্র, সাম্যবাদ, ধর্ম্মসংঘ এবং রাষ্ট্রের স্বাতন্ত্র্য, নারীগণের সামাজিক ও রাজনীতিক অবস্থার উন্নতিসাধন প্রভৃতি বিষয়ে লেখনী চালনা করিতেন। Heine, Kühne, Mundt, Wienborg, Laube, Gutzkaw প্রভৃতি এই সম্প্রদায়ের প্রধান লেখক। **Young Ireland**—ইংলণ্ডের অধীনতাপাশ ছেদনের উদ্দেশ্যে ১৮৪১ খৃঃ অব্দে আয়র্লণ্ডের গঠিত সম্প্রদায়বিশেষ। উক্ত উদ্দেশ্য সাধনের জন্য এই সম্প্রদায় আয়র্লণ্ডের রোম্যান ক্যাথলিক ও প্রোটেষ্ট্যান্ট দিগের মধ্য ঐক্যসাধনের চেষ্টায় প্রবৃত্ত হয়। ১৮৪৮ খৃঃ অব্দে ব্রিটিশ গভর্ণমেন্ট সম্প্রদায়ের কএক জন নেতাকে নির্ব্বাসিত করেন। এই ঘটনার কিছুকাল পরেই এই সম্প্রদায় বিলুপ্ত হয়। **Young-Italy** — অষ্ট্রিয়ার অধীনতাপাশ হইতে ইতালীর উদ্ধারসাধনের এবং সমগ্র ইতালী দেশে প্রজাতন্ত্র শাসনপ্রণালী প্রতিষ্ঠার উদ্দেশ্যে ম্যাটিসিনির নেতৃত্বাধীনে ১৮৩১ খৃঃ অব্দে প্রতিষ্ঠিত সম্প্রদায়বিশেষ, নব্যইতালী। **Youngman**—যুবক; প্রণয়ী, নাগর। **Young-Norway**—নরওয়ের শাসনপদ্ধতির আমূল পরিবর্ত্তনের উদ্দেশ্যে Henrik Wergeland এর নেতৃত্বে গঠিত কৃষকদিগের সম্প্রদায়বিশেষ। **Young Pretender**—চার্লস এডোয়ার্ড ষ্টুয়ার্ট। ১৭৪৫ খৃঃ অব্দের বিদ্রোহ ইঁহার নেতৃত্বাধীনে সংঘটিত হয়। **Young Switzerland** — সুইজরলণ্ড, টাইরল, সেভয়, প্রভৃতি Alps পার্ব্বত্যাঞ্চলের প্রদেশসমূহের অধিবাসিগণের মধ্যে ঐক্যস্থাপনের উদ্দেশ্যে উনবিংশ শতাব্দীর মধ্যভাগে প্রতিষ্ঠিত সমিতিবিশেষ, নব্য সুইজরলণ্ড। **Young thing** — ছেলেমানুষ **Young-Turkey**—তুরস্ক সাম্রাজ্যের রাজনীতিক এবং সামাজিক সংস্কারসাধনের জন্য প্রতিষ্ঠিত সম্প্রদায়বিশেষ, নব্যতুর্কি। **Young-woman**—যুবতী, তরুণী; প্রণয়িনী। **Old head on young shoulders**—Wise though young in age: বয়সে তরুণ হইলেও জ্ঞানে প্রবীণ। **In my young days**—While I was young; যৌবনে। **Young Men's Christian Association**—খৃষ্টীয় যুবক-সমিতি। যুবক-সমাজের সামাজিক, মানসিক, এবং আধ্যাত্মিক উন্নতি সাধনের উদ্দেশ্যে প্রতিষ্ঠিত সমিতিবিশেষ। ১৮৪৪ খৃঃ অব্দে George William কর্ত্তৃক লণ্ডননগরীতে এই সমিতি প্রতিষ্ঠিত হয়। বর্ত্তমানে পৃথিবীর সকল প্রধান প্রধান নগরীতে 'খৃষ্টীয় যুবক-সমিতি' প্রতিষ্ঠিত হইয়াছে। **Young Women's Christian Association** — খৃষ্টীয় মহিলা-সমিতি। **With young**—Pregnant; গর্ভবতী, অন্তঃসত্ত্বা, সসত্ত্বা।

young'-stêr (yŭng-), A young person; a lad; যুবক; ছোকরা, ছোড়া।

youn'-kêr (yŭng-), *n.* **1.** (*Colloq.*) Same as YOUNGSTER. **2.** Same as JUNKER.

your (yŏr), *poss. pron.* Pertaining, or belonging to, you; আপনার, তোমার (in addressing equals and Gods), তোর (used in addressing inferior persons), আপনাদের (pl. used in addressing superiors), তোমাদের (pl., in addressing equals), তদীয়, তোদের (used in addressing inferiors).

yours (yörs), *pron.* & *adj.* That or those which belongs to you; as, my house and *yours*; তোমার জিনিষ, তদীয় বস্তু, তোমার কোনকিছু। *Adj.* Belonging to yours; আপনার, তোমার, তদীয়, তব, তোর, আপনাদের, তোমাদের, তোদের। **Ever yours**—চিরদিন আপনার। **You and yours**—তুমি এবং তোমার। **Yours obediently**—আপনার অনুগত (পত্রে নাম স্বাক্ষরের উপরে ব্যবহৃত হয়)। **Yours faithfully**—আপনার বিশ্বস্ত। (পত্রে নাম স্বাক্ষরের উপরে ব্যবহৃত হয়)।

your'-sĕlf (yör-) *Pron.* (*Pl. yourselves*), **1.** A compound of *your-* and *self* used to express distinction emphatically; আপনি স্বয়ং, তুমি নিজে, স্বয়ং তোমাকেই, স্বয়ং আপনাকেই।

youth (yōth), *n.* **1.** The state or time of being young; যৌবন' যৌবনকাল, নবযৌবন, তারুণ্য, যৌবন বয়স, নবীন বয়স, কৈশোর (দশ হইতে পঞ্চদশ বর্ষ পর্য্যন্ত)। [উজ্জ্বল নীলমণিতে নারীর নব-যৌবনের এইরূপ সংজ্ঞা দেওয়া হইয়াছে:—"দরোদ্ভিন্নস্তনং কিঞ্চিৎ চলাক্ষং মেদুরস্মিতম্। মনাগ্‌ভিন্ন রুভাবং নব্যং যৌবনং উচ্যতে"।] **2.** A young person; যুবক, যুবতী। **3.** Young persons generally or collectively; as, the *youth* of India; যুবকবৃন্দ, যুবতীবৃন্দ, যুবজন (গীতঃ), যুবকসমাজ। **Youth'-ful,** *adj.* Belonging to the early stge of life; তরুণবয়স্ক। **2.** Suitable or pertaining to youth; যৌবনসমুচিত,

যৌবনসুলভ, যৌবনসম্বন্ধীয়। **3.** Fresh or vigorous, as in youth ; তরুণ, নবীন, সতেজ। **Youth'-ful-ness,** *n.* The state of being youthful; যৌবনসম্পন্নতা, তারুণ্য, তরুণিমা **The youth of the worlds**—পৃথিবীর শৈশব।

yowl, Same as YAWL (which see).

ỹt'-têr'-bi-ŭm, *n.* (*Chem.*) A rare metal ; (রসায়নশাস্ত্র) একপ্রকার দুষ্প্রাপ্য ধাতু।

ỹt'-tri-ă (-rĭ-), A fine white powder, insoluble in water and infusible ; একপ্রকার অদ্রাব্য এবং জলে অমুলনীয় সূক্ষ্ম শ্বেতচূর্ণ।

ỹt'-tri-ŭm (-rĭ-), *n.* The base of yttria ; একপ্রকার দুষ্প্রাপ্য ধাতু, ইত্রিক (সাঃ পঃ)।

yŭc'-că, *n.* Kinds of American white flowering liliaceous plant ; আমেরিকাদেশীয় শ্বেতপুষ্পপ্রসূ বিভিন্ন প্রকার স্থলকুমুদজাতীয় ক্ষুপের নাম।

yūle, *n.* Christmas ; খৃষ্টমাস, বড়দিন। **Yule-tide**—বড়দিনের সময়। **Yule-log**—খৃষ্টমাস দিনের পূর্ব্ববর্ত্তী দিবস যে বৃহৎ কাষ্ঠখণ্ড প্রজ্বালিত করা হয়।

yŭnx (yŭngks), *n.* Same as WRYNECK (bird.)

Z

Z, **1.** The last letter of the English alphabet : ইংরাজী বর্ণমালার সর্ব্বশেষ অক্ষর। **2.** The third unknown quantity ; (বীজগণিত) তৃতীয় অজ্ঞাত রাশি।

zā'-bă-ĭsm, —ĭst, *ns.* Same as SABIANISM (which see).

zăc'-chō, *n.* The lowest part of the pedestal of a column ; স্তম্ভপীঠের নিম্নতম অংশ।

zăf'-fre (-fêr), **zăf'-fêr,** *ns.* A substance obtained from cobalt, used by enamellers as a blue colour ; কোবাল্ট হইতে প্রাপ্ত দ্রব্য বিশেষ—যাহা মিনাকরেরা নীলা রঙ্গ রূপে ব্যবহার করে।

zăn'-tă cŭr'-rant (-ănt), *n.* A kind of seedless grape or raisin ; একপ্রকার বীচিশূন্য আঙ্গুর বা কিসমিস।

zā'-nỹ, *n.* **1.** A subordinate buffoon or merry-andrew ; অপ্রধান ভাড়, উপবিদূষক। **2.** A simpleton ; বোকা।

Zăn'-zi-bă-ri, *n.* & *adj.* **1.** A [na]tive of Zanzibar ; জেন্‌জিবারের বাসী। *Adj.* Pertaining to Zanzibar ; অফ্রিকার অন্তর্গত জেন্‌জিবার প্রদেশসম্বন্ধীয়।

ză-pō'-tĕc', *n.* A civilized Indian of Ancient Mexico ; প্রাচীন মেক্‌সিকোর সভ্য অধিবাসী। **—an,** *adj.*

zăp'-tī-ah (-ă), *n.* A Turkish policeman; তুরস্কদেশের পুলিশ কনেষ্টবল।

Zăr-ă-thûs'-tr-, *n.* Same as ZOROASTR-. **—tri-an, —tric,** *adjs.*

ză-rē'-bă, *n.* In the Soudan a temporary camp guarded by a fence of bushes etc. ; আফ্রিকার সুদান প্রদেশে কণ্টকগুল্মাদি দ্বারা বেষ্টিত অস্থায়ী শিবির।

zeal (zēl), *n.* Passionate ardour in the pursuit of anything ; আগ্রহ, উৎসাহ, উদ্যম। **Zeal'-ous,** *adj.* Possessing zeal ; উৎসাহসম্পন্ন, উৎসাহপূর্ণ। **zeal'-ous-ly,** *adv.* **zeal'-ous-ness** *n.*

zeal'-ŏt (zĕl-) *n.* **1.** A fanatic ; a bigot ; ধর্ম্মোন্মত্ত ; গোঁড়া, ধর্ম্মান্ধ **2.** (*Cap.*) One of a fanatical sect who resisted the Roman occupation of Palestine ; প্যালেষ্টাইন প্রদেশে রোমীয়দিগের অধিকারস্থাপনে বাধাপ্রদানকারী ধর্ম্মান্ধ সম্প্রদায় বিশেষের লোক। **—ism,** *n.*

zē'-bĕc, —bĕk, *ns.* Same as XEBEC (which see).

zē'-bră, *n.* A slight graceful quadruped of Southern Africa with striped body ; জেব্রা [চিত্রাশ্ব জেব্রা, চিত্রগর্দ্দভ, চিত্ররাসভ।] **Zebra-wood**—একপ্রকার ডোরাকাটা দৃঢ়কাষ্ঠ কাঁকড়াশিঙ্গী [Syn. কর্কটশৃঙ্গী (খারী) কর্কটাখ্যা, মহাঘোষা, শৃঙ্গী, কুলীরশৃঙ্গী, চক্রাঙ্গী, কুলিঙ্গী, কাসনাশিনী, ঘোষা, চক্রা, বনমূর্দ্ধজা, শিখরী, কর্কটাঙ্গা, কর্কটী, বিষাণিকা, কৌলীরা, বলাঙ্গা]।

zē'-bū, *n.* The humped ox of India ; বৃষ, বৃষভ, ককুদ্মান।

zĕd, *n.* The letter Z ; ইংরাজী Z অক্ষর।

zĕd'-ō-ă-rỹ, *n.* A medicinal root, belonging to a plant, *curcuma zedoria*, growing in the East Indies, and of a pungent and tonic quality ; শুণ্ঠী, শুঁঠ, শটী [Syn. নাগর, বিশ্বা, মহৌষধি, বিশ্বভেষজ বিশ্বা, মহৌষধী, ইন্দ্রভেষজ, মেষজ,

বিশ্বৌষধ, কটুষণ, কটুভদ্র, কটুগ্রন্থি, সৌপর্ণ, শৃঙ্গবের, কফারি, নাগরাহ্ব, শোষণ, চান্দ্রক, শুণ্ঠা, কচূর্রক, কর্বুরক, বেধমুখ্যক, দ্রাবিড়ক, কাল্প, কাল্পক, সুস্পলুষ্ঠ।] [Arab. *zerukbad, jadwar* ; Chin. *tien-chuh-kan-kyang* ; Fr. *zedoaire* ; Germ. *zittwer* ; It. *zedoaria, zettovario,* Portug. *zedoaria* ; Sp. *cedoaria* ; Pers. *zerumbad* ; Tam. *pulang-kalangu*; *kasturi manjal, kapurkichili* ; Teleg. *kichili-gadda, kusthuri pasupu.*] **Wild** or **yellow zedoary**—বন হলদী।

zē'-ïne *n.* A substance of yellow colour, soft, insipid and elastic produced from Indian corn ; ভুট্টা হইতে প্রাপ্ত একপ্রকার কোমল, নীরস, স্থিতিস্থাপক পীতবর্ণ পদার্থ।

zeitgeist, *n.* Spirit of the times ; কালধর্ম্ম।

Zē-lă'-nĭ-ăn, *adj.* Pertaining to New Zealand ; নবজিলণ্ডসম্বন্ধীয়।

zĕ-mĭn-dâr', *n.* (India) The holder of large portion of land under the government ; জমিদার। **–y,** *n.*

zĕm'-stvō, *n.* A Russian district council composed of landed proprietors and representatives of artisans and peasants ; শিল্পী, ভূস্বামী, কৃষকগণের প্রতিনিধিবর্গদ্বারা গঠিত রুশদেশের জেলা সমিতি।

zĕ-nä'-nă, *n.* **1.** The part of a house in India reserved for women ; অন্তঃপুর, অন্দরমহল, শুদ্ধান্ত, অবরোধ। **2.** A kind of stuff woven with silk on one side and woollen on the other side; একপ্রকার কাপড়—যাহার এক দিক পশম এবং অপর দিক রেশমে বোনা হয়। **Zenana mission**—অন্তঃপুরিকাদিগের মধ্যে ধর্ম্ম, স্বাস্থ্যতত্ত্ব, প্রভৃতি বিষয়ে শিক্ষাপ্রদানের জন্য খৃষ্টীয় প্রচারিকাগণ কর্ত্তৃক পরিচালিত প্রচারসমিতিবিশেষ, অন্তঃপুর প্রচারসমিতি।

zĕnd, *n.* The ancient language of the Iranian family, allied to Sanskrit ; প্রাচীন ইরাণীগণের ভাষা। [এই ভাষাতে Zoroasterএর জেন্দাবস্তু নামক প্রসিদ্ধ ধর্ম্মগ্রন্থ রচিত হইয়াছে।]

Zĕnd-A-vĕs'-tă (-ă-), *n.* The sacred books of Zoroastrians, Magians, Gubers or Parsees ascribed to Zoroaster himself ; পারসীকদিগের প্রধান ধর্ম্মগ্রন্থ, জেন্দোবস্তু, আবেস্তা।

zē'-nĭth, *n.* **1.** The point in the visible celestial hemisphere which is vertical to the spectator, and from which a direct perpendicular line passing through the spectator would proceed to the centre of the earth ; দ্রষ্টার মস্তকের ঠিক উর্দ্ধস্থ আকাশের বিন্দুর নাভিমধ্য (আর্য্যঃ), খস্বস্তিক, খমধ্য (সাঃ পঃ), সম (ঐ), উর্দ্ধস্বস্তিক (ঐ), শিরোবিন্দু। 2. Highest point সর্ব্বোচ্চ মাত্রা, পরাকাষ্ঠা, চরমসীমা। 2. Time or place of greatest power or prosperity or happiness ; as, he rose to the *zenith* of prosperity ; চরম সুখসমৃদ্ধি বা ক্ষমতাভোগের কাল বা স্থান। **–al,** *adj.* **Zenith distance**—কোন বস্তু এবং খমধ্য এতদুভয়ের মধ্যবর্ত্তী চাপ বা বৃত্তখণ্ড, নত (zenith-distance at meridian transit—সূঃ সিঃ), নতভাগ (*ib.*), নতাংশ (*ib.*)। **Zenith sector**—খমধ্যের নিকট দিয়া যে সকল নক্ষত্র অতিক্রম করে ঐ বিন্দু হইতে তাহাদের দূরত্ব সূক্ষ্মভাবে নির্ণয়ের জন্য যন্ত্রবিশেষ, সমচ্ছেদ। **The cosine of the zenith distance or the sine of the highest** or **central point of the ecliptic at a given time**—দৃগ্গতি (আর্য্যঃ), দৃগ্গতিজীবা (সূঃ সিঃ), দৃগ্গতিজ্যা (আর্য্যঃ—টীকা)। **The sine of the zenith distance** or **the cosine of the altitude**—দৃগ্জ্যা। **The sine of the zenith distance of the highest** or **central point of the ecliptic at a given time**—দৃক্ক্ষেপ (সূঃ সিঃ)। **Zenith-distance of a body in any other position**—দৃক্ (সাঃ পঃ)।

zē'-ō-lĭte, *n.* An extensive family of minerals, so called from their frothing or intumescing into a whitish spongy enamel under the blow-pipe ; একজাতীয় খনিজ পদার্থ। **–lit'-ic, –lit-i-form,** *adj.*

zĕph'-yr (-ẽr), *n.* **1.** The west wind ; পশ্চিমানিল। **2.** (*Poet.*) A soft, mild, gentle breezes ; মৃদু পবন, মন্দপবন, ধীরসমীর (গীত), মন্দানিল, মৃদুমারুত, মন্দমারুত, মলয়ানিল। **2.** An athelet's jersey made of a thin gauzy cloth ; পাতল কাপড়ে প্রস্তুত মল্লদের একপ্রকার আঁটসাট জামা। **3.** Same as ZEPHYR-CLOTH. **4.** (*Entom.*) A genus of Lycaenidae ; (কীটতত্ত্ব) একজাতীয় পতঙ্গ। **Zephyr-cloth**—একপ্রকার অতি সূক্ষ্ম পশমী কাপড়, হাওয়ার কাপড়।

zĕph-ŷ-rŭs, *n.* The west wind or zephyr personified (*cap.*) ; গ্রীক-পুরাণোক্ত পশ্চিম পবনদেবতা।

zē'-rō, *n.* **1.** The figure o ; ০ শূন্য। **2.** The lowest point in thermometer ; তাপমান প্রভৃতি যন্ত্রের সর্ব্ব নিম্ন বিন্দু। **3.** (*Astron.*) The first point of Aries ; মেষরাশির প্রথম বিন্দু। **Absolute zero**—273° C তাপমাত্রা—যাহাতে যে সকল কণিকার গতি দ্বারা তাপ উৎপন্ন হয় তাহারা অচঞ্চল থাকে, নির্ব্বিকল্প শূন্য। **Zero-point**—যে বিন্দু হইতে কোন কিছুর মাত্রা গণনা আরম্ভ হয়, শূন্যবিন্দু।

zĕst, *n.* **1.** (*Obs.*) Orange or lemon peal, used to flavour liquor ; (অপ্রঃ) মদ্যাদি সুগন্ধ করার জন্য ব্যবহৃত লেবু বা কমলালেবুর খোসা। **2.** Something which gives a relish or pleasant taste ; রুচিকর বস্তু, রুচিবর্দ্ধক বস্তু। **3.** Piquancy ; relish : "Liberality of disposition and conduct gives the highest *zest* and relish to social intercourse" ; সরসতা, রুচিজনকতা ; স্বাদ, রস। **4.** Keen enjoyment; gusto; "They joined and partook of the rude fare with the *zest* and fatigue of youth" ; তীব্র রসাস্বাদ ; রুচি।

zē'-tā, *n.* The Greek letter corresponding to English Z ; ইংরাজী Z অক্ষরের প্রতিরূপ গ্রীক অক্ষর, জেটা।
zē-tēt'-ic, *adj.* (*Rare*) Proceeding by inquiry ; (কচিদ্ ব্যবহৃত) প্রশ্নাত্মক।
zeu'-glō-dōn (zü-), *n.* A fossil mammal of the whale kind of great size ; তিমিজাতীয় অতি বৃহৎ শিলীভূত জন্তুবিশেষ।
zeug'-mā (züg-), *n.* (*Gram.*) The connection of two nouns with an adjective or verb suitable to one of them but suggesting another verb suitable to the other noun ; এমন কোন বিশেষণ বা ক্রিয়া দ্বারা বিশেষণদ্বয়ের সংযোজন, যাহা কেবলমাত্র একটীর পক্ষে প্রযোজ্য হইয়া থাকে এবং অপর বিশেষ্যের পক্ষে উপযোগী অনুক্ত অন্য ক্রিয়া ইঙ্গিতে ব্যক্ত করে, পদলোপালঙ্কার [cf. I hate you and you (hate) me] ; **—mat'-ic**, *adj.*
Zeus, (züs), *n.* **1.** The supreme divinity among the Greeks ; গ্রীকপুরাণোক্ত দেবরাজ। [ইঁহার পিতার নাম Cronus এবং জননীর নাম Rhea দেবী। বিদ্যুৎ বজ্র ইঁহার ইঙ্গিতে চালিত হয়। Thessaly প্রদেশের অন্তর্গত Olympus পর্ব্বতে অন্যান্য দেবগণেরসহিত ইনি বাস করেন।] **2.** (*l. c.*) A genus of fishes remarkable for their oval compressed form ; গোলাকার বা ডিম্বাকৃতি একজাতীয় দৃঢ়াঙ্গ মৎস্য।
zib'-ēt, *n.* Same as CIVET (which see.)
zig'-zāg, *adj.*, *n.*, *adv.*, *v. t.* & *v. i.* Having sharp or quick turns or flexures ; আঁকাবাঁকা, টের্‌া-বাঁকা। ***Noun.*** A zigzag line or road or set of trenches ; আঁকাবঁকা রেখা, সর্পিল রেখা, আঁকাবাঁকা পথ, আঁকাবাঁকা পরিখাশ্রেণী। ***Adv.*** With a zigzag course ; আঁকিয়া বাঁকিয়া। ***Verb t. & i.*** To form or move with sharp turns or angles ; as, the river *zigzags* through the meadow ; আঁকিয়া বাঁকিয়া যাওয়া, টেরা বাঁকা হওয়া।
zimb (zĭm), *n.* An insect obnoxious to cattle ; গোমহিষাদির অনিষ্টকর একপ্রকার কীট।
zinc (zĭngk), *n.* & *v. i.* A metel of a brilliant white colour, with a shade of blue somewhat like tin ; দস্তা [Syn. খর্পর (ধাঃ রঃ প্রঃ), চর্ম্মক (ধাঃ প্রঃ), জসদ (সাঃ পঃ), জাসত্ব (ধাঃ প্রঃ), ত্রোটক (ঐ), রসক (ঐ), রসকসত্ব (সাঃ পঃ), রসবর্দ্ধক (ঐ), রূপ্যভ্রাতা (ঐ), রাজত (ঐ), যশোদায়ক (ঐ), রঙ্গাভ (ঐ)] [Dutch. *spelter* ; It. & Sp. *zinco*, *chinck* ; Russ. *schpaater* ; Chin. *peh-yuen*, *peht'ung* ; Tam. *tulanagam.*] ***Verb i.*** To coat with zinc ; দস্তার পাত দ্বারা আচ্ছাদিত করা। **Zinc'-ic, Zinc-if'-er-ous, Zinc'-oid**, *adjs.* **Zinc-i-fi-ca'-tion**, *n.* **Zinc'-i-fy**, *v. t.* **Zinc'-ous, Zinc'-y**, *adjs.* **Flowers of zinc, Zinc-oxide**—মলম, বিলাতী মাটি, শ্বেতবর্ণ রঞ্জক পদার্থ, প্রভৃতি রূপে ব্যবহৃত চূর্ণ বিশেষ, খর্পরপুষ্প। **Zinc-amalgam**—রসক (সাঃ পঃ)। **Zinc-amyl**—এমিল এবং দস্তার সংমিশ্রণে প্রস্তুত একপ্রকার স্বচ্ছ অবর্ণ তরল পদার্থ। **Zinc-blende**—দস্তা এবং গন্ধকের মিশ্র। **Zinc-bloom**—দস্তা, অঙ্গারাম্ল, অক্‌সাইড অব জিঙ্কের সংমিশ্রণে গঠিত একপ্রকার হরিদ্বর্ণ খনিজ পদার্থ। **Zinc-ethyl** — এথিল এবং দস্তার মিশ্রণে গঠিত একপ্রকার স্বচ্ছ, অবর্ণ এবং বিষাক্ত তরল পদার্থ। **Zinc-methyle** — অঙ্গার, উদজান এবং দস্তাদ্বারা গঠিত একপ্রকার উদ্বায়ী এবং পূতিগন্ধ তরল পদার্থ। **Zinc-white**—শ্বেতবর্ণ রঞ্জকপদার্থ বিশেষ, জসদশ্বেত (হিঃ কোঃ)।
zinc-īte (zĭngk-), *n.* A name for red zinc of iron ; লৌহমিশ্রিত রক্তবর্ণ দস্তা, আয়স-খর্পর।
zincke (zĭnk), *n.* A small horn pipe or whistle of German origin ; একপ্রকার ক্ষুদ্র শিঙ্গা, শিটি।
zin'-cō (zĭng-), *n.* & *v. t.* Same as ZINCOGRAPH.
zinc'-oid (zĭngk-ōyd), *n.* The positive pole of a voltaic battery ; ভলটেয়িক তাড়িত ঘটশ্রেণীর ধন ধ্রুব।
zin'-cō-grăph, (zĭng-), *n.*, *v. t.* & *i.* **1.** An etching on zinc ; দস্তার ফলকের উপর ক্ষোদিত চিত্র, ক্ষোদিত দস্তাফলক। **2.** An impression obtained by zincography ; ক্ষোদিত দস্তার ফলক হইতে গৃহীত চিত্র। ***Verb t. & i.*** To etch on zinc ; দস্তার ফলকের উপর ক্ষোদাই করা। **—cog'-ra-phy, —cog'-ra-pher**, *ns.* **—graph'-ic**, *adj.*
zin'-cō-tȳpe, (zĭng-), *n.* Same as ZINCOGRAPH.
zingaro, *n.* Same as GIPSY (which see).
zin'-ni-ā (-ĭ-), *n.* A genus of plants with six or seven species ; ক্ষুপবিশেষের গণ।
Zī'-ōn, *n.* The holy hill of Ancient Jerusalem ; প্রাচীন জেরুজেলেমের পবিত্রগিরি। **2.** Ancient Jerusalem ; প্রাচীন জেরুজেলেমনগরী। **3.** The theocracy or church of God ; দেবতন্ত্র, খৃষ্টীয় ধর্ম্মসংঘ। **4.** The heavenly Jerusalem or the kingdom of heaven ; নিত্য জেরুজেলেম (cf. নিত্য বৃন্দাবন)। **5.** The Israelites ; এশ্রায়েলের বংশধরগণ। **6.** A dissenting chapel ; খৃষ্টধর্ম্মের উপাসকসম্প্রদায় বিশেষের ভজনালয়। **Zion-ward**—নিত্য জেরুজেলেমের অভিমুখে।
Zī-ōn'-ist, *n.* One who advocates the colonising of Palestine by the Jews ; প্যালেষ্টাইন প্রদেশে ইহুদীগণের উপনিবেশস্থাপনের পক্ষপাতী ব্যক্তি, জেরুজেলেমপন্থী। **—ism**, *n.*
zir'-cōn (zēr), *n.* A hard lustrous mineral forming one of the gems ; গোমেদ, গোমেদমণি। [Syn. গোমেদক রাহুরত্ন, তমোমণি, স্বর্ভানব, পিঙ্গস্ফটিক, পীতমণি,] [রাজনির্ঘণ্টগ্রন্থে এই মণির এইরূপ গুণ উল্লিখিত আছে :—"অম্লত্বম্, উষ্ণত্বম্। বাতকোপবিকারনাশিত্বম্। দীপনত্বম্, পাচনত্বম্।" যুক্তিকল্পতরুগ্রন্থে

এই মণির পরীক্ষা ও শ্রেণীবিভাগ সম্বন্ধে লিখিত হইয়াছে। যথা :—হিমালয়ে বা সিন্ধৌ বা গোমেদমণিসম্ভবঃ। স্বচ্ছকান্তি-গুরুঃস্নিগ্ধো বর্ণাঢ্যো দীপ্তিমানপি ॥ বলক্ষঃ পিঞ্জরোধস্মো গোমেদ ইতি কীর্তিতঃ। চতুর্দ্ধা জাতিভেদস্তু গোমেদোऽপি প্রকাশ্যতে। ব্রাহ্মণঃ শুক্লবর্ণঃ স্যাৎ ক্ষত্রিয়ো রক্ত উচ্যতে আপীতো বৈশ্যজাতিস্তু শূদ্রস্থানীল উচ্যতে। ছায়া চতুর্বিধা শ্বেতা রক্তা (hyacinth), পীতা হসিতা তথা। * * * পরীক্ষ বহ্নিতঃ কাষা শাণে বা রত্নকোবিদৈঃ। স্ফটিকেনৈব কুর্ব্বন্তি গোমেদ প্রতিরূপিণম্।"]

zir-cō′-ni-ŭm (zêr-), *n.* A metal found chiefly in zircon; গোমেদ মণিতে প্রাপ্ত একপ্রকার ধাতু। **—con′-ic,** *adj.*

zith′-ẽr (tsĭt-), **zith′-ẽrn** (tsĭt-), *ns.* A stringed musicul instrument; একপ্রকার তন্ত্রীবিশিষ্ট বাদ্যযন্ত্র। **—ist,** *n.*

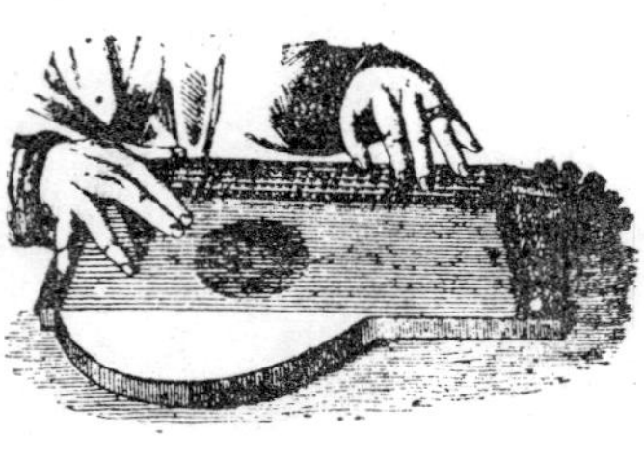

Zither.

Zō′-ăr, *n.* A place of refuge; আশ্রয়স্থান, আশ্রয়স্থলী (*Gen.* xix).

zō′-di-ăc, *n.* **1.** An imaginary belt or zone in the heavens, divided into twelve equal parts or signs, within which the apparent motions of the sun, moon and principal planets are confined; রাশিচক্র, জ্যোতিশ্চক্র, ভচক্র (সাঃ পঃ) ভগণ (ঐ), রাশিমণ্ডল (প্রপঞ্চঃ) **2.** (*Rare*) Complete course (কচিদ্ ব্যবহৃত) আবর্ত্তন। **—di′-a-cal,** *adj.* **Zodiacal light** -জ্যোতির্ম্ময় ত্রিকোণাকার নভোখণ্ড—যাহা কখন কখন সূর্য্যোদয়ের প্রাক্কালে পূর্ব্বে এবং সূর্য্যাস্তের পর পশ্চিমে দৃষ্ট হয়।

zō′-ē-trōpe, *n.* Wheel of life; বৈজ্ঞানিক ক্রীড়নকবিশেষ—যাহাতে কোন ব্যক্তি বা বস্তুর বিভিন্ন ভঙ্গীতে অঙ্কিত কতিপয় চিত্র দ্রুত ঘূর্ণিত হইলে, উহারা সম্মিলিত হইয়া সেই ব্যক্তি বা বস্তুর একই সচল চিত্ররূপে প্রতিভাত হয়।

zō′-ic, *adj.* Of, or pertaining, to animals; জন্তুসম্পর্কীয়।

Zō′-lă-iṡm, *n.* Realistic description of obscene, which is the chief characteristic of the French novelist Emile Zola; অশ্লীল বিষয়ের বাস্তব বর্ণনা—যাহা ফরাসী ঔপন্যাসিক জোলার রচনার একটী প্রধান বিশেষত্ব। **—is′-tic, —esque′,** *adjs.*

zollverein, *n.* A customs union; শুল্কসম্পর্কীয় ব্যাপারে কতিপয় রাষ্ট্রের সম্মিলন যদ্দ্বারা সংঘের বহির্ভূত রাষ্ট্রসমূহের উপর এক সাধারণ বাণিজ্য-শুল্ক স্থাপন এবং সংঘভুক্ত রাষ্ট্র সকলের মধ্যে অবাধ বাণিজ্যের প্রতিষ্ঠা করা হয়।

zōne, *n.* & *v. t.* **1.** A girdle or belt; কটিবন্ধনী, মেখলা, রশনা, চন্দ্রহার, কাঞ্চী। **2.** (*Fig.*) Any encircling band, stripe, or girdle; as, a *zone* of trees; কটিবন্ধ, মেখলা। **3.** (*Geog.*) One of the five great divisions of the earth, bounded by circles parallel to the equator; (ভূগোল) বিষুবরেখার সহিত সমান্তরাল বৃত্তসমূহ দ্বারা বেষ্টিত ভূমণ্ডলের পঞ্চ বিভাগের অন্যতম, মণ্ডল, বলয়। **4.** The area included between two exact or approximate concentric circles; যথার্থ বা প্রায় এককেন্দ্রিক বৃত্তদ্বয়ের মধ্যবর্ত্তী স্থান। **5.** Any area or part of a region characterised by uniform or similar animal or plant life; as, Littoral *zone*; পৃথিবীর যে অঞ্চলে বা অংশে একরূপ জন্তু বা উদ্ভিদ দৃষ্ট হয়। **7.** (*Geol.*) Particular beds in the stage or divisions of a certain geological formation; (ভূবিদ্যা) পাষাণাদির বিভিন্ন অবস্থা বা বিভাগ স্তর, স্তরবলয়। **8.** (*Math.*) The portion of the surface of a sphere included between two parallel planes; (গণিতশাস্ত্র) গোলকের যে অংশ সমান্তরাল ধরাতল (plane) দ্বয়ের মধ্যে থাকে। ***Verb t.*** To encircle with or as with zone; কটিবন্ধবৎ বেষ্টিত করা, কটিবন্ধ দ্বারা, বেষ্টিত করা। **Zon′-al, Zon′-a-ry, Zo′-nu-lar, Zon′-ule,** *adjs.* **Zon′-al ly.** *adv.* **Frigid zone**—হিমমণ্ডল, হিমবলয়, হিমালয়। **Maiden**

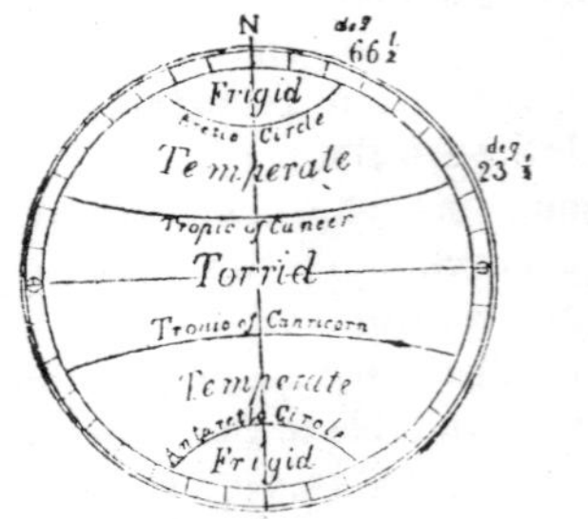

Zone.

or virgin-zone — কৌমার্য্য চিহ্ন। **North frigid zone** – উত্তর হিমবলয় (সাঃ পঃ)। **North temperate zone** – উত্তর মন্দোষ্ণ বলয় (সাঃ পঃ)। **South frigid zone** – দক্ষিণ হিমবলয় (সাঃ পঃ)। **South temperate zone**—দক্ষিণ মন্দোষ্ণ বলয় (সাঃ পঃ)। **Temperate zone** — মন্দোষ্ণবলয়। **Torrid zone**—গ্রীষ্মমণ্ডল (সাঃ পঃ), উষ্ণবলয় (ঐ)। **To loose the maiden zone** — To deprive of virginity; কৌমার্য্য হরণ করা।

zōō′, *n.* (*colloq.*) Zoological garden; (চলিত ভাষায়) চিড়িয়াখানা, পশুশালা।

zō-ō-c͟hĕm′-is-trȳ, *n.* A branch of chemistry dealing with the constituents of animal bodies; পশুরসায়ন।

zō-ō-cœ′-nō-cȳte (-sē-.) *n.* (*Bot.*) One of the peculiar reproductive bodies in the alga *vancheria*; (উদ্ভিদ্‌বিদ্যা) জন্তুসমষ্টি জৈবনিক।

zō-ō-dȳ-năm′-ic, *n.* Animal physiology; জন্তুশারীরবিজ্ঞান।

zō-og′-ă-mȳ, *n.* The sexual reproduction of animals; যৌন-উৎপাদন।

zō-oġ′-ē-nȳ, *n.* Formation of animal organs; জীবাঙ্গউৎপাদন, জীবোৎপত্তি।

zō-ō-ġē-ŏg′-ră-phȳ, *n.* The science of the distribution of animals on the earth's surface ; পৃথিবীতে জন্তু সমূহের সংস্থানসম্বন্ধীয় বিজ্ঞান, জন্তুভূগোল। **–o-graph'-ic, –o-graph'-i-cal,** *adjs.* **–pher,** *n.*

zö-ö-gloe'-ă (-glē-), *n.* Colony or mass of bacteria caused by the swelling of the cell membranes through the absorption of water, যোজনরস (সাঃ পঃ)।

zö-ŏg'-ră-phy̆, *n.* A description of animals, their forms and habits ; জন্তুবর্ণনবিদ্যা, প্রাণিবর্ণন। **–o-graph'-ic, –o-graph'-i-cal,** *adjs.* **–phist,** *n.*

zö'-oid (-ŏyd), *adj.* & *n.* A term used to denote organic bodies, sometimes free and locomotive, which may resemble, but are not animals or plants ; অসম্যক্-ধর্ম্মী। ***Noun.*** **1.** An organic product capable of more or less independent existence ; যে জৈব পদার্থ অল্পাধিক পরিমাণে স্বাধীন সত্তা রক্ষা করিতে পারে। **2.** Any member of a compound organism ; মিশ্র অঙ্গীর অন্তর্ভুক্ত কোন প্রাণী।

zö-ŏl'-ă-trȳ, *n.* Religious worship of animals ; জন্তুপূজা।

zö'-ŏ-lite, *n.* **1.** A fossil animal ; শিলীভূত জন্তু। **2.** Fossilised animal-substance ; শিলীভূত জান্তব দ্রব্য।

zö-ŏl'-ŏ-ğȳ, *n* The science of the natural history of animals ; জন্তুবিদ্যা, জন্তুবিজ্ঞান, প্রাণিবিদ্যা। **–gist,** *n.* One who is well versed in zoology ; জন্তুতত্ত্ববিদ্, পশুতত্ত্ববিদ্। **–o-log'-i-cal,** *adj.* **–o-log'-i-cal-ly,** *adj.* **Zoological society**— জন্তুবিদ্যা অনুশীলনের জন্য ১৩২৬ খৃঃ অব্দে লণ্ডন নগরীতে প্রতিষ্ঠিত সম্প্রদায় বিশেষ।

zö-ŏ-măg'-nĕt-ĭsm, *n.* Same as ANIMAL-MAGNETISM (which see).

zö'-ŏ-măn-cy̆, *n.* The art of divination from animals ; জন্তুদের আকৃতি বা আচরণ দর্শনে ভবিষ্যকথন, জন্তুজ্যোতিবিদ্যা।

zö'-ŏ-mē-chăn-ĭcs, zö-ŏ-dȳ-năm'-ĭcs, *ns.* The measuremet of animals ; পশুমিতি, জন্তুমিতি।

zö-ŏ-mŏr'-phĭc, *adj.* **1.** Pertaining to, or exhibiting, animal forms ; জন্তুরূপী, জন্তুরূপ প্রদর্শক। **2.** (*Anthrop.*) Representing a God or other supernatural being under the form of one of the lower animals ; (নৃতত্ত্ব) দেবতাদিগকে জন্তুরূপে প্রদর্শী। **–phism,** *n.* **1.** (*Rare*) The transformation of man into animals ; (কচিদ্ব্যবহৃত) মানবের পশুদেহে রূপান্তর। **2.** The representation of a god or man under the form of a beast ; মানব অথবা দেবতাকে পশুরূপে প্রদর্শন, জন্তুরূপপ্রদান। **3.** The ascription to beings animal in form of divine or human qualities ; জন্তুতে দেব বা মানবের আরোপ।

zö'-ŏn, *n.* The product of a fertilized ovum ; পুংবীজনিষিক্ত অণ্ডক হইতে উৎপন্ন বস্তু।

zö-ŏn'-ŏ-my̆, zö-ŏ-nō-mĭ-ă *ns.* The laws of animal life ; the science that treats of animal life ; জন্তু জীবনের নিয়মনিচয় ; পশুবিজ্ঞান।

zö-ŏ-phy̆s'-ĭcs, *n.* The study of physical structure of animals ; জন্তুর অঙ্গবিন্যাস সম্বন্ধীয় বিদ্যা, জন্ত্বঙ্গ-সংস্থানবিদ্যা।

zö'-ŏ-phȳte, *n.* **1.** A term applied to simple polyps and compound individuals consisting of many polyps united togeter, thus forming the connecting link between plants and animals, as corals, sponge, etc. ; বিভিন্ন প্রকার উদ্ভিদ্‌ধর্ম্মী জন্তুর সাধারণ নাম। **–phy'-ic,** *adj.* **–phy-tol'-o-gy,** *n.* **–phy-to-log'-i-cal,** *adj.* **–phy-tol'-o gist,** *n.*

zö'-ŏ-plăs-ty̆, *n.* The grafting of a piece of living tissue from a lower animal on to a hnman being; কোন সজীব জন্তুর দেহের বিধানতন্তু মানব দেহে স্থানান্তর।

zö-ŏ-psy-chŏl'-ŏ-ğȳ (-sī-), psychology of animals othe men ; জন্তুমনস্তত্ত্ব, জন্তুমনোবিজ্ঞান

zö'-ŏ-spĕrm, *n.* **1.** One of the spermatic particles or spermatozoa of an animal ; জন্তুর শুক্রাণু **2.** same ZOOSPORE.

zö'-ŏ-spōre, *n.* The spore of a cryptogamic plant, so called because it moves as if alive after it is discharged from the spore-case ; অবীজদল পুষ্পের রেণুকা। এই সকল রেণু রেণুস্থলী হইতে চ্যুত হইলে সজীবৎ চলিয়া থাকে বলিয়া এই নাম, জঙ্গরেণু (সাঃ পঃ)। **–spor'-ic,** *adj.*

zö'-ŏ-tăx-y̆, *n.* Classification of animals ; প্রাণীবিভাগ।

zö'-ŏ-thĕ-ĭsm, *n.* Beast worship পশুপূজা। **–is'-tic,** *adj.*

zö-ŏt'-ŏ-mȳ, *n.* **1.** The dissection of animals other than men ; জন্তুদেহ ব্যবচ্ছেদ। **–mist,** *n.*

zŏr'-ĭl, *n.* A South African animal about the size of polecat ; দক্ষিণ আফ্রিকার একপ্রকার গন্ধমার্জ্জারবৎ জন্তু।

Zö-rō-ăs'-tĕr, *n.* The founder of the Parsee religion who probably lived about 800 B. C. ; পারসীক ধর্ম্মের প্রবর্ত্তক জরোয়াষ্টার, জরাথুস্ত্র, জরসস্ত (ভবিষ্যপুরাণ—১৩৭), জরসথ (ঐ)। **–tri-an,** *adj.* & *n.* **–tri-an-ism** *n.* The religion of the Persians introduced by Zoroaster ; জোরোয়াস্তারের প্রবর্ত্তিত ধর্ম্ম খৃঃ পূঃ ৫৫০ হইতে খৃষ্টোত্তর ৭ম শতাব্দী পর্য্যন্ত পারস্যের জাতীয় ধর্ম্ম ছিল। খৃষ্টীয় সপ্তম শতাব্দীতে মুসলমানগণ পারস্যদেশ আক্রমণ করে। ঐ সময়ে কতিপয় জোরয়াস্তার ধর্ম্মাবলম্বী ভারতবর্ষে পলায়ন করেন। এই ধর্ম্মে পরমেশ্বরের নাম জারুণ আকরণ (অনন্তকাল)। ধর্ম্মেশ্বর আউর মজদা (Ahura Mazda) এবং অধর্ম্মেশ্বর আংরো মেইন্যু (Angra Mainyu) এই উভয় ঈশ্বর ইহা হইতে উদ্ভূত হয়। আউর মজদা আলোকের এবং আংরোমেইন্যু অন্ধকারের স্রষ্টা। এই উভয় ঈশ্বর যুগপ্রলয় পর্য্যন্ত পরস্পরের বিরুদ্ধাচরণ করিতেন। এই ধর্ম্মে

...তর প্রাণীর প্রতি দয়া, এবং নৈতিক ...ত্রর উৎকর্ষ সম্বন্ধে উৎকৃষ্ট [বিধান ...হইয়াছে। জরসথের ধর্ম্মের প্রধান অঙ্গ অগ্নিপূজা। জরসথের মতে প্রত্যেক ব্যক্তির স্বাধীন ইচ্ছা, ধর্ম্ম-বুদ্ধি, আত্মা, এবং স্বর্গধামে স্বীয় আধ্যাত্মিক প্রতিরূপ রহিয়াছে। মৃত্যুর পর শ্রেয়স্ (Sraosha) নামক দেবতা মৃতব্যক্তির আত্মাকে লইয়া উর্দ্ধে ধাবিত হয়। স্বর্গ এবং পৃথিবীর মধ্যবর্ত্তী সেতুতে উপস্থিত হইলে মিত্র এবং রসন নামক দেবতাদ্বয় জীবাত্মার নিকট পাপ ও পুণ্য কর্ম্মের হিসাব উপস্থিত করেন। অতঃপর পাপ-কর্ম্মের প্রায়শ্চিত্তের পর জীবাত্মা ঐ সেতু অতিক্রম করে। জীবাত্মা স্বর্গবাসের উপযুক্ত হইলে সেই সেতু সুপ্রশস্ত ও সুখগম্য হয়, অন্যথায় উহা কেশের মত সূক্ষ্ম আকার ধারণ করে। স্বর্গবাসের অযোগ্য আত্মা তখন অতল-স্পর্শখাতে পতিত হয়। যে আত্মা সেতু অতিক্রমে সমর্থ হয় সে এক অনন্ত আলোকের রাজ্যে প্রবিষ্ট হয়]।

Zouave.

zou′-ave (zô-âv *or* zwâv), *n.* A soldier of the French light infantry crops; মুরদিগের পরিচ্ছদ ধারী ফরাসী পদাতিক সৈনিক বিশেষ।

zounds (zownds), *interj.* An exclamation contracted from "*God's wounds*" and much used as an oath; অধঃপাতে যাও।

zuc′-chět-tă (tsô-), **-tō** *ns.* A skull-cap worn by Roman Catholic ecclesiastics, black by priests, purple by bishops, red by Cardinals and white by Popes; রোমানক্যাথলিক ধর্ম্মযাজক প্রভৃতির কিনারাবিহীন টুপি (এই টুপি সাধারণ যাজকদিগের পক্ষে কাল, বিশপদিগের পক্ষে মেজেন্টা, কার্ডিন্যালগণের পক্ষে লাল ও পোপদিগের পক্ষে শ্বেতবর্ণের হইয়া থাকে)।

Zû′-lû (*or* zô-lô), *n.* **1.** A member of a South African people belonging to the Banta stock; দক্ষিণ আফ্রিকার জাতিবিশেষের লোক, জুলু। **2.** The language of the Zulus; জুলুজাতির ভাষা।

zwieback, *n.* A biscuit rusk, or a sweet spiced cake toasted; পাউরুটি হইতে ছিন্ন খণ্ড বিশেষ—যাহা পুনরায় সেঁকিয়া লওয়া হয়, ভর্জ্জিতমান রুটিখণ্ড, মিষ্ট পিষ্টক।

Zwing′-li-an, *n.* **1.** Of, or pertaining to, the Swiss religious reformer Zwingli; সুইজরলণ্ডের ধর্ম্মপ্রচারক Zwingli সম্বন্ধীয়। **2.** A follower of Zwingli; Zwinglির মতাবলম্বী ব্যক্তি।

zȳ′-găl, *n.* H-shaped; as, *zygal* fissuress; H অক্ষরাকৃতি।

zȳg-ă-pŏph′-ȳ-sis, *n.* One of the processes on a vertebra as articulation with another; মেরুদণ্ডের সন্ধিপর্ব্বের প্রবর্দ্ধন বিশেষ—যদ্দ্বারা উহার একটী অপরটীর সহিত সংযুক্ত হয়।

zȳ′-gite, *n.* A rower in the middle bank of a trireme; প্রাচীন-গ্রীসের পোতের মধ্যের সারির দাঁড়ী।

zȳ-gō-dăc′-tȳl, *adj.* & *n.* Having the toes disposed in pairs, two forward and two backwards; সম্মুখদিকে এবং পশ্চাদ্দিকে যুগ্মপদাঙ্গুলীবিশিষ্ট। *Noun.* A bird with toes so arranged; যে পক্ষীর পদাঙ্গুলী চতুষ্টয়ের মধ্যে দুইটী সম্মুখের দিকে এবং অপর দুইটী পশ্চাদ্দিকে থাকে। **-ty-lous** *adj.* Same as ZYGODACTYL, *adj.*

zȳ-gō′-mă, *n.* The bony arch of the cheek; গণ্ডের তোরণাকৃতি অস্থি, গণ্ডাস্থির যুগবৎ প্রবর্দ্ধন। এতদ্দ্বারা শঙ্খাস্থি ও গণ্ডাস্থি সংযুক্ত আছে। **—mat′-ic,** *adj.*

zȳ-gō-mŏr′-phous (-fŭs), *adj.* Divisible into similar halves only in one plane; as, a *zygomorphous* flower; সমযুগ্মক (সাঃ পঃ) একমাত্রিক (ঐ)।

zȳ-gō′-sis, *n.* Same as CONJUGATION 3.

zȳ′-gō-spōre, *n.* (*Bot.*) A spore formed by conjugation of two similar gametes or sexual cells; (উদ্ভিদ্‌বিদ্যা) যুগ্মজরেণু (সাঃ পঃ)।

zȳ′-gōte, *n.* (*Bot.*) Any spore formed by the conjugation of two gametes; যুক্তবোধ (সাঃ পঃ)।

zȳ-mō′-sis, *n.* **1.** Fermentation; অন্তরুৎসেক, গাঁজন। **2.** A contagious disease due to some morbific agent fermenting in the system; একপ্রকার সংক্রামক রোগ-যাহা দেহে কোনরূপ রোগজনক বস্তু গাঁজন হইতে উপজাত হয়।

zȳ-mŏt′-ic, *adj.* Pertaining to fermentation; গাঁজনসম্বন্ধী। **Zymotic disease** — Same as ZYMOSIS *n.* 2.

Additional List of Familiar Phrases, Proverbs, Maxims, Quotations and Mottoes.

A bas—Down ! down with ! (Fr.) ; ভূপাতিত কর, পাতয়, মারয়।

Ab irato— In a fit of passion (L.) ; রাগের মাথায়।

. **bon droit**—Justly ; according to reason (Fr.) ; ন্যায়তঃ ; ন্যায়সঙ্গতরূপে, যুক্তিসিদ্ধরূপে।

. **bon marche**—Cheap (Fr.) ; সস্তা।

.. **origine**—From the beginning (..) ; আদি হইতে।

. **ovo usque ad mala**—From the beginning to the end (lit. from the egg to the apples) (L.) ; আদি হইতে অন্ত পর্য্যন্ত, আদ্যন্ত।

brege—Abridgment (Fr.) ; সংক্ষেপ।

bsit invidia—Envy apart (L.) ; বিদ্বেষের কথা না ধরিলে।

b uno disce omnes — From a single instance you may infer the whole (L.) ; একটী ঘটনা হইতেই সমস্ত .দয়ঙ্গম হয়।

capite ad calcem—From head heel (L.) ; আপাদমস্তক।

compte—In part payment (lit. account) (Fr.) ; কতক টাকা ..শিলস্বরূপ।

couvert — Under cover (Fr.) ; ছাদনে, আবরণে।

.uce salus—Salvation from the .oss (L.) ; ক্রুশ হইতে মুক্তি।

aperturam—Wherever a book .y be opened (L.) ; পুস্তকের যে .াই খোলা যাউক না কেন।

arbitrium—At pleasure (L.) ; .চ্ছাক্রমে।

avizandum—Into considera-.on (Scots Law) (L.) ; বিবেচনাধীন।

A Deo et rege—From God and the king (L.) ; রাজা এবং পরমেশ্বরের নিকট হইতে।

Ad extremum — At last (L.); সর্ব্বশেষে।

Ad finem—To the end (L.); শেষ পর্য্যন্ত।

Ad Græcas kalendas — At the Greek calends, *i. e.* never (L.) ; কখনও না।

Adhuc sub judice lis est—The affair is not yet decided (L.) ; ব্যাপারটী এখনও মীমাংসিত হয় নাই।

A discretion — Without any restriction (lit. at discretion) (Fr.) ; নির্ব্বিশেষে।

Ad majorem Dei gloriam—To the greater glory of God (L.) ; ভগবানের উচ্চতর মহিমায়।

Ad patres—Dead; to death (lit. to the fathers) (L.) ; মৃত ; মৃত্যুপর্য্যন্ত।

Ad quod damnum — To what damage (L.) ; কি ক্ষতিতে।

A droit—To the right (Fr.) ; দক্ষিণদিকে, ডাইনে, দক্ষিণে।

Ad utrumque paratus—Prepared for either case (L.) ; উভয় ঘটনার জন্য প্রস্তুত।

Ad vivum—To the life (L.) ; জীবন পর্য্যন্ত।

Ægrescit medendo—The remedy is worse than the disease (lit. the disorder increases with the remedy) (L.) ; পীড়ার চেয়ে ঔষধ অধিক অনিষ্টজনক।

Æquam servare mentem — To preserve an even temper (L.) ; মানসিক স্থৈর্য্য রক্ষা করা।

Æquo animo—With an even or equable mind (L) ; ধীর এবং প্রশান্ত চিত্তে।

Affaire d'amour—(Fr.) Same as AFFAIR OF LOVE.

Affaire d'honneur—An affair of honour ; a duel (Fr.) ; সম্মানের বিষয় ; দ্বন্দ্বযুদ্ধ।

Affaire du cœur—An affair of the heart (Fr.) ; ভালবাসার ব্যাপার।

A gauche—To the left (Fr.) ; বামে, বামদিকে।

Age quod agis—Attend to (lit. do) what you are doing (L.) ; নিজের চরকায় তৈল দেও।

A grands frais—At great expense (Fr.) ; বহু ব্যয়ে।

Aide-toi, le Ciel t'aidera — Help yourself and Heaven will help you (Fr.) ; উদ্যমের সহিত কর্ম্মে প্রবৃত্ত হও তবেই পরমেশ্বরের সাহায্য পাইবে।

A l'abandon—At random ; little cared for (Fr.) ; যদৃচ্ছাক্রমে ; বিশেষ মনোযোগ না দিয়া।

A la bonne heure—Well-timed (Fr.) ; সময়োচিত।

A l'abri—Under shelter (Fr.) ; আশ্রয়ে।

A la derobee—By stealth (Fr.) ; চুপে চুপে।

Alea est jacta—The die is cast ; the step is taken (L.) ; পাশার দান ফেলা গিয়াছে ; যা করিবার তাহা করা হইয়াছে।

Alere flammam—To feed the flame (L.) ; অগ্নিতে ঘৃতাহুতি প্রদান করা

Alieni appetens, sui profusus—Covetous of other men's property, prodigal of his own (L.) ; নিজের অর্থ ব্যয়ে মুক্তহস্ত এবং পরের অর্থে লোভী।

A l'improviste—Unawares (Fr.) ; আচম্বিতে, আচম্‌কা।

Aliquando bonus dormitat Homerus—Sometimes even the good Homer nods (L.) ; হোমারকেও কখনও কখনও নত হইতে হয়।

Alter idem—Another exactly similar (L.) ; অবিকল প্রতিরূপ।

Alter ipse amicus—A friend is a second self (L.) ; বন্ধু অভিন্নস্বরূপ অথবা দ্বিতীয় প্রতিরূপ।

A main armee—By force of arms (Fr.) সবলে।

A mensa et thoro—From bed and board ; divorced (L.) ; শয্যা এবং ভোজন হইতে ; বিবাহবিচ্ছিন্ন।

A merveille—To a wonder (Fr.) ; আশ্চর্য্যজনকভাবে।

Amicus humani generis—A friend of the human race (L.) ; মানবজাতির বন্ধু, বিশ্ববন্ধু, জগদ্বন্ধু, জনবন্ধু।

Amicus Plato, sed magis amica veritas—Plato is my friend, but truth is my divinity (lit. more a friend) (L.); প্লেটো আমার বন্ধু কিন্তু সত্য আমার উপাস্য দেবতা।

Amor patriæ—The love of our country (L.) ; স্বদেশপ্রীতি, স্বদেশানুরাগ, স্বদেশপ্রেম।

Anguis in herba—A snake in the grass (L.) ; ঘাসের ভিতর সাপ, ক্ষীরের ভিতর হীরার ছুরী।

Animo et fide—By courage and faith (L.) ; সাহস এবং বিশ্বাসের বলে।

Animo, non astutia—By courage not by craft (L.); সাহসে, কৌশলে নহে।

A perte de vue—Beyond the range of vision (Fr.) ; দৃষ্টির বাহিরে, দৃষ্টিসীমাতীত।

A point—To a point exactly (Fr.); সূক্ষ্মভাবে, সঠিকভাবে।

A posse ad esse—From possibility to actuality (L.) ; সম্ভাবনা হইতে বাস্তবিকতায়।

Aquila non capit muscas—An eagle does not catch flies (L.) ; ঈগল পক্ষী মাছি ধরে না (cf. মাছি মেরে হাত কাল করা।)

Arbiter elegantiarum—(L.) Same as THE MASTER OF THE CEREMONIES (see CEREMONY).

Argumentum ad invidiam—An argument which appeals to low passions ; (L.) ; লোকের রাগদ্বেষের নিকট আবেদন।

Ars longa, vita brevis—Art is long, life is short (L.) ; কাজ অনন্ত কিন্তু জীবন সীমাবদ্ধ। (cf. অনন্ত শাস্ত্রং বহু বেদিতব্যং স্বল্পশ্চ আয়ুঃবহবশ্চ বিঘ্নাঃ)।

Artis est celare artem—The perfection of art is to conceal art (L.); কলাকৌশলের প্রচ্ছন্নতাই চারুশিল্পের চরমোৎকর্ষ।

Assumpsit—An action on a verbal promise (L. Law); মৌখিক প্রতিশ্রুতির উপর যে কার্য্য করা হয়।

Au courant—Perfectly acquainted with (Fr.) ; অভিজ্ঞ, বিশারদ, কুশল, সিদ্ধহস্ত।

Audi alteram partem—Hear the other party ; hear both sides (L.) ; অপর পক্ষের কথা শোন ; উভয় পক্ষের কথা শোন।

Au pis aller—At the worst (Fr.) ; মন্দের পক্ষে।

Aura popularis—Popular favour (lit. breeze) (L.) ; জনপ্রীতি।

Aut vincere aut mori—Either to conquer or die (L.); হয় বিজয়লক্ষ্মীকে অঙ্কগত করিব নতুবা যুদ্ধে প্রাণ বিসর্জ্জন করিব।

A verbis ad verbera—From words to blows (L.) ; কথা হইতে হাতাহাতিতে।

A votre sante—To your health (Fr.) ; তোমার স্বাস্থ্য কামনায়।

Bel esprit—A person of genius ; a brilliant mind (Fr.) ; প্রতিভাবান ব্যক্তি ; বুদ্ধিদ্বারা উদ্ভাসিত মন।

Bon gre, mal gre—Whether willing or not (Fr.) ; স্বেচ্ছায়ই হউক বা অনিচ্ছায়ই হউক।

Bon jour—Same as GOOD DAY (Fr.)

Bon soir—Good evening (Fr.) ; শুভসায়াহ্ন (অভিবাদনার্থে ব্যবহৃত হয়)।

Brevete—Patented (Fr.); পেটেণ্টকৃত।

Campus Martius—A place of military exercise (lit. field of Mars) (L.) ; অস্ত্রচালানাদি অভ্যাসের স্থান, শরচালনক্ষেত্র।

Canaille—Same as RABBLE (Fr.)

Candide et constanter—With candour and constancy (L.); নিষ্ঠা এবং সরলতার সহিত।

Carpe diem—Make a good use of the present (L.) ; বর্ত্তমান সময়ের সদ্ব্যবহার কর।

Cedant arma togæ—Let the military yield to the civil power (lit. arms to the gown) (L.) ; সামরিক শক্তি অসামরিক শক্তির অধীনে থাকুক।

Ce n'est que le premier pas qui coute—It is only the first step that is difficult (lit. costs) (Fr.) ; কার্য্যের প্রারম্ভই কঠিন।

Chef de cuisine—A head cook (Fr.) ; প্রধান সূপকার, প্রধান পাচক।

Ci git—Here lies (Fr.) ; এই স্থানে শায়িত।

Clarum et venerabile nomen—An illustrious and honoured name (L.) ; সুবিখ্যাত এবং সম্মানিত ব্যক্তি।

Cogito, ergo sum—I think, therefore I am (L.) ; আমি চিন্তা করিতেছি অতএব আমি বর্ত্তমান আছি।

Commune bonum—A common good (L.) ; সাধারণের উপকার, জনহিত, লোকোপকার।

Communi consensu—By common consent (L.) ; সর্ব্বসম্মতিক্রমে।

Compagnon de voyage—A fellow-traveller (Fr.) ; সহযাত্রী।

Consuetudo pro lege servatur—Custom is observed as law (L.) ; দেশাচার আইনের মত অনুসৃত হইয়া থাকে।

Contra bonos mores—Against good morals (L.) ; সুনীতির বিরুদ্ধে।

Cordon bleu—A skilful cook (lit. a blue ribbon) (Fr.) ; রন্ধনকুশল পাচক।

Corps diplomatique.—The diplomatic body (Fr.) ; কুট রাজনীতিক সম্প্রদায়।

Couleur de rose—A flattering representation (Fr.) ; মনোরম বর্ণনা, মনোমতভাবে প্রদর্শন।

Coup d' essai—First attempt (Fr.) ; প্রথম উদ্যোগ।

Coup de soleil—SUNSTROKE (Fr.)

Coup de theatre — Theatrical effect (Fr.) ; নাটুকেভাব।

Courage sans peur — Courage without fear (Fr.) ; শৌর্য্য।

Coute qu'il coute—Let it cost what it may (Fr.) : যতই ব্যয় হউক না কেন।

Crux criticorum—The puzzle of critics (L.); সমালোচকদের হতবুদ্ধিতাজনক বিষয়।

Crux medicorum—The puzzle of physicians (L.) ; চিকিৎসকের হতবুদ্ধিতাজনক বিষয়।

Cui bono ?— Whom does it benefit (L) ; কাহার উপকারার্থে।

Cul de sac—A street or lane that has no outlet (Fr.) ; আঁধা গলি।

Cum grano salis—With a grain of salt, *i.e.*, with some allowance (L.) ; কিছু বাদ সাদ দিয়া।

Cum privilegio—With privilege (L.) ; বিশেষ সুবিধার সহিত।

De bonne grace—(Fr.) WITH A GOOD GRACE (See GRACE).

Deceptio visus—Optical illusion (L.) ; দৃষ্টিবিভ্রম।

De die in diem—From day to day (L.) ; দিনের পর দিন, দিন দিন।

De mortuis nil nisi bonum—Let nothing be said of the dead but what is favourable (L.) ; মৃতের সম্বন্ধে কোনরূপ গ্লানিজনক কথা বলা অনুচিত

De nihilo nihil fit—From nothing nothing is produced (L.) ; অসৎ হইতে কোন বস্তু জাত হয় না, নাসতঃ সজ্জায়তে।

Deo favente—With God's favour (L.) ; ঈশ্বরানুগ্রহে, দেবানুগ্রহে।

Deo gratias—Thanks to God (L.) ; পরমেশ্বরকে ধন্যবাদ।

Deo juvante—With God's help (L.) ; ভগবানের সাহায্যে।

Desunt cætera—The remainder is wanting (L.) ; অবশিষ্টের অভাব।

Dieu et mon droit—God and my right (Fr.) ; ভগবান এবং আমার ন্যায়সঙ্গত অধিকার।

Die Wacht am Rhein — "The watch on the Rhine," a German national song (Ger.) ; "রাইনের প্রহরা" (জর্ম্মণদিগের জাতীয় সঙ্গীত)।

Dii penates — Household gods (L.) ; গৃহদেবতাগণ।

Disponendo me, non mutando me—By disposing of me, not by changing me (L.) ; আমাকে বিনাশ করিয়া পরিবর্ত্তন করিয়া নয়।

Divide et impera—Divide and govern (L.); ভেদনীতি অবলম্বনে শাসন কর।

Docendo discimus—We learn by teaching (L.) ; শিক্ষা দানের সঙ্গে সঙ্গে আমরা শিক্ষা করি।

Dominus providebit—The Lord will provide (L.) ; ঈশ্বর আমাদের জন্য ব্যবস্থা করিবেন।

Domus et placens uxor— Thy house and pleasing wife (L.) ; তোমার গৃহ এবং তোমার মনোরমা ভার্য্যা।

Double entendre — A double meaning (Fr.) ; দ্ব্যর্থ।

Double entente — Double signification (Fr.) ; দ্ব্যর্থবোধকতা।

Droit des gens — The law of nations (Fr.) ; জাতিসমূহের আইন।

Dulce domum—Sweet home (L.) ; মধুময় গৃহ।

Dulce est desipere in loco—It is pleasant to jest at the proper time (L.) ; সময়োচিত পরিহাস অতি মনোরম।

Dulce et decorum est pro patria mori—It is sweet and glorious to die for one's country (L.) ; স্বদেশের জন্য প্রাণ দান করা কি গৌরবের বিষয়।

Dum spiro, spero—While I breathe, I hope (L.) ; যতক্ষণ শ্বাস ততক্ষণ আশ।

Dum vivimus, vivamus—Let us live while we live (L.) ; যতদিন দেহে প্রাণ আছে ততদিন মানুষের মত জীবন যাপন করিব।

Durante beneplacito — During good pleasure (L.) ; যতদিন মনস্তুষ্টি থাকে।

Durante vita—During life (L.) ; জীবদ্দশায়।

E contra—On the other hand (L.) ; পক্ষান্তরে।

E contrario—On the contrary (L.) ; পক্ষান্তরে।

Ego et rex meus—I and my king (L.) ; আমার রাজা এবং আমি।

Eloignement—Estrangement(Fr.); মনোবাদ, মনোমালিন্য।

En ami—As a friend (Fr.); বন্ধুস্বরূপ।

En attendant—In the meantime (Fr.) ; ইতঃমধ্যে।

En famille—In a domestic state (Fr.) : গৃহপালিত অবস্থায়।

Enfants de famille—Children of the family (Fr.) ; পরিবারের বালক বালিকা।

Enfants perdus — Same as FORLORN HOPE. (Fr.)

Enfant gate — A spoiled child (Fr.) ; নষ্ট ছেলে।

Enfant trouve — Same as FOUNDLING. (Fr.)

En foule—In a crowd (Fr.); জনতার মধ্যে।

En grande tenue—In full dress (Fr.) ; পূর্ণপরিচ্ছদে।

En rapport—In relation ; in connection (Fr.) ; সম্পর্কে ; বিষয়ে।

Ense et aratro—With sword and plough (L.) ; তরবারী ও লাঙ্গলের সাহায্যে।

En suite — In company (Fr.) সহযাত্রিরূপে।

En verite—In truth (Fr.) ; বাস্তবিক পক্ষে, প্রকৃতপক্ষে।

Epicuri de grege porcus — A pig of the flock of Epicurus (L.) ; এপিকিউরাসের শূকর সমূহের মধ্যে একটী।

Errare humanum est—It is human to err (L.); ভুল মানুষেরই হয়।

Esperance en Dieu — Hope in God (Fr.); ঈশ্বরের উপর ভরসা।

Esse quam videri—To be rather than to seem (L.); প্রতিভাত হওয়ার চেয়ে বরং হওয়া।

Est modus in rebus—There is a mean in everything (L.); প্রত্যেক বিষয়েরই একটা মধ্যাবস্থা আছে।

Esto perpetua—Let it be perpetual (L.); ইহা চিরস্থায়ী হউক।

Et hoc genus omne—And everything of this kind (L.); এবং ঐ জাতীয় প্রত্যেক বস্তু।

Et sic de ceteris—And so of the rest (L.); অবশিষ্টের পক্ষেও এইরূপ।

Et tu, Brute—And you, Brutus (L.); ব্রুটাস তুমিও (সীজরের উক্তি। সীজর পুত্রবৎ প্রিয় ব্রুটাসকে তদীয় হত্যাকারগিণের মধ্যে দর্শনে আক্ষেপের সহিত এই উক্তি করিয়াছিলেন। See Shakespeare's *Julius Cœsar.*)

Ex abrupto—Without preparation (L.); বিনা আয়োজনে।

Ex æquo—By right (L.); অধিকারবলে।

Ex animo—From the soul; heartily (L.); অন্তর হইতে; আন্তরিকভাবে।

Exceptio probat regulam—Same as EXCEPTION PROVES THE RULE (under EXCEPTION.)

Exceptis excipiendis — The requisite exceptions being made (L.); বর্জ্জিত বিষয় সমূহ বাদ দিলে।

Ex concesso — Admittedly (L.); সর্ব্বস্বীকৃতভাবে।

Ex curia—Out of court (L.); আদালতের বাহিরে।

Ex delicto—From the crime (L.); ঐ অপরাধ হইতে।

Exempli gratia—By way of example (L.); দৃষ্টান্তস্বরূপ।

Ex mero motu—From one's own free will (L.); কাহারো স্বাধীন ইচ্ছা হইতে।

Ex nihilo nihil fit — Nothing produces nothing (L.); অবস্তু হইতে কোন বস্তু উৎপন্ন হয় না, নাসতঃ সজ্জায়তে, কথং অবস্তুনা বস্তু সিদ্ধিঃ।

Ex opere operato—By the external act (L.); বাহিরের কার্য্য দ্বারা।

Ex pede Herculem—We judge of the size of the statue of Hercules by the foot (L.); আমরা পদদৃষ্টে হার্কিউলিসের (ভগ্ন) পাষাণমূর্ত্তির আয়তন নির্ণয়ের চেষ্টা করিতে পারি।

Experimentum crucis—A decisive experiment (L.); নিশ্চায়ক পরীক্ষা।

Experto crede—Believe one who has had experience (L.); অভিজ্ঞলোকের উপর আস্থা স্থাপন করিও।

Ex professo—Like one who knows (L.); জ্ঞাতসার ব্যক্তির মত।

Extra muros—Beyond the walls (L.); প্রাচীরের বাহিরে।

Ex ungue leonem—The lion may be known by his claw (L.); থাবা দ্বারাই সিংহের পরিচয় পাওয়া যায়।

Ex uno disce omnes—From one judge of all (L.); একজনকে দেখিলে সকলের সম্বন্ধেই বিচার করা যায়।

Faber suæ fortunæ—The maker of his own fortune (L.); আত্মচেষ্টায় সমৃদ্ধি লাভকারী।

Facile princeps—The admitted chief; with ease at the top (L.); সর্ব্বজন স্বীকৃত নায়ক; অনায়াসে সর্ব্বোচ্চ শিখরে উপনীত।

Facilis est descensus Averni—The descent to hell is easy; the downward road is an easy one (L.); অবতরণের পথ অতি সহজ; অধঃপতনের রাস্তা অতি সহজ।

Facit indignatio versum — Indignation gives spirit to a song (L.); ক্রোধ সঙ্গীতে প্রাণসঞ্চার করে।

Fæx populi — The dregs of the people (L.); ইতর লোক, ওঁছা লোক।

Fama clamosa—A current scandal (L.); যে কেলেঙ্কারির কথা লইয়া বর্ত্তমানে আলোচনা চলিতেছে।

Fas est et ab hoste doceri—It is right to derive instruction even from an enemy (L.); শত্রুর নিকট হইতেও উপদেশ লাভ করা সঙ্গত।

Fata obstant—The fates oppose it (L.); অদৃষ্ট ইহার পরিপন্থী (cf. অদৃষ্ট আমার বাদী)।

Faux pas—A false step (Fr.); অন্যায়ের পথে পদবিক্ষেপ।

Fiat justitia, ruat cœlum—Let justice be done, though the heavens should fall in (L.); যদ্যপি আকাশ ভাঙ্গিয়া পড়ে তথাপি ন্যায়সঙ্গত কার্য্য সম্পাদনে শিথিলপ্রযত্ন হইও না।

Fiat lux—Let there be light (L.); আলো আসুক।

Filius nullius—The son of nobody (L.); কাহারো পুত্র নয়।

Filius terræ—Son of the earth, one low born (L.); ভূমিজীবী; হীনবংশজাত ব্যক্তি।

Finis coronat opus — The end crowns the work (L.); পরিসমাপ্তি কার্য্যের মুকুটস্বরূপ।

Flagrante bello—During the war (L.); যুদ্ধকালে।

Flagrante delicto—In the very act (L.); হাতেনাতে।

Fortuna favet fortibus—Same as FORTUNE FAVOURS THE BRAVE (L.)

Frangas, non flectes—You may break, but you will not bend me (L.); তুমি আমাকে ভাঙ্গিতে পার কিন্তু নোয়াইতে পারিবে না। (অর্থাৎ তুমি আমাকে বিনাশ করিতে পার, কিন্তু কখনও পদানত করিতে পারিবে না)।

Fronti nulla fides—There is no trusting to appearances (L.); বাহির দেখিয়া ভুলিও না।

Furor loquendi — A rage for speaking (L.); রসনাকণ্ডুয়ন।

Furor poeticus—The poet's frenzy (L.); কবির উন্মাদনা।

Furor scribendi — A rage for writing (L.); লিখিবার জন্য উৎকট আকাঙ্ক্ষা, করকণ্ডুয়ন।

Garde du corps — Same as BODYGUARD (L.)

Gaudeamus—Let us have a joyful time (L.); চল আমরা আনন্দ করি।

Gens de guerre—Soldiers (Fr.) সৈনিকবৃন্দ।

Gens de lettres—Literary people (Fr.) ; সাহিত্যিক-সমাজ।

Genus irritabile vatum — The irritable tribe of poets (L.); কোপনস্বভাব কবিসম্প্রদায়।

Gutta cavat lapidem non vi, sed semper cadendo — The drop hollows the stone not by force, but by constant falling (L.); ক্রমাগত বারিবিন্দু পতনে প্রস্তরও ক্ষয় প্রাপ্ত হয়, ঘষিতে ঘষিতে প্রস্তরও ক্ষয় পায়।

Hannibal ante portas — The enemy at the gates (L.) ; শত্রু দ্বারে।

Helluo librorum—A devourer of books (L.) ; গ্রন্থপাঠানুরাগী।

Heureka—I have found it out (Gr.) ; পেয়েছি।

Hoc loco — In this place (L.) ; এইস্থানে।

Hoi polloi—The multitude (L.) ; লোকসংঘ।

Homme d'affaires — A business man (Fr.) ; ব্যবসায়ী।

Homme d'esprit— A witty man (Fr.) ; সুরসিক মানুষ।

Honi soit qui mal y pense—Evil be to him that evil thinks (Fr.) ; শত্রুর মুখে ছাই পড়ুক।

Humanum est errare—To err is human (L.) ; মুণীনাঞ্চ মতিভ্রমঃ।

Ich dien—I serve (Ger.) ; আমি সেবা করি।

Ignorantia legis excusat neminem — Ignorance of the law excuses nobody (L.) ; আইনের বিষয় অজ্ঞাত এই ওজর খাটে না।

Il penseroso— The pensive man (It.) ; বিষণ্ণ ব্যক্তি।

Imo pectore—From the bottom of the heart (L.) ; হৃদয়ের অন্তঃস্তল হতে।

In æternum—For ever (L.) ; চিরদিনের জন্য।

In capite—In chief (L.) ; প্রধানতঃ।

In cauda venenum—Poison lurks in the tail, or there is a sting in the tail (L.) ; লাঙ্গুলে বিষ আছে, লাঙ্গুলে হুল আছে।

In cœlo quies—There is rest in heaven (L.) ; স্বর্গে শান্তি আছে।

In commendam — In trust or recommendation (L.) ; বিশ্বাসের উপর বা সুপারিসের উপর।

In curia—In the court (L.) ; আদালতে।

In extenso—At full length (L.) ; সবিস্তারে।

In forma pauperis—As a poor man (L.) : দরিদ্ররূপে।

Infra dignitatem—See INFRADIG.

In hoc signo vinces—By this sign thou shalt conquer (L.) ; এই চিহ্ন দ্বারা তুমি জয়ী হইবে।

In limine—At the threshold (L.) ; প্রবেশদ্বারে।

In nomine—In the name of (L.) ; নামে।

In nuce—Same as IN A NUTSHELL under NUT (L.)

In præsenti — At present (L.) ; বর্ত্তমানে।

In propria persona—In person (L.) : স্বয়ং।

In re—In the matter of (L.) ; বিষয়ে।

In transitu — In passing (L.) ; গমনকালে।

In vacuo—In empty space (L.) ; বায়ুশূন্য স্থানে।

In vino veritas—There is truth in wine ; that is, the truth comes out under its influence (L.) ; সুরায় সত্য বিদ্যমান ; অর্থাৎ লোক মাতাল হইলে সত্য কথা বলিয়া ফেলে।

Ipso jure — By the law itself (L.) ; আইনের দ্বারা।

Ira furor brevis est—Anger is a short madness (L.) ; রাগ ক্ষণিক উন্মত্ততা মাত্র।

Ita lex scripta—Thus the law is written (L.) ; এই ভাবে বিধি লিখিত আছে।

Jeu de main—A practical joke (Fr.) ; কার্য্য দ্বারা ঠাট্টা।

Jure divino—By divine law (L.) ; ঈশ্বরের বিধি দ্বারা, দেববিধি দ্বারা।

Jure humano—By human law (L.) ; মানবীয় বিধি দ্বারা।

Jus civile—The civil law (L.) ; লৌকিক আইন।

Jus divinum—Divine law (L.) ; দেববিধি, ঈশ্বরবিধি।

Jus gentium—The law of nations (L.) ; জাতিসংঘের আইন।

Juste milieu—The golden mean (Fr.) ; শ্রেয়ঃ মধ্য পন্থা।

Kalendæ Græcæ — See GREEK CALENDS under CALENDS (L.)

Laborare est orare—To labour is to pray (L.) ; শ্রমই উপাসনা।

Labore et honore — By labour and honour (L.) ; শ্রম এবং সম্ভ্রমবুদ্ধি দ্বারা।

Labor ipse voluptas — Labour itself is pleasure (L.) ; শ্রমই আনন্দ।

Labor omnia vincit — Labour conquers everything (L.) ; শ্রমসর্ব্বজয়ী।

Laisser faire—To let things alone and take their course (Fr.) ; কোন বিষয়ে হস্তক্ষেপ না করিয়া যেমন চলিতেছে তেমনি চলিতে দেওয়া।

L'allegro—The merry man (It.) ; হর্ষোৎফুল্ল ব্যক্তি।

Langage des halles—Language of the fish market (Fr.) ; মেছোহাটের ভাষা, নীচ মেছো ভাষা।

Lapsus memoriæ—A slip of the memory (L.) ; স্মৃতির ভুল।

Lares et penates—Same as THE LARES AND PENATES under LAR.

Laus Deo—Praise to God (L.) ; ঈশ্বরকে ধন্যবাদ।

Le grand monarque—Louis XIV. the grand monarch (Ft.) ; ফরাসীরাজ চতুর্দ্দশ লুই।

Le pas—Precedence in place or rank (Fr.) ; স্থান বা পদবী সম্পর্কে অগ্রগণ্যতা।

Lese majeste—Same as HIGH TREASON (see under TREASON)(Fr.)

Le tout ensemble— The whole together (Fr.) ; সর্ব্বশুদ্ধ, সর্ব্বসাকল্য, সর্ব্বমোট।

Lettres de cachet—Private sealed letters from the king (L.); গালামোহর দেওয়া রাজকীয়পত্র এবং সরকারী চিঠি।

Lex terræ—The law of the land (L.) দেশের আইন।

Liberum arbitrium—Free will (L.); স্বাধীন ইচ্ছা।

Lite pendente—During the law suit (L.); মোকদ্দমা বিচারাধীন থাকা কালীন।

Litera scripta manet — The written letter remains (as proof) (L.); তাহার হাতের লিখা চিহ্ন রহিয়াছে (প্রমাণস্বরূপ)।

Locus sigilli—The place of the seal (L.); সীল মোহরের স্থান।

Lucidus ordo—A lucid arrangement (L.); পরিস্কার ব্যবস্থা।

Lusus naturæ—A monstrosity a freak of nature (L.); অপরূপ জীব; বিকটজীব।

Ma foi—My faith (Fr.); আমার বিশ্বাস।

Magnum bonum—A great good (L.); পরমমঙ্গল, পরমশুভ।

Maison de sante—A madhouse (Fr.); বাতুলালয়, উন্মাদাগার।

Maison de ville—A town house (Fr.); নগরবাটীকা, পুরবাটীকা।

Maitre d'hotel—A house steward (Fr.); বড় লোকের বাটীর প্রধান ভাণ্ডারী।

Maladie du pays — Home-sickness (L.); গৃহের জন্ম আকুলতা।

Malis avibus—Under bad omens (L.); অশুভ সূচনার মধ্যে।

Mea culpa—By my fault (L.); আমার দোষে।

Medio tutissimus ibis—The medium is the safest course (L.); মধ্য পথই সর্ব্বাপেক্ষা নিরাপদ পথ।

Me judice—I being judge; in my opinion (L.); আমি বিচারক হওয়ায়; আমার মতে।

Mens sana in corpore sano—A sound mind in a sound body (L.); শরীর সুস্থ থাকিলে মনও সুস্থ থাকে।

Menus plaisirs — Pocket-money (Fr.); হাত খরচের টাকা।

Meum et tuum—(L.) Same as MEUM AND TUUM (See under MEUM.)

Mezzo termine—A middle course (It.); মধ্য পথ।

Mirabile dictu—Wonderful to tell (L.); বর্ণন করিতে বিস্ময়জনক।

Mise en scene—The getting up or putting in preparation for the stage (Fr.); রঙ্গমঞ্চের জন্য প্রস্তুত করা।

Modo et forma—In manner and form (L.); প্রকারে এবং আকারে।

Monstrum horrendum—A horrible monster (L.); বিকট জীব।

Mont de piete—Same as PAWNSHOP. (Fr.)

Mors omnibus communis—Death is common to all (L.); একদিন সকলকেই মরিতে হইবে।

Mot du guet—Same as WATCHWORD (Fr.)

Motu proprio—Of his own accord (L.); স্বেচ্ছায়।

Mutato nomine, de te fabula narratur—Change the name, and the story will apply to yourself (L.); শুধু নামটী পরিবর্ত্তন করিলেই গল্পটী তোমার সম্পর্কেও খাটিবে।

Natio comœda est—The nation is a company of players (L.); জাতি ক্রীড়কসংঘ ভিন্ন আর কিছুই নহে।

Naturam expellas furca, tamen usque recurret—You may drive out nature by violence (lit. with a pitchfork but she will ever come rushing back again (L.); তুমি বলপূর্ব্বক প্রকৃতিকে পুনঃ পুনঃ বিতাড়িত করিতে পার কিন্তু সে তোমার দিকে পুনঃ পুনঃ ধাবিত হইবে।

Nec cupias nec metuas—Neither desire nor fear (L.); যাহার বাসনা নাই তাহার ভয়ও নাই।

Ne cedas malis—Do not yield to misfortunes (L.); দুর্দ্দিনে হৃদয়ের বল হারাইও না।

Necessitas non habet legem—See NECESSITY HAS NO LAW (L.)

Nec placida contentus quiete est—Nor is he contented with quiet repose (L.); কিম্বা শান্তিপূর্ণ বিশ্রামেও সে সন্তোষলাভ করিতে পারে না।

Nec prece nec pretio—Neither by entreaty nor a bribe (L.); উৎকোচেও নহে উপরোধেও নয়।

Nec quærere nec spernere honorem—Neither to seek nor despise honours (L.); সম্মান কামনাও করিও না পায়েও ঠেলিও না।

Nec scire fas est omnia—The gods do not permit us to know everything (L.); দেবতারা আমাদিগকে সকল বিষয় জানিতে দেন না।

Nec temere nec timide—Neither rashly nor timidly (L.); ভীরুর মতও নয় কিম্বা হঠকারিতার সহিতও নয়।

Ne fronti crede—Trust not to appearances (L.); বাহির দেখিয়া ভুলিও না।

Ne Jupiter quidem omnibus placet—Not even Jupiter pleases everybody (L.); দেবরাজ জুপিটারও সকলকে তুষ্ট করেন না।

Nemo mortalium omnibus horis sapit—No man is wise at all times (L.); সকল সময়ে কোন ব্যক্তি সুবিবেচকের মত কাজ করিতে পারে না।

Ne quid nimis—Shun extremes; not too much (L.); সর্ব্বমত্যন্ত-গর্হিতং।

Ne sutor ultra (properly **supra**) **crepidam** — Let not the shoemaker go beyond his last (L.); Same as A COBBLER MUST STICK TO HIS LAST (see under LAST).

N'importe—It matters not (Fr.); এতে কিছু আসে যায় না।

Nisi Dominus frustra — Unless the Lord be with us, we strive in vain (L.); ভগবান সহায় না হইলে আমাদের সকল চেষ্টাই বৃথা।

Nobilitatis virtus non stemma character—Virtue, not pedigree should characterize nobility (L.); উপাধি নয়, সদ্‌গুণই সম্ভ্রান্তবংশীয় লোকগণের ভূষা হওয়া উচিত।

Non compos mentis – Not sound in mind (L.) ; বিকৃতমনাঃ।

Non constat – It does not appear (L.) ; এরূপ বোধ হয় না।

Non est vivere, sed valere vita—Life is not mere existence, but the enjoyment of health (L.) ; জীবন কেবল সত্তামাত্র নহে—স্বাস্থ্যভোগই প্রকৃত জীবন।

Non fumum ex fulgore, sed ex fumo dare lucem—Not to elicit smoke from splendour, but light from smoke (L.) ; আলোক হইতে ধূম বাহির করিতে হইবে না কিন্তু ধূম হইতে আলোক বাহির করিতে হইবে।

Non generant aquilæ columbas—Eagles do not bring forth pigeons (L.) ; ঈগল পাখী ঘুঘু শাবক প্রসব করে না, সিংহী কি শৃগাল শাবক প্রসব করে।

Non obstante—Notwithstanding (L.) ; স্বত্বেও।

Non omnia possumus omnes—We cannot all of us do everything (L.) ; আমরা সকলে সকল কাজ করিতে পারি না।

Non omnis moriar—I shall not altogether die (L.) ; আমি একেবারে মরিব না।

Non sibi, sed patriæ—Not for himself, but for his country (L.) ; তাহার নিজের জন্য নয়—কিন্তু তাহার দেশমাতৃকার জন্য।

Nosce te ipsum—Know thyself (L.); আপনাকে জান, নিজের স্বরূপ অবগত হও, আত্মজ্ঞান লাভ কর।

Noscitur ex sociis—He is known by his companions (L.) ; সে যে সব লোকের সঙ্গ করে—তদ্দ্বারাই সে কিরূপ লোকে তাহা বুঝা যায়।

Notre Dame—Our Lady (Fr.) ; আমাদের উপাস্যা দেবী (কুমারী মেরী)।

Nous verrons — We shall see (Fr.) ; দেখা যাউক।

Novus homo — A new man ; a man risen from obscurity (L) ; ন লোক ; ভুঁইফোঁড় লোক।

[illegible]lli secundus—Second to none [illegible].) ; অদ্বিতীয়, অপ্রতিম।

Nullum numen abest si sit prudentia—Where there is prudence, a protecting divinity is not far away (L.) ; যেখানে বিজ্ঞতা, রক্ষাকারী দেবতাও সেখান হইতে দূরে নহেন।

Nunc aut nunquam—Same as NOW OR NEVER (L.)

Nunquam aliud natura, aliud sapientia dicit — Nature never says one thing, and wisdom another (L.) ; প্রকৃতি এমন কোন কথা বলেন না যাহা আমাদের প্রজ্ঞা সমর্থন না করে।

Obscurum per obscurius—Explaining something obscure by what is more obscure (L.) ; কোন অস্পষ্ট বিষয় তদপেক্ষা অস্পষ্টতর বিষয় দ্বারা ব্যাখ্যা করা।

Obsequium amicos, veritas odium parit — Obsequiousness procures us friends, truth enemies (L.); হীনানুগত লোকের বন্ধুর অভাব নাই কিন্তু স্পষ্টবাদী লোকের শত্রুর সংখ্যা নাই।

Omne ignotum pro magnifico—Everything unknown is thought to be magnificent (L.); প্রত্যেক অজ্ঞাত বস্তুই মহান্ বলিয়া মনে হয়।

Omne solum forti patria—To a brave man every soil is his country (L.) ; পৃথিবীর সকল দেশই বীরের স্বদেশ।

Omne tulit punctum qui miscuit utile dulci—He has gained every point who has combined the useful with the agreeable (L.) ; কার্য্যকারিতা এবং প্রীতিজনকতা এই উভয় গুণের সম্মিলন যে ব্যক্তির চরিত্রে তাহার পক্ষে কোন কার্য্যই অসাধ্য নয়।

Omnia bona bonis — All things are good with good men (L.) ; যে নিজে ভাল তাহার কাছে জগতই ভাল।

Omnia mutantur, nos et mutamur in illis—All things change and we along with them (L.); জগতের সকল বস্তুরই নিত্য পরিবর্ত্তন হইতেছে এবং সঙ্গে সঙ্গে আমাদেরও হইতেছে।

Optimates — Men in the highest position (L.) ; সর্ব্বোচ্চ পদস্থ ব্যক্তি।

Ora et labora—Pray and labour (L.); প্রার্থনা কর এবং কর্ম্ম কর।

Ora pro nobis—Pray for us (L.) ; আমাদের জন্য প্রার্থনা কর।

Origo mali—The origin of the evil (L.) ; অশুভের উৎপত্তি।

O tempora, O mores! — O the times and the manners! (L) ; সে রামও নাই—সে অযোধ্যাও নাই।

Ouvriers—Artizans (Fr.) ; শিল্পী, কারিকর, কারুশিল্পী।

Pacta conventa—Terms agreed on (L.) ; স্বীকৃত সর্ত্ত সমূহ।

Palma non sine pulvere — The palm is not gained without labour (L.) ; বিনা আয়াসে জয় লাভ হয় না।

Par nobile fratrum — (Ironically) a noble pair of brothers (L.) ; মাণিকযোড়।

Particeps criminis—An accomplice (L.) ; সহাপরাধী।

Parturiunt montes, nascetur ridiculus mus—The mountain is in labour, and a ridiculous mouse will be brought forth (L.) ; পর্ব্বতের মূষিক প্রসব।

Parva componere magnis—To compare small things with great ; (L.) ; বৃহতের সহিত ক্ষুদ্রের তুলনা করিতে গেলে।

Parvum parva decent — Little things are suitable to a little man (L.) ; ক্ষুদ্র ক্ষুদ্র বিষয় ক্ষুদ্র লোকেরই উপযোগী।

Passato il pericolo, gabbato il santo—When the danger is past, the guardian saint is derided (It) ; বিপদ পার হইয়া গেলে দেবতাকে বৃদ্ধাঙ্গুষ্ঠ প্রদর্শন করা, নদী পার হইলে খেয়ানী কোন শালা।

Pater patriæ—The father of his country (L.) ; দেশবাসীর পিতৃস্থানীয়।

Patience passe science—Patience surpasses knowledge (Fr.) ; জ্ঞান অপেক্ষা ধৈর্য্য বরণীয়।

Patria cara, carior libertas—My country is dear but liberty is dearer (L) ; জননী জন্মভূমি আমার প্রিয় কিন্তু স্বাধীনতা তদপেক্ষাও প্রিয়তর।

Patriæ pietatis imago—An image of paternal tenderness (L.); পিতৃবাৎসল্যের প্রতিমূর্ত্তি।

Pax in bello—Peace in war (L.); সমরে শান্তি।

Pede pœna claudo—Punishment follows crime with a slow foot (L); কুকর্ম্মের শাস্তি একদিন ভোগ করিতেই হইবে।

Per ardua libertas — Freedom through difficulties (L); নানাপ্রকার বিপদের ভিতর দিয়া স্বাধীনতা লাভ।

Per fas et nefas—Through right and wrong (L); ন্যায় অন্যায়ের ভিতর দিয়া।

Per il suo contrario—By its reverse or opposite (It.); ইহার বিপরীত বিষয় দ্বারা।

Per mare. per terras—By sea and land (L); জলে স্থলে।

Philosophia stemma non inspicit—Philosophy does not look into genealogies (L); দর্শনশাস্ত্র বংশের দিকে লক্ষ্য করে না।

Pleno jure—With full authority (L); পূর্ণক্ষমতায়।

Pluries — At several times (L. Law.); কয়েকবার।

Poco a poco—Little by little (It.); অল্পে অল্পে।

Poeta nascitur, non fit—Nature, not study, forms the poet (lit. a poet is born not made) (L); কবি প্রকৃতি দেবীরই সৃষ্টি, গ্রন্থ পাঠে কেহ কবি হইতে পারে না।

Point d'appui—Point of support; a rallying point (Fr.); আশ্রয় স্থান।

Pondere, non numero—By weight, not by number (L); গুরুত্ব দ্বারা—সংখ্যায় নহে।

Post cineres gloria sera venit—Fame comes too late to our ashes (L); মানুষের মৃত্যুর পরই সাধারণতঃ তাহাদের কীর্ত্তি প্রচারিত হয়।

Post tot naufragia portum—After so many shipwrecks, a port (L.); বহুবার পোত ভগ্ন হওয়ার পর অবশেষে বন্দরে আশ্রয় পাওয়া গেল।

Pour passer le temps—To pass the time (Fr.); সময় কাটান।

Pour prendre conge—To take leave (Fr.); বিদায় লওয়া।

Præmonitus, præmunitus—Same as FOREWARNED, FOREARMED (L.)

Prendre la lune avec les dents—To aim at impossibilities (lit. to seize the moon with the teeth) (Fr.); আকাশ হইতে চাঁদ পাড়িতে চেষ্টা করা বামন হইয়া চাঁদে হাত দেওয়া।

Pret d'accomplir—Ready to perform (Fr.); সম্পাদনে উদ্যত।

Pret pour mon pays—Ready for my country (Fr.); দেশের কাজের জন্য প্রস্তুত।

Pro aris et focis—For our altars and our hearths (L): আমাদের বেদীর জন্য এবং আমাদের গৃহপীঠের জন্য।

Probatum est — It has been proved (L.); ইহা প্রমাণিত হইয়াছে।

Probitas laudatur et alget—Honesty is praised and is left to starve (L); সাধু লোককে সকলেই প্রশংসা করে কিন্তু সে অনাহারে মরিলেও কেহ তাহার দিকে ফিরিয়া চায় না।

Probum non pœnitet—Honesty repents not (L.); সাধু লোককে কখনও অনুতপ্ত হইতে হয় না।

Pro Deo et ecclesia—For God and the Church (L); ঈশ্বরের নিমিত্ত এবং ধর্ম্মসংঘের জন্য।

Pro et con—For and against (L); Same as PROS & CONS.

Projet de loi—A legislative bill (Fr.); ব্যবস্থাপকসভায় প্রস্তাবিত আইনের পাণ্ডুলিপি।

Pro rege, lege, et grege—For the king, the law, and the people (L.); রাজা, রাজবিধি এবং জনসাধারণের জন্য।

Pro salute animæ — For the health of the soul (L); আত্মার স্বাস্থ্য কামনায়।

Punica fides — Same as PUNIC FAITH (L.)

Quæ fuerunt vitia mores sunt—What were vices once are now manners (L.); একসময়ে যাহা পাপচার ছিল আজকাল তাহা দেশাচারে পরিণত হইয়াছে।

Quanti est sapere—How valuable is wisdom (L.); জ্ঞান অমূল্য ধন।

Quantum mutatus ab illo!—How changed from what he once was (L.); তাহার আজ কত পরিবর্ত্তন।

Quid novi—What news (L.); কি খবর?

Quis custodiet ipsos custodes?—Who shall guard the guards themselves (L)? রক্ষীদিগকে কে রক্ষা করিবে।

Quo animo?—With what purpose, or intention (L)? কি উদ্দেশ্যে, কি অভিপ্রায়ে।

Quocunque trahunt fata, sequamur—Wherever the Fates direct us, let us follow (L); চল আমরা নিয়তির অনুসরণ করি।

Quod di omen avertant—May the gods avert this (L); ঈশ্বর না করুন।

Quod scripsi, scripsi — What I have written, I have written (L) আমি যাহা লিখিয়াছি তাহার বিন্দুমাত্র পরিবর্ত্তন হইবে না।

Quod semper, quod ubique, quod ab omnibus—What has been believed always, everywhere and by all (L); সর্ব্বদা সর্ব্বত্র সর্ব্বলোক যাহা বিশ্বাস করিয়াছে।

Quos Deus vult perdere, prius dementat—Those whom God has a mind to destroy, he first deprives of their senses (L); ভগবান যাহাদের বিনাশ কামনা করে অগ্রে তাহাদের বুদ্ধি লোপ পায়।

Quot homines, tot sententiæ—So many men, so many opinions (L); ভিন্নরুচির্হি লোকঃ।

Quo warranto?—By what warrant (A legal writ) (L.): কিসের বলে।

Recte et suaviter—Justly and mildly (L.); ন্যায়সঙ্গত ভাবে ও মৃদুতার সহিত।

Redeunt saturnia regna — The golden age (lit. the age of Saturn returns (L); সত্যযুগ সমাগত হইল

Regium donum—A royal gift (L); রাজকীয় দান।

Rem acu tetigisti—You have hit the nail on the head (lit. touched it with a needlepoint) (L) ; তুমি ঠিক জায়গায় ঘা দিয়াছ।

Respublica—The commonwealth (L.) ; সাধারণতন্ত্র, গণতন্ত্র।

Resurgam—I shall rise again (L); আমি পুনরায় উত্থিত হইব।

Revenons a nos moutons—Let us return to our subject (Fr.) ; আমরা পুনরায় সে বিষয়ে পুনরালোচনায় প্রবৃত্ত হই।

Rien n'est beau que le vrai—Nothing so lovely as truth (Fr.) ; সত্যের মত সুন্দর কিছুই নাই।

Risu inepto res ineptior nulla—Nothing is more contemptible than silly laughter (L.) ; নির্ব্বোধের হাসির মত হেয় অন্য কিছুই নাই।

use contre ruse—(Fr.) Same as DIAMOND CUT DIAMOND (See nder DIAMOND.)

ise de guerre — Same as TRATAGEM (Fr.)

l atticum — (L.) Same as TTIC SALT.

alus populi suprema est lex—The supreme law is the welfare of the people (L.) ; লোকের কল্যাণই শ্রষ্ঠতম বিধি।

lvo jure—Saving the right (L) ; য় ব্যতিরেকে।

vo pudore—Without offence to odesty (L) ; লজ্জাশীলতায় আঘাত করিয়া।

s Dieu rien—Nothing without God (Fr.) ; ভগবান সর্ব্বত্রই বিদ্যমান।

artor resartus — The tailor patched (L.) ; দর্জ্জি তালি দিয়াছে।

atis verborum — Enough of words (L.) ; কথা অনেক হইয়াছে।

emper avarus eget—The covetous man is ever in want (L.) ; অর্থগৃধ্নু লোক সর্ব্বদাই অভাবগ্রস্ত।

emper idem—Always the same (L.) ; নিয়ত একরূপ।

mper paratus—Always ready L.) ; সর্ব্বদাই প্রস্তুত।

Sempre il mal non viene per nuocere—Evil does not always come to injure (It.) ; অশুভ ঘটনায় সকল সময়ই আমাদের অনিষ্ট হয় না।

Se non e vero, e ben trovato—If not true, it is well invented (It.); যদিও ইহা সত্য না হয় তথাপি ইহা সুকল্পিত।

Servabo fidem—I will keep faith (L.) ; আমি কখনও বিশ্বাসঘাতকতা করিব না।

Sic itur ad astra—This is the way to immortality (lit. to the stars) (L.): ইহাই অমরত্বের পথ, ইহাই অমৃতের বর্ত্ম।

Sic passim—So everywhere (L.) ; সর্ব্বত্রই এইরূপ।

Sic transit gloria mundi—Thus passes away the glory of the world (L.) ; পৃথিবীর গৌরব এইরূপেই লুপ্ত হয়।

Silent leges inter arma—Laws are silent in the midst of arms (L.) ; অস্ত্রের ঝঞ্ঝনার মধ্যে আইন নীরব থাকে।

Simel et simul—Once and together (L.) ; একবার এবং একত্রে।

Similis simili gaudet—Like rejoices in like (L.) ; চোরে চোরে মাসতুত ভাই।

Si monumentum quæris, circumspice—If you seek his monument, look around (L.) ; যদি তাহার কীর্ত্তিস্তম্ভ দেখিতে চাও তবে চতুর্দ্দিকে দৃষ্টিপাত কর।

Simplex munditiis—Simple and elegant (L.) ; সাদাসিধা অথচ শোভাসম্পন্ন।

Siste, viator—Stop, traveller (L.) ; পান্থ থাম।

Si vis me flere—If you wish me to weep (L.) ; আমি অশ্রুপাত করি ইহা যদি তোমার ইচ্ছা হয়।

Si vis pacem, para bellum—If you wish peace, prepare for war (L.) ; যদি শান্তি চাও তবে যুদ্ধের জন্য প্রস্তুত হও।

Sola nobilitas virtus — Virtue alone is true nobility (L.) ; সদ্‌গুণ প্রকৃত কুলীনত্ব।

Sola virtus invicta — Virtue alone is invincible (L.) ; ধর্ম্ম একমাত্র সর্ব্বজয়ী।

Solvuntur tabulæ—The defendant is acquitted (L.) ; প্রতিবাদীকে বেকসুর খালাস দেওয়া হইল।

Spectemur agendo—Let us be tried by our actions (L.) ; আমাদের কার্য্য দ্বারা আমাদের বিচার হউক।

Spero meliora—I hope for better times (L.) ; আমি সুদিনের আশা করি।

Spes mea in Deo—My hope is in God (L.) ; ঈশ্বরই আমার একমাত্র আশা।

Spes tutissima cœlis—The safest hope is in heaven (L.) ; আমাদের সব চেয়ে নিশ্চিত আশা স্বর্গে অবস্থিত।

Sponte sua—Of one's own accord (L.) ; স্বেচ্ছায়।

Status quo ante bellum — The state in which both parties were before the war (L.) ; উভয় পক্ষ যুদ্ধের পূর্ব্বে যে অবস্থায় ছিল সেই অবস্থায়।

Suaviter in modo, fortiter in re—Gentle in the manner but vigorous in the deed (L.) ; স্বভাব শান্ত কিন্তু কর্ম্মে তেজস্বী।

Sublata causa, tollitur effectus—When the cause is removed, the effect ceases (L.) ; কারণ না থাকিলে কার্য্যও থাকেনা।

Sufficit—It is enough (L.) ; ঢের হয়েছে, যথেষ্ট হয়েছে, প্রচুর হয়েছে।

Suivez raison — Follow reason (Fr.) ; বিচারবুদ্ধির অনুসরণ কর।

Summum jus summa injuria—The rigour of the law is the height of oppression ; the excess of justice is the excess of injustice (L) ; আইনের কঠোরতাই অত্যাচারের চরমমাত্র ; অতি মাত্র ন্যায়বিচার এবং অতিমাত্র অন্যায় এই উভয়ে কোন প্রভেদ নাই।

Sum quod eris, ful quod es—I am what thou wilt be ; I have been what thou art (L.) ; তুমি এখন যেমন আমিও একদিন তেমন ছিলাম।

Sunt superis sua jura—The gods have their own laws (L.); দেবতাদের স্বতন্ত্র বিধি রহিয়াছে।

Suo Marte—By his own exertion (L.); নিজের চেষ্টায়, নিজের উদ্যমে, আত্ম চেষ্টায়।

Supersedeas—A writ to stay proceedings (L. Law); মোকদ্দমার কার্য্য স্থগিত রাখার জন্য পরওয়ানা।

Sursum corda—Keep up your heart (L.); হৃদয়ের বল হারাইওনা।

Suum cuique — Let every man have his own (L.); কোন ব্যক্তিকে তাহার প্রাপ্য বস্তু হইতে বঞ্চিত করিবে না।

Suus cuique mos—Everyone has his own habit (L.); প্রত্যেক লোকেরই একটী বিশিষ্ট অভ্যাস আছে।

Talis pater, qualis filius — Such a father such a son (L.); যেমন পিতা তেমন পুত্র, যেমন বাপ তেমন ছেলে।

Tam Marte quam Minerva—As much by his courage as genius (L.); তাহার প্রতিভা দ্বারা যতটুকু তাহার সাহস দ্বারাও ততটুকু।

Tantæne animis cœlestibus iræ?—Do the gods harbour such resentment? (Fr.); দেবতারা কি এরূপ আক্রোশ পোষণ করেন?

Tant mieux—Same as SO MUCH THE BETTER (Fr.)

Tant pis—Same as SO MUCH THE WORSE (Fr.)

Tel maitre, tel valet—(Fr.) Same as LIKE MASTER, LIKE MAN (under LIKE.)

Tempora mutantur, nos et mutamur in illis—The times are perpetually changing, and we with the times (L.); কালচক্র নিত্য ঘূর্ণিত হইতেছে এবং আমরাও তৎসঙ্গে আবর্ত্তিত হইতেছি।

Tempus edax rerum—Time that devours all things (L.); কাল সর্ব্বগ্রাসী।

Tempus fugit, et nunquam revertitur—Time flies, and never returns (L.); সময় চলিয়া গেলে আর ফিরিয়া আসে না।

Tempus omnia revelat—Time discloses all things (L.); সময়ে সবই প্রকাশ পায়।

Teres et rotundus—Smooth and round (L.); মসৃণ এবং সুগোল।

Tiens ta foy—Preserve thy faith (Fr.); বিশ্বাস অক্ষুণ্ণ রাখিও।

Timeo Danaos et dona ferentes—I distrust the Greeks, even when they offer gifts (L.); গ্রীকদিগকে আমি কদাচ বিশ্বাস করি না এমন কি তাহারা যখন কোন উপহার দিতে আসে তখনও আমি তাহাদিগকে বিশ্বাস করি না।

Tot homines, tot sententiæ.—So many men, so many opinions (L.); নানা মুনির নানা মত।

Tout-a-fait—Quite (Fr.); সম্পূর্ণরূপে, পুরা।

Tout bien ou rien—The whole or nothing (Fr.); সবটা অথবা কিছুই নয়।

Tria juncta in uno—Three joined in one (L.); এক দেহে তিন।

Troja fuit—Troy was (L.); ট্রয় নগরী আর নাই, সে রামও নাই সে অযোধ্যাও নাই।

Tua res agitur—It is a matter that concerns you (L.); ইহা তোমার সম্পর্কীয় বিষয়।

Tu ne cede malis—Yield not to misfortune (L.); দুর্ব্বিপাকে মনের বল হারাইও না।

Tu quo que!—You too! (L.); তুমিও!

Tutte quanti — Same as ET CETERA (It.)

Ubi jus incertum, ibi jus nullum—Where the law is uncertain, there is no law (L.); যেখানে বিধি অনিশ্চিত সেখানে কোন বিধি নাই বলিলেও চলে।

Ubique—Everywhere (L.); সর্ব্বত্র।

Una voce—With one voice (L.); একবাক্যে।

Unguibus et rostro — With talons and beak (L.); কামড়াইয়া আঁচড়াইয়া।

Unum et idem — One and the same (L.); অভিন্ন।

Urbi et orbi—For the Rome (lit. the city) and the world (L.); রোম সাম্রাজ্যের জন্য—তথা জগতের জন্য।

Utile dulci—The useful with the agreeable (L.). প্রীতিপ্রদ এবং কার্য্যকরী।

Ut prosim—That I may do good (L.); যাহাতে আমি লোকের উপকার করিতে পারি।

Utrum horum mavis accipe—Take whichever you prefer (L.); তোমার যেটী ইচ্ছা লও।

Vacuus cantat coram latrone viator—The traveller who has an empty purse sings in the face of the robber (L.); নিঃসম্বল পথিক দস্যুর সম্মুখেও গান গাইতে পারে।

Vade in pace—Go in peace (L.); শান্তিতে চলিয়া যাও।

Vade retro—Same as AVAUNT (L.)

Væ victis! — Woe to the vanquished! (L.); পরাজিতগণ অধঃপাতে যাও!

Vanitas vanitatum — Vanity of vanities (L.); দম্ভের উপরে দম্ভ।

Variæ lectiones — (L.) See VARIALECTO.

Variorum notae—Notes of various authors (L.); বহু গ্রন্থকারের টীকা।

Veluti in speculum—As if in a mirror (L.); নখদর্পণের মত।

Veni, vidi, vici—I came, I saw, I conquered (L.); আমি আসিলাম, আমি দেখিলাম, আমি জয় করিলাম।

Velis et remis—With sails and oars (L.); পাইল ও দাঁড়ের সাহায্যে।

Ventis secundis—With favouring winds (L.); অনুকূল বায়ুতে।

Ventre affame n'a point d'oreilles—A hungry belly has no ears (Fr.); ক্ষুধিত ব্যক্তি কোন কথায় কর্ণপাত করে না।

Verbatim et literatim — Same as WORD FOR WORD (L.)

Verbum sat sapienti—A word is enough to a wise man (L.); জ্ঞানী লোকের পক্ষে একটী কথাই যথেষ্ট।

Veritas parit odium — Truth begets hatred (L.); সত্য কথা বলিলেই লোকের বিদ্বেষভাজন হইতে হয়।

Ver non semper viret—Spring does not always flourish (L.); বসন্ত চিরদিন থাকে না।

Vexata quaestio—A much-debated question (L.); বহু আলোচিত প্রশ্ন।

Victis honos — Honour to the conquered (L.); পরাজিত ব্যক্তিরা সম্মান লাভ করুক।

Vide ut supra—See the preceding statement (L.); পূর্ব্বের উক্তি দেখ।

Video meliora proboque, deteriora sequor—I see and approve of the better, and I follow the worse (L.); আমি উভয়ের মধ্যে যেটী ভাল তাহা অনুমোদন করি কিন্তু মন্দটীকে অনুসরণ করি।

Vincit amor patriæ—The love of our country prevails (L.); আমাদের স্বদেশপ্রীতি সর্ব্বোপরি প্রভাব বিস্তার করে।

incit veritas—Truth conquers (L.); সত্য সর্ব্বজয়ী।

Vires acquirit eundo—She acquires strength in her progress (spoken of Fame.) (L.); কীর্ত্তি দিন দিনই পুষ্টিলাভ করে।

Virtus laudatur et alget—Virtue is praised and is left to starve (L.); লোকেরা ধার্ম্মিককে শতমুখে প্রশংসা করে কিন্তু অনশনে কষ্ট পাইলেও কেহ তাহার দিকে ফিরিয়া চায় না।

Virtus semper viridis—Virtue is ever green (L.); ধর্ম্ম চিরনবীন।

Virtute et fide — By virtue and faith (L.); ধর্ম্ম দ্বারা এবং ঈশ্বরনিষ্ঠা দ্বারা।

Virtuti nihil obstat et armis—Nothing can resist valour and arms (L.); অস্ত্রধারী বীরকে কিছুতেই প্রতিরোধ করিতে পারে না।

Virtuti non armis fido—I trust to virtue and not to arms (L.); আমি ধর্ম্মের উপরেই নির্ভর করি অস্ত্রের উপর নয়।

Virtutis amor—The love of virtue (L.); ধর্ম্মানুরাগ।

Vitam impendere vero—To consecrate his life to truth (L.); সত্যের জন্য তাহার জীবন উৎসর্গ করিতে।

Vive la republique—Long live the republic (Fr.); আমাদের গণতন্ত্র চিরকাল বর্ত্তমান থাকুক।

Vive le roi—Long live the king (Fr.); রাজা দীর্ঘায়ু হউন।

Vivida vis animi—The lively vigour of genius (L.); প্রতিভার প্রদীপ্ত প্রভা।

Vivit post funera virtus—Virtue survives the grave (L.); সদ্গুণ মৃত্যুর পরেও বিরাজমান থাকে।

Voila une autre chose—That's quite another matter (Fr.); এটা সম্পূর্ণ স্বতন্ত্র বিষয়।

Volo non valeo—I am willing but unable (L.); আমি ইচ্ছুক কিন্তু অসমর্থ।

Zonam solvere—To unloose the virgin zone (L.); কুমারীর নীবিবন্ধ শিথিল করা (অর্থাৎ তাহার কৌমার্য্য হরণ করা)।

Prefixes and Suffixes.

PREFIXES.

(A. S.) on or in; as, abed, shore, afield.

(A. S. *and*) over, against; , along.

A. S. *a*) used as an intensive fix to verbs; as, arise, abide, right.

A. S.) of or from; as, own, anew.

A. S. *ge*) as, aware.

ld sign of *inf.*; as, ado.

(G.) without, denoting ion; as, apathy, without feeling; anarchy, without government.

a, ab, abs (L.) from or away; as, avert, abhor, abstain, abstract.

ad (L.) to, at; with its different forms **a, ac, af, ag, al, an, ap, ar, as, at**; as, adhere, ascend, accept, affect, aggravate, allot, announce, appear, arrest, assent, attend.

all (A. S.) all; as, almighty, altogether.

amb, ambi, am (L.) on both sides around; as, ambient, ambition, ambidexter, amputate.

amphi (G.) both, round about; as, amphibious, amphitheatre.

an (F. *en*, L. *in*) as anoint.

ana (G.) through, back, up; as, anatomy, analyse.

ante, anti, anci, ant, an (L.) before; as, antecedent, anticipate, ancient, antique, ancestor.

anti, ant (G.) opposite to, against, as, antipathy, antipodes, antagonist

apo (G.) from ; as, apostasy, apostate ; **aph,** in aphelion.

arch, archi, arche (G.) first, chief; as in archangel, architect, archetype.

at (E.) nearness ; as in atone.

auto, auth, (G.) self ; as, autobiography, authentic.

be (A. S.) causative ; as, becloud ; privative, as, behead ; intensive, as, bespatter, bespeak, etc.

bis, bi, bin (L.) twice, double ; as, biscuit, biennial, binocular.

by (A. S.) near, beside ; as, bystander, bypath.

cata, cat, cath (G.) down, downwards, according to; as, cataract, catechism, catholic.

circum,. circu (L.) round about ; as, circumscribe, circumfluent, circumspect, circuit.

cis (L.) on this side ; as, cisalpine.

con (L.) with its forms **co, col, com, cor, coun,** together, with ; as, connect, cohere, collect, compose, correct, council.

contra (L.) against ; as, contradict, controvert.

counter (F. *contre*) against ; as, counteract.

de (L.) down, from, or off ; as, deject, deter, defend.

demi (F.) half ; as, demigod.

dia (G.) through ; as, diameter, diaphanous.

di (G.) double ; as, dilemma.

dis (L.) with its forms **diff** and **di,** off, asunder, away, out ; as, dispel, disarm, dishonest, diffuse, divert.

dis (G.) two, twice ; as; dissyllable.

dys (G.) ill, difficult ; as dysentery.

e, *See* EX.

e (A.S. *ge*) enough.

e (French phonetic addition) as in esquire.

ec (G) out of ; as, eccentric

emb (A. S. *ymb-ryne*) a circuit ; as ember-days.

en, em, and **im** (F., L., and G.) in or on, also to make ; as, encircle, encaustic, enfeeble, embark, immerge.

enter (F.) between, among ; as, entertain.

ep, eph, epi (G.) upon ; as, epoch, ephemeral, epitaph.

es (F.) out ; as, escape.

eso (G.) in, into ; as, esoteric.

eu, ev (G.) well ; as euphony, evangelist.

ex (L.) with its forms **e, ef,** etc., out, from ; as, exclaim, evade, effuse, effulgence.

ex (G.) from, out of ; as, exodus.

exo (G.) without ; as, exotic.

extra (L.) on the outside, beyond ; as, extramural, extraordinary, extradition.

for (A. S.) in place of ; as, forasmuch.

for (A.S.) from, away, against; as, forswear, forbid.

for (F., L.) out of doors, outside ; as, foreclose, forfeit.

fore (A. S.) before ; as, forerun, foretell.

forth (A. S.) forth ; as, forthwith.

fro (Scand.) from ; as, froward.

gain (Scand.) against ; as, gainsay.

hemi (G.) half ; as, hemisphere.

hetero (G.) other ; as, heterodox.

holo (G.) entire ; as, holograph.

homo (G.) same; as, homœopathy.

hyper (G.) over, above ; as, hypercritical, hyperborean.

hypo, hyph, hyp (G.) under ; as, hypocrite, hyphen, hypallage.

i (L.) not ; as, ignoble.

i, y (A. S. *ge*) yclept, handywork.

in (L.) with its forms **il, im, in, ir,** in, into, upon ; as, inter, illumine, impend, include, irrigate.

in (L.) with its forms **il, im, ir,** negative ; as, infirm, illegal immortal, irregular.

in, im (A. S.) in, on ; as, inwrap, inward, imbed.

inter (L.) between ; as, intercept, interpose, interval.

intra (L.) in the inside of, within ; as, intramural.

intro (L.) into; within ; as, introduce.

iss (F., from L. *ex*) out of ; as, issue.

juxta (L.) close to, near ; as, juxtaposition.

l, curtailment of *all* ; as lone.

l (Ar.) the ; as in lute.

male, mal, mau (L.) badly ; as malefactor, maladroit, maugre.

meta, meth, met (G.) change ; as metamorphose, method, meteor.

mid (A. S.) with ; as midwife.

mis (A. S. and Icel.) wrongly ; as, misdeed, mistrust.

mis (F., L.) badly ; as, mischief.

mono, mon (G.) single ; as, mono graph, monk.

multi, mult (L.) many ; a multiply.

n, as in newt, *i. e.,* an ewt, nick name (an ekename).

ne (L.) not; as, nefarious, neuter

ne (G.) not ; as, nepenthe.

nec (L.) not ; as, neglect, negative

non (L.) not ; as, nonsense, nonage

ob (L.) with its forms **o, oc, o op, os,** against, in front, in or or as, obloquy, omit, occur, offe oppose, ostensible.

off (A. S.) off, trom, away ; a offal, offset.

on (A. S.) on ; as, onlooker.

or (A. S.) out ; as, ordeal.

out (A. S.) beyond ; as, outd outrun.

over (A. S.) eminence or exces as, overtop, overthrow.

palim, palin (G.) against ; palimpsest, palindrome.

pon, panto (G.) all ; as, pana pantomime.

para, par, pa (G.) alongside, beyond, against; as, paradigm, parody, palsy.
pel, *see* PER.
pene (L.) almost; as, peninsula.
per, par, pel, pil (L.) through, thoroughly; as, perfect, parson, pellucid, pilgrim.
peri (G.) round; as, perimeter, periphrasis, period.
pol, por, pour, pur (F.) other forms of L. *pro*; as, pollute, portend, pourtray, purvey.
post (L.) after, hehind; as, postpone.
pre (L.) before; as, predict, precede, prevail.
preter (L.) beyond; as preternatural.
pro (L.) forth, forward, for; as, proceed, proconsul, provoke, pronoun.
pros (G.) towards; as, proselyte.
proto, prot (G.) first; as, prototype, protoxide.
re, red, ren (L.) back; as, retract, redeem, render.
retro (L.) going backwards; as, retrograde, retrospect.
s, for **se**; as in sober.
s, for **dis**; as in spend.
s, for **ex**; as in sample.
se, sed (L.) literally by itself, without, aside: as, seclude, sedition.
semi (L.) half; as, semitone.
sine (L.) without; as, sinecure.
sub (L.) with its forms **s, su, suc, suf, sug, sup, sus, so,** under or after; as, subject, sombre, suspect, succeed, suffuse, suggest, suppose, sustain, sojourn.
subter (L.) under; as, subterfuge, subterraneous.
super (L.) over, above, beyond; as, superstructure, superfine, superadd.
supra (L.) over, above; as, superabundance, supernumerary, supra mundane.
sur (F., L. *super*) as, surmount, surprise.
syn (G.) with its forms **sy, syl, sym,** together, with; as, syntax, system, syllogism, sympathy.
t at; as, in twit.
thorough (A. S.) through; as, thoroughfare.
to (A. S.) together; as in to-day.
to (A. S.) asunder as, in the biblical to-brake.
trans, tran, tra, tres, tre (L.) beyond, over, through; as, transit, transcend, traduce, trespass, treason.
u (G.) not; as, Utopia.
ultra (L.) beyond; as, ultra-marine.
um (L.) Same as NON, not; as umpire.
un (A.S.) not; as, unable, unseen; before a verb, to do the opposite; as, unloose, untie, unfetter.
under (A. S.) under, below; as, underprop, undersell.
un, uni (L.) one; as, unanimous, unicorn.
up (A. S.) high, over; as, uplift, upset.
ve (L.) apart from; as, vestibule.
vis, vice (F., L.) in place of; as, viscount, viceroy.
wan (A. S.) wanting; as, wanton (wanting education).
with (A. S.) against, back; as, withstand, withdraw.
y, *see under* I.

SUFFIXES.

ble (L. *abilis*) fit to be; as, portable.
c (G.) pertaining to; as, elegiac.
ceous (L. *aceus*) having the qualities of; as, herbaceous.
cious (L. *ox, acis*) full of; as, audacious.
city (L. *acitas*) power, abundance; as, capacity, loquacity.
y (L.) act of doing; as, conspiacy; state; as, celibacy.
le (F.) relating to, pertaining to; as, decade.
(L. *aticus*, F. *age*) act of ing, or thing done, locality; as passage, parentage, postage, parsonage.
al (L. *alis*) belonging to; as, bridal, criminal, nuptial.
an, ain (L. *anus*) belonging or pertaining to, one who; as, guardian, human, librarian.
ana (L.) things belonging to, sayings; as, Johnsoniana.
ance, ancy (L. *antia*) state or being; as, ignorance, abundance, constancy, occupancy.
and, end (L. *andus, endus*) as, viand, legend.
aneous (L. *aneus*) belonging to; as, extraneous.
ant (L. *ans, antis*) equivalent of E. *ing*; as, assistant, pleasant.
ar (L. *aris*) of or belonging to; as, globular, angular; one who; as, beggar.
ard (F.) one who; as, drunkard.
ary (L. *arius*) agent or doer, one who; as, secretary, missionary, lapidary;—(L. *arium*) place where; as, seminary.
ass, ace (L. *aceus acius*) cuirass pinnace.

aster (L. *aster*) implying contempt; as, poetaster.
ate (L. *atus, ata, atum*) to make; as, regulate, deliberate; one who; as, delegate, potentate; office, thing; as, consulate, duplicate; having, full, as, animate, adequate.
ative (L. *ativus*) having power; as, vegetative, creative.
atory (L. *atorius*) relating to, being; as, predatory, transitory.
ature (L. *atura*) state, form; as, creature.
ble, *see* ABLE.
ble, ple (L. *plus*) fold; as, double, quadruple.
bund and **cund** (L. *bundus* and *cundus*) moribund, rubicund.
celli, cello (L. *culus* and *ellus*) diminutive; as, violoncello.
ch, augmentative; as, blotch.
cle, cule (L. *culus*) particle, animalcule.
craft (A. S. *craft*) skill; bookcraft, priestcraft.
cy (L. *tia*) being or state of being; as, clemency, delicacy, intimacy, infancy.
d, t, or **ed,** suffix of past tense; did, felt, loved.
d, ed, denotes possession; in nouns with passive meanings, as, deed, seed; in adjectives formed from nouns; as, booted, feathered; in past participles, as, loved.
dom (A. S.) state, power; as, kingdom, earldom, dukedom.
ed (E.) having, action done; as, landed, finished.
ee (F., from L. *atus*) one who; as, lessee, trustee, referee, refugee.
eer, (F. *ier*, L. *arius*) one who, agent or doer; as, muleteer, charioteer, mutineer, engineer.
el (L. *ellus*, or *illus*) diminutive; as, damsel.
el (A.S.) instrument; as, shovel.
en (A.S.) made of or belonging to; as wooden, golden; to make; as, lengthen, strengthen.
en (A. S. *en*) diminutive; as, maiden.
en (A.S. *en*) vixen.
en (A.S. *n, ne, en*) *pp.*; woven.
en (A. S. *an*) oxen, kine.
en (A. S.) to make; darken.
ence, ency (L. *entia*) action, state or being; as, leniency, consistence, tendency, indolence, complacency.
ent (L. *ens*) being; as, president, opponent, different.
eous (L. *eus*) pertaining to, containing; as, aqueous.
er (A. S. *ere*) one who; as, maker, singer, writer.
er (A. S. *erian*) frequentative; as, flicker.
er, more; in comparative of adjectives; as greater.
erel (O. F.) little; as pikerel, cockerel.
erie (L. *arium*) place where; as, menagerie.
erly (*ern, ly*) direction to or from; as, southerly.
ern (L. *erna*) noun suffix; cistern.
ern (A. S.) direction to or from; as, eastern, western; or belong-to; as, modern.
ery (F. *erie*) place, act, state; as, brewery, bribery, waggery.
es, or **s** (A. S. *as*) *pl.* suffix; as, foxes, boots.
escent (L. *escens*) growing, becoming; as, convalescent.
ese (L. *ensis*) belonging to; as, Japanese.
ess (F. *esse*, L. *issa*) *fem.* suffix of nouns; as, tigress, lioness.
est (A. S.) bringest, lovest.
est (A. S. *est*) *superl.* suffix in *adj.*; as, youngest.
et (F.) little; as, casket, tablet, floweret, rivulet.
etic (G. *etikos*) relating to; as, pathetic.
ette, (F.) little; as coquette.
ety (L. *etas*) state of; as, sobriety, anxiety.
ever (A.S.) every, any; as, whosoever, whoever.
ey (A. S. *ig*) consisting of; as, clayey.
fare, way; as, welfare.
fast (A. S. *faest*) firm, fast; as, steadfast.
fold (A. S. *feald*) *adj.* suffix; as, fourfold.
ful (A.S.) full of; as, joyful, usefull, painful, delightful.
fy (F. *fier*, L. *facere*) to make; as, purify, fortify, diversify.
head or **hood** (A. S. *had*, state) state or being; as, manhood, priesthood, neighbourhood.
i, *pl.* suffix of nouns, through Italian; banditti.
ian (L. *ianus*) *adj.* suffix; as, Arabian, Canadian.
ible (F., L. *ibilis*) able to be; as, flexible, accessible, possible.
ic (L. and G.) belong to; as, gigantic, angelic, cubic.
ical, *adj.* suffix, belonging to; as, cubical, comical.
ice (L. *itium*) thing done; as, service. notice.
ice, ish (L. *ix, icis*) as, pumice radish.
icle (A. S. *gicel*, a piece of ice) as, icicle.
ics (G *ika*) in names of science; as, pneumatics, mathematics.
id (L. *idus*) belonging to; as, rabid, fervid.
ide (G. *eidos*, form) as, bromide.
ie, y diminutive; as, lassie.
ier (F. *ier*) one who; as, cavalier, hosier.
il, ile (L. *ilis*) able; as, civil, ductile.
ile (L. *ilis*) belonging to; as, juvenile, mercantile, gentile.
im *pl.* suffix; as, cherubim.
ina, *fem.* suffix; as, Czarina.

ine (L. *inus*) belonging to ; as, divine, genuine, feline.
ine (F. *ine*, L. *ina*) *fem.* suffix ; as, heroine.
ing (A.S. *ende*) suffix of *ppr.* coming.
ing (A. S. *ung, ing*) noun suffix : as, learning, dwelling.
ng (A. S. *ing*) son of ; as, Manning, Harding ; also in names of animals ; herring ; in coins, as, farthing.
ion, (L. *io*) being or state of being : as, creation.
ior, (L.) more, as, superior, inferior.
ique (F., L. *iquus*) belonging to ; antique.
ish (A. S. *isc*) like : as, childish, girlish, foolish ; little, as, brownish ;—(F. *iss*, L. *esc*) to make as, establish, finish.
ism, asm (G. *ismos, asmos*) act, being, or state of being ; as, atheism, pleonasm.
ist, ast (G. *istes, astes*) one who ; as, atheist, gymnast.
ite (G. *ites*) belonging to, one who ; as, anchorite, dymamite.
ity (L. *itas*) being or state ; as, ability, capability, inability.
ve (L. *ivus*) belonging to, having the power to ; as, native, active, expansive, persuasive.
x (L.) as, executrix, testatrix.
ze (G. *izein*) to make , as, fertilize, realize, equalize, canonize, epitomize.
k, a verbal suffix ; as, walk, talk.
kin (A. S.) little ; as, lambkin, manikin.
kind (A.S.) race, sort ; as, womankind, humankind, mankind.
le, as verb suffix ; as, kneel, drizzle.
el (A. S.) denoting instrument, etc. ; as, needle, navel.
a, at ont (L. *lentus*) full of ; as, bene-
a, an olent, redolent, violent, virulent,
privat corpulent.

less (A. S. *leas*) without as, useless, worthless, valueless, tenantless.
let (*el, le,* and *et*) diminution, little ; as, eaglet, streamlet.
like (A. S. *lic*) like ; as, warlike, saintlike, godlike.
ling (A.S.) little, young ; as, darkling, codling, darling ; sometimes depreciatory , as, hireling, groundling.
ling, long (A. S. *lunga, linga*) *adv.* suffix ; as, sidelong, darkling.
lock (A. S. *lac*) noun suffix ; wedlock.
lock, lick (A. S. *leac*) a leek ; garlic, hemlock.
ly (A.S. *lic*) like , as, lordly, friendly, kindly, manly.
meal (A. S. *mælum*) *adv.* suffix ; as piecemeal.
men (L. *men*) state, that which ; as, regimen, acumen.
ment (F. L. *mentum*) act or state of ; as, treatment, excitement, advancement, nourishment.
mony (F. *monie*, L. *monium, monia*) act or state of ; as, parsimony, testimony, matrimony.
most (*ma* and *est*) greatest ; as, uppermost, endmost, topmost.
n, in participles, denoting possession ; as, broken, hewn.
nd (A. S.) *ppr.* suffix ; friend.
ness (A. S.) being or state of being ; as, madness, blindness, kindness.
ock (A. S. *uc*) little ; as, hillock.
oid, oidal (G. *oeides*) colloid.
om (A. S. *um*) old dative ; as whilom.
on (L. *onem*) as felon.
on, one, oon (F. *on*, It. *one*) augmentative ; as, balloon, flagon, trombone.
or (L.) one who ; as, imitator, persecutor, author, factor.
ory (L. *orius*) belonging to or place where : as, olfactory, purgatory, prefatory, piscatory.

ose (L. *osus*) full of ; as, verbose, jocose.
osity (L. *ositas*) abundance, state ; as, verbosity, curiosity.
ot (F.) little ; as, ballot, pivot ;—(G. *otes*) one who ; as, patriot, zealot.
our (F. *eur*, L. *or*) state of being ; as, honour, favour.
ous (L. *us*) full of ; as, prosperous, lustrous, nervous, dubious, fibrous.
ow, w (A. S. *u, we, wa*) meadow, sparrow, straw.
r, er, verb suffix ; as, chatter, titter.
re (A. S.) place ; as, here, there.
red (A. S. *ræd*) implying number ; as, hundred.
red (A. S. *ræden*, rule) state, those who ; as, kindred.
ric (A. S. *rice*, dominion) dominion, region ; as, bishopric.
right (A. S. *riht*) as upright, downright.
ry, ery, (F. *rie, erie*) art, place ; as, masonry, foundry : also the result of action ; as, poetry ; action ; as, sorcery ; condition ; as, slavery ; forming collective noun ; as, infantry.
s (A. S. *es*) marking the genitive case.
se (A.S. *sian*) to make ; as, cleanse.
ship (A. S. *scipe*) state or quality ; as, hardship, friendship.
sis (G.) action or state ; as, thesis.
some (A. S.) full of ; as, tiresome, quarrelsome, gladsome.
son, son ; as, Johnson.
ster (A. S. *estre*) agent or doer ; as, punster, gamester.
stress (A. S.) as, songstress.
sy, se (G. *sis*) state ; as, dropsy, eclipse.
t (L. *tus*) *adj.* and noun suffix ; as, fact, exact.
t, for **th,** as, height.

teen (A. S. *tyne*) ten to be added ; as, fifteen, sixteen.
ter, tre (G. *tron*) meter, centre.
ter, ther (A. S. *der, ter*) thither, after.
th, or **t** (A. S.) state or thing ; as, birth, broth, light.
ther, ter, der (A. S. *dor, ther, der*) the agent, action ; as, father, mother, slaughter, rudder.
tude (L. *tudo*) being or state of being; as, solitude, altitude, gratitude.
ty (A. S. *tig*) ten to be multiplied ; as, seventy.
ty (F. *te*, L. *tas*) being or state of being ; as, captivity, poverty, rapidity.
ule, le (L. *ulus*) little ; as, globule, circle.
und, ond (L. *undus*, F. *ond*) jocund, vagabond.
ure (L. *ura*, F. *eur*) act or state ; as, verdure, mixture, capture, exposure.
urn (L. *urnus*) taciturn.
urnal (L. *urnus*) belonging to ; as, diurnal
ward (A. S.) in the direction of ; as, hitherward, homeward, eastward.
ways (A. S.) way, manner ; as, sideways, bye-ways, wrong-ways.
wise (A. S.) way, manner ; as, likewise.
y (A. S. *e*) place ; as, smithy ;—(A. S. *ig*) as mighty ;—(A. S. *i-an*) as ferry.
y (F. *ie*, L. *ia*) abbey ;—(L. *ivus*) study —(L. *ies*) progeny ;—(L. *ivus*, F. *if*) massy ;—(G. *ia*) academy.
yer (A. S.) one who ; as, lawyer.

Abbreviations and Contractions Commonly used.

A. or *ans.* Answer.
a. or @ (L. *ad*). To or at.
A. B. or *B. A.* (L. *Artium Baccalaureus*), Bachelor of Arts.
Abbr. Abbreviated.
Abp. Archbishop.
A. C. (L. *Ante Christum*) Before Christ.
a/c., Acct. Account.
acad. Academy.
A. C. P. Associate of the college of Preceptors.
A. D. (L. *Anno Domini*) In the year of our Lord.
A. D. C. Aide-de-camp.
ad inf. (L. *ad infinitum*) To infinity.
ad init. (L. *ad initium*) At the beginning.
Ad lib, or *Ad libit.* (L. *ad libitum*) At pleasure.
Advt. Advertisement.
A. G. Adjutant-General ; Artorney General.
A. H. (L. *Anno Hegiræ*) In the year of the Hegira.
A.M. (L. *Anno Mundi*) In the year of the world ; (L. *Ante Meridiem*) before noon ; (L. *Artium Magister*), Master of Arts.
Anon. Anonymous.
Ans. Answer.
Antiq. Antiquities.
Ap. (L. *Apud.*) According to ; in the writings of.
App. Appendix.
Aq. (L. *aqua*) Water.
A. R. A. Associate of the Royal Academy.
A. R. C. S. Associate of the Royal College of Science.
A. S., A. -Sax. Anglo-Saxon.
A. S. C. Army Service Corps.
At. Wt. Atomic Weight.
A. U. C. (L. *Anno Urbis Conditæ* or *Ab Urbe Condita*) In the year from the building of the city (= Rome).
A. V. Artillery Volunteers ; also Authorized Version (of the Bible).
b. Born.
B. A. Bachelor of Arts.
Bart. or *Bt.* Baronet.
Batt. Battalion.
B. C. Before Christ.
B. C. L. Bachelor of Civil Law.
B. D. Bachelor of Divinity.
B. E. Bachelor of Engineering.
b. l. Bill of lading.
B. L. Bachelor of Law.
B. Mus. Bachelor of Music.
Bp. Bishop.
Brit. Britain, British.
B. S. Bachelor in Surgery.
b. s. Bill of sale.
B. Sc. Bachelor of Scince.
B. Th. Bachelor of Theology.
B. V. Blessed Virgin.—*B. V. M.* Blessed Virgin Mary.
B. W. T. A. British Women's Temperance Association.
C or *Cent.* Centigrade.
C or *Cap* (L. *caput*) Chapter.
C. A. Chartered Accountant.
Cal. Calcutta.
Cantab. (L. *Cantabrigiensis*) Of Cambridge.
Cantuar. (L. *Cantuariensis*) Of Canterbury.
Cap. Capital.
Capt. Captain.
C. B. Companion of the Bath.
C. C. Cricket (or Cycling) Club ; County Court (or Councillor).

C. C. C. Corpus Christi College.
C. D. V. Carte-de-visite.
C. E. Civil Engineer.
Cent. (L. *centum*) A hundred.
Cf. (L. *confer*) Compare.
C. G. Centre of gravity.
cg. Centigramme.
Ch. Chapter ; Church.
Ch. B. Bachelor of Surgery.
C. I. Order of the Crown of India.
Cicestr. (*Cicestrensis*) Of Chichester.
C. I. E. Companion of the Order of the Indian Empire.
C. J. Chief Justice.
C. M. (L. *Chirurgiæ Magister*) Master in Surgery.
cm. Centimetre.
C. M. G. Companion of the Order of St. Michael and St. George.
C. M. S. Church Missionary Society.
Co. Company ; County.
c/o. Care of.
C. O. S. Charity Organisation Society.
Cp. Compare.
C. P. C. Clerk of the Privy Council.
C. P. S. (L. *Custos Privati Sigilli*) Keeper of the Privy Seal.
Cr. Credit or Creditor.
Cr. 8 vo. Crown octavo.
C. S. Civil Service ; Clerk to the Signet ; Court of Session.
C. S. I. Companion of the Star of India.
Curt. Current ; this month.
C. V. O. Commander of the Royal Victorian Order.
Cwt. (L. *centum*, a hundred, and Eng. *weight*). A hundredweight or hundredweights.
d. (L. *denarius, denarii*) A penny or pence ; died.
D. C. L. Doctor of Civil Law.
D. D. Doctor of Divinity.
D. D. S. Doctor of Dental Surgery.
D. G. (L. *Dei Gratiâ*) By the Grace of God ; Dragoon Guards.
D. L. Deputy Lieutenant.
D. Litt. (or *Lit*). Doctor of Literature.
Do (It. *ditto*) The same.
Doz. Dozen.
Dol. or *Dols.* Dollars.
D. P. H. Diploma in Public Health.
Dr. Debtor ; Doctor ; Dram or drams.
D. Sc. Doctor of Science.
D. S. O. Distinguished Service Order.
D. T. (L. *Doctor Theologiæ*) Doctor of Theology or Divinity.
D. Th. Doctor of Theology.
D. V. (L. *Deo volente*) God willing.
Dwt. (L. *denarius*, penny and Eng. *weight*) A pennyweight or pennyweights.
E. East or eastern ; English.
E. C. U. English Church Union.
Ed. Edition or editor.
E. E. Errors excepted ; Early English.
e. g. (L. *exempli gratiâ*) For example.
E. I. R. East Indian Railway.
E. N. E. East-north-east.
E. R. I. (L. *Eduardus Rex et Imperator*) Edward King and Emperor.
E. S. E. East-south-east.
Esq. Esquire.
et al (L. *et alibi*, or *alii*) And elsewhere, or others.
Etc. (L. *et cœteri, cœteræ*, or *cœtera*) And others; and so forth.
Et. seq. or *et sqq.* (L. *et sequentes* or *sequentia*) And the following.
E. & O. E. Errors and omissions excepted.
F. Fahrenheit.
f. Feminine
F. C. Free Church (of Scotland).
Fcp. Foolsc–
F. C. S. Fellow of the Chemical Society.
F. D. (L. *Fidei Defensor* or *Defensatrix*) Defender of the Faith.
F. F. P. S. Fellow of the Faculty of Physicians and Surgeons (Glas.)
F. G. S. Fellow of the Geological Society.
F. I. C. Fellow of the Institute of Chemistry.
F. M. Field-marshal.
Fo. Folio.
f. o. b. Free on board (goods delivered).
F. P. S. Fellow of the Philological Society.
F. R. A. S. Fellow of the Royal Astronomical Society.
F. R. C. I. Fellow of the Royal Colonial Institute.
F. R C. P. Fellow of the Royal College of Physicians.
F. R. C. S. Fellow of the Royal College of Surgeons.
F. R. C. S. L. Fellow of the Royal College of Surgeons, London.
F. R .G. S. Fellow of the Royal Goographical Society.
F. R. Met. S. Fellow of the Royal Meteorological Society.
F. R. S. Fellow of the Royal Society.
Ft. Foot or feet.
F. T. C. D. Fellow of Trinity College, Dublin.
F. Z. S. Fellow of the Zoological Society.
G. German.
G. C. B. Knight Grand Cross of the Bath.
G. C. H. Knight Guard Cross of Hanover.
G. C. I. E. Knight Grand Cross of the Indian Empire.
G. C. L. H. Grand Cross of the Legion of Honour.
G. C. M. Greatest Common Measure.

G. C. M. G. Knight Grand Cross of St. Michael and St. George.
G. C. S. I. Knight Grand Commander of the Star of India.
G. C. V. O. Knight Grand Cross of the Royal Victorian Order.
gm. Grammes.
G. M. Grand Master.
G. O. M. Grand Old man (W. E. Gladstone).
Gov. Government, Governor.
G. P. O. General Post-office.
G. P. R. Great Peninsular Railway.
gr. Grain or Grains.
H. B. M. His (or Her) Britannic Majesty.
H. C. F. Highest Common Factor.
H. C. S. Home Civil Service.
H. E. His Excellency.
H. H. His (or Her) Highness.
Hhd. Hogshead or Hogsheads.
H. I. H. His (or Her) Imperial Highness.
H. I. M. His (or Her) Imperial Majesty.
H. M. His (or Her) Majesty.
H. M. S. His (or Her) Majesty's Service ; His (or Her) Majesty's Ship.
Hon. Honourable.
H. P. Horse-power.
H. R. H. His (or Her) Royal Highness.
H. S. H. His (or Her) Serene Highness.
Ib. or *ibid.* (L. *ibidem*) In the same place.
I. C. S. Indian Civil Service.
Id. (L. *idem*) The same.
i. e. (L. *id est.*) That is.
I. F. A. Indian Football Association.
I. H. P. Indicated Horse-Power.
Imp. (L. *imperator*) Emperor ; Imperial.
I. M. S. Indian Medical Service.
In. Inch or inches.
Incog. (It. *incognito, incognita*) Unknown.
In loc. (L. *in loco*) In its place.
In loc. cit. (L. *in loco citato*) In the place cited.
I. N. R. I. (L. *Iesus Nazarenus Rex Judæorum*) Jesus of Nazareth, King of the Jews.
intro. introd. Introduction.
Inst. Instant ; the present month.
I. O. U. I owe you—an acknowledgment for money.
J. C. Jesus Christ.
J. P. Justice of the peace.
K. B. Knight of the Bath ; Bachelor King's Bench.
K. C. King's Counsel.
K. C. B. Knight Commander of the Bath.
K. C. I. E. Knight Commander of the Indian Empire.
K. C. M. G. Knight Commander of St. Michael and St. George.
K. C. S. I. Knight Commander of the Star of India.
K. C. V. O. Knight Commander of the Royal Victorian Order.
kg. Kilogramme.
K. G. Knight of the Garter.
K. L. H. Knight of the Legion of Honour.
km. Kilometre.
K. P. Knight of St. Partrict.
Kt. Knight.
L., *l.*, or £ (L. *libra*) Pound or pounds (sterling).
L. lb or ℔ Pound or pounds (weight).
L. Latin ; Liberal.
Lat. Latitude, Latin.
lc. (L. *loco citato*), in the place quoted ; also lower-case (in printing).
L. Ch. Licentiate in Lurgery.
L. C. J. Lord Chief justice.
L. C. M. Least (or lowest) common multiple.
L. C. P. Licentiate of the College of Preceptors.
L. Div. Licentiate in Divinity.
L. D. S. Licentiate of Dental Surgery.
L. F. P. S. Licentiate of the Faculty of Physicians and Surgeons.
L. H. D. (L. *Literarum humaniorum doctor*) Doctor of Literature.
Lib. (L. *liber*) Book.
Lieut ; *Lt.* Lieutenant.
Lit. D. Doctor of Literature.
LL. B (L. *Legum Baccalaureus*) Bachelor of Laws. [LL. is written because the word is plural.]
L. L. D. (L. *Legum Doctor*) Doctor of Laws. [see *LL. B.*]
LL. M. (L. *Legum Magister*) Master of Laws. [See *LL. B.*]
L. M. S. London Missionary Society.
L. R. C. P. Licentiate of the Royal College of Physicians.
L. R. C. S. Licentiate of Royal College of Surgeons.
L. S. D. (L. *Libræ, Solidi, Denarii*) Pounds, shillings, pence.
L. Th. Licentiate in Theology.
M. (F. *mille*) Thousand ; (L. *meridies*), noon ; mile or miles ; Monsieur.
m. Minute or minutes.
M. A. Master of Arts. See *A. M.*
M. B. (L. *Medicinæ Baccalaureus*) Bachelor of Medicine.
M. C. Master of Ceremonies Member of Congress ; Master in Surgery. See *C. M.*
M. D. (L. *Medicinæ Doctor*) Doctor of Medicine.
Mdlle. Mademoiselle or Miss.
M. E. Middle English.
Messrs. Messieurs, Gentlemen.
M. ft. (*L. Mistura fiat*) Let a mixture be made.
Mgr. Monsignor.

H. S. Member of the Historical Society.
I. C. E. Member of the Institu-on of Civil Engineers.
I. E. E. Member of the insti-ıte of Electric Engineer.
I. M. E. Memeer of the insti-te of mining Engineers.
I. Mech. E. Member of the stitution of Mechanical Engi-ers.
L. C. Member of the Legislative ouncil.
'e. Mademoiselle or Miss.
. Millimetres.
f. Messieurs.
ıe. Madame.
l. wt. Molecular weight.
P. Member of Parliament.
P. S. Member of the Philo-ɔgical Society.
r. Master (pron. *Mister*).
. R. A. S. Member of the Royal ıcademy of Science; Member of the Royal Asiatic Society.
'. R. C. P. Member of the Royal College of Physicians.
f. R. C. S. Member of the Royal College of Surgeons.
'Irs. Mistress.
MM. Manuscript; *MSS.* Manuscripts.
f. Sc. Master of Science.
Noon; North; Northern; ote.
A. North America or North ınerican.
B. (*L. Nota bene*) Note well take notice.
D. No Date.
/. E. North-east; North-eastern.
ı. con. (L. *nemine contra-cente*) No one contradicting; unanimously.
Nem. dis. (L. *nemine dissentiente*) No one dissenting.
V. H. New Hemisphere.
/. N. E. North-north-east.
N. N. W. North-north-west.
No. (L. *numero*) Number.
Non. seq. (L. *non siquitur*) It does not follow.
N. P. Notary-public.
N. S. New Style: Nova Scotia; National Society.
N. T. New Testament.
N. W. North-west; North-western.
N. Y. New York.
Ob. (L. *obiit*). Died.
O. E. Old English.
O. F. Old French.
O. H. G. Old High Germany.
O. H. M. S. On his Majesty's Service.
O. P. Out of print; Order of Preachers (Dominicans).
O. S. Old Style.
O. S. A. Order of St. Augustine.
O. S. B. Order of St. Benedict.
O. S. F. Order of St. Francis.
O. T. Old Testament.
Oxon (L. *Oxoniensis*) Of Oxford.
Oz. Ounce, [*Note,* The z, as in *viz.*, represents an old symbol for a terminal contraction].
p. page; *pp* pages.
P. & O. Co. Peninsular and Oriental Steam Navigation Company.
Per cent. or *per ct.* (L. *per centum*) By the hundred.
Ph. D. (L. *Philosophiœ Doctor*) Doctor of Philosophy.
P. M. (L. *post meridiem*) Afternoon; Past Master; Post master.
P. M. G. Postmaster-general.
P. O. Post office; postal order.
Pp. Pages.
P. P. C. (Fr. *pour prendre conge*) To take leave.
Pro tem. (L. *pro tempore*) For the time being.
Prox. (L. *proximo*) Next or of the next month.
P. R. S. President of the Royal Society.
P. R. S. A. President of the Royal Scottish Academy.
P. S. (L. *post scriptum*) Postscript.
P. S. Privy Seal.
P. T. O. Please turn over.
P. W. D. Public Works Department.
Q. Query or question.
Q. B. Queen's Bench.
Q. C. Queen's College; Queen's Counsel.
Q. E. D. (L. *quod erat demonstrandum*) Which was to be demonstrated.
Q. E. F. (L. *quod erat faciendun*) Which was to be done.
Q. E. I. (L. *quod erat invenien-dum*) Which was to be found out.
Q. M. Quarter-master.
Q. M. G. Quartermaster-general.
Q. S. Quarter Sessions.
q. v. (L. *quod vide*) Which see.
R. (L. *Rex*). King (*Regina*). Queen; Reaumur; Radical.
R. A. Royal Academician; Royal Artillery.
R. A. S. Royal Asiatic Society; Royal Astronomical Society.
R. C. Roman Catholic.
R. C. A. Royal College of Art.
R. C. M. Royal College of Music.
R.C.P. Royal College of Physicians.
R. C. S. Royal College of Surgeons (or of Science).
R. C. V. S. Royal College of Veterinary Surgeons.
R. E. Royal Engineers.
Rev. Reverend.
R. F. A. Royal Field Artillery.
R. G. A. Royal Garrison Artillery.
R. G. S. Royal Georgraphical Society.
R. H. G. Royal Horse Guards.
R. I. P. (L. *requiescat in pace*), May he (or she) rest in peace!
R. M. Royal Mail; Royal Marines; Resident Magistrate (Irel.)

R. M. A. Royal Military Academy, Royal Marine Artilley.

R. M. C. Royal Military College.

R. M. S. Royal Mail Steamer; Royal Microscopical Society.

R. N. Royal Navy.

R. S. Royal Society.

R. S. V. P. (Fr. *Repondez, s'il Vous plait*) Answer if you please.

Rt. Hon. Right Honourable.

Rt. Rev. Right Reverend.

R. V. Rifle Volunteers; Revised Version.

R. W. Right Worshipful or Right Worthy.

S. Saint; Signor; south; southern; Socialist.

s. Second or seconds; shillings.

S. A. South Africa, South Australia or South America.

Sc. (L. *scilicet*). To wit; namely; being understood; (L. *sculpsit*), He or she) engraved it.

Sc. B. (L. *Scientiœ Baccalaureus*) Bachelor of Science.

Sc. D. (L. *Scientiœ Doctor*) Doctor of Science.

S. D. F. Social Democratic Federation.

S. E. South-east; south-eastern.

Seq. or *Sqq.* (L. *sequentes* or *sequentia*) The following or the next.

S. G. Solicitor-general.

S. J. Society of Jesus.

S. P. C. A. Society for the Prevention of cruelty to Animals.

S. P. C. C. Society for the Prevention of cruelty to children.

S. P. C. K. Society for the promotion of Christian knowledge.

S. P. G. Society for the propagation of the Gospel.

S. S. E. South-south-east.

S. S. W. South-south-west.

Stg. Sterling.

S. T. P. (L. *Sacrœ Theologiœ Professor*) Professor of Divinity.

s.v. (L. *sub voce*) Under the word or title.

S. W. Southwest; south-western.

T. O. Turn over

T. U. Trade union.

U. F. C. United Free Church (of Scotland).

Ult. (L. *ultimo*) Last, or of the last month.

U. S. United States.

U. S. A. United States of America, or United States Army.

V. (L. *versus*). Against; (L. *vide*).

V. C. Vice Chancellor; Victoria Cross.

V. G. Vicar-general.

Vid. (L. *vide*) See.

Viz. (L. *videlicet*) Namely; wit. See note under *Oz.*

V. P. Vice president.

V. R. (L. *Victoria Regina*) Queen Victoria.

V. S. Veterinary Surgeon.

W. West; Western.

W. A. West Africa; Wes Australia.

W. C. Water-closet.

W. C. T. U. Women's Chr- Temperance Union.

w. f. Wrong fount (in prir

W. I. West Indies.

W. N. W. West-north-wes.

W. S. W. West-south-west.

X. Christ. (*Note*—The *X* r sents the Greek X (= CH) a *Christos.*

Xm. or *Xmas.* Christmas.

Xn. Christian.

Xnty. Christianity.

Xt. Christ.

Xtian. Christian.

Y. Year.

Y. M. C. A. Young Men's Cl tian Association.

Y. W. C. A. Young Women' Christian Association.

Z. S. Zoological Society.

Derivation of Geographical Names

Ab, Aub (Per.) water; as Doab, two rivers; Punjaub, five rivers.

Abad (Per., Hind., &c.), house, town; as Hyderabad, town of Hyder.

Abbas (Per.), father; Abbasabad, paternal town or abode.

Aber (Celt.), mouth of river; Aberdeen, town at the mouth of the Dee.

Adel (G.), noble; Adelsberg, noble's mountain.

Agoa (Pg.), **Agua** (Sp.), water; Agoa Fria, cold water; Aguas Calientes, warm waters.

Ain (Ar.), a spring; Ain Moosa, spring of Moses.

Ak (Turk.), white; Ak-Serai, white palace; Ak-su, white river.

Al, El (Ar.), the or a; Alcant the bridge; Alcazar, palace.

Allah (Ar), God; Allahabad, town of God.

Alp, Alb (Celt.) an elevated place Alpnach, high waters.

Alt (G.), old; Altdorf (or Altorf), old village; Altenkirchen, old churches.

.ta, Alto (Sp., It., Pg.), high ; Tierra Alta, high land (Sp.).
rd (Celt.), high, height ; Ardglass, green height.
Arl, Adler (G.), eagle ; Arlberg, Adlerberg, eagle's mountain.
rroyo (Sp.), rivulet ; Arroyo de 'erco, rivulet of the hog.
Aue (G.), meadow ; Reicnau, rich meadow ; Golden ie, golden meadow.
en, Avon (Celt.), flowing water ; -nnmore, great water ; Strat-n, valley of the river.
(Ar., Chal.), gate, court ; el-Mandeb, gate of tears.
, (Turk.), father ; Babadagh, er mountain.
1 (G.), brook, rivulet ; Fisch-ach, fish brook.
.d (G.), bath ; Baden, the baths ; Carlsbad, Charles' bath.
ahr (Ar.), sea, river ; Bahr Lut, sea of Lot, the Dead Sea ; Bahr-el-Abiad, the white river (White Nile).
Bal Bally (Celt.) town ; Ballin-y, town of the oak wood ; allyclare, town on the plain.
.nya (Hung.), a mine ; Banya-Nagy, great mine ; Banya-Felsö, upper mine.
Bar (Hind.), country ; Malabar, mountainous country.
Bazar, Basar (Turk.) market-own ; Novi-Bazar or Yeni-Bazar, new market-town.
au, Bel (Fr.) beautiful ; Beau-u (—Beauly), beautiful place ; elmont, beautiful mountain.
éla, Bielo (Rus.) white ; Belgrade, white town ; Bielaya, white stream.
eled, Bilad (Ar.), country, town ; Biledulgerid, country of dates.
Bello, Bella (It., Sp., Pg.), beautiful ; Portobello, beautiful port.
Ben (Celt.), hill ; Ben More, the great hill.

Bender (Turk., Per.), port ; Bender-Abbaz (Persia).
Berg (G.), hill, mountain ; Carlsberg, Charles' hill.
Beth (Heb.), house ; Bethel, house of God.
Bhum, Bhoom (Hind.) land, country ; Birbhum, land of heroes.
Bir (Ar.), well ; Bir-es-seba, well of seven (—Beersheba).
Bischof (G.), bishop ; Bischofsheim, bishop's home.
Blanc, Blanche (Fr.), white ; Mont Blanc ; Dent Blanche, white tooth (mountain peak).
Blanco (Sp.) white ; Cabo Blanco, white cape.
Bocca (It.), **Bocr** (Sp., Pg.), mouth ; Boca Chica, little mouth.
Borg (Sw., Dan.) castle ; Aalborg, eel town ; Frederiksborg.
Bosch (D.) wood ; Hertogenbosch, duke's wood (Bois-le-duc).
Bouroun, Bournu (Turk.) cape Narat-Bourun, cape of firs.
Bruck (G.) bridge ; Innsbrück, the bridge over the inn.
Brugg (Swiss.), bridge; Glattbrugg.
Brunn, Brunnen (G.), well ; Schönbrunn, beautiful well.
Bueno, Buena (Sp.), good ; Buenos Ayres, fine airs ; Buena Vista, fine view.
Burg (G.,) castle, fortified place ; Rothenburg, red castle ; Augsburg, castle of Augustus.
By (Dan.) town ; Sunby, town on the sound ; Ashby, ash town ; Kirkby, church town.
Caer, Car (Celt.), fortified place, fortified town ; Caer-Caradoc, fort of Caradoc or Caractacus ; Carnarvon, fort in Arvon.
Casa (Sp.), house ; Casas-Crandes, the great houses.
Cerro (Sp.), mountain peak, rugged hill ; Cerro de Pasco.

Chang, Chung (Chinese), middle ; Chang-choo foo, Chang-chuen.
Chow (Chinese), island ; second-class city ; Hang-chow.
Cidade (Pg.), city ; Cidade do Recife, city of the reef.
Cima (It.), mountain peak ; Cima Nove, new peak.
Citta (It.), city, town ; Chitta-di-Castello, town of the castle.
Ciudad (Sp.), city ; Ciudad Real royal city ; Ciudad-Rodrigo, city of Roderick.
Civita (It.), town ; Civita Vecchia, old town.
Col (Fr.), pass, elevated pass ; Col de Geant, giant's pass.
Croce (It.), cross ; Santa Croce the holy cross.
Croix (Fr.), cross ; Sainte Croix, the holy cross.
Cruz (Sp.), cross ; Vera Cruz, the true cross ; Santa Cruz, the holy cross.
Cumbre (Sp.), mountain peak ; Cumbres Altas, the high peaks.
Czerna, Czerny, Cherni (Slav.), black ; Czernagora, the black mountain (—Montenegro) ; Czernamore, the Black Sea.
Dagh. Tagh (Per., Turk.), mountain or mountain range ; Babadagh, father mountain.
Dal (Dan., Sw.), valley, dale ; Da Elf, valley river.
Dam (D.), dam , Amsterdam, the dam of the Amstel ; Rotterdam, dam of the Rotte.
Daria, Darya (Per.), sea, river ; Amu Darya, Sir Darya.
Diva, Diu (Hind.), island ; the Maldives ; Laccadives.
Dun (Celt.), fort ; Dundee, the fort on the Tay.
Eisen (G.), iron ; Eisenberg, iron mountain ; Eisenstadt, iron town.

El, Al (Ar.), the or a ; El Kantara, the bridge. See Al. (El is also Spanish for the.)

Elf (Sw.), river ; Göta Elf ; Dal Elf, river of the dale.

Eski (Turk.), old ; Eski-Hissar, old castle ; Eski-Stambul, old Constantinople.

Feld (G.), field ; Feld church ; Hirschfeld, field of the stag.

Fels, Felsen (G.), rock ; Drachenfels, dragon rock.

Felso (Hung.) upper ; opposite of Alsó, lower ; Felsö Lendva.

Fjeld, Field (Dan.), **Fjall** (Sw.), mountain, mountains, as the Dovrefjeld, the Fillefjeld.

Foo (Chinese), a first-class city ; Tse-nan-foo.

Frey, Frei (G.), free ; Freiburg, free castle or town.

Fried, Frieden (G.), peace ; Friedland, land of peace.

Furst (G.), prince ; Fürstenwalde, princes's wood.

Gamla (Sw.), Gamla Karleby, old Charles-town.

Garh Gurh, Ghur (Hind.), fort, castle ; Futtehgurh, fort of victory.

Gawa (Japanese), river ; Sakadagawa ; Shinanogawa.

Gebirge (G.), mountains ; Riesengebirge, giant mountains.

Ghaut, Ghat (Hind.), a mountain pass, also a landing-place or flight or steps on the side of a river.

Giri (Hind.), mountains ; Nilgiri (Neilgherry), blue mountains.

Gora (Slav), mountain ; Czernagora, black mountain (—Montenegro).

Gorod, Grad (Slav.) town ; Novgorod, new town.

Graf, Grafen (G.), count ; Grafenberg, count's hill.

Grande (Sp., It., Pg.), great ; Rio Grande, great river.

Groote (D.), great : Groote Aa, great river.

Gross (G.), great ; Gross-Glogau ; Gross-Biberan.

Gunong (Malay), mountain ; Gunong Tebu- ; Gunong Api.

Hafen (G.), **Havn** (Dan.), port ; Bremerhafen, port of Bremen ; Kjöbenhavn, merchant's haven (Copenhagen).

Hai (Chi.), sea ; Whang-hai, Hoang-hai, yellow sea.

Ham, Hamn (Sw.), port ; Carlshamn, Charles' haven.

Haus (G.), house ; Neuhaus, new house ; Oberhausen, upper houses.

Havn (Dan.), port. See HAFEN, HAM.

Hegy (Hung.), mountain ; Hegyallya.

Heilige, Heiligen (G.), holy, saint ; Heiligenstadt, holy town.

Heim (G.), home (—E. ham) ; Bischofsheim, bishop's home.

Hissar (Turk.), castle ; Ak-Hissar, white castle ; Kara-Hissar, black castle.

Ho (Chinese), river, canal ; Hoang-ho, yellow river ; Pei-ho, white river.

Hoang (Chinese), yellow ; Hoang-ho, yellow river, Hoang-choo, yellow town.

Hoch (G.), high ; Hochkirch, high church ; Hochberg, high mountain.

Hof (G.), court, farm, estate ; Hof-wyl.

Hohe (G.), height ; Hohenzollern, the height of the Zoller family.

Holm (Sw., Dan.), small island ; Bornholm, Island of Burgundians.

Hondo, Honda (Sp.), deep ; Rio Honde, deep river.

Ile, Isle (Fr.), Island ; Belle isle, beautiful island; Lisle (l'isle), the island.

Inver (Celt.), mouth of a ri Inverness, mouth of the Ness.

Irmak (Turk.), river ; K Irmak, red river (the an Halys).

Isola (It.), **Isla** (Sp.), **Ilha** (island ; Isola Bella, beautil island ; Ilha Grande, great isl

Jebel, Djebel (Ar.), mounta Jebel Moosa, mount of Moses the modern Arabic name of Mt. Sinai ; Gibraltar, corrupted from Jebel Tarik, mount of Tarik.

Jeni (Turk.), new. See YENI.

Jezireh (Ar.), island ; Al Jezir the name of the region betwe the Euphrates and Tigris.

Kafir (Ar.), infidel ; Kafiristan land of infidels.

Kaiser (G.), emperor ; Kaiserstuhl, emperor's chair or throne ; Kaiserstadt, emperor's town.

Kale (Turk.), castle ; Yeni-kal new castle ; Kale Dagh, c hill.

Kand, Khand, Kund (Hind land, country ; Khokand, land o mountains ; Bundelkhand.

Kara (Turk.), black ; Kara-Su, black river ; Kara-Hissar, black fortress.

Kiang (Chinese), river ; Yang-tse-kiang, son of the sea river ; Ta-kiang, great river; Pe-kiang north river.

Kil (Celt.), cell, church ; Kilpatrick, church or cell of St. Patrick, Kilkenny, church of St. Kenny ; Kildare, church of the oaks.

Kin (Celt.), head, upper part ; Kinloch, head of the loch.

King (Chinese), town ; Pe-king, northern city ; Nan-king, southern city.

Kio, Kei (Japanese), town ; Tokio, same as YEDO.

Kirche (G.), church ; Kirchdorf church village.

(Hung.), little ; Kis-barath ; ..s-ber.

..l, **Kysyl** (Turk.), red ; Kizil-..mak, red river.

..n (G.), little ; Klein-Glogau, distinguished from Gross-..gau.

..h, **Kuh** (Per.), mountain ; ..du-Koh, Indian mountain.

..oi, **Kul** (Tart.); lake ; Kara Kul, black lake ; Issikol or Issikul.

..onig (G.), king ; Königsberg, king's mountain.

..pf (G.), head ; Schneekopf, ..ow-head, snow-capped moun-..in.

..oping (Dan., Sw.), market-town ; Nyköping, new market-town.

..rasnoe (Rus.), pretty : Krasnoe-selo, pretty village.

Krasnoi (Rus.), red ; Krasnoiarsk, town of the red cliff.

..eis (G.), circle, district forming administrative division.

.. (It., Sp., Pg.), lake ; Lago ..aggiore, the greater lake.

..guna (It., Sp.), marsh, lagoon.

..angen, Lange (G.), long ; Lang-enberg, long mountain.

..auter (G.), clear ; Lauterbrun-nen, clear fountains.

Levante (It.), east, eastern region ; hence the Levant.

..icht (G.), light ; Lichtenstein, ..ear stone or rock.

..ieu (Fr.), place ; Beaulieu, fine place.

..aha (Hind.), great ; Mahanadi, Mahanuddy, great river.

Mark (G.), boundary, march ; Mark lorf, boundary village.

Mark (Scand.), territory ; Lapp-mark, territory of the Lapps.

..arkt (G.), market ; Neumarkt, new market ; Markt Oberhausen.

..avros, Mavron, Mavro (Gr.), black ; Marvon Oros, black mountain.

Meer (G.), sea ; Schwarzes Meer, the black sea.

Meer (D.), lake ; Borkumnar Meer, lake of Borkum.

Mer (Fr.), sea ; Mer Morte, the Dead Sea.

Mezo, Meso (Hung.), field ; Mezo-Careny.

Mittel (G.), middle ; Mittelwalde, middle wood.

Mond, Monde (D.), mouth Dendermonde, town at the mouth of the Dender.

More (Celt.), great ; Glen More, the great glen ; Ben More, the great mountain.

Muhl (G.), mill ; Altmühl, the old mill ; Mühlhausen, mill-houses.

Mund (G.), mouth ; Warnem-ünde, town at the mouth ; of the Warnow.

Munster (G.) monastery, minster ; Munsterberg, minster mountain

Nagor, Nagar, Naggur (Hind.), town ; Ahmednagar, town of Ahmed.

Nagy (Hung.), great : Nagy-Varad, same as GROSSWARDEIN.

Nahr (Ar.) river ; Nahr el Asy, the Orontes (in Syria).

Nan (Chinese), Southern ; Nan-king, southern city (opposite of Pe-king).

Negro (It., Sp., Pg.), black ; Rio Negro, black river ; Negro-Cerro, black mountain.

Neu (G.), new ; Neuhaus, new house.

Nevado, Nevada (Sp.), snowy ; Sierra Nevada, snowy chain of mountains.

Nieder (G.), lower ; Neiderbronn, lower well ; Neiderlande, the Netherlands.

Nieuw, Nieu (D.), new ; Nieuw-poort, Nieuport, new port.

Nijnei, Nizhnei (Rus.), lower ; Nijnei-Novgorod.

Nor (Mong.), lake Koko Nor ; Lob Nor.

Nov, Novoi, Novaia (Rus.), new ; Novgorod, new town ; Novoi-Cherkask Novaia Semlia (Nova Zembla).

Nuevo, Nueva (Sp.), new ; Villa Nueva, new town.

Nuovo, Nuova (It.), new.

Ny (Sw.), new; Nyborg, new town; Nyköping, new market.

O (Hung), Old O-Becse.

O, Oe (Dan., Sw.), island ; Sandö, sand island ; Samsö, Lessö.

Ober (G.), upper ; Oberkirch, upper church.

Ola, Oola (Mongolian), mountain ; Bogdo-Oola, holy mountain.

Oost (D.), east ; Oostburg, east town.

Ost, Oster, Oester (G.), east ; Oesterreich, eastern empire, Austria

Ostrog (Rus.), fortress, as the town Ostrog in Volhynia.

Oud, Oude (D.), old; Oudenbosch, old wood ; Oudewater, old water.

Ozero (Rus.), lake ; Bielozersk, town on Lake Bielo.

Patam (Hind.), town ; Seringa-patam, town of sriringa or Vishnu

Pe (Chinese), north, northern ; Peking, the northern city.

Pei (Chinese), white ; Pei-ho, the white river.

Pico (Sp., Pg.), mountain peak ; Pico de Ten eriffe, peak of Teneriffe.

Piz (Rumonsh), mountain peak ; (It. Pizzo ; Sp. Pico).

Pol, Poli, Polis, Ple (Gr., Rus. Turk.), town ; Sevastopol, city o Augustus ; Tripoli, the three cities; Nicopolis, city of victory ; Con-stantinople, city of Constantine.

Pont (Fr.), **Ponte** (It., Pg.), **Puente** (Sp.), bridge ; Pont-du Château, bridge of the castle; Ponte-San-Pietro, St. Peter's bridge.

Poor, Pore, Pur (Hind.), town ; Cawnpoor, city of the khan or chieftain ; Jeypore, Jypoor, city of victory.

Porto (It., Pg.), harbor ; Portobello, beatiful harbor.

Puerto (Sp.), harbor ; Puerto Rico, rich port, Porto Rico.

Pulo (Malay), Island ; Pulo Penang, Areca Island, Penang or Prince of Wales' Island.

Ras (Ar.), cape, promontory; Ras-el-had, cape of danger.

Reich (G.), kingdom, monarchy, dominion ; Oesterreich, Austria.

Rio (Sp., Pg.), river ; Rio Grande, great river.

Roth (G.), red ; Rothwasser, red wate. ; Rothenburg, red castle.

Rud Rood (Per.), river ; Heri-rud, Keshef-rud.

Saki, Misaki (Japanese), cape ; Idsumo-saki, Kona-saki.

Salz (G.), salt ; Salzburg, salt castle.

San, Santo, Santa (Sp., Pg., It.), saint ; San-Juan, San-Miguel, Santo-Domingo, Santa-Rosa.

Schnee (G.), snow ; Schneekopf, snow-head, snow-capped mountain.

Schwarz (G.), black ; Schwarzwald, the Black Forest.

See (G.), lake ; Thunersee, the lake of Thun.

Serai, Sarai (Turk.), palace ; Akserai, white palace ; Baktchiserai, place of the gardens.

Serra (Pg.), **Sierra** (Sp.), mountain range ; Sierra Nevada, snowy range ; Sierra Morena, black range.

Shan (Chinese), mountain ; Thian-shan, mountains of heaven.

Shehr (Turk., Per.), city, house ; Eski-shehr, old city.

Sima, Shima (Japanese), island ; Tsu-sima, Tanega-sima.

Sk (Rus.), town ; Tobolsk, town on the Tobol.

Ski, Skoi, Skoe, Skaia (Rus.), cape ; Chukotskoi, Kromskaia.

Sneeuw (D.), snow ; Sneeuwbergen, snowy mountains.

Stadt (G.), **Stad** (Dan., Sw., D.), town ; Friedrichstadt, Frederikstad, Frederick's town.

Stan (Per.), country ; Afghanistan, land of the Afghans.

Stein (G.), stone, rock ; Konigstein, stone of the king.

Stor (Sw.), great ; Stor Skar, great island.

Su, Soo (Turk.), lake, river ; Ak-su, white river.

Sul (Pg.), south ; Rio Grande do Sul, grand river of the south.

Tag, Tagh (Turk., Per.), mountain; Agri Tagh, (Dagh is another form of this word).

Tau (Turk.), mountain ; Koshtan-Tau, peak of Caucasus.

Tell (Ar.), hill; Tel-el-kebir, great hell.

Terra (Pg., It.), **Tierra** (Sp.), earth, land; Tierra del Fuego, land of fire.

Thal (G.), valley ; Rheinthal, valley of the Rhine.

Unter (G.), under, lower ; Ur waldon, under or below t. woods ; Unter Ammergau.

Valle (Sp., It. Pg.) valley ; Va Hermoso, beautiful valley ; Rio-del Valle, river of the valley.

Var, Varos (Hung.), fortress, town ; Temesvar, castle or f tress on the river Temes.

Veld (D.) field ; Roggeveld, fielc or plain of rye.

Villa (It., Sp., Pg.), town ; Villa Nova, Villa Nuova, new town.

Ville (Fr.), town ; Villeneuve, nev town ; Abbeville, abbot's town.

Vorder (G.), in front ; Vorderrhein, one of the head-waters of tl Rhine.

Wady (Ar.), valley, a valley with a river in it, a river ; Wady Moosa, valley of Moses ; Wad el-Kebir, great river (hence Guadalquivir).

Wald (G.), forest ; Schwarzwald the Black Forest.

Weiler (G.), village ; Badenweller, village of baths.

Weiss (G.), white ; Weisskirch white church ; Weissenburg white castle.

Wiese (G.), meadow ; Wiesenthal meadow valley.

Yama (Japanese), mountain ; Fusi-Yama, the great mountain.

Zee (D.), sea ; Zuider Zee, the south sea.

Zwart, Zwarte (D.), black ; (Zwarte-berg, the black mountain.

Forms of Address in ceremonious communications with persons of title or official position.

..bassador—The title 'Excel-lency' belongs specially to ambassadors, as well as to governors of colonies, and the Lord-lieutenant of Ireland. Address letters His Excellency (with name or distinctive title following) His Britannic Majesty's Ambassador and Minister Plenipotentiary to the Court of—'. Begin: 'Sir,' 'My Lord,' according as the ambassador possesses title or not. When personal reference is made say 'Your Excellency.'

..chbishop — Address: 'His Grace the Lord Archbishop of—' Begin. 'My Lord Archbishop' Refer to as 'Your Grace.' The most formal method of addressing the Archbishop of Canterbury is as follows: 'The Most Reverend Father in God, Frederick (or whatever the Christian name is), by Divine Providence Lord Archbishop of Canterbury, Primate of All England and Metropolitan'. An Irish archbishop is now addressed as 'The Most Reverend the Archbishop of —'. In America the common from of address is 'The Most Reverend A—B—, D.D.' The wife of an Archbishop has no special title in right of her husband's dignity, being only plain Mrs.

..hdeacon — An archdeacon is called 'Venerable': 'The Venerable the Arbhdeacon of—'. Begin 'Venerable Sir', or 'Reverend Sir', or 'Mr. Archdeacon' (especially in speaking).

Baron—Address: 'The Right Hon. Lord —'; less formally 'The Lord —'. Begin. 'My Lord.' Refer to as 'Your Lordship.'

Baron's Daughter — Barons' daughters are all entitled to be called 'Honourable'. Unmarried they are addressed as 'The Hon. A—B—', with Christian and surname. They retain the title 'Hon.' after marriage, the wife of a commoner being 'The Hon. Mrs.' with husband's surname, the wife of a knight or baronet being 'The Hon. Lady,' with husband's surname. Begin 'Madam'; refer to as 'Your Ladyship' if so entitled by marriage. If a higher rank is conferred by the husband the title of course corresponds.

Baron's Son—All the sons are 'Hononrable,' with Christian name and surname. In Scotland the eldest son is addressed as 'The Hon. the Master of' (peerage title), or 'The Hon. (John), Master of.' Begin: 'Sir.' The wife of a baron's son is 'The Hon Mrs,' with husband's surname or both Christian name and surname. Begin: 'Madam.' If the daughter of an earl, marquis, or duke, she must be addressed accordingly.

Baroness—Address: 'The Right Hon. the Baroness—', or 'The Right Hon. Lady—', or 'The Lady—'. Begin: 'Madam'; refer to as 'Your Ladyship.'

Baronet—Address: 'Sir A—B—, Bart.' giving Christian name and surname. The Christian name *must* be given; it is quite wrong to speak, for instance, of 'Sir Vernon Harcourt' where 'Vernon' is merely one of the surnames. Begin; 'Sir.' A baronet's wife is addressed as 'Lady' with husband's surname (her Christian name would also be used if the daughter of a duke, marquis, or earl, and in this case she would also be 'Right Hon.') Begin 'Madam'; refer to as 'Your Ladyship.'

Bishop—Address: 'The Right Rev. the Lord Bishop of—', or 'The Right Rev. A—B—, Lord Bishop of—', or simply 'The Lord Bishop of—'. Begin: 'My Lord Bishop'; refer to as 'Your Lordship.' In formal documents a bishop is styled 'The Right Reverend Father in God, John, by Divine Permission, Lord Bishop of—'. Begin: 'Right Rev. Sir.' Bishops' wives have no share in their husbands' titles.

In Ireland the bishops of the Protestant church are now most correctly addressed as 'The Right Reverend the Bishop of—' Begin 'Right Rev. Sir.' In Scotland the usage is the same. Neither Irish nor Scottish bishops can claim to be spoken of as 'Lord Bishop,' 'Your Lordship,' though this is sometimes done.

A retired bishop is still addressed as 'Right Reverend'; 'The Right Reverend Bishop—', 'Right Rev. Sir.' In America the form of address to a bishop is generally 'The Right Rev. A—B—'.

[Romen Catholic bishops in Ireland are addressed as 'Most Reverend.']

Canon— Address: 'The Rev. Canon—'. Begin: 'Reverend Sir.'

Cardinal—The special title of a cardinal as such is 'His Eminence.' Begin: 'Your Eminence.'

Charge d'Affaires—See AMBASSADOR.

Clergy—The general form of address is 'The Reverend A—B—'. Begin: 'Rev. Sir' or simply 'Sir.' If a clergyman is the son of a duke or marquis he is to be addressed as 'The Rev. Lord A—B—'; if the son of an earl, viscount, or baron: 'The Rev. the Honourable A—B—', or 'The Hon. and Rev. A—B—.' If he is a baronet, 'The Rev. Sir A—B—, Bart.'

Congress, Members of (U. S.). Addressed generally 'The Honourable A—B—'.

Consul—There is no special form of address to a person as such. 'A—B—, Esq., H. B. M.'s Consul', 'Consul-general', or as the case may be. In the U. States, however, a consul is commonly called 'Honourable.'

Countess—Address: The Right Honourable the Countess of—'. Begin: 'Madam'; refer to as 'Your Ladyship'.

Dean—Address: The Very Reverend the Dean of—'. Begin: 'Very Rev. Sir'; more familiarly 'Mr. Dean' (used in oral communications).

Doctor—The initials denoting the particular degree are placed after the usual form of address, whether D. D., LL. D., M. D., D.Sc., &c. 'The Rev. A—B—, D. D.'; 'A—B—, Esq., M. D.' Less formally: 'The Rev. Doctor A—B—'.

Dowager—When the holder of a title marries, the widow of a previous holder of the same title becomes 'dowager', this being often inserted in addressing her: 'The Right Hon. the Dowager Countess of—'; 'The Dowager Lady—'. Instead of 'Dowager', to which some ladies object, the Christian name may be used: 'The Right Hon. Mary Countess of—'. Begin: 'Madam'; refer to as 'Your Ladyship.'

Duchess—Address: 'Her Grace the Duchess of—'. Begin: 'Madam'; refer to as 'Your Grace.'

Duke—Address: 'His Grace the Duke of—'. Begin: 'My Lord Duke'; refer to as 'Your Grace'. All the children of a duke are entitled to be called 'Right Honourable.' Royal dukes are different. See PRINCE.

Duke's Daughter—Address: 'The Right Hon. Lady,' with Christian name and surname, or 'The Lady', with Christian name and surname. Begin: 'Madam'; refer to as 'Your Ladyship.' If married to a commoner or a peer by courtesy, the surname is derived from the husband's name or title; if to a peer, the wife takes a title corresponding to her husband's.

Duke's Son—A duke's eldest son takes by courtesy one of his father's secondary titles, and is thus usually a marquis or an earl, being addressed exactly as if really a peer with the respecti[ve] rank. His wife receives the co[r]responding title, being th[e] marchioness or countess, [and] their eldest son takes al[so a] courtesy title belonging to [the] family, being thus either a v[is]count or a baron.

A duke's younger son is ad[d]ressed similarly to his siste[rs] 'The Right Honourable Lor[d] A—B—', or 'The Lord A—B—'. Begin: 'My Lord'; refer to a[s] 'Your Lordship.' Their wiv[es] are treated in a correspondin[g] manner: 'The Right Honourable Lady A—B—', or 'The Lad[y] A—B—'; 'Your Ladyship.'

Earl—Address: 'The Righ[t] Honourable the earl of—', o[r] 'The Earl of—', Begin: 'My Lord'; refer to as 'Your Lordship'. The wife of an earl is a countess. (See above.)

Earl's Children—The eldest son of an earl (like the eldest son of a duke) takes a courtesy title from his father and thus ranks either as a viscount or a baron, being treated as if really a pee[r] and his wife as a peeress. The younger sons of an earl are all called 'Honourable' (their eldest brother 's 'Right Honourable')—'The Hon. A—B—', the same as the sons of a baron. (See above).

The daughters of an earl are all 'Right Honourable', and are addressed as the daughters of a duke. (See above.)

Envoy—See AMBASSADOR.

Executive Council, Members of (in colonial governments). Generally addressed as 'The Honourable A—B—.'

Governor of Colony — Colo[nial] governors have the title o[f] xcellency' in virtue of their office. ldress : 'His Excellency A— –, Esq. (Sir A—B—, The t Honourable the Earl of, Governor of —'. Begin rding to rank ; refer to as r Excellency.' A duke holding such a position would, how-, be 'His Grace,' 'Your Grace.' governor's wife does not have claim to be called 'Her Ex-ency.' Lieutenant-governors, n India and the Dominion of nada, are styled 'Honourable,' s Honour,' 'Your Honour.'

ernor of State—(U.S.)Usually ressed as 'His Excellency.' s Excellency A—B—, Gover- of —', or 'His Excellency the vernor of —'. A lieutenant-vernor is called 'Honour-ble.'

dge—This in Britain has not very distinctive meaning. In ngland and Ireland the judges f the supreme courts are called ords Justices and Justices ; in cotland the judges are the rds of Session. (See JUSTICE, JUSTICE, LORD OF SESSION.) gland the county court s, however, are regularly ed 'Judge.' 'His Honour ige—' (surname) ; on the ch referred to as 'Your onour.'

In many British colonies the members of the higher courts e called judges and addressed 'The Honourable A—B—'. the U. States the term judge regularly applied to all such tionaries ; and all are ad-sed in the same way.

ce — Judges of the High rt of Justice in England, in Chancery and other divisions, called justices. Address : 'The Honourable Mr. Justice—' ; or if a knight, 'The Hon. Sir A—B—'. Begin in both cases 'Sir.' On the bench he is addressed as 'My Lord' ; and referred to as 'Your Lordship.'

Justice of peace—In England is formally addressed in documents as 'The Worshipful,' and on the bench is referred to as 'Your Worship.'

King—To be addressed as 'The King's Most Excellent Majesty.' Begin : 'Sire,' or 'May it please Your Majesty' ; refer to as 'Your Majesty.'

King's Counsel—Ordinary address with the addition of K. C.

Knight Bachelor—Treated as a baronet, but 'Kt.' is not usually appended to the name in addressing a letter. As in the case of a baronet, carefully avoid using a surname instead of a Christian name.

Knight of the Bath, St Michael and St. George, Star of India, Indian Empire—Address : 'Sir A—B—, G. C. B.', or K. C. B., K. C. M. G., K. C. S. I., K. C. I. E, as the case may be. Begin : 'Sir'.

Knight of the Garter, Thistle, St. Patrick- As above, with the initials K. G., K. T., K. P. respectively following the name.

Knight' Wife (of any class)—As baronet's wife.

Legislative Council, Members of—Those (who belong to colonial governments) are generally addressed as the 'Honourable A—B—'.

Lieutenant Governor. See GOVERNOR.

Lord Advocate of Scotland—Address : 'The Right Honourable the Lord Advocate'. Begin : 'My Lord' ; refer to Lordship'.

Lord Chancellor—Address Right Hon. the Lord High Chancellor' ; or 'The Right Hon. Earl——(or as the case may be), Lord High Chancellor'. Begin : 'My Lord' ; refer to as 'Your Lordship'.

Lord Chief Justice—(England) Address : 'The Right Honourable the Lord Chief Justice', or 'The Right Honourable Sir A—B—, Lord Chief Justice'. Begin : 'My Lord' or 'Sir', as the case may be.

Lord Justice— (English Supreme Court of Appeal). Address : 'The Right Honourable the Lord Justice——', or 'The Right Honourable Sir A—B'. Begin : 'Sir'. When on the bench they are addressed 'My Lord', 'Your Lordship'.

Lord-Lieutenant of Ireland. Address : 'His Excellency the Lord-Lieutenant', or if a duke, 'His Grace the Lord-Lieutenant'. How to begin and refer will also be determined by rank ('My 'Lord Duke', 'My Lord Marquis').

Lord Mayor — Only London, York, and a few other cities have a Lord Mayor. Address : 'The Right Honourable the Lord Mayor of——', or 'The Right Hon. A—B, Lord Mayor of—'. Begin : 'My Lord'; refer to as 'Your Lordship'.

The Lord Mayor's wife is addressed : 'The Right Honourable the Lady Mayoress of—'. Begin : 'My Lady' ; refer to as 'Your Ladyship'.

Lord Provost.—Address : 'The Right Hon. the Lord Provost of Edinburgh' ; 'The Hon. the

Provost of Glasgow. 'The Provost of Aberdeen', ..., or 'Dundee'. Begin: 'My Lord'. or 'My Lord Provost'; refer to as 'Your Lordship'. The Lord Provost's wife has no share in the title.

Lords of Appeal (in Ordinary). These are judicial members of the House of Lords who rank as barons and are so addressed. Their wives are baronesses; their children are not specially distinguished.

Maid of Honour — Address: 'The Honourable Miss——'. Begin: 'Madam'.

Marchioness — Address: 'The Most Honourable the Marchioness ——'. Begin: 'Madam'; refer to as 'Your Ladyship'.

Marquis—Address: 'The Most Hon. the Marquis of——'. Begin: 'My Lord Marquis'; refer to as 'Your Lordship'.

Marquis's Children—All are 'Right Honourable' like those of a duke. The eldest son take a courtesy title like the eldest son of a duke, and is similarly addressed. Younger sons and daughters are like those of a duke.

Mayor — Address 'The Mayor of——', or in formal documents 'The Right Worshipful the Mayor of——', Address: 'Sir'; refer to as 'Your Worship'.

In the United States mayors are usually styled 'Honourable'; 'The Honourable A—B—Mayor of'.

Member of Parliament - Not specially recognized except by adding, M. P.' to ordinary address; 'A—B, Esq., M. P.'; 'Sir A—B—, Bart., M. P'.

Minister — See AMBASSADOR CLERGY.

Moderator of General Assembly (Scotland) – The Right Rev.': the Assembly itself is 'The Venerable'.

Officers, Military and Naval. Their professional rank is put before any title they may independently possess: 'General' or 'Admiral the Right Hon. the Earl of——'; 'Colonel the Honourable A—B—'.

Premier—No special title or address as such.

President—(U.S.) Address: 'His Excellency the President of the United States'; 'His Excellency A—B, President of the U. States'. The Vice President and ex-presidents are 'Honourable'; 'The Honourable the Vice-President'; 'The Honourable A—'.

Prince—Address: 'His Royal Highness the Prince of Wales'; 'His Royal Highness Prince A——' (Christian name). If a royal duke: 'His Royal Highness the Duke of——'. Begin in any case: 'Sir'; refer to as 'Your Royal Highness'.

Princess—Address: 'Her Royal Highness the Princess of Wales'; 'Her Royal Highness the Princess A—(Christian name); or if a duchess: 'Her Royal Highness the Duchess of——'. Begin: 'Madam'; refer to as 'Your Royal Highness'.

Principal of a Scottish University—If a clergyman, address as 'The Very Rev. the Principal of——'; or 'The Very Rev. Principal (surname)'.

Privy-Councillor—All members of the privy-council are entitled to be addressed as 'Right Honourable'; 'The Right Honourable A—B—, P. C. (omit 'Esq'). Otherwise according to rank.

Queen—Address: 'The Queen's Most Excellent Majesty'; Begin 'Madam', or "May it please your Majesty; refer to as 'Your Majesty'.

Recorder—Addressed as 'The Worshipful'; in London 'The Right Worshipful'. Begin 'Sir'; refer to as 'Your Worship'.

Secretary of State—Address: 'His Majesty's Principal Secretary of State for the—Department'.

Senators – (Canada and U. States) Addressed as 'The Honourable A—B—'.

Serjeant-at-law—Address: 'Serjeant——', or 'Mr. Serjeant——'.

Sheriff of London. As recorder of London.

Viscount—Address: 'The Hon. the Lord Viscount——' 'The Right Hon. Lord——'. 'The Lord Viscount——', Begin 'My Lord'; refer to as 'Your Lordship'.

Viscountess — Address: 'The Right Honourable the Viscountess——', or 'The Viscountess——' 'The Right Hon. Lady——' Begin: 'Madam'; refer to 'Your Ladyship'.

Viscount's Children—Are addressed in the same way those of a baron.